The Directory of World Museums

The Directory of World Museums

Edited by

KENNETH HUDSON

and

ANN NICHOLLS

COLUMBIA UNIVERSITY PRESS
NEW YORK 1975

Published in Great Britain in 1975
under the title *The Directory of Museums* by
THE MACMILLAN PRESS LTD

Library of Congress Catalog Card Number 74–21772

ISBN 0–231–03907–7

Printed in Great Britain by
UNWIN BROTHERS LIMITED

Contents

The Museum World Today

'ANYONE WHO SETS out to talk about museums', wrote Richard Grove recently,[1] 'is instantly faced with the task of trying to figure out just what sort of creature this is. It is a nearly unique peculiarity. A hospital is a hospital. A library is a library. A rose is a rose. But a museum is Colonial Williamsburg, Mrs Wilkerson's Figure Bottle Museum, the Museum of Modern Art, the Sea Lion Caves, the American Museum of Natural History, the Barton Museum of Whiskey History, The Cloisters, and Noell's Ark Chimpanzee Farm and Gorilla Show'.

The United States has something like a quarter of all the museums in the world and the sheer exuberance and fertility of the situation there within the museum field makes any attempt to sift, define and classify this great range of institutions exceptionally difficult, a fact well realised by the American experts who have the unenviable task of visiting museums, normally in teams, in order to decide whether this or that collection should be officially accredited as a museum. Does it have a permanent collection? Can it be said to have a professional staff? Is it coping satisfactorily with the presentation of its paintings or machinery or animals to the public? Is it fair or reasonable to allow accreditation to a museum which employs a qualified staff to look after its large and valuable assets in a manner which attracts only specialists, and to deny such recognition to a lively place, always full of visitors and with an enthusiastic staff, merely because it has, in the accepted sense, no permanent collection? How does one draw the line between a museum and an exhibition? Who benefits by such a distinction? Has the word 'museum' outlived its usefulness?

Few words have been more argued about, especially during the past quarter of a century, when the developing countries have shown themselves increasingly unwilling to be patronised or fettered by concepts and philosophies which are irrelevant to their special needs and conditions. ICOM, the International Council of Museums, does its tactful best to keep the museum people of widely different cultures in communication with one another and to present a broad museum front to the world, but the task is far from easy and ICOM conferences are characterised by the kind of rumblings and explosions which make the organisers all too clearly aware that the word 'museum' contains a considerable quantity of dynamite.

ICOM, which has its headquarters in Paris and is consequently exposed to the continuous benefits of the French longing for perfect and aesthetically satisfying definitions, is constantly revising and refining its phrases. By 1971, it came up with the following delightful and, one might think, foolproof, attempt to satisfy all parties, from Canada to the Congo, as to what could and could not be legitimately described as a museum.

No translation can do justice to the beauties of the French, but the following version conveys the substance, if not the spirit, of the original.

> The museum [ICOM suggests] is an institution which exists to serve the community. It acquires, preserves, makes intelligible and, as an essential part of its function, presents to the public the material evidence concerning man and nature. It does this in such a way as to provide opportunities for study, education and enjoyment.[2]

Or, as the Boston Museum of Fine Arts described itself:

THIS IS

..... a recreation center
..... a place to learn
..... a collector's paradise
..... a research laboratory
..... a craftsman's mecca
..... a 'World's Fair' of art

THIS is YOUR family's PERSONAL Museum of Fine Arts.[3]

The differences between the ICOM definitions of 1971 and 1957 are interesting. In 1951, the Executive Committee decided that ICOM would recognise as a museum 'any permanent institution which conserves and displays, for purposes of study, education and enjoyment, collections of objects of cultural or scientific significance'. Within this definition would fall

(*a*) exhibition galleries permanently maintained by public libraries and collections of archives;
(*b*) historical monuments and parts of historical monuments or their dependencies, such as cathedral treasuries, historical, archaeological and natural sites, which are officially open to the public, botanical and zoological gardens, aquaria, vivaria, and other institutions which display living specimens, natural reserves.

The main omission in 1957, by comparison with the 1971 definition, is the important phrase 'which exists to serve the community'. The 1971 version would, for this reason, be much more acceptable to the socialist countries of the world, but not only to the socialist countries. During the past twenty years a feeling has become increasingly apparent that museums should not exist, attract public funds and demand entrance fees without making a serious effort to meet the cultural needs of as wide a cross-section of the public as possible. Unless it does, in the broadest sense, 'serve the community', it will have no generally acceptable measure of its success. Any institution which consciously and deliberately sets out to 'serve the community' will necessarily be sensitive to what its customers think about what is being offered to them. It will be involved in both market research and in marketing, a fact of which the best of today's museum curators are certainly well aware.

An American, Dr Alma S. Wittlin, who has given a great deal of thought to the communication-function of museums, noting with approval the ICOM view that a museum is essentially an establishment in which objects are the main means of communication, writes:

> If we agree with this definition, establishments in which objects are not used at all or are not used as main carriers of messages are not museums, whatever their qualities may be otherwise. A place in which people are exposed to changing lights or to a galaxy of light and sound unrelated to objects may offer a new kind of symphony or a carnival, according to its quality, but it is not a museum. If a few objects provided by a museum or by any source are used in a club or a recreation center among other items on the program, such as dancing or discussions of current problems and of vocational opportunities, the place still retains its identity. The term museum is neither better nor worse than the term club or center. We dim the outlook on our goals if we instill terms with connotations of borrowed status. . . .
>
> There is considerable scope [she concludes] for a combination of objects with other media, with brief motion pictures illustrating a single concept or with appropriately designed (and not overdesigned), suitably sized and placed graphics, but objects have to remain the stars of the cast.[(4)]

This is well said, and one finds little difficulty in agreeing with Dr Wittlin's point of view. A serious difficulty arises, however, when one considers the word 'object'. Can a living cactus or goldfish or lion be reasonably called an object? Might it not, perhaps, be carrying tolerance, broad-mindedness or empire-building too far to call a botanical garden, or an aquarium, or a zoo a museum? As Dr Wittlin rightly reminds us, 'the term museum is neither better nor worse than the term club or center'. It is equally neither better nor worse than the perfectly good and well-understood terms, botanical garden, aquarium, zoo, or, for that matter, library. A library could not unreasonably be described as a museum of books, but it somehow seems more suitable to continue to call it a library. And both ICOM and Dr Wittlin would be unlikely to include Thomas Marioni's San Francisco Museum of Conceptual Art, a museum which describes itself as functioning on two levels—'as a storehouse and library for documentation of events and happenings and conceptual art projects from all over the world, but primarily as a place where these may take place and be witnessed'.

Whatever definition of a museum is followed, it is certain that museums are very unevenly distributed between the rich countries and the poor. In 1965 the American Association of Museums revealed the interesting and possibly frightening fact that between 1960 and 1963 a new museum was established somewhere in the United States every 3.3 days. Between 1940 and 1949 the rate of increase had been one every 10.5 days.

In 1932 [reported the Director of the Association] there were over eleven museums for every million of the population, in a total population of approximately 134 million for the United States and Canada. Today, there are more than twenty-one museums for every million of the population, in an estimated total of 194 million for the United States and Canada.[(5)]

Attendances at American museums have been equally remarkable. The statistics can be presented in many different ways. The Director of the New York Historical Society, Mr James J. Heslin, has observed[(6)] that the number of people visiting American museums and art galleries 'is more than the number attending the baseball games of all the major league teams in a year'.

The post-war growth of museums in Japan, too, has been spectacular, with the total number doubling between 1951 and 1971. Elsewhere, however, the story is different. In 1936, when S. F. Markham published his book, *The Museums of India*, he pointed out that a nation with a sixth of the world's population had only 105 museums. The figure had risen to only 274[(7)] by 1967. This, a leading American authority has commented,[(8)] is both extraordinary and a wasted opportunity. 'Museums', Dr Ripley notes, 'could be the most important single educational tool in India today. With a population problem and a language problem combined, here is the perfect opportunity for the development of imaginative new techniques, using displays and objects to communicate and to teach'.

It could be, however, that in a poor and still largely peasant country, the answer does not lie in a proliferation of museums on the American pattern. It may be cheaper and more effective to use television as the means of communication, drawing the programme material from a relatively few well-stocked and well-staffed museums. The real problem in that case is to collect and preserve the evidence of local and regional cultures before it disappears for ever. Such evidence may take the form of objects, films, photographs or recordings, but, given the very limited public funds available in such countries as India and China, it would seem more sensible to devote what money is available to the urgent task of collecting highly perishable material while it is still there to collect, rather than to the relative luxury of building, staffing and equipping centres where such collections can be made available to the public. In the social and financial circumstances of the developing countries, the non-proliferation of museums could be a sign of political wisdom, rather than of conservatism and backwardness. What André Malraux has called[(9)] 'the museum without walls' is a force and an opportunity which the educational planners have to reckon with.

There are, even so, serious disadvantages to be found in the large, centralised collection. They were indicated forty years ago in the United States by Paul Marshall Rea. Rea produced evidence to show that the larger the museum, the more it costs to increase the attendance figures.

> From a social point of view [he insisted] it is impossible to face with equanimity the expenditure of steadily mounting millions of dollars for progressively diminishing increments in attendance, which is the underlying reason for the rising cost per visitor. If it were possible to include in these costs the interest on the investment in buildings and collections, they would be increased to still more disturbing magnitudes.[(10)]

The solution, Rea believed, 'is to decrease, rather than increase, size, and to decentralise the museum by establishing conveniently located neighbourhood branches in all the larger cities'.[11] The idea was not new. Fifteen years earlier, another American, Margaret Talbot Jackson, had protested against the current notion that size meant efficiency. In due course, she hoped,

> we shall learn that economy in running a large plant is not the only consideration. Such monstrosities as the Louvre in Paris, the South Kensington in London, and the Metropolitan in New York, will no longer be possible, but their place will be taken by museums of moderate size, devoted not to all art from earliest times to the present day, but to different periods of classes of material, and we shall then have museums dotted about in different quarters of the city where they will reach a larger number of people and where one can spend, in intimate association with a series of objects, a number of hours without the overwhelming sense of fatigue that comes to the weary visitor who knows that although he is now in gallery number 22, there are fifty-seven that he has not seen and through which he may possibly have to pass before emerging from the building. It is very much more interesting to go to ten different places than it is to go to the same place ten times.

It is quite possible that the overwhelming and sometimes stupefying size of the large, centralised museum has produced its own reaction and that the increasing popularity of small, house-size museums is due to a wish to visit places which are on a human scale. The steady growth in numbers of what may be called the historic house museum appears to be strong evidence in this direction. Throughout the world, but especially in the United States, these miniature museums, sometimes the former homes of the great and famous, sometimes distinguished survivals of the architecture of a past age, have great popular appeal. They are frequently, perhaps usually, restored, furnished and arranged to a high standard, and their contents are, for the most part, presented more informally and less didactically than in most large museums. They are museums without pressure and without salesmanship, welcome oases in a world which gives such exaggerated prestige to the large institution and the complex organisation.

> Houses [wrote the American author of the house-museum curator's Bible] appeal partly to the emotions, and this – their power for museum purposes – deserves to be strengthened by developing atmosphere. One of the commonest remarks of visitors in any well-appointed house is that they enjoy being there because the place is like a home and not like an institution. Whatever meaning this may have for other museums is beside the point; the implication for historic house museums is plain. Historic houses must be made to live again.[12]

There were, he went on, simple and proved ways of achieving this. 'Clocks that run, wall hangings, table coverings, cushions, and rugs are among the accessories that give feeling. Clothes in closets, dishes in cupboards, and objects in drawers contribute to the same end'.[13]

Labelling 'destroys illusion'. 'Labels are part of the apparatus of formal museum exhibits, and in the furnished rooms of a house they testify either to the presence of alien material or to some recognized inadequacy of curatorial services'.[14]

But, he emphasised,

> however convincing all other arrangements may be, the illusion is still far from complete unless visitors have a chance to sit down. In some houses a few chairs – strong pieces, or perhaps reproductions – are provided for use. The best place for these seats is in the room where newcomers are grouped to hear the curator's introductory remarks. This method of making visitors at home is used effectively in Longfellow's Wayside Inn, South Sudbury, and in Hawthorne's Wayside at Concord.

The visitor to what Coleman has pleasantly termed 'the little institution' is less likely to become exhausted and more likely to find himself personally involved in what is put before him than the person who crosses the entrance-hall of the large museum, which holds the challenge, and often the threat, of a labyrinth of rooms beyond. The house where Lenin stayed for a year, the Tchekov family mansion, the peasant cottage where Mao tse-Tung had his headquarters, Queen Victoria's apartments at Osborne, all these are agreeable places in which to spend an hour and to absorb the atmosphere. They are also very cheap to run, especially when, as is often the case, the staff is largely composed of public-spirited volunteers.

An important reason for the increased numbers and popularity of museums away from city centres, and especially those in small towns and villages, is the widespread, but certainly not yet universal, growth of car-ownership. The ranch-museums, the archaeological sites, the open-air museums, the abandoned Gold Rush towns, the early forges and mills, the country houses and estates of the rich and famous can now be visited without difficulty, even by people who live many miles away. It consequently becomes worthwhile to restore, equip and promote such places, in the knowledge that the investment can probably be recouped within a comparatively few years. But – and the proviso has to be stressed – the job has to be done with thoroughness and imagination. It is no great hardship, although it may be a disappointment, to discover that a city museum is not what one expected it to be, but to drive fifty or a hundred miles and to find something unintelligible or unappealing at the end of the journey is another matter.

During the past twenty-five years, the museum-going public has changed a great deal, and is still changing. Its range of interests has widened, it is far less reverent and respectful in its attitudes, it expects to find electronic and other modern technical facilities adequately used, it considers the intellect to be no more prestigious or respectable than the emotions, and it is suspicious, if not scornful, of the subject-divisions and specialisms so precious to academics.

The new context within which museums are required to operate was well illustrated at a seminar held in 1967 at the Museum of the City of New York. The seminar was concerned with the 'ways, means and values of museum communication with the viewing public', and among those who took part was Dr Marshall McLuhan.

All the conventions of the museum and art gallery world were treated as at least potentially obsolete, irrelevant and expendable. What was described as the 'story-line approach' – using the artifacts to illustrate a story or a theme – met with particularly rough handling. Dr McLuhan was full of praise for Expo 67, on the grounds that it was the first world fair to have no story-line whatever:

> It was [he said] just a mosaic of discontinuous items in which people took an immense satisfaction precisely *because* they weren't being told anything about the overall pattern or shape of it, but they were free to discover and participate and involve themselves in the total overall thing. The result was also that they never got fatigued.(15)

At this point, Dr McLuhan dug into his own past.

> I remember as a youngster being familiar with a phrase, which I may have invented, 'that museum feeling', a kind of claustrophobia and exhaustion which settles upon you as soon as you get inside those straightened avenues and alleyways. Once you move into a world of continuous, connected space – visual space – you quickly discover exhaustion setting in, because there is no means of participation.(16)

During the seminar, the general outline of the 'participating museum' emerged. It would ask the visitor questions, rather than give him answers.(17) It would accept the touching of objects as normal. It would recognise that understanding through the ear was a different process from understanding through the eye, but equally valid. The man or the child 'who lives in an oral world, that is, where the primary method of communication is by mouth to ear, lives at the center of a sphere where communication comes into him simultaneously from all sides, banging at him'.

It appeared that, in today's terms, what the amateur small-town museum is doing is often excellent and 'what we high-priced professionals are doing to the museums is bad'. In other words, said a curator who took part in the seminar, 'We go to one of the small-town museums and say, "You're doing the wrong thing", and "You're not doing anything with these articles. You're simply exposing them to the local townspeople. You're not doing a full job." Then the local townspeople say back to us, "We like it that way".'(18)

This, if it is true, puts official, professional bodies in a most difficult position. 'No collection of objects, haphazardly displayed, can nowadays be accepted as a museum', declared W. T. O'Dec in an ICOM report published in 1962.(19) Except, apparently, by the public, which may on occasions react in ways which the professionals would consider perverse, obstinate or even ungrateful.

NOTES

1. 'Some problems in museum education', contribution to *Museums and Education*, ed. Eric Larrabee (Washington, 1968) p. 79.
2. The French version runs: 'Le musée est une institution au service de la communauté, qui acquiert, conserve, communique, et notamment expose, à des fins d'étude, d'éducation et de délectation, des témoins matériels de l'évolution de la nature et de l'homme.'
3. Quoted by Walter Muir Whitehill, *Independent Historic Societies: An enquiry into their research and public functions, and their financial future* (Boston: The Boston Athenaeum; distributed by the Harvard University Press, 1962) p. 539.
4. *Museums in Search of a Usable Future* (1970) pp. 203–4.
5. Quoted by Alma S. Wittlin, *Museums in Search of a Usable Future*, p. 174.
6. 'Does the Museum of History Teach History?' in *Museums and Education*, ed. Larrabee, p. 153.
7. India and Pakistan combined.
8. Dillon Ripley, *The Sacred Grove* (1969) p. 89.
9. *The Voices of Silence* (1954) p. 16.
10. *The Museum and the Community* (Lancaster, Pennsylvania, 1932).
11. Ibid., p. 173.
12. Laurence Vail Coleman, *Historic House Museums* (Washington: American Association of Museums, 1933) pp. 34–5.
13. Ibid., p. 67.
14. Ibid.
15. *Exploration of the ways, means and value of Museum Communication with the viewing public*, Seminar, 1967, at the Museum of the City of New York (New York, 1969) p. 3.
16. Ibid.
17. Most museum labels are answers. But not in the Museum of Childhood in Edinburgh.
18. *Exploration . . . the viewing public*, p. 3.
19. *Science Museums in Developing Countries*, ed. Frank Greenway (ICOM, 1962) p. 39.

Criteria for the Directory

THE PRESENT EDITORS have worked to a simple basic principle – to use all available sources in order to discover as many museums as possible and then to decide which of these museums should reasonably be excluded from the final list. In carrying out this task we have been obliged to assume that museum administrators have been providing reliable and truthful information, although there is unfortunately good reason to believe that this is not always the case. The temptation to grade up one's museum for outside consumption appears sometimes to be irresistible, and the official jargon of the museum world makes this all too easy to do with a good conscience.

Consider, for instance, those two rather grand and scientific-sounding words, 'mineralogy' and 'ethnography'. They can, and should indicate that a museum possesses properly classified, arranged and presented collections of mineral specimens or of the material culture of a particular region. What, one fears, they not infrequently glorify are a few haphazardly laid out and largely meaningless bits of stone on the one hand and of feathers, pots and pans and boomerangs on the other. Occasionally, a museum may feel that 'ethnography' is too strong a term to describe its little hoard and it will write back to report, more honestly and helpfully, that its collections include a folklore collection. Eventually, we have found, one develops something of a sixth sense in these matters and puts down 'folklore' and 'rocks' for a small local museum and 'ethnography' and 'mineralogy' for a large museum, unless one has positive evidence to the contrary.

It is possible to be blinded with science in other ways, too. We have cynically learnt never to take statistics at their face value. In many countries, curators are much given to publicising the number of objects the museum, or a particular department, contains. We may be told, for instance, that there are 10,000 butterflies, 50,000 coins or 2000 agricultural implements. Such figures give no idea of the size, character or interest of the agricultural implements – they may be dibbers or they may be combine-harvesters – or of the number of duplicates among the coins or the butterflies. Statistics of this kind can all too easily transform a small and unimportant museum into something much more impressive, which may benefit the morale of the curator and his committee, but confuses the outside world.

An ideal solution, no doubt, would be to subject every museum to a personal inspection, but, with something like 25,000 museums involved, this is a little difficult to accomplish, although one does one's best to discover the reality behind the phrases and the figures, both by seeing as many museums as possible oneself and by encouraging one's friends and acquaintances to send in reports. A museum directory should improve edition by edition in much the same way as a hotel and restaurant directory, and for the same reasons. No one is more likely to write to the editor than a customer who has been led, guide in hand, to expect one kind of restaurant or museum and who has discovered something quite different when he gets there. But, in order to evaluate a complaint, one has to know something about the customer as well as about his unfortunate experience, and supplementary information of this kind is rarely provided.

An enormous list of museums, such as the one we print below, will inevitably be used in a great many different ways. In choosing and setting out our material we have tried to imagine the people who might consult it. We came to feel that they would probably fall into seven main categories.

(A) PEOPLE PROFESSIONALLY ENGAGED IN MUSEUM WORK.

Here we distinguish between two quite separate interests. One, very human and often highly subjective and irrational, is to discover what details are given about one's own museum and about those of one's friends and enemies. Has this part of the museum or the collection been given what the curator feels to be its correct emphasis and prominence? Why has Museum X received more space than Museum Y?

The second motive which members of museum staffs might have in turning to our work is to look for collections, either at home or abroad, which contain material with a special professional interest to them. One agricultural or medical or wine museum might be expected to welcome the opportunity to check up or correspond with similar museums throughout the world. We have tried to give the kind of information which will encourage this.

(B) LIBRARIANS

These may need a quick reference-source to particular museums or to types of museum.

(C) RESEARCH WORKERS

These might range from the postgraduate student writing a thesis about banknotes to the author of a new standard work on the history of polo. There must be remarkably few specialities not catered for by one museum or another and, equally, there must be many approaches to almost any potential subject for research which have not so far manifested themselves. However, research workers, in our experience, include both those who intend to devote a minimum amount of personal effort to a project and those who are happy to work hard at following up clues. The first category of researcher will almost certainly be dissatisfied with the information we give, but to the second we think we have a good deal to offer.

(D) PEOPLE WITH HOBBIES AND ENTHUSIASMS

These passionate concerns might be railways, postage stamps, covered bridges, lace, wrought iron, coins, early broadcasting or circuses. Their devotees correspond frequently and intensively with like-minded, or supposedly like-minded (museum curators are, alas, by no means always enthusiastic about their collections) enthusiasts elsewhere and are known to build their holidays around visits to places where they can find fresh nourishment for their special interests.

(E) ORGANISERS OF CONFERENCES AND COURSES, AND SALESMEN OF OTHER TYPES OF PRODUCT, INCLUDING LECTURERS

They may see a directory of this kind primarily as the raw material of an up-to-date mailing list.

(F) PEOPLE WHOSE MAIN INTEREST IS TOURISM OR TRAVEL

These may be entrepreneurs, looking for new items to add to their programme, or, on the other hand, private individuals or groups wanting to find out interesting places to visit within a particular area or country.

(G) EXPERTS IN NATIONAL PRESTIGE AND INTERNATIONAL TROUBLE-MAKING

People professionally engaged in promoting the image of their country abroad, quick to notice omissions or alleged insults in any work of reference and anxious to make full use of any propaganda advantage which an author or editor may have unwittingly presented.

It would not be at all difficult, for instance, to use the obvious fact that the United States has a large number of military, naval and air force museums in order to prove that the United States is a violently militaristic nation and a menace to world peace. Or, considering the vast total of art museums in the same country, to declare that the appreciation of art in the United States is more widespread, and on an altogether higher level, than in China, where there are very few art museums. Both conclusions would, however, be of very doubtful value.

It is evident that one cannot give equal satisfaction to such a wide variety of people. It is probably unwise to make the attempt. On the other hand, there is no reason whatever to consider any one of the categories mentioned above as essentially more or less worthy of attention than any other. Just as universities are not the sole concern of the people employed in them, or railways of railwaymen, so, without question, museums and their contents are not the exclusive preserve and interest of museum specialists. The more the citizens of one country know about what is done abroad, the better the chance they have to see their own country's achievements in proper proportion.

With these considerations, and the great bulk of our material in mind, it seemed reasonable to follow these principles of selection:

No museum without a permanent collection. We are not altogether happy about this, partly because it meant the exclusion of a number of excellent exhibition centres and galleries, in, for example, China and Czechoslovakia, and partly because we could never be satisfied that all our informants were telling us the truth, or at least the whole truth about their collections. If, to be officially acceptable, a museum has to possess a permanent collection, then it is prudent to possess a permanent collection, at least on paper.

No zoos or botanical gardens. This, we admit, may be a confession of either conservatism or prejudice, or possibly both. None the less, and with all the broadmindedness that studying the particulars of 25,000 museums must bring, we find ourselves unable to regard either a zoo or a botanical garden or an aquarium as a museum. Each of these admirable institutions is a collection in its own right, and we are not convinced that anything is gained by calling it a museum.

No historic houses without appropriate furnishings, or without a deliberate attempt to make the building and its contents significant to visitors. This rules out, and, in our opinion, quite rightly, any establishment, however important, which the public is permitted to visit, but on a strictly take-it-or-leave-it basis.

No historic site which is merely an historic site. To merit inclusion in our list, there must be some kind of visitor centre, orientation exhibition, or other method of explaining the site.

No collection which exists solely for the purpose of propaganda. This excludes, for example, the Turkish Museum of Greek Atrocities in Cyprus or the Museum of the Berlin Wall, at Checkpoint Charlie, in West Berlin.

No collection without a serious theme of some kind. This seemed to us to be the only sensible and fair way to strike out, for example, Ripley's 'Believe it or Not' museums in the United States, and most of the waxworks museums. But we saw no reason to refuse to admit a museum to our canon merely because it is run for commercial gain.

Having pruned our list in these various ways, we had to decide how much or how little we could say about each museum within the space that was possible. What should go out in order that other information should remain?

After considerable heart-searching and discussion, we settled for the name and address of the museum, a brief guide to its contents, and the opening times. The amount of the entrance-fee, if any, seemed to be of no particular consequence, except possibly to museum politicians, and an extra line devoted to the contents looked like a very fair exchange for the name of the director who might, in any case, have been replaced by the time the directory appeared.

This work is, obviously, intended for people who can read English. The interests of most of our readers appeared, therefore, to be best served by putting the name of the museum in English, with the native title in parentheses in those few cases where this might be felt to be necessary in order to avoid confusion or where a translation presented unusual difficulty. To include both the English and the foreign name in every case would, in our judgement, have been unnecessary pedantry and it would certainly have added considerably to the cost. We saw no reason to introduce such a complication and extra expense, particularly since our own experience of writing many thousands of letters to museums abroad had proved to us that an enquiry was just as likely to be answered, usually in the respondent's own language, or in some all-purpose language such as French or German, if both our letter and the name of the museum on the envelope were in English.

For the present work, as for a previous one involving a considerable amount of letter-writing around the world, we have found that different countries vary enormously as correspondents. The Russians are, beyond all question, the worst and, like most other researchers, we have found exceptional difficulties in getting the information we needed about the Soviet Union. The other Eastern European countries, by contrast, have been most helpful and one hopes that, in due course, their excellent example will spread its influence to the north and east of their frontiers. There are, however, consolations to be found in other directions. Two years ago we would have rated the French very low as correspondents, almost at the Russian level, but recently they have improved to an amazing degree. We have no idea why, but we are grateful for the change. On the other hand, the Scandinavians, previously admirable, have become somewhat less satisfactory.

Our general experience is that museum directors and curators reply reasonably promptly and that women are much better than men in this respect. Academics everywhere, and of both sexes, require an abnormal amount of prodding before they can be persuaded to commit information to a piece of notepaper and to put that piece of paper in an envelope, even a stamped addressed envelope. To answer letters is to destroy the myth of extreme busyness and total devotion to scholarship. We have been interested to observe that our very simple enquiry, usually about the scope of a collection or about opening times, appears to produce a response from small museums in cases where the elaborate questionnaires sent out by more ambitious researchers, including national associations of museums, have apparently met with silence. The replies we have received from local museums in such areas as the American mid-West suggest that many of these museums are looked after by devoted but unsophisticated people, not given to attending museum conferences or to subscribing to professional journals, to whom letter-writing does not come easily and who are easily and understandably frightened off by a four-page questionnaire, containing questions which must seem irrelevant, if not incomprehensible, to the person who receives them.

It would be arrogant and absurd to claim that we have located and described every museum in all five continents. We are quite certain we have not. Our mail brings us details every day of a newly-established or an unsuspected old museum in one country or another. It is impossible to keep up to date with what has for many years been one of the world's major growth industries. Museums also have a way of fading away, dying or catching fire. This is especially true of smaller museums which depend for their continued existence and success on the energy, personal presence and vigilance of a single public-spirited enthusiast. When he or she dies or becomes ill, the museum not infrequently closes its doors until a successor can be found, which may well be never. For this reason, too, no directory can be fully accurate or up-to-date.

We have made no more than incidental attempts to evaluate museums, partly because we are well aware that one man's meat is another's poison, partly because different museums are trying to do different things and have to be measured against their own scale of values, and partly because museums exist and function within such a wide range of cultural contexts. Even so, it will usually be sufficiently clear from the kind of details we provide if a particular museum or collection is of more than average interest or importance. Where we believe this to be so, our opinion is reflected in the inclusion of the museum in the classified index. We shall, of course, be exceedingly grateful to those of our readers who take the trouble to communicate with us about any errors, omissions, inadequacies or mistakes of emphasis which they may have noticed. These matters will be put right in a future edition.

These reflections are continued in greater detail in the introductions which precede each national list of museums given below. The museums a country has are no bad guide to its priorities, traditions and ambitions. It is certainly as reasonable to look for significant clues to the philosophy and way of life of, say Australia or Brazil in their museums as in their shops, their newspapers and magazines and in the utterances of their public figures. From this point of view, what is not represented in a museum is often quite as important as what is. There is, for example, something strange and probably suicidal about a twentieth-century nation which excludes industry and technology from its definition of culture and consequently from its museums. The decision that certain historical events and personalities shall be officially regarded as disreputable and not suited to museum displays is also of great interest. So, too, is the fairly widespread feeling in many parts of Africa, Asia and America that museums are part of a white man's plot to force his discredited point of view on coloured men.

We do not claim, in these brief introductions, to do anything more than indicate certain features of the context within which museums operate and which we feel to be important and, for anyone who may feel so inclined, worth devoting more time and care to following up. We have not presented these necessarily very concentrated and, in some cases, very generalised opinions with an conscious or deliberate wish to please the government or régime concerned. We realise that some countries may feel flattered by our comments and others very annoyed. We can only attempt to meet either of these reactions by saying that we have been living with a good many thousands of museums for a long time and we think as a result that we may be well placed to distinguish strengths and weaknesses which are not always apparent to the people on the spot. We know, too, from our experiences in preparing other works of an international character, that many of the details and opinions one has tried hard to extract during the research period flow in quite naturally and easily once the first edition of the book has appeared. People are stimulated to write more by errors, omissions and alleged slights than they are by polite and repeated letters requesting information. We have no reason to believe that the present work will prove an exception to the general rule, and we are greatly looking forward to the correspondence we think we shall be receiving from all over the world. The international community of scholars and experts is a very real thing and today's violent and aggrieved critics have a way of turning into tomorrow's friends.

The index of Specialised Collections may call for a special word of explanation. When we began to plan *The Directory of Museums* we toyed with the idea of attempting some kind of evaluation, either in the form of stars or code letters, along the lines of the *Guides Michelin* to hotels or restaurants, or by weaving in adjectives or intensitives to indicate our feelings about a particular museum or section of the contents. We soon came to realise that such a scheme was quite impracticable, partly because we were so dependent on what the administrators and curators said about their own collections, and partly because, where the institution is a museum, any reliable assessment of its quality must be based to a great extent on the opinions of its customers.

We therefore decided to do two things – to write another book,* in which we would try to discover, from all the evidence we could marshal, what the public has thought about museums during the past two hundred years or so, and, more immediately, to discriminate in the present book very broadly between collections which appeared to us to be of greater and lesser importance. We have carried out this unenviable task by compiling a selective index. The museums which are in it – sometimes more than once, if they have several specialities – can be assumed to be, in our view, more important than the museums which are not in it. Beyond this, we felt we could not and should not go.

* *A Social History of Museums: What the Visitors Thought* (Macmillan, 1975).

Acknowledgements

IT WOULD NEED many pages of small print to list all the individuals, museums and government bodies, from Ulan-Bator to Dublin and from Calgary to Budapest, who have helped us in one way or another to obtain, amplify or check information; and to attempt to make a selection from such a list would be unfriendly and absurd. We are very grateful to the many busy people who have somehow found time to write to us, to meet us and, not infrequently, to entertain us during our travels.

It does, however, seem entirely appropriate to thank Hugues de Varine-Bohan* and his super-competent, tolerant and always approachable staff at ICOM in Paris. Without them and their magnificent library and card-index, we should have abandoned the chase at an early stage.

The co-editors also hope that they will be permitted the eccentricity of expressing their gratitude to one another for the mutual patience and encouragement they have shown throughout what has frequently seemed an impossible task.

* Succeeded as Director, in June 1974, by Luis Monreal.

Glossary

ANTIQUITIES

Remains, relics or monuments of antiquity, in a general sense and with no restriction as to period. Often used, however, to refer exclusively to the antiquities of Greece, Rome and Egypt.

APPLIED ART(S)

Art put to some practical use. 'Applied art' frequently and inevitably overlaps 'decorative art' and 'industrial art'. A British advertisement of December 1972 invited applications for the post of 'Keeper of Decorative Arts' at Leicester Museums, and went on to say that 'the successful candidate will be responsible for all the important applied arts collections'.

ARTIFACTS

Objects made by man. Usually, within the museum field, applied only to objects created by some form of manual or artistic skill.

BYGONES

A helpful word, for a long time out of favour with the more scientifically-minded museum professionals, but now showing some signs of a revival. It describes a wide range of objects, from mousetraps to corset-bones, which were once in everyday use, especially during the nineteenth century. 'Bygones' implies a degree of fondness or nostalgia for the objects in question and probably became suspect for this reason.

CASTLE

A simple-looking word which gives rise to major translation problems. We have to consider buildings of three types:

(*a*) the fortress, planned, built and occupied entirely for defence;

(*b*) the fortified city (German *burg*, Czech *hrad*);

(*c*) the palace-type residence, which may occupy the site of a former fortress, but which, as a result of subsequent rebuilding or remodelling, has long since lost any appearance of a building created for defence.

Where we believe ourselves to be concerned mainly with (*a*) or (*b*) we call the building a castle and where we are faced with (*c*) we call it a palace. So far as we are concerned, 'palace' is merely a piece of shorthand. It implies no estimate of size or quality, although clearly it never describes a cottage. A palace, for us, is something larger and grander than a house. 'Mansion' seems less appropriate, as a general and international term, and *château*, which would have done very well, is not yet an English word and might quite reasonably have been considered precious.

CERAMICS

A word greatly loved by museum people. It is, except to specialists in archaeology, much more impressive than 'pottery', but beyond this we can see little difference between the two. Left to ourselves we should have used 'pottery' consistently and all the time, but we were forced to realise that some curators used 'ceramics' in a wider sense than others. To some, it apparently means any object made of baked clay, to others it means pottery, porcelain and tiles, to others again pottery and porcelain, but not tiles. Until some international standard of meaning for pottery and ceramics can be agreed on, we must, unless we can organise visits of investigation to all museums, continue to use both words, in full knowledge of the fact that we are not giving as precise a description of a collection as we should like.

CHILDREN'S MUSEUMS

These are of two types – museums which contain material, such as toys or dolls, reckoned to be of special interest to children, and museums which present their collections in a way likely to make an appeal to children. Sometimes known, for reasons of flattery, as 'junior museums', although, to the purists, 'junior museums' aim at teenagers and 'children's museums' at a rather younger age-group.

COLONIAL

Used widely throughout the world to describe the period during which a particular country was governed from abroad. One may therefore speak of 'colonial art' in Mexico or 'colonial furniture' in the United States, and it is not difficult to envisage what is meant. There are, however, two problems of which it is well to be aware. The first is that, in the United States, the word 'colonial' can have strong emotional overtones, exactly as 'Georgian' and 'Elizabethan' have in England. For many people, it implies 'hand-made, craftsmen-built, of yesterday's never-to-be-seen-again high quality'. Over much of the rest of the world, in Africa for example, it has a pejorative flavour, recalling the bad old days of oppression and exploitation. Even in the United States, it is not a word calculated to build a bridge of brotherhood between whites and blacks.

COSTUMES

'Costumes' often means no more than yesterday's clothing. Museums tend to fight shy of 'clothing', possibly on the grounds that to admit having collections of clothing might suggest they were in the ready-to-wear business. Collections of costumes sound more prestigious and valuable than collections of clothing. There are some signs of a change, possibly in order to keep 'costumes' for ceremonial or exceptionally fine and beautiful garments and 'clothing' for the everyday items. Our use of 'costumes' does not, however, necessarily mean that we are referring to expensive, elaborate or splendid clothes. We are, like the museum curators, the victims of a convention.

CRAFTS

Some museums report their collections as including 'crafts' and others, 'handicrafts'. It does not appear to be either possible or necessary to make a clear distinction between the two words, and, in any case, an editor and his publishers will always bend to prefer 'crafts', because it saves five precious letters. It has been suggested to us that 'crafts' implies a rather higher artistic quality, smaller-sized products and less elaborate equipment than 'handicrafts', but we have reservations about this.

CULTURAL HISTORY

A term not greatly beloved by the English-speaking countries, but, in various translations, exceedingly common elsewhere. It includes the artistic achievements of a country or region, customs, traditions, religion – anything in fact which is supposed to enshrine the finest qualities of the race. A mystical and potentially very dangerous phrase, to be avoided or broken down into more precise and more communicable elements wherever possible.

DECORATIVE ARTS

Almost, but not quite, a synonym for 'applied arts'. There is considerable controversy here. Should a bed-coverlet, a vase or a piece of tapestry, for example, be regarded as examples of decorative art or applied art? The truth of the matter is that the two terms have become almost interchangeable. The only distinction between them would seem to be that the decorative arts place a rather smaller emphasis on the usefulness of this or that item.

EARLY HISTORY

This is a difficulty created, and one hopes regretted, by the German-speaking countries, which, for some reason best known to themselves, are not content to speak and write of 'prehistory' and 'history'. They have, instead, 'primeval history', 'prehistory', 'early history' and 'history', which seems to complicate matters unnecessarily, especially since no two countries, even German-speaking countries, agree as to when, in their own particular case, early history ends and history begins. We take 'history' to imply that there are some written records and 'prehistory' that there are none, and we have tried to simplify the position accordingly. On onc or two occasions we have, however, and for highly subjective reasons, made minor concessions to the German-speaking world on this point.

ETHNOLOGY, ETHNOGRAPHY

These two words are very commonly confused, and perhaps it is already too late to restore the original distinction. Ethnology is, or was, the scientific study of races and peoples and especially of their distinctive physical characteristics and forms of behaviour. Ethnography could be defined as applied ethnology, the scientific description of the customs and habits of nations and races. Museum collections may be concerned with either ethnography or ethnology, but we have reason to believe that the two words are often used almost as synonyms, which is unhelpful, especially at a distance.

FINE ART(S)

An absurd phrase, which one is still compelled to use. It means, in the opinion of the most respected judges, paintings, drawings, prints, sculpture which have only their beauty to recommend them. Fine Art items are essentially useless items, to be appreciated essentially through the eye. But the definition is not by any means foolproof. How sure can one be, for instance, that a Ming vase would never be used for umbrellas or a Japanese porcelain bowl for sweets? Or, for that matter, a Rembrandt and its frame as a tray? Most things have their uses, however perverted and unlikely those uses may be. The criterion is presumably the answer to the question, 'Would the creator of the Ming vase have expected his masterpiece to have been used as an umbrella container or as an object of contemplation?' The object of contemplation is Fine Art, the umbrella container is Applied Art.

FOLK ART

A cosy, patronising term for which no satisfactory equivalent exists. The fact that it is a literal translation from the German makes it no better. It covers the various forms of painting, carving and ornamental crafts carried out by the common people (another inevitable but unfortunate label) in their spare time. 'Popular art' (a literal translation from the French) has become barely usable since the universal acceptance of Pop Art as a recognised genre. To find Popular Art in one's local museum of ethnography and Pop Art in the Museum of Modern Art round the corner would be to confuse both curators and the public unreasonably. So, for all its folksy connotations, Folk Art has to stay until something a good deal better turns up.

FOLKLORE

The traditional beliefs, legends and customs of, once again, the common people. The study of these traditional beliefs, legends and customs. A museum cannot, in the strict sense, contain folklore collections, although it can find ways of illustrating and reflecting these, mainly through such artifacts as *ex voto* tablets, handicrafts, paintings and records of witch-burnings. We use 'folklore' as an abbreviation for 'the tangible evidence of folklore'. It is hard to draw a line between folklore and ethnography. One shades off into the other. In general, however, ethnography is a more systematic and scientific affair than folklore.

FURNITURE, FURNISHINGS

Exactly what the official dividing line between furniture and furnishings is, we have not been able to discover. Broadly speaking, we take furniture to be objects one sits at or on, or lies on, or keeps one's possessions in, and furnishings to be everything else in the room. Tables and chairs are furniture, curtains and carpets and mirrors are furnishings. 'Household equipment', sometimes referred to, for the sake of variety, as 'domestic equipment' is the housewife's collection of working tools.

HOUSE-MUSEUM

This usually means the Great Man's former home, or one of his former homes, in which visitors can see a collection of his possessions and, if he was an artist, musician or writer, of his works. Not infrequently, however, the name is all and the contents of the museum may have no direct connexion with the poet or composer. This can cause disappointment to people who have been misled by the museum's title.

HUNTING

Very difficult, and a cause of serious international misunderstanding for many years. No single English word translates the French *chasse*, which goes perfectly well into most other languages. In English, *chasse* has to be 'hunting and shooting' – one cannot hunt pheasants or rabbits in England – but, for brevity, what should be, for English readers, a Hunting and Shooting Museum has become in the present work, simply a Hunting Museum. The editors hope they will be forgiven for something which they realise is normally unpardonable.

INDUSTRIAL ART

A term much used in the later nineteenth century and still found. It originally meant applied art produced by machinery, or on a mass-production basis. A wide range of metalware, pottery and textiles received the accolade of 'industrial art', as a reward for being better-looking than the average. Nowadays, with most things made by machinery, the phrase is of small value, but some curators appear to need or like it.

NATIONAL MUSEUM

A 'national museum' is always an important museum, but after that the term ceases to have much precision. It may mean that it is financed by the state, that it is a country's main or only effort in this particular direction, or that it is the central mother-museum, controlling the activities of provincial museums in the same field. Not all national museums, in whichever sense one understands the term, include the word 'national' in their title. Similar complications occur in the case of 'state' and 'provincial' museums. In Germany, for instance, 'state museum' is a relic of the former kingdoms, such as Prussia and Bavaria, which were eventually united to form the German Reich. A 'state museum' in France, on the other hand, would mean a nationally financed and controlled museum. A 'provincial museum' in Spain or Romania is an important institution, the spearhead of museum activity in a province. A provincial museum in England, on the other hand, is no more than a museum in the provinces. These terms have to be understood in their national contexts.

NATURAL HISTORY

This, in its various translations, originally meant the systematic study of all natural objects, whether animal, vegetable or mineral. It included rocks equally with snakes and insects. More recently it has tended to become restricted to the study of living creatures and to acquire something of a popular and non-scientific flavour. When an institution describes itself as a museum of natural history or says it has natural history collections, it is often difficult to decide what is meant. Unless we have been provided with further guidance, we have assumed that the term is being used in its narrower sense, and that only the animal and vegetable kingdoms are involved.

NATURAL SCIENCE(S)

Originally no more or less than the study of nature and its phenomena. Now frequently reserved for the sciences, such as chemistry and physics, which do not involve the study of living matter, although a wider definition includes the biological sciences as well. Wherever possible, we have tried to use 'natural sciences' as a portmanteau equivalent of chemistry, physics and the mathematics group.

OPEN-AIR MUSEUM

Sometimes known as a 'Skansen-type' museum, after the first example of the type to be established, in Stockholm, although by no means all open-air museums follow the original pattern. In the museum world, an open-air museum generally means a collection of peasant houses, farm-buildings, rural churches, workshops and mills, re-erected on the museum site. There are, however, a number of other kinds of museum, ranging from industrial archaeology sites to Shaker villages, and from sculpture-parks to excavated Roman towns, which seem equally deserving of the title 'open-air museum'. They, however, will probably have to be called 'outdoor museum', leaving 'open-air' and 'Skansen-type' for the rural-building variety.

PALAEONTOLOGY

The scientific study of fossil animals and plants. The key element in the definition is 'scientific study'. Many museums contain fossils, but what they have cannot be reasonably described as palaeontology.

PEASANT

Nowadays there are supposed to be no peasants in either Britain or North America, although personal observation suggests the belief may be a little rash. It is certain, however, that, in the English-speaking world, farming families, no matter how small their scale of operations, do not enjoy being called peasants. One cannot even get away with it, as the Germans can, by calling someone a Great Peasant. Or by reminding him that, in the Communist countries, everybody is a worker, a soldier or a peasant. On the other hand, one does desperately need a general word meaning a person who lived and worked in a rural community before, say, 1920, and whose income came mainly from agricultural work. 'Farmer' will not do, because, rightly or wrongly, it connotes someone who lives by other people's work. So, with many apologies to those present-day members of the agricultural classes who may feel themselves insulted, we have used 'peasant', and such compounds as 'peasant houses', 'peasant handicrafts', 'peasant furniture'.

PHARMACY

The English study pharmacy, qualify as pharmaceutical chemists and then set up in business as chemists. Their working premises are nowadays known as chemists' shops, not as pharmacies. In the nineteenth century the term 'medical hall' was also frequently found. To the rest of the world, however, 'pharmacy' and 'pharmacist' have always been the normal words. We have tried to steer our way round this problem by using 'pharmacy' for everything except an English pharmacy in the nineteenth and twentieth centuries.

PIONEER

A favourite word in the United States and Canada and one also found in Australia and New Zealand, although not with quite the same overtones. It is an emotionally-charged word which makes Americans feel good. It means, usually, 'first-generation white settler'. A great many Chinese were to be found among the early settlers and workers of the Pacific West, but they are not normally thought of as pioneers. The original inhabitants of these new American territories, the Indians, are certainly never included in the definition of 'pioneer'. We have fallen in with the American habit, mainly because 'pioneer' is a conveniently short word.

PRIMITIVE ART

Artistic creations produced by allegedly simple and uneducated people of any race or period who have received no professional training. For some reason, the art of the Mayas or Benin bronzes rank as 'primitive art', whereas Roman or Greek figurines or vases are 'art'. There is no logic about this, but if a museum wants to feel that it owns items of primitive art, we are content to oblige them.

REGIONAL MUSEUM

Many languages have a word which corresponds fairly exactly to the German word *Heimat*. English, perhaps fortunately, does not, and a satisfactory translation of *Heimatmuseum* and its equivalent in other languages is consequently impossible. The root of the problem is that *Heimat* contains both a patriotic and a cosy element. A *Heimatmuseum* is both a Little-Grey-Home-in-the-West museum and a Fatherland or Motherland Museum. It means 'museum of the area in which I live, which is in its turn part of the country which has achieved glorious feats of arms in the past'; and, if any reader is aware of an English word which performs that little service, we shall be more than usually pleased to hear from him or her.

A further complication is that *Heimatmuseums* were greatly beloved and favoured by the Hitler régime. A *Heimatmuseum* was a deliberate method of spreading the Aryan gospel to every town and area in the land. For this reason alone, we could not entertain the idea of Fatherland or Motherland museums. We had to go for something neutral, non-political, non-emotional, cold. We eventually decided on 'Regional Museum' although we realised that, in other situations, 'regional museum' is an administrative, organisational or status label. It covers a wide range of collections and certainly flatters quite a few, but we feel it matches up to reality fairly well. Visitors to a European Regional Museum, particularly in Germany, might expect to find any type of collection reflecting the history, archaeology, natural history, occupations or social conditions of the area. There is no stereotype.

VISITOR CENTRES

Also known as 'orientation centres'. These are interesting American creations, essentially buffers, airlocks or compression chambers between the museum and the outside world. The idea behind them is that, before being let loose on the museum proper, the visitor shall be put in the right mind to appreciate what the museum is trying to do. An efficient visitor centre provides a preview of the exhibits ahead and tells the visitor what to look for and at. This, it is felt, saves time and effort and prevents frustration and misunderstanding. Some people have been known to say that they find the visitor centre more interesting than the museum itself.

WORKERS' MOVEMENT

A general term, much used in the Communist countries, to describe the forces and activities leading towards the establishment of the present socialist régime. By no means all the people involved were, in the strictest sense of the word, workers, although most of them, no doubt, could be described as workers for socialism. The term 'workers' movement' looks strange in English, as indeed does 'revolutionary movement', but we have not been able to think of a better alternative.

Afghanistan

Afghanistan, with about 12 million people, a population density roughly equal to that of the United States, has seven museums, concerned entirely with the country's past. Agriculture is unrepresented, except indirectly in the ethnographical collections, and there is nothing to reflect or support the considerable industrial development since 1945, nor the political developments which led up to the present interesting and somewhat complicated dependence on both Russia and America.

BAMYAN

BAMYAN MUSEUM
Bamyan
Local history. Ethnography.
On request.

GHAZNI

GHAZNI MUSEUM
Ghazni
Local history. Ethnography.
On request.

HERAT

HERAT MUSEUM
Herat
Local history. Ethnography.
On request.

KABUL

KABUL MUSEUM
Darul Aman, Kabul
Ancient articles of clothing, weapons, national costumes, embroidery, utensils, war flags, manuscripts. Silver, gold and copper coins. Archaeology. Library contains collections of handwritten manuscripts.
Mar. 22 - Oct. 22, 8-12, 1-4.30. Oct. 23 - Mar. 20, 9-12, 1-3.30. Closed Th. and F. afternoon.

KANDAHAR

KANDAHAR MUSEUM
Kandahar
Local history. Ethnography.
On request.

MAIMANA

MAIMANA MUSEUM
Maimana
Local history. Ethnography.
On request.

MAZAR-I-SHARIF

MAZAR-I-SHARIF MUSEUM
Mazar-i-Sharif
Local history. Ethnology.
On request.

Albania

Albania is celebrated among the Communist countries for maintaining diplomatic relations with China, but not with the Soviet Union. Its museums illustrate the curious and often turbulent history of the country, with some good archaeological material and a number of ethnographical collections dealing with the recent past of a country where industrialisation is only just beginning and where agriculture and forestry still form the mainstay of the economy.

BERAT

LOCAL MUSEUM
Berat
Local history. Archaeology. Historical documents.
On request.

BRITRINTI

BRITRINTI MUSEUM (REGIONAL)
Britrinti
Historic site. Prehistory. Classical archaeology. Local history.
Tu.-Su. 9-5.

DURRËSI

LOCAL MUSEUM
Durrësi
Historic site. Prehistory. Classical archaeology. Local history.
On request.

ELBASAN

LOCAL MUSEUM
Elbasan
Historical and natural history collections. Medieval art and archaeology. Ethnography. Local and military history.
On request.

FIER

FIER MUSEUM
Fier
Historic site. Prehistory. Classical archaeology. Ethnography.
Tu.-Su. 9-5.

GJIROKASTËR (ARGYROCASTRO)

LOCAL MUSEUM
Gjirokastër
Natural history. Ethnography. Local history. Military history.
On request.

KORÇA

LOCAL MUSEUM
Korça
Archaeology. Natural history. Ethnography. Local history. Military history.
On request.

KRUJA

LOCAL MUSEUM
Kruja
Archaeology. Natural history. Military history (War of Independence). Local history.
On request.

POJANI (APOLONIA)

POJANI MUSEUM
Pojani
Historic site. Prehistory. Classical archaeology.
Tu.-Su. 9-5.

SHKODRA (SCUTARI)

LOCAL MUSEUM
Shkodra
Prehistory. Classical, medieval archaeology. Ethnography. Local history. Military history.
Tu.-Su. 9-5.

TIRANA

LENIN-STALIN MUSEUM
Tirana
Collections illustrating life and work of Lenin and Stalin, and of the workers' and revolutionary movements.
Tu.-Su. 9-5.

MUSEUM OF ARCHAEOLOGY AND ETHNOGRAPHY
Institute of Scientific Research in History and Linguistics, State University, Tirana
Exhibits of the Palaeolithic, Neolithic and Bronze Ages. Objects of the Illyrian culture, Iron Age and Greek and Roman periods of colonisation. Albanian exhibits from the Middle Ages. Agricultural tools, stock-breeding equipment, interiors and exteriors and household objects, textiles. Costumes. Local crafts. Ceramics.
Tu.-Su. 9-5.

MUSEUM OF NATURAL HISTORY
State University, Tirana
Geology. Botany. Zoology.
Tu.-Su. 9-5.

MUSEUM OF THE STRUGGLE FOR NATIONAL LIBERATION
Tirana
Exhibits trace the history of the Albanian people from the struggles against the Ottomans to the present day.
Tu.-Su. 9-5.

VLORA

LOCAL MUSEUM
Vlora
Archaeology. Local and military history. Historical documents.
On request.

Algeria

Algeria is well stocked with former royal palaces, some of which have made acceptable museums. They are best viewed as museums of royalty and royal taste and, as such, they help explain why revolutions take place. Most of Algeria's museums, however, are concerned with the archaeology of the earlier cultures which have existed within its boundaries - Phoenician, Greek, Roman and Byzantine. These, like the ethnographical collections, have to be supplemented by the material transferred to Paris by the country's former rulers. The Sahara Museum is imaginative and excellent. North Africa could do with more like it.

ALGIERS

LE BARDO MUSEUM OF ETHNOGRAPHY AND PREHISTORY
3 rue F. D. Roosevelt, Algiers
Stone-Age implements. Anthropology. Pottery. Rock paintings. Jewellery. Toureg handicrafts. Algerian domestic life. Collections of African art and weapons, especially from the Cameroons and the Ivory Coast.
Daily ex. M. 9-12, 2.30-5.30.

MONT RIANT CHILDREN'S MUSEUM
Parc du Mont Riant, Algiers
One section devoted to paintings and handicrafts by children. In the building of the former Mont Riant archaeological museum.
Daily ex. M. 9-12, 2.30-5.30.

MUSEUM OF THE PALACE OF THE DEY
Palais du Dey, Algiers
Historical collections.
Daily ex. M. 9-12, 2.30-5.30

MUSEUM OF POPULAR ARTS AND TRADITIONS
Rue Soggéma-Casbah, Algiers
In former house of Princess Nefissa. Costumes. Furniture. Textiles. Jewellery. Metalwork. Pottery.
Daily ex. M. 9-12, 2.30-5.30.

MUSEUM OF THE REVOLUTION
2 rue du 20 août, Algiers
Collections relating to the struggle for national liberation.
Daily ex. M. 9-12, 2.30-5.30.

NATIONAL MUSEUM OF ANTIQUITIES
Parc de la Liberté, Algiers
Formerly Stéphane Gsell Museum. Greco-Roman sculpture, Mosaics, Bronzes, Phoenician and Roman pottery. Christian reliquaries and epitaphs. Vandal tablets. Phoenician, Numidian, Roman and Byzantine coins. Islamic sculpture, faience, pottery, jewels, carpets and furniture. Local handicrafts.
Summer: Daily ex. M. and Su. morning, 9-12, 2.30-6. Winter: Daily ex. M. and Su. morning, 9-12, 2-5. Closed public holidays.

NATIONAL MUSEUM OF FINE ART
Jardin d'Essai, Algiers
Paintings by Islamic masters. European paintings of the 16th-19th centuries. Graphics. Contemporary Algerian art. Collection on the theme of Art and Revolution in Algeria. Engravings showing Algiers from 16th century onwards.
Daily ex. M. 9-12, 2.30-5.30.

ZOOLOGICAL PARK
Le Hamma, Algiers
Zoological and botanical collections.
Daily ex. M. 9-12, 2.30-5.30.

ANNABA

HIPPONE MUSEUM
Route d'Hippone, Annaba
Collection of Greek and Roman antiquities.
Daily ex. M. 9-12, 2.30-5.30.

BEDJAIA (Formerly BOUJIE)

BEDJAIA MUSEUM
Place de Gueydon, Bedjaia
Greek and Roman archaeology. Berber pottery. Natural science collections.
Daily ex. M. 9-12, 2.30-5.30.

BENI-ABBES

BOTANICAL AND ZOOLOGICAL COLLECTIONS
Beni-Abbes
Botanical and zoological collections.
Daily ex. M. 9-12, 2.30-5.30.

BOU ISMAIL

AQUARIUM
Institut des Pêches, Bou Ismail
Study collections of marine life.
Daily ex. M. 9-12, 2.30-5.30.

CHERCHELL (EL-ASNAM)

CHERCHELL MUSEUM
Place de la Mairie, Cherchell
The Roman Caesarea. Roman copies of Greek statues. Mosaics. Egyptian and Greek antiquities.
Daily ex. M. 9-12, 2.30-5.30.

OPEN-AIR MUSEUM
Parc Bocquet, Cherchell
Mosaics. Antiquities excavated from the area.
Daily ex. M. 9-12, 2.30-5.30.

CONSTANTINE

CONSTANTINE MUSEUM
Plateau du Coudiat, Constantine
Formerly Musée Gustave-Mercier. Archaeology, including 500 stelae, and other material from local excavations. History of Algeria. Tiddis site museum. Paintings.
Daily ex. M. 9-12, 2.30-5.30.

DJEMILA

DJEMILA MUSEUM
Wilaya de Sétif, Djemila
Mosaics and other material from the Roman town (Cuicul).
Daily ex. M. 8-11.30, 2.30-5.

EL BIAR

MUSEUM OF THE REVOLUTION, 1954-62
El Biar
Items relating to the contemporary history of Algeria.
Daily ex. M. 9-12, 2.30-5.30.

EL OUED

EL OUED MUSEUM
El Oued
Prehistory. Ethnography of the area. Local crafts.
Daily ex. M. 9-12, 2.30-5.30.

GHARDAIA

GHARDAIA MUSEUM OF FOLKLORE
Ghardaia
Folklore of the district. Local crafts.
Daily ex. M. 9-12, 2.30-5.30.

GUELMA

MUSEUM OF THE GUELMA THEATRE
Roman Theatre, Guelma
Sculpture. Numismatics.
Daily ex. M. 9-12, 2.30-5.30.

LAMBERE

TAZOULT SITE MUSEUM
Lambere
Epigraphy of Numidian military life.
Daily ex. M. 9-12, 2.30-5.30.

ORAN

MUNICIPAL MUSEUM
Boulevard Zabana, Oran
Prehistory. Roman and Punic archaeology. Ethnography. Zoology. Geology. Botany. Painting and sculpture.
Daily ex. M. 9-12, 2.30-5.30.

OUARGLA

SAHARA MUSEUM
Ouargla
Ethnography of the Sahara. Prehistory. Local crafts.
Daily ex. M. 9-12, 2.30-5.30.

PHILIPPEVILLE (SKIJDA)

MUNICIPAL MUSEUM
Rue du Sphinx, Philippeville
Local antiquities.
Daily ex. M. 9-12, 2.30-5.30.

SÉTIF

SÉTIF MUSEUM
Tribunal, Sétif
Formerly Archaeological Museum. Roman antiques. Ethnographical collections.
Daily ex. M. 9-12, 2.30-5.30.

SKIKDA

SKIKDA MUSEUM
Skikda
Punic and Roman antiquities. Modern art.
Daily ex. M. 9-12, 2.30-5.30.

TAZOULT

TAZOULT MUSEUM
Tazoult
Greek and Roman antiquities.
Daily ex. M. 9-12, 2.30-5.30.

TEBESSA (THEVESTE)

MUSEUM OF THE TEMPLE OF MINERVA
Place de Minerve, Tebessa
Prehistory. Antiquities. Local art.
Daily ex. M. 9-12, 2.30-5.30.

TIMGAD

TIMGAD MUSEUM
Wilaya des Aurès, Timgad
Formerly Archaeological Museum. Collections of mosaics, funerary stelae and excavated objects from the old town.
Daily except W. 8-12, 2-6.

TIPASA

ANTIQUARIAN MUSEUM OF THE TIPASA EXCAVATIONS
Tipasa
On site of the Roman town. Exhibits from the excavations which have taken place over the last 50 years, including ancient glassware, Punic and Roman funerary furniture, mosaics and marble sarcophagi.
Daily ex. M. and public holidays 9-12, 2-5.

TLEMCEN

MUSEUM OF TLEMCEN
Mosquée de Sidi Bel Hacène, Tlemcen
Antiquities. Moslem art.
Daily ex. M. 9-12, 2.30-5.30.

Angola

This Portuguese colony, important especially for its coffee and minerals, is exceptional among African countries in that its museums are more concerned with natural resources and the economy than with the native culture, although this, too, is represented.

CARMONA

CONGO MUSEUM
Carmona
Ethnography. Native art.
M.-F. 9-12, 3-5. Sa.-Su. 3-5.

LUANDA

ANGOLA MUSEUM
Rua de Nossa Senhora Da Muxima, Luanda
Natural sciences. Ethnography. History. Portuguese and African art and furniture. Religious art. Industry.
M.-Sa. 9-12, 2.30-5; Su. 3-5.

COFFEE MUSEUM
Avenida Paulo Dias de Novais 101, P.O. Box 342, Luanda
History and techniques of the local coffee industry. Photographs. Advertisements. Packaging.
By appointment: M.-Sa. 9-12.30, 2.30-5; Su. 9-12.30.

MUSEUM OF GEOLOGY, PALAEONTOLOGY AND MINERALOGY
Direccao Provincial dos Servicos de Geologia e Minas, Avenida Paulo Dias de Novais 105, Luanda
Geology, palaeontology and mineralogy collections.
Daily 9-12.

MUSEUM OF MINERALOGY AND GEOLOGY
Universidade de Luanda, Avenida Paulo Dias de Novais, 78A, Luanda
General collection of minerals and ores, minerals and rocks of Angola, as well as a collection of palaeontology.
M.-F. 8.30-12.30, 2-5; Sa. 8.30-12.30.

LUNDA

DUNDO MUSEUM
Companhia de Diamantes de Angola, Lunda
Ethnographical and archaeological collections of the Lunda district. Folklore. Musical instruments. African flora and fauna.
M.-Sa. 7.30-11; 12.30-3.30.

MOÇAMEDES

MUSEUM OF THE FISHING INDUSTRY
Moçamedes
History of the fishing industry in Moçamedes and other fishing ports of Angola.
M.-Sa. 8-11, 12.30-3.30.

NOVA LISBOA

MUNICIPAL MUSEUM
Avenue Paiva Couceiro, Nova Lisboa
Ethnographical and historical material relating to the Huambo region. Geography. Photographs.
Daily 5-8.30. Su. 10-12, 5-8.30.

SÁ DE BANDEIRA

HUILA MUSEUM
P.O. Box 445, Sa da Bandeira
Natural sciences. History. Ethnography. Musical instruments.
M.-Sa. 9-12, 2-5.

Argentina

Only Argentina, to the best of our belief, has a museum of caricatures of people once prominent in public life - an admirable institution, which would do a great deal of good if it were reproduced, and kept up to date, elsewhere. Such a museum is not, of course, an indication that Argentina is a country without heroes. On the contrary, it has taken great pains to see that its Great Men - to judge by its museums, Argentina does not appear to have had any Great Women - are properly celebrated in memorial collections. In the case of the nineteenth-century makers of the revolution and fighters for independence this has gone so far that, to commemorate one notability, the museum has acquired the furniture and even the front door of the house in which he breathed his last in far-away Boulogne. There is, too, a museum, somewhat on the Irish model, in the notorious prison where many subsequently prominent Argentine citizens were at one time incarcerated.

There are excellent art museums, especially for contemporary paintings, well distributed over the country; and many museums, both in Buenos Aires and in provincial towns, have rich collections of the work produced by goldsmiths, silversmiths and other craftsmen during the colonial period. A high proportion of these items were originally made for churches and monasteries, and one is, indeed, constantly reminded of the extent to which the history of Argentina is at the same time the history of the Catholic Church. Not by any means all the national treasure is or has been in religious keeping. One of the striking features of Argentinian museums is the number which are still, or have only very recently ceased to be, private collections. Money talks in another way, too, in the museum world of Argentina. All the major banks have museums to illustrate their history and development, which is a useful way of reminding members of the public that they are dealing with a solidly based, old-established institution.

One is given many reminders of Argentina's wide-ranging cultural roots. There is, for example, a special local museum devoted to its Welsh community and another to the English naturalist and writer, W. H. Hudson. The museum which emphasises the debt to Europe most dramatically, however, is that in the former home of Bishop Colombres. The Bishop was no mere cleric. He was, as the museum makes clear, responsible for introducing sugar cane to his province of Tucumán, and in his garden there stands as his memorial a huge steam-driven sugar press imported from France in 1883.

ALTA GRACIA

MANUEL DE FALLA MUSEUM
Alta Gracia
In former home of the composer, with his furniture, library and other material illustrating his life and work.
Tu.-Su. 9-12, 2-5.

AVELLANEDA

MUSEUM OF HISTORY AND POPULAR TRADITIONS
Beruti 216, Avellaneda
Collections illustrating regional history. Folk-lore. Handicrafts.
Sa., Su. 5-8.

AZUL

ENRIQUE SQUIRRU ETHNOGRAPHICAL MUSEUM
San Martin, esquina Alvear, Azul
History of Azul and its region. Handicrafts, especially silver, textiles. Weapons. Archaeology. Palaeontology.
Tu.-Su. 2-6.

BERNAL

ADMIRAL BROWN MUSEUM
25 de Mayo, No. 198, Bernal
Collections illustrating naval career of Admiral Brown, with personal possessions and campaign mementoes. History, archaeology, rural life of the province.
Daily 1-6.

BOLIVAR

FLORENTINO AMEGHINO MUSEUM
Bolivar
Paintings. Sculpture. Furniture. Silver.
Winter: M.-Sa. 10-12, 2-5; Su., public holidays 10-12, 2-5. Summer: M.-Sa. 10-12, 3-6; Su., public holidays 10-12, 3-6.

BUENOS AIRES

JUAN B. AMBROSETTI MUSEUM OF ETHNOGRAPHY
Morena 350, Buenos Aires
Archaeology of Central and South America, and particularly of Argentina. Ethnography of the Americas, Africa, Asia and Oceania. Anthropology of Argentina.
Daily 1-5.

ARCHITECTURAL MUSEUM
Esquina noreste de Alsina y Defensa, Buenos Aires
Paintings, drawings illustrating architectural history of Buenos Aires. Architectural items from buildings demolished in the city.
Daily 2-5.

ARGENTINE NATIONAL BANK MUSEUM OF HISTORY AND NUMISMATICS
Bartolomé Mitré 326, Buenos Aires
Collections illustrating history of banking in the Argentine. Argentine coins, currency notes.
M.-F. 12-5.30.

BANK OF LONDON AND SOUTH AMERICA MUSEUM
Corner of Bartolomé Mitré and Reconquista, Buenos Aires
Old notes, ledgers, scales, pictures and mementoes of the history of the Bank since it was founded in 1862.
12-4 each working day.

ISAAC FERNÁNDEZ BLANCO MUSEUM OF SPANISH-AMERICAN ART
Suipacka 1422, Buenos Aires
Colonial art. Paintings. Sculpture. Silver. Ceramics.
Th.-Tu. 3-7.

CASEROS HISTORICAL MUSEUM
Terrenos del Colegio Militar de la Nación, Buenos Aires
19th-20th century history of Argentina.
Sa. 9-12.

COLÓN THEATRE MUSEUM
A. Toscanini 1150, Buenos Aires
Collections illustrating history of the Colón Theatre. Portraits. Photographs, prints, paintings illustrating performances. Costumes and costume designs. Stage designs. Programmes. Posters.
M.-Sa. 12-6.

DE LA BOCA MUSEUM OF FINE ART
Pedro de Mendoza 1835, Buenos Aires
Paintings. Sculpture. Engravings. Maritime exhibits. Works by Argentinian artists, "belonging to all the social and cultural levels of the population".
Daily 9-12, 3-6.

FORENSIC MUSEUM
Junín 7760, Buenos Aires
Collections illustrating methods used by criminals and the measures available to detect them.
By appointment.

FRIGATE 'PRESIDENTE SARMIENTO' NAVAL MUSEUM
Dársena Norte, Buenos Aires
Sailing frigate, built at Birkenhead (1896), and used by Argentine government as training ship until 1961. Now preserved, fully fitted as naval museum.
Sa., Su. 2-5.

GENERAL SAN MARTIN MUSEUM OF THE REGIMENT OF MOUNTED GRENADIERS
Avenida Luis María Campos, Buenos Aires
Collections illustrating history of the Regiment since 1812.
By appointment.

JOSÉ HERNÁNDEZ MUSEUM
Chacra Pucyrredon, Buenos Aires
Local history. Paintings by Argentinian artists.
Sa., Su., public holidays 2-5.

JOSÉ HERNÁNDEZ MUSEUM OF POPULAR ART
Avda. del Libertador 2373, Buenos Aires
Precolonial art, including pottery, textiles. Costumes. Collections illustrating traditions, cultures, religious superstitions and folk art of Argentina.
Tu.-Su. 2-6.

HISTORICAL MUSEUM OF THE BANK OF THE PROVINCE OF BUENOS AIRES
Córdoba 934, Buenos Aires
19th century bank furniture, equipment, documents. Coins and currency notes.
Tu.-F., Su. 2-6.

JEWISH MUSEUM
Libertad 773, Buenos Aires
History of the Jewish community in Argentina.
M. 9.30-12, 3-5.30; W. 3-5; Th. 9.30-12, 3-5.30; Su. 10.30-12.30.

ENRIQUE LARRETA MUSEUM OF SPANISH ART
Obligado 2139, Buenos Aires
Former home of the writer, E. Larreta. Collection illustrating his life and work. Paintings of the Spanish school (16th-17th centuries). 16th century woodcarvings. Gilt objects. Tapestries.
F.-W. 3-7.45.

MITRÉ MUSEUM
San Martin 336, Buenos Aires
Former home of General Bartolomé Mitré, furnished as it was when he lived there. Manuscripts, documents and printed works illustrating Argentina's political development.
M.-F., Su. 3-7.

MUSEUM OF BOTANY AND PHARMACOLOGY
Junin 956, Buenos Aires
Botany of America, especially Argentina. History of pharmacology.
M.-F. 9-12.

MUSEUM OF ENGRAVINGS
Florida 588, Buenos Aires
Works by foreign and Argentinian artists, mainly 18th-20th century.
M.-F. 4-8; Sa. 11-1.

MUSEUM OF FINE ARTS
Yerbal 2370, Buenos Aires
In General Urquiza School. Paintings, drawings by Argentinian artists.
M.-F. 8.30-12, 2.30-5.

MUSEUM OF GEOLOGY AND MINERALOGY
Perú 562, Buenos Aires
Geology and mineralogy of Argentina.
M.-F. 12.30-6.30.

MUSEUM OF THE GOVERNOR'S HOUSE
Hipoleto Yrigoyen 219, Buenos Aires
Historical material, especially of former Presidents of Argentina. Parts of earlier building revealed by excavations.
Tu.-F. 9-4; Th. 9-7; Su. 3-6.

MUSEUM OF THE INSTITUTE OF THE ANTARCTIC
Cerrito 1248, Buenos Aires
Oceanography. Geophysics. Ionospherics. Glaciology. Microbiology. Geology. Palaeontology. Biology. Exploration of the Antarctic.
M.-F. 7-4; Sa. 7-2.

MUSEUM OF MARITIME ART
Calle O'Higgins 2135, Buenos Aires
Paintings, drawings, prints, tapestry, literature on maritime subjects.
Tu.-F., Su. 2-6.

MUSEUM OF MINERALS
Jubo A. Roca 651, Buenos Aires
Geology and mineralogy of the Argentine.
M.-F. 3-7.

MUSEUM OF MODERN ART
Corrientes 1530, Buenos Aires
20th century works by Argentinian artists. Paintings. Sculpture. Drawings. Collages. Engravings. Tapestry.
Tu.-Su. 4-10.

MUSEUM OF THE NATIONAL INSTITUTE OF MICROBIOLOGY
Vélez Sarsfield 563, Buenos Aires
Collections illustrating the scope and techniques of microbiology.
M.-F. 10-5.

MUSEUM OF TECHNOLOGY
Escuela Industrial de la Nacion, Paseo Colón 650, Buenos Aires
Collections illustrating development of industry and technology, especially in Argentina.
Tu.-F. 9-11.

MUSEUM OF THE TORCUATO DI TELLA INSTITUTE
Florida 936, Buenos Aires
Paintings. Handicrafts. Local history.
Tu.-Th., Sa., Su. 12-8; F. 12-10.

NATIONAL AVIATION MUSEUM
Avenida Rafael Obligado 4550, Buenos Aires
History of aviation, especially in the Argentine. Original aircraft and models. Photographs. Personal possessions of flying notabilities.
Th., Sa., Su.: Winter 2-5; Summer 4-7.

NATIONAL HISTORICAL MUSEUM
Defensa 1600, Buenos Aires
History of Argentina. Memorabilia of San Martin, including uniforms and the original furniture and door of the house in which he died at Boulogne.
W.-F., Su. 2-6.

NATIONAL HISTORICAL MUSEUM OF THE MAY REVOLUTION
Bolivar 65, Buenos Aires
Paintings, documents and furniture recording the May (1810) Revolution. Altar from the church of San Nicolas, where Moreno was baptised and the first national flag dedicated. Hall in which the first Junta met (May 1810).
Su.-F. 3-5.30.

NATIONAL MUSEUM OF THE CITY HALL OF BUENOS AIRES
Bolivar 65, Buenos Aires
History of Buenos Aires. Religious art. Furniture.
F., Su. 3-5.30.

NATIONAL MUSEUM OF DECORATIVE ART
Avenida del Libertador 1902, Buenos Aires
In the Palacio Errázuriz. 18th century French furniture, decorative arts.
W.-M. 2-7.

NATIONAL MUSEUM OF FINE ART
Avenida del Libertador 1473, Buenos Aires
Modern Argentine, American and European paintings. Old masters. Paintings representing the conquest of Mexico (15th-16th centuries). Wooden carvings from Argentine hinterland.
Th.-Tu. 3-7.

NATIONAL MUSEUM OF ORIENTAL ART
Avenida del Libertador 1902, Buenos Aires
In the Palacio Errázuriz. Art of the Far East and Near East, especially China, Japan, Persia. Ceramics. Religious art. Woodcarving. Bronzes.
Tu., Th. 3-7.

NATIONAL MUSEUM OF WEAPONS
Santa Fé 750, Buenos Aires
Weapons of the Indians of N. and S. America. Firearms. Uniforms. Oriental and African weapons. Chemical, biological and nuclear weapons.
Tu.-Su. 2-5.

NATIONAL NAVAL MUSEUM
Centro Naval, Esquina de Florida y Cordoba, Buenos Aires
Models, paintings illustrating history of navigation. Weapons. Ships' furnishings. Navigational instruments. Maps. Charts. Flags.
M.-F. 9-1; Sa., Su. 2-6.

NATIONAL SAN MARTIN MUSEUM
Sanchez de Bustamente and Avenida A. M. de Aguado, Buenos Aires
Personal possessions and portraits, including daguerrotypes of San Martin.
M.-F. 9-12, 2-5; Sa., Su. 2 5.

NATIONAL THEATRE MUSEUM
Avenida Cordoba 1199, Buenos Aires
Collections illustrating history of the theatre in Argentina, 1853-1910. Models of theatres and stage settings. Manuscripts. Paintings. Posters. Photographs.
M.-Sa. 12-6.

NUMISMATICS MUSEUM OF THE CENTRAL BANK
Reconquista 266, Buenos Aires
Coins and currency-notes of Argentina.
M.-F. 12-6.30.

POLICE MUSEUM
San Martin 353, Buenos Aires
History of the police force in Argentina. Police uniforms. Water-colours showing uniforms. Weapons and other equipment used by criminals. Forgery.
Tu., Th., 2-5.30; Sa., Su. 2-7.30.

POSTAL MUSEUM
Palacio Central de Correos y Telecommunicaciones, Sarmiento 151, Buenos Aires
History of the postal services in Argentina.
M.-F. 11-6.

BERNARDINO RIVODAVIA MUSEUM OF NATURAL SCIENCES
Angel Galiardo 470, Buenos Aires
Palaeontology. Zoology. Mineralogy. Botany. Archaeology. Marine section.
Tu., Th., Sa. 2-6.

ROCA MUSEUM
Calle Vicente Lopez 2220, Buenos Aires
Collections illustrating the military, political and administrative activities of General Julio Argentino Roca.
M.-F. 9-1.

RICARDO ROJAS HOUSE
Charcas 2837, Buenos Aires
Former home of Rojas, the "Prince of Argentine Letters", containing his library, souvenirs of his travels. Literary and historical curios.
W., Sa. 3-6.

CORNELIO SAAVEDRA HISTORICAL MUSEUM
Parque General Paz, Avenida General Paz y Repubrliquetas 6309, Buenos Aires
Paintings. Furniture. Gold and silver work. Coins. Watches. Fans. Hair-combs. Religious art. Textiles. Porcelain.
Tu.-F. 3-6; Sa. 8-12 p.m.; Su. 3.30-7.30.

SAN ROQUE MUSEUM
Basilica de San Francisco, Buenos Aires
Art of the colonial period. Religious art.
F., Sa. 3.30-7; Su. 11-1, 3.30-7.

SARMIENTO HISTORICAL MUSEUM
Cuba 2079, Buenos Aires
Collections illustrating life and work of Domingo Faustino Sarmiento.
W.-F. 2.30-6.30; Sa., Su. 3-5.

EDUARDO SIVORI MUSEUM OF THE PLASTIC ARTS
Corrientes 1530, Buenos Aires
Sculpture, paintings, drawings, engravings by Argentinian artists.
Tu.-Su. 4-10.

SEVERO VACCARO MUSEUM OF CARICATURE
Estador Unidos 2162, Buenos Aires
19th-20th century caricatures and drawings of people prominent in Argentine life.
M.-Sa. 3-5.

YRURTIA HOUSE
O'Higgins 2830, Buenos Aires
Sculpture and paintings by Yrurtia in his former home.
W.-F. 3-6; Sa., Su. 2-6.30.

CARMEN DE PATAGONES

FRANCISCO DE VIEDMA REGIONAL HISTORICAL MUSEUM
Palacio Municipal, Suipacha 265, Carmen de Patagones
Regional and military history. Archaeological material from Patagonia.
Summer: Su.-Th. 8.30-10.30; 6.30-8.30. Winter: Su.-Th., public holidays 2.30-4.30.

CATAMARCA

MUSEUM OF THE "ESQUIÚ" CULTURAL INSTITUTE
Sarmiento 450, Catamarca
Archaeology. Colonial history. Iconography. Mineralogy.
M.-F. on request.

CHASCOMÚS

PAMPEANO MUSEUM
Avenidas Lastra y Francisco Javier Muñez, Chascomús
Archaeology. Regional history. Pre-colonial art. Agricultural implements. Weapons. Coins. Medals. Religious art and liturgical items. Currency notes.
Winter: M.-Sa. 10-12, 2-5; Su., public holidays 10-4.
Summer: M.-Sa. 10-12, 3-6; Su., public holidays 10-6.

CONCEPCIÓN DE URAGUAY

EL PORVENIR MUSEUM
San Martin 782, Concepción del Uraguay
Local history.
Tu.-Sa. 8-11.30, 2.30-5.

CÓRDOBA

BOTANICAL MUSEUM
Universidad Nacional de Córdoba, Casilla de Correo 495, Córdoba
Herbaria of Argentina and adjacent countries.
By appointment.

HISTORICAL MUSEUM OF THE HOUSE OF THE VICEROY SOBREMONTE
Rosario de Santa Fé 213, Córdoba
18th century house. 18th-19th century furniture, pictures, silver. Porcelain. Weapons.
Tu.-Su. 9-2; Tu.-F. also 3.30-6.30.

LEOPOLDO LUGONES MUSEUM
Avenida H. Yrigoyen 645, Córdoba
Collections illustrating life and work of the writer, L. Lugones, in the family home. Household equipment of the colonial period. Paintings.
Tu.-Su. 9-12.

MUSEUM OF FINE ARTS
Plaza Centenario, Córdoba
Argentine and foreign paintings, sculptures, drawings and engravings.
Daily ex. M. 9-12, 3-6.

PROVINCIAL MUSEUM
Cabildo, Plaza San Martin, Córdoba
Natural history exhibits.
Daily ex. M. 9-12, 3-6.

CORRIENTES

COLONIAL, HISTORICAL AND FINE ARTS MUSEUM
Calle 9 de Julio No. 1044, Corrientes
Pictorial and period exhibits relating to the province. Architectural items from demolished 18th-19th century buildings. Religious art.
Tu.-Su. 3-7.

FATHER JOSÉ DE LA QUINTANA MUSEUM
Dirección de Cultural, Corrientes
In former Franciscan monastery. Collections illustrating life and work of Father José.
Tu.-Su. 3-7.

NATURAL HISTORY MUSEUM
Salta y San Martin, Corrientes
Regional geology, botany, zoology.
Tu.-Su. 3-7.

DOLORES

LOS LIBROS DEL SUR MUSEUM
Dolores
18th-19th century regional history. Furniture. Weapons. Memorabilia of 19th century revolutionaries. Plants and wildlife of the region.
Winter: M.-Sa. 10-12, 2-5; Su., public holidays 11-5.
Summer: M.-Sa. 10-12, 3-6.

EL PALOMAR D CASEROS

HISTORICAL MUSEUM
Casa de Caseros, El Palomar de Caseros
Collections illustrating the Battle of Caseros. Weapons. Uniforms. Documents.
M.-Sa. 9-12.

ENTRE RIOS

MARTINIANO LEGUIZAMÓN HISTORICAL MUSEUM
Calles Buenos Aires y Laprida, Urquiza 1214, Entre Rios
Local history. Military relics. Silver.
Tu.-Sa. 9-12, 4-7; Su. 9-12.

PROVINCIAL HISTORICAL MUSEUM
Rivadavia 226, Entre Rios
Archaeology, history and folklore of the province.
Tu.-Su. 8-12, 2-5.

PROVINCIAL MUSEUM
Urquiza 608, Entre Rios
Ethnographical material from the province. Pre-colonial art. Handicrafts.
Tu.-Su. 8-12, 2-5.

PROVINCIAL MUSEUM OF FINE ART
Rivadavia 77, Entre Rios
Paintings, sculpture by Argentinian artists.
Tu.-Su. 8-12, 2-5.

ESPERANZA

MUSEUM OF THE COLONIES
Intendencia Municipal, Esperanza
Collections illustrating the problems and achievements of the early European settlers of the Argentine. Furniture. Domestic equipment. Agricultural implements. Weapons. Horse-drawn vehicles.
Daily 9-12.30, 2.30-6.

FLORENCIA VARELA

BIRTHPLACE OF W. H. HUDSON
Florencia Varela, near Quilmes
Birthplace of the naturalist, W. H. Hudson (1841-1922), restored to its original appearance and containing collections illustrating his life and work.
Sa., Su., public holidays 1-4.30.

GAIMAN

MUSEUM OF THE WELSH COLONY
Gaiman, nr. Trelew
History of the Welsh community in Gaiman.
Daily 9-12.

GENERAL PAZ

RANCHOS HISTORICAL MUSEUM
General Paz
History of the former fortress town of Ranchos. Local history. Handicrafts. Weapons. Maps. Fauna of the region.
Tu., Th., Sa., Su. 2-5.

GODOY CRUZ

FERNANDO FADER MUNICIPAL MUSEUM OF FINE ART
Saenz Peña y Biritos, Godoy Cruz
19th-20th century paintings, drawings, sculpture by Argentinian artists.
Tu.-Su. 9-12, 3-6.

GUALEGUAYCHÚ

ANDRADE HOUSE-MUSEUM
Gualeguaychú
In former house of the poet, Olegario V. Andrade. Collection illustrating his life and work. Family furniture.
Tu.-Su. 9-12.

MAGNASCO MUSEUM OF FINE ART
Camila Nieves 78, Gualeguaychú
19th-20th century paintings, sculpture by Argentinian artists.
Tu.-F. 8-12, 3-6; Su. 8-12.

JESUS MARIA

JESUIT MUSEUM
Convento de San Isidro, Jesus Maria
Collections illustrating history and work of the Society of Jesus. 17th-18th century furniture. Regional archaeology. Religious art. Handicrafts.
Daily 9-12.

LA PLATA

ALMAFUERTE MUSEUM
Calle 68, No. 530, La Plata
Local history. Archaeology. Handicrafts.
M.-F. 2-6.

LA PLATA MUSEUM OF NATURAL SCIENCES
Paseo del Bosque, La Plata
Anthropology. Archaeology. Botany. Geology. Mineralogy. Comprehensive palaeontological collection, including Patagonian mammalia. Ethnographical collections include human skulls, mummies and prehistoric implements. Reconstructed skeletons of giant prehistoric animals.
Daily ex. public holidays 2-6.

POLICE MUSEUM
Calle 54, No. 393, La Plata
History of the police and of the methods used by criminals.
M.-Sa. 2-6.

PROVINCIAL MUSEUM OF FINE ART
Calle 51, No. 525, La Plata
Paintings, sculpture by Argentinian artists.
Tu.-Su. 2-8.

DARDO ROCHA MUSEUM
Calle 50, No. 933, La Plata
In former home of Dr. Dardo Rocha, with his furniture, library, art collection, personal possessions and correspondence.
Winter: M.-Sa. 9-12, 2-5; Su., public holidays 9-12, 2-3.
Summer: M.-Sa. 9-12, 3-6; Su., public holidays 9-12, 3-6.

LA RIOJA

INCA-HUASI ARCHAEOLOGICAL MUSEUM
Calle Juan B. Alberdi 650, La Rioja
Collections illustrating prehistory of N. E. Argentina. Religious art. Regional history. Spurs.
Apr.-Nov., M.-F. 9.15-1; Sa., Su., public holidays 10-12.
Dec.-Mar., M.-F. 9-1, 5-7; Sa., Su., public holidays 10-12.

PROVINCIAL HISTORICAL MUSEUM
Calle Adolfo Davila 85, La Rioja
History of the province from the colonial period onwards. Paintings. Portraits. Silver. Furniture. Documents.
M.-F. 9-1, 5-7.

LAS HERAS

MUSEUM OF FINE ART
San Miguel y Rivadavia, Las Heras
19th-20th century paintings, graphics by S. American, especially Argentinian, artists.
Tu.-Su. 10-12, 3-6.

LOMAS DE ZÁMORA

AMERICAN MUSEUM OF ANTHROPOLOGY, HISTORY, NUMISMATICS AND NATURAL SCIENCE
Manuel Castro 254, Lomas de Zámora
Geology, botany, zoology and anthropology of S. America, especially Argentina. History of Argentina.
M., W., Th. 9-12; Su. 2-6.

LOSA CORRAL

FERNANDO FADER HOUSE-MUSEUM
Losa Corral
Former home of the artist, F. Fader, with his library, furniture, art collections, and personal possessions.
Tu.-F. 9-12, 3-5.

LOS COCOS

MUSEUM
Hotel Gran Mansion El Desconso, Los Cocos, Cruz Chica
Imitation Roman statuary. Patriotic exhibits. Local history.
M.-Sa. 2-6.

LOS CORRALES

CREOLE MUSEUM
Avenida de Los Corrales 6476, Los Corrales
History of cattle-ranching in the Argentine. Equipment. Weapons. Paintings.
Sa. 9-12.

LÚJAN

MUSEUM OF FINE ART
Parque Ameghino La Cupula, San Martin y Lavalle, Lújan
Paintings, sculpture, graphics by Argentinian artists.
W.-Su. 12.30-5.

TRANSPORT MUSEUM
Avenida Nuestra Senõra, Lújan
History of Argentine transport from pre-Conquest times to the present day.
W.-Su. 12.30-5.

ENRIQUE UDSONDO MUSEUM OF HISTORY AND THE COLONIAL PERIOD
Lavalleja 917, Lújan
In former prison (18th century) in which many leading Argentinians were incarcerated. Furniture. Jewellery. Goldsmith's work. Portraits. Horse-drawn vehicles. Early motor cars. The aeroplane, 'Plusultra' and the first locomotive to run in Argentina.
Winter: M.-Sa. 12-5; Su., public holidays 10-5. Summer: M.-Sa. 12.30-5.30; Su., public holidays 10-6.

MAR DEL PLATA

MUSEUM OF FINE ART
Correo Central, Mar del Plata
19th-20th century paintings, sculpture by Argentinian artists.
Tu.-Su. 2-5.

NATURAL HISTORY MUSEUM
Mar del Plata
Palaeontology. Zoology.
Tu.-Su. 2-5.

MAYOR DRUMMOND

E. GUIÑAZÚ MUSEUM
Lujan de Cuyo, San Martin 3651, Mayor Drummond
Local history. Handicrafts.
Tu.-F. 9-12, 2-5; Sa., Su. 9-12.

MENDOZA

MOYANO MUSEUM OF NATURAL HISTORY
Calle Belgrano, Mendoza
Argentine plants and animals. Some Colonial exhibits. Palaeontology. Anthropology. Archaeology. Geology. Folklore.
Daily 8-12, 3-7.

MUSEUM OF THE ANCIENT PROVINCE
Montividea 544, Mendoza
In former Governor's residence. 19th century furniture. Paintings by Argentinian artists. Coins. Weapons.
Daily 8-12.

MUSEUM OF MODERN ART
Municipalidad de la Ciudad de Mendoza, Mendoza
20th century paintings, drawings, graphics by S. American, especially Argentinian artists.
Daily 8-12.

SAN MARTIN HISTORICAL MUSEUM
R. E. de San Martin 1843, Mendoza
Collections illustrating 19th-20th century history of the province, especially struggle for national independence.
Daily 8-12, 3-7.

MORENO

ALMANCIA ALCORTA MUNICIPAL HISTORICAL MUSEUM
Diagonal Coleta Palacio, Moreno
History of Moreno and district.
Tu.-Su. 9.30-11, 2.30-5.30.

MUSEUM OF THE PLASTIC ARTS
Joly y Núñez, Moreno
Sculpture, paintings by Argentinian artists.
M.-F. 8-6.

MORÓN

GENERAL SAN MARTIN MUSEUM OF HISTORY AND ART
Sarmiento y Casullo, Morón
Religious paintings and sculpture. Miniatures. Porcelain. Millstones. Coins. Archaeological collection of Peruvian material.
Summer: Tu.-F. 8-12, 3.30-7.30; Sa., Su. 3.30-7.30. Winter: Tu.-F. 8-12, 2.30-6.30; Sa., Su. 2.30-6.30.

DOMINGO VITTORIA MUSEUM
Calles José M. Torres y Salvador del Carril, Morón
In Vittoria's former home and studio. Collections illustrating his life and work.
Daily 9-12, 3-5.

OLAVARRIA

DÁMASO ARCE ETHNOGRAPHICAL MUSEUM
Olavarria
Collections illustrating the cultural history of the region.
Tu.-Su. 2-5.

PARANÁ

HISTORICAL MUSEUM
Calle Buenos Aires y Laprida, Paraná
History. Folklore. Archives. Numismatics.
Daily 9-12, 3-6.

DR. PEDRO MARTINEZ MUSEUM OF FINE ART
Laprida 333, Paraná
19th-20th century paintings, drawings, sculpture, graphics by Argentinian and European artists.
Daily 9-12, 3-6.

PIGÜÉ

REGIONAL MUSEUM
Parque Provincial, Pigüé
Pre-colonial art. Material illustrating life in the colonial period. Revolutions of the 1890s.
M.-Sa. 2-7; Su. 12-8.

POSTA DE SINSACATE

MUSEUM OF RURAL LIFE
Posta de Sinsacate
Collections illustrating 18th-19th century rural life in the region. Furniture. Tools. Agricultural implements. Handicrafts.
Daily 9-12, 2-5.

QUILMES

MUSEUM OF THE HISTORY OF TRANSPORT
Quilmes
Collections illustrating development of road, rail and air transport in Argentina.
M., Th. 10-12; Tu., W. 2-4.

RAFAELA

MUNICIPAL MUSEUM OF FINE ART
San Martin 555, Rafaela
19th-20th century paintings, drawings by Argentinian artists.
Tu.-Su. 9-12, 3-5.

ROSARIO

A. GALLARDO MUSEUM OF NATURAL SCIENCES
Moreno 965, Rosario
Geology, palaeontology, botany and zoology of Argentina.
Tu.-Su. 3-6.

MUNICIPAL MUSEUM
Santa Fé 748, Rosario
Paintings by Goya, El Greco, David, Boucher, Van Dyck, Ribera. Antique glass, ivories, ceramics. 16th-18th century furniture. Silver.
Tu.-Su. 3-6.

MUSEUM OF FINE ARTS
Avenida Pellegrini 2202, Rosario
Paintings include works by El Greco, Goya, Titian, José de Ribera. European and American paintings and sculpture from 16th century to the present day.
W.-Sa. 4-7; Su. and holidays 10-12, 4-7.

MUSEUM OF MARINE BIOLOGY
Parque Leandro Alem, Rosario
Marine biology of S. America, especially Argentina.
Tu.-Su. 3-6.

PROVINCIAL HISTORICAL MUSEUM
Parque Independencia, Rosario
Local and national history collections. Spanish American art of the colonial period. Silver. Woodcarving. Furniture. Textiles. Feather-work. Folklore. Coins. Porcelain.
Tu., Th., Sa., Su. 3-6.

DR. BARTOLOMÉ VASALIO MUSEUM
Avenida Cordoba 501, Rosario
Colonial art. Religious art. Handicrafts.
Sa., Su., public holidays 2-5.

SALLIQUELÓ

REGIONAL HISTORICAL MUSEUM
Salliqueló
History and archaeology of the region.
Winter: M.-F. 2-7; Sa., Su., public holidays 2-8. Summer: M.-Sa. 9-12, 5-8; Su., public holidays 9-12.

SALTA

HOUSE OF PRESIDENT JOSÉ E. URIBURU
Caseros 421, Salta
House (1773). Uriburu family home. History and relics of the War of Independence. Weapons. Collections illustrating career of General Arenales. Archaeology of N. E. Argentina. Coins.
Daily 9-12, 3.30-7.30.

NORTHERN HISTORICAL MUSEUM
Cabildo de Salta, Calle Caseros, Salta
Regional history and archaeology. Paintings. Uniforms. 18th-19th century religious art. Folk art. Handicrafts. Coins. Medals. Horse-drawn vehicles.
Tu.-Su. 12.30-7.

PROVINCIAL MUSEUM
Caseros 712, Salta
Ethnography. Archaeology. Pre-Colonial art.
Tu.-Su. 12.30-7.

JUAN DE TEJEDA MUSEUM OF ART
Salta
In former Carmelite monastery. Religious art. Paintings, goldsmiths' work, paintings of the colonial period.
Tu.-Su. 9-2.

SAMAY HUASI

REGIONAL MUSEUM "MIS MONTAÑAS"
Samay Huasi, La Rioja Province
In house formerly belonging to the writer and statesman, Joáquin V. Gonzalez. Collections illustrating his life and work. Paintings, sculpture illustrating local subjects. Flora, fauna, archaeology and geology of the province. Dioramas.
Daily 8-12, 2-6.

SAN ANTONIO DE ARECO

RICARDO GUIRALDES GAUCHO MUSEUM
San Antonio de Areco
In typical late 19th century estancia. Creole history. Works of Guiraldes, writer who described Gaucho life. 18th century furniture, religious art. Clothing. Tools. Weapons. Handicrafts.
Tu.-Su. 9.30-11, 2.30-5.30.

SAN CARLOS DE BARILOCHE

DR. FRANCISCO MORENO PATAGONIAN MUSEUM
Centro Civico, San Carlos de Bariloche
History of Patagonia, especially the conquest and religious conversion. Weapons. Paintings. Life and work of Dr. Moreno. Indian ethnography. Regional plants, wildlife, geology.
Summer: daily 10-12, 3-6. Winter: W., F., Su., 10-12, 2-5.

GENERAL VINTTER MUSEUM
Fuerte General Roca, San Carlos de Bariloche
Military history. Collections illustrating career of General Vintter.
On request.

SAN ISIDRO

BRIGADIER GENERAL JUAN MARTIN DE PUEYRREDÓN MUSEUM
Saenz Peña y Rivera Indalle, San Isidro
In former-home of General Martin (d.1850). His furniture, paintings, documents, weapons, illustrating the life and taste of the period.
Tu., Th., Sa., Su. 2-6.

SAN JOSÉ

REGIONAL HISTORICAL MUSEUM
Urquiza 378, San José
Regional history. Agricultural implements. Handicrafts. Weapons. Horse-drawn vehicles. Early cars. Religious art.
Winter: Tu.-Su. 8-12, 2-5.30; Summer: Tu.-Sa. 3-7.

REGIONAL MUSEUM
Palacio San José, San José
Former palace of General Urquiza. Paintings of Urquiza's battles. Military relics. Furniture. Personal possessions.
Daily 9-6.

SAN JUAN

INCA HOUSE MUSEUM
San Juan
Indian skulls. Fine collection of funerary urns, and "pregnant pots" or jars thought to belong to the Florescent Era, 300 B.C./A.D. 400.
Tu.-Su. 3-6.

SAN JUSTO

MUSEUM OF VISUAL ARTS
9 de Julio, San Justo
Paintings. Sculpture. Religious art.
Daily 8-12, 3-6.

SAN MARTIN

JOSÉ HERNÁNDEZ-CHACRA DE PUEYRREDÓN MUSEUM
San Martin
Birthplace of the poet, J. H.-C. de Pueyrredón (1806), furnished to illustrate the life of a rural family of the period.
Winter: Sa., Su. 2-5. Summer: Sa., Su. 3-6.

SAN MARTIN (JUJUY)

ROOM OF HISTORIC FLAGS
Government House, Entre Gorriti y Sarmiento, San Martin (Jujuy)
Flags illustrating the military campaigns, battles and the units involved. Collections illustrating struggle for independence.
Daily 8-12, 4-6.

SAN MIGUEL DE TUCUMÁN

MUSEUM OF THE HISTORIC HOUSE OF THE INDEPENDENCE
Calle Congreso 151, San Miguel de Tucumán
Meeting place of the congress which declared National Independence (1816). Portrait of the Congress. Furniture. Historical relics.
Daily 8-6.

SAN NICOLAS DE LOS ARROYOS

HOUSE OF THE AGREEMENT (CASA DEL ACUERDO) MUSEUM
San Nicholas de los Arroyos
House in which General de Urquiza secured agreement between the provincial governors (1852). Display illustrating the event and its background.
Tu.-Su. 2-6.

SAN RAFAEL

MUSEUM OF FINE ART
B. de Irigoyen 138, San Rafael
19th-20th century paintings, graphics, sculpture by Argentinian, especially regional, artists.
Daily 9-12, 3-7.

SAN SALVADOR

JUJUY HISTORICAL MUSEUM
Lavalle 256, San Salvador
House of the colonial period. Regional history. Religious art. Archaeology. Handicrafts, especially silver.
Daily 8-12, 4-7.

SANTA FÉ

ROSA GALISTEO DE RODRIGUEZ MUSEUM OF FINE ARTS
Calle General Lopez, Santa Fé
Exhibitions of work by local painters. Contemporary Argentine and foreign art.
Tu.-Su. 10-12, 4-7.

MUSEUM OF ETHNOGRAPHY
San Martin 1498, Santa Fé
Handicrafts, folk art of the region.
Tu.-Su. 10-12, 4-7.

NATURAL HISTORY MUSEUM
Moreno No. 2557, Santa Fé
Botany. Zoology. Flora and fauna of Argentina.
Tu.-Su. 10-12, 4-7.

PROVINCIAL MUSEUM OF HISTORY
San Martin 1480, Santa Fé
Local history collections. 17th-18th century woodcarvings, paintings. 19th century primitive paintings by Argentinian artist. Silver.
Tu.-Su. 10-12, 4-7.

SANTIAGO DEL ESTERO

MUSEUM OF FINE ART
Independencia 222, Santiago del Estero
19th-20th century paintings, drawings, graphics by Argentinian artists.
May-Sept., Tu.-F. 9-12, 3-6. Oct.-Apr., M.-F. 8-1.

PROVINCIAL HISTORICAL MUSEUM
Urquiza 354, Santiago del Estero
Folk art. Handicrafts, especially silver, leather, textiles. History of the province.
May-Sept., Tu.-F. 9-12, 3-6. Oct.-Apr., M.-F. 8-1.

WAGNER ARCHAEOLOGICAL MUSEUM
Rivadavia esquina Cordoba, Santiago del Estero
Archaeological finds of the Chaco-Santiagueno culture and finds of later cultures. Ceramics. Musical instruments. Ceremonial objects.
May-Sept., Tu.-F. 9-12, 3-6; Oct.-Apr., M.-F. 8-1.

TANDIL

MUNICIPAL MUSEUM OF FINE ARTS
Chacubuco 357, Tandil
Argentinian paintings of the Classic, Impressionist, Cubist and Modern schools.
Tu.-Sa. 9-2, 4-6; Su. 9-2.

TAPELQUÉ

MUSEUM OF CULTURE
Tapelqué
Regional history. Folk art. Religious art.
Winter: M.-Sa. 1-7; Su., public holidays 10-12, 2-6. Summer: M.-Sa. 9-12, 5-8; Su., public holidays 9-12.

TIGRE

MUSEUM OF THE RECONQUEST
Tigre, nr. Buenos Aires
Story of the reconquest of Buenos Aires from the British. Relics and souvenirs.
M.-Sa. 9-12, 1-4; Su., public holidays 10-4.

NAVAL MUSEUM
Tigre, nr. Buenos Aires
Models of ships. Navigational instruments. Flags and banners. Paintings of naval battles. History of Argentine Navy.
Daily ex. M. 8-6.

TILCARA

ARCHAEOLOGICAL MUSEUM
Calle Belgrano, Tilcara
Archaeological and ethnographical material from N. E. Argentina, and from Chile, Peru and Bolivia. Menhirs. Petroglyphs. Pottery.
Daily 8-12, 2.30-6.

TRENQUE LAUQUEN

PROVINCIAL MUSEUM
Trenque Lauquen
Provincial history, art. Handicrafts.
Winter: daily 1.30-5.30. Summer: daily 9-12, 3-6.

REGIONAL HISTORICAL MUSEUM
Almafuerte 150, Trenque Lauquen
Aboriginal material. Collections illustrating wars against the Indians and life of early settlers. Natural history. Archaeology.
Tu.-Su. 1.30-5.

TUCUMÁN

BISHOP COLOMBRES' HOUSE
Parque 9 de Julio, Tucumán
Home of Bishop Colombres, who introduced the sugar cane to Tucumán in the early 19th century, and containing his first crude attempt at a pressing machine. The back garden contains a gigantic steam-press imported from France in 1883. Educational history. Memorabilia of Bishop Colombres.
Tu.-Su. 8-12, 3-5.

MUSEUM OF ANTHROPOLOGY
Buenos Aires 260, Tucumán
Anthropological collections covering the provinces of Argentina.
Tu.-Su. 3-5.

MUSEUM OF ARGENTINE FOLKLORE AND HANDICRAFTS
24 de septiembre 565, Tucumán
Pre-colonial art. 19th-20th century folk art, handicrafts, costumes.
Tu.-Su. 9-12, 3-5.

MUSEUM OF FINE ART
Avenida Sarmiento 655, Tucumán
19th-20th century paintings, drawings, sculpture by Argentinian artists.
Tu.-Su. 3-5.

MUSEUM OF HISTORY: HOUSE OF INDEPENDENCE
Calle Congreso 141, Tucumán
Contains room where, in 1816, the Congress of the United Provinces of Rio de la Plata met to draft and proclaim Argentina's Declaration of Independence. Chair used by President of the Congress. Portraits. 17th-18th century furniture. Seals and mementoes of the signing of the Act of Independence.
Daily 8-12, 3-6.

MUSEUM OF THE MIGUEL LILLO INSTITUTE
Miguel Lillo 205, Tucumán
Animals and insects. Herbarium. Original edition of Von Humboldt's travels in Spanish America.
Tu.-Su. 9-12, 3-5.

MUSEUM OF NATURAL HISTORY AND ANTHROPOLOGY
Miguel Lillo y San Lorenzo, Tucumán
Natural history, anthropology of Argentina.
Tu.-Su. 9-12, 3-5.

VICENTE LOPEZ

MUSEUM OF FINE ART
Vicente Lopez
Art collection in private house. Paintings by Argentinian artists.
By appointment.

Australia

A fairly high proportion of Australian museums have a certain unsophisticated quality about them, strongly reminiscent of the American mid-West. One, more forthright than the average, describes itself, in the best eighteenth-century fashion, as a Museum of Wonders, with the charmingly hotch-potch collection of old guns, vases, faded photographs, shells and stuffed birds that delights children and other unspoilt people and brings dismay to the heart of the international museum world. These small-town Australian museums have some remarkable Wonders in their care - knuckledusters made from the metal tips of pearl-divers' boots, an 80-year-old vacuum cleaner, the only dinosaur egg found in Australia, an early pill-making machine, the skeleton of a whale known as Tom, and 'the anatomy of the platypus'. They include 'old-world bedrooms' and they are liable to go for such arresting titles as 'Land of the Beadies History House Museum'.

Australian museums, and presumably their visitors, are unique in their extraordinary love of bottles. Taking the country as a whole, at least one museum in six announces that it has a bottle collection. A more ambitious establishment than most is called Frankie's Bottle Bonanza, another merely claims that it has a million bottles, and a third beats all its rivals by pointing out that the museum itself is constructed of bottles. Shell museums are also popular.

It is not easy to gather by correspondence what many of the smaller art galleries, particularly in Adelaide, contain, because thay have a way of describing their collections as merely 'art', in the same undiscriminating way as Americans call whisky just 'Scotch', apparently unaware that there are different kinds of Scotch and that they taste different. One must emphasise, on the other hand, that the major Australian cities have highly professional museums which give visitors an excellent opportunity to look at their national traditions and achievements in their world context, and which could not be described by even the most hostile and prejudiced observer as unsophisticated. One thinks, for instance, of the excellent displays illustrating the culture of the aborigines, of the exhibits intended to give a balanced picture of the early settlement of the continent, and of the collections of European art in Sydney and Melbourne. It would be difficult for Australian museums to be dull, reflecting as they do the kind of population-mix which is illustrated by the Chinese Joss House Museum, by the Mosque restored as a memorial to pioneer Afghan cameldrivers, and by Albany Old Jail, where employers hired convicts to work for them.

ADELAIDE

ADELAIDE POTTERS CLUB
15 Liston Street, Parkside, Adelaide, South Australia
Pottery. Paintings.
M.-F. 11-4.

APPLIED SCIENCE MUSEUM
South Australia Institute of Technology, North Terrace, Adelaide, South Australia 2601
Anatomy. Nutrition. Ethnology.
Daily 9-5; Su. 2-5. Public holidays 10-4.30. Closed Christmas Day and Good F.

ART GALLERY OF SOUTH AUSTRALIA
North Terrace, Adelaide, South Australia 5000
19th-20th century paintings, drawings and prints, and sculpture by Australian artists. Works by European artists from the 15th century onwards (including St. Martin and St. Nicholas of Tours by the Master of the Uttenheim Altarpiece). European and Asian (particularly Thai) ceramics. Silver. Furniture. Weapons and armour. Coins and medals.
M.-Sa. 10-5; Su. 2-5. Closed Christmas Day and Good F.

AURORA GALLERY
64a Semaphore Road, Semaphore, Adelaide, South Australia
Paintings, sculpture by Australian artists.
W.-F. 12-3; Sa., Su. 2-5.

BONYTHON GALLERY
88 Jerningham Street, North Adelaide, South Australia
Paintings, prints by Australian artists.
Tu.-Sa. 11-6.

BOTANIC MUSEUM
Adelaide, South Australia
Economic plants and their products. Fruits and seeds (carpological collection). Botany. Practical horticulture.
Daily 9-4.

CAPTAIN STURT'S HOUSE
Grange, Adelaide, South Australia
Local history.
W.-Su. and public holidays, 1-5.

CONTEMPORARY ART SOCIETY
14 Porter Street, Parkside, Adelaide, South Australia
Contemporary art, especially of Australia.
W.-Su. 2-6.

FINCHLEY CRAFT WORKSHOP
59 Shakespeare Avenue, Magill, Adelaide, South Australia
Paintings. Crafts.
Daily ex. Tu. morning, 10-4.30; Su. 11-5.

GALLERY CURIO
177 O'Connell Street, North Adelaide, South Australia
Art collections.
W. 5-8; Sa. 12-5; Su. 2-5.

GALLERY 45
45 George Street, Norwood, Adelaide, South Australia
Art collections.
Tu.-F. 11-5.30; Sa. 9-2; Su. 2-5.

GILBERTON GALLERY
2-4 Walkerville Terrace, Gilberton, Adelaide, South Australia
Art collections.
M.-F. 10-5.30; Su. 2-5.30.

GLENELG HISTORICAL MUSEUM
Esplanade, Glenelg, Adelaide, South Australia
Historical collections.
M.-F. 9.30-3.30; Sa. 9.30-4; Su. 11-5.

HABITAT GALLERY
75 Melbourne Street, North Adelaide, South Australia
Art collections.
M.-F. 9.30-5; Sa. 9.30-12.

KING WILLIAM STREET GALLERY
126 King William Road, Goodwood, Adelaide, South Australia
Art collections.
M.-F. 10-5.30; Sa. 10-12.30.

KINGSTON HOUSE GALLERY
Kingston Park, Adelaide, South Australia
Art collections.
Daily 9-6.

LIDUMS ART GALLERY
The Common, Beaumont, Adelaide, South Australia
Art collections.
M.-Sa. 11-6; Su. and public holidays 1-5.

LLEWELLYN GALLERY
16 Swift Street, Dulwich, Adelaide, South Australia
Art collections.
M.-Sa. 11-6.

LOMBARD STREET GALLERY
Lombard Street, North Adelaide, South Australia
Art collections.
Sa. 11-6; Su. 2-5.

MAX ADAMS GALLERY
113 Melbourne Street, North Adelaide, South Australia
Art collections.
M.-F. 11-5.30; Sa. 10-12.

MUSEUM OF NATURAL HISTORY
North Terrace, Adelaide, South Australia
Australian fauna and ethnology.
M.-Sa. 10-5; Su. and public holidays 2-5.

NAUTICAL MUSEUM
135 St. Vincent Street, Port Adelaide, South Australia
Nautical collections. Ships models. Maps.
W. 10.30-4; Sa. 10-12; Su. 2-4.

OFF THE BEATEN TRACK GALLERY
16 Sydenham Road, Norwood, Adelaide, South Australia
Art collections.
Tu.-Sa. 2-5.

OSBORNE ART GALLERY
13 Leigh Street, Adelaide, South Australia
Art collections.
M.-F. 10-5.30.

RAILWAY MUSEUM
Railway Terrace, Mile End South, Adelaide, South Australia
History of the railways in Australia. Rolling stock, equipment.
1st and 3rd Su. in month, 2-5.

ROYAL SOUTH AUSTRALIAN SOCIETY OF ARTS GALLERY
Institute Building, North Terrace, Adelaide, South Australia
Paintings, sculpture, drawings, prints by Australian and European artists.
M.-Sa. 10-5.

SHELL MUSEUM
47 Malwa Street, Osborne, Adelaide, South Australia
Shell collection.
M.-Sa. 10-5.

THE SOUTH AUSTRALIAN MUSEUM
North Terrace, Adelaide, South Australia
Anthropology. Vertebrates and invertebrates. Molluscs. Palaeontology. Mineral collections, including australites. Archaeology. Aboriginal material.
M.-Sa., holidays, 10-5; Su. 2-5. Closed Good F. and Christmas Day.

THORNGATE GALLERY
Basement, 57 Pulteney Street, Adelaide, South Australia
Art collections.
M.-F. 9-5.30; Sa. 9-12.

WALKERVILLE GALLERY
111 Walkerville Terrace, Walkerville, Adelaide, South Australia
Art collections.
M.-F. 9-5.30.

ADVANCETOWN

PIONEER HOUSE
Numinbah Valley Road, Advancetown, Gold Coast, Queensland
Iron-bark cottage, reconstruction of original pioneer house. Relics of pioneer days.
Daily 10-4.30.

ALBANY

ALBANY OLD JAIL
Stirling Terrace, Albany, Western Australia
Originally the convict hiring depot (1851-1905). Cells and warders' quarters. Aboriginal weapons and artifacts. Maritime history. Armed Services room. History of Albany.
W., Su. 2-4.15.

THE OLD FARM
Strawberry Hill, Albany, Western Australia
Where farming was first carried out in Western Australia. Restored farm buildings.
Daily 2-5.

PATRICK TAYLOR COTTAGE MUSEUM
31 Duke Street, Albany, Western Australia
Cottage (c.1832). Period furniture. Relics of early Albany. Barrett collection of silver. Coins of Henry VIII, George II, III and IV. Kitchenware.
Daily 2-4.30. Evenings by appointment (tel: 41376).

ALBURY

MUSEUM OF APPLIED ARTS AND SCIENCES, ALBURY BRANCH
Wodonga Place, Albury, New South Wales 2640
Decorative arts. Science. Gold finds. Communications. 16th century armour. Early Australian coinage. Iron treasure chest.
Daily except W. 10-5; Su. 2-5. Closed Christmas Day and Good F.

ARMIDALE

ART GALLERY
Armidale, New South Wales
Paintings. Sculpture, graphic arts by Australian and European artists.
Daily ex. Sa. 8.30-5.30; Sa. 8.30-12.

ARMIDALE FOLK MUSEUM
Armidale, New South Wales
Aboriginal culture. Pastoral life. Squatting life in N.S.W. since the 1830s. Mining life. Agriculture. Firearms. Clothing. Home crafts. Laundry equipment. Victorian parlour, bedroom and kitchen. Transport and communication section includes bullock dray, horse drays, drag, wool waggon, wheelwright's implements. Commercial life is illustrated by early typewriters, copy presses, letter-books, invoices, shop scales, cash registers, mechanical change-carrier.
Daily 2-5 and also 7.30-8.30 p.m. (except Su.); Sa. 9.30-12 and 7.30-8.30.

ARMIDALE MUSEUM OF EDUCATION
Teachers' College, Mossman Street, Armidale, New South Wales
Classroom furnished as in the 1880s. Photographs of schools and school life. School textbooks. Teaching aids. Children's work.
By arrangement with the College Office between 9 and 5 during normal College terms.

ATHERTON

FRANKIE'S BOTTLE BONANZA
1 Cook Street, Atherton, Cairns Region, Queensland
Late 19th century and early 20th century bottles.
Daily 10-5.

BALLARAT

BALLARAT ART GALLERY
40 Lydiard Street North, Ballarat, Victoria 3350
Australian painting from 1840 to present day. Examples of English Victorian painting from the Royal Academy, brought to Australia in the 1880s when the Gallery opened. Australian drawings and prints of the same period. European porcelain, silver and glass. English furniture, 1780-1880. Medieval manuscripts.
M.-F. 10.30-4.30; Sa. 11-4.30; Su. 2-4.30.

BALLARAT HISTORICAL MUSEUM
Barkly Street, Ballarat, Victoria
Local history.
Mon.-Sat. 10-5.

MONTROSE COTTAGE AND EUREKA MILITARY MUSEUM
Ballarat, Victoria 3350
Authentic mining cottage. Museum of Eureka stockade uniforms and equipment.
Daily ex. F. 10-4.30.

SOVEREIGN HILL HISTORICAL PARK
P.O. Box 294, Ballarat, Victoria 3350
Open-air Museum depicting a goldmining township, 1851-1860. Reconstruction of diggings; colonial public buildings; commercial centre; company quartz mine with underground workings.
Daily 10-5.

BATHURST

ART GALLERY
Bathurst, New South Wales
Paintings by N.S.W. artists.
M.-F. 10-12, 2-5. Sat. 10-1.

FOLK MUSEUM
Macquairie House, 1 George Street, Bathurst, New South Wales
Relics of the pioneering days of the district. Early farm and household implements. Tools and equipment used in the gold rush era. Gold scales and specimens. Clothing, paintings, photographs and personal items of the early settlers. Aboriginal artifacts and weapons. Cottage (1817) - "Government House" - with furniture and utensils of the early pioneering era.
Weekdays 2-5; Sa. 10-12; Su. 2.30-5. Holidays 2.30-5. Closed Christmas Day, Good F. and Anzac Day.

MUSEUM OF APPLIED ARTS AND SCIENCES
William Street, Bathurst, New South Wales
Applied arts and sciences. Original Cobb & Co. coach. Engineering. Porcelain. Pottery. Glassware. Mechanical and musical instruments. Numismatics. Mineral industries of the Bathurst area.
Tu., W. and F. 2-5. Sa., Su. and public holidays, 2-5. Closed M., Th., Christmas Day and Good F.

THE REGIONAL GALLERY
Civic Centre, Bathurst, New South Wales
Collections of paintings, many by Australian artists, acquired by the City of Bathurst.
M.-F. 8.30-4.30; Sa. 9.30-12.30.

BATTERY POINT

VAN DIEMEN'S LAND MEMORIAL FOLK MUSEUM
'Narryna', 103 Hampden Road, Battery Point, Tasmania 7000
House (1836). Furniture. China. Glass. Silver. Paintings. Historical records of the early sailing ships. Costumes and parasols.
Tu.-F. 10-5; Sa., Su. 2-5. Jan.-Mar., also M. 10-5, Tu.-Th. 7.30-9.30 p.m. Closed mid. July-Aug., also Christmas Day, Good F. and Anzac Day.

BEECHWORTH

BURKE MEMORIAL MUSEUM
Loch Street, Beechworth 3747, Victoria
Early gold-rush souvenirs, including tools, photographs and newspapers. Items relating to Ned Kelly and his gang, including the dock in which he stood (1870), and a replica of his armour, weighing 95 lbs. The Chinese community at Beechworth is represented by relics of their Joss House. Pair of boots belonging to the dwarf, General Tom Thumb, who came to Beechworth in 1870. Stuffed animals and birds. Aboriginal weapons exhibited at the Paris Convention, 1879. Gem stones found in the area. Guns and relics of the Boer War. Silver.
Afternoons: 1.30-4.30. Mornings by appointment. Public Holidays 10-5.

BEGA

BEGA VALLEY HISTORICAL MUSEUM
49 Church Street, Bega, New South Wales
Early pioneering relics. History of Bega. Aboriginal artifacts.
M.-F. 11-4; Sa. 10-12.

BELAIR

OLD GOVERNMENT HOUSE
National Park, Belair, South Australia
Local history.
W.-Su. and public holidays, 1-4.30.

BELLAMBI

STARR SHELL MUSEUM
159 Rothery Road, Bellambi, New South Wales
Shell collection.
Tu.-Th., Sa., Su. 10-4.

BENALLA

BENALLA ART GALLERY
Benalla Memorial Hall, Benalla, Victoria 3672
Modern paintings by Australian artists.
M.-F. 2-5; W. evening, 7-9; Sa. 10-12.

PIONEERS MUSEUM
16 Mair Street, Benalla, Victoria 3672
Aboriginal artifacts. Uniforms. Antique silver and china. Period clothing and furniture. Coins. Stamps. Material relating to Ned Kelly. Pioneer relics. Photographs. Maps. Documents.
One afternoon a week, by appointment. Open daily at Easter and holiday times.

BENDIGO

BENDIGO ART GALLERY
View Street, Bendigo, Victoria
Australian paintings. Neptune Scott collection of French impressionists. 19th century European works by Courbet, Boudin, Harpignes, Corot, Sisley and Remond. 19th century sculpture. Etchings, wood cuts, lithographs and serigraphs. Ceramics. Porcelain, 1750 - early 1900s.
M.-F. 10-12.30, 1.30-5; Sa. 10-12; Su. and public holidays, 2.30-5. Closed Good F., Anzac Day, Christmas Day.

CENTRAL DEBORAH GOLD MINE
Bendigo, Victoria
Working gold mine, open to tourists.
Daily 8-5.

COBB & COMPANY HISTORICAL FOLK MUSEUM
Bendigo, Victoria
Carriages. Gold mining equipment. Tools.
M.-F. 10-6.

BERRIMA

MUSEUM OF BAKING
Wingcarribee Street, Berrima, New South Wales
In old Bakehouse. Ovens and bakery are restored. Old photographs of baking processes.
By appointment.

BEVERLEY

BEVERLEY AERONAUTICAL MUSEUM
Vincent Street, Beverley, Western Australia
History of aviation in Western Australia.
F. 2.30-4.30; Sa. 3-4; Su. 11-12, 2-4.30.

BEXLEY

LYDHAM HALL
Lydham Avenue, between Herbert and Clarence Streets, Bexley, New South Wales
Furnished rooms, 1870-1880. Photographs of early St. George district. Early clothing, lamps, china.
Sa., Su. 2-4.

BIRDWOOD

BIRDWOOD HILL MUSEUM
Birdwood, South Australia
Folk art. Pioneer relics.
Daily 9.15-5.

BLACKWOOD

HILLS KITCHEN GALLERY
Shiraz Court, Blackwood, South Australia
Art collections.
Daily 12-11.

BOGGABRI

HISTORICAL MUSEUM
Boggabri, New South Wales
History of the area.
By arrangement.

BOWEN

SHELL AND BOTTLE MUSEUM
Don River, via Bowen, Townsville Region, Queensland
Shells, bottles. Dolls. Lamps.
M., W., Th., Sa. 2-5.

BOWRAVILLE

FOLK MUSEUM
High Street, Bowraville, New South Wales
Exhibits depicting provincial life. Farm equipment. Pioneer cottage, re-erected inside museum. Paintings by local artists.
Su. 2-4. Extended hours during holiday periods.

BRADBURY

DAVAAR GALLERY
Longwood Road, Bradbury, South Australia
Art collections.
Tu.-Su. 10-8.

BRIDGEWATER

OLD MILL GALLERY
Bridgewater Institute, Bridgewater, South Australia
Art collections.
Tu.-F. 2.30-4.30; Sa. 1-5; Su. 10-5.

BRIGHT

BRIGHT AND DISTRICT HISTORICAL SOCIETY MUSEUM
c/o Shire Offices, Bright, Victoria 3741
Local history. Mining exhibits: models of dredges used in the valley; maps and charts showing location of gold mines; tools; illustrations of sluicing operations. Heavy machinery used in gold industry. Vehicles for transport and farming. Saddlery.
Variable according to time of year: displayed outside Museum.

BRISBANE

EARLY STREET
75 McIlwraith Avenue, Norman Park, Brisbane, Queensland 4000
Pioneer town with old pub, settlers' cottage, coach house and Aboriginal gunyah. Coaches, household and farming implements of the day.
Daily 2-5.

HIGH BARBAREE
109 Albany Creek Road, Aspley, Brisbane, Queensland 4000
Mid. 19th century house, furnished in period style. Coach house. Local history.
Su. 11-5.

MIEGUNYAH
31-35 Jordan Terrace, Bowden Hills, Brisbane, Queensland 4000
Home restored as memorial to the pioneer women of Queensland. Period furniture. Costumes. Utensils. Historic photographs. Aboriginal relics.
Tu. 10.30-3; Sa., Su. 10.30-4.30.

OLD COURT HOUSE
Cleveland, Brisbane, Queensland 4000
Building (1853), subsequently restored. China. Cooking utensils. Historical paintings and documents.
Su. 1.30-5.

ORMISTON HOUSE
Wellington Street, Ormiston, Brisbane, Queensland 4000
On site of Australia's first commercial sugar plantation. Original section of the house made from bricks baked on the property, cedar and hand-made nails.
Su. and public holidays, 10-5.

QUEENSLAND ABORIGINAL CREATIONS GALLERY
135-137 George Street, Brisbane, Queensland 4000
Aboriginal art.
M.-F. 9-4.30.

QUEENSLAND NATIONAL ART GALLERY AND MUSEUM
Gregory Terrace and Bowen Bridge Road, Brisbane, Queensland 4000
Australian paintings and drawings. European paintings and sculpture. Asian art. Wildlife. Aboriginal relics. Historic documents.
M.-Sa. 10-5; Su. 2-5.

REDBANK RAILWAY MUSEUM
Redbank, Brisbane, Queensland 4000
Open-air museum housing a variety of steam locomotives which ran on the Queensland railway system for more than a century.
Tu.-Su. 10-5.

REDLANDS MUSEUM
Cleveland Showgrounds, Cleveland, Brisbane, Queensland 4000
Agricultural implements and coaches of pioneer days.
W. 9-12.30.

ROYAL HISTORICAL SOCIETY OF QUEENSLAND MUSEUM
Newstead House, Newstead Park, Brisbane, Queensland 4000
House (1840). Paintings by Oscar Fristrom. Relics of shipwrecks. Photographs of aeroplanes. First passenger ticket issued by Qantas (1922). Washing machine of 1879. Period furniture and kitchen of 1846.
M.-F. 12-3.30; Su. 2-4.30.

SHELL BUNGALOW
58 Beaufort Place, Deception Bay, Brisbane, Queensland 4000
Collection of over 1 million shells from the Moreton Bay region.
Daily 10-5.

WOLSTON HOUSE
Wacol, Brisbane, Queensland 4000
Building (1852), of local freestone and hand-made bricks. Period furniture. Own butcher's shop and grain storage room.
Su. 1.30-5.

BROADBEACH

CASTLE OF YESTERYEAR
Nerang Road, Broadbeach, Gold Coast, Queensland
Australian antiques, including bottles, Aboriginal tools, household items, lamps, sewing machines and farm implements.
Daily 9-5.

BROKEN BAY

HENRY KENDALL'S COTTAGE
West Gosford, Broken Bay, New South Wales
Preserved as a memorial to the famous Australian poet. Houses a museum of local history.
On request.

BROKEN HILL

AFGHAN MOSQUE
Corner William Street and Racecourse Road, Broken Hill, New South Wales
Mosque restored as memorial to pioneer Afghan camel drivers who helped to open up the West Darling Region. Walking stick and vestments belonging to the Mullah. Stepping stones used by the faithful to reach the Mosque. Inner prayer room is carpeted and furnished with prayer rugs, texts and copies of the Koran.
Su. 2.30-4.

MUSEUM OF APPLIED ARTS AND SCIENCES
Technical College Building, Argent Street, Broken Hill, New South Wales
Geology and mineralogy of the area. Silver and silver coinage. Ceramics. Oriental art. Cloissoné work. Firearms. Lace.
M.-F. 10-5; Sa., Su., public holidays 2-5. Closed Christmas Day, Good F.

"PRO" HART'S ART GALLERY AND MUSEUM
108 Wyman Street, Broken Hill, New South Wales
Art collections. Local history.
M.-F. 10-5; Sa., Su. 2-5.

SILVERTON GAOL AND HISTORICAL MUSEUM
Silverton, nr. Broken Hill, New South Wales
Gaol buildings. Local history. Pioneer relics.
Daily 9.30-12, 1.30-3.

BROOME

MUSEUM OF FIREARMS
Police Station, Broome, Roebuck Bay, Western Australia 6725
Firearms. Chains. Handcuffs. Old type police batons. Knuckledusters made from the metal tips of boots belonging to the pearl divers. Material on the pearling riots.
At any time.

BRUNI ISLAND

BLIGH MUSEUM OF PACIFIC EXPLORATION
Adventure Bay, Bruni Island, Tasmania
Relics of the island's early days. Historical volumes on early voyages. Sketches by artists on these voyages, notably Webber's engravings of Cook's voyages - the Tasmanian Opossum and Tobin's water-colours of Adventure Bay done in 1792. Aboriginal artifacts. Material relating to explorers, including Fuchs, Hilary, Scott, Mawson and Amundsen.
Sept.-May Daily ex. W. 1.30-3.

BUDERIM

HOUSE OF TREASURES MUSEUM
Buderim, Sunshine Coast, Queensland
Furniture. Native relics of Australia and New Guinea. Oriental tapestries. Porcelain. English newspapers dating from 16th century.
Daily 9.30-4.

MOVIE MUSEUM
Burnett Street, Buderim, Sunshine Coast, Queensland
Early model film cameras in working order. Film projectors.
30-minute inspection and commentary is given, and short sequences of early films are shown.
M.-Sa. 9.30-5; Su. 2-5.

PIONEER COTTAGE
Ballanger Crescent, Buderim, Sunshine Coast, Queensland
Original home of pioneer settler, restored and furnished to display pioneer relics.
Daily 10-12, 2-4.

BUGALDIE

THE CEDARS MUSEUM
Coonabarabran - Baradine Road, Bugaldie, New South Wales
Geology of the district. 19th century bedroom, kitchen. Bottles. Bushman's camp. Machinery.
Sa. 2-5; Su. 10-5. Weekdays 9-5 by arrangement only.

BUNBURY

ART GALLERY
Prinsep Street, Bunbury, Western Australia
Works by Australian artists, including Albert Namitjira, Kathleen O'Connor, Hans Heysen and Marcus Clark. Collections relating to the town of Bunbury.
M.-F. 9-5; Sa. 9-12.

SHELL MUSEUM
108 Mangles Street, Bunbury 6230, Western Australia
Sea shells. Mineralogy. Antique bottles. Natural history. Cyp friendi. Local birds' eggs.
Afternoons and weekends.

BUNDARRA

ANDERSON'S BOTTLE COLLECTION
Muirhead Street, Bundarra, New South Wales
Reputed to be the largest bottle collection in Australia.
Daily 8-6, or by arrangement.

BURNIE

THE PIONEER VILLAGE MUSEUM
High Street, Burnie, Tasmania
Reconstructed street of a typical North-Western Tasmanian town at the turn of the century. Buildings include blacksmith's shop, a printer's, general store, Post and Telegraph office, Saddler's, bootmaker's shop, inn, carpenter's shop, butter factory and a typical home. Local history material. 19th century crafts.
M., W., Th. and F. 11-4; Su. 1.30-4.30. Other times by arrangement.

BURRA

FOLK MUSEUM
Burra, South Australia
Collection illustrating 19th century rural life.
F., Su. 2-4 or by appointment.

BURRADOO

BARBICAN MUSEUM
Toogoon Road, Burradoo, New South Wales
Military history from 17th century onwards.
Sa., Su. 12-4. Other times by appointment.

BURTONVILLE

BURTON GALLERY ANTIQUES
Burtonville, nr. Carroll, New South Wales
Victorian silver, brassware, porcelain, cedar and rosewood. Small furnishings. Paintings.
By arrangement.

BUSSELTON

LOCAL MUSEUM
Prospect Villa, Busselton, Western Australia 6280
Articles used by pioneers, including chairs, books, china and tools.
M.-F. 9-5; Sa. 9-12.

CAIRNS

HOUSE OF 10,000 SHELLS
60 Shields Street, Cairns, Queensland
Shells from the Great Barrier Reef and other parts of the world.
May-Sept., daily 9-8.30. Christmas and New Year, daily 9-8.30. Easter 9-1. Other times, daily 6 a.m.-8.30 p.m.

CAMDEN

CAMDEN MUSEUM OF AVIATION
Hangar 57, Camden Airport, Camden, New South Wales
Military aircraft and aircraft engines. Exhibits include a Bristol Beaufighter, Vultee Vengeance dive-bomber, Sea Venom, Fairey Firefly and Avro Anson. Scale models. Photographs.
Su. and public holidays, 10.30-5.

HISTORICAL SOCIETY MUSEUM
John Street, Camden, New South Wales
History of Camden and district. Pioneer relics.
Sa. and public holidays, 11-4.30; Su. 12-4.30. Other times by arrangement.

CAMPERDOWN

CAMPERDOWN HISTORICAL MUSEUM
218 Manifold Street, Camperdown, Victoria 3260
Australian aboriginal artifacts. Side-saddles and other riding equipment. Cooking utensils. Silver. China. Needlework. Business and legal records. Letters, extracts from diaries, photographs and drawings.
Key on request.

CANBERRA

AUSTRALIAN INSTITUTE OF ANATOMY
McCoy Circuit, Acton, Canberra City, A.C.T. 2601
Anatomical and biological material explaining the general function of the human body, together with a display covering the evolution of Man. Anatomy of the platypus.
Ethnographic material from the National Ethnographic Collections.
M.-Sa. 9-5; Su. 2-5. Public holidays 10-4.30. Closed Christmas Day and Good F.

AUSTRALIAN WAR MEMORIAL
Top of Anzac Parade, Reid, P.O. Box 345, Canberra City, A.C.T. 2601
Wartime relics, records, paintings, dioramas and models. Work of the Australian navy and air force and of the medical and women's services.
Daily 9-4.45. Closed Christmas Day.

BILLABONG PARK HORSE ERA MUSEUM
Stirling Avenue, Watson (North), Canberra City, A.C.T.
Colonial-style coach house. Horsedrawn vehicles. Saddlery and harness, including side-saddles, child's basket saddle, military saddles. Household appliances. Farming equipment.
Daily 9-5.

BLUNDELL'S COTTAGE
Wendouree Drive, Canberra City, A.C.T. 2601
Restored settler's cottage (1858). Period furnishings.
Daily 2-4. Also W. mornings, 10-12. Closed Christmas Day. Good F.

NATIONAL LIBRARY OF AUSTRALIA
King Edward Terrace Parkes, Canberra City, A.C.T. 2601
Historic manuscripts, including Captain Cook's Journal, diaries from the Burke & Wills expedition, and the papers of Australia's first Prime Minister.
M.-F. 9 a.m. - 10 p.m.; Sa., public holidays 9-4.45. Closed Christmas Day, Good F. and Anzac Day.

REGATTA POINT MUSEUM
Commonwealth Park, Canberra City, A.C.T. 2601
Models, diagrams and pictures showing present and future development of Canberra.
Daily 9-12.30, 1.30-5.

CASINO

HISTORICAL MUSEUM
Walker Street, Casino, New South Wales
Pioneer culture. Aboriginal artifacts. Cedar timber-cutting industry. Period furniture. Early agricultural implements and tools.
F., Su. 2-4.30.

CASTLEMAINE

CASTLEMAINE ART GALLERY AND HISTORICAL MUSEUM
Lyttleton Street, Castlemaine 3450, Victoria
Paintings, prints and drawings by Australian artists from the early days to the present time. Artists represented include Louis Buvelot, members of the Heidelberg Impressionist School, Rupert Bunny and Phillips Fox, Sir William Dobell, Sir Russell Drysdale, Charles Blackman, John Perceval and Fred Williams.
Documents, photographs and articles relating to the early gold rush era of Castlemaine and district.
M.-Sa. and public holidays: 10-12, 1-5. Su. 2-5. Closed Good F. and Christmas Day.

CHILTERN

CHILTERN ATHENAEUM AND MUSEUM
Conness Street, Chiltern, Victoria 3683
History of Chiltern and the surrounding district. Sections on squatting, pioneers, mining, gold-field artists, authors, manufacture, local government.
During school holidays, 10-5. Other times by arrangement with the Chiltern Shire Secretary.

COBAR

COBAR PASTORAL, MINING AND TECHNOLOGICAL MUSEUM
Barrier Highway, Cobar, New South Wales
Local history. Mining in the area. Technology.
Su.-F. 9-11.30, 3-5; Sa. 2-4.

COFFS HARBOUR

JARRETT'S NATURELAND MUSEUM
Bennetts Road Ph., Coffs Harbour 73, New South Wales
Sea shells. Antique rifles. Minerals. Stuffed animals and birds.
Daily 9-5.30.

COOKTOWN

JAMES COOK HISTORICAL MUSEUM
Cooktown, North Queensland
In former convent and girls' high school. Church and school material. Chinese joss house. Reconstruction of old Cooktown temple (1878), with gods, carvings, altar, drum and bells. Aboriginal collection. Life history of James Cook. Plants and animals of the area. Barrier Reef shell collection. Local history.
M.-F. 10-12, 2-4; Sa. 10-12, 7.30-9.30. Closed Su.

COOLANGATTA

VINTAGE AND VETERAN CAR MUSEUM
Coolangatta, Gold Coast, Queensland 4225
Veteran, Edwardian and Vintage cars, both Australian and foreign. Commercial vehicles dating from 1908. Fire engines; tractors and farm equipment; horsedrawn delivery vans; cycles and motorcycles, including a 1870 Boneshaker; locomotives; aircraft and aircraft engines. 1904 Darracq, "Genevieve", which starred in the film of the same name.
Daily 8.15-5. Closed Good F., Christmas Day and Sa. mornings during winter season.

COOLGARDIE

GOLDFIELDS EXHIBITION
Bayley Street, Coolgardie, Western Australia
History of Coolgardie, especially the gold rush days of the 1890s.
Daily 9-5. Other times by arrangement with the caretaker.

COOMA

COOMA MONARO FOLK MUSEUM
Snowy Mountains Highway, Cooma, New South Wales
3 miles west of Cooma. Folklore. Local history. Guns. Kitchen (1860s). Carriages and coaches. Blacksmith's shop.
Daily 8-6.

RAGLAN GALLERY
11 Lambie Street, Cooma, New South Wales
Art collections.
F.-M. 9-6.

COONAMBLE

COONAMBLE HISTORICAL MUSEUM
Aberford Street, Old Police Building, Coonamble, New South Wales
Local historical collections.
By arrangement.

COWELL

FRANKLIN HARBOR MUSEUM
Cowell, South Australia
Colonial exhibits.
On request: enquiries to District Council office during office hours.

COWRA

HISTORICAL MUSEUM
Olympic Way - Railway Institute Building, Cowra, New South Wales
Local history. Photographs.
Sa., Su. 2-4.30.

CRADLE MOUNTAIN

CRADLE MOUNTAIN TRAILSIDE MUSEUM
Lake St. Clare National Park, Cradle Mountain, Tasmania
Geology. Local wildlife, botany.
Daily 9-12, 2-5.

CURRUMBIN

SEA SHELL MUSEUM
Gold Coast Highway, Currumbin, Gold Coast, Queensland
Shells and marine specimens.
Daily 10-4.

DALBY

DALBY MUSEUM
22 Drayton Street, Dalby, Darling Downs Region, Queensland
Antique bottles. Early farming equipment. Telephones. Household utensils.
Sa., Su. 2-5.

DAYLESFORD

DAYLESFORD AND DISTRICT HISTORICAL SOCIETY MUSEUM AND CULTURAL CENTRE
Daylesford, Victoria 3460
Aboriginal, gold mining and pioneer artifacts. Local records, photographs and curios.
Sa., Su., Holidays, and by appointment.

DEE WHY

HISTORICAL MUSEUM
92 McIntosh Road, Dee Why, New South Wales
Local history. Pioneering relics.
Su. 11-5.

DONGARA

RUSS HISTORICAL COTTAGE
Dongara, near Geraldton, Western Australia
Named after original owner. Building (c.1870). Local history. Period furnishings.
Su. 2-4.

DRAYTON

DRAYTON FOLK MUSEUM
8 Parker Street, Drayton, nr. Toowoomba, Queensland
Collection of Australian rural-life exhibits.
By appointment (tel: 30 1278, Mr. and Mrs. Gardner).

DUBBO

HISTORICAL MUSEUM
Macquarie Street, Dubbo, New South Wales
Local history. 19th century drawing room. Colonial bedroom. Philately. War relics. 19th century bridal and Valentine mementoes. Blacksmith's forge. Aboriginal artifacts.
M.-F. 10-1, 2-5.

DUNGOG

HISTORIC MUSEUM
School of Arts Building, Dowling Street, Dungog, New South Wales
Local history. Dairy implements dating from 1885. Agricultural machinery. Early pill-making machine. 19th century surgical instruments.
Su. 1-5.

EDEN

EDEN MUSEUM
Imlay Street, Eden, New South Wales
Material connected with the whaling industry in Eden. Skeleton of killer whale known as Tom (1930).
Daily 2-5 or by appointment.

EL DORADO

EL DORADO MUSEUM
El Dorado, Victoria 3746
Mining relics and history. Farm machinery and vehicles. Gem stones. Bottles. Household articles. Old newspapers and photographs.
Su. 2-5. Public holidays 10-5. Other times by appointment.

ELIZABETH

ELIZABETH GALLERY
Prince Charles Walk, Elizabeth Town Centre, Elizabeth, South Australia
Art collections.
M.-F. 9-5.30; Sa. 9-12.

EUGOWRA

HISTORIC MUSEUM
Norton Street, Eugowra, New South Wales
Early life of the settlers in the Lachlan Valley. Personal possessions of the bushranger, Ben Hall.
Sa., Su. 10-5.

EUNGELLA

DOLL MUSEUM
Dalrymple Heights, Eungella, Mackay Region, Queensland
International doll collection.
On request.

FORBES

FORBES FOLK MUSEUM
Cross Street, Forbes, New South Wales
Relics of bushranger Ben Hall. Local history, including photographs, newspapers. Pioneer household equipment. Farm machinery.
M.-Sa. 10-12, 2-5.

FORTITUDE VALLEY

QUEENSLAND ART GALLERY
Gregory Terrace, Fortitude Valley, Brisbane, Queensland
Australian paintings, with some English and French works, including "Hollandaise à la Coiffe" (1905). Sculpture, including works by Dégas, Despiau, Rodin, Greco, Plazzotta and Epstein.
M.-Sa. 10-5; Su. 2-5. Closed Christmas Day, Good F. and Anzac Day.

QUEENSLAND MUSEUM
Gregory Terrace, Fortitude Valley, Brisbane, Queensland 4006
Natural science. Australian and Melanesian anthropology. History. Technology. Avro Avian single-engined bi-plane used by Bert Hinkler on his pioneering solo flight from England to Australia in 1928.
M.-Sa. 10-4.55; Su. 2-4.55. Closed Christmas Day, Good F. and Anzac Day.

FRANKSTON

BALLAM PARK HOMESTEAD AND HISTORICAL MUSEUM
Cranbourne Road, Frankston, Victoria 3199
House (c.1843). Furniture, bric-a-brac and clothing of the period 1850-1910. Photographs. Early farm implements and horse-drawn vehicles - buggies, sulkies, drays and ploughs.
Sa. and Su. 1.30-5. Open public holidays and also during the week, by appointment.

McCLELLAND GALLERY
Box 121, Studio Park, Boundary Road, Frankston, Victoria 3199
19th and 20th century Australian paintings, prints, drawings, sculpture.
Tu.-Th., Sa., Su. 12-5.

FREMANTLE

MARITIME AND HISTORICAL MUSEUM
Finnerty Street, Fremantle, Western Australia
In building constructed by convicts in the 1860s as a Lunatic Asylum. State history from the earliest voyages of discovery by Dutch sailors in the 17th century. Establishment of the Swan River Colony. Early history of Fremantle and its harbour. Sailing ships, early steamers, paddle boats. History of pearling and whaling. Weapons. Navigational instruments.
M.-Sa. 10.30-5; Su. 1-5; public holidays 9.30-5. Closed Christmas Day, Good F. and Anzac Day.

GAWLER

FOLK MUSEUM
Old Telegraph Building, Murray Street, Gawler, South Australia
Collection illustrating 19th century rural life.
Su. 2-5.

GEELONG

GEELONG ART GALLERY
Little Malop Street, Geelong 3220, Victoria
Paintings by early Australian artists, including Piguinet, Buvelot and von Guerrard. The Heidelberg School is represented by Roberts, Streeton and Conder Withers. Works by contemporary Australian painters, printmakers and sculptors.
M.-F. 11-5; Sa. 10-12; Su. 2-5.

GERALDTON

GERALDTON SHELL MUSEUM
114 North-West Coastal Highway, Geraldton, Western Australia
Shells. Gem Stones. Native art work. Coral formations.
Daily 9-5.

GLENBAWM DAM

HUNTER VALLEY MUSEUM OF RURAL LIFE
Glenbawm Dam, near Scone, New South Wales
Collections illustrating rural life. "Bone shaker" bicycle, 80-year-old vacuum cleaner.
W., Sa., Su., public holidays, 10-4.

GLEN INNES

BALD NOB HOTEL MUSEUM
Glen Innes, New South Wales
Staging depot, 16 miles east of Glen Innes on Gwyder Highway. Local history.
Sa., Su. 2-5.

LAND OF THE BEADIES HISTORY HOUSE MUSEUM
Glen Innes, New South Wales
Historic house (1874). Period furnishings. Local history. Minerals. Ceramics. Implements of pioneering days.
Sa., Su., public holidays 2-5.

GOOLWA

GOOLWA SOUTH COAST MUSEUM
Goolwa, South Australia
Colonial exhibits.
Public holidays 11-4. Weekdays during school holidays 1-4. W., Th. 1-4; Sa. and Su. 11-4.

GOSFORD WEST

KENDALL COTTAGE
Kendall Street, Gosford West, New South Wales
Home of Henry Kendall, poet. Memorabilia of Kendall.
W., Sa., Su., public holidays 10-4.

GOULBURN

MUSEUM OF APPLIED ARTS AND SCIENCES
Montague Street, Goulburn, New South Wales
Engineering and ship models. Pottery, porcelain, glassware. Rocks and minerals. Wool. History of the bicycle.
M.-F. 2-5; Sa. 9-12. Closed Su., Christmas Day, Good F.

MUSEUM OF HISTORIC ENGINES
Marsden Bridge, Crookwell Road, Goulburn, New South Wales
Exhibits include original pumping engine last used in 1918; 30-ton ploughing engine from the Murrumbidgee Irrigation Area; 1923 steam engine; working models of steam engines.
Daily 10-5.

RIVERSDALE
Goulburn, New South Wales
Colonial Georgian house (c.1840). Period furniture and furnishings.
Daily 10-5. Closed Christmas Day, Good F.

GRAFTON

SCHAEFFER HOUSE
Fitzroy Street, Grafton, New South Wales
House (1906), former home of the Government Architect. Furniture and furnishings, including original paintings and a section devoted to the early days on the Clarence.
Tu. 2-4; Th. 7-9 p.m. Other times by arrangement with Grafton Municipal Council.

GRENFELL

HISTORICAL MUSEUM
Municipal Library, Grenfell, Mid-Western Highway, New South Wales
Period bedroom of the 1880s. Dentist's surgery of 1910-15. Gold-rush history. Photographs and documents illustrating the history of the area. Aboriginal artifacts. Local gemstones. Section devoted to the poet, Henry Lawson, born in Grenfell in 1867.
Open public holidays. Other times by arrangement with the Local Municipal Council.

GRIFFITH

PIONEER PARK MUSEUM
Griffith, New South Wales
Open-air museum of Australia's pioneering life.
M.-Sa. 2-4; Su. 1-5.

GULGONG

PIONEERS' MUSEUM
Gulgong, nr. Mudgee, New South Wales
Relics of the gold-rush which hit Gulgong in the 1870s. Tools. Utensils. Vehicles. Engines. History of the town made famous by the $10 note.
M.-F. 2-5; weekends and public holidays 9.30-5.

GUNDAGAI

HISTORICAL MUSEUM
Homer Street, Gundagai, New South Wales
Pioneer and bushranging relics. Aboriginal curios. Domestic equipment, including a rare swinging water jug and a wooden washing machine of the 19th century. Aboriginal material includes cooking implements, nardoo stones, message stick, tribal weapons and copper medallions with chains inscribed and given to Aboriginal chieftains for services rendered. Gold-mining display. Early horse-drawn agricultural implements, steam and oil engines, bullock and horse waggons. Blacksmith's shop.
Daily 9-6. Other times by request.

GYMPIE

GYMPIE AND DISTRICT HISTORICAL MUSEUM
Brisbane Road, Gympie, Queensland
Relics and photographs of the district in its gold rush days. Gold scales, rock samples, journals and newspapers, mining share registers and mining equipment.
Daily 10-5.

HADSPEN

ENTALLY HOUSE
Hadspen, Bass Highway, nr. Launceston, Tasmania
Early Colonial home furnished with antiques.
Daily 10-12.30, 1-5. Closed Christmas Day, Good F., and July.

HAHNDORF

HAHNDORF ACADEMY
Princes Highway, Hahndorf, South Australia
Art collection. Exhibits illustrating 19th century rural life.
Daily 10-5.30.

HAMILTON

HAMILTON ART GALLERY
Hamilton, Victoria
Art collections.
On request.

HILL END

NATIONAL PARKS AND WILDLIFE VISITATION CENTRE
High Street, Hill End, New South Wales
History of Hill End, first Government controlled village in N.S.W. for preservation and restoration. Natural history.
Daily 9.30-1, 2-5.

HOBART

ALLPORT LIBRARY AND MUSEUM OF FINE ARTS
State Library of Tasmania, 91 Murray Street, Hobart, Tasmania 7001
18th century paintings and prints relating to Australia and the Pacific. Furniture. Silver and glass (mostly 18th century.)
M.-F. 10.30-4.30. Closed public holidays.

TASMANIAN MUSEUM AND ART GALLERY
G.P.O. Box 1164M, 5 Argyle Street, Hobart, Tasmania 7001
Natural history, zoology and early art of the State. Material on Tasmanian aborigines. Development of Tasmania.
M.-F. 10-5; Sa. 10-4; Su. 2.30-5. Closed Christmas Day and Good F.

HUNTERS HILL

HISTORIC MUSEUM
Hunters Hill Town Hall, Alexandra Street, Hunters Hill, New South Wales
Local history. Photographs. Paintings. Model of the local Roman Catholic church, "Villa Maria".
M.-F. 9-4.

ILFRACOMBE

ILFRACOMBE FOLK MUSEUM
Ilfracombe, Queensland
Relics of pioneer days, including restored waggons, buggies and drays.
M.-F. 8.30-5.

IMBIL

MUSEUM OF WONDERS
Island Road, Imbil, Queensland
Guns. War-time service rifles, helmets, swords and medals. Antique lamps. Sea shells. Wood carvings. Bottles.
Daily 10-12, 2-4, 7-8.

INNISFAIL

CHINESE JOSS HOUSE
Earnest Street, Innisfail, Cairns Region, Queensland
Collection of Chinese idols, carvings and brassware.
Daily 10-5.

JAMESTOWN

JAMESTOWN FOLK MUSEUM
Jamestown, South Australia
Exhibits illustrating 19th century rural life.
Su. 2-4.

JENOLAN CAVES

113 m. west of Sydney and 48 m. south-west of Katoomba, New South Wales
Series of limestone caves. Eight 'dark' caves have been developed for tourists and are lit by electricity to show the fantastic forms and subtle colours of the calcite deposits - stalactites, stalagmites, pillars, shawls, canopies and nodules.
Inspections: mornings, 10.00, 10.15, 10.30, 11.00. Afternoons, 1.30, 1.45, 2.00, 4.00. Evenings, 7.30.

JEPARIT

AGRICULTURAL MUSEUM
Jeparit, Victoria
Pioneering agricultural implements and tools from the Wimmera and Mallee areas.
Daily 10-5.

JINDERA

PIONEER MUSEUM
Jindera, nr. Albury, New South Wales
Local history. Pioneering relics. District general store (1880s) with goods of the day.
Tu., Th., Sa., Su. 2-5.30. School holidays, daily 2-5.30.

KADINA

NATIONAL TRUST MUSEUM
Matta House, Kadina, York Peninsula, South Australia
Furniture and household articles dating back to the area's early days. Agricultural material. Implements, machinery and tools. Copper mining relics and history, 1859-1923.
W., Sa., Su. and public holidays (ex. Christmas Day) 2-5.

KALBARRI

SHELL, MARINE AND MINERAL MUSEUM
Grey Street, Kalbarri, Western Australia
Fish and sea life. Sponges, coral and star fish. Harpoons and other fishing gear. Rocks and minerals. Shells. Local history.
M.-F. 9-5. Sa. 9-12.

KALGOORLIE

GOLDEN MILE MUSEUM
Kalgoorlie, Western Australia
History of Mining.
Mon.-Sa. 10-1, 2-5.

SCHOOL OF MINES MUSEUM
British Arms Hotel, Kalgoorlie, Western Australia
Geology. History of mining and of mining techniques.
M.-F. 10-5.

KAPUNDA

KAPUNDA HISTORICAL SOCIETY MUSEUM
Hill Street, Kapunda, South Australia
Colonial exhibits. Local history.
Su. and public holidays 2-5.

KATANNING

KATANNING HISTORICAL MUSEUM
Town Hall, Katanning, Western Australia
Firearms. Aboriginal relics, including spear heads, throwing stones, rasps, hammers, scrapers, meeros, spears and boomerangs. Period dresses; 250-year-old spinning wheel; gold-weighing scales; blacksmiths' bellows; original Edison gramophone and records which were played in 1897. Charter and seal of Sir Richard Spencer. Farming relics include shepherds' crooks, an early shearing machine handpiece, butter pats, the horns of a working bullock, cowbells, buggy lamps and hand-carved gambells.
1st and 3rd Su. in month, 2-4. Other times by arrangement.

KATOOMBA

PYALA MUSEUM
Echo Point, Katoomba, New South Wales
Captain Cook relics. Aboriginal and convict relics. Stone Age cultures in the Pacific. Shell work from different countries. Handcraft of the old sailing days. Dioramas illustrating native customs.
Summer: W.-M. 10-5. Winter: Sa., Su. 10-5.

KEMPSEY

GILL'S BOTTLE MUSEUM
Bloomfield Street, South Kempsey, New South Wales
Bottle collection. 19th century bedroom and kitchen. Dray carts, sulky, old delivery van, bullock gear.
Holidays, and by arrangement with the Information Centre.

MACLEAY RIVER HISTORICAL MUSEUM
Elbow Street, West Kempsey, New South Wales
Macleay River Historical Society's collection of local history exhibits.
Sa., Su. 2-5.

KINGSCOTE

NATIONAL TRUST MUSEUM
Kingscote, South Australia
Exhibits illustrating colonial history.
M. 2-4; Tu. 10-12, 2-4; Th.-Sa. 10-12, 2-4. W. and Su. by appointment.

KIRRA

GILLTRAP'S AUTO MUSEUM
Gold Coast Highway, Kirra, Gold Coast, Queensland
Vintage and veteran cars; early model trucks; cycles; motor cycles; horse-drawn vehicles; aircraft and general machinery.
Daily ex. Sa., commentary and show at 9.45, 11.30, 1.30 and 3.

KOROIT

NATURAL HISTORY CENTRE
Koroit, Victoria
Natural history collections, housed in building in volcanic crater.
Daily 9.30-12.30, 1.30-4.30.

KURNELL

CAPTAIN COOK'S LANDING PLACE MUSEUM
Kurnell, New South Wales
Exhibits covering the discovery of Botany Bay on April 29, 1770 by Captain James Cook on board H.M.S. 'Endeavour'. Cannon from the 'Endeavour'. Replica of Cook's sword. Model of the 'Endeavour'.
Daily 10-30-4.30. Closed Christmas Day, Good F.

KYNETON

KYNETON HISTORICAL MUSEUM
Piper Street, Kyneton, Victoria 3444
19th century relics of the goldfields. China. Glass. Silver. Costumes. Colonial kitchen (19th century). Bottles. Pioneers' room. Rooms furnished in colonial style. Slab hut, original 'Theaden' homestead, 1841, with furnishings of the period. Coach house, with horse-drawn vehicles and early farm equipment. Goose house.
M.-Sa. 1.30-4.30; Su. and holidays 10.30-12.30, 1.30-4.30.

LAKES ENTRANCE

ABORIGINAL ART MUSEUM
Lakes Entrance, Gippsland Lakes, Victoria
Aboriginal artifacts.
Daily 10-8.

LANE COVE

CARISBROOK HISTORIC HOUSE AND MUSEUM
Lane Cove, New South Wales
Home and museum illustrating local life in the 1860s.
W.-Sa. 11.30-4; Su. 1.30-4.

LA PEROUSE

BARE ISLAND MUSEUM
La Perouse, New South Wales
In old Fort at entrance to Botany Bay. Local history. Convicts' relics.
M.-F. 10.30-3.30; Sa., Su. 11-5.

LAUNCESTON

FRANKLIN HOUSE
nr. Launceston, Tasmania
House (1838), built for Mr. Britton Jones, an early Launceston brewer and innkeeper, which became a school in 1842. Period furnishings. Situated on main highway to Hobart.
Daily 9.30-12.30, 1.30-5. Closed Christmas Day, Good F.

QUEEN VICTORIA MUSEUM AND ART GALLERY
Wellington Street, Launceston, Tasmania 7250
Natural history. Social sciences. Fine arts. Chinese Joss House from colonial mining settlement; the original flag first incorporating the Australian design; Tasmanian anthropological and zoological collections. Planetarium.
M.-Sa. 10-5; Su. 2.30-4.30. Closed Christmas Day, New Year's Day, Good F. and Anzac Day.

LENAH VALLEY

LADY FRANKLIN MUSEUM
Lenah Valley Road, Lenah Valley, Tasmania
Art collections.
Su. 2-4.30.

LEURA

EVERGLADES
Denison Street, Leura, New South Wales
House (1933). International dolls and handicrafts collection.
Daily 10-4. Closed Christmas Day, Good F.

LIGHTNING RIDGE

BOTTLE HOUSE MUSEUM
Opal Street, Lightning Ridge, New South Wales
Constructed of numerous bottles and containing early opal mining and historical artifacts, mineral specimens.
Daily 10-5.

MICK'S MUSEUM
Pandora Street, Lightning Ridge, New South Wales
Opal mining artifacts. Mineral specimens.
Daily 10-5.

LISMORE

ART GALLERY
Arts Trust, Molesworth Street, Lismore, New South Wales
Paintings by local artists.
On request.

RICHMOND RIVER HISTORICAL SOCIETY MUSEUM
135 Molesworth Street, Lismore, New South Wales 2480
Aboriginal artifacts. Silver and glassware. Household items. Agricultural implements. Photographs. Furniture. Arts and crafts. History of the Richmond River.
Tu. 10-1, 2-4; W. 12-3; Th. and F. 1-4; Sa. 10-12. Closed Su. and M. During 6 weeks of Christmas school vacation, open daily 10-4.

LITHGOW

ESK BANK HOUSE
Inch Street, Lithgow, New South Wales
House (1841), restored and furnished in period style. Pioneer history. Minerals and fossils. Hansom cab. Old steelworks locomotive.
Daily ex. Th. 10-12, 2-4.

LITTLEHAMPTON

BADERLOO COACH AND RAILWAY MUSEUM
Balhannah Road, Littlehampton, South Australia
Railway collections.
Su. 10-5 or by appointment.

LOBETHAL

LOBETHAL MUSEUM
Main Road, Lobethal, South Australia
Colonial exhibits.
Su. 1.30-5; Tu. 2-3.

LOFTUS

TRAMWAY MUSEUM
Royal National Park, Loftus, New South Wales
Historic trams.
Su. and public holidays, 10.30-5.

LONG JETTY

WONDERS OF THE SEA AND GEMSTONE HOUSE
54 Grandview Street, Shelley Beach, Long Jetty, nr. Gosford, New South Wales
World-wide collection of sea shells, corals and marine life.
Daily 9.30-5.

LUCAS HEIGHTS

AUSTRALIAN ATOMIC ENERGY COMMISSION RESEARCH ESTABLISHMENT VISITORS CENTRE
New Illawarra Road, via Menai, Lucas Heights, New South Wales
Activities of the Research Establishment, including production and use of radio isotopes and research connected with nuclear power.
M.-F. 9-5; Sa., Su. 10-5.

MAITLAND

FOLK MUSEUM
Grossman House, Church Street, Maitland, New South Wales 2320
Period furnishings (1860): paintings, objets d'art, photographs, old kitchen utensils and needlework, including patchwork quilts, doll's and children's clothing. Furniture and, notably, a ceramic item composed of seven fitting pieces, called "Pagoda", "Bachelor's Toddy" or "Bachelor's Nightcap".
Sa. 1.30-4.30; Su. 10.30-4.30. Weekday visits by arrangement: tel. 336452.

MALDON

FOLK MUSEUM
High Street, Maldon, Victoria 3463
Mining tools. Agricultural implements. Early air compressor. Local history. Collection of flat irons. Bottles used in local breweries and cordial factories. Edison Cylindrical Gramophone (1890). Early wireless sets, sewing machines. Paintings. Collection of lamps.
Sa. and Su., public holidays, 2-6. Other times by arrangement.

MANNUM

MARION PADDLEWHEEL MUSEUM
Mannum, Murray River District, South Australia 5236
Anchored at a permanent dock on the river, the museum contains relics of the early days on the Murray. Photographs of the paddle steamer "Marion" during its working life, and of an old steam-car (early 20th century) built by David Shearer at Mannum.
Daily 10-5.

MAROOCHYDORE

COX MUSEUM AND ANTIQUES
Sixth Avenue, Maroochydore, Sunshine Coast, Queensland
Veteran cars. Antique furniture, washing machines and gramophones.
Daily 9-5.30.

McLAREN VALE

THE BARN GALLERY AND MUSEUM
South Road, McLaren Vale, South Australia
Art collections. Local history.
M.-Sa. 9-9.

MELBOURNE

GEOLOGICAL MUSEUM
University of Melbourne, Parkville N.2, Melbourne, Victoria 3052
Palaeontological exhibits of the Palaeozoic, Mesozoic and Cainozoic eras. Local material includes Archaeocyathidae, "Hydroids", Gastropods and plants. Victorian Ordovician-Silurian graptolites and ammonoid caphelopods. Meteorites and australites, the major attraction being the main mass of the Cranbourne No. 7 Meteorite (1941).
M.-F. 9-5.

LEIGHTON GALLERY OF ART
Leighton House, 346 Little Collins Street, Melbourne, Victoria
Paintings, sculpture by Australian, especially local artists.
M.-Sa. 10-5.

MUSEUM OF MODERN ART AND DESIGN OF AUSTRALIA
180 Flinders Street, Melbourne, Victoria
Paintings by Australian artists. Applied arts.
M.-Sa. 10-5. Su. 2-5. Closed Dec. 25, Good F., Anzac Day.

NATIONAL GALLERY OF VICTORIA
180 St. Kilda Road, Melbourne, Victoria 3004
European and Australian paintings, prints and drawings. Oriental art. Costumes. Furniture. Decorative artifacts. Ceramics. Bronzes. Silver. Glass.
Tu.-Su. 10-5; W. 10-9. Closed M. except when public holiday. Also closed Christmas Day, Good F. and Anzac Day.

NATIONAL MUSEUM OF VICTORIA
285-321 Russell Street, Melbourne C.1, Victoria 3000
Natural history. Zoology. Geology. Anthropology. Aboriginal art and artifacts.
M.-Sa. 10-5; Su. 2-5. Closed Christmas Day, Good F. and Anzac Day.

OLD MELBOURNE GAOL AND PENAL MUSEUM
Russell Street, Melbourne, Victoria 3000
Former gaol (1880s). Scaffold. Methods of corporal punishment.
Daily 10-5.

RAILWAY MUSEUM
Champion Road, North Williamstown, Melbourne, Victoria 3000
Rolling stock of the steam era.
Sa., Su. 2-5.

SCIENCE MUSEUM OF VICTORIA
304-328 Swanston Street, Melbourne, Victoria 3000
Engineering. Applied physics, chemistry, biology and geology. Public health. Communications. Transport. H. V. McKay planetarium. The Thomson Steam Motor Car, the first motor vehicle to be made in Australia, and the Duigan Bi-plane, the first Australian-designed and built aircraft to fly.
Tu.-Sa. 10-5; Su. 2-5; M. 12-5.

O. W. TIEGS MUSEUM
Zoology Department, University of Melbourne, Parkville, Victoria 3052
Specimens covering the various phyla. Skeletal material. Embryological models. Specimen of *Dinornis robustus*.
On request during University term-time.

TRAMWAY MUSEUM SOCIETY OF VICTORIA LTD.
Union Lane, Bylands, Victoria 3600
Former Bylands station and track on branch-line to Heathcote. Specimens of all Victorian tramway operators. Traction: horse, cable and electric. Different kinds of body-type, e.g. enclosed both ends (Victoria), open drop-end (California). Quarter of a mile double-track 'street environment', with period shops housing tramwayana.
Su. 10-5.

UNIVERSITY MUSEUM
University of Melbourne, Parkville N.2, Melbourne, Victoria 3052
Australian paintings, water colours, drawings and sculpture. Silver. Glass. Print collection, mainly European. Greek and Roman pottery, artifacts and coins. Ethnographical collection of major works of primitive art.
During exhibitions: Tu.-F. 12-6. At other times by appointment with the Curator's office.

MELROSE

COURT HOUSE MUSEUM
Melrose, South Australia
Exhibits of 19th century rural life.
Daily 2-5 or by appointment.

MERRIWA

COLONIAL COTTAGE
Bettington Street, Merriwa, New South Wales
Cottage (c.1857). Parlour and bedroom furnished in style of 1880. Rifles. Bottles. Maps. Chinaware. Telephones. Tools, farming equipment, harness and saddles on display in cellar.
Tu., F. 2-4; Sa., Su. 11-12, 2-4.

HISTORIC MUSEUM
Merriwa, New South Wales
In convict-built sandstone building. Early history of the district.
Daily 10-5.

MILDURA

MILDURA ARTS CENTRE ART GALLERY
199 Cureton Avenue, Mildura, Victoria 3500
English paintings, including murals and figure sketches by Sir Frank Brangwyn and portraits and satirical paintings by Sir William Orpen. Jacob Epstein bronze. Augustus John portraits. Dégas pastel. Australian artists include Sir Arthur Streeton, Frederick McCubbin, Elioth Gruner, Sydney Long, Penleigh Boyd and Percy Lindsay. Australian and New Zealand sculpture.
M.-F. 9-4.30; Sa. and Su. 2-4.30.

MUSEUM OF LOCAL HISTORY
Mildura Arts Centre, 199 Cureton Avenue, Mildura, Victoria 3500
In former home of "W.B." Chaffey, the co-founder of Mildura. Original furniture and wall-panelling (1890s). Aboriginal artifacts. Local flora and fauna. Early Mallee transport. Documents connected with Australia's first irrigation project. Early telecommunications. Domestic equipment.
M.-F. 9-4.30; Sa. and Su. 2-4.30.

MILLICENT

MILLICENT HISTORICAL MUSEUM
Millicent, South Australia
Colonial exhibits.
Daily 1-5.

MILLTHORPE

HISTORICAL MUSEUM
Millthorpe, nr. Orange, New South Wales
Collections of bottles and farm machinery, as well as local history items. Interiors, with period furniture.
Sa. and Su. 2-5. Public holidays 10-5. Other times on request to Mr. S. Bryant, back of shop opposite school.

MILTON

FOLK MUSEUM
Watson Street, Milton, New South Wales
Folklore. Local history. Pioneer relics, including kitchen and laundry articles. Bottles, lamps and lanterns. Aboriginal artifacts. Items relating to the dairy industry.
Summer: daily 10-5. Othertimes by arrangement.

HISTORICAL MUSEUM
Milton, New South Wales
Period rooms. Clothing of the 1850s. Kitchen utensils. Hardware.
Su. 2-5.

MOE

FOLK MUSEUM
Moe, Latrobe Valley, Victoria
Original houses from Gippsland area. Implements. Domestic equipment. Railway vehicles.
Daily 9-5.

MOLONG

MOLONG HISTORICAL MUSEUM
Molong, New South Wales 2866
Building (1856). Local history.
Su. 2.30-5.30.

MONTVILLE

ELANDS OLD CLOCK DISPLAY AND MINI MUSEUM
Main Street, Montville, Sunshine Coast, Queensland
Early clocks and other antiques.
Daily 10-5.

MOONTA

NATIONAL TRUST MUSEUM
Moonta Mines Primary School, Moonta, York Peninsula, South Australia
The collections include working models of the mines; pioneer relics; curiosities; historic documents; antiques. The Trust also owns an early miner's cottage, furnished in authentic style.
Museum and cottage: Sa., Su., W., public holidays and school holidays, 2-4.

MOORA

BERKSHIRE VALLEY FOLK MUSEUM
Moora, Western Australia
12 miles east of Moora. Museum housed in Clinch's mill house (original mill can still be viewed). Folk exhibits.
Apr. 4 - July 31, Su. 2.30-5, also public holidays ex. Good F. Aug. 1 - Nov. 20, Sa., Su., public holidays 2.30-5.

MOREE

LOCAL ARTS MUSEUM
25 Iris Street, Moree, New South Wales
Rough and polished gemstones. Bullets, cartridges, antique pistols, rifles. Aboriginal weapons and relics.
Weekdays after 4 p.m., all day Sa., Su.

MORNINGTON

OLD MORNINGTON POST OFFICE MUSEUM
Cr. Main Street and The Esplanade, Mornington, Victoria 3931
Local history, including household utensils, clothing, school work, and official registers, certificates and advertising matter. Aboriginal artifacts. Photographs of early residents and their homes.
Dec.-Feb., Tu., Th., Sa., Su. 2-5. Feb.-Apr. Sa., Su. 2-5. Apr.-Nov., Su. 2-5. Other times by appointment.

MORPHETT VALE

PIONEER VILLAGE MUSEUM
Morphett Vale, South Australia
Folk collections, arranged in reconstruction of pioneer village.
Tu.-Su. 10-5.

MORWELL

LATROBE VALLEY ARTS CENTRE
138-140 Commercial Road, Morwell, Victoria 3840
Paintings in oils and water-colours, prints and drawings by contemporary Australian artists.
M. 1.30-4.30; Tu.-F. 10-4.30; Tu. and Th. 7-9 p.m.; Sa. 10-12.30; Su. 3-5.

MOUNT GAMBIER

SIMPSONS MUSEUM
27 Vansittart Road, Mount Gambier, South Australia
Colonial exhibits.
Daily ex. Th. 11-5.

MOUNT MORGAN

MOUNT MORGAN HISTORICAL MUSEUM
East Street, Mount Morgan, Rockhampton Region, Queensland
Relics from the early days of the Mount Morgan gold and copper mine. Photographs.
M.-F. 11.30-1.30; Su. 2-4.

MOUNT VICTORIA

DISTRICT HISTORICAL MUSEUM
Railway Station, Mount Victoria, New South Wales
History of the district.
Sa., Su., public and school holidays, 2-5.

MOUNT YORK

NATURAL MUSEUM
Mount York Reserve, Mount York, New South Wales
Moths and butterflies. Aboriginal artifacts. Egyptian archaeology. Fossil dinosaur and marsupial remains, including the only dinosaur egg found in Australia.
Daily 9-5.

MUDGEE

COLONIAL INN MUSEUM
Market Street, Mudgee, New South Wales
Colonial relics. Local history.
Sa., Su. 2-5; public holidays 10-12, 2-5. Closed Good F. and Christmas Day.

MURRAY BRIDGE

MURRAY BRIDGE MUSEUM
12 Thomas Street, Murray Bridge, South Australia
Colonial exhibits.
M.-Sa. 10-4; Su. 10-5. Evenings by arrangement.

NARACOORTE

NARACOORTE MUSEUM AND GALLERY
Naracoorte, South Australia
Colonial exhibits. Paintings. Sketches.
W., F. and Sa. 2-5.

NAGAMBIE

NAGAMBIE FOLK MUSEUM
344 High Street, Nagambie, Victoria 3608
Antique furniture. Domestic utensils. Nursery, with old pram and cradle. Bottles. Lamps. Steam engines. Horse-drawn vehicles. Harness.
Su. 2-5.

NAMBUCCA HEADS

HISTORICAL MUSEUM
The Headland, Nambucca Heads, New South Wales
History of the Nambucca district over the past 100 years.
Sa., Su. 2-4.

ORANA MINERAL AND ART MUSEUM
Seaview Street, Nambucca Heads, New South Wales
Minerals and fossils. Paintings by local artists.
Afternoons, except M. and F.

NARRANDERA

NARRANDERA AND STURT HISTORICAL SOCIETY'S MUSEUM
87 East Street, Narrandera, New South Wales
Local history.
M.-Th. 2-5; F. and Sa., 2-5, 7-9.

NELSON BAY

GEMSTONE HOUSE
Shoal Bay Road, Nelson Bay, New South Wales
World-wide display of rough and polished gemstones.
Daily 9-5.

HISTORIC MUSEUM
43 Donald Street, Nelson Bay, New South Wales
Local history.
M., Tu., F. 1-4.

NEWCASTLE

CITY ART GALLERY
Cultural Centre, Laman Street, Newcastle, New South Wales 2300
Paintings by Conrad Martens, Joseph Lycett, Sir Arthur Streeton, Rupert Bunny, Roland Wakelin, Fred Williams, Sir Russell Drysdale, Sidney Nolan, Godfrey Miller, Arthur Boyd, Sydney Ball and Alun Leach-Jones. Collections of prints, drawings and ceramics, together with contemporary sculpture and Australian aboriginal art. Works by Sir William Dobell, who was born in Newcastle.
M.-F. 10-5; W. 10-9; Sa. 10-1, 2-5. Su. and public holidays, 2-5. Closed Christmas Day and Good F.

MUSEUM
Pitt Street, Newcastle, New South Wales 2300
Local history.
Sa., Su. 10-4.30.

NEW TOWN

RUNNYMEDE
61 Bay Road, New Town, Tasmania
House (1844), furnished in the style of the 1860s. Memorial rooms to previous owners of the house.
Tu.-Su. 2-5.

NOOSAVILLE

HOUSE OF SHELLS
5 Edward Street, Noosaville, Sunshine Coast, Queensland
Miniature house of shells, coral gardens, shell collections and displays of coloured sands in bottles and paintings.
Daily 10-5.

NURIOOTPA

ANTIQUE BOTTLE MUSEUM
Coulthard House, Nuriootpa, South Australia
Bottle collection.
By arrangement.

OVERLAND CORNER

OVERLAND CORNER HOTEL MUSEUM
Overland Corner, South Australia
Folk exhibits.
Su.-F. 9.30-12, 1-5; Sa. 1-5. Closed Th.

PARKES

HENRY PARKES MUSEUM
316 Clarinda Street, Parkes, New South Wales
Local history. Memorabilia of the founder of the town, Henry Parkes.
Daily 10-5.

PARRAMATTA

EXPERIMENT FARM COTTAGE
9 Ruse Street, Parramatta, New South Wales
Cottage (1798). Agricultural history. Implements.
M.-Th. 10-12.30, 2-4; Sa. 2-4.30; Su. and holidays 10-12.30, 2-4.30.

HAMBLEDON COTTAGE
Hassall Street, Parramatta, New South Wales
Cottage (1824), with period furnishings.
W., Th., F., Sa., Su. and public holidays, 10-5. Closed Good F. and Christmas Day.

LINDEN HOUSE
Lancer Barracks, corner Smith and Station Streets, Parramatta, New South Wales
Collections illustrating military history of Australia.
Su. and public holidays 11-4.

OLD GOVERNMENT HOUSE
Parramatta Park, Parramatta, New South Wales
Vice-Regal home, 1799-1855. Period furnishings.
Tu.-Th., 10-12, 1.30-3.30; Su. and public holidays 10-12, 2-4.

STEAM TRAM AND RAILWAY MUSEUM
Parramatta National Park, Parramatta, New South Wales
Trams and railway engines, including Australia's oldest operating tram.
3rd Su. in month, 1.30-4.45 (weather and circumstances permitting).

PENNESHAW

NATIONAL TRUST MUSEUM
Penneshaw, South Australia
Folk exhibits.
Tu., Th. 2-4.

PERTH

OLD MILL
Narrows Bridge, South Perth, Western Australia
Mill (1835), restored to original appearance. Relics of pioneering days.
M., W., Th. 1-5; Sa. 1-4; Su. 1-5.

STIRLING HOUSE MUSEUM
Broadway, Nedlands, Perth, Western Australia
Relics and literature of the State's early history.
M.-Th. 2-4. Also open one Su. afternoon each month.

VINTAGE CAR MUSEUM
Wembley, Perth, Western Australia
Collection of vintage and veteran cars, 'all in perfect mechanical condition.'
Sa. and Su. 2-5.

WESTERN AUSTRALIAN ART GALLERY
Beaufort Street, Perth, Western Australia 6000
Australian art and aboriginal art. English and European art, ranging from 18th century to the present day. Prints, drawings. Antique and modern furniture. Coins. Medals. Stamps. Silver and gold ware. Ceramics. Glass. Pottery. Sculptures.
M.-F. 10.30-5; Sa. 9.30-5; Su. 2-5. W. also 7.30-10 p.m.

WESTERN AUSTRALIAN MUSEUM
Francis Street, Perth, Western Australia 6000
Collections of mammals, reptiles, fish, molluscs, fossils, insects, anthropology, archaeology, history, marine archaeology and technology. Emphasis on Australian and, in particular, Western Australian material.
M.-F. 10.30-5; Sa. 9.30-5; Su. 2-5. Closed Good F. and Anzac Day.

PORT ADELAIDE

PORT ADELAIDE NAUTICAL MUSEUM
St. Vincent Street, Port Adelaide, South Australia 5015
Maritime museum, featuring ships' relics, figureheads, bells. Ships' models. Photographic collection.
W. 11.30-4; Sa. 11-12; Su. 2.30-4.

PORT ARTHUR

PORT ARTHUR MUSEUM
Arthur Highway (Route 7), Port Arthur, Tasmania
Pioneer relics. Relics from convict establishments.
May-Nov., daily 9-4. Dec.-Apr., daily 9-5.

PORT AUGUSTA

CURDNATTA ART AND POTTERY GALLERY
105 Commercial Road, Port Augusta, South Australia
Art. Pottery.
M.-Sa. 9-5.

PORT DOUGLAS

BARRIER REEF SHELL COLLECTION
Macrossan Street, Port Douglas, Cairns Region, Queensland
Shell and coral collections.
Daily 9.30-5.30.

RANDALL'S SHELLS
Murphy Street, Port Douglas, Cairns Region, Queensland
Shell collection.
Daily 10-5.

PORT ELLIOT

PORT ELLIOT ART POTTERY
Port Elliot, South Australia
Art collection.
M.-Sa. 8-5; Su. 1-5. Closed Christmas Day, Good F.

PORT KENNEDY

QUETTA MEMORIAL MUSEUM
Cathedral, Thursday Island, Port Kennedy, Queensland
Memorial collection to the Quetta earthquake.
Daily, 9-5.

PORTLAND

CARL F. KURTZE MUSEUM
78 Wellington Road, Portland, Victoria 3305
Sea shells and coral from all over the world. Aboriginal artifacts. Gem stones of Australia. Mineral collection. Dolls in international costumes. Bottles. Stone jars. Earthenware.
Daily 8-12, 1-5.30. Also evenings during peak periods.

PORT LINCOLN

OLD MILL MUSEUM
Mill Hill, Port Lincoln, South Australia 5606
Documents and photostat copies of photographs, stories of early pioneer families. Working model exhibits of early farm machinery. Ships' models. Candlemoulds. Tricycle with wooden wheels. Old clocks, irons and washing machines.
Sa. and Su. 2-5. W. 2-5 Sept.-May only.

PORT MACQUARIE

HASTINGS DISTRICT HISTORICAL MUSEUM
Clarence Street, Port Macquarie, New South Wales
Local history.
M.-Sa. 9.30-12, 2-5; Su. 2-5. School holidays also 7-9 p.m.

PORT PIRIE

NATIONAL TRUST MUSEUM
Ellen Street, Port Pirie, South Australia
Colonial exhibits.
Daily 1-4; Sa. 10-4.

PORT STEPHENS

SHELL MUSEUM
Soldiers Point Road, Port Stephens, New South Wales
Shell collection.
Tu.-Su. 9.30-5.

PROSERPINE

PROSERPINE FOLK MUSEUM
57 Marathon Street, Prosperpine, Mackay Region, Queensland
Late 19th century furniture and household items.
Daily ex. Th. 9.30-12, 2-5. Sa. and Su. also 7.30-9.30 p.m.

QUORN

QUORN MILL MUSEUM AND ART GALLERY
Quorn, South Australia
Folk exhibits. Paintings.
Daily 9-7.

RENMARK

RENMARK HISTORICAL MUSEUM
Renmark, South Australia
Colonial exhibits.
Su. 2-4; holidays and weekends by arrangement.

ROBE

ROBE GALLERY AND ART CENTRE
Robe, South Australia
Colonial exhibits. Paintings.
M.-F. 9.30-4; Sa. 9.30-12; Su. 2-4.

ST. KILDA

ELECTRICAL TRANSPORT MUSEUM
St. Kilda, South Australia
History of electrical transport. Models.
Su. 2-5.

SALE

SALE ART GALLERY
142 MacAlister Street, Sale, Victoria
Paintings, prints by Australian artists.
M.-Sa., 10-4.

SCONE

HISTORICAL MUSEUM
Kingdom Street, Scone, New South Wales
Local history.
Sa. 3-5 in summer. Winter: Su. 3-5; Sa. 2-4, 7-9.

HUNTER VALLEY MUSEUM OF RURAL LIFE
Scone, New South Wales
Pioneer relics. Domestic equipment. Agricultural tools.
M.-F. 10-5, Sa.-Su. 10-12.

SHEPPARTON

SHEPPARTON ART GALLERY
Shepparton, Victoria
Paintings, drawings by Victoria artists.
On request.

SHOALHAVEN

FOLK PIONEER MUSEUM
Nowra School of Arts, Shoalhaven, New South Wales
Local history.
M.-F. 9-4, during school term.

SINGLETON

HISTORICAL MUSEUM
Court House, Singleton, New South Wales
Housed in the gaol cell block built in 1841 by Benjamin Singleton, the founder of the town. Cell in its original state, with iron bed, restraining rings and double doors. Colonial kitchen, with open fire, bread-baking oven and period furnishings. Early history of Australia, including documentary material. Photography. Lamps and lighting. Bottles. Aboriginal artifacts. Display of early farm machinery and vehicles.
Su. afternoon and public holidays. Other times by arrangement.

SOUTH ESK

CLAREDON HOUSE
South Esk, Tasmania
House (1830s) with extensive formal garden. Period furnishings. Paintings.
Daily ex. Tu. and W., 10.30-12.30, 1.30-5.

STIRLING

LIGHT CASTLE ART GALLERY
Milan Terrace, Stirling, South Australia
Art collections.
Daily 11-10.

SURFERS PARADISE

AUSTRALIAN PIONEERS' MUSEUM
Wax Museum Arcade, Gold Coast Highway, Surfers Paradise, Gold Coast, Queensland
Relics of the pioneer days.
Daily 10-10.

LONDON'S WAX MUSEUM
Wax Museum Arcade, Gold Coast Highway, Surfers Paradise, Gold Coast, Queensland
Historical and contemporary figures in wax. Replicas of the Crown Jewels.
Daily 10-10.

SWAN HILL

INTERNATIONAL MILITARY MUSEUM
Swan Hill, Victoria
Military uniforms and arms from all countries.
Daily 9.30-5.30, 7-9.

SWAN HILL FOLK MUSEUM
Horseshoe Bend, Swan Hill, Victoria
A recreated display of early pioneer life in Australia. Authentic buildings have been removed from their surroundings and reassembled and displayed with period furnishings of pioneer life. Machines (man, horse and power operated) are displayed, together with articles of everyday life.
Daily 8.30-5.30 (until 7.30 in summer). Son et Lumière performances each evening after dark.

SWANSEA

GOOD OLD DAYS FOLK MUSEUM
Swansea, Tasmania 7275
Agricultural and domestic articles used by pioneers in the area: personal effects and equipment of Dr. G. F. Story, the first medical practitioner; anvil from a nearby convict Probation Station; whaling harpoons; a settler's slab hut; early engines; Huon pine furniture and locally-made Oyster Bay pine furniture. Steam car, built in Tasmania in 1900.
Dec.-Easter and during school holidays. Other times on application.

SYDNEY

ART GALLERY OF NEW SOUTH WALES
Art Gallery Road, Domain, Sydney, New South Wales 2000
Australian art. Primitive art, Australian aboriginal, including burial posts and bark paintings. European collection, especially 19th century British art. Prints and drawings. Oriental art: Chinese ceramics and bronzes; Tibetan, Japanese and Chinese paintings; Japanese ceramics; Japanese woodcuts; Thai sculpture; Persian ceramics; Persian and Indian miniatures. Decorative arts: 17th-18th century English pewter; 18th century and Victorian English porcelain; contemporary tapestries by Lurcat and Matisse.
M.-Sa. 10-5; Su. 2-5. Closed Christmas Day, Good F.

AUSTRALIAN MUSEUM
6-8 College Street, Sydney, New South Wales 2000
The collections cover all fields of natural history of the Australian continent, except botanical collections, which are housed elsewhere. Anthropological collections of the Australian Aboriginal people and Melanesian races.
Tu.-Sa. daily 10-5; M. 12-5; Su. 2-5. School holidays, M. 10-5. Closed Christmas Day and Good F.

BOTANICAL MUSEUM AND NATIONAL HERBARIUM
Sydney, New South Wales
Plants of Australia, especially New South Wales.
M.-F. 9.30-5. Sat., Public holidays 11-4. Sun. 2-5. Closed Dec. 25, Good F.

FORT DENISON
Sydney Harbour, Sydney, New South Wales
Fort (1857) built as a precaution during Crimean War in the event of Sydney Harbour being invaded. Relics and mementoes of the fort's early years.
Tours: (times given are for departure times of ferry), Tu.-F. 10.15-12.15, 1-3, 2.30-4.30. Sa. 8.45-10.45, 10.15-12.15, 1-3, 2.30-4.30. Closed public holidays.

HASWELL ZOOLOGICAL MUSEUM
University of Sydney, Sydney, New South Wales
Zoology of Australia.
M.-F. 10-4.30. Closed public holidays.

MACLEAY MUSEUM OF NATURAL HISTORY
University of Sydney, Sydney, New South Wales 2006
Collections of zoology and anthropology: mammals, birds, reptiles, fish, fossils, shells, crustaceans. A mummy collected from Danley Island (New Guinea) in 1875.
M.-F. 8-5.

MINING AND GEOLOGICAL MUSEUM
36 George Street North, Sydney, New South Wales 2000
Geological displays of rocks, minerals and fossils. Mining production and exploration methods.
M.-F. 9.30-5; Sa. and public holidays 11-4; Su. 2-5. Closed Christmas Day and Good F.

MUSEUM OF APPLIED ARTS AND SCIENCES
659-695 Harris Street, Broadway, Sydney, New South Wales 2007
Applied arts and sciences: ceramics, glassware, gemstones (including opal collection), oriental crafts, furniture, musical instruments, costumes, engineering, shipping, lighting and heating. The aircraft section assembles nearly all the surviving models constructed by Hargrave (1850-1915), who invented the rotary engine and whose experiments showed the way to the builders of the earliest biplanes. A beam engine built by James Watt in 1785 may be inspected on request.
M.-Sa. 10-5; Su. 2-5. Closed Christmas Day and Good F.

NICHOLSON MUSEUM OF ANTIQUITIES
University of Sydney, Sydney, New South Wales 2006
Collections of Near Eastern, Egyptian, Greek, Cypriot, Roman, Etruscan and European antiquities.
M.-F. 10-4.30. Closed public holidays.

OUR YESTERDAY'S MUSEUM
Argyle Arts Centre, 18 Argyle Street, Sydney, New South Wales 2006
Pioneer history, 1788-1900. Original convict and period clothing.
Daily 10-6.

RAIL TRANSPORT MUSEUM
Enfield Locomotive Depot, Sydney, New South Wales
The collection contains 35 steam locomotives, 15 of which are in working order, and one diesel, as well as various passenger and goods rolling stock. Signalling equipment, ways and works tools, photographs, tickets. 'O' gauge model railway.
Weekend and public holidays, 10-4. Other times by prior arrangement.

J. L. SHELLSHEAR MUSEUM OF COMPARATIVE ANATOMY AND PHYSICAL ANTHROPOLOGY
Department of Anatomy, University of Sydney, Sydney, New South Wales
Comparative racial series of human skulls, skeletons, brains and marsupials.
By written appointment.

WILLIAM DIXSON GALLERY AND MITCHELL LIBRARY
Macquarie Street, Sydney, New South Wales 2000
Paintings. Drawings. Prints. Photographs. Stamps. Coins. The whole collection relates to Australia and the South-West Pacific.
M.-Sa. 10-5; Su. 2-6.

TAMWORTH

TAMWORTH ART GALLERY AND MUSEUM
Tamworth, New South Wales
Australian paintings, including items by Ashton, Hyson, Turner and Lyndsay. Early Australian silverware. Comprehensive coin and postage stamp collections. Military and civil medals. Local pottery. Dickens collection, including books, manuscripts, etchings, paintings and pottery.
M.-F. 10-2, 3.30-6, 7-8; Sa. 10-12.

TANUNDA

BAROSSA VALLEY MUSEUM
47 Murray Street, Tanunda, South Australia
History of the Barossa Valley, a wine-making area. Dresses and personal possessions. Farm implements, tools and household utensils. The area was settled by German peasants from Silesia and the display of typical early church furniture shows the influence of the Lutheran church.
Daily 1-4.30. Other times by appointment.

TEA TREE GULLY

OLD HIGHERCOMBE HOTEL MUSEUM
Perseverance Road, Tea Tree Gully, South Australia
Folk exhibits.
Sa., Su. 2-5.

TEMORA

ROCK AND MINERAL MUSEUM
Council Chambers, Temora, New South Wales
Specimens of gold from the Temora district. Silver and lead from Trungby Hill. Tin from Ardlethan. Mineral samples from all parts of Australia, as well as other countries.
During Council office hours.

TENTERFIELD

SIR HENRY PARKES MEMORIAL MUSEUM
School of Arts, Rouse Street, Tenterfield, New South Wales
Historical relics and records associated with Sir Henry Parkes, Premier of N.S.W.
During library hours.

TEWANTIN

HOUSE OF BOTTLES
Miles Street, Tewantin, Sunshine Coast, Queensland
Collection of bottles ranging from fingernail size to ten gallons.
Daily 9-5.

PALMGROVE
Cooroy Range Road, Tewantin, Sunshine Coast, Queensland
Marine exhibits. Shells. Arts and crafts.
Daily 8.30-5.

THIRROUL

VALS GALLERY
271 Main Road, Thirroul, New South Wales
Works by local artists, including paintings, pottery, weaving, wood carvings.
M.-F. 10-4; Sa. 9-12.

TINGHA

SMITH'S MINING AND NATURAL HISTORY MUSEUM
Tingha, New South Wales
Minerals and gemstones from all over Australia. Coins and banknotes. Ethnographical section on Aborigines and inhabitants of the Pacific Islands. Crustacea. Local history of the area. Early farming and mining equipment. Clothing. Bottle collection. Taxidermy section, with many animal mutations. Chinese wood carvings from the Chinese joss house, once used by miners at the turn of the century.
Daily 9-12, 1-5. Closed Christmas Day.

TOODYAY

TOODYAY GAOL HISTORICAL MUSEUM
Toodyay, Western Australia
Housed in a gaol erected in 1862, the museum contains material on the early history of the Avon Valley. At the rear of the premises is a display of old farm machinery.
Sa. 2-4; Su. 10-12, 2-4. Public holidays 10-12, 2-4.

TOOWOOMBA

ART GALLERY AND GEM COLLECTION
2 St. Louis Street, Toowoomba, Queensland
"World's Original Opal Gemstone oil paintings" by Louis H. Gauvin. Displays of Queensland precious opal from the rough uncut state to the finished product. Australian gemstones and fashion jewellery pieces.
Tu.-Sa. 10-4 or by appointment.

COBB & COMPANY AUSTRALIAN MUSEUM
James and Water Streets, Toowoomba, Queensland
Horse-drawn vehicles and articles associated with the coaching era in Australia, including two Cobb coaches, and a landau built for the visit of the Duke of Edinburgh in 1867. Plants and trees in the adjacent garden have historical associations.
M.-F. 10-12, 1.30-4; Su. 2.30-5.

CREATIVE 92 ART CENTRE
Perth Street, Toowoomba, Queensland
Aboriginal birch carvings. Enamels. Pottery. Weaving. Paintings by Queensland artists. Downs District works of art.
Enquire locally.

DENNIS HILL ANTIQUES COLLECTION
80 Margaret Street, Toowoomba, Queensland
Georgian and Victorian furniture, silver and porcelain.
M.-F. 9.30-5; Sa. 9.30-12.30.

LIONEL LINDSAY ART GALLERY
1 Godsall Street, Toowoomba, Queensland
Australian art, including works by Lionel Lindsay. Etching plates and wood blocks. Historical books on early exploration and discovery.
M.-F. 2.15-5; Su. 2-5.

TAWA PIONEER COTTAGE
9 Boulton Street, off Campbell Street, West Toowoomba, Queensland
Restored home of the mid-1880s, with period furnishings.
Tu.-F. 11-3; Sa., Su. and public holidays 11-3.

TIA GALLERY
Toowoomba, Queensland
2 miles from Toowoomba, on the Old Western Highway. Sculptures in timber and stone. Paintings and pottery by Queensland artists.
Daily 9-6.

TOOWOOMBA ART GALLERY
Council Chambers, Ruthven Street, Toowoomba, Queensland
Works of Queensland artists as well as general Australian paintings.
M., W. and F. 11-3.

TOWNSVILLE

KENNEDY ANTHROPOLOGICAL MUSEUM
Rose Street and Esplanade, North Ward, Townsville, North Queensland
Primitive and Barbaric musical instruments. Complete collection of aboriginal stone artifacts from the Townsville district. Shells. Botanic exhibits, including ferns. Anthropological material from Australia, New Zealand, New Guinea, the Pacific Islands, South Africa, Rhodesia, Kenya, India, China, Thailand and New Mexico.
Daily 3.15-4.15.

TUMBY BAY

KOPPIO SMITHY MUSEUM
Tumby Bay, South Australia
Folk exhibits.
Sa. 3-5; Su. and public holidays 11-5.

URAIDLA

YUREILLA GALLERY
Uraidla, South Australia
Art collections.
Daily ex. F. 10.30-5.30.

URALLA

ROCK HUNTER'S RENDEZVOUS
New England Highway, Uralla, New South Wales
Cut and uncut gemstones. Mineral samples.
Daily 9-5.

VAUCLUSE

VAUCLUSE HOUSE
Wentworth Road, Vaucluse, New South Wales
Colonial mansion, once the home of William Charles Wentworth. Period furniture, china and family mementoes belonging to Wentworth.
Daily 10-4.45. Closed Good F., Christmas Day.

VICTOR HARBOR

CORNHILL MUSEUM AND ART GALLERY
Cornhill Road, Victor Harbor, South Australia
Art collections. Local history.
M.-Sa. 9-5; Su. 1-6.

MUSEUM OF HISTORICAL ART
Yankalilla Road, Victor Harbor, South Australia
Art collections.
Daily 10-5 ex. M.

WHALERS HAVEN MUSEUM
Victor Harbor, South Australia
Whaling collections.
Daily 10.30-5. Closed Christmas Day.

WAGGA WAGGA

HISTORICAL MUSEUM
Urana Street, Wagga Wagga, New South Wales
Local history.
Sa., Su., public holidays 2-5. School holidays 9.30-12.30, 2-5.

WAIKERIE

LYNDLEY'S WORKSHOP GALLERY
Peake Terrace, Waikerie, South Australia
Arts and crafts.
Daily 10-5.30.

WALCHA

FOLK MUSEUM
Derby Street, Walcha, New England, New South Wales
A pioneer home maintained by the local historical society.
Weekends 11-4.

WARRNAMBOOL

HISTORY HOUSE
Warrnambool and District Historical Society, Gilles Street, P.O. Box 359, Warrnambool, Victoria 3280
Local history and folk collections. Maps. Documents. Photographs. Household relics.
First Su. in month, 2-5. Also open during holiday periods.

WARWICK

PRINGLE COTTAGE HISTORICAL MUSEUM
81 Dragon Street, Warwick, Darling Downs Region, Queensland
Historic records. Period costumes and furniture. Antique bottles. Household utensils. Pioneer relics.
W. 7.30-9.30 p.m. Sa., Su. 2-5.

WATSON'S BAY

BRONKS MOTOR MUSEUM
17 Military Road, Watson's Bay, New South Wales
Veteran and vintage cars ranging from 1905 single cylinder Jackson to 1930 8-cylinder Packard. Motor cycles. 1922 vintage Garford fire engine. Old-fashioned radiators.
W.-M. 10-5.30.

WEDDERBURN

GENERAL STORE MUSEUM
Wedderburn, Calder Highway, Victoria
Original general store with old-time products. Carriages.
Daily 9-5.

WELLINGTON

WELLINGTON MUSEUM
Warne and Percy Streets, Wellington, New South Wales
Housed in original Bank of New South Wales, contains material illustrating the early history of the area. Official records, other documents, letters and photographs covering a period from the time of John Oxley's discovery of the district in 1817 and the first settlement in 1823, up to recent times. Collection of items covering all aspects of domestic, farming, transport and industrial development of Wellington and district. Early settler's cottage.
Sa. and Su. 2-5. Public and school holidays, 10-12, 2-5.

WENTWORTH

FOLK MUSEUM AND ARTS CENTRE
Wentworth, New South Wales 2648
Historical revolvers and pistols. Australia's largest collection of photographs of river paddle steamers. Machinery and farm equipment. Domestic utensils. Stones, gems and minerals. Photographs of early Wentworth. Murals by local artists.
Daily 10-5. Closed Christmas Day and Good F.

WEST GOSFORD

KENDALL COTTAGE
Henry Kendall Street, West Gosford, New South Wales
Original treadle lathe used by James Dunlop (Australia's first astronomer) and many of his instruments (1831-47). Convict relics. Plate presented by Queen Victoria to one of her staff (c.1830). Photographs of sporting events and early settler days. Bullock yokes and waggons, smoothing irons, clothing, tools and domestic equipment used by pioneers. Books, verse and photographs of Henry Kendall.
W., Sa., Su. and bank holidays, 10-4.

WEST WYALONG

HISTORICAL MUSEUM
Wyalong Memorial Hall, Neeld Street, West Wyalong, New South Wales
History of West Wyalong and the Bland Shire.
By arrangement with the Secretary (tel: 429).

WILBERFORCE

AUTHENTICATED AUSTRALIAN SETTLERS VILLAGE
Wilberforce, New South Wales
Open-air museum with reconstruction of early pioneer homes. Domestic equipment. Agricultural implements.
Tu.-Su. 10-5. Also M. during school and public holidays.

WILLIAMSTOWN

MUNICIPAL MUSEUM
Williamstown, Victoria 3016
Relics and bygones illustrating the development of the town, as the former main port of Melbourne and the original landing place (1835) for passengers and stock. Exhibits on the gold-rush of the 1850s, when the town was a penal station. Imperial and Australian naval relics. Ship models, rope-making machines, shipwrights' tools, sail-making tools and breeches buoy apparatus.
Su. 10-5. Weekdays: conducted tours by arrangement with the Williamstown Historical Society.

WILLUNGA

OLD POLICE STATION AND COURT HOUSE
Willunga, South Australia
Local history. Pioneer relics.
W., Sa. and public holidays 10-4; Su. 1-5.

WILLUNGA HOUSE
Willunga, South Australia
Art collections.
Tu.-Su. 10-5.

WILSON'S PROMONTORY

WILSON'S PROMONTORY MUSEUM
Wilson's Promontory, Victoria
Pioneer life. Household and agricultural equipment.
On request.

WINDSOR

HAWKESBURY MUSEUM
90 The Terrace, Windsor, Upper Hawkesbury, New South Wales
Relics of the Hawkesbury district from 1794: documents, photographs, clothing, household utensils and farm equipment (1800-1900).
Daily 10-4.

WINGHAM

MANNING VALLEY HISTORICAL MUSEUM
Farquhar Street, Wingham, New South Wales
Life in the Manning Valley during the early years of the district's settlement.
W., S., Su. 2-4. Daily during school holidays.

WOLLONGONG

ILLAWARRA HISTORICAL MUSEUM
11 Market Street, Wollongong, New South Wales
Early pioneering history of the district.
Summer: daily 2-5. Winter: Tu., Th., Sa. and Su. 2-5.

YASS

HISTORICAL MUSEUM
Yass, New South Wales
Local history. Pioneer relics.
On request.

YEPPOON

YEPPOON SHELL MUSEUM
James Street, Yeppoon, Rockhampton Region, Queensland
International shell collection.
Daily 9-5.

YOUNG

LAMBING FLAT HISTORICAL MUSEUM
Corner Lynch and Marina Streets, Young, New South Wales
Early history of the district.
F., Sa., Su. 2-5; M.-Th. 3-5 (January).

ZEEHAN

WEST COAST PIONEERS' MEMORIAL MUSEUM
P.O. Box 70, Zeehan, Tasmania
Collection of old Zeehan School of Mining and Metallurgy: samples of Crocoite, Cerussite and Dundasite; early tools, assay equipment, mementoes of the Mount Lyell Mine disaster; working model of the Mount Bischoff treatment plant; diorama of an old mine 'face'. Modern mining techniques; four locomotives and mining equipment, including a 'bogger' and Jumbo drill. Daimler Rail Car, used by the General Manager of the Mount Lyell Mining and Railway Co. and restored to its original condition. Tasmanian animals and birds. Tasmanian aboriginal collection.
Daily 8.30-dusk.

Austria

Austria's museums rely heavily on her past and on her geology, the first of which has proved both a blessing and a nuisance. The grandeurs and wealth of the former Imperial Court made it possible to accumulate magnificent collections of art and to encourage the most talented musicians in Europe to settle in places convenient to their patrons and their market; but these solid advantages of money and prestige also produced the monumental museum-palaces from which curators have suffered ever since - inflexible morgues for pictures, statues and suits of armour, which cost an annual fortune to heat and maintain and which drained away so much money to restore after extensive war-damage. After toiling up the great staircases and through the pompous marble halls of the nineteenth-century court museums in Vienna, one turns to the lighter touch, humanity and shorter journeys of the modern Museum of the City of Vienna with a relief which is not easy to communicate to anyone who has not been tested in the same fire.

This is, however, to pay a poor tribute to the immense and successful efforts made by a far from rich state to repair the appalling damage brought about by the hostilities of 1939-45. Everything, to outward appearances, at least, is now as it was before and, in many instances, a great deal better. The little museums especially - the houses where Beethoven and Haydn composed and Mozart died and where Goethe stayed - are miraculously there again, with only photographs to show the condition they were in twenty-five years ago. The Museum of Horse-Drawn Cabs is there to show the splendid old vehicles that had their own way of surviving the bombings and the burning, and the restorers have worked wonders with the paintings that spent the war years in the salt mines.

Apart from the musical shrines and the art galleries, there are perhaps three kinds of collection which combine to give a special quality to Austrian museums as a whole: the monastery collections, to be found in a quantity not equalled elsewhere; the mining museums and, one regrets to have to say it, the torture-chambers and torture-instruments in an abundance quite unparalleled in other countries.

ADMONT

MUSEUM OF ART HISTORY
Benediktinerabtei, 8911 Admont, Bezirk Liezen, Steiermark
11th-20th century religious art. 17th-18th century embroidery by lay-brothers of Monastery. Sculpture by J. T. Stammel (1695-1765). 'Fathers of the Church' series of paintings by G. B. Goetz. Frescoes, religious paintings, landscapes by A. Kurtz (d.1916). Applied art. Goldsmiths' work. Pewter. Glass. Coins. Medals.
By appointment.

NATURAL HISTORY MUSEUM
Benediktinerabtei, 8911 Admont, Bezirk Liezen, Steiermark
Mineralogy. Fossils. Fish. Molluscs. Snakes. Birds (especially humming birds and birds of Paradise). Mammals, including Australian collection. Insects.
June-Sept. Daily 10-12, 2-4. Other months by appointment.

REGIONAL MUSEUM. FLOIGMAYER COLLECTION
8911 Admont, Bezirk Liezen, Steiermark
Regional history.
By appointment.

AIGEN

COLLECTIONS OF SCHLÄGL MONASTERY
4160 Aigen, Upper Austria
Portraits and other paintings. Calligraphy. Incunabuli.
On request.

ALPL

PETER ROSEGGEN'S BIRTHPLACE
Kluppeneggerhof, 8671 Alpl, Bezirk Mürzzuschlag, Steiermark
House (1744) was birthplace of the writer, Peter Roseggen (1843-1918). Original and period furnishings. Memorabilia of Roseggen.
Daily 8-6.

ALTAUSSEE

SALTMINE
8992 Altaussee, Bezirk Bad Aussee, Steiermark
Salt-mine and visitor centre, with displays illustrating history and techniques of local salt-production. Mining equipment, including Austria's oldest mine-locomotive (1897). St. Barbara Chapel, with votive pictures and paintings of the Bad Aussee Fire of 1742.
May-Sept. Daily 8-4. Other times by appointment.

ALTENBURG

COLLECTIONS OF BENEDICTINE MONASTERY
3591 Altenburg, Lower Austria
Austrian Baroque paintings and furnishings.
By appointment.

ALTENMARKT

ETHNOLOGICAL COLLECTION
Heimatstube, Schulhaus, 8934 Altenmarkt, Bezirk Radstadt, Steiermark
Local history and folklore.
By appointment.

AMSTETTEN

MUNICIPAL COLLECTION
Neues Stadthaus, Hauptplatz 29, 3300 Amstetten, Nieder Osterreich
Local and regional history. Palaeolithic, Neolithic and Bronze Age tools. Roman material, mostly copies, from Mauer-an-der-Ure. (originals in Kunsthistorisches Museum, Vienna).
M.-F. 8.30-5.

ANZENAU

ANZENAU MILL OPEN-AIR MUSEUM
Anzenau, Bezirk Bad Ischl, Oberösterreich
In restored farm buildings. Watermill. Bakehouse. Stables. Agricultural tools, implements. Peasant handicrafts.
By appointment.

ARNFELS

MUSEUM OF CLOCKS, MUSICAL INSTRUMENTS AND FOLKLORE
Maltschach 3, 8454 Arnfels, Bezirk Leibnitz, Steiermark
Clocks, including 16th-17th century water-clocks. Hourglasses. Mechanical musical instruments. Popular art, including drinking glasses, pipes, coffins. Religious art. Weapons. Coins. Agricultural tools and implements.
By appointment.

ARNSDORF

FRANZ XAVIER GRUBER MUSEUM
Arnsdorf 9, Bezirk Salzburg-Land, Salzburg
Home of Franz Xavier Gruber, composer of 'Stille Nacht, Heilige Nacht' (1818). Original furnishings. Memorabilia of Gruber. Manuscripts.
By appointment.

ARZBERG

REGIONAL MUSEUM
Passail, Arzberg, Bezirk Weis, Steiermark
Peasant household equipment. Thatching and roof-shingling tools. Tools and equipment of the flax and wool textile industries, including 17th century loom. Scythemaking and mining equipment.
By appointment.

ASPARN

LOWER AUSTRIA MUSEUM OF PREHISTORY
2151 Asparn-an-der-Zaya, Bezirk Mistelbach, Niederösterreich
Prehistory and early history of Lower Austria. Open-air museum, with reconstructions of prehistoric dwellings.
Apr.-Oct. Tu.-Sa. 9-5.

WEINLAND MUSEUM
Minoritenkloster, 2151 Asparn-an-der-Zaya, Bezirk Mistelbach, Niederösterreich
Geology. Palaeontology. Prehistory and early history of the region. Botany. Zoology. Ethnography. Local history. Agriculture.
Apr.-Oct., Su. 10-12. Other times by appointment.

BAD AUSSEE

AUSSEE REGIONAL MUSEUM
Kammerhofgebäude, Chlumetzkyplatz 1, 8990 Bad Aussee, Steiermark
Costumes. Aussee Fasching masks. Early forestry tools. Mineralogy. Local history.
May-June and Sept. Tu., Th., Sa. 4-6. July-Aug. M.-Sa. 10-12, 4-6.

BAD DEUTSCH ALTENBURG

AFRICAN MUSEUM
Schloss Ludwigstorff, 2405 Bad Deutsch Altenburg, Bezirk Bruck an der Leitha, Niederösterreich
Castle (17th century). Ethnographical and zoological collections from E. Africa. Dioramas. *May-Sept. Daily 8-4. Other times by appointment.*

CARNUNTIUM MUSEUM
Badgasse 42, 2405 Bad Deutsch Altenburg, Bruck an der Leitha, Niederösterreich
Material (1st-4th centuries) from excavations at the Roman town of Carnuntium and the nearby legionary camp. Monuments. Mosaics. Statues. Gold and silver ornaments. Pottery. Glass. Bronzes. Coins. Architectural items.
Daily 9-5.

CARL LEOPOLD HOLLITZER MUSEUM
2405 Bad Deutsch Altenburg, Bezirk Bruck an der Leitha, Niederösterreich
Home of artist, Carl Leopold Hollitzer. Works by Hollitzer. Figurines for the theatre. Portraits and caricatures of artists and of famous contemporaries. Drawings of uniforms.
By appointment.

BADEN

EMPEROR FRANZ JOSEPH MUSEUM
Hochstrasse 51, 2500 Baden, Niederösterreich
Crafts and craftsmen's tools, especially wrought iron, pottery, clock-making, instrument-making, weaving, candle-making. Lighting equipment. Woodcarving. Religious art.
May-Oct. Tu.-Su. 9-5. Nov.-Apr, Tu.-Su. 9-4.

ROLLETT MUSEUM
Weikersdorfer Platz 1, 2500 Baden, Niederösterreich
Geology. Palaeontology. Mineralogy. Herbarium. Insects. Prehistoric and Roman material from local sites. Skulls. Mask of Napoleon I. Biedermeier period watercolours, handicrafts, fabrics. History of Baden. Memorabilia of Grillparzer and Beethoven. Works of the sculptor, Josef Müllner.
May-Oct. Su. 9-12; W., Sa. 5-6. Other months by appointment.

BADGASTEIN

REGIONAL MUSEUM
5640 Badgastein, Bezirk St. Johann im Pongau, Salzburg
Roman coins. Minerals from local mines. 1690 map of goldmine. History of spa. Costumes.
May-Sept. M.-F. 9.30-11. Other times on request.

BAD GOISERN

GOISERN REGIONAL MUSEUM
Haus der Kurverwaltung, Gottlieb-Oberhauser Strasse, 4822 Bad Goisern, Bezirk Gmunden, Oberösterreich
Works and memorabilia of the 'peasant philosopher', Konrad Deubler. Paintings by local artists. Household equipment. Handicrafts. Musical instruments. Prehistoric and early historical material from local sites. The last local water-driven forge-hammer is set up in the Kurpark.
Sa., W. 2-6; Su., public holidays, 9-12.

BAD HALL

REGIONAL MUSEUM
Tassilo-Quelle, Sulzbachtal, 4540 Bad Hall, Oberösterreich
History of Bad Hall. Handicrafts. Agricultural implements. Household equipment. Furnished peasant room. History of the spa.
F. 3-5. Other times by appointment.

BAD ISCHL

LEHAR VILLA
Franz Lehar Kai 8, 4820 Bad Ischl, Oberösterreich
House-museum of the composer, Franz Léhar. Personal possessions and memorabilia. Original scores. Paintings. Furniture.
May 15 - Sept. 30, daily 9-12, 2-5.

MUSEUM OF ETHNOLOGY
Riedlerhäusl, Engleithen, 4820 Bad Ischl, Oberösterreich
Ethnographical material from the Salzkammergut.
By appointment.

MUSEUM OF THE HAENEL AND PANCERA FAMILIES
Villa Haenel, Concordiastrasse 3, 4820 Ischl-Kaltenbach, Oberösterreich
Paintings by 17th-19th century European artists, including Rembrandt, Caravaggio, Frans Hals. Sculpture, especially copies of Greek, Roman and Renaissance originals. Porcelain. Glass. Carpets. Clocks. Oriental objets d'art. Memorabilia of the pianist. Ella Pancera. Autographed letters of famous 19th century people.
May 15- Oct. 1, Daily 9-12, 2-4.

REGIONAL MUSEUM
Franz Lehar Kai 8, 4820 Bad Ischl, Oberösterreich
Models, plans, pictures, illustrating development of Bad Ischl. Furniture. Household equipment. Cribs. History of local mining and saltworks. Paintings, drawings, photographs showing 19th-20th century life in the Salzkammergut.
May 15- Sept. 30, Daily 9-12, 2-6.

VILLA OF THE EMPEROR
Jainzen 38, 4820 Bad Ischl, Oberösterreich
Summer residence of the Emperor Franz Joseph I. Original furnishings. Memorabilia of the Imperial Family. Hunting trophies. Paintings by 19th century Austrian and European artists. Sculpture. Porcelain.
Easter- Oct. 31, Daily 8-5.30.

BAD LEONFELDEN

REGIONAL MUSEUM
4190 Bad Leonfelden, Oberösterreich
In former church. Local history. Craftsmen's tools, especially weaving. Peasant life. Costumes.
Su. 9-5.

BAD TATZMANNSDORF

BURGENLAND OPEN-AIR MUSEUM
7431 Bad Tatzmannsdorf, Bezirk Oberwart, Burgenland
17th-18th century peasant houses, workshops, farm buildings.
Daily 9-6.

BAD VÖSLAU

REGIONAL MUSEUM
Schloss, 2540 Bad Vöslau, Bezirk Baden, Niederösterreich
History of Vöslau and its spa. Furniture. Household equipment. Paintings. Fossils. Palaeontology. Vineyard equipment. Techniques and tools of the pitch industry. Austrian postage stamps. Weapons. Hunting trophies.
May-Sept. Sa. 2-6; Su., public holidays 9-12. Other times by appointment.

BAD WIMSBACH-NEYDHARTING

BUDWEIS COLLECTION
Paracelsus Haus, 4654 Bad Wimsbach-Neydharting, Bezirk Wels, Oberösterreich
History of the Nudweis Forestry School. Mementoes of its establishment in 1865.
Daily 2-4.

INTERNATIONAL PEAT-BOG MUSEUM
Paracelsus Haus, 4654 Bad Wimsbach-Neydharting, Bezirk Wels, Oberösterreich
Extraction and uses of peat. Settlements. Archaeological discoveries.
Daily 9-12, 3-5.

JUNGSCHÜTZEN MUSEUM
Stiftungshaus, 4654 Bad Wimsbach-Neydharting, Bezirk Wels, Oberösterreich
Memorial museum of the K. K. Freiwilligen Oberösterreichischen Schützenregiments and of the campaigns in the S. Tyrol (1914-18). Weapons and equipment. Flags.
Emergency money, 1918-20.
Daily 10-12, 2-4.

PENTAGRAM MUSEUM
Kurhaus, 4654 Bad Wimsbach-Neydharting, Bezirk Wels, Oberösterreich
World collection of pentagrams, from Neolithic times onwards.
By appointment.

REGIONAL MUSEUM
Paracelsus Haus, 4654 Bad Wimsbach-Neydharting, Bezirk Wels, Oberösterreich
Prehistoric material from the peat-bog near Bad Meydharting. Neolithic and Bronze Age earthenware vessels. 12th-17th century Austrian pottery.
Daily 10-12, 4-6.

TRANSPORT MUSEUM
Paracelsus Haus, 4654 Bad Wimsbach-Neydharting, Bezirk Wels, Oberösterreich
Mementoes of the oldest Austrian railway, Budweis-Gmunden. Models. Original locomotive and coach.
Daily 3-4.

BERNSTEIN

PALACE MUSEUM
7434 Bernstein, Bezirk Oberwart, Burgenland
13th century castle, remodelled in 16th-17th centuries. Neolithic, Bronze and Iron Age tools. Punishment cell, with medieval instruments of torture. Weapons. 17th century alchemists' equipment. *May-Oct. Daily 8-12, 1-5. Nov.-Apr. by appointment.*

BEZAU

REGIONAL MUSEUM
Ellenbogen 181, 6870 Bezau, Bezirk Bregenz, Vorarlberg
Life and history of the Bregenzer Wald. Craftsmen's tools. Furniture. Household equipment. Portraits. Religious art.
Tu.-Sa. 9-11, 2-5. Su., public holidays, 2-4.

BLEIBURG

WERNER BERG GALERIE
Stadtplatz, 9150 Bleiburg, Bezirk Völkermarkt, Kärnten
Paintings and sketches by Werner Berg.
May 20- Oct. 15, 10-12, 4-6.

BLUDENZ

REGIONAL MUSEUM
Kirchgasse 9, 6700 Blundenz, Vorarlberg
Local and regional history and folklore. Religious art, including Muttersberg altar. Plague cross (c.1500). Drawings by T. Leu (1752-1802).
May-Oct. W., Sa. 2-4; Su. 10-12. Other times by appointment.

BRAMBERG

REGIONAL MUSEUM
Gemeindeamt, 5733 Bramberg, Bezirk Zell am See, Salzburg
Peasant furniture, tools and implements. Knives. Glass paintings. Local minerals.
July-Aug., Su. 9.30-11.30; Th. 4-6. Other times by appointment.

BRANDHOF

ARCHDUKE JOHANN HUNTING MUSEUM
Jagdschlösse am Seeberg, Bezirk Bruck an der Mur, Steiermark
House-memorial to the Archduke. Portraits. Writing-room, with original furnishings. Personal possessions and memorabilia of the Archduke. Hunting trophies and weapons.
June-Sept. Daily 9-12, 2-5.

BRAUNAU AM INN

DISTRICT MUSEUM
Johann Fischer Gasse 18 und 20, 5282 Braunau am Inn, Oberösterreich
Local history and folklore. Prehistoric material. Peasant furniture, household equipment, tools, handicrafts. Popular art. 16th century bell-founder's workshop. 19th century sitting room. Coins.
Tu.-Su. 9-11, 3-5.

BREGENZ

VORARLBERG MUSEUM
Kornmarkt 1, 6900 Bregenz, Vorarlberg
Regional history. Prehistoric material. Roman archaeological discoveries from Brigantium (Bregenz). Alemannic and Rhaetoromannic artifacts. Costumes. Religious art. Musical instruments. Weapons. Instruments of torture. Tapestries. 19th-20th century paintings, sculpture, applied art. Coins. Porcelain.
Tu.-Su. 9-12, 2-5.

BREITENAU

VOTIVE COLLECTION OF ST. ERHARD'S CHURCH
2624 Breitenau, Niederösterreich
14th century painted glass. Wood and wax votive objects.
On request.

BRUCK AN DER LEITHA

REGIONAL MUSEUM
Johnstrasse 1, 2460 Bruck an der Leitha, Niederösterreich
Prehistoric and Roman archaeology. Coins. Fossils. Display illustrating local cement production. Weapons. Craftsmen's tools. Household equipment.
Su. 10-12. Other times on request.

BRUCK AN DER MUR

REGIONAL MUSEUM
Am Grazertor 1, 8600 Bruck an der Mur, Steiermark
Local and regional history. Folklore. Art. Natural history.
Apr.-Oct., M., Th., F., Sa., Su. 9-12, 2-6.

DEUTSCH WAGRAM

REGIONAL MUSEUM
Gemeindeamt, Bahnhofstrasse, 2232 Deutsch Wagram, Bezirk Gänserndorf, Niederösterreich
Napoleonic history and relics. Mementoes, dioramas, relics of the Battle of Wagram. History of the Emperor Ferdinand Northern Railway (1837). Memorabilia of the physicist and inventor, Dr. J. Sahulka (d.1927).
Apr.-Oct., 1st, 3rd, 5th Su. in month, 10-12. 2nd, 4th Su. in month, 3-5.

DÖLLACH

REGIONAL AND GOLDMINING MUSEUM
Schloss Grosskirchheim, 9843 Döllach, Bezirk Spittal an der Drau, Kärnten
Local history. Furniture. Household equipment. Tools. Ceramics. Weapons. Minerals and ores. Goldmining equipment and techniques.
By appointment.

DÖLSACH

AGUNTINUM MUSEUM
9991 Dölsach, Bezirk Lienz, Tirol
Site museum (reconstruction of Tuscan open-roofed atrium) with material from excavations at Roman town of Aguntum and at Lavant. Mosaics. Mithras altar. Pottery. Jewellery.
May-Oct. Daily 8-12, 1-7. Nov.-Apr., by appointment.

DORNBIRN

LANDSCAPE AND ECOLOGY OF THE VORARLBERG
Marktstrasse 33, 6850 Dornbirn, Bezirk Feldkirch, Vorarlberg
Displays showing changes in the Vorarlberg landscape, in its plants and wildlife. Herbarium. Dioramas. Forestry. Agriculture. Water resources and their application. Geology. Glaciers. Mineralogy. Palaeontology.
Mar.-Oct. Tu.-Su. 9-12, 2-5.

DREISTETTEN

SCHERRER INN REGIONAL MUSEUM
Post Piesting, Dreistetten, Bezirk Wiener Neustadt, Niederösterreich
Minerals. Fossils. Local and regional history. Peasant furnishings, household equipment. Costumes. Weapons.
Daily, during opening hours of inn.

DROSENDORF

FRANZ KIESSLING MUSEUM
Drosendorf 17, 2095 Drosendorf, Bezirk Horn, Niederösterreich
Prehistoric material from local sites. Local history. 19th-20th century craftsmen's tools and equipment, especially colour printing. Writings of Franz Kiessling.
Sept.-June Daily 10-12. July-Aug. Daily 9-12.

DÜRNSTEIN

DÜRNSTEIN REGIONAL MUSEUM
Klarissinenkloster, 3601 Dürnstein 25, Bezirk Krems, Niederösterreich
Local history. 16th-19th century peasant furniture, household equipment, tools. Weapons. Costumes. 16th century brass-founder's equipment.
By appointment.

EBENAU

REGIONAL MUSEUM
5323 Ebenau, Bezirk Salzburg Land, Salzburg
In administrative building of former brassworks. Water-driven hammers. 16th century brass foundry equipment. Peasant furniture, including 16th-17th century chests. Costumes. Weapons, including flint-lock guns.
Daily 10-10.

EFERDING

MUNICIPAL MUSEUM, STARHEMBERG FAMILY MUSEUM, REGIONAL MUSEUM
Schloss Starhemberg, Kirchplatz 1, 4070 Eferding, Oberösterreich
In castle (1416, remodelled 1600). Prehistoric and Roman archaeology. Local history. Altar paintings. Guild-chests. Weapons. Starhemberg family possessions and memorabilia.
May-Sept. Su., public holidays 9-12. Other times by appointment.

EGG

REGIONAL MUSEUM
6863 Egg, Bezirk Bregenz, Vorarlberg
Folklore. Costumes. Jewellery and ornaments. Clothes' cupboards. Garlands. Votive pictures. Paintings showing local costumes. Furnished peasant rooms. Guild pictures and archives. Weapons. Agricultural implements.
Tu. 11-12; F., Su. 11-12. Other times by appointment.

EGGENBURG

KRAHULETZ MUSEUM
Krahuletzplatz 1, 3730 Eggenburg, Bezirk Horn, Niederösterreich
Geology. Palaeontology. Fossils. Prehistoric archaeology, including bridle (4th century B.C.). Displays illustrating peasant life. Furnished interiors. Glass. Porcelain. Clocks. Weapons. Wrought-iron. Ornaments. Costumes.
Tu.-Su. 9-11, 2-4.

EIBENSTEIN

OPEN-AIR MUSEUM
Naturpark Blockheide, Eibenstein, Bezirk Gmünd, Niederösterreich
Local types of commercially useful stones, as quarried and dressed.
Daily, dawn-dusk.

EIBISWALD

KLOEPFER MUSEUM
8552 Eibiswald 36, Bezirk Deutschlandsberg, Steiermark
Birthplace and house-museum of the local doctor and poet, Hans Kloepfer, (d.1944). Manuscripts, personal possessions and memorabilia of Kloepfer.
Daily 8-12, 3-6.

REGIONAL MUSEUM
8552 Eibiswald 36, Bezirk Deutschlandsberg, Steiermark
Peasant household equipment. Tools. Handicrafts and applied art, especially keys, locks. Furnished interiors. Relics of the local mining and scythe-making industries.
Daily 8-12, 3-6.

EISBACH

COLLECTION OF REIN CISTERCIAN MONASTERY
Eisbach, Bezirk Deutschlandsberg, Steiermark
Illuminated manuscripts. Incunabula and other books from the library of Archduke Ferdinand. Gold and silversmiths' work. Musical instruments.
Guided tours, M.-Sa. 9 and 2; Su., public holidays, 2. Other times by appointment.

EISENERZ

MINING MUSEUM
Tullstrasse 17A, 8790 Eisenerz, Bezirk Leoben, Steiermark
History and techniques of local iron-mining. Models. Minerals. Tools and equipment. Mine transport. Lighting equipment. Flags. Paintings. Drawings. Material from excavation of 4th century smelting furnace.
M.-Sa., 8-4; Su., public holidays 8-12.

REGIONAL MUSEUM
Museumstiege 2, 8790 Eisenerz, Bezirk Leoben, Steiermark
History of local iron-ore mining. Local history. Folklore. Early 19th century clockwork marionettes and pictures made by the Tendler family. Weapons. Targets. Wrought-iron. Glass. Majolica. Musical instruments. Coins.
Tu.-Sa. 9-12, 2-6. Su., public holidays, 9-12.

EISENSTADT

BURGENLAND MUSEUM
Museumgasse 1-5, 7000 Eisenstadt, Burgenland
Geology. Mineralogy. Geology. Archaeology of Hallstatt period. Roman mosaics. Folklore. Art history. Judaica collection.
Special exhibitions only during rebuilding of museum.

HAYDN MUSEUM
Joseph Haydn Gasse 21, 7000 Eisenstadt, Burgenland
House was Haydn's home, 1766-78. Memorabilia of Haydn and his times. Musical instruments. Portraits. Paintings. Autograph letters and manuscripts. Material relating to Franz Liszt and to the dancer, Fanny Eisler.
M.-F. 9-12, 1-5; Sa., Su. 9-12. Easter-Nov. 1, also Sa., Su. 1-5.

ELBIGENALP

FALGER MUSEUM
Schnitzerfachschule, 6652 Elbigenalp, Tyrol
Local history. History of woodcarving. Works and personal possessions of the lithographer, J. A. Falger (d.1876).
By appointment.

ENNS

MUNICIPAL MUSEUM
Hauptplatz 19, 4470 Enns, Bezirk Linz-Land, Oberösterreich
In old Town Hall (1547). Local and regional history. Prehistoric and Roman material from local sites. Medieval sculpture, weapons. Furniture. Costumes. Wrought-iron. Town views, 1593 onwards. Coins from Enns mint, 1294 onwards. Oldest Austrian town charter (1212).
Daily 1.30-4. Su. also 10-12.

ERNSTBRUNN

PALACE MUSEUM
2115 Ernstbrunn, Bezirk Mistelbach, Niederösterreich
Collection illustrating 18th-19th century domestic life.
By appointment.

FELDBACH

REGIONAL MUSEUM
Im Tabor, 8330 Feldbach, Steiermark
Regional handicrafts. Agricultural implements. Water-driven oil-mill and corn-mill. Mural paintings. Local history material. Representation of the Battle of St. Gotthard (1664).
Tu., F. 9-12; Su., public holidays 8-11, 3-6.

FELDKIRCH

REGIONAL MUSEUM IN THE SCHATTENBURG
6800 Feldkirch, Vorarlberg
In 13th-14th century castle. History of local life. 12th century sculpture. Applied art. Locks. Weapons. Coins. Targets.
Daily 9-11, 2-5.

FESTENBURG

KERNSTOCK MUSEUM
Schloss Festenburg, Bezirk Hartberg, Steiermark
House-museum of the priest and poet, Dr. Ottokar Kernstock (d.1928). Original furnishings. Books, memorabilia and personal possessions of Dr. Kernstock.
M.-Sa. 8-10, 1-5. Su. 1-5.

FISCHAMEND

REGIONAL MUSEUM
Im Marktturm, Hauptplatz 5, 2401 Fischamend, Bezirk Wien-Umgeburg, Niederösterreich
Prehistory and early history, especially material from the Roman town, Alquinoctium (Fischamend). Peasant furnishings, household equipment, craftsmen's tools and equipment, especially relating to milling. Pictures and documents illustrating events of 1848.
May-Oct., Su., public holidays 10-12. Other times on request.

FORCHTENSTEIN

COLLECTIONS AT FORCHTENSTEIN CASTLE
Neustift an der Rosalia, Forchtenstein, Burgenland
Weapons and armour. Shields. Morions. Hunting equipment. Military equipment of the Esterházy units. War trophies. Flags. Battle pictures. Family portraits.
Daily 8-12, 1-5.

FRAUENBERG

ROMAN MUSEUM
Altes Schulhaus, Frauenberg, Bezirk Leibnitz, Steiermark
4th century Roman temple site, covered by late 17th century school building, of which the cellar serves as museum. Architectural details. Sculpture. Roman tools and utensils.
On request.

FREISTADT

MÜHLVIERTEL REGIONAL MUSEUM
Schloss, 4240 Freistadt, Oberösterreich
Peasant paintings on glass. Handicrafts. Collections illustrating the history, people and life of the Mühlviertel.
May-June, Sept.-Oct., guided tours daily at 2. July-Aug. guided tours daily at 9 and 2.

FRESACH

EVANGELICAL DIOCESAN MUSEUM
9712 Fresach, Bezirk Villach-Land, Kärnten
History of the Reformation and the Evangelical Church in Austria-Hungary. Documents. Books, including Slovenian Protestant Bible (1584) and Catechism (1580). Chancel altar (1785).
Easter-Nov. 1, daily 9-12, 3-6. Other times on request.

FRIESACH

REGIONAL MUSEUM
Fürstenhofgasse 115, 9712 Friesach, Bezirk St. Viet an der Glan, Kärnten
Local and regional history and folklore. Medieval sculpture, including late Gothic altar-shrine by Konrad von Friesach. Costumes. Coins. Guild badges and tokens. Weapons. Engravings and drawings of Friesach. *May-Oct. Tu., Th., F. 3-5. Other times on request.*

FÜRSTENFELD

MUNICIPAL MUSEUM
8280 Fürstenfeld, Steiermark
Local history and folklore.
On request.

FROHNLEITEN

RABENSTEIN CASTLE COLLECTIONS
8130 Frohnleiten, Styria
Castle, partly 12th century. Weapons. Military equipment.
On request.

GAADEN

FERDINAND RAIMUND MEMORIAL MUSEUM
Heiligenkreuzer Strasse 1, 2531 Gaaden, Bezirk Mödling, Niederösterreich
Summer home of the composer, Ferdinand Raimund. Furniture, autograph manuscripts, paintings, scores and other memorabilia.
Daily 9-6.

GALLNEUKIRCHEN

PREHISTORIC COLLECTION
Hauptschule, 4210 Gallneukirchen, Bezirk Urfahr, Oberösterreich
Prehistoric material from local sites.
By appointment.

GARS AM KAMP

REGIONAL HISTORY COLLECTION
Apoigergasse 90, 3571 Gars am Kamp, Niederösterreich
Local and regional history.
By appointment.

GLEISDORF

REGIONAL MUSEUM
Rathaus, Florianiplatz, 8200 Gleisdorf, Bezirk Weis, Steiermark
Regional history. Material from 1st-2nd century A.D. Roman temple. Peasant furnishings, household equipment. Craftsmen's tools, especially for comb-making industry.

Display illustrating 18th century Gleisdorf postal service. 17th-18th century paintings of hunting scenes. Dioramas showing changes in local geography and landscapes.
Apr.-Oct. Su. 9-12. Other times by appointment.

GMÜND

MUNICIPAL MUSEUM
Altes Rathaus, Stadtplatz, 3950 Gmünd, Niederösterreich
History of Gmünd and the surrounding area. Minerals. Local crafts, especially wrought-iron, weaving, pottery. Religious sculpture. History of local guilds. Weapons.
W. 2-6; Su., public holidays, 8-12.

MUSEUM OF GLASS
Rathaus, Stadtplatz 34, 3950 Gmünd, Niederösterreich
Displays showing history and techniques of regional glassworks, 16th-19th centuries. Examples of glassware produced. Tools and equipment. Salzburg crystal. Nitreous glazes. Glass from Schnegattein. Glass ornaments from Watten. Present-day glassmaking in Austria. Quarrying and masonry in the region.
Su., public holidays 9-12. May-Oct. also W. 2-6. Other times by appointment.

REGIONAL MUSEUM
Schloss, 9853 Gmünd, Bezirk Spittal an der Drau, Kärnten
Mineralogy. Agricultural implements. Peasant household equipment. Wedding garments. History of Gmünd. Views of the town.
May-Oct. M., W., F. 5-6. Other times on request.

GMÜNDEN

TOWN MUSEUM
Kammerhofgasse, 4810 Gmünden, Oberösterreich
Local history. Folklore. Pottery. Woodcarving. Sculpture. Paintings. Drawings. Brahms and Hebbel Collections.
On request.

GNAS

REGIONAL MUSEUM
Rathaus, Hauptplatz, 8342 Gnas, Bezirk Feldbach, Steiermark
Local history and folklore. Peasant craft tools. Locks. Pewter. Guild jugs. Models and pictures of regional house-types. Items from prehistoric burial mounds.
On request.

GOBELSBURG

PALACE MUSEUM
3551 Gobelsburg, Bezirk Krems, Niederösterreich
18th century castle. 17th-19th century painted furniture. Paintings of peasant houses and peasant life. 18th-19th century Austrian and Italian majolica. Popular art.
May-Oct. Tu.-Su. 9-5.

GÖTTWEIG

MONASTERY GRAPHICS COLLECTION
Furth, Göttweig, Bezirk Krems, Niederösterreich
16th-18th century German, Dutch, Flemish, Italian, French prints and drawings. 17th-18th century copper plates. Portraits. Landscapes.
Apr.-Nov. Daily 9.30-12, 2-5.30.

GRAZ

BAROQUE MUSEUM
Schloss Eggenberg, Eggenberger Allee 90, 8020 Graz, Steiermark
Paintings by J. A. Raunacher (d.1768). 18th century stoves. 17th-18th century carpets. Chinese porcelain, silk and scroll paintings. Outdoor collection of Roman stone inscriptions and other monuments and architectural items.
Daily 9-12. May-Oct. also Daily 2-6, rest of year 2-4.

DIOCESAN MUSEUM
Hoforatorium, Domkirche, 8010 Graz, Steiermark
Religious art from the diocese of Seckau.
On request.

GRAZ SCHOOL MUSEUM
Schloss Eggenburg, Eggenberger Allee, 8020 Graz, Steiermark
Educational history. Local history.
Daily 9-12. M., Tu., F. also 3-6.

JOANNEUM PROVINCIAL MUSEUM OF CULTURAL HISTORY AND APPLIED ART
Neutorgasse 45, 8010 Graz, Steiermark
History of Graz and Steiermark, medieval times to 19th century. Wrought and cast iron. Renaissance and Baroque period rooms. History of craft guilds in Steiermark. Religious art. Johannes Kepler room. Sun dials. Stone calendars. Costumes. Textiles. Ceramics. Glass. Pewter. Musical instruments.
M.-F. 9-5; Sa., Su. 9-12.

JOANNEUM PROVINCIAL MUSEUM OF THE HISTORY OF GRAZ
Schloss Eggenberg, Eggenberger Allee 90, 8020 Graz, Steiermark
History of Graz and of early settlements in the area. 17th-19th century models, paintings, engravings, showing development of Graz. Theatre, opera and musical history of Graz. Special collections illustrating life and work of Joseph Marx, Hugo Wolf, Robert Hamerling, Peter Rosegger and Bruno Ertler.
Daily 9-12, 2-5.

JOANNEUM PROVINCIAL MUSEUM OF THE ETHNOLOGY AND FOLKLORE OF STEIERMARK
Paulustorgasse 13, 8010 Graz, Steiermark
Furnished rooms from peasant houses. Painted furniture. Development of ploughs. Costumes. Masks. Musical instruments. Exhibits showing scenes from religious plays. Wrought-iron votive plaques.
Apr.-Nov. Daily 9-12, M., W., F. also 2-5.

JOANNEUM PROVINCIAL MUSEUM OF MINERALOGY
Raubergasse, 8010 Graz, Steiermark
Mineralogy, especially of Steiermark. Industrial uses of minerals. Sample of Coelestin sent by Goethe to Archduke Johann.
Daily 9-12. M., Tu., F. also 3-6.

JOANNEUM PROVINCIAL MUSEUM OF MINING, GEOLOGY AND TECHNOLOGY
Raubergasse 10, 8010 Graz, Steiermark
Geology. Palaeontology. Fossils, including mastodons, dinotheria. Dioramas. Models showing early mining and smelting methods. Demonstration coalmine.
Daily 9-12. M., Tu., F. also 3-6.

JOANNEUM PROVINCIAL MUSEUM: NEW GALLERY
Stadtpalais Eggenberg-Herberstein, Sackstrasse 16, 8010 Graz, Steiermark
19th-20th century paintings, sculpture, especially by Austrian artists. Special collection of works by Wilhelm Thony.
Daily 9-12. M., Tu., F. also 3-5.

JOANNEUM PROVINCIAL MUSEUM: OLD GALLERY
Neutorgasse 45, 8010 Graz, Steiermark
Medieval paintings, sculpture, drawings, especially from Steiermark. Austrian, German, Italian, Dutch, Flemish Renaissance paintings, sculpture. Austrian, German, Italian Baroque paintings, engravings. 13th-15th century glass paintings. Baroque sketches in oils, especially by Martin Johann Schmidt.
Daily 9-12. M., Tu., F. also 3-5.

JOANNEUM PROVINCIAL MUSEUM OF PREHISTORY AND EARLY HISTORY
Schloss Eggenberg, 8010 Graz, Steiermark
Archaeological material from sites in Steiermark, Palaeolithic to medieval. Strettweg Bronze Age cart. Roman archaeology. Mesopotamian, Egyptian, Greek antiquities. World-wide collection of coins.
Daily 9-12. M., Tu., F. also 3-6.

JOANNEUM PROVINCIAL MUSEUM OF WEAPONS AND ARMOUR
Herrengasse 16, 8010 Graz, Steiermark
16th-18th century weapons and armour.
Apr.-Nov. Daily 9-12. M., W., F. also 2-5. July-Aug. also Tu., Th. 2.30-5.

JOANEUM PROVINCIAL MUSEUM FOR ZOOLOGY AND BOTANY
Raubergasse 10, 8010 Graz, Steiermark
World-wide collections of zoology and botany. Dioramas, showing local landscapes and wildlife. Extinct animals. Aquarium. Herbarium. Fruits and seeds. Tree-sections. Alpine plants.
M.-Sa. 9-12. Easter-Nov., M., Tu., F., also 3-6, and Su. 9-12.

SCHLOSSBERG MUSEUM
Glockenturm, Schlossberg, 8010 Graz, Steiermark
History of the Schlossberg, its fortress and subsequent buildings.
Easter-Nov. 1, Daily 8-6.

STEIERMARK HUNTING MUSEUM
Schloss Eggenberg, Eggenberg Allee 90, 8020 Graz, Steiermark
Paintings, sculpture, prints with hunting as subject. Weapons. Trophies. History and techniques of hunting. Specimens of abnormal wild creatures. Dioramas.
Daily 9-12, 2-5.

GRAZ-MARIA TROST

MAURACH MUSEUM
Hans Mauracher Strasse 29, 8044 Graz-Maria Trost, Steiermark
Works by the local sculptor, Hans Maurach (d.1957).
Tu.-Th., Su. 10-6.

GRIEFENSTEIN

CASTLE MUSEUM
3422 Burg Greifenstein, Bezirk Tulln, Niederösterreich
11th century castle, rebuilt 1670. Renaissance and Baroque rooms. Paintings. Glass paintings. Weapons.
May-Oct. Daily 8-6.

GREILLENSTEIN

CRIMINAL LAW COLLECTION OF THE PROVINCIAL MUSEUM OF LOWER AUSTRIA
Schloss, Röhrenbach, Greillenstein, Bezirk Horn, Niederösterreich
Collection illustrating development and application of the criminal law, 16th-19th centuries. Reconstruction of law court. Infliction of punishment. Instruments of torture.
Mar. 15- Nov. 15, Tu.-Su., guided tours 9-dusk.

PALACE MUSEUM
Röhrenbach, Greillenstein, Bezirk Horn, Niederösterreich
16th century castle, remodelled late 17th century. Kuefstein family papers. Memorabilia of the ambassador, Hans Ludwig Kuefstein and his journey to Constantinople (1628).
Mar. 15- Nov. 15, Tu.-Su., guided tours 9-dusk.

GRESTEN

REGIONAL MUSEUM
Rathausplatz, 3264 Gresten, Bezirk Scheibbs, Niederösterreich
Local history and folklore. Peasant furniture and household equipment. Weapons. Guild jugs and chests. Crafts, especially wrought-iron and woodcarving. Religious art. Engravings by Matthäus Vischer of castles in the Erlauftal.
June-Sept. Tu., Th., Sa., Su. 8-11. Other times by appointment.

GRIESKIRCHEN

REGIONAL MUSEUM
4710 Grieskirchen, Oberösterreich
Local history and folklore.
By appointment.

GROSSENGERSDORF

REGIONAL MUSEUM
2212 Grossengersdorf, Bezirk Gänserndorf, Niederösterreich
Local history and folklore.
By appointment.

GÜNDORF

MUSEUM OF LOCAL LIFE
11 Gündorf bei St. Johann im Saggautal, Bezirk Leibnitz, Steiermark
House (c.1706). Peasant furnishings and tools.
On request.

GÜSSING

REGIONAL AND CASTLE MUSEUM
Schloss, Güssing, Burgenland
Prehistoric material from local sites. Weapons. Shields. Relics of the Crusades. Instruments of torture. Peasant tools. Glass. 15th century organ. Batthyány family papers.
By appointment.

GUTENBRUNN

BAROQUE MUSEUM
Schloss Heiligenkreuz, Post Reidling, 3665 Gutenbrunn, Bezirk St. Pölten, Niederösterreich
Baroque paintings by local artists. Glass. Pewter. Majolica. Costumes. Sculpture. Drawings. Engravings.
Mar. 15- Nov. 15, Tu.-Su. 8.30-5. Other times on request.

GUTENSTEIN

'ALTE HOFMÜHLE' REGIONAL MUSEUM
Markt 31, 2770 Gutenstein, Bezirk Wiener Neustadt, Niederösterreich
In restored grist-mill. Displays showing local crafts: forestry and timber industries, with models, tools, paintings and drawings.
May-Sept. Tu., Th., Su. 10-12, 2-5. Other times by appointment.

HUNTING COLLECTION
2770 Schloss Gutenstein, Bezirk Wiener Neustadt, Niederösterreich
Game animals of Central Asia and big game of Africa, North America, Greenland.
By appointment.

HAAG

HAAG MUSEUM OF LOCAL LIFE AND HISTORY
Schloss Starhe-berg, 4680 Haag, Bezirk Grieskirchen, Oberösterreich
Local history. Mining. Peasant life and crafts, especially flax processing, spinning, weaving. Guilds.
May-Sept. Su. 3-5. July-Aug. also Th. 3-5. Other times by appointment.

HABACH

EMERALD MINING MUSEUM
Gasthaus Alpenrose, Habachtal, Bezirk Zell am See, Salzburg
History of local emerald mining, from Roman times onwards. Old mining tools, equipment. Maps. Photographs.
May 25- Sept. 25, Daily 8-7.

HADERSDORF

REGIONAL MUSEUM
Rathaus, 3493 Hadersdorf, Bezirk Krems, Niederösterreich
Local history and prehistory. Urns from cinerary burials, 700 B.C. Handicrafts.
Daily 10-12. Other times by appointment.

HAINBURG

MUNICIPAL MUSEUM
Wienertor, 2410 Hainburg, Bezirk Bruck an der Leitha, Niederösterreich
Prehistoric, Roman and medieval material from local excavations. Flags. Guild collection. Models of boat-mills.
Apr.-Nov., Tu., Th. 3.30-5.30; Sa. 10-11.30, 1-3; Su., public holidays 10-11.30, 1-3.

HALLEIN

MUNICIPAL MUSEUM
Pflegerplatz, 5400 Hallein, Salzburg
Prehistory, especially La Tène. Minerals. Fossils. Paintings of local scenes. Sculpture. Handicrafts and applied art, especially 15th century Guild crosses. Mining and salt-production. Flags. Local history. Memorabilia of Franz Xavier Gruber, composer of 'Stille Nacht, Heilige Nacht'. 18th century furnished interiors.
May-Sept. Daily 8.30-12, 1-6. Other months by appointment.

HALLSTATT

LOCAL MUSEUM
Markt, 4830 Hallstatt, Bezirk Gmunden, Oberösterreich
In former prison (14th century). Prehistory, especially Hallstatt culture, and history of the district. Saltmining displays, with dioramas, tools. Roman archaeology. Musical instruments. Peasant rooms, costumes, handicrafts, tools. Minerals. Local wildlife. Memorabilia of the naturalist, Friedrich Simony.
May-Oct., Daily 9-5. Other months by appointment.

HARD

MITTELWEIBERBURG REGIONAL MUSEUM
Wasserschloss, 6971 Hard, Bezirk Bregenz, Vorarlberg
Local history and handicrafts, especially weaving and textile printing. Peasant furniture.
May-Oct. M.-Sa. 10-12; Su. 2-5.

HASLACH

MUSEUM OF LOCAL HISTORY AND FOLKLORE
Im Alten Turm, 4170 Haslach, Bezirk Rohrbach, Oberösterreich
Local history. History and techniques of local linen weaving industry. Models. Equipment. Costumes. Household equipment. Tools.
Apr.-Oct. Tu., Su., guided tours 9.30.

HEILIGENKREUZ

MONASTERY COLLECTIONS
2532 Stift Heiligenkreuz, Bezirk Baden, Niederösterreich
In Cistercian monastery (1135). 13th-18th century sculptures. 15th century German paintings. Paintings of Biedermeier period. Glass. Gobelins tapestries. Painted wall-hangings. Coins. Workshop and models of the sculptors Martin Altomontes and Johannes Giulianis.
Daily, on request.

HERBERSTEIN

PALACE MUSEUM
Herberstein, Bezirk Hartberg, Steiermark
Furnishings, household equipment of the Herberstein family. Herbersteiner font (16th century). 17th century painted chests and processional organ. Weapons. In chapel, mid-14th century frescoes.
By appointment (written application).

HERMAGOR

GAITAL REGIONAL MUSEUM
Bahnhofstrasse 128, 9620 Hermagor, Kärnten
Local history. Furniture. Pottery. Kitchen equipment. Costumes. Musical instruments. Baroque and Biedermeier furnished interiors. Glass paintings. Religious books, including Lutheran Bible (1541).
June 15- Sept. 1, Daily 10-12.

HERRNBAUMGARTEN

LOCAL MUSEUM
Volkschule, Hauptstrasse 39, 2171 Herrnbaumgarten, Bezirk Mistelbach, Niederösterreich
Prehistoric material from local sites.
By appointment.

HERZOGENBURG

COLLECTIONS OF THE MONASTERY
3130 Stift Herzogenburg, Bezirk St. Pölten, Niederösterreich
Picture gallery (c.1737) with 17th-18th century pictures hung in original way. 14th-16th century paintings, sculpture, from former monasteries and churches. 14th-15th century stained glass. Musical instruments. Weapons. Glass. Religious ornaments, and liturgical items, mainly 18th century. Coins. Prehistoric archaeology.
Apr.-Oct. Daily 9-12, 1-5.

HOCHOSTERWITZ

CASTLE COLLECTIONS
Osterwitz-Launsdorf, Carinthia
Weapons. Armour. Khevenhüller family portraits. History of the Castle.
By appointment.

HOHENAU

REGIONAL MUSEUM
Hauptschule, Hauptstrasse 34-6, 2273 Hohenau, Bezirk Gänserndorf, Niederösterreich
Palaeontology. Remains of mammoths and woolly rhinoceros. Neolithic and Hallstatt material. Peasant furniture, tools, household equipment. Plans, photographs, paintings illustrating history of Hohenau.
1st and 3rd Su. in month, guided tours at 11. Other times by appointment.

HOHENBRUNN

HUNTING MUSEUM OF UPPER AUSTRIA
Schloss Hohenbrunn, Bezirk Linz-Land, Oberösterreich
In castle (1722-32). Weapons. Tapestries. Falconry and hunting equipment. Paintings with hunting themes. Hunting mementoes of Emperor Franz Joseph I. Dioramas showing history of hunting costumes and wildlife of Upper Austria.
Apr.-Oct. Tu.-Su. 10-12, 2-5.

HOLLABRUNN

MUNICIPAL MUSEUM
Hölzlgasse 13, 2020 Hollabrunn, Niederösterreich
Palaeontology. Ice-Age mammals. Neolithic tools. Bronze Age, Iron Age and Migration material. Medieval and Renaissance pottery, sculpture, carving. Glass pictures. Coins and medals. Wine museum. Coats of arms.
Apr.-Nov. Sa., Su. 10-12, 2-5.

HOLLENEGG

PALACE COLLECTION
Hollenegg, Steiermark
Furniture, paintings and other material from the 15th-17th century castle at Riegersburg and Limburg.
By appointment (written application).

HOLLERSBACH

REGIONAL MUSEUM
Gemeindehaus, 5731 Hollersbach, Bezirk Zell am See, Salzburg
Minerals of the region. Emeralds. Peasant furniture, tools, wedding and baptismal costumes. Church furnishings. Votive tablets.
Daily 5-6. Other times by appointment.

HORN

HÖBARTH MUSEUM
Wiener Strasse 4, 3580 Horn, Niederösterreich
Geology. Mineralogy. Natural science. Prehistory. History of Horn, especially during Reformation. Religious art.
Mar. 15- Nov. 15, Daily 9-12, 2-5.

IMST

REGIONAL MUSEUM
Rathaus, Ballgasse 1, 6460 Imst, Tirol
History of Imst and its region from prehistoric times. Tools, utensils, ornaments from Höttinger sites (1200-800 B.C.). 15th-19th century carved and painted chests. Kitchen equipment. Locks. Keys. Tools. Mining equipment. Birdcatchers' equipment. Costumes. Masks. Local history and archives. Religious paintings, sculpture.
Tu., Th. 8-12, 2-4. Other times by appointment.

INNSBRUCK

AMBRAS CASTLE COLLECTION
6020 Innsbruck, Tirol
Weapons. Armour. History of jousting. Portraits, especially of Archduke Ferdinand II and his family. Tapestries. Natural curiosities. Minerals. Gold and silverwork. Games. Drinking customs. Coins, including coin cabinet of 1592. 16th-17th century musical instruments.
May 15- Oct. 15, Daily 9-12, 2-5, guided tours only.

APOTHECARY MUSEUM
Herzog Friedrich-Strasse 25, 6020 Innsbruck, Tirol
Apothecary's shop (c.1700), with original furnishings, equipment.
Daily 9-12, by appointment.

ART COLLECTION OF THE SERVITEN MONASTERY
Theresienstrasse 42, 6020 Innsbruck, Tirol
Items illustrating history of the monastery. Religious painting, sculpture. Liturgical objects.
Guided tours daily, 10-12, 3-5.

BERG ISEL MUSEUM OF THE TYROLEAN KAISERJÄGER REGIMENT
Berg Isel 3, 6020 Innsbruck Tirol
19th-20th century Austrian and foreign guns. Uniforms and equipment of the Austrian army, 1683-1900. Flags, weapons, portraits recalling the Tyrolean Rebellion (1809). History of the Kaiserjäger regiment.
May-Oct. Daily 8-6. Nov.-Apr. Daily 9-5.

'FERDINANDEUM', TIROL MUSEUM
Museumstrasse 15, 6020 Innsbruck, Tirol
14th-16th century gravestones and memorials from the Tirol. 11th-17th century weapons, ivories, goldsmith's work. Austrian, German porcelain. 15th-19th century German, Bohemian, Venetian glass. 16th century painted windows. 12th-20th century paintings and sculpture of the

Tirol. Prehistoric, Celtic, Roman archaeology, art. 16th-17th century Dutch, Flemish paintings. 17th-18th century Italian paintings. 15th-16th century Limoges enamels. Minerals of the Tirol.
May-Sept. M.-Sa. 9-5; Su. 9-12. Oct.-Apr. M.-Sa. 9-12, 2-4; Su. 9-12.

MUSEUM OF THE KAISERSCHÜTZEN REGIMENT
Schloss Ambras, 6020 Innsbruck, Tirol
History of the Tyrol Landes and Kaiserschützen regiments. Paintings. Relics and mementoes of campaigns.
June 15 - Sept. 30, Sa., Su. 3-6.

MUSEUM OF TYROLEAN POPULAR ART
Universitätsstrasse 2, 6020 Innsbruck, Tirol
Models showing house-types in Tyrol. Peasant and bourgeois rooms, household equipment, pottery, glass, stoves. Carved and painted peasant furniture. Religious art. Agricultural implements. Cow-bells. Models of farm carts and waggons. Spinning and weaving equipment. Masks.
M.-Sa. 9-12, 2-5; Su., public holidays 9-12.

MUSEUM OF THE WILTEN PRAEMONSTRATENSIAN CHORAL FOUNDATION
Klostergasse 7, 6020 Innsbruck, Tirol
Gothic and baroque paintings, sculpture, including Gothic altar. Habsburg portraits. Roman archaeology. Pewter.
By appointment.

PALACE, SILVER CHAPEL AND PALACE CHURCH
Hofburg, Rennweg 1, 6020 Innsbruck, Tirol
Hofburg has furnished interiors of the Imperial Palace, with 17th-19th century furniture, tapestries, portraits and paintings of historic scenes. Silver Chapel and Palace Church have statues of the Imperial family and other historic personages, together with tombs of the Emperors and their relatives and of Andreas Hofer.
May 15 - Oct. 15, daily 9-12, 2-5. Oct. 16 - May 14, M.-Sa. 9-12, 2-4.

SCHWARZKOPF COLLECTION
6020 Innsbruck, Tirol
History of hairdressing.
By appointment.

UNIVERSITY ARCHAEOLOGICAL COLLECTION
Leopold-Franzens Universität, Inrain 52, 6020 Innsbruck, Tirol
Prehistoric and Roman archaeology, particularly from sites in the Tirol and Austria.
By appointment.

JEDENSPEIGEN

REGIONAL MUSEUM
Schulhaus, 2264 Jedenspeigen, Niederösterreich
Local and regional history.
By appointment.

JUDENBURG

TOWN AND DISTRICT MUSEUM
Rathaus, Kaserngasse, 8750 Judenburg, Steiermark
Landscapes by the local painter, Ignaz Raffalt. Historical maps, models. Commercial history of Judenburg. Coins.
Tu., W., Th. 9-11. Other times by appointment.

KAPFENBERG

CAVE MUSEUM
Hauptplatz, 8605 Kapfenberg, Steiermark
Local history. Archaeological material from local caves. Industrial history of the area.
On request.

KINDBERG

HUNGARIAN MUSEUM IN WESTERN EUROPE
8650 Schloss Hart, Bezirk Mürzzuschlag, Steiermark
Castle (1523). History, applied art and folklore of Hungary.
May-Nov. Daily 9.30-11.45, 4-5. Other months by appointment.

KIRCHBERG AM WALDE

HAMERLING MEMORIAL MUSEUM
3932 Kirchberg am Walde, Niederösterreich
Works and memorabilia of the poet Robert Hamerling (d.1889), born in Kirchberg.
By appointment.

KITZBÜHEL

REGIONAL MUSEUM
Alter Getreidekasten, Hinterstadt 32, 6370 Kitzbühel, Tirol
Display illustrating history of local mining. Paintings and drawings by the Kitzbühel painter, Alfons Walde (d.1958). History of Kitzbühel as a skiing resort.
M.-F. 9-12, 2-5.

KLAGENFURT

CARINTHIAN GALLERY
Burgstrasse 8, 9020 Klagenfurt, Kärnten
19th-20th century paintings, sculpture by artists from Carinthia, especially of the 1920s. Woodcarvings.
Tu.-Sa. 9-12, 1-4; Su., public holidays, 10-12.

CARINTHIA PROVINCIAL MUSEUM
Museumgasse 2, 9020 Klagenfurt, Kärnten
Dioramas showing wild-life of Carinthia. Geology. Palaeontology. Botany. Zoology. Entomology. History of mining in Carinthia. Prehistoric and Roman archaeology. Gothic altars. Peasant costumes, furniture, tools, household equipment.
Tu.-Sa. 9-4; Su. 10-12.

DIOCESAN MUSEUM
Residenz Mariannengasse 2, 9020 Klagenfurt, Kärnten
Religious art, especially from Carinthia. Ornaments. Altars. Church windows. Sculpture. Manuscripts. Incunabula. Liturgical objects.
Apr.-Oct. Tu.-Th., guided tours 10-12.

KOSCHAT MUSEUM
Viktringerring 17, 9020 Klagenfurt, Kärnten
Memorial museum to the composer, Thomas Koschat (d.1914). Furniture, manuscripts, scores, pictures and other memorabilia of Koschat.
May 15 - Sept. 30, Daily 10-12.

KLAM

KLAM CASTLE MUSEUM
4352 Klam, Bezirk Grein, Oberösterreich
Castle (1150). In chapel, frescoes of c.1380. Furniture. Meissner and Alt-Wiener porcelain. Sculpture. Religious ornaments. Weapons. Uniforms. Decorations awarded to the Clam-Martinic family.
May-Oct. daily 10-12, 2-6. Other months by appointment.

KLEINENGERSDORF

"DER BISAMBERG UND DER WEINVIERTLER" MUSEUM
70 and 31 Kleinengersdorf, Bezirk Wien-Umgeburg, Niederösterreich
Geology. Palaeontology. Prehistoric and Roman archaeology from local sites. 15th century weapons, coins. Relics of the Turkish siege of Vienna (1683). History of lighting. Glass paintings. 18th-19th century furniture, costumes, ornaments. Collection of walking-sticks and pipes. Vineyard and asparagus-growing implements. Locks. Coins. Paintings. Manuscripts of Grillparzer and Wilczer.
Daily on request.

KLEINWETZDORF

HEROES' MEMORIAL
Kleinwetzdorf, Bezirk Hollabrunn, Niederösterreich
Memorial, 1848-49, to Fieldmarshals Radetzky and Wimpffen. In the Memorial Park, monuments and busts of Austrian military leaders.
May-Sept. M.-Sa. 9-5; Su., public holidays 8-6. Oct.-Apr. Tu.-Su. 8-6.

KLOSTERNEUBURG

MUSEUM OF THE AUGUSTINIAN MONASTERY
Stiftsplatz 1, 3400 Klosterneuburg, Niederösterreich
Roman and medieval sculpture and architectural features. 14th-16th century paintings by Austrian, Italian, Dutch and Flemish artists. 14th-16th century Italian sculpture. Glass paintings. 10th-18th century ivories. Clocks. Glass.
Sa., Su. 9-12, 1-6. Other times by appointment.

KORNEUBURG

TOWN MUSEUM
Stockerauerstrasse 10. Korneuburg, Niederösterreich
Local history.
On request.

KREMS

MUNICIPAL MUSEUM
Minoritenkirche, Stein, 3500 Krems, Niederösterreich
13th-17th century religious art. Wood sculpture. Altars. Paintings. Peasant art and handicrafts. Glass. Bottles. Glass-paintings. Pottery. Prehistoric and Roman archaeology. History of Krems. Guild relics. Furniture and furnished interiors, including furnishings of the rooms of the Krems physician and apothecary, Wolfgang Kaepler (early 16th century).
Apr.-Oct. Tu.-Sa. 9-12, 2-5. Su., public holidays, 9-12.

WINE MUSEUM
Theaterplatz 8-9, 3500 Krems, Niederösterreich
Displays illustrating vineyard techniques and the production and storage of wine. Cultivating tools. Winepresses. Casks. Inn furnishings and equipment. Glasses. Bottles. Pewter. Cooper's tools. History of wine production.
Apr.-Oct., Tu.-Sa. 9-12, 2-5. Su., public holidays 9-12.

KREMSMÜNSTER

MONASTERY COLLECTIONS
Benediktinerstift, 4550 Kremsmünster, Bezirk Kirchdorf an der Krems, Oberösterreich
14th-19th century Austrian paintings, sculpture. 16th-17th century Dutch, Flemish, German, Italian paintings. Snuff-boxes. Glass. Gold and silversmith's work. Ivories. Weapons. Armour. 8th-14th century religious art. Geology. Mineralogy. Palaeontology. Physics. Zoology. Ethnography. Astronomical instruments.
Guided tours only. Easter-Apr. 30, Su., public holidays, 9.15-3. May 1 - Oct. 1, Daily 9.15-3.

KREUZENSTEIN

CASTLE AND CASTLE COLLECTIONS
Leobendorf, Kreuzenstein, Bezirk Korneuburg, Niederösterreich
Medieval and Renaissance furnished interiors. Weapons. Armour. Medieval bathroom, with Moorish faience bath. 8th-15th century religious art. Sculpture. Paintings. Altars. Local history.
May-Oct. Tu.-Su. 8-5. Nov.-Apr. 8-dusk.

KRIEGLACH

PETER ROSEGGER MUSEUM
Roseggerstrasse 223, 8670 Krieglach, Bezirk Mürzzuschlag, Steiermark
Rosegger's house, with his work room and the room where he died. Portraits, manuscripts, books and other memorabilia.
Guided tours, daily 8-5.

KUCHL

REGIONAL MUSEUM
5431 Kuchl, Bezirk Hallein, Steiermark
Local history. Celtic and Roman archaeology from local sites. Costumes. Furnishings and household equipment. Weapons.
May-Oct. Daily 9.30-11.30, 4-6.

KUFSTEIN

REGIONAL MUSEUM
6330 Burg Kufstein, Tirol
Prehistoric material from local sites. Wildlife, especially birds of the region. Furnished interiors of peasant homes. Musical instruments. Costumes. Religious art. History and activities of local guilds. Memorabilia of J. Madesperger, inventor of the sewing machine, born in Kufstein. Military history of Kufstein.
Guided tours, Apr.-Oct. 9-11, 2-5.

LAA

REGIONAL MUSEUM
Rathaus, 2136 Laa, Bezirk Mistelbach, Niederösterreich
Local history.
By appointment.

LAMBACH

COLLECTIONS OF THE BENEDICTINE MONASTERY
4650 Lambach, Oberösterreich
History of monastery. Monastery theatre (1746-1770). Engravings. Sculpture.
By appointment.

LANDECK

DISTRICT MUSEUM
Schloss Landeck, 6500 Landeck, Tirol
Local history.
By appointment.

LANGENLOIS

REGIONAL MUSEUM
Rathuasstrasse 13, 3550 Langenlois, Bezirk Krems, Niederösterreich
Palaeontology. Prehistoric archaeology from local sites. Furnished interiors. Painted furniture. Clocks. Guild pictures. 15th century painting on wood. Lead church ornaments. Peasant art, handicrafts. Coins. Seals. Guild and regimental flags. Targets.
By appointment.

LANGENZERSDORF

REGIONAL MUSEUM
Hauptplatz 1, 2103 Langenzersdorf, Bezirk Wien-Umgebung, Niederösterreich
Prehistoric material from local sites. Local history and industry, including collection of cooper's tools. Works and memorabilia of the sculptor, Anton Hanak (d.1934).
Apr.-Sept., 2nd Su. in month, 10-12. Other times by appointment.

LEOBEN

MINING MUSEUM
Münzenbergstrasse 1, 8706 Leoben, Steiermark
History of local mines and iron-works.
By appointment.

MUNICIPAL MUSEUM
Kirchgasse 6, 8700 Leoben, Steiermark
Prehistoric material from local sites, including items relating to early mining and ironworking. Displays illustrating later history of local iron industry. Tools and equipment. Wrought ironwork. Weapons. Miners' costumes. Local history. 15th-16th century sculpture.
Daily 9-12, 3-5.

LEOBEN-GÖSS

GÖSS BREWERY MUSEUM
Gösser Platz 1, 8707 Leoben-Göss, Bezirk Leoben, Steiermark
Brewing tools and equipment. History of the former Göss monastery. Flags and banners.
By appointment.

LICHTENEGG

JOHANN JAKOB TSCHUDI MEMORIAL MUSEUM
Tschudihof, 2813 Lichtenegg, Steiermark
Former home of the physician and naturalist, J. J. Tschudi. Natural science collection. Manuscripts and other memorabilia. Watercolours of Peruvian archaeology.
By appointment.

LIEFERING

MISSION MUSEUM
Liefering
Ethnography of the Pacific.
On request.

LIENZ

EAST TIROL REGIONAL MUSEUM
Schloss Bruck, 9900 Lienz, Tirol
18th-20th century paintings, drawings, sculpture by Tyrolean artists. 14th-18th century wood sculptures, carving. Paintings by Albin Egger-Lienz (d.1926). Peasant furniture, costumes, handicrafts, craftsmen's tools. Material from Roman town of Aguntum. Prehistoric archaeology from local sites. Geology. Mineralogy. Zoology. Botany. Mementoes of the struggle for Tyrolean independence. Weapons. Flags. Portraits.
Tu.-Su. 9-12, 2-6.

KLÖSTERLE SMITHY OPEN-AIR MUSEUM
9900 Lienz, Tirol
16th century smithy, restored to give original appearance. Viewed from outside, through windows.
At all times.

LILIENFELD

MONASTERY COLLECTIONS
3180 Stift Lilienfeld, Bezirk St. Pölten, Niederösterreich
Paintings. Engravings.
By appointment.

MUSEUM OF LOCAL LIFE
Dörfl, 3180 Lilienfeld, Bezirk St. Pölten, Niederösterreich
Local history and ethnography. Natural history, especially insects. History of the mining and iron industries of the Traisental.
On request.

LINZ

DIOCESAN MUSEUM
Herrenstrasse 36, 4020 Linz, Oberösterreich
Religious art.
By appointment.

MUSEUM OF THE CITY OF LINZ
Hauptplatz 8, 4020 Linz, Oberösterreich
History of Linz. Roman and prehistoric material from Linz area. Paintings, drawings, prints by Linz artists. Furniture. Craftsmen's tools. Costumes. Guild history.
By appointment.

NEW GALLERY OF THE TOWN OF LINZ AND WOLFGANG GURLITT MUSEUM
Hauptplatz 8, 4020 Linz, Oberösterreich
19th-20th century German and Austrian paintings, sculpture. Drawings. Prints.
M.-Sa. 10-6; Su. 10-1.

STIFTER MEMORIAL ROOM
Adalbert Stifter Institut, Untere Donaulände 6, 4020 Linz, Oberösterreich
Material relating to the poet, Adalbert Stifter (d.1868). Furniture. Manuscripts. Personal possessions. Portraits.
Daily 8-1, 2-6.

UPPER AUSTRIA PROVINCIAL MUSEUM
Schloss, Tummelplatz 10 and Muzeumstrasse 14, 4020 Linz, Oberösterreich
Stone Age, Bronze Age and Roman material from local sites. Medieval coats of arms. 9th-19th century weapons, armour. 10th-15th century wood and stone sculpture, paintings. Medieval and Renaissance religious art, including textiles, ornaments, liturgical items. 17th-18th century sculpture. 16th-18th century Italian, Dutch, Flemish, Austrian paintings. 19th century Austrian paintings. 17th-18th century musical instruments. Peasant life, handicrafts, costumes, toys. Transport, including railway collection, horse-drawn vehicles, sledges. Military history. Historical display showing preparation and storage of fruit juice. Geology. Mineralogy. Botany. Zoology.
In Schloss: Tu.-Sa. 10-1; Su. 9-12.30. F., Sa. also 2-6. W. 2-8.
At Muzeumstrasse 14 (natural history): M.-Sa. 9-12, Tu., Th. also 2-5.

LOCKENHAUS

SCHOOL MUSEUM
Schloss, Hauptplatz, 7442 Lockenhaus, Bezirk Oberpullendorf, Burgenland
Natural history. Dioramas. Ethnography. Reproductions of portraits of artists.
Daily 8-12, 1-5.

LOICH

LOICH REGIONAL ROOM
Loichgegend 13, 3211 Loich, Bezirk St. Pölten, Niederösterreich
Peasant furniture, household equipment, craftsmen's tools. Coal-mining tools, equipment.
By appointment.

LOOSDORF

CASTLE COLLECTIONS
2133 Loosdorf, Bezirk Mistelbach, Niederösterreich
18th century period rooms. Chinese porcelain.
May-Oct., Su. 2-6. Other times by appointment.

LOSENSTEIN

REGIONAL MUSEUM
Schulhaus, 4460 Losenstein, Bezirk Steyr, Oberösterreich
Local history. Tools and products of local nailsmiths. Memorabilia of the Losenstein poet, Anton Schosser (d.1849).
May-Sept. W. 3-5. Other times by appointment.

LUNZ

AMON HOUSE MUSEUM
3293 Lunz, Bezirk Scheibbs, Niederösterreich
Geography and resources of the Upper Ybbstal. Furniture and household objects of the Amon family. Chiselled locks. History of local iron-forges. Tools. Equipment. Peasant kitchen.
June-Sept. Tu.-Su. 10-12.

MARCHEGG

HUNTING MUSEUM OF LOWER AUSTRIA
Schloss, 2294 Marchegg, Bezirk Gänserndorf, Niederösterreich
Dioramas and other displays illustrating hunting in Lower Austria. Animals. Weapons and equipment. Paintings of hunting scenes. Hunting music.
Apr.-Nov. 1, Daily 9-12, 1-5.

MARIA LANGEGG

TREASURY OF THE PILGRIMAGE CHURCH
Aggsbach-Dorf, Maria Langegg, Bezirk Krems, Niederösterreich
Religious art. Ornaments. Votive tablets and offerings.
On request.

MARIA SAAL

CARINTHIAN OPEN-AIR MUSEUM
9063 Maria Saal, Bezirk Klagenfurt-Land, Kärnten
Peasant houses and farm buildings from Carinthia.
May-Oct. Su.-F. 8-12, 2-5; Sa. 2-5.

MONASTERY CHURCH MUSEUM
9063 Maria Saal, Bezirk Klagenfurt-Land, Kärnten
Religious art. Liturgical objects. Ornaments. Sculptures.
By appointment.

MARIA STEIN

PALACE MUSEUM
Burg, 7433 Maria Stein, Bezirk Kufstein, Tirol
15th-17th century religious art, ornaments. Schurff family portraits. 17th century votive and miracle pictures.
On request.

MARIA TAFERL

TREASURY OF THE PILGRIMAGE CHURCH
3672 Maria Taferl, Bezirk Krems, Niederösterreich
Religious art. Votive offerings.
On request.

MARIAZELL

TREASURY OF THE BASILICA OF GOD'S GRACE
Kardinal Eugène Tisserand Platz 1, 8630 Mariazell, Bezirk Bruck an der Mur, Steiermark
14th-18th century religious art, votive offerings. Gold and silver liturgical items given by members of the Imperial family.
May-Oct. Daily 8-12, 2-5. Other times on request.

MATTSEE

MONASTERY COLLECTIONS
5163 Mattsee, Bezirk Salzburg-Land, Salzburg
14th-17th century tombstones. Religious art.
By appointment.

REGIONAL MUSEUM
5163 Mattsee, Bezirk Salzburg-Land, Salzburg
Peasant furnished rooms. Domestic equipment. Costumes. Fishing equipment. Locks. Fossil animals. Material from Celtic and Roman sites in the area.
July-Aug., Daily 10-12, 3-5. Other times by appointment.

MAUTERN

TOWN MUSEUM
Frauenhofgasse 55-56, 3512 Mautern, Bezirk Krems, Niederösterreich
Prehistoric, Roman and early medieval material from local excavations.
Apr. 1-Oct. 3, W., Su. 10-12. Other times by appointment.

MAUTHAUSEN

REGIONAL MUSEUM
Schloss Pragstein, 4310 Mauthausen, Bezirk Perg, Oberösterreich
Local history. Prehistoric material from local sites. History of lighting.
By appointment.

MELK

BENEDICTINE ABBEY COLLECTION
3390 Melk, Niederösterreich
Memorabilia of Abbot Berthold Dietmayr (d.1739), largely responsible for building the Abbey. Religious art, including Cranach's *Madonna in the Vine-Arbour*.
Daily 9-12, 2-4.

REGIONAL MUSEUM
Linzer Strasse 3-5, 3390 Melk, Niederösterreich
In former post office (1792). Prehistoric, Roman and medieval material from local sites. Peasant household equipment.
By appointment.

MICHAELBEUERN

ABBEY REGIONAL MUSEUM
Benediktinerabtei, 5152 Michaelbeuern, Bezirk Salzburg-Land, Salzburg
Paintings and sculpture by Austrian baroque artists. Furniture. Peasant art, handicrafts.
On request.

MIESENBACH

GAUERMANN MEMORIAL MUSEUM
Scheuchenstein, 2761 Miesenbach, Niederösterreich
House (c.1800), was home of Gauermann family. Paintings, drawings, engravings by Jakob and Friedrich Gauermann. Memorabilia of the Gauermanns.
On request.

MISTELBACH

MUNICIPAL MUSEUM OF REGIONAL LIFE
Museumgasse 4, 2130 Mistelbach, Niederösterreich
Fossils of mastodon, dinotherium and other animals. Prehistoric and early historical material from local sites. Guild relics. 18th century religious paintings, sculpture. History of Mistelbach fire-brigade. Grape-processing and coopers' tools.
Su., public holidays 10-12. Other times by appointment.

MITTELBERG

REGIONAL MUSEUM
6993 Mittelberg, Vorarlberg
Regional life and history.
By appointment.

RIEZLERN REGIONAL MUSEUM
Riezlern 14, 6993 Mittelberg, Vorarlberg
Regional life and history. Peasant furnishings, household equipment, tools. Religious art.
M.-Sa. 2-5.

MITTERNDORF

MUSEUM OF REGIONAL LIFE
2441 Mitterndorf, Bezirk Liezen, Steiermark
Mineralogy. Peasant household equipment. Painted furniture. Costumes. Ornaments. Coins. Paintings. Masks for the Nikolosspiel.
On request.

MITTERSILL

REGIONAL MUSEUM
5730 Mittersill, Bezirk Salzburg-Land, Salzburg
Minerals of the Pinzgau and adjacent areas. Emeralds and epidotes. Local history and ethnography.
Th.-Tu. 9-12, 2-5. Other times by appointment.

MÖDLING

MUNICIPAL MUSEUM
Museumsplatz 2, 2340 Mödling, Niederösterreich
Natural history of the region. Economic geography. Prehistoric and early historical material. 15th-18th century paintings, wrought iron. Costumes. Household equipment. Beethoven memorabilia.
Apr.-Oct. Th., Sa. 3-6; Su., public holidays, 10-12, 3-6. Other times by appointment.

ST. GABRIEL'S MISSION MUSEUM
Missionshaus St. Gabriel, Gabrielerstrasse 171, 2340 Mödling, Niederösterreich
Ethnographical material collected by missionaries from many parts of the world, especially New Guinea, Japan, China and Africa.
Su. 10-6. Other times by appointment.

MONDSEE

'MONDSEE RAUCHHAUS' OPEN-AIR MUSEUM
Mariahilferberg, Mondsee, Bezirk Vöcklabruck, Oberösterreich
Farm house and outbuildings, including mill, granary, fruit store, with tools and equipment.
May-Sept. Daily 8-6. Apr. and Oct., Sa., Su. 8-6. Other times by appointment.

REGIONAL MUSEUM
Klosterbibliothek, Mondsee, Bezirk Vöcklabruck, Oberösterreich
Neolithic - Bronze Age pottery. 18th century sculpture from the Benedictine Abbey. Photographs of 12th century Mondsee book-illustrations. Local history. Mondsee handicrafts. Peasant costumes, household equipment. Charcoal-burning. Fishing. Transport, including locomotive from former Salzkammergut narrow-gauge railway.
May-Sept. Daily 8-12, 2-6. Other times on request.

MOOSHAM

PALACE COLLECTIONS
Unternberg, Moosham, Bezirk Tamsweg, Salzburg
Period rooms. Furniture. Porcelain. Faience. Pewter. Paintings. Engravings. Sculpture. Stoves. Horse-drawn vehicles. Sledges. Harness.
By appointment.

MURAU

MUNICIPAL MUSEUM OF LOCAL LIFE
Anna Neumann Strasse 34, 8850 Murau, Steiermark
In former Apothecary's shop (c.1500). 19th century paintings. Peasant tools, implements, furniture, transport. 18th-19th century fire-fighting equipment. Wrought iron-work. Locks. Musical instruments. Glass-paintings. 17th-18th century wood carving, sculpture. Coins. Seals. Civil and military uniforms, weapons.
Guided tours, M., Th. 4. Other times by appointment.

PALACE MUSEUM
8850 Murau, Steiermark
Local iron-mining and iron-working.
June-Sept. W., F., guided tours at 4.

MÜRZZUSCHLAG

WINTER SPORTS AND REGIONAL MUSEUM
Wiener Strasse 79, 8680 Mürzzuschlag, Steiermark
History of winter sports. Skis and skiing equipment from Europe and USA. Sleighs and sledges. Toboggans. Ice-hockey. Curling. Skating. Memorabilia of Viktor Kaplan, inventor of turbine named after him.
Su.-Th. 9-12, 2-5.

MURAU-KENDLBRUCK

SMELTER
8850 Murau-Kendlbruck, Steiermark
19th century kiln and refining furnace.
At all times.

MURECK

MUSEUM
Rathaus, 8480 Mureck, Steiermark
Local history. Weapons. Coins.
On request.

NEULENGBACH

REGIONAL MUSEUM
Bezirksgericht, 3040 Neulengbach, Bezirk St. Pölten, Niederösterreich
Local history. Literary memorabilia of Fritz Habeck and Josef Weinheber. Paintings by local artists.
May-Oct., Su., public holidays 10-11.30. Other times on request.

NEUNKIRCHEN

REGIONAL MUSEUM
Dr. Stockhammergasse 13, 2620 Neunkirchen, Niederösterreich
Prehistoric and Roman material from local excavations. Copper smelting site (1000 B.C.). Coins. Peasant rooms. House and shop signs. Guild material. Costumes. Wood sculpture, carvings. Turpentine production. Shingle-making tools. Agricultural implements. Mineralogy.
Tu., Su. 9-12. F. 2-5. Other times by appointment.

NEUSIEDL

LAKE MUSEUM
7100 Neusiedl, Burgenland
Wildlife and flora of Neusiedler See area.
Easter - Oct. Daily 9-12, 1-6.

NIEDERLEIS

CASTLE MUSEUM
2116 Niederleis, Bezirk Mistelbach, Niederösterreich
Greek, Roman, Lombard, medieval, Renaissance and 18th century sculpture, mostly from N. Italy. 15th-19th century leather wall-hangings. Medieval and baroque altar furnishings. Tapestry. Furniture. Faience. Majolica. Glass.
Apr. 1 - Nov. 15, guided tours only, Sa., Su. 1-6. Other times on request.

OBERNBERG

REGIONAL MUSEUM
Gurtentor, 4982 Obernberg, Bezirk Ried im Innkreis, Oberösterreich
Local handicrafts. Medicine. Weapons. Fire-protection. Paintings, drawings, plans illustrating navigation of the Inn. Sculpture by local artists. Paintings showing development of Obernberg. Guild and craftsmen's signs. Coins. Brewery history. Peasant room, with furniture, tools. Gold-washing equipment.
On request.

OBERNDORF

REGIONAL MUSEUM
Schulweg 77, 5110 Oberndorf, Bezirk Salzburg-Land, Salzburg
Utensils, equipment of the Salzach salt-boatmen and their Guild. Uniforms. Flags. Boat-models. Peasant room, with domestic utensils, tools.
May-Oct. Daily 2-5. Other times by appointment.

OBERPERFUSS

ANICH-HUEBER MUSEUM
Schulhaus, 6173 Oberperfuss, Bezirk Innsbruck-Land, Tirol
Memorabilia, especially maps, of the cartographers, Peter Anich and Blasius Hueber. Geodetic instruments. Globes.
Daily, by appointment.

OBERZEIRING

DEMONSTRATION MINE AND MUSEUM
8762 Oberzeiring, Bezirk Judenburg, Steiermark
Silvermine, restored to give original 13th century appearance. Minerals. Archaeological material. Mining tools, equipment.
M.-Sa. 8-5; Su., public holidays 9-5.

ORTH

FISHING MUSEUM
Schloss, 2304 Orth, Bezirk Gänserndorf, Niederösterreich
Fishing equipment, techniques. History of local fishing industry.
Apr.-Oct. Daily 8-dusk.

REGIONAL MUSEUM
Schloss, 2304 Orth, Bezirk Gänserndorf, Niederösterreich
Prehistoric material. Mineralogy. Natural history. Local history. Peasant household equipment.
Tu.-Su. 8-12, 1-6.

OTTMANACH

MUSEUM OF THE MAGDALENSBERG EXCAVATIONS
Ottmanach, Bezirk Klagenfurt-Land, Kärnten
Excavated ruins of Roman colony on the Magdalensberg, with museum in the restored Repräsentationshaus. Agricultural tools. Sculpture. Writing equipment. Pottery. Coins. Tools. Toys. Ornaments.
May 1 - Oct. 15, guided tours only, 8-6.

PEGGAU

MUSEUM OF THE LUR CAVES
8120 Peggau, Steiermark
Archaeological material from caves in the Peggau area.
On request.

PERSENBURG

REGIONAL MUSEUM
Gemeindeamt, 3680 Persenburg, Bezirk Melk, Niederösterreich
Local history. Weapons.
May-Sept. by appointment.

PETRONELL

CARNUNTUM OPEN-AIR MUSEUM
2404 Petronell, Bezirk Bruck an der Leitha, Niederösterreich
Excavated site of Roman colony and military camp. Carnuntum Amphitheatre. Baths. Mosaics. Houses. Commercial premises.
At all times.

DANUBE MUSEUM
Schloss, 2404 Petronell, Bezirk Bruck an der Leitha, Niederösterreich
Geography, history and economic importance of the Danube, especially in Austria. Roman material from Carnuntum, including statue of the god, Danuvius. Geology. Wildlife dioramas. Fishing. History of navigation. Boat-mills. Guild flags. Weapons. Paintings and drawings of Danube scenes.
Apr.-Oct. Daily 8-dusk.

MUSEUM OF APPLIED ART
2404 Schloss Petronell, Bezirk Bruck an der Leitha, Niederösterreich
17th-early 19th century furniture and applied art. Porcelain. Faience. Glass. Ivory carvings. Goldsmiths' work. Pewter. Pottery. Locks and keys. Portraits.
Mar.-Oct. Daily 8-5.

PFAFFSTÄTTEN

REGIONAL MUSEUM
Dr. Dolp-Strasse, 2511 Pfaffstätten, Bezirk Baden, Niederösterreich
Fossils. Roman archaeology. Medieval coins. Agricultural and vineyard implements. Local history. Resin industry.
M.-Sa. 9-12. Other times on request.

PINKAFELD

REGIONAL MUSEUM
Rathaus, Hauptplatz, 7423 Pinkafeld, Bezirk Oberwart, Burgenland
Local history. Development of agriculture and industry. Guild flags and signs. Peasant household equipment. Popular art. Biedermeier crib.
Apr.-Oct., M.-F. 7-12, 1-4. Other times on request.

PISCHELSDORF

REGIONAL MUSEUM
8212 Pischelsdorf, Bezirk Weiz, Steiermark
Local history, mostly items collected by schoolchildren. Neolithic and medieval material. Coins. Peasant household equipment, tools, glass paintings. 17th century weapons.
F. 3-5; Su. 10-12.

PÖCHLARN

REGIONAL MUSEUM
Welserturm, 3380 Pöchlarn, Bezirk Melk, Niederösterreich
Neolithic, Bronze Age and Roman material from local sites. Furnished peasant rooms. Stations of the Cross from the Ordninger Chapel.
On request.

PÖGGSTALL

REGIONAL MUSEUM
Schloss Rogendorf, 3650 Pöggstall, Bezirk Melk, Niederösterreich
Local and regional history. Wood sculpture. Torture chamber, with original equipment. Peasant furniture. Spinning wheels. Loom.
Daily 9-6.

PÖLLAU

REGIONAL MUSEUM
8225 Pöllau, Steiermark
Local history. Handicrafts.
By appointment.

PÖLS-ENZERSDORF

HUSSLIK REGIONAL MUSEUM
8761 Pöls-Enzersdorf, Bezirk Judenburg, Steiermark
Locally made furniture. Glass. Porcelain. Household equipment. Clocks with wooden gears. Locks. Firearms. Costumes. Paintings.
By appointment.

POPPENDORFBERG

VINTNER'S HOUSE
Poppendorfberg, Bezirk Feldbach, Steiermark
Peasant furniture, household equipment. Pottery. Weapons.
On request.

POTTENBRUNN

MUSEUM OF TIN FIGURES
3140 Pottenbrunn, Bezirk St. Pölten, Niederösterreich
Dioramas with tin figures, illustrating Austrian history, especially military history.
Apr.-Oct. Tu.-Su. 8-5.

POYSDORF

REGIONAL MUSEUM
Volkschule, 2170 Poysdorf, Bezirk Mistelbach, Niederösterreich
Fossil animals. Articles used in wine-making, including stone press and carved casks. Firearms. 19th century fire-fighting equipment. 19th century furniture.
May-Oct. Su. 10-12. Other times by appointment.

PRESSBAUM

REGIONAL MUSEUM
3021 Pressbaum, Bezirk St. Pölten, Niederösterreich
Geology. Local wildlife and flora. Peasant furniture, household equipment.
Su. 9-11.

PÜRGG

FAHRINGER REGIONAL MUSEUM
8981 Pürgg, Steiermark
Local history. Tools. Handicrafts.
By appointment

PULKAU

REGIONAL MUSEUM
3741 Pulkau, Bezirk Hollabrunn, Niederösterreich
Local history.
On request.

PURGSTALL

REGIONAL MUSEUM
Rathaus, 3251 Purgstall, Bezirk Scheibbs, Niederösterreich
Neolithic, Roman and medieval material from local sites. Targets.
Daily 8-12, 2-6.

RAABS

DR. JOSEF GRASSL REGIONAL MUSEUM
Schloss, 3820 Raabs, Bezirk Waidhofen an der Thaya, Niederösterreich
History of Raabs. Local costumes. Weapons. Peasant tools. Guild history.
By appointment.

RABENSTEIN

PIELACHTAL REGIONAL MUSEUM
Gemeindeamt, 3203 Rabenstein, Bezirk St. Pölten, Niederösterreich
Agricultural implements, including wooden ploughs. Peasant household equipment, costumes, ornaments. Pottery. Looms. Linen and woollen textiles. Weapons. 15th century wooden sculpture. 17th century votive pictures.
Su. 9-12. Other times by appointment.

RADKERSBURG

TOWN MUSEUM OF REGIONAL LIFE
Emmenstrasse 9, 8490 Radkersburg, Steiermark
In former 16th century arsenal. Local history. Roman material from local sites. Negau helmet (800 B.C.). 16th century oath-board and judge's sword.
On request.

RAIDING

FRANZ LISZT MUSEUM
Liszt Strasse 41, Raiding, Bezirk Oberpullendorf, Burgenland
Birthplace of Liszt. Portraits, letters and other memorabilia of the composer.
Daily 7 a.m. - 9 p.m.

RAMSAU

REGIONAL ROOM
8972 Ramsau, Bezirk Liezen, Steiermark
Household equipment. Costumes. Craftsmen's tools.
M.-Sa. 8-12. Other times by appointment.

RANKWEIL

OPEN-AIR MUSEUM
Römervilla, bei Brederis, 6830 Rankweil, Bezirk Feldkirch, Vorarlberg
Excavated and preserved site of Roman villa.
At any time.

RAURIS

RAURIS GOLD-MINING MUSEUM
Markt 9, 5661 Rauris, Bezirk Zell am See, Salzburg
History and techniques of local goldmining. Mining tools, equipment. Memorabilia of the last mine-owner, Ignaz Rojacher (d.1891). Geological maps. Minerals. Watercolours of local flora and insects. Models of peasant houses. Costumes.
Tu., F. 10-12, 3-5. Other times on request.

REICHENAU AN DER RAX

MUSEUM OF MINING AND REGIONAL LIFE
Hauptstrasse 28, 2651 Reichenau an der Rax, Niederösterreich
Mining and smelting since prehistoric times. Natural history. Local history and folklore.
July-Sept. Tu.-F. 2.30-4.30; Sa. 10-12. Other times by appointment.

REICHENAU NATURAL HISTORY MUSEUM
Rathaus, Talhofstrasse 6, 2651 Reichenau an der Rax, Niederösterreich
Geographical features of Lower Austria. Alpine flowers and fungi. Austrian birds.
Apr. 15-Oct. 15, Daily 9-2

REICHERSBERG

MONASTERY MUSEUM
Augustiner Chorherrenstift, 4981 Reichersberg, Bezirk Ried im Innkreis, Oberösterreich
Monastery (17th century). History of monastery. 17th-18th century sculpture, painting, weapons. 12th-18th century gravestones.
Daily 2-5.

RENNWEG

VILLAGE MUSEUM
9863 St. Peter Rennweg, Bezirk Spittal an der Donau, Kärnten
Bronze Age material. Peasant household equipment, tools. Mining equipment. Coins.
May-Sept. Daily 10-1.

RETZ

MUNICIPAL MUSEUM
Altes Bürgerspital, Znaimer Strasse 7, 2070 Retz, Bezirk Hollabrunn, Niederösterreich
Palaeontology. Mineralogy. Prehistory of Retz area. Peasant household equipment. Pottery. Wrought iron. Displays showing grape-growing, wine production and the wine trade.
May-Oct. Su., public holidays 9-12. Other times on request.

MUSEUM OF TOWN HISTORY
Rathaus, Hauptplatz, 2070 Retz, Bezirk Hollabrunn, Niederösterreich
History of Retz. Archives. Insignia. Guild material. Weapons. Religious art. Views of the town. Biedermeier room (1830).
May-Oct. Su., public holidays, 9-12. Other times by appointment.

REUTTE

REGIONAL MUSEUM
Untermarkt 24, 6600 Reutte, Tirol
Baroque paintings. Late 18th century woodcarving of the Last Supper. 18th century glass paintings. Furniture. Clocks. Spinning wheels. Folk art. Paintings, engravings of Reutte. Court and prison antiquities.
M.-Sa. 10-12, 3-5. Su. 10-12. Closed April, Nov.

RIED

ETHNOLOGICAL MUSEUM OF THE INNVIERTEL
Kirchenplatz 13, 4910 Ried, Oberösterreich
Folk art of the Innviertel. Popular remedies. Costumes.

Ornaments. Painted furniture. Pipes. Pottery. Glass. Toys. Clocks. Weapons. Targets. 16th-19th century engravings, woodcuts. Sculpture. 'Stille Nacht' crib. Paintings by the Ried artist, Wilhelm Dachauer (d.1951).
Tu.-Sa. 9-12, 2-6; Su., public holidays, 9-12

RIEGERSBURG

CASTLE MUSEUM
8333 Riegersburg, Bezirk Feldbach, Steiermark
Firearms. Powder horns. 17th century flamethrower. Swords. Daggers. Instruments of torture. Lithographs by Kriehuber. Woodcarving (c.1500) of Crucifixion.
May-Sept. Daily 8-12, 1.30-6. Mar. 15- Apr. 30, Oct. 1- Nov. 15, Daily 10-12, 1.30-5.

CASTLE MUSEUM
8333 Riegersburg, Bezirk Hollabrunn, Niederösterreich
Castle (early 18th century). 18th-19th century furniture. French, Chinese, wallpaper. Family history of the Counts of Khevenhüller-Metsch. History of the castle.
Apr. 15- Oct. 15, Tu.-Su. 9-12, 1-5.

ROHRAU

FAMILY COLLECTION OF COUNT HARRACH
Schloss Rohrau, Bezirk Bruck an der Leitha, Niederösterreich
Paintings, especially 17th-18th century Spanish, Neapolitan, Dutch, Flemish. 17th-18th century furniture, applied arts.
Mar.-Nov., Tu.-Su. 9-5.

HAYDN MUSEUM
Rohrau, Bezirk Bruck an der Leitha, Niederösterreich
Haydn's birthplace. Memorabilia of the composer. Musical instruments. Scores. Early editions. Paintings. Engravings. Figurines. Recordings of Haydn's works.
Mar. 15- Nov. 15, Tu.-Su. 9-6.

ROSENBURG

CASTLE MUSEUM
3573 Burg Rosenburg, Bezirk Horn, Niederösterreich
16th-17th century furniture. Weapons. 15th-18th century wrought-iron work, including spurs, locks, pistols, daggers. Majolica. Pewter. 15th-16th century religious paintings. Prehistoric artifacts.
Daily 8-6.

RÖTHELSTEIN

PALACE COLLECTION
Röthelstein, Steiermark
Local history. Ethnography.
By appointment.

SAALFELDEN

MUSEUM OF LOCAL LIFE AND OF CRIBS
Schloss Ritzen, 5760 Saalfelden, Bezirk Zell am See, Steiermark
17th-20th century cribs. 17th century peasant room, with painted furniture. Costumes. Ornaments. Spinning and weaving equipment. Pottery. Popular religious art. Mineralogy.
W., Sa., Su. 2-4. Other times on request.

SALZBURG

CASTLE MUSEUM
Festung Hohensalzburg, 5020 Salzburg
Furniture. Flags. Weapons. Wrought-iron work. Craftsmen's tools.
Mar. 15- Oct. 31, daily 9-7. Nov. 1- Mar. 4, daily 9.30-5.

COLLECTIONS OF THE BENEDICTINE ABBEY OF ST. PETER
5020 Salzburg
Paintings. Coats of arms. Engravings. Gold and silversmiths' work.
By appointment.

COLLECTION OF THE NONNBERG BENEDICTINE MONASTERY
Nonnberggasse 2, 5020 Salzburg
Religious sculpture and applied art, including 13th century folding chair.
Daily 9-11, 2-4.

FATHER PETER SINGER MUSEUM
Franzirkanerkloster, Hofstallgasse, 5020 Salzburg
Memorabilia of Father Singer. Pansymphonicon (1845).
On request.

FRANK COLLECTION OF THE HISTORY OF PHOTOGRAPHY
Reichenhaller Strasse 18, 5020 Salzburg
History of photography from its beginnings to the present day. Daguerre camera (1839). Daguerrotypes (c.1850). Lenses. Shutters. Reconstruction of studio and darkroom (1870). Light and exposure meters. Stereoscopic equipment.
Tu.-Su. 3-6.

MOZART MUSEUM
Getreidegasse 9, 5020 Salzburg
Mozart's birthplace. Portraits and memorabilia of Mozart and his family. Letters. Musical autographs. Musical instruments, including Mozart's first Clavichord (1760), and his first violin.
Oct.-May, daily 9-6. June and Sept. daily 9-7. July-Aug. daily 8-8.

MOZART'S HOUSE
Markartplatz 8, 5020 Salzburg
18th century musical instruments. Autograph manuscripts of Mozart's works.
July-Aug. daily 9-6.

MUSEUM OF ETHNOLOGY
Monatsschlösschen, Hellbrunn, 5020 Salzburg
Furnished interiors. Painted furniture. Faience. Pottery. Household equipment. Tools. Costumes. Waggons. Carriages. Sleighs. Bottles. Glass. Toys. Weapons. Popular art. Votive pictures.
Apr.-May and Sept. daily 9-5.30. June-Aug. daily 8-6.

NATURE HOUSE
Museumsplatz 5, 5020 Salzburg
Dioramas, displays illustrating man's dependence on nature. Biology. Minerals. Coral. Fungi. European wildlife. Animals of Africa, America, Asia, Australasia. Life in the Ice Age. Domestic animals. Achievements of Aristotle Lamarck, Darwin, Mendel, Haeckel.
Apr.-Sept. Tu.-Su. 9-5. Oct.-Mar. Tu.-Su. 10-4.

RAINER REGIMENT MUSEUM
Festung Hohensalzburg
Schwarzstrasse 33
5020 Salzburg
History of the Rainer Regiment, established 1682. Weapons. Equipment. Paintings.
May 1 - Sept. 15, daily 9-5. Other months by appointment.

RESIDENZ GALERIE
Residenzplatz 1, 5020 Salzburg
16th-18th century German, Dutch, Flemish paintings. 17th century Italian, Dutch, Flemish paintings, including works by Rembrandt, Ruisdael, Rubens, Brueghel. 17th-18th century French paintings. 17th-18th century Italian, Austrian Baroque paintings. 19th-20th century Austrian paintings.
June-Sept. Daily 9-6.

SALZBURGER MUSEUM, CAROLINO AUGUSTEUM
Museumsplatz 6, 5020 Salzburg
Art and history of the city and province of Salzburg. Prehistoric material. Roman and medieval archaeology. Memorabilia of Paul Hofhaymer, Hans Baumann, Paracelsus, Georg Trakl. Musical instruments. 19th century portraits. Costumes. Drawings. Prints. Weapons. Coins. Furniture. Household equipment. Stoves. Faience. Pewter. Clocks. Religious art. 18th-20th century paintings by Austrian artists.
Daily 9-5.

ST. ERHARD

VOTIVE COLLECTION IN THE PILGRIMS' CHURCH
8615 St. Erhard, Bezirk Bruck an der Mur, Steiermark
Animal votive-offerings in iron, wood, wax.
On request.

ST. FLORIAN

COLLECTIONS OF THE AUGUSTIAN MONASTERY
4490 St. Florian, Bezirk Linz-Land, Oberösterreich
15th-18th century paintings, sculpture. 13th-15th century glass paintings. Wood statues of St. Florian (c.1300). Botany. Zoology. Mineralogy. Anton Bruckner memorial room.
Guided tours, Nov.-Mar. daily 11 and 3. Apr.-Oct. 10, 11, 2, 3, 4.

ST. GEORGEN

PALACE MEMORIAL MUSEUM
8413 St. Georgen, Bezirk Leibnitz, Steiermark
Castle was home of the poet, Paul Ernst (d.1933). Furniture, works and personal possessions of Ernst. Sculpture and paintings by Barbara Ernst.
May-Oct., on request.

ST. LAMBRECHT

COLLECTIONS OF THE BENEDICTINE MONASTERY
8813 St. Lambrecht, Bezirk Murau, Steiermark
Tools. Toys. Cribs. Votive offerings. Glass paintings. Natural history. Roman sculpture, inscriptions. 15th-18th century religious paintings, sculpture.
June 15- Sept. 15, daily, guided tours 10.30, 2.30. Other months by appointment.

ST. MARGARETHEN

OPEN-AIR MUSEUM IN ROMAN QUARRY
7062 St. Margarethen, Bezirk Eisenstadt, Burgenland
Quarry worked since Roman times, used for many important buildings in Vienna. Now contains works by sculptors from many countries who have visited the quarry each year since 1959.
At all times.

ST. MARTIN

VOTIVES COLLECTION OF THE PILGRIMS' CHURCH OF MARIA KIRCHENTAL
5092 St. Martin, Bezirk Zell am See, Salzburg
1500 votive pictures, 1690 - present day.
Daily 8-dusk.

ST. PAUL

MONASTERY ART COLLECTIONS
9470 St. Paul, Bezirk Wolfsberg, Kärnten
15th-17th century German, Dutch, Flemish and Italian paintings, drawings, engravings, lithographs, woodcuts. Sculpture, including ivory relief (c.900). 11th-15th century religious ornaments, lithurgical objects. 18th century porcelain figures. 12th-13th century Romanesque embroidered pictures. Faience. Glass. Medals. Coins.
May-Oct. Daily 10.30-12, 2-4.

ST. PETER

TEURNIA MUSEUM
St. Peter, Bezirk Spittal an der Drau, Kärnten
Romano-Celtic sculpture and architectural items from excavations at Teurnia and Upper Carinthia. Mosaics.
On request.

ST. PÖLTEN

DIOCESAN MUSEUM
Domplatz 1, 3104 St. Pölten, Niederösterreich
Prehistoric and Roman material from local sites. Roman pottery, especially sigillata. Coins. Medals. Seals. Mineralogy. Palaeontology. Botany. Religious art. Liturgical objects. Baroque furniture. Sculpture. Glass paintings. Engravings.
On request.

MUNICIPAL MUSEUM
Prandtauerstrasse 2, 3104 St. Pölten, Niederösterreich
Local history. Prehistoric and Roman material from local sites. Commercial and industrial development of region. Theatre history. Coins.
On request.

ST. ULRICH

LAVANTTAL MUSEUM OF LOCAL LIFE
Post Eitweg, 6393 St. Ulrich, Bezirk Wolfsberg, Kärnten
Household equipment and popular art of the Laventtal. Costumes. Handicrafts, especially spinning, weaving. Biedermeier room. Peasant kitchen.
Daily 8-12, 2-4.

ST. VEIT

REGIONAL MUSEUM
Alte Herzogburg, Hauptplatz 1, 9300 St. Veit, Kärnten
Targets, with historical scenes. Coins. Seals. Weapons. History of St. Veit and surrounding area. Guild chests.
On request.

SCHÄRDING

MUNICIPAL MUSEUM
Schlossgasse, Schärding, Oberösterreich
History of Schärding and surrounding area. Prehistoric material. Peasant furniture, tools, handicrafts. Beliefs and superstitions. Agriculture. Granite-quarrying. 15th-17th century wood sculpture, carvings. Historical views of Schärding.
M., Sa., Su., public holidays 10-12. Tu., Th. 2-4.

SCHEIBBS

HOTTENROTH COLLECTION
Heroksiedlung 218, 3270 Scheibbs, Niederösterreich
Peasant furniture, art and household equipment. Handicrafts. Wool and linen processing. Weaving. Agricultural implements. Woodworking tools. Equipment for butter-making and honey extraction. Religious art. Targets.
By appointment.

REGIONAL MUSEUM
Rathausplatz 75, 3270 Scheibbs, Niederösterreich
Local history. Weapons, especially from time of Peasants' War. Instruments of torture. Targets.
M.-F. 8-11.

SCHLÄGL

COLLECTIONS OF THE PREMONSTRATENSIAN ABBEY
Aigen, Schlägl, Bezirk Rohrbach, Oberösterreich
15th-16th century German, Austrian paintings. 17th-18th century Italian, Austrian, Dutch, Flemish paintings. Codices. Incunabula. Portraits.
May-Sept. daily 9-11, 2-5. Other times by appointment.

SCHLAINING

CASTLE MUSEUM
Schlaining, Bezirk Oberwart, Burgenland
Artistic cast-iron work, mostly Mariazell, 1600 - present day. 17th-19th century paintings. Weapons. Musical instruments. Carpets. Objets d'art. Household equipment.
May 1 - Oct. 15, Tu.-Su. 8-12, 2-6.

SCHRUNS

MONTAFON REGIONAL MUSEUM
Silvrettastrasse, 6780 Schruns, Bezirk Bludenz, Vorarlberg
House (1609) with original Montafor furniture. Peasant household equipment, tools, weapons. Costumes. Popular religious art. Local animals.
June-Sept. daily 10-1, 4-5. Other months by appointment.

SCHWANENSTADT

REGIONAL MUSEUM
Rathaus, Stadtplatz 54, 4690 Schwanenstadt, Bezirk Vöcklabruck, Oberösterreich
History of the Schwanenstadt area. Roman material from local excavations. Agricultural implements. Craftsmen's tools, equipment.
By appointment.

SCHWARZENBERG

COMMUNITY MUSEUM
Kleberhaus, 6867 Schwarzenberg, Bezirk Bregenz, Vorarlberg
Local history, folklore. 18th century peasant rooms. Weapons. Costumes. Religious art. Pottery. Pewter. Portraits of local personalities. Memorial room to Angelica Kauffmann, and to the Schwarzenberg painters, Jakob Fink and Bartle Kleber.
Tu.-Sa. 2-6; Su. 3-6. Other times by appointment.

SECKAU

ABBEY MUSEUM
8732 Seckau, Steiermark
Religious art. Liturgical objects. Coins.
Su., guided tours 10.45, 2.45.

SEEBENSTEIN

CASTLE MUSEUM
Burg, 2824 Seebenstein, Bezirk Neunkirchen, Niederösterreich
Furniture. Period rooms. Chinese, Japanese porcelain. 15th-17th century weapons. Paintings. Sculpture.
Easter-Nov. 1, guided tours, Tu., W., F., Sa., Su. 9, 11, 2, 4.

SEEKIRCHEN

REGIONAL MUSEUM
Markt 73, 5201 Seekirchen, Salzburg
Furniture and furnishings. 18th-20th century costumes. Pottery. Tools and equipment used in agriculture, fishing, joinery, blacksmith's shop. 11th-18th century religious art. Crib-figures. Weapons. Coins. Stone Age, Bronze Age, Celtic, Roman and medieval material from local excavations.
Daily 8-6.

SEITENSTETTEN

COLLECTIONS OF THE BENEDICTINE ABBEY
3353 Seitenstetten, Bezirk Amstetten, Niederösterreich
15th-18th century religious paintings, sculpture, wood carving and ivory carving. Glass paintings. 15th-19th century South German, Dutch, Flemish, Austrian, Italian paintings. Prehistoric, Roman material from local sites. Mineralogy. Zoology.
May-Nov. guided tours 10.30, 2.30. Other months by appointment.

SOLBAD HALL

MINING MUSEUM
Fürstengasse, 6060 Solbad Hall, Bezirk Innsbruck-Land, Tirol
Models of local salt-mine workings. Maps. Minerals.
June-Sept. Su.-F. 9-12, 2-5; Sa. 9-12.

MUNICIPAL MUSEUM
Rathaus, Oberer Stadtplatz, 6060 Solbad Hall, Bezirk Innsbruck-Land, Tirol
Local history. Saltmining. Glass-making. Coins. Relics of the Tyrolean revolt (1809). Religious art. Portraits.
May-Sept. daily 10-12. Other times by appointment.

SALTMINE AND BOILING PLANT
Saline 17, 6060 Solbad Hall, Bezirk Innsbruck-Land, Tirol
Saltmine. Machinery and equipment. Models of salt boiling house.
May-Sept. guided tours, M.-Th. 9-5.

SONNTAGBERG

TREASURY OF THE PILGRIMS' CHURCH
Sonntagberg, Bezirk Amstetten, Niederösterreich
Church ornaments. Votive pictures. Gold and silversmiths' work.
On request.

SPARBEREGG

REGIONAL MUSEUM
Sparberegg, Bezirk Hartberg, Steiermark
In restored farmhouse. Peasant furniture, household equipment. Agricultural implements.
Daily 8-6.

SPITAL

REGIONAL MUSEUM
Stift, 4582 Spital, Bezirk Kirchdorf an der Krems, Oberösterreich
Geology. Palaeontology. History of the monastery, the town and the area. Prehistoric bears' skulls. History and archaeology of Roman road over the Pyhrn Pass. Household equipment. Tools. Display showing production of scythes.
On request.

SPITTAL

MUSEUM OF LOCAL LIFE
Schloss Porcia, Edlingerstrasse 13, 9800 Spittal, Kärnten
16th century rooms, with original furniture. History and folklore of Upper Carinthia. Agricultural implements and machinery. Hunting weapons, traps. Fishing equipment. Skis. Sleighs. Mining equipment. Reconstruction of 17th century schoolroom. Cribs. Religious art. Paintings by Karl Truppes.
May 15 - Oct. 1, daily 9-6. Other months on request.

SPITZ

MUSEUM OF NAVIGATION
Schloss Erlahof, 3620 Spitz, Bezirk Krems, Niederösterreich
History of Danube navigation. Models. Documents. Equipment.
Apr.-Oct. Tu.-Su. 10-12, 2-4.

STADL-PAURA

MUSEUM OF SHIPPING
Pfarrhof, 4651 Stadl-Paura, Bezirk Wels, Oberösterreich
History and commercial importance of shipping on the Traun. Ship models. Harbours. Salt-trade. Local history. Peasant furniture.
On request.

STAMS

MONASTERY COLLECTIONS
Zisterzienstift und Stiftsammlungen, 6422 Stams, Tirol
Baroque statues. Ironwork. Frescoes.
By appointment.

STANS

PALACE COLLECTION
Schloss Tatzberg, Jenbach, 6135 Stans, Tirol
14th-16th century furniture. Mural of Hapsburg family tree (c.1500). Weapons. Armour.
By appointment.

STEGERSBACH

SOUTH BURGENLAND COUNTRYSIDE MUSEUM
7551 Stegersbach, Bezirk Güssing, Burgenland
Geology. Mineralogy. Prehistoric material. Local history. Industrial and commercial development of area. Folklore. Peasant furniture. Household equipment.
Apr.-Oct. daily 8-12, 1-3.

STEYR

REGIONAL MUSEUM
Grünmarkt 26, 4400 Steyr, Oberösterreich
In former granary (1612). History of iron-working. Scythe-making. Neolithic and Bronze Age material. History of Steyr. Weapons. Guns. 15th-18th century sculpture. 17th-18th century paintings. Folklore. Furniture. Costumes. Toys. Dolls. Birds of Upper Austria.
Apr.-Dec. Tu.-Su. 9-12; Tu., Th. also 2-5. Jan.-Mar. M.-Sa. 9-12, Tu., Th. also 2-5.

STEYRERMÜHL

STEYRERMÜHL PAPER-MILL MUSEUM
4662 Steyrermühl, Bezirk Gmunden, Oberösterreich
Equipment and processes for the production of hand-made paper. Collection of watermarks.
M.-F. 8-12, 1-3.

STILLFRIED

MUSEUM OF PREHISTORY AND EARLY HISTORY
Schule, 2262 Stillfried, Bezirk Gänserndorf, Niederösterreich
Prehistoric and medieval material from sites in Lower Austria. Mammoth skull. Neolithic painted pottery. Stone-working implements.
Su. 11-12. Other times by appointment.

STOCKERAU

DISTRICT MUSEUM
Kirchengasse 2, 2000 Stockerau, Bezirk Korneuburg, Niederösterreich
Palaeontology, including lower jaw of woolly rhinoceros. Local history and folklore. Community chests. Clocks. Coins. 17th-18th century altar paintings. Wood sculpture. Glass paintings. Memorabilia and work of the poet, Nikolaus Lenau.
Easter-Christmas, Su., public holidays, 9-11. Other times by appointment.

STRASSBURG

DIOCESAN AND REGIONAL MUSEUM
Schloss, 9341 Strassburg, Bezirk St. Veit an der Glan, Kärnten
Religious art. Sculpture. Liturgical objects. Church furnishings. Peasant household equipment. Craftsmen's tools. South German carved chests.
Apr.-Nov. daily 8-6.

STÜBING

AUSTRIAN OPEN-AIR MUSEUM
8114 Stübing, Bezirk Graz-Umgebung, Steiermark
Peasant houses, farm-buildings and workshops from all parts of Austria.
Apr.-Oct. Tu.-Su. 9-5.

TAMSWEG

LUNGAU REGIONAL MUSEUM
Nr. 133, 5580 Tamsweg, Steiermark
Peasant furniture, household equipment, tools. Chests. Glasses. Bottles. Pewter. Stoneware. Glass paintings. Paintings. Iron cemetery crosses. Weapons. Weaving equipment. Neolithic, Bronze Age and Roman archaeology.
June-Oct. Tu.-Su. 8-12, 2-6. Other times by appointment.

TAUFKIRCHEN

REGIONAL ROOM
Hauptschule, 4775 Taufkirchen, Bezirk Schärding, Oberösterreich
Zoology. Prehistoric archaeology. Local history. Household equipment. Farm implements. Flax processing and linen manufacture. Hunting. Fishing. Weapons.
Daily, on request.

TELFS

REGIONAL MUSEUM
Altes Zollhaus, Untere Marktstrasse 18, 6410 Telfs, Bezirk Innsbruck-Land, Tirol
Prehistoric archaeology. Local history. Peasant art, household equipment, tools, cribs. Masks. Votive tablets. 18th-20th century paintings, sculpture by local artists.
June-Sept. daily 10-12, 3-5. Other months on request.

THALGAU

REGIONAL COLLECTION
5303 Thalgau, Oberösterreich
Local and regional history.
On request.

TIESCHEN

REGIONAL MUSEUM
8355 Tieschen, Steiermark
Prehistory.
On request.

TRAISMAUER

REGIONAL MUSEUM
Florianplatz 13, 3133 Traismauer, Bezirk St. Pölten, Niederösterreich
Prehistoric and Roman material from local sites. Industrial and commercial history. Coins. Coats of arms. Weapons.
Apr.-Oct., Su. 9-11.

TRAUN

REGIONAL HOUSE
Schloss, 4050 Traun, Bezirk Linz-Land, Oberösterreich
Relics and history of Traun fishing industry. Furniture. Locks and keys.
M.-F. 11-12.

TRAUTENFELS

COUNTRYSIDE MUSEUM
8951 Schloss Trautenfels, Bezirk Liezen, Steiermark
Mineralogy. Fossils. Dioramas and mounted specimens of local animals. Prehistoric material. Local history. Dairying and bee-keeping equipment. Peasant furniture, handicrafts. Masks. Weapons.
Easter-Nov. 2, daily 8.30-12, 1.30-4.30. Other times by appointment.

TULLN

REGIONAL MUSEUM
Wiener Strasse 24-26, 3430 Tulln, Niederösterreich
Geology, mineralogy of area. Mastodon and mammoth teeth. Prehistoric, Roman and medieval material from local sites. Coins. Local history. Folklore. Craftsmen's tools. Guild relics. Drawings, prints by Egon Schiele.
Apr.-Nov., 1st, 3rd, 5th Su. in month, 9-11. 2nd and 4th Su. in month, 3-5. Other times by appointment.

VIGAUN

REGIONAL MUSEUM
Heimathaus, 5752 Vigaun, Bezirk Hallein, Steiermark
Peasant furniture, household equipment, furnished interiors. Prehistoric material. Fossils.
Apr.-Oct., by appointment.

VILLACH

MUNICIPAL MUSEUM
Widmanngasse 38, 9500 Villach, Kärnten
Prehistoric, Roman, Lombard, medieval material from local sites. 15th-18th century paintings, sculpture. Mineralogy. Leadmining. Paracelsus section.
May 1-Oct. 15, M.-Sa. 9-12, 2-5; Su., public holidays 9-12. Other months on request.

RELIEF MAP OF CARINTHIA
Peraustrasse, Schillerpark, 9500 Villach, Kärnten
200 sq. m. relief map of Carinthia, to scale of 1:10,000.
May 1-Oct. 15, M.-Sa. 9-12, 2-5; Su., public holidays 9-12.

VILLACH-WARMBAD

ARCHAEOLOGICAL COLLECTION
Kurhaus, 9504 Villach-Warmbad, Villach, Kärnten
History of the Baths. Roman material.
During opening times of Baths.

VÖCKLABRUCK

REGIONAL HOUSE
Hinterstadt 19, 4840 Vöcklabruck, Oberösterreich
Furnished rooms of peasant houses. 16th-18th century paintings, sculpture. Memorabilia of Anton Bruckner. Prehistoric, Roman and medieval archaeology, including discoveries at lake villages.
Guided tours, W., Sa. 10. Other times by appointment.

VORDERNBERG

WATER-POWERED IRONWORKS AND FORGE
Hauptplatz, Vordernberg, Bezirk Leoben, Steiermark
Early ironworks and its equipment. Blast furnace. Hammer.
Daily 9-12, 2-4.

WAIDHOFEN AN DER THAYA

REGIONAL MUSEUM
Wiener Strasse 14, 3830 Waidhofen an der Thaya, Niederösterreich
18th-19th century household equipment. Agricultural implements. Bee-keeping. Weaving. Flax growing, processing. Guild chests. Glass paintings.
Su., public holidays 10-12. Other times on request.

VIENNA

ALBERTINA GRAPHICS COLLECTION
Augustinerstrasse 1, 1010 Vienna 1
European drawings of the 15th-20th centuries. Among the artists represented are Albrecht Dürer, Holbein the Elder and the Younger, Cranach the Elder, Kremser Schimdt, Fra Angelico, Filippino Lippi, Bellini, Michelangelo, Tintoretto, Veronese, Tiepolo, Canaletto, Rubens, Breughel, Rembrandt, Poussin, Lorrain, Hogarth, Reynolds, Romney, Picasso, Matisse, Chagall. Special displays of Japanese woodcuts, views of Vienna, posters, illustrated books, maps.
M., Tu., Th., F. 10-4; W. 10-6; Sa., Su. 10-1.

ALSERGRUND DISTRICT MUSEUM
Währinger Strasse 43, 1090 Vienna 9
History of the Alsergrund district. Paintings. Engravings. Photographs. House-signs. Mementoes of notable residents, including Mozart, Beethoven, Johann Strauss, Bruckner. Industrial history.
Tu. 5-7; Su. 10-12.

ART COLLECTIONS OF THE SCHWARZENBERG PALACE
Rennweg 2, 1030 Vienna 3
Palace (1697-1705). Furniture. Paintings. Sculpture.
Apr.-Oct. Tu., W., Th., Sa., Su. 10-12, 3-6.

AUSTRIAN GALLERY: AUSTRIAN BAROQUE MUSEUM
Unteres Belvedere, Rennweg 6, 1030 Vienna 3
18th century portraits of members of the Imperial family. Paintings and sculpture by the principal Austrian baroque artists. Frescoes. Original lead figures from the fountain in the Neuer Markt (1739). Mirrors. Chinese vases.
Tu.-Sa. 10-4; Su., public holidays 10-1.

AUSTRIAN GALLERY: MUSEUM OF MEDIEVAL AUSTRIAN ART
Orangerie des Unteren Belvedere, Rennweg 6, 1030 Vienna 3
14th-16th century wood and stone sculpture. Altar paintings, carvings.
Tu.-Sa. 10-4; Su., public holidays 9-1.

AUSTRIAN MUSEUM OF APPLIED ART
Stubenring 5, 1010 Vienna 1
13th-15th century church vestments, furniture. 14th-16th century Italian, French, German, Flemish furniture, tapestry, ceramics. 16th century enamels, majolica. 17th century German goldsmiths' work, pewter, scientific apparatus. 18th-19th century French, Austrian furniture. Chinese porcelain, painting. Persian and Turkish carpets. 18th century European porcelain. Coptic textiles. Engravings.
Tu.-F. 9-4; Sa., Su. 9-1.

AUSTRIAN MUSEUM OF ETHNOLOGY
Laudongasse 18, 1080 Vienna 8
In Schönborn Palace (1706-10). Peasant furniture, household equipment, furnished rooms. Models of houses. Popular religious art. Sleighs. Costumes. Ornaments. Votive offerings. Handicrafts. Pottery. Wooden masks and other material for folk-plays. Musical instruments. Cribs. Dolls. Toys. Guild material.
Tu.-F. 9-2; Sa. 9-12; Su. 9-1.

AUSTRIAN MUSEUM OF INDUSTRY AND COMMERCE
Vogelsanggasse 36, 1050 Vienna 5
Displays showing development and organisation of Austrian industry, transport and commerce. Population statistics. Banking. Exports.
M.-F. 8-4.

AUSTRIAN GALLERY OF THE 19th AND 20th CENTURIES
Oberes Belvedere, Prinz Eugen Strasse 27, 1030 Vienna 3
19th century portraits, landscapes, historical scenes, watercolours by Austrian artists. Major collections of paintings by F. G. Waldmüller, Hans Makart, Anton Romako. Frescoes. Miniatures. The 20th century sections emphasise works by Gustav Klimt, Egon Schiele, Richard Gerstl, Gerhard Frankl, Herbert Boeckl, Wilhelm Thöny, Oskar Kokoschka.
Tu.-Sa. 10-4; Su., public holidays 9-1.

AUSTRIAN RAILWAY MUSEUM
Technisches Museum, Mariahilferstrasse 212, 1140 Vienna 14
Historic locomotives and coaches. Models. Pictures and plans of tunnels, bridges. Dioramas of Alpine routes. Railway workshops. Signalling. Telegraph. Tramways.
Tu.-F. 9-4; Sa. and Su. 9-1.

BEETHOVEN MEMORIAL ROOMS
Pasqualatihaus, Mölkerbastei 8, 1010 Vienna 1
Beethoven's home, 1804-15, in which he wrote the 4th, 5th, 7th symphonies. Memorabilia include Streicher piano (1821), deathmask, portraits, personal possessions.
Tu.-Sa. 9-4; Su., public holidays, 9-1.

FRIEDRICH JULIUS BIEBER MUSEUM
Tuersgasse 21, 1130 Vienna 13
Ethnographical collections from Ethiopia and the Sahara.
By appointment.

BRIGITTENAU DISTRICT MUSEUM
Raffaelgasse 13, 1200 Vienna 20
History of the district. Pictures. Maps. Press cuttings. Watercolours showing destruction, 1940-45, and subsequent rebuilding. Literary works dealing with Brigittenau. Memorabilia of Robert Blum and Lorenz Böhler.
Su. 10-11.30

CABINET OF ENGRAVINGS OF THE ACADEMY OF FINE ARTS
Schillerplatz 3, 1010 Vienna 1
Drawings, watercolours and engravings, mostly by Austrian artists. Medieval architectural drawings from the Stephanskirche. Special collection of engravings by Dürer.
Aug. 16-July 14, M.-F. 10-4; Sa. 9-12.

CATHEDRAL AND DIOCESAN MUSEUM
Rotenturmstrasse 2, 1010 Vienna 1
Medieval sculpture, paintings, textiles. 17th-18th century religious ornaments, liturgical objects.
Tu.-Su. 10-1.

CLOCK MUSEUM OF THE CITY OF VIENNA
Schulhof 2, 1010 Vienna 1
Clocks and earlier devices for measuring time. Hourglasses. Sundials. Astronomical clocks. Peasant clocks. Musical clocks.
Tu.-Su. 9-1.

COLLECTIONS OF THE ADLER SOCIETY FOR HERALDRY AND GENEALOGY
Haarhof 4A, 1010 Vienna 1
Coats of arms. Pedigrees. Death announcements. Seals, 1825 onwards.
W. 5-7.

COLLECTION OF HISTORIC CARRIAGES
Schloss Schönbrunn, 1130 Vienna 13
130 carriages for ceremonial purposes and everyday use, 1690-1917. Harness. Equipment. Costumes. Imperial coach and hearse. Napoleon II's perambulator. Sleighs. Paintings of stallions from the stud of Emperor Karl VI.
Daily 10-4. May-Sept. 10-5.

COLLECTION OF THE INSTITUTE OF THE HISTORY OF MEDICINE
Währinger Strasse 25, 1090 Vienna 9
History of the Vienna Medical School. Instruments. Pictures. Photographs. Documents. Coins. Medals.
Tu., Th. 9-3.

COLLECTIONS OF THE MARKETS AUTHORITY OF THE CITY OF VIENNA
Rathausstrasse 14-16, 1010 Vienna 1
Displays illustrating the methods of adulterating food and of giving false weight. Collection of wax models of edible and non-edible fungi. History of the Vienna markets since 1860.
M.-Sa. 8-6; Su. 8-11.

COLLECTION OF POPULAR RELIGIOUS ART
Johannesgasse 8, 1010 Vienna 1
In former Convent apothecary's shop (18th century) with original furnishings and equipment. 17th-19th century popular religious art. Wood sculpture and relief. Devotional paintings. Wax models.
Su. 9-1.

COSTUME COLLECTION OF THE ACADEMY OF FINE ARTS
Schillerplatz 3, 1235 Vienna 23
Uniforms. Regional costumes. Texiles.
By appointment.

COUNT HARRACH'S PICTURE GALLERY
Freyung 3, 1010 Vienna 1
16th-17th century Dutch, Flemish, Italian, German paintings. 18th century French, Italian paintings. 17th-18th century Neapolitan paintings.
Apr.-Oct. M., F., Sa. 10-1, 3-6; W., Th. 10-1; Su. 3-6.

DÖBLING DISTRICT MUSEUM
Döblinger Hauptastrasse 96, 1190 Vienna 19
In Wertheimstein villa (1835). History of the present Döbling district. Prehistoric, Roman and medieval material from local sites. Memorial rooms to Eduard von Bauernfeld (d.1890) and Ferdinand von Saar (1906).
Sa. 3-6; Su. 9.30-12. During Vienna Festival, also Tu., Th. 5-7.

DOG MUSEUM
Karl Schweighofer Gasse 3, 1070 Vienna 7
Paintings, prints, photographs illustrating breeds of dog. Dogs' skulls.
Apr.-Oct., 1st and 3rd F. in month, 5-6.

ELECTROPATHOLOGICAL MUSEUM
Selzergasse 19, 1010 Vienna 1
Exhibitions illustrating damage caused by electricity to organic and inorganic substances.
By appointment.

EXHIBITION OF THE FORMER COURT COLLECTIONS OF TABLEWARE AND SILVER
Batthyanstiege, Hofburg, 1010 Vienna 1
18th-19th century silver, bronze, glass and porcelain table services from the Imperial household. Chocolate beakers. 'Panorama plates' of Vienna and Meissen porcelain. 'Vermilion' service for 140 persons.
Tu., F., Su. 9-1.

FEDERAL COLLECTION OF PERIOD FURNITURE
Mariahilfer Strasse 88, 1070 Vienna 7
18th-19th century furniture, including a number of pieces originally belonging to members of the Imperial family. Biedermeier rooms.
Tu.-F. 9-12, 2-4; Sa., Su. 9-12. Guided tours only.

FIRST AUSTRIAN-SILESIAN MUSEUM IN VIENNA
Singerstrasse 13/3/14, 1010 Vienna 1
Folklore. Costumes. Furniture. Porcelain. Objets d'art. Views of former Austrian Silesia. Pencil drawings by Carl Riedl (d.1914).
W. 10-5; Sa. 2-5; Su. 10-12.

FLORISDORF DISTRICT MUSEUM
Prager Strasse 33, 1210 Vienna 21
History of the 11 village communities which developed into Florisdorf. Geology. Mineralogy. Flora. Fauna. Prehistoric and Roman material. Furniture. Household equipment. Cooper's tools. Pictures and plans showing old and new course of the Danube. Danube navigation. Boat-mills. Weapons. Uniforms. Memorabilia of writers and composers who lived in Florisdorf.
Sa. 4-6; Su. 10-12. During Vienna Festival, Sa. 4-9.

FRANCISCAN MONASTERY MUSEUM
Franziskanerplatz 4, 1010 Vienna 1
History of the Franciscan Order.
By appointment.

GALLERY OF PAINTINGS OF THE ACADEMY OF FINE ARTS
Schillerplatz 3, 1010 Vienna 1
14th-18th century Italian paintings. 15th-17th century Dutch, Flemish paintings. 17th century Spanish paintings. 16th century German, Dutch, Flemish portraits. 18th-19th century French paintings. German paintings of the early Renaissance.
Tu., Th., F. 10-2; W. 10-1, 3-6; Sa., Su., public holidays 9-1.

HAYDN MUSEUM
Haydngasse 19, 1060 Vienna 6
House where Haydn lived, 1797-1809, and where he composed *The Seasons* and *The Creation.* Autograph manuscripts, scores. Haydn's death-mask. Mementoes of Haydn's period and portraits of his contemporaries.
Tu.-Sa. 9-4; Su., public holidays 9-1.

HERNALS DISTRICT MUSEUM
Hernalser Hauptstrasse 72-74, 1170 Vienna 17
Prehistoric and Roman material from local sites. Paintings, prints, models, plans showing development of district. Household equipment. Flags. Religious art. Memorabilia of noted local residents, including the Schrammel brothers, inventors of lithography.
Su. 9.30-12.

HETZENDORF PALACE COLLECTION
Hetzendorfer Strasse 79, Vienna
Vienna fashions, mainly 19th century.
Tu.-Sa. 10-3; Su. 9-1.

HIETZING DISTRICT MUSEUM
Am Platz 2, 1130 Vienna 13
History of the district and especially of Schönbrunn. Memorabilia of Emperor Franz Joseph I, of famous Viennese actresses, of artists who lived in the district. Collections and memorabilia of Rudolf Freiherr von Slatin and of the African explorer, Dr. Emil Holub. Prehistoric artifacts. Geology. Palaeontology.
Su. 9-12. During Vienna Festival Week, daily 10-12. Closed July 1 - Aug. 31.

HISTORICAL MUSEUM OF THE CITY OF VIENNA
Karlsplatz, 1040 Vienna 4
Vienna in prehistoric times. Roman pottery, sculpture, household objects. Medieval sculpture, architectural features, paintings. Plans, models and views of Vienna, 15th century onwards. Siege of Vienna by the Turks. Weapons. Armour. Portraits. Freemasonry in Vienna. Furniture. Vienna porcelain, silver and industrial art. Costumes. Rooms from the house of Grillparzer. Theatre history.
Tu.-F. 9-4; Sa. 2-6; Su., public holidays 9-1.

HOUSE WHERE SCHUBERT DIED
Kettenbrückengasse 6, 1040 Vienna 4
Memorabilia of the last year of Schubert's life, 1828.
Tu.-Sa. 9-4; Su., public holidays 9-1.

HOUSE OF THE SEA
Flakturm, Esterházypark, 1060 Vienna 6
Ethnographical material from New Guinea. World-wide collection of molluscs. Aquaria. Specimens of sea-creatures.
Daily 9-6.

JEWISH MUSEUM
Tempelgasse 2, 1010 Vienna 1
History of Judaism and of the Jewish Community in Vienna. Liturgical objects. Manuscripts. Portraits. Coins and medals.
By appointment.

LANDSTRASSE LOCAL MUSEUM
Sechskrügelgasse 2, 1030 Vienna 3
Paintings and photographs showing history and development of the Third District. Diorama of the Landstrasse in 1900. Roman remains from local sites. Mozart's gravestone from St. Mark's Cemetery.
Nov.-June, Su. 10-12.

LEOPOLDSTADT DISTRICT MUSEUM
Karmelitergasse 9, 1020 Vienna 2
History and topography of the Second District of Vienna. Paintings. Drawings and architectural features of the former North Station. Judaica. Theatre and circus history.
W. 5-7; Sa. 2.30-5; Su. 9-12.

LIESING DISTRICT MUSEUM
Perchtoldsdorfer Strasse 2, 1235 Vienna 23
History of Liesing district. Paintings. Drawings. Engravings. Craftsmen's tools. Pottery. Palaeontological and prehistoric material from local sites.
W., Sa. 9-12.

MECHINARIST MUSEUM
Mecharistengasse 4, 1070 Vienna 7
Material relating to history of this Armenian sect. Manuscripts. Coins. Paintings, drawings of Armenian scenes.
On request.

MEIDLING DISTRICT MUSEUM
Nymphengasse 7, 1120 Vienna 12
History of the former villages of Altmannsdorf, Gaudenzdorf, Hetzendorf, Meidling. Geology. Remains of Roman water-system. Paintings, engravings, photographs illustrating local history. Industry. Theatre history. Works by artists who lived in the district.
Su. 9-12. Other times by appointment.

MONASTERY MUSEUM OF THE BROTHERS OF MERCY
Taborstrasse 16, 1010 Vienna 1
Religious art. Weapons. Coins. Medals.
On request.

MOZART MEMORIAL ROOM
Figarohaus, Schulerstrasse 8, 1010 Vienna 1
Mozart's house, 1784-87, where the *Marriage of Figaro* was written. Manuscripts. Scores. Portraits of Mozart and his family. Mementoes of visitors to the house, including Haydn and Beethoven.
Tu.-Sa. 9-4; Su., public holidays 9-1.

MUSEUM OF THE AUSTRIAN POST OFFICE SAVINGS BANK
Georg Coch Platz 2, 1010 Vienna 1
History of the leading part played by Austria in the development of the credit-transfer system. Memorabilia of Georg Coch (d.1890). Bank books of Franz Joseph I and other distinguished people.
M.-F. 8-3.

MUSEUM OF THE BÖHMERWALD
Ungargasse 3, 1030 Vienna 3
History of the Böhmerwald. Coats of arms. Paintings. Models of houses. Household equipment. Memorabilia of Adalbert Stifter and other famous residents.
Th. 10-12, 2-5; Sa., Su., public holidays 9-12.

MUSEUM OF THE CITY FUNERAL ORGANISATION
Goldeggasse 19, 1040 Vienna 4
Equipment for important ceremonies. Hearses. Ornaments. Franz Schubert's death certificate.
M.-F. 7.30-4.30, by appointment.

MUSEUM OF ETHNOLOGY
Heldenplatz 3, Neue Burg, 1010 Vienna 1
Monuments from Ephesus. African handicrafts, utensils, tools, ornaments, carvings. Benin bronzes (12th-19th centuries). Mexican archaeology, ornaments. Cult objects, weapons. Collections of material from Oceania, made by Captain Cook.
M., W., Th., Sa. 10-1; F. 2-7; Su. 9-1. May-Sept. Su. 9-4.

MUSEUM OF THE FARRIER'S ART
Tierärztliche Hochschule, Linke Bahngasse 11, 1030 Vienna 3
Development of the horseshoe. Farriers' tools. Methods of curing injured and diseased hoofs.
M.-F. 8-12, 2-4.

MUSEUM OF THE FEDERAL GEOLOGICAL INSTITUTE
Rasumofskygasse 23, Vienna
Geology. Palaeontology.
By appointment.

MUSEUM OF THE FIRST AUSTRIAN SAVINGS BANK
Graben 21, 1010 Vienna 1
History of the Savings Bank. Collections illustrating development of money and tokens.
M.-F. 9-3; Sa. 2-6; Su. 10-1. July-Aug. closed Sa., Su.

MUSEUM OF HARNESS AND SADDLERY
Tierärztliche Hochschule, Linke Bahngasse 11, 1030 Vienna 3
Development of harness for horses and oxen. Specialist harness for troikas, sledges. Saddle-types. Postage stamps depicting horses.
M.-F. 8-12, 2-4.

MUSEUM OF THE HISTORY OF ART: COLLECTION OF ANTIQUES
Burgring 5, 1010 Vienna 1
Greek vases, utensils, paintings, ornaments, reliefs. 3rd-5th century statues, pottery, carvings from Lower Italy. Statues, pottery from Cyprus. Greek and Roman sarcophagi. Etruscan pottery, portraits, sculpture, lamps. Roman mosaics, sculpture, jewellery, ornaments. Terra sigillata. Glass. Inscriptions. Pottery. Votive objects. Byzantine, Old Bulgarian gold- and silver-smiths' work.
Tu.-Sa. 10-3; Su. 9-1.

MUSEUM OF THE HISTORY OF ART: COLLECTION OF OLD MUSICAL INSTRUMENTS
Neue Burg, 1010 Vienna 1
Old musical instruments. 17th-18th century clavichords. 18th century pianofortes, especially by Vienna makers. 15th-19th century violins, violas, violoncellos. Guitars. Zithers. Harps.
Su. 9-2; M. 10-3.

MUSEUM OF THE HISTORY OF ART: COIN, MEDAL AND CURRENCY COLLECTIONS
Burgring 5, 1010 Vienna 1
History of money, from its beginnings to the present day. European, African, American and Asian examples. Paper money. Comprehensive collection of Austrian money. European medals, from Roman times onwards.
Tu.-Sa. 10-3; Su. 9-1.

MUSEUM OF THE HISTORY OF ART: EGYPTIAN AND ORIENTAL COLLECTION
Burgring 5, 1010 Vienna 1
Temple columns and other fragments. Statues. Sarcophagi. Inscriptions. Wood, stone and faience statuettes. Mummies of human beings, animals, birds. Scarabs. Seals. Jewels and ornaments.
Tu.-Sa. 10-3; Su. 9-1.

MUSEUM OF THE HISTORY OF ART: GALLERY OF PAINTINGS
Burgring 5, 1010 Vienna 1
15th-19th century European paintings. Among the artists particularly strongly represented are Dürer, Holbein the Younger, Rubens, Rembrandt, Van Dyck, Titian, Velasquez, Canaletto.
Tu.-Sa. 10-3; Su. 9-1.

MUSEUM OF THE HISTORY OF ART: MUSEUM OF AUSTRIAN CULTURE
Neue Burg, 1010 Vienna 1
History of the Austrian territories. Settlement patterns. Town development. Maps. Models. Geographical features. Wine and sugar production. Transport. Trade and industry. Geology. Mining. Salt-production. Paper. Wool.
Su. 9-1; M. 10-3.

MUSEUM OF THE HISTORY OF ART: SCULPTURE AND APPLIED ART COLLECTION
Burgring 5, 1010 Vienna 1
14th-16th century Venetian, Spanish, English sculpture. 15th-16th century German, Italian, Dutch, Flemish sculpture. 14th-18th century ivory carvings. 16th-17th century clocks. Musical automata. Scientific instruments. 16th-17th century German, Italian, French, tableware, glass, drinking vessels.
Tu.-Sa. 10-3; Su. 9-1.

MUSEUM OF THE HISTORY OF ART: TREASURY
Hofburg, 1010 Vienna 1
Imperial insignia (9th century onwards). Insignia of the Order of the Golden Fleece, Order of Maria-Theresa, Order of St. Stephen. Memorial room to the Duke of Reichstadt and his mother, Marie Louise. Religious ornaments, liturgical objects.
M., W., Sa. 9.30-3; Tu., Th. 2-7; Su. 9-1.

MUSEUM OF THE HISTORY OF ART: WEAPONS COLLECTION
Neue Burg, 1010 Vienna 1
14th-20th century weapons, armour, for warfare, jousting, ceremonial occasions, especially belonging to historic figures. Turkish weapons. 17th-18th century German, French, Spanish firearms. Paintings.
Su. 9-1; M. 10-3.

MUSEUM OF HORSE-DRAWN CABS
Veronikagasse 12, 1170 Vienna 17
History of the Vienna cab-trade. Paintings. Prints. Engravings. Photographs. Press cuttings. Models. Pictures of noted cab-drivers.
May-Oct. W. 8-1. Nov.-Apr., 1st W. in month, 8-1.

MUSEUM OF INDUSTRY AND TECHNOLOGY
Mariahilferstrasse 212, 1140 Vienna 14
Development of motive power, illustrated by models and original machines. Bicycles, motor cycles, motor-cars. History of ships. Industrial art. Craftsmen's workshops. Mining, including replica of part of coal mine. Smelting. Machine tools. Agricultural implements. Woodworking. Aviation. Gas. Electricity. Chemistry. Paper. Textiles. Printing. Photography. Building. Bridges. Glass. Ceramics. Clocks. Nuclear energy. Musical instruments. Fire-fighting equipment.
Tu.-Su. 9-1. May-Sept., Tu.-F. also 2-4.

MUSEUM OF THE INSTITUTE OF FORENSIC MEDICINE
Sensengasse 2, 1090 Vienna 9
Prepared specimens illustrating death from drinking, drowning, burning and various forms of violence. Murder weapons.
By appointment.

MUSEUM OF THE JOSEFSTADT DISTRICT
Zeltgasse 7, 1080 Vienna 8
History of the district. Engravings. Plans. House-signs. Manuscripts and memorabilia of Edmund Eysler. The first Bösendorfer grand piano, once owned by Franz von Suppé.
W. 6-8; Su. 10-12.

MUSEUM OF THE JOSEFSTADT DISTRICT, 'OLD BAKEHOUSE'
Langegasse 34, 1080 Vienna 8
Restored bakehouse (1701), with original oven, utensils, weights and measures. History of the house and of the Punzmann family.
Daily 10-12.

MUSEUM OF THE LIFE OF THE BLIND
Wittelsbachstrasse 5, 1020 Vienna 2
Development of teaching methods and teaching material for the blind. Paintings, drawings, prints, with blind people as subjects. Casts of gravestones of blind organists and other musicians of the Middle Ages.
On request.

MUSEUM OF THE MARIAHILF DISTRICT
Gumpendorferstrasse 4, 1060 Vienna 6
History of the Mariahilf district. Paintings. Prints. Theatre history, especially of the Viennese operetta and the works of Johann Strauss. Memorabilia of Haydn, Fanny Elssler, and other noted local residents. Handicrafts. Popular art.
Sa. 3-6; Su. 9.30-12.

MUSEUM OF MILITARY HISTORY
Objekt 1, Arsenal, 1030 Vienna 3
Portraits and memorabilia of Austrian military leaders. Paintings of scenes from military history. Weapons. Uniforms. Orders. Motorcar in which Archduke Franz Ferdinand was assassinated, 1914. Models and paintings of warships.
Sa.-Th. 10-4.30.

MUSEUM OF POSTAL AND TELECOMMUNICATION SERVICES
Technischesmuseum, Mariahilferstrasse 212, 1140 Vienna 14
History of the postal services in Austria. Roman and medieval postal systems. Postal vehicles. Uniforms. Letterboxes. Franking machines. Production of postage stamps. Development of electric and electronic forms of communication.
Tu.-Fr. 9.30-1; Sa., Su. 9-1.

MUSEUM OF THE PROVINCE OF LOWER AUSTRIA
Herrengasse 9, 1010 Vienna 1
Landscape, geology, flora and fauna of Lower Austria. Production of timber, coal, minerals, petroleum, gold. Hunting, fishing. Fossil animals. Skeletons of prehistoric animals. Paintings of provincial scenes. Religious paintings, sculpture. Votive offerings. Cribs. Tools. Wine-making equipment. Clothing. Costumes. Painted and carved furniture. Models of peasant house-types. Roman and medieval tools, ornaments, pottery, coins.
Tu.-Sa. 9-5; Su., public holidays 8-1.

MUSEUM OF THE TOBACCO MONOPOLY
Porzellangasse 51, 1090 Vienna 9
History of the Austrian tobacco monopoly and of smoking customs. Products of the Austrian tobacco industry since 1865. Paintings, watercolours, engravings with smoking as subject. Pipes. Cigar holders. Tobacco boxes.
M.-F. 9-12, 2-4. Other times by appointment.

MUSEUM OF THE 20th CENTURY
Schweizergarten, 1030 Vienna 3
20th century paintings, sculpture, including works by Munch, Picasso, Kokoschka, Marc, Mondrian, Kandinsky, Klee, Ernst, Moore, Giacometti. Architectural models, including buildings by Le Corbusier and Lloyd Wright.
M., Tu., Th., Sa. 10-4; F. 2-9; Su. 10-1.

MUSEUM OF THE VIENNA HAIRDRESSERS' ASSOCIATION
Mollardgasse 1, Vienna
History of hairdressing. Wig collection.
By appointment.

MUSEUM OF THE VIENNA VETERINARY INSTITUTE
Viehmarkt 5-7, 1030 Vienna 3
Displays showing animal diseases, ailments and parasites.
M.-F. 9-2.

NATURAL HISTORY MUSEUM: DEPARTMENT OF ZOOLOGY
Burgring 7, 1010 Vienna 1
World collections, illustrating the development of living creatures.
M., W., F. 9-1.

NATURAL HISTORY MUSEUM: GEOLOGY AND PALAEONTOLOGY COLLECTIONS
Burgring 7, 1010 Vienna 1
Fossil plants, animals, fish, reptiles. Mounted skeletons of prehistoric animals and of the moa. Skeletons of cave-bears, mammoths and woolly-rhinoceros from Austrian Ice Age sites.
Th., Sa., Su. 9-1.

NATURAL HISTORY MUSEUM: MINERALOGICAL-PETROGRAPHICAL SECTION
Burgring 7, 1010 Vienna 1
Origins and structures of minerals. Commercial and industrial minerals. Precious and semi-precious stones. The Petersburg Eggs (hen's egg sized gems), belonging to Tsar Nicholas II. Meteorites. Emperor Franz I Stephan's machine illustrating the Copernican system.
Th., Sa., Su. 9-1.

NATURAL HISTORY MUSEUM: PREHISTORIC DEPARTMENT
Burgring 7, 1010 Vienna 1
Prehistoric material from excavations in the territory of former Austria - Hungary. Stone Age artifacts. Bronze Age tools, ornaments, utensils. Weapons. Metal smelting and working equipment. Iron Age weapons, utensils, tools, remnants of clothing.
Th.-Sa., Su. 9-1.

NEW GALLERY OF THE MUSEUM OF THE HISTORY OF ART
Stallburg, Reitschulgasse 2, 1010 Vienna 1
19th-20th century paintings by other than Austrian artists. German and French Romantics, including Millet, Courbet, Rodin, Böcklin. French and German Impressionists. Post-Impressionists.
Su. 9-1; M. 10-3.

OTTAKRING DISTRICT MUSEUM
Richard Wagner Platz 19, 1160 Vienna 16
History of Ottakring. Industry and handicrafts, including button maker's workshop. Material illustrating history of the workers' movement. Period room (1910), with original furnishings.
Su. 10-12, except during school holidays.

PENZING DISTRICT MUSEUM
Penzinger Strasse 59, 1140 Vienna 14
History of the Penzing district. Furniture. Household equipment. Industry. Handicrafts. Art.
Su. 10-12. Closed July-Aug.

PRATERMUSEUM
Planetarium, Praterstein, 1020 Vienna 2
History of the Prater, its activities and institutions. Memorabilia of the Basilio Calafatis family. Paintings and drawings of the Prater. History of the Rotunda.
Tu.-Su. 4-8; Su., public holidays 2-8.

REMAINS OF ROMAN BUILDINGS
Am Hof 9, 1010 Vienna 1
Remains of Roman tower and drainage channel, with drawings and reconstructions.
W., Su., guided tours, 10.

ROMAN RUINS
Hoher Markt 3, 1010 Vienna 1
Parts of two houses, probably legionary officers' quarters. Displays, with casts of architectural features. Legionary relics.
Tu.-Su. 9-1.

SAMPLES COLLECTION OF THE REVENUE AND MONOPOLY DEPARTMENT
Kriehubergasse 26, 1050 Vienna 5
Exhibition of monopoly-commodities and others liable for duty. Spirits. Wine. Beer. Mineral oils. Tobacco. Salt. Playing-cards.
By appointment.

SCHLUMBERGER WINE MUSEUM
Heiligenstädter Strasse 43, 1190 Vienna 19
Vineyard and cellar equipment. Drinking vessels.
By appointment.

SCHOTTEN ABBEY COLLECTION
Freyung 6, 1010 Vienna 1
16th-19th century German, Austrian, Dutch, Flemish, Italian paintings.
By appointment.

SIMMERING DISTRICT MUSEUM
Enkplatz 2, 1110 Vienna 11
History of Simmering and Kaiser-Ebersdorf. Prehistoric, Roman and medieval material from local sites. Furniture. Household equipment. Local industry.
Sa. 3.30-5.30; Su. 9-12. Closed Jan. and during school holidays.

SOBEK COLLECTION
Geymüller Schlössel, Khevenhüllerstrasse 2, 1180 Vienna 18
House (1810), with Empire and Biedermeier furniture. 18th-19th century clocks.
Mar.-Nov. Tu., Th., Su., guided tours 11, 3. Other times by appointment.

ADALBERT STIFTER MUSEUM
Pasqualatihaus, Mölkerbastei 8, 1010 Vienna 1
Paintings, drawings by Adalbert Stifter. Stifter memorabilia, manuscripts.
Tu.-Sa. 9-4; Su., public holidays 9-1.

TREASURY OF THE GERMAN ORDER
Singerstrasse 7, 1010 Vienna 1
Insignia of the Order, 13th century onwards. Ceremonial vessels. 17th-18th century glasses. Furniture. Clocks. Astronomical instruments. Oriental weapons. Portraits of Grand Masters and Knights of the Order. Manuscripts of two marches written by Beethoven and dedicated to the Order.
Apr.-Oct. Tu.-Sa. 10-12, 3-5; Su. 10-12. Nov.-Mar., Tu., Th., Sa. 10-12, 3-5; Su. 10-12.

UNIVERSITY MUSEUM
Universitätogabäude, Dr. Karl Lueger Ring 1, 1010 Vienna 1
History of the University of Vienna, and of its students. Paintings. Portraits. Documents. Academic diploma of Anton Bruckner, and presentation copy of his 1st Symphony dedicated to the University.
M.-F. 9-4.30.

VIENNA GOETHE MUSEUM
Augustinerstrasse 1, 1010 Vienna 1
Portraits and busts of Goethe and his friends. Manuscripts. Editions of Goethe's works published in his lifetime. Drawings by Goethe. Dr. Vogel's report on Goethe's last illness.
M., Tu., Th., F. 10-4; W. 10-6; Sa., Su. 10-1. June 1-Sept. 15, closed Sa., Su.

VIENNA INTERNATIONAL ESPERANTO MUSEUM
Hofburg, Batthyanstiege, 1010 Vienna 1
Memorabilia of Dr. Ludwig Lazarus Zamenhof, founder of Esperanto, including pictures, letters, manuscripts. Books in and about Esperanto. Stamps. Conference reports. Press cuttings.
M., W., F. 9-3.45.

VÖCKLAMARKT

WALCHEN CASTLE
4870 Vöcklamarkt, Oberösterreich
Local and regional history. 16th-20th century furniture, household equipment.
May-Oct., daily 10-12, 3-6.

WAIDHOFEN AN DER YBBS

PIATY PRIVATE COLLECTION
Unterer Stadtplatz 39, 3340 Waidhofen an der Ybbs, Niederösterreich
Original Ybbstal peasant-room, with carved ceiling (1614). Wax figures. Door-knockers. Agricultural implements. Craftsmen's tools.
On request.

REGIONAL MUSEUM
Obererstadtplatz 32, 3340 Waidhofen an der Ybbs, Niederösterreich
16th-18th century crafts, especially ironwork. Paintings, prints, models showing development of Waidhofen. Prehistoric and Roman archaeology. Weapons. Armour. 17th-19th century rooms, with furniture, household equipment. Costumes. Religious and popular art. Geology, flora and fauna of the Ybbstal.
Apr. 1 - Oct. 1, Tu. 9-12; Th., Sa. 2-5; Su., public holidays 9-1.

WAIZENKIRCHEN

WILHELM KIENZ BIRTHPLACE
Gasthof Mayerhuber, 4730 Waizenkirchen, Bezirk Grieskirchen, Oberösterreich
Memorabilia of the composer, Wilhelm Kienz (d.1941).
On request.

WALCHEN

PAULI HANREICH-LUDWIG COLLECTION
Schloss Walchen, Bezirk Vöcklabruck, Oberösterreich
Castle (16th century). 16th-18th century furniture. Collection of popular art, costumes, dolls, wax-models, household equipment. Gmund majolica, glass, birdcages. Wrought-iron. 17th-18th century sculpture. 19th century paintings.
By appointment.

WALDING

LOCAL MUSEUM
Volksschule, 4111 Walding, Bezirk Vöcklabruck, Oberösterreich
Local history. Prehistoric archaeology. 13th-14th century weapons. Peasant household equipment.
Daily, on request.

WARTBERG

REGIONAL MUSEUM AT THE RUINS OF LICHTENEGG CASTLE
8661 Wartberg, Bezirk Mürzzuschlag, Steiermark
In tower of castle. Local history and folklore. Peasant household equipment. Geology.
Daily 3-5, during good weather. Other times by appointment.

WATTENS

REGIONAL MUSEUM
Schulhaus, 6112 Wattens, Bezirk Innsbruck-Land, Tirol
Prehistoric material from local sites. Folklore. Local industry.
By appointment.

WEIKENDORF

MARCHFELD MUSEUM
Pfarrhof, 2253 Weikendorf, Bezirk Gänserndorf, Niederösterreich
History of local rural life. Costumes. Agricultural implements. Craftsmen's tools. Furniture. Memorabilia of the composer and choir master, Franz Mair (d.1853).
Su. 9-2. Other days by appointment.

WEISSENKIRCHEN

WACHAU MUSEUM
Teisenhoferhof, 3610 Wiessenkirchen, Bezirk Krems, Niederösterreich
Local history. 19th-20th century views of the Wachau. Landscapes by Kremser Schmidt. Weapons. 18th century wine-press.
May-Oct. Tu.-Su. 10-12, 2-5. Mar. 15- Apr. 30, Nov. 1-15, Sa., Su. 10-12, 2-5.

WELS

CASTLE MUSEUM
4600 Wels, Oberösterreich
Agricultural history and implements. 18th century painted furniture. Spinning and weaving equipment. Craftsmen's tools. Fishing and hunting equipment. Carved fruit-presses. Festival bread, cakes. History of the Wels agricultural fair. Emperor Maximilian I.
May-Oct. daily 10-12, 2-5; Su. 10-12. Nov.-Apr. daily 2-5; Su. 10-12.

MUNICIPAL MUSEUM
Pollheimerstrasse 17, 4600 Wels, Oberösterreich
Prehistoric archaeology from local sites. Roman material from Ovilava (Wels). Christian epitaph (early 4th century). 16th-17th century pottery. Popular religious art. Biedermeier period applied art. Habsburg portraits. Geology. Mineralogy. Palaeontology.
Daily 8-12, 2-5; Su. 9-12.

WENIGZELL

REGIONAL HOUSE
Pfarrermühle, 8254 Wenigzell, Bezirk Hartberg, Steiermark
Local industries and handicrafts. Agricultural implements. Painted furniture. Costumes. Peasant household equipment.
June 1 - Oct. 1, Su. 9.30-12, 3-6; Tu., Th. 10-12, 3-5.

WIENERBRUCK

TRÜBENBACH SCHOOL MUSEUM
3223 Wienerbruck, Bezirk Lilienfeld, Niederösterreich
Household equipment. Products of local linen industry. Mining tools.
M.-F. 8-6.

WIENER NEUSTADT

MUNICIPAL MUSEUM
Wienerstrasse 63, 2700 Wiener Neustadt, Niederösterreich
Palaeolithic, Bronze Age and Iron Age material from local sites. Medieval sculpture. Paintings of Wiener Neustadt. Craftsmen's tools, records. Industrial history. Weapons. Flags. Religious art. Biedermeier room.
Apr.-Oct. W., F. 2- 30; Su. 9-12.

MUSEUM OF THE THERESIAN MILITARY ACADEMY
Burgplatz 1, 2700 Wiener Neustadt, Niederösterreich
History of the Academy. Pictures. Flags.
On request.

WIESELBURG

STEFAN MEMORIAL COLLECTION
Rathaus, Hauptplatz 26, 3250 Wieselburg, Bezirk Scheibbs, Niederösterreich
Prehistoric, Roman and medieval material from local sites. Local history.
M.-F. 8-5.

WILDALPEN

FORESTRY MUSEUM
8924 Wildalpen, Bezirk Liezen, Steiermark
Peasant household equipment. Craftsmen's tools. Minerals. History of Wildalpen iron-forge.
May 15- Sept. 30, Su., public holidays 10-12. Other times by appointment.

WILHERING

MONASTERY COLLECTION
Zisterzienserstift, 4073 Wilhering, Bezirk Linz-Land, Oberösterreich
Baroque paintings by Austrian artists. Coins.
By appointment.

YBBS

LOCAL MUSEUM
Kirchengasse, 3370 Ybbs, Niederösterreich
Local history. Industry. Commerce.
By appointment.

ZELL AM MOOS

IRRSEE REGIONAL MUSEUM
4893 Zell am Moos, Bezirk Vöcklabruck, Oberösterreich
Peasant rooms. Furniture. Household equipment. Mill, with original machinery and equipment. Fruit presses.
By appointment.

ZWENTENDORF

LOCAL MUSEUM
Amtshaus, 3435 Zwentendorf, Bezirk Tulln, Niederösterreich
Roman, Lombard and medieval material from local excavations.
Apr.-Sept. M., W., F. 8-12, 2-6; Tu., Th. 8-12; Sa., Su. on request.

ZWETTL

ANTON MUSEUM
Landstrasse 65, 3910 Zwettl, Niederösterreich
Sculpture. Glass paintings. Weapons. Instruments of torture. Furniture. Household equipment. 18th century fire engine.
Daily, on request.

ART GALLERY AND TREASURY OF ZWETTL MONASTERY
Zisterzienserstift, 3910 Zwettl, Niederösterreich
Religious art. Coins.
Daily 8-12, 1-5.

ZWICKLEDT

KUBIN HOUSE
Zwickledt, Bezirk Schärding, Oberösterreich
House of the artist, Alfred Kubin (d.1959). Original furnishings, paintings, drawings. Memorabilia of Kubin.
May-Sept. daily 10-12. 2.30-5.30. Apr. and Oct. daily 10-12, 2-5. Guided tours only.

Bahamas

One of our correspondents in the Bahamas informed us that the museum was 'Temporarily closed. Owner away' - a situation which reflects the as yet somewhat unprofessional flavour of the island's museums. This is not likely, however, to cause very much worry to the tourists on whom the economy so greatly relies. Of the non-tourist aspects of local life, fishing and sponging are the only occupations so far to receive any serious museum attention.

NASSAU

BAHAMIA MUSEUM
P.O. Box 1247, Nassau
Old photographs of Nassau. Boat-building. Sponging. Fishing. Rope-making and straw-work. Bush medicine exhibits. Items illustrating Bahamian life in the past, including irons, grindstones, outdoor Dutch oven. Cotton. Bahamian stamps. Shells. Costumes.
By appointment.

GOVERNMENT MUSEUM
Public Library, Nassau
Local collections, including maps, prints, arawak artifacts, letters from governors, coins and stamps. Paintings.
On request.

HISTORICAL SOCIETY MUSEUM
P.O. Box 981, Nassau
Bahamian artifacts. Prints. Old photographs.
By appointment.

SAN SALVADOR

NEW WORLD MUSEUM
San Salvador
Arawak potsherds. Local artifacts, including mortars and pestles, gourds and conch shells. Coins. Stamps. Charts.
By appointment.

Bahrain

Bahrain's one museum is so far restricted to history and archaeology, but the growing wealth of the area, under the nourishing influence of petroleum, will no doubt produce in a short time the kind of expansion of amenities which has been found in other oil-bonanza states.

MANAMA

BAHRAIN NATIONAL MUSEUM
Ministry of Education, Antiquities Division, P.O. Box 43, Manama
Archaeological material dating from the Stone Age. Flint tools. Finds from ancient burial mounds of the early Dilman period (2800-1500 B.C.), consisting of bronze weapons, pottery, an ostrich egg, gold chain and an ivory statuette. Seals, bronze figures and alabaster vases from the temples of Barbar (c.2500 B.C.). Finds from the city excavations at Qala'at al Bahrain include pottery, seals, weapons, statuettes and cuneiform tablets. Snake skeletons as well as coffins and bowls for human burials. 11th century inscriptions.
Daily ex. F. 8-1.30.

Bangladesh

As the following list makes clear, a very high proportion of the museums of Bangladesh are on university and college premises. The collections exist primarily for teaching and research purposes and public admission is normally restricted to those persons who can produce evidence of some more serious purpose than the wish to escape from the heat or the outside world for an hour. If these, mainly scientific, museums are removed from the list, it will be noticed that Bangladesh has, in fact, few museums and that those which do exist are concerned almost entirely with archaeology, art and the various aspects of ethnography.

It should perhaps be mentioned that, with very few exceptions, the museums Bangladesh has today are ones which were already there when the British departed in 1950.

BARISAL

BARISAL MEDICAL COLLEGE MUSEUM
Barisal
Anatomy. Physiology. Biology.
By appointment.

CHITTAGONG

ETHNOLOGICAL MUSEUM
Chittagong
Regional ethnography, handicrafts, folk-art. Agricultural implements.
Sa.-Th. 10-5.

MEDICAL COLLEGE MUSEUM
Chittagong
Biology. Anatomy. Physiology.
By appointment.

UNIVERSITY HISTORY MUSEUM
Chittagong
Archaeological collections.
By appointment.

COMILLA

RAMMALA MUSEUM
Comilla
Regional archaeology. Memorabilia of distinguished people who lived in the Comilla area, or who were associated with it.
Sa.-Th. 9-1, 3-5.

DACCA

BANGLA ACADEMY MUSEUM
Dacca
Collections illustrating folk art and literature of Bangladesh.
By appointment.

BOTANY MUSEUM
University of Dacca, Dacca
Botanical collections, representing flora of Bangladesh.
By appointment.

COLLEGE OF MUSIC MUSEUM
Dacca
Collection of Oriental and Western musical instruments.
By appointment.

DACCA MUSEUM
Ramna, Dacca
Art and archaeology of Bengal, in particular of Bangladesh. Sculpture. Coins. Inscriptions. Copper-plates. Medieval arms and weapons, manuscripts and documents. Porcelain. Metal work and wood work. Miniatures and modern paintings. Folk life material.
Sa.-W. 10-4.30; F. 8-11.30. Closed Th.

EPSIC DESIGN CENTRE
Dacca
Dolls. Crafts. Textiles.
Daily 9-5, ex. F.

GEOGRAPHY MUSEUM
University of Dacca, Dacca
Geography of Bangladesh.
By appointment.

GEOLOGY MUSEUM
University of Dacca, Dacca
Geology of Bangladesh and adjacent countries.
By appointment.

LALBAGH FORT SITE MUSEUM
Dacca
Moghul art, mainly sculpture.
Daily 9-5.

MEDICAL COLLEGE MUSEUM
Dacca
Biology. Anatomy.
By appointment.

MUSEUM OF ART AND ARCHAEOLOGY
Islamic History Department, University of Dacca, Dacca
Regional archaeology. Folk-art. Religious sculpture.
By appointment.

POSTAL MUSEUM
Dacca
Philately and the history of the postal service in Bangladesh.
Sa.-Th. 9-5.

SALIMULLAH MEDICAL COLLEGE MUSEUM
Dacca
Anatomy. Biology. Physiology.
By appointment.

SOCIOLOGY MUSEUM
University of Dacca, Dacca
Sociology. Art. Ethnographical material from all the regions of Bangladesh. Collections illustrating fields and methods of sociological enquiry.
By appointment.

SOIL SCIENCE MUSEUM
University of Dacca, Dacca
Geology and soils of Bangladesh. Collections illustrating methods of testing and analysing soil structure.
By appointment.

ZOOLOGY MUSEUM
University of Dacca, Dacca
Zoology, especially of Bangladesh.
By appointment.

DINAJPUR

DINAJPUR MUSEUM
Dinajpur
Archaeological material from excavations in the Dinajpur region.
Sa.-Th. 9-1, 3-6.

TAXIDERMY MUSEUM
Dinajpur
Zoological collections, illustrating methods of taxidermy.
Sa.-Th. 9-1, 3-5.

HABIGANJ

AHARANI MUSEUM
Habiganj, Sylhet district
Art. Archaeology. Natural history.
Sa.-Th. 9-5.

KISHOREGANJ

KISHOREGANJ MUSEUM
Kishoreganj, Mymensingh district
Archaeology.
Sa.-Th. 9-5.

MAHASTANGARH

ARCHAEOLOGICAL MUSEUM
Mahastangarh, Bogra district
Regional archaeological material.
Sa.-Th. 10-5.

MAINAMATI

ARCHAEOLOGICAL MUSEUM
Mainamati, Comilla district
Regional archaeology.
Sa.-Th. 10-1, 3-6.

MYMENSINGH

DEPARTMENTAL MUSEUMS
E.P. Agricultural University, Mymensingh
Anatomy. Botany. Entomology. Fisheries. Soil science. Plant pathology. Zoology.
By appointment during term-time.

MEDICAL COLLEGE MUSEUM
Mymensingh
Biology. Anatomy.
By appointment.

MYMENSINGH MUSEUM
Mymensingh
Applied arts. Archaeology. Handicrafts.
Sa.-Th. 10-5.

PAHARPUR

ARCHAEOLOGICAL MUSEUM
Paharpur, Rajshahi district
Archaeology.
Sa.-Th. 10-5.

RAJSHAHI

DEPARTMENTAL MUSEUMS
University of Rajshahi, Rajshahi
Botany. Geography. Zoology. Art and archaeology.
By appointment during term-time.

RAJSHAHI MEDICAL COLLEGE MUSEUM
Rajshahi
Biology. Anatomy.
By appointment.

RANGAMATI

RANGAMATI MUSEUM
Rangamati
Ethnography of the Rangamati region.
Su.-Th. 10-5.

SILAIDAHA

SILAIDAHA KUTHIBARI MUSEUM
Silaidaha, Kushtia district
Memorabilia of distinguished people associated with the Kushtia district.
Su.-Th. 10-5.

SYLHET

MEDICAL COLLEGE MUSEUM
Sylhet
Biology. Anatomy.
By appointment.

Barbados

It may or may not be significant that the only museum in Barbados is in the former military prison; but to collect material documenting the history of the Barbados sugar industry and then to display it in an old prison is certainly an economical and artistically satisfying way of making the point that in the old days the production of sugar was not a wholly voluntary activity on the part of the men, women and children who carried out the work. The association of sugar with the forces of law and order is an imaginative piece of museum planning.

BARBADOS

BARBADOS MUSEUM
St. Ann's Garrison, Barbados, Windward Islands
Housed in former military prison, with original cell. Prehistory of the island. History, natural history and marine life. Archaeology. The Jews in Barbados. Furniture. Silver. China. Glass. Collection of West Indian prints. Children's gallery. Drax Gallery, containing exhibits relating to the sugar industry.
M.-Sa. 10-6; Su. 2.30-6.

Belgium

Belgian museums, as a group, are solid, sober and lacking in eccentricity. There are practically no museums devoted to off-beat subjects, such as one commonly finds among Belgium's neighbours. Germany would certainly have set up museums of gingerbreads and billiard balls, had these happened to be German specialities, but Belgium goes for less frivolous things. In the Belgian museum-world, the scholar is still much more important than the impresario, and certain national traditions and achievements are apparently more reputable than others. It is extraordinary, for instance, that a country which was industrialised so early and which depends so much on its manufacturing enterprises should have no national or general museum of industry and technology, although the history of science is properly looked after and transport is strong. There are, however, many local museums which deal with particular crafts and industries, such as brewing, tanning, glass-making and pottery. Oddly enough, there is no museum of brick and tile-making, important features of the Belgian landscape and economy for centuries.

The tourist's Belgium quite rightly includes the great art galleries, the guild houses and halls, the homes and workshops of Plantin, Rubens and other famous craftsmen-entrepreneurs, and the splendid town-houses, with their paintings and period furnishings. The Belgians do this kind of museum very well; with history their touch is perhaps a little less sure. One tires rather easily nowadays of the two World Wars and Napoleon, important though these subjects no doubt are.

There can be no question, however, about the quality of the major ethnographical collections. These are concerned mainly with Belgium itself and with its African colonies, and there is great pleasure to be found in them. To anyone who complains that the Belgians are a prosaic people and that all the energy they have to spare from money-making is devoted to quarrels about language and religion, one might reply that the national memorial collection to the great violinist, Ysaye, includes an urn containing his embalmed heart. No Polish museum could go further.

AALST

ACADEMY COLLECTION
Hospitaal van O. L. Vrouw, Aalst, East Flanders
Paintings and furniture from the former hospital.
On application, one week in advance.

LOCAL MUSEUM
Schepenhuis, Aalst, East Flanders
Local history. Folklore. Belgo-Roman and French archaeology.
June-Aug., M.-Sa. 10-12, 2-5; Su. 10-12. Other months: Sa. 1-5; M., Th. 10-12, 1-5; Su. 10-12.

AARSCHOT

REGIONAL MUSEUM
Drossaarde, Aarschot, Brabant
Local history. Folklore. Local trades and customs.
Daily 10-12, 2-4.

ANDENNE

LOCAL MUSEUM
Ancien Hôtel de Ville, Andenne, Namur
Medieval ceramics. Pottery. Faience.
On request.

ANTWERP

ARCHIVES AND MUSEUM OF FLEMISH CULTURAL LIFE
Minderbroedersstraat 22, Antwerp
Collections relating to Flemish culture from 1750 onwards: music, theatre, plastic arts. Records of the Flemish Movement. Documents.
Tu.-Su. 10-5. Closed M. ex. holidays, also Jan. 1-2, May 1, Ascension Day, Nov. 1-2, Dec. 25-26.

BREWERS' HOUSE
Adriaan Brouwerstraat 20, Antwerp
16th century installations for water-supply to breweries. Council chamber.
Tu.-Su. 10-5. Closed M. ex. holidays, also Jan. 1-2, May 1, Ascension Day, Nov. 1-2, Dec. 25-26.

CITY PRINT-ROOM
Vrijdagmarkt 23, Antwerp
Prints and drawings, especially by Antwerp artists.
By appointment only.

COOPERS' MUSEUM
Suikerrui 20, Antwerp
Collection of old coopers' tools, housed in wine cellar dating partly from 12th century.
Daily 10-5.

ETHNOGRAPHICAL MUSEUM
Kloosterstraat 11, Antwerp
Arts and crafts of pre-literate and non-European peoples.
Tu.-Su. 10-5. Closed M. ex. holidays, also Jan. 1-2, May 1, Ascension Day, Nov. 1-2, Dec. 25-26.

FLAT IRON MUSEUM
Vosstraat 87, Borgerhout, Antwerp
Historical collection of flat irons.
4th Su. of each month, 10-4.

FOLK-LORE MUSEUM
Gildekamerstraat 2-6, Antwerp
Folk-lore of the Flemish provinces, especially folk art and crafts.
Tu.-Su. 10-5. Closed M. ex. holidays, also Jan. 1-2, May 1, Ascension Day, Nov. 1-2, Dec. 25-26.

MAAGDENHUIS MUSEUM
Lange Gasthuisstraat 33, Antwerp
Housed in part of ancient orphanage for girls. 15th century paintings. Sculpture. Furniture. Liturgical objects. Copper. Bronzes. Antwerp pottery (16th century). Pewter.
M.-F. 8.30-4.30. Closed holidays. Sa. and Su. by appointment only.

MAYER VAN DEN BERGH MUSEUM
Lange Gasthuisstraat 19, Antwerp 2000
Paintings, including works by Breughel, Quinten Metsys, Broederlam, de Vos, Van Cleve. Medieval sculpture, ivories. Breviary dating from 1500.
Tu.-Su. 10-5. Closed M. ex. holidays, Jan. 1-2, May 1, Ascension Day, Nov. 1-2, Dec. 25-26.

MUSEUM OF CONCHOLOGY
Suikerrui 22, Antwerp
Shells from all over the world. Minerals, precious stones, fossils.
Easter-Sept. Daily ex. F. 10-6. Oct.-Easter, W. and Sa., 10-6.

MUSEUM OF NATURAL HISTORY
Koningin Astridplein 26, Antwerp
Natural history collections of the Royal Society of Zoology. Mammals. Birds. Reptiles. Fishes.
M.-F. 10-11.30, 2-4. Closed Sa., Su., holidays, and for 3 weeks in Aug.

NATIONAL MARITIME MUSEUM
Steenplein 1, Antwerp
Maritime history, with particular reference to Belgium. Ships' models, navigational instruments, nautical charts, ships' decorations, fishing craft, inland craft.
Tu.-Su. 10-5. Closed M. ex. holidays, also Jan. 1-2, May 1, Ascension Day, Nov. 1-2, Dec. 25-26.

OLD BUTCHERS' HALL
Vleeshouwersstraat 38, Antwerp
Building dates from 1500, built for the Butchers' Corporation. Prehistory. Local history. Egyptian, Greek and Roman antiquities. Numismatics. Sculpture. Applied art. Furniture. Arms. Musical instruments.
Tu.-Su. 10-5. Closed M. ex. holidays, also Jan. 1-2, May 1, Ascension day, Nov. 1-2, Dec. 25-26.

OPEN-AIR MARITIME MUSEUM
Thonetlaan, Antwerp
Situated next to the floating bridge. Collections relating to navigation, shipping.
At any time.

OPEN-AIR MUSEUM OF SCULPTURE
Middelheim, Antwerp 2020
Contemporary sculpture, including works by Rodin, Maillol, Zadkine, Marini, Manzu, Gargallo and Moore, exhibited in a large park.
Mar. 15- Oct. 14 and during biennials from 10-sunset. Oct. 15- Mar. 14, 10-4.

PLANTIN-MORETUS MUSEUM
Vrijdagmarkt 22, Antwerp
16th-19th century printing house and foundry. Engravings on copper and wood. Drawings. Illuminated manuscripts. Paintings include 18 canvases by Rubens. Period furniture.
Tu.-Su. 10-5. Closed M. ex. holidays, also Jan. 1-2, May 1, Ascension Day, Nov. 1-2, Dec. 25-26.

POLDER MUSEUM
Tolhuisstraat 14-16, Lillo (3rd district), Antwerp
Collections illustrating life in the Antwerp polders. Interiors. Domestic equipment. Folk-lore.
Apr.-Oct. Su. and holidays 1-7. Other times on request, Omwentelingstraat 4.

PROVINCIAL INSTITUTE FOR SAFETY
Jezusstraat 28-30, Antwerp
Permanent exhibition on the prevention of accidents and occupational diseases. Safety in industry, on the roads and in the home.
Daily ex. Su. and holidays, 1-5.

PROVINCIAL MUSEUM OF INDUSTRIAL ART
Hooftvunderlei 160, Deurne, Antwerp
In 14th century chateau. Ethnology. Objects in copper, tin, iron, glass. Calico-printing. Coins and medals. Weights and measures.
Daily ex. F. 10-5. Closed Nov. 1 - Palm Su.

RIDDER SMIDT VAN GELDER MUSEUM
Belgiëlei 91, Antwerp
Chinese and European porcelain. Dutch 17th century paintings. 18th century French furniture. Sèvres and Dresden china. Jewellery (16th-19th centuries).
Tu.-Su. 10-5. Closed M. ex. holidays, Jan. 1-2, May 1, Ascension Day, Nov. 1-2, Dec. 25-26.

ROCKOX'S HOUSE
Keizerstraat 10, Antwerp
16th century patrician house, containing period rooms. Paintings include portraits of the former owner, Burgomaster Nikolaus Rockox, by Rubens and Van Dyck.
Daily 10-6. Evening visits on request.

ROYAL MUSEUM OF FINE ARTS
Place Leopold de Wael, 2000 Antwerp
Works by Flemish artists, including Van Eyck, Van der Weyden, Memling, Massys, Fouquet, Rubens, Van Dyck, Jordaens, Rembrandt and Frans Hals. Works of Belgian artists of 19th and 20th centuries, including De Braekeleer, Ensor, Wouters, Permeke. Paintings of the Italian, German, French and Dutch schools.
Apr. 15- Sept. 30, 10-5. Oct. 1- Nov. 14, 10-4. Nov. 15- Jan. 1, 10-2. Feb. 1- Apr. 14, 10-4. Closed Tu., also Jan. 1, May 1, Ascension Day, Christmas Day.

RUBENS' HOUSE
Rubensstraat 9-11, Antwerp 1
Reconstruction of Rubens' house and studio. Original 17th century portico and pavilion. Paintings by P. P. Rubens, his collaborators and pupils. 17th century furnishings.
Tu.-Su. 10-5. Closed M. ex. holidays, also Jan. 1-2, May 1, Ascension Day, Nov. 1-2, Dec. 25-26.

ARLON

ARCHAEOLOGICAL MUSEUM
Place de Diekirch 18, Arlon, Luxembourg
Archaeology. Local history. Folklore. Roman sculpture. Glass. Pottery, including pot of the early 1st century. Frankish antiquities. Local Luxembourg interiors. Collection of firebacks (1570-1818), jacks, spits and other ironwork.
Daily 10-12, 2-4.

ATH

ARCHAEOLOGICAL SOCIETY MUSEUM
Rue de Pintamont 54, Ath, Dendre
Collection of coins and medals. Paintings.
By appointment.

ATTRE

LOCAL MUSEUM
Château, Attre, Hainault
Building (1752-56). Original furnishings. Paintings by Watteau, Snyders, Hubert Robert and La Tour.
Easter- mid. Nov., Su. and holidays 10-12, 2-7. Weekdays on request.

BELOEIL

CASTLE MUSEUM
Castle of the Princes de Ligne, Beloeil, Hainault
Furniture, arms, portraits, paintings, miniatures, tapestries, china. Family archives dating from 12th century. Souvenirs of Prince Charles-Joseph de Ligne (1735-1814), Field-marshal in the Austrian Army.
Daily 9-7.

VAN WEST MUSEUM
Rue du Moulin 18, Beloeil, Hainault
Local history.
Daily 10-12, 2-4.

BINCHE

MUNICIPAL MUSEUM
Hôtel de Ville, Binche, Hainault
Local history. Archaeology. Mementoes of the local Carnival.
On request.

BLANKENBERGE

FOLK MUSEUM
Town Hall, Blankenberge, West Flanders
Folklore.
Tu., Th. 10-12.

BORNEM

FOLKLORE MUSEUM
Bornem, Flanders
Archaeology. Local history. Folklore. Material on dialects.
Daily ex. Su. 10-12, 4-6.

BOUILLON

BOUILLON MUSEUM
Bouillon, Semois Valley
Historical manuscript and documents. Archaeology. Folklore. Exhibition of the history of Godefroy de Bouillon.
March-Oct., daily 10-12, 2-4.

BOUVIGNES

LOCAL MUSEUM
Spanish House, Bouvignes, Namur
Local history.
Daily 10-12, 2-4.

BRECHT

CAMPINE MUSEUM
Brecht, Campine
Archaeology. Prehistory. Folklore.
By written appointment.

BRUGES

ARCHERS GUILD OF ST. SEBASTIAN
Carmersstraat, Bruges
Architectural complex. Paintings. Silverware. Archives. Souvenirs of the Guild membership of Belgian and British sovereigns.
Daily 9-12, 1.30-7.

BÉGUINE'S HOUSE
Béguinage, Bruges
The "Princely Béguinage of the Vineyard" was founded in 1245. Present-day nuns are no longer Béguines, but Benedictine Sisters, who have kept the 15th century costume. The house gives a good idea of how the Béguines lived.
Apr.-Sept., M.-Sa. 9.15-7; Su. and public holidays 10.30-7. Oct.-Mar. M.-Sa. 9.30-1, 1.30-6; Su. and public holidays 10.30-6.

BRANGWYN MUSEUM
Dyver 16, Bruges
Oil paintings, water-colours and etchings by Frank Brangwyn (1867-1965). Views of Bruges.
Mar.-Sept. 9.30-12, 2-6; Su. and public holidays 9.30-12, 2-6. Oct.-Feb. Daily ex. Tu. 10-12, 2-5; Su. and public holidays 10-12, 2-5. Closed Jan. 1.

CATHEDRAL MUSEUM
St. Saviour's Church, Rue des Carmes, Bruges
Paintings by Flemish artists, including D. Bouts, H. van der Goes. Polychrome tombstones. Reliquaries. Church ornaments.
Apr.-Sept., M.-Sa. 10-12, 3-5; Su. and public holidays 3-5. Oct.-Mar. M.-Sa. 10-12, 3-5. Closed W.

FOLKLORE MUSEUM
Tour des Halles, Market, Bruges
Domestic equipment. Reconstruction of typical tavern and kitchen.
Palm Su. - 3rd Su. in May, and July 1 - Sept. 15, daily 2-5. Su. only, mid-May - June.

GUIDO GEZELLE MUSEUM
nr. Rolweg, Bruges
Birthplace of the Flemish poet, Guido Gezelle (1830-1899). Memorabilia. Photographs. Documents. Manuscripts.
Apr.-Sept. Daily 10-12, 2-5. Oct.-Mar. Daily ex. Su. and M. 10-12, 2-5.

GRUUTHUSE MUSEUM
Dyver 17, Bruges
Originally Palace of the Lords of Gruuthuse. Sculpture. Goldsmiths' work. Guild insignia. Weapons. Musical instruments. Pottery. Lace. Coins and medals. Tapestries.
Mar.-Sept. Daily 9.30-12, 2-6; Su. and public holidays 9.30-12, 2-6. Oct.-Feb. Daily ex. Tu. 10-12, 2-5; Su. and public holidays 10-12, 2-5. Closed Jan. 1.

MEMLING MUSEUM
St. John's Hospital, Mariastraat 38, Bruges
Paintings by Jan Memling and other artists. Furniture and household utensils. Old dispensary.
Mar. 15- Oct. 15, M.-Sa. 9-12.30, 2-6; Su. and public holidays 9-12.30, 2-6. Oct. 16- Mar. 14, M.-Sa. 9.30-12, 2-4; Su. and public holidays 9.30-12, 2-4. Closed Jan. 1.

MUNICIPAL ART GALLERY
12 Dyver, Bruges
Paintings, including works by Jan van Eyck, Hieronymus Bosch, Hugo van der Goes, Jan Memling, Gerard David. Ancient and modern works.
Mar.-Sept. 9.30-12, 2-6; Su. and public holidays 9.30-12, 2-6. Oct.-Feb. daily ex. Tu. 10-12, 2-5; Su. and public holidays 10-12, 2-5. Closed Jan. 1.

MUSEUM OF THE COURTS OF JUSTICE
Hoogstrasse, Bruges
Exhibits include chimney piece (oak, alabaster and black marble, 1529) conceived in honour of Emperior Charles V. Royal portraits.
Apr.-Sept. 9.30-12, 2-6. Oct.-Mar. 10-12, 2-4. Closed M., Tu., W. and Th. afternoons. Closed Su. afternoons in March.

MUSEUM OF THE CROSS GATE
Cross Gate, Bruges
Military history of Belgium (1830-1945). History of Bruges.
Daily 9-12, 2-6.

MUSEUM OF FOLKLORE
Halles, Bruges
Reconstruction of the life of the Guilds. Folklore of West Flanders. Popular art and customs.
Daily 10-12, 2-5 during Easter period and 1st week in May, then Su. only. Daily July 1 - Sept. 15.

MUSEUM OF THE HOLY BLOOD
Basilica of the Holy Blood, Dijver Rozenhoed Kaai, Bruges
Contains the golden reliquary (1617), silver reliquary, wrought copper and paintings.
Apr.-Sept. Daily 9-12, 2.30-6. Oct.-Mar. Daily 9.30-12, 2.30-4.30. Closed W. afternoons from Nov. 1 - Palm Su.

MUSEUM OF THE POTTERY HOSTEL
Quai de la Poterie, Bruges
Church ornaments. Furniture. Paintings. 16th century tapestry.
Apr.-Sept. M.-Sa. 9-12, 2-6; Su. and public holidays 9-12, 2-6. Oct.-Mar. Daily 10-12, 2-4. Closed Jan. 1.

STORIE HOUSE
Steenhouwersdijk, Bruges
15th century Bruges house, home of the portrait painter, Jose Storie (1899-1961). Historical collection of Belgian lace (16th-20th centuries).
Apr.-Sept. M.-Sa. 9.30-12, 2.30-7; Su. 10-12, 2.30-7. Other times by appointment.

BRUSSELS

ALBERT I ROYAL LIBRARY
Boulevard de l'Empereur 4, 1000 Brussels
Reconstructions of the studies of the poets Emile Verhaeren, Max Elskamp, Henri van de Velde and Michel de Ghelderode. Documents and literary memorabilia.
M., W. and Sa. 2-5. Closed Su., public holidays and the week before Easter.

ATOMIUM
Heysel, 1020 Brussels
Exhibition illustrating the peaceful uses of atomic energy.
Daily 9.30-6; Sa. and Su. 9.30-7. Easter-Sept. also 7-10.

BELGIAN RAILWAYS MUSEUM
Gare du Nord, (entrée rue du Progrès), 1000 Brussels
Historic documents, stamps and coins illustrating the evolution of Belgian railways. Maps. Models.
M.-F. 9-5. Closed public holidays.

BELLONA HOUSE
Rue de Flandre 46, 1000 Brussels
Home of the "Ommegang", best known of the city's historical processions. Mementoes connected with this ancient Brussels tradition.
Apr. 15- Sept. 30, M.-F. 10-12, 2-5.

BREWERY MUSEUM
Maison des Brasseurs, Grand'Place 10, 1000 Brussels
Collections relating to the brewing industry.
Daily ex. Sa. afternoon and Su., 9.30-12, 2-5.

BREUGHEL MUSEUM
Rue Haute 132, 1000 Brussels
Paintings, documents and memorabilia of Breughel.
June 24- Sept. 24, Tu., Th. and Sa. 2.30-6.

CABINET OF PRINTS AND DRAWINGS
Bibliothèque Royale Albert Ier, Boulevard de l'Empereur 4, 1000 Brussels
Engravings. Drawings.
M.-Sa. 9-1, 2-5. Closed Su., public holidays, the week before Easter, Nov. 2, 15, December 26.

CHARLIER MUSEUM
Avenue des Arts 16, 1040 Brussels
19th century paintings, furniture, silverware.
Su. 9.30-12.30. On request during the week.

CHINESE PAVILION
Avenue Van Praet 44, 1020 Brussels
Collection of porcelain from the Far East.
Daily ex. M. and public holidays, 9.30-12, 1-5.

ERASMUS' HOUSE
Rue du Chapitre 31, 1070 Brussels
Documents, paintings, early editions and manuscripts relating to Erasmus and other Humanists of the 16th century. Period furniture and decorations.
Daily ex. Tu. and F. 10-12, 2-5.

HORTA MUSEUM
Rue Americaine 25, 1050 Brussels
Mementoes connected with the architect's life.
Daily ex. Tu. 1-5; W. 1-8.

INTERNATIONAL PRESS MUSEUM
Mundaneum, Chaussée de Louvain 696, 1030 Brussels
Collection of periodicals from all over the world. Documents, photographs and postcards.
Daily ex. Sa. afternoon and Su., 9-12, 2-5.

IXELLES FINE ARTS GALLERY
Rue Jean Van Volsem 71, 1050 Brussels
Paintings. Water-colours. Drawings. Engravings. Sculpture. French and Belgian works of the Impressionist school (early 20th century).
Tu.-Sa. 10-5; Su. 10-1. Closed public holidays.

CAMILLE LEMONNIER MUSEUM
Maison des Ecrivains, Chaussée de Wavre 150, 1050 Brussels
Documents relating to the writer, Camille Lemonnier. Objets d'art. Memorabilia of Lemonnier.
Tu. and Th. 3-5. Closed July and Aug.

MANNEKIN PIS COSTUME COLLECTION
Maison du Roi, Grand'Place, 1000 Brussels
Costumes and uniforms worn in the city since the 18th century.
Oct.-Mar. Daily 10-12, 1-4. Apr.-Sept. Daily 10-12, 1-5. Sa., Su. and public holidays, 10-12. Closed Jan. 1, May 1, Nov. 1, 11, Dec. 25.

MANUSCRIPTS ROOM
Bibliothèque Royale Albert Ier, Mont des Arts, 1000 Brussels
Permanent display of manuscripts.
M., W. and Sa. 2-5. Closed public holidays, Nov. 2, 15, Dec. 26.

MARIONETTE MUSEUM
Petite Rue des Bouchers 21-23, 1000 Brussels
Collection of marionettes.
Daily, 9-5.

CONSTANTIN MEUNIER MUSEUM
Rue de l'Abbaye 59, 1050 Brussels
Housed in the home built by the painter-sculptor Constantin Meunier at the end of the 19th century. Sculpture. Paintings.
Su. 9.30-12.30. M., W., F. and Sa. 9-12, 2-5.

MUNICIPAL MUSEUM OF THE CITY OF BRUSSELS
'Maison du Roi', Grand'Place, 1000 Brussels
History and archaeology of Brussels. Local arts and industries, including tapestries, faience and porcelain, lace, jewellery.
Oct.-Mar. daily 10-12, 1-4. Apr.-Sept. daily 10-12, 1-5. Sa., Su. and public holidays, 10-12. Closed Jan., May 1, Nov. 1, 11, Dec. 25.

MUSEUM OF ART
Rue de la Régence 3, 1000 Brussels
15th-18th century paintings and drawings, including works by Breughel, Rubens and Van Dyck. Sculpture.
Tu.-Su. 10-5. Closed Jan. 1, Nov. 1 and 11, and election days.

MUSEUM OF THE DYNASTY
Rue de Bréderode 21, 1000 Brussels
Documents relating to the Belgian Royal House from 1830 to the present day.
W. and Sa. 2-5; Su. and public holidays, 10-5.

MUSEUM OF MODERN ART
Place Royale 1, 1000 Brussels
Paintings, drawings and sculpture of the 19th and 20th centuries, mainly of French and Belgian schools.
Tu.-Su. 10-12.30, 1.30-5. Closed Jan. 1, Nov. 1 and 11, and election days.

MUSEUM OF THE POOR LAW ADMINISTRATION
Hôpital St. Pierre, Rue Haute 298a, 1000 Brussels
15th-18th century paintings, sculptures, tapestries, jewellery and furniture from the main charitable institutions in Brussels under the Ancien Régime.
M. 9-12; W. 2-6. Closed public holidays.

MUSEUM OF THE ROYAL BELGIAN INSTITUTE OF NATURAL SCIENCES
Rue Vautier 31, 1040 Brussels
Zoology. Palaeontology. Mineralogy. Botany. Anthropology. Prehistory.
Sa.-Th. 9.30-12.30, 2-5. Oct.-Feb. 9.30-12.30, 2-4. Closed Jan. 1, Nov. 11.

MUSEUM OF THE SPOKEN WORD
Mont des Arts, 1000 Brussels
Collection of recordings of over 5,000 famous voices.
Weekdays, by appointment only.

THE OLD BÉGUINAGE AT ANDERLECHT
4 rue du Chapelain, Brussels
Founded 1252 by the Dean of the Anderlecht Chapter, the convent has been restored to its original appearance. Mother Superior's room, kitchen, oratory and other buildings.
On request.

PANORAMA OF WATERLOO MUSEUM
1420 Braine l'Alleud, Brussels
Panorama showing the battlefield at Waterloo.
Summer: daily 8-sunset. Winter: daily 9-sunset.

LE PÉRUCHET
50 avenue de la Forêt, Brussels
Puppet collection.
By appointment.

PORTE DE HAL MUSEUM
Boulevard de Waterloo, 1000 Brussels
Military history from the Middle Ages to the 18th century. Ancient artillery; arms and armour.
Tu.-Su. 9.30-12.25, 1.30-4.50. Closed Jan. 1, May 1, Nov. 11.

POSTAL MUSEUM
Petite rue des Minimes 2, Place du Grand Sablon 40, 1000 Brussels
Complete collection of Belgian postage stamps, and stamps from other parts of the world. Original designs for postage stamps. History of the postal services in Belgium. Ancient and modern telegraphic and telephone equipment.
Tu.-Sa. 10-4; Su. and public holidays 10-12.30.

ROYAL ARMY MUSEUM
Avenue de Tervueren, Parc du Cinquantenaire, 1040 Brussels
Military history of Belgium from 18th century onwards. Arms. Uniforms. Decorations. Paintings. Sculpture. Maps. Navigation cabin of Zeppelin. Posters of the First World War.
Tu.-Su. 10-12, 1.30-5. Closed Jan. 1 and May 1.

ROYAL CONSERVATORY OF MUSIC: COLLECTION OF MUSICAL INSTRUMENTS
Place du Petit Sablon 17, 1000 Brussels
Collection of musical instruments from all over the world and of all periods. Organ folding into shape of a book. Complete set of Javanese orchestral instruments. Aztec whistles. Pyramid piano. Organ to the sounds of which painted figures mime the extraction of teeth.
Su. 10.30-12.30. Tu., Th., Sa. 2.30-4.30. W. 8-10 p.m. with concert. Tu., Th. and holiday Sa. 10.30-12.30. Closed public holidays.

ROYAL MUSEUM OF ART AND HISTORY
Avenue des Nerviens, 1040 Brussels
Collections illustrating the ancient civilisations of Europe, Asia, Oceania and Africa. Greek, Roman and Egyptian antiquities. Prehistory. American ethnography and archaeology. Art, ethnography and folklore of the Far East. Belgian folklore.
"Even days" 9.30-12.25, 1.30-4.50. Closed M., Jan. 1, May 1 and Nov. 11.

SCHOTT MUSEUM
Rue du Chêne 27, 1000 Brussels
15th and 17th century sculptures in wood. Statues. Miniatures. Furniture.
Tu. and Th. 2-5. Closed public holidays.

TOWN HALL
Grand'Place, Brussels
Brussels tapestries.
Apr.-Sept. M.-F. 9-5 (last visit 4.30). Oct.-Mar. 9-4 (last visit 3.30). Sa., Su. and public holidays 10-12 (last visit 11.30). Closed Jan. 1, May 1, Nov. 1, 11, Dec. 25.

TRAMWAY MUSEUM
Chaussée de Ninove 184, 1750 Schepdaal, nr. Brussels
Collection of 30 vehicles, tracing the history of the tramway system from 1894-1935.
Easter-Oct. 31, Sa., Su. and public holidays, 2-6.

VEHICLE MUSEUM
Parc du Cinquantenaire, 1040 Brussels
Collection of vehicles of 19th and 20th centuries.
Odd dates, 9.30-12.25, 1.30-4.50. Closed M., Jan. 1, May 1, Nov. 11.

WIERTZ MUSEUM
Rue Vautier 62, 1040 Brussels
Workshops of the romantic painter, Antoine Wiertz, containing examples of his work.
Daily 10-5. Nov. 16-Feb. 15, 10-4. Closed M., Jan. 1, Nov. 1, 11.

CHARLEROI

MUNICIPAL PICTURE AND SCULPTURE GALLERY
Hôtel de Ville, Charleroi, Hainault
Paintings and sculpture, including works by P. J. Navez (17871869), born in Charleroi.
On request.

COMBLAIN-AU-POINT

REGIONAL MUSEUM
Grand-Place, Comblain-au-Point, Liège
Regional history and customs. Folklore.
Daily 10-12, 2-4.

COURTRAI

MUSEUM OF ARCHAEOLOGY AND INDUSTRIAL ART
Marché-aux-Avoines, Courtrai, Flanders
Archaeological collections. Industrial art.
By appointment.

MUSEUM OF PAINTING
Rue du Béguinage 1, Courtrai, Flanders
Works by local painters: Roeland Savery, Bernard de Ryckere, Alfred Verwee, Jozef de Coene, Emil Claus. Archaeology. Courtrai damasks. Relics of the battle of 1302.
Su. 10-1, 2-5; M., W., Sa. 10-12.30, 2-5; Th. 2-5.

DAMME

ARCHAEOLOGICAL MUSEUM
Hôpital Saint-Jean, Damme, Flanders
Art. Archaeology. Folklore.
On request.

VAN MAERLANT MUSEUM
Sint Jan Mansion, Damme, Flanders
Works and personal possessions of Jacob Van Maerlant (c.1235-1300), the 'father of Flemish poetry', who died and is buried at Damme.
Daily 10-12, 2-4.

DEINZE

LOCAL MUSEUM
Hôtel de Ville, Deinze, Flanders
Folklore. Archaeology.
On request.

DENDERMONDE

MUSEUM OF ANTIQUITIES
Vleeshalle, Dendermonde, East Flanders
Building (1460). Local history.
Su. 10-12, 3-6.

PICTURE GALLERY
Town Hall, Dendermonde, East Flanders
Paintings by local artists.
On request.

DEURNE

STERCKHOF
Hooftvunderlei, Deurne
Collections illustrating Flemish life.
On request.

DIEST

MUSEUM OF THE BÉGUINAGE
Diest, Campine
Local history. Folklore.
Daily 10-12, 2-4.

DINANT

MUSEUM OF ARMS AND ARMOUR
Citadel, Dinant, Namur
Souvenirs of Waterloo and of Sedan. 17th-19th century arms and armour.
Daily 9-7. Winter 9-5.

DIXMUDE

LOCAL MUSEUM
Stadhuis, Dixmude, West Flanders
Local history. Fragments of rood-loft.
Daily 10-12, 2-4.

ECAUSSINNES

CASTLE
Ecaussinnes, Hainault
12th century castle, with 15th century kitchen practically unchanged. 19th century salon. Furniture and furnishings.
Summer: daily ex. F. 9-12, 2-6.

ENGHIEN

ARCHAEOLOGICAL MUSEUM
Rue d'Argent, Enghien, Dendre
Archaeology. History. Paintings. Folklore.
Daily 10-12, 2-4.

EREZÉE

LOCAL MUSEUM
School of Fisenne, Erezée, Luxembourg
Local history. Folklore. Art.
By appointment.

EUPEN

REGIONAL MUSEUM
Gres de Raeren, Eupen, Liège
Textiles. Folklore. Local history.
Daily 10-12, 2-4.

FRANC-WARET

CHÂTEAU
Franc-Waret, Namur
17th century château. Furnishings and furniture of the French and Dutch styles (17th and 18th centuries). 16th century tapestries.
Mid. June - mid. Sept., Su. 2-6.

FURNES

MUSEUM OF ART AND ARCHAEOLOGY
Hôtel de Ville, Furnes, West Flanders
Archaeology. Modern art. Documents. Coins.
Summer: daily 9-12, 2-5.

PALAIS DE JUSTICE
Grand-place, Furnes, West Flanders
Antiquities. Coins and medals.
On request.

GAASBEEK

CHÂTEAU MUSEUM
Gaasbeek, Brabant
Local history. Furniture. Paintings. Tapestries. Objets d'art.
Nov. 1-Jan. 31, Tu., Th. and Su. 10-3. Feb. 1-Mar. 31 and Sept. 1-Oct. 31, Tu., Th. and Su. 10-5.

GERAARDSBERGEN

LOCAL MUSEUM
Abbey of St. Adrian, Geraardsbergen, East Flanders
Local history. Folklore.
Sa. 2-7; Su. 10.30-12.30, 2.30-7.30.

GHENT

BELFRY MUSEUM
Limburgstrasse, Ghent
Collections illustrating the history of the Belfrey (c.1300). Bells.
Daily 8.30 onwards.

CASTLE OF THE COUNTS OF FLANDERS
Ghent
Built 1180 on foundations of 10th century fortress. Furniture and furnishings. Collection of instruments of torture. Weavers' looms, including the famous Lieven Bauwens "spinning jenny".
Daily 9-6. Oct.-Mar. 9-4.

FINE ARTS MUSEUM
Citadelpark, Ghent
Paintings. Sculpture. Tapestries. Drawings. Etchings. Old masters include Jerome Bosch, G. Hoorenbaut, Engebrechtsz, Pourbus, Ysenbrandt, Breughel, Rubens, Jordaens, Van Dijck, De Crayer, Frans Hals, Tintoretto, Reynolds, Hogarth, Chardin. Modern works, especially of the Belgian school: Evenepoel, Claus, Permeke, George Minne. Collection of etchings by Jules de Bruycker. French School: Gericault, Corot, Millet, Boudin, Fantin-Latour, Rouault, Dufresne. Sculptures by Delvaux, De Vigne, C. Meunier, Vincott, G. Minne, Bourdelle, Rodin, Renoir.
Daily 9-12.30. Oct.-Mar. 9-12.

FOLKLORE MUSEUM
Kraanlei 63, Ghent
Objects and collections illustrating the customs and traditions of the city of Ghent and the Flemish people. Marionette theatre. 19th century kitchen. Home weaving loom. Sweet shop. 16th century candlestick-maker's workshop. Printing shop. Distillery (16th, 18th, 19th centuries). Transport. Children's toys. Picture books. Fashion. Tobacco pipes.
Daily ex. Tu. 10-12, 1.30-5.

MUSEUM OF ANTIQUITIES
Godshuizenlaan 2, 9000 Ghent
Housed in ancient abbey of the Byloke, 13th century. Furniture of the Chamber of the Governors of the Poor, originally in Town Hall. Paintings by Gillis Leplat (1691) and Jan Van Cleef. 18th century tapestries and Brussels carpets. 14th century frescoes. Religious objects of art. Ironwork. Decorative and domestic copper, brass, bronze and pewter objects, including the City of Ghent's weights and measures of 1281. Flemish pottery, faience, porcelain and crystal. Ancient garments and uniforms. Weapons. Gothic room with souvenirs of the Ghent merchant and craft guilds. Rooms furnished in 17th, 18th and 19th century style. Silverware and paintings. 17th century Abbess's house. Insignias of the Corporation of the City of Ghent.
Jan.-Mar. and Oct.-Dec. Daily 10-12, 1.30-4.30. Apr.-Sept. Daily 10-12, 1.30-5.30.

MUSEUM OF DECORATIVE ARTS AND INDUSTRIAL DESIGN
The de Coninck Mansion, J. Breydelstrasse, Ghent
Mansion (1752), containing model craftwork and furniture, grouped according to style.
By appointment.

MUSEUM OF THE HISTORY OF SCIENCE
Korte Meer 9, Ghent
Pioneer work accomplished by Ghent scholars: John Palfijn, inventor of the forceps; Joseph Plateau, forerunner of the cinema; D. van Monckhoven, pioneer of the photographic industry; Kekulé van Stradonitz, who helped define the molecule; Leo Baekeland, inventor of bakelite; Victor Deneffe, who, in 19th century, assembled a collection of surgical equipment going back to antiquity.
M. and W. 2-5; Sa. 9-12. Other days on request.

MUSEUM OF THE TREATY OF GHENT
Veldstraat, Ghent
Material relating to the Treaty of Ghent (1814) and its period. Documents. Portraits. Medals. Drawings. Empire furniture. Collection of Chinese and Japanese porcelain, jades and prints. Room devoted to Lievin Bauwens, with original sketches of textile machinery. Souvenirs of Wellington's stay in Ghent in 1815 at the time of the "Hundred Days".
By appointment.

MICHEL THIERY SCHOOL MUSEUM
Sint-Pietersabdij, Sint-Pietersplein 14, Ghent
Geology. Mineralogy. Palaeontology. Invertebrates. Molluscs. Insects.
Tu.-F. 9-12, 2-5. Sa. and Su. 9-12. Closed M.

HAN-SUR-LESSE

GROTTO MUSEUM
Han-sur-Lesse, nr. Dinant, Namur
Local antiquities. Fossils. Minerals. Rock crystals.
Easter-Oct. 15, Daily.

HANZINELLE

CHÂTEAU
Hanzinelle, Namur
Château dates from 1681. Woodcarvings from the period of Louis XV. 18th century paintings. Paintings depicting the life of Don Quixote.
Enquire locally.

HASSELT

OPEN-AIR MUSEUM
Bokrijk Park, Hasselt, Limburg
Exhibits include a reconstruction of the old abbey farm of Tongerlo (early 17th century); small Campine farmhouses; Windmill (1788) from Mol-Millegem.
Daily 10-6.

PROVINCIAL MUSEUM
Begijnhof, Hasselt, Limburg
Paintings. Coins and medals. Statues. Folklore. Local history.
Su. 11-1; M., Th. and Sa. 2-4.

E. P. VALENTIN MUSEUM
Hasselt, Limburg
Local history.
Daily 10-12, 2-4.

HERCHIES

LOCAL MUSEUM
Castle, Herchies, Hainault
Local history. Folklore.
Daily 9-12, 2-6, Easter-Oct.

HERENTALS

FRAIKIN MUSEUM
Hôtel de Ville, Herentals, Antwerp
Sculptures by Ch.-R. Fraikin.
M.-Sa. 8-12, 1-4; Su. and holidays 11-12.

HOOGSTRATEN

SAINT-SANG MUSEUM OF FOLK-LORE AND FOLK-ART
Hoogstraten, Antwerp
Folk-art. Handicrafts. Ethnography.
Daily 10-12, 2-4.

TOWN HALL MUSEUM
Hoogstraten, Antwerp
Local crafts and industries. Trade guilds.
On request.

HOUTHALEN

PROVINCIAL AUTOMUSEUM
Domein Kelchterhoef, B-3530 Houthalen, Limbourg
Motor vehicles, all in working order, dating from a 1899 Dion-Bouton tricycle to a 1939 Délage. Models from many European countries and from America.
Apr.-Oct. Daily 10-7. Nov.-Mar. Daily 10-5. Closed Dec. 23-Jan. 7.

HUY

DISTRICT MUSEUM
Ruelle des Frères-Mineurs, Huy, Liège
Local industries, including cultivation of the vine.
On request.

TREASURY OF THE COLLEGIATE CHURCH OF NOTRE-DAME
Huy, Liège
Religious art. Shrines, including those of St. Domitian and St. Mengold, both by Godefroid de Huy (1173, 1177). Chalice, from grave of Bishop Dietwin of Liège, dates from 1100.
Daily 10-12, 2-4.

JABBEKE

LOCAL MUSEUM
Jabbeke, West Flanders
Collection of the works of Constant Permeke (1886-1952), who had his studio here.
Daily ex. F. 10-12, 2-4. Winter: Su. 10-12, 2-4.

LAVAUX-SAINTE-ANNE

BELGIAN MUSEUM OF HUNTING AND NATURAL CONSERVATION
Feudal Castle, Lavaux-Sainte-Anne, Namur
Ornithology. Works of art. Antique furniture. Hunting, past and present. Hunting attire. Butterfly and insect collection.
Daily 10-12, 2-4.

LIÈGE

ANSEMBOURG MUSEUM
114 Féronstrée, Liège
In former Hôtel d'Ansembourg, built for the banker, Michel Willens (1735-41). 18th century decorative arts of Liège. Reconstructions of interiors. Tapestries. Glass. Wrought-iron. Wood-carvings.
Daily ex. Tu., Su. and public holidays, 11-12.30, 2-5. Also open Th. 7-10 p.m. Closed Jan. 1, May 1, Nov. 1 and Dec. 25.

ARCHAEOLOGICAL BASEMENT
Place Saint-Lambert, Liège
Annexe of the Musée Curtius, containing the remains of a Roman villa. Hypocaust.
June-Sept. Su. and public holidays 10-12. July and Aug. also M. 2-5.

CABINET OF PRINTS AND DRAWINGS
Parc de la Boverie, Liège
Drawings and engravings. Artists represented include Dürer, Lucas, Leyde, Lombard, Bry, Demarteau, Valdor, Varin, Lairesse. 17th-18th century French works. Contemporary works by local artists.
W. and F. 11-12.30. Other times by appointment.

CURTIUS MUSEUM
13 quai de Maastricht, Liège
Prehistory. Romano-Belgian and Frankish history and archaeology. Liège coins. Decorative arts from Middle Ages to 19th century.
Daily ex. Tu., Su. and public holidays, 11-12.30, 2-5. Also open W. 7-10 p.m. Closed Jan. 1, May 1, Nov. 1, Dec. 25.

DIOCESAN MUSEUM AND CATHEDRAL TREASURY
Rue Bonne-Fortune, Liège
Paintings of the Liège school, and by Flemish, German and Italian artists. Wooden sculpture. Statues. Jewellery. Gothic and Renaissance furnishings. Fabrics. Roman tombs. Ironwork of the 13th century. Reliquaries. Ivories. Statues. Vestments.
Sa. 3-5; Su. 10-12.

GLASS MUSEUM
13 quai de Maastricht, Liège
Glassware from the main centres of production, from earliest times to the present day. Examples from Europe and the Mediterranean, from the Middle Ages and the Italian Renaissance.
Daily ex. Tu., Su. and public holidays, 11-12.30, 2-5. Closed Jan. 1, May 1, Nov. 1, Dec. 25.

GRÉTRY MUSEUM
34 rue des Récollets, Liège
Birthplace of Grétry, and now preserved as a memorial to the musician. Memorabilia. Manuscripts. Portraits and busts.
Daily ex. Tu., Su. and public holidays, 11-12.30, 2-5. Closed Jan. 1, May 1, Nov. 1, Dec. 25.

LAPIDARY GALLERY
Place Saint-Lambert, Liège
Annexe of the Musée Curtius. Lapidary collection.
Daily 11-12.30, 2-5.

MUSEUM OF FINE ART
rue de l'Académie 34, Liège
Paintings of the Belgian school. French paintings from Ingrès to Picasso. Sculpture.
Daily ex. Tu., Su. and public holidays, 11-12.30, 2-5. Closed Jan. 1, May 1, Nov. 1 and Dec. 25.

MUSEUM OF WALLOON ART
3 parc de la Boverie, Liège
Sculpture. Engravings. Paintings by Patenier, Blès, Lombard, Douffet, Lairesse, Bertholet, Flémalle, Damery and Carlier. Léonard Defrance, Léon Philippet, Auguste Donnay and Richard Heintz.
Daily ex. Tu., Su. and public holidays, 11-12.30, 2-5. Closed Jan. 1, May 1, Nov. 1 and Dec. 25.

MUSEUM OF WALLOON LIFE
Cour des Mineurs, Liège
Ethnography, folklore, arts and crafts and history of southern Belgium.
Daily ex. Tu., Su. and public holidays, 11-12.30, 2-5. Also open F. (Oct.-Mar.) 7.30-10 p.m. Closed Jan. 1, May 1, Nov. 1, Dec. 25.

MUSEUM OF WEAPONS
Quai de Maastricht 8, Liège
History of portable firearms from 1350 to the present day.
Daily ex. Tu., Su. and public holidays, 11-12.30, 2-5. Closed Jan. 1, May 1, Nov. 1, Dec. 25.

TCHANTCHÈS MUSEUM
56 rue Surlet, Liège
Folklore. Costumes. Reconstructions of interiors. Domestic equipment. Trades. Marionettes from the Imperial theatre of Roture.
On request to Mr. Chalant, quai de Longdoz, 60 (tel: 42.53.30).

WITTERT MUSEUM
1 Place Cockerill, Bibliothèque de l'Université, 4000 Liège
15th and 17th century paintings. Prints. Coins. Collection of Congolese art and craft.
Daily ex. Tu., Su. and public holidays, 11-12.30, 2-5. Closed Jan. 1, May 1, Nov. 1, Dec. 25.

YSAYE'S STUDIO
Conservatoire Royal, 14 rue Forgeur, Liège
Reconstruction of the studio of the violinist, Eugène Ysaye. Memorabilia. Busts, portraits. Urn containing the embalmed heart of the artist.
Tu. and Th. 3-5.

ZOOLOGICAL MUSEUM
l'Université, Quai Van Beneden, Liège
Aquarium. Zoological specimens from all over the world.
Daily 2-6; Su. and public holidays, 10.30-12.30, 2-6.

LIERRE

ASTRONOMICAL CLOCK
Zimmertoren, Zimmerplein, Lierre, Liège
Astronomical Clock (1930-31) by Louis Zimmer, with 13 dials on the tower face and another 57 in the studio. The mechanism records the time of day, phases of the moon and the seasons, and operates models of kings and burgomasters in medieval costume.
Museum of Folklore in adjoining building.
Daily 9-12, 2-7 (2-4 in winter).

WUYTS VAN CAMPEN MUSEUM
Rue F. Van Cauwenbergh, Lierre, Liège
Flemish and Dutch paintings by Rubens, Van Dyck, Teniers. Faience. Sculptural fragments.
Daily 10-4.

LESSINES

LOCAL MUSEUM
Hôpital Notre-Dame à la Rose, Lessines, Hainault
Local history.
Daily 9-12, 2-4.

LO

MUSEUM OF RELIGIOUS ART
Convent of the Grauwe Zusters, Lo, West Flanders
Church art.
Daily 10-12, 2-4.

LOKEREN

DISTRICT MUSEUM OF ARCHAEOLOGY
Hôtel de Ville, Grand-Place, Lokeren
Archaeology. Local history.
On request.

LOUVAIN

MUSEUM OF ART AND ARCHAEOLOGY
Hôtel van der Kelen-Mertens, Rue de Savoie 12, Louvain, Brabant
Archaeology. Paintings. Sculpture. Drawings. Coins. Ceramics. Period furniture.
M.-Sa. 10-12, 2-4; Su. 10-1.

MUSEUM OF RELIGIOUS ART
Béguinage, Groot Beginhof, Louvain, Brabant
Religious art.
Apply at no. 11 or 12.

SPOELBERCH DE LOVENJOEL MUSEUM
Rue de Namur 40, Louvain, Brabant
Porcelain. Furniture. Paintings.
Daily 10-12, 2-4.

TOWN HALL MUSEUM
Louvain, Brabant
Fragments of original sculptures on façade. Sketch by Josse Massys (1507) of his proposed completion of the west tower of St. Pieter.
M.-Sa. 9-12, 2-5.

MAASEIK

CHURCH TREASURY
Maaseik, Limburg
10th century gold and silver work. 14th century Agnus Dei. The Eyck Gospels of early 8th century.
On request.

MALMÉDY

ABBEY MUSEUM
Malmédy, Liège
Folklore. Souvenirs of the Princes-Abbots. Local industries which have died out. Manufacture of 'couques' and dominoes.
On request.

MARIEMONT-MORLANWELZ

MUSEUM OF ART AND OF THE HISTORY OF ARCHAEOLOGY
Domaine de Mariemont-Morlanwelz, Hainault
Antiquities from Greece, Rome, France, India, China and Japan. Porcelain from Tournai and Brussels. Bronzes and marbles by Rodin, V. Rousseau, J. Lambeaux, C. Meunier, Devreese. 17th-19th century lace. Paintings. Coins and medals. Statues.
Nov.-Jan. Sa.-Th. 9-3. Feb.-Mar. and Oct., Sa.-Th. 9-4. Apr.-Sept., Sa.-Th. 9-5.

STATE MUSEUM
Rue Warocqué, Mariemont-Morlanwelz, Hainault
Collections relating to the history and government of Belgium.
M.-Sa. 8-8; Su. 8-12.

MARTELANGE

LOCAL MUSEUM
Martelange, Luxembourg
Folklore. Local crafts and traditions.
Daily 10-12, 2-4.

MECHELEN (MALINES)

MUSEUM OF APPLIED ART
De Zalm, Mechelen (Malines), Antwerp
Applied art.
Sa.-M. 10-12, 2-4.

MUSEUM OF ART AND ARCHAEOLOGY
Hôtel de Ville, Grand-Place, Mechelen (Malines), Antwerp
Paintings. Sculpture. Local history. Contemporary art.
Daily 10-12, 2-5.

DIOCESAN MUSEUM
Rue de l'Ecoutète, Mechelen (Malines), Antwerp
Archaeology. Religious art.
Daily ex. Tu. 10-12, 2-4.

MUSEUM
Hospital of Our Lady, Korte Maagdenstraat, Mechelen (Malines), Antwerp
"Besloten Hofjes", a series of small glazed shrines (15th or early 16th century), adorned with embroidery, woodcarving and painted images.
On application, 10-12, 2-4.

MODAVE

CASTLE MUSEUM
Modave, Namur
Collection of armour. Tapestries.
Summer: daily 10-12, 2-4.

MONS

CANON PUISSANT MUSEUM
"Vieux Logis", rue Notre-Dame Debonnaire, Mons
Civil and religious antiquities. Incunabula. Manuscripts, paintings. Drawings. Engravings. Lace. Textiles.
Daily ex. M. 10-12, 2-6.

CERAMICS MUSEUM
Centennial Museums, Jardin du Mayeur, Mons
Ceramics, 17th-19th centuries.
Daily 10-12, 2-6.

COLLEGIATE CHURCH OF ST. WAUDRU: TREASURY
Square Roosevelt, Mons
Religious art.
Treasury: on request.

ICONOGRAPHIC MUSEUM OF MONS
Square du Château, Mons
Iconography of Mons and Hainault from the 9th century until 1436.
Daily 10-12, 2-6.

INDUSTRIAL MUSEUM
Institut Supérieur de Commerce de la Province de Hainault, 17 place Warocqué, Mons
Manufactured products. Iron and steel. Chemical products. Exhibits connected with the former Belgian Congo are housed in the same building.
On request.

JEAN LESCARTS MUSEUM
Rue Neuve, Mons
Collections relating to Mons. Folklore. Antiquities. Faience. Porcelain. Glass. Coins. Prehistory. Military collection.
Daily 10-6.

MUSEUM OF FINE ART
Rue Neuve, Mons
Paintings. Sculpture. Archaeology of the Belgo-Roman period. Faience, porcelain and stoneware, from Belgium, Holland and France.
Daily ex. M. 10-12, 2-6.

MUSEUM OF NATURAL HISTORY
Rue des Gaillers, Mons
Geology. Mineralogy. Palaeontology. Zoology. Botany. Osteology.
Daily ex. M. 10-12, 2-6.

MUSEUM OF NUMISMATICS AND PREHISTORY
Centennial Museums, Jardin du Mayeur, Mons
Collections of coins and medals from various countries and of the prehistoric, Roman and Frankish periods.
Daily 10-12, 2-6.

ROYAL CONSERVATORY OF MUSIC
Salle Camille Bouillot, Rue de Nimy, Mons
Furniture. Engravings. Musical instruments. Porcelain.
On request.

WAR MUSEUM
Centennial Museums, Jardin du Mayeur, Mons
Souvenirs of the two World Wars. British relics of the 1914-18 war on the continent, including 26 British regimental drums.
Daily 10-12, 2-6.

NAMUR

ARCHAEOLOGICAL MUSEUM
Rue du Pont, Namur
Occupies former Meat Market (1560). Gallo-Roman, Merovingian and Medieval antiquities. Objects from the Belgo-Roman villa at Anthée and from the cemetery at La Plante. Faience from Hastière and Huy. 13th century reliquaries. 15th century sculpture. Ivories. Statues. Retables. Ceramics.
Daily ex. F. and holidays, 10-12, 2-5.

THE DE CROIX MUSEUM
Rue Joseph Saintraint, Namur
18th century mansion. Paintings. Necklaces and plates. 18th and 19th century local crafts (chinaware, porcelain, cutlery and glass-ware). 18th century kitchen.
Daily ex. F. and holidays, 10-12, 2-5.

DIOCESAN MUSEUM
Place du Chapitre, Cathedral of St. Aubain, Place St. Aubain, Namur
Relics and ornaments from the old collegiate church. Objects from sanctuaries and monasteries abolished during the French Revolution, and from the St. Pierre-au-Château church. The collection includes a 10th century Gospel-book on which the Counts took oaths; portable altar (12th century); golden crown set with two thorns from the crown of Christ; the Cross of Brogne (1505) containing a piece of the Cross of Christ.
Daily ex. F. and holidays, 10-12, 2-5.

FORESTRY MUSEUM
Route Merveilleuse, Citadelle, Namur
Collections of the flora and fauna of the Ardennes. Diagrams showing the formation and growth of all the species of the forests. Damage resulting from disease or parasites and the appropriate remedies. Lepidoptera.
Daily ex. F. and holidays, 10-12, 2-5.

MUSEUM OF WEAPONS
Château des Comtes, Route Merveilleuse, Namur
Weapons of the First and Second World Wars. Hunting and

fencing weapons. Military history of the province. Sieges of Namur (1692, 1695, 1746). European military history. Weapons of the Orient and the Far East.
Museum: Daily ex. F. and holidays, 10-12, 2-5.

NAMUR MUSEUM OF ARTS AND CRAFTS
Rue de Fer, Namur
18th century mansion. Arts and crafts of the Middle Ages and the Renaissance. Meuse region gold plate of 12th and 13th centuries. Wooden statues (13th-15th centuries). Bas-relief and stone statues of 15th century. Bronze, copper, and glass objects, embroidered liturgical ornaments of 15th and 16th centuries. 15th-16th century carved reredoses and painted panels. Copper-ware of 17th and 18th centuries. Works of the Meuse Valley painter, Félicien Rops (1833-1898).
Daily ex. F. and holidays, 10-12, 2-5.

THE HUGO D'OIGNIES GOLD PLATE COLLECTION
Rue Julie Billiart, Namur
In the Convent of the Soeurs de Notre Dame. Liturgical objects enriched with enamel and precious stones. Reliquary of St. Peter's rib (1228). Chalices. Phylacteries.
M.-F. 10-12, 2-5.

NEDER-OVER-HEEMBEEK

FOLKLORE MUSEUM
Church of St. Nicolas, Neder-over-Heembeek
Local crafts. Reconstructions of interiors of peasant houses and workshops.
Daily 10-12, 2-4.

NIEUWPOORT

MUSEUM OF HISTORY AND FOLKLORE
Kokstraat 18, Nieuwpoort, West Flanders
Historical objects. Maps. Documents. Photographs. Folklore collection, including a typical fisherman's kitchen.
Easter holidays, July and Aug., weekdays 10-12, 2-6.

MUSEUM OF ORNITHOLOGY
Market Place 6, Nieuwpoort, West Flanders
Stuffed seabirds and crustaceans, in their natural environment. As background, a painting (60 x 3.5 m.) of Nieuwpoort, designed by Bastien and painted by Wattecamps.
Easter holidays, July and Aug., weekdays 10-12, 2-6.

PIETER-BRAECKE MUSEUM
Hoogstraat 2, Nieuwpoort, West Flanders
Plaster models by the Nieuwpoort sculptor, Pieter Braecke (1859-1938).
Easter holidays, July and Aug., weekdays 10-12, 2-6.

WAR MUSEUM "NIEUWPOORT 1914-1918"
Hoogstraat 2, Nieuwpoort, West Flanders
Arms, paintings, photographs and souvenirs of the 1st World War. Records of the flooding in October 1914.
Easter holidays, July and Aug., weekdays 10-12, 2-6.

NISMES

FOLKLORE MUSEUM
Town Hall, Nismes, Namur
Folklore. Local history. Art. Archaeology. Numismatics. Mineralogy. Colonial section.
Daily 10-12, 2-4.

NIVELLES

ARCHAEOLOGICAL MUSEUM
Place St. Paul, Nivelles, Brabant
Archaeology. Folklore. Local history.
Daily ex. Tu. 9.30-12.30, 2.30-5.30.

OLLOY

LOCAL MUSEUM
Olloy, Hainault
Local history.
Daily 10-12, 2-4.

OP-HEYLISSEM

SCHOOL MUSEUM
Op-Heylissem, Liège
Local industries. Former weaving industry. Folklore.
On request.

OSTEND

CITY ART GALLERY
Festival Hall, Wapenplein, Ostend
Collections of contemporary art, including works by Ensor, a native of Ostend.
Daily ex. Tu. 10-12, 2-5. Closed October.

JAMES ENSOR MUSEUM
27 Vlaanderenstraat, Ostend
House of the painter James Ensor (1860-1949), a native of Ostend. Selection of his works.
Daily 9-12, 4-6.

FISHERY MUSEUM
6 Handelsplein, Ostend
Local history of the fishing industry.
Daily 9.30-12, 2-6.

FOLKLORE MUSEUM
Festival Hall, Ostend
Folklore collections.
July-Aug. M.-Sa. 10-12, 2.30-4.30. Sept.-June, Sa. 10-12.

'MERCATOR'
Mercator Yacht Dock, Ostend
Training ship and museum.
June-Sept. Daily 10-5. May and Oct. Sa. and Su. 10-5. Nov.-Apr. Su. 10-5.

WAR MUSEUM
Fortuinstraat 17, Ostend
Relics of the 1939-45 war.
By appointment.

OUDENARDE

ARCHAEOLOGICAL MUSEUM
Hôtel de Ville, Oudenarde, East Flanders
Coins and medals. Paintings. Statues. Archaeology. Local folklore. Collection of crossbows. 12 pewter jugs, which the authorities used to present, filled with wine, to important persons passing through the town.
On request.

RENAIX (RONSE)

MUSEUM OF FOLKLORE AND LOCAL HISTORY
15 Priesterstraat, Renaix (Ronse), Flanders
Local history, in old canons' houses.
Daily 9.30-12.30, 2.30-5.30.

RIJKHOVEN

CHÂTEAU OF OUDE BIEZEN
Rijkhoven, Limburg
Château (1280). Portraits of Grand Commanders of the Order of Teutonic Knights. Panelled Ceilings. 17th century tapestries.
Daily 11-12, 2.30-5.30.

ROBERTVILLE

LOCAL MUSEUM
Robertville, Liège
Local history.
Daily 10-12, 2-4.

LA ROCHE-EN-ARDENNE

WAR MUSEUM
La Roche-en-Ardenne, Namur
War relics.
Summer: daily 10-12, 2-4.

ROCLENGE-SUR-GEER

STRAW MUSEUM
Hôtel de l'Union, Roclenge-sur-Geer
Industries in the Geer area using straw as raw material.
On request.

LE ROEULX

CASTLE MUSEUM
au Château, Le Roeulx, nr. Mons, Hainault
Art collections.
Apr.-Oct. Daily ex. Tu. 10-6.

SINT-NIKLAAS WAAS

ARCHAEOLOGICAL MUSEUM
Zaman Street, Sint-Niklaas Waas, East Flanders
Archaeology. Paintings. Sculpture. Flemish room. Guilds room. Folklore. Atlases. Maps. Two globes (terrestrial and celestial) made by Mercator (1512-94).
M.-Sa. 9-11, 1-4; Su. 10-1.

FINE ARTS GALLERY
Mercator Hall, Sint-Niklaas Waas, East Flanders
Art collections.
Daily 10-12, 2-4.

SAINT-TROND

BÉGUINAGE MUSEUM
Begijnhof, Saint-Trond, Brabant
14th-18th century frescoes. Religious objects. Local history. Astronomical clock (1942) by K. Festraets, with the 'Fantastic Ship' behind it.
Summer: Su. and holidays 8.45-12, 1.45-7, or by appointment to No. 40 Begijnhof.

SAINT-VITH

REGIONAL MUSEUM
Saint-Vith
Furnished interiors.
On request.

SOIGNIES (ZINNIK)

ARCHAEOLOGICAL MUSEUM
Rue Henry-le-Roi, Soignes (Zinnik), Hainault
Archaeology. Folklore. Lapidary collection.
Summer: 1st and 3rd Su. in month, 10-12, 2-4, or on application.

SPA

DISTRICT MUSEUM
Waux-Hall, Avenue de la Géronstère, Spa, Liège
History. Folklore. Painted wood, "boîtes de Spa". Charts. Paintings. Drawings. Coins and medals.
Su. 2-5.

SPONTIN

CASTLE
Spontin, Namur
12th-16th century castle, with period furnishings. Paintings. Tapestries. Furniture.
Easter-Sept. Daily 10-12.30, 2-6.30.

STAVELOT

ARCHAEOLOGICAL MUSEUM
Town Hall, Stavelot, Liège
Belgo-Roman antiquities. Medieval art archaeology. Folklore.
Daily 10-12, 2-4.

TANNERY MUSEUM
Gate-Tower, Stavelot, Liège
History of the tanneries which operated in the district until 1939.
July-Sept., 10-12, 2.30-5.30. June: 2.30-5.30.

TREASURY
Parish Church, Place St. Remácle, Stavelot, Liège
Shrine of St. Remaclus (1263) in gilt and enamelled copper, with reliefs and statuettes. Reliquaries. Vestments.
On application to the sacristan, at 4 Place St. Rémacle.

TERVUEREN

ROYAL CENTRAL AFRICAN MUSEUM
Leuvensesteenweg 13, 1980 Tervueren
Prehistory. Ethnography. Native arts and crafts. Geology. Mineralogy. Palaeontology. Zoology. Entomology. Ornithology. History. Economics.
Daily ex. F. 9.30-12.30, 2-5 (Oct.-Feb. 2-4). Closed Jan. 1, Nov. 11.

TIRLEMONT

ARCHAEOLOGICAL MUSEUM
Hôtel de Ville, Tirlemont
Archaeological collections.
On request.

TONGRES

ARCHAEOLOGICAL MUSEUM
Société Scientifique et Littéraire du Limbourg, Rue des Dominicains, Tongres, Limburg
17th century paintings and sculptures. Antiquities.
By appointment.

GALLO-ROMAN MUSEUM
Grote Markt, Tongres, Limburg
Roman glass, ceramics, bronzes and grave-goods (mainly 1st-3rd century). Roman graves with their contents as found.
Daily 9-12, 2-5.30.

TREASURY OF THE BASILICA OF ONZE LIEVE VROUW
Tongres, Limburg
Reliquaries of 10th-13th centuries. Monstrances. Shrines (13th-15th centuries).
On request.

TOURNAI

ARMOURY
Tower of Henry VIII, Avenue Leray, Tournai
Collection of weapons used in the two World Wars.
Apr.-Sept. Daily 10-12, 2-6. Oct.-Mar., Su. and public holidays, 10-12.30, 2.30-5.30.

ART ASSOCIATION
Rue Clairisses, Tournai
Collections of paintings, sculpture.
Apr.-Sept. Daily 10-12, 2-6. Oct.-Mar. Su. and public holidays 10-12.30, 2.30-5.30.

CATHEDRAL TREASURY
Marché aux Poteries, Tournai
Relics. Ornaments. Psalters. Ivory seals. Byzantine cross-reliquary (6th or 7th century). Vestments. Tournai and Brussels tapestries.
Daily ex. during services.

FINE ARTS MUSEUM
Rue de l'Enclos Saint-Martin, Tournai
Collection of paintings, from 15th century to the present day.
Apr.-Sept. Daily 10-12, 2-6. Oct.-Mar., Su. and public holidays, 10-12.30, 2.30-5.30.

FOLKLORE MUSEUM
Réduit des Sions, Tournai
Crafts. Jewellery. Domestic articles. Traditional costumes. Folk-art. Local porcelain (1740-1891).
Apr.-Sept. Daily 10-12, 2-6. Oct.-Mar. Su. and public holidays, 10-12.30, 2.30-5.30.

MUSEUM OF HISTORY AND ARCHAEOLOGY
Mont de Piété, Rue des Carmes 8, Tournai
Art from Tournai, from the Gallo-Roman period to the Renaissance. Manuscripts. Coins. Tapestries. Porcelain. Goldsmiths' work.
Apr.-Sept. Daily 10-12, 2-6. Oct.-Mar., Su. and public holidays, 10-12.30, 2.30-5.30.

MUSEUM OF NATURAL HISTORY
Cour Hôtel de Ville, Tournai
Geology. Palaeontology. Botany. Zoology.
Apr.-Sept. Daily 10-12, 2-6. Oct.-Mar. Su. and public holidays, 10-12.30, 2.30-5.30.

MUSEUM OF PALAEONTOLOGY AND PREHISTORY
Mont de Piété, Rue des Carmes 8, Tournai
Crystals. Rocks. Minerals. Collections illustrating the evolution of life and man.
Apr.-Sept. Daily 10-12, 2-6. Oct.-Mar. Su. and public holidays, 10-12.30, 2.30-5.30.

WAR MUSEUM
Tour Henri VIII, Tournai
Material relating to the Resistance and the clandestine Press during the German occupation.
Daily 10-12, 2-4.

TURNHOUT

TAXANDRIA MUSEUM OF ARCHAEOLOGY
Société Archéologique Taxandria, Rue Meermans, Turnhout, Antwerp
Local history and industry. Popular arts. Playing cards. Antiquities of the Celtic period of the Campine, including Merovingian grave.
Su.-F. 10-12, 2-5.

VERVIERS

MUSEUM OF ARCHAEOLOGY AND FOLKLORE
Rue des Raines 42, Verviers, Liège
Paintings. Archaeology. Folklore. Local history. Ceramics. Glass. Local furniture and woodwork.
May-Sept. M.-Th. 9-12, 2-5; Sa. 9-12, 2-5; Su. and public holidays 10-1, 3-6. Oct.-Apr. M.-Th. 2-5; Sa. 9-12, 2-5; Su. and public holidays, 10-1, 3-6.

MUSEUM OF FINE ART
Rue Renier 17, Verviers, Liège
Sculpture. Paintings. European and Asian ceramics.
May-Sept. M.-Th. 9-12, 2-5; Sa. 9-12, 2-5; Su. and public holidays 10-1, 3-6. Oct.-Apr. M.-Th. 2-5; Sa. 9-12, 2-5; Su. and public holidays, 10-1, 3-6.

RENIER MUSEUM
Rue Renier 15, Verviers, Liège
Archaeology. Folklore of the Verviers district. Paintings. Porcelain. Lace. Coins and medals.
M., Th., Su. and public holidays, 10-1, 2-6. Other days 10-12 on application to the Curator.

VIRTON

GAUMAIS MUSEUM
40 rue d'Arlon, Virton, Luxembourg
Metallurgy. Pottery. Sabot-making. Basket-making. Reconstructions of workshops and household interiors.
Daily 10-12, 2-4.

VRESSE-SUR-SEMOIS

TOBACCO MUSEUM
Vresse-sur-Semois, Namur
History of tobacco.
On request.

WATERLOO

MUSEUM OF CAILLIOU
Chaussée de Bruxelles, Vieux Grenappe, Waterloo
On the battlefield of Waterloo. The last headquarters of Napoleon. Panorama of the Battle. Relics.
Daily ex. Tu. 9-6.

WATERMAEL-BOISSFORT

LOCAL MUSEUM
Watermael-Boissfort, Brabant
Local history.
On request.

WULVERINGEM

CHÂTEAU OF BEAUVOORDE
Wulveringem, West Flanders
Moated château, rebuilt 1591-1617. Furniture. Paintings.
July-Sept., daily 9-12, 2-5.

YPRES

"BELLE GODSHUIS"
Rijsselstraat 38, Ypres, West Flanders
Oldest almshouse in Europe (13th century). Council Chamber, with seven Commemoration Books showing all Irish soldiers killed in World War I. Paintings. Furniture.
M.-F. 9-12, 2-5; Sa. 9-12.

MERGHELYNCK MUSEUM
4 Merghelynckstraat, Ypres, West Flanders
Mansion, furnished in Louis XV and Louis XVI style and painted in Versailles colours.
M.-F. 10-12, 2-5. Closed July 15-31.

MUNICIPAL MUSEUM
Kloostergebouw, Ypres, West Flanders
Local history and art.
May-Sept., Su. 10-12, 2-5.

SALIENT MUSEUM
Stadhuis, Boomgaardstraat, Ypres, West Flanders
Souvenirs of the 1939-45 war.
Easter-Sept., daily 10-6.

YZERTOREN

MUSEUM OF THE YSER BATTLE
Yzertoren, West Flanders
Mementoes of the Yser battle, 1914.
Apr. - mid. Oct., daily 9-12, 2-7.

ZEEBRUGGE

ZEEBRUGGE MUSEUM
Zeebrugge, Flanders
Historical relics and souvenirs of World Wars 1 and 2. Special section devoted to the Battle of Zeebrugge (23 April 1918).
May 1 - Sept. 15, Daily 10-12.30, 2-6. Also open at Easter.

Bermuda

Bermuda is in the fortunate position of having much nostalgic material to offer both to Americans and to the visiting British, and this fact is well reflected in its museums. In addition to the shipping history which was fundamental to the development of the island, one also finds suitably selected and displayed treasure from the many shipwrecks which took place around the coasts of the island and, slightly less in place in this Caribbean island, a set of full-scale replicas of the British Crown Jewels. The Museum of Horse-Drawn Carriages has the great advantage of being reproduced on the streets of the island in the form of very similar vehicles plying for hire - an excellent and original example of a living museum.

FORT ST. CATHERINE

FORT ST. CATHERINE
St. George
Fort (1866) on site of earlier fortifications. Dioramas illustrating Bermuda's history, ranging from the wrecking of the 'Sea Venture' in 1609 to the romance between Tom Moore and Nea Tucker in 1804. Replicas of the Crown Jewels of England. Replica of Officers' Duty Room, c.1870. Cookhouse. Magazines for storing powder, shells and cartridges. Regiment room. Wax figures.
Daily 10-4.30.

HAMILTON PARISH

BERMUDA MUSEUM
P.O. Box 145, The Flatts, Hamilton Parish
Natural history of Bermuda. The Teddy Tucker Treasure, which includes an emerald studded cross and pieces of eight, found in shipwrecks in 17th century.
Daily 9-5. Closed Christmas Day.

HAMILTON

PAR-LA-VILLE MUSEUM
Bermuda Historical Society, Par-la-Ville, Hamilton
Artifacts relating to Bermuda's history, including portraits of Sir George Somers and Lady Somers, and Sir George Somers' lodestone and seachest.
Daily ex. Th. and Su., 10-5.

ST. GEORGE'S

THE CARRIAGE MUSEUM
Water Street, St. George's
Collection of carriages and other horse-drawn vehicles.
By appointment.

THE CONFEDERATE MUSEUM
The King's Parade, St. George's
Collections illustrating events in Bermuda during the American Civil War. One room furnished as a pre-1865 Victorian parlour.
Daily 10-12, 1-5.

THE "DELIVERANCE" REPLICA
Ordnance Island, St. George's
Replica of the sailing ship "Deliverance" (built 1609), with period furniture. Memorabilia of Sir George Somers. Flora and fauna of the area. Galley contains the sort of food eaten during voyages.
Daily 10-4.

PRESIDENT HENRY TUCKER HOUSE
Water Street, St. George's
Named after Henry Tucker, President of the Council and sometime acting Governor, who lived there during the American Revolutionary War. Furnishings (18th century), many of Bermuda cedar.
Daily 10-12, 1-5.

ST. GEORGE'S HISTORICAL SOCIETY MUSEUM
Kent Street, St. George's
Typical Bermuda house of the early 1700s, with period furnishings, pictures and documents.
Daily ex. Su. 10-4.

SOUTHAMPTON

MARINE MUSEUM
Gibbs Hill Lighthouse, Southampton
Maritime collections. Ships models. Documents.
Daily 10-1, 2-5.

SMITH'S PARISH

VERDMONT
Smith's Parish
17th century house containing furnishings of 1815, many of them pieces of Bermuda cedar, made in Bermuda.
Daily 10-5, with variable closing hour for lunch.

Bhutan

This small country on the fringe of India, with a population of about 800,000 earns a living by exporting timber, cereals and the products of its cottage industries. Its single museum mirrors this.

PARO

TA-DZONG MUSEUM
Paro
History and ethnography of Bhutan. Natural history.
Daily 10-1, 2-5.

Bolivia

Bolivia's artists and craftsmen, sophisticated and unsophisticated, are well represented in the country's museums and galleries. If one had only the evidence of museum collections as a guide, however, it would not be easy to deduce that Bolivia was a major world producer of tin and petroleum, or a considerable exporter of a wide range of agricultural products. Science and technology collections are to be found only at Bolivia's seven universities and we have no information to suggest that they should be regarded as museums within our present definition.

LA PAZ

"CASA DE MURILLO" MUSEUM
Calle Jaen 666, La Paz
Folk-art of Bolivia.
Tu.-Sa. 10-1, 3-6; Su. 10-1.

CENTRAL BANK COLLECTION
Colón, La Paz
Bolivian paintings of the colonial period.
M.-F. 9-12, 2-5.

MUNICIPAL ART GALLERY
Colón, La Paz
Bolivian paintings, applied art, folk art of the colonial period. 19th-20th century paintings, graphics, sculpture by Bolivian artists.
M.-Sa. 10-12.30, 3-7.

NAIRA GALLERY
Sagárnaga, La Paz
19th-20th century paintings, graphics by South American, especially Bolivian, artists.
By appointment.

NATIONAL MUSEUM
Prado, La Paz
Arts and crafts of ancient Tiahuanaco.
Tu.-F. 9-12, 2-6; Sa. 9-12; Su. 10.30-12.30. Closed M.

NATIONAL MUSEUM OF ARCHAEOLOGY
Calle Tihuanacu 93, Casilla oficial 64, La Paz
Archaeological and ethnographical collections. Lake Titicaca district exhibits. Anthropology. Zoology. Numismatics. Folklore. Traditional native arts and crafts. Colonial art.
Tu.-F. 9-12, 2-6; Sa. 9-12; Su. 10.30-12.30.

NATIONAL MUSEUM OF ART
Calle Socabaya 485, La Paz
European and Bolivian paintings, sculpture, graphics, mostly 18th-19th century. 20th century Bolivian paintings, graphics. Ceramics. Silver. Furniture.
M.-F. 10-1, 3-7; Sa. and Su. 10-12.30.

POTOSI

NATIONAL MUSEUM OF THE POTOSI MINT
Casilla 39, Potosi
Colonial art. 18th century wooden machinery. Coins. Historical archives. Mineralogy. Weapons. Indian ethnography. Archaeology. Contemporary Bolivian paintings, graphics.
M.-F. 10-1, 3-6; Sa., Su. 10-1.

PALACE OF THE MARQUESS OF VILLAVERDE
Potosi
Bolivian paintings of the colonial period. 18th-19th century furniture, decorative arts.
On request.

SUCRE

ANTHROPOLOGICAL MUSEUM
Apto. Postal 212, Universidad Mayor, Real y Pontificia de San Francisco Xavier de Chuquisaca, Sucre
Archaeology. Ethnography. Folklore. Exhibits include items relating to the pre-Inca civilisations.
By appointment.

ART GALLERY
Sucre
Paintings, graphics by 19th-20th century Bolivian artists.
Tu.-Su. 10-1.

CATHEDRAL TREASURY
Sucre
Religious paintings, sculpture. Vestments. Ornaments. Liturgical items.
Daily 9-5.

CHARCAS MUSEUM
Universidad de San Francisco Xavier de Chuquisaca, Apto. 212, Sucre
Regional history.
By appointment.

COLONIAL MUSEUM
Sucre
Collections illustrating art, handicrafts, life of the colonial period. Furniture. Household equipment.
M.-F. 10-12.30, 3-6; Sa., Su. 10-12.30.

HISTORICAL MUSEUM
Casa de la Independencia, Sucre
Historical material, including the Bolivian Declaration of Independence.
M.-F. 10-1, 3-5.

MUSEUM OF FINE ART
Sucre
Paintings, graphics, sculpture by Bolivian artists. Portraits.
M.-F. 10-12.30, 3-6; Sa., Su. 10-12.30.

Botswana

This thinly populated country, formerly the British Protectorate of Bechuanaland, has two museums, both in the capital. Their main interest is the people, the plants and the wildlife of the country, with good ethnographical collections. The important mineral discoveries recently made within Botswana's territory are certain to bring considerable changes to the national economy and prosperity, and the resulting educational and technical developments are very likely to be reflected in interesting developments in the museum field.

GABERONES

NATIONAL MUSEUM AND ART GALLERY
Churchill Road, Independence Avenue, P.O. Box 131, Gaberones
Ethnography, history and natural history. Ecological aspects of wildlife in Botswana.
Daily 9-1, 2-5 (2-6 in summer). Closed Christmas and Easter.

KANYE

KGOSI BATHOEN II MUSEUM
Private Bag 2, Kanye
Ethnographic collection from all over the country. Archaeology. Natural history.
On request to Local District Council.

Brazil

The fact that the museum of one of Brazil's Agricultural High Schools contains a small historical collection of instruments of torture may or may not tell us anything significant about the Agricultural High School. What it does illustrate, however, is the interesting way in which the Brazilian past and the Brazilian present flow into each other. The crimes of the colonial rulers and the achievements of the nineteenth-century liberators are never far away from the work of the twentieth-century scientists and economists.

The first Europeans to invade Brazil went there for gold and silver, and, perhaps incidentally, to convert the natives to Christianity. Both themes are clearly shown in the museums, where the interweaving of European and Indian cultures to produce the present remarkable Brazilian mélange is reflected in art, in religion, in attitudes to authority, to suffering, to material possessions, to comfort and to power.

There is a new-nation simplicity, charm and vigour about museums which preserve, as a shrine, the mud-hut in which Pedro I spent the night before uttering his famous cry of "Iparanga" -Independence or Death - and the urn used to receive the votes cast at the election of Bento Gonçalves. Our feet are firmly back on the ground, however, with the Diamond Museum, the exhibits of scales and weights for weighing gold, the Bank Museum of safes, ledgers and early telephones, and the Museum of Taxation.

What might be called the Museums-Inward are mostly concerned with people - "Contributions made by immigrants to the national culture" while the Museums-Outward tend to confine themselves to things - "Museum of the Exportable Products of the Region". Despite Pedro I's mud-hut and the many museums of art, especially contemporary art, the list of the museums of Brazil has a solidly commercial flavour about it. The heroes commemorated are overwhelmingly the heroes of national unification and independence, of wise investment and financial success. There is one notable exception, the pioneer aviator, Santos Dumont, who has, quite rightly, a museum to himself.

AMERICANA

AMERICANO MUSEUM
Americana, São Paulo
History of the War of Secession. Personal possessions of the Confederates and their family.
Tu.-Sa. 8-5; Su. 1-5.

APARECIDA

MUSEUM OF OUR LADY OF APARECIDA
Galeria do Hotel Becseio, Praça N. S. Aparecida, Aparecida, São Paulo
Coins. Seals. Jewellery. Liturgical items.
M.-Sa. 8-5; Su. 7-4.30.

MUSEUM OF OUR LADY OF APARECIDA
Museum in the Tower of the New Church, Basilica de Aparecida, Aparecida, São Paulo
Collection illustrating local customs and traditions.
M.-Sa. 8-5; Su. 7-4.30.

ARACAJÚ

MUSEUM OF ART AND POPULAR TRADITIONS
Av. Barão de Marium 629, Aracajú, Sergipé
Palaeontology. Anthropology. Ethnography. Religious art. Furniture. Paintings. Zoology.
Daily 10-5.

MUSEUM OF THE HISTORICAL AND GEOGRAPHICAL INSTITUTE
Rua Itabaianinha 41, Aracajú, Sergipé
Collections of fossils, coins, old maps of Sergipé.
M.-Sa. 9-12, 2-5.

ARARAQUARA

HISTORICAL MUSEUM OF THE PATRIOTIC VOLUNTEERS
Av. Espanha 437, Araraquara, São Paulo
Domestic equipment. Religious art. Indian material. Medals. Collections relating to the war with Paraguay and to the Revolution of 1932.
M.-F. 12.30-5.30; Su. 8-12.

ARAXÁ

DONA BEJA REGIONAL MUSEUM OF ART
Praça Coronel Adolfo 78, Araxá, Minas Gerais
Paintings, sculpture by Portuguese artists.
Tu.-Su. 10-12, 2-5.

ARCOLEZO

ARCOLEZO ALDEIRA
Arcolezo, Rio de Janeiro
Religious art. Popular art. Handicrafts.
By appointment.

AREIA

PEDRO AMÉRICO MUSEUM
Rua Pedro Américo 66, Areia, Paráiba
Collection of art, including paintings, drawings by Pedro Américo (1843-1906), born in Areia.
M.-Sa. 1-5.

ATIBAIA

JOÃO BATISTA CONTI MUNICIPAL MUSEUM
Praça Bento Pais, Atibaia, São Paulo
Local history, ethnography.
Tu.-Su. 12-5.

AVARÉ

HISTORICAL MUSEUM
Avaré, São Paulo
Historical collections.
By appointment.

BAGÉ

PATRICIO CORREA DA CAMARA MUSEUM
Parque do Forte Santa Tecia, Bagé, Rio Grande do Sul
Ethnography. 18th century Portuguese and Spanish material from excavations at Forte de Santa Lucia.
Daily 9-6.

DIOGO DE SOUZA MUSEUM
Av. Maréchal Floriano Peixoto 2171, Bagé, Rio Grande do Sul
Collections illustrating history of Brazil. Numismatics.
Daily 2-5.

MUSEUM OF THE FORTE DE SANTA TECLA
Bagé, Rio Grande do Sul
In ruins of 18th century fort. Ethnographical collection.
Daily 9-6.

BARBACENA

GEORGES BERNANOS HISTORICAL MUSEUM
Bairro da Cruz das Almas, Barbacena, Minas Gerais
Local history.
M.-Sa. 9-12, 2-5.

BARBALHA

HISTORICAL MUSEUM OF THE READING ROOMS
164 Rua Pero Coelho, Barbalha, Ceará
Local history.
On request.

BARRETOS

ANA ROSA HISTORICAL MUSEUM
Colégio Estadual Mário Viera, Barretos, São Paulo
Local history.
On request.

BATATAIS

DR. WASHINGTON LUIZ HISTORICAL MUSEUM
Praça Anita Garibaldi, Batatais, São Paulo
Historical and art collections of Dr. Washington Luiz.
M.-F. 12-6; Sa. 8-4.

BATURITÉ

HISTORICAL MUSEUM
Avenida Dom Bosco, Baturité, Ceará
Local history.
M.-Sa. 9-5.

BELÉM

EMÍLIO GOELDI PARÁ MUSEUM
Avenida Independência 364, Belém, Pará
Natural history, anthropology and ethnography of the Amazon region. Collections of Marajó and Santarem ceramics.
Tu.-F. 8-11.30, 1.30-5; Su. 8-12, 2-6.

MUNICIPAL ART GALLERY
Belém, Pará
Paintings, drawings by Brazilian artists.
Tu.-F. 8-11.30, 1.30-5; Su. 8-12, 2-6.

BELO HORIZONTE

ANTHROPOLOGICAL MUSEUM OF THE FACULTY OF PHILOSOPHY
Rua Carangola, Belo Horizonte, Minas Gerais
Anthropology. Ethnography.
By appointment.

ABILIO BARRETO HISTORICAL MUSEUM
Rua Bernardo Mascarenhas, Belo Horizonte, Minas Gerais
History of Belo Horizonte.
M.-Su. 12-5.

LEOPOLDO CATHOND TEACHING COLLECTIONS
Colégio Santo Antônio, Rua Pernambuco 880, Belo Horizonte
Minas Gerais
Local history, ethnography, natural history.
By appointment.

HISTORICAL MUSEUM OF BELO HORIZONTE
Cidade Jardim, Belo Horizonte, Minas Gerais
History of Belo Horizonte and its region.
Tu.-F. 1-5; Sa., Su. 11-5.

MUSEUM OF ART
Lago da Pampulha, Belo Horizonte, Minas Gerais
Painting, sculpture by Brazilian and European artists.
M.-Sa. 12-6; Su. 2-6.

MUSEUM OF COLONIAL ART
Escuela de Arquitetura de Minas Gerais, Belo Horizonte, Minas Gerais
Brazilian art of the colonial period.
By appointment.

MUSEUM OF THE FACULTY OF MEDICINE
Av. Mantiqueira, Belo Horizonte, Minas Gerais
Collections illustrating history of medicine. Anatomical and physiological collections.
By appointment.

MUSEUM OF THE 5th BATALLION OF CACADORES
Av. Amazonas, Bairro Gameleira, Belo Horizonte
Minas Gerais
Collections illustrating history of the Batallion.
Daily 10-12, 2-5.

MUSEUM OF THE PUBLIC ARCHIVES
Av. João Pinheiro 372, Belo Horizonte, Minas Gerais
Collections illustrating history of Minas Gerais.
Tu.-F. 10-5.

POLICE MUSEUM OF CRIMINOLOGY
Dep. Inst. da Polícia Militar, Belo Horizonte, Minas Gerais
Collections illustrating techniques used by criminals.
On request.

RACIOPPI MUSEUM OF ART AND HISTORY
Rua Padre Eustáquio 1442, Belo Horizonte, Minas Gerais
Religious art. Paintings by Estēves, Murta, Neves.
By appointment.

BERTIOGA

JOÃO RAMALHO MUSEUM
Forte de São João, Bertioga, São Paulo
Local history, ethnography. Religious art.
M.-Sa. 10-12, 2-5; Su. 8-11.

BLUMENAU

FRITZ MUELLER MUSEUM
Rua Minas Gerais, Blumenau, Santa Catarina
Historical collections. The museum is named after the German physicist and naturalist and supporter of Darwin, who was professor of mathematics at the Jesuit College and did much of his research on bio-genetics at Blumenau (1821-97).
M.-Sa. 8-12, 2-5.

MUSEUM OF A COLONIAL FAMILY
Alamêda Duque de Caxias, Blumenau, Santa Catarina
Furniture, household equipment, books, illustrating life of a local family in the Colonial period.
M.-Sa. 8-11.45, 1.30-5.30.

BOITUVA

HISTORICAL MUSEUM
Rua Expedicionário Boituvense 41, Boituva, São Paulo
Prehistoric and Indian material. Ethnography. Handicrafts. Numismatics. Postage stamps.
M.-F. 12-6.

BOTUCATU

FATHER VINCENTE PIRES DA MOTA HISTORICAL MUSEUM
Rua João Passos 251, Botucatu, São Paulo
Minerals. Military history. Domestic equipment. Brazilian and foreign coins.
Tu.-F. 1-5.

BRODÓSQUI

PORTINARI HOUSE-MUSEUM
Praça Cândido Portinari, Brodósqui, São Paulo
Former home of the painter, Cândido Portinari. Collections of his works, equipment and personal possessions.
Daily 8-12, 1-5.

BRUSQUE

ARCHDIOCESAN MUSEUM
Praça de Azambuja, Brusque, Santa Catarina
Religious art. Local history and traditions.
Daily 8-5.

CAÇAPAVA

MUSEUM OF THE IPIRANGHA BATALLION OF THE 1/6th REGIMENT
Rua José Bonifacio 33, Caçapava, São Paulo
Trophies. Weapons. Medals. Flags.
M.-F. 8-11, 2-4; Sa., Su., public holidays by appointment.

CACHOEIRA

NOBRE HOUSE MUSEUM
Praça da Aclamação, Cachoeira, Bahia
Collections illustrating life and work of the writer, Nobre, in his former home.
Daily 8-12, 1-5.

PARISH MUSEUM
Igreja Matruz de N.S. do Rosario, Cachoeira, Bahia
Religious art, especially gold vessels and 17th-18th century images.
Tu.-Su. 9-12, 2-5; closed public holidays.

CAETÉS

REGIONAL MUSEUM
Caetés, Minas Gerais
Regional history, ethnography.
M.-F. 10-12, 2-6; Sa., Su. 2-6.

CAMPANHA

DOM INOCÊNCIO MUSEUM
Rua João Luis Alves 76, Campanha, Minas Gerais
Mineralogy. Medals. Manuscripts.
Daily 8-10, 12.30-4.

CAMPINAS

ARCHDIOCESAN MUSEUM
Rua Aquidabâ 734, Campinas, São Paulo
Religious art. History of the Church in Brazil.
Sa., Su. 1-5.

CARLOS GOMES MUSEUM
Rua Bernardino de Campos 989, Campinas, São Paulo
Collections illustrating life and work of the musicians, Carlos and Sant'Anna Gomes.
M.-Sa. 2-6.

HISTORICAL AND ANTHROPOLOGICAL MUSEUM OF THE CATHOLIC UNIVERSITY
Rua Marechal Deodoro, Campinas, São Paulo
Teaching collections of Brazilian history and anthropology.
By appointment.

MUNICIPAL MUSEUM
Bosque dos Jequitibás, Campinas, São Paulo
Mineralogy. Fossils. Zoology. Anthropology.
Tu., Th., Su., public holidays 8-5.

MUSEUM OF CONTEMPORARY ART
Avenida Saudade 1004, Campinas, São Paulo
Paintings, sculpture, photographs, jewellery by contemporary Brazilian artists.
M.-F. 12-6.

RAILWAY MUSEUM
Rua Sales de Oliveira 1380, Campinas, São Paulo
Collections illustrating Brazilian railway history, especially of the Mogina Railway Company.
Daily 9-11, 1-5.

CAMPO GRANDE

DOM BOSCO REGIONAL MUSEUM
Avenida President Kennedy, Campo Grande, Mato Grosso
Ethnographical and entomological collections.
Daily 8-11, 2-5.

CAMPOS

MUSEUM OF DOCTOR BARBOZA GUERRA
Campos, Rio de Janeiro
Historical collections.
By appointment.

MUSEUM OF DOCTOR IZIMBARDO PEIXOTO
Praça São Salvador, Campos, Rio de Janeiro
General collections.
By appointment.

CAMPOS DO JORDÃO

GOVERNOR'S PALACE MUSEUM
Palacio Boa Vista, Alto da Jordão, Campos do Jordão, São Paulo
Furniture. Porcelain. Brazilian and foreign paintings. Persian carpets. Religious art.
W., Sa., Su., public holidays 10-12, 2-5.

CAPIVARI

CESARIO MOTA HISTORICAL MUSEUM
Praça José Zuza, Capivari, São Paulo
Documents, paintings and other material relating to the history of Capivari.
Tu.-F. 9-11, 12-6; Sa. 8-12.

CARPINA

MUSEUM OF THE HISTORICAL INSTITUTE
Praça Carlos Pena 94, Carpina, Pernambuco
Religious art. Coins. Weapons. Handicrafts.
Tu.-Su. 8-12, 2-6.

CARUARU

MUSEUM OF POPULAR ART
Caruaru, Pernambuco
Regional folk art, handicrafts.
Tu.-Su. 12-5.

VITALINO HOUSE MUSEUM
Caruaru, Pernambuco
In former home of the writer, Vitalino. Collections illustrating his life and work.
On request.

CATAGUESES

MUSEUM OF FINE ART
Chácara da Granjaria, Catagueses, Minas Gerais
Brazilian paintings, sculpture.
M.-Sa. 7-12, 1-6; Su. 1-6.

CATANDUVA

GOVERNOR PEDRO DE TOLEDO HISTORICAL MUSEUM
Rua Alagoas 32, Catanduva, São Paulo
Local history. Indian material. Military relics. Religious art.
Tu.-F. 1-5; Sa., Su., public holidays 8-11.

CAXIAS DO SUL

MUSEUM OF POPULAR TRADITIONS
Estrada Federal Getúlio Vargas, Caxias do Sul, Rio Grande do Sul
Regional geology. Agricultural implements. Craftsmen's tools, equipment. Costumes. Indian pottery.
Daily 1-5.30.

CÊRRO

OTTONI HOUSE
Cêrro, Minas Gerais
Collection illustrating life and work of the Ottoni family.
On request.

CORUMBÁ

REGIONAL MUSEUM
Rua Delamare 939, Corumbá, Mato Grosso
Regional history, natural history.
Daily 9-5.

CORUPÁ

SEMINARY MUSEUM
Corupá, Santa Catarina
Mounted animals. Local history.
Daily 9-11, 1-5.

CRATO

ITAYTERA MUSEUM
Rua Amaripe, Crato, Ceará
Local history.
M.-F. 10-12, 2-5; Sa., Su. 8-11.

CUIABÁ

RAMIS BUCAIR MUSEUM
Rua Coronel Pedro Celestino 213, Cuiabá, Mato Grosso
Archaeological collections.
M.-F. 8-12, 2-5.

MUSEUM OF HISTORY, GEOGRAPHY AND ETHNOLOGY
Av. Fernando Costa, Cuiabá, Mato Grosso
Regional collections of history, geography and ethnography.
M.-F. 9-12, 2-5.

CURITIBA

ALFREDO ANDERSEN MUSEUM
Rua Mateus Leme 336, Curitiba, Paraná
Paintings, including works by the Norwegian artist, Alfredo Andersen, who settled in Curitiba and died there in 1935.
M.-F. 8-6.30.

DAVID CARNEIRO MUSEUM
Rua Brigadeiro Franco, Curitiba, Paraná
Coins. Weapons. Historical paintings. Engravings. Miniatures. Silver. Furniture.
By appointment.

MUSEUM OF MAN
Rua General Carneiro 460, Curitiba, Paraná
Palaeontology. Prehistoric archaeology. Indian ethnography. Folk art. Handicrafts.
M., F. 9-5.

PARANÁ MUSEUM
Praça Generoso Marques, Curitiba, Paraná
Archaeology. Ethnography. History.
M.-F. 8.30-6; Sa., Su., public holidays 12-5.

DIAMANTINA

DIAMOND MUSEUM
Rua Direita 14, Diamantina, Minas Gerais
Collections of deposits, formations and specimens of diamonds occuring in Brazil. Objects of historical or artistic value connected with the mining industry.
Tu.-Su. 8-11, 12-6.

FEIRA DE SANTANA

REGIONAL MUSEUM
Rua Gemini and Costa, Feira de Santana, Bahia
Paintings by contemporary Brazilian and English artists.
Tu., F.-Su. 2-6; M. 10-12, 2-6.

FLORIANÓPOLIS

FOLKLORE MUSEUM
Rua Tenente Silveira 69, Florianópolis, Santa Catarina
Popular art, handicrafts.
M.-F. 2-6.

INDIAN MUSEUM
Rua Pedro Soares 20, Florianópolis, Santa Catarina
Regional history, zoology, archaeology.
M.-F. 1-5.30.

MAJOR LARA RIBAS MUSEUM
Polícia Militar do Estado, Praça Getulio Vargas, Florianópolis, Santa Catarina
Portuguese military history. Weapons. Equipment.
M.-F. 8-11.30, 2-6.

VITOR MEIRLES HOUSE MUSEUM
Rua Saldanha Marinho 3, Florianópolis, Santa Catarina
Paintings, drawings, watercolours by Meirles, in the house where he was born.
Daily 2-6.

MUSEUM OF THE HISTORICAL AND GEOGRAPHICAL INSTITUTE
Florianópolis, Santa Catarina
Regional collections of history and geography.
M.-F. 10-5.

MUSEUM OF MODERN ART
Av. Rio Branco 160, Florianópolis, Santa Catarina
20th century paintings by Brazilian and foreign artists.
M.-F. 9-9; Sa. 1-6.

MUSEUM OF THE SANTA CATARINA HIGH SCHOOL
Florianópolis, Santa Catarina
History. Archaeology. Natural history.
On request.

POLICE DEPARTMENT MUSEUM
Florianópolis, Santa Catarina
Collections illustrating types of crime and techniques used by criminals.
By appointment.

SAMBAGUI MUSEUM OF MAN
Rua Estéves Júnior 159, Florianópolis, Santa Catarina
Geology, mineralogy, zoology of Brazil. Archaeology. Indian artifacts. Ethnography.
Daily 2-6.

FORTALEZA

GUSTAVO BAIROSO MUSEUM
Colégio Militar, Praça da Bandeira, Fortaleza, Ceará
History of the Military College and of its leading personalities.
M., W., F. 8-11.

DIAS DA ROCHA MUSEUM
214 Rua Tristão Gonçalves, Fortaleza, Ceará
Geology. Palaeontology. Botany. Zoology. Archaeology. Ethnography of Ceará. Plates manufactured by the Royal Plate Factory of Lisbon (18th century).
M.-Sa. 1-5.

ARTUR RAMOS MUSEUM
Rua Barão do Rio Branco 1321, Fortaleza, Ceará
Collections made by Prof. Ramos. Ethnography. Folk art. Religious art. Prehistory. Archaeology.
M.-Sa. 1-5.

UNIVERSITY MUSEUM OF ANTHROPOLOGY
Fortaleza, Ceará
Anthropology of S. America, especially Brazil.
By appointment.

UNIVERSITY MUSEUM OF ART
Reitoria da Universidade do Ceará, Fortaleza, Ceará
European and Brazilian paintings, sculpture.
By appointment.

FRANCA

HISTORICAL MUSEUM
Praça Cel. Francisco Martins, Franca, São Paulo
Mineralogy. Ethnography. Religious art. Horse-drawn vehicles. Numismatics. Postage stamps.
M.-F.9-11, 2-6; Sa. 6-9; Su. 9-12.

GOIÂNIA

MUSEUM OF MODERN ART
Av. Anhangüera, Goiânia, Goiás
19th-20th century paintings by Brazilian artists.
M.-Sa. 2-6.

MUSEUM OF ORNITHOLOGY
Av. Para, Goiânia, Goiás
Complete collection of the birds of Goiás, with some examples from the rest of Brazil.
Daily 8-9.

PROFESSOR ZOROASTRO ARTIAZA MUSEUM
Praça Cívica, Goiânia, Goiás
Geology. Mineralogy. Botany. Zoology. Anthropology. Ethnography. Archaeology. Furniture. Costumes. Paintings. Sculpture.
Tu.-Su. 8-5. Closed public holidays.

GOIANA

RELIGIOUS ART MUSEUM
Igreja de Nossa Senhora de Amparo, Goianâ, Pernambuco
Paintings. Ornaments. Images. Liturgical items.
Daily 9-5.

GOIÁS

MUSEUM OF THE BANDEIRAS
Praça Dr. Brasil, Goiás
18th-19th century religious art. Scales and weights for weighing gold. Indian bows and arrows, pottery.
Tu.-F. 1-4; Sa., Su. 9-11.

GUAIRA

MUSEUM OF NATURAL HISTORY
Av. Joaquim Dorneeles Vargas 479, Guaira, Paraná
Mineralogy. Zoology. Botany. Archaeology. Ethnography. Numismatics.
M.-Sa. 2-5.

GUARAPUAVA

VISCONDE DE GUARAPUAVA MUNICIPAL MUSEUM
Rua Visconde de Guarapuava 288, Guarapuava, Paraná
Indian material. Paintings.
M.-F. 8-12, 1-5.

IGARAÇU

COLLECTIONS OF THE HISTORICAL INSTITUTE
Rua Dr. Barbosa Lima, Igaraçu, Pernambuco
History of Brazil.
By appointment.

MUSEUM OF RELIGIOUS ART
Convento de São Francisco, Igaraçu, Pernambuco
Paintings. Sculpture. Liturgical items.
Daily 10-5.

IJUÍ

MUSEUM OF ANTHROPOLOGY
Rua São Francisco 509, Ijuí, Rio Grande do Sul
Palaeontology, anthropology, and ethnography of Brazil.
M.-F. 8.30-11.30, 2.30-5.30.

ILHÉUS

MUSEUM OF THE CHURCH OF ST. GEORGE
Ilhéus, Bahia
17th-18th century religious art.
Daily 9-11, 2-5.

ITABAIANA

LOCAL MUSEUM
Rua Padre Felesmino 546, Itabaiana, Sergipé
Weapons. Religious art. Furniture. Household equipment. Saddles and harness.
Su., public holidays 8-12, 3-6.

ITABIRITO

MUSEUM OF THE IRON AND STEEL INDUSTRY
Itabirito, Minas Gerais
History and technology of the iron and steel industry in Brazil.
M.-F. 8-12, 2-5.

ITAPECERICA DA SERRA

MESTRE TONICO HISTORICAL MUSEUM
Rua Luis Gama 31, Itapecerica da Serra, São Paulo
Local history.
Th., Sa., Su., public holidays 9-12, 2-5.

ITAPETININGA

HISTORICAL MUSEUM
Rua Silva Jardim 675, Itapetininga, São Paulo
Local history.
M.-F. 12-5.

ITAPORANGA D'AJUDA

MUSEUM OF ART AND POPULAR TRADITIONS
Rua Prefeito Manuel Sobral, Itaporanga D'Ajuda, Sergipé
Brazilian paintings. Folk art.
By appointment.

ITATAIA

REGIONAL MUSEUM OF ITATAIA NATIONAL PARK
Itataia, Rio de Janeiro
Local flora, wildlife.
Daily 8-4.30.

ITU

MUSEUM OF THE REPUBLICAN CONVENTION
Rua Barão do Itaim 69, Itu, São Paulo
18th-19th century paintings. Furniture. Bronzes.
Tu.-Th. 9-11, 12-6; F.-Su. 1-6.

JAGUARÃO

ALFRÊDO VARELA MUSEUM, Avenida 20 de setembro 348, Jaguarão, Rio Grande do Sul
18th-19th century religious art. Porcelain. Coins. Paintings. Weapons. Uniforms.
M., Tu., Th.-Su. 2-6.

JOÃO PESSOA

DR. LEON CLEROT'S NATURAL HISTORY MUSEUM
João Pessoa, Paraíba
Natural history. Paintings.
By appointment.

EDUCATIONAL MUSEUM
Praça São Francisco, João Pessoa, Paraíba
Collections available for teaching purposes. Natural history. Local history. Geography. Anthropology. Ethnography. Religious art. Fishing.
Tu.-Su. 8-11, 2-5.

JOINVILLE

NATIONAL MUSEUM OF IMMIGRATION AND COLONISATION
Rua Rio Branco 229, Joinville, Santa Catarina
Paintings. Furniture. Weapons. Uniforms. Horse-drawn vehicles.
Tu.-Su. 8-12, 1.30-5.30.

SAMBAQUI MUSEUM
Rua Rio Branco 229, Joinville, Santa Catarina
Regional prehistory and ethnography. Skeletons. Stone axes. Bows and arrows. Arrowheads. Pestles and mortars.
Tu.-Su. 8-12, 1.30-5.30.

JUAZEIRO DO NORTE

FATHER CÍCERO MUSEUM
Rua São José 224, Juazeiro do Norte, Ceará
Ethnography, folk art, natural history of the Amazon.
Daily 8-11, 2-5.

VILAS BOAS PORTUGAL MUSEUM
512 Avenida Dr. Floro, Juazeiro do Norte, Ceará
General collections.
M.-F. 8-12, 2-5.

JUIZ DE FORA

MARIANO PROCÓPIO MUSEUM
Juiz de Fora, Minas Gerais
Paintings by Pedro Américo, Vitor Meirelles, Antonio Parreiras. Sculpture by Bernardelli and others. Medals. Engravings. Furniture. Ceramics.
Tu.-Su. 1-5.

MUSEUM OF THE ROYAL BANK OF MINAS GERAIS
Rua Halfeld 50H, Juiz de Fora, Minas Gerais
Safes, scales, telephones, ledgers and other equipment used by the Bank since its foundation. Brazilian and foreign coins, seals.
M.-F. 1-4.30.

LAGUNA

ANITA GARIBALDI MUSEUM
Praça da Bandeira, Laguna, Santa Catarina
Documents, furniture and personal effects of the Brazilian wife of the man who unified Italy.
Tu.-Sa. 10-5.

PIUS X PAROCHIAL MUSEUM
Sede Distrital de Pexaria Brava, Laguna, Santa Catarina
Religious art.
M.-F. 9-5; Sa., Su. 12-5.

LAJES

TIAGO DE CASTRO HISTORICAL MUSEUM
Rua Hercilio Luz, Lajes, Santa Catarina
Local history.
M.-F. 12-5; Sa., Su. 10-5.

LAPA

CARMELITE CONVENT MUSEUM
Largo da Lapa, Lapa, Rio de Janeiro
Ecclesiastical art and history.
On request.

FEDERALIST REVOLUTION (GENERAL CARNEIRO) MUSEUM
Avenida Doctor David Carneiro, Lapa, Paraná
Historical collections.
By appointment.

LARANJEIRAS

HORÁCIO HERA MUSEUM
Rua Coronel Freitas 19, Laranjeiras, Sergipé
Local history. Paintings. Ethnography.
Daily 9-12, 2-5, 7-9.

LAVRAS

HISTORICAL MUSEUM
Escola Superior de Agricultura, Lavras, Minas Gerais
Instruments of torture. Handicrafts. Lamps.
M.-Sa. outside college hours.

LENÇÓIS

AFRÂNIO PEIXOTO HOUSE OF CULTURE
Praça Afrânio Peixoto, Lençóis, Bahia
In former home of the writer, A. Peixoto, with his personal possessions and collections illustrating his life and work.
Daily 9-12, 2-6.

LIMOEIRO

SEVERINO ARAGÃO RURAL MUSEUM
Rua Vigário Pinto 420, Limoeiro, Pernambuco
Collections illustrating rural life and occupations. Weapons. Domestic equipment.
By appointment.

MACAPÁ

AMAPÁ TERRITORIAL MUSEUM
Fortaleza de S. José de Macapá, Macapá, Territorio do Amapá
Zoology. Archaeology. Ethnography. Numismatics. Costumes. Paintings. Engravings.
Daily 7-5.

JOAQUIM CAETANO DA SILVA MUSEUM
Macapá, Territorio Federal do Amapá
Brazilian trees and their products. Medicinal plants. Oilseeds. Minerals. Handicrafts. Industrial products. Indian material. Regional ceramics. Numismatics.
M.-F. 7-5.

MACEIÓ

COMMERCIAL AND ARCHAEOLOGICAL MUSEUM OF THE COMMERCIAL EMPLOYEES' SYNDICATE
418 Rua João Pessoa, Maceió, Alagôas
General collections, particularly Negro art.
M.-F. 8-5.

DOM RANULFO MUSEUM OF RELIGIOUS ART
Igreja do Rosario, João Pessoa 270, Maceió, Alagoas
Images. Paintings. Jewellery. Liturgical items.
W.-Su. 3-6.

MUSEUM OF THE ALAGOAS HISTORICAL INSTITUTE
382 Rua João Pessoa, Maceió, Alagoas
History of the region.
Tu.-Sa. 9-12, 2-5.

MANAUS

AMAZONAS CHAMBER OF COMMERCE MUSEUM
Rua Guilhermo Moreira 281, Manaus, Amazonas
Collections showing the exportable products of the region. Raw materials.
By appointment.

ART GALLERY
Altos de Biblioteca Pública, Manaus, Amazonas
Paintings by Brazilian artists.
M.-Sa. 9-6.

MUSEUM OF THE HISTORICAL AND GEOGRAPHICAL INSTITUTE OF AMAZONAS
Rua Bernardo Ramos 131, Manaus, Amazonas
Regional geography and history.
M.-F. 10-12, 2-5.

MUSEUM OF INDIAN CULTURE
Rua Duque de Caxias, Manaus, Amazonas
Exhibits of Indian culture in Amazonas. Ceramics. Sculpture.
M.-Sa. 8-11, 2-5; Su. 8-11.

MUSEUM OF NUMISMATICS
Palacio Rio Branco, Av. D. Pedro II, Manaus, Amazonas
World collection of coins, including Roman and Byzantine examples.
M.-F. 8-12.

MARIANA

ARCHDIOCESAN MUSEUM
Rua Frei Durão 49, Mariana, Minas Gerais
18th century Brazilian and European paintings. Furniture. Vestments. Liturgical items.
Su.-M. 9-11, 12-5.

MESSEJANA

ALENCAR MUSEUM
Messejana, Ceará
Collections illustrating life and work of the Brazilian Romantic novelist, José de Alencar (1817-77), born in Messejana.
M.-Sa. 9-12, 2-5.

MIRACATU

PEDRO LARAGNOIT MUSEUM
Rua Dr. João Mendes 5, Miracatu, São Paulo
Laragnoit family possessions, including furniture, paintings.
By appointment.

MIRASSOL

MUNICIPAL MUSEUM
Rua Campos Sales, Mirassol, São Paulo
Mineralogy. Fossils. Zoology. Silkworm breeding. Paintings. Drawings. Local history.
Tu.-Sa. 2-5, 7.30-9.30; Su., public holidays 7.30-9.30.

MOGI-MISIM

DR. JOÃO TEODORO XAVIER HISTORICAL MUSEUM
Rua Dr. José Alves, Paço Municipal, Mogi-Misim, São Paulo
Coins. Seals. Musical instruments. Indian material.
Tu.-F. 12-5.

MOSSORÓ

MUNICIPAL MUSEUM
Rua Almiro Afonso, Mossoró, Rio Grande do Norte
Local history.
Tu.-Sa. 8-12, 2-5.

MURITIBA

MUSEUM OF THE CASTRO ALVES HISTORICAL PARK
Muritiba, Bahia
Collections illustrating life and work of the poet, Castro Alves, in reconstruction of his former home.
Daily 2-5.

NATAL

MUSEUM OF ART AND HISTORY
Rua de Conceição 601, Natal, Rio Grande do Norte
Furniture. Household equipment. Photographs. Paintings. Religious art. Folk art. Weapons.
Tu.-Su. 1-6.

MUSEUM OF THE CAMARA CASCUDO INSTITUTE OF ANTHROPOLOGY
Av. Hermes da Fonseca 1398, Natal, Rio Grande do Norte
Geology. Palaeontology. Speleology. Displays illustrating history of mining and industry in the region. Handicrafts.
Daily 8-11, 2-5.

MUSEUM OF THE HISTORICAL AND GEOGRAPHICAL INSTITUTE
Rua da Conceição 628, Natal, Rio Grande do Norte
Material illustrating history of the Rio Grande do Norte. Folk art.
M.-F. 8-11, 1-6.

MUSEUM OF THE INSTITUTE OF MARINE BIOLOGY
Praia de Mãe Luisa, Natal, Rio Grande do Norte
Collections illustrating marine biology of Brazil.
Daily 8-11, 2-5.

MUSEUM OF THE PÃMPONO SPORTING CLUB
Praça dos Heróis, Natal, Rio Grande do Sul
Animals of the region.
Sa. 2-5; Su. 10-5.

MUSEUM OF POPULAR ART
Fortaleza dos Reis Magos, Rua Trairi 558, Natal, Rio Grande do Norte
Furniture. Sculpture. Handicrafts. Harness. Costumes. Toys.
Daily 1.30-5.30.

NITERÓI

CRIME MUSEUM
Rua Coronel Gomes Machado, Niterói, Rio de Janeiro
Weapons used by criminals. Types of crime. Techniques of criminals.
By appointment.

MUSEUM OF PUBLIC HEALTH
Rua Coronel Gomes Machado 226, Niterói, Rio de Janeiro
Collections illustrating aims and techniques of public health.
M.-F. 12-6.

MUSEUM OF RELIGIOUS ART
Catedral de São João Batista, Praça Pedro II, Niterói, Rio de Janeiro
Religious art. Liturgical items.
Daily 10-5.

ANTÓNIO PARREIRAS MUSEUM
47 Rua Tiradentes, Niterói, Rio de Janeiro
Works of António Parreiras, housed in his former house. 17th century French, Dutch, Flemish, Italian paintings. 19th century Brazilian paintings.
M.-Sa. 12-5.

NOVA ERA

MUNICIPAL MUSEUM
Praça da Matruz, Nova Era, Minas Gerais
Collections illustrating history and function of art.
Tu.-Su. 12-5. Closed public holidays.

OLINDA

OLINDA REGIONAL MUSEUM
Rua do Amparo 128, Olinda, Pernambuco
Historical exhibits. Regional art. Furniture. Religious images. Antiques.
Tu.-Su. 8-12, 2-6.

PERNAMBUCO MUSEUM OF CONTEMPORARY ART
Rua 13 de Maio, Olinda, Pernambuco
Paintings, drawings, engravings by contemporary Brazilian and foreign artists.
Tu.-Su. 8-12, 2-6.

OLIVEIRA

DIOCESAN HISTORICAL MUSEUM
Praça Manvelita Chagas 40, Oliveira, Minas Gerais
History of the diocese.
Daily 10-5.

ORLEANS

MUSEUM OF IMMIGRATION
Rua Rio Belo, Instituto São José, Orleans, Santa Catarina
Collections of art, handicrafts, books and other material, showing contribution made by immigrants to the national culture.
By appointment.

OURO PRÊTO

MUSEUM OF THE HISTORY OF DEMOCRATIC IDEALS AND CULTURE IN MINAS GERAIS
Ouro Prêto, Minas Gerais
Building dates from 1784. Objects of various kinds relating to the historic events of the *Inconfidencia Mineira* and to those who took part in them. Sepulchres where the bones of the conspirators are laid. Furniture. Pictures. Religious statuary. Implements. Regional works of art.
Tu.-Su. 11-5.

MUSEUM OF PHARMACY
Escola de Farmácia, Ouro Prêto, Minas Gerais
Collections illustrating history of pharmacy, especially in Brazil.
M.-F. 10-5.

PALMEIRA DOS ÍNDIOS

GRACILIANO RAMOS HOUSE MUSEUM
Palmeira dos Índios, Alagoas
In former home of the writer, G. Ramos. Collections illustrating his life and work.
On request.

PARAIBUNA

PARAIBUNA MUSEUM OF ROAD TRANSPORT
Paraibuna, Rio de Janeiro
History of horse-drawn transport in the region. Carriages. Diligences. Road-maps. Models.
M.-F. 9-5; Sa., Su. 2-5.

PARANAGUA

MUSEUM OF ARCHAEOLOGY AND POPULAR ART
Rua Quinze de Novembro 567, Paranagua, Paraná
Prehistoric archaeology. Folk-art. Handicrafts.
Daily 12-6.

PELOTAS

LOCAL MUSEUM
Praça Coronel Pedro Osório 103, Pelotas, Rio Grande do Sul
Mineralogy. Palaeontology. Botany. Zoology. Archaeology. Ethnography. Local history. Coins.
M.-F. 9-11.30, 2-5.

PENEDO

MUSEUM OF FOLK ART AND FOLK CULTURE
Praça Marechal Floriano Peixoto 237, Penedo, Alagoas
Ethnography, folk art, furniture and handicrafts of the region.
M.-F. 10-12, 2-5; Sa., Su. 10-5.

PETRÓPOLIS

SANTOS DUMONT'S HOUSE
Rua do Encanto 22, Petrópolis, Rio de Janeiro
Housed in former residence of the Brazilian pioneer airman. Material illustrating the history of aviation.
Tu.-Sa. 9-5; Su. 11-5.

IMPERIAL MUSEUM
Avenida 7 de Setembro 94 and 220, Petrópolis, Rio de Janeiro
Exhibits of Brazilian Empire and Petrópolis history, 1808-89, notably imperial regalia, jewels and apparel. Library on the history of Brazil.
Daily ex. M. 12-5.

PINDAMONHANGABA

LEOPOLDINA HISTORICAL MUSEUM
Rua Marechal Deodoro 260, Pindamonhangaba, São Paulo
Regional history.
Daily 1-5.

LOCAL MUSEUM
Casa de Cultura, Pindamonhangaba, São Paulo
In 19th century palace. Paintings. Furniture. Decorative arts.
Daily 9-12, 2-5.

PIRACICABA

MUSEUM OF THE AGRICULTURAL HIGH SCHOOL
Piracicaba, São Paulo
Zoology of Brazil. Anatomy of farm animals.
Daily 8-11, 1-5.

PRUDENTE DE MORAES HISTORICAL MUSEUM
Rua Santo Antônia 641, Piracicaba, São Paulo
Collections relating to President Prudente de Moraes and his family and contempories. Palaeontology. Archaeology. Numismatics.
Tu.-F. 1-5; Su. 9-12.

PIRAPÓRA

MUSEUM OF THE PREMONSTRATENSIAN SEMINARY
Pirapóra, São Paulo
Religious art, including terracotta statues of the colonial period.
Su. 10-12, 1-4.

PIRASSUNUNGA

FERNANDO COSTA HISTORICAL MUSEUM
Institúto de Educação, Pirassununga, São Paulo
Local history.
By appointment

PIRATINI

FARROUPILHA HISTORICAL MUSEUM
Rua Coronel Manuel Pedroso 77, Piratini, Rio Grande do Sul
Local history. Weapons. Paintings. Urn used to receive votes cast at the election of Bento Gonçalves.
M.-F. 8-11, 1-5.

PÔRTO ALEGRE

GENERAL OSÓRIO ARMOURY MUSEUM
130 Rua Nossa Senhora da Aparecida, Pôrto Alegre, Rio Grande do Sul
Arms and military equipment.
By appointment.

JULIO DE CASTILHOS STATE HISTORICAL MUSEUM
Rua Duque de Caxias 1931, Pôrto Alegre, Rio Grande do Sul
Exhibits of national history, including the 1835 Revolutionary period, the Paraguayan War, and collection of Indian pieces. Armoury. Furniture. Zoology. Palaeontology. Mineralogy. Natural history. Historical documents, maps. Jesuit art.
M.-F. 2-5.

MUSEUM OF THE POLICE ACADEMY
Pôrto Alegre, Rio Grande do Sul
Collections illustrating types of crime and methods used by criminals.
By appointment.

MUSEUM OF THE PÔRTO ALEGRE INSTITUTE OF GEOGRAPHY AND HISTORY
Av. Sete de Setembro 94, Pôrto Alegre, Rio Grande do Sul
Regional geography, history, ethnography. Indian art. Coins. Weapons.
Daily 2-5.

MUSEUM OF RELIGIOUS ART
Catedral Metropolitani, Pôrto Alegre, Rio Grande do Sul
Paintings. Sculpture. Images. Liturgical items.
Daily 9-5.

NATURAL HISTORY MUSEUM
Av. Nilo Peçanha 1521, Pôrto Alegre, Rio Grande do Sul
Natural history of the Rio Grande do Sul. Fossils. Shells. Geology. Birds. Insects.
M.-F. 2-5.30; Sa., Su. 3-6.

RIO GRANDE MUSEUM OF THE NATURAL SCIENCES
Av. Mauá 1855, Pôrto Alegre, Rio Grande do Sul
Mineraiogy. Palaeontology. Zoology. Botany.
M.-F. 1.30-6.

RIO GRANDE DO SUL MUSEUM OF ART
Praça Mal. Deodoro, Pôrto Alegre, Rio Grande do Sul
Paintings, drawings, sculpture by Brazilian and foreign artists.
*M.-F. 1-6; Sa., Su., when the Teatro S*ao Pedro is open.*

STATE ART GALLERIES
Pôrto Alegre, Rio Grande do Sul
Portraits, including some by the Santa Catarina artist, Vitor Meirelles (1831-1902).
M.-F. 1-6.

VARIG MUSEUM
Rua Dezoito de Novembro, Esquina de Augusto Severo, Pôrto Alegre, Rio Grande do Sul
History of the Brazilian airline, Varig, since its establishment in 1927.
Th. 8-10; F., Su. 9-11.

PEDRO ZATTI MUSEUM
Pôrto Alegre, Rio Grande do Sul
Weapons. Hunting trophies.
By appointment.

PÔRTO FELIZ

HISTORICAL MUSEUM
Praça Cel, Esmedio 31, Pôrto Feliz, São Paulo
Local history. Portraits of local notabilities. Coins. Folklore.
Tu.-Th. 1-5; Sa., Su., public holidays 8-10, 12-5.

PÔRTO UNIÃO

MUNICIPAL MUSEUM
Rua Prudente de Morais 117, Pôrto União, Santa Catarina
Local history.
Sa. 2-6; Su. 9-12, 2-6. Other days by appointment.

PÔRTO VELHO

HISTORICAL MUSEUM OF THE MADEIRA-MAMORÉ RAILWAY
Pôrto Velho, Territorio de Rondônia
In former railway station. Collections illustrating history of the railway.
Tu.-F. 1-5; Sa., Su. 10-5.

RONDON MUSEUM
Av. Presidente Dutra, Pôrto Velho, Territorio de Rondônia
Minerals. Forestry. Regional history. Indian material.
Tu.-F. 9-12, 2-5; Sa., Su. 2-5.

RECIFE

MUSEUM OF THE ABOLITION
Rua do Benfica, Madalena, Recife, Pernambuco
18th-19th century Brazilian history.
By appointment.

MUSEUM OF ANTHROPOLOGY
Instituto Joaquim Nabuco de Pesquisas Sociais, Av. 17 de Agosto 2, Recife, Pernambuco
Material from demolished buildings in the region. Folk art, especially ceramics, ex-votos. Furniture. Clothing. Craftsmen's equipment. Agricultural implements.
M.-F. 12-6.30.

MUSEUM OF ARCHAEOLOGY
Cidade Universitária, Engenlio do Mero, Recife, Pernambuco
Archaeology of Brazil.
By appointment.

MUSEUM OF NATURAL SCIENCES OF THE FEDERAL RURAL UNIVERSITY OF PERNAMBUCO
Dois Irmãos, Recife, Pernambuco
Birds, animals, insects, reptiles of Brazil, mainly from the Amazon and Central Brazil. Mineralogy of the whole of Brazil.
M.-F. 7-1.

MUSEUM OF THE PERNAMBUCO INSTITUTE OF ARCHAEOLOGY, HISTORY AND GEOGRAPHY
Rua do Hospicio 130, Recife, Pernambuco
Historical objects. Manuscripts. Maps. Paintings. Material connected with the history and art of Pernambuco.
M.-Sa. 10-12, 2-5.

MUSEUM OF POPULAR ART
Hôrto Dois Irmãos, Recife, Pernambuco
Pottery, paintings, ex-votos from N. E. Brazil.
Tu.-Su. 10-5.

MUSEUM OF RELIGIOUS ART OF THE MATRIZ DA CONCEIÇÃO DOS MILITARES
Rua Nova, Recife, Pernambuco
Furniture. Images. Ornaments. Early books.
Daily 8-11, 2.30-5.

STATE MUSEUM
Avenida Rui Barbosa 960, Recife, Pernambuco
Local history. Paintings by the 19th century landscape painter, Teles Junior. Furniture, porcelain and ceramics of local and foreign origin. Religious sculpture of the colonial period. Lithographs showing the history of Recife from the Dutch occupation to the present day. Archaeology. Ethnography.
Tu.-Su. 9-5.

SUGAR MUSEUM
Av. 17 de Agôsto 2223, Monteiro, Recife, Pernambuco
Models of Colonial mills. Devices for torturing slaves. Collections of antique sugar bowls.
Tu.-Su. 10-5.

RECONCAVO

WANDERLEY PINHO MUSEUM
Engenho da Freguesia, Reconcavo, Bahia
In 18th century house, former home of the Wanderley Pinho family. Furniture. Porcelain. Jewellery.
By appointment.

RESENDE

MUSEUM OF THE MILITARY ACADEMY
Resende, Rio de Janeiro
Military history.
By appointment.

MUSEUM OF MODERN ART
Resende, Rio de Janeiro
19th-20th century paintings, drawings, engravings by Brazilian and foreign artists.
Tu.-Su. 10-5.

RIBEIRÃO PRÊTO

FRANCESCO SCHMIDTH MUSEUM
Bairro de Monte Alegre, Ribeirão Prêto, São Paulo
History and methods of coffee-growing. Exhibits showing importance of coffee to the national economy.
M.-Sa. 8-5; Su. 1-5.

DR. PLINIO TRAVASSOS DOS SANTOS MUSEUM
Bairro de Monte Alegre, Ribeirão Prêto, São Paulo
Mineralogy. Botany. Zoology. Ethnography. Local history. Paintings. Sculpture.
M.-Sa. 8-5; Su. 1-5.

RIO BRANCO

ACRE MUSEUM
Rio Branco, Acre Territory
Documents and relics dealing with the incorporation of Acre as an integral part of Brazil. Local history, ethnography.
Tu.-Su. 9-12, 2-5.

RIO CLARO

AMADOR BUENO DA VEIGA MUSEUM OF HISTORY AND PEDAGOGY
Av. Dois, Esquina da Rua Sete, Rio Claro, São Paulo
Local history, ethnography.
Tu.-Su. 12-5.

ARGEMIRO M. DIAS MUSEUM
1693 Rua Oito, Rio Claro, São Paulo
Geological collections.
By appointment.

NAVARRO DE ANDRADE FORESTRY MUSEUM
Companhia Paulista de Estradas de Ferro, Rio Claro, São Paulo
Zoology. Botany. Collections relating to the eucalyptus.
M.-Sa. 7.30-11, 12.30-5; Su., public holidays 7.30-6.

RIO GRANDE

OCEANOGRAPHIC MUSEUM
Praça Tamandaré, Rio Grande, Rio Grande do Sul
Oceanography. Icthyology. Malacology. Algology. Large shell collection.
Tu.-Su. 2-4.

RIO DE JANEIRO

ARMY MUSEUM
Praça Duque de Caxias, Rio de Janeiro
Military history.
Tu.-Su. 11-4.

CARPOLOGICAL MUSEUM
Rua Jardim Botânico 1008 and Pacheco Leão 915, Rio de Janeiro, Guanabara
Brazilian and foreign plants, fruits.
Tu., F. 2-5.

CHILDHOOD MUSEUM
90 Rua Moncorvo Filho, Rio de Janeiro, Guanabara
Pediatrics.
Daily 10-12, 2-5.

COIN AND POSTAGE STAMP MUSEUM
Praça Duque de Caxias, Rio de Janeiro
Coins. Medals. Seals. Postage stamps.
Tu.-Su. 9-12, 2-5.

BENJAMIN CONSTANT HOUSE-MUSEUM
Rua Monte Alegre 255, Rio de Janeiro, Guanabara
Collection illustrating life and work of Constant, in the house where he died.
M.-Sa. 9-12, 2-6.

CURRENCY MUSEUM OF THE BANK OF BRAZIL
Avenida Rio Branco 30, Rio de Janeiro, Guanabara
Brazilian and foreign coins and medals. Brazilian paper money.
Tu.-F. 10.30-4.30; Sa. 10.30-2.30; Su. 12-4.

FORESTRY MUSEUM
Rua Major Rubens Vaz 122, Rio de Janeiro, Guanabara
Specimens of forest timbers. Furniture and other objects made of wood.
Daily 1-4.

GEOGRAPHICAL MUSEUM OF BRAZIL
Avenida Beira Mar 436, Rio de Janeiro, Guanabara
Collection of Brazilian products and the artifacts. Physical, human and economic geography of Brazil.
M.-F. 9-6.

ITAMARTY MUSEUM OF HISTORY AND DIPLOMACY
Av. Marechal Floriano 196, Rio de Janeiro, Guanabara
In 19th century Itamarty Palace. Furniture. Paintings. Sculpture. Collections of objects formerly belonging to prominent Brazilians and to foreigners having diplomatic contacts with Brazil. Tapestries. Miniatures. Drawings. Engravings.
M.-F. 10-4.

JOCKEY CLUB COLLECTION
Av. Rio Branco 93, Rio de Janeiro, Guanabara
Racing trophies. Coins. Early books about horse racing.
M.-F. 12-6.

KUHLMANN BOTANICAL MUSEUM
Rua Jardim Botânico 920, Rio de Janeiro, Guanabara
Herbaria and other exhibits, illustrating botany of Brazil.
M.-F. 9-5.

ANTÔNIO LAGO MUSEUM
Rua dos Andradas 96, Rio de Janeiro, Guanabara
History of pharmacy in Brazil. 17th-18th century pharmaceutical equipment, manuscripts.
M.-F. 2-5.

MUSEUM OF THE AUTOMOBILE
Rua Marquês de São Vicente, Rio de Janeiro, Guanabara
Collections illustrating development of motor transport.
M.-F. 10-5; Sa., Su. 12-4.

MUSEUM OF THE BANK OF BRAZIL
Av. Presidente Vargas 328, Rio de Janeiro, Guanabara
Brazilian and foreign coins, medals, seals.
M.-F. 9.30-5.

MUSEUM OF BLACK MAGIC
47 Rua da Relacão, Rio de Janeiro, Guanabara
Variety of objects used in black magic at the illegal ceremonies of Voodooism known as *candomblés.*
Tu.-Su. 9-12, 2-5.

MUSEUM OF THE BRAZILIAN HISTORICAL AND GEOGRAPHICAL INSTITUTE
Avenida Augusto Severo 8, Rio de Janeiro
History. Geography. Ethnography. Coins and medals.
By appointment.

MUSEUM OF THE CITY OF RIO DE JANEIRO
Estrada Santa Marinha, Parque da Cidade, Gávea, Rio de Janeiro, Guanabara
Art and history of the city. Portuguese-Brazilian furniture, porcelain, pictures, gold and silverware, and coins.
Th. 1-5; Sa., Su. 11-5.

MUSEUM OF DENDROLOGY
631 Estrada Castorina, Gávea, Rio de Janeiro, Guanabara
Botany, especially the study of trees.
By appointment.

MUSEUM OF THE FIRE BRIGADE
Praça da Republica 45, Rio de Janeiro, Guanabara
Collections illustrating history of fire-fighting in Rio de Janeiro. Early fire-engines and other equipment.
Daily 9-4.

MUSEUM OF FOLK-LORE
Parque Palácio do Catete, Rio de Janeiro, Guanabara
Collection illustrating ethnography and folk art of the whole of Brazil.
Tu.-F. 12-6; Sa., Su. 3-6.

MUSEUM OF THE GEOLOGICAL AND MINERALOGICAL DIVISION OF THE MINISTRY OF MINES AND ENERGY
Avenida Pasteur 404, Praia Vermelha, Rio de Janeiro, Guanabara
Collections of rocks, minerals and fossils of Brazil.
M.-Sa. 10-5.

MUSEUM OF THE HUNTERS' CLUB
Rua São Geraldo 38, Rio de Janeiro, Guanabara
Wildlife of Brazil. Hunting weapons, equipment.
M., Tu., Th.-Sa. 8-12; W. 6-10.

MUSEUM OF THE INDEPENDENT COMPANY OF GUARDS OF THE PALACE OF GUANABARA
Rua Cardoso Junior 479, Rio de Janeiro, Guanabara
History of the Independent Company. Weapons. Equipment.
Daily 8-4.

MUSEUM OF THE INDIAN
Rua Mata Machado 127, Maracaña, Rio de Janeiro, Guanabara
Collections illustrating the life and traditions of the Brazilian Indians.
M.-F. 11-5.

MUSEUM OF THE INSTITUTE OF FORENSIC MEDICINE
Rua dos Invalidos 152, Rio de Janeiro, Guanabara
Material illustrating cases referred to the Institute.
By appointment.

MUSEUM OF MILITARY HEROES
Praça General Tiburcio 83, Rio de Janeiro, Guanabara
Weapons. Uniforms. Medals. Documents. Photographs.
Daily 8-6.

MUSEUM OF MUSICAL INSTRUMENTS
Rua do Passeio 98, Rio de Janeiro, Guanabara
Musical instruments from all the regions of Brazil.
Daily 1-5.

MUSEUM OF THE NATIONAL ACADEMY OF MEDICINE
Av. General Justo 365, Rio de Janeiro, Guanabara
Collections illustrating history of medicine and public health in Brazil.
Th. 3-6.

MUSEUM OF THE NATIONAL PRINTING WORKS
Avenida Rodrigues Alves 1, Rio de Janeiro, Guanabara
Printing machinery. Display of works produced at the National Printing Works.
M.-Sa. 9-6.

MUSEUM OF THE NATIONAL WAR MEMORIAL
Av. Infante D. Henrique 75, Rio de Janeiro, Guanabara
Collections relating to the part played by Brazilian forces in the 2nd World War. Weapons. Medals. Uniforms. Paintings. Documents.
Tu.-Su. 10-5.

MUSEUM OF THE NAVAL SCHOOL
Ilha de Villegaignon, Rio de Janeiro, Guanabara
Brazilian naval history. Trophies. Medals. Ethnographical material brought back from training voyages.
M.-F. 9-4.

MUSEUM OF NUMISMATICS AND PHILATELY
Casa da Molda, Praça da República 173, Rio de Janeiro, Guanabara
Coins. Medals. Local history. Postage stamps.
M.-Sa. 8-12, 2-5; Su. 2-5.

MUSEUM OF THE ORDER OF OUR LADY OF MOUNT CARMEL
Rua do Carmo 46, Rio de Janeiro, Guanabara
Religious art. Gold liturgical items.
Tu.-F. 11-4.

MUSEUM OF THE ORDER OF ST. FRANCIS
Largo da Carisca 5, Rio de Janeiro, Guanabara
History of the order. Religious art. Furniture. Porcelain.
1st and 3rd Su. in month, 8-10.

MUSEUM OF OUR LADY OF GLORY OF OUTEIRO
Praça Nossa Senhora da Gloria 135, Rio de Janeiro, Guanabara
Paintings. Jewellery. Ornaments. Furniture. Porcelain. Bronzes. Medals. Manuscripts. Liturgical items.
M.-F. 8-12, 2-5.

MUSEUM OF PICTURES AND SOUND
Praça Marechal Ancora 1, Rio de Janeiro, Guanabara
Engravings, photographs illustrating history of Brazil. Recordings and scores of Brazilian folk music.
Tu.-Sa. 12-6; Su. 2-6.

MUSEUM OF PICTURES OF THE UNCONSCIOUS
Rua Ramiro Magalhães 521, Rio de Janeiro, Guanabara
Paintings, models, drawings, made spontaneously by psychiatric patients in the Pedro II Psychiatric Centre.
F. 10-12.

MUSEUM OF THE POLICE ACADEMY
Rua Frei Caneca, Rio de Janeiro, Guanabara
Collections illustrating different types of crime.
M.-F. 8-5.

MUSEUM OF POPULAR ART AND TRADITIONS
Parque do Flamengo, Av. Rui Barbosa, Rio de Janeiro, Guanabara
Folk art of Brazil, with comparative examples from Portugal, Spain, Africa.
Tu.-Su. 12-5.

MUSEUM OF THE PORT OF RIO
Av. Rodrigues Alves, Rio de Janeiro, Guanabara
History of the port, with early equipment, documents, paintings.
M.-F. 1-5; Sa., Su., public holidays 2-5.

MUSEUM OF THE RAYMUNDO OTTONI DE CASTRO FOUNDATION
Rua Murtinho Nobre 93, Rio de Janeiro, Guanabara
Oriental and European paintings, sculpture. Furniture. Oriental porcelain. Persian, Turkish, Caucasian carpets.
By appointment.

MUSEUM OF THE REPUBLIC
Catete Palace, Rua do Catete, Rio de Janeiro, Guanabara
Formerly the residence of the Barão de Nova Friburgo, and containing the bedroom in which President Getulio Vargas shot himself. Collections illustrating history of Brazil.
Tu.-F. 12-5.30; Sa., Su., public holidays 3-6.

MUSEUM OF THE RUI BARBOSA FOUNDATION
Rua São Clemente 134, Rio de Janeiro, Guanabara
Furniture, costumes, paintings formerly the property of Rui Barbosa, Governor of the Republic (d.1923).
Tu.-F. 12.30-7; Sa., Su. 3-7.

MUSEUM OF TAXATION
Rua Araújo Pôrto Alegre, Palácio da Fazenda, Rio de Janeiro, Guanabara
Collections illustrating history and methods of taxation in Brazil, especially during the colonial period.
M.-F. 11-5.

MUSEUM OF THE TECHNOLOGICAL DEPARTMENT OF THE FORESTRY SERVICE
Rua Major Rubéns Vaz 122, Gávea, Rio de Janeiro, Guanabara
Wood technology. Samples of wood from Brazil and other countries. Displays of forestry products and hand-made wood objects.
By appointment.

NATIONAL HISTORICAL MUSEUM
Praça Marechal Ancora, Rio de Janeiro, Guanabara
Colonial sculpture and furniture. Maps. Paintings. Weapons. Armour. Silver. Porcelain. The building was once the old War Arsenal of the Empire.
Daily ex. M. 12-5.

NATIONAL MUSEUM
Quinta da Boa Vista, Rio de Janeiro
In the entrance hall is the ''Bendego'' meteorite, found in the state of Bahia in 1888 (original weight 5,360 kilos). Brazilian ethnographic collections of Indian weapons, dresses, utensils. Mineral collection. Birds, mammals, fish and butterflies.
Daily ex. M. 12-4.30.

MUSEUM OF FAUNA
Quinta da Bõa Vista, São Cristovão, Rio de Janeiro, Guanabara
Birds, mammals and reptiles of Brazil.
Tu.-F. 12-5; Sa., Su. 10-5.

NATIONAL MUSEUM OF FINE ART
199 Avenida Rio Branco, Rio de Janeiro, Guanabara
Paintings. Sculpture. Works by contemporary Brazilian artists. Furniture. Graphic arts. Numismatics. Posters. Photographs.
Daily ex. M. and national holidays, 12-9.

NAVAL MUSEUM
Rua Dom Manoel 15, Rio de Janeiro, Guanabara
History of the Brazilian navy. Ship models. Equipment. Weapons. Paintings.
Daily 12-5.

PATHOLOGY MUSEUM
Instituto Oswaldo Cruz, Manguihos, Rio de Janeiro, Guanabara
In former study and laboratory of the Institute's founder, Oswaldo Cruz, with its original furniture and equipment. Manuscripts, diplomas, medals and other material illustrating life and work of Cruz.
M.-F. 11-5.

PRESS MUSEUM
Rua Araújo Pôrto Alegre 71, Rio de Janeiro, Guanabara
Maintained by the Brazilian Press Association.
Daily 9-12, 2-5.

RIO DE JANEIRO MUSEUM OF MODERN ART
Avenida Beira Mar, Atêrro, Rio de Janeiro, Guanabara
World-wide collections of 20th century paintings, sculpture, drawings, including works by Dali, Klee, Matisse, Rouault.
Tu.-F. 12-7; Sa., Su. 2-7.

SANTA CASA DA MISERICÓRDIA: MUSEUM OF PHARMACY
Rua Santa Luzia 206, Rio de Janeiro, Guanabara
Early pharmaceutical equipment.
M.-F. 8-12, 2-4.

SANTA CASA DA MISERICÓRDIA DO RIO DE JANEIRO: MUSEUM OF RELIGIOUS ART
Rua Santa Luzia 206, Rio de Janeiro, Guanabara
Religious paintings, sculpture, liturgical items.
Daily 8-6.

CLÁUDIO DE SOUZA HOUSE-MUSEUM
Praça Rui Barbosa, Rio de Janeiro, Guanabara
Collections illustrating life and work of de Souza.
Tu.-Sa. 9-12, 2-5.

THEATRE MUSEUM
Avenida Rio Branco, Rio de Janeiro, Guanabara
Buildings of Brazilian theatre. Costume. Stage designs. Posters. Programmes.
M.-F. 1-5.

VILLA LOBOS MUSEUM
Rua Da Imprensa 16, Rio de Janeiro, Guanabara
Musical scores. Concert programmes. Photographs.
M.-F. 11-4.

RIO PARDO

BARON SANTO ANGELO HISTORICAL MUSEUM
155 Rua Andrade Neves, Rio Pardo, Rio Grande do Sul
Material relating to Baron Santo Angelo (1807-1879), born in Rio Pardo, and known as a painter, architect, poet, playwright and critic. Local history.
M.-Sa. 12-5.

RUSSAS

FATHER JULIO MARIA MUSEUM
Rua Mons João Luis 759, Russas, Ceará
Local history.
Tu.-Su. 9-12, 2-5.

SABARÁ

MUSEUM OF GOLD MINING
Intendencia de Ouro, Sabará, Minas Gerais
Collections illustrating gold mining in the area in the 18th century. Early methods of gold mining and smelting. 18th century furniture. Handicrafts of the mining districts.
Tu.-Su. 12-5.

SALVADOR

CASTRO ALVES MUSEUM
Colégio Ipiranga, Rua do Sodré, Salvador, Bahia
Collection illustrating life and work of the poet, Castro Alves.
M.-Sa. 8-12, 2-5.

BAHIA MUSEUM OF ART
Av. Joana Angélica 198, Salvador, Bahia
17th-19th century works by artists from Bahia and abroad. Paintings. Porcelain. Furniture.
Tu.-F. 8-12, 2-6; Sa., Su. 3-6.

BAHIA MUSEUM OF MODERN ART
Rua Desembargador Castelo Branco 1, Salvador, Bahia
19th-20th century works by Brazilian artists. Paintings. Sculpture. Engravings. Tapestries.
Tu.-Su. 2-6.

HOUSE OF THE SEVEN CANDEEIROS
Rua São Francisco 32, Salvador, Bahia
17th century house. Furniture. Religious art. Paintings.
M.-F. 2-5.

MUSEUM OF ART
Rua Monsenhor Flaviano 2, Salvador, Bahia
Jacaranda furniture. Paintings. Porcelain. Cut glass. Costumes. Jewellery.
By appointment.

MUSEUM OF THE BAHIA INSTITUTE OF GEOGRAPHY AND HISTORY
Avenida Sete de Setembro 94, Salvador, Bahia
Mineralogy. Geography. History. Folklore. Negro art.
Daily 2-5.

MUSEUM OF CAMPAIGN TROPHIES
Salvador, Bahia
Historic material relating to the various military campaigns in which the forces of Bahia took part.
M.-F. 9-12, 2-5.

MUSEUM OF THE CARLOS COSTA PINTO FOUNDATION
Avenida Sete de Setembro 389-391, Salvador, Bahia
17th-19th century Brazilian furniture. 18th-19th century Chinese and European porcelain. Brazilian and European jewellery. Baccarat cut-glass. Paintings. Religious art.
M., W.-Su. 3-7.

MUSEUM OF THE CARMELITE CONVENT
Ladeira do Carmo, Salvador, Bahia
17th-19th century furniture, goldsmiths' work. Sculptures by Francisco Manoel das Chagos.
Daily 9-12, 2-5.

MUSEUM OF MODERN ART
Rua Des. Castelo Branco 1, Salvador, Bahia
Handicrafts and folk art from N.E. Brazil.
Tu.-Su. 2-6.

MUSEUM OF THE NINA RODRIGUES INSTITUTE
Rua Alfredo Brito, Salvador, Bahia
Forensic medicine. Anthropology. Negro art.
M.-F. 2-5.

MUSEUM OF POPULAR ART
Rua Monsenhor Flaviano 2, Salvador, Bahia
Embroidery. Carvings. Jewellery. Ceramics.
M.-F. 9-12, 2-5.

MUSEUM OF RELIGIOUS ART
Terreiro de Jesus, Salvador, Bahia
Images. Vestments. 17th-19th century gold ornaments, liturgical items.
Daily 9-5.

MUSEUM OF RELIGIOUS ART
Monastery and Church of Santa Tereza, Ladeira de Santa Tereza, Rua do Sodré, Salvador, Bahia
Carvings, including some of local origin. Silver and gold reliquaries. Gilded wooden reliquary by the Brazilian sculptor, Aleijadinho.
Daily 9-5.

RUI BARBOSA HOUSE-MUSEUM
Rua Rui Barbosa 12, Salvador, Bahia
House in which Barbosa was born. Furniture. Personal possessions. Photographs. Books and articles by Barbosa.
M.-Sa. 9-12, 2-5.

SANTA CASA DO MISERICÓRDIA
Rua da Misericórdia 6, Salvador, Bahia
Religious art. Paintings. Images. Furniture.
M.-F. 8-12, 2-5.

NELSON DE SOUSA OLIVEIRA COLLECTION
Av. 7 de Setembro 172-4, Salvador, Bahia
Home of Prof. de Sousa, with his collections of paintings, sculpture, Jacaranda furniture, porcelain, peasant pottery, coins, medals, fossils, shells.
Daily 9-12, 2-8.

SANTA LEOPOLDINA

COLONIAL MUSEUM
Rua Presidente Vargas, Santa Leopoldina, Espirito Santo
Museum illustrating life during the colonial period. Paintings. Furniture. Handicrafts. Musical instruments.
Tu.-Su. 8-11, 12-6.

SANTA LUZIA

DOLABELA MUSEUM
621 Rua Direita, Santa Luzia, Maranhão
Historic documents relating to the Liberal Revolution of 1842. Regional furniture. Costumes.
By appointment.

SANTA MARIA

VICTOR BERSANI MUSEUM
Praça Saldanha Marinho, Santa Maria, Rio Grande do Sul
Historical exhibits. Collections of applied art from the region.
M., Tu., Th., F. 8 p.m.-10; W. 2-5.30.

MUSEUM OF THE ANTONIO ALVER RAMOS AGRICULTURAL ESTATE
Santa Maria, Rio Grande do Sul
Palaeontology. Archaeology. Herbarium. Ceramics. Coins.
Daily 8-5.

SANTANA DO IPANEMA

MUNICIPAL MUSEUM OF HISTORY AND ART
Av. N. S. de Fátima 181, Santana do Ipanema, Alagoas
Local history. Brazilian paintings. Folk art.
Tu.-F. 8-12; Sa., Su. 2-5.

SANTANA DO LIVRAMENTO

DAVID CANABARRO MUNICIPAL MUSEUM
Rua Manduca Rodrigues, Santana do Livramento, Rio Grande do Sul
Minerals of the region. Weapons. Regional history.
M.-F. 9-11.30, 1.30-5; Sa. 8-11.30.

SANTA RITA DO PASSA QUATRO

ZEQUINHA DE ABREU HISTORICAL MUSEUM
Rua Prudente de Morais 85, Santa Rita do Passa Quatro, São Paulo
Paintings. Sculpture. Personal possessions and musical collections of the composer, Zequinha de Abreu.
M.-F. 8-11, 1-5.

SANTA ROSA

VICENTE CARDOSO MUNICIPAL MUSEUM
Rua Borges de Medeiros, Santa Rosa, Rio Grande do Sul
Local history, ethnography.
Tu.-Su. 10-12, 2-5.

SANTA TEREZA

MELO LEITÃO MUSEUM OF BIOLOGY
Santa Tereza, Espirito Santo
Botany.
M.-F. 9-5.

SANTO ÂNGELO

MUSEUM OF THE MISSIONS
Santo Ângelo, Rio Grande do Sul
Religious art. Vestments. Liturgical items.
On request.

SANTOS

MUSEUM OF THE HISTORICAL AND GEOGRAPHICAL INSTITUTE
Av. Conselheiro Nebias 689, Santos, São Paulo
History and geography of Brazil, especially the São Paulo region.
Daily 8-11, 2-5.

MUSEUM OF THE SEA FISHERIES INSTITUTE
192 Avenida Bartolomeu de Gusmao, Santos, São Paulo
Applied zoology. Specimens of marine creatures.
Tu.-Su. 1-6.

SANTOS DUMONT

SANTOS DUMONT MUSEUM
Fazenda de Cabangu, Santos Dumont, Minas Gerais
Birthplace of the aviator, Alberto Santos Dumont. Collections illustrating his life and work.
Daily 10-5.

SÃO BORJA

MUNICIPAL MUSEUM
Travessa Albino Pfeiffer 49, São Borja, Rio Grande do Sul
Religious art of the missionary period. Regional geology, archaeology, ecology.
M.-F. 8-11, 2-5.30.

SÃO CARLOS

HISTORICAL MUSEUM
Rua Sete de Setembro 2078, São Carlos, São Paulo
Paintings. Handicrafts. Ethnography. Material relating to the Constitutional Revolution of 1832.
M., W., F. 12-6; Tu., Th. 6-10; Sa. 9-3.

SÃO CRISTÓVÃO

SERGIPÉ MUSEUM
Praça São Francisco, São Cristóvão, Sergipé
Religious art. 19th century Brazilian paintings. Weapons. Furniture. Images. Coins.
Tu.-F. 9-11, 2-5; Sa., Su. 2-6.

SÃO GABRIEL

JOÃO PEDRO NUNES MUSEUM
412 Rua João Manoel, São Gabriel, Rio Grande do Sul
Historical documents relating to the Revolutions of 1893 and 1923. Applied art.
By appointment.

SÃO JOÃO DA BOA VISTA

DR. ARMANDO DE SALLES OLIVEIRA HISTORICAL MUSEUM
Praça Gov. Armando Sales 122, São João da Boa Vista, São Paulo
Porcelain. Costumes. Furniture. Weapons. Religious art.
Tu., Th., Sa. 2-5; W., F. 9-11.30.

SÃO JOÃO DEL REI

MUNICIPAL MUSEUM
Praça Frei Orlando 90, São João del Rei, Minas Gerais
Natural history. Local history.
Daily 8-5.

MUSEUM OF THE WAR VETERANS OF BRAZIL
Area do Circulo Militar, São João del Rei, Minas Gerais
Material relating to campaigns in Italy. Weapons. Trophies. Medals.
On request.

REGIONAL MUSEUM
Rua Marechal Deodoro 12, São João del Rei, Minas Gerais
18th century house. Regional history. Furniture.
Tu.-Su. 10-6.

SÃO JOSÉ DO RIO PARDO

EUCLIDES DA CUNHA MUSEUM
Rua Marechal Floriano 105, São José do Rio Pardo, São Paulo
Named after the author of 'Trouble in the Backlands'. Collections illustrating life, work and times of da Cunha.
M.-F. 8-11, 2-6; Sa.-Su. 9-11, 3-5.

RIO PARDO MUSEUM
Rua Marechal Florianó 105, São José do Rio Pardo, São Paulo
Local history.
M.-F. 8-11, 2-5; Sa., Su. 9-11, 3-5.

SÃO LEOPOLDO

MUSEUM OF THE ANTÔNIO VIEIRA LITERARY SOCIETY
São Leopoldo, Rio Grande do Sul
General collections. The society is named after Father Antônio Vieira, eminent Jesuit preacher, writer and diplomatist, born in Portugal but educated in Brazil (1608-97).
By appointment.

VISCOUNT SÃO LEOPOLDO COLONIAL MUSEUM
São Leopoldo, Rio Grande do Sul
Housed in old trading post (1824). Collection relating to German colonisation in South America.
Tu.-Su. 2-5.30.

SÃO LUIS

FLORY GAMA MUSEUM
121 Rua Coronel Colares Moreira, São Luis, Maranhão
Collection of sculpture.
By appointment.

MUSEUM OF THE HISTORICAL INSTITUTE
São Luis, Maranhão
History. Ethnography. Art.
M.-Sa. 9-12, 2-5.

PIUS XII MUSEUM
Rua 13 de Maio 500, São Luis, Maranhão
Religious art.
Daily 9-5.

SÃO MIGUEL

MUSEUM OF THE JESUIT MISSIONS
Praça das Missões, São Miguel, Rio Grande do Sul
Works of art and objects of historical interest connected with the Seven Peoples of the Eastern Missions founded by the Company of Jesus.
By appointment.

SÃO PAULO

ART MUSEUM OF SÃO PAOLO
Avenida Paulista 1578, São Paulo
Paintings of the Italian, Spanish, Dutch, Flemish and French schools. Works by Portinari and Lasar Segall.
Tu.-Su. 2-6.

DR. JOÃO BARBOSA RODRIGUES BOTANICAL MUSEUM
Av. Miguel Estefano, São Paulo
Plants, fruits, seeds and trees of São Paulo.
Daily 9-12, 1-5.

JOSÉ BONIFACIO MUSEUM
Rua Benjamin Constant 158, São Paulo
Collections illustrating history of Brazil.
M.-F. 1.30-5.

BOTANICAL MUSEUM
Av. Miguel Estefano, São Paulo
Botany of the São Paulo region.
Daily 9-12, 1-5.

CASA DO GRITO
Parque do Ipiranga, São Paulo
Early 19th century house, with period furniture, domestic equipment.
Tu.-Su. 12-5.

DR. RAUL DA CUNHA MUSEUM
284 Rua dos Apeninos, São Paulo
Historical documents and photographs.
By appointment.

OSWALDO CRUZ MUSEUM
Rua Helvétia 694, São Paulo
Pathological collection.
By appointment.

ECCLESIASTICAL MUSEUM
37 Rua Santa Teresa, São Paulo
Religious works of art, mostly of the colonial period. Coins. Medals. Jewellery. Paintings of the 18th century São Paulo artist, the Carmelite Friar Jesuino.
Daily 9-5.

ETHNOGRAPHICAL MUSEUM OF THE FACULTY OF PHILOSOPHY, SCIENCE AND LETTERS
Universidade de São Paulo, Caixa Postal 8105, São Paulo
Brazilian Indian cultures, including Canella and Bororo collections. Tupi ceramics. Rio Negro wooden signal drums.
By appointment.

FORESTRY MUSEUM
Caixa Postal 1322, São Paulo
Forestry and timber technology. Collections of local timber.
M.-Sa. 8-5.

GEOGRAPHICAL AND GEOLOGICAL MUSEUM
Rua Antonio de Godói 122, São Paulo
Geology. Mineralogy. Limestone caves.
M.-F. 9-11, 1-5.

MANOR HOUSE MUSEUM
Praça Monteiro Lobato, São Paulo
18th century house, with period furniture, domestic equipment.
Tu.-Su. 11-5.30.

METROPOLITAN SYNOD MUSEUM
Praça Clovis Bevilacqua 37, São Paulo
Religious art. Numismatics.
By appointment.

MUNICIPAL PLANETARIUM
Parque do Ibirapuera, São Paulo
Planetarium. Astronomical instruments.
Sa., Su., public holidays 10-8.

MUSEUM OF AERONAUTICS
Ibirapuera Park, São Paulo
History of aviation. Historic aeroplanes include the Santos Dumont aircraft.
Tu.-Su. 2-6.

MUSEUM OF THE BUTANTÃ INSTITUTE
Avenida Vital Brasil, São Paulo
Snakes. Snakebite poisoning and preparation of vaccines.
Daily 8-4.

MUSEUM OF CONTEMPORARY ART
Ibirapuera Park, São Paulo
19th century paintings by European and Brazilian artists.
Tu.-Su. 2-7.

MUSEUM OF FOLKLORE
Rua Catão 611, São Paulo
Folklore collections.
M.-Sa. 9-5.

MUSEUM OF HUNTING AND FISHING
Avenida Francisco Matarazzo 455, São Paulo
Hunting and fishing equipment, trophies.
Daily 9-12, 2-5.

MUSEUM OF THE IMPERIAL CHAPEL
São Paulo
Religious art.
Tu.-Su. 1-5.

MUSEUM OF THE INSTITUTE OF BIOLOGY
Av. Conselheiro, Rodrigues Alves 1252, São Paulo
Botany. Zoology. Paintings of agricultural and forest scenes.
M.-F. 9-11, 2-6.

MUSEUM OF THE OSCAR FREIRE INSTITUTE
Rua Teodoro Sampaio 115, São Paulo
Anatomical collections.
M.-F. 8-4, by appointment.

MUSEUM OF RELIGIOUS ART
Avenida Tiradentes 676, São Paulo
Sculpture. Paintings. Furniture. Gold ornaments, liturgical objects.
Tu.-Su. 1-5.

MUSEUM OF RELIGIOUS ART: COLLECTION OF SHRINES
Marquise do Parque Ibirapuera, São Paulo
17th-19th century shrines from Europe and Brazil.
Tu.-Su. 1-5.

MUSEUM OF SCIENCE
Ibirapuera Park, São Paulo
Apparatus, equipment, models illustrating scientific principles and phenomena.
Daily 2-5.

PAULISTA MUSEUM
Ipiranga, São Paulo
Documents describing life in São Paulo State. Furniture, carriages, pictures, engravings. Religious art. Ethnography. Paintings by the São Paulo artist, Almeida Junior (1857-1899). The mud hut in which Dom Pedro I spent the night before his famous cry of ''Ipiranga'' - Independence or Death - is preserved in the park.
Tu., Th. and Su., also holidays, 12-4.

REPUBLICAN CONVENTION MUSEUM
67 Rua Barão de Itaim, São Paulo
Paintings and other material relating to republican propaganda. Engravings by Rugendas. Brazil in the 19th century.
Daily 10-5.

SÃO PAULO MUSEUM OF MODERN ART
Parque Ibirapuera, São Paulo
19th-20th century paintings, sculpture, drawings, engravings by Brazilian and foreign artists.
Tu.-Sa. 3.30-10; Su. 11.30-6.

SERTÃO HOUSE
Praça Paulo, São Paulo
Ethnography. Indian pottery, weapons, handicrafts. 19th century applied, decorative art.
Tu.-Su. 12.30-5.30.

STATE ART GALLERY
Praça da Luz 2, São Paulo
Paintings by Brazilian artists of 19th and 20th centuries. Photographs. Plaster casts.
M., W., Sa. 12-6; Tu., Su., public holidays 2-5.

UNIVERSITY MUSEUM OF ARCHAEOLOGY AND ETHNOGRAPHY
Edificio de Geografia e Historia, Cidade Universitarío, São Paulo
Archaeological and ethnographical material from Italy, Egypt, Mesopotamia, Andes, Amazon, Africa.
Tu.-F. 10-8; Sa. 2-6.

ZOOLOGICAL MUSEUM
Universidade de São Paolo, Avenida Nazareth 481, São Paulo
Collections of Brazilian and world fauna.
By appointment.

SÃO VICENTE

MUSEUM OF ART
São Vicente, São Paulo
Paintings, sculpture by Brazilian artists.
M.-F. 12-6; Sa., Su. 2-6.

SOBRAL

DIOCESAN MUSEUM
Rua Senador Paulo, Sobral, Ceará
Furniture. Ceramics. Jewellery. Coins. Religious art.
Daily 8-4.

SOROCABA

BRIGADIER RAFAEL TOBIAS DE AGUIAR HISTORICAL MUSEUM
Rua da Penha 681, Sorocaba, São Paulo
Brazilian history, especially 1750-1850.
W.-F. 1-5; Sa., Su., public holidays 9-3.

HISTORICAL MUSEUM
Rua Teodoro Kaysel, Sorocaba, São Paulo
Local archaeology, history. Transport. Costumes. Iron-founding. Ethnography. Religious art. Numismatics.
Tu.-F. 12-6; Sa., Su., public holidays 9-6.

TATUÍ

MARQUÊS DE MONTE ALEGRE HISTORICAL MUSEUM
Praça Manuel Guedes, Tatuí, São Paulo
Brazilian and foreign coins and medals.
Tu.-F. 6-12, 2-6; Sa. 8-12.

TAUBATÉ

HISTORICAL MUSEUM
996 Rua Quinze de Novembro, Taubaté, São Paulo
Regional history.
Tu.-Su. 9-12, 2-5.

TERESINA

ANISIO BRITO'S HOUSE
Rua Coelho Rodrigues 1016, Teresina, Piauí
Local history.
Tu.-Su. 9-4.

PIAUÍ MUSEUM OF ART
Praça Marechal Deodoro 900, Teresina, Piauí
Paintings. Sculpture. Porcelain. Pottery. Metal-work.
M.-F. 8-11.30.

TERESÓPOLIS

VON MARTIUS MUSEUM
Parque Nacional da Serra dos Orgaos, Teresópolis, Rio de Janeiro
Posters. Manuscripts of Dr. von Martius. Paintings.
Tu.-Th., Sa., Su. 9-4.

TIRADENTES

MUSEUM OF RELIGIOUS ART
Igreja do Rosario, Tiradentes, Minas Gerais
Regional religious art.
Daily 9-5.

TRAMANDAÍ

GENERAL OSÓRIO MUSEUM
Parque General Osório, Tramandaí, Rio Grande do Sul
Birthplace of General Osório. Collections illustrating his life and work.
M.-F. 9-5; Sa., Su. 11-5.

TRIUNFO

FARROUPILHA MUSEUM
Rua Luís Barreto 17, Triunfo, Rio Grande do Sul
Natural history. Weapons. Local history.
On request.

TUPÃ

ÍNDIA VANUIRE HISTORICAL MUSEUM
Rua Aimore 1367, Tupã, São Paulo
Indian material. Handicrafts. Weapons.
W.-Su. 1-5.

UBATUBA

HISTORICAL MUSEUM
Av. Iperoig 214, Ubatuba, São Paulo
Paintings, lithographs of local scenes. Weapons. Agricultural implements.
Tu.-F. 12-6; Sa. 9-12; Su. 12-6.

VALENÇA

ESTÊVES ESTATE (FAZENDA) MUSEUM
Fazenda de Estêves, Valença, Rio de Janeiro
Collections illustrating the Estêves estate during the period of slavery.
Daily 1-5.

VASSOURAS

CASA DA HERA MUSEUM
Rua Dr. Fernandes Júnior 89, Vassouras, Rio de Janeiro
In group of early 19th century buildings, with furniture, faience, cut-glass, paintings, costumes of the period.
Tu.-Su. 12-5.

VENÂNCIO AIRES

HISTORICAL MUSEUM
Venâncio Aires, Rio Grande do Sul
Local history.
M.-Sa. 9-12, 2-5; Su. 10-2.

VICOSA DO CEARÁ

AMELIA BEVILACQUA MUSEUM
Curso Bevilacqua, Viçosa do Ceará, Ceará
House where the Brazilian jurist and writer, Clovis Bevalicqua, was born in 1853. Furniture. Objects relating to the foundation of the town in 1759. Numismatics. Ethnography.
Tu.-F. 9-12, 2-5; Sa.-Su. 2-5.

VITÓRIA

MUSEUM OF THE FEDERAL UNIVERSITY OF THE HOLY SPIRIT
Barão de Monjardim, Av. Paulino Müller, Jucutuquara, Vitória, Espirito Santo
Archaeology. History. Furniture. Agricultural implements.
M.-F. 1-5.

VITÓRIA DE SANTO ANTÃO

COLLECTIONS OF THE HISTORICAL AND GEOGRAPHICAL INSTITUTE
Vitória de Santo Antão, Pernambuco
History and geography of Brazil.
By appointment.

Brunei

The former British dependency of Brunei, with its long coastline, its 115,000 people and 5800 sq. km. of territory, did not join the Federation of Malaysia in 1963. Its single museum illustrates the Malay culture and the military and maritime history of the area, and there are also collections of plants and wildlife of both the coastal and inland regions.

KOTA BATU

BRUNEI MUSEUM
Kota Batu, Brunei, Borneo
Archaeology. Ethnography. Natural history. Brassware made in Brunei. Brass cannons.
Tu.-Su. 10-5.30.

Bulgaria

A high proportion of Bulgaria's museums take the form of memorials to partisan heroes, workers' leaders, poets and other literary figures of the past thirty years. These museums are often in the former homes of the distinguished people whose careers are commemorated, which is an economical, sensible and attractive way of going about the business. Not all of the one-time residences of the great, however, contain items as impressive or spectacular as one displayed with pride in the house of Aleko Konstantinov, who was murdered in 1897. Here one can see, safely preserved, his heart, "showing the fatal wound".

Apart from these house-museums, the Bulgarians have given much attention to recalling the people who made major contributions to the long process of getting rid of the Turks and the subsequent oppressors of the country and to the eventual establishment of a socialist state with a scientific education and modern industries. Museums offer the full range of mementoes, from collections documenting the tobacco-workers' strike of 1872 and the annihilation of a village by the Turks in 1876 to the Nazi methods of 1939-45.

Bulgaria has good open-air museums, to safeguard and exhibit her peasant buildings, watermills and agricultural bygones and many well-arranged collections of folk art and handicrafts. The abundant archaeological material from Greek and Roman sites is a feature of many museums, some of them on the site where the excavations have taken place. A number of monasteries have valuable works of art and furnishings, which can be seen by visitors, and one such establishment has the useful feature of special exhibitions to illustrate the life lived in the monastery, both by monks and by laymen.

The most surprising museum in Bulgaria is probably the first modern-type school to be set up there, in 1862. Teaching was in the Bulgarian language and the school was organised on the English Bell and Lancaster monitorial system. The original equipment is still there, a distinction shared by no school in England.

ARTEMIDA

ARTEMIDA MUSEUM
Artemida
Greek and Roman antiquities.
Daily 10-1, 3-5.

ASENOVGRAD

NATIONAL MUSEUM
Asenovgrad
Ethnography. History of town and surrounding area.
Tu.-Su. 10-5.

BANSHO

NIKOLA VAPKAROV HOUSE-MUSEUM
Bansho
Birthplace and home of the revolutionary poet, Nikola Vapkarov. Furnishings. Personal possessions. Exhibits illustrating his life and work.
On request.

BĂCKOV

MUSEUM OF THE MONASTERY
Băckov
Displays illustrating life lived in the monastery, by both monks and laymen.
On request.

BATAK

'ANTON IVANOV' MUSEUM
Batak
Collections illustrating the annihilation of the population of Batak by the Turks (1876) and partisan activities, 1940-45.
On request.

MUSEUM OF HISTORY AND ARCHAEOLOGY
Batak
Prehistory, archaeology and history of Batak. Ethnography. Folk art.
Daily 9-5.

BERKOVICA

IVAN VAZOV MUSEUM
Berkovica
Former home of the poet, Ivan Vazov. Collections illustrating his life and work.
On request.

BIALA CERKOVA

MEMORIAL MUSEUM OF THE POET ZANKO ZERKOVSKY
Biala Cerkova
Collections illustrating life and work of Zerkovsky.
On request.

BLOGOEVGRAD

BLOGOEVGRAD MUSEUM
Blogoevgrad
History of Blogoevgrad since Roman times. Special section illustrating activities of the resistance, 1941-45.
Tu.-Su. 10-5.

BOTEVGRAD

HISTORY MUSEUM
Botevgrad
History and archaeology for the Botevgrad area.
Daily 9-12, 3-5.

BOURGAS

REGIONAL MUSEUM OF HISTORY
Lenin 21, Bourgas
Archaeology. Ethnography. Natural sciences. Social history. History of the Revolution.
Tu.-Su. 9-12, 3-7.

BRACIGOVO

HISTORICAL MUSEUM
Bracigovo
History and archaeology of the Bracigovo region.
Tu.-Su. 9-5.

DIMOVO

MAGURATA CAVE MUSEUM
Dimovo
Bronze Age rock-paintings. Weapons, utensils, ornaments from the Bronze Age, and from the Roman and Slav periods. Mementoes of the resistance movement, 1941-44.
Daily 10-5.

ETARA

OPEN-AIR MUSEUM
Etara
Rural houses, farm-buildings, mills from the Etara region-
Daily 10-5.

GORA LIPNICA

ZORA MUSEUM
Gora Lipnica
Ethnography of the Gora Lipnica region.
Daily 10-5.

HASKOVO

NATIONAL MUSEUM
Haskovo
History of the workers' movement, beginning with the tobacco-workers' strike of 1872.
Tu.-Su. 10-5.

HISARJA

DISTRICT MUSEUM
Hisarja
Material from excavations on site of Roman town of Augusta. Inscriptions. Statues. Coins. Gold vases and other items from tomb of the Duvanii, from Thracian tomb and Bronze Age burial site.
M.-Su. 9-12, 3-6.

KALOFER

HRISTO BOLEV HOUSE-MUSEUM
Kalofer
Birthplace of the revolutionary, Hristo Bolev.
Daily 10-12, 2-6.

KARNOBAT

NATIONAL MUSEUM
Karnobat
Archaeology. History of Karnobat and its area since medieval times. Furnishings. Handicrafts. Costumes.
Tu.-Su. 10-6.

KAZANLUK

NATIONAL MUSEUM
Kazanluk
Art. Archaeology. Natural history. Ethnography.
Tu.-Su. 10-5.

KJUSTENDIL

VLADIMIR DIMITROV-MAJSTORA GALLERY
Kjustendil
Paintings by Dimitrov-Majstora.
Tu.-Su. 9-5.

DISTRICT MUSEUM
Kjustendil
History of Kjustendil and the surrounding area. Handicrafts. Furniture. Folk art.
Daily 10-1, 3-5.

KOBEL

NATURAL HISTORY MUSEUM
Kobel
Natural history of the Kobel region.
Tu.-Su. 9-12, 2-5.

KOLAROVGRAD

ARCHAEOLOGICAL MUSEUM
Kolarovgrad
Local history and archaeology.
Daily 10-5.

LAJOS KOSSUTH MUSEUM
Kolarovgrad
Kossuth's home during his exile from Hungary. Kossuth memorabilia.
Tu.-Su. 9-12, 3-5.

KOPRIVSHTIŹA

GEORGI BENKOVSKI HOUSE-MUSEUM
Koprivshtiźa
Birthplace of the revolutionary, Benkovski. Exhibits illustrating his life and work.
On request.

TODOR KABLEŠOV HOUSE-MUSEUM
Koprivshtiźa
House (1850). Furnishings. Personal possessions and memorabilia of the revolutionary, Kablešov.
On request.

LJUBEN KARAVELOV HOUSE-MUSEUM
Koprivshtiźa
Former home of the revolutionary poet, Karavelov. Exhibits illustrating his life and work.
On request.

OSLEKOV ETHNOGRAPHICAL MUSEUM
Koprivshtiźa
Former home of Nenco Nikolov Oslekov, built (1856) with materials brought from Constantinople. Original furnishings. Ethnographical collections made by Oslekov during his travels.
Tu.-Su. 10-1, 3-5.

KOPRIVŠTICA

DIMČO DEBELJANOV HOUSE-MUSEUM
Doganska ul., Koprivštica
Former home of the poet, Dimčo Debeljanov. Local history. Ethnography. Reconstruction of the poet's room.
On request.

JAKO DOROSSIEV HOUSE-MUSEUM
Koprivštica
Former home of the writer and revolutionary, J. Dorossiev. Exhibits illustrating his life and work.
On request.

NAJDEN GEROV HOUSE-MUSEUM
Koprivštica
Former home of the writer, Najden Gerov. Collections illustrating his life and work.
On request.

LOM

DISTRICT MUSEUM
Lom
History of Lom, especially of early 19th century cultural activities.
Tu.-Su. 10-5.

LOVEČ

VASIL LEVSKI MUSEUM
Loveč
House in which the revolutionary, V. Levski often sought refuge. Life and work of Levski, with some of his personal possessions.
On request.

REGIONAL MUSEUM OF HISTORY
H. Kărpačev 17, Loveč
Archaeology. Ethnography. History of the Revolution.
Daily 9-5.

MADARA

RAFAIL POPOV MUSEUM
Madara
Prehistoric material from local excavations, especially flint implements, weapons.
Tu.-Su. 10-5.

MELNIK

JANE SANDANSKI MUSEUM
Melnik
Memorabilia of Jane Sandanski.
On request.

MIHAJLOVGRAD

HRISTO MIHALJOV HOUSE-MUSEUM
Mihajlovgrad
Former home of the resistance leader, Hristo Mihaljov (d.1944). Collections illustrating his life and work.
On request.

MUSEUM OF THE SEPTEMBER UPRISING
V. Kolarov 3, Mihajlovgrad
Objects associated with the rising of September 1923. Photographs.
Daily 10-5.

NOVA ZAGORA

HISTORICAL MUSEUM
Nova Zagora
History of the town of Nova Zagora.
Daily 10-1, 3-5.

PANAGIOURISTE

RAJNA KNIAGJANIA REGIONAL MUSEUM
Panagiouriste
Ethnography, especially handicrafts, costumes. Local history.
Tu.-Sa. 10-5; Su. 10-1.

PAZARDŽIK

REGIONAL MUSEUM OF HISTORY
A. Zlatarov 5, Pazardžik
History of Pazardžik and its region, housed in former synagogue. Struggle for national liberation.
Tu.-Su. 10-5.

STANISLAV DOSPEVSKY MUSEUM
B. G. Dimitrov 50, Pazardžik
House where the painter lived and worked, containing documents, personal effects and an exhibition of paintings and icons.
On request.

HADJI STOIANOVATA HOUSE-MUSEUM
Pazardžik
Former home of the workers' leader, Hadji Stoianovata, with collections illustrating his life and work.
On request.

PLEVEN

MUSEUM OF MILITARY HISTORY
Bul. G. Dimitrov 157, Pleven
History of warfare and the army in Bulgaria.
Daily 10-6.

NATIONAL ART GALLERY
Ul. V. Kolarov 15, Pleven
Paintings by Bulgarian artists. Reproductions. Posters.
Tu.-Su. 10-6.

REGIONAL MUSEUM OF HISTORY
G. Dimitrov 104, Pleven
Archaeology. Ethnography. History of the Revolution.
Daily 10-6.

PLOVDIV

ART GALLERY
Ul. Kolarov 15, Plovdiv
19th-20th century paintings by Bulgarian artists, especially Georgi Bojadžiev, who attempted to adapt religious themes to the revolutionary ideology.
M.-F. 9-5; Sa., Su. 10-6.

BUKURESCHLIEV HOUSE-MUSEUM
Ulica K. Raitcho 7, Plovdiv
Former home of the composer and poet, Bukureschliev. Exhibits showing his life and work.
On request.

DISTRICT NATIONAL MUSEUM
Plovdiv
Collections illustrating the way of life of the people of the district and in the Rhodope Mountains.
Daily 9-5.

MUSEUM OF SOCIALIST CONSTRUCTION
Ul. Ivan Vasov 47, Plovdiv
History of the revolutionary and workers' movements and of the development of Bulgaria since 1945.
Daily 9-5.

NATURAL SCIENCE MUSEUM
Ul. General Zaimov 34, Plovdiv
Exhibits showing history and achievements of the natural sciences.
Tu.-Su. 10-5.

REGIONAL MUSEUM OF ARCHAEOLOGY
Pl. Săedinenie 1, Plovdiv
Prehistory. Classical and medieval archaeology. Numismatics. Panagyurishté Gold Treasure, consisting of vessels dating from 4th century B.C. History of Plovdiv in the Thracian period and under Macedonian and Roman rule. The classless society and the formation of classes: the Slave-owning Society; Feudal Society.
Tu.-Su. 10-5.

REGIONAL MUSEUM OF ETHNOLOGY
Dr. Čomakov 2, Plovdiv
Mural paintings and wood carvings. Implements and tools of different periods. National costumes. Embroideries. Interior arrangements. Furniture and furnishings from houses in Thrace and the Rhodope Mountains region. Attar of roses distillery. Agricultural implements. Reproductions of craftsmen's workshops.
Tu.-Su. 10-6.

REGIONAL MUSEUM OF THE REVOLUTIONARY MOVEMENT
A. Bukoreštliev 14, Plovdiv
History of Capitalism, the Uprising and Socialism. Murals and wood carvings. Activities of Dimitras Blagoev (1885-1903). Risings of 1876, 1923. Resistance movement, 1941-44.
Daily 9-5.

PRESLAV

ARCHAEOLOGICAL MUSEUM
Preslav
Near excavations of the capital of the first Bulgarian kingdom (893-972). Model of palace of King Simeon. Pottery. Inscriptions. Architectural items.
Daily 10-5.

RAJKOVO

NATIONAL MUSEUM OF THE RHODOPE
Rajkovo
Reconstruction of 18th century Rhodope house. Furnishings, Handicrafts. Gold and silver jewellery. Carpets, blankets, cushions. Costumes. History of struggle against the Turks. Resistance movement, 1941-44.
Tu.-Su. 9-12, 2-5.

RAZGRAD

NATIONAL MUSEUM
Razgrad
Material discovered during excavations at Roman town of Abritus.
Tu.-Su. 9-12, 2-6.

RAZLOG

MUSEUM OF THE LOCAL REVOLUTIONARY MOVEMENT
Razlog
History of the local workers' and revolutionary movements. Includes also material on the Balkan War.
On request.

NAKOLAJ PARAPUNOV HOUSE-MUSEUM
Razlog
Former home of the resistance leader, and opponent of the monarchy, N. Parapunov.
On request.

RILA

RILA MONASTERY NATIONAL MUSEUM
Rila
Historical development of Bulgarian art and architecture during the Ottoman period. Bulgarian history. History of the monastery. Manuscripts. Early printed books. First Bulgarian terrestrial globe. Early charters.
Daily 9-5.

RUSE

REGIONAL MUSEUM OF HISTORY
Ruse
History. Archaeology. Ethnography. Natural history. Renaissance art and history. Regional social history. Art gallery. History of Ruse and of the workers' and revolutionary movements.
Tu.-Su. 10-5.

SAMOKOV

NATIONAL MUSEUM
Samokov
History and archaeology of Samokov and its region.
Tu.-Sa. 10-5; Su. 2-5.

SAMOKOV MOSQUE (BAJRAKLI DŽAMIJA)
Samokov
Restored and modified architecturally in 1840, when the present internal decorations were carried out. Museum illustrating history of the mosque.
Daily 9-5.

SANDANSKI

REGIONAL MUSEUM
Sandanski
Thracian and Roman material from local excavations. History of Sandanski since medieval times, and of the workers' and revolutionary movements.
Tu.-Sa. 9-1, 3-6; Su. 10-1.

ŠČRAKLEVO

MUSEUM OF REGIONAL HISTORY AND ETHNOGRAPHY
Ščraklevo
Archaeology. Local history. Handicrafts. Folk art. Furniture.
Daily 9-12, 2-5.

SLIVEN

NATIONAL MUSEUM
Sliven
History and ethnography of Sliven and its region. Handicrafts. Industries. Folk art.
Tu.-F. 9-5; Sa., Su. 10-4.

SOFIA

DIMITER BLAGOEV MUSEUM
33 L. Kossouth Street, Sofia
House of the founder of the Bulgarian Communist Party, containing documents and personal effects.
By arrangement.

BOYANA CHURCH NATIONAL MUSEUM
Bǎkston 53, Sofia
Religious art. Vestments.
Daily 9-5.

GEORGI DIMITROV CENTRAL MUSEUM
1 Gourko Street, Sofia
Material illustrating the life and work of the Communist leader.
By arrangement.

GEORGI DIMITROV MUSEUM
Opǎlčenska 66, Sofia
House where the leader of the Communist Party lived from 1888 to 1912. Furniture and personal belongings. Library. Political documents.
By arrangement.

P. K. JAVOROV HOUSE-MUSEUM
Rakovski ulica 136, Sofia
Life and work of the writer, P. K. Javorov, in his former home.
On request.

VASSIL KOLAROV MUSEUM
5 Assen Zlatarov Street, Sofia
History of the life and work of Vassil Kolarov, the Bulgarian revolutionary and leader of the international workers' movement.
By arrangement.

V. KOLAROV NATIONAL LIBRARY
Bd. Tolbukin 11, Sofia
Early Bulgarian books, manuscripts.
M.-Sa. 10-5.

MUSEUM OF THE REVOLUTIONARY MOVEMENT
Pl. Narodno Sabranie 11, Sofia
Photographs, documents and other material illustrating history of the working-class and socialist movements in Bulgaria.
Daily 9-5.

MUSEUM OF THE REVOLUTIONARY MOVEMENT IN BULGARIA
14 Rousski Boulevard, Sofia
Exhibits from the revolutionary movement, and the history of the Bulgarian Communist Party.
Daily ex. Sa. 12-7; F. 8-1.

MUSEUM OF SOFIA'S HISTORY
27 Exarch Yossif Street, Sofia
Material relating to the history of the capital from the Neolithic Age to the present day.
Daily ex. M. 10-12, 2-5.

NATIONAL ARCHAEOLOGICAL MUSEUM
A. Stambolisky 2, Sofia
Archaeological and artistic relics of Bulgaria from the Palaeolithic Age to the late Feudal Epoch.
Daily ex. Tu. 10-5.30.

NATIONAL ART GALLERY
Ninth of September Square, Sofia
National and foreign art. Icons and medieval ecclesiastical art. Works by Bulgarian painters, graphic artists and sculptors from the National Revival Period to the present day.
Daily ex. Tu. 10-5.30; M. 9-2.30.

NATIONAL ETHNOGRAPHICAL MUSEUM
Mosckovska 6A, Sofia
Ethnography. Folklore. Costumes. Fabrics. Ornaments. Crafts.
Daily ex. Tu. 10-6; M. 9-3.

NATIONAL MUSEUM OF ECCLESIASTICAL HISTORY AND ARCHAEOLOGY
Pl. Lenin 19, Sofia
In former Great Mosque. Prehistory. Bulgaria in Roman times. Parchment manuscripts, gospels, icons, prints, mural paintings and articles of arts and crafts. Early charters.
Daily ex. Su. 9-12, 2-5.30; Sa. 9-1.

NATIONAL MUSEUM OF BULGARIAN-SOVIET FRIENDSHIP
K. Gotvald 4, Sofia
Material illustrating the political, economic and cultural relations between the Bulgarian and Soviet people. Historical background and development of Bulgaro-Soviet friendship.
Daily 9-6; Su. 9-3.

NATIONAL MUSEUM OF MILITARY HISTORY
Skobelev 23, Sofia
Military relics, documents, battle-paintings related to the Bulgarian People's Army and Bulgaro-Russian friendship throughout the ages.
Daily ex. Sa. 9-12, 2-6; Su. 1-7.

NATIONAL POLYTECHNIC MUSEUM
Rakovski 108, Sofia
History of technology in Bulgaria. Industrial developments and techniques. Machines. Scientific equipment. Photographs.
Tu.-Su. 10-5.

NATIONAL ZOOLOGICAL MUSEUM
Bulgarian Academy of Sciences, Ruski 1, Sofia
Vertebrates and invertebrates. Insects. Birds. Mammals. Freshwater and sea fauna. Geology. Palaeontology. Skeletons of mammals of the Tertiary and Quaternary periods.
Daily ex. M. and F. 9-12, 3-6. Open 9-1, 3-7 on days preceding holidays, and on holidays.

PETKO AND PENCHO SLAVEIKOV MUSEUM
138 Rakovski Street, Sofia
Material illustrating the life and work of Petko Slaveikov (poet, journalist, teacher, patriot-democrat, political worker) and Pencho Slaveikov (lyricist, epic poet, literary critic and folklorist).
By arrangement.

HRISTO SMYRNENSKI MUSEUM
116 E. Shekerdjiiski Street, Sofia
Material illustrating the life and work of Hristo Smyrnenski, proletarian poet and representative of socialist realism.
By arrangement.

ALEXANDER STAMBOLISKY MUSEUM
Suhudol 44, Sofia
Exhibits illustrating the life of Stambolisky (1879-1923). Documents relating to the Agrarian Union Government of 1920-23 and to the Peasant Uprising in Pazardjik led by Stambolisky.
By arrangement.

NIKOLA VAPTSAROV MUSEUM
37 Angel Kunchev Street, Sofia
House in which the poet Nikola Vaptsarov lived and worked from 1940 to 1942. Personal possessions. Manuscripts.
By arrangement.

IVAN VASOV MUSEUM
Ul. I. Vasov 10, Sofia
Attached to the Institute of Literature, Bulgarian Academy of Sciences; the house in which the Bulgarian poet lived.
By appointment.

P. K. YAVOROV MUSEUM
136 Rakoski Street, Sofia
House containing personal possessions of the poet, playwright and revolutionary, P. K. Yavorov.
By arrangement.

STARA ZAGORA

ARCHAEOLOGICAL MUSEUM
Stara Zagora
Prehistoric material from excavations in the Stara Zagora area. Medieval archaeology.
Daily 9-12, 2-5.

GEO MILEV HOUSE-MUSEUM
Geo Milev ulica, Stara Zagora
Life and work of the poet and translator, Geo Milev (d.1915).
On request.

REGIONAL MUSEUM OF HISTORY
Ruski 42, Stara Zagora
Archaeology. History. Ethnography. Documents, photographs and other material illustrating history of Stara Zagora, its cultural development and revolutionary activity.
Daily 9-5.

SVIŠTOV

HISTORY MUSEUM
Svištov
In former home of the writer, Aleko Konstantinov (murdered 1897). His heart, showing the fatal wound, is preserved in the museum. Collection illustrating life and work of Konstantinov.
On request.

TARGOVIŠČE

PROVINCIAL HISTORICAL MUSEUM
Hadzàngelovata kasća, Targovišce
History and archaeology of the Targovišce area. Furniture. Household equipment. Folk art.
Tu.-Su. 9-12, 2-5.

TARNOVO

PROVINCIAL MUSEUM
Tarnovo
History of Tarnovo. Material illustrating Tarnovo before the Turkish occupation. Tools. Ornaments. Pottery. Frescoes. Mosaics. Tarnovo during the Ottoman period. Handicrafts. Struggle for national emancipation. History of the workers' and resistance movements.
Tu.-Su. 10-6.

TURKISH PRISON
Tarnovo
Prison (1864). Cells, with beds and straitjackets. Dungeon where Bačo Kiro Petrov was imprisoned (1876). Torture chamber.
M., Tu., Th.-Sa. 8-11.30, 2-5.30; Su. 9-11.30, 2-5.30.

TETEVEN

NATIONAL MUSEUM
Teteven
History of the local workers, revolutionary and resistance movements, and especially of the fighting which has taken place in the neighbouring mountains.
Tu.-Su. 9-1, 3-6.

TRJAVNA

MUSEUM OF WOOD CARVING AND MURAL PAINTINGS
P. Slavejkov 27, Trjavna
Carved wooden ceilings and other wood-carvings. Handicrafts. Local history.
Tu.-Sa. 9-1, 2-5; Su. 9-1.

TRJAVNA MUSEUM
Trjavna
History and archaeology of Trjavna and its area. Paintings. Folk art.
Daily 9-12, 2-5.

TROJAN

MUSEUM OF APPLIED ARTS AND CRAFTS
Pl. N. Vlaskovski, Trojan
19th-20th century Bulgarian paintings, sculpture. Furniture. Ceramics. Silver.
Tu.-Su. 10-5.

VARNA

ARCHAEOLOGICAL MUSEUM
Sejnovo 5, Varna
Archaeological material illustrating the civilisations - Thracian, Greek, Roman, Byzantine, Turkish, Bulgarian - which have existed in the Varna area. Medieval tools, utensils, ornaments, religious art. Pottery. Coins.
May-Sept., Su.-F. 9-11, 3-6; Oct.-Apr., Su.-F. 9-11, 3-5.30.

ART GALLERY
Bul. Lenin 65, Varna
19th-20th century Bulgarian paintings, sculpture. 17th-19th century European paintings, especially German, Dutch.
May 30- Sept. 30, daily 9-11, 3-6; Oct. 1- May 29, daily 9-12, 2.30-6.

MUSEUM OF ICON-PAINTING
Ignatiev ulica 19, Varna
In Sveti Athanas church. 16th-19th century Bulgarian icons. 17th-19th century engravings, lithographs, missals.
Tu.-Sa. 9-11, 3-6.30; Su. 9-11.

MUSEUM OF THE NATIONAL REBIRTH
27 Juli ulica 7, Varna
In the first Bulgarian school (1862), organised on the Bell and Lancaster system, with its original equipment. History of the Bulgarian struggle for independence. Icons.
May 30-Sept. 30, M., W., F. 9-11, 3-6.30; Su. 3-6.30. Oct. 1-May 29, M., W., F. 9-11, 3-5.30; Su. 3-5.30.

MUSEUM OF THE REVOLUTIONARY MOVEMENT
ulica 8 November 7, Varna
History of the revolutionary movement in Varna, 1818-1944, against the background of the development of the city. Careers and activities of the leading figures in the movement.
May 30- Sept. 30, M.-Sa. 9-11, 4-6.30; Su. 3-6.30. Oct. 1- May 29, M.-Sa. 9-11, 4-5.30; Su. 3-5.30.

NATURAL HISTORY MUSEUM
Varna
Geology, botany and zoology of the Varna region. Palaeography. Black Sea and tropical marine life. Coral. Parrots. Tropical butterflies.
May-Sept., Su.-F. 9-11, 3-6. Oct.-Apr., Su.-F. 9-11, 3-5.30.

NAVAL MUSEUM
Bul. Tschervenoarmejski 2, Varna
History of shipping on the Danube and the Black Sea Fleet. Museum includes the gunboat and later training-ship, 'Drăjski' and the 'Amalia', the first ship built in Bulgaria. Special exhibit devoted to Ivan Zabulanov who, in 1900, organised the distribution of Lenin's newspaper *Iskra* to Odessa.
May 30- Sept. 30, Tu., W., F.-Su. 9-12, 3-7. Oct. 1- May 29, Tu., W., F.-Su. 9-12, 2-6.

PARK-MUSEUM OF THE BROTHERHOOD OF ARMS
Varna
Site-museum commemorating battle of Varna (1444). Exhibits illustrating the battle and its historical context.
May 30- Oct. 30, Tu.-W., F.-Su. 9-5; Th. 11-5. Nov. 1- May 29, Tu.-W., F.-Su. 9-5.

REGIONAL MUSEUM OF HISTORY
Varna
Archaeology. History. Ethnography.
May-Sept., Su.-F. 9-11, 3-6. Oct.-Apr., Su.-F. 9-11, 3-5.30.

GEORGI VELČEV HOUSE-MUSEUM
Schetschka-Karamfilova ulica 8, Varna
In birthplace, home and studio of the marine painter, G. Velčev (d.1955). Works by Velčev, with exhibits illustrating his life.
Sa.-M., W., Th. 10-12, 4-7.

VASOVGRAD (formerly SOPOT)

IVAN VAZOV HOUSE-MUSEUM
Vasovgrad
Birthplace of the writer, Ivan Vasov (1850-1921). Collections illustrating his life and work.
On request.

VELIKO TĂRNOVO

REGIONAL MUSEUM OF HISTORY
I Boteva 1, Veliko Tărnovo
History of Veliko Tărnovo and its region.
Daily 9-5.

VIDIN

ARCHAEOLOGICAL MUSEUM
Vidin
Archaeological material, especially Roman, from local sites and excavations.
Tu.-Su. 10-1, 3-6.

MUSEUM OF THE REVOLUTIONARY YOUTH MOVEMENT
Vidin
In former home of Bojan Čonos, victim of the resistance movement in Vidin. Collections illustrating the history of the revolutionary and resistance movements, and of the life of Čonos.
Daily 9-5.

REGIONAL MUSEUM OF HISTORY
G. Dimitrov 55, Vidin
Archaeology. Ethnography. Folklore. History of the Revolution. Agriculture.
Daily 9-5.

VRATSA

NATIONAL MUSEUM
Vratsa
History and archaeology of the Vratsa area. Ethnography.
Tu.-Su. 10-1, 3-5.

YAMBOL

NATIONAL MUSEUM
Yambol
History and archaeology of Yambol and its region.
Tu.-Su. 9-12, 3-5.

ZHERAVNA

TORDAN YOVKOV HOUSE-MUSEUM
Zheravna
Former home of the writer, Tordan Yovkov, with furnishings and his personal possessions. Examples of his work.
On request.

Burma

The museums of this largely agricultural country are devoted mainly to its history and religion, with little about agriculture, although the Natural History Museum in Rangoon has a section devoted to Burma's very important forestry and timber industry. As in all Buddhist countries, the dividing line between temples and pagodas on the one hand and museums on the other is not always easy to establish, especially when the pagoda is a museum exhibit in its own right.

KYAUKPYU

STATE LIBRARY AND MUSEUM
Kyaukpyu
History. Silver coins. Costumes.
Daily ex. F. 10-3.

MANDALAY

STATE LIBRARY AND MUSEUM
Mandalay
History of the 19th century city of Mandalay and its former ruling dynasty. History. Architectural fragments from palace buildings. Art objects (19th century).
Daily ex. F. 10-3.

MOULMEIN

STATE LIBRARY AND MUSEUM
Moulmein
History of Moulmein and the surrounding district. Art objects. Architectural fragments.
Daily ex. F. 10-3.

PAGAN

ARCHAEOLOGY MUSEUM
Pagan
On site of many 11th-13th century temples and other buildings, many with murals. Archaeology of the area. Inscriptions.
Daily ex. F. 10-3.

PEGU

SHWENAWDAW PAGODA MUSEUM
Pegu
Bronzes. Modern religious items.
Daily ex. F. 10-3.

RANGOON

BOGYOKE AUNG SAN MUSEUM
25 Tower Lane, Rangoon
Collection illustrating the life and work of General Aung San.
Daily ex. F. 10-3.

INTERNATIONAL INSTITUTE OF ADVANCED BUDDHIC STUDIES MUSEUM
Kaba-aye Pagoda Compound, Rangoon
Buddhist art and archaeology. Manuscripts dealing with history of pagodas in Burma.
By appointment.

NATIONAL MUSEUM OF ART AND ARCHAEOLOGY
Jubilee Hall, Pagoda Road, Rangoon
Paintings. Replica of King Mindon's Mandalay Palace. Traditional handicrafts. Ethnology. Contemporary paintings. Mandalay court regalia, including the Lion Throne.
Daily ex. F. 10-3.

NATURAL HISTORY MUSEUM
Former Boat Club, Royal Lake, Rangoon
Mammals. Fish. Geology. Forestry, including section on the timbers of Burma.
Daily ex. F. 10-3.

Burundi

Administered, before gaining independence in 1962, first by Germany and then Belgium, and then, after 1962, the victim of much internal plotting, coups and blood-letting, Burundi has not had a great deal of energy to spare for museums. The three which exist do, however, contain interesting collections to show the traditional life of the people, and are particularly strong on handicrafts and household utensils.

ASTRIDA

ETHNOGRAPHIC MUSEUM
Astrida
Folklore and ethnography. Costumes. Domestic equipment. Handicrafts. Tools.
Daily 9-5.

BUJUMBURA

MUSEUM OF AFRICAN CIVILISATION
Bujumbura
Collections illustrating African arts and handicrafts. Paintings.
Daily 9-5.

KITEGA

NATIONAL MUSEUM
Place de la Révolution, Kitega
History and art. Collections of musical instruments, weapons and witchcraft utensils.
Daily 7-4.30.

Cameroun

The Federal Republic of Cameroun includes East Cameroun formerly French) and West Cameroun (formerly British). Its museums are devoted almost entirely to art and handicrafts, with some particularly good collections of carvings, sculpture and masks.

BAFOUSSAM

BAFOUSSAM MUSEUM
Bafoussam
Local history. Ethnography.
Daily 9-12, 2-5.

BAMENDA

MANKON MUSEUM
Mezam Division, Bamenda
Local history. Ethnography.
Daily 9-12, 2-5.

DOUALA

DOUALA MUSEUM
P.O. Box 1271, Douala
Ethnography and traditional art. Prehistory, zoology, mineralogy and geology.
Daily 9-12, 2-5.

DSCHANG

BAMILIKE MUSEUM
Dschang
Traditional art museum, containing sculptures, masks, skulls and pottery.
Daily 8-12, 2.30-6.

FOUMBAN

MUSEUM OF ETHNOGRAPHY AND ART
Centre Ifan, Foumban
Ethnography. Art. Handicrafts.
Daily 9-12, 2-5.

MUSEUM OF THE BAMOUN ROYAL PALACE
Palais du Sultanat Bamoun, Foumban
Archaeology. History. Ethnography. Skulls. Hand-carved thrones. Handicrafts.
Daily 7-12, 2-5.30.

GUIDER

GUIDER MUSEUM
Guider
Local history. Ethnography.
Daily 9-12, 2-5.

KOUSSÉRI

KOUSSÉRI MUSEUM
Kousséri
Local history. Ethnography.
Daily 9-12, 2-5.

MAROUA

MAROUA MUSEUM
B.P. 36, Maroua
Local history. Ethnography.
Daily 9-12, 2-5.

MOKOLO

MUNICIPAL MUSEUM
Mokolo
History of Mokolo and the surrounding district. Ethnography, including costumes.
Daily 9-12, 2-5.

YAOUNDÉ

MUSEUM OF CAMEROUN ART
B.P. 1178, Yaoundé
Paintings and sculpture by Cameroun artists.
Daily 9-12, 2-5.

MUSEUM OF NEGRO ART
c/o Centre Catholique, B.P. 876, Universitaire de Yaoundé, Yaoundé
Traditional art. Archaeology. Prehistory. Ancient objets d'art of different African regions. Coins from Ethiopia dating back to early Christian times. Ceramics.
Daily 8-12, 3-6. Also 8-10 p.m. by arrangement.

Canada

Canadian museums are, one might say, the same as those to be found across the border in the United States, but different. The similarities are in the National Park Centres - a splendid North American invention - in the restored forts and schoolhouses, in the university museums and art galleries, in the museums devoted to lumbering, mining and pioneer life, in the Indian collections - although the Canadian collections tend to be less patronising - and in the former palaces of millionaires. The differences are equally significant and not difficult to observe - the absence of the colonial house-museums, which are such a successful feature of the museum landscape in the United States; the small amount of early manufacturing industry to record and document; the need to reflect two cultures, the English and the French, in a way that avoids political problems; and the very minor scale of the negro contribution to the national life.

Canada has a number of excellent museums illustrating the history of the agricultural and fishing industries, and both the Royal Canadian Mounted Police and the army are well supplied with museums to prevent their traditions from being forgotten. Open-air museums are increasingly popular, but they have to contend with the Canadian winter.

Certain special features of Canadian museums should be mentioned. One is the trouble which has been taken to give adequate representation to the art and handicrafts of the Eskimos. This, especially the sculpture, lends itself very well to museum displays, and, in several instances, the Eskimo material forms one of the most attractive sections of the museum. One should also notice the development, especially in Nova Scotia, of a type of country-house museum which is rather different from anything one is accustomed to in England or the United States, a medium-sized country mansion, usually of the first half of the nineteenth century, which is used to display not so much fine furniture or works of art as collections illustrating the history and occupations of the district.

In 1967, the centenary of the founding of Canada in its present political form, many towns set up what are described as Centennial Museums. This was done with the encouragement and help of the Government and the Provinces. The Centennial Museums are still young, and they are certainly very mixed in quality. At their worst, they provide repositories for interesting local material which might otherwise have disappeared for ever, and at their best they present exhibitions of history, bygones, handicrafts, photographs and personal relics which increase local patriotism and help to make sense of the settlement and growth of the area. The Centennial Museums are a peculiarly Canadian institution, corresponding most nearly to the *Heimatmuseums* in Germany and the *Vlastivedne* museum in Czechoslovakia. Fortunately, one is not required to find a translation for "Centennial Museum".

ADOLPHUSTOWN

UNITED EMPIRE LOYALIST MUSEUM
Adolphustown Park, Adolphustown, Ontario
Story of the Loyalists' emigration to the Province and the contribution they made to its early development. Documents. Maps. Pioneer furnishings, tools, household utensils.
June 1 - 30: W., Sa., Su. 2-5.30. July 1 - Aug. 31: Tu.-Su. 2-5.30.

ALBERTA BEACH

GARDEN PARK FARM MUSEUM
Alberta Beach, Alberta
Agricultural history. Implements. Machinery.
Daily 9-5.

ALBERTON

ALBERTON MUSEUM
Poplar Street, Alberton, Prince Edward Island
In reconstruction of early 19th century house. Period furnishings. Local history.
July 1 - Aug. 31: M.-Sa. 10-5.

ALERT BAY

ALERT BAY PUBLIC LIBRARY AND MUSEUM
Alert Bay, British Columbia
Kwawkewith Indian material. Masks. Clothing. Tools. Utensils.
M. 7.30 p.m.-9.30; Sa. 2-4.

KWAKWALA ARTS AND CRAFTS ASSOCIATION MUSEUM
Alert Bay, British Columbia
Indian museum. Reconstruction of Community House. Costumes. Masks. Totems.
May 1 - Oct. 10, 1.30-4.30.

ALGONQUIN

ALGONQUIN PIONEER LOGGING EXHIBIT
Algonquin Park, Highway 60, Algonquin, Ontario
History of logging in the area.
May 9 - June 7, Sept. 14 - Oct. 18: Sa., Su., public holidays 10-6. June 8-26, Sept. 7-13, daily 10-6. June 27 - Sept. 6, daily 9.30-8.

ALGONQUIN PROVINCIAL PARK VISITOR CENTRE
Highway 60, Algonquin, Ontario
Geology, fish and wildlife of Park. Archaeology.
May 9 - June 7: Sa., Su., public holidays 10-6. June 8-26, Sept. 7 - Oct. 18, daily 10-6. June 27 - Sept. 6, daily 9.30-8.

ALLISTON

SOUTH SIMCOE PIONEER MUSEUM
Riverdale Park, Alliston, Ontario
In pioneer log cabin (1851). Pioneer household equipment and agricultural implements. Furniture. Guns.
July 1 - Sept. 30: Tu.-Sa. 12-8.

ALMONTE

MILL OF KINTAIL MUSEUM
Rural Route 1, Almonte, Ontario, KOA 1AO
In mill (1830). Sculpture by Dr. Robert Tait McKenzie, in his former home and studio. Pioneer relics from Ottawa Valley region.
June 1 - Oct. 15: Su. 2-6; M., W.-Sa. daily 10-12, 2-6.

AMELIASBURGH

AMELIASBURGH MUSEUM
Between Highways 33 and 14, Ameliasburgh, Ontario, KOK 1AO
Log cabin, furnished in 1850 period. Pioneer material. Indian artifacts.
May 16 - June 29, Aug. 29 - Oct. 12: Sa., Su. 1-5, 7-9. June 30 - Aug. 28, daily 2-5, 7-9.

AMHERST

CENTENNIAL CENTRE
City Hall, Amherst, Nova Scotia
Local history.
M.-F. 9-5.

AMHERSTBURG

FORT MALDEN NATIONAL HISTORIC PARK
E. Bank of Detroit River, Amherstburg, Ontario
Fort (1797-9). Objects associated with history of the fort and the region. History of fugitive slaves.
Daily 9-6.

ANNAPOLIS ROYAL

FORT ANNE NATIONAL HISTORIC PARK
St. George Street, Annapolis, Nova Scotia
Remains of fort (1797). Displays illustrating Acadian settlement and hostilities between English and French.
Apr. 1 - June 14, Labour Day - Nov. 30, daily 10-5.

ARICHAT

LENOIR FORGE
Arichat, Nova Scotia
Restored French-style forge (c.1867). Museum collections of anchor-making and ships' chandlery.
June 1 - Sept. 30, dawn-dusk.

ARNPRIOR

ARNPRIOR AND DISTRICT MUSEUM
John and Madawaska Streets, Arnprior, Ontario
Local history. Fur trade. Lumber industry. Agriculture. Household equipment.
May 12 - Sept. 30: Tu.-Sa. 2-5; F. also 7 p.m.-8.30; Su. 2-4.

ARTHABASKA

LAURIER MUSEUM
16 Avenue Laurier, Arthabaska, Quebec
Formerly residence (1867-96) of Sir Wilfrid Laurier. Period furnishings. Paintings by Suzor Côté. Sculpture by Alfred Laliberté. Engravings by Henry Julien.
W.-F. 9-12, 1.30-5; Sa., Su. 1-5.

ASHCROFT

ASHCROFT MUSEUM
Railway Avenue, Ashcroft, British Columbia
Local history. Mineralogy. Freight waggons. Indian material.
June 1 - Sept. 30, 10-5. Other months by appointment.

ATIKOKAN

ATIKOKAN CENTENNIAL MUSEUM
Civic Centre, Atikokan, Ontario
History of area. Logging equipment, including restored logging engine and train. Fur trade. Iron-ore industry.
M.-F. 1-5, 7-9; Sept. 1 - June 30, also Sa. 2-5. July 1 - Aug. 31, also Sa., Su. 11-3.

QUETICO PROVINCIAL PARK MUSEUM
Dawson Trail Camp Grounds, Highway 11, French Lake, Atikokan, Ontario
Flora, fauna and history of Quetico Park.
June 15 - 30, Sa., Su. 10-5. July 1 - Sept. 13, daily 10-5.

AULAC

FORT BEAUSEJOUR NATIONAL HISTORIC PARK MUSEUM
Aulac, New Brunswick
History of Albert, Chigneto and Westmorland Counties, New Brunswick, and Cumberland County, Nova Scotia.
Apr. 1 - June 15 and Labour Day - Nov. 30, daily 10-5. June 15 - Labour Day, daily 9-8. Closed Dec.-Mar.

AUSTIN

MANITOBA AGRICULTURAL MUSEUM
Trans-Canada and No. 34 Highways, Austin, Manitoba, ROH OCO
Agricultural implements. Horse-drawn implements. Old cars. Pioneer furniture and utensils. Indian artifacts. Pioneer town of buildings moved to museum site.
May 1 - Oct. 31, 9-9. Other months by appointment.

AYLESFORD

AYLESFORD MUSEUM OF CANADIANA
Aylesford, Nova Scotia
19th century Nova Scotia furniture, domestic equipment, utensils. Glass. Coins.
June 1 - Oct. 31, daily 9-6.

AYLMER EAST

CANADIAN GOLF MUSEUM
Kingsway Park, Mountain Road, Aylmer East, Quebec
Collections showing development of golf clubs and balls, 1830s onwards. Prints. Portraits.
May 1 - Oct. 31, daily 10-5.

BADDECK

ALEXANDER GRAHAM BELL MUSEUM
Baddeck, Nova Scotia
Scientific achievements of Dr. Bell and his associates. Tetrahedral kites. Powered aircraft and the hydrofoil. Helicopters. Jet propulsion. Solar stills. Air-conditioning. Mulberry harbour. Sheep-breeding. Genetics. Telephones.
Apr. 1 - June 14, daily 10-5. June 15 - Labour Day, 9-8. Day after Labour Day - Nov. 30, 10-5.

BAIE COMEAU

CÔTE-NORD HISTORICAL SOCIETY MUSEUM
Centre Culturel, Baie Comeau, Quebec
Local history. Indian artifacts. Tools. Household equipment. Snowshoes. Guns. Photographs.
M.-Sa. 9-12, 1-5.

BALDWIN TOWNSHIP

BEAVER VALLEY MUSEUM
Beaver Valley Park, Baldwin Township, Ontario
History of early settlement in the area. Development of pulp and paper industries.
July 1 - Aug. 31: M.-Sa. 10-9; Su. 1-9.

BALMORAL

BALMORAL GRIST MILL
Balmoral via Tatamagouche, Nova Scotia
Restored grist mill (1831), operational for 1 hour morning and afternoon.
May 15 - Oct. 15, daily 9-5.

BANCROFT

BANCROFT HISTORICAL MUSEUM
Station Street, Bancroft, Ontario, KOL ICO
In log house (1897), moved to site. Local history. Pioneer relics.
July 1 - Aug. 31, daily 1-5. Labour Day - Thanksgiving: Sa., Su. 1-5. Other times by appointment.

BANFF

BANFF NATIONAL PARK NATURAL HISTORY MUSEUM
Banff Avenue, Banff, Alberta, TOL OCO
Botany, animals, birds, fishes of the Canadian Rockies.
May 1 - Sept. 30, daily 11-8. Oct. 1 - Apr. 30, Th.-M. 10-6. Closed Christmas, New Year.

LUXTON MUSEUM
Banff, Alberta, TOL OCO
Mounted birds, animals. Tools, utensils, weapons, costumes of the Plains and Woodland Indians.
Oct. 1 - Apr. 30. Tu.-Su. 10-12, 1.30-5. May 1 - Sept. 30, daily 9-9. Closed Dec. 24-25, Jan. 1.

MUSEUM OF ARCHIVES OF THE CANADIAN ROCKIES
Box 160, Banff, Alberta, TOL OCO
History of mountaineering, especially in the Rockies. Paintings. Prints.
M.-F. 10-5; Sa. 1-5. Closed Christmas.

BARKERVILLE

BARKERVILLE HISTORIC PARK
Barkerville, British Columbia
Restoration of Gold Rush town (1869-85), with houses, stores, workshops and public buildings. Displays of mining techniques.
Apr. 1-30, daily 8-5. May 1 - Oct. 15, daily 8-8.

BARLOCHAN

WOODWINDS HISTORICAL MUSEUM
Barlochan, Ontario
Log building, with pioneer furnishings. Frame building, with Indian artifacts, glass. Logging equipment. Agricultural implements.
June 1 - Aug. 31, daily 10-5.

BARRHEAD

BARRHEAD AND DISTRICT CENTENNIAL MUSEUM
Box 546, Barrhead, Alberta, TOG OEO
Local history. Mineralogy. Pioneer life. Indian artifacts.
June 1 - Oct. 31: Sa. 2-5. Other times by appointment.

BARRINGTON

OLD MEETING HOUSE
Barrington, Nova Scotia
Oldest non-conformist church in Canada (1765). Local history.
July 1 - Labour Day: Tu.-Sa. 10-12, 1.30-5.30; Su. 1-5.30.

OLD WOOLLEN MILL MUSEUM
Barrington, Nova Scotia
Restored water-powered mill (1882). Displays showing method of wool production and processing in Nova Scotia fishing community.
June 15 - Sept. 15: daily 9.30-5.30.

BATOCHE

BATOCHE NATIONAL HISTORIC SITE
Batoche, Saskatchewan, SOK OKO
Material concerning rebellion of the Metis (1885). Archaeology. Anthropology. Ethnology. Agriculture. Industry.
July 1 - Aug. 31, daily 10-9. May 1 - June 30, Sept. 1 - Oct. 31: M.-Sa. 9-5; Su. 2-dusk.

BATTLEFORD

FORT BATTLEFORD NATIONAL HISTORIC PARK
Battleford, Saskatchewan, SOM OEO
5 restored buildings (1877-98) of N.W. Mounted Police district headquarters. Displays relating to N.W. Territorial Government, N.W. Mounted Police, N.W. Rebellion and Plains Indians.
July 1 - Aug. 31, daily 10-9. May 1 - June 30, Sept. 1 - Oct. 31: M.-Sa. 9-5; Su. 2-dusk.

BEAVERLODGE

SOUTH PEACE CENTENNIAL MUSEUM
Beaverlodge, Alberta
Local history.
M.-Sa. 9-5; Su. 10-4.

BELLEVILLE

HASTINGS COUNTY MUSEUM
257 Bridge Street East, Belleville, Ontario, K8N IP4
History of area. Victorian furnishings. 19th century European paintings. Lamps. Furniture, china, silver and oils from the Couldery Estate, formerly of Ventnor, Isle of Wight.
Tu.-F. 9-4; Sa. 10-4; Su. 1-4. Closed M.

BLIND RIVER

TIMBER VILLAGE MUSEUM
Park Street, Blind River, Ontario
History of lumbering and agriculture in the area. Models. Implements and equipment. Replicas of lumber camp buildings, including blacksmith's shop.
May 1 - Oct. 31: M.-F. 10-8; Sa., Su. 12-5.

BOISSEVAIN

CENTENNIAL HISTORICAL MUSEUM
Boissevain, Manitoba, ROK OEO
Local history. Pioneer life.
By appointment.

BONAVENTURE

BONAVENTURE ACADIAN MUSEUM
Avenue Grand-Pré, Bonaventure, Quebec
Geology and fossils of the area. Local history and archaeology. Acadian history.
Daily 8.30-8.

BONSHAW

CAR LIFE MUSEUM
Bonshaw, Prince Edward Island
Early cars. 19th - early 20th century agricultural machinery.
May 20 - June 30, Sept. 1 - Oct. 15: daily 10-6. July 1 - Aug. 31, daily 9-9.

BORDEN

CANADIAN FORCES INTELLIGENCE AND SECURITY MUSEUM
Canadian Forces Base, Borden, Ontario
History of Canadian military intelligence. Escape kits. Maps. Propaganda.
M.-F. 8-4; Sa., Su. by appointment.

ROYAL CANADIAN ARMY SERVICE CORPS MUSEUM
Canadian Forces Base, Building S-89, Ortona Road and Lundy's Lane, Borden, Ontario
History of Corps. Weapons.
M.-F. 9-4; W. 9-12; Sa., Su., public holidays 2-4.

WORTHINGTON MUSEUM
Canadian Forces Base, Combat Arms School, Borden, Ontario
Canadian military history. Weapons. Equipment. Special collection illustrating history of Royal Canadian Electrical and Mechanical Engineers.
M.-F. 8-4.30; Sa., Su. 1-5.

BOTHWELL

FAIRFIELD MUSEUM
Highway 2, Bothwell, Ontario, NOP ICO
Story of Moravians and of their missionary work (1735 onwards) with Delaware Indians, especially Indian refugees from the U.S. Relics of Fairfield (burnt by U.S. invaders, 1813). Indian artifacts.
M.-Sa. 9-5; Su. 1.30-7.

BOWDEN

BOWDEN CENTENNIAL CENTRE
Bowden, Alberta
History of the Bowden area.
Daily 9-4.

BOWMANVILLE

BOWMANVILLE MUSEUM
37 Silver Street, Bowmanville, Ontario
House (1861). Victorian period rooms. Early trades and crafts. Musical instruments. Toys. Costumes.
May 25 - Oct. 15, daily 2-5.

THE PIONEER HOUSE
Darlington Provincial Park, Bowmanville, Ontario
2 storey log-house, restored and furnished in style of 1820-40.
June 15 - Sept. 15: Sa. 1-5; Su., public holidays 9-12.

BRAMPTON

PEEL COUNTY MUSEUM AND ART GALLERY
7 Wellington Street E., Brampton, Ontario
History of Peel County. Agriculture. Industry. Transport. Paintings by Canadian artists.
Jan. 3 - Nov. 29: Sa., Su. 1.30-4.30. May 26 - Oct. 9 also Tu.-F. 1.30-4.30.

BRANDON

B. J. HALES MUSEUM OF NATURAL HISTORY
Brandon University, 270 18th Street, Brandon, Manitoba, R7A 5A7
Birds and mammals of Manitoba. Indian artifacts.
Daily 2-5.

BRANTFORD

ART GALLERY OF BRANT
20 Ava Road, Brantford, Ontario, N3T 1A1
Worldwide collection of prints, drawings. Paintings by Canadian artists.
Tu.-F. 2-8; Sa., Su. 2-6. Closed Dec. 24-25, 31, Jan. 1, Good F.

BELL HOMESTEAD
94 Tutela Heights Road, Brantford, Ontario, N3T 1A1
Formerly home of Alexander Graham Bell, where the first long-distance telephone call was made. Period furnishings. Exhibits of telephones and other inventions by Bell.
June 1 - Sept. 30: Tu.-Su. 9-9. Oct. 1 - May 31, daily 9-6.

BRANT COUNTY HISTORICAL MUSEUM
57 Charlotte Street, Brantford, Ontario, N3T 2W6
Early pioneer life in Brant County. Displays illustrating lives of some of the area's prominent historical figures, including Alexander Graham Bell.
May 1 - Aug. 31: Tu.-Su. 2-5. Sept. 1 - Apr. 30: Tu., Th., Sa., 1st and 3rd Su. in month, 2-5.

BRIDGEWATER

DES BRISAY MUSEUM
Municipal Park, Bridgewater, Nova Scotia
History of Lunenburg County. Collections illustrating contributions of Micmac Indians, French, English and German communities.
June 1 - Sept. 30: Tu.-Su. 10-12, 2-5, 7-9. Oct. 1 - Apr. 30: Tu.-Sa. 10-12, 2-5; Su. 2-4.30.

BRIGHTON

PRESQU'ILE PROVINCIAL PARK MUSEUM
R.R.5, Brighton, Ontario, KOK 1HO
In former lighthouse keeper's house. Geology, botany, animals, birds and fish of the area. Relics of early settlers.
May 15 - June 27, Sept. 2-15: Sa., Su. 10-5. June 28 - Sept. 1, daily 10-6.

BROUGHAM

PICKERING TOWNSHIP MUSEUM
Highway 7, Brougham, Ontario
Museum complex, with buildings including school (1859) log cabin and barn (1830), blacksmith's shop and display barns, with collections of steam and petrol engines, pioneer tools and household equipment. Indian artifacts.
May 16 - June 26, Sept. 19 - Oct. 18: Sa., Su. 2-6. June 27 - Sept. 18: M.-F. 2-5; Sa., Su. 2-6.

BRUCE MINES

BRUCE MINES MUSEUM
Highway 17, Bruce Mines, Ontario
In former church. Local history. Household equipment. Agricultural implements. Indian artifacts. History of Bruce Mines. Rock specimens.
June 1 - Sept. 10, daily 9-8.

BULYEA

LAKESIDE MUSEUM
Bulyea, Saskatchewan, SOG 0L0
Indian artifacts. Pioneer tools, household equipment. Dinosaur bones.
Daily, on request.

BURLINGTON

JOSEPH BRANT MUSEUM
1240 N. Shore Boulevard E., Burlington, Ontario
Replica of last home of the Mohawk Indian Chief, Captain Joseph Brant. Indian artifacts. Pioneer history of Southern Ontario. Memorabilia of Captain Brant and his family.
M.-Sa. 10-5; Su. 1-5. Other times by appointment. Closed Christmas, New Year.

BURNABY

BURNABY ART GALLERY
6344 Gilpin Street, Burnaby, British Columbia
Etchings, prints, drawings by contemporary Canadian artists.
M.-F. 1-5; W., also 7-9; Sa. 10-5; Su. 1-5. Closed public holidays.

CALGARY

ART GALLERY OF THE UNIVERSITY OF CALGARY
29th Avenue and 29th Street N.W., Calgary, Alberta
Paintings by contemporary Canadian artists.
M.-F. 8.30-11; Sa. 8.30-4.30.

CALGARY ALLIED ARTS CENTRE
830 9th Avenue S.W., Calgary, Alberta, T2P 1L7
Works by 20th century Canadian artists. Drawings. Prints.
M.-Sa. 9 a.m.-10.30 p.m.; Su. 2-9.

CALGARY BREWERY HORSEMAN'S HALL OF FAME
1892 15th Street S.E., Calgary, Alberta, T2G 3M2
History of pioneer ranching families of Alberta Foothills.
July 1-31: daily 10-8; Aug. 1-June 30: daily 10-5.

CALGARY CENTENNIAL PLANETARIUM
Mewata Park, Calgary, Alberta, T2P 2M5
Astronomy. Planetarium. Aircraft. Aeroplane engines.
W.-Su., daily 1.30-10.30.

CALGARY ZOOLOGICAL GARDENS, PALAEONTOLOGICAL PARK
St. George's Island, Calgary, Alberta
Fossils. 50 life-sized replicas of dinosaurs.
May 1 - Sept. 30, daily 8-dusk.

GALLERY OF ALBERTA COLLEGE OF ART
1301 16th Avenue N.W., Calgary, Alberta, T2M 0L4
Works by 20th century Canadian artists. Paintings. Sculpture. Prints. Drawings.
Sept. 1 - May 31: M.-Th. 12-1, 7-10.

GLENBOW-ALBERTA INSTITUTE
902 11th Avenue S.W., Calgary, Alberta, T2R 0E7
Mineralogy. History and ethnology of Western Canada. Coins.
Tu.-F. 10-9; M., Sa. 10-5; Su., public holidays 11.30-6.

GLENBOW FOUNDATION, ALBERTA GOVERNMENT MUSEUM
7th Avenue and 5th Street S.W., Calgary, Alberta
Natural history. Local and military history. Pioneer life. Indian material. Paintings, prints related to history of Canadian Northwest.
By appointment.

HERBARIUM
University of Calgary, Calgary, Alberta
Botany of Canada, especially Alberta.
By appointment during University terms.

HERITAGE PARK
82nd Avenue and 14th Street S.W., Calgary, Alberta
Pioneer village illustrating life in early 20th century. 45 buildings moved to site. Operating steam locomotive. Paddle wheel steamer.
Daily, 9-dusk.

LORD STRATHCONA'S HORSE (ROYAL CANADIAN MUSEUM)
Sarcee Camp, Calgary, Alberta
History of the regiment. Weapons. Equipment. Photographs. Documents.
May-Oct., M.-Sa. 10-4.

MUSEUM OF ZOOLOGY
University of Calgary, Calgary, Alberta
Zoology of North America.
M.-Sa. 9-5, during University terms.

THE QUEEN'S OWN RIFLES OF CANADA REGIMENTAL MUSEUM
Currie Barracks, Calgary, Alberta
History of the Regiment. Uniforms and equipment. Weapons. Medals. Photographs.
M.-F. 10-4.30; Su., public holidays by appointment.

REGIMENTAL MUSEUM OF PRINCESS PATRICIA'S CANADIAN LIGHT INFANTRY
Currie Barracks, Calgary, Alberta, T3E 1T8
History of the Regiment. Uniforms. Weapons. Equipment. Photographs. Paintings.
M.-F. 8-4.30; Sa., Su. by appointment.

CALUMET

CIP NATURE CENTRE
R.R.2, Calumet, Quebec
Natural history. Herbarium. Transport. Technology. Tree breeding and propagation.
Daily 8.30-5.

CAMPBELL RIVER

CAMPBELL RIVER CENTENNIAL MUSEUM
1235 Island Highway, Campbell River, British Columbia
Indian material, chiefly from Kwakintl tribe. Handicrafts. Masks. Pioneer artifacts.
May 15 - Sept. 30: Tu.-F. 1-5, 7-9, Sa. 10-12, 1-5. Oct. 1 - May 14: Tu., F., Sa. 3-5. Closed public holidays, Christmas, New Year.

CAMPOBELLO

CAMPOBELLO LIBRARY ASSOCIATION
Campobello, New Brunswick
Memorabilia and personal possessions of Owen family, original owners of the Island.
Tu.-F. 2-4.30.

ROOSEVELT SUMMER HOUSE AND PARK
Campobello, New Brunswick
Franklin D. Roosevelt's summer estate. Original and period furnishings. Roosevelt memorabilia.
May 15 - Sept. 30, daily 9-5.

CAMROSE

CAMROSE AND DISTRICT MUSEUM
52nd Street and 45th Avenue, Camrose, Alberta
Regional history. Exhibits illustrating pioneer life.
June 1 - Sept. 14: Tu.-Su. 2-9. Sept. 15 - Oct. 31: Su. 2-6.

CANNIFTON

O'HARA MILL
Box 68, Cannifton, Ontario
Sawmill and farmhouse (1848). Log schoolhouse (1861). Logging and lumber industry. Agriculture. Costumes. Furnishings.
May 20 - Labour Day, daily 9-dusk.

CANNINGTON

HEWETT HOME
Cannington, Saskatchewan
Pioneer house.
Daily 10-4.

CAPE SPEAR

CAPE SPEAR NATIONAL HISTORIC SITE
Cape Spear, Newfoundland
Lighthouse.
Daily 9-dusk.

CARAQUET

ACADIAN MUSEUM
Route 11, Caraquet, New Brunswick
Fossils. Acadian household objects and handicrafts. Agriculture.
May 15 - Aug. 31: M.-Sa. 10-9; Su. 1-5. Sept. 1 - Oct. 15: M.-Sa. 10-5.

CARBON

SIR JOHN A. MACDONALD MUSEUM
Carbon, Alberta, T0M 0L0
Regional history. Pioneer life. Agricultural implements and machinery. Tradesmen's tools.
By appointment.

CARDSTON

C.O. CARD HOME AND MUSEUM
Main Street, Cardston, Alberta, T0K 0K0
House (1887), former home of the Mormon pioneer, C. O. Card. Early history of Cardston.
July 1 - Aug. 31, daily 9-12, 1-5.

CARIK

PRAIRIE PIONEER MUSEUM
Box 273, Carik, Saskatchewan
Pioneer history. Tools. Machines. Clothing. Indian artifacts.
Apr.-Oct., F.-Su., public holidays, 2-5, 7-9. Other times by appointment.

CARMAN

DUFFERIN HISTORICAL PIONEER SETTLEMENT MUSEUM
Carman, Manitoba, R0G 0J0
Local history. Pioneer life. Furniture. Household equipment. Farm tools. Indian artifacts. Water colours showing pioneer farm life before 1900.
May 15 - Oct. 15: M.-Sa. 2.30-5; Su. 2-9.

CARILLON

ARGENTEUIL MUSEUM
Carillon, Quebec
In old Carillon Barracks (1829). Local history. Household utensils. Indian artifacts. Paintings. Memorabilia of Sir John Abbott.
May 1 - Oct. 31, daily 1-6.

CASTLEGAR

CASTLEGAR AND DISTRICT MUSEUM
Castlegar, British Columbia
Local history. Arrow Lakes steam boat relics. Mining. Industry. Blacksmith's shop. Camera collection. Doukhobor material.
June 1 - Sept. 30, daily 2-8.

CAUGHNAWAGA

KATERI TEKAKWITHA MUSEUM
Mission Saint François Xavier, Caughnawaga, Quebec
Religious history. Life and achievements of Kateri Tekakwitha (1656-80). Paintings.
Daily 9-9.

MUSEUM OF THE MISSION OF FORT ST. LOUIS
Caughnawaga, Quebec
Indian culture, and artifacts.
On request.

CAYUGA

HALDINAND HISTORICAL SOCIETY MUSEUM
Munsee Street, Cayuga, Ontario, N0A 1E0
In old County Court House. Pioneer material. Natural history. Indian artifacts. Log cabin, furnished in style of 1830s.
June 15 - Sept. 15: M.-Sa. 8-5; Su. 2-5. Log cabin open Su. only.

CHAMBLY

FORT CHAMBLY NATIONAL HISTORIC PARK
Richelieu and Fort Streets, Chambly, Quebec
French fort (1709). Displays illustrating military history.
Daily 9-5.

CHARLOTTETOWN

CONFEDERATION ART GALLERY AND MUSEUM
P.O. Box 848, Charlottetown, Prince Edward Island
Paintings by Canadian artists. Contemporary Canadian crafts. Pioneer history and relics.
Sept. 1 - June 30: Tu.-Sa. 10-5; Th. also 6 p.m.-8; Su., public holidays 2-5. July 1 - Labour Day: M.-Su. 10-9. Closed Christmas, New Year, Easter.

PRINCE EDWARD ISLAND HERITAGE FOUNDATION
P.O. Box 922, Charlottetown, Prince Edward Island
History of Prince Edward Island.
M.-F. 9-5.

CHATHAM

MIRAMICHI NATURAL HISTORY MUSEUM
149 Wellington Street, Chatham, New Brunswick
Birds and animals of New Brunswick. Pioneer history.
June-Oct., M.-Sa. 9-12, 1.30-5.

CHATHAM-KENT MUSEUM
59 William Street N., Chatham, Ontario, N7M 4L3
Pioneer life. Indian material. Memorabilia of Rev. Josiah Henson ('Uncle Tom, of *Uncle Tom's Cabin*). Birds.
Tu., Th., Sa. 2-5. 1st and 3rd Su. each month 2-5.

CHEAPSIDE

WILSON MACDONALD MEMORIAL SCHOOL MUSEUM
Rainham and Cheapside Roads, Cheapside, Ontario
School (1872) where the poet, Wilson MacDonald, received his early education. 19th century school furnishings, equipment. Pioneer life.
June 1 - Oct. 15: Su., public holidays 2-5. Other days by appointment.

CHETICAMP

ACADIAN MUSEUM
Cheticamp, Nova Scotia
French Acadian artifacts. Furniture. Spinning-wheels and looms. Glass. Farm tools and implements.
June 1 - Oct. 15: M.-Sa. 8-9; Su. 11-5.

CHICOUTIMI

SAGUENAY MUSEUM
Séminaire de Chicoutimi, Chicoutimi, Quebec
Local history and archaeology. Saguenay Indian material. Costumes. Agricultural implements. Coins.
Daily 10-12, 1.30-5. Th. also 8 p.m.-10.

LA SOCIÉTÉ DES ARTS
305 Hôtel de Ville Street, Chicoutimi, Quebec
Paintings. Graphics. Sculpture. Ceramics.
Sept.-May, daily 1.30-5.

CHILLIWACK

WELLS CENTENNIAL MUSEUM
209 S. Corbould Street, Chilliwack, British Columbia
Local history. Agriculture. Archaeology. Indian artifacts.
W.-Sa. 1.30-4.30.

CHURCHILL

ESKIMO MUSEUM
Catholic Church, Churchill, Manitoba, R0B 0E0
Eskimo artifacts, art, handicrafts.
M.-Sa. 9-12, 1-5, 7-8.30; Su. 1-4.

FORT PRINCE OF WALES NATIONAL HISTORIC PARK
Churchill, Manitoba, R0B 0E0
Ruins of Hudson's Bay Company fortress (1771). History of fortress.
By appointment.

CLARESHOLM

CLARESHOLM MUSEUM
Canadian Pacific Railway Station, Claresholm, Alberta, T0L 0T0
Exhibits illustrating local pioneer life.
By appointment.

CLEMENTSPORT

OLD ST. EDWARD'S CHURCH MUSEUM
Clementsport, Nova Scotia
In Church (1795). Furniture. Household equipment. Agriculture.
May-Sept., daily 9-5.

CLINTON

SOUTH CARIBOO HISTORICAL MUSEUM
Cariboo Highway, Clinton, British Columbia
Natural history. Anthropology. Pioneer history. Archaeology.
Easter Sa. - Nov. 30, daily 9-6. Other times by appointment.

CLOVERDALE

SURREY CENTENNIAL MUSEUM
17679 60th Avenue, Cloverdale, British Columbia
Local history. Early agricultural implements. Pioneer furniture and household equipment. Carpenter's tools. Indian handicrafts.
Daily 1-4.30.

COBALT

NORTHERN ONTARIO MINING MUSEUM
Silver Street, Cobalt, Ontario
Mineralogy. History of local silver mines. Early mining equipment. Silver.
June 1 - Oct. 31: M.-Sa. 9-5; Su. 10-5. Other times by appointment.

COBOURG

COBOURG PUBLIC LIBRARY ART GALLERY
18 Chapel Street, Cobourg, Ontario, K9A 1H9
Works by Canadian artists. Paintings. Drawings. Prints. Sculpture.
M.-Sa. 9-5.

COLINTON

KINNOUL HISTORICAL MUSEUM
Colinton, Alberta, T0G 0R0
In former pioneer home (1905). Pioneer furnishings, domestic equipment, handicrafts and clothing.
M.-Sa., 7-10.30 p.m. Su. 10 a.m.-10.30 p.m.

COLLINGWOOD

COLLINGWOOD MUSEUM
St. Paul Street, Collingwood, Ontario
In former railway station. Local history. Pioneer life. Shipbuilding. Maritime history, 1850 onwards. Indian artifacts.
May 19 - June 23, Sept. 5 - Oct. 9: Sa., Su. 9-5.30. June 24 - Sept. 4, Daily 9-5.30.

COMBER

TILBURY WEST AGRICULTURAL MUSEUM
Highway 77, Comber, Ontario, N0P 1J0
Local history. Agricultural development of the area. Agricultural implements, machinery.
May 16 - Oct. 15: Th.-Tu. 9-5.

CONSORT

CONSORT MUSEUM
Canadian Legion Recreation Centre, Consort, Alberta, T0C 1B0
Local pioneer history. Letters. Diaries. Documents.
Summer: daily 9-5.

CORNWALL

UNITED COUNTIES MUSEUM
731 2nd Street W., Cornwall, Ontario, K6J 1H5
In Wood House (1840). Furniture. Indian artifacts. Household equipment. Clothing. Tools. Toys. Electrical equipment installed in Stormont Mill by Thomas Edison.
May 15 - Oct. 15: M.-Sa. 10-12, 1-5. Su. 2-5.

CORUNNA

PILOT HOUSE MUSEUM
Highway 40, Corunna, Ontario, N0N 1G0
Centre castle ('pilot house') of S.S. 'Imperial Hamilton' (1916), Great Lakes and coastal oil tanker. Includes officers' and captain's quarters, bridge and equipment, engine room. Ship models. Photographs.
June 1 - Sept. 30: Sa., Su. 2-4. Other times by appointment.

COTEAU-DU-LAC

FORT COTEAU-DU-LAC
Coteau-du-Lac, Quebec
Ruins of fort buildings and canal (c.1812). Museum, with displays showing local military and transport history.
May 1 - Oct. 30, daily 9-6.

COURTENAY

COURTENAY AND DISTRICT MUSEUM
Cliffe Avenue, Courtenay, British Columbia
Relics of early settlers. Indian material. Early logging equipment.
July 1 - Sept. 15, 1-5. Rest of year by appointment.

COWANSVILLE

COWANSVILLE ART CENTRE
225 Main Street, Cowansville, Quebec
Paintings by Canadian artists.
Tu., Th., Sa., Su. 2-5; F. 7 p.m.-9.

CRAIK

PRAIRIE PIONEER MUSEUM
Highway 11, Craik, Saskatchewan, S0G 0V0
Pioneer history.
June 1 - Sept. 30, daily 8-9.

CUMBERLAND

MUNICIPAL MUSEUM
Tourist Bureau, Cumberland, British Columbia
Local history. Coal mining. Chinese material.
July 1 - Aug. 31: M.-F. 9-5.

CZAR

PRAIRIE PANORAMA MUSEUM
Chorncliffe Park, Box 156, Czar, Alberta, T0B 0Z0
Local history and archaeology. Pioneer household equipment. Costumes. Toys.
June 1 - Sept. 30, Su. 2-8.

DALHOUSIE

CHALEUR AREA HISTORICAL MUSEUM AND LIBRARY
Adelaide Street, Dalhousie, New Brunswick
Local history. Pioneer tools, utensils. Displays illustrating domestic life and the development of local industries.
July 1 - Aug. 31, daily 9-9. Other times by appointment.

DARTMOUTH

DARTMOUTH HERITAGE MUSEUM
Wyse Road, Dartmouth, Nova Scotia
History and development of Dartmouth.
Sept. 1 - June 30: M.-Sa. 1-5, W. also 6-9, Su., public holidays 2-5. July 1 - Aug. 31, M.-F. 9-9, Sa. 9-5, Su. 2-9. Closed Good Friday, Christmas.

DAWSON CITY

S.S. 'KENO'
Dawson City, Yukon Territory
Old Yukon River sternwheeler. History of river navigation.
M.-S. 9-5; Su. 10-1.

PALACE GRAND
Dawson City, Yukon Territory
Restored Palace Grand Theatre (1898). History of the Theatre.
Daily 9-4.

DAWSON CREEK

DAWSON CREEK MUSEUM AND ART GALLERY
13th Street and Alaska Avenue, Dawson Creek, British Columbia
Geology. Natural history. Local history. Industry. Paintings by British Columbia artists. Indian and Eskimo handicrafts. Agriculture.
June 1 - Sept. 30, M.-Sa. 9-9; Su., public holidays 1-9. Rest of year M.-F. 9-5.

DENARE BEACH

NORTHERN GATEWAY MUSEUM
Denare Beach, Saskatchewan, S0P 0B0
Geology. Mining. Local history. Indian artifacts.
Sept. 1 - May 31, W., Sa., Su. 1-6. June 1 - Aug. 31 by appointment.

DOON

HOMER WATSON GALLERY
Doon, Ontario
Paintings by Homer Watson.
Daily 10-8.

DORCHESTER

HEILLOR HOUSE MUSEUM
Route 6, Dorchester, New Brunswick
House (1813). 19th century furnishings. Pioneer history. Tools.
June-Aug., M.-Sa. 9-5; Su. 1-5. Labour Day-Thanksgiving, Sa., Su. 1-5. Other times by appointment.

DOWNSVIEW

BLACK CREEK PIONEER VILLAGE
Jane Street and Steeles Avenue, Downsview, Ontario
20 restored village buildings (1793-1867), including town hall, flour mill, church, shops and workshops. 19th century toys. Horse-drawn vehicles.
Apr. 1 - May 31: M.-F. 9.30-5; Sa., Su. 10-6. June 1-30: M.-F. 9.30-5; Sa., Su. 10-6.30. July 1 - Aug. 31: M.-F. 10-6; Sa., Su. 10-6.30. Sept. 1 - Oct. 31: M.-F. 9.30-5; Sa., Su. 10-6. Nov. 1-30: M.-F. 9.30-4; Sa., Su. 10-5.

DRESDEN

UNCLE TOM'S CABIN
Rural Route 5, Dresden, Ontario, N0P 1M0
House (c.1842), former home of Rev. Josiah Henson,

'Uncle Tom' of Harriet Beecher Stowe's novel. Mementoes of Henson's life. Negro history. Pioneer relics. Agricultural tools, implements.
May 1 - Oct. 31, daily 10-dusk.

DRUMHELLER

DRUMHELLER AND DISTRICT MUSEUM
335 1st Street, E., Drumheller, Alberta, T0J 0Y0
Geology. Palaeontology. Fossils. Archaeology. Indian stone implements. Local history. Children's museum.
June 1 - Oct. 31, daily 9-8. Apr. 1 - May 31, daily 10-5. Winter by appointment.

HOMESTEAD ANTIQUE MUSEUM
Drumheller, Alberta, T0J 0Y0
Local history. Agricultural implements and household equipment used by Alberta pioneers.
May 15 - Oct. 15, daily 9-9.

DRYDEN

DRYDEN AND DISTRICT MUSEUM
Tourist Bureau, Highway 17 E., Dryden, Ontario
Local history. Trapping. Pioneer tools, household equipment. Minerals.
May 17 - Sept. 12, daily 9-7.30. Sept. 13 - May 16: M.-F. 9-4.30.

DUCK LAKE

DUCK LAKE HISTORICAL MUSEUM
Duck Lake, Saskatchewan, S0K 1J0
Restored N.W. Mounted Police jail. Pioneer history. Indian artifacts. Hudson's Bay Company material. Riel Rebellion relics.
June 1 - Sept. 30, daily 9-9. Other months by appointment.

DUNCAN

COWICHAN VALLEY FOREST MUSEUM
Highway 1, Duncan, British Columbia
Logging museum. Dioramas. Photographs. Operating steam railway.
May 15 - Sept. 30, daily 9-5.

DUNDAS

DUNDAS HISTORICAL SOCIETY MUSEUM
139 Park Street W., Dundas, Ontario
Local history. Pioneer relics. Costumes. Toys. Glass.
M.-F. 10-12, 1-4. May 1 - Oct. 31 also Su. 2-5.

DUNVEGAN

MISSION ST. CHARLES
Dunvegan, Alberta
Log-built church and rectory (1885). Natural history. Pioneer tools. Indian material.
On request.

GLENGARRY MUSEUM
Dunvegan, Ontario, K0C 1J0
In former Star Inn (c.1835). Pioneer history. Handicrafts. Agricultural implements and machinery. Early maps.
June 15 - Oct. 14: Tu.-Su. 2-6.

EAR FALLS

EAR FALLS HISTORICAL MUSEUM
Highway 105, Ear Falls, Ontario
Log building, with displays illustrating history of transport in N. Ontario.
June 1 - Sept. 30, daily 10-5.

EASTEND

EASTEND SCHOOL MUSEUM
1 Eastend Street, Eastend, Saskatchewan, S0N 0T0
Dinosaur remains. Fossils.
Daily 9-4. Closed school vacations.

EATON

COMPTON COUNTY HISTORICAL MUSEUM
Eaton, Quebec
In old Eaton Church (c.1835). Pioneer history. Household equipment. Agricultural implements.
July 1 - Aug. 31, Su. 2-4.

EDMONTON

ALBERTA GOVERNMENT TELEPHONES HISTORIC EXHIBIT
Edmonton, Alberta
Communications museum. History of telephony in Alberta.
M.-Sa. 9-5.

EDMONTON ART GALLERY
2 Sir Winston Churchill Square, Edmonton, Alberta, T5J 2C1
Works by Canadian artists. Paintings. Prints. Drawings. Sculpture. Silver. Children's gallery.
M., Tu., F., Sa. 10-5; W., Th. 10-10; Su., public holidays 1-5. Closed Christmas, New Year.

FOLSON'S EDMONTON HOUSE
12040 104th Avenue, Edmonton, Alberta, T5K 0T2
Log fort. Relics of early settlers in Canadian West.
July 1 - Aug. 31, daily 1-5. Rest of year: Tu., Th., Sa. 1-5.

FORT EDMONTON HISTORIC PARK
Whitemud Creek, Edmonton, Alberta
Pioneer village of reassembled early Edmonton buildings. Living history museum of history and future of Edmonton.
May 1 - Sept. 30, daily 9-9.

HERBARIUM
Biological Sciences Building, University of Alberta, Edmonton, Alberta
Flora of North America, especially Canada.
M.-F. 9-4.

HISTORICAL EXHIBITS BUILDING
10105 112th Avenue, Edmonton, Alberta, T5G 0H1
History of Edmonton. Pioneer life. Indian artifacts. Fur trade.
M.-F. 10-5; Sa., Su., public holidays 11-6.

GEORGE MCDOUGALL MUSEUM AND SHRINE
101 Street and 100th Avenue, Edmonton, Alberta
In former church, built by the missionary Rev. George McDougall. History of early missions in Western Canada.
June 1 - Sept. 30: Tu.-Sa. 2-5.

MINERALOGY AND PALAEONTOLOGY MUSEUM OF THE UNIVERSITY OF ALBERTA
Agriculture Building, 112th Street and Saskatchewan Drive, Edmonton, Alberta
Geology. Mineralogy. Palaeontology.
M.-F. 9-12, 1-4.30.

OBLATE ARCHIVES
9916 110th Street, Edmonton, Alberta, T5K 1J3
Material relating to early Catholic missionaries. Indian artifacts.
By appointment.

PRINCESS PAT'S LIGHT INFANTRY REGIMENTAL MUSEUM
Hamilton Gault Barracks, Edmonton, Alberta
History of the Regiment.
Th. 2-4. Other times by appointment.

PROVINCIAL MUSEUM AND ARCHIVES OF ALBERTA
12845 102nd Avenue, Edmonton, Alberta, T5N 0M6
Natural and human history of Alberta. Geology. Palaeontology. Botany. Zoology. Ethnology. Archaeology. History.
June 16 - Sept. 14: M.-Sa. 9-9; Su., public holidays 1-9. Rest of year: M.-Th., Sa. 9-5; F. 9-9; Su., public holidays 11-6.

QUEEN ELIZABETH PLANETARIUM
137 Street and 114th Avenue, Edmonton, Alberta
Astronomy. Meteorites. Planetarium.
June 30 - Sept. 1: M.-Sa. 3 p.m. and 8 p.m.; Su., public holidays 2, 4, 8 p.m. Sept. 2 - June 30: Tu.-F. 8 p.m.; Sa. 3.30 p.m., Su., public holidays 3, 8 p.m.

UKRAINIAN ARTS AND CRAFTS MUSEUM
10611 110th Avenue, Edmonton, Alberta, T5R 3R8
Folk museum of the Ukrainian community in Alberta. Costumes. Weaving. Embroidery. Pottery. Easter eggs. Beadwork.
Su. 2-5. Other times by appointment.

UNIVERSITY ART GALLERY AND MUSEUM
University of Alberta, Ring House 1, Edmonton, Alberta, T6G 2F2
Works by Canadian artists. Paintings. Sculpture. Graphics. Indian artifacts. Anthropology.
M.-Tu. 10-4; W., F. 12-4; Th. 12-8. Closed public holidays.

UNIVERSITY OF ALBERTA GEOLOGY MUSEUM
Room 91, Agriculture Building, 112th Street and Saskatchewan Drive, Edmonton, Alberta
Mineralogy. Petrology. Palaeontology.
M.-F. 9-4.30.

JOHN WALTER HISTORICAL SITE
10627 93rd Avenue, Edmonton, Alberta, T6E 2V9
Houses (1874 and 1886), built by John Walter, sawmill and ferry operator. Period furnishings. Memorabilia of John Walter and his activities.
June 16 - Sept. 4: Daily 10-9.

EDMUNTON

AUTOS OF YESTERYEAR MUSEUM
Route 2, Edmunton, New Brunswick
Old cars.
Daily 9-4.

ELKHORN

MANITOBA AUTOMOBILE MUSEUM
Elkhorn, Manitoba, R0M 0N0
Old cars. Agricultural implements and machinery.
May 1 - Oct. 31, daily 9-9.

ELK ISLAND

ELK ISLAND NATIONAL PARK
Highway 16, Elk Island, Alberta
Folk museum. Buildings of early Ukrainian settlers. Household equipment. Costumes. Tools.
M.-F. 10-6; Sa., Su. 10-8.

ELK POINT

FORT GEORGE MUSEUM
Elk Point, Alberta
Military history.
Daily 9-5.

ELLIOT LAKE

ELLIOT LAKE MINING AND NUCLEAR MUSEUM
Highway 108, Elliot Lake, Ontario
Models and displays illustrating uranium mining and processing. Energy, especially nuclear. Natural history. Pioneer life.
Jan. 1 - May 30, Oct. 1 - Dec. 31: M.-F. 8.30-5. June 1 - Sept. 30, daily 9-8.

ELORA

WELLINGTON COUNTY MUSEUM
Mill Street, Elora, Ontario, N0B 1S0
Pioneer history of County. Furniture. Tools. Handicrafts. Household equipment. China. Glass. Agricultural implements.
June 1 - Sept. 30: M., W., F. 1-6; Sa., Su., public holidays 1-9.

EMERSON

GATEWAY STOPPING PLACE MUSEUM
Highway 75, Emerson, Manitoba, R0A 0L0
Customs House (c.1870). Jail (c.1879). Local history. Indian artifacts.
July 1 - Aug. 31: M.-Sa. 2-6; Su. 2-8.

EMO

EMO AND DISTRICT MUSEUM
Highway 11, Emo, Ontario
Pioneer life.
Daily 2-5, 7-9. Closed Sa. June 1 - Sept. 30.

ESTEVAN

LIONS NORTH WEST MOUNTED POLICE MUSEUM
Estevan, Saskatchewan
Restored N.W. Mounted Police barracks (1887). Natural history. Pioneer relics. Indian material.
June 1 - Sept. 30, daily 9-5.

FALKLAND

VALLEY MUSEUM
Falkland, British Columbia
Geology. Mineralogy. Pioneer material.
June 1 - Sept. 30, daily 9-5.

FANSHAWE

FANSHAWE PIONEER VILLAGE
Fanshawe, Ontario
Reproduction of 19th century cross-roads village of the pre-railway period. Log cabins, workshop, stores and public buildings.
May 18 - Sept. 2: M.-F. 10-5; Sa., Su. 10-7.

FENELON FALLS

FENELON FALLS MUSEUM
Fenelon Falls, Ontario, K0M 1N0
In Maryborough Lodge (1837). Pioneer history. Indian artifacts.
May 14 - Oct. 31, daily 1-5. July 1 - Aug. 31, also W., Su. 7 p.m.-9.

FOAM LAKE

FOAM LAKE PIONEER MUSEUM
Box 163, Foam Lake, Saskatchewan, S0A 1A0
Natural history. Pioneer relics. Local history.
Tu. 2.30-5.30. Th. 7-9. Sa. 2-5.30, 7-9.

FONTHILL

MOUNTAIN MILLS MUSEUM
Rural Route 1, Fonthill, Ontario
Watermill (1872), in operating condition with original machinery.
June 5 - Sept. 14, Tu.-F. 1-5; Sa., Su., public holidays 12-5. May 15 - June 14, Sept. 15 - Oct. 14, Sa., Su. 12-5.

FOREST

FOREST-LAMBTON MUSEUM
S. Broadway Street, Forest, Ontario, N0N 1J0
In former pioneer house. Fossils. Country schoolroom. Pioneer history and artifacts.
May 24 - Labour Day: W., Sa., Su. 2-5. Other times by appointment.

FORT ERIE

OLD FORT ERIE
Government Park, Fort Erie, Ontario
Restored fort (1804-14). Museum of military equipment and relics.
May 1 - Oct. 31, daily 10-6. Nov. 1 - Apr. 30, daily 12-5.

FORT FRANCES

FORT FRANCES MUSEUM
Public Library, 363 Church Street, Fort Frances, Ontario
Local history. Indian life. Fur trade. Early settlers. Industrial development. Lumbering.
Sept. 1 - June 30: M., W., F. 2-5. Tu. also 7 p.m.-9. July 1 - Aug. 31: M.-F. 10-5.

FORT LANGLEY

BRITISH COLUMBIA FARM MACHINERY MUSEUM
Fort Langley, British Columbia
Pioneer material. Early agricultural tools and machinery.
July 1 - Aug. 31, daily 1-4. Sept. 1 - Nov. 30, Mar. 1 - June 30, Tu.-Su. 10-5.

FORT LANGLEY NATIONAL HISTORIC PARK
Mavis Street, Fort Langley, British Columbia
Restoration of part of Hudson's Bay Company Fort (1858). Museum illustrating history of the Fort and the area.
July 1 - Sept. 15, daily 10-9. Sept. 16 - June 30, daily 10-5.

LANGLEY CENTENNIAL MUSEUM
Mavis Street, Fort Langley, British Columbia
Local history. Handicrafts. Costumes. Indian artifacts. Agriculture.
Oct. 1 - Dec. 15, Mar. 1 - Apr. 30: Th., Sa. 10-5; Su. 2-5. May 1 - Sept. 30: M.-Sa. 10-5, Su. 2-5.

FORT MACLEOD

FORT MACLEOD HISTORICAL MUSEUM
Box 776, Fort MacLeod, Alberta, T0L 0Z0
Exhibits illustrating history of N.W. Mounted Police. Indian material. Pioneer life. History of Fort MacLeod.
May 1 - Oct. 14, daily 8-8.

FORT QU'APPELLE

FORT QU'APPELLE MUSEUM
Fort Qu'appelle, Saskatchewan, S0G 1S0
Restored Hudson Bay Company trading post. History of post. Indian material.
June 1 - Sept. 30, daily 9-5.

FORT ST. JOHN

PEACE ISLAND PARK MUSEUM
Fort St. John, British Columbia
Local history. Pioneer tools, furniture and household equipment. Costumes.
On request.

FORT SASKATCHEWAN

FORT SASKATCHEWAN MUSEUM
10102 100th Avenue, Fort Saskatchewan, Alberta, T0B 1P0
In pioneer house. Local history. Items illustrating pioneer life.
Tu.-W., F.-Sa., public holidays 2-4. Su. 2-5.

FORT STEELE

FORT STEELE HISTORIC PARK
Fort Steele, British Columbia
Reconstruction of buildings brought to site to form village of c.1900. Park museum has exhibits showing history of E. Kootenay district and includes reconstruction of first N.W. Mounted Police fort (1887) in British Columbia.
June 16 - Aug. 31, daily 9-9. May 1 - June 15, Sept. 1 - Oct. 31, daily 9-5.

FORT WILLIAM

FOUNDERS MUSEUM
Highway 61, Fort William, Ontario
Stoves. Internal combustion engines. Agricultural implements.
Sa., Su. 10-8.

LOGGING MUSEUM
Centennial Park, Fort William, Ontario
Reconstruction of logging camp. Logging tools and equipment.
May 15 - June 15: M.-F. 12-6; Sa., Su. 10-8. June 15 - Sept. 15: daily 10-8. Sept. 15 - Oct. 15: M.-F. 12-6; Sa., Su. 11-7.

THUNDER BAY HISTORICAL SOCIETY MUSEUM
219 May Street, Fort William, Ontario
Mineralogy. Local history. Pioneer life. Fur trade. Indian material.
Sept. 1 - June 30: M., W., F. 2-5. Tu. also 7 p.m.-9. July 1 - Aug. 31: M.-F. 10-5.

FRANKVILLE

KITLEY HISTORICAL SOCIETY MUSEUM
Highway 29, Frankville, Ontario, K0E 1H0
Log house (1840), furnished as early 19th century pioneer house. Barn, with display of early agricultural implements and machinery.
Sa., Su. nearest to May 23 and June 27 - Sept. 1: Sa., Su. 1-5.

FREDERICTON

BEAVERBROOK ART GALLERY
Queen Street, Fredericton, New Brunswick
English paintings, prints and porcelain. Canadian paintings.
May 1 - Sept. 30: Tu.-Sa. 10-9, Su.-M. 2-9. Oct. 1 - Apr. 30: daily 2-9. Closed Christmas, New Year.

BRYDONE JACK OBSERVATORY
Fredericton, New Brunswick
First astronomical observatory in Canada (1851).
By appointment.

BURDEN SCHOOL
University of New Brunswick, Fredericton, New Brunswick
One-room schoolhouse (c.1850), moved from original site near Mactaquac Dam. Period furnishings.
On request.

THE GUARD HOUSE
Carleton Street, Fredericton, New Brunswick
Military historical restoration (part of the Military Compound).
June-Sept., see locally.

MILITARY COMPOUND
Queen Street, Fredericton, New Brunswick
Restored officers' quarters, barracks and guard house. Exhibits illustrating military history of area.
Daily 10-4.

PROVINCIAL PORTRAIT GALLERY
Legislative Building, Fredericton, New Brunswick
Portraits, including works by Sir Joshua Reynolds. Audubon prints.
July 1 - Sept. 15: M.-F. 8.30-5, 7-9.30. Sept. 16 - June 30: M.-F. 8.30-5.

UNIVERSITY OF NEW BRUNSWICK ART CENTRE
Fredericton, New Brunswick
Works by Canadian and European artists. Paintings. Drawings. Prints. Sculpture.
Sept. 1 - May 31: M.-F. 10-5; Su. 2-5.

YORK SUNBURY HISTORICAL MUSEUM
Queen Street, Fredericton, New Brunswick
In former officers' quarters of Military Compound (1839). Pioneer history. Household equipment. Military history.
May 1 - Sept. 30: M.-Sa. 10-8; Su. 2-8.

GAGETOWN

SIR LEONARD TILLEY HOUSE
Route 102, Gagetown, New Brunswick
House (1786, with additions by Tilley family 1817). Early 19th century furnishings. Local history.
May 1 - Sept. 30, daily 9-7. Oct. 1 - Apr. 30, daily 1-5.

GANANOQUE

GANANOQUE HISTORICAL SOCIETY MUSEUM
10 King Street, Gananoque, Ontario, K0H 1R0
Local history. Pioneer tools, household equipment. Agricultural implements. China. Glass. Costumes. Period rooms. Geology. Zoology. Junior museums.
June 1-30, Sept. 1-30, M.-Sa. 2-5. July 1 - Aug. 31, M.-Sa. 2-5. 7-9.

GANDER

CONQUEST OF THE ATLANTIC MUSEUM
Gander Airport, Gander, Newfoundland
Aviation history, 1919-45.
Daily, at all times.

GIBSONS

ELPHINSTONE PIONEER MUSEUM
Municipal Hall, S. Fletcher Road, Gibsons, British Columbia
Pioneer clothes, tools, furniture. Logging. Eskimo carvings. Mining equipment. Shells. Molluscs.
July 1 - Sept. 30: Tu., Th., Sa. 2-4.

GILFORD ISLAND

NA WA LA GWA TSI
Simoom Sound, Gilford Island, British Columbia
Restored Indian Community House. Indian artifacts.
Daily 10-4.

GIROUXVILLE

GIROUXVILLE MUSEUM
Girouxville, Alberta
Local history.
M.-Sa. 10-1, 2-5; Su. 10-1.

GLACE BAY

MINERS' MUSEUM
Quarry Point, Glace Bay, Nova Scotia
History of coal-mining, especially in Nova Scotia. Demonstrations of mining techniques in workings attached to Museum.
June 15 - Sept. 14: daily 9-9. Sept. 15 - June 14: M.-Sa. 10-5. Su., public holidays 1-5.30.

GLOUCESTER

ACADIAN MUSEUM
Caraquet, Gloucester, New Brunswick
Local history. Agriculture.
June-Sept., M.-Sa. 9-5; Su. 1-5.

GODERICH

HURON COUNTY PIONEER MUSEUM
110 North Street, Goderich, Ontario, N7A 2T8
History of motive power. Early industry and industrial techniques. Milling. Lumbering. Pioneer history. Indian artifacts. Horse-drawn vehicles.
Apr. 1 - Oct. 31: M.-Sa. 9-5.30; Su. 1-5.30. Closed Su. in Apr. Other times by appointment.

GOLDEN LAKE

ALGONQUIN MUSEUM
Highway 60, Golden Lake, Ontario, K0J 1X0
Mineralogy. Natural history. Pioneer and Indian artifacts. Costumes.
May 25 - Labour Day: M., W., Sa. 10-6; Su. 1-8. Other times by appointment.

GRAFTON

BARNUM HOUSE MUSEUM
Highway 2, Grafton, Ontario, K0K 2G0
House (1817). Period rooms. Early agricultural tools, implements.
July 1 - Aug. 31: daily 1-5. May, June, Sept., Oct., Su., public holidays, 1-5. Other times by appointment.

GRAND BEND

EISENBACH MUSEUM
Highway 21, P.O. Box 448, Grand Bend, Ontario, N0M 1T0
Museum of local and pioneer history, in complex of five 19th century buildings. Household equipment. Agriculture.
May 1 - Oct. 31: M.-Sa. 10-8; Su. 1-8.

GRAND HARBOUR

GRAND MANAN MUSEUM
Grand Harbour, Grand Manan Island, New Brunswick
Natural history. Material illustrating early settlement of Island. Geology. Birds of Grand Manan.
July 1 - Labour Day, daily 2-5. F. also 7 p.m.-9.30. Other times by appointment.

GRANDE PRAIRIE

GRANDE PRAIRIE PIONEER MUSEUM
Grande Prairie, Alberta
Geology. Fossils. Mounted birds and animals. Material illustrating pioneer life.
Oct. 1 - Apr. 30, daily 10-4. May 1 - Sept. 30, daily 10-5.

GRAND PRÉ

GRAND PRÉ NATIONAL HISTORIC PARK MUSEUM
Grand Pré, Nova Scotia
Life and history of the Acadians and of the New England planters.
June 16 - Labour Day, daily 9-8. May 15 - June 15: daily 10-5.

GRAND FORKS

BOUNDARY MUSEUM
Central Avenue and S.E. 9th Street, Grand Forks, British Columbia
Local history.
May 15 - June 28: Sa., Su. 10-6. June 29 - Labour Day, daily 9-9. Labour Day - Sept. 30, daily 9-5.

GRAVENHURST

WOODWINDS HISTORICAL MUSEUM
Highway 69, Gravenhurst, Ontario
Log building, containing furniture and furnishings of pioneers and early settlers. Log church and new museum building house collections illustrating agriculture, hunting and trapping, logging and steamboating.
May 15 - June 30, Sa., 11-5; Su. 1-5. July 1 - Aug. 31: Tu.-Sa. 11-5; Su. 1-5. Sept. 1 - Oct. 31, by appointment.

'SEGWUN' STEAMBOAT MUSEUM
Bay Street, Muskoka Bay, Gravenhurst, Ontario
Steamship 'Segwun' (1887). Displays illustrating early navigation and logging on the Muskoka Lakes. Vintage outboard motors. Pioneer household equipment. Paintings by local artists.
May 18 - June 30, Sept. 3 - Oct. 14: Sa., Su. 11-5; July 1 - Sept. 2: M.-Sa. 11-5; Su. 1-5.

GREENWOOD

GREENWOOD MUSEUM
Greenwood Street, Greenwood, British Columbia
Local history. Pioneer life. Household equipment. Costumes. Japanese collection. Logging and mining equipment.
June 16-30, daily 10-6; July 1 - Sept. 14, daily 10-8.

GRIMSBY

STONE SHOP MUSEUM
271 Main Street W., Grimsby, Ontario
House (c.1800). Local history. Mementoes of War of 1812.
May 9 - Oct. 10, daily 1-5.

GUELPH

GUELPH CIVIC MUSEUM
Gordon and Waterloo Streets, Guelph, Ontario
Local history. Pioneer life. Agriculture. Industry.
Sept. 1 - May 31: Sa., Su. 2-4.30. June 1 - Aug. 31: Tu.-Su. 2-4.30.

COLONEL JOHN McCRAE MUSEUM
102 Water Street, Guelph, Ontario, N1G 1A6
House (1872) was birthplace of the doctor, poet and artist, Col. John McCrae. Personal possessions, sketches, manuscripts of Col. McCrae. McCrae family memorabilia, furnishings.
May 14 - Oct. 15: Tu.-Su., public holidays 2-5. Oct. 16 - May 13: Su. 2-5. Other times by appointment.

HALIBURTON

HALIBURTON HIGHLANDS PIONEER MUSEUM
Haliburton, Ontario, K0M 1S0
Pioneer household equipment. Tools and equipment used in lumbering, agriculture, trapping.
May 24 - June 22: Sa., Su. 1-5. June 28 - Labour Day, daily 1-5. Labour Day - Thanksgiving: Sa., Su. 1-5.

HALIFAX

THE ARMY MUSEUM
The Citadel, Halifax, Nova Scotia
Military history. Uniforms. Weapons.
June 1 - Sept. 30, daily 9-8. Oct. 1 - May 31, M. Sa. 10-5, Su. 12-5. Closed Christmas, New Year.

CENTENNIAL ART GALLERY
Halifax Citadel, P.O. Box 2262, Halifax, Nova Scotia
Paintings by Canadian artists.
Oct.-Apr., Tu.-Sa., public holidays 10-5; Su. 12-5. May-Sept., daily 10-5. Closed Christmas, New Year.

DALHOUSIE ART GALLERY
University Drive, Halifax, Nova Scotia
Persian and Chinese ceramics. Pre-Inca pottery. Paintings, prints and drawings by Canadian and American artists.
M.-F. 10-4; Su. 2-5.

HALIFAX CITADEL NATIONAL HISTORIC PARK
Sackville Street, Halifax, Nova Scotia
Fort and moat (1828). Local and military history. Paintings. Graphics. Sculpture.
Sept. 7 - June 14, daily 10-5; June 15 - Sept. 6, daily 9-8. Closed Christmas.

NOVA SCOTIA MUSEUM
1747 Summer Street, Halifax, Nova Scotia
Natural history. Maritime and provincial history. Furniture. Handicrafts. Musical instruments. Agricultural implements.
M.-F. 1-9; Sa., Su. 9-5.

PUBLIC ARCHIVES OF NOVA SCOTIA
Dalhousie Campus, Coburg Road, Halifax, Nova Scotia
Maritime history. Paintings. Prints. Coins. Stamps. Maps.
M.-F. 8.30-10. Sa. 9-6. Su. 1-10. Closed public holidays.

SCIENCE MUSEUM
5410 Spring Garden Road, Halifax, Nova Scotia
Mineralogy. Palaeontology. Astronomy. Planetarium. Biology. Entomology.
Daily 9-5; Su. 2-5.

TELEPHONE MUSEUM
1484 Hollis Street, Halifax, Nova Scotia
Development of telephone industry, especially in Nova Scotia. Life and achievements of Graham Bell.
By appointment.

YORK REDOUBT NATIONAL HISTORIC SITE
Halifax, Nova Scotia
Restored late 18th century Martello tower. Gun emplacements. Military history of Halifax.
June 1-14, M.-Sa. 10-5, Su. 12-5. June 15 - Sept. 7, daily 9-8.

HAMILTON

ART GALLERY OF HAMILTON
Main Street W. and Forsyth Street, Hamilton, Ontario
Works by Canadian, American, British and French artists. Paintings. Prints. Drawings. Sculpture.
Tu.-Sa. 10-5; Th. also 8 p.m.-10; Su. 2-5. Closed July, Good Friday, July 25 - Aug. 8.

DUNDURN CASTLE
Dundurn Park, York Boulevard, Hamilton, Ontario
Castle (1832). Furnishings, décor as when occupied by Sir Allan MacNab, Canadian Prime Minister, 1854-6. Culinary demonstrations in restored 19th century kitchen.
Labour Day - June 30, daily 1-4. Rest of year, daily 10-5. Closed Christmas, New Year.

MCMASTER UNIVERSITY PLANETARIUM
King Street W., Hamilton, Ontario
Astronomy. Planetarium.
By appointment.

ROYAL BOTANICAL GARDENS
Plains Road W., Hamilton, Ontario
Herbarium.
M.-F. 9-5.

HAMPTON

KINGS COUNTY HISTORICAL SOCIETY MUSEUM
Centennial Building, Hampton, New Brunswick
22 miles north of St. John. Natural history. Pioneer life. County history.
June 1 - Sept. 30: M.-Sa. 10-5; Su. 2-5.

HANEY

DYCH'S DINOSAUR PARK
20492 Lougheed Highway, Haney, British Columbia
Fossil plants and animals. Life-sized reproductions of extinct animals.
Apr. 1 - Oct. 31, daily 9-9.

HANNA

HANNA PIONEERS MUSEUM
Hanna, Alberta, T0J 1P0
In former schoolhouse (c.1900). Local history. Ranching and farming. Indian artifacts.
May 1 - Nov. 30: M.-Sa. 9-5; Su. 1-5. Other times by appointment.

HARTLAND

CIVIC HISTORICAL COLLECTION
Town Hall, Hartland, New Brunswick
Pioneer life. Tools, furniture, household utensils.
M.-F. 9-5.

HARTSPORT

CHURCHILL HOUSE AND MARINE MEMORIAL ROOM
Hartsport, Nova Scotia
Shipbuilder's house (1860). Ship models. Paintings. Prints. Ship building tools. Nautical instruments. Ships' logs.
House: July 1 - Aug. 31, W. 2-5.
Marine memorial: daily 2-5.

HAVELOCK

TRENT RIVER MUSEUM
R.R.2, Havelock, Ontario, K0L 1Z0
Displays in eleven early 19th century buildings, illustrating farming and home life of pioneer settlers of Trent River region.
June 15 - Sept. 15, F. 1.30-5; Su. 6.30-8.

HAZELTON

KSAN INDIAN VILLAGE AND MUSEUM
Box 326, Hazelton, British Columbia
Replica of cedar-built Indian community house. Indian artifacts and history. Ethnology.
Jan. 1 - Sept. 30, daily 2-4, 7-9. Oct. 1 - Dec. 31, Sa., Su. 2-4, 7-9.

HIGH PRAIRIE

CENTENNIAL LIBRARY AND MUSEUM
High Prairie, Alberta, T0G 1E0
Local history. Agricultural tools, implements. Pioneer furniture, utensils. Early land survey plans. Maps. Indian artifacts.
M.-Sa. 9-5.

HIGH RIVER

MEDICINE TREE POW WOW MUSEUM
High River, Alberta, T0L 1B0
Exhibits illustrating early pioneer life.
May 1 - Sept. 30: M.-Sa. 2-5.

HOPEWELL CAPE

ALBERT COUNTY MUSEUM
Route 114, Hopewell Cape, New Brunswick
In former Jail (1846). Furniture and other items belonging to early settlers.
June 15 - Sept. 30, M.-Sa. 10-6; Su. 12-8.

HULL

CANADIAN GOLF MUSEUM
Mountain Road, Hull, Quebec
History of golf.
Apr.-Oct., M.-Sa. 9-9; Su., public holidays 2-9.

OTTAWA PUBLIC LIBRARY
Chemin Freeman, P.O. Box 938, Hull, Quebec
Paintings. Graphics. Sculpture.
M.-F. 9-5.

HUNTSVILLE

MUSKOKA MUSEUM
Huntsville Park, Brunel Road, Huntsville, Ontario
Museum complex includes 7 pioneer houses moved to the Park. History of Huntsville and Muskoka area. Local fish and birds.
June 15 - Sept. 15, F. 1.30-5. Su. 6.30 p.m.-8.

IDDESLEIGH

RAINY HILLS HISTORICAL MUSEUM
Iddesleigh, Alberta, TOJ 1TO
Local history. Pioneer life. Farming tools.
Oct. 1 - Apr. 30, daily 10-4. May 1 - Sept. 30, daily 9-5.

ILE-AUX-NOIX

FORT LENNOX NATIONAL HISTORIC PARK
Saint Paul, Ile-aux-Noix, Quebec
Restored buildings of fort (1820-9). Military history. Local history. Coins.
May 1 - Oct. 31, daily 9-6.

INVERMERE

MUSEUM OF WINDERMERE DISTRICT HISTORICAL SOCIETY
Invermere, British Columbia
In 2 pioneer log cabins. Artifacts, pictures and histories of local pioneer families.
June 1 - Aug. 31, daily 2-4.

IONA

NOVA SCOTIA HIGHLAND VILLAGE MUSEUM
Barra Glen, Route 2, Iona, Nova Scotia
Artifacts and memorabilia of pioneer settlers from Scotland.
July 10 - Sept. 15, daily 10-5.

IROQUOIS

CARMEN HOUSE MUSEUM
Carman Road, Iroquois, Ontario, KOE 1KO
House (c.1825), with original furnishings.
Apr. 1 - Oct. 31, daily 10-10.

ISLAY

MORRISON MUSEUM OF THE COUNTRY SCHOOL
Islay, Alberta
In school building of c.1860. 19th century school books, furnishings. Photographs.
On request.

JOLIETTE

JOLIETTE ART MUSEUM
455 Boulevard Base de Roc, Joliette, Quebec
Paintings by European and Canadian artists. Religious decorative art. Natural history.
By appointment.

JORDAN

BALL'S FALLS MUSEUM
R.R.I., Jordan, Ontario
Museum complex based on restored buildings of the late 18th - early 19th century. Glen Elgin pioneer settlement. These include a grist mill and lime-kiln (c.1810) and 2 log cabins (c.1780).
May 18 - Sept. 30: daily 8.30-11.

JORDAN HISTORICAL MUSEUM OF THE TWENTY
Jordan, Ontario
Museum of local history, based on Vintage House (1815), Jacob Fry House (1815) and early 19th century schoolhouse. Exhibits of farm implements, furniture, kitchen equipment, guns.
May 9 - Oct. 25, daily 12-6.

KAMLOOPS

FORT KAMLOOPS
Riverside Park, Kamloops, British Colombia
Replica of Hudson's Bay Company fort, with factor's cabin and trading post. Exhibits of horse-drawn vehicles and early agricultural machinery.
July 1 - Sept. 30: M.-Sa. 2-8.

KAMLOOPS MUSEUM
207 Seymour Street, Kamloops, British Columbia
Geology. Mineralogy. Palaeontology. Natural history. Ethnology. Indian material. Pioneer items.
July 1 - Aug. 30: M.-F. 10-9; Sa. 10-5. Sept. - June 30: M.-F. 3-5, 7-9; Sa. 10-5.

KAPUKASING

KAPUKASING AND DISTRICT HISTORICAL MUSEUM
Government Road, Kapukasing, Ontario
In 2 railway coaches, with Canadian National engine. Local and pioneer history. Logging.
May 24 - Sept. 15: M., Tu., Th., F. 3-6, 7-9; Sa. 3-6.

KASLO

KOOTENAY LAKE HISTORICAL SOCIETY MUSEUM
Kaslo, British Columbia
Museum of lake navigation and local history in last of the British Columbia inland waterway stern-wheelers.
Apr. 15 - Oct. 15, daily 10-5.

KELOWNA

OKANAGAN MUSEUM AND ARCHIVES ASSOCIATION
470 Queensway, Kelowna, British Columbia
Natural history and history of the Okanagan Valley. Replica of Hudson's Bay store. Period rooms.
May 1 - Sept. 30, daily 10-5, 7-9. Oct. 1 - Apr. 30, daily 2-5, 7-9.

KENORA

LAKE OF THE WOODS MUSEUM
Water Street, Box 497, Kenora, Ontario
Mineralogy. Pioneer history. Indian artifacts.
June 1-12, Sept. 15-30: M.-F. 1-5. June 15 - Sept. 15: M.-Sa. 1-5, 7-9.

KILLARNEY

KILLARNEY MUSEUM
414 Williams Avenue, Killarney, Manitoba, ROK 1GO
Local history. Pioneer tools. Domestic equipment. Musical instruments. Butterflies. Insects.
M.-Sa. 1-5. Su. by appointment. Closed public holidays.

KINDERSLEY

KINDERSLEY CENTENNIAL MUSEUM
905 1st Street W., Kindersley, Saskatchewan, SOL 1SO
Local history and archaeology. Pioneer relics. Agricultural tools, implements. Indian material.
Tu.-Sa. 2-5, 7-9.

KINDERSLEY PLAINS

KINDERSLEY PLAINS MUSEUM
Kindersley Plains, Saskatchewan
Regional history.
Tu.-Sa. 2-5, 7-9.

KINGSTON

'BELLEVUE HOUSE' NATIONAL HISTORIC PARK
35 Centre Street, Kingston, Ontario, K7L 4E5
House (c.1840) was home of Canada's first Prime Minister, John A. MacDonald. Furnished in style of 1840s. Exhibits relating to MacDonald's life and career.
Daily 9-6. Closed Christmas, New Year, public holidays.

AGNES ETHERINGTON ART CENTRE
Queen's University, Kingston, Ontario
Works by Canadian and European artists. Paintings. Prints. Sculpture.
Su.-F., daily 2-5; M.-Th. also 7 p.m.-9; F. 9-5.

GEOLOGICAL MUSEUM
Miller Hall, Queen's University, Kingston, Ontario
Mineralogy. Palaeontology. Zoology.
M.-F., daily 9-5. Other times by appointment.

MURNEY TOWER MUSEUM
Macdonald Park, King Street W., Kingston, Ontario
British Martello Tower (1846). Exhibits illustrating local and military history.
May 15 - June 30, Sept. 1 - Oct. 15: Sa., Su. 11-6. July 1 - Aug. 31, daily 11-6.

OLD FORT HENRY
Highways 2 and 15, Box 213, Kingston, Ontario
Restored 19th century fort. Barracks, officers' quarters and tradesmen's workshops furnished in style of period. 19th century military and naval weapons, equipment, uniforms.
May 15 - June 14, Labour Day - Sept. 15, daily 9.30-5. June 15 - Labour Day, daily 9.30-6.30.

PUMP HOUSE AND STEAM MUSEUM
23 Ontario Street, Kingston, Ontario
In 1849 Pump House, enlarged 1890. Main pump-room, restored to 1895 condition. Contains its two original engines, one built in 1891, by the Osborne-Killey Co. of Hamilton, and the other (1897) by the John Inglis Co. of Toronto. Other steam engines and scale models have been added to the collection. All the engines are working.
June 4 - Sept. 15, daily 10-5.

ROYAL CANADIAN SIGNALS MUSEUM
Vimy Barracks, Highway 2, Kingston, Ontario
History of military communications.
Jan. 12 - May 25, Oct. 5 - Dec. 21: Tu.-F., Su. 2-4. May 31 - Sept. 28: M.-F. 1-5; Sa., Su. 1-4.

ROYAL MILITARY COLLEGE MUSEUM
Fort Frederick, Kingston, Ontario
In Martello Tower (1846). History of the College, Fort Frederick and the Naval Dockyard. Weapons. Uniforms. Maps.
June 1 - Sept. 7, daily 9-9.

KIRKLAND LAKE

MUSEUM OF NORTHERN HISTORY
24 Duncan Street N., Kirkland Lake, Ontario
Early mining and settlement in the area. Indian artifacts. Agriculture.
June 1 - Sept. 30, daily 9-5. Oct. 1 - May 31: M.-F. 9-5.

KITCHENER

DOON PIONEER VILLAGE
R.R.2, Kitchener, Ontario
19th century pioneer buildings moved to site, including church, general store, blacksmith's and cooper's shops. Farm implements. Horse-drawn vehicles. Conestoga wagons. Roller flour mill. First production car built in Canada.
May 1 - Oct. 31, daily 10-5.

KITCHENER-WATERLOO ART GALLERY
43 Benton Street, Kitchener, Ontario, N2G 1E3
Works by Canadian and European artists. Paintings. Graphics. Sculpture.
Wed.-Sa. 10.30-5; W., Th., F. also 7-9; Su. 1-5. Closed public holidays.

WOODSIDE NATIONAL HISTORIC PARK
528 Wellington Street N., Kitchener, Ontario, N2H 5L5
House (c.1870), boyhood home of W. L. Mackenzie King, Canadian Prime Minister. Original and period furnishings.
Daily 9-6. Closed public holidays.

KLEINBERG

MCMICHAEL CONSERVATION COLLECTION OF ART
Kleinberg, Ontario
Paintings especially landscape by Canadian artists. W. Coast Indian carvings. Eskimo sculpture. Pioneer artifacts.
Feb. 1 - Nov. 30: Tu.-Su., public holidays 1-5.30.

KNOWLTON

BROME COUNTY HISTORICAL SOCIETY MUSEUM
Knowlton, Quebec
In former Knowlton Academy (1854). History of Brome County and Knowlton. Pioneer artifacts. Tibbits Hill Schoolhouse (1844) is also in the care of the Society.
July 1 - Sept. 30, daily 10-5.

LACHINE

LACHINE CULTURAL CENTRE
100 La Salle Road, Lachine, Quebec
In former home of Robert Cavalier; period local furnishings. Natural history. Restored fur trade post (1671-80).
Daily 2-5, 7-11.30.

SAINTE-ANNE MUSEUM
Collège Sainte-Anne, 1250 Rue Saint-Joseph, Lachine, Quebec
Geology. Mineralogy. Palaeontology. Botany. Zoology. Ornithology. Entomology.
On request.

LADYSMITH

CROWN ZELLERBACH CANADA ARBORETUM AND MUSEUM
Ladysmith, British Columbia
Locomotives and other equipment used in timber haulage. Specimens of timber trees.
Daily, round-the-clock.

LANG

CENTURY VILLAGE
Lang, Peterborough County, Ontario
Pioneer village of 13 19th century buildings moved to site.
Mar. 22 - June 30, Sept. 1 - Oct. 9, M.-Sa. 2-5; Su. 2-6. July 1 - Aug. 31, M.-Tu., Th., F. 2-4; W., Sa. 2-5; Su. 2-6.

LANG MILL MUSEUM
Keene Road, Lang, Peterborough County, Ontario
Restored and operational grist mill (1826).
May 1 - Oct. 14, daily 9-5.

LA POCATIÈRE

MUSEUM OF THE COLLEGE OF SAINTE-ANNE
Avenue Painchaud, La Pocatière, Quebec
Ornithology. Entomology. Conchology. Local history. Maps. Coins.
Sept. 1 - June 30: Su., public holidays 2-5.

LA SARRE

MUSEUM OF ABITIBI HISTORICAL SOCIETY
Fort Iberville, Chalet du Lac, La Sarre, Quebec
Local history.
M., W., F. 7 p.m.-10; Su. 2-3. Closed public holidays.

LATCHFORD

LATCHFORD HOUSE OF MEMORY
Highway 11, Latchford, Ontario
Geology. Early 19th century household equipment. Lumbering tools. Horse-drawn vehicles.
May 15 - Sept. 15, daily 2-5, 7-9.

LAURENTIDE

SIR WILFRED LAURIER HOUSE
Laurentide, Quebec
House (1840). Memorabilia, personal possessions of Sir Wilfred Laurier.
Feb.-Dec., daily 9-6. Closed public holidays.

LEAMINGTON

POINT PELEE NATIONAL PARK NATURE CENTRE
Leamington, Ontario
Natural history of Point Pelee.
Daily 9-6.

LETHBRIDGE

FORT WHOOP-UP
Lethbridge, Alberta
Restored pioneer fort (c.1830). Pioneer and military history.
May-Oct., daily 10-5.

SIR ALEXANDER GALT MUSEUM
Lethbridge, Alberta
Early development of Lethbridge and Southern Alberta. Mining museum, including reconstructed entrances to 2 drift-mines (1882).
June 1 - Sept. 30, daily 10-5. Oct. 1 - May 31: Su. 2-5.

UNIVERSITY OF LETHBRIDGE ART GALLERY
Lethbridge, Alberta
Paintings, sculpture, drawings, prints by Canadian artists.
M.-Sa., 10-5, during University terms.

GENEVIEVE YATES MEMORIAL CENTRE
Civic Centre, Lethbridge, Alberta
Paintings by Canadian artists.
M.-Sa. 10-6.

LINDSAY

VICTORIA COUNTY HISTORICAL SOCIETY MUSEUM
Highway 7, Lindsay, Ontario
Local history. Indian and pioneer material. Agricultural implements. Pioneer furnishings.
June 15 - Sept. 15: Tu.-Su. 2-5.

LIVERPOOL

SIMEON PERKINS HOUSE
420 Main Street, Liverpool, Nova Scotia
House (1766), former home of Nova Scotia diarist, Simeon Perkins. 18th century furnishings. 18th-19th century household equipment.
May 1 - Sept. 30, daily 9-5.

QUEENS COUNTY HISTORICAL SOCIETY MUSEUM
420 Main Street, Liverpool, Nova Scotia
History of Queen's County.
May 15 - Oct. 31, daily 9-5.

LLOYDMINSTER

BARR COLONY MUSEUM
5011 49th Avenue, Lloydminster, Saskatchewan, S9V OT8
Natural history. Paintings by Canadian artists.
Daily 9-9. Closed Christmas, New Year.

LONDON

ELDON HOUSE
481 Ridout Street N., London, Ontario, N6A 2P8
House (1834). Period furnishings.
Feb. 1 - Nov. 30, daily 2-5. Closed Good Friday.

FANSHAWE PIONEER VILLAGE
London, Ontario
Village of pioneer buildings moved to site. Period furnishings. Tools. Agricultural implements.
Victoria Day - Labour Day: M.-F. 10-5; Sa., Su. 10-7.

HISTORICAL MUSEUM
325 Queen's Avenue, London, Ontario, N6B 1X2
History of London and the Lake Erie region. Household equipment, utensils. Medals. Costumes.
M.-F. 9-9; Sa. 9-6; Su. 2-5. Closed Good Friday, Dec. 1 - Jan. 31.

LONDON PUBLIC LIBRARY AND ART MUSEUM
305 Queen's Avenue, London 14, Ontario, N6B 1X2
20th century paintings and sculpture by Canadian artists.
M.-F. 9.30-9; Sa. 9.30-6; Su. 2-5. Closed public holidays.

MCINTOSH MEMORIAL ART GALLERY
University Campus, University of Western Ontario, London, Ontario
17th-19th century European paintings. Canadian paintings, prints, drawings. English watercolours and drawings.
M.-F. 12-5; Sa., Su. 1-5. W. also 7 p.m.-10. Closed public holidays.

MUSEUM OF INDIAN ARCHAEOLOGY AND PIONEER LIFE
Middlesex College, University of Western Ontario, London, Ontario
Displays illustrating Indian village life. Early Ontario pioneer artifacts. Guns.
M.-F. 9-5.

ROYAL CANADIAN REGIMENT MUSEUM
Wolseley Barracks, Elizabeth Street, London, Ontario
History of the Regiment.
M.-Th. 9-12, 2-4.30; W. 7-9. Closed Aug. 18-31, Dec. 31 - Jan. 2, Mar. 15-31.

LONGUEUIL

CHARLES LEMOYNE HISTORICAL MUSEUM
4 est Rue Saint-Charles, Longueuil, Quebec
Local history. Memorabilia of LeMoyne family. Military relics. Prints. Maps. Coins. Banknotes.
M.-F. 10-6. Closed public holidays.

LONGUEUIL COLLEGE MUSEUM
147 Chemin Chambly, Longueuil, Quebec
Ornithology. Entomology.
Daily 9-9.

LOUGHEED

IRON CREEK MUSEUM ASSOCIATION
Lougheed, Alberta
Local history. Tools. Domestic equipment. Costumes.
May-Sept., M.-Sa. 10-1, 3-5. Other times by appointment.

LOUISBOURG

FORTRESS OF LOUISBOURG NATIONAL HISTORIC PARK
P.O. Box 160, Louisbourg, Nova Scotia
Restored French fortress (1720-40). Material relating to French occupation. Military and maritime history. Transport.
May 15 - June 15, Labour Day - Oct. 15, daily 10-5. June 15 - Labour Day, daily 9-8.

LUNENBURG

LUNENBURG FISHERIES MUSEUM
Lunenburg, Nova Scotia
'Theresa E. Connor', last of the Lunenburg salt tankers. Maritime history, especially Nova Scotia schooners and their crews.
June 1 - Sept. 30, daily 10-8.

MADOC

O'HARA MILL
O'Hara Mill Conservation Area, Madoc, Ontario
Restored and operational water-powered saw-mill (1840). O'Hara House (1848), with period furnishings. Log schoolhouse (1861). Horse-drawn vehicles.
May 1 - Sept. 30, 9-dusk.

MAITLAND

W. D. LAWRENCE HOUSE
Maitland, Nova Scotia
House (1870), formerly home and office of the shipbuilder, W. D. Lawrence. Original furnishings.
By appointment.

MA-ME-O BEACH

LAKESIDE MUSEUM
Ma-Me-O Beach, Alberta
Local natural history, Indian and pioneer relics.
Apr.-Oct., daily 9-5.

MANITOULIN ISLAND

ASSIGINACK MUSEUM
Manitowaning, Manitoulin Island, Ontario
In former jail. Pioneer and Indian material. Blacksmith's shop.
June 1 - Sept. 30: M.-Sa. 10-5; Su. 2-5.

LITTLE CURRENT-HOWLAND CENTENNIAL MUSEUM
Highway 68, Shequiandah, Manitoulin Island, Ontario
Indian culture. Pioneer life.
June 15 - Sept. 25, daily 10-9.

LITTLE RED SCHOOLHOUSE MUSEUM
Southbaymouth, Manitoulin Island, Ontario
Building (1898) with original furnishings. Local history.
June 1 - Sept. 30, 10-5.

MANITOULIN HISTORICAL MARINE MUSEUM
Meldrum Bay, Manitoulin Island, Ontario
Mineralogy. Underwater archaeology.
May 1 - Nov. 8, daily 8 a.m.-9 p.m.

NED SHED MUSEUM
Meldrum Bay, Manitoulin Island, Ontario
Furnishings. Household equipment. Farm implements. Fishing. Lumbering. Costumes. Buttons.
June 15 - Sept. 1: M.-Sa. 2-5, 7-9.

WESTERN MANITOULIN HISTORICAL MUSEUM
Old Jail, Dawson Street, Gore Bay, Manitoulin Island, Ontario
Pioneer life. Indian material. Mounted birds.
May 1 - Sept. 2: M.-Sa. 1-6.

MANNING PARK

MANNING PARK PROVINCIAL NATURE HOUSE
Highway 3, Manning Park, British Columbia
Nature interpretation centre. Exhibits illustrating botany and natural history of Park area.
July 1 - Aug. 31, daily 9.30-8.

MANOTICK

LONG ISLAND MILL
Highway 16, Manotick, Ontario
Operational water-powered grist and flour mill (1860).
May 1 - Sept. 30: M.-F. 9-5; Sa., Su. 1-6; public holidays 10-6.

MAPLE CREEK

CYPRESS HILLS PIONEER MUSEUM
Jasper Street, Maple Creek, Saskatchewan, SO9 1NO
Local history. Indian material. Fossils. Dinosaur bones.
Daily 11-12, 2-5.30.

MARGAREE CENTRE

MARGAREE SALMON MUSEUM
Margaree Forks, Margaree Centre, Nova Scotia
Life cycle of the salmon. Fishing equipment. Poachers' techniques and equipment.
June 15 - Oct. 15, daily 9-5.

MARSHALL

DELP'S MINERAL MUSEUM
Marshall, Saskatchewan, SOM 1R0
Minerals from all parts of the world.
Daily 8-5.

MASSEY

MASSEY PIONEER MUSEUM
Public Library, Highway 27, Massey, Ontario
History of Massey and Fort Lacloche. Indian material. Lumbering.
June 15 - Labour Day: M.-Sa. 10.30-8.30.

MCBRIDE

OSCAR'S WILDLIFE MUSEUM
McBride, British Columbia
Natural history of British Columbia. Mounted animals and animal heads.
Su.-F. by appointment.

MEAFORD

MEAFORD MUSEUM
Bayfield and Collingwood Streets, Meaford, Ontario, NOH 1YO
Local history. Pioneer items.
June 15 - Sept. 15. Daily 2-5, 7-9.

MEDICINE HAT

MEDICINE HAT ART CLUB
Public Library, Medicine Hat, Alberta
Paintings by Alberta artists.
M.-F. 10-9; Sa. 10-6.

MEDICINE HAT HISTORICAL AND MUSEUM FOUNDATION
1302 Bomford Crescent, Medicine Hat, Alberta, T1A 5E6
Pioneer artifacts of Western Canada. Plains Indian material. Archives.
June 1 - Aug. 31, M.-F. 9-9. Rest of year, M.-F. 2-5. Closed Christmas, New Year, Good Friday.

MERRICKVILLE

BLOCKHOUSE MUSEUM
Merrickville, Ontario
Fort (1826). Displays showing history of Merrickville area.
July 1 - Aug. 31, daily 1-6. June 15 - Sept. 15 also Sa. Su. 1-6.

MIDDLEPORT

CHIEFSWOOD
Highway 54, Six Nations Reserve, Middleport, Ontario
House was birthplace of Indian poetess, E. Pauline Johnson. Memorabilia of Pauline Johnson.
May 1 - Oct. 30: M.-F. 10-12, 1-4; Sa., Su. 10-12, 1-6.

MIDLAND

HURONIA MUSEUM
Little Lake Park, Midland, Ontario
Indian life. Pioneer and maritime history.
May 24 - Oct. 4: M.-Sa. 10-5; Su. 1-5.

HURON INDIAN VILLAGE
Little Lake Park, Midland, Ontario
Reconstruction of Huron Indian Village. Long houses. Sweat bath. Medicine Man's Lodge. Smoke house. Sleeping shelter.
May 18 - Oct. 12: M.-Sa. 9-5; Su. 1-5.

MARTYR'S SHRINE MUSEUM
Highway 12, Midland, Ontario
On site of Fort Sainte Marie (1639-49), former Jesuit centre. Huron Indian pottery, tools. Items from French missions, 1625-50.
May 1 - Oct. 31, daily 10-5.

SAINTE MARIE AMONG THE HURONS
R.R.I, Midland, Ontario
Reconstruction of Ontario's first European community, 1639-49. Palisaded compound with European and Indian dwellings.
May 18 - Sept. 2, daily 10-6. Sept. 3 - Oct. 14, daily 10-5.

MILTON

HALTON COUNTY MUSEUM
Kelso Conservation Area, Milton, Ontario
Life in Halton County, 1800-1900. Furnishings. Household equipment. Agricultural implements. Handicrafts. Exhibits include farm forge, water-powered turbine and Alexander Homestead (c.1836).
May 1 - Oct. 31, M., W.-F. 2-5. Sa. 2-5.30. Su. 2-6.

MINESING

SIMCOE COUNTY MUSEUM
Rural Route 2, Minesing, Ontario
Local history, up to 1900. Indian archaeology and culture. Spearin House (1834) and Marvin Barn (1856) are in the care of the Museum.
Jan. 1 - Mar. 31: Sa. 10-12, 1-5; Su. 1-5. Apr. 1 - May 31, Sept. 1 - Dec. 31: Tu.-Sa. 1-5; Su. 1-5. June 1-30: M.-Sa. 9-5; Su. 1-9. July 1 - Aug. 31: M.-Sa. 9-9; Su. 1-9.

MINNEDOSA

MINNEDOSA AND DISTRICT PIONEER CO-OP MUSEUM
57 2nd Avenue N.W., Minnedosa, Manitoba
Furnished rooms of the pioneer period. Agricultural implements. Indian collection.
May 21 - Sept. 30, Tu., Th., Sa. 2-5, 7.30-9; Su. 2-9.

MIRACLE BEACH

MIRACLE BEACH PROVINCIAL PARK NATURE HOUSE
E. of Island Highway, Miracle Beach, British Columbia
Nature interpretation centre. Exhibits illustrating botany and natural history of Park area.
June 20 - Labour Day, daily 10-9.

MISCOUCHE

ACADIAN MUSEUM
Miscouche, Prince Edward Island
Household equipment. Agricultural tools, equipment. Furniture.
May 1 - Sept. 30: M.-Sa. 10-12, 1-7. Su. 1-6.

MISSISSAUGA

LEWIS BRADLEY PIONEER MUSEUM
Meadow Wood and Orr Roads, Mississauga, Ontario
House (c.1830), moved to present site. Period furnishings and household equipment.
May 1 - Oct. 31: F., Su. 1-5; Sa. 10-5.

MISTASSINI

CONFEDERATE CULTURAL CENTRE
219 boulevard Panoramique, Mistassini, Quebec
Local history.
W.-Sa. 9-5; M., Tu., Su. 2-5.

MONCTON

FREE MEETING HOUSE
Moncton, New Brunswick
Church (1821), built to provide place of worship for all denominations. Original furnishings. Local history.
By appointment.

MONCTON CIVIC MUSEUM
Mountain Road at Belleview Avenue, Moncton, New Brunswick
History of Greater Moncton area from 18th century to present day.
Daily 10-8.30.

UNIVERSITY OF MONCTON ART GALLERY
Moncton, New Brunswick
Paintings. Prints. Sculpture.
Sept. 1 - July 3, daily 2-4. M., W. also 7 p.m.-9. Closed Christmas, New Year, Easter.

UNIVERSITY OF MONCTON MUSEUM
Moncton, New Brunswick
Acadian history, furniture, handicrafts.
Sept. 1 - June 30, M.-Sa. 2-4. Mornings by appointment. July 1 - Aug. 31, Su. F. 2-4. M.-Th. 2-4, 7-9.

MONTAGUE

GARDEN OF THE GULF MUSEUM
Montague, Prince Edward Island
Pioneer history. Household equipment. Industry. Agricultural implements.
July 1 - Sept. 30: M.-Sa. 9-6; Su. 1-6.

MONTREAL

ALCAN MUSEUM
1 Place Ville Marie, Montreal 113, Quebec
History of the aluminium industry.
M.-F. 9-5.

ART GALLERY OF SIR GEORGE WILLIAMS UNIVERSITY
Henry F. Hall Building, 1455 De Maisonneuve Boulevard, Sir George Williams University, Montreal, Quebec
Works by contemporary Canadian artists. Paintings. Drawings. Prints. Sculpture, including primitive sculpture.
M.-F. 11-9; Sa. 11-5.

ART NOVA ET VETERA GALLERY
625 Boulevard Sainte-Croix, Montreal 279, Quebec
Traditional Quebec art. Contemporary paintings, graphics, sculpture.
Sept.-May, daily 10-4.

BANK OF MONTREAL MUSEUM
Bank of Montreal Building, Place d'Armes, Montreal, Quebec
Replica of Canada's first banking office. Collection of historic banking items. Coins.
M.-F. 10-3.

MARGUERITE BOURGEOYS MUSEUM
Church of Notre Dame de Bon Secours, 400 E. Saint Paul Street, Montreal, Quebec
Miniature dioramas illustrating life of the nun, Marguerite Bourgeoys.
Daily 9-11.30, 1-7.

CALVET HOUSE
Bonsecours and Saint Paul Streets, Montreal, Quebec
Restored house of Pierre Calvet. Early Quebec furnishings and paintings.
M.-F. 10-4; Sa., Su. 12-5.

CANADA RAILWAY MUSEUM
122A St. Pierre Street, Montreal, Quebec
History of Canadian railways. Locomotives. Coaches. Trams. Operating equipment.
May 1 - Oct. 31, daily 10-5.

CANADIAN GUILD OF CRAFTS
2025 Peel Street, Montreal, Quebec
Permanent collection of Canadian handicrafts. Rugs. Woven and needlework bedspreads. Woodcarving. Metalwork. Pottery. Indian basketry, beadwork, porcupine quill and moose-hair embroidery.
M.-F. 9-5; Sa. 9-1. Closed public holidays.

CHAPEL OF NOTRE DAME DE BONSECOURS
400 St. Paul Street E., Montreal 127, Quebec
Early history of Montreal. History of the Chapel.
Tu.-Su. 9-11.30, 1-5.

CHÂTEAU DE RAMEZAY
290 Notre Dame Street E., Montreal, Quebec
Former home (1705) and administrative headquarters of Claude de Ramezay, Governor of Montreal. Local history. Indian artifacts. Portraits.
Tu.-Sa. 10-5; Su. 2-5. Closed Christmas, New Year, Easter.

DEAF-MUTE MUSEUM
7400 Saint-Laurent Boulevard, Montreal, Quebec
Museum attached to Institution des Sourds-Muets. Children's museum. Natural history collections.
On request.

DOCUMENTATION CENTRE OF SAINT-JOSEPH ORATORY
3800 Reine-Marie Road, Montreal, Quebec
Religious history, especially the cult of St. Joseph. Paintings.
Daily 9-5.

DOW PLANETARIUM
1000 St. Jacques Street W., Montreal, Quebec
Astronomy. Meteorology. Space science. Planetarium.
M.-Su. 12-5; Tu., Su. also 7.45 p.m.-10.30.

LA SAUVEGARDE
160 E. Notre Dame Street, Montreal, Quebec
House (1800). Contemporary paintings, graphics, sculpture by Canadian artists.
Daily 12-6. Closed Dec. 25-Jan. 1.

LOYOLA COLLEGE MUSEUM
7141 W. Sherbrooke Street, Montreal, Quebec
Paintings. Sculpture.
On request.

MCCORD MUSEUM
690 Sherbrooke Street W., Montreal, Quebec
Canadian pre-history and history. 18th-20th century furniture, furnishings. Decorative arts. Handicrafts. Paintings. Prints. Guns. Costumes.
Tu.-Sa. 10-5. Su. 2-5.

MONTREAL BOTANICAL GARDEN
4101 Sherbrooke Street E., Montreal 406, Quebec
Herbarium.
Daily 10-dusk.

MONTREAL MUSEUM OF FINE ART
1379 Sherbrooke Street W., Montreal 109, Quebec
13th-20th century European paintings, sculpture, decorative arts. Oriental art. Canadian paintings, sculpture.
Tu., Th.-Sa. 10-4.45; W. 10-9.45; Su. 1-4.45. Closed public holidays.

MONTREAL MUSEUM OF PRIMITIVE ART
Collège Sainte-Marie, 1180 Bleury Street, Montreal Quebec
Primitive art of Mexico, Oceania and Africa. Separate collection of Oriental art.
On request.

MUSEUM OF CONTEMPORARY ART
Cité du Havre, Montreal, Quebec
Canadian and foreign art since 1940. Paintings. Graphic arts. Sculpture. Tapestry.
Tu.-Su. 10-6. Closed Dec. 25-26, Jan. 1-2.

MUSEUM OF THE CHURCH OF NOTRE DAME
430 Saint-Sulpice, Montreal, Quebec
Religious history. Paintings. Vestments. Silver.
Sept. 1-May 31: M.-Sa. 10-4.30; Su. 1-5. June 1-Aug. 31: M.-Sa. 9-5; Su. 1-6.

MUSEUM OF THE INSTITUTE OF APPLIED ARTS
1430 Saint-Denis Street, Montreal, Quebec
Historical collections of applied arts in Quebec, especially furniture.
W., Th. 2-4. Other times by appointment.

MUSEUM OF THE MILITARY AND MARITIME SOCIETY OF MONTREAL
The Old Fort, St. Helen's Island, Montreal, Quebec
Fort (c.1820). Items and displays illustrating military and maritime history, 1500 onwards, especially Canadian. Firearms. Costumes and uniforms. Prints. Documents.
May 1-Sept. 30, daily 10-5.

MUSEUM OF QUEBEC FEDERATION OF CULTURAL CENTRES
3100 rue Saint Donat, Montreal 429, Quebec
Paintings. Graphics. Sculpture. Theatre history.
Daily 10-4.

REDPATH MUSEUM
805 Sherbrooke Street, Montreal 110, Quebec
Geology. Palaeontology. Zoology.
M.-Sa. 9-5; Su. 2-5.

ROYAL CANADIAN ORDNANCE CORPS MUSEUM
6560 Hochelaga Street, Montreal 427, Quebec
History of the Regiment and the Canadian Army.
M.-F. 10-12, 2-4; Sa., Su., public holidays, by appointment.

VILLA MARIA
4245 Décarie Boulevard, Montreal, Quebec
House, formerly official residence of the Governors-General of Canâda.
On request.

WISER'S CANADIAN MUSEUM
3411 Drummond Street, Montreal, Quebec
Late 18th-19th century Canadian furniture.
M.-F. 9-4.30.

MOOSE FACTORY

MOOSE FACTORY MUSEUM PARK
Moose Factory, Ontario
Site of first English settlement and trading post in Ontario. Restoration of powder magazine (c.1830), log fort and blacksmith's shop (c.1812). Displays illustrating development of Hudson's Bay and James Bay areas.
June 9-Sept. 30: M.-Sa. 10.30-12, 1.30-5, 7-8; Su. 2-5, 7-8.

MOOSE JAW

MOOSE JAW ART MUSEUM
Centennial Building, Crescent Park, Moose Jaw, Saskatchewan
Local history and archaeology. Indian artifacts. Paintings by Saskatchewan artists.
May 1-Sept. 30, Tu.-Sa. 2-9. Oct. 1-Apr. 30, Tu.-Sa. 2-10. Closed public holidays.

MORPETH

RONDEAU PROVINCIAL PARK INTERPRETIVE CENTRE
Rondeau Provincial Park, Rural Route 1, Morpeth, Ontario, NOP 1XO
Geology. Natural history. Local history.
May 1-Sept. 30, M.-F. 10-6; Sa., Su. 10-9. Oct. 1-Apr. 30, M.-F. 10-6.

MORRISBURG

UPPER CANADA VILLAGE
Crysler Farm Battlefield Park, Highway 2, Morrisburg, Ontario, KOC 1XO
Reconstruction of 19th century village, with 40 Ontario buildings (1784-1867) restored and furnished to show provincial life. Craft workshops, with demonstrations.
May 15-June 14, daily 9.30-5. June 15-Sept. 2, daily 9.30-6.30. Sept. 3-Oct. 15, daily 9.30-5.

MOUNT UNIACKE

SOUTH RAWDON MUSEUM
R.R.I., Mount Uniacke, Nova Scotia
In Sons of Temperance Hall (1867). Period furnishings. Industry. Local history. Costumes.
June-Sept., daily 2-5.

UNIACKE HOUSE
Mount Uniacke, Nova Scotia
House (1813). Uniacke family furnishings.
June 1-Sept. 30, daily 9.30-5.30.

MUNDARE

MUSEUM OF THE BAZILIAN FATHERS
Mundare, Alberta, TOB 3HO
History of Bazilian Order in Canada. Paintings. Documents. Coins. Military history. Indian artifacts.
May 1-Oct. 31, M.-Sa. 10-6.

NANAIMO

NANAIMO CENTENNIAL MUSEUM
100 Cameron Road, Piper Park, Nanaimo, British Columbia
Local history. Fishing. Pioneer life. Coal mining. Chinese settlement. Indian collection.
May 15-Sept. 15, daily 10-5. Sept. 16-May 14: Tu.-Su. 1-4.

NANTON

CANADIANA MUSEUM
Nanton, Alberta
Collections illustrating Canadian social history. Pioneer tools, equipment, furniture. Photographs.
May-Oct., daily 10-5. Other months by appointment.

NAPANEE

ALLAN MACPHERSON HOUSE
Macpherson Street, Box 342, Napanee, Ontario, KOK 2RO
House (1837), restored and furnished to reflect the period of MacPherson's occupation, 1820-40.
May 16-Oct. 31: Tu.-Su. 12-5, 1-8.

LENNOX AND ADDINGTON HISTORICAL MUSEUM
County Memorial Building, Dundas Street, Napanee, Ontario, KOK 2RO
Indian and pioneer life of area.
June 1-Sept. 30, daily 2-5.

NARAMATA

NARAMATA PUBLIC LIBRARY AND MUSEUM
Naramata, British Columbia
Local history.
M.-Sa. 9-7.

NELSON

KOOTENAY MUSEUM
618 Blake Street, Nelson, British Columbia
Geology. Mining. Doukhobor art and handicrafts. Early exploration of British Columbia. Indian material.
June 1-Sept. 30, daily 1-9. Rest of year by appointment.

KOOTENAY SCHOOL OF ART
Box 480, Silver King Road, Nelson, British Columbia
Contemporary Canadian paintings, graphics, sculpture.
M.-F. 8.30-4; Sa., Su. by appointment. Closed public holidays.

NEW DENMARK

NEW DENMARK MEMORIAL MUSEUM
New Denmark, New Brunswick
Household articles, documents, machinery belonging to original settlers from Denmark.
17th June and other times by appointment.

NEW GLASGOW

PICTOU COUNTY HISTORICAL MUSEUM
86 Temperance Street, New Glasgow, Nova Scotia
County history. Glass. Household equipment. Farm tools and implements. 'Samson' locomotive (1839).
July 1-Aug. 31, daily 2-4, 7-9. Other months by appointment.

NEW LONDON

LUCY MAUD MONTGOMERY BIRTHPLACE
New London, Prince Edward Island
House. Period furnishings. Memorabilia of Lucy Maud Montgomery.
June 15-Sept. 30, daily 10-8.

NEW ROSS

ROSS FARM AGRICULTURAL MUSEUM
New Ross, Nova Scotia
Building (1817). Agricultural history of Nova Scotia. Farm tools, implements.
May 15-Oct. 15, daily 9.30-5.30.

NEW WESTMINSTER

IRVING HOUSE HISTORIC CENTER
302 Royal Avenue, Westminster, British Columbia
House (1862), with original and period furnishings. Local history. Indian material.
Oct. 1-Apr. 30, Sa.-Su. 2-4. May 1-Aug. 31, Sa.-Su. 11-5. Closed public holidays.

ANTIQUE AUTO MUSEUM
Niagara Falls, Ontario
Vintage cars, shown in period settings.
June 1-Sept. 30, 8.30 a.m.-12.30 a.m. Oct. 1-May 31, 10-10.

NIAGARA FALLS

HYDRO HALL OF MEMORY
Sir Adam Beck Generating Station, Niagara Parkway, Niagara Falls, Ontario
History of development and use of hydro-electric power in Ontario.
Sept. 1-June 30, daily 9-4. July 1-Aug. 31, daily 9-7. Closed Dec. 25, 26, 31 and Good Friday.

LUNDY'S LANE HISTORICAL MUSEUM
Ferry Street, Niagara Falls, Ontario
On site of Battle of Lundy's Lane (1812). Military and naval relics. Indian artifacts. Pioneer tools, household equipment, agricultural implements.
May 15 - Sept. 15, daily 12.30-4.30.

NIAGARA FALLS MUSEUM
Rainbow Bridge, Niagara Falls, Ontario
Local history. Chinese ivories. Japanese armour, swords. Indian artifacts. Equipment used to carry men over Horseshoe Falls. Local wildlife.
Daily 9-9.

OAK HALL
Portage Road S., Niagara Falls, Ontario
House (mainly 1898-1928, with some earlier parts), formerly home of the millionaire Schoellkopf and Oakes families. Many original furnishings. Panelling from Hampton Court, England. Gallery of early prints.
Last Sa. in June - Labour Day, daily 12-8.

POTVIN MUSEUM
Queen Victoria Park, Niagara Falls, Ontario
Woodcarvings.
May 1 - Sept. 30, daily 10 a.m.-midnight. Oct. 1 - Nov. 30, 12-10.

SCHOOL OF HORTICULTURE HERBARIUM
Botanical Garden, Niagara Falls, Ontario
Plants of N.E. America.
Daily, dawn-dusk.

WILLOUGHBY TOWNSHIP HISTORICAL MUSEUM
Niagara Parkway and Weaver Road, Niagara Falls, Ontario
Life of early settlers.
May 17 - June 22, Sept. 6 - Oct. 12: Sa., Su., public holidays 2-5. June 23 - Sept. 1, daily 2-5.

NIAGARA-ON-THE-LAKE

FORT GEORGE
Niagara Parkway, Niagara-on-the-Lake, Ontario
Restored buildings of British military post (1796-9). Furnishings of period of British occupation (1797-1813). Items recovered from excavations of fort ruins. Paintings, prints illustrating early development of Canada.
May 15 - Sept. 15, daily 9-6.

MCFARLAND HOUSE
Niagara Parkway, Niagara-on-the-Lake, Ontario
House (1800, with additions of 1892), furnished in style of 1820-45.
May 18 - Sept. 29, daily 10-6.

NAVY HALL
Niagara-on-the-Lake, Ontario
Building (1775-87), site of first Parliament in Upper Canada. Military history. Guns. Uniforms. Badges.
May 11 - June 30, Sept. 1 - Oct. 14, daily 10-6. July 1 - Aug. 31, daily 10-7.

NIAGARA HISTORICAL SOCIETY MUSEUM
43 Castlereagh Street, Niagara-on-the-Lake, Ontario
Early Niagara history. Indian material. Pioneer furnishings, costumes. Documents and artifacts relating to War of 1812. Relics of local shipbuilding industry.
May 15 - June 15, Sept. 3 - Oct. 14: Sa. 12-5; Su. 1-5. June 16 - Sept. 2, daily 12-5.

NICOLET

NICOLET SEMINARY MUSEUM
Nicolet, Quebec
Mineralogy. Zoology. Local history. Religious art. Coins.
Daily 8.30-6.

NORTH BATTLEFORD

WESTERN DEVELOPMENT MUSEUM AND PIONEER VILLAGE
Highways 5 and 40, North Battleford, Saskatchewan
Reconstruction of pioneer village, containing 19th and early 20th century buildings moved to site. Period furnishings. Steam tractors. Old cars. Horse-drawn vehicles. Agricultural implements and machinery.
May 1 - Oct. 31, 9 a.m.-dusk.

NORTH BUXTON

RALEIGH TOWNSHIP MUSEUM
County Road 6, North Buxton, Ontario
Displays showing Elgin settlement and work of Rev. William King in educating and rehabilitating freed slaves.
May 1 - Oct. 31: Tu., Th., Sa. 1-5. Other times by appointment.

NORWICH

NORWICH AND DISTRICT HISTORICAL SOCIETY MUSEUM
Stoner Street, Norwich, Ontario, NOJ 1PO
Displays illustrating the emigration of Quakers from Dutchen County, Pennsylvania and the establishment of Norwich (1810). Pioneer life. Quaker culture. Indian artifacts. Drug store. Period rooms. Agricultural implements.
May 1 - Oct. 31: W., Sa., Su., public holidays 2-5. Other times by appointment.

NORWICH PIONEERS' SOCIETY MUSEUM
Post Office Building, Norwich, Ontario, NOJ 1PO
Natural history. Mastodon bones. Local history. Indian material. Household equipment. Costumes. Agricultural implements.
Sa. 2-4.

OAKVILLE

OLD POST OFFICE AND THOMAS HOUSE MUSEUM
Lakeside Park, Oakville, Ontario
The old Post Office (1835) contains pioneer farm tools from Halton County. Thomas House (1827) has period furnishings, including some of the original household items. Maritime history. Ship-building tools.
May 15 - Oct. 17: Tu.-F. 2-5; Sa., Su. 1.30-5.

TARAS H. SHEVCHENKO MUSEUM
1363 Dundas Street, Oakville, Ontario
Material illustrating life of the Ukrainian poet, Shevchenko. Copies of his literary works. Ukrainian Canadian handicrafts. Relics of early Ukrainian pioneer life in Western Canada.
June 1 - Aug. 31: Sa., Su. 12-5. Rest of year by appointment.

ODANAK

ODANAK MUSEUM
Abenaki Indian Reserve, Odanak, Quebec
Material relating to the Indian tribes of Quebec, especially the Abenaki. Natural history. Dioramas. Handicrafts.
May 1 - Oct. 31: Sa., Su. 1-6. June 15 - Sept. 7, daily 10-6.

OHSWEKEN

COUNCIL HOUSE
Six Nations Reserve, Ohsweken, Ontario
Building (1864). Indian history.
By appointment.

OIL SPRINGS

OIL MUSEUM OF CANADA
Kelly Road, Oil Springs, Ontario, NON 1PO
History of the first commercial oil well in N. America. Early techniques of prospecting, drilling, refining. Replica of 1858 oil well. Life in an oil town of the 1860s. Uses of oil.
May 18 - Oct. 13, daily 10-6. Oct. 14-31, daily 10-5. Nov. 1-30: Sa., Su. 1-5.

OKANAGAN MISSION

FATHER PANDESY MISSION
Okanagan Mission, British Columbia
Restored log buildings (1859) of Oblate Mission. 3 other early settlers' houses moved to site and furnished in style of 1870-1900. Farm implements. Horse-drawn vehicles.
May 24 - Sept. 15, dawn-dusk.

INDIAN VILLAGE
Okanagan Mission, British Columbia
Reconstruction of Salish Indian encampment. Displays showing Indian life.
May 24 - Sept. 15, 9-dusk.

ORILLIA

STEPHEN LEACOCK MEMORIAL HOME
Old Brewery Bay, Atherley Road, Orillia, Ontario
House, 'Old Brewery Bay' (1927) was Leacock's summer home. Some original furniture. Leacock's correspondence, manuscripts and personal possessions.
June 1 - Labour Day: daily 10-8. May 1-31, Labour Day - Oct. 15, by appointment.

OROMOCTO

CANADIAN FORCES BASE, GAGETOWN MUSEUM
Combrai Barracks, Oromocto, New Brunswick
Military history.
M.-F. 8-12, 1-4; Sa., Su., public holidays by appointment.

FORT HUGHES BLOCKHOUSE
Off Route 2, Oromocto, New Brunswick
8 m. east of Fredericton. Military historical reconstruction.
July 1 - Sept. 4, daily 1-8.

OSHAWA

CANADIAN AUTOMOTIVE MUSEUM
99 Simcoe Street S., Oshawa, Ontario
History of Canadian-built cars.
Jan. 1 - June 30, Sept. 1 - Dec. 31: M.-F. 9-5; Sa. 10-6. July 1 - Aug. 31: M.-F. 9-9; Sa. 10-9; Su. 12-9.

CANADIAN CABIN MUSEUM
Macdonald-Cartier Freeway and Courtice Road, Oshawa, Ontario
Settler's cabin of 1830s, moved to site. Period furnishings.
May 1 - Sept. 30, daily 9-5.

HENRY HOUSE MUSEUM
Lakeview Park, Oshawa, Ontario
House (1846). Collections illustrating local life 1850-1880. Furnishings. Household equipment. Agricultural implements. Tradesmen's tools. Costumes.
May 15 - Oct. 15: Tu.-Su., public holidays 2-5. Other times by appointment.

ROBERT MCLAUGHLIN GALLERY
Civic Centre, Oshawa, Ontario
Canadian paintings, graphics, sculpture, 1920-40. Japanese wood-block prints.
M.-F. 12-5, 7-9; Sa. 12-5; Su. 2-5.

ROBINSON HOUSE MUSEUM
Lakeview Park, Oshawa, Ontario
House (1846). Collections illustrating history of Oshawa area. Maritime history. Development of lighting.
May 15 - Oct. 15: Tu.-Su., public holidays 2-5.

OSOYOOS

OSOYOOS MUSEUM
Rural Route 1, Osoyoos, British Columbia
Local history museum in former jail, school, church and customs house (all c.1890). Room of original log Government administration building. Relics of first settlers in area (c.1860). Gold mining. Arts and crafts from Indian Reserve, Ikameep Band. Fossils. Marine specimens. Natural history.
July 1 - Aug. 31, daily 10-8. Other times by appointment.

OTTAWA

BYTOWN MUSEUM
Canal Locks, Rideau Canal, Ottawa, Ontario
In Commissariat building (1826), built by Col. John By during construction of Rideau Canal. Collections relating to Col. By, the Canal and the history of the Ottawa area.
May 1 - Oct. 15: M., Tu., Th.-Su. 2-5; W. 12-5.

CANADIAN FILM ARCHIVES
1762 Carling Street, Ottawa, Ontario
History of film in Canada. Film equipment. Stills. Films. Recordings.
M.-F. 8.30-4.30. Closed public holidays.

CANADIAN WAR MUSEUM
330-350 Sussex Drive, Ottawa, Ontario
Weapons. Uniforms. Equipment. Medals. Maps. Photographs. Flags. Models.
May 15 - Sept. 14, M.-Sa. 9-9; Su. 1-9. Sept. 15 - May 14, Tu.-Sa. 9-5; Su. 12-5.

COLLECTIONS OF PLANT RESEARCH INSTITUTE
Central Experimental Farm, Ottawa, Ontario, K1A OC6
Mycology. Herbarium of vascular plants.
M.-F. 8.15-4.30.

GOVERNOR GENERAL'S FOOTGUARDS MUSEUM
Drill Hall, Cartier Square, Ottawa, Ontario
In Drill Hall (1879). History of regiment since 1872. Weapons. Uniforms. Medals. Photographs.
Tu., F. 8 p.m.-10. Other times by appointment.

LAURIER HOUSE
335 Laurier Avenue E., Ottawa, K1N 6R4
House (1878) was home of 2 Canadian Prime Ministers, Sir Wilfred Laurier and W. L. MacKenzie King. Period furnishings. Paintings. Memorabilia of the Prime Ministers.
Tu.-Sa. 10-5; Su. 2-5. Closed Christmas, New Year, Good Friday.

MUSEUM OF CANADIAN SCOUTING
1345 Base Line Road, Ottawa, Ontario, K2C OA7
Life of Lord Baden-Powell. History of Scouting in Canada.
M.-F. 9-4. Sa. by appointment.

MUSEUM OF NATIONAL HISTORIC SITES SERVICE
National and Historic Parks Branch, Department of Indian Affairs and Northern Development, Ottawa, Ontario
History. Technology. Industry. Aeronautics. Maritime history. Science.
June 15 - Labour Day, daily 9-8. Apr. 1 - June 14, day following Labour Day - Nov. 30, M.-Sa. 10-5; Su. 12-5. Closed public holidays.

NATIONAL AERONAUTICAL COLLECTION
Rockcliffe Airfield, Ottawa, Ontario
80 aircraft, illustrating world development of aviation, with particular emphasis on Canadian achievements.
May 1 - Oct. 31, daily 9-9. Nov. 1 - Apr. 30: Tu.-Su. 9-9.

NATIONAL FILM BOARD MUSEUM
Still Photography Division, Tunny's Pasture, Ottawa, Ontario
Works by Canadian photographers.
M.-F. 10-6; Sa., Su. 12-6. Closed Christmas, New Year, Good F.

NATIONAL GALLERY OF CANADA
Lorne Building, Elgin Street, Ottawa 4, Ontario
16th-18th century European paintings. 19th-20th century European paintings, sculpture. 19th-20th century Canadian prints, drawings. 18th-20th century Canadian paintings, sculpture.
M., W., F., Sa. 10-6; Tu., Th. 10-10; Su., public holidays 2-6. Sept. 1 - Apr. 30, closed M.

NATIONAL MUSEUM OF MAN
Victoria and Metcalfe Streets, Ottawa, Ontario, K1A OM8
Anthropology. Ethnology. Folklore. History. Folk-song collections.
May 1 - Sept. 30: Tu.-Sun. 9-9. Oct. 1 - Apr. 30: M.-Sa. 9-5; Su. 2-5. Closed Christmas.

NATIONAL MUSEUM OF NATURAL SCIENCES
Victoria Memorial Building, McLeod and Metcalfe Streets, Ottawa, Ontario
Herbarium. Zoology. Oceanography. Palaeontology. Mineralogy.
May 1 - Sept. 30: Tu.-Su. 9-9. Oct. 1 - Apr. 30: Tu.-Su. 9-5. Closed Christmas.

NATIONAL MUSEUM OF SCIENCE AND TECHNOLOGY
St. Laurent Boulevard and Russell Road, Ottawa, Ontario, K1A OM8
Canadian development of technology and the physical sciences. Land and air transport. Agriculture. Communications. Chemistry. Astronomy. Energy. Mining. Industry. Forestry. Marine technology.
May 15 - Sept. 14: daily 9-9. Sept. 15 - May 14: Tu.-Su. 9-9.

PUBLIC ARCHIVES OF CANADA
395 Wellington Street, Ottawa, Ontario, K1Y 2Y1
Material illustrating Canadian history. Documents. Paintings. Photographs. Maps. Medals.
M.-Th. 9-5; F.-Sa. 9-9; Su., public holidays 1-9.

OTTERVILLE

SOUTH NORWICH HISTORICAL MUSEUM
Municipal Building, Otterville, Ontario, NOJ 1RO
Local history. Household equipment. Agricultural implements.
M.-F. 9-5. Other times by appointment.

OWEN SOUND

COUNTY OF GREY AND OWEN SOUND MUSEUM
975 6th Street E., Owen Sound, Ontario, N4K 1G9
Mineralogy. Fossils. Indian and pioneer life. Furnishings. Local flax industry. Log cabins. Blacksmith's shop.
July 1 - Aug. 31, M.-Sa. 9-8; Su. 1-5. Sept. 1 - June 30: Tu.-Su. 1-5.

TOM THOMSON MEMORIAL GALLERY AND MUSEUM OF FINE ART
840 1st Avenue W., Owen Sound, Ontario, N4K 4K4
Canadian paintings. Memorabilia of Tom Thomson.
Sept. 1 - June 30. Tu.-Su. 12-5. July 1 - Aug. 31: M., Tu., Th., Sa., Su. 12-5. W.-F. 7-9. Closed New Year, Good Friday.

PAKAN

FORT VICTORIA MUSEUM
Pakan, Alberta
Early 19th century fort. Pioneer history. Indian material.
Apr.-Sept., daily 9-5.

PARKDALE

PARKDALE MAPLEWOOD COMMUNITY MUSEUM
Route 3, Parkdale, Nova Scotia
Local history. Pioneer life.
June 1 - Sept. 30, daily 9-5.

PARRSBORO

MINERAL AND GEM GEOLOGICAL MUSEUM
Tourist Bureau, Parrsboro, Nova Scotia
Geology. Minerals. Pioneer tools.
June 1 - Sept. 30, M.-Sa. 8.30-8.30; Su. 10-8.

PATRICIA

DINOSAUR PROVINCIAL PARK
Patricia, Alberta, TOJ 2KO
Open air museum of palaeontology, including in situ fossils of dinosaurs.
Daily 9-5.

PEACE RIVER

PEACE RIVER CENTENNIAL MUSEUM
Peace River, Alberta, TOH 2XO
Natural history. Local history. Pioneer material.
May 1 - Oct. 31, daily 9-5.

PEMBROKE

CHAMPLAIN TRAIL MUSEUM
Highway 17, Pembroke, Ontario
In schoolhouse (1838) and pioneer house (1872). History of early settlement of area. Period furnishings. Indian material. Lumbering. Hunting equipment. Farm implements.
June 1-30, Sept. 1-30: M.-Sa. 2-5, 7-9. July 1 - Aug. 31, daily 10-12, 1-5, 7-9.

PENETANGUISHENE

BRITISH NAVAL AND MILITARY ESTABLISHMENT MUSEUM
Penetanguishene, Ontario
Reconstruction of British Establishment on Lake Huron (1814-56). Museum in former officers' quarters contains contemporary furniture, uniforms, military equipment and pictures. U.S. Schooner 'Tigress' and H.M. Schooner 'Tecumseth' raised from Georgian Bay.
May 1 - Oct. 31, daily 9-6.

PENETANGUISHENE CENTENNIAL MUSEUM
Burke Street, Penetanguishene, Ontario
Local history. Transport, including 1903 Oldsmobile, the first car to be used in the area.
May 24 - July 1: Sa., Su. 2-5. July 2 - Sept. 2: M.-Sa. 10-5; Su. 2-5.

PENTICTON

PENTICTON MUSEUM AND ARCHIVES
785 Main Street, Penticton, British Columbia
Geology. Natural history. Local history. Pioneer tools and furniture. Indian artifacts. Guns.
June 16 - Sept. 15, daily 1-9. Rest of year Tu.-Sa. 2-5.

PERIBOUKA

LOUIS HÉMON - MARIA CHAPDELAINE MUSEUM
Peribouka, Quebec
House, was home of the writer, Louis Hémon. Early 20th century furnishings. Hemon memorabilia.
May 1 - Oct. 31, daily 8-8.

PERTH

ARCHIBALD CAMPBELL MEMORIAL MUSEUM
Gore and Foster Streets, Perth, Ontario
In Matheson House (1840). Period rooms. History of Perth area. Indian artifacts. Natural history.
May 5 - Nov. 1: M.-Sa. 10-12, 1-5; Su. 2-5.

PETERBOROUGH

CENTURY VILLAGE
Keene Road, Peterborough, Ontario
12 restored 19th century buildings moved to site. They include a blacksmith's shop, store, shingle mill and church.
May 15 - Sept. 2: Tu.-Su. 1-7. Sept. 3 - Oct. 14: Sa., Su. 1-7.

PETERBOROUGH CENTENNIAL MUSEUM
Armour Hill, Peterborough, Ontario
Pioneer life. Industrial history of Peterborough area.
May 1 - Sept. 30: Tu.-Sa. 10-5; Su. 1.30-5. Oct. 1 - Apr. 30, Tu.-Su. 1.30-5.

PICKERING

PICKERING TOWNSHIP MUSEUM
1710 Kingston Road, Pickering, Ontario
Main museum is in former schoolhouse (1859). Pioneer tools, furniture, clothing and farm implements. Other 19th century buildings moved to site include houses, barns, workshops, a hotel and a church. Some contain period furnishings and there are also collections of early petrol and steam engines.
Daily 10-5. Closed Christmas, Easter.

PICTON

MIC MAC MUSEUM
Rural Route 1, Picton, Nova Scotia
Ethnology. Indian burial mounds (on site). Pioneer relics.
May 1 - Sept. 30, daily 8-10.

NORTH MARYSBURGH MUSEUM
Rural Route 4, Picton, Ontario
Restored settler's house (1850). Period furniture. Pioneer documents.
July 1 - Sept. 4, daily 1.30-5.30.

PINCHER CREEK

PINCHER CREEK HISTORICAL PARK
Pincher Creek, Alberta
Outdoor museum, illustrating pioneer and Indian life.
Apr.-Oct., daily 9-5.

PLACENTIA

CASTLE HILL MUSEUM
Placentia, Newfoundland
On site of former French capital. Exhibits illustrating period of French occupation.
June 1 - Labour Day, daily 9-8. Closed public holidays.

POINTE-AU-PIC

LAURE CONAN MUSEUM
Place Roland, Pointe-au-Pic, Quebec
History of Charlevoix County and Murray Bay. Memorabilia of prominent residents. Life and writings of the novelist Laure Conan. Indian artifacts.
M.-Sa. 9-6; Su. 1-6.

PONOKA

ALBERTA HOSPITAL MUSEUM
Ponoka, Alberta
History of medicine and medical care in Alberta.
M.-Sa. 10-5.

FORT OSTELL MUSEUM
Ponoka, Alberta
Local pioneer life. Military and Indian history.
May-Oct., daily 9-5.

PORCUPINE

PORCUPINE MINING MUSEUM
Highway 101, Porcupine, Ontario
Open-air museum. Early history of mining in Porcupine. Equipment on display includes 'Little Giant' drill and steam locomotive.
May 24 - Sept. 15, daily, dawn-dusk.

PORT ARTHUR

LOGGING MUSEUM
Centennial Park, Port Arthur, Ontario
Logging tools and equipment. Replica of logging camp, with living accommodation, cookhouse, blacksmith's shop.
May 15 - June 15: M.-F. 12-6; Sa., Su. 10-8. June 15 - Sept. 15: daily 10-8. Sept. 16 - Oct. 15: M.-F. 12-6; Sa., Su. 11-7.

PORT CARLING

PORT CARLING PIONEER MUSEUM
Port Carling, Ontario
Local history. Pioneer life.
Sept. 1 - Oct. 31: Sa., Su. 2-5. July 1 - Aug. 31: M.-Sa. 11-5, 7-9; Su. 2-5.

PORT ROWAN

THE BACKHOUSE (BACKUS) MILL AND BACKUS AGRICULTURAL MUSEUM
Backus Conservation Area, Port Rowan, Ontario, NOE 1MO
Grist Mill (1798), in continuous operation until 1955. Agricultural implements. Horse-drawn vehicles.
May 15 - Oct. 15: Sa., Su. 1-7. June 1 - 30, also W., 1-7.

PORT ROYAL

PORT ROYAL NATIONAL HISTORIC PARK
Port Royal, Nova Scotia
Reconstruction of Port Royal Habitation (1605), with reproduction of original interior and furnishings.
June 16 - Sept. 7, daily 9-9. Sept. 8 - June 15: M.-F. 9-5; Su. 2-5.

PORTAGE LA PRAIRIE

CENTENNIAL MUSEUM
113 Dufferin Avenue E., Portage La Prairie, Manitoba, R1N OV3
Local history.
May 1 - Sept. 30, daily 10-5. Other months on request.

FORT LA REINE MUSEUM
35 Tupper Street S., Portage La Prairie, Manitoba
Replica of fort. Pioneer and Indian artifacts.
By appointment.

POWELL RIVER

POWELL RIVER HISTORICAL MUSEUM
Centennial Buildings, Powell River, British Columbia
History of the Powell River area.
Tu.-Su., public holidays, 2-4.

PRESCOTT

FORT WELLINGTON NATIONAL HISTORIC PARK
Dibble Street E., Prescott, Ontario, KOE 1TO
Fort (1812-60). Restored blockhouse, officers' quarters (1840) and Guard House (1800). Period furnishings.
May 1 - Oct. 31, daily 9-6.

PRINCE ALBERT

LUND WILDLIFE EXHIBIT
River Park, Prince Albert, Saskatchewan
Natural history of Saskatchewan.
June 1 - Sept. 30, daily 10-10.

PRINCE RUPERT

MUSEUM OF NORTHERN BRITISH COLUMBIA
1st Avenue and McBride Street, Prince Rupert, British Columbia
Fossils. Mounted fish. Local history. Industries. Indian material. Guns.
May 1 - Sept. 30: M.-Sa. 9-9; Su. 2-5. Oct. 1 - Apr. 30: Tu.-Sa. 9-4.

PRINCETON

PRINCETON AND DISTRICT PIONEER MUSEUM
Princeton, British Columbia
Local pioneer history. Gold and copper mining.
Tu.-Su. 1-5, 7-9.

PRINCE WILLIAM

KINGS LANDING HISTORICAL SETTLEMENT
Prince William, New Brunswick
Restoration of settlement, 1790-1870, on Trans-Canada Highway 23m. west of Fredericton West.
June-Sept., daily 10-7.

PUBNICO

DE LA TOUR MUSEUM
Middle West Pubnico, Nova Scotia
Local history. Acadian household equipment, utensils.
Daily 9-5.

QUEBEC

CENTRE OF MARY OF THE INCARNATION
Monastère des Ursulines, 12 Donnacona Street, Quebec 4, Province of Quebec
In Maison de Madame de la Peltrie (1644). 17th-18th century furniture. Musical instruments. Handicrafts. Religious history. Skull of Montcalm.
May 1 - Oct. 31: M.-Sa. 10.30-12, 2-5; Su. 2-5.

CONVENT OF THE AUGUSTINES
32 Charlevoix Street, Quebec, Province of Quebec
Building (1696). History of the Order of the Augustines. 17th-19th century furniture. Handicrafts. Paintings. Engravings.
Daily 9-11, 2-5; Su. 2-5. Other times by appointment. Closed Carnival.

JESUITS' OLD HOUSE
2320 Chemin des Foulons, Quebec, Province of Quebec
Building (1702). History of the Jesuits in Canada, 17th-18th century. 19th century furniture.
June 1 - Oct. 15, daily 9 a.m. - 10 p.m.

LAVAL UNIVERSITY
School of Visual Arts, 2e Tour, Cité Universitaire, Quebec 10, Province of Quebec
Works by Canadian artists. Paintings. Graphics. Sculpture.
M.-F. 9-5.

MAILLOU HOUSE
17 Saint-Louis Street, Quebec, Province of Quebec
House (1754-6). Period furniture.
M.-F. 9-5.

MUSEUM OF MINERALOGY AND GEOLOGY
Laval University, Quebec 10, Province of Quebec
Geology. Mineralogy. Palaeontology.
M.-F. 9-5.

MUSEUM OF QUEBEC
Parcs des Champs de Bataille, Quebec 6, Province of Quebec
Works by French Canadian artists. Paintings. Sculpture. Furniture. Gold. Decorative arts.
Tu.-Sa. 9-5; W. also 7 p.m.-10; Su. 1-5.

QUEBEC CHAMBER OF COMMERCE
17 St. Louis Street, Quebec, Province of Quebec
In Maillou House (1734). Period furniture.
M.-F. 9-5.

QUEBEC SEMINARY MUSEUM
6 University Street, Quebec 4, Province of Quebec
Furniture. European and Canadian paintings. Gold. Coins. Stamps.
Sept. 1 - June 30: M.-F. 10-12, 1-4. July 1 - Aug. 31: Sa. 1-4.

MUSEUM OF THE ARCHIVES OF QUEBEC
Hôtel du Governement, Parc des Champs de Bataille, Quebec, Province of Quebec
Paintings. Engravings. Costumes. Handicrafts. Coins and medals. Documents.
M.-Sa. 9-5; Su. 1-5.

MUSEUM OF THE ROYAL 22ND REGIMENT
Citadel, Quebec, Province of Quebec
History of the Regiment since 1914.
June 1 - Sept. 30, daily 9-8. Rest of year, daily 10-5.

JEAN TALON VAULTS
1033 des Prairies, Quebec 2, Province of Quebec
Building (1668) was first brewery in Canada. Furniture. Guns. 17th century tools, domestic equipment.
June 15 - Aug. 31: M.-F. 10-4.

QUESNEL

QUESNEL HISTORICAL MUSEUM
Carson Street, Quesnel, Britisn Columbia
Local history. Agricultural implements. Pioneer items. Indian handicrafts.
May 15 - Oct. 16, daily 8.30-8.30.

QUIDI VIDI

MILITARY BATTERY
Quidi Vidi, Newfoundland
Restored fort (c.1812).
June 1 - Sept. 30, Daily 10-5.

RAYMORE

PIONEER MUSEUM
1st Avenue, Raymore, Saskatchewan, S0A 3J0
Pioneer history. Costumes. Indian material.
June 1 - Oct. 31: Sa. 8 p.m.-10; Su. 1-6. Other times on request.

REGINA

DIEFENBAKER HOMESTEAD
Wascana Centre, Regina, Saskatchewan
Restored boyhood home of Canadian Prime Minister, J. G. Diefenbaker. Furnishings and personal possessions of Diefenbaker family.
June 1 - Sept. 30, daily 9-5.

NORMAN MACKENZIE ART GALLERY
University of Saskatchewan, Regina S4S 0A2, Saskatchewan
Works by European, Canadian and American artists. Paintings. Sculpture. Prints. Drawings.
M.-Th. 12-5, 7-10; F., Sa. 12-5; Su. 1-5, 7-10. Closed public holidays.

REGINA PUBLIC LIBRARY ART GALLERY
2311 12th Avenue, Regina, S4P 0N3, Saskatchewan
Paintings, graphics, sculpture, crafts by Canadian artists.
M.-F. 9.30-9; Sa. 9.30-6; Su. 2-5. Closed public holidays.

ROYAL CANADIAN MOUNTED POLICE MUSEUM
Depot Division, Regina S4P 3J7, Saskatchewan
History of Royal Canadian Mounted Police. Indian and Eskimo material.
June 1 - Sept. 15, daily 8 a.m.-9p.m. Sept. 16 - June 14, daily 8-5.

SASKATCHEWAN MUSEUM OF NATURAL HISTORY
Wascana Park, Regina, Saskatchewan
Palaeontology. Zoology. Specimens of birds, mammals, insects. Anthropology. Ethnology. Archaeology. N. American Indian exhibits.
May 1 - Sept. 30, daily 9-9. Oct. 1 - Apr. 30: M.-F. 9-5; Sa., Su., public holidays, 2-6.

TELORAMA
Saskatchewan Government Telephones, 2350 Albert Street, Regina S4P 2Y4, Saskatchewan
Development of telecommunications.
May 1 - Sept. 30, daily 1.15-4.30, 7-8.30. Oct. 1 - Apr. 30: M.-Sa. 1.15-4.30; Su. 1.15-4.30, 7-8.30.

RENFREW

MCDOUGALL MILL MUSEUM
O'Brien Park, Renfrew, Ontario
Grist mill (1855). Early farming implements and dairy equipment. Household items.
June 1 - Thanksgiving, daily 1-5, 7-9.

REVELSTOKE

REVELSTOKE MUSEUM
Mackenzie Avenue, Revelstoke, British Columbia
Local history.
May 16 - Sept. 14, M.-Sa. 2-5, 7-9.

RICHARD'S LANDING

SAINT JOSEPH'S ISLAND MUSEUM
Richard's Landing, Ontario
Local history. Pioneer relics. Indian material.
July 1 - Aug. 31, Tu.-Su. 12-5.30. June 1-30, Sept. 1-30, F.-Su. 2-5.30.

RICHMOND

MUSEUM OF RICHMOND ART CENTRE
767 Minoru Gate, Richmond, British Columbia
Local, military and maritime history. Aeronautics.
M.-F. 2-5, 7-9; Sa., Su. 7-9. Closed public holidays.

RIGAUD

BOURGET COLLEGE MUSEUM
65 rue St. Pierre, Rigaud, Quebec
Mineralogy. Palaeontology. Zoology. Canadian antiquities. Weapons. Coins and medals. Sculpture.
Su. 3.45-4.45 and 8-9; Tu. 12.30-1.15; W. 7 p.m.-8. Other times on request.

RIMBEY

PAS-KA-POO HISTORICAL PARK
Rimbey, Alberta, T0C 2J0
Reconstructed early local buildings, including schoolhouse, church, town office. Pioneer exhibits.
May 1 - Sept. 30, daily 9-8.

RIMOUSKI

RIMOUSKI SEMINARY MUSEUM
Avenue du Séminaire, Rimouski, Quebec
Mineralogy. Botany. Zoology.
Daily 10-6.

RIVERHURST

F. T. HILL MUSEUM
Riverhurst, Saskatchewan, S0H 3P0
Pioneer relics. Indian artifacts. Firearms.
July 1 - Aug. 31, daily 2-5, 7-9. Sept. 1 - June 30, daily 2-5.

ROCANVILLE

ROCANVILLE AND DISTRICT MUSEUM
Rocanville, Saskatchewan, S0A 3L0
Pioneer relics. Steam and gas engines. Tractors.
Su. 1-5.

ROCK FOREST

MUSEUM OF PICE DORÉS NATURALIST YOUTH CLUB
Galt Street W., Rural Route 1, Sherbrooke, Rock Forest, Quebec
Rock and ore specimens. Insects. Birds. Mammals. Butterflies.
Daily 8-8.

ROCK ISLAND

BARN MUSEUM
Lee Farm, 1 Boulevard Notre Dame, Rock Island, Quebec
Local history.
July-Aug., Su. 2-4.

ROCKTON

WESTFIELD PIONEER VILLAGE
Highway 52, Rockton, Ontario
Re-creation of 19th century village, with buildings moved to site. History of rural community life in Western Canada.
May 20 - June 30, Sept. 1 - Oct. 31: Sa. 11-5.30. July 1 - Aug. 31: M.-Sa. 11-5.30; Su. 12-6.

ROCKY POINT

FORT AMHERST NATIONAL HISTORIC PARK
Rocky Point, Prince Edward Island
Military history.
Apr. 1 - June 14, day following Labour Day - Nov. 30, daily 10-5. June 15 - Labour Day, daily 9-8.

ROSE BAY

THE OVENS NATURAL PARK AND MUSEUM
Route 3, Rose Bay, Nova Scotia
Caverns. Geological formations. Early mining equipment and agricultural implements.
June 1 - Oct. 31, 8-10.

ROSEBUD

ROSEBUD CENTENNIAL MUSEUM
Rosebud, Alberta, T0J 2T0
Local history. Exhibits illustrating life of early settlers.
Oct. 1 - Apr. 30, M.-Sa. 10-4. May 1 - Sept. 30, daily 10-5.

ROSSLAND

ROSSLAND HISTORICAL MUSEUM
P.O. Box 26, Rossland, British Columbia
Local history. Salish Indian camp. Industry. Restored underground gold-mine workings.
May 15 - Sept. 15, daily 9-5.

SAANICHTON

SAANICH PIONEER MUSEUM
E. Saanich Road, Saanichton, British Columbia
Pioneer tools, furniture, household equipment. Indian material. Agricultural implements.
July 1 - Aug. 31, Sa. 2-5. Other times by appointment.

SABREVOIS

MUSEUM OF RICHELIEU VALLEY HISTORICAL SOCIETY
Sabrevois, Quebec
House was birthplace of Honoré Mercier, Prime Minister of Quebec, 1887-91. Furniture, library and personal possessions of the Prime Minister.
July 1 - Aug. 31: M.-Sa. 9-6; Su. 1-6.

SACKVILLE

OWENS ART GALLERY
York Street, Sackville, New Brunswick
Prints. Drawings. Canadian paintings, 17th century - present day.
M.-F. 10-5; Sa. 9-12; Su. 2-5. Closed university holidays.

ST. ALBERT

FATHER LACOMBE MUSEUM
3 St. Vital Avenue, St. Albert, Alberta
In former Oblate mission church (1861). Local history. Indian material. Memorabilia of Father Lacombe and Oblate missionaries. Tools. Early church furniture.
On request, M.-Sa. 9-9; Su. 1-9.

ST. ANDREWS

BLOCK HOUSE HISTORIC SITE AND CENTENNIAL PARK
St. Andrews, New Brunswick
Restored fort (1812). Displays illustrating military history of the area. Agricultural implements.
May 15 - Sept. 15, daily 9-8.

CHARLOTTE COUNTY HISTORICAL SOCIETY MUSEUM
Water Street, St. Andrews, New Brunswick
19th century furniture, household equipment, books, tools. School desks and bells. Pictures. Clothing.
June-Sept., M.-Sa. 10-5; Su. 2-5.

SUNBURY SHORES ARTS AND NATURE CENTRE
139 Water Street, St. Andrews, New Brunswick
Arts. Crafts. Natural history.
July-Aug., daily 9-5.

ST. ANNS

GIANT MACASKILL HIGHLAND PIONEERS MUSEUM
Craft Centre Building, Gaelic College, St. Ann's, Nova Scotia
History of early settlement by pioneers frcm Scottish Highlands. Clothing and other articles belonging to Angus MacAskill, who was 8 feet tall.
May 24 - Oct. 14, daily 9-6.

SAINT BONIFACE

SAINT BONIFACE MUSEUM
494 Tache Avenue, Saint Boniface, Manitoba
Restored Chapel of the Grey Nuns (1846). Dioramas of the Nuns' life. Pioneer life.
June 1 - Aug. 31: M.-F. 11-5, 7-9; Su. 1-6. Sept. 1 - Nov. 1: M.-F. 11-5. Feb. 1 - May 30: Su. 1-6.

ST. CATHERINES

MUSEUM OF ST. CATHERINES AND DISTRICT ARTS COUNCIL
109 St. Paul Crescent, St. Catherines, Ontario
In Rodman Hall (1753). Contemporary Canadian paintings, graphics.
Tu.-Sa. 1-5; Su. 1-5, 7-9. Closed Dec. 25-26, Good F.

ST. CATHERINES HISTORICAL MUSEUM
343 Merritt Street, St. Catherines, Ontario
In former Merriton Town Hall. Local history. War of 1812. Agriculture. Industry. History of Welland Canal.
Daily 2-5. Closed Christmas, New Year, Good Friday.

ST. CONSTANT

CANADIAN RAILWAY MUSEUM
St. Constant, Quebec
History of Canadian railways. Locomotives. Rolling stock. Equipment.
Apr. 1-30, Sa. 10-6. May-Aug., daily 10-6. Sept.-Oct., Sa., Su. 10-6.

SAINTE-ANNE-DE-BEAUPRÉ

HISTORICAL MUSEUM AND ART GALLERY
10,018 avenue Royale, Basilique Sainte-Anne, Sainte-Anne-de-Beaupré, Quebec
Religious history. Life of St. Anne.
June 1 - Sept. 30, daily 9-6.

SAINT-JEAN

ROYAL MILITARY COLLEGE
Saint-Jean, Quebec
History of Fort Saint-Jean, and of the regiments which served there. Weapons. Uniforms.
Daily 9-6.

SAINT JOHN

BARBOUR'S GENERAL STORE
King Street E., Saint John, New Brunswick
Restored store (C.1867). Period furnishings, equipment and merchandise.
May 1 - Sept. 30: M.-Sa. 10-9; Su., public holidays 12-9.

LOYALIST HOUSE
120 Union Street, Saint John, New Brunswick
House (1810-17). Period furnishings. Children's museum.
June 1-30, Sept. 1-30: M.-Sa. 10-5; Su. 2-5. July 1 - Aug. 31, M.-Tu., Th.-F. 10-8; W. 10-5; Sa. 10-6; Su. 2-6. Closed July 1, Labour Day.

MARTELLO TOWER
Charlotte Street, Extension W., Saint John, New Brunswick
Fort (1812-14). History of War of 1812. Uniforms. Weapons. Paintings. Drawings.
June 1-30, Sept. 1-30: M.-Sa. 10-5; Su. 2-5. July 1 - Aug. 31: M.-Sa. 9-9; Su. 1-9.

THE NEW BRUNSWICK MUSEUM
277 Douglas Avenue, Saint John, New Brunswick
Geology and natural history of New Brunswick. Social, military and maritime history. Paintings by New Brunswick artists. Applied arts. Children's museum.
June 1 - Sept. 30: daily 10-9. Oct. 1 - May 31, daily 2-5. Closed public holidays.

PLEASANT VILLA SCHOOL
Carmarthen Street, Saint John, New Brunswick
Schoolhouse (c.1876), formerly at Pleasant Villa on the St. John River, with original furniture.
May-Oct., daily 9-9.

ST. JOHNS

MEMORIAL UNIVERSITY ART GALLERY
St. Johns, Newfoundland
Works by contemporary Canadian artists, displayed throughout university. Paintings. Prints. Sculpture. Rotating exhibitions from University's permanent collection are in the Arts and Culture Centre.
M.-Sa. 10 a.m. - 10.30 p.m.; Su. 10.30 a.m. - 10.30 p.m.

NEWFOUNDLAND MUSEUM
Duckworth Street, St. Johns, Newfoundland
Viking artifacts. Beothuck Indian, Eskimo and Nascapi material. History of early settlement of Newfoundland. Maritime, whaling and fishing history. Pulp and paper industries.
M.-Sa. 10-12.30, 2.30-5.

NEWFOUNDLAND NAVAL AND MILITARY MUSEUM
Confederation Building, St. Johns, Newfoundland
Naval and military history of Newfoundland. Ship models. Uniforms. Weapons. Models of fortifications.
M.-F. 9.30-5; Sa., Su. 2.30-5.

SIGNAL HILL NATIONAL HISTORIC PARK
P.O. Box 5879, St. Johns, Newfoundland
Remains of fort (1762). Cabot Tower (1897), commemorating first transatlantic wireless message. Displays illustrating history of Newfoundland and Signal Hill.
June 16 - Sept. 7, daily 9-8. Sept. 8 - June 15, daily 10-5.

ST. JOSEPH ISLAND

ST. JOSEPH ISLAND MUSEUM
St. Joseph Island, Ontario
History of settlement of the Island. Pioneer life.
May 24 - June 30, Sept. 1-30: W., F.-Su. 2-5.30. July 1 - Aug. 31: Tu.-Su. 2-5.30.

ST. GEORGE

ADELAIDE HUNTER HOODLESS HOMESTEAD
Rural Route 1, St. George, Ontario
House was home of Adelaide Hunter Hoodless, founder of the Women's Institute movement. Furnished in style of 1857-81.
Mar. 1 - Jan. 31, daily 2-5. Other times by appointment.

SAINT-LAURENT

MUSEUM OF THE NUNS OF THE HOLY CROSS
815 boulevard Sainte-Croix, Saint-Laurent, Quebec
Geology. Mineralogy. Palaeontology. Botany. Zoology.
On request.

NOVA ET VETERA GALLERY
Collège Saint-Laurent, 1025 boulevard Sainte-Croix, Saint-Laurent, Quebec
Works, especially sculpture and furniture, by Quebec artists and craftsmen.
On request.

SAINT-LIN

LAURIER HOUSE
Avenue Laurier, Saint-Lin, Quebec
House (1841-2), formerly home of Sir Wilfrid Laurier, Canadian Prime Minister. French Canadian country furnishings of the period.
Daily 9-5. Closed Christmas, New Year.

SAINTE-LUCE

SAINTE-LUCE HISTORICAL MUSEUM
Sainte-Luce, Quebec
Local history.
May 1 - Oct. 31. Tu.-Sa. 10-5; Su. 10-1. Nov. 1 - Apr. 30. Tu.-Sa. 9-5; Su. 10-1.

ST. MARY'S

ST. MARY'S DISTRICT MUSEUM
177 Church Street S., Cadzow Park, St. Mary's, Ontario N0M 2V0
Displays illustrating early settlement of the area. Household equipment. Tools. Musical instruments. Costumes. Natural history. Transport.
June 1 - Oct. 31: M.-Sa. 2-5. Other times by appointment.

ST. PETER'S

NICOLAS DENYS MUSEUM
St. Peter's, Nova Scotia
Local history. Memorabilia of Nicolas Denys. Paintings by Robert Harris.
Daily 9-5.

ST. THOMAS

ELGIN COUNTY PIONEER MUSEUM
32 Talbot Street, St. Thomas, Ontario
House (1848-9) was home and surgery of Dr. Charles Duncombe. Period rooms. Pioneer history. Life and career of Col. Thomas Talbot, founder of Talbot Settlement.
M.-F. 10-5; Sa., Su. 2-5. May 1 - Oct. 31 also M.-F. 7-9.

SALMON ARON

SALMON ARON MUSEUM
Salmon Aron, British Columbia
Local history. Natural history. Pioneer life. Costumes. Guns. Indian material.
July 1 - Aug. 31, daily 9-9. Sept. 1 - June 30: Tu. 2-4.30 and 7-9; Sa. 2-4.30.

SANGUDO

LAC SAINTE ANNE AND DISTRICT HISTORICAL SOCIETY
Pioneer Museum, Highway 43, Sangudo, Alberta, T0E 2A0
Local history. Pioneer artifacts.
June 1 - Sept. 30, daily 9-5, 7-9.

SARNIA

BAYVIEW RAILROAD MUSEUM
Point Edward, Bayview, Sarnia, Ontario
Canadian railway history, especially railway development in Lambton County.
May 1 - Oct. 14, daily 10-8.

PILOT HOUSE MUSEUM
18 St. Clair Parkway, Sarnia, Ontario
Maritime history. Ship models, equipment. Paintings.
W., Th., Sa., Su. 2-4. Closed public holidays.

SARNIA PUBLIC LIBRARY AND ART GALLERY
124 Christina Street S., Sarnia, Ontario, N7T 2M6
Paintings and sculpture by Canadian artists. Eskimo sculpture.
M.-F. 9-9. Sa. 9-5.30. Oct. 1 - May 31 also Su. 2-5. Closed public holidays.

SASKATOON

W. P. FRASER MEMORIAL HERBARIUM
University Campus, Saskatoon, Saskatchewan
Herbarium. Vascular plants. Bryophytes. Lichens.
M.-F. 8.30-5.

MARQUIS HALL ART GALLERY
University Campus, Saskatoon, Saskatchewan
19th-20th century Canadian and European paintings, sculpture, drawings, prints.
M.-F. 8.30-5; Sa., Su. 2-5.

MUSEUM OF UKRAINIAN CULTURE
202 Avenue M. South, Saskatoon, Saskatchewan, S7M 2K4
18th-20th century Ukrainian life and culture. Pioneer tools, implements. Costumes. Tapestries.
Tu., Th., Su., public holidays 2-5. Other times by appointment.

MUSEUM OF THE UKRAINIAN WOMEN'S ASSOCIATION
1240 Temperance Street, Saskatoon, Saskatchewan, S7N 0P1
Pioneer household equipment. Ukrainian handicrafts, costumes.
May-Sept., Tu., Th., Su. 2-5. Rest of year by appointment.

NUTANA COLLEGIATE LIBRARY AND ART GALLERY
11th Street E., Saskatoon, Saskatchewan
Paintings by Canadian artists.
Sept. 1 - June 30 M.-F. 9-3.30. Closed college holidays.

SASKATOON GALLERY AND CONSERVATORY
950 Spadina Crescent E., Saskatoon, Saskatchewan, S7K 3H6
Works by Canadian and European artists. Paintings. Drawings. Prints. Sculpture. Eskimo sculpture.
M.-Sa. 9-9; Su., public holidays 2-9.

VICTORIA SCHOOLHOUSE
University Campus, Saskatoon, Saskatchewan
Restored schoolhouse (1887). Replicas of original furnishings and equipment.
Daily 8.30-5.

VIGFUSSON MUSEUM
Room 69, Arts Building, University Campus, Saskatoon, Saskatchewan
World-wide collections of archaeological, anthropological and ethnological material, with special emphasis on the Saskatchewan Cree Indians.
M.-F. 8 a.m.-10 p.m.

WESTERN DEVELOPMENT MUSEUM
Saskatoon, Saskatchewan, S7M 1J1
Mailing address: P.O. Box 1910, 2610 Lorne Avenue South, Saskatoon, Saskatchewan
Agricultural, transport and pioneer history. Steam and gasoline tractors. Old cars. Reconstruction of street in pioneer town, c.1910. Railway locomotives, coaches. Horse-drawn vehicles.
May-Sept., daily 9-9. Oct.-Apr., daily 9-5.

SAULT STE. MARIE

THE OLD STONE HOUSE (ERMATINGER HOUSE)
831 Quillen Street, Sault Ste. Marie, Ontario
House (c.1814). Regional pioneer furnishings.
June 18 - Sept. 30, daily 10-5.

WOSGUHAEGUN
Sault Ste Marie, Ontario
Reconstruction of early fur trade post.
June 15 - Sept. 2, daily 10-8.

SAWYERVILLE

COMPTON COUNTY HISTORICAL MUSEUM
Sawyerville, Quebec
In former Congregational Church (1834). Early pioneer life.
July-Aug., Su. 2-5. Other times by appointment.

SAYWARD

LINK AND PIN LOGGING AND PIONEER MUSEUM
Sayward, British Columbia
Early logging equipment. Pioneer items.
May 1 - Sept. 30, daily 10-6.

SCARBOROUGH

CORNELL HOUSE
Bromley Road and Lawrence Avenue, Thomson Memorial Park, Scarborough, Ontario
House (c.1890). Rural type period furnishings. Local history. Clothing. Household, especially kitchen equipment.
May 17 - Oct. 13: W., Sa. 1.30-5, 7-9; Su. 1.30-5. Other times by appointment.

SELKIRK

LOWER FORT GARRY NATIONAL HISTORIC PARK
Box 7, Group 342, R.R.3, Selkirk, Manitoba
Reconstructed Fort buildings. Hudson Bay Company collection, illustrating early history of the fur trade.
May 1 - June 30, Sept. 1 - 30, Oct. 1 - Apr. 30, daily 9-6. July 1 - Aug. 31, daily 9-9.

SEPT-ILES

SEPT-ILES OLD POST
Sept-Iles, Quebec
House (1890), with period furnishings. Powder magazine. Store. Indian encampment.
June-Sept., daily 10-8.

SHARON

TEMPLE OF PEACE
40 Eglington Avenue E., Sharon, Ontario
Sharon Temple (1825) contains displays relating to pioneer life in York County and to the Children of Peace, who built the Temple. Adjoining the Temple are 2 houses (1819, 1850) and the Study (1829) of David Wilson, leader of the sect.
May 24 - Oct. 1, Daily 10-5. Rest of year by appointment.

SHAUNAVON

GRAND COTEAU MUSEUM
Centre Street, Shaunavon, Saskatchewan, S0N 2M0
Geology. Archaeology. Natural history. Pioneer history. Indian relics.
Mar. 1 - Oct. 31, W., Sa. 2-4.

SHELBURNE (NOVA SCOTIA)

ROSS-THOMSON HOUSE
Shelburne, Nova Scotia
House (1783). Shipbuilding tools. Agricultural implements. Household equipment.
June 15 - Sept. 15: Daily 9-5.

SHELBURNE (ONTARIO)

DUFFERIN COUNTY HISTORICAL MUSEUM
Hiland Park, Shelburne, Ontario
Log house (c.1875), with period furniture. Barn, with display of tools and agricultural implements. Blacksmith's shop. Orangemen's Hall. Railway flag station.
July 1 - Sept. 30: Tu.-F. 10-5; M., Sa. 10-4; Su. 2-5.

SHERBROOKE (NOVA SCOTIA)

SHERBROOKE VILLAGE PROJECT
Sherbrooke, Nova Scotia
Restored buildings of village (1870).
May 15 - Oct. 15, daily 9.30-5.30.

SHERBROOKE (QUEBEC)

SHERBROOKE UNIVERSITY ART GALLERY
Sherbrooke, Quebec
Modern paintings, sculpture, decorative arts by Canadian artists.
M.-Th. 12-9.30. Su., public holidays 1-5. Closed Dec. 22 - Jan. 5, Easter week.

SHILO

ROYAL CANADIAN ARTILLERY MUSEUM
Canadian Forces Base, Shilo, Manitoba, R0K 2A0
Regimental history.
M.-F. 10.30-4.30.

SHUSWAP LAKE

SHUSWAP LAKE PROVINCIAL PARK NATURE HOUSE
Shuswap Lake, British Columbia
Natural history.
July 1 - Labour Day, daily 1-9.

SIMCOE

EVA BROOK DONLY MUSEUM
109 Norfolk Street S., Simcoe, Ontario, N3Y 2W3
Fossils. Pioneer relics. Indian artifacts. Paintings by W.E. Cantelon, portraying pioneer life in Norfolk County. Forge. Paintings by Eva Brook Donly.
May 15 - Oct. 15: W.-Su. 1.30-5. Oct. 16 - May 14: Sa., Su. 10-5.

SIOUX LOOKOUT

SARAH VAUGHAN LIBRARY AND MUSEUM
5th Avenue, Sioux Lookout, Ontario
Local history.
M. 3-5; Tu. 3-5, 7-9; W. 7-9; Th. 3-5; F. 3-5, 7-9; Sa. 7-9; Su. 2-4. Other times by appointment.

SMITHERS

BUCKLEY VALLEY HISTORICAL SOCIETY MUSEUM
Main Street, Smithers, British Columbia
Local history. Minerals and mining. Pioneer tools.
Tu. 7 p.m.-9; W. 2-4; F. 7 p.m.-9; Sa. 2-4. Other times by appointment.

SMOKY LAKE

FORT VICTORIA MUSEUM
Box 178, Smoky Lake, Alberta, T0A 3C0
In log building (1890). Local history. Pioneer furniture, household equipment, farm implements. Model of Hudson Bay Company's Fort Victoria (1864). Mounted fish, birds and animal heads.
Daily 9-5.

SOMBRA

SOMBRA TOWNSHIP MUSEUM
Highway 40, P.O. Box 99, Sombra, Ontario, N0P 2H0
History of Sombra and the St. Clair River. Pioneer furniture and household equipment. Indian material. Military and maritime history.
May 24 - Sept. 2, daily 2-5: Su., public holidays 2-8. Sept. 3 - Oct. 14, Su., public holidays 2-9.

SOUTHAMPTON

BRUCE COUNTY MUSEUM
Southampton, Ontario, N0H 2L0
In former schoolhouse (1875). History of Bruce County. Pioneer tools, household equipment. Indian artifacts.
May 20 - June 30, Sept. 1-30: daily 2-5. July 1 - Aug. 31: M.-F. 10.30-5; Su. 1.30-5.

SOUTH BAY

MARINERS MEMORIAL LIGHTHOUSE PARK
County Roads 9 and 13, South Bay, Ontario
Maritime history, illustrated by items salvaged from local waters. Light from False Duck Island Lighthouse (1828-9).
Daily, dawn-dusk.

SOUTH RAWDON

SOUTH RAWDON MUSEUM
South Rawdon, Nova Scotia
Local history. Pioneer relics.
Daily 2-5.

STANBRIDGE EAST

CORNELL MILL MUSEUM
Stanbridge East, Quebec
Mill (1830). Agricultural implements. Furniture. Household equipment. China. Glass. Costumes. Toys.
May 1 - Oct. 31: M.-Sa. 10-5; Su. 11-6.

STANSTEAD

BARN MUSEUM
Rock Island, Stanstead, Quebec
Agricultural tools, implements. Waggons. Sleighs. Looms. Stoves.
July 1 - Aug. 31, daily 2-5.

STANSTEAD COUNTY MUSEUM
100 Dufferin Road, Stanstead, Quebec
Local history. Furniture. Tools. Musical instruments.
July 1 - Aug. 31, Su. 2-4. Other times by arrangement.

STAVELY

WILLOW CREEK HISTORICAL MUSEUM
Stavely, Alberta, T0L 1Z0
Local history. Material associated with Willow Creek Cattle Association.
May 1 - Oct. 31, 9-5. Other months by appointment.

STEINBACH

MENNONITE VILLAGE MUSEUM
Highway 12, P.O. Box 1136, Steinbach, Manitoba, R0A 2A0
Folk museum, containing restored buildings (c.1874) of Mennonite community. These include cheese factory, grist mill, sawmill and blacksmith's shop.
May 1 - June 30, Oct. 1 - 31, Sa.-Su. 2-6. July 1 - Sept. 30, daily 2-6.

STELLARTON

MINERS' MUSEUM
Allan Centennial Park, Stellarton, Nova Scotia
Mining techniques and equipment. Underground mine.
June 1 - Sept. 30. M.-Sa. 10-12, 1-4, 6-8.

STONEY CREEK

GAGE HOUSE
Highway 20 and King Street, Stoney Creek, Ontario
In former Gage homestead (1795). Furnishings of 1770-1830. Local history.
May 20 - Sept. 4: W.-Su. 2-6.

STRATFORD

BROCKSDEN SCHOOL MUSEUM
Vivian Street extension, Stratford, Ontario
School building (1853). Period furnishings. Local history.
June 1 - Sept. 30: Sa., Su., public holidays 2-5.

MINNIE THOMSON MEMORIAL MUSEUM
186 Vivian Street, Stratford, Ontario, N5A 5E1
Household equipment. Agricultural machinery and tractors. Operating steam calliope (1857). Operating narrow gauge steam railway.
May 1 - Oct. 30, daily 1-6. Other times by appointment.

ROTHMANS ART GALLERY OF STRATFORD
54 Romeo Street S., Stratford, Ontario, N5A 4S9
Contemporary Canadian and American paintings, prints.
May 1 - Sept. 30, M.-Sa. 11-8. Su., public holidays 12-6. Oct. 1 - Apr. 30, Tu.-Th. 10-10; Sa., Su. 10-6. Closed Good Friday, Christmas.

STURGEON FALLS

STURGEON RIVER HOUSE MUSEUM
166 King Street, Sturgeon Falls, Ontario
House (1867). Period furnishings. Local history. Pioneer material. Indian artifacts. History of fur trade.
June 15 - Sept. 15, daily 9-5.

SUDBURY

MUSEUM OF THE JESUIT ARCHIVES
University of Sudbury, Ramsey Lake Road, Sudbury, Ontario
Geology. Local and regional history. Agriculture. Indian history. Ethnology. Archaeology.
Sept. 1 - June 30, M.-Sa. 9-5. Su. by request.

SUDBURY CENTENNIAL MUSEUM AND ART GALLERY
Laurentian University, John and Nelson Streets, Sudbury, Ontario
Local history. Paintings, sculpture, prints by Canadian artists.
Tu.-Su. 1.30-5. Closed public holidays.

SUNDRE

SUNDRE AND DISTRICT HISTORICAL SOCIETY MUSEUM
Sundre, Alberta
Local history.
On request.

SUTTON

SIBBALD MEMORIAL MUSEUM
Sibbald Provincial Park, Sutton, Ontario
In Eildon Hall (1820). Memorabilia of Sibbald family. Furniture. Local history. Chinese ceramics, bronzes. Indian miniatures.
May 20 - June 15: Sa., Su. 10-6. June 16 - Labour Day: daily 10-6.

SWIFT CURRENT

SWIFT CURRENT MUSEUM
2nd Avenue N.E., Swift Current, Saskatchewan, S9H 2E2
Natural history of S.W. Saskatchewan. Pioneer history.
June 15 - Labour Day, daily 2-5, 7-9. Labour Day - June 14: Sa., Su., M. 2-5.30; Tu.-F. also 7 p.m.-9. Closed Christmas, New Year, Good Friday.

SYDNEY

ST. PATRICK'S CHURCH MUSEUM
Esplanade Street, Sydney, Nova Scotia
Building (1828). Artifacts of the early settlement of Cape Breton.
June 15 - Sept. 7, daily 12-8.

TADOUSSAC

CHAUVIN HOUSE
Tadoussac, Quebec
House, on site of Chauvin's house, first white man's dwelling in Quebec. Indian relics. 17th century Canadian furniture, pewter, kitchen equipment.
June 15 - Sept. 15, daily 9-5.

TATAMAGOUCHE

SUNRISE TRAIL MUSEUM
Tatamagouche, Nova Scotia
Pioneer household equipment, tools, guns. Clothing belonging to Annie Swan, who was 8 feet tall.
June 24 - Sept. 30, M.-Sa. 9-5; Su. 1-5. July 1 - Sept. 4 open until 9 M.-Sa.

TATLA LAKE

TATLA LAKE CENTENNIAL MUSEUM
Tatla Lake, British Columbia
In restored log schoolhouse. Pioneer history. Indian handicrafts and artifacts. Mineralogy. Natural history.
Daily 10-4.

TAYLOR

PEACE ISLAND PARK MUSEUM
Taylor, British Columbia
Fossils. Pioneer history.
May 15 - Sept. 15, daily 10-8.

TEETERVILLE

WINDHAM TOWNSHIP PIONEER MUSEUM
Teeterville, Ontario, N0E 1S0
Pioneer log cabin (1849). Period furnishings.
May 16 - Oct. 14, W., Sa., Su., public holidays 1.30-5.

THE PAS

THE SAM WALLER LITTLE NORTHERN MUSEUM
1359 Gordon Avenue, The Pas, Manitoba
Local history.
Daily 9-9. Other times by appointment. Closed Christmas.

THUNDER BAY

MUSEUM OF THUNDER BAY HISTORICAL SOCIETY
Thunder Bay, Ontario
Mineralogy. Archaeology. Anthropology. Maritime history. Transport. Indian artifacts. Paintings. Graphics.
July-Aug., daily 10-5.

TOBERMORY

PENINSULA AND ST. EDMUNDS TOWNSHIP MUSEUM
Highway 6, Tobermory, Ontario, N0H 2R0
Pioneer history. Furniture. Agricultural implements. Indian material.
May 20 - June 24, Sept. 9 - Oct. 9, Sa., Su. 1-9. July 1 - Sept. 4, daily 1-9.

TOFIELD

TOFIELD HISTORICAL MUSEUM
Tofield, Alberta, T0B 4J0
Local history. Pioneer life. Tools. Farm implements. Household equipment. Maps. Indian material.
By appointment.

WILDLIFE EXHIBIT
Tofield, Alberta
Botany, wildlife of Alberta.
May-Sept., daily 9-5.

TORONTO

ART GALLERY OF ONTARIO
317 Dundas Street W., Toronto 133, Ontario
15th-18th century Italian paintings, drawings. 17th century Dutch paintings. 17th-20th century French paintings. 18th-20th century English paintings, drawings. 19th-20th century Canadian and American paintings, sculpture, drawings, prints.
M.-Sa. 10.30-5.30; Su., public holidays 1.30-5.30. Oct. 1-Apr. 30 also W. 5.30-10.30. Closed Christmas, New Year, July.

COLBORNE LODGE
Howard Road, High Park, Toronto 138, Ontario
House (1836), built by John G. Howard. Original Howard furnishings, personal possessions and paintings of Canadian subjects by Mr. and Mrs. Howard.
May 1-Oct. 31: M.-Sa. 9.30-5; Su. 12-5. Nov. 1-Apr. 30: Sa., Su. 12-5.

H.M.C.S. 'HAIDA'
Pier 6, York Street, Toronto, Ontario
Former Naval destroyer. Contains museum display showing activities of R.C.N. ships in World War II.
May 1-Nov. 30, daily 10 a.m.-dusk.

HISTORIC FORT YORK
Fleet Street and Strachan Avenue, Toronto, Ontario
Military post, established 1793. 8 restored buildings (1812). 19th century military, social and domestic life. Period furnishings. Displays illustrating early history of Upper Canada and the town of York. History of the Canadian militia.
May 1-Labour Day, daily 9.30-5. July 1-Aug. 31 also W., Su. 5-9.30 p.m. Labour Day-Apr. 30: Tu.-Sa. 9.30-5; Su. 12-5.

MACKENZIE HOUSE
82 Bond Street, Toronto, Ontario
Home of W. L. Mackenzie, first Mayor of Toronto. Period furnishings. Memorabilia of Mackenzie. Printing shop owned by Mackenzie.
May 1-Labour Day: M.-Sa. 9.30-5; Su. 12-5. Labour Day-Apr. 30: Tu.-Sa. 9.30-5; Su. 12-5.

MARINE MUSEUM OF UPPER CANADA
Exhibition Park, Toronto 138, Ontario
In former officers' quarters of Stanley Barracks (1840). Displays showing exploration of central Canada and navigation on the inland waterways of the St. Lawrence River and Great Lakes Basin.
M.-Sa. 9.30-5; Su. 12-5. Closed Dec. 25-6, Good Friday, New Year.

MCLAUGHLIN PLANETARIUM
100 Queen's Park, Toronto 181, Ontario
Astronomy. Planetarium.
Tu.-F. 3.30-8.30; Sa. 11-8; Su. 2-5.

ONTARIO SCIENCE CENTRE
Don Mills Road and Eglinton Avenue E., Toronto, Ontario
Physical sciences. Life sciences. Engineering. Communications. Industry. Maritime history. Transport.
M.-Th. 10-6; F. 10-10. Sa., Su. 10-6. July 1-Aug. 31, M.-F. 10-10. Closed Christmas.

ROYAL CANADIAN MILITARY INSTITUTE
426 University Avenue, Toronto, Ontario
Military history. Uniforms. Medals. Paintings. Prints. Photographs.
M.-F. 9.5, by appointment. Closed public holidays.

ROYAL ONTARIO MUSEUM
100 Queen's Park, Toronto 5, Ontario
Greek, Roman, European and Far Eastern, especially Chinese, archaeology, art. Ethnology, mainly N. American Indian artifacts. Costumes. Canadian history. Geology. Mineralogy. Palaeontology. Zoology. Astronomy. Children's Museum.
M. 10-5; Tu-Sa. 10-9; Su. 1-9. Closed Christmas, New Year.

SCADDING CABIN
Exhibition Park, Toronto, Ontario
18th century pioneer loghouse (1794), moved to site. Period furnishings, household equipment.
July 1-Aug. 15: Sa., Su., public holidays 3-9. Aug. 16-Sept. 2: daily 10-9.

SIGMUND SAMUEL CANADIANA MUSEUM
14 Queen's Park Crescent, Toronto, Ontario
Canadian fine, applied and decorative arts, mostly before 1867. Paintings, water colours. Prints. Silver. Glass. Coins and medals. Wood sculpture.
M.-Sa. 10-5; Su. 1-5. Closed Christmas.

TARAS H. SHEVCHENKO MUSEUM
42 Roncesvalles Avenue, Toronto 156, Ontario
Ukrainian handicrafts. Tools used by Ukrainian pioneers in Western Canada.
Last Su. in June, and July-Aug., Su. 12-5. Other times by appointment.

TODMORDEN MILLS MUSEUM PARK
67 Pottery Road, Toronto 6, Ontario
Parshall Terry House (c.1794) and Helliwell House (c.1821), both with period furnishings. Restored 19th century paper mill. Former brewery building contains collection of maps, pictures, documents, illustrating history of the lower Don valley, especially Todmorden Mills.
Tu.-Su. 1-dusk.

UKRAINIAN ARTS AND CRAFTS MUSEUM
404 Bathurst Street, Toronto 12, Ontario
Ukrainian handicrafts, costumes, dolls.
On request.

TROIS RIVIÈRES

PIERRE BOUCHER MUSEUM
Séminaire Saint-Joseph, Trois Rivières, Quebec
Quebec history. Paintings. Decorative arts.
On request.

INTERNATIONAL PHILATELIC GALLERIES
950 Notre Dame Street, Trois Rivières, Quebec
History of postage stamps.
M. 2-5; Tu., W., Sa. 10-5; Th., F. 2-9.

MUSEUM OF PREHISTORIC ARCHAEOLOGY
1260 rue Royale, Trois Rivières, Quebec
Collections of palaeontology, anthropology and archaeology relating to Europe and Quebec. Quebec history.
M.-F. 9-5; Sa. 2-5.

TROIS-RIVIÈRES ART CENTRE
1580 rue Des Cheneaux, Trois Rivières, Quebec
Works by local artists.
Daily 9-10.

VILLAGE OF ST. MAURICE IRONWORKS
Rue des Forges, Trois Rivières, Quebec
Restored 18th-19th century ironworking village.
June 15-Sept. 15, daily 9-5.

UPPER WOODSTOCK

OLD CARLETON COUNTY COURT HOUSE
Upper Woodstock, New Brunswick
Restoration of first Court House (1883). Period furnishings. Local history.
July 1-Nov. 30: M.-Sa. 2-5.

UXBRIDGE

COUNTRY HERITAGE MUSEUM
Uxbridge, Ontario
In former Scott Township Municipal Hall (1860), moved to site. Local history.
May 16-Nov. 1: Sa., Su., public holidays 10-5.

VANCOUVER

CENTENNIAL MUSEUM
1100 Chestnut Street, Vancouver 9, British Columbia
Mineralogy. Natural history. History of Western British Columbia. Northwest American Indian material. Children's museum.
May 1-Sept. 30, daily 10-10. Oct. 1-Apr. 30, daily 12-10.

FINE ARTS GALLERY
University of British Columbia, Vancouver, British Columbia
Paintings, graphics, sculpture, especially by Canadian artists.
Tu.-Sa. 10-30-5. Closed public holidays.

LIPSETT COLLECTION
British Columbia Building, Vancouver, British Columbia
Indian material. Historical paintings by John Innes.
Daily 11-5. Evenings by appointment.

MARITIME MUSEUM
1905 Ogden Street, Vancouver 9, British Columbia
Local maritime history. Ship models. Paintings. Documents. Includes Royal Canadian Mounted Police Schooner, 'St. Roch'.
M. 12-6, Tu.-F. 12-9, Sa., Su. 10-9.

OLD HASTINGS MILL STORE MUSEUM
1575 Alma Road, Vancouver 8, British Columbia
In former sawmill store (1865). Material illustrating early history of Vancouver and British Columbia.
June 1-Sept. 15: daily 10-4. Sept. 16-May 31: Sa., Su. 1-4. Closed Christmas, New Year.

PACIFIC NATIONAL EXHIBITION
British Columbia Pavilion, Exhibition Park, Vancouver, British Columbia
Natural history. Big game trophies.
M.-F. 11-5; Su. 1-5.

THE VANCOUVER ART GALLERY
1145 W. Georgia Street, Vancouver 5, British Columbia
18th-20th century European, especially British, paintings. Paintings and sculpture by Canadian artists.
M.-Tu., Th.-Sa. 10-5; W.-F. 10-10; Su. 2-5.

UKRAINIAN FOLK ART MUSEUM
154 E. 10th Avenue, Vancouver, British Columbia
Ukrainian handicrafts. Costumes.
By appointment.

UNIVERSITY OF BRITISH COLUMBIA, ANTHROPOLOGY MUSEUM
Library Building, University of British Columbia, Vancouver 9, British Columbia
Anthropological and ethnographical collections. Canadian North-West, Eskimoes, Plains Indians. Oceania.
Sept. 21-Apr. 14, M.-W., F., Sa. 1-5; July 3-Aug. 20, M.-Sa. 10-5.

UNIVERSITY OF BRITISH COLUMBIA, HERBARIUM
Biological Sciences Building, University of British Columbia, Vancouver, British Columbia
Plants of North-West America and British Columbia.
M.-F. 9-5. Closed May 1-June 30, Sept. 1-30, public holidays.

UNIVERSITY OF BRITISH COLUMBIA, VERTEBRATE MUSEUM
Department of Zoology, University of British Columbia, Vancouver, British Columbia
British Columbia, with some foreign, vertebrate material. Skins and hides. Skeletons. Eggs.
M.-F. 9-4.

M. Y. WILLIAMS GEOLOGICAL MUSEUM
Geological Sciences Centre, University of British Columbia, Vancouver 8, British Columbia
Geology. Palaeontology. Mineralogy. Meteorites. Fossils of birds, reptiles, fish, dinosaurs, bison, elk. Mounted heads of modern game animals.
M.-F. 9-5.

VAUDREUIL

VAUDREUIL HISTORICAL MUSEUM
31 rue Du Bois Vert, Vaudreuil, Quebec
Local history. Agricultural implements. Household equipment. Furniture. Decorative arts.
Daily 1-6.

VEDDER CROSSING

R.C.E. MILITARY MUSEUM
Canadian Forces Base, Chilliwack, Vedder Crossing, British Columbia
History of the Canadian Army, especially the Corps of Canadian Engineers.
May 1-Sept. 30: Su.-F. 1-4.30. Oct. 1-Apr. 30: Su. 2-4.

VEREGIN

VEREGIN DOUKHOBOR PRAYER HOUSE
Veregin, Saskatchewan, S0A 4H0
Restored mid-19th century Doukhobor meeting house. Natural history. Local history. Horse-drawn vehicles.
June 1-Oct. 31, daily 10-5.

VERNON

HISTORIC O'KEEFE RANCH
Highway 97, Box 29, Vernon, British Columbia
Restoration of late 19th century ranch complex. Buildings include Church (1887), blacksmith's shop, store and man-

sion (c.1900). O'Keefe family history. Victorian furnishings. Costumes. Indian artifacts.
Apr. 1 - Oct. 31, daily 9-9.

VERNON MUSEUM
Library Building, Vernon, British Columbia
Natural history. Pioneer life. Horse-drawn vehicles. Salish Indian artifacts, including dug-out canoe. Paintings by Canadian artists.
M.-Sa. 10-1, 2-5; Tu., F. also 7-9; Su. 2-5.

VICTORIA

ART GALLERY OF GREATER VICTORIA
1040 Moss Street, Victoria, British Columbia
European and Canadian paintings, prints, drawings, decorative arts.
Tu.-Sa. 11-5; Th. also 7.30 p.m.-9.30; Su. 2-5.

BRITISH COLUMBIA FOREST SERVICE MUSEUM
Department of Lands, Forests and Water Resources, Parliament Buildings, Victoria, British Columbia
History of the British Columbia Forest Service since it was established in 1911.
M.-F. 8.30-5.

BRITISH COLUMBIA MINERAL MUSEUM
Department of Mines and Petroleum Resources, Douglas Building, Victoria, British Columbia
Rocks and minerals of British Columbia. Mining and oil-well models.
M.-F. 8.30-5. Closed public holidays.

EMILY CARR HOUSE
207 Government Street, Victoria, British Columbia
Former home of the Canadian painter and author, Emily Carr.
By appointment.

CRAIGFLOWER MANOR
110 Island Highway, Victoria, British Columbia
House (1853), with original and period furnishings.
May 1 - Sept. 30, Tu.-Su. 10-5. Oct. 1 - Apr. 30, Tu.-Su. 12-4.

FRANCIS PARK NATURE HOUSE
541 McKenzie, Victoria, British Columbia
Natural history of Park area.
Daily 9.30-7.30.

FORT RODD HILL NATIONAL HISTORIC PARK
604 Belmont Road, Victoria, British Columbia
Restored fort. Includes Fisgard lighthouse.
Daily, 9-1 hour before sunset.

HELMCKEN HOUSE
638 Elliott Street, Victoria, British Columbia
House (1852), with original furnishings. Local history. Early medical instruments.
May 1 - Sept. 30: Tu.-Su. 10-5. Oct. 1 - Apr. 30, Tu.-Su. 1-5. Closed public holidays.

MALTWOOD MEMORIAL MUSEUM OF HISTORIC ART, UNIVERSITY OF VICTORIA
4509 W. Saanich Road, Victoria, British Columbia
Canadian crafts and decorative arts, 1860 onwards.
June 1 - Sept. 1: Tu.-Sa. 10-5; Su. 1-5. Closed University vacations.

MARITIME MUSEUM OF BRITISH COLUMBIA
28 Bastion Square, Victoria, British Columbia
Naval and Merchant Service history and trade of British Columbia. Ship models. Figureheads. Paintings. Weapons. Uniforms.
July 1 - Sept. 14, daily 10-9. Sept. 15 - June 30: M.-Sa. 10-5; Su. 1-5.

POINT ELLICE HOUSE
2612 Pleasant Street, Victoria, British Columbia
House (c.1860), former home of O'Reilly family. Original furnishings. Early history of British Columbia and Canada.
Sept. 1 - May 31, daily 9-5. June 1 - Aug. 31, Su. 9-9.

PROVINCIAL MUSEUM
Belleville Street, Victoria, British Columbia
Natural and human history of British Columbia. Dioramas showing ecology of the Province. Indian cultures. N.W. coast Indian art. Reconstructions of street, sawmill, mine shaft, fish-packing house, gold diggings.
Apr. 1 - Sept. 30, daily 10-8.30. Oct. 1 - Mar. 31, 10-4.30.

OLD CRAIGFLOWER SCHOOLHOUSE MUSEUM
2765 Admirals Road, Victoria, British Columbia
Schoolhouse (c. 1855). History of the school and of settlement in the area.
Tu., Su. 12-5.

THUNDERBIRD PARK
Belleville and Douglas Streets, Victoria, British Columbia
Kwakiutl Indian Dance House. Totem poles (1850-90) and carvings of other Indian coastal tribes.
All hours.

VIKING

VIKING HISTORICAL SOCIETY MUSEUM
Viking, Alberta, T0B 4N0
History of early settlement of area. Model of first Viking gas well (1913).
M.-Sa. 9-1, 2-5. Su. 2-4.

WAINWRIGHT

BATTLE RIVER HISTORICAL MUSEUM
Wainwright, Alberta, T0B 4P0
Local history. Pioneer material.
Tu.-Su. 10-5.

WALTON

WOMEN'S INSTITUTE HISTORICAL MUSEUM
Walton, Nova Scotia
Pioneer relics.
By appointment.

WASAGA BEACH

MUSEUM OF THE UPPER LAKES
Nancy Island, Wasaga Beach, Ontario
Maritime history of the Upper Great Lakes, and of the War of 1812. Hull and other relics of the British schooner 'Nancy' sunk in 1812.
May 16 - Sept. 7, daily 10-6. Sept. 8 - Oct. 12, daily 10-5.

WASAGAMING

RIDING MOUNTAIN NATIONAL PARK MUSEUM
Wasagaming, Manitoba, R0J 2H0
Botany. Natural history.
May 1 - Sept. 30, daily 10-10.

WASKESIU

PRINCE ALBERT NATIONAL PARK MUSEUM
Waskesiu Lake, Waskesiu, Saskatchewan, S0J 2H0
Natural history of Park. Geology. Botany. Mounted birds and mammals. Indian artifacts.
July 1 - Aug. 31, daily 12-9.

WATERLOO

GALLERY OF THE THEATRE OF THE ARTS
University of Waterloo, Waterloo, Ontario
Contemporary Canadian paintings, sculpture.
M.-F. 9-5; Su. 2-5.

WAUPOOS

MARYSBURGH MUSEUM
Waupoos, Ontario
History of settlement and subsequent development of Marysburgh.
June 1-30, by appointment. July 1-31, daily 2-5, 7-9. Aug. 1 - Sept. 3, daily 2-5. Sept. 3-30: Sa., Su. 2-5.

WELLINGTON

WELLINGTON COMMUNITY HISTORICAL MUSEUM
411 Main Street, Wellington, Ontario, K0K 3L0
History of Wellington and surrounding area. Furnishings.
May 24 - June 30, Sept. 15 - Thanksgiving: Sa., Su., public holidays 1-5. July 1 - Sept. 14: Tu.-F. 1-5; Sa., Su. 1-5, 7-9. Other times by appointment.

WEST KILDONAN

SEVEN OAKS HOUSE
Ruperts Land Avenue E., West Kildonan, Manitoba
House (c.1851), built by pioneer fur-trader and merchant. Original furnishings.
May 15 - June 14: Sa., Su. 2-4.30. June 15 - Labour Day, daily 2-4.30, 7-8.30.

WESTLOCK

WESTLOCK AND DISTRICT HISTORICAL SOCIETY MUSEUM
Westlock, Alberta
Local history. Agriculture. Pioneer life.
May-Oct., daily 10-5.

WESTPORT

RIDEAU DISTRICT MUSEUM
Bedford and Westport Streets, Westport, Ontario, K0G 1X0
In former blacksmith's shop and carriage works (c.1870). Local history and pioneer life.
June 1 - Sept. 30, daily 1.30-4.30.

WETASKIWIN

REYNOLDS MUSEUM
Highway 2A, Wetaskiwin, Alberta
Local history. Pioneer furnishings. Guns. Indian and Eskimo material. Farm tools, implements, machinery. Early motor-vehicles, tractors and aeroplanes.
May 1 - Sept. 30, daily 10-5.

WEYBURN

500 LINE HISTORICAL MUSEUM
Gout Road S. and 4th Avenue S., Weyburn, Saskatchewan
Local history. Agricultural implements. Household equipment. Horse-drawn vehicles.
June 1 - Aug. 31: M., Tu., Th.-Su. 2-5, 7-9.

WHITBY

WHITBY HISTORICAL SOCIETY MUSEUM
Centre Street S., Whitby, Ontario
Reproduction of early country store. Local history.
June 1 - Sept. 30: Sa., Su. 2-5.

WHITEHORSE

S.S. 'KLONDIKE'
South Whiskey Flats, Whitehorse, Northwest Territories
Sternwheeler, restored to original condition, with period furnishings.
May 1 - Oct. 31, daily 9-5.

MCBRIDE CENTENNIAL MUSEUM
First Avenue and Steele Street, Whitehorse, Northwest Territories
Local history, especially relating to the Gold Rush. Natural history of the area. Indian handicrafts. Museum housed in log cabin (1900) featured by Robert Service, in his poem, *The Cremation of Sam McGee.*
May 20 - Sept. 30, daily 1-4, 7-9.

WHITE LAKE

MCNAB WABA COTTAGE MUSEUM
McNab Waba Park, White Lake, Ontario
Reconstruction of home of Archibald McNab, responsible for settlement of McNab Township. Pioneer furnishings.
May 16 - Sept. 6, M.-F. 1-5. Sept. 7 - Oct. 11, Sa.-Su. 1-5.

WHITNEY

ALGONQUIN PARK VISITOR CENTRE
Box 219, Whitney, Ontario
Herbarium. Natural history. Archaeology of Grand Lake and Lake Traverse. Logging.
May-June, Sept.-Oct., daily 10-6. July-Aug., daily 9.30-8.

WILLIAMSTOWN

NORTH WEST AND LOYALIST MUSEUM
Williamstown, Ontario, K0C 2J0
Building (1842). History of North West Company and the fur trade.
June 1 - Oct. 13: Tu.-Su. 1.30-5.30. Closed Tu. and open M., when M. is public holiday.

WILLINGDON

HISTORIC VILLAGE AND PIONEER MUSEUM
Willingdon, Alberta, T0B 4R0
Reconstructed buildings of early settlers. Farm tools, implements. Clothing. Furniture. Handicrafts.
May 1 - Oct. 31, daily 9-5.

WINDSOR

HALIBURTON MEMORIAL MUSEUM
Clifton Avenue, Windsor, Nova Scotia
House (1833), was home of the author, Thomas Chandler

Haliburton. Period furnishings. Illustrations by C. W. Jefferys to Haliburton's stories.
May 15 - Oct. 15, daily 9.30-5.30.

HIRAM WALKER HISTORICAL MUSEUM
254 Pitt Street-W., Windsor 12, Ontario
House (1811). History of Essex, Kent and Lambton Countries. Indian material. Pioneer relics and handicrafts. Guns.
Jan. 2 - Nov. 30 and Dec. 26-31: Tu.-Sa. 10-5; Su., public holidays 2-5. Closed Easter.

WILLISTEAD ART GALLERY OF WINDSOR
Willistead Park, Windsor 15, Ontario
Works by Canadian artists. Paintings, sculpture, decorative arts.
M.-W. 10-5, 7-9; Th.-Sa. 10-5; Su. 2-5. Closed public holidays.

WINNIPEG

GALLERY 111, UNIVERSITY OF MANITOBA
University Campus, Winnipeg R3T 2N2, Manitoba
Paintings and prints by contemporary Canadian and foreign artists.
May 1 - Sept. 15: M.-F. 8.30-4.30. Sept. 16 - Apr. 30, M., Th., F. 9-5; Tu., W. 9-5, 6-9; Sa. 9-12.

MANITOBA MUSEUM OF MAN AND NATURE
Rupert and Main Streets, Winnipeg, Manitoba
Geology. Palaeontology. Botany. Zoology. Ecology. Ethnology. Archaeology. Manitoba history. Planetarium.
Tu.-Sa. 10-9, Su. 12-9. Closed Christmas, New Year.

MUSEUM OF UKRAINIAN WOMEN'S ASSOCIATION
1175 Main Street, Winnipeg, Manitoba, R2W 3S4
Ukrainian arts and crafts.
Daily 9-5.

PROVINCIAL ARCHIVES OF MANITOBA
Legislative Building, Winnipeg, Manitoba
History of Manitoba, illustrated by pictures, maps, manuscripts and public records.
M.-F. 10-5.

ROSS HOUSE MUSEUM OF MANITOBA HISTORICAL SOCIETY
176 Higgins Avenue, Winnipeg, Manitoba, R3B 0B9
Log-house (1852-5), first post office in Western Canada. Relics of early Red River settlement.
M.-Sa. 10-6; Su. 1-5.30.

TRANSCONA MUSEUM
Public Library, Transcona, Winnipeg, Manitoba
Local history. Pioneer material.
During library hours.

UNIVERSITY OF MANITOBA, MINERALOGY MUSEUM
Department of Mineralogy, University Campus, Winnipeg, Manitoba
Geology. Mineralogy.
M.-F. 8.30-5.30.

UNIVERSITY OF MANITOBA, NATURAL HISTORY MUSEUM
Department of Zoology, University Campus, Winnipeg, Manitoba
Invertebrate zoology.
M.-F. 9-5.

WINNIPEG ART GALLERY
Civic Auditorium, 300 Memorial Boulevard (1), Winnipeg R3C 1V1, Manitoba
Medieval European panel paintings. 18th-19th century English paintings, drawings. 19th-20th century Canadian paintings. Contemporary paintings, sculptures, graphics from a number of countries.
M., W., F.-Sa. 10-6. Tu., Th. 10-10. Su. 12-6. Closed national holidays.

WOLFVILLE

ACADIA UNIVERSITY ART GALLERY
P.O. Box 28, Wolfville, Nova Scotia
Paintings, graphics by Canadian artists.
M.-F. 9.30-9.30.

WOLFVILLE HISTORICAL MUSEUM
Wolfville, Nova Scotia
In Randall House (1814). Household equipment. Furnishings. Paintings. Prints.
June 22 - Aug. 30, daily 10-5.

WOODSTOCK

OXFORD MUSEUM
City Square, Woodstock, Ontario
Collections illustrating settlement and development of Oxford County. Natural history. Indian artifacts.
July-Aug., Tu.-F. 10-12, 2-5. Sept.-June, Tu., Th., Sa. 2-5. Closed public holidays.

YARMOUTH

FIREMEN'S MUSEUM
601-603 Main Street, Yarmouth, Nova Scotia
History of local firefighting. Old fire-engines. Photographs.
June 1 - Sept. 30, M.-Sa. 10-12, 1-3, 7-9. Rest of year by appointment.

YARMOUTH COUNTY HISTORICAL SOCIETY MUSEUM
22 Collins Street, Yarmouth, Nova Scotia
Maritime history. Ship models. Household equipment.
June 15 - Sept. 30, daily 9.30-5; Oct. 1 - June 14, daily 10-12, 2-4. July 1 - Aug. 31 also Tu.-Th. 7 p.m.-9 and Su. 2-5.

YELLOWKNIFE

MUSEUM OF THE NORTH
Yellowknife, Northwest Territories, X0E 1H0
History of Northwest Territories. Geology. Mineralogy. Indian handicrafts, birch canoes. Eskimo sculpture and artifacts. Mounted animals of the Territories. Relics of exploration and fur-trade.
June 1 - Sept. 30: M.-Sa. 10-7.

YORKTON

WESTERN DEVELOPMENT MUSEUM
Yorkton Airport, Yorkton, Saskatchewan
Ethnology and historical background of national groups making up population of Yorkton area. Agricultural implements. Steam, gas and petrol engines. Old cars.
May 1 - Sept. 30, 9-9. Rest of year, 10-5. Evenings by appointment.

Central African Republic

This now independent state, formerly part of French Equatorial Africa, has its main museum base in the capital, Bangui, where great efforts are being made to collect and preserve material relating to the traditional local culture. Much of this has to be stored for the time being and some of the most valuable, including the recordings of folk-songs, could never become exhibits in the normal museum sense.

BANGUI

BARTHÉLÉMY BOGANDA MUSEUM
B.P. 349, Bangui
Ethnography, including 1500 folk songs on magnetic tape. National history. Archaeology. Handicrafts. Statues and masks.
Daily except M., 8.30-12, 2.30-5; Sa. 8.30-12.30; Su. 9.30-12, 2.30-5.

BOUAR

DISTRICT MUSEUM
Bouar
Local history. Folklore and traditions.
Daily ex. M. 9-12, 2.30-5.

Chad

The Chad National Museum was established when Chad was still part of French Equatorial Africa. Its two branches, one at Fort Lamy and the other at Fort Archambault, have excellent collections of the natural history, archaeology and ethnography of Chad.

FORT ARCHAMBAULT

CHAD NATIONAL MUSEUM
(Annexe of National Museum, Fort Lamy), Fort Archambault
History. Archaeology. Ethnography. Prehistory.
Daily 7-1, 4-6; Su. 10-12, 4-6. Closed public holidays.

FORT LAMY

CHAD NATIONAL MUSEUM
Place de l'Indépendence, B.P. 503, Fort Lamy
Palaeontology. Prehistory. Zoology. Mineralogy. Ethnography and handicrafts. Fossils of the quaternary period. Ceramics of the later Stone Age. Statues, masks. Arms. Musical instruments.
Daily 7-1, 4-6; Su. 10-12, 4-6. Closed public holidays.

Chile

Chile, to most informed people, means copper, gold, iron and fertilisers. Its museums refuse to be so conservative, and go for natural history, the Indians and the handicrafts and folklore of the country. They also have a good deal to show of the history of Chile in its colonial period and during the years of struggle for national independence.

ANGOL

DILLMAN S. BULLOCK MUSEUM
Casilla 2-D, Angol
General local flora and fauna. Birds, mammals, reptiles, insects. Local archaeology.
Tu.-Su. 9-1, 3-5.

CHUQUICAMATA

MUSEUM OF THE AMERICAN SCHOOL
Chuquicamata
Mounted animals and birds. Indian artifacts.
By appointment.

CONCEPCIÓN

CONCEPCIÓN MUSEUM
Edmundo Larenas 420, Casilla 1054, Concepción
Local and Araucanian Indian items.
Tu.-Sa. 9-5; Su. 9-12.

HUALPEN

HUALPEN MUSEUM
Hualpen, Concepción
Roman, Greek and Egyptian archaeology. Chilean weapons and numismatic collections. Oriental art. Chilean and American folk art. Chilean archaeology. 18th-19th century furniture.
Tu.-Su. 9-5.

LA SERENA

LA SERENA ARCHAEOLOGICAL MUSEUM
Casilla 117, La Serena
Archaeology. Prehistory. Physical anthropology. Colonial history. Ethnography. Palaeontology. Diaguito Indian exhibits. Pottery.
Tu.-Su. 9-5.

PUNTA ARENAS

SALESIAN REGIONAL MUSEUM
Instituto 'Don Bosco', Avenida Bulnes 374, Casilla 347, Punta Arenas
Scientific and ethnographical exhibits, including relics of extreme South American and Tierra del Fuegan tribes.
On request.

SAN PEDRO DE ATACAMA

ARCHAEOLOGICAL MUSEUM
San Pedro de Atacama, near Calama
Indian skulls and artifacts.
Tu.-Su. 10-5.

SANTIAGO

ANATOMICAL MUSEUM
Universidad Catolica de Chile, Santiago
Human and comparative anatomy collections.
By appointment.

CONTEMPORARY ART MUSEUM
Universidad de Chile, Quinta Normal, Casilla 5627, Santiago
Collection of paintings, sculpture, graphics by 20th century Chilean artists.
By appointment.

INDIAN HISTORIC MUSEUM
Basement, Hidalgo Castle, Santiago
Ethnographical material relating to the Indian tribes of Chile.
Tu.-Su. 10-5.

MUSEUM OF THE ART OF THE AMERICAN PEOPLES
Casilla 10-D, Universidad de Chile, Santiago
Traditional minor arts and industries. Ritual and folklore of the Americas. Araucanian silverware. Pottery. Textiles.
By appointment.

MUSEUM OF NATURAL HISTORY
Avenida Matucana, Santiago
Natural history collections, including the mummy of an Inca child found on the summit of El Plomo, 17,710 ft., 25 miles from Santiago.
Tu.-Su. 10-5.

NATIONAL HISTORICAL MUSEUM
Mireflores 50, Casilla 9764, Santiago
Conquest, Colonial, Independence, Republican periods. Military exhibits. Numismatics.
Tu.-Su. 9-5.

HISTORICAL MUSEUM
National Library, Avenida O'Higgins, Santiago
Collections illustrating history and archaeology of Chile.
Tu.-Su. 9-12, 3-5.

NATIONAL MUSEUM OF FINE ARTS
Parque Forestal, Santiago
Paintings, engravings, etchings, sculpture, mostly by Chilean artists.
Tu.-Su. 9-1, 3-6.

NATIONAL MUSEUM OF NATURAL HISTORY
Casilla 787, Santiago
Vertebrates. Invertebrates. Entomology. Hydrobiology. Botany. Cryptogams. Phanerogams. Mineralogy and geology. Palaeontology. Anthropology. Herpetology.
Tu.-Su. 9-5.

NATURAL HISTORY MUSEUM
Huérfanos 669, Casilla 525, Santiago
Natural history of Chile. Geology. Palaeontology. Zoology. Botany.
Tu.-Su. 9-5.

PEDAGOGICAL MUSEUM
Cienfuegos 59, Santiago
Collections illustrating the educational history of Chile.
Tu.-Sa. 9-12, 3-5.

EMILIO AND DUNCAN WAGNER ARCHAEOLOGICAL MUSEUM
Santiago
Archaeology. Anthropology. Ethnography. Mineralogy. Palaeontology.
Daily 9-4.

TALCA

O'HIGGINS AND FINE ARTS MUSEUM
1 Norte, 2 Oriente No. 875, Talca
Paintings. Stained glass. Weapons.
Daily 9-12.

TEMUCO

ARAUCANIAN MUSEUM
Avenida Alemania 084, Casilla 481, Temuco
Artistic and folklore exhibits of the Araucanian Indians of South Chile and others relating to the conquest and pacification of Araucania.
Daily 8-12, 3-5.

VALPARAISO

MUSEUM OF FINE ARTS
Valparaiso
Paintings, sculpture, graphics, mostly 19th-20th century and by Chilean artists.
Daily 9-12.30, 3-5.

NATURAL HISTORY MUSEUM
Calle Errazuriz 254, Playa Ancha, Valparaiso
Geology, zoology, botany of Chile.
Daily 9-12.30, 3-5.

VICUNA

GABRIELA MISTRAL MUSEUM
Vicuna, near La Serena
Memorabilia of the Chilean Nobel Prize poet, Gabriela Mistral.
Tu.-Su. 9-5.

VIÑA DEL MAR

ARCHAEOLOGICAL AND NATURAL SCIENCES MUSEUM
Palacio Rioja, Quinta Riojo, Casilla 18, Viña del Mar
Archaeology of Chile. Geology. Palaeontology.
Tu.-Su. 9-5

INSTITUTE OF OCEANOGRAPHY
Montemar, Viña del Mar
Marine biology.
By appointment.

MUSEUM OF COMPARATIVE MARINE ZOOLOGY
Casilla 13-D, Viña del Mar
Large collections of fish, birds and molluscs from the coastal regions.
By appointment.

MUSEUM OF NAVAL HISTORY
The Castle, Viña del Mar
Collections illustrating naval and maritime history of Chile. Models. Paintings. Photographs. Equipment.
Daily 10-5.

China, The People's Republic of

Until very recently, only Peking and those cities which lie along the coast of China and which had had links with the West for many generations contained establishments which would be generally regarded as museums by the outside world. Under the old order, the museum was not an institution which grew naturally in Chinese soil. Individual households would have their own works of art, which took their place among the other family possessions, and in the temples and shrines there were paintings, sculpture and other works of art related to ritual observances and to the religious functions of the buildings. To most Chinese, the notion of moving manuscripts, paintings, porcelain or furnishings from the place where they properly belonged and into an alien, impersonal setting would have seemed strange, disturbing and pointless. Consequently, after more than a century of purchasing and looting, there are now almost certainly far more Chinese artistic masterpieces in foreign museums than in Chinese museums.

Despite remarkable progress during the past twenty-five years, China is still, by Western standards, a poor country, in which the investment of money, skill and human effort has had to be planned with the greatest prudence. Especially since the Cultural Revolution, the criteria by which every project has had to be judged have been, "Will this improve the living standards and morale of our people?"; or "Will this help to defend us against foreign aggression?" If the answer was no, the proposal went no further. The effect on museums of this policy has been interesting.

All citizens of the People's Republic must be made aware of the history and achievements of their country. Since museums can help to create this awareness, they clearly have a part to play in the educational process. Mao tse-Tung himself has said quite plainly that the business of museums is to present their material in a way that makes sense to ordinary men and women. The rather slow reopening of museums since the Cultural Revolution has been due mainly to the need to fulfil Mao's demands. Nevertheless, museums are expensive places to build and run, and each province and town consequently has to ask itself if, at least for the time being, its resources might not be more usefully and sensibly devoted to, say, an exhibition of modern machinery or industrial products or public health, or whether a better plan might not be to provide buses to take people to visit the museums in the nearest major city, rather than to try to establish something locally.

For these reasons, the museums which have been set up during the past twenty years or so have been of three types:

(*a*) site museums, to preserve newly discovered archaeological material;

(*b*) exceptionally important temples and shrines, which are no longer in use;

(*c*) historic buildings or sites connected with recent Chinese history.

When reference is being made to our list of museums, two points should be kept in mind. The first is that, except in Peking, no foreigner would normally visit a museum except with a guide and as an honoured guest. The museum would be open to meet his convenience; and "on request" therefore seemed the correct way to indicate the opening hours. The second point concerns temples, shrines and caves. Here we felt obliged to use the same yardstick as for any other country. We had to ask, "Has this place been merely opened to the public, or have pains been taken to explain the significance of its contents to visitors?" If we had no evidence that more than just opening was involved, we excluded the item from our list. In due course, no doubt, we shall be told where we were wrong.

AMOY (XIAMEN)

OVERSEAS CHINESE MUSEUM
Amoy, Fukien province
Photographs of conditions in which Chinese have lived overseas. Bronzes. Pottery. Handicrafts of the Ming and Qing Periods.
On request.

ANTUNG (ANDONG)

PROVINCIAL MUSEUM
Antung, Liaoning province
History of agriculture and lumber industry. Archaeology. Regional cultural history. History of workers' movement.
On request.

CANTON (GUAN DONG)

HISTORY MUSEUM
Canton, Kwantung province
Prehistory. Tomb figurines. Bronzes. Lacquerware. Introduction of cotton by Moslems. Pottery. Steles. Engraved bricks. History of Guang Dong. Industrial development. Porcelain. 19th century Chinese astronomy, medicine. Anti-Manchu and anti-European movements.
On request.

PALACE OF SCIENCE
Canton, Kwantung province
Educational museum for children. Natural and physical sciences.
On request.

CHANGCHUN

PROVINCIAL MUSEUM
Changchun, Kirin province
Prehistory. Archaeology. Industrial development of Changchun and the province. History of workers' and revolutionary movements.
On request.

CHANG SHA (ZHEN ZHOU)

MUSEUM OF THE COMMUNIST PARTY COMMITTEE
Chang sha, Honan province
In former office of the Honan Communist Party Committee. Includes meeting-rooms used by Mao and other leaders. Collections illustrating Communist Party history since 1921, political organisation and the education of the workers.
On request.

OLD NORMAL SCHOOL
Chang sha, Honan province
School attended by Mao, 1912-18, now a museum. Photographs of his teachers. Books he enjoyed. Articles written by him. Exhibits illustrating his political activities, 1912-20.
On request.

PROVINCIAL MUSEUM
Chang Sha, Honan province
Prehistory and early history of the area. Carvings. Tomb figurines. Lacquer-ware. Pottery. Bronzes. History of the period of revolution, 1920s onwards.
On request.

CHENG TU (CHEN DU)

CINNAMON TREE LAKE MEMORIAL
Cheng tu, Szechuan province
Memorial hall to the scholar, Yang Shen (d.1559). Copies of his works and some of his personal possessions.
On request.

FU'S COTTAGE
Cheng tu, Szechuan province
Cottage of the poet, Tu Fu (d.772). Paintings which inspired his poems. His works and commentaries on them. Memorabilia.
On request.

CHINCHOW (JINZHOW)

PROVINCIAL MUSEUM
Chinchow, Liaoning province
Sculpture. Porcelain. Jade. Lacquer-ware. Weapons. History and industrial development of the province. Archaeology.
On request.

CHINGTEHCHEN (TSINGTAO)

CERAMICS MUSEUM
Chingtehchen, Chekiang province
Porcelain. Pottery.
On request.

CHOUKOUTIEN

MUSEUM OF PALAEONTOLOGY
Choukoutien, Hopeh province
Site of discovery of the bones of Peking Man. Museum illustrating significance of the discovery.
On request.

CHUNKING

MUNICIPAL MUSEUM
Chunking, Szechwan province
Agricultural history and development. Workers' and revolutionary movement. Archaeology.
On request.

FOOCHOW (FUZHOU)

PROVINCIAL MUSEUM
Foochow, Fukien province
Prehistory. Archaeology. Material illustrating contacts of Foochow with the West, as a former treaty-port. Tea-growing and exporting.
On request.

GUAN XIAN

DAM MUSEUM
Guan xian, Szechuan province
Museum illustrating the dam and irrigation system (c.250 B.C.), made by Li Bing. Models. Plans. Maps.
On request.

HANGCHOW (HAN ZHOU)

CHEKIANG PROVINCIAL MUSEUM
Hangchow, Chekiang province
Botany. Zoology. Physical geography. Natural resources. Prehistory. History. Folk art. Early iron tools. Mirrors. Bronze cannon. Silk manufacture. Porcelain.
On request.

XI LING BRIDGE MUSEUM
Hangchow, Chekiang province
Gardens, with collection of epigraphs.
At any time.

HARBIN

PROVINCIAL MUSEUM
Harbin, Heilungkiang province
History of Harbin and its industrial development. Harbin as a treaty-port. Agricultural history. Archaeology. Paintings. Porcelain. Pottery.
On request.

HO FEI

PROVINCIAL MUSEUM
Ho fei, An wei province
Archaeology and history of the province. History of the revolutionary movement.
On request.

JING GANG SHEN

REVOLUTIONARY BASE MUSEUM
Jing gang shen, Kiangsi province
In December 1927 the Revolutionary Army of peasants and workers, led by Mao, settled here. 4th Army was founded here. Some of the buildings used by the army are now a museum of the Revolution.
On request.

KAIFENG

PROVINCIAL MUSEUM
Kaifeng, Honan province
Prehistoric and early historical material from local excavations. Tomb figurines. Sculpture. Paintings. Furnishings. Agricultural history, especially cotton.
On request.

KUEILIN

PROVINCIAL MUSEUM
Kueilin, Nan Ling province
Industrial development of the region, especially textiles, sugar, timber. Archaeology. Sculpture. Cultural history.
On request.

KUN MING

PROVINCIAL MUSEUM
Kun ming, Yun nan province
History and archaeology of the province. Bronze drums. Weapons. Exhibits illustrating non-Chinese cultures in the province.
On request.

KWANCHOW

MUSEUM OF THE HISTORY OF KWANCHOW FOREIGN TRADE
Kwanchow, Kwantung province
In Great Hall of former Kai yuan si Temple. Development of the city's overseas trade, 11th century onwards. Steles with foreign language inscriptions.
On request.

MUSEUM OF THE INSTITUTE OF THE PEASANT MOVEMENT
Kwanchow, Kwantung province
The Institute trained peasant leaders. Mao tse-Tung lectured there and was Dean for a while. Chou en-lai also lectured there. After the death of Sun yat-sen (1926) it was closed. Now a museum, showing the Institute as it was before 1926 and illustrating the history of the Peasant Movement.
On request.

MUSEUM OF KWANCHOW'S FAMOUS MEN
Kwanchow, Kwantung province
Sections devoted to Yu Da xian (d.1579), who fought the Japanese, to the philosopher, Li Zhuo wu (d.1602), to Zheng Ching gong (d.1662), and to Qui En liang (d.1855), who led a peasant revolt.
On request.

KWEIYANG (GUIJANG)

PROVINCIAL MUSEUM
Kweiyang, Kweichow province
Prehistory and cultural history of the province. Industrial and commercial development. Revolutionary movement.
On request.

LANCHOW (LANZHOU)

PROVINCIAL MUSEUM
Lanchow, Kansu province
Archaeology and history of the province. Paintings. Furnishings. Applied arts. Handicrafts, industry and agriculture, especially tea, silk, tobacco.
On request.

LHASA

LHASA MUSEUM
Lhasa, Tibet province
History of Lhasa and Tibet.
On request.

LUCHOU

LOCAL MUSEUM
Luchou, Szechwan province
Development of the area since the 1920s. Early history of the city and the area. Handicrafts. Furnishings.
On request.

LUO YANG

TOWN MUSEUM
Luo Yang, He Nan province
In former Guan di temple. Historical development of the area. Fossil animals. Pottery. Bronzes. Tomb figurines. Jades. Sculpture. Mirrors.
On request.

MUKDEN (SHENYIANG)

IMPERIAL PALACE
Mukden, Liao ning province
Early 17th century palace of the Qing rulers. Collections of porcelain, furniture, paintings.
On request.

INDUSTRIAL EXHIBITION
Mukden, Liaoning province
Permanent exhibition of the industrial products of Shen Yang, and of the province of Liaoning. Diagrams, models, products, illustrating the principal industries.
On request.

NORTH EAST MUSEUM
Mukden, Liaoning province
Archaeology and cultural development, history of the North Eastern part of the province. Its historical functions as a commercial, educational and transport centre.
On request.

NAN CHANG

BA DA SHAN REN MUSEUM
Nan chang, Kiangsi province
Memorial museum to Ba da Shan ren, 17th century painter who refused to recognise the Zing dynasty and spent most of his life in monasteries.
On request.

MUSEUM OF THE NAN CHANG RISING
Zhong shan lu, Nan chang, Kiangsi province
History and mementoes of the rising of August 1, 1927, in buildings which were the rebels' headquarters.
On request.

QING YUN PU MONASTERY
Nan chang, Kiangsi province
Monastery in which the painter, Ba da Shan ren, lived, 1661-87. His rooms. Paintings by him, by his pupils and followers and by painters who were influenced by him.
On request.

NANKING (NAN JING)

KIANG SU PROVINCIAL MUSEUM
Nanking, Kiang su province
Prehistory and history of the province. Pottery. Bronzes. Lacquer-ware. Early iron agricultural implements. Tomb sculpture. Wall-paintings. Handicrafts. Furniture. Model of machine designed by Huang Dao po (early Ming period) for weaving cloth.
On request.

MUSEUM OF THE HEAVENLY KINGDOM OF GREAT PEACE
Nanking, Kiang su province
History of the Tai ping rebellion against the Manchu, of the new administration and of the Tai ping movement.
On request.

PEKING

CULTURAL PALACE OF THE MINORITIES
Fu xing men nei da je, Peking
Natural resources, history, ethnography of the region where the 54 national minorities live. Their historical problems and how the have been solved.
Daily 8.30-5.

HSU PEI HUNG MUSEUM
16 Dong shou lu, Peking
Home of the painter, Hsu Pei Hung (d.1953), the famous painter of horses. His living quarters, library, furniture. Portraits. Collections illustrating development of his work.
Daily 8.30-5.

IMPERIAL PALACE
Peking
Most of the buildings are 18th century, some earlier. Collections of works of art, Neolithic times onwards. Imperial collection of clocks, clockwork figures. 18th-19th century furniture. Sculpture. Ceramics. Bells. Fabrics, especially silk. Imperial table-ware. Artificial flowers. Imperial thrones, with surrounding furniture, screens, incense burners.
Winter: daily 8.30-4. Summer: daily 8.30-5.30.

LU HSUN MUSEUM
Xi san tiao, Peking
Life, literary career, travels and influence of Lu Xun (Lu Hsun) (d.1936). Manuscripts. Documents. Photographs. Personal possessions.
Daily 8.30-5.

MILITARY MUSEUM OF THE CHINESE PEOPLE'S REVOLUTION
Peking
Sections cover the Second Internal Revolutionary War, the War against Japan, the Third Internal Revolutionary War, the Defence of Socialist Construction, Aid to Korea, the Militia.
Daily 8.30-5.

MUSEUM OF CHINESE HISTORY
Tian an men, Peking
History of China, from the earliest times to 1840. Collections illustrate 3 periods - Primitive Society, Slave Society, Feudal Society. A large proportion of the items displayed are copies.
Daily 8.30-5.

MUSEUM OF THE INSTITUTE OF MUSICOLOGY
Xue yuan lu shu, Peking
Collections illustrating evolution of Chinese musical instruments.
Daily 8.30-5.

MUSEUM OF THE REVOLUTION
Tian an men, Peking
History of the Revolutionary Movement in China, from the Opium Wars to the founding of the People's Republic.
Daily 8.30-5.

NATURAL HISTORY MUSEUM
Peking
Geology. Palaeontology. World flora. Zoology.
Daily 8.30-5.

OLD OBSERVATORY
Peking
17th century observatory, with collections of astronomical instruments made by European missionaries.
Daily 8.30-5.

PLANETARIUM
Peking
Planetarium. Astronomical instruments. Photographs.
Daily 8.30-5.

SUN YAT SEN MUSEUM
Peking
Life and achievements of Dr. Sun Yat Sen, revolutionary and founder and first President of the Chinese Republic (1912).
Daily 8.30-5.

TEMPLE OF THE SOURCE OF THE LAW
Peking
Now houses Buddhist College. Manuscripts. Paintings. Bronzes. Statues and statuettes of the Buddha. Ritual vessels. Robes.
By appointment.

QING DAO

TOWN MUSEUM
Qing dao, Shan dong province
Local history and archaeology.
On request.

QIU JIN

REVOLUTIONARY BASE MUSEUM
Qiu jin, Kiangsi province
Important revolutionary base during 2nd Civil War. The Workers' and Peasants' Central Democratic Government was established in the nearby village of Ye ping. Restored buildings used by revolutionaries can be visited.
On request.

QU FU

RESIDENCES OF THE DESCENDANTS OF CONFUCIUS
Qu Fu, Shan dong province
Furnishings. Archives. Paintings. Clothes belonging to members of the Kong family. Dinner services.
On request.

TEMPLE OF CONFUCIUS
Qu Fu, Shan dong province
Imperial steles. Manuscripts. Musical instruments. Confucius' tree. Statues of Confucius, of the Four Companions and of the Twelve Disciples. Engraved stones, bearing the Legend of Confucius. Altars. Sacrificial vases.
On request.

SHANGHAI

ART AND HISTORY MUSEUM
Shanghai, Kiangsu province
Collections illustrating evolution of Chinese art. Painted pottery. Bronzes. Weapons. Clay tomb-figurines. Sculpture. Steles. Mirrors. Porcelain. Jade. Lacquer-ware. Shadow puppets.
On request.

THE INDUSTRIAL EXHIBITION
Shanghai, Kiangsu province
Chinese products, from jade, coral and ivory carvings, to the largest and most sophisticated machinery.
Daily 8.30-5.30.

LU XUN (LU HSUN) MUSEUM
Shanghai, Kiangsu province
House in which the writer, Lu Xun, died (1936). Collections illustrating his life and work, his revolutionary activities and his contacts with foreign writers, including Shaw and Gorki.
On request.

MEMORIAL HALL OF REVOLUTIONARY HISTORY
Shanghai, Kiangsu province
History of revolutionary and workers' movements in Shanghai and Kiangsu province.
On request.

MUSEUM OF NATURAL SCIENCES
Shanghai, Kiangsu province
Geology. Palaeontology. Botany. Zoology.
On request.

SHAO SHAN

BIRTHPLACE OF MAO TSE TUNG
Shao Shan, Honan province
Farmhouse where Mao was born (1893), now a museum. Original family furnishings. Agricultural implements. Photographs.
On request.

MAO TSE TUNG MUSEUM
Shao Shan, Honan province
Exhibits illustrating Mao's life, education and political career.
On request.

SHAO SHING

LU HSUN MUSEUM
Shao shing, Chekiang province
House in which the novelist, Lu Hsun lived as a child. Collection illustrating his life and work.
On request.

QIU JIN MUSEUM
Shao shing, Chekiang province
Memorial museum to Qiu Jin, revolutionary heroine, who edited a newspaper at Shanghai and was shot by the Emperor's supporters (1907).
On request.

SIAN (XIAN)

MUSEUM OF HEADQUARTERS OF 8TH ROUTE ARMY
Sian, Shensi province
Building used as office (1937-46) for organising the 8th Route Army against the Japanese and against the Kuo Min Tang who ostensibly controlled Sian. Displays illustrating the work of the office and the campaigns of the Army.
On request.

PANPO VILLAGE
Sian, Shensi province
Neolithic village, discovered during housing-site excavations (1963). 3,000 sq. m. roofed over and displayed. Adjoining museum shows photographs of excavation and reconstruction, pottery, stone and bone tools, ornaments. Relics and other evidence of agriculture, domestication of animals, fishing, weaving, cotton cultivation.
Daily 8.30-4.30.

SHENSI PROVINCIAL MUSEUM
Sian, Shensi province
Prehistory and history of the province. Steles, both memorials and with engraved inscriptions used for teaching purposes. Bronzes. Porcelain. Documents. Weapons. Animal figures from tombs. Tools. Early polo mementoes.
On request.

SUCHOW (SU ZHOU)

HISTORY MUSEUM
Suchow, Kiangsu province
Prehistory. Bronze and iron implements, weapons. Documents illustrating early gold-mining and canal-building. Silk manufacture and silkworm rearing. Porcelain. Steles. Portraits.
On request.

TAI YUAN

SHAN XI MUSEUM
Tai yuan, Shansi province
Sutras engraved and printed under the rule of the Jin. Stone carvings. Stone and clay animals. Tomb frescoes.
On request.

TIENSIN (TIANJING)

CITY MUSEUM OF HISTORY
Tiensin, Hopeh province
Exhibits illustrating cultural and political history of Tiensin. Handicrafts. Industrial development in present century.
On request.

PEOPLE'S HALL OF SCIENCE
Tiensin, Hopeh province
Physical and natural sciences. Scientific equipment. Technology. Industry.
On request.

PROVINCIAL MUSEUM
Tiensin, Hopeh province
History of the province since prehistoric times. Paintings. Sculpture. Furnishings. Part played by the province in the workers' and revolutionary movements. Local industries, especially tractors, food-processing.
On request.

TSINAN (JI NAN)

LI QING ZHAO MUSEUM
Tsinan, Shantung province
Portraits and early editions of the works of Li Qing zhao, the most famous of China's poetesses, born in Ji nan (1084).
On request.

PROVINCIAL MUSEUM
Tsinan, Shantung province
Archaeology. Prehistory and history of the province. Ethnography. Political history. Industrial development, especially gem-stones, textiles.
On request.

TSINGTAO (QINGDAO)

MARITIME MUSEUM
Tsingtao, Shantung province
History of shipping, trade and commerce between the former treaty-port and the outside world.
On request.

URUMCHI (WULUMUCHI)

REGIONAL MUSEUM
Urumchi, Sinkiang Autonomous Region
Ethnography and history of the region. Crafts. Recent industrial development. Revolutionary history.
On request.

WACHANG (WU HAN)

PROVINCIAL MUSEUM
Wachang, Hopeh province
Prehistory, especially pottery. History of the province up to the time of the Opium War. History of the Revolution, from the Opium War to 1949. Memorial exhibition to the poet, Qu yuan.
On request.

YENAN (YAN AN)

MAO'S HOUSE
Yenan, Shensi province
House, with its own air-raid shelter, in which Mao lived, 1935 onwards. Posters, books, photographs and other items illustrating this period in his life.
On request.

MUSEUM OF THE REVOLUTION
Yenan, Shensi province
Exhibits documenting the arrival of the Communist armies, Oct. 1935, after the Long March, and previous risings at the end of the Ming dynasty and in 1911.
On request.

ZUN YI

MAO TSE TUNG MUSEUM
Zun yi, Yun nan province
Town where Mao became leader of the Party. The house in which the meeting was held is now a museum.
On request.

China, Republic of (Taiwan)

The museums of a country of fourteen million people which claims to contain the true and legitimate government of a country of seven hundred million are almost bound to have a certain atmosphere of unreality about them. The ethnographical and artistic collections of Taiwan are culturally Chinese, but the Little England atmosphere in which they are presented gives them an additional quality which they would not have on the mainland of China. They are the nostalgic museums of exiles. A Museum of Chinese Postal Services in Peking is one thing; but a Museum of Chinese Postal Services in Taipei is something rather different. The time may well come, however, when both the world and the Chinese People's Republic will be grateful for the patriotic, if xenophobic, care which has been devoted to the creation of museum collections in Taiwan during the past quarter of a century.

NANKING

EXHIBITION ROOM OF THE ARCHAEOLOGICAL SECTION
Academia Sinica, Institute of History and Philology, Nanking, Taiwan
Exhibits of Shang, Chou and other Bronze Age material. Clay making and bronze casting equipment.
By appointment, M.-F. 9-4.50. Closed holidays.

TAINAN CITY

CHIHKAN TOWER MUSEUM
Tainan City, Taiwan
Formerly Fort Providentia (built 1650). Collection of documents, weapons and other historical material.
Daily 9-5.

TAIPEI

NATIONAL ART GALLERY OF TAIWAN
Nan Hai Road, Taipei, Taiwan
Collects works of art mainly for international exhibitions.
Daily 9-5.

NATIONAL MUSEUM OF HISTORY
49 Nan Hai Road, Taipei, Taiwan
Chinese bronzes and pottery. Chinese costume, embroidery, paintings, historical documents. Hsi-ping classical stone carvings. Stone pagoda. Exhibits from Japan after the Sino-Japanese war. Modern Chinese paintings.
Daily 9-5.

NATIONAL PALACE MUSEUM AND NATIONAL CENTRAL MUSEUM
Wai-shuang-hsi, Shih-lin, Taipei, Taiwan
Collections of Chinese objets d'art. Bronzes, jade, porcelain, lacquer, enamel ware, carvings, calligraphy, paintings, books and documents. Items dating from the Shang Dynasty (1522-1028 B.C.) to the Ch'ing Dynasty (A.D. 1644-1911).
Daily 9-5.

NATIONAL TAIWAN SCIENCE HALL
41 Nan-Hai Road, Taipei, Taiwan
Biology. Physics. Chemistry. Physiology. Astronomical models, specimens, pictures.
Daily 9-12, 1-5.

POSTAL MUSEUM
50 Shihtow Road, Sintien, Taipei, Taiwan
Documents and objects relating to the history of the Chinese postal service and the UPU. Complete collection of Chinese postage stamps. Proofs and engravings. Books, catalogues and periodicals connected with philately.
Daily 9-5.

RAN-IN-TING MUSEUM
11-124 Fulin Road, Shihlin, Taipei, Taiwan
Collection of the works of the painter, Ran-In-Ting. Memorabilia.
By appointment.

TAIWAN PROVINCIAL MUSEUM
No. 2 Siangyang Road, Taipei, Taiwan
Anthropology. Zoology. Botany. Oceanography.
Daily 9-5 except M. and W. afternoon and the day after public holidays.

Colombia

Since 1819, when the present territories of Panama, Venezuela and Colombia became independent of Spain, what is now Colombia has had a complicated history and it is not always easy to decide from printed museum literature exactly which revolution or year of liberation is being referred to. The collections in Colombia's large and wide-ranging network of museums provide an excellent body of illustrative material to the whole process, beginning with 1819 and ending in 1863. As one might expect, special attention is paid to Simon Bolívar, but there are in addition a number of house-museums commemorating patriots and popular heroes of lesser size than Bolívar. The heroes are not all political. The Museum of Colombian Aviation, for instance, gives prominence to the Colombians who pioneered flying and, in Bogota, the Museum of Bull-Fighting commemorates another type of national superman.

There are many archaeological and ethnographical collections which preserve the artifacts of the native Indian culture, and the art of the colonial period, especially its furniture, its pottery and its goldsmiths' work, is to be found in the majority of the country's museums.

The Museum of Numismatics is pleasantly and appropriately housed in a former Mint.

ARMENIA

ARCHAEOLOGICAL MUSEUM
Carrera 17, Calles 20-21, Armenia, Quindio
Ceramics. Goldsmith's work. Archaeological finds excavated in the area.
Tu.-Su. 10-12, 3-6.

BARRANQUILLA

ARCHAEOLOGICAL MUSEUM
Universidad del Atlántico, Barranquilla, Atlántico
Archaeological finds from sites in the area.
M.-F. 10-12, 2-6.

BOGOTA

BOLÍVAR MUSEUM
Calle 20, No. 3-23, Bogota
Former possessions of the Liberator of Colombia, Simon Bolívar and of other leaders of the Independence Movement. Paintings. Furniture. Weapons. Medals.
Tu.-Su. 10-6.

ETHNOGRAPHICAL MUSEUM OF THE CARO AND CUERVO INSTITUTE
Carrera Central del Norte, K. 32, Hacienda Yerbabuena, Bogota
Colombian folk art, handicrafts. Domestic equipment.
Tu.-F. 8.30-12, 1.30-4.

JORGE ELIECER GAITAN MUSEUM
Calle 42, No. 15-52, Bogota
In former home of Gaitan, assassinated 1948. Furniture, paintings and personal possessions of Gaitan. His death mask.
Tu.-Sa. 10-6; public holidays 10-2.

HISTORICAL MUSEUM
Carrera 7, Calles 28-66, Bogota
Spanish flags. Colonial history. Portraits. Collections illustrating struggle for national independence. Coins. Medals. Uniforms. Weapons.
Tu.-Sa. 10-6; public holidays 10-2.

MUSEUM OF AVIATION
Instituto Militar Aeronáutico, Ciudad Kennedy, Bogota
Collections illustrating Colombian aviation history and its pioneers.
M.-F. 7-2; public holidays 9-4.

MUSEUM OF BULL-FIGHTING
Plaza de Toros de Santamaria, Bogota
Collections illustrating history of bull-fighting in Colombia. Posters. Bull-fighters' costumes, equipment. Photographs.
W.-Su. 9-12, 2-6.

MUSEUM OF COLONIAL ART
Carrera 6, No. 9-77, Bogota
Paintings by Colombian artists of the Colonial period. Gilt and polychromed wood-carvings. Furniture. Decorative arts. Silver. Mirrors.
Tu.-Sa. 10-6; public holidays 10-2.

MUSEUM OF CONTEMPORARY ART
Carrera 74 and Calle 83, Bogota
Paintings, drawings, engravings, sculpture, photographs by 20th century American, European, Colombian artists.
Tu.-Sa. 10-1.

MUSEUM OF ETHNOGRAPHY
Carrera 7, Calles 28-66, Bogota
Collections illustrating arts and handicrafts of the people and tribes of Colombia. Ceramics. Musical instruments. Ornaments. Religious art. Tools, weapons. Governor's cloak of woven feathers.
Tu.-Sa. 10-6; public holidays 10-2.

MUSEUM OF FINE ART
Carrera 7, Calles 28-66, Bogota
Paintings, sculpture by Colombian and foreign artists. Drawings by Colombian artists.
Tu.-Sa. 10-6; public holidays 10-2.

MUSEUM OF GOLD
Carrera 6 and Carrera 16, Bogota
Goldsmiths' work of the pre-Hispanic period.
Tu.-Sa. 9-5; public holidays 10-1.

MUSEUM OF GRAPHIC ART
Av. 1 and Carrera 15, Bogota
Old printing presses, woodcuts, typographical equipment. Lithography. Currency notes. Stamps.
M.-F. 8-5.

MUSEUM OF LITERATURE
Carretera Central del Norte, K 32, Hacienda Yerbabuena, Bogota
19th Century hacienda-style furniture. Manuscripts, portraits, memorabilia of Colombian writers.
Tu.-F. 8.30-12, 1.30-4.

MUSEUM OF MODERN ART
Carrera 10 and Calle 28, Bogota
Sculpture by Alexander Calder. Paintings by Picasso, Chagall.
Tu.-Su. 10-7.

MUSEUM OF MUSEUMS
Av. Jimenez 17-23, Academia de la Lengua, Piso 3, Bogota
Reproductions of paintings, tapestries, cartoons by Goya.
Tu.-Sa. 10-7; Su. 10-1.

MUSEUM OF NATURAL HISTORY
Planetario Distrital, Bogota
Galleries arranged in sequence from top to bottom of the building, following Colombia's climatic levels. Geography. Geology. Mammals. Birds. Fish. Botany.
Tu.-Sa. 9-9; public holidays 11-7.

MUSEUM OF NUMISMATICS
Calle 11, No. 4-93, Bogota
In former 18th century Mint. Colombian coins, from Colonial period to present day. Commemorative medals.
Tu.-F. 8.30-12, 1.30-4.

MUSEUM OF POPULAR ARTS AND TRADITIONS
Carrera 8 and Calle 7, Bogota
Handicrafts. Ancient crafts.
Tu.-Su. 10-7.

MUSEUM OF PRE-COLOMBIAN CERAMICS
Carrera 6 and Calle 8, Bogota
Ceramics of all the pre-Hispanic cultures of Colombia.
Tu.-Su. 10-7.

MUSEUM OF THE 20TH OF JULY, or HOUSE OF THE FLOWER VASE
Calle 11, No. 6-86, Bogota
Collections illustrating the independence movement and its leaders.
Tu.-Sa. 10-6; public holidays 10-2.

MUSEUM OF THE URBAN DEVELOPMENT OF BOGOTA
Calle 10, 4-21, Bogota
Maps, plans, photographs, models illustrating growth of Bogota. First Bogota tram. Early telephones.
Tu.-Sa. 10-1, 3-6; Su. 11-7.

ANTONIO NARIÑO MUSEUM
Calle 10 Sur. Cra. 38, Bogota
Collections illustrating life and work of the journalist and patriot, Antonio Nariño.
W.-Su. 9-12, 2-6.

NATIONAL MUSEUM
Carrera 7, Calles 28-66, Bogota
Crude sculptures from the Valley of the Statues, San Agustin. National history, pre-Conquest days onwards. Metal and ceramic Indian artifacts. Quesada's coat of mail. Pizarro's flag. State robe belonging to the Inca Atahualpa's queen. Ethnography. Natural sciences.
Tu.-Sa. 10-6; public holidays 10-2.

NATIONAL MUSEUM OF ANTHROPOLOGY
Carrera 7, Calles 28-66, Bogota
Collections illustrating the cultures of Colombia. Ceramics. Stone carvings. Goldsmiths' work. Textiles.
Tu.-Sa. 10-6; public holidays 10-2.

POLICE MUSEUM
Carrera 7, Calles 28-66, Bogota
History of the Colombian police. Uniforms, weapons, equipment of the police forces of 22 countries.
Tu.-Sa. 10-6; public holidays 10-2.

MERCEDES SIERRA DE PEREZ MUSEUM
Carrera 7, 94-17, Bogota
Colombian paintings of the Colonial and modern periods. European furniture, paintings. Porcelain. Oriental art.
Tu. 2.30-5.30; W.-Sa. 10-12.30, 2.30-5.30; public holidays 10-5.30.

SANTA CLARA MUSEUM
Calle 9, 8-31, Bogota
Paintings by Portuguese and foreign artists. Altars. Polychrome carvings. Images. Colonial furniture. Bells.
W.-Sa. 10-1, 3-5.30; Su. 10-1.

BUCARAMANGA

BOLÍVAR HOUSE-MUSEUM
Calle 37, 12-15, Bucaramanga, Santander
House in which Bolívar died. Regional art, history.
Tu.-Su. 10-12, 3-5.

PERU DE LA CROIX HOUSE-MUSEUM
Bucaramanga, Santander
Former home of the writer, Peru de la Croix, friend of Bolívar.
Tu.-Su. 10-12, 3-6.

GARCÍA ROVIRA HOUSE-MUSEUM
Calle 35, 8-68, Bucaramanga, Santander
Birthplace of García Rovira. Art, furnishings of the Colonial period.
Tu.-Su. 10-12, 3-6.

CALI

MUSEUM OF ANTIQUITIES
Av. 4, 10-42, Cali, Valle del Cauca
Incunabula. Coins. Arms. Weapons. Books.
Tu.-Su. 10-12, 3-6.

MUSEUM OF THE FRANCISCAN FATHERS
Calle 9 and Carrera 6, Cali, Valle del Cauca
Incunabula. Paintings. Religious art.
Tu.-Su. 10-12, 3-6.

MUSEUM OF NATURAL HISTORY
Avenida 2, Oeste 4-82, Cali, Valle del Cauca
Regional history, archaeology. Natural history.
Tu.-Su. 10-12, 3-6.

LA TERTULIA MUSEUM OF ART
Avenida Colombia 5-105 Oeste, Cali, Valle del Cauca
Modern paintings, graphics, especially by Colombian artists. Sculpture.
Tu.-Su. 10-12, 3-6.

CARTAGENA

ANTHROPOLOGICAL MUSEUM
Palacio de la Inquisición, Plaza de Bolívar, Cartagena, Bolívar
Anthropology of Colombia.
M.-F. 10-12, 2-6.

COLONIAL MUSEUM
Palacio de la Inquisición, Plaza de Bolívar, Cartagena, Bolívar
Colonial history, art.
M.-F. 10-12, 2-6.

RAFAEL NUÑEZ HOUSE-MUSEUM
Barrio del Cabrero, Cartagena, Bolívar
Collections illustrating life and work of Rafael Nuñez.
M.-F. 10-12, 2-6.

CENTROS CULTURALES

MUSEUM OF THE SCHOOL OF FINE ART
Calle 68 Carrera 53, Centros Culturales, Atlántico
Paintings. Sculpture. Ceramics.
M.-F. 10-12, 2-6.

COLOSO

PRIVATE MUSEUM
Coloso, Sucre
Art and handicrafts of the Pre-Colombian period.
By appointment.

DUITAMA

MUSEUM OF RELIGIOUS ART
Hacienda Colonial de San Rafael, nr. Duitama, Boyaca
Religious art, from churches in the diocese.
Tu.-Su. 10-12, 2-6.

EL CERRITO

EL PARAISEO
nr. El Cerrito, Valle del Cauca
Scene of the novel, *Maria*, by Jorge Isaacs.
Tu.-Su. 10-12, 3-6.

FLORENCIA

FABIO SANCHEZ MUSEUM
El Paujil, nr. Florencia, Intendencia del Caqueta
Local history.
On request.

GUADUAS

EZPELETA MUSEUM
Guaduas, Cundinamarca
Founded by the historian, Alberto Hincapié Espinosa. Collections illustrating local history.
Tu.-Su. 10-12, 3-6.

LA POLA HOUSE-MUSEUM
Guaduas, Cundinamarca
Former home of the patriot, La Pola. Collections illustrating his life and work.
Tu.-Su. 10-12, 3-6.

INZA

MUSEUM OF ARCHAEOLOGY
Inza, nr. Popayan, Cauca
Pre-Colombian art, archaeology.
Tu.-Su. 10-12, 3-6.

MANIZALES

MUSEUM OF ANTHROPOLOGY
Palacio de Bellas Artes, Universidad de Caldas, Manizales, Caldas
Ceramics of the Quimbaya, Calima and Tayrona cultures.
Tu.-Su. 9-12, 3-6.

MUSEUM OF NATURAL SCIENCES
Instituto Universitario de Caldas, Manizales, Caldas
Regional flora, fauna.
Tu.-Su. 9-12, 3-6.

MUSEUM OF PRE-COLOMBIAN CERAMICS
Banco de Republica, Carrera 23, Calle 23, Manizales, Caldas
Pre-Colombian ceramics.
M.-Sa. 9-12, 3-6.

MEDELLÍN

COLTEJER MUSEUM OF MODERN ART
Calle 52 and Carrera 49, Medellín, Antioquia
Modern art, especially by Colombian artists.
M.-F. 10-12, 2-6.

JUAN DEL CORRAL MUSEUM
Santa Fe de Antioquia, nr. Medellín, Antioquia
82 km. from Medellín. Collections illustrating life and work of Juan del Corral.
M.-Sa. 10-12, 2-6.

MAESTRO PEDRO NEL GOMEZ HOUSE-MUSEUM
Carrera 51B, 85-24, Medellín, Antioquia
Collections illustrating life and work of Maestro Pedro Nel Gomez.
M.-F. 10-12, 2-6.

INDIAN MUSEUM
Transv. 92, 33B-21, Belencito, Medellín, Antioquia
Indian artifacts.
M.-F. 10-12, 2-6.

MINERALOGICAL MUSEUM
Facultad de Minas, Robledo, Calle 76, 76-7, Medellín, Antioquia
Mineralogy.
M.-F. 10-12, 2-6.

MUSEUM OF ANTHROPOLOGY
Calle 48, 42-16, Ciudad Universitaria, Universidad de Antioquia, Bloque 15, Medellín, Antioquia
Anthropology. Pottery.
M.-F. 9-12, 2-6; Sa. 9-12.

MUSEUM OF ETHNOGRAPHY
Belencito, Calle 48, 42-17, Universidad de Antioquia, Medellín, Antioquia
Colombian handicrafts, especially ceramics.
M.-F. 10-12, 2-6.

MUSEUM OF FOLKLORE
Calle 44, 66-50, Tejicondor, Medellín, Antioquia
Colombian folk art, handicrafts, especially of the Antioquia region.
M.-F. 10-12, 2-6.

MUSEUM OF NATURAL SCIENCES
Colegio de San José, Carrera 30, 50-55, Medellín, Antioquia
Natural sciences. Zoology. Botany. Mineralogy.
M.-F. 10-12, 2-6.

MUSEUM OF PRE-COLOMBIAN CERAMICS
Hacienda Fizebad, nr. Medellín, Antioquia
29 km. from Medellín. Pre-Colombian ceramics.
M.-Sa. 10-12, 2-6.

SANTA FÉ MUSEUM
Zoologico Santa Fé, Carretera Guayabal, Salida al Aeropuerto, nr. Medellín, Antioquia
Zoology.
M.-F. 10-12, 2-6.

ZEA MUSEUM
Carrera 53, 51-74, Medellín, Antioquia
Local history, ethnography.
M.-F. 10-12, 2-6.

MONTERIA

UNIVERSITY MUSEUM
Universidad de Córdoba, Monteria, Córdoba
Paintings, sculpture by Colombian artists.
M.-F. 10-12, 2-6.

NEIVA

DEPARTMENTAL MUSEUM
Neiva, Huila
Pre-Colombian ceramics, art.
Tu.-Sa. 10-12, 3-6.

PAMPLONA

COLONIAL MUSEUM
Calle 6, 2-56, Pamplona, Norte de Santander
Regional history. Paintings.
W.-Sa. 9-12, 2-6.30; public holidays 9-12.

PASTO

DELFIN GUAYASAMIN MUSEUM
Carrera 18-54, Pasto, Nariño
Collections illustrating life and work of Delfin Guayasamin.
Tu.-Su. 10-12, 3-6.

LA MERCED MARIADIAZ MUSEUM
Calle 18, 32A-39, Pasto, Nariño
Local history, ethnography.
Tu.-Su. 10-12, 3-6.

JOSÉ IGNACIO OBANDO MUSEUM
Carrera 30, 21-33, Pasto, Nariño
Collections illustrating life and work of José Ignacio Obando.
Tu.-Su. 10-12, 3-6.

TAMINANGO MUSEUM
Pasto, Nariño
Colonial period house with period furnishings.
Tu.-Su. 10-12, 3-6.

ALFONSO ZAMBRANO MUSEUM
Calle 20, 29-78, Pasto, Nariño
Collections illustrating life and work of Alfonso Zambrano.
Tu.-Su. 10-12, 3-6.

PEREIRA

ARCHAEOLOGICAL MUSEUM
Avenida Circunvalar 11-08, Pereira, Risaralda
Archaeological finds from excavations in the area.
Tu.-Su. 10-12, 3-6.

POPAYAN

COLONIAL MUSEUM
Calle 4, 9-13, Popayan, Cauca
Paintings, handicrafts of the Colonial period.
Tu.-Su. 10-12, 3-6.

MARTÍNEZ MUSEUM
"El Refugio", Via Moscopan, nr. Popayan, Cauca
Life and achievements of the painter, Efraín Martínez, in his former home.
Tu.-Su. 10-12, 2-6.

MUSEUM OF COLONIAL HISTORY AND ART
Casa de Mosquera, Calle 3, 5-14, Popayan, Cauca
Colonial history, art, ethnography.
Tu.-Su. 10-12, 2-6.

MUSEUM OF RELIGIOUS ART
Calle 4, Carrera 9, Popayan, Cauca
Religious paintings, ornaments.
Tu.-Su. 10-12, 2-6.

NATURAL HISTORY MUSEUM
Carrera 3, Calle 3N, Popayan, Cauca
Flora and fauna of Colombia.
Tu.-Su. 10-12, 3-6.

VALENCIA HOUSE-MUSEUM
Carrera 6, 2-69, Popayan, Cauca
In former home of the poet, Guillermo Valencia. Collections illustrating his life and work. Sculptures by Victorio Macho.
Tu.-Su. 10-12, 2-6.

RIOHACHA

GUAJIRO MUSEUM OF PRE-COLOMBIAN ART AND CULTURE
Calle de la Marine, Riohacha, Guajira
Pre-Colombian art and culture.
Tu.-Su. 10-12, 3-6.

MUSEUM OF THE SCHOOL OF ART
Riohacha, Guajira
Paintings by regional artists.
On request.

SOCORRO

MUSEUM OF PRE-COLOMBIAN ART
Socorro, Santander
Pre-Colombian art.
Tu.-Su. 10-12, 3-6.

SAN PEDRO ALEJANDRINO

LOCAL MUSEUM
San Pedro Alejandrino, nr. Santa Maria, Magdalena
Place where Bolívar spent his last days. Memorabilia.
Tu.-Su. 10-12, 3-6.

SANTA MARIA

ETHNOGRAPHICAL MUSEUM
Carrera 2, Calles 16-17, Santa Maria, Magdalena
In former Convent of Santo Domingo. Ethnographical collections.
Tu.-Su. 10-12, 3-6.

SOGAMOSO

ARCHAEOLOGICAL PARK
Sogamoso, Boyaca
On site of the Chibcha Temple of the Sun, destroyed by the Spanish conquerors in 1537. Chibcha archaeology.
Tu.-Su. 10-12, 2-6.

TUNJA

HOUSE OF JERONIMO DE HOLGUIN
Carrera 10, Calles 20-21, Tunja, Boyaca
Former home of Jeronimo de Holguin. Memorabilia and paintings.
Tu.-Su. 10-12, 2-6.

HOUSE OF THE FOUNDER
Carrera 9, Calles 19-20, Tunja, Boyaca
16th century house, with period furnishings.
Tu.-Su. 10-12, 2-6.

HOUSE OF RUIZ DE MANCIPE
Calle 19, Carreras 11-12, Tunja, Boyaca
Former home of Ruiz de Mancipe. Memorabilia. Furnishings.
Tu.-Su. 10-12, 2-6.

HOUSE OF BERNARDINO DE MUJICA Y GUEVARA
Carrera 7, Calles 19-20, Tunja, Boyaca
Paintings.
Tu.-Su. 10-12, 2-6.

JUAN DE VARGAS HOUSE MUSEUM
Calle 20, Carreras 8-9, Tunja, Boyaca
Former home of the writer, Juan de Vargas. Memorabilia.
Tu.-Su. 10-12, 2-6.

VILLA DE LEYVA

COLONIAL MUSEUM
Villa de Leyva, Boyaca
Paintings by Vásquez Ceballos, Gaspar Figueroa. Woodcarvings and paintings by Joaquín Gutierrez.
Tu.-Su. 10-12, 2-6.

HOUSE OF RICAURTE
Villa de Leyva, Boyaca
Weapons, portraits, memorabilia of the heroes of San Mateo.
Tu.-Su. 10-12, 2-6.

VILLANUEVA

MUSEUM OF NATIVE ART AND CULTURE
Villanueva, Guajira
Colombian native art and culture.
Tu.-Su. 10-12, 3-6.

Congo

This former French territory produces lead and a certain amount of gold. Apart from that its economy is entirely based on agriculture and forestry. Its three museums attempt to show something of the traditional life of the people, especially during the past hundred years, and to explain its political development.

BRAZZAVILLE

MUSEUM OF EARTH SCIENCES
Ecole Supérieure des Sciences, Brazzaville
Geological and mineralogical specimens.
By appointment.

MUSEUM OF THE REVOLUTION
B.P. 2271, Brazzaville
History of the Congo. Items include the guns used by Mabiala Mangangade.
Daily 7.30-12, 2.30-5.

NATIONAL MUSEUM OF THE CONGO
Avenue Patrice Lumumba, B.P. 459, Brazzaville
History and ethnography. Wooden bottle gourd of Mfoati. Ivory sculptures.
Daily 7.30-12, 3-5.30. Sa. and Su. only 7.30-12.30.

Costa Rica

Economists think of Costa Rica in terms of coffee, bananas and timber. The museum-world has a different country in mind, characterised by archaeology, ethnography and handicrafts. The two viewpoints add up to Costa Rica as it really is.

SAN JOSÉ

ART GALLERY
Casa del Artista, San José
19th-20th century paintings, sculpture, drawings by Costa Rican artists.
Tu.-Su. 9-5.

GALLERY OF THE FACULTY OF FINE ARTS
Universidad de Costa Rica, San José
Paintings, drawings, graphics, sculpture by American and European artists.
By appointment.

GOLD MUSEUM
Banco Central de Costa Rica, San José
Collection of gold and jade artifacts from aboriginal tribes.
W. and Sa. 9-12.

MUSEUM OF MUSICAL HISTORY
Sala de Conciertos Tassara, Calle 14, No. 944, San José
Collections illustrating musical history of Costa Rica.
On request.

NATIONAL MUSEUM
Apto. 749, San José
Archaeology of Costa Rica. History. Ethnography. Botany. Zoology.
Tu.-Su. 9-5.

NATIONAL THEATRE GALLERY
Teatro Nacional, San José
Collections illustrating history of the National Theatre, its performances and its actors.
Tu.-Su. 10-4.

NATIVE MUSEUM
Seminario Central, San José
Ethnography. Folk art. Handicrafts.
On request.

ZOOLOGICAL MUSEUM
Departamento de Biología, Universidad de Costa Rica, Ciudad Universitaria "Rodrigo Facio", San José
Collections illustrating animal life in Costa Rica and on the coast.
By appointment.

Cuba

Apart from a brief British interval in 1762-3, Cuba was a Spanish possession from 1492, when it was discovered by Columbus, until 1898, when it became an independent republic. The country's museums document a large part of these 400 years, and all of the turbulent twentieth century. Colonial furniture and paintings and the art of the Catholic religion are displayed more or less side-by-side with the equipment of witchcraft and of the Cuban negroes' secret society, *nanquismo.* As one would expect from the museums of a modern Communist state, there is great emphasis on the aims and history of the revolution; and, perhaps unique in the world, there is what is encouragingly called a Museum of Literacy, an exhibition of what has been achieved and what is still to be achieved in the campaign against illiteracy. Equally belonging to today is a museum of agriculture and mining, organised and presented to show the development and potential of Cuba's two main industries. To preserve an atmosphere of continuity, an old sugar-mill of colonial days is displayed as an open-air exhibit.

In the midst of all the public pressure to create a new socialist Cuba, reminders of the United States and of capitalism seem slightly out of place. But the Ernest Hemingway museum is still there, open and presented with some pride, in the writer's former home.

BANES

MUSEUM OF THE CUBAN INDIANS
General Marrero 26, Banes
Pre-Colombian Cuban archaeology.
M.-F. 10-6; Sa. 10-2.

BAYAMO

CARLOS MANUEL DE CESPEDES BIRTHPLACE
Bayamo
Furniture and personal possessions of C. M. de Cespedes, in the house where he was born.
M.-F. 10-6; Sa. 10-2.

CAMAGUEY

IGNACIO AGRAMONTE MUSEUM
Avenida de los Martires 2, Camaguey
Art, history and natural history of Cuba.
M.-F. 10-6; Sa. 10-2.

GIBARA

NATURAL HISTORY MUSEUM
Gibara
Mammals, birds, fish, reptiles and crustaceans of the region.
M.-F. 10-6; Sa. 10-2.

GUANABACOA

HISTORICAL MUSEUM
Marti 108, Versalles y San Antonio, Guanabacoa
Ethnography. Afro-Cuban collection relating to the Abakua-Yoruba y Palo Monte rituals. 19th century furnishings. Colonial sugar mill in garden.
Tu.-Su. 4-10.

HABANA

AGRICULTURAL MUSEUM
Ministerio de Agricultura, Habana
Main products of Cuba, especially agriculture and mining.
By appointment.

CARLOS J. FINLAY MUSEUM OF MEDICAL SCIENCE
Calle Cuba 460, Amargura y Tte. Rey, Habana
Collections illustrating history and practice of medicine in Cuba.
M.-F. 10-6; Sa. 10-2.

HEMINGWAY MUSEUM
Finca La Vigia, San Francisco de Paula, Habana
Books and personal items of Ernest Hemingway, in his former home. Furniture.
W.-Sa. 9-12, 2-6; Su. 9-1.

JOSÉ MARTI BIRTHPLACE
Léonor Perez 314 esq. a Egido, Habana
Manuscripts, personal possessions and other material illustrating life and work of Marti.
Tu.-Su. 9-5.

MONTANÉ ANTHROPOLOGICAL MUSEUM
Plaza Cadenas, Universidad de la Habana, Habana
Ethnography of America and Cuba. Cuban Indian archaeology. Objects connected with Cuban ritual, magic, witchcraft, *nanquismo* (Cuban Negroes' secret society) and folklore.
M.-F. 10-6; Sa. 10-2.

MUSEUM OF THE CITY OF HABANA
Palacio de los Capitanes Generales, Plaza de Armas Tacón 1, O'Reilly y Obispo, Habana
In historic Cuban palace. Historical material from earliest times to the present day. Paintings. Emblems. Carriages.
M.-F. 2-5, 8-10.30; Sa. 8-10.30.

MUSEUM OF COLONIAL ART
Plaza de la Catedral, Habana
Furniture. Architectural items. Collections illustrating Cuba in the Colonial period.
Tu.-Sa. 3-10.30; Su. 2-6.

MUSEUM OF DECORATIVE ARTS
Calle 17, esq. a E., Vedado, Habana
World-wide collections of decorative arts, especially from France, Japan, China. Porcelain. Bronzes. Gold and silver work. Tapestries. Furniture. Fans.
Tu.-Sa. 3-10.30; Su. 2-6.

NAPOLEONIC MUSEUM
San Miguel y Ronda, Habana
Furniture, weapons and other material of the Napoleonic period.
Tu.-Sa. 3-10.30; Su. 2-6.

NATIONAL MUSEUM
Palacio de Bellas Artes, Calle Trocadero e Zuelta y Monserrate, Habana
Works of art from Egypt, Greece, Italy (Renaissance and 17th-18th century), the Low Countries, France, England and Spain. Cuban art from the Colonial period to the present day.
Tu.-Sa. 3-10.30; Su. 2-6.

FELIPE POEY MUSEUM
Capitolio Nacional, Habana
Mineralogy. Archaeology. Physical and natural sciences. Zoology.
Tu.-Su. 6-11 p.m.

POSTAL MUSEUM
Ministerio de Communicaciones, Plaza de la Revolución, Habana
Complete collection of postage stamps of Cuba. History of the postal service. Postal equipment.
M.-F. 10-6; Sa. 10-2.

HOLGUÍN

CARLOS DE LA TORRE NATURAL HISTORY MUSEUM
Apartado 216, Holguín
Natural history.
M.-F. 10-6; Sa. 10-2.

MARIANAO

MUSEUM OF LITERACY
Ciudad Libertad, Marianao
Collections illustrating the Campaign against Illiteracy.
M.-F. 10-6; Sa. 10-2.

MATAZANAS

ARCHAEOLOGICAL MUSEUM
Matazanas
Finds from excavations in the area.
M.-F. 10-6; Sa. 10-2.

MATANZAS

MUSEUM OF PHARMACY
Milanes 49-51, Matanzas
Furnishings and equipment of old Cuban pharmacy.
M.-F. 10-6; Sa. 10-2.

PINAR DEL RIO

MUSEUM OF MARINE FAUNA
Naval Academy, Mariel, Pinar del Rio
Rare specimens of deep-sea fish.
By appointment.

REMEDIOS

JOSÉ M. ESPINOSA MUSEUM
Maceo 56, Remedios, Las Villas
Local history. Furniture.
M.-F. 10-6; Sa. 10-2.

SANCTI-SPIRITUS

PALACIO VALLE IZNAGA COLONIAL MUSEUM
Plácido 74, Sancti-Spiritus, Las Villas
Furniture and other material of the Colonial period.
M.-F. 10-6; Sa. 10-2.

SANTA CLARA

HISTORICAL MUSEUM
Parque Vidal, Santa Clara, Las Villas
Weapons, photographs and other collections illustrating the aims and history of the Revolution.
M.-F. 10-6; Sa. 10-2.

SANTIAGO DE CUBA

EMILIO BACARDI MUSEUM
Aguilera y Pío Rosado, Santiago de Cuba, Oriente
Archaeology, history and art of Cuba.
M.-F. 10-6; Sa. 10-2.

COLONIAL MUSEUM
Parque Céspedes, Santiago de Cuba, Oriente
Furniture and other material of the Colonial period.
M.-F. 10-6; Sa. 10-2.

FRANK PAIS BIRTHPLACE
Santiago de Cuba, Oriente
Manuscripts, personal possessions and other material illustrating life and work of Pais, in the house where he was born.
M.-F. 10-6; Sa. 10-2.

SCIENCE MUSEUM
Santiago de Cuba, Oriente
Ethnography. Archaeology. Natural and physical sciences.
M.-F. 10-6; Sa. 10-2.

SIBONEY BARN
Santiago de Cuba, Oriente
Building used as a base by the men preparing to attack the Moncada. Weapons and uniforms used in the attack.
M.-F. 10-6; Sa. 10-2.

Cyprus

The museum tradition of Cyprus was established in the pre-1914 days of British rule, when a museum in the Middle East meant antiquities and archaeology and practically nothing else. The Cyprus Museum, its colonial charm now sadly dwarfed by greedy and ill-sited modern office blocks, has remained firmly in this tradition, as the main treasurehouse of the prehistoric, Greek and Roman material which has been discovered in such impressive abundance at many points in the island. Since 1945, however, the field has been widened by a small group of museums designed to preserve and display the evidence of the rapidly disappearing rural culture, and by a single Turkish museum, which has the original dancing floor of the Whirling Dervishes as its central showpiece. Private collections are now very active in Cyprus and it is quite likely that one or two or these hoards will become accessible to the public within the next few years.

EPISKOPI

CURIUM MUSEUM
Episkopi
Finds from local excavations, including statuary from the Roman villa of Curium. This includes figures of Hermes in his role as Pastor or Protector of Shepherds, and of Asclepios, the God of Medicine, as well as a head of Aphrodite crowned with a diadem.
Daily 8-1, 4-6; Su. 10-1. Sept. 21-May 15, daily 8.30-1, 2.30-4.30; Su. 10-1.

FAMAGUSTA

FAMAGUSTA ARCHAEOLOGICAL MUSEUM
Famagusta Town
Antiquities found in the district, dating from Neolithic times.
Daily 8-1, 4-6; Su. 10-1. Sept. 21-May 15, daily 8.30-1, 2.30-4.30; Su. 10-1.

KTIMA

PRIVATE COLLECTION OF PROFESSOR ELIADES
1 Exo Vrysis Street, Ktima
Collection of early pottery, and small folk museum.
On request.

KYRENIA

FOLK ART MUSEUM
Kyrenia
Objects of folk art. Embroideries, woodcarvings, modern pottery and silversmiths' work from various parts of the island. Bridal costumes. Kitchen utensils.
Daily 8-1, 4-6; Su. 10-1. Sept. 21-May 15, Daily 8.30-1, 2.30-4.30; Su. 10-1.

SHIPWRECK MUSEUM
Kyrenia Castle, Kyrenia
Remains of a 4th century B.C. Greek ship salvaged off Kyrenia, in 1968. Amphorae. Grain mills. Timbers of ship's hull are now on display in tanks of preservative liquid.
May 15-Sept. 15, daily 7-7. Sept. 16-May 14, daily 7.30-dusk.

LARNACA

LARNACA ARCHAEOLOGICAL MUSEUM
Kilkis Street and Kimonos Street, Larnaca
Antiquities dating from Neolithic times discovered in the district. Tools, ornaments from Khirokitia, dating from 5800-5250 B.C. Late Bronze Age (14th century B.C.) vases. Jewellery. Statuary, mostly from Arsos.
Daily 8-1, 4-6; Su. 10-1. Sept. 21-May 15, daily 8.30-1, 2.30-4.30; Su. 10-1.

LIMASSOL

NATURAL HISTORY MUSEUM
Zoological Gardens, Limassol
Flora and fauna, especially of Cyprus.
M.-Sa. 10-12, 2-5.

MUNICIPAL FOLK ART MUSEUM
Heroes Square, Limassol
Folk art objects from various parts of the island.
On application to the Library in Ayios Andreas Street.

NICOSIA

THE CYPRUS MUSEUM
P.O. Box 2024, Nicosia
Pottery from Neolithic and Chalcolithic periods to the Roman period. Medieval pottery. Terracotta figures from Bronze Age to Roman times. Limestone and marble sculpture. Jewellery, especially of the Mycenean period (1400-1200 B.C.). Coins. Inscriptions (Phoenician, Cypriot and Greek). Bronzes. Glass. Alabaster. Bone. Room of reconstructed tombs.
M.-Sa. 8-1, 4-6; Su. 10-1. Sept. 21-May 15, M.-Sa. 8.30-1, 2.30-4.30; Su. 10-1.

LAPIDARY MUSEUM
Yeni Djami Street, Nicosia
Medieval tombstones, marble lintels, carved stones of palaces and churches, housed in old Venetian house.
Apply to custodian at Selimiye Mosque.

MUSEUM OF BYZANTINE ICONS
Varnava Street, Nicosia
Collections of icons from 11th century onwards.
May 15-Sept. 15, M.-Sa. 8-1, 4-6; Su. 10-1. Sept. 16-May 14, M.-Sa. 8.30-1, 2.30-4.30; Su. 10-1.

THE MUSEUM OF FOLK ART
P.O. Box 1436, Varnava Street, Nicosia
Cyprus arts and crafts from early to recent times; mainly Greek Cypriot items. Village arts and crafts. Bridal costumes. Silk sheets, weaving and embroidery. Carvings.
May 15-Sept. 15, M.-Sa. 8-1, 4-6; Su. 10-1. Sept. 16-May 14, M.-Sa. 8.30-1, 2.30-4.30; Su. 10-1.

TEKKÉ OF THE MEVLEVI DERVISHES
Enia Avenue, Nicosia
Originally a monastery of the Whirling Dervishes sect, now houses a collection of Turkish arts and crafts.
M.-Sa. 8-5.

PALAEPAPHOS

PALAEPAPHOS MUSEUM
Palaepaphos
Site museum containing antiquities excavated in the area.
Daily 8-1, 4-6; Su. 10-1. Sept. 21-May 15, daily 8.30-1, 2.30-4.30; Su. 10-1.

PAPHOS

PAPHOS MUSEUM
Grivas Dighenis Avenue, Paphos
Antiquities dating from Neolithic times discovered locally. Amphorae, Roman glass and fragments of statuary. Objects from the House of Dionysus.
Daily 8-1, 4-6; Su. 10-1. Sept. 21-May 15, daily 8.30-1, 2.30-4.30; Su. 10-1.

Czechoslovakia

Both in the Czech and the Slovak provinces, Czechoslovakia has an exceptionally long and honourable tradition of museum-keeping and the average standard of its museums is high. There is a marked tendency for the two national cultures to keep themselves separate in the organisation of museums, as in most other matters, but, since the field is so rich, this appears to have done no great harm.

In looking at the great range of museums in Czechoslovakia, it is logical to think first of the many splendid collections which concern themselves with rocks and minerals. The Bohemian silver and lead mines pioneered techniques for extracting and processing ores which later spread all over Europe. The museums have much to tell us about this, and about the life and traditions of the mining communities. The rocks and ores themselves are often very beautiful and it needs no technical knowledge or interest to appreciate their appearance, or to enjoy a visit to one of the Museums of Stalactites. Mining and geological museums are a Czechoslovak speciality, but much attention is given to other kinds of industry as well. The most frequently represented in museum collections are glass, porcelain, textiles and iron, all products for which Czechoslovakia has long been famous. Shoemaking and wine also have interesting collections devoted to them.

Some of the most attractive museums are in former castles and châteaux, with which the western part of the country particularly is generously supplied. This kind of building provides a very suitable environment for the Czech hunting collections, which have a great reputation among connoisseurs, of stags' heads, stuffed wild boars and albino hares, and for the valuable furniture, tapestries and porcelain amassed by the aristocracy of the old Austro-Hungarian empire.

Museums in the former homes of distinguished people are much favoured, especially in the case of writers and musicians. The brothers Čapek, Dvořak, Smetana and Fibich, for example, are all commemorated by intimate museums of this kind.

Taken as a whole, the museums of Czechoslovakia reflect, inevitably, both the country's great cultural and international traditions - one thinks, for instance, of the collections devoted to Comenius - and its more recent political upheavals. There are many exhibits recalling the atmosphere and the details of the years of German occupation and, as the following list makes clear, numerous examples of museums of the Struggle against Fascism, museums of Socialist Construction, and collections illustrating the emergence of a particular district from capitalism to socialism. When one visits the museum in question, these descriptions sometimes turn out to be a little highly coloured and not always in strict accordance with the facts. One has to realise that in the Communist countries "history of the post-war period" would be regarded as sadly lacking in purposeful dynamism, just as "collections illustrating the national fight for full employment" would seem overdramatised in cynical, jaded Britain or America. The art of translation has to be constantly practised both ways across the Iron Curtain, to the benefit of all concerned.

Politics are not omnipresent, however. The Spa Museum at Pieštany contains, among other historical material, a collection of crutches left behind by patients who needed them when they arrived, but not when they went away.

ANTOL

FORESTRY AND HUNTING MUSEUM
Antol
In 18th century castle, with period rooms, including Marie Antoinette's room, brought from France. Development of the forestry and timber industries in Slovakia. Tools and equipment. Hunting weapons, equipment. Game animals, birds. Trophies.
Nov. 1-Mar. 15, M.-Sa. 7-4. Mar. 16-Oct. 31, M.-Sa. 7-5; Su., public holidays 9-5.

AŠ

MUNICIPAL MUSEUM
Mikulášska ulica č. 3, Aš
Mineralogy. Natural history. Textiles. Porcelain. Furniture. Exhibits illustrating the struggle against the German forces of occupation.
M.-F. 9-12, 2-5; Sa. 9-12.

BANSKÁ BYSTRICA

MUSEUM OF THE HISTORY OF SLOVAKIA
namestí Slovenského národného povstania, Banská Bystrica
In house (1479) known as House of King Matthias. Natura history, especially minerals, butterflies. Prehistory and his tory of the region. Religious art. Mining. Handicrafts. Cos

tumes. Folk art. History of the revolutionary and socialist movements in central Slovakia.
May-Oct., Tu.-Sa. 8-12, 1-4; Su. 9-12, 1-4. Nov.-Apr., Tu.-Su. 9-12, 1-4.

SLOVAKIAN MUSEUM OF THE NATIONAL RISING
Banská Bystrica
In Old Town Hall (1510). Collections illustrating the struggle against the German occupation, 1939-45.
May-Sept., Tu.-F. 7.30-12, 12.30-4.15. Sa. 7.30-3.30; Su. 8-2.

BANSKÁ ŠTIAVNICA

MINING MUSEUM
Banská Štiavnica
(a) in Trojiče námesti (Trinity Square). Geology. Mining models, equipment. Miners' handicrafts. Paintings of mining scenes. Coins. Medals.
(b) in Star zámek (the old Castle). Mining history. Ethnography. Weapons. Pipe-maker's workshop.
(c) in the Kammerhof. Mining techniques and machinery.
M.-Sa. 7-5; Su., public holidays 9-5.

BARDEJOV

MUSEUM OF URBAN HANDICRAFTS
Vila Rákoczi, Bardejov
Handicrafts and tools of urban craftsmen.
Tu.-Su. 8-12, 1-4.

OPEN-AIR MUSEUM OF FOLK-ARCHITECTURE
Bardejovských kúpelov, Bardejov
In park surrounding the Spa. Houses and other rural buildings from upper Šariš and Zemplin.
Tu.-Su. 8-12, 1-4.

ŠARIŠ MUSEUM
Radnica and Rhódino ulica, Bardejov
In 16th century Town Hall (Radnica): 15th-16th century religious art. 16th-18th century weapons, paintings, household equipment. Handicrafts, especially lace, pottery, glass, iron, locks, gold. Sculpture. Local history.
In Ródy ulice: Geology, botany, zoology of the region.
Tu.-Su. 8-12, 1-4.

BECHYNĚ

CERAMICS MUSEUM
Náměsti Rudé armády č. 140 Bechyně
Geology. Archaeology. Folk art. Local history. Bechyně ceramics.
May-Sept., daily 8.30-12.30, 1-5. Public holidays 9-12, 2-5.

BĚLÁ POD BEZDĚZEM

REGIONAL MUSEUM
Zámek č. 1, Bělá pod Bezdězem
Geology. Social and cultural history of the region. Ethnography.
By appointment.

BENÁTKY NAD JIZEROU

MUNICIPAL MUSEUM
Zámek č. 1, Benátky nad Jizerou
Geology, botany, ornithology of the region. Ethnography. Local history. Archaeology.
Tu.-F., Su. 8-12, 1-4; Sa. 8-12.

BEROUN

DISTRICT MUSEUM
1 Gottwaldovo nám. č. 87, Beroun
Mineralogy. Palaeontology. Archaeology. Local history.
May-Oct., Tu.-Su. 9-5; Nov.-Dec. 9-4.

BETLIAR

STATE PALACE
Betliar
18th century palace (with later modifications). Period rooms. 18th century library. Viennese, English and local furniture. Medieval - 19th century weapons. Hunting trophies. Slovakian, Egyptian, Roman antiquities. European paintings. Andrássy family portraits.
Apr.-Sept., daily 8-1, 2-6. Oct.-Mar., daily 9-12, 1-4.

BÍLÁ TŘEMEŠNÁ

JAN AMOS KOMENSKY (COMENIUS) MEMORIAL MUSEUM
č. 217, Bílá Třemešná
Collections illustrating life and work of J. A. Komensky, in his former home.
Daily 8-4.

BÍLINA

BÍLINA MUSEUM
Zámek, Bílina
Archaeology.
By appointment.

BÍLOVEC

MUNICIPAL MUSEUM
Zámecká ul. č. 5, Bílovec
Local history. Ethnography. Natural history.
M.-F. 9-4; Sa. 9-12.

BLANSKO

BLANSKO REGIONAL MUSEUM
Zámek, Blansko
Regional history. Folklore. Industry. Artistic cast-iron products from the local iron-works.
Tu.-F. 9-4; Sa. 9-3; Su. 9-5.

BLOVICE

DISTRICT MUSEUM
Tř. Rudé armády č. 148, Blovice
Archaeology. History. Literature.
M.-F. 8-5; Sa., Su. 10-12.

BOJKOVICE

LOCAL MUSEUM
Zámek Nový Světlov, Bojkovice
Geology. Zoology. Local history. Archaeology. Mining.
Tu.-Su. 9-12, 1-5.

BOJNICE

REGIONAL MUSEUM
Bojnice
In Bojnice Castle (13th century and later). Geology, archaeology and history of the Horná Nitra region. Guilds and crafts. Furniture. Contemporary Slovakian art.
Apr.-Oct., 8-4.

BOSKOVICE

REGIONAL MUSEUM
Zámek, Hradní ulica č. 42, Boskovice
Prehistory. Archaeology. Regional history and ethnography.
May-Oct., Tu.-Su. 9-5.

BOUZOV

REGIONAL CENTRE
Státní hrad Bouzov, Bouzov
Period rooms. Furnishings. Paintings, especially medieval. Handicrafts.
Apr.-Oct., daily 8-5.

BRANDÝS NAD LABEM-STANÁ BOLESLAV

PRAGUE-VÝCHOD DISTRICT MUSEUM
Zámek, Č. 402, Brandýs nad Labem-Staná Boleslav
Geology. Zoology. Prehistory. Archaeology. Ethnography.
May-Oct., M.-Th. 1-5; Sa., Su. 9-12, 1-5.

BRATISLAVA

ETHNOGRAPHICAL MUSEUM
Vajnory, Bratislava
Furniture. Household equipment.
Tu.-F. 10-5; Sa., 9-5.

J. N. HUMMEL MUSEUM
Klobučnická ulice 2, Bratislava
Life and work of the composer, J. N. Hummel, in the house where he was born. His spinet and piano. Scores. Medals. Death-mask.
Tu.-F. 10-5; Sa., Su. 9-5.

JANKO JESENSKÝ MUSEUM
Somolického ulice 4, Bratislava
Life and work of the writer, J. Jesenský, in his former home.
Tu.-F. 10-5; Sa., Su. 9-5.

MUNICIPAL MUSEUM
Stará radnica and Apponyiho palác, Bratislava
In the Stará radnica (old Town Hall): History of Bratislava, since prehistoric times. Furniture. Tools. Paintings. Religious art. Textiles. Musical and scientific instruments. History of law-enforcement.
In the Apponyiho palác (Apponyi Palace): History of wine-production. History of the Town Hall.
Tu.-F. 10-5; Sa., Su. 9-5.

MUSEUM OF PHARMACY
Michalska ulice 24, Bratislava
In 18th century Pharmacy, with original furnishings and equipment. Collections illustrating history of medicine and pharmacy.
Tu.-F. 10-5; Sa., Su. 2-5.

SLOVAKIAN NATIONAL MUSEUM: HISTORICAL COLLECTIONS
Hrad, Bratislava
In Bratislava castle. Prehistoric and Roman archaeology. Slovakian religious, political, social history from the medieval period to the present day. History of the workers' movement. Ceramics. Painted glass. Majolica. Folk-art.
Tu.-Su. 9-5.

SLOVAKIAN NATIONAL MUSEUM: NATURAL HISTORY COLLECTIONS
Vajanského nábrežié, Bratislava
Geology, palaeontology, petrography, botany, zoology and anthropology of Slovakia.
Tu.-Su. 9-5.

BŘECLAV-POHANSKO

POHANSKO ARCHAEOLOGICAL MUSEUM
Zámek, Břeclav-Pohansko
Pottery and other prehistoric material from local excavations, especially at Pohansko.
Apr.-Oct., Tu.-Su. 9-4.

BŘEZNICE

MUNICIPAL MUSEUM AND LUDVÍKA KUBA GALLERY
Zámek, Březnice
Archaeology. Local and natural history. Ethnography. Paintings by Ludvíka Kuba.
May-Sept., Tu.-Su. 8-12, 1-6. Apr., Oct., Tu.-Su. 9-12, 1-4.

BRNO

MORAVIAN MUSEUM: ANTHROPOLOGICAL MUSEUM
Pisárky, Brno
Palaeontology and anthropology collections relating to Moravia.
Tu.-Su. 8.30-5.

MORAVIAN MUSEUM: BOTANICAL AND ENTOMOLOGICAL COLLECTIONS
Preslova ul. č. 1, Brno
Plants and insects of Moravia. Entomological collections also from New Guinea, Afghanistan, Cuba.
Tu.-Su. 8.30-5.

MORAVIAN MUSEUM: ETHNOGRAPHICAL COLLECTIONS
Gagarinova tř. č. 1, Brno
Archaeology. Ethnography. Agricultural implements, techniques.
Tu.-Su. 8.30-5.

MORAVIAN MUSEUM: GREGOR MENDEL MEMORIAL MUSEUM
Nám. G. Mendela, Brno
History of the science of genetics, and of Mendel's contribution to it.
Tu.-Su. 8.30-5.

MORAVIAN MUSEUM: MUSICAL COLLECTIONS
Smetanova ul. č. 14, Brno
Musical instruments. Manuscripts. Portraits. Documents.
Tu.-Su. 8.30-5.

MORAVIAN MUSEUM: NATURAL HISTORY AND HISTORY COLLECTIONS
Nám 25, února č. 8 and Kapucínské nam., Brno
Geology. Palaeontology. Mineralogy. Petrography. Zoology. Prehistory. History. Coins.
Tu.-Su. 8.30-5.

MUSEUM OF THE CITY OF BRNO
Hrad 1, Brno
Social and cultural history of Brno. Paintings. Drawings. Prints. Furniture. Porcelain. Faience. Costumes. Plans and documents illustrating growth of the city.
Apr.-Sept., daily 7.30-5. Oct.-Mar., daily 8.30-5.

MUSEUM OF HISTORICAL MOVEMENTS
Nám. Rudé armády c. 1A, Brno
Collections illustrating Czech movements for national liberation, from Hus onwards.
M.-Sa. 8-5; Su. 8-12.

TECHNICAL MUSEUM
Ortí ul. č. 20 (offices, library, meeting rooms) and, Josefská ul. č. 1 (museum), Brno
Historical collections specialising in the production of energy. Water-power, including Kaplan turbines. Internal combustion engines. Electricity.
Tu.-Th., Su. 9-6; F. 9-5; Sa. 9-3.

BROUMOV

REGIONAL MUSEUM
Býv. klášter gymnasium č. 1, Broumov
Natural history and history of the Broumov region. Ethnology.
May-Sept., Tu.-Su. 8-12, 1-5.

BRUNTÁL

REGIONAL MUSEUM
Zámek, Bruntál
Natural history and history of the Bruntál region.
Tu.-Su. 8-12, 1-5.

BUČOVICE

MUNICIPAL MUSEUM
Zámek, Bučovice
Local mineralogy, archaeology, history, folklore. Paintings. Ceramics. Natural history.
Tu.-F. 9-12, 2-4; Sa. 9-12; Su. 9-12, 1.30-5.

BUDYNĚ NAD OHŘÍ

MUNICIPAL MUSEUM
Náměstí, Zámek, Budyně nad Ohří
Palaeontology. Archaeology. Folk art. Natural history.
Th.-Tu. 8-11, 2-5.

BYSTŘICE NAD PERNŠTEJNEM

MUNICIPAL MUSEUM
Náměstí, Bystřice nad Pernštejnem
Local history. Natural sciences. Natural history.
Tu.-Su. 8-5.

ĆÁSLAV

MUNICIPAL MUSEUM
Ul. Protifašist, bojovníkú čp. 291, Čáslav
Geology. Mineralogy. Botany. Zoology. Local archaeology, history. coins. Porcelain. Industrial ceramics.
Tu.-Sa. 9-5; Su. 9-12.

ČÁSLAVICE

DR. BEDŘICH VÁKLAV MEMORIAL MUSEUM
Č. 23, Čáslavice
Collections illustrating life and work of Dr. Váklav, in his former home.
Daily 8-3.

ČECHY POD KOSÍŘEM

JOSEF MÁNESA MEMORIAL MUSEUM
Zámek, Čechy pod Kosírem
Collections illustrating life and work of the painter, Josef Mánesa, in his former home.
Apr.-Oct., daily 8-3.

ČELÁKOVICE

MUNICIPAL MUSEUM
Tirz, Čelákovice
Local archaeology, history. Plants and wildlife of the region. Paintings by local artists.
May-Oct., Th.-Su. 9-12, 2-5.

ČELČICE

ČELČICE MUSEUM
Čelčice
Mineralogy. Archaeology. Local history.
By appointment.

ČERVENÝ HRÁDEK

MEMORIAL TO THE STRUGGLE AGAINST FASCISM
Státni zámek, Červený Hrádek
Exhibits recalling the agreement between Henlein and Lord Runciman (1938) over the Sudetenland, and the subsequent resistance movement under the German occupation.
Sa. 1-5; Su. 9-12, 1-5.

ČERVENÝ KAMEŇ

MUSEUM OF FURNITURE
Červený Kameň
In 16th century castle. 16th century Italian furniture. Italian, Persian, Chinese, German majolica. Hunting weapons. Portraits of Turkish sultans.
Tu.-Su. 8-5.

ČERVENÝ KLÁŠTOR

MONASTERY MUSEUM
Červený Kláštor
Carthusian Monastery (1319). History of the monastery. Religious art. Furniture. Natural history and ethnography, especially costumes, crafts of the Piening region. Agriculture.
Tu.-Su. 8-12, 2-6.

ČERVENÝ KOSTELEA

BOŽENA NEMCOVA MEMORIAL MUSEUM
Červený Kostelea
Memorial of the writer, Božena Nemcova and of her residence in Červený Kostelea.
By appointment.

ČESKÁ LÍPA

REGIONAL MUSEUM
Komenského nám. č. 297, Česká Lípa
Natural history. Local history. Handicrafts.
Tu.-Su. 9-4.

ČESKA SKALICE

BOŽENY NÉMCOVA MUSEUM
Museum: Česka Skalice 11; School: Ul. Boženy Némcové, Česka Skalice
Local history. Paintings by local artists. Porcelain. Collections illustrating life and work of the writers, Boženy Némcova and Václava Řesnícka. 100 year-old school building, with collections illustrating its history.
Museum: Apr.-Sept., Tu.-Sa. 8-5; Su. 7-5.
School: Apr.-Sept., Tu.-Sa. 8-12, 2-5; Su. 7-12, 1-5.

ČESKÁ TŘEBOVÁ

MUNICIPAL MUSEUM
Náměsti, býv. radnice, Česká Trebová
Local history. Handicrafts. Pottery. Paintings showing the town.
W. 1-4; Th.-Sa. 9-12.

ČESKE BUDĚJOVICE

MUSEUM OF SOUTHERN CZECHOSLOVAKIA
Dukelská č. 1, Česke Budějovice
Geology. Mineralogy. Botany. Archaeology. Ethnography. Local history. Coins. Drawings, prints by local artists. Regional literature.
Tu.-Su. 9-5.

ČESKÝ BROD

MUSEUM OF LOWER LIPAN
Ulice 5, kvetna č. 761, Český Brod
Local archaeology, natural history, ethnography.
Tu.-F. 9-4; Sa., Su. 9-12, 1-4.

ČESKÝ DUB

KAROLINY SVĚTLÉ MUSEUM
č. 31/IV, Český Dub
Geology. Mineralogy. Archaeology. Local history. Costumes. Ornaments. Collections illustrating literary history of Czechoslovakia.
Daily 9-4.

ČESKÝ KRUMLOV

REGIONAL MUSEUM
Horní ul. č. 152, Český Krumlov
Geology. Mineralogy. Palaeontology. Archaeology. Local history. Ethnology. Folk art. Gothic and Renaissance sculpture.
Tu.-Su. 9-12, 1-4.

ČESKÝ TĚŠIN

REGIONAL CENTRE
Revoluční ul. 13, Český Těšin
Local history. Ethnography. Natural history. Furniture. Handicrafts. Costumes.
M.-Sa. 8-4.

CHEB

REGIONAL MUSEUM
Nám. krále Jiřího z Poděbrad č. 3, Cheb
Natural history, especially ornithology. Regional archaeology, history. Sculpture. History of the Resistance Movement.
M.-F. 9-5; Sa. 9-12.

CHLUM

MUSEUM OF THE WAR OF 1866
Č. 66, Chlum
Mementoes of the Austro-Prussian War and of the Battle of Hradec Králové.
Daily 9-5.

CHLUMEC NAD CIDLINOU

MUSEUM OF THE PEASANTS' REVOLT AND V. K. KLICPERA MEMORIAL
Zámek, Chlumec nad Cidlinou
Local history. History of the Peasants' Revolt. Collections illustrating development of the regional theatre. Life and work of V. K. Klicpera.
By appointment.

CHLUMEC U ÚSTÍ NAD LABEM

LOCAL MUSEUM
Chlumec u Ústí nad Labem
Botany. Ornithology. Entomology. Palaeontology. Archaeology. Ethnography.
By appointment.

CHOCERADY

LOCAL MUSEUM
č. 24, Chocerady
Local history.
By appointment.

CHOELŃ

ORLICKÝ MUSEUM
Zámek, Stalingradské nábřeží, Choelň
Palaeontology. Ornithology. Entomology. Archaeology. Ethnography. History of the Resistance Movement, 1939-45.
Su., public holidays 9-12. Other times by appointment.

CHOMUTOV

REGIONAL MUSEUM
Náměsti 1, máje č. 1, Chomutov
Geology. Mineralogy. Archaeology. 16th-18th century sculpture. Lace.
Tu.-F. 9-5; Sa. 9-12.

CHOTĚBOŘ

MUNICIPAL MUSEUM
Riegrova ul. č. 1 - zámek, Chotěboř
Regional geology, mineralogy. Local history.
May-Oct., Tu.-Su. 10-3. Nov.-Apr., Tu.-Su. 10-2.

JINDŘICH PRUCHY GALLERY
Riegrova ul. č. 1 - zámek, Chotěboř
Paintings, graphics, sculpture by Jincřich Pruchy, Zděňky Rykry and Karl Opatrny.
May-Oct., Tu.-Su. 10-3. Nov.-Apr., Tu.-Su. 10-2.

CHRAST U CHRUDIMÉ

MUNICIPAL MUSEUM
Gottwaldovo nám č. 1 - zámek, Chrast u Chrudimé
Geology. Mineralogy. Local history. Handicrafts. Paintings.
May-Oct., Su., public holidays 9-12, 2-5. Other times by appointment.

CHROPYNÉ

DR. EMIL AXMAN MEMORIAL
Zámek, náměstí č. 30, Chropyně
Local history, ethnography. Emil Filly room. History and development of Chropyně.
On request.

CHRUDIM

REGIONAL MUSEUM
Chrudim IV, Obránců míru 86, Chrudim
Geology. Mineralogy. Zoology. Archaeology. Ethnography. Local history.
Tu.-F. 7.30-4; Sa. 8.30-12; Su. 9-12, 2-4.

CHUDENICE

JOSEF DOBROVSKY AND JAROSLAV KVAPILA MUSEUM
Stary zámek, Chudenice
Local history. Memorabilia of the writers and patriots, Jaroslav Kvapila and Josef Dobrovsky.
Sa., Su., public holidays 10-12, 2-5. Other times by appointment.

DAČICE

MUNICIPAL MUSEUM
Býv. klášter, Jemnická ul. 21, Dačice
Local and regional archaeology, history. 16th century European paintings. 20th century Czech. paintings, graphics, especially by Max Svabinsky and Michael Florian.
Tu.-Su. 9-11, 1-4.

DAŠICE

JOSEF HYBEŠE MEMORIAL MUSEUM
č. 2, Dašice
Memorial collection illustrating life and work of the politician and workers' leader, Josef Hybeše.
By appointment.

DĚČÍN

DISTRICT MUSEUM
IV tř Československé mládeže 1-31, Děčín
Natural history, especially geology, entomology. Paintings. Sculpture. Graphics. Furniture. Porcelain. Pottery. Musical instruments. Relics and history of the German concentration camp at Rabštejn.
Tu.-Su. 9-12, 1-5. Concentration camp buildings: Apr.-Sept., W. 9-1, Sa., 1-5, Su. 10-5.

DĚDICE U VYŠKOVA

KLEMENT GOTTWALD HOUSE-MUSEUM
Revoluční 16-102, Dědice u Vyškova
Collections illustrating life and work of Klement Gottwald, in his former home.
Tu.-Su. 8-6.

DIVÁKY

MEMORIAL MUSEUM TO THE MRŠTÍKŮ BROTHERS
Č. 57, Diváky
Life and writings of the Mrštíků brothers, in their former home. Original furnishings.
May-Oct., Tu.-Su. 9-4.

DOBŘÍŠ

MUNICIPAL MUSEUM
Dvořákova č. 275 a náměstí č. 68, Dobříš
Local history. Ethnography. Folk art.
On request.

DOBŘÍV

FORGE MUSEUM
Dobřív
Forge, with water-driven hammer, c.1702. Museum describing history and working of the forge.
May-Sept., Sa., Su. 10-4. Other times by appointment.

DOBRUŠKA

MUNICIPAL MUSEUM
Šubertovo náměstí č. 53, Dobruška
Local and regional history. Exhibits illustrating political development of the area and leading personalities associated with it.
Tu.-Su. 8-12, 1-4.

DOKSY

DISTRICT MUSEUM
Lípove náměstí č. 150, Doksy
Books published by K. H. Máchy. Local history. Paintings, drawings of local scenes.
Daily 9-5.

DOLÍNEK

VÍTEZSLAV HÁLEK MEMORIAL MUSEUM
Býv. hostinec, Dolínek
In former inn. Collections illustrating life and work of Czech. writers, especially Vítezslav Hálek.
By appointment.

DOLNI DOMASLOVICE

DOMASLOVICE AND DISTRICT MUSEUM
Skolo u kostela, Dolni Domaslovice
Local history. Ethnography. Costumes. Furniture. Handicrafts.
June-Aug., W., Su. 9-1. Other times by appointment.

DOLNÝ KUBÍN

P.O. HVIEZDOSLAVA MUSEUM
Čaplovičovej knižnice, Dolný Kubín
In Čaplovic Library. Life and work of the writer, P. O. Hviezdoslava.
Tu.-Sa. 8-4; Su. 8-2.

DOMAŽLICE

DOMAŽLICE MUSEUM
Chodské náměsti č. 96 - Chodský hrad, Domažlice
History of Domažlice. Regional ethnography. Furnished interiors. Paintings.
May-Sept., 8-12, 1-5. Oct.-Apr., 10-12, 1-3.

JINDŘICHA JINDŘICHA MUSEUM
Dolejsi předm. č. 61 (náměsti Svobody), Domažlice
Regional ethnography, handicrafts. Furniture. Costumes. Pottery. Coins. Paintings by regional artists. Literary and musical manuscripts.
By appointment.

DUCHOV

MANOR HOUSE MUSEUM
Zámek, Duchov
Local history. Paintings. Graphics. Memorial collection to the organist and composer, Narciso Casanovas (d.1799).
Tu.-Su. 8-11, 1-3.

DVUR KRÁLOVÉ NAD LABEM

TEXTILE MUSEUM
Nejedlého ul. 1029, Dvur Králové nad Labem
History of textile manufacturing in Czechoslovakia.
Daily 9-5.

FIL'AKOVO

MUNICIPAL MUSEUM
Fil'akovo
In former Franciscan monastery (16th century). Local archaeology, history. 16th century Turkish weapons.
Tu.-Sa. 10-4; Su. 10-2.

FRANTIŠKOVY LÁZNĚ

MUNICIPAL MUSEUM
Ul. Dr. Pohoreckého č. 8, Františkovy Lázně
Local history.
M.-F. 9-12, 2-5.

FRENŠTÁT POD RADHOŠTĚM

MUNICIPAL MUSEUM
Nám míru č. 1, radnica, Frenštát pod Radhŏstĕm
Local history. Folk art. Folklore. Natural history.
M.-F., Su. 9-4; Sa. 8-12.

FRÝDEK-MÍSTEK

REGIONAL MUSEUM
Zámek, Frýdek-Místek
Regional natural history, history, ethnography. Folk art.
Tu.-F. 8-4; Su. 1-5. Sa. by appointment.

FRÝDLANT V ČECHÁCH

MUNICIPAL MUSEUM
Náměsti, radnice, Frýdlant v Čechách
Geology. Botany. Local history. Furniture. Pottery. Handicrafts. Collection illustrating the Peasants' Revolt of 1679.
Daily 8-5.

FULNEK

JAN AMOS KOMENSKY (COMENIUS) MEMORIAL
Storová ulica č. 1, býv. Bratrský sbor, Fulnek
Collection of documents, books, photographs and personal possessions illustrating the life and work of J. A. Komensky (Comenius).
Oct.-Mar., Su. 8-12. Other times by appointment. Apr.-Sept., M., W., F. 9-4; Su. 8-12.

GELNICA

MINING MUSEUM
Gelnica
Minerals. Development and techniques of the local mining industry. History of Gelnica.
Tu.-Su. 10-4.

GOTTWALDOV

GOTTWALDOV MUSEUM OF SOUTHERN MORAVIA
Soudni ulica č. 1, Gottwaldov
Geology. Zoology. Entomology. Ethnography. Archaeology. Local history. Emergence of the district from capitalism to socialism.
M.-F. 9-12, 1-5; Sa., Su. 9-12.

MUSEUM OF SHOE-MAKING
Svit, Gottwaldov
History of shoe-making. Footwear collections. Manufacturing techniques.
M.-F. 7-3; Sa., Su. by appointment.

HAVÍŘOV

MUSEUM OF SOCIALIST CONSTRUCTION
Havírov IV, Bl. 63, Havířov
History and development of the district.
Daily 8-12, Tu.-F. also 1-3.

HAVÍŘOV-ŽIVOTICE

MUSEUM OF THE STRUGGLE AGAINST FASCISM
Havírov XI - Životice (zaňek), Havířov-Životice
History of the German occupation and local resistance movement.
Tu.-F. 8-12, 1-3.

HAVLÍČKOVA BOROVA

KARL HAVLÍCKY BOROVSKY MEMORIAL
čp. 163, Havlíckova Borova
Collections illustrating life and work of K. H. Borovsky, in his former home.
Tu.-Su. 8-12, 2-6.

HAVLÍČKŮV BROD

KARL HAVLÍCKY BOROVSKY MEMORIAL
Nám čs. armady č. 19, Havlíckuv Brod
Collections illustrating life and work of K. H. Borovsky.
May-Sept., Tu.-Su. 8-12, 1-4. Oct.-Apr., Tu.-F. 8-12, 1-4; Sa., Su. by appointment.

OTAKAR ŠTÁFLY MEMORIAL
Havlíckovy sady-basťa, Havlíčkuv Brod
Collections illustrating life and work of the painter, Otakar Štáfly.
May-Sept., Tu.-Su. 8-12, 1-5.

HLINSKO

REGIONAL MUSEUM AND ART GALLERY
Havlíckova 675, Hlinsko
Geology. Mineralogy. Regional history, ethnography, archaeology. Folk art. Textiles. Pottery. Paintings. Sculptures.
M.-Sa. 9-12, 1-4; Su. 9-12.

HLUBOKÁ NAD VLTAVOU

MUSEUM OF THE COUNTRYSIDE
Zámek Ohrada, Hluboká nad Vltavou
Forestry and timber. Lumbering. Fishing. Hunting. Birds. Insects. Animals.
Apr.-Oct., Tu.-Sa. 8-5.

HODONÍN

DISTRICT MUSEUM
Zámecké náměsti 9 - zámeček, Hodonín
Local history, ethnography, natural history.
Daily 8-4.

HODSLAVICE

FRANTIŠEK PALACKY MEMORIAL
č. 108, Hodslavice
Life and work of Palacky, in his former home.
Daily 7-7.

HOLEŞOV

MUNICIPAL MUSEUM
Zámek, Richtrovo náměsti 190, Holešov
Local archaeology, history. Ethnography. Paintings.
Tu.-F. 8-3; Sa. 9-12; Su. 9-12.

HOLICE V ČECHÁCH

AFRICA MUSEUM; DR. EMIL HOLUB MEMORIAL
Kulturni dům, Holubova ulica 1/768, Holice v Čechách
Natural history. Art and ethnography of Africa, based on the collections of the explorer and travel-writer, Emil Holub (d.1902).
Apr.-Oct., Tu.-Su. 9-12, 1-4.

HORAŽĎOVICE

REGIONAL MUSEUM
Zámek, Horažďovice
Geology. Mineralogy. Local history, archaeology, ethnography.
Su., public holidays, by appointment.

HORNÍ BRANNÁ

JAN AMOS KOMENSKY (COMENIUS) MEMORIAL MUSEUM
Zámek, Horní Branná
Collections illustrating the life and work of Komensky.
By appointment.

HORNI PLANÁ

ADALBERT STIFTER MEMORIAL
Horni Planá
Collections illustrating life and work of Stifter, in his former home.
On request.

HOŘOVICE

MUNICIPAL MUSEUM
11 č. 1, tzu. novy zámek, Hořovice
Geology. Palaeontology. Mineralogy. Zoology. Archaeology. Renaissance, Baroque, Empire and Czech furniture. Ethnography.
Apr.-Aug., Tu.-Su. 8-12, 2-6. Sept.-Oct., Tu.-Su. 9-12, 2-4. Other times by appointment.

HORŠOVSKY TÝN

REGIONAL MUSEUM
Zámecký park č. 5, Horšovsky Týn
Local history and archaeology. Natural history. Ethnography. Handicrafts. Coins.
May-Sept., daily 8-5. Oct.-Apr., Daily 9-4.

HOSTINNÉ

MUSEUM OF ANTIQUE ART
Byv františkánský kostel, Hostinné
Greek and Roman sculpture and casts.
May-Sept., Tu.-Su. 9-12, 1-5.

HRADEC KRÁLOVÉ

REGIONAL MUSEUM: DEPARTMENT OF ARCHAEOLOGY AND HISTORY
Nabřeží protifašist bojovníků č. 465, Hradec Králové
Regional archaeology, history. History of the revolutionary movement. Ceramics. Illuminated manuscripts. Coins.
Tu.-F., Su. 9-12, 1-5; Sa. 9-12.

REGIONAL MUSEUM: DEPARTMENT OF NATURAL HISTORY
Husovo náměsti č. 124, Hradec Králové
Geology. Palaeontology. Mineralogy. Entomology. Zoology.
Tu.-F., Su. 9-12, 1-5; Sa. 9-12.

HRANICE NA MORAVĚ

MUSEUM OF CENTRAL MORAVIA
Janáčkova ul. č. 1, Hranice na Moravě
Geology. Zoology. Local archaeology and ethnography. Pewter. Ceramics. Coins. Faience.
W. 2-5; Su. 9-12. Other times by appointment.

HRONOV

JIRÁSKŮV MUSEUM
Náměsti, budova Jiráskova divadla, Hronov
Collections illustrating life and work of Aloise Jiráskův, in his former home. Local history. Natural history.
May-Sept., Tu.-Su. 8-12, 1-5.

HUDLICE

JOSEF JUNGMANN MEMORIAL
Rodný domek č. 43, Hudlice
Collections illustrating life and work of Jungmann, in his former home. Natural history.
Daily 8-5.

HUKVALDY

LEOŠ JANÁČEK MEMORIAL
č. 79, Hukvaldy
Collections illustrating history of music, especially life and work of Leoš Janáček.
Daily 8-4.

HUMPOLEC

DR. ALEŠE HRDLIČKY MUSEUM
Horní náměsti, Humpolec
Local history, ethnography. Anthropology. Textiles. Paintings. Coins.
Tu.-Sa. 9-11, 2-4; Su. 9-11.

HUSINEC

JAN HUS MEMORIAL
Rodný domek, Husinec
Life and work of Jan Hus, in his former home.
May 1 - Nov. 15, Tu.-Su. 8-12, 1-5.

HYNIČE-VRAŽNÉ

J. GREGOR MENDEL MEMORIAL
Č. 120, Hyniče-Vražné
Collections illustrating Mendel's life and work.
Daily 9-4.

IVANČICE

DISTRICT MUSEUM
Palackéhv nám č. 6, Ivančice
Archaeology. Local history. Ceramics. Ethnography. Paintings.
Daily 8-4.

JABKENICE

SMETANA MEMORIAL MUSEUM
Č. 32, Jabkenice
Collections illustrating life and work of Smetana.
May-Oct., Tu.-Su. 9-1, 2-6. Nov.-Apr., Tu.-Su. 9-1, 2-4.

JABLONEC NAD NISOU

MUSEUM OF GLASS AND JEWELLERY
Jiráskova ul. č. 4, Jablonec nad Nisou
16th-19th century European, especially Czech, glass, jewellery.
Tu.-Su. 8-4.

JÁCHYMOV

MUNICIPAL MUSEUM
Náměsti Republiky č. 37 - mincovna, Jáchymov
Geology. Mineralogy. Uranium and radium mining. Atomic energy. Local history. Early printed books. Library of 16th century Latin school at Jáchymov. History of the Spa.
May-Sept., Tu.-Sa. 9-12, 2-4; Su. 9-12. Oct.-Apr., M., Th. 9-12, 2-4; Tu., W., F. 9-12.

JAROMĚŘ

MUNICIPAL MUSEUM AND ART GALLERY
Husova tř. 295, Jaroměř
Archaeology. Ethnography. Collection illustrating life and work of O. Španiela. Paintings, sculpture by Španiela and A. J. Wágner. Local history. Coins.
Apr.-Oct., Tu.-F. 9-4; Sa. 9-12.

JAVOŘÍČKO

CAVE MUSEUM
Javořičko
Geological and prehistoric collection in the Javořičko caves.
Apr.-Oct., daily 8-5. Other months by appointment.

JEMNICE

JEMNICE MUSEUM
Náměsti svobody č. 31, Jemnice
Local history. Mining. Ceramics. Furniture. Handicrafts. Paintings by local artists.
June-Oct., Su., public holidays 9-12. Other times by appointment.

JEMNIŠTĚ U BENEŠOVA

DISTRICT MUSEUM
Zámek, pošta Postupice, Jemniště u Benešova
Geology. Archaeology. Local history and ethnography.
Apr.-Oct., Tu.-Su. 8-12, 1-5.

JESENICE U RAKOVNÍKA

JESENICE REGIONAL MUSEUM
Dům osvěty, Jesenice u Rakovníka
Archaeology. Local history. Ceramics.
W. 4-6; Su. 2-6, on request. July-Aug. daily 2-6.

JESENÍK

REGIONAL MUSEUM
Zámecké nam. č. 1, Jeseník
Geology. Mineralogy. Archaeology. Glass. Porcelain. Paintings on glass.
Apr.-Oct., Tu.-F. 10-12, 1-3; Sa., Su. 9-12, 1-3.

JIČÍN

DISTRICT MUSEUM
Gottwaldovo nám č. 1 - zámek, Jičín
Geology. Mineralogy. Archaeology. Local history. Ethnography.
M.-F. 8-4; Sa., Su. 8-12.

JIHLAVA

VYSOČINY MUSEUM
Nám Míru č. 57 a 58, Jihlava
Geology. Mineralogy. Regional history. Ethnography. Folk art.
Tu.-F. 9-5; Sa. 8-12, Su. 9-5.

JILEMNICE

KRKONOŠ MUSEUM
Býv. Havrachovský zámek, č. 75, Jilemnice
Geology. Period rooms. Furniture. Textiles. Costumes. Paintings by Fr. Kaván.
Tu.-F. 8-12, 2-6; Sa., Su. 8-12.

JILOVÉ U PRAHY

MUSEUM OF THE PRODUCTION AND PROCESSING OF GOLD
Náměsti č. 16, Jilové u Prahy
Local history, ethnography. Archaeology. History and techniques of the local mining industry.
May-Sept., W., Su. 9-12, 2-5.

JINDŘICHŮV HRODEC

REGIONAL MUSEUM
Balbínovo náměsti č. 19/1, Jindřichův Hrodec
Memorabilia of Smetana, Rákoczy, Destinovou. Paintings. Ethnography. Czech glass. Gothic and Baroque sculpture. Ceramics. Folk art.
Tu.-Su. 8-12, 1-5.

JUR PRI BRATISLAVE

PETRA JILEMNICKÝ MUSEUM
Jur pri Bratislave
Collections illustrating life and work of the writer, P. Jilemnický, in his former house.
Tu.-Su. 9-4.

KAČINA U NOVÝCH DVORŮ

MUSEUM OF AGRICULTURE
Zámek, Kačina u Nových Dvorů
Collections illustrating history of agriculture and horticulture in the region. Wine-production.
Tu.-Su. 8-5.

KADAŇ

MUNICIPAL MUSEUM
Náměsti č. 115, Kadaň
Local archaeology, history.
Th. 2-5; Su. 9-12, 2-5.

KAMENICE NAD LIPOU

REGIONAL MUSEUM
Palackého ul. 75, Kamenice nad Lipou
Mineralogy. Zoology. Local history. Ethnology. Furniture. Glass. Coins. History of partisan activities, 1939-45.
Daily 9-5.

KAMENICKÝ ŠENOV

MUSEUM OF GLASS
Ul. Osvobození č. 69, Kamenický Šenov
Czech. glass, 17th century - present day.
Tu.-Su. 8-4.

KARLOVY VARY

KARLOVY MUSEUM
Zámecký vrch č. 22, Karlovy Vary
Geology. Mineralogy. Petrography. Botany. Entomology. Local history. Drawings, prints by local artists.
Tu.-Su. 2-5.

KARL MARX MUSEUM
Ul. Karla Marxe č. 3, Karlovy Vary
Local history. Collections illustrating period spent by Marx in Karlovy Vary.
Tu.-Su. 9-12, 2-5.

KARLOVY VARY - BŘEZOV

MUSEUM OF KARLOVY PORCELAIN
Tovární ulice, Karlovy Vary - Březov
History of the porcelain factory at Březov. Collection of local porcelain.
M.-F. 8-3. Closed public holidays.

KARLOVY VARY - DVORY

MUSEUM OF GLASS
Tř. kapitána Jaroše 19, Karlovy Vary - Dvory
History and products of the former Moser glass factory.
M.-F. 7-3; Sa. 7-12. Closed public holidays.

KAŠPERSKÉ HORY

ŠUMAVY MUSEUM
Náměstí č. 140, Kašperské Hory
Natural history of the Sumavy region. Industry, especially mining, paper, glass. Sculpture. Paintings of local scenes. Local history. Folk art.
May-Sept., Daily 8-5. Oct.-Apr., M.-Sa. 8-4, by appointment, Su. 9-12.

KELČ

KELČ MUSEUM
Kelč
Palaeontology. Archaeology. Coins.
By appointment.

KEŽMAROK

MUNICIPAL MUSEUM
Kežmarok
In Tököly Castle. Local archaeology, ethnography, crafts. Pictures illustrating history of Kežmarok.
Tu.-Su. 9-4.

KLADNO

DISTRICT MUSEUM
Ulica Dělnického hnutí, Zámek č. 1, Kladno
Geology. Mineralogy. Archaeology. Ethnography. Fabrics. Prints. Posters.
Tu.-Su. 9-5.

KLÁŠTEREC NAD OHŘÍ

MUSEUM OF CZECH PORCELAIN
Státni zámek č. 1, Klášterec nad Ohří
18th-20th century Czech porcelain.
Tu.-Su. 8-12, 2-6.

KLATOVY

REGIONAL MUSEUM
Ul. dr. Karla Hostaše č. 1/IV, Klatovy
Geology. Mineralogy. Botany. Zoology. Ornithology. Regional prehistory, history. Medicine and pharmacy. Ethnography, including furnished interiors.
May-Sept., Tu.-F. 8-5; Sa. 8-12; Su. 9-12. Oct.-Apr., Tu.-F. 8-4.

KLENČÍ POD ČERCHOVEM

J. Š. BAAR MUSEUM
Nám Jindř Jinřicha č. 140, Klenčí pod Čerchovem
Local and regional history, ethnography. Collections illustrating life and work of J. S. Baar.
Apr.-Oct., daily 8-5.

KLOBOUKY U BRNA

MUNICIPAL MUSEUM
Zámek, Klobouky u Brna
Local history, ethnography. Paintings on glass. Costumes. Archaeology. Glass. Ceramics. Coins.
May-Oct., Tu., Th., Sa., Su. 10-12, 2-4. Other months and times by appointment.

KOJETIN

MARIE GARDAVSKA MUSEUM
Husovo ul. č. 64, Kojetin
Ceramics. Glass. Ethnography. Archaeology. Paintings.
Su. 10-12. Other times by appointment.

KOLÍN

REGIONAL MUSEUM
Nám Obránců míra č. 8 and Brandlova ul. č. 24,27,35, Kolín
Regional archaeology, history. Paintings. Ethnography. Coins.
Tu.-F. 9-4; Sa., Su. 9-12, 1-4.

KOMÁRNO

DANUBE MUSEUM
Komárno
In the Palace of Culture. Stone and Bronze Age material from local excavations.
Tu.-Su. 8-4.

MUSEUM OF RELIGIOUS ART
Ulice G. Steinera 32, Komárno
In Orthodox Church. Religious art. Liturgical objects.
Tu.-Su. 8-6.

PODUNAJSKA REGIONAL MUSEUM
Komárno
Archaeology, especially Roman. Sculpture. Terra sigilata. Glass. Pottery. Bronzes. Coins. History of the town and castle. Tartar and Turkish invasions. Crafts. Gold-extraction from the Danubian sands.
Tu.-Sa. 8-6.

KOMÁROV

MUSEUM OF IRON
Budova býv zámku, dnes pošty, Komárov
History of Komárov ironworks. Examples of their products. Artistic iron-work.
On request.

KOPLIDNA

MUSEUM COLLECTIONS
Ul. Fri. Hilmara č. 86, Koplidna
Regional archaeology, history. Coins.
By appointment.

KOPŘIVNICE

TECHNICAL MUSEUM
Janáčkovy sady č. 226, Kopřivnice
Local history, ethnography. History of automobiles and automobile engineering, with special reference to the Tatra works. Kopřivnice ceramics industry.
Apr.-Oct., daily 8-4. Nov.-Mar., Tu.-Su. 8-4.

KOŠICE

MUSEUM OF EASTERN SLOVAKIA
náměsti Maratónu mieru and Miklušova Väsnica, Košice
At náměsti Maratónu mieru: Geology. Mineralogy. Wildlife. Archaeology. Religious art. Handicrafts. Folk-art. In museum courtyard are 2 bell-towers and the wooden church from Kozuchoviec.
In Miklušova Väsnica: history of Košice.
Tu.-Su. 8-12, 2-6.

TECHNICAL MUSEUM
Leninova ulice 94, Košice
Metallurgy, including production of wrought-iron. Aviation. Railways. Telecommunications. Textile manufacture. Photography. Physics. Clock-making. Astronomy. Map-making. Mining. Water, steam and electric power.
Tu.-F. 9-5.30; Sa., Su. 8-1.

KOSTELEC NAD ČERNÝMI LESY

CENTRAL CZECHOSLOVAKIAN MUSEUM OF POTTERY AND CERAMICS
Náměsti č. 41, Kostelec nad Černými Lesy
Pottery and ceramics from central Czechoslovakia.
M.-F. 8-12, 1-4; Sa., Su. by appointment.

KOSTELNEC NA HANÉ

PETR BEZRUČ MEMORIAL
Bezručova ul. 256, Kostelnec na Hané
Collections illustrating life and work of the poet, Petr Bezruč.
May-Sept., daily 9-11.30, 1-5.30. Other months by appointment.

KOUŘIM

KOUŘIM MUSEUM
Náměsti č. 1, Kouřim
Geology. Palaeontology. Archaeology. Ethnography.
Tu.-F. 9-4; Sa., Su. 9-12, 1-4.

KOŽLANY

MUNICIPAL MUSEUM
Kožlany
Local history. Pottery. Memorabilia of President Beneš and other notabilities who lived in Kožlany.
By appointment.

KRÁLÍKY

MUNICIPAL MUSEUM
Náměstí čs. armády 365, Králíky
Regional history, ethnography.
By appointment.

KRÁLŮV DVŮR

LOCAL MUSEUM
Králův Dvůr
Geology. Palaeontology. Local history.
By appointment.

KRÁSNA HÔRKA

CASTLE MUSEUM
Krásna Hôrka
Furniture. 16th century weapons. Music room. Portraits of castle musicians and other servants. Stoves.
Apr.-Sept., 8-1, 2-6. Oct.-Mar., 9-12, 1-4.

KRAVAŘE

PALACE MUSEUM
Alejní č. 8, Kravaře
Building (1721-28). Period furniture. Open-air museum of ethnography.
Tu.-Su. 9-5.

KREČOVICE U SEDLČAN

JOSEF SUK MEMORIAL
Č. 3, Krečovice u Sedlčan
Memorabilia, personal possessions and furniture of Suk, in his former home.
Tu.-Su. 9-12, 2-5.

KREMNICA

MUNICIPAL MUSEUM
Hellensteinovský dom, náměsti I maja, Kremnica
History of Kremnica. Special exhibition illustrating the art of minting coins and medals.
M.-Sa. 8-4.

KRNOV

MUNICIPAL MUSEUM
Revolučné ul. č. 20, Krnov
Local archaeology, history. Ethnography. Textiles. Modern Czech paintings, graphics.
M.-Sa. 8-12, 1-5.

KROMĚŘÍŽ

DISTRICT MUSEUM
Státni zámek, Sněmovní ul. č. 1, Kroměříž
Archaeology. Ethnography. Porcelain. Pewter. Paintings. Coins.
Tu.-Su. 8-5.

KRUPKA

MUNICIPAL MUSEUM
Husitská 21, Krupka
Applied art. Weapons. Pewter.
W., F., Su. 9-12, 1-5.

KUBLOV

J. L. ZOONAŘA MEMORIAL
Č. 14, Kublov
Collection illustrating life and work of Josef Leopold Zoonařa.
By appointment.

KUTNÁ HORA

DISTRICT MUSEUM: JENEWEIN GALLERY
Vlašsky dvûr, Kutná Hora
Paintings by Felix Jenewein. Paintings, engravings, drawings of Kutná Hora.
Tu.-Su. 8-12, 1-5.

DISTRICT MUSEUM: HRADKU COLLECTIONS
Barboiská č. 28, Kutná Hora
History and techniques of local mining industry.
Tu.-Su. 8-12, 1-5.

DISTRICT MUSEUM: KAMENNÝ HOUSE
Náměsti 1, máje 183, Kutná Hora
Archaeological material from prehistoric settlements.
Tu.-Su. 8-12, 1-5.

DISTRICT MUSEUM: TYLA MEMORIAL
Tylova ulica č. 507, Kutná Hora
Life and work of J. K. Tyla.
Tu.-Sa. 8-12, 1-5.

KYJOV

LOCAL MUSEUM
Palackého ul. č. 70 - zámeček, Kyjov
Palaeontology. Botany. Entomology. Archaeology. Ethnography.
M.-F. 8-12, 1-4; Sa., Su. 10-12.

LANŠKROUN

MUNICIPAL MUSEUM
Zámek, Lanškroun
Geology. Palaeontology. Ethnology. Local history.
By appointment.

LÁZNĚ BĚLOHRAD

K. V. RAISE MEMORIAL
Zámek, Lázně Bělohrad
Collections illustrating life and work of Karl Vaclav Raise.
May-Sept., M.-F. 8-5; Su. 9-12. Other months by appointment.

LEDEČ NAD SÁZAVOU

MUNICIPAL MUSEUM
Hrad, Ledeč nad Sázavou
Local history. Ethnography. Ceramics.
July-Aug., daily 9-12, 2-5. Other months by appointment.

LEDNICE NA MORAVĚ

MUSEUM OF AGRICULTURE
Zámek, Lednice na Moravě
History and technique of agriculture, fruit-growing, vineyard cultivation. Agricultural products. Models of farm-buildings. Hunting.
Apr.-Oct., Tu.-Su. 8-4. Other months by appointment.

LEŠKOVICE

LOCAL MUSEUM
Býv. škola, č. 38, Leškovice
History of the partisan brigade led by M. J. Husa.
By appointment.

LETOHRAD

PETR JILEMNICKÝ MEMORIAL
Zámek, Letohrad
Collections illustrating the life and work of Jilemnický, in his former home.
By appointment.

LEVICE

TEKOV MUSEUM
Levice
In Levice Castle. Natural history, archaeology and history of the region. Ethnography. Paintings. Sculpture. Coins.
M.-F. 8-4; Sa. 8-1.

LEVOČA

SPIŠ MUSEUM
Radnice and Mäsiarska ulice 17, Levoča
In the old Town Hall. Collections illustrating history of Levoča. Weapons. In Mäsiarska ulice 17: Natural history. 18th century Spiš furniture. Paintings by local artists. Pewter. Copper. Clocks.
May-Oct., daily 8-12, 1-5. Nov.-Apr., daily 8.30-2.30.

LEŽÁKY

MUSEUM OF THE STRUGGLE AGAINST FASCISM
Ležáky
Display illustrating the Nazi massacre in Ležáky, June 24, 1942.
May-Sept., daily 8-6.

LIBÁŇ

LOCAL MUSEUM
Č. 96, Libáň
Local history.
By appointment.

LIBEREC

MUSEUM OF NORTHERN CZECHOSLOVAKIA
Liberec
Regional geology, zoology, entomology. History of Liberec, 17th century - 1945. European tapestries, glass, paintings, furniture, porcelain.
Tu.-Su. 9-5.

LIDICE

MEMORIAL TO THE TRAGEDY OF LIDICE
Lidice
History of Lidice. Photographs and other material illustrating the Nazi massacre and destruction.
Apr.-Sept., daily 8-4. Other months by appointment.

LIPNICE NAD SÁZAVOU

JAROSLAV HAŠK MEMORIAL
Č. 185, Lipnice nad Sázavou
Collections illustrating life and work of the satirist, Jaroslav Hašk.
Apr.-Oct., Tu.-Su. 9-12, 1-4. Feb.-Mar., Tu.-Su. 9-12, 2-4.

LIPNÍK NAD BEČVOU

ZÁHOŘÍ MUSEUM
Piaristický klášter and Bratrská 353, Lipník nad Bečvou
19th-20th century furnished interiors, with paintings, glass, ceramics, sculpture. Renaissance and Baroque paintings, sculpture.
May-Sept., Su. 9-12.

LIPOVÁ LÁZNĚ

REGIONAL MUSEUM
Lipová Lázně
Local history, including display illustrating the Hunger March of 1931. In nearby caves, stalactites.
Apr.-Oct., daily 8-5. Other months by appointment.

LIPTOVSKÝ MIKULÁŠ

PETER MICHAL BOHÚŇ GALLERY
Tranovská, Liptovský Mikuláš
Paintings, drawings, prints by Slovak artists.
M.-Sa. 7-4; Su. 9-3.

JANKO KRÁL MUSEUM OF LITERATURE
Liptovský Mikuláš
Collections illustrating literary past of the Liptov region, with material relating to writers who were born or who worked here.
M.-Sa. 7-4; Su. 9-3.

MUSEUM OF THE SLOVAKIAN LIMESTONE FORMATION
Liptovský Mikuláš
Exhibition showing distribution and characteristics of the limestone caverns. Dioramas of caverns, inhabited during the Neolithic and Palaeolithic periods. Archaeological material. Stalagmites and stalactites.
M.-Sa. 7-4; Su. 9-3.

LITEŇ

MEMORIAL TO THE MASSACRE AT LITEŇ AND TO V. B. TŘEBÍZSKY
Ulica liteňského zámku, tzo Čechovna, Liteň
Local history.
Su. 9-12, 1-5.

LITOMĚŘICE

DISTRICT MUSEUM
Mírové náměsti č. 171/40, Litoměřice
Geology. Mineralogy. Botany. Entomology. Local history. Ethnography. Handicrafts. Fruit-growing. Vineyard cultivation.
Tu.-Sa. 10-12, 1-5; Su. 9-5.

LITOMYŠL

DISTRICT MUSEUM
Jiráskova ulica č. 6, Litomyšl
Local history, archaeology, ethnography. Coins. Paintings. Posters. Educational history.
May-Sept., daily 8-5. Other months by appointment.

LITOVEL

REGIONAL MUSEUM
Ulica Boženy Němcové č. 199, Litovel
Local history. Litovel pottery.
W. 9-12, 1-3; Sa. 8-12, 1.30-3; Su. 9-12, 2-4.

LITVINOV

LOCAL MUSEUM
Tř. Sovětské armády č. 1, Litvinov
Geology. Botany. Entomology. Ethnography. Local history. Industries, especially textiles.
Tu.-F., Su. 2-5.

LOMNICE NAD POPELKOU

MUNICIPAL MUSEUM
Náměsti č. 43, Lomnice nad Popelkou
Local history. Ethnography. Textile industry.
Tu.-F. 8-11, 4-6; Sa. 9-12; Su. 2-6.

LOŠTICE

REGIONAL MUSEUM
Ulica muzea č. 8, Loštice
15th-19th century Loštice pottery. Local history.
Apr.-Oct., daily 10-12.

REGIONAL MUSEUM AND ADOLF KAŠPAR MEMORIAL
Palackého ul. č. 343, Loštice
Life and work of Adolf Kašpar, in his former home.
Apr.-Oct., daily 10-12, 1-5. Other months by appointment.

LOUNY

REGIONAL MUSEUM
Pivoskarská ul. č. 43, Louny
Geology. Archaeology. Ethnography. Local history.
Su.-F. 2-4.

LUKAVEC U PACOVA

ANTONÍN SOVY MEMORIAL
Zámek, Lukavec u Pacova
Collections illustrating life and work of the poet, Antonín Sovy.
By appointment.

LUŽANY U PŘEŠTIC

LOCAL MUSEUM
Zámek, Lužany u Přeštic
Collection of literature, music, paintings, graphics by local writers, artists and composers.
May-Sept., Tu.-Su. 9-11, 2-4.

LYSÁ NAD LABEM

MUSEUM OF ANCIENT ORIENTAL CULTURE
Náměsti Dr. Hrozného č. 265, Lysá nad Labem
Collections of oriental art, ethnography made by Dr. Bedrich Hrozný.
Su. 10-12.

MALEČ

FRANTIŠEK PALACKÝ AND FRANTIŠEK RIEGER MEMORIAL
Zámek, č. 1, Maleč
In former summer residence of Fr. Rieger and of his father-in-law, Fr. Palacký. Furniture. Library.
Tu.-Su. on request.

MALÉ SVATOŇOVICE

MUSEUM OF THE BROTHERS ČAPEK
Náměsti, Malé Svatoňovice
In former home of Karl Čapek. Collections illustrating life and work of Josef and Karl Čapek.
Daily 9-12, 1-6.

MANĚTÍN

REGIONAL MUSEUM
Zámek, Manětín
Local history. Paintings, sculpture by Czech artists, especially 18th century.
Su., public holidays 10-3. Other days by appointment.

MARIANSKÁ TYNICE-KRALOVICE

DISTRICT MUSEUM
Býv. klášter, Marianská Tynice - Kralovice
Archaeology. Ceramics. Folk art. Ethnography. Costumes. Collections illustrating life under the German occupation.
Daily 8-6.

MARIÁNSKE LÁZNĚ

MUNICIPAL MUSEUM
Gottwaldovo nám. č. 11, Mariánske Lázne
Geology. Mineralogy. Ethnography. Coins. Pewter. Porcelain. Goethe, Chopin and Gorki collections.
May-Oct., Tu.-Su. 10-12, 2-4. Nov.-Apr., Tu., Th., F., Su. 10-12, 2-4.

MARKUŠOVCE

MUSEUM OF FURNITURE
Markušovce
15th-19th century furniture by Slovakian makers. Portraits. Porcelain. Glass. Venetian mirrors.
Dec.-Mar., Tu.-Su. 8-12. Apr.-Nov. Tu.-Su. 8-12, 2-4.

MARTIN

SLOVAKIAN NATIONAL MUSEUM: ETHNOGRAPHICAL COLLECTIONS
Martin
Prehistory of Central and Western Slovakia. Collections illustrating the life and work of the Slovak people, 15th-20th centuries. Folk-art. Handicrafts. Costumes. Embroidery. Lace. Fabrics. Open-air museum, with buildings from the different regions of Slovakia.
May-Aug., daily 8-6. Sept.-Apr., daily 8-4.

MĚLNÍK

DISTRICT MUSEUM
Zámek, Mělník
Palaeontology. Archaeology. Ethnography. Industrial art. Exhibits illustrating local wine industry. Manuscripts of the politician and journalist, Viktor Dyk (d.1931).
By appointment.

MĚSTEC KRÁLOVE

MUNICIPAL MUSEUM
Náměsti, Městec Králove.
Archaeology. Handicrafts. Ethnography.
Su., public holidays 10-12.

MICHALOVCE

ZEMPLIN MUSEUM
Michalovce
In Sztáray Castle. Geology. Mineralogy. Botany. Zoology. Prehistory, history and economic development of the region. Religious art. Costumes. Agricultural implements. Pottery. History, equipment and techniques of wine-production.
Tu.-Sa. 9-4; Su. 9-1.

MIKULČICE

NATIONAL CULTURAL MEMORIAL
Mikulčice
Archaeological material from excavations at local Slavonic sites.
Apr.-Oct., Tu.-Su. 9-5.

MIKULOV

REGIONAL MUSEUM
Zámek, Mikulov
Geology. Mineralogy. Botany. Zoology. Archaeology. Local history. Ethnography. Coins. Medals. Ceramics. Glass. Porcelain. Paintings.
Apr.-Oct., Tu.-Su. 9-12, 1-5. Other times by appointment.

MILETÍN

KARL JAROMÍR ERBEN MEMORIAL
Ulica Barbory Cinkové č. 142, Miletín
Collections illustrating life and work of Erben in his former home. Local history, ethnography.
By appointment.

MILEVSKO

MUNICIPAL MUSEUM
č. 563, býv. klášter, Milevsko
Local archaeology, history. Handicrafts. Ethnography. Pottery.
Su.-F. 9-11.

MIROTICE

MIKOLÁŠ ALŠE MEMORIAL
Mirotice
Collections illustrating life and work of Alše.
Tu.-Su. 9-4.

MLADÁ BOLESLAV

DISTRICT MUSEUM
Českobratrské náměsti, Mladá Boleslav
Local history, archaeology. Ceramics. Glass. Coins. Ethnography.
Tu.-Su. 8-5.

MLADÁ VOŽICE

LOCAL MUSEUM
Žižkovo náměsti č. 190, Mladá Vožice
History of the town and district. Ethnography.
Su. 9-12.

MLADEČ

CAVE MUSEUM
Mladeč
Complex system of underground passages and caves. Prehistoric human and animal remains.
Apr.-Sept., daily 8-5.

MNICHOVO HRADIŠTĚ

MUNICIPAL MUSEUM
Státni zámek, Davidova ulica č. 148, Mnichovo Hradiště
Regional archaeology, history, ethnography. Sculpture. Collection illustrating local struggle against German occupation.
Apr.-Oct., Tu.-Sa. 8-12, 1-5; Su. 8-12, 1-5.

MOHELNICE

LOCAL MUSEUM
Kostelní náměsti č. 3, Mohelnice
Local archaeology, history.
Apr.-Oct. Th., Su. 10-12, 1-3.

MORAVSKÁ TŘEBOVA

MUNICIPAL MUSEUM
Třída Osvoboditelů 281, Moravská Třebova
Paintings. Oriental and Czech textiles. Handicrafts. Coins.
Tu. 8-12; W.-Sa. 8-12, 1.30-3.30; Su. 9-11.30, 2.30-3.30.

MORAVSKÉ BUDĚJOVICE

MUSEUM OF WESTERN MORAVIA
Zámek, náměsti, Moravské Budějovice
Regional handicrafts, especially weaving, mother-of-pearl work, file-making, stove-making, pottery, wrought-iron, furniture-making, dyeing, saddlery.
On request.

MORAVSKÝ KRUMLOV

MUNICIPAL MUSEUM
Hlavní náměsti č. 321, Moravský Krumlov
Collections illustrating Paracelsus at Moravský Krumlov. Prehistory of the region.
Apr.-Oct., on request.

MOST

DISTRICT MUSEUM
Švermova ulica č. 187, 188, 216, Most
Geology. Archaeology. Local history. Mining. Coins.
Tu. 2-5; Sa. 9-1.

MŠENO

J. L. PÍČE MEMORIAL MUSEUM
Mšeno
Collections illustrating life and work of the historian and archaeologist, Josef Ladislav Píce.
May-Sept., on request.

NÁCHOD

DISTRICT MUSEUM
Státni zámek, Náchod
Archaeology. Ethnography. Glass. Ceramics. Coins. Paintings.
Apr. 1-30, Sept. 1- Oct. 31, Tu.-Su. 9-12, 1-4. May-Aug. Tu.-Su. 8-12, 1-5.

NÁCHOD GALLERY
Státní zámek, Náchod
19th-20th century Russian paintings. 19th-20th century Czech paintings, graphics.
Apr., Sept.-Oct., Tu.-Su. 9-12, 1-4. May-Aug., Tu.-Su. 8-12, 1-5.

NÁMEŠŤ NA HANÉ

REGIONAL MUSEUM
Zámek, Náměšt na Hane´
18th century rooms. 19th century Czech paintings. Historical collection relating to the bishops and archbishops of Olomouci.
Apr.-Oct., daily 8-5.

NELAHOZEVES

ANTON DVOŘÁK MUSEUM
Proti nádrazí č. 12, Nelahozeves
Collections relating to the composer, Anton Dvořak, in his former home.
W., Th., Sa.-M. 9-12, 2-5.

NEPOMUK

LOCAL MUSEUM
Přesanické náměsti č. 1, Nepomuk
History of the town and district. 18th century paintings, sculpture. Collections illustrating life and work of the painter, Augustin Němejcld, (d.1938).
May-Sept., Su., public holidays 9-11.

NETOLICE

MUNICIPAL MUSEUM
Náměsti č. 248, Netolice
Archaeology. Local history. Ethnography.
May 15- Oct. 31, W.-Su. 9-12, 2-3.30.

NETVOŘICE

MUNICIPAL MUSEUM
č. 46, Netvořice
Archaeology. Local history. Ceramics.
Mar. 15- Nov. 15, daily 9-5. Other times by appointment.

NITRA

AGRICULTURAL MUSEUM
Nitra
In former Franciscan monastery (17th century). History of agriculture and horticulture in Slovakia. Implements and implement-makers' workshops. Cultivation techniques. Crops. Farm animals. Bee-keeping. Fruit-growing.
Tu.-Su. 8-4.

NOVÁ PAKA

MUSEUM OF GEM-STONES
Náměsti, budova MNV, Nová Paka
Regional geology. Display of local semi-precious stones.
Apr.-Oct., Tu.-Su. 8-5. Other months by appointment.

REGIONAL MUSEUM
Suchardova ulica č. 68, Nová Paka
Local and regional history. Mineralogy.
By appointment.

NOVÉ MEŠTA NA MORAVĚ

HORÁKÉ MUSEUM AND ART GALLERY
Náměsti Dr. I. Sekaniny 114, Nové Mešta na Moravě
Regional history, ethnography.
Daily 8-4.

NOVÉ MESTO NAD VÁHOM

MUSEUM OF THE LOWER JAVA
Nové Mesto nad Váhom
In 1740 house. Natural history. Local history. Ethnography.
M., W.-Sa. 8-4; Su. 8-12.

NOVÉ STRAŠECÍ

REGIONAL MUSEUM
Č. 123, Nové Strašecí
Local archaeology, history, folk art. Ethnography.
Su., W. 9-12.

NOVÝ BOR

MUSEUM OF GLASS
Náměstí míru Č. 105, Nový Bor
History, technology and products of local glass industry, including optical glass.
Tu.-Su. 9-12, 1-6.

NOVÝ BYDŽOV

MUNICIPAL MUSEUM
Mírové náměstí č. 2, Nový Bydžov
Local and regional history, ethnography.
May-Oct., Su. 10-12. Other times by appointment.

NOVÝ JIČIN

DISTRICT MUSEUM
Ulica 28 řijna č. 12, Nový Jičin
Mineralogy. Palaeontology. Entomology. Botany. Ornithology. Zoology. Archaeology. History. Ethnography. Rural architecture. Peasant handicrafts. Folk art. Paintings. History of the German occupation.
Su.-F. 9-4; Sa. 8-12.

MUSEUM OF HAT-MAKING
Ulica 28 řijna č. 12, Nový Jičin
History and products of the local hatting industry.
Su.-F. 9-4; Sa. 9-12.

MUSEUM OF LIGHTING AND REFRIGERATION
Ulica 28 řijna č. 12, Nový Jičin
History of lighting and refrigeration, including products from local factories.
Su.-F. 9-4; Sa. 9-12.

NYMBURK

REGIONAL MUSEUM
Eliščina tř. 154/22, Nymburk
Regional botany, entomology, zoology. Archaeology. Ethnography. Ceramics.
W. 9-4; Sa. 9-12; Su. 9-12.

OBŘÍSTVÍ

BEDŘICH SMETANA MEMORIAL MUSEUM
Obříství
Collection illustrating life and work of the composer, Bedřich Smetana.
By appointment.

OLOMORIC

REGIONAL ART GALLERY
Hynaisova č. 13, Olomoric
19th-20th century drawings, prints by Czech artists.
Tu.-Su. 9-5.

OLOMOUC

ART GALLERY
Náměsti Rudé armády č. 7, Olomouc
16th-18th century European paintings, drawings, sculpture. 19th-20th century Czech paintings, graphics.
Tu.-Sa. 11-5, Su. 9-12.

GALLERY OF FINE ART
Hynaisova ulica č. 13, Olomouc
19th-20th century Czech paintings. 15th-17th century European paintings.
Tu.-Sa. 9-5; Su. 9-12.

REGIONAL MUSEUM
Náměsti Republiky 5/6, Olomouc
Geology. Petrography. Palaeontology. Botany. Entomology. Zoology. Regional archaeology, history, ethnography. Paintings. Coins.
Tu.-Su. 9-5.

OLOMUČANY

CERAMICS MUSEUM AND MUSEUM OF THE WORKERS' MOVEMENT
MNV č. 123, Olomučany
Ceramics, mainly 19th century, produced at the local factory. History of the local workers' movement.
Daily 8-12, 2-6.

OPAVA

PETR BEZRUČ MEMORIAL
Ostrozná ul. č. 35, Opava
Manuscripts, books, memorabilia of regional writers.
Tu.-Su. 9-6.

SILESIAN MUSEUM: COLLECTIONS OF PREHISTORY AND PHOTOGRAPHY
Komenského ulica č. 8, Opava
Czechoslovakia in prehistoric times. Collections illustrating history of photography.
Apr.-Oct., Su.-F. 9-6.

SILESIAN MUSEUM: ETHNOGRAPHY AND ART COLLECTIONS
Sněmovni ulica č. 1, Opava
Costumes. Handicrafts. Paintings on glass. Furniture. Household equipment. Paintings, sculpture, ceramics, porcelain from the region. Czech glass. Italian and German paintings of the Renaissance.
Apr.-Oct., Su.-F. 9-6.

SILESIAN MUSEUM: HISTORY COLLECTIONS
Tyršova ulica č. 1, Opava
Regional prehistory, history. Pottery, bronzes, tools and other material from excavations in the Opava region. Musical history of the region. Coins.
Apr.-Oct., Su.-F. 9-6.

SILESIAN MUSEUM: NATURAL HISTORY COLLECTIONS
Tř. Vítěz února 35, Opava
World-wide collection of geology, mineralogy, palaeontology, botany, zoology.
Apr.-Oct., Su.-F. 9-6.

ORAVSKY PODZÁMOK

ORAVA MUSEUM
Oravský Podzámok
In Orava Castle. Regional geology, botany, zoology. Prehistory. History. Ethnography. Furniture. Celtic coins. Gregory's telescope. Paintings by Slovak artists.
May-Oct., daily 7-5.

OSTRAVA

ART GALLERY
Dům umění, Jurečkova ulica č. 9, Ostrava
Paintings, graphics by European and Czech artists, mostly 19th-20th century.
Tu.-Su. 9-5.

MUSEUM OF SOCIALISM AND THE REVOLUTION
Dimitrovova 10, Ostrava
Collections illustrating history of Communist Party in Ostrava.
By appointment.

OSTRAVA MUSEUM
Nám. lidových milicí č. 1, Ostrava
Geology. Mineralogy. Palaeontology. Entomology. Ornithology. Archaeology. Ethnography of the Ostrava region. Folk art. Wood-carving. Paintings on glass.
Tu.-F. 8-4; Sa. 8-12; Su. 9-12.

OSTRAVA-VÍTKNOVICE

MUSEUM OF THE VÍTKOVICE IRON-WORKS
Zámek VŽKG, Výstavní č. 99, Ostrava-Vítkovice
History and technology of iron-working. History of the local workers' movement.
M.-F. 8-5.

OSTŘEDEK

SVATOPLUKA ČECHA MUSEUM
Ustav sociálni péče pro dospělé zámek č. 1, Ostředek
Literary works and mementoes of Svatopluka.
Daily 9-4.

OSTROV NAD OHRI

ART GALLERY
Letohrádek u zámeckém parku, Ostrov nad Ohri
Paintings, graphics by regional artists.
May-Oct., Su.-F. 10-12, 2-6. Nov.-Apr., Su.-F. 9-12, 1-2.

PACOV

ANTONIN SOVA MUNICIPAL MUSEUM
Hronova ulica č. 274, Pacov
Local history. Collections relating to local writers and artists.
M.-F. 8-4; Sa., Su. 9-12.

PARDUBICE

ART GALLERY OF EASTERN CZECHOSLOVAKIA
Státni zámek č. 3, Pardubice
20th century paintings, sculpture, drawings by Czech artists.
Daily 9.30-6.

MUSEUM OF EASTERN CZECHOSLOVAKIA
Zámek č. 1, Pardubice
Mineralogy. Palaeontology. Botany. Ornithology. Archaeology. Ethnography. Folk art. Local history.
May-Oct., Tu.-Su. 9-5.

PASEKY NAD JIZEROU

ZAPADLÝ VLASTENCA MUSEUM
Škola, Paseky nad Jizerou
Violins. Books. Notebooks. Manuscripts.
On request.

PECKA

CASTLE MUSEUM
Pecka
Local history. Ethnography. Rural handicrafts. Medieval archaeology.
May-Sept., Tu.-Su. 8-4.

PEČKY

MEMORIAL MUSEUM OF THE PEČKY WORKERS' MOVEMENT
Budova MNV, náměsti, Pečky
History of the workers' movement in the Pečky region.
By appointment.

PELHŘIMOV

DISTRICT MUSEUM
Mírové náměsti č. 12, Pelhřimov
Archaeology. History. Ethnography, especially costumes, household equipment. Peasant art. Applied arts.
May-Oct., M.-F. 8-4; Sa., Su. 8-12.

PEZINOK

JAN KUPECKÝ HOUSE-MUSEUM
Kupecký ul. 18, Pezinok
Life and work of the 18th century portrait painter, Jan Kupecký.
On request.

MUNICIPAL MUSEUM
Pezinok
Local history and ethnography.
Tu.-Su. 8-5.

PIEŠTANY

SPA MUSEUM
Pieštany
Palaeolithic, Neolithic, Bronze Age and Roman archaeology. Coins, including series from the time of the 30 Years War. Painted glass. Wooden statuettes. Embroidery. Costumes. Crutches presented by patients healed at Pieštany.
Tu.-Su. 8-12, 2-5.

PÍSEK

ADOLF HEYDUK MEMORIAL
Tyršova ulica č. 438, Písek
Collections illustrating life and work of the Czech poet, Adolf Heyduk.
On request.

REGIONAL MUSEUM
Leninovo náměsti č. 114, Písek
Geology. Mineralogy. Archaeology. Memorabilia of local painters, musicians, writers. Costumes. Furniture. Peasant art. Paintings by local artists. Local textiles.
May-Sept., M.-F. 9-5; Oct.-Apr. 3, M.-F., Sa., Su. 9-12.

PLÁNICE

DR. FRANTIŠKY KŘIŽÍK MEMORIAL MUSEUM
Křižíkova ulica č. 86, Plánice
Collections illustrating life and work of the electrical engineer, Dr. Křižík.
Daily 10-5.

PLASY

MUNICIPAL MUSEUM
Konvent, Plasy
Geology. Local history.
June-Oct., Su., public holidays 10-12, 2-4. Other times by appointment.

PLZEŇ

ART GALLERY OF WESTERN CZECHOSLOVAKIA
Kopeckého sady č. 2, Plzeň
Paintings, sculpture, drawings, graphics (mostly 19th century) by Czech artists.
Tu.-F. 9-5; Sa. 9-12.

MUSEUM OF WESTERN CZECHOSLOVAKIA
Kopeckého sady č. 2, Plzeň
Collections illustrating cultural, political and economic history of Czechoslovakia.
Tu.-F., Su. 9-5; Sa. 9-12.

MUSEUM OF WESTERN CZECHOSLOVAKIA: ARCHAEOLOGICAL COLLECTIONS
Františkánská ulica č. 13, Plzeň
Archaeological material from 28 sites in Western Czechoslovakia, covering the Bronze Age, Halstadt and Slavonic periods.
Tu.-F., Su. 9-5; Sa. 9-12.

MUSEUM OF WESTERN CZECHOSLOVAKIA: ETHNOGRAPHICAL COLLECTION
Náměsti Republiky č. 13, Plzeň
Ethnography of Western Czechoslovakia, mostly 19th-20th century.
Tu.-F., Su. 9-5; Sa. 9-12.

MUSEUM OF WESTERN CZECHOSLOVAKIA: JULIUS FUČIK MEMORIAL COLLECTION
Havlíckova ulica č. 17, Plzeň
Collections illustrating life and work of the composer, Julius Fučik.
Tu.-F., Su. 9-5; Sa. 9-12.

MUSEUM OF WESTERN CZECHOSLOVAKIA: MUSEUM OF BREWING
Veleslavínova ulica č. 6, Plzeň
In former brewery with original equipment. History and technology of brewing.
Tu.-F., Su. 9-5; Sa. 9-12.

MUSEUM OF WESTERN CZECHOSLOVAKIA: NATURAL HISTORY COLLECTIONS
Veleslavínova ulica č. 6, Plzeň
Geology, palaeontology, zoology, entomology of Western Czechoslovakia.
Tu.-F., Su. 9-5; Sa. 9-12.

POČÁTKY

OTOKARA BŘEZINY HOUSE-MUSEUM
Ul. Otokara Březiny č. 224, Počátky
Collections illustrating life and work of the poet, Otokara Březiny.
By appointment.

MUNICIPAL MUSEUM
Palackého nám č. 27, Počátky
Local archaeology, history, ethnography. Memorabilia of local writers, artists.
On request.

PODĚBRADY

DISTRICT MUSEUM
Palackého tř. č. 68/III, Poděbrady
Geology. Palaeontology. Botany. Zoology. Local history. Ethnography. 18th-20th century sculpture, paintings by Czech artists. Coins and medals. Memorabilia of local artists.
Apr.-Oct. Tu.-Su. 9-12, 1-4.

POHANSKO U BŘECLAVĚ

ARCHAEOLOGICAL SITE MUSEUM
Býv lovecky zámeček Lichtenštejnů, Pohansko u Břeclavě
Material from excavation of early Slovakian fortress.
May-Oct., Tu.-Su. 8-4.

POLICE NAD METUJI

MUNICIPAL MUSEUM
Býv klášter, Police nad Metuji
Local and regional history. Memorabilia of local writers and artists.
May-Sept., Su., public holidays 9-12, 2-4. Other days by appointment.

POLIČKA

MUNICIPAL MUSEUM AND ART GALLERY
Tylova ul č. 112/113, Polička
Regional history, ethnography. Paintings. Glass. Folk art. Bohuslav Martinů memorial collection.
Apr.-Sept., daily 9-12, 2-4.

POLNÁ

LOCAL MUSEUM
Zámek č. 485, Polná
Paintings. Decorative and applied art. Old Polná school. Works by the sculptor, J. Vitka. Local history.
May-Sept., Tu.-F. 8-12, 1-5; Sa. 8-12; Su. 9-5.

POPRAD

TATRA MUSEUM
Poprad
Material from the Tatra National Park. Geology. Mineralogy. Palaeontology. Botany. Zoology. Archaeology. History. Roman coins.
Tu.-Su. 9-4.

POTŠTEJN

JIRÁSKUV 'POKLAD' MEMORIAL MUSEUM
Potštejn
History and products of the Poklad linen-factory.
May-Sept., Sa., Su. by appointment.

PRACE

MOHYLA MIRU (MOUND OF PEACE) MEMORIAL
Prace
History of the Napoleonic wars, especially Battle of Slavkov.
Tu.-Su. 8-6; M. 10-4.

PRACHATICE

DISTRICT MUSEUM
Gottwaldovo náměsti č. 13, Prachatice
Regional history, ethnography. Bank notes of the Austro-Hungarian empire. Paintings. Graphics. Sculpture. Furnished interiors.
Tu.-Su. 9-12, 1-4.

PRAGUE

CZECH MUSEUM OF AGRICULTURE
Vinahrady, Na Kozačce 3, Prague 2
Agricultural products and techniques. Implements and machinery. Livestock. Veterinary medicine.
By appointment.

CZECH MUSEUM OF MEDICINE AND HEALTH
Sokolská 31, Prague 2
History of medicine and pharmacy, especially in Czechoslovakia. Paintings, coins with medicine as subject. Portraits. Documents.
By appointment.

ANTONÍN DVOŘÁK MUSEUM
Nové Město čp. 462, Ke Karlovu 20, Prague 2
Collections illustrating the life and work of the composer. His furniture, viola, piano and other personal possessions. Concert programmes, posters. Photographs. Documents. Manuscripts.
Daily 10-5.

ETHNOLOGICAL COLLECTIONS
Petřínské sady, Praha-Smíchov č. 98, Prague
Cultural history of the Czech and Slovak peoples. Furniture. Household and agricultural equipment. Folk art. Pottery. Handicrafts. Open-air museum of houses, mills, workshops, farm buildings.
Daily 10-6.

KLEMENT GOTTWALD MUSEUM
Rytírska 29, Prague 1
History of Marxism-Leninism, and of the establishment of socialism in Czechoslovakia, including the part played by K. Gottwald.
Tu.-Su. 9-6.

HUSSITE COLLECTION
Jungmannova 9, Prague 1
History of the Evangelical church and the Reformation in Czechoslovakia.
By appointment.

JEWISH MUSEUM
Jáckymova 3, Prague 1
Vestments, books, manuscripts and liturgical objects from synagogues in Czechoslovakia, originally brought to Prague by Nazi looters. The museum administers a number of other buildings on the site of the former Prague ghetto, including a 13th century synagogue and an old Jewish cemetery.
Su.-F. 9-5.

ALOIS JIRÁSEK AND MIKOLÁŠ ALŠE MUSEUM
Liboc, Letohrádek Hvězda, Prague 6
Books and photographs on art, ethnology and history collected by A. Jirásek and M. Alše.
May-Oct., Tu.-Sa. 9-5; Su. 9-6. Nov.-Apr., Tu.-Sa. 9-4; Su. 9-5.

J. B. KOMENSKY (COMENIUS) MUSEUM OF EDUCATION
Malá Strana, Valdštejnský palác, Prague 1
History of the aims, methods and organisation of education in Czechoslovakia.
M.-Sa. 9-5.

V. I. LENIN MUSEUM
Hybernská 7, Prague 1
Documents, photographs and other material illustrating the history of the revolutionary and socialist movements in Czechoslovakia.
Tu.-Su. 9-6.

MILITARY MUSEUM
Hradčanské nám 2, Schwarzenberský palác, Prague 1
Departments at ul. Památníku 2, Prague 3; letiště Kbely, Prague 9; Na Karlově, Horska ul.
History of the Czechoslovak army, of Czechoslovak contributions to the Austro-Hungarian armies and of military forces and warfare on Czechoslovak territory. Weapons. Equipment. Paintings. Photographs. Documents.
May-Oct., M.-F. 9-3.30; Sa., Su. 9-5.

MUSEUM OF ANTHROPOLOGY
Vinicna 7, Prague 2
Charles University teaching collections of anthropological material.
By appointment.

MUSEUM OF THE CITY OF PRAGUE
Nové Město, Svermovy sady čp. 1554, Departments at Dejvice, Sárecká 29, Prague 6; Hradčany, Loretánské nám. 7; Nové Město, Nabř. B. Engelse 42; Nové Město, Vinična 2, Prague 2
Architecture, archaeology, prehistory, history and art of Prague.
Tu.-Sa. 9-12, 1-5.

MUSEUM OF THE CULTURES OF ASIA, AFRICA AND AMERICA
Staré Město, Betlémské náměsti 1, Prague 1
Ethnographical collections, photographs, documents illustrating the native cultures of Asia, Africa, North, Central and South America and Oceania.
Daily 3-6.

MUSEUM OF CZECH LITERATURE
Strahovské nádvori čp. 132, Prague
First editions, manuscripts of books by Czech authors. Correspondence, including letters by Pushkin, Goethe, Gorki, Kafka, Maupassant. Portraits.
Daily 9-5.

MUSEUM OF THE DEFENCE OF THE CZECH FRONTIER
Horská ul. 7, Prague 2
History of the changes in the boundaries of Czechoslovakia. Frontier-guards and their equipment. Techniques of frontier-control.
Tu.-Th., Sa., Su. 10-5.

MUSEUM OF POSTAL SERVICES AND TELECOMMUNICATIONS
Smichov, Holečkova 10, Prague 5
History of the postal services and telecommunications in Czechoslovakia. Equipment. Photographs. Documents. Postage stamps.
M.-F. 8-3. Sa., Su. by appointment.

MUSEUM OF SPORT
Malá Strana, Újerd 450, Prague 1
History of sport and gymnastics in Czechoslovakia. Photographs. Mementoes. Films.
F.-W. 9-5.

NATIONAL MUSEUM: COLLECTIONS OF THE HISTORY OF MUSIC
Malá Strana, Velkopřevorské náměsti 4, Prague 1
Portraits and memorabilia of composers, especially Czech and including Smetana, Dvořak, Fibich. 16th-19th century musical instruments.
Daily 10-12, 2-5.

NATIONAL MUSEUM: MUSEUM OF HISTORY
Václavské náměsti 1700, Prague 1
Prehistory. Archaeology. History. Coins. Manuscripts. Lapidarium.
M.-Sa. 9-4. W., Su. also 4-6.

NATIONAL MUSEUM: MUSEUM OF NATURAL HISTORY
Václavské náměsti 1700, Prague 1
Mineralogy. Petrography. Geology. Palaeontology. Botany. Entomology. Zoology. Anthropology.
M.-Sa. 9-4; W., Su. also 4-6.

NATIONAL TECHNICAL MUSEUM
Letná, Kostelní 42, Prague 7
Mechanical engineering. Iron-founding, forging. Road, rail, air transport. Photography. Film. Radio. Television. Astronomy.
Daily 10-5.

PHARMACEUTICAL MUSEUM
Malá Strana, Nerudova ulica č. 219, Prague
Equipment, documents, paintings, prints illustrating history of pharmacy in Czechoslovakia.
Tu., Th., F. 2.30-6.

BEDŘICH SMETANA MUSEUM
Staré Město, Novotného lávka 1, Prague 1
Smetana manuscripts. Articles and books about his music. Documents illustrating his work and career.
Tu.-Su. 10-6.

PŘELOUČ

MUNICIPAL MUSEUM
Náměsti Rudé armády, Přelouč
Ornithology. Local archaeology, history. Ethnography. Coins.
By appointment.

PŘEROV

J. A. KOMENSKY MUSEUM
Horní náměsti č. 1, Přerov
Collection illustrating life and work of Komensky (Comenius). Mineralogy. Zoology. Entomology. Archaeology. Coins. Optical instruments. Glass. Ceramics. Paintings. Sculpture. Fabrics.
W. 9-12, 2-5; Tu., Th., F. 2-5; Su. 9-12.

PŘEROV NAD LABEM

MUSEUM OF ETHNOGRAPHY
Přerov nad Labem
Open-air museum of 18th-19th century rural buildings from the region. Peasant furniture, household equipment, tools. Folk-art. Textiles.
Tu.-F. 2-4; Sa. 1-6; Su. 10-12, 1-6.

PREŠOV

MUSEUM OF THE SLOVAK REPUBLIC
Prešov
In Rakoczi House. Geology, botany, zoology, ecology of the region. Dioramas. Prehistoric material. History of Prešov.
Tu.-F. 10-4; Sa. 10-2; Su. 8-2.

PŘIBOR

PŘIBOR MUSEUM AND SIGMUND FREUD MEMORIAL
Piaristická ulica č. 1-3, Přibor
Local history. Collections illustrating Freud's life and work.
Tu.-Th. 8-12, 2-4.30; Su. 9-12.

PŘIBRAM

DISTRICT MUSEUM
Březové Hory, Příbram
Geology. Mineralogy. Mining history. Life of local mining community. Handicrafts.
Tu.-Su. 9-4.

PŘIBYSLAV

MUNICIPAL MUSEUM
Husova ulica č. 300, Přibyslav
Local history. Handicrafts. Guilds. Textiles.
Su., public holidays 9-12. Other times by appointment.

PŘIMĚTICE

PROKOP DIVIŠ MEMORIAL
Přimětice
Collections illustrating the life and work of the naturalist, Prokop Diviš (d.1765).
Apr.-Oct., on request.

PROSEČ U SKUTČE

TERÉZA NOVÁKOVÁ MEMORIAL MUSEUM
Náměsti č. 61, Proseč u Skutče
Collections illustrating life and work of the writers, Teréza Nováková and Thomas Mann, who lived at Proseč u Skutče.
Su. 11-12. Other times by appointment.

PROSTĚJOV

DISTRICT MUSEUM
Náměsti 9 května č. 2, Prostějov
Entomology. Botany. Archaeology. History. Ethnography.
Apr.-Nov., Tu.-Su. 9-4.

PROTIVÍN

MUNICIPAL MUSEUM
Náměsti č. 19, Protivín
Local history, ethnography. Rural architecture. Handicrafts.
May-Oct., Su. 9-11. Other times by appointment.

RADNICE

MUNICIPAL MUSEUM
Leninova ulica č. 84, Radnice
Mineralogy. Palaeontology. Botany. Local history, ethnography.
May-Oct., Tu.-Su. 9-12.

RAKOVNÍK

DISTRICT MUSEUM
Náměsti obětovaných č. 1/1, Rakovník
Regional geology, mineralogy, palaeontology. Archaeology. Ethnography. Local history. Handicrafts. Ceramics.
Tu.-F. 8-4; Sa., Su. 9-12.

RIMAVSKÁ SOBOTA

GEMER MUSEUM
Rimavská Sobota
Prehistory and history of the region. 11th-13th century religious art, jewellery. Coins. Furniture. Household equipment. Craftsmen's tools, equipment. Woodcarving.
M.-Sa. 8-12, 1-4; Su. 10-12.

ROKYCANY

DISTRICT MUSEUM
č. 141/1 u kostela, Rokycany
Palaeontology. Local history. Handicrafts. Furniture.
May-Oct., M.-F. 8-4; Sa., Su. 8-12.

RONOV NAD DOUBRAVOU

ANTONÍN CHITTUSSIKY MEMORIAL MUSEUM
Časlavská ulica 309, Ronov nad Doubravou
Collections illustrating life and work of the painter, Antonín Chittussiky, in his former home.
May-July, Tu.-Su. 8-12, 2-5.

ROŠTEJN

VYSOČINY MUSEUM
Obec Doupě č. 1, Hrad, Roštejn
Local flora. History of the castle. Paintings. Ceramics. Pewter. Wrought-iron.
May-Sept., Tu.-Su. 8-12, 1-5.

ROUDNICE NAD LABEM

DISTRICT GALLERY OF FINE ART
Očkova ulica č. 5, Roudnice nad Labem
Paintings, mostly 19th-20th century, by Czech artists.
Tu.-Su. 10-5.

ROUSÍNOV

KLEMENT GOTTWALD MEMORIAL
Rousínov
Mementoes of Gottwald's residence in Rousínov.
Tu.-Su. 8-6.

ROŽĎALOVICE

JIŘÍ MELANTRICH MEMORIAL MUSEUM
Husova ulice, Rožďalovice
Collections illustrating literary works of Czechoslovakia.
Su., public holidays, 10-12. Other times by appointment.

ROŽMITAL POD TŘEMŠÍNEM

MUNICIPAL MEMORIAL AND JAKUB JAN RYBY MEMORIAL
Stará škola na náměsti, Rožmital pod Třemšinem
Collection illustrating life and work of J. J. Ryby. Local history.
By appointment.

ROŽŇAVA

MINING AND METALWORKING MUSEUM
Rožňava
Geology. Natural history. Mining history and equipment. Measuring tools used by miners.
Daily 8-5.

ROŽNOV POD RADHOŠTĚM

VALASKIAN MUSEUM OF ETHNOGRAPHY
Rožnov pod Radhoštěm
Open-air museum, with 17th-19th century rural buildings from the Carpathian region. Furnishings. Household equipment. Folk art.
May 1-15, daily 8-6. May 16-Aug. 31, daily 7-7. Sept. 1-Oct. 15, daily 8-6.

ROZTOKY U PRAHY

REGIONAL MUSEUM
Zámek, Roztoky u Prahy
Natural history. Archaeology. Handicrafts. Folk art. Early printed books.
M.-F. 9-12, 2-6; Sa., Su., public holidays 9-6.

RTYNĚ V PODKRKONOŠÍ

MEMORIAL OF THE PEASANT REVOLT OF 1777
Býv. rychta, Rtyně v Podkrkonoší
Open-air museum. Rural buildings, furnishings, household equipment.
On request.

RUMBURK

REGIONAL MUSEUM
Vraní ulica č. 10/401, Rumburk
18th century paintings. Pewter. Glass. Porcelain. Folk art. Coins.
Tu.-F. 9-12, 1-3; Su. 8-1.

RUŽINOV

MUSEUM OF THE ILLEGAL SLOVAKIAN COMMUNIST PARTY
Priekopy 73, Ružinov
Collection illustrates underground activities of the Party, 1941-42.
Tu.-F. 10-5; Sa., Su. 9-5.

RUŽOMBEROK

LIPTOV MUSEUM
Ružomberok
Geology, mineralogy, botany, zoology, history and ethnology of the region. Religious art. Paintings by local artists. Agriculture. Mining. Fishing. Bee-keeping. Cheese-moulds. Embroidery.
Tu.-Sa. 8-12, 1-4; Su., public holidays 8-12.

RYCHNOV NAD KNĚŽNOU

ORLICKÁ GALLERY
Státni zámek, Rychnov nad Kněznou
Paintings by artists from the region, or of subjects connected with it.
Apr.-Oct., daily 9-5.

RYCHNOV NAD KNĚŽNOU

ORLICKÉ HORY MUSEUM
Státni zámek 1, Rychnov nad Kněznou
Archaeology. Ornithology. Ethnography. Handicrafts.
Apr.-Sept., Tu.-Su. 9-12, 2-4.

SABINOV

MUNICIPAL MUSEUM
Sabinov
Natural history. Archaeology. History. Ethnography.
Tu.-Su. 10-4.

SADSKÁ

MUNICIPAL MUSEUM
Náměsti č. 258, Sadská
Archaeology. Ethnography. Local history.
By appointment.

SÁZAVA

MUSEUM OF GLASS TECHNOLOGY
Zámek, Sázava
History and techniques of local glass-making.
Apr.-Oct., Tu.-Su. 8-12, 1-5.

SEDLČANY

MUNICIPAL MUSEUM
Zámek Červený Hrádek, Sedlčany
Local archaeology, history, ethnography. Josef Suk memorial collection.
By appointment.

SEMILY

MUNICIPAL MUSEUM AND ANTAL STAŠEK AND IVAN OLBRACHT MEMORIAL
Hurova ul. č. 2, Semily
Local history. Handicrafts. Collections illustrating life and work of Antal Stašek and Ivan Olbracht.
Tu.-F. 9-12, 1-4.30; Sa. 9-12.

SEZIMOVO ÚSTI

JOSEF ŠVEHLY MEMORIAL
Budova Městnu, Sezimovo Ústi
Archaeological collections from the town and region made by Josef Švehly.
M.-F. 8-12, 1-4; Sa. 8-12. Apr.-Sept., Su., public holidays 9-12, 1-4.

SKALICA

ZAHORA MUSEUM
Skalica
Natural history. Archaeology. History. Ethnography. Slovak pottery.
Tu.-Sa. 8-12, 1-4; Su. 9-2.

SKÁLY

ALOIS JIRÁSEK MEMORIAL MUSEUM
Teplice nad Metiyí IV, Zámeček, Skály
Collections illustrating life and work of the writer, Alois Jirásek.
May-Sept., Tu.-Su. 9-6.

SKRYJE

REGIONAL MUSEUM
Zákl. devítiletá škola, Skryje
Palaeontology. Archaeological material from local excavations.
On request.

SKUTEČ

MUNICIPAL MUSEUM
Rybičkova ul. č. 364, Skuteč
Geology. Natural history. Shoe-making. Toyshop. Tobacconist's shop. Cultural history of the district.
Th.-F. 8-11.30, 1-4; Sa. 8-11.15; Su. 9.30-11.30. Other times by appointment.

VITĚZSLAV NOVAK MUSEUM
Rybičkova ul. č. 364, Skuteč
Collections illustrating life and work of Vitězslav Novak. Memorabilia of his musical salon.
Th.-F. 8-11.30, 1-4; Sa. 8-11.30; Su. 9.30-11.30. Other times by appointment.

SLANÝ

REGIONAL MUSEUM
Náměsti 9, května č. 159, Slaný
Regional geology, palaeontology, entomology, ornithology. Ethnography. Folk art. Handicrafts. Russian and Czech pewter. Glass. Porcelain. Paintings. Sculpture.
Tu., Th., Sa., Su., Public holidays 9-12. W., F. 1-5.

ŠLAPANICE

REGIONAL MUSEUM
Náměsti 1, máje č. 4, Šlapanice
Geology. Local history, ethnography. Costumes. Paintings by Alois Kalvody.
Sa. 7-1; Su. 7.30-11.30, 1-4.

SLATIŇANY

MUSEUM OF THE HORSE
Zámek, Slatiňany
Anatomy. Breeding. Harness and equipment. Paintings and sculpture depicting horses.
Apr.-Oct., Tu.-Su. 8-12, 2-6.

SLAVKOV

MUSEUM OF THE NAPOLEONIC WARS
Státni zámek, Palackého nám. č. 1, Slavkov
Local history. Exhibits and relics illustrating Napoleon's life and campaigns. History of the French Revolution. Archaeology. Ethnography. Furniture.
Tu.-Su. 8-5.

ŠLUKNOV

MUNICIPAL MUSEUM
Zámecká ul. č. 642, Šluknov
Regional history, ethnography.
W. 2-4; Su. 10-12.

SMIŘICE

HISTORICAL COLLECTION
Smiřice
Local archaeology and history.
By appointment.

SOBĚSLAV

MUSEUM OF SOUTHERN CZECHOSLOVAKIA
Rožmberský dům, tr. č. armády č. 152, Soběslav
Regional geology, mineralogy, botany, zoology. Folk art. Folklore. Ceramics. 15th-18th century paintings, sculpture. Pewter. Glass. Coins.
May-Sept., Tu.-Su. 9-12, 1-4.

MUSEUM OF SOUTHERN CZECHOSLOVAKIA
Department of Ethnography, Cerný orel, náměsti č. 117, Soběslav
Regional ethnography.
May-Sept., Tu.-Su. 9-12, 1-4.

MUSEUM OF SOUTHERN CZECHOSLOVAKIA
Department of Religious Art, Hřbitovní kostel sv Marka, Soběslav
Paintings. Sculpture. Textiles.
May-Sept., Tu.-Su. 9-12, 1-4.

SOBOTKA

MUSEUM OF LITERARY HISTORY
Zámek Humprecht, Sobotka
Regional history, Literary memorabilia of Turnovský, Šolc, Šrámek. Collections illustrating life and work of Josef Haken. Ethnography.
Apr.-Oct., daily 7.30-11.30, 1.30-5.30. Other months by appointment.

FRA. ŠRÁMEK HOUSE-MUSEUM
Náměsti č. 3, Sobotka
Collections illustrating life and work of the writer, Fran Šrámek, in his former home. Original furnishings, library. Manuscripts. Correspondence.
Daily, on request.

SOKOLOV

MINING MUSEUM
Zámek, Sokolov
Geology. Mineralogy. Palaeontology. Regional ethnography, history. History and techniques of local mining industry.
Tu.-F. 9-5; Sa. 10-5. Su. 11-5.

SPIŠSKÁ NOVÁ VES

REGIONAL MUSEUM
Spišská Nová Ves
Natural history. Archaeology.
Tu.-Sa. 10-12, 4-6; Su. 10-12.

STARÁ HUŤ U DOBŘÚŠE

KAREL ČAPEK MEMORIAL MUSEUM
Na Strži č. 125, Stará Huť u Dobřúše
Collections illustrating life and work of Karel Capek, in his former home. Original furnishings. Collections illustrating life and work of Olga Scheinpflug.
Tu.-Su. 8-12, 1-5.

STARÁ L'UBOVŇA

MUNICIPAL MUSEUM
Stará L'ubovňa
In Stará L'ubovňa Castle. History of the Castle and the town. Ethnography.
Tu.-Su. 10-4.

STARÉ MĚSTO

LOCAL MUSEUM
Radnice, Staré Město
Archaeological material from local excavations, especially at Valách, Špitálkách and Modré u Velehradu.
By appointment.

ŠTERNBERK

MUSEUM OF MUSIC
Bezručova ul. č. 1, Šternberk
Regional history. Collections illustrating musical history.
Tu.-Su. 8.30-4.30.

ŠTERNBERK STATE CASTLE
Státni hrad, Šternberk
13th century castle, remodelled in 16th century. Czech and Moravian Gothic paintings, sculpture. Folk art, Handicrafts. 11th-17th century tapestries. European furniture.
Apr.-Oct., daily 8-5.

STRAKONICE

FR. L. ČELAKOVSKÝ HOUSE MUSEUM
Čelakovského ulice č. 252, Strakonice
Collections illustrating life and work of the poet, Fr. L. Čelakovský, in his former home.
Sa., Su. 10-12, 2-4.

MUSEUM OF HISTORY AND ETHNOGRAPHY
Hrad, Strakonice
Local history, ethnography. Paintings. Sculpture. Coins. Archaeology.
Tu.-Su. 7-12, 1-4.

ŠTRAMBERK

MUNICIPAL MUSEUM
Na bráně č. 144, Štramberk
Regional geology, palaeontology, history, ethnography.
May-Oct., daily 9-12, 2-6. Other months by appointment.

STRÁŽNICI

REGIONAL MUSEUM OF FOLK ART
Zámek, Strážnici
Musical instruments. Costumes. Folk art.
May-Nov., daily 9-12, 2-5.

STŘÍBRO

REGIONAL MUSEUM
Radnice, Stříbro
Mineralogy. Palaeontology. Local history. Local mining industry.
June 15- Sept. 15, Tu.-F. 7.30-4; Sa., Su. 7.30-12.

STUDÉNKA

CARRIAGE MUSEUM
Býv. zámek hrabete Blüchera, dnes majetek Městnv, Studénka
Horse-drawn vehicles. Models.
May-Sept., M.-F. 8-1; Su. 10-4.

SUCHDOL NAD LUŽNICI

LOCAL MUSEUM
Národní výbor č. 9, Suchdol nad Lužnici
Geology. Regional history. Stoves. Furniture. Household equipment.
On request.

SUŠICE

ŠUMAVY MUSEUM
Nám. Klementa Gottwalda č. 2, Sušice
Local history, archaeology. Local glass, furniture.
May-Sept., Tu.-Sa. 8-5; Su. 8-12. Oct.-Apr., daily 8-12, 2-4.

SVIDNÍK

MUSEUM OF THE BATTLE OF DUKLA
Svidník
Reconstruction of the Battle of Dukla (1944), one of the key events in the liberation of the country from the Germans.
Tu.-Su. 8-5.

TÁBOR

MUSEUM OF THE HUSSITE REVOLT
Žiřkovo nám. č. 1; Hlavni budova-radnice; Bechyňská brána, Tábor
Collections illustrating life of the religious reformer, John Hus (martyred 1415) and the civil war which followed his death.
Zirkovo nám. and Hlavni budova, Apr.-Sept. 8-12, 1-5. Bechynská brána, May-Sept. 8-12, 1-5.

TACHOV

DISTRICT MUSEUM
Na tř. Míru č. 447, Tachov
In 15th century Franciscan monastery. Regional natural history, ethnography, paintings, handicrafts. Hussite movement.
Apr. 15-Oct. 15, Tu.-F. 8-4; Sa., Su. 9-1.

TATRANSKÁ LOMNICA

MUSEUM OF THE TATRA NATIONAL PARK (TANAP)
Tatranská Lomnica
Mineralogy, botany, zoology of the National Park area. History of tourism, recreation and sport in the mountain area. Ethnography.
M.-F. 8-12, 1-5. Sa., Su. 8-12.

TELČ

TELČ MUSEUM
Zámek, Telč
Economy and cultural history of the Telč district. Paintings of local scenes. Development of the town. Folk art. African sculpture.
Apr.-Sept., Tu.-Su. 9-12, 1-4.30.

TEPLICE

REGIONAL MUSEUM
Zámecké nám. 14, Teplice
Regional geology, mineralogy, zoology, history. Handicrafts. Porcelain. Pewter. Glass. Mementoes of Ludwig van Beethoven. 17th-19th century paintings.
Tu.-Su. 10-12, 1-6.

TEPLICE NAD BEČVOU

REGIONAL MUSEUM
Teplice nad Bečvou
Collections illustrating the geysers and hot mineral springs at Aragontinova.
Apr.-Sept., daily 8-5. Other months by appointment.

TEREZÍN

MEMORIAL OF THE NATIONAL SUFFERING
Malá pevnost, Terezín
Documents and other material illustrating the German concentration camp at Terezín.
May-Oct., daily 7-7. Nov.-Apr., daily 8-4.

TIŠNOV

REGIONAL MUSEUM
Porta coeli č. 2, Tišnov
Geology. Mineralogy. Palaeontology. Zoology. Archaeology. Ethnology. Coins.
Tu.-F. 8-4; Sa. 8-12; Su. 8-2.

TOVAČOV

MUSEUM OF ETHNOGRAPHY
Zámek, Tovačov
Regional ethnography. Costumes. Glass. Ceramics.
W., Su. 9-12, 2-5; Sa. 9-12. Other times by appointment.

TŘEBECHOVICE POD OREBEM

MUNICIPAL MUSEUM
Náměsti č. 40, Třebechovice pod Orebem
Local and regional history.
Su., public holidays 10-12. Other times by appointment.

TŘEBENICE

MUSEUM OF GARNETS
Loucka ulice, Třebenice
History of mining, processing and utilisation of garnets. Mining techniques. Life of mining community.
By appointment.

TŘEBÍČ

MUSEUM OF WESTERN MORAVIA
Podklášteří, tř. 9 května, Zámek č. 1, Třebíc
Natural history. Archaeology. Ethnography. Sculpture. Graphics.
Tu.-Su. 8-12, 1-5.

DR. BOHUMÍR ŠMERALA MEMORIAL MUSEUM
Nové Dvory, Třebíc
Collection illustrating life and work of Dr. Šmerala, in his former home.
On request.

TŘEBÍZ

V. B. TŘEBIZSKY MEMORIAL MUSEUM
Č. 19, Třebíz
In former home of Třebizsky. Collections illustrating his life and work. Regional literature.
Su. 9-12. Other times by appointment.

TRENČÍN

TRENČÍN MUSEUM
Hrad and Župrom dome, Trenčín
In Castle (Hrad): Prehistory, Roman and Slav archaeology. History of the region. Turkish relics. Handicrafts. Costumes. Housing.
In the 18th century County House (Župrom dome): Natural history. History of the workers' movement.
Tu.-Su. 8-5.

TŘEŠŤ

LOCAL MUSEUM
Zámek, Třešt
Local history. Handicrafts. Paintings. Ceramics. Folk art.
On request.

TRHANOV

JAROSLAV ŠPILLAR GALLERY
Zámek č. 1, Trhanov
Paintings by J. Špillar (d.1917).
May-Sept., daily 8-12, 1-5.

TRNAVA

MUSEUM OF WESTERN SLOVAKIA
Kláštorik, Sladovnícka 1, Trnava
Natural history, archaeology. ethnography and history of Western Slovakia. Slovakian ceramics. Painted glass. Oriental art, especially ceramics, bronzes. Samurai weapons and armour. Early 18th century Japanese artistic cast-iron from the Imperial foundry.
Tu.-Su. 10-4.

TROCNOV

JAN ŽIŽKY MEMORIAL MUSEUM
Bývala hájovna, Trocnov
Collections illustrating life of Jan Žižky at Trocnov.
Daily 8-4.

TRUTNOV

MUSEUM OF LOWER KRKONIA
Školni ulice č. 9, Trutnov
Geology. Mineralogy. Palaeontology. Botany. Archaeology. Regional history.
By appointment.

TURNOV

DISTRICT MUSEUM
Ulica č. armády č. 71, Turnov
Geology. Mineralogy. Petrography. Palaeontology. Local prehistory, history. Ethnography. 18th century music. Paintings. Coins.
Tu.-Su. 9-12, 2-5.

TÝNEC NAD SÁZAVOU

TÝNEC MUSEUM OF CERAMICS
Nádvoří Adama Hodějovského č. 48, Týnec nad Sázavou
History and manufacture of Týnec ceramics. Cotton spinning. Archaeology. Local history.
Mar. 15-Oct. 31, Su. 9-12. Other times by appointment.

TÝN NAD VLTAVOU

MUNICIPAL MUSEUM
Stalingradské náměsti č. 1, Týn nad Vltavou
Natural history. Ethnography. Coins. Popular musical instruments.
Daily 8-12, 1-6.

UHERSKÝ BROD

JAN AMOS KOMENSKY (COMENIUS) MUSEUM
Ulica Přemysla Otakara 11, č. 38-9, Uherský Brod
Collections illustrating life and work of Komensky (Comenius). Regional geology, mineralogy, zoology, archaeology, ethnography.
Su.-M. 8-12, 2-5; Sa. 8-12.

UHERSKÉ HRADIŠTĚ

GALLERY OF FINE ART
Otakarova ulica č. 103, Uherské Hradiště
Paintings, drawings, graphics, sculpture, especially by Slovak artists.
Apr.-Oct., Tu.-Su. 9-12, 1-5. Other months by appointment.

SLOVAK MUSEUM
Smetanovy sady č. 178, Uherské Hradiště
Ethnography of Slovakia. Regional archaeology, history.
Tu.-Su. 10-6.

UHLIŘSKÉ JANOVICE

MUSEUM OF HISTORY
Gottwaldovo náměsti č. 168, Uhlířské Janovice
Local archaeology, ethnography, handicrafts, folk art.
By appointment.

UHROVEC

STÚR MUSEUM
Uhrovec
Birthplace of the 19th century Slovak leader, Ludovíc Stúr. Stúr memorial collection, History of Uhrovec.
Tu.-Su. 8-12, 2-4.

ÚJEZD

J. S. KOZINY MEMORIAL MUSEUM
Kozinův statek č. 3, Újezd
Regional ethnography.
May-Sept., daily 8-5.

UNHOŠŤ

MELICHAR MUNICIPAL MUSEUM
Karlovarská ul. č. 104, Unhošt
Local archaeology, history, ethnography. Paintings. Handicrafts.
By appointment.

UNIČOV

REGIONAL MUSEUM
Nám 9 května č. 21, Uničov
Archaeology. Geography. Local history.
Tu., Th. 8-11, 1-5.

ÚPICE

MUNICIPAL MUSEUM
Náměsti míru, stará radnice č. 30, Úpice
Ethnography. Local history. Memorabilia of Josef and Karl Čapek.
Sa., Su. 9-11.30; W. 2-6. Other times by appointment.

ÚSOV

REGIONAL MUSEUM
Zámek, Úsov
Hunting trophies, equipment. Forestry. Woodland insects.
Apr.-Oct., daily 8-6.

ÚSTÍ NAD LABEM-TRMICE

DISTRICT MUSEUM
Denisovy sady č. 189, Ústí nad Labem-Trmice
Geology. Palaeontology. Botany. Archaeology. Ethnography. Paintings. Local history. Coins.
By appointment.

VALAŠSKÉ KLOBOUKY

MUNICIPAL MUSEUM
Náměsti míru, stará radnice, Valašské Klobouky
Natural history. Archaeology. Ethnography. Pottery.
May-Oct., M., Tu., Th., F. 11-3; Sa. 10-12; Su. 9-11. Other times by appointment.

VALAŠSKÉ MEZIŘÍČÍ

LOCAL MUSEUM
Leninova č. 3, Valašske Meziříčí
Geology. Botany. Ornithology. Ethnography. Paintings on glass. Ceramics. Textiles. Paintings. Sculpture.
Daily 9-5.

VAMBERK

MUNICIPAL MUSEUM
Husovo náměsti č. 84, Vamberk
Regional history. Ethnography, especially costumes.
June-Aug., Tu.-Su. 8-12, 1-5. Other times by appointment.

VARNSDORF

MUNICIPAL MUSEUM
Tř. Národní revoluce č. 415, Varnsdorf
Natural history. Local history. Local and Coptic textiles.
Su., public holidays 9-12.

VELKÁ BÍTEŠ

MUNICIPAL MUSEUM
Náměsti Rudé armády č. 5, Velká Bíteš
Local history.
Daily 9-11, 2-4.

VELKÁ NAD VELIČKOU

LOCAL MUSEUM
Velká nad Veličkou
Ethnography. History of art.
By appointment.

VELKÉ KARLOVICE

KARLOVICE MUSEUM
č. 267, Velké Karlovice
Local history, ethnography.
Daily 10-6.

VELKE MEZIŘÍČÍ

MUNICIPAL MUSEUM
Zámek, Velke Meziříčí
Mineralogy. Ornithology. Zoology. Ethnography. Ceramics. Textiles.
Tu.-F., Su. 8-6; Sa. 8-1.

VELVARY

MUNICIPAL MUSEUM
Náměsti č. 10, Velvary
Archaeology. Ethnography. Glass. Porcelain. Pewter.
May-Oct., Su. 2-6. Other times by appointment.

VERELI NAD LUŽNICÍ

REGIONAL MUSEUM
Náměsti č. 111/1, Vereli nad Lužnicí
Paintings. Sculpture. Ceramics. Glass. Fabrics.
June-Aug., Tu.-Su. 9-12, 1-4.

VESELI NAD MORAVOU

LOCAL MUSEUM
Stalingradské nám č. 41, Veseli nad Moravou
Geology. Palaeontology. Archaeology. Local history. Ethnography.
Tu., W. 8-4. Other times by arrangement.

VIMPERK

MUNICIPAL MUSEUM AND ŠUMAVY GALLERY
Zámek, Vimperk
Natural history. Local history. Vimperk glass and printing industries. Fabrics.
May 1 - Nov. 15, Tu.-Su. 9-12, 2-4.

VLASTĚJOVICE

LOCAL MUSEUM
Škola č. 56, Vlastějovice
Geology. Local history. Ethnography. Handicrafts. Applied arts. History of local mining industry and mining community.
July-Aug., daily 9-12. Other times by appointment.

VODŇANY

MUNICIPAL MUSEUM AND ART GALLERY
Družstevni ul. č. 153/1, Vodňany
Local history, archaeology, paintings. Memorabilia and works of writers and artists associated with the area. Ethnography.
Tu.-Su. 9-4.

VRCHLABÍ

KRKONOŞ MUSEUM (ASSOCIATED WITH KRKONOŞSKÝ NATIONAL PARK)
Husova ul. č. 213, Vrchlabí
Geology. Mineralogy. Botany. Zoology. Peasant handicrafts. Sculpture. Paintings on glass. Coins. Paintings. Local history, ethnography.
Tu.-Su. 9-5.

VRCHOTOVY JANOVICE

R. M. RILKE MEMORIAL MUSEUM
Zámek č. 1, Vrchotovy Janovice
Memorabilia and works of the poet, R. M. Rilke.
Apr.-Oct., Tu.-Su. 8-12, 1-5.

VRÚTKY

KLEMENT GOTTWALD MUSEUM OF THE REVOLUTIONARY PRESS
Vrútky
History of the press of the Slovak workers' movement and Communist Party.
Tu.-Sa. 8-12, 2-5; Su. 8-12, 1-5.

VŠEBOŘICE

ZDEŇKO FIBICH MEMORIAL MUSEUM
Všebořice u Dolních Kralovic, myslivna, Všebořice
Collections illustrating life and work of the composer, Fibich (d. 1900), in his former home.
July-Aug., daily 8-1, 2-6. May-June, Sept.-Oct., Sa., Su. 10-5.

VSETIN

LOCAL MUSEUM
Horni náměstí č. 2 - zámek, Vsetin
Agriculture. Domestic industries. Drawings.
Daily 9-5.

VYSOKÁ U PŘIBRAMI

ANTON DVOŘÁK MEMORIAL MUSEUM
Zámeček, č. 69, Vysoká u Přibrami
Collections illustrating the life and work of Dvořak, in his former home.
Tu.-Su. 10-5.

VYŞKOV

VYŞKOV MUSEUM
Náměsti čs. armády č. 2, Vyškov
Regional geology, palaeontology, botany, zoology. Archaeology. Paintings. Peasant pottery. Textiles. Coins. Local history. History of local workers' and socialist movements.
Tu.-F. 9-6; Su., public holidays 9-12, 2-5.

VYSOKÉ MÝTO

A. V. ŠEMBERY DISTRICT MUSEUM
Šemberova ul. č. 125/1, Vysoké Mýto
Archaeology. Ethnography. Folk art. Ceramics. Glass. Coins. Memorabilia, manuscripts and printed works of regional writers.
M.-Sa. 9-6; Su. 9-12.

OTMAR VAŇORNY MEMORIAL MUSEUM
Náměsti, býv. radnice, Vysoké Mýto
Correspondence, library and memorabilia of Otmar Vaňorny.
By appointment.

VYSOKÉ NAD JIZEROU

REGIONAL MUSEUM
Vysoké nad Jizerou
Paintings of local scenes. Folk art. Local byegones.
Tu.-Su. 9-11, 2-6.

ZÁBŘEH NA MORAVĚ

REGIONAL MUSEUM
Žižkova ul. č. 1, Zábřeh na Moravě
Textiles. Paintings on glass. Ceramics. Engravings by Hollar.
Apr.-Oct., Tu.-F. 10-12, 1-5; Sa. 10-12. Other months by appointment.

ZÁHLINICE

FR. SKOPALÍK MEMORIAL MUSEUM
Č. 24, Záhlinice
Collections illustrating life and work of Františk Skopalík, in his former home.
Su. 9-12. Other times by appointment.

ZÁLÁNICE

LOCAL MUSEUM
Zámek, Zálánice
Archaeology. Ceramics. Folk art. Handicrafts. Furniture.
Su. 9-12, 2-4. Other times by appointment.

ŽAMBERK

PROKOP DIVIŠ MEMORIAL MUSEUM
Ulice č. armády, Žamberk
Collections illustrating life and work of the naturalist, Prokop Diviš (d.1765), in his former home.
By appointment.

MUNICIPAL MUSEUM
Zámek, Žamberk
Ethnography. Memorabilia of Prokop Diviš and Eduard Albert.
By appointment.

ŽAROŠICE

LOCAL MUSEUM
Žarošice
Local history, ethnography.
By appointment.

ŽATEC

K. A. POLÁNEK MUNICIPAL MUSEUM
Husova ulica č. 678, Žatec
Palaeontology. Archaeology. Paintings. Sculpture.
Tu.-Sa. 9-12, 2-5; Su., public holidays 9-12.

ZBIROH

MUNICIPAL MUSEUM
Náměsti č. 41, Zbiroh
Local history, natural history.
May-Sept., Tu.-Su. 10-12. Other months by appointment.

JOSEF VÁCLAV SLÁDEK MEMORIAL MUSEUM
Náměsti č. 28, Zbiroh
Collections illustrating life and work of the journalist and teacher, J. V. Sládek (d.1912).
Su. 10-12. Other times by appointment.

ŽĎÁR NAD SÁZAVOU

MUSEUM OF THE BOOK
Zámek, Žďár nad Sázavou
Early printed books. Printing inventions. History of printing technology. Illustration processes.
Tu.-Su. 8-5.

ŽĎÁR MUSEUM AND ART GALLERY
Zámek, Ždár nad Sázavou
Geology. Mineralogy. Botany. Ethnography. Local history. Paintings. Memorabilia, manuscripts, printed works of local writers. Early 19th century textiles.
Apr.-Oct. daily 8-5.

ŽEBRAK

MUNICIPAL MUSEUM
č. 89, Žebrak
Local archaeology, history. Memorabilia of local writers.
On request.

ŽELEZNÁ RUDA

ŠUMAVY MUSEUM
Železná Ruda
History and products of local glass industry. Paintings on glass.
W.-Sa. 8-5; Su. 8-12.

ZELEZNICE

MUNICIPAL MUSEUM AND T. F. SIMON ART GALLERY
Muzejní náměsti č. 181, 94, Zeleznice
Geology. Mineralogy. Palaeontology. Archaeology. Folk art. Ethnography. Paintings.
June-Sept., Su. 8-12. Other months by appointment.

ŽELEZNÝ BROD

MUNICIPAL MUSEUM
Velké náměsti č. 197, Železný Brod
Folk art. Handicrafts. Local glass.
Su.-F. 10-12, 2-4.

ŽILINA

POVAŽIA MUSEUM AND ART GALLERY
Žilina
In 16th century Budatin Castle. Geology. Botany. Zoology, especially rare butterflies, of the region. Archaeology. Prehistory and history. Baskets, vases, cages, sculpture and other objects made by Slovak craftsmen from iron-wire. Paintings by local artists.
Tu.-Su. 8-5.

ŽIROVNICE

REGIONAL MUSEUM
Zámek, Žirovnice
Local history. Special collection of objects made of mother-of-pearl.
Tu.-Su. 8-12, 1-5.

ZLONICE

DVOŘÁK MEMORIAL MUSEUM
Bývalý špitál, Zlonice
Memorabilia of Anton Dvořak.
Su. 9-12. Other times by appointment.

ŽLUTICE

MUSEUM OF THE HUSSITE REVOLT
Náměsti Rudé armády č. 147, Žlutice
History of the Hussite movement. Archaeology. Local history.
By appointment.

ZNOJMO

MUSEUM OF SOUTHERN MORAVIA
Ulica Hradní č. 10, Znojmo
Mineralogy. Botany. Zoology. Archaeology. Handicrafts. Textiles. Coins. Local history.
Apr.-Oct., daily 8-4.

Dahomey

An agricultural country, trying to improve its economy by the cultivation of cotton and coffee, Dahomey has four museums, all established during the period of French administration. The collections are almost entirely ethnographical.

ABOMEY

HISTORICAL MUSEUM
Siège Annexe de l'I.R.A.D., B.P. 25, Abomey
Local history collections.
Daily 9-12, 3-6.

OUIDAH

HISTORICAL MUSEUM
Fort Portugais, Ouidah
Local history museum. Collections illustrate the history of the colonial period (1420-1960) and the discovery of the Gulf of Guinea.
Daily 9-12, 3-7.30.

PARAKOU

OPEN-AIR MUSEUM OF ETHNOGRAPHY AND NATURAL SCIENCES
Parakou
Open-air collections showing life in Dahomey. Natural history exhibits. Flora and fauna of the region.
Daily 9-12, 3-6.

PORTO-NOVO

ETHNOGRAPHICAL MUSEUM
I.R.A.D., B.P. 6, Porto-Novo
Ethnographical material on the tribes of Dahomey.
Daily 9-12, 4-8.

Denmark

By English and American, but not by Finnish standards, Denmark has a remarkable number of open-air museums. Most are of what might be termed the traditional type, collections of rural buildings moved to the museum grounds from their original sites, but there are other kinds too, including an open-air museum of sculpture and an open-air laboratory for archaeological experiments, such as building houses by old and, in some cases, prehistoric methods, and carrying out farming operations with reconstructions of prehistoric implements. One of the most interesting Danish contributions to the development of the rural, if not exactly open-air, museum concept has been the creation of watermill and windmill museums in which milling operations are carried on in the traditional manner but as a business, not merely as a display for the benefit of visitors. The miller, whose family has often run the mill for generations, is subsidised by the government in order to produce flour and animal feed in the old, but now uneconomic, way. This system, which has proved very popular with the public, and not unpopular with millers, allows the museum to earn a substantial part of its own living, which is in accordance with the current fashion for maximising investment.

Hunting, fishing and shipping are well represented, and so is agriculture, where a special effort has been made to locate and preserve early buildings, machinery and equipment connected with Denmark's long-important dairying industry. One cannot, unfortunately, say the same about another leading national speciality, furniture-making, which is poorly represented in museum collections. Its post-war contribution to the national export trade might seem to entitle it to a museum to itself.

Some of the most interesting archaeological material is the wide range of items recovered from peat-bogs, much of it in an extraordinarily good state of preservation. These discoveries include Viking ships, weapons and, most noteworthy of all, human beings, complete with their clothing and the contents of their stomachs, invaluable evidence of the Danish diet of many centuries ago.

Among the notabilities commemorated in museum collections are Tycho Brahe, the astronomer, and Hans Andersen, whose relics include the length of rope he always carried with him on his travels, to allow him to escape in case the hotel in which he was staying should happen to catch on fire.

ÅBENRÅ

ABENRÅ MUSEUM
33 H.P. Hanssens Gade, Åbenrå, S. Jutland
Prehistory, cultural history. Maritime collection. Ethnography, especially Chinese objects. Danish art, 19th and 20th centuries.
Daily except M. 2-4. Summer 10-12, 2-5.

ÅLBORG

ÅLBORG ART GALLERY
48 Algade, Ålborg, N. Jutland
19th-20th century Danish paintings, sculpture, drawings.
Summer: Daily 10-12, 2-5. Winter: W., Sa. and Su. 1-3. Closed M.

ÅLBORG HISTORICAL MUSEUM
48 Algade, Ålborg, N. Jutland
Prehistory. Cultural history. Reconstruction of Neolithic house from Ferslev (Himmerland, c.2000 B.C.).
Summer: Daily 10-12, 2-5. Winter: W., Sa. and Su. 1-3.

ÅRHUS

ÅRHUS KUNSTMUSEUM
(Århus Art Museum), Vennelystparken, Århus, E. Jutland
Danish painting, sculpture, graphic arts, c.1750 to present time. European graphics, paintings.
Tu.-F. 10-4; Sa., Su. 10-5. Closed M.

ÅRHUS MUSEUM
Vester Allé, Århus, E. Jutland
Antiquities, including Rune stones, Iron Age cauldron found at Braa, Roman swords and other objects from a bog at Illerup. Iron Age Grauballe Man, discovered in the Nebelgaards Mose and believed to be a nobleman who voluntarily offered himself as a sacrifice to the goddess of fertility. Danish paintings. Modern French paintings.
Daily 10-3 or 5. Closed M. in Winter.

DANISH PRESS MUSEUM
90 Strandvejen, Århus, E. Jutland
Collections illustrating the history of the Danish Press, from its early days. Technical developments. Censorship during the occupation (1940-45). Maps of the World Press. Economic basis of the Press 1900-1960. Sales and production. History of a century as recorded by the Press through hand-bills, headlines, and advertisements. Caricatures of well-known journalists.
M.-Sa. 12-4.

DEN GAMLE BY
(The Old Town), Vesterbrogade, Århus, E. Jutland
Open air museum. Town-houses, some with furnished interiors, workshops and handicrafts.
Opening hours of the houses: Summer, Daily 10-5. Winter: Weekdays 11-1, Su. 10-3 (these hours are extended at certain periods.)

MUSEUM OF PREHISTORY
Vester Allé, Århus, E. Jutland
Danish prehistory. Ethnography. Collections of the Bahrain expeditions.
Summer: Daily 10-5. Winter: Daily 10-3, closed M.

NATURAL HISTORY MUSEUM
Universitetsparken, Århus, E. Jutland
Zoology. Geology. Danish and foreign animals. African dioramas. Origins and development of life. Prehistoric skeletons. Denmark after the Ice Age.
Daily 10-5.

ARS

VESTHIMMERLAND MUSEUM
Ars
Prehistory. Cultural history. Folk collections, including finds from the Borremose.
May-Oct. Su. 4-6. Other times on application.

ALS

LOCAL HISTORY MUSEUM
Als Østj, Als, Hadsund
Cultural history. Old farmhouse, dating from the middle of the 19th century equipped with tools and furniture. Handicraft equipment.
On application.

ASSENS

WILLEMOES MEMORIAL ROOMS
36 Østergade, Assens, W. Funen
Cultural history. Memorial rooms of the naval hero, Peter Willemoes, in half-timbered building (1675).
Summer: Daily 10.30-12 and 2-5.

AUNING

GAMMEL ESTRUP
Jyllands Herregårdsmuseum, Auning
Former manor-house (17th century). Furniture, tapestries and portraits.
Daily 9-5.

BOGENSE

MUSEUM OF NORTH FUNEN
Rådhuset, Bogense, N. W. Funen
Prehistory. Cultural history. Costumes and crafts of North Funen.
Su. and W. 3-5.

BOVBJERG

JENS SØNDERGAARD MUSEUM
Bovbjerg, N.W. Jutland
House where the artist, Jens Sondergaard lived, with a collection of his paintings.
Daily 9-11, 2-4.

BRANDE

BRANDE MUSEUM
Godsbanegade, Brande
Prehistory. Cultural history.
Su. 3-5. Other times on request.

BREGNINGE

HJEMSTAVNMUSEUM
Bregninge, S. Funen
Half-timbered house of 1826, containing furniture, costumes, textiles and bygones from the island.
May-Sept. 10-6 or 8.

CHRISTIANSFELD

BRØDREMENIGHEDENS MUSEUM
Nørregade, Christiansfeld, S. Jutland
Ethnographical and folk collections. Historical relics of the Moravian brotherhood in the town.
Apr.-Sept. daily 10-5.

CHRISTIANSØ

CHRISTIANSØ MUSEUM
Christiansø
History of the fortifications 1685-1857. Local history since 1945.
Summer: Daily 1-4.

CLAUSHOLM

CLAUSHOLM CASTLE
nr. Randers, E. Jutland
Built 1694-99. Interiors from the time of Queen Anne Sophie, who died here 1743.
Usually open Apr.-Oct. daily 10-12, 2-5.

COPENHAGEN

AGRICULTURAL MUSEUM
79 Kongevejen, Lyngby, nr. Sorgenfri, Copenhagen
Danish agriculture. Implements, machinery.
May-Sept. Daily 10-6. Oct. Daily 10-4. Nov.-Jan. Su. 10-3. Feb.-Mar. Su. 10-5. Apr. Sa. and Su. 10-5.

AMAGER MUSEUM
Store Magleby, Copenhagen
Cultural history. Old farmhouse, containing rooms with furniture, implements and costumes showing influences from the Dutch immigration to Amager. Danish paintings of Amager.
May 15-Sept. 15 Daily 10-5. Sept. 16-May 14, W. and Su. 11-3.

ASTRONOMY MUSEUM
Rundetårn, Copenhagen K
History of Danish astronomy (Tycho Brahe, Ole Romer). Entrance from 'The Round Tower', built 1642 as observatory.
Su. 12-4.

BAKKE HOUSE MUSEUM
23 Rahbeks Allé, Copenhagen V
Building (1764). Memorial rooms of K.L. and Kamma Rahbek, who lived here 1802-30, and their circle of Danish poets. Collections illustrating Danish literature and culture, 1780-1850.
W., Th., Sa. and Su. 11-3.

BIOLOGICAL COLLECTION
5 Håbets Allé, Brønshøj, Copenhagen
Natural history collection for the use of Copenhagen schools and for adult education.
M., W. and F. 2-5.

BURMEISTER AND WAIN MUSEUM
4 Strandgade, Copenhagen K
Shipbuilding. Technical Museum owned by the firm of Burmeister & Wain (shipyard). History of Diesel engines.
Weekdays 10-1; Sa. 10-12.

CARL CLAUDIUS' MUSICAL COLLECTION
3 Carit Etlars Vej, Copenhagen V
Old musical instruments.
Guided tours W. and Sa. at 2.

CARLSBERG MUSEUM
1 Valby Langgade, Valby, Copenhagen
History of the Carlsberg Breweries and the Jacobsen family. Technical collections illustrating brewing processes.
Weekdays 12-3. Closed Sa.

CHRISTIANSBORG PALACE
Royal Reception Rooms, Copenhagen
Rooms equipped with paintings and furnishings of the period 1920-30.
Apr.-Oct. Daily ex. M. Nov.-Mar. Daily ex. M. and Tu. Guided tours at 12, 1, 2, 3, 4 p.m.

DANISH FILM MUSEUM
St. Søndervoldstraede, Copenhagen K
History of film, including a large collection of press cuttings and programme leaflets, as well as prints and negatives, books and periodicals, stills and posters. Film apparatus.
Daily M.-F. 12-4. Aug. 15-June 1, also Tu. and Th. evenings, 6.30-9.30. Sept.-May film shows M.-F. at 5, 7 and 9.

DANISH POST AND TELEGRAPH MUSEUM
59 Vesterbrogade, Copenhagen V
History of Danish postal service (collection of stamps), telegraphy and broadcasting.
Su. and Th. 10-4. Winter 1-3.

C. L. DAVID'S COLLECTION
30 Kronprinsessegade, Copenhagen K
Medieval Islamic art. Danish and foreign fine and applied art of 18th century.
Daily ex. M. 1-4.

FISHERIES MUSEUM
7 Nørregade, Copenhagen K
History of the Danish fishing industry. Models of old boats. Nets and fishing tackle from Denmark and foreign countries.
W. and Sa. 1-3.

GUNPOWDER FACTORY MUSEUM
Frederiksvaerk, Copenhagen
Museum of Gunpowder Factory for black gunpowder (1756-1965). Old mill houses with a working watermill and other machines.
Apr.-Oct. Daily 11-5.

HIRSCHSPRUNG COLLECTION
20 Stockholmsgade, Copenhagen Ø
Danish paintings, sculptures and drawings of the 19th century.
Daily 1-4. Closed M. Oct.-Mar. also Tu. 7-9.

MINERALOGICAL MUSEUM
7 Østervoldgade, Copenhagen
Minerals, fossils and meteorites. Geology of Denmark and Greenland.
Su. 10-12. M.-F. (from May 1 Tu.-Sa.) 1-4.

MUSEUM OF THE CITY OF COPENHAGEN
59 Vesterbrogade, Copenhagen V
History of Copenhagen. Soren Kierkegaard collection.
Daily 10-4. Nov.-Mar. 1-4, Closed M. Tu. also 7-9.

MUSEUM OF THE DANISH RESISTANCE MOVEMENT
Churchillparken, Copenhagen
Collections illustrating the work of the Danish Resistance Movement, 1940-45.
Su. 12-5; Weekdays 11-3 (June 15-Sept. 15, Daily 10-4; Su. 10-5; Tu. also 7-9 p.m.). Closed M.

MUSEUM OF DECORATIVE ART
Bredgade 68, Copenhagen K
Danish and foreign decorative art from the Middle Ages to the present day. Furniture. Carpets. Tapestries. Pottery. Porcelain. Silverware. Jewellery. Textiles. Bookbindings. Chinese and Japanese art and handicrafts.
Daily 1-4. Sept.-May, Tu. also 1-9.

MUSEUM OF THE HISTORY OF MEDICINE
62 Bredgade, Copenhagen K
Medical history, including exhibits on surgery, folk medicine, alchemy, vaccination, stethoscopy, octo-rhino-laryngology, ophthalmology, obstetrics and gynaecology, psychiatry, odontology and epidemics. Documents relating to Niels Ryberg Finsen and Wilhelm Conrad Röntgen.
June 1-Sept. 15, M.-F. 11-3.

MUSEUM OF THE HISTORY OF MUSIC
Åbenrå 34, Copenhagen K
Housed in the Reformed Church's former parsonage (1730). European musical instruments and musical history. Non-European instruments. Dutch paintings giving an impression of musical activity during the Renaissance and Baroque periods.
Daily ex. M. and Th. 1-4.

MUSEUM OF THE MOSAIC CONGREGATION
6 Ny Kongensgade, Copenhagen K
History of the Mosaic congregation in Denmark.
Su. 10-12.

NATIONAL MUSEUM
12 Frederiksholms Kanal, Copenhagen K
Danish civilisation from Stone Age to modern times. Ethnography. Royal Coin and Medal Collection. Oriental and Classical Antiquities. Prehistoric and Greenland sections.
Mid. June-mid. Sept. Daily 10-4. Mid. Sept.-mid. June Su. 1-5. Weekdays alternating departments 11-3 or 1-3. See locally for individual departments.

NEW CARLSBERG GALLERY
Dantes Plads, Copenhagen V
Egyptian, Greek, Etruscan and Roman classical art. Danish and French art of 19th century.
May-Sept. Daily 10-4. Oct.-Apr. Su. 10-4, Weekdays 12-3. Oct.-Mar. also Th. 7-10 p.m. Closed M. whole year.

NYBODEN MUSEUM
20 Skt. Pauls Gade, Copenhagen K
Furnished residence of ship-builder (Royal Dockyard), built c.1630.
Su. 2-4.

ORDRUPGAARD
110 Vilvordevej, Charlottenlund, Copenhagen
19th century French paintings.
May-Sept. Daily ex. M. 2-5. Oct.-Apr. Sa. and Su. 2-4.

ØREGÅRD MUSEUM
2 Ørehøj Allé, Hellerup, Copenhagen
Local history and topography of the municipality of Gentofte. Country house built 1806.
Su. and W. 2-5.

RAILWAY MUSEUM
40F Sølvgade, Copenhagen K
History of Danish railways. Collection of locomotives dating from 1868, as well as models of engines, ferries and ships.
Apr.-Oct. W. 12-4.

ROSENBORG PALACE
4A Øster Voldgade, Copenhagen K
Royal Castle (1606-34). Crown jewels and treasures of the royal family (15th-19th century). Silver. China. Paintings. Furniture.
May-Oct. Daily 11-3. Nov.-Apr. Su. 11-2; Tu. and F. 11-1.

ROYAL ARSENAL MUSEUM
3 Tøjhusgade, Copenhagen K
International collections of weapons, uniforms and weapons in Christian IV's armoury (1598-1604).
May-Sept. Weekdays 1-4; Su. 10-4. Oct.-Apr. Weekdays 1-3; Su. 10-4.

ROYAL LIBRARY
8 Christians Brygge, Copenhagen K
Illuminated manuscripts; Chinese, Indian, Islamic, Jewish manuscripts. Incunabula; Book-bindings.
Weekdays 9-6.

ROYAL MUSEUM OF FINE ARTS
1307 Sølvgade, Copenhagen
Danish paintings, sculpture 18th-20th century. Scandinavian paintings, 19th and 20th century. Italian, Flemish, Dutch, German and French paintings, 16th-20th centuries.
Department of Prints and Drawings in annexe at 18 Kastelsvej, Copenhagen O. (W. 10-10, Th.-Su. 10-4. Closed M. and Tu.)
Tu., Th.-Su. 10-5; W. 10-10. Closed M.

ROYAL NAVAL MUSEUM
St. Nicolai Kirke, Copenhagen K
History of the Royal Danish Navy. Ship models, weapons and other relics.
June-Aug. Daily 11-4. Sept.-May Daily 1-4. Closed M.

STATE ARCHIVES MUSEUM
Tøjhusgade, Copenhagen K
Exhibition of Danish historical documents from the public record office.
Su. 10-12.

THEATRE MUSEUM
18 Christiansborg Ridebane, Copenhagen K
History of the Danish theatre from the time of Holberg to the present day. In former Royal Court Theatre (1766).
Su. and W. 2-4.

THORVALDSEN MUSEUM
Slotsholmen, Copenhagen K
Paintings and classical antiquities collected by Thorvaldsen. His sculptures and paintings.
Daily 10-3. May 1 - Sept. 30, 10-4.

TS MUSEUM
15 Struenseegade, Copenhagen N
History of mechanical sound. Musical boxes, radios. Museum owned by the Tage Schouboe electro-technical wholesale business.
Su. 10-1.

WESSEL MUSEUM
3 Gråbrødretorv, Copenhagen K
Memorial rooms of the poet, J. H. Wessel, who lived here 1761-77. Building 1732.
Apr.-Oct. W. 2.30-5.

ZOOLOGICAL MUSEUM
15 Universitetsparken, Copenhagen
Modern exhibitions on animal life, with dioramas, working models and sound effects. Prehistoric animals from Denmark and from South Africa.
May-Oct. Daily 10-5. Nov.-Apr. M.-F. 1-5; Sa. and Su. 10-5.

DRAGØR

AMAGER MUSEUM
Store Magleby, Dragør, Amager
Amager furniture, dresses and needlework, displayed in an half-timbered farmhouse. Life and traditions of the district.
W. and Su. 10-5 (winter 11-3). Mid. June- mid. Aug. other days 1-3.

DRAGØR MUSEUM
Havnen, Dragør, Amager
History of the old fishing village and its shipping trade. Furniture, costumes. Model Ships. Architectural drawings.
Summer: Daily 3-5. Winter: Su. 3-5.

DRONNINGMØLLE

RUDOLPH TEGNER MUSEUM
Kildekrog, Dronningmølle
Works of the sculptor Rudolph Tegner (1873-1950).
Daily 9-12 and 2-sunset.

EBELTOFT

DYER'S HOUSE
Adelgade, Ebeltoft, E. Jutland
17th century craftsman's house, with its original dyeing plant and homemade tools.
Whit. - Oct. daily 10-6.

FRIGATE 'JYLLAND'
Ebeltoft, E. Jutland
Wooden man-of-war in the harbour of Ebeltoft (known from the Battle of Helgoland, 1864).
May-Sept. Daily 10-5.

MUSEUM
Raadhus, Adelgade, Ebeltoft, E. Jutland
Building (1789). Historical relics from the town and district. Prehistory. Old utensils.
Daily 9-12, 1-6.

POST HOUSE
Nedergade, Ebeltoft, E. Jutland
Archaeological and ethnographical collections from Thailand and Malaya.
Whit.-Oct. daily 10-6.

EMBORG

ØM MONASTERY
Emborg, nr. Skanderborg
Ruins of monastery. Archaeological and medical history museum. Medieval skeletons.
Apr. 9-5. May-Aug. 9-6. Sept.-Oct. 9-4.30.

ENGESVANG

KLOSTERLUND MUSEUM
Engesvang
Prehistory. Cultural history.
Su. 3-5. Other times on request.

ESBJERG

ESBJERG ART GALLERY
The Art Pavilion, Byparken, Esbjerg, W. Jutland
20th century Danish art.
Daily 10-12, 2-6. Closed M.

ESBJERG MUSEUM
1 Finsensgade, Esbjerg, W. Jutland
Prehistory, especially Iron Age. Cultural history. Folklore. Fishery collections.
Summer: Daily 2-5. Closed M. Su. also 10-12. Winter: Tu., Sa. and Su. 2-5; Su. also 10-12.

FISHING AND MARITIME MUSEUM
1 Finsensgade, Esbjerg, W. Jutland
Collections illustrating fishing and navigation.
Summer: Daily 2-5. Closed M. Su. also 10-12. Winter Tu., Sa. and Su. 2-5. Su. also 10-12.

ESPERGAERDE

TIKOB SOGN'S EDUCATIONAL COLLECTION
Stokholmsvej, Espergaerde, Zealand
Cultural history. Collections particularly for use in the teaching of history in local schools.
By appointment.

FAABORG

FAABORG MUSEUM
Østergade, Faaborg, S.W. Funen
Paintings, sculptures and drawings by artists of the Funen School (c.1885-1915).
Daily 10-12, 1.30-4. (Apr.-Sept. until 5).

KALEKO MILL MUSEUM
Holstenshuus Godskontor, 5600 Faaborg, S.W. Funen
On site of a medieval water mill (c.1440). The present building dates from 1650 and was last used as a mill in 1912. It has been converted into a museum of Danish rural life. The rooms are furnished and equipped with household articles to create a picture of how people lived and worked in the house last century.
Apr. 15- June 15, Sa., Su. and public holidays, 2.30-5.30. June 15- Aug. 31, Daily 10-1, 2.30-5.30. Sept. 1-30 Sa. and Su. 2.30-5.30. Closed Oct.-Apr. 15.

THE OLD HOUSE
Holkegade, Faaborg, S.W. Funen
Cultural history.
Summer: Daily 10-12, 2-5.

FÅREVEJLE

FÅREVEJLE MUSEUM
Esterhøj, Fårevejle
Cultural history. Local history and customs.
Apr.-Sept. daily on request.

FERRING

SØNDERGAARD'S MUSEUM
Bovbjerg, Ferring
Paintings by Jens Sondergaard (1895-1957).
Summer: Daily 9-12, 2-5.

FREDENSBORG

OLAF POULSEN MUSEUM
Slotsgade, Fredensborg, N. Zealand
House of the actor Olaf Poulsen (1849-1923), with memorial rooms.
Summer: Daily 2-4.

PALACE OF FREDENSBORG
Fredensborg, N. Zealand
Palace built 1719-32. Paintings. Ceilings in Louis XIV style. Furniture and furnishings. Chapel contains sculptures by Johannes Wiedewelt. The Normandsdalen contains 69 sandstone figures of peasants from Norway, Iceland and the Faeroes in national costume.
Daily 10-6, in the absence of the royal family.

FREDERICIA

FREDERICIA MUSEUM
Jernbanegade, Fredericia, E. Jutland
Cultural history. Building c.1720. Paintings. Relics from 1848-49 war.
Daily 1-5. Su. and weekdays June-Aug. also 10-12. Closed M.

FREDERIKSHAVN

BANGSBO MUSEET
Frederikshavn, N. Jutland
In 18th-century manor house. Cultural history, especially shipping and fishing. Examples of ships from Viking times and the Middle Ages. Resistance movement 1940-45. Danish paintings.
Daily 10-12, 2-6.

KRUDTTÅRN MUSEUM
nr. Harbours, Frederikshavn, N. Jutland
Collections of weapons and uniforms in tower (1686), a remnant of an old fortress.
June-Sept. Daily 10-12, 2-5.

FREDERIKSSUND

J. F. WILLUMSEN MUSEUM
Omkørselsvej, Frederikssund, Zealand
Paintings and sculptures by J. F. Willumsen (1863-1958), one of the founders of the Symbolist movement.
Apr.-Sept. Su. 10-5; Weekdays 10-12, 2-5. Oct.-Mar. Su. 10-4; Weekdays 1-4.

FREDERIKSVAERK

FREDERIKSVAERK AND DISTRICT MUSEUM
Torvet, Frederiksvaerk, N. Zealand
Cultural history. History of the town and its old armament industry. Housed in the previous arsenal (c.1800).
Mid. June-Aug. Daily 10-12, 3-5. May and Sept. W. 3-5, Su. 10-12 and 3-5.

FUR

FUR MUSEUM
Nederby Fur, Fur
Prehistory. Cultural history. Geology. Fossils.
Summer: Daily 10-11.30, 1.30-5.

GAMMEL ESTRUP

JYLLANDS HERREGAARDSMUSEUM
Gammel Estrup, nr. Randers, Jutland
Mansion on site of 14th century house. Collections illustrate old manor-house life in Jutland. 17th century Flemish tapestries depicting noted Danish manor houses (including Gammel Estrup). Portraits of the Empress Catherine II of Russia (by Vigilius Erichsen) and Count A. P. Bernstorff (by Jens Juel).
Daily 9-5.

GAVNØ

GAVNØ CASTLE
Gavnø, nr. Naestved
Former Dominican nunnery, founded 1402. Portraits of Danish noblemen. German and Dutch paintings.
Summer: daily 10-12, 2-5.

GILLELEJE

GILLELEJE MUSEUM
Main Street, Gilleleje, N. Zealand
Cultural history, especially fishing. Objects recovered from an old fishing hamlet, covered by sand 1500-1700. Instruments used by the lighthouse, buoys, pilot and customs authorities. Pottery and stoneware found in the sea. Material relating to the privateer war (1807-14), the wars against Prussia (1848-50 and 1864) and the two World Wars. Animal and plant life on the coast and in the sea.
June-Aug. Daily ex. M. 10-12, 2-5. Other times by arrangement (tel. 30-01-92 or 30-04-44 after 4 p.m.).

GLUD

GLUD MUSEUM
Glud, nr. Horsens, E. Jutland
Open air museum. Rural buildings. Prehistory. Cultural history.
May-Sept. daily 10-6. See locally for winter times.

GRENÅ

DJURSLAND MUSEUM
1 Søndergade, Grenå, E. Jutland
Prehistory. Cultural history. Weapons. Handicrafts. Coins.
Summer: Daily 10-11, 2-5.

GRINDSTED

GRINDSTED AND DISTRICT MUSEUM
Borgergade, Grindsted
Prehistory. Cultural history. Jutland pots.
May-Sept. 10-11, 2-5.

GUMMERUP

VESTFYNS HJEMSTAVNSGÅRDEN
Gummerup, 5620 Glamsbjerg
Farmhouse, furnished in the style of the 1880s. Furniture. Clothing. Tools. Forge.
Daily Apr.-Oct. 10-5.30.

HADERSLEV

HADERSLEV MUSEUM
Åstrupvej, Haderslev, S. Jutland
Prehistory. Open-air department with furnished farmhouses and mill. Antiquities include two Bronze Age sacrificial bowls of gold.
Daily 10-12, 2-5. Closed Th.

HELSINGØR

DANISH MARITIME MUSEUM
Kronborg Castle, Helsingør, N. Zealand
Collections illustrating the history of Danish merchant shipping and colonies. Ship models. Old prints and charts. Instruments. Model of Viking Gokstad ship at Oslo.
May-Sept. Daily 10-5; Apr. and Oct. Daily 11-4; Nov.-Mar. Daily 11-3.

DANISH TECHNICAL MUSEUM
Ndr. Trandvej 23, 3000 Helsingør, N. Zealand
Collections show the development and significance of natural sciences, techniques, industry, transport and means of communication from the early days to the present time. Professor Kratzenstein's electrostatic apparatus (1780). Christian Sørensen's linotype press (1855). Ball-typewriter of 1867-75. Hammel-car (1886). Early aeroplanes, motorcars, cycles, tramcars and an entire railway train (1868-69). Electric machines. Physics apparatus. Engines. Telephones. Electro-chemistry.
Daily 10-5.

HELSINGØR TOWN AND HAMLET MUSEUM
Marienlyst Palace, Helsingør, N. Zealand
Palace (1587). History of Helsingør. Paintings. Relics from Sound Toll period. Hamlet collection. Statues.
May-Sept., Daily 1-3.

KRONBORG CASTLE
Helsingør, N. Zealand
Fortified royal castle (late 16th century). Royal Apartments with furniture, tapestries. Chapel. Casemates.
Daily May-Sept. 10-5. Nov.-Mar. 11-3. Apr. and Oct. 11-4.

MUSEUM
West Wing, Karmeliterklostret, (Carmelite Monastery), St. Annagade, Helsingør, N. Zealand
Local relics. Hospital room.
Apr. 15- Sept. 15, daily 10-4.

HERNING

HERNING MUSEUM
Museumsgade, Herning, Mid. Jutland
Prehistory. Cultural history. Open-air department (farmhouses). Textile machinery.
Apr.-Sept. Daily 9-12, 1-6. Oct.-Mar. Daily 10-3.

HILLERØD

AEBELHOLT MONASTERY
nr. Hillerød, N.W. Jutland
Ruins of monastery 4 miles outside the town. Museum of human osteology (medieval skeletons).
May-Aug. Daily 10-5. Sept.-Oct. Daily 1-5. Nov.-Apr. Sa. and Su. 1-4.

NATIONAL HISTORICAL MUSEUM
Frederiksborg Castle, Hillerød, N. Zealand
Museum of national history in former royal castle (built c.1600). Historical paintings, portraits, furniture, and objects of art (Middle Ages to present day). Coronation chapel.
Daily May-Sept. 10-5. Apr. and Oct. 11-4. Nov.-Mar. 11-3.

NORTH ZEALAND MUSEUM ASSOCIATION
Sdr. Banevej 4, Hillerød, N. Zealand
Folk museum with collections of farming implements and tools. Furniture and craft exhibits. Local history.
Apr.-Aug. Daily 2-5.

HJERL HEDE

HJERL HEDE OPEN-AIR MUSEUM
Sevel, nr. Vinderup, Jutland
Old farmhouses, mills, dairy. Reconstructions of Iron Age house and church c.1100.
Apr.-Oct. Daily 8-sunset.

HJØRRING

VENDSYSSEL HISTORICAL MUSEUM
Museumsgade, Hjørring, N. Jutland
Prehistory. Cultural history. Bog and grave finds of Early Iron Age. Ecclesiastical art.
Daily 10-12, 1-4.

HOBRO

HOBRO MUSEUM
21 Vestergade, Hobro, N.E. Jutland
Prehistory. Cultural history. Townhouse built 1820. China. Relics of S. S. Blicher.
Daily 2-4.30; Su. and Sa. only 3-4.

HOLBAEK

HOLBAEK AND DISTRICT MUSEUM
16 Klosterstraede, Holbaek, N.W. Zealand
Prehistory. Cultural history. Buildings 1660 and later, with interiors arranged to show the former life and work of the town.
Daily 2-5. May-Oct. also 10-12.

HOLSTEBRO

DRAGOON AND FREEDOM MUSEUM
Holstebro, W. Jutland
Development of the Jutland Dragoons, as shown by arms and uniforms, 1679 - present day. Resistance material and weapons (1940-45).
Summer: Th.-Tu. 2-5; Su. 10-12, 2-5. Winter: Su. 10-12, 2-5.

HOLSTEBRO MUSEUM
Lystanlaegget, Holstebro, W. Jutland
Prehistory. Cultural history. Goldsmith's workshop. Domestic utensils.
Daily except M. 3-6.

HORNBAEK

RUDOLPH TEGNER'S MUSEUM
Kildekrog, Hornbaek, N. Zealand
Sculptures and paintings by R. Tegner. Park contains 14 bronze statues.
Daily 9-12, 2-sunset.

HORNSLET

ROSENHOLM
Hornslet
Manor house, built 1559-96. Portraits. Furniture. Tapestries.
Usually open daily during summer, 10-11.30 and 2-5.

HORSENS

HORSENS MUSEUM
1A Sundvej, Horsens
Collections of prehistory and cultural history. Danish art 19th-20th centuries.
Annexe at 31 Norregade, a furnished town house built 1740.
Daily 2-4. Closed M. Su. also 10-12.

HUMLEBAEK

LOUISIANA ART GALLERY
Humlebaek, nr. Copenhagen
Contemporary Danish fine and applied art.
Daily July 1-August 31, 10-7. Sept. 1-June 30, Daily 10-5.

HUNDESTED

KNUD RASMUSSEN'S COTTAGE
Hundested, N. Zealand
Arranged as it was when the arctic explorer lived in the cottage. Arctic equipment. Greenland women's dresses. Hunting implements. Pictures of Eskimoes.
Apr. 15- Oct. 15, daily 11-4. Oct. 16- Dec. 15 and Feb. 15- Apr. 14, daily 11-2.30.

HØJBY SJ.

STENSTRUP MUSEUM
4573 Højby Sj., Odsherred
Old farm sitting room from the early 19th century, with period furniture. Items from the warship "Prins Christian Frederik", destroyed by the English in 1808. One of the oldest typewriters in the world, made by a Dane, R. Malling Hansen (1870). Costume collection; Stone Age items. Tools. Watches.
Daily ex. M. 10-4.

HØJERUP

STEVNS MUSEUM
Højerup, nr. Store Heddinge
Prehistory and cultural history. Peasant rooms and clothing from Stevns.
Su. 3-5. Other times by arrangement.

HØRSHOLM

HØRSHOLM MUSEUM
2 Søndre Jagtvej, Hørsholm, N. Zealand
Cultural history. History of Horsholm.
May-Sept. Daily 11-4.

HUNTING AND FORESTRY MUSEUM
Hørsholm, N. Zealand
Collections are arranged in 18th century buildings which formed part of the Royal Horsholm Palace, demolished in 1810-12. Displays are devoted to the history of sport and forestry, sporting guns and hunting implements, Danish game species, collections of trophies, hunting in the Faroes and Greenland, cultivation of the heath, the giant oaks, the timber industry, and forestry tools.
Mar.-Nov. Daily 10-5. Dec.-Feb. Sa., Su. and holidays 10-4. Closed Dec. 24 and 31.

HØVE

LOCAL HISTORY MUSEUM
Høve, nr. Asnaes, N.W. Zealand
Cultural history. Costumes. Peasant furniture.
M.-Sa. 2-4; W. also 7-9; Su. 10-12, 3-6.

JAEGERSPRIS

JAEGERSPRIS CASTLE
Jaegerspris, N. Zealand
Former royal palace (17th-18th century). Memorial rooms to King Frederik VII.
May-Sept. Daily 10-12, 1-5. Apr. and Oct. Su. 10-12, 1-5.

KALUNDBORG

KALUNDBORG AND DISTRICT MUSEUM
Lindegården, Kalundborg, W. Zealand
Prehistory, cultural history. Town-house built 1620-1785. Furniture. Costumes.
Daily 9-12, 2-6 (winter until sunset).

KERTEMINDE

KERTEMINDE MUSEUM
Langegade, Kertminde, N.E. Funen
Cultural history. Paintings.
Daily 10-4. Closed M.

KILDEKROG

MUSEUM
Kildekrog, Helsingør
Sculptures and paintings by Rudolph Tegner (1873-1950).
Daily 9-12, 2-dusk.

KJELLERUP

TORNING MUSEUM
nr. Kjellerup, Mid. Jutland
Local culture. Material on St. Blicher, the poet.
Mar.-Oct., daily 10-12, 2-4.

KOLDING

KOLDING ART GALLERY
Koldinghus Castle, Kolding, E. Jutland
Danish art, mainly 20th century. Housed in a wing of Koldinghus Castle.
Daily. May-Sept. 9-6. Nov.-Mar. 10-3. Apr. and Oct. 10-4.

KOLDINGHUS MUSEUM
Koldinghus Castle, Kolding, E. Jutland
Prehistory. Cultural history. Furniture, silver, porcelain, arms and uniforms. Housed in the castle of Koldinghus destroyed by fire in 1808 and still partly a ruin.
Daily. May-Sept. 9-6. Nov.-Mar. 10-3. Apr. and Oct. 10-4.

KØGE

KØGE MUSEUM
Nørregade, Køge, Zealand
17th century house, with historical collections from the town and neighbourhood. Costumes. Memorials of the German occupation. Grundtvig's writing table.
May 15-Sept. 15, daily 10-12, 2-4 or 5. Other periods Tu., Th., Sa. and Su. 2-4.

LADBY

VIKING SHIP
nr. Kerteminde Fjord, Ladby, N.E. Funen
Viking burial ship of a 10th century chieftain, together with his arms and personal ornaments, four hunting dogs, warhorse and ten other horses.
Daily 10-6 (Oct.-Mar. 10-3).

LEJRE

RESEARCH CENTRE FOR HISTORY AND ARCHAEOLOGY
Lejre
Open-air laboratory for archaeological experiments (housebuilding and farming with pre-historic implements).
Summer: Daily 10-sunset.

LEMVIG

LEMVIG AND DISTRICT MUSEUM
Vesterhus, Lemvig
Cultural history. History of the North Sea Lifeboat Service. Paintings by local artists.
W. and Su. 3-5. June-Aug. also F.

LERCHENBORG

LERCHENBORG MANOR
nr. Kalundborg
18th century manor-house, privately owned. A few rooms open to visitors. Memorial room to Hans Andersen.
Summer: Daily 11-5.

LISELUND

OLD CASTLE
Liselund, nr. Borre
Park with château, 1792. Park contains Swiss cottage, Norwegian house, and Chinese summer-house. Furnishings.
Summer: Daily at any time.

LYNGBY

AGRICULTURAL MUSEUM
Lyngby
Agricultural tools, implements.
May-Oct. Daily 10-6 (to 4 in Oct.). Nov.-Jan., Su. and holidays 10-3. Feb.-Apr. 10-5.

OPEN-AIR MUSEUM
Lyngby
Rural buildings from many parts of Denmark and former Danish provinces in S. Sweden and re-erected here in natural surroundings. Mostly 18th-19th century, the buildings are furnished as far as possible in their original styles.
May-Oct. Daily 10-6 (to 4 in Oct.). Nov.-Jan. Su. and holidays, 10-3. Feb.-Apr. 10-5.

LYSGÅRD

BLIONER MEMORIAL MUSEUM
E. Bindstouw, Lysgård
House dedicated to the author, S. S. Blioner, who wrote short stories in Jutland dialect. Period furniture. The house formed a meeting place for artists and writers.
Daily 10-5.

LAESØ

LAESØ LOCAL HISTORY MUSEUM
Byrum, Laesø
Cultural history. 18th century farmhouse.
May-Oct., Su. 3-5. Other times on request.

MARIAGER

MARIAGER AND DISTRICT MUSEUM
Kirkegade, Mariager, E. Jutland
Prehistory. Cultural history. Domestic utensils. Furniture.
Summer: Daily 9.30-3.30.

MARIBO

DIOCESAN MUSEUM
Jernbanegade, Maribo, Lolland
Historical collection. Picture gallery. Polish collection.
Mar.-Oct., daily 10-12, 2-6. Nov.-Feb., daily 2-4.

LOLLAND AND FALSTER MUSEUM
22 Jernbanegade, Maribo, Lolland
Danish art, 18th-20th century. Prehistory, cultural history. Relics of Polish immigration.
Annexe: Open-air museum at Bangshave. Old rural buildings from the islands of Lolland and Falster.
Museum: Mar.-Oct. Daily except M. 10-12, 2-6. Nov.-Feb. Daily except M. 2-4; Th. also 7-9. Annexe: May-Sept. Daily 10-12, 1.30-5.

MARSTAL

MARSTAL AND DISTRICT MUSEUM
4 Prinsengade, Marstal, Aerø
Prehistory, cultural history. Shipping. Ships' models. Old prints. Nautical instruments. Local costumes.
June-Aug. Daily 9.30-5. May and Sept. Daily 10-12, 2-5.

MIDDLEFART

MIDDLEFART MUSEUM
6 Brogade, Middlefart, N.W. Funen
Cultural history. Local history. Copy of a bridal crown of the time of Christian II (1513-23).
Summer: Daily 10-12, 2-5.

MØN

MØN MUSEUM
Empiregaarden, Møn
Finds from prehistoric sites in the area. History of the island.
May-Oct. daily ex. Sa. 10-12, 2-4.

NIVÅ

NIVAAGAARD ART GALLERY
Nivaagaard, Nivå, nr. Copenhagen
Italian, French and Dutch paintings. 19th century Danish paintings, sculpture.
May-Sept. Tu., Th. and Sa. 1-4; Su. 1-5.

NORDBY

FANØ MUSEUM
Skolevej, Nordby, Fanø
Cultural history. Fano house.
June-Aug. 10-12, 2-4.

NYBORG

MADS LERCHES HOUSE
Kongegade, Nyborg, Funen
Half-timbered house (1601). Danish interiors. Folk collection.
Daily 9-12, 2-6. Winter: daily ex. W. 10-12, 2-3.30.

NYBORG CASTLE
Nyborg, Funen
Medieval royal castle, now a state-owned castle museum. Furnishings. Paintings. Weapons. Armour.
May-Sept. Daily 9-6. Feb.-Apr. and Oct.-Nov. Daily 10-3. Dec.-Jan. Closed.

NYKØBING (FALSTER)

ANNEBERG COLLECTION
Nykøbing, Falster
Collection of Roman-19th century glass.
Summer: Daily 10-12, 2-4.

FALSTERS MINDER MUSEUM
Faergestraede, 4800 Nykøbing F., Falster
Collections date back to 1500 and consist of national costumes, household articles from farmsteads and provincial towns on Falster, faience, pottery, tin and copper. Goldsmith's shop and workshop from 1800. Middle-class town sitting-room dating from about 1860-70.
Weekdays 10-4; Su. 10-12.

NYKØBING (MORS)

MORSLAND HISTORICAL MUSEUM
Dueholmgade, Nykøbing, Mors
Prehistory. Cultural history. Ecclesiastical art. Furniture. Agricultural implements.
Th. and Su. 3-5. Winter 2-4.

NYKØBING (ZEALAND)

ODSHERRED FOLK MUSEUM
Kirkestraede, Nykøbing, N.W. Zealand
Cultural history. Antiquities. Furniture and fittings from rural dwellings.
Summer: Weekdays 10-12, 2-4.

NAERUM

SØLLERØD DISTRICT MUSEUM
Naerum Ungdomsgård, Naerum
Prehistory. Cultural history.
Su. 2-4; W. 7-9.

NAESTVED

GAVNØ
Naestved, S.E. Zealand
Manor house (1755, partly c.1400) 4 miles from town. Collection of paintings.
Summer: Daily except F., 10-5.

MUSEUM OF ANTIQUITIES
Helligaandshuset, Naestved, S.E. Zealand
Collection of antiquities, housed in part of medieval hospital.
Daily 2-4.

NAEVSTED AND DISTRICT MUSEUM
4 Ringstedgade, Naestved, S.E. Zealand
Prehistory. Cultural history. Building 15th century, originally a religious hospital.
Daily 2-4.

NØRRE LYNDELSE

CARL NEILSEN'S HOUSE
Nørre Lyndelse
Childhood home of the Danish composer, Carl Nielsen (1865-1931). Mementoes. Period furnishings.
Apr.-Sept. daily 10-5.

ODDER

MUSEUM
5 Møllevej, Odder, nr. Horsens, E. Jutland
Housed in old water-mill. Costumes and peasant furniture. Dug-out boat carved with runes. Medieval pottery from the now-demolished Bjornkaer castle, nr. Hov.
M.-Sa. 2-4; W. also 7-9; Su. 10-12, 3-6.

ODENSE

H.C. ANDERSEN'S CHILDHOOD HOME
Munkemøllestraede 3-5, Odense, Funen
The house where Andersen lived with his parents during most of his childhood.
Apr.-Sept. Daily 10-5. Oct.-Mar. Daily 12-3.

THE FUNEN VILLAGE
Sejerskovvej, Hjallese, Odense, Funen
Open-air museum of 20 old rural buildings with furniture and implements; Smithy, toll-house, prison-house, windmill, inn, farmhouses; parsonage.
Apr.-Oct. Daily 10-sunset (Apr. 5.30. June-July 8.30, Oct. 4.30). Winter: Su. 10-4 (Dec.-Jan. 10-3.30). Weekdays closed.

HANS ANDERSEN'S HOUSE
Hans Jensensstraede 39-43, Odense, Funen
Birthplace of Hans Christian Andersen. Portraits, letters, orders conferred on Andersen, first editions of the *Fairy Tales,* translations into 50 languages. Drawings made by Andersen. Furniture and personal belongings, including his travelling equipment - trunks, hat case, umbrella, walking stick and the length of rope which he always carried in the event of fire at his hotel.
June-Aug. daily 9-9. Apr., May and Sept. daily 10-5. Oct.-Mar., Su. 10-12, 2-5; weekdays 10-3.

CARL NIELSEN'S CHILDHOOD HOME
Nørre Lyndelse, Odense, Funen
House where Carl Nielsen lived for some years when a child. Relics of the composer's childhood.
Apr.-Sept. Daily 10-5.

ODENSE MUNICIPAL MUSEUMS
Funen Museum, 3 Jernbanegade, Odense, Funen
Danish art, 18th-20th century, especially works by Funen artists. Archaeological finds from Funen, especially Iron Age. Prehistoric collections. Natural history. Numismatics.
Apr.-Sept. Daily 10-5. Oct.-Mar. Su. 10-12, 2-4, Weekdays 10-3.

ODENSE MUNICIPAL MUSEUMS
Møntestraede Museum of Cultural History, 48-50 Overgade, Odense, Funen
Cultural history, especially history of Odense and local corporations. Buildings 1547-1646. Ecclesiastical exhibits. Faience. Church plate. Costumes. Relics of old Odense.
Apr.-Sept. Daily 10-5. Oct.-Mar. Su. 10-12, 2-5; Weekdays 10-3.

OTTERUP

OTTERUP MUSEUM
Otterup
History of the town and the district. Objects found in the area round "The Plain" (the reclaimed land between Odense and Otterup).
Apr.-Sept. Daily 10-5.

ØLGOD

ØLGOD MUSEUM
Vestergade 49, Ølgod
Collections illustrate the history of the district from antiquity to the present time, special importance being attached to things which belonged to the common people between 1700 and 1800.
Branches of the museum are to be found in the town: a School Museum, and a Dairy Museum, (the first cooperative dairy in Denmark).
May-Nov. 1, W. 3-5; Su. 2-5.

PEDERSTRUP

REVENTLOW MUSEUM
Pederstrup, nr. Torrig, Lolland
Former manor-house (built 1813-22), now a memorial museum of the Reventlow family. Furniture, objects of art, portraits, chiefly 18th century.
Mid. April-Sept. Daily 1-6. Mid. June-mid. Aug. also 10-12. Oct.-mid. Apr. Daily 1-3.

PRAESTØ

THORVALDSEN COLLECTION
Nysø Manor House, Praestø, S.E. Zealand
Sculptures and sketches by Thorvaldsen, made during his stays 1830-33 at Nysø (manor house, built 1671-73).
Apr.-Sept. W. and Sa. 2-5; Su. 10-5.

RANDERS

RANDERS ART GALLERY
Fischersgade, Randers, E. Jutland
18th-20th century Danish art.
Daily 1-4. Closed M.

MUSEUM OF CULTURAL HISTORY
Stemannsgade 2, Randers, E. Jutland
Prehistoric and historical remains from the surrounding area. General outline of the prehistoric archaeology of the area. Local church history. Period rooms from the early 17th century up to 1912.
Tu., Th. and F. 2-6; W. 2-10; Sa. 10-2; Su. 2-5. Closed M.

REBILD BAKKER

FOLK ART AND SPILLEMAEND MUSEUM
Rebild Bakker, nr. Skørping, N. Jutland
Folk collection from the district, including instruments and relics of the wandering fiddlers ('spillemaend'), formerly to be seen all over Denmark.
Summer: daily 10-6.

THE LINCOLN LOG CABIN MUSEUM
Rebild Bakker, nr. Skørping
Souvenirs of Danish emigrants. The Cabin is built of logs from every original state in the union.
Summer: daily 10-6. Key at cottage near the kiosks.

REERSØ

REERSØ MUSEUM
Reersø
Local history and traditions.
Summer: daily 10-6.

RIBE

ANTIQUARIAN COLLECTION
Quedens' Gaard, Ribe, S.W. Jutland
Cultural history. Original interiors (Renaissance, 19th century). Prehistory. Renaissance furniture. Church fittings.
Summer: Daily 10-12, 2-6. Winter: Daily 11-12, 3-6. Porsborg: Daily except M. 3-6. Both Departments also F. 7-8.

HANS TAUSEN'S HOUSE
Skolegade, Ribe, S.W. Jutland
Prehistoric and medieval collections. Carved furniture from S.W. Jutland.
May-Sept. daily 10-12, 2-6.

RIBE ART MUSEUM
Skt. Nicolaj Gade, Ribe, S.W. Jutland
18th-20th century Danish art.
Apr.-Oct. Daily 2-5. Nov.-Mar. Daily 1-3.

RIBE TOWN HALL COLLECTION
Town Hall, Ribe, S.W. Jutland
Collection of the Corporation's arms, documents and silver. Old instruments of torture.
On application.

RINGE

RINGE MUSEUM
58 Algade, Ringe, Funen
Prehistory. Cultural history.
Summer: daily.

RINGKØBING

RINGKØBING MUSEUM
Museumspladsen, Ringkøbing, W. Jutland
Prehistory, especially Iron Age. Cultural history. Coins. Ecclesiastical exhibits. Objects from Greenland.
Daily.

RONAES

OLD PARSONAGE
Ronaes, nr. Odense, Funen
Far Eastern antiquities and costumes.
May-Sept. daily 10-8.

ROSENHOLM

ROSENHOLM CASTLE
Rosenholm, nr. Aarhus, E. Jutland
Moated Renaissance castle (c.1560). French and Flemish tapestries. Spanish furniture.
mid. Mar. - Oct. daily 10-12, 1-5.30.

ROSKILDE

ROSKILDE MUSEUM
18 St. Olsgade, Roskilde, Zealand
Prehistory. Cultural history. History of the town. Furniture. Costumes.
Daily 2-4. June-Aug. 2-5.

VIKING SHIP MUSEUM
Roskilde, Zealand
Five Viking ships dating from 1000 A.D.
June-Aug. Daily 10-8. Sept.-Oct. Daily 10-6. Nov. Mar. Daily 10-4. Apr.-May Daily 10-6.

RUDKØBING

LANGELAND MUSEUM
Jens Winthers Vej, Rudkøbing, Langeland
Prehistory. Cultural history. Finds from Stone Age settlements at Lindø and Treldebjerg, and from Viking graves.
June-Aug. Daily except M. 10-4. Sept.-May Daily except M. 2-4.

RØMØ

COMMANDER'S HOUSE
Toftum, Rømø
Furnished house, built 1748 for one of the sea-captains of the island.
May-Sept. Daily 10-7.

RØNNE

BORNHOLM MUSEUM
29 Skt. Mortens Gade, Rønne, Bornholm
Works of art chiefly by artists native to the island of Bornholm or who have worked there. Historical collections. Prehistory, cultural history. Annexe: 'Erichsens Gård'. Furnished house of well-to-do Ronne family (1807).
June-Aug. Daily 10-12, 2-5. May and Sept.-Oct. Su. 1-4, Weekdays 2-5. Nov.-Apr. Su., Tu. and Th. 1-4. Annexe: same hours.

SAEBY

VOERGÅRD CASTLE
Saeby
Paintings, Sculpture, Porcelain. Furniture. China used by Marie Antoinette and Louis XVI during their imprisonment in Tour de Temple in Paris during the French Revolution. Dinner set ordered by Napoleon I in the 100 Days period. Paintings by Rubens, Raphael, Goya and Corot. Altar with Catholic relics, including the Virgin Mary with the Infant Jesus by Della Robbia. Remnants of Ingeborg Skeel's grave-clothes and coffin furnishings.
Easter holidays, 10-5; Easter Sa. 2-5. May 11 - Sept. 17, Sa. 2-5; Su. 10-5. June 19 - Aug. 18, Weekdays 2-5; Su. 10-5.

SAMSØ

SAMSØ MUSEUM
Samsø
Built and established about 1830 as a farm and now containing a collection of objects from the Stone Age.
May-Oct. 10-12, 2-5.

SILKEBORG

SILKEBORG MUSEUM
Hovedgårdsvej and, 36 Hostrupsgade (new section), Silkeborg, Mid. Jutland
Old section: prehistory; cultural history. Danish art, mainly 20th century, housed in former manor-house c.1770.
New section: Modern international non-figurative art (especially Asger Jorn, Jean Dubuffet).
Daily May-Oct. 10-12, 2-5. Nov.-Apr. W., Sa. and Su. 10-12, 2-4.

SKAGEN

SKAGEN BYGONES
P.K. Nielsens Vej, Skagen, N. Jutland
Open-air museum of old Skagen buildings. Exhibits illustrating fishing and life-saving.
June-Sept. Daily 10-12, 1-6.

SKAGEN MUSEUM
Brøndumvej, Skagen, N. Jutland
Collections of paintings by Scandinavian artists working in Skagen (The Skaw) from 1870s onwards.
Mid. June-Aug. Daily 10-6 (in June and after Aug. 15 closed 12-2). Mid. May-mid. June and Sept. Daily 2-6. Oct.-mid. May, Su. only 2-5 (Nov.-Mar. 1-3).

SKIVE

SKIVE MUSEUM
Skive, Jutland
Archaeological and cultural collections from the region, including the largest find of amber (beads) in Denmark. Modern Danish art.
May-Oct. Daily ex. M. 2-5. Oct.-May, W., Sa. and Su. 2-5.

SKJERN

SKJERN MUSEUM
Skjern, W. Jutland
Prehistory; cultural history.
May-Oct. Su. 3.30-5.30.

SLEGE

SLEGE MUSEUM
Slege
Local history museum, including costumes, furniture and collections illustrating different styles of living over the past six centuries.
Summer: Daily ex. M. 10-12, 2-4. Other times by arrangement with the custodian.

SORØ

ACADEMY MUSEUM
Danneskjold's Avenue, Sorø, Zealand
Physics. Natural history. Ethnology.
Apr. 15- Oct. 15, Su. 2-4.

SORØ ART GALLERY
9 Storgade, Sorø, Zealand
Danish art from about 1300 to the present day.
May-Sept. Daily 2-5 (June 15- Aug. 15 also 10-12). Oct.-Apr. Su. 11-12, 1-3 (Mar.-Apr. to 4).

SORØ DISTRICT MUSEUM
17 Storgade, Sorø, Zealand
Cultural history. Memorial room to the poet B. S. Ingemann, who lived in Soro 1822-62. 19th century peasant interiors. Paintings by Chr. Dalsgaard.
Summer: Daily 2-4.

SPØTTRUP

SPØTTRUP CASTLE
Spøttrup, N. Jutland
Fortified castle built in the Middle Ages by the bishop of Viborg. Furnishings. Weapons.
June-Aug. Daily 10-6. May and Sept. Daily 10-12, 2-6.

STEGE

MØNS MUSEUM
75 Storegade, Stege, Møn
Prehistory, cultural history.
May-Oct. Daily 10-12, 2-4.

STRUER

STRUER MUSEUM
23 Søndergade, Struer, N. Jutland
Cultural history. Annexe: house of the poet Johs. Buchholtz (1882-1940). Costumes. Furniture. Domestic implements. Ships' models.
W., Sa. and Su. 3-5.

SVENDBORG

SVENDBORG DISTRICT MUSEUM
Fruestraede 3, Svendborg, S. Funen
Cultural history. Historical and maritime collections.
Su., W. and Sa. (mid. June-mid. Aug. daily) 2-4.

ZOOLOGICAL MUSEUM
Dronningemaen, Svendborg, S. Funen
Danish birds and their eggs. Fishes. Butterflies. Beetles. Mammals.
Daily 10-4 or 6.

SAEBY

SAEBY MUSEUM
3 Søndergade, Saeby, N. Jutland
Cultural history.
Mid. June-mid. Sept. Daily 9-12, 2-5.

SØNDERBORG

SCHOOL OF ATHLETICS
Sønderborg, S. Jutland
Modern Danish sculpture.
Mid. May- mid. Sept. daily ex. M. at 10.15 and 3.15.

MUSEUM
Sønderborg Castle, Sønderborg, S. Jutland
Prehistoric and medieval collections. Relics from the old Augustenborg. Exhibits illustrating the town's history. Military collections, including a model of the Dybböl fortifications and mementoes of the engagements of 1848-49 and 1864. Folk collection.
Mid. May- Aug. daily 10-6. Other periods 1-4.

TERSLØSE

TERSLØSE HOUSE
nr. Dianalund
Former manor house (1737) with memorial rooms to the author Ludvig Holberg, owner of the manor 1745-54. Mementoes and relics. Danish and foreign editions of his works.
Apr.-Oct. M.-Sa. 10-11, 2-4; Su. 9-11, 2-6.

THISTED

THISTED MUSEUM
4 Jernbanegade, Thisted, N.W. Jutland
Prehistory, especially Bronze Age. Cultural History. Memorial rooms to the poet J. P. Jacobsen and the folk high school pioneer Kr. Kold.
Summer: Daily 3-5 except M. (mid. June-mid. Aug. also Su. 10-12, W. and F. 7.30-9). Winter: Su. and W. 3-5.

TINGBAEK

BUNDGÅRD MUSEUM
Tingbaek Limemine, Tingbaek, nr. Skørping, N. Jutland
Quarry converted into a museum of the works of the sculptor, A. J. Bundgård.
Summer: daily 10-8.

TÓRSHAVN

FAROES HISTORICAL MUSEUM
Tórshaven, Faroe Islands
Archaeological finds of Viking period and Middle Ages. Cultural history. Fishing. Navigation.
Annexe: Dúvugarðar, Saksun. Old farmhouses.
Su. 3-5.

TRANEBJERG

SAMSØ MUSEUM
Tranebjerg
Prehistory; cultural history. Farmhouse, with furnished interiors.
Apr.-Oct. Daily 9-11, 2-5.

TROENSE

MARITIME MUSEUM
Old School, Troense
Maritime exhibits. Ships models. Maps and documents.
May-Sept. daily 8-6.

TRY

ØSTVENDSYSSEL LOCAL HISTORY MUSEUM
Try, nr. Dronninglund
Cultural history. Local traditions.
Summer: daily 11-12, 2-4.

TØNDER

TØNDER MUSEUM
Tønderhus, Uldgade, Tønder, S. Jutland
Furniture and ceramics from N. and S. Slesvig. Tönder lace. English porcelain. Dutch faience and furniture. Silver. Copper. Pewter.
Daily ex. M. 10-12, 1-4 or 6.

UDBY

GRUNDTVIG MEMORIAL MUSEUM
Udby Praestegård, Udby, nr. Lundby, S. Zealand
Memorial rooms to the clergyman and poet N. F. S. Grundtvig (1783-1872) who was born in the parsonage of Udby. Collections include several original manuscripts and first editions of Grundtvig's works, a collection of portraits of himself and his friends, furniture and oil paintings. The rectory itself is well preserved and unaltered since Grundtvig's time.
Apr.-Oct. 10-4. Other times on request.

VAERLØSE

VAERLØSE MUSEUM
3500 Vaerløse
Regional museum with collections of archaeology, textiles, peasant furniture, tools, documents and photographs.
1st and 3rd Su. of month and by previous arrangement.

VANDEL

RANDBØL SOGNS MUSEUM
Vandel
Prehistory; cultural history. Local traditions.
Summer: daily 11-12, 2-4.

VARDE

VARDE AND DISTRICT MUSEUM
Lundvej, Varde, W. Jutland
Prehistory. Cultural history. Church fittings from Middle Ages and Renaissance. Agricultural and fishing implements. Fano room and clothing. Numismatics. Paintings. Industrial art.
Su.-F. 2-5 (winter 2-4); Su. also 10-12.

VEJEN

VEJEN MUSEUM
4 Østergade, Vejen, S. Jutland
Sculpture and ceramics by N. Hansen Jacobsen. Danish aft of 20th century.
Daily 2-5. Apr.-Sept. also 10-12.

VEJLE

VEJLE MUSEUM
16 Flegborg, Vejle, E. Jutland
Danish art, mainly 20th century. Danish and foreign prints and drawings, 17th-20th centuries. Prehistory and cultural history.
Daily 10-5.

VIBORG

SKOVGAARD MUSEUM
3 Mogensgade, Viborg, Jutland
Works of art by Joakim Skovgaard and other members of his family.
Daily 1.30-5. Summer also 10-12. Closed M.

VIBORG MUSEUM
Gammel Torv, 8800 Viborg, Jutland
Regional museum, with collections relating to the cultural history of the area with special emphasis on the Bronze Age, the Middle Ages and the 18th century.
15 km. north of Viborg the museum has an open-air excavation area, Hvolris, with remnants of Stone Age, Iron Age and medieval settlements.
May-Oct. Daily 10-12, 1.30-5. Nov.-Apr. Daily 1.30-5.
Hvolris: May 15- Sept. 15, Daily 9-5.

VOERGÅRD

VOERGÅRD
nr. Praestbo, N. Jutland
Manor house, built 1590. Paintings. Furnishings. Open to visitors.
Summer: daily 10-12, 2-5.

VORDINGBORG

SOUTH ZEALAND MUSEUM
Algade, Vordingborg, S. Zealand
Prehistory; cultural history. History of Vordingborg castle, the ruins of which surround the museum. Peasant collections. Mementoes of M. A. Goldschmidt (1819-97), the novelist, born in Vordingborg.
June-Sept. Daily 9-12, 1-5. Oct.-May Daily except Sa. 9-12, 1-4.

AERØSKØBING

AERØ MUSEUM
5 Brogade, Aerøskøbing
Cultural history. Housed in former residence of a ducal magistrate (built c.1750).
Summer: Daily 9-11.30, 1.30-5. Spring and autumn: Daily 10-11.30, 2-4.

COLLECTIONS OF BOTTLE AND MODEL SHIPS
Smedegade, Aerøskøbing
Collection of 500 ship models, all inside bottles. Collection of pipes. Local bygones.
Daily 10-4.

HAMMERICH HOUSE
Gyden, Aerøskøbing
Half-timbered house c.1700 with collection of furniture, faience, tiles.
Summer: Daily 11-12, 2-3.

ØLGOD

ØLGOD MUSEUM
Ølgod
Cultural history. Local history and bygones.
Summer: daily 11-12.30, 2-4.

Dominican Republic

Discovered by Columbus in 1492, Dominica has over four million people of mixed European, African and Indian blood, mostly trying to make a living out of agriculture, and with something like half of them unemployed. This is a good environment for museums which concern themselves with natural history and with art; but very unsatisfactory for a museum with relevance to the present, unless it is a crusading one. Dominica concentrates on the first alternative.

SANT DOMINGO

NATIONAL FINE ARTS GALLERY
Santo Domingo
Later paintings and sculptures previously exhibited at the National Museum.
Daily 9-12, 2.30-5.30.

NATIONAL MUSEUM
Centro de los Héroes, Santo Domingo
Pre-Columbian exhibits. Indian, archaeological, anthropological and ethnographical collections. Ceramics, wooden objects, idols, amulets, charms, weapons and tools, pots, including some of Maya origin from Mexico and Guatemala; Weapons. Armour. Parts of ships. Ceramics. Bells. Contemporary paintings, drawings. Photographs. Numismatics.
Daily 9-12, 2.30-5.30.

Ecuador

Ecuador is a largely non-industrialised country, dependent on agriculture and forestry. Until very recently it had a high rate of illiteracy. In these circumstances it would have been unreasonable to expect much money to have been spent on museums, and it will be noticed that the majority of the museums which do exist belong either to educational or research institutions or to banks.

CUENCA

MUNICIPAL MUSEUM
Cuenca
Local history, ethnography. Paintings, furniture, handicrafts of the colonial period.
M.-Sa. 10-12.30, 3-6; Su. 10-12.30.

GUAYAQUIL

TOWN MUSEUM
Avenida 10 de Agosto, Calle Pedro Carbo, Guayaquil
Historical, ethnographical, palaeontological, geological exhibits. Colonial and modern paintings. Numismatics.
M.-F. 9-5.

QUITO

ARCHAEOLOGICAL MUSEUM
Banco Central del Ecuador, Quito
Archaeology of Ecuador.
M.-F. 9-5.

CENTRAL UNIVERSITY MUSEUMS
Ciudadela Universitaria, Quito
Sections on Anthropology, Archaeology and Ethnography.
By appointment.

CIVIC MUSEUM OF ARTS AND HISTORY
Calle Espejo 1147, Apdo. 399, Quito
Sculptures. Paintings. Documents illustrating history of Quito.
Tu.-Sa. 9-12, 3-6. Su. 9-12.

FRANCISCAN MUSEUM
Quito
Religious art.
Daily 9-5.

JIJÓN Y CAAMAÑO ARCHAEOLOGICAL AND HISTORICAL MUSEUM
12 de Octubre y Ladron de Guevara, Apto. 2184, Quito
Archaeology. Historical documents. Portraits. Uniforms.
By appointment, daily 10-1.

LA SALLE MUSEUM
Caldas 587, Apdo. 329, Quito
Natural science collections.
By appointment.

MUSEUM OF ARCHAEOLOGY AND ETHNOLOGY
Instituto Ecuatoriano de Anthropologia y Geografia, Casilla 2258, Quito
Prehistoric sculpture. Ceramics. Precious stones.
By appointment.

MUSEUM OF BOTANY AND FORESTRY
Servicio Forestal, Grecia 190, La Carolina, Quito
Herbarium. Equatorial trees and forest products.
By appointment.

MUSEUM OF COLONIAL HISTORY AND RELIGIOUS ART
Banco Central del Ecuador, Quito
Religious paintings, sculpture. Documents, handicrafts, art of the colonial period.
M.-F. 9-4.

MUSEUM OF THE MONASTERY OF SANTO DOMINGO
Monastery of Santo Domingo, Quito
Religious art.
On request.

MUSEUM OF MUSICAL INSTRUMENTS
Avenida 6 de Diciembre 332, Apdo. 67, Quito
European instruments. Pre-Inca and colonial examples from Ecuador.
Tu.-Su. 9-12, 3-5.

NATIONAL MUSEUM OF COLONIAL ART
Calle Cuenca and Calle Mejia, Quito
16th-18th century Ecuadorean sculpture, paintings.
Tu.-Su. 10-1, 3-5.

NATURAL HISTORY MUSEUM
Escuela Militar "Eloy Alfaro", Avenida Orellana, La Pradera 400, Quito
Geological specimens and fauna from the Galapagos Islands. Taxidermy and anatomy, especially of mammals and birds.
M.-F. 9-5.

PETROGRAPHICAL MUSEUM
Carrion 1016, Quito
Minerals found in Ecuador. Collections of the National Geological and Mineralogical Service.
By appointment.

PICTURE GALLERY
Casa de la Cultura Ecuatoriana, Parque de Mayo, Quito
18th-20th century paintings by Ecuadorean artists.
Tu.-Sa. 10-5; Su. 10-1.

ANTONIO SANTIANA ANTHROPOLOGICAL MUSEUM
Universidad Central del Ecuador, Quito
Anthropological collections from Central and S. America, especially Ecuador.
By appointment.

Egypt

There are few more famous museums in the world than the National Museum in Cairo, with its remarkable collections of antiquities, including most of the Tutankhamun material. But the National Museum is in urgent need of money and modernisation, and presents a distinctly nineteenth-century appearance to the visitor who goes there today, and the Tutankhamun relics certainly looked a good deal better when they were shown in London than they normally do in Cairo.

The Egyptians are not always the best publicists in their own cause, at least where museums are concerned. The excellent and lively Science Museum and the Agricultural and Cotton Museum in Cairo and the Fine Arts Museum in Alexandria, for instance, show much more evidence of modern museum thinking than most of the archaeological museums do. The Science Museum, however, appears in no tourist literature that the present editors have seen and few tours find time for the Agricultural and Cotton Museums, which seems a great pity.

ALEXANDRIA

FINE ARTS MUSEUM AND CULTURAL CENTRE
18 Sharia Menashe, Alexandria
Permanent collection of modern Egyptian painting and sculpture. Temporary exhibitions of European art.
Daily ex. M. 9-1, 5-8.

GRECO-ROMAN MUSEUM
Museum Street 5, Alexandria
Exhibits from the Coptic, Roman and Greek eras. Roman and Ptolemaic sculpture. Mosaics. Sarcophagi. Tombstones and funerary stelae. Egyptian monuments and mummies. Pottery. Lamps. Cinerary urns. Terracotta statuettes. Tanagras. Jewellery. Christian antiquities.
Daily 9-4. Closed F., 11.30-1.30.

MONTAZAH PALACE MUSEUM
Montazah, Alexandria
19th century royal palace, with original furnishings and family possessions.
Daily 8-sunset.

MARITIME MUSEUM
Quait Bey Fort, Alexandria
Egyptian naval and maritime history.
Daily 8-3. Closed F. 11.30-1.30.

OCEANOGRAPHY AND AQUARIUM MUSEUM
Anfushy, Alexandria
Dioramas, showing Mediterranean fish and underwater life. Skeleton of whale.
Daily 9-2.

CAIRO

ABDINE PALACE MUSEUM
El Goumhouria Square, Cairo
Former royal palace (19th century) with original furnishings and family possessions.
Daily 9-5.

AGRICULTURE MUSEUM
El Dokki, Giza, Cairo
History of Egyptian agriculture. Seeds and other food crops from pyramids and other tombs. Implements. Irrigation methods. Botany. Zoology.
Daily ex. M., public holidays, 9-4.

AL GAWHARA PALACE MUSEUM
Citadel, Cairo
Built 1811, on the Ottoman style. Original interiors. Oriental and French furniture, including gilded throne, Turkish paintings, exhibitions of clocks, glass, 19th century costumes.
Daily 9-4.

AL MANIAL PALACE MUSEUM
Isle of Rodah, Cairo
Former royal palace, with original furnishings.
Daily 9-5.

ANDERSON MUSEUM
Beside Ibn Tulun Mosque, Beit el-Kretlia, Cairo
Private collections of Oriental art objects bequeathed to Egypt by R. G. Gayer Anderson Pasha in 1936.
Daily 8.30-4. Closed F. 11.15-1.

COPTIC MUSEUM
St. George Street, Old Cairo
Sculpture. Architecture. Ivory. Pottery. Glass. Manuscripts. Textiles. Icons. Metalwork.
Summer: daily 8-1. Winter: daily 9-4.

ARAB POST MUSEUM
Arab League Building, Midan Al Tahir, Cairo
Collections illustrating history of the Arab Post.
Daily ex. F., public holidays, 10-1.

COTTON MUSEUM
Agricultural Society, Gezira, Cairo
All aspects of cotton growing, diseases, pests, and methods of spinning and weaving are shown.
Daily 8-1.30.

EGYPTIAN ANTIQUITIES MUSEUM
Mariette Pasha Street, Cairo
Material from pre-dynastic and Pharaonic sites. Paintings, statues, reliefs. Objects from the tomb of Tutankhamen. Royal mummies.
Daily 8.30-4; closed F. 11.15-1.

EGYPTIAN NATIONAL MUSEUM
Midan-el-Tahrir, Kasr El-Nil, Cairo
Collections from prehistoric times until 6th century A.D., excluding Coptic and Islamic periods.
Winter: daily 9-4. Summer: daily 9-1.

GEOLOGICAL MUSEUM
Sharia El Sheikh Rihan 15, Cairo
Geological specimens, mostly Egyptian. Exhibits illustrating all branches of geology, especially recent acquisitions connected with revival of industry.
Daily ex. F., public holidays, 9-1.

GEZIRA MUSEUM
Gezira, Cairo
History of the Pyramids. Material found during excavations.
Daily 9-3.

HELWAN PALACE MUSEUM
Helwan, Cairo
Former royal palace, with original furnishings.
Daily 9-5.

MILITARY MUSEUM
The Citadel, Cairo
History of the Egyptian army.
Daily 9-4. Closed F., 11.15-1.

MOHAMED MAHMRUD KHALIL MUSEUM
St. Saray el Guezired, Zamalak, Cairo
Collections illustrating life and achievements of M. M. Khalil.
Daily 9-2.

MOUSTAFA KAMEL MUSEUM
The Citadel Area, Cairo
Collections illustrating life and achievements of Moustafa Kamel.
Daily 9-5.

MUKHTAR MUSEUM
El Gezira, Cairo
Archaeological and ethnographical collections.
Daily 9-2.

MUSEUM OF EGYPTIAN CIVILISATION
Agricultural Society, Giza, Cairo
Arts, crafts and technology of Egypt. Textiles. Pottery. Glass. Transport. Dioramas. Dams and irrigation.
Daily ex. F., public holidays, 9-4.

MUSEUM OF HYGIENE
Midan-el-Gamhouria, Cairo
Exhibits illustrating history and techniques of public health.
Sa.-Th. 9-4. F. 1-4.

MUSEUM OF ISLAMIC ART
Ahmed Maher Square, Cairo
Collection of objects representing the evolution of Islamic art from the spread of Islam till 1879.
Daily 9-4. Closed F., 11.15-1.

MUSEUM OF MODERN ART
4 Sharia Kasr, El-Nil, Cairo
Paintings, sculpture, graphics by 20th century artists, mostly Egyptian.
Winter: daily 9-4. Summer: daily 9-1.

POSTAL MUSEUM
General Post Office, Ataba, Cairo
History of the Egyptian postal services. Postage stamps.
Daily ex. F., public holidays, 8.30-1.

SCIENCE MUSEUM
Cairo
Principles of science, illustrated by working models and displays. Development of communications. Public health. Science and handicraft clubs.
Daily 8.30-5.

STATE RAILWAYS MUSEUM
Central Station, Bab el Hadid, Cairo
Models of foreign and Egyptian railways, and technical information and statistics of the evolution and development of the Egyptian railway services.
Daily 8.30-2.

WAX MUSEUM
Helwan, Cairo
Wax figures and dioramas illustrating Egypt's history.
Daily 9-4.

El Salvador

El Salvador is distinguished as the main world source of the gum obtained from balsam trees. This by itself makes an inadequate basis for the collections of its two museums, which are necessarily supplemented by material illustrating the country's great timber resources, its agriculture and its folklore and handicrafts.

SAN SALVADOR

NATIONAL MUSEUM DAVID J. GUZMAN
Carretera Internacional Franklin Delano Roosevelt, San Salvador
History. Archaeology. Ethnography. Linguistics.
Daily ex. M. 9-12, 2.30-5.30.

NATURAL HISTORY MUSEUM
Parque Zoologico Nacional, "Finca Modelo", San Salvador
Natural history collections. Birds, mammals of El Salvador.
Daily ex. M. 9-12, 2.30-5.30.

Equatorial Guinea

The solitary museum of Equatorial Guinea concentrates its attention on the ethnography of the country, especially its art and handicrafts. Much of this material is at present being stored as it is collected, awaiting the time when display facilities become available.

SANT ISABEL

MUSEUM OF ETHNOGRAPHY
C.M.F., Apartado 10, Santa Isabel
Prehistory and ethnography of Fernando Pó and Rio Muni. Nature art of the Bubus. Sculptures, wooden columns of totemistic importance, wooden bells.
By arrangement.

Ethiopia

The five museums of Ethiopia are concerned almost entirely with religious art and with the prehistory of the country. There has been, as yet, little attempt to create exhibits of the natural history of Ethiopia, which is one of its most remarkable features.

ASMARA

ARCHAEOLOGICAL MUSEUM
Liceo Martini, Asmara
Archaeological finds from excavations in the area.
M.-Sa. 9-12, 3-6; Su. 9-12.

ADDIS ABABA

INSTITUTE OF ETHIOPIAN STUDIES MUSEUM
Haile Selassie I University, Addis Ababa
Collection of Ethiopian church art, including icons, crosses and manuscripts. Ethiopian ethnography. Complete set of coins from Harar. Musical instruments. Ceremonial dresses. Crown and stool of the Kings of Kaffa.
M.-F. 8.30-12.30, 2.30-5.30; Sa. and Su. 9-1.

MUSEUM OF THE HOLY TRINITY CHURCH OF ETHIOPIA
Like Sultinate Hapte Mariam, Addis Ababa
Religious art. Liturgical objects.
M.-Sa. 8.30-1, 3-6.

NATIONAL MUSEUM
King George VI Street, P.O. Box 2065, Addis Ababa
Prehistory of the Omo Valley. Archaeological finds from Axum and Matara. Historical material includes photo-murals of Lalibela rock churches, and portraits of Emperors. Inscriptions of the first Ethiopian writings. Room devoted to the contemporary artist, Afewrk Tekle.
M.-Sa. 9-1, 3-6; Su. 2-6.

NATURAL HISTORY MUSEUM
Haile Selassie I University, P.O. Box 1176, Addis Ababa
Displays of natural history of Ethiopia: birds, mammals, flora and fauna.
M.-F. 8.30-12.30, 2.30-5.30.

Falkland Islands

The Falkland Islands have only one museum, largely the result of the enthusiasm of a single man. Apart from general material related to the natural history and history of the Islands the collection is noteworthy for a number of relics of the S.S. *Great Britain*, which was stranded here for many years before its ultimate return to Britain.

PORT STANLEY

FALKLAND ISLANDS MUSEUM
Port Stanley, Falkland Islands, South Atlantic
Historical collection of Falkland Island exhibits, including early colonial and maritime objects. Geological and botanical specimens. Relics of *S.S. Great Britain* and its stranding in Port Stanley.
On request. Keys available at Police Station.

Fiji

Fiji means above all things the sea, and the island's museum has constructed its collections around the long-established and fundamental activities of fishing and sailing and rowing boats, with sufficient about living conditions and handicrafts to balance the picture.

SUVA

FIJI MUSEUM
Botanical Gardens, Suva
Emphasis on Melanesian material and in particular that of Fiji from 1836 onwards. Weapons, pottery, bark cloth, headrests from the 1870-1880 period which are associated with Ratu Cokobau who ceded Fiji to Great Britain. Solomon Islands material includes barava plaques, clam shell work, carved house posts and musical instruments. Masks, pottery and tree gongs from the New Hebrides; fishing gear, weapons and other artifacts from the Gilbert and Ellice Islands. New Guinea collection. Maritime exhibits.
M.-F. 8.30-5; Sa. 8.30-12; Su. 2-5.

Finland

It has been said, unkindly but not altogether untruthfully, that the Finnish recipe for a museum is to buy a small field, scatter old wooden cottages, pig-houses, sauna-baths and cowsheds over it, with a windmill and a rural distillery for good measure, and then to open the results to the public between the beginning of May and the end of September. This is a fair description of the raw material of at least a third of all the museums in Finland, but it ignores two important facts; one, that the task can be carried out either with or without skill and imagination; and the other, that all or any of these wooden buildings house historical collections of one kind or another. Good or less good, however, these open-air museums are popular, non-sensational and non-vulgar and they allow a lot to be done on a small budget, an important advantage in a far from wealthy country. Summertime visitors who wonder why these museums tend to be a little bare and primitive should try to think of them in December and January, closed, unheated and covered in snow, conditions which are liable to be a little hard on all but the most robust museum objects and displays. That said, it would be both ungracious and unjust not to emphasise that the Finns have shown what is, by world standards, an exceptional concern for preserving the evidence of their rural and agricultural past and that many of the collections are exceedingly well presented.

Relics of Finland's maritime history are to be found in a number of museums, the most impressive single exhibit being the understandably cherished windjammer *'Pommern'*, which for many years earned her living carrying grain from Australia to England. Looking through the list of Finnish museums one is reminded frequently of the fact that all this was once Russian territory, with the Czar's fishing lodge, a museum in a former Russian military church and, inevitably, a Lenin Museum, all available for public inspection.

There are several bank museums - Finland and the Argentine are the great countries for bank museums - and, quite properly, two Sibelius museums and three glass museums. Less to be expected, perhaps, but agreeably original, is a Customs Museum, "illustrating the methods of the Customs and Revenue Departments".

ALAJÄRVI

NELIMARKKA MUSEUM
Pekkola, Alajärvi
Paintings. Drawings. Applied arts. Memorabilia of Eero Nelimarkka.
M.-Sa. 10-4; Su., public holidays 12-6.

ANJALA

ANJALA MANOR-HOUSE MUSEUM
Anjala
18th-19th century period rooms. Applied arts. Paintings. Graphics.
Tu.-F. 12-6; Sa. 12-4; Su. 11-7.

ARTJÄRVI

DISTRICT MUSEUM
Ratula, Artjärvi
Early 18th century house and outbuildings, including sauna. Windmill. Local history. Handicrafts. Agricultural implements.
By appointment.

ASIKKALA

URAJÄRVI FARM MUSEUM
Urajärvi, Asikkala
Farmhouse (1740-50). Furnishings. Agricultural implements, equipment.
May 15- Sept. 15, daily 10-5. Other times by appointment.

ASKAINEN

LOUHISAAREN FARM MUSEUM
Askainen
Manor-house (1655). Period furnishings, household equipment. Agricultural implements.
May 15- Sept. 15, daily 12-5.

BILLNÄS

IRON MUSEUM
Billnäs
Museum of the Oy Fiskars Company, showing history of the iron-industry at Billnäs. Collection of axes, spades and other tools made at the forge.
On request.

ELIMÄKI

MUSEUM OF THE CORPS OF PIONEERS
Koria, Varuskunta, Elimäki
Collections illustrating history and work of the Army Corps of Pioneers.
Su. 10-4.

ESPOO

CLOCK MUSEUM
Opintie 5, Tapiola, Espoo
Clocks and watches. Clock-maker's workshop.
By appointment.

DISTRICT MUSEUM
Glims, Espoo
18th century house, subsequently inn, with stables and other outbuildings, including dairy. Agricultural implements, equipment.
W. 10-4; Su. 12-4.

GALLEN-KALLELAN MUSEUM
Tarvaspää, Leppövaara, Espoo
Paintings, graphics, sculpture. Early paintings, graphics by Gallen-Kallelan.
Tu.-Sa. 12-4.

MUSEUM OF THE GEOLOGICAL INSTITUTE
Otaniemi, Espoo
Geology. Mineralogy. Palaeontology.
Su. 12-3.

EVIJÄRVI

LAKE MUSEUM
Kerttuankylä, Evijärvi
Open-air museum of houses and other rural buildings, including a church and distillery. Handicrafts. Agricultural implements.
June-Aug., daily 12-6.

FORSSA

NATURAL HISTORY MUSEUM
Kartanonkatu 10A, Forssa
Flora and fauna of the Forssa region.
Tu., Th., Su. 1-5.

SOUTH-WEST HÄME MUSEUM
Teatteritalo, Forssa
Local history. Handicrafts, especially textiles. Furniture. Household equipment.
Su. 1-4.

HÄMEENLINNA

ART MUSEUM
Viipurcntie 2, Hämeenlinna
Paintings, graphics, sculpture, especially by Finnish artists.
Tu., W., F. 10-3, 5-8; Th. 10-1, 3-5; Sa. 10-1; Su. 12-5.

HÄMEENLINNA MUSEUM
Lukiokatu 6, Hämeenlinna
Local history. Furniture. Household equipment. Paintings. Handicrafts. Toys.
Su.-F. 12-4; W. also 6-8.

MILITARY MUSEUM
Parolo, Hämeenlinna
Military history of Finland.
May-Oct., daily 9-9.

HAMINA

CITY MUSEUM
Kadettikoulunkatu 2, Hamina
History of Hamina. Shipping. Commerce. Military history.
May-Sept., Tu.-Sa. 12-2; Su. 12-3. Oct. Apr., Su. 12-3.

HANKASALMI

PIENMÄEN HOUSE-MUSEUM
Niemisjärvi, Hankasalmi
Pienmäen house, with wood-shed, sauna and other outbuildings. Furniture. Household equipment.
On request.

HANKO

HANKO MUSEUM
Kaupungintalo, Hanko
History of Hanko and its region. Furnishings. Handicrafts. Shipping history.
Th., Su. 2-4.

HARJAVALTA

EMIL CEDERCREUTZIN MUSEUM
Harjula, Harjavalta
Regional history. Agriculture. Craftsmen's tools, equipment. Paintings. Drawings. Graphics. Sculpture.
M.-F. 5-7; Su. 12-5.

HARTOLA

EAST HÄME MUSEUM
Koskopää, Hartola
Cultural history of the area. Paintings. Furnishings. Costumes. Agriculture. Household equipment. Folk art.
Daily 12-4.

HATTULA

MUSEUM OF ARMOURED VEHICLES
Parolannummi, Hattula
Tanks, rocket-launchers and other armoured vehicles.
May 1-31, daily 9-9.

HAUHO

HAUHO MUSEUM
Hauho
Open-air museum, with houses, mill and other rural buildings (1700-1850).
Su. 11-2. Other times by appointment.

HEINOLA

HEINOLA MUSEUM
Siltakatu 20, Heinola
Local history. Agriculture. Folklore. Handicrafts.
Su. 4-7; Tu.-Th. 6-8.

HELSINKI

AMOS ANDERSON MUSEUM OF ART
Yrjönkatu 27, Helsinki 10
Paintings. Graphics. Religious art.
Th.-Su., Tu. 11-4; W. 11-8.

ARABIA MUSEUM
Hämeentie 135, Helsinki 56
Products of local industries, especially ceramics, textiles.
On request.

ARMFELT MUSEUM
Suomenlinna A5, Helsinki 19
Local history. Period rooms.
May 1-31, Sept. 1-30, daily 12-4; June-Aug., daily 12-5.

ARCHITECTURAL MUSEUM OF FINLAND
Puistokatu 4, Helsinki
Drawings, models, photographs illustrating history of Finnish architecture.
M.-F. 10-4; Sa. 1-3.

ATENEUM ART GALLERY
Kaivokatu 2-4, Helsinki 10
16th-20th century European paintings, drawings, engravings. 19th-20th century works by Finnish artists.
Tu.-Sa. 10-4; W. also 6-8; Su. 11-4.

CUSTOMS MUSEUM
Unionkatu 5, Helsinki 13
Collections illustrating history and methods of the Finnish Customs and Revenue departments.
W. 6-7. Other times by appointment.

CYGNAEUKSEN GALLERY
Kalliolinnant 17, Helsinki 14
European paintings, drawings, especially Finnish, German.
W.-Su. 12-2; W. also 6-8.

DIDRICHSEN MUSEUM OF ART
Kuusilahdenkuja 3, Helsinki 34
Paintings. Handicrafts. Applied art and folk art of Asia, Central and South America.
W., Su. 2-4. Other times by appointment.

FINNISH NATIONAL MUSEUM
Mannerheimintie 34, Helsinki 10
Prehistory, history of Finland. Ethnographical collection covering the whole world, especially N. Africa, Central Europe and Balkans, Siberia, Mongolia, Tibet, N. and S. America.
June-Aug., daily 11-3. Sept.-May, Tu.-Su. 12-3. F. also 6-8.

GALLEN-KALLELA MUSEUM
Leppävaara, Tarvaspää, Helsinki
Former home of the artist, Gallen-Kallela. Collection of his paintings.
M., W., F. 12-4; Tu.-Th. 12-8; Su. 10-5.

HELSINKI MUNICIPAL MUSEUM
Karamsininkatu 2, Helsinki 10
History of Helsinki. Furniture. Paintings. Drawings. Prints. Archives. Literature relating to Helsinki.
Su.-F. 12-4; Th. also 6-8.

HELSINKI TELEPHONE MUSEUM
Korkeavuorenk 35, Helsinki 13
Collection illustrating development of the telephone system and of communications technology.
On request.

HELSINKI THEATRE MUSEUM
Aleksanterink 12, Helsinki 10
History of the theatre in Finland. Drawings. Paintings. Photographs. Stage and costume design. Programmes.
Su. 12-4; W., F. 5-7.

MANNERHEIM MUSEUM
Kaivopuisto, Kalliolinnantie 22, Helsinki 14
Former home of Marshal Mannerheim. Original furnishings. Personal possessions and war-mementoes of the Marshal.
Tu.-Sa. 11-3; Su. 11-4.

MILITARY MUSEUM
Maurinkatu 1, Helsinki 17
History and campaigns of the Finnish army. Uniforms. Weapons. Equipment.
Su.-F. 11-3; F. also 6-8.

MISSIONARY MUSEUM
Tähtitorninkatu 16A, Helsinki 14
Ethnographical material collected by Finnish missionaries, especially in Africa, China.
Su. 1.30-3. Other times by appointment.

MUSEUM OF THE CO-OPERATIVE BANK
Arkadiankatu 23, Helsinki 10
History of the bank. Records. Equipment. Photographs.
Daily, during banking hours.

MUSEUM OF THE CO-OPERATIVE SOCIETY
Marjaniemi, Helsinki 82
Collections illustrating history and development of the Society. Documents. Photographs. Equipment.
By appointment.

MUSEUM AT THE COURTS OF JUSTICE
Thomarinkylän kartano, Helsinki
In former law-courts building (1780). Early fire-fighting equipment. Agricultural implements. Furniture. Pewter. Pottery. Textiles.
Su.-F. 12-4; Th. also 6-8.

MUSEUM OF THE NATIONAL BANK
Aleksanterink 42, Helsinki 10
Bank furniture, equipment of the 1890s. Coins.
M. 2-3. Other times by appointment.

MUSEUM OF POSTAL SERVICES AND COMMUNICATIONS
Tehtaankatu 21B, Helsinki 15
History of Finnish postal, telephone and telegraph services. Postage stamps.
Tu., F. 12-3; W. 6-8.

MUSEUM OF SPORT
Stadion, Helsinki
Sports equipment, especially skis. Photographs. Medals. Sports-club insignia.
Su.-F. 12-2.

MUSEUM OF THE UNITED BANK
Aleksanterinkatu 30, Helsinki 10
History of the Bank and of banking. 19th century bank furniture, equipment. Documents.
Tu. 2-3. Other times by appointment.

NAVAL MUSEUM
Suomenlinna B40, Helsinki 19
Paintings, prints, documents, relics illustrating Finnish naval history.
May, Sept., daily 12-4. June-Aug., daily 12-5. Oct.-Apr., Su. 12-3.

PAPER MUSEUM
Helsinki
In building of Finnish Pulp and Paper Research Institute. History of paper and paper-making material, mainly in Finland.
M.-F. 8-4, on request.

RAILWAY MUSEUM
Rautatieasema, Helsinki 10
History of railways in Finland. Original locomotives, rolling-stock. Models. Operating equipment. Documents. Photographs. Originals of locomotives and coaches are stored in the old engine sheds at Kaipiainen, Myllmäki, Hyoinkää and Karjaa.
Su.-F. 12-3.

SAFETY AT WORK MUSEUM
E. Esplanaadi 4, Helsinki
Public health. Occupational diseases. Safety devices. Rehabilitation methods.
Su.-F. 11-5.

SEURASAARI OPEN-AIR MUSEUM
Seurasaari, Helsinki 25
Farm buildings and rural housing from all regions of Finland. Windmills. Fishermen's houses, with fishing equipment.
June-Sept., Su.-F. 11.30-5.30; Sa. 11.30-3.30.

PAUL AND FANNY SINEBRIJ CHOFFIN ART COLLECTION
Bulevardi 40, Helsinki 12
17th century French, Dutch, Italian paintings. 17th-18th century Swedish portraits. Miniatures. Glass. Porcelain.
W., Sa., Su. 12-4; W. also 6-8.

UNIVERSITY AGRICULTURAL MUSEUM
Viikin Roetila, Helsinki 17
Implements, tools. Stockbreeding. Farm buildings.
Su. 12-4. Other times by appointment.

UNIVERSITY MUSEUM OF BOTANY
Unioninkatu 44, Helsinki 17
World-wide collections, including Scandinavia, Finland, Central Europe, Caucasia, Canada, Patagonia, Soviet Asia.
F., Su. 1-3. Other days by appointment.

UNIVERSITY MUSEUM OF THE HISTORY OF MEDICINE
Kasarminkatu 11-13, Helsinki 13
Collections illustrating history of medicine and nursing in Finland. Instruments and equipment. Paintings. Prints. Photographs. Documents.
By appointment.

UNIVERSITY MUSEUM OF ZOOLOGY
P. Rautatienkatu 13, Helsinki 10
Palaeontology. World-wide zoological collections, especially of Finland and Scandinavia.
W. 9-3; Su. 12-4.

HYVINKÄÄ

ART GALLERY
Hyvinkää
Paintings, graphics, sculpture by Finnish artists.
Tu.-Sa. 10-6.

IISALMI

JUHANI AHO MUSEUM
Mansikkaniemi, Iisalmi 2
Life and work of the author, Juhani Aho.
June-Sept., daily 8-8.

MUSEUM OF HISTORY
Iisalmi
Local history.
Daily 12-8.

ILMAJOKI

ILMAJOKI MUSEUM
Ilmajoki
Furniture. Domestic equipment. Religious art. Agricultural implements, equipment.
Su. 12-6. Other times by appointment.

IMATRA

MUSEUM OF ART
Imatra
Paintings, drawings, graphics, sculpture by Finnish artists.
May-Sept., Su. 2-6; Th. 2-6.

INARI

LAPP OPEN-AIR MUSEUM
Inari
Buildings from Lapland villages and settlements, including meat-storehouse, fodder-house, dwelling-house.
June-Aug., daily 8-8.

ISOKYRÖ

REGIONAL MUSEUM
Taipale, Isokyrö
Rural buildings (1850-1910), moved to museum-site.
Daily 8-5.

JALASJÄRVI

DISTRICT MUSEUM
Jalasjärvi
Local history. Handicrafts. Religious art. Textiles.
M.-F. 12-6. Other times by appointment.

JANAKKALA

REGIONAL MUSEUM
Janakkala
Houses, stables and other rural buildings moved to museum site.
May-Sept., Sa. 2-7; Su., public holidays 11.30-7.

JÄRVENPÄÄ

AINOLA
Järvenpää
Former home of the composer, Sibelius. Furnishings. Personal possessions. Grave of Sibelius.
W., Su. 12-5.

PEKKA HALONEN HOUSE-MUSEUM
Fauniland, Järvenpää
Life and work of the artist, Pekka Halonen, in his former home. Local history.
On request.

JOENSUU

ART GALLERY
Rantakatu 8, Joensuu
Paintings, sculpture, graphics by Finnish artists.
Sept. 16-May 14, Su. 12-3, 6-8; Tu., W., Th. 6-8. May 15-Sept. 15, daily 11-6; Su., Tu., W., Th. also 6-8.

MUNICIPAL MUSEUM AND KARELIA HOUSE
Karjalan Talo, Joensuu
Local history. Ethnology and art of Karelia.
Sept. 16-May 14, Su. 12-3, 6-8; Tu.-Th. 6-8. May 15-Sept. 15, daily 11-4. Su., Tu., W., Th. also 6-8.

JOKIOINEN

PARSONAGE MUSEUM
Jokioinen
Mid-19th century parsonage, with period furnishings and household equipment.
By appointment.

JUVA

REGIONAL MUSEUM
Juva
Storehouse (1835), from which seed was loaned to farmers. Windmill (1866). Handicrafts. Folk art.
Su., public holidays, May-Sept., 12-2.

JYVÄSKYLÄ

MUSEUM OF CENTRAL FINLAND
Ruuspuisto, Jyväskylä
Housing. Folk-art. Paintings. Handicrafts. Costumes. Furnishings. Tools.
Tu.-Su. 12-3. May-Sept., W. also 6-8.

UNIVERSITY MUSEUM
Yliopisto, Jyväskylä
History. Natural history. Ethnography. History of the university.
Daily 12-3, during university terms.

KAARLELA

LOCAL MUSEUM
Kaarlela
Folk art. Handicrafts. Local history.
June-Aug., on request.

KAJAANI

KAINUU MUSEUM
Väinämöisenk 16, Kajaani
Local history. Industry. Watercolours and drawings by Louis Sparren.
Su. 2-4. Other times by appointment.

KALAJOKI

HISTORICAL MUSEUM
Kalajoki
Collections illustrating local life and trades, especially fishing, seal-hunting.
May-Sept., daily 12-5. Other times by appointment.

KALANTI

OSKARI RAULAN REGIONAL MUSEUM
Kalanti
Saw-mill, sauna, blacksmith's shop, granary and other rural buildings, moved to museum site.
Su. 12-3. Other times by appointment.

KARHULA

MUSEUM OF GLASS
Karhula
Company Museum. 19th-20th century glass, mostly of local manufacture.
M.-F. on request.

KASKINEN

KASKINEN MUSEUM
Kaskinen
In old windmill. Local history.
Tu.-Sa. 10-6.

KAUHAJOKI

LOCAL MUSEUM
Kauhajoki
Windmill and other rural buildings. Furniture. Handicrafts. Carpenter's, tanner's, shoemaker's tools.
Su. 3-6. Other days by appointment.

KEMI

ART GALLERY
Kaupungintalo, Kemi
19th-20th century paintings, sculpture by Finnish artists.
W. 6-8; Su. 12-4.

KEMI MUSEUM
Meripuisto, Kemi
Local archaeology, history. Mid.-19th century period rooms. Household equipment. Handicrafts. Forestry. Timber industry.
W. 2-4; Su. 1-4.

KEMIÖ

REGIONAL MUSEUM
Kemiö
18th-19th century cottages, mills, farm buildings, brought to site. Material illustrating social and educational history of the district.
May 10-Sept. 10, Tu.-Su. 11-4. Other times by appointment.

KESÄLAHTI

LOCAL MUSEUM
Kesälahti
18th-19th century rural buildings. Agricultural implements. Local history.
May-Sept., daily 9-7. Other times by appointment.

KEURUU

LOCAL MUSEUM
Keuruu
Local history. Folk art. Handicrafts.
June-Aug., daily 11-6.

KIHNIÖ

LOCAL MUSEUM
Kihniö
Local history. Agricultural history, equipment.
May 15-Aug. 31, Su. 11-1.

KIURUVESI

REGIONAL MUSEUM
Kiuruvesi
Windmill. Rural buildings. Furniture. Domestic equipment. Agricultural implements.
Daily 7-8.

KOKEMÄKI

AGRICULTURAL MUSEUM
Kokemäki
Local collections illustrating history of agriculture and rural life. Farm implements, equipment. Blacksmith's, carpenter's, cooper's tools.
Su. 12-4.

OPEN-AIR MUSEUM
Kokemäki
17th-19th century houses, farm buildings, mills. Furniture. Domestic equipment. Tools.
Su. 12-4.

KOKKOLA

K. H. RENLUNDIN MUSEUM
Pitkänsillankatu 28, Kokkola
Local history. Shipping. Trade. Industry. 19th-20th century paintings, drawings, sculpture by Finnish artists.
Tu.-F. 6-7; Su. 3-6.

KOTKA

CZAR'S FISHING LODGE
Langinkoski, Kotka
Built (1889) for Czar Alexander III. Mementoes of the Czar and Czarina.
May-Aug., daily 10-7. Other times by appointment.

KRISTIINANKAUPUNKI

LEBELL MUSEUM
Rantakatu, Kristiinankaupunki
Local history. Handicrafts. Household equipment. Costumes. Maritime history.
Daily 12-2.

KUHMOINEN

HISTORICAL MUSEUM
Kuhmoinen
Local history. Handicrafts and trades, especially weaving, carpentry and joinery, distilling.
Su. 12-1.

KULLAA

LOCAL MUSEUM
Kullaa
Local history. Open-air section, with rural buildings, agricultural implements.
By appointment.

KUOPIO

KUOPIO MUSEUM
Kauppakatu 23, Kuopio
Local history. Costumes. Furniture. Craftsmen's tools. Paintings by Juho Rissasen. Natural history.
Tu.-F. 12-3; W. also 6-8; Su. 12-4.

MUSEUM OF THE ORTHODOX CHURCH
Sinauskappelintie 1, Kuopio
History of the Orthodox Church. Liturgical objects. Icons. Vestments.
W. 1-3, 6-8; Sa. 6-8; Su. 1-3. Other times by appointment.

KUOREVESI

REGIONAL MUSEUM
Lahdenkylä, Kuorevesi
19th century rural buildings moved to site. Furniture. Handicrafts.
June-Aug., Tu.-Su. 12-6; May 20-31, Sept. 1-10, Tu.-Su. 11-3.

KUORTANE

KLEMETTI MUSEUM
Kuortane
In former home of Prof. Heikki Klemetti, with his furniture, personal possessions and examples of his work.
June-Aug., Su. 11-5.

MUSEUM OF BUILDINGS
Kuortane
Houses, mills, workshops and other rural buildings moved to museum site.
June-Aug., Su. 11-5.

KURIKKA

LOCAL MUSEUM
Kurikka
Furniture. Religious art. Handicrafts.
Su. 12-2. Other times by appointment.

LAHTI

ART GALLERY
Vesijärvenkatu 11, Lahti
Paintings, graphics, sculpture by Finnish artists.
Tu.-Sa. 10-3; W. also 6-8; Su. 12-4.

MUSEUM OF HISTORY
Lahdenkatu 4, Lahti
History of Lahti. Furniture. Household equipment. Costumes. Tools. Handicrafts. Industrial development. Italian majolica, Dutch faience. Paintings.
Tu., Th. 12-4, 6-8. F. 12-4. Sa. 12-3.

LAMONI

LOCAL MUSEUM
Lamoni
Agricultural implements, tools, especially those connected with cultivation of flax. Sawmilling and lumbering. Horse-drawn vehicles. Granary.
Su. 12-1. Other times by appointment.

LAPINJÄRVI

PORLAMMI REGIONAL MUSEUM
Porlammi, Lapinjärvi
Farm-buildings. Granary. Collections illustrating rural handicrafts, trades.
Su. 12-3. Other times by appointment.

LAPPEENRANTA

MUSEUM OF SOUTHERN KARELIA
Linnoitus, Lappeenranta
History and ethnography of S. Karelia. Religious history, art.
M.-F. 11-3; W.-F. also 6-8; Su. 12-4, June-Aug. also 10-3.

LAUKAA

VILLAGE MUSEUM
Laukaa
Churches, mills, houses and other rural buildings moved to museum site.
May 15-Aug. 31, M.-Sa. 11-3; Su. 4-6.

LEPPÄVIRTA

REGIONAL MUSEUM
Leppävirta
Local industries, especially mining. Collections illustrating local life, art, handicrafts.
M.-Sa. 11-1; Su. 12-3. Other times by appointment.

LIEKSA

MUSEUM OF HISTORY
Lieksa
History and ethnology of the Lieksa region. Open-air museum of rural houses, workshops. Furniture. Handicrafts.
Indoor Museum: June-Aug., Su. 12-3.
Open-Air Museum: June-Aug., Su. 12-6. Other times by appointment.

LIETO

VANHALINNA MUSEUM
Vanhalinna, Lieto
Open-air museum at the Vanhalinna farm, with houses and farm buildings (1860-1927).
Su. 1-4. Other times by appointment.

LOHJA

HISTORY MUSEUM
Laurinkatu, Lohja
Local history. Collections illustrating traditions and culture of the area. Furniture.
June-Aug., Su. 11-3.

LOVIISA

MUNICIPAL MUSEUM
Komendantintalo, Loviisa
Local and military history. Shipping. Navigation. Furnishings and equipment of 19th century stationery-shop.
June-Aug. Tu.-Sa. 12-3; W. also 6-8; Su. 12-3.

LUHANKA

PELTOLA MOUNTAIN VILLAGE MUSEUM
Tammijärvi, Luhanka
Cottages, farm-buildings moved to site to give impression of village.
M.-Sa. 10-7.

LUOPIOINEN

LOCAL MUSEUM
Luopioinen
18th-19th century mills, workshops, houses, farm-buildings moved to museum site.
Su. 9.30-12.

MAARIANHAMINA

ÅLANDS MUSEUM
Torikatu 5, Maarianhamina
Archaeology and history of the province.
Tu., Th., Sa. 1-3.

ÅLANDS MUSEUM OF ART
Maarianhamina
Paintings by Finnish artists.
Tu., Th., Sa. 1-3.

MARITIME MUSEUM
Maarianhamina
Seafaring history of the Åland Islands. Includes the sailing ship 'Pommern', which carried grain from Australia to England. Log books. Ships' documents. Navigational instruments. Saloon of the 'Herzogin Cecilien'.
M.-Sa. 12-4; Su. 1-4.

MÄNTTÄ

MUSEUM OF THE GÖSTA SERLACHIUKSEN ART INSTITUTE
Mänttä
16th-18th century Italian, Spanish paintings. 19th-20th century Finnish paintings, drawings, graphics, sculpture.
Su. 1-3. Other times by arrangement.

MIKKELI

SOUTH SAVO PROVINCIAL MUSEUM
Otavankatu 11, Mikkeli
Regional history. Coins.
Apr.-Sept., M.-F. 11-3; Su. 12-4, 6-8. Oct.-Mar., W. 6-8; Su. 12-4.

MUHOS

REGIONAL MUSEUM
Muhos
Local history, crafts, industries, especially charcoal-burning.
June-Aug., daily 12-3.

NAANTALI

LOCAL MUSEUM
Museokatu, Naantali
Mills, workshops, cottages, farm buildings moved to museum site.
M., W., Th., Sa. 12-3; Tu., F. 5-8; Su. 12-4.

NÄRPIÖ

REGIONAL MUSEUM
Närpiö
Windmill, cottages and farm-buildings, moved to museum site. Tools. Furniture. Household equipment.
May-Sept., daily 12-6.

NASTOLA

REGIONAL MUSEUM
Nastola
Cottages and other rural buildings, mostly 19th century, moved to site. Furniture. Household equipment. Coins.
Su. 11-1. Other days by appointment.

NIVALA

LOCAL MUSEUM
Nivala
Rural cottages and farm-buildings moved to site. Household equipment. Furniture. Agricultural implements.
Su. 12-2. Other times by appointment.

NOKIA

REGIONAL MUSEUM
Kankaantaka, Nokia
Open-air museum of rural buildings, moved to museum site.
M.-Sa. 4-6.

NURMIJÄRVI

REGIONAL MUSEUM
Nurmijärvi
Agricultural implements. Ecclesiastical history. J. F. Berghiin and Bernard Cruselliin collections.
By appointment.

INDUSTRIAL MUSEUM
Rajamäki, Nurmijärvi
At distillery. History, technology and products of the local distilling industry.
By appointment.

RAJAMÄKI HOUSE
Rajamäki, Nurmijärvi
Peasant house and outbuildings (1828), with household and agricultural equipment.
By appointment.

ORIMATTILA

AGRICULTURAL MUSEUM
Orimattila
18th century farm buildings. Agricultural implements.
M.-Sa. 6-8; Su. 12-2, 6-8.

ORWESI

DISTRICT MUSEUM
Orwesi
Watermill, farm buildings, cottages. Craftsmen's tools. History of the Orwesi army reserve company.
May 15-Aug. 31, daily 12-6.

OULU

MUSEUM OF ART
Torikatu 4, Oulu
Paintings, drawings, graphics, sculpture by Finnish, especially regional, artists.
Tu.-Sa. 11-3; Su. 12-4.

MUSEUM OF NORTH OSTROBOTHNIA
Ainola, Oulu
History and ethnography of Ostrobothnia and Lapland. Charcoal-burning. Wood-tar production. Maritime history.
Tu.-Sa. 11-3; W. also 6-8; Su. 12-4.

TURKANSAARI OPEN-AIR MUSEUM
Oulusuu, Oulu
Church, parsonage, farm-buildings, mills and other rural buildings.
May-Sept., daily 11-9.

UNIVERSITY BOTANICAL COLLECTIONS
Torikatu 15, Oulu
Herbaria of Finland.
M.-F. on request.

UNIVERSITY ZOOLOGICAL MUSEUM
Linnarkatu 5, Oulu
Zoology of Finland and the surrounding countries.
M.-Sa. 11-3.

PALLASTUNTURI

NATURAL HISTORY MUSEUM
Pallastunturi
In annexe of hotel. Minerals, animals, birds, flowers of Finnish Lapland.
On request.

PALTAMO

HISTORICAL MUSEUM
Paltamo
School and church history. Local history, handicrafts. Shoemaker's tools.
On request.

PARAINEN

REGIONAL MUSEUM
Parainen
17th-19th century houses and farm-buildings, moved to museum site.
Daily 12-5.

PERNIÖ

LOCAL HISTORY MUSEUM
Perniö
Local, especially educational history.
Su. 12-2; W., F. 2-4. Other days by appointment.

PIEKSÄMÄKI

LOCAL MUSEUM
Tasakatu 4-6, Pieksämäki
Local history. Forestry. Agriculture. Paintings by local artists.
M. 6-8; Su. 1-3.

PIETARSAARI

J. L. RUNEBERG MUSEUM
Westmansmors stuga, Pietarsaari
School attended by the poet, J. L. Runeberg, with collections illustrating his life and work.
Sa.-Th. 1-4; Th. also 6-9.

STRENGBERG'S TOBACCO MUSEUM
Koulukatu, Pietarsaari
Museum of the Strengberg Company. History of the company and of tobacco manufacturing in Finland. Pipes and other smoking requisites.
By appointment, M.-F. 7-4.

TOWN MUSEUM
Isokatu 2, Pietarsaari
Local history, ethnography. Handicrafts, especially ceramics, textiles.
Sa.-Th. 1-4; Th. also 6-9.

PORVOO

ALBERT EDELFELT MUSEUM
Haikko, Porvoo
Former home of the painter, Albert Edelfelt. Collections illustrating his life and work.
On request.

MUSEUM OF NATURAL HISTORY
Kaivokatu 40, Porvoo
Regional natural history. Geology. Mineralogy. Mammals. Birds. Reptiles. Plants. Lichens.
Tu.-Su. 12-4.

J. L. RUNEBERG HOUSE-MUSEUM
Runebergink 20, Porvoo
Collections illustrating life and work of the poet, J. L. Runeberg, in the house where he lived, 1860-70.
May-Sept., M.-Sa. 11-4; Su., public holidays 12-5. Oct.-Apr., M.-Sa. 11-3; Su., public holidays 12-4.

WALTER RUNEBERG SCULPTURE COLLECTION
Aleksanterink 5, Porvoo
Sculptures by Runeberg.
May-Sept., M.-Sa. 11-4; Su., public holidays 12-5. Oct.-Apr., M.-Sa. 11-3. Su., public holidays 12-4.

PÖYTYÄ

MUSEUM OF THE PÖYTYÄ HISTORICAL SOCIETY
Pöytyä
Parsonage, windmill and 18th-19th century farm-buildings, houses, moved to site. Collections illustrating local and agricultural history.
May-Sept., Su. 12-3.

PUNKAHARJU

REGIONAL MUSEUM
Hiukkajoki, Punkaharju
Farm-buildings, houses, windmills, moved to museum site.
May-Sept., daily 12-3.

PUNKALAIDUN

LOCAL MUSEUM
Yli-Kirra, Punkalaidun
19th century rural buildings moved to museum site. Collections illustrating history and techniques of agriculture, forestry.
May-Sept., Su. 12-3. Other times by appointment.

PYHÄJOKI

REGIONAL MUSEUM
Pyhäjoki
Windmill, farm-buildings, workshops moved to museum site. Furniture. Tools. Household equipment.
May-Sept., Su. 12-3. July 1-31 also M.-Sa. 12-3.

RAAKE

MUNICIPAL MUSEUM
Kauppatorinanta, Raake
Regional history. Handicrafts. Maritime history. Industry. Commerce. Religious art.
Su.-M. 1-3.

RANTASALMI

REGIONAL MUSEUM
Rantasalmi
Windmill, fisherman's house, farm-buildings. Craftsmen's tools.
June-Aug., daily 12-3. Other months by appointment.

RAUMA

TOWN MUSEUM
Eteläpitkäkatu 10, Rauma
In old Town Hall. Lace. Maritime history. Paintings of sailing ships. Furniture.
June-Aug., M.-Sa. 12-2, 6-8; Su. 2-5. Sept-May, Th. 12-3; Su. 2-5.

RAUTALAMPI

LOCAL MUSEUM
Rautalampi
Collections illustrating local occupations. Paintings by local artists.
Daily 11-3.

RIIHIMÄKI

FINNISH GLASS MUSEUM
Allinna, Riihimaki
Collections illustrating history and products of the Finnish glass-industry.
M.-Sa. 3-6; Su. 12-6.

REGIONAL MUSEUM
Etelöinen kansakoulu, Riihimäki
Collections illustrating local occupations, handicrafts.
W., Su. 2-4.

ROVANIEMI

REGIONAL MUSEUM
Pöykkölä, Rovaniemi
19th century farm and village buildings, brought to site. Collection illustrating local occupations.
June-Aug., Su.-F. 12-3. Other months by appointment.

MUNICIPAL NATURAL HISTORY MUSEUM
Hallituskatu 9, Rovaniemi
Animals, birds and plants of the region.
Tu.-Sa. 12-8; Su. 12-6.

RUOKOLAHTI

REGIONAL MUSEUM
Ruokolahti
19th century farm buildings. Folk art. Religious art.
June-Aug., W. 4-6; Sa. 2-6; Su. 9-10, 11.30-6.

RUOTSINPYHTÄA

STRÖMFORS MUSEUM
Strömfors, Ruotsinpyhtäa
19th century ironworks. Collections of tools, nails.
By appointment.

RUOVESI

REGIONAL MUSEUM
Ruovesi
16th-19th century farm and village buildings moved to site. Craftsmen's tools. Household equipment.
May 15- July 30, M.-Sa. 10-4; Su. 10-6.

SÄÄKSMÄKI

EMIL WIKSTRÖMIN MUSEUM
Visavuori, Tarttila, Sääksmäki
Former home and studio of the sculptor, Emil Wikströmin, with collections illustrating his life and work.
May-Sept., M.-Sa. 12-8; Su. 10-8. Oct.-Apr., M.-Sa. 12-4; Su. 12-5.

SÄKYLÄ

LOCAL MUSEUM
Säkylä
Farm and village buildings. Local history, occupations.
By appointment.

SAMMATTI

LOHILAMPI MUSEUM
Lohilampi, Sammatti
Farm buildings. Collections illustrating local occupations, handicrafts.
June-Aug., Su. 12-3.

PAIKKARI FARM
Paikkari, Sammatti
Early 19th century farm, former home of Elias Lönrotin, with his personal possessions.
By appointment.

SEINÄJOKI

GUNPOWDER MUSEUM
Seinäjoki
In former laboratory (1840) of gun-powder mill. Exhibits illustrating history and Technology of manufacturing gunpowder, on this estate which also carried on an iron-foundry and iron-forging business.
On request.

MUSEUM OF SOUTH OSTROBOTHNIA
Törnävä, Seinäjoki
Open-air museum of 19th century rural buildings, with furniture and agricultural implements.
Tu.-F. 6-7; Sa., Su. 1-6.

SIMO

HISTORICAL MUSEUM
Simo
Local history. Industries. Handicrafts.
May-Sept., Su. 12-2.

SOMERO

LOCAL MUSEUM
Somero
17th-19th century farm and village buildings, moved to museum site.
June-Aug., daily 12-3. Other months by appointment.

SUND

JAN KARLS FARM
Kasteholm, Sund
19th century farm, with cottages, outbuildings and mills.
May-Sept., daily 11-4.

TAMMELA

MUSTRALA MUSEUM OF AGRICULTURAL HISTORY
Mustrala, Tammela
Collections illustrating history of regional agriculture, occupations and rural life.
Su. 1-3. Other times by appointment.

TAMMISAARI

MUNICIPAL MUSEUM
Kustaa Vaasankatu 13, Tammisaari
Furnished interiors, showing home of well-to-do tradesman of the early 19th century. Coins. Medals.
Su. 1-4.

TAMPERE

ART GALLERY
Puutarhakatu 34, Tampere
Paintings, drawings, graphics, sculpture by 19th-20th century Finnish artists.
Tu.-Su. 11-8.

FINNISH SCHOOL MUSEUM
Tammelan kansakoulu, Tampere
Exhibits illustrating development of schools in Finland since the Middle Ages.
Su. 1-3; May 1-31, daily 12-4.

GALLERY OF MODERN ART
Palomäentie 23, Tampere
Paintings, prints, sculpture by contemporary Finnish artists.
M.-Th., Sa. 11-8; Su., public holidays 12-8.

HAIHARA DOLL MUSEUM
Kaukajärvi, Tampere
19th-20th century dolls from Finland and countries abroad.
Tu.-Su. 11-8.

HÄME MUSEUM
Häsilinna, Tampere
Local history, ethnography. Handwoven rugs, tapestries. Chimneyless cottage.
F.-W. 11-3; W. also 5-8.

HIEKKA MUSEUM OF ART
Pirkankatu 6, Tampere
Paintings, sculpture, graphics by regional artists.
W., Su. 12-3. Other times by appointment.

LENIN MUSEUM
Hallituskatu 19, Tampere
Collections illustrating life and work of Lenin.
Tu.-Sa. 11-3; Su. 11-4.

NATURAL HISTORY MUSEUM
Pirkankatu 2, Tampere
Palaeontology. Geology. Botany. Zoology. Entomology.
Tu.-Su. 11-2; W. also 6-8.

TECHNICAL MUSEUM
Puutarhakatu 2, Tampere
In former shoe-factory. Development of technology and history of local industries. Includes carding machine installed at Tampere by James Finlayson in 1824.
Tu.-F., Su. 1-4; Tu., F. also 6-8.

TENHOLA

LOCAL MUSEUM
Tenhola
Farm building (c.1850). Collections illustrating local life and occupations.
May 15- Sept. 15, Su. 12-1.

TORNIO

TORNIO VALLEY MUSEUM
Keskikatu 22, Tornio
Former Russian military church. Now contains historical and ethnographical collections connected with northern Ostrobothnia and Lapland.
Su. 2-5. June 15- Aug. 15, also Tu.-F. 6-8.

TURKU

WÄINÖ AALTOSEN MUSEUM
Itäinen Rantakatu 38, Turku
Paintings, drawings, graphics, sculpture in the possession of W. Aaltosen.
Tu.-Su. 11-3; W. also 6-8.

ART GALLERY
Puolalanmäki, Turku
19th-20th century Finnish paintings, drawings, prints, sculpture. International print collection.
M.-Sa. 10-4; Sept.-May, closed M.

BIOLOGICAL MUSEUM
Neitsytpolku 1, Turku
Fauna of Finland.
May, daily 9-2. June 1- Aug. 8, daily 11-3.

CITY MUSEUM
Turun linna, Turku
In 13th-16th century castle. 17th-19th century European furniture, porcelain, tapestries. Silver. Pewter. Glass. Local history.
May 2- Aug. 31, daily 10-4. Sept. 1- Apr. 4, daily 11-3.

"ETT HEM" MUSEUM
Piispankatu 14, Turku
House (1828-31). Portraits. Paintings. Ceramics. Silver. Pewter. Rugs. Porcelain. Glass.
Tu.-Su. 1-3.

MARITIME MUSEUM
Gezeliuksenkatu 2, Turku
Ship-models. Paintings. Portraits. Navigation equipment. Ships' documents.
Tu.-Su. 1-4.

MONASTERY MUSEUM OF HANDICRAFTS
Luostarinmäki, Turku
Finnish arts and crafts. Furnished interiors.
May 2- Aug. 31, daily 10-4. Sept.-Apr., daily 11-3.

MUSEUM OF BIOLOGY
Neitsytpolku 1, Turku
Collections illustrating the fauna of Finland.
Tu.-Su. 1-4.

MUSEUM OF PHARMACOLOGY
Läntinen Rantakatu 13B, Turku
History of pharmacology. 18th-19th century pharmacy furnishings, equipment.
May 2- Aug. 31, Su.-F. 12-5. Sept.-Apr., Su.-F. 11.30-3.30.

SIBELIUS MUSEUM
Piispankatu 17, Turku
Collections relating to Sibelius and to the history of Finnish music. Musical instruments.
Tu.-Su. 12-3.

UNIVERSITY BOTANICAL MUSEUM
Kasvilteen laitos, Turku 2
World-wide botanical collections, especially Scandinavia, N. and S. America.
M.-Sa. 12-2.

TUUSULA

MUSEUM OF ANTI-AIRCRAFT DEFENCE
Ilmatorjuntakoulu, Hyrylä, Tuusula
Anti-aircraft equipment. Photographs. Drawings.
By appointment.

URJALA

FARMHOUSE MUSEUM
Urjalankylä, Urjala
Manor-house (early 19th century), and farm buildings. Windmill. Furniture. Agricultural implements.
May-Sept., daily 6-8; Su. 2-8.

NUUTAJÄRVI GLASS MUSEUM
Nuutajärvi, Urjala
Collections of locally-made 19th-20th century glass.
By appointment.

UUSIKAARLEPYY

MUNICIPAL MUSEUM
Uusikaarlepyy
Local history. Furniture. Costumes.
Tu.-Su. 12-5.

ZACHARIAS TOPELIUS HOUSE-MUSEUM
Kuddnäs, Uusikaarlepyy
In former home of the poet, Z. Topelius (d.1898). Empire and Biedermeier furniture. Personal possessions of Topelius.
Tu.-Su. 12-5.

UUSIKAUPUNKI

MUSEUM OF CULTURAL HISTORY
Ylinenkatu 11, Uusikaupunki
Maritime history. Navigational instruments. Handicrafts. Textiles. Coins.
Sa. 10-12; Su. 12-4.

WINDMILLS MUSEUM
Uusikaupunki
Windmills brought to museum site from different parts of Finland.
Sa. 10-12; Su. 12-4.

VAASA

BRAGE OPEN-AIR MUSEUM
Vaasa
Rural buildings moved to museum site. Farmhouse (1810), with outbuildings. Blacksmith's shop. Stables. Pig-houses.
Daily 4-7.

EAST BOTHNIA AUSTRALIS MUSEUM
Kirkkopuistikko 21, Vaasa
World-wide botanical collections, especially Scandinavia, Finland, Siberia, Madeira, Italy, Egypt. Geology. Mineralogy. Botany. Zoology.
Th. 4-5; Su. 2-3.

EAST BOTHNIA MUSEUM
Koulukatu, Vaasa
In former Wasastjern mansion (1780). Period rooms. Furniture. Ceramics. Lace. Paintings by Dutch, Flemish, Italian, German, Finnish artists. History of the region, especially War of Independence.
May-Sept., Tu.-Su. 12-2, Tu., W. also 6-8. Oct.-Apr., Tu.-Su. 11-2; W. also 6-8.

TIKANOJA ART GALLERY
Hovioikeudenpolku 4, Vaasa
Paintings, sculpture by Finnish artists.
Tu.-Su. 12-4.

VALKEAKOSKI

KAIPPILANMÄKI
Open-Air Museum, Rinnekatu 5, Valkeakoski
Collection showing traditional buildings and building methods of the region. Timber and heather houses, farm-buildings and out-buildings.
May-Sept., Su. 12-8; W., F. 4-8. Other times by appointment.

VALTIMO

MURTOVAARA HOUSE MUSEUM
Murtovaara, Valtimo
19th century manor house and farm buildings. Furniture. Household equipment. Agricultural implements.
By appointment.

VAMMALA

TYRVÄA MUSEUM
Jaatsink 1, Vammala
In former parsonage barn, and outbuildings. Collections illustrating local occupations, crafts. Craftsmen's tools, including those of a potter, tailor, shoe-maker and chimney sweep. Collections of pottery, glass, weapons. Agricultural implements. Dairying equipment.
Su.-F. 3-6.

VARKAUS

LOCAL MUSEUM
Veritorni, Varkaus
Local history. Works by local artists. Agriculture, especially flax-growing. Handicrafts. Finnish postage stamps.
M.-F. 3-7; Su. 2-7.

VETELI

LOCAL MUSEUM
Veteli
Windmill, Collections illustrating local life and history.
By appointment.

VIHANTI

LOCAL MUSEUM
Vihanti
Local history. Furnishings. Household equipment. Tools.
June 1 - Sept. 9, daily 12-2. Other times by appointment.

YLÄNE

LOCAL MUSEUM
Yläne
19th century farm and village buildings. Collections illustrating local life.
June-Aug., Su. 12-3.

ÄHTÄRI

LOCAL MUSEUM
Ähtäri
Houses, windmill and other rural buildings.
June-Aug., daily 10-2.

France

'The Louvre,' we were assured by a noted French museologist, 'is the curse of French museums, and the 'Mona Lisa' is the curse of the Louvre.' This appalling double heresy contains much good sense. The huge Palace of the Louvre, with its never-ending rooms and collections, both exhausts the visitor and allows him to feel that once he has done the Louvre he has carried out his duty towards museums in France. Equally, with the 'Mona Lisa' safely seen and behind him, he is in a fit condition to talk to other people about the Louvre. He does not need to remember anything else, because nobody he is likely to talk to will remember anything else either.

This perfectly understandable attitude does great injustice to the rest of French museums, many of which, both in Paris and in the provinces, present their material in a considerably more humane and intelligible manner and in premises which, financially and in other ways, are more appropriate to the age in which we live. One could go even further than our French expert chose to do, and say that the Louvre has been an international curse, as well as a French curse, since it has encouraged generations of museum administrators elsewhere, and their governments and backers, to believe that museums should be housed in grand buildings, which have subsequently been discovered to be inconvenient, inflexible, difficult to light and to police and extremely expensive to heat.

France spends a great deal of public money on its major museums. Whether the money is always spent to the best advantage is another matter. One thinks, for instance, of the great ethnographical and anthropological collections displayed by the Musée de l'Homme in Paris, set out in a new building in the mid-1930s and still to be seen in their original outmoded state, complete with the original and now yellowing labels. There is, one is told, no money with which to put matters right. The Musée de l'Homme, like many others in France (and in the rest of the world), is the victim of its own size and magnificence.

But Paris, whatever governments and tourist agencies may think, is not France, a fact which we hope our list makes clear. Away from the expense and the clogging bureaucracy of Paris, there are many admirable and exciting museums, especially of archaeology, art, handicrafts, agriculture and ethnography. There are, unfortunately, very few museums run by industrial or commercial companies. Such museums are not in the French tradition. The French industrialist is notoriously self-contained and secretive about his affairs. Old tools and machinery and old records are usually destroyed, with little or no thought for the needs of posterity.

To be specially sought out are the numerous small museums devoted to individual writers, artists and musicians, both French and foreign. France is strong in this type of museum, just as it is weak in open-air museums and site museums. French administrators like to get their material domesticated and under proper control in buildings firmly and unmistakably registered as museums. But the situation is changing.

And where else but in France would one find, as at the Orléans Natural History Museum, a 'collection of minerals, shells, butterflies and exotic birds, selected for their beauty', or at Villeneuve-Loubet, a Museum of the Art of Cookery, in the former home of the great chef, Auguste Escoffier, with a signed portrait of Nellie Melba, presented to Escoffier as a token of esteem for his invention of Peach Melba? At Villeneuve-Loubet one is thousands of psychological kilometres away from the Louvre.

ABBEVILLE

BOUCHER-DE-PERTHES MUSEUM
Rue du Beffroi, 80100 Abbeville, Somme
Prehistory. Traditional industries of the Somme Valley and north of France. Archaeology. Brussels tapestries. Furniture, ceramics from the north of France. 15th-16th century carvings, paintings. Portraits by Largillière, Greuze and Lépicié. Engravings.
May-Sept. Daily 2-6. Apr., Oct. and Nov. Th. and Su. 2-6.

AGDE

AGDE MUSEUM
5 and 7 rue de la Fraternité, 34300 Agde, Herault
Local history collection, including folklore, faience, glass-making. Section on the Mediterranean, including many ship-models. Wine museum. Under-water archaeology.
Daily 10-5.

AGEN

MUNICIPAL MUSEUM
Place de l'Hôtel de Ville, 47000 Agen, Lot-et-Garonne
Paintings by Goya. Works by Impressionist painters. Celtic, Gallo-Roman and Merovingian archaeology. Ceramics.
Nov. 1-Mar. 31. Daily 10-12, 2-4. Apr. 1-Sept. 30. Daily 10-12, 2-6. Closed Tu.

AIGUILLES

OLD QUEYRAS MUSEUM
Place de la Mairie, 05470 Aiguilles, Hautes-Alpes
Local folklore. The collection includes everyday articles, furniture, local handicrafts, popular art.
Summer: Daily 9-12, 3-6

AIME

ARCHAEOLOGICAL MUSEUM
73210 Aime, Savoie
Gallo-Roman archaeology. Roman pottery. Objects found during excavations of the Forum Claudii Ceutronum.
By appointment. Daily 9-12, 2-6

AIX (ÎLE D')

AFRICAN MUSEUM
Fondation Gourgaud, 17123 Île d'Aix, Charente-Maritime
The collection includes the dromedary ridden by Bonaparte during his Egyptian Campaign, as well as trophies and ethnographic documents collected by Baron Gourgaud.
Daily 10-12, 2-6

NAPOLEONIC MUSEUM
Maison de l'Empereur, Fondation Gourgaud, 17123 Île d'Aix, Charente-Maritime
Napoleon's first place of retreat in France, 12-15th July 1815. Relics of Napoleon and souvenirs of Marie-Louise and Josephine, and his faithful companions Bertrand, Gourgaud and Montholon.
Daily 10-12, 2-6.

AIX-EN-PROVENCE

PAUL ARBAUD MUSEUM
2A rue du 4-Septembre, 13100 Aix-en-Provence, Bouches-du-Rhône
Paintings. Drawings. Objets d'art, including collection of faience of Moustiers, Apt and Marseille. Archive material concerning the Félibrige (literary society of Provençal writers).
Daily except W. 9-12, 2-5. Closed Oct.

CÉZANNE'S STUDIO
Avenue Paul-Cézanne, 13100 Aix-en-Provence, Bouches-du-Rhône
Personal possessions and memorabilia of the artist.
Daily except Tu. and public holidays, 10-12, 2-5 (2.30-6 in summer).

DOBLER MUSEUM
Pavillon de Vendôme, 32 rue Cellony, 13100 Aix-en-Provence, Bouches-du-Rhône
17th century house, furnished in the style of the time.
Daily ex. M. 10-12, 2-5

GRANET MUSEUM
Place Saint-Jean-de-Malte, Ancien Prieuré des Chevaliers de Malte, 13100 Aix-en-Provence, Bouches-du-Rhône
Paintings of the French, Italian and Spanish Schools. Works by Dutch and Flemish painters, including Rembrandt, Rubens. Roman and Gothic sculptures. Archaeology. Furniture, tapestries, objets d'art, ceramics and weapons from the Middle Ages to 17th century. Engravings. Postage stamps.
Daily 9-12, 2-5 (2-6 in summer). Closed Tu., Jan. 1, May 1, Ascension, July 14, Aug. 15, Nov. 1, 11, Christmas, Su. and M. before Shrove Tu.

MUSEUM OF OLD AIX
17 rue de Saporta, 13100 Aix-en-Provence, Bouches-du-Rhône
Local history and folklore. Collection of marionettes, santons (small coloured clay figures used to group round the Christmas crib in Provence) and cribs. Documents concerning Mirabeau.
Daily except Tu. 10-12, 2-5.

MUSEUM OF TAPESTRY AND FURNITURE
Palais de l'ancien Archevêché, Place des Martyrs-de-la-Résistance, 13100 Aix-en-Provence, Bouches-du-Rhône
Furniture and religious paintings, 17th-18th centuries, formerly the property of the Archbishops of Aix. 17th-18th century tapestries.
Daily except Tu. 10-12, 2-5.

SAINT-SAUVEUR CATHEDRAL
Rue de Saporta, 13100 Aix-en-Provence, Bouches-du-Rhône
Triptych by Nicolas Froment. 15th century tapestries.
Any time.

AIX-LES-BAINS

DOCTEUR FAURE MUSEUM
Boulevard des Côtes, 73100 Aix-les-Bains, Savoie
Impressionist paintings, including works by Carot, Fantin-Latour, Jongkind, Boudin, Sisley, Pissarro, Dégas and Cézanne. Sculptures and water-colours by Rodin.
Mid. Apr.-mid. Oct. Daily except Tu. 9-12, 2-6. Remainder of the year, Th., Sa. and Su. 10-12, 2-4.

MUSEUM OF ARCHAEOLOGY
Place Maurice-Mollard, 73100 Aix-les-Bains, Savoie
Archaeology of the region. Gallo-Roman sculptures, pottery and inscriptions.
Easter-Oct. Daily 10-12, 2-6.

AJACCIO

FESCH MUSEUM
Rue Fesch, 20000 Ajaccio, Corsica
14th-18th century Italian paintings. Works of the Schools of Rimini, Fabriano, Venice and Florence. Paintings by Rossei, Piero di Cosimo, Giovanni Boccati, Botticelli and Titian. Spanish paintings, including works by Pereda and Vélasquez.
Summer: Daily 10-12, 3-6. Winter: M.-Sa. 9-11, 2-5.

NAPOLEONIC MUSEUM
Hôtel de Ville, 20000 Ajaccio, Corsica
Material relating to the Emperor and his family.
Summer: Daily 10-12, 3-6. Winter: M.-Sa. 9-11, 2-5.

NATIONAL MUSEUM OF THE HOUSE OF THE BONAPARTES
Rue Saint-Charles, 20000 Ajaccio, Corsica
Birthplace of Napoleon. Furniture acquired by the Bonaparte family after the pillage of 1793 and used in 1799 by Napoleon on his return from Egypt. Memorabilia, arms, portraits and historical documents relating to the Bonaparte family from its earliest days to the end of 19th century.
June 21-Sept. 21, Daily 9-12, 2-6. Sept. 22-June 20, Daily 10-12, 2-5. Closed Su. afternoon and Jan. 1, May 1, Nov. 1, 11, Dec. 25.

ALBERTVILLE

CONFLANS MUSEUM
Maison Rouge, 73200 Albertville, Savoie
Local history and folklore. Portraits of the Princes of Savoy. Wooden religious sculptures, 16th-18th centuries. Furniture and interiors of houses in Savoy.
May-Sept. Daily 9-12, 2-6.

ALBI

TOULOUSE-LAUTREC MUSEUM
Place de l'Archevêché, 81000 Albi, Tarn
Birthplace of Toulouse-Lautrec. Collection of his works, including paintings, engravings, prints and book illustrations. Contemporary art, including works by Vuillard, Bonnard, Matisse, Rouault, Marquet, Friesz, Dufy, Valadon, Dunoyer de Segonzac, Rodin and Bourdelle.
Winter: Daily 10-12, 2-5. Summer: Daily 9-12, 2-6. Closed Tu., Oct. 1 and Palm Su.

ALENÇON

MUSEUM OF PAINTING
Hôtel de Ville, place Foch, 61000 Alençon, Orne
Triptych by Massone (late 15th century). Collection of Alençon lace. Paintings by Jean Jouvenet, Ribera, Philippe de Champaigne, Géricault and Courbet.
Daily ex. M. 10-12, 2-6 (2-4 in winter).

D'OZÉ MUSEUM
Place de la Magdeleine, 61000 Alençon, Orne
Drawings and sketches by Poussin, Greuze, Boucher, Watteau, Fragonard and Géricault. Material from Oceania and Cambodia, including clothes, jewels and weapons.
Oct.-Easter, Daily except Tu. 10-12, 2-4. Easter-Oct. Daily except Tu. 10-12, 2-6.

ALÉRIA

JÉRÔME CARCOPINO MUSEUM OF ARCHAEOLOGY
Fort de Matra, 20270 Aléria, Corsica
Excavated objects from a pre-Roman Necropolis and from the Roman town of Aléria. These include ceramics, bronzes, arms, jewellery, coins and inscriptions.
July-Sept. 8-12.30, 2-7. Oct.-June Daily 8-12, 2-6.

ALÈS

ALÈS MUSEUM
Château du Colombier, 30100 Alès, Gard
Regional archaeology. Material from the Bronze Age, Iron Age, Gallo-Roman period and the Middle Ages. Geology, Mineralogy, Palaeontology. 17th-18th century paintings of Flemish, Dutch, Italian and Spanish Schools. French paintings of 17th-20th centuries, including a triptych by Jean Bellegambe.
Winter: Daily 10-12, 2-4. Summer: Daily 10-12, 3-7. Closed Tu. and public holidays.

ALISE-SAINTE-REINE

MUNICIPAL AND ALÉSIA MUSEUM
Alise-Sainte-Reine, 21150 Les Laumes, Côte d'Or
Gallo-Roman antiquities. Alésia (now Alise-Sainte-Reine) was the scene of Vercingetorix's defeat by Caesar.
Easter-Nov. 1, Daily 9-11.45, 2-6.

ALLAUCH

MUSEUM OF OLD ALLAUCH
Place Pierre-Bellot, 13190 Allauch, Bouches-du-Rhône
Neolithic pottery and flints. Ceramics, Coins, Glass. Geology. Palaeontology. Ornithology.
Th. and Sa. afternoon, Su. 10-5.30.

ALTKIRCH

SUNDGAU MUSEUM
Rue de l'Hôtel de Ville, 68130 Altkirch, Haut-Rhin
Local archaeology, prehistory, engravings, weapons. History and traditions of Sundgau. Paintings by local artists.
Su. 3-5. Aug. Daily except M. 3-5. By appointment at other times.

AMBERT

MUSEUM OF THE HISTORY OF PAPER-MAKING
Moulin Richard de Bas, 63600 près d'Ambert, Puy-de-Dôme
Housed in a mill which has been in operation since the 14th century, the museum displays all aspects of the production of paper. History of paper-making.
Daily 9-12, 2-5.

PEASANT MUSEUM OF THE VALLORGUE AND 'FOURME' MUSEUM
La Jasserie du Coq Noir, Saint-Anthème-en-Vallorgue, 63600 Ambert, Puy-de-Dôme
Folklore museum illustrating peasant life in the area. Local produce, including cheese (fourme) and brezou (soup with milk and rye bread).
June 1-Sept. 30. Daily 9-5.

AMBIERLE

FORÈZE MUSEUM
42820 Ambierle, Loire
Ethnography of the region, including reconstructions of house interiors.
Mar., Apr., May, Sept. and Oct. Daily 10-12, 2-5. Open until 6 June, July and Aug. Closed Nov.-Feb.

AMBOISE

LEONARDO DA VINCI MUSEUM
Le Clos Lucé, 37400 Amboise, Indre-et-Loire
At one time the home of Leonardo da Vinci. Period rooms.
Sa. before Easter-Dec. Daily 9-12, 2-7. Jan. and Mar. 1 - F. before Easter, daily 9-12, 2-5. Closed Feb.

POSTAL MUSEUM
6 rue Joyeuse, 37400 Amboise, Indre-et-Loire
Postal documents. First stamp printed in France. Chappe's optical telegraph. Microfilms describing the siege of Paris (1870-1871). Transport, including horse diligence, coach and barouche. Models, posters, route-maps.
Apr.-Sept. Daily ex. Th. 9.30-12.30, 3-7. Oct.-Mar. Daily ex. Th. 10-12, 2-5. Closed Jan. 1, Mar. 1, Ascension, Nov. 1 and Dec. 25.

TOWN HALL MUSEUM
La Mairie, 37400 Amboise, Indre-et-Loire
Aubusson tapestries. Portraits of the Duke of Choiseul. Signatures of the kings of France on documents relating to Amboise.
Daily 9-12, 2-5. Closed public holidays.

AMIENS

CHARLES DE L'ESCALOPIER COLLECTION
Bibliothèque Municipal, 50 rue de la République, 80000 Amiens, Somme
Ancient bronzes. Gold and silver ware. Ivories. Wooden sculptures. Textiles.
By appointment only. The library in which the collection is housed is open daily except M. 9-7. Closed Aug. and Easter.

MUSEUM OF REGIONAL ART AND HISTORY
Fondation Gérard de Berny, 36 rue Victor-Hugo, 80000 Amiens, Somme
Furniture belonging to the Hôtel de Berny. Rooms devoted to Marshal Leclerc, Choderlos de Laclos, Jules Verne, Parmentier.
Th., Sa. and Su. 2-6.

PICARDY MUSEUM
48 rue de la République, 80000 Amiens, Somme
Archaeological collections, Roman period onwards. Paintings by the Brotherhood of Puy-Notre-Dame, 15th-16th century, in praise of the Virgin Mary. Flemish paintings. 18th century paintings. Collection of contemporary art. Objets d'art from Egyptian times to the France of Louis XII.
Daily except Tu. 10-12, 2-6.

ANCY-LE-FRANC

CHÂTEAU
89160 Ancy-le-Franc, Yonne
The drawing rooms and smaller rooms are decorated with panelling and paintings by Primaticcio and Niccolo dell'Abbate. Frescoes. Furniture. Books. Tapestries.
Daily 10-11, and at 3, 4, 5 and 6.

ANDILLAC

EUGÉNIE AND MAURICE DE GUÉRIN MUSEUM
Château du Cayla, Andillac, 81480 Cahuzac sur Vère, Tarn
Living rooms and kitchen restored to their original state. Memorabilia of the Guérin family.
Winter: Daily 9-4. Summer: Daily 9-6.

ANGERS

CATHEDRAL TREASURY
Cathédrale d'Angers, 49000 Angers, Maine-et-Loire
Fabrics. Reliquaries. 12th and 15th century croziers. Gold and silver plate. Gifts made to the Cathedral by King René.
Daily ex. Tu. 10-12, 2-5.

MUSEUM OF FINE ART
12 rue du Musée, 49000 Angers, Maine-et-Loire
Sculptures by David d'Angers. Italian primitives. 17th century Dutch and Flemish paintings. Works by Greuze, Watteau, Fragonard, Chardin, Houdon.
Apr.-Sept. Daily 9-12, 2-6. Oct.-Mar. Daily 10-12, 2-4. Closed Tu.

MUSEUM OF PALAEONTOLOGY AND NATURAL HISTORY
Place Louis Imbach, 49000 Angers, Maine-et-Loire
Palaeontology. Geology. Mineralogy. Botany. Zoology.
Apr.-Sept. W., Th., Sa. and Su. 2-6.

SAINT-JEAN MUSEUM OF ARCHAEOLOGY
Hôpital Saint-Jean, 4 boulevard Arago, 49000 Angers, Maine-et-Loire
Collection of glassware from Gallo-Roman period to the present day. Limoges enamels.
Winter: Daily 10-12, 2-4. Summer: Daily 9-12, 2-6. Closed Tu.

TAPESTRY MUSEUM
Château d'Angers, 49000 Angers, Maine-et-Loire
French tapestries, including the 77 Apocalyptic Tapestries, woven by Nicholas Bataille.
Daily 9-12, 2-6.

TURPIN DE CRISSÉ MUSEUM
32b rue Lenepveu, Hotel Pincé, 49000 Angers, Maine-et-Loire
Egyptian antiquities. Greek vases and statues. Limoges ceramics. Japanese engravings. European paintings.
Daily except Tu. 10-12, 2-6. (2-4 in winter).

WINE MUSEUM
Greniers Saint Jean, 49000 Angers, Maine et Loire
Collections illustrating the production of the wines of Anjou.
Daily ex. M. 10-12, 2-6 (2-4 in winter).

ANGLARDS-DE-SALERS

CHÂTEAU
15380 Anglards-de-Salers, nr. Mauriac, Cantal
Collection of La Marche tapestries (16th century).
Enquire locally.

ANGOULÊME

MUNICIPAL MUSEUM
1 rue de Friedland, 16000 Angoulême, Charente
Prehistory. Archaeology. Regional history. Paintings of the Italian, Dutch, Flemish and French Schools. 18th century faience. African and Oceanic ethnography. Tapestries.
Daily except Tu. 10-12, 2-5.

MUSEUM OF THE CHARENTE ARCHAEOLOGICAL AND HISTORICAL SOCIETY
44 rue de Montmoreau, 16000 Angoulême, Charente
Prehistoric archaeology. Roman and Renaissance sculpture. Original sculptures from the cathedral of Angoulême (12th century). Pottery, faience of Angoulême. Popular art. Engravings.
Sept. Daily except M. 10-12, 2-5. Apr. Daily 9-12, 2-6.

ANNECY

CHÂTEAU D'ANNECY
Place du Château, 74000 Annecy, Haute-Savoie
Archaeology. Regional sculpture, from Middle Ages to the present day, including fragments from the ancient sepulchre of Annecy. Popular art of Savoy.
Easter-Oct. Daily 10-12, 2-7. Evening visits in summer.

CHÂTEAU DE MONTROTTIER
Lovagny, 74000 Annecy, Haute-Savoie
Tapestries. Furniture. Ceramics. 4 bas-reliefs in bronze by Peter and Hans Vischer of Nuremberg (16th century). Armour. Weapons.
Easter-Oct. 15, Daily 8-12, 2-7.

MUNICIPAL MUSEUM
Hôtel de la Ville, 74000 Annecy, Haute-Savoie
Local history.
Daily ex. M. 10-5.

PALAIS DE L'ISLE MUSEUM
Palais de l'Isle, 74000 Annecy, Haute-Savoie
Local history.
Daily ex. M. 10-5.

ANNONAY

OLD ANNONAY MUSEUM
07100 Annonay, Ardèche
Regional archaeology and ethnography. Faience of Vivarais. Documents on 18th century muleteers and watermen. Portraits and memorabilia of Marc Séguin and Montgolfier.
On request.

ANTIBES

GRIMALDI MUSEUM
Château d'Antibes, 06600 Antibes, Alpes-Maritimes
Home of Picasso in 1946 and containing the works he finished during his stay, including paintings, sculptures, engravings, a tapestry and lithography. Bronzes. Woodcarvings. Roman antiquities.
Summer: Daily 10-12, 3-7. Winter: Daily except Tu. 10-12, 3-5.

MUSEUM OF LAND AND UNDERWATER ARCHAEOLOGY
Bastion Saint André, 06600 Antibes, Alpes-Maritimes
Excavated material from different periods in the history of the town. Amphora. Etruscan vases. Roman mosaics. Fragments of murals. Pottery. Ceramics.
Daily ex. Tu. 9-12, 2-6.

NAVAL AND NAPOLEONIC MUSEUM
Batterie de Grillon, Cap d'Antibes, 06600 Antibes, Alpes-Maritimes
Collections illustrating the landing of the Emperor on 1st March 1815.
Winter: Daily 10-12, 2-4. Summer: 10-1, 3-7. Closed Tu. and from Nov. 15 to Dec. 15.

ANZIN

THÉOPHILE JOUGLET MUSEUM
Avenue Anatole-France, 59410 Anzin, Nord
Regional art and sculpture. Portraits of generals in the First World War by Lucien Jonas. Sketches by Fontanarosa (illustrations to Zola's *Germinal*). Fossils.
On demand.

AOSTE

MUSEUM OF GALLO-ROMAN ANTIQUITIES
38810 Aoste, Isère
Roman and Gallo-Roman antiquities, excavated in the area, including ceramics, glassware, coins and medals.
Daily (mornings only).

APT

ARCHAEOLOGICAL MUSEUM
Rue Scudery, 84400 Apt, Vaucluse
Local archaeology, prehistory, inscriptions, sculptures and Gallo-Roman ceramics. Medals.
M.-Sa. 9-12, 3-6.

SAINTE-ANNE'S CATHEDRAL
84400 Apt, Vaucluse
Limoges enamels. Illuminated books. Arab textiles.
Daily 9-12, 2.30-7 except during services.

ARBOIS

MUSEUM OF THE PASTEUR FAMILY HOME
83 rue de Courcelles, 39600 Arbois, Jura
The family home of Pasteur, as it was at his death. Furniture. Personal relics. Office. Library. Laboratory where he worked during the holidays.
Apr. 15- Sept. 30 Daily (including public holidays) 10-12, 2-6 (until 5 Su.). Oct. - Apr. 15, Daily 2-4.

ARCACHON

ARCACHON AQUARIUM MUSEUM
2 rue du Professor Jolyet, 33120 Arcachon, Gironde
Migratory birds. Sea birds. Birds of prey. Fish. Sharks. Crustaceans. Shells. Molluscs.
Easter - Oct. 1, Daily 10-12, 2-7.

ARGENTEUIL

OLD ARGENTEUIL MUSEUM
5 rue Pierre-Guierme, Argenteuil sur Armançon, 89160 Ancy le Franc, Yonne
Archaeology. Memorabilia of Héloise, abbess of Argenteuil. History of Jansenism. Folklore. Mirabeau collection.
Th., Sa. and Su. afternoons. Closed Aug.

ARLANC-EN-LIBRADOIS

MUSEUM OF HANDMADE LACE
63220 Arlanc-en-Libradois, Puy-de-Dôme
Collection of old lace. Displays illustrating lace-making, and differences of style.
June 1 - Sept. 30. Daily 9-5.

ARLES

ARLES MUSEUM
42 rue de la République, 13200 Arles, Bouches-du-Rhône
Founded in 1899 by Frédéric Mistral, who donated the money from his Nobel Prize to the museum. Ethnographic collection illustrating daily life and customs in Provence.
Winter: Daily except Tu. 9-12, 2-4. Summer: Daily 9-12,

LAPIDARY MUSEUM OF CHRISTIAN ART
Rue Balze, 13200 Arles, Bouches-du-Rhône
4th and 5th century marble sarcophagi. Ceramics. Coinage minted in Arles under Constantine. Fragments of Roman and Gothic sculptures.
Winter: Daily 9-12, 2-4. Summer: 8.30-12, 2-7.

LAPIDARY MUSEUM OF PAGAN ART
Place de la République, 13200 Arles, Bouches-du-Rhône
The archaeological collection includes four large mosaics, sarcophagi, friezes, a large statue of Augustus. Portrait of Octavius. Copy in marble of the *clipeum virtutis* of Augustus.
Daily 9-12, 2-4 (winter); 8.30-12, 2-7 (summer).

REATTU MUSEUM
Rue du Grand-Prieuré, 13200 Arles, Bouches-du-Rhône
16th century Arras tapestries. 18th century paintings. Sculpture. Contemporary paintings, including works by Picasso, Lurçat.
Winter: Daily 9-12, 2-4. Summer: daily 8.30-12, 2-7.30.

ARRAS

MUSEUM OF THE FORMER ABBEY OF SAINT-VAAST
62000 Arras, Pas-de-Calais
Sculpture, including a collection of stone funerary monuments from Tournai. Wooden sculptures (15th-18th centuries). 17th and 18th century French paintings. Paintings of Italian, Dutch and Flemish Schools. Tournai and Arras porcelain.
Daily except Tu. 10-12, 2-4 (winter); 9-12, 2-5.30 (summer).

ARROMANCHES-LES-BAINS

MUSEUM OF THE NORMANDY LANDINGS
14117 Arromanches-les-Bains, Calvados
Documents and dioramas illustrating the 1944 landings at Arromanches.
Daily 9-12, 2-6 (2-7 in summer).

ARUDY

MUSEUM OF THE PYRÉNEES OCCIDENTALES
Potz Mansion, 64260 Arudy, Pyrénées-Atlantiques
Flora and fauna of the region surrounding the National Park.
Enquire locally.

OSSAU MUSEUM
64260 Arudy, Pyrénées-Atlantiques
17th century building, containing collection of palaeontology and prehistory. Material on the Parc National des Pyrénées - geology, fauna and flora, the layout of the Parc and its objectives.
July and August, Daily 10-12, 2-6.

AUCH

MUSEUM OF ART AND ARCHAEOLOGY
32000 Auch, Gers
American and colonial collections (17th-18th centuries). Objets d'art. Sculpture, including a bust of Louis XVI attributed to Houdon. Gascon history.
Daily except M. 9-12, 2-5.

MUSEUM OF THE GERS DEPARTMENTAL ARCHIVES
14 rue Edgar-Quinet, 32000 Auch, Gers
Local and regional history.
Daily ex. M. morning, 10-12, 2-5. Closed public holidays and from 1-15 Aug.

AUMONT

HENRI BARBUSSE MUSEUM
Villa Sylvie, Aumont, 60300 Senlis, Oise
Museum devoted to Henri Barbusse, poet and essayist, in his former home. Documents and material on his life. Manuscripts. Correspondence with his friends, including Edmond Rostand, Gorki and Lenin. The original military citations he received.
Daily ex. Tu. 9-12, 2-6.

AURILLAC

HIPPOLYTE DE PARIEU MUSEUM
8 place de la Paix, 15000 Aurillac, Cantal
Bust of Victor Hugo by Rodin. 17th-18th century portraits of Cantal personalities. 19th-20th century French paintings.
M. and Th. 2-5. July 15 - Sept. 15, Daily 2.30-5.30. Su. on application to the caretaker.

JEAN-BAPTISTE RAMES MUSEUM
8 pavillon de l'Horloge, 15000 Aurillac, Cantal
Local archaeology collection of the geologist, J. B. Rames. Coins. Bronzes. Pottery. Iron articles.
Daily 9-12, 2-6 on application to the caretaker.

AURIOLLES

ALPHONSE DAUDET COLLECTION
Mas de la Vignasse, Auriolles, 07120 Ruoms, Ardèche
Collections illustrating life and work of Alphonse Daudet, in his family home. The Mas de la Vignasse inspired the young poet to write the works to be found in his first book, *Les Amoureuses* (1858). Family portraits, including 200 of Alphonse Daudet.
Daily: no fixed hours.

AUTUN

AUTUN NATURAL HISTORY MUSEUM
14 rue St. Antoine, 71400 Autun, Saône-et-Loire
Rocks and minerals of Morvan. Fossils. European birds. Eggs. Philibert mosses.
By appointment.

ROLIN MUSEUM
3 rue des Bancs, 71400 Autun, Saône-et-Loire
Archaeological collection. Romanesque sculpture. Burgundian statuary of 15th century. French primitive paintings. 15th-20th century paintings, sculpture and furniture.
Oct.-Mar. 15, Daily except Tu. and public holidays, 10-12, 2-4. Mar. 16-Sept. 30, Daily 9.30-12, 2.30-7.

SAINT-NICOLAS LAPIDARY MUSEUM
10 rue Saint-Nicolas, 71400 Autun, Saône-et-Loire
Gallo-Roman and medieval archaeology, from 12th century chapel.
Daily except Tu. on application to the caretaker.

AUVILLAR

OLD AUVILLAR MUSEUM
Place du Palais, 82340 Auvillar, Tarn-et-Garonne
Archaeology. Local history and folklore. Faience of Auvillar (18th-19th centuries). Wrought iron. Paintings and views of the region. Weapons.
Daily, afternoons in summer. Su. in winter.

AUXERRE

LAPIDARY AND ARCHAEOLOGICAL MUSEUM
Rue de Paris, 89000 Auxerre, Yonne
In 18th century Chapel of Visitandines, called the Soufflot chapel. Archaeology.
On request.

LEBLANC-DUVERNOY MUSEUM
Rue d'Egleny, 89000 Auxerre, Yonne
18th century tapestries. Regional faience. Decorative art. Memorabilia of Louvois.
Oct.-June 15, Daily except Tu. 2-5. June 16-Sept. 30, Daily 1.30-6.

MUSEUM OF ART AND HISTORY
Place du Maréchal-Leclerc, 89000 Auxerre, Yonne
16th-19th century paintings. Egyptian, Greek and Estruscan archaeology. History of Auxerre. Napoleonic souvenirs belonging to Marshal Davout.
Oct.-June 15, Daily except Tu. 2-5. June 16-Sept. 30, Daily 1.30-6.

SAINT-GERMAIN ABBEY
89000 Auxerre, Yonne
Religious sculptures. Carolingian frescoes (in crypt).
Apr. 15-Oct. 30, Daily 9-12, 2-6.

AUXONNE

BONAPARTE MUSEUM
Rue Lafayette, 89000 Auxonne, Côte d'Or
Gallo-Roman and prehistoric archaeology. Local folklore. Memorabilia left by Napoleon during his stay at Auxonne between June 1788 and June 1791.
May-Oct. 15, Daily. Closed Oct. 16-Apr. 30. Application should be made to the caretaker.

AVALLON

AVALLON MUSEUM
7 rue des Odebert, 79200 Avallon, Yonne
Local prehistoric collection. Gallo-Roman archaeology. Sculpture and furniture from villas in the region. Group of statues by Montmarte (early 2nd century). Religious and popular art. Weapons and jewels from the cemetery at Vaux-Donjon. 19th and 20th century paintings.
Oct. 11-June 14, first Su. in month, from 2-5. June 15-Sept. 9, Daily except M. and Tu., 2-6. Closed Sept. 10-Oct. 10.

AVESNES-SUR-HELPE

ARCHAEOLOGICAL SOCIETY MUSEUM
59440 Avesnes-sur-Helpe, Nord
Collection of Gallo-Roman archaeology, including coins, jewels, pottery and bronze statuettes. 15th-17th century sculpture. Local history. Folk art. Coloured prints.
June-Oct. Su. 3-6. Other times by request.

AVIGNON

CALVET MUSEUM
65 rue Joseph-Vernet, 84000 Avignon, Vaucluse
14th-15th century Italian primitives. Paintings of the Avignon School. Collection of French and foreign paintings (16th-20th centuries). 15th and 19th century wrought iron work. Egyptian, Greek and Roman antiquities.
Winter: Daily 9-12, 2-5. Summer: Daily 9-12, 2-6.

LAPIDARY MUSEUM
27 rue de la République, 84000 Avignon, Vaucluse
Gallic sculptures. Tombs of Cardinal de Lagrange and Cardinal de Brancas. Effigies of Urbain V and Clement VII, popes of Avignon.
Daily except Tu. 9-12, 2-6 (2-5 Oct.-Mar.). Closed Jan. 1, May 1, Aug. 15, Nov. 1, 11, Dec. 25.

RÉQUIEN MUSEUM OF NATURAL HISTORY
67 rue Joseph Vernet, 84000 Avignon, Vaucluse
Collection of mammals, birds and fish. Molluscs. Fossils. Rocks and minerals. Grasses and plants.
By appointment, M.-F. 8.30-12, 2-7.

AVRANCHES

LOCAL MUSEUM
Bibliothèque de Ville, 50300 Avranches, Manche
Manuscripts from the Abbey of Mont-Saint-Michel. Ethnography of Lower Normandy.
Easter-Sept. Daily, except Tu. 9-12, 2-6.

AZAY-LE-FERRON

CHÂTEAU MUSEUM
Azay-le-Ferron, 36290 Mézières en Brenne, Indre
Main building (16th-18th centuries) contains furniture and works of art.
Apr.-Sept. Daily 10-12, 2-6. Oct. and Mar. Daily except Tu., 10-12, 2-5. Nov. and Jan. Daily except Tu., 10-12, 2-4.30. Closed Feb.

AZAY-LE-RIDEAU

CHÂTEAU
37190 Azay-le-Rideau, Indre-et-Loire
16th century house, arranged as museum. Contemporary furniture and objets d'art. Flemish tapestries.
Sa. before Easter-Sept. 15, Daily 9-12, 2-6.30. Sept. 16-Nov. 15, Daily 9-12, 2-4.30. Nov. 16-F. before Easter, Daily 10-12, 2-4.30.

BAGNÈRES-DE-BIGORRE

MUNICIPAL MUSEUM
Boulevard de Casino, 65200 Bagnères-de-Bigorre, Hautes-Pyrénées
Archaeology. Numismatics. Paintings by Murillo, Philippe de Champaigne, Salvator Rosa, Jordaens.
Daily ex. Sa. 10-12, 3-5. Winter: Th. and Su. 10-12, 2-4.

BAGNÈRES-DE-LUCHON

LUCHON REGIONAL MUSEUM
Château de Lassus-Nestier, 31110 Bagnères-de-Luchon, Haute-Garonne
In château of 1772. Archaeology. Ethnography. Iconography. History of the monuments and sites of the Pyrénées-Orientales. Local Gallo-Roman antiquities.
June-Oct. Daily 10-12, 2-6. Other times by request.

BAGNOLS-SUR-CÈZE

LÉON ALÈGRE MUSEUM
Mairie, 30200 Bagnols-sur-Cèze, Gard
Collection of contemporary paintings formed by the painter, Albert André. Works by Renoir, Berthe Morisot, Monet, Signac, Vuillard, Bonnard, Marquet, Matisse, Valtat, Albert André, Boudin, Pissarro, Gauguin, Picasso. Faience. Archaeology.
Mar. 15-Oct. 15, Daily 10-12, 2-6. Oct. 15-Mar. 15, Su. only.

BAILLEUL

BENOÎT DE PUYDT MUSEUM
Bue du Musée, 59270 Bailleul, Nord
Ceramics from Delft, Strasbourg, Rouen, Tournai, Saint-Omer and Bailleul. Lace. Tapestries. Paintings. Wooden sculptures. Chinese and Japanese porcelain.
Easter-Oct. Su. 10-12, 3-5.30. By appointment at other times.

BARBEZIEUX

GETRAUD MUSEUM
Place de Verdun, 16300 Barbezieux, Charente
Folklore. Paintings. Water-colours by Harpignies.
On request.

BARBIZON

AUBERGE GANNE MUSEUM
77630 Barbizon, Seine-et-Marne
Memorabilia of the painters of the Barbizon School.
Summer: Daily except W. 10-6. Winter: Su., Tu. and Th. 12-6.

MILLET MUSEUM
77630 Barbizon, Seine-et-Marne
Exhibition room and shop for works by local artists, housed in the former studio of the painter, Millet.
Daily 9.45-6.30 except for W., from Su. before Easter to Nov. 15. Winter: Tu., F. and Su.

THÉODORE ROUSSEAU MUSEUM
77630 Barbizon, Seine-et-Marne
Works by painters of the Barbizon School, housed in the studio of the artist, Théodore Rousseau.
Daily 10-6.

BARCELONNETTE

CHABRAND MUSEUM
Avenue de la Libération, 04400 Barcelonnette, Alpes-de-Haute-Provence
Local art of the Ubaye valley. Natural history. Birds.
June-Sept., daily 3-5. Other times on application to caretaker.

TOWN HALL MUSEUM
04400 Barcelonnette, Alpes-de-Haute-Provence
Archaeology (Gallo-Roman). Works by local artists; Ethnography. Mexican folk art.
June-Sept. Daily 3-5 on application to the caretaker.

BARENTIN

MUNICIPAL MUSEUM
Hôtel de Ville, 76360 Barentin, Seine-Maritime
Archaeological material from local excavations. Exhibits illustrating the construction of the Barentin viaduct.
Daily 9-12, 2-6 on application to the caretaker. Closed Sa. afternoon, Su. and public holidays.

BAR-LE-DUC

BARROIS MUSEUM
Hôtel de Ville, 55000 Bar-le-Duc, Meuse
Prehistoric, protohistoric and Gallo-Roman archaeology. Paintings. Argonne ceramics.
Daily 9-12, 2-6. Closed Jan. 1, May 1, July 14, Nov. 11, Christmas.

BARR

LA FOLIE MARCO MUSEUM
30 rue du Dr. Sultzer, 67140 Barr, Bas-Rhin
Furniture from the Renaissance to the Restoration. Collection of 18th and 19th century faience. Porcelain of the same period, from Strasbourg and Frankenthal, Meissen and Niderviller. 18th century pewter-ware from Alsace and neighbouring regions.
Pentecost-Last Su. in June, Sa., Su. and public holidays. Last Su. in June-first Su. in October, Daily except Tu. 10-12.30, 2.30-6. Oct. Sa. and Su. only, 10-12.30, 2.30-6.

BASTIA

MUSEUM OF CORSICAN ETHNOGRAPHY
Palais des Gouverneurs Génois, 20200 Bastia, Corsica
Prehistory. Greek and Roman archaeology. Collection of amphora. Corsican ethnography. Geology. Botany. Paintings, drawings of local scenes.
Daily except Sa. afternoon and Su., 9-12, 2-5. Easter-Oct. open Daily 9-12, 3-6.

BAVAY

ARCHAEOLOGICAL MUSEUM
Porte de Valenciennes et 49 Grande Rue, 59570 Bavay, Nord
Material from excavations at Bagacum, city of the Nervii. Sculpture. Utensils. Implements. Jewellery.
Daily ex. Tu. 8-12, 2-5; Su. 2-7.

BAYEUX

MUSEUM OF PAINTING
Cour des Tribunaux, 14400 Bayeux, Calvados
Paintings, especially Italian, French. Ceramics. Bayeux porcelain. Gobelins tapestries.
Summer: Daily 9-12, 2-6. Winter: Daily 10-12, 2-4.30.

QUEEN MATHILDA'S MUSEUM
Rue Léonard-Leforestier, 14400 Bayeux, Calvados
Contains Bayeux Tapestry, woven after the Battle of Hastings, 1066, on the order of Odon, Bishop of Bayeux and half-brother of William the Conqueror, to decorate the nave of the cathedral. It is 70 m. long, and 50 cm. wide, depicting the principal events in the conquest of England.
Summer: Daily 9-12, 2-6.30. Winter: Daily 10-12, 2-4.30.

BAYONNE

BASQUE MUSEUM
1 rue Marengo, 64100 Bayonne, Pyrénées-Atlantiques
Folklore. Local handicrafts. Models of Basque homesteads. Sports. Dances. Witchcraft. Archaeology and prehistory. Pelota.
Daily except Su. and public holidays, 10-12, 2.30-5.30 (winter), 9.30-12.30, 2.30-6.30 (summer).

BONNAT MUSEUM
5 rue Jacques-Laffitte, 64100 Bayonne, Pyrénées-Atlantiques
Collection formed by Léon Bonnat and presented to his native town. Paintings by El Greco, Goya, Rembrandt, Rubens, Veronese, Van Dyck, Dégas, Lawrence, Reynolds and others. Drawings. Roman, Greek and Italian sculpture.
Oct.-June. Daily 10-12, 2-5. July-Sept. Daily 10-12, 2-6. Closed Tu. and public holidays.

NATURAL HISTORY MUSEUM
rue Jacques Laffitte, 64100 Bayonne, Pyrénées-Atlantiques
Zoology. Botany. Mineralogy. Local prehistory. Ornithology.
Su. and Th. 2-4. Other days on request.

BAZEILLES

MUSEUM OF THE LAST CARTRIDGE
Route de Sedan, Bazeilles, 08140 Douzy, Ardennes
Memorabilia of Marshal Gallieni.
Apr.-Sept. Daily 8-12, 1.30-7. Oct.-Mar. Daily 9-12, 2-5.

BEAUFORT-EN-VALLÉE

JOSEPH DENAIS MUSEUM
5 place Notre-Dame, 49250 Beaufort-en-Vallée, Maine-et-Loire
Prehistory. Archaeology. Ethnography. Ceramics. Medieval sculptures. Paintings. Natural sciences. Arms. Costumes.
Su. 2-5. Other days on request.

BEAUGENCY

DUNOIS MUSEUM
Château Dunois, 45190 Beaugency, Loiret
In 15th century château. Folklore collections relating to the Orléans region. Costumes. Furniture. Rooms devoted to vineyard cultivation and wine-production and to the Loire.
Winter: Daily 9-11, 2-4. Summer: Daily 9-11, 2-6.

BEAUJEU

MARIUS AUDIN MUSEUM OF POPULAR TRADITIONS
Place de l'Hôtel de Ville, 69430 Beaujeu, Rhône
Local history and ethnography. Collection of old dolls.
Easter-Nov. 1, Su. 10-1, 2-7; other days except Tu. 2.30-6. July and Aug. also open 10-12.

BEAULIEU-SUR-MER

THÉODORE REINACH FOUNDATION
Villa "Kerylos", 06310 Beaulieu-sur-Mer, Alpes-Maritimes
Reconstruction of an ancient Greek villa, containing furniture and objets d'art. Mosaics. Sculpture.
Sept.-June. Daily except M., 2-6. July-Aug. Daily 3-7. Closed Nov.

BEAUMONT-EN-AUGE

LAPLACE MUSEUM AND MUSEUM OF PAINTING
14950 Beaumont-en-Auge, Calvados
Paintings by Laurens, Puvis de Chavannes, Bonnat and Langlois. History. Local folklore. Works of Pierre-Simon Laplace, astronomer and mathematician.
Easter-Sept. on request.

BEAUNE

BELFRY MUSEUM
Place Monge, 21200 Beaune, Côte d'Or
Archaeology. Mineralogy. Local history.
Daily ex. M. 10-5.

CATHEDRAL TREASURY
Place Maufoux, 21200 Beaune, Côte d'Or
Five tapestries (1474-1500) portraying the life of the Virgin.
On request.

CHARITÉ HOSPICE
Rue de Lorraine, 21200 Beaune, Côte d'Or
Wrought-iron. Tomb in copper of the founders of the Hospice. Collections of furniture, tapestries, objets d'art and pewter.
Su. 9-12, 2-4 (2-5 in summer).

COLLÈGE OF NOTRE-DAME
21200 Beaune, Côte d'Or
15th century tapestries commissioned by Cardinal Jean Rolin. In eight sections, they tell the story of the life of the Virgin.
On request.

HÔTEL-DIEU
Rue de l'Hôpital, 21200 Beaune, Côte d'Or
The Last Judgement by Roger Van der Weyden, in the place for which it was commissioned. Collections of tapestries, furniture, statuettes, pewter, 15th-16th century ivories.
Daily 9-11, 2-4.15.

MUSEUM OF BURGUNDIAN CRAFTS
Hôtel de Ville, 21200 Beaune, Côte d'Or
Works by painters and sculptors of Beaune, notably Félix Ziem. Antiquities.
Su. 9-12, 2-4 or 5.

MUSEUM OF FINE ART
Place de l'Hôtel de Ville, 21200 Beaune, Côte d'Or
Paintings by De Troy, Le Brun, Jean Maigeon, Prud'hon, Corot, Ziem. Local Gallo-Roman archaeology. Furniture and objets d'art from the Middle Ages to the Renaissance. Local history. Chromophotography by Dr. E.-J. Marey.
Easter-Nov. 1, Daily except Tu. 10-12, 2-6.

MUSEUM OF THE WINE OF BURGUNDY
Rue d'Enter, 21200 Beaune, Côte d'Or
Historical background of the industry. Displays devoted to cultivation; historical development; making and completion of casks; social structure of vignerons and vineyard owners, dealers and related trades and professions. Room dedicated to wine drinking. 13th century vatting room with traditional presses, decorated with a Burgundy tapestry by André Lurçat (1947).
Daily 9-12, 1-5.45.

BEAUVAIS

CATHEDRAL TREASURY
Cathédrale St. Pierre, 60000 Beauvais, Oise
Woodcarvings; liturgical vestments. Illuminated manuscripts. Tapestries. Gold and silverware. Stained-glass. Statues.
Daily 2.15-3.15, 4.15-5.15 on application to the caretaker.

MUSEUM OF THE OISE DEPARTMENT
Palais de Justice, 60000 Beauvais, Oise
Regional archaeology collection. Romanesque and Gothic sculptures, 16th century wooden sculptures. 12th-13th century Italian art. 18th century furniture. Beauvais ceramics. 15th-17th century tapestries. 16th-20th century French paintings.
Nov.-Mar. Daily except Tu. 10-12, 2-5. Mar. 2-Oct. Daily 10-12, 2-6.

BELFORT

BELFORT MUSEUM
4 rue du Général-Roussel, 90000 Belfort, Territoire de Belfort
Paintings. Local history. Numismatics. Collection of regional archaeology. Merovingian gold and silver ware. Figurines.
Daily except Tu. 10-12, 2-6.

BENDOR

MARITIME MUSEUM
Ile de Bendor, Bendor, Ile de Var
Maritime collections. Ship-models. Local history.
Daily ex. M. 10-5.

BERGERAC

TOBACCO MUSEUM
Hôtel de Ville, 24100 Bergerac, Dordogne
History of tobacco trade and industry. Tobacco in art, including *Intérieur d'une Tabagie* by Teniers, *Les Fumeurs* by Meissonier, and *Le Fumeur* by Charlot.
There is a small local history museum in the same building.
Daily except M. 9-12, 2-6; Su. 2-7. May-Nov. also M. 2-7.

BERGUES

MUNICIPAL MUSEUM
Mont-de-Piété, 59380 Bergues, Nord
Paintings from the ancient Abbey of Saint-Winoc, including works by Bruegel, Jordaens, Rubens, Van Dyck, Georges de la Tour and Ribera. Drawings by Hubert Robert, Pieter Quast and Largillière. Manuscripts of Lamartine. Flemish ethnographical material.
A small natural history museum in the same building has a bird collection and over 3,000 butterflies from Europe and America.
Daily except F. 10-12, 2-5.

BERNAY

MUNICIPAL MUSEUM
27300 Bernay, Eure
Flemish and Spanish paintings. Collection of Rouen ceramics, notably enamelled tiles from the Château of Ecouen, made in Rouen in the middle of the 16th century, by Masseot Abaquesne.
Su. 2-4. On request at other times. Closed M. and All Saints' Day.

BESANÇON

FOLK MUSEUM
Citadelle de Besançon, 25000 Besançon, Doubs
Ethnography. Rural traditions and occupations. Folk theatre. Agriculture.
Nearby is an open-air museum, *la Maison de Petite Chaux*, near Mouthe (Doubs).
On request.

HISTORICAL MUSEUM
94-96 Grande-Rue, 25000 Besançon, Doubs
Local history from the Renaissance to 19th century. Memorabilia of Victor Hugo. Bruges tapestries. Portraits by Antonio Moro. Rooms dealing with the Revolution in Franche-Comté.
May-Nov. 1, Daily except Tu., 11-12, 2-6.

LAPIDARY MUSEUM
25000 Besançon, Doubs
Gallo-Roman, medieval and Merovingian architectural remains. Collection of tombstones. 13th-18th century armorial bearings.
May-Oct. Daily 10-12, 2-6.

MUSEUM OF CLOCKS AND WATCHES
1 place de la Révolution, 25000 Besançon, Doubs
Collection of ancient and modern clocks, including a clock belonging to Cardinal Granvelle (1564) and the Leroy watch, the most complicated model in the world (1900).
Daily except Tu., 9.30-12, 2-5.30.

MUSEUM OF FINE ART
1 place de la Révolution, 25000 Besançon, Doubs
European, especially French, drawings, sketches, watercolours, including works by Filippo Lippi, Carragio, Tiepolo, Fragonard, Gros, David, Géricault and Courbet. Paintings by Clouet, Georges de la Tour and Largillière. Prehistoric and Gallo-Roman collection.
Daily, except Tu., 9.30-12, 2-5.30.

MUSEUM OF THE RESISTANCE
Place Granvelle-Besançon, 25000 Besançon, Doubs
Collections showing the rise of the Nazi régime and its subsequent defeat. Resistance efforts. Collection of drawings, paintings and sculptures carried out in the German prisons and camps.
Summer: Daily ex. Tu. 9-11.30, 1.30-7. Winter: Th., Sa. and Su. 9-11.30, 1.30-5.

SAINT-JACQUES HOSPITAL
25000 Besançon, Doubs
One of the oldest hospital pharmacies in France, containing a collection of 17th and 18th century jars, equipment.
Daily except Su., 2-4.

BÉZIERS

LAPIDARY MUSEUM
Cloître de l'église Saint-Nazaire, 34500 Béziers, Hérault
Gallo-Roman sarcophagi. Medieval archaeology.
Always open.

MUSEUM OF ARCHAEOLOGY
7 rue Massol, 34500 Béziers, Hérault
Underwater archaeology, including collection of bronze objects and copper ingots. Many Greek wrecks, one of which contained 3rd century amphora from Marseilles. Sailing ship belonging to Colbert.
Winter: Daily except M. 2-6. Summer: Daily except M. 10-12, 2-6.

MUSEUM OF FINE ART
Hôtel Fabregat, Place de la Révolution, 34500 Béziers, Hérault
Collection of Greek vases. Paintings by Martin Schaffner, Holbein, Bourdon, Géricault, Delacroix and Corot.
Daily except M. and Su. morning, 9-12, 2-6.

MUSEUM OF NATURAL HISTORY
15 Place Pierre Semart, 34500 Béziers, Hérault
The collections include Mediterranean and exotic shellfish; birds; entomology; botany; regional geology; zoology; mineralogy. Local pre-history.
W., Th. and F. 2.30-5.30. Sa. by appointment only. Closed July 15- Aug. 15.

BIARRITZ

MUSEUM OF THE SEA
Esplanade du Rocher-de-la-Vièrge, 64200 Biarritz, Pyrénées-Atlantiques
Aquarium. Zoological and geological collections. Ethnology. Deep-sea fishing. Regional fauna.
Oct.-May Daily 9-12, 2-6. June 9-12, 2-7. July-Sept. 9-7.

BIÈVRES

MUSEUM OF PHOTOGRAPHY
Mairie, 91570 Bièvres, Essonne
Collections illustrating the history of photography from its earliest times. Permanent exhibition of contemporary photographs.
Daily except Tu. 2.30-5.30.

BIOT

FERNAND LÉGER MUSEUM
06410 Biot, Alpes-Maritimes
The works of Fernand Léger, 1905-1955. Paintings. Drawings. Gouaches. Bronzes. Ceramics. Sculpture. Mosaics. Tapestries.
Oct. - Mar. 15, Daily 10-12, 2-5. Mar. 16- Sept. Daily 10-12, 3-7.

LE BLANC

MUSEUM OF BIRDS
Mairie, 36300 Le Blanc, Indre
Collections of birds from the area, and from other parts of the world. Birds' eggs. Nests.
Daily except Sa. p.m. and Su., 9-11.30, 2-5.30.

BLAYE

REGIONAL MUSEUM OF HISTORY AND ART
Citadelle de Blaye, 33390 Blaye, Gironde
Collection illustrating life of the Duchess of Berry, during her captivity in the convent of Minimes. Personal relics of the Duchess.
Daily 9-6.

BLÉRANCOURT

NATIONAL MUSEUM OF FRANCO-AMERICAN FRIENDSHIP
Château de Blérancourt, Blérancourt, 02300 Chauny, Aisne
Collection telling the story of Franco-American friendship. Souvenirs of the War of Independence, portraits and busts of Franklin, Washington, La Fayette, Jefferson. American weapons. French troops in America. Literary, artistic and technical co-operation between France and America.
Daily 10-12, 2-5.30 (to 4.30 in winter).

BLESLÉ-SUR-VILAINE

CHURCH OF SAINT-PIERRE
Beslé-sur-Vilaine, 44290 Guémené Penfao, Loire-Atlantique
In the Choeur des Dames there are canonesses' stalls and a collection of religious ornaments of the 17th and 18th centuries.
On request.

BLOIS

CHÂTEAU MUSEUM
Château, 41000 Blois, Loir-et-Cher
Italian and French paintings. Sculpture of the Renaissance and Romantic periods. Tapestries. Regional religious art. Archaeology. Natural history.
Mid.-Mar. - Oct. 1, Daily 9-12, 2-6.30. Oct. 2 - Jan. Daily 9-12, 2-5. Feb.-mid. Mar. Daily 9-12, 2-5.30.

ROBERT HOUDIN MUSEUM
5 Voûte du Château, 41000 Blois, Loir-et-Cher
Sculpture of the Renaissance and Romantic periods.
Daily 10-12, 2.30-6.30.

BONNEVAL

BONNEVAL MUSEUM
Mairie, 28800 Bonneval, Eure-et-Loir
Local history and folklore.
By appointment.

BONNIÈRES-SUR-SEINE

MUSEUM OF BURIALS
Bonnières-sur-Seine, 60112 Milly sur Therain, Oise
Neolithic burial site. Skeletons. Flint implements. Bone and shell ornaments.
M.-F. 8-12, 1.30-5.30; Sa. 8-11. Su. by appointment only.

BORDEAUX

AQUITAINE MUSEUM
20 cours d'Albret, 33000 Bordeaux, Gironde
Prehistoric collections from the Bordelais and Perigord areas. Gallo-Roman architectural fragments, Roman inscriptions. Reliefs. Medieval sculpture. Funerary statue of Marshal Ornano. Fragments of the mausoleum of the Dukes of Epernon by Pierre Biard. Regional ethnography.
Open on request for groups.

HISTORICAL COLLECTION OF THE CONSEIL INTERPROFESSIONAL DU VIN DE BORDEAUX
1 Cours du XXX Juillet, 33000 Bordeaux, Gironde
Wine in art. Tapestry by Saint-Saëns: 'the ardent rays of Phoebus shine on a langorous allegory of the Garonne depicted as a siren. The majestic river links the white and red vineyards, represented by two vine stocks heavy with bunches of grapes.' Paintings. Stained-glass window. Roman wine goblets and bowls. Charters. Letters patent relating to wine trade and cultivation of the vine.
By appointment only, M.-Sa.

MARITIME MUSEUM
Place de la Bourse, Pavillon Central, 33000 Bordeaux, Gironde
Models, portraits, documents and other exhibits illustrating maritime and local history.
Daily except Tu. and W., 10-12, 3-6.

JEAN MOULIN MUSEUM
30 rue des Frères Bonie, 33000 Bordeaux, Gironde
Collections relating to the 1939-45 war, the Resistance movement in France, and the activities of the Free French forces.
Tu.-Sa. 2-6. Closed Su. and M.

MUNICIPAL COLLECTION OF COINS AND MEDALS
Bibliothèque Municipale, 33000 Bordeaux, Gironde
Currency of Aquitaine. Weights and measures from 13th to 18th century.
During library hours.

MUSEUM OF DECORATIVE ARTS
39 rue Bouffard, 33000 Bordeaux, Gironde
In 18th century Hôtel de Lalande. European ceramics of the 17th and 18th centuries. 12th-18th century enamels. Glass. Silver. Furniture. 18th century locks made in Bordeaux. Local history.
Daily except Tu. 2-6.

MUSEUM OF FINE ART
Jardin de la Mairie, cours d'Albret, 33000 Bordeaux, Gironde
Works by Veronese and Rubens. 18th-19th century French painting and sculpture, especially Chardin, Corot, Delacroix and Rodin.
Daily except Tu. 10-12, 2-6.

TREASURY OF CATHEDRAL OF SAINT-ANDRÉ
33000 Bordeaux, Gironde
Miniatures. Gold plate. Italian primitives. Embroidery.
Daily on request.

BORMES-LES-MIMOSAS

CHARLES CAZIN MUSEUM
Hôtel de Ville, 83230 Bormes-les-Mimosas, Var
Collection of works of the painter Gazin. Works by Cross, Luce, Benezit. Two terra cotta by Rodin.
Daily 8.30-12, 2-6.

BOUGES-LE-CHÂTEAU

COLLECTION OF CARRIAGES AND HARNESS
Château de Bouges, 36560 Bouges-le-Château, Indre
The Château itself contains a collection of 18th century furniture and rooms with period furnishings. In the 19th century stables is a collection of saddles, harnesses and boots. Barouches. Berceuses. Broughams. Spring-van. Mail coach. Dog-carts.
June-Sept. Daily 9-12, 2-6. May and Oct. Daily ex. Tu. 10-12, 2-6. Nov.-Apr. Th., Sa. and Su. 10-12, 2-5.

BOULOGNE-SUR-MER

MUSEUM OF FINE ART AND ARCHAEOLOGY
34b Grande-Rue, 62200 Boulogne-sur-Mer, Pas-de-Calais
Greek and Peruvian vases. Egyptian collection. Satirical English engravings about Napoleon. Paintings by Lastman, Guérin, David, Boudin, Corot, Fantin-Latour, Vlaminck, Mathieu, Sisley. Ceramics. Geology. Prehistory. Archaeology.
May 2- Oct. 31, Daily except M., Tu. and Su. morning, 10-12, 2-6. Nov.-Apr. Th. and Su. only, 10-12, 2-6. Closed Jan. 1, May 1, July 14, Nov. 1, 11, Dec. 25.

BOULOGNE BILLANCOURT

PAUL LANDOWSKY MUSEUM
14 rue Max-Blondat, 92100 Boulogne Billancourt, Hauts-de-Seine
Works of the sculptor Paul Landowsky, including bronzes, marbles, plasters, ivories, drawings and rough models. Bust of Paul Valéry. The museum is housed in the former home of the sculptor.
Sa. and Th. 10-5; Tu. 2-5; Su. 3-5. Closed Dec. - Mar. 1 and Aug.

BOURBON LANCY

MUNICIPAL MUSEUM
Eglise Saint Nazaire, 71140 Bourbon Lancy, Saône-et-Loire
Sculpture, particularly by local artists. Paintings. Stone, Bronze and Iron Age material. Gallo-Roman items found in the area, including pottery, figurines, bronze and glassware, vases and amphorae. Stones and fossils. Coins. Sèvres vases and porcelain. Wooden dug-out canoe. Stone sarcophagi, one of which contains a skeleton (probably of a pilgrim of St. James of Compostella).
May-Sept. Tu., Th., Sa. and Su. 4-6.

BOURBON-L'ARCHAMBAULT

AUGUSTIN BERNARD MUSEUM
03160 Bourbon-l'Archambault, Allier
Local prehistory. Roman pottery. Folklore. Collection of pharmaceutical jars from Nevers.
May 10- Oct. 1, Tu., Th. and Su., 3-6.

BOURBONNE-LES-BAINS

MUNICIPAL MUSEUM
Parc de la Mairie, 52400 Bourbonne-les-Bains, Haute-Marne
Prehistory. Gallo-Roman, Roman and Celtic antiquities. Coins.
On request.

BOURG-EN-BRESSE

AIN MUSEUM
65 boulevard de Brou, 01000 Bourg-en-Bresse, Ain
Regional archaeology and prehistory. Paintings, including landscapes by Lyonnais artists of the 19th century. Poultry in art. Regional ethnography, including the reconstruction

of a Bresse house. History of lighting, including a collection of 260 lamps. 16th-18th century furniture.
Oct.-Mar. 15, Daily 10-12, 2-4.30, Mar. 16-June, Daily 8.30-12, 2-6. July-Sept. 8-12, 1.30-6.30.

BOURGES

DU BERRY MUSEUM
Maison du Berry, 4-6 rue des Arènes, 18000 Bourges, Cher
Built c.1515. Collection of pre-Roman and Roman archaeology. Ceramics. Bronzes. Religious and funerary sculpture. Folklore and popular art of Berry. Paintings of Fontainebleau School, and by Poussin, Greuze, Fragonard.
Daily except Tu. Apr.-mid. Sept. 10-12, 2-6. Mid. Sept.-Mar. 10-12, 2-5.

HÔTEL JACQUES COEUR
Place Jacques Coeur, 18000 Bourges, Cher
Built 1440-50. Romanesque and Gothic sculpture. Reliefs from rood-screen of the Cathedral (14th century). Statues from the Bourges Sainte Chapelle (15th century). Figures of mourners from tomb of Duc Jean de Berry (14th-15th centuries). Tapestries.
Daily except Tu. Mar. 22-Oct. 9-12, 2-6. Nov.-Mar. 21, 10-12, 2-6.

HÔTEL LALLEMANT
Rue Bourbonnaux, 18000 Bourges, Cher
Merchant's house (1487-1518). Furniture. Tapestries. Faience. Enamels. Clocks. Pewter of 16th-19th centuries.
Daily except W. Apr.-mid. Sept. 10-12, 2-6. Sept. 16-Mar. 3, 10-12, 2-5.

BOURGNEUF-EN-RETZ

RETZ REGIONAL MUSEUM
Mairie, 44580 Bourgneuf-en-Retz, Loire-Atlantique
Collections illustrating the lives of peasants, artisans and sailors. Costumes. Furniture. History and geology of the district.
June-Sept. Daily except Tu. 10-12, 2-5. Oct.-May, Th., Sa., Su. 10-12, 2-5.

BOURGOIN-JALLIEU

VICTOR CHARRETON MUSEUM
15 rue Victor-Hugo, 38300 Bourgoin-Jallieu, Isère
Paintings by Victor Charreton. 19th and 20th century paintings. History. Local folklore. Furniture. Medals. Coins. Historic documents. Engravings. Textiles. Weapons.
Th. 3-6; Sa. 11-12, 3-5; Su. 11-12, 3-6. Other times by request.

BOUSSY-SAINT-ANTOINE

DUNOYER DE SEGONZAC MUSEUM
Place André-Dunoyer-de-Segonzac, Boussy-Saint-Antoine, 91800 Brunoy, Essonne
Birthplace of André Dunoyer de Segonzac, restored and containing an important collection of engravings, posters, books, catalogues, documents, illustrating his life. The installation of this material was supervised by the artist himself.
Th. afternoons.

BOUXWILLER

BOUXWILLER MUSEUM
Hôtel de Ville, Place du Château, 67330 Bouxwiller, Bas-Rhin
History and ethnography of Hanau-Lichtenberg, including paintings, furniture, costumes and folklore. Collection of petrified objects from Bastberg.
Daily except Sa. afternoon, Su. and public holidays, 9-12, 2-6, on application to the Town Hall.

BRANTÔME

FERNAND DESMOULINS MUSEUM
Hôtel de Ville, 64310 Brantôme, Dordogne
Prehistoric remains from the region. Paintings by Desmoulins. Ceramics.
June 15-Sept. 15, Daily 9-12, 2-6.

BREIL-SUR-MERIZE

SARTHOIS MUSEUM
Domaine de Pescheray, 72370 Breil-sur-Merize, Sarthe
Domestic and agricultural items, typical of the area.
Daily 9-5.

BREST

MARITIME MUSEUM
Château, 29200 Brest, Finistère
Maritime history from the 16th century to the present day.
Daily except M. morning and public holidays, 9-12, 2-6.

MUNICIPAL MUSEUM
22 rue Traverse, 29200 Brest, Finistère
French and Italian paintings.
Daily except Tu. 10-12, 2-7.

BRIARE

AUTOMOBILE MUSEUM
45250 Briare, Loiret
History of the motor-car. Early models.
Sa. before Easter-Nov. 15, Daily 9-6.

BRICQEBEC

MUNICIPAL MUSEUM
Tour de l'Horloge, 50260 Bricqebec, Manche
Folklore. Tools. Furniture. Pottery. Handicrafts. Minerals.
On request.

BRIENNE-LE-CHÂTEAU

NAPOLEONIC MUSEUM
Rue de l'Ecole-Militaire, 10500 Brienne-le-Château, Aube
Napoleonic material, including manuscripts and letters about the youth of Napoleon I at Brienne-le-Château.
Daily 9-11, 2-6.

BRIGNOLES

BRIGNOLES MUSEUM
Place des Comtes-de-Provence, 83170 Brignoles, Var
Gallo-Roman archaeology. Paintings. Ethnography.
Mar.-Oct., Th., Sa. and Su. 9-12. Winter: Su. only, 9-12, 3-5.

BRIVE-LA-GAILLARDE

ERNEST RUPIN MUSEUM
15 rue du Docteur-Massenat, 19100 Brive-la-Gaillarde, Corrèze
Prehistory. Gallo-Roman antiquities. Sculpture. Paintings. Engravings. Coins. Religious and military art. Furniture. Objets d'art. Ethnography. Natural history.
Daily 10-12, 2-5.

LE BRUSC

MUSEUM OF THE MARINE OBSERVATORY
Ile des Embiez, 83000 Le Brusc, Var
Specimens of fish and other marine life. Shells. Sponges. Coral. Starfish.
Daily 9-6.

LE BUGUE-SUR-VÉZÈRE

BARA-BOU CAVE
24260 le Bugue-sur-Vézère, Dordogne
Prehistoric cave drawings of bears, bison, wild oxen and ibex. They appear to date from the Aurignacian Age.
Palm Su.-Oct. 31, 8-7.

LA BUSSIÈRE

MUSEUM OF FISHING
La Bussière, 45230 Chatillon Coligny, Loiret
Collections relating to every aspect of fishing, housed in a château which is furnished in period styles: 16th century, Napoleon III, 19th century. Fishing in art, in history and in poetry, as well as purely technical aspects.
Daily 9-12, 2-5.

BUSSY-LE-GRAND

CHÂTEAU DE BUSSY-RABUTIN
Bussy-le-Grand, 21150 Les Laumes, Côte d'Or
Weapons. Memorabilia of Roger de Rabutin. Military history.
Summer: Daily except Tu. 9-11, 2-6. Winter: Daily except Tu. 10-11, 2-4.

CABRERETS

MUSEUM OF PREHISTORY AND AFRICAN ETHNOLOGY
46330 Cabrerets, Lot
Prehistoric collections, attached to the prehistoric grotto of Pech-Merle. African ethnography.
Mar. 15-Nov. 15, daily 9-6.

CAEN

MUSEUM OF FINE ART
Château de Caen, 14000 Caen, Calvados
Paintings of the Italian, French, Flemish Schools. Ceramics. Dutch paintings of 17th century. Engravings by Dürer, Rembrandt, Callot. Regional archaeology, prehistory. Manuscripts.
Mar. 16-Sept. 30, Daily ex. Tu. 10-12, 2-6. Oct. 1-Mar. 15, Daily ex. Tu. 10-12, 2-5 (2-6 Su.).

NORMANDY MUSEUM
Château de Caen, 14000 Caen, Calvados
History, ethnography and archaeology of Normandy.
Oct.-Mar. 15, Daily except Tu. and public holidays, 10-12, 2-5 (2-6 Su.). Mar. 16-Sept., Daily except Tu. and public holidays, 10-12, 2-6.

CAGNES-SUR-MER

CASTLE MUSEUM
The Castle, 06800 Cagnes-sur-Mer, Alpes-Maritimes
Paintings by Chagall, Kisling, Carzou and Seyssaud. Ethnographical collection dealing with life in the region of Nice in earlier days, and in particular with the cultivation of the olive and the crafts connected with it.
Daily ex. Tu. 10-12, 2-6 (2-5 in winter).

RENOIR HOUSE-MUSEUM
aux Collettes, 06800 Cagnes-sur-Mer, Alpes-Maritimes
Paintings, sculptures and souvenirs of Auguste Renoir, who lived in Cagnes from 1900-1919.
Daily except Tu. 2-5 or 6.

CAHORS

MUNICIPAL MUSEUM
54 rue Emile-Zola, 46000 Cahors, Lot
Archaeology. Objets d'art. Medieval sculptures. Portraits of Catherine de Medici, Philip II. Paintings by Vlaminck, Dufy, Lurçat, Bissière, Cottavoz. Memorabilia of Gambetta, who was born at Cahors.
Daily except Su. 3-6.

CALAIS

NEW MUSEUM
25 rue Richelieu, 62100 Calais, Pas-de-Calais
Dutch and Flemish paintings (16th-18th centuries). Italian (18th century) and French (18th-19th centuries) paintings. English and French water-colours of 19th century. Local history. Room devoted to the machine-made lace of Calais.
Daily except Tu. and public holidays, 10-12, 2-6.

CAMARET-SUR-MER

MARITIME MUSEUM
Tour de Vauban, 29129 Camaret-sur-Mer, Finistère
Maritime history from the 16th century to the present day.
May-Sept. Daily 10-7. Oct.-Apr. Th., Sa., Su. and public holidays, 2-6. Closed Nov. 15-Dec. 15 and Jan. 15-Feb. 15.

CAMBO-LES-BAINS

EDMOND ROSTAND MUSEUM
Villa 'Arnaga', 62450 Cambo-les-Bains, Pyrénées-Atlantiques
In house where Rostand lived and died. Personal souvenirs of the writer.
July-mid. Sept. Daily 10-12, 2.30-6.30. Oct. Su. only 2.30-6. Easter, Whitsun and mid. Sept. to end of Sept. 2.30-6.

CAMBRAI

MUNICIPAL MUSEUM
15 rue de l'Epée, 59400 Cambrai, Nord
Gallo-Roman remains. Roman sculptures from the north of France. Sculptures from the old cathedral. 16th-20th century paintings. Drawings by Pissarro, Maillol, Matisse, Despiau. Souvenirs of Fénelon, Archbishop of Cambrai. Sculptures by Rodin, Bourdelle, Gimond.
Daily except Tu., 10-12, 2-5.

CANNES

LYCKLAMA MUSEUM
La Castre, Le Suquet, 06150 Cannes, Alpes-Maritimes
Pre-Colombian archaeology. Mexican pottery. Masks. Ethnography of Oceania. Persian and Middle East art of the 17th-early 19th centuries. Roman archaeology.
Winter: Daily 10-12, 2-5. Summer: Daily 10-12, 3-6. Closed M.

CARCASSONNE

CATHEDRAL MUSEUM
11000 Carcassonne, Aude
18th century paintings by Jacques Gamelin. Fabrics. Gold and silver objects.
July-Sept. 15, Daily 9-7. At other times, on application to the caretaker.

MUSEUM OF FINE ARTS
1 rue de Verdun, 11000 Carcassonne, Aude
17th-20th century French paintings. Dutch paintings. Faience. André Chénier collection.
Daily 8-12, 2-6.

MUSEUM OF THE WALLED CITY
Château Comtal, 11000 Carcassonne, Aude
Sculpture from the town and the area, from the time of the Roman Conquest to the 16th century. Archaeology and documents relating to the history of the city and its restoration. Frescoes.
Winter: Daily 9-12, 2-5. Summer: Daily 8-12, 2-6.

CARENTAN

WAR MUSEUM
50500 Carentan, Manche
Documents and souvenirs of the 1939-45 War.
Daily ex. M. 10-5.

CARNAC

MUSEUM OF PREHISTORY
Miln-le-Rouzic, 56340 Carnac, Morbihan
Prehistoric collection. Ceramics. Necklaces. Gold jewels and other objects found in and around Carnac.
Summer: Daily 8-7.

CARPENTRAS

COMTADIN MUSEUM
Boulevard Albin-Durand, 84200 Carpentras, Vaucluse
Ethnography. Paintings by local and regional artists. Provençal folklore.
Daily 10-12, 2-4 (2-6 in summer).

DUPLESSIS MUSEUM
Boulevard Albin-Durand, 84200 Carpentras, Vaucluse
Works by Bidauld and by Duplessis, portrait painter of Louis XVI, both of whom were born at Carpentras.
Paintings by artists of the French School, including Rigaud, Le Brun and Ingres. Bronzes. Ivories.
Daily except W. 10-12, 2-4 (2-6 in summer).

MUSEUM OF ARCHAEOLOGY
Rue des Saintes-Maries, 84200 Carpentras, Vaucluse
Gallo-Roman, Palaeochristian and Medieval material, including inscriptions, altar votives and tombs, all found in the region. Mosaics, glassware and pottery, especially urns and lamps. Remains of sculpture from the Romanesque cathedral of Saint Siffrein. Mineralogical collection.
Daily except W. 10-12, 2-4 (2-6 in summer).

MUSEUM OF RELIGIOUS ART
Cathédrale Saint-Siffrein, 84200 Carpentras, Vaucluse
16th-18th century wooden statues. Ivory crosses and other religious objects, including a 13th century enamelled cross.
On application to the verger.

SOBIRATS MUSEUM
11 rue du Collège, 84200 Carpentras, Vaucluse
In 18th century manor house. Louis XV and Louis XVI period rooms with tapestries and furniture. Faience from Marseille and Moustiers. Renaissance room. Regency and Louis XVI bedchambers. Library of the Comte de Sobirats.
Daily ex. W. 10-12, 2-4 (2-6 in summer).

CASSEL

MONT CASSEL MUSEUM OF LOCAL LIFE
12 Grande-Place, 59670 Cassel, Nord
Souvenirs of Marshal Foch, including his writing desk which he used during his stay at the house in 1914/15. Period rooms. Porcelain. Faience. Geology. Fossils.
June 15-Sept. 15, Daily.

CASSIS

MUNICIPAL MUSEUM
Mairie, 13260 Cassis, Bouches-du-Rhône
Roman antiquities from the ancient Carsicis Portus, on which the modern town is built. Roman coins. Paintings.
Daily except Su. and public holidays, 9.30-12, 3-6.

CASTRES

GOYA MUSEUM
Hôtel de Ville, 81100 Castres, Tarn
Four portraits by Goya and also his *Junta of the Philippines.* 1820 drawing of the eighty *Caprices.*
Spanish primitives. Works by Murillo, Valdès Léal, Arellano, Ribera, Vélasquez. 19th-20th century paintings.
Daily except M. 9-12, 2-6 (opens at 10 Su. and public holidays).

JAURÈS MUSEUM
Hôtel de Ville, 81100 Castres, Tarn
Collections illustrating life and work of the Socialist political leader, Jean Jaurès, assassinated 1914.
Daily ex. Tu. 9-12, 2-6.

LE CATEAU

HENRI MATISSE MUSEUM
Hôtel de Ville, 59360 Le Cateau, Nord
Works by Henri Matisse, presented by the artist to the town where he was born. Stained-glass window by Matisse, 1954, the year of his death.
Works by Vlaminck, Guérin, Yves Brayer, Oudot and Gromaire. Room devoted to the paintings of Auguste Herbin, born in this region.
Sa., Su. and public holidays, 3-5.

CAUDEBEC-EN-CAUX

BIOCHET MUSEUM
Rue de la Boucherie, 76490 Caudebec-en-Caux, Seine-Maritime
Architecture, sculptures from churches and houses which have been demolished. Engravings of old Caudebec. Local history and prehistory.
Tu. and Th. 3-5. June-Aug. 3-6. Closed at other times.

CAVAILLON

ARCHAEOLOGICAL MUSEUM
Place Jean-Bastide, 84300 Cavaillon, Vaucluse
Housed in the chapel of an 18th century hospital, the collections comprise local prehistoric and Gallo-Roman remains.
Apr.-Sept. Daily except Tu. and F., 9-12, 2-7. Oct.-Mar. Daily except Tu. and F., 10-12, 2-5.

OLD CAVAILLON MUSEUM
84300 Cavaillon, Vaucluse
Local folklore. Reconstruction of an 18th century bourgeois home.
Apr.-Sept. Daily except Tu. and F. 9-12, 3-7. Oct.-Mar. Th., Su. and M. 10-12, 2-4. At other times, apply to the caretaker.

SYNAGOGUE
Rue Hébraïque, 84300 Cavaillon, Vaucluse
Synagogue (1772-74) which has been preserved exactly as it was when it was built, a vestige of the Israelite communities who lived in the area from the Middle Ages to the Revolution, under the protection of the pontifical authority of Avignon. Judeo-Comtadin museum of Jewish history is in one of the annexes.
Daily except W. 9-12, 2-6.

CÉRET

MUSEUM OF MODERN ART
Rue Joseph-Parayre, 66400 Céret, Pyrénées-Orientales
Cubist paintings. Déodat de Severac, Manolo, Burty, Picasso, Braque, Max Jacob, Kisling, Juan Gris. Room devoted to works given by Picasso.
Daily except Tu. 9-12, 2-4 (2-7 in summer).

CERISY-LA-FORÊT

ABBOT'S HOUSE
50680 Cerisy-la-Forêt, Manche
Architectural items. Sculpture from the former abbey.
On request.

CHAÂLIS

JACQUEMART-ANDRÉ MUSEUM
Abbaye de Chaâlis, Chaâlis, Oise
Collection of ancient Egyptian, Greco-Roman and Medieval material. Paintings of the French, Flemish, Catalan and Italian Schools.
17th and 18th century, Renaissance furniture. Busts and memorabilia of J.-J. Rousseau. 18th century portraits. Tapestries.
Mar.-Nov. 1, M., Th., Sa. and Su. 2-5.30.

CHÂLONS-SUR-MARNE

CATHEDRAL OF ST. ETIENNE
51000 Châlons-sur-Marne, Marne
The Treasury contains a collection of Romanesque art.
On request.

GARINET MUSEUM
13 rue Pasteur, 51000 Châlons-sur-Marne, Marne
Memorabilia of Schiller and Goethe, including furniture and documents belonging to Schiller and his family. Material concerning Goethe and the battle of Valmy (1792).
Th. and Su., 2-6 on request.

MUNICIPAL MUSEUM
Place Godart, 51000 Châlons-sur-Marne, Marne
Images of Indian deities. Archaeology from the Stone Age to the Gallo-Roman period. 15th century head of Christ in wood. Paintings. Two bronzes by Rodin.
Su. and Th. 2-6 and on request.

SCHILLER-GOETHE MEMORABILIA
13 rue Pasteur, 51000 Châlons-sur-Marne, Marne
Furniture of the 18th century and Empire. Clothes, jewellery and other objects belonging to the poet Schiller and his family. Material concerning Goethe and the Battle of Valmy.
Su. and Th. 2-6 on request.

CHALON-SUR-SAÔNE

DENON MUSEUM
Place de l'Hôtel de Ville and rue Biochot, 71100 Chalon-sur-Saône, Saône-et-Loire
Prehistory. Gallo-Roman and Merovingian material. Paintings of the French, Flemish, Dutch and Italian Schools. Drawings by Greuze and Fragonard.
Room devoted to Vivant-Denon, engraver, Director General of French museums in 1802; another to Niepce, inventor of photography, born at Chalon in 1765; a third to H. de Chardonnet, inventor of artificial silk; a fourth to the Sâone and river transport.
Daily except Tu. 9.30-11.30, 2.30-5.30.

CHAMBÉRY

CHARMETTES MUSEUM
73000 Chambéry, Savoie
In 17th century country house where Jean-Jacques Rousseau lived with Mme. de Warens from 1735 to 1740. Furniture, prints and documents of that period.
Apr.-Sept. Daily except Tu. 10-12, 2-6. Oct.-Mar. 2-4.30, Th. and Su. 10-12.

MUSEUM OF FINE ART
Place du Palais-de-Justice, 73000 Chambéry, Savoie
Primitives of the Italian and Savoy Schools, including *Portrait of a Young Man* by Paolo Uccello. Italian and Renaissance paintings. Italian faience.
Apr.-Sept. Daily except Tu. 10-12, 2-6. Oct.-Mar. 2-4.30, Th. and Su. 10-12.

MUSEUM OF NATURAL HISTORY
2 Avenue de Lyon, 73000 Chambéry, Savoie
Mineralogy, including minerals found in Savoy. Crystallography. Mosses and lichens. Mammals and birds. Botany. Lepidoptera. Palaeontology. Dioramas.
Daily ex. Tu. 9-12, 2-6.

MUSEUM OF SAVOY
Square de Lannoy-de-Bissy, 73000 Chambéry, Savoie
Archaeology, including collection of prehistoric objects from the lake-dwellings of Bourget. Art and traditions of the Savoy district. Local history and documents relating to the House of Savoy.
Daily 9-12, 2-5.

CHAMBORD

CHÂTEAU DE CHAMBORD
Chambord, 41250 Bracieux, Loir-et-Cher
Historic portraits. Gobelins tapestries, including 18th century hunting scenes.
Apr.-Sept. Daily 9-11, 2-6.30. Oct. Daily 9-11, 2-5. Nov.-Mar. Daily 10-11.45, 2-4.

CHAMPIGNY-SUR-MARNE

MUNICIPAL MUSEUM
104 avenue Jean-Jaurès, Champigny-sur-Marne, 51500 Rilly la Montagne, Val-de-Marne
Prehistory. Local history. Furniture belonging to the poetess, Juliette de Wills.
Daily ex. M. 10-5.

CHAMPLITTE-ET-LE-PRÉLOT

DEPARTMENTAL MUSEUM OF HISTORY AND ETHNOGRAPHY
Château de Champlitte, 70600 Champlitte-et-le-Prélot, Haute-Saône
17th-19th century paintings. 18th century furniture. Folk art. Reconstructions of country interiors, including workshops, school, grocer's shop and inn.
Daily except Su. morning, 9-12, 2-6.

CHAMPS-SUR-MARNE

CHÂTEAU DE CHAMPS-SUR-MARNE
77420 Champs-sur-Marne, Seine-et-Marne
18th century furniture and wood carvings. Paintings by French artists.
Park open: Feb. 20-Mar. 20, Daily 10-5. Mar. 21-Sept. 30, Daily 10-6.30. Oct. Daily 10-5.30. Nov. 1-Feb. 20, Daily 10-4.30. Closed Tu.
Château: same dates and times as park, but closed between 12 and 1.30 and half an hour before the park closes each evening.

CHANCELADE

DIOCESAN MUSEUM OF ART
Abbaye de Chancelade, Chancelade, 24000 Périgueux, Dordogne
Ecclesiastical art. Religious objects, including reliquaries, chalices, 17th-19th century chasubles, and statuettes in natural and gilded wood (16th and 18th centuries).
Easter-June, Su. 2-6.30. June-Nov. 1, Daily 2-6.30. Rest of year on request.

CHANTILLY

CONDÉ MUSEUM
Château de Chantilly, 60500 Chantilly, Oise
Historic apartments belonging to the Grand Condé. 18th century furniture. Chantilly porcelain. Château.
French, Flemish and Italian paintings, including works by Giotto, Clouet, Memling, Raphael and Poussin. Miniatures by Fouquet for his *Heures dEtienne Chevalier*. Drawings by Poussin, Clouet, Carmontelle, Claude Lorrain.
1st Su. in Mar. - Nov. 1, Daily except Tu., 1.30-5.30. Open every day in July and Aug.

LA CHARITÉ-SUR-LOIRE

LOCAL MUSEUM
Hotel Adam, 58400 La Charité-sur-Loire, Nièvre
Ethnography and local history.
Easter-Oct. Daily 10-12, 2-6.

CHARLEVILLE-MÉZIÈRES

ARDENNES AND RIMBAUD MUSEUM
Au Vieux-Moulin, 08000 Charleville-Mézières, Ardennes
Ethnography. Memorabilia of Rimbaud.
May-Sept. Daily except F. 10-12, 2-6.

MUNICIPAL MUSEUM
2 rue du Musée, 08000 Charleville-Mézières, Ardennes
Archaeology. Numismatics. Paintings. Documents relating to the history of Charleville and of Mézières.
Daily except M. 10-12, 2-6; Su. 2-6.

CHAROLLES

RENÉ DAVOINE MUSEUM
32 rue René-Davoine, 71120 Charolles, Saône-et-Loire
Works of the sculptor, René Davoine.
Easter- Nov. 1, Daily except Tu.

JEAN LARONZE MUSEUM
Rue du Château, 71120 Charolles, Saône-et-Loire
Prehistory. Paintings by Jean Laronze. Furniture. Engravings.
Apr.-Sept. Su. and Th. 9-11, 1-5. Oct.-Mar. Su. and Th. 9-11, 1-4. Open on public holiday afternoons.

CHARROUX

ABBEY MUSEUM
86250 Charroux, Vienne
Statues from the end of 13th century, and 13th-14th century shrines to be found in the chapter-house of this ruined abbey, which was built between 12th and 15th centuries and, after Cluny, was one of the largest in the Christian world.
Daily 9-11.30, 2-6.30; Su. 3-6.30.

CHARTRES

JEAN MOULIN MUSEUM
Place Châtelet, 28000 Chartres, Eure-et-Loir
Collections describing the life, work and death of Jean Moulin (1899-1943), Head of the French Resistance movement during the occupation of France during World War II, and former Administrator of the Eure-et-Loir area.
Apr. 1- Nov. 11, Th., Sa. and Su. 2-5.

MUNICIPAL MUSEUM
29 Cloître de Notre Dame, 28000 Chartres, Eure-et-Loir
Medieval sculpture. French and Italian paintings of 15th-18th centuries. Tapestries, including some from the Choir of the Cathedral. Arms and armour. Greek ceramics. Enamels. Faience. Porcelain. Folklore.
Daily excluding Tu. and W., 10-12, 2-6 (2-9 in summer).

TREASURY
Cathédrale, 28000 Chartres, Eure-et-Loir
Triptych: 'Chasse de Saint-Aigan'. Gold and silver items. Vestments.
Mar.-Nov. Daily 10-12, 2-6. Dec.-Feb. Su. 2-6.

CHÂTEAU-DU-LOIR

HEURTELOUP-CHEVALLIER MUSEUM
14 rue Jean-Jaurès, 72500 Château-du-Loir, Sarthe
Roman archaeology. Local history and folklore. Furniture. Weapons.
Th. 3-6; Sa. 3-5; Su. 10.30-12.30.

CHÂTEAUDUN

CHÂTEAU DE CHÂTEAUDUN
28200 Châteaudun, Eure-et-Loir
15th-16th century building. Collection of tapestries and sculpture.
Sa. before Easter- Nov. 1, Daily 9.30-11.45, 2-6. Nov. 2- F. before Easter, Daily except Tu. 10-11.45, 2-4.45.

MUNICIPAL MUSEUM
Rue Toufaire, 28200 Châteaudun, Eure-et-Loir
Prehistory. Egyptology. Ornithology.
Sa. before Easter- Sept. 15, Tu.-Su. 9.30-11.30, 2-6. Sept. 16- F. before Easter, Tu.-Su. 10-11.30, 2-5.

CHÂTEAU-GOMBERT

MUSEUM OF PROVENÇAL ART
5 place des Héros, Château-Gombert, Bouches-du-Rhône
Faience from Marseilles and Moustiers. Costumes, Furniture. Paintings. Sculptures by Puget. Provençal head-dresses.
Th., Sa. and Su. 2-6.

CHÂTEAU-GONTIER

MUNICIPAL MUSEUM
Rue de la Poste, 53200 Château-Gontier, Mayenne
Italian, French and Dutch paintings. Greek and Roman archaeology. 15th century wooden statuette of St. Martha.
Daily 10-12, 2-6.

CHÂTEAUMEILLANT

ÉMILE CHENON MUSEUM OF ARCHAEOLOGY
Rue de la Victoire, 18370 Châteaumeillant, Cher
Collections illustrating the history of the district since prehistoric times. Pottery. France before and after the Roman conquest.
Daily 10-12, 2-6.

CHÂTEAUNEUF-SUR-LOIRE

MUNICIPAL MUSEUM
Château de Châteauneuf, 45110 Châteauneuf-sur-Loire, Loiret
Collection illustrating the maritime life of the Loire.
Sa. before Easter- Apr. 19, Daily except Tu., 10-12, 2-5. Apr. 20- May 29, Sa., Su. and public holidays 10-12, 2-5. May 30- Sept. 1, Daily except Tu. 10-12, 2-6. Sept. 2- Oct. 2, Sa., Su. 10-12, 2-5.

CHÂTEAUPONSAC

LOCAL MUSEUM
87290 Châteauponsac, Haute Vienne
Prehistory. Polished axes and prehistoric bola found locally. Tools, bones of humans and animals. Flint ploughshare found in the region. Gallo-Roman material, including urns and other items from a chieftain's grave. Medieval and 17th/ 18th century exhibits. Revolutionary material includes General Desverine's uniform and Commandant Borrianne's sword (both natives of Châteauponsac). Paintings and sketches.
Daily 9-12, 2-6.

CHÂTEAUROUX

BERTRAND MUSEUM
2 rue Descente des Cordeliers, 36000 Châteauroux, Indre
House of General Bertrand (1753-1844). Napoleonic relics, bequeathed by Bertrand (who followed Napoleon to St. Helena and brought his ashes back to Paris). Italian and French paintings, engravings and drawings. Furniture. Reconstruction of kitchen of Berry region.
June-Sept. Daily except M. and July 14, 9.30-12, 2-6. Oct.-May Daily except M. and Jan. 1, May 1, Nov. 1 and 12, Dec. 25, 2-5.

MUSEUM OF ARCHAEOLOGY
Place Saint-Hélène, 36000 Châteauroux, Indre
Celtic and Gallo-Roman lapidary collection, including Gallic altar dedicated to the god Cernunos. Medieval fragments (tympanum and capitals) from the Abbey of Déols.
On request at the Musée Bertrand.

CHÂTEAU-THIERRY

JEAN DE LA FONTAINE MUSEUM
12 rue Jean-de-la-Fontaine, 02400 Château-Thierry, Aisne
Manuscripts, engravings and portraits of the fable-writer. Editions of his works, and a library of books about him.
Summer: Daily except Tu. 10-12, 2.30-6.30. Winter: Sa., Su. and M. 10-12, 2-5.

CHÂTELLERAULT

PAUL CHÉRON DE LA MARTINIÈRE MUSEUM
12 rue Gaudeau-Lerpinière, 86100 Châtellerault, Vienne
17th and 18th century paintings. Wood sculpture. Ceramics. Souvenirs of "Le Chat Noir" tavern. Armour. Cutlery. Locksmith's work.
Daily 2-6 on application. Closed Su. and public holidays.

CHÂTILLON-SUR-SEINE

MUSEUM OF ARCHAEOLOGY
21400 Châtillon-sur-Seine, Côte d'Or
Prehistoric, Celtic, Greek, Gallo-Roman archaeology, including the treasure of Vix, which was found in 1953 at the foot of Mount Lassois in the tomb of a Celtic princess buried in the 6th century A.D. Gold diadem. Bronze bowl with frieze. Souvenirs of Marshal Marmont.
Daily including public holidays, 9-12, 2-6.

LA CHÂTRE

MUSEUM OF GEORGE SAND AND OF THE VALLÉE NOIRE
71 rue Venôse, 36400 La Chatre, Indre
Souvenirs and documents relating to George Sand and other writers and artists who stayed at Nohant. Head-dresses, costumes and embroidery of Bas-Berry. Collection of birds from all over the world.
Daily except Sa. 10-12, 2-6.

CHAUMONT

CHAUMONT MUSEUM
Place du Palais, 52000 Chaumont, Haute-Marne
Archaeology collection. 15th-18th century sculptures. Fragments of the mausoleums of Claude de Guise and the Duke of Vitry. 17th-19th century paintings.
Nov.-Mar. Th. 10-12, 2-5; Su. 2-6. Apr.-Oct. Th., Sa. and Su. 10-12, 2-6.

CHAUMONT-SUR-LOIRE

MUSEUM IN THE STABLES
Château, Chaumont-sur-Loire, 41150 Onzain, Loir-et-Cher
15th-16th century château, residence of Catherine de Medici, widow of Henry II and then of Diane de Poiters. Furnishings. Tapestries.
Sa. before Easter- Sept. 15, daily ex. Tu. 9-11.45, 2-6.30. Sept. 16- Nov. 15, 9-11.45, 2-5. Nov. 16- F. before Easter, 10-11.45, 2-4.

CHAUNY

LOCAL MUSEUM
Mairie, 02300 Chauny, Aisne
Palaeontology. Prehistory, Gallo-Roman and Merovingian

archaeology. Manuscripts and writings of Victor Leduc. Local history. Coin collection. Faience.
Th. 3-5.30; Sa. 4-6.30. Closed Aug.

CHAUVIGNY

FOLKLORE AND ETHNOGRAPHIC MUSEUM
86300 Chauvigny, Vienne
Collections illustrating history and ethnography of the region. Lapidary collection.
Holiday periods: daily 9-12, 2-6. Winter: Su. 2-6.

CHELLES

ALFRED BONNO MUSEUM
Place de la République, 77500 Chelles, Seine-et-Marne
Regional prehistory. Gallo-Roman, Merovingian and medieval archaeology. Documents relating to the Abbey of Chelles.
Th. and Sa. 2-5 or by appointment.

CHERBOURG

THOMAS HENRY MUSEUM
Hôtel de Ville, 50100 Cherbourg, Manche
Italian paintings, including works by Filippo Lippi, Caravaggio. Spanish paintings by Murillo and Ribera. Flemish paintings by Van Eyck, Van Dyck. Dutch, German, French paintings. J. F. Millet room.
Daily except Tu. 10-12, 2-6.

MUSEUM OF LOCAL AND REGIONAL ART
Château de Tourlaville, 50100 Cherbourg, Manche
Paintings, drawings, sculpture by local artists.
May 1 - Sept. 30. Daily 2-7.

MUSEUM OF NATURAL HISTORY AND ETHNOGRAPHY
Parc Emmanuel Liais, 50100 Cherbourg, Manche
In the former home of Emmanuel Liais, 19th century astronomer, naturalist and explorer. Geology. Palaeontology. Mammals. Birds. Reptiles. Entomology. Ethnography. Prehistory.
Daily ex. Tu. 10-12, 2-5. Winter: 2-5. On request only in the mornings.

MUSEUM OF THE WAR AND THE LIBERATION
Fort du Roule, 50100 Cherbourg, Manche
History of Cherbourg since the Middle Ages. Paintings. Engravings. Seals. Medals. History of the Occupation and the liberation of Cotentin. Map room. Armament room (allied and German weapons). Posters and leaflets.
Daily 9.30-12, 2-6. Closed Tu. Oct.-Mar.

CHEVERNY

CHÂTEAU DE CHEVERNY
Cheverny, Val de Loire
17th century Château. Armour. Gobelins and other tapestries. Family portraits. Furniture.
Daily 8.30-12, 2-5 (2-7 in summer).

CHINON

JEAN D'ARC MUSEUM
Tour de l'Horloge, Château de Chinon, 37500 Chinon, Indre-et-Loire
Relics and memorabilia of the life of the Maid of Orleans. Weapons. Children's drawings.
Winter: Daily 9-12, 2-5. Summer: Daily 9-12, 2-6.30.

OLD CHINON MUSEUM
8 rue Voltaire, 37500 Chinon, Indre-et-Loire
Collections of archaeology and ethnography. Medieval sculptures. Portrait of Rabelais, by Delacroix.
Daily except Tu., 1-6.

CHOLET

CHOLET MUSEUM
Avenue Gambetta, 49300 Cholet, Maine-et-Loire
Relics and mementoes of the war in Vendée.
By appointment.

LA CIOTAT

LA CIOTAT MUSEUM
Rue des Poilus, 13600 La Ciotat, Bouches-du-Rhône
Local archaeology and ethnography. Models of ships. Nautical instruments. Natural history. Paintings.
Sa. 5-7; Su. and public holidays 10-12.

CIVRAY

MUNICIPAL MUSEUM
Mairie, 86400 Civray, Vienne
Archaeological material from the caves at Le Chaffaud and other nearby caves.
Daily 9-12, 2-6.

CLAMECY

MUNICIPAL MUSEUM
Hôtel de la Bellegarde, 58500 Clamecy, Nièvre
Paintings of the Flemish School (17th century) and of the French School (18th-19th centuries). Faience from Nevers. Ethnography. History of timber-floating.
Daily 10-12, 2-6.

CLÈRES

MOTOR MUSEUM
76690 Clères, Seine-Maritime
50 vintage cars, including the Delaunay of the Bonnot team, a 40 horse-power Renault, velocipides of "the heroic ages", armoured car and a self-propelled gun of the second World War.
Daily ex. M. 10-5.

CLERMONT-EN-BEAUVAISIS

LIBRARY AND MUSEUM
Donjon de l'Hôtel de Ville, 60600 Clermont-en-Beauvaisis, Oise
Portraits of local personalities. Drawings and engravings of the old city.
Daily, on application.

CLERMONT-FERRAND

BARGOIN MUSEUM
45 rue Ballainvilliers, 63000 Clermont-Ferrand, Puy-de-Dôme
Gallo-Roman and prehistoric archaeology. Paintings. Sculpture.
Daily except M. 10-12, 2-5.

LECOQ MUSEUM
15 rue Bardoux, 63000 Clermont-Ferrand, Puy de Dôme
Natural sciences. Collections of rocks and minerals of Auverne.
Daily ex. M. 2-5. Th. and Su. also 10-12.

RANQUET MUSEUM
1 petite rue Saint-Pierre, 63000 Clermont-Ferrand, Puy-de-Dôme
The collection includes Pascal's calculating machine, souvenirs of Desaix, objets d'art. Weapons. Glass. Faience. Enamels. Regional ethnography.
Daily except M. 10-12, 2-5.

CLOS-LUCÉ

LEONARDO DA VINCI MUSEUM
Clos-Lucé, Indre-et-Loire
Collections illustrating life and work of Leonardo da Vinci. Exhibition of sketches made by I.B.M. on the plans of machines designed by Leonardo.
Daily 9-12, 2-7. Closed Feb.

CLUNY

CELLAR MUSEUM
Ećole Nationale des Arts et Metiers, 71250 Cluny, Saône-et-Loire
Cellar with a collection of sculptures, 12th to 18th centuries.
Term-time: Weekdays 2.15-5; Su. 9-12, 2-5 in summer; Su. 10-12, 2-4 in winter. Vacation: Daily 9-12, 2-5.

FLOUR-MERCHANT'S MUSEUM
École Nationale des Arts et Metiers, 71250 Cluny, Saône-et-Loire
Roman cornices from the chancel of the abbey church, sculpted in 1095. Tomb stone of Saint Hugues. Altar used in the consecration of Cluny.
Term-time: Weekdays 2.15-5; Su. 9-12, 2-5 in summer; Su. 10-12, 2-4 in winter. Vacation: Daily 9-12, 2-5.

OCHIER MUSEUM
Rue de l'Abbatiale, 71250 Cluny, Saône-et-Loire
Documents relating to the consecration of the Benedictine order and its growth during the medieval period. Paintings and drawings by Prud'hon, a native of Cluny. Objects from the Abbey, including furniture, chalices, Easter candlesticks.
Apr.-Sept. Daily except Tu. 9.30-12, 2-6. Oct.-Mar. Daily except Tu. 10-12, 2-4.

LA CLUSE-ET-MIJOUX

CHÂTEAU DE JOUX MUSEUM
Près de Pontarlier, La Cluse-et-Mijoux, Doubs
Weapons. Military headgear of the First Empire, the Restoration and the Second Empire.
Su. from Easter onwards and daily from July 1 - Oct. 1, 9-12, 2-6.

CLUSES

MUSEUM OF THE NATIONAL SCHOOL OF WATCH AND CLOCKMAKING
Grand-Rue, 74300 Cluses, Haute-Savoie
Collection of old time-pieces.
By appointment.

COGNAC

MUNICIPAL MUSEUM
Boulevard Denfert-Rochereau 34, 16100 Cognac, Charente
Regional prehistoric archaeology, ethnography. French paintings (16th-20th centuries). Agricultural and vineyard implements, including harrows and ploughs, as well as hand tools. Sulphators. Presses. Copper measures. Cooper's implements.
Summer: daily ex. Tu. 10-12, 2.30-6. Remainder of year, M., Tu., Sa., Su. 2.30-5.30.

COLMAR

BARTHOLDI MUSEUM
30 rue des Marchands, 68000 Colmar, Haut-Rhin
Works. Memorabilia and personal belongings of the sculptor, Bartholdi. Reconstruction of his Paris studio.
Daily 9-12, 2-4; Su. 9-12.

UNTERLINDEN MUSEUM
1 place d'Unterlinden, 68000 Colmar, Alsace
Housed in a Dominican monastery, the exhibits include furniture, porcelain, weapons and armour, sculptures and paintings. Replica of an Alsatian wine-cellar. Wine presses and casks.
Daily 9-12, 2-5 (2-6 in summer). Closed Jan. 1, May 1, Nov. 1, Dec. 25. Closed Tu. from Nov.-Mar.

COMMANA

OPEN-AIR MUSEUM
Commana 29-N, Brittany
The whole village, with 17th-19th century houses, two water-mills, stables and two farmhouses, is preserved as a museum. Another feature is the last tan mill in Britanny, with one of the last tan yards.
May 1 - Sept. 30, daily 10-6.

COMMERCY

LOCAL MUSEUM
Hôtel de Ville, 55200 Commercy, Meuse
Collection of faience and ivories from the Far East.
Daily 8.30-12, 2-6 on application to the caretaker.

COMPIÈGNE

COMPIÈGNE PALACE NATIONAL MUSEUM
60200 Compiègne, Oise
Royal and imperial apartments. Restored royal apartments, with original décor, furniture and works of art. Rooms of the First and Second Empire, and the 'salon de jeux' of Marie-Antoinette. The rooms devoted to Napoleon III's time contain a collection of contemporary documents, furniture and works of art, including paintings by Winterhalter, Meissonier, Alfred Stevens, Boudin, and the paintings and sculptures by Carpeaux. The five rooms of the Empress contain personal possessions of the Imperial family.
Daily 9.45-12, 2-5.30 (4.30 in winter). Closed Nov. 1, Dec. 25 and Jan. 1.

NATIONAL MUSEUM OF ROAD TRANSPORT AND TOURISM
Palais de Compiègne, 60200 Compiègne, Oise
Land transport. 18th century travelling coaches. 19th century carriages for long journeys, for use in the town and for sport. Collection of sleighs. Litters and palanquins. Early cycles and motor-cars, models. Documents.
Daily 9.45-12, 2-5.30 (4.30 in winter). Closed Nov. 1, Dec. 25 and Jan. 1.

MUSEUM OF HISTORIC MODEL FIGURES
Annexe de l'Hôtel de Ville, 60200 Compiègne, Oise
Collection of model soldiers, in lead, wood and cardboard (90,000 items).
Dioramas and panoramas. French sovereigns and their families in gala costumes from Charlemagne to Napoleon III.
Daily 9-12, 2-6.

VIVENEL MUSEUM
Hôtel de Songeons, Hôtel de Ville and Hôtel-Dieu Saint Nicholas, 60200 Compiègne, Oise
At Hôtel de Songeons: Greek vases. Prehistory. Egyptian antiquities. Ivories and enamels. Medals. 16th century glass, faience. Sculpture. Weapons. 16th-20th century drawings, including two by Dürer and one by Rembrandt.
At Hôtel de Ville: Woodwork. Paintings. Tapestries. 15th and 18th century furniture. Reredos in alabaster from Saint-Germain-l'Auxerrois (15th century).
At Hôtel-Dieu Saint Nicholas: Wooden reredos (17th century). Wood carvings, statues and religious paintings (12th-13th centuries).
Daily ex. Tu. 9-12, 2-6.

CONCARNEAU

MUSEUM OF FISHING
rue Vauban, Ville Close, 29110 Concarneau, Finistère
Models of fishing boats, together with three full-sized vessels. Methods of catching different fish. Ship-building. Sailmaking. Special exhibits include a coelacanth, a giant Japanese crab, and stuffed fish and animals. History of the town of Concarneau.
Easter holiday, then May 15 - Sept. 30, 10-12, 2-6.

CONDÉ-SUR-L'ÉSCAUT

MUNICIPAL MUSEUM
Château, Place Verte, 59163 Condé-sur-l'Éscaut, Nord
Paintings, drawings, water-colours of the Fontainebleau School. History of water-transport.
Tu. and F. 7-8 p.m. Su. 10-12.

CONDOM

ARMAGNAC MUSEUM
32100 Condom, Gers
Agricultural implements, including a swing plough of an extremely rare type made entirely of wood except for the share. Grape harvesting equipment. Cooper's tools. Techniques of conservation.
Daily on application.

CONFLANS-SAINTE-HONORINE

MUSEUM OF WATER TRANSPORT
Château du Prieuré, 78700 Conflans-Sainte-Honorine, Yvelines
Inland waterways. Local history. Ethnography. Technology.
Th., Sa. and Su. 2-5.

CONQUES

CONQUES ABBEY MUSEUM
Conques, 12320 St. Cyprien sur Dourdou, Aveyron
Shrine of Pepin d'Aquitaine (838-871), with statue studded with precious stones. Two portable altars, made of gold, depicting Saint Foy. 12th century vestments, shrines, enamels and jewellery.
Easter - Nov. 1, 10-12, 2-6.

CORCELLE

FRANCHE-COMTÉ MUSEUM
Courcelle, 25590 Rigney, Doubs
Tools. Agricultural implements. Wooden plough shares. Basketwork. Pottery. Domestic equipment. Images. Interiors of peasant homes.
Apr. 1 - Dec. 1, Su. 2-6. June 1 - Oct. 21, also Sa. 2-6.

CORDES

CHARLES PORTAL MUSEUM
au Portail-peint, 81170 Cordes, Tarn
History of old Cordes. The 'Livre Ferrat', which contains the laws of the city from 1273 to 1623. Local antiquities from Neolithic times to the Middle Ages. The Cordes well, 113,4 m. deep.
Daily 9-6.

CORTE

MUSEUM OF CORSICAN HISTORY
Palais National, 20250 Corte, Corsica
History of the island, from Prehistoric times to the period Napoleon III spent in Corsica.
Daily 10-12, 3-6 in Summer; 9-11, 2-5 in Winter.

COSNE-SUR-LOIRE

MUNICIPAL MUSEUM
58200 Cosne-sur-Loire, Nièvre
Material illustrating the life and traditions of the bargemen on the Loire.
Daily ex. M. 10-5.

COSSÉ-LE-VIVIEN

ROBERT TATIN MUSEUM
53230 Cossé-le-Vivien, Mayenne
Paintings and watercolours by Robert Tatin. Drawings and embroidery designed by the artist. Pottery exhibited in Brazil by Robert Tatin, where he was a prize-winner in São Paulo (1951). In the middle of the Museum is an open space containing a pool, around which stand 12 statues, one for each month of the year. The entrance to the Musuem is flanked by more statues - "the way of the Giants".
Mar.-Jan. 6, Daily. Visitors from abroad welcome at any time.

LA CÔTE-SAINT-ANDRÉ

BERLIOZ MUSEUM
69 rue de la République, 38260 La Côte-Saint-André, Isère
Collection illustrating the life and work of Berlioz, in his birthplace.
Mar.-Dec. Daily except M. 9-12, 3-6. Feb. M.-Sa. 3-6; Su. 9-12, 3-6. Closed Jan.

COUILLY PONT-AUX-DAMES

THEATRE MUSEUM
77740 Couilly Pont-aux-Dames, Seine-et-Marne
Portraits, busts and souvenirs of famous actors and actresses.
Apr. 1 - Sept. 30. Daily 2-5. Oct. 1 - Mar. 31. Sa., Su. and M. 2-5. On request for groups of at least ten people.

COULOMMIERS

MUNICIPAL MUSEUM
Ancienne Église des Capucins, Parc du Château, 77120 Coulommiers, Seine-et-Marne
Prehistoric archaeology. Paintings relating to the ancient château of the Duchess of Longueville. 13th century sculptures. Manuscripts, including one by Bossuet.
Apr. 15 - Oct. 15, Su. 2-5. Other times on request.

COURBEVOIE

ROYBET-FOULD MUSEUM
178 boulevard Saint-Denis, 92400 Courbevoie, Hauts-de-Seine
Sculptures, paintings and drawings by Carpeaux. Paintings by Roybet.
Th., Sa., Su. and public holidays, 2-6.

COUR-CHEVERNY

CHÂTEAU COLLECTIONS
Cour-Cheverny, 41700 Contres, Loir-et-Cher
Château (1634). Furniture and decorations. Tapestries. Paintings by Jean Mosnier (1600-56). Hunting collection.
Sa. before Easter - Sept. 15, daily 8.30-11.45, 2-6. Sept. 16 - F. before Easter, daily 8.30-11.45, 2-5.

COUTANCES

MUNICIPAL MUSEUM
2 rue Quesnel-Morinière, 50200 Coutances, Manche
Gallo-Roman archaeology. 17th-19th century paintings including works by Rubens, Le Sueur. Collection of Normandy pottery.
Daily 2-4 on application.

LA COUTURE-BOUSSEY

MUSEUM OF INDUSTRY AND INSTRUMENTS
Mairie, 27750 La Couture-Boussey, Eure
Old musical instruments (originals and copies). Models. Flutes, oboes, clarinets. Local industry.
Daily on request.

CRÉCY-EN-BRIE

MUNICIPAL MUSEUM
Mairie, 77580 Crécy-en-Brie, Seine-et-Marne
Plans and drawings of the town. Portrait of the Duke of Penthièvre, benefactor of the town. Objets d'art.
Daily 9-5, except for Sa. afternoon, Su. and public holidays.

CREIL

GALLÉ JUILLET MUSEUM
Cour du Château, 60100 Creil, Oise
A 19th century middle-class family's home, with a British flavour (the first owner was British). Period rooms. Costumes. Photographs. Shells. Toys. Room devoted to the paintings and drawings of Lernercier and Cossard.
Daily ex. Tu. 2-6.

CRÉPY-EN-VALOIS

MUSEUM OF THE VALOIS AND OF ARCHERY
au Château, 60800 Crépy-en-Valois, Oise
Prints. Engravings. Provincial flower vases. Company flags. Large collection of material connected with the cross-bow and the long-bow.
Easter-Nov. 11-12, 2-5. Closed Tu. and F.

LE CREUSOT

MUSEUM OF MAN AND INDUSTRY
Château de la Verrerie, Le Creusot, Saone-et-Loire
Headquarters of 'fragmented' or 'eco' museum, covering ecology and history of the area.
Enquire locally

LE CROISIC

MARITIME MUSEUM
Mairie, 44490 Le Croisic, Loire-Atlantique
History of shipping, navigation.
June 25 - Sept. 7, Daily except M., Th. mornings, 10-12, 3-7.

CROISSET

PAVILLON FLAUBERT
18 quai Gustave-Flaubert, Croisset, Seine-Maritime
Memorabilia of Flaubert, including furniture and personal belongings. His library is to be found at the Mairie.
Daily except Tu. and W. morning, 10-12, 2-6. Closed Jan. 1, May 1, Nov. 1, 11. Also closed last three F. in Jan; last three F. in Nov.; first two F. in Dec.

CROIX-DE-VIE

MARAICHIN MUSEUM
Croix-de-Vie, Vendée
Local peasant culture. Furniture. Utensils. Costumes. Interiors of the houses of Vendée peasants.
July-mid. Sept. 2-5.

DENAIN

MUNICIPAL MUSEUM
Place Wilson, 59220 Denain, Nord
Neolithic and Gallo-Roman archaeological remains. Documents on local history, mining, metallurgy. Room devoted to the poet of mining, Jules Mousscron. Paintings.
Su. and public holidays, 10-1, 4-7. Weekdays 4-7. Closed Tu. Other times on application.

DIE

MUNICIPAL MUSEUM
11 rue Camille-Buffardel, 26150 Die, Drôme
Local archaeology of the Roman period, including epigraphs, sculptures, ceramics, glassware and metallic objects. Sculptures. Ethnography.
June 15 - Aug. 31, Tu., Th. and Sa. 2-5.

DIEPPE

CHÂTEAU MUSEUM
76200 Dieppe, Seine-Maritime
Paintings, including works by Courbet, Boudin, Pissarro, Sisley, Sickert, Dufy. Pottery. Room devoted to Camille Saint-Saëns. Souvenirs of the composer. Maritime collection, including 16th and 17th century sea charts and harbour maps. Compasses. 18th and 19th century models of ships in wood and ivory. Ivory trinkets.
June 15 - Sept. 15, Daily except Tu. 10-12, 2-6.

DIGNE

MUNICIPAL MUSEUM
Boulevard Gassendi, 04000 Digne, Alpes-de-Haute-Provence
Prehistory. Gallo-Roman archaeology. 19th-20th century paintings, especially by local artists. Regional history.
Winter: Daily 2-4. Summer: Daily 3-5.

DIJON

ARCHAEOLOGICAL MUSEUM
5 rue Docteur-Maret, 21000 Dijon, Côte d'Or
Sculptures. Gallo-Roman objects, including bas-relief of wine shop. Wooden sculptures found near the source of the Seine. Medieval and Renaissance sculpture. Busts of Christ
Daily except Tu. 9-12, 2-5. Closed Dec. 25 and Jan. 1.

CHAMPMOL CHARTERHOUSE
21000 Dijon, Côte d'Or
Remains of the gate-house of the church, which includes five statues by Claus Sluter and *Le Puits de Moise.*
Daily 8.30-11.30, 2-5.30.

MAGNIN MUSEUM
5 rue des Bons-Enfants, 21000 Dijon, Côte d'Or
Paintings including works by Poussin, Vouet, Vignon, Restout, Fragonard, Prud'hon, David, Magnasco, Jerome Bosch, Van der Helst. Furniture. Drawings by Primatice, Pisanello, Mantegna.
Daily except Tu. 9-12, 2-5.

MUSEUM OF FINE ART
Place de la Sainte-Chapelle, 21000 Dijon, Côte d'Or
The chief works of art from the Charterhouse of Champmol. Tomb of Philippe le Hardi by Claus Sluter and Claus Werwe, and of Jean sans Peur and Marguerite of Bavaria. 15th and 16th century paintings and tapestries, including Flemish, Swiss and German primitives. Paintings by Rubens and Franz Hals. Italian, French paintings of 16th-19th centuries. Ivories. Enamels. Gold and silver ware. Medieval sculpture. Wood carvings and furniture of the French Renaissance period. 15th and 16th century Burgundian sculptures. 19th-20th century French paintings.
Daily 9-12, 2-6 (2-4 in winter). Apr. - Nov. 15, open Sa. also 7-8 p.m. Tu. on application.

MUSEUM OF NATURAL HISTORY
1 Avenue Albert I, 21000 Dijon, Côte d'Or
Geology. Fauna of the Côte d'Or region. Entomology. Shells. Birds' eggs. Stuffed birds.
Th., F., Sa., Su. and public holidays, 2-5.

PERRIN DE PUYCOUSIN MUSEUM
40 rue des Forges, 21000 Dijon, Côte d'Or
Burgundian folklore. Reconstructions of the interior of Burgundian houses. Furniture, costumes, tools.
July 1 - Sept. 15, 9-12, 2-5; Th. and Su. 2-5 (Sept 15 - July 1).

REGIONAL HOSPITAL MUSEUM
2 rue de l'Hôpital, 21000 Dijon, Côte d'Or
Sculptures, including a 15th century *Mise au Tombeau* and a 14th century *Trinité* by the Sluter School. Tombstones. Paintings. Documents.
Daily except Sa. afternoon and Su., 8-12, 2-6.

RUDE MUSEUM
Rue Vaillant, 21000 Dijon, Côte d'Or
Casts of sculpture by Rude, notably the *Marseillaise*, a high-relief 13 metres high which decorates the *Arc de Triomphe* in Paris.
Summer: Daily except Tu. 10-12, 2-5. Winter: Su. 10-12, 2-5. On weekdays apply to the caretaker.

DINAN

MUNICIPAL MUSEUM
Château de Dinan, 22100 Dinan, Côtes-du-Nord
Military architecture. Ethnography. History.
Summer: Daily 9-12, 1-7. Winter: Daily except M. 9-12, 2-5. Closed Nov.

DINARD

MARITIME MUSEUM
35800 Dinard, Ille-et-Vilaine
Maritime history. Souvenirs of the polar expeditions commanded by Charcot.
Pentecost - Oct. 1, Daily 10-12, 2-6. (Su. until 7).

DIORS

BERRICHON MUSEUM OF THREE WARS
Château, Diors, 36130 Déols, Indre
Devoted to the wars of 1870, 1914 and 1939. Medals, flags, tracts and newspapers.
Mar.-Apr. Weekdays 8-12, 2-6; Su. and public holidays, 1.30-6. May-Sept. Weekdays 8-12, 2-6; Su. and public holidays, 1.30-7.

DOLE

JULIEN FEUVRIER MUSEUM OF ARCHAEOLOGY
Chapelle du College de l'Arc, 39100 Dole, Jura
Material from local excavations: Gallic, Gallo-Roman and Merovingian collections. Egyptology. 15th century sculptures. Natural history. Furniture.
Easter-Oct. Daily ex. M. 2-5.

MUSEUM OF FINE ART
College de l'Arc, 39100 Dole, Jura
Collections include paintings by Simon Vouet and Courbet. Sculptures. 16th and 17th century works of the French School.
Daily except M. 2-5.

PASTEUR MUSEUM
43 rue Pasteur, 39100 Dole, Jura
House where Louis Pasteur was born. Collections illustrating his life and work.
Daily 10-12, 2-6 (2-4 in winter).

DOMFRONT

MUNICIPAL MUSEUM
Mairie, 61700 Domfront, Orne
Paintings and items of local interest. Drawings by the caricaturist, Léandre.
On request.

DOMRÉMY LA PUCELLE

JEANNE D'ARC MUSEUM
annexe de la maison de Jeanne d'Arc, Domrémy la Pucelle, 88300 Neufchâteau, Vosges
Next door to her birthplace, this small museum contains memorabilia of Joan of Arc and her times.
On request.

DOUAI

MUNICIPAL MUSEUM
a l'ancienne Chartreuse, 59500 Douai, Nord
Gallo-Roman and medieval archaeology. Paintings of the Flemish, Dutch and Italian Schools. 18th-19th century French paintings, including works by Chardin, David, Corot, Boudin, Courbet, Sisley, Pissarro and Bonnard.
Daily except Tu. 10-12, 2-5.

DOULLENS

LOMBARD MUSEUM
7 rue du Musée, 80600 Doullens, Somme
18th and 19th century French paintings. Flemish paintings. Coloured lithographs and posters by Francis Poulbot (1879-1946). 18th and 19th century engravings. Sculpture. Japanese engravings. Far Eastern ceramics. Ethnography of Picardy.
Tu. and Su. 2-6.

DRAGUIGNAN

MUNICIPAL MUSEUM
9 rue de la République, 83000 Draguignan, Var
Gallo-Roman archaeology. Paintings by artists of the Italian and Flemish Schools.
M. and during month of Aug. 2-4.

DREUX

BELFRY MUSEUM
Grande-Rue Maurice Viollette, 28100 Dreux, Eure-et-Loir
Local history. Folklore.
July-Sept. 9, Daily except Tu. and W., 10-12, 2-6. Easter Su. - June 30 and Sept. 16 - Nov. 30, Sa., Su. and Th. 10-12, 2-6. Dec. 1 - Easter Sa. 10-12, 2-5.

MUNICIPAL MUSEUM
7 place du Musée, 28100 Dreux, Eure-et-Loir
20th century French painting. 18th century French furniture. Medieval sculpture. Collections relating to general and local history, especially to the Orleans family.
Th., Su. 10-12, 2-5. Sa. 2-5.

DUNKERQUE

DUNKERQUE MUSEUM
Place du Général-de-Gaulle, 59140 Dunkerque, Nord
Flemish, Dutch and German paintings. Ship models.
Daily except Tu. 10-12, 3-6.

EAUZE

ARCHAEOLOGICAL MUSEUM
Mairie, 32800 Eauze, Gers
Steles. Ceramics. Sculpture. Souvenirs of the sculptor Félix Soulès, who worked on the façade of the Grand Palace.
On request.

EMBRUN

CATHEDRAL OF NOTRE-DAME
05200 Embrun, Hautes-Alpes
15th and 18th century religious ornaments. Gold and silver ware. Books and sacred vessels. Paintings.
Daily 9-7.

ENSÉRUNE

ARCHAEOLOGICAL MUSEUM
Ensérune, 34440 Nissan-lez-Ensérune, Hérault
Celtic material from excavations in the area.
Daily ex. Tu. Oct.-Easter, 9-12, 2-5.

ÉPERNAY

CHAMPAGNE MUSEUM
Château-Perrier, 13 avenue de Champagne, 51200 Épernay, Marne
History of the Champagne district and its wines. Tools. Costumes. Presses. Bottles. Glasses. Documents. Models to illustrate the various processes of wine-making.
Daily except Tu. 9-12, 2-5.30.

MUSEUM OF FINE ART
Château-Perrier, 51200 Épernay, Marne
Paintings. Ceramics. Sculptures. Furniture.
Daily except Tu. 9-12, 2-5.30.

REGIONAL MUSEUM OF PREHISTORY
13 avenue de Champagne, 51200 Épernay, Marne
Prehistoric collection, ranging from the Stone Age to the Gallo-Roman period.
Daily except Tu. 9-12, 2-5.30.

ÉPINAL

INTERNATIONAL MUSEUM OF RELIGIOUS IMAGES
Musée Départemental, Place Lagarde, 88000 Épinal, Vosges
Images from Epinal dating from image-making centres in France, Italy, England, Spain, Holland, Greece, Switzerland, Germany.
Oct.-May. Daily except Tu. 10-12, 2-5. Open until 6 in June and Sept., until 7 in July and Aug.

VOSGES MUSEUM
Place Lagarde, 88000 Épinal, Vosges
Gallo-Roman and medieval sculptures. Gallo-Roman and Merovingian archaeology. Vosges ethnography. 16th-20th century paintings, including Rembrandt's *Portrait of a Woman* (1661). 18th century drawings including works by Boucher, Fragonard, Greuze.
Oct.-May Daily except Tu. 10-12, 2-5. Open until 6 in June and Sept., until 7 in July and Aug.

EPINEUIL-LE-FLEURIEL

ALAIN-FOURNIER MUSEUM
School, Epineuil-le-Fleuriel, 18360 Saulzais le Potier, Cher
The school where Alain Fournier spent 7 years and which was described in his novel, *Le Grand Meaulnes*, under the pseudonym of Ste. Agethe. The school is as it was in 1890, with the classrooms, kitchen, staircase to the attics and corn-loft. Collections illustrating the writer's life and works.
Daily, except during school hours, on application.

EQUEURDREVILLE-HAINNEVILLE

TOWN-HALL MUSEUM
Hôtel de Ville, 50120 Equeurdreville-Hainneville, Manche
Paintings, sculptures, drawings and engravings of the 19th and 20th centuries, including works by Boudin.
M.-Sa. 9-12, 2-6. Su. 9-11.

ÉTAMPES

MUNICIPAL MUSEUM
Hôtel de Ville, 91150 Étampes, Essonne
Gallic and Gallo-Roman objects, especially sculptures. Mosaic by Souzy. Iron gate from the Abbey of Marigny (12th century). Head of the king of Notre-Dame d'Étampes (12th century). Paintings. Natural history.
Oct. - Mar. 15, Daily 10-12, 2-4. Closed Tu. Mar. 16-Sept. 30, Daily except Tu. 9.30-12, 2.30-7.

ETAPLES

MUNICIPAL MUSEUM
62630 Etaples, Pas-de-Calais
Palaeolithic, Mesolithic, Neolithic and Iron Age archaeology. Gallo-Roman collections from the first, second and third centuries. Material covering the Merovingian and Carolingian periods. Historical items from 15th-17th centuries. Geology. Terra Sigillata.
July 1 - Sept. 15, Daily ex. Tu. Open Th. and Su. rest of year.

ÉVIAN-LES-BAINS

MUSEUM OF SAVOY
Rue Nationale, 74500 Évian-les-Bains, Haute-Savoie
Regional folklore. At the Town Hall are to be found souvenirs of Anna de Noailles.
July and Aug.

ÉVREUX

MUNICIPAL MUSEUM
Rue Charles-Corbeau, 27000 Évreux, Eure
Regional archaeology, includes Stone and Bronze Age and Gallo-Roman material. Enamels and objets d'art from the Middle Ages, including the mitre of Jean de Marigny. 18th century furniture and marquetry. Paintings. Ceramics.
Oct. - Palm Sa. Daily except Tu. 10-12, 2-5. Palm Su. - Sept. 30, Daily 9.30-12, 2.30-7.

SAINT-TAURIN CHURCH
27000 Évreux, Eure
Well-known 14th century silver-gilt shrine.
Daily.

LES EYZIES-DE-TAYAC

NATIONAL MUSEUM OF PRE-HISTORY
Dépôt-laboratoire au Château, 24620 Les Eyzies-de-Tayac, Dordogne
Collection of objects in flint and bone recovered from the area during the last fifty years. Weapons. Carvings on stone, bone. Sculpture. Copies of the bas-reliefs of human figures at Laussel. Magdalenian tombs.
Oct.-Mar. Daily 10-12, 2-4. Apr.-May Daily except Tu. 9-12, 2-6. June-Sept. Daily 9-12, 2-6.

EZE

CHÂTEAU MUSEUM
Eze, 06360 Eze Bord de Mer, Alpes-Maritimes
The ruins of the medieval Château contain an exhibition of local handicrafts, including pottery and wrought iron work.
Enquire locally.

FÉCAMP

BENEDICTINE ABBEY MUSEUM
110 rue Alexandre-Le Grand, 76400 Fécamp, Seine-Maritime
Items from the old abbey, including sculpture. 14th century alabasters, fragments of the rood-screen, haut-relief of 16th century, wrought-iron work.
Easter-Sept. Daily 9-11.30, 2-5.30. Winter: M.-F. 9-11.30, 2-5.30.

MUNICIPAL MUSEUM
21 rue Alexandre-Legros, 76400 Fécamp, Seine-Maritime
Faiences. Porcelain. 16th century portraits "aux trois crayons", representing the famous people of the day. Marine collection. Folklore. Local history. Archaeology and religious art. Paintings.
Daily except Tu. 10-11.30, 2-5.30 (4 in winter).

MUSEUM OF CHILDHOOD
Rue Alexandre-Legros, 76400 Fécamp, Seine-Maritime
Collection of objects of all ages relating to childhood.
Daily ex. M. 10-12, 2-5 (2-4 in winter).

LA FÈRE

JEANNE D'ABOVILLE MUSEUM
Place de l'Esplanade, 02800 La Fère, Aisne
Paintings, especially primitives, German, Dutch and 17th-18th century French works.
June-Sept. Daily except M. and Tu. 2-6. Oct.-Mar. Su. and Th. 2-4. Apr.-May Su. and Th. 2-6.

FERRETTE

MUNICIPAL MUSEUM
Hôtel de Ville, 68480 Ferrette, Haut-Rhin
Prehistoric archaeology. Sketches by Gustave Moreau.
On request.

FEURS

MUNICIPAL MUSEUM
Route de Saint-Etienne, 42110 Feurs, Loire
Weapons. Local history.
Daily 10-12, 3-6.

FIGEAC

CHAMPOLLION MUSEUM
Hôtel de la Monnaie, Place Vival, 46100 Figeac, Lot
Prehistory. Inscriptions from the Gallo-Roman age to the end of the Middle Ages. Numismatics. History of Champollion.
May-Sept. Daily. Other times by request.

FIXIN

NOISOT NAPOLEONIC MUSEUM
Maison du gardien du Parc Noisot, 21710 Fixin, Côte d'Or
Engravings and reproductions of paintings relating to the Emperor. Medals. Flag of the first regiment of Grenadiers of the Guard, carried during the retreat from Fontainebleau. Correspondence of Claude Noisot, officer of the Imperial Guard.
Daily on request.

LA FLÈCHE

SOUVENOR BRUTION MUSEUM
Prytanée militaire, 72200 La Flèche, Sarthe
Portraits of outstanding former pupils of the Military Academy including the philosopher, René Descartes. Uniforms of various periods in the school's history. Swords of the Prince de Condé and of the Duc de Berry. Medals. Picture commemorating the young St. Cyr officers who charged the enemy in 1914, wearing their full dress uniforms.
Daily, on application.

FLERS

CHÂTEAU MUSEUM
Château Flers, 61100 Flers, Orne
16th century château. Paintings. Local history.
Apr.-Sept. 7-dusk. Oct.-Mar. 7-7.

FOIX

ARIÈGE MUSEUM
Château des Comtes de Foix, 09000 Foix, Ariège
Prehistory. Roman, Merovingian and medieval antiquities. Ethnography. Folk-art.
June 15- Sept. 15, Daily 8-12, 2-7. Snpt. 16- June 14, Daily 9-12, 2-6. Closed Tu. from Sept. 16- June 14.

FONTAINEBLEAU

FAR-EASTERN MUSEUM
au Palais, 77300 Fontainebleau, Seine-et-Marne
Chinese and Indo-Chinese collections. Golden belt given by Louis XV to the Siamese ambassadors. Gold crown of the King of Siam.
Apr.-Oct. Daily 10-12, 1.15-5. Oct.-Apr. Daily 10-12, 1.15-4. Closed W.

MUNICIPAL MUSEUM OF MILITARY UNIFORMS AND EQUIPMENT
15 rue Royale, 77300 Fontainebleau, Seine-et-Marne
Collections of arms and uniforms of the Revolutionary period, First Empire, Second Empire and of the Army in Africa, 1830-1870.
Apr.-Sept. Daily 10-12, 1.30-5. Oct.-Mar. Daily 1.30-4.

PALACE OF FONTAINEBLEAU
77300 Fontainebleau, Seine-et-Marne
Royal château, dating from the 12th century and reconstructed by Francis I in 1528-47. 16th-18th century French and Italian decorations. The furnishings, which were scattered after the Revolution, were restored as far as possible on the orders of Napoleon I. Louis XVI furniture, including a bureau encrusted with mother-of-pearl which belonged to Marie-Antoinette. Tapestries by Oudry. Second Empire theatre.
Apr.-Oct. 10-12, 1.15-5. Oct.-Apr. 10-12, 1.15-4. Closed W.

FONTAINE-DE-VAUCLUSE

PETRARCH MUSEUM
Fontaine-de-Vaucluse, 84800 L'Isle sur la Sorgue, Vaucluse
Collections of prints, brochures and books relating to Petrarch and his stay in the area.
Daily 10-5.

FONTENAY-LE-COMTE

VENDÉE MUSEUM
Place du 137e, 85200 Fontenay-le-Comte, Vendée
Regional ethnography. Prints and paintings by Vendean artists and of regional subjects. Numismatics. Neolithic and Paleolithic collections. Gallo-Roman archaeology. Medieval sculpture.
July-Aug. Daily 2-5. Rest of the year: Tu. and Su. 2-5.

FONTVIEILLE

ALPHONSE DAUDET MUSEUM
Moulin de Daudet, 13990 Fontvieille, Bouches-du-Rhône
It was here that Daudet had the idea for his *Lettres de Mon Moulin.* Collections illustrating his life and works.
Daily 9-12, 2-7 (summer), 10-12, 2-4 (winter).

FORCALQUIER

MUNICIPAL MUSEUM
Place du Bourguet, 04300 Forcalquier, Alpes-de-Haute-Provence
Prehistory. Objets d'art. Faience. Provincial furniture. Pottery. Portraits of local personalities. Natural history. Geology.
Daily except M., on request.

FRÉJUS

ARCHAEOLOGICAL MUSEUM
Cloître de la Cathédrale, 83600 Fréjus, Var
Regional archaeology, including sculptures, ceramics, mosaics, coins, Gallo-Roman material.
Apr.-Sept. Daily except Tu. 9-12, 2-6. Oct.-Mar. Daily except Tu. 9.30-12, 2-4.30.

FRESNAY-SUR-SARTHE

MUSEUM OF HEADDRESSES
Château, 72130 Fresnay-sur-Sarthe, Sarthe
Headdresses and costumes of the area.
July-Aug. Daily 9-12, 2-6. Mar.-June and Sept. Su. 9-12, 2-6.

GAILLAC

CHÂTEAU MUSEUM
Cayla, nr. Gaillac, Lot
Museum dedicated to the poet, Maurice de Guérin, and to his sister, Eugénie, famous for her journal and correspondence.
Daily 2-5 (2-4 in winter).

GAILLAC MUSEUM
Château de Foucaud d'Alzon, Gaillac, Lot
Paintings and watercolours by local painters of the late 19th and early 20th centuries, including works by Salabert, Loubat, Durel.
May 1- Sept. 30. Daily 2-5. Winter: Th. and Su. 2-4.

NATURAL HISTORY MUSEUM
Place Philadelphe Thomas, Gaillac, Lot
Minerals and rocks. Wild and domestic animals of the region. Sea and river fish. Palaeontology. Birds. Eggs. Butterflies. Reptiles. Tools. Prehistoric objects. Animal skeletons.
Th. and Su. 2-5 (2-4 in winter).

GANNAT

DELARUE MUSEUM
Jardin Delarue, 03800 Gannat, Allier
Gallo-Roman archaeology. Paintings. Drawings. Furniture.
June-Sept. Daily 10-12, 2-6.

GAP

MUSEUM OF THE HAUTES-ALPES DEPARTEMENT
4 avenue du Marechal-Foch, 05000 Gap, Hautes-Alpes
The main feature of the museum is the mausoleum of the Duke of Lesdiguières, by Jacob Richier. Ethnography of the Alps. Wooden objects from Queyras. Lace. Headdresses.
June-Sept. Daily except F. 10-12, 2-5. Sept.-June, Tu., Th., Sa. and Su. 2-4.

GARGILESSE DAMPIERRE

GEORGE-SAND HOUSE-MUSEUM
'Algira', Gargilesse Dampierre, 36190 Orsennes, Indre
Furniture, manuscripts, tableaux and souvenirs of George Sand and her son, Maurice.
Sa. before Easter- Oct. 1, daily except W., F. morning, 9-12, 2-7.

GIEN

INTERNATIONAL MUSEUM OF HUNTING
Château de Gien, 45500 Gien, Loiret
Weapons, including sporting guns used by Louis XIV and Napoleon. Hunting scenes shown in tapestries, manuscripts, engravings, paintings, especially 100 works by Desportes, painter to Louis XIV.
Su. before Easter- Nov. 1, Daily 8.30-12, 2.15-6.30. Nov. 1- Sa. before Easter, 9-12, 2.15-5.30.

GORDES

CHÂTEAU MUSEUM
84220 Gordes, Vaucluse
This 16th century château houses paintings by Vasarély, donated by the artist.
Daily ex. Tu. 10-12, 2-6.

LE GRAND-PRESSIGNY

MUSEUM OF PREHISTORY
Château, 37350 Le Grand-Pressigny, Indre-et-Loire
Palaeolithic collection. In Neolithic times this was a centre of production of the flint industry, and the museum contains more than 3,000 items found in the area.
Daily 9-12, 2-7 (to 5 in winter).

GRANVILLE

MUSEUM OF OLD GRANVILLE
Rue Lecarpentier, 50400 Granville, Manche
Local folklore and history. Headdresses and costumes of Basse-Normandie. Newfoundland collection.
July-Sept. Daily 10-12, 2-6. Easter Su. - July 1, and Oct., Su. and Tu. 10-12, 2-6. Closed Nov. 1 - Easter Su.

GRASSE

ADMIRAL DE GRASSE MEMORIAL MUSEUM
9 rue Gazan, 06130 Grasse, Alpes-Maritimes
Room devoted to Malta (Admiral de Grasse was a Chevalier of Malta). Model of an 18th century galley. Views of Malta. Model of the cruiser 'Jeanne d'Arc' and also of a sloop. Career of the Admiral from 1737 until 1782. His family tree and certificates of baptism, marriage and death, together with illustrations of the châteaux in which he lived. Photographs, documents, and portraits.
Tu.-Sa. 2.30-5.30. Last Su. in each month, 2.30-5.30.

FRAGONARD MUSEUM
2 rue Mirabeau, 06130 Grasse, Alpes-Maritimes
History and art of Lower Provence. Furniture. Costumes. Ceramics. Works by Fragonard (b. Grasse 1732). Archaeology. Naval collection.
Summer: Daily except Su. and M. 2-6. Winter: 10-12, 2-5. Closed Nov.

GRAVELOTTE

MILITARY MUSEUM
Gravelotte, 57130 Ars sur Moselle, Moselle
Relics of the wars of 1870. Collection of popular engravings relating to the battles.
Daily 8-8.

GRAY

BARON MARTIN MUSEUM
Château, 70100 Gray, Haute-Saône
Flemish and Dutch paintings. 18th century French paintings. 19th century paintings, drawings, including drawings and pastels by Prud'hon.
Daily 8-12, 2-6 (until sunset in winter).

GRENOBLE

DAUPHINÉ MUSEUM
30 rue Gignoux, 38000 Grenoble, Isère
Archaeology, history and ethnography of the Dauphiné. Pottery. Grenoble faience.
Daily except Tu. and W. 2-6.

FANTIN LATOUR MUSEUM
1 rue Général de Beylié, 38000 Grenoble, Isère
Collection illustrating life and work of the painter, Fantin-Latour, born at Grenoble in 1836.
Daily ex. Tu. 10-12, 2-5.

MUSEUM OF PAINTING AND SCULPTURE
Place de Verdun, 38000 Grenoble, Isère
19th-20th century paintings, including works by Gauguin, Monet, Boudin, Renoir, Bonnard, Matisse, Derain, Dufy, Picasso, Juan Gris, Utrillo, Modigliani, Chagall. 15th-18th century Italian paintings. 17th-18th century Dutch, Flemish, French paintings.
Daily ex. M. and public holidays, 10-12, 2-5.

STENDHAL MUSEUM
Ancien Hôtel de Ville, 38000 Grenoble, Isère
Portraits of Stendhal. Engravings and manuscripts of the writer. Collection of drawings of various periods.
Daily ex. M. and Tu. morning, 9-12, 2-5.

GREZOLLES

MUSEUM OF HISTORY
Grezolles, 42260 St. Germain Laval, Loire
Local history and folklore. Documents on the old families of the area and on Father François de la Chaise, confessor to Louis XIV, born at the Château d'Aix.
Daily 9-12, 2-5.

GRIGNAN

CABROL MUSEUM
Château, 26230 Grignan, Drôme
Souvenirs of the different owners of the Château from 12th to 19th century. Furniture. Tapestries. Souvenirs of the Marquise de Sévigné.
June 20 - Sept. 15, Daily 10-12, 2-6. From Sept. 15 only open Su. and public holidays.

GROSBOIS

CHÂTEAU DE GROSBOIS
Boissy-Saint-Léger, Grosbois, Val-de-Marne
Paintings by Winterhalter, Carie Vernet and Gros. Empire furniture. Gold and silver work by Thomire.
Sa., Su. and public holidays, 2-5.30. Apr. 6 - Sept. 14, also Th., 2-5.30.

GUEBWILLER

FLORIVAL MUSEUM
Ancienne Église des Dominicains, 68500 Guebwiller, Haut-Rhin
Local history and folklore. Ceramics. Sculpture. Archaeological material from local excavations.
Oct.-Apr. Su. 9-12, 2-6. July-Aug. Tu., Th. and Sa. 2-6.

GUÉRANDE

PORTE SAINT-MICHEL MUSEUM
44350 Guérande, Loire-Atlantique
Rood-screen of a 16th century chapel. Rood-screen doors of College of Guérande (17th century). Local ethnography.
Su. before Easter - Sept. 30, Daily 9-12, 2-7.

GUÉRET

MUNICIPAL MUSEUM
Avenue de la Sénatorerie, 23000 Guéret, Creuse
Prehistoric and Gallo-Roman collections. Limoges enamels. 17th and 18th century Aubusson and Flanders tapestries. Ceramics. Dolls. Zoology. Mineralogy. Weapons. Coptic fabrics. Drawings by Ingres, Matisse, La Fresnaye, Jongkind, Delacroix, Tiepolo and Veronese. French, Dutch and Flemish paintings of the 18th and 19th centuries. 19th and 20th century French paintings.
Daily 10-12, 2-5 (until 6.30 in summer).

GUIDEL

MARITIME MUSEUM
56520 Guidel, Morbihan
Maritime history from the 16th century to the present day. Pouldu signal-post.
June-Sept. 15, Daily 10-12, 2-7.

GUIRY-EN-VEXIN

ARCHAEOLOGICAL MUSEUM
Guiry-en-Vexin, 95450 Vigny, Val-d'Oise
Prehistoric, Gallo-Roman and Merovingian collections. 2nd century Gallo-Roman sculptures from Genainville. Gallo-Roman funerary furniture from Maule. Merovingian steles.
Sa. 2-6. Su. and public holidays 10-12, 2-6.

HAGUENAU

HAGUENAU MUSEUM
9 rue du Marechal-Foch, 67500 Haguenau, Bas-Rhin
Bronze Age archaeology. Roman sculptures, coins and medals from Alsace. Furniture and weapons from Alsace.
Tu.-F. 9-12, 2-6; Su. 2-5.

HAMBYE

ABBEY MUSEUM
50650 Hambye, Manche
Tapestries. Local paintings. Furniture. Archaeological material from excavations in the area.
Daily ex. M. 10-5.

HASPARREN

FRANCIS JAMMES MUSEUM
64240 Hasparren, Pyrénées-Atlantiques
House in which the poet, Francis Jammes, lived and died. Memorabilia. Manuscripts. Paintings.
On request.

LE HAVRE

GRAVILLE ABBEY
Rue de l'Abbaye, 76600 Le Havre, Seine-Maritime
Architecture of the 13th, 17th and 18th centuries. The abbey contains a collection of 11th-18th century sculpture, including the famous *Princesse de Cour* (end of 14th century). 150 models of homes, 13th to 17th centuries, from different regions of France.
June 15 - Sept. 14, Daily except M. and Tu. 10-12, 2-7. Sept. 15 - June 14, Th., Sa., Su. and public holidays, 10-12, 2-7. Closed July 14, Nov. 11, December 25, Jan. 1 and May 1.

MUSEUM OF FINE ART
Boulevard J. F. Kennedy, 76600 Le Havre, Seine-Maritime
French, Dutch, Flemish and Italian paintings of the 16th, 17th and 19th centuries, including works by Corot, Boudin, Dégas, Pissarro, Monet, Sisley, Dufy.
June 15 - Sept. 14, Daily except Tu. 10-12, 2-7. Sept. 15 - June 14, Daily except M., Tu. 10-12, 2-7. Closed July 14, Nov. 11, Dec. 25, Jan. 1, May 1.

MUSEUM OF NATURAL HISTORY
Place du Vieux-Marché, 76600 Le Havre, Seine-Maritime
Ornithology. Regional prehistory. Vertebrates. Mineralogy. Palaeontology. Ethnography.
M.-F. 10-12, 2-6 (2-5 in winter).

MUSEUM OF OLD LE HAVRE
1 rue Jerome-Bellarmato, 76600 Le Havre, Seine-Maritime
Gallo-Roman and Merovingian archaeology. History of Le Havre. Engravings. Paintings. Ship models. 16th-19th century glassware, from France and elsewhere.
June 15 - Sept. 14, Daily except M. and Tu. 10-12, 2-7. Sept. 15 - June 14, Th., Sa. and Su. and public holidays, 10-12, 2-7. Closed July 14, Nov. 11, Dec. 25, Jan. 1 and May 1.

L'HAY-LES-ROSES

MUSEUM OF THE ROSE
à la Roseraie, 94240 L'Hay-les-Roses, Val-de-Marne
Collection of objects inspired by the rose: Jouy linen, porcelain, book bindings, pewter, cloth, painted paper. Documents and objects relating to the rose in pharmacy, literature, perfumery and confectionery.
Daily except Tu. 10-6.

HAZEBROUCK

MUNICIPAL MUSEUM
Place Georges-Degroote, 59190 Hazebrouck, Hord
Paintings. Drawings. Ceramics. Folklore.
Th., Sa. and Su. 10-12, 2-5.

HÉRICOURT

MINAL MUSEUM
Place de l'Église, 70400 Héricourt, Haute-Saône
19th century paintings. Modern jewellery.
Th., Su. 2-4.

HESDIN

TOWN HALL
62140 Hesdin, Pas-de-Calais
17th century Flemish tapestries.
Daily 9-12, 2-6.

HIRSON

HIRSON MUSEUM
Ancien Château, 02500 Hirson, Aisne
Local archaeology and folklore. War relics.
Apr.-Oct. 1st and 3rd Su. in the month, 2-5. Nov.-Mar. 1st Su. in month, 2-5. Other days on request.

HONFLEUR

EUGÈNE BOUDIN MUSEUM
Rue Albert-Ier, 14600 Honfleur, Calvados
17th century paintings by Van Dyck, Mignard, Sebastian Bourdon. 19th and 20th century works of the Honfleur School, including works by Boudin, Jongkind, Monet, Dufy, Villon and Renouf. 18th and 19th century headdresses and costumes. Engravings. Furniture.
Easter - Oct. 15, Daily except Tu. 10-12, 2-6. Closed May 1 and July 14.

NORMANDY MUSEUM OF ETHNOGRAPHY AND FOLK ART
Quai Saint-Etienne, 14600 Honfleur, Calvados
Reconstruction of Normandy interiors. Furniture. Costumes. Souvenirs of the privateers and slave ships.
Daily 10-12.30, 3-6.30. Closed in Jan.

HYÈRES

MUNICIPAL MUSEUM
Jardin Alphone Denis, Place Georges Clémenceau, 83400 Hyères, Var
Greek and Roman archaeological exhibits from excavations at Olbia. Local industries of salt, cane and cork. 18th-20th century paintings.
Daily ex. Tu. and holidays 3-6.

ILLIERS COMBRAY

PIÉ-CATELAN
Rue des Vièrges, 28120 Illiers Combray, Eure-et-Loir
The garden of 'M. Jules Amiot', the husband of 'Tante Leonie'. In this garden Marcel Proust met Gilbert.
On request.

MARCEL PROUST HOUSE-MUSEUM
Maison de Tante Léonie, 28120 Illiers Combray, Eure-et-Loir
Personal possessions of the writer, Marcel Proust.
By appointment.

L'ISLE-ADAM

MUSÉE SEULECQ
46 Grand-Rue, 95290 L'Isle-Adam, Val-d'Oise
Local history. Works of artists who have stayed at L'Isle-Adam. Paintings by Dupré, Vlaminck. Engravings by Willette.
May-Sept. Sa. 3-5; Su. 10-12, 3-5.

ISSOUDUN

MISSION MUSEUM
38 Place du Sacré Coeur, 36100 Issoudun, Indre
Collection designed to promote knowledge and appreciation of the work of the Church in the mission field, especially in New Guinea and the neighbouring islands. Life at mission stations. Ethnology of native peoples. Masks. Weapons.
Apr.-Sept. Daily 9-11, 2.30-6. Other times by appointment only.

SAINT-ROCH HOSPITAL MUSEUM
Hôpital Saint-Roch, 36100 Issoudun, Indre
Complete laboratories and dispensaries of 17th-19th centuries.
Daily except Tu. 10-12, 2-7.

ISTRES

MUSEUM OF OLD ISTRES
9 rue Portail Neuf, 13800 Istres, Bouches-du-Rhône
Gallo-Roman archaeology. Prehistory. Provençal folklore.
Oct.-Mar. Th. and Su. 2-5. Apr.-Sept. Daily 2-6. Apply to the caretaker opposite the Museum.

IZERNORE

MUSEUM OF ARCHAEOLOGY
01580 Izernore, Ain
Gallo-Roman antiquities. Weapons. Pottery. Ex-votos. Coins and medals.
On request.

JARVILLE-LA-MALGRANGE

MUSEUM OF THE HISTORY OF IRON
Route de Fléville, 54140 Jarville-la-Malgrange, Meurthe-et-Moselle
Iron-ore. History of iron-smelting and iron-working.
Daily except Tu. 2-5.

JEUMONT

LOCAL MUSEUM
6 rue de Soire-le-Château, 59460 Jeumont, Nord
Faience. Manuscripts. Weapons.
On application to the Town Hall.

JOINVILLE

HOSPITAL MUSEUM
Rue Irma-Masson, 52300 Joinville, Haute-Marne
Portraits. Objets d'art. Tapestries. Sculpture. Faience.
Daily 10-12, 2-6.

JUMIÈGES

LAPIDARY MUSEUM
Ruines de l'Abbaye, 76118 Jumièges, Seine-Maritime
13th century tomb of Enerves. Tomb housing the heart of Agnes Sorel (15th century).
Summer: Daily 9-12, 2-6. Winter: Daily except Tu. 10-12, 1-4.

KERJEAN

BRETON MUSEUM
Château de Kerjean, Saint Vougay, Kerjean, Finistère
Breton art. Furniture, including box beds and chests.
Daily 9-12, 2-6.

LAGHET

SANCTUARY MUSEUM
Sanctuaire de Notre-Dame de Laghet, Laghet, Alpes-Maritimes
Votive drawings and paintings, mid-17th century onwards, on the subject of the Virgin of Laghet. The collection of folk-art illustrates the tribulations which afflict mankind.
Daily 8-7.

LAGNY-SUR-MARNE

MUNICIPAL MUSEUM
Mairie, 77400 Lagny-sur-Marne, Seine-et-Marne
Collections include prehistory, mineralogy, local history and palaeontology.
On request.

LAMBESC

OLD LAMBESC MUSEUM
Cours Gambetta, 13410 Lambesc, Bouches-du-Rhône
Prehistory. Gallo-Roman archaeology. Local history and folklore. In the 18th century church is to be found an organ by J. Isnard (1788).
The two last Sun. in each month, in the afternoon, on demand.

LANGEAIS

CHÂTEAU
37130 Langeais, Indre-et-Loire
Renaissance furniture. Flemish tapestries. The château is one of the oldest in the Loire Valley.
Sa. before Easter-Sept. 15, Daily except M. morning, 9-12, 2-6.30. Sept. 16-F. before Easter, Daily except M. 9-12, 2-4.30.

LANGRES

HÔTEL DU BREUIL DE SAINT-GERMAIN MUSEUM
52200 Langres, Haute-Marne
Collection of Aprey faience. Incunabula and manuscripts. Book bindings. Furniture. Pewter. Cutlery. Memorabilia of Diderot, born at Langres.
Daily 9-12, 2-6.

SAINT-DIDIER MUSEUM
Place Saint-Didier, 52200 Langres, Haute-Marne
Regional palaeontology. Archaeology. Gallery of paintings.
Daily 9-12, 2-6.

LANQUAIS

CHÂTEAU DE LANQUAIS
Lanquais, 24150 Lalinde, Dordogne
Building of 14th-17th centuries. 17th century furniture.
Easter-All Saints' Day. Daily 9-12, 2-6. All Saints' Day-Easter Su., public holidays and by appointment for groups on other days.

LAON

MUNICIPAL MUSEUM OF ARCHAEOLOGY
Rue Georges-Ermant, 02000 Laon, Aisne
Regional archaeology, prehistory. Ceramics. Glass. Gallo-Roman and Merovingian jewellery. Medieval sculpture. Paintings include the fragment of a diptych on wood by Maître des Heures de Rohan. Faience of Sinceny. Egyptian vases and figurines. Cypriot, Greek and Roman vases, glassware. Roman bronzes.
Daily except Tu. 10-12, 2-5.

LAVAL

CHÂTEAU MUSEUM
Château, 53000 Laval, Mayenne
Prehistory. Gallo-Roman, Merovingian and medieval archaeology. Ceramics. Ironwork. Natural history. Palaeontology.
Daily except Tu. 10-12, 2-5.30.

MUSEUM OF FINE ART
Place de Hercé, 53000 Laval, Mayenne
Oriental antiquities. Medieval sculpture. Fire-backs. Jouy linen. Pictures of old Laval.
Daily 10-12, 2-5 (2-6 in summer).

HENRI ROUSSEAU MUSEUM OF PRIMITIVE ART
53000 Laval, Mayenne
Modern primitive paintings, especially by Rousseau.
On request.

LAVAUR

VAURAIS MUSEUM
Rue de la Mairie, 81500 Lavaur, Tarn
Prehistory. Gallo-Roman antiquities. Numismatics. Sundials, thought to be Roman. Local history.
Apr.-Oct. Sa. 2-5; Su. 10-12, 2-5.30. In winter, apply to the caretaker.

LECTOURE

EUGÈNE CAMOREYT MUSEUM
Hôtel de Ville, 32700 Lectoure, Gers
Series of altars (3rd and 4th century), Commemorating the sacrifice of bulls or of rams to the goddess Cybele, particularly honoured at Lectoure. Bronzes, pottery, coins, funerary half-columns. Statues from the Gallo-Roman period.
Daily except Su. 9-12, 2-6, on application to the caretaker.

LEZOUX

MUSEUM OF GALLO-ROMAN POTTERY
à la Mairie, 63190 Lezoux, Puy-de-Dôme
In the Gallo-Roman period Lezoux was a centre for ceramics, with 160 kilns, and the museum contains many specimens of the art.
Daily (Easter-Oct. 15) 2.30-7.

LIBOURNE

RENÉ PRINCETEAU MUSEUM
Mairie de Libourne, 33500 Libourne, Gironde
Regional archaeology and Gallo-Roman collections. 16th-19th century paintings.
Oct.-May M.-Sa. 10-12, 2-6. June-Sept. 9-12, 2-7.

LILLE

DIOCESAN MUSEUM OF RELIGIOUS ART
Cryptes de la Cathédrale, 59000 Lille, Nord
Roman remains. Gold and silver ware. Carved wood and polychromes. Paintings.
Th. 2-5. Other days on request to the Conservateur, 32 rue dAngleterre.

MUSEUM OF THE COMTESSE HOSPICE
32 rue de la Monnaie, 59000 Lille, Nord
In 15th century hospital ward. Kitchen with Lille and Delft tiles. Furniture. Tapestries. Sculptures. Paintings. Flemish ceramics of 17th and 18th century. History and ethnography of the north of France.
Th., Sa. and Su. 10-12.30, 2-5. Closed public holidays.

MUSEUM OF INDUSTRY, COMMERCE, TECHNOLOGY AND AGRICULTURE
2 rue du Lombard, 59000 Lille, Nord
Collections of different types of wood. Flax. Photography. Electricity. Agriculture. Wine making. Clocks and timepieces. Musical instruments. Paper-making. Chemistry and physics. Mechanics (including steam engines).
Tu.-Sa. 10-12, 2-6; Su. 10-12, 2-5. Closed M., New Year's Day, May 1, July 14, Nov. 1, Dec. 25.

MUSEUM OF THE LILLE BATALLION OF CANONNIERS SÉDENTAIRES
Hôtel militaire des Canonniers, 44 rue des Canonniers, 59000 Lille, Nord
Material relating to the Bataillon des Canonniers Sédentaires de Lille, the oldest artillery unit in France, created in 1483.
Tu., Th., Sa. afternoon, or on request.

MUSEUM OF NATURAL HISTORY
19 rue de Bruxelles, 59000 Lille, Nord
Zoology collection, including rare mammals, European birds, reptiles, amphibians, fish and molluscs. Entomology as it affects agriculture.
The geology section is housed in the Musée Charles Barrois (or Musée Houiller) of the University, and in the Musée

Jules Gosselet (or Musée de Géologie Régionale). Rock collections. Plant and animal fossils recovered from French coal-mines, especially in the North. Mineralogical specimens. Exhibits relating to the finding of water underground. Rocks from the Ardennes.
Th. and Su. 10-4. Students are admitted at other times on written application to the curator.

PALACE OF FINE ART
Place de la République, 59000 Lille, Nord
Paintings of the Flemish and Dutch Schools: Rubens, Van Dyck, Jordaens, Van Ostade, Van Goyen, Ruysdael, De Witte, Franz Hals. Spanish and German Schools. French School: David, Boilly, Delacroix, Courbet. Impressionist works by Monet, Sisley, Renoir and Lebourg. Ceramics. Ivories. Enamels. Gold and silverware. Collection of drawings by Raphaël and Michelangelo.
Daily 10-12.30, 2-5. Closed Tu., May 1, Nov. 1, Christmas and New Year, W. following Easter, July 14, Pentecost, the Fête de Lille, Assumption, Nov. 11 and the W. before Ascension.

LILLEBONNE

MUNICIPAL MUSEUM
Hôtel de Ville, 76170 Lillebonne, Seine-Maritime
Local history from antiquity to the 19th century. Gallo-Roman objects excavated in the city. Faience. Objets d'art. Furniture. Documents. Ornithology.
Daily 10-12, 2-6.

LIMERAY

MUSEUM OF POSTAL HISTORY
Le Haut Chantier, Limeray, 37400 Amboise, Indre-et-Loire
History of the postal service. Stamps. Transport.
On request.

LIMOGES

ADRIEN DUBOUCHE NATIONAL MUSEUM
Place Winston-Churchill, 87000 Limoges, Haute-Vienne
Ceramics.
Nov. 2- Apr. 1, Daily except Tu. and public holidays, 10-12, 1.30-5. Apr.-Oct. Daily except Tu. and public holidays, 10-12, 1.30-6.

MUNICIPAL MUSEUM
Place de la Cathédrale, 87000 Limoges, Haute-Vienne
Egyptian antiquities. Gallo-Roman material. Fresco decorated with animals (late 1st or early 2nd century), found in Limoges in 1962. Enamels. Paintings, include works by Renoir, who was born at Limoges. Drawings by Léger, Chagall, Matisse and Laurens. Costumes and objects relating to the local Brotherhood of Penitents. Mineralogical collection.
Daily except Tu. Open on Tu. July-Sept.

LIMOUX

PETIET MUSEUM
Promenade de Tivoli, 11300 Limoux, Aude
Prehistory. Archaeology. Collections illustrating the "Belle Epoque".
June and Oct. Sa., Su. and M. 2-6. July, Aug. and Sept. Daily except Tu. 2-6.

LIRÉ

JOACHIM DU BELLAY MUSEUM
49530 Liré, Maine-et-Loire
History of Liré. Local art and folklore. Collections relating to Bellay and his family.
Jan. 16- Dec. 12, daily except M., 9-12, 2-6. Closed Dec. 15- Jan. 15.

LISIEUX

MUSEUM OF PAINTINGS
38 boulevard Pasteur, 14100 Lisieux, Calvados
European paintings, including an Italian primitive attributed to Antonio di Calvis.
M.-Sa. 2-7 (to 5 in winter).

LISLE-SUR-TARN

RAIMOND LAFAGE MUSEUM
81310 Lisle-sur-Tarn, Tarn
Archaeology of the Gallo-Roman and prehistoric periods. Medieval archaeology. Local paintings.
Each Su. morning except Easter Su.

LOCHES

LANSYER MUSEUM
Rue Lansyer, 37600 Loches, Indre-et-Loire
Far East Collection. Works of the painter Lansyer. Engravings by J.-B. Piranese. Regional ethnography.
Daily except F. Mar. 1- F. before Easter, Oct. 1-31, 9-11.45, 2-4.45. Sa. before Easter- Sept. 30, 9-11, 2-5.45. Oct. 1- Feb. 28, 9-11.45, 2-3.45.

LOCRONAN

MUNICIPAL MUSEUM
annexe de la Mairie, Locronan, 29136 Plogonnec, Finistère
Works of painters and contemporary sculptors dedicated to Brittany. Folklore.
June 15- Sept. 15, Daily 9-6.30.

LODÈVE

MUSEUM OF NATURAL HISTORY
8 rue République, 34700 Lodève, Hérault
Prehistory. Zoology. Palaeontology. Mineralogy. Fossils include tracks of Stegocephanes, found in the ground at Permien. Ammonites. Pottery. Vases. Funerary urns. Statuettes.
Daily ex. M. 10-12, 2-5.

LONGWY

MUNICIPAL MUSEUM
rue de la Manutention, 54400 Longwy, Meurthe-et-Moselle
Archaeology. History. Cast-iron plates.
Sa. 2-4. Other times on request.

LONS-LE-SAUNIER

MUSEUM OF FINE ART AND PREHISTORY
Hôtel de Ville, 39000 Lons-le-Saunier, Jura
Prehistoric collection from the lake at Chalain. Gallo-Roman and Merovingian collections. Paintings of the Flemish and Italian Schools; French works of the 17th and 18th centuries, including works by Bruegel, Simon Vouet and Courbet. Sculptures by Perraud. Palaeontology.
Daily except Tu. 2-5. W. and Th. mornings, 10-12 also.

PHARMACY
39000 Lons-le-Saunier, Jura
Ancient pharmaceutical jars.
On request.

LORIENT

NAVAL MUSEUM
l'Arsenal, 56100 Lorient, Morbihan
Models of sailing ships. Porcelain from the India Company.
July- Sept. 15, Daily except Su. 9.30-10.30.

LOUDUN

CHARBONNEAU-LASSAY MUNICIPAL MUSEUM
Rue de Martrey, 86200 Loudun, Vienne
Egyptian, Gallic and Gallo-Roman antiquities. Collection of weapons of all periods. Museum of African art.
June-Sept. Daily 2-6. Oct.-May Th. and Su. 2-5. Outside these hours, on request.

LOURDES

BERNADETTE MUSEUM
65100 Lourdes, Hautes-Pyrénées
Twenty-eight scenes representing the life of St. Bernadette.
Easter- Oct. 15, daily 9-11.45, 2-6.45.

BOLY MILL
Rue Bernadette-Soubirous, 65100 Lourdes, Hautes-Pyrénées
Birthplace of St. Bernadette (1844). The mill was her mother's dowry.
Easter-Oct. daily 8-7.30.

MUSEUM OF OUR LADY OF LOURDES
65100 Lourdes, Hautes-Pyrénées
Mementoes of the Revelations of St. Bernadette.
M.-Sa. 9-12, 2-7.

MUSEUM OF THE PYRENEES
au Château, 65100 Lourdes, Hautes-Pyrénées
Local ethnography, art and traditions. Regional faience. Alpine plants. Mementoes of the discovery of the summits of the Pyrenees, and the great ascents.
Summer: Daily 9-7. Winter: Daily 9.30-12, 2-5.

LOUVIERS

MUNICIPAL MUSEUM
Place Ernest-Thorel, 27400 Louviers, Eure
Faience from Rouen, Strasbourg and Nevers. Local and regional history. Archaeology. Furniture. Paintings.
Daily except Tu. 2-7.

LOVAGNY-GORGES-DU-FIER

LÉON MARÈS COLLECTION
Château de Montrottier, Lovagny-Gorges-du-Fier, 74330 La Balme de Sillingy, Haute-Savoie
Weapons. Armour. Religious art. Furniture. Tapestries. Ceramics. Lace.
Easter-Oct. 15, Daily 8.30-12, 1.30-7.

LUNÉVILLE

MUNICIPAL MUSEUM
Château de Lunéville, 54300 Lunéville, Meurthe-et-Moselle
18th century faience of Lunéville and Saint-Clément. Documents on the reign of King Stanislas. Military history.
Daily except Tu. 9-12, 2-6 (until 5 in winter).

LUXEUIL-LES-BAINS

MUSEUM OF THE ECHEVINS TOWER
Thermal Establishment, 70300 Luxeuil-les-Bains, Haute-Saône
Archaeology. Collection of funerary steles of the Gallo-Roman period. Altar dedicated to Apollo. Ceramics from Luxeuil, Lezoux, Reimzabern and Graufesenque. Room devoted to Jules Adler, born at Luxeuil in 1865 and containing many of his paintings. Self-portrait of Courbet, a pastel by Vuillard. Local history.
Daily ex. Su., the same times as the Establishment.

LUZECH

ARCHAEOLOGICAL MUSEUM
Hôtel de Ville, 46140 Luzech, Lot
Archaeological material found in the neolithic dwellings at Pêche de la Nène. Exhibits illustrating siege of Uxellodunum by Julius Caesar.
Daily on request.

LUZ-SAINT-SAUVEUR

LOCAL MUSEUM
Chapelle de l'église, 65120 Luz-Saint-Sauveur, Hautes-Pyrénées
Archaeology. Local ethnography. Religious objects and religious paintings of the 16th and 17th centuries. Statues of the 12th-16th centuries.
Daily on request.

LYON

AMPÈRE MUSEUM
Poleymieux-au-Mont-d'Or, 69001 Lyon, Rhône
Memorabilia of the physicist, Ampère, in the house where he spent his early days.
Daily ex. Tu. 9-12, 2-6.

BERLIET MUSEUM
69 Venissieux, 69001 Lyon, Rhône
Museum of transport, with examples of cars and vans built by Berliet from 1894 to the present day.
M.-F. 8-11, 2-4.

CANUT MUSEUM
12 rue d'Ivry, 69001 Lyon, Rhône
History of silk manufacture in the area.
Daily 8.30-12, 2-6. Closed Su. mornings.

CATHEDRAL TREASURY MUSEUM
Cathédrale, 69001 Lyon, Rhône
Ecclesiastical vestments. Gold and silver ware. Documents.
Easter-Sept., Su. 2-6.

CRIME MUSEUM
Ecole de Police, Saint-Cyr-au-Mont-d'Or, 69001 Lyon, Rhône
Uniforms. Weapons. Documents and souvenirs of famous crimes.
On request.

FOURVIÈRE MUSEUM OF ARCHAEOLOGY
Montée de l'Antiquaille, 69001 Lyon, Rhône
Gallo-Roman archaeology.
Closed for reconstruction until 1974.

FRENCH MOTOR MUSEUM
Château de Rochetaillée, 69001 Lyon, Rhône
Vintage motorcars (1890-1956). Car models. Posters. Drawings. Photographs. Cycles and bicycles (1819-1920). Motorcycles (1898-1935).
Mar. 15- Oct. 31, daily 9-12, 2-7. Nov. 1- Mar. 14, daily 9-12, 2-6.

GUIMET MUSEUM
20 boulevard des Belges, 69001 Lyon, Rhône
Assyrian frescoes. Greek and Roman antiquities. Egyptian gallery. Buddhist and Islamic art from India. Khmer, Siamese, Chinese and Japanese art.
W.-Su. 2-5.

EDOUART HERRIOT MUSEUM
Hôtel de Ville, 69001 Lyon, Rhône
Local history.
On request.

LYON MUSEUM OF DECORATIVE ARTS
30 rue de la Charité, 69001 Lyon, Rhône
Cabinet work and chairs of the 18th century, carrying the signatures of the best Parisian craftsmen. Bronzes. Clocks. Objets d'art. Gobelins, Aubusson and Flanders tapestries. French silver of the 18th century. Porcelain from Saint-Cloud, Sèvres and Tournai. 16th-18th century French faience. Italian majolica of the 15th and 16th centuries. Limoges enamels.
Daily 10-12, 2-5. Closed M., Tu. morning and public holidays.

MUSEUM OF CASTS OF ANTIQUE, MEDIEVAL AND MODERN ART
15 quai Claude-Bernard, 69001 Lyon, Rhône
Casts of sculptures and architectural features.
M.-F. 9-12, 2-6. Closed school holidays.

MUSEUM OF THE CIVILIAN HOSPITALS OF LYON
Place de l'Hôpital, 69001 Lyon, Rhône
Art collections housed in three rooms richly decorated with wood carvings, (12th-13th centuries). Bust of Cousteau. 16th and 17th century furniture, tapestries. Collection of 16th-19th century pharmaceutical pottery. Documents on the history of medicine at Lyon. 18th and 19th century surgical instruments.
Daily except M. 2-5; Su. 10.30-12, 2-5.

MUSEUM OF FINE ART
Palais Saint-Pierre, 69001 Lyon, Rhône
Sculpture. Paintings by Quentin Metzys, Pérugin, Tintoretto, Cranach, Sébastien Stoskopf, Greco, Zurbaran, David, Prud'hon, Delacroix. *La Jeune Fille en blanc* by Manet; *Nava Nave Mahana* by Gauguin; *Portrait de la Princesse Cantacuzène* by Puvis de Chavannes; *la Guitariste* by Renoir. Illustrations of contemporary books by Picasso, la Fresnaye, Delaunay, Matisse, Max Ernst, Villon, Dufy, Marquet, Dubuffet. Objets d'art from the Middle Ages, the Renaissance to the present day. Oriental and Moslem art. Paintings of the Lyon School. Medals.
Daily 10-12, 2-6.

MUSEUM OF FORENSIC MEDICINE
Faculté de Médécine, 8 avenue Rockefeller, 69001 Lyon, Rhône
Collections illustrating the history of forensic medicine.
On request.

MUSEUM OF THE HISTORY OF LYON
10 rue de Gadagne, 69001 Lyon, Rhône
Romanesque sculptures from churches and abbeys of the Lyon region. 18th century Lyon furniture and pottery. Manuscripts relating to the French Revolution and the siege of Lyon (1793). Napoleonic souvenirs. Nevers ceramics. Renaissance Lyon. Plans and maps. Pewter collections and manuscripts concerning the ancient trade guilds.
Daily ex. Tu. 10-12, 2-6.

MUSEUM OF THE HISTORY OF TEXTILES
34 rue de la Charité, 69001 Lyon, Rhône
Collection of textiles from all the principal centres of production, both in the Orient and in Europe. Coptic, Byzantine, Moslem, Egyptian, Persian and Sicilian material. 16th and 17th century Persian carpets. Lyon textiles since the 17th century. Italian and Spanish textiles of the Renaissance. Far Eastern cloth.
Daily 10-12, 2-5. Closed M. and Tu. morning and public holidays.

MUSEUM OF THE LYON AFRICAN MISSIONS
150 cours Gambetta, 69001 Lyon, Rhône
Collections from West Africa. Sculptures from the Ivory Coast, masks, weights for measuring gold. Sculptures, masks, copper from Dahomey and Nigeria. Egyptian collection.
Daily except M. 9-11, 2-5.

MUSEUM OF NATURAL HISTORY
28 boulevard des Belges, 69001 Lyon, Rhône
Large animals, extinct and still in existence. Deep sea creatures. Fossils. Minerals. Geological history of the district. Fauna. Birds of the Dombes region. Palaeontology, with specimens of the major French and European vertebrates.
W.-Su. 2-6.

MUSEUM OF PRINTING AND PAPER-MONEY
13 rue de la Poulaillerie, 69001 Lyon, Rhône
History of printing, including 17th century printing press. Origins of the book. Fragment of the Gutenberg Bible. Books printed in Lyon. Collections illustrating the development of paper money and the problems of counterfeiting. Engraving processes.
W.-Su. 9.30-12, 3-6. Closed M. and Tu.

MUSEUM OF THE PROPAGATION OF THE FAITH
12 rue Sala, 69001 Lyon, Rhône
Ethnography of the Far East and of Africa. Items brought back by missionaries.
Daily except M. and Tu. 10-12, 2-5.

MUSEUM OF RELIGIOUS ART
12 rue de la Poulaillerie, 69001 Lyon, Rhône
Religious art.
Th. and Sa., 3-6.

MUSEUM OF THE RESISTANCE
5 rue Boileau, 69001 Lyon, Rhône
Mementoes of the transportation camps. Underground material. Photographs of landings. Mementoes of Jean Moulin and General Brossette.
Daily 2-6. Closed Jan. 1, May 1, Ascension, Aug. 15, Nov. 11 and Dec. 25.

PUPPET MUSEUM
Hôtel de Gadagne, Rue de Gadagne, 69001 Lyon, Rhône
Lyon puppets made by Laurent Mourguet, creator of Guignol. Glove puppets from Paris theatres, and from England, Holland and Russia. Marionettes moved by a rod, from Brussels, Liège, Venice, Amiens. Wire puppets from shows and shadow theatres originating from Turkey or the Far East (Cambodia, Java, Siam).
Daily ex. Tu. 10-12, 2-6.

LE PUYLATA MUSEUM
4 montée Saint-Barthélémy, 69001 Lyon, Rhône
Roman ruins.
Sa. 5-7. Closed July-Aug.

SEWING MACHINE MUSEUM
79 rue de Bourgogne, 69001 Lyon, Rhône
History of the sewing machine.
On request (tel: 83-73-65, afternoons).

MÂCON

LAMARTINE MUSEUM
Hôtel Senecé, 21 rue Sigorgne, 71000 Mâcon, Saône-et-Loire
Furniture. Tapestries. Ceramics. Paintings. Section devoted to the life of Alphonse de Lamartine, poet and statesman, who was born in Mâcon in 1790.
Apr. 1- Nov. 1, Daily ex. M. 10-12, 2-6. Su. and public holidays 2-6. Closed May 1 and July 14.

MUNICIPAL MUSEUM OF THE URSULINES
5 rue des Ursulines, 71000 Mâcon, Saône-et-Loire
Prehistory. Archaeology. Paintings by Titian, including *Portrait d'un Doge*. Works by Le Brun, Coypel, Greuze, Courbet, Monet. Paintings of the Dutch and Flemish Schools. African ethnography. Chinese porcelain. Costumes and headdresses of the Mâcon region. Local crafts. History of the province.
Daily except M. 10-12, 2-6. Su. and public holidays, 2-6. Closed May 1, July 14 and Nov. 11.

MUSEUM OF ARCHAEOLOGY AND FINE ART
Hôtel de Ville, 71000 Mâcon, Saône-et-Loire
Paintings. Prehistory. African ethnography.
Daily ex. Su. afternoon and M., 10-12, 2-5.

MAGNY-LES-HAMEAUX

NATIONAL MUSEUM OF THE GRANGES DE PORT-ROYAL
Maison des Petites Écoles, Magny-les-Hameaux, 78470 Saint-Remy-les-Chevreuse, Yvelines
Engravings. Paintings by Philippe de Champaigne (1602-1674), giving a complete history of Port-Royal monastery and the Jansenist movement. Collections relating to Blaise Pascal and Jean Racine.
Daily ex. Tu. and W. 10-11.30, 2.30-5.30 (until 5 Nov.-Feb.)

MAILLANE

FRÉDÉRIC MISTRAL MUSEUM
13910 Maillane, Bouches-du-Rhône
The house, furniture, library and correspondence of Mistral.
Daily except Tu. and public holidays, 8-12, 2-6.

MAISONS-ALFORT

ANATOMICAL MUSEUM OF THE SCHOOL OF VETERINARY SCIENCE
7 rue Jean Jaurès, Maisons-Alfort, Seine
Anatomical collections, embracing medical pathology, surgery and bacteriology. Superintendence of meat. Farriery. Parasites affecting animals.
By appointment.

MAISONS-LAFFITTE

CHÂTEAU
78600 Maisons-Laffitte, Yvelines
Built in 12th century by Francois Mansart, and decorated with sculptures by Sarrazin, Buyster, Houdon, Clodion. Gobelins tapestries. 17th and 18th century paintings of the French and Italian Schools.
Conducted tours: Th. and Sa. at 3.30; Su. at 3 and 4.30.

MALAKOFF

TRANSPORT MUSEUM
150 boulevard Gabriel-Péri, 92240 Malakoff, Hauts-de-Seine
Public transport vehicles. Omnibuses. Trams. Railway engines.
First Su. in month, 3-6. May-July Daily 3-6.

MANDELIEU-LA NAPOULE

CHÂTEAU DE MANDELIEU-LA NAPOULE
06210 Mandelieu-la Napoule, Alpes-Maritimes
19th century building, with three surviving towers of the 14th century castle. Restored 1919 by the American sculptor, Henry Clews. Works by Clews.
June-Oct. Daily 3-6. Nov.-May, Sa., Su., 3-6. Closed Nov. 15- Dec. 15.

LE MANS

AUTOMOBILE MUSEUM
Les Raineries, Route d'Angers, 72000 Le Mans, Sarthe
Collection of motor cars, in Museum situated within the Le Mans 24 Hours circuit.
Mar. 16- Nov. 11, Daily 9-12, 2-7. Nov 12- Mar. 15, 9-12, 2-7. Closed Tu.

QUEEN BERENGARIA MUSEUM
9 et 11 rue de la Reine-Bérengère, 72000 Le Mans, Sarthe
18th and 19th century pottery from the workshops at Ligron and Malicorne. Ethnography. Local history.
Daily except Tu. 10-12, 2-5.

DE TESSÉ MUSEUM
Avenue de Paderborn, 72000 Le Mans, Sarthe
Paintings, including works by Lorenzetti, Pisanello, Kalf, Boucher, Delacroix, Constable. Goldsmiths' work. Enamel recumbent figure of Geoffrey Plantagenet, Duke of Normandy, Anjou and Touraine (c. 1145-1150). Tapestries. The museum also houses material relating to mineralogy, palaeontology, ornithology, archaeology, ethnography and weapons.
Daily 8-12, 2-6.

MARCIGNY

RÉGIONAL MUSEUM
à la Tour du Moulin, 71110 Marcigny, Saône-et-Loire
French and foreign faience. Greek and Roman sculpture.
Daily 9.30-12, 2-6.

MARLY-LE-ROI

OLD MARLY MUSEUM
au Chénil, place du Général-de-Gaulle, 78160 Marly-le-Roi, Yvelines
History of the Marly district. Furniture. Ancient musical instruments.
Mar.-Sept. Su. and public holidays, 3-6.30. Oct.-Feb. Su. and public holidays, 2-6.

MARQUÈZE

OPEN-AIR MUSEUM OF THE LANDES DE GASCOIGNE
Marquèze, Landes
In the Regional Natural Park of the Vallées de la Leyre and the Val de l'Eyre. Peasant buildings - shepherds' huts and sheep folds; piggery; bread oven; chicken house. Illustrations of rural economy and crop production.
Summer: daily 9-dusk. Winter: enquire locally.

MARSAC-EN-LIVRADOIS

CHAPEL-MUSEUM OF THE WHITE PENITENTS
63940 Marsac-en-Livradois, Puy-de-Dôme
Housed in 11th century church, the museum depicts the life and rites of the Penitents in the 15th century. With the help of a diorama the spectator can follow the Good Friday procession.
Daily June-Sept. 9-10, 2-6. Also open Easter Su. and M.

JASSERIE DU COQ NOIR
Col des Supeyres, 63940 Marsac-en-Livradois, Puy-de-Dôme
The "jasserie" (temporary accommodation used by animals and shepherds during the summer months) has been converted into a rural museum, where visitors can sample local cheeses, rye bread and "brezou", a bowl of milk straight from the cow and into which bread has been crumbled.
June-Sept. Daily 10-12, 2-6.

MARSEILLE

CANTINI MUSEUM
19 rue Grignan, 13001 Marseille, Bouches-du-Rhône
Provençal faience. Decorative objets d'art. Collection of contemporary paintings, prints.
Daily except Tu. and F. morning, 10-12, 2-6.

GROBET-LABADIE MUSEUM
140 boulevard Longchamp, 13001 Marseille, Bouches-du-Rhône
Flemish, German and Italian Primitives. Paintings and drawings by Claud Lorrain, Puget, Fragonard, Grueze, Ingres, Corot, Géricault, Delacroix, Daumier, Rodin and Daubigny. Sculptures of the Middle Ages and the Renaissance. French and Flemish tapestries of 16th-18th centuries. Eastern carpets. Furniture. Faience. Wrought-iron. Musical instruments.
Daily except Tu. and F. morning, 10-12, 2-6.

MARSEILLE MARITIME MUSEUM
Palais de la Bourse, 13001 Marseille, Bouches-du-Rhône
History of the port of Marseille and its ships. Models. Paintings. Drawings. Documents.
Daily except Tu. 10-12, 2-6.30.

MUSEUM OF ARCHAEOLOGY
Château Borely, 13001 Marseille, Bouches-du-Rhône
Greek ceramics. Sarcophagi. Egyptian collection. 18th century French drawings.
Daily except Tu. and F. morning, 10-12, 2-6.

MUSEUM OF THE BLACK PENITENTS
6 rue du Bon Jésus, 13001 Marseille, Bouches du Rhône
History and relics of the Confraternity.
Su. and holidays 7-11 a.m.

MUSEUM OF FINE ART
Palais de Longchamp, 13001 Marseille, Bouches-du-Rhône
Paintings of the Flemish and Italian schools. French paintings, including works by Philippe de Champaigne, Chardin, Granet, Daumier, Courbet, Millet, Corot, Dufy. Drawings.
Winter: Daily 9-12, 2-5. Summer: Daily except F. morning and Tu., 9-12, 3-6.

MUSEUM OF OLD MARSEILLE
Maison Diamantée, rue de la Prison, 13001 Marseille, Bouches-du-Rhône
Popular art. History. Provençal furniture. Ships' figureheads; Plans, medals, engravings and domestic items of the 17th and 19th centuries.
Daily except Tu. and F. morning, 10-12, 2-6.

MUSEUM OF PROVENÇAL ART
Château Gombert, 5 place des Héros, 13001 Marseille, Bouches du Rhône
Costumes. Silver plate. Agricultural implements. Furniture. Objets d'art.
M., Sa. and Su. 2-5. Parties at other times by appointment.

NATURAL HISTORY MUSEUM
Palais de Longchamp, 13001 Marseille, Bouches du Rhône
Natural history collections: vertebrates, mammals, birds, reptiles.
Daily ex. Tu. and F. mornings, 10-12, 2-5.

ROMAN DOCKS MUSEUM
Annexe du Musée Borely, place Vivaux, 13001 Marseille, Bouches-du-Rhône
Roman harbour installations. Archaeological material from under-water excavations.
Daily except Tu., Fr. morning and public holidays, 10-12.

MARS LA TOUR

FALLER MILITARY MUSEUM
Place Jeanne d'Arc au Presbytère, Mars La Tour, 54800 Jarny, Meurthe-et-Moselle
Items relating to the war of 1870, including arms, uniforms and correspondence.
Daily 9-12, 2-6; Su. 9-11, 2-6.

MARTAINVILLE EPREVILLE

DEPARTMENTAL MUSEUM OF HAUTE-NORMANDIE
Château, 76124 Martainville Epreville, Seine-Maritime
Folklore of Haute-Normandie.
On application.

MARTEL

LOCAL MUSEUM
Hôtel de Ville, 46600 Martel, Lot
Gallic and Gallo-Roman archaeology material from Puy d'Issolud, the old Gallic town of Uxellodunum. Prehistory. Historical material on the town of Martel. Collection of pharmaceutical jars.
Daily 8-12, 2-6. Closed public holidays.

MARTIGUES

MUSEUM OF OLD MARTIGUES
Rue Colonel-Denfert-Rochereau, 13500 Martigues, Bouches-du-Rhône
Gallo-Roman archaeology. Mementoes of the Penitents. River transport and fishing. Room devoted to the founder of the Order of the Chevaliers de Malte. Paintings and drawings by Félix Ziem.
Th., Su. and public holidays, 10-12, 2-6. Open every day in July, Aug. and Sept.

FÉLIX ZIEM MUSEUM
rue du Colonel-Denfert, 13500 Martigues, Bouches-du-Rhône
Paintings by Félix Ziem.
Th., Su. and public holidays, 10-12, 2-6. Open every day in July, Aug. and Sept.

MARZY

FOLKLORE MUSEUM
Mairie, Marzy, 58000 Nevers, Nièvre
Local history and folklore. Views of the region. Old musical instruments. Geology. Prehistory. Coins.
On request.

LE MAS D'AZIL

LADEVÈZE MUSEUM
Mairie, 09290 Le Mas d'Azil, Ariège
Excavated remains of animals from the Grottoes of Mas d'Azil, including mammoth, rhinoceros, bear, hyena and bison. Flint and bone tools. Spears. Fossils. Objects from the Neolithic and Bronze Ages.
Apr. 1-July 1, Daily 2-6 and mornings by appointment. Su. and public holidays, 10-12, 2-6. July 1-Oct. 1, Daily 10-12, 2-6.

LE MAS-SOUBEYRAN

DESERT MUSEUM
Le Mas-Soubeyran, 30140 Anduze, Gard
Protestant museum housed in the family home of Roland Laporte, one of the leaders of the Camisard Revolt (1702). The Laporte family kitchen has been preserved intact, so too has the cupboard that conceals the hiding place, Roland's bible, the sword of Jean Cavalier, and other mementoes.
Mar.-Nov. Daily 9-12, 2-6.

LES MATELLES

MUSEUM OF THE CENTRE FOR PREHISTORIC STUDIES AT THE UNIVERSITY OF MONTPELLIER
Les Matelles, 34270 St. Mathieu de Tréviers, Hérault
Prehistoric material from local excavations. Crematory furnace. Neolithic temple.
Dec. 15-Mar. 15. Daily 9-12, 2-5. Rest of year, 9-12, 2-6. Closed M., W. and F.

MAUBEUGE

FERCOT DELMOTTE MUSEUM
9 rue du Chapitre, 59600 Maubeuge, Nord
In chapter-house (17th century). Gallo-Roman archaeology. Sculpture. Paintings, 17th century to the present day. Faience from Ferrière-la-Petite. Local history and folklore.
July-Sept. Daily except Tu. 2.30-5.30. Dec.-Mar. Th. and Su. 2.30-5.30. Other months, Su., M., W. and Th. 2.30-5.30.

MAULE

VICTOR AUBERT MUSEUM
Rue Quincampoix, 78580 Maule, Yvelines
Prehistory. Local folklore. Costumes. Tools.
Daily, on request.

MAUVEZIN

CHÂTEAU MUSEUM
Mauvezin, 65130 Capvern les Bains, Hautes-Pyrénées
10th century castle, housing collections of folklore and local history.
June-Sept. Daily 9-12, 2-7. Oct.-May, Su. and public holidays 2-7. Weekdays, apply to the keeper.

MAYENNE

MUNICIPAL MUSEUM
13 rue Dupont-Grandjardin, 53100 Mayenne, Mayenne
Local and prehistoric archaeology. Roman coins. Furniture. Sculpture.
Su. and Th. except public holidays, 9-12.

MAZÉ

CHÂTEAU DE MONTGEOFFROY
Mazé, 49250 Beaufort en Vallée, Maine-et-Loire
18th century château, with original furniture and woodwork. Constructed in 1775 for the Marshal de Contades, it has always belonged to the same family.
Su. after Easter-Nov. 1, Daily 9.30-12, 2.30-4.

MEAUX

BOSSUET MUSEUM
Place de la Libération, 77100 Meaux, Seine-et-Marne
Gems. Paintings. Furnishings. Roman sculpture-portrait, said to be of Ogier the Dane. Ethnography of Brie. Memorabilia of Bossuet, bishop of Meaux.
Winter: Su., M., Th., Sa. 2.30-4.30 (Summer until 6.30). July-Sept. Daily 2.30-6.30.

LE MÉE-SUR-SEINE

CHAPU MUSEUM
334 rue Chapu, 77350 Le Mée-sur-Seine, Seine-et-Marne
Sculpture including items by Chapu, who was born at Mée.
On request.

MEHUN-SUR-YÈVRE

CHÂTEAU CHARLES VII MUSEUM
Place du Général-Leclerc, 18500 Mehun-sur-Yèvre, Cher
Antiquities. Mehun porcelain.
Daily except Tu. 2-6. Easter-Oct., Su. and public holidays, also 10-12. Closed M. afternoon of Pentecost.

MELUN

MELUN MUSEUM
5 rue du Franc-Murier, 77000 Melun, Seine-et-Marne
Prehistory. Gallo-Roman inscriptions. Sculpture of the Middle Ages. Objets d'art. Ceramics. Faience from Rubelles. Paintings. Furniture. Sculptures by H. Chapu.
Daily ex. M. 10-12, 2-5.

MENDE

MUSEUM OF THE LOZÈRE SOCIETY OF LETTERS, SCIENCES AND ARTS
Avenue du Musée, 48000 Mende, Lozère
Prehistoric, Gallo-Roman and Gothic archaeology. Collec-

tion of sigillata from Banassac. Ethnography. Numismatics. Rocks, minerals and fossils.
Daily 9-12, 2-5.

MENTON

COCTEAU MUSEUM
Le Bastion au Port, 06500 Menton, Alpes-Maritimes
Collection of designs, pastels, tapestries and ceramics belonging to the poet. Works of his friends Picasso, Mac Avoy, Vasquez.
Winter: Daily except M., Tu. and public holidays 9-12, 2-6. Summer: Daily except M., Tu. and public holidays 9-12, 3-6.

MARRIAGE HALL
Mairie, 06500 Menton, Alpes-Maritimes
Collection of paintings by Cocteau.
Daily except Su. and public holidays, 9-12, 2-6.

MUNICIPAL MUSEUM
Rue Lorédan-Larchey, 06500 Menton, Alpes-Maritimes
Prehistoric objects from the excavations at Rochers-Rouges. Skull of the Menton Man, discovered in 1884. Objects from the Lazaret Grotto (Nice) and from various sites in the Alpes maritimes. Paintings by Camoin, Dérain, Dufy, Picabla, Valadon and Vlaminck. Works of the Italian, Flemish, Spanish and Dutch Schools (14th-17th centuries). History and folklore of the Menton area.
Daily except M., Tu. and public holidays, 9-12, 2-6 (3-7 in summer).

METZ

CENTRAL MUSEUM
2 rue du Haut-Poirier, 57000 Metz, Moselle
Archaeological specimens are grouped to illustrate the theme of water. Room devoted to daily life in the Gallo-Roman period. Collection of Merovingian and Carolingian sculptures, including fragments of the chancel of the Abbey of Saint-Pierre-aux-Nonnains. Paintings by Clouet, Jouvenet, Hubert Robert, Greuze, Largillière, Nattier, Duplessis, Delacroix, Chasseriau, Corot, Vuillard, Dufy, Marquet, Bazaine and Bissière. Paintings of the German, Flemish and Dutch Schools. Medieval collections are in a nearby corn-loft (15th century).
Daily except M. and Su. morning, 10-12, 2-6.

MEUDON

MEUDON MUSEUM
Maison d'Armande Béjart, 11 rue des Pierres, 92190 Meudon, Hauts-de-Seine
Local history. Technology, especially that connected with local industry. Astronomy. Aeronautics. Glass. Ceramics.
Apr.-Oct. Daily except Tu. 2-6.

MUSEUM OF AVIATION
Parc de l'O.N.E.R.A., 2 rue des Vertugadins, 92190 Meudon, Hauts-de-Seine
History of aviation from Montgolfier to the present day. Exhibits include full-size flying machines, mock-ups of aeroplanes and balloons; motors and 'nacelles'.
Winter: Sa., Su. and public holidays 10-12, 2-5. Summer: Sa., Su. and public holidays 10-12, 2-6. Other days 9-5.

RODIN MUSEUM
Villa des Brillants, 92190 Meudon, Hauts-de-Seine
Annexe of the Musée Rodin in Paris, containing his plaster-work and rough sketches. In the park, the tomb of Rodin carries *le Penseur* and antique marble sculptures from the collection gathered together by the artist.
Apr.-Nov. Su. 1-6; Sa. and M. 1.30-5.30.

MIALET

'DESERT' MUSEUM
Le Mas Soubeyran, Mialet, 30140 Anduze, Gard
Collection relating to the period of the 'Desert' (1685-1787) when Protestant Churches were obliged to lead an underground life in consequence of the revocation of the Edict of Nantes. Rooms are dedicated to the Camisard War, to the Protestants sentenced to row in galleys because of their faith, to women imprisoned in the Tower of Constance, and to the Churches of 'Refuge'.
Mar.-Nov. Daily 9.30-12, 2.30-6.

MILLAU

GRAUFESENQUE MUSEUM
Rue Antoine-Guy-Millau, 12100 Millau, Aveyron
Housed in an old mill, the archaeological collections comprise material on the Gallo-Roman period in the Graufesenque region, and Neolithic relics from the Causses area.
July-Sept. 15, 9-12, 4-7. Closed Su. Outside these times open only on written application.

MILLY-LA-FORÊT

CHAPELLE
91490 Milly-la-Forêt, Essonne
Chapel decorated by Jean Cocteau.
Daily except Tu. 10-12, 2-6. Nov 1 - Su. before Easter, open only on Sa., Su. and public holidays.

MIRABEL

OLIVIER DE SERRES MUSEUM
Domaine du Pradel, Mirabel, 07170 Villeneuve-de-Berg, Ardèche
Portraits of the contemporaries of the agriculturist, Olivier de Serres. Manuscripts. Fine edition his *Theâtre d'Agriculture.* Collections illustrating life and work of de Serres.
Daily except Su. and public holidays, 9-11, 2.30-5.

MIRANDE

LOCAL MUSEUM
Salle de la Mairie, 32300 Mirande, Gers
Paintings relating to the town of Mirande.
Daily.

MUSEUM OF THE MINOR PAINTERS OF MIRANDE
Boulevard Alsace-Lorraine, 32300 Mirande, Gers
Italian primitive paintings. Dutch Renaissance works. Portraits of the French School, 17th-19th centuries. 18th century ceramics. Gallo-Roman pottery and busts, mainly from local excavations.
Th. and Su. 2-4. Other times by appointment.

MOISSAC

MONASTERY MUSEUM
au Chapelle, 82200 Moissac, Tarn-et-Garonne
Archaeology. Religious art. Lapidary collections.
Daily 9-12, 2-6.

MUSEUM OF THE POPULAR ARTS AND TRADITIONS OF BAS-QUERCY
Rue de l'Abbaye, 82200 Moissac, Tarn-et-Garonne
Collections illustrating peasant life in the valley of the Garonne, in the Bas-Quercy area. Examples of craftsmen's work.
Daily except Tu. and Su. morning, 9-12, 2-6.

MOLSHEIM

MUSEUM OF ART AND HISTORY
Les Grandes Boucheries, Metzig, 67120 Molsheim, Bas-Rhin
Prehistoric archaeology. Local history and folklore. Locks and ironwork on furniture. 16th century clock.
July-Sept. 15, 9-12, 3-6.

LE-MONASTIER-SUR-GAZEILLE

ABBEY CHURCH
43150 Le-Monastier-sur-Gazeille, Haute-Loire
Bust of Saint Chaffre (11th century) in silver-plated wood, embellished with precious stones. Byzantine fabrics.
Any time.

MONSIREIGNE

MUSEUM OF PROTESTANTISM IN WESTERN FRANCE
Le Bois-Tiffrais, 85930 Monsireigne, Vendée
History of Protestantism in western France. Engravings. Manuscripts. Medals. Books. Gold and silver.
Apr. 1 - Sept. 30.

MONTAIGU

MUSEUM OF THE NORTHERN VENDÉE
au Château, 86500 Montaigu, Vendée
Prehistory. Medieval and Gallo-Roman archaeology. Folklore. Paintings. Sculpture.
M.-Sa. 2.30-4. Su. and public holidays 10-12.

MONTARGIS

GIRODET MUSEUM
Hôtel de Ville, 45200 Montargis, Loiret
Local archaeology. 18th and 19th century sculpture. 16th-19th century French paintings. Drawings. Objets d'art. Ethnography.
Daily except Tu. 10-12, 2-5.

MONTAUBAN

VICTOR BRUN MUSEUM OF NATURAL HISTORY
Place Antoine Bourdelle, 82000 Montauban, Tarn-et-Garonne
Prehistoric archaeology. Local palaeontology, consisting of many specimens of mammals from Quercy. General ornithology. The Orgueil meteorite.
Daily ex. M. and Su. morning, 10-12, 2-6.

INGRÈS MUSEUM
19 rue de la Mairie, 82000 Montauban, Tarn-et-Garonne
Four thousand drawings and paintings left by Ingrès to his native town, including *The Dream of Ossian.* Antique and medieval archaeology. Room devoted to the Black Prince. Paintings by Masolino, Poussin, David, Delacroix, Géricault, Chassériau and Ribera. Sculptures and drawings by Antoine Bourdelle. Paintings by François Desnoyer.
Su. before Easter - Sept. Daily 10-12, 2-6. Oct. - Su. before Easter Daily except M. and Su. morning, 10-12, 2-5.

MONTBARD

MUSEUM
au Château, 21500 Montbard, Côte d'Or
Prehistory. Medieval statues. Paintings and sculptures of 19th and 20th centuries by Burgundian artists.
Daily except W. 9-5.

BUFFON MUSEUM
Tour St. Louis, Parc Buffon, 21500 Montbard, Côte d'Or
Collections illustrating the life and work of Georges Louis Leclerc de Buffon (1707-88), the naturalist, born in Montbard.
Daily ex. M. 10-12, 2-5.

MONTBÉLIARD

CHÂTEAU MUSEUM
25200 Montbéliard, Doubs
Natural history. Archaeology, especially of the Gallo-Roman period. Collection devoted to Albert André and his friends. History of science.
Daily except Tu. 10-12, 2-5.

HISTORICAL MUSEUM OF OLD MONTBELIARD
Hôtel Beurnier, 1778 place Saint-Martin, 25200 Montbéliard, Doubs
Regional history. Ethnography. Furniture. Memorabilia of the naturalist, Georges Cuvier, born at Montbeliard.
Daily except Tu. and public holidays, 2-5.

MONTBRISON

ALLARD MUNICIPAL MUSEUM
Boulevard de la Préfecture, 42600 Montbrison, Loire
Medals. Ornithology. Mineralogy. Dolls.
Th. and Su. afternoon, 2-4 (until 5 in summer).

MONTCARET

PIERRE TAUZIAC MUSEUM
Montcaret, 24230 Vélines, Dordogne
Local archaeology, including sculptures from 5th-11th centuries, sarcophagi. Roman remains.
Daily mid. Mar. - mid. Nov. 3-7. Closed mid. Nov. - mid. Mar.

MONT-DE-MARSAN

DAUBALEN MUSEUM
Hôtel de Ville, Place Pascal-Duprat, 40000 Mont-de-Marsan, Landes
Prehistory. Regional archaeology. Ethnography. Natural history.
Oct.-Mar., M. 4-6, Tu., Th. and F. 10-12, Apr.-Sept. Tu., Th. and F. 9-12, M. 4-7.

MONTÉLIMAR

LOCAL MUSEUM
Château des Adhémar, 26200 Montélimar, Drôme
Prehistory. Modern paintings. Numismatics. Natural history.
On request.

MONTFORT-L'AMAURY

MAURICE RAVEL MUSEUM
5 rue Maurice-Ravel, 78490 Montfort-l'Amaury, Yvelines
Collection illustrating life and work of the composer.
Daily except Tu., 2-6.

MONTIGNAC-LASCAUX

LASCAUX GROTTO
24290 Montignac-Lascaux, Dordogne
Prehistoric rock-paintings.
By appointment.

MONTLUÇON

MUNICIPAL MUSEUM
03100 Montluçon, Allier
Regional collections of natural history, history and ethnography. Room devoted to history and to the stringed-instrument trade of the town. Collection of 17th-19th century French faiences.
Daily except Tu. 10-12, 2-6.

MONTMAURIN

ARCHAEOLOGICAL MUSEUM
Mairie, Montmaurin, 31350 Boulogne sur Gesse, Haute-Garonne
Gallo-Roman and prehistoric archaeology.
During hours when the Town-Hall is open.

MONTMORENCY

JEAN-JACQUES ROUSSEAU MUSEUM
5 rue J.-J.-Rousseau, Montmorency, Val-d'Oise
Le Montiouis, the house which the philosopher occupied from 1757 to 1762. Engravings, manuscripts and other material relating to Jean-Jacques Rousseau's stay at Montmorency.
Apr.-Oct. Daily except Tu. 2-6.

MONTPELLIER

ARCHAEOLOGICAL SOCIETY MUSEUM
5 rue des Trésoriers-de-France, Hôtel de Lunaret, 34000 Montpellier, Hérault
Regional archaeology. Prehistory and protohistory. Etruscan and Greek ceramics. Bronzes. Glass of the Gallo-Roman period. Local ceramics. Sculptures by Saint-Guilhem-le-Desert.
On request.

ATGER MUSEUM
Faculté de Médecine, 2 rue de l'Ecole-de-Médecine, 34000 Montpellier, Hérault
Collection of drawings left to the Medical Faculty by Xavier Atger at the beginning of the 19th century. 16th-18th century works of the French, Italian and Flemish Schools.
Opening restricted to university vacations. Closed at Easter and Christmas. July-Sept. generally open from 2-6 except on Sa.

FABRE MUSEUM
Rue Montpellieret, 34000 Montpellier, Hérault
Paintings of the Italian School, including works by Brescianino and Veronese, the Spanish School and the Flemish and Dutch Schools. Paintings by Reynolds. French paintings by Sébastien Bourdon, (a native of Montpellier), Aved, Greuze, David, Géricault, Delacroix, Courbet, Berthe Morisot, Marquet, Matisse and La Patellière. Sculptures by Houdon. Drawings include three by Raphaël.
Daily except M. and public holidays, 9-12, 2-5.

HÔTEL DE CABRIÈRES-SABATIER D'ESPEYRAN
34000 Montpellier, Hérault
Napoleon III, Louis XV and Louis XVI furniture. Furniture with the trademarks of Fromageot, Claude I Sené, Turcot, Jacob, Befort, Pillot. Aubusson and Gobelins tapestries. Busts by Pajou. Vases by Gouthières. 16th-18th century jewellery.
Daily except M. and public holidays, 9-12, 2-5.

MONTPEZAT-DE-QUERCY

CHURCH MUSEUM
82270 Montpezat-de-Quercy, Tarn-et-Garonne
16th century tapestries. Gold and silver. Sculptures.
Daily.

MONTREUIL

MUSEUM OF LIVING HISTORY
Château de Montreau, 21 boulevard Théophile-Sueur, 93100 Montreuil, Seine-Saint-Denis
Engravings and manuscripts illustrating the revolutions of 1789, 1830, 1848 and the Commune. Rooms devoted to Marx and Engels, the 3rd Republic, Jean Jaurès, the first World War and to the events of the period 1918-1939. History of the Resistance in Montreuil.
Tu., Th., Sa. and Su. 10-12, 2-6 (2-5 in winter). Closed during August. During public holidays, enquire locally.

MONTRICHARD

PORT-CHER CASTLE MUSEUM
The Keep, 41400 Montrichard, Loir-et-Cher
12th century Keep, housing folklore collections.
Easter Su. - Nov. 1, Daily 9-12, 2-6. Nov. 2 - Sa. before Easter, Su. 2-6.

MONT-SAINT-MICHEL

MUSEUM OF HISTORY
Mont-Saint-Michel, Manche
15th, 16th and 18th century paintings on copper made by the monks. Bas-reliefs in alabaster. Collection of weapons. Copper portraits. Under-water periscopes.
Mar.-Oct. Daily 8-6.30.

MONTSOREAU

GOUMS MUSEUM
Château de Montsoreau, 49730 Montsoreau, Maine-et-Loire
Memorabilia of the Goumiers and their leaders, displayed in the Château Liautey. de Lattre de Tassigny collections. 1939-45 war exhibits.
Daily 9-12, 2-7.30 (to 5 in winter).

MOREZ

JOURDAIN MUSEUM
Place Jean-Jaurès, 39400 Morez, Jura
17th and 18th century French and Scandinavian paintings.
Daily except M. on request.

MORLAIX

MUSÉE MUNICIPAL
Rue des Vignes, 29210 Morlaix, Finistère
Art and ethnography of Leon. Religious sculpture and iconography. Maritime collection. Ship-models. Contemporary paintings and drawings.
Daily except M. 10-12, 2-6.

MOROSAGLIA

PASCAL PAOLI MUSEUM
20261 Morosaglia, Corsica
Birthplace of Pascal Paoli. Collection illustrating his life and work.
Summer: Daily 10-12, 3-6. Winter: Daily 9-11, 2-5.

MORTAGNE-AU-PERCHE

PERCHERON MUSEUM
Porte Saint-Denis, rue du Portail-Saint-Denis, 61400 Mortagne-au-Perche, Orne
Regional history and folklore. Drawings. Paintings. Engravings. Prints by Chaplain.
July 15- Sept. 15, Su. 2.30-5.30. Apr. 1 - July 15 and Sept. 15- Oct. 31, first Su. in the month, 2.30-5.30.

MORTAIN

TREASURY OF THE COLLEGIATE CHURCH
50140 Mortain, Manche
Religious art. Liturgical items, including an 8th century Anglo-Saxon holy oil container.
On request.

MOUILLERON-EN-PAREDS

MUSEUM OF THE TWO VICTORIES
Mairie, 85390 Mouilleron-en-Pareds, Vendée
Memorabilia of Clemenceau and Maréchal de Lattre de Tassigny.
Daily 10-5.

MOULINS

CATHEDRAL
03000 Moulins, Allier
Paintings, including one of the most celebrated French primitives, the triptych of Maître de Moulins, *The Virgin in Glory.*
Daily.

MUNICIPAL AND REGIONAL MUSEUM
Place de Colonel-Laussedat, 03000 Moulins, Allier
Regional archaeology. German primitive paintings. Sculptures. Tapestries. Objets d'art. Faience of Moulins, Nevers, Rouen, Moustiers. Weapons.
Daily except Tu. 10-12, 2-6 (2-5 Sept. 16- Apr. 30).

MUSEUM OF FOLKLORE AND OF OLD MOULINS
6 place de l'Ancien-Palais, 03000 Moulins, Allier
Costumes from Bourbon. History of the town of Moulins.
Daily 8-7.

MOUSTIERS-SAINTE-MARIE

FAIENCE MUSEUM
Mairie, 04360 Moustiers-Sainte-Marie, Alpes-de-Haute-Provence
Moustiers faience, including moulds and other objects concerned with their manufacture.
Daily 9-12, 2-6 (2-7 June-Aug.). Nov. 1 - Mar. 31, open only Sa. afternoon, Su. and public holidays.

MOUTIERS

MUSEUM OF THE ACADEMY OF THE VAL D'ISÈRE
Eveché, Place St. Pierre, 73600 Moutiers, Savoie
History of the town and of the Tarentaise Valley from prehistoric times to 1860. Bronze Age bracelets and anklets. Roman terra cotta ware. Coins. Souvenirs of the Salines Royales of the town. Minerals and fossils.
By appointment with M. Allemmoz, 52 grand'rue, Moutiers.

MOZAC

LAPIDARY MUSEUM
Salle annexe de l'Eglise, Mozac, 36200 Riom, Puy-de-Dôme
Lapidary collections. Treasury includes shrine of St. Calmin (1168) and the painted shrine of St. Austremoine (16th century).
Daily ex. M. 10-12, 2-5.

MULHOUSE

MUSEUM OF FINE ART
3 rue des Bonnes-Gens, 68100 Mulhouse, Haut-Rhin
Paintings and drawings. Lithographs.
Daily except W. 10-12, 2-5.

MUSEUM OF HISTORY
Ancien Hotel de Ville, Place de la Réunion, 68100 Mulhouse, Haut-Rhin
Furniture, banners, arms, portraits and documents relating to the old republic of Mulhouse. 14th and 15th century religious sculpture. 18th and 19th century costumes. Regional archaeology. Painted room from Sundgau.
Daily except W. 10-12, 2-5. Open until 6 from June 15- Oct. 1, and also Th. 8-10 p.m.

MUSEUM OF TEXTILE PRINTING
3 rue des Bonnes-Gens, 68100 Mulhouse, Haut-Rhin
Collection of textiles from all over the world, dating from the Middle Ages to the present day. Patterns. Prints. Designs. Printing equipment. Costumes. Collection of cloth from Jouy. 18th century materials from India and Persia.
Daily except F. morning, 10-12, 2-5. June-Sept. 8-10 p.m.

RAILWAY MUSEUM
Mulhouse Nord, 68100 Mulhouse, Haut-Rhin
Situated in a roundhouse of the former steam locomotive depot at Mulhouse-Nord, the museum contains historic locomotives and coaches, 1844-1937. They include the Buddicom engine from the former Paris-Rouen Company, the 3.1192 "Chapelon Nord", a Pullman Car and a Dining Car from the International Sleeping Car Company.
Apr.-Oct. Daily 10-6. Nov.-Mar. Sa. and Su. 10-dusk. Parties by appointment during week.

SAINT-JEAN CHAPEL MUSEUM
Grand-Rue, 68100 Mulhouse, Haut-Rhin
16th century murals. Sculptures.
May-Sept. Daily except W. 10-12, 2-5.

MURAT

PRIORY CHURCH
Bredons Dyke, 15300 Murat, Cantal
Religious art.
Any time.

MURET

CLÉMENT ADER MUSEUM
Maison des Jeunes, Rue Clément-Ader, 31600 Muret, Haute-Garonne
Material relating to the battle of Muret. Memorabilia of Marshal Niel and Clément Ader, the aviation pioneer.
Daily except Su. 9-12, 2-6.

MUROL

ARCHAEOLOGICAL MUSEUM
Mairie, 63790 Murol, Puy-de-Dôme
Neolithic and Mesolithic material. Gallo-Roman pottery fragments. Coins. Local folklore. Paintings by contemporary local artists.
M.-Sa. 9-12, 2-6.

MURVIEL-LÈS-MONTPELLIER

ARCHAEOLOGICAL MUSEUM
Mairie, Murviel-lès-Montpellier, 34570 Pignan, Hérault
Material from the excavations of the Roman oppidum at Castellas. Chronologically arranged material from 3rd century B.C. to 3rd century A.D., including ceramics, glassware, coins, metallic objects, bones, fragments of sculpture and architecture.
By appointment: daily 9-12, 2-6.

NANCY

CHURCH OF THE CORDELIERS
54000 Nancy, Meurthe-et-Moselle
Effigy of Philippe de Gueldre by Ligier Richier. Tombs of the Dukes of Lorraine.
On request.

LORRAINE MUSEUM OF HISTORY
Grand-Rue, 54000 Nancy, Meurthe-et-Moselle
Gallo-Roman and Merovingian archaeology. Medieval and Renaissance art. Tapestries. Collections illustrating 30 Years' War. Works by Lorraine artists (17th century), especially Jacques Callot, Georges de la Tour. 18th-19th century ironwork, furniture, ceramics and glass. Religious sculpture.
Daily ex. Tu. 10-12, 2-5 (2-6 in summer). Closed Jan. 1, Easter Su., Nov. 1 and Dec. 25.

MUSEUM OF DECORATIVE ARTS
38 rue du Sergent-Blandan, 54000 Nancy, Meurthe-et-Moselle
Majorelle and Vallin furniture. French art-nouveau. Posters and contemporary paintings of the movement by Lautrec, Cheret, Ibelo, Beardsley and Schwabe.
Nov.-Apr. Daily 10-12, 2-5 (open 2-6 Apr.-Nov.).

MUSEUM OF EARTH SCIENCES
École Nationale Supérieure de Géologie Appliquée et de Prospection Minière, P.O. Box 452, 94 avenue de Lattre de Tassigny, 54000 Nancy, Meurthe-et-Moselle
Fossils. Distribution of animal and vegetable life. Changes in the structure of the earth. Geology and related disciplines.
Th. 9-12, 2-6; Su. 2-6.

MUSEUM OF FINE ART
3 place Stanislas, 54000 Nancy, Meurthe-et-Moselle
14th-18th century Italian paintings; 16th-17th century Flemish paintings. Dutch 16th-17th century paintings. German and Alsatian paintings of the 16th century. French 16th-19th century paintings, including works by Poussin, Boucher, Greuze, Prud'hon, Gérard, Vuillard, Matisse, Vlaminck, Derain, Dufy, Segonzac, Modigliani, Utrillo and Lurçat. Drawings by Ingres and Grandville. Engravings by Jacques Callot.
Daily ex. Tu. 10-12, 2-6 (2-5 in winter).

UNIVERSITY AND CITY MUSEUM OF ZOOLOGY
30 rue Ste. Catherine, 54000 Nancy, Meurthe et Moselle
General and local zoological collections, including fauna of Lorraine.
Th., Sa., Su. and public holidays, 2-6. July-Sept. 15, Daily 2-6.

NANTES

DOBRÉE MUSEUM
Place Jean-V, 44000 Nantes, Loire-Atlantique
Archaeology, including Egyptian and Gallo-Roman. Greek and Etruscan ceramics. Ivories. Illuminated manuscripts. Sculpture. Paintings. Furniture. Engravings. History of the war in Vendée.
Daily except Tu., 10-12, 2-6.

MUSEUM OF DECORATIVE ARTS
Château, 44000 Nantes, Loire-Atlantique
In 15th century castle of Dukes of Brittany. Local history. Peasant culture of Nantes region. Costumes. Furniture. Ceramics. Breton handicrafts. Toys.
Daily except Tu. Apr.-Sept. 10-12, 2-6. Oct.-Mar. 10-12, 2-5. Temporarily closed for reorganisation.

MUSEUM OF FINE ART
10 rue Georges Clemenceau, 44000 Nantes, Loire-Atlantique
Paintings of Italian, French and Spanish Schools. French sculpture. 19th and 20th century engravings, including complete works of the Nantes engraver, Phélippes-Beaulieux.
Apr.-Sept. Weekdays 9-12, 2-6; Su. 10-12, 2-5. Oct.-Mar. Weekdays 9-12, 2-5; Su. 10-12, 2-5.

MUSEUM OF NATURAL HISTORY
12 rue Voltaire, 44000 Nantes, Loire-Atlantique
Geology. Mineralogy. Mammals and birds, both general and regional. Entomology. Malacology. Grasses, algae and lichen. Comparative anatomy. Vivarium.
Tu., Th., F., Sa. and Su., 2-6. Th. also 10-12. Closed during public holidays.

MUSEUM OF PICTURES OF NANTES
Porte St. Pierre, 44000 Nantes, Loire Atlantique
History of the city of Nantes, as shown by paintings, drawings, prints, photographs.
By appointment.

MUSEUM OF REGIONAL POPULAR ART
Château, 44000 Nantes, Loire-Atlantique
Ethnography. Sculpture. Furniture.
Daily except Tu. Apr.-Sept. 10-12, 2-6. Oct.-Mar. 10-12, 2-5.

MUSEUM OF RELIGIOUS ART
La Psalette, 44000 Nantes, Loire-Atlantique
Housed in 15th century chapter house. Religious art.
On request.

SALORGES MUSEUM
Château, 44000 Nantes, Loire-Atlantique
Collections illustrating the slave trade. Local maritime history. Regional industries.
Su. 10-12, 2-6.

JULES VERNE MUSEUM
Bibliothèque, 44000 Nantes, Loire Atlantique
Memorabilia of Jules Verne, including manuscript letters from Verne to his family. Books by and about Verne, in French and foreign languages. First editions.
Daily 9.30-12, 2-6.30.

NARBONNE

LAPIDARY MUSEUM
Place Lamouguié, 11100 Narbonne, Aude
Gallo-Roman lapidary collection illustrating 500 years of life in the area. Architectural fragments.
Oct.-May 14, Daily except M. 10-12, 2-5. May 15-Sept. 30, Daily 10-12, 2-6. Closed Jan. 1, May 1, July 14, Dec. 25.

MUNICIPAL MUSEUM
Palais des Archêveques, 11100 Narbonne, Aude
Bust of Louis XIV by Pierre Puget. Paintings, including works by Bruegel, Titian, Boucher, Ribera, Tintoretto, Veronese. Ceramics. Palaeolithic, Mesolithic, Neolithic, Chalcolithic and Bronze Age collections. Iron Age funerary urns.
Oct.-May 14, daily ex. M. 10-12, 2-5. May 15-Sept. 30, daily 10-12, 2-6. Closed Jan. 1, May 1, July 14, Dec. 25.

MUSEUM OF NARBONNE PREHISTORY AND ANTIQUITIES
Palais des Archevêques, 11100 Narbonne, Aude
Collections covering the period from early man to the coming of the Barbarians. Evolution of industries, religions and arts.
Oct.-May 14, Daily ex. M. 10-12, 2-5. May 15-Sept. 30, Daily 10-12, 2-6. Closed Jan. 1, May 1, July 14 and Dec. 25.

NEMOURS

CHÂTEAU MUSEUM
Rue Gautier-Ier, 77140 Nemours, Seine-et-Marne
Palaeolithic, Neolithic and Gallo-Roman archaeology. Paintings, sculptures and drawings of the 15th-20th centuries. Numismatics. Ornithological collection.
Nov. - Mar. 15, Daily except F. 10-12, 2-4. Mar. 16- Oct. 31, Daily except F. 10-12, 2-5. Apply to the caretaker, on the left-hand side of the courtyard.

NÉRAC

CHÂTEAU HENRI IV MUSEUM
47600 Nérac, Lot-et-Garonne
Mementoes of the court of Henri IV and Queen Marguerite de Valois. Paintings. Prehistory. Local archaeology.
Daily, on request.

NÉRIS-LES-BAINS

RIECKOTTER MUNICIPAL MUSEUM
Centre Thermal, 03310 Néris-les-Bains, Allier
Prehistoric and Gallo-Roman objects. Coins. Jewels. Ceramics.
Daily 4-6.

NEUFCHÂTEL-EN-BRAY

MATHON MUSEUM
Rue Saint-Pierre, 76270 Neufchâtel-en-Bray, Seine-Maritime
17th and 19th century ceramics. 18th century weapons. Open-air museum contains a cider mill, well and a press-house (18th and 19th century).
Su. 2-5; Sa. 2-4. Closed Tu. Other days apply to the caretaker.

NEVERS

FAIENCE MUSEUM
21 rue Saint-Martin, 58000 Nevers, Nièvre
Nièvre faience. 16th century Flanders tapestry. Paintings by Suzanne Valadon, Picabia, Gromaire and Dufy.
Daily ex. Tu. 10-12, 2-6. Closed Jan.

NIÈVRE MUSEUM OF ARCHAEOLOGY
Porte de Croux, 58000 Nevers, Nièvre
Greek sculpture. Celtic archaeology. Medieval sculptures from the old churches of Nevers.
Daily 2-6, including public holidays in summer. Open only Th. and Su. in winter.

NICE

CHÉRET MUSEUM
33 avenue des Baumettes, 06000 Nice, Alpes-Maritimes
Gobelins tapestries. Italian primitives. Paintings of the French school, including works by Fragonard, Matisse, Dufy. Chinese and Japanese sculpture. History of Nice Carnival.
Daily except M. and public holidays, 10-12, 2-5.

INTERNATIONAL MUSEUM OF MALACOLOGY
3 cours Salaya, 06000 Nice, Alpes-Maritimes
Zoology. Palaeontology. Shell collections, both of exotic species and Mediterranean varieties. Land and fresh water fauna, both present day and fossil, as well as sea fauna. A lithography press, dating from Daumier's day, recalls the technical processes once used for illustrating works of conchology.
Summer: M.-Sa. 10-12, 3-7. Winter: Tu.-Su. 10-12, 2-6.

MARITIME MUSEUM
Tour Bellanda, 06000 Nice, Alpes-Maritimes
Maritime collection. Models of ships. Navigational instruments. Weapons.
Nov.-Dec. Daily 10-1, 2-5. Feb. Daily 10-1, 2-6. Mar.-Oct. Daily 10-1, 2-7.

MASSÉNA MUSEUM
65 rue de France and 35 promenade des Anglais, 06000 Nice, Alpes-Maritimes
House (1900) built for Victor Masséna, Prince of Essling. Local history and folklore. Armour. Weapons. Jewellery. Pottery and faience. Primitives by Nice artists. Impressionist paintings.
Daily except M. and public holidays, 10-12, 2-5.

MATISSE MUSEUM
Villa des Arènes de Cimiez, 06000 Nice, Alpes-Maritimes
Paintings, drawings, models and sculptures by Matisse. Personal possessions and furniture illustrating his early life.
Summer: Daily 10-12, 2-7. Winter: Daily 2-5. Closed M. except during July-Sept.

MUSEUM OF ARCHAEOLOGY
164 avenue des Arènes de Cimiez, 06000 Nice, Alpes-Maritimes
On site of 3rd century Roman baths. Collection of items from the archaeological site of Cemenelum, including ceramics, glass, jewels, tools and inscriptions. Greek vases.
Summer: Daily ex. M. 10-12, 2-7. Open M. July-Sept. Winter: Daily ex. M. 2-5. Closed Nov.

MUSEUM OF MUSICAL INSTRUMENTS
Conservatoire Regional de Musique, d'Art Dramatique et de Danse, 24 boulevard Cimiez, 06000 Nice, Alpes Maritimes
Collection of ancient musical instruments, including violins, guitars, mandolins, harps, trombones and other wind instruments. Items from Japan, China, India, Tunisia, Persia and Senegal.
Open to students only by written appointment.

NATURAL HISTORY MUSEUM
60b boulevard Risso, 06000 Nice, Alpes-Maritimes
Casts in painted plaster of mushrooms and fungi of the Alpes-Maritimes. Collection of marine and other shells.

Palaeontological collection, including ammonites. Fossils. Vivarium.
Daily ex. M. 9-12, 2-5.30.

PALAIS LASCARIS
15 rue Droite, 06000 Nice, Alpes-Maritimes
17th and 18th century décor and painted ceilings. 18th century pharmacist's shop.
Th., Sa. and Su. 10-3. Mardi-Gras, Easter and Christmas: Daily 10-3.

VIEUX-LOGIS PRIORY MUSEUM
59 avenue Saint-Barthélémy, 06000 Nice, Alpes-Maritimes
Reconstruction of a medieval priory. 15th-16th century furniture, paintings and sculpture.
Th., Sa. and first Su. in month, 3-5 (4-6 in summer).

NÎMES

ARCHAEOLOGICAL MUSEUM
17 Grande-Rue, 30000 Nîmes, Gard
Roman, Gallo-Roman and Celtic antiquities.
Su. and Th. 1-5 (1-4 in winter).

MUSEUM OF ANTIQUITIES
à la Maison Carrée, 30000 Nîmes, Gard
Ruins of Gallo-Roman temple. Inscriptions and mosaics illustrating the importance of Nîmes in Roman times.
Daily 9-12, 2-5 (2-7 in summer).

MUSEUM OF FINE ART
Rue Cité-Foulc, 30000 Nîmes, Gard
Works by painters of the French School, including Greuze, Poussin, Boucher, Claude Lorrain. Flemish, Dutch and Italian paintings. Sculpture. 16th-18th century drawings.
Daily except Tu. 9-12, 2-4 (2-5 in summer).

MUSEUM OF OLD NÎMES
Place de la Cathédrale, 30000 Nîmes, Gard
Local history. Regional ethnography. Ceramics. History of Protestantism in the area. Documents on Provençal and Spanish bullfighting.
Daily except Su. morning, 9-12, 2-5 (3-6 in summer).

NIORT

MUSEUM OF FINE ART
3 rue du Musée, 79000 Niort, Deux-Sèvres
17th and 18th century Aubusson tapestries. Objets d'art. Wood carvings. Paintings by Miéris, Coypel, Steenwyck, Nattier, Huet and Grimou.
Daily 10-12, 2-6.

PILORI MUSEUM
Rue Mathurin-Berthomé, 79000 Niort, Deux-Sèvres
Prehistory. Numismatics. Stone inscriptions.
Daily 2-6.

POITEVIN MUSEUM OF COSTUME
Donjon, 79000 Niort, Deux-Sèvres
Ethnography. Headdresses and costumes.
Daily 10-12, 2-6.

TAIRE MUSEUM
2 rue Pasteur, 79000 Niort, Deux-Sèvres
Works by local artists.
By appointment.

NISSAN-LEZ-ENSÉRUNE

CHURCH TREASURY
34440 Nissan-lez-Ensérune, Hérault
Vestments. Sculptures. Paintings. Liturgical items. Archaeological material from local excavations.
On request.

LOCAL MUSEUM
34440 Nissan-lez-Ensérune, Hérault
Material from local excavations, giving a picture of life in the area at the time of the Roman conquest.
Daily 8-12, 2-6. Oct.-Easter, closed Tu., Daily 9-12, 2-5.

NOGENT-LE-ROTROU

MUNICIPAL MUSEUM
au Château St. Jean, 28400 Nogent-le-Rotrou, Eure-et-Loir
Prehistoric archaeology of the region. Iconography of Nogent and of Perche. Headdresses and costumes. Ceramics. Fragments of sculptures.
Daily except Tu. 10-12, 2-5.

NOGENT-SUR-MARNE

MUSEUM OF THE SMITH-LESOUËF FOUNDATION
14b rue Charles VII, Nogent-sur-Marne, Val-de-Marne
Engravings. Drawings, including two by Victor Hugo. Paintings. Greco-Roman antiquities. Chinese exhibits. Furniture.
Th. 2-6. Closed Aug.-Sept.

NOGENT-SUR-SEINE

PAUL DUBOIS AND ALFRED BOUCHER MUSEUM
Rue Paul-Dubois, 10400 Nogent-sur-Seine, Aube
Copies of the work of the sculptors Paul Dubois and Alfred Boucher, who were both born in the area.
Daily ex. M. 10-12, 2-5.

NOHANT-VIC

GEORGE SAND HOUSE-MUSEUM
Nohant-Vic, 36400 La Châtre, Indre
Memorabilia of the writer and of her friends: Chopin, Liszt, Balzac, Musset, Delacroix.
On request.

NOIRMOUTIER EN L'ILE

CHÂTEAU MUSEUM
Château Fort, 85330 Noirmoutier en l'Ile, Vendée
Natural history, especially conchology and ornithology. Local history and prehistory. Staffordshire pottery.
May-mid. Sept. Daily 9-11, 2-5. Mid. Sept.-Apr. by appointment Su. Oct. 15-Nov. 1, from Dec. 20-Jan. 10 and from Feb. 1-May 1.

NOYON

CALVIN MUSEUM
6 place Aristide-Briand, 60400 Noyon, Oise
Engravings, tableaux, documents and books relating to Calvin. 16th century editions of his works. 16th and 17th century documents. Revocation of the Edict of Nantes; Spread of Calvanism in the 17th century. The Museum is in Calvin's birthplace.
Daily except M., 10-12, 2.30-5.30.

NOYON REGIONAL MUSEUM
rue de l'Evéché, 60400 Noyon, Oise
Local history. Memorabilia of Calvin (1509-64), born at Noyon.
Daily ex. M. 10-12, 2-5.

OIRON

CHÂTEAU
Oiron, 79100 Thouars, Deux-Sèvres
Frescoes and murals based on the Eneïde (Fontainebleau School). Coffered ceiling in wood. Louis XIII plaster ceilings and carved or gilded wooden ceilings. Faience tiles with monochrome paintings, from Nevers.
May-Oct. 15, Daily 9-12, 2-7. Oct. 16-Apr. 30, 10-12, 2-4.

ORANGE

LOCAL MUSEUM
Place des Frères-Mounet, 84100 Orange, Vaucluse
Gallo-Roman collection, including fragments of statues, inscriptions and a Roman land register. Furniture belonging to the Gasparin family. Paintings. Local history.
Daily 8-12, 2-5 (2-6 in summer).

ORLÉANS

MUSEUM OF FINE ART
1 place de la République, 45000 Orléans, Loiret
French sculpture. Paintings of French, Spanish, Dutch, Flemish and Italian Schools. 17th-19th century drawings, pastels and engravings.
Daily except Tu. Apr. Sept. 10-12, 2-6. Oct.-Mar. 10-12, 2-5.

MUSEUM OF HISTORY AND ARCHAEOLOGY
Hôtel Cabin, Square Abbé Desnoyers, rue Sainte-Catherine, 45000 Orléans, Loiret
Gallo-Roman bronzes from Neuvy en Sullias. Figurines, Animal figures. Wooden ex-voto carvings from Montbouy. Medieval archaeology. Religious images from the Orléans region.
Th., Su. 10-12, 2-6. Closed Tu. Other days 2-6.

MUSEUM OF NATURAL SCIENCE
2 rue Marcel-Proust, 45000 Orléans, Loiret
General and local prehistory. Ornithology, including a supplementary section on birds in painting. Dioramas of European mammals. Petrology. Palaeontology. Terrariums and aquariums. Collection of minerals, shells, butterflies and exotic birds, selected for their beauty.
Th. and Su. 10-12, 2-6. Other days 2-6. Closed Tu.

PÉGUY MUSEUM
11 rue du Tabour, 45000 Orléans, Loiret
Life and career of Charles Péguy, the politician and writer. Portraits, manuscripts, newspaper articles, letters and other mementoes.
Daily except Su., M. and public holidays, 2-6.

ORNANS

GUSTAVE COURBET'S BIRTHPLACE
25290 Ornans, Doubs
Memorabilia of the painter, Gustave Courbet, in his birthplace.
Easter-Nov. 1, Daily ex. Tu. 10-12, 2.30-6.30.

COURBET MUSEUM
Hôtel de Ville, 25290 Ornans, Doubs
Paintings by Gustave Courbet, born at Ornans.
Easter-Nov. 1, Daily 10-12, 2-6.

HOSPITAL PHARMACY
25290 Ornans, Doubs
Hospital pharmacy, built in 1719, with collection of 18th century ceramics and other equipment.
On request.

OUARVILLE

MILL MUSEUM
Ouarville, 28150 Voves, Eure-et-Loir
Medieval, possibly 14th century, post-mill, restored 1958. Oak-framed, with a centre post timber measuring 0.65 metres across.
Daily 2-5. Grinds corn on summer Sundays.

OUESSANT

OPEN-AIR MUSEUM
Ouessant Island, Brittany
Branch of the Regional Park of Armorique, which concentrates on rural and maritime life of the area. Domestic life and cultural history.
Daily 9-12, 2.30-8.

PARAY-LE-MONIAL

HIÉRON EUCHARISTIC MUSEUM
Route de Charolles, 71600 Paray-le-Monial, Saône-et-Loire
12th century Tympanum from the priory of Anzy-le-Duc. Paintings by Guido Reni, Tiepolo, Le Brun and Mignard.
Daily from Palm Su. until Oct. 17, 9-12, 2-6.

PARIS

ARC DE TRIOMPHE MUSEUM
Place d'Étoile, 75001 Paris 1e
History of the Arc de Triomphe. Documents and mementoes of the Napoleonic wars. Records of famous visitors to the tomb of the Unknown Soldier.
Daily except Tu. 10-4 (10-6 summer). Closed Jan. 1, May 1, Nov. 2, 11, Dec. 25.

JACQUEMART ANDRÉ MUSEUM
158 boulevard Haussmann, 75008 Paris 8e
Painting, sculpture, furniture and objets d'art, mainly of 18th century France and the Italian Renaissance. Works by Rembrandt.
Daily ex. M., Tu. Closed public holidays. 1.30-5.

ARMENIAN MUSEUM IN FRANCE
59 avenue Foch, 75016 Paris 16e
Collections illustrating Armenian life from 12th-17th century. Manuscripts. Religious works of art. Ceramics.
Winter: Su. 1-4. Summer: Su. 1-5.

ARMY MUSEUM
Hôtel National des Invalides, 75007 Paris 7e
Weapons. Armour. Military relics from Henri IV to Louis XVI. Mementoes of Napoleon. Trophies, flags, standards. Room devoted to the Second World War.
Daily 10-12.15, 1.30-5. Open until 6 on Th., Sa. and Su. Closed Tu.

ASTRONOMICAL MUSEUM OF THE PARIS OBSERVATORY
61 avenue de l'Observatoire, 75014 Paris 14e
Astronomical instruments of the 16th, 17th, 18th and 19th centuries. Statues and pictures of celebrated astronomers. Sundials.
1st Su. in each month, 2.30.

AVIATION MUSEUM
91 boulevard Pereire, 75007 Paris 7e
Engravings and paintings inspired by Montgolfier and balloons. Models of early aeroplanes, airships and balloons. Posters, documents and photographs.
By appointment.

BALZAC MUSEUM
47 rue Raynouard, 75016 Paris 16e
House in which Balzac wrote (1840-47) part of his *Comédie Humaine*. Material connected with Balzac and his times.
Daily except Tu. and public holidays 10-6 (10-5 in winter).

BOIS-PRÉAU NATIONAL MUSEUM
1 avenue de l'Impératrice Josephine, 92 Rueil-Malmaison, 75000 Paris
Napoleonic history. Court and military clothes and weapons. Mementoes of Sainte Helena, Marie-Louise and the King of Rome.
Daily ex. Tu. 10-12, 2-5.

ANTOINE BOURDELLE MUSEUM
16 rue Antoine Bourdelle, 75015 Paris 15e
Works by the sculptor Antoine Bourdelle and his pupils. Paintings. Pastels. Water-colours. Frescoes. Manuscripts. Studio preserved with original Gothic furniture.
Daily except Tu. 10-12, 2-5.

BRANLY MUSEUM
Institut Catholique, 21 rue d'Assas, 75006 Paris 6e
Museum built on the site of the old laboratories of Branly. Collections illustrating his life and work.
M.-Sa. 9-12, 2-6. Closed Su. and public holidays.

CABINET OF COINS
Bibliothèque Nationale, 58 rue de Richelieu, 75001 Paris 1e
Collections of currency, coins and medals. 3 paintings by Dürer. Greek vases and bronzes. Throne of King Bagobert from Saint-Denis. Cameo of Saint-Chapelle. Draughtboard belonging to Charlemagne.
Daily except Su. 10-4. Closed day after public holidays if this falls on a Su. (except Nov. 11, Jan. 2, Dec. 31, when Jan. 2 falls on Su.); Sa. before Easter, Whit. M., Nov. 2, and Nov. 3 when Nov. 2 is a Su.; the fortnight beginning 2nd M. after Easter.

CARNAVALLET MUSEUM
23 rue de Sévigné, 75003 Paris 3e
History of Paris. Paintings, drawings and engravings of the City from 16th century onwards. Portraits of famous Parisians. The Revolutionary period. Napoleon. Madame de Sévigné. George Sand. Inn and shop signs.
Daily except M., Tu. and public holidays, 10-12, 2-5 (2-6 in summer).

CERNUSCHI MUSEUM
7 avenue Vélasquez, 75008 Paris 8e
Chinese art. Pottery and porcelain. Bronzes. Jade. Buddhist sculptures. Paintings.
Daily except M., Tu. and public holidays, 10-5.30.

CITY OF PARIS MUSEUM OF MODERN ART
11 avenue du Président-Wilson, 75016 Paris 16e
Situated next to the National Museum of Modern Art, the museum complements its collection with works of Fauvism, Cubism and Orphism. Paris School. Paintings by Rouault, Gromaire, Braque, Delaunay, Picasso, Léger, Chagall, Pascin, Soutine, Villon, Dufy, La Patellière, Derain. *La Fée Electricité* by Dufy, 60 m. long and 10 m. high.
Daily except M. and Tu. 10-6.

CLEMENCEAU MUSEUM
9 rue Franklin, 75016 Paris 16e
Former apartment belonging to Clemenceau, containing his library and collections relating to his life and work.
Tu., Th., Sa. and Su. and public holidays, 2-5. Closed Aug.

CLUNY MUSEUM
6 place Paul-Painlevé, 75005 Paris 5e
Medieval art, furniture and objets d'art. Collection of Limoges enamels. The collection of Tapestries include *La Vie Seigneuriale* series, and *La Dame à la Licorne* series.
Daily except Tu. 9.45-12.45, 2.00-5.15.

COGNACQ JAY MUSEUM
25 boulevard des Capucines, 75002 Paris 2e
Collection of 17th-18th century art, including early works by Rembrandt. Furniture. Porcelain, figurines and jewels. Drawings by Watteau. Gouaches by Millet.
Daily except M., Tu. and public holidays, 10-6.

COMÉDIE FRANÇAISE MUSEUM
12 Galérie du Theâtre-Française, 75001 Paris 1er
Collection of paintings, drawings and statuary. Portraits, theatre scenes, busts and statues illustrating history of the theatre. The focal point is the armchair from ''*Le Malade imaginaire*'', in which Molière sat when he felt the first attack of the illness which was to cause his death a few hours later. Portrait of Molière by Mignard, showing the actor-playwright in the tragic role of César, in *La mort de Pompée*. Marble bust of Piron by Caffieri. Busts of 17th and 18th century playwrights by Houdon, Le Moyne, Pajou, Berruer and Foucou.
By appointment only. Guided tours on Su. only, 10.30-12.

CONCIÈRGERIE MUSEUM
1 quai de l'Horloge, 75004 Paris 4e
Relics of famous prisoners. Inscriptions, engravings, documents and other material.
Apr.-Sept. Daily ex. Tu. and W. 10-12, 1.30-6. Oct., Feb. and Mar. Daily ex. Tu. and W. 10-12, 1.30-5. Nov.-Jan. Daily ex. Tu. and W. 10-12, 1.30-4.

COSTUME MUSEUM
11 avenue du Président-Wilson, 75016 Paris 16e
French costumes from the 18th century to the present day. Rooms furnished in the style of 16th and 17th centuries.
Daily except Tu. and public holidays, 10-12, 2-6.

EUGÈNE DELACROIX MUSEUM
6 place de Fürstenberg, 75006 Paris 6e
Annual exhibitions depicting different aspects of the work of Eugène Delacroix. House, garden and studio of the artist.
Oct.-Apr. 10-12, 2-5. Apr.-Oct. 10-5.

ENNERY MUSEUM
59 avenue Foch, 75016 Paris 16e
Art of China and Japan. Ceramic, wood and ivory sculptures. Ceramic and inlay work.
Su. 1-5.

FAUCHARD DENTAL MUSEUM
45 rue de la Tour d'Auvergne, 75009 Paris 9e
Historical collection of dental instruments, including those belonging to Charles X's dentist. Reproductions of Egyptian and Persian instruments. Specimens of apparatus since earliest times. Anatomical and pathological sections.
Daily except Sa. afternoon, 9-11.30, 2.30-6.

FORNEY LIBRARY
Hôtel des Archevêques de Sens, 1 rue du Figuier, 75004 Paris 4e
History of the fine arts and decorative arts. Handicrafts and industrial techniques. Sale catalogues.
Tu., W., Th., F. 1.30-8.30. Sa. 10-8.30.

FRENCH POSTAL MUSEUM
4 rue Saint-Romain, 75007 Paris 7e
Collection of documents, uniforms, engravings, stamps, cards and other postal material relating to the history of the French postal system.
Daily ex. Tu. 2-6.

FOCH MUSEUM
École Militaire, place de l'École Militaire, 75007 Paris 7e
History of the French Army. Career of Marshal Foch.
By written appointment.

GOBELINS MUSEUM
42 avenue des Gobelins, 75013 Paris 13e
Gobelins and Beauvais tapestries, mostly 18th century and made under the direction of Le Brun. Carpets: 16th century Persian; 17th century Savonnerie made at Chaillot, and a Savonnerie made at the Gobelins.
W., Th. and F. 2-4.

GRÉVIN MUSEUM
10 boulevard Montmartre, 75009 Paris 9e
Collection of waxworks. Founded by the caricaturist, Grévin, in 1882, it includes scenes from the history of France and figures of present-day persons of note.
M.-F. 2-7; Sa. and Su. 1.30-8.

GUIMET MUSEUM
6 place d'Iéna, Annexe at 10 avenue d'Iéna, 75016 Paris 16e
Chinese art, including jade, sculpture, furniture and ceramics; Thai, Indonesian, Korean and Japanese art, including pottery and engravings. Collection of medieval sculptures in stone and bronze.
Daily except Tu. 9.45-12, 1.30-5.15.

VALENTIN HAÜY MUSEUM
3-9 rue Duroc, 75007 Paris 7e
Historical and technical material relating to blindness. Specimens of the first trials of relief printing by Valentin Haüy and his emulators. ''Night writing'' of Captain Charles Barbier. Process for writing words, music and plainsong by means of points, by Louis Braille, Paris, 1829: variations of this system (New York point, Wait system). Writing tablets, typewriters and stereotype plates. Hand-guides, maps, geometrical figures, scientific diagrams, games and tools adapted for the blind. Collection of pictures showing the blind at different periods.
First Th. of each month, 3 p.m.

JEAN-JACQUES HENNER MUSEUM
43 avenue de Villiers, 75017 Paris 17e
In the house where the painter died in 1905. Works from every phase of the artist's career, originating from his studio and his house at Bernwiller in Alsace.
Daily except M. 2-5.

HERMES MUSEUM
24 rue du Faubourg-Saint Honoré, 75008 Paris 8e
Private collection relating to the horse, hunting and carriages. Paintings by Alfred de Dreux and Constantin Guys. Carriages and their history. Saddles. Stirrups. Spurs. Miniatures of 18th-19th century carriages. Travelling sets from 18th century to 1850.
M.-Sa. 9.30-1.15, 2.15-6.

HÔTEL DE CLUNY MUSEUM
6 place Paul Painlevé, 75005 Paris 5e
Art. Archaeology. Costumes. Tapestries. Weaving. Collections illustrating different aspects of medieval life: domestic, war, hunting, court life.
Daily except Tu. 10-12.45, 2-5. Closed some public holidays.

VICTOR HUGO MUSEUM
Maison Victor-Hugo, Hôtel de Rohan-Guéménée, 6 place des Vosges, 75004 Paris 4e
Portraits and personal relics of Hugo and his family. Illustrations to his work by contemporary artists. Documents and manuscripts. Engravings. Library.
Daily except Tu. and public holidays, 10-12.30, 2-6.

PAUL LANDOWSKI MUSEUM
12 rue Max-Blondat, Boulogne-sur-Seine, 75000 Paris
Works, studies and drawings of the sculptor, Paul Landowski.
Sa. 10-12, 2-5; Su. 3-5; Th. 2-5.

THE LOUVRE
Palais du Louvre, Paris 3e
Former Royal palace. Middle-Eastern, Roman, Greek, Etruscan, Moslem, early Christian antiquities. Medieval and modern sculpture. Ceramics. Tapestries. Enamels. Clocks and watches.
Paintings of the French, Dutch, Flemish, German, Spanish and Italian schools. Drawings. Engravings.
Tu.-Su. 10-5. Closed public holidays.

MARITIME MUSEUM
Palais de Chaillot, place du Trocadéro, 75016 Paris 16e
Paintings by Joseph Vernait. Models of 17th-19th century ships. Galleys. Sailing ships.
Mid. Oct.-Apr. Daily except Tu. 10-5 (10-6 May-mid. Oct.). Closed May 1 and public holidays.

MARMOTTAN MUSEUM
2 rue Louis-Boilly, 75016 Paris 16e
Empire furniture. Flemish and Burgundian tapestries. German wood-sculptures. Impressionist paintings, including 65 by Monet.
Daily ex. Tu. 10-6.

FRÉDÉRIC MASSON MUSEUM
27 place St. Georges, 75009 Paris 9e
Napoleonic material.
By appointment.

MEMORIAL OF THE ORDER OF THE LIBERATION
Hôtel National des Invalides, Pavillon Robert de Cotte, 51b boulevard Latour-Maubourg, 75007 Paris 7e
History of the Free French forces and the Resistance movement.
M.-F. 2-5.

ADAM MICKIEWICZ MUSEUM
6 quai d'Orléans, 75004 Paris 4e
Portraits, sculptures, manuscripts and souvenirs of the poet,

his Polish and French associates, and of the Romantic period.
Th. (not public holidays) 3-6. Closed Dec. 23 - Jan. 3, 2 weeks at Easter and July 15 - Sept. 15.

GUSTAVE MOREAU MUSEUM
14 rue de la Rochefoucauld, 75009 Paris 9e
Paintings, water-colours, sketches and rough drawings by Gustave Moreau. The luxuriousness of the rooms gives a good idea of the interior of an 'artist painter's' home in 19th century.
M., W.-Sa. 10-1, 2-5. Closed Su., Tu., public holidays and month of August.

MUSEUM OF THE ARMY MEDICAL SERVICES
Val-de-Grace, 277b rue Saint-Jacques, 75005 Paris 5e
Models illustrating methods of transporting the wounded since the days of the First Empire, together with surgical exhibits and descriptions of preventive measures. The historical part of the Museum contains pictures and souvenirs of doctors in the service (Larrey, Percy, Desgenettes). Uniforms. Pharmaceutical and scientific displays. Room devoted to the medical corps.
M.-F. 9-11, 1.30-5. Closed public holidays.

MUSEUM OF THE BIBLE AND THE HOLY LAND
Institut Catholique, 21 rue d'Assas, 75006 Paris 6e
Material from the Bronze and Iron Ages, including ceramics and weapons. Roman glassware, ceramics, bones and inscriptions. Two jars from Qumran containing fragments of scrolls, papyruses. Collection of Roman, Byzantine and Arabic lamps. Coins.
Th. and Sa. 3-6.

MUSEUM OF COINS AND MEDALS
Hôtel de la Monnaie de Paris, 11 quai de Conti, 75006 Paris 6e
Currency and medals from the Middle Ages to the present day.
M.-F. 11-5. Closed public holidays. Guided tours of the workshops at 2 and 3.30, Tu. and Th.

MUSEUM OF DECORATIVE ARTS
Pavillon de Marsan, 107-109 rue de Rivoli, 75001 Paris 1e
Furniture and decorative arts from the Middle Ages to the present day. Complete reconstructions of ancient interiors, arranged chronologically. Rooms devoted to the art of 1900.
Daily except M., Tu. and public holidays, 11-12, 2-5. Su. 10-5.

MUSEUM OF THE DUKE OF ORLEANS
45b rue de Buffon, 75005 Paris 5e
Collection bequeathed to France by the Duke of Orleans in 1928. Natural history, especially zoology. Dioramas.
Th., Sa., Su. 1.30-5. Closed public holidays.

MUSEUM OF THE FACULTY OF PHARMACY
4 avenue de l'Observatoire, 75005 Paris 5e
Historic instruments, pharmaceutical jars. History of the Faculty of Pharmacy.
By appointment only.

MUSEUM OF FORGERY
16 rue de la Faisanderie, 75016 Paris 16e
Small collection formed by the Union of Manufacturers to show their activities in the field of combatting forgery and pirating of designs and exclusive models.
M.-F. 8.30-5.

MUSEUM OF THE FRENCH OVERSEAS TERRITORIES
293 avenue Daumesnil, 75012 Paris 12e
History of French colonies. Paintings. Sculpture. Documents. Ethnology. Archaeology.
Daily except Tu. 2-5.30 (2-6 in summer).

MUSEUM OF THE HIGHER NATIONAL CONSERVATORY OF MUSIC
14 rue de Madrid, 75008 Paris 8e
Musical instruments of all periods, including lutes, harpsichords and spinets, clavichords and small organs.
Th. and Sa. 2-4. By appointment other days. Closed public holidays and during August.

MUSEUM OF THE HIGHER SCHOOL OF FINE ART
14 rue Bonaparte, 75006 Paris 6e
Paintings, sculpture, engravings.
Daily 2-6 on request.

MUSEUM OF THE HIGHER SCHOOL OF MINES
60 boulevard Saint-Michel, 75000 Paris
Collection of mineralogical specimens. Meteorites. Palaeontology.
Tu.-F. 2.30-4. Sa. 3-5.30. Closed July 14 - Aug. 15, 2 weeks Jan./Feb. and public holidays.

MUSEUM OF THE HISTORY OF THE CHÂTEAU DE VINCENNES
75000 Paris
History of the Château from 18th century to the present day.
Daily except Tu. 10-5.30 (10-4.30 in winter).

MUSEUM OF THE HISTORY OF EDUCATION
29 rue d'Ulm, 75005 Paris 5e
Collections illustrating the history of teaching methods and education, provision and theory.
M.-F. 9-12, 2-6. Closed public holidays.

MUSEUM OF THE HISTORY OF FRANCE
Hôtel de Soubise, 60 rue des Francs-Bourgeois, 75003 Paris 3e
History of France, as shown by original documents, from the Merovingian period to 1815, displayed in the apartments of the Princes de Soubise.
Daily except Tu. 2-5.

MUSEUM OF THE HISTORY OF FRENCH PROTESTANTISM
54 rue des Saints-Pères, 75006 Paris 6e
History of French Protestantism up to the present day. Manuscripts. Books.
Tu. and Sa. 2-6. Only open Tu. from Aug. 1 - Sept. 15.

MUSEUM OF THE HOSPITALS OF PARIS
47 quai de la Tournelle, 75005 Paris 5e
Paintings, engravings, sculpture, manuscripts and relics relating to the history of the Charity and of the Paris hospitals. Collection of pharmacists' utensils.
Daily except Tu. 10-12, 2-5.

MUSEUM OF HUNTING
Hôtel de Guénégaud, 60 rue des Archives, 75000 Paris
Weapons, equipment and objets d'art relating to hunting and shooting. Paintings on sporting subjects.
Daily except Tu. and public holidays, 10-5 (10-6 summer).

MUSEUM OF IMPRESSIONNISM
Place de la Concorde, 75001 Paris 1er
The collections include the forerunners of the Impressionists and the late 19th century innovators up to Van Gogh, Seurat and Henti Rousseau, as well as Impressionist masterpieces. These include Manet's *The Balcony*; Renoir's *Le Moulin de la Galette* and *The Swing*; Monet's *La Gare Saint-Lazare* and Cézanne's *L'Estaque*. 18th century furniture. *Absinth* and *The Dancing Lesson* by Dégas. Works by Toulouse Lautrec, painted for la Goulue's bar. Sculpture by Dégas. Paintings by Gauguin and reliefs in wood, with which the artist decorated his house in the South Pacific.
Daily except Tu., 10-12, 2-5.

MUSEUM OF JEWISH ART
42 rue des Saules, 75000 Paris
Objects of worship and popular art. Models of synagogues and tombstones. Religious paintings and mosaics. Works by contemporary Jewish artists.
Tu., Th., Su. 3-6. Closed Sept. and public holidays.

MUSEUM OF THE LEGION OF HONOUR
Hôtel de Salon, 2 rue de Bellechasse, 75007 Paris 7e
History of the Order, from the Middle Ages to the present day. French and foreign decorations. Badges. Costumes. Paintings. Collection relating to Napoleon.
Daily except Tu. 2-5. Closed Jan. 1, May 1, July 14, Dec. 25.

MUSEUM OF THE LIBERATION
51b boulevard de Latour Maubourg, 75007 Paris 7e
Souvenirs of those who participated in the Resistance movement in France, and who were deported.
Daily ex. Sa. and Su., 1.45-5.

MUSEUM OF MAN
Place du Trocadéro, 75016 Paris 16e
Anthropology. Physical types since prehistoric times. Material culture and artistic creativity of Africa, Oceania, New Guinea, South America. Aztec skull in rock crystal. Physical malformations.
Daily except Tu. 10-5. Public holidays open Su.

MUSEUM OF MATERIALS
Palais de Chaillot, Aile, 75016 Paris 16e
Collections dealing with different kinds of building materials and methods of construction. The information in the section on stone helps present-day architects and builders in restoring historic monuments. Collection of specimens of French marble. Tiles. Slates.
By appointment.

MUSEUM OF MINERALOGY
National School of Mining, 60 boulevard Saint Michel, 75005 Paris 5e
Mineralogy. Geology. Fossils.
Tu.-F. 2.30-5; Sa. 3-5.30. Closed Aug. 1 - Sept. 1.

MUSEUM OF THE MONUMENTS OF FRANCE
Palais de Chaillot, 75016 Paris 16e
Casts of Roman, Gothic, Renaissance and Classical architecture. Reproductions of mural paintings and frescoes.
Daily except Tu. 9.45-12.30, 2-5.45. Closed between Dec. 25 and Jan. 1; Easter M., May 1, Whit. M., July 14, Aug. 15, Nov. 1 and 11.

MUSEUM OF MUSICAL INSTRUMENTS
14 rue de Madrid, 75016 Paris 16e
Housed in the Conservatory of Music, the 2,000 musical instruments are built up from the collection of Clapisson, the composer (1808-1866), who was the museum's founder.
Th. and Sa. 2-4.30. Closed from July 15 - Oct. 10.

MUSEUM OF NATURAL HISTORY
57 rue Cuvier, 75000 Paris
In the garden there is a cedar from Jussieu (1734), a maple from Crete (1702), a Robinia or false cedar (first planted in Europe in 1601). Piece of the trunk of a sequoia which is more than 2000 years old. Anatomy and palaeontology sections. Fossils, skeletons of a mammoth and of prehistoric animals. Mineralogical specimens.
Garden: *Jan. 1 - Feb. 28 from 8 a.m. Rest of year open at 7.15. Closes 10 minutes before sunset.* Galleries: *Daily except Tu. and public holidays in the week, 1.30-5. Su. 10.30-5.*

MUSEUM OF OLD MONTMARTRE
17 rue St. Vincent, 75018 Paris 18e
History of the Montmartre district. Paintings. Engravings. Architectural details from demolished buildings.
Daily except Tu. 2-5.

MUSEUM OF THE PARIS MINT
Hôtel de la Monnaie, 11 quai Conti, 75006 Paris 6e
Coins and medals from the Middle Ages to the present day.
Daily except Sa., Su. and public holidays, 11-5.

MUSEUM OF PLANS AND MODELS
Hôtel des Invalides, 75007 Paris 7e
Collection of models of fortified towns, made between 1668 and 1870. Models and reliefs of fortifications. Topographical material.
Daily except Tu. and public holidays, 10-12.15, 1.30-6. Closed Su. morning. M., W. and F. closes at 5.

MUSEUM OF POPULAR ARTS AND TRADITIONS
Route de Madrid, 75016 Paris 16e
Ethnography of France, including homes, costumes, tools, trades, pastimes and beliefs.
Daily except Tu. 10-12, 2-5.

MUSEUM OF PUBLIC ASSISTANCE
47 quai de la Tournelle, 75005 Paris 5e
History of Paris hospitals. Paintings of the French School. Collection of 18th century pharmaceutical jars.
Daily except Tu. 10-12, 2-5. Closed public holidays.

MUSEUM OF SWEDISH ART
Institut Tessin, 11 rue Payenne, 75003 Paris 3e
Relations between France and Sweden, especially in 18th century. Paintings by 18th century Swedish artists who worked in France, and by French artists who painted in Sweden. Material relating to the Royal Swedish Regiment, which fought in the French Army from the reign of Louis XIV until the Revolution. Costumes from different regions of Sweden. Scandinavian books.
M.-F. 2-5.

MUSEUM OF THE TWO WORLD WARS
Château de Vincennes, Pavillon de la Reine, 75000 Paris
Collections illustrating 1914-18 and 1939-45 wars. International politics. Paintings, drawings, water-colours, engravings, photographs, films, medals and other material.
By appointment.

MUSEUM OF URBAN, INTERURBAN AND RURAL TRANSPORT
5 rue de la Santé, 75013 Paris 13e
The museum has branches at 150 boulevard Gabriel-Péri, 92-Malakoff, and at 45-Pithiviers (station). Collection of urban transport vehicles, including the omnibus, tram, trolley-car and locomotive. Photographs and models, as well as authentic vehicles.
Apr.-July, Su. 3-6. Aug.-Mar. first Su. in month, 3-6. (at 150 boulevard Gabriel-Peri).

NATIONAL CONSERVATORY OF ARTS AND CRAFTS
292 rue Saint-Martin, 75016 Paris 16e
Housed in the former priory of Saint-Martin-des-Champs, the museum traces the entire history of mechanics and machines. Collections of glass, clocks and watches, and automata.
Daily except M. 1.30-5.30.

NATIONAL MUSEUM OF AFRICAN AND OCEANIC ART
293 avenue Daumesnil, 75012 Paris 12e
Collection devoted to African and Maghreb art, and to the art of Oceania.
Daily ex. Tu. and public holidays, 10-12, 1.30-5.

NATIONAL MUSEUM OF MODERN ART
13 avenue du Président-Wilson, 75016 Paris 16e
Works by artists of the Paris School as well as by Matisse, Braque, Bonnard, Juan Gris. Paintings by Kandinsky, Modigliani. Sculptures by Moore, Hajdu, César and Arp. Tapestries.
Daily except Tu. 10-5.15.

NATIONAL OPERA MUSEUM
1 place Charles-Garnier, 75009 Paris 9e
Collections illustrating ballet and opera history. Mementoes of ballet dancers and opera singers.
M.-Sa. 10-5.

NATIONAL MUSEUM OF ROAD TRANSPORT AND TOURISM
hâteau de Compiègne, 75000 Paris
ld carriages. Sedan chairs. Development of the bicycle nd the automobile.
aily ex. Tu. 10-12, 2-5.

ATIONAL TECHNICAL MUSEUM
92 rue Saint-Martin, 75003 Paris 3e
istory of science and technology. Early motor cars and ying machines. Locomotive models. Scientific instru-ents. Development of photography, the cinema, radio and levision, recording machines, electricity, the telephone.
u.-Sa. 1.30-5.30; Su. 10-5. Closed public holidays except aster Su. and Whitsun.

ISSIM DE CAMONDO MUSEUM
rue de Monceau, 75008 Paris 8e
e French home in the 18th century. Furniture, including ms which bear the signatures of some of the great binet-makers. Aubusson and Savonnerie tapestries. Col-ction of Chinese porcelain.
aily except Tu. and W., 10-12, 2-5.

PERA MUSEUM
place Charles-Garnier, 75009 Paris 9e
tached to the 'grand theatre lyrique' in Paris, the museum ntains documentary material on all the theatrical produc-ns since its foundation in 1669. Portraits of musicians d instrumentalists, including Renoir's portrait of Wagner, esented to the museum by Alfred Cortot.
ily except Su. and public holidays, 10-5.

ANGERIE MUSEUM
lace de la Concorde, 75001 Paris 1er
o rooms devoted to the *Nymphéas* by Claude Monet.
ily except Tu. 10-12, 2-5.

FILA MUSEUM
ulté de Médicine, 45 rue des Saints-Pères, 75006 is 6e
nan anatomy, anthropology, embryology.
ly on application to the curator. Closed public holidays months of July and Aug.

ACE OF DISCOVERY
nd Palais des Champs-Elysées, avenue Franklin D. sevelt, 75008 Paris 8e
cientific cultural centre'', a ''dynamic museum'', with tific experiments and demonstrations usually involving a full range of modern equipment, continuously in progress for the benefit of visitors. Planetarium. Computer. 300,000 volt electrostatic machine.
Daily except M., 10-6.

PASTEUR MUSEUM
Institut Pasteur, 25 rue du Docteur-Roux, 75014 Paris 14e
Apartment formerly lived in by the Pasteurs, containing personal items, original scientific instruments, papers and historic photographs.
By appointment: M., W. and F. 2-6; Tu. and Th. 9-12.

PETIT PALAIS MUSEUM
Avenue W-Churchill, 75008 Paris 8e
18th century French painting. Furniture, porcelain and tapestries, objets d'art from the medieval period onwards. Engravings by Dürer, J. Callot and Rembrandt.
Daily except M., Tu. and public holidays, 10-5.50.

POLICE MUSEUM
36 quai des Orfèvres, 75001 Paris 1er
History of the French police from 16th century to the present day. Engravings; archives; medals. Revolutionary material, including orders or arrest. Police force reorganised by Bonaparte. Documentation of famous cases.
Th. 2-5 except public holidays.

RODIN MUSEUM
Hôtel Biron, 77 rue de Varenne, 75007 Paris 7e
Works by Rodin in marble, stone, bronze and wax. Engravings. Water-colours. Rodin's personal collection, including works by Van Gogh, Monet, Renoir. Greek, Roman and medieval sculptures.
Daily except Tu. 10-12.15, 2-5.

TENNIS COURT MUSEUM
Salle du Jeu de Paume, place de la Concorde et rue de Rivoli, 75001 Paris 1er
Collection of 19th-20th century paintings, with works ranging from those by Manet and the Impressionists, to Van Gogh and Douanier Rousseau.
Daily except Tu. 10-5. Closed public holidays except Easter M. and Whit M. and also Aug. 15 if this is a Su.

TREASURY OF NOTRE DAME
Cathédrale Notre Dame, Place du Parvis, 75004 Paris 4e
Relics of the Passion, given in 1238 by Baudouin II, Emperor of Constantinople, to St.-Louis, who built Sainte-Chapelle to house them and where they remained until the Revolution. Reliquaries. Sacred vases, Chalices. Crufixes in silver and ivory. Books with fine bindings. Souvenirs of the coronation of Napoleon I.
Daily 10-5. Closed Su., meeting days of the chapter and religious festivals.

VAL DE GRACE MUSEUM
227b rue Saint Jacques, 75005 Paris 5e
Medical material. Portraits of military doctors. Uniforms. Letters. Documents relating to Ambroise Paré.
M.-F. 9-12, 1.30-5. Closed public holidays and Nov.

PAU

BÉARNAIS MUSEUM
3rd floor, Château Henry IV, 64000 Pau, Pyrénées-Atlantiques
History and folklore of Béarn.
Winter: Daily 10.30-11.30, 2.30-4.30. Summer: Daily 9.30-11.30, 2-5.30.

BERNADOTTE MUSEUM
8 rue Tran, Pau, Basses Pyrénées
House where Marshal Bernadotte (Charles XIV of Sweden) was born. Documents and relics relating to Bernadotte.
Daily 10-12, 2-6. Closed M. in winter.

HENRI IV NATIONAL MUSEUM
Château de Pau, 64000 Pau, Pyrénées-Atlantiques
Replicas of royal apartments. Historical material relating to the d'Albret family and to Henry IV, including the tortoise-shell reputed to have been his cradle. Tapestries.
Winter: Daily 9.30-12, 2-5. Summer: Daily 9.30-12, 2-6.30.

MUSEUM OF FINE ART
Cours Bosquet, 64000 Pau, Pyrénées-Atlantiques
Paintings, including works by Tintoretto, Romney, Rubens, Boudin and Degas. Sculpture. Engravings. Drawings. Coins. Prehistory.
May-Sept. Daily except Tu. 10-12, 2-6. Oct.-Apr. 10-12, 2-5.

PAUILLAC

MOUTON-ROTHSCHILD MUSEUM OF WINE
au Château, 33250 Pauillac, Gironde
Collection illustrating the iconography of the vine in art. Tapestries representing the different stages in the production of wine (Strasbourg or Nederweiler, c.1500). Arts of the ancient Near East, including a relief from Sakkhara, from the Fifth Dynasty, and a Sassanian drinking-bowl, c. A.D. 425. The cult of wine in Greece. Gold and silverware. Glass-ware. 19th century French sculpture. Modern works include a gouache, *L'Ivrogne*, by Rouault.
Daily 9-12, 2-6. Closed Sa. afternoon and M. morning.

PÉRIGUEUX

MILITARY MUSEUM
23 rue des Farges, 24000 Périgueux, Dordogne
Collection illustrating military history of Périgord. Prints. Portraits. Weapons. Flags. Uniforms.
Daily 2-5 on request.

PÉRIGORD MUSEUM
Cours Tourny, 24000 Périgueux, Dordogne
Prehistory. Skeleton of the Chancelade Man. Quaternary tomb of Reymonden. Bison frieze from l'Abri Blanchard. Flemish, Dutch and Italian paintings, including Luca Giordano, *St. Paul on the road to Damascus*.
Daily except Tu., 10-12, 2-5.

PÉRONNE

DANICOURT MUSEUM
Mairie, 80200 Péronne, Somme
Gallic, Greek and Roman coins. Intaglios and scarabs. 5th and 6th century Merovingian jewellery.
Tu., Th. and Sa. 2-6.

PÉROUGES

OLD PÉROUGES MUSEUM
Cité des Pérouges, Pérouges, 01800 Meximieux, Ain
Archaeology. Regional faience and furniture. Documents concerning the history of the town and its surroundings. Weapons.
Daily 8-7.

PERPIGNAN

MUSEUM OF NATURAL HISTORY
12 rue Fontaine-Neuve, 66000 Perpignan, Pyrénées-Orientales
Natural history collections.
Th., Su. and public holidays 2-5. Other days on request.

JOSEPH PUIG MUSEUM OF NUMISMATICS
Villa des Tilleuls, 66000 Perpignan, Pyrénées-Orientales
World-wide collection of coins and medals.
Th., Sa. and Su. 2-6.

HYACINTHE RIGAUD MUSEUM
1 rue du Musée, 66000 Perpignan, Pyrénées-Orientales
Paintings by Rigaud (born at Perpignan), Ingres, Saint-Aubin. Spanish and Italian paintings. Catalan primitives. 13th-16th century Spanish-Moorish faience, and 13th-18th century Catalan faience. Archaeological remains from excavations in the area.
Daily except Tu. Oct.-Mar. 9.30-12, 2-5. Apr.-Sept. 9-12, 2-5.

LE PETIT-COURONNE

CORNEILLE MUSEUM
502 rue Pierre-Corneille, 76650 Le Petit-Couronne, Seine-Maritime
Manuscripts, iconography and early editions of works of the poet, housed in his 'Maison des Champs'.
Daily 10-12, 2-5 (2-7 in summer).

PÉZENAS

VULLIOD SAINT-GERMAIN MUSEUM
3 rue A.-P.-Allies, 34120 Pézenas, Hérault
16th-19th century paintings. 17th and 18th century furniture. Aubusson tapestries. Memorabilia of Molière; Regional ethnography. Faience. Old pharmacy of the Hôtel-Dieu. Folklore.
Daily except Tu. and F. 10-12, 2-5.

PHALSBOURG

MUSEUM OF HISTORY AND ART
57370 Phalsbourg, Moselle
Local history. Material relating to the sieges of 1814, 1815, 1870. Memorabilia of Erckmann-Chatrian. Weapons.
Daily 8-12, 2-5 (2-9 Su.).

PITHIVIERS

MUNICIPAL MUSEUM
Rue de la Poste, 45300 Pithiviers, Loiret
Kanaka ethnography collection, brought back from Oceania by Admiral Gourdon, 1843-1913.
M.-F. 2-4, Sa. and Su. 2-4.

TRANSPORT MUSEUM
Rue Carnot, près de la Gare S.N.C.F., 45300 Pithiviers, Loiret
Steam locomotives. Trams. Railway coaches. Railway lamps. Demonstration line 4 km. long which is used on Sunday afternoons and public holidays by a steam train.
May 1 - last Su. in October and every Su. and public holiday, 2.30-6.

PLESSIS-LES-TOURS

MUSEUM CHÂTEAU
Château, Plessis-les-Tours, Indre-et-Loire
Relics of Louis XI (who died here, 1483) and of St. François de Paul. Material illustrating local industries, especially silks and braids.
Apr.-Sept. Daily except May 1, July 14, 10-12, 2-6. Oct.-Mar. Daily except Tu., Nov. 11, Dec. 25 and Jan. 1, 10-12, 2-5.

PLOMBIÈRES-LES-BAINS

LOUIS FRANÇAIS MUSEUM
30 avenue Louis-Français, 88370 Plombières-les-Bains, Vosges
In the summer residence of the painter Louis Français (1814-1897). Paintings, watercolours, drawings and souvenirs, together with material relating to his family and friends. Two rooms are devoted to the history of Plombières.
May 10 - Sept. 30, Daily ex. Tu. 3-6.

POËT-LAVAL

MUSEUM OF PROTESTANTISM IN THE DAUPHINÉ
Temple du Vieux Village, Poët-Laval, Drome
16th-19th century documents, pictures and other material illustrating the history of the Protestant movement in the region. The Museum building includes part of a 7th century church.
Public holidays, 3-6.30. Other times by appointment.

POITIERS

RUPERT DE CHIÈVRES MUSEUM
9 rue Victor Hugo, 86000 Poitiers, Vienne
Decorative and industrial arts. Regional history. Folklore. Coins and medals.
Daily ex. Tu. 10-12, 2-6 (2-5 in winter).

L'ÉCHEVINAGE MUSEUM
Passage de l'échevinage, 86000 Poitiers, Vienne
Prehistory and regional antiquities. Material from excavations at Père de la Croix.
Daily ex. Th. 10-12, 2-6.

HYPOGEUM OF THE DUNES
Rue Père de la Croix, 86000 Poitiers, Vienne
Early Christian archaeology.
Daily except Tu. 10-12, 2-5 (2-6 in summer).

MUSEUM OF THE BAPTISTRY OF ST. JOHN
Rue Jean-Jaurès, 86000 Poitiers, Vienne
4th and 6th century baptistry of St. John, one of the most ancient Christian monuments in France. Merovingian antiquities.
Daily except W. 10-12, 2-6. Closed Jan. 15 - Feb. 15.

MUSEUM OF FINE ART
Place du Maréchal-Leclerc, Hôtel de Ville, 86000 Poitiers, Vienne
Sculpture. Romanesque columns from the old churches of Poitou. Paintings, including works attributed to Bruegel de Velours and Ruysdael, and works by Chasseriau, Fromentin, Courbet and G. Moreau.
Daily except Tu. 10-12, 2-5 (2-6 in summer).

POLEYMIEUX AU MONT D'OR

AMPÈRE HOUSE AND MUSEUM OF ELECTRICITY
Poleymieux au Mont d'Or, 69250 Neuville sur Saône, Rhône
Memorabilia of A. M. Ampère, in his former home, and of his son, Jean-Jacques-Antoine, author and historian. Documents. Displays, including working models, demonstrating the fundamental principles of electrodynamics and electromagnetics. 18th-19th century apparatus showing the history of electricity.
Daily ex. Tu. 8-12, 2-7.

PONS

ARCHAEOLOGICAL MUSEUM
17800 Pons, Charente-Maritime
Prehistoric tools. Roman pottery, jewellery, amphorae. Medieval exhibits. Paintings by Barthélémy Gautier.
Daily 9.30-12, 3-6. Closed Sept.-June.

PONT-L'ABBÉ

BIGOUDEN MUSEUM
Château des Barons du Pont, 29120 Pont-l'Abbé, Finistère
History and art of the Bigouden area. Maritime activities. Furniture. Local crafts. Costumes. Embroidery.
June 15 - Sept. 15, Daily except Su. 9-12, 2-7.

PONT-AUDEMER

CANEL MUSEUM
64 place de la République, 27500 Pont-Audemer, Eure
Prehistory. Paintings. Drawings. Sculpture. Entomological collection.
Su. 9.30-12; Th. 2-5.

PONT-AVEN

PONT-AVEN MUSEUM
à la Mairie, 29123 Pont-Aven, Finistère
Paintings by artists of the School of Pont-Aven.
June 15 - Sept. 15, Daily 9.30-12, 2-5.

PONTÉCOULANT

CHÂTEAU DE PONTÉCOULANT MUSEUM
au Château, Pontécoulant, 14110 Condé sur Noireau, Calvados
Collections of furniture.
Daily ex. M. 10-12, 2-5.

PONT-DE-VAUX

CHINTREUIL MUSEUM
01190 Pont-de-Vaux, Ain
Gallo-Roman archaeology. 16th-18th century paintings. Local history. Folklore. Costumes. Ceramics. Wrought-iron.
On request.

PONTOISE LES NOYON

TAVET-DELACOUR MUSEUM
4 rue Lemercier, Pontoise les Noyon, 60400 Noyon, Oise
16th 20th century paintings. 13th-16th century sculpture. Drawings. Regional history.
Daily except Tu. 10-12, 2-6. Closed Jan. 1, May 1 and Dec. 25.

PORT-LOUIS

MARITIME MUSEUM
Tour de Vauban, 56290 Port-Louis, Morbihan
Maritime history from the 16th century to the present day.
May-Sept. Daily 10-7. Oct.-Apr. Th., Sa., Su. and public holidays, 2-6. Closed Nov. 15 - Dec. 15 and Jan. 15 - Feb. 15.

PORT-ROYAL DES CHAMPS

LOCAL MUSEUM
Port-Royal des Champs, Yvelines
Museum in the ruins of the ancient abbey of Port-Royal des Champs. Relics and documents relating to the history of the monastery.
Daily except Tu.

PROVINS

TITHE-BARN MUSEUM
4 rue Saint Jean, 77160 Provins, Seine-et-Marne
Prehistory. Gallo-Roman archaeology. Wooden and stone sculpture of the Middle Ages and the Renaissance. Medieval pottery.
Summer: Daily 9-12, 2-6. Winter: Weekdays 2-5; Su. 9-12.

LE PUY-EN-VELAY

CATHEDRAL OF NOTRE DAME TREASURY
43000 Le Puy-en-Velay, Haute-Loire
Collection of relics and ornaments, including the Carolingian Bible of Theodulphus, written on purple vellum and white parchment. The Chapel of Relics is decorated with a fresco of the Liberal Arts (late 15th century).
On request.

CROZATIER MUSEUM
Jardin Henri-Vinay, 43000 Le Puy-en-Velay, Haute-Loire
History and art of Velay. Collections of local mineralogy, petrography, palaeontology, prehistory. Roman, Carolingian, Romanic and Gothic material. Local crafts and arts, including lace and gold and silver work. Local sculptures and paintings. Paintings. Primitives. Collection of working machinery.
Daily except Tu. and Feb. 10-12, 2-4 (2-6 in summer).

QUIMPER

BRITTANY MUSEUM
Rue du Roi-Gradion, 29000 Quimper, Finistère
History, archaeology and ethnography. 16th century tomb of Troilus de Mondragon. Carved wooden facade of a Quimper house of the 15th century. 16th-18th century chests; Breton saints in wood and stone. Furniture from Cornouailles. Breton costumes. Faience from Quimper.
Nov.-Mar. Daily 10-12, 2-4. Open until 5 Apr.-Oct. and until 6 July-Sept. 15. Closed Tu. July-Sept. 15.

MUSEUM OF FINE ART
Hôtel de Ville, Place Saint-Corentin, 29000 Quimper, Finistère
Paintings, including works by Rubens, Fragonard, Greuze, Lancret, Boucher, Corot, Boudin. Paintings of the Pont-Aven school. Works by Max Jacob, born at Quimper.
Nov.-Mar., daily 10-12, 2-4. Open till 5, Apr.-Oct. and till 6, July-Sept. 15. Closed Tu., July-Sept. 15.

RAMBOUILLET

CHÂTEAU DE RAMBOUILLET
78120 Rambouillet, Yvelines
Furniture. Tapestries. Carvings.
Daily except Tu., in the absence of the President of the Republic, 11-12, 2-4 (Oct.-Mar.) and until 5, (Apr.-Sept.)

REMIREMONT

MUNICIPAL MUSEUM
70 Grand-Rue, 88200 Remiremont, Vosges
Ethnography of the Vosges. 17th-19th century paintings. Drawings.
Oct.-May, Daily except Tu. 10-12, 2-5. Open until 6 in June and Sept. and to 7 in July and Aug.

RENNES

AUTOMOBILE MUSEUM OF BRITTANY
Route de Fougeres, 35000 Rennes, Ille-et-Vilaine
Collection of motor cars.
Daily 9-12, 2-6.

BRITTANY MUSEUM
20 quai Emile-Zola, 35000 Rennes, Ille-et-Vilaine
Prehistory and early history. Models of megalithic monuments. Gallo-Roman Armorica. Romanesque architecture. 15th century Breton art. Brittany during the Ancien Regime. Furniture. Collections representing the period from 1789-1914, including costumes.
Daily except Tu. 10-12, 2-6.

MUSEUM OF ARCHAEOLOGY AND FINE ART
20 quai Emile-Zola, 35000 Rennes, Ille-et-Vilaine
Paintings, including works by Veronese, Tintoretto, Carragio, Rubens, Le Nain. Works by Impressionist painters and artists of the School of Pont - Aven-Gauguin, Bernard, Vlaminck, Dufy, Picasso, Rouault. Sculptures by Coysevox and Rodin. 15th-18th century drawings by Dürer, Leonardo, Rembrandt, Puget and Watteau. 17th-19th century French ceramics and Faience. Egyptian, Greek and Etruscan antiquities.
Daily except Tu. 10-12, 2-6.

RHEIMS

HALL OF SURRENDER
10 rue Franklin-Roosevelt, 51100 Rheims, Marne
Room, papered with operational maps of the end of the 1939-45 war, in which the Armistice was signed on May 7, 1945.
Daily ex. W. 10-12, 2-6.

OLD RHEIMS MUSEUM
36 place du Forum, 51100 Rheims, Marne
Iconography of the history of Rheims, and its monuments. Memorabilia of the coronations of the kings of France. Drawings by Albert Dürer.
Daily except W., 2-6.

SAINT-DENIS MUSEUM
9 rue Chanzy, 51100 Rheims, Marne
18th-19th century French paintings, including works by Corot, Delacroix, Millet, Boudin, Daumier, Renoir, Pissarro, Vuillard, Monet, Gauguin, Matisse, Dufy, Picasso, Poussin, David, Boucher. Portraits by Cranach. Series of paintings representing scenes from the Old and New Testaments (1460-1520). 13th century statues of musicians. French and foreign ceramics. 15th century tapestries.
Daily except Tu. 10-12, 2-6.

SAINT-RÉMI MUSEUM
53 rue Simon, 51100 Rheims, Marne
Archaeology. Collections cover the prehistory, Gallo-Roman, Barbarian and medieval periods.
Daily except Tu. 10-12, 2-6.

TREASURY
Cathedral, 51100 Rheims, Marne
Collection of sacerdotal ornaments and silverware which were used in the coronation ceremonies of the French kings.
On request.

RIBEAUVILLÉ

HOSPICE MUSEUM
41 Grand-Rue, Hôtel de Ville, 68150 Ribeauvillé, Haut-Rhin
Archaeology. Folklore. Jewellery. Paintings by Marcel Lenoir.
July-Sept. 15, Daily 10-11, 3-4. Rest of the year, apply to the Mairie.

RICHELIEU

MUSEUM OF THE 17th CENTURY
Mairie, 37120 Richelieu, Indre-et-Loire
Collections from the 17th century, particularly concerning Cardinal Richelieu and his family. Tapestries. Bust of the Cardinal by Warin. J.-M. de Heredia collection.
July 1 - Aug. 31, Daily 9-12, 2-5. Sa. before Easter - June 30, and Sept. 1-15, Daily except Tu. 9-12, 2-5. Nov. 16 - F. before Easter, 10-12, 2-4.

RIOM

AUVERGNE REGIONAL MUSEUM OF FOLKLORE
10b rue Delille, 63200 Riom, Puy-de-Dôme
Arts and popular traditions of the province of Auvergne. The collection is in an 18th century mansion.
Apr.-Sept. Daily except Tu. 10-12, 2-5.30. Oct.-Mar. Daily except M. and Tu., 10-12, 2-4.30.

JOAN OF ARC MUSEUM
Town Hall, 63200 Riom, Puy-de-Dôme
History of the town. Relics of Joan of Arc.
On request.

FRANCISQUE MANDET MUSEUM
Rue de l'Hôtel de Ville, 63200 Riom, Puy-de-Dôme
Paintings, including works by Franz Hals, Bruegel, Le Nain. Wood carvings.
Apr.-Sept. Daily except Tu. 10-12, 2-5.30. Oct.-Mar. Daily except M. and Tu. 10-12, 2-4.30.

RIQUEWIHR

MUSEUM OF HISTORY AND ARCHAEOLOGY
68340 Riquewihr, Haut-Rhin
Ethnography of Alsace. Torture chamber in the Tour des Voleurs. Weapons.
During vacations, Daily 8-12, 2-6.

REGIONAL POSTAL AND TELECOMMUNICATIONS MUSEUM
Château des Montbeliard-Wurtemberg, 68340 Riquewihr, Haut-Rhin
Collections illustrating the evolution of postal services and telecommunications in the north-east region. Material includes photographs, documents, uniforms and postage stamps. The coming of the railways. The Montgolfier balloon. The postal service during the two World Wars. Telegraphic and telephonic exhibits.
Apr.-Oct. Daily including Su. and public holidays, 10-12, 2-6. Nov.-Mar. on application.

ROANNE

JOSEPH DECHELETTE MUSEUM
Ancien Hôtel Valence de la Minardière, 42300 Roanne, Loire
Prehistory. Rock carvings; Egyptian, Celtic and Gallo-Roman antiquities found locally. Medieval and Renaissance sculpture. Carved wooden panels. 15th-20th century paintings. Scandinavian and Spanish primitives. Oriental, European and local ceramics. Faience from Roanne. 16th-19th century furniture.
Daily except Tu. and public holidays, 10-12, 2-5.

ROCHECHOUART

A. ET P. MASFRAND MUNICIPAL MUSEUM
Château, 87600 Rochechouart, Haute-Vienne
Prehistory. Gallo-Roman archaeology. Ceramics. Mural paintings of the beginning of the 16th century.
Mar.-Nov. 15, Sa., Su. and public holidays, 10-12, 2-6. Outside these hours, apply to the curator.

ROCHECORBON

ESPELOSIN MUSEUM
Château des Basses-Rivières, Rochecorbon, 37210 Vouvray, Indre-et-Loire
Wine and wine production. Paintings and other works of art relating to wine. Wallpaper depicting vineyard landscapes. In the cellars, built into the rock, wine-presses, replica of ancient treading vat, collection of barrels and bottles.
Daily except Tu. and the day after public holidays, 9-12, 2-5 (winter), 2-6 (summer). Closed during Dec.

ROCHEFORT

MUSEUM OF FINE ART
63 rue de l'Arsenal, 17300 Rochefort, Charente-Maritime
Paintings of the Italian, French and Flemish Schools. Drawings by Rubens. Far Eastern objets d'art. Items from New Zealand, Oceania. Local history.
Mar.-Oct. Daily 1.30-5.30. Nov.-Feb. Daily 1.30-4.30. Closed mornings except M. 10-12.

NAVAL MUSEUM
Place de la Galissonnière, 17300 Rochefort, Charente-Maritime
Models of ships built at Rochefort. The oldest, the "Louis le Grand" and "Royal" date from the reign of Louis XIV. Wood carvings from ships of the 17th, 18th and up to mid-19th centuries, including prows, caryatids and surrounds of portholes. Allegorical figures, eagles, winged monsters, mythological and official heads.
By appointment.

LA ROCHELLE

LAFAILLE AND FLEURIAU MUSEUM
28 rue Albert Ier, 17000 La Rochelle, Charente-Maritime
Ethnography. Natural sciences. Collection of Negro art. Objects from Oceania, Easter Island. Prehistory.
Daily except M. 10-12, 2-5. Closed Su. morning.

MUSEUM OF FINE ART
Rue Gargolleau, 17000 La Rochelle, Charente-Maritime
Paintings, ranging from primitives to the present day, including 19th century landscapes by Corot. Glass. Paintings and drawings by Marinot. Copies of busts by Despiau.
Daily except Tu. and Su. morning, 10-12, 2-4 (6 in summer).

ORBIGNY MUSEUM
2 rue Saint-Côme, 17000 La Rochelle, Charente-Maritime
Local and regional history. Historical documents, notably those relating to the siege of La Rochelle. 18th century faience. Rochelle plates. Display showing one hundred years of pharmaceutical jars. Archaeology.
Daily except Tu. and Su. morning, 10-12, 2-5 (6 in summer).

PROTESTANT MUSEUM
Rue Saint-Michel, 17000 La Rochelle, Charente-Maritime
Documents relating to the history of Protestantism in the region at Aunis, Saintonge and Poitou.
Daily except Su., on request.

LA ROCHE-SUR-YON

MUSEUM OF ART AND ARCHAEOLOGY
Rue Jean-Jaurès, 85000 La Roche-sur-Yon, Vendée
Prehistory. Gallo-Roman collection. Paintings and sketches by local artists.
Tu.-Sa. 2-5. Closed public holidays.

LA ROCHE-TAILLÉE

AUTOMOBILE MUSEUM
Château, La Roche-Taillée, 69270 Fontaines sur Saône, Rhône
Collection of cars, cycles and motor-cycles.
Daily 9-12, 2-6.

RODEZ

FÉNAILLE MUSEUM
Rue Saint-Just, 12000 Rodez, Aveyron
Prehistoric art, especially menhirs. Collections of Gallo-Roman ceramics from Graufesenque.
Daily except Su. and M. 2-6 from July-Oct. and during Easter holidays.

MUSEUM OF FINE ART
Terrasse du Point de vue Sainte-Catherine, 12000 Rodez, Aveyron
17th century Italian and Flemish paintings. Architectural drawings. Contemporary works by Vlaminck, Picabia, Limouse, Desnoyer, Rohner, Humblot. Sculptures by Denys Puesch and his friends, Despiau, Bouret, Gimond, Volti and Poisson.
Every afternoon, on request.

ROMANÈCHE-THORINS

GUILLON MUSEUM
71720 Romanèche-Thorins, Saône-et-Loire
The museum houses the works of Pierre François Guillon.
Su. and public holidays.

BENOÎT RACLET MUSEUM
71720 Romanèche-Thorins, Saône-et-Loire
Material relating to Benoît Raclet and to his work in safeguarding vines against disease. Implements used in the cultivation of vines.
On request.

ROMANS-SUR-ISÈRE

REGIONAL MUSEUM AND INTERNATIONAL MUSEUM OF FOOTWEAR
5-7 côte de Chapelier, 26100 Romans-sur-Isère, Drôme
Local history and folklore. Four thousand years of footwear.
Daily except M. 10-12, 3-6.

ROMENAY-EN-BRESSE

MUSEUM OF BRESSAN FOLKLORE
à la Mairie, Romenay-en-Bresse, 71470 Montpont-en-Bresse, Saône-et-Loire
Archaeology. Local folklore. Costume collection.
Daily, on request.

ROMORANTIN-LANTHENAY

SOLOGNE MUSEUM
Hôtel de Ville, 41200 Romorantin-Lanthenay, Loir-et-Cher
Local folklore and ethnography.
Daily except Tu. 10-12, 2-6. Dec. 1 - Feb. 28. closed on Su. and public holidays.

ROQUEBRUNE-CAP-MARTIN

CHÂTEAU DE ROQUEBRUNE
06190 Roquebrune-Cap-Martin, Cap-Martin, Alpes-Maritimes
History of Roquebrune district. Medieval and Renaissance furniture, armour, weapons and domestic equipment. Folklore.
Daily 9-12, 2-5.

ROUEN

CORNEILLE MUSEUM
4 rue de la Pie, 76000 Rouen, Seine-Maritime
Birthplace of Pierre Corneille. Collection of books and engravings.
Daily except Tu., W. morning and public holidays, 10-12, 2-6. Closed Jan. and Nov. (the three last Fridays) and the first two Fridays in Dec.

FLAUBERT MUSEUM
51 rue Lecat, 76000 Rouen, Seine-Maritime
Birthplace of Gustave Flaubert, containing memorabilia of the writer. History. Medicine.
Daily except Tu. and W. morning, 10-12, 2-6.

MUSEUM OF ANTIQUITIES OF THE DEPARTMENT OF THE SEINE MARITIME
198 rue Beauvoisine, 76000 Rouen, Seine-Maritime
Gallic and Gallo-Roman sarcophagi, bronzes, glassware, ceramics. Merovingian mosaics. Viking jewellery and weapons. Pottery. Ivories. Enamel-ware. Gold and silver. Alabaster. Wood carvings. Tapestries. Stained-glass. Egyptian, oriental, Greek and Etruscan antiquities. Italian and Spanish-Moorish ceramics.
Daily except W. and public holidays, 10-12, 2-5.

MUSEUM OF FINE ARTS AND CERAMICS
Square Verdrel, 76000 Rouen, Seine-Maritime
Paintings, including works by Gérard David, Rubens, Veronese, Caravaggio and Guardi. Works of the French School - Poussin, Fragonard, Lancret, Delacroix, Ingres, Corot. Impressionists - Monet, Sisley and Renoir. Sculpture, including works by Pierre Puget.
Oct. 15 - Apr. 15, daily ex. Tu. and W. morning, 10-12, 2-4.30. Open until 6, Apr. 16 - Oct. 14.

MUSEUM OF NATURAL HISTORY, ETHNOGRAPHY AND PREHISTORY
Square André Maurois, 76000 Rouen, Seine-Maritime
Collections of natural history, ethnography and prehistory.
W.-Su. 10-12, 2-6 (2-4 in winter). Closed M. and Tu.

LE SECQ DES TOURNELLES MUSEUM
Rue de la Bibliothèque, 76000 Rouen, Seine-Maritime
Wrought-ironwork, including medieval gates, signs, lecterns, banisters of staircases, door knockers, keys and locks, tools.
Daily except Tu. and W. morning, 10-12, 2-4 (until 6 in summer).

RUEIL-MALMAISON

CHÂTEAU DE BOIS-PRÉAU
92500 Rueil-Malmaison, Hauts-de-Seine
The salon of the king of Rome. Memorabilia of the Empress Marie-Louise, of the son of the Emperor and of the Napoleonic legend.
Daily except Tu. 10-12, 1.30-4.30 (to 5.30 in summer). Closed Jan. 1, May 1, July 14, Nov. 1 and 11, Dec. 25.

MALMAISON NATIONAL CHÂTEAU
92500 Rueil-Malmaison, Hauts-de-Seine
Art and history of the Napoleonic period in France. The rooms include the Emperor's study, the Council room, dining room, the 'gilded salon', music gallery, the Empress's bedroom, with furniture, hangings, musical instruments, art and domestic objects and carpets from Imperial residences which have since vanished (Tuileries, Saint-Cloud). Paintings, sculptures and drawings representing the Emperor, the Empress, the members of their families and of their entourage, or of events which interested them, as well as documents and manuscripts. This was Bonaparte's favourite residence (1800-1809) and the place where the Empress Josephine stayed after her divorce. She died here in 1814.
Daily except Tu. 10-12, 1.30-4.30 (to 5.30 in summer). Closed Jan. 1, May 1, July 14, Nov. 1 and 11, Dec. 25.

RUMILLY

CHÂTEAU DE CLERMONT-EN-GENEVOIS
74150 Rumilly, Haute-Savoie
Religious ornaments and paintings. Furniture. Wood carvings. Church plate.
July and Aug. Su. 2-6.

MUNICIPAL MUSEUM
Rue d'Hauteville, 74150 Rumilly, Haute-Savoie
Local and regional collections. Pottery. Costumes. Coins, drawings, plans, furniture, weapons.
July, Aug. and Sept. Daily 5-7.30 p.m.

LES SABLES D'OLONNE

MUNICIPAL MUSEUM
Rue de Verdun, 85100 Les Sables d'Olonne, Vendée
Prehistory. Headdresses and costumes. Tools and furnishings. Paintings.
Daily except Tu. Sa. before Easter - Sept. 30, 10-11.30, 2.30-6. Nov. 1 - F. before Easter, 2.30-5. Closed Jan. 1, May 1, 20, July 14, Aug. 15, Nov. 1, 11, Dec. 12 and Oct. 1-31.

SACHÉ

BALZAC MUSEUM
Château de Saché, Saché, 37190 Azay le Rideau, Indre-et-Loire
Saché is the setting Balzac used for *Lys dans la Vallée*. The author's apartments are intact, and he wrote a large part of *la Comédie Humaine* here. First editions, manuscripts, portraits. Material relating to Romantic period.
Mar. 15 - Oct. 14, Daily 9-12, 2-6.45. Oct. 15 - Nov. 30 and Jan. 1 - Mar. 14, Daily 9-11.45, 2-4.45. Closed Dec.

SAINT-AMAND-LES-EAUX

CARILLON MUSEUM
Grand-Place
59230 Saint-Amand-Les-Eaux, Nord
Thirty-eight carillon bells dating from 1784. Collection of faience and porcelain from Saint-Amand. Regional archaeology.
Daily except Tu. 9-12, 2-5.

SAINT-AMAND-MONTROND

SAINT VIC MUSEUM
Cours Manuel, 18200 Saint-Amand-Montrond, Cher
Paintings. French 18th century drawings. Regional folklore and popular art. Regional archaeology.
June - Sept. Daily except M. 10-12, 3-7. Oct. - May Th., Sa., Su. 2-5.

SAINT-AMARIN

SERRET MUSEUM
33 Grande Rue, 68550 Saint-Amarin, Haut Rhin
Collections describing the First World War especially fighting in the Vosges. Textiles, weaving frames and fabric printing. Local history, including the glass trade in Wildenstein (1699-1880). Religious art. 16th-19th century sculpture.
May-Sept. Su. 2-6.

SAINT-ANTONIN-NOBLE-VAL

MUSEUM OF PREHISTORY, ARCHAEOLOGY AND ETHNOGRAPHY
Hôtel de Ville, 82140 Saint-Antonin-Noble-Val, Tarn-et-Garonne
Prehistory. Palaeontology. Entomology. Local folklore. Archaeology.
On request.

SAINT AUBIN-DE-LOCQUENAY

ART GALLERY
Mairie de Fresnay, Saint Aubin-de-Locquenay, 72130 Fresnay sur Sarthe, Sarthe
Wood carvings and sculpture.
Su., public holidays, 9-12, 2-7.

SAINT-BERTRAND-DE-COMMINGES

COMMINGES MUSEUM
Saint-Bertrand-de-Comminges, 31510 Barbazan, Haute-Garonne
The Roman town of Lugdunum Convenarum. Material excavated since 1919 includes mosaics, sculptures and trophies.
Daily 8-6.

SAINT BRIEUC

HÔTEL DE VILLE MUSEUM
Place du Général de Gaulle, 22000 St. Brieuc, Côtes du Nord
Collection of ethnographical material. Tombstones. Polychrome statues, in particular that of St. Giles of Brittany (15th century). Paintings. Local history.
Daily on request.

SAINT-CANNAT

SUFFREN MUSEUM
Mairie, 13760 Saint-Cannat, Bouches-du-Rhône
Portraits of the Bailiffs of Suffren. Local history and folklore.
First Su. in each month, 10-12.

SAINT-CLAUDE

MUNICIPAL MUSEUM
2 place des Halles (first floor), 39200 Saint-Claude, Jura
Paintings, including works by Auguste Lançon. Portrait of M. Bertin, founder of *Le Figaro*. Miniature of the tomb of Auguste Lançon, at Père la Chaise. Natural history section, including butterflies and mammals. Local history.
On request.

SAINT-CLOUD

MUSEUM OF LOCAL HISTORY
Mairie, 92210 Saint-Cloud, Hauts-de-Seine
Local history. Porcelain and faience from the Saint-Cloud factory. History of the Franco-Prussian War of 1870-1.
Tu. and Th., 2-3.30 and by appointment.

SAINT-CYR-AU-MONT-D'OR

NATIONAL POLICE MUSEUM
l'Ecole National de Police, 69450 Saint-Cyr-au-Mont-d'Or, Rhône
Historic documents and of photographs of famous criminals. Collections illustrating celebrated criminal cases.
On written application.

SAINT-CYR-SUR-MER

ARCHAEOLOGICAL MUSEUM
Ruines de Tauroentum, Route de la Madrague, 83270 Saint-Cyr-sur-Mer, Var
Greek and Roman archaeology, including vases and amphorae. Local ceramics.
Daily, including public holidays, 8-12, 2-6.

SAINT-DENIS

MUNICIPAL MUSEUM
4 place de la Légion-d'Honneur, 93200 Saint-Denis, Seine-Saint-Denis
Local art and history. Archaeology. Merovingian jewellery, Gallo-Roman and medieval pottery, sculpture. Collections from the old Hôtel-Dieu: apothecary's wares, furniture, 18th century wood carvings, ironwork. Local 19th century crafts: printing on cloth and glass. Memorabilia of Paul Eluard, including his workroom and many manuscripts, personal items and works of art which belonged to him. Paintings and drawings by Pissarro, Signac, Dufy, Léger, Pignon and Picasso.
Daily except Su. morning and Tu., 10-12, 2-6.

SAINT-DIÉ

LOCAL MUSEUM
Hôtel de Ville, 88100 Saint-Dié, Vosges
Memorabilia of Jules Ferry and his family. Collection of arms and uniforms from wars between France and Germany, 1800-1944.
On request.

SAINT-DIZIER

MUNICIPAL MUSEUM
52100 Saint-Dizier, Haute-Marne
Prehistory. Sculptures and antiquities from Carthage. Ethnography. Petrography. Mineralogy. Ornithology. Paintings.
M.-F. 9-12; Sa. 2-6.

SAINT-ÉMILION

ARCHAEOLOGICAL MUSEUM
33330 Saint-Émilion, Gironde
Prehistoric, Gallo-Roman and medieval archaeology. Local history and folklore. Archives from the Middle Ages to the Revolutionary period.
On request.

MUSEUM OF WINE
33330 Saint Émilion, Gironde
Exhibits include old wine receptacles, tools and implements, wooden ploughs and sulphators, wine storage, vatting and coopering instruments, agricultural implements. Collections of blown bottles, labels and tasting glasses.
Enquire locally.

SAINTES

ARCHAEOLOGICAL MUSEUM
1 rue Gautier, 17100 Saintes, Charente-Maritime
Gallo-Roman inscriptions and remains. Much of the material has been recovered from an old Gallo-Roman wall, the materials for which had been taken from the Roman town of Mediolanum Santonum. Collection of ceramics from prehistoric times to the present day.
On request.

DUPUY-MESTREAU MUSEUM
18 rue Monconseil, 17100 Saintes, Charente-Maritime
Regional folklore. Ceramics.
Summer: Daily except M. 2-6. Winter: on demand.

MUSEUM OF FINE ART
Ancien Présidial, Rue Victor-Hugo, 17100 Saintes, Charente-Maritime
Paintings include *L'Automne* by Bruegel; *Portrait de Vauban* by Rigaud, and works by Lesueur, Beerstraten, Wlerick and Jongkind. Ceramics; faiences from Saintonge, 11th century to the present day.
Daily except Su. and public holidays, 9-12, 2-6.

SAINTES-MARIES-DE-LA-MER

CAMARGUE MUSEUM
13460 Saintes-Maries-de-la-Mer, Bouches-du-Rhône
Local folklore. Roman archaeology. Birds. Views of the Camargue.
May-Sept. Daily 9-7. Oct.-Apr. Su. only, 9-7.

SAINTE-MARIE-DU-MONT-UTAH-BEACH

LOCAL MUSEUM
Sainte-Marie-du-Mont-Utah-Beach, Manche
Collections commemorating the Allied landings of 1944 at Utah-Beach.
Daily ex. M. 10-12, 2-5.

SAINTE-MÈRE-EGLISE

AIRBORNE TROOPS MUSEUM
50480 Sainte-Mère-Eglise, Manche
Collections commemorating the place where the first allied airborne troops were dropped on June 5, 1944.
Daily ex. M. 10-12, 2-5.

ST. ÉTIENNE

MUSEUM OF ART AND INDUSTRY
Place Louis Comte, 42000 St. Étienne, Loire
Sections representing the traditional industries of the town. Mine gallery, with models and tools. Weapons, including firearms dating from the 15th century. Cloth, ribbons and lace-making. Enamels and ceramics. Paintings and sculpture: Rubens, Boucher, Greuze, David, Gros, Monet, Rodin, Vuillard, Matisse, Picasso, Mondrian, Arp, Calder. Collages. Lyonnais artists from 18th century onwards: Pillement, Boissieu, Chinard, Ravier. Tapestries of Lurçat and Corbusier.
Daily except Tu., and W. morning, 10-12, 2-5.

FOLKLORE MUSEUM
13b rue Gambetta, 42000 St. Étienne, Loire
17th century woodwork and ironwork. Statues, 15th-18th centuries. Collections illustrating the industry of the town; cycles, ribbons, arms, coal-mining. Memorabilia of local personalities.
Tu. and Sa., 2-5. Closed Aug. and Sept.

SAINT ETIENNE LE MOLARD

BASTIE D'URFÉ MUSEUM
Château, Saint Etienne le Molard, 42130 Boën, Loire
Château in Italian Renaissance style. Period rooms. Aubusson tapestries and 17th century tapestries by the Ateliers de Bruges.
Daily 9-12, 2-6.

SAINT-FLOUR

HAUTE-AUVERGNE MUSEUM
Ancien Palais Épiscopal, 1 place d'Armes, 15 Saint-Flour, Haute-Auvergne
Housed in the former Archbishop's Palace. Religious art. Items from the cathedral of Saint-Flour. Art and traditions of the Haute-Auvergne area; paintings by Onslow and Charbonnel. Prehistoric and Gallo-Roman archaeology.
Daily 9-12, 2-6. Closed Sa. and Su. Oct.-May.

MUSEUM OF THE CONSULAR HOUSE ALFRED DOUET
Hôtel de Ville, Saint-Flour, Haute-Auvergne
Built in 1760 as a consular house. Period rooms. Aubusson tapestry (16th century). Powder boxes. Religious art. Paintings. Sculptures. Weapons.
Easter school holidays and May 1-Oct. 15, Daily 9-12, 2-7.

SAINT-GERMAIN-EN-LAYE

MUNICIPAL MUSEUM
Place Maurice-Berteaux, 78100 Saint-Germain-en-Laye, Yvelines
16th and 17th century Flemish and French paintings. Drawings. Local history. In the garden stands *Hommage à Claude Debussy* by Maillol.
Daily except Tu. 2-7; Su. 10-12.

MUSEUM OF NATIONAL ANTIQUITIES
Château de Saint-Germain, 78100 Saint-Germain-en-Laye, Yvelines
The museum is concerned with the history of France from the beginning to the year 800. Prehistory. Cut and polished stone. Bone tools. Palaeolithic objets d'art. Items from the Bronze and Iron Ages. Weapons, jewellery, and tombs of the Gallo-Roman period, and of the Barbarian and Merovingian periods. Bronze scythes. Benin bronzes.
Daily except Tu. 9.45-5.

ST. GERMAIN LAVAL

MUNICIPAL MUSEUM
Mairie, 42260 St. Germain Laval, Loire
Tapestries. Louis XV furniture. Miniatures.
Apr.-Nov. Daily on request.

ST. GERMAIN RIMOUSKI

RIMOUSKI REGIONAL MUSEUM
35 Ouest, St. Germain Rimouski, G5L 4B4
In restored church (1824). European art. Wooden sculptures. Silversmiths' work.
Winter: daily 2-6; F.-M. also 7-10 p.m. Summer: M.-F. 10-10; Sa., Su. 2-10.

ST. GILLES DU GARD

ARCHAEOLOGICAL MUSEUM
Maison romaine, 30800 St. Gilles du Gard, Gard
Fragments of ancient architecture. Collection of birds from the Camargue and of species which are extinct.
Daily on request.

SAINT-GUÉNOLÉ-PENMARCH

FINISTÈRE MUSEUM OF PREHISTORY
Université de Rennes Faculté des Sciences, 29131 Saint-Guénolé-Penmarch, Finistère
Museum devoted to the prehistoric and protohistoric antiquities found in the Finistère region.
Apr.-Sept. 10-12, 2-6. Oct.-Mar. on request.

SAINT-JEAN-CAP-FERRAT

EPHRUSSI DE ROTHSCHILD FOUNDATION
Musée Ile de France, 06290 Saint-Jean-Cap-Ferrat, Alpes-Maritimes
Varied collection, specialising in the 18th century. Beauvais and Aubusson tapestries. Furniture. Paintings by Boucher, Fragonard, Vincennes, Sèvres and Saxe porcelain. Far Eastern objets d'art. Impressionist paintings, especially by Monet, Renoir and Sisley.
Sept.-June: Daily except Tu. 2-6. July-Aug. Daily except M. 3-7.

ST. JEAN D'ANGELY

MUSEUM OF THE ARCHAEOLOGICAL SOCIETY
Hôtel d'Hausen, 17400 St. Jean d'Angely, Charente-Maritime
Weapons from many different periods and countries. Naval mementoes. Local history. Regional iconography.
Th. and Su. afternoons, including public holidays. Other days on request.

SAINT-JEAN-DE-LUZ

HOUSE OF MEMORIES
Parc Ducontenia, 64500 Saint-Jean-de-Luz, Pyrénées-Atlantiques
History of Saint-Jean-de-Luz and of life in the Basque country. Furniture. Prints.
Daily on request.

SAINT-JULIEN-EN-BEAUJOLAIS

CLAUDE BERNARD MUSEUM
Hameau de Chatenay, Saint-Julien-en-Beaujolais, 69640 Denicé, Rhône
Manuscripts, diplomas and laboratory equipment of the physiologist, Claude Bernard.
Daily on request.

SAINT LAURENT DE LA PLAINE

MUSEUM OF THE OLD TRADES OF ANJOU
Salle Saint-Laurent, Saint Laurent de la Plaine, 49290 Chalonnes sur Loire, Maine-et-Loire
Collection of tools and equipment of old-established trades. From the Cognac region: two old 18th century stills and other equipment. Tarn: copper-working tools, including a tilt-hammer operated by water-power. Normandy: two old cider mills (one stone, one wooden). Oise: button-maker's tools and samples of his work. Many examples of workmanship from the Anjou region, including material on miners, stone masons, carpenters. Old corn mills and windmills. Lace. Embroidery. Church ornaments.
July-Oct. Su. 10-7; Sa. 2-7. Weekdays by appointment.

SAINT-LÔ

SAINT-LÔ MUSEUM
Hôtel de Ville, 50000 Saint-Lô, Manche
Tapestry (16th century Bruges), in eight pieces, called *Les Amours de Gombaut et de Macée.* Paintings by Corot. Drawings. Miniatures by Daniel Saint, a local artist.
July-Sept. 15, Daily except Su. Sept. 16-June 30, Daily except M. and F.

SAINT-MALO

INTERNATIONAL MUSEUM OF THE CAPE HORN ROUTE
Tour Solidor, Saint-Servan, 35400 Saint-Malo, Ille-et-Vilaine
History of voyages round the world since Henry the Navigator. History of the big ships of the member countries of the Association of Captains of the Cape Horn Route. Manuscripts, cards, printed material, models, paintings and other material illustrating round-the-world voyages.
Apr.-Oct. Daily 10-12, 2-6.30. Guided tours from 2-4 in winter.

QUIC-EN-GROIGNE GALLERY
Château, 35400 Saint-Malo, Ille-et-Vilaine
History of Saint-Malo and its famous men, illustrated by interiors and dioramas. Wax images of persons of note.
Pentecost-Sept. 15, Daily 9-12, 2-6.

SAINT-MALO MUSEUM
Château, 35400 Saint-Malo, Ille-et-Vilaine
History of Saint-Malo from its origins to the present day. Privateering, deep-sea fishing and naval construction are all illustrated. Local personalities, including Jacques Cartier, Duguay-Trouin, Surcouf, Chateaubriand and Lamennais.
Apr.-Oct. Daily 10-12, 2-6.30. Guided tours from 2-5 during the other months.

SAINT-MARTIN-DE-RÉ

ERNEST COGNACQ MUSEUM
Place de la République, 17410 Saint-Martin-de-Ré, Charente-Maritime
Prehistory. Local history. Faience. Coins. Sea-charts. Natural history. Weapons.
On request.

MARITIME MUSEUM
Hôtel de Clerjotte, 17410 Saint-Martin-de-Ré, Charente-Maritime
History of the sea and shipping from the 16th century to the present day.
May-Sept. Daily 10-1, 3-7. Oct.-Apr. Th., Sa., Su. and public holidays, 2-6. Closed Nov. 15-Dec. 15 and Jan. 15-Feb. 15.

SAINT-MAUR-DES-FOSSÉS

MUNICIPAL MUSEUM
23 avenue Henri-Martin, Saint-Maur-des-Fossés, Val-de-Marne
Prehistoric and Gallo-Roman archaeology. 9th and 13th century fragments of inscriptions. Contemporary paintings.
M., Th., Sa. 2-5 (2-4 in winter).

SAINT-MIHIEL

LIGIER RICHIER MUSEUM
Bibliothèque Municipale, 55300 Saint-Mihiel, Meuse
Casts of sculpture by Ligier Richier. Prehistoric collection.
On request.

SAINT-OMER

HENRI DUPUIS MUSEUM
9 rue Henri-Dupuis, 62500 Saint-Omer, Pas-de-Calais
Natural history. Collection of European and exotic birds (humming birds, birds of paradise). Shells. Fossils. Mineralogy. Ethnography. Faience. Reconstruction of a Flemish kitchen.
Daily except Tu. 10-12, 2-6. Closed Jan.

HÔTEL SANDELIN MUSEUM
14 rue Carnot, 62500 Saint-Omer, Pas-de-Calais
Wood carvings. Furniture. Flemish and German primitive paintings. 17th century Flemish and Dutch paintings. French paintings of 18th century: Lépicié, Greuze, Nattier, Boilly, Fragonard, Girodet, Prud'hon. 20th century German paintings. Ceramics. Porcelain. 12th-16th century objets d'art. Greek, Roman, Gallo-Roman and medieval archaeology. Weapons.
Daily ex. Tu. 10-12, 2-5.

SAINT-PAUL-DE-VENCE

MAEGHT FOUNDATION
06570 Saint-Paul-de-Vence, Alpes-Maritimes
Architecture. Mosaics by Chagall and Tal Coat, sculptures and ceramics by Miró. Sculpture by Calder, Giacometti, Hepworth. 20th century paintings, including works by Braque, Chagall, Kandinsky, Miró, Giacometti, Bonnard, Dérain, Léger.
June-Sept. Daily 10-12.30, 3-7. Oct.-May Daily 10-12.30, 2.30-6.

SAINT-PAULIEN

MUSEUM OF ANTIQUITIES
École de Filles, 43350 Saint-Paulien, Haute-Loire
Large fragments of mosaics, stèles, Romanesque columns. Gallo-Roman utensils. Pottery. Funerary urns.
On request.

SAINT-PÈRE

REGIONAL ARCHAEOLOGICAL MUSEUM
Depôt Archéologique, Saint-Père, 89450 Vézelay, Yonne
Roman, Merovingian archaeology. Sculptures from the Gothic church of Saint-Père.
Daily 9-12, 2-7.

SAINT-PIERRE-DE-CHARTREUSE

LA CORRERIE CHARTERHOUSE MUSEUM
Saint-Pierre-de-Chartreuse, 38380 St. Laurent du Pont, Isère
History and development of the monastery. Life of Saint Bruno. 15th century triptych.
Su. before Easter to Nov. 2, Daily 9-12, 2-6.30. Su. and public holidays 10-12, 2-6.30. Apr. and Oct. 9-12, 2-6.

ST. PIERRE D'OLÉRON

ALIENOR D'AQUITAINE MUSEUM
25 rue Pierre-Loti, 17310 St. Pierre d'Oléron, Charente-Maritime
Room devoted to Pierre Loti, whose family came from Oléron. Collection of costumes and headdresses. Local industries and handicrafts, including agriculture, wine-production, salt, with model of a salt marsh.
June 1 - Sept. 15, Daily ex. Su. morning, 10-12, 2.30-4.30.

SAINT-POINT

CHÂTEAU
Saint-Point, 71630 Tramayes, Saône-et-Loire
Partly medieval château, remodelled in the mid-19th century. Lamartine's study and private room.
Daily 9-12, 2-6. Closed Su. morning.

SAINT-QUENTIN

CHILDREN'S MUSEUM
École de la Tour, 02100 Saint-Quentin, Aisne
Displays, grouped according to period, of objects of interest to children.
Th. and Su. 2.30-5. In the week open on request 8 days in advance.

A. LÉCUYER MUSEUM
Rue Antoine-Lécuyer, 02100 Saint-Quentin, Aisne
Paintings by Maurice Quentin de La Tour, including a self-portrait, and portraits of Mlle. Fels, Rousseau, Alembert, Marshal de Saxe, the Marquis d'Argenson, the Queen, the Dauphin, Mme. de Pompadour, the King. 18th century ceramics, ivories, enamels and faience.
Daily except M. 10-12, 2-5. Closed Jan. 1 and July 14.

SAINT-RAMBERT-SUR-LOIRE

SAINT-RAMBERT-SUR-LOIRE MUSEUM
Ancien Prieuré, 42170 Saint-Rambert-sur-Loire, Loire
11th century liturgical items. Anthropological collections. Regional history. Prehistoric, Gallic and Gallo-Roman archaeology. Displays illustrating water transport of the Loire.
Mar.-Nov. Th., Sa., Su. and public holidays, 2.30-6.30.

SAINT-RAPHAEL

MUSEUM OF UNDER-WATER ARCHAEOLOGY
Place de la Vieille Église, 83700 Saint-Raphael, Var
Collection of archaeological remains found off the coast and dating from 4th century B.C. to 5th century A.D. Amphorae material from shipwrecks, fragments of anchors.
Summer: Daily ex. M. 10-12, 3-7; Sa. and Su. also 8-10 p.m. Winter: Daily ex. M. 2-5.

SAINT-RÉMY-DE-PROVENCE

ARCHAEOLOGICAL CENTRE
Hôtel de Sade, Rue du Parage, 13210 Saint-Rémy-de-Provence, Bouches-du-Rhône
Objects from the ancient Greek city, then the Roman city of Glanum. Funerary furniture. Pre-Roman sculpture.
Mar.-Oct. Daily including public holidays, 9-12, 2-6. Nov.-Apr. on request.

PIERRE DE BRUN MUSEUM OF PROVENÇAL FOLKLORE
Lou, Planet, place Favier, 13210 Saint-Rémy-de-Provence, Bouches-du-Rhône
Local iconography, and sculpture. Geology.
Mar.-Oct. Daily including public holidays, 9-12, 2-6. Nov.-Apr. On request.

SAINT-SAUVEUR-LE-VICOMTE

BARBEY-D'AUREVILLY MUSEUM
au Château, 50390 Saint-Sauveur-le-Vicomte, Manche
Dedicated to the memory of the writer, Jules Barbey d'Aurevilly (d.1889), and containing his personal possessions and manuscripts, including the original copy of *Disjecta Membra.* Archives and documents.
Nov.-Mar. Daily 10-12, 2-5. Mar. 2-Oct. 31, Daily 9.30-12, 2-6. Apply to the caretaker.

SAINT-SAVIN-SUR-GARTEMPE

ABBEY CHURCH
86310 Saint-Savin-sur-Gartempe, Vienne
11th and 13th century frescoes.
Daily.

LOCAL MUSEUM
Capitular Room of the Abbey, 86310 Saint-Savin-sur-Gartempe, Vienne
Medieval sculptures, statues of the Virgin. Shrines and reliquaries.
Daily 9-12, 1-6.

SAINT-SEVER

MUNICIPAL MUSEUM
Hôtel de Ville, Saint-Sever, Landes
Gallo-Roman cornices. Sculpture. Paintings.
Tu.-Sa. 9-12, 2-5.30. On request.

SAINT-SYMPHORIEN-SUR-COISE

COLIN MUSEUM
La Neylière, 69590 Saint-Symphorien-sur-Coise, Rhône
Dedicated to Père Jean-Claude Colin (1790-1875), founder of the Maristes, who spent his last years here. Collections illustrate his life and work. Missionary activity.
May 1 - Sept. 15, Daily 9-12, 2-6. Remainder of the year, Sa. and Su. afternoons.

LA NEYLIÈRE OCEANIC MUSEUM
La Neylière, 69590 Saint-Symphorien-sur-Coise, Rhône
Contains collection of objects from Oceania brought back by Mariste missionaries in the 19th century. Material from New Caledonia, the Hebrides, Solomon Islands, Wallis Islands, Samoa and Fiji. Introduction of Christian culture. Models and documents illustrating the voyages of the missionaries.
May 1 - Sept. 15, Daily 10-12, 2-6. Remainder of the year, Sa. afternoons and Su. all day.

SAINT-TROPEZ

MARITIME MUSEUM
à la Citadelle, 83990 Saint-Tropez, Var
History of the sea and shipping from 16th century to the present day.
Daily 10-6.

MUSEUM OF THE ANNUNCIATION
Place Georges-Grammont, 83990 Saint-Tropez, Var
Modern paintings, including works by Seurat, Vlaminck, Derain, Marquet, Rouault, Matisse, Bonnard, Vuillard, Signac, Dunoyer de Segonzac, Braque, Friesz and Manguin. Sculptures by Maillol and Despiau.
Daily except Tu. 10-12, 2-6 (3-7 June-Sept.). Closed Nov.

SAINT VINCENT-SUR-JARD

PRESIDENT CLEMENCEAU HOUSE-MUSEUM
Saint Vincent-sur-Jard, 85520 Jard sur Mer, Vendée
Clemenceau's house, as it was at his death.
Su. before Easter - Oct. 15, Daily 9-12, 2-6. Oct. 16 - Sa. before Easter, Daily except Tu. 9-12, 2-6.

SALINS-LES-BAINS

HOSPITAL
39110 Salins-les-Bains, Jura
The pharmacy laboratory contains faience from Moustiers and wood carvings of the 17th century.
Daily in summer. Th. and Su. in winter.

SALON-DE-PROVENCE

L'EMPÉRI MUSEUM
Château, 13300 Salon-de-Provence, Bouches-du-Rhône
History of the French army from 1700-1918. Flags. Weapons. Uniforms. Equipment. Paintings. Drawings. Engravings. Decorations. Books. Manuscripts.
Daily except Tu. 10-12, 2.30-6.30, from Easter-mid. Nov.

SAMADET

MUSEUM OF FAIENCE
Château de l'Abbé Marquis de Roquépine, Baron de Samadet, 40340 Samadet, Landes
Collection of faience from the area. Folk-art and popular traditions. Interiors of bourgeois and peasant dwellings. Tools of trades which have now died out.
Daily 9-12, 2-7, including Su. and public holidays.

SARREBOURG

REGIONAL MUSEUM
Chapelle des Cordeliers, 57400 Sarrebourg, Moselle
Gallo-Roman and Merovingian archaeology. Collection of 14th century terra-cotta vases and figurines, of local workmanship.
Apr. 15 - Sept. 30. Daily except W. 11-12, 2-5; Su. 2-5.

SARS-POTERIES

GLASS MUSEUM
Château Imbert, 59216 Sars-Poteries, Nord
The exhibits, mostly 19th century, are objects made by glass-blowers in their leisure-time, and called 'bousillés'. These items were never sold, but were always given by the workers to their families and friends.
Sa. and Su. 2-7. Holiday periods (Summer, Easter, Christmas) Daily 2-7.

SAULGES

PREHISTORIC CAVE DWELLINGS AND ROCK-PAINTINGS
Saulges, 53340 Ballée, Mayenne
Two prehistoric caves, containing rock paintings, are open to the public and it is hoped to open a third.
Admission from hotel near entrance.

SAULIEU

FRANÇOIS POMPON MUSEUM
Place de la Fontaine, Saulieu, Côte-d'Or
Regional archaeology, including Gallo-Roman funerary steles. Religious art. Works of the animal painter and sculptor, Pompon. Rural crafts and folklore of Morvan. Gastronomy of Saulieu.
July-Sept. Daily except Su. 10-12, 2-6. Outside these hours, apply to the Mairie.

SAUMUR

CHURCH OF NOTRE DAME DE NANTILLY
49400 Saumur, Maine-et-Loire
15th-17th century tapestries, including the 15th century 'Dance of St. Anthony's Fire'.
Daily.

MUSEUM OF DECORATIVE ARTS AND MUSEUM OF THE HORSE
Château des ducs d'Anjou, 49400 Saumur, Maine-et-Loire
16th-18th century French faience and porcelain. 13th century Limoges enamels. French and foreign sculpture. 13th-18th centuries liturgical ornaments, tapestries, furniture. Local archaeology. History of the horse and of horsemanship; harness. English engravings of equine subjects.
July-Aug. Daily 9-7.30. Apr.-June and Sept. Daily 9-12, 2-6. Oct.-Mar. Daily except Tu. 10-12, 2-5. Late evening visits July-Aug.

SAVERNE

MUNICIPAL MUSEUM
Château (South Wing), 67700 Saverne, Bas-Rhin
Early and Gallo-Roman archaeology. Sculptures from 12th to 17th centuries. 18th century art. Alsace paintings of the 19th century. Regional ethnography.
May-Sept. Su. and public holidays, 10-12, 3-5. July and Aug. Daily except M. 3-5.

SCEAUX

ILE-DE-FRANCE MUSEUM
Château de Sceaux, 92330 Sceaux, Hauts-de-Seine
History and art of the Paris region. Prototype of an 1869 velocipede. Tapestries. Ceramics.
Winter: M., W., Th., F. 2-5. Summer: 2-6. Public holidays 10-12, 2-5 (winter); 10-12, 2-7 (summer).

SEDAN

SEDAN MUSEUM
Château Fort, 08200 Sedan, Ardennes
In 15th century military fort. Collection of Gallo-Roman archaeology. Souvenirs of the first World War. Objects excavated from the Château.
Easter-Sept. Daily 10-12, 2-5.

SÉLESTAT

TOWN MUSEUM
Halle aux Blés, Place Gambetta, 67600 Sélestat, Bas-Rhin
Prehistoric and Gallo-Roman antiquities. 15th century sculpture. Faiences.
Daily except Sa. afternoon, Su. and public holidays, 8-12, 2-6. Open on request for groups.

SEMUR-EN-AUXOIS

SEMUR MUSEUM
Rue Jean-Jacques Collenot, 21140 Semur-en-Auxois, Côte-d'Or
Paintings by Corot. Local archaeology: prehistoric, Gallic and Gallo-Roman. Geology and palaeontology. Medieval sculpture.
Th., Sa. and Su. 2-5 and on request at the Mairie.

SENLIS

HAUBERGIER MUSEUM
10 rue du Haubergier, 60300 Senlis, Oise
Regional archaeology: prehistoric, Gallic and Gallo-Roman. Collection of ex-votos from a temple in the forest of Halatte. Merovingian objects. Medieval sculpture. Regional history. Enamels. Drawings. Paintings.
Daily except Tu. 10-12, 2-6.

MUSEUM
Château Royal, 60300 Senlis, Oise
Hunting scenes by Desportes, Oudry, Paul de Vos. Sculpture. Hunting weapons, equipment.
Apr.-Sept. Daily except Tu. and W. morning, 10-12, 2-6 (2-5 Oct.-Mar.).

SENS

CATHEDRAL TREASURY
Place de la République, 89100 Sens, Yonne
Tapestries. Altar ornaments (15th century). Byzantine shrouds (7th-10th centuries); Vestments of St. Thomas Becket, Archbishop of Canterbury (12th century); and also of St. Edme, also Archbishop of Canterbury (13th century). Byzantine casket in ivory of the 10th century. Liturgical comb of St. Loup in ivory and silver (7th century). Enamels. Manuscripts.
Daily except Tu., Su. and feast days during services, 10-12, 2-6 (2-4 in winter).

JEAN COUSIN MUSEUM
8 rue Jean-Cousin, Sens, Yonne
Local history museum.
Apr.-Nov. Daily 1-5.

MUNICIPAL MUSEUM
5 rue Rigault, 89100 Sens, Yonne
Gallo-Roman archaeology. Mosaics. Local prehistory. Paintings of the Italian and French Schools of the 17th, 18th and 19th centuries.
Mar.-Oct. 1, Daily except Tu. 9-12, 2-6 (2-5 in winter). Closed May 1.

OFFICIALITÉ
89100 Sens, Yonne
Sculpture, some of which come from the Cathedral. Gallo-Roman mosaics; 16th century tapestry, *Judith and Holopherne*, which belonged to Thomas Wolsey, Chancellor of England.
Daily except Tu. 9-12, 2-6 (2-4 in winter).

SEPT-FONTAINES

SEPT-FONTAINES ABBEY MUSEUM
Sept-Fontaines, Haute-Marne
Faience. Sèvres porcelain. Furniture. Statuettes. Jewellery.
On request.

SÉRIGNAN-DU-COMTAT

HENRI FABRE MUSEUM
l'Harmas de J.-H. Fabre, Sérignan-du-Comtat, 84100 Orange, Vaucluse
Collections illustrating life and work of the naturalist, in his former home. 'Mushroom room'. Work-room.
Nov.-Mar. Daily except Tu. 9-11.30, 2-4 (2-6 Apr.-Sept.). Closed Oct.

SERRIÈRES

MUSEUM OF RHÔNE SHIPPING
Ancien Eglise Saint-Sornin, 07340 Serrières, Ardèche
The collections are slanted towards the activities of the bargemen, not of their boats. Navigational instruments and measuring instruments of the 18th and 19th centuries. Crosses which decorated the barges, and which were carried in procession on feast days. Décor of bargemen's homes on land (many of them were wine-growers). Boat-building.
Apr., May, June, Sept. 15-30, Oct. Sa., Su. and public holidays 2-6.30. July, Aug., Sept. 1-15, Sa., Su., M. and public holidays 2-6.30.

SESSENHEIM

GOETHE MEMORIAL
67770 Sessenheim, Bas-Rhin
Memorabilia of Goethe and of Frédérique Brion. Material illustrating the time Goethe spent in Alsace. Documents.
Daily Apr.-Sept. 9-12, 2-7.

SÈTE

PAUL VALÉRY MUNICIPAL MUSEUM
34200 Sète, Hérault
19th and 20th century paintings. Memorabilia of Paul Valéry, including drawings, watercolours, letters and manuscript of *Le Cimetière Marin*. Collection relating to naval battles.
Daily except Tu. 10-12, 2-4 (2-5 in summer).

SEUILLY-LA-DEVINIÈRE

RABELAIS MUSEUM
La Devinière, Seuilly-la-Devinière, 37500 Chinon, Indre-et-Loire
François Rabelais' farm. Memorabilia of Rabelais.
Mar. 15-Oct. 15, Daily 9-11.45, 2-6.45.

SÈVRES

SÈVRES NATIONAL MUSEUM OF CERAMICS
92310 Sèvres, Hauts-de-Seine
History of ceramics from prehistoric times to the present day.
Daily except Tu. 10-12, 1-5.30 (Su. until 6).

SIGEAN

MUNICIPAL MUSEUM
44 Grand-Rue, 11130 Sigean, Aude
Ceramics from Greece, Campania, Spain and Aude. Bronzes. Gallo-Roman furniture.
Daily except Tu. 2-5.

SISTERON

SISTERON MUSEUM
Rue de Provence, 04200 Sisteron, Alpes-de-Haute-Provence
Local prehistory. Roman sculpture. Wooden statues. Folklore. Numismatics.
Daily on request 10-12, 2-5. Open from 4-9 during Aug.

SOISSONS

MUNICIPAL MUSEUM
Ancienne Abbaye Saint-Léger, 02200 Soissons, Aisne
Prehistoric, Gallic, Roman, Gallo-Roman and medieval archaeology. Paintings by Francken, Largillière and Boudin. Sculpture, including *Tête de Négresse* by Houdon.
Daily except Tu. 10-12, 2-5.

SOLLIÉS-PONT

JEAN AICARD MUSEUM
83210 Solliés-Pont, Var
Furniture, personal possessions of the poet, Jean Aicard (d.1921). Paintings.
Daily 9-12, 2-6.

SOLUTRÉ-POUILLY

MUSEUM OF PREHISTORY
Route de Maçon, Solutré-Pouilly, 71910 Dauagé, Saône-et-Loire
Neolithic and Aurignacian skeletons. Collection of flints from different periods.
Permanently open.

SOUVIGNY

LAPIDARY MUSEUM
Église Saint-Pierre, 03210 Souvigny, Allier
Tombs of the Dukes of Bourbon. Medieval sculptures, including the 12th century *Souvigny Calendar.*
On request.

SOYONS

MUSEUM OF ARCHAEOLOGY
Soyons, 07130 St. Péray, Ardèche
Excavated material from the Mousterian grottos at Soyons and from the oppidum at Malpas.
Daily on request.

STRASBOURG

ALSACE MUSEUM
23 quai Saint-Nicolas, 67000 Strasbourg, Bas-Rhin
Art, furniture, costumes and ceramics from different parts of Alsace. Agriculture and vine-growing.
Apr.-May: Daily 10-12, 2-5. June-Sept. Daily 10-12, 2-6. Oct.-Mar. Daily except Tu. 10-12, 2-4. Closed Good F., Christmas Day, Easter Su., Pentecost, May 1, July 14, Nov. 1 and Jan. 1.

CHÂTEAU DES ROHAN
2 place du Château, 67000 Strasbourg, Bas-Rhin
The Château (18th century), was the old palace of the Princes/ Bishops of Strasbourg. Bedroom and salon of the King. Cardinals' library. The royal apartments were occupied by Louis XV, Marie-Antoinette, Napoleon I.
Apr.-May 10-12, 2-5. Closed Good F. and Easter Su., Pentecost and May 1. June-Sept. Daily 10-12, 2-6. Closed July 14. Oct.-Mar. Daily 10-12, 2-4. Closed Tu., Nov. 1, Dec. 25 and Jan. 1.

COIN CABINET
Bibliothèque Nationale et Universitaire, 6 place de la République, 67000 Strasbourg, Bas-Rhin
Coins and medals from Alsace, Lorraine, France, Europe and the East.
Tu. afternoon, 2-5. Closed from July 13-Sept. 15.

HISTORICAL MUSEUM
Pont du Corbeau, 67000 Strasbourg, Bas-Rhin
Documents and collections relating to the political, military and topographical history of Strasbourg. Large relief map of the town, made by military engineers in 1727. Memorabilia of the Marshal of Saxe and of General Kléber. Arms, uniforms, military and family mementoes.
Apr.-May: Daily 10-12, 2-5. June-Sept. Daily 10-12, 2-6. Oct.-Mar. Daily except Tu. 10-12, 2-4. Closed Good F., Christmas Day, Easter Su., Pentecost, May 1, July 14, Nov. 1 and Jan. 1.

MUSEUM OF ARCHAEOLOGY
Château des Rohan, 67000 Strasbourg, Bas-Rhin
Collections illustrating the history of Alsace from the paleolithic period to the invasions during the early period of Christianity. Prehistoric habitations and tombs, presented as they were found. Collections of ceramics, weapons, jewellery, pottery. Gallo-Roman sculpture.
Apr.-May: Daily 10-12, 2-5. June-Sept. Daily 10-12, 2-6. Oct.-Mar. Daily except Tu. 10-12, 2-4. Closed Good F., Christmas Day, Easter Su., Pentecost, May 1, July 14, Nov. 1 and Jan. 1.

MUSEUM OF CASTS
Université de Strasbourg, Place de l'Université, 67000 Strasbourg, Bas-Rhin
Collection of casts of classical Greek statues and architecture. Several pediments of temples, some complete and some partly complete (Elgin, the Parthenon). Sculptures and frieze elements are to be seen around the walls. The Museum has examples of Assyrian and Roman architecture, not on display.
By appointment.

MUSEUM OF THE CATHEDRAL WORKSHOPS
3 place du Château, 67000 Strasbourg, Bas-Rhin
Houses dating from 14th, 16th and 17th centuries, grouped round the workshops. 11th and 12th century sculpture. The *Tête du Christ* by Wissembourg, the oldest known figura-

tive stained-glass window (c.1070). The originals of 13th century sculptures in the cathedral, the Church and the Synagogue, statues from the rood-screen which is now no longer in existence. Drawings (13th-15th century) made during work on the cathedral. Room showing the huts of the masons and stone cutters (1580) with the originals of the sculptures on the Saint-Laurent door (1495-1505). 15th century exhibits include sculptures, stained glass, paintings from Alsace. Graphic arts and book illustrations (1500-1600). Paintings, designs and stained-glass by Hans Baldung-Grien and his followers. Meeting room of the administrators of the work of Notre-Dame. Furniture and sculpture of the Renaissance. Still life exhibits include the works of the Strasbourg painter, Sebastian Stosskopff (1597-1657). Evolution of Strasbourg gold and silver ware from 15th-19th centuries. Glassware.
Apr.-May: Daily 10-12, 2-5. June-Sept. Daily 10-12, 2-6. Oct.-Mar. Daily except Tu. 10-12, 2-4. Closed Good F., Christmas Day, Easter Su., Pentecost, May 1, July 14, Nov. 1 and Jan. 1.

MUSEUM OF DECORATIVE ARTS
Château des Rohan, 67000 Strasbourg, Bas-Rhin
Collection of faience from the factory of Hannong, which operated at Strasbourg from 1721 to 1782, with a branch at Haguenau from 1742. General history of ceramics. Manufacture and history of European porcelain. Collection of old time-pieces: dials, mechanisms and automatic figures from the astronomical clocks of the cathedral, dating from 1354 and 1574. Watches. Wrought-iron. Pewter.
Apr.-May: Daily 10-12, 2-5. June-Sept. Daily 10-12, 2-6. Oct.-Mar. Daily except Tu. 10-12, 2-4. Closed Good F., Christmas Day, Easter Su., Pentecost, May 1, July 14, Nov. 1 and Jan. 1.

MUSEUM OF FINE ART
Château des Rohan, 67000 Strasbourg, Bas-Rhin
Paintings of the Italian School, including works by Filippino Lippi, Corregio, Veronèse, Tintoretto, Tiepolo and Guardi. Spanish works by Greco, Zurbaran and Goya. The Dutch School is represented by Memling, Lucas de Leyde, Martin van Heemskerk, Rubens, Van Dyck and Pieter de Hooch. French School: works by Simon Marmion, Valentin, Simon Vouet, Jean Tassel, Watteau, Boucher, Chardin, Fragonard, Corot, and Théodore Rousseau. Impressionist paintings from the end of the 19th century and beginning of the 20th century.
Apr.-May: Daily 10-12, 2-5. June-Sept. Daily 10-12, 2-6. Oct.-Mar. Daily except Tu. 10-12, 2-4. Closed Good F., Christmas Day, Easter Su., Pentecost, May 1, July 14, Nov. 1 and Jan. 1.

MUSEUM OF THE FORMER CUSTOMS HOUSE
Pont du Corbeau, 67000 Strasbourg, Bas-Rhin
Paintings from the Impressionist period to the present day. Artists represented include Gauguin, Manet, Sisley, Renoir, Marquet, Dufy, Marinot, Braque, Lurçat, Arp, Sophie Taeuber, Zadkin, Archipenko, Klee, Klimt, Campendonk and Monet. Stained glass windows (1900) by Theo Doesburg, Dülberg, Bissière and Poliakoff.
Apr.-May Daily 10-12, 2-5. June-Sept. Daily 10-12, 2-6. Oct.-Mar. Daily except Tu. 10-12, 2-4. Closed Good F., Christmas Day, Easter Su., Pentecost, May 1, July 14, Nov. 1 and Jan. 1.

SURESNES

MUNICIPAL MUSEUM
34 avenue Franklin-Roosevelt, 92150 Suresnes, Hauts-de-Seine
Local history. History of the Rosière, and of vine-growing in the Suresnes area.
Oct.-June: W., Sa. and Su. 2-5. Closed July-Sept. and public holidays.

TALCY

CHÂTEAU DE TALCY
Talcy, 41370 Marchenoir, Loir-et-Cher
Contemporary decorations. Original 16th-18th century furniture. Tapestries.
Daily except Tu. Apr.-Sept. 9-11.45, 2-6.30. Oct. 9-11.45, 2-5. Nov.-Mar. 10-11.45, 2-4.

TANLAY

CHÂTEAU TANLAY
89430 Tanlay, Yonne
Long gallery ornamented with Italian cameos and collection of old furniture. Frescoes reproducing in allegorical form the political and religious problems of the 16th century.
Palm Sunday - Oct. 1, Daily 9.30-12, 2-7. Oct. 1 - Palm Su. Daily ex. Tu. 9-12, 1.30-4.

TARADEAU

MUSÉE PROVENÇAL ET FOLKLORIQUE
Taradeau, 83460 Les Arcs, Var
Domestic, agricultural and workmen's tools and articles. Roman remains.
Daily 10-4 (10-6 in summer).

TARBES

BIRTHPLACE OF MARSHAL FOCH
65000 Tarbes, Hautes-Pyrénées
Paintings and sculptures relating to Marshal Foch and the 1914-18 war. Personal possessions of the Marshal, dating from this period.
Daily except Tu. 9-12, 2-5.

MASSEY MUSEUM
Jardin Massey, 65000 Tarbes, Hautes-Pyrénées
16th-19th century paintings. History of the Hussars from 15th century to the present day. Uniforms.
Daily except M., Tu. and public holidays, 10-12, 2-6.

THANN

MUSEUM OF THE FRIENDS OF THANN SOCIETY
Halle au Blé, 68800 Thann, Haut-Rhin
14th-18th century wooden and stone sculptures. Local history and craftsmanship. Mineralogical collection. Relics of the 1914-18 war.
May, June, Sept. and Oct., Th. and Sa. 4-6; Su. 10-12, 2-6. July and Aug. Daily 10-12, 2-6.

THIERS

FONTENILLE MONDIÈRE MUSEUM
10 rue de Barante, 63300 Thiers, Puy-de-Dôme
Cutlery. Paintings, 17th century to the present day. Children's toys.
Jan.-May and Oct.-Dec. Daily except M. and Tu., 2-5. June, July and Sept. M. 10-12, 2-5, Tu.-Su. 2-5. Aug. Daily 10-12, 2-5.

THÉSÉE-LA-ROMAINE

EXCAVATIONS MUSEUM
Mairie, Thésée-la-Romaine, Loir-et-Cher
Gallo-Roman archaeological remains, including local pottery, decorated ceramics, objects and tools in iron and bronze, coins. Model of a potter's oven. Photographs of excavations.
Sa. before Easter - Nov. 1, Daily 2-6.

THOUARS

LOCAL MUSEUM
Rue Henri-Barré, 79100 Thouars, Deux-Sèvres
Coins. Ceramics by Bernard Palissy. Relics of wars in Vendée.
Daily ex. Tu. 1-4.

THÔNES

THÔNES MUSEUM
Rue Blanche, 74230 Thônes, Haute-Savoie
Local history. Firemen's uniforms. Paintings. Furniture. Furnished interiors.
June 15 - Sept. 15, Daily 3-7 (Su. also 10-12). On request other months.

THONON-LES-BAINS

CHABLAIS MUSEUM OF FOLKLORE
Place de l'Hôtel de Ville, 74200 Thonon-les-Bains, Haute-Savoie
Regional archaeology. Local history. Ethnography of Chablais. Portrait of Vaugelas, the French grammarian. Engravings. Portraits of the Savoie family.
Nov.-June 15, Tu., Th. and Sa. 2.30-5.30. June 15 - Sept. 15, Daily except Tu. 9.30-11.30, 3-5.30.

TIGY

MUSEUM OF RURAL CRAFTS
Rue de Sully, 45510 Tigy, Loiret
Collections of workmen's tools of dying rural crafts. Reconstructed workshops of locksmith, saddle-maker, smith, cooper, carpenter, mason and wheelwright. Agricultural tools which have now fallen out of use.
July-Sept. Su. 9.30-12, 3-7.

TONNERRE

HOSPITAL
40 rue de l'Hôpital, 89700 Tonnerre, Yonne
Hospital ward of the latter part of the 13th century.
On request.

MUNICIPAL MUSEUM
22 rue Rougemont, 89700 Tonnerre, Yonne
Sculptures ranging from the Middle Ages to the Renaissance. Memorabilia of the Chevalier d'Eon. Natural history.
Th. and Sa. 2-4. Closed on public holidays and during Oct.

TORIGNI-SUR-VIRE

LOCAL MUSEUM
Town Hall, 50160 Torigni-sur-Vire, Manche
Tapestries from the old castle of the Matignon family.
On request.

TOULON

MUSEUM OF ART AND ARCHAEOLOGY
20 boulevard du Maréchal-Leclerc, 83100 Toulon, Var
Egyptian, Greek, Roman and Gallo-Roman archaeology. Art of the Near and Far East. Paintings of the French and other Schools of the 13th-19th centuries. Modern paintings.
Daily except M. and W. 10-12, 3-6.

NATURAL HISTORY MUSEUM
20 boulevard Marechal Leclerc, 83100 Toulon, Var
Geological collections, including petrography, mineralogy and palaeontology. Zoology exhibits include mammals, birds and shells.
Daily ex. M. and W. 10-12, 3-6.

NAVAL MUSEUM
Mairie de Toulon, 83100 Toulon, Var
Models of warships. Armament. Figureheads. Portraits of famous sailors.
Daily except M. 10-12, 3-6.

OLD TOULON MUSEUM
69 cours Lafayette, 83100 Toulon, Var
History of the town and region. Religious art. Engravings and drawings.
Daily except M. and W. 10-12, 3-6.

TOULOUSE

PAUL DUPUY MUSEUM
13 rue de la Pleau, 31000 Toulouse, Haute-Garonne
Applied art, 11th century to the present day. Enamels. Glass. Ceramics. Locks. Tapestries. Drawings and engravings. Medals. Seals. Weights and measures. Clocks. Costumes. Weapons. Ethnography and history of Languedoc and the Pyrenees.
Daily except Tu. 2-5; Su. and Th. 10.30-12 and 2-5 (2-6 Apr.-Sept.).

FÉLIX DÜRRBACH MUSEUM
Collection de Moulages, Faculté des Lettres, Annexe, 56 rue du Tour, 31000 Toulouse, Haute Garonne
Museum of sculpture-casts, installed in a Carmelite Chapel. Restoration in 1751 included in particular a group of decorative paintings by Despax.
On request.

GEORGES LABIT MUSEUM
43 rue des Martyrs-de-la-Libération, 31000 Toulouse, Haute-Garonne
Wooden chariot, bronzes and miniatures from India. Engravings, paintings and weapons from Japan. Paintings, neolithic ceramics, bronzes and porcelain from China. Paintings, sculptures and cultural objects from Tibet. Khmer sculptures. Items from Java. Egyptian archaeology.
Daily except Tu. 10-12, 2-5 (2-6 in summer).

MUSEUM OF THE AUGUSTINIANS
2 rue d'Alsace-Lorraine, 31000 Toulouse, Haute-Garonne
Paintings include works by Rubens, Delacroix, Philippe de Champaigne, Murillo, Boucher, Gérard, Gros, Ingres, Corot, Courbet, Toulouse-Lautrec, Vuillard. The classic school of Toulouse is represented by Chalette, Tournier, Fredeau, Lèbre, Rivalz, Subleyras, Gamelin and Roques. Collection of Romanesque sculpture, including statues, bas-reliefs and other items from the churches of Daurade, Saint-Etienne and Saint-Sernin. Contemporary paintings.
Daily except Tu. 10-12, 2-5 (2-6 in summer).

MUSEUM OF NATURAL HISTORY
Jardin des Plantes, Allée Jules Guesde, 31000 Toulouse Haute Garonne
Collection of palaeontology, prehistory and ethnography of tertiary and quaternary sites. Ornithology.
Daily ex. M. 10-12, 2-5.

OLD TOULOUSE MUSEUM
7 rue Dumay, 31000 Toulouse, Haute-Garonne
History of the city. Regional art. Ethnography.
Every afternoon except Tu.

SAINT-RAYMOND MUSEUM
Place Saint-Sernin, 31000 Toulouse, Haute-Garonne
Replicas of Greek and Roman statues. Etruscan, Greek and Roman ceramics. Coins. Roman inscriptions. Ornaments. Medieval ivories.
Daily except Tu. 10-12, 2-6 (2-5 Oct.-Mar.).

TOURCOING

BELL-TOWER MUSEUM
Tour de l'Eglise Saint-Christophe, 59200 Tourcoing, Nord
Folklore and local history.
Daily.

MUNICIPAL MUSEUM OF FINE ART
2 rue Paul-Doumer, Square Winston-Churchill, 59200 Tourcoing, Nord
Flemish and Dutch paintings of the 18th century. Engravings from 17th-20th centuries. Contemporary paintings. Pottery. Medals. Sculpture.
Oct.-Mar. Sa. 2.30-4.30; Su. 10-12, 2.30-4.30. Open until 6 April-Oct. Closed Aug.

MUSEUM OF THE CHURCH OF SAINT CHRISTOPHE
59200 Tourcoing, Nord
Religious art. Sculpture.
Sa. and Su. 4-7 on request.

MUSEUM OF COSTUMES AND FABRICS
Chambre de Commerce, 59200 Tourcoing, Nord
5000 samples of material ranging from Italian velvet of 15th century to the present day materials. 18th century costumes.
On request.

TOURNON-SUR-RHÔNE

RHÔNE MUSEUM
Château de Tournon, 07300 Tournon-sur-Rhône, Ardèche
Geography, ethnography and economy of the Rhône basin. Mementoes of old-time river transport.
Daily 9-11, 3-5. Closed Th. all day and Su. morning; Feb. Dec. 25 and Jan. 1.

TOURNUS

GREUZE MUSEUM
Rue du Collège, 71700 Tournus, Saône-et-Loire
Paintings and drawings by Greuze. Prehistory. Local archaeology.
Palm Sunday-Nov. 1, Daily except Tu. morning, 10-12, 2-6.

HÔTEL-DIEU
Rue de l'Hôpital, 71700 Tournus, Saône-et-Loire
Apothecary with a collection of 17th and 18th century faience jars.
Daily 10-12, 2-6.

PERRIN DE PUYCOUSIN MUSEUM
8 place de l'Abbaye, 71700 Tournus, Saône-et-Loire
Folklore. Reconstructions of local interiors. Furniture and Costumes of Burgundy.
Daily 10-12, 2-6.

TOURS

ESPELOSIN MUSEUM
Château de Basses-Rivières, 37000 Tours, Indre-et-Loire
Home, cellar and vineyard of a vine-cultivator. The collection includes presses, antique amphorae, bottles. In the main salon is an example of Directoire wallpaper, the design depicting casks being loaded onto sailing ships. Ceremonial model of screw press carried by a confraternity of Tourraine vignerons in a procession on St. Vincent's Day. Implements.
By appointment.

MUSEUM OF ARCHAEOLOGY AND ANCIENT ART
Hôtel Babou de la Bourdaisière, 8 place de la Foire-du-Roi, 37000 Tours, Indre-et-Loire
Prehistory. Archaeology. Coins.
Apr.-Sept. Tu.-Su. 10-12, 2-6. Oct.-Mar. Th. and Su. 10-12, 2-5.

MUSEUM OF THE COMPAGNONNAGE
Cloître Saint Julien, 8 rue Nationale, 37000 Tours, Indre-et-Loire
Paintings, drawings, flags, tools, documents and other objects relating to the history of the Compagnonnage, an Association founded in 1480 by members of the working class (probably the men who worked on the building of cathedrals). Customs and rites of the Association, a forerunner of craft unions and friendly societies.
F. before Easter-Nov. 11, daily except Tu. 10-12, 2-6.

MUSEUM OF FINE ART
18 place François-Sicard, 37000 Tours, Indre-et-Loire
In 17th-18th century Archbishop's Palace. French and Italian paintings, including Mantegna's 'Christ in the Garden of Olives' and 'Resurrection' and Boucher's 'Sylvia fleeing from the Wolf'. Works by Vignon and Bosse. Sculpture, including works by Houdon and Rodin. Furniture. Bookbindings, with armorial bearings.
Daily except Jan. 1, May 1, July 14, Nov. 11, Dec. 25. Apr.-May and Sept. 13-30. 9-12, 2-6. June-Sept. 12. 9-12, 2-6, 9-11 p.m. Oct.-Mar. 9-12, 2-5.

MUSEUM OF MEDIEVAL ART AND OF THE RESISTANCE
Hôtel Gouin, 25 rue du Commerce, 37000 Tours, Indre-et-Loire
Sculptures and decorative art of the Middle Ages and the Renaissance. Mementoes of the Resistance.
Nov.-Feb. Th., Su. and public holidays, 10-12, 2-6. Mar.-Oct. Daily except Tu. 10-12, 2-6.

MUSEUM OF THE WINES OF TOURAINE
Celliers Saint Julien, 14 rue Nationale, 37000 Tours, Indre-et-Loire
Collections illustrating the history of wine and wineyards in Touraine, from classical times to the present day. Tools. Methods of cultivation. Fraternities. Bottles. Glasses. Objets d'art connected with wine. Folk art.
W.-Su. 10-12, 2-6. Closed the day following public holidays.

PRIORY OF ST. COSME
La Riche, 37000 Tours, Indre-et-Loire
The priory contains the tomb of Ronsard, and visitors can see the refectory and the guest-house.
Mar. 15-Oct. 15, Daily 9-12, 2-7. Oct. 16-Mar. 14, Daily 9-12, 2-5.30.

TOURS-LA-RICHE

CHÂTEAU DE PLESSIS-LÈS-TOURS
Tours-la-Riche, Indre-et-Loire
Louis XI died here in 1483. Memorabilia of Saint François de Paule. Objects relating to local industries, notably the silk and lace-making trades, with specimens of ancient work (15th-18th centuries). Faience and enamels. Pottery. Folklore. Basket-making.
Daily 10-12, 2-5 (2-6 in summer). Closed Jan. 1, May 1, July 14, Nov. 11, Dec. 25. Also closed Tu. from Sept. 15 to the Tu. before Palm Su.

TRÉGASTEL

MUSEUM OF PREHISTORY
près de Sainte-Anne-en-Trégastel, 22730 Trégastel, Côtes-du-Nord
The Museum is located in a natural cave near the beach of 'Coz Pors', and was used as a chapel in the 19th century, hence its name in the Breton language of 'Coz Ilis', or old church. Prehistoric tools. Ancient pottery. Rocks. Local marine flora and fauna (sea weeds, fish and crayfish).
Easter-Oct. 10-12, 3-6 (July and Aug. open till 10).

TRÉGUIER

ERNEST RENAN'S BIRTHPLACE
Rue Ernest-Renan, 22220 Tréguier, Côtes-du-Nord
Birthplace of Renan, with mementoes of his childhood. Memorabilia of Ernest and Michel Psichari, grandsons of Renan.
Easter-Oct. Daily 9-12, 2-7.

TROUVILLE-SUR-MER

MUSEUM OF LOCAL AND REGIONAL ART
Casino Municipal (West Wing), 14360 Trouville-sur-Mer, Calvados
Paintings and engravings illustrating local history and the history of sea-bathing.
June-Sept. Daily 10-12, 2-7.

TROYES

CATHEDRAL OF SAINT-PIERRE-ET-SAINT-PAUL
10000 Troyes, Aube
13th-16th century stained glass. Treasury contains Byzantine ivory coffer of the 11th century, as well as reliquaries in enamelware and in gold and silver. The Chapel of the Colbert de Villacerf family contains Limoges enamels of the 16th century.
Any time.

MUSEUM OF FINE ART
21 rue Crétien-de-Troyes, 10000 Troyes, Aube
Archaeological collections. Arms and gold jewellery found at Pouan (Aube) in the sepulchre of a contemporary of Attila. Paintings include works by Philippe de Champaigne, Rigaud, Watteau, Boucher, Prud'hon. Collection of Limoges enamels. Furniture. Natural science section.
Daily except Tu. 10-12, 2-6 (2-5 in winter). Closed Jan. 1, May 1, July 14, Nov. 1 and 11.

MUSEUM OF THE HISTORY OF TROYES AND CHAMPAGNE
Hôtel de Vauluisant, 4 rue de Vauluisant, 10000 Troyes, Aube
15th and 16th century sculptures and paintings on wood. Local history. Iconography of old Troyes. Faience. Rural tools. Hosiery industry: looms, stockings and caps.
Daily except Tu. 10-12, 2-6 (2-5 in winter). Closed Jan. 1, May 1, July 14, Nov. 1 and 11.

TULLE

CLOISTER MUSEUM
Place Zola, 19000 Tulle, Corrèze
Archaeology. Wood sculptures. Faiences. Local history. Collection of hearth plates, 15th-18th centuries. Weapons.
Daily 10-12, 2-5. Closed Tu.

LA TURBIE

MUSEUM OF THE ALPINE VICTORY MONUMENT
Tour d'Auguste, 06630 La Turbie, Alpes-Maritimes
Documents and other material relating to the Tower of Augustus, built in 6 B.C. to celebrate the victory of Augustus over the Alpine tribes.
Summer: Daily 8-midnight. Winter: Daily 9-5. Illuminated from mid. May-mid. Sept.

UZÈS

LOCAL MUSEUM
Hôtel de Ville, 30700 Uzès, Gard
Prehistoric and Gallo-Roman archaeology. Local history. Local pottery. Memorabilia of André and Charles Gide. Botany of the Garrigue. Conchology.
Summer: Daily 10-12, 2-5. In winter apply to the caretaker. Closed Dec. 25, Jan. 1, Easter and Aug. 15.

DI RODO MUSEUM
3b Route de Nîmes, 30700 Uzès, Gard
Paintings. Engravings. Ceramics. Cars. Bicycles. Railway engines and Motor cycles. Collection of objects and models illustrating railway history. "0" gauge layout with more than 1000 feet of tracks. Scale models.
Su. before Easter-Nov. 1, Daily 10-12, 3-7. Winter: Su. and holy days 10-12, 3-7.

VAISON-LA-ROMAINE

ARCHAEOLOGICAL MUSEUM
Quartier de Puymin, 84110 Viason-la-Romaine, Vaucluse
Material from local excavations, including a bust in silver of the owner of a Roman villa (2nd century). Head of Venus, crowned with laurels, in marble. Statues of the Emperors Augustus, Tiberius and Hadrian. Religious and funerary inscriptions, bas-reliefs and sculptures. Ornaments. Ceramics. Lamps. Objects in bronze and iron. Coins.
Daily 9-12, 2-6.

VALENÇAY

GALLERY OF MEMENTOES OF PRINCE DE TALLEYRAND
Commun du Château, 36600 Valençay, Indre
Historical collection relating to the Prince, including a reconstruction of his room, with portraits of the Princess de Talleyrand by Mme. Vigée-Lebrun, of the Duchess of Dino, niece of the Prince by Prud'hon, and of King Ferdinand VII of Spain. Swords. Miniatures. Seals. Paintings. Furniture.
Sa. before Easter-Oct. 31, Daily 9-12, 2-7. Nov. 1-F. before Easter, Su. and public holidays, 10-12, 2-7.

VALENCE

MUSEUM OF FINE ART AND NATURAL HISTORY
4 place des Ormeaux, 26000 Valence, Drôme
15th and 17th century painted ceilings. 18th century woodcarvings. Red chalk ('sanguine') drawings by Hubert Robert. Paintings, including works by Rubens, Gérard, Fragonard, Boudin, Dufy. The natural history section includes exotic birds, mammals, reptiles, shells, insects and butterflies. Minerals. Palaeontology. Gallo-Roman archaeology.
Daily ex. public holidays, 9-11.45, 2-5.45.

VALENCIENNES

MUSEUM OF FINE ART
Boulevard Watteau et Place Verte, 59300 Valenciennes, Nord
Works by Watteau, Pater, Harpignies and Carpeaux, all born at Valenciennes. Flemish paintings. Large religious works by Rubens and a series of lesser known works by him. Portraits by Pourbus. 16th century Tournai tapestry. 17th and 19th century earthenware from Avesnois and the north.
Daily except Tu. 10-12, 2-5. Closed May 1, Nov. 1 and Dec. 25.

VALLAURIS

NATIONAL MUSEUM
Place de la Mairie, 06220 Vallauris, Alpes-Maritimes
The museum contains a large mural by Picasso, entitled *La Guerre et la Paix*, in three panels (1952). Local history.
Oct.-May: Daily 10-12, 2-5. June-Oct. Daily 10-12, 2-7.

VALOGNES

CIDER MUSEUM
Halles, 50700 Valognes, Manche
Grinders, presses and other equipment used in the cider industry. Shells. Fossils. Minerals. Prehistoric objects.
Daily ex. M. 10-12, 2-5.

VANNES

LIMUR MUSEUM
31 rue Thiers, 56000 Vannes, Morbihan
Paintings, especially French, from 1850 to the present day. Prints by Géricault, Delacroix, Charlet, Charrériau, Bonnard, Derain, Maillol.
July-Sept. Daily 10-12, 2-7.

MUSEUM OF THE MORBIHAN POLYMATHIC SOCIETY
2 rue Noé, 56000 Vannes, Morbihan
Prehistory and local archaeology. Natural science.
Daily except Su. 9-12, 2-6.

VARZY

MUNICIPAL MUSEUM
58210 Varzy, Nièvre
16th and 17th century Flemish paintings. 18th and 19th century French works. Red chalk ('sanguine') drawing by Boucher. Watercolours by Natoire, David. Faience from Nevers. Gallo-Roman and Egyptian archaeology. Furniture. Musical instruments, including a spinet by J. Denis.
Daily except Tu. 10-12, 2-5.

VAUCOULEURS

MUNICIPAL MUSEUM
Hôtel de Ville, 55140 Vaucouleurs, Meuse
Paintings. Local history. Material relating to Joan of Arc.
Easter-Oct. 1, Daily 8-12, 2-6.

VAUX-LE-VICOMTE

CHÂTEAU
Vaux-le-Vicomte, Seine-et-Marne
Paintings by Le Brun. Sculptures by Girardon and Houdon. Gobelins tapestries. Savonnerie carpet. Period furniture. The gardens were laid out by Le Nôtre, with fountains and water-jets.
Apr.-Nov. 11: Daily except W. 10-12, 2-5.30.

VENCE

CHAPEL OF THE ROSARY
Avenue Henri-Matisse, 06140 Vence, Alpes-Maritimes
Mural paintings by Matisse.
Tu. and Th. 10-11.30, 2.30-5.30.

VENDÔME

MUNICIPAL MUSEUM
Cloître de l'Abbaye, 41100 Vendôme, Loir-et-Cher
In 17th century Abbey of the Trinity. Medieval and Renaissance statues and tombstones. Rouen ware. Queen Marie-Antoinette's harp.
Daily except Tu. 9.30-10.30, 2-4. Closed Oct. 20-Nov. 20.

VERDUN

UNDERGROUND CITADEL
55100 Verdun, Meuse
An important part of the defence of Verdun, these underground tunnels sheltered the civilian population and off-duty soldiers. Relics of 1914-18 War.
Pentecost-Sept. Daily 8-12, 2-6.

FORT DE VAUX AND FORT DE DOUAUMONT
55100 Verdun, Meuse
These two forts played an important role in the defence of the city during the First World War. Visitors can see the corridors, the keeps, casemates and magazines.
Easter-Sept. Daily 8-7.

PRINCERIE MUSEUM
16 rue de la Belle-Vièrge, 55100 Verdun, Meuse
Local archaeology. Prehistoric, Egyptian, Etruscan, Greek, Gallo-Roman and Merovingian objects. Faience from Argonne.
May-Oct. 1, Daily except Tu. 9-12, 2-6.

WAR MUSEUM
Hôtel de Ville, 55100 Verdun, Meuse
Collections and documents relating to the 1914-18 war and to the generals who liberated Verdun. Resistance movement, 1940-5.
Easter-Nov. 11, Daily 10-12, 2-6.

VERSAILLES

CHÂTEAU
Versailles, Seine-et-Oise
Visitors can see the chapel, Opéra, Galérie des Glaces and royal apartments. 17th and 18th century mural decorations and royal furniture. Painted ceilings by Le Brun and his pupils. Paintings by Veronese and Bernin. The park was laid out by Le Nôtre.
Daily 10-5.

GRAND TRIANON
Versailles, Seine-et-Oise
Louis XIV woodcarvings. Paintings commissioned by Louis XIV. Furniture.
Daily except Tu. 10-5.

LAMBINET MUSEUM
54 boulevard de la Reine, Versailles, Seine-et-Oise
Medieval religious art, including Abbesses' crosses and liturgical objects. Regional history, including material relating to General Hoche, the musician Delalande, the manufacture of arms at Boutet, education at Saint-Cyr. Works of the sculptor Houdon, a native of Versailles, notably his busts of Voltaire and Rousseau. 18th century furniture and objets d'art. Revolutionary relics. Rooms devoted to Charlotte Corday and Marat. Representation of Versailles donated by Dunoyer de Segonzac. Paintings by Eugène Delaporte, and André Surera.
Tu., Th., Sa., Su. 2-6. Closed on public holidays.

MUSEUM OF HISTORY
Versailles, Seine-et-Oise
Portraits, both painted and sculpted. Historical tableaux (16th-19th centuries). Paintings by Cranach, Corneille de Lyon, Clouet, Philippe de Champaigne, Le Brun, Van der Meulen, Rigaud, Largillière, Vanloo, Natoire, Nattier, Oudry, Vigée-Lebrun, David, Gérard, Ingres, Delacroix and Winterhalter. Sculptures by Coysevox, Coustou, Girardon, Bouchardon, Pigalle, Pajou and Houdon.
Daily except Tu. 2-5.

MUSEUM OF HORSE-DRAWN VEHICLES
Parc de Versailles, Versailles, Seine-et-Oise
Collection of state coaches, including one used in 1821 for the baptism of Henri-Dieudonné de France, Duke of Bordeaux and better known as Comte de Chambord. This coach was modified for use at the marriage of Napoleon III and the Empress Eugénie. Most of the collection dates from the 19th century, but there are some earlier examples.
Apr.-Sept. Daily 2-5.30. Closed Tu. Oct.-Mar. Daily ex. Tu. 1-5.

PETIT TRIANON
Versailles, Seine-et-Oise
Collection of wood carvings and furniture of the end of the 18th century.
Daily except Tu. 2-5.

VERVINS

MUSEUM OF ARCHAEOLOGY AND HISTORY
3 rue du Traité-de-Paix, 02140 Vervins, Aisne
Palaeontology. Prehistory. Gallo-Roman, Merovingian and medieval antiquities. Furniture.
On request.

VESOUL

GARRET MUSEUM
Mairie de Vesoul, 70000 Vesoul, Haute-Saône
Celtic, Gallo-Roman. Neolithic and Merovingian archaeology. Flemish and French paintings of the 17th-20th centuries.
Th. and Sa. afternoon. Other days on request.

VEZELAY

LOCAL MUSEUM
Mairie, 89450 Vezelay, Yonne
Gallo-Roman archaeology. Ceramics. Seals. Masonic insignia. Weapons.
Easter-Sept. Daily 9-12, 2-6.

VICHY

MUSEUM OF ART AND HISTORY
3 rue Verrier, 03200 Vichy, Allier
Gallo-Roman antiquities. History of Vichy. Mementoes of famous visitors to the town.
May 15-Sept. 30: Daily except M. 2.30-6.

VIENNE

LAPIDARY MUSEUM
Église Saint-Pierre, 38200 Vienne, Isère
Sarcophagi of Saint Léonien and Saint Mamert. Bust of Magnentia; heads of Augustus and Apollo. Mosaics and sculptures.
Apr.-Oct. 15, Daily 9-12, 2.30-6.30. Oct. 16-Mar. 31, Daily except Tu. 10-12, 2-4.

MUSEUM OF CHRISTIAN ART
Cloître de Saint-André-le-Bas, 38200 Vienne, Isère
Merovingian, Carolingian, Romanesque and Gothic sculptures. Early Christian inscriptions. Altar of 7th century. 6th century altar table. Decorated sarcophagi of 4th and 6th centuries.
Apr.-Oct. 15, Daily 9-12, 2.30-6.30. Oct. 16-Mar. 31, Daily except Tu. 10-12, 2-4.

MUSEUM OF FINE ART
38200 Vienne, Isère
Paintings. Faience. Pharmaceutical jars. Archaeology. Bronzes. Jewels. Ceramics. Numismatics.
Apr.-Oct. 15, Daily 9-12, 2.30-6.30. Oct. 16-Mar. 31, Daily except Tu. 10-12, 2-4.

VIERZON

LOCAL MUSEUM
Mairie, 18100 Vierzon, Cher
16th and 17th century woodcarvings. Sculptures. Faience. Folklore.
On request.

LE VIGAN

CÉVENNE MUSEUM
1 rue des Calquieres, 30120 Le Vigan, Gard
Local handicrafts. Tools. Room devoted to André Chamson.
Apr.-Nov. 1, Daily except Tu. 10-5. Other months: Th. 10-5.

VILLEDIEU-LES-POËLES

LOCAL MUSEUM
50800 Villedieu-les-Poëles, Manche
Copper and brass ware.
On request.

VILLEFRANCHE-DE-ROUERGUE

CABROL MUSEUM
Rue du Sergent-Bories, 12200 Villefranche-de-Rouergue, Aveyron
Local folklore. Archaeology of the Iron Age, the Bronze Age and the Gallo-Roman period.
By appointment.

VILLEFRANCHE-SUR-MER

CHAPEL OF SAINT-PIERRE
06230 Villefranche-sur-Mer, Alpes-Maritimes
Fishermen's chapel, decorated with frescoes by Jean Cocteau.
Daily 9-12, 2-7.

VILLEFRANCHE-SUR-SAÔNE

MUNICIPAL MUSEUM
Place Fiaubert, 69400 Villefranche-sur-Saône, Rhône
Paintings. Engravings. Geological collection.
Th. and Sa. 2-4.

VILLENEUVE-LÈS-AVIGNON

HOSPICE MUSEUM
30400 Villeneuve-lès-Avignon, Gard
Paintings, including the primitive, *Coronation of the Virgin* by Enguerrand Charonton. Tomb of Pope Innocent VI.
Daily except Tu. 10-11.30, 2-5 (2-6 in summer).

VILLENEUVE-SUR-LOT

GASTON RAPIN MUSEUM
Avenue Ernest-Lafon et Boulevard Voltaire, 47300 Villeneuve-sur-Lot, Lot-et-Garonne
Archaeological collection, including Gallo-Roman remains from Excisum. Sculptures and Romanesque columns. Paintings and sculpture by regional artists. Religious art. Local ethnography.
May-Sept. Tu., Th., Sa. and Su. 2-6. Oct.-Apr. 2-4.

VILLENEUVE-LOUBET

MUSEUM OF THE ART OF COOKERY
Fondation Auguste Escoffier, Rue Escoffier, 06270 Villeneuve-Loubet, Alpes-Maritimes
In the house of Auguste Escoffier. Memorabilia of Escoffier, including a portrait of the prima donna, 'Melba', which she dedicated to him in acknowledgement of his creating 'Peach Melba'. Each room contains sugar works of art, given by the Pastry Chefs' Association. Paintings by restaurateurs and chefs. Reconstructed Provençal kitchen, typical of 18th and 19th centuries when simmering was predominant. Mementoes of great chefs and gastronomes all over the world, including a gold watch and chain from Russia, engraved with the coat of arms of Tzar Nicholas II, presented to Louis Cubat, chef to the court of Siam. Room devoted to menus from all over the world, mostly written in French.
Tu.-Su. 2-6. Closed M. and public holidays, also for the month of November.

VILLENEUVE-DE-MARSAN

CHÂTEAU DE RAVIGNAN
40190 Villeneuve-de-Marsan, Landes
Building of 16th century. Collections of engravings of Henry IV. Men's costumes of reign of Louis XVI.
By arrangement.

VILLEQUIER

VICTOR HUGO MUSEUM
Villequier, 76490 Caudebec en Caux, Seine-Maritime
In the old home of the family of Léopoldine Hugo, containing some of the original furnishings. Memorabilia of the poet and his family. Letters. Drawings. Portraits.
Daily except W. and public holidays, 10-12, 2-6 (2-7 in summer). Closed for one month during the winter.

VILLERS-COTTERÊTS

ALEXANDRE DUMAS MUSEUM
24 rue Démoustier, 02600 Villers-Cotterêts, Aisne
Memorabilia and manuscripts of the writer.
Daily except M. morning and all day Tu. 2-4.30. Closed 2nd Su. in each month from Oct.-Mar.

VILLESAVIN

COLLECTION OF HORSE-DRAWN VEHICLES
Commun du Château, Villesavin, Loir-et-Cher
Old carriages in coach-house. Furnished rooms, with old serving dishes, jugs, pitchers and plates.
Sa. before Easter-Sept. 15, Daily 9-12, 2-7. Sept. 16-Dec. 20, Jan. 20-F. before Easter, 9-12, 2-5. Closed Dec. 20-Jan. 20.

VILLEVENARD

MARAIS DE SAINT-GOND MUSEUM OF PREHISTORY
Villevenard, 51270 Montmort, Marne
Prehistoric archaeology. Weapons, tools and other objects from the Neolithic caves of the region.
On request.

VILLIERS-SAINT-BENOÎT

MUNICIPAL MUSEUM
89119 Villiers-Saint-Benoît, Yonne
Faience from factories at Ancy-le-Franc, Montigny-sous-Perreux, Arthé, Vausse, Chevannes, Auxerre, Foulnier d'Ancy-le-Franc and Les Cornes. Burgundian medieval sculpture.
Daily ex. Tu. 9.30-12, 2-5 (until 6 in summer).

VINCENNES

HISTORICAL MUSEUM OF THE CHÂTEAU DE VINCENNES
Donjon et Saint Chapelle du Château, 94300 Vincennes, Val de Marne
The story of this fortress in which Henry V of England died is told by exhibits in the Keep.
On request.

KODAK MUSEUM
24 avenue du Petit Parc, 94300 Vincennes, Seine
Collection of Kodak equipment since its beginnings, together with examples of different photographic processes: daguerrotypes, ambrotypes, ferrotypes and calotypes.
By appointment only, in writing.

VIRE

MUNICIPAL MUSEUM
Ancien Hôtel-Dieu, Rue Emile-Chénel, 14500 Vire, Calvados
Paintings. Furniture. Local history.
On request.

VITRÉ

CHÂTEAU MUSEUM
au Château, 35500 Vitré, Ille-et-Vilaine
Tapestries. Faience. 15th and 16th century archaeology. History of Vitré. Local ethnography.
Daily except Tu. 10-12, 2-5.

VIZILLE

CHÂTEAU DE VIZILLE
38220 Vizille, Isère
Paintings. Sculpture. 17th century tapestries.
Apr.-Sept. Daily except Tu. 9-12, 1.30-6. Oct.-Mar. Daily except Tu. 10-12, 1.30-4.

VOIRON

MAINSSIEUX COLLECTION
Bâtiment du Jardin de Ville, 38500 Voiron, Isère
19th century paintings. Impressionist works, and works of the Lyonnais and local Schools. Paintings by Mainssieux.
Th. and Sa. afternoons.

WALDERSBACH

OBERLIN MUSEUM
Presbytère, Waldersbach, 67130 Schirmeck, Bas-Rhin
Memorabilia of J. J. Oberlin. Collection of folk art.
On request.

WISSEMBOURG

WESTERCAMP MUSEUM
Rue du Musée, 67160 Wissembourg, Bas-Rhin
Furniture. Regional costumes. Prehistoric and Gallo-Roman archaeology. Merovingian sarcophagi. Sculpture. Ironwork of the Middle Ages and the Renaissance. Ceramics. Collection of weapons and uniforms. History of the war of 1870-71.
Daily 10-12, 2-5. Su. and public holidays, 2-5.

YVETOT

MUNICIPAL MUSEUM
Hôtel de Ville, 76190 Yvetot, Seine-Maritime
Carved ivory. Terra-cotta ware.
On request.

YZEURE

HISTORICAL MUSEUM OF THE BOURBONNAIS
Annexe des Archives départementales de l'Allier, Chapelle du Château de Bellevue, 03400 Yzeure, Allier
Documents relating to the history of the Bourbonnais. Maps. Drawings. Photographs. Original documents.
Daily except Sa. 2-6. Closed during winter.

French Guiana

Nearly half of the population of French Guiana lives in the chief town, Cayenne. Until 1945 there was a notorious penal settlement here, many prisoners being employed on forestry work. The single museum reflects the natural resources of Guiana, but had little to say about its colonial and penal history.

CAYENNE

LOCAL MUSEUM
2 avenue du Général-de-Gaulle, Cayenne
Flora and fauna of Guiana. Historical documents. Paintings. Maps of old Cayenne. Indian ethnography. Zoology. Conchology. Botany. Mineralogy.
Daily 10-5.

French Polynesia

The five island groups which comprise the administrative unit known as French Polynesia derive their income almost equally from tourists and from agricultural products, mainly coffee and vanilla, and mother-of-pearl. The two museums, both on Tahiti, illustrate this and pay proper homage to the man who has done more than anyone else to publicise Tahiti, the painter Paul Gauguin.

TAHITI

PAUL GAUGUIN MUSEUM
P.O. Box 536, Papeari, Tahiti
Collection illustrating Gauguin's life and work. Library of unpublished documents. Paintings by R. Delaunay, S. Delaunay, Buffet and others.
Daily 9-5.

PAPEETE MUSEUM
P.O. Box 110, Rue Bréa, Tahiti
Ethnography of French Polynesia. Historical souvenirs. Natural history.
A Tahitian temple ('marae') is in the care of the museum.
M.-Th. 1.30-5.30; F. 9-5.30; Sa. 9-12. Closed Su., holidays.

Gabon

This is a part of Africa long exposed to French culture and methods of organisation. It is not surprising, therefore, that the country's single museum should be entirely devoted to native arts and traditions, with present-day commerce and industry kept severely at a distance.

LIBREVILLE

GABON MUSEUM OF ARTS AND TRADITIONS
B.P. 3115, Avenue de Générale de Gaulle, Libreville
Ethnography. Prehistory. Musicology. Musical instruments. Jewellery. Masks. Statues. Handicrafts.
Daily except Su. 10-12, 4-6.30.

Germany, Democratic Republic of

The detached observer is able to take a view of German museums which is perhaps denied to the Germans themselves and to say that in both East and West Germany the museum-going public benefitted a good deal from the 1939-45 war, simply because the division of the country into two parts, hermetically sealed off from one another, produced a far better distribution of museums than would otherwise have been possible. A unified Germany had, and would certainly still have had, for example, only one National Railways Museum and one National Postal Museum. A divided Germany, inevitably, has two.

After the end of the war, and the division of Berlin, the G.D.R. found itself endowed or cursed, according to one's point of view, with the terrifyingly huge mass of Prussian masonry on Berlin's Museum Island which had previously contained the cultural loot of most of the civilisations of the world. The West Germans must often have been exceedingly grateful, at least in private, that the burden of doing something about this shattered mountain of Imperial prestige had been laid on other shoulders; and, very sensibly, the East Germans have decided to give a low priority to dealing with the worst of the ruins and to make their museum investment in more promising quarters, such as in the development of the Museum of German History, which West Germans find it politic to sniff at, but which is, in fact, one of the most interesting and professional pieces of museum creation of the post-1945 European world.

The G.D.R. is, of course, a German country and, as such, it recognises its duty to preserve and present the traditional material of what the Germans take an extraordinary and possibly perverted pride in calling Cultural History; but they have added new elements to the cultural mix. One finds now such Russian-like combinations of collections within the same museum as paintings and machine tools and, hardly possible in West Germany, a Bone-Mill Cultural Centre. New folk-heroes have been admitted to the Pantheon, so that Clara Zetkin and Karl Liebknecht have their museums, as well as the more-securely established Bach and Goethe. There is, too, a stronger emphasis on industrial history, industrial archaeology and industrial techniques than one finds in the West, and even the smallest and most unlikely museum feels obliged to include a section on the History of the Workers' Movement, and to present "seventeenth-century music and musicians in their social context".

But the German love of highly specialised museums knows no Iron Curtain. The German Two-Stroke Motor Cycle Museum happens to be in the G.D.R., but one can be sure that the G.F.R. would be equally proud to give it a home.

ADORF

REGIONAL MUSEUM
Stadttor, Freibergerstrasse, Adorf
Geology and wildlife of the area. Local history. Industrial and commercial development of Adorf and surrounding district.
M.-F. 10-12, 2-4; Su. 10-12.

AKEN

REGIONAL MUSEUM
Köthener Strasse 15, Aken
Natural history, prehistory of the area. History of Aken. Craftsmen's tools, equipment. Local handicrafts. River and canal navigation.
Sa. 3-5; Su. 10-12. Other times by appointment.

ALLSTEDT

THOMAS MÜNTZER MEMORIAL
Wigberti Kirche, Allstedt
In tower of church (c.1200). Memorabilia of the theologian, Thomas Müntzer (d.1525). History of the Peasants' War.
Apr.-Sept. daily 9-5. Other months by appointment.

REGIONAL MUSEUM
Rathaus, Allstedt
Geology, especially local slates and shales and their working. Local and regional prehistory and history.
Apr.-Sept. daily 9-5. Rest of year by appointment.

ALTENBURG

CASTLE MUSEUM AND PLAYING CARDS MUSEUM
Schloss Altenburg, Altenburg
Prehistory of the Altenburg district. Local history, 10th-19th century. Peasant furniture, household equipment, craftsmen's tools, costumes. Weapons. Documents. 17th-19th century porcelain. History of the workers' movement. Industrial development of the area. History of playing cards in Germany and abroad.
Apr.-Sept. daily 9-5. Oct.-Mar. daily 10-4.

LINDENAU STATE MUSEUM
Ernst Thälmann Platz 5, Altenburg
Greek and Etruscan vases. 11th-20th century European, especially Italian, German sculpture. 13th-16th century panel paintings. Drawings. Prints.
Tu.-Su. 9.30-6.

'MAURITIANUM' MUSEUM OF NATURAL HISTORY
Park des Friedens, Schlossgarten, Altenburg
Geology, birds and animals of the Altenburg area.
Tu.-F. 9-5; Sa. 9-12; Su. 9-5.

ORE-CRUSHING AND TINWASHING PLANT
Technisches Museum, Altenburg
History of local tin-mining. Water-driven machinery, including original washing-plant (1513).
Daily 9-4.

RED PINNACLES
Berggasse 15, Altenburg
In towers of 12th century church. 14th-18th century religious sculpture, applied art, inscriptions.
Apr.-Sept. daily 9-5. Oct.-Mar. daily 10-4.

ALT SCHWERIN

OPEN-AIR MUSEUM OF AGRICULTURAL HISTORY
Alt Schwerin
Agricultural history and ethnography of Mecklenburg.
May-Oct., Tu.-Su. 9-5.

ANGERMÜNDE

REGIONAL MUSEUM
Berliner Strasse 72, Angermünde
Geology, prehistory and history of the Angermünde district.
Tu., F. 9-12, 2-5.

ANKLAM

REGIONAL MUSEUM
Rudolf Breitscheid Platz 4, Anklam
Prehistoric material from local sites. 13th-20th century history of Anklam. Handicrafts. Memorabilia of the glider-constructor, Otto Lilienthal (d.1896).
Tu.-Sa. 10-1, 4-6; Su. 9-1.

ANNABERG-BUCHHOLZ

ERZGEBIRG MUSEUM: DEPARTMENT OF CULTURAL HISTORY
Grosse Kirchgasse 16, Annaberg-Buchholz
13th-16th century mining history, techniques, equipment. Local crafts, 17th-19th centuries. 16th-19th century lace-making. Silk weaving. Religious ornaments. 18th-19th century peasant household equipment, tools. Pewter. History of the local workers' movement.
Daily 9-4.30.

ERZGEBIRG MUSEUM: DEPARTMENT OF NATURAL HISTORY
Kupferstrasse 20, Annaberg-Buchholz
Botany of the district, especially mosses and lichens. Rocks and minerals. Local birds, insects, butterflies.
Daily 9-4.30.

APOLDA

BELL AND REGIONAL MUSEUM
Bahnhofstrasse 41, Apolda
Examples of bells, 1st century B.C. onwards. Techniques and history of bellfounding. History of Apolda. Development of local knitting industry, with models and equipment.
Tu.-F. 9-12, 2-5; Sa., Su. 9-12.

ARENDSEE

REGIONAL MUSEUM
Am See 3, Arendsee
In former hospital of the monastery (1184). Prehistoric material from local sites. Botany. Fishing industry.
May-Sept., Tu.-Su. 9-12, 2-7. Oct.-Apr. Tu.-F., Su. 9-12, 2-5.

ARNEBURG

REGIONAL MUSEUM
Karl Marx Strasse 14, Arneburg
Prehistory of the area. Botany. Wildlife. History of Arneburg. Handicrafts. Pottery. Elbe navigation.
M.-F. 9-11, 3-4.30; Sa. 9-12; Su. 3-5.

ARNSTADT

BACH MEMORIAL
Bahnhofstrasse 2A, Arnstadt
Material illustrating Bach's period as organist in Arnstadt. The Bach family in Arnstadt and Thuringia.
Daily 8-5.

PALACE MUSEUM
Schlossplatz 1, Arnstadt
In Castle (1732). 16th-20th century paintings. Tapestries. Handicrafts. Porcelain. Pottery. Faience. 18th century dolls houses.
Daily 8-5.

REGIONAL MUSEUM
Schlossplatz 1, Arnstadt
Prehistory of the area. History of Arnstadt. Wildlife, especially birds. Handicrafts. 15th-17th century pottery, religious art.
Daily 8-5.

ASBACH

FINSTERTAL DEMONSTRATION MINE IN THE KOHLBERG
Asbach
Demonstration of old and modern mining methods.
May-Oct., daily 9.30-4, by appointment.

ASCHERSLEBEN

REGIONAL MUSEUM
Markt 21, Aschersleben
In former (1788) Masonic Lodge building. Geology, palaeontology of district. Local potash and brown coal mining. History of Aschersleben. Furniture. Household equipment. Weapons. Coins.
Tu.-F., Su. 9-12, 2-5.

AUE

REGIONAL COLLECTION
Stadthaus, Aue
Local geology, geography, history. Ethnography. Mining. Popular art.
Tu.-Th. 11-3.

AUERBACH

REGIONAL ROOM
Rathaus, Auerbach
Minerals. Prehistoric material from local excavations. Butterflies. History of Auerbach.
On request.

AUGUSTUSBURG

GERMAN TWO-STROKE MOTOR CYCLE MUSEUM
Schloss Augustusburg, Augustusburg
International development of two-stroke motorcycle. Original machines. Models. History of motor-cycle racing. 18th-19th century historic coaches.
Daily 8-12, 1-5.

REGIONAL MUSEUM
Schloss Augustusburg, Augustusburg
Castle (1572), formerly hunting lodge of Prince August of Saxony. History of the Castle, and the town. History of hunting. Industrial development of the district. Musical instruments. Natural history.
Daily 8-12, 1-5.

BAD BLANKENBURG

FRIEDRICH FRÖBEL MUSEUM
Goetheweg 15, Bad Blankenburg
Memorial museum to Fröbel, who established his first kindergarten in Bad Blankenburg (1840). Material relating to Fröbel's life and work.
M.-F. 9-12, 2-5; Sa. 10-12.

BAD DOBERAN

DISTRICT MUSEUM
Grosser Tempel, Bad Doberan
Prehistory and early history of the area. History of Doberan Monastery. Development of Doberan as a lake resort. Fishing industry. 19th century lithographs.
Tu.-F. 9.30-11.30, 3-5; Su. 9.30-11.30.

BAD DÜBEN

DÜBEN HEATH MUSEUM
Burg Düben, Bad Düben
Geology and prehistory of the area. History of the castle and the town, 10th-19th centuries. Handicrafts. Models of mills.
May-Sept., daily 8-12, 2-5. Oct.-Apr. daily 9-12, 2-4.

BAD DÜRRENBERG

BORLACH MUSEUM
Borlach Platz, Bad Dürrenberg
History of the Dürrenberg salt industry. Geology. Models. Plans. Tools. Dürrenberg as a spa.
May-Oct., Sa. 2-6; Su. 9-12, 2-5.

BAD ELSTER

REGIONAL ROOM
Kurhaus, Bad Elster
Local history. Development of the spa. Pearl-oyster industry. Minerals. Drinking glasses. 18th-19th century popular art.
Daily 9.30-12, 3-6.

BAD FRANKENHAUSEN

DISTRICT MUSEUM
Schloss, Bad Frankenhausen
Geology, palaeontology, botany, wildlife, prehistory of the Artern district. History of Bad Frankenhausen. Industrial development. Medieval pottery. Coins. Diorama showing Thomas Müntzer and the Battle of Frankenhausen.
Tu.-F. 10-12, 3-5; Sa. 2-5; Su. 10-12.

BAD FREIENWALDE

ODERLAND MUSEUM
Uchtenhagenstrasse 2, Bad Freienwalde
Prehistory. Geography. History of the town. 18th-19th century peasant furniture, household equipment. Astronomy. Space travel.
Tu.-Sa. 2-5; Su. 10-12, 2-5.

BAD KÖSEN

REGIONAL MUSEUM
Romanisches Haus, Bad Kösen
History of the Pforte Cistercian monastery. Architectural details. Gravestones. History of the spa and the saltworks.
Tu.-F. 10-12, 2-4.30, Sa., Su. 9-12.

BAD KÖSEN-SAALECK

SAALECK CASTLE
Bad Kösen-Saaleck
In towers of 12th century castle. History of the castle. Display illustrating founding and growth of the Turingia and Saxony History Society.
Apr. 15- Oct. 15, daily 9-5.

BAD KÖSTRITZ

HEINRICH SCHÜTZ MEMORIAL
Thälmanstrasse 1, Bad Köstritz
Birthplace of the composer, Heinrich Schütz (d.1672). Life and work of Schütz. 17th century music and musicians in their social context.
W. 9-11, 2-6; Su. 9-12. Other times by appointment.

BAD LANGENSALZA

REGIONAL MUSEUM
Thälmannplatz 7, Bad Langensalza
In former Augustinian monastery. Prehistoric material. Local history. Handicrafts.
Tu.-Su. 10.30-12; F. 4.30-6. Other times by appointment.

BAD LAUCHSTÄDT

GOETHE THEATRE AND PAVILION
Kurpark, Bad Lauchstädt
Theatre (1802), built at the instigation of Goethe. The Pavilion has material illustrating the 18th-19th century development of the town and spa, and the history of the Goethe Theatre.
Su. 10-12. Other times by appointment.

BAD LIEBENWERDA

MUSEUM OF LIEBENWERDA DISTRICT
Dresdener Strasse 15, Bad Liebenwerda
Local geology, prehistory. History of Bad Liebenwerda. Handicrafts. Agriculture.
Tu., F., Su. 2-6. Other times by appointment.

BAD SCHANDAU

REGIONAL MUSEUM
Badallee 10-11, Bad Schandau
Geology. Natural history. Mining. Quarrying. Local history. Handicrafts. Elbe navigation.
M.-F. 10-12, 3-5; Sa., Su. 10-12.

BAD SULZA

SALTWORKS MUSEUM
Verwaltungsgebäude, VEB Saline Neusulza, Bad Sulza
History of the saltworks. Prehistoric material found in the saltmine. Weapons and relics of the Battle of Auerstedt (1806).
Tu., Th. 2.30-4.30; Su. 9.30-11.30. Other times by appointment.

BAD SÜLZE

SALT MUSEUM
Sanatorium, Bad Sülze
History of the spa and the saltworks.
On request.

BALLENSTEDT

REGIONAL MUSEUM
Goetheplatz 1, Ballenstedt
Geology. Prehistory. History of Ballenstedt, 11th-20th centuries. Handicrafts. Costumes. Peasant furniture, household equipment, tools.
Tu.-Sa. 9-12, 3-5; Su. 9-12.

BARLEBEN

COLLECTION OF PREHISTORY AND EARLY HISTORY
Rothenseer Strasse 25, Barleben
Prehistory and early history of the Barleben area.
By appointment.

BAUERBACH

SCHILLERHAUS
Bauerbach
House where Schiller lived, 1782-83, and where he wrote *Kabale und Liebe*, *Fiesko* and the first draft of *Don Carlos*. Memorabilia of his visit.
Mar.-Oct., daily 9-1, 2-5. Nov.-Feb., Tu.-Su. 9-1, 2-4.

BAUTZEN

MUSEUM OF ART AND CULTURAL HISTORY
Platz der Roten Ammee 1A, Bautzen
Geology. Botany. Zoology. 16th-20th century paintings. Medieval and Baroque sculpture, woodcarvings. 19th-20th century sculpture. Drawings. Prints. 17th-20th century furniture, handicrafts. Faience. Porcelain. Costumes. Toys. 18th-19th century children's books. 18th-19th century bookbindings. Prehistory of the area. History of Bautzen.
Tu., Th., Sa., Su. 10-12, 2-5; Nov.-Mar. also W. 10-12, 2-5.

MUSEUM OF SORBIAN LITERATURE
Sorbenhaus am Postplatz, Bautzen
Development of Sorbian literature since the 16th century. Documents. Paintings. Engravings. Sculpture.
M.-F. 12-5; Sa., Su. 9-1.

OLD WATERWORKS TECHNICAL MUSEUM
Wendischer Kirchof 7, Bautzen
In 16th century fortification and waterworks. Display illustrating history and technical features of the equipment.
May-Oct., Tu., Th., Sa., Su. 9-12, 2-5.

BEESKOW

REGIONAL MUSEUM OF BIOLOGY
Frankfurter Strasse 23A, Beeskow
Geology, wildlife and prehistory of the area. Memorabilia of L. Leichardt (d.1948). History of Beeskow.
Tu.-Sa. 9-12, 2-5; Su. 2-6.

BELGERN

REGIONAL MUSEUM
Oschatzer Strasse 11, Belgern
In former town prison. Prehistoric material. Local history. Handicrafts.
Su. 2-4. Other times by appointment.

BELZIG

REGIONAL MUSEUM
Burg Eisenhardt, Belzig
Prehistory. Local history. 19th century craftsmen's tools, equipment; peasant furniture, household equipment.
Sa. 1-5; Su. 9-6. Other times by appointment.

BERLIN

ANTHROPOLOGICAL COLLECTION OF HUMBOLDT UNIVERSITY
Mauerstrasse 69-75, Berlin 108
Anthropological material from Europe, Asia, Africa, South America.
By appointment.

JOHANNES R. BECHER HOUSE
Majokowski Ring 34, Berlin
House of the 20th century poet, Johannes R. Becher, with original furnishings. Pictures, books, manuscripts, and other memorabilia of the poet, author of the text of the national anthem of the GDR.
Tu., F. 2-7; Th. 8-1.

BODE MUSEUM: COIN COLLECTION
Bodestrasse 1-3, Museuminsel, Berlin 102
Worldwide coin collection, especially Greek, Roman, Oriental, 12th-19th century European. Paper money. Seals. Medals, including 16th century German wood and stone examples. Displays showing currencies and prices. Dies.
Tu., Th.-Sa. 9-5; W. 12-8; Su. 10-6.

BODE MUSEUM: COLLECTION OF EARLY CHRISTIAN AND BYZANTINE ART
Bodestrasse 1-3, Museuminsel, Berlin 102
3rd-18th century works from countries surrounding the Mediterranean. Portraits and architectural sculptures. Icons. Woollen and silk fabrics from Egyptian graves. Ceramics. Gravestones, especially Italian. Panel paintings. Coptic art. Sarcophagi.
M., Th.-Sa. 9-5; W. 12-8; Su. 10-6.

BODE MUSEUM: COLLECTION OF PAINTINGS
Bodestrasse 1-3, Museuminsel, Berlin 102
14th-18th century Dutch, Flemish, German, Italian, English, French paintings, including works by Filippino Lippi, Cranach, Poussin, Gainsborough. 15th-16th century German, Dutch sketches. 18th century Berlin portraits.
M., Th.-Sa. 9-5; W. 11-7; Su. 10-6.

BODE MUSEUM: DEPARTMENT OF PRINTS AND DRAWINGS
Bodestrasse 1-3, Museuminsel, Berlin 102
Miniatures, drawings, woodcuts, etchings, from 15th century to present day. Botticelli's illustrations to Dante's *Divine Comedy.* Drawings by Edvard Munch. Modern French, German engravings. Illustrated books.
M., Th.-Sa. 9-5; W. 12-8; Su. 10-6.

BODE MUSEUM: EGYPTIAN MUSEUM
Bodestrasse 1-3, Museuminsel, Berlin 102
Egyptian art and history in the time of the Pharaohs and in the Hellenistic period. Mummy portraits. Tomb-paintings. Gold jewellery.
M., Th.-Sa. 9-5; W. 11-7; Su. 10-6.

BODE MUSEUM: PAPYRUS COLLECTION
Bodestrasse 1-3, Museuminsel, Berlin 102
Papyri. Parchments. Wax and wood tablets. Literary texts, stories and legends of ancient Egypt. Greek, Latin, Hebrew, Aramaic, Persian, Syrian, Ethiopian, Nubian documents.
M., Th.-Sa. 9-5; W. 11-7; Su. 10-6.

BODE MUSEUM: SCULPTURE COLLECTION
Bodestrasse 1-3, Museuminsel, Berlin 102
14th-17th century Italian sculpture. 14th-18th century French, German, Dutch, Flemish sculpture.
M., Tu.-Sa. 9-5; W. 12-8; Su. 10-6.

CENTRAL COLLECTION OF THE STATE GEOLOGICAL MUSEUM
Invalidenstrasse 44, Berlin
Stratigraphy. Fossils. Sedimentary rocks. Petrography. Mineralogy. Cores.
By appointment.

HUGUENOT MUSEUM
Französicher Dom, Platz der Akademie, Berlin
History of the Reformed Church and of the French Protestant community in Prussia. Register of Huguenot settlers. Memorabilia of Theodor Fontane.
On request.

HUMBOLDT UNIVERSITY: MUSEUM OF MINERALOGY AND PETROGRAPHY
Museum für Naturkunde, Invalidenstrasse 43, Berlin 104
Minerals, arranged according to chemical composition. Crystallography. Evolution of crystals.
Tu., Su. 10-2; W., Th. 3-7.

HUMBOLDT UNIVERSITY: MUSEUM OF PALAEONTOLOGY
Museum für Naturkunde, Invalidenstrasse 43, Berlin 104
Animal and plant fossils. Skeletons of Sauria, including Brachiosaurian. Ammonites. Fossilised fish. Geology. Geotechnics.
Tu., Su. 10-2; W., Th. 3-7.

HUMBOLDT UNIVERSITY: ZOOLOGICAL MUSEUM
Museum für Naturkunde, Invalidenstrasse 43, Berlin 104
Evolution of species. Mounted specimens of animals. Special collection of the wild-life of Germany. Dioramas. Memorial exhibition to Professor Walter Arndt.
Tu., Su. 10-2; W., Th. 3-7.

ROBERT KOCH MUSEUM
Humboldt Universität, Clara Zetkin Strasse 96, Berlin
In former Physiological Institute. Memorabilia of the bacteriologist and Nobel Prize winner, Robert Koch.
M.-F. 9-4.

MUSEUM OF CULTURAL HISTORY
Am Köllnischen Park 5, Berlin 102
History of Berlin, from prehistoric times. Documents. Prints. Paintings. Furniture. Science and literature in Berlin. Memorabilia of the novelist, Theodor Fontane, of the playwright Gerhart Hauptmann and of the artist, Heinrich Zillé. Theatre history. Berlin porcelain. Mechanical musical instruments.
Tu., Th.-Su. 9-4; W. 9-7.

MUSEUM OF GERMAN HISTORY
Unter Den Linden 2 und Clara Zetkin Strasse 26, Berlin 108
In former Arsenal (1705). History of the German people, 1789-present day. Unified displays, showing historical process at different stages and making use of posters, photographs, furniture, clothing, tools, industrial products, weapons, machines, household equipment.
Tu.-Sa. 8-7; Su. 9-4.

MUSEUM OF POSTAL HISTORY
Mauerstrasse 69-75, Berlin
History of German postal and telecommunication services. Documents. Models. Equipment and apparatus. Postal vehicles.
Tu.-F. 10-6; Sa. 10-5.

MUSEUM OF PREHISTORY AND EARLY HISTORY
Bode Museum, Bodestrasse 1-3, Museuminsel, Berlin 102
Material illustrating early history and culture of Europe and Asia.
Special exhibitions from permanent collections.

NATIONAL GALLERY
Bodestrasse 1-3, Museuminsel, Berlin 102
18th-20th century European paintings, sculpture, especially works by French and German artists.
Tu.-Sa. 9-5; Su. 10-6; W. 12-8.

PERGAMON MUSEUM: COLLECTION OF GREEK AND ROMAN ANTIQUITIES
Bodestrasse 1-3, Museuminsel, Berlin 102
Hellenistic architecture, from Priene, Magnesia, Miletus. The Pergamon Altar. Greek sculpture, vases, objets d'art, especially terracottas. Roman sculpture and copies of Greek originals. Roman portrait sculpture, mummy portraits, mosaics.
Tu.-Sa. 9-5; Su. 10-6.

PERGAMON MUSEUM: FAR EASTERN COLLECTION
Bodestrasse 1-3, Museuminsel, Berlin 102
Late Stone Age - 20th century Chinese ceramics. 18th-19th century woven silk fabrics, embroideries. Enamels. Jades. Lacquerwork. Contemporary Chinese and Indian ink paintings. Japanese coloured woodcuts.
Tu., Th.-Sa. 9-5; W. 12-8; Su. 10-6.

PERGAMON MUSEUM: ISLAMIC MUSEUM
Bodestrasse 1-3, Museuminsel, Berlin 102
Art and cultural history of the Moslem world, 8th-19th centuries. Calligraphy. Persian and Indian miniatures. Façade of desert palace of Mshatta. Prayer niche from Maydân mosque. Wood carvings.
Tu.-Sa. 9-5; Su. 10-6.

PERGAMON MUSEUM: MUSEUM OF ETHNOGRAPHY
Bodestrasse 1-3, Museuminsel, Berlin 102
Textiles and textile manufacturing equipment. 18th-20th century costumes. Pottery. Stoneware. Furniture. Woodcarvings. Agricultural implements. Craftsmen's tools. Peasant ornaments.
Tu., Th.-Sa. 9-5; Su. 10-6.

PERGAMON MUSEUM: NEAR EASTERN MUSEUM
Bodestrasse 1-3, Museuminsel, Berlin 102
Art and architecture of the Near East. Babylonian architecture of the period of Nebuchadnezzar. Assyrian reliefs, sculptures. Ceramics. Glass. Cuneiform clay tablets. Mosiacs. Metal artifacts.
Tu., Th.-Sa. 9-5; W. 9-7; Su. 10-6.

OLD MUSEUM
Lustgarten, Berlin
19th-20th century drawings, sketches, especially German. 20th century German paintings, prints.
W.-M. 9-5; Su. 10-6.

STATE MUSEUM OF ARTS AND CRAFTS
Schloss Köpenick, Berlin-Köpenick, Berlin 117
German baroque and Italian Renaissance furniture. Jewellery. Berlin and Meissen porcelain. Silver. Pewter. Glass. Medieval - 19th century textiles.
W.-M. 9-5; Su. 10-6.

BERNAU

REGIONAL MUSEUM
Steintor, Bernau
In tower (1420-50). Local history. Handicrafts. 15th-16th century weapons, armour.
Tu.-F., Su. 9-12, 2-5; Sa. 9-12.

BERNBURG

BERNBURG CASTLE MUSEUM
Schlossstrasse 24, Bernburg
Geology of the Bernburg area. Potash and salt industries. Local birds, insects. History of Bernburg. 17th-19th century furniture, household equipment. 18th century handicrafts. Coins.
W., F., Su. 10-1, 2-5.

BIRKENWERDER

CLARA ZETKIN MEMORIAL
Summter Strasse 4, Birkenwerder
Life and achievements of Clara Zetkin (d.1933), in the house in which she lived. Paintings. Photographs. Documents. Memorabilia.
Tu.-Su. 9-6.

BITTERFELD

DISTRICT MUSEUM
Kirchplatz 3, Bitterfeld
Geology, prehistory and history of the district. Local brown coal industry. Palaeontology. Ornithology. Development of film technology.
M.-F. 10-12, 1.30-6.30; Su. 9-12.30.

BLANKENBURG

REGIONAL MUSEUM
Schnappelberg 6, Blankenburg
Prehistoric and medieval material from local excavations. Pottery. Religious ornaments. 17th-18th century furnishings. Costumes. Weapons. Handicrafts.
Tu.-Sa. 9-12, 2-5; Su. 9-12.

BLANKENHAIN

REGIONAL MUSEUM
Schloss, Blankenhain
Local history. 18th century Blankenhain porcelain. Peasant tools, handicrafts.
Tu., F., Sa. 1-5. Other times by appointment.

BLANKENSEE

VILLAGE MUSEUM
Blankensee
Local history and prehistory. Peasant handicrafts, tools, costumes.
By appointment.

BOIZENBURG

REGIONAL MUSEUM
Kleine Wallstrasse 7, Boizenburg
Local history. Peasant tools, handicrafts. Pottery.
W. 2-5; Su. 10-12. Other times by appointment.

BORNA

REGIONAL MUSEUM
Karl Marx Platz 3, Borna
Local history and prehistory. Handicrafts. Development of industry and brown coal industry since 1799. Animal fossils.
Su. 10.30-12. Other times by appointment.

BRANDENBURG

DISTRICT MUSEUM
Hauptstrasse 96, Brandenburg
Geology, prehistory and history of the district. 17th-19th century furniture, household equipment. 16th-20th century European drawings, prints. 16th-18th century embroidery.
Tu.-Sa. 3-6; Su. 10-1.

BRAND-ERBISDORF

REGIONAL MINING MUSEUM
Huthauz zum Reussen, Brand-Erbisdorf
Local history. Silver and lead mining, 17th-20th centuries, with models and original equipment. Ores.
Su. 10-12.

BRÜSSOW

REGIONAL MUSEUM
Rathaus, Brüssow
Local history.
Su. 2-4.

BUCHENWALD BEI WEIMAR

NATIONAL BUCHENWALD MEMORIAL
Buchenwald bei Weimar
On the site of former concentration camp. Museum of Buchenwald camp and resistance movement. Ernst Thälmann memorial room.
Apr.-Sept. daily 8-5.30. Oct.-Mar. Tu.-Su. 8-5.

BÜRGEL

CERAMICS MUSEUM
Altes Badertor, Bürgel
Ceramics from the Bürgel factory.
By appointment.

BÜTZOW

REGIONAL MUSEUM
Schlossplatz, Bützow
Local history. 17th-20th century handicrafts. 19th-20th century furnishings. Butterflies.
2nd Su. in month, 10-12. Other times by appointment.

BURG BEI MAGDEBURG

DISTRICT MUSEUM
Platz des Friedens 26, Burg bei Magdeburg
Local history, prehistory. Costumes. Uniforms. Weapons. Ceramics.
Tu.-F. 3-5; Su. 10-12, 3-6.

BURGK

REGIONAL AND CASTLE MUSEUM
Schloss Burgk, Burgk
In castle (1403). 18th century furnished rooms. Local history. Weapons. Silbermann organ.
Daily 9-1, 2-6.

BUTTSTÄDT

REGIONAL MUSEUM
Altes Vogtshaus, Freiheitstrasse, Buttstädt
Local history, prehistory. Handicrafts. Household equipment. Costumes. Development of fire-fighting equipment.
Su. 3-6. Other times by appointment.

CAMBURG

REGIONAL MUSEUM
Amtshof 1-2, Camburg
Geology. Prehistory. 17th-20th century history of Camburg.
Tu.-Th. 2-6. Other times by appointment.

CARLOW

REGIONAL ROOM
Rathaus, Carlow
Local history. Ethnography.
On request.

COLDITZ

REGIONAL MUSEUM
Kurt Böhme Strasse 1, Colditz
Local history, prehistory. Handicrafts. Pottery. Porcelain. Coins. Butterflies.
Tu.-Th. 9-12, 2-4; Sa., Su. 9-12.

COSPEDA

1806 MEMORIAL
Gasthaus 'Zum Grünen Baum', Cospeda
Displays illustrating the Battle of Jena, 1806. Dioramas. Drawings. Prints. Weapons.
May-Oct., Tu.-Su. 9-5.

COSWIG

CERAMICS FACTORY MUSEUM
Rosa Luxemburg Platz 13, Coswig
In former ceramics factory. Development of pottery techniques. Original machines and models. Ceramics for the chemical and building industries.
W., Su. 10-12, 2-6; Sa. 2-6.

REGIONAL MUSEUM
Kirchstrasse 6, Coswig
Local history and prehistory.
1st and 3rd Su. in month, 10-12, 3-5.

COTTBUS

BLECHEN MEMORIAL
Bezirksmuseum, Schloss Branitz, Cottbus
Memorial room to the painter, Carl Blechen (d.1840).
Tu.-Su. 10-6.

DISTRICT MUSEUM
Schloss Branitz, Cottbus
In castle (1772). 12th-19th century history of Cottbus. Handicrafts. Furniture. Costumes. 16th-18th century wrought iron. 18th-19th century pewter. Paintings.
Tu.-Su. 10-6.

CRIMMITSCHAU

REGIONAL MUSEUM
Strasse der Befreiung 1, Crimmitschau
Geology. Mineralogy. Wildlife of the region. Local history. Handicrafts. Costumes. Pewter. Porcelain.
M.-F., Su. 10-12. Other times by appointment.

CROSTAU

REGIONAL ROOM
Im Hofe 1, Crostau
Local history. Materials from excavations on the site of Crostau Castle (destroyed 1350). Local weaving industry.
By appointment.

CUMLOSEN

REGIONAL ROOM
Cumlosen 113
Local history. Birds of the region.
By appointment.

DAHLEN

REGIONAL ROOM
Wurzener Strasse 1, Dahlen
Geology of the area. Local and regional history.
Tu., Th. 3-5; Su. 10-12.

DAHME

REGIONAL MUSEUM
Am Kloster 2, Dahme
Local history, prehistory. Handicrafts. 19th century furnishings, clothing. Coins. Medals.
Tu.-Su. 10-12, 2-5.

DELITZSCH

DISTRICT MUSEUM
Schloss, Delitzsch
Prehistory and history of the district. 11th-17th century history of Delitzsch. 16th-19th century furniture. Clocks and watches. Craftsmen's tools. Agricultural implements. Papers of the naturalist, C. G. Ehrenberg.
Tu., Th. 9-12, 3-5; Su. 3-5.

DEMMIN

DISTRICT MUSEUM
Ernst Thälmann Strasse 23, Demmin
Local history, prehistory. 13th-18th century painting, sculpture, crafts. Wrought iron. Pewter. Porcelain. 17th-18th century Louis XVI and Biedermeier furniture. 14th-20th century coins, manuscripts.
M.-Sa. 9-12, 4-5; Su. 10-12.

DERMBACH

DISTRICT MUSEUM
Bahnhofstrasse 16, Dermbach
Geology. Local history, prehistory. Wildlife of the district, especially birds. Handicrafts. Industry. Glass. Porcelain. Woodcarving.
Tu.-F. 9-11, 2-5; Su. 10-12.

DESSAU

LUISIUM CASTLE
Dessau-Waldersee, Dessau
18th-19th century German paintings, drawings. Special collection of 18th century Frankfurt painters.
Tu.-Su. 10-6.

MOGISKAU PALACE STATE MUSEUM
Dessau-Mogiskau, Dessau
In castle (1757). 17th-18th century furnishings, paintings, porcelain, faience, glass.
Tu.-Su. 10-6.

MUSEUM OF NATURAL HISTORY AND PREHISTORY
August Bebel Strasse 32, Dessau
Geology. Mineralogy. Local wildlife, especially birds. Local history. 13th-16th century handicrafts. Ceramics.
Tu.-Su. 9-6.

STATE GALLERY: GEORGIUN PALACE
Puschkindallee 100, Dessau
In castle annexe (1780). 15th-18th century German, Dutch, Flemish paintings. 18th century portraits. 19th-20th century German, French paintings.
Tu.-Su. 10-6.

DIESDORF

ALTMARK REGIONAL MUSEUM
Diesdorf
Farmhouse (1787). Bakehouse. 18th century granary. 17th-19th century local history.
Tu.-Sa. 9-12, 2-5.

DOBERLUG-KIRCHHAIN

TAWERS' MUSEUM
Potsdamer Strasse 18, Doberlug-Kirchhain
In former taw-maker's workshop (1788). Tools, equipment.
On request.

DÖMITZ

REGIONAL MUSEUM
Festungshof, Dömitz
In former fortress (1569). Local history. Handicrafts. Elbe navigation. 19th-20th century household equipment.
Tu.-F. 10-12, 2-4; Sa. 10-1; Su. 10-12, 2-5.

DOHNA

REGIONAL MUSEUM
Pfarrstrasse 6, Dohna
Local history, prehistory. History of Dohna Castle, until its destruction (1402). Photographic collection showing 19th-20th century development of Dohna.
May-Oct., Tu. 4-6; Su. 2-4.

DORFCHEMNITZ, KREIS BRAND-EIBISDORF

DORFCHEMNITZ FORGE HAMMER
Dorfchemnitz, Kreis Brand-Eibisdorf
18th-19th century forge hammer.
M.-F. 1-5; Sa., Su. 10-12, 1-5.

DORFCHEMNITZ, KREIS STOLBERG

BONE-MILL CULTURAL CENTRE
Am Anger 1, Dorfchemnitz, Kreis Stolberg
Bonemill and barkmill. Stocking works. Insects. Butterflies. Birds. Popular art.
On request.

DORNBURG

DORNBURG CASTLES
Dornburg
16th-17th century castle contains Goethe Memorial Room, with personal possessions recalling his stay in the castle. 18th century castle has period rooms, with porcelain collection.
Tu.-Su. 9-1, 2-5.

DRESDEN

MARTIN ANDERSEN NEXÖ MEMORIAL
Collenbuschstrasse 4, Dresden-Weisser Hirsch, Dresden
House and memorabilia of M. A. Nexö (d.1954).
Tu., Th., F. 10-3; W. 2-8; Su. 10-1.

BOTANICAL INSTITUTE OF DRESDEN TECHNICAL UNIVERSITY
Zellescher Weg 40, Dresden
Herbaria, especially of Saxony. European lichens and the potentilla family.
On request.

CARL MARIA VON WEBER MEMORIAL
Dresdenerstrasse 44, Dresden-Hosterwitz, Dresden
Exhibits illustrating life and work of the composer, Carl Maria von Weber (d.1826), and especially his period as conductor of the orchestra in Dresden, 1817-26.
M., Sa., Su. 10-7. Tu., Th., F. 1-7.

GERMAN MUSEUM OF HEALTH EDUCATION
Zentralinstitut für Medizinische Aufklärung, Lingner Platz 1, Dresden
Displays illustrating methods of achieving personal and public health.
Daily 9-6.

INSTITUTE AND MUSEUM OF THE HISTORY OF THE CITY OF DRESDEN
Ernst Thälmann Strasse 2, Dresden 801
History of Dresden and of the Dresden workers' movement. 18th-20th century paintings. 16th-20th century drawings, prints. Furniture. Weapons. Coins. Medals.
M.-Th., Sa. 10-6; Su. 10-4.

INSTITUTE OF PRECISION INSTRUMENT-MAKING OF THE TECHNICAL UNIVERSITY OF DRESDEN
Barkhausen Bau, Helmholtzstrasse 18, Dresden
Development of the typewriter since 1864.
By appointment.

KRASZEWSKI HOUSE
Nordstrasse 28, Dresden
House in which the Polish artist, Josef Ignacy Kraszewski (d.1887) spent a period of exile.
M.-Sa. 10-6; Su. 10-4.

LEONHARDI MUSEUM
Grundstrasse 62, Dresden-Loschwitz, Dresden
Memorabilia of the painter, E. Leonhardi (d.1905), in his former home.
May-Sept., Th. 3-5; Su. 10-12. Other times by appointment.

MARCOLINI PALACE
Friedrichstrasse 41, Dresden
Exhibition in entrance hall of Palace (1745), where Napoleon's meeting with Metternich took place. Memorabilia of Napoleon's visit.
On request.

MUSEUM OF PHOTOGRAPHY
Käthe Kollwitz Ufer 76, Dresden
Development of cameras, lenses and photographic equipment since 1860.
By appointment.

MUSEUM OF POPULAR ART
Köpckestrasse 1, Dresden 806
Popular art of Saxony, especially from the Lausitz, Vogtland and Erzgebirge areas. Furniture. Kitchen equipment. Pottery. Costumes. Toys. Woodcarving and turning.
Tu.-Sa., 10-5; Su. 10-4.

POLYTECHNIC MUSEUM
Friedrich Engels Strasse 15, Dresden 8060
History of electro-technics and photography.
M., Tu., W., F. 9-4; Th. 9-7.

PROVINCIAL MUSEUM OF PREHISTORY
Japanisches Palais, Karl Marx Platz, Dresden
Prehistory and early history of Saxony. Archaeological material, especially from hut-sites.
By appointment.

PUPPET THEATRE COLLECTION
Barkengasse 6, Radebeul, Dresden
19th-20th century marionettes and puppets from many countries. 18th-19th century Saxony marionette theatre. Puppet collections of the DEFA film studios and of the television service.
By appointment.

SCHILLER'S COTTAGE
Schillerstrasse 19, Dresden
House in which Schiller completed *Don Carlos* (1787). Schiller memorabilia.
W., Su. 11-6.

STATE ART COLLECTIONS: DEPARTMENT OF COINS
Güntzstrasse 34, Dresden 8016
Coins. Medals. Seals. Dies. Paper money. Important collection of Saxony coins, medals. Greek and Roman coins and medieval German coins.
Special exhibition of material from permanent collection.
May-Oct., M., W., F.-Su. 9-6; Tu. 9-8; Th. 2-6. Nov.-Apr., M., W., F.-Su. 10-6; Tu. 10-8.

STATE ART COLLECTIONS: DEPARTMENT OF PRINTS AND DRAWINGS
Güntzstrasse 34, Dresden 8016
15th-20th century European prints, drawings, watercolours. Japanese woodcuts. Photography. History of the 17th-18th century theatre. Illustrated books.
Special exhibition of material from permanent collection.
May-Oct. M., W., F.-Su. 9-6; Tu. 9-8; Th. 2-6. Nov.-Apr., M., W., F.-Su. 10-6; Tu. 10-8.

STATE ART COLLECTIONS: GALLERY OF MODERN PAINTINGS
Albertinium, Georg Treu Platz 3, Dresden 801
19th-20th century European paintings, including works by French, Polish, Hungarian and Belgian artists. German Impressionists and Expressionists. Contemporary socialist paintings, portraits.
May-Oct., M., W., F.-Su. 9-6; Tu. 9-8; Th. 2-6. Nov.-Apr., M., W., F.-Su. 10-6; Tu. 10-8.

STATE ART COLLECTIONS: GREEN VAULT
Albertinium, Georg Treu Platz, Dresden 801
14th-18th century European jewellery, goldsmiths' work. 16th-18th century glass, enamel. 16th century bronzes.
May-Oct., M., W., F.-Su. 9-6; Tu. 9-8; Th. 2-6. Nov.-Apr., M., W., F.-Su. 10-6; Tu. 10-8.

STATE ART COLLECTIONS: HISTORICAL MUSEUM
Semper Galerie, Zwinger, Dresden 801
16th-18th century weapons. Armour for men and harness, including 16th-18th century ceremonial armour of the Court of Saxony. Helmets. Shields. Hunting weapons, equipment.
Th.-Tu. 9-5.

STATE ART COLLECTIONS: MUSEUM OF ARTS AND CRAFTS
Wasserpalais, Schloss Pillnitz, Dresden 8057
Applied art, medieval period - present day. Furniture. Musical instruments. Glass. Metalwork. German, Dutch, French faience. Stoneware. Pewter. Textiles. 20th century industrial design.
M.-F. 10-4; Tu., Th. also 4-7; Sa. 10-1.

STATE ART COLLECTIONS: OLD MASTERS GALLERY
Semper Galerie, Zwinger, Sophienstrasse, Dresden 801
15th-18th century Italian paintings. 17th century Flemish, Dutch, Spanish paintings. 16th century German paintings. 17th-18th century French paintings. 18th century paintings by Saxony artists.
May-Oct., Tu., Th.-Su. 9-6; M. 2-6; W. 9-9. Nov.-Apr. Tu.-Su. 10-6; W. 10-8.

STATE ART COLLECTIONS: PEWTER COLLECTION
Zwinger, Dresden
15th-19th century European, especially German, Pewter.
Daily 9-4.

STATE ART COLLECTIONS: PORCELAIN COLLECTION
Zwinger, Dresden 801
Chinese pottery of the Han, Wei and Tang periods. Chinese porcelain of the Sung periods and of the 15th-18th centuries. 17th-18th century Japanese porcelain. 18th century Meissen porcelain.
Sa.-Th. 9-5.

STATE ART COLLECTION: SCULPTURE GALLERY
Albertinum, Georg Treu Platz, und Schloss Pillnitz, Dresden 801
Greek, Etruscan and Roman sculpture, objets d'art (in Albertinum). 15th-20th century German, French sculpture (in Schloss Pillnitz). Egyptian sculpture.
May-Oct., M., W., F.-Su. 9-6; Tu. 9-8; Th. 2-6. Nov.-Apr., M., W., F.-Su. 10-6; Tu. 10-8.

STATE HALL OF MATHEMATICS AND PHYSICS
Zwinger, Dresden 801
Historic instruments and equipment used in the natural sciences, watchmaking, precision engineering, surveying, cartography. Calculating machines. Weights and measures.
Daily 9-5.

STATE MUSEUM OF ETHNOLOGY
Japanisches Palais, Karl Marx Platz, Dresden 801
World-wide collections of ethnographical material, including skulls.
By appointment.

STATE MUSEUM OF MINERALOGY AND GEOLOGY
Augustusstrasse 2, Dresden
Palaeontology, palaeobotany and mineralogy of Saxony.
By appointment.

STATE MUSEUM OF ZOOLOGY
Augustusstrasse 2, Dresden
Displays illustrating evolution and development in the animal world.
Daily 9-4.

TRANSPORT MUSEUM
Johanneum, Augustusstrasse 1, Dresden 801
History of railways, shipping, motor transport. Models. Paintings. Drawings. Prints. Original vehicles and equipment.
Tu.-Su. 9-5.

ZOOLOGICAL INSTITUTE OF DRESDEN TECHNICAL UNIVERSITY
Zellescher Weg, Dresden
Study collections of birds, reptiles, amphibians, fish, insects.
By appointment.

EBERSBACH

REGIONAL MUSEUM
Humboldt Baude, Schlechteberg, Ebersbach
Local geology, prehistory, history. Furniture. Costumes. Ceramics. Glass.
Apr.-Nov., Tu., Su. 2.30-6. July-Aug. also Th. 2.30-6.

EBERSWALDE

DISTRICT AND REGIONAL MUSEUM
Kirchstrasse 8, Eberswalde
Prehistoric material. Local history.
Tu.-F., Su. 10-12, 2-5. Sa. 10-12.

ECKARTSBERGA

MUSEUM OF REGIONAL LIFE
Eckartsburg, Eckartsberga
Local and regional history. Diorama of the Battle of Auerstedt (1806).
On request.

EGELN

MUNICIPAL MUSEUM
Moritz Wiener Strasse 3, Egeln
Prehistory and early history of the district.
W. 8 p.m.-10, Su. 3-7. Other times by appointment.

EHRENFRIEDERSDORF

GREIFENSTEIN MUSEUM
Ehrenfriedersdorf
Local history. 16th-19th century tin mining. Furniture. Wood carving.
M.-W., F.-Su. 9-12, 2-5.

EIBAU

REGIONAL AND HUMBOLDT MUSEUM
Beckenberg, Eibau
Local and regional history. Furniture. Wood carving. Ceramics. Glass.
Apr.-Oct., Su., public holidays 2-6. Other times by appointment.

EIBENSTOCK

MUNICIPAL EXHIBITION OF REGIONAL LIFE
Eibenstock
Geology. Regional history. Industry and technology.
May-June, Sept. Su. 10-12, W. 10-12, 2-5. July-Aug. Su. 10-12, Tu., Th. 10-12, 2-5, Sa. 2-5.

EILENBURG

DISTRICT AND MUNICIPAL MUSEUM
Schlossberg 7, Eilenburg
Local history and prehistory.
W. 2-4, Su. 10-12. Other times by appointment.

EISENACH

BACH HOUSE
Frauenflan 21, Eisenach
Home of the Bach family, with original household equipment. Material relating to the Bachs and their circle. 16th-19th century musical instruments.
Apr-Sept., M.-Sa. 9-5, Su. 9-1, 2.30-5. Oct.-Mar., M.-Sa. 9-5, Su. 9-1.

1869 EISENACH PARTY CONGRESS MEMORIAL
Marienstrasse 45, Eisenach
History of the German Workers' Movement, with special reference to Eisenach.
M.-F. 9-12.30, 2.30-5, Sa. 9-5, Su. 9-12.30. July-Aug. also Su. 9-12.30, 2.30-5.

LUTHER HOUSE
Lutherplatz 8, Eisenach
History of the Reformation. Portraits. Manuscripts. Medals. Books. Special collection of material relating to Martin Luther.
Daily 9-1, 2-6.

REUTER HOUSE
Reuterweg 2, Eisenach
In former home of the artist, Fritz Reuter (d.1868). Paintings and drawings by Reuter. Memorabilia of him, and of his friends. Collection illustrating life and work of Richard Wagner.
Tu.-Su. 9-12.30, 2.30-5.

SCULPTURE COLLECTION
Predigerplatz 4, Eisenach
In former 13th-14th century Dominican Church. Merovingian tombstones. Romanesque sculpture. Medieval religious sculpture.
Tu.-Su. 9-12.30, 2.30-5.

TEA-HOUSE IN THE KARTAUSGARTEN
Kartausgarten, Eisenach
18th century garden pavilion, with period furnishings, decorative arts.
Tu.-Th., Sa., Su. 9-12.30, 2.30-5. F. 9-12.30, 2.30-6.

THURINGIA MUSEUM
Market 24, Eisenach
Local history, prehistory. Glass, medieval - present day. Pottery. Porcelain. Faience. Wrought-iron. 18th-19th century furniture, household equipment. Local handicrafts. 19th century German paintings.
Tu.-Th., Sa., Su., 9-12.30, 2.30-5. F. 9-12.30, 2.30-6.

WARTBURG
Eisenach
14th-18th century furniture. 15th-18th century applied arts. 16th century paintings. 14th-15th century sculpture.
Daily 8.30-4.

EISENBERG

DISTRICT AND REGIONAL MUSEUM
Schloss Friedrichstanneck, Eisenberg
History and prehistory of the town and region. Local handicrafts. 19th century peasant furniture, household equipment, costumes.
Tu.-Su. 8-12, 1-5.

EISFELD

OTTO LUDWIG REGIONAL MUSEUM
Schloss Eisfeld, Eisfeld
Prehistoric material from local excavations. Geology, flowers and butterflies of the region. History of Eisfeld. Handicrafts. 17th-19th century peasant furniture, household equipment, tools, costumes. 20th century applied art. Development of the porcelain industry. Memorabilia of Otto Ludwig (d.1865).
M.-F. 8-12, 2-5. Su. 10-12, 2-5.

EISLEBEN

BÜRGERGARTEN MEMORIAL TO THE MANSFELD WORKERS' MOVEMENT
Nicolaistrasse 20, Eisleben
In the oldest meeting place of the Eisleben workers. History of the local workers' movement.
Tu. 10-12, F. 3-5, Su. 10-12.

DISTRICT AND REGIONAL MUSEUM
Andreaskirchplatz 7, Eisleben
Prehistory of the region. History of Eisleben. Mansfeld mining industry since 1200. Mansfeld Miners' movement 1891-1945. 17th-19th century handicrafts. Religious textiles. Coins.
Tu.-Sa. 9-12, 3-5. Su. 10-12.

HOUSE WHERE LUTHER DIED
Andreaskirchplatz 7, Eisleben
Memorabilia of Luther. Portraits. Letters. Documents.
Tu.-Sa. 9-12, 3-5. Su. 10-12.

LUTHER'S BIRTHPLACE
Lutherstrasse 16, Eisleben
Luther's life and work. Leaflets. Bibles. Coins and medals of the Reformation.
Tu.-Sa. 9-12, 3-5. Su. 10-12.

NATURAL HISTORY COLLECTION
Lutherstrasse, Eisleben
Rocks. Minerals. Local birds, beetles. Mosses.
Tu., W. 10-12, 3-5. Th. 3-5. F. 10-12.

ELLRICH

REGIONAL MUSEUM
Nicolaiplatz 12, Ellrich
Regional history. History of the workers' movement.
Apr.-Nov., Su. 3-6.

ERFURT

ANGER MUSEUM OF ART
Anger 18, Erfurt
14th-16th century German sculpture, panel paintings. Medieval glass paintings. 18th-20th century German paintings. Medieval-Renaissance applied art. Furniture. 14th-20th century wrought iron. Faience. Porcelain. 17th-20th century drinking glasses.
Tu., Su. 10-1. W.-Sa. 10-5.

FOLK-LORE MUSEUM
Juri Gagarin Ring 140A, Erfurt
Antiquities from village churches in Thuringia. Peasant furniture, household equipment, tools, costumes. Handicrafts. Glass. Faience. Porcelain. Toys.
Tu., Th., F. 10-1. W. 10-1, 2-5. Sa. 10-4. Su. 10-12.

MEMORIAL TO THE ERFURT PARTY CONGRESS OF 1891
Futterstrasse 15-16, Erfurt
History of the German workers' movement, especially in Erfurt.
M.-F. 10-1, 2-6. Sa. 10-2.

MOLSDORF MUSEUM
Schloss Molsdorf, Erfurt
Period rooms.
W.-Su. 2-5.

MUNICIPAL HISTORY MUSEUM
Juri Gagarin Ring 140A, Erfurt
Prehistory. History of Erfurt since 1742. View of the town. 14th-16th century seal-stamps. 16th-17th century coin dies. Municipal collection of silver.
Tu., Th., F. 10-1, W. 10-1, 2-5, Sa. 10-4, Su. 10-12.

NATURAL SCIENCE MUSEUM
Leninstrasse 169, Erfurt
Geology. Biology. Astronomy.
Tu., Th., F. 10-1. W. 10-12, 1-5. Sa. 10-4. Su. 10-12.

ERKNER

GERHART HAUPTMANN MEMORIAL
Gerhart Hauptmann Strasse 1-2, Erkner
Memorabilia of Gerhart Hauptmann (d.1946) and his association with Erkner.
1st Su. in month 10-12; Th. 2-5; Sa. 9-12.

FALKENSEE

REGIONAL ROOM
Thalmannplatz, Falkensee
Geology and wildlife of the district. History of Falkensee.
Apr.-Sept., Sa. 2-5.

FALKENSTEIN

REGIONAL MUSEUM
Platz der Deutsch-Sowjetischen Freundschaft, Falkenstein
13th-19th century history of Falkenstein. Handicrafts. Wood carvings. Costumes. Local tin and iron mining, 1469-1800.
May-Sept., Tu.-Sa. 9-12, 2-4.30; Su. 9-12. Oct.-Apr., M.-F. 9-12, 2-4.30; Sa. 9-11.

FINSTERBERGEN

REGIONAL MUSEUM
Lindenstrasse 112, Finsterbergen
Local and regional history.
By appointment.

FINSTERWALDE

LOCAL STUDIES CENTRE
Schloss, Finsterwalde
Prehistoric material. Local history. Rocks.
Su. 10-12. Other times by appointment.

FRANKENBERG

EXHIBITION OF REGIONAL LIFE
Hainicher Strasse 5A, Frankenberg
Local history. Industry. Handicrafts. Transport.
W., F., Su. 10-12; M. 2-4. Other times by appointment.

FRANKFURT AN DER ODER

DISTRICT MUSEUM
Emanuel Bach Strasse 11, Frankfurt an der Oder
Prehistory of the area. History of Frankfurt.
Tu.-Sa. 10-5; Su. 10-12, 2-6.

GALLERY OF MODERN ART
Rathaus, Frankfurt an der Oder
Paintings, drawings, prints, sculpture by contemporary German artists.
Tu.-Sa. 10-6. Su., public holidays 11-5.

KLEIST MEMORIAL
Stadtarchiv, Julian Marchlewski Strasse 17-18, Frankfurt an der Oder
Material relating to Heinrich von Kleist (d.1811) and his time.
M.-F. 10-1, 3-5. Su. by appointment.

FRAUENSTEIN

REGIONAL MUSEUM
Schloss, Frauenstein
In 16th century castle. History of the citadel. 14th-15th century religious sculpture.
Daily 9-12, 2-5.

FREIBERG

GEOLOGICAL INSTITUTE
B. von Cotta Strasse, Freiberg
Geology. Palaeontology.
By appointment.

INSTITUTE OF FUEL
B. von Cotta Strasse, Freiberg
Fuels, especially those found in Germany.
By appointment.

MUNICIPAL AND MINING MUSEUM
Am Dom 1-3, Freiberg
History of Freiberg and of the local workers' movement. Paintings. Sculpture. Handicrafts. Applied art. Furniture. Glass. Pottery. Faience. Wrought iron. 16th-19th century weapons. Life and work of Lommossov.
Tu.-Sa. 8.30-12.30, 1.30-4.30; Su. 8.30-1.30.

MUSEUM OF NATURAL HISTORY
Waisenhausstrasse 10, Freiberg
Minerals. Rocks. Evolution of plants and animals. Nuclear physics.
May-Sept., M.-Sa. 8.30-12.30, 1.30-4.30; Su. 8.30-12, 1.30-5. Oct.-Apr., M.-Sa. 8-12.30; Su. 9-12, 2-5.

SCIENTIFIC COLLECTION OF FREIBERG MINING ACADEMY
Brennhausgasse 14, Freiberg
Geology. Mineralogy. Crystallography. Mining technology.
M.-F. 8-11, 2-4; Sa. 8-11.

FREITAL

REGIONAL HOUSE
Schloss Burgker Strasse 61, Freital
Geology. Mineralogy. History of Freital. Development of local mining industry.
Tu.-Su. 10-4.

FREYBURG

JAHN MUSEUM
Schlossstrasse 1, Freyburg
Former home of Friedrich Ludwig Jahn (d.1852). Jahn memorabilia.
Tu.-Su. 9-12, 2-6.

NEUENBURG CASTLE MUSEUM
Freyburg
Geology. Local history and prehistory.
Tu.-Su. 8-12, 1-5.

FRIEDLAND

REGIONAL MUSEUM
Neubrandenburger Stadttor, Friedland
Local and regional history.
By appointment.

FROHBURG

ALTE FARBE REGIONAL MUSEUM
Teichgasse, Frohburg
Local history. Peasant handicrafts, tools.
Sa. 1-4, Su. 9.30-12. Other times by appointment.

FROHNAU

FROHNAU FORGE
Frohnau, Kreis Annaberg, Erzgebirge
In disused forge (1436) and in former house of the smith. History of the forge and of the local iron industry. Tools. Equipment.
Daily 9-12, 1-5.

FÜRSTENWALDE

MUNICIPAL AND REGIONAL MUSEUM
Holzstrasse 1, Fürstenwalde, Spree
Geology. Prehistory. Local history.
Tu., Th.-Sa. 9-1; W. 2-5; Su. 9-12. Other times by appointment.

GADEBUSCH

REGIONAL MUSEUM
Amtstrasse, Gadebusch
Local and regional history.
Sa. 4-6; Su. 10-12.

GARDELEGEN

MEMORIAL MUSEUM
Philipp Müller Strasse 22, Gardelegen
History of the local workers' movement.
Always.

REGIONAL MUSEUM
Philipp Müller Strasse 16, Gardelegen
Local history. Handicrafts. Peasant tools, implements, equipment. Costumes.
Tu.-Sa. 10-12, 3-5.

GARZ

ERNST MORITZ ARNDT MUSEUM
Garz auf Rügen
Regional history. Collection illustrating life and work of Arndt (d.1860). Memorabilia. Portraits. Manuscripts. First editions.
Daily 9-12, 2-6.

GEISA

REGIONAL MUSEUM
Schloss, Geisa
Handicrafts. 17th-18th century furniture. Memorial room to the Jesuit, Father A. Kircher, born in Geisa and founder of the Museo Kircheriano, Rome.
Su. 10-1. Other times by appointment.

GENTHIN

DISTRICT AND REGIONAL MUSEUM
Mützelstrasse 22, Genthin
Prehistory of the Elb-Havel area. Peasant handicrafts, tools, equipment. Coins.
M.-F. 8-12, 2-5; Su. 10-12.

GEORGENTHAL

GEORGENTHAL REGIONAL MUSEUM
Kornhaus, Georgenthal
History of Georgenthal Monastery. Medieval paintings.
Tu., Th., F., Su. 3-5.

GERA

MUSEUM OF CULTURAL HISTORY
Strasse der Republik 2, Gera
In former Arsenal (1732-8). Prehistory and history of Gera and its region. Handicrafts. Industry. Gera porcelain, glass. Prussian coins. Furniture from Osterstein Castle. Medieval art of East Thuringia.
Tu.-Su. 9-12, 2-5.

NATURAL HISTORY MUSEUM
Am Nicholaiberg 3, Gera
Geology of E. Thuringra. Pleistocene animals. Development of biological studies. Life and work of the Thuringian ornithologists, Brehm, Engelmann, Hennicke, Liebe. Molluscs of America. Birds of Asia, Africa, America.
Tu.-Su. 9-12, 2-5.

GERSTUNGEN

REGIONAL MUSEUM
Sophienstrasse 2, Gerstungen
In former castle (16th century). Local history. 18th-19th century peasant furnishings, tools, handicrafts.
May-Sept., M.-F. 9-12, 1-5. Mar.-Apr., Oct., Tu.-Th. 2-5. Other months on request.

GEYER

REGIONAL MUSEUM
Wachtturm, Geyer
In 13th century watch-tower. Local history. 17th-19th century history of local tin mining. Minerals and rocks. Pewter. Gold and silver lace, made in Geyer.
Tu.-Su., 9-12, 2-5.

GLAUCHAU

MUNICIPAL MUSEUM AND ART COLLECTION
Schloss Hinterglauchau, Glauchau
Geology. Mineralogy. Plants and wildlife of the region. 17th-19th century furniture, paintings. 16th-20th century drawings, engravings, prints. Local history and handicrafts, especially weaving. Pewter. Porcelain.
M.-F. 8-12, 1-5; Sa. 9-12; Su. 2-4.

GNANDSTEIN

REGIONAL MUSEUM
Burg Gnandstein
Local history. Peasant furnishings, tools, handicrafts, costumes. Paintings. Memorabilia of Theodor Korner's residence in Gnandstein.
Tu.-Su. 9-12, 2-6.

GOHREN

MÖNCHGUTER REGIONAL MUSEUM
Strandstrasse, Gohren
Local history.
May-Sept., Daily 9-12, 3-6. Oct.-Apr., Tu., F., 9-12, 3-6.

GÖRLITZ

KAISERTRUTZ: STATE ART COLLECTION
Demianiplatz 1, Görlitz
Local history. Handicrafts, industry, commerce. 14th-16th century paintings, sculpture. 18th-19th century German paintings. 20th century applied art.
Tu.-Sa. 10-1, 3-6; Su. 10-4.

REICHENBACK TOWER
Demianiplatz, Görlitz
Tower (15th century). Medieval - 18th century weapons.
Tu.-Sa. 10-1, 3-6; Su. 10-4.

STATE ART MUSEUM: HAUS NEISSSTRASSE MUSEUM
Neissstrasse 30, Görlitz
Local history, prehistory. Industry and commerce of the region. Furniture. Crafts. Applied art. Coins. Drawings. Prints.
Tu.-Sa. 10-1, 3-6; Su. 10-4.

STATE MUSEUM OF NATURAL HISTORY
Am Museum 1, Görlitz
Geology. Mineralogy. Wildlife of the world, with special local collection. Evolution.
Tu., F. 10-1, 3-6. Other times by appointment.

GOLDBERG

DISTRICT MUSEUM
Müllerweg 2, Goldberg
Geology, prehistory and history of the Goldberg district. Handicrafts. Industry.
Su. 10-12.30, 3-5.30. Other times by appointment.

GOTHA

CASTLE MUSEUM
Schloss Friedenstein, Gotha
Castle (1656) of the Dukes of Saxe-Gotha. 14th-17th century painting, sculpture. 15th-18th century engravings. Coins, especially Roman. 17th-19th century German applied art. Greek, Roman, Chinese art.
May-Sept., Daily 8-6. Oct.-Apr., Tu.-Su. 9-5.

EKHOF THEATRE
Schloss Friedenstein, Gotha
Oldest surviving German theatre in original condition. Theatre history. Music.
Daily 9-5.

1875 GOTHA PARTY CONGRESS MEMORIAL
Cosmarstrasse 24-5, Gotha
History of the workers' movement, with special reference to Gotha.
Daily 10-12, 3-6.

MUSEUM OF REGIONAL HISTORY AND FOLKLORE
Schloss Friedenstein, Gotha
Local history. Costumes. Weapons.
May-Sept., daily 9-5. Oct.-Apr., Tu.-Su. 9-5.

NATURAL HISTORY MUSEUM
Parkallee 15, Gotha
Geology. Palaeontology. Mineralogy. Zoology.
Daily 9-5.

GOTHA-SIEBLEBEN

GUSTAV FREYTAG MEMORIAL
Weimarer Strasse 145, Gotha-Siebleben
In former home of the writer and art historian, Gustav Freytag (d.1895). Work and memorabilia of Freytag.
By appointment.

GRABOW

REGIONAL MUSEUM
Kirchenstrasse 14, Grabow
Regional history, prehistory. Handicrafts.
Su. 10.30-12. Other times by appointment.

GRAUPA

RICHARD WAGNER AND REGIONAL MUSEUM
Graupa
Regional history. Peasant tools. Hunting equipment. Memorial room to Wagner, who composed part of *Lohengrin* in Graupa. Wagner memorabilia, pictures.
Su., M., Tu., Th., 9-12, 2-6; Sa. 3-6.

GREIFSWALD

COLLECTIONS OF THE ERNST MORITZ ARNDT UNIVERSITY: ANATOMICAL INSTITUTE AND MUSEUM
Friedrich Loeffler Strasse 23C, Griefswald
Comparative anatomy. Skeleton and skull collections.
By appointment.

COLLECTIONS OF THE ERNST MORITZ ARNDT UNIVERSITY: ARCHAEOLOGICAL INSTITUTE
Lonsstrasse 20, Greifswald
Casts of Greek and Roman sculpture, with some original sculpture.
By appointment.

COLLECTIONS OF THE ERNST MORITZ ARNDT UNIVERSITY: INSTITUTE OF AGRICULTURAL BIOLOGY
Ludwig Jahn Strasse 15A, Greifswald
Herbarium.
By appointment.

COLLECTIONS OF THE ERNST MORITZ ARNDT UNIVERSITY: INSTITUTE FOR PREHISTORY AND EARLY HISTORY
Domstrasse 11, Greifswald
Archaeological material from Pomerania.
By appointment.

COLLECTIONS OF THE ERNST MORITZ ARNDT UNIVERSITY: BOTANICAL INSTITUTE
Grimmerstrasse 88, Greifswald
Herbaria. Microscope preparations.
By appointment.

COLLECTION OF THE ERNST MORITZ ARNDT UNIVERSITY: GEOLOGICAL AND PALAEONTOLOGICAL INSTITUTE
Ludwig Jahn Strasse 176, Greifswald
Historical geology. Vertebrate and invertebrate fossils. Fossils from Scandinavia. Micropalaeontology.
By appointment.

COLLECTION OF THE ERNST MORITZ ARNDT UNIVERSITY: MINERALOGICAL AND PETROGRAPHICAL INSTITUTE
Ludwig Jahn Strasse 17, Greifswald
Minerals, Rocks, Meteorites. Gem-stones.
By appointment.

COLLECTIONS OF THE ERNST MORITZ ARNDT UNIVERSITY: ZOOLOGICAL INSTITUTE AND MUSEUM
Johann Sebastian Bach Strasse 11-12, Greifswald
Biology. Ecology. Ornithological collection. Skeletons.
By appointment.

GREIFSWALD MUNICIPAL MUSEUM
Theodor Pyl Strasse 1-2, Greifswald
Prehistory and history of the Greifswald region. History of the University. 13th-14th century architectural items. 17th-19th century pewter, copper, silver. 19th-20th century paintings by Greifswald artists. Memorial rooms to C. D. Friedrich and E. M. Arndt.
Tu.-Sa. 10-5; Su. 10-1, 2-5.

GREIZ

DISTRICT AND REGIONAL MUSEUM
Unteres Schloss, Burgplatz 12, Greiz
History of Greiz. Popular art. Furniture. Household equipment. Costumes.
Tu.-F. 9-12.30, 2-5; Sa. 9-12.30; Su. 10-5.

STATE COLLECTION OF BOOKS AND ENGRAVINGS
Sommerpalais, Leninpark, Greiz
Development of the illustrated book since 1500. Prints and engravings. English etchings, caricatures, maps.
Tu.-F. 10-4; Sa., Su. 10-1.

GREUSSEN

REGIONAL MUSEUM
Rathaus, Greussen
Geology. Regional history. Local handicrafts.
W., Su. 4-6. Other times by appointment.

GRIMMA

DISTRICT MUSEUM
Paul Gerhard Strasse 43, Grimma
Geology and prehistory of the district. History of Grimma. Peasant handicrafts, tools, furniture, household equipment. Toys.
Tu.-F. 10-12, 2-4; Su. 12.30-4.30. Other times by appointment.

GÖSCHEN HOUSE
Schillerstrasse 25, Grimma
Formerly home of Göschen, the publisher (d.1828). Local history. Furniture and paintings of the Empire and Biedermeier periods.
On request.

MILL MUSEUM
Grossmühle 2, Grimma
In mill (1725). History of mills since earliest times. Grain processing. Milling equipment.
On request.

GRÖBZIG

LOCAL COLLECTION
Ernst Thälmann Strasse, Gröbzig
In former Synagogue (1780). Prehistoric material. Local history. 18th-19th century history of the Gröbzig Jewish community. Birds of the region.
1st Su. in month 2-5.

GROSSBEEREN

GROSSBEEREN 1813 MEMORIAL
Dorfstrasse, Grossbeeren
Display illustrating the Battle of Grossbeeren (1813). Causes of the Battle. Plans. Views. Weapons.
Apr.-Oct., daily 10-12, 2-6.

GROSSENGOTTERN

REGIONAL ROOM
Langensalzaer Strasse, Grossengottern
Prehistoric material from local sites. Local history. Peasant tools, furnishings and household equipment. Natural history.
Su. 2-5. Other times by appointment.

GROSSENHAIN

DISTRICT MUSEUM
Kirchplatz 4, Grossenhain
Local history and prehistory. Peasant furnishings. Weapons. Toys. Engravings. Coins.
Tu.-F. 9-12, 2-5; Su. 9-12.

GROSSKOCHBERG

GOETHE MEMORIAL
Schloss, Grosskochberg
Memorabilia of Goethe and of Charlotte von Stein.
Tu.-Su. 9-12, 2-4.

GROSSROHRSDORF

REGIONAL MUSEUM
Mühlstrasse 5, Grossrohrsdorf
Local history. Peasant handicrafts, tools. 19th century hunting equipment. 19th century ceramics, jewellery.
Tu., Th., Su. 3-6. Other times by appointment.

GROSSSCHÖNAU

OBERLAURITZ REGIONAL AND DAMASK MUSEUM
Kupperjaus, Schenaustrasse, Grossschönau
In former damask mill. Damask-making machines, equipment. Local handicrafts. Religious art. Birds and rocks of the district.
Apr. 15- Oct. 31, M.-F. 9-12, 2-5. Nov. 1 - Apr. 14, by appointment.

GÜSTROW

ERNST BARLACH MEMORIAL
Getrudenkapelle, Güstrow
In 15th century chapel. Sculpture by Barlach.
Su. 10-6.

DISTRICT MUSEUM
Franz Parr Platz 7, Güstrow
Prehistory of the district. History of Güstrow. Furniture. Household equipment. Collection of Güstrow theatre tickets since 1740.
Tu.-Su. 10-6.

HAINICHEN

REGIONAL MUSEUM
Platz der Deutsch-Sowjetischen Freundschaft 9, Hainichen
Life and work of the writer, C. F. Gellert (d.1769). Memorabilia of F. G. Keller (d.1895). Local handicrafts. Pewter. Sculpture.
W. 3-5; Su. 9-12. Other times by appointment.

HALBERSTADT

CATHEDRAL COLLECTION
Dom, Halberstadt
12th-16th century ornaments, vestments. 13th-14th century sculpture, panel-paintings. Reliquaries. Liturgical objects. Medieval manuscripts.
Guided tours only. Tu.-Sa., 10, 12, 3. Su. 11.30.

GLEIN HOUSE
Domplatz 31, Halberstadt
Displays illustrating career of J. W. L. Glein and spiritual life of 18th century. Portraits. Manuscripts. Letters. Books.
Tu.-Sa. 9-12, 3-6; Su. 10-3.

MUNICIPAL MUSEUM
Domplatz 36, Halberstadt
Natural sciences. Prehistory. History of Halberstadt. 16th-18th century furniture. Peasant costumes, tools, handicrafts. Religious sculpture. Paintings.
Tu.-Sa. 9-6; Su. 9-1.

HALDENSLEBEN

DISTRICT MUSEUM
Breitergang, Haldensleben
Geology. Zoology. Prehistory. History of Haldensleben. Local ceramics industry. Household equipment. Costumes. Weapons. Paintings. Prints.
M.-F. 9-12, 2-5. Su. 10-12.

HALLE

BOTANICAL INSTITUTE OF MARTIN LUTHER UNIVERSITY
Neuwerk 21, Halle
Herbarium, with particularly important collections from Central Germany, S. America, S. Africa, Australia.
By appointment.

COLLECTION OF THE DEPARTMENT OF MINERALOGY AND PETROLOGY OF MARTIN LUTHER UNIVERSITY
Domplatz 1, Halle
Geology. Mineralogy.
By appointment.

FRANCKES FOUNDATION NATURAL HISTORY AND HISTORICAL COLLECTIONS
Franckeplatz 1, Halle
Collection of A. H. Franckes. History of the Franckes Foundation, 1698-1945. Portraits. Bible collection.
By appointment.

HALLOREN MUSEUM
Mansfelder Strasse 52, Halle
History of the Halle salt-industry. Collection of silversmiths' work.
By appointment.

HÄNDEL HOUSE
Grosse Nicolai Strasse 5, Halle
In birthplace of G. F. Händel. Life and work of the composer. Collection of musical instruments.
Tu.-Sa. 3-6. Su. 10-6.

MARTIN LUTHER UNIVERSITY MUSEUM OF THE GEISEL VALLEY
Domstrasse 5, Halle
Geology. Fossils from brown-coal beds and from the copper

shales. Historical development of brown coal. Local mining industry.
M.-F. 8-12, 2-5.

MORITZBURG STATE GALLERY
Friedemann Bach Platz 5, Halle
Decorative arts. Meissen porcelain. Glass. Faience. Pottery. Gold- and silversmiths' work. Carpets. German paintings, especially Impressionist and Expressionist. 12th-17th century architectural sculpture from Halle. Contemporary sculpture. 15th-20th century prints, drawings.
Tu.-Su. 10-1, 3-5.

MUSEUM OF THE DEPARTMENT OF ARCHAEOLOGY AT MARTIN LUTHER UNIVERSITY
Universitätsplatz 12, Halle
Greek and Roman small works of art. Casts of Greek and Roman sculpture.
By appointment.

MUSEUM OF THE DEPARTMENT OF ZOOLOGY OF MARTIN LUTHER UNIVERSITY
Domplatz 4, Halle
Mammals. Birds. Molluscs.
By appointment.

PROVINCIAL MUSEUM OF PREHISTORY
Richard Wagner Strasse 9-10, Halle
Archaeological material of the Palaeolithic, Bronze and Iron ages. Special collection relating to the Halle region before 961.
Tu.-Su. 10-1, 3-5.

REGIONAL MUSEUM
Grosse Märkerstrasse 10, Halle
History of Halle and of the local Workers' Movement.
Tu.-Sa. 10-12, 3-6; Su. 10-6.

WALDKATER REGIONAL MUSEUM
An der Heide, Halle
Wildlife and plants of the Dölaner Heath.
M., Tu., Th. 9-1. W., Sa. 2-6; Su. 10-6.

HARTENSTEIN

REGIONAL MUSEUM
Burg Stein, Hartenstein
History of the Castle and its occupants, 12th century onwards. Weapons. Execution equipment. Local history, especially mining.
May-Sept., Tu.-F. 9-12, 1-4. Oct.-Apr., Tu.-F. 9-12, 1-3.

HAVELBERG

PRIGNITZ MUSEUM
Am Dom, Havelberg
Prehistory. Regional history. Architectural items from the Cathedral. Shipbuilding. Navigation. Fishing.
Tu.-F. 9-12, 2-5; Sa. 9-12; Su. 10-12, 2-4.

HEILIGENSTADT

EICHFELD REGIONAL MUSEUM
Collegienstrasse 10, Heiligenstadt
Local geology, prehistory, birds. Regional history. Peasant handicrafts, furnishings, costumes. 15th century religious sculpture.
Tu., Th. 2.30-4.30; Su. 10.30-12.30. Other times by appointment.

HERRNHUT

'ALT HERRNHUTER STUBE' REGIONAL MUSEUM
Löbauer Strasse 18, Herrnhut
In 18th century town-house. 2 fully furnished and equipped rooms of the early Biedermeier period.
Th.-M. 10-12, 2-5.

ETHNOGRAPHICAL MUSEUM
Löbauer Strasse 18, Herrnhut
World-wide ethnographical collections.
Tu. 10-12; Th. 2-5; Sa. 10-12; Su. 10.30-12, 2-5.

HIDDENSEE

BIOLOGICAL RESEARCH INSTITUTE OF THE ERNST MORITZ ARNDT UNIVERSITY, GREIFSWALD: BIRD-WATCHING STATION
Kloster, Hiddensee
Palaeontology. Ornithology.
By appointment.

GERHART HAUPTMANN MEMORIAL
Kloster, Hiddensee
In former home of Gerhart Hauptmann (d.1946). Life and work of the author.
May-Sept., daily 10-5.

HIDDENSEE ISLAND REGIONAL MUSEUM
Kloster, Hiddensee
History of the Island and the region. Wildlife. Coastal protection.
May-Sept., daily 9-4.

HILDBURGHAUSEN

REGIONAL MUSEUM
Rathaus, Marx-Engels Platz, Hildburghausen
Local history. Handicrafts. 19th century furnishings. Collection relating to the publisher and bookseller, Joseph Meyer, and to the foundation of the Bibliographical Institute.
Daily 10-1, 2-5.

HINZDORF

REGIONAL ROOM
Hinzdorf
Prehistoric material from local sites. 19th century peasant furnishings.
By appointment.

HOHENLEUBEN

HOHENLEUBEN - REICHSFELS MUSEUM
Burg Reichenfels, Hohenleuben
Geology, minerals and wildlife of the area. Prehistory and early history. Handicrafts. Weapons. Armour.
Tu.-F. 8-6; Su. 8-4.

HOHNSTEIN

CONCENTRATION CAMP MEMORIAL IN HOHNSTEIN CASTLE
Jugendburg Ernst Thälmann, Hohnstein
Site of the 1st German concentration camp. Memorial exhibition to the victims.
Daily 8-12, 1-5.

HOLZHAUSEN

BURGMUSEUM
Veste Wachrenburg, Holzhausen
Geology. Wildlife. History of the castle. Peasant furnishings, tools.
Daily 9.30-5.

HOYERSWERDA

DISTRICT MUSEUM
Platz des Friedens 1, Hoyerswerda
Geology, zoology, prehistory, history of the district. Pewter. Costumes.
W., Su. 10-12, 2-6.

ILMENAU

REGIONAL MUSEUM
Markt 7, Ilmenau
Local history. Handicrafts. Porcelain. Glass. Peasant furnishings, costumes. Goethe Room, with material relating to Goethe's life and work, especially his period in Ilmenau, 1776 - his death. Goethe's geological collection.
M. 9-12, 2-4; Su. 9-12.

ILSENBURG

REGIONAL MUSEUM
Marienhof Ernst Thälmann Strasse 9, Ilsenburg
In 18th century manorhouse. Local geology, prehistory, history. Quarrying and processing of granite and quartz. Mining history. Paintings, drawings, watercolours.
May-Sept., M.-F. 9-12, 2-4; Su. 10-12. Oct.-Apr., Tu., F. 9-12, 2-4.

JARMEN

MILL MUSEUM
Jarmen
Dutch windmill. History and techniques of milling. 17th-19th century peasant tools.
On request.

JENA

COLLECTION OF THE ANTHROPOLOGICAL AND ETHNOLOGICAL DEPARTMENTS, FRIEDRICH SCHILLER UNIVERSITY
Kollegiengasse 10, Jena
Anthropological collection, medieval period - present day. Ethnology.
By appointment.

COLLECTION OF THE ARCHAEOLOGICAL DEPARTMENT OF THE FRIEDRICH SCHILLER UNIVERSITY
Ernst Thälmann Ring 24A, Jena
Greek and Roman sculpture, coins. Oriental coins.
By appointment.

COLLECTION OF THE DEPARTMENT OF GEOLOGY AND PALAEONTOLOGY OF THE FRIEDRICH SCHILLER UNIVERSITY
Fraunhofer Strasse 6, Jena
Geology of Germany and adjoining territories. Historical geology of Thuringia. European palaeontology, petrography. Mineralogy.
By appointment.

COLLECTION OF THE DEPARTMENT OF MINERALOGY AND PETROGRAPHY OF THE FRIEDRICH SCHILLER UNIVERSITY
Sellierstrasse 6, Jena
Rocks. Minerals. Textiles. Meteorites.
By appointment.

GOETHE MEMORIAL
Goethe Allee 26, Jena
House in which Goethe stayed during his visits to Jena (1817, 1822). Memorabilia of the poet and of his friends.
Apr. 16- Oct. 14, Tu.-Sa. 2-5; Su. 10-12.

ERNST HAECKEL HOUSE
Berggasse 7, Jena
In former home of the zoologist, Ernst Haeckel (d.1919). Life and work of Haeckel. Personal possessions. Letter. Manuscripts. Portraits.
M.-F. 9-5; Sa., Su. 9-2.

HAUSKNECHT HERBARIUM: COLLECTION OF THE BOTANICAL DEPARTMENT OF THE FRIEDRICH SCHILLER UNIVERSITY
Goetheallee 1, Jena
Herbarium of the flora of Thuringia and Central Europe. Phanerogamae of the Far East.
By appointment.

HILPRECHT COLLECTION OF NEAR EASTERN ANTIQUITIES OF THE FRIEDRICH SCHILLER UNIVERSITY
Professor Ibrahim Strasse 24, Jena
Cuneiform texts, 3000 B.C. - A.D. 300. Aramaic inscriptions.
Daily 9-1, 3-5.

KARL LIEBKNECHT HOUSE
Zwätzengasse 16, Jena
Memorial to Karl Liebknecht. 19th-20th century history of the German workers' movement.
M.-Sa. 10-5.

MUNICIPAL MUSEUM
Am Planetarium 12, Jena
In former summer residence (1784) of Professor J. F. Griesbach. History of Jena and the university. Local handicrafts, industry. Religious sculpture, drawings. Pewter. Porcelain. Textiles.
Tu.-Su. 10-5.

OPTICAL MUSEUM
Am Planetarium 7, Jena
History and technology of the optical industry. Life and work of Carl Zeiss.
Tu.-Su. 9-4.30.

PHYLETIC MUSEUM
Vor dem Neutor 1, Jena
Comparative anatomy and embryology. Anthropology. Palaeontology. Anatomical preparations. Genetics.
Th.-Tu. 9-2; W. 9-5.

SCHILLER MEMORIAL
Schiller Gässchen, Jena
House in which Schiller lived (1797-1802). Original furnishings. Schiller memorabilia.
Apr. 16- Oct. 15, Tu.-Sa. 10-2; Su. 10-12, 2-4.

JÜTERBOG

DISTRICT MUSEUM
Planeberg 9, Jüterbog
In former Abbot's residence (15th century) of Zinna Monastery. Local history and prehistory. Handicrafts. Costumes.
W., Sa., Su. 10-12, 2-6.

KAHLA

LEUCHTERBURG REGIONAL MUSEUM
Kahla
In 13th century castle. Geology. Prehistory. Local history. Weapons. Hunting techniques and equipment. Peasant and ruling-class furnishings. Porcelain from Thüringia and Kahla. Exhibits illustrating life of the porcelain workers.
Tu.-Sa. 8-12, 2-5; Su. 8-6.

KAMENZ

LESSING MUSEUM
Lessingplatz 3, Kamenz
Life and work of G. E. Lessing (d.1781). Theatre history.
Tu.-Sa. 8-12, 1-5.

WEST LAUSITZ MUSEUM
Pulsnitzer Strasse 16, Kamenz
Geography, botany, wildlife, prehistory and history of West Lausitz. Pewter. Handicrafts. Household equipment.
Tu., Th., Sa. 9-12, 1.30-3.30; Su. 9-12.

KAPELLENDORF

CASTLE MUSEUM
Wasserburg, Kapellendorf
Local geology, prehistory, history. Peasant ethnography. Agricultural implements.
Tu.-Su. 9-5.

KARL MARX STADT

"THE FIGHTER" MEMORIAL
Karl Immermann Strasse 23, Karl Marx Stadt
History of local workers' movement.
Tu.-Su. 9-5.

MUNICIPAL ART COLLECTION
Theaterplatz 1, Karl Marx Stadt
18th-19th century German, especially Saxon, paintings. 19th-20th century German sculpture. 18th-20th century German drawings, prints, engravings. Applied arts. Lace. Silk. Embroidery. 19th-20th century German furnishing, decorative arts.
Tu.-Su. 10-12.30, 2-4.30 (Tu., Th. 2-6.45).

NATURAL HISTORY MUSEUM
Theaterplatz 1, Karl Marx Stadt
Regional geology, mineralogy, palaeontology, zoology.
Tu.-Su. 10-12.30, 2-4.30 (Tu., Th. 2-6.45).

RABENSTEIN CASTLE
Oberfrohnaer Strasse, Karl Marx Stadt
Part of castle (12th century). Animal frescoes (1624). History of castle, with exhibition of material found during site excavations.
May-Oct., Tu.-Su. 9-12, 12.30-5.

RABENSTEIN UNDERGROUND ROCK CATHEDRAL
Rabenstein, Karl Marx Stadt
Limestone workings. Exhibition showing methods of quarrying and transporting the stone.
May-Oct., 8-5. Nov.-Apr., 9-4.

RED TOWER
Wilhelm Pieck Strasse 12, Karl Marx Stadt
Tower (13th century). Local history collection.
May-Oct., Tu., Th., F. 2-6.30; W., Sa. 11-6.30; Su. 9.30-1.

SCHLOSSBERG MUSEUM: MUNICIPAL AND CULTURAL HISTORY COLLECTION
Schlossberg 12, Karl Marx Stadt
Local history. Industrial development of former city of Chemnitz, now Karl Marx Stadt. History of German workers' movement. Fritz Heckert memorial room. Peasant handicrafts, furnishings, domestic equipment. Wrought-iron. 13th-18th century sculpture. 18th-19th century paintings by Chemnitz artists. 13th-17th century architectural items.
Tu. 10-12.30, 2-6.30; W.-Su. 10-12.30, 2-4.30.

KIRSCHAU

CASTLE MUSEUM
Am Schlossberg 21, Kirschau
Material from excavations at Körse Castle (destroyed 1352). Weapons. Ceramics. Textiles.
May-Oct., W. 3-5.

KLOSTER ZINNA

REGIONAL MUSEUM
Neue Abtei, Kloster Zinna
In part of former Cistercian abbey (15th century). Weaving. History of the Abbey, 1170-1553.
By appointment.

KÖLLEDA

REGIONAL MUSEUM
Thälmannstrasse 10, Kölleda
Geology. Local prehistory, history, wildlife, handicrafts. Coins. Medals. Seals.
Su. 10-12, 3-5. Other times by appointment.

KÖNIGSTEIN

KÖNIGSTEIN FORTRESS
Königstein
13th century fortress, later Saxony state prison. Old Arsenal (1594) contains weapons collection and August Bebel room.
Daily 8-6.

KÖTHEN

JOHANN FRIEDRICH NAUMANN MUSEUM
Schloss Köthen
Naumann's collecton of birds. Memorabilia of the naturalist.
W. 2-5, Su. 10-5.

REGIONAL MUSEUM
Museumstrasse 4-5, Köthen
Local prehistory, history, handicrafts. Religious art, especially 12th-16th century bells. Furniture. Household equipment. Display illustrating the first German Language Association (1618-50), in Köthen. Bach Memorial Room. Collection relating to scientists and artists connected with Köthen.
Tu., F. 2-5; Su. 10-5.

KOHREN

SCHWIND PAVILLON
Ortsteil Rüdigsdorf, Kohren
Garden-room in Rüdigsdorf Park, with frescoes by Moritz Schwind and L. Schulz (1838).
W., Sa. 2-4; Su. 10-12, 2-4.

KOHREN-SAHLIS

POTTERY MUSEUM
Ernst Thälmann Strasse 14, Kohren-Sahlis
Pottery (1763), with workshop. Collection of everyday Kohren tableware, 17th-19th century.
Mar.-Oct., Tu.-Su. 10-12, 1-5.

KRAKOW AM SEE

MILL MUSEUM
Blechern-Krug, Krakow am See
Dutch-type windmill. History of milling. Milling tools, equipment.
June-Sept., daily 10-12, 3-5. Other times by appointment.

KRIEBSTEIN

KRIEBSTEIN CASTLE DISTRICT MUSEUM
Kriebstein
14th century castle. Chapel with 1425 frescoes. Museum illustrating history of castle and of Kriebstein. 15th-17th century religious sculpture.
Daily 9-5.

KYFFHÄUSER

CASTLE MUSEUM
Kyffhäuser
Ruins of 11th-12th century castle. Museum illustrating history of the castle. Material from site excavations.
Daily 8-5.

LANDSBERG

'BERNHARD BRÜHL' REGIONAL MUSEUM
Bahnhofstrasse, Landsberg
Local prehistory, history, wildlife. Handicrafts. Industrial development of Landsberg.
Mar.-Oct., W., Su. 2-6; F. 9-1.

LANDWÜST

VOGTLAND PEASANT MUSEUM
Landwüst 48
Folklore. Peasant life, Middle Ages - present day. Carved butter moulds.
M.-W., F.-Su., 8.30-12, 1.30-5.

LAUCHA

BELL MUSEUM
Glockenmuseumstrasse 1, Laucha
18th century bellfoundry. Tools and equipment. Displays showing techniques of bell-founding. 15th-19th century bells.
Tu.-Su. 8-12, 2-5.

LAUENSTEIN

CASTLE AND REGIONAL MUSEUM
Schloss, Lauenstein
In 13th-14th century castle. History of the castle and the town. 17th-18th century furniture. Peasant handicrafts.
May-Sept., M.-Sa. 9-12, 2-6; Su. 10-12. Oct.-Apr., W., F. 2-6; Su. 10-12.

LAUSCHA

GLASS MUSEUM
Oberlandstrasse 10, Lauscha
History of the glass industry in Thuringia. Glass technology. Optical uses of glass.
Daily 8-5.

LEHDE

OPEN-AIR MUSEUM
Lehde 31
Farm (1800), with buildings, installations, tools, implements and costumes of the period.
Apr. 15-Oct. 30, Tu.-Su. 9-5. Nov. 1-Apr. 14, by appointment.

LEIPZIG

ARCHAEOLOGICAL MUSEUM
Archäologisches Institute, Karl-Marx Universität, Universitätstrasse 3-5, Leipzig
Roman, Greek, Near-Eastern prehistoric archaeology.
By appointment.

BACH MUSEUM
Menckestrasse 23, Leipzig
Documents, books and pictures relating to the life and work of Bach. Manuscripts. Recordings.
M., F. 1-5; W. 1-8; Tu., Th., Sa. 9-1.

BOOK AND WRITING MUSEUM OF THE GERMAN BOOK-TRADE
Deutscher Platz, Leipzig
History of books, writing and writing materials. Bindings. Watermarks.
M.-Sa. 9-6.

BOTANICAL INSTITUTE
Karl Marx Universität, Talstrasse 33, Leipzig
World botanical collection, with special emphasis on Germany.
By appointment.

GEORGI DIMITROFF MUSEUM
Georgi Dimitroff Platz 1, Leipzig
Displays illustrating life and political career of Dimitroff. The Reichstag Fire Trial.
Tu.-F. 8-5; Sa., Su. 8-2.

EGYPTIAN MUSEUM
Ägyptologisches Institut der Karl-Marx Universität, Schillerstrasse 6, Leipzig
Egyptian objets d'art. Material from tomb excavations.
By appointment.

ETHNOLOGICAL MUSEUM
Johannisplatz, Leipzig
World-wide ethnographical collections. Housing. Furniture. Food and its preparation. Tools. Handicrafts. Cloth-

ing. Weapons. Musical instruments. Paintings. Sculpture. Masks.
Tu.-F. 9.30-6; Sa. 10-4; Su. 9-1.

GEOGRAPHICAL MUSEUM OF THE GERMAN ACADEMY OF SCIENCES, BERLIN
Grassimuseum, Johannisplatz 5/11, Leipzig
Displays illustrating world physical and economic geography. Climate. Polar research. Resources and problems of tropical countries. Development of the Central Asian Republic of the U.S.S.R. Alexander von Humboldt memorial exhibition.
Tu.-F. 9.30-6; Sa. 10-4; Su. 9-1.

GERMAN GEOGRAPHICAL INSTITUTE
Georgi Dimitroff Platz 1, Leipzig
Exploration records. Maps. Documents.
By appointment.

INSTITUTE OF GEOLOGY AND PALAEONTOLOGY
Karl Marx Universität, Talstrasse 35, Leipzig
Geology and palaeontology of Germany.
By appointment.

INSTITUTE OF MINERALOGY AND PETROGRAPHY
Karl Marx Universität, Scharnhorststrasse 20, Leipzig
Mineralogy and petrography of Saxony and Central Germany. Crystallography.
On request.

INSTITUTE OF ZOOLOGY
Karl Marx Universität, Talstrasse 33, Leipzig
Historical development of animals and humans.
On request.

ISKRA MEMORIAL
Russenstrasse 48, Probstheida, Leipzig
House in which *Iskra* was printed, 1900-1. Displays showing organisation, preparation and production of *Iskra* and its historical and political importance. Reconstruction of the printing room and its equipment.
Tu.-Sa. 9-5; Su. 9-1.

KARL LIEBKNECHT HOUSE
Braustrasse 15, Leipzig
Liebknecht family house, 1865-81, and birthplace of Karl Liebknecht, 1871.
Tu., F., Sa. 11-5; W. 4-7; Su. 10-1.

LENIN MEMORIAL
Rosa Luxemburg Strasse 19-21, Leipzig
Headquarters of the *Leipziger Volkeszeitung* since 1900. Museum contains displays showing Lenin's political achievements. Furniture from house, 45 Bernhard Göring Strasse, in which Lenin lived in 1914.
Tu.-Sa. 9-5; Su. 9-1.

KARL MARX UNIVERSITY MUSEUM OF MUSICAL INSTRUMENTS
Täubchenweg 2e, Leipzig
16th-late 18th century musical instruments, including oldest clavichord and oldest grand piano. Complete range of instruments of the time of Bach. 19th-20th century European orchestral instruments. Popular and non-European instruments.
Tu.-Th. 3-6; F. 10-1; Sa. 10-3; Su. 10-1.

MEMORIAL TO THE PEOPLE'S BATTLE
Wilhelm Külz Park, Leninstrasse, Leipzig
Site of the battle where Napoleon was defeated in 1813. Memorial (1857). Museum illustrating history and results of the battle.
Tu.-Su. 9-4.

MUSEUM OF ARTS AND CRAFTS
Johannisplatz 5/11, Leipzig
13th-19th century German pottery, stoneware. Oriental stoneware, faience. 15th-18th century Spanish majolica. 17th-18th century European faience. European, oriental porcelain. Glass. Pewter. Ironwork. Medals. 16th-20th century goldsmiths' work. Ivories. Enamels. Late medieval, especially German, wood sculpture. 15th-19th century furniture. Textiles. Costumes.
Tu.-F. 9-30-6; Sa. 10-4; Su. 9-1.

MUSEUM OF THE HISTORY OF THE CITY OF LEIPZIG
Altes Rathaus, Markt, Leipzig
History of the workers' movement in Leipzig. Musical life of the city, 18th-19th century. Local architecture. Development of Leipzig. Portraits. Relics of battle of 1813. Railway history. Medieval pottery, stoneware. 15th-16th century printing.
Tu.-Sa. 9-6; Su. 9-1.

MUSEUM OF THE HISTORY OF THE LEIPZIG WORKERS' MOVEMENT
Georgi Dimitroff Platz 1, Leipzig
History of the workers' movement in Leipzig, 1830 to the present day.
Tu.-Su. 9-6.

MUSEUM OF NATURAL SCIENCES
Lortzingstrasse 3, Leipzig
Astronomy. Planetarium. Geology. Prehistory. Palaeontology. Wildlife of the Leipzig region. Local industries, especially brown coal.
Tu.-Sa. 9-6; F. 9-7.

MUSEUM OF PICTORIAL ART
Georgi Dimitroff Platz 1, Leipzig
15th-18th century Italian paintings. 17th century Dutch, Flemish paintings. 18th-19th century German paintings. 17th-19th century French, Spanish paintings. German, Italian, Dutch, Flemish drawings, prints. 19th century European sculpture.
Tu.-F. 9-6; Sa. 9-5; Su. 9-1.

SCHILLER'S COTTAGE
Menckestrasse 42, Leipzig
Mementoes of Schiller's stay (1785) in the summer cottage of Göschen, the publisher.
Tu., F., Sa. 11-5; Su. 9-12, W. 3-6.

KARL SUDHOFF INSTITUTE FOR THE HISTORY OF MEDICINE AND THE NATURAL SCIENCES
Karl Marx Universität, Talstrasse 33, Leipzig
Medical equipment and instruments from Europe, Asia, Africa. Superstitions and folk cures. Herbarium of medicinal plants. Drugs. Pictures.
By appointment.

LEISNIG

MILDENSTEIN CASTLE DISTRICT MUSEUM
Burglehn 6, Leisnig
In former granary and residence of 14th century castle. Prehistory and history of the district. Industrial development. Workers' movement. 19th century peasant household equipment, tools. Guild history. Handicrafts. Religious wood sculpture. Weapons. Coins.
M.-F. 8-12, 1-5; Su. 8-12, 1-6.

LENGENFELD

REGIONAL ROOM
Otto Nuschke Strasse 3, Lengenfeld
Geology. Local history. Handicrafts. 19th-20th century costumes.
Su. 9-12, 3-6.

LENZEN

REGIONAL MUSEUM
Burghof, Lenzen
Prehistoric material from local sites. History of Lenzen. Local handicrafts.
Su. 2-4. Other times by appointment.

LICHTENSTEIN

REGIONAL MUSEUM
Ernst Thälmann Strasse 29, Lichtenstein
In former Town Hall (1709). Geology. Regional history. Industrial development. Guild history. Local handicrafts.
Sa. 4-6; Su. 10-12.30.

LIEBSTADT

CASTLE KUCKUCKSTEIN REGIONAL MUSEUM
Liebstadt
In 18th century restoration of 15th century castle. Regional geology, flora, wildlife. Local history.
W., F., Sa. 2-5; Su. 9-12, 2-5.

LIMBACH-OBERFROHNA

REGIONAL MUSEUM
Chemnitzer Strasse 9, Limbach Oberfrohna
Geology and birds of the region. Local history, handicrafts, industry, especially textiles.
W., Th. 2-6; Su. 10-12. Other times by appointment.

LÖBAU

MUNICIPAL MUSEUM
Löbau
Prehistory of the region. History of Löbau. Furniture, household equipment. Handicrafts. 18th century religious sculpture.
Th.-F. 3-5; Su. 10-12.

LOMMATZCH

REGIONAL MUSEUM
Rathaus, Markt 1, Lommatzch
Prehistory of the region. History of Lommatzch. Peasant handicrafts, tools.
1st and 3rd Su. in month, 9-12.

LÜBBENAU

LÜBBENAU MUSEUM IN THE SPREEWALD
Volkspark, Lübbenau
Prehistory. History of Lübbenau. History of Sorbian culture and literature. Luther's works. Controversial writing of the Reformation period. Local handicrafts. Costumes. 17th-19th century paintings, drawings, prints. Glass. Porcelain. Pottery.
May-Oct., Tu.-Su. 9-5. Nov.-Apr., Tu.-F. 9-5.

LUCKAU

REGIONAL MUSEUM
Langestrasse 71, Luckau
Prehistory and wildlife of the region. Peasant furniture, household equipment, costumes, tools. Handicrafts. Coins.
M. 8-12; Tu.-Sa. 9-12, 2-5.

LUCKENWALDE

DISTRICT MUSEUM
Platz der Lugend 11, Luckenwalde
Prehistory of the district. History of Luckenwalde. Industrial development.
W. 2-6; Su. 3-7. Other times by appointment.

LÜTZEN

GUSTAVUS ADOLPHUS MEMORIAL
Svenskön Blockhaus, Schwedeninsel, Lützen
Constructed (1932) by the Swedish Government, on site of Battle of Lützen (1632), where the Swedish king, Gustavus Adolphus, was killed. History and relics of the battle.
May-Sept., M. 8-12; Tu.-Su. 8-12.30, 1.30-6. Oct.-Apr., Tu.-Su. 9-12.30, 1.30-4.

REGIONAL MUSEUM
Schloss, Thälmann Park, Lützen
History of Lützen. Material and displays illustrating 30 Years War, especially Battle of Lützen.
Tu.-F. 10-12, 2-4; Sa., Su. 10-12.

MAGDEBURG

LIFE AND RESOURCES OF THE WELTALL
Weitlingstrasse 1A, Magdeburg
Geology, geography, population, life of the Weltall area.
Tu.-Su. 10-6.

MONASTERY OF OUR LADY
Magdeburg
Medieval sculpture and handicrafts.
On request.

MUSEUM OF CULTURAL HISTORY
Otto von Guericke Strasse 68-73, Magdeburg
Regional geology, mineralogy, wildlife, prehistory. History of Magdeburg. Ceramics. Faience. Enamels. Wrought-iron. Table-ware. Paintings, drawings, prints, sculpture, expecially by 19th-20th century German and Dutch artists. Machine-tools since 1847.
W.-Su. 10-6; Tu. 1-9.

ERICH WEINERT MEMORIAL
Theimstrasse 7, Magdeburg Buckau
Birthplace of Erich Weinert (1890-1953). Weinert's life and work.
M.-Sa. 10-7.

MALCHIN

REGIONAL MUSEUM
Rathaus, Platz der Freundschaft, Malchin
Prehistory of the region. History of Malchin.
W. 4-6; Su. 10-12.

MARIENBERG

REGIONAL MUSEUM
Karl Marx Strasse 12, Marienberg
History of Marienberg. Tin and silver mining. Wildlife of the region. Paintings of local subjects.
Tu.-Sa. 3-6; Su. 10-12, 2-5.

MARKKLEEBERG

REGIONAL MUSEUM
Markkleeberg-Mitte
Local and regional history.
Su. 10-1. Other times by appointment.

MARKNEUKIRCHEN

MUSEUM OF MUSICAL INSTRUMENTS
Bienengarten 2, Markneukirchen
Local history. World-wide collection of musical instruments. Mechanically operated musical instruments.
Tu.-Su. 10-12, 2-5.

MARKRANSTÄDT

PEACE ROOM
Schloss Altranstädt, Markranstädt
Room in which treaty of peace between Sweden and the Elector of Saxony was signed. Exhibition illustrating the war and the peace.
Su. 10-12. Other times by appointment.

REGIONAL MUSEUM
Platz des Friedens 5, Markranstädt
Geology. Mineralogy. Prehistory of the region. Local history. Handicrafts. Weapons. History and techniques of brown-coal mining.
Su. 10-12. Other times by appointment.

MEERANE

REGIONAL MUSEUM
Rathaus, Platz der Roten Armee 3, Meerane
In 1572 Town Hall. Geology, prehistory and history of the region. Ethnographical material from Africa, Asia, South America.
M., W., F. and 2nd, 4th Su. in month, 2-5. Other times on request.

MEININGEN

BAUMBACH HOUSE
Burgstrasse 22, Meiningen
Former home of the poet, Rudolf Baumbach (d.1905). Memorabilia of Baumbach and of the author, Ludwig Bechstein (d.1860). 19th century furniture, furnishings.
Tu.-Su. 9-5.

MEININGEN MUSEUM
Schloss Elisavethenburg, Meiningen
In former castle residence (1692). 18th-19th century European paintings, religious sculpture, furniture. 20th century drawings, paintings. 19th-20th century theatre history. History of music. 17th-19th century musical instruments. History of early 18th century Italian opera in contemporary documents.
Tu.-Su. 9-5.

TEACHING DISPLAY FOR THE PROTECTION OF BIRDS
Am Bibrasberg, Meiningen
Birds of the region.
By appointment.

MEISSEN

ALBRECHTSBURG
Domplatz 1, Meissen
In former Residence of the Electors of Saxony. Period rooms. 15th-16th century religious sculpture. History of the Meissen porcelain factory.
May-Oct., daily 8-5. Nov.-Apr., daily 8-4.

DISPLAY HALL OF THE MEISSEN STATE PORCELAIN FACTORY
Talstrasse 9, Meissen
Models showing development of Meissen porcelain factory from beginning to present day. Modern production techniques.
Apr.-Oct., daily 8-4. Nov.-Mar., M.-F. 9-4; Sa. 9-12.

MUNICIPAL AND DISTRICT MUSEUM
Rathausplatz 3, Meissen
In 13th-15th century Franciscan Church. Prehistory. History of Meissen, medieval - modern times. Wine industry. 17th-19th century period rooms. Clocks. 18th-19th century Meissen porcelain.
Daily 10-5 (W. 10-6).

MERSEBURG

DISTRICT MUSEUM
Schloss Merseburg
Local prehistory and history.
Daily 10-12, 2-5.

MITTWEIDA

REGIONAL MUSEUM
Kirchberg 3-5, Mittweida
History, especially architectural, of Mittweida. Guild history. Handicrafts. History of local mining industry. 15th-17th century paintings, drawings, religious sculpture.
Tu., Th. 6-9; Su. 9-12.

MOLCHOW-STENDENITZ

MUSEUM IN THE FOREST
Zermützelsee, Molchow-Stendenitz
Regional flora, wildlife, history.
May-Sept., Tu.-Su. 11-1, 2-5.

MORITZBURG

MORITZBURG CASTLE BAROQUE MUSEUM
Moritzburg
Castle (1545, restored 1732-6). Period rooms. 17th-19th century handicrafts, porcelain, glass, portraits. 18th century carts, carriages. Käthe Kollwitz memorial collection.
May-Oct., daily 8-12, 1-5. Nov.-Apr. by appointment.

MUSEUM OF BIRDS AND BIRD PROTECTION
Fasanenschlösschen, Moritzburg
In 1769-82 building. Birds of the region. Protection of birds.
Apr.-Oct., daily 8-11, 1-4; Sa. 8-5. Other times by appointment.

MÜHLBERG

REGIONAL MUSEUM
Museumstrasse 9, Mühlberg
In 16th century monastery. Prehistory of the region. History of Mühlberg. Religious sculpture. Navigation. Fishing.
Apr.-Oct., Su. 10-12.30. Other times by appointment.

MÜHLHAUSEN

DISTRICT MUSEUM
Leninstrasse 61, Mühlhausen
Geology, mineralogy, palaeontology and wildlife of the district. Ethnography of Africa and the S. Pacific. History of Mühlhausen. Handicrafts. Costumes. Pewter. Faience. Porcelain. Coins. Locks. Thomas Müntzen Memorial Room.
Tu.-Sa. 8-12, 1-5; Su. 10-12, 2-4.

RAVENS' TOWER AND PARAPET WALK
Mühlhausen
Section of the town wall (13th-14th century). Museum of furnishings, local history.
Tu.-Su. 10-12, 2-4.

MÜLLROSE

REGIONAL MUSEUM
Rathaus, Platz der Freihert, Müllrose
Prehistory. Local handicrafts. Peasant furnishings, household equipment, art.
Tu.-F. 3-5; Su. 9-11.

MUTZSCHEN

REGIONAL ROOM
Berggasse 21, Mutzschen
Regional and local prehistory, history. Local stove manufacturing industry.
M.-F. 8-5. Other times on request.

MYLAU

REGIONAL MUSEUM
Burg Mylau
In late 12th century castle. Regional geology, zoology, mining history. History of Mylau. Local textile industry.
Tu.-Th. 9-5.

NAUMBURG

REGIONAL MUSEUM
Grochlitzer Strasse 49-50, Naumburg
Regional prehistory. History of Naumburg, 11th century - 1848. Local wildlife, handicrafts. Documents and photographs illustrating history of the workers' movement, 1920-45.
Tu.-F. 9-12, 2-4; Sa., Su. 9-12.

FRITZ RENTSCH MEMORIAL
Neidschützerstrasse 19, Naumburg
Home of the painter, Fritz Rentsch. Works by Rentsch.
W., Sa. 11-1. Other times on request.

NAUMBURG-GROSSJENA

MAX KLINGER MEMORIAL
Naumburg-Grossjena
Summer residence of the artist, Max Klinger. Life and work of Klinger.
Tu.-Sa. 2-6. Other times by appointment.

NEIDERCUNNERSDORF

'OLD WEAVERS' ROOM' REGIONAL MUSEUM
Niedercunnersdorf
Local and regional history.
By appointment.

NEIDERLEHME-ZIEGENHALS

ERNST THÄLMANN MEMORIAL
Birkenweg, Neiderlehme-Ziegenhals
Memorabilia of Ernst Thälmann and of his fellow members of the Central Committee of the German Communist Party at its last meeting on Feburary 7, 1933.
Daily 10-7.

NIEDER-NEUNDORF

REGIONAL ROOM
Dorfstrasse 45, Nieder-Neundorf
Local rocks, prehistory, history. 19th century peasant household equipment.
By appointment.

NERCHAU

REGIONAL ROOM
Karl Marx Platz 3, Nerchau
Regional prehistory. History of Nerchau. 18th-19th century peasant tools, equipment. Textiles. Embroidery. Development of local industry.
Su. 10-12. Other times by appointment.

NESCHWITZ

BIRD PROTECTION STATION
Neschwitz
Displays illustrating local wildlife, especially birds. Collection of birds.
By appointment.

NEUBRANDENBURG

MUSEUM OF CULTURAL HISTORY
Treptower Strasse 38, Neubrandenburg
Prehistory of the district. 13th-20th century history of Neubrandenburg. Medieval weapons. 13th-15th century ceramics. Local handicrafts. Religious applied art. 19th-20th century German painting, sculpture, graphics. Natural history. Memorabilia of Fritz Reuter and Arnold Eckelmann.
Tu.-F. 8-12, 2-4; Su. 10-30-12, 2-4.

NEUGERSDORF

REGIONAL MUSEUM
Goethestrasse 2, Neugersdorf
17th-19th century history of Neugersdorf. Birds, rocks of the region. Working-class life in the 19th century. History of the workers' movement.
Tu.-F. 10-12, 2-5; Su., public holidays 9-12.

NEUHAUS-SCHIERSCHNITZ

REGIONAL ROOM
Burg, Neuhaus-Schierschnitz
In 16th century castle. Collection of local birds. History of regional mining industry, 1756-1911. 19th century peasant life. Furniture. Household equipment. Costumes. Local porcelain industry.
On request.

NEUKIRCH

REGIONAL MUSEUM
Lessingschule, Hauptstrasse 24, Neukirch
Geology, birds, prehistory and history of the region. 19th century handicrafts, especially pottery, weaving. 18th-19th century peasant life. Costumes.
2nd Su. in month, 3-6. Other times by appointment.

NEURUPPIN

DISTRICT MUSEUM
August Bebel Strasse 14-15, Neuruppin
House (1790). Regional natural history, prehistory, history. History of Neuruppin. Fontane and Schinkel memorial rooms.
Tu.-F. 8.30-6; Sa. 8.30-12; Su. 10-12, 3-5.

NEUSTADT

REGIONAL MUSEUM
Rathaus, Neustadt
17th-19th century history of Neustadt. 18th-19th century industry, handicrafts.
Tu., F., Su. 10-12, 2-4. Other times by appointment.

NORDHAUSEN

MEYENBURG MUSEUM
Alexander Puschkin Strasse 31, Nordhausen
Local geology, prehistory, history. 15th-19th century furniture. Porcelain. Coins. African ethnography.
Tu.-Su. 9-12, 1-5.

NOSSEN

REGIONAL MUSEUM
Schloss, Nossen
In 16th century castle. Prehistory. Rocks. Zoology, especially birds, beetles. History of Nossen. 18th-19th century furniture, household equipment. Pewter.
On request.

ODERBERG

REGIONAL MUSEUM
Ernst Thälmann Strasse 31, Oderberg
Geology, prehistory, history of the region. Development of agriculture. Handicrafts. River and canal navigation. Ship models.
Tu.-F. 2-6; Su. 9-1.

OEDERAN

REGIONAL MUSEUM
Pfarrgasse 5, Oederan
History of Oederan and of the local workers' movement. Popular art of the Erzgebirge area. Handicrafts.
May-Oct., M.-Sa. 9-12, 2-5; Su. 10-12, 2-5. Other times by appointment.

OELSNITZ

REGIONAL MUSEUM
Karl Marx Platz, Oelsnitz
13th-20th century regional history. Local weaving industry.
Daily 9-8.

OHRDRUF

REGIONAL MUSEUM
Schloss Ehrenstein und Thüringer Hof, Ohrdruf
Regional geology, wildlife, history. Local handicrafts and industry, especially mining, wooden toys, porcelain.
Su. 10-12, 3-6. Other times by appointment.

OLBERNHAU

ALTHAMMER
VEB Blechwalzwerk, Olbernhau
Forge hammer in the former Grünthal copper works (1537). Manager's office. Smiths' workshop.
Daily 9-5.

REGIONAL HOUSE
Ernst Thälmann Platz, Olbernhau
Regional geology, wildlife, history. Handicrafts, especially pewter, wood-carving.
Tu.-Su. 10-6.

ORANIENBAUM

DISTRICT MUSEUM
Schloss, Oranienbaum
Regional history. Handicrafts. Industry and technology.
Tu.-F. 9-12, 1-4.30; Sa., Su. 8.30-12, 1-5.30.

ORANIENBURG

DISTRICT MUSEUM
Breitestrasse 1, Oranienburg
Local prehistory, history, birds. 18th-19th century handicrafts. River and canal navigation. Memorial room to the chemist F. F. Runge (d. 1867).
Tu.-Th., 10-4; Sa., 8-5; Su. 8-12.

OSCHATZ

REGIONAL ROOM
Frongasse 1, Oschatz
Prehistory material from local excavations. History of Oschatz. 19th century peasant furniture, household equipment.
Tu., Th. 9-12, 3-5; Su. 10-12.

OSSMANNSTEDT

WIELAND MEMORIAL
Ossmannstedt
Former home of the poet, C. M. Wieland (d.1813). Memorabilia of Wieland.
May-Sept., daily 9-5. Oct.-Apr., daily 9-4.

OSTERBURG

DISTRICT MUSEUM
Strasse des Friedens 21, Osterburg
Regional geology, prehistory, history, wildlife. Industry. Material from castle excavations (1935).
M.-Th. 9-1, 2-6; F. 9-1, 2-8; Sa., Su. 10-1. Other times by appointment.

OSTERWIECK

REGIONAL MUSEUM
Alte Rathaus, Markt 11, Osterwieck
Regional geology, prehistory, zoology. Handicrafts. 16th-18th century theological writings.
Su. 10-12. Other times by appointment.

OSTRITZ

REGIONAL MUSEUM
Brauhausstrasse, Ostritz
Regional and local history.
Su. 10-12.

OYBIN

MUSEUM AUF DEM BERG OYBIN
Oybin
Local history.
M.-Sa. 10-12, 2-4; W. 2-6; Su. 10-12.

PARCHIN

REGIONAL MUSEUM
Thälmann Platz 3, Parchin
Local prehistory, history. 18th-19th century products of Mecklenburg glassworks.
W., F., Su. 3-5.

PEGAU

REGIONAL MUSEUM
Ernst Thälmann Strasse 16, Pegau
Regional geology, prehistory, history. Transport. History of postal services. Diorama of Battle of Grossgörschen.
Su. 10-12.

PERLEBERG

DISTRICT MUSEUM
Mönchort 7-9, Perleberg
Local prehistory, history, handicrafts. Peasant furniture, household equipment, tools.
Tu.-F. 10-12, 3-5; Sa. 10-12; Su. 10-1.

PIRNA

DISTRICT MUSEUM AND POLYTECHNIC MUSEUM OF ARTIFICIAL SILK
Klosterhof, Pirna
Local prehistory, history, rocks. History of production of artificial silk.
Tu.-F. 9-12, 2-4; Sa. 2-4; Su. 10-12.

PLAUEN

HERMANN VOGEL HOUSE
Plauen-Kreber
Former home of the artist, Hermann Vogel. Original furnishings. Studio. Drawings by Vogel.
On request.

VOGTLAND DISTRICT MUSEUM
Nobelstrasse 9-13, Plauen
In 3 houses (1780-90). Rococo, Biedermeier and Louis XVI rooms. Local geology, prehistory, history. Mining. Forestry. Water resources. Handicrafts and industry, especially lace, blinds. Peasant furniture, household equipment, costumes.
M., Tu., Th., F. 7.30-4.30; W. 7.30-6; Sa. 7.30-1.30; Su. 10-1.

POBERSHAU

DEMONSTRATION MINE
Amtsseile 32, Pobershau
Tin and silver mine (1484). Miners' tools.
June-Aug., M.-Sa. 9-12, 2-5; Su. 9-5. Other times by appointment.

POSTERSTEIN

DISTRICT MUSEUM
Burg, Posterstein 83
History of the town and the castle. Handicrafts. Peasant household equipment.
Tu.-Sa. 8-5. Other times by appointment.

POTSDAM

CECILIENHOF PALACE
Neuer Garten, Potsdam
Palace (1913-16). Meeting place of Potsdam Conference, 1945. Exhibition relating to Potsdam Agreement.
May-Sept., daily 8-6. Oct.-Apr., daily 9-5.

DISTRICT MUSEUM
Wilhelm Külz Strasse 10-11, Potsdam
Building (1770). Local geology, plants, wildlife, history. Glass. Faience. Pewter. Wrought iron. Furniture. Coins.
Tu.-Sa. 10-12, 2-6. Su. 11-5.

GERMAN ARMY MUSEUM
Marmor Palais, Neuer Garten, Potsdam
History of the German Army. Weapons. Uniforms. Flags. Paintings. Photographs. Documents. Military links between the E. European countries.
Tu.-Su. 10-5.

SANSSOUCI PALACE: CHARLOTTENHOF PALACE
Park Sanssouci, Potsdam
Built (1826-8) as royal summer residence. 18th-19th century furnishings, paintings, decorative arts.
May-Sept., Tu.-Su. 10-6. Oct.-Apr., Tu.-Su. 10-5.

SANSSOUCI PALACE: CHINESE TEAHOUSE
Park Sanssouci, Potsdam
Tea-house (1747-57). 18th century Chinese porcelain, furnishings, objets d'art.
May-Sept., daily 10-6.

SANSSOUCI PALACE: NEW PALACE
Park Sanssouci, Potsdam
Building (1763-9). German rococo furnishings, decorative arts, paintings, sculpture. 17th-18th century French, Italian paintings.
May-Sept., daily 10-6. Oct.-Apr. 10-5.

SANSSOUCI PALACE: NEW ROOMS
Park Sanssouci, Potsdam
Built as Orangery (1747), remodelled 1772. 18th century German paintings, reliefs, furnishings. Berlin and Meissen porcelain.
May-Sept., Tu.-Su. 10-6. Oct., Mar. 15- Apr. 30, Tu.-Su. 10-5.

SANSSOUCI PALACE: ORANGERY
Park Sanssouci, Potsdam
Building (1851-60). Mid 19th century furnishings, decorative arts. Copies of paintings by Raphael.
May-Sept., daily 10-6. Oct., Mar. 15- Apr. 30, daily 10-5.

SANSSOUCI PALACE: PARK SCULPTURE
Park Sanssouci, Potsdam
Temples and garden pavilion. 18th-19th century sculpture in marble and sandstone.
May-Sept., daily 10-6. Oct.-Apr., daily 10-5.

SANSSOUCI PALACE: PICTURE GALLERY
Park Sanssouci, Potsdam
Gallery (1755-63). 17th century Flemish, Italian, French paintings. 17th-18th century paintings from various European countries.
May-Sept., W.-Su. 10-6. Oct., Mar. 15- Apr. 30, W.-Su. 10-5.

SANSSOUCI PALACE: ROMAN BATHS
Park Sanssouci, Potsdam
Reproduction (1829-35) of Roman baths. 19th century portraits. 18th century painted wallhangings.
May-Sept., Tu.-Su. 10-6. Oct., Mar. 15- Apr. 30. Tu.-Su. 10-5.

POTSDAM-BABELSBERG

BRUNO H. BÜRGEL MEMORIAL
Merkurstrasse 10, Potsdam-Babelsberg
Home of the scientist, Bruno H. Bürgel. Life and scientific work of Bürgel. Memorabilia, personal possessions.
By appointment.

MUSEUM OF PREHISTORY AND EARLY HISTORY
Schloss Babelsberg, Potsdam-Babelsberg
Prehistory and early history of the Potsdam Havelland.
Tu., Th., F. 2-5. W. 10-1, 2-5. Sa. 11-1, 2-6. Su. 10-1, 2-6.

PRENZLAU

DISTRICT MUSEUM
Uckerwiek 813A, Prenzlau
In former Dominican monastery (1275-1343). Local botany, zoology, prehistory, history. Agricultural development, implements.
Tu. 10-12, 2-4. F. 10-12, 4-6. Su. 10-12.

PREROW

DARSS REGIONAL MUSEUM
Deichhaus, Prerow
Regional geology, botany. Forestry. Fishing. Navigation.
May-Sept., 9-5. Oct.-Apr., by appointment.

PRIEROS

REGIONAL MUSEUM
Am Dorfanger 1, Prieros
Regional prehistory, history.
May-Sept., Tu.-Su. 10-12, 2-5.

PRITZWALK

DISTRICT MUSEUM
Karl Liebknecht Platz 10, Pritzwalk
Regional and local history.
Tu., F. 9-12, 3-5. Su. 3-5.

PULSNITZ

REGIONAL MUSEUM
Platz der Befreiung, Pulsnitz
In town hall (1550). Regional and local history.
M., Tu., F., Sa., 2-4. 2nd and 4th Su. in month, 10-11.30.

QUEDLINBURG

CASTLE MUSEUM
Schlossberg 1, Quedlinburg
In former residence (996) of the Abbesses of Quedlinburg. Renaissance and baroque period rooms. Rocks. Minerals. Prehistory. Handicrafts. Guild history. History of Quedlinburg. 18th-19th century costumes. 16th-19th century paintings, drawings, prints.
Tu.-Su. 9-12, 2-5.

KLOPSTOCK MUSEUM
Schlossberg 12, Quedlinburg
16th century house, birthplace of the poet, F. G. Klopstock (d.1803). Life and work of Klopstock. In the same house are memorial rooms to the first German woman doctor, Dorothea Christiana Erxleben (d.1762), the gymnastic instructor, J. C. F. GutsMuth (d.1839) and the geographer, Carl Ruter (d.1859).
Tu.-Su. 9-12, 2-6.

MUSEUM BEHIND THE KLOPSTOCK HOUSE
Schlossberg 12, Quedlinburg
German and foreign animals. Ethnography. Animal and plant protection.
Tu.-Su. 9-12, 2-6.

QUERFURT

DISTRICT MUSEUM
Burg, Querfurt
In former granary and armoury (1535). Prehistory. History of the castle and the town.
Tu. 9-12, 2-6. W.-F. 9-12, 2-5. Sa. 10-12. Su. 9-12, 2-4.

RABENAU

REGIONAL COLLECTION
Schulstrasse, Rabenau
Regional botany, zoology. History of Rabenau. Local chairmaking industry.
May-Sept., 1st Su. in month. Other times by appointment.

RADEBERG

REGIONAL MUSEUM
Schlossstrasse 6, Radeberg
In former hunting-lodge (1546). Regional geology, prehistory. History of Radeberg. Pewter. Locks.
Tu.-Su. 9-12, 2-5.

RADEBEUL

INDIAN MUSEUM
Hölderlinstrasse 15, Radebeul
19th century N. American Indian collection. Weapons. Costumes. Tools. Ornaments. Trophies. Religious items.
May-Oct., Tu.-Su. 9-12, 2-5. Nov.-Apr., Tu., F., Su. 10-1. Other times by appointment.

REGIONAL MUSEUM
Schloss Hoflössnitz, Knohlweg 37, Radebeul
Castle (1649). Regional geology, history, wine-production.
W., Sa. 2-6. Su. 9-12, 2-6. Other times by appointment.

RADEBURG

REGIONAL MUSEUM
Heinrich Zille Strasse 9, Radeburg
Regional prehistory, history. Local handicrafts, industry. Drawings by the Radeburg artist, Heinrich Zille (d.1929).
W., Su. 3-6.

RAMMENAU

FICHTE MUSEUM
Schloss Rammenau
Memorial-museum to the writer, Johann Gottlieb Fichte (d.1814). Portraits. Letters. Works.
Tu. 9-12; F. 2-5; 1st and 3rd Su. in month 9-12; 2nd and 4th Su. 1.30-4.30.

RANIS

DISTRICT MUSEUM
Burg Ranis
Geology. Prehistory, with Palaeolithic, Neolithic, Bronze Age and La Tène period material from local excavations. 10th-19th century history of the castle.
Apr.-Sept., daily 8-12, 1-6. Oct.-Mar., 8-12, 1-5.

RAVENSBRÜCK

NATIONAL RAVENSBRÜCK MEMORIAL
Ravensbrück
Site of Ravensbrück concentration camp. Cells. Crematorium.
Tu.-Su. 8-5.

REGENSTEIN

RUINS OF REGENSTEIN CASTLE
Regenstein
Ruins and surviving sections of castle of the Counts of Regenstein (remodelled 1671).
May-Sept., daily 8-5. Oct.-Apr., daily 9-4.

REICHENAU

REGIONAL MUSEUM
Reichenau 90
Regional and local history.
By appointment.

REICHENBACH/OLDENBURG

REGIONAL MUSEUM
Gersdorfer Strasse 9, Reichenbach, Oldenburg
Regional and local history.
Su. 10-12.

REICHENBACH/VOGTLAND

NEUBER MEMORIAL
Johanninplatz 3, Reichenbach, Vogtland
Birthplace of the actress Karoline Neuber (d.1760). Life and work of Karoline Neuber.
By appointment.

RENTHENDORF

BREHM MEMORIAL
Renthendorf 22
Former home of the naturalist, A. E. Brehm (d.1884). Memorabilia. Manuscripts. Scientific preparations. Working library.
May-Sept., Tu.-Su. 9-12, 2-5. Oct.-Apr., Tu.-Su. 9-1.

RERIK

REGIONAL MUSEUM
Leuchtturmstrasse 11, Rerik
Prehistory. Local history. Fishing equipment.
By appointment.

REUTERSTADT STAVENHAGEN

FRITZ REUTER LITERATURE MUSEUM
Markt 1, Reuterstadt Stavenhagen
Birthplace of the writer, Fritz Reuter (d.1874). Reuter's life and literary work.
Tu.-F. 9-12, 2-5. Sa. 9-12. Su. 10-12, 2-4.

RIBNITZ-DAMGARTEN

DISTRICT MUSEUM
Klosterstrasse 12, Ribnitz-Damgarten
Regional prehistory, history. Navigation. Shipbuilding. Fishing.
Su.-F. 2-6.

RIESA

REGIONAL MUSEUM
Poppitzer Platz 3, Riesa
Geology. Prehistory. History of Riesa. Handicrafts. Industry, especially steel. Shipping. Transport.
W., Su. 1-5. Other times by appointment.

RIETSCHEN

REGIONAL ROOM
Görlitzer Strasse, Rietschen
Regional history and ethnography.
Su., public holidays 1-5.

ROCHLITZ

REGIONAL MUSEUM
Schloss, Rochlitz
In castle (12th-13th century, remodelled 16th century). Regional geology, history. Flax processing. Textile industry. Ceramics.
Tu.-F., Su. 8-12, 1-5; Sa. 8-12.

ROCHSBURG

CASTLE MUSEUM
Rochsburg
In castle (12th century, remodelled 16th century). Rooms furnished in baroque, rococo, Empire and Biedermeier styles.
Tu.-Su. 8-12, 1-5.

RODEWISCH

GÖLTZSCH MUSEUM
Strasse der Jugend 2, Rodewisch
Geology. Prehistoric material from local excavations. 13th-16th century tools. Ceramics. Industrial history, especially spinning, knitting.
Tu.-Th., Sa. 2-5; Su. 10-12, 2-5.

RÖMHILD

STEINSBURG MUSEUM
Römhild
Prehistory. Local history.
M.-Sa. 9-5.

ROSSLA

REGIONAL MUSEUM
Kulturhaus, Rossla
Local prehistory, history. Baroque and Empire furniture. Pewter.
On request.

ROSTOCK

ART GALLERY
Am Schwanenteich, Rostock
Paintings. Drawings. Prints. Sculpture.
Tu., Th.-Su. 9-6; W. 9-10.

COLLECTION OF THE DEPARTMENT OF BOTANY
Universität Rostock, Doberaner Strasse, Rostock
Herbarium of Mecklenburg plants.
By appointment.

COLLECTION OF THE DEPARTMENT OF GEOLOGY AND PALAEONTOLOGY
Universität Rostock, Wismarsche Strasse 8, Rostock
Geology. Palaeontology. History of the earth.
By appointment.

COLLECTION OF THE DEPARTMENT OF MINERALOGY AND PETROGRAPHY
Universität Rostock, Wismarsche Strasse 8, Rostock
Minerals. Rocks. Gemstones. Meteorites.
By appointment.

COLLECTION OF THE DEPARTMENT OF ZOOLOGY
Universität Rostock, Universitätsplatz 2, Rostock
Wildlife of the Region.
By appointment.

MUSEUM OF CULTURAL HISTORY
Steintor, Rostock
Prehistory and early history, including material dredged from Warnow River. History of Rostock and of the Hanseatic League. Shipping. Shipbuilding. Ships' models. Handicrafts. Industrial development. Paintings. Prints and drawings. Weapons.
Tu.-F., Su. 8-1, 2-6. Sa. 10.30-1, 2-6.

MUSEUM OF SHIP-BUILDING
Rostock-Schmare
History of the Rostock ship-building industry.
Tu.-F., Su. 8-1, 2-6; Sa. 10.30-1, 2-6.

SHIPPING MUSEUM
August Bebel Strasse 1, Rostock
History of Baltic navigation, especially in relation to Rostock. Models. Equipment. Paintings. Prints. Charts.
Tu.-F., Su., 8-1, 2-6; Sa. 10.30-1, 2-6.

ROSTOCK-WARNEMÜNDE

WARNEMÜNDE REGIONAL MUSEUM
Theodor Körner Strasse 31, Rostock-Warnemünde
In late 18th century fisherman's house. Local history. Fishing. Navigation. Ships' models. 19th century costumes.
May-Oct., Tu.-Su. 9-1, 2-5.

ROTHENBURG

REGIONAL MUSEUM
Rathaus, Karl Marx Platz, Rothenburg
Local and regional history.
Su. 10-12. Other times by appointment.

ROTTLEBEN

BARBAROSSA CAVERN
Rottleben
Gypsum cavern, with lakes, gypsum formations.
Daily 8-6.

RUDOLSTADT

HEIDECKSBURG STATE MUSEUM
Schlossbezirk 1-3, Rudolstadt
18th century castle. Rooms furnished in Renaissance, baroque, classical and Biedermeier styles. 17th-19th century European paintings. Religious sculpture. Pewter. Copper. Ceramics. Porcelain. 15th-19th century weapons, uniforms. 18th century ceremonial sleighs. Prehistory and early history of the region. Minerals. Rocks. Botany. Zoology. Geography.
Period rooms: May-Oct., Tu.-Su. 8-6; M. 10-6. Nov.-Apr., Tu.-Su. 9-4. Picture gallery: Apr.-Oct., Tu.-Su. 8-6. Remainder of collections: May-Oct., daily 9-1, 2-6. Nov.-Apr., Tu.-Su. 9-1, 2-5.

MUSEUM OF ETHNOLOGY: THURINGIAN PEASANT HOUSES
Grosse Wiese 2, Rudolstadt
Open-air museum, based on 2 Thuringian half-timbered houses (1667 and 1700). Peasant furniture, household equipment, tools, handicrafts.
May-Aug., Tu.-F., Su. 8-12, 2-6; Sa. 8-12. Oct.-Apr., Tu.-F., Su. 9-12, 2-4; Sa. 9-12.

RÜBELAND

RÜBELAND STALACTITE CAVERNS
Blankenburger Strasse 34, Rübeland
In two limestone caverns. Displays showing formation of the caverns and history of their discovery. Material from excavations, including bones of cave-bears.
May 15-Oct. 1, daily 8.30-5. Oct. 2-May 14, daily 9-12, 2-4.

RUHLA

REGIONAL MUSEUM
Obere Lindenstrasse 29-31, Ruhla
In house (1600). Geology. History of local mining, metal, clockmaking, cutlery industries. Wrought-iron. Tobacco pipes. Peasant furniture, costumes.
May-Sept., Tu.-F. 9.30-12, 2-4.30; Sa., Su. 10-12. Oct.-Apr., Tu.-F. 10-12, 2-4.

SAALFELD

THURINGIA REGIONAL MUSEUM
Minzplatz 5, Saalfeld
In former Franciscan monastery (c.1270). Medieval history of monastery. Religious sculpture, decorative arts. Geology. Minerals. History of Saalfeld. Peasant furniture, household equipment, costumes, tools, handicrafts. Coins.
May-Oct., daily 8-12.30, 2-5. Nov.-Apr., M.-Sa. 8-12.30, 2-5.

SACHSENHAUSEN BEI ORANIENBURG

NATIONAL MEMORIAL
Sachsenhausen bei Oranienburg
Museum of site of former Sachsenhausen concentration camp. Cell block. Pathology, with medical instruments. Museum of European anti-fascist resistance. Museum of Jewish persecution by the Nazis.
Apr.-Sept., daily 8-5.30. Oct.-Mar., daily 8-5.

SALZWEDEL

JOHANN FRIEDRICH DANNEIL MUSEUM
An der Marienkirche 3, Salzwedel
Prehistory and early history of Altmark. 12th-15th century history of the Hansa town of Salzwedel. Handicrafts. Pewter. 13th-18th century religious sculpture. Memorial room to the historian, J. F. Danneil.
M.-Sa. 9-12, 2-5. May-Sept., also Su. 2-6.

JENNY MARX MUSEUM
Jenny Marx Strasse 20, Salzwedel
Material relating to the Marx family, 1805-48.
Tu.-Su. 9-12, 2-5.

SANGERHAUSEN

SPENGLER MUSEUM
Strasse der opfer des Faschismus 33, Sangerhausen
Regional geology. Fossil animals. Prehistory and history of the region. Local birds, butterflies, molluscs. Mining industry.
Tu.-F., Su. 10-12, 2.30-5. Sa. 10-12.

SCHIRGISWALDE

REGIONAL MUSEUM
Hentschelgasse am Markt, Schirgiswalde
Geology. Local history.
May-Oct., Tu.-F. 3-6.

SCHKEUDITZ

REGIONAL MUSEUM
Mühlstrasse 50, Schkeuditz
Prehistory. Local history.
Su. 10-12. Other times on request.

SCHLETTAU

CASTLE MUSEUM
Schloss, Schlettau
13th century castle, converted to hunting lodge. Period rooms. Religious ornaments. 18th-19th century peasant furniture. 16th-18th century weapons, armour.
M.-Sa. 9-12, 1-5. Su. 11-6.

SCHLEUSINGEN

REGIONAL MUSEUM
Bertholdsburg, Schleusingen
Geology. Mineralogy. History of Schleusingen. Glass technology. Glass blowing. Paper industry. History of writing and books. Beidermeier furnishings.
M. 9-12. Tu.-Sa. 9-12, 2-5. Su. 10-12.

SCHMALKALDEN

DISTRICT MUSEUM
Schloss Wilhelmsburg, Schmalkalden
Castle 1585-9. Geography, geology and mineralogy of the district. Local history. Handicrafts. Iron industry. Stove collection. Costumes. Uniforms. Peasant furniture. Coins.
Daily 9-5.

SCHMÖLLN

REGIONAL MUSEUM
Schloss, Schmölln
Castle (1748-50). Prehistoric material from local excavations. History of Schmölln. Local birds. Peasant houshold equipment, handicrafts.
Tu., F. 3-5. 1st Su. in month 10-12.

SCHNEEBERG

MUSEUM FOR POPULAR ART OF THE MINING COMMUNITY
Rosa Luxemburg Platz 1, Schneeberg
Local minerals and ores. History of Schneeberg and the mining industry. Handicrafts. 17th-18th century popular religious art.
Tu.-Su. 10-12, 2-6.

SCHÖNBERG

REGIONAL MUSEUM
An der Kirche 8-9, Schönberg
Regional prehistory, history. Handicrafts. Pewter. Brass. Peasant furniture, household equipment, tools, costumes.
Tu.-Su. 10-12, 3-5. Other times by appointment.

SCHÖNEBECK

DISTRICT MUSEUM
Pfännerstrasse 41, Schönebeck
In old Salzelmen Town Hall (15th century). Geology. Mineralogy. Local prehistory and history. Archaeological material from 6th century cemetery. History of local salt industry. Handicrafts. Guild history. Elbe navigation. Furniture. Household equipment. Costumes.
Tu.-Su. 10-1, 3-6.

SCHÖNEICHE

REGIONAL MUSEUM
Dorfaue 8, Schöneiche
In farmhouse (1643). Regional and local history.
W. and 1st Su. in month 11-4.

SCHWARZENBERG

MUSEUM OF THE ERZGEBIRGE IRON INDUSTRY
Obereschlossstrasse 36, Schwarzenberg
History of iron-mining, smelting and forging.
Tu.-F. 9-12, 2-5. Sa., Su. 9-12.

SCHWERIN

MUSEUM OF PREHISTORY AND EARLY HISTORY
Alter Garten, Schwerin
Prehistory and early history of Mecklenburg.
Tu.-Su. 9.30-1, 2-5.

SCHWERIN STATE MUSEUM
Am Alten Garten, Schwerin
17th century Dutch, Flemish paintings. 18th century European paintings. 15th-19th century German paintings. 20th century European paintings, drawings, prints, sculpture. 18th-20th century Mecklenburg popular art. Local history. Peasant furniture, household equipment, tools, costumes, ornaments. Handicrafts. Guild history. Glass. Ceramics. Faience. Porcelain. Textiles.
Tu.-Su. 9.30-1, 2-5.

SCHWERIN HISTORICAL MUSEUM
Strasse der Nationalen Einhert 28, Schwerin
History of the workers' and peasants' movements in Mecklenburg.
M.-F. 9-5. Sa. 9-12.

SEBNITZ

REGIONAL MUSEUM
Bergstrasse 9, Sebnitz
History of Sebnitz. 17th-19th century pewter. Local industries, especially manufacture of paraffin lamps and artificial flowers.
May-Oct., Tu., F. 10-12, 3-5; W. 3-5; Su. 10-12 (guided tours only).

SEEBACH

SEEBACH BIRD-PROTECTION STATION
Seebach
Local birds. Display illustrating aims and methods of bird-protection.
On request.

SEEBAD HERINGSDORF

MAXIM GORKI MEMORIAL
Villa Irmgard, Maxim Gorki Strasse 20, Seebad Heringsdorf
In Gorki's former home. Memorabilia of Gorki, with library and recordings of his works.
Daily 9-12, 2-5.

SEIFFEN

ERZGEBIRGE TOY MUSEUM
Ernst Thälmann Strasse 73, Seiffen
Development of local toy-making industry, 17th century - present day. Demonstration workshop.
Daily 9-12, 2-5.

SEIFHENNERSDORF

NATURAL HISTORY AND REGIONAL MUSEUM
Nordstrasse 30, Seifhennersdorf
Regional geology, birds, nature protection. Local history. 19th century peasant furniture, household equipment.
F. and 2nd Su. in month, 2-6.

SENFTENBERG

DISTRICT MUSEUM
Schloss Senftenberg
Prehistory. History of the Castle and town since 13th century. Brown-coal mining. Fossil flora. 16th century religious art. Peasant handicrafts, household equipment.
Tu.-Su. 10-12, 2-5.

SERRAHN

SERRAHN BIOLOGICAL STATION
Serrahn
Displays illustrating methods and aims of wildlife, especially bird, protection.
M.-Sa. 9-3.

SIEBENLEHN

REGIONAL MUSEUM
Otto Altenkirch Strasse 44, Siebenlehn
Botany. Zoology. History of Siebenlehn. Memorabilia of the naturalist, Amalie Dielrich.
W. 3-5, 2nd Su. in month 2-4. Other times by appointment.

SOHLAND

REGIONAL HOUSE
Lessingstrasse 19, Sohland
18th century weaver's house. Local history.
May-Oct., Su. 9-12, W. 3-5.

SONDERHAUSEN

STATE REGIONAL AND CASTLE MUSEUM
Schloss, Sonderhausen
In former Residence (16th-19th century) of Princes of Schwarzburg-Sonderhausen. 17th-19th century furniture, paintings, decorative arts. Geology. Palaeontology. Prehistory. History of Sonderhausen. Coins. Medals. Ceramics. Faience. Glass. Costumes. History of music.
Tu.-Su. 10-12, 2-5.

SONNEBERG

GERMAN TOY MUSEUM
Beethovenstrasse 10, Sonneberg
Regional and local history. Handicrafts. Guild history. Costumes. Porcelain. Faience. Worldwide collection of toys. Production of toys by handicraft and factory methods.
Tu.-Su. 9-4.

STADTILM

REGIONAL MUSEUM
Rathaus, Strasse der Einhert 1, Stadtilm
In former Cistercian Abbey (13th century). Geology. Early history of region. Local handicrafts. Leather, porcelain and textile industries. 17th-19th century furnishings.
On request.

STADT WEHLEN

REGIONAL MUSEUM
Lohmenstrasse 18, Stadt Wehlen
Local geology, botany, history, handicrafts, industry. Elbe navigation.
Apr.-Oct., daily 9-12, 2-5. Nov.-Mar., on request.

STECKBY

STECKBY BIRD PROTECTION STATION
Steckby
Techniques and aims of bird protection. Pest control.
On request.

STENDAL

ALTMARK MUSEUM: COLLECTION AT THE CATHEDRAL
Winckelmannstrasse 36, Stendal
In Cathedral. Medieval ceramics, faience, porcelain. 18th century prints. Peasant furniture, household equipment.
Tu.-Su. 10-12, 3-5.

ALTMARK MUSEUM: MÖNCHSKIRCHOF COLLECTION
Mönchskirchof 1, Stendal
Medieval bronze and wood sculpture. Architectural features from local 12th-14th century brick buildings.
By appointment.

ALTMARK MUSEUM: WEBERSTRASSE COLLECTION
Weberstrasse 18, Stendal
Prehistory and early history of the area.
Tu.-Su. 10-12, 3-5.

WINCKELMANN MEMORIAL MUSEUM
Winckelmannstrasse 36, Stendal
Birthplace of the archaeologist, J. J. Winckelmann (d.1768). Memorabilia. Letters. Collection of African material. Local history. Handicrafts. Coins. Medals. Costumes. 18th-20th century drawings, prints.
Tu.-Su. 10-12, 3-5.

STOLBERG

OLD STOLBERG TOWN-HOUSE
Stolberg
House (1450). 16th-18th century furniture.
Tu.-Sa. 8-12.

REGIONAL MUSEUM
Thomas Müntzer Gasse 19, Stolberg
In house (1535). Geology. Local mining industry. History of Stolberg. Mint. Coins. Handicrafts. Thomas Müntzer Memorial room.
Tu.-F. 8-12, 2-6; Sa. 8-12, 2-5. Apr.-Oct., also Su. 9.30-12.

STOLPEN

STOLPEN CASTLE
Schlossstrasse 10, Stolpen
15th-16th century weapons and instruments of torture. Models of cannon. Firefighting equipment.
May-Sept., daily 9-12, 1-4. Oct.-Apr., Tu.-Su. 9-12, 1-4.

STRALSUND

MUSEUM OF CULTURAL HISTORY
Mönchstrasse 25-7, Stralsund
In former Dominican monastery (14th-16th century). Prehistory and history of the area. Medieval religious sculpture, paintings, liturgical items. Handicrafts. Navigation. Fishing. Wrought-iron. Faience. Playing cards. 17th-19th century tools, costumes, toys. Coins. Medals. 16th-17th century European paintings, drawings, prints. 18th-20th century paintings, drawings, prints by N.E. German artists. Views of Stralsund. Ernst Moritz Arndt collection.
Tu.-Sa. 10-5; Su. 10-12.30, 2-5.

MUSEUM OF THE SEA
Katharinenberg 14A, Stralsund
Geographical history of Mecklenburg. Hydrography of the Baltic. Plants and wildlife of the coastal region. Aquarium.
Daily 10-5.

STRAUSBERG

DISTRICT MUSEUM
Georg Kurtze Strasse 35, Strausberg
Regional and local history.
Tu.-Sa. 10-5; Su. 10-12.30, 2-5.

STUTZERBACH

GOETHE HOUSE AND GLASS MUSEUM
Sebastian Kneipp Strasse 18, Stutzerbach
Mementoes of Goethe's visits to Stutzerbach. History and technology of glassmaking.
Tu.-Su. 9-12, 1-5.

SUHL

REGIONAL AND WEAPONS MUSEUM
Malzhaus am Herrenteich, Suhl
In house (17th century). History of Suhl. Prehistoric weapons, tools from local excavations. 16th-20th century manufacture of weapons. Collection of guns, pistols.
Tu.-Sa. 9-12, 2-5. Su. 9-12.

TANGERMÜNDE

REGIONAL MUSEUM
Am Markt, Tangermünde
In old Town Hall (15th century). Regional prehistory, history. 19th-20th century industrial development. Elbe navigation, fishing. Peasant handicrafts, furniture, household equipment.
Tu.-Su. 9-12, 2-4. Other times by appointment.

TAUCHA

REGIONAL MUSEUM
Schlossstrasse 13, Taucha
Regional geology, wildlife, prehistory. History of Taucha. Handicrafts.
Su. 10-12; W. 3-6. Other times by appointment.

TEMPLIN

MUSEUM OF ETHNOLOGY
Prenzlauer Tor, Templin
Regional and local history.
Tu.-Th. 9-12; F. 3-6; 1st Su. in month 3-6.

THALE

WALPURGIS HALL
Hexenplatz, Thale
Timber hall in old Germanic style. Representation of the Walpurgis story from Goethe's *Faust*. Geology, plants, wildlife, prehistory of the region.
May-Sept., 10-6.

THARANDT

GRILLENBURG CASTLE
Tharandt
Hunting lore. Trophies. Equipment. Game birds.
By appointment.

INSTITUTE OF FORESTRY BOTANY
Dippoldiswalder Strasse 7, Tharandt
Species and varieties of timber trees.
By appointment.

INSTITUTE OF FOREST PRODUCTS
Dippoldiswalder Strasse 8, Tharandt
German and foreign timber. Faults in timber.
By appointment.

INSTITUTE OF FORESTRY ZOOLOGY
Dippoldiswalder Strasse 8, Tharandt
Entomology. Insect pests. Amphibians. Reptiles. Forest animals. Trophies.
By appointment.

THEMAR

REGIONAL MUSEUM
Markt 1, Themar
Regional prehistory, birds, handicrafts. 13th-14th century material from excavations on the Osterburg. History of Themar. Local industries, especially furniture.
On request.

TORGAU

DISTRICT MUSEUM
Schloss Hartenfels, Torgau
Local prehistory, history. History of the Castle. Weapons. Armour. Model of Battle of Torgau. Stoneware production.
Tu.-Su. 10-12, 2-5. (May-Sept., 8-6.).

UMMENDORF

WANZLEBEN DISTRICT MUSEUM
Burg, Ummendorf
Local geology, prehistory, history. Peasant furniture, household equipment, tools, costumes, ornaments. Collection of fungi.
Tu.-F. 8-5; Su. 10-5.

VELTEN

MUNICIPAL AND CERAMICS MUSEUM
Karl Marx Strasse 79, Velten
Regional and local history. 17th-20th century development of Velten stove-manufacturing industry.
Tu., F. 2-4; Su. 10-12.

WALDENBURG

REGIONAL MUSEUM AND NATURAL HISTORY COLLECTION
Geschwister Scholl Platz 1, Waldenburg
Local history. Handicrafts, especially pottery. Pipes. 15th-19th century religious art. Peasant furniture, household equipment. Mineralogy. Palaeontology. Herbaria. Zoology. Entomology. Butterflies.
M.-F. 7.30-12, 1.30-5; Sa. 7.30-12; Su. 8.30-12, 1.30-6.

WALLDORF

QUARRY
Walldorf
Sandstone quarry. Display of tools used during excavation of stone.
May-Sept., daily 9-5.

WALTERSDORF

REGIONAL MUSEUM
Waltersdorf 120
In watermill (c.1400), with machinery of 1800. Local history. Display showing historical development of milling equipment. Peasant household equipment.
M.-W. 9-12; Th., F. 2-5. Other times by appointment.

WALTERSHAUSEN

REGIONAL MUSEUM
Schloss Tenneberg, Waltershausen
In castle (1720). Local history. Costumes. Ornaments. Peasant furniture, household equipment. Toy industry. Pipes. 17th-19th century seals.
Apr.-Dec., M.-Th., Sa., Su. 10-5.

WALTERSHAUSEN-SCHNEPPENTHAL

GUTSMUTH MEMORIAL
Waltershausen-Schneppenthal
Building (1784-93), formerly school run by C. G. Salzmann. Life and work of the teacher, J. C. GutsMuth.
By appointment.

WANDLITZ

REGIONAL MUSEUM
Breitscheidstrasse 8, Wandlitz
Regional geology, wildlife. Local history. Peasant furniture, household equipment, tools.
Tu.-Su. 9-12.

WAREN AN DER MÜRITZ

MÜRITZ MUSEUM
Friedenstrasse 5, Waren an der Müritz
Geology, botany, wildlife, prehistory, history of the region. Local history. Fishing. Hunting. Peasant handicrafts, costumes. 18th-19th century products of Mecklenburg glassworks. History of land reform and the workers' movement.
Tu.-Sa. 8-5; Su. 10-12, 2-4.

WASCHLEITHE

HERKULES FRISCH GLÜCK DEMONSTRATION MINE
Waschleithe
Silver mine, with displays of tools, mining methods.
Apr.-Oct., daily 9-4. Nov.-Mar., M.-F. 9-4.

WEESENSTEIN

CASTLE MUSEUM
Burg Weesenstein
Castle (13th century, with 1575 additions). Empire and Biedermeier period rooms. Hunting equipment, trophies. French, Chinese, leather tapestries.
Th.-Tu., 8-4.

WEIDA

DISTRICT MUSEUM
Osterburg, Weida
Castle (12th century, remodelled 17th-19th century). Regional, local history. Handicrafts. History of guilds.
Tu.-Su. 9-12, 2-5. (July, Aug., 1-6).

WEIMAR

BELVEDERE PALACE ROCOCO MUSEUM
Weimar
Art of the period 1700-60. Paintings. Porcelain. Faience. Glass. Textiles.
May-Oct., daily 10-1, 2-6. Nov.-Apr., W.-M. 10-1, 2-6.

CASTLE MUSEUM
Burgplatz, Weimar
Palace (mid-17th century, remodelled 1792-1803). Period rooms. 16th-20th century European paintings. 15th-19th century drawings, prints. 18th-19th century porcelain. Coins. Medals.
F.-W. 9-1, 2-5.

GERMAN BEE MUSEUM
Ilmstrasse 3, Weimar
History of bees and bee-keeping. Biology of bees.
M., Tu., Th.-Su., 9-11, 1.30-3.30.

GOETHE'S GARDEN HOUSE
Corona Schröter Strasse, Weimar
House lived in by Goethe, 1776-82. Original furnishings. Memorabilia of the poet.
May-Oct., Tu.-Su. 9-12, 1-5. Nov.-Feb., Tu.-Su. 9-12, 1-4.

KIRMS KRACKOW HOUSE
Jakobstrasse 10, Weimar
Medieval house, once the property of Franz Kirms. Late 18th-early 19th century furnishings, decorative arts. Memorial rooms and memorabilia of Herder, Falk and Musäu.
Mar.-Oct., Tu.-Su. 9-12, 1-5. Nov.-Feb., Tu.-Su. 9-12, 1-4.

LISZT HOUSE
Marienstrasse 17, Weimar
Former house of the composer, Franz Liszt. Portraits. Sculpture. Manuscripts. First editions of Liszt's music. Memorabilia.
Mar.-Oct., Tu.-Su. 9-1, 2-5. Nov.-Feb., Tu.-Su. 9-1, 2-4.

MUSEUM OF NATURAL HISTORY
Am Herdeplatz 14, Weimar
Palaeontology. Zoology. Evolution.
Tu.-Su. 9-12, 2-5.

MUSEUM OF THE PREHISTORY AND EARLY HISTORY OF THURINGIA
Humboldstrasse 11, Weimar
Evolution. Anthropology. Prehistory and early history of Thuringia.
Tu.-Sa. 8-12, 2-4. Su. 10-12, 2-4.

NATIONAL GOETHE MUSEUM
Frauenplan 1, Weimar
In Goethe's former home (1709). Life and work of Goethe. The poet's art collection.
House: Mar.-Oct., Tu.-Su. 9-1, 3-5; M. 1-5. Nov.-Feb., Tu.-Su. 9-1, 2-4; M. 1-4.
Museum: Tu.-Su. 9-1, 2-6; M. 1-6; Th. 1-10.

ORANGERY
Schloss Belvedere, Weimar
Carriages. Coaches. Sleighs.
May-Oct., daily 10-1, 2-6. Nov.-Apr., W.-M. 10-1, 2-6.

REGIONAL MUSEUM OF NATURAL HISTORY, HISTORY AND POPULAR ART
Karl Liebknecht Strasse 7-9, Weimar
Local history. Handicrafts. Industrial history. Peasant furniture, household equipment, costumes. Military history.
Tu.-Su. 9-12, 2-6.

RÖMISCHES HOUSE
Im Park, Weimar
Summer residence (1792-6) of Duke Karl August. Display illustrating history of Weima Park. Period furnishings, decorative arts.
On request.

SCHILLER'S HOUSE
Schillerstrasse 12, Weimar
Life and work of Schiller, with part of his library.
Mar.-Oct., Tu.-Su. 9-1, 2-5. Nov.-Feb., Tu.-Su. 9-1, 2-4.

TIEFURT PALACE
Haupstrasse 14, Weimar
18th century house, formerly summer residence of the Duchess Amalia. 18th-mid 19th century furniture, porcelain.
Mar.-Oct., Tu.-Su. 9-1, 2-5. Nov.-Feb., Tu.-Su. 9-1, 2-4.

WITHUM PALACE
Am Palais 3, Weimar
House (1767). 18th-early 19th century furnishings. Wieland Memorial.
Mar.-Oct., daily 9-12, 1-5. Nov.-Feb., Tu.-Su. 9-12, 1-4.

WEISSENBERG

'OLD SPICE BREAD BAKERY' REGIONAL MUSEUM
August Bebel Platz 34, Weissenberg
18th century bakery, with original equipment. Local history. Prehistoric material from local sites.
Su. 9.30-11.30; W. 4-6.

WEISSENFELS

GUSTAVUS ADOLPHUS MEMORIAL
Grosse Burgstrasse 22, Weissenfels
House (1552). Material relating to Gustavus Adolphus and the 30 years War. Diorama of the Battle of Lützen.
By appointment.

MUNICIPAL MUSEUM
Langendorferstrasse 33, Weissenfels
Geology, mineralogy, wildlife, plants, prehistory, history of the region. Handicrafts. Guild history. Development of local shoe industry. Shoe collection. Glass. Artistic cast iron. Educational and musical history of Weissenfels.
M.-F. 8-4; Sa. 8-11; Su. 10-1.

HEINRICH SCHÜTZ MEMORIAL
Nicolaistrasse 13, Weissenfels
16th century house, formerly home of the composer, Heinrich Schütz. Memorabilia of Schütz.
By appointment.

WERDAU

REGIONAL MUSEUM
Uferstrasse 1, Werdau
Regional geology, mineralogy, prehistory, history. Peasant household equipment, handicrafts, costumes. History of local textile industry, with spinning machinery and steam-engine for driving mill. Pewter. Mechanical musical instruments.
Tu.-Su. 10-12. Tu. also 3-6.

WERDER

ORCHARD MUSEUM
Karl Marx Platz, Werder
Geology, soil, climate of local fruit-growing area. History of fruit growing.
By appointment.

WERMSDORF

REGIONAL ROOM, WITH BEBEL AND LIEBKNECHT MEMORIALS
Schlosshubertusburg, Wermsdorf
In former royal hunting lodge (1724), subsequently prison. Regional and local history. History of German workers' movement. Memorabilia of Karl Liebknecht and August Bebel, who were imprisoned here.
Daily 9-11, 2-4.

WERNIGERODE

FEUDAL MUSEUM
Schloss, Wernigerode
12th century castle. 17th-19th century furniture. 13th-18th century religious art. Faience. Porcelain. Glass. Goldsmiths' work. Paintings. Weapons. Instruments of torture. Regional history.
May-Oct., daily 9-6. Nov.-Apr., Tu.-Su. 9-1, 1.30-5.30.

HARZ MUSEUM
Klint 10, Wernigerode
Local prehistory, history, geology. 19th century industrial history, especially mining. Peasant handicrafts, furniture, household equipment.
Tu.-Sa. 10-4; Su. 10-1.

WIEDERAU

CLARA ZETKIN MEMORIAL
Wiederau 190
Birthplace of Clara Zetkin (1857-1933). Memorabilia of Clara Zetkin and her friends.
On request.

WILDSRUFF

REGIONAL COLLECTION
Gezinge, Wildsruff
Regional prehistory, wildlife, history. Peasant handicrafts, household equipment. 19th century woodcarving.
May-Sept., 2nd Su. in month, 2-4. Other times by appointment.

WILHELM PIECK STADT (formerly GUBEN)

WILHELM PIECK MEMORIAL
Helmut Just Strasse, Wilhelm Pieck Stadt
Life and work of Wilhelm Pieck (d.1960). History of the Guben workers' movement.
Tu.-F. 10-12, Sa. 2-5.

WILTHEN

REGIONAL ROOM
Bahnhofstrasse 130C, Wilthen
19th century weavers' room. Tools and equipment for flax-processing and linen-weaving.
May-Sept., Sa. 3-5.

WISMAR

SCHABBELT HOUSE REGIONAL MUSEUM
Schweinsbrücke 8, Wismar
Regional prehistory, history. 17th-19th century painting. Costumes.
Tu.-Su., 10-12, 3-5.

WITTENBERGE

REGIONAL MUSEUM
Amtshof 5, Wittenberge
In 13th century tower. Regional prehistory, history, minerals, rocks. Elbe navigation and fishing.
June 1-Sept. 15, W., F., Su. 10-12, 3-5. Sept. 16-May 31, W., F., Su. 3-5.

WITTENBERG LUTHERSTADT

LUTHER MUSEUM
Collegienstrasse 54, Wittenberg Lutherstadt
In Luther's house. Life and work of Martin Luther. History of the Reformation.
May-Oct., M.-Sa. 9-6, Su. 10-6. Nov.-Apr., M.-Sa. 9-5, Su. 10-5.

JULIUS RIEMER MUSEUM OF NATURAL HISTORY AND ETHNOLOGY
Schloss, Wittenberg Lutherstadt
Evolution of animals and men. Prehistoric and early historical material from local excavations.
Tu.-Su. 9-5.

REGIONAL MUSEUM AND MELANCTHON HOUSE
Collegienstrasse 60, Wittenberg Lutherstadt
House (1535) was home of Melancthon. Life and work of Melancthon. Local history. Weapons. Medals.
Tu.-Su. 10-12, 3-5.

WÖBBELIN

KÖRNER MEMORIAL
Wöbbelin
Life and work of the writer, Theodor Körner (d.1813). Engravings. Weapons.
On request.

WOLDEGK

REGIONAL ROOM
Woldegk
Local prehistory, history. Milling.
On request.

WOLGAST

REGIONAL MUSEUM
Karl Liebknecht Platz 6, Wolgast
In 15th century house. Regional prehistory, history.
M.-F. 9-4. May-Oct., also Sa. 9-12.

WOLKENSTEIN

REGIONAL ROOM
Schloss Wolkenstein
Regional history. Current affairs.
June-Oct., Su. 9-12.

WOLMIRSTEDT

DISTRICT MUSEUM
Glindenbergstrasse 9, Wolmirstedt
Prehistoric and early historical material from local excavations. Regional history, birds.
Tu.-Sa. 10-12, 2-4; Su. 10-12.

WORBIS

REGIONAL MUSEUM
Amtstrasse 1, Worbis
In 17th century house. Regional geology, wildlife, prehistory, history. Agriculture. Forestry. Potash industry. Textiles.
Tu., Th., F., 10-12, 2-4.

WÖRLITZ

STATE PALACES
Wörlitz
18th century palace and temples, built for Prince Franz von Anhalt Dessau. Period rooms. 16th-18th century German, Dutch, Flemish, Italian paintings. 17th-18th century engravings. 15th-17th century Swiss glass paintings. China. Porcelain. Glass.
Daily 9-6, guided tours only.

WURZEN

DISTRICT MUSEUM
Domgasse 2, Wurzen
Geology. Prehistory. Local history. Birds. Peasant handicrafts.
Tu.-F. 9-12, 1-4; Su. 10-12.

WUSTERHAUSEN

KYRITZ DISTRICT MUSEUM
Roter Platz 20, Wusterhausen
Local prehistory, ethnography, popular art, history.
Tu. 4-6; Sa. 10-12, 2-4; Apr.-Sept., Su. 10-12.

ZEITZ

MUNICIPAL MUSEUM
Schloss Moritzburg, Zeitz
In 17th century castle. Regional geology, prehistory, history, industry. 14th-20th century paintings, sculpture. 16th-19th century glass, pewter, porcelain, faience. Coins. Medals. Costumes.
Tu.-F. 10-12, 2-4.30; Sa. 10-12.30; Su. 9-1.

ZELLA-MEHLIS

REGIONAL MUSEUM
Thälmannstrasse, Zella Mehlis
Geology, ethnography and industry of the region.
Su. 9-12, 2-5. Other times by appointment.

ZERBST

REGIONAL MUSEUM
Weinberg 1, Zerbst
In former Franciscan monastery, subsequently school. Regional geology, prehistory, history. Pewter. Faience.
Tu.-Su. 10-12.

ZEULENRODA

MUNICIPAL MUSEUM OF INDUSTRIAL ART AND REGIONAL LIFE
Aumaische Strasse 30, Zeulenroda
Local history. History of local education, handicrafts and industry, especially furniture, stockings. Peasant furniture, household equipment, costumes. Pewter. Ceramics. Faience. Coins. Locks.
M.-F., Su. 9-12, 2-6.

ZIEGENRÜCK

MUSEUM OF WATER-POWER
Lobensteiner Strasse 6, Ziegenrück
History and technology of water-power.
On request.

ZINGST

REGIONAL HOUSE
Prerowerstrasse 4, Zingst
18th century ship-owner's house. History of local navigation. Ships' models. Memorabilia of local shipping notabilities. Local history.
June-Sept., M.-Th., Sa., Su. 2-6.

ZITTAU

DR. CURT HEINKE MUSEUM
Thälmannring, Zittau
Geology and prehistory of Lansitz.
M. 11-1, 4.30-6.30; Th. 4.30-6.30.

MUNICIPAL MUSEUM
Klosterstrasse 3, Zittau
In former Franciscan Monastery. Local history. Religious sculpture. 18th-20th century paintings, drawings, prints. Weapons. Coins. Musical instruments. Pewter. Embroidery. Woodcarving. Toys. Glass paintings. Artistic cast iron. 18th-19th century peasant furniture, household equipment. Ceramics. Stoneware. Faience.
M., Tu., Th.-Sa. 10-12, 2-4; W. 2-6; Su. 10-12.

MUSEUM ON OYBIN HILL
Zittau
Local history. History of the Castle and of Oybin Monastery.
May-Sept., Daily 9-1, 2-5.

ZÖRBIG

REGIONAL MUSEUM
Am Schloss 10, Zörbig
Regional prehistory, history. Peasant furniture, household equipment, handicrafts.
Tu.-F. 9-12, 2-4; W. 8 p.m.-10; Sa. 9-12; 1st Su. in month 2-5.

ZWICKAU

MUNICIPAL MUSEUM
Lessingstrasse 1, Zwickau
Geology. Mineralogy. History of Zwickau. Coal-mining and life of mining community. Medieval ceramics. 16th-19th century pewter, porcelain. 13th-18th century religious sculpture. Portraits of the Electoral Princes of Saxony. Drawings. Prints.
Tu.-Su. 10-1, 3-5.

ROBERT SCHUMANN HOUSE
Hauptmarkt 5, Zwickau
Birthplace of Robert Schumann (1810-56). Life and work of the composer. Original furnishings. Portraits. Manuscripts. First editions of Schumann's music. Clara Wieck-Schumann's programme collection.
Tu.-Sa. 10-12, 3-5.

Germany, Federal Republic of

West Germany suffered serious and widespread damage to its museum buildings between 1940 and 1945 but, twenty-five years later, one can see that the War brought benefits as well. Foremost among these was the ending of the previous over-dependence on Berlin, which had always, since the mid-nineteenth century, had more than its fair share of cultural importance and of the great national collections. The immense scale of the destruction in Berlin, the cutting of the city into two halves and the difficulties of travel to and from the rest of the Federal Republic combined to bring about a marked decentralisation of political and cultural life, evidenced in our particular field by the strengthening of museums and galleries in the major cities, such as Hamburg, Düsseldorf and Munich, and in the development of many small, specialised, and often very attractive museums elsewhere.

West German museums, even the largest, are financed for the most part either from *Land* (Provincial) or municipal funds, although Federal subsidies are available in certain cases. Germans traditionally expect a substantial proportion of their taxes to be devoted to cultural enterprises and, although there is never, of course, as much money available for the theatre, the opera and the other arts as their administrators would wish, it would be fair to say that the larger museums and galleries in Germany have an income which very few other European countries can match.

The results of such prestige and official favour are not always wholly good. There is a regrettable tendency in Germany to worship size for its own sake, which causes many of the best-known museums to be dauntingly monumental and all-embracing. The decision to restore these giants to their pre-war proportions may, in some cases, have turned out to be unfortunate. Not infrequently, too, the scholarly function of museums appears to have been overemphasised, so that younger people are frightened off and the adult visitor is liable to feel that he may be required to sit for an examination at any moment.

Having said this, one should add, as a counterweight, that the Federal Republic contains a remarkable number of second- and third-size establishments where great professional skill and imagination have produced museums of notable charm, lightness of touch and effectiveness on such unscholarly subjects as bread, bicycles and hats. A study of our index and list will show the range and quantity of these specialised museums. One might also draw attention to the excellent and numerous museums maintained by industrial and commercial firms, to the opportunities for seeing the work of contemporary artists and designers, and to the variety of interesting experiments with the presentation of archaeological and architectural material.

AACHEN

AACHEN MUSEUM OF THE INTERNATIONAL PRESS
Pontstrasse 13, 5100 Aachen, Nordrhein-Westfalen
In Frosses Haus von Aachen (c.1495). Newspapers and periodicals from the whole world. History of newspapers, 16th century - present day, especially in Germany.
M.-F. 9.30-1; M., W.-F. also 2.30-5.

CATHEDRAL TREASURY
Domhof 6, 5100 Aachen, Nordrhein-Westfalen
Religious art and liturgical objects, especially 10th-16th century.
May-Sept., M.-Sa. 9-1, 2-6; Su. 10.30-1, 2-5. Oct.-Apr., M.-Sa. 9-1, 2-5; Su. 10.30-1, 2-5.

COUVEN MUSEUM
Hühnermarkt 17, 5100 Aachen, Nordrhein-Westfalen
In Haus Monheim (late 17th century). 18th - early 19th century furniture, decorative arts.
M., W.-F. 10-5; Th., Sa., Su. 10-1.

REGIONAL MUSEUM AND COLLECTION OF INDUSTRIAL ART
Burg Frankenburg, 5100 Aachen, Nordrhein-Westfalen
Local history. Folklore of the Aachen region. Industrial art.
M.-F. 10-5; Sa., Su. 10-1.

SUERMONDT MUSEUM
Wilhelmstrasse 18, 5100 Aachen, Nordrhein-Westfalen
Greek, Roman art. Medieval sculpture, decorative arts. 15th-19th century Dutch, German paintings. Contemporary paintings, stained glass.
Tu.-F. 10-5; Sa., Su. 10-1.

AALEN

LIMES MUSEUM
St. Johanastrasse 5, 7080 Aalen, Baden-Württemberg
Collections illustrating the Roman occupation of S. Germany. Roman art, household equipment, weapons, armour, coins, medals. Dioramas.
Tu.-Su. 10-12; W., Sa., Su. also 3-6.

REGIONAL AND SCHUBART MUSEUM
Hampstrasse 1, 7080 Aalen, Baden-Württemberg
Life and work of the writer and composer, C. F. D. Schubart. Greek, Roman, medieval antiquities. Peasant household equipment, tools.
M.-Sa. 2-4; Su. 11-12.

ABENSBERG

AVENTINUS MUSEUM
Karmelstenplatz 5, 8423 Abensberg, Bayern
In former Carmelite convent. Local prehistory, history, geology, folklore. Weapons.
M.-Sa. 10-12, 2-5; Su. 8-10, 1-5.

AHLEN

REGIONAL MUSEUM
Wilhelmstrasse, 4730 Ahlen, Nordrhein-Westfalen
Collections illustrating 19th - early 20th century town and country life in S.E. Germany.
W. 2-5; Su. 10-12.

AHRENSBURG

AHRENSBURG CASTLE MUSEUM
2070 Ahrensburg, Schleswig Holstein
In castle (1596, remodelled late 18th century). 18th-19th century furnishings. Paintings. Portraits. 18th-19th century Meissen porcelain.
Tu.-Sa. 10-6.

AHRWEILER

AHRGAU MUSEUM
Altenbaustrasse, 5482 Ahrweiler, Rheinland-Pfalz
Local prehistory, history, folklore. 11th-15th century religious art.
Tu.-Sa. 10-5.

AICHACH

REGIONAL MUSEUM
Schulstrasse, 8890 Aichach, Bayern
Regional prehistory, history. Peasant handicrafts, furniture, household equipment. Costumes. Religious art. Liturgical objects.
M.-Sa. 10-12, 2-5.

ALFELD

REGIONAL MUSEUM
Kirchhof 4-5, 3220 Alfeld, Niedersachsen
In carved half-timbered house (1610). Local geology, wildlife, history.
M. 10-1, 4-6; Su. 10-12.

ALHAUSEN

WEBER'S BIRTHPLACE
3491 Alhausen-Bad Driburg, Niedersachsen
Collections illustrating the life and work of the poet, F. W. Weber.
Daily 9-12, 3-6.

ALSFELD

REGIONAL MUSEUM
Hochzutshaus am Marktplatz, 6320 Alsfeld, Hessen
Museum building (1570). Local prehistory, history. Religious art. Furnishings. Costumes. Industrial development of the area. Musical instruments. Weapons. Coins.
Daily 9-11, 3-6.

ALTENA

MUSEUM OF THE COUNTY OF MARK, WITH THE GERMAN BLACKSMITH'S MUSEUM AND WIRE MUSEUM
Burg Altena, 5990 Altena, Nordrhein-Westfalen
Local geology, prehistory. History of technology. Wrought-iron. Weapons.
Tu.-Sa. 9.30-5; Su. 9.30-6.

ALTENBEKEN

EGGE MUSEUM
Bahnhofstrasse 5A, 4791 Altenbeken, Nordrhein-Westfalen
House (1583, enlarged 1789). Stove collection. Furniture. Household equipment. Agricultural implements. Tools. Maps. Local history and geology.
Tu.-Sa. 9-5; Su. 9-1.

ALTENHOF

ALTENHOF MANORHOUSE
2330 Altenhof, Niedersachsen
House (1722-8). Louis XV and XVI period furnishings. Porcelain. Paintings.
May-Sept., Tu.-Su. 2-5.

ALT-FRESENBURG

MENNONITE AND MENNO SIMONS MEMORIAL
2061 Alt-Fresenburg, Niedersachsen
Manuscripts, books and other items relating to Menno Simons and the Mennonites.
By appointment.

ALTÖTTING

MUNICIPAL MUSEUM OF REGIONAL LIFE
Kapellplatz 2A, 8262 Altötting, Bayern
Local wildlife, prehistory, history. Pilgrimages. Paintings. Sculpture. Votive and In Memoriam pictures. Peasant furnishings. Biedermeier furniture.
By appointment.

TREASURY
Kapellplatz 4, 8262 Altötting, Bayern
Liturgical objects. Devotional gifts. Altar (c.1600). Religious sculpture.
May-Sept., daily 10.15-2, 3.30-5. Oct.-Apr., on request.

ALTWIEDERMUS

RONNEBURG CASTLE MUSEUM
Burg, 6451 Alwiedermus, Hessen
Craftsmen's tools. Agricultural implements. Peasant furnishings. Weapons. Prehistoric, medieval archaeology.
Daily 9-6.

ALZEY

ALZEY MUSEUM
Schloss, 6508 Alzey, Rheinland-Pfalz
Local geology, prehistory (especially La Tène), history. Ceramics. Porcelain.
Sa., Su. 10-12.

AMBERG

REGIONAL MUSEUM
Eichenforstgasse 12, 8450 Amberg, Bayern
Local pre-history, history. Peasant tools, handicrafts, agricultural implements. Costumes. Furniture. Faience. House-chapel (14th century), with painted glass.
1st Su. in month, 10-12, 2-5.

AMORBACH

AMORBACH COLLECTIONS OF PRINCE ZU LEININGEN
Kellereigasse, 8762 Amorbach, Bayern
Local handicrafts, folk-art. Medieval pottery.
M.-Sa. 9-12.30; Su. 12-6.30.

ANDECHS

PILGRIMAGE AND MONASTERY CHURCH
8131 Andechs, Bayern
Religious art. Liturgical objects. Reliquaries. Votive gifts.
By appointment.

ST. HEDWIG'S MUSEUM
Erling-Andechs
In the former apothecary's room of the Monastery (1763-7). Exhibits illustrating life and work of Duke Hedwig of Silesia, canonised 1267.
Daily 9-5.

ANDERNACH

MUNICIPAL MUSEUM
Hochstrasse 97, 5470 Andernach, Rheinland-Pfalz
Regional pre-history, history.
By appointment.

ANHOLT

CASTLE MUSEUM
4294 Anholt, Nordrhein-Westfalen
Castle (13th century, with subsequent restorations). 17th-18th century Flemish tapestries. 18th century leather wall-hanging. Paintings. Sculpture. Furniture.
May-Sept., Tu.-Su. 10-6. Oct.-Apr., Tu.-Su. 2-6.

ANSBACH

ANSBACH MANSION
8800 Ansbach, Bayern
17th-18th century furnishings. Porcelain. Paintings.
May-Sept., daily 9-12, 2-5. Oct.-Apr., daily 10-12, 2-4.

COLLECTION OF ANSBACH PORCELAIN
8800 Ansbach, Bayern
Ansbach porcelain, faience.
M.-Sa. 10-12, 2-5; Su. 10-12.30.

DISTRICT AND MUNICIPAL MUSEUM
Schaitberger Strasse 10, 8800 Ansbach, Bayern
Local prehistory, history. History of the Princes of Ansbach. Natural sciences. Ansbach porcelain, faience. Punch and Judy collection.
M.-Sa. 10-12, 2-5; Su. 10-12.30.

RESIDENZ STATE ART GALLERY
8800 Ansbach, Bayern
17th-18th century European paintings.
May-Sept., daily 9-12, 2-5. Oct.-Apr., daily 10-12, 2-4.

ARNSBERG

SAMERLAND MUSEUM
Landsberger Hof, Alter Markt 26, 5770 Arnsberg, Nordrhein-Westfalen
Local prehistory, geology. Social history of Arnsberg and its region. 16th-19th century religious art. Birds.
Tu.-Sa. 10-1, 3-5; Su. 10-1.

AROLSEN

KAULBACH MUSEUM
Residenzschloss, 3548 Arolsen, Hessen
Works by members of the Kaulbach family. Paintings. Drawings. Engravings. Casts of sculpture.
May-Sept., daily 9-12, 2-5. Oct.-Apr., by appointment.

REGIONAL MUSEUM
Hauptstrasse 27, 3548 Arolsen, Hessen
Geology. Mineralogy. Botany. Local history. Costumes. Weapons. Armour.
Daily 10-12.

ASCHACH

COUNT VON LUXBURG MUSEUM
Schloss, 5464 Aschach, Rheinland-Pfalz
Furniture. Paintings. 16th-19th century goldsmith's work. Chinese ceramics. Carpets. Folklore.
May-Oct., 3-6.

ASCHAFFENBURG

ASCHAFFENBURG MUNICIPAL MUSEUM
Stiftsplatz, 8750 Aschaffenburg, Bayern
Prehistoric and early historical material from local excavations. 12th-17th century architectural sculptures. Faience. Spessart glass. Ceramics.
May-Sept., Tu.-Su. 10-1, 2-5.

NATURAL HISTORY MUSEUM
8750 Aschaffenburg, Bayern
Mineralogy. Botany. Zoology.
Public holidays 10.30-12.30. Other times by appointment.

STATE COLLECTION OF GRAPHICS
Stiftsplatz, 8750 Aschaffenburg, Bayern
15th-18th century English, German paintings.
By appointment.

ASCHHAUSEN

COUNT VON ZEPPELIN MUSEUM
7109 Aschhausen, Baden-Württemberg
Local history. Collections made by members of the Zeppelin family, 1803-1953.
By appointment.

ASSENHEIM

PALACE MUSEUM
Hauptstrasse 40, 6361 Assenheim, Hessen
Local prehistory, history, folklore.
By appointment.

ATTENDORN

REGIONAL MUSEUM
Marktplatz 1, 5952 Attendorn, Nordrhein-Westfalen
Geology. Archaeological material from local excavations. Household equipment. Religious art.
Tu.-F. 9-1, 3-5; Sa. 9-1; Su. 11-1.

AUGSBURG

GERMAN GALLERY OF THE BAROQUE
Maximilianstrasse 46, 8900 Augsburg, Bayern
In the Schaezler Palace (1765-7). Baroque paintings by German, Swiss, Austrian artists.
May-Sept., Tu.-Su. 10-5; Oct.-Apr., daily 10-4.

GRAPHICS COLLECTION
Maximilianstrasse 46, 8900 Augsburg, Bayern
In Schaezler Palace (1765-7). 15th-17th century drawings, prints by Augsburg artists.
May-Sept., Tu.-Su. 10-5. Oct.-Apr., daily 10-4.

MAXIMILIAN MUSEUM
Phil Weiser Strasse 24, 8900 Augsburg, Bayern
In 2 houses (15th, 16th century). History of Augsburg and its handicrafts. South German and Austrian sculpture in wood and stone. Works by Augsburg craftsmen in metal, faience, wood.
May-Sept., Tu.-Su. 10-5. Oct.-Apr., daily 10-4.

MOZART MEMORIAL
Frauentorstrasse 30, 8900 Augsburg, Bayern
House (17th century) was birthplace of Leopold Mozart. Memorabilia of Leopold and W. A. Mozart.
Tu.-F. 10-12, 2-5; Sa. 10-12; Su. 10-1.

NATURAL HISTORY MUSEUM
Fuggerhaus, Maximilianstrasse 36, 8900 Augsburg, Bayern
Geology. Palaeontology. Mineralogy. Botany. Zoology, especially European birds.
Tu., F. 9-12, 5-8; W., Th., Sa. 9-12, 2-5; Su. 9-12.

ROMAN MUSEUM
Dominikanergasse 15, 8900 Augsburg, Bayern
In former Dominican church (1515). Prehistory and early history, especially Roman material from sites in Bavaria.
May-Sept., Tu.-Su. 10-5. Oct.-Apr., daily 10-4.

STATE GALLERY
Maximilianstrasse 46, 8900 Augsburg, Bayern
Swabian paintings of the late Gothic period.
May-Sept., Tu.-Su., 10-5. Oct.-Apr., daily 10-4.

AUMÜHLE-FRIEDRICHSRUH

BISMARCK MUSEUM
2055 Aumühle-Friedrichsruh, Niedersachsen
Collections illustrating life and work of Otto von Bismarck.
May-Sept., Tu.-Su. 9-6; M. 1-6. Oct.-Apr., Tu.-Sa. 9-4; Su. 10-4.

AUTENRIED

ICON MUSEUM
Schloss, 8871 Autenried, Bayern
Religious art and liturgical objects of the Orthodox Church. Icons. Gold. Embroidery. Ivories. Manuscripts.
Daily 10-12, 2-5.

BABENHAUSEN

FUGGER MUSEUM
Schloss, 8943 Babenhausen, Bayern
Glass. Porcelain. Ivories. Miniatures. Gold. Religious art. Folk art. Weapons.
Mar. 16- Nov. 20, daily 10-12, 2-5; Su. 10-12, 1-6.

BACHARACH

STAHLECK
6533 Bacharach, Rheinland-Pfalz
Local and regional history.
By appointment.

BACKNANG

HELFER HOUSE MUSEUM
Stiftshof 11, 7150 Backnang, Baden-Württemberg
Local history. Prints. Drawings. Roman archaeology. Peasant furnishings, crafts.
W. 6.30 p.m.-8.30; Su. 10.30-12.30, 3-6.

BADEN-BADEN

MUNICIPAL HISTORY COLLECTIONS
Neues Schloss, 7570 Baden-Baden, Baden-Württemberg
Local prehistory and early history. Roman material from local sites. Medieval collection.
Daily 10-1, 3-6.

MUNICIPAL MUSEUM
Neues Schloss, Schlossstrasse 22, 7570 Baden-Baden, Baden-Württemberg
Local and regional history.
Daily 10-1, 3-6.

ZÄHRINGER MUSEUM
Neues Schloss, 7570 Baden-Baden, Baden-Württemberg
17th-18th century furnishings, paintings, drawings, decorative art. Period rooms, once in possession of the Grand Dukes of Baden.
By appointment.

BAD AIBLING

REGIONAL MUSEUM
Wilhelm Leibl Platz 2, 8202 Bad Aibling, Bayern
Local prehistory, history. Folklore. Popular art. Room of the painter, Wilhelm Leibl.
Daily 9-5.

BAD BUCHAU

FEDERSEE MUSEUM
7952 Bad Buchau, Baden-Württemberg
Geology. Botany. Zoology. Prehistory and early history of Upper Swabia.
On request.

BAD DRIBURG

MISSION MUSEUM
Dringenbergerstrasse 19, 3490 Bad Driburg, Nordrhein-Westfalen
In Steyler Mission. Ethnology. Zoology. Local history.
On request.

REGIONAL COLLECTION
Jahnstrasse, 3490 Bad Driburg, Nordrhein-Westfalen
History of Bad Driburg and its region.
On request.

ST. XAVIER MISSION MUSEUM
Dringenbergerstrasse 32, 3490 Bad Driburg, Nordrhein-Westfalen
Collections made by members of the Mission in the Far East. Tapestry. Embroidery. Porcelain. Lacquerware. Masks. Carvings. Weapons. Idols. Prehistoric tools. Zoology. Bird-cages.
Daily 8-6.

BAD DÜRKHEIM

REGIONAL MUSEUM
Eichstrasse 22, 6702 Bad Dürkheim, Rheinland-Pfalz
Geology. History of Bad Dürkheim and its region. Zoology.
On request.

BAD EMS

LOCAL HISTORY COLLECTION
Rathaus, 5427 Bad Ems, Rheinland-Pfalz
Geology. Prehistory, early history (especially Roman), history, of the Bad Ems area.
Tu., F. 9-12.

BAD GANDERSHEIM

REGIONAL MUSEUM
Markt 10, 3353 Bad Gandersheim, Niedersachsen
Local and regional history. Furnishings. Household equipment. Paintings. Decorative arts.
Su., Th. 10-1.

BAD HERSFELD

MUNICIPAL MUSEUM
Im Stift 6A, 6430 Bad Hersfeld, Hessen
Fossils. Prehistory and early history of the area. Agricultural implements. Industry and handicrafts, especially dyeing. Town seals, coins.
M.-Sa. 9-1, 3-5; Su. 10-12.

BAD HOMBURG

LOCAL HISTORY AND HAT MUSEUM
Promenade 103, 6380 Bad Homburg, Hessen
Local history. Hat collections. History of local hatmaking industry. Daguerreotypes.
Tu., F. 4.30-6.30; Su. 10-12.

BAD KISSINGEN

REGIONAL MUSEUM
Rathausplatz 1, 8730 Bad Kissingen, Bayern
History of Bad Kissingen and its region. 16th-17th century material from local excavations.
By appointment.

BAD KREUZNACH

KARL GEIB MUSEUM
Kreuzstrasse 69, 6550 Bad Kreuznach, Rheinland-Pfalz
Geology. Palaeontology. Local prehistory, early history.
May-Sept., M.-F. 9-12.30, 2.30-6. Oct.-Apr., M.-F. 9-12.30, 2-4; Su. 10.30-12.30.

MAX PLANCK INSTITUTE FOR AGRICULTURE AND AGRICULTURAL TECHNOLOGY
6550 Bad Kreuznach, Rheinland-Pfalz
Historical development of agricultural and gardening implements and equipment.
By appointment.

BAD MERGENTHEIM

MUSEUM OF THE TEUTONIC ORDER AND REGIONAL MUSEUM
Schloss, 6990 Bad Mergentheim, Baden-Württemberg
In former castle of the Teutonic Order. History of the Order. Local prehistory, history. Folklore. Religious art.
Daily, on request.

BAD MÜNSTEREIFEL

REGIONAL MUSEUM
Rathaus, 5338 Bad Münstereifel, Nordrhein-Westfalen
In Town-Hall (1350). History of Bad Münstereifel and its region.
Daily 9-12.

BAD NAUHEIM

SALT MUSEUM
Ludwigstrasse 20-22, 6350 Bad Nauheim, Hessen
Prehistoric and medieval salt-industry in Bad Nauheim. Local history.
W., F., Sa. 3.30-6.

BAD NEUSTADT

BAD NEUSTADT DISTRICT MUSEUM
Landratsamt, 8740 Bad Neustadt, Bayern
In former administrative offices of the Episcopal Palace. Folk art. Wood-carvings.
Tu., Th. 3-4.30; Su. 2-4.

BAD OEYNHAUSEN

DISTRICT MUSEUM
Schützenstrasse 35A, 4970 Bad Oeynhausen, Nordrhein-Westfalen
Local and regional history. 18th-19th century peasant furniture, household equipment, agricultural implements. Craftsmen's tools.
Daily 9-5.

BAD OLDESLOE

REGIONAL MUSEUM
Mühlenstrasse 22, 2060 Bad Oldesloe, Schleswig-Holstein
Local prehistory, history.
Sa. 9-12, 3-6.

BAD ORB

BAD ORB REGIONAL MUSEUM
Kurparkstrasse 2, 6482 Bad Orb, Hessen
Birds. Local history. History of the local salt industry.
Th. 3.30-5; Su. 10-12.

SPESSART MUSEUM
Villbacherstrasse 8, 6482 Bad Orb, Hessen
Rocks, minerals, fossils of Europe, Africa, N. America. History of the Bad Orb area.
By appointment.

BAD PYRMONT

REGIONAL MUSEUM
Am Hylligen Born, 3280 Bad Pyrmont, Niedersachsen
History of Bad Pyrmont. Paintings. Engravings.
Tu., Th. 10-12, 3.30-5.30; Sa. 3.30-5.30; Su. 9.30-12.

BAD REICHENHALL

MUNICIPAL MUSEUM
Getreidegasse 4, 8230 Bad Reichenhall, Bayern
Local prehistory, history. Peasant furnishings, household equipment. Folk-art. 13th-18th century sculpture.
May-Oct., Tu.-F. 2-4. 1st Su. in month, 10-12.

BAD ROTHENFELDE

REGIONAL MUSEUM
Ferdinandstrasse, 4502 Bad Rothenfelde, Niedersachsen
Regional prehistory, history. Peasant handicrafts, furniture, household equipment.
Tu., F. 4-6.

BAD SALZUFLEN

MUSEUM OF THE SPA AND THE TOWN
Kurverwaltung, 4902 Bad Salzuflen 1, Nordrhein-Westfalen
Geology. Prehistory. History of the saltworks, the spa and the town. Folklore.
W., F. 3-5.30; Su. 10-12.

BAD SCHWARTAU

REGIONAL MUSEUM
Augusstrasse 34, 2407 Bad Schwartau, Schleswig-Holstein
Natural history, especially birds. Prehistory. Folklore. Furniture. Domestic equipment.
Tu.-Sa. 2-5.

BAD SEGEBERG

OLD SEGEBERG TOWN HOUSE
Lübecker Strasse 15, 2360 Bad Segeberg, Schleswig-Holstein
Local anhydrite industry. Shoemaking. 17th-19th century furniture, household equipment, decorative arts.
Mar.-Oct., Tu., W., F., Sa., 10-12, 2-6. Nov., Jan., Tu., W., F., Sa. 10-12, 3-6; Su. 10-12, 2-4.

BAD SOODEN-ALLENDORF

BAD SOODEN REGIONAL MUSEUM
Vor dem Tor, 3437 Bad Sooden-Allendorf, Hessen
Local and regional history.
On request.

BAD TÖLZ

BAD TÖLZ MUSEUM
Schlossplatz 2, 8170 Bad Tölz, Bayern
Regional history, geology. Furniture, especially Empire and Biedermeier. Household equipment. Handicrafts. Costumes. Popular religious art. 16th and 18th century sculpture.
May-Sept., daily 10-12, 2-6. Oct.-Apr., M.-Sa. 10-12, 2-5; Su. 10-12.

BAD VILBEL

REGIONAL AND MINERAL SPRINGS MUSEUM
6368 Bad Vilbel, Hessen
In former castle (15th century) of the Knights of Vilbel. Prehistoric, Roman and Medieval material from Bad Vilbel. History of the local mineral springs.
W., Sa. 3-5; Su. 10-12, 2-5.

BAD WALDSEE

BAD WALDSEE REGIONAL MUSEUM
Spitalhof, 7967 Bad Waldsee, Baden-Württemberg
18th century furniture, household equipment. 14th-18th century sculpture.
On request.

SMALL GALLERY
Elisabethenbad, 7967 Bad Waldsee, Baden-Württemberg
Paintings. Sculpture.
M.-Sa. 9-7.

BAD WIESSEE

CERAMICS MUSEUM
Anton von Rieppel Strasse 21, 8182 Bad Wiessee, Bayern
Ceramics. History of pottery-making.
By appointment.

BAD WILDUNGEN

ASIATIC MUSEUM
Laustrasse 26, 3590 Bad Wildungen, Hessen
Art of China, Japan, Korea.
Tu.-Su. 2.30-6.

BAD WILDUNGEN REGIONAL MSEUM
Lindenstrasse 9, 3590 Bad Wildungen, Hessen
History of Bad Wildungen and its region. Prehistoric and medieval material from local sites.
On request.

BAD WIMPFEN

STEINHAUS MUSEUM
7107 Bad Wimpfen, Baden-Württemberg
Local history. Peasant furniture, tools, handicrafts. Coins. Weapons.
By appointment.

BAD WINDSHEIM

REGIONAL MUSEUM
Schumbergstrasse 4, 8532 Bad Windsheim, Bayern
Local wildlife, prehistory, history. Pottery. Weaving. Pipes. Costumes.
Daily 9.30-11, 2-4.

BAD WÖRISHOFEN

KNEIPP MUSEUM
Kloster der Dominikanerinnen, Klostenhof 1, 8937 Bad Wörishofen, Bayern
Memorabilia of the priest and doctor, Sebastian Kneipp (d.1897).
M., W., F. 3-6.

BAD ZWISCHENAHN

AMMERLAND REGIONAL MUSEUM
2903 Bad Zwischenahn, Niedersachsen
Local and regional prehistory and history.
On request.

BALDERN

CERAMICS COLLECTION
Schloss, 7081 Baldern, Baden-Württemberg
Ceramics. Faience.
By appointment.

BALINGEN

MUSEUM OF WEIGHING EQUIPMENT
Zollernschloss, 7460 Balingen, Baden-Württemberg
Collections and displays illustrating development of weighing equipment since prehistoric times.
M., W., F. 2-4. Other times by appointment.

REGIONAL MUSEUM
Zollernschloss, 7460 Balingen, Baden-Württemberg
In 15th century castle. Geology. Prehistory and history of the Balingen area. Handicrafts. Dyer's workshop. Peasant furniture, household equipment.
M., W., F. 4-6. Other times by appointment.

BALVE

REGIONAL MUSEUM OF PREHISTORY AND CAVE ARCHAEOLOGY
Volksschule, 5983 Balve, Nordrhein-Westfalen
Local prehistory, history. Material from palaeolithic cave-dwellings.
Tu., W., F. 2-5. Other times by appointment.

BAMBERG

BAMBERG STATE GALLERY
Neue Residenz, 8600 Bamberg, Bayern
15th-18th century European paintings.
Daily 10-12, 2.30-6; Su. 10-1.

BEER MUSEUM
Alte Hofhaltung, 8600 Bamberg, Bayern
Collections and displays illustrating history of brewing, especially in Germany.
M.-Sa. 9-12, 2-5; Su., public holidays 10-1.

BÖTTINGER HOUSE MUSEUM
8600 Bamberg, Bayern
17th-18th century furniture, decorative arts.
May-Sept., M.-Sa. 10-12.

DIOCESAN MUSEUM
Kapitelhaus, 8600 Bamberg, Bayern
In Cathedral chapter-house (1733). 11th-19th century religious art. Vestments. Altar-hangings. Liturgical objects.
M.-Sa. 10-12, 2.30-6; Su. 10-1.

J. HELLER COLLECTION OF GRAPHICS
Neue Residenz, 8600 Bamberg, Bayern
16th-18th century German drawings, engravings, prints.
Daily 10-12, 2.30-6; Su. 10-1.

HISTORICAL MUSEUM
Alte Hofhaltung, Domplatz 7, 8600 Bamberg, Bayern
Local prehistory, history. The Bamberg Idols. 12th-18th century sculpture, applied arts. Clocks. Astronomical instruments.
May-Sept., M.-Sa. 9-12, 2-5; Su., public holidays 10-1.

HISTORY MUSEUM
Domplatz 7, 8600 Bamberg, Bayern
Folklore. Paintings. Drawings. Decorative arts. Handicrafts.
Tu.-Sa. 9-12, Su. 10-1.

E.T.A. HOFFMAN HOUSE AND MUSEUM
Schillerplatz 26, 8600 Bamberg, Bayern
In former home of the writer and composer, E.T.A. Hoffmann (d.1822). Memorabilia of Hoffmann. Manuscripts. 1st editions.
M.-Sa. 4.30-5.30; Su. 9.30-10.30.

KARL MAY MUSEUM
E.T.A. Hoffmannstrasse 2, 8600 Bamberg, Bayern
Collections illustrating Indian life in N. and S. America. Costumes. Weapons. Artifacts. Study, library and memorabilia of the writer, Karl May.
M.-F. 10-12, 2-4; Sa. 10-12.

NATURAL HISTORY MUSEUM
Fleischstrasse 2, 8600 Bamberg, Bayern
Geology. Palaeontology. Mineralogy. Herbarium. Birds.
F. 2-6. Other times by appointment.

NEW RESIDENCE
Domplatz, 8600 Bamberg, Bayern
17th-early 19th century furniture, decorative arts. Paintings.
Daily 10-12, 2.30-6; Su. 10-1.

TEXTILE MUSEUM
Domplatz 5, 8600 Bamberg, Bayern
11th-19th century European and Byzantine vestments, altar-hangings, ritual items.
M.-Sa. 10-12, 2.30-6.

BANZ

COLLECTION OF PETRIFIED OBJECTS
Benediktinerstift, 8621 Banz, Bayern
Geology. Palaeontology.
M.-Sa. 8-12, 1-6; public holidays 11-6.

BARMSTEDT

RANTZAU COUNTY MUSEUM
Am Markt 13, 2202 Barmstedt, Schleswig-Holstein
Local prehistory, history. Peasant furniture, household equipment. Costumes. Weapons. Folklore. Handicrafts. Apothecary's equipment. Guild material. Prints.
May-Oct., 4-6. Other times by appointment.

BAUSCHLOTT

GALLERY OF THE BUSLAT GUILD OF ARTISTS
Schloss, Hauptstrasse 70, 7531 Bauschlott, Baden-Württemberg
20th century paintings, prints, sculpture.
By appointment.

BAYREUTH

BRANCH GALLERY OF THE BAVARIAN STATE COLLECTIONS OF PAINTINGS
Neues Schloss, Ludwigstrasse, 8580 Bayreuth, Bayern
16th-18th century paintings.
Apr. Sept., daily 10-12, 1-5. Oct.-Mar., daily 10-12, 1.30-3.30.

COLLECTION OF AGRICULTURAL IMPLEMENTS AND EQUIPMENT
Adolf Wächter Strasse 3, 8580 Bayreuth, Bayern
Agricultural and forestry tools, equipment. Craftsmen's equipment, especially brewing, charcoal-burning, linen-weaving.
By appointment.

GERMAN MUSEUM OF FREEMASONRY
Im Hofgarten 1, 8580 Bayreuth, Bayern
Masonic ritual objects. Porcelain, glass, medals, prints, containing masonic emblems and themes. Documents.
M.-Sa. 9-11. Other times by appointment.

HERMITAGE
St. Johannis, 8580 Bayreuth, Bayern
Period rooms. Bayreuth rococo art. Hermits' cells. Grotto.
Apr.-Sept., daily 9-12, 1-5. Oct.-Mar., daily 10-12, 1-3.

MUNICIPAL MUSEUM
Neues Schloss, Ludwigstrasse, 8580 Bayreuth, Bayern
Local prehistory, history. Furniture. Decorative arts. Ceramics. Faience. Fichtelgeburg glass. Stage décors by Carlo Bibiena.
July-Aug., daily 10-12, 2-5.

MUSEUM OF HISTORIC TYPEWRITERS
Luitpoldplatz 3, 8580 Bayreuth, Bayern
Collection illustrating development of the typewriter.
By appointment.

NEW PALACE
Ludwigstrasse 21, 8580 Bayreuth, Bayern
Period rooms. Paintings.
May-Sept., daily 10-12, 2-5. Oct.-Apr., 10-12, 1-4.

JEAN PAUL ROOM
Königsallee 84, 8580 Bayreuth, Bayern
Memorial exhibition to the poet, Jean Paul Friedrich Richter (d.1825), in his former home.
By appointment.

SANSPAREIL
Burg Zwernitz, 8580 Bayreuth, Bayern
18th century period rooms. 18th century rock-gardens.
Apr.-Sept., daily 9-6. Oct.-Mar., daily 10-4.

RICHARD WAGNER MEMORIAL
Neues Schloss, Glasenappweg 2, 8580 Bayreuth, Bayern
Collections illustrating life and work of Richard Wagner. History of Bayreuth Festival.
M.-F. 9-12, 2-5. During Festival, 9-5.

BEBENHAUSEN

STATE COLLECTION OF MEDIEVAL ART IN CISTERCIAN ABBEY
Kloster, 7401 Bebenhausen, Baden-Württemberg
In 13th-15th century abbey. Medieval religious art.
May-Sept., daily 8-12, 2-6. Oct.-Apr., daily 10-12, 2-4.

BENEDIKTBEUERN

FRAUNHOFER GLASSWORKS
Fraunhofer Strasse 126, 8174 Benediktbeuern, Bayern
Displays illustrating techniques and processes of local glass industry, especially production of optical glass.
M.-Sa. 10-12, 2-5; Su. 1-5.

BENSBERG

TOWN MUSEUM
Burggraben 17, 5060 Bensberg, Nordrhein-Westfalen
Geology. Early history, folklore, furnishings, household equipment of Bensberg area. Local paper and leather industry.
Tu.-Sa. 10-5; Su. 11-5.

BENSHEIM

BERGSTRÄSSER REGIONAL MUSEUM
Klosterhof, 6140 Bensheim, Hessen
Prehistory, history of Bensheim and its region. Handicrafts. Guilds. Furnishings, household equipment.
Sa. 2-4; Su. 9-12, 2-4.

BENSHEIM-AUERBACH

FÜRSTENLAGER TOWN PARK
6142 Bensheim-Auerbach, Hessen
In former summer residence of the Grandukes of Hessen-Darmstadt. Local history. 18th-19th century furnishings, decorative arts.
Tu., F. 4.30-6.30; Su. 10-12.

BENTHEIM

REGIONAL MUSEUM
Schloss Bentheim, 4442 Bentheim, Niedersachsen
Geology. Mineralogy. Local prehistory, history. Folklore. Weapons. Armour. Sculpture. Prints. Drawings.
Daily 8-6.

BERATSHAUSEN

REGIONAL MUSEUM
Bischof Weig Strasse 26, 8411 Beratshausen, Bayern
Local history. Costumes. Folklore. Peasant tools, equipment.
Su. 10-12.

BERCHTESGADEN

GERMAN MUSEUM OF COATS OF ARMS
Salzburger Strasse, 8240 Berchtesgaden, Bayern
Coats of arms of German towns and of families.
M.-Sa. 10-1, 2-5. Other times by appointment.

PALACE MUSEUM
Schlossplatz 2, 8240 Berchtesgaden, Bayern
Art collections of the Wittelsbach family. Furniture. Tapestries. Porcelain. Glass. Sculpture. Weapons.
May-Sept., daily 10-1, 2-5. Oct.-Apr., M.-F. 10-1, 2-5.

REGIONAL MUSEUM
Schloss Adelsheim, 8240 Berchtesgaden, Bayern
In castle (1614). Folk-art. Furniture. Household equipment. Tools. Woodturning and carving. Pipes. Masks. Sculpture.
M.-F. 10-3.

SALT MUSEUM
Bergwerkstrasse, 8240 Berchtesgaden, Bayern
In saltmine, operational since 1517. Techniques of salt-mining, processing. Tools, costumes, customs of salt-miners.
May-Sept., daily 8-5. Oct.-Apr., M.-Sa. 1-4.

BERGEN

RÖMSTEDT HOUSE REGIONAL MUSEUM
Am Friedensplatz 7, 8221 Bergen, Bayern
Prehistoric material. Agricultural implements. Peasant furnishings. Household equipment. Beekeeping. Flax-processing, spinning.
M.-Sa. 9-11.30, 3-5.30, Su., public holidays, by appointment.

BERGHEIM

REGIONAL MUSEUM
Hauptstrasse 99, 5150 Bergheim, Nordrhein-Westfalen
History of Bergheim and its region.
On request.

BERGKAMEN-OBERADEN

DISTRICT MUSEUM
Jahnstrasse 31, 4619 Bergkamen-Oberaden, Nordrhein-Westfalen
Roman and Germanic material from local excavations. Geology. Mineralogy. Local history, folklore.
W. 3-5; Sa. 9-12; Su. 10-12.

BERLEBURG

BERLEBURG PALACE
592 Berleburg, Nordrhein-Westfalen
16th century buildings, remodelled in 18th and 19th centuries. Weapons. Uniforms. Hunting equipment and trophies. 16th-18th century furniture. 18th century German porcelain, glass. Portraits of the Sayn-Wittgenstein, Berleburg family.
By appointment.

WITTGENSTEIN DISTRICT MUSEUM
Goethe Platz 2, 592 Berleburg, Nordrhein-Westfalen
Local history. 19th century furniture, household equipment. Rural crafts, especially spinning, cabinet-making, wrought-iron work, woodturning. Toys.
Tu.-Su. 3-6.

BERLIN

ACADEMY OF ART
Hanseatenweg 10, 1000 Berlin 21
Documents, literature relating to German artists.
Sa.-Th. 10-7; F. 10-10.

AVIATION MUSEUM
Schütte Lanz Strasse 45-9, 1000 Berlin
History of aviation. Models. Original components. Documents. Paintings. Photographs. Medals.
Tu.-Su. 10-4.

BELLEVUE PALACE COLLECTIONS
Tiergarten, 1000 Berlin
Paintings. Furniture. Decorative arts.
Su. 10-4.

BERLIN MUSEUM
Lindenstrasse 14, 1000 Berlin 61
History of Berlin since c.1650. Paintings. Drawings. Prints. Sculpture.
Tu.-Sa. 11-6.

BERLIN POSTAL AND TELECOMMUNICATIONS MUSEUM
An der Urania 15, 1000 Berlin 30
History of the German postal, telegraph, radio and telephone services. Postage stamps.
Tu.-F. 10-4; Sa., Su. 10-1.

BERLIN TRANSPORT MUSEUM
Kleiststrasse 14, An der Urania, 1000 Berlin 30
History of transport. Roads. Railways. Aviation. Space travel.
Tu.-Su. 10-5.

BOTANICAL GARDEN AND MUSEUM
Königin Luise Strasse 6-8, 1000 Berlin 33
History, propagation and cultivation of plants. Native fungi. Commercial plants. Trees growing in streets of Berlin. Stamps showing plants. Plants found in Egyptian tombs. Herbarium.
Tu., Th.-Sa. 10-5; W. 10-7.

BRÜCKE MUSEUM
Bussardsteig 9, 1000 Berlin 33
Works by the Brücke group of artists, founded in Dresden in 1905. Paintings. Watercolours. Drawings. Engravings. Prints. Sculpture.
M., W.-Su. 11-5.

CHARLOTTENBURG PALACE
19 Luisenplatz, 1000 Berlin
Frederich the Great's picture collection. 18th century French paintings. Early 19th century European paintings, applied art.
Tu.-Su. 9-5.

DEPARTMENT OF ENGRAVINGS
Arnimallee 23-27, 1000 Berlin 33
15th-18th century European prints, engravings, woodcuts. Incunabula.
Tu.-F. 9-5; Sa., Su. 10-5.

DEPARTMENT OF PLASTER-CASTS
Sophie Charlotte Strasse 17-18, 1000 Berlin 19
Exhibition of moulds and plaster casts from the Department's collection.
M.-F. 9-4.

DEPARTMENT OF SCULPTURE
Arnimallee 23-27, 1000 Berlin 33
3rd-18th century Western and Byzantine religious sculpture. 12th-18th century Italian, Spanish, German, French, Dutch, English sculpture. Figurines.
Tu.-F. 9-5; Sa., Su. 10-5.

EGYPTIAN MUSEUM
Schlossstrasse 70, 1000 Berlin 19
Egyptian life and art. Sculpture. Grave-gifts. Weapons. Seals. Amulets. Masks. Agricultural implements. Household equipment. Papyri. Architectural items.
M., W.-F. 9-5; Sa., Su. 10-5.

EMIL FISCHER REGIONAL MUSEUM
Ganghofer Strasse 3-5, 1000 Berlin 44
Geology and history of the Neukölln area.
W., Th., Sa. 9-1.

GALLERY OF PAINTINGS
Arnimallee 23/27, 1000 Berlin 33
Medieval - early 19th century European paintings.
Tu.-F. 9-5; Sa., Su. 10-5.

GERMAN CARBURETTOR MUSEUM
Heidestrasse 52, 1000 Berlin 21
Development of the carburettor since 1865.
By appointment.

GERMAN RADIO AND TELEVISION MUSEUM
Hammerskjüldplatz 1, 1000 Berlin 19
History and technical development of German radio and television.
Tu.-Sa. 10-5; Su., public holidays 10-4.

GLIENICKE PALACE
Königsstrasse, Berlin-Wannsee, 1000 Berlin
17th-19th century period rooms.
Tu.-Su. 10-6.

GREEK AND ROMAN DEPARTMENT
Schlossstrasse 1, 1000 Berlin 19
Greek and Roman objets d'art. Attic vases, glass, ornaments, votive figures. Roman silver. Mummy portraits.
M., Th., F. 9-5; W. 2-7.

GRUNEWALD HUNTING LODGE COLLECTIONS
Berlin-Grunewald, 1000 Berlin
15th-19th century German, Dutch paintings. Contemporary furniture, furnishings. Hunting trophies, equipment.
Tu.-Su. 10-6.

GEORG KOLBE MUSEUM
Sensburger Allee 25, 1000 Berlin 19
Home and studio of the artist, Georg Kolbe. Drawings, sketches, sculpture by Kolbe. Kolbe's private collection of Impressionist and Expressionist paintings.
May-Sept., W., Su. 10-5. Oct.-Apr., W., Su. 10-4.

MUSEUM OF APPLIED ART
Schloss Charlottenburg, 1000 Berlin 19
Medieval - 18th century European applied art. 13th-19th century religious art.
M., W., F., Sa. 9-5; Su. 10-5.

MUSEUM OF THE BLIND
Rothenburgstrasse 14, 1000 Berlin 41
History of Braille and of machines for producing it. Methods of teaching Braille.
F. 1-4.

MUSEUM OF ETHNOLOGY
Arnimallee 23-27, 1000 Berlin 33
Ethnological collections from Africa, North and South America, Asia, Europe (except Germany).
Tu.-F. 9-5; Sa., Su. 10-5.

MUSEUM OF FAR EASTERN ART
Takustrasse 40, 1000 Berlin 33
Chinese, Japanese ceramics, paintings, lacquerware, jades.
Tu.-F. 9-5; Sa., Su. 10-5.

MUSEUM OF FREEMASONRY
Emser Strasse 12-13, 1000 Berlin 31
History of Freemasonry. Masonic regalia, paintings, ritual equipment.
By appointment.

MUSEUM OF GERMAN FOLKLORE
Gardeschützenweg 71-101, 1000 Berlin 45
German popular art and handicrafts. Furnishings. Household equipment. Costumes. Ornaments. Guilds. Toys. Popular customs.
Tu.-F. 9-5; Sa., Su. 10-5.

MUSEUM OF INDIAN ART
Takustrasse 40, 1000 Berlin 33
Art of the Indian peninsula, Central Asia, Indonesia. Paintings. Sculpture. Wood-carving. Bronzes. Applied art.
Tu.-F. 9-5; Sa., Su. 10-5.

MUSEUM OF ISLAMIC ART
Takustrasse 40, 1000 Berlin 33
Islamic art, 8th-18th century. Miniatures. Ceramics. Glass. Ivory. Iron. Brass. Gold. Silver. Carpets. Illuminated manuscripts of the Koran.
Tu.-F. 9-5; Sa., Su. 10-5.

MUSEUM OF MUSICAL INSTRUMENTS
Bundesallee 1-12, 1000 Berlin 15
Collections showing development of musical instruments in all parts of the world. Portraits of musicians.
Tu., Th.-Sa. 9-5; W. 11-8; Su. 10-2.

MUSEUM OF PREHISTORY AND EARLY HISTORY
Schloss Charlottenburg, 1000 Berlin 19
European and Oriental prehistory, early history. Life and artifacts of hunting, farming and fishing communities.
Tu.-F. 9-5; Sa., Su. 10-5.

NATIONAL GALLERY
Potsdamer Strasse 50, 1000 Berlin 90
19th-20th century European paintings, drawings, sculpture, especially French and German.
W.-Sa. 9-5; Su. 10-5.

NEUKÖLLN LOCAL MUSEUM
Ganghofer Strasse 3-5, 1000 Berlin 44
Displays illustrating history of Neukölln. Dioramas.
W., Th., Sa. 9-1.

PLÖTZENSEE MEMORIAL
Jugendstrafanstaet, Saatwinkler Damm, 1000 Berlin
In former prison. Memorial exhibition to victims of the Hitler régime, 1932-45.
On request.

REINICKENDORF LOCAL MUSEUM
26 Eichborndamm, 1000 Berlin
History of Reinickendorf and the surrounding district.
Tu.-F. 9-3; Sa. 10-2.

SCHÖNEBERG LOCAL MUSEUM
John F. Kennedy Platz 1, 1000 Berlin 62
History of Schöneberg. Changes in the local landscape since prehistoric times.
Tu.-F. 9-3; Su. 10-2.

SPANDAU LOCAL MUSEUM
Zitadelle Haus 2, 1000 Berlin 20
In Spandau Citadel (12th and 16th century). Prehistory, history of the Spandau area. Handicrafts. Guilds. Furnishings. Household equipment. Views of old Spandau. Portraits of Spandau personalities.
Tu.-F. 9-4; Sa. 2-5; Su. 10-1.

STATE PORCELAIN FACTORY
Wegelystrasse und Budapesterstrasse, 1000 Berlin 48
Berlin porcelain.
M.-Sa. 9-5.

STAUFFENBERGSTRASSE MEMORIAL
Bendlerblock, 1000 Berlin
Memorial exhibition to the victims of the revolt in July 20, 1944.
M.-F. 9-7; Sa. 8-3; Su. 9-1.

STEGLITZ LOCAL MUSEUM
Drakestrasse 64A, 1000 Berlin 45
History of Steglitz.
Tu.-F. 9-4; Sa. 10-5; Su. 10-1.

STUCCO MUSEUM
Karl Marx Strasse 17, 1000 Berlin 44
Architectural stucco decoration, especially 19th century.
M.-F. 9-5.

SUGAR MUSEUM
Amrumer Strasse 32, 1000 Berlin 65
History of sugar. Sugar chemistry. Sugar by-products. Model of the first beet-sugar factory. Sugar-bag collection.
M.-F. 9-4.

TEGEL PALACE
Adelheidallee 19-21, 1000 Berlin 27
Former home of Wilhelm and Alexander von Humboldt. Greek and Roman art, especially sculpture.
W., Sa., Su., public holidays, 2-6.

TEMPELHOF LOCAL MUSEUM
Alt-Mariendorf 43, 1000 Berlin 42
History of Tempelhof and Marienhof.
W. 1-6; Sa. 11-3.

ZILLE EXHIBITION
Alboinstrasse 36, 1000 Berlin 42
Drawings and prints by Heinrich Zille.
On request.

BERNKASTEL-KUES

ST. NIKOLAUS HOSPITAL
Cusanusstrasse, 5550 Bernkastel-Kues, Rheinland-Pfalz
Hospital (1401-64). Paintings. Sculpture. Manuscripts. Incunabula.
May-Oct., Tu.-F., guided tour at 10 a.m.

BERSENBRÜCK

DISTRICT MUSEUM
Stiftshof 4, 4558 Bersenbrück, Niedersachsen
Local geology, zoology, history. Peasant furnishings, household equipment, tools. 13th-18th century religious art. Paintings. Watercolours. Handicrafts. Costumes.
Tu.-Sa. 2-5; W., F. also 9-12; Su. 10-1.

BERTOLDSHEIM

PICTURE GALLERY
Schloss, 8859 Bertoldsheim, Bayern
17th-18th century German, Dutch paintings. Furniture. Decorative arts.
By appointment.

BERUMERFEHN

WOODLAND AND MOOR MUSEUM
2981 Berumerfehn, Niedersachsen
Local history, wildlife, plants. Timbers. Ecology.
Apr.-Sept., W., Su. 3-6.

BEURON

BIBLE MUSEUM
Erzabtei, 7207 Beuron, Baden-Württemberg
Collection of material for Biblical research. Ceramics. Papyri. Cuneiform inscriptions. Water-skins.
By appointment.

BEXBACH

REGIONAL AND MINING MUSEUM
6652 Bexbach, Saarland
Local prehistory, history. Mining. Forge and foundry work.
May-Sept., daily 9-7.

BIBERACH

BRAITH-MALI MUSEUM
Museumstrasse 2, 7950 Biberach, Baden-Württemberg
Natural history. Prehistory. History. Handicrafts. 15th-20th century sculpture. Bequests and studios of the painters of animals, Anton Braith (d.1905) and Christian Mali (c.1906), with paintings by their Munich contemporaries.
Tu.-Su. 10-12, 2-5; W. also 5-9.

WIELAND MUSEUM
Saudengasse 10, 7950 Biberach, Baden-Württemberg
Life and work of the poet, Christoph Martin Wieland (d.1813).
By appointment.

BIEDENKOPF

REGIONAL MUSEUM
Schloss, Nikolauskirchstrasse 8, 3560 Biedenkopf, Hessen
Geology. Mineralogy. Ornithology. Peasant tools, handicrafts. Costumes. Weapons. Armour.
Mar.-Oct., daily 8-6.

BIELEFELD

BIELEFELD MUNICIPAL ART GALLERY
Artur Ladebeck Strasse 5, 4800 Bielefeld, Nordrhein-Westfalen
20th century paintings, drawings, prints, sculpture.
Tu., W., F. 11-6; Th. 11-8; Su. 10-6.

FARMHOUSE OPEN-AIR MUSEUM
Dornberger Strasse 82, 4800 Bielefeld, Nordrhein-Westfalen
Farmhouses. Barns. Mills. 16th-19th century folk-art. Costumes. Furniture. Tools.
Tu.-Su. 10-1, 2-6.

GERMAN PLAYING CARD MUSEUM
Sparrenburg, 4800 Bielefeld, Nordrhein-Westfalen
World wide collection of playing cards and card games. Production of playing cards.
W.-M. 11-5.

MUSEUM OF CULTURAL HISTORY
Welle 61, 4800 Bielefeld, Nordrhein-Westfalen
Paintings, graphics, sculpture by artists of the Bielefeld region. Silver. Pewter. Glass. Furniture. Porcelain.
Tu.-Sa. 12-6; Su. 10-1.

NATURAL HISTORY MUSEUM
Stapenhorststrasse 1, 4800 Bielefeld, Nordrhein-Westfalen
Geology. Mineralogy. Geography. Botany. Zoology.
Tu.-Su. 11-5; W. also 8 p.m.-10.

BINGEN

REGIONAL MUSEUM
Burg Klopp, 6530 Bingen, Rheinland-Pfalz
Local prehistory, history. Greek and Roman art, utensils. Folklore. Musical instruments. Coins. Weapons. Armour. Glass. History of wine and wine-production.
M.-F. 9-12, 2-5; Sa. 9.30-12, 2-5; Su., public holidays 9.30-12.

BIRKENFELD

REGIONAL MUSEUM
6588 Birkenfeld, Rheinland-Pfalz
Archaeology, folklore, and history of Birkenfeld and the Rhineland.
Su. 10-1. Other times by appointment.

BISCHOFSHEIM

REGIONAL MUSEUM
Theodor Heuss Schule, Friedrich Ebert Platz, 6451 Bischofsheim, Hessen
Local and regional history.
On request.

BLANKENHEIM

DISTRICT MUSEUM
Johannesstrasse 6, 5378 Blankenheim, Nordrhein-Westfalen
Zoology. Local prehistory, history. Furniture. Household equipment. Folklore. Folk-art.
May-Sept., Tu.-F., Su. 11-1. Oct.-Sept., Tu.-F. 2-5.

BLAUBEUREN

MUSEUM OF PREHISTORY
Karlstrasse 21, 7902 Blaubeuren, Baden-Württemberg
Neolithic material from local excavations.
Daily 10.30-12, 2-4.

REGIONAL MUSEUM
Klosterhof, 7902 Blaubeuren, Baden-Württemberg
Zoology. Palaeolithic material from local sites. History of Blaubeuren and its region. 14th-17th century wood and stone sculpture. Pewter. Copper. Peasant costumes. Agricultural implements.
Daily 9-12, 2-5.

BOCHOLT

MUNICIPAL ART GALLERY
Salierstrasse 6, 429 Bocholt, Nordrhein-Westfalen
Paintings, drawings, watercolours by contemporary local and regional artists. Maps and town-views of East and Central Germany. Spinning, weaving and dyeing equipment. Engravings by Israbel van Meckenem (d.1503).
Daily 10-1, 3-6.

BOCHUM

BOCHUM MUSEUM
Kortumstrasse 147, 4630 Bochum, Nordrhein-Westfalen
History of Bochum. Peasant life. Contemporary German art.
Tu., Th.-Sa. 10-1.30, 3-6; W. 10-1.30, 3-9; Su. 10-2.

GEOLOGICAL MUSEUM OF THE RUHR MINING DISTRICT
Hernerstrasse 45, 4630 Bochum, Nordrhein-Westfalen
Geology and mineralogy, especially of the Ruhr.
M.-F. 9-4; Su. 9-1.

LOCAL HISTORY COLLECTIONS
An der Kemnade 10, 4630 Bochum, with branch at Oberburg, 4324 Blankenstein 2, Nordrhein-Westfalen
Prehistory, history of the Ruhr. Folk-art. 18th century farmhouse. Peasant furniture, tools, agricultural implements.
M.-Sa. 9-5; Su. 9-1.

MINING MUSEUM
Vödestrasse 28, 4630 Bochum, Nordrhein-Westfalen
History of mining techniques. Art, customs, housing, furnishings of the mining community. Demonstration mine.
Tu.-F. 8.30-5.30. Sa., Su., public holidays 9-1.

BODENWERDER

BARON MÜNCHHAUSEN MUSEUM
3452 Bodenwerder, Niedersachsen
Memorabilia of Baron von Münchhausen, in the house where he was born (1720).
Tu.-Su. 10-5.

BOGENBERG

REGIONAL MUSEUM
Alter Pfarrhofstadel, Bogenberg
Peasant furniture, tools. Folk-art. 13th-18th century sculpture. Costumes.
By local announcement.

BONN

BEETHOVEN HOUSE - MUSEUM
Bonngasse 20, 5300 Bonn
Collections illustrating life and work of Ludwig van Beethoven in his former home. Manuscripts. Paintings. Musical instruments. Memorabilia.
May-Sept., daily 9-1, 3-6. Oct.-Apr., daily 9-1, 3-5; Su. 9-1.

BONN MUSEUM OF PAINTINGS: KASIMIR HAGEN COLLECTION
Wilhelmstrasse 34, 5300 Bonn
German Jugendstil and Expressionist paintings.
Tu.-Sa. 10-5; Su. 10-1.

INSTITUTE OF ZOOLOGICAL RESEARCH AND ALEXANDER KOENIG MUSEUM
Adenauerallee 150-164, 5300 Bonn
Zoological collections, including birds, fish, snakes.
Tu.-Su. 9-12.30, Tu.-F. 1.30-5; W. also 7.30 p.m.-9.30.

ERNST MORITZ ARNDT HOUSE MUSEUM
Adenauerallee 79, 5300 Bonn
Home of E. M. Arndt (d.1860). 16th-19th century views of Bonn and Rhineland landscapes. History of Bonn.
Tu.-Sa. 10-5; Su. 10-1.

MUNICIPAL ART COLLECTIONS
Rathausgasse 7, 5300 Bonn
20th century German paintings, sculpture. Contemporary prints, drawings. Local and regional history.
Tu.-Su. 10-5; W., also 5-9.

RHINELAND MUSEUM
Colmanstrasse 14-16, 5300 Bonn
Prehistory of the Rhineland. Roman, early Christian, Frankish, Medieval archaeology. Art of the region from prehistoric times. Handicrafts. Coins.
Tu.-Su. 10-5; W. also 5-9.

UNIVERSITY MUSEUM OF ART
Am Hofgarten, 5300 Bonn
Casts of Greek and Roman sculpture. Greek and Roman terra cotta, vases, bronze tools, coins, glass. Coptic textiles.
M.-F. 10-1, 4-7.

UNIVERSITY MUSEUM OF MINERALOGY AND PETROLOGY
Poppelsdorfer Schloss, 5300 Bonn
Minerals and rocks, including local collections. Meteorites. Gemstones.
W. 3-5; Su. 10-12.

BOPPARD

BOPPARD REGIONAL MUSEUM
Burgstrasse, 5407 Boppard, Rheinland-Pfalz
Local prehistory, history. Geology. Mineralogy. Handicrafts. Costume ornaments. Weapons. Coins.
Tu., Th., Su. 10.30-12.30.

FOREST AND TIMBER MUSEUM
Burgstrasse, 5407 Boppard, Rheinland-Pfalz
Varieties of timber-trees. Timber processes. Butterflies.
June-Sept., daily 10.30-12.30, 3-5.

BORKEN

REGIONAL MUSEUM
Heilig Geist Kirche, Heilig Geist Strasse, 4280 Borken, Nordrhein-Westfalen
Local geology, prehistory, history. Furnished 19th century living room. Peasant furniture, household equipment. Portraits of distinguished local people.
Su. 10-12; other days by appointment.

BORKUM

REGIONAL MUSEUM
2972 Borkum, Niedersachsen
Local and regional history. Folklore. Coastal shipping. Fishing industry.
M.-Sa. 9-5; Su. 10-2.

BORTFELD

FARM-HOUSE MUSEUM
3301 Bortfeld
Farmhouse (1724), with furniture, household equipment, implements.
Tu.-Th. 10-5; F. 10-4; Su. 10-1.

BOTTROP

REGIONAL MUSEUM
Im Stadtgarten 20, 4250 Bottrop, Nordrhein-Westfalen
Mineralogy. Palaeontology. Biology. Folklore. History of Bottrop and the Ruhr.
Tu. 2-5; W.-Sa. 9-1, 2-5; Su. 11-1, 3-6.

BOXBERG

REGIONAL MUSEUM
Hauptstrasse 138, 6973 Boxberg, Hessen
Regional life. Folklore. Folk-art.
M.-Sa. 10-5; Su. 10-1.

BRAKE

MUSEUM OF SHIPPING AND NAVIGATION OF THE OLDENBURG RIVER PORTS
Mitteldeichstrasse 36, 2800 Brake, Niedersachsen
History of sailing ships. Development of the Weser ports. Pilotage. Sailors' art. Charts. Ship-models.
Tu.-Su. 9-12, 2-6.

BRAUBACH

MARKSBURG CASTLE MUSEUM
5423 Braubach, Rheinland-Pfalz
13th-14th century castle. History of Braubach and the Rhineland. Folklore. Folk-art. Medieval furnishings, domestic utensils. Weapons.
Daily 9-7.

BRAUNFELS

DR. KANNGIESSER'S WOODLAND MUSEUM
6333 Braunfels, Hessen
Natural history. Botany.
On request.

PALACE MUSEUM
Schloss, 6333 Braunfels, Hessen
Local and regional history. Furnishings. Household utensils, equipment. Handicrafts. Folk-art.
M.-Sa. 9-5; Su. 10-1.

BRAUNLAGE

REGIONAL MUSEUM
3389 Braunlage, Niedersachsen
Natural history. Local and regional history.
Daily 10-12.

BRAUNSCHWEIG

BRUNSWICK PROVINCIAL MUSEUM OF HISTORY AND LOCAL LIFE
An der Agidienkuche, 3300 Braunschweig, Niedersachsen
Regional prehistory, history. Folklore. Social, economic and cultural history.
Tu.-Th. 10-5; F. 10-4; Su. 10-1.

COLLECTION OF THE SCHOOL OF DESIGN
Boitzemer Strasse 230, 3300 Braunschweig, Niedersachsen
Development of craftsmen's and industrial tools and equipment used to produce everyday goods. Industrial design.
During times when School of Design is open.

COUNT ANTON ULRICH MUSEUM
Museumstrasse 1, 3300 Braunschweig, Niedersachsen
14th-18th century paintings, applied art. Bronzes. Ivory. Textiles. 16th-20th century drawings, prints, engravings.
Tu.-F. 11-4; Sa. 10-4; Su. 10-2.

DANKWARDEROBE CASTLE
3300 Braunschweig, Niedersachsen
Collections of the Guelphs. Decorative and applied arts. Furnishings. Paintings. Weapons.
Tu.-F. 11-4; Sa. 10-4; Su. 10-4.

MUNICIPAL MUSEUM
Steintorwall 14, 3300 Braunschweig, Niedersachsen
History of Braunschweig and its area. Folklore. Ethnology. Furniture. Household equipment. Applied art. Coins.
M.-W., F. 11-4; Th. 1-8.

WILHELM RAABE HOUSE - MEMORIAL
Leonlardstrasse 29A, 3300 Braunschweig, Niedersachsen
Life and work of the poet, Wilhelm Raabe (d.1910), in the house where he lived.
M., W., F. 11-2, and by appointment.

SALVE HOSPES HOUSE
Lessingplatz 12, 3300 Braunschweig, Niedersachsen
Paintings. Graphics.
On request.

STATE MUSEUM OF NATURAL HISTORY
Pockelsstrasse 10A, 3300 Braunschweig, Niedersachsen
Zoology. Dioramas of local wildlife.
Tu., Th., F. 9-5; W. 9-9; Su. 10-1.

BREISACH

KAISERSTUHL MUSEUM
7814 Breisach, Baden-Württemberg
History of the town and region. Roman material from local excavations.
On request.

BREMEN

BREMEN MUSEUM OF THE ARTS
Am Wall 207, 2800 Bremen
15th-20th century European paintings. 17th-20th century European sculpture, prints, drawings.
Tu.-F. 10-4; Tu. and F. also 7 p.m.-9; Sa., Su. 10-2.

COLLECTION OF PAINTINGS IN THE PAULA BECKER MODERSOHN HOUSE
Böttcherstrasse 8-10, 2800 Bremen
Collections of paintings made by Paula Becker Modersohn (d.1907) and Heinrich Vegeler (d.1942).
M.-F. 10-4; Sa. 10-2; Su. 11-1.

FOCKE MUSEUM
Schwachhausen Heerstrasse 240, 2800 Bremen
Local prehistory, history. Folklore. Shipping.
Tu., Th., Sa. 10-4; W. 10-6; Su. 10-2.

'LEAD-CELLAR' IN ST. PETER'S CATHEDRAL
Am Markle, 2800 Bremen
In former chapel of St. Peter's Cathedral (c.1050), called the 'lead-cellar' from the sheets of lead in it, which preserved and mummified bodies. Religious art, including sculptures of the Evangelists (c.1700).
M.-Sa. 8-5.

GERHARD MARCKS FOUNDATION
Am Wall 208, 2800 Bremen
Sculpture, drawings, woodcuts by Gerhard Marcks.
M.-F. 10-4; Sa. 10-2; Su. 11-1.

OVERSEAS MUSEUM
Bahnhofsplatz 13, 2800 Bremen
Geology. Mineralogy. Zoology. Ethnology. Trade goods. Reproductions of Japanese temple garden, Japanese and Chinese houses.
Tu.-Sa. 10-4; Su. 10-2.

OVERSEAS MUSEUM: CHILDREN'S MUSEUM
Bahnhofsplatz 13, 2800 Bremen
Dioramas showing wildlife of the woods and dunes. Working models of plants, animals.
Tu.-Sa. 10-4; Su. 10-2.

LUDWIG ROSELIUS COLLECTION
Böttcherstrasse 4, 2800 Bremen
12th-18th century paintings, sculpture, furniture, textiles, gold, silver, ceramics, coins, medals.
M.-F. 10-4; Sa. 10-2; Su. 11-1.

LUDWIG ROSELIUS HOUSE OF PREHISTORY
Worpswede, 2800 Bremen
Regional prehistory.
M.-F. 10-4; Sa. 10-2; Su. 11-1.

VEGESACK REGIONAL MUSEUM
Weserstrasse 7, 2800 Bremen
Regional prehistory, history. Peasant tools, equipment, utensils.
M.-F. 10-4; Sa. 10-2; Su. 11-1.

WEAPON COLLECTION OF THE BÖTTCHERSTRASSE COMPANY
Böttcherstrasse 4, 2800 Bremen
Weapons and equipment.
M.-F. 10-4; Sa. 10-2; Su. 11-1.

BREMERHAVEN

GERMAN MUSEUM OF SHIPPING AND NAVIGATION
Georgstrasse 19, 2850 Bremerhaven, Bremen
History of shipping, navigation.
Tu.-F. 10-4; Sa. 10-1; Su. 10.30-12.30.

MORGENSTEIN MUSEUM
Kaistrasse 5-6, 2850 Bremerhaven, Bremen
Prehistory. History of Bremerhaven. Folklore.
Tu.-F. 10-4; Sa. 10-1; Su. 10.30-12.30.

NORTH SEA MUSEUM
Am Handelshafen 12, 2850 Bremerhaven, Bremen
Flora and fauna of the North Sea and Atlantic.
M.-F. 8-6; Sa. 9-1; Su., public holidays 10-1.

SPECKENBÜTTEL OPEN-AIR MUSEUM
Parkstrasse 9, 2850 Bremerhaven, Bremen
Local life and folklore. Furniture. Household equipment. Tools. Agricultural implements. Fire-fighting equipment.
F.-W. 9-11, 3-5.

BREMERVÖRDE

DISTRICT MUSEUM
Vorwerkstrasse 19 und Wesermünder Strasse 20, 2140 Bremervörde, Niedersachsen
Natural history, especially geology. Local prehistory, history, folklore.
Su. 10-12. Other times by appointment.

BRENZ

REGIONAL MUSEUM
Schloss Brenz, 7927 Brenz, Baden-Württemberg
Local and regional history.
By appointment.

BRETTEN

MELANCTHON MUSEUM
Melancthonstrasse 1, 7518 Bretten, Baden-Württemberg
Life and work of the religious reformer, Philipp Melancthon, born in Bretten (1497). Collection illustrating history of the Reformation.
On request.

BRILON

REGIONAL MUSEUM
Rathaus, 5790 Brilon, Nordrhein-Westfalen
Local and regional history. Handicrafts. Peasant art.
On request.

BRUCHSAL

MUNICIPAL COLLECTIONS
Rathaus, 7520 Bruchsal, Baden-Württemberg
Prehistory, history of Bruchsal and its region. Coins.
On request.

PALACE
7520 Bruchsal, Baden-Württemberg
Palace (1722 onwards). Period rooms. 16th-18th century paintings, tapestries.
On request.

BRÜCKENAU

REGIONAL HOUSE
8788 Brückenau, Bayern
Local history collection. Documents. Paintings. Drawings.
Tu., Th., Sa. 3-5.

BRÜHL

AUGUSTUSBERG PALACE
5040 Brühl, Nordrhein-Westfalen
Palace (1725-8), with period furnishings.
Daily 10-12, 2-4.

BUCHAU

FEDERSEE MUSEUM
7952 Buchau, Baden-Württemberg
Prehistoric material from local sites. Local and regional history.
Tu.-Sa. 10-5; Su. 10-12.

BUCHEN

STEINERNES HOUSE REGIONAL MUSEUM
Kellereistrasse 29, 6967 Buchen, Baden-Württemberg
Prehistory. Early history, especially Roman. Peasant furniture, household equipment. Folk-art. Faience. Costumes. Religious art. Weapons.
By appointment and local announcement.

BÜCKEBURG

GALLERY OF PAINTINGS
Schloss, 4967 Bückeburg, Nordrhein-Westfalen
17th-19th century furniture, decorative arts, paintings.
By appointment.

REGIONAL MUSEUM OF SCHAUMBURG-LIPPISCH
Lange Strasse 22, 4967 Bückeburg, Nordrhein-Westfalen
Palaeontology. Prehistory. Furniture. Household equipment. Costumes. Mining. History of the House of Schaumburg Lippe.
May-Sept., 10-5.

BÜDINGEN

HEUSON MUSEUM
Rathaus, 6470 Büdingen, Hessen
Early history, especially Roman. History of Büdingen. Folk-art. Ceramics. Craftsmen's workshops.
M.-Sa. 10-5; Su. 11-12.

PALACE MUSEUM
Schloss, 6470 Büdingen, Hessen
Furniture. 16th century murals. Porcelain. Glass. Weapons.
Apr.-Nov., Tu.-F., Su., guided tours 10-12, 2-5.

BÜHL

REGIONAL MUSEUM
7580 Bühl, Baden-Württemberg
Local and regional history. Folk-art. Peasant tools, implements, household equipment.
M.-Sa. 9-5; Su. 10-12.

BÜNDE

DISTRICT MUSEUM
Fünfhausenstrasse 10-12, 4980 Bünde, Nordrhein-Westfalen
Geology. Fossils. Peasant furniture, household equipment. Costumes. Ornaments. Folk-art. Religious art.
M.-Sa. 10-12; W., Sa. also 3-5; Su. 11-12.30.

GERMAN TOBACCO AND CIGAR MUSEUM
Fünfhausenstrasse 10-12, 4980 Bünde, Nordrhein-Westfalen
World-collection of tobacco pipes, smoking equipment. Displays showing production of cigars. Advertisements. Smoking rooms, with period furniture.
M.-Sa. 10-12; W., Sa. also 3-5; Su. 11-12.30.

BÜNZEN

THE OLD HOUSE
2356 Bünzen, Schleswig-Holstein
18th-20th century peasant furniture, household equipment.
Su. 3-6. Other times by appointment.

BURGAU

REGIONAL MUSEUM
Schloss, 8872 Burgau, Bayern
Regional prehistory, history. Handicrafts. Guilds. Folk-art. Furniture. Household equipment. Flax-processing, spinning, weaving equipment. Costumes. Glass. Faience.
By appointment.

BURG-DITHMARSCHEN

WOODLAND MUSEUM
Obere Waldstrasse, 2224 Burg-Dithmarschen, Schleswig-Holstein
Plants and wildlife of the region.
Apr. 15 - Oct. 15, daily 10-4.

BURGDORF

REGIONAL MUSEUM
Markstrasse 13, 3167 Burgdorf, Niedersachsen
Regional prehistory, folklore. Military history.
By appointment.

BURG-FEHMARN

FEHMARN REGIONAL MUSEUM
2449 Burg-Fehmarn, Schleswig-Holstein
Geology. Prehistory. History of Burg-Fehmarn and its region. Social life. Folklore. Costumes. Handicrafts. Shipping. Weapons. Hunting. Coins. Paper-money.
June-Sept., M., W., Sa. 2-6.

BURGHAUSEN

CASTLE
8263 Burghausen, Bayern
Period rooms. Paintings.
May-Sept., 9-6. Oct.-Apr., 9-12, 1-4.

BURGHAUSEN STATE GALLERY
Burg, 8263 Burghausen, Bayern
15th-18th century German paintings, especially 15th-16th century Bavarian.
May-Sept., daily 9-6. Oct.-Apr., daily 9-12, 1-4.

MUSEUM OF THE HISTORY OF BURGHAUSEN
Burg 48, 8263 Burghausen, Bayern
Castle (13th-15th century). Birds. Local prehistory, history. Folklore. Folk-art. Handicrafts. 14th-18th century sculpture. Furniture. Decorative arts. Weapons.
Mar. 16 - Nov. 15, daily 9-dusk.

BURG RHEINECK

CASTLE MUSEUM
Auf der Burg, 5481 Burg Rheineck, Nordrhein-Westfalen
Local and regional history.
By local announcement.

BURG-WUPPER

MUSEUM OF THE COUNTS VON BERG
Schloss, 5652 Burg-Wupper, Nordrhein-Westfalen
Local prehistory, history. History of the Castle and its inhabitants, 13th-17th century. Paintings by J. P. Hasenclever. Household equipment. Coins.
Mar.-Oct., Tu.-Su. 9-6; M. 1-6. Nov.-Feb., Tu.-Su. 10-5.

BÜSUM

WILDLIFE PARADISE
2242 Büsum, Schleswig-Holstein
Dioramas of regional birds. Mounted specimens of animals. Pictures showing local landscape.
Apr.-Oct., daily 10-12, 2-6.

BUTZBACH

REGIONAL MUSEUM
Griedelerstrasse 20-22, 6308 Butzbach
Prehistory, early history of the Butzbach region. Roman material from local excavations.
M.-Sa. 9-12, 2-5; Su. 10-12.

BUXTEHUDE

REGIONAL MUSEUM
St. Petri Platz, 2150 Buxtehude, Niedersachsen
Local, regional prehistory, history. Goldsmiths' work. Folk-art.
May-Sept., Tu., W., F., Sa. 10-1, 3-5; Su. 10-1. Oct.-Apr., M., W., Sa. 11-12; Su. 3-4.

CALW

CALW REGIONAL MUSEUM AND HERMANN HESSE MEMORIAL
Bischofstrasse 58, 7260 Calw, Baden-Württemberg
Peasant furniture. Pewter. Religious art. Folk-art. Empire furniture. Near-Eastern archaeology. Memorabilia of the writer, Herman Hesse.
May-Oct., M.-F. 2-3.30; 1st and 3rd Su. in month, 10-30-12.30.

CASTROP-RAUXEL

CASTROP-RAUXEL REGIONAL MUSEUM
Ickerner Strasse 56, 4620 Castrop-Rauxel, Nordrhein-Westfalen
Local history, geology, mineralogy. Folklore.
On request.

CELLE

BOMANN MUSEUM
Schlossplatz 7, 3100 Celle, Niedersachsen
Prehistory, history of the Celle region. Peasant furniture, art, handicrafts.
M.-Th. 10-5; Sa., Su. 10-1.

DUCAL PALACE
Schlossplatz 1, 3100 Celle, Niedersachsen
History of Celle. Period rooms.
By appointment.

CHAM

REGIONAL MUSEUM
Ludwigstrasse 1, 8490 Cham, Bayern
History of Cham and its region. Furniture. Handicrafts. Household utensils. Religious art.
On request.

CLAUSTHAL-ZELLERFELD

COLLECTIONS OF THE GEOLOGICAL INSTITUTE: CLAUSTHAL TECHNICAL UNIVERSITY
Leibnizstrasse, 3392 Clausthal-Zellerfeld, Niedersachsen
Geology, palaeontology, especially of the Harz and N. Germany.
By appointment.

MINERAL COLLECTION OF THE ACADEMY OF MINES
Technische Universität, 3392 Clausthal-Zellerfeld, Niedersachsen
Mineralogy. Stratigraphy. Petrography.
M.-F. 8-1, 3-6.

UPPER HARZ REGIONAL AND MINING MUSEUM
Bornhardtstrasse 16, 3392 Clausthal-Zellerfeld, Niedersachsen
16th-19th century mining. Regional prehistory, history. Coins.
Daily 9-1, 2-5.

CLOPPENBURG

VILLAGE MUSEUM
Museumstrasse, Burg Arkenstede, 4590 Cloppenburg, Niedersachsen
Rural buildings, furniture, household equipment from Lower Germany. Crafts and workshops.
May-Oct., M.-Sa. 8-6; Su. 9-6. Nov.-Apr., M.-Sa. 8-5; Su. 10-5.

COBURG

DR. OTTO BLOSS MEMORIAL COLLECTION
Callenbergen Strasse 70, 8630 Coburg, Bayern
Paintings, watercolours, pastels by Otto Bloss, in his former home and studio.
May-Sept., daily 9-11.30, 2-4. Oct.-Apr., Tu.-Su. 2-4.

EHRENBURG PALACE MUSEUM
8630 Coburg, Bayern
History of Coburg. 19th century furniture, decorative arts.
May-Sept., daily 9-11.30, 2-4. Oct.-Apr., Tu.-Su. 2-4.

MUNICIPAL ART COLLECTIONS
8630 Veste Coburg, Bayern
Medieval sculpture. 16th-20th century glass. Engravings. Weapons. Luther room.
May-Sept., daily 9-11.30, 2-4. Oct.-Apr., Tu.-Su. 2-4.

MUSEUM OF NATURAL SCIENCE
Park 6, 8630 Coburg, Bayern
Mineralogy. Gemstones. Historical geology and geography. Coral. Wildlife, especially birds. Birds' eggs.
M.-Sa. 9-12, 2-6; Su. 9-6.

COESFELD

REGIONAL MUSEUM
Letter Strasse, 4420 Coesfeld, Nordrhein-Westfalen
Regional geology, palaeontology, mineralogy, archaeology, history, folklore. 18th-19th century furniture, decorative arts. Costumes. Glass. Coins. Paintings. Sculpture. Drawings. Prints. Wood-carving.

CRAILSHEIM

FRANKEN-HOHENLOHE REGIONAL MUSEUM
Langestrasse, 7180 Crailsheim, Baden-Württemberg
In 14th century chapel. Local history. Handicrafts. Faience.
On request.

CREUSSEN

MUSEUM OF CREUSSEN JUGS
Hinteres Tor, 8581 Creussen, Bayern
History of pottery. Collection of jugs.
On request.

CUXHAVEN

CUXHAVEN REGIONAL MUSEUM
Schloss Ratzebuhl, 2190 Cuxhaven, Niedersachsen
In 13th century castle. History of Cuxhaven. Peasant furniture, household equipment. Local industries. Shipping.
M.-F. 9.30-12.30, 3-5.30; Sa., Su. 9.30-12.30.

KARL WALLER MUSEUM
Seedeich 23, 2190 Cuxhaven, Niedersachsen
Prehistory, history of the Cuxhaven region.
May-Sept., Tu.-Su. 10-12, 3-5. Oct.-Apr., Sa. 9-5; Su. 10-12.

DACHAU

CONCENTRATION CAMP MEMORIAL
Alte Romerstrasse 75, 8060 Dachau, Bayern
History of Nazi concentration camps, especially Dachau, 1933-45.
Daily 9-5.

DACHAU PALACE
8060 Dachau, Bayern
Remaining wing of late 16th century palace. Paintings.
By appointment.

REGIONAL MUSEUM
8060 Dachau, Bayern
Regional prehistory, history. Folk-art. Handicrafts. 19th-20th century paintings, drawings by Dachau artists.
By appointment.

DAHLENBURG

REGIONAL MUSEUM
3148 Dahlenburg, Niedersachsen
Local history. Diorama of the Battle of Göhrde (1813).
By appointment.

DANNENBERG

REGIONAL MUSEUM
Am Amtsberg, 3138 Dannenberg, Niedersachsen
Local and regional history.
By local announcement.

DARMSTADT

ART GALLERY
Steubenplatz, 6100 Darmstadt, Hessen
16th-20th century European paintings.
Tu.-Sa. 10-1, 3-6; Su. 10-1.

BAUHAUS COLLECTIONS
Ernst Ludwig Haus, Mathildenhöhe, 6100 Darmstadt, Hessen
Collections illustrating work of the Bauhaus in design, architecture and art-teaching.
Daily 9-12.

DARMSTADT MUSEUM
Grosse Bachstrasse 2, 6100 Darmstadt, Hessen
History of Darmstadt.
Tu.-Sa. 10-1, 3-6; Su. 10-1.

EXHIBITION OF LITERARY AND MUSICAL MANUSCRIPTS
Hessische Landes- und Hochschulbibliothek, Schloss, 6100 Darmstadt, Hessen
Literary and musical manuscripts. Incunabula. Letters from musicians.
M.-F. 9-12.30, 2-4.30.

HESSE MUSEUM
Friedenplatz 1, 6100 Darmstadt, Hessen
Regional geology, mineralogy, palaeontology, zoology, prehistory, history. Egyptian, Greek, Roman collection. Paintings. Sculpture. Drawings. Engravings. Prints. Glass paintings. Handicrafts.
Tu.-Sa. 10-5; Su. 10-1, 2.30-5; W. also 7 p.m.-9.

KRANICHSTEIN PALACE MUSEUM OF HUNTING
Kranichsteinerstrasse, 6100 Darmstadt, Hessen
16th-19th century hunting weapons, equipment, trophies. Paintings of hunting scenes.
Tu.-Su. 10-1, 2-5.

PALACE MUSEUM
Residenzschloss, 6100 Darmstadt, Hessen
17th-20th century furniture. Carriages. Sleighs. Court costumes, uniforms. Decorative arts. Paintings, including 'Madonna' by Holbein the Younger.
M.-Th., Sa. 10-1, 2-5; Su. 10-1.

PORCELAIN COLLECTION OF THE GRAND DUKES
Prinz Georgs Palais, Schlossgarten, 6100 Darmstadt, Hessen
18th-19th century European faience, porcelain, especially Russian and Kelsterbach.
M.-Th. 10-1, 2-5; Sa., Su. 10-1.

DATTELN

HERMANN GROCHTMANN MUSEUM
Lohstrasse 20A, 4354 Datteln, Nordrhein-Westfalen
Geology. Palaeontology. Natural history. Local prehistory, history. Folklore. Heraldry. Coins. Peasant furniture, tools.
May 1-Oct. 31, W. 4-6, Su. 10-1, 4-6. Other times by appointment.

DAUN

REGIONAL MUSEUM
Burg Daun, 5568 Daun, Rheinland-Pfalz
Geology. Palaeontology. History of Daun.
On request.

DAVENSBERG

DAVERT BURGTURM
Mühlendamm, 4715 Davensberg, Nordrhein-Westfalen
Local history, folklore.
By appointment.

DEGGENDORF

REGIONAL MUSEUM
Schlachterhausgasse 1, 8360 Deggendorf, Bayern
Local pre-history, history. Furniture, household equipment. Handicrafts. Ceramics. 15th-18th century sculpture. Guild history. 18th-19th century painted furniture, glass-paintings.
M., W. 9-12, 2-5.

DEIDESHEIM

MUSEUM OF MODERN CERAMICS
6705 Deidesheim, Rheinland-Pfalz
20th century German ceramics.
M.-Sa. 9-12, 2-6; Su. 11-12, 2-5.

DETMOLD

BREAD MUSEUM
Am Schützenberg 9, 4930 Detmold, Nordrhein-Westfalen
History and techniques of breadmaking.
On request.

LIPPE MUSEUM
Ameide 4, 4930 Detmold, Nordrhein-Westfalen
Ethnology and folklore, especially of Peru and Lippe. Local and regional history. Archaeology. 16th-20th century portraits. Uniforms. Flags. Decorations. History of the Detmold Court Theatre. Craftsmen's workshops, tools. Peasant costumes.
Tu.-F. 9-12, 2-5; Sa. 9-12.

OPEN AIR MUSEUM
Krummes Haus, 4930 Detmold, Nordrhein-Westfalen
Rural houses, farm buildings, workshops, agricultural implements.
Tu.-Su. 10-5.

PALACE OF THE PRINCES OF LIPPE
Schloss, 4930 Detmold, Nordrhein-Westfalen
Palace (13th century, rebuilt 16th-18th centuries). Paintings. European and Oriental porcelain. Brussels Tapestries. Weapons. Venetian and Bohemian glass. Family portraits.
Apr. 1-Oct. 15, daily 9-1, 2-6. Oct. 16-Mar. 31, M.-F. 10-3. Other times by appointment.

DIEBURG

DIEBURG AND DISTRICT MUSEUM
Schloss Fechenback, 6110 Dieburg, Hessen
Prehistoric material from local sites. Collections from the former Roman town of Vetus Ulpius. Alemannic-Frankish archaeology. Remains of Dieburg Mithräum. Local history, folklore.
Apr.-Oct., Su. 10.30-12, 3.30-5.30. Other times by appointment.

DIESSEN-AM-AMMERSEE

REGIONAL MUSEUM
Klosterhof 1, 8918 Diessen-am-Ammersee, Bayern
Local history. Handicrafts. Folk-art.
Tu.-Sa. 9-5; Su. 12-5.

DIEZ/LAHN

NASSAU REGIONAL MUSEUM
Am Guckenberg 8, 6252 Diez/Lahn, Rheinland-Pfalz
Geology. Prehistory. Folklore. Paintings.
May-Sept., Tu., Th., Sa., Su. 9-11, 2-5.

ORANIENSTEIN NASSAU MUSEUM
Am Guckenberg 8, 6252 Diez/Lahn, Rheinland-Pfalz
Orange-Nassau family collections. Paintings. Manuscripts. Coins. Medals.
M.-F. 10.30-3; Sa., Su., public holidays 9-12, 2-3.30.

SCHAUMBURG PALACE
6252 Diez/Lahn, Rheinland-Pfalz
Furniture. Decorative arts.
Mar.-Oct., M.-F. 10.30-3; Sa., Su., public holidays 9-12, 2-3.30.

DILLENBURG

MUSEUM OF ORANGE-NASSAU
Wilhelmsturm, 6340 Dillenburg, Hessen
Early history of Dillenburg region. Weapons. Pottery. Porcelain. Pewter. Engravings. Prints.
Tu.-F. 9-12, 2-6; Sa. 9-12; Su. 9-12, 1-6.

DILLINGEN AN DER DONAU

MUSEUM OF DILLINGEN HISTORICAL SOCIETY
Lammstrasse, 8880 Dillingen an der Donau, Bayern
Local prehistory, history. Folklore. Coins.
By appointment.

DINGOLFING

REGIONAL MUSEUM
Herzogsburg, 8312 Dingolfing, Bayern
Local and regional history. Folk-art. Votive pictures. Sculpture. Paintings.
Apr.-Oct., Tu., Th. 2-4; Su. 10-12.

DINKELSBÜHL

MUSEUM OF HISTORY
Dr. Martin Luther Strasse 6, 8804 Dinkelsbühl, Bayern
Local prehistory, history. Handicrafts. Folk-art. Furniture. Household equipment. Costumes. Guild collection.
Easter- Oct. 31, Tu.-Su. 10-12, 2.30-5.

DINSLAKEN

REGIONAL HOUSE
Brückstrasse 31, 4220 Dinslaken, Nordrhein-Westfalen
Local and regional history.
By appointment.

DONAUESCHINGEN

COLLECTIONS OF THE PRINCES OF FÜRSTENBERG
Kariplatz 7, 7710 Donaueschingen, Baden-Württemberg
Regional geology, palaeontology, mineralogy, prehistory, history. 15th-16th century German paintings.
Tu.-Su. 9-12, 2-5.

PALACE OF THE PRINCES OF FÜRSTENBERG
7710 Donaueschingen, Baden-Württemberg
Palace (1722). 16th-18th century furniture, decorative arts.
Apr.-Sept., daily 9-5.

DONAUWÖRTH

REGIONAL MUSEUM
Museumgasse, Im Ried 103, 8850 Donauwörth, Bayern
In late 15th century house. Local and regional history. Handicrafts. Furniture. Household equipment. 18th century sculpture. Glass-paintings. Votive-tablets.
May-Sept., W. 2-4. Other times by appointment.

DORSTEN

REGIONAL MUSEUM
Gertrudistrasse 1, 4270 Dorsten, Nordrhein-Westfalen
In the old Weighhouse (1567). Local geology, prehistory, history. Handicrafts, especially textile-printing, clog-making, ship-building. Shipping. Coins.
Tu., F. 3-6.

DORTMUND

KHAYON FOUNDATION FOR INDO-ASIAN RESEARCH
Am Knappenberg 92, 4600 Dortmund, Nordrhein-Westfalen
Indian art and culture.
By appointment.

MUSEUM ON THE EAST WALL
Ostwall 7, 4600 Dortmund, Nordrhein-Westfalen
19th-20th century sculpture, paintings, graphics, especially works by German Expressionists.
Tu., Th.-Sa. 10-6; W. 10-9; Su. 10-1.

MUSEUM OF THE HISTORY OF ART AND CULTURE
Ritterhausstrasse 34, 4600 Dortmund, Nordrhein-Westfalen
Prehistory, archaeology, history of the Dortmund region. History of Dortmund.
Tu.-F., Su. 10-5.

NATURAL HISTORY MUSEUM
Balkenstrasse 40, 4600 Dortmund, Nordrhein-Westfalen
Zoology. Maps. Foodstuffs.
Tu.-Sa. 10-6; Su. 10-1.

WESTPHALIAN SCHOOL MUSEUM
Gnadeort 3-5, 4600 Dortmund, Nordrhein-Westfalen
History of education in Westphalia.
Tu., F. 11-1; W. 4-6.

DREIEICHENHAIN

DREIEICH MUSEUM
Fahrgasse 52, 6072 Dreieichenhain, Hessen
Geology. Local prehistory and history. Medieval material from local excavations. Peasant furnishings, household equipment, handicrafts.
Tu.-F. 9-12, 2-7; Sa. 12-6; Su. 9-12.30, 2.30-6.

DREVENACK

OTTO PANKOK MUSEUM
Haus Esselt, 4231 Drevenack, Nordrhein-Westfalen
Former house of the painter and sculptor, Otto Pankok. Paintings. Drawings. Charcoal-drawings, prints, sculpture by Otto Pankok.
F.-Su. 10-1, 3-8.

DUDERSTADT

EICHSFELD REGIONAL MUSEUM
Oberkirche 3, 3428 Duderstadt, Niedersachsen
Local prehistory, history. Peasant furniture, household equipment. Costumes. Handicrafts. Religious art.
Tu.-Sa. 9-12, 2-6; Su. 11-1.

TOWN HALL
3428 Duderstadt, Niedersachsen
Town Hall (13th century, with later remodelling). Salt-room. Torture chamber. Glass. Medieval antiquities.
On request. Guided tours only.

DUISBURG

KÖNIGSBERG HOUSE
Mühlheimer Strasse 39, 4100 Duisburg, Nordrhein-Westfalen
History, social and domestic life of pre-1945 Königsberg. Amber.
Tu., W. 10-5; Th., F. 10-4; 1st Su. in month, 10-4.

WILHELM LEHMBRUCK MUSEUM
Düsseldorfer Strasse 51, 4100 Duisburg, Nordrhein-Westfalen
20th century German paintings, prints, engravings. 20th century sculpture. Works by Wilhelm Lehmbruck (d.1919).
Tu., Th.-Su. 10-5; W. 10-1, 3-8.

MUSEUM OF THE LOWER RHINE
Friedrich Wilhelm Strasse 64, 4100 Duisburg, Nordrhein-Westfalen
History of Duisburg. Prehistory. Roman material from Asberg (Asciburgium). History of cartography. Work of Mercator.
Tu., Th.-Su. 10-5; W. 10-1, 3-8.

DÜLKEN

DÜLKEN REGIONAL MUSEUM
Rathaus, 4052 Dülken, Nordrhein-Westfalen
History of Dülken and its region.
On request.

DÜLMEN

MUNICIPAL MUSEUM
Kulturamt, Rathaus, 4408 Dülmen, Nordrhein-Westfalen
Local prehistory, history. Peasant tools, household equipment.
M.-Th. 5.15 p.m.-7.15; F. 4.30-6.30; Su. 8-1.

DURBACH

STAUFENBERG PALACE
7601 Burbach, Baden-Württemberg
Local and regional history.
On request.

DÜREN

LEOPOLD HOESCH MUSEUM
Hoeschplatz 1, 5161 Düren, Nordrhein-Westfalen
19th-20th century paintings. 14th-20th century sculpture, applied art, handicrafts.
Daily 10.30-1, 2.30-5.

REGIONAL MUSEUM
Hoeschplatz 1, 5161 Düren, Nordrhein-Westfalen
Regional pre-history, history. Roman provincial art. Lapidarium. Eifel fire-backs.
Daily 10.30-1, 2.30-5.

DÜSSELDORF

ART COLLECTION OF NORDRHEIN-WESTFALEN
Schloss Jägerhof, Jacobistrasse 2, 4000 Düsseldorf, Nordrhein-Westfalen
20th century paintings.
Tu.-Su. 10-5; W. also 5-8.

BENRATH NATURAL HISTORY MUSEUM
Benrather Schlossallee 102, 4000 Düsseldorf, Nordrhein-Westfalen
Botany and zoology of the Lower Rhine area.
Tu.-Su. 9-5.

BENRATH PALACE
Benrather Schlossallee, 4000 Düsseldorf, Nordrhein-Westfalen
Rococo and late Baroque furnishings. Frankenthal porcelain.
Tu.-Su. 9-5.

CITY MUSEUM OF ART
Ehrenhof 5 und Schulstrasse 5, 4000 Düsseldorf, Nordrhein-Westfalen
16th-20th century paintings. Engravings. Drawings. Prints. Medieval and Baroque sculpture. Applied art. Glass.
Tu.-Sa. 10-6.

CONZEN COLLECTION
Bilker Strasse 5, 4000 Düsseldorf, Nordrhein-Westfalen
History of Düsseldorf. 16th-19th century paintings.
Tu.-Su. 9-5.

DUMONT-LINDEMANN COLLECTION
Ehrenhof 3, 4000 Düsseldorf, Nordrhein-Westfalen
Theatre-history collection of the founders of the Düsseldorf Theatre, Louise Dumont and G. Lindemann.
M.-F. 9-2.

DÜSSELDORF MUSEUM OF PHOTOGRAPHY
Florastrasse 68, 4000 Düsseldorf, Nordrhein-Westfalen
History of photography. Early photographic equipment.
On request.

GOETHE MUSEUM
Jägerhofstrasse 1, 4000 Düsseldorf, Nordrhein-Westfalen
Life and work of J. W. von Goethe. Manuscripts. Portraits. 1st editions. Porcelain. Glass.
Tu.-Su. 10-5.

HALL OF THE ARTS
Grabbeplatz 4, 4000 Düsseldorf, Nordrhein-Westfalen
20th century paintings, graphics, sculpture, posters.
Tu.-Su. 10-8.

HEINE COLLECTION
Universitäts Bibliothele, Grabbeplatz 5-7, 4000 Düsseldorf, Nordrhein-Westfalen
Heine manuscripts, books, portraits and other paintings.
By appointment.

HETJENS MUSEUM
Palais Nesselrode, Schulstrasse 4, 4000 Düsseldorf, Nordrhein-Westfalen
World-wide ceramics collections. Porcelain. Faience. Stoneware.
Tu.-Su. 10-5.

HOUSE OF THE EASTERN GERMAN TERRITORIES
Bismarckstrasse 90, 4000 Düsseldorf, Nordrhein-Westfalen
History and life of the German Eastern Provinces. Furniture. Household equipment. Decorative arts. Coats of arms.
Daily 10-1, 3-9.

KALKUM PALACE MUSEUM
Kaiserswerth, 4000 Düsseldorf, Nordrhein-Westfalen
History of Nordrhein-Westfalen. Religious history of late Middle Ages. Heraldry. Genealogy.
Tu.-Sa. 9-5; Su. 10-12.

LAND MUSEUM OF THE PEOPLE AND THE ECONOMY
Ehrenhof 2, 4000 Düsseldorf, Nordrhein-Westfalen
Exhibition illustrating the German and international economies and their links with society and social organisations. Trade. Nutrition.
M.-F. 9-5; Sa. 9-1; Su. 10-6.

LÖBBECKE MUSEUM
Brehmstrasse, 4000 Düsseldorf, Nordrhein-Westfalen
Geology. Palaeontology. Molluscs. Lepidoptera. Animal sculpture by Josef Pallenberg.
Daily 10-6.

MUSEUM OF THE HISTORY OF DÜSSELDORF
Bäckerstrasse 7-9, 4000 Düsseldorf, Nordrhein-Westfalen
Local prehistory, history. Paintings. Sculpture. Applied art. Coins. Medals. Costumes. Weapons. Rhine shipping. Furniture. Household equipment. Trade and industry.
Tu.-Su. 10-5.

DR. ERNST SCHNEIDER COLLECTION
Jacobistrasse 2, 4000 Düsseldorf, Nordrhein-Westfalen
18th century applied arts, especially Meissen porcelain.
Tu.-Su. 9-5.

VESTER'S ARCHIVE
Schloss Kalkum, 4000 Düsseldorf, Nordrhein-Westfalen
History of pharmacy. Drugs. Advertisements. Woodcuts. Engravings.
Tu.-Sa. 9-5; Su. 10-12.

EBERMANNSTADT

REGIONAL MUSEUM
Rathaus, 8553 Ebermannstadt, Bayern
Local and regional history. Folk-art. Costumes.
By appointment.

EBINGEN

EBINGEN REGIONAL MUSEUM
Rathaus, 7470 Ebingen, Baden-Württemberg
Local history. Folk-art.
Tu.-Sa. 9-5; Su. 10-12.

EHINGEN

REGIONAL MUSEUM
Kasernengasse 2, 7930 Ehingen, Baden-Württemberg
17th-18th century paintings, sculpture. Regional prehistory, early history. Views of Ehingen. Guild material.
May-Oct., Su. 10-12, 2-4.

EICHENZELL

FASANERIE PALACE MUSEUM
Adolphseck, 6411 Eichenzell, Hessen
Local prehistory, history.
By local announcement.

EICHSTÄTT

BENEDICTINE ABBEY OF ST. WALBURG
8833 Eichstätt, Bayern
In Church Treasury. Medieval - 19th century religious art. Reliquaries. Monstrances.
On request.

BERGÉR MUSEUM
Harthof, 8833 Eichstätt, Bayern
Fossils. Insects. Saurians. Sea-creatures. Ornaments. Jewellery.
M.-Sa. 1-5; Su. 10-5.

CATHEDRAL TREASURY
Kapitelsakristei, 8833 Eichstätt, Bayern
Religious art, especially 18th century. Embroidery. Vestments. Carpets. Gold.
By appointment.

DIOCESAN MUSEUM
Osternstrasse 26, 8833 Eichstätt, Bayern
Liturgical items. 15th-18th century sculptures from churches in the Eichstätt diocese.
M.-Sa. 9-5; Su. 9-12.

NATURAL SCIENCE COLLECTIONS
Leonrodplatz 3, 8833 Eichstätt, Bayern
Geology. Palaeontology. Fossils. Mineralogy. Petrography. Botany. Zoology.
By appointment.

WILLIBALD CASTLE MUSEUM
8833 Eichstätt, Bayern
Castle (1350-1535, remodelled 17th century). Palaeontology. Local prehistory (especially palaeolithic), early history (especially Roman), history. 15th-18th century paintings, sculpture. Religious art. Folk art.
May-Oct., daily 9-12, 1-5. Nov.-Apr., daily 10-12, 2-4.

EINBECK

MUNICIPAL MUSEUM
Steinweg 11, 3352 Einbeck, Niedersachsen
History of the Einbeck area. Handicrafts. Brewing.
Tu.-F. 10-12, 2-4; Sa., Su. 10-12.

ELLINGEN

ELLINGEN PALACE
8836 Ellingen, Bayern
18th-19th century period rooms, in classical and Empire styles. History of the Teutonic Order.
May-Oct., daily 9-12, 1-5. Nov.-Apr., daily 10-12, 1-4.

ELLWANGEN

PALACE MUSEUM
7090 Ellwangen, Baden-Württemberg
Regional prehistory, history. Religious art. Schrezheim faience. Wasseralfing cast-iron work. Early printers' tools. 17th-18th century drawings. Folk-art.
Daily 9-12, 2-5.

ELMSHORN

KONRAD STRUVE MUSEUM
Drückhaumers Gang, 2200 Elmshorn, Schleswig-Holstein
Historical geology. Prehistory. History of Elmshorn. Furniture. Household equipment.
Su. 10-12.

EMDEN

LAND MUSEUM OF OSTFRISIEN
Neutorstrasse, 2970 Emden, Niedersachsen
Regional history. Paintings. Decortive arts. Household equipment.
Tu.-F. 11-1, 3-6.

MUNICIPAL MUSEUM
Neutorstrasse, 2970 Emden, Niedersachsen
History of Emden. Medieval sculpture, paintings. Weapons.
Tu.-F. 11-1, 3-6; Sa., Su. 11-1.

EMMENDINGEN

REGIONAL MUSEUM
Markgrafenschloss, Kirchstrasse 7, 7830 Emmendingen, Baden-Württemberg
History of Emmendingen and its region. Handicrafts. Guilds. Memorabilia of Goethe. Work of the painter, Fritz Boehle (d.1916).
May-Oct., Su. 11-12.

EMMERICH

RHINE MUSEUM
4240 Emmerich, Nordrhein-Westfalen
History of Rhine shipping and navigation. Ship and shipyard models, equipment. Views of Emmerich.
Tu.-F. 10-12, 2-5; Sa., Su. 10-12.

EMSDETTEN

AUGUST HOLLÄNDER MUSEUM
Frauenstrasse 20, 4407 Emsdetten, Nordrhein-Westfalen
Regional geology, mineralogy, palaeontology, archaeology. Crafts, especially weaving, clog-making. Costumes. Household equipment.
Su. 10.30-12, 4-6.

ENGER

WIDUKIND MEMORIAL MUSEUM
Kirchplatz 10, 4904 Enger, Nordrhein-Westfalen
History of Enger and its region. Material relating to Widukind (Weitekind), who fought against Charlemagne and is probably buried at Enger.
Tu.-Su. 9-12, 3-6.

ENNEPETAL-VOERDE

WILHELM CRONE MUSEUM
Loherstrasse 115, 5828 Ennepetal-Voerde, Nordrhein-Westfalen
Local and regional history. Folklore.
By appointment.

EPPSTEIN

REGIONAL MUSEUM
Eppstein Burg, 6239 Eppstein, Hessen
History of Eppstein and its castle. Architectural sculpture. Furniture. Decorative arts. Ceramics. Household equipment. Tools. 17th-20th century views of Eppstein. Weapons.
Apr.-Oct., Su. 2.30-5.30.

ERBACH

COLLECTIONS OF COUNT ZU ERBACH-ERBACH
Schloss, 6122 Erbach, Hessen
Medieval weapons. Armour. Firearms. Busts of Roman and Greek emperors and generals. Stags' antlers.
Daily 8-12, 1-5.

ERBACH IVORY MUSEUM
Otto Glenz Strasse 1, 6122 Erbach, Hessen
18th-20th century German carved ivory.
M., W.-Sa. 10-12, 2-5; Su., ublic holidays 10-12, 2-4.

ERDING

REGIONAL MUSEUM
Rathaus, 8058 Erding, Bayern
Local prehistory, history. 14th-18th century sculpture. Folk-art. Guilds. Handicrafts. Peasant furniture, household equipment. Musical instruments.
1st Su. in month 10-12, 2-4. Other times by appointment.

ERFELDEN

REGIONAL MUSEUM
Wilhelm Leuschnes Strasse 28, 6081 Erfelden, Hessen
Local prehistory, history. Applied arts.
M.-Sa. 9-5; Su. 2-5.

ERLANGEN

ARCHAEOLOGICAL COLLECTION OF THE UNIVERSITY OF ERLANGEN-NÜRNBERG
Kochstrasse 4, 8520 Erlangen, Bayern
Casts of Greek and Roman sculpture. Objets d'art.
By appointment.

BRIX-KOMOTEN REGIONAL MUSEUM
Loewenichstrasse 1, 8520 Erlangen, Bayern
Local and regional history.
Tu.-Sa. 9-5; Su. 2-5.

CITY ART COLLECTIONS
Rathaus, Marktplatz 1, 8520 Erlangen, Bayern
16th-20th century paintings, graphics, sculpture.
Tu.-Sa. 9-5; Su. 2-5.

CITY MUSEUM
Altstädter Rathaus, Martin Luther Platz 9, 8520 Erlangen, Bayern
Local prehistory, history. Handicrafts. Toys. Dolls. Works by the painter, Hans Barthelmess (d.1916) and the sculptor, Karl May (d.1961).
M.-F. 9-5; Su. 10-1.

GEOGRAPHICAL AND ETHNOLOGICAL COLLECTIONS OF THE UNIVERSITY OF ERLANGEN-NÜRNBERG
Kochstrasse 4, 8520 Erlangen, Bayern
Geography. Ethnology.
By appointment.

GEOLOGICAL COLLECTION OF THE UNIVERSITY OF ERLANGEN-NÜRNBERG
Schlossgarten 5A, 8520 Erlangen, Bayern
Geology. Historical geology. Stratigraphy. Mineralogy.
By appointment.

GRAPHICS COLLECTION OF THE LIBRARY OF THE UNIVERSITY OF ERLANGEN-NÜRNBERG
Universitätsstrasse 4, 8520 Erlangen, Bayern
Drawings. Engravings. Woodcuts, including self-portraits by Albrecht Dürer, Mathias Grunwald. Coins. Medals.
By appointment.

MINERALOGICAL COLLECTION OF THE UNIVERSITY OF ERLANGEN-NÜRNBERG
Schlossplatz 4, 8520 Erlangen, Bayern
Minerals, especially of Germany.
By appointment.

MUSICAL INSTRUMENTS COLLECTION OF THE UNIVERSITY OF ERLANGEN-NÜRNBERG
Schlossplatz 4, 8520 Erlangen, Bayern
History of musical instruments.
By appointment.

PAINTINGS COLLECTION OF THE UNIVERSITY OF ERLANGEN-NÜRNBERG
Schlossgarten 1, 8520 Erlangen, Bayern
Paintings, graphics, sculpture.
By appointment.

PREHISTORY AND EARLY HISTORY COLLECTION OF THE UNIVERSITY OF ERLANGEN-NÜRNBERG
Kochstrasse 4, 8520 Erlangen, Bayern
Palaeolithic - medieval collections. Cultures of American Indians. Pottenstein forgeries.
By appointment.

TEACHING COLLECTION OF PAINTINGS OF ERLANGEN FOLK HIGH SCHOOL
Friedrichstrasse 17, 8520 Erlangen, Bayern
History of European art.
By appointment.

ZOOLOGICAL COLLECTION OF THE UNIVERSITY OF ERLANGEN-NÜRNBERG
Universitätsstrasse 19, 8520 Erlangen, Bayern
History of zoology.
By appointment.

ESCHERSHAUSEN

RAABE MEMORIAL MUSEUM
Raabestrasse 5, 3457 Eschershausen, Niedersachsen
Life and work of the poet, Wilhelm Raabe (d.1910), in the house where he was born.
By appointment.

ESCHWEGE

REGIONAL MUSEUM
Vor dem Berge 14A, 3440 Eschwege, Hessen
Palaeontology. Local prehistory, history. Folklore. Botany. Zoology. Trade and industry. History of photography. Weapons.
By appointment.

ESSEN

CATHEDRAL TREASURY
Burgplatz 2, 4300 Essen, Nordrhein-Westfalen
In Cathedral Treasury (1000). Religious art. Liturgical items.
Tu.-Su. 10-4.

FOLKWANG MUSEUM
Bismarckstrasse 64-66, 4300 Essen, Nordrhein-Westfalen
Sculpture. Medieval - 18th century religious art. Ceramics. Porcelain. Glass. Silhouette figures from Java. 19th century drawings, engravings. 19th-20th century paintings, sculpture, especially French, German. Graphics.
Tu.-Su. 10-6.

GERMAN POSTER MUSEUM
Alfredisstrasse 2, 4300 Essen, Nordrhein-Westfalen
International collection of posters, especially French, 1875-1908, Polish, 1945-65. Variety theatre and circus posters, 1880-1920.
Tu.-Sa. 10-6.

RUHR AND REGIONAL MUSEUM
Bismarckstrasse 62, 4300 Essen, Nordrhein-Westfalen
Natural sciences. Regional prehistory, archaeology, history.
Tu.-Su. 10-6.

VILLA HÜGEL
4300 Essen, Nordrhein-Westfalen
German industrial history. Paintings. Sculpture. Graphics. Applied art.
Tu.-Su. 10-6.

ESSLINGEN AM NECKAR

TOWN MUSEUM
Rathausplatz 1, 7300 Esslingen am Neckar, Baden-Württemberg
Local and regional history. Paintings. Sculpture. Graphics.
M.-Sa. 9-5; Su. 2-5.

ETTLINGEN

ALBGAU MUSEUM
Schloss, 7505 Ettlingen, Baden-Württemberg
Local and regional history.
Sa. 3-5; Su. 10.30-12. Other times by appointment.

EUTIN

DISTRICT MUSEUM
St. Georgs Hospital, Lübecker Strasse 17, 2420 Eutin, Schleswig-Holstein
Folklore. Peasant furniture, household equipment. Handicrafts and industry, especially flax, linen, pottery.
Tu.-Sa. 4-6; Su. 11-1, 4-6.

EUTIN PALACE
2420 Eutin, Schleswig-Holstein
Medieval castle, remodelled as palace in 17th-18th century. 16th-19th century portraits, landscapes, historical paintings. 17th - early 19th century furniture, decorative arts. Tapestries. Porcelain. Early 18th century shipmodels, formerly in the possession of Tsar Peter III.
May 15 - Oct. 30, Tu.-Su., guided tours at 11, 3, 4.

EVERSBERG

REGIONAL MUSEUM
Mittelstrasse 12, 5779 Eversberg, Nordrhein-Westfalen
Local and regional history.
Tu., Th., Sa., Su. 9-12, 3-6.

FALLERSLEBEN

HOFFMANN VON FALLERSLEBEN MUSEUM
Hoffmannstrasse 5, 3183 Fallersleben, Niedersachsen
Paintings, graphics, sculpture bequeathed by Hoffmann von Fallersleben, including works by his son.
By appointment.

FEUCHTWANGEN

REGIONAL MUSEUM
Museumstrasse 19, 8805 Feuchtwangen, Bayern
Furniture. Household equipment. Decorative arts. Craftsmen's workshops. 18th century farmhouse rooms. Porcelain. Faience. Pewter. Costumes. Folk-art. Folklore. 18th century firefighting equipment.
May-Oct., daily 8-1, 2-7. Nov.-Apr., daily 9-1, 2-4.

FISCHERHUDE

IRMINTRUT REGIONAL MUSEUM
2801 Fischerhude, Niedersachsen
In 16th century house. Period furniture, household equipment, decorative arts.
M.-Su. 9-5.

FLADUNGEN

RHÖN MUSEUM
8741 Fladungen, Bayern
Regional wildlife. History of Fladungen. Guilds. Folk-art. Furniture. Household equipment. Wood-carving. Wooden masks.
Apr.-Oct., daily 8-11, 1-5.

FLENSBURG

FLENSBURG MUNICIPAL MUSEUM
Lutherplatz 1, 2390 Flensburg, Schleswig-Holstein
Cultural history of Schleswig-Holstein. Paintings. Sculpture. Folk-art. Applied art. Shipping and navigation. Regional history, prehistory.
Tu.-Sa. 10-1, 3-5; Su. 10-1.

REGIONAL MUSEUM OF NATURAL HISTORY
Süderhofenden 40-42, 2390 Flensburg, Schleswig-Holstein
Regional geology, botany, wildlife. Hunting.
Tu.-F. 10-12, 3-5; Su. 10-1.

FLÖRSHEIM

REGIONAL MUSEUM
Mainturm, Konrad Adenauer Ufer, 6093 Flörsheim, Hessen
Local and regional history.
Tu.-Sa. 10-1, 3-5; Su. 10-1.

FORCHHEIM

PFALZ MUSEUM
Kapellenstrasse 16, 8550 Forchheim, Bayern
Local prehistory, history.
May-Oct., Tu.-Sa. 10-12, 2-5. Nov-Apr., by appointment.

FRANKENBERG

DISTRICT MUSEUM
Bahnhofstrasse 10, 3558 Frankenberg, Hessen
Local history, prehistory.
Tu.-Sa. 10-1, 2-5; Su. 10-12.

FRANKENTHAL

ERKENBERT MUSEUM
Städtliche Verwaltungsgebäude, 6710 Frankenthal, Rheinland-Pfalz
Local prehistory, history. 16th-17th century paintings by Frankenthal artists. 18th century porcelain.
Su. 11-1, 3-5; W. 4-5.

MUNICIPAL PORCELAIN COLLECTION
Rathaus, 6710 Frankenthal, Rheinland-Pfalz
18th-20th century European porcelain.
Tu.-Sa. 10-1, 3-5; Su. 10-1.

FRANKFURT

AIRPORT EXHIBITION OF MODELS
Rhein-Main Flughafen, 6000 Frankfurt, Hessen
Models, diagrams illustrating history of flying and airline operations.
Daily 10-5.

COIN COLLECTION OF THE GERMAN FEDERAL BANK
Taunusanlage 4-6, 6000 Frankfurt, Hessen
Medieval - 20th century coins. Paper money.
M.-F. 10-5.

GOETHE HOUSE AND MUSEUM
Grosser Hirschgraben 23, 6000 Frankfurt, Hessen
Life and work of J. W. von Goethe. Late 18th - early 19th century German paintings, sculpture, drawings, engravings. German literary manuscripts, 1750-1850.
M.-Sa. 9-6; Su. 10-1.

HISTORY MUSEUM
Untermainkai 14, 6000 Frankfurt, Hessen
Cultural and artistic history of Germany, especially Frankfurt. Greek, Roman, German coins, medals.
Tu., Sa. 10-4; Su. 10-1.

LIEBIGHAUS MUNICIPAL GALLERY
Schaumainkai 71, 6000 Frankfurt, Hessen
Chinese, Japanese, Indian sculpture. Egyptian, Greek, Roman art. Medieval, Renaissance, Baroque and 18th century art.
M., Tu., Th.-Su. 10-5; W. 10-8.

MODEL RAILWAY MUSEUM
Neue Mainzer Strasse 18, 6000 Frankfurt, Hessen
18th-19th century model railway locomotives, rolling stock, operating equipment.
M.-Sa. 10-5; Su. 10-1.

MUSEUM OF APPLIED ART
Schaumainkai 15, 6000 Frankfurt, Hessen
Medieval - 20th century applied art. Chinese, Japanese, Indian, Islamic art. Manuscripts. Incunabula. Genealogies.
M., Tu., Th.-Sa. 10-4; W. 10-7; Su. 10-1.

MUSEUM OF ETHNOGRAPHY
Schaumainkai 29, 6000 Frankfurt, Hessen
Ethnographical collections from America, Africa, Australia, Oceania, Indonesia.
Tu.-Sa. 10-4; Su. 10-1.

MUSEUM OF THE FEDERAL POSTAL SERVICES
Schaumainkai 53, 6000 Frankfurt Hessen
History of postal communications. Post vehicles, uniforms. Telegraph, telephone, radio equipment. Paintings. Drawings. Prints.
Tu.-Sa. 10-3; Su. 10-1.

MUSEUM OF PREHISTORY AND EARLY HISTORY
Justinianstrasse 5, 6000 Frankfurt, Hessen
Prehistory and early history of the Frankfurt region. Greek and Roman small sculpture, applied art.
M., Tu., Th.-Su. 10-5; W. 10-8.

SENCKENBERG NATURAL HISTORY MUSEUM AND RESEARCH INSTITUTE
Senckenberg Anlage 25, 6000 Frankfurt, Hessen
Palaeontology. Marine biology.
By appointment.

STÄDEL INSTITUTE OF ART
Schaumainkai 63, 6000 Frankfurt, Hessen
14th-20th century European paintings, sculpture, especially Dutch, Flemish, Italian, German.
Tu.-Sa. 10-5; Su. 10-1.

FRAUENWÖRTH

FRAUENCHIEMSEE EXHIBITION OF PAINTINGS
8211 Frauenwörth, Bayern
Paintings, especially by local artists.
Tu.-Sa. 10-1, 3-5; Su. 10-1.

FREIBURG IM BREISGAU

AUGUSTINER MUSEUM
Augustinerplatz, 7800 Freiburg im Breisgau, Baden-Württemberg
Medieval and 18th century art. 19th-20th century paintings by local artists. Glass-paintings. Applied art.
Tu.-Sa. 10-5; Su. 10-1.

GERMAN LIBRARY AND MUSEUM OF FOLK-SONG
Silberbachstrasse 13, 7800 Freiburg im Breisgau, Baden-Württemberg
Collections illustrating development of German folksong and folkdance. Prints. Drawings. Leaflets.
M.-F. 9-12, 2-5; Su. 10-12.

MINSTER MUSEUM
Schoferstrasse 4, 7800 Freiburg im Breisgau, Baden-Württemberg
Sculpture and architectural items from Freiburg Minster.
M.-F. 9-12, 2-5; Su. 10-1.

MUSEUM OF ETHNOGRAPHY
Adelhauser Strasse 33, 7800 Freiburg im Breisgau, Baden-Württemberg
In former 17th century convent. Ethnography, especially of former German colonies.
Tu.-Sa. 10-5; Su. 10-1.

MUSEUM OF PREHISTORY AND EARLY HISTORY
Gerberau 32, 7800 Freiburg im Breisgau, Baden-Württemberg
Prehistoric and early historical material from local sites.
Tu.-Sa. 10-5; Su. 10-1.

NATURAL HISTORY MUSEUM
Gerberau 32, 7800 Freiburg im Breisgau, Baden-Württemberg
Regional and foreign wildlife. Forestry. Herbarium. Minerals. Gemstones.
Tu.-Sa. 10-5; Su. 10-1.

PEWTER-FIGURES ROOM
Schwabentor, 7800 Freiburg im Breisgau, Baden-Württemberg
18th-20th century miniature pewter figures, illustrating German history. Costumes.
May-Oct., Tu.-Sa. 10-5; Su. 10-1.

FREISING

CATHEDRAL TREASURY
Dom, 8050 Freising, Bayern
8th-19th century religious art.
By appointment.

MUSEUM OF FREISING HISTORICAL ASSOCIATION
Marienplatz, 8050 Freising, Bayern
Local prehistory, history, folklore. 14th-18th century sculpture. Paintings. Engravings.
Su. 11-12.

SEMINARY ART COLLECTION
Domberg 27, 8050 Freising, Bayern
12th-20th century religious art. 15th-19th century paintings, sculpture by artists from the Tyrol.
Tu.-Sa. 10-5.

FREUDENSTADT

REGIONAL MUSEUM
7290 Freudenstadt, Baden-Württemberg
Local and regional history.
By appointment.

TAXATION MUSEUM
Musbacher Strasse 33, 7290 Freudenstadt, Baden-Württemberg
History of taxation since 3000 B.C.
M.-Sa. 10-5.

FREYUNG

WOLFSTEIN DISTRICT MUSEUM
Schloss Wolfstein, 8393 Freyung, Bayern
History of Freyung area. Peasant household equipment,

furnishings, tools. Handicrafts, especially linen weaving. Glass-painting. Natural history.
May-Oct., Tu.-F. 3-5; 1st and 3rd Su. in month, 3-5.

FRIEDBERG (HESSEN)

FRIEDBERG CASTLE
6360 Friedberg, Hessen
Local, regional history. Furniture. Decorative arts.
Tu.-Sa. 10-5; Su. 2-5.

WETTERAU MUSEUM
Haagstrasse 16, 6360 Friedberg, Hessen
Local prehistory, history, especially Roman. Folk-art.
M.-F. 9-12, 2-5; Sa., Su. 10-12.30.

FRIEDBERG (SCHWABEN)

REGIONAL MUSEUM
Schloss, 8904 Friedberg, Schwaben
Regional prehistory, history. 15th-18th century sculpture. Furniture. Decorative arts. Folk-art. Faience. Pottery. Clocks by Friedberg makers.
Sa. 2-5.

FRIEDRICHSDORF

PHILIPP REIS MEMORIAL
Hauptstrasse 93, 6382 Friedrichsdorf, Hessen
Memorabilia of Philipp Reis (d.1874), inventor of the telephone. History of communications.
On request.

FRIEDRICHSHAFEN

MUNICIPAL MUSEUM OF LAKE CONSTANCE
Kirchplatz 2, 7990 Friedrichshafen, Baden-Württemberg
Neolithic material from local sites. Paintings, sculpture from the Lake Constance area. Life and work of Count Zeppelin. Zeppelin collections.
Tu.-Su. 10-12, 2-5.

FRIEDRICHSRUH

BISMARCK MUSEUM
2055 Friedrichsruh, Baden-Württemberg
Life and work of the Imperial Chancellor, Prince Otto von Bismarck. Orders and decorations. Paintings. Manuscripts.
May-Oct., M. 2-6; Tu.-Su. 9-6. Nov.-Apr., Tu.-Su. 9-4.

FRITZLAR

CATHEDRAL MUSEUM
Dr. Jestädt Platz 11, 3580 Fritzlar, Hessen
Religious art. Liturgical objects.
May-Sept., daily 9-12, 2-6. Oct.-Apr., daily 10-12, 2-4.

FRITZLAR MUSEUM
Hochzeitshaus, 3580 Fritzlar, Hessen
In 16th century house. Geology. Prehistory. Early history. Peasant household equipment, tools. Handicrafts.
M.-F. 10-12, 3-6; Sa. 10-12; Su. 3-6.

FÜRSTENFELDBRUCK

REGIONAL MUSEUM
Altes Rathaus, 8080 Fürstenfeldbruck, Bayern
Local history. Peasant art. Handicrafts. Agricultural history.
Su. 11-12.

FULDA

CATHEDRAL MUSEUM
Domplatz 1, 6400 Fulda, Hessen
Religious art. Tomb of St. Boniface. History of art in the Fulda area.
M.-Sa. 9-5.

EXHIBITION COLLECTION OF THE HESSE LAND LIBRARY AT FULDA
Heinrich von Bibra Platz 12, 6400 Fulda, Hessen
History of western writing and book-illumination, 11th-20th century. Beginnings of printing and binding.
M.-Sa. 9-6.

GERMAN MUSEUM OF FIRE-FIGHTING
Stadtschloss, 6400 Fulda, Hessen
History of fire-fighting. Original equipment. Models. Fire-prevention.
By appointment.

VONDERAU MUSEUM
Stadtschloss und Universitätsplatz, 6400 Fulda, Hessen
Natural history. Local prehistory, folklore. Handicrafts. Coins. Paintings. Sculpture. Drawings. Prints. Furniture. Decorative arts. Porcelain. Faience.
Daily 10-12.30, 2.30-5.

FÜRTH

TOWN MUSEUM
Schloss Burgfarrnbach, 8510 Fürth, Bayern
Local history. Folklore. Folk-art. Goldbeating. Paintings, especially 18th-19th century. 17th-20th century coins, medals, graphics.
Tu.-Sa. 10-5; Su. 10-1.

FURTH IM WALD

TOWN TOWER MUSEUM
Schlossplatz, 8492 Furth im Wald, Bayern
Local history. Guilds. Handicrafts. 18th century sculpture. Glass-paintings.
W. 4-6; Su. 11-12.

FURTWANGEN

HISTORIC CLOCK COLLECTION
Gerwigstrasse, 7743 Furtwangen, Baden-Württemberg
History of the measurement of time. Black Forest clocks.
Apr. 1 - Dec. 15, daily 9-12, 2-5.

FÜSSEN

FÜSSEN STATE GALLERY
Hohes Schloss, Magnusplatz 10, 8958 Füssen, Bayern
15th-18th century paintings by S. German artists.
Tu.-Sa., daily 10-5; Su. 10-1.

REGIONAL MUSEUM
Lechhalde 3, 8958 Füssen, Bayern
History of Füssen, shown in drawings, watercolours, lithographs, engravings. Madonnas. Handicrafts, especially violins, lutes. Peasant furniture. Glass-paintings.
May-Oct., daily 10.30-5.

GAMMERTINGEN

REGIONAL MUSEUM
Rathaus, 7487 Gammertingen, Baden-Württemberg
Local and regional history.
On request.

GARDING

THEODOR MOMMSEN MEMORIAL
Schliessfach 48, 2256 Garding, Schleswig-Holstein
In birthplace of the historian, Theodor Mommsen (1817-1903). Collections illustrating Mommsen's life and work.
On request.

GARMISCH-PARTENKIRCHEN

SCHACHEN HUNTING LODGE
8100 Garmisch-Partenkirchen, Bayern
Local history.
Tu.-F. 10-1, 3-5; Sa. 10-1; Su. 10-12.

RICHARD STRAUSS MUSEUM
8100 Garmisch-Partenkirchen, Bayern
In house of Richard Strauss. Life and work of the composer (d.1949).
Tu.-F. 10-1, 3-5; Sa. 10-1; Su. 10-12.

WERDENFELSER MUSEUM
Rathausplatz 13, 8100 Garmisch-Partenkirchen, Bayern
Agriculture. Handicrafts. Peasant furniture, household equipment. Costumes. Ceramics. Glass. Graphics. 16th-18th century sculpture.
Tu.-F. 10-1, 3-5; Sa. 10-1; Su. 10-12.

GEILENKIRCHEN

REGIONAL MUSEUM
Vogteistrasse 2, 5130 Geilenkirchen, Nordrhein-Westfalen
Geology. Natural history. Regional prehistory, history. Folklore.
1st and 3rd Su. in month, 11-12, 4-6.

GEISLINGEN

REGIONAL MUSEUM
7340 Geislingen, Baden-Württemberg
Local and regional history.
On request.

GELDERN

DISTRICT MUSEUM
Weselerstrasse, 4170 Geldern, Nordrhein-Westfalen
Local and regional history.
On request.

GELNHAUSEN

IMPERIAL PALACE
Schloss, 6460 Gelnhausen, Hessen
In castle (12th century). Local and regional history.
On request.

REGIONAL MUSEUM
Kirchgasse 2, 6460 Gelnhausen, Hessen
Prehistoric material from local excavations. History of Gelnhausen. Collection illustrating history and life of the E. German territories.
Tu.-Sa. 10-12.

GELSENKIRCHEN

MUNICIPAL ART COLLECTION
Horster Strasse 5-7, 4660 Gelsenkirchen-Buer, Nordrhein-Westfalen
20th century art.
Tu.-Su. 10-1, 3-6.

MUNICIPAL MUSEUM
Horster Strasse 5 und Bredde Strasse 23, 4660 Gelsenkirchen-Buer, Nordrhein-Westfalen
Natural history. History of Gelsenkirchen and its region.
Tu.-Su. 10-1, 3-6.

GENGENBACH

CHURCH MUSEUM
Pfarrei, 7614 Gengenbach, Baden-Württemberg
Religious art. Liturgical objects.
On request.

GERNSHEIM

REGIONAL MUSEUM
Realgymnasium, 6084 Gernsheim, Hessen
Local and regional history.
Tu.-Sa. 9-5; Su. 10-1.

GEROLSTEIN

DAUN DISTRICT MUSEUM
Sarresdorfer Strasse, 5530 Gerolstein, Rheinland-Pfalz
Geology. Minerals. Local and regional history. Peasant furnishings. Medieval ceramics.
M.-Sa. 10.30-12.30. May-Sept., also 2-5.

VILLA SARABODIS MUSEUM
Sarresdorfer Strasse, 5530 Gerolstein, Rheinland-Pfalz
Prehistory. Roman and Frankish material from excavations in the Eifel.
May-Oct., M., F. 11-12; W. 8-12, 2-6; Th. 3-4. Nov.-Apr., W. 8-12, 2-6. Other times by appointment.

GEROLZHOFEN

REGIONAL MUSEUM
Rathaus, 8723 Gerolzhofen, Bayern
Local and regional history. Armour.
By appointment.

GERSFELD

PALACE MUSEUM
Schlossstrasse 1, 6412 Gersfeld, Hessen
17th-18th century furniture, decorative arts. Fulda porcelain.
By appointment.

GESEKE

MUNICIPAL HELLWEG MUSEUM
Hellweg 13, 4787 Geseke, Nordrhein-Westfalen
House (1664). Local and regional history. Palaeontology. Religious art. Furniture. Household equipment. Craftsmen's tools, workshops. Coins.
M.-Sa. 10-5; Su. 10-1.

GIESSEN

LIEBIG MUSEUM
Liebigstrasse 12, 6300 Giessen, Hessen
In 'Chemical Laboratory' (1824), with original equipment. Collection illustrating life and work of the chemist, Justus von Liebig (d.1873).
M.-W., F., Sa. 10-12, 2-4; Su. 11-1.

UPPER HESSE MUSEUM
Asterweg 9, 6300 Giessen, Hessen
Regional prehistory, early history. Folklore. 19th-20th century paintings, graphics. Engravings by J. G. Wille (d.1808).
Tu.-Su. 9-12.

GIFHORN

DISTRICT MUSEUM
Schloss, 3170 Gifhorn, Niedersachsen
In palace (1526-68) of the Dukes of Celle. Geology. Natural history. Folklore. Costumes. Handicrafts. Industry.
Tu.-Su. 10-1.

GLADBECK

GLADBECK TOWN MUSEUM
Burgstrasse 64, 4390 Gladbeck, Nordrhein-Westfalen
In Wittringen Castle (c.1200). Geology. Natural history. Local prehistory, history. Folklore. Life and work of the cabinet-maker, Jean-Henri Riesener (d.1806), born in Gladbeck.
Tu.-F., 9-1, 2-5; Sa. 9-12; Su. 11-1, 3-4.

GLADENBACH

REGIONAL MUSEUM
Am Bornrain 7, 3568 Gladenbach, Hessen
Prehistory, including material from local excavations. History of Gladenbach.
Daily 10-12, 3-6.

GLÜCKSBURG

PALACE MUSEUM
Schloss, 2392 Glücksburg, Schleswig-Holstein
History of Schleswig-Holstein. 17th-19th century furniture, decorative arts. Paintings. Tapestries. Leather wall-hangings. Applied art.
Tu.-Su. 10-12, 2-5.

GLÜCKSTADT

DETLEFSEN MUSEUM
Am Fleth 43, 2208 Glückstadt, Schleswig-Holstein
In Brockdorff Palace (1631-2). History of Gluckstadt. Folklore. Handicrafts. Whaling. Shipping and navigation.
Sa. 3.30-5.30; Su. 10-12, 3-6.

GOCH

GATE-HOUSE MUSEUM
4180 Goch, Nordrhein-Westfalen
Prehistoric material from local excavations. Roman archaeology. Medieval pewter. Religious art. Wood sculpture. Glass pictures.
Daily 10-12, 3-5.

GODDELAU

REGIONAL MUSEUM
Bahnhofstrasse 1, 6086 Goddelau, Hessen
Local and regional prehistory, history.
Daily 10-5.

GÖPPINGEN

DR. ENGEL MUSEUM
Boller Strasse 102, 7320 Göppingen, Baden-Württemberg
Building (1610), was former visitors' lodgings at Jebenhausen Spa. Geology, palaeontology of the Swabian Alps.
W., F.-Su., public holidays 10-12, 2-5.

MUNICIPAL MUSEUM
Wühlestrasse 36, 7320 Göppingen, Baden-Württemberg
In former palace (1535). Local prehistory and history. Folklore. Religious art.
W. 2-5; Sa., Su., public holidays 9-12, 2-5.

GÖSSWEINSTEIN

REGIONAL MUSEUM
Burgring 70, 8551 Gössweinstein, Bayern
Regional fossils, natural history.
Tu., F., Su. 10-12, 2-7.

GÖTTINGEN

ART COLLECTION OF THE UNIVERSITY OF GÖTTINGEN
Kurze Geismarstrasse 40, 3400 Göttingen, Hessen
14th-18th century Italian, 16th-17th century Dutch, Flemish, 15th-20th century German paintings, graphics, sculpture.
M.-F. 11-1, 2-4; Su. 10-1.

COLLECTIONS OF THE ARCHAEOLOGICAL INSTITUTE OF THE UNIVERSITY OF GÖTTINGEN
Nikolausbergerweg 15, 3400 Göttingen, Hessen
Greek, Roman vases, coins. Casts of Greek, Roman sculpture.
During hours when Institute is open.

COLLECTIONS OF THE ETHNOGRAPHICAL INSTITUTE OF THE UNIVERSITY OF GÖTTINGEN
Theaterplatz 15, 3400 Göttingen, Hessen
Ethnography, especially of Africa and Oceania.
During hours when Institute is open.

COLLECTIONS OF THE ZOOLOGICAL INSTITUTE OF THE UNIVERSITY OF GÖTTINGEN
Berliner Strasse 28, 3400 Göttingen, Hessen
Zoological study-collections.
During hours when Institute is open.

MUNICIPAL MUSEUM
Ritterplan 7, 3400 Göttingen, Hessen
In Hardenberger Hof, former Renaissance palace. Regional prehistory, history. History of the University and of student life. Folklore. Handicrafts. Munich faience. Fürstenberg porcelain. Waygang pewter. Furniture. Decorative arts. 12th-18th century religious art. Jewish history. Musical instruments. Prints. Drawings.
Tu.-Su. 10-1; Tu.-F. also 3-5.

GOSLAR

CATHEDRAL ANTECHAMBER
3380 Goslar, Niedersachsen
Architectural items from 11th century Goslar Cathedral (demolished 1819). Tomb-stones. Sculpture in stone and bronze.
May-Sept., M.-Sa. 10-1, 2.30-4.30. Oct.-Apr., daily 10.30-12.30.

COLLECTION ILLUSTRATING THE CULTURAL HISTORY OF GERMANY AND EUROPE
Gemeindehof 1, 3380 Goslar, Niedersachsen
Natural sciences. Prussian history. Manuscripts. Paintings. Drawings. Coins. Mining. Smelting. Metal-working.
M.-Sa. 10-12.

GOSLAR MUSEUM
Königstrasse 1-2, 3380 Goslar, Niedersachsen
Prehistory, historical geography, wildlife and cultural history of the Harz. Coins.
June-Sept., M.-Sa. 9-1, 2.30-5. Oct.-May, M.-Sa. 10-1, 3-5; Su. 10-1.

HALL OF HOMAGE
Rathaus, 3380 Goslar, Niedersachsen
Late medieval wall-paintings. 15th century goldsmiths' work. 13th century Gospels.
May-Oct., daily 9-6. Nov.-Apr., 10-4.30.

IMPERIAL PALACE
3380 Goslar, Niedersachsen
History of Goslar.
May-Sept., daily 9-6. Mar.-Apr., Oct., daily 10-4.30. Nov.-Feb., daily 10-3.30.

MÖNCHEHAUS HUNTING AND FORESTRY MUSEUM
Mönchestrasse, 3380 Goslar, Niedersachsen
History of hunting and forestry. Paintings depicting animals and hunting scenes.
June-Sept., Tu.-Sa. 10-1, 3-5; Su. 10-1. Oct.-May, Tu.-Su. 10-1.

MUSEUM OF NATURAL HISTORY
Münzstrasse, 3380 Goslar, Niedersachsen
Natural history specimens from non-European countries. Birds. Butterflies. Molluscs. Corals. Mammals.
June-Sept., Tu.-Sa. 10-1, 3-5; Su. 10-1. Oct.-May, Tu.-Su. 10-1.

GRAFENWÖHR

REGIONAL MUSEUM
8484 Grafenwöhr, Bayern
Building (1532). Local history. Natural history. Folklore. Handicrafts. Religious art. Clocks. Coins. Uniforms. Weapons.
Apr.-Oct., 1st and 3rd Su. in month, 3-5.

GRAFING BEI MÜNCHEN

REGIONAL MUSEUM
8018 Grafing bei München, Bayern
Local history. Costumes. Folk-art. Industry.
1st Su. in month, 2-4.

GREBENSTEIN

DIEMEL HOUSE AGRICULTURAL MUSEUM
3523 Grebenstein, Niedersachsen
In 15th century house. Local history. Peasant tools, handicrafts.
M.-Sa. 10-4; Su. 10-1.

GREVENBROICH

GEOLOGICAL MUSEUM
Schloss, 4048 Grevenbroich, Nordrhein-Westfalen
Regional geology, palaeontology.
By appointment.

GRONAU

REGIONAL MUSEUM
Bahnhofstrasse 8, 4432 Gronau, Nordrhein-Westfalen
Regional and local history.
By appointment.

GROSS-GERAU

REGIONAL MUSEUM
6080 Gross-Gerau, Hessen
Prehistoric and medieval material from local excavations. History of Gross-Gerau. Furniture. Household equipment.
1st and 3rd Su. in month. Other times by appointment.

GÜNZBURG

REGIONAL MUSEUM
Rathausgasse 2, 8870 Günzburg, Bayern
Regional prehistory, history. History of Günzburg. Religious art. 17th-18th century sculpture. Ceramics.
On request.

GUNZENHAUSEN

REGIONAL MUSEUM
Marktplatz 49, 8820 Gunzenhausen, Bayern
Regional prehistory, history. History of Gunzenhausen. Handicrafts. 16th-18th century furniture. Ceramics.
W., Sa. 9-11, 1-5; Su. 10-11.

GUTACH

BAILIFF'S FARM OPEN-AIR MUSEUM
7611 Gutach, Baden-Württemberg
Peasant household equipment, implements, tools. Chapel with painted glass.
Apr.-Oct., daily 8.30-6.

GÜTERSLOH

REGIONAL MUSEUM
Domhof 5, 4830 Gütersloh, Nordrhein-Westfalen
Local and regional prehistory, history. Peasant furnishings, household equipment. Textile manufacture. Religious art.
By appointment.

HACHENBURG

PALACE MUSEUM
5238 Hachenburg, Rheinland-Pfalz
History of Hachenburg and the Westerwald. Weapons. Military equipment.
On request.

HACHTEL

OTTMAR MERGENTHALER'S BIRTHPLACE
6991 Hachtel, Hessen
Memorabilia of Ottmar Mergenthaler (d.1899), inventor of linotype.
By appointment.

HAGEN

KARL ERNST OSTHAUS REGIONAL MUSEUM
Hochstrasse 73, 5800 Hagen, Nordrhein-Westfalen
20th century German art, especially Expressionist and Jugendstil. 20th century drawings, prints, engravings. Regional geology, prehistory. History of Hagen. Furniture. Handicrafts, decorative arts. Porcelain, especially 18th century German.
Tu., W., F., Sa. 10-6; Th. 10-8; Su. 10-1.

PLAYING CARD COLLECTION
Birkenstrasse 39, 5800 Hagen, Nordrhein-Westfalen
World-wide collection of playing-cards.
M.-Sa. 10-5.

WESTPHALIAN OPEN-AIR MUSEUM OF TECHNICAL MONUMENTS
Mäckingerbach, 5800 Hagen-Selbecke, Nordrhein-Westfalen
History of handicrafts and technology from prehistoric times to the early industrial period.
Tu.-Su. 9-7.

HAIGERLOCH

WECKENMANN MUSEUM
7452 Haigerloch, Baden-Württemberg
Religious art.
By appointment.

HALLIG HOOGE

THE KING'S PARLOUR
Hanswarft, 2251 Hallig Hooge, Schleswig-Holstein
House (1776). 18th century furniture, household equipment, decorative arts.
Daily 10-12, 2-5.

HALLSTADT

TOWN MUSEUM
Marktplatz 2, 8605 Hallstadt, Bayern
Prehistory. History of Hallstadt. Handicrafts. Industry.
Mar.-Oct., Su. 10-12, 1st Su. in month also 2-4.

HALTERN

ROMAN AND GERMANIC MUSEUM
Goldstrasse 1, 4358 Haltern, Nordrhein-Westfalen
Prehistory. Germanic history. Material from excavations at Roman military station.
Tu.-Sa. 8.30-1.

HAMBURG

AIRPORT EXHIBITION OF MODELS
Flaghafen, 2000 Hamburg-Fuhesbüttel
History of aviation. Airport operational techniques.
M.-Sa. 9-5.

ALTONA MUSEUM
Museumstrasse 23, 2000 Hamburg
Shipping and navigation. Fishing industry. Ship-models. Geology of the North-German coastal area. Zoology. Botany. Folklore. Folk-art. Costumes. Toys. Paintings. Drawings. Prints.
Tu.-F., Su. 10-5; Sa. 10-1.

ERNST BARLACH HOUSE
Jenischpark, 2000 Hamburg
Life and work of the artist, Ernst Barlach (d.1938). Sculpture, drawings, prints by Barlach.
Tu.-Sa. 11-1, 3-6; Su. 11-5.

BERGEDORF AND VIERLAND MUSEUM
80 Bergedorfer Schloss, 2000 Hamburg
History of Bergedorf and the Vierland.
Tu.-Sa. 10-5; Su. 10-3.

EXHIBITION IN THE PLANETARIUM
39 Im Stadtpark, 2000 Hamburg
Paintings, prints illustrating history of astrology and astronomy.
Su.-F. 10-4.

HAMBURG HALL OF THE ARTS
1 Glockengiesserwall, 2000 Hamburg
15th-20th century paintings. 19th-20th century sculpture. 16th-20th century coins. Watercolours. Drawings. Prints. Engravings.
Tu.-Su. 10-5; W. 10-7.

HAMBURG MUSEUM OF ETHNOLOGY AND PREHISTORY
Binderstrasse 14, 2000 Hamburg
Prehistory, ethnology, popular art of Africa, America, East Asia, Near and Middle East, Indian, Oceania.
Tu.-F., Su. 10-4; Sa. 10-1.

HAMBURG STATE ARCHIVES: COLLECTION OF SEALS AND COATS OF ARMS
Rathaus, 2000 Hamburg
N. German seals, coats of arms. Paintings, prints, documents illustrating history of Hamburg and the Hanseatic League.
Daily 9-3.30.

HELMS MUSEUM
90 Knoopstrasse 12-14, 2000 Hamburg
Prehistory, early history of the northern Lüneburg Heath. Geology. Geography. History of Hamburg.
Tu.-F. 10-5; Sa. 10-1; Su. 10-5.

JENISCH HOUSE
52 Jenisch Park, Baron Voght Strasse, 2000 Hamburg
N. German town-house furniture, especially from Hamburg. Louis XVI and Jugendstil furnishings.
Tu.-Sa. 2-5; Su. 11-5.

KIEKEBERG OPEN-AIR MUSEUM
90 Ehestorf, 2000 Hamburg
18th-19th century farmhouses. Peasant furniture, household equipment from Lüneburg Heath.
Tu.-F. 10-5; Sa. 10-1; Su. 10-5.

MILK MUSEUM AND WILHELMSBURG REGIONAL MUSEUM
93 Kirchdorfer Strasse 163, 2000 Hamburg
Local history. 18th century peasant furnishings. History of the regional dairying and market-gardening industries.
Su. 4-6. Other times by appointment.

MUSEUM OF ARTS AND CRAFTS
1 Steintorplatz, 2000 Hamburg
Art of Egypt, Asia, Greece, Etruria, Rome. European crafts, from prehistoric times to present day. Ceramics. Furniture. Gold. Textiles. Paintings. 20th century applied arts, expecially posters, advertisements, books illustrations.
Tu.-Su. 10-5; W. also 5-7.

MUSEUM OF THE HISTORY OF HAMBURG
36 Holstenwall 24, 2000 Hamburg
History of Hamburg. Guilds. Trade. Transport, especially railways, shipping. Coins. Folklore.
Tu.-F., Su. 10-5; Sa. 10-1.

POSTAL MUSEUM
36 Stephansplatz, 2000 Hamburg
Postal history. Stamps. Franking equipment. Telegraph and telephone equipment.
Tu.-F. 10-2; Th. 10-6.

REEMTSMA COLLECTION OF THE HISTORY OF TOBACCO
Parkstrasse 51, 2000 Hamburg
History of tobacco processing. Tobacco pipes. Paintings. Caricatures. Taxation. Anti-smoking campaign.
By appointment.

RIECK HOUSE: VIERLAND OPEN-AIR MUSEUM
Curslacker Deich, 2000 Hamburg
16th-19th century rural houses from the Vierland. Peasant furniture, household and farm equipment.
Tu.-F., Su. 10-4; Sa. 10-1.

SCHWARZKOPF COLLECTION
Hohenzollernring 127-129, 2000 Hamburg
History of hairdressing. Fashions. Techniques.
By appointment.

THEATRE COLLECTION OF THE UNIVERSITY OF HAMBURG
Rothenbaumchausee 162, 2000 Hamburg
Theatre history. Stage designs. Tickets. Posters. Programmes. Photographs of stage-sets and of actors and actresses.
Tu.-Sa. 9-4.30.

UNIVERSITY OF HAMBURG: ECONOMIC BOTANY COLLECTION
36 Bei den Kirchöfen 14, 2000 Hamburg
Commercially useful plants, especially tropical and subtropical fruits and plants from which sugar is obtained. Models, diagrams, photographs showing methods of cultivation and harvesting.
M.-F. 9-4.

VOLKSDORF VILLAGE MUSEUM
67 Im Alten Dorfe 46, 2000 Hamburg
17th-19th century farmhouses, with furnishings, farm implements, equipment. Handicrafts.
W.-M. 9-12, 2-6.

ZOOLOGY MUSEUM
Bornplatz 5, 2000 Hamburg
Zoological specimens.
During hours when University is open.

HAMBURG-BRUNSBÜTTEL

BRUNSBÜTTEL REGIONAL MUSEUM
Am Markt 12, 2212 Hamburg-Brunsbüttel, Schleswig-Holstein
In 18th century house. Local history. 18th-19th century woodcarvings. History of the Brunsbüttel religious drama. Drawings. Prints.
Daily 8-8.

HAMELN

REGIONAL MUSEUM
Osterstrasse 9, 3250 Hameln, Niedersachsen
Local history. Collections illustrating history of the Pied Piper Legend.
May-Oct., Tu.-F. 10-4; Su.-M. 10-1. Nov.-Apr., daily 10-1.

HAMM

GUSTAV LÜBCKE MUNICIPAL MUSEUM
Museumsstrasse 2, 4700 Hamm, Nordrhein-Westfalen
Egyptian, Greek and Roman antiquities. Prehistory and history of the region. 15th-19th century applied art. Furniture. Porcelain. Faience. Medieval miniatures, sculpture. 17th century Dutch, Flemish paintings. Coins.
Tu.-Sa. 10-4; Su. 10-1.

HAMMELBURG

REGIONAL MUSEUM
8783 Hammelburg, Bayern
Local and regional history.
Tu.-Sa. 10-4; Su. 10-1.

HANAU

HISTORY MUSEUM
Schloss Philippsruhe, 6450 Hanau, Hessen
In Philippsruhe Palace (1701-13). Local prehistory, history. Paintings. Sculpture. Applied art.
May-Oct., daily 3-5; Su. also 10-12.

HOUSE OF GERMAN GOLDSMITHS' WORK
Altstätter Markt 6, 6450 Hanau, Hessen
History of goldsmiths' work.
By appointment.

HANNOVER

WILHELM BUSCH MUSEUM
Georgengarten 1, 3000 Hannover, Niedersachsen
Paintings, drawings by Wilhelm Busch (d.1908). Memorabilia and manuscripts of the artist.
Apr.-Sept., Su.-F. 10-5; Sa. 10-1. Oct.-Mar., Su.-F. 10-4; Sa. 10-1.

CITY ART GALLERY AND LAND ART GALLERY OF LOWER SAXONY
Am Maschpark 5, 3000 Hannover, Niedersachsen
11th-20th century European paintings, drawings, sculpture.
Tu.-Sa. 10-4; F. 4-9; Su. 9-2.

HERRENHAUSEN MUSEUM
Alte Herrenhäuser Strasse 14, 3000 Hannover, Niedersachsen
In 17th century palace. Furniture and paintings from collections of the House of Brunswick-Lüneburg.
Apr.-Sept., daily 10-6; Oct.-Mar., daily 10-4.

HISTORY MUSEUM ON THE HIGH BANK
Pferdestrasse 6, 3000 Hannover, Niedersachsen
History of Hannover and of the former Kingdom of Hannover. Regional history in the pre-industrial age. Folklore.
Tu. 10-9; W.-F. 10-4; Sa. 10-6; Su. 10-1.

KESTNER MUSEUM
Trammplatz 3, 3000 Hannover, Niedersachsen
Egyptian, Greek, Cypriot, Etruscan, Roman art. Medieval religious art. Applied art. Coins. Jewels. 15th-20th century drawings, woodcuts, engravings, prints. Manuscripts.
Tu., Th., F. 10-4; W. 10-9; Sa. 10-6; Su. 10-1.

LAND MUSEUM OF LOWER SAXONY: DEPARTMENT OF ETHNOLOGY
Am Maschpark 5, 3000 Hannover, Niedersachsen
Ethnography of Europe, Asia, Africa, America, Australia, Oceania.
Tu.-Sa. 10-4; F. 4-9; Su. 9-2.

LAND MUSEUM OF LOWER SAXONY: DEPARTMENT OF NATURAL HISTORY
Am Maschpark 5, 3000 Hannover, Niedersachsen
Geology. Palaeontology. Mineralogy. Zoology. Hunting.
Tu.-Th., 10-4; F. 10-9; Sa., Su. 10-2.

LAND MUSEUM OF LOWER SAXONY: DEPARTMENT OF PREHISTORY
Am Maschpark 5, 3000 Hannover, Niedersachsen
Prehistory, especially of the Hannover region.
M.-W. 10-4; F. 10-9; Sa. 10-4; Su. 9-2.

HANNOVERSCH MÜNDEN

REGIONAL MUSEUM
Schlossplatz, 3510 Hannoversch Münden, Niedersachsen
In Palace of the Guelphs (15th-18th century). Local and regional history.
Tu.-Sa. 10-4; Su. 10-1.

HARBER

GERMAN ARMY MUSEUM
Hasenheide 3, 3041 Harber, Niedersachsen
Documents illustrating the political and military history of Germany, 1933-45. Uniforms. Military equipment.
By appointment.

HARBURG

LIBRARY AND ART COLLECTION OF THE PRINCES OF OETTINGEN-WALLERSTEIN
Schloss, 8856 Harburg, Bayern
8th-16th century illuminated manuscripts. Incunabula. Enamels. Ivories. Gold. 15th-16th century tapestries, wood-sculpture.
Mar. 16- Nov. 30, daily 9-12, 1-6.

HASELÜNNE

REGIONAL MUSEUM
Lingener Strasse, 4473 Haselünne, Nordrhein-Westfalen
House (1749). Neolithic, Mesolithic archaeology. Household equipment. Coins.
Su. 3-6.

HASLACH

HANSJAKOB AND REGIONAL MUSEUM
Kapuzinerkloster und Freihof, 7612 Haslach, Baden-Württemberg
History of Haslach and its region. Painting. Sculpture, especially Roman, early Gothic, Baroque. Prints. Drawings. Applied art. Costumes.
M.-W., F. 10-12, 3-6; Su. 11-12, 3-6.

HATTINGEN

REGIONAL MUSEUM
Altes Rathaus, Untermarkt 2, 4320 Hattingen, Nordrhein-Westfalen
Local and regional history. Folklore. Furniture. Household equipment. Pewter. Coins.
W., Sa. 4-6. Su. 10-1, 4-6.

SIEBENBURG REGIONAL ROOMS
Heimathaus, Haldenplatz 1, 432 Hattingen, Nordrhein-Westfalen
Folk art from the Siebenburg area.
Su. 10-12.

HAUSEN

BISMARCK'S RESIDENCE
7831 Hausen, Baden-Württemberg
House (1767-70). Bismarck's study, drawing room, bedroom. Memorabilia of the Chancellor.
On request.

HECHINGEN

HOHENZOLLERN LAND-COLLECTION
7450 Hechingen, Baden-Württemberg
Prehistory and early history of the Hohenzollern territories.
By appointment.

HOHENZOLLERN MUSEUM
Burg, 7450 Hechingen, Baden-Württemberg
In the Zollern Palace (1847-67). Collections illustrating the history of the House of Hohenzollern.
On request.

MUNICIPAL MUSEUM
Altes Rathaus, 7450 Hechingen, Baden-Württemberg
Local and regional history.
Tu.-Sa. 10-5; Su. 10-1.

OELS REGIONAL ROOM
Schlossplatz 5, 7450 Hechingen, Baden-Württemberg
Local and regional history.
On request.

TOWN MILITIA MUSEUM
Zollerstrasse, 7450 Hechingen, Baden-Württemberg
Collection illustrating the history of the Hechingen Town Militia.
On request.

HEIDE

KLAUS GROTH MUSEUM
Lüthenheid 48, 2240 Heide, Schleswig-Holstein
House was birthplace of the writer, Klaus Groth (d.1899). Manuscripts, library and memorabilia of Groth.
Daily 8-12; M., Tu., Th., F. also 2-4.

MUSEUM OF DITHMARSCHEN PREHISTORY
Brahmsstrasse 8, 2240 Heide, Schleswig-Holstein
Geology. Botany. Zoology. Local prehistory, history. Folklore. Handicrafts. Memorabilia of the sculptor and painter, Nicolaus Bachmann and of the musician, Arnold Ebel.
May-Sept., Tu.-F. 9-12, 2-5; Su. 10-5. Oct.-Apr., W. 2-5; Su. 10-12, 2-5.

HEIDELBERG

COLLECTIONS OF GREEK AND ROMAN MINOR ART AND SCULPTURE CASTS
Marstallhof, 6900 Heidelberg, Baden-Württemberg
Greek and Roman minor sculpture.
During University terms, W. 3-7.

COLLECTION OF THE UNIVERSITY SEMINAR OF MUSIC
Augustinergasse 7, 6900 Heidelberg, Baden-Württemberg
History of music. Musical instruments.
By appointment.

EGYPTOLOGY COLLECTION OF HEIDELBERG UNIVERSITY
Marstallhof, 6900 Heidelberg, Baden-Württemberg
Egyptian art and everyday utensils from prehistoric times to the Coptic period.
By appointment.

ETHNOLOGY MUSEUM OF THE J. AND E. VON PORTHEIM FOUNDATION
Hauptstrasse 235, 6900 Heidelberg, Baden-Württemberg
In former Palais Weiman. Ethnography of Africa, Asia, Oceania. Amulets. Musical instruments.
Tu.-Sa. 3-5; Su. 11-1.

GERMAN APOTHECARY MUSEUM
Friedrich Ebert Anlage 23A, 6900 Heidelberg, Baden-Württemberg
Apothecaries' equipment. Medicaments. S. German monastery pharmacy. Witches' kitchen.
Apr.-Nov., daily 10-5; Dec.-Mar., Sa., Su. 11-5.

PALATINE MUSEUM
Hauptstrasse 97, 6900 Heidelberg, Baden-Württemberg
In Morass Palace (1710). Prehistory, history of the Palatinate. 14th-18th century paintings, sculpture, applied art. 17th-18th century Dutch, Italian, French paintings. Late 18th-early 19th century European paintings, drawings. Engravings. Coins. Medals.
Tu.-Su. 10-1, 2-5.

UNIVERSITY COLLECTION OF FOLK ART
Augustinerstrasse 7, 6900 Heidelberg, Baden-Württemberg
Folklore. Folk-art.
By appointment.

UNIVERSITY MUSEUM OF ZOOLOGY
Berliner Strasse 15, 6900 Heidelberg, Baden-Württemberg
Birds of New Guinea. Extinct and rare animals. Comparative anatomy, morphology.
By appointment.

HEIDENHEIM

REGIONAL MUSEUM
Schloss Hellenstein, 7920 Heidenheim, Baden-Württemberg
Palaeolithic and Alemannic archaeology. Folklore. Local industries. Beetles. Indian art. Horse-drawn vehicles.
M.-Sa. 2-4; Su. 11-12, 2-4.

HEILBRONN

HEILBRONN COLLECTION OF MUSIC
Klarastrasse 10-12, 7100 Heilbronn, Baden-Württemberg
16th-17th century music.
M.-F. 8-12, 2-4.

HISTORY MUSEUM
Kramstrasse 1, 7100 Heilbronn, Baden-Württemberg
In former courthouse (1600). Local prehistory, history. Folklore. Wine-production. Paintings. Weights and measures. History of local postal services.
Tu.-Su. 10-12, 3-5.

HEILIGENHAFEN

REGIONAL MUSEUM
Lauritz Massmann Strasse, 2447 Heiligenhafen, Schleswig-Holstein
Natural history. Local prehistory, history. Memorabilia of Theodor Storm and W. Jensen.
July-Aug., daily 4-6. Sept.-June, Tu., F. 4-6.

HEILSBRONN

REGIONAL MUSEUM
8802 Heilsbronn, Bayern
Peasant furniture, costumes, household equipment.
By appointment.

HEINSBERG

REGIONAL MUSEUM
Hochstrasse 21, 5138 Heinsberg, Nordrhein-Westfalen
In 16th century Gate-house. Prehistory. Early history. Religious sculpture. Paintings, especially by the Begas family of court-painters. Furniture. Basketmaking. Clog-making. Velvet-ribbon weaving. Agricultural implements.
Su. 11-12.30, 1st and 3rd Su. in month, 5-7.

HELMBRECHTS

REGIONAL MUSEUM
Münchberger Strasse 17, 8662 Helmbrechts, Bayern
Local history, minerals. Folklore. Weaving. Guilds.
M.-Sa. 10-5.

HELMSTEDT

DISTRICT MUSEUM
Bötticherstrasse 2, 3330 Helmstedt, Niedersachsen
Palaeontology. Prehistory. Folklore. Early medieval sculpture. Coins. Peasant art. Costumes. Handicrafts.
By appointment.

MUSEUM OF ST. MARIENBERG MONASTERY
Kloster, 3330 Helmstedt, Niedersachsen
In 12th century monastery. Medieval religious ornaments. 20th century religious art.
By appointment.

HEMER

REGIONAL MUSEUM
Dulohstrasse 22, 5870 Hemer, Nordrhein-Westfalen
Local and regional geology, archaeology, history.
On request.

HEPPENHEIM

FOLKLORE MUSEUM
Amtsgasse 5, 6148 Heppenheim, Hessen
Local and regional history.
Easter- Oct. 15, W. 3-5; Su., public holidays 10-12.30.

HERBORN

REGIONAL MUSEUM
6348 Herborn, Hessen
Local and regional history.
On request.

HERFORD

MUNICIPAL MUSEUM
Deichtorwall 2, 4900 Herford, Nordrhein-Westfalen
History of the town and abbey of Herford. 16th-19th century furniture. Portraits of abbesses and canonesses. Memorial room to M. D. Pöppelmann, architect of the Zwinger, Dresden.
Tu., Th., F. 10-1, 3-5; W. 3-5; Sa., Su. 10-1.

HERMANNSBURG

MISSIONARY AND REGIONAL MUSEUM
3102 Hermannsburg, Niedersachsen
Ethnographical material from Africa, Australia. Costumes and agricultural implements from the Lüneburg Heath.
June-Sept., Tu., Th., 10-5.

HERNE

EMSCHERTAL MUSEUM
Schloss, Strunkede Strasse 77A, 4690 Herne, Nordrhein-Westfalen
Regional prehistory, history. Geology. Palaeontology. Natural history. Folklore. Furniture. Stoves. Pewter. Sundials.
Tu.-Su. 10-1, 2-6.

HERRENALB

REGIONAL ROOM
Rathaus, 7506 Herrenalb, Baden-Württemberg
Relics and documents of the former monastery. Collection of handmade and dated roofing-tiles.
M. 10-12.

HERRENCHIEMSEE

NEW PALACE AND LUDWIG II MUSEUM
8210 Herrenchiemsee, Bayern
In palace (1876-86), built for Ludwig II of Bavaria on the model of Versailles. Paintings and applied art from the royal collections. History of the palace. Pictures illustrating performances of Wagner's operas.
May-Oct., daily 8.30-5.30. Nov.-Apr., daily 9-4.

HERSBRUCK

REGIONAL AND HUNTING MUSEUM
Eisenhüttlein 7, 8562 Hersbruck, Bayern
History of Hersbruck. Furniture. Handicrafts. Hunting.
Daily 9-11, 3-5.

HERZOGENAURACH

REGIONAL MUSEUM
Am Markt, 8522 Herzogenaurach, Bayern
Local and regional history.
On request.

HILCHENBACH-ALLENBACH

SCHOOL AND REGIONAL MUSEUM
Hof Stöcken Weg 13, 5912 Hilchenbach-Allenbach, Nordrhein-Westfalen
Agricultural implements. Dairying equipment. Collections illustrating local iron-ore mining and iron-working. Clocks. Portraits.
3rd Su. in month, 1-4. Other times by appointment.

HILCHENBACH-GRUND

JUNG-STILLING MEMORIAL ROOM
Jung-Stilling Strasse 16, 5912 Hilchenbach-Grund, Nordrhein-Westfalen
Memorabilia of the writer and Marburg professor, J. H. Jung-Stilling (b.1740 in Grund). Portraits of his contemporaries.
On request.

HILDEN

REGIONAL MUSEUM
Elberfelder Strasse 24, 4010 Hilden, Nordrhein-Westfalen
Local and regional history.
On request.

HILDESHEIM

ROEMER-PELIZAEUS MUSEUM
Am Steine 1, 3200 Hildesheim, Niedersachsen
Geology. Palaeontology. Mineralogy. Botany. Zoology. Archaeology. Egyptology. Folklore. Paintings. Prints. Drawings. Coins.
Tu.-F. 10-4.30; Sa., Su. 10-1.

HILTRUP

COLLECTIONS OF THE HILTRUP MISSION HOUSE
Hammerstrasse 213, 4403 Hiltrup, Nordrhein-Westfalen
Ethnological material from Africa, Oceania and the Far East. History of the Mission.
On request.

COLLECTIONS OF THE HOUSE OF MISSIONARY NUNS
Hammerstrasse 109, 4403 Hiltrup, Nordrhein-Westfalen
History of the Mission.
On request.

HINDELANG

REGIONAL COLLECTION
Rathaus, 8973 Hindelang, Bayern
Paintings and models showing history of Hindelang. Drawings. Documents, illustrating history of local salt and nail-making industries.
By appointment.

HIRSAU

MONASTERY MUSEUM
7262 Hirsau, Baden-Württemberg
Religious paintings, sculpture.
On request.

HITZACKER

REGIONAL MUSEUM
3139 Hitzacker, Niedersachsen
Prehistory. History of Hitzacker. Local shipping and fishing industries. Furniture, decorative arts.
Tu. 9.30-11.30; F. 3.30-5.30.

HÖCHSTADT-AISCH

REGIONAL MUSEUM
8552 Höchstadt-Aisch, Bayern
Local prehistory. History. Handicrafts. Guilds. Agricultural implements, equipment.
Daily 8-12, 3-6.

HÖCHSTÄDT-DONAU

REGIONAL MUSEUM
Oberer Waberberg, 8884 Höchstädt-Donau, Bayern
Local and regional history. Mementoes of the Battles of Höchstädt (1703 and 1704), and of the Napoleonic period. Handicrafts. Guilds.
By appointment.

HOF

MUNICIPAL MUSEUM
Hallplatz 3, 8670 Hof, Bayern
Natural history. Local and regional history. Furniture. Decorative arts. Guilds. Paintings, drawings by J. C. Reinhart (d.1847) and K. von Enhuber (d.1867).
W., Sa. 2-5; Su. 10-12.

HOFGEISMAR

REGIONAL MUSEUM
Markt 1, 3520 Hofgeismar, Hessen
House (1621). Geology. Prehistory. History. Folklore. Paintings. Sculpture. Drawings. Prints. Military history.
Apr.-Sept., Su. 10.30-12.30.

HOHENBURG

SPÖRER MUSEUM OF CULTURAL HISTORY
8451 Hohenburg, Bayern
Prehistory, early history. Folklore. Folk-art. Costumes. Weapons. Postage stamps.
By appointment.

HOHENLIMBURG

REGIONAL MUSEUM
Schloss, 5850 Hohenlimburg, Nordrhein-Westfalen
In 13th century castle (remodelled in 18th century). Geology. Regional prehistory, history. Furniture, decorative arts, paintings, applied art from the collections of the Princes of Bentheim-Tecklenburg. Weapons. Coins.
Oct.-Mar., daily 10-4; Apr.-Sept., daily 10-6.

HOHENSCHWANGAU

HOHENSCHWANGAU PALACE
8959 Hohenschwangau, Bayern
Palace (1833-38). Period furniture, decorative arts.
Oct.-Mar., daily 10-4. Apr.-Sept., daily 8.30-5.30.

HOHENWESTEDT

REGIONAL MUSEUM
Friedrichstrasse 11, 2354 Hohenwestedt, Schleswig-Holstein
Natural history. Regional history. Folklore.
W., Sa. 2-4; Su. 10-12.

HÖHR-GRENZHAUSEN

GRENZAU CASTLE
5410 Höhr-Grenzhausen, Rheinland-Pfalz
Castle (1181-1222). Regional history. Handicrafts. Stone Age and Medieval pottery. 16th-18th century stoneware. Artistic cast-iron.
By appointment.

HOISDORF

STORMARN VILLAGE MUSEUM
Alte Schule, 2071 Hoisdorf, Niedersachsen
Geology. Local prehistory, history. Folklore.
By appointment.

HOLZMADEN-TECK

HAUFF MUSEUM
7331 Holzmaden-Teck, Baden-Württemberg
Early historical material from local excavations.
Tu.-Su. 9-12, 1-5.

HOLZMINDEN

REGIONAL MUSEUM
Oberbachstrasse, 3450 Holzminden, Niedersachsen
Local and regional history. Folk-art.
On request.

HOMBERG

REGIONAL MUSEUM
Hochzeitshaus, 3588 Homberg, Hessen
House (1517). Folklore. Local history. Guilds. Collection of stoves.
Sa. 10-5; Su. 10-1.

HOMBURG

REGIONAL MUSEUM
Kaiserstrasse 41, 6650 Homburg, Saarland
Local and regional prehistory, history. Early historical material from local excavations. Maps. Paintings. Engravings.
Daily 8-12, 2-4.

HORB

HORB PEASANT MUSEUM
Ihlingerstrasse, 7240 Horb, Baden-Württemberg
Agricultural implements. Peasant furniture, household equipment.
By appointment.

REGIONAL MUSEUM
Neckarstrasse 74, 7240 Horb, Baden-Württemberg
Local and regional history.
On request.

HORN-BAD MEINBERG

CASTLE MUSEUM
4934 Horn-Bad Meinberg, Nordrhein-Westfalen
Castle (1348, remodelled 1656-59). Weapons. Paintings of the Town. Furniture. Handicrafts. Archaeology. Geology. Paintings, sculpture by Robert and Karl Henckel.
By appointment.

HÖXTER

HÖXTER-CORVEY MUSEUM
Schloss Corvey, 3470 Höxter, Nordrhein-Westfalen
In former 9th century Benedictine abbey, with 9th century Carolingian murals. Prehistory. Folklore. Natural history. Portraits. Weapons. Furniture. Craftsmen's workshops, tools. Memorabilia of the writers, H. von Fallersleben (d.1874), F. W. Weber (d.1894) and Peter Hille (d.1904).
Apr.-Oct., daily 9-6.

HÜCKESWAGEN

REGIONAL MUSEUM
5609 Hückeswagen, Nordrhein-Westfalen
In 13th century castle. 18th-19th century furniture, decorative arts, household equipment. Agricultural implements, equipment.
Th. 4-6; Su. 11-12.30.

HÜLLHORST

REGIONAL MUSEUM
Schulweg 162, 4971 Hüllhorst, Nordrhein-Westfalen
Regional prehistory, history. Peasant furniture, household equipment. Guilds. Costumes. Ornaments. Coins.
By appointment.

HÜLS

REGIONAL MUSEUM
Rathaus, 4153 Hüls, Nordrhein-Westfalen
Local and regional history.
By appointment.

HÜNFELD

REGIONAL MUSEUM
6418 Hünfeld, Hessen
Local and regional history.
On request.

HUSUM

NISSEN HOUSE
Herzog Adolf Strasse 25, 2250 Husum, Schleswig-Holstein
Geology. Natural history. Local prehistory, history. Industrial and commercial development of the area. Folklore. Paintings. Drawings. Sculpture.
By appointment.

OSTENFELD FARMHOUSE OPEN-AIR MUSEUM
Nordhusumer Strasse 11, 2250 Husum, Schleswig-Holstein
In 17th century hall-type house and half-timbered barn. Peasant furniture, household equipment, Handicrafts.
May-Oct., daily 8-12.30. Nov.-Apr., daily 9-12, 2-5.

IBBENBÜREN

ART GALLERY AND MUSEUM
Alpenstrasse 142, 453 Ibbenbüren, Nordrhein-Westfalen
Local geology, archaeology, history. 19th-20th century graphics.
M.-Sa. 8-5. Other times by appointment.

IDAR-OBERSTEIN

EXHIBITION OF GEM-STONES
Gewerbehalle, Dr. Liesegangstrasse, 6580 Idar-Oberstein, Rheinland-Pfalz
International collection of gemstones, in their cut and uncut states.
By appointment.

MINERAL MUSEUM
Hauptstrasse 62, 6580 Idar-Oberstein, Rheinland-Pfalz
Gem-stones.
Daily 9-12, 2-4.

REGIONAL MUSEUM
Hauptstrasse 440, 6580 Idar-Oberstein, Rheinland-Pfalz
Mineralogy. Biology. Zoology. Local history. History of the local jewellery industry.
Apr.-Sept., daily 8-5.30. Oct.-Mar., daily 9-12, 1.30-5.

IDSTEDT

IDSTEDT MEMORIAL HALL
2381 Idstedt, Schleswig-Holstein
Documents relating to the war of 1848-51. Military equipment.
Apr.-Sept., daily 8-6. Oct.-Mar., Su.-F. 9-5.

IGGELHEIM

REGIONAL MUSEUM
Altes Rathaus, 6731 Iggelheim, Baden-Württemberg
In Town Hall (1569). Peasant furniture, household equipment, handicrafts. Equipment for flax-processing and dyeing.
By appointment.

ILLEBEUREN

FARMHOUSE MUSEUM
Haus Nr. 11, 8941 Illebeuren, Bayern
18th-19th century peasant furniture, decorative arts, household equipment. Tools, equipment for flax-processing and linen-weaving. House-brewery.
Daily 8-12, 1-3.

ILSFELD

LIEBENSTEIN CASTLE
7129 Ilsfeld, Baden-Württemberg
Local history. Folk-art.
By appointment.

IMMENSTADT

REGIONAL MUSEUM
Klosterplatz 3, 8970 Immenstadt, Bayern
Local history. Folk-art. Sculpture. 18th century painted glass. Engravings.
M.-Sa. 2-6, public holidays 9-12.

INGELHEIM

CARLO FREIHERR VON ERLANGER MUSEUM
6507 Ingelheim, Rheinland-Pfalz
The collection of the ornithologist and African explorer, Carl Freiherr von Erlanger (d.1904). Zoology, especially birds and mammals of Germany and North Africa.
By appointment.

HISTORY MUSEUM
Rathausplatz, 6507 Ingelheim, Rheinland-Pfalz
Regional and local history.
On request.

INGOLSTADT

BAVARIAN ARMY MUSEUM
Neues Schloss, Paradeplatz 4, 8070 Ingolstadt, Bayern
History of the Bavarian Army. Weapons and uniforms, 16th-19th century Paintings. Prints. Drawings. Model soldiers. Musical instruments. Military equipment.
Tu.-Sa. 10-5; Su. 10-1.

MUNICIPAL MUSEUM
Esplanade 1, 8070 Ingolstadt, Bayern
Local and regional history. Views of Ingolstadt. History of the University of Ingolstadt. Prehistoric and early historical material from local excavations, especially the Celtic town of Manching. 16th century paintings. 15th-18th century printed books. Guilds.
By appointment.

ISERLOHN

REGIONAL HOUSE
Altstadt, 5860 Iserlohn, Nordrhein-Westfalen
Local geology, palaeontology, history. Folk-art.
On request.

ISNY

ISNY REGIONAL MUSEUM
Rathaus, 7920 Isny, Baden-Württemberg
Local history. Folk-art.
By appointment.

ITZEHOE

GERMANIC GRAVE
Lornsenplatz, 2210 Itzehoe, Schleswig-Holstein
Bronze-Age grave-mound, now roofed over.
By appointment.

PRINZESSHOF REGIONAL MUSEUM
Viktoriastrasse 20, 2210 Itzehoe, Schleswig-Holstein
17th century house. Geology. Prehistoric material from local excavations. Regional history. Folklore. Handicrafts.
Su. 10-12; W., Sa. 2-4.

JAGSTHAUSEN

PALACE MUSEUM
Götzenburg, 7109 Jagsthausen, Baden-Württemberg
Local history. Weapons. The 'Iron Hand' of Götz von Berlichingen.
Apr.-Sept., daily 9-6.

JEVER

PALACE AND REGIONAL MUSEUM
Schloss, 2942 Jever, Niedersachsen
Regional prehistory. Furniture. Handicrafts. Porcelain. Clocks.
Tu.-Sa. 10-1, 3-5; Su. 11-1, 3-5.

JUGENHEIM

CASTLE MUSEUM
Heiligenberg, 6104 Jugenheim, Hessen
Local and regional history.
M.-Sa. 9-5; Su. 10-1.

JUIST

COASTAL MUSEUM
2983 Juist, Niedersachsen
History of chart-making, navigation and time-reckoning. Marine biology.
M.-Sa. 9-12, 3-6.30.

JÜLICH

ROMAN AND GERMANIC MUSEUM
Rathaus, 5170 Jülich, Nordrhein-Westfalen
Roman and Frankish material from local excavations.
Su. 11-1.

KAISERSLAUTERN

PALACE GALLERY AND ARTS AND CRAFTS COLLECTION
Museumplatz 1, 6750 Kaiserlautern, Rheinland-Pfalz
19th-20th century paintings, drawings, prints, sculpture. Arts and crafts.
Tu.-Sa. 10-1, 2-4.30.

KAISERLAUTERN

THEODOR ZINK MUSEUM
Rathaus, 6750 Kaiserlautern, Rheinland-Pfalz
History of Kaiserlautern. Folklore of the Palatinate.
Tu.-Sa. 10-1, 2-4.30.

KALKAR

ART COLLECTION OF THE NICOLAI CHURCH
4192 Kalkar, Nordrhein-Westfalen
Religious art, especially 15th-16th century woodcarvings and paintings by Kalkar artists.
M.-Sa. 9-4; Su. 9-12.

KAMEN

MUNICIPAL MUSEUM
Sesekedamm 10, 4618 Kamen, Nordrhein-Westfalen
History of Kamen and Westphalia. Development of local mining and other industries.
Tu.-Sa. 10-5; Su. 10-1.

KAPELLEN-STOLZENFELS

STOLZENFELS CASTLE
Auf der Burg, 5401 Kappellen-Stolzenfels, Rheinland-Pfalz
Regional history.
On request.

KARLSRUHE

BADEN MUSEUM
Schloss, 7500 Karlsruhe, Baden-Württemberg
In 18th century palace. Egyptian, Greek, Etruscan, Roman art. European, especially German sculpture and crafts, medieval - 20th century. Prehistory, early history and folklore of Baden. Weapons. Trophies brought back by Margrave Ludwig Wilhelm von Baden from wars with Turks. Coins.
Apr.-Sept., M., W., F.-Su. 10-5; Th. 10-5, 8 p.m.-10. Oct.-Mar., M., W., F.-Su., 10-4; Th. 10-4, 7-9.

CITY ART COLLECTION
7500 Karlsruhe, Baden-Württemberg
European, especially German, paintings, sculpture, engravings.
Tu.-F. 2-5; Sa., Su. 10-12.30, 1-5.

CITY HISTORY COLLECTIONS
Zähringer Strasse 96-98, 7500 Karlsruhe, Baden-Württemberg
History of Karlsruhe and of Baden.
Tu.-F. 2-5; Sa., Su. 10-12.30, 1-5.

CARPATHIAN ROOM
Kaiserallee 8, 7500 Karlsruhe, Baden-Württemberg
History and culture of the former German-speaking areas of Slovakia.
M.-F. 9-5.

LAND NATURAL HISTORY COLLECTIONS
1 Erbprinzenstrasse 13, 7500 Karlsruhe, Baden-Württemberg
Geology. Palaeontology. Mineralogy. Botany. Zoology.
Tu.-F. 2-5; Sa., Su. 10-12.30, 1-5.

PFINZGAU MUSEUM
Pfinztalstrasse 9, 7500 Karlsruhe-Durlach, Baden-Württemberg
History of Karlsruhe and Baden.
Tu.-F. 2-5; Sa., Su. 10-12.30, 1-5.

STATE HALL OF ARTS
Hans Thoma Strasse 2-6, 7500 Karlsruhe, Baden-Württemberg
14th-20th century European paintings, drawings, engravings, woodcuts.
Apr. 1 - Oct. 15, daily 10-5. Oct. 16 - Mar. 31, 10-4.

WRITERS' MUSEUM OF THE UPPER RHINE
Rontgenstrasse 6, 7500 Karlsruhe, Baden-Württemberg
Paintings. Literary manuscripts. Books. Book illustrations.
M.-F. 9-12, 2-5; Sa. 10-12.

KASSEL

GERMAN TAPESTRY MUSEUM
Schloss Wilhelmshöhe, 3500 Kassel, Hessen
World-wide collections of tapestries and wall-hangings.
Apr.-Sept., daily 10-6. Oct.-Mar., daily 10-4.

MUNICIPAL ART COLLECTION
Schöne Aussicht 2, 3500 Kassel, Hessen
19th-20th century European paintings, drawings, engravings, prints.
Tu.-Su. 10-5.

MUSEUM OF THE BROTHERS GRIMM
Brüder Grimm Platz 4A, 3500 Kassel, Hessen
Manuscripts and printed works of Jacob, Wilhelm and Emil Grimm. Paintings. Prints. Drawings. Books and articles about the brothers Grimm.
M.-F. 9-7; Sa. 9-1; Su. 10-1.

NATURAL HISTORY MUSEUM
1 Steinweg 2, 3500 Kassel, Hessen
In the Ottoneum, the earliest surviving German theatre. Geology. Palaeontology. Mineralogy. Botany. Zoology. Ratzeberg Herbarium (1556).
Tu.-F. 10-4.30; Sa., Su. 10-1.

RHEINSTAHL-HENSCHEL WORKS MUSEUM
Henschelstrasse, 3500 Kassel, Hessen
History of German iron and steel-making, especially of the firm, Rheinstahl-Henschel.
By appointment.

LOUIS SPOHR MEMORIAL AND RESEARCH INSTITUTE
Brüder Grimm Platz 4A, 3500 Kassel, Hessen
Life and work of the composer, Louis Spohr (d.1859). Musical instruments. Furniture. Portraits of musicians. 1st editions of printed music.
F. 3-6. Other times by appointment.

STATE ART COLLECTIONS
Schloss Wilhelmshöhe, 3500 Kassel, Hessen
Regional prehistory, history. Greek and Roman archaeology. Folklore. Paintings. Drawings. Sculpture. Applied arts. Astronomy. Physics.
Tu.-Su. 10-5; Apr.-Sept. also W. 10-10.

WILLHELMSHÖHE PALACE AND STATE PARK
Schloss Wilhelmshöhe, 3500 Kassel, Hessen
History of Hessen.
Daily 9-5.

KAUB-RHEIN

BLÜCHERMUSEUM
Metzgergasse 6, 5425 Kaub-Rhein, Rheinland-Pfalz
Memorabilia of Field-Marshal Blücher.
Daily 10-12, 2-6.

KAUFBEUREN

REGIONAL MUSEUM
Kaisergässchen 12-14, 8950 Kaufbeuren, Bayern
Regional prehistory, history. Furniture. Decorative arts. Paintings. Sculpture. Folkart. Ceramics. Handicrafts. Crucifix collection. Ganghofen memorial collection.
Tu.-Sa. 9-12, 1-4; Su. 9-12.

KAUFBEUREN-NEUGABLONZ

GABLONZ ARCHIVES AND MUSEUM
Gustav Leutelt Schule, 8950 Kaufbeuren-Neugablonz, Bayern
Regional folklore and industrial history.
Th. 3-4.

GABLONZ GALLERY
Neue Zeile 11, 8950 Kaufbeuren-Neugablonz, Bayern
Works by local artists.
By local announcement.

KEHL

HANAU MUSEUM
Friedhofstrasse 2, 7640 Kehl, Baden-Württemberg
Regional prehistory, history. Geology. Palaeontology. Costumes.
1st and 3rd Su. in month, 10-1.

KEITUM-SYLT

OLD FRISIAN HOUSE
2286 Keitum-Sylt, Schleswig-Holstein
Local furniture, household equipment.
May-Oct., daily 10-12, 2-5.

SYLT REGIONAL MUSEUM
2286 Keitum-Sylt, Schleswig-Holstein
Local prehistory, history, folklore, folk-art, wildlife, shipping.
May-Oct., daily 10-12, 2-5.30. Other times by appointment.

KELHEIM

HALL OF LIBERATION
8420 Kelheim, Bayern
Material illustrating 19th century movement for German unification. Sculpture by Ludwig Schwartaler, in his studio.
May-Oct., daily 8-6. Nov.-Apr., daily 10-12, 2-4.

TOWN MUSEUM
Deutscher Hof, 8420 Kelheim, Bayern
Natural history. Local and regional prehistory, history. Folklore.
May-Oct., daily 8-12, 2-6.

KELLINGHUSEN

REGIONAL MUSEUM
Rathaus, 2217 Kellinghusen, Schleswig-Holstein
Regional prehistory, history. Peasant furniture, household equipment, tools, implements. Pottery. Costumes. Memorabilia of local personalities, including the writer, Detlef Freiherr von Liliencron (d.1909).
1st and 2nd Su. in month 9.30-12.

KEMPEN

KRAMER MUNICIPAL MUSEUM
Burgstrasse 19, 4152 Kempen, Nordrhein-Westfalen
13th-19th century German paintings, sculpture, applied arts.
Tu.-F. 10-12, 3-5; Sa. 3-5.

KEMPTEN

ALLGAU REGIONAL MUSEUM
Grosser Kornhausplatz 1, 8960 Kempten, Bayern
Regional history. Folk-art. Paintings. Coins.
M.-Sa. 2-4; Tu., F., Su. 10-12.

CAMBODUNUM ROMAN COLLECTION AND NATURAL SCIENCES COLLECTION
Residenzplats 31, 8960 Kempten, Bayern
Roman material from local excavations. Natural sciences.
M.-Sa. 2-4; Tu., F. also 10-12; Su. 10-12.

KEVELAER

FOLKLORE MUSEUM OF THE LOWER RHINE
Hauptstrasse 18, 4178 Kevelaer, Nordrhein-Westfalen
Regional prehistory. Folklore. Applied arts and sculpture by regional artists.
May-Oct., daily 10-12, 1-5; Nov.-Apr., M.-F., Su. 1-5.

KIEL

COLLECTION OF THEATRE HISTORY AND HEBBEL COLLECTION
Dänische Strasse 15, 2300 Kiel, Schleswig-Holstein
Theatre history. Scenic design. Promptbooks. Tickets. Programmes. Portraits of actors and actresses. Memorabilia of Friedrich Hebbel (d.1863) and his circle.
Tu.-Sa. 10-5; Su. 10-1.

HISTORY COLLECTION OF THE SCHLESWIG-HOLSTEIN LAND LIBRARY
Schloss, 2300 Kiel, Schleswig-Holstein
History of Kiel and Schleswig-Holstein. Paintings. Drawings. Prints. 19th century weapons and uniforms. Coins and medals.
Tu.-Th., 10-1, 3-7; W. 10-1; 1st and 3rd Su. in month, 11-1.

INSTITUTE AND MUSEUM OF MINERALOGY, PETROLOGY, GEOLOGY AND PALAEONTOLOGY
Olshausenstrasse 40-60, 2300 Kiel, Schleswig-Holstein
Geology. Palaeontology. Mineralogy. Petrography.
By appointment.

KIEL MUSEUM OF FIRE PREVENTION
Gartenstrasse 4, 2300 Kiel, Schleswig-Holstein
Methods of fire-prevention. Fire-prevention regulations. Damage done by fire.
M.-F. 9.30-12.30.

MUSEUM OF ETHNOGRAPHY
Hegenischstrasse 3, 2300 Kiel, Schleswig-Holstein
Art and ethnography of Africa, the Far East and the Pacific. Musical instruments.
Su., Th., F. 10-1; W., Th., 10-4; Sa. 2-5.

PICTURE GALLERY AND GRAPHICS COLLECTION OF THE KIEL KUNSTHALLE
Düsternbrocker Weg 1-7, 2300 Kiel, Schleswig-Holstein
19th-20th century German, especially Schleswig-Holstein, paintings, sculpture. Coins. German drawings, prints, engravings from the time of Dürer onwards.
Tu.-Su. 10-1; W., Sa. also 4-7.

SCHLESWIG-HOLSTEIN OPEN-AIR MUSEUM
2300 Kiel, Schleswig-Holstein
Peasant houses, mills, barns, workshops and other rural buildings from Schleswig-Holstein.
Apr. 1 - Nov. 15, Tu.-Su. 9-5.

SCHLESWIG-HOLSTEIN TRAVELLING MUSEUM
Projensdorferstrasse 324, 2300 Kiel, Schleswig-Holstein
Collections illustrating natural sciences, especially connected with Schleswig-Holstein.
By local announcement.

ZOOLOGY MUSEUM OF THE UNIVERSITY OF KIEL
Hegenischstrasse 3, 2300 Kiel, Schleswig-Holstein
World-wide collection of animals, sea-creatures. Dioramas.
Tu.-Sa. 10-5; Su. 10-1.

KIRCHHEIM

REGIONAL MUSEUM
Kornhaus, Max Eyth Strasse 19, 7312 Kirchheim, Hessen
Local history. Alemannic material from local excavations. Petrified material. Memorabilia of Max Eyth (d.1906).
M.-Sa. 9-5; Su. 10-1.

KIRCHHEIMBOLANDEN

REGIONAL MUSEUM
Amtstrasse 14, 6719 Kirchheimbolanden, Rheinland-Pfalz
Regional prehistory, history. Furniture. Household equipment. Wrought-iron. agricultural implements. Pottery. Natural science.
May-Sept., Su. 10-12.

KISSLEGG

WOLFEGG CASTLE
7967 Kisslegg, Baden-Württemberg
Local history.
By appointment.

KITZINGEN

GERMAN FASCHING MUSEUM
8710 Kitzingen, Bayern
Collection illustrating German carnival. Masks. Costumes. Paintings. Literature relating to carnival.
Sa., Su. 2-5.

MUNICIPAL ARCHIVES
Landwehrstrasse 23, 8710 Kitzingen, Bayern
Local prehistory, history. Handicrafts. Furniture.
W. 10-12; Sa. 3-5; Su. 10-12.

MUNICIPAL MUSEUM
Stadtverwaltung, 8710 Kitzingen, Bayern
Local prehistory, history. Wine-production. Agriculture.
W. 10-12; Sa. 3-5; Su. 10-12.

KLEVE

HAUS KOEKKOEK MUNICIPAL MUSEUM
Kavarinerstrasse, 4190 Kleve, Nordrhein-Westfalen
Flemish and Dutch painting, Middle Ages - 19th century.
Tu.-Su. 3-6.

KNITTLINGEN

FAUST MEMORIAL
Rathaus, 7134 Knittlingen, Baden-Württemberg
Origins and development of the Faust legend. The Faust story in plays, music, films, ballet, Faust-marionettes. Paintings, drawings, prints, illustrating the Faust story.
M.-Sa. 8-5; Su., public holidays on request.

KOBLENZ

MUSEUM OF THE MIDDLE RHINE
Florinmarkt 15, 5400 Koblenz, Rheinland-Pfalz
Regional prehistory, history. Medieval art from the region. 18th-20th century Rhineland paintings. 20th century graphics.
M.-Sa. 10-1, 2.30-6; Su. 10-1.

POSTAL MUSEUM OF THE MIDDLE RHINE
Friedrich Ebert Ring 14, 5400 Koblenz, Rheinland-Pfalz
History of the postal and telecommunications services. Postage stamps. Coins.
W., F. 9-1, 2-6. Other times by appointment. Closed public holidays.

RHINE MUSEUM
Festung Ehrenbreitstein, 5400 Koblenz, Rheinland-Pfalz
Ship-models. Paintings and engravings showing the Rhine landscape and fishing scenes. Hydrography. Methods of water-control and water-extraction.
M.-Th., Sa., Su. 10-6.

STATE COLLECTIONS OF PREHISTORY AND FOLKLORE
Festung Ehrenbreitstein, 5400 Koblenz, Rheinland-Pfalz
Prehistory, early history and folklore of the Koblenz and Montabaur regions.
M.-Th., Sa., Su. 10-6.

KOHLGRUB

REGIONAL MUSEUM
Lüssweg 1, 8112 Kohlgrub, Bayern
Peasant furnishings, household equipment, wood-carving.
M.-Sa. 9-12.

KÖLN

CUSTOMS MUSEUM
1 Nord-Süd Fahrt 1, 5000 Köln, Nordrhein-Westfalen
History of the German Customs and their administration. Smuggling.
M.-Sa. 10-12, 2-4.

CUTLERY MUSEUM
1 Burgmauer 68, 5000 Köln, Nordrhein-Westfalen
World-wide collection of eating implements.
M.-Sa. 9-6.30.

DIOCESAN MUSEUM
1 Roncalliplatz 2, 5000 Köln, Nordrhein-Westfalen
Religious applied art.
M.-Sa. 9-5; Su. 12.30-5.

MUSEUM OF ARTS AND CRAFTS
Eigebsteintorburg, 5000 Köln, Nordrhein-Westfalen
European arts and crafts and textiles, especially 16th century.
Daily 10-5.

MUSEUM OF THE CITY OF COLOGNE
Zeughausstrasse 1-3, 5000 Köln, Nordrhein-Westfalen
History of Cologne. Folklore. History of local trade and commerce. Coins. Drawings, prints, engravings.
Daily 10-5; Th. also 5 p.m.-10.

MUSEUM OF FIRE-FIGHTING
Melchiorstrasse 3, Altstadt, 5000 Köln, Nordrhein-Westfalen
History of fire-fighting methods and equipment.
M.-Sa. 10-5.

MUSEUM OF ORIENTAL ART
Kattenburg 18-24, 5000 Köln, Nordrhein-Westfalen
Art of China, Korea, Japan.
Daily 10-5.

RAUTENSTRANCH-JOEST MUSEUM
Ubierring 45, 5000 Köln, Nordrhein-Westfalen
Art and culture of non-European countries.
Daily 10-5; M., Th. also 7-10.

ROMAN AND GERMANIC MUSEUM
1 Roncallplatz 2, 5000 Köln, Nordrhein-Westfalen
Roman and Germanic material from excavations in Cologne. Special collections of Roman glass and lamps.
Daily 10-5.

SCHNÜTGEN MUSEUM
Cöcilienstrasse 29, 5000 Köln, Nordrhein-Westfalen
Religious art, from the Middle Ages to the 18th century.
Daily 10-5; W. also 7 p.m.-10.

TREASURY
Trankgasse, 5000 Köln, Nordrhein-Westfalen
Religious art. Liturgical objects.
Daily 9-5; Su. 12.30-5.

WALLROF RICHARTZ MUSEUM
An der Rechtschule 7, 5000 Köln, Nordrhein-Westfalen
European art. Paintings, 14th-20th century. Drawings, woodcuts, engravings, prints, 15th-20th century. Sculpture, 19th-20th century.
Daily 10-5; Tu.-F. also 10-10.

KÖLN-BIKKENDORF

HERBIG HAARHAUS MUSEUM OF LACQUERWARE
Vitalisstrasse, 5000 Köln-Bikkendorf, Nordrhein-Westfalen
Ming period Chinese lacquerware. Chinoiserie.
M.-Sa. 9-5; Su. 10-1.

KÖLN-MERHEIM

GERMAN MUSEUM OF HEALTH
Ostmerheimer Strasse 200, 5000 Köln-Merheim, Nordrhein-Westfalen
Collection illustrating the anatomy and working of the human body.
M.-Sa. 9-5.

KOMMERN

LAND MUSEUM OF FOLKLORE
Gielstrasse, 5351 Kommern, Nordrhein-Westfalen
Folk-art and handicrafts of the Rhineland. Pottery. Artistic cast-iron. Furniture-making. Toys. Dolls' houses.
Apr.-Oct., daily 9-6. Nov.-Mar., daily 10-4.

RHINE OPEN-AIR MUSEUM
Gielstrasse, 5351 Kommern, Nordrhein-Westfalen
Rural houses, workshops, mills from the Rhineland.
Apr.-Oct., daily 9-6. Nov.-Mar., daily 10-4.

KÖNIGHEIM

DR. ARTHUR BECHTOLD'S COLLECTION OF PAINTINGS
Rathaus, 7201 Königheim, Baden-Württemberg
16th-19th century European paintings.
By appointment.

KÖNIGSHOFEN

REGIONAL MUSEUM
Im Grobfeld, 8742 Königshofen, Bayern
Local and regional history. Furniture. Costumes.
By appointment.

KÖNIGSLUTTER

KLAGES COLLECTION
Sack 1, 3307 Königslutter, Niedersachsen
In former brewery (1670). Minerals. Fossils.
Tu.-Sa. 9-5; Su. 10-1.

KÖNIGSWINTER

SIEBENGEBIRGE MUSEUM
Klotzstrasse 11, 5330 Königswinter, Niedersachsen
Geology and history of the Siebengebirge region.
Tu.-Sa. 9-5; Su. 10-1.

KONSTANZ

LAKE CONSTANCE MUSEUM OF NATURAL HISTORY
Katzgasse 5-7, 7750 Konstanz, Baden-Württemberg
Geology. Palaeontology. Mineralogy. Botany. Zoology.
Tu.-Sa. 10-12, 3-5; Su. 10-12.

ROSGARTEN MUSEUM
Rosgartenstrasse 3-5, 7750 Konstanz, Baden-Württemberg
Regional prehistory, history. Folk-art. Handicrafts. Coins.
Tu.-Sa. 9-12, 2-5. Su. 10-1.

VON WESSENBERG PICTURE GALLERY
Wessenbergstrasse 41, 7750 Konstanz, Baden-Württemberg
19th-20th century paintings, graphics by local artists. 20th century German drawings.
Tu. 10-12, 2-5; Su. 11-1.

KORBACH

KORBACH REGIONAL MUSEUM
3540 Korbach, Hessen
Geology. Zoology. Regional prehistory, history. Handicrafts. Furniture. Household equipment. Agricultural implements. Costumes. German culture of the Eastern (Polish) territories.
Apr.-Oct., Tu.-Su. 9-12, 2-5.

KRAIBURG

REGIONAL MUSEUM
8261 Kraiburg, Bayern
Local and regional history.
By appointment.

KRANENBURG

KATHARINENHOF MUSEUM
Mühlenstrasse 7, 4193 Kranenburg, Nordrhein-Westfalen
In former convent (1460). 14th-19th century religious art. Paintings, Engravings. Sculpture.
Daily 3.30-5.30.

REGIONAL MUSEUM
Mühlenstrasse, 4193 Kranenburg, Nordrhein-Westfalen
Popular religious art.
Daily 3.30-5.30.

KREFELD

CENTRAL RESEARCH INSTITUTE FOR THE RESTORATION OF HISTORIC TEXTILES
Frankenring 20, 4150 Krefeld, Nordrhein-Westfalen
Collection illustrating methods of restoring old textiles.
Tu.-Su. 10-6.

KAISER WILHELM MUSEUM
Karlsplatz 35, 4150 Krefeld, Nordrhein-Westfalen
16th-20th century European paintings, graphics, sculpture. Special collections of Jugendstil, Rhineland Expressionism, Pop Art and Minimal Art. Chinese scroll paintings.
Daily 10-6.

REGIONAL MUSEUM OF THE LOWER RHINE
12 Burg Linn, 4150 Krefeld, Nordrhein-Westfalen
In castle (1740) and former air-raid shelter. Prehistory, history, folklore of Krefeld and the Lower Rhine.
Daily 11-1, 3-6.

TEXTILE COLLECTION
Frankenring 20, 4150 Krefeld, Nordrhein-Westfalen
World-wide collection of textiles. Costumes. Ornaments. Pattern-books.
Tu.-Th. 10-4; F. 10-2.

KREMPE

TOWN HALL
Am Markt 1, 2209 Krempe, Schleswig-Holstein
Townhall (1570). Furniture. Household equipment. Guilds. Local history.
By appointment.

KRONACH

FRANKENWALD REGIONAL MUSEUM
Festung Rosenberg, 8640 Kronach, Bayern
History of Kronach. 18th-19th century furniture, decorative arts. Craftsmen's workshops. Keys and bolts. Costumes. Ceramics. Glass. Sculpture. Religious art. Paintings, engravings by Onghers and Lorenz Karon.
M.-Sa. 10-5; Su. 10-1.

KRONBERG

FASANERIE PALACE MUSEUM
6411 Kronberg, Hessen
Early 18th century palace, remodelled early 19th century. 17th-19th century furniture, porcelain. Greek and Roman sculpture.
Apr.-Oct., Tu.-Su. 10-12, 2-6.

KRUMBACH

REGIONAL MUSEUM
Heinrich Sinzstrasse 5, 8908 Krumbach, Bayern
In 18th century town-house. Local and regional prehistory, history. Peasant furnishings. Handicrafts. Folk-art. Pewter. Ceramics.
1st Su. in month 10-12.

KULMBACH-PLASSENBURG

GERMAN MUSEUM OF TIN FIGURES
Bauergasse 2, 8650 Kulmbach-Plassenburg, Bayern
Miniature tin-figures. Dioramas.
Apr.-Sept., Tu.-Su. 9-12, 1-5. Oct.-Mar., Tu.-Su. 10-12.30, 1.30-3.30.

MUNICIPAL COLLECTIONS
8650 Kulmbach-Plassenburg, Bayern
Paintings. Butterflies. Weapons.
Apr.-Sept., daily 9-12, 1-5. Oct.-Mar., daily 10-12, 1.30-3.30.

PLASSENBURG
8650 Kulmbach-Plassenburg, Bayern
In 16th century castle. Period rooms. Weapons. Coins.
May-Oct., daily 8-6. Nov.-Apr., 10-12, 2-4.

PLASSENBURG STATE GALLERY
8650 Kulmbach-Plassenburg, Bayern
17th-18th century battle-paintings.
May-Oct., daily 8-6. Nov.-Apr., 10-12, 2-4.

UPPER MAIN REGIONAL MUSEUM
Bauergasse 2, 8650 Kulmbach-Plassenburg, Bayern
Natural sciences. Prehistory. History. Folk-art. Handicrafts. Furniture.
Apr.-Sept., Tu.-Su. 9-12, 1-5. Oct.-Mar., Tu.-Su. 10-12.30, 1.30-3.30.

KÜNTZELSAU

REGIONAL MUSEUM
7118 Küntzelsau, Baden-Württemberg
Local and regional history. Religious life. Costumes. Handicrafts. Implements, tools. Farmhouse kitchen. Sitting-room.
M., F. 1-5.

KÜRNBACH

THATCHED HOUSE
7953 Kürnbach, Baden-Württemberg
House (1663-5). Peasant household equipment. Agricultural implements.
Su., public holidays 10-5.

LABOE

NAVAL MEMORIAL
2304 Laboe, Schleswig-Holstein
Paintings, drawings illustrating history of navigation and the sea-battles in both World Wars. Ship-models.
Daily 9-5.

LADBERGEN

REGIONAL MUSEUM
Hermann Löns. Mailing address: Kattenvenner Strasse 1, 4544 Ladbergen, Nordrhein-Westfalen
Prehistory. Folklore. Handicrafts. Peasant furnishings. Hunting trophies.
Daily 9-12, 3-6.

LADENBURG

LOBDENGAU MUSEUM
Im Bischofshof, 6802 Ladenburg, Nordrhein-Westfalen
Regional prehistory, early history, especially Roman material from excavations at Lopodunum. History of Ladenburg. 18th-19th century folk-art, especially from the Odenwald.
Sa. 2.30-5.30; Su. 11-12.30, 2.30-5.30.

LAGE

LOCAL, REGIONAL AND TILE-MAKING MUSEUM
Schulstrasse 11, 4910 Lage, Nordrhein-Westfalen
Geology. Regional prehistory, history. Handicrafts. Flax-processing, spinning, weaving. Brick and tilemaking.
Tu., Th., Sa., Su. 10-12; Tu. also 3-5; F. 4-5.

LAHR (SCHWARZWALD)

GEROLDSECKER MUSEUM
Im Storchenturm, Marktstrasse, 7630 Lahr (Schwarzwald), Baden-Württemberg
History of Lahr and of the owners of Geroldseck.
Apr.-Sept., M.-Sa. 5-7; Su., public holidays 11-12, 5-7.

LOWER BREISGAU MUSEUM OF PREHISTORY AND EARLY HISTORY
Dinglinger Hauptstrasse 54, 7630 Lahr (Schwarzwald), Baden-Württemberg
Prehistory and early history of the Breisgau region.
W., Sa. 4-6; Su., public holidays 10-12.

MUSEUM IN THE TOWN PARK
Kaiserstrasse 101, 7630 Lahr (Schwarzwald), Baden-Württemberg
Minerals. Birds. History of Lahr. Folklore.
W. 3-5; Sa. 3-6; Su., public holidays 10.30-12.30, 2-5.

LAICHINGEN

LAICHINGEN CAVE MUSEUM
Beurer Steig 47, 7903 Laichingen, Baden-Württemberg
Stalactites. Cave animals. Calcified objects.
May-Oct., daily 10-5. Nov.-Apr., Su. 10-5.

LAMPERTHEIM

REGIONAL MUSEUM
6840 Lampertheim, Hessen
Local and regional history.
M.-Sa. 9-12, 2-5; Su. 2-5.

LANDAU (ISAR)

REGIONAL MUSEUM
Höckingerstrasse 9, 8380 Landau (Isar), Bayern
Local and regional history. Folk-art. Peasant furniture, implements, tools. Pottery. Coins.
Daily 8-6.

LANDAU IN DER PFALZ

LANDAU REGIONAL MUSEUM
Sudring 20, 6740 Landau in der Pfalz, Rheinland-Pfalz
In former Town Arsenal. Regional prehistory, history. Medieval pottery. Furniture. Handicrafts.
M., Tu., Th. 10-12, 2-5; Su. 10.30-12.

LANDSBERG AM LECH

HERHOMER COLLECTION
Altes Rathaus, 8910 Landsberg am Lech, Bayern
Local history. Paintings.
M.-Sa. 9-5; Su. 10-1.

TOWN MUSEUM
8910 Landsberg am Lech, Bayern
Bronze Age archaeology. Local history. Handicrafts.
M.-Sa. 9-5; Su. 10-1.

LANDSHUT

LANDSHUT RESIDENCE
Altstadt 79, 8300 Landshut, Bayern
In former palace (1536-43) of Ludwig X of Bavaria. 18th century furniture, decorative arts. 16th-18th century paintings.
Apr.-Sept., daily 9-12, 1-5. Oct.-Mar., Tu.-Su. 9-12, 1-4.

TOWN AND DISTRICT MUSEUM
Altstadt 79, 8300 Landshut, Bayern
Local and regional prehistory, history. Furniture. Decorative arts. Paintings. Sculpture. Ceramics. Folklore.
Daily 9-12, 1-4.

TRAUSNITZ CASTLE
8300 Landshut, Bayern
Renaissance furniture, decorative arts. Tapestries.
Oct.-Mar., Tu.-Su., daily 9-12, 1-4. Apr.-Sept., daily 9-12, 1-5.30.

LANDSTUHL

NAUSTEIN CASTLE
6790 Landstuhl, Rheinland-Pfalz
Local history.
On request.

LANGENARGEN

MONTFORT PALACE
7994 Langenargen, Baden-Württemberg
Local and regional history.
On request.

LANGENAU

REGIONAL MUSEUM
7907 Langenau, Baden-Württemberg
Regional prehistory, history, folklore. Peasant furniture, household equipment. Guilds. Handicrafts. Costumes.
By appointment.

LANGENBURG

PALACE MUSEUM
7183 Langenburg, Baden-Württemberg
Regional history. Furniture. Decorative arts.
On request.

HALLIG LANGENESS

HONKENSWARF FRISIAN ROOM
2251 Hallig Langeness, Schleswig-Holstein
Frisian furniture, household equipment. Costumes.
By appointment.

LANGERWEHE

POTTERY MUSEUM
5163 Langerwehe, Nordrhein-Westfalen
History and techniques of local pottery-making. 18th century furniture, decorative arts.
Tu.-F. 9-12, 2-5; Sa. 9-12; Su. 10-12.

LAUDA

REGIONAL MUSEUM
Philipp Adam Ulrich Haus, 6970 Lauda, Baden-Württemberg
History of Lauda. Handicrafts. Folklore. Wine-production.
Su. 3-5. Other times by appointment.

LAUDENBACH

PALACE MUSEUM
8761 Laudenbach, Bayern
In wing of 18th century palace. Furniture. Decorative and applied arts. Sculpture.
Tu.-Th., 3-6. Other times by appointment.

LAUENBURG

ELBE SHIPPING MUSEUM
Elbstrasse 59, 2058 Lauenburg, Schleswig-Holstein
Local history. History of Elbe navigation.
Tu., Th., Sa. 10-1, 2-4.30.

LAUF AN DER PEGNITZ

CASTLE
Schlossinsel 1, 8560 Lauf an der Pegnitz, Bayern
Local history. Coats of Arms.
W., Sa., by appointment.

MUNICIPAL COLLECTIONS
Spitalstrasse 5, 8560 Lauf an der Pegnitz, Bayern
In 14th century castle. Local and regional history. Handicrafts. Industry. Guilds. 15th century sculpture. Drawings, engravings. Folklore.
By appointment.

LAUINGEN

REGIONAL HOUSE
Herzog Georgstrasse 57, 8882 Lauingen, Bayern
Regional prehistory, history. 15th-18th century paintings. 18th-19th century views. Folk-art.
Mar.-Oct., Su., public holidays 10-12.

LAUPHEIM

REGIONAL MUSEUM
Schillerstrasse 3, 7958 Laupheim, Baden-Württemberg
Local and regional history.
On request.

LAUTERBACH

HOHLHAUS MUSEUM
Stadtschloss, 6420 Lauterbach, Hessen
In 18th century palace. History of Lauterbach. Material from local excavations. Folklore. Furniture. Decorative arts. Costumes. Coins. Porcelain. Pewter. Craftsmen's tools and equipment. Oriental collection.
Tu.-F. 9-11, 2-4; Sa. 2-4; Su. 11-12.

LEER

REGIONAL MUSEUM
Neue Strasse 14, 2950 Leer, Niedersachsen
Regional prehistory, history. Natural history. East Frisian furniture, household equipment. Shipping. Paintings. Drawings. Engravings.
Tu.-Th., 10-12; Su. 11-12.30.

LEHRTE

MUNICIPAL MUSEUM
3160 Lehrte, Niedersachsen
Local and regional history.
M.-Sa. 9-5; Su. 10-1.

LEIHGESTERN

HÜTTENBERG REGIONAL MUSEUM
Altes Rathaus, 6301 Leihgestern, Hessen
In former Town Hall (1772). Peasant furniture, household equipment. Costumes.
M.-F. 8-12, 1.30-4.30.

LEINFELDEN BEI STUTTGART

MUSEUM OF THE ASSOCIATED ALTENBURG AND STRALSUND PLAYING CARD FACTORIES
Fasanenweg 5, 7022 Leinfelden bei Stuttgart, Baden-Württemberg
World-wide collection illustrating history of playing-cards.
M.-F. 8-4.

LEINSWEILER

SLEVOGTHOF NEUCASTEL
6741 Leinsweiler, Hessen
Former home of the painter, Max Slevogt (d.1932). Works by Slevogt.
On request.

LEMBRUCK

DÜMMER MUSEUM
2841 Lembruck, Niedersachsen
Prehistoric material from local excavations. Regional wildlife, especially birds, fish. Crafts. History of watersports.
Feb. 16 - Apr. 30, Oct. 1 - Dec. 15, daily 9-6. May 1 - Sept. 30, 9-8.

LEMBECK ÜBER DORSTEN

LEMBECK PALACE MUSEUM
4274 Lembeck über Dorsten, Nordrhein-Westfalen
17th century palace. 18th-19th century furniture. Glass. Porcelain. 17th century Flemish tapestries.
Daily 10-6.

LEMGO

HOUSE OF THE WITCHES' MAYOR
Breitestrasse 19, 4920 Lemgo, Nordrhein-Westfalen
Local history. Material relating to 16th-17th century witchcraft-trials. Crafts. Guilds. 16th-19th century maps. Coins. Incunabulae. Oriental antiquities.
Tu.-F., Su. 9-1, 3-6.

LEMKENHAFEN

MUSEUM OF WINDMILLS AND AGRICULTURE
2449 Lemkenhafen, Niedersachsen
In windmill (1787). History of windmills. Milling equipment. Agricultural implements. Craftsmen's tools. Local history. Botany.
June-Sept., M., W., Sa. 2-6. Other times by appointment.

LENDRINGSEN

REGIONAL ROOMS
Villa von Dücker, 5757 Lendringsen, Nordrhein-Westfalen
Local and regional geology, archaeology, history. Household equipment. Craftsmen's tools. Stoves. Folk-art. Maps. Coins.
Su. 11-12.30. Other times by appointment.

LENNGRIES

REGIONAL MUSEUM
Rathausplatz 1, 8172 Lenngries, Bayern
Local and regional history. Costumes. Agricultural implements. Craftsmen's tools.
M.-F. 9-5.

LEONBERG

MUSEUM OF GEOLOGY AND PALAEONTOLOGY
Glemseckstrasse 36, 7250 Leonberg, Baden-Württemberg
Geology. Palaeontology. Mineralogy.
W. 2-6; Sa. 9-12, 2-6; 1st and 2nd Su. in month, 9-12, 2-6. Other times by appointment.

LETMATHE

REGIONAL MUSEUM
Am Langen Kummer, 5868 Letmathe, Nordrhein-Westfalen
Prehistory. Geology. Folklore. History of regional industries.
Su. 11-12.

LETMATHE-GRÜNE

MUSEUM OF THE STUDENTS' ARCHAEOLOGICAL AND SPELEOLOGICAL SOCIETY
Düsingstrasse 2, 5868 Letmathe-Grüne, Nordrhein-Westfalen
Fossils. Skeletons and bones of prehistoric animals. Prehistoric tools.
Su. 11-1. Other times by appointment.

LETMATHE-OESTRICH

OESTRICH REGIONAL MUSEUM
Grürmannsheiderstrasse, 5868 Letmathe-Oestrich, Nordrhein-Westfalen
Peasant kitchen, living-room, bedroom. Household equipment. Clothing. Craftsmen's tools. Agricultural equipment. Geology. Mineralogy. Archaeology.
Su., public holidays 11-12.30.

LEUTKIRCH

REGIONAL MUSEUM
Kornhaus, Marktplatz, 7970 Leutkirch, Baden-Württemberg
Building (c.1500). Regional history. Industry, especially glass, linen. Early 19th century furniture, decorative arts.
May-Oct., M., W., Su. 9-5. Nov.-Apr., 1st Su. in month, 9-5.

LEVERKUSEN

MUNICIPAL MUSEUM
Schloss Morsbroich, 5090 Leverkusen, Nordrhein-Westfalen
20th century paintings, drawings, prints, sculpture.
M.-F. 10-8; Su. 11-5.

LICHTENBERG (ODENWALD)

LICHTENBERG PALACE MUSEUM
Lichtenberg, 6101 Odenwald, Hessen
History of N.W. Odenwald.
M.-Th., Sa., Su. by appointment.

LICHTENSTEIN

PALACE MUSEUM
Schloss, 7410 Lichtenstein, Baden-Württemberg
Paintings. Glass. Weapons. 14th-16th century painted glass.
Mar.-Nov., daily 9-5.

LIESBORN

BECKUM DISTRICT MUSEUM
Abteiring 8, 4725 Liesborn, Nordrhein-Westfalen
In former Abbey (1735). Prehistory, history of the Beckum district. Collection illustrating development of the Cross as a symbol. Crafts. Contemporary paintings, sculpture.
Tu.-Sa. 9-12, 2-6; Su. 2-6.

LIMBURG (LAHN)

LIMBURG CATHEDRAL TREASURY
Rossmarkt, 6250 Limburg (Lahn) Hessen
12th-20th century religious art.
By appointment.

LIMBURG DIOCESAN MUSEUM
Burg, 6250 Limburg (Lahn), Hessen
Religious art from churches in the diocese of Limburg.
M.-Sa. 9-5.

MISSION MUSEUM
Wiesbadener Strasse 1, 6250 Limburg (Lahn), Hessen
Mission history. Ethnographical and zoological material from S. Africa, the Cameroons, N.W. Australia, N. and S. America.
Daily 8-8.

REGIONAL MUSEUM
Fahrgasse, 6250 Limburg (Lahn), Hessen
Regional history. Local industries. Crafts.
M.-Sa. 9-5; Su. 10-1.

LINDAU

MUNICIPAL ART COLLECTIONS
Marktplatz 6, 8990 Lindau, Bayern
Local prehistory, history. 15th-20th century paintings, drawings, engravings, sculpture. Furniture. Decorative arts. Coins. Seals.
Tu.-Sa. 9.30-12, 1.30-5; Su. 10-12.

LINDERHOF

PALACE
8103 Linderhof, Bayern
Collections illustrating history of the times of Ludwig II of Bavaria.
May-Sept., 8.30-5.30; Oct.-Apr., 9-12, 1-4.

LINGEN

DISTRICT MUSEUM
Nordstrasse 9A, 4450 Lingen, Niedersachsen
Local and regional history.
On request.

LIPPSTADT

DISTRICT MUSEUM
Rathausstrasse 13, 4780 Lippstadt, Nordrhein-Westfalen
Prehistory, history of the Lippstadt district. 14th-19th century religious art. Folklore. Agricultural implements, equipment.
Tu.-Sa. 10-12, 3-6; Su. 10-1.

LÖFFINGEN

REGIONAL MUSEUM
Schulhaus, Löffingen, Baden-Württemberg
History of Löffingen and its region. Craftsmen's tools. Costumes. Weapons. Coins.
W., Su. 10.30-11.30.

LOHR AM MAIN

REGIONAL AND SPESSART MUSEUM
Schlossplatz 1, 8770 Lohr am Main, Bayern
In 13th century castle. History of Lohr and the Spessart region. Furniture. Household equipment. 16th-19th century glass. 18th century mirrors. 17th-19th century pottery. Weapons. Shipbuilding.
Apr.-Oct., W., Su., public holidays 10-12.

LÖRRACH

REGIONAL MUSEUM
Burghof 5, 7850 Lörrach, Baden-Württemberg
Geology. Mineralogy. Regional prehistory, history. 17th-20th century paintings. Cartography. Coins. Weapons. Pottery. Porcelain.
Su. 10-12; W. 10-8.

LORSCH

HOUSE OF THE ELECTORAL PRINCES
Kloster, 6143 Lorsch, Baden-Württemberg
Carolingian architectural items. Sculpture.
By appointment.

REGIONAL MUSEUM
Rathaus, 6143 Lorsch, Baden-Württemberg
Regional prehistory, history. Roman material from local excavations. Memorial collection of the former German district of Steinberg, in Sudetenland.
M.-Sa. 9-5; Su. 10-1.

LOSSBURG

BLACK FOREST MUSEUM
7291 Lossburg, Baden-Württemberg
In 19th century granary. Peasant furnishings. Craftsmen's tools. Black Forest clocks, 1650 onwards. Costumes. Paintings. Weapons.
Daily 9-8.

LÜBBECKE

DISTRICT MUSEUM
Burgmannshof, Markt 19, 4990 Lübbecke, Nordrhein-Westfalen
Local and regional archaeology, history. Fossils. Craftsmen's tools. Peasant furniture. Costumes.
M.-Sa. 9-5; Su. 10-1.

LÜBECK

BEHNHAUS MUSEUM
Königstrasse 11, 2400 Lübeck, Schleswig-Holstein
In 18th century house. 19th-20th century German paintings.
Oct.-Mar., Tu.-Sa. 10-4; Su. 11-4. Apr.-Sept., Tu.-Sa. 10-5; Su. 11-5.

ETHNOGRAPHY COLLECTION
Duvekenstrasse 21, 2400 Lübeck, Schleswig-Holstein
Ethnography of Africa, Far East.
By appointment.

HOLSTENTOR MUSEUM
Holstentor, 2400 Lübeck, Schleswig-Holstein
Early historical material from local excavations. History of Lübeck, illustrated by models and views. Ship-models.
Oct.-Mar., Tu.-Sa. 10-4; Su. 11-4. Apr.-Sept., Tu.-Sa. 10-5; Su. 11-5.

MUNICIPAL COLLECTION OF COINS AND MEDALS
Mühlendamm 1-3, 2400 Lübeck, Schleswig-Holstein
Coins and medals of Lübeck and its region.
M.-F. 8-4.

NATURAL HISTORY MUSEUM
Mühlendamm 1-3, 2400 Lübeck, Schleswig-Holstein
Geology. Palaeontology. Mineralogy. Botany and zoology of Schleswig-Holstein. Dioramas.
Apr.-Sept., Tu.-Sa. 10-5; Su. 11-5. Oct.-Mar., Tu.-Sa. 10-4; Su. 11-4.

ST. ANNEN MUSEUM
St. Annen Strasse 15, 2400 Lübeck, Schleswig-Holstein
Medieval art by Lübeck artists. Lübeck furniture, decorative arts.
Oct.-Mar., Tu.-Sa. 10-4. Su. 11-4. Apr.-Sept., Tu.-Sa. 10-5. Su. 11-5.

ST. CATHERINE'S CHURCH
Königstrasse, 2400 Lübeck, Schleswig-Holstein
Collection of casts of medieval sculpture.
May-Oct., by appointment.

STUDY COLLECTION OF THE CITY OF LÜBECK DEPARTMENT OF PREHISTORY AND EARLY HISTORY
Miesenring 8, 2400 Lübeck, Schleswig-Holstein
Early historical and medieval material from Lübeck exhibitions.
By appointment.

LUCHOW

REGIONAL MUSEUM
Dr. Lindemann Strasse 27, 3130 Luchow, Niedersachsen
Regional prehistory, history. Costumes. Folklore.
Su. 2-6. Other times by appointment.

LÜDENSCHEID

MUNICIPAL MUSEUM
Liebigstrasse 11, 5880 Lüdenscheid, Nordrhein-Westfalen
Local and regional history. Maps. Button collection. Industry. Handicrafts. Early airship engine, built in Lüdenscheid. Train from the former Lüdenscheid-Altena line. Agricultural implements.
Apr.-Sept., Tu.-Sa. 10-5; Su. 11-5. Oct.-Mar., Tu.-Sa. 10-4; Su. 11-4.

LÜDINGHAUSEN

VISCHERING CASTLE
4710 Lüdinghausen, Nordrhein-Westfalen
13th century castle, with later remodelling. Furnishings. Paintings. Portraits. Weapons. Hunting equipment. Local history.
Tu.-Sa. 10-5; Su. 10-1.

LUDWIGSBURG

PALACE MUSEUM
7140 Ludwigsburg, Baden-Württemberg
In former palace (1704-33). Local history. Paintings. Baroque art. Ludwigsburg porcelain.
Tu.-Sa. 10-4; Su. 10-1.

REGIONAL MUSEUM
Brenzstrasse 21, 7140 Ludwigsburg, Baden-Württemberg
Local and regional history. Württemberg antiquities. Drawings. Engravings.
M.-Sa. 10-5; Su. 10-1.

STATE MUSEUM OF NATURAL HISTORY
Arsenalplatz 3, 7140 Ludwigsburg, Baden-Württemberg
Geology. Palaeontology. Mineralogy. Botany. Zoology. Entomology.
M.-F. 10-4; Su. 10-12.

LUDWIGSHAFEN

K. O. BRAUN REGIONAL MUSEUM
Rathaus, 6700 Ludwigshafen-Oppau, Rheinland-Pfalz
Prehistory. Furniture. Decorative arts. Folklore. Folk-art. Weapons.
Su. 10-12, 2-5.

CITY MUSEUM
Rottstrasse 17, 6700 Ludwigshafen, Rheinland-Pfalz
Prehistory. History of Ludwigshafen and the Palatinate. History of chemistry. Coins.
M.-F. 10-4; Su. 10-12.

MUNICIPAL ART COLLECTIONS
Raschighaus, Jubiläumstrasse 5, 6700 Ludwigshafen, Rheinland-Pfalz
Expressionist and contemporary art.
M.-F. 10-1, 3-7; Sa. 10-1, 3-5; Su. 11-4.

SCHILLER HOUSE MUSEUM
Schillerstrasse 6, 6700 Ludwigshafen-Oggersheim, Rheinland-Pfalz
Schiller's former home. Portraits, letters, memorabilia of the poet. First editions of his works.

LUDWIGSSTADT

LAUENSTEIN CASTLE
8642 Ludwigsstadt, Bayern
Local and regional history.
Apr.-Sept., daily 9-6. Oct.-Mar., 1-4.

LÜGDE

REGIONAL MUSEUM
Am Markt 1, 3283 Lügde, Nordrhein-Westfalen
Local and regional prehistory, history.
By appointment.

LÜNE

ART COLLECTIONS OF LÜNE MONASTERY
Kloster, 3140 Lüne, Niedersachsen
Religious art. 15th-16th century carpets, rugs.
By appointment.

LÜNEBURG

MUSEUM OF THE PRINCIPALITY OF LÜNEBURG
Wandrahmstrasse 10, 3140 Lüneburg, Niedersachsen
Local and regional prehistory, history. Religious art. Peasant rooms. Early scientific equipment. Bookprinting and bookbinding. Cabinet of rarities.
Tu.-F. 10-4; Sa., Su. 10-1.

REGIONAL MUSEUM
3140 Lüneburg, Niedersachsen
Local and regional history.
Tu.-F. 10-5; Sa., Su. 10-1.

LÜNEN

MUNICIPAL MUSEUM
Coppenberger Strasse 62, 4628 Lünen, Nordrhein-Westfalen
Regional geology. Coal fossils. History of Lünen. Castironwork. Westphalian pottery.
Th. 3-5. Other times by appointment.

MUSEUM OF ART AND CULTURAL HISTORY OF DORTMUND
Schloss Coppenberg, 4628 Lünen, Nordrhein-Westfalen
12th century castle, remodelled 1816-31. History of Dortmund. Folk-art of Westphalia. 18th-19th century paintings, crafts.
Apr.-Oct., M.-Th., Sa., Su. 10-6.

MAINBURG

HOLLEDAU REGIONAL MUSEUM
Rathaus, Marktplatz 1, 8302 Mainberg, Bayern
Local and regional prehistory, history. Furniture. Decorative arts. Handicrafts. Folk-art.
By appointment.

MAINHARDT

REGIONAL MUSEUM
Hauptstrasse, 7173 Mainhardt, Baden-Württemberg
Roman material from local excavations.
By appointment.

MAINZ

BOOK-BINDERS' MUSEUM
Liebfrauenplatz 5, 6500 Mainz, Rheinland-Pfalz
History of the production of books.
Tu.-Sa. 9.30-1, 2.30-5.

CATHEDRAL AND DIOCESAN MUSEUM
Domstrasse 3, 6500 Mainz, Rheinland-Pfalz
Religious art from the Cathedral and from churches in the Diocese of Mainz. 15th-16th century tapestries.
M.-Sa. 10-12, 2-5.

CENTRAL MUSEUM OF ROMAN AND GERMANIC ANTIQUITIES
Kurfürstliches Schloss, Ernst Ludwig Platz 2, 6500 Mainz, Rheinland-Pfalz
European prehistory. Roman and Greek antiquities.
Tu.-Su. 10-1, 3-5.

COIN CABINET
Stadtbibliothek, Rheinallee 3B, 6500 Mainz, Rheinland-Pfalz
Coins and medals, especially Roman, medieval, and from Mainz.
M.-F. 9-12.30, 2-6; Sa. 9-12.30.

GUTENBERG MUSEUM
Liebfrauenplatz 5, 6500 Mainz, Rheinland-Pfalz
15th-20th century book-printing, binding. Gutenberg's printing shop. 19th-20th century posters, prints, engravings.
May-Oct., Tu.-Sa. 10-1, 3-6; Su., public holidays 10-1. Nov.-Apr., Tu.-Sa. 9.30-1, 2.30-5, Su., public holidays 10-1.

KUPPERBERG COLLECTION
Kupperberg Terrasse 19, 6500 Mainz, Rheinland-Pfalz
History of champagne and of the Kupperberg Company. Old cellars. 19th-20th century engravings. Wine-casks. Glasses.
Apr. 15 - Oct. 15, 9.30-11.30, 2.30-3.30.

LAND MUSEUM OF THE MIDDLE RHINE
Grosse Bleiche 49-51, 6500 Mainz, Rheinland-Pfalz
Prehistory of the Middle Rhine area. Roman and Frankish material. Medieval paintings, sculpture. Flemish, Dutch, French paintings. Porcelain.
Tu.-Sa. 10-1, 3-6; Su., public holidays 10-1.

NATURAL HISTORY MUSEUM
Reichsklarastrasse 1, 6500 Mainz, Rheinland-Pfalz
Geology and palaeontology of the Mainz area. Mineralogy. Botany. Zoology. Ice-Age fossils.
Tu.-Sa. 10-1, 3-6; Su., public holidays 10-1.

PRINZ JOHANN GEORG MUSEUM
Binger Strasse 26, 6500 Mainz, Rheinland-Pfalz
Late Greek and Roman and early Christian antiquities. Icons.
M.-F. 10-12, 2-5. Other times by appointment.

RESEARCH INSTITUTE FOR THE HISTORY OF PAPER
Liebfrauenplatz 5, 6500 Mainz, Rheinland-Pfalz
History of paper and its manufacture.
M.-F. 10-12, 2-5.

MALENTE-GREMSMÜHLEN

REGIONAL HOUSE
Sebastian Kneipp Strasse, 2427 Malente-Gremsmühlen, Schleswig-Holstein
Craftsmen's workshops, tools, equipment. Agricultural implements.
May-Aug., daily 9-6.

MANNHEIM

MANNHEIM CITY HALL OF THE ARTS
Moltkestrasse 9, 6800 Mannheim, Baden-Württemberg
19th-20th century paintings, sculpture, drawings, engravings, prints.
Tu.-Th., Sa. 10-1, 2-5; F. 2-8; Su. 10-5.

MANNHEIM PALACE
6800 Mannheim, Baden-Württemberg
Period rooms. History of the Palace and of Mannheim.
May-Oct., daily 8-6. Nov.-Apr., daily 9-5.

REISS CITY MUSEUM
1 Zeughaus, 6800 Mannheim, Baden-Württemberg
In former Arsenal (1777-9). Prehistory, history of Mannheim and its region. Medieval and baroque sculpture. 17th-18th century paintings. Folk-art. Frankenthal porcelain. Faience. 17th-18th century furniture, glass, silver. World-wide collection of ethnography. History of the theatre in Mannheim.
Tu.-Th., Sa. 10-1, 2-5; F. 2-8. Su. 10-5.

MARBACH

NATIONAL SCHILLER MUSEUM AND GERMAN LITERARY ARCHIVES
Schillerhöhe, 7142 Marbach, Baden-Württemberg
18th-19th century manuscripts and books by Swabian writers. Portraits.
May-Oct., daily 8-6. Nov.-Apr., daily 9-5.

SCHILLER'S BIRTHPLACE
Nikolastorstrasse 31, 7142 Marbach, Baden-Württemberg
Collections illustrating the life and work of Friedrich von Schiller (d.1805).
May-Oct., daily 8-6. Nov.-Apr., daily 9-5.

MARBURG (WÜRTTEMBERG)

ETHNOGRAPHICAL COLLECTION OF MARBURG UNIVERSITY
Gutenbergstrasse 18, 7142 Marburg, Baden-Württemberg
World-wide ethnographical collections.
Daily 8-12, 3-5, on request.

MARBURG (HESSEN)

PHILIPPS UNIVERSITY COLLECTION OF GREEK AND ROMAN SCULPTURE AND CASTS
Ernst von Hülsen Haus, Biegenstrasse, 3550 Marburg, Hessen
Greek and Roman minor art, especially pottery, terracottas. Casts of Greek and Roman sculpture.
Apr.-Sept., daily 10-1, 3-5. Oct.-Mar., daily 11-1, 3-5.

UNIVERSITY COLLECTION OF MATERIAL RELATING TO RELIGION
Schloss 1, 3550 Marburg, Hessen
Art and liturgical objects of the non-Christian religions.
M.-F. 9-4 on request.

UNIVERSITY OF MARBURG MUSEUM OF ART AND CULTURAL HISTORY
Biegenstrasse 11, 3550 Marburg, Hessen
History of North Hessen. 19th-20th century paintings, drawings, engravings, prints.
Apr.-Sept., daily 10-1, 3-5. Oct.-Mar., daily 11-1, 3-5.

MARGRETHAUSEN

REGIONAL MUSEUM
7471 Margrethausen, Baden-Württemberg
Local and regional history.
M.-Sa. 9-5; Su. 10-1.

MARKTL

REGIONAL MUSEUM
8261 Marktl, Bayern
Local history. Handicrafts.
By appointment.

MARKTOBERDORF

COLLECTIONS OF LOCAL LIFE AND HISTORY
Rathaus, Eberle Kögl Strasse 20, 8952 Marktoberdorf, Bayern
Folk-art and ethnography of the East Allgau.
By appointment.

RIESENGEBIRGE COLLECTION
St. Martins Heim, Eberle Kögl Strasse, 8952 Marktoberdorf, Bayern
Folk-art from the Riesengebirge.
By appointment.

MARL

REGIONAL MUSEUM
Am Mühlenwall, Museumsgasse 14, 4370 Marl, Nordrhein-Westfalen
In former 16th century mill-house. Geology. Mineralogy. Regional prehistory, history. Folklore. Furniture. Costumes. Weapons.
M.-Sa. 10-12, 3-5; Su. 10-12.

MARNE

SKAT CLUB MUSEUM
Museumsstrasse 2, 2222 Marne, Schleswig-Holstein
Local prehistory, history. Folklore.
By appointment.

MARQUARTSTEIN

MARQUARTSTEIN CASTLE
8215 Marquartstein, Bayern
Period rooms. History of Marquartstein and of the Castle.
By appointment.

MASSING

FARM MUSEUM OF LOWER BAVARIA
Schusteröderhof, 8332 Massing, Bayern
Peasant tools, furniture, household and farm equipment.
M.-F. 10-12, 2-6; Sa., Su., public holidays 2-6.

MAULBRONN

ART COLLECTIONS
Kloster, 7133 Maulbronn, Baden-Württemberg
In former Cistercian abbey. Medieval religious art.
On request.

MAXBERG

SOLENHOFER COMPANY MUSEUM
8831 Maxberg, Bayern
History of lithography. Use of Solenhof stone for building, sculpture, lithography. Geology. Botany. Zoology.
Daily 8-12, 1-5.

MAYEN

EIFEL MUSEUM
Genovevaburg, 5440 Mayen, Rheinland-Pfalz
Geology, history and folklore of the Eifel region.
Tu.-Sa. 9-1, 3-6; Su., public holidays 10-1.

MEERSBURG

DROSTE MUSEUM
Fürstenhäuschen, 7758 Meersburg, Baden-Württemberg
House (1595, remodelled 1843). Furnishings, manuscripts and personal possessions of the writer, Annette Droste zu Hülshoff, and her family.
Apr.-Oct., 9-12.30, 2-6.

MEERSBURG PALACE
7758 Meersburg, Baden-Württemberg
Castle (700, remodelled 16th century). Furniture. Decorative arts. Paintings. Sculpture. Weapons. Hunting trophies. Annette Droste zu Hülshoff (d.1848) memorial collection.
Daily 9-6.

NEW PALACE
7758 Meersburg, Baden-Württemberg
History of the palace. Period rooms. Local history.
Daily 9-6.

MELDORF

DITHMARSCH FARMHOUSE MUSEUM
Jungfernstieg 4A, 2223 Meldorf, Schleswig-Holstein
Peasant implements, tools, furniture, household equipment.
Apr.-Sept., Tu.-Sa. 9-6; Su. 10-4.

DITHMARSCH LAND MUSEUM
Bütjestrasse 4, 2223 Meldorf, Schleswig-Holstein
History of the Dithmarsch region. Peasant furniture, household equipment. Costumes. Ornaments. Toys. Views of the area. Religious art. Shipping.
Tu.-Sa. 9-6; Su. 10-4.

MELLE

GRÖNEGAU MUSEUM
Wallgarten 2, 4520 Melle, Niedersachsen
History of Melle. Peasant furnishings, implements. Handicrafts. Costumes. Silver. Porcelain. Liturgical objects.
Tu.-Su. 3-5.

MEMMINGEN

MUNICIPAL MUSEUM
Zangmeisterstrasse 8, 8940 Memmingen, Bayern
In mid-18th century palace. Prehistory. History of Memmingen, illustrated by 17th-19th century models and 16th-20th century views. Guilds. Crafts. Religious art. 17th-19th century paintings. Faience. Dolls.
May-Nov., 1st and 3rd Su. in month 10-12, 2-4; Tu. 10-12.

REGIONAL ROOM
Zangmeisterstrasse 8, 8940 Memmingen, Bayern
History of the Freudenthal district and of the Teutonic Order.
May-Nov., 1st and 3rd Su. in month, 10-12, 2-4.

MENDEN

MENDEN REGIONAL MUSEUM
Marktplatz 3, 5750 Menden, Nordrhein-Westfalen
Local geology, mineralogy, prehistory. Folklore. 16th-19th century furniture, household equipment.
Tu.-F. 9-12, 3-5; Sa. 9-12; Su. 11-12.

MENGEN

REGIONAL MUSEUM
In der alten Post, 7947 Mengen, Baden-Württemberg
Local and regional history.
On request.

METTINGEN

TÜÖTTEN MUSEUM
Gasthof Telsemeyer, Sunderstrasse 2, 4532 Mettingen, Nordrhein-Westfalen
History of 17th century pedlars of materials and equipment for household flax industry. Peasant furniture, household equipment.
M.-Th., Sa., Su., 9-dusk.

METTMANN

NEANDERTAL MUSEUM
Düsseldorfer Strasse 26, 4020 Mettmann, Nordrhein-Westfalen
Prehistory.
Apr.-Sept., Tu.-Su. 10-6. Oct.-Mar., Tu.-Su. 10-5.

MICHELAU

BASKETRY AND WICKERWORK MUSEUM
Bismarckstrasse 4, 8626 Michelau, Bayern
Basketry and wickerwork.
M.-F., daily 9-12, 2-5.

MICHELSTADT

ODENWALD MUSEUM
Braunstrasse 7, 6120 Michelstadt, Hessen
In 16th century inn. Furniture. Household equipment. Handicrafts. Folklore. Guilds. Toys. Weapons. Coins. Clocks.
May-Oct., daily 9-12, 2-5.

REGIONAL MUSEUM
Kellerei, 6120 Michelstadt, Hessen
Peasant furniture, household equipment. Handicrafts. Guilds. Folklore.
On request.

MIESBACH

REGIONAL MUSEUM
8160 Miesbach, Bayern
Peasant furnishings. Handicrafts. Folklore.
By appointment.

MILTENBERG

REGIONAL MUSEUM
8760 Miltenberg, Bayern
House (1590). Regional prehistory, history. Furnishings. Ceramics. Spessart glass. Pewter.
Tu.-Su. 10-12.

MINDELHEIM

MINDELHEIM REGIONAL MUSEUM
Hauberstrasse 2, 8948 Mindelheim, Bayern
Regional prehistory, history. Crafts. Applied art. 15th-18th century paintings, sculpture. Furniture. Household equipment. Costumes. Folk-art.
Daily 9-11, 2-4, on request.

MINDEN

CATHEDRAL TREASURY AND ARCHITECTURAL MUSEUM OF THE OLD CATHEDRAL
Grossen Domhof 10, 8950 Minden, Nordrhein-Westfalen
9th-12th century Cathedral destroyed in 1939-45 war, subsequently rebuilt. Religious art, liturgical items. Architectural details from the old cathedral.
By appointment.

MINDEN MUSEUM OF HISTORY, ETHNOLOGY AND REGIONAL STUDIES
Rutterstrasse 23-27, 4950 Minden, Nordrhein-Westfalen
In 17th century house. Geology. Palaeontology. Prehistory. History of Minden and its region. Panorama of Battle of Minden. 17th-18th century peasant furniture, household equipment, costumes. Craftsmen's workshops. Folk-lore.
Tu. 10-1, 3-7.30; W.-Sa. 10-1, 3-5; Su. 10.30-1.

MINDEN TOWN LOCKS EXHIBITION HALL
Wasser- und Schiffahrtsamt Am Hohen Ufer 1, 4950 Minden, Nordrhein-Westfalen
Models of local locks and docks. Maps. Examples of goods carried on local canal and river system.
Apr.-Oct., daily 9-5.

MITTENWALD

REGIONAL MUSEUM AND MUSEUM OF VIOLIN MAKING
Ballenhausgasse 3, 8102 Mittenwald, Bayern
Violin-making in the Mittenwald region. Musical instruments. Peasant furniture, household equipment.
Dec. 15-Mar. 31, May 15-Oct. 10, M.-F. 10-12, 2-5.

MOERS

COUNTY MUSEUM
Schloss, 4130 Moers, Nordrhein-Westfalen
Local and regional history.
Tu.-F. 10-1, 3-5; Sa., Su. 10-1.

MOLLENFELDE

BREAD AND CAKE MUSEUM
Altes Forsthaus, 3511 Mollenfelde, Niedersachsen
History and techniques of baking.
M.-Sa. 9-5; Su. 10-1.

MÖLLN

REGIONAL MUSEUM
Am Markt 2, 2410 Mölln, Schleswig-Holstein
Regional prehistory, history. Crafts. Folklore. Eulenspiegel collection.
May 1-Oct. 15, Tu.-F., Su. 9-12, 2-5; Sa. 9-12, 1.30-3.30.

MÖNCHENGLADBACH

MUNICIPAL MUSEUM
Bismarckstrasse 97, 4050 Mönchengladbach, Nordrhein-Westfalen
Local prehistory, history. Crafts. Textiles. 20th century art.
Tu.-F. 10-1, 3-5; Sa., Su. 10-1.

MONSCHAU

MUSEUM OF THE SCHEIBLER FOUNDATION
Laufenstrasse 10, 5108 Monschau, Nordrhein-Westfalen
In the 18th century Rotes Haus. Furniture. Decorative arts.
Mar.-Nov., Tu.-Su. 10-12, 2-5.

MONTABAUR

DISTRICT MUSEUM
Kehreinstrasse, 5430 Montabaur, Rheinland-Pfalz
Furniture. Decorative arts. Ceramics. Pewter. Weapons.
Tu.-F. 9-4; Sa., Su. 10-1.

MOOSBURG

REGIONAL MUSEUM
Stadtplatz 13, 8052 Moosburg, Bayern
Regional prehistory, history. Crafts. Folk-art. Religious art. Peasant furnishings. Weapons.
Su. 10-12. Other times by appointment.

MÖRNSHEIM

MUSEUM OF PETRIFIED OBJECTS
8837 Mörnsheim, Bayern
At site of discovery of the bird-ancestor, Archae Opteryx. Fossils. Petrified birds, animals, plants.
By appointment.

MOSBACH

REGIONAL MUSEUM
Rathaus, 6950 Mosbach, Baden-Württemberg
Roman material from local excavations. Folklore. Crafts.
By appointment.

MÜHLACKER

MÜHLACKER REGIONAL MUSEUM
Stuttgarter Strasse 5, 7130 Mühlacker, Baden-Württemberg
Local and regional history.
M.-F. 9-5; Sa., Su. 10-1.

MÜHLDORF

DISTRICT MUSEUM
Fragnergasse 7, 8260 Mühldorf, Bayern
Prehistory, history of the Mühldorf district. Crafts. Folk-art. Weapons. Inland shipping.
Daily 9-4.

MÜLHEIM

MUNICIPAL MUSEUM
Leineweberstrasse 1, 4330 Mülheim, Nordrhein-Westfalen
History of Mülheim. Crafts. Costumes.
On request.

MÜNCHBERG

REGIONAL MUSEUM
8660 Münchberg, Bayern
Regional history. Crafts. Industries.
M.-F. 9-5; Sa., Su. 10-1.

MÜNCHEN

ARCHITECTURAL COLLECTION OF THE TECHNICAL UNIVERSITY
2 Arcisstrasse 21, 8000 München, Bayern
Architectural features, especially from buildings in S. Germany.
On request.

BAVARIAN NATIONAL MUSEUM
22 Prinzregentenstrasse 3, 8000 München, Bayern
9th-20th century arts and crafts. Glass paintings. Ivories. Miniatures. 18th century sketches in oils. Clocks and automata. Costumes. Porcelain. Faience. Folklore. Folk-art.
Apr.-Sept., Tu.-F. 9.30-4.30. Oct.-Mar., Tu.-F. 9-4; Sa., Su., 10-4.

BAVARIAN STATE COLLECTIONS OF GENERAL AND APPLIED GEOLOGY
19 Luisenstrasse 37, 8000 München, Bayern
Geology of the alps and of the Munich region. Geology of former German colonies in E. and S.W. Africa.
By appointment.

BAVARIAN STATE COLLECTION OF PALAEONTOLOGY AND HISTORICAL GEOLOGY
2 Richard Wagner Strasse 10, 8000 München, Bayern
Rocks, especially of Bavaria. Palaeontology. Palaeozoology. Fossils, including specimens from S. Africa, S. America.
M.-F. 8-4.

BAVARIAN STATE SCIENCE COLLECTIONS
19 Menzinger Strasse 71, 8000 München, Bayern
Natural sciences.
Tu.-Su. 9.30-4.30.

BMW MUSEUM
13 Leichenauer Strasse 76, 8000 München, Bayern
Vehicles made by BMW. Motor-cycles. Passenger cars. Sports cars. Racing-cars. Aero-engines.
M.-F. 8-3.30. Guided tours of the BMW works, daily 9-1.

CITY COLLECTION OF MUSICAL INSTRUMENTS
2 St. Jakobs Platz 1, 8000 München, Bayern
World-wide collection of musical instruments.
Tu.-Su. 9-4.

EXHIBITION COLLECTIONS OF THE BAVARIAN STATE LIBRARY
19 Schloss Nymphenburg, 8000 München, Bayern
Portraits, especially of scientists and technologists. Manuscripts. Commemorative coins.
Daily 9-6.

FILM AND PHOTOGRAPHY MUSEUM IN MUNICH CITY MUSEUM
2 St. Jakobs Platz 1, 8000 München, Bayern
History of film-making, film-techniques, and of photography.
Tu.-Su. 9-4.30.

GERMAN MUSEUM
Museum Insel, 8000 München, Bayern
Natural sciences and technology. Geology. Mining. Petroleum. Transport. Shipbuilding. Aviation. Physics. Chemistry. Printing. Textiles. Agriculture. Photography. Astronomy. Planetarium.
Daily 9-5.

GERMAN MUSEUM OF BREWING
2 St. Jakobs Platz 1, 8000 München, Bayern
History of brewing, especially in Germany.
Tu.-Su. 9-4.

GLYPOTHEK
2 Königsplatz 3, 8000 München, Bayern
Greek and Roman sculpture.
Tu.-Su. 10-4; W. also 7 p.m.-9.

HUNTING MUSEUM
2 Neuhauserstrasse 53, 8000 München, Bayern
Hunting trophies, equipment. Wildlife dioramas. Paintings, engravings, drawings, coins with hunting themes.
Tu.-Su., by appointment.

KRAUSS-MAFFEI COMPANY ART EXHIBITIONS AND COLLECTION
Krauss-Maffei Strasse 2, 8000 München, Bayern
Contemporary paintings, sculpture.
M.-F. 8-4.

LENBACH HOUSE MUNICIPAL GALLERY
19 Luisenstrasse 33, 8000 München, Bayern
12th-20th century paintings by Munich artists. Works by Lenbach.
Tu.-Su. 9-4.30.

MINERALOGY COLLECTION
19 Luisenstrasse 37, 8000 München, Bayern
Minerals, especially of Germany and the surrounding countries.
By appointment.

MODERN ART MUSEUM
Arabellapark, Bogenhausen, 8000 München, Bayern
20th century paintings, graphics.
Daily 9-4.30.

MUNICH CITY MUSEUM
2 St. Jakobs Platz 1, 8000 München, Bayern
History of Munich. Paintings. Sculpture. Porcelain. Applied art. Costumes. Fashions. Toys. Portraits. Views of Munich. Posters. Coins. Medals.
Tu.-Su. 9-4.30.

MUSEUM OF CASTS OF CLASSICAL SCULPTURE
2 Meiserstrasse 10, 8000 München, Bayern
Casts of Greek and Roman sculpture.
Tu.-Th. 10-12. Other times by appointment.

THE NEW COLLECTION
22 Prinzregentenstrasse 3, 8000 München, Bayern
19th-20th century applied and industrial art. Industrial design.
Tu.-Su. 10-5.

NEW GALLERY
19 Haus der Kunst, Westflügel, Prinzregentenstrasse 1, 8000 München, Bayern
19th century European paintings, sculpture.
Daily 9-4.30.

NEW STATE GALLERY
19 Haus der Kunst, Westflügel, Prinzregentenstrasse 1, 8000 München, Bayern
20th century European paintings, sculpture.
Daily 9-4.30.

OLD GALLERY
2 Barerstrasse 27, 8000 München, Bayern
14th-18th century European paintings, especially German, Flemish, Dutch, Spanish.
Daily 9-4.30; Tu., Th. also 8 p.m.-10.

PROBST COLLECTION
Ebenböckstrasse 11, Pasing, 8000 München, Bayern
Prints, drawings, engravings illustrating the topography and cultural history of Munich.
W., F., Su. 9-4.30.

PUPPET THEATRE COLLECTION
2 St. Jakobs Platz 1, 8000 München, Bayern
Theatre puppets. Shadow-puppets. Mechanical figures. Posters, prints, drawings relating to puppetry.
Tu.-Su. 9-4.30.

RESIDENCE MUSEUM
22 Max Joseph Platz 3, 8000 München, Bayern
In former Residence of the Dukes of Bavaria. 17th-19th century furnishings. Silver. Porcelain. Majolica. Liturgical items. Carpets. Paintings. Sculpture.
Apr.-Sept., Tu.-Sa. 9-5. Oct.-Mar., 10-4.

ROYAL STABLES
19 Schloss Nymphenburg, 8000 München, Bayern
Ceremonial carriages. State-coaches. Sleighs. Harness.
Summer: daily 9-5. Winter: daily 10-4.

SCHACK GALLERY
19 Prinzregentenstrasse 9, 8000 München, Bayern
19th century German paintings.
Daily 9-4.30.

STATE ANTHROPOLOGICAL COLLECTION
2 Richard Wagner Strasse 10-11, 8000 München, Bayern
Collections illustrating human development. Morphology.
By appointment.

STATE BOTANICAL COLLECTION
19 Menzingerstrasse 67, 8000 München, Bayern
Herbaria of plants of the whole world.
By appointment.

STATE COLLECTIONS OF CLASSICAL ART
2 Königsplatz 1, 8000 München, Bayern
Greek, Etruscan, Roman bronze and terracotta statuettes. Greek vases. Greek, Etruscan gold ornaments. Greek and Roman glass.
Tu.-Su. 10-4; W. also 7 p.m.-9.

STATE COLLECTION OF COINS
2 Residenzstrasse 1, 8000 München, Bayern
Coins. Medals. Tokens. Engraved stones.
Tu.-Sa. 10-4; Su., public holidays 10-1.

STATE COLLECTION OF EGYPTIAN ART
2 Meiserstrasse 10, 8000 München, Bayern
Statues. Reliefs. Monuments. Papyri. Coffins. Mummies. Grave gifts. Artistic objects of glass, metal. Ceramics.
Tu.-Su. 10-4; Tu. also 8 p.m.-10.

STATE GRAPHICS COLLECTION
2 Meiserstrasse 10, 8000 München, Bayern
15th-20th century drawings, woodcuts, engravings, prints.
Tu.-Su. 9-4.30.

STATE MUSEUM OF ETHNOGRAPHY
22 Maximilianstrasse 42, 8000 München, Bayern
Art and handicrafts of non-European peoples.
Tu.-Su. 9.30-4.30.

STATE PREHISTORICAL COLLECTION
22 Prinzregentenstrasse 3, 8000 München, Bayern
Prehistory and early history, especially of Bavaria.
M.-F. 8-4.

STUCK MUSEUM OF ART NOUVEAU
80 Prinzregentenstrasse 60, 8000 München, Bayern
In home of the artist, Franz von Stuck (d.1928). Paintings. Graphics. Applied art. Furniture. Glass.
Tu.-Su. 10-5.

THEATRE MUSEUM
22 Galeriestrasse 4A, 8000 München, Bayern
History of the theatre throughout the world. Models. Paintings, drawings, photographs of performances, stage-design. Costumes and costume-design. Manuscripts. Recordings. Portraits.
Tu.-Sa. 10-4; Su. 10-1.

TREASURY OF THE MUNICH RESIDENCE
22 Max Joseph Platz 3, 8000 München, Bayern
11th-19th century European goldsmiths' work. Jewels. Carved ivory.
Tu.-Sa. 9-5; Su. 10-1.

VALENTIN MUSEUM
24 Tal 43, 8000 München, Bayern
Works by Kurt Valentin and Liesl Karlstadt.
Daily 11-5.30.

WERNER VON SIEMENS INSTITUTE FOR THE HISTORY OF THE HOUSE OF SIEMENS
2 Prannerstrasse 10, 8000 München, Bayern
Development of electro-technics, illustrated by the history of the firm of Siemens.
M.-F. 9-4; Sa., Su. 10-2.

MÜNNERSTADT

REGIONAL MUSEUM
Rathaus, 8732 Münnerstadt, Bayern
Regional prehistory, history. Household equipment. Sculpture. Folk-art.
By appointment.

MÜNSINGEN

MÜNSINGEN REGIONAL MUSEUM
Schlosshof 2, 7420 Münsingen, Baden-Württemberg
Local and regional history.
M.-Sa. 10-5; Su. 10-1.

MÜNSTER

ARCHAEOLOGICAL MUSEUM
Fürstenberghaus, Domplatz 20-22, 4400 Münster, Nordrhein-Westfalen
Greek and Roman ceramics, sculpture. Egyptian and Cypriot ceramics.
Tu., Th. on request.

CATHEDRAL MUSEUM AND TREASURY
Domplatz 32, 4400 Münster, Nordrhein-Westfalen
Religious art. 13th-17th century sculpture.
M.-Sa. 9-5.

HALL OF THE PEACE
Prinzipalmarkt, 4400 Münster, Nordrhein-Westfalen
In rebuilt 14th century Town Hall, where peace was concluded between Spain and the Netherlands (1648). Portraits. Weapons. Armour. Archives.
M.-F. 9-5; Sa. 9-4; Su. 10-1.

LAND MUSEUM OF ART AND CULTURAL HISTORY
Domplatz 10, 4400 Münster, Nordrhein-Westfalen
Local and regional history. Maps. Views. Architectural drawings. Portraits. Crafts. Religious art. Medieval paintings, sculpture. 19th-20th century German paintings. Coins.
Tu.-Sa. 10-1, 2-5; Su. 10-1. W. also 5 p.m.-8.

LAND MUSEUM OF NATURAL HISTORY
Himmelreichallee 50, 4400 Münster, Nordrhein-Westfalen
Mammals. Birds. Insects. Snails.
Mar.-Oct., Tu.-Su. 10-6; M. 1-6. Nov.-Feb., Tu.-Su. 10-5.

LAND MUSEUM OF PREHISTORY AND EARLY HISTORY
Rothenburg 30, 4400 Münster, Nordrhein-Westfalen
Prehistory and early history of Westphalia.
Tu.-Su. 10-1, 2-5; Su. 10-1.

MILL MUSEUM
Sentruper Strasse, 4400 Münster, Nordrhein-Westfalen
In late 18th century mill. Milling history and equipment.
Apr. 1-Oct. 31, 9.30-12.30, 2.30-5.30. Nov. 1-Mar. 31, 2.30-5.30.

MUSEUM OF CRYSTALS AND ROCKS
Hüfferstrasse 1, 4400 Münster, Nordrhein-Westfalen
Rocks. Minerals. Ores. Synthetic crystals.
W. 3-6; Su. 10.30-12.30.

UNIVERSITY OF MÜNSTER MUSEUM OF ARCHAEOLOGY
Domplatz 20-22, 4400 Münster, Nordrhein-Westfalen
Greek vases. Greek, Roman, Egyptian, Cypriot minor art. Casts of Greek and Roman sculpture.
Tu., Th., by appointment.

UNIVERSITY OF MÜNSTER MUSEUM OF GEOLOGY AND PALAEONTOLOGY
Pferdegasse 3, 4400 Münster, Nordrhein-Westfalen
General, applied and historical geology. Complete mammoth skeleton. Palaeontology.
Su. 11-12.30. W. 3-5. Other times by appointment.

MÜNSTERSCHWARZACH

BENEDICTINE ABBEY
8711 Münsterschwarzach, Bayern
Religious art. Local history.
By appointment.

MURRHARDT

CARL SCHWEIZER MUSEUM
Am Klostersee, 7157 Murrhardt, Baden-Württemberg
Dioramas of European wildlife. Local histor.
Apr.-Oct., M.-Sa. 11-12, 4-6; Su., public holidays 11-6.

MÜSEN

MINING AND REGIONAL MUSEUM
Hauptstrasse 145, 5912 Müsen, Nordrhein-Westfalen
Mining in Siegerland. Folklore.
4th Su. in month, 10.30-12.

NEBEL

AMRUNER MUSEUM
2279 Nebel, Schleswig-Holstein
In store-rooms of 1771 windmill. Regional botany, zoology, prehistory, history.
M.-W. 10-12; Th.-Su. 3-6.

NECKARMÜHLBACH

GUTTENBERG CASTLE
6951 Neckarmühlbach, Baden-Württemberg
15th century castle. 15th century manuscripts, incunabula. Family possessions. Paintings of hunting scenes.
Easter-Oct. 31, daily guided tours, 10-4.30.

NECKARSULM

GERMAN BICYCLE MUSEUM
7101 Neckarsulm, Baden-Württemberg
In former castle of the Teutonic Order. Collections illustrating development of the bicycle and motorcycle.
Mar.-Nov., daily 9-12, 1.30-5.

NEHEIM-HÜSTEN

GERMAN MUSEUM OF BIRDCAGES
Cäcilienstrasse 13, 5760 Neheim-Hüsten, Nordrhein-Westfalen
Old bird-cages. Paintings, engravings, showing bird-cages.
M.-F. 8-5.

LIGHTING MUSEUM
Gebr. Kaiser U. Co., Mohnestrasse 55, 5760 Neheim-Hüsten, Nordrhein-Westfalen
History of artificial light.
M.-F. 8-12, 2-4.

NENNIG

ROMAN VILLA
6641 Nennig, Saarland
On site of large Roman villa. Mosaic. Archaeological material. Decorated Frankish coffins.
Apr.-Sept., Tu.-Su. 8.30-12, 1-6. Oct.-Mar., Tu.-Su. 9-12, 1-4.30.

NENTERSHAUSEN

TANNENBERG MUSEUM
Burg Tannenberg, 6441 Nentershausen, Saarland
Regional history. Folk-art.
On request.

NEUBURG

REGIONAL MUSEUM
Amalienstrasse 4-9, 8858 Neuburg, Bayern
Regional prehistory, history. Crafts. Paintings. Sculpture. Applied art. Furniture. Household equipment. Weapons.
Su., public holidays 10-12, 2-4. Other times by appointment.

STATE GALLERY
Amalienstrasse A9, 8858 Neuburg, Bayern
17th century Flemish and German paintings.
Tu.-Su. 10-4.

NEUENBURG

RAUCHKATE REGIONAL MUSEUM
2934 Neuenburg, Niedersachsen
In 17th century farmhouse. Peasant furnishing, household equipment. 18th-19th century craftsmen's tools and agricultural implements.
May 15-Sept. 15, Su. 4-6.

NEUENSTEIN

HOHENLOHE MUSEUM
Schloss Neuenstein, 7113 Neuenstein, Baden-Württemberg
Palace (1555-64). Roman and Celtic material from local excavations. Regional history. 16th-19th century furnishings, decorative arts. Minerals. Natural history. Engravings. Coins. Seals.
Daily 9-5.

NEUMARKT

REGIONAL MUSEUM
8430 Neumarkt, Bayern
Local and regional history.
On request.

NEUMÜNSTER

TEXTILE MUSEUM
Parkstrasse 17, 2350 Neumünster, Schleswig-Holstein
History of spinning, weaving. Bronze-and Iron-Age clothing.
M.-F. 7.30-5.30; Su. 10-1.

NEUNBURG VOR WALD

DISTRICT MUSEUM
8462 Neunburg vor Wald, Bayern
Regional prehistory, history. Weapons. Furniture. Guilds. Wrought-iron. Glass paintings.
July-Sept., W., Su. 10-12.

NEUNHOF

KNOBLAUCHLAND REGIONAL MUSEUM
Am Schlosshof, 8501 Neunhof, Bayern
Local history. Crafts. Costumes. Folk-art.
Mar.-Oct., Su. 1-5. Other times by appointment.

NEUNHOF PALACE
8501 Neunhof, Bayern
16th century palace. Old hunting equipment. Household equipment.
May-Sept., Sa., Su. 10-4.

NEUSCHWANSTEIN

PALACE
8959 Neuschwanstein, Bayern
Palace (1869-86) of Ludwig II of Bavaria. Murals. Furniture. Decorative arts.
May-Oct., daily 8.30-5.30. Nov.-Apr., 10-4.

NEUSES

RÜCKERT MEMORIAL
8631 Neuses, Bayern
Study of Friedrich Rückert (d.1866), with his books, furniture and personal possessions.
Daily 9-5.

NEUSS

CLEMENS SELS MUSEUM
Im Obertor, 4040 Neuss, Nordrhein-Westfalen
Roman material from local excavations. History of Neuss. 14th-19th century paintings, sculpture. Folk-art.
Tu.-Sa. 10-5; Su. 10-1.

NEUSTADT AN DER AISCH

MUSEUM OF THE LOCAL HISTORY SOCIETY
Untereschlossgasse 8, 8530 Neustadt an der Aisch, Bayern
In former Albrecht Achilles Palace. Natural history. Local

and regional history. Crafts.
2nd Su. in month, 9.30-11.30.

NEUSTADT AN RÜBENBERGE

DISTRICT MUSEUM
3057 Neustadt am Rübenberge, Niedersachsen
Regional prehistory, history. Handicrafts. Furniture. Household equipment.
On request.

NEUSTADT AN DER WALDNAAB

LOCAL MUSEUM
Altes Schloss, 8482 Neustadt an der Waldnaab, Bayern
Local history, folklore, folk-art.
M.-Sa. 9-5; Su. 9-1.

NEUSTADT BEI COBURG

MUSEUM OF COSTUMES AND DOLLS
Hindenburgplatz, 8632 Neustadt bei Coburg, Bayern
Neustadt toys. Costume-puppets from European and non-European countries.
Daily 8-6.

NEUSTADT (HOLSTEIN)

DISTRICT MUSEUM
Kremper Tor, 2430 Neustadt, Schleswig-Holstein
Local geology, prehistory, history. Furnishings. Fishing. Shipping.
May-Oct., M.-Sa. 2-5; Su. 10-12.

NEUSTADT (ODENWALD)

BREUBERG MUSEUM
Burg Breuberg, 6129 Neustadt, Odenwald
In castle (1613). Regional history. Folklore.
Daily 9-5.

NEUSTADT (SCHWARZWALD)

REGIONAL ROOMS
Scheuerlenstrasse 31, 3057 Neustadt, Schwarzwald
Local and regional history. Peasant furnishings, household equipment. Clock-maker's workshop. Painted glass.
W.-F. 2-5.

NEUSTADT-WEINSTRASSE

NATURAL HISTORY MUSEUM
Am Weissenhaus 1, 6730 Neustadt-Weinstrasse, Rheinland-Pfalz
Regional geology, botany, wildlife.
M.-Sa. 9-5; Su. 10-1.

REGIONAL AND WINE MUSEUM
Villa Böhm, Maximilianstrasse 25, 6730 Neustadt-Weinstrasse, Rheinland-Pfalz
Local and regional history. History of wine-production.
M.-Sa. 9-5; Su. 10-1.

NEU-ULM

NEU-ULM REGIONAL MUSEUM
Augsburgerstrasse 15, 7910 Neu-Ulm, Bayern
Regional prehistory, history. Furnishings. Folk-art.
By appointment.

NEUWIED

DISTRICT MUSEUM
Raiffelsenplatz, 5450 Neuwied, Rheinland-Pfalz
Roman and Frankish material from local excavations. 18th century furniture, clocks. Medieval paintings, religious art. Artistic cast-iron. Folk-art. Coins.
M.-F. 10-1, 2-5; Su. 10.30-1.

NEUWEIER

PALACE
7571 Neuweier, Baden-Württemberg
Local and regional history.
On request.

NIEBÜLL

NIEBÜLL FRISIAN MUSEUM
Osterweg 76, 2260 Niebüll, Schleswig-Holstein
Natural history. Prehistory. Folklore.
By appointment.

NIEDERALTAICH

BENEDICTINE ABBEY
8351 Niederaltaich, Bayern
Religious art and monuments of Lower Bavaria.
Daily 8-12, 1.30-5.30.

NIEDERBÜHL-FÖRCH

FAVORITE PALACE
7551 Niederbühl-Förch, Baden-Württemberg
Palace (1711). Early 18th century furniture, decorations. Glass. Ceramics.
Mar.-Nov., daily 8-12, 2-5.

NIEDERMARSBERG

REGIONAL MUSEUM
Lillerstrasse, 3558 Niedermarsberg, Nordrhein-Westfalen
Geology. Fossils. Prehistory. Models of Celtic and Saxon earthworks. Regional history. Religious art. Coins, including examples made by Marsberg mint.
W. 10-12, by appointment.

NIENBERGE

DROSTE MUSEUM
4401 Nienberge, Nordrhein-Westfalen
Rooms lived in by the writer, Annette von Droste-Hülshoff (d.1848). Collection of sections of timber-trees.
Daily 9-12, 2.30-4.45.

NIENBURG

MUSEUM OF THE COUNTIES OF HOYA, DIEPHOLZ, WÖLPE
Leinestrasse 4, 3070 Nienburg, Niedersachsen
Prehistoric and early historical material from local sites. History of Nienburg and its region.
On request.

NÖRDLINGEN

TOWN MUSEUM
Vordere Gerbergasse 1, 8860 Nördlingen, Bayern
In former hospital (1518-64). Local prehistory, history. 15th-19th century paintings. Late Gothic panel-paintings. Crafts. Peasant furnishings. Costumes.
Tu.-Su. 9-12, 2-5.

NORDEN

REGIONAL MUSEUM
Altes Rathaus, Am Markt 36, 2980 Norden, Niedersachsen
In former Town Hall (1540). Views of Old Norden. Furnishings, domestic equipment.
May-Oct., M. 9-12; Tu.-Th. 3-5.

NORDESEIF

FISHERMAN'S HOUSE MUSEUM
Nordeseif
In Replica of fisherman's house. Life and history of the Frisian Islands. History of the local fishing industry. Molluscs.
May-Oct., daily 10-12, 3-6.

NORTHEIM

NORTHEIM MUSEUM
Markt 13-14, 3410 Northeim, Niedersachsen
Local and regional history.
Tu.-Sa. 9-5; Su. 10-1.

NÜMBRECHT

MUSEUM OF THE OBERBERG REGION
Schloss Homburg, 5223 Nümbrecht, Nordrhein-Westfalen
In medieval castle, with 17th century additions. Regional geology, botany, zoology, prehistory, history. 18th century furniture, decorative arts. Heraldry. Weapons. Coins.
Apr.-Nov., daily 9.30-6. Other times by appointment.

NÜRNBERG

CITY ART COLLECTIONS
Lorenzer Strasse 32, 8500 Nürnberg, Bayern
19th-20th century paintings, drawings, engravings, prints, sculpture.
Tu.-F. 10-5; Sa., Su. 10-1.

DUNGEON PRISON IN THE OLD TOWN HALL
Rathausplatz 2, 8500 Nürnberg, Bayern
Medieval interrogation prison. Cells. Torture-chamber.
May 2- Sept. 30, M.-F. 10-4; Sa., Su. 10-1.

ALBRECHT DÜRER HOUSE
Albrecht Dürer Strasse 39, 8500 Nürnberg, Bayern
15th century house, formerly home of Dürer, with his personal possessions. Works by Dürer.
Daily 9-11, 1-5.

FEMBO HOUSE CITY MUSEUM
Burgstrasse 15, 8500 Nürnberg, Bayern
History of Nürnberg. 16th-19th century furnishings. Paintings. Prints. Views and plans of the city.
Daily 9-5.

GERMAN NATIONAL MUSEUM
Kornmarkt 1, 8500 Nürnberg, Bayern
German art and cultural history. Paintings. Engravings. Sculpture. Crafts. Tapestries. Peasant furniture. Costumes. Musical instruments. Toys. Weapons. Hunting equipment. Coins. Medals.
Apr.-Sept., M.-Sa. 10-5; Su. 10-4. Oct.-Mar., Tu.-Sa. 10-4; Su. 10-1; Th. also 8 p.m.-9.30.

MAN AND NATURE MUSEUM
Gewerbemuseumsplatz 4, 8500 Nürnberg, Bayern
Geology. Speleology. Natural history. Local prehistory, early history. Ethnography.
M., Tu., F., 1-6.45; Th. 9-1; Sa. 9-12.

MUSEUM OF APPLIED ARTS
Gewerbemuseumsplatz 2, 8500 Nürnberg, Bayern
Ceramics. Porcelain. Silver. Jewellery. Glass. Metalwork. Oriental art.
Tu.-F. 10-5; Sa., Su. 10-1.

NEUPERT PIANO MUSEUM
Kornmarkt 1, 8500 Nürnberg, Bayern
Development of the piano, 16th-19th century.
Apr.-Sept., M.-Sa. 10-5; Su. 10-4. Oct.-Mar., Tu.-Sa. 10-4; Su. 10-1; Th. 8-9.30.

NÜRNBERG IMPERIAL CASTLE
Auf der Burg 13, 8500 Nürnberg, Bayern
Castle (1050). History of the castle. Furnishings. Paintings. Weapons.
May-Oct., daily 9-5. Nov.-Apr., daily 10-12, 1-4.

NÜRNBERG MUSEUM OF TRANSPORT
Lessingstrasse 6, 8500 Nürnberg, Bayern
Railway and postal history. Original and model locomotives. Locomotive building and repair. Model railway systems. Operating equipment. Postage stamps.
Oct.-Mar., M.-Sa. 10-4; Su. 10-1.

TOY MUSEUM
Karlstrasse 13, 8500 Nürnberg, Bayern
Medieval - 20th century Nürnberg toys.
Apr.-Sept., Tu.-Sa. 10-1, 2-5; Su. 10-4. Oct.-Mar., Tu.-Sa. 10-12, 2-4; Su. 10-1.

OBERAMMERGAU

OBERAMMERGAU REGIONAL MUSEUM
8103 Oberammergau, Bayern
14th-18th century sculpture. Woodcarving. Folk-art. Cribs. Painted glass.
May-Sept., daily 9-12, 2-6.

OBERGÜNZBURG

REGIONAL MUSEUM
Altes Pfarrhaus, 8953 Obergünzburg, Bayern
Local history. Crafts. Peasant implements. Religious art. 18th century paintings, sculpture. Folk-art. Costumes.
By appointment.

SOUTH SEAS COLLECTION
Pfarrstadel, 8953 Obergünzburg, Bayern
Zoology and ethnology of the S. Pacific, India and Sumatra.
By appointment.

OBERHAUSEN

MUNICIPAL GALLERY
Schloss, Sterkrader Strasse 48, 4200 Oberhausen, Nordrhein-Westfalen
Contemporary paintings, sculpture, glass.
Tu., Th., F., 10-1, 2-5; W. 10-1, 4-7; Sa., Su. 10-5.

OBERHEINING

BRECHELBAD MUSEUM
8229 Oberheining, Bayern
Peasant crafts, tools, household equipment. Folk-art.
On request.

OBERKAUFUNGEN

REGIONAL MUSEUM
Leipziger Strasse 45, 3504 Oberkaufungen, Hessen
In 11th century monastery. Local and regional history. Agricultural implements. Craftsmen's tools. Mining. Glass-blowing. Folklore. Coins.
9-4.30, on request.

OBERKIRCHEN

MINERALOGICAL MUSEUM
Bahnhofstrasse 3, 6691 Oberkirchen, Nordrhein-Westfalen
Mineralogy.
Daily 9-6.

OBERLAHNSTEIN

BODEWIG MUNICIPAL MUSEUM
5420 Oberlahnstein, Rheinland-Pfalz
Local prehistory, early history. History of Oberlahnstein.
M.-Sa. 9-5; Su. 10-1.

OBERNBURG

ROMAN HOUSE
Mainstrasse 1, 8753 Obernburg, Bayern
Roman material from local excavations.
M., W.-F., 8-12; Tu. 2-5.

OBERNDORF

REGIONAL MUSEUM
Kameralstrasse 8, 7238 Oberndorf, Baden-Würthemberg
History of Oberndorf. Household equipment. Craftsmen's tools. Weapons.
W., Sa. 2-4; Su. 10-12.

OBERNZELL

REGIONAL MUSEUM
Schloss, 8391 Obernzell, Bayern
In 15th-16th century castle. History of Obernzell. Models and displays showing history, techniques and products of local graphite industry.
M.-Sa. 9-12. Other times by appointment.

OBER-RAMSTADT

REGIONAL MUSEUM
Altes Rathaus, Grafengasse, Kirchstrasse, 6105 Ober-Ramstadt, Hessen
In old Town Hall (1732). Regional prehistory, early history, especially Roman. Local history. Crafts. Dollmaker's tools. Memorabilia of the physicist and writer, G. C. Lichtenberg (d.1799).
1st and 3rd Su. in month, 10-1.

OBERRIEXINGEN

ROMAN WINE CELLAR
Weilerstrasse 12, 7141 Oberriexingen, Baden-Württemberg
In former wine-cellar of Roman villa. Pictures and documents illustrating Roman production of wine. Objects discovered during excavation of Roman graves.
By appointment.

OBERSTDORF

REGIONAL MUSEUM
Oststrasse 13, 8980 Oberstdorf, Bayern
Regional prehistory, history. Crafts. 18th century peasant furnishings, costumes. Folk-art. Paintings, drawings, especially by 19th century Oberstdorf artists.
May-Nov., daily 8-12. Other times by appointment.

OCHSENFURT

TOWN MUSEUM
Hauptstrasse 42, 8703 Ochsenfurt, Bayern
In 14th century bridge-fortification. Rocks. Crafts. Weapons. Costumes.
Daily 10-12, 2-6.

ÖHRINGEN

WEYGANG MUSEUM
Karlsvorstadt, 7110 Öhringen, Baden-Württemberg
Roman material from local excavations. Peasant living-room, furnishings. Crafts. Pewter. Faience.
Tu.-Su. 9-11, 2-4. Closed 2nd Su. in month.

OELDE

GÖTZ ARCHIVES
Brüggenfeld 11, 4740 Oelde, Nordrhein-Westfalen
Documents, prints and other material illustrating practice of magic.
By appointment.

OERLINGHAUSEN

GERMANIC FARMHOUSE OPEN-AIR MUSEUM
Barkhauser Berg, 4811 Oerlinghausen, Nordrhein-Westfalen
Reconstruction of Germanic farmhouse (c.A.D.100), and the contents. Material from site excavation of the farmhouse and farmbuildings.
Apr.-Sept. daily 8-12.30, 1.30-6. Oct. 1-31, daily 1.30-5.

REGIONAL MUSEUM
Barkhauser Berg, 4811 Oerlinghausen, Nordrhein-Westfalen
Regional prehistory, especially Mesolithic, Neolithic.
Apr.-Sept. daily, 8-12.30, 1.30-6. Oct. 1-31, daily 1.30-5.

OESTRICH-LETMATHE

REGIONAL MUSEUM
6227 Oestrich-Letmathe, Hessen
Local and regional history.
On request.

OETTINGEN

REGIONAL MUSEUM
Rathaus, Schlossstrasse 36, 8867 Oettingen, Bayern
Regional prehistory, history. Crafts. Guilds. Ceramics. Furnishing, especially Biedermeier. Weapons.
May-Sept., Su. 10.45-12. Other times by appointment.

OEVENTROP

SOUTH SEAS MUSEUM
Missionshaus, 5777 Oeventrop, Rheinland-Pfalz
Botany and wildlife of the S. Pacific. Costumes. Ornaments. Witchcraft. Ancestor worship.
By appointment.

OFFENBACH

GERMAN MUSEUM OF LEATHER
Frankfurter Strasse 86, 6050 Offenbach, Hessen
Production of leather. Leather-work. Tools and equipment. Leather wall-hangings.
Daily 10-5.

GERMAN SHOE MUSEUM
Frankfurter Strasse 86, 6050 Offenbach, Hessen
History of footwear. Mexican leatherwork.
Daily 10-5.

KLINGSPOR MUSEUM
Herrnstrasse 80, 6050 Offenbach, Hessen
20th century book production, calligraphy. Bindings. Graphics.
Daily 10-12; M.-F. also 3-5.

OFFENBURG

HOUSE OF THE KNIGHTS MUSEUM
Ritterstrasse 10, 7600 Offenburg, Baden-Württemberg
House (1775). Regional natural history, prehistory, history. Crafts. Folk-art. Hunting trophies. Ethnology, especially of the former German colonies.
W., Sa. 2-4; Su. 10-12.

MUNICIPAL GALLERY
Ritterstrasse 10, 7600 Offenburg, Baden-Württemberg
18th-20th century paintings by Offenburg artists.
W., Sa. 2-4; Su. 10-12.

OLDENBURG

LAND MUSEUM OF ART AND CULTURAL HISTORY
Schloss, 2900 Oldenburg, Niedersachsen
Regional history. Greek, Roman minor art. Medieval sculpture, applied art. 15th-17th century European paintings. 20th century paintings, crafts. Folklore. Coins. Medals.
Tu., Th., F., Sa., Su. 10-1; W. 3-5.

MUNICIPAL ART COLLECTIONS
Raiffeisenstrasse 32-3, 2900 Oldenburg, Niedersachsen
Greek, Roman minor art. Paintings, graphics, sculpture by Oldenburg artists. 20th century paintings, sculpture, prints, drawings.
Sa., Su. 10-1; Tu.-F. 10-1, 3-5; W. also 5-7.30.

STATE MUSEUM OF NATURAL HISTORY AND PREHISTORY
Damm 40, 2900 Oldenburg, Niedersachsen
Geology. Palaeontology. Mineralogy. Botany. Zoology. Geography of N.W. Lower Germany, shown by models, maps, aerial photographs. Ethnology.
Tu.-F. 10-1; W. 3-6; Su. 10-1.

OPPENAU

RENCHTAL REGIONAL MUSEUM
Rathaus, 7603 Oppenau, Baden-Württemberg
Geology. History of Oppenau. Furniture. Costumes. Religious art. History of mills, milling.
W. 2-6; F. 2-6.

ORTENBERG

CASTLE MUSEUM
Schloss, 6474 Ortenberg, Nordrhein-Westfalen
Local and regional history.
By appointment.

OSNABRÜCK

DIOCESAN MUSEUM
Hasestrasse 40A, 4500 Osnabrück, Niedersachsen
Medieval sculpture. Pewter. Religious ornaments.
By appointment.

MUNICIPAL MUSEUM
Heger Tor Wall 27, 4500 Osnabrück, Niedersachsen
Geology. Mineralogy. Botany. Zoology. Roman, Greek sculpture. Prehistory and history of Osnabrück. Costumes. Weapons. Armour. Paintings. Graphics. Sculpture. Applied art. Glass. Coins. Medals.
Tu.-F. 8-1, 2-6; Sa. 8-5; Su. 10-1.

ST. JOHN'S CHURCH TREASURY
Johannisstrasse, 4500 Osnabrück, Niedersachsen
Religious art.
On request.

OSTERHOLZ-SCHARMBECK

REGIONAL MUSEUM
Bördestrasse 43, 2860 Osterholz-Scharmbeck, Niedersachsen
Regional prehistory, history. Crafts. Paintings by local artists. Local cigar-industry.
M.-Sa. 9-12, 3-6; Su. 10-12.

OSTERODE

OSTERODE REGIONAL MUSEUM
Am Rollberg 32, 3360 Osterode, Niedersachsen
History of Osterode and the Harz.
M.-Sa. 9-12, 2-5; Su. 10-1.

OSTHEIM

REGIONAL MUSEUM
Kirchenburg, Kirchstrasse, 8745 Ostheim, Bayern
Local and regional history. Peasant furniture, household equipment. Costumes.
M.-Sa. 9-5; Su. 9-1.

OTTERNDORF

KRANICH HOUSE DISTRICT MUSEUM
Reichenstrasse, 2178 Otterndorf, Niedersachsen
History and folklore of the Otterndorf district.
By appointment.

OTTOBEUREN

ABBEY MUSEUM
8942 Ottobeuren, Bayern
Natural history, especially molluscs, birds. Religious art. Architectural items from Ottobeuren Abbey. Peasant furnishings, household equipment.
Daily 10-12, 2-6.

PADERBORN

CATHEDRAL TREASURY
Domplatz 3, 4790 Paderborn, Nordrhein-Westfalen
13th-19th century religious art. liturgical items. 10th century portable altar. Goldsmiths' work, especially 11th century.
M.-F. 10-11. Other times by appointment.

DIOCESAN MUSEUM
Domplatz 3, 4790 Paderborn, Nordrhein-Westfalen
Religious art. Art and liturgical items of the Byzantine Church. Vestments. 9th-19th century sculpture.
M.-F. 10-12, 3-5; Sa. 3-5; Su. 10-12.

MUSEUM OF THE HISTORICAL SOCIETY
4790 Paderborn, Nordrhein-Westfalen
Local prehistory, early history, folklore.
By appointment.

REGIONAL MUSEUM OF NATURAL HISTORY
Dörenerweg 20, 4790 Paderborn, Nordrhein-Westfalen
Geology. Palaeontology. Mineralogy. Botany. Zoology.
Su. 10-1; W. 3-6.

PAPENBURG

SHIPPING AND MOOR MUSEUM
Hauptkanal Links 65, 4490 Papenburg, Niedersachsen
History of local shipping, fishing and peat industries.
On request.

PARSBERG

REGIONAL MUSEUM
8161 Parsberg, Bayern
Local and regional history. Folklore.
On request.

PASSAU

LOWER BAVARIA MUSEUM OF FIRE-FIGHTING
Schloss Oberhaus, 8390 Passau, Bayern
In the castle vaults. 18th-20th century fire-fighting methods and equipment.
Mar.-Oct., M.-Sa. 9-5.

MUSEUM OF THE BÖHMERWALD
Schloss Oberhaus, 8390 Passau, Bayern
Mementoes of Southern Bohemia. Memorial collections to the writers, Adalbert Stifter and Hans Watzlik.
Mar.-Oct., M.-Sa. 9-5.

NEW COLLECTION
Oberhaus Museum, Schloss Oberhaus, 8390 Passau, Bayern
20th century paintings, sculpture by Passau artists.
Mar.-Oct., M.-Sa. 9-5.

OBERHAUS MUSEUM
Schloss Oberhaus, 8390 Passau, Bayern
Natural history. Craftsmen's workshops, tools. Guilds. 15th-20th century paintings, drawings, engravings of Passau. Peasant furnishings. Porcelain. Pottery. 15th-16th century paintings, sculpture. Religious art. Shipping and navigation.
Mar.-Oct., M.-Sa. 9-5.

PASSAU HISTORICAL MUSEUM
Schloss Oberhaus, 8390 Passau, Bayern
Local prehistory, history.
Mar.-Oct., M.-Sa. 9-5.

STATE GALLERY
Oberhaus Museum, Schloss Oberhaus, 8390 Passau, Bayern
16th-20th century European paintings.
Mar.-Oct., M.-Sa. 9-5.

PEINE

REGIONAL MUSEUM
Spittastrasse 9, 3150 Peine, Niedersachsen
Local and regional history.
By appointment.

PERSCHEN

PEASANT MUSEUM OF THE UPPER PALATINATE
Edalmannshof, 8470 Perschen, Bayern
In 12th century farmstead. Peasant furniture, household equipment, Agricultural implements. Models show types of farmhouses in the Upper Harz.
Tu.-Su. 9-5.

PEWSUM

EAST FRISIAN OPEN-AIR MUSEUM
2974 Pewsum, Niedersachsen
In windmill (1843), farmhouse (1863) and 15th century moated castle. Farm implements. Milling history, techniques, Peasant crafts. Display showing castles of Ostfriesland. 12th-19th century gravestones.
W., S. 4-6. Other times by appointment.

PFAFFENHOFEN

REGIONAL MUSEUM
Rathaus, Hauptplatz, 8068 Pfaffenhofen, Bayern
Regional prehistory, history. Crafts. Folk-art.
By appointment.

PFARRKIRCHEN

ROTTAL REGIONAL MUSEUM
Altes Rathaus, 8340 Pfarrkirchen, Bayern
In old Town Hall (c.1550). History of Pfarrkirchen and its region. Weaving and dyeing equipment. Peasant furniture. Folk-art. Painted glass. Ceramics.
On request.

PFORZHEIM

JEWELLERY MUSEUM
Reuchlinhaus, Jahnstrasse 42, 7530 Pforzheim, Baden-Württemberg
World-wide collection of jewellery. Special collection of Pforzheim jewellery.
Tu.-Sa. 10-6; W. also 8-10; Su. 10-1, 3-5.

REGIONAL MUSEUM
Jahnstrasse 42, 7530 Pforzheim, Baden-Württemberg
Regional prehistory, history.
Tu.-Sa. 10-6; W. also 8 p.m.-10; Su. 10-1, 3-5.

PIDING

STAUFENECK PALACE
Schlossweg 15, 8229 Piding, Bayern
History of the Berchtesgaden region.
Tu.-Sa. 10-5; Su. 10-1.

PIRMASENS

REGIONAL MUSEUM
Hauptstrasse 26, 6780 Pirmasens, Rheinland-Pfalz
Regional prehistory, history. Paintings. Sculpture.
Th. 3-6; Su. 10-1.

SHOE MUSEUM
Altes Rathaus, 6780 Pirmasens, Rheinland-Pfalz
World-wide historical collection of footwear and shoemaking techniques.
Th. 3-6; Su. 10-1.

PLÖN

PLÖN DISTRICT MUSEUM
Schlossberg 3, 2320 Plön, Schleswig-Holstein
Prehistory, history of the Plön district. Crafts. Pewter. Glass.
Daily 2-6.

PLÖSSBERG

REGIONAL MUSEUM
8591 Plössberg, Bayern
Prehistory, history of the Plössberg district.
On request.

POLLING

REGIONAL MUSEUM
Schulhaus, 8121 Polling, Bayern
Local history.
On request.

POMMERSFELDEN

WEISSENSTEIN PALACE
8602 Pommersfelden, Bayern
Baroque furnishings. Porcelain. Glass. Paintings.
Apr.-Oct., daily 8-12, 2-5.

PORZ-WAHN

THEATRE MUSEUM
Schloss, 5050 Porz-Wahn, Rheinland-Pfalz
Theatre history. Stage-designs. Photographs. Films. Paintings. Prints. Porcelain. Masks. Puppets.
M.-F. 9-5.

POTTENSTEIN

POTTENSTEIN CASTLE
8573 Pottenstein, Bayern
Castle (c.900). Local history. Paintings.
Mar.-Oct., daily 9-6.

REGIONAL MUSEUM
Forcheimer Strasse 57, 8573 Pottenstein, Bayern
Natural history, prehistory and history of the Pottenstein region. Crafts. Peasant furnishings, household equipment. Ceramics.
W., F. 10-12.

PRESSATH

PRESSATH MUSEUM OF THE REGIONAL PROTECTION SOCIETY
8481 Pressath, Bayern
Local and regional history.
By appointment.

PRIEN

REGIONAL MUSEUM
Friedhofweg 1, 8210 Prien, Bayern
Furniture. Decorative arts. Costumes. Craftsmen's workshops. Folk-art. Paintings by Chiemgau artists. Fishing industry.
M.-F. 10-11, 3-6.

PRUNN

PALACE
8421 Prunn, Rheinland-Pfalz
Local history. Furniture. Tapestries. Paintings.
May-Oct., daily 9-6. Nov.-Apr., daily 9-4.

RADOLFZELL

REGIONAL MUSEUM
Rathaus, Marktplatz 8, 7760 Radolfzell, Baden-Württemberg
Local and regional history. Archaeological material from local excavations.
By appointment.

RAESFELD

REGIONAL MUSEUM
Alte Schule, Weselerstrasse, 4281 Raesfeld, Nordrhein-Westfalen
Regional prehistory, early history. 17th century weapons.
By appointment.

RAHDEN

RAHDEN FARM MUSEUM
4993 Kleinendorf bei Rahden, Nordrhein-Westfalen
Farm-buildings and craftsmen's workshop brought to site from Rahden area. Craftsmen's tools, equipment. Flax-processing and linen weaving. Local costumes.
Apr.-Sept., Tu.-Su. 9-6. Oct., Mar. Tu.-Su. 9-5.

RAIN

LOCAL MUSEUM
Kirchplatz 143, 8852 Rain, Bayern
Local history. Folklore. Handicrafts. Natural history.
July-Aug., Su. 10-12. Other times on request.

RAMSDORF

RAMSDORF CASTLE REGIONAL MUSEUM
Burgplatz, 4285 Ramsdorf, Nordrhein-Westfalen
Local and regional history.
By appointment.

RASTATT

MUSEUM OF MILITARY HISTORY
Schloss, 7750 Rastatt, Baden-Württemberg
Military history from the Middle Ages to modern times. Weapons. Uniforms. Flags. Orders. Medals. Paintings. Models.
Apr. 15- Oct. 15, Tu.-Sa. 10-12, 3-5; Su., public holidays, 10-12, 2-5.

PALACE
Schloss, 7750 Rastatt, Baden-Württemberg
Period rooms. Paintings.
By appointment.

REGIONAL MUSEUM
Herrnstrasse, 7750 Rastatt, Baden-Württemberg
Local and regional history.
Apr.-Sept., Su. 10-12.

RATINGEN

MUSEUM OF THE HISTORY OF RATINGEN
Speestrasse 21, 4030 Ratingen, Nordrhein-Westfalen
Furniture. Porcelain. Regional history.
Daily 9-12, 2-5.

RATZEBURG

ERNST BARLACH MEMORIAL
Baslachplatz 3, 2418 Ratzeburg, Schleswig-Holstein
House (1840) was former home of Ernst Barlach. Bronzes, drawings, lithographs and woodcuts by Barlach. Letters and other documents illustrating the artist's life and work.
Tu.-Su. 9.30-12, 3-6.

DISTRICT MUSEUM
Domhof 13, 2418 Ratzeburg, Schleswig-Holstein
Regional prehistory, history. 18th-19th century furnishings. Folk-art.
M.-F. 9-1, 3-5; Sa., Su. 2-5.

RAVENSBURG

REGIONAL MUSEUM
Rathaus, 7980 Ravensburg, Baden-Württemberg
Building (1470) has 16th century wall and ceiling paintings. Paintings, prints, household equipment and other material illustrating the history of Ravensburg and its region.
W.-Sa. 2-4; Su. 10-12, 2-4.

RECHTENFLETT

HERMANN ALLMER HOUSE AND REGIONAL MUSEUM
2851 Rechtenflett, Niedersachsen
Local and regional history. Life and work of Hermann Allmer (d.1902).
Tu.-Sa. 9-5; Su. 10-1.

RECKLINGHAUSEN

ICON MUSEUM
Kirchplatz 2A, 4350 Recklinghausen, Nordrhein-Westfalen
Icons from Byzantium, Russia, Italy and the Balkans. Coptic sculpture, glass, bronzes, vestments. Liturgical items of the Orthodox Church.
Tu.-Sa. 10-6; Su., public holidays 11-1, 3-6.

MUNICIPAL HALL OF THE ARTS
Franz Grosse Perdekamp Strasse, 4350 Recklinghausen, Nordrhein-Westfalen
International art since 1945. Paintings. Sculpture. Graphics. 20th century works by Westphalian artists.
Tu.-Sa. 10-6; Su. 11-1, 3-6.

VESTISCH MUSEUM
Franz Grosse Perdekamp Strasse, 4350 Recklinghausen, Nordrhein-Westfalen
Regional geology, prehistory, early history. Furniture. Household equipment. Agricultural implements. Paintings, sculpture by artists from Westphalia and the Lower Rhine. Weapons. Armour. Folk-art.
By appointment.

REGENSBURG

EAST GERMAN FOUNDATION GALLERY
Dr. Johann Maier Strasse 5, 8400 Regensburg, Bayern
Paintings, prints, engravings, illustrating the history and culture of the former German eastern provinces.
Tu.-Sa. 10-12, 2-4; Su. 10-1.

GALLERY OF THE 20th CENTURY
8400 Regensburg, Bayern
20th century paintings, graphics by artists from Regensburg, Lower Bavaria and the Upper Palatinate.
Tu.-Sa. 10-1, 2-5; Su. 10-1.

KEPLER HOUSE MEMORIAL
Keplerstrasse 5, 8400 Regensburg, Bayern
House (c.1500) in which Johann Kepler died (1630). Collections illustrating Kepler's life and work.
Tu.-Su. 10-12; M.-Sa. 2.30-4.30.

MUSEUM OF THE PALACE OF THE PRINCES OF THURN AND TAXIS
Emmeramsplatz, 8400 Regensburg, Bayern
Furnishings, paintings, sculpture and decorative arts from the Princes' palaces in Brussels and Frankfurt. Special collection of 17th century Brussels tapestries.
M.-F. 2-4; Su. 10-12.

NATURAL HISTORY MUSEUM
Prebronntor 4, 8400 Regensburg, Bayern
Natural history of Upper Bavaria. Geology. Mineralogy. Zoology.
Apr.-Sept., W., Sa. 2-6; Su. 10-12.

PARLIAMENT MUSEUM
Rathausplatz 4, 8400 Regensburg, Bayern
Documents, views and memorabilia illustrating the history of the Parliaments which met in Regensburg.
M.-Sa. 9.30-12, 2-5; Su. 10-1.

REGENSBURG CITY MUSEUM
Dachauplatz 2-4, 8400 Regensburg, Bayern
In former convent (1226) of Minorite nuns. Local prehistory, history. Peasant furnishings, household equipment. Folklore. Costumes. Fashions. Religious folk-art. 14th-19th century paintings, graphics. 11th-19th century sculpture. 15th-19th century furniture. Medieval - 19th century glass, ceramics, wrought-iron, bronze, copper, brass, pewter. Musical instruments.
Tu.-Sa. 10-1, 2-5; Su. 10-1.

STABLES MUSEUM OF THE PRINCES OF THURN AND TAXIS
Emmeramsplatz, 8400 Regensburg, Bayern
18th-20th century coaches, carriages, sleighs.
Guided tours only. M.-F. 2 and 3; Su. 10 and 11.

STATE GALLERY
Dachauplatz 2-4, 8400 Regensburg, Bayern
16th-18th century European paintings.
Tu.-Su. 11-12, 2-5.

TREASURY OF ST. EMMERAN'S CHURCH
8400 Regensburg, Bayern
Religious art and liturgical objects, 11th-19th century.
By appointment.

REINFELD

REINFELD REGIONAL MUSEUM
Neuer Garten 9, 2067 Reinfeld, Schleswig-Holstein
History of Reinfeld Palace. Ceramics. Roofing tiles. Paintings. Letters and other writings by and about Matthais Claudius.
Su. 11-12.30.

REINHEIM

REGIONAL MUSEUM
Kirchstrasse 41, 6101 Reinheim, Hessen
Local and regional history.
On request.

REKEN

MUSEUM IN THE OLD CHURCH
Hauptstrasse, 4421 Reken, Nordrhein-Westfalen
In former 15th century parish church. Religious paintings, sculpture, ornaments, vestments, service-books from churches and museums in the district. Exhibits illustrating architectural history of the church.
By appointment.

REMAGEN

ROMAN AND FRANKISH MUSEUM
5480 Remagen, Rheinland-Pfalz
In former chapel (15th century) of Knechtstetten Abbey. Roman and Frankish material from local excavations. Pottery. Terracotta. Bronze and iron objects. Glass. Coins. Inscriptions.
By appointment.

REMSCHEID

GERMAN TOOL MUSEUM
Hasten, Cleffstrasse 2-6, 5630 Remscheid, Nordrhein-Westfalen
History and development of tools, from Palaeolithic times to the present day.
Tu.-Sa. 9-12, 3-6; Su. 3-6.

GERMAN X-RAY MUSEUM
Schweimer Strasse, 5630 Remscheid-Lennep, Nordrhein-Westfalen
History, applications and techniques of X-rays.
M.-F. 9-5; Sa. 10-12.

REGIONAL MUSEUM
Hasten, Cleffstrasse 2-6, 5630 Remscheid, Nordrhein-Westfalen
Regional history. Furnishings. Household equipment.
Tu.-Sa. 9-12, 3-6; Su. 3-6.

RENDSBURG

MUSEUM OF ARTISTIC CASTS
Ahlmann-Carlshütte K.G., Glück-Auf Allee, 2370 Rendsburg, Schleswig-Holstein
Artistic cast iron. Portraits. History of the Carlshütte works.
Sa. 3-6. Other times by appointment.

REGIONAL MUSEUM
Altes Rathaus, 2370 Rendsburg, Schleswig-Holstein
In old Town Hall (1446). Biology. Prehistoric material from local excavations. Medieval history of Rendsburg. Ceramics. Faience. Folklore. Peasant rooms. Coins.
Tu.-Sa. 10-12, 3-5.

REUTLINGEN

MUSEUM OF NATURAL HISTORY
Spendhausstrasse 8, 7410 Reutlingen, Baden-Württemberg
Wildlife of the region. Petrified material.
W. 3-5; Sa. 2-5; Su. 10.30-12, 2-5.

REGIONAL MUSEUM
Oberamteistrasse 22, 7410 Reutlingen, Baden-Württemberg
Regional prehistory, history. Crafts. Industry. Guilds. Period rooms. Costumes. Adam Müller Guttenbrunn memorial room.
W., Sa. 2-5; Su. 11-12, 2-5.

SPENDHAUS ART EXHIBITION
Spendhausstrasse 8, 7410 Reutlingen, Baden-Württemberg
Paintings. Water-colours. Drawings.
By appointment.

RHEINBACH

GLASS MUSEUM
Vor dem Voigtstor 23, 5308 Rheinbach, Nordrhein-Westfalen
History of glass-making. Collection of glasses.
Tu.-Su. 10-12, 3-6.

RHEINBERG

REGIONAL MUSEUM
Kamperstrasse 8, 4134 Rheinberg, Nordrhein-Westfalen
Ceramics. Pewter. Engravings.
By appointment.

RHEINE

FALKENHOF MUSEUM
Tiefe Strasse, 4440 Rheine, Nordrhein-Westfalen
15th-20th century paintings, sculpture, graphics. History, folklore of the Rheine area. Weapons and military equipment. Coins.
M.-F. 9-12; Tu., Th. also 4-6; Su. 10.30-12.30.

RHEINHAUSEN

HEHL COLLECTION
Händelstrasse 8, 4140 Rheinhausen, Nordrhein-Westfalen
Pottery and ceramics by Josef Hehl.
Tu.-Sa. 9-5; Su. 10-1.

MUNICIPAL COLLECTIONS
Händelstrasse 8, 4140 Rheinhausen, Nordrhein-Westfalen
Roman and Frankish material from excavations in the Rheinhausen area. Folklore.
Tu.-Sa. 9-5; Su. 10-1.

RHEYDT

MUNICIPAL MUSEUM
Schloss Rheydt, 4070 Rheydt, Nordrhein-Westfalen
16th-18th century paintings, graphics, sculpture, applied art, weapons. Prehistoric and early historical material from local excavations.
May-Oct., Tu.-Sa. 11-1, 3-6.

RIEDENBURG

MUNICIPAL MUSEUM
Schloss Rosenburg, 8422 Riedenburg, Bayern
History of Riedenburg. Folklore. Furniture. Applied art.
Tu.-Sa. 10-5; Su. 10-1.

RIEDLINGEN

REGIONAL MUSEUM
Am Wochenmarkt, 7940 Riedlingen, Baden-Württemberg
in 14th century hospital. Prehistory, history of Riedlingen area. Painted glass. Coins.
Daily 9-6.

RIETBERG

MISSION MUSEUM
Missionshaus St. Joseph, 4835 Rietberg, Nordrhein-Westfalen
Ethnological material from Africa and S. Pacific.
On request.

RINTELN

SCHAUMBURG REGIONAL MUSEUM
Eulenburg, 3260 Rinteln, Niedersachsen
Prehistory and history of Rinteln and its region. Crafts. Industry. Religious art. Costumes.
Mar.-Oct., daily 10-12, 3-5. Nov.-Feb., daily 10-12.

RISSTISSEN

ROMAN FORT MUSEUM
Neue Schule, 7931 Risstissen, Baden-Württemberg
Roman material from local excavations.
By appointment.

ROCKENHAUSEN

NORTH PALATINATE REGIONAL MUSEUM
6760 Rockenhausen, Rheinland-Pfalz
Minerals. Regional prehistory, history. Agricultural implements. Craftsmen's tools. Coins.
By appointment.

ROSENHEIM

MUNICIPAL ART COLLECTIONS
Max Bram Haus, Max Bram Platz 2, 8200 Rosenheim, Bayern
19th-20th century paintings, sculpture, graphics by Munich artists.
Tu.-Su. 9-5.30.

REGIONAL MUSEUM
Ludwigsplatz, 8200 Rosenheim, Bayern
Regional prehistory, history. Folklore. Crafts. Inland shipping.
Tu.-Su. 9-12, 2-4.

ROTENBURG-FULDA

DISTRICT MUSEUM
Schloffhof, 6442 Rotenburg-Fulda, Hessen
Local and regional history.
Tu.-Sa. 10-12, 2-4.

ROTENBURG-WÜMME

REGIONAL MUSEUM
Burgstrasse, 2130 Rotenburg-Wümme, Niedersachsen
In former farmhouse (1695). Regional prehistory, history. Furnishings. Folklore.
Daily 9-12, 3-6.

ROTH

REGIONAL MUSEUM
Schloss Ratibor, 8542 Roth, Bayern
In Ratibor Palace (1535). History and crafts of the Roth area. Farmhouse living room. Biedermeier room. Weapons. Toys. Copper and ceramic tableware.
Sa. 2-4; Su. 10.30-12, 2-4.

ROTHENBURG OB DER TAUBER

HISTORICAL COLLECTION OF MEDIEVAL LAW ENFORCEMENT
Klostergasse 1-3, 8803 Rothenburg ob der Tauber, Bayern
Collection illustrating 13th-19th century law enforcement. Medieval torture-chamber.
Daily 10-2.

HISTORY MUSEUM
Rathaus, 8803 Rothenburg ob der Tauber, Bayern
Collection illustrating Rothenburg as it was in the early 17th century.
Daily 10-2.

MUSEUM OF THE IMPERIAL CITY
8803 Rothenburg ob der Tauber, Bayern
In former 15th century Dominican monastery. Prehistory. History. Furniture. Craftsmen's tools, equipment.
Daily 10-2.

ROTHENBURG AND WASSE GALLERIES
Klosterhof, 8803 Rothenburg ob der Tauber, Bayern
19th-20th century paintings.
Daily 10-2.

ROTTACH-EGERN

REGIONAL MUSEUM
Hauptstrasse, 8183 Rottach-Egern, Bayern
Local and regional history.
On request.

ROTTENBURG AM NECKAR

DIOCESAN MUSEUM
7407 Rottenburg am Neckar, Baden-Württemberg
Religious art, especially late Gothic panel-paintings, wood-sculpture. Glass reliquaries.
By appointment.

SÜLCHGAU MUSEUM
Bahnhofstrasse, 7407 Rottenburg am Neckar, Baden-Württemberg
Local prehistory, history. Folklore. Crafts.
Sa. 3-5; Su. 11-12.

ROTTHALMÜNSTER

REGIONAL MUSEUM
Rathaus, 8399 Rotthalmünster, Bayern
Regional wildlife, prehistory, history. Painted furniture. Household equipment. Spinning. Weaving. Paintings. Graphics. Folk-art.
M.-F. 7.30-12, 1.30-5.

ROTTWEIL

ART COLLECTION OF THE LORENZKAPELLE
7210 Rottweil, Baden-Württemberg
14th-16th century paintings, sculpture. Panel-paintings. Wood-sculpture.
Daily 10-12, 2-5.

ROTTWEIL MUNICIPAL MUSEUM
Hauptstrasse 21, 7210 Rottweil, Baden-Württemberg
Roman and Alemannic archaeology. Local history. Carnival collection. Paintings. Applied art.
M.-Sa. 9-12, 2-5; Su. 10-12.

RÖTZ

RÖTZ REGIONAL MUSEUM
Rathaus, 8463 Rötz, Bayern
Local and regional history. Folklore. Folk-art. Crafts. Commerce. Costumes. Weapons.
On request.

ROXEL

DROSTE ZU HÜLSHOFF MUSEUM
Burg Hülshoff, 4401 Roxel, Nordrhein-Westfalen
13th century castle, birthplace and family home of the writer, Annette von Droste zu Hülshoff. 16th-19th century furniture. Paintings. Family portraits. Porcelain. Glass. Cameos. Engravings. Miniatures. Carpets.
By appointment.

RÜDESHEIM

RHEINGAU AND WINE MUSEUM
Brömserburg, Rheinstrasse 2, 6220 Rüdesheim, Hessen
Regional prehistory, history. Local wine-production.
Daily 9-6.

RUHPOLDING

BARTHOLOMÄUS SCHMUCKER REGIONAL MUSEUM
Jagdschloss, Schlossstrasse, 8222 Ruhpolding, Bayern
18th-19th century peasant furniture. Crafts. Folk-art. Guild material. Religious art. Votive tablets.
M.-F. 9-12.

RUNKEL

RUNKEL CASTLE
Schlossplatz, 6251 Runkel, Hessen
17th-20th century furnishings, weapons.
Apr.-Oct., daily 10-5.

RÜSSELSHEIM

LOCAL MUSEUM
Darmstädter Strasse 27, 6090 Rüsselsheim, Hessen
Minerals. Fossils. Prehistory. History of the Roman, Frankish, medieval periods. Farmhouse living room.
Tu., Th. 9-12; F., Su. 1-5.

SAALBURG-KASTELL

SAALBURG MUSEUM
6381 Saalburg Kastell, Hessen
Prehistoric art. Roman material from local excavations.
Daily 8-5.

SAARBRÜCKEN

LAND MUSEUM OF PREHISTORY AND EARLY HISTORY
Ludwigsplatz 15, 6600 Saarbrücken, Saarland
In Freithal Palace (late 18th century). Prehistoric and early historical material from local sites.
Tu.-F. 10-4; Sa. 10-2; Su. 10-6.

SAARLAND MUSEUM
Altes Haus, St. Johanner Markt 24, und Moderne Galerie, Bismarckstrasse 11-15, 6600 Saarbrücken, Saarland
In Altes Haus: 18th century art, applied art.
Moderne Galerie: 19th-20th century paintings, sculpture, graphics.
Altes Haus: Tu.-Sa. 10-4; Su. 10-6.
Moderne Galerie: Tu.-Su. 10-6.

SAARLOUIS

REGIONAL MUSEUM
6630 Saarlouis, Saarland
Regional natural history, prehistory, history. Folklore. Industry. Transport.
Daily 9-12, 2-5.

SÄCKINGEN

UPPER RHINE MUSEUM
Schloss, 7880 Säckingen, Baden-Württemberg
Minerals. Palaeontology. Prehistory. History of Säckingen. Costumes. Coins. Paintings. Prints.
Tu., Th., Su. 3-5.

SAFFERSTETTEN

MUSEUM OF PEASANT LIFE
8399 Safferstetten, Bayern
Peasant furnishings, household equipment.
Tu.-Sa. 10-5; Su. 10-11.

SALZGITTER-SALDER

TOWN MUSEUM
Schloss, 3321 Salzgitter-Salder, Niedersachsen
In 17th-18th century palace. Local and regional history. Folk-art.
Tu.-Sa. 3-5; Su. 10-12, 3-5.

ST. ANDREASBERG

REGIONAL MUSEUM AND HISTORIC SILVER MINE
Grube Samson, 3424 St. Andreasberg, Niedersachsen
At Samson silvermine. Local history. History of silvermining in the Upper Harz.
Daily 10-4.

ST. BLASIEN

REGIONAL MUSEUM
7822 St. Blasien, Baden-Württemberg
Local and regional history.
By appointment.

ST. GEORGEN

REGIONAL MUSEUM
Rathaus, 7742 St. Georgen, Baden-Württemberg
Peasant furnitur. Costumes. Clocks.
M.-F. 8-12.30, 2-5.

ST. GOAR

REGIONAL COLLECTION
Burg Rheinfels, 5407 St. Goar, Rheinland-Pfalz
Archaeological material from local excavations. Local history. Drawings and plans of Rheinfels Castle. Engravings. Coats of arms.
May-Oct., daily 10-5.

ST. OTTILIEN

MISSION MUSEUM
8917 St. Ottilien, Bayern
Botany and zoology of E. Africa. Ethnological material from E. Africa, Zululand, Korea, Manchuria. History of the mission.
Apr.-Sept., 10-6.30. Oct.-Mar., 10-5.

ST. PETER-ORDING

EIDERSTEDT REGIONAL MUSEUM
Oldsdorfer Strasse 6, 2252 St. Peter Ording, Schleswig-Holstein
In 18th century farmhouse. Regional history. Folklore. Crafts. Shipping and fishing industries.
May-Sept., Tu.-Sa. 10-12, 3-5. Oct.-Apr., Tu.-Su. 10-12.

ST. WENDEL

ETHNOLOGICAL COLLECTION OF THE STEYL MISSIONARIES
Missionshaus, 6691 St. Wendel, Saarland
Ethnology. History of the mission.
M.-Sa. 10-5; Su. 10-1.

REGIONAL MUSEUM
Rathaus, 6691 St. Wendel, Saarland
Local and regional history.
M.-Sa. 10-5; Su. 10-1.

SCHACHEN-GARMISCH PARTENKIRCHEN

HUNTING PALACE
8100 Schachen-Garmisch Partenkirchen, Bayern
Palace (1870). 19th century furnishings.
May-Oct., daily 8-1, 2-6.

SCHEESSEL

REGIONAL HOUSE
Zevener Strasse, 2138 Scheessel, Schleswig-Holstein
Local and regional history.
On request.

SCHIFFERSTADT

REGIONAL MUSEUM
Bleichstrasse 8, 6707 Schifferstadt, Rheinland-Pfalz
Regional prehistory, history. Biedermeier room. Reproduction of inn. Weapons. Pewter.
Apr.-Oct., 1st Su. in month 10-12, 2-4.

SCHLEISSHEIM

SCHLEISSHEIM NEW PALACE AND STATE GALLERY
Max Emanuel Platz 1, 8042 Schleissheim, Bayern
Castle (c.1700). 17th-18th century Dutch, Italian, German paintings.
May-Oct., Tu.-Su. 10-12.30, 1.30-5. Nov.-Apr., Tu.-Su. 1.30-4.

SCHLESWIG

LAND MUSEUM OF SCHLESWIG-HOLSTEIN
Schloss Gottorf, 2382 Schleswig, Schleswig-Holstein
18th century palace. Medieval paintings, sculpture. 16th-17th century furnishings. Applied art. Peasant crafts, implements. Faience. Empire and Biedermeier period rooms. Folk-art. Toys. Drawings. Prints.
Apr.-Oct., Tu.-Su. 9-5. Nov.-Mar., Tu.-Sa. 10-4; Su. 9.30-5.

MUNICIPAL MUSEUM
Friedrichstrasse 7-11, 2380 Schleswig, Schleswig-Holstein
History of Schleswig. Schleswig faience, silver, pewter. Paintings by local artists.
M., W., Sa. 9-5; Su. 9-1.

SCHLESWIG-HOLSTEIN MUSEUM OF PREHISTORY AND EARLY HISTORY
Schloss Gottorf, 2380 Schleswig, Schleswig-Holstein
Prehistoric and early historical material from excavations in Schleswig-Holstein.
Apr.-Oct., Tu.-Su. 9-5. Nov.-Mar., Tu.-Sa. 10-4; Su. 9.30-5.

SCHLIERSEE

REGIONAL MUSEUM
8162 Schliersee, Bayern
15th century farmhouse, with 17th-19th century furnishings.
M., W., F. 9-5.

SCHLITZ

REGIONAL MUSEUM
6407 Schlitz, Hessen
Local and regional history. Furniture. Crafts. Weapons. Costumes. Linen-weaving.
Tu., Th., Sa. 2-4; Su. 11-12.

SCHLOSS MESPELBRUNN

PALACE MUSEUM
8751 Schloss Mespelbrunn, Bayern
16th-19th century furniture, paintings, applied arts, weapons. 15th-17th century glass painting. Porcelain.
Daily 9-12, 1.30-6.

SCHLÜCHTERN

BERGWINKEL MUSEUM
Schlossstrasse, 6490 Schlüchtern, Hessen
In Castle (1440). Local pottery. Memorabilia of the Brothers Grimm and of Ulrich von Hutten.
By appointment.

MUSEUM OF WOODEN TOOLS AND EQUIPMENT
Burg Brandenstein, 6490 Schlüchtern, Hessen
Wooden tools, equipment.
Daily 9-5.

SCHNAIT

SILCHER MUSEUM
7051 Schnait, Baden-Württemberg
Memorabilia of F. Silcher.
Easter-Nov. 14, daily 10-12, 2-5.

SCHNAITTACH

REGIONAL MUSEUM
8563 Schnaittach, Bayern
Regional furniture, household equipment. Prehistoric material. Religious art.
Daily 9-5.

SCHONGAU

TOWN MUSEUM
Blumenstrasse 2, 8920 Schongau, Bayern
Local and regional prehistory, history. Crafts. 17th-18th century paintings, sculpture. Peasant furnishings.
Su. 2-4. Other times by appointment.

SCHÖNINGEN

REGIONAL MUSEUM
Markt 33, 3338 Schöningen, Niedersachsen
In former school (1638). Regional geology, prehistory, history. Agriculture. Industry.
Sa., Su. 10.30-12.30.

SCHÖPPENSTEDT

TILL EULENSPIEGEL MUSEUM
Nordstrasse, 3307 Schöppenstedt, Niedersachsen
Material relating to the Till Eulenspiegel story. Literature. Music. Plays. Paintings. Sculpture. Drawings. Prints.
Sa., M. 9-12, 2-5; Su. 9-1.

SCHORNDORF

REGIONAL MUSEUM
Kirchplatz 9, 7060 Schorndorf, Baden-Württemberg
House (1648). Local history, Roman times - present day. Local pewter. Guild material.
Sa. 3-5; Su. 11-12, 3-5.

SCHÖTMAR

REGIONAL MUSEUM
4903 Schötmar, Nordrhein-Westfalen
Local and regional history.
On request.

SCHOTTEN

VOGELSBERG REGIONAL MUSEUM
Hauptstrasse 23, 6479 Schotten, Hessen
Local prehistory, history.
By appointment.

SCHRAMBERG

TOWN MUSEUM
7230 Schramberg, Baden-Württemberg
History of Schramberg.
By appointment.

SCHROBENHAUSEN

LENBACH MUSEUM
Ulrich Peisser Gasse 1, 8898 Schrobenhausen, Bayern
Life and work of Frans von Lenbach (d.1904). Paintings by J. B. Hofner.
Daily 8-5.

REGIONAL MUSEUM
Lenbachstrasse 22, 8898 Schrobenhausen, Bayern
Local prehistory, history. Crafts. Furniture. Sculpture. Costumes. Medals.
By appointment.

SCHUSSENRIED

FARMHOUSE MUSEUM
7953 Schussenried, Baden-Württemberg
Local history. Peasant furniture, household equipment.
On request.

SCHWABACH

TOWN MUSEUM
Pfarrgasse 8, 8540 Schwabach, Bayern
Regional natural history, history. Crafts. 16th century paintings. Folk-art. Local book-printing. Needle-maker's and goldbeater's workshops. Forge-hammer.
W., Sa., Su. 10-5.

SCHWÄBISCH-GMÜND

SCHWÄBISCH-GMÜND MUSEUM
Rektor Klaus-Strasse 100, 7070 Schwäbisch-Gmünd, Baden-Württemberg
Regional geology, palaeontology, history, wildlife, plants. 18th century furnishings, decorative arts. 18th-20th century crafts. 19th-20th century sculpture, paintings by regional artists.
On request.

SCHWÄBISCH HALL

KECKENBURG MUSEUM
Untere Herrengasse 8-10, 7170 Schwäbisch Hall, Baden-Württemberg
Regional prehistory, history. Religious art.
Tu.-Sa. 10-5; Su. 10-1.

SCHWABMÜNCHEN

REGIONAL MUSEUM
Museumstrasse 18, 8930 Schwabmünchen, Bayern
Regional mineralogy, palaeontology, prehistory, history. Crafts. Peasant furniture. Applied art. Sculpture. 19th century paintings.
May-Oct., 3rd Su. in month, 10-1.

SCHWANDORF

REGIONAL MUSEUM
Rathausstrasse, 8460 Schwandorf, Bayern
Peasant living-room (1828). Crafts. Applied art. Folklore. Costumes. History of Schwandorf.
1st Su. in month 10-12.

SCHWARZENAHER

OPEN-AIR ROMAN MUSEUM
6651 Schwarzenaher, Hessen
Roman material from local excavations.
Daily 9-5.

SCHWEINFURT

MUNICIPAL MUSEUM
Martin Luther Platz 12, 8720 Schweinfurt, Bayern
In former school (1582). Local and regional natural history, prehistory, history. Folk-art. Crafts. Furniture. 15th-18th century scientific instruments. Weapons.
W. 2-3; 2nd Su. in month 2-5; 2nd Su. in month 10-5.

SCHWELM

SCHWELM MUNICIPAL MUSEUM
Schloss Martfeld, 5830 Schwelm, Nordrhein-Westfalen
In 17th century castle. History of Schwelm. Views. Models. 16th-19th century furniture, household equipment, applied art. History of local societies and organisations.
W. 4.30-6.30; Sa. 10-12.

SCHWENNINGEN

HELLMUT KIENZLE CLOCK MUSEUM
7220 Schwenningen, Baden-Württemberg
History of clocks, clockmaking.
W. 2-6.

SCHWENNINGEN REGIONAL MUSEUM
7220 Schwenningen, Baden-Württemberg
Natural history, especially geology. Regional prehistory, history. Local crafts, agriculture. Clocks. Clock-making tools.
Tu., W., Sa., 1st Sun. in month, 10-12, 2-6.

SCHWERTE

MUSEUM OF THE RUHR VALLEY
Altes Rathaus, 5840 Schwerte, Nordrhein-Westfalen
Regional geology, prehistory, history. Pewter. Coin-forgeries, 1620-1815. Postal history. History of shooting clubs and gymnastic societies.
W., F. 3-6; Su. 10-1.

SCHWETZINGEN

PALACE
6830 Schwetzingen, Baden-Württemberg
18th-19th century furnishings, decorative arts. Paintings.
Tu.-Sa. 10-1, 2-5.

SEEBÜLL

ADA AND EMIL NOLDE SEEBÜLL FOUNDATION
2261 Seebüll, Schleswig-Holstein
Former home and studio of the painter, Emil Nolde

(d.1956). Paintings, watercolours, prints, applied arts by Nolde.
Mar.-Nov., daily 10-6.

SELIGENSTADT

REGIONAL MUSEUM
Am Klosterhof 1, 6453 Seligenstadt, Hessen
Local and regional history.
On request.

SESSLACH

REGIONAL MUSEUM
Marktplatz 98, 8601 Sesslach, Bayern
History of Sesslach and its region. Crafts. Applied arts. Peasant furniture. Household equipment. Agricultural implements. Costumes. Folk-art. Weapons.
On request.

SIEGBURG

COLLECTION OF THE HISTORY OF TAXATION
Michaelsberg, 5200 Siegburg, Nordrhein-Westfalen
History of Taxation from early historical times to the present day. Adminstrative and technical equipment.
By appointment.

SIEGBURG REGIONAL MUSEUM
Grimmelgasse, 5200 Siegburg, Nordrhein-Westfalen
Regional prehistory, historical geography. History of Siegburg. Folklore. Ceramics. Peasant living room. Furniture. Household equipment. Guild chests. Stoneware. Engravings. Paintings. Maps. Coins. Humperdinck collection.
M. 5-7; Tu., Th., F. 10-12, 3-5; W., Su. 10-12.

SIEGEN

SIEGERLAND MUSEUM
Oberes Schloss, 5900 Siegen, Nordrhein-Westfalen
In 13th century castle. Early history of the Siegerland. Portraits of members of the House of Orange-Nassau. Commerce and economics. Artistic cast-iron. Minerals. Demonstration mine.
Tu.-Su. 10-12.30, 2-5.

SIGMARINGEN

HOHENZOLLERN MUSEUM
Schloss, 7480 Sigmaringen, Baden-Württemberg
Prehistory, early history of the region. 17th-19th century furnishings. Paintings. Hohenzollern portraits. 15th-19th century weapons. Collection of coaches and carriages.
Daily 8-6.

SIMBACH

TOWN MUSEUM
Innstrasse 14, 8265 Simbach, Bayern
History of Simbach. 18th-19th century peasant furniture, household equipment. Folklore. Folk-art.
By appointment.

SIMMERN

HUNSRÜCK MUSEUM
Schlossplatz, 6540 Simmern, Rheinland-Pfalz
Local prehistory, history. Folklore. Peasant household equipment. Costumes.
May-Oct., Tu.-F. 10-12, 3-6; Su. 10-12.

SINDELFINGEN

TOWN MUSEUM
Altes Rathaus, Langestrasse 13, 7032 Sindelfingen, Baden-Württemberg
Local prehistory, history. Regional folklore.
Tu.-Th. 9-12; W. 2-5; 1st Su. in month (not Aug.) 11-12.

SINGEN

HEGAU MUSEUM
Gräfliches Schloss, 7700 Singen, Baden-Württemberg
Local prehistory, history.
W., Sa. 2-5; Su. 10-1.

SINSHEIM

REGIONAL MUSEUM
Kirchplatz 16, 6920 Sinsheim, Baden-Württemberg
Weapons. Pewter. Crafts. Apothecary's utensils, equipment. Collections relating to Dean Wilhemi and General Frans Sigel.
Tu. 2-4; 1st Su. in month, 10.30-12.0.

SINZIG

REGIONAL MUSEUM
Schloss, 5485 Sinzig, Rheinland-Pfalz
In 19th century palace. Prehistoric material from regional excavations. Locally made terra sigillata. 15th-19th century sculpture. 17th-19th century paintings. Furniture. Porcelain. Pewter.
Su. 10-12.

SOEST

BURGHOF MUSEUM
Burghofstrasse 22, 4770 Soest, Nordrhein-Westfalen
In 16th century castle. Prehistory and history of Soest Furnishings. Religious history.
Tu.-Sa. 10-12, 3-5; Su. 11-1.

WILHELM MORGNER HOUSE
Thomästrasse, 4770 Soest, Nordrhein-Westfalen
Paintings. Sculpture. Graphics, including almost complete collection of Heinrich Aldergrev engravings.
Tu.-Sa. 10.30-12, 4-5; Su. 10.30-12.30.

MUSEUM OF ST. PATROKLUS' CATHEDRAL
4700 Soest, Nordrhein-Westfalen
Medieval architectural fragments. Religious ornaments, embroidery. 13th-19th century gold and silversmiths' work. Exhibits illustrating architectural history of the cathedral.
By appointment.

SÖGEL

EMSLAND MUSEUM
Schloss Clemenswerth, 4475 Sögel, Niedersachsen
In palace pavilions (c.1740). Regional prehistory, history, folklore. History of hunting. Hunting equipment.
Daily 10-1, 3-5.

SOLINGEN

GERMAN MUSEUM OF CUTTING IMPLEMENTS
Wuppertalerstrasse 160, 5650 Solingen, Nordrhein-Westfalen
Prehistoric - 20th century swords, daggers, knives.
Tu., Th., Sa., 10-1, 3-5; F. 10-1, 3-8.

SOLTAU

MUSEUM IN REGIONAL HOUSE
Poststrasse 11, 3040 Soltau, Niedersachsen
Regional geology, prehistory, folklore, handicrafts.
By appointment.

SONTHOFEN

REGIONAL MUSEUM
Sonnenstrasse 1, 8972 Sonthofen, Bayern
Regional prehistory, history. Folklore. Costumes. Peasant furnishings.
On request.

SPAICHINGEN

MUSEUM OF GEOLOGY AND PREHISTORY
Bahnhofstrasse, 7208 Spaichingen, Baden-Württemberg
Geology. Botany. Zoology. Prehistory. Early history.
By appointment.

SPEYER

DIOCESAN MUSEUM
Grosse Pfaffengasse 7, 6720 Speyer, Rheinland-Pfalz
Liturgical objects, medieval period - 18th century. Manuscripts. Prayerbooks. Historical material from tombs of the German Emperors.
Daily 9-12, 2-5.

MUSEUM OF THE HISTORY OF THE PALATINATE
Grosse Pfaffengasse 7, 6720 Speyer, Rheinland-Pfalz
Prehistory, history of the Palatinate. Wine-production.
Daily 9-12, 2-5.

SPRINGE

REGIONAL MUSEUM
Friedrichstrasse 17D, 3257 Springe, Niedersachsen
Regional prehistory, history, folklore.
M.-Sa. 10-5; Su. 10-1.

STADE

MUSEUM OF PREHISTORY
Eisenbahnstrasse 21, 2160 Stade, Niedersachsen
Regional geology, prehistory, early history.
Tu.-Sa. 10-1, 2-4.

OPEN-AIR MUSEUM
Auf der Insel, 2160 Stade, Niedersachsen
Farmhouses (1841 and 1733), from Cheessel and Huttfleth, with furnishings, household equipment. Agricultural implements. Other rural buildings moved to site include late 17th century windmill.
Daily 10-12, 2-5.

REGIONAL MUSEUM
Inselstrasse, 2160 Stade, Niedersachsen
History and folklore of the Stade region.
Tu.-Su. 10-1, 2-4.

STADT BLANKENBERG

TOWER MUSEUM
5201 Stadt Blankenberg, Rheinland-Pfalz
Local geology, archaeology, history. Crafts. Religious art. Weapons.
Sa., Su. 11-1.

STADT SCHOPFHEIM

REGIONAL MUSEUM
Flurgstrasse, 7860 Stadt Schopfheim, Baden-Württemberg
Local and regional history.
On request.

STAFFELSTEIN

REGIONAL MUSEUM
Marktplatz 1, 8623 Staffelstein, Bayern
Natural history. Prehistory, early history of Staffelstein region. Crafts. Applied arts.
M.-F. 8-12, 1.30-5; Sa., Su. 10-12.

STARNBERG

MUNICIPAL MUSEUM
Possenhofenerstrasse 9, 8730 Starnberg, Bayern
Prehistory, early history of Starnberg and its region. Crafts. Sculpture. Applied arts. Folk-art. Peasant furniture, household equipment. Agricultural implements. Costumes. Religious art.
Mar.-Oct., Tu.-Su. 9-12, 2-5.

STAUFEN

REGIONAL AND COSTUME MUSEUM
7813 Staufen, Baden-Württemberg
Local and regional history. Costumes.
On request.

STEINAU

PALACE MUSEUM
6497 Steinau, Hessen
Renaissance palace. Furnishings. Memorial collection to the Brothers Grimm.
Tu., F. 4.30-6.30; Su. 10-12.

STEINHEIM AM MAIN

MUNICIPAL MUSEUM
Schloss, 6452 Steinheim am Main, Hessen
Bronze Age and Roman material from local excavations. Coats of arms, seals of the Archbishops of Eppstein and Mainz. Models showing development of Steinheim. Weapons.
Tu., Th., F. 10-1; Su. 3-6.

STEINHEIM-MURR

MUSEUM OF PRIMITIVE MAN
Hans Trautwein Haus, 7141 Steinheim-Murr, Nordrhein-Westfalen
Prehistory, especially Homo Steinheimensis. Early history.
Daily 10-5.

STEINHUDE

PALACE MUSEUM
Festung Wilhelmstein, 3053 Steinhude, Niedersachsen
In 18th century palace. Memorabilia of Count Wilhelm zu Schaumburg-Lippe. 18th-19th century weapons.
Apr. 1 - Oct. 15, daily 9-1, 2-6.

STRAUBING

GÄUBODEN AND STRAUBING MUSEUM
Fraunhoferstrasse 9, 8440 Straubing, Bayern
Regional prehistory, early history. History of Straubing. 12th-18th century church sculpture. Furniture. Ceramics. Copper. Pewter. Portraits. Folk-art. Roman material from local site.
Daily 10-12.

STUTTGART

DAIMLER BENZ MUSEUM
Mercedes Strasse, 7000 Stuttgart, Baden-Württemberg
History of motor-vehicles.
M.-F. 8.30-4.30; Sa. 8.30-1.

FEUERBACH REGIONAL MUSEUM
Wiener Strasse 157, 7000 Stuttgart, Baden-Württemberg
Local and regional history. Folklore.
Tu.-Su. 10-5.

HOHENHEIM MODEL COLLECTION
Garbenstrasse 9, 7000 Stuttgart, Baden-Württemberg
Models of agricultural implements.
By appointment.

LGA DESIGN CENTRE
1 Kanzleistrasse 19, 7000 Stuttgart, Baden-Württemberg
International product design.
Tu.-Su. 11-6.

LINDEN MUSEUM
Hegelplatz 1, 7000 Stuttgart, Baden-Württemberg
World-wide ethnographical collections.
Tu.-Su. 10-5; F. also 7-10.

MUSEUM OF THE HISTORY OF STUTTGART
1 Konrad Adenauer Strasse 2, 7000 Stuttgart, Baden-Württemberg
Cultural history of Stuttgart.
M.-F. 10-6; Sa., Su. 10-4.

POSTAL MUSEUM
1 Lautenschlagerstrasse 17, 7000 Stuttgart, Baden-Württemberg
History of postal services and telecommunications.
M., W., F. by appointment.

REGIONAL MUSEUM
Wilhelmstrasse 7, 7000 Stuttgart-Bad Cannstatt, Baden-Württemberg
History of the Stuttgart area.
Tu.-Su. 10-5.

OSKAR SCHLEMMER COLLECTION
Konrad Adenauer Strasse, 7000 Stuttgart, Baden-Württemberg
Paintings, graphics by Oskar Schlemmer (d.1943).
W., F., Sa., Su. 10-4; Tu., Th. 10-9.

STATE GALLERY
Konrad Adenauer Strasse 32, 7000 Stuttgart, Baden-Württemberg
European paintings, Middle Ages - present day. 19th-20th century sculpture. Drawings, engravings.
W., F., Sa., 10-4; Tu., Th. 10-9.

STATE MUSEUM OF NATURAL HISTORY
1 Schloss Rosenstein, 7000 Stuttgart, Baden-Württemberg
World-wide natural history collections. Geology. Palaeontology. Mineralogy. Botany. Zoology.
Tu.-Sa. 10-4; Su., public holidays 10-5.

STUTTGART CITY GALLERY
Bolzstrasse 2, 7000 Stuttgart, Baden-Württemberg
19th-20th century paintings, sculpture, drawings, prints by Swabian artists.
Tu., Th., F. 10-6; Sa., Su. 10-4.

WÜRTTEMBERG MUSEUM
Schillerplatz 6, 7000 Stuttgart, Baden-Württemberg
Prehistory. Early history. Greek and Roman antiquities. Crafts. Folk-art. Paintings. Sculpture. Graphics. Applied arts. Clocks. Musical instruments. Coins. Weapons.
Tu.-Su. 10-4.

SÜCHTELN

SUCHTELN REGIONAL MUSEUM
Probsteinstrasse 1, 4053 Süchteln, Nordrhein-Westfalen
Local and regional history.
Tu.-Su. 10-5.

SULZBACH-ROSENBERG

REGIONAL MUSEUM
8458 Sulzbach-Rosenberg, Bayern
History of Sulzbach-Rosenberg. Mining. Furniture. Militia and police. Law enforcement. Fire fighting. Weapons. Majolica. Faience. Costumes. Guilds.
Su. 10-12, 2-4.

SULZBÜRG

LOCAL MUSEUM
8431 Sulzbürg, Bayern
Natural history. Local history. Crafts. Agricultural implements. Costumes.
On request.

SURWOLD

WOODLAND MUSEUM
4491 Surwold, Nordrhein-Westfalen
Woodland plants and pests. Animals and birds of local woodland areas.
May-Sept., Su., public holidays 2-7. Other days by appointment.

SYKE

DISTRICT MUSEUM
Herrlichkeit 65, 2818 Syke, Niedersachsen
Local prehistory, early history. Folklore.
W. 10-3; Sa., Su. 10-12, 3-6.

TAUBERBISCHOFSHEIM

KURMAINZ OLD PALACE
6972 Tauberbischofsheim, Baden-Württemberg
15th century castle. Prehistory. Early history. Folklore.
On request.

TAUBERFRANKEN REGIONAL MUSEUM
Schloss, 6972 Tauberbischofsheim, Baden-Württemberg
Folklore. Prehistory. Furniture. Household equipment.
Sa., Su. 10-1, 2-5.

TECKLENBURG

DISTRICT MUSEUM
Am Wellenberg, 4542 Tecklenburg, Nordrhein-Westfalen
In 17th century house. Rooms furnished to show domestic conditions in 18th and 19th centuries. Geology. Prehistory. Mining history, with mine-models. Craftsmen's tools. Hemp and flax-processing.
Tu., Th., F. 9.30-12.30, 2.30-5; W. 9.30-12.30; Sa., Su. 3-5.

TEGERNSEE

TEGERNSEE REGIONAL MUSEUM
Rosenstrasse 24, 8180 Tegernsee, Bayern
Regional history. Folklore. Folk-art.
May 15- Oct. 15, daily 9-5.

TELGTE

MÜNSTERLAND REGIONAL HOUSE
4404 Telgte, Nordrhein-Westfalen
In 16th century farmhouse. Religious folk-art. Christmas cribs. Folk-art (paintings, textiles). 19th-20th century furniture, crafts.
Tu.-Su. 9.30-12.30, 1.30-5.30.

TETTNANG

MONTFORT MUSEUM
Altes Schloss, 7992 Tettnang, Baden-Württemberg
In gatehouse of former 17th century palace. Family history of the Counts of Montfort. Regional history.
W., Sa. 2-5.

THAINING

REGIONAL HOUSE
8911 Thaining, Bayern
Agricultural implements, equipment. Craftsmen's tools.
By appointment.

TIENGEN

NATURAL HISTORY MUSEUM
7897 Tiengen, Baden-Württemberg
Local wildlife. Botany.
On request.

TITTMONING

REGIONAL MUSEUM
Burg, 8261 Tittmoning, Bayern
Agricultural implements. Wrought-iron grave-crosses. Crafts. Furniture. Decorative arts.
F.-Tu. 9-5.

TRABEN-TRARBACH

MUSEUM OF THE CENTRAL MOSEL AREA
Moselstrasse, 5580 Traben-Trarbach, Rheinland-Pfalz
House (1750). Regional prehistory, history. 17th-18th century furniture, decorative arts. History of wine-production. Paintings. Prints. Drawings. Coins. Weapons.
W. 6-8; Su. 11-1.

TRAUNSTEIN

REGIONAL MUSEUM
Stadtplatz, 8220 Traunstein, Bayern
In 15th century inn. Regional natural history, prehistory, history. Crafts. Applied art. Folk-art. 17th-18th century paintings. 16th-19th century furniture. Sculpture. Coins.
Apr.-Oct., daily 10-12, 3-5.

TRECHTLINGHAUSEN

RHEINSTEIN PALACE ART COLLECTIONS
6531 Trechtlinghausen, Rheinland-Pfalz
Local history. Folklore. Paintings. Prints. Drawings.
Tu.-Sa. 10-5; Su. 10-1.

TREMSBÜTTEL

HILLERS MUSEUM OF AUTOMOBILES
Schlossstrasse, 2071 Tremsbüttel, Schleswig-Holstein
History of automobile construction. Motorcycles. Cars.
Apr.-Nov., daily 11-8. Dec.-Mar., Su. 11-8.

TRIBERG

REGIONAL MUSEUM
Wallfahrtstrasse 4, 7740 Triberg, Baden-Württemberg
Minerals. Craftsmen's workshops. Wood-carving. Glass. Operating Black Forest model-railway. Clocks. Costumes.
May-Oct., daily 8-6. Nov.-Apr., 9-12, 2-5.

TRIER

CATHEDRAL AND DIOCESAN MUSEUM
Konstantiplatz 4-5, 5500 Trier, Rheinland-Pfalz
Early Christian material from local excavations. 11th-19th century sculpture, paintings. 14th-19th century religious ornaments.
Daily 10-1.

CATHEDRAL TRESURY
Dom, 5500 Trier, Rheinland-Pfalz
Gold ornaments, liturgical objects. The Holy Shroud. Late medieval manuscripts. Carved ivory.
Daily 10-1.

KARL MARX HOUSE
Brückenstrasse 10, 5500 Trier, Rheinland-Pfalz
House in which Karl Marx was born (1818). Collection illustrating life of Marx.
By appointment.

MUNICIPAL MUSEUM
Simeonstift, 5500 Trier, Rheinland-Pfalz
History of Trier. 16th-18th century Dutch, Flemish paintings. 19th century paintings by Rhineland artists. Medieval sculpture, paintings. Coptic textiles.
Tu.-Su. 10-6; M. 10-5.

RHINELAND MUSEUM
Ostallee 44, 5500 Trier, Rheinland-Pfalz
Regional prehistory, early history, especially Roman. Medieval, 19th-20th century paintings, sculpture.
M.-Sa. 10-1, 2-5; Su. 9-1.

TROSSINGEN

FRITZ BEHN MUSEUM
7217 Trossingen, Baden-Württemberg
Life and work of Fritz Behn.
On request.

TROSTBERG

TROSTBERG MUNICIPAL MUSEUM
Schedling 9, 8223 Trostberg, Bayern
Regional history. 17th-19th century crafts, applied art. 17th-18th century furniture, decorative arts.
1st Su. in month, 1-4.

TÜBINGEN

STUDY-COLLECTIONS OF THE UNIVERSITY INSTITUTE OF ANTHROPOLOGY
Schloss, 7400 Tübingen, Baden-Württemberg
Anthropological collections.
By appointment.

COLLECTION OF THE UNIVERSITY INSTITUTE OF ARCHAEOLOGY
Nauklerstrasse 2, 7400 Tübingen, Baden-Württemberg
Greek, Roman, Etruscan objets d'art. Casts of Greek and Roman statues.
Tu.-F. 4-6. During University terms also 1st and 3rd Su. in month 11-12.30.

COLLECTION OF THE UNIVERSITY INSTITUTE OF EGYPTOLOGY
Correnstrasse 12, 7400 Tübingen, Baden-Württemberg
Egyptian art and antiquities.
By appointment.

COLLECTION OF THE UNIVERSITY INSTITUTE OF ETHNOLOGY
Schloss, 7400 Tübingen, Baden-Württemberg
Ethnography of the S. Pacific area.
By appointment.

COLLECTION OF THE UNIVERSITY INSTITUTE OF GEOLOGY AND PALAEONTOLOGY
Sigwartstrasse 10, 7400 Tübingen, Baden-Württemberg
Geology, especially of S.W. Germany. Palaeontology, especially vertebrates.
M.-F. 8-12, 2-6.

COLLECTIONS OF THE UNIVERSITY INSTITUTE OF THE HISTORY OF ART
Schloss Bebenhausen, 7400 Tübingen, Baden-Württemberg
Medieval - 19th century European paintings.
By appointment.

COLLECTIONS OF THE UNIVERSITY INSTITUTE OF PREHISTORY AND EARLY HISTORY
Schloss, 7400 Tübingen, Baden-Württemberg
European, especially German, prehistory, early history.
By appointment.

THEODOR HEARING HOUSE
Neckarhalde 31, 7400 Tübingen, Baden-Württemberg
History of Tübingen and the university. Paintings, drawings, engravings, especially views of the city. Book-printing, publishing, selling. Writers, philosophers, musicians with Tübingen connexions.
W., 1st and 3rd Su. in month 10-12, 3-6.

HÖLDERLIN MEMORIAL
Bursagasse 6, 7400 Tübingen, Baden-Württemberg
Life and work of Friedrich Hölderlin (1843).
Daily 10-12, public holidays 3-6.

MUSEUM OF THE UNIVERSITY INSTITUTE OF MINERALOGY AND PETROGRAPHY
Wilhelmstrasse 56, 7400 Tübingen, Baden-Württemberg
Mineralogy. Petrography. Meteorite science.
By appointment.

MUSEUM OF THE UNIVERSITY INSTITUTE OF ZOOLOGY
Nauklerstrasse, 7400 Tübingen, Baden-Württemberg
General zoological collections.
By appointment.

TUTTLINGEN

REGIONAL MUSEUM
Donaustrasse 50, 7200 Tuttlingen, Baden-Württemberg
Regional prehistory, history, ethnography. Commercial and industrial development of the area.
Su. 1.30-4.30. Other times by appointment.

TUTZING

G. FREY MUSEUM
Entomologisches Institut, Hofrat Beisele Strasse 6, 8132 Tutzing, Bayern
Coleopterae.
Tu.-Sa. 8-5.30, by appointment.

ÜBERLINGEN

REGIONAL MUSEUM
7770 Überlingen, Baden-Württemberg
Local history. Paintings and sculpture. Folklore. Puppet collection.
Tu.-Sa. 9-12, 2-6; Su. 10-12.

UELZEN

REGIONAL MUSEUM
Hoefftstrasse 3, 3110 Uelzen, Niedersachsen
Regional prehistory, cultural history.
W. 3-5; Sa., Su. 10.30-12.30.

UETERSEN

MUSEUM OF MILITARY AVIATION
Fliegerborst, 2082 Uetersen, Schleswig-Holstein
History of flying, especially military. Models of aircraft types, 1914-45. Original aeroplanes.
M.-F. 5-6; Sa. 3-5.30; Su., public holidays 9-4.

UFFENHEIM

REGIONAL MUSEUM
Albrecht Dürer Strasse 10, 8704 Uffenheim, Bayern
In tower (c.1387) of medieval town fortifications. Regional prehistory, history. Furniture. Household equipment. Apothecary's shop. Porcelain. Faience.
May-Oct., 8-12, 1-6.

ULM

GERMAN BREAD MUSEUM
Fürsteneckerstrasse 17, 7900 Ulm, Baden-Württemberg
History of breadmaking. Exhibition illustrating world-nutrition at the present time.
Daily 10-12, 3-5.30.

ULM MUSEUM
Neue Strasse 92, 7900 Ulm, Baden-Württemberg
Medieval art of Upper Swabia. Late 19th century - contemporary prints, watercolours, drawings, collages.
Tu.-Sa. 10-12, 2-5; Su. 10-1, 2-5.

UNNA

HELLWEG MUSEUM
Burgstrasse 8, 4750 Unna, Nordrhein-Westfalen
In 15th century castle. Local geology, prehistory, history. Folklore. Household equipment. Craftsmen's tools. Coins. Commercial and economic development of the Unna region.
Tu.-F. 10-1, 3-5; Sa., Su. 11-1.

UNTERRODACH

FLÖSSER MUSEUM
Kirchplatz 4, 8641 Unterrodach, Bayern
Pottery-manufacture. Models of types of pottery. Tools. equipment.
Daily 8-12, 2-5.

UNTERUHLDINGEN

OPEN-AIR MUSEUM OF GERMAN PREHISTORY
Standpromenade 6, 7777 Unteruhldingen, Baden-Württemberg
2 reconstructed prehistoric villages (Stone and Bronze Age), with furnishings, equipment. Prehistoric material from site excavations.
May-Oct., daily 8-6.

URACH

URACH CASTLE ALPINE MUSEUM
Schloss, 7417 Urach, Baden-Württemberg
History of Urach. Weapons.
May-Oct., Tu.-Sa. 10-12, 2-6; Su. 10-12, 1-6. Nov.-Apr., Tu.-Sa. 2-5; Su. 1-5.

USINGEN

WILHELM AND REGIONAL MUSEUM
Schlossplatz 4, 6390 Usingen, Hessen
Regional prehistory, history. Folklore.
Tu.-Sa. 10-12, 2-5; Su. 10-12.

VAREL

REGIONAL MUSEUM
2930 Varel, Niedersachsen
Local and regional history.
M.-F. 9-12, 2-5; Sa., Su. 10-12.

VEITSHÖCHHEIM

SUMMER PALACE
8702 Veitshöchheim, Bayern
17th-19th century palace. 18th - early 19th century period rooms. Tapestries. Paintings. Engravings.
May-Oct., Tu.-Su. 9-12, 1-6. Nov.-Apr., Tu.-Su. 10-12, 1-5.

VELBERT

GERMAN MUSEUM OF LOCKS AND FASTENINGS
Rathaus, 5620 Velbert, Nordrhein-Westfalen
Locks. Keys. Bolts. Furniture showing fitting and techniques of different types of fastening. Catalogues of engravings, woodcuts illustrating locks and fastenings.
Tu.-F. 9-5; Sa. 9-12.30; Su. 11-12.30.

VELBURG

REGIONAL MUSEUM
Burgstrasse 8, 8436 Velburg, Bayern
Natural history. Local and regional history. Handicrafts.
On request.

VERDEN

GERMAN MUSEUM OF THE HORSE
Kreishaus, 3090 Verden, Niedersachsen
Collections and displays illustrating the development of the horse and the horse in the history of mankind.
On request.

REGIONAL MUSEUM
Grosse Fischerstrasse 10, 3090 Verden, Niedersachsen
In early 18th century house. Regional prehistory, history. Folklore. Crafts.
W. 10-6; Su. 10-1.

VERINGENSTADT

REGIONAL MUSEUM
Rathaus, Hauptstrasse, 7481 Veringenstadt, Baden-Württemberg
Early history of the area. Roman tools. Documents relating to witchcraft trials. History of Veringenstadt.
On request.

VIERNHEIM

REGIONAL MUSEUM
Schlossstrasse 9, 6806 Viernheim, Baden-Württemberg
Local and regional history.
Tu.-Sa. 10-12, 2-5; Su. 10-1.

VIETZE

REGIONAL MUSEUM
3131 Vietze, Niedersachsen
Local and regional history.
On request.

VILLINGEN

BLACK FOREST COLLECTION
Rietstrasse 39, 7730 Villingen, Baden-Württemberg
Folklore of the Black Forest.
May-Oct., Tu.-F. 10-12. Nov.-Apr. by appointment.

VILLINGEN MUSEUM
Münsterplatz, 7730 Villingen, Baden-Württemberg
In medieval Town Hall. Local prehistory, early history. Paintings. Sculpture. Furniture. Crafts.
May-Oct., Tu.-Sa. 10-12. Other months by appointment.

VILSIBURG

REGIONAL MUSEUM
Stadtplatz 40, 8313 Vilsiburg, Bayern
Regional prehistory, history. Ceramics.
By appointment.

VOHENSTRAUSS

VOHENSTRAUSS REGIONAL MUSEUM
Marktplatz 9, 8483 Vohenstrauss, Bayern
Natural history. Crafts. Folk-art. History of local militia.
Daily 8-5.

VOLKACH

SCHELF HOUSE
Schelfengasse 1, 8712 Volkach, Bayern
House (1719-20), built by J. A. G. Schelf. 18th-19th century furniture, household equipment, decorative arts.
M.-F. 8-5.

VON DER HEYDT

GEOLOGICAL COLLECTION OF THE SAARBRÜCKEN SCHOOL OF MINING
Von der Heydt 22, 6601 Von der Heydt, Hessen
Geology. Mineralogy. Flora and fauna of the Saarland coal region.
W. 9-6; Su. 10-6.

VREDEN

HAMALAND MUSEUM
Gasthausstrasse 356, 4426 Vreden, Nordrhein-Westfalen
Local and regional geology, prehistory, history. Peasant household equipment, costumes, agricultural tools and equipment. Horse-drawn vehicles. Local pottery.
Tu.-Su. 9-12.30, 2.30-6.

WACHENDORF

PALACE MUSEUM
Schloss, 7241 Wachendorf, Baden-Württemberg
Local history. Crafts. Folklore.
By appointment.

WAIBLINGEN

REGIONAL MUSEUM
Rathaus, Schmiedener Strasse 51, 7050 Waiblingen, Baden-Württemberg
Prehistory of the region. History of Waiblingen. Agricultural implements. Crafts. History of local industry.
Sa., Su. 10-1. Other times by appointment.

WALDBURG

CASTLE MUSEUM
Burg, 7980 Waldburg, Baden-Württemberg
Furniture. Family history.
On request.

WALDECK

CASTLE MUSEUM
Burg, 3592 Waldeck, Hessen
Local and regional history. History of the castle.
May-Oct., 10-5.

WALDERBACH

REGIONAL MUSEUM
8411 Walderbach, Bayern
In former Cistercian monastery (12th century). Peasant house. Handicrafts. Agricultural history.
By appointment.

WALDSHUT

REGIONAL MUSEUM
Kaiserstrasse, 7890 Waldshut, Baden-Württemberg
Building (1588). Regional prehistory, history. Folklore. Paintings. Drawings. Prints. Sculpture. Applied art.
Su. 10-12.30.

WALDSRODE

REGIONAL MUSEUM
Hermann Löns Strasse 2, 3030 Waldsrode, Niedersachsen
Regional geology, prehistory, history. 17th-19th century crafts. 19th century portrait, medallions.
Apr.-Oct., M.-Sa. 9-12, 2-6; Su. 9-1.

WALLDÜRN

REGIONAL AND PILGRIMAGES MUSEUM
Haus 'Zum Goldenen Engel', 6968 Walldürn, Baden-Württemberg
House (1588). Folk-art, costumes, pottery, household equipment of the Odenwald. Craftsmen's tools. Agricultural implements. Walldürn pilgrimage mementoes. Religious folk-art.
W., Su. 2-4. Other times by appointment.

WALLDÜRN MUSEUM OF IVORY
Burgstrasse 24, 6968 Walldürn, Baden-Württemberg
12th-20th century carved ivory.
By appointment.

WALLERSHAUSEN

REGIONAL COLLECTION
6479 Wallershausen, Hessen
Regional history. Folklore.
By appointment.

WANFRIED

WANFRIED REGIONAL MUSEUM
Rathaus, Marktstrasse, 3442 Wanfried, Niedersachsen
Local and regional history.
On request.

WANGEN

GUSTAV FREYTAG MUSEUM AND ARCHIVES
Atzenberg 27, 7988 Wangen, Baden-Württemberg
Material relating to Gustav Freytag. Portraits. Manuscripts. Letters.
Tu. 3-6.

GERMAN EICHENDORFF MUSEUM
Atzenberg 31, 7988 Wangen, Baden-Württemberg
Life and work of Joseph Freiherr von Eichendorff (d.1857).
By appointment.

HERMANN STEHR MUSEUM
Atzenberg 29, 7988 Wangen, Baden-Württemberg
Life and work of Hermann Stehr (d.1940).
By appointment.

WANGEN REGIONAL MUSEUM
Haus Sonnenhalde, 7988 Wangen, Baden-Württemberg
Folklore. Regional history. Folk-art.
By appointment.

WANNE-EICKEL

REGIONAL MUSEUM
Unser Fritz Strasse 108, 4680 Wanne-Eickel, Nordrhein-Westfalen
Geology. Palaeontology. Regional history, ethnography. Peasant furniture, household equipment
Tu.-F. 8-12, 3-7; Sa., Su. 10-1.

WARBURG

REGIONAL MUSEUM
Sternstrasse 35, 3530 Warburg, Nordrhein-Westfalen
Prehistoric, early historical material from local excavations. History of Warburg. Furniture. Household equipment.
Daily 8-12, 3-5.

WARENDORF

DISTRICT MUSEUM
Münsterstrasse 12, 4410 Warendorf, Nordrhein-Westfalen
Local and regional prehistory, history. Furniture. Textiles. 18th-19th century sculpture, ceramics. Church pewter. Maps.
On request.

WARSTEIN

HAUS KUPFERHAMMER MUNICIPAL MUSEUM
Belecker Landstrasse, 4788 Warstein, Nordrhein-Westfalen
Regional geology, natural history, prehistory, history. Furniture. Craftsmen's tools. Agricultural equipment. 18th-19th century period rooms.
W., Sa. 4-6; Su. 10-12. Other times by appointment.

WARTHAUSEN

PALACE MUSEUM
Schloss, 7951 Warthausen, Baden-Württemberg
18th-19th century furniture, paintings, decorative arts.
By appointment.

WASSERBURG

WASSERBURG REGIONAL MUSEUM
Herrengasse, 8090 Wasserburg, Bayern
History of Wasserburg and its region. Folklore. Folk-art. 15th-19th century peasant furniture, household equipment. Agricultural implements. Religious art.
M.-W., F., Sa. 2-4; Su., public holidays 10-12.

WASSERTRÜDINGEN

SCHWARZKOPF COLLECTION
8822 Wassertrüdingen, Bayern
History of hairdressing and cosmetics.
By appointment.

WEENER

REGIONAL MUSEUM
2952 Weener, Niedersachsen
In former Old People's Home (1750). Agriculture. Household equipment. Nail-making. Tile-making. Social and cultural history of the region.
May-Sept., daily 3-5.

WEIDEN

TOWN MUSEUM
Unterer Markt 23, 8480 Weiden, Bayern
House (1536). Local prehistory, history. Crafts. Applied art. Furniture. Household equipment. Costumes. 17th-19th century pottery. Memorabilia of the composer, Max Reger.
By appointment.

WEIKERSHEIM

PALACE MUSEUM
6992 Weikersheim, Baden-Württemberg
Renaissance palace. 16th-18th century furniture, tapestries, paintings, porcelain, cut-glass.
May-Oct., daily 8-6. Nov.-Apr., Tu.-Su. 10-12, 2-4.

WEIL DER STADT

KEPLER MUSEUM
Kepler Gasse 2, 7252 Weil der Stadt, Baden-Württemberg
Religious history. History of science.
On request.

REGIONAL MUSEUM
Storchenturm, 7252 Weil der Stadt, Baden-Württemberg
Local and regional history.
On request.

WEILBURG

MUNICIPAL AND MINING MUSEUM
Schlossplatz 1, 6290 Weilburg, Hessen
Local prehistory, history. Mining and ore-processing. Furniture. Household equipment. Crafts. Commerce. Transport, especially airships. Paintings by Heinrich Heinlein. Weapons. Coins.
Apr.-Sept., Tu.-F., Su. 10-12, 2-5. Oct.-Mar., M.-F. 10-12; Th., F. also 2-4.

PALACE
6290 Weilburg, Hessen
16th-18th century palace. Furniture. Paintings. Decorative arts.
Tu.-F. 10-12.

WEILER

WEST ALLGAU REGIONAL MUSEUM
8999 Weiler, Bayern
Regional prehistory, history. Furniture. Costumes. Religious art. 15th-18th century sculpture.
W. 2-4; Su. 10-12.

WEILHEIM

TOWN MUSEUM
8120 Weilheim, Bayern
In old Town Hall (1533). Local prehistory, history. Local handicrafts. Medieval - 18th century sculpture. Paintings.
By appointment.

WEINGARTEN

WEINGARTEN MUSEUM OF PREHISTORY
7987 Weingarten, Baden-Württemberg
Prehistory of Weingarten and its region.
By appointment.

WEINHEIM

REGIONAL MUSEUM
Amtsgasse 2, 6940 Weinheim, Baden-Württemberg
In former House of the Teutonic Order. Regional prehistory, history. 19th century period rooms.
W., Sa. 2-4; Su. 10-12, 2-4.

WEINSBERG

JUSTINUS KERNER HOUSE
Ohringerstrasse 3, 7102 Weinsberg, Baden-Württemberg
Memorabilia of Justinus Kerner and his circle. Kerner's collection of paintings, drawings, sculpture.
Daily 9-12, 2-5.

WEISMAIN

REGIONAL MUSEUM
Am Markt 19, 8621 Weismain, Bayern
Handicrafts. Folk-art. Applied art. Weapons, especially cannon and culverins of the 30 Years War. Coins.
M., Th. 8-6; F. 8-5.

WEISSENBURG

REGIONAL MUSEUM
Martin Luther Platz 3, 8832 Weissenburg, Bayern
Regional prehistory, history. Folklore. Crafts. Peasant furniture, household equipment.
Tu.-F. 10-12, 2-4; Sa., Su. 10-12.30.

WEISSENHORN

REGIONAL MUSEUM
7912 Weissenhorn, Baden-Württemberg
15th-18th century sculpture. Paintings. Drawings. Furniture. Household equipment. Crafts. Religious art. Liturgical objects.
May-Oct., 1st Su. in month 2-4.

WEMDING

REGIONAL MUSEUM
Marktplatz 3, 8853 Wemding, Bayern
Regional prehistory, history. Peasant furniture, household equipment.
July-Aug., W. 2-5.

WERL

MISSION MUSEUM
Meisterstrasse 15, 4476 Werl, Nordrhein-Westfalen
Ethnographical material from Japan, China, New Guinea, Brazil and the Near East. Chinese coins. Babylonian cuneiform tablets.
Daily 9-6.

WERNE

REGIONAL MUSEUM
Kirchhof 13, 4712 Werne, Nordrhein-Westfalen
Fossils. Palaeolithic tools. Bronze Age pottery. Craftsmen's tools. Peasant domestic equipment.
Tu. 3-6; F., Sa. 9-12.

WERTACH

REGIONAL MUSEUM
8965 Wertach, Bayern
Regional wildlife. Paintings, sculpture, drawings by local artists. Agriculture. Weapons.
W., Sa. 2-5.

WERTINGEN

REGIONAL MUSEUM
Marktplatz 1, 8857 Wertingen, Bayern
Regional prehistory, history. Crafts. Peasant furniture, household equipment. Sculpture. Folk-art.
By appointment.

WESEL

SCHILL MUSEUM
Zitadelle, 4230 Wesel, Niedersachsen
Local history. Crafts.
On request.

WESSELBUREN

HEBBEL MUSEUM
Oesterstrasse 6, 2244 Wesselburen, Schleswig-Holstein
Life and work of C. F. Hebbel. Manuscripts. Engravings. Busts. First editions of Hebbel's works. Documents relating to his career.
May-Oct., daily 10-12, 2-6. Nov.-Apr., Tu., F. 3-6. Other times by appointment.

WESTRHAUDERFEHN

OSTFRIESLAND AND SATERLAND FEN AND SHIPPING MUSEUM
Rajen 120, 2953 Westerhauderfehn, Niedersachsen
Art Nouveau building. Prehistory. Settlement in the fens and moors. Shipping history. Memorial tablets to sailors lost at sea. Marine biology. Art of Africa, India, China, Japan. Coins.
Tu.-Sa. 10-12, 3-5; Su. 11-12, 3-5.

WETTELSHEIM

LOCAL COLLECTION
Amtshof, 8831 Wettelsheim, Bayern
Natural history. Local prehistory, history. Crafts. Folk-art. Costumes. Peasant furniture.
By appointment.

WETZLAR

FURNITURE COLLECTION
6330 Wetzlar, Hessen
16th-17th century furniture, household equipment.
By appointment.

JERUSALEM HOUSE
Schillerplatz, 6330 Wetzlar, Hessen
Memorabilia of K. W. Jerusalem, original of Goethe's Werther, who shot himself 1772.
M.-F. 10-12, 3-5; Sa. 10-12.

LOTTE'S HOUSE
Lottestrasse 8-10, 6330 Wetzlar, Hessen
Building was (1600 onwards) residence of the Steward of the Order of Teutonic Knights and in late 18th century of the Steward, Adam Buff, whose daughter was original of Lotte in Goethe's 'Werther'. Furniture. Memorabilia of Goethe. Werther collection.
Tu.-Sa. 10-1, 3-6; Su. 10-1.

MUNICIPAL MUSEUM
Lottestrasse 8-10, 6330 Wetzlar, Hessen
Local prehistory, history. Paintings. Mementoes and history of the Supreme Court (held at Wetzlar). Peasant art, furnishings.
Tu.-Sa. 10-1, 3-6; Su. 10-1.

PAPIUS MANSION
Kornblumengasse 1, 6330 Wetzlar, Hessen
European furniture. 16th-18th century applied art, especially bronzes, enamels, faience, lustreware.
Tu.-Sa. 10-12, 3-5; Su. 10-12.

WEWELSBURG

DISTRICT MUSEUM
Burg, 4791 Wewelsburg, Nordrhein-Westfalen
In 12th century castle. Local geology, prehistory, history. 15th-18th century furniture, household equipment. Agricultural implements. Religious art. Crafts. Wood carving. Weapons.
Tu.-Sa. 9-12, 3-5; Su. 11-12, 3.30-5.

WIESBADEN

NATURAL SCIENCES COLLECTION
Rheinstrasse 10, 6200 Wiesbaden, Hessen
Geology. Botany. Zoology, especially rare and extinct animals.
Tu.-Su. 10-4; Tu. also 5-9.

WIESBADEN MUNICIPAL MUSEUM
Friedrich Ebert Allee 2, 6200 Wiesbaden, Hessen
Natural sciences. Paintings. Engravings. Furniture. Applied arts.
Tu.-Su. 10-4; Tu. also 5-9.

WIESMOOR

MOOR MUSEUM
2954 Wiesmoor, Niedersachsen
History of the local peatmoors. Wildlife. Plants. Peat industry.
On request.

WILFINGEN

PALACE MUSEUM
Schloss, 7941 Wilfingen, Baden-Württemberg
Local history. Paintings. Furniture. Personal possessions of the von Stauffenberg family.
By appointment.

WILHELMSDORF

MAYOR'S OFFICES
7983 Wilhelmsdorf, Baden-Württemberg
Local history. Furniture. Documents.
By appointment.

WILHELMSHAVEN

COASTAL AND SHIPPING MUSEUM
Rheinstrasse 95, 2940 Wilhelmshaven, Niedersachsen
Regional geology, archaeology, history. Shipping and navigation, with special reference to the German Navy.
M.-F. 9-12, 3-5; Su. 10-1; May-Sept. also 10-1.

COLLECTION OF THE INSTITUTE FOR ORNITHOLOGICAL RESEARCH
2940 Wilhelmshaven, Niedersachsen
Birds of the North Sea coast. Bird-protection methods.
By appointment.

WILHELMSTHAL

PALACE
3520 Wilhelmsthal, Niedersachsen
18th century palace. Furniture. Decorative arts.
On request.

WILSEDE

HEATH MUSEUM
Ole Hus, 3041 Wilsede, Niedersachsen
Local and regional history.
M.-Sa. 10-5; Su. 10-12.

WILSTER

OLD TOWN HALL
Op de Goten 8, 2213 Wilster, Schleswig-Holstein
Building (1585). Regional history.
Tu.-Sa. 3-5.

WINDECK

WINDECK REGIONAL MUSEUM
5227 Windeck, Rheinland-Pfalz
Local history. Craftsmen's tools. Agricultural implements. Stove-plates.
Apr.-Sept., W., Sa. 2-6; Su. 10-12, 2-6.

WINNENDEN

REGIONAL MUSEUM
Torturm, 5057 Winnenden, Rheinland-Pfalz
Local and regional history.
M.-Sa. 10-12, 2-5.

WINSEN

MUSEUM ST. GEORG
2090 Winsen, Niedersachsen
Local and regional folklore.
Daily 9-12.

WITTEN

REGIONAL MUSEUM
Husemannstrasse 12, 5810 Witten, Nordrhein-Westfalen
Geology. Palaeontology. Mineralogy. Petrography. Local history. Folklore. Furniture. Household equipment. Medieval sculpture. German paintings, prints, drawings, since 1900. Coins.
Tu.-Sa. 10-1, 2-5; Su. 11-1.

WITTMUND

KARL BÖSCH COLLECTION
Osterstrasse 46, 2944 Wittmund, Niedersachsen
Paintings by Karl Bösch.
By appointment.

WOCKLUM

LUISENHÜTTE IRONWORKS MUSEUM
5759 Helle über Fröndenberg, Wocklum, Nordrhein-Westfalen
Early 19th century furnace and ironworks, with machinery and equipment.
May-Oct., M. 1-6; Tu.-Sa. 10-6; Su. 11.30-6. Nov.-Apr., M.-Sa. 10-6; Tu.-F. 3-6. Closed first Su. in month.

WOLFACH

WOLFACH REGIONAL MUSEUM
7620 Wolfach, Baden-Württemberg
Regional prehistory, history. Mineralogy. Mining. Folklore. Furniture. Decorative and applied arts. Paintings. Sculpture. Musical instruments. Costumes. Weapons. Armour.
W., Su. 10-12, 3-5.

WOLFEGG

WOLFEGG PALACE
7962 Wolfegg, Baden-Württemberg
17th century palace. Paintings, especially by Swabian artists. 16th-18th century furniture. Weapons.
M.-Sa. 9-12, 1.30-5.

WOLFENBÜTTEL

LAND MUSEUM OF HISTORY AND TRADITION
Kanzleistrasse 3, 3340 Wolfenbüttel, Niedersachsen
Prehistory and early history of Lower Saxony.
M., F., Sa. 10-1.

LESSING HOUSE
Lessingplatz 1, 3340 Wolfenbüttel, Niedersachsen
Lessing and his time. The German Enlightenment.
Apr.-Sept., daily 10-12, 2-4. Oct.-Mar., daily 10-12, 3-5.

WOLFENBÜTTEL DISTRICT MUSEUM
Schloss, 3340 Wolfenbüttel, Niedersachsen
In 15th-18th century palace. History of Wolfenbüttel area. 17th-18th century furnishings, paintings.
Tu.-Su. 9.30-12.30. Apr.-Sept. also Tu.-F., Su. 3-6. Oct.-Mar. also W., Su. 3-5.

WOLFHAGEN

REGIONAL MUSEUM
3549 Wolfhagen, Hessen
Regional prehistory, early history. Folklore. Religious history. Ceramics.
Su. 11-1, on request.

WORMS

HEYLSHOF GALLERY
Stephansgasse 9, 6520 Worms, Rheinland-Pfalz
15th-19th century Italian, French, Flemish, Dutch, German paintings. Painted glass. 16th-18th century ceramics. 17th-18th century glass. 16th-18th century Flemish, Dutch, French, German drawings.
Tu.-Su. 10-12, 2-4.

WORMS TOWN MUSEUM
Weckerlingplatz 7, 6520 Worms, Rheinland-Pfalz
Local and regional prehistory, history. Paintings. Drawings. Prints.
May-Oct., daily 9-12, 2-5. Nov.-Apr., daily 10-12, 2-4.

WORPSWEDE

MUSEUM AMONG THE TREES
2862 Worpswede, Niedersachsen
In the Art Nouveau style Café Verrückt. Prehistory, early history.
M.-F. 10-4; Sa. 10-2; Su. 11-1.

WÜLFRATH

NIEDERBERG REGIONAL MUSEUM
Bergstrasse 22, 5603 Wülfrath, Nordrhein-Westfalen
Regional geology, mineralogy, wildlife. Folklore. Limestone industry.
W., Sa. 3-6; Su. 11-12.30, 3-6.

WUNSIEDEL

WUNSIEDEL MUSEUM OF THE FICHTELGEBIRG REGION
Spitalhof 1-2, 8592 Wunsiedel, Bayern
Regional prehistory, history. Minerals. Crafts. Peasant furniture. Cribs. Costumes. Weapons.
Tu.-Sa. 8-12, 2-6; Su. 9-12.

WUPPERTAL

FRIEDRICH ENGELS MEMORIAL
5600 Wuppertal, Nordrhein-Westfalen
Life and work of Friedrich Engel.
M.-Sa. 10-5; Su. 10-1.

MISSION MUSEUM
Missionsstrasse 7, 5600 Wuppertal, Nordrhein-Westfalen
Ethnography. History of the Mission.
On request.

MUNICIPAL MUSEUM
Haus der Jugend, Geschwister Scholl Platz 6, 5600 Wuppertal, Nordrhein-Westfalen
Local and regional history.
M.-F. 10-12, 2-6; Su. 11-1.

MUSEUM OF KITSCH
Alarichstrasse 49, 5600 Wuppertal, Nordrhein-Westfalen
Kitsch art, crafts, curiosities.
Su. 10-1.

VON DER HEYDT MUSEUM
Turmhof 8, 5600 Wuppertal, Nordrhein-Westfalen
17th-20th century paintings, drawings, prints, sculpture.
Tu. 10-1, 5-9; Su. 10-1.

WUPPERTAL CLOCK MUSEUM
Poststrasse 11, 5600 Wuppertal, Nordrhein-Westfalen
Clocks, watches and other methods of measuring time. Paintings, engravings, coins, medals with the measurement of time as their subject.
M.-F. 10-12, 4-6; Su. 11.30-1.

WÜRZBURG

CITY GALLERY
Hofstrasse 3, 8700 Würzburg, Bayern
19th-20th century paintings, graphics, sculpture by artists living in the Würzburg region, or with local associations.
M., W.-Sa. 10-5; Su. 10-1.

FRANKISH MUSEUM
Festung Marienberg, 8700 Würzburg, Bayern
Frankish art. Applied arts. Sculpture by Peter Wagner and Ferdinand Tietz. 17th-18th century paintings. Tomb-sculpture.
May-Oct., daily 10-5; Nov.-Apr., 10-4.

MACROSCOPIC ANATOMY COLLECTION
Koellikerstrasse 6, 8700 Würzburg, Bayern
Comparative anatomy.
By appointment.

MARIENBERG CASTLE
8700 Würzburg, Bayern
Castle (partly 8th century), residence (13th-18th century) of the Bishops of Würzburg. Period rooms. Paintings.
May-Oct., daily 9-5. Nov.-Apr., Tu.-Su. 10-4.

RESIDENCE
Residenzplatz 2, 8700 Würzburg, Bayern
Late 19th century building. Period furnishings. Paintings. Tapestries.
May-Oct., daily 9-5. Nov.-Apr., Tu.-Su. 10-4.

UNIVERSITY OF WÜRZBURG COLLECTION OF MINERALOGY AND PETROGRAPHY
Pleichertorstrasse 34, 8700 Würzburg, Bayern
Historical geology.
By appointment.

MARTIN VON WAGNER MUSEUM OF THE UNIVERSITY OF WÜRZBURG
Residenz, 8700 Würzburg, Bayern
Greek and Roman ceramics (especially Greek vases), sculpture. 15th-19th century European drawings, engravings, prints, woodcuts. 14th-19th century European paintings. 14th-19th century German sculpture.
Greek and Roman department: Tu.-Sa. 2-5.30; Su. 10-1. Paintings: Tu.-Sa. 9.30-1; Su. 10-1. Graphics: Tu., Th. 4-6.

WYK

FÖHR ISLAND MUSEUM SOCIETY
Rebbelstieg, 2270 Wyk, Schleswig-Holstein
Local prehistory, history, wildlife. Folklore. Costumes. Crafts. Shipping, navigation. Whaling. Development of Wyk as seaside resort.
May-Oct., daily 10-12, 3-6. Nov.-Apr., 10-12, 2-4.

XANTEN

CATHEDRAL MUSEUM
Dom, 4232 Xanten, Nordrhein-Westfalen
Paintings. Sculpture. 1st-19th century liturgical objects. Religious ornaments.
Daily 10-12, 2-5.

ZIEGENHAIN

SCHWALM MUSEUM
Kleiner Pardeplatz, 3579 Ziegenhain, Hessen
Geology. Prehistory. History. Folklore. Agriculture. Crafts. Costumes. Household equipment.
Daily 10-12, 3-5.

ZÜLPICH

ZÜLPICH REGIONAL MUSEUM
5352 Zülpich, Nordrhein-Westfalen
Prehistory. Roman and medieval material from local excavations. Development of Zülpich since medieval times.
By appointment.

ZWEIBRÜCKEN

REGIONAL MUSEUM
Herzogstrasse 9, 6660 Zweibrücken, Rheinland-Pfalz
Local and regional history.
On request.

ZWIESEL

TOWN MUSEUM
Rathaus, 8372 Zwiesel, Bayern
Local history. Woodland and timber. Roots as natural sculpture. History of glass and glassmaking.
M.-Sa. 10-12, 2-5; Su. 10-12.

Ghana

Ghana is rightly proud of its museums. It has tried very hard since achieving independence to create not only museum institutions but a museum style and philosophy that will allow its more recent history to be seen in a reasonable perspective. The collections of ethnography and archaeology are presented for the most part in a pleasant way, with the regalia of chiefs supplemented by material showing the part that Ghana has played in the trading pattern of Europe and Africa.

ACCRA

DEPARTMENT OF ARCHAEOLOGY
University of Ghana, P.O. Box 3, Legon, Accra
Archaeology. Ethnography - mainly pottery, some brass work, basketry, wood carving. Some archaeological material from other parts of Africa. Collection of stone tools and fossil hominid casts.
M.-F. 8.30-3.

ETHNOGRAPHIC COLLECTION
Institute of African Studies, University of Ghana, Maintenance Road, Legon, Accra
Ethnography. Visual arts.
Daily 8-12, 2-4 by arrangement.

GHANA NATIONAL MUSEUM
Barnes Road, P.O. Box 3343, Accra
Archaeological collections illustrating the history and achievements of man in Africa, with some exhibits from Ancient Egypt and the classical world, and the bulk from Ghana. Ethnographical collections illustrate the traditional way of life of Ghanaian societies in all their aspects, Domestic religious and economic. Modern paintings and sculpture.
Tu.-Su. 9-6.

MUSEUM OF SCIENCE AND TECHNOLOGY
Liberia Road, P.O. Box 3343, Accra
The permanent exhibits include models and parts of the human body; models and parts of cars, including a demonstration of the working parts; project on studies of the life of clams of Battor; local herbs and flowers.
Daily ex. M. 9.30-6.

CAPE COAST

CAPE COAST HISTORICAL MUSEUM
c/o University College of Cape Coast, Cape Coast
Collections illustrating European/African trading on the west coast of Africa from 15th century to the present day.
By appointment.

KUMASI

MILITARY MUSEUM
The Fort, Kumasi
The collection includes a portrait of Yaa Asantewaa, leader of the 1900 Ashanti War; the rifle taken from a British Officer by Yaa Asantewaa, and two cannons used in the 1900 war.
Daily 7.30-5; closed 12-12.30.

MUSEUM OF NATURAL HISTORY
Department of Biological Sciences, University of Science and Technology, Kumasi
The collections include mounted study-skins and preserved specimens of mammals, birds, reptiles, fishes and insects.
Daily 7.30-12.30, 1.30-4.30.

PREMPEH II JUBILEE MUSEUM
National Cultural Centre, P.O. Box 3085, Kumasi, Ashanti
Collections comprise mainly Chiefs' Regalia, such as stools, gold arm bangles, finger rings, bracelets, treasure containers, weights and balances. Textiles and pottery.
Tu.-Sa. 9-5.30; Su. 1-5.30. Public holidays 1-5.30.

Gibraltar

Gibraltar's one museum features, it will be noticed, Barbary Apes and the history of the naval and military base. There is not a great deal more to feature.

GIBRALTAR

GIBRALTAR MUSEUM
Bomb House Lane, Gibraltar
Geology, botany and zoology of the Rock, including bones of animals which formerly lived in Gibraltar: lion, leopard, wolf, rhinoceros. Stuffed local birds. Display on the Barbary Apes. Old and New Stone Age material found in Gibraltar Caves. Phoenician pottery, scarabs, glass and jewellery. Roman exhibits. History and topography of Moorish and Spanish Gibraltar. History of the Rock since the British occupation in 1704: everyday life, portraits of Governors, early paintings and prints, model of the Rock. Military collections, including naval and army equipment and prints, material on the Great Siege of Gibraltar (1779-1783) and Lord Nelson (1758-1805).
Weekdays 11-1, 3-6.

Great Britain

Museums in Britain have always been handicapped by a chronic shortage of money. This is symbolised by the ludicrously inadequate headquarters of the central organisation, the Museums Association. A comparison between these wretched premises and the managerial splendours of the American Association of Museums in Washington drives the point home. Museum curators in Britain achieve wonders with resources that are a disgrace to a civilised community. Salaries are very low, secretarial and other forms of technical support on a pitiful scale, money for purchases laughable, even in the case of major national institutions, such as the Science Museum and the National Gallery.

Some of the younger and more enterprising curators have come to believe, however, that this impossible poverty may not necessarily be a bad thing, because it is gradually forcing museums to realise that it is futile to expect to get enough money from either national or central government, and that financial support has to be attracted, in one way or another, directly from the public. To achieve this, a museum must make sense by today's standards. It must have, not merely something, but a lot to offer to people of all ages and educational backgrounds, who are used to television styles, who are not afraid to be brutally rude when they are not interested, and who, most important, do not keep their knowledge and enthusiasms in the watertight compartments beloved of old-type museum administrators and scholars.

The museums in Britain which nowadays attract most people in relation to their size and, if one dare use the word, investment, and which are most written about in foreign periodicals and foreign professional journals are those which specialise and which have discovered how to promote their speciality - the Castle Museum at York, Tolgus Tin at Redruth, the new Museum of Man in London, the Ironbridge Gorge Museum in Shropshire, the County Museum in Dorchester, the Montagu Motor Museum at Beaulieu. It is probably true to say that the people who have done more than anybody else to push and haul British museums into the modern world are those once (but no longer) scorned Dukes and Earls, who have learnt how to become impresarios of their great mansions and estates. Whether Longleat or Woburn or Wilton or Blenheim have become museums in the process is difficult to say. We think they have, just as we are sure that the house which is graciously open to the public on two weekends a year remains firmly and unmistakably a house.

Of one thing there can be no mistake, that the Marquis of Bath, the Duke of Bedford, the Earl of Pembroke and their professional advisers have taught British museum curators some invaluable lessons about public relations, about advertising and about the willingness of the British public to spend large sums of money on educating itself, provided the word education is never used or hinted at.

The controversy about museum charges is political and irrelevant. If people are interested and feel they are being given good value, they will pay. If they are not being given good value, by modern standards, the museum in question should reform itself - which may involve moving out of its present embarrassing building - reshape itself into an efficient filing system for scholars; or close.

ABERDEEN

ABERDEEN ART GALLERY AND MUSEUM
School Hill, Aberdeen, Aberdeenshire
Oil paintings, water-colours, drawings and prints. Applied arts. History, especially maritime, of north-east of Scotland.
Weekdays 10-5; Sunday 2-5.

THE GORDON HIGHLANDERS SERVICE MUSEUM
Viewfield Road, Aberdeen, Aberdeenshire
Uniforms, old arms, awards, campaign medals, regimental colours, pictures, trophies and souvenirs illustrating history of the regiment.
W. and Su. 2-5.

PROVOST SKENE'S HOUSE
Guestrow, City Centre, Aberdeen, Aberdeenshire
17th century house, restored and maintained as a Museum of local history and domestic life.
Daily 10-5.

ABERDEEN UNIVERSITY ANTHROPOLOGICAL MUSEUM
Aberdeen, Aberdeenshire
Archaeology and ethnography. Classical, Eastern, Egyptian, American and Pacific collections. Local antiquities and skeletal remains of the Short Stone Cist (Beaker) people.
M.-F. 9-4 (W. 9-5, 6-9.30); Sa. 9-12, 2.30-5.30; Su. 2.30-5.30.

ABERDEEN UNIVERSITY NATURAL HISTORY MUSEUM
Zoology Department, Tillydrone Avenue, Aberdeen, Aberdeenshire
Natural history.
By appointment.

ABERFORD

LOTHERTON HALL
Aberford, Yorkshire
Paintings. Furniture. Silver race cups (1776-1842). Costumes.
Daily 10.30-6.15 or dusk. May-Sept. also Th. 10.30-8.30.

ABERGAVENNY

ABERGAVENNY AND DISTRICT MUSEUM
Castle House, Abergavenny, Monmouthshire
Border kitchen. Bygones. Prints. Photographs. Rural craft tools. Costumes. Archaeology. Harness. Postal history.
Weekdays 11-1, 2-5; Su. 2.30-5. Apr.-Sept.

ABERGELE

GARTHEWIN
nr. Abergele, Denbighshire
House (1730-1772). 18th century barn, now used as a theatre. Furniture and family portraits.
Easter-Sept. Daily 2.30-5.30.

ABERYSTWYTH

CEREDIGION MUSEUM
14 Vulcan Street, Aberystwyth, Cardiganshire, SY23 1JH
Folk material from the Cardiganshire area. Industrial archaeology. Archaeology.
M.-Sa. 2-6.

NANTEOS MANSION
Aberystwyth, Cardiganshire
Mansion (1739). Paintings. Victorian and Regency furniture. 17th-18th century books. Domestic utensils.
June-Sept., Th.-Tu. 1-10. Oct.-May, daily 1-5.30.

NATIONAL LIBRARY OF WALES
Aberystwyth, Cardiganshire
Books, manuscripts and records relating to Wales and the Celtic countries. Topographical prints, maps, drawings.
Weekdays 9.30-6; Sa. 9.30-5.

UNIVERSITY COLLEGE OF WALES GALLERY
Aberystwyth, Cardiganshire
Paintings. Sculpture. Pottery.
Verify opening times locally: normally Tu.-Sa. 10-5.

UNIVERSITY COLLEGE OF WALES, MUSEUM AND ART GALLERY
Aberystwyth, Cardiganshire
Crafts, principally pottery and wooden items.
M.-F. 10-5; Sa. 10-12.30 during term. By appointment during vacation.

ABINGDON

BOROUGH MUSEUM
County Hall, Abingdon, Berkshire
17th century building. Local fossil remains. Archaeological material, especially Anglo-Saxon. Local history. Prints. Charters. Documents.
Daily 2-5.

GUILDHALL
Abingdon, Berkshire
Building (15th - 19th century). Paintings, including works by Gainsborough, Lely. Corporation silver and plate, 16th-20th century.
Daily (unless in use) 9-5.

THE PENDON MUSEUM OF MINIATURE LANDSCAPE AND TRANSPORT
(The Pendon Museum Trust Limited), Long Wittenham, Abingdon, Berkshire
Historically accurate reproductions in miniature (1/76 scale) of country scenes of c. 1930, including Great Western trains (running) and thatched village. Railway relics, 1812 to present day.
Sa., Su., Bank Holidays (except Christmas Day and Boxing Day), 2-6.

ACCRINGTON

HAWORTH ART GALLERY
Haworth Park, Accrington, Lancashire
Early English water-colours. Tiffany glass.
Daily 2-5, also 6-8 on Su. April-Oct.

ACHARN

LOCHTAYSIDE CRAFTS
The Old Mill, Acharn, by Aberfeldy, Perthshire
Household equipment and agricultural implements used by Highland crofters in the 18th and 19th centuries.
By appointment.

AIRDRIE

AIRDRIE PUBLIC MUSEUM
Wellwynd, Airdrie, Lanarkshire
Local history.
Weekdays 10-9.

ALCESTER

COUGHTON COURT
Alcester, Warwickshire
Jacobite relics. Furniture, porcelain, portraits and personal possessions of the Throckmorton family.
Apr. and Oct., Sa. and Su. (Easter week daily except Good F.). May-Sept., W., Th., Sa., Su. and Bank Holiday M. and Tu. following 2-6.

RAGLEY HALL
Alcester, Warwickshire
Paintings. China. Furniture.
Mid.-Apr. - end Sept. Tu., W., Th., Sa., Su. and Bank Holiday M. 2-6.

ALDBOROUGH

ALDBOROUGH ROMAN MUSEUM
Boroughbridge, Aldborough, Yorkshire
Archaeological material, including pottery, glass, metalwork and coins, from the Roman town.
Mar., Apr. and Oct. 9.30-5.30 (Sun. 2-5.30); May- Sept. 9.30-7 (Su. 2-7); Nov. - Feb. 9.30-4 (Su. 2-4).

ALDEBURGH

THE MOOT HALL
Aldeburgh, Suffolk
Ship models and other items illustrative of the town's maritime history. Material from the Snape Ship Burial.
Summer only: M.-Sa. 10-12.30, 2-5; Su. 2.30-6.

ALDERSHOT

AIRBORNE FORCES MUSEUM
Browning Barracks, Queens Avenue, Aldershot, Hampshire
Development of British airborne forces, 1940 to the present day.
M.-F. 9-12.30, 2-5; Sa. 9.30-12.30; Su. 10-12.30, 2-4.30.

ARMY PHYSICAL TRAINING CORPS MUSEUM
A.S.P.T., Queen's Avenue, Aldershot, Hampshire
Uniforms, weapons, awards, campaign medals, regimental colours, pictures, trophies and souvenirs illustrating history of the Corps.
M.-F. by appointment 10-4.30.

QUEEN ALEXANDRA'S ROYAL ARMY NURSING CORPS SERVICE MUSEUM
The Royal Pavilion, Farnborough Road, Aldershot, Hampshire
Uniforms, awards, medals, pictures, trophies and souvenirs illustrating history of the Corps.
M.-F. 8-4.30.

ROYAL ARMY DENTAL CORPS MUSEUM
Duke of Connaught's Road, Aldershot, Hampshire
Dental instruments and other items of professional interest.
By written appointment only.

ROYAL ARMY MEDICAL CORPS HISTORICAL MUSEUM
Keogh Barracks, Ash Vale, Aldershot, Hampshire
History of Royal Army Medical Corps.
By appointment.

ROYAL ARMY VETERINARY CORPS MUSEUM
Thornhill, Aldershot, Hampshire
History of Royal Army Veterinary Corps.
By appointment.

ROYAL CORPS OF TRANSPORT MUSEUM
Queen Elizabeth Barracks, Crookham, nr. Aldershot, Hampshire
Uniforms, weapons, awards, campaign medals, regimental colours, pictures, trophies and souvenirs illustrating history of the Corps.
M.-F. 10-12.30, 2-4.

ALEXANDRIA

CAMERON HOUSE
Alexandria, Dumbartonshire
House (1412, rebuilt 1865). Furniture. Porcelain. Toys. Memorabilia of Tobias Smollett.
Easter-Sept., daily 11-6.

ALLOWAY

BURNS' COTTAGE AND MUSEUM
Alloway, Ayrshire
Thatched cottage in which Robert Burns was born (1759). Burns' relics.
M.-Sa. 9-7; Su. 2-7. Nov.-Mar. closes at dusk.

ALNWICK

ALNWICK CASTLE
Alnwick, Northumberland
Castle (12th century). Heirlooms of Percy family. State coach. British and Roman antiquities.
May-Sept. Daily (except F. and Sa.) 1-5. No admission after 4.30.

ALTON

ALLEN GALLERY
12 Church Street, Alton, Hampshire
Curtis family portraits and mementoes. Local topographical paintings and drawings.
M., Tu., Th. and F. 2-5; Sa. 10-1, 2-5. Closed W., Bank and public holidays.

CURTIS MUSEUM
High Street, Alton, Hampshire
Hampshire craft tools and domestic bygones. Local geology, natural history, archaeology. English porcelain, pottery. Glass relics of Fanny Adams.
M., Tu., Th. and F. 2-5, Sa. 10-1, 2-5. (Closed W., Bank and Public Holidays).

C. G. VOKES GALLERY OF SPORTING FIREARMS
Curtis Museum Annexe, 10 Church Street, Alton, Hampshire
Firearms and accessories illustrating the development of gun-making from 14th to 20th centuries. Collection includes items from Europe, the United States and Japan.
M.-F. 2-5; Sa. 10-1. Closed Su. and W.

ALTRINCHAM

ART GALLERY AND MUSEUM
George Street, Altrincham, Cheshire
Local history. Paintings.
M., Tu., Th. and F. 10-7.30; W. 10-1; Sa. 10-5.

AMBLESIDE

RYDAL MOUNT
Ambleside, Westmorland
Home of William Wordsworth, 1813 until his death in 1850. Family portraits. Furniture. Memorabilia of the poet. First editions of his works.
Mar. 1 - Jan. 2, daily ex. Tu. 10-12.30, 2-5.30.

ANDOVER

TASKERS OF ANDOVER LIMITED
Waterloo Iron Works, Anna Valley, Andover, Hampshire
Tasker collection of agricultural machinery, traction engines and rural engineering.
Collection held by Hampshire County Museum Service, Chilcomb House, Chilcomb Lane, Winchester, Hampshire.
By appointment.

ANNAN

ANNAN MUSEUM
Moat House, Annan, Dumfries
Natural history. Archaeological. Local history. Shipping. Thomas Carlyle and Dr. Arnott material.
Weekdays 9-5.

ANSTRUTHER

SCOTTISH FISHERIES MUSEUM
St. Ayles, Harbourhead, Anstruther, Fife
Marine aquarium. Fishing. Ships' gear. Navigation equipment, model fishing vessels.
June-Sept. Weekdays 10-12.30, 2-6; Su. 2-5. Oct.-May, Daily 2.30-4.30 (Closed Tu.).

ARBORFIELD

ROYAL ELECTRICAL AND MECHANICAL ENGINEERS MUSEUM
Moat House, Arborfield, Berkshire
Uniforms, weapons, awards, campaign medals, regimental colours, pictures, trophies and souvenirs.
By appointment.

ARBROATH

ARBROATH ABBEY MUSEUM
Arbroath, Angus
Architectural and historical exhibits primarily connected with the Abbey.
Apr.-Sept., Daily 9.30-7 (Su. 2-7); Oct.-Mar., Daily 10-4.30 (Su. 2-4.30).

ARBROATH ART GALLERY
Public Library, Hill Terrace, Arbroath, Angus
Paintings and drawings, mainly by local artists. Pastels and water colours by J. W. Herald.
Weekdays 11-1, 2.30-6. Closed Th.

ST. VIGEANS MUSEUM
Arbroath, Angus
Sculptured monuments of the Celtic Christian period, including the Drosten stone.
Apr.-Sept., Weekdays 9.30-7; Oct.-Mar., Weekdays 10-4.30.

ARDRESS

ARDRESS
County Armagh, Northern Ireland
House (1660, remodelled 1770s). 18th century plasterwork, furnishings. Paintings.
Apr.-Sept., W.-M. 2-6.

ARGYLL

INVERARAY CASTLE
Argyll, Argyllshire
18th century castle. 18th century furniture. Paintings. Tapestries. Domestic utensils. Armour.
M.-Th., Sa. 10-12.30, 2-6; Su. 2-6. July-2nd Su. in Oct., M.-Sa. 10-6; Su. 2-6.

ARMAGH

ARMAGH COUNTY MUSEUM
The Mall, Armagh, Northern Ireland
Local antiquities, prehistoric weapons, implements. Costumes, uniforms. Natural history. Bygones.
Weekdays 10-1, 2-5. Closed Bank Holidays.

THE ROYAL IRISH FUSILIERS MUSEUM
Sovereign's House, The Mall, Armagh, Northern Ireland
Uniforms, weapons, awards, campaign medals, regimental colours, pictures, trophies and souvenirs illustrating the history of the Regiment.
M.-F. 10-12.30, 2-4.30.

ARRETON

ARRETON MANOR
Arreton, Isle of Wight
17th century manor house. Early and late Stuart furniture. Domestic and agricultural bygones. Children's toys. Dolls and dolls' houses.
April-Oct., Weekdays 10-6; Su. 2.30-6.

ARUNDEL

ARUNDEL CASTLE
Arundel, Sussex
Portraits and furniture, 15th century onwards.
Mid-Apr. - mid June, M.-Th. 1-4.30. Mid-June - 1st Oct. M.-F. 12-4.30 (also in Aug. Su. 12-4.30).

ASHBURTON

ASHBURTON MUSEUM
1 West Street, Ashburton, Devon
Local antiquities, weapons, period costumes, lace, implements, lepidoptera. American Indian antiques. Bygones.
May-Sept. Tu. and Sa. 2.30-5. Other times by appointment.

ASHFORD

GODINTON PARK
Ashford, Kent
Jacobean house. Furniture. China. Portraits. Panelling and wood carvings.
Easter Sa.-M. 2-5. June-Sept., Su. and Bank Holidays 2-5.

THE INTELLIGENCE CORPS MUSEUM
Templer Barracks, Ashford, Kent
History of British military intelligence in memento, document and pictorial form, from Elizabethan times to present day.
M.-F. 10-12, 2-4.

WYE COLLEGE AGRICULTURAL MUSEUM
Wye College, Wye, Ashford, Kent
Farm tools and implements. Farm wagons and carts.
W. June-Sept. 2-5. Sa. (Aug. only) 2-5.

ASHWELL

ASHWELL VILLAGE MUSEUM
Swan Street, Ashwell, Hertfordshire
Life and work in the village from the Stone Age to the present day.
Su. 2.30-5 or any time by appointment.

ASTON MUNSLOW

WHITE HOUSE COUNTRY LIFE MUSEUM
Nr. Craven Arms, Ashton Munslow, Shropshire
Agricultural tools and implements, dairy and domestic utensils. Cart shed, granary, cider house, stable, tools, kitchen. Carts, traps, ploughs.
Early Apr. - late Oct., W., Sa. 11-6; mid-July - early Sept. M., Tu. and W. 2-6. Good Friday 2-6. Easter, Spring and late Summer Holiday weeks, Daily except Th. and Su. 11-6.

AVEBURY

ALEXANDER KEILLER MUSEUM
Avebury, Wiltshire
Pottery and other objects of the Neolithic and Bronze Ages and later date from the excavations at Avebury and Windmill Hill.
Mar. and Oct. 9.30-5.30 (Su. 2-5.30); Apr. 9.30-5.30 daily; May-Sept. 9.30-7 daily; Nov.-Feb. 9.30-4 (Su. 2-4).

AXBRIDGE

AXBRIDGE CAVING GROUP AND ARCHAEOLOGICAL SOCIETY
The Museum, Town Hall, Axbridge, Somerset
History and pre-history of the Axbridge-Banwell-Cheddar areas.
By appointment.

AYLESBURY

BUCKINGHAMSHIRE COUNTY MUSEUM
Church Street, Aylesbury, Buckinghamshire
County archaeology and history. Local crafts. Costumes. Natural history. Paintings.
M.-F. 9.30-5; Sa. 9.30-12.30, 1.30-5.

WADDESDON MANOR
nr. Aylesbury, Buckinghamshire
French decorative art 17th-18th centuries. English, Dutch, Flemish and Italian paintings. French drawings, textiles, costumes, lace. Family mementoes.
Apr.-Oct. W.-Su. 2-6, also Bank Holidays, 11-6.

AYLSHAM

BLICKLING HALL
Aylsham, Norfolk
Jacobean house, altered 1765-70. State rooms contain furniture, pictures, tapestries.
House and Gardens, April - early Oct. W., Th., Sa., Su. and Bank Holiday M., 2-6 (Gardens open at 11, Spring Bank Holiday Su. to end Sept.).

AYOT ST. LAWRENCE

SHAW'S CORNER
Ayot St. Lawrence, Hertfordshire
Home of George Bernard Shaw from 1906-1950. Manuscripts and other relics of the author.
All the year, Daily (except Tu.), 11-1, 2-6 or dusk. Closed Good F., the last 2 weeks in Dec. and first 2 weeks in Jan.

AYR

AYR MUSEUM
12 Main Street, Ayr, Ayrshire
Local history.
Weekdays 10-7.

AYRSHIRE YEOMANRY SERVICE MUSEUM
Yeomanry House, Ayr, Ayrshire
Regimental uniforms, weapons, awards, campaign medals, regimental colours, pictures, trophies and souvenirs.
By appointment.

BACUP

BACUP NATURAL HISTORY SOCIETY'S MUSEUM
24 Yorkshire Street, Bacup, Lancashire
Natural history. Local geology. Domestic bygones.
By appointment.

BADMINTON

BADMINTON HOUSE
Badminton, Gloucestershire
17th century house. Italian, Dutch and English paintings. 18th and 19th century furniture.
Early Spring Bank Holidays, then May 30 - early Sept., W. only 2.30-5.

BAGSHOT

ROYAL ARMY CHAPLAINS' DEPARTMENT CENTRE
Bagshot Park, Surrey
Uniforms, awards, campaign medals, pictures, trophies and souvenirs of the Corps.
M., Tu., Th. and F.

BAKEWELL

CHATSWORTH
Bakewell, Derbyshire
Built for 1st Duke of Devonshire 1687-1707. Pictures. Drawings. Books. Furniture.
Apr.-Oct. 3, W., Th. and F. 11.30-4; Sa. and Su. 2-5.30; Bank Holiday M. and Tu. and Good F., 11.30-5.30.

OLD HOUSE MUSEUM
Cunningham Place, Bakewell, Derbyshire
Medieval house with original wattle and daub interior walls and open-timbered chamber. Industrial archaeology collection including early Arkwright machinery.
Easter Sa. - Sept. 30, daily 2.30-5.

BAMBURGH

GRACE DARLING MUSEUM
Bamburgh, Northumberland
Grace Darling relics. Life-boat history.
Easter - mid-Oct., Weekdays 11-12.30, 2-5; Su. 3-5. Other times by arrangement.

BANBURY

SULGRAVE MANOR
Banbury, Northamptonshire
House (1560) was home of ancestors of George Washington. Portraits of Washington. Old kitchen equipment.
Daily (except W.) Apr.-Sept. 10.30-1, 2-5.30. Oct.-Mar 10.30-1, 2-4.

BANBURY PUBLIC MUSEUM AND GLOBE ROOM
Marlborough Road, Banbury, Oxfordshire
Local history.
M., W., Th., F. 3-5; Sa. 9.30-12.30, 2-5.

BROUGHTON CASTLE
Banbury, Oxfordshire
Relics of English Civil War.
Apr.-Sept. W., Su. (see local press). Also Bank Holiday M. 2-5.30.

CHACOMBE PRIORY
nr. Banbury, Oxfordshire
Priory dates from 1066. Picture gallery and silver room. Furniture.
Apr., May and Sept., Su. and Bank Holiday weekends including Good F. June and July Sa. and Su., Aug. F., Sa. and Su. 2.30-6.30.

BANCHORY

CRATHES CASTLE
Banchory, Kincardineshire
16th century castle. Painted ceilings. Furniture.
May-Sept. Daily 2-7. Oct. and Apr. W. and Su. 2-7.

BANFF

BANFF MUSEUM
Banff, Banffshire
Local and natural history.
By appointment.

BANGOR

BANGOR ART GALLERY
Bangor, Caernarvon
Contemporary painting and sculpture.
Weekdays 10.30-5.30.

MUSEUM OF WELSH ANTIQUITIES
University College of North Wales, College Road, Bangor, Caernarvon
History of North Wales. Welsh prehistoric and Roman antiquities, furniture, domestic objects, textiles, ceramics and clothing.
Nov. - Mar., M.-F. 1-4; Apr. - Oct., Weekdays 10-4.

PENRHYN CASTLE
Bangor, Caernarvon
Castle 1827-40. Dolls. Locomotives and rolling stock. Stuffed animals, birds, butterflies and insects.
Apr.-Oct. M.-F. 11-5; Sa., Su. 2-5.

BARNARD CASTLE

BOWES MUSEUM
Barnard Castle, Co. Durham
European art, late medieval - 19th century. Tapestries, furniture, porcelain, glass, jewellery, sculpture and metalwork. Paintings by Italian, Spanish, Flemish, Dutch, French and English artists.
Weekdays, 10-5.30 (10-5 Oct., Mar., Apr. 10-4 Nov.-Feb.). Su. 2-5 (2-4 in winter).

BARNSLEY

CANNON HALL ART GALLERY AND MUSEUM
Barnsley, Yorkshire
18th century country house museum containing furniture, paintings, china, silver, in period rooms. Military section showing the history of the 13th/18th Royal Hussars.
Weekdays 10.30-5; Su. 2.30-5 (dusk in winter).

COOPER ART GALLERY
Church Street, Barnsley, Yorkshire
17th-19th century European paintings. English drawings. Sadler collection
Weekdays 11.30-5 (closed Su.).

BARNSTAPLE

ARLINGTON COURT
Barnstaple, Devon
Regency furniture. Shells. Pewter. Model ships. Horse-drawn vehicles.
Apr.-mid Oct. Daily 11-1 (last admission 12.30); 2-6 (last admission 5.30).

NORTH DEVON ATHENAEUM
The Square, Barnstaple, Devon
North Devon geological specimens. Cryptograms. Local antiquities.
M.-F. 10-1, 2-6; Sa. 10-1.

ST. ANNE'S CHAPEL MUSEUM
St. Peter's Churchyard, High Street, Barnstaple, Devon
Local history.
Whitsun-Michaelmas 10-1, 2-5.

BARROW-IN-FURNESS

BARROW-IN-FURNESS MUSEUM
Ramsden Square, Barrow-in-Furness, Lancashire
History of the Furness area. Vickers-Armstrong collection of ship models. Finds from prehistoric sites, chiefly Bronze Age. Lake District bygones.
Weekdays 10-7. Closed Bank Holidays.

BASINGSTOKE

WILLIS MUSEUM
New Street, Basingstoke, Hampshire
Geology, archaeology and history of Hampshire. Costumes. Horology, including watchmakers' tools. Numismatics. Local topographical prints and drawings.
M. 1.30-5.30; Tu.-Sa. 10-12.30, 1.30-5.30. Closed Bank and Public Holidays.

BATH

AMERICAN MUSEUM IN BRITAIN
Claverton Manor, nr. Bath, Somerset
American decorative arts, late 17th-mid 19th century. Furnished rooms. Paintings. Furniture. Glass. Woodwork. Metal work. Textiles. Miniature rooms. Marine room. American gardens.
Easter-mid Oct. Daily (exc. M.) 2-5. Bank Holidays 2-5. During winter on application only.

BATH ROMAN MUSEUM
Abbey Churchyard, Nr. Bath Abbey, Bath, Somerset
Adjoins the extensive remains of the Roman Baths, and includes material from that and other Roman sites, including architectural fragments, inscriptions.
Winter: Weekdays 9-5; Su. 11-5. Summer: Daily 9-6.

HOLBURNE OF MENSTRIE MUSEUM
Great Pulteney Street, Bath, Somerset
Paintings. Drawings. Silver. Porcelain. Glass. Furniture. Miniatures.
Apr.-Oct., Weekdays 11-1, 2-5; Su. 2.30-5.30. Nov.-Mar. Weekdays (exc. W.) 11-1, 2-5.

MUSEUM OF COSTUME
Assembly Rooms, Bath, Somerset
Every aspect of fashion, 17th century to the mode of the current year.
Winter: Weekdays 10-5; Su. 11-5. Summer: Weekdays 9.30-6; Su. 11-6.

NO. 1 ROYAL CRESCENT
Bath, Somerset
Georgian House as it was when built by John Wood the Younger, 1767. Furniture of that period.
Mar.-Oct. Tu., W., Th., F. and Sa. 11-5; Su. 2-5.

VICTORIA ART GALLERY
Bridge Street, Bath, Somerset
18th century and modern paintings. Early water-colour drawings. Etchings. Ceramics. Coins of Bath mint and Bath tokens. Glass. Watches.
Weekdays 10-6. Closed Su., Good Friday, Christmas Day and Boxing Day. Display rooms also at 18 Queen Square: Geology (Moore Collection) and local history. Tu.-Sa. 10-1, 2.30-6.

BATLEY

ART GALLERY
Market Place, Batley, Yorkshire
Contemporary paintings and drawings.
Weekdays 11-6 (closed 5 Sa., 8 F.). Closed Tu. and Su.

BAGSHAW MUSEUM
Wilton Park, Batley, Yorkshire
Natural history. Local history. Ethnography. Applied arts. Oriental antiquities. Textile industry bygones. Victoriana.
M. 1.30-6 (1.30-5.30 in winter); other weekdays 11-6, Sa. 11-6 (11-5.30 in winter); Su. 2-7 (12-4.30 in winter).

OAKWELL HALL
Birstall, Batley, Yorkshire
16th century house with Bronte associations. Wall earth closet or "secret passage". Period furniture.
Daily 2-7 (12-5 winter). Closed F. (Summer opening April 1-Oct. 31).

BATTLE

BATTLE MUSEUM
Langton House, Battle, Sussex
Battle of Hastings diorama. Roman-British remains from local sites. Sussex iron industry collection.
Easter-Oct.: Weekdays 10-1, 2-5; Su. 2.30-5.30.

BEAMISH

NORTH OF ENGLAND OPEN AIR MUSEUM
Beamish Hall, Stanley, Co. Durham
All aspects of the industry of the North-East.
May-Oct. F., Sa., Su. 11-8.

BEAULIEU

MARITIME MUSEUM
Buckler's Hard, Beaulieu, Hampshire
Ships and shipping history.
Apr.-Oct. Daily 10-6. Nov.-Mar. Sa. and Su. 10-5.

NATIONAL MOTOR MUSEUM
Palace House, Beaulieu, Hampshire
Veteran and Vintage Motor Car and Motor Cycle collection.
Daily 10-6 (winter 10-5).

BECKINGTON

THE MIN LEWIS PERAMBULATOR MUSEUM
Beckington, Bath, Somerset
17th century house. Eighty vintage baby-carriages, early 19th century to the present day, with a large bisque doll dressed in period costume in each perambulator. Wall decoration of Victorian park scene.
Daily except F. 11-1, 2-5.30 or by appointment.

BEDALE

BEDALE HALL
Bedale, Yorkshire
Georgian mansion. Domestic and craft exhibits.
Mar.-Sept. Tu. 2-4.30 or by appointment at other times.

BEDFORD

BEDFORD MUSEUM
The Embankment, Bedford, Bedfordshire
Local history. Natural history. Coins. Maps. Prints.
Weekdays 11-5; Su. 2-5.

BUNYAN COLLECTION
Public Library, Harpur Street, Bedford, Bedfordshire
Library and exhibition devoted to life and works of John Bunyan.
Weekdays 10-6.

BUNYAN MEETING LIBRARY AND MUSEUM
Mill Street, Bedford, Bedfordshire
Contains the surviving personal relics of John Bunyan. Collection of Bunyan's works in over 150 languages.
Tu.-F. 10-12, 2.30-4.30.

CECIL HIGGINS ART GALLERY
Castle Close, Bedford, Bedfordshire
English and Continental porcelain. English glass, furniture, water-colours, prints and silver.
Weekdays 11-6; Su. 2.30-5.

ELSTOW MOOT HALL
Bedford, Bedfordshire
Medieval market hall containing 17th century collection associated with John Bunyan.
Tu.-Sa. 11-5; Su. 2.30-5.30. Open Summer Bank Holidays.

BELFAST

QUEEN'S UNIVERSITY
Department of Geology, Elmwood Avenue, Belfast, Northern Ireland
Fossils, minerals and rocks.
By appointment only.

THE ROYAL ULSTER RIFLES MUSEUM
Waring Street, Belfast, Northern Ireland
Uniforms, old arms, awards, campaign medals, regimental colours, pictures, trophies and souvenirs associated with the regiment.
M.-F. 10-4; Sa. 9.30-12.30. Closed Bank Holidays.

TRANSPORT MUSEUM
Witham Street, Newtownards Road, Belfast, Northern Ireland
Steam locomotives and railway carriages. Steam, electric and horse trams. Coaches, carriages and vans. Early cars, motor bicycles and pedal cycles. Fire appliances. Ship models. Railway relics and equipment. Prints and photographs.
Weekdays 10-6 (W. 10-9).

ULSTER MUSEUM
Stranmillis, Belfast, Northern Ireland
Irish antiquities. Local history. Industrial technology and natural history of Ireland. Ethnography. Spinning wheels. Cycles. Art Gallery contains contemporary paintings and sculpture, old masters, water colours and Irish silver, glass and pottery. Treasure from Spanish Armada galleass *Girona.*
M., Tu., F., Sa. 11-6; W. and Th. 11-9; Su. 2.30-5.

ULSTER FOLK MUSEUM
Cultra Manor, Craigavad, Belfast, Northern Ireland
Indoor and outdoor exhibits. Craftsmen's tools, equipment. Furnishings. Domestic equipment. Costumes. The outdoor museum features several traditional buildings reconstructed in natural settings, including an operative 19th century water-powered spade mill from Co. Tyrone.
Summer: Daily 2-9. Winter: Daily 2-5.

BEMBRIDGE

RUSKIN GALLERY
Bembridge School, Isle of Wight
Pictures and manuscripts by Ruskin and his contemporaries.
By appointment.

BERKELEY

BERKELEY CASTLE
Berkeley, nr. Bristol
Castle (1153), scene of the murder of King Edward II (1327). Paintings. Furniture. Tapestries. Berkeley collection of silver.
Apr.-Sept. Daily (except M.) 2-5.30, also Bank Holiday M. 11-5.30. Su. only in Oct., 2-4.30.

BERWICK-ON-TWEED

BERWICK-ON-TWEED MUSEUM AND ART GALLERY
Marygate, Berwick-on-Tweed, Northumberland
Ceramics and brasswork. Special collection of local antiquities. Paintings by Dégas, Daubigny, Boudin and Opie.
M., W. and F. 10-7; Tu., Th. and Sa. 10-5.

THE KING'S OWN SCOTTISH BORDERERS SERVICE MUSEUM
The Barracks, Berwick-on-Tweed, Northumberland
Uniforms, old arms, awards, campaign medals, regimental colours, pictures, trophies and souvenirs associated with the Regiment.
M.-F. 9.15-12.30, 2-4.30; Sa. 9.15-12.30. Su. by appointment.

BEVERLEY

BEVERLEY ART GALLERY AND MUSEUM
Champney Road, Beverley, Yorkshire
Art Gallery includes paintings by the Beverley artist F. W. Elwell. Local antiquities.
Weekdays 10-6 (10-1 W.).

THE EAST YORKSHIRE REGIMENT SERVICE MUSEUM
Beverley, Yorkshire
Amherst Flag 1751-57. Dioramas. Uniforms, weapons, awards, campaign medals, pictures, trophies and souvenirs associated with the regiment.
W.-F. 2-4.

BEWDLEY

BEWDLEY MUSEUM
The Shambles, Townhall, Bewdley, Worcestershire
In the town's lockups (late 18th-early 19th centuries).

Local history. Natural history. Handicrafts. Rope-walk. Demonstrations by potters, smiths and glass-blowers.
Apr.-Oct. Tu.-F. 2-6; Sa. 10-6; Su. 2.30-6. Other times by appointment.

BEXHILL

BEXHILL MUSEUM
Egerton Park, Bexhill, Sussex
Natural history and archaeology of district.
Weekdays, except F. 10-5.

BIBURY

ARLINGTON MILL
Bibury, Gloucestershire
17th century Mill. Rural crafts and industries. Old mill machinery. Staffordshire china. Furniture by Peter Waals. Victorian costumes and furniture.
All the year, Daily, 11.30-1, 2-7, or dusk if earlier.

BICTON

BICTON COUNTRYSIDE MUSEUM
Bicton Gardens, East Budleigh, Bicton, Devon
Farm wagons, implements, tools. Cider making. Old tractors. Traction engines.
Easter-May: Daily 2-6; June-mid Sept. Daily 10-6; mid Sept.-beginning Oct. 2-6; also some Su. in Oct. 2-6.

BIDEFORD

BIDEFORD MUSEUM
Municipal Buildings, Bideford, Devon
North Devon pottery. Shipwrights' tools. Geology. Maps. Prints.
Weekdays 10-5 (Sa. 10-12.45).

BURTON ART GALLERY
Victoria Park, Kingsley Road, Bideford, Devon
Paintings. Drawings. Prints. Sculpture.
Daily 10-1, 2-5. Closed M. afternoon.

BIGGAR

GLADSTONE COURT
Biggar, Lanarkshire
Indoor street of bygone shops including Ironmonger, Druggist, Printer, China Merchant, Watchmaker, Shoemaker, Grocer and Dressmaker. Schoolroom. Bed used by Cargill the Covenanter (1681).
May-Oct., Th., F. and Sa. 2-5. Other times by arrangement.

BIGGLESWADE *(See Old Warden)*

SHUTTLEWORTH COLLECTION
Old Warden Aerodrome, Biggleswade, Bedfordshire
Aeronautics. Road Transport.
Summer 10-5; Winter 10-4.

BIGNOR

BIGNOR ROMAN VILLA COLLECTION
Bignor, Sussex
Samian pottery. Wall plaster. Coins. Jewellery. Models of Villa. Maps of Roman roads. Roofing tiles.
Mar.-Oct. Tu.-Su. 10-6.30 or one hour before sunset; Bank Holidays and M. during Aug. and Su. in Nov.

BIRCHINGTON

POWELL-COTTON MUSEUM
Quex Park, Birchington, Kent
Zoological specimens. African and Indian jungle scenes. Native arts, crafts. Household objects.
Th. all the year round, also W. from June-mid July. Daily (except M. and Sa.) from mid July-mid Sept. 2.30-6.

BIRCHOVER

HEATHCOTE MUSEUM
Nr. Matlock, Derbyshire
Finds from Bronze Age barrows on Stanton Moor.
By appointment.

BIRKENHEAD

WILLIAMSON ART GALLERY AND MUSEUM
Slatey Road, Birkenhead, Cheshire
Water-colours. Applied arts include Della Robbia (Birkenhead) pottery and Liverpool porcelain. Shipping gallery. Local exhibits.
Weekdays (except Th.) 10-5; Th. 10-9; Su. 2-5.

BIRMINGHAM

THE ASSAY OFFICE
Newhall Street, Birmingham, B3 1SB, Warwickshire
Old Birmingham and other silverware, coins, tokens and medals. Correspondence of Matthew Boulton, 1760-1810.
By appointment.

ASTON HALL
Frederick Road, Aston, Birmingham, Warwickshire
Jacobean house, 1618-35, once the home of the Holte family. Noteworthy oak staircase and panelled Long Gallery. 17th-18th century English furniture.
Apr.-Sept., M.-Sa. 10-5; Su. 2-5. Oct.-Mar., M.-Sa. only 10-5 (or dusk if earlier). Closed 1-2. Closed Good Friday, Christmas Day and Boxing Day.

AVERY HISTORICAL MUSEUM
Soho Foundry, Birmingham 40, Warwickshire
Machines, instruments, weights, records, relating to the history of weighing.
During factory hours by appointment.

BARBER INSTITUTE OF FINE ARTS
The University, Birmingham, B15 2TS, Warwickshire
Paintings. Drawings. Prints. Sculpture.
Open normally to individual visitors M.-F. 10-5; Sa. 10-1, except when the University is closed.

BIRMINGHAM CITY MUSEUM AND ART GALLERY
Congreve Street, Birmingham 3, Warwickshire
Department of Archaeology, Ethnography and Birmingham History-Material from Nineveh, Ur, Vinca on the Danube, Mexico, Cyprus, Kish and Midland sites. Greek vases. Rings and jewellery. Roman glass. Egyptian, Indian, Chinese and Persian art and antiquities from the South Seas and Peru. Wooden Bygones.
M.-Sa. 10-6; Su. 2-5.30. Closed Good Friday, Christmas Day and Boxing Day.

BIRMINGHAM CITY MUSEUM AND ART GALLERY
Congreve Street, Birmingham 3, Warwickshire
Department of Art-Old master paintings. English water-colours. Italian 17th century paintings. 19th century English paintings including *The Blind Girl* by Millais and *The Last of England* by Ford Madox Brown. Sculpture. Costumes. Ceramics. Silver.
M.-Sa. 10-6; Su. 2-5.30. Closed Good Friday, Christmas Day and Boxing Day.

BIRMINGHAM CITY MUSEUM AND ART GALLERY
Congreve Street, Birmingham 3, Warwickshire
Department of Natural History-British birds. Herbaria. Lepidoptera. Gemstones.
M.-Sa. 10-6; Su. 2-5.30. Closed Good Friday, Christmas Day and Boxing Day.

BLAKESLEY HALL
Blakesley Road, Yardley, Birmingham, Warwickshire
Timber-framed house of c.1550-1600, containing exhibits dealing with archaeology and the history of Birmingham and district.
M.-Sa. 9.30-6; Su. 2-5. Closed Good Friday, Christmas Day and Boxing Day.

CANNON HILL MUSEUM
Pershore Road, Birmingham, Warwickshire
Various leisure time pursuits including bird watching, bee-keeping, fishing and pets. Dioramas of bird life, safari hut with sights, sounds and smells of the African bush.
M.-Sa. 10-8; Su. 2-5. Winter: M.-Sa. 10-5; Su. 2-5. Closed Good Friday, Christmas Day and Boxing Day.

GEOLOGICAL DEPARTMENT MUSEUM
The University, Edgbaston, Birmingham 15, Warwickshire
Palaeontology. Stratigraphy. Petrology. Mineralogy and Physical Geology. Fossils. Graptolites.
Daily 9-5 by arrangement.

MUSEUM OF SCIENCE AND INDUSTRY
Newhall Street, Birmingham 3, Warwickshire
General industrial and scientific collections, including steam engines, machine tools, small arms and scientific instruments.
M.-F. 10-5; Sa. 10-5.30; Su. 2-5.30. 1st W. in each month 10-9. Closed Good Friday, Christmas Day and Boxing Day.

SAREHOLE MILL
Cole Bank Road, Hall Green, Birmingham, Warwickshire
18th century water powered corn mill used by Matthew Boulton for metal working and later for blade grinding. Now restored to working order.
Open until late Nov. Daily 2-7 (Sa. 11-7).

UNIVERSITY MEDICAL SCHOOL MUSEUM
Hospitals Centre, Birmingham 15, Warwickshire
Anatomical and pathological specimens. General ethnographical material.
Weekdays 9-5, by appointment only, to bona fide Medical Students or Medical graduates.

WEOLEY CASTLE
Alwold Road, Birmingham, Warwickshire
Former fortified moated dwelling house, 1100-1320 A.D. Contains small museum of local history.
W. 2-8 (or dusk if earlier); Sa. 10-5; Th., F. and Su. 2-5. Closed M., Tu., Good Friday, Christmas Day and Boxing Day.

BISHOP'S STORTFORD

RHODES MEMORIAL MUSEUM
Bishop's Stortford, Hertfordshire
Collections illustrating life of Cecil Rhodes. Illustrations of Southern and Central African history.
M.-Sa. 10-4.

BLACKBURN

BLACKBURN MUSEUM AND ART GALLERY
Library Street, Blackburn, Lancashire
Local geology and mineralogy. General natural history. Coins. Porcelain. Pottery. Glass. Paintings. Water-colours. Japanese prints. Industrial art. Watches.
M.-F. 9.30-8; Sa. 9.30-6.

LEWIS MUSEUM OF TEXTILE MACHINERY
Blackburn, Lancashire
Development of spinning and weaving industries. Machine demonstrations.
Weekdays 10-5 (10-7.30 W. and F.).

SAMLESBURY HALL
Preston New Road, Nr. Preston, Lancashire
Medieval half-timbered Manor House, c.1340. Furniture.
Easter-Sept., Su. afternoons with conducted tours at 2.30, 3.30 and 4.30.

BLACKPOOL

GRUNDY ART GALLERY
Queen Street, Blackpool, Lancashire
Paintings and drawings by 19th and 20th century British artists.
Weekdays 10-5; Su. 2-5 (Summer).

BLAIR ATHOLL

BLAIR CASTLE AND ATHOLL MUSEUM
Blair Atholl, Perthshire
Collections of arms and armour. Portraits. Jacobite relics. China. Lace.
Easter weekend then Apr., Su., M. 10-6. May 1-Oct. 14, M.-Sa. 10-6; Su. 2-6.

BLANDFORD FORUM

ROYAL SIGNALS MUSEUM
Blandford Camp, nr. Blandford Forum, Dorset
Uniforms, old arms, awards, campaign medals, regimental colours, pictures, trophies and souvenirs associated with the Corps.
M.-F. 10-12.30, 2-5; Sa. 10-12.

BLANTYRE

SCOTTISH NATIONAL MEMORIAL TO DAVID LIVINGSTONE
Blantyre, Lanarkshire
Collection of personal relics, tableaux and working models in the birth-place of the missionary-explorer.
Weekdays 10-6; Su. 2-6.

BLITHFIELD

MUSEUM OF CHILDHOOD AND COSTUME
Blithfield Hall, Nr. Rugeley, Staffordshire
Children's toys, books, furniture and costumes. Georgian

costumes and uniforms. Needlework figures. Toys. Miniature theatres.
Good Friday to 1st Su. in Oct., W., Th., Sa. and Su. 2.30-6, also Easter, Spring and Late Summer Bank Holiday M. 12-7, Tu. following 2.30-6.

BODIAM

BODIAM CASTLE MUSEUM
Bodiam, Sussex
Relics found during excavations of medieval castle.
Daily: Apr.-Sept. 10-7; Weekdays: Oct.-Mar. 10-dusk.

BODMIN

THE DUKE OF CORNWALL'S LIGHT INFANTRY SERVICE MUSEUM
The Keep, Bodmin, Cornwall
Uniforms, old arms, awards, campaign medals, regimental colours, pictures, trophies and souvenirs of the regiment.
M.-F. 9-12.30, 2-4.45 (Sa. 10-12.30 1st Apr. - 30th Sept.) Closed Public Holidays.

LANYDROCK
nr. Bodmin, Cornwall
17th century picture gallery. Plaster ceilings. Family portraits, 17th-20th centuries.
Apr.-mid Oct. Daily (except Su.) 2-6. Last admission 5.30.

PASSMORE EDWARDS PUBLIC LIBRARY AND MUSEUM
Lower Bore Street, Bodmin, Cornwall
Local history.
On application: M.-F. 10-1, 2-5; Sa. 10-1.

BOGNOR REGIS

GUERMONPREZ MUSEUM
Lyon Street, Bognor Regis, Sussex
Natural Science, Archaeology. Local history.
M.-F. 10-4; Sa. 10-1.

BOLTON

HALL I'TH'WOOD MUSEUM
Bolton, Lancashire
16th century Manor House, home of Crompton, inventor of spinning mule. Local and industrial history. Furniture.
Weekdays (exc. Th.) 10-6 (Oct. - Mar. 10-5); Su. (Apr. - Sept.) 2-6. Closed Good Friday, Christmas Day, Boxing Day and New Year's Day.

MUSEUM AND ART GALLERY
Civic Centre, Bolton, Lancashire
Botany. Zoology. Geology. Prehistory. Egyptian collection. Paintings and sculpture of English and European schools. English water-colours. 18th century English pottery.
M.-F. 10-6; Sa. 10-5.30. Closed all Bank Holidays and New Year's Day.

SMITHILLS HALL
Smithills Dean Road, Bolton, Lancashire
Manor house, 14th-16th century. Tudor panelling, 17th century furniture.
Weekdays ex. Th. 10-6 (Oct.-Mar. 10-5); Su. (Apr.-Sept.), 2-6. Closed Good F., Christmas Day, Boxing Day and New Year's Day.

TONGE MOOR TEXTILE MACHINERY MUSEUM
Tonge Moor Road, Bolton, Lancashire
Historic textile machines, including Crompton's Mule, Hargreave's Jenny and Arkwright's water frame.
M., Tu., Th. and F. 9.30-7.30; W. 9.30-1; Sa. 9.30-5.30. Closed Bank Holidays.

BOOTLE

BOOTLE MUSEUM AND ART GALLERY
Oriel Road, Bootle, L20 7AG, Lancashire
English figure pottery. Liverpool pottery.
M.-F. 9-7; Sa. 9-1.

BOSTON

BOSTON MUSEUM
The Guildhall, South Street, Boston, Lincolnshire
15th century building associated with the early Pilgrim Fathers, 1607. Local history and archaeology. Local prints and pictures.
M.-F. 9.30-12, 1.30-4.30; Sa. 9.30-12 (1.30-4.30 May-Sept.).

BOSTON SPA

BRAMHALL PARK
Boston Spa, Yorkshire
Collection of sporting pictures.
Easter Su. - end Sept. Su. and each Bank Holiday M. and Tu., 2-6.

BOURNEMOUTH

BOURNEMOUTH NATURAL SCIENCE SOCIETY'S MUSEUM
39 Christchurch Road, Bournemouth, Hampshire
Local natural history and archaeology. Fossils from Barton Beds and Bournemouth leaf-beds.
By arrangement.

BRITISH TYPEWRITER MUSEUM
'The Beeching Collection', 137 Stewart Road, Bournemouth, Hampshire
Collection illustrating 100 years of typewriter production. Exhibits include two Remington Sholes, the first typewriters produced on a production line (1873).
M.-Sa. 9-1, 2-5.30.

ROTHESAY MUSEUM
8 Bath Road, Bournemouth, Hampshire
Italian paintings and pottery. English porcelain. 17th century furniture. Victorian bygones and pictures. Ethnography. Arms and armour. Maritime rooms containing ship models, shells and pictures; Local and exotic butterflies and moths.
Apr. - Oct. Weekdays 10-6; Su. 2.30-5. Nov. - Mar. Weekdays 10-5; Su. 2.30-5.

RUSSELL-COTES ART GALLERY AND MUSEUM
East Cliff, Bournemouth, Hampshire
17th-20th century oil paintings. Tempera, water-colours. Sculpture. Miniatures. Ceramics. Japanese, Chinese, Burmese, theatrical material. Collection of "Pictures You May Borrow". Geological terrace.
Apr. - Oct. Weekdays 10-6; Su. 2.30-5. Nov. - Mar. Weekdays 10-5; Su. 2.30-5.

BRADFORD

BOLLING HALL
Bolling Hall Road, Bradford, Yorkshire
Illustrates Yorkshire domestic life, 15th-late 18th century.
Daily 10-8 (Apr. and Sept. 10-7, Jan.-Mar., Oct.-Dec. 10-5).

BRADFORD INDUSTRIAL MUSEUM
Moorside Mills, Moorside Road, Bradford, Yorkshire, BD2 3HP
Machinery from local industries, especially textiles. Transport, including a Bradford tram and trolley bus. Social, economic and technological background of Bradford and district. Motive power gallery, with steam and gas engines, water wheel, and single beam engine.
Daily 10-5.

CITY ART GALLERY AND MUSEUM
Cartwright Hall, Bradford, Yorkshire
16th-18th century European paintings. 19th-20th century British paintings. Chinese ceramics. Natural history, archaeology and geology of the West Riding.
Daily 10-8 (Apr. and Sept. 10-7, Jan.-Mar., Oct.-Dec. 10-5).

BRADING (HAMPSHIRE)

NUNWELL HOUSE
Brading, Hampshire
House (1522). Family collection of paintings, furniture, silver.
Mid-June - mid-Sept., Su., W. and Th., 2.30-6.30.

BRADING (ISLE OF WIGHT)

OSBORN-SMITH'S WAX MUSEUM
Brading, Isle of Wight
House (1499). Island history. Costumes. Wax figures. Period furniture.
Open every day of the year 10-10 (10-9 Oct.-Apr.).

ROMAN VILLA
Morton, Brading, Isle of Wight
Remains of a Roman villa with mosaic pavements *in situ*, hypocaust. Utensils. Coins.
May-Oct. Weekdays 9.30-6; Su. 3-6. Winter months by appointment only.

BRAMBER

POTTER'S MUSEUM
Bramber, Sussex
Exhibits illustrating the art of the taxidermist.
Daily 11-8.

ST. MARY'S
Bramber, Sussex
15th century timber-framed house. Panelling. Handicrafts.
Good F. - mid-Oct. Weekdays (except M.) 11-6; Su. 2-6. Bank Holidays 11-6.

BRAMHALL

BRAMALL HALL
Bramhall, Cheshire
15th and 18th century house with timber and plaster work. Furniture. Domestic equipment. Paintings.
Daily 11-1, 2-7. (Oct.-Mar. 11-1, 2-4).

BRECHIN

BRECHIN MUSEUM
Mechanics Institute, Brechin, Angus
Local antiquities.
Tu. and W. 2-5; Sa. 10.30-12.30.

BRECON

BRECKNOCK MUSEUM
Glamorgan Street, Brecon
Natural history. Local antiquities and archaeology. Folk material. Coins. Costumes. Pottery and porcelain. Arms. Paintings. Prints.
M. 10-12; Tu.-Sa. and Bank Holidays 10-12, 1-4. Closed Good Friday, Christmas Day and Boxing Day.

BRECON BEACONS NATIONAL PARK MOUNTAIN CENTRE
Brecon
Display of maps, photographs and other material illustrating Brecon Beacons National Park and how it can be enjoyed.
Nov.-Feb. M.-F. 9.30-5; Sa., Su. and Bank Holidays 9.30-5.30. Mar. and Oct. M.-F. 9.30-6; Sa., Su. and Bank Holidays 9.30-6.30. Apr. and Sept. M.-F. 9.30-7; Sa., Su. and Bank Holidays 9.30-7.30. May-Aug. M.-F. 9.30-8; Sa., Su. and Bank Holidays 9.30-8.

THE SOUTH WALES BORDERERS MUSEUM
The Barracks, Brecon
Uniforms, old arms, awards, campaign medals, regimental colours, pictures, trophies and souvenirs associated with the regiment.
Daily 9-5.

BRENTFORD

BRITISH PIANO MUSEUM
368 High Street, Brentford, Middlesex
Automatic musical instruments. Pianos.
Mar.-Nov. Th., Sa. and Su. 2.30-6.

LONDON TRANSPORT COLLECTION OF HISTORIC VEHICLES
Syon Park, Brentford, Middlesex
Historic buses, trams, trolleybuses, locomotives, rolling stock, posters, signs, tickets and other exhibits.
Apr.-Sept., daily 10-7. Oct.-Mar., daily 10-5 or dusk (whichever is earlier). Last tickets sold one hour before closing time.

BRENTWOOD

THE ESSEX REGIMENT SERVICE MUSEUM
Eagle Way, Warley, Brentwood, Essex
Uniforms, old arms, awards, campaign medals, regimental colours, pictures, trophies and souvenirs associated with the regiment.
M.-F. 10-12, 2-4; Sa. and Su. by appointment.

BRIDGWATER

ADMIRAL BLAKE MUSEUM
Blake Street, Bridgwater, Somerset
Reputed birthplace of Admiral Blake, containing Blake relics and exhibits relating to the Battle of Sedgemoor. Archaeology and local history.
Daily 10-1, 2-5 (closes Tu. at 1 p.m.).

BRIDLINGTON

BRIDLINGTON ART GALLERY AND MUSEUM
Sewerby Hall, Bridlington, Yorkshire
Amy Johnson exhibition. Local and natural history and archaeology.
Easter-Sept., Su.-F. 10-12.30, 1.30-6; Sa. 1.30-6.

BURTON AGNES HALL
Bridlington, Yorkshire
House (1598-1610). Furniture. French impressionist paintings. Oriental china.
Easter M., then early May-mid. Oct. Daily (except Sa.) 1.45-5; Su. 1.45-6.

BRIDPORT

BRIDPORT MUSEUM AND ART GALLERY
South Street, Bridport, Dorset
Local antiquities and natural history. Paintings, drawings and sketches. History of local rope and netting industries.
Summer: weekday mornings. Winter: Tu., W. and F. Or by appointment.

BRIGHOUSE

BRIGHOUSE ART GALLERY
Halifax Road, Brighouse, Yorkshire
Paintings and water-colours, mainly 19th century.
Weekdays 10-8 (10-5 Sa.).

BRIGHTON

BOOTH MUSEUM OF BRITISH BIRDS
Dyke Road, Brighton, Sussex
Comprehensive display of birds mounted in their natural habitat. Reference collection of eggs, butterflies and moths.
Weekdays 10-5; Su. 2-5. Winter closing 4.30.

BRIGHTON MUSEUM AND ART GALLERY
Church Street, Brighton, Sussex
16th-20th century European paintings. English water-colours, drawings and miniatures. Archaeology. Natural history. Musical instruments. Sussex history. Ceramics. Glass. Jewellery.
Weekdays 10-7; Sa. 10-5; Su. 2-5 (Summer 2-6).

CREED AND COMPANY LIMITED
Brighton, Sussex
Company Museum. Telecommunications and transport.
By appointment.

GRANGE ART GALLERY AND MUSEUM
Rottingdean, Brighton, Sussex
Georgian house, adjacent to Kipling's home, displays letters, books and illustrations of the author. Sussex folk life collection. Toys.
Weekdays 10-7 (Sa. 10-5); Su. 2-5 (Summer 2-6). Closed Good F., Christmas Day and Boxing Day.

PRESTON MANOR
Preston Park, Brighton, Sussex
The Thomas-Stanford Museum. Georgian house with 18th century furnishings, silver and china. English period furniture.
Weekdays 10-5; Su. 2.30-5. Closed Good F., Christmas Day and Boxing Day.

ROYAL PAVILION
Brighton, Sussex
King George IV's seaside palace. 23 State Rooms displaying original furniture and interior decoration, including the King's Apartments, Banqueting Room, Great Kitchen.
Oct.-June, daily 10-5. July-Sept., daily 10-8.

BRISTOL

BLAISE CASTLE HOUSE MUSEUM
Henbury, Bristol
Collections in 18th century house of objects illustrating English life in former days. Folk Park exhibits (on view May-Sept.) include a reconstructed corn-mill and dairy.
May-Sept., Weekdays 2-5.30; Su. 3-5. Oct.-Apr. Weekdays 2-5; Su. 3-4.30 excluding Dec., Jan. and Feb.

BRISTOL CITY ART GALLERY
Queen's Road, Bristol 8
Paintings. Applied art, with particular emphasis on English and Oriental ceramics.
Weekdays 10-5.30.

BRISTOL CITY MUSEUM
Queen's Road, Bristol 8
Classical and British archaeology. Ethnography. Industrial history. Technology. Natural history. Geology. History of the West of England.
Weekdays 10-5.30.

BRISTOL WATERWORKS COMPANY
Barrow Gurney Filtration Works, Barrow Gurney, Bristol
Company museum. Waterworks equipment. Two beam engines preserved at Blagdon waterworks.
By appointment.

G. B. BRITTON AND SONS LIMITED
Kingswood, Bristol, BS15 1JB
Company Museum. Shoemaking equipment.
Collection at present in store.

CHATTERTON HOUSE
Redcliffe Way, Bristol 1
Birthplace of the poet Thomas Chatterton. Life and work of Chatterton.
W. and Sa. 3-5.

DYRHAM PARK
nr. Bristol
Furniture. Paintings, especially Dutch.
Easter Sa. to Sept. Daily (except M. and Tu.), 2-6; Bank Holidays 12-6. March-Easter, Oct., Nov. W., Sa., Su. 2-6 or dusk. Closed Dec., Jan., Feb.

GEORGIAN HOUSE
7 Great George Street, Bristol 1
Georgian House, exhibiting furniture and fittings of that period.
Weekdays 11-5.

HARVEYS WINE MUSEUM
12 Denmark Street, Bristol 1
Company Museum. Bristol wine trade. Bottles. Wine-making.
By appointment only, M.-F., 2.30 and 6.30, conducted tours.

THE RED LODGE
Park Row, Bristol 1
Elizabethan house, with early 18th century alterations, and furnishings of these periods.
Weekdays 1-5.

ST. NICHOLAS CHURCH MUSEUM
Baldwin Street, Bristol 1
Medieval - recent local church art, especially plate. Bristol topography. History of medieval Bristol.
M.-Sa. 10-5.15.

BRIXHAM

BRIXHAM MUSEUM
Higher Street, Brixham, Devon
Maritime and folk museum dealing with merchant schooners, trawlers, fisheries, ship-building and allied trades. Local geology, archaeology and history.
Whitsun-Sept., Weekdays 10-1, 2.30-5.30, 7.15-9; Su. 2.30-5.30. Oct. and Easter-Whitsun: W. and Su. 2.30-5.

BROADSTAIRS

DICKENS HOUSE MUSEUM
Victoria Parade, Broadstairs, Kent
House and its owner used by Dickens as model for Betsy Trotwood and her home in *David Copperfield.* Parlour furnished as described by Dickens. Memorabilia of Dickens, including letters, furniture, writing box. Prints. Costumes.
Apr.-Sept., daily 2.30-5.30.

BROADWAY

SNOWSHILL MANOR
Broadway, Gloucestershire
Tudor house with front of about 1700. Collections of musical instruments, clocks, toys, bicycles.
May-Sept., W., Th., Sa., Su. and Bank Holidays M. 11-1, 2-6; Apr. and Oct.: Sa., Su. 11-1, 2-6 (closes dusk if earlier).

BROKERSWOOD

THE PHILLIPS COUNTRYSIDE MUSEUM OF NATURAL HISTORY AND FORESTRY
The Woodland Park, Brokerswood, nr. Westbury, Wiltshire
Natural history and forestry. Birds' eggs. Mounted birds and small animals. Nests. Production of honey.
Daily 10.30-dusk.

BROMSGROVE

AVONCROFT MUSEUM OF BUILDINGS
Stoke Prior, Bromsgrove, Worcestershire
Open-air museum including a 15th century timber-framed merchant's house, 18th century post-mill and 19th century chainmaking and nailmaking workshops. The Guesten Hall Roof, a 14th century timber roof from Worcester, has also been preserved.
Mid-Mar. - mid-Oct. W. and Th. 2-5; Sa., Su. and Bank Holidays, 11-6.

PLAYTHINGS PAST MUSEUM
Beaconwood, Beacon Hill, nr. Bromsgrove, Worcestershire
Antique and period dolls, dolls' houses, toys and automata.
By written application for appointment. Children under 12 not admitted.

BRYNSIENCYN

SNAKES' PATH MUSEUM
Brynsiencyn, Anglesea
Antique furniture, stuffed birds and items of local interest.
Tu. and Th. at any time. Also by appointment.

BUCKFASTLEIGH

BUCKFASTLEIGH FARM MUSEUM
Dial Court, Buckfastleigh, Devon, TQ11 0BU
Large collection of vintage tractors. Steam traction engines, waggons, ploughs, barn machinery, hand tools dating back to the Stone Age. Old kitchen equipment.
Daily from 10 a.m.

BUCKLAND ABBEY

BUCKLAND ABBEY
nr. Yelverton, Devon, PL20 6EY
Maritime and Sir Francis Drake collections. Ship models. Agricultural implements. Building construction.
Easter-Sept. Weekdays 11-6; Su. 2-6. Winter W.-Sa. 11-6; Su. 3-5.

BURFORD

TOLSEY MUSEUM
High Street, Burford, Oxfordshire
Charters, maces and seals of the Corporation of Burford, 13th to 18th century. Manuscripts and folios on local history. Dolls' house, replica of late 18th century house, with period furnishings and costumes. Cotswold stone display.
Apr.-mid-Oct. Daily 2.30-5.30.

BURNLEY

TOWNELEY HALL ART GALLERY AND MUSEUM
Towneley Hall, Burnley, Lancashire
Paintings. Water colours. Period furniture. Ivories. 18th century glassware. Chinese pottery. Archaeology. Geology. Natural history. East Lancashire Regimental Room.
Weekdays 10-5.30; Su. 2-5.

BURTON-ON-TRENT

HOAR CROSS HALL
nr. Burton-on-Trent, Staffordshire
Arms and armour. 17th-19th century furniture and paintings. Victorian ball gowns. Vintage motor cycles.
Good F. to mid-Oct. W., Th., Sa. and Su. 2-6. Good F., Bank Holiday M. and Tu., 12-7. Other times by appointment.

MUSEUM AND ART GALLERY
Guild Street, Burton-on-Trent, Staffordshire
Local history. British and foreign birds.
M.-F. 11-6; Sa. 11-5. Closed Su. and Bank Holidays.

BURWASH

BATEMAN'S, RUDYARD KIPLING'S HOME
Burwash, Sussex
17th century house, home of Rudyard Kipling from 1902 until 1936, with his study as he used it.
Mar.-Oct., Sa., Su. and Good Friday 2-6; M., Tu., W. and Th. 11-12.30, 2-6.

BURY

BURY ART GALLERY AND MUSEUM
Moss Street, Bury, Lancashire
Paintings. Water-colours. Local history.
Weekdays 10-6 (Sa. 10-5).

BURY TRANSPORT MUSEUM
Castlecroft Road, Bury, Lancashire
Fire engines. Steam roller. Double-decker buses. Narrow gauge diesel locomotive. Hand crane (1894). Lancashire and Yorkshire Railway van. Railway coaches and rolling stock.
Sa., Su., Bank Holidays, 10-5.

THE LANCASHIRE FUSILIERS SERVICE MUSEUM
Lancashire Headquarters, The Royal Regiment of Fusiliers, Wellington Barracks, Bury, Lancashire
Uniforms, old arms, awards, campaign medals, regimental colours, pictures, trophies and souvenirs of the regiment.
M.-F. 9-5; Sa. 9-12.

BURY ST EDMUNDS

GERSHOM-PARKINGTON MEMORIAL COLLECTION OF CLOCKS AND WATCHES
8 Angel Hill, Bury St. Edmunds, Suffolk
Collection of clocks and other instruments for recording time from 16th century onwards.
Weekdays 10-1, 2-5.

ICKWORTH
nr. Bury St. Edmunds, Suffolk
House (1794-1830). Contents include late Regency and 18th century French furniture. Silver. Family portraits.
Rotunda, corridors and gardens open Apr.-mid. Oct., W., Th., Sa., Su. and Bank Holidays 2-6.

MOYSE'S HALL MUSEUM
Cornhill, Bury St. Edmunds, Suffolk
12th century dwelling house containing local antiquities, natural history.
Weekdays 10-1, 2-5.

THE SUFFOLK REGIMENT MUSEUM
Gibraltar Barracks, Bury St. Edmunds, Suffolk
Uniforms, old arms, awards, campaign medals, regimental colours, pictures, trophies and souvenirs associated with the regiment.
Weekdays 9-4.30.

BUXTON

BUXTON MUSEUM
Terrace Road, Buxton, Derbyshire
Local history. Pleistocene and later animal remains from local caves. Local rocks, minerals, fossils and stones. Blue John and Ashford Marble ornaments. Paintings. Prints. Pottery. Glass.
M.-F. 10-7; Sa. 10-5.

CAERLEON

LEGIONARY MUSEUM
Caerleon, Monmouthshire
Display of the more important material found on the site of the Roman Legionary Fortress of Isca and in the immediate neighbourhood.
Apr.-Sept. Weekdays 11-5; Su. 2-5. Other times on application.

CAERNARVON

THE ROYAL WELCH FUSILIERS MUSEUM
Queen's Tower, Caernarvon Castle, Caernarvon
Uniforms. Hat ribbon worn by King William of Orange, 1690. Keys of Corunna; Gold Peninsula War medals. Royal and other portraits by Dennis Fields, Oswald Birley, Gerald Kelly.
Weekdays 9.30-7 (closes 5.30 Mar., Apr. and Oct. and at 4 Nov.-Feb.); Su. opening 9.30 in Summer.

SEGONTIUM ROMAN FORT AND MUSEUM
Caernarvon, Caernarvonshire
Site of one of the principal Roman forts in the region. Roman antiquities from the fort itself and from other sites in North Wales.
Mar.-Apr. M.-Sa. 9.30-5.30; Su. 2-5.30. Oct. M.-Sa. 9.30-7; Sa. 2-7. Oct. M.-Sa. 9.30-5.30; Su. 2-5.30. Nov.-Feb. M.-Sa. 9.30-4; Su. 2-4. Closed Christmas Day and Boxing Day.

CALSTOCK

COTEHELE HOUSE
Calstock, Cornwall
Medieval house (1485-1539). Armour. Furniture. Tapestries. 17th-18th century needlework.
Apr.-mid. Oct. Daily (except M. but inc. Bank Holiday M.) 11-1 (last admission 12.30), 2-6 or dusk if earlier. Last admission to house 5.30.

CAMBERLEY

CAMBERLEY MUSEUM
Knoll Road, Camberley, Surrey
Natural history, history and archaeology of the area.
Th., F. and Sa. 2-5.

NATIONAL ARMY MUSEUM
Royal Military Academy, Sandhurst, Camberley, Surrey
History of British and Indian Army for last 300 years, shown in pictures, relics, silver, medals, uniforms and colours.
Weekdays 10-5; Su. 11-5.

ROYAL ARMY ORDNANCE CORPS MUSEUM
Deepcut, Camberley, Surrey
Uniforms, old arms, awards, campaign medals, regimental colours, pictures, trophies and souvenirs associated with the Corps.
Weekdays 10-12, 2-4 or by appointment.

CAMBO

WALLINGTON
Cambo, Northumberland
House (1688, altered 18th and 19th centuries). 18th century plasterwork. Furniture. Paintings. Portraits.
Hall: Apr.-Sept., M., W., Th., Sa. Su. and Good Friday 2-6; Oct., Sa. and Su. 2-5. Gardens open daily 10-6 (7 weekends and Bank Holidays. Oct. closed at 5).

CAMBORNE

CAMBORNE SCHOOL OF METALLIFEROUS MINING MUSEUM
Camborne, Cornwall
Collection of minerals and ores.
M.-F. 9-4.30; Sa. 9-12. Closed Bank Holidays.

CORNISH ENGINES
East Pool Mine, Pool, Camborne, Cornwall
30-in. rotative beam winding engine (1887) and 90-in. beam pumping engine (1892), complete in their houses. Also engines at Levant Mine, St. Just and South Crofty Mine, Camborne.
Apr.-mid.-Oct. M.-F. 11-1, 2-6 (last tour 5.30).

HOLMAN BROTHERS LIMITED
Holman Museum, Camborne, Cornwall
Company Museum. Mining engineering. Local history.
M.-F. 9-4.

PUBLIC LIBRARY AND MUSEUM
Cross Street, Camborne, Cornwall
Archaeology. Mineralogy. Local history and antiquities.
Weekdays 10-6.

CAMBRIDGE

ANGLESEY ABBEY
nr. Cambridge, Cambridgeshire
Founded 1236. An Elizabethan manor was created from the remains by the Fokes family. European paintings and objets d'art.
Principal rooms and gardens, Apr.-early Oct. W., Th., Sa., Su. and Bank Holiday M. 2-6 (Gardens open at 12, end May-end Sept.).

CAMBRIDGE AND COUNTY FOLK MUSEUM
2-3 Castle Street, Cambridge, Cambridgeshire
Museum in former White Horse Inn. Domestic and agricultural bygones. Toys. Pictures. Trade exhibits.
Tu.-Sa. 10.30-1, 2-5; Su. 2.30-4.30 (open all Bank Holidays).

FITZWILLIAM MUSEUM
Trumpington Street, Cambridge, Cambridgeshire
15th-20th century paintings. Archaeology. Glass. Ceramics. Coins. Drawings. Prints. Music. Medieval manuscripts.
Weekdays 10-5; Su. 2.15-5. Closed Good Friday, Christmas Day and Boxing Day.

SEDGWICK MUSEUM OF GEOLOGY
Downing Street, Cambridge, Cambridgeshire
Fossils. Collections of rocks, building stones and ornamental marbles.
M.-F. 9-1, 2.15-5; Sa. 9-1. Closed 1 week at Easter and 1 week at Christmas.

THE SCOTT POLAR RESEARCH INSTITUTE
Lensfield Road, Cambridge, Cambridgeshire
Current scientific work in the Arctic and Antarctic. Expedition relics and equipment. Eskimo and general polar art collections.
M.-Sa. 2.30-4.

UNIVERSITY COLLECTION OF AERIAL PHOTOGRAPHS
11 West Road, Cambridge, Cambridgeshire
Aerial photographs illustrating different aspects of agriculture, archaeology, geography, geology, history, vegetation and the social and economic past and present of the United Kingdom.
By appointment.

UNIVERSITY MUSEUM OF ARCHAEOLOGY AND ETHNOLOGY
Downing Street, Cambridge, Cambridgeshire
Archaeological collections illustrating the Old Stone Age in Europe, Asia and Africa, Britain from Pre-historic to Medieval times, Prehistoric America. Ethnographical material from America, Africa and Oceania.
Weekdays 2-4. Mornings by appointment.

UNIVERSITY ARCHIVES
The Old Schools (behind Senate House), Cambridge, Cambridgeshire
Manuscripts dating from 13th century. Charters of privilege, statutes, Royal letters and mandates, Grace books, matriculation books, university accounts and many other classes of records.
Weekdays during term, M.-F. 10-1, 2.30-5; Sa. 10-12.30. Other times by appointment.

UNIVERSITY MUSEUM OF CLASSICAL ARCHAEOLOGY
Little St. Mary's Lane, Cambridge, Cambridgeshire
Casts of Greek and Roman sculpture.
M.-F. 9-1, 2.15-5; Sa. 9-1.

UNIVERSITY MUSEUM OF MINERALOGY AND PETROLOGY
Downing Street, Cambridge, Cambridgeshire
Geology. Mineralogy. Petrology.
By appointment. Closed in vacations.

UNIVERSITY MUSEUM OF ZOOLOGY AND COMPARATIVE ANATOMY
Downing Street, Cambridge, Cambridgeshire
Zoology.
By appointment.

WHIPPLE MUSEUM OF THE HISTORY OF SCIENCE
Free School Lane, Cambridge, Cambridgeshire
Collection of historic scientific instruments, mainly of 16th-18th centuries.
M.-F. 9.30-1, 2-5. By appointment during vacations.

CAMPBELTOWN

CAMPBELTOWN MUSEUM
Campbeltown, Argyllshire
Archaeological, geological and natural history of Kintyre.
Weekdays 10.15-6 (10.15-1 W.). Open till 9 during summer.

CANTERBURY

BATTLE OF BRITAIN MUSEUM
Chilham Castle, nr. Canterbury, Kent
Most of the exhibits cover the period July-Oct. 1940, and include aircraft engines (British and German); airframe parts, instruments, radios, navigational aids, maps, cannons, machine guns, bombs and ammunition. Three full-sized aircraft: a Spitfire, Hurricane and Me 109 of 1940. Small section devoted to the R.F.C.
Easter-Oct. Last Su. in month, 10-6.

THE BUFFS REGIMENTAL MUSEUM
Poor Priests Hospital, Stour Street, Canterbury, Kent
Uniforms, old arms, awards, campaign medals, regimental colours, pictures, trophies and souvenirs associated with the regiment.
Weekdays: Summer 10-1, 2-5; Winter, 2-4.

CANTERBURY ROYAL MUSEUM
Beaney Institute, High Street, Canterbury, Kent
Local archaeological material. Natural history collection. Mineralogical exhibits. Pottery. Porcelain. Local and other prints, engravings and pictures.
Weekdays 9.30-5.30.

THE QUEEN'S REGIMENT MUSEUM
Howe Barracks, Canterbury, Kent
Exhibits from Queen's Royal Regiment (West Surrey); The Buffs; Royal East Kent Regiment; The East Surrey Regiment; The Queen's Own Royal West Kent Regiment; The Royal Sussex Regiment and the Middlesex Regiment (Duke of Cambridge's Own).
M.-Sa. 10-12, 2-4; Su. 10-12. Other times by appointment.

ROMAN PAVEMENT
Butchery Lane, Canterbury, Kent
Foundations of Roman Villa including 2 coloured mosaic floors and hypocaust.
Weekdays: Summer 10-1, 2-6; Winter 2-4. Su.: Summer 2-6.

THE WESTGATE
Canterbury, Kent
Museum of arms and armour housed in 14th century city gate house.
Weekdays: Summer 10-1, 2-6; Winter 2-4.

CARDIFF

NATIONAL MUSEUM OF WALES
(Amgueddfa Genedlaethol Cymru), Cathays Park, Cardiff
Geology, botany, zoology, archaeology, industry and art of Wales.
Weekdays 10-5 (10-6 Apr.-Sept. and Bank Holidays and Tu. following); Su. 2.30-5.

ST. FAGANS CASTLE
Cardiff, Glamorgan
Folk Museum, including farmhouses, workshops, cottages, chapel and cockpit. Gallery of Material Culture.
Daily (except M.) and Bank Holidays. Apr.-Sept. 11-7; Su. 2.30-7. Oct.-Mar. 11-5; Su. 2.30-5. Closed Christmas Eve, Christmas Day, Boxing Day and New Year's Day.

THE WELCH REGIMENT MUSEUM
Maindy Barracks, Cardiff, Glamorgan
Uniforms, old arms, awards, campaign medals, regimental colours, pictures, trophies and souvenirs associated with the regiment.
M.-F. 10-4.

CARLISLE

THE BORDER REGIMENT SERVICE MUSEUM
The Keep, The Castle, Carlisle, Cumberland
Officer's Grenadier cap, Cumberland Militia, c.1745. V.C. of Major Elton, 55th Regiment and V.C. of Private Coffey, 34th Regiment. Uniforms, records and documents from 1702.
Nov.-Feb. 9.30-4 (Su. 2-4); Mar. and Apr. 9.30-5.30 (Su. 2-5.30); May-Sept. 9.30-7 daily; Oct. 9.30-5.30 (Su. 2-4).

MUSEUM AND ART GALLERY
Tullie House, Castle Street, Carlisle, Cumberland
Jacobean mansion with Victorian extension housing regional collection of prehistoric and Roman remains. Lakeland birds, mammals and geology. Pre-Raphaelite paintings. English porcelain.
Weekdays 9-8 (9-5 Oct.-Mar.); Su. June, July and Aug. 2.30-5.

CARMARTHEN

COUNTY MUSEUM
Quay Street, Carmarthen
Archaeology of Carmarthenshire from the Stone Age to medieval period. Collections of Roman gold and jewellery and other antiquities found in the county.
Summer: M.-Sa. 10-6. Winter: M.-Sa. 10-5. Closed Su.

CARRICKFERGUS

5TH ROYAL INNISKILLING DRAGOON GUARDS MUSEUM
Carrickfergus Castle, Co. Antrim, Northern Ireland
Uniforms, old arms, awards, campaign medals, regimantal colours, pictures, trophies and souvenirs associated with the regiment.
Oct.-Mar. Weekdays 10-1, 2-4; Su. 2-4. Apr.-Sept. Weekdays 10-1, 2-6; Su. 2-6.

NORTH IRISH HORSE SERVICE MUSEUM
Carrickfergus Castle, Co. Antrim, Northern Ireland
Uniforms, old arms, awards, campaign medals, regimental colours, pictures, trophies and souvenirs associated with the regiment.
Weekdays 10-1, 2-4; Su. 2-4 (Oct.-Mar.). Weekdays 10-1, 2-6; Su. 2-6 (Apr.-Sept.).

QUEEN'S ROYAL IRISH HUSSARS SERVICE MUSEUM
Carrickfergus Castle, Co. Antrim, Northern Ireland
Uniforms, old arms, awards, campaign medals, regimental colours, pictures, trophies and souvenirs associated with the regiment.
Oct.-Mar. Weekdays 10-1, 2-4; Su. 2-4. Apr.-Sept. Weekdays 10-1, 2-6; Su. 2-6.

CASTLECOOLE

CASTLECOOLE
County Fermanagh, Northern Ireland
House (1798), by James Wyatt. Original furnishings.
Apr.-Sept., W.-M. 2-6.

CASTLE DOUGLAS

CASTLE DOUGLAS ART GALLERY
Castle Douglas, Kirkcudbrightshire
Collection of paintings by Ethel S. G. Paterson.
Open daily.

CASTLEFORD

CASTLEFORD PUBLIC LIBRARY AND MUSEUM
Carlton Street, Castleford, Yorkshire
Roman remains found in Castleford (Legiolium). Castleford pottery. Glassware from local works.
Weekdays 9.30-6 (9.30-12 Th., 9.30-5.30 Sa.).

CASTLE HOWARD

CASTLE HOWARD COSTUME GALLERY
Castle Howard, Yorkshire
Period dresses, 17th-20th centuries.
Easter Su.- early Oct. Tu., W., Th., Sa. and Su. 1.30-5; Easter, Spring and Late Summer Holiday M. 11.30-5.30.

CASTLETOWN

NAUTICAL MUSEUM
Bridge Street, Castletown, Isle of Man
Contains the schooner-rigged armed yacht "Peggy", built 1789, preserved in her original boathouse; papers and personalia of the Quayle family (her builders). Sailmaker's loft. Ship models. Nautical gear. Early photographs of Manx maritime trade and fishing.
Early June- mid. Sept. Weekdays 10-1, 2-5.

CASTLE WARD

CASTLE WARD
County Down, Northern Ireland
House (1765), with 18th century plasterwork, furnishings. Ward family portraits.
Apr.-Sept., W.-M. 2-6.

CAWTHORNE

CANNON HALL
Cawthorne, Yorkshire
House (18th century). Furniture. Glassware. Dutch and Flemish paintings. Regional museum of the 13th-18th century Royal Hussars.
M.-Sa. 10.30-5.

VICTORIA JUBILEE MUSEUM
Cawthorne, Yorkshire
Local natural history, geology, history.
Weekdays 10-7.

CHALFONT ST GILES

MILTON'S COTTAGE
Chalfont St. Giles, Buckinghamshire
Life and times of John Milton. Furniture. First editions of *Paradise Lost* and *Paradise Regained.* Portraits and busts of Milton.
Feb.-Oct. Weekdays (except Tu.), 10-1, 2.15-6; Su. 2.15-6. Nov.-Jan. Sa. 10-1, 2.15-dusk; Su. 2.15-dusk.

CHARD

FORDE ABBEY
Chard, Dorset
12th century Cistercian Monastery. Mortlake tapestries.
Early May- Sept. W., also frequent summer Su. (check locally).

CHATHAM

ROYAL ENGINEERS MUSEUM
Brompton Barracks, Chatham, Kent
Relics of General Gordon.
M.-F. 9-12.30, 1.30-4.30; Sa. by previous arrangement 9-12.

CHAWTON

JANE AUSTEN'S HOME
Chawton, Hampshire
Personal possessions of Jane Austen and her family.
Daily 11-4.30 (inc. Su. and Bank Holiday). Closed M. and Tu. Nov.-Mar. and Christmas Day and Boxing Day.

CHEDDAR

CHEDDAR MOTOR AND TRANSPORT MUSEUM
The Cliffs, Cheddar, Somerset
Cars, motor cycles, cycles, steam engines and motoring accessories. Caves exhibition.
Daily 10- dusk. Closed Christmas Day.

GOUGH'S CAVES MUSEUM
Cheddar, Somerset
Upper Palaeolithic remains including almost complete skeleton. Flints. Amber. Engraved stones.
Weekdays 9-7.30; Su. 10-7.30. Closes 5 in winter.

CHEDWORTH

CHEDWORTH ROMAN VILLA AND MUSEUM
Chedworth, Gloucestershire
Villa A.D. 150-350 with mosaic pavements.
Daily (except M.) 10-1, 2-7 or dusk if earlier. Closed Oct. 1-15 and Jan. Open Bank Holiday Monday.

CHELMSFORD

CHELMSFORD AND ESSEX MUSEUM
Oaklands Park, Chelmsford, Essex
Collections relating to Roman Essex. Bygones. Coins. Costumes. Paintings. British birds.
Weekdays 10-5; Su. 2-5.

CHELTENHAM

CHELTENHAM ART GALLERY AND MUSEUM
Clarence Street, Cheltenham, Gloucestershire
Paintings, especially Dutch. Water-colours. Etchings. Local prints. English pottery and porcelain. Local geology, natural history, archaeology. Cotswold bygones. Edward Wilson memorabilia. Georgian room. Victorian kitchen. Cotswold furniture. Chinese Porcelain.
Art Gallery 10-6 (W. 10-7); Museum 10-1; 2.15-5. Closed Su.

COLLEGE MUSEUM
Cheltenham, Gloucestershire
Natural history. Geology. Antiquities. Coins. Medals, including Waterloo medals.
During term by appointment.

SKYFRAME AIRCRAFT MUSEUM
Gloucester and Cheltenham Airport, Staverton, Cheltenham, Gloucestershire
Aeronautics.
Apr.-Oct. W.-Su. 2-6. Nov.-Mar. W.-Su. 2-5.

CHEPSTOW

THE MUSEUM
Bridge Street, Chepstow, Monmouthshire
Chepstow Society collection of local antiquities, prints and photographs.
Summer: Daily 2-5.

CHERTSEY

CHERTSEY MUSEUM
The Cedars, Windsor Street, Chertsey, Surrey
18th and 19th century costumes and furniture. Ceramics. Local history and archaeology.
Tu.-F. 2-5; Sa. 10-1, 2-5.

CHESTER

THE CHESHIRE REGIMENT SERVICE MUSEUM
The Castle, Chester, Cheshire
Uniforms, old arms, awards, campaign medals, regimental colours, pictures, trophies and souvenirs associated with the regiment.
Daily (except M.) 10.30-12.30, 2-6 (2-4 in winter).

GROSVENOR MUSEUM
Grosvenor Street, Chester, Cheshire
Roman antiquities from the legionary fortress, including a large number of inscribed and sculptured stones. Special gallery illustrating the Roman army. Natural history. Bygones.
Weekdays 10-5; Su. 2-5.

KING CHARLES'S TOWER
City Walls, Chester, Cheshire
Dioramas and exhibits illustrating Chester in the Civil War.
May-Sept. M.-F. 10-6.30; Sa. 10-7; Su. 2.30-6.30.

3RD CARABINIERS (PRINCE OF WALES'S DRAGOON GUARDS) SERVICE MUSEUM
The Dale, Liverpool Road, Chester, Cheshire
Exhibits illustrating history of 3rd Dragoon Guards, 6th Carabiniers, 3rd Carabiniers and 25th Dragoons. Uniforms, old arms, awards, campaign medals, regimental colours, pictures, trophies and souvenirs associated with the regiment.
M.-F. 10.30-8. Sa. and Su. by appointment.

WATER TOWER
City Walls, Chester, Cheshire
Dioramas and exhibits illustrating Chester in the Middle Ages.
May-Sept., M.-F. 10-6.30; Sa. 10-7; Su. 2.30-6.30.

CHESTERFIELD

HARDWICK HALL
nr. Chesterfield, Derbyshire
Built 1591-1597 by "Bess of Hardwick". Period furniture, needlework, tapestries. Portraits.
Easter Sa. to end of Oct., W., Th., Sa., Su. and Bank Holiday M. 2-6 (or dusk if earlier).

LIBRARY CENTRE
New Square, Chesterfield, Derbyshire
Paintings. Water colours. Photographs.
Mar. 1 - Sept. 30, M.-Sa. 10-5.

REVOLUTION HOUSE
Old Whittington, Chesterfield, Derbyshire
Old inn connected with the plotting of the 1688 Revolution, with 17th century furnishings.
Good Friday - September 30: Daily 11-12.30; 2-5, 6-dusk.

CHESTERS

CLAYTON COLLECTION
Hadrian's Wall, nr. Chollerford, Chesters, Northumberland
Roman inscriptions, sculpture, weapons, tools and ornaments from the forts at Chesters, Carrawburgh, Housesteads, Great-chesters and Carvoran.
Mar.-Apr. 9-5; Su. 2-4.30. May-Sept. 9-5.30; Su. 2-5. Oct.-Feb. 9.30-4; Su. 2-4.

CHICHESTER

CHICHESTER CITY MUSEUM
29 Little London, Chichester, Sussex
Local history and archaeology.
Tu.-Sa. 10-6 (Oct.-Mar. 10-5).

CORPS OF ROYAL MILITARY POLICE SERVICE MUSEUM
Roussillon Barracks, Chichester, Sussex
Uniforms, old arms, awards, campaign medals, regimental colours, pictures, trophies and souvenirs associated with the corps.
M.-F. 9-6, Sa. and Su. by appointment.

GOODWOOD HOUSE
Chichester, Sussex
House (1780-1800). Gobelin tapestries. English and European porcelain. Paintings by Lely, Stubbs, Reynolds, Canaletto, Van Dyck. Clocks and watches.
Late May - late Oct. Su. only. Tickets by reservation only. May-Nov., also 2nd W. in month. Times subject to alteration.

ROMAN PALACE
Salthill Road, Fishbourne, Chichester, Sussex
The largest Roman residence yet found in Britain. Thought to be the palace of the local King, Tiberius Claudius Cogidubnus. Site-museum, with material found during excavations.
June, July and Aug. Daily 10-7. May and Sept. Daily 10-6. Mar., Apr. and Oct. Daily 10-4. Nov. weekends only, 10-4.

THE ROYAL SUSSEX REGIMENT MUSEUM
Chichester City Museum, Chichester, Sussex
Uniforms, old arms, awards, campaign medals, regimental colours, pictures, trophies and souvenirs associated with the regiment.
Tu.-Sa. 10-6 (Oct.-Mar. 10-5).

THE WEALD AND DOWNLAND OPEN AIR MUSEUM
nr. Chichester, Sussex
Open-air museum. Collection includes two medieval farmhouses, 16th century treadwheel, granary and toll cottage.
End May - end Oct. W., Th., Sa. and Su. 11-6.

CHIPPENHAM

CORSHAM COURT
Chippenham, Wiltshire
Elizabethan (1582) and Georgian (1760-70) house. 18th century furniture. Italian and Flemish paintings.
State Rooms open all year Su. Apr.-Oct. W., Th. and Su. Daily mid-July to mid-Sept. except M. and F. Also Bank Holiday M. and during Bath Festival. 11-12.30, 2-6 (closes 4.30 mid-Oct.).

CHIPPING SODBURY

DODINGTON HOUSE
Chipping Sodbury, Gloucestershire
Architect James Wyatt. Parkland landscaped by "Capability" Brown. Carriage museum - coaches and horse-drawn vehicles.
Good F. - end Sept. Daily Oct. Sa. and Su. only. House, 1.30-5.30. Other amenities 12.30-6.

CHIRK

CHIRK CASTLE
nr. Wrexham, Denbighshire
State rooms provide examples of 16th-19th century decoration and furnishings.
Easter Sa. and Su., then Su. until May, 2-5. May-Sept. Tu., Th., Sa. and Su., also Easter M., Whitsun and Aug. Bank Holiday 11-5.

CHORLEY

ASTLEY HALL, ART GALLERY AND MUSEUM
Astley Park, Chorley, Lancashire
Paintings. Furniture. Collections of glass, Leeds pottery.
Weekday afternoons, also Su. afternoon, Apr.-Sept.

CHRISTCHURCH

RED HOUSE MUSEUM AND ART GALLERY
Quay Road, Christchurch, Hampshire
Regional museum for natural history and antiquities. 19th century fashion plates. Costumes. Dolls. Bygones.
Weekdays 11-1, 2.15-5 (6 in Summer); Su. 2.15-5.

CIRENCESTER

CORINIUM MUSEUM
Park Street, Cirencester, Gloucestershire
Roman antiquities, found locally on the site of Corinium Dubunnorum. Mosaic pavements. Provincial Roman sculpture. Architectural details.
Weekdays: July-Sept. 10-1, 2-5.30; Oct.-June 10-1, 2-4.30. Su. during Summer only, 2-4.30. Closed Christmas Day, Boxing Day and Good Friday.

CLACTON

ST. OSYTH'S PRIORY
nr. Clacton, Essex
Chinese jade and ceramics.
Gardens and Ancient Monuments: Easter weekend, then May-Sept. Daily 10-6. Aug., daily 2.30-4.30.

CLAYTON-LE-MOORS

MERCER MUSEUM AND ART GALLERY
Mercer Park, Rishton Road, Clayton-le-Moors, Lancashire
Personal relics of the late John Mercer. Collections of coal and coke products, sea shells and the fine arts.
By appointment, Weekdays 9-4.30.

CLEVEDON

CLEVEDON COURT
nr. Clevedon, Somerset
Collections of Nailsea glass and Elton ware.
Apr.-Sept. W., Th. and Su., also Bank Holiday M., 2.30-5.30.

CLITHEROE

BROWSHOLME HALL
near Clitheroe, Lancashire
House (1507 with additions 1604). Elizabethan and Stuart panelling. Tapestries. Paintings. Furniture.
Good F. - mid. Oct., Tu., Sa., Su., Bank Holidays 2-6.30.

CLUN

CLUN TOWN TRUST MUSEUM
Clun, Shropshire
Flint implements. Local archaeology.
Mar.-Oct. Tu. 2-5 or by appointment.

COALBROOKDALE

MUSEUM OF IRONFOUNDING
Coalbrookdale, Shropshire
History of iron smelting and casting. Abraham Darby Furnace. Locomotives. Art castings. Street furniture. Bridge castings. Missionary pots.
Mar.-Oct. M.-F. 10-12, 2-4; Sa. and Su. 2-4. Closed Good Friday.

COCKERMOUTH

WORDSWORTH HOUSE
Main Street, Cockermouth, Cumberland
House (1745), where Wordsworth was born in 1770. Period furniture.
Easter Sa. - Sept. 30, Daily ex. F. and Su. 10.30-12.30, 2-4.30.

COLCHESTER

COLCHESTER AND ESSEX MUSEUM
Colchester, Essex
The Castle-Norman Keep standing on foundations of a Roman temple, and containing archaeological material of all kinds from Essex and finds from Roman Colchester.
The Holly Trees-House (1718) used as museum of later social history, including costume.
Museum of Natural History, All Saints Church, High Street-Natural history of Essex.
Weekdays 10-5. Castle only, Su. Apr.-Sept. 2.30-5.

MINORIES ART GALLERY
High Street, Colchester, Essex
Georgian house, with period rooms.
Weekdays 10-1, 2-5. Su., or by appt.

COLNE

BRITISH IN INDIA MUSEUM
Sun Street, Colne, Lancashire
Life and work of the British in India. Paintings. Photographs. Uniforms. Coins. Medals. Stamps. Working model of Kalka-Simla Railway.
Apr.-Sept. W. 2-8, Sa. 10-6; Su. 2-6. Rest of year Sa. 10-5; Su. 2-5.

COLNE MUSEUM
Public Library, Colne, Lancashire
Local geological, natural history, geographical and historical displays.
M., W., Th. and F. 9-7.30; Tu. and Sa. 9-5.

CONISTON

ART GALLERY MUSEUM
Brantwood, East of Lake Road, Coniston, Lake District, Lancashire
Home of John Ruskin (1872-1900), containing pictures by Ruskin and contemporary artists, Ruskin's furniture, part of his library, his boat and coach.
M.-F., Su. 10-4.30; Sa. 2-4.30. Oct.-Mar. by appointment only.

RUSKIN MUSEUM
Coniston, Lancashire
Life and work of John Ruskin. Local history, scenery and industries.
Daily 10-6.

CONWY

ABERCONWY HOUSE
Castle Street, Conwy, Caernarvonshire
Merchant's house of early 16th century. Furniture.
Summer: M.-F. Su. and Bank Holidays 10-5.30. Closed Sa. and in winter.

ROYAL CAMBRIAN ACADEMY OF ART
Plas Mawr, High Street, Conwy, Caernarvonshire
Elizabethan mansion, housing collection of works by Welsh artists.
Oct.-Mar. 10-4, closed Su. Apr.-Sept. M.-Sa. 10-5.30; Su. 2.30-5.30.

COOKHAM-ON-THAMES

STANLEY SPENCER GALLERY
King's Hall, Cookham-on-Thames, Berkshire
Paintings, drawings and personal effects of the artist.
Easter-Oct. Daily 10.30-6.30. Nov.-Mar. Sa. and Su. only 11-5.

COOKSTOWN

WELLBROOK BEETLING MILL
Cookstown, Co. Tyrone, Northern Ireland
A water-powered mill built in 18th century, with 19th century modifications.
Apr.-Sept. Daily (except Tu.) 2-6.

CORBRIDGE

CORBRIDGE ROMAN SITE
Corbridge, Northumberland
Roman pottery, sculpture, inscribed stones.
March and Oct. 9.30-5.30 (Su. 2-5.30); Apr. 9.30-5.30 daily; May-Sept. 9.30-7 daily; Nov.-Feb. 9.30-4 (Su. 2-4).

CORRIS

CORRIS RAILWAY MUSEUM
Station Yard, Corris, Merioneth
Equipment, pictures and mementoes of the now closed Corris Railway.
July, Aug. and Bank Holidays, Sa. and Su. 10-5. Other days as advertised locally or on application at the Station.

CORSLEY

THE LONGHEDGE COLLECTION
Longhedge Farm, Corsley, Wiltshire
Old farm machinery and tools, including corn machinery, a cider mill and press, cake crackers and root pulpers. Dairy equipment. Blacksmith's shop. Wheelwright's shop. Forestry equipment. Horseshoes. Traps. Carts and waggons. Tractors. Ploughs. 18th century steam-driven flour mill.
Sa., Su. 10.30-5. Weekdays by arrangement.

COVENTRY

HERBERT ART GALLERY AND MUSEUM
Jordan Well, Coventry, Warwickshire
Natural history. Local industry. Paintings illustrating the theme of *British Life and Landscape.* Water-colours of Warwickshire. Topography and portraiture of local interest. Works by local artists. Figure drawings by 20th century British artists. Sketches for the Coventry Cathedral tapestry.
M., Th., F. and Sa. 10-6; Tu. and W. 10-8; Su. 2-5.

LUNT ROMAN FORT
Coventry, Warwickshire
Roman archaeology.
Summer only. Sa. and Bank Holidays 2-6; Su. 11-6.

WHITEFRIARS MUSEUM OF LOCAL HISTORY
Coventry, Warwickshire
Local history.
F; and Sa. 10-6; Su. 2-5.

CRANFIELD

COLLEGE OF AERONAUTICS
Department of Flight, Cranfield, Bedfordshire
History of aeronautics.
By appointment.

CREGNEASH

MANX VILLAGE FOLK MUSEUM
Cregneash, Isle of Man
Group of thatched buildings in Cregneash village, including traditionally-furnished crofter-fisherman's cottage, weaver's shed, turner's shop, smithy and outbuildings of a farmstead.
Early June - mid-Sept. Weekdays 10-1, 2-5.

CRICH

TRAMWAY MUSEUM
Cliff Quarry, Matlock Road, Crich, Nr. Matlock, Derbyshire
Collection of horse, steam and electric tramcars and associated equipment.
Sa., Su. and all Bank Holidays (except Christmas) during the hours of daylight or by appointment.

CRICKHOWELL

WELSH BRIGADE MUSEUM
Cwrt-y-Collen, Crickhowell, Breconshire
Uniforms, old arms, awards, campaign medals, regimental colours, pictures, trophies and souvenirs associated with the Regiment.
Th.-M. 9-4.30; Tu. 9-1.

CROMARTY

HUGH MILLER'S COTTAGE
Cromarty, Ross
Birthplace of the geologist, containing relics and geological specimens.
Apr.-Oct. Weekdays 10-12, 1-5 (Su. 2-5 from June).

CULLEN

CULLEN HOUSE
Cullen, Banffshire
Portraits. Furniture. Tapestries.
June, W., Th., Su. 2-5. July-Aug., W., Th., Su. 2-5. Sept., W., Su. 2-5.

CULROSS

DUNIMARLE MUSEUM
Culross, Fife
Napoleonic furniture. Paintings. Ceramics. Glass. Silver.
Apr.-Oct. Daily 2-6.

DARLINGTON

DARLINGTON ART GALLERY
Crown Street, Darlington, Co. Durham
Paintings, drawings, water-colours.
M.-F. 10-8; Sa. 10-7.

DARLINGTON MUSEUM
Tubwell Row, Darlington, Co. Durham
Local history. Natural history. Model engines and machinery.
M., Tu., W., F. and Sa. 10-6; Th. 10-1.

RABY CASTLE
Staindrop, Darlington, Co. Durham
Principally 14th century. Alterations made 1765 and mid-19th century. English, Dutch and Flemish pictures.
Easter Sa., Su. and M., then Su. to end of May and Spring Bank Holiday weekend. W., Sa. and Su. June and July. Also daily (except F.) from Aug.-early Sept., then W., Sa. and Su. to end of Sept., 2-5.

DARTFORD

DARTFORD BOROUGH MUSEUM
Market Street, Dartford, Kent
Local geology. Roman, Saxon and other archaeological specimens. Local antiquities, industries and natural history.
M., Tu., Th. and F. 12.30-5.30, Sa. 9-5.

DEAL

DEAL MUSEUM
Town Hall, High Street, Deal, Kent
Local prehistory, history. Complete robes of a Baron of the Cinque Ports.
By appointment.

DEDHAM

CASTLE HOUSE
Dedham, Essex
Home of the late Sir Alfred Munnings. The house and two studios contain many of his paintings, drawings, sketches and other works.
Mid-May- mid. Oct. W. and Su. 2-4.30.

DENBIGH

DENBIGH CASTLE MUSEUM
Denbigh
Local history. Model of the cottage, originally home of Henry Morton Stanley, African explorer.
M.-Sa. 10-5. Su. 2-5.

DERBY

DERBY MUSEUM AND ART GALLERY
Strand, Derby, Derbyshire
Archaeology. Natural history. Technical and industrial section includes scale working layout of Midland Railway. Porcelain. Paintings by Wright of Derby.
M.-F. 10-6; Sa. 10-5; Su. 2.30-4.30.

ELVASTON CASTLE COUNTRY PARK MUSEUM
Thulston, Derby, Derbyshire
Local natural history. Rural crafts. Agriculture. Household utensils.
Winter: daily 10-4. Summer: M.-F. 10-4; Sa., Su. 10-6.

KEDLESTON HALL
Derby, Derbyshire
Robert Adam house. Contemporary furniture, pictures.
Easter Su. and M., then Su. from Apr.-end Sept., also Bank Holiday M. 2-6. Gardens 2-7.

MUSEUM OF INDUSTRY AND TECHNOLOGY
Silk Mill Lane, off Full Street, Derby, Derbyshire
On site of Lombe's silk mill and housing the Rolls-Royce collection of aero engines. Material relating to the industries of Derby and Derbyshire.
Provisionally Tu.-Sa. 10-6.

DERRYMORE

DERRYMORE
County Armagh, Northern Ireland
Thatched manorhouse (1776). Period furnishings.
By appointment.

DEVIZES

DEVIZES MUSEUM
Long Street, Devizes, Wiltshire
Archaeological and geological collections concerned with Wiltshire, including Sir Richard Colt-Hoare's Stourhead collection of prehistoric material.
Tu.-Sa., Summer 11-5; Winter 11-4.

THE WILTSHIRE REGIMENT MUSEUM
Le Marchant Barracks, Devizes, Wiltshire
Uniforms, old arms, awards, campaign medals, regimental colours, pictures, trophies and souvenirs associated with the regiment.
M.-F. 9.30-4.30.

DEWSBURY

DEWSBURY MUSEUM AND ART GALLERY
Crow Nest Park, Dewsbury, Yorkshire
History of Dewsbury. British natural history.
Oct.-Mar. Tu. and Sa. 2.30-dusk; Apr.-Sept. Tu., W., Th., Sa. and Su. 2.30-7.30. Closed Boxing Day.

DIDSBURY

FLETCHER MOSS
Didsbury, nr. Manchester, Lancashire
English watercolours, including a group by J. M. W. Turner.
All the year, Daily. Nov.-Feb. Weekdays 10-4, Su. 2-4. May-Aug. Weekdays 10-8, Su. 2-8. Mar., Apr., Sept. and Oct. Weekdays 10-6, Su. 2-6. Closed Good Friday and Christmas Day.

DISLEY

LYME PARK
Disley, Cheshire
House (1541), with Palladian exterior (1720) by Giacomo Leoni. Grinling Gibbons carvings. State rooms with period furniture and tapestries.
House: *Daily (inc. Su.). Guided Tours May-Aug., 1.30, 3, 4.30, 6.15. Sept., Oct., Mar., Apr. 2, 3, 4, 5. Su. and Bank Holidays 1 p.m. and every half hour.* Park and Gardens: *All the year, daily 8 to dusk.*

DODDINGTON

DODDINGTON HALL
Doddington, Lincolnshire
Manor (1593-1600), built by Robert Smythson. Paintings. Furniture. Tapestries. Porcelain.
May-Sept., W. 2-6.

DONCASTER

DONCASTER MUSEUM AND ART GALLERY
Chequer Road, Doncaster, Yorkshire
British natural history. Prehistory and Romano-British exhibits. Local history. Costumes. Paintings. Drawings. Watercolours. Sculpture.
Daily 10-5.30; Su. 2-5.

DORCHESTER

DORSET COUNTY MUSEUM
Dorchester, Dorset
Dorset geology, natural history, prehistory and history. Thomas Hardy Memorial room. Pictures of Dorset or by Dorset artists.
Weekdays 10-1, 2-5. Closed Christmas Day, Boxing Day and Good Friday.

THE DORSET MILITARY MUSEUM
The Keep, Dorchester, Dorset
Documents, uniforms and weapons illustrating Dorset military history from 1660 to present day. Dorset Militia. Volunteers and Queen's Own Dorset Yeomanry. World War II exhibits include Hitler's desk from Berlin Chancellery.
M.-F. 9-5; Sa. 9-12 (July-Sept. 9-5).

DORKING

POLESDEN LACEY
nr. Dorking, Surrey
Greville collection of paintings, tapestries, furniture.
Mar.-mid. Dec. Sa., Su. and Bank Holiday M. 11-12.45, 2-6 or dusk if earlier. W. 2-6 or dusk if earlier, also Tu. May-Aug. 2-6 (except May 25).

DOUGLAS

MANX MUSEUM
Douglas, Isle of Man
Collections illustrating Manx archaeology, folk life and natural history. Art Gallery devoted to Manx paintings and works by Manx artists. Memorial Room to T. E. Brown, the Manx poet. Reconstructed 19th century farmhouse, barn, dairy.
Weekdays 10-5.

DOVER

DOVER CORPORATION MUSEUM
Ladywell, Dover, Kent
British and foreign lepidoptera. Ceramics. Roman pottery. Natural history. Local history dioramas. Horology.
Weekdays 10-5 (except W.).

DRIFFIELD

SLEDMERE HOUSE
Driffield, Yorkshire
House (1751, enlarged 1787). Chippendale, Sheraton and French furniture. Porcelain.
Easter Su. and M., then Su. only to mid. May. Mid. May-mid.-Sept. Daily (except M. and F.) also Spring and Late Summer Bank Holiday M. 1.30-5.30.

DUDLEY

BLACK COUNTRY MUSEUM
Dudley, Worcestershire
Open-air museum in course of arrangement, illustrating development of Black Country industries, expecially coal, iron and the metal trades. Site contains part of Dudley Canal, including tunnel, and groups of late 18th century limekilns.
M.-Sa. 10-6. Closed Easter and Christmas.

BRIERLEY HILL GLASS MUSEUM AND ART GALLERY
Moor Street, Dudley, Worcestershire
Collection of local (Stourbridge) and foreign glass.
Weekdays (closed W.) 2-5; Sa. 10-1, 2-5.

DUDLEY MUSEUM AND ART GALLERY
St. James's Road, Dudley, Worcestershire
Geology, especially of local limestone and coal measure fossils. Reconstructed Black Country Nail Forge. Adjacent Brooke-Robinson Museum shows benefactor's personal collection of fine art.
Weekdays 10-6. Closed Bank Holidays.

DUMFRIES

DUMFRIES BURGH MUSEUM
The Observatory, Corberry Hill, Dumfries, Dumfriesshire
Natural history, archaeological and ethnographical collections.
Apr.-Sept. Weekdays 10-1, 2-5; Su. 2-5. Oct.-Mar. Weekdays only 10-1, 2-5.

FOLK MATERIAL COLLECTION
Ellisland Farm, nr. Dumfries, Dumfriesshire
In Burns' former granary.
May-Sept. Weekdays 10-1, 2-6.

OLD BRIDGE HOUSE MUSEUM
Old Bridge Street, Dumfries, Dumfriesshire
17th century house, with period rooms. Local history.
Closed Tu. Apr.-Sept. Weekdays 10-1, 2-5; Su. 2-5. Oct.-Mar. Weekdays only 10-1, 2-5.

DUNBLANE

DUNBLANE CATHEDRAL MUSEUM
The Cross, Dunblane, Perthshire
Pictures of Cathedral before restoration. Communion tokens. Reproductions of Bishops' seals. Leightoniana. Medieval carving. Local history.
Late May-early Oct. 10.30-12.30, 2.30-4.30. Other times on request.

DUNDEE

BARRACK STREET MUSEUM
Ward Road, Dundee, Angus
Museum of Dundee shipping and industries. Gallery of art and photography.
Weekdays 10-5.30; Sa. 10-1, 2-5. Closed F. Summer only, Su. 2-5.

BROUGHTY CASTLE MUSEUM
Broughty Ferry, Dundee, Angus
Relics of local and military history. Natural history of the Tay. Whaling gallery.
Weekdays (except F.) 10-1, 2-5; Su. 2-5.

DUNDEE CITY MUSEUM AND ART GALLERIES
Albert Square, Dundee, Angus
Regional collection of archaeological, historical, natural history, botanical and geological material. Flemish, Dutch, French and British painting, particularly Scottish schools.
Weekdays 10-5.30.

ORCHAR ART GALLERY
Broughty Ferry, Dundee, Angus
Paintings and water-colours, mostly by Scottish artists of the 19th century. Etchings include 36 by Whistler.
Sa. and Su. 2-5.

ST. MARY'S TOWER
Nethergait, Dundee, Angus
Tower of St. Mary's Church. Site museum relating to ecclesiastic and local history.
M.-Th. 10-1, 2-5; Sa. 10-1, 2-5. Closed F. Summer only, Su. 2-5.

SPALDING GOLF MUSEUM
Camperdown House, Camperdown Park, Dundee, Angus
Representing nearly three centuries of golf history. Oldest item in collection is an iron club, made c.1680 and used by Robert Clark, probably the first writer on golf.
M.-Th. 12-7; Sa. and Su. 1-7.

DUNFERMLINE

ANDREW CARNEGIE BIRTHPLACE MEMORIAL
Junction of Moodie Street and Priory Lane, Dunfermline, Fife
The Weaver's Cottage, where Carnegie was born and the Memorial Hall reflecting his many benefactions.
Weekdays 11-1, 2-8 (Summer); 11-1, 2-6 (Winter); Su. 2-6.

DUNFERMLINE MUSEUM
Viewfield, Dunfermline, Fife
Local history and natural history of the region.
M., W., Th. and F. 11-1, 2-7.30; Sa. 11-1, 2-5; Su. 2-5.

PITTENCRIEFF HOUSE MUSEUM
Pittencrieff Park, Dunfermline, Fife
Costume collection c.1800 to present day.
Weekdays 11-1, 2-dusk; Su. 2-dusk.

DUNKELD

THE SCOTTISH HORSE MUSEUM
The Cross, Dunkeld, Perthshire
Uniforms, old arms, awards, campaign medals, regimental colours, pictures, trophies and souvenirs associated with the Regiment.
Easter-Oct. daily 2-4, 6-7.30.

DURHAM

DORMITORY MUSEUM
The Cathedral, Durham, Co. Durham
The relics of St. Cuthbert. Anglo-Saxon sculptured stones. Medieval seals. Vestments. Manuscripts.
Weekdays 10-5; Su. 1-5.

DURHAM LIGHT INFANTRY MUSEUM AND ARTS CENTRE
Nr. County Hall, Durham, Co. Durham
Uniforms, models, weapons and illustrations showing the County Regiment's 200 years of history.
Weekdays (except M.) 10-5; Su. 2-5. Closed Christmas and Boxing Day.

GULBENKIAN MUSEUM OF ORIENTAL ART AND ARCHAEOLOGY
Elvet Hill, Durham, Co. Durham
Egyptian and Mesopotamian antiquities. Chinese pottery, porcelain, jade and other hard stone carvings, ivories. Chinese textiles. Near-Eastern pottery. Indian sculpture. Japanese and Tibetan art. Oriental coins.
M.-F. 9.30-1, 2.15-5, Sa. 9.30-12, 2.15-5; Su. 2.15-5. Closed Sa. and Su. afternoons between Christmas and Easter and Bank Holiday weekends.

DURSLEY

R. A. LISTER AND COMPANY LIMITED
Dursley, Gloucestershire
Company Museum. Agricultural machinery and miscellaneous products of the company since 1867.
By appointment.

EARDISLAND

BURTON COURT
Eardisland, Herefordshire
14th century Great Hall. Costumes. Furnishings.
Whitsun-Aug., Su., W., Th., Sa. and Bank Holiday M., 2.30-6.

EASTBOURNE

ROYAL NATIONAL LIFEBOAT INSTITUTION MUSEUM
Grand Parade, Eastbourne, Sussex
Lifeboats from the earliest date to the present time. Items used in lifeboat service.
Daily 9.30-5 (Winter 9-1).

TOWER 73 (THE WISH TOWER)
Eastbourne, Sussex
Restored Martello Tower. Displays show the historical background, disposition, building and manning of these defence forts built during the Napoleonic war, together with examples of equipment, weapons, uniforms and documents relating to the building.
Late May-early Oct. Daily 10-5.30.

TOWNER ART GALLERY
Manor House, 9 Borough Lane, Eastbourne, Sussex
19th and 20th century British painters. Contemporary prints. Sussex paintings. Georgian caricatures. Original drawings by British book illustrators. British butterflies.
Weekdays 10-6 (10-5 Oct.-Mar.); Su. 2-6 (2-5 Oct.-Mar.).

EAST COWES

OSBORNE HOUSE
East Cowes, Isle of Wight
Queen Victoria's favourite residence, showing her private rooms, the State Apartments and Swiss Cottage.
Easter M.-early Oct., M.-F. 11-5.30.

ECCLEFECHAN

CARLYLE'S BIRTHPLACE
The Arched House, Ecclefechan, Dumfriesshire
House where Carlyle was born in 1795, containing personal relics and manuscript letters.
Weekdays Mar.-Oct. 10-6.

ECCLES

MONKS HALL MUSEUM
42 Wellington Road, Eccles, Lancashire, M30 0NP
Nasmyth machinery (including steam hammer). Gardner engine (1903). Browett Lindley steam engine (1930).
M., Tu., W., F. 10-6; Sa. 10-5.

PROTECTOR LAMP AND LIGHTING COMPANY LIMITED
Lansdowne Road, Monton, Eccles, Manchester, M30 9PH
Company Museum. Miners' lamps.
By appointment.

EDENBRIDGE

CHIDDINGSTONE CASTLE
nr. Edenbridge, Kent
Stuart and Jacobite collection. Egyptian antiquities. Japanese lacquer, swords, netsuke.
Easter Sa. to Oct., Daily (except M.) 2-5.30, Sa., Su. and Bank Holiday M. 11.30-5.30; open Su. 2-4 in winter (except Dec., Jan. and Feb.).

HEVER CASTLE
nr. Edenbridge, Kent
Formal Italian garden, with collection of Greek and Roman statuary and sculpture.
Castle and Gardens open Easter S.-mid. Oct., W., Su. and Bank Holidays. Gardens 1-7 (no admittance after 6). Castle 2-7 (no admittance after 6.15).

EDGEHILL

UPTON HOUSE
Edgehill, Oxfordshire
Brussels tapestries. Sèvres porcelain. Chelsea figures. 18th century furniture and pictures.
May-Sept. W. and Sa. 2-6. Oct.-Apr. W. only 2-6 or dusk.

EDGWARE

THE MIDDLESEX REGIMENT SERVICE MUSEUM
Regimental Headquarters, T.A. Centre, Deansbrook Road, Edgware, Middlesex
Uniforms, old arms, awards, campaign medals, regimental colours, pictures, trophies and souvenirs associated with the Regiment.
By appointment.

EDINBURGH

CANONGATE TOLBOOTH
Canongate, Edinburgh, Midlothian
Burgh courthouse and prison for more than 300 years. Collection of Highland dress and tartan.
Weekdays 10-5. During Festival only, Su. 2-5.

EDINBURGH CASTLE
Castlehill, Edinburgh, Midlothian
Uniforms. Military history. Scottish Crown jewels and regalia.
May-Oct. 9.30-6; Su. 11-6. Precincts only, daily 6-9. Nov.-Apr. 9.30-5.15, Su. 12.30-4.30.

HUNTLY HOUSE
Canongate, Edinburgh, Midlothian
Local history and topography; Edinburgh glass. Scottish pottery. Reconstruction of an old Scots kitchen. Original copy of the "National Covenant" of 1638. Personal possessions of Field Marshal Earl Haig.
Weekdays 10-5 (also W. evenings June-Sept.). Festival only Su. 2-5.

LADY STAIR'S HOUSE
Lady Stair's Close, Lawnmarket, Edinburgh, Midlothian
Reconstructed town house dating from 1622. Relics connected with Robert Burns, Sir Walter Scott and R. L. Stevenson.
M.-F. 10-4; Sa. 10-1. During Festival only, Su. 2-5.

LAURISTON CASTLE
Cramond Road South, Edinburgh, Midlothian
16th century house with 19th century additions. Period furniture. Ceramics. Tapestries. Wool Mosaics.
Apr.-Oct. Daily (except F.) 11-1; 2-5. Nov.-Mar. Sa. and Su. only 11-1, 2-5.

MUSEUM OF CHILDHOOD
38 High Street, (opposite John Knox's house), Edinburgh, Midlothian
Games. Toys. Books. Costumes. Health and education.
Weekdays 10-5. During Festival only, Su. 2-5.

MUSEUM GALLERY
18 Shandwick Place, (West end of Princes Street), Edinburgh, Midlothian
History of Scottish daily life. 18th-19th century costumes. Agriculture. Handicrafts.
Weekdays 10-5 (10-8 during Festival). Closed Su.

MUSEUM OF THE ROYAL COLLEGE OF SURGEONS OF EDINBURGH
18 Nicholson Street, Edinburgh, Midlothian
Exhibits of surgical, dental, pathological and historical interest.
By appointment.

NATIONAL GALLERY OF SCOTLAND
The Mound, Edinburgh, EH2 2EL, Midlothian
European paintings, sculpture, drawings and prints, 14th-19th centuries. Scottish art up to 1900.
Weekdays 10-5; Su. 2-5. Open until 8 weekdays during Festival.

NATIONAL MUSEUM OF ANTIQUITIES OF SCOTLAND
Queen Street, Edinburgh 2, Midlothian
Collections cover the whole of Scotland from the Stone Age to recent times. Prehistoric and Roman material. Sculptured stones. Relics of the Celtic Church. Scottish coins and medals. Stuart relics. Highland weapons, domestic life.
Weekdays 10-5 (10-8 during Festival); Su. 2-5.

PALACE OF HOLYROOD HOUSE
Canongate, Edinburgh, Midlothian
Relics of Mary Queen of Scots.
May-Oct. Weekdays 9.30-6; Su. 11-6. Nov.-Apr. Weekdays 9.30-5.15 Su. 12.30-4.30. Closed at short notice when the Royal Family is in residence and for State Visits.

THE ROYAL SCOTS (THE ROYAL REGIMENT) MUSEUM
The Castle, Edinburgh, Midlothian
Uniforms, old arms, awards, campaign medals, regimental colours, pictures, trophies and souvenirs associated with the Regiment.
June-Sept. Daily 9.30-6; Oct.-May, M.-F. 10-4.

ROYAL SCOTTISH MUSEUM
Chambers Street, Edinburgh, EH1 1JF, Midlothian
Paintings. Drawings. Water-colours. Prints. Scottish archaeology. Natural History. Geology. Mineralogy. Technology with accurate scale models operated by viewer. Shipping. Mining. Navigation gallery. Glass. Children's museum.
Weekdays 10-5; Su. 2-5.

RUSSELL COLLECTION OF HARPSICHORDS AND CLAVICHORDS
St. Cecilia's Hall, Niddry Street, Cowgate, Edinburgh, Midlothian
Keyboard instruments, including harpsichords, clavichords, fortepianos, regals, spinets, virginals and chamber organs. Paintings (Pannini, Ruysdael). Tapestries and textiles.
Sa. 2-5 throughout year. Daily during Festival (afternoons).

SCOTTISH NATIONAL GALLERY OF MODERN ART
Royal Botanic Garden, Edinburgh, EH3 5LR, Midlothian
20th century paintings and sculpture, including works by Picasso, Matisse, Leger, Aep, Giacometti. Modern Scottish painting.
Weekdays 10-6 or until dusk. Su. 2-6 or dusk.

SCOTTISH NATIONAL PORTRAIT GALLERY
Queen Street, Edinburgh, EH2 1JD, Midlothian
Portraits of famous Scottish men and women from 16th century to modern times.
Weekdays 10-5; Su. 2-5. Open till 8 Weekdays during Festival.

SCOTTISH UNITED SERVICES MUSEUM
Crown Square, Edinburgh Castle, Edinburgh, Midlothian
Illustrates by its display of uniforms, head-dress, arms and equipment, medals, portraits and models, the history of the armed forces of Scotland. Prints of uniforms.
Weekdays 9.30-6 (9.30-5.15 Nov.-Apr.); Su. May-Oct. only 11-6.

TRANSPORT MUSEUM
Shrubhill, Leith Walk, Edinburgh, Midlothian
Relics of Edinburgh cable-car tramways. Development of public transport system in Edinburgh. Horse-trams. Early steam road roller. Static and working models. Displays of historical maps, photographs, uniforms, tickets, information bills, posters, bus stop plates.
M.-Sa. 10-5.

EGHAM

PICTURE GALLERY
Englefield Green, Egham, Surrey
Paintings, mainly British, of the late 18th and early 19th centuries.
By appointment.

ELGIN

ELGIN MUSEUM
1 High Street, Elgin, Morayshire
Collections of reptile and fish fossils, prehistoric stone and Bronze Age weapons, lepidoptera.
Weekdays (Oct.-Mar.) except Tu. 10-12.30, 2-5; Tu. 10-1.

ENFIELD

FORTY HALL
Forty Hill, Enfield, Middlesex
Mansion (1629 with 18th century modifications). 17th-18th century furniture, paintings, ceramics and glass.
Easter-Sept., Tu.-F. 10-8; Sa., Su. 10-6. Oct.-Easter, Tu.-Su. 10-5.

ENNISKILLEN

THE ROYAL INNISKILLING FUSILIERS MUSEUM
The Keep of the Castle, Castle Barracks, Enniskillen, Co. Fermough, Northern Ireland
Uniforms, old arms, awards, campaign medals, regimental colours, pictures, trophies and souvenirs associated with the regiment.
By appointment only.

ETON

ETON COLLEGE NATURAL HISTORY SOCIETY MUSEUM
Eton, Buckinghamshire
Collection of British birds, ethnological and entomological specimens, mammals, reptiles and fossils.
By appointment.

EVESHAM

ALMONRY MUSEUM
Vine Street, Evesham, Worcestershire
Romano-British, Anglo-Saxon, medieval and monastic remains. Agricultural implements. Local history.
Mar.-Sept. Daily (except M., W.) 2.30-6.30.

EXETER

THE DEVONSHIRE REGIMENT SERVICE MUSEUM
Wyvern Barracks, Exeter, Devon
Uniforms, old arms, awards, campaign medals, regimental colours, pictures, trophies and souvenirs associated with the Regiment.
M.-F.

EXETER MARITIME MUSEUM
International Sailing Craft Association, The Quay, Exeter, EX2 4AN, Devon
Collection of about 40 boats, mostly sail or man propelled, from all over the world. Steam tug built in Denmark in 1931 and a Brunel steam dredger (1843).
May-Oct. Daily 10-6; Nov.-Apr. 10-5.

ROUGEMONT HOUSE MUSEUM
Castle Street, Exeter, Devon
Archaeology and local history of Exeter and Devon.
M.-Sa. 10-5.30.

ROYAL ALBERT MEMORIAL MUSEUM AND ART GALLERY
Queen Street, Exeter, Devon
English paintings, watercolours, ceramics and glass. Exeter silver. Costumes. Natural history. Ethnography.
M.-Sa. 10-5.30.

TOPSHAM MUSEUM
25 The Strand, Topsham, Exeter, Devon
History of the port and trade of Topsham.
M., W. and Sa. 2-5.

FALKIRK

FALKIRK BURGH MUSEUM
Dollar Park, Falkirk, Stirlingshire
Local history.
By appointment.

SCOTTISH RAILWAY PRESERVATION COLLECTION
Wallace Street, Falkirk, Stirlingshire
Steam locomotives, coaches and wagons, maintained in working order.
Sa. 11-5.

FARLEIGH HUNGERFORD

FARLEIGH CASTLE
Farleigh Hungerford, Somerset
In the former Castle Chapel. Arms and armour, largely of civil war period. Medieval stained glass.
Mar., Apr. and Oct. 9.30-5.30 (Su. 2-5.30); May-Sept. 9.30-7 (Su. 2-7); Nov.-Feb. 9.30-4 (Su. 2-4).

FARNHAM

PITT RIVERS MUSEUM
Farnham, Dorset
Ancient glass from Eastern Mediterranean. Archaeology.
By appointment.

FARNHAM MUSEUM
Wilmer House, 38 West Street, Farnham, Surrey
Early Georgian (1718) façade of cut and moulded brick. Carving and panelling. Local history.
Tu.-Sa. 11-5; Su. and Bank Holiday M. 2.30-5. Closed M.

FAVERSHAM

MAISON DIEU
Ospringe, Faversham, Kent
In 13th century building. Material from Roman cemetery discovered at Ospringe.
Mar., Apr. and Oct. 9.30-5.30; Su. 2-5.30. May-Sept. 9.30-7; Su. 2-7. Nov.-Feb. 9.30-4; Su. 2-4.

FILKINS

FILKINS AND BROUGHTON POGGS MUSEUM
Filkins, nr. Letchlade, Gloucestershire
Folklore. Tools. Household equipment.
Daily by appointment.

FIFE

CULROSS PALACE
Culross, Fife
Palace 1597-1611. Contains series of paintings on wooden walls and ceilings. Furnishings.
Apr.-Sept. 9.30-7; Su. 2-7. Oct.-Mar. 10-4.30; Su. 2-4.30.

FLORENCE COURT

FLORENCE COURT
County Fermanagh, Northern Ireland
House (1764). 18th century furnishings.
Apr.-Sept., W.-M. 2-6.

FOLKESTONE

FOLKESTONE MUSEUM AND ART GALLERY
Grace Hill, Folkestone, Kent
Local history. Archaeology. Natural science.
Weekdays 10-1, 2.30-5.30.

FORDINGBRIDGE

BREAMORE HOUSE
nr. Fordingbridge, Hampshire
Elizabethan manor house (1583) with collections of paintings, tapestries, furniture. Carriage collection.
Apr.-Sept. Daily (except M. and F.) and all Bank Holidays, 2-5.30.

HALE PARK
nr. Fordingbridge, Hampshire
House (c.1715). Family portraits. Aubusson tapestries.
July-mid-Sept., W., Th., Su. and Late Summer Bank Holiday, 2.30-6.

FORFAR

MEFFAN INSTITUTE MUSEUM
Forfar, Angus
Collections of archaeological, historical, geological and natural history material.
Weekdays 10-12, 2-4; Sa. 10-12.

FORRES

FALCONER MUSEUM
Centre of Forres, Forres, Moray
Fossils, arrowheads from Culbin sands.
Summer 10-5; Winter 10-3.

FORT GEORGE

SEAFORTH HIGHLANDERS; THE QUEEN'S OWN CAMERON HIGHLANDERS AND QUEEN'S OWN HIGHLANDERS (SEAFORTH AND CAMERONS) MUSEUM
Fort George, Invernesshire
Uniforms, old arms, awards, campaign medals, regimental colours, pictures, trophies and souvenirs associated with the Regiment.
Weekdays (Apr.-mid. Oct.) 10-7; Su. 2-7; mid. Oct.-Mar. M.-F. 10-4; Sa. 12-4.

FORT WILLIAM

WEST HIGHLAND MUSEUM
Cameron Square, Fort William, Inverness
Historical, natural history and folk-lore exhibits. Local history. Tartans. Processing of aluminium.
Weekdays Sept.-May 9.30-5. June-Aug. 9.30-9.

FOWEY

NOAH'S ARK FOLK MUSEUM
27-35 Fore Street, Fowey, Cornwall
Period rooms, 1457-1914. Marine cellar with shipbuilding exhibits. Early photography. Domestic irons. Local history.
M.-Sa. 10-5.30. Su. and evenings by appointment.

GAINSBOROUGH

GAINSBOROUGH OLD HALL
Parnell Street, Gainsborough, Lincolnshire
15th century black and white manor house, now used as Folk Museum. Handicrafts. Costumes. Domestic equipment.
Weekdays 2-5; Su. 2-5 (Easter-Oct.).

GATESHEAD

SALTWELL PARK MUSEUM
Saltwell Park, Gateshead, Co. Durham
Local natural history. Prints. Pottery. Glass. Wood carving. Dolls.
By appointment.

SHIPLEY ART GALLERY
Prince Consort Road South, Gateshead, Co. Durham
Paintings. Water-colours.
Weekdays 10-6; Su. 3-5.

GLAMIS

ANGUS FOLK COLLECTION
Kirkwynd, Glamis, Angus
Collection of early furnishings, clothing, domestic utensils and agricultural implements from County of Angus.
Daily, early Apr.-mid. Oct. 1-6.

GLASGOW

CITY OF GLASGOW CORPORATION ART GALLERY AND MUSEUM
Kelvingrove, Glasgow, Lanarkshire
Italian, Dutch, Flemish, French, British paintings, 16th century to present day and 19th-20th century French paintings, European and Oriental art-objects. Arms and Armour. Neolithic, Bronze Age and Roman archaeology. Egyptian, Greek and Cypriot collections. Scottish bygones. Engineering exhibits and collection of ship models including *Queen Mary*. Ethnography. Animals of Scotland, Polar Regions, Africa, India and Australia. British birds. Geology. Zoology. Tapestries. Furniture. Porcelain. Stained glass. Silver.
Weekdays 10-5; Su. 2-5.

CAMPHILL MUSEUM
Queen's Park, Glasgow, Lanarkshire
Paintings. Art-objects. Natural history.
Weekdays 11-5; Su. 2-5 (Winter 2-dusk).

HUNTERIAN MUSEUM
Glasgow University, Glasgow W.2, Lanarkshire
Geological, archaeological, historical and ethnographical material. Hunterian coin cabinet, books and manuscripts. Fine art collection of the University, including works by Whistler and Chardin.
M.-F. 9-5; Sa. 9-12.

MUSEUM OF TRANSPORT
25 Albert Drive, Glasgow S.1, Lanarkshire
Land transport. Glasgow tramcars from 1894 horse-drawn to electric 1937. Veteran and vintage cars with emphasis on Scottish motor production up to present day. Passenger and commercial horse-drawn vehicles. Development of the bicycle. Railway locomotives.
Weekdays 10-5; Su. 2-5.

OLD GLASGOW MUSEUM
People's Palace, Glasgow, Lanarkshire
Development of Glasgow. Domestic life through the centuries. Royal portraits from James VI to George III commissioned by the Town Council. Paintings and prints illustrating places and buildings of interest in Glasgow or associated with City's history. 16th century Bible belonging to the last Pre-Reformation Archbishop of Glasgow. Yachting Trophies. Fulton Orrery.
Weekdays 10-5; Su. 2-5.

POLLOK HOUSE
Pollok Park, Glasgow S.3, Lanarkshire
Spanish paintings. Silver. Porcelain.
Weekdays 10-5; Su. 2-5.

PROVAND'S LORDSHIP
3 Castle Street, Glasgow C.4, Lanarkshire
17th and 18th century furniture. Domestic equipment.
Apr.-Sept. Daily (except Su.) 10-5. Oct.-Mar. 11-4.

THE ROYAL HIGHLAND FUSILIERS MUSEUM
518 Sauchiehall Street, Glasgow, Lanarkshire
Princess Margaret's Own Glasgow and Ayrshire Regiment. Uniforms, old arms, awards, campaign medals, regimental colours, pictures, trophies and souvenirs associated with the regiment.
M.-F.

TOLLCROSS MUSEUM
Tollcross Park, Glasgow, Lanarkshire
Children's Museum. Zoology. Dolls.
Weekdays 11-5 (Winter 11-dusk); Su. 2-5 (Winter 2-dusk).

GLASTONBURY

GLASTONBURY LAKE VILLAGE MUSEUM
The Tribunal, High Street, Glastonbury, Somerset
Prehistoric material from Glastonbury Lake Village.
Daily 10-1, 2.15-5.15. Closed Christmas Day.

GLENESK

GLENESK FOLK MUSEUM
The Retreat, Glenesk, Angus
Period rooms. Costumes. Local history, folklore. Agriculture.
Su. from Easter. Daily June-Sept. 2-6.

GLOUCESTER

BISHOP HOOPER'S LODGING
99-103 Westgate Street, Gloucester, Gloucestershire
Group of three Tudor timber-framed buildings. Collections illustrate bygone crafts and industries of the county, agriculture, Severn fishing, local history and history of the Gloucestershire Regiment.
Weekdays 10-5.30.

CITY MUSEUM AND ART GALLERY
Brunswick Road, Gloucester, Gloucestershire
Local archaeology, natural history, geology. Numismatics. English period furniture. Barometers. Pottery. Glass. Silver. Costumes.
Weekdays 10-5.30.

THE GLOUCESTER REGIMENT SERVICE MUSEUM
103 Westgate Street, Gloucester, Gloucestershire
Uniforms, old arms, awards, campaign medals, regimental colours, pictures, trophies and souvenirs associated with the Regiment.
By appointment.

GODALMING

CHARTERHOUSE SCHOOL MUSEUM
Godalming, Surrey
Carthusiana. Prehistoric and Roman archaeology. Greek and Peruvian pottery. Medals. Household equipment. Ethnography. Natural history.
Tu., Sa. and Su. 2.30-4.30. Closed during vacations.

GODALMING BOROUGH MUSEUM
Old Town Hall, Godalming, Surrey
Local geology, antiquities and bygones.
Tu., F., Sa. 3-5 or by appointment.

GOLCAR

COLNE VALLEY MUSEUM
Cliffe Ash, Golcar, Huddersfield, Yorkshire
Group of weavers' cottages. The living room and weaving workshop have been restored in one of these, and a cobbler's and clog-maker's shop in another. Collections of local and industrial history.
Sa. 2-5.

GORDON

MELLERSTAIN
Gordon, Berwickshire
Adam mansion, with original interiors and furniture. Paintings.
May-Sept. Daily (except Sa.) 2-5.30.

GOSPORT

SUBMARINE MUSEUM
H.M.S. Dolphin, Gosport, Hampshire
Medals, pictures and trophies of the submarine command.
End May-mid. Sept. Sa. and Su. conducted tours 2-5. Closed Late Summer Bank Holiday.

GRANTHAM

BELVOIR CASTLE
nr. Grantham, Leicestershire
Rebuilt by Wyatt 1816. Pictures by Holbein, Reynolds, Gainsborough, Poussin. Gobelin tapestries.
Early Apr.-Sept. W., Th., Sa. 12-6, Su. 2-7; Good F. and Bank Holiday M. and Tu. 11-7; also Su. only during Oct. 2-6.

17TH/21ST LANCERS SERVICE MUSEUM
Belvoir Castle, nr. Grantham, Leicestershire
Mementoes of the regiment, including the original bugle sounded at the famous Charge of the Light Brigade.
Summer only: W., Th. and Sa. 12-6; Su. 2-7; Bank Holidays 11-7.

BELTON HOUSE
Grantham, Lincolnshire
Grinling Gibbons carvings. Paintings. Duke of Windsor souvenirs.
Easter- early Oct., Tu., W., Th., Su. and Bank Holidays 12-6.

GRASMERE

DOVE COTTAGE
Grasmere, Westmorland
Early home of Wordsworth (1799-1808), with mementoes of the Wordsworth family and their friends.
Oct.-Easter Weekdays 10-4.30; Easter-Oct. Weekdays 10-6. Closed mid.-Jan. - March 1.

WORDSWORTH MUSEUM
Grasmere, Westmorland
Manuscripts and objects illustrative of rural life in Wordsworth's time.
Easter-Oct. only, weekdays 10-6.

GRAYS

THURROCK LOCAL HISTORY MUSEUM
Central Library, Orsett Road, Grays, Essex
Prehistoric, Romano-British and Pagan Saxon archaeology. Social, agricultural and industrial history of locality.
Weekdays 10-8; Sa. 10-6.

GREAT HAYWOOD

SHUGBOROUGH
Great Haywood, Staffordshire
Local history. 18th century French furniture. 19th century estate laundry and brewery.
Mid.-Mar. - mid. Oct. Daily (except M.) but including Bank Holiday M., 11-5.30; Su. 2-5.30. Closed Good Friday.

GREAT YARMOUTH

CAISTER CASTLE
Great Yarmouth, Norfolk
Early motor cars.
Mid.-May to last Su. in Sept., Daily 10-5.

MARITIME MUSEUM FOR EAST ANGLIA
Marine Parade, Great Yarmouth, Norfolk
Maritime history of the area. Fishing. North Sea oil and gas. Lifesaving.
May-Sept. Daily 10-1, 2-8.

MUSEUM OF DOMESTIC LIFE
4 South Quay, Great Yarmouth, Norfolk
Tudor house. Furniture. Domestic equipment.
June-Sept. Daily (except Sa.) 10-1, 2-5.30.

OLD MERCHANT'S HOUSE
Row 117, Great Yarmouth, Norfolk
Collection of domestic ironwork from 17th-19th centuries, in early 17th century house.
Mar., Apr. and Oct. 9.30-5.30 (Su. 2-5.30); May-Sept. 9.30-7 (Su. 2-7); Nov.-Feb. 9.30-4 (Su. 2-4).

THE TOLHOUSE
Tolhouse Street, Great Yarmouth, Norfolk
Medieval building. Local history.
May-Sept. Daily (except Sa.) 10-1, 2-5.30.

GREENHAM

COTHAY MANOR
Greenham, Somerset
15th century manor house. Furniture. Collection of war decorations.
By written appointment only. For special open days see local press.

GREENOCK

GREENOCK MUSEUM AND ART GALLERY
9 Union Street, West End, Greenock, Renfrewshire
Picture gallery and comprehensive natural history, geology and shipping exhibits. Relics of James Watt.
M.-Sa. 10-5.

GRIMSBY

DOUGHTY MUSEUM
Town Hall Square, Grimsby, Lincolnshire
Model ships, especially fishing vessels. Porcelain.
Tu., F. and Sa. 10-12.30, 2-5.30. W. and Th. 10-12.30, 2-8.

GUERNSEY

GUILLE ALLES MUSEUM
St. Peter Port, Guernsey, Channel Islands
Natural history. Farming implements. Photographs connected with German occupation.
Weekdays 10.30-12.30, 2-4 (Th. 10.30-12.30 only).

HAUTEVILLE HOUSE
38 Hauteville, St. Peter Port, Guernsey, Channel Islands
Victor Hugo's house. Collections of china, furniture, tapestries and Hugo relics.
Weekdays 10-12, 2-4.30 (except Th. afternoon).

LUKIS AND ISLAND MUSEUM
St. Barnabas, Cornet Street, St. Peter Port, Guernsey, Channel Islands
Channel Islands archaeology and anthropology. Chinese porcelain.
Weekdays (except W.). Closed Bank Holidays.

GUILDFORD

CLANDON PARK
nr. Guildford, Surrey
Built 1731-35 by Giacomo Leoni. Furniture. Porcelain. 19th century kitchen, with original equipment.
May-Oct. Tu., W., Th., Sa., Su. and Bank Holiday M. 2-6.

GUILDFORD MUSEUM
Castle Arch, Guildford, Surrey
Archaeological and historical museum for the county, especially West Surrey and Guildford Borough. Needlework.
Weekdays 11-5.

LOSELEY HOUSE
near Guildford, Surrey
Mansion (1562). Tapestries. Furniture. Inlaid cabinets. Paintings.
Spring Bank Holiday- Sept., Th., F., Sa. 2-5.

WATTS GALLERY
Compton, Guildford, Surrey
Memorial collection of paintings of G. F. Watts.
Daily (except Th.) 2-6; (Oct.-Mar. 2-4). W. and Sa. 11-1 also.

WOMEN'S ROYAL ARMY CORPS MUSEUM
WRAC Centre, Queen Elizabeth Barracks, Guildford, Surrey
Uniforms, awards, campaign medals, pictures, trophies and souvenirs associated with the Corps.
By appointment. Weekdays 8.30-5.

HAILSHAM

MICHELHAM PRIORY
Upper Dicker, nr. Hailsham, Sussex
Priory, founded (1229). Furniture. Tapestries. Stained glass. Sussex ironwork. Forge and wheelwright's shop. Farm waggons. Musical instruments.
Apr. 20- Oct. 21, daily 11-5.30.

HALESWORTH

HEVENINGHAM HALL
nr. Halesworth, Suffolk
Georgian mansion. Original furniture by James Wyatt.
Apr.-mid.-Oct. W., Th., Sa., Su. and Bank Holidays (also Tu. in Aug.). House: 2-5.30. June-Aug., also Tu., 2-5.30. Gardens 2-7 Su. and Bank Holidays.

HALIFAX

BANKFIELD MUSEUM AND ART GALLERY
Akroyd Park, Halifax, Yorkshire
Textile machinery. Textiles. Costumes. Archaeology. Local history. Natural history.
Weekdays 11-5 (11-7 Apr.-Sept.); Su. 2.30-5.

THE DUKE OF WELLINGTON'S REGIMENT SERVICE MUSEUM
Bankfield Museum, Ackroyd Park, Halifax, Yorkshire
Personal relics of the first Duke of Wellington.
Weekdays 11-5 (11-7 Apr.-Sept.); Su. 2.30-5.

4TH/7TH ROYAL DRAGOON GUARDS SERVICE MUSEUM
Bankfield Museum, Halifax, Yorkshire
Uniforms, weapons, awards, campaign medals, regimental colours, pictures, trophies and souvenirs associated with the Guards.
Weekdays 11-5 (11-7 Apr.-Sept.); Su. 2.30-5.

WEST YORKSHIRE FOLK MUSEUM
Shibden Hall, Shibden Park, Halifax, Yorkshire
1420 half-timbered hall with 17th century furniture. 17th century barn. Early agricultural implements. Coaches and harness. Craft workshops.
Apr.-Sept. Weekdays 11-7; Su. 2-5. Oct. and Mar. Weekdays 11-5; Su. 2-5. Feb. Su. 2-5. Closed Nov., Dec. and Jan.

HALSTEAD

BLUE BRIDGE HOUSE
Halstead, Essex
Home and memorabilia of 'England's remarkable butcher' John 'Carcase' Morley, 1655-1732.
May- mid.-Oct. Th., F., Sa., Su., Bank Holiday M., 2.30-6.

HAMILTON

THE CAMERONIANS (SCOTTISH RIFLES) SERVICE MUSEUM
129 Main Street, Hamilton, Lanarkshire
Uniforms, old arms, awards, campaign medals, regimental colours, pictures, trophies and souvenirs associated with the Regiment.
Daily ex. W. 10-5; Su. 12-5.

HARLYN BAY

HARLYN BAY PREHISTORIC BURIAL GROUND AND MUSEUM
nr. Padstow, Cornwall
Prehistoric remains, skeletons, skulls, slate implements.
Daily: Summer 10.45-12.30, 2.30-6 (closed F. and Sa.) Winter: by appointment.

HARROGATE

CORPORATION ART GALLERY
Library Building, Victoria Avenue, Harrogate, Yorkshire
Paintings. Water-colours.
Weekdays 9.30-7; Su. 2-5.

RIPLEY CASTLE
near Harrogate, Yorkshire
Paintings. Furniture. Weapons of the Civil War period.
May-Sept., Su. 2-6. Easter, Spring and Late Summer Bank Holiday M. 2-6.

ROYAL PUMP ROOM MUSEUM
opp. Valley Gardens, Harrogate, Yorkshire
Victoriana, local history, archaeology, pottery, costume.
Summer: Weekdays 11-7; Su. 2-5. Winter: Weekends only. Closed Christmas to Easter.

RUDDING PARK
Harrogate, Yorkshire
Tapestries. China. Furniture. Miniature figures.
Easter Sa. - early Oct. Daily (except F.) 2-6. Also Easter, Spring and Late Summer Bank Holiday Su. and M. 11-7.

HARTLEBURY

WORCESTERSHIRE COUNTY MUSEUM
Hartlebury Castle, nr. Kidderminster, Worcestershire
Worcestershire industry, including needles, carpets, scythes, gloves, cider. Transport.
Feb.-Nov., M.-Th. 10-6; Sa., Su. 2-6. Closed F.

HARTLEPOOL

GRAY ART GALLERY AND MUSEUM
Clarence Road, Hartlepool, Co. Durham
Paintings. British birds. Chinese porcelain. Indian idols. Local industries - shipbuilding, engineering, timber.
Weekdays 10-5.30; Su. 3-5.

HARTLEPOOL MARITIME MUSEUM
Northgate, Hartlepool, Co. Durham
Fishing and ship-building industries of the town. Simulated fisherman's cottage and ship's wheelhouse. World's earliest gas illuminated lighthouse.
Daily 10-5.

HASLEMERE

HASLEMERE EDUCATIONAL MUSEUM
High Street, Haslemere, Surrey
British birds, geology, zoology, botany. Local industries.
Weekdays 10-5 (10-4 Nov.-Mar.); Su. Apr.-Oct. only 2-5. Closed Boxing Day and Good Friday.

HASTINGS

THE FISHERMAN'S MUSEUM
Rock-a-nore, Hastings, Sussex
Maritime exhibits, including a large picture of the presentation to Sir Winston Churchill of a golden winkle at the *Enterprise* on Winkle Island, September 1955.
Apr.-Sept. Daily 10-6.

MUSEUM OF LOCAL HISTORY
Old Town Hall, High Street, Hastings, Sussex
Local history. Cinque Ports relics. Ships' models.
Easter-Sept. M., Tu., W., F. and Sa. 9-12.30, 2-5.30. Th. 9-12.30. Closed Su.

PUBLIC MUSEUM AND ART GALLERY
John's Place, Cambridge Road, Hastings, Sussex
Local natural history, bygones. Sussex ironwork. Ceramics, including Sussex and Kent pottery. Ethnographical collection.
Weekdays 10-1, 2-5; Su. 3-5.

HATFIELD

HATFIELD HOUSE
Hatfield, Hertfordshire
Childhood home of Queen Elizabeth I. Built by Robert Cecil, first Earl of Salisbury, 1607-11. Portraits, furniture and relics of Queen Elizabeth I.
House and West Gardens: *mid. Apr. - end of Apr., Weekdays also Easter Su. and M., May 1 - early Oct. Daily (except M.) but including Spring and Late Summer Bank Holidays Su. and M., 12-5 (Su. 2-5.30).* East and West Gardens only: *May-Sept., M. 2-5 (excluding Bank Holiday M.).*

HAVERFORDWEST

PEMBROKESHIRE COUNTY MUSEUM AND ART GALLERY
The Castle, Haverfordwest, Pembrokeshire
Archaeological and other material from the county's past. Folklore. Local industry. Works of art.
Summer: M.-Sa. 10-6. Winter: M.-Sa. 10-5.30. Closed Su.

HAWICK

WILTON LODGE MUSEUM
The Park, Hawick, Roxburgh
Geology. Natural history. Coins. Medals and church tokens. Local history. Hosiery machinery section.
Apr.-Oct. Weekdays 10-5; Su. 2-5. Nov.-Mar. Weekdays only 10-4. Closed F.

HAWORTH

BRONTE PARSONAGE MUSEUM
Haworth, Yorkshire
Bronteana and the Bonnell Collection of manuscripts. Toys, books, clothes, portraits, samplers and drawings.
Apr.-Sept., M.-Sa. 11-5.30; Su. 2-5.45. Oct.-Mar., M.-Sa. 11-4.30; Su. 2-4.45.

HEBDEN BRIDGE

HEPTONSTALL OLD GRAMMAR SCHOOL
Hebden Bridge, Yorkshire
17th century grammar school. School furniture (17th century). Agricultural implements. Domestic equipment.
Apr.-Sept., Sa., Su., public holidays 2-6.

HELSTON

BOROUGH MUSEUM
Old Butter Market, Church Street, Helston, Cornwall
Agriculture. Fire appliances. Cider making. Grist mill. Early radio. Lifesaving. Clay pipe making. Netting loom. Farm vehicles.
Weekdays 10.30-12.30, 2.30-4.20.

HEMEL HEMPSTEAD

PICCOTTS END MEDIAEVAL MURALS
138 Piccotts End, Hemel Hempstead, Hertfordshire
15th century wall paintings in building believed to have been pilgrims' hospice. Elizabethan painted room.
May-Sept. Daily 10-7.30; Oct.-Apr. Daily 10-6.

HENLEY-ON-THAMES

GREYS COURT
Henley-on-Thames, Oxfordshire
Tudor donkey wheel for raising well water. 18th century plasterwork and furniture.
House: *Apr.-Sept. M., W. and F.* Grounds: *Apr.-Sept., M.-Sa. 2.15-6.*

HEREFORD

CHURCHILL GARDENS MUSEUM
Venn's Lane, Hereford, Herefordshire
Costumes. Furniture. Water-colours and paintings by local artists.
Daily 2-5.

HEREFORD CITY MUSEUM AND ART GALLERY
Broad Street, Hereford, Herefordshire
Archaeology. Natural history. Costumes. Toys. Embroidery. Textiles. Military equipment. Agricultural bygones. Pictures by local artists. Applied art. Silver. Pottery. Porcelain.
Weekdays 10-6.30 (10-5 Th. and Sa.); Su. 2-5.30.

HEREFORDSHIRE LIGHT INFANTRY REGIMENTAL MUSEUM
Harold Street, Hereford, Herefordshire
Uniforms. Weapons. Campaign medals. Regimental colours. Pictures. Trophies. Souvenirs.
M.-F. 9.30-12.30, 2-4.30; Sa. and Su. by appointment.

KENTCHURCH COURT
Hereford, Herefordshire
14th century manor house altered by Nash. Paintings. Grinling Gibbons carving.
Parties only, by appointment.

THE OLD HOUSE
High Town, Hereford, Herefordshire
Preserved as a Jacobean Period Museum, with furniture of the period.
Apr.-Sept., Weekdays 10-1, 2-5.30; Su. 2-5.30. Oct.-Mar. M.-F. 10-1, 2-5.30; Sa. 10-1.

HERNE BAY

HERNE BAY MUSEUM
High Street, Herne Bay, Kent
Exhibits of local or Kentish interest. Stone, Bronze and Early Iron Age archaeology. Roman material from Reculver. Pictures, maps and bygones.
Weekdays 9.30-7 (9.30-1 W. and 9.30-5 Sa.).

HERTFORD

HERTFORD MUSEUM
18 Bull Plain, Hertford, Hertfordshire
Early scientific apparatus. Local archaeology, history, geology, natural history.
M.-Sa. 10-5.

HIGH WYCOMBE

ART GALLERY AND MUSEUM
Castle Hill, High Wycombe, Buckinghamshire
Collection of chairs of most periods, but mainly devoted to the Windsor Chair. Tools and equipment. Lace.
M., Tu. and Th. 10-8; F. and Sa. 10-6. Winter closes at 5.30.

DISRAELI MUSEUM
Hughenden Manor, High Wycombe, Buckinghamshire
Home of Benjamin Disraeli, Earl of Beaconsfield (1847-81). Relics, furniture, pictures and books.
Feb. 1-Dec. 31 Daily (except Tu.) incl. Su. and Bank Holiday M. 2-6; Sa. and Su. 12.30-6. Closed Jan. 1-31, Good Friday and Christmas Day.

PARKER-KNOLL LIMITED
Temple End, High Wycombe, Buckinghamshire
Company museum. Chairs and chair manufacture covering period from 1600-1900.
By appointment.

HITCHIN

HITCHIN MUSEUM
Paynes Park, Hitchin, Hertfordshire
Archaeology. Local history. Natural history, costume. Paintings by Samuel Lucas.
Weekdays 10-5.

HOCKLEY HEATH

PACKWOOD HOUSE
Hockley Heath, Warwickshire
Tapestry. Needlework. Formal garden and yew garden of c. 1650 representing the Sermon on the Mount.
Apr.-Sept. Tu., W., Th., Sa. and Bank Holiday M. 2-7; Su. 2.30-7. Oct.-Mar. W., Sa. and Bank Holidays 2-5; Su. 2.30-5. Closed Christmas Day.

HOLLINGBOURNE

EYHORNE MANOR
Hollingbourne, Kent
Early 15th century timber-framed manor house. Collection of domestic irons.
May, June, July- W., Th., Sa. and Su. 2-6. Other times by arrangement.

HOLLINWOOD

FERRANTI LIMITED
Hollinwood, Lancashire
Company Museum. Electrical engineering. Steam engine.
By appointment with the company archivist.

HONITON

HONITON AND ALLHALLOWS PUBLIC MUSEUM
High Street, Honiton, Devon
Collection of local interest including Honiton lace, and a complete Devon kitchen. Bones of hippopotamus, straight-tusked elephant, ox and red-deer.
Weekdays, Apr.-Nov. 10-5.

HORSHAM

HORSHAM MUSEUM
Causeway House, Horsham, Sussex
In 16th century gabled building. Local history. Costumes. Toys. Early bicycles. Domestic and rural life, crafts and industries of Sussex, including reconstructed blacksmith's forge, wheelwright's and saddler's shops.
Tu., W., Th. and Sa. 2.30-4.30; F. 12-4.

HOUSESTEADS

HOUSESTEADS MUSEUM
Haydon Bridge, Housesteads, Northumberland
Roman pottery. Inscribed stones. Sculpture.
Mar. and Oct. 9.30-5.30 (Su. 2-5.30); Apr. 9.30-5.30 daily; May-Sept. 9.30-7 daily; Nov.-Feb. 9.30-4 (Su. 2-4).

HOVE

HOVE MUSEUM OF ART
Central Library, Church Road, Hove, BN3 2EG, Sussex
Collections of English ceramics, glass, silver, watches, pictures and prints, period furniture, medals and medallions, children's toys, dolls and doll's houses.
M.-Sa. 10-5.

HUDDERSFIELD

HUDDERSFIELD ART GALLERY
Princess Alexandra Walk, Huddersfield, Yorkshire
Paintings. Water-colours. Drawings. Sculpture.
Weekdays 10-5.30 (F. 10-7.30).

TOLSON MEMORIAL MUSEUM
Ravensknowle Park, Wakefield Road, Huddersfield, Yorkshire
Collections illustrating the natural history and human history of the Huddersfield district. Displays of geology, botany, zoology, prehistory, history, bygones, toys and local industries, horsedrawn vehicles.
Weekdays 10.30-5; Su. 2-5.

HULL

4TH BATTALION THE EAST YORKSHIRE REGIMENT (T.A.) SERVICE MUSEUM
Londesborough Barracks, Hull, Yorkshire
Uniforms. Weapons, awards. Campaign medals. Regimental colours. Pictures. Trophies. Souvenirs.
M.-F. 9.15-12.30, 2.15-4.30.

FERENS ART GALLERY
Queen Victoria Square, Hull, Yorkshire
English 18th and 19th century portraits. Painting of Humberside scenes.
Weekdays 10-5.30; Su. 2.30-4.30.

HULL CORPORATION WATER DEPARTMENT
Springhead Pumping Station, Kingston-upon-Hull, Yorkshire
Waterworks equipment. 90-in. Cornish beam engine.
By appointment.

MARITIME MUSEUM
Pickering Park, Hull, Yorkshire
Exhibits of fishing and shipping industries, including relics of whaling days.
Weekdays 10-5; Su. 2.30-4.30. Closed Christmas Day, Boxing Day and Good F.

TRANSPORT AND ARCHAEOLOGY MUSEUM
36 High Street, Hull, Yorkshire
Collection of coaches and motor-cars. Archaeology of East Yorkshire.
Weekdays 10-5; Su. 2.30-4.30. Closed Christmas Day, Boxing Day and Good Friday.

WILBERFORCE HOUSE
25 High Street, Hull, Yorkshire
Early 17th century mansion, birthplace of William Wilberforce, the slave emancipator. Now local historical museum and memorial to Wilberforce. Furnished period rooms.
Weekdays 10-5; Su. 2.30-4.30. Closed Christmas Day, Boxing Day and Good Friday.

HUNTINGDON

CROMWELL MUSEUM
Market Square, Huntingdon, Huntingdonshire
History of Cromwellian period. Contemporary portraits. Cromwelliana. Documents.
Tu.-Sa. 11-1, 2-5; Su. 2-4.

HUTTON-LE-HOLE

RYEDALE FOLK MUSEUM
Hutton-le-Hole, Yorkshire
Prehistoric and Roman antiquities. Tools of 19th century crafts. Furniture and domestic equipment. Folk Park, housing blacksmith's shop, wagon park, Elizabethan glass furnace and medieval longhouse.
Open Easter-Oct. Daily (except Tu. and F. in Apr. and May) 2-6 (11-6 mid.-July and Aug.).

HYTHE

HYTHE (KENT) BOROUGH MUSEUM
Oaklands, Stade Street, Hythe, Kent
Local antiquities.
Weekdays, when Library is open.

ILFRACOMBE

CHAMBERCOMBE MANOR
Ilfracombe, Devon
14th-15th century house. Private Oratory. Mainly Tudor and Jacobean furniture. Benz motor car, c.1889.
House and Garden: Easter- mid.-Oct. Daily 9.45-6.30.

ILFRACOMBE MUSEUM
Wilder Road, Ilfracombe, Devon
Botany, North Devon birds, mammals, reptiles and insects. Early engravings, paintings, maps. Marine life. Weapons.
Weekdays 10-1, 2-5. Spring-Sept. Closed Good Friday.

ILKLEY

MANOR HOUSE MUSEUM
Castle Yard, Ilkley, Yorkshire
In Tudor manor house, collections illustrating the town's history, Prehistoric, Roman, Saxon, to the present day, exhibitions.
Daily (except M.) 10.30-12.30, 2-5 (Oct.-Apr. 2-5 only).

INGATESTONE

INGATESTONE HALL
(North Wing and Long Gallery), Ingatestone, Essex
Exhibitions of Essex documents, paintings, water-colours, prints.
Apr.- beginning of Oct. Tu.-Sa. and Bank Holiday M. 10-12.30, 2-4.30.

INNERLEITHEN

TRAQUAIR HOUSE
Innerleithen, Peeblesshire
Embroidery. Glass. Silver. Paintings. 18th century brewhouse and brewing equipment, including copper installed in 1739.
June, W., Sa. 2-5.30. July-Sept. Daily 2-5.30 (except F.). Spring Bank Holiday 2-5.30.

INVERNESS

INVERNESS MUSEUM AND ART GALLERY
Castle Wynd, Inverness, Inverness-shire
Highland and Jacobite collection.
Weekdays 9-5 (W. 9-1, 2.15-5).

INVERURIE

INVERURIE MUSEUM
Public Library Building, Inverurie, Aberdeenshire
Collection of local prehistoric material. Geology. Natural history. Bygones. Coins.
Weekdays 9.30-12, 3-5. Closed Su.

IPSWICH

CHRISTCHURCH MANSION
Christchurch Park, Ipswich, Suffolk
Begun 1548, altered 17th and early 18th centuries. Period rooms. Paintings, including works by Gainsborough, Constable, Steer. 20th century prints. 18th century wine glasses. Ship models. Local history collections. Costumes.
Daily, Weekdays 10-5; Su. 3-5. Closed Christmas Day and Good Fri.

IPSWICH MUSEUM
High Street, Ipswich, Suffolk
Geology. Prehistory. Archaeology of Suffolk from earliest times to medieval period. Natural history. Ethnography.
Weekdays 10-5; Su. 3-5.

ISLE OF MULL

DUART CASTLE
Isle of Mull, Argyll
Jacobite and Maclean relics. Scout exhibition.
May-Sept. M.-F. 10.30-6. Su., July and Aug. 2.30-6.

JEDBURGH

MARY, QUEEN OF SCOTS' HOUSE
Queen Street, Jedburgh, Roxburgh
Collections dealing with the life of Mary, Queen of Scots. Paintings. Engravings.
Apr.-Oct. only: Weekdays 10-12, 1-5, 6-8; Su. 1-5.

JERSEY

GOREY CASTLE MUSEUM
Gorey District, Jersey, Channel Islands
Pottery. Coins. Fragments of glass clay pipes. Regimental buttons.
Daily from 10 a.m. Closed for 4 months during Winter.

ST. PETER'S BUNKER MUSEUM OF NAZI GERMAN EQUIPMENT AND OCCUPATION RELICS
St. Peter's Parish, Jersey, Channel Islands
History of German occupation.
Apr.-Nov. Daily 10-5.

JODRELL BANK

MUSEUM OF DEPARTMENT OF RADIO ASTRONOMY
University of Manchester, Concourse Building, Jodrell Bank, Macclesfield, Cheshire, SK11 9DL
Astronomy. Radio telescopes. Planetarium.
Easter-Oct. Daily 2-6.

KEIGHLEY

KEIGHLEY ART GALLERY AND MUSEUM
Cliffe Castle, Keighley, Yorkshire
Pictorial art. Sculpture. Applied arts. Domestic and agricultural bygones. Natural history. Archaeology. Geology. Reconstructed craft workshops. Clog-iron and nailmaking. Textiles. Children's toys and games.
Weekdays 10.30-5.30 or dusk; Su. 2-5 or dusk (May-Aug. open until 8 on Tu., Sa. and Su.).

KENDAL

ABBOT HALL ART GALLERY
Kendal, Westmorland
18th century furnished rooms. Paintings. Sculpture. Furniture. Pottery.
Weekdays 10.30-5.30; Sa. and Su. 2-5. Closed for 2 weeks at Christmas.

ABBOT HALL MUSEUM OF LAKELAND LIFE AND INDUSTRY
Kendal, Westmorland
Period rooms. Costumes. Printing. Weaving. Local industries.
Weekdays 10.30-12.30, 2-5; Sa. and Su. 2-5.

KENDAL BOROUGH MUSEUM
Station Road, Kendal, Westmorland
Natural history. Local history. Domestic equipment.
Weekdays 10-4.30.

SIZERGH CASTLE
Kendal, Westmorland
14th-15th century castle. English and French furniture. Silver. China. Family portraits. Stuart portraits. Stuart and Jacobean relics.
Apr.-Sept. W. 2-5.45. Garden only, Tu. and Th. 2-5.45.

KESWICK

FITZ PARK MUSEUM AND ART GALLERY
Station Road, Keswick, Cumberland
Original Southey, Wordsworth and Walpole manuscripts. Local geology and natural history.
Weekdays 10-12, 2-5 (except July and Aug. 10-12, 2-7).

PENCIL MUSEUM
Cumberland Pencil Company Limited, Greta Bridge, Keswick, Cumberland
Pencil manufacturing methods from 1558 to the present day. Specimens of pure Borrowdale plumbago.
May-Sept. M.-F. 9-12.30, 1.30-5.30.

KETTERING

ALFRED EAST ART GALLERY
Sheep Street, Kettering, Northamptonshire
Paintings, water-colours and etchings by Sir Alfred East.
Weekdays 10-8 (during loan exhibitions, Su. 2-6).

WESTFIELD MUSEUM
West Street, Kettering, Northamptonshire
Archaeological and natural history material from Kettering and the vicinity. Collections of footwear, shoe-making tools, bygones.
Weekdays 10-5 (W. and F. in summer 10-8); Su. 2-6.

KIDDERMINSTER

ART GALLERY
Market Street, Kidderminster, Worcestershire
Brangwyn etchings. Paintings.
M.-F. 10-12, 2.30-6; Sa. 10-12, 2.30-5.

KIDDERMINSTER MUSEUM
Kidderminster, Worcestershire
Local studies and archaeology.
M.-F. 10-12, 2.30-6; Sa. 10-12, 2.30-5.

WORCESTERSHIRE COUNTY MUSEUM
Hartlebury Castle, Hartlebury, nr. Kidderminster, Worcestershire
Displays of archaeology, geology, crafts and industries of the county. Restored cider mill. Furniture. Glass. Costumes. Horse-drawn vehicles, including gypsy caravans.
Feb.-Nov. M.-Th. 10-6; Sa. and Su. 2-6.

KILBARCHAN

WEAVER'S COTTAGE
The Cross, Kilbarchan, Renfrewshire
18th century craftsman's house, containing traditional weaving and domestic exhibits.
Tu., Th. and Sa. 2-5; also Su. (May-Oct.) 2-5.

KILMARNOCK

BURNS' MONUMENT AND MUSEUM
Kay Park, Kilmarnock, Ayrshire
Holograph manuscripts dealing with the poet Robert Burns. Burns' original first edition. McKie Burnsiana.
Mid.-Apr. - mid.-Sept. 12.30-4, 5-8.30; Mid-Sept. mid.-Apr. 10-12, 1-5.

DICK INSTITUTE MUSEUM
Elmbank Avenue, Kilmarnock, Ayrshire
Geological, ornithological, archaeological and ethnological collections. Weapons, especially Scottish basket-hilted swords. Documents of the Boyd family; Incunabula. Early Bibles. Children's Museum. Paintings, including works of the Glasgow School.
Oct.-Apr. 10-5; May-Sept. 10-8 (W. and Sa. 10-5).

KINGSBRIDGE

WILLIAM COOKWORTHY MUSEUM
Old Grammar School, 108 Fore Street, Kingsbridge, Devon
Life history of William Cookworthy (1705-80), discoverer of china clay and the method of making true porcelain from it. Development of china clay industry and uses to which the material is put. Commercial, natural, agricultural, maritime and social history of the South Hams. 17th century panelled school room. Victorian kitchen and scullery.
M.-Sa. 11-6.

KING'S LYNN

KING'S LYNN MUSEUM AND ART GALLERY
Market Street, King's Lynn, Norfolk
Natural history, archaeology and folk material, particularly of N.W. Norfolk. Coins. Costumes. Paintings. Water-colours. Local prints. English drinking glasses and pottery.
Weekdays 10-5.

KINGSTON-UPON-THAMES

THE QUEEN'S ROYAL SURREY REGIMENT SERVICE MUSEUM
T. & A.V.R. Centre, Surbiton Road, Kingston-upon-Thames, Surrey
Uniforms, old arms, awards, campaign medals, regimental colours, pictures, trophies and souvenirs associated with the regiment.
M.-F. 10-12.30; 2-4 (Su. 10-12 by arrangement).

KINGUSSIE

HIGHLAND FOLK MUSEUM
Kingussie, Inverness-shire
Comprehensive collection of old Highland material, including examples of craft-work and tools, household equipment, tartans. Furnished farm-cottage, with mill and farming shed.
May-Sept. Weekdays 10-4.

KIRKCALDY

INDUSTRIAL MUSEUM
Forth House, Kirkcaldy, Fife
Local industries, including forge, horsedrawn vehicles, linoleum exhibits, cooper's shop.
May-Sept. M.-Sa. 2-5.

KIRKCALDY MUSEUMS AND ART GALLERY
War Memorial Square, Kirkcaldy, Fife
Art Collection (Sickert, Peploe, McTaggart, Camden Town Group). Geology. Natural history. Prehistory and history of Fife. Annexe for industrial exhibits includes a forge, wheelwright's shop, horse-drawn vehicles and the history of Fife Linoleum.
M.-Sa. 11-5; Su. 2-5.

KIRKCUDBRIGHT

BROUGHTON HOUSE
Kirkcudbright, Kirkcudbrightshire
Burns collection. Paintings by Hornel and other artists. Furniture.
Apr.-Sept. M.-F. 11-1, 2-4; Oct.-Mar. Tu. and Th. 2-4.

STEWARTRY MUSEUM
St. Mary Street, Kirkcudbright, Kirkcudbrightshire
Regional museum depicting the history and culture of Galloway.
Daily 10-5.

KIRKOSWALD

SOUTER JOHNNIE'S HOUSE
Kirkoswald, Ayrshire
Home of John Davidson on whom Burns modelled Souter Johnnie in his narrative poem, 'Tam O'Shanter'. Life-sized sculptured figures of Souter, Tam, the Innkeeper and his wife.
Apr.-Sept. Daily 2.30-8.

KIRRIMUIR

BARRIE'S BIRTHPLACE
Kirrimuir, Angus
Mementoes and manuscripts of Sir James Barrie.
Apr.-Oct. Weekdays 10-12.30, 2-6; Su. 2-6.

KNEBWORTH

KNEBWORTH HOUSE
Knebworth, Hertfordshire
Tudor mansion, started in 1492. Paintings and historic relics of 16th-19th centuries.
Early Apr. - early May, Sa., Su., Good Friday and Easter M. Early May - early Oct. Daily (except M. but open Spring and Late Summer Bank Holiday M. and closed Tu. following), 2-5.

KNUTSFORD

TATTON PARK
Knutsford, Cheshire
Georgian house by Samuel and Lewis Wyatt. Collection of furniture, pictures, china, silver, formed by Egerton family. Museum of sporting trophies.
Early Apr. - mid.-Oct. Daily (except M. but open Bank Holiday M. and Good Friday). House, 2-5.15 (2-5.45 early May - early Sept.). Gardens 2-6 (2-6.30 early May - early Sept.). Park 11-6.30 (11-8 early May - early Sept.).

LACOCK

LACKHAM COLLEGE OF AGRICULTURE
Lacock, Wiltshire
Agricultural implements and tools.
By appointment only.

LAMBOURN

ASHDOWN HOUSE
nr. Lambourn, Berkshire
Late 17th century house, built by first Lord Craven for Elizabeth of Bohemia. Contains Craven family portraits associated with Elizabeth of Bohemia.
Apr. W. only. May-Sept. W. and 1st and 3rd Sa. in month, 2-6. Courtyards and grounds open and access to roof of house.

LANCASTER

THE KING'S OWN REGIMENTAL MUSEUM
Lancaster Museum, Old Town Hall, Market Square, Lancaster, Lancashire
Uniforms, old arms, awards, campaign medals, regimental colours, pictures, trophies and souvenirs.
Weekdays 10-5.30.

LANCASTER MUSEUM
Old Town Hall, Market Square, Lancaster, Lancashire
Prehistoric, Roman and Medieval archaeology. Bygones.
Weekdays only, 10-5.30.

LEAMINGTON SPA

LEAMINGTON SPA ART GALLERY AND MUSEUM
Avenue Road, Leamington Spa, Warwickshire
Paintings by Dutch and Flemish masters. 20th century paintings and water-colours, mainly English. 18th-19th century pottery and porcelain. 18th century and modern English glass.
Weekdays 10.45-12.45, 2.30-5; also Th. 6-8; Su. 2.30-5. Closed W. afternoons.

LECHLADE

KELMSCOTT MANOR
nr. Lechlade, Gloucestershire
Cotswold-style manor of 16th and 17th century. Summer home of William Morris from 1871 until his death in 1896. Original Morris possessions and examples of his designs.
By written application, giving at least 2 weeks' notice. Apr.-Sept., 1st W. in each month, 11-6.

LEDBURY

EASTNOR CASTLE
nr. Ledbury, Herefordshire
19th century castle, containing armour, paintings, tapestries.
Easter M., Spring Bank Holiday Su. and M., and late Summer Bank Holiday M. and Tu. (but from mid.-July - mid.-Sept. daily) 2.30-5.30. June-Sept. 2.15-6.

LEEDS

ABBEY HOUSE MUSEUM
Kirkstall, Leeds, Yorkshire
Folk museum illustrating the life and work of the people of Yorkshire over the last 300 years. Three full-sized 19th century streets of houses, shops and workplaces.
Apr.-Sept. Weekdays 10-6; Su. 2-6. Oct.-Mar. Weekdays 10-5; Su. 2-5.

CITY ART GALLERY
Leeds, Yorkshire
Old Masters. English watercolours. 19th and 20th century British and French paintings. Modern paintings and sculpture. Leeds and Staffordshire pottery. English silver.
Weekdays 10.30-6.30; Su. 2.30-5.

CITY MUSEUM
Municipal Buildings, Leeds 1, Yorkshire
Natural history. Ethnography. Archaeology. Although the collections are world-wide, they particularly concern the Yorkshire region.
Weekdays 10-6.30.

HAREWOOD HOUSE
Leeds, Yorkshire
Furniture by Robert Adam and Thomas Chippendale. Sèvres porcelain. Oriental china. English and Italian paintings.
Good F. - Sept. Daily 11-6, then Su. in Oct. 11-6.

LIBRARY OF THE THORESBY SOCIETY
23 Clarendon Road, Leeds, LS2 9NZ, Yorkshire
Collection of books, manuscripts, pictures, medals, coins, maps and relics of old Leeds.
Tu. and Th. 10-2.

LOTHERTON HALL
Aberford, nr. Leeds, Yorkshire
Built round an earlier house dating from the mid-18th century, extensions added in 1896 and 1903. Furniture. Paintings. Silver.
Daily 10.30-6.15 (or dusk); Th. (May-Sept.) 10.30-8.30.

MUSEUM OF THE HISTORY OF EDUCATION
University of Leeds, Leeds, LS2 9J2, Yorkshire
Textbooks, exercise books, practical work, administrative documents and photographs illustrating the history of education.
By appointment (tel. Leeds 31751, ex. 6159, mornings).

TEMPLE NEWSAM HOUSE
nr. Leeds, Yorkshire
Tudor and Jacobean house with Georgian decorations. 17th and 18th century English furniture. Collections include European paintings. Chinese ceramics. English silver.
Daily 10.30-6.15 (or dusk); also W. (May-Sept.) 10.30-8.30.

LEEK

CHEDDLETON FLINT MILL
near Leek, Staffordshire
Twin water wheels on River Churnet operate flint grinding plant. Museum collection of machinery used in pottery milling includes 100 h.p. steam engine.
Sa. and Su. afternoons Apr.-Oct. (and often in other months).

LEEK ART GALLERY
Nicholson Institute, Leek, Staffordshire
Paintings, water-colours, drawings, mainly by British artists.
Daily 10-9 (Sa. 10-5).

LEICESTER

BELGRAVE HALL
Thurcaston Road, Leicester, Leicestershire
Furnished Queen Anne house (1709-13) and gardens. Stables with coaches and agricultural collection.
Weekdays 10-5 (Apr. and Sept. 10-6, May-Aug. 10-7); Su. 2-5.

GUILDHALL
Guildhall Lane, Leicester, Leicestershire
Medieval Guildhall and later Town Hall of Leicester. Hall, Mayor's Parlour, library and cells.
Weekdays 10-5 (Apr. and Sept. 10-6, May-Aug. 10-7).

JEWRY WALL MUSEUM
St. Nicholas Street, Leicester, Leicestershire
Museum of archaeology. The Roman Jewry Wall and Baths. Mosaic pavement in situ.
M.-F. 10.30-7; Sa. 9.30-7; Su. 2-5.

MUSEUM AND ART GALLERY
New Walk, Leicester, Leicestershire
Art, archives (including Brough and Archdeaconry records), biology and geology. Aquarium.
M.-F. 10-5 (Apr. and Sept. 10-6, May-Aug. 10-7); Sa. 10-7; Su. 2-5.

MUSEUM OF TECHNOLOGY
Abbey Pumping Station, Corporation Road, Leicester, Leicestershire
Road transport, including horse-drawn vehicles, cycles, motor-cycles and cars. Local industries.
Weekdays ex. Tu. 10-5; Su. 2-5.

NEWARKE HOUSES MUSEUM
The Newarke, Leicester, Leicestershire
Social history of the city and county from 1500 to present day. Period street scene. Costumes. Local clocks. History of the hosiery industry.
Weekdays 10-5 (Apr. and Sept. 10-6; May-Aug. 10-7); Su. 2-5.

RAILWAY MUSEUM
London Road, Stoneygate, Leicester, Leicestershire
Items relating to local railway history, including four locomotives.
Th. and F. 2-5; Sa. and Su. 11-5.

THE ROYAL LEICESTERSHIRE REGIMENT SERVICE MUSEUM
Newarke Houses, Leicester, Leicestershire
Uniforms, old arms, awards, campaign medals, regimental colours, pictures, trophies and souvenirs associated with the Regiment.
Weekdays 10-5 (Apr. and Sept. 10-6; May-Aug. 10-7); Su. 2-5.

LEIGH

PENNINGTON HALL MUSEUM AND ART GALLERY
Pennington Hall, Leigh, Lancashire
Natural history. Machinery and products of the former local silk industry. Water colours.
By appointment only.

LEOMINSTER

EYE MANOR
Leominster, Herefordshire
Built in 1680 by Barbados slave trader Ferdinando Gorges. Costumes. Corn dollies. Private press books. Costume dolls.
Apr.-June, Su., W., Th., Sa., 2.30-5.30. July-Sept., daily 2.30-5.30. Bank Holiday M. and Tu., 2.30-5.30.

LETCHWORTH

LETCHWORTH MUSEUM AND ART GALLERY
Town Square, Letchworth, Hertfordshire
Collections include N. Herts. archaeological material. Natural history. History of first Garden City.
Weekdays 10-5.30 (F. 10-7; Sa. 10-6). Closed Bank Holidays.

LEWES

ANNE OF CLEVES HOUSE
High Street, Southover, Lewes, Sussex
Half-timbered Tudor house containing collection of bygones, furniture, costumes, household equipment. Ironwork and firebacks. Chalk fossils.
Weekdays 10.30-1, 2-5.30.

BARBICAN HOUSE MUSEUM
High Street, Lewes, Sussex
Prehistoric, Romano-British and Medieval antiquities relating to Sussex. Prints and water-colours of Sussex.
Weekdays 10-1, 2-5.30.

FIRLE PLACE
nr. Lewes, Sussex
Collection of Italian, Dutch and English paintings. Sèvres china. French and English furniture. Relics of American War of Independence.
June-Sept. W. and Th. 2.15-5.30. Su. 3-6 (also Easter Su. and M., Spring Bank Holiday Su. and M. and Late Summer Bank Holiday 3-6).

GLYNDE PLACE
nr. Lewes, Sussex
Collection of paintings, includes works by Rubens, Kneller, Hoppner, Lely and Zoffany. Soldani bronzes. Needlework.
Easter Sa., Su. and M., then May-early Oct., Th., Sa. and Su., also Spring and Late Summer Bank Holidays, 2.15-5.30.

LICHFIELD

DR. JOHNSON'S BIRTHPLACE
Bread Market Street, Lichfield, Staffordshire
Relics and pictures of Dr. Johnson and his contemporaries.
Apr.-Oct. Weekdays (except M.), late Summer Bank Holiday 10-1, 2-5. Nov.-Mar. Weekdays (except M., Christmas Day and Boxing Day) 10-1, 2-4. June-Sept. Su. 2.30-5.

LICHFIELD ART GALLERY AND MUSEUM
Bird Street, Lichfield, Staffordshire
Local history. Paintings, drawings, watercolours by local artists.
M., Tu., Th. and F. 10-6; W. and Sa. 10-5.

THE STAFFORDSHIRE REGIMENT (THE PRINCE OF WALES'S) MUSEUM
Whittington Barracks, Lichfield, Staffordshire
Uniforms, old arms, awards, campaign medals, regimental colours, pictures, trophies and souvenirs associated with the Regiment.
M.-F. 9-4.30; Sa. Su. and Bank Holidays by arrangement.

LINBY

NEWSTEAD ABBEY
Linby, Nottinghamshire
Relics of Lord Byron. Pictures. Furniture.
Good F. to end Sept. Tours at 2, 3, 4, 5 daily. Oct.-Easter by arrangement.

LINCOLN

LINCOLN CATHEDRAL TREASURY
The Cathedral, Lincoln, Lincolnshire
Gold and silver plate from the Diocese. Magna Carta.
Easter-Sept. Weekdays 2.30-4.30; Su. 2.15-3.30.

LINCOLN CITY AND COUNTY MUSEUM
Broadgate, Lincoln, Lincolnshire
Local collections with emphasis on Prehistoric, Roman and Medieval antiquities, arms and armour, natural history.
Weekdays 10-5.30; Su. 2.30-5.

MUSEUM OF LINCOLNSHIRE LIFE
Lincolnshire Association, County Centre, Burton Road, Lincoln, Lincolnshire
Displays of material illustrating life in Lincolnshire from Elizabethan times to present day. Ruston and Hornsby collection of oil, gas and aero engines.
Daily 2-5 (except M.).

ROYAL ANGLIAN REGIMENT (LINCOLNSHIRE) SERVICE MUSEUM
Sobraon Barracks, Burton Road, Lincoln, LN1 3PY, Lincolnshire
Uniforms, old arms, awards, campaign medals, regimental colours, pictures, trophies and souvenirs associated with the Regiment.
M.-Th. 9.30-12.30; F. 9.30-12.30. Closed Sa., Su. and Bank Holidays.

USHER GALLERY
Lindum Road, Lincoln, Lincolnshire
Antique watches. Miniature portraits. Porcelain. European 17th century glass. Works by the water-colourist, Peter de Wint. Paintings, water colours and drawings of the City.
Weekdays 10-5.30; Su. 2.30-5.

LINDISFARNE

LINDISFARNE PRIORY
Holy Island, Lindisfarne, Northumberland
Anglo-Saxon sculpture. Reproduction of the Lindisfarne gospels. Medieval pottery.
Mar. and Oct. 9.30-5.30 (Su. 2-5.30); Apr. 9.30-5.30 daily; May-Sept. 9.30-7 daily; Nov.-Feb. 9.30-4 (Su. 2-4).

LINGFIELD

PUTTENDEN MANOR
nr. Lingfield, Surrey
Four-poster bedsteads. Copper and wooden baths. Handmade dolls. Romany caravans.
Good F. - end Sept. W. and Sa. 2-6; Su. and Bank Holidays 2-6.

LISS

ARMY TRANSPORTATION AND MOVEMENT CONTROL MUSEUM
Longmoor, Liss, Hampshire
Uniforms, old arms, awards, campaign medals, regimental colours, pictures, trophies and souvenirs associated with the Regiment.
By appointment.

LITTLE GADDESDEN

THE MANOR HOUSE
Little Gaddesden, Hertfordshire
Early keyboard instruments. Wall paintings, including picture of Elizabeth I. Furniture.
Good F. to late Sept., Su. and Bank Holidays, also W. July and Aug., 2-6.

LITTLEHAMPTON

LITTLEHAMPTON MUSEUM
12A River Road, Littlehampton, Sussex
Collections of old sailing and marine material and objects of local interest, including paintings.
Summer: M., W., F. and Sa. 10.30-1, 2.15-4.30. Winter: M., W. and Sa. 10.30-1, 2.15-4.30.

LITTLE RISSINGTON

CENTRAL FLYING SCHOOL MUSEUM
RAF Little Rissington, Cheltenham, Gloucestershire
History of aeronautics.
M.-F. 8.30-5 by appointment.

LIVERPOOL

CITY OF LIVERPOOL MUSEUMS
William Brown Street, Liverpool, Lancashire
Egyptian, Oriental, Roman and Greek antiquities. Anglo-Saxon jewellery. Porcelain. Limoges enamels. Medieval and classical ivories. Weapons, armour. Historical musical instruments. English silver. Liverpool pottery. African masks and figures. Natural history displays include *Life in the Sand Dunes*, an ecological gallery based on the National Nature Reserve at Ainsdale, and *Earth Before Man*, a geological gallery with an evolutionary series of dioramas. Land transport of the Liverpool region including horsedrawn and steam road vehicles. Ship models. Social, industrial and commercial background of the port. Planetarium. History of time-keeping. Space exploration.
Weekdays 10-5, Su. 2-5 (closed Good Friday and Christmas Day).

DENTAL HOSPITAL MUSEUM
Pembroke Place, Liverpool, Lancashire
Dental pathology and collections of historical dental items.
Available for members of profession and research workers on written application.

HORNBY LIBRARY
William Brown Street, Liverpool, Lancashire
Prints, manuscripts, fine bindings and illustrated and rare books illustrating the art of printing and book production throughout the ages. Autographs. Private press books.
M.-F. 9-9; Sa. 9-5.

THE KING'S REGIMENT COLLECTIONS
Liverpool City Museums, William Brown Street, Liverpool 3, Lancashire
Uniforms, old arms, awards, campaign medals, regimental colours, pictures, trophies and souvenirs associated with the Regiment.
Weekdays 10-5; Su. 2-5 (Closed Good Friday and Christmas Day).

MORATH BROS.
71 Dale Street, Liverpool, L2 2HT, Lancashire
Company Museum. Horology.
Weekdays 2-5.

MUSEUM OF THE SCHOOL OF HYGIENE
126 Mount Pleasant, Liverpool, Lancashire
Collection of public health exhibits, mainly of interest to students.
M.-F. 9-4.30.

SPEKE HALL
Liverpool, Lancashire
16th century half-timbered building. Furniture. Paintings. Decorative and applied arts.
Weekdays 10-7; Su. 2-7 (Oct.-Mar. Weekdays 10-5; Su. 2-5).

SUDLEY ART GALLERY AND MUSEUM
(Emma Holt Bequest), Mossley Hill Road, Liverpool, Lancashire
18th and 19th century paintings, mainly English, including works by Turner, Gainsborough, Romney and Holman Hunt. Pottery. Costumes.
Weekdays 10-5; Su. 2-5. Closed Boxing Day.

TATE AND LYLE REFINERIES LIMITED
Love Lane Refinery, Liverpool 3, Lancashire
Company Museum. Sugar-making equipment.
9-5 on application.

WALKER ART GALLERY
William Brown Street, Liverpool, Lancashire
Early Italian and Flemish paintings. The later Italians, Dutch and Germans and the English School from Holbein onwards. Paintings by the Liverpool School and the Pre-Raphaelites. Late Victorian academic paintings. 20th century paintings and sculpture.
Weekdays 10-5; Su. 2-5. Closed on Boxing Day.

LLANBERIS

NORTH WALES QUARRYING MUSEUM
(Amgueddfa Chwareli Gogledd Cymru), Llanberis, Caernarvonshire
Housed in workshop complex of former Dinorwic Slate

Quarries Company. Original machine tools, including lathes, drilling machines, shaping machines, forging hammers. Foundry. Blacksmiths' hearths. Slate dressing machines. Waterwheel (1870), 50 ft. 5 ins. in diameter.
May-Sept., daily 9.30-7.

LLANDRINDOD WELLS

AUTOMOBILE PALACE VETERAN CYCLE COLLECTION
Automobile Palace Limited, Llandrindod Wells, Radnorshire
Collection of old cycles and tricycles from 1869-1938.
Weekdays 8-8; Su. 10-7.

RADNORSHIRE COUNTY MUSEUM
Public Library, War Memorial Gardens, Temple Street, Llandrindod Wells, Radnorshire
Archaeological material, mainly from Castell Collen excavations (Roman). Doll Collection.
Weekdays 10-5. Closed Bank Holidays.

LLANDUDNO

RAPALLO HOUSE MUSEUM AND ART GALLERY
Fferm Bach Craig-Y-Don, Llandudno, Caernarvonshire
Collection of paintings, prints, water-colour drawings, pastels. Porcelain. Sculpture. Bronzes. Armour and Weapons. Roman relics. Welsh kitchen.
May-Aug. Weekdays (except Tu.) 10-1, 2-5. Sept.-Apr. Weekdays (except Tu.) 10-1, 2-4. Closed Boxing Day.

LLANELLI

PARC HOWARD MUSEUM AND ART GALLERY
Llanelli, Carmarthenshire
Collection of Llanelli pottery. Paintings by Welsh artists. Local history.
Winter: M.-F. 10-4.30. Summer, inc. Bank Holidays, 10-8.

LLANFAIR P.G.

PLAS NEWYDD
Llanfair P.G., Anglesey
Furniture. Porcelain. Paintings, including Rex Whistler murals.
By appointment.

LLANGOLLEN

PLAS NEWYDD MUSEUM
Llangollen, Denbighshire
Home (1780-1831) of the "Ladies of Llangollen". Wood carvings. Stained glass. Cordovan leather.
May-Sept. Weekdays 10.30-7.30; Su. 11-4. Oct.-Apr. Weekdays by arrangement.

LLANIDLOES

MUSEUM OF LOCAL HISTORY AND INDUSTRY
Market Hall, Llanidloes, Montgomeryshire
Local history and industry.
Easter-Sept. Weekdays 11-1, 2-5.

LLANRWST

GWYDIR CASTLE
nr. Llanrwst, Denbighshire
16th and 17th century furniture.
Easter-Oct. Daily 10-6.

LLANVAPLEY

RURAL CRAFTS MUSEUM
nr. Llanvapley, Monmouthshire
Collection of old agricultural tools, items from the farmhouse kitchen and the implements used in country crafts, such as thatching, smithing, milling.
Su. 3-6 or dusk.

LLANYSTUMDWY

LLOYD GEORGE MEMORIAL MUSEUM
Llanystumdwy, Caernarvonshire
Caskets, deeds of Freedom, documents, scrolls and other mementoes of Earl Lloyd George of Dwyfor.
Spring Bank Holiday-Sept. 30, also Easter M.-Sa. 9.30-6. Closed Su. and winter.

LONDON

ABBEY ART CENTRE AND MUSEUM
89 Park Road, New Barnet, Hertfordshire
Ethnology and art of Africa, Asia, Oceania and pre-Columbian America.
By appointment.

APSLEY HOUSE
Wellington Museum, 149 Piccadilly, Hyde Park Corner, London W.1
House (1771-8). Paintings. Porcelain. Silver-plate. Personal relics of first Duke of Wellington.
Daily, Weekdays and Bank Holidays 10-6; Su. 2.30-6.

ARTILLERY MUSEUM
The Rotunda, Woolwich Common, London S.E.18
Collection of guns, muskets, rifles.
M.-F. 10-12.45, 2-5 (2-4 in winter); Sa. 10-12; Su. 2-4 (2-4 in winter).

BADEN-POWELL HOUSE
Queen's Gate, London S.W.7
Mementoes of Baden-Powell. Historical records of the Scout Movement.
Daily 9-6.

BARNET MUSEUM
31 Wood Street, Barnet, Hertfordshire
Archaeological and historical exhibits relating to the area. Bygones and miscellaneous.
Tu. and Th. 2.30-4.30. Sa. 10-12.30, 2.30-4.30.

BETHNAL GREEN MUSEUM
Cambridge Heath Road, London E.2
British paintings, domestic pottery, porcelain, glass and silver. Children's section, with toys, games, dolls and dolls' houses. Spitalfields silks and Costumes.
Weekdays 10-6; Su. 2.30-6.

BEXLEY LONDON BOROUGH MUSEUM
Hall Place, Bourne Road, Bexley
Local history. Paintings. Prints.
Weekdays 10-5; Su. 2-6.

BLINDIANA MUSEUM
224-8 Great Portland Street, London W.1
International collection of current and historic aids used by blind people.
By appointment only.

BRITISH DENTAL ASSOCIATION MUSEUM
63-4 Wimpole Street, London W1M 8AL
History of dental surgery.
By appointment.

BRITISH MUSEUM
Great Russell Street, London W.C.1
Comprising the National Museum of Archaeology, Art and Ethnography, the collection of Prints and Drawings and the National Library. The Museum departments are - Coins and Medals, Egyptian Antiquities, Western Asiatic Antiquities, Greek and Roman Antiquities, British and Medieval Antiquities (including Ceramics) and Oriental Antiquities (including Ceramics). The Department of Ethnography is at 6 Burlington Gardens, W.1.
Weekdays 10-5; Su. 2.30-6.

BRITISH MUSEUM (NATURAL HISTORY)
Cromwell Road, South Kensington, London S.W.7
National collections of animals and plants, extinct as well as existing, and of the rocks and minerals which make up the earth's crust.
Weekdays 10-6; Su. 2.30-6.

BRITISH PIANO MUSEUM
Brentford, Middlesex
Automatic, old and odd musical instruments.
Mar. 1 - Nov. 30. Demonstrations Th., Sa. and Su. 2.30-6.

BRITISH THEATRE MUSEUM
Leighton House, 12 Holland Park Road, Kensington, London W.14
A selection from British Theatre Archives and personal theatre collections.
Tu., Th., Sa. 11-5; closed Bank Holidays.

BROOMFIELD MUSEUM
Broomfield Park, Palmers Green, London N.13
Local antiquities and bygones. Natural history. Pottery. Paintings.
Easter-Sept. Tu.-F. 10-8; Sa. and Su. 10-6. Oct.-Easter Daily (except M.) 10-5 (or park closing time).

BRUCE CASTLE MUSEUM
Lordship Lane, Tottenham, London N.17
Local history. Postal history.
Daily except W. and Su. 10-12.30, 1.30-5.

BUCKINGHAM PALACE
The Queen's Gallery, Buckingham Palace Road, London S.W.1
Exhibitions from the Royal Collection of paintings, furniture and other works of art.
Tu.-Sa. and Bank Holiday M. 11-5; Su. 2-5.

BUTLER MUSEUM
Harrow School, Harrow-on-The-Hill, Middlesex
Natural history. Herbarium. British and tropical lepidoptera, British birds.
By appointment.

CARLYLE'S HOUSE
24 Cheyne Row, Chelsea, London S.W.3
Portraits, letters, furniture, prints, manuscripts and a small library of books belonging to Thomas Carlyle.
Weekdays (except Tu.) 10-1, 2-6; Su. 2-6 (or dusk). Closed Good Friday, Christmas Day and Boxing Day.

CHARTERED INSURANCE INSTITUTE'S MUSEUM
20 Aldermanbury, London E.C.2
Collection of Insurance Companies' fire marks, fire fighting equipment, helmets, medals indicating the part played by insurance companies in lessening the dangers of fire.
Open during office hours, M.-F.

CHISWICK HOUSE
Burlington Lane, Chiswick, London W.4
Villa designed by the Earl of Burlington, 1725, and derived from Palladio's Villa Capra. William Kent decorations. Period furniture. Paintings.
Apr. Daily 9.30-5.30; May-Sept. Daily 9.30-7. Oct. and Mar. Weekdays (except M. and Tu.) 9.30-5.30; Su. 2-5.30. Nov.-Feb. Weekdays 9.30-4; Su. 2-4.

CHURCH FARM HOUSE MUSEUM
Church End, Hendon, London NW4 4JR
Local history. Period rooms.
Weekdays except Tu. 10-12.30, 1.30-5.30; Tu. 10-1; Su. 2.30-6.

CLOCKMAKERS' COMPANY MUSEUM
Guildhall Library, London E.C.2
Horology. Library and archives of Clockmakers' Company.
M.-F. 9.30-5; Sa. 9.30-12, 2-5.

COMMONWEALTH INSTITUTE
Kensington High Street, London W.8
Life, scenery and resources of the Commonwealth. Art and social development of Commonwealth peoples.
Weekdays 10-5.30; Su. 2.30-6. Closed Christmas Eve, Christmas Day and Good Friday.

COURTAULD INSTITUTE GALLERIES
Woburn Square, London W.C.1
The Galleries of the University of London. Paintings, especially Impressionist and Post-Impressionist. Watercolours. Drawings. Prints.
Weekdays 10-5; Su. 2-5.

THE CRICKET MEMORIAL GALLERY
(Marylebone Cricket Club), Lord's Ground, London N.W.8
Pictures, objets d'art, trophies and bygones illustrating the history of cricket. The Ashes.
Match days 10.30 to close of play. Off season: M.-F. 9.30-4.30.

CUMING MUSEUM
Walworth Road, Southwark, London S.E.17
History of Southwark and district. Roman and Medieval remains from archaeological excavation, Dickensian Marshalsea Prison Pump and Dog and Pot shop sign. Examples of George Tinworth's modelling. Collection illustrating London Superstitions.
Weekdays 10-5.30 (Th. 10-7, Sa. 10-5) Closed Su.

THE "CUTTY SARK"
Cutty Sark Gardens, Greenwich Pier, London S.E.10
Last and most famous of all tea clippers, now permanently in a riverside berth at Greenwich. Refitted and rigged as she would be in harbour in the heyday of her sea-going career. She also holds two exhibitions - the story of the "Cutty Sark" and figureheads from the "Long John Silver" collection.
Weekdays 11-6; Su. 2.30-6. (Closes at 5 in winter).

DANOR ENGINEERING LIMITED
170 Pentonville Road, London N1 9JN
Company Museum. Smoothing, pressing and goffering irons.
M.-F. 8-5.

DARWIN MUSEUM
Down House, Downe, Kent
Home of Charles Darwin. His study and drawing room. Collections illustrating his life and work.
Daily (except F.) 10-5; Nov.-Mar. 11-5.

DICKENS HOUSE
48 Doughty Street, London WC1N 2LF
House occupied by Dickens and his family 1837-39. Relics displayed include manuscripts, furniture, autographs, portraits, letters and first editions.
Weekdays 10-5. Closed Bank Holidays.

DOLLOND AND AITCHISON LIMITED
1A-3 Westville Road, London W.12
Company Museum. Optics. Scientific instruments.
Collection in store.

DULWICH COLLEGE PICTURE GALLERY
College Road, London S.E.21
European paintings, including works by Rembrandt, Rubens, Claude, Poussin, Gainsborough, Watteau.
Weekdays (except M.) 10-6. Closes at 5 Sept. - mid.-Oct. and mid.-Mar. - end of Apr. and at 4 mid.-Oct. to mid.-Mar. Su. (Summer only) 2-6 (2-5 in Apr. and Sept.).

EPPING FOREST MUSEUM
Queen Elizabeth's Hunting Lodge, Chingford, London E.4
Exhibits of animals, bird and plant life in Epping Forest and man's association with them.
W.-Su. 2-6.

ERITH MUSEUM
Walnut Tree Road, Erith, Kent
Local geology, archaeology, industrial products, fauna, minerals, bygones.
On request. Weekdays 10-5 (Th. 10-1).

FENTON HOUSE
The Grove, Hampstead, London N.W.3
House (1693). Early keyboard musical instruments. Porcelain. Furniture.
Weekdays (except Tu.) and Bank Holidays 11-5; Su. 2-5 or dusk. Closed Christmas Day and Boxing Day.

FLEET BUILDING TELECOMMUNICATIONS MUSEUM
40 Shoe Lane, London EC4 A3DD
Telecommunications.
M.-F. 10-4.30.

FOUNDLING HOSPITAL ART TREASURES
40 Brunswick Square, London W.C.1
English paintings, including works by Hogarth, Gainsborough, Kneller. Sculpture by Rysbrack and Reubiliac. Handel relics.
M. and F. only except Bank Holidays 10-12, 2-4. Closed on all other days.

GEFFRYE MUSEUM
Kingsland Road, Shoreditch, London E2 8EA
Period rooms show the development of the middle-class English home from about 1600.
Tu.-Sa. 10-5; Su. 2-5. Closed M. (except Bank Holiday), Christmas Day, Boxing Day and Good Friday.

GEOLOGICAL MUSEUM
Exhibition Road, South Kensington, London S.W.7
Earth history and the general principles of geological science. Regional geology of Great Britain. Economic geology and mineralogy of the world. Gemstones.
Weekdays 10-6; Su. 2.30-6. The Library is open for free public reference M.-Sa. 10-4.30.

"GIPSY MOTH IV"
Greenwich Pier, London S.E.10
The yacht in which Sir Francis Chichester made his single-handed voyage round the world in 1966-7. Exhibits illustrating the voyage.
Weekdays 11-6; Su. 2.30-6. Closes at 5 in winter.

GOLDSMITHS' HALL
Foster Lane, Cheapside, London E.C.2
Antique plate, including some pieces with interesting historical associations. Modern silver and jewellery.
By appointment or written application. Occasionally open to the public - see local announcement.

GORDON MEDICAL MUSEUM
St. Thomas Street, London S.E.1
Guy's Hospital Medical School. Collection of specimens of disease in humans. Anatomical and dermatological models in wax.
Weekdays 9-5 by application to Dean of Medical School or Curator.

GREENWICH BOROUGH MUSEUM
232 Plumstead High Street, London S.E.18
Natural and local history. Commercial and industrial development of the district.
M., Th., F. and Sa. 10-5; Tu. 2-8.

GUILDHALL ART GALLERY
King Street, Cheapside, London E.C.2
Paintings, mainly by British artists.
Weekdays 10-5.

GUILDHALL MUSEUM
Gillett House, 55 Basinghall Street, London E.C.2
History and archaeology of the City from Roman times. Museum of Leathercraft. Glass excavated from City; fragments and entire specimens from Roman times to 18th century.
Weekdays 10-5. Closed Bank Holidays and religious days.

GUNNERSBURY PARK MUSEUM
Gunnersbury Park, London W.3
Local history, archaeology, bygones, including the Rothschilds' coaches, prints and maps, in the Rothschilds' late Regency mansion.
Apr.-Sept. M.-F. 2-5; Sa. and Su. 2-6. Oct.-Mar. Daily 2-4.

HALL PLACE
Bourne Road, Bexley, Kent
Local history.
Weekdays 10-5; Su. 2-6.

HAM HOUSE
Petersham, Richmond, Surrey
Built 1610 and altered at various times in 17th century. Period furniture.
Apr.-Sept. Tu.-Su. and Bank Holidays 2-6. Oct.-Mar. Tu.-Su. and Bank Holidays 12-4.

HAMPTON COURT PALACE
Hampton Court
Royal Palace begun in 1514 by Wolsey, addition by Henry VIII and later by Wren for William and Mary. Staterooms. Tapestries. Pictures. Furniture.
Mar., Apr. and Oct. 9.30-5 (Su. 2-5); May-Sept. 9.30-6 (Su. 11-6). Nov.-Feb. 9.30-4 (Su. 2-4).

THE HAMSON MUSEUM
Uxbridge Library, High Street, Uxbridge, Middlesex
Items relating to the history of the town and district.
Weekdays 9-8 (W. and Sa. 9-5).

HAYES AND HARLINGTON MUSEUM
Golden Crescent, Hayes, Middlesex
Local history.
M., Tu., Th. and F. 9-8; W. 9-1; Sa. 9-5.

HEALTH EXHIBITION CENTRE
90 Buckingham Palace Road, London S.W.1
Public health.
M.-F. 10-5.

HMS BELFAST
Symans Wharf, London E.C.3
British warship of the early 19th century.
Sa. and Su. 11-6.

HOGARTH'S HOUSE
Hogarth Lane, Chiswick, London W.4
The artist's country house for 15 years. Copies of Hogarth's paintings, impressions from engravings and relics.
Weekdays 11-6 (Winter 11-5, closed Tu.); Su. 2-6 (Winter 2-5).

HONOURABLE ARTILLERY COMPANY SERVICE MUSEUM
Armoury House, Finsbury, London E.C.1
Uniforms, old arms, awards, campaign medals, regimental colours, pictures, trophies and souvenirs associated with the regiment.
By appointment only.

HORNIMAN MUSEUM
London Road, Forest Hill, London SE23 3PQ
Ethnographical museum dealing with the study of man and his environment. Natural history collections. Musical instruments from all parts of the world.
Weekdays 10.30-6; Su. 2-6. Open Good Friday. Closed Christmas Eve and Christmas Day.

I.T.A. TELEVISION GALLERY
70 Brompton Road, London S.W.3
History of television, both international and British. Television techniques.
By appointment during office hours. Minimum age 16.

IMPERIAL WAR MUSEUM
Lambeth Road, London S.E.1
Illustrates and records all aspects of the two world wars and other operations involving Britain and the Commonwealth since 1914. Exhibits include aircraft, weapons, uniforms, decorations, models and dioramas.
Weekdays 10-6; Su. 2-6. Reference Departments Tu.-F. 10-5. Closed Christmas Eve, Christmas Day, Boxing Day and Good Friday.

INDUSTRIAL HEALTH AND SAFETY CENTRE
97 Horseferry Road, London S.W.1
Methods, arrangements and appliances for promoting the safety and health of industrial workers.
M.-F. 10-4.30. Closed Bank Holidays.

THE IVEAGH BEQUEST
Kenwood, Hampstead, London N.W.3
Paintings include Rembrandt self-portrait, Vermeer's "Lady Playing a Guitar" and works by Van Dyck, Hals and Cuyp, as well as English 18th century paintings by Reynolds, Romney and Gainsborough.
Weekdays 10-5; Su. 2-5. Open until 7 Apr.-Sept. (Closed Good Friday, Christmas Eve and Christmas Day).

JEWISH MUSEUM
Woburn House, Upper Woburn Place, London W.C.1
Jewish antiquities illustrating the public and private worship of the Jews.
M.-Th. 2.30-5; F., Su. 10.30-12.45. Closed Bank and Jewish Holidays.

JOHN EVELYN SOCIETY'S MUSEUM
Village Club, Ridgway, Wimbledon, London S.W.19
Water-colours, prints and photographs of Wimbledon's historic buildings and worthies.
Sa. 3-5.

DR. JOHNSON'S HOUSE
17 Gough Square, London E.C.4
Home of Samuel Johnson from 1748-59. Relics and small library.
Weekdays 10.30-5 (10.30-4.30 Oct.-Apr.). Closed Su. and Bank Holidays.

KEATS HOUSE AND MUSEUM
Wentworth Place, Keats Grove, Hampstead, London N.W.3
Former home of John Keats. Regency home. Relics and manuscripts of the poet.
Weekdays 10-6. Closed Su., Christmas Day, Boxing Day, Good Friday and Christmas Eve.

KENSINGTON PALACE
Kensington, London W.8
Bought by William III, 1689. Altered and added to by Wren and later alterations. Part open as London Museum. Furniture. Paintings.
Mar.-Sept. 10-6, Su. 2-6. Oct.-Feb. 10-4; Su. 2-4. Closed Good F., Christmas Eve and Christmas Day.

KEW PALACE
Kew, (Dutch House), nr. Richmond, Surrey
Palace (1631). Souvenirs of George III. Furniture. Paintings.
Apr.-Sept. Weekdays 11-6; Su. 1-6.

KINGSTON-UPON-THAMES MUSEUM AND ART GALLERY
Fairfield West, Kingston-upon-Thames, Surrey
Local archaeology (especially Bronze Age and Anglo-Saxon), history and natural history. Also "Zoopraxiscope" of Edweard Muybridge.
Museum: Weekdays 9-5. Art Gallery: hours vary (advertised locally).

KODAK MUSEUM
Wealdstone, Harrow, Middlesex
History of photography and cinematography.
By appointment only M.-F. 9-12, 1.30-4.30.

LANCASTER HOUSE
Stable Yard, St. James's, London S.W.1
Town mansion of the early Victorian period. Period furnishings.
Easter Eve to mid.-Dec. Sa., Su. and Bank Holidays 2-6. Occasionally closed to the public at short notice.

MARBLE HILL HOUSE
Twickenham, Middlesex
English Palladian villa. Early Georgian paintings and furniture.
Weekdays (except M.) 10-5; Su. 2-5. Closed Good Friday, Christmas Eve and Christmas Day. Open Bank Holiday.

MUSEUM OF LEATHERCRAFT
at the Guildhall Museum, 55 Basinghall Street, London E.C.2
Exhibits of the wares of the leather-using guilds of the City of London.
M.-Sa. 10-5.

LEIGHTON HOUSE ART GALLERY AND MUSEUM
12 Holland Park Road, Kensington, London W14 8LZ
Home of Frederic, Lord Leighton, 1866-1896. Contains an Arab Hall, with tiles from Rhodes, Damascus, Cairo. Exhibition of High Victorian Art, includes paintings, drawings and sculpture by Leighton, Burne-Jones, Alma-Tadema, Millais, Poynter, Stevens, Watts and other contemporaries and friends. Period rooms.
Weekdays 11-5 (11-6 during exhibitions). Garden open Apr.-Sept. Children under 16 must be accompanied by an adult. Closed Bank Holidays.

LONDON IRISH RIFLES MUSEUM (T.A.)
Duke of York Headquarters, Sloane Square, London S.W.3
Uniforms, old arms, awards, campaign medals, regimental colours, pictures, trophies and souvenirs associated with the regiment.
By arrangement with the Adjutant.

LONDON MUSEUM
Kensington Palace, The Broad Walk, Kensington Gardens, London W.8
History of London from the earliest times, illustrated by antiquities, paintings, drawings, costume and domestic articles of all kinds. Adjoining the museum and also open to the public are the state apartments of Kensington Palace.
Weekdays 10-6; Su. 2-6 (except Oct. and Feb., closing 5 and 4 between Nov. and Jan.). Closed Christmas Eve, Christmas Day, Boxing Day and Good Friday.

LONDON SCOTTISH REGIMENTAL MUSEUM (T.A.)
59 Buckingham Gate, London S.W.1
Uniforms, old arms, awards, campaign medals, regimental colours, pictures, trophies and souvenirs associated with the regiment.
By appointment.

MARTINWARE POTTERY COLLECTION
Public Library, Osterley Park Road, Southall, Middlesex
Large collection of Martinware, including birds, face mugs, grotesques.
M.-F. 9-8; Sa. 9-5.

MELTONIAN WREN LIMITED
Oxgate Lane, London N.W.2
Company Museum. Footwear.
By appointment.

MUSEUM OF BRITISH TRANSPORT
Clapham High Street, London S.W.4
Transport. Road and rail vehicles. Railway equipment. Paintings. Posters. Photographs.
Weekdays 10-5.30.

MUSEUM OF MANKIND
Ethnography Department of the British Museum, 6 Burlington Gardens, London, W1X 2EX
World ethnography exhibitions from the permant collections, to be changed yearly. Current displays include Eskimo art; costumes of Palestine; spinning and weaving in Palestine; turquoise mosaics from Mexico; the tribal image (Africa, Oceania, Asia, America, including Hawaii); the Javanese orchestra; Malay shadow puppets; Australian aborigines; Solomon islanders; the potter's art in Africa; divine kingship in Africa; hunters and gatherers - the material culture of the nomadic Hadza tribe of Tanzania.
Weekdays 10-5; Su. 2.30-6. Closed Good F., Dec. 24-26.

NATIONAL ARMY MUSEUM
Royal Hospital Road, London S.W.3
Objects relating to the history of the British standing army and auxiliary forces to 1914, the East India Company and the Indian Armies to 1947, and the land forces of Britain's overseas possessions up to their dates of independence. Uniforms, medals, decorations, weapons, works of art, silver, ceramics and personal relics. Documents, Prints. Photographs. Paintings.
M.-Sa. 10-5.30; Su. 2-5.30. Closed Christmas Day, Christmas Eve and Good Friday. Any variation to these arrangements will be published in the national press.

NATIONAL GALLERY
Trafalgar Square, London W.C.2
Founded 1824 as the National collection of European paintings. Representative collection of Italian, Dutch, Flemish, Spanish, German Schools; French painting up to 1900. British paintings from Hogarth to Turner.
Weekdays 10-6; Su. and Boxing Day 2-6. Closed Christmas Eve, Christmas Day and Good Friday.

NATIONAL MARITIME MUSEUM
Romney Road, Greenwich, London S.E.10
Portraits. Paintings of maritime interest. Ship models. Navigational instruments and charts. Uniforms. Medals. Documents.
Weekdays 10-6; Su. 2.30-6. Closed Christmas Eve, Christmas Day, Boxing Day and Good Friday.

NATIONAL PORTRAIT GALLERY
St. Martin's Place, London W.C.2
Collection of portraits of the famous and infamous in British history, including paintings, sculpture, miniatures and engravings.
Twentieth century annexe for film and photography is at 15 Carlton House Terrace, London S.W.1.
M.-F. 10-5; Sa. 10-6; Su. 2-6. Closed Christmas Eve, Christmas Day, Boxing Day, New Year's Day and Good Friday.

NATIONAL POSTAL MUSEUM
King Edward Building, King Edward Street, London E.C.1
British and foreign postage stamps.
M.-F. 10-4.30; Sa. 10-4.

INSTITUTE OF OPHTHALMOLOGY
Judd Street, London W.C.1
Specimens illustrating the morphology and pathology of the eye.
Weekdays 9-5.30. Open to undergraduate and postgraduate students only.

ORLEANS HOUSE GALLERY
Riverside, Twickenham, Middlesex
In James Gibbs' baroque Octagon Room (1720). 18th and 19th century paintings, watercolours and engravings of Richmond and Twickenham.
Weekdays ex. M. 1-5.30 (Oct.-Mar. 1-4). Su., Spring and Late Summer Bank Holidays 2-5 (Oct.-Mar. 2-4).

OSTERLEY PARK HOUSE
Isleworth, Middlesex
House by Robert Adam with original furniture and decorations.
Apr.-Sept. Tu.-Su. and Bank Holidays 2-6. Oct.-Mar. Tu.-Su. and Bank Holidays 12-4.

PASSMORE EDWARDS MUSEUM
Romford Road, Stratford, London E15 4LZ
Collections of Essex archaeology, local history, geology and natural history.
Weekdays 10-6 except Th. 10-8 and Sa. 10-5. Closed Sa. 1-2.

PERCIVAL DAVID FOUNDATION OF CHINESE ART
53 Gordon Square, London W.C.1
Chinese ceramics.
M. 2-5; Tu.-F. 10.30-5; Sa. 10.30-1. Closed Bank Holidays.

PHARMACEUTICAL SOCIETY'S MUSEUM
17 Bloomsbury Square, London W.C.1
Collection of crude drugs of vegetable and animal origin used in the 17th century. Early printed works, manuscripts and prints relating to pharmacy. English Delft drug jars, leech jars, bell-metal mortars, medicine chests, dispensing apparatus.
By arrangement.

PUBLIC RECORD OFFICE AND MUSEUM
Chancery Lane, London WC2A 1LR
Contains the national archives. William the Conqueror's Domesday Book. Signatures of the Kings and Queens of England, Shakespeare, Milton and Guy Fawkes; Wellington's despatch from Waterloo. Marlborough's despatch from Blenheim and the log of Nelson's *Victory.*
M.-F. 1-4. Closed Bank Holidays.

ROYAL AIR FORCE MUSEUM
Hendon, London N.W.9
Military and civil aviation, with special emphasis on the work of the Royal Air Force. Original aircraft. Technical equipment. Armaments. Uniforms. Decorations. Personalia. Paintings, drawings and sculptures. Documents, photographs, maps, plans and sound recordings.
M.-Sa. 10-6; Su. 2-6.

ROYAL ARTILLERY REGIMENTAL MUSEUM
Royal Military Academy, Academy Road, Woolwich, London S.E.18
Uniforms, old arms, awards, campaign medals, regimental colours, pictures, trophies and souvenirs associated with the regiment.
Weekdays 10-12.30, 2-4.

ROYAL BOTANIC GARDENS
(Kew Gardens), near Richmond, Surrey
Herbaria. Museum illustrating history of the Gardens.
Museum open at 10, Houses at 1. Closing times vary according to season but never open later than 4.50 weekdays or 5.50 Su.

ROYAL COLLEGE OF MUSIC
Prince Consort Road, South Kensington, London S.W.7
Musical instruments.
M. and W. during term-time, 10-30-4.30 by appointment.

ROYAL COLLEGE OF SURGEONS' MUSEUM
Lincoln's Inn Fields, London W.C.2
The Hunterian Collection and other items of interest in medical history.
By appointment.

THE ROYAL FUSILIERS MUSEUM
Tower of London, Tower Hill, London E.C.3
Dioramas of famous battles. Paintings (including George V by Oswold Birley). Uniforms worn by George V. Medals.
Weekdays 10-5 (winter 10-4); Summer: Sundays only 2-5.

ROYAL HOSPITAL MUSEUM
Royal Hospital, Royal Hospital Road, Chelsea, London S.W.3
Pictures, plans and maps, medals and uniforms connected with the Royal Hospital.
Weekdays 10-12, 2-5; Su. 2-5 except Good Friday, Easter Sunday and Christmas Day.

OLD ROYAL OBSERVATORY
National Maritime Museum, Greenwich Park, London S.E.10
The buildings, including Flamsteed House which was designed by Wren, form a part of the National Maritime Museum for the exhibition of astronomical and navigational instruments, many of the former being exhibited in their original settings. The Greenwich Meridian can be seen marked across the courtyard and in the pathway outside the wall.
Weekdays 10-6; Su. 2.30-6. Closed Christmas Eve, Christmas Day, Boxing Day and Good Friday.

ROYAL MEWS
Buckingham Palace Road, London S.W.1
Royal horses and equipages. Vintage Royal cars.
W. and Th. 2-4.

ST. BARTHOLOMEW'S HOSPITAL PATHOLOGICAL MUSEUM
West Smithfield, London E.C.1
Pathological specimens.
By appointment. M.-F. 9-5; Sa. 9-12.

ST. BRIDE'S CRYPT MUSEUM
St. Bride's Church, Fleet Street, London E.C.4
During excavations made prior to rebuilding over 1,000 years of unrecorded history were revealed. Roman pavement and remains of seven previous churches on site (dating from 6th century) can be seen together with permanent display of history of site.
Daily 9-4.30.

ST. GEORGE'S HOSPITAL MEDICAL SCHOOL PATHOLOGICAL MUSEUM
Hyde Park Corner, London S.W.1
Pathological specimens.
By appointment.

ST. JOHN'S GATE
St. John's Square, Clerkenwell, London E.C.1
Early 16th century gate-house containing silver, furniture, pictures and other treasures of the Knights of St. John.
By appointment with the Curator.

SCIENCE MUSEUM
Exhibition Road, South Kensington, London S.W.7
Historical collection portraying the sciences of mathematics, physics and chemistry and their applications, and the development of engineering, transport and communications, mining and industries generally from early times to the present day.
Weekdays 10-6; Su. 2.30-6. Closed Good Friday, Christmas Eve, Christmas Day and Boxing Day. The Science Library is open Weekdays 10-5.30.

SIR JOHN SOANE'S MUSEUM
13 Lincoln's Inn Fields, London W.C.2
Museum built by Sir John Soane, R.A. in 1812-13 as his private residence. Contains his collection of antiquities and works of art.
Tu.-Sa. 10-5 (lecture tours Sa. 2.30). Closed Bank Holidays and during Aug.

SOUTH LONDON ART GALLERY
Peckham Road, London S.E.5
Collection of 17th-20th century paintings, oil and watercolours. 20th century prints.
Weekdays 10-6; Su. 3-6.

TATE GALLERY
Millbank, London SW1P 4RG
The British Collection: works from the 16th century up to about 1900. Paintings, sculpture, watercolours, drawings and engravings.
The Modern Collection: works by British artists born after 1850, together with foreign paintings from the Impressionists onwards.
M.-Sa. 10-6; Su. 2-6. Closed Christmas Eve, Christmas Day, Boxing Day, New Year's Day and Good Friday.

TOWER OF LONDON
Tower Hill, London E.C.3
Crown jewels. Historic relics. Uniforms. Armouries. Dungeons.
Weekdays Mar.-Oct. 9.30-5. Nov.-Feb. 9.30-4. Su. Mar.-Oct. 2-5.

UNIVERSITY COLLEGE ANATOMY MUSEUM
Gower Street, London W.C.1
Anatomical and anthropological specimens.
By appointment.

UNIVERSITY COLLEGE DEPARTMENT OF EGYPTOLOGY MUSEUM
Gower Street, London W.C.1
Egyptian archaeology.
M.-F. 10-5.

UNIVERSITY COLLEGE MUSEUM OF ZOOLOGY AND COMPARATIVE ANATOMY
Gower Street, London W.C.1
Collection of zoological material.
By appointment.

VALENCE HOUSE MUSEUM
Becontree Avenue, Dagenham, Essex
17th-century manor house, still partly moated. Local history. Fanshawe family portraits. Furniture.
M.-F. 9.30-12, 2-4 or by appointment.

VICTORIA AND ALBERT MUSEUM
Cromwell Road, South Kensington, London S.W.7
Fine and applied art of all countries, periods and styles. Collections of sculpture, furniture, tapestries, pottery, porcelain, glass, musical instruments, silver, jewellery, costume and miniatures and the arts of Islam, India and China. The finest works in all media are grouped by date and style, including study collections where work in a particular medium can be seen in depth. Masterpieces in the Museum include the Raphael Cartoons, Bernini's *Neptune and a Triton*, the Devonshire Hunting Tapestries and the Gloucestershire candlestick. There is also a comprehensive collection of paintings by John Constable.
Weekdays 10-6; Su. 2.30-6.

WALLACE COLLECTION
Hertford House, Manchester Square, London W.1
Paintings of the French, Spanish, Italian, Flemish, Dutch and British Schools. Miniatures. Sculpture. Furniture. Armour. Glass. Goldsmiths' work. Ceramics.
Weekdays 10-5; Su. 2-5. Closed Christmas Eve, Christmas Day and Good Friday.

WALTHAMSTOW MUSEUM
Vestry House, London E.17
Early 18th century workhouse. Local history.
Weekdays 10-12, 1-5 (until 8 M. and W.). Closed Bank Holidays.

WELLCOME INSTITUTE OF THE HISTORY OF MEDICINE
The Wellcome Building, Euston Road, London N.W.1
Collections illustrate the history of medicine and allied sciences from the earliest times to the present century.
M.-Sa. 10-5. Closed Bank Holidays.

WESLEY'S HOUSE AND MUSEUM
47 City Road, London E.C.1
The house in which John Wesley lived and died. Collection of his personal possessions.
Weekdays 10-1, 2-4 and by arrangement. Closed Bank Holidays.

R. WHITE AND SON LIMITED
Albany Road, London S.E.5
Company Museum. Mineral water bottles.
By appointment.

WILLIAM MORRIS GALLERY
Water House, Lloyd Park, Forest Road, Walthamstow, London E.17
18th century house, the boyhood home of William Morris. Collections include textiles, wall-papers, designs etc. by Morris, the pre-Raphaelites and contemporaries. Pictures and sculpture by 19th-20th century artists.
Weekdays 10-1, 2-5 (Tu. and Th. 10-1, 2-8 in Summer). Su. first Su. in each month 10-12, 2-5. Closed Bank Holidays.

"WOODLANDS" LOCAL HISTORY CENTRE AND ART GALLERY
90 Mycenae Road, London S.E.3
Built 1774 for John Julius Angerstein, founder of Lloyds and patron of the arts. Material relating to Greenwich.
Weekdays ex. W. 10-7.30; Sa. 10-6; Su. 2-6.

LONDON COLNEY

PROTOTYPE DE HAVILLAND MOSQUITO
Salisbury Hall, London Colney, Hertfordshire
Historic aircraft, including prototype of the de Havilland Mosquito aircraft designed and built at Salisbury Hall during 2nd world war, D.H. Vampire and Venom.
Easter Su. to Sept. Su. (also Th. July-Sept.) 2-6; Bank Holidays 10.30-5.30. Other times by appointment.

LOOE

THE CORNISH MUSEUM
Lower Street, East Looe, Cornwall
Life and culture of Cornwall: arts, crafts, folklore, mining, fishing, early travel, games and pastimes. Collection of relics dealing with witchcraft, charms and superstitions.
May-Sept. Daily 10-9.

LOWESTOFT

EAST ANGLIA TRANSPORT MUSEUM
Chapel Road, Carlton Colville, Lowestoft, Suffolk
Tramcars, trolleybuses, buses, cars and commercial vehicles. Miniature railway. Operating tramcar service.
Spring Holiday - Sept. 30, 2-6.

SOMERLEYTON HALL
near Lowestoft, Suffolk
16th century building with 1844 additions. Tapestries. Grinling Gibbons carving. Paintings.
Easter-May 31, Su., Th. 2-6. Also Tu. and W. until Sept. 30 and Bank Holidays.

LUDLOW

LUDLOW MUSEUM
Butter Cross, Ludlow, Shropshire
Fossils. Collections of prehistoric, Roman and Medieval material, including arms and armour.
Easter-Sept. M., Tu., W., F. and Sa. 10.30-12.30, 2-5. Oct.-Easter, M., Tu., W. and F. 2-5; Sa. 10.30-12.30, 2-5. Closed Th. and Su.

LUTON

WERNHER COLLECTION
Luton Hoo, Luton, Bedfordshire
Paintings. Furniture. English china. Portraits and memorabilia of the Russian Imperial Family. Park landscaped by Capability Brown.
Apr. 20 - Sept. 30, M., W., Th., Sa. 11-6; Su. 2-6.

LUTON MUSEUM AND ART GALLERY
Wardown Park, Luton, Bedfordshire
Bedfordshire archaeology and history. Rural trades and crafts, particularly the straw hat and pillow lace industries. Furniture. Decorative and fine arts. Costumes. Needlework. Doll and toy collection.
Weekdays 10-6; Su. 2-6 (closed at 5, Oct.-Mar.). Closed Christmas Day and Boxing Day and Su. Dec. and Jan.

VAUXHALL MOTORS LIMITED
Kinipton Road, Luton, Bedfordshire
Company collection. Vauxhall cars, 1904-1926.
Not normally accessible except by previous arrangement.

LYME REGIS

THE PHILPOT MUSEUM
Bridge Street, Lyme Regis, Dorset
Old prints and documents, fossils and coins. Sun Fire Engine of 1710.
Summer: Daily 10-1, 2.30-5.30. Winter: Tu. 10.30-12.30; Th. 2.30-4.30; Sa. and Su. 10.30-12.30, 2.30-4.30.

MACCLESFIELD

CAPESTHORNE
Macclesfield, Cheshire
Built by John Wood of Bath in 1722. Pictures. Furniture.
March 28 - Sept. 26, Su., Also Good F. and Bank Holiday M. (also W. from early May), 2-5.30. May-Aug. Sa. 2-4.

WEST PARK MUSEUM AND ART GALLERY
Prestbury Road, Macclesfield, Cheshire
Egyptian collection. Local paintings and water-colour drawings, including sketches by Landseer, and oil paintings and sketches by C. F. Tunnicliffe.
Oct.-Mar. Daily 9.30-4.30; Apr.-Sept. Daily 9.30-5.30; Su. 2-5.

MAIDENHEAD

CLIVEDEN
Maidenhead, Buckinghamshire
Tapestry. Furniture. Gardens contain temples by Giacomo Leoni.
House: end Mar. - near end Oct. W., Sa. and Su. 2.30-5.30; Su. 2.30-5.30. Gardens: end Mar. - near end Oct. W., Th., F., Sa. and Su. Also Bank Holidays, 11-6.30.

HENRY REITLINGER BEQUEST
Oldfield, Riverside, Maidenhead, Berkshire
Chinese, European, Italian, Persian pottery. Paintings. Sculpture and Glass.
Tu. and Th. 10-12.30, 2.15-4.30.

MAIDSTONE

ALLINGTON CASTLE
nr. Maidstone, Kent
Crenellated castle surrounded by moat. Jacobean, Queen Anne furniture.
All the year, Daily 2-4. Other times by appointment.

THE FRIARS
Aylesford, nr. Maidstone, Kent
Restored 13th century Friary. Sculpture and ceramics by contemporary artists.
All the year, Daily 9-dusk.

MUSEUM AND ART GALLERY
St. Faith's Street, Maidstone, Kent
16th century Manor House containing local archaeological, art and natural history collections. Pacific and Oriental section. William Hazlitt relics. Costume gallery. Bygones. Ceramics. 17th century Dutch and Italian oil paintings.
Weekdays Oct.-Mar. 10-5; Apr.-Sept. 10-6. Closed Bank Holidays.

THE QUEEN'S OWN ROYAL WEST KENT REGIMENTAL MUSEUM
Maidstone, Kent
First Colour carried by the Regiment in 1763. Items relating to the 50th and 97th Foot and West Kent Militia.
Weekdays Oct.-Mar. 10-5; Apr.-Sept. 10-6. Closed Bank Holidays.

TYRWHITT-DRAKE MUSEUM OF CARRIAGES
Archbishop's Stables, Mill Street, Maidstone, Kent
Horse-drawn vehicles, including most types of state, official and private carriages. Models.
Weekdays 10-1, 2-5. Closed Bank Holidays.

MALMESBURY

ATHELSTAN MUSEUM
Cross Hayes, Malmesbury, Wiltshire
History of Malmesbury. Coins. Household equipment. Old fire engine.
Daily 10-4.

MALTON

ROMAN MALTON MUSEUM
Milton Rooms, Market Place, Malton, Yorkshire
Romano-British collections from the Malton district. Prehistoric and medieval material.
Daily (except Th.) 2-4 (at other times M.-F. apply Town Hall).

MANCHESTER

ATHENAEUM ANNEXE
Princess Street, Manchester, Lancashire
Ceramics.
Weekdays 10-6; Su. 2.30-5.

CITY ART GALLERY
Mosley Street, Manchester, Lancashire
European and British paintings. Sculpture. English silver and pottery.
Weekdays 10-6; Su. 2.30-5.

FLETCHER MOSS MUSEUM
The Old Parsonage, Wilmslow Road, Didsbury, Manchester, Lancashire
18th-20th century English water-colours and drawings, including a group by Turner.
Nov.-Feb. Weekdays 10-4; Su. 2-4. May-Aug. Weekdays 10-8; Su. 2-9. Other times: Weekdays 10-6; Su. 2-6.

GALLERY OF ENGLISH COSTUME
Platt Hall, Rusholme, Manchester, Lancashire
House (c.1764). Collection of English clothing from 17th century to the present.
Nov.-Feb. Weekdays 10-4; Su. 2-4. May-Aug. Weekdays 10-8; Su. 2-9. Other periods: Weekdays 10-6; Su. 2-6.

HEATON HALL
Heaton Park, Manchester, Lancashire
Former home of the Egerton family, re-built in the late 18th and early 19th century to a design of 1772 by James Wyatt. Contemporary furniture, paintings and sculpture.
Nov.-Feb. Weekdays 10-4; Su. 2-4. May-Aug. Weekdays 10-8; Su. 2-9. Other periods Weekdays 10-6; Su. 2-6.

MANCHESTER MUSEUM
The University, Oxford Road, Manchester, Lancashire
Geology. Botany. Zoology. Entomology. Egyptology. Classical archaeology. Ethnology. Numismatics.
Weekdays 10-5 (W. 10-9). Closed a few days at Christmas and on Good Friday.

MANCHESTER MUSEUM OF SCIENCE AND TECHNOLOGY
97 Grosvenor Street, Manchester, Lancashire
Industry and technology of Manchester area. Textiles. Scientific instruments.
M.-F. 10-5.

THE MANCHESTER REGIMENT SERVICE MUSEUM
Queen's Park Art Gallery, Manchester, Lancashire
Uniforms, old arms, awards, campaign medals, regimental colours, pictures, trophies and souvenirs associated with the regiment.
Nov.-Feb. Weekdays 10-4; Su. 2-4. May-Aug. Weekdays 10-8; Su. 2-9. Other periods: Weekdays 10-6; Su. 2-6.

MANCHESTER SHIP CANAL COMPANY MUSEUM
Ship Canal House, King Street, Manchester 2, Lancashire
Company museum. Material relating to the history of the canal.
By appointment. Apply to public relations officer.

QUEEN'S PARK ART GALLERY
Rochdale Road, Harpurhey, Manchester, Lancashire
Victorian paintings and sculpture. 20th century British paintings.
Nov.-Feb. Weekdays 10-4; Su. 2-4. May-Aug. Weekdays 10-8; Su. 2-9. Other periods: Weekdays 10-6; Su. 2-6.

WHITWORTH ART GALLERY
Oxford Road, Manchester, Lancashire
English water-colours. Old Master drawings. Post-Impressionist and 20th century European drawings. Contemporary paintings and sculpture. Prints, Renaissance - present day, including Japanese colour wood-cuts. Coptic and Peruvian textiles. Spanish and Italian embroideries. Damasks and velvets. Near Eastern embroideries. Contemporary fabrics.
Weekdays 10-5 (Th. 10-9).

WYTHENSHAWE HALL
Northenden, nr. Manchester, Lancashire
Half-timbered manor house. Furniture. Paintings, mainly the 17th century. Royal Lancastrian pottery. Local history.
Nov.-Feb. Weekdays 10-4, Su. 2-4; May-Aug. Weekdays 10-8, Su. 2-8. Mar., Apr., Sept. and Oct. Weekdays 10-6; Su. 2-6. Closed Good F. and Christmas Day.

MANSFIELD

MANSFIELD MUSEUM AND ART GALLERY
Leeming Street, Mansfield, Nottinghamshire
Zoology. Lustre ware. Water-colours of old Mansfield.
Weekdays 10-6.

MARGAM

MUSEUM OF STONES
Margam Abbey, Margam, Glamorgan
Collection of early Christian memorial stones and Roman milestone from vicinity.
Mar.-Oct. W., Sa., Su. 2-5. Nov.-Feb. W., Sa., Su. 2-4. Open Bank and Public Holidays exc. Christmas Day.

MARGATE

MARGATE MUSEUM
Public Library, Victoria Road, Margate, Kent
Saxon, Roman and other antiquities. Local history.
Weekdays 10-6. Closed W.

MARKET HARBOROUGH

MARKET HARBOROUGH ARCHAEOLOGICAL AND HISTORICAL SOCIETY MUSEUM
The County Library, Market Harborough, Leicestershire
Contains the collections of the Market Harborough Archaeological and Historical Society.
M.-F. 10-12.30, 1.30-5; Sa. 10-5.

SYMINGTON MUSEUM OF PERIOD CORSETRY
R. & W. H. Symington and Company Limited, P.O. Box 5, Market Harborough, Leicestershire
Company Museum. Corsetry since 1856. Evolution of the liberty bodice.
By appointment.

MARLBOROUGH

AVEBURY MANOR
near Marlborough, Wiltshire
House mainly 16th century. Furniture. Porcelain.
May-Aug., W.-M. 2-6. Apr. and Sept., Sa., Su. 2-6; Bank Holidays 10-6.

MEIGLE

MEIGLE MUSEUM
Meigle, Perth
25 sculptured monuments of the Celtic Christian period.
Apr.-Sept. Weekdays 9.30-7; Oct.-Mar. Weekdays 10-4.30. Closed Su.

MELBOURNE

MELBOURNE HALL
Melbourne, Derbyshire
Paintings. Furniture. Ceramics. Glass.
Hall and Gardens: early Apr. - end Sept. (including Easter and Bank Holidays) daily except M. and F., then Su. Oct. 1st and 2nd weeks, 2-6. Bank Holiday M. 11-6.

MELROSE

ABBOTSFORD HOUSE
Melrose, Roxburghshire
Home of Sir Walter Scott, containing many historical relics collected by him.
Late Mar. - end Oct. Weekdays 10-5; Su. 2-5.

MELROSE ABBEY MUSEUM
Melrose, Roxburghshire
In Commendator's House. Architectural and sculptural details and other items associated with the Abbey.
Apr.-Sept. Weekdays 9.30-7; Su. 2-7. Oct.-Mar. Weekdays 10-4.30; Su. 2-4.30.

MELTON MOWBRAY

STAPLEFORD PARK
nr. Melton Mowbray, Leicestershire
Miniature railway and miniature liners. Paintings. Tapestries, furniture. Staffordshire Portrait Figures.
Easter Su. and M., then May-Sept., W., Th., Su. also Spring Bank Holiday M. and Tu., and Late Summer Bank Holiday M., 2.30-6.30.

MERE

STOURHEAD
Stourton, nr. Mere, Wiltshire
House (1722). Chippendale furniture. Paintings, especially landscapes and portraits of members of the Hoare family.
House: *Easter Sa. - Sept., W. and Th., Sa., Su. and Bank Holidays. Mar. - Easter, Oct. and Nov., W., Sa. and Su. 2-6 or dusk if earlier. Closed Dec.-Feb.* Pleasure grounds: *daily 11-7 or dusk if earlier.*

MERTHYR TYDFIL

ART GALLERY AND MUSEUM
Cyfarthfa Castle, Merthyr Tydfil, Glamorgan
Collections include paintings, ceramics, coins and medals, silver and other art objects, natural history and local history. Welsh kitchen.
Weekdays 10-1, 2-6.30 (Oct.-Mar. 10-1, 2-5). Su. 2-5.

MIDHURST

RICHARD COBDEN COLLECTION
Dunford, Midhurst, Sussex
Portraits and library of Richard Cobden and family.
By appointment.

MILLPORT

ROBERTSON MUSEUM AND AQUARIUM
Marine Station, Millport, Isle of Cumbrae
Marine life of the Clyde Sea area.
Weekdays 9.30-12.30, 2-5. Closed Sa. during winter.

MONEYMORE

SPRINGHILL
Moneymore, County Derry, Northern Ireland
17th century house, with 18th-early 19th century additions. 18th-19th century paintings, furniture. Gun room. Costume collection.
Apr.-Sept., W.-M. 2-6.

MONMOUTH

NELSON MUSEUM
The Market Hall, Priory Street, Monmouth
Relics of Admiral Lord Nelson, his contemporaries and Lady Hamilton. Local history. Archives. Maps.
Apr.-Oct. Weekdays 10.15-1, 2.15-5.15 (July and Aug. 10-6). Su. July and Aug. 2.30-5.30. Easter and Whit Su. 2.30-5.30.

MONTROSE

MONTROSE MUSEUM
Panmure Place, Montrose, Angus
Regional collection of archaeological, historical, natural history and geological exhibits, including sculptured stones and collection of Scottish coins and medals.
Daily 10-1, 2.30-4.30.

MORETON-IN-MARSH

CHASTLETON HOUSE
near Moreton-in-Marsh, Oxfordshire
House (1603). Original furniture, tapestries.
M., Tu., Th.-Sa. 10.30-1, 2-5.30 (dusk in winter); Su. 2-5 (or dusk in winter).

MORWELLHAM

MORWELLHAM QUAY
Morwellham, nr. Tavistock, Devon
Museum of industrial archaeology; copper port of the 19th century with incline planes, harbours, quays and water wheels. Natural history.
Summer 10-7; Winter 10-dusk.

MUCH MARCLE

HELLEN'S
Much Marcle, Herefordshire
Manorial house (1292). Furniture of 16th and 17th centuries. 19th century carriages.
Easter Su. - Sept. Sa. and Su. and Bank Holidays, 2-6.

NARBERTH

BLACKPOOL MILL
Narberth, Pembrokeshire
19th century corn mill.
Apr.-Sept. Daily 2-6.

NEAR SAWREY

HILL TOP
Near Sawrey, nr. Hawkshead, Lancashire
Home of Beatrix Potter, with contemporary furnishings and

the original illustrations of her books.
Easter Sa. - Oct. 31, M.-Sa. 11-5.30; Su. 2-5.30.

NETHER ALDERLEY

ALDERLEY OLD MILL
Nether Alderley, Cheshire
15th century corn mill in use until 1939, and subsequently restored.
Apr.-Oct., W., Su. 2-5.

NETHER STOWEY

COLERIDGE COTTAGE
Nether Stowey, Somerset
Home of S. T. Coleridge from 1797-1800. Coleridge museum and relics.
Mar.-Oct. Daily (except F. and Sa.) 11-1, 2-5.

NEWARK-ON-TRENT

MUSEUM AND ART GALLERY
Appleton Gate, Newark-on-Trent, Nottinghamshire
Local archaeology and history. Natural history. Paintings.
Weekdays 10-1, 2-5; Su. (Apr.-Sept.) 2-5.

NEWBURY

NEWBURY BOROUGH MUSEUM
Wharf Street, Newbury, Berkshire
Local history and archaeology. Natural history.
Weekdays (except W.) Apr.-Sept. 10-12.30, 1.30-5. Oct.-Mar. 10-12.30, 1.30-4, W. 10-12.30.

NEWCASTLE-UNDER-LYME

NEWCASTLE-UNDER-LYME BOROUGH MUSEUM AND ART GALLERY
Brampton Park, Newcastle-under-Lyme, Staffordshire
Collections of local history including Royal charters. Natural history. Textiles. Geology. General science. Ceramics. 18th and 19th century English water-colours. Arab and Oriental collection.
Weekdays 10-1, 2-6; Su. (May-Sept.) 2-5.30.

NEWCASTLE-UPON-TYNE

THE BAGPIPE MUSEUM
The Black Gate, Newcastle-upon-Tyne, Northumberland, NE1 1RQ
Almost 100 sets of bagpipes, from Northumbria, Scotland and Ireland. Foreign pipes from France, Italy, Spain, India, Egypt, Greece and Bulgaria. Only known example of the English Shuttle Bagpipe. English and Scottish Border pipes. Recordings. Musical boxes. Photographs. Manuscripts. Paintings. 19th century Shepherd's Cottage Room, where the various stages of drone and chanter reed making can be seen. Tools and implements from a pipe maker's workshop.
M. 2-5; Tu.-Sa. 10-5 (10-4 Oct.-Mar.). Closed Su., Christmas Day, New Year's Day and Good F.

HIGHAM PLACE GALLERY
8 Higham Place, Newcastle-upon-Tyne, Northumberland
British water colour drawings, prints.
Weekdays 10-1, 2.30-6.

JOHN GEORGE JOICEY MUSEUM
City Road, Newcastle-upon-Tyne, Northumberland
Housed partly in the former Holy Jesus Hospital (history of Newcastle from Roman times to the present day) and partly in the medieval Austin Friars' Tower (arms and armour).
Weekdays 10-1, 2-6.

THE KEEP MUSEUM
St. Nicholas Street, Newcastle-upon-Tyne, Northumberland
The keep of the "New Castle" built by Henry II in 1170. Collections of medieval material.
By appointment.

LAING ART GALLERY AND MUSEUM
Higham Place, Newcastle-upon-Tyne, Northumberland
British paintings and water-colours, 17th century - onwards. Egyptian and Greek antiquities. Pottery and porcelain. Glass. Silver. Ironwork. Arms and armour. Costumes. Textiles. Local history.
Weekdays 10-6 (Tu. and Th. 10-8); Su. 2.30-5.30.

MUSEUM OF SCIENCE AND ENGINEERING
Exhibition Park, Great North Road, Newcastle-upon-Tyne, Northumberland
Engineering, shipbuilding, mining, transport, electrical and other industries, with special reference to the North East.
Summer: Weekdays 10-6 (Tu. and Th. 10-8); Su. 2.30-5.30. Winter: Weekdays 10-4.30; Su. 1.30-4.30.

PLUMMER TOWER
Croft Street, Newcastle-upon-Tyne, Northumberland
18th century period room and City archives.
Weekdays 10-1, 2.30-6.

THE ROYAL NORTHUMBERLAND FUSILIERS MUSEUM
The Armoury, Fenham Barracks, Newcastle-upon-Tyne 2, Northumberland
Uniforms, old arms, awards, campaign medals, regimental colours, pictures, trophies and souvenirs associated with the regiment.
M.-F. 9-4.30 or by appointment.

UNIVERSITY OF NEWCASTLE-UPON-TYNE
Border Forest Park Museum, Lewisburn, Kielder, Northumberland
Natural history, geology and human history of the Forest Park area.
Weekends and Bank Holidays from Easter-Sept. Daily during Aug.

UNIVERSITY OF NEWCASTLE-UPON-TYNE
Greek Museum, Percy Building, The Quadrangle, Newcastle-upon-Tyne, Northumberland
Collection of ancient Greek and Etruscan art, Minoan to Hellenistic times; vases, terracottas, bronzes, gems and armour.
M.-F. 10-5 and by appointment.

UNIVERSITY OF NEWCASTLE-UPON-TYNE
Hancock Museum, Barras Bridge, Newcastle-upon-Tyne, Northumberland
Natural history, especially British birds and of plant and animal fossils. Ethnographical section. Original drawings by Thomas Bewick.
Weekdays 10-5; Su. (Easter-Sept.) 2-5.

UNIVERSITY OF NEWCASTLE-UPON-TYNE
The Hatton Gallery, The Quadrangle, Newcastle-upon-Tyne, Northumberland
Collection of Italian and other paintings.
Weekdays 10-6.

UNIVERSITY OF NEWCASTLE-UPON-TYNE
Museum of Antiquities, The Quadrangle, Newcastle-upon-Tyne, Northumberland
Prehistoric, Roman and Anglo-Saxon antiquities, chiefly from Northumberland. Scale models of Hadrian's Wall and full scale reconstruction of a temple of Mithras.
Weekdays 10-5. Closed Good Friday, December 24-6 and New Year's Day.

UNIVERSITY OF NEWCASTLE-UPON-TYNE
Museum of the Department of Mining Engineering, Queen Victoria Road, Newcastle-upon-Tyne, Northumberland
Mine safety lamps and other exhibits illustrating history of mining. Water-colours of Northumberland and Durham mines, 1838-42, by T. H. Hair.
M.-F. 9-5.

NEWENT

THE FALCONRY CENTRE MUSEUM
Newent, Gloucestershire, GL18 1JJ
History of hawking. Various types of hoods from all over the world; other hawking equipment. Applications of falconry: hunting, sport, clearing birds from airfields. Hawking training methods. Copies and originals of old prints and pictures of hawing. Hawk speedometers. Photographs of birds of prey. Collection of eggs of raptors.
Daily ex. Tu., 10.30-5.30 (or dusk if earlier).

NEWPORT (ISLE OF WIGHT)

CARISBROOKE CASTLE MUSEUM
Newport, Isle of Wight
Isle of Wight County Museum - collection illustrating history of the island and also relics of Charles I. Contains the oldest organ in the country still in playing order. Working donkey wheel of 1857. Records of Marconi's experiments.
Mar., Apr. and Oct. Weekdays 9.30-5.30. May-Sept. Weekdays 9.30-7. Weekdays Nov.-Feb. 9.30-4. Su. Easter-Sept. 2-7.

NEWPORT (MONMOUTHSHIRE)

NEWPORT MUSEUM AND ART GALLERY
John Frost Square, Newport, Monmouthshire
Natural history. English water-colours. Roman remains from Venta Silurum (Caerwent). Pontypool Japan ware.
Weekdays 10-5.30.

NEWTONMORE

CLAN MACPHERSON HOUSE AND MUSEUM
Newtonmore, Inverness-shire
Clan relics and memorials, including Black Chanter, Green Banner and Charmed Sword.
Easter-Sept. Weekdays 10-12, 2-6.

NEWTOWN

NEWTOWN WOOLLEN INDUSTRY MUSEUM
Commercial Street, Newtown, Montgomeryshire
The process of wool from sheep to handloom. Newtown as a woollen town from c.1790 to 20th century.
Apr.-Sept. Tu.-Sa. 2-4.30.

THE ROBERT OWEN MEMORIAL MUSEUM
Broad Street, Newtown, Montgomeryshire
Books, documents, relics, relating to Robert Owen.
Daily 2-4.

NORTHAMPTON

ABINGTON MUSEUM
Abington Park, Northampton, Northamptonshire
Manor house (15th century, partly rebuilt 1745). Period rooms, including Victorian "street". Chinese ceramics. Ethnographical and natural history material.
Apr.-Sept. Weekdays 10-12.30, 2-6; Su. 2.30-5. Oct.-Mar. Weekdays 10-12.30, 2-5. Su. closed.

ALTHORP
Northampton, Northamptonshire
House (16th century, with alterations 1670, 1790 and 1877). European paintings. Portraits. Porcelain, both Oriental and European. 18th century furniture.
May, Su. only, then June-Sept., Su., Tu. and Th., also Easter Su. and M., Spring and Late Summer Bank Holidays, 2.30-6.

CASTLE ASHBY
Northampton, Northamptonshire
Elizabethan house with Inigo Jones (1635) front. Italian Renaissance, English 18th century and Dutch 17th century paintings. 17th century tapestries and furniture.
Good F. to Easter M., then May-Aug., Th., Sa. and Bank Holidays, also Su. June-Aug. 2-5.30.

CENTRAL MUSEUM AND ART GALLERY
Guildhall Road, Northampton, Northamptonshire
Collections of footwear through the ages. Cobbler's shop. Local archaeological material. English ceramics. Paintings. Water-colours.
M., Tu., W., F. 10-6; Th. and Sa. 10-8.

THE NORTHAMPTONSHIRE REGIMENT SERVICE MUSEUM
Gibraltar Barracks, Barrack Road, Northampton, Northamptonshire
Uniforms, old arms, awards, campaign medals, regimental colours, pictures, trophies and souvenirs associated with the regiment.
Tu.-Sa. 9.30-12.30, 2-4.30.

ROYAL PIONEER CORPS MUSEUM
Simpson Barracks, Wootton, Northampton, Northamptonshire
Uniforms, old arms, awards, campaign medals, regimental colours, pictures, trophies and souvenirs associated with the Corps.
M.-F. 9-5.

NORTH BERWICK

THE BURGH MUSEUM
The Old Public School, North Berwick, East Lothian
Archaeological and historical sections. Natural history.
May-Sept. Daily 10-1, 2-5.

NORTHENDEN

WYTHENSHAWE HALL
Northenden, Lancashire
17th century paintings, furniture. Local history. Royal Lancastrian pottery.
Nov.-Feb., M.-Sa. 10-4; Su. 2-4. May-Aug., M.-Sa. 10-8; Su. 2-8. Mar.-Apr., Sept.-Oct., M.-Sa. 10-6; Su. 2-6. Closed Good F. and Christmas Day.

NORWICH

BRIDEWELL MUSEUM
Bridewell Alley, St. Andrew's Street, Norwich, NOR 02H, Norfolk
Scientific instruments. Weights and measures. Timekeeping. Milling. Engineering. Transport. Leather. Textiles.

Building materials. Agricultural implements.
Weekdays 10-5.

LAWRENCE SCOTT AND ELECTROMOTORS LIMITED
Permanent Company Exhibition, Norwich, N0R 85A, Norfolk
Electric motors; control gear.
By appointment.

NORWICH CASTLE MUSEUM
Norwich, Norfolk
Paintings and water-colours (particularly of the Norwich School). Local archaeology and natural history. Dioramas.
Weekdays 10-5; Su. 2.30-5.

THE ROYAL NORFOLK REGIMENT MUSEUM
Britannia Barracks, Norwich, Norfolk
Uniforms, old arms, awards, campaign medals, regimental colours, pictures, trophies and souvenirs associated with the regiment.
M.-F. 9.30-4.30. Other times by appointment.

ST. PETER HUNGATE CHURCH MUSEUM
Princes Street, Norwich, Norfolk
15th century church used for display of ecclesiastical art and East Anglian antiquities.
Weekdays 10-5.

STRANGERS' HALL
Charing Cross, Norwich, Norfolk
Late medieval mansion furnished as a museum of 16th-19th century urban domestic life.
Weekdays 10-5.

NOTTINGHAM

INDUSTRIAL MUSEUM
Wollaton Hall Stables, Nottingham, Nottinghamshire
Nottingham industry, with special reference to lace-making.
Apr.-Sept. Th. and Sa. 10-7. Oct.-Mar. Th. and Sa. 10-5.30. Nov.-Feb. Th. and Sa. 10-4.30. Mar.-Oct. Su. 2-5. Nov.-Feb. Su. 2-4.30.

NATURAL HISTORY MUSEUM
Wollaton Hall, Wollaton Park, Nottingham, Nottinghamshire
In Elizabethan mansion. Zoology. Botany. Geology. British and foreign herbaria. Cycling history room.
Apr.-Sept. M.-Sa. 10-7. Oct. and Mar. M.-Sa. 10-5.30. Nov.-Feb. M.-Sa. 10-4.30. Su. (summer) 2-5; (winter) 1.30-4.30. Closed Good Fri. and Christmas Day.

NEWSTEAD ABBEY
Linby, nr. Nottingham, Nottinghamshire
Byron relics, pictures and furniture, manuscripts and first editions.
Good F. to Sept., Su. and Bank Holidays, 2-6.30. Other days: tours at 2, 3, 4, 5. On application during winter.

NOTTINGHAM CITY MUSEUM AND ART GALLERY
The Castle, Nottingham, Nottinghamshire
Ceramics (emphasising medieval earthenware, Nottingham stoneware and Wedgwood). Glass, Silver. Woodwork. Ironwork. Costumes. Textiles and lace. 17th and 18th century vehicles. Nottingham medieval alabaster carving. Paintings and drawings (mainly English), 14th century to present day. Works by the Nottingham-born artists Thomas and Paul Sanby, and R. P. Bonington.
Apr.-Sept. Weekdays 10-6.45 (10-5.45 on F.); Su. 2-4.45. Oct.-Mar. Weekdays 10-dusk. Su. 2-4.45.

THE SHERWOOD FORESTERS MUSEUM
The Castle, Nottingham, Nottinghamshire
Uniforms, old arms, awards, campaign medals, regimental colours, pictures, trophies and souvenirs associated with the regiment.
Apr.-Sept. Weekdays 10-6.45 (10-5.45 F.); Su. 2-4.45. Oct.-Mar. Weekdays 10-dusk; Su. 2-4.45.

WOLLATON HALL
Nottingham, Nottinghamshire
Late Elizabethan Renaissance architecture. Furniture. Natural history.
Apr.-Sept. 10-7; Su. 2-5. Oct.-Mar. 10-dusk; Su. 2-5. Closed Good F. and Christmas Day.

NUNEATON

NUNEATON MUSEUM AND ART GALLERY
Riversley Park, Nuneaton, Warwickshire
Prehistory archaeology (including Roman and medieval Nuneaton). Geology. Mining. Ethnography and anthropology. Paintings. Engravings. Coins and medals. George Eliot memorabilia.
M.-F. 12-7; Sa. and Su. 10-7 (closes 5, Dec.-Feb.).

OAKHAM

RUTLAND COUNTY MUSEUM
Catmos Street, Oakham, Rutland
Archaeology. Local history. Craft tools. Agricultural implements.
Oct.-Apr., Weekdays (except M.) 10-12, 2-4. May-Sept. Weekdays (except M.) 10-12, 2-5; Su. 2-5.

OLDHAM

ART GALLERY AND MUSEUM
Union Street, Oldham, Lancashire
Early English water-colours. 19th and 20th century British paintings. British glass. Oriental collection.
M.-F. 10-7; Sa. 10-5.

LOCAL INTEREST CENTRE
Greaves Street, Oldham, Lancashire
Local history. Environmental problems.
M.-F. 10-7; Sa. 10-5.

WERNETH PARK STUDY CENTRE
Werneth Park, Frederick Street, Oldham, Lancashire
Natural history.
M.-Th. 1.30-9; F. and Sa. 9-5.

OLD WARDEN

THE SHUTTLEWORTH COLLECTION
The Aerodrome, Old Warden, Biggleswade, Bedfordshire
Early civil and military aircraft and motor cars. Blériot Type XI (1909). Deperdussin (1910). Replica of Avro Triplan (1909). Blackburn monoplane (1912). English Daimler (1857). Bicycles. Motor cycles. Fire engines.
Daily 10-5. Closed Christmas. Flying demonstrations on last Sundays of Mar., Apr., June, July, Aug. and Sept. Check locally.

OLLERTON

THORESBY HALL
near Ollerton, Nottinghamshire
Mansion (1864). Furniture. Paintings. Toy and model theatres.
Good F. - Sept. 30, Su. 2.30-6. Bank Holiday Su., M. 12.30-6. Tu. following Bank Holiday, W., Th., Sa. 2.30-6.

OLNEY

COWPER AND NEWTON MUSEUM
Market Place, Olney, Buckinghamshire
Personal belongings of William Cowper and Rev. John Newton. Manuscripts and items of local interest.
Tu.-Sa. 10-12, 2-5.

OXFORD

ASHMOLEAN MUSEUM OF ART AND ARCHAEOLOGY
Beaumont Street, Oxford, Oxfordshire
British, European, Mediterranean, Egyptian and Near Eastern Archaeology. Italian, Dutch, Flemish, French and English paintings. Old Master and modern drawings, water-colours and prints. Miniatures. European ceramics. Sculpture and bronzes. English silver. Applied art. Engraved portraits. Coins and medals of all countries and periods. Casts from the antique. Chinese and Japanese porcelain, painting and lacquer. Chinese bronzes. Tibetan art. Indian sculpture and painting. Islamic pottery and metalwork.
Weekdays 10-4; Su. 2-4. Closed at Christmas and Easter. Open Easter M.

CHRIST CHURCH LIBRARY
Peckwater Quadrangle, Oxford, Oxfordshire
Statuary. Music. Carrolliana. Manuscripts and printed books.
M.-F. during most part of University vacations, 2-4.30.

CHRIST CHURCH PICTURE GALLERY
Canterbury Quadrangle, Oxford, Oxfordshire
Old master paintings and drawings.
Weekdays 2-4.30. Closed Dec. 24 - Jan. 1 and week before Easter Su.

MUSEUM OF THE HISTORY OF SCIENCE
Broad Street, Oxford, Oxfordshire
Collection of early scientific instruments (astrolabes, armillary spheres, sundials, microscopes, astronomical, medical and chemical apparatus).
M.-F. 10.30-1, 2.30-4; Sa. 10.30-1.

MUSEUM OF MODERN ART
Pembroke Street, Oxford, Oxfordshire
Contemporary British painting, prints and sculpture.
Tu.-Sa. 10-6; Su. 3-5.

OXFORD UNIVERSITY MUSEUM
Parks Road, Oxford, Oxfordshire
Zoological, entomological, geological and mineralogical collections of the University.
Weekdays 10-4.

PITT RIVERS MUSEUM
Parks Road, Oxford, Oxfordshire
Ethnology and prehistoric archaeology of the peoples of the world, arranged typologically. Musical instruments.
M.-Sa. 2-4.

THE ROTUNDA
Grove House, 44 Iffley Turn, Oxford, Oxfordshire
Early dolls' houses, 1700-1885 and contents (furniture, silver, dinner services, dolls, etc.).
May - mid. Sept. Su. 2.15-5.15 and other times for 6 persons or more by written appointment.

PADIHAM

GAWTHORPE HALL
Padiham, Lancashire
Manor house (17th century). Kay-Shuttleworth collection of lace and embroidery.
Easter-Sept., M., W., Sa. 2-6.

PAIGNTON

TORBAY AIRCRAFT MUSEUM
Barton Pines, nr. Paignton, Devon
Aircraft dating from 1929, with documents, photographs, medals and uniforms illustrating history of aviation.
Daily 10-6.

PAISLEY

PAISLEY MUSEUM AND ART GALLERIES
High Street, Paisley, Renfrewshire
Paisley shawls. Renfrewshire history, geology and natural history. Scottish paintings. Ceramics.
Weekdays 10-5 (10-8 Tu. and 10-6 Sa.).

PEEBLES

CHAMBERS INSTITUTION
High Street, Peebles, Peeblesshire
Local flora, fauna, geology. Local history.
Weekdays 10-7 (10-12 W.).

PEMBROKE DOCK

PEMBROKESHIRE MOTOR MUSEUM
Pembroke Dock, Pembrokeshire
Collection of mechanical road transport.
Easter-Sept. Daily 10-6.

PENARTH

TURNER HOUSE GALLERY
A branch art gallery of the National Museum of Wales
Plymouth Road, Penarth, Glamorgan
16th-20th century paintings. Applied art.
Weekdays (except M.) 11-12.45, 2-5; Su. 2-5. Bank Holiday M. as weekdays.

PENICUIK

SCOTTISH INFANTRY DEPOT (GLENCORSE) MUSEUM
Glencorse Barracks, Penicuik, Midlothian
Uniforms, old arms, awards, campaign medals, regimental colours, pictures, trophies and souvenirs associated with the Scottish Infantry regiments.
M.-F. 9-4.30 or by appointment.

PENZANCE

PENZANCE NATURAL HISTORY AND ANTIQUARIAN MUSEUM
Penlee Park, Penzance, Cornwall
Archaeological, antiquarian and tin mining exhibits.
Daily 12.30-4.30.

PERTH

THE BLACK WATCH (R.H.R.) SERVICE MUSEUM
Balhousie Castle, Perth, Perthshire
Uniforms, old arms, awards, campaign medals, regimental colours, pictures, trophies and souvenirs associated with the regiment.
M.-F. 10-12, 2-5; Su. 2-5, May-Sept.

PERTH ART GALLERY AND MUSEUM
George Street, Perth, Perthshire
Paintings, mainly of the Scottish School. Regional natural history. Ethnographical, geological and antiquarian exhibits.
M.-F. 10-1, 2-5 (also 6-8 W. and F.); Sa. 10-1, 2-5; Su. 2-4.

SCONE PALACE
Perth, Perthshire
Collections of French furniture, china, ivories and Vernis Martin vases and objets d'art.
Apr. 22- Oct. 8, M.-Sa. 10-6; Su. 2-6.

PETERBOROUGH

PETERBOROUGH MUSEUM AND ART GALLERY
Priestgate, Peterborough, Huntingdonshire
Local archaeology, history and natural history. Paintings. Ceramics.
Weekdays 10-1, 2-5 (M. 2-5).

PETERHEAD

ARBUTHNOT MUSEUM
St. Peter Street, Peterhead, Aberdeen
Local history. Whaling. Arctic exploration. Coins.
Weekdays 10-12, 2-5.

PETERSFIELD

UPPARK
South Harting, nr. Petersfield, Sussex
House (1690). Interior decoration, including wallpapers, and furnishings unaltered since 18th century.
Apr.-Sept. W., Th., Su. and Bank Holiday M. 2-6.

PETWORTH

PETWORTH HOUSE
Petworth, Sussex
Paintings. Carvings by Grinling Gibbons.
Apr.-Oct. W., Th., Sa. and Bank Holiday M., 2-6.

PLYMOUTH

BUCKLAND ABBEY
Plymouth, Devon
Home of Sir Richard Grenville, bought by Sir Francis Drake. Drake's relics. Ships' models.
Good F. - Sept. Weekdays 11-6; Su. 2-6. Oct. - Good F., W., Sa. and Su. 3-5.

CITY MUSEUM AND ART GALLERY
Drake Circus, Plymouth, Devon
Paintings. English porcelain. English and Italian drawings, Reynolds family portraits. Local and natural history. Ships' models.
Weekdays 10-6 (10-8 F.); Su. 3-5.

ELIZABETHAN HOUSE
32 New Street, Plymouth, Devon
16th century house in Plymouth's historic quarter, with period furniture.
Weekdays 10-1, 2.15-6 (dusk in winter); Su. (Summer only) 3-5.

SALTRAM HOUSE
Plymouth, Devon
George II house. Two rooms by Robert Adam. Furniture. Paintings (some by Reynolds). 18th century plasterwork and woodwork.
Apr. - mid. Oct. Daily 2-6.

POCKLINGTON

BURNBY HALL GARDENS
Pocklington, Yorkshire
Hunting trophies. African, Indian art and ethnography.
Apr.-Sept. Gardens daily 2-6. Stewart Collection: Weekends 2-6 (Summer daily).

POLEGATE

WILMINGTON PRIORY MUSEUM OF AGRICULTURAL IMPLEMENTS
Near Polegate, Sussex
Agricultural history.
M.-Th. 10-6; Su. (May-Sept.) 2-5.

PONTEFRACT

CASTLE MUSEUM
Pontefract Castle, Pontefract, Yorkshire
Roman pottery. Medieval weapons and armour. Siege coins. Local history.
Weekdays 9-dusk; Su. 10-dusk.

THE KING'S OWN YORKSHIRE LIGHT INFANTRY SERVICE MUSEUM
Wakefield Road, Pontefract, Yorkshire
Uniforms, old arms, awards, campaign medals, regimental colours, pictures, trophies and souvenirs associated with the regiment.
M.-F. 9-12, 2-4.

POOLE

OLD TOWN HOUSE
Scaplen's Court, High Street (adjoining Quay), Poole, Dorset
Poole's first Guildhall and headquarters of the pre-Reformation "Guild of St. George". Exhibits of local historic interest - china, pottery, ships and shipping, industrial archaeology. Bronze-age dug-out canoe, found in Poole Harbour in 1964.
Mid. May- Sept. Daily (inc. Su. and Bank Holidays) 10-7.

POOLE MUSEUM
South Road, Poole, Dorset
Local Roman antiquities, pottery and coins. Local fauna (specialising in sea-birds). Maritime history. Local pottery and trade tokens. Arms and armour. Local history.
Weekdays 10-5.

PORT ERIN

MARINE BIOLOGICAL STATION
Port Erin, Isle of Man
Marine biology.
Weekdays 10-5 (Su. in summer 2-5).

PORTHMADOG

FESTINIOG RAILWAY MUSEUM
Harbour Station, Porthmadog, Caernarvonshire
Museum illustrating the past history and present activity of the Festiniog Railway. Exhibits include early rail specimens, slate wagon No. 79 and the unique Hearse Van.
Summer: Daily 9-9.30. Winter: Daily 9-5.30.

PORTLAND

PORTLAND ISLAND MUSEUM
Avice's Cottage, Wakeham, nr. Easton, Dorset
Local history. Natural history.
Summer 10-5; Winter, M., W., Th. and Sa. 10-5. Closed Su.

PORTMEIRION

PORTMEIRION
Penrhyndeudraeth, Cardigan Bay, Merionethshire
This architectural museum ranging from 17th century to present day, includes barbican gate-house, town hall, campanile, lighthouse, cloisters, hotel, shops, cafe and various re-erected historic buildings. Buildings of all periods collected by architect Clough Williams-Ellis.
Daily 10-7, Easter-Oct.

PORTSMOUTH

CITY MUSEUM AND ART GALLERY
Alexandra Road, Portsmouth, Hampshire
English furniture, pottery and glass. Contemporary and topographical paintings and prints.
Nov.-Feb. Daily 10-5. Mar., Apr., Sept. and Oct. 10-6. May-Aug. Daily 10-9.

CUMBERLAND HOUSE MUSEUM AND ART GALLERY
Eastern Parade, Southsea, Portsmouth, Hampshire
Natural history. Collection of English furniture.
Nov.-Feb. Daily 10-4; Mar., Apr., Sept., Oct. Daily 10-6. May-Aug. Daily 10-9.

DICKENS' BIRTHPLACE MUSEUM
393 Commercial Road, Mile End, Portsmouth, Hampshire
The house where Charles Dickens was born in 1812. Dickensiana including personal items, holograph letters, first editions, prints and portraits.
Nov.-Feb. Daily 10-4. Mar., Apr., Sept., Oct. Daily 10-6; May-Aug. Daily 10-9.

NEW BEAM ENGINE HOUSE
Eastney, Portsmouth, Hampshire
Two Boulton and Watt Reciprocal Beam Engines (1887). Restored Beam Engine House. Pumps.
Sa. Su. 9-5.

PORTSMOUTH ROYAL NAVAL MUSEUM
HM Naval Base, Portsmouth, Hampshire
Nelson's personal possessions, furniture, crockery, miniatures. Ships' figureheads, prints, paintings, ship models, navigational instruments and documents relating to Nelson's time. Panorama of the Battle of Trafalgar by W. L. Wylie.
M.-Sa. 10.30-5.30; Su. 1-5.

SOUTHSEA CASTLE
Clarence Esplanade, Portsmouth, Hampshire
Local and military history of Portsmouth. Archaeology.
Nov.-Feb. Daily 10-4. Mar., Apr., Sept., Oct. Daily 10-6. May-Aug. Daily 10-9.

PORT SUNLIGHT

THE LADY LEVER ART GALLERY
Port Sunlight, Cheshire
Paintings, water colours, engravings and miniatures, mainly of the British School. Antique, Renaissance and British sculpture. Chinese pottery and porcelain. Wedgwood ware. English furniture.
Weekdays 10-5; Su. 2-5.

PRESTON

THE EAST LANCASHIRE REGIMENT SERVICE MUSEUM
Fulwood Barracks, Preston, Lancashire
Uniforms, old arms, awards, campaign medals, regimental colours, pictures, trophies and souvenirs associated with the regiment.
By appointment only. M.-F. 9.30-12, 2-4.

HARRIS MUSEUM AND ART GALLERY
Market Square, Preston, PR1 2PP, Lancashire
Ceramics. Glass. Costumes. Dolls and games. Colour prints. Victoriana, including collections of scent bottles, card cases. Local history and archaeology. Devis Family of Painters (pictures and relics); 19th and 20th century paintings, drawings, sculpture. Prints.
Weekdays 10-5.

THE LANCASTRIAN BRIGADE MUSEUM
Fulwood Barracks, Preston, Lancashire
Uniforms, old arms, awards, campaign medals, regimental colours, pictures, trophies and souvenirs associated with the Brigade.
M.-F. 9-12; by appointment 2-4.

THE LOYAL REGIMENT (NL) SERVICE MUSEUM
Fulwood Barracks, Preston, Lancashire
Uniforms, old arms, awards, campaign medals, regimental colours, pictures, trophies and souvenirs associated with the regiment.
M.-F. 9-12, 2-4.30 or by appointment.

PRESTWICH

HEATON HALL
Prestwich, nr. Manchester, Lancashire
House (1772), with some original Etruscan decorations. Organ by Samuel Green. 18th century furniture. Paintings.
Nov.-Feb. Weekdays 10-4; Su. 2-4; May-Aug. Weekdays 10-8, Su. 2-8. Mar., Apr., Sept. and Oct. Weekdays 10-6, Su. 2-6. Closed Good F., Christmas Day.

PULBOROUGH

PARHAM
Pulborough, Sussex
Elizabethan, Jacobean and Georgian portraits, furniture and needlework.
Easter Su. - early Oct., Su., W., Th. and Bank Holidays 2-5.30.

PURSE CAUNDLE

PURSE CAUNDLE MANOR
Purse Caundle, nr. Sherborne, Dorset
Medieval manor house. Period furniture.
All the year, W., Th., Su. and Bank Holidays, 2-5.

RADCLIFFE

RADCLIFFE LOCAL HISTORY MUSEUM
Stand Lane, Radcliffe, Lancashire
History of Radcliffe and district from prehistoric times to the present day.
By appointment M.-F. 9-8; Sa. 9-5.

RAVENGLASS

MUNCASTER CASTLE
Ravenglass, Cumberland
Seat of the Pennington family since 13th century. 16th and 17th century furniture, pictures and embroidery. Porcelain. Tapestries.
Grounds: *Easter Sa. to end June, Daily, then July-Aug. W., Th., Su. and Bank Holiday 1-6.* Castle: *Easter Sa. - Sept., W., Th., Sa., Su. and Bank Holiday 2-5.*

RAWTENSTALL

MUSEUM AND ART GALLERY
Whitaker Park, Rawtenstall, Lancashire
Fine arts. Natural history. Bygones.
Weekdays 2-dusk; Sa. 10-5.

READING

COLE MUSEUM OF ZOOLOGY
University of Reading, Whiteknights Park, Reading, Berkshire.
Specialist collection for teaching purposes. Dissections, skeletons and models.
By appointment.

MUSEUM AND ART GALLERY
Blagrave Street, Reading, Berkshire
Natural history. Local archaeology. Roman collection from Silchester. Prehistoric and medieval metalwork. Delft ware.
Weekdays 10-5.30.

MUSEUM OF ENGLISH RURAL LIFE
Whiteknights Park, University of Reading, Reading, Berkshire
National collection of material relating to the history of the English countryside, including agriculture, crafts, domestic utensils and village life.
Tu.-Sa. 10-1, 2-4.30. Closed Su., M. and Bank Holidays.

MUSEUM OF GREEK ARCHAEOLOGY (FACULTY OF LETTERS)
University of Reading, Whiteknights Park, Reading, Berkshire
Greek antiquities, mainly pottery.
By appointment.

THE ROYAL BERKSHIRE REGIMENT
Brock Barracks, Reading, Berkshire
Uniforms, old arms, awards, campaign medals, regimental colours, pictures, trophies and souvenirs associated with the regiment.
By appointment only.

REDHILL

ROYAL EARLSWOOD HOSPITAL MUSEUM
Redhill, Surrey
History of the Hospital, with sections dealing with early history and development, finance, elections, medical and nursing, education, training and occupation, entertainment, building, farm and engineering.
M.-F. 9-5 by appointment with the Hon. Curator.

REDRUTH

TOLGUS TIN
Portreath Road, Redruth, Cornwall
Working Cornish tin streams. 12-headed set Cornish stamps, driven by water-wheel. Round frames; rag frames; dipper wheels. water-wheels.
M.-F. 10-5.30; also Su. in summer. Closed Christmas Day, Boxing Day and Good F.

REIGATE

HOLMESDALE NATURAL HISTORY CLUB MUSEUM
14 Croydon Road, Reigate, Surrey
Collection of British birds, insects, plants, fossils, minerals and mammals.
By appointment.

REPTON

REPTON SCHOOL MUSEUM
Repton, Derbyshire
Collections illustrate history of Repton village and Repton School.
By appointment.

RIBCHESTER

RIBCHESTER MUSEUM OF ROMAN ANTIQUITIES
Ribchester, Lancashire
Remains from the Roman site of Bremetennacum, including an excavated area adjoining the museum revealing part of the Granaries, North Wall and Gateway.
May-Aug. Weekdays 2-5.30. Sept.-Nov. and Feb.-Apr. Weekdays (except F.) 2-5. Closed 1st week in Oct. Dec. and Jan. Sa. 2-5 only for parties by prior arrangement.

RICHBOROUGH

RICHBOROUGH CASTLE
Richborough, Kent
Objects found during excavation of the site. Roman pottery, coins and other small objects.
Mar. and Oct. Weekdays 9.30-5.30; Su. 2-5.30. Apr. Daily 9.30-5.30. May-Sept. Daily 9.30-7. Nov.-Feb. Weekdays 9.30-4; Su. 2-4.

RICHMOND

THE GREEN HOWARDS SERVICE MUSEUM
Gallowgate, Richmond, Yorkshire
Uniforms, old arms, awards, campaign medals, regimental colours, pictures, trophies and souvenirs associated with the regiment.
Weekdays 9-12, 2-5; Su. 2-4.30.

RIPON

NEWBY HALL
Ripon, Yorkshire
Adam house. Gobelin tapestries. Statuary. Furniture. Chamber pots.
Easter Sa. - mid. Oct. House: *W., Th., Sa. and Su., also Bank Holiday M. and Tu. 2-6.30.* Gardens: *Daily 2-7.*

ROCHDALE

ART GALLERY
Esplanade, Rochdale, Lancashire
Paintings and water-colours by British artists.
M.-F. 10-8; Sa. 10-5; Su. 2.30-5.

ROCHDALE CO-OPERATIVE MUSEUM
Toad Lane, Rochdale, Lancashire
The original store of the Rochdale Co-operative Pioneers containing documents, pictures and other material of British and international co-operative interest.
By appointment.

ROCHESTER

ROCHESTER PUBLIC MUSEUM
Eastgate House, Rochester, Kent
Local history and natural history, archaeology, costumes, manuscripts, coins, local bygones. Fine collection of clocks. Charles Dickens chalet and relics. Large models of ships and models of seaplanes.
Daily (except F.) 2-5.30.

ROTHERHAM

ROTHERHAM CORPORATION DEPARTMENT OF TRADING STANDARDS
Weights and Measures Office, Station Road, Rotherham, Yorkshire
Weighing and measuring equipment.
M.-F. 8.30-5.30.

ROTHERHAM MUSEUM AND ART GALLERY
Clifton Park, Rotherham, Yorkshire
Antiquities from Roman forts at Templebrough. Gem stones and jewellery. Rockingham porcelain. Natural history.
Apr.-Sept. Weekdays (excluding F.) 10-6 (10-8 Th.); Su. 2.30-5. Oct.-Mar. Weekdays (excluding F.) 10-5; Su. 2.30-4.30.

ROTHESAY

BUTESHIRE NATURAL HISTORY SOCIETY MUSEUM
Stuart Street, Rothesay, Bute
Collections of the natural history, archaeology, geology and history of the county of Bute.
Apr.-Oct. Weekdays 10.30-12.30, 2.30-4.30 (also Su. June-Sept. 2.30-4.30). Nov.-Mar. Weekdays 2.30-4.30.

RUDDINGTON

RUDDINGTON AND DISTRICT LOCAL HISTORY SOCIETY VILLAGE MUSEUM
The Hermitage, Wilford Road, Ruddington, Nottinghamshire
Local history and archaeology. Material from Iron Age, Roman and medieval sites. 18th-20th century domestic and agricultural bygones.
The Society is also responsible for the Museum of Framework Knitting in Chapel Street, Ruddington.
Tu. 10.30-12.30. First F. in each month: 7.30-9 p.m. Other times by arrangement.

RUFFORD

RUFFORD OLD HALL
Rufford, nr. Ormskirk, Lancashire
Half-timbered hall with 15th century screen. Local history. Furniture. Applied art.
Weekdays (except M.), including Bank Holiday M. and Good F., 12-8 or dusk if earlier. Su. 1-8 or dusk if earlier. Closed Th. in Dec. and Jan.

RUGBY

STANFORD HALL
nr. Rugby, Leicestershire
Paintings. Furniture. 1898 Flying Machine. Motor Cycle and Car Museum. Kitchen utensils.
Easter Su. - end Sept. Th., Sa. and Su. 2.30-6. Also Easter, Spring and Late Summer Bank Holiday M. and Tu., 12-6.

RUGELEY

BLITHFIELD HALL
nr. Rugeley, Staffordshire
Stuart relics. Georgian costumes. Toy museum. Collection of coaches. Needlework figures. Toy and model theatres.
Good F. to early Oct., Good F., W., Th., Sa. and Su. 2.30-6, also Easter, Spring and Late Summer Bank Holiday M. 12-7, Tu. 2.30-6.

RUNCORN

THE SHAW MUSEUM
Cross Street, Runcorn, Cheshire
Pictures and photographs of Runcorn. Local history and archaeology.
Tu. and Th. 2-5; Sa. 10-12.

RUSHOLME

PLATT HALL
Rusholme, nr. Manchester, Lancashire
English Costumes, 17th century - present day.
Nov.-Feb. Weekdays 10-4, Su. 2-4. May-Aug. Weekdays 10-8, Su. 2-8. Mar., Apr., Sept. and Oct. Weekdays 10-6, Su. 2-6. Closed Good Friday and Christmas Day.

RYE

RYE MUSEUM
Ypres Tower, Rye, Sussex
Local history collections housed in a 13th century tower. Medieval pottery from the Rye kilns. Cinque Ports material, Victoriana.
Easter - mid. Oct. Weekdays 10.30-1, 2.15-5.30; Su. 11.30-1, 2.15-5.30.

RYHOPE

RYHOPE PUMPING STATION AND MUSEUM
Ryhope, Sunderland, County Durham
History of pumping and water supply. The Pumping Station dates from 1865 and contains two double compound rotative engines, with Watts parallel motion and centrifugal over speed cut-outs.
Apr. 1 - Sept. 30 Sa. and Su. 10-6. Other times by appointment.

ST. ALBANS

CITY MUSEUM
Hatfield Road, St. Albans, Hertfordshire
County archaeological and natural history collections. Biology. Geology. Tools to illustrate local crafts and trades. 19th century glass and pottery.
Summer: Weekdays 10-5. Winter: Weekdays 10-5 (closed M. and Tu.).

CLOCK TOWER
Market Place, St. Albans, Hertfordshire
Erected 1402-11. The tower stands 77 ft. high with five storeys. Display of medieval pottery and glass. Prints of the history of the Tower and the City.
Summer: M.-Sa. 10-5.30; Su. 2-5.30. Winter: M.-Sa. 10-4; Su. 2-4.

VERULAMIUM MUSEUM
St. Michael's, St. Albans, Hertfordshire
On the site of the Roman city of Verulamium and houses all the material from the Roman and Belgic cities, including several of the finest mosaics in Britain, one of which is preserved in situ in the Hypocaust annexe.
Summer: Weekdays 10-5.30; Su. 2-5.30. Winter: Weekdays 10-4; Su. 2-4.

ST. ANDREWS

ST. ANDREWS CATHEDRAL MUSEUM
St. Andrews Cathedral and Priory, St. Andrews, Fife
Collection of early Christian and medieval monuments, also pottery, glass work and other relics discovered on the site.
Apr.-Sept. Daily 9.30-7 (Su. 2-7). Oct.-Mar. Daily 10-4.30 (Su. 2-4.30).

ST. FAGANS

WELSH FOLK MUSEUM
St. Fagans, Glamorgan
The Castle, a 16th-century house within curtain wall of 13th century castle, the re-erected buildings and folk life exhibits, illustrate the pattern of the social structure of Wales, especially in rural areas.
Apr.-Sept. Weekdays 11-7; Su. 2.30-7. Oct.-Mar. Weekdays 11-5; Su. 2.30-5. Closed M. except Bank Holiday M.

ST. HELENS

PILKINGTON GLASS MUSEUM
Pilkington Brothers Limited, Prescot Road, St. Helens, Lancashire
History of glass. Evolution of glass making techniques.
M.-F. 10-5 (W. Mar.-Oct. 10-9); Sa. and Su. 2-4.30.

PUBLIC ART GALLERY AND MUSEUM
Central Library, St. Helens, Lancashire
British birds. Corals. Local history and manufactures.
Daily 10-5.

ST. IVES

BARNES MUSEUM OF CINEMATOGRAPHY
Fore Street, St. Ives, Cornwall
Cinematography; photographic processes.
June-Sept. Weekdays 11-5.

NORRIS LIBRARY AND MUSEUM
The Broadway, St. Ives, Huntingdonshire
Local collections. Prehistory to bygones. Local literature.
M., W., F. and Sa. 10-12, 2-4. Tu. 10-12. Su. 2-4. Closed Th.

SAFFRON WALDEN

SAFFRON WALDEN MUSEUM
Museum Street, Saffron Walden, Essex
Local archaeology, geology and natural history, bygones, ceramics and glass. Ethnology.
Winter: Weekdays 11-1, 2-4. Summer: Weekdays 11-1, 2-5; Su. 2.30-5.

SALCOME

SHARPITOR
Salcombe, Devon
Local history.
Apr. - mid. Oct. Daily (except Sa.), 11-1, 2-6.

SALFORD

MUSEUM AND ART GALLERY
The Crescent, Peel Park, Salford, Lancashire
L. S. Lowry Collection of paintings; "Lark Hill Place" (a 19th century 'street').
Weekdays 10-6 (10-5 Oct.-Mar.); Su. 2-5. Closed Good F., Christmas Day, Boxing Day and New Year's Day.

SCIENCE MUSEUM
Buile Hill Park, Salford, Lancashire
"Buile Hill No. 1 Pit", Coal Mining exhibits. Natural history.
Weekdays 10-6 (10-5 Oct.-Mar.); Su. 2-5 (Apr.-Sept.) Closed Good Fr., Christmas Day, Boxing Day and New Year's Day.

SALISBURY

SALISBURY AND SOUTH WILTSHIRE MUSEUM
St. Ann Street, Salisbury, Wiltshire
Natural and social history of Salisbury and south Wiltshire in all periods. Models of Stonehenge and Old Sarum. Local guild and craft relics, pottery and costumes. Archaeology.
Weekdays Oct.-Apr. 10-4; May-Sept. 10-5.

WILTON HOUSE
Salisbury, Wiltshire
In present form work of Inigo Jones (c.1650) and James Wyatt (1810). Paintings. Kent and Chippendale furniture. Collection of 19th century model soldiers.
Apr.-Sept. Tu.-Sa. and Bank Holidays 11-6; Su. 2-6.

SALTCOATS

NORTH AYRSHIRE MUSEUM
Kirkgate, Saltcoats, Ayrshire
History, industry and life in North Ayrshire.
Summer: Weekdays 10-9; Su. 2-5. Winter: Sa. 11-5.

SANDFORD ORCAS

THE MANOR HOUSE
Sandford Orcas, Dorset
Tudor mansion furnished with antiques, period furniture, pictures, silver, glass, rugs and china.
Mid. March - end Oct. Daily 11-5; end Oct. to mid. March F., Sa. and Su. 11-4 or by appointment.

SANDOWN

MUSEUM OF ISLE OF WIGHT GEOLOGY
High Street, Sandown, Isle of Wight
Fossils from Secondary and Tertiary strata of the Isle of Wight.
Apr.-Oct. Weekdays (except W.) 10-1, 2-5.30. Oct.-Mar. M.-F. (except W.) 2-4; Sa. 10-12, 2-4.

SANDRINGHAM

THE SANDRINGHAM ESTATE MUSEUM
Estate Office, Sandringham, Norfolk
Collection of big game heads and trophies. Local archaeology. Cars belonging to British monarchs, including a 1900 Daimler Tonneau.
April, May and Sept.: Tu., W., Th. 11-5. June, July, Aug.: Tu., W., Th., F. 11-5. Easter M., Apr. 23, Spring Bank Holiday, May 28, Late Summer Bank Holiday, Aug. 27, 11-5. Closed July 24, 26, 27, and when H.M. the Queen or any member of the Royal Family is in residence.

SANDTOFT

SANDTOFT TRANSPORT CENTRE
Sandtoft, nr. Doncaster, Lincolnshire
Trolleybuses from towns and cities all over Britain.
On request.

SANDWICH

THE GUILDHALL MUSEUM
Sandwich, Kent
Local history and archaeology.
Daily 10.30-12.30, 2-4.

SCARBOROUGH

ST. THOMAS'S MUSEUM
East Sandgate, Scarborough, Yorkshire
Local history and bygones, in former St. Thomas's Church.
May-Sept. Weekdays 10-5; Su. (from Spring Bank Holiday) 2-5.

SCARBOROUGH ART GALLERY
The Crescent, Scarborough, Yorkshire
Works by local artists. Laughton Collection (English School).
Weekdays 10-1, 2.30-5; Su., Spring Bank Holiday to Sept., 2-5.

SCARBOROUGH MUSEUM OF LOCAL HISTORY AND BYGONES
Vernon Road, Scarborough, Yorkshire
Archaeological collections of all periods represented in N.E. Yorkshire. Scarborough bygones. Local transport during 19th and 20th centuries. Inventions of two local men, Sir George Cayley (aeronautics) and Dr. William Harland (steam carriages).
Weekdays 10-1, 2.30-5; Su. Apr.-Sept. 2-5.

SCARBOROUGH MUSEUM OF NATURAL HISTORY
Wood End, The Crescent, Scarborough, Yorkshire
Formerly the home of the Sitwell family; two rooms are devoted to paintings and first editions of this famous literary family. British and foreign natural history. Yorkshire geological material.
Weekdays: Summer 10-5; Winter 10-1, 2.30-5. Su., Spring Bank Holiday to Sept. 2-5.

SCUNTHORPE

BOROUGH MUSEUM AND ART GALLERY
Oswald Road, Scunthorpe, Lincolnshire
The Regional Museum for North Lincolnshire. Prehistoric collections. Roman and later archaeology. Geology. Natural history. Local industry. Bygones. Period rooms. John Wesley collection.
Weekdays 10-5; Su. 2-5.

NORMANBY HALL
Scunthorpe, Lincolnshire
Regency mansion by Sir Robert Smirke, furnished and decorated in period. Costume displays. Paintings.
Nov.-Mar., M.-F. 10-5; Su. 2-5. Apr.-Oct. Weekdays (except Tu.) 10-5.30; Su. 2-5.30.

SELBORNE

GILBERT WHITE MUSEUM
The Wakes, Selborne, Hampshire
Relics of Gilbert White, pioneer naturalist, and of Capt. L. E. G. Oates, Antarctic explorer.
Daily (except F.): Weekdays (11-1 Apr.-Oct.) 2.30-5.30; Su. 2.30-5.30.

SELKIRK

SELKIRK MUSEUM
Ettrick Terrace, Selkirk, Selkirkshire
Collection of items relating to Mungo Park, explorer; James Hogg (Ettrick Shepherd), J. B. Selkirk. Local crafts.
Weekdays 9-6 (Sa. 9-4).

SETTLE

PIG YARD CLUB MUSEUM
Settle, Yorkshire
Bones and artifacts found in Victoria Cave, some dating from the Ice Age.
Enquire locally.

SEVENOAKS

KNOLE
Sevenoaks, Kent
Collection of 17th and 18th century furniture. Sackville family portraits. Charles II silver and furniture.
All the year (except Jan. and Feb.) W., Th., F., Sa. and Bank Holidays, 10-12, 2-5 (closes 3.30 in winter). Closed Boxing Day.

SHAFTESBURY

ABBEY RUINS MUSEUM
Park Walk, Shaftesbury, Dorset
Objects from excavations of the Church of the Benedictine Nunnery founded by Alfred the Great. Tiles. Worked stones. Models of church and pre-Dissolution town.
Easter-Sept. 10-12.30, 2-dusk; Su. 2-dusk.

GALLERY 24
Bimport, Shaftesbury, Dorset
Modern paintings.
Daily 2-6 (except M.). Other times by arrangement.

LOCAL HISTORY MUSEUM
Gold Hill, Shaftesbury, Dorset
Local history.
See local notice board.

SHEFFIELD

ABBEYDALE INDUSTRIAL HAMLET
Abbeydale Road South, Sheffield, Yorkshire
18th century scytheworks comprising a Huntman's type crucible steel furnace, tilt-hammers, grinding shop and hand-forges.
Weekdays 11-5; Su. 2-5 (end May - end Aug. Weekdays 11-8; Su. 2-8).

GRAVES ART GALLERY
Surrey Street, Sheffield 1, Yorkshire
British portraits. European paintings. Artists include Leonardo da Vinci, Murillo, Ribera, Cezanne, Corot, in addition to a collection of English water-colours. Chinese, Indian and Islamic art. African art.
Weekdays 10-8; Su. 2-5.

MAPPIN ART GALLERY
Weston Park, Sheffield, Yorkshire
Paintings and sculpture, mainly representative of the British School of the 18th-20th centuries, including pictures by Turner, Wilson, Gainsborough, Constable and the Pre-Raphaelites.
Weekdays 10-5 (June-Aug. 10-8.30); Su. 2-5.

SHEFFIELD CITY MUSEUM
Weston Park, Sheffield 10, Yorkshire
General collections of natural history, geology, ceramics, coins and bygones. Specialised collections of cutlery, Old Sheffield Plate, local archaeology and local history.
Weekdays 10-5 (June-Aug. 10-8.30); Su. 2-5.

SHEPHERD WHEEL
Witeley Wood, Sheffield, Yorkshire
A Sheffield "Little Mesters" water-powered grinding shop.
Times of admission from City Museum.

THE YORK AND LANCASTER REGIMENT MUSEUM
Regimental Headquarters, Endcliffe Hall, Sheffield, Yorkshire
Uniforms, old arms, awards, campaign medals, regimental colours, pictures, trophies and souvenirs associated with the regiment.
M.-F. 9-12, 2-4. Sa., Su. and Bank Holidays by appointment.

SHEPTON MALLET

SHEPTON MALLET MUSEUM
Market Place, Shepton Mallet, Somerset
Bronze Age, Iron Age, Roman and Medieval archaeology. Mendip geological, palaeontological and ornithological collections.
M.-F. 9-1, 2-5.

SHERBORNE

SHERBORNE CASTLE
Sherborne, Dorset
16th century mansion built by Sir Walter Raleigh. Furniture. Porcelain. Pictures by Van Dyke, Gainsborough, Reynolds, Lely.
Easter Sa. - end Sept. Th., Sa. and Su., also Bank Holiday M., 2-6.

SHERBORNE MUSEUM
Abbey Gate House, Sherborne, Dorset
Exhibits illustrating local geology and history, including Abbey, founded 705 AD, Sherborne Missal 1400 AD and 18th century local silk industry. Model and plans of Norman and Elizabethan castles, Victorian dolls' house.
Easter-Oct. Weekdays except M. 10.30-12.30, 3-4.30. Su. 3-5. Winter: Tu. and Sa. 10.30-12.30, 3-4.30; Su. 3-5.

SHIFNAL

WESTON PARK
nr. Shifnal, Shropshire
House (1671). English, Flemish and Italian pictures. Gobelin and Aubusson tapestries. Disraeli letters.
Easter Sa. - mid. Sept. Daily except M. and F., also Easter, Spring and Late Summer Bank Holiday M. and Su. Weekdays, House and Grounds 2-6; Su. and Bank Holidays, Grounds open 11-6, House 1.30-6.

SHOREHAM

THE MARLIPINS MUSEUM
High Street, Shoreham, Sussex.
Early 12th century building housing collections of ship models, paintings and photographs of the locality, geological specimens, old maps, household articles and coins. Local archaeology.
Easter and May-Oct. Daily 10-12.30, 2-5.

SHREWSBURY

CLIVE HOUSE
College Hill, Shrewsbury, Shropshire
Georgian house containing art, ceramics, geological specimens and furniture.
Weekdays: M. 12-6; Tu.-Sa. 10-6. Closes 4.30 in Winter.

COLEHAM PUMPING STATION
Old Coleham, Shrewsbury, Shropshire
Contains two compound rotative beam engines of 1900.
W. and F. 2-5.

1ST THE QUEEN'S DRAGOON GUARDS SERVICE MUSEUM
Clive House, College Hill, Shrewsbury, Shropshire
Uniforms, old arms, awards, campaign medals, regimental colours, pictures, trophies and souvenirs associated with the regiment.
May-Oct. M. 12-6; Tu.-Sa. 10-6; Nov.-Apr. M. 12-4.30; Tu.-Sa. 10-4. Public Holidays excepting Good Friday and Christmas Day.

THE KING'S SHROPSHIRE LIGHT INFANTRY SERVICE MUSEUM
Sir John Moore Barracks, Shrewsbury, Shropshire
Uniforms, old arms, awards, campaign medals, regimental colours, pictures, trophies and souvenirs associated with the regiment.
By appointment weekdays 10-4.

ROWLEY'S HOUSE MUSEUM
Barker Street, Shrewsbury, Shropshire
Roman material from Viroconium (Wroxeter). Prehistoric and medieval archaeology.
Weekdays 10-1, 2-5 or by appointment.

SHREWSBURY ART GALLERY
Castle Gates, Shrewsbury, Shropshire
Paintings. Drawings. Graphics.
Daily 10-6.

SHROPSHIRE YEOMANRY MUSEUM
Territorial House, Sundorne Road, Shrewsbury, Shropshire
Uniforms, old arms, awards, campaign medals, regimental colours, pictures, trophies and souvenirs.
M.-F. 9-5.

SHUGBOROUGH

STAFFORDSHIRE COUNTY MUSEUM AND MANSION HOUSE
Museum of Staffordshire Life, Shugborough, Great Hayward, nr. Stafford, Staffordshire
Horse-drawn vehicles. Farm equipment. Railway and industrial exhibits. Firearms. Domestic life. Pottery. Silver. Costumes. Geology. 18th century French furniture. Paintings. Porcelain. Silver. Brew-house. Laundry.
Weekdays (except M.) 11-5.30; Su. and Bank Holidays 2-5.30. Closed late Oct. - late Mar. except for organised school parties.

SIDMOUTH

SIDMOUTH MUSEUM
Woolcombe House, Woolcombe Lane, Sidmouth, Devon
Medieval hall. Local history. Furniture. Household equipment.
July-Sept. Weekdays 10.30-12.30, 2.30-4.30. Oct.-Mar. Th. and Sa. 2.30-4.30. Apr.-June Th. and Sa. 10.30-12.30, 2.30-4.30; Su. 2.30-4.30.

SILCHESTER

CALLEVA MUSEUM
Rectory Grounds, Silchester Common, Silchester, Hampshire
Roman objects from site of nearby Calleva.
Daily 10-dusk.

SINGLETON

WEALD AND DOWNLAND OPEN AIR MUSEUM
Singleton, nr. Chichester, Sussex
Historic buildings which have been threatened with demolition, moved to site. Early crafts and industries from the Weald and Downland of Kent, Surrey, Sussex and eastern Hampshire.
May-Oct., Tu., W., Th., Sa., Su., Bank Holidays, 11-6.

SKIPTON

CRAVEN MUSEUM
Public Library and Museum, High Street, Skipton, Yorkshire
Craven antiquities, including remains from Elbolton Cave, the Iron Age settlements, and Elslack Roman fort. Bygones. Geology. Natural history.
Su., M., W., Th. and F. 2-5; Sa. 10-12, 1.30-4.30.

SOUTH MOLTON

SOUTH MOLTON MUSEUM
Town Hall, Guildhall, South Molton, Devon
Local history. Documents. Pewter. Weights and measures. Bygones.
M.-Sa. 11-12.30, 2.30-4.30; Su. 2.30-4.30.

SOUTHAMPTON

BARGATE GUILDHALL MUSEUM
High Street, Southampton, Hampshire
Local historical exhibits, housed in the former hall of guilds above the medieval north gate.
Weekdays 10-12, 1-5; Su. 2.30-4.30.

GOD'S HOUSE TOWER MUSEUM
Town Quay, Southampton, Hampshire
Early 15th century fortification, now a museum of local archaeology.
Weekdays 10-5; Su. 2.30-4.30.

MARITIME MUSEUM
Wool House, Bugle Street, Southampton, Hampshire
14th century wool store, now museum of shipping.
Weekdays 10-5; Su. 2.30-4.30.

SOUTHAMPTON ART GALLERY
Civic Centre, Southampton, Hampshire
British paintings, particularly contemporary. European paintings, especially 19th century French.
Weekdays 10-7; Su. 2-5.

TUDOR HOUSE MUSEUM
St. Michael's Square, Southampton, Hampshire
16th century mansion. Local history. Bygones.
Weekdays 10-5; Su. 2.30-4.30.

SOUTHEND-ON-SEA

BEECROFT ART GALLERY
Station Road, Westcliffe-on-Sea, nr. Southend-on-Sea, Essex
Paintings, drawings, graphics, mainly English.
Weekdays 10.30-5.30; Su. 2-5.30.

HISTORIC AIRCRAFT MUSEUM
Cherry Orchard Lane, Southend Airport, Southend, Essex
The collection of thirty aircraft ranging from 1925 to the present day includes the Beverley.
Daily 10-7.

PRITTLEWELL PRIORY MUSEUM
Priory Park, Southend-on-Sea, Essex
Originally a Cluniac Monastery. Local history. Natural history.
Apr.-Sept. Weekdays 11-6; Su. 2.30-6. Oct.-Mar. Weekdays 11-4.30.

SOUTHPORT

ATKINSON ART GALLERY
Lord Street, Southport, Lancashire
Paintings, water-colours and sculpture.
Weekdays 10-5; Su. 3-5.

BOTANIC GARDENS MUSEUM
Churchtown, Southport, Lancashire
Local and natural history. Victorian period room.
Weekdays 10-5 (Summer 10-6); Su. 2-5 (dusk in Winter).

SOUTH QUEENSFERRY

BURGH MUSEUM
Burgh Chambers, High Street, South Queensferry, West Lothian
Manuscripts, prints, photographs, exhibits illustrative of local social history. Early charters.
M.-Th. 2-4 or by arrangement with the Curator.

HOPETOUN HOUSE
South Queensferry, West Lothian
Adam house. Collections of pictures and furniture.
May-Sept. Daily (except Th. and F.) 1.30-5.30.

SOUTHSEA

ROYAL MARINES MUSEUM
Eastney Barracks, Southsea, Hampshire
Uniforms, old arms, awards, campaign medals, regimental colours, pictures, trophies and souvenirs.
M.-F. 10-4; Sa. and Su. 10-12.

SOUTH SHIELDS

ROMAN FORT AND MUSEUM
Baring Street, South Shields, County Durham
Memorial Stones and other material found on the site of the Roman Fort.
May-Sept. Weekdays 10-7.30; Su. 11-7.30. Oct.-Apr. M.-F. 10-4; Sa. 10-12.

SOUTH SHIELDS LIBRARY AND MUSEUM
Ocean Road, South Shields, County Durham
Natural history. Local glass. Ship models. Original model of first lifeboat, invented by W. Wouldhave (1789).
Weekdays 10-7; Sa. 10-5.

SOUTHWOLD

SOUTHWOLD MUSEUM
St. Bartholomew's Green, Southwold, Suffolk
Local archaeology, natural history and bygones.
Summer: Tu., W. and F. 2.30-4.30. Other times by appointment.

SPALDING

AYSCOUGHFEE HALL
Churchgate, Spalding, Lincolnshire
British Birds.
Weekdays 10-6 (10-5 in Winter). Su. by arrangement.

BRITISH VINTAGE WIRELESS MUSEUM
Homa House, Quadring, Watergate, Spalding, Lincolnshire
Wireless receivers and transmitters from the beginning of the century to the present day. Television sets.
By appointment.

SPALDING MUSEUM
Broad Street, Spalding, Lincolnshire
Bygones. Ceramics. Glass. Coins. Medals. Prehistoric material.
By appointment.

STAFFORD

IZAAK WALTON COTTAGE
Shallowford, Stafford, Staffordshire
The angler Izaak Walton's restored country cottage.
Daily (except Tu.) 10-1, 2.30-4.30.

STAFFORD MUSEUM
The Green, Stafford, Staffordshire
Collections relating to the history, social life, art and industry of the locality.
M.-F. 10-7; Sa. 10-5.

STALYBRIDGE

THE ASTLEY CHEETHAM ART GALLERY
Trinity Street, Stalybridge, Cheshire
Egyptian, Greek and Roman antiquities. Paintings.
M.-F. 10-4 (10-1 on W.); Sa. 10-4. Closed Bank Holidays and during winter months.

STAMFORD

BURGHLEY HOUSE
Stamford, Northamptonshire
Elizabethan house. State Apartments. Pictures. Furniture. Silver fireplace. Painted ceilings. Tapestries.
Early Apr. - early Oct. Tu., W., Th., Sa. and Bank Holidays, 11-5; Good F. and Su. 2-5.

STEEPLE ASTON

ROUSHAM HOUSE
Steeple Aston, Oxfordshire
17th century house, with contemporary furniture. Portraits and miniatures.
June-Aug. W. and Bank Holidays 2-6. Su. gardens only, 2-6.

STEVENAGE

STEVENAGE MUSEUM
Lytton Way, New Town Centre, Stevenage, Hertfordshire
Local archaeology and history. General natural history with special local displays.
Weekdays 10-6; Su. 2-6.

STICKLEPATH

STICKLEPATH MUSEUM OF RURAL INDUSTRY
Sticklepath, Okehampton, Devon
Nineteenth century edge tool works containing water-powered tilt-hammers, shears, grindstone and blower, all in working order, driven by three separate water-wheels. Collection of tools made or used on the premises and other examples of bygone domestic and agricultural implements.
Daily 11-5.

STIRLING

ARGYLL AND SUTHERLAND HIGHLANDERS SERVICE MUSEUM
Stirling Castle, Stirling, Stirlingshire
Uniforms, old arms, awards, campaign medals, regimental colours, pictures, trophies and souvenirs.
Apr.-Sept. Weekdays 10-6; Su. 11-1, 2-6.

SMITH ART GALLERY AND MUSEUM
Albert Place, Stirling, Stirlingshire
Paintings. Water colours. Natural history. Household equipment. Archaeology. Ethnology.
Weekdays 10-5.

UNIVERSITY OF STIRLING
Department of Biology Museum, Stirling, Stirlingshire
Skeletal material. Specimen dissections. Anatomical and Embryological models. Representations of plant tissues and structures. Animal histology. Plant anatomy.
By appointment.

STOCKPORT

MUNICIPAL MUSEUM
Vernon Park, Turncroft Lane, Stockport, Cheshire
Local history. Natural history. Geology. Ceramics. Victoriana.
Weekdays 10-6 (closes at 5 Oct.-Feb.); Su. 2-5 (closed Nov.-Feb.).

WAR MEMORIAL ART GALLERY
Wellington Road South, Stockport, Cheshire
British paintings, mainly water-colours. Epstein head of Yehudi Menuhin.
M.-F. 12-6; Sa. 10-12, 2-6.

STOKE BRUERNE

WATERWAYS MUSEUM
Stoke Bruerne, Nr. Towcester, Northamptonshire, NN12 7SE
Canal transport. On Grand Union Canal. Boats. Cast-iron lock gate. Life of the men and women who worked on the canals.
Daily 10-12.30; 2-5, 6-8. Closed M. winter and at 5 each day. Closed Christmas Day and Boxing Day.

STOKE-ON-TRENT

ARNOLD BENNETT MUSEUM
205 Waterloo Road, Cobridge, Stoke-on-Trent, Staffordshire
Arnold Bennett's early home, with two rooms devoted to drawings and personal relics.
M., W., Th. and Sa. 2-5.

CITY MUSEUM AND ART GALLERY
Broad Street, Hanley, Stoke-on-Trent, Staffordshire
Staffordshire pottery and porcelain. European, South American, Near Eastern and Oriental pottery. 18th century English water-colours. English paintings since 1900; Sculpture. The natural history collection includes Staffordshire birds and mammals.
Weekdays 10-6; Su. 2.30-5.

FORD GREEN HALL
Smallthorne, Stoke-on-Trent, Staffordshire
16th century timber-framed manor house containing furniture and domestic utensils. Associations with Isaak Walton and the early Quakers.
Weekdays (except Tu. and F.) 10-12.30, 2-6 (closes 4.30 in Winter); Su. 2-5.

SPODE-COPELAND MUSEUM AND ART GALLERY
Church Street, Stoke-on-Trent, Staffordshire
Collections of early Spode blue-printed ware, bone china and stone china and wares of Copeland and Garrett.
M.-F. 10-4. By appointment only.

THE WEDGWOOD MUSEUM
Josiah Wedgwood and Sons Limited, Barlaston, Stoke-on-Trent, Staffordshire
Early Wedgwood ware.
By appointment.

STOWMARKET

THE ABBOT'S HALL MUSEUM OF RURAL LIFE OF EAST ANGLIA
Stowmarket, Suffolk
Collections relating to the rural life of the area, agriculture, crafts and domestic utensils.
Apr.-Oct. 2-5.

STRABANE

PRINTING PRESS
Main Street, Strabane, Co. Tyrone, Northern Ireland
18th century printing shop.
Daily (except Th. and Su.) 2-6.

STRANGFORD

CASTLE WARD
Strangford, nr. Downpatrick, Co. Down, Northern Ireland
Laundry Museum.
Apr.-Sept. Daily (except Tu.) 2-6.

STRANRAER

WIGTOWN COUNTY MUSEUM
The County Library, London Road, Stranraer
Local history.
During library hours.

STRATFORD-UPON-AVON

ANNE HATHAWAY'S COTTAGE
Shottery, Stratford-upon-Avon, Warwickshire
Furniture and Hathaway heirlooms from Tudor period onwards.
Apr.-Oct. Weekdays 10-6; Su. 2-6. Nov.-Mar. Weekdays 9-12.45, Su. 2-4.30. June-Sept. and Th. and Sa. during Season, Weekdays till 7.

HARVARD HOUSE
High Street, Stratford-upon-Avon, Warwickshire
Home of the mother of John Harvard, founder of the American University. 17th century furnishings.
Apr.-Sept. 9-1, 2-6; Su. 2-6. Oct.-Mar. Weekdays only 10-1, 2-4.

HALL'S CROFT
Old Town, Stratford-upon-Avon, Warwickshire
Tudor town house containing Elizabethan and Jacobean furniture. Exhibition room devoted to the story of the Stratford Shakespeare Festival.
Apr.-Oct. Weekdays 9-6; Su. 2-6. Nov.-Mar. Weekdays 9-12.45, 2-4.

MARY ARDEN'S HOUSE
Wilmcote, Stratford-upon-Avon, Warwickshire
Home of Shakespeare's mother, with a farming museum in the barns.
Apr.-Oct. Weekdays 9-6, Su. 2-6; Nov.-Mar. Weekdays only 9-12.45, 2-4.

NEW PLACE AND NASH'S HOUSE
Stratford-upon-Avon, Warwickshire
Contains material illustrative of the background of Shakespeare's England, together with local historical exhibits including Roman and Anglo-Saxon antiquities and David Garrick exhibits.
Apr.-Oct. Weekdays 9-6; Su. 2-6. Nov.-Mar. Weekdays 9-12.45, 2-4.

THE QUEEN'S OWN WARWICKSHIRE AND WORCESTERSHIRE YEOMANRY SERVICE MUSEUM
T. and A.V.R. Centre, New Broad Street, Stratford-upon-Avon, Warwickshire
Uniforms, old arms, awards, campaign medals, regimental colours, pictures, trophies and souvenirs.
M.-F. 9-5; Sa. and Su. by arrangement.

ROYAL SHAKESPEARE THEATRE PICTURE GALLERY
Stratford-upon-Avon, Warwickshire
Original costumes and designs, portraits of famous actors and actresses. Exhibition of Shakespeare portraits and the X-Ray radiographs of the "Flower" and "Venice" portraits, also wig, mask and headdress exhibition.
Apr.-Nov. Daily 10-1, 2-6; Su. 2-6. Matinees 10-6 (Nov. close at 4). Nov.-Mar. Sa. 10-1, 2-4; Su. 2-4.

SHAKESPEARE'S BIRTHPLACE
Henley Street, Stratford-upon-Avon, Warwickshire
Shakespearian exhibits.
Apr.-Oct. Weekdays 9-6 (9-7 Th. and Sa.), also 9-7 on all weekdays during June, July, Aug. and Sept. Su. 10-6. Nov.-Mar. Weekdays 9-4 (Mar. 9-5); Su. 2-4.30.

STRATHAVEN

JOHN HASTIE MUSEUM
Strathaven, Lanark
Local history collection.
Weekdays 2-8. Oct.-Mar. 2-4.

STREET

SHOE MUSEUM
C. and J. Clark Limited, Street, Somerset
Shoes, shoe-making machinery, advertising material of C. and J. Clark Limited, from the mid-19th century onwards. Documents illustrating the company's history, 1825 to the present day. Non-Clarks shoes, 350 A.D. to present, as well as Clarks shoes.
M.-F. 10-4.45; Sa. 10-1.

STRENSALL

YORKSHIRE REGIMENT'S MUSEUM
Queen Elizabeth Barracks, Strensall, Yorkshire
Uniforms, old arms, awards, campaign medals, regimental colours, pictures, trophies and souvenirs associated with the regiment.
M.-F. by appointment.

STROMNESS

ORKNEY NATURAL HISTORY MUSEUM
52 Alfred Street, Stromness, Orkney
Collections of ethnology, zoology, geology, botany, ship models and Orkney bygones.
Weekdays 11-5 (Th. 11-1). Open at 10 July-Aug.

STROUD

STROUD MUSEUM
Lansdown, Stroud, Gloucestershire
Collections covering geology, archaeology, local crafts and industrial archaeology, farming and household equipment, ceramics, dolls. Paintings, photographs and records of local houses and mills.
Weekdays 10.30-1, 2-5.

SUDBURY

GAINSBOROUGH'S HOUSE
Sudbury, Suffolk
Gainsborough's birthplace, containing portraits, landscapes, drawings by him.
Tu.-Sa. 10.30-12.30, 2-5; Su. 2-5. Closed M. and Bank Holidays.

MELFORD HALL
nr. Sudbury, Suffolk
Paintings. Furniture. Chinese porcelain.
Apr.-Sept. W., Th., Su. and Bank Holidays 2.30-6.

SULGRAVE

SULGRAVE MANOR
Sulgrave, Northamptonshire
Early home of ancestors of George Washington. Kitchen and kitchen equipment of period. 17th century furnishings. Washington memorabilia.
Daily (except W.) 10.30-1, 2-5.30. Closes at 4 Oct.-Mar.

SUNDERLAND

GRINDON CLOSE BRANCH MUSEUM
Grindon Close, Grindon Lane, Sunderland, County Durham
Situated on the first floor of an Edwardian house, the collections comprise a cobbler's workshop; dentist's surgery (c.1910); a chemist's shop; general dealer's shop. Living room, bedroom, nursery and kitchen set out in period style, c.1910.
M., W. and F. 9.30-7.30. Th. and Sa. 9.30-5. Closed Su., Bank Holidays and preceding Saturdays, Christmas and Boxing Days, New Year's Day and Good F.

MONKWEARMOUTH STATION MUSEUM
North Bridge Street, Sunderland, County Durham
Station (1848). Exterior and North Eastern Railway ticket office have been restored. Local history. Displays of local land transport, including models, uniforms, prints, photographs.
M.-Sa. 9.30-12.30, 1.30-5.30. Closed Su. and bank holidays.

SUNDERLAND CENTRAL MUSEUM AND ART GALLERY
Borough Road, Sunderland, SR1 1PP, County Durham
Collections include examples of Sunderland lustreware pottery and local glass; English 16th-19th century silver. Shipping. Industry. Archaeology. Costumes. Bygones. Natural history. Local history exhibits. Paintings. Watercolours. Graphics art, mainly English 19th and 20th century.
M.-F. 9.30-6; Sa. 9.30-5; Su. 3-5. Bank Holidays 10-5. Closed Christmas and Boxing Days, New Year's Day and Good F.

SWANSEA

GLYNN VIVIAN ART GALLERY
Alexandra Road, Swansea, Glamorgan
British paintings, drawings and sculpture, ceramics, including Welsh pottery and porcelain. Glass.
Weekdays 10.30-5.30. Closed Su., Good F. and Boxing Day.

INDUSTRIAL MUSEUM OF SOUTH WALES
Victoria Road, Swansea, Glamorgan
Industrial relics and displays of local industry covering steel, copper, aluminium, oil, light industries and transport.
Weekdays 10-5.

ROYAL INSTITUTION OF SOUTH WALES MUSEUM
Victoria Road, Swansea, Glamorgan
Collections of local antiquarian interest. Archaeology. Ceramics. Welsh folk culture. Ornithology. Botany. Zoology. Geology. Numismatics. Industry.
Weekdays 10-5.

SWINDON

GREAT WESTERN RAILWAY MUSEUM
Faringdon Road, Swindon, Wiltshire
Originally a model lodging house for employees of the railway works. Replica, including some original parts, of 'North Star'. 'City of Truro' (1903), 'Lode Star' (1907). Mementoes of Brunel, Churchward, Good. Early posters, handbills, tickets, notices and maps. Engravings and coloured lithographs illustrating railway history.
Weekdays 10-5; Su. 2-5.

RICHARD JEFFERIES MUSEUM
Coate, Swindon, Wiltshire
Personal items, manuscripts, first editions relating to Richard Jefferies and Alfred Williams.
W. and Sa. 2-5 Oct.-Mar. W., Sa. and Su. 2-5 (Apr.-Sept.).

SWINDON MUSEUM AND ART GALLERY
Bath Road, Swindon, Wiltshire
Archaeology, natural history, botany and geology of Wiltshire. Local bygones. Roman and English coins. Paintings.
Weekdays 10-6; Su. 2-5.

TALGARTH

HYWEL HARRIS MUSEUM
Trefaca, Talgarth, Breconshire
Books, furniture, prints and articles associated with Hywel Harris's 18th century Trefaca religious community.
M.-F. 10-5. Weekends by appointment.

TAMWORTH

TAMWORTH CASTLE
Tamworth, Staffordshire
Houses a museum of early English coins of the Tamworth mint.
Mar.-Oct. Weekdays 10-8 or one hour before sunset. Su. 2-8 or one hour before sunset. Nov.-Feb. Weekdays (except F.) 10-4, Su. 2-4. Closed Christmas Day.

TARBOLTON

BACHELORS CLUB
Tarbolton, Ayrshire
17th century house named after the literary society founded by Robert Burns and his friends there in 1780. Contains facsimiles of letters and poems from the poet's Lochlie period.
See notice on property. Key from caretaker.

TAUNTON

SOMERSET COUNTY MUSEUM
Taunton Castle, Taunton, Somerset
Local and natural history. Insects and extinct mammals from the Mendip Caves. Local geology, natural history, archaeology, pottery, pewter, glass, dolls, bygones and folk collection. Meare Lake Village material.
M.-F. 9.30-1, 2.15-5.30; Sa. 9.30-5.30.

SOMERSET LIGHT INFANTRY MUSEUM
14 Mount Street, Taunton, Somerset
Uniforms, old arms, awards, campaign medals, regimental colours, pictures, trophies and souvenirs.
M.-F. 10-12, 2-4; Sa. 9-12.

TEESSIDE

CAPTAIN COOK MUSEUM
Stewarts Park, Marton, Middlesbrough, Teesside
Collection illustrating Captain Cook's life and connections with Middlesbrough.
Tu.-Sa. 10-1, 2-6.

DORMAN MUSEUM
Linthorpe Road, Middlesbrough, Teesside
Collections illustrating the ecology, geology and natural history of the region.
Weekdays 10-6.

MIDDLESBROUGH ART GALLERY
Linthorpe Road, Middlesbrough, Teesside
Contemporary British paintings.
Weekdays 10-6.

PRESTON HALL MUSEUM
Preston Park, Eaglescliffe, Preston, Teesside
Weapons. Armour. Local pottery. Toys. Ivory. Period rooms.
Weekdays 10-6.

TEESSIDE MUSEUMS AND ART GALLERIES SERVICE
Redcar Museum of Fishing and Shipping, Redcar, Teesside
Graphic and three-dimensional material, illustrating the history of Tees shipping and fishing, including model ships and *The Zetland*, the oldest lifeboat in the world.
Tu.-Sa. 10-1, 2-6.

STOCKTON AND DARLINGTON RAILWAY MUSEUM
Stockton, Teesside
Historic pictures and relics from the world's first paid-passenger railway, and sited where the first ticket office once stood.
Tu.-Sa. 10-1, 2-6.

TELFORD

IRONBRIDGE GORGE MUSEUM
Southside, Church Hill, Ironbridge, Telford, Shropshire
Open-air museum, illustrating development of local coal, iron and pottery industries. Coal mines of different periods, blast furnaces, including Abraham Darby's (1777) at Coalbrookdale, and its associated museum. Hay inclined plane (1793). Coalport China Works. The Iron Bridge (1779).
M.-F. 9-1, 2-5 or by arrangement.

TENBY

TENBY MUSEUM
Castle Hill, Tenby, Pembrokeshire
Collections of local geology, archaeology, history and natural history, maps, pictures and bygones.
June-Sept. M.-Sa. 10-6; Su. 2-6. Oct.-May M.-Sa. 10-1, 2-4. Closed Su.

TUDOR MERCHANT'S HOUSE
Quay Hill, Tenby, Pembrokeshire
Late 15th century merchant's house, with period furniture.
Easter-Sept. M.-F. 10-1, 2-5; Su. 2-6. Bank Holidays 10-6. Closed Sa.

TENTERDEN

ELLEN TERRY MEMORIAL MUSEUM
Smallhythe Place, Tenterden, Kent
Timbered house (1480), home of Dame Ellen Terry, 1899 until her death in 1928. Memorabilia of Ellen Terry, Sir Henry Irving and Mrs. Siddons.
Mar.-Oct., W., Th., Sa.-M. 2-6 or dusk.

TETBURY

LASBOROUGH MANOR
Tetbury, Gloucestershire
Cotswold manor, 1609. Family pictures, furniture and old fireplaces.
House and Garden open Spring Bank Holiday, Sa., Su. and M. and Late Summer Bank Holiday, Su. and M. Other dates by appointment.

TEWKESBURY

TEWKESBURY MUSEUM
Barton Street, Tewkesbury, Gloucestershire
Archaeology. Costumes. Furniture. Military history and local history.
Whitsun - Sept. 30, M.-Sa. 10-5.

THETFORD

THE ANCIENT HOUSE MUSEUM
White Hart Street, Thetford, Norfolk
15th century timbered house. Collections of archaeology, numismatics, botany, entomology, geology and zoology. Saxon pottery.
Apr.-Sept. Daily 2-5; Sa. 10-5. Oct.-Mar. Tu., Th. and Su. 2-4; Sa. 10-4.

DULEEP SINGH COLLECTION
The Guildhall, Thetford, Norfolk
Gallery of Norfolk and Suffolk portraits.
Weekdays 10-5.

THURSO

THURSO MUSEUM
The Library, Thurso, Caithness
Zoological, geological and botanical collections. Plants and mosses.
Weekdays 10-12, 2-5, 6-8 (Th. 10-12 only).

TILFORD

OLD KILN AGRICULTURAL MUSEUM
The Reeds Road, Tilford, Farnham, Surrey
Blacksmith's forge. Wheelwright's shop. Barn machinery in working order. Hand tools. Dairy equipment. Horse-drawn implements.
Apr.-Sept., 1st and last weekends in each month, 1-7. Also open Bank Holiday weekends.

TIVERTON

TIVERTON CASTLE
Tiverton, Devon
Castle (1106). Portraits of Joan of Arc. Clock collection.
By previous written appointment only, Su.-F., June-Aug. and Oct.

TONBRIDGE

PENSHURST PLACE
Tonbridge, Kent
House dates from 1340. Period furniture, furnishings. China. Glass. Paintings. Toy collection.
Easter Sa. - Apr. 30, Sa., Su. 2-6. May, W., Th., Sa., Su. 2-6. June, Tu.-Th., Sa., Su. 2-6. July-Sept. 17, Tu.-Th., Sa., Su. 1-6. Bank Holidays, 11.30-6. Times subject to alteration.

TORPOINT

ANTONY HOUSE
Torpoint, Cornwall
House (1711-1721). Family portraits, some by Reynolds. Furnishings.
Apr.-Sept. Tu., W. and Th., also Bank Holiday M. 2-6.

TORQUAY

TORQUAY NATURAL HISTORY SOCIETY MUSEUM
Babbacombe Road, Torquay, Devon
Collections illustrate Kents Cavern and other caves, Devon natural history, local folk culture.
Weekdays 10-5.

TORRE ABBEY
Torquay, Devon
Ruins of abbey founded 1196, and early 18th century mansion, housing Art Gallery. Paintings. Drawings.
Daily all the year, 10-1, 2-5.30. Closed Sa. and Su. from end Oct. - Easter.

TOTNES

THE ELIZABETHAN HOUSE
70 Fore Street, Totnes, Devon
Period furniture and costumes. Local tools, toys, domestic articles. Archaeology. Documents from local collections.
Apr.-Sept. Weekdays 10.30-1, 2-5.30.

TRE'R DDOL

TRE'R DDOL MUSEUM
Tre'r Ddol, Cardiganshire
Rural crafts and folk culture.
June-Oct. Tu.-Sa. 12-4.

TRESCO

VALHALLA MARITIME MUSEUM
Tresco Abbey, Tresco, Isles of Scilly
Figureheads and ships' ornaments from ships wrecked in the Isles of Scilly.
Weekdays 10-4.

TRING

ZOOLOGICAL MUSEUM
Akeman Street, Tring, Hertfordshire
Mounted specimens of animals from all parts of the world. British butterflies, moths, shells and birds' eggs.
Daily 2-5. Bank Holidays 10-5.

TROUTBECK

TOWNEND
Troutbeck, Westmorland
House built c.1626, containing carved woodwork, books, papers and furniture collected by the yeoman family which lived here from that date until 1944.
Easter-Sept. 30, Daily ex. Sa. and M. 2-6 or dusk if earlier. Open Bank Holiday M. Oct.-Easter. W. 2-6 or dusk if earlier.

TRURO

COUNTY MUSEUM AND ART GALLERY
River Street, Truro, Cornwall
Local antiquities and history. Ceramics and art. Cornish minerals.
Nov.-Mar. 10-4; Apr.-Oct. 10-5. Closed Bank Holidays.

TUNBRIDGE WELLS

PENSHURST PLACE
Tunbridge Wells, Kent
Collections of arms and armour, furniture, pictures, silver. Toy Museum.
Easter Sa. - mid. Apr. Sa. and Su. 2-6. End Apr. - end May W., Th., Sa. and Su. 2-6. June 1-27, Tu., W., Th., Sa. and Su. 2-6. June 29 - mid. Sept. Tu., W., Th., Sa. and Su., 12.30-6. Bank Holidays 11.30-6.

ROYAL TUNBRIDGE WELLS MUSEUM AND ART GALLERY
Civic Centre, Tunbridge Wells, Kent
Prints of Old Tunbridge Wells. Domestic and agricultural bygones. Dolls. Toys. Natural history. Geology. Wealden prehistory. Coins. Tunbridge ware. Victorian paintings.
Weekdays 10-5.30. Closed Bank Holidays and Sa. prior to them.

TURTON

THE ASHWORTH MUSEUM
Turton Tower, Chapletown Road, Turton, Lancashire
Items of local interest including furniture, brass, weapons and local records.
W. and Sa. 2-sunset. Su. Apr.-Oct. 10-sunset.

TWICKENHAM

ROYAL MILITARY SCHOOL OF MUSIC MUSEUM
Kneller Hall, Twickenham, Middlesex
Old instruments of a military nature. Uniforms. Music. Accoutrements.
Open for 2 hours before each Summer Concert. Other times by appointment only.

TYWYN

NARROW GAUGE RAILWAY MUSEUM
Tywyn, Merioneth
Locomotives, rolling stock and exhibits representing the narrow gauge railways of the British Isles.
Whitsun-Sept. Daily 10-6 or by appointment.

WADDESDON

WADDESDON MANOR
Waddesdon, Buckinghamshire
Built 1880-89 by Baron Ferdinand de Rothschild. French 18th century decorative art, furniture, carpets, tapestries, porcelain; Dutch 17th century and French 18th century paintings. English 18th century portraits.
Apr.-Oct. W., Th., F. (inc. Good F.), Sa. and Su. 2-6 (Su. grounds open from 11.30); Bank Holiday M. 11-6. Children under 12 not admitted to house.

WAKEFIELD

CITY ART GALLERY
Wentworth Terrace, Wakefield, Yorkshire
Paintings. Sculpture. Drawings. Prints. 18th century English water-colours and drawings.
Weekdays 11-5; Su. 2-5.

CITY MUSEUM
Wood Street, Wakefield, Yorkshire
Costumes. Bygones. Local and natural history. Silver. Glass. Ceramics. Victorian and Jacobean rooms. Period shops.
Weekdays 11-6; Su. 2.30-5.30.

HEATH HALL
near Wakefield, Yorkshire
Mansion (18th century). Impressionist paintings. Rockingham porcelain. 18th and early 19th century inkwells.
May-Sept., W. 2-5.

NOSTELL PRIORY
Wakefield, Yorkshire
Chippendale furniture. Motor cycle museum.
Easter Sa. - mid. Oct. W., Sa., Su. (and Tu. after Bank Holidays), 2-6. Bank Holiday M. and Su. 11-6. Daily Aug. - mid. Sept. 2-6.

WALL

LETOCETUM MUSEUM
Wall, Staffordshire
Archaeological material from the excavated Roman military station Letocetum.
Mar., Apr. and Oct. 9.30-5.30; Su. 2-5.30. May-Sept. 9.30-7; Su. 2-7. Nov.-Feb. 9.30-4; Su. 2-4.

WALSALL

E. M. FLINT ART GALLERY
Lichfield Street, Walsall, Staffordshire
Paintings. Leathercraft.
M.-Sa. 10-7 (Su. 10-5.30).

MUSEUM OF LEATHERCRAFT
Central Library and Art Gallery, Lichfield Street, Walsall, Staffordshire
"Leather in Life" permanent exhibition.
Daily 10-7; Sa. 10-5.30.

WAREHAM

ROYAL ARMOURED CORPS TANK MUSEUM
Bovington Camp, Wareham, Dorset
Uniforms, old arms, awards, campaign medals, regimental colours, pictures, trophies and souvenirs.
Weekdays 10-12.30, 2-4.45. Weekends and Bank Holidays 10.30-12.30, 2-4.

SMEDMORE
nr. Wareham, Dorset
18th century manor house. Antique dolls.
Early June - early Sept. W., 2.30-5.45.

WARMINSTER

LONGLEAT HOUSE
Warminster, Wiltshire
Built 1566-1580 with later alterations 1801-11. State rooms. Furnishings. Paintings. Books.
Daily (including Su.) 10-6. Winter 10-4. Closed Christmas Day.

WARRINGTON

THE LANCASHIRE REGIMENT (P.W.V.) SERVICE MUSEUM
Peninsula Barracks, Orford, Warrington, Lancashire
Uniforms, old arms, awards, campaign medals, regimental colours, pictures, trophies and souvenirs.
M.-F. 9-12, 2-4 or any time by appointment.

MUNICIPAL MUSEUM AND ART GALLERY
Bold Street, Warrington, Lancashire
Natural history. Botany. Geology. Ethnology. Anthropology. Bygones. Early English water colours. Pottery. Porcelain. Local glass.
M.-F. 10-7; Sa. 10-5. Closed Bank Holidays.

WARWICK

DOLL MUSEUM
Oken's House, Castle Street, Warwick, Warwickshire
Antique and period dolls and toys.
Weekdays 10-6; Su. 2.30-5.

LORD LEYCESTER HOSPITAL
West Gate, Warwick, Warwickshire
Group of halls and residences, 1383. Includes Guildhall Museum. Local history.
Weekdays 10-6 (Summer), 10-4 (Winter). Closed Su., Good F. and Christmas Day.

THE QUEEN'S OWN HUSSARS SERVICE MUSEUM
Lord Leycester Hospital, High Street, Warwick, Warwickshire
Uniforms, old arms, awards, campaign medals, regimental colours, pictures, trophies and souvenirs.
Weekdays 10-6 (Summer); 10-4 (Winter).

THE ROYAL WARWICKSHIRE REGIMENT MUSEUM
St. John's House, Warwick, Warwickshire
Uniforms, old arms, awards, campaign medals, regimental colours, pictures, trophies and souvenirs associated with the regiment.
Weekdays (except Tu.) 10-12.30, 1.30-5.30; Su. (May-Sept.) 2.30-5.

ST. JOHN'S HOUSE
Coten End, Warwick, Warwickshire
Warwickshire bygones. Period costumes. Furniture.
Weekdays (except Tu.) 10-12.30, 1.30-5.30; Su. (May-Sept.). 2.30-5.

WARWICK CASTLE
Warwick, Warwickshire
State Apartments. Furniture. Paintings, including works by Holbein, Reubens and Van Dyck.
Good F. - mid. Sept. Daily 10-5.30. Shorter hours out of season. Closed Nov.-Feb.

WARWICK COUNTY MUSEUM
Market Place, Warwick, Warwickshire
Natural history, geology, archaeology and history of Warwickshire.
Weekdays (except F.) 10-5.30; Su. (May-Sept.) 2.30-5.

WATFORD

WATFORD ART COLLECTION
Central Public Library, Hempstead Road, Watford, Hertfordshire
Local prints. Paintings. Fossils.
Daily 9-8 (9-1 W. and 9-5 Sa.).

WELLINGBOROUGH

HINWICK HOUSE
nr. Wellingborough, Northamptonshire
Queen Anne house. Pictures by Van Dyck, Lely, Kneller. Tapestries and needlework. Furniture.
Easter M., Spring Bank Holiday M., Late Summer Bank Holiday M. Otherwise by written appointment.

WELLS

HOLKHAM HALL
Wells, Norfolk
Palladian mansion. Pictures. Tapestries. Statuary. Furnishings.
June-Sept. Th., 2-5, also M. in July and Aug. 2-5.

WELLS MUSEUM
Cathedral Green, Wells, Somerset
Local bygones. Prehistoric cave finds. Coins. Natural history, Mendip rocks, fossils and minerals.
Weekdays: Apr.-Sept. 10-6; Oct.-Mar. 2-4.30. Su., July, Aug. and Sept. 2.30-5.30.

WELSHPOOL

POWIS CASTLE
Welshpool, Montgomeryshire
Plasterwork. Murals. Furniture. Paintings. Tapestry. Lead statuary. Animals and birds.
Castle: *June-Sept. Daily (except M. and Tu.) 2-6 (10.30-5.30 on Spring and Late Summer Bank Holiday M.).*

WEST BROMWICH

OAK HOUSE MUSEUM
Oak Road, West Bromwich, Staffordshire
15th century half-timbered house, furnished in period style. 16th - early 18th century furniture.
Apr.-Sept. M.-Sa. 10-5; Su. 2.30-5. Oct.-Mar. M.-Sa. 10-4. Closed Th. afternoon.

WEST CLANDON

CLANDON PARK
West Clandon, Guildford, Surrey
House (1730s). Furniture. Porcelain. 19th century domestic equipment. Pictures.
Apr. 1 - Oct. 14, Tu.-Th., Sa., Su. and Bank Holiday M. 2-6. Closed Tu. after Bank Holidays.

WESTERHAM

CHARTWELL
Westerham, Kent
The home for many years of Sir Winston Churchill. Rooms with original furnishings and Churchill mementoes.
Mar.-Nov. (Gardens and Studio Apr. - mid. Oct.), W. and Th. 2-6 or dusk if earlier; Sa., Su. and Bank Holiday M. 11-6 or dusk.

KENT AND COUNTY OF LONDON YEOMANRY (SHARPSHOOTERS) SERVICE MUSEUM
Squerryes Court, Westerham, Kent
Uniforms, old arms, awards, campaign medals, regimental colours, pictures, trophies and souvenirs associated with the regiment.
House open Mar.-Oct. inclusive. W., Sa. Su. and Bank Holidays 2-6.

QUEBEC HOUSE
Westerham, Kent
Relics of General Wolfe.
Mar.-Oct., Tu., W. and Su. 2-6. Bank Holiday M. 10-1, 2-6.

SQUERRYES COURT
Westerham, Kent
William and Mary manor house (1681). Period furniture. Dutch pictures. Tapestries. Military uniforms and relics.
Mar.-Oct. W., Sa., Su. and Bank Holidays, 2-6.

WESTER ROSS

EILEAN DONAN CASTLE
Wester Ross, Ross and Cromarty
Jacobite relics - mostly with Clan connections.
Apr.-Oct. Weekdays only, 10-12.30, 2-6.

WEST HOATHLY

PRIEST HOUSE
West Hoathly, Sussex
Collection of old furniture, bygones, dolls and embroidery.
Easter-Sept. Weekdays (except F.) 10-6; Su. 2-5.

WESTON-SUPER-MARE

MUSEUM AND ART GALLERY
The Boulevard, Weston-super-Mare, Somerset
Local history including archaeology and folk life material. Collection of Somerset birds.
M.-F. 10-6; Sa. 10-5.

WEST WYCOMBE

WEST WYCOMBE PARK
West Wycombe, Buckinghamshire
Palladian house with frescoes and painted ceilings. Original furniture. Picture collection.
June, Tu. and W. 2.15-6. July and Aug. Daily except M. but including Late Summer Bank Holiday, 2.15-6.

WEYBRIDGE

WEYBRIDGE MUSEUM
Church Street, Weybridge, Surrey
Local exhibits of archaeology, costume and local history.
M.-F. 2-5; Sa. 10-5.

WEYMOUTH

NO. 3 TRINITY STREET
Weymouth, Dorset
Tudor house. 17th century furnishings.
Easter Sa. - beginning of Oct., W. and Sa. and Bank Holiday M., 2.30-5.

WHITBY

WHITBY MUSEUM AND ART GALLERY
Pannett Park, Whitby, Yorkshire
Early and contemporary English water-colours and paintings, including works by Turner, Bonington, David Cox, Peter de Wint and the Weatherills. Maritime exhibits. Scoresby's magnetic experiments.
May-Sept. 9-1, 2-5.30; Su. 2-5. Oct.-Apr. Weekdays 10.30-1 also W. and Sa. 2-4; Su. 2-4.

WHITBY LITERARY AND PHILOSOPHICAL SOCIETY MUSEUM
Pannett Park, Whitby, Yorkshire
Fossils. Flint weapons. Relics of Roman occupation. Model of Whitby Abbey. Captain Cook relics. Shipping Gallery. Exhibits of local natural history and local industries.
May-Sept. 9-1, 2-5.30; Su. 2-5. Oct.-Apr. Weekdays 10.30-1, also W. and Sa. 2-4; Su. 2-4.

WHITHORN

WHITHORN PRIORY MUSEUM
Whithorn Priory, Whithorn, Wigtownshire
Early Christian monuments including the Latinus stone (5th century) and the St. Peter Stone, showing a late form of the Chrism or Chi-Rho monogram.
Apr.-Sept. Daily 9.30-7; Su. 2-7. Oct.-Mar. Daily 10-4.30; Su. 2-4.30.

WICK

CARNEGIE LIBRARY AND MUSEUM
Wick, Caithness
Local antiquities and natural history.
Weekdays 10-5.

WIGAN

WIGAN ART GALLERY AND MUSEUM
Station Road, Wigan, Lancashire
Collections include geology, mineralogy, coins, medals, bygones, local industries.
Weekdays 10-5.

WILLENHALL

UNION WORKS
Gower Street, Willenhall, Staffordshire, WV13 1JX
Company Museum. Locks.
By appointment.

WILMINGTON

WILMINGTON MUSEUM
Wilmington Priory, Wilmington, Sussex
Collection of old agricultural implements and farmhouse utensils.
Apr.-Sept. Weekdays (except F.) 10-6; Su. 2-5.

WIMBORNE MINSTER

PRIEST'S HOUSE MUSEUM
High Street, Wimborne Minster, Dorset
Local archaeology and history.
Easter M. - Sept. Weekdays 10.30-12.30, 2.30-4.30. Other dates as announced locally.

WIMBORNE ST. GILES

ST. GILES' HOUSE
Wimborne St. Giles, Dorset
Home of the Earls of Shaftesbury. Jacobean mansion. Tapestries. 18th century Shell Grotto.
By appointment.

WINCHCOMBE

FOLK MUSEUM
Town Hall, Winchcombe, Gloucestershire
Local history.
By appointment.

HAILES ABBEY MUSEUM
Hailes Abbey, Winchcombe, Gloucestershire
Medieval sculpture and other architectural fragments found in the ruins of the Abbey.
Mar., Apr. and Oct. 9.30-5.30; Su. 2-5.30. May-Sept. 9.30-7; Su. 2-7. Nov.-Feb. 9.30-4; Su. 2-4.

SUDELEY CASTLE
Winchcombe, Cheltenham, Gloucestershire
Castle (12th century), home of Queen Katherine Parr. Royal relics. Needlework. Furniture. Tapestries. Picture collection, including works by Constable, Rubens, Turner and Van Dyke.
Mar. 24 - May 26, Tu.-Sa., 2-5.30; Su. 12-5.30. May 29 - Sept. 23, Tu.-Su. 12-5.30. Sept. 25 - Oct. 14, Tu.-Sa. 2-5.30; Su. 12-5.30.

WINCHELSEA

WINCHELSEA MUSEUM
Court Hall, Winchelsea, Sussex
Collection illustrating the history of the Cinque Ports. Handicrafts, archaeological specimens, models, maps, documents.
Whitsun - Sept. 30.

WINCHESTER

THE ROYAL GREEN JACKETS MUSEUM
Peninsula Barracks, Winchester, Hampshire
Incorporating 1st Battalion (43rd and 52nd); 2nd Battalion (The King's Royal Rifle Corps); 3rd Battalion (The Rifle Brigade). Regiment's history over past 200 years, including collection of medals of the Peninsular and Waterloo Campaigns.
M.-F. 10-4; Sa. (Apr.-Sept. only) 2.30-4.30.

THE ROYAL HAMPSHIRE REGIMENT SERVICE MUSEUM
Series House, Southgate Street, Winchester, Hampshire
Uniforms, old arms, awards, campaign medals, regimental colours, pictures, trophies and souvenirs associated with the regiment.
M.-F. 10-12.30, 2-4.

THE WESTGATE MUSEUM
High Street, Winchester, Hampshire
Medieval west gate of the city. Exhibits illustrate the civic history of Winchester. City moot horn (13th century). Medieval and later weights and measures.
Weekdays 10-4, 5 or 6 according to the season. Su. 2-4.30.

WINCHESTER CITY MUSEUM
The Square, Winchester, Hampshire
Archaeology of Winchester and central Hampshire.
Weekdays 10-4, 5 or 6 according to the season. Su. 2-4.30.

WINCHESTER COLLEGE MUSEUM
Winchester, Hampshire
Collections of Greek pottery, English water-colours.
By appointment.

WINDSOR

THE GUILDHALL EXHIBITIONS
High Street, Windsor, Berkshire
Collections include implements, Charters and documents, pictures and dioramas. The Guildhall, dating from 1689, contains a collection of Royal portraits.
Aug.-Oct. Daily 1-5.30.

THE HOUSEHOLD CAVALRY MUSEUM
Combermere Barracks, Windsor, Berkshire
General exhibits of The Life Guards and Royal Horse Guards (The Blues).
M.-F. 10-1, 2-5; Su. 11-1, 2-5.

WINDSOR CASTLE
Windsor, Berkshire
Royal Residence. The Castle is now largely medieval, Stuart and Regency. The State Apartments contain many examples of the work of Van Dyck. Furniture. Porcelain. Armour. Queen Mary's Dolls' House and Exhibition of Dolls.
Castle Precincts: *Daily 10-sunset.* State Apartments: *Weekdays (subject to requirements of court), Nov.-Feb. 11-3; Mar.-Apr. 11-4; May-Sept. 11-5; Oct. 11-4; also Su. (Apr.-Oct.) from 1.30.* St. George's Chapel: *Weekdays 11-3.45 (F. 1-3.45). Closed Jan. Su. 2.30-4.* Queen Mary's Dolls' House and Exhibition, Old Master Drawings: *Daily all year. Not Su. Nov.-Apr., Christmas Day or Good F. Hours as for State Apartments. State Apartments usually closed 6 weeks for Easter, 3 weeks for Ascot and 3 weeks Christmas.*

WING

ASCOTT
Wing, Buckinghamshire
Paintings. French and Chippendale furniture. Oriental porcelain of the Ming, K'ang Hsi and Chun ware of the Sung Dynasties.
Apr.-Sept. W., Sa. and Bank Holiday M., also some Su. in July and Aug. 2-6.

WINSLOW

CLAYDON HOUSE
nr. Winslow, Buckinghamshire
Built 1752-68 on site of an earlier house. Rococo staterooms including Florence Nightingale Museum, with her bedroom and sitting room.
Mar.-Oct. Daily except M. but open Bank Holiday M., 2-6. Closed Tu. following Bank Holiday M. Closed Good Friday and Christmas Day. Nov.-Feb. by appointment only.

WISBECH

WISBECH AND FENLAND MUSEUM
Museum Square, Wisbech, Cambridgeshire
Fenland and Natural History. Archaeological and antiquarian collections. Pottery and porcelain, bygones. Library of books and manuscripts including that of Dickens' "Great Expectations".
Tu.-Sa. and Bank Holidays 10-1, 2-5. Winter 10-1, 2-4.

WOBURN

WOBURN ABBEY
Woburn, Bedfordshire
18th century mansion. Paintings by Canaletto, Rembrandt, Van Dyck, Cuyp, Teniers, Gainsborough, Reynolds, Velazquez, Holbein. French and English 18th century furniture. 18th century silver. State Apartments.
Apr.-Aug. M.-Sa. 11.30-6; Su. 11.30-7. Sept.-Oct. Su. 11.30-6.30. Nov.-Mar. M.-Sa. 1-4.30; Su. 1-4.

WOLVERHAMPTON

BANTOCK HOUSE
Bantock Park, Wolverhampton, Staffordshire
Early Worcester porcelain. Chinese ivories. Wolverhampton bygones.
Weekdays 10-7; Su. 2-5.

BILSTON MUSEUM AND ART GALLERY
Mount Pleasant, Wolverhampton, Staffordshire
Collections illustrating the life and activities of Bilston and the Black Country.
M., Tu., Th. and F. 10-7; W. and Sa. 10-5.

MOSELEY OLD HALL
Wolverhampton, Staffordshire
17th century furniture. Documents, portraits, relics, relating to Charles II.
Mar.-Nov. W., Th., Sa. and Su. 2-6 (or dusk if earlier). Bank Holiday M. and Tu. 10.30-12.30, 2-6. First three Su. in Dec. 2-4.30 or by appointment.

MUNICIPAL ART GALLERY AND MUSEUM
Lichfield Street, Wolverhampton, Staffordshire
English enamels. Staffordshire pottery. English watercolours and paintings. Sculpture by local artists.
Weekdays 10-6.

WIGHTWICK MANOR
Wolverhampton, Staffordshire
William Morris wallpaper, tapestries, curtains, embroidery. Pre-Raphaelite pictures, tiles and stained glass.
Tu., Sa., Bank Holidays, 2.30-5.30. Also May-Sept. W. 2-6 (last party 4.30).

WOODBRIDGE

GLEMHEM HALL
nr. Woodbridge, Suffolk
Brick Elizabethan house, altered early 1700. Panelled rooms, Queen Anne furniture.
Mid. Apr. - end Sept. W., Su. and Bank Holidays 2-6.

WOODSTOCK

BLENHEIM PALACE
Woodstock, Oxfordshire
House by Sir John Vanbrugh (1705-22). Collection of pictures and tapestries.
Apr. 2 - Oct. 25, daily ex. F. 1-6. Closed Spring Bank Holiday.

OXFORD CITY AND COUNTY MUSEUM
Fletcher's House, Woodstock, Oxfordshire
Crafts, industries, domestic life of Oxford City and County.
May-Sept. M.-F. 10-5; Sa. 10-6; Su. 2-6. Oct.-Apr. Weekdays 10-5.

WOOKEY HOLE

WOOKEY HOLE
Somerset
The earliest known home of man in Great Britain. Animal remains of the newer Pilocene period. Relics of the late Celtic and Romano-British civilisation including tools, ornaments, pottery, coins, etc.
Summer: Daily 9-dusk. Winter: Daily 10-12, 1.30-5.

WORCESTER

CITY MUSEUM
Foregate Street, Worcester, Worcestershire
Folk life material, archaeology, geology and natural history illustrating man and his environment in the Severn Valley region with particular reference to the City of Worcester.
M.-Sa. 9.30-6. Closes at 5 Th. and Sa.

THE DYSON PERRINS MUSEUM OF WORCESTER PORCELAIN
The Royal Porcelain Works, Severn Street, Worcester, Worcestershire
Worcester porcelain.
M.-F. 10-1, 2-5. (Sa., May-Sept.).

TUDOR HOUSE FOLK MUSEUM
Friar Street, Worcester, Worcestershire
Museum of folk life, illustrating the domestic life of the city of Worcester. History of the river Severn.
M.-Sa. 9.30-6. Closes at 5 Th. and Sa.

THE WORCESTERSHIRE REGIMENT MUSEUM
Norton Barracks, Worcester, Worcestershire
Uniforms, old arms, awards, campaign medals, regimental colours, pictures, trophies and souvenirs.
M.-F. 9-12.30, 2-4. Weekends by appointment.

WORKINGTON

HELENA THOMPSON MUSEUM
Park End Road, Workington, Cumberland
Local history.
Tu.-Sa. 10-12, 2-4.

WORKSOP

WORKSOP MUSEUM
Memorial Avenue, Worksop, Nottinghamshire
Local archaeological and historical display. Bygones and Victoriana. Local birds, butterflies and moths.
Daily (except Th. and Su.) 10-4.

WORTHING

WORTHING MUSEUM AND ART GALLERY
Chapel Road, Worthing, Sussex
Collections of archaeological material, geology, costumes. Sussex bygones and pottery, works of art including Early English water-colours. Dolls. Jewellery.
Weekdays 10-7; 10-5 Oct.-Mar.

WREXHAM

CHIRK CASTLE
nr. Wrexham, Denbighshire
Built 1310. Portraits, tapestries and furniture of the 17th, 18th and early 19th centuries.
Easter-Sept., Tu., Th., Sa., Su. 2-5. Bank Holidays, 11-5.

WREXHAM EXHIBITION HALL AND WREXHAM ROOM
Public Library, Queen Square, Wrexham, Denbighshire
Printed books and manuscripts relating to Wrexham.
M.-F. 10.30-7; Sa. 10.30-5.

WROXETER

VIROCONIUM MUSEUM
Wroxeter, Shropshire
Objects found during the excavation of the site. Roman inscriptions, pottery, coins.
Mar., Apr. and Oct. 9.30-5.30; Su. 2-5.30. May-Sept. 9.30-7; Su. 2-7. Nov.-Feb. 9.30-4; Su. 2-4.

WYE

AGRICULTURAL MUSEUM
Wye College, University of London, Court Lodge Farm, Brook, Wye, Kent
Agricultural implements, machinery, hand tools and other farming equipment.
June-Sept. W. 2-5 (also Sa. during Aug.), and by appointment with the Curator.

YEOVIL

BOROUGH MUSEUM
Hendford Manor Hall, Yeovil, Somerset
Local history and archaeology. Fire-arm collection. Costumes.
Weekdays (except Th.) 10.30-1, 2.15-5.

MONTACUTE HOUSE
Yeovil, Somerset
House (1588). Heraldic glass. Tapestries. Panelling. Furniture.
Easter Sa. - Sept. Daily except M. and Tu., but open Bank Holiday M., 12.30-6. Mar. - Easter and Oct. and Nov., W., Sa. and Su. 2-6 or dusk if earlier. Other times by written application.

YEOVILTON

FLEET AIR ARM SERVICE MUSEUM
Royal Naval Air Station, Yeovilton, Somerset
Uniforms, old arms, awards, campaign medals, regimental colours, pictures, trophies and souvenirs associated with the RNAS.
Apr. - Oct. Weekdays 10.30-5; Su. 2-5.

YORK

CASTLE HOWARD
York, Yorkshire
Designed by Vanbrugh (1699-1726). Paintings, statuary, tapestries and furniture. Costume Galleries in the Stables.
Easter Su. - early Oct. Tu., W., Th., Sa. and Su. 1.30-5 (Grounds open 12.30-6.30). Bank Holiday M. 11.30-5.30.

CITY OF YORK ART GALLERY
Exhibition Square, York, Yorkshire
Collection of Old Master and modern English and European paintings. Ceramics. Topographical watercolours and prints.
Weekdays 10-5; Su. 2.30-5.

RAILWAY MUSEUM
Queen Street, York, Yorkshire
Locomotives. Coaches. Operating equipment. Documents illustrating railway history.
Weekdays 10-5.

YORK CASTLE MUSEUM
Tower Street, York, Yorkshire
Folk Museum of Yorkshire Life. Bygones. Period rooms. Domestic and agricultural equipment. Early crafts. Costumes. Toys. Yorkshire militaria, an Edwardian street, water-driven corn mill.
Apr.-Sept. Weekdays 9.30-7.30; Su. 10-7.30. Oct.-Mar. Weekdays 9.30-4.30; Su. 10-4.30.

THE YORKSHIRE MUSEUM
Museum Street, York, Yorkshire
Natural history. Archaeology. Geology. Pottery. Coins. Medieval Architecture Museum. A subsidiary Roman collection is housed in the Hospitium.
Weekdays 10-5; Su. 1-5.

ZENNOR

WAYSIDE MUSEUM
Old Mill House, Zennor, Cornwall
Archaeology of West Cornwall. Folk collections include domestic, mining, quarrying, agricultural, milling and blacksmithing exhibits.
Whit.-Oct. 10-dusk.

Greece

Greece has a slowly changing economy, based on a moderate expansion of manufacturing industry, and an unsatisfied demand for scientists, economists and technical people of all kinds. One would never suspect this from a list of its museums, which could be fairly labelled "splendid, but completely out of balance". Throughout the country, there are dozens of museums devoted to archaeology, folk art, folklore and the Hellenistic Past, and, with one or two academic exceptions in Athens, none to science, contemporary history, industry, transport. So far as Greek museums are concerned, the modern world does not exist, a fact which must make for great frustration among the many Greek teachers and parents who are trying to prepare children to earn a skilled living in the last quarter of the twentieth century. Such a completely unsatisfactory situation can hardly continue for much longer, and one knows from the conversations one has had in Greece in recent years that there are tentative plans to bring about an improvement. It could well be that the next ten years will see some very interesting experiments aimed at developing museums of science and technology on a small budget. Meanwhile, however, the situation can only be described as it is, with a thought as to the possible reasons for this museum backwardness.

The main reasons, as always, are both political and financial. Greece is not, by European standards, a rich country, although in 1945 it was certainly no poorer than its neighbour, Bulgaria, which now has an excellent, well-balanced system of museums, including several interesting examples of open-air museums, which, for some inexplicable reason, have not been established in the equally sunny Greece. It is easy, and no doubt partly true, to say that museums which deal with the modern world may, to some kinds of régime, be politically dangerous and that museums of archaeology and folklore are politically safe; but this is not the whole story. Greece still has more reason to be proud of its distant past, when it was a great nation, than of its recent past and its present, when it has been of small significance in the world; and it is human and natural to wish to draw attention to one's strong points and to play down one's weaknesses, especially when the strong points are so attractive, both to scholars and to tourists.

AEGINA

MUSEUM
Aegina
Site of Temple of Aphaia. Sculpture. Torso of Amazon. Early Corinthian vases. Vases of Attica. Coins. Sphinx of Attic workmanship contemporary with Kalamis. Inscribed anchors. Local pottery (neolithic to archaic).
Summer: Daily 8-1, 3-6; Su. and holidays 10-1, 3-6. Winter: Daily 9-1, 2.30-5; Su. and holidays 10-1, 2.30-5. Closed Jan. 1, Mar. 25, Good F. (until noon), Easter Su. and Christmas Day. Closed M.

AFANDOU

E. KANDIS PRIVATE COLLECTION
Afandou, Rhodes
Ornamental plates.
By written appointment.

AGIA

ARCHAEOLOGICAL COLLECTION
Gymnasium (secondary school), Agia
Architectural fragments and inscriptions of the Hellenistic and Roman periods. Post-Byzantine icons and crosses.
During school hours, on request.

AGIASSOS

CHURCH OF THE PANAGIA
Agiassos, Lesvos
Hanging lamps (votive offerings), icons, vestments, church plate, manuscripts (some illuminated) and many old documents.
Daily 9-4.

AGION OROS

MONASTERY SACRISTY
Agion Oros
All the monasteries of Agion Oros have sacristies, where they keep valuable works of Byzantine and post-Byzantine art: icons, church plate, embroidered vestments, wood-carvings, reliquaries, illuminated manuscripts and other relics.
Enquire locally. Women not admitted.

AGIOS KIRYKOS

ARCHAEOLOGICAL COLLECTION
Gymnasium (secondary school), Agios Kirykos, Ikaria
Pottery from the archaic to the Roman period.
During school hours, on request.

AGIOS NIKOLAOS

ARCHAEOLOGICAL MUSEUM
Konstantinou Paleologou Street, Agios Nikolaos, Crete
Contains finds from eastern Crete. Comprehensive and important collection of pottery from all the periods of the Minoan civilisation; sarcophagi. Figurines. Stone vases and tools. Bronze weapons. Pottery, statuettes and figurines of the geometric, archaic, classical and hellenistic periods. Coins and inscriptions. A few 19th century weapons.
Temporarily closed: enquire locally.

TOURING CLUB COLLECTION
Agios Nikolaos, Crete
Mainly local woven materials and a few embroideries.
By written appointment.

AGRINION

ARCHAEOLOGICAL MUSEUM
Agrinion
Finds from Aetolia and Akarnania. Prehistoric spearheads, sculpture (notably the grave reliefs and inscribed stelae from Astakos), vases, statuettes and terracotta architectural fragments. Bronzes. inscriptions.
Summer: Daily 8-1, 3-6; Su. and holidays 10-1, 3-6. Winter: Daily 9-1, 2.30-5; Su. and holidays 10-1, 2.30-5. Closed Jan. 1, Mar. 25, Good F. (until noon), Easter Su. and Christmas Day, also M.

AIANI

ARCHAEOLOGICAL AND FOLKLORE COLLECTION
Village Hall, Aiani, Kozani
Bronze Age and Iron Age pottery and weapons. Geometric bronze jewellery; classical, Hellenistic and Roman vases and statuettes. Hellenistic and Roman coins and inscriptions. Post-Byzantine icons, wood-carvings, local costumes and jewellery.
Summer: Daily 8-1, 3-6; Su. and holidays 10-1, 3-6. Winter: Daily 9-1, 2.30-5; Su. and holidays 10-1, 2.30-5. Closed Jan. 1, Mar. 25, Good F. (until noon), Easter Su. and Christmas Day.

AIGINA

ARCHAEOLOGICAL MUSEUM
Eynardeion, Aigina
Neolithic, Middle Helladic, Mycenean and Minoan pottery, tools and stone utensils. Sculpture and architectural fragments from the archaic to the Roman period. Terracotta architectural fragments from the temple of Aphaia, archaic and classical vases and statuettes. Lamps and bronzes. Some early Christian and Byzantine sculpture. Inscriptions.
Summer: Daily 8-1, 3-6; Su. and holidays 10-1, 3-6. Winter: Daily 9-1, 2.30-5; Su. and holidays 10-1, 2.30-5. Closed Jan. 1, Mar. 25, Good F. (until noon), Easter Su. and Christmas Day.

AIGION

MONASTERY OF THE TAXIARCHS
Aigion
Vestments, post-Byzantine church embroideries and plate, manuscripts and documents.
Enquire locally at Metropolis of Kalavryta (at Aigion).

ALEXANDROUPOLIS

ARCHAEOLOGICAL COLLECTION
Town Hall, Alexandroupolis
Hellenistic and Roman sculpture; prehistoric, Hellenistic and Roman sherds.
Summer: Daily 8-1, 3-6; Su. and holidays 10-1, 3-6. Winter: Daily 9-1, 2.30-5; Su. and holidays 10-1, 2.30-5. Closed Jan. 1, Mar. 25, Good F. (until noon), Easter Su. and Christmas Day.

E. FILIPPIDIS PRIVATE COLLECTION
33 Proussis Street, Alexandroupolis
Woven materials, embroideries, gold embroideries, aprons, knitted material, woodcarvings and silverware, from the biggest Sarakatsan 'tselingata' (communities of nomadic shepherds) in the prefectures of Evros and Rodopi.
By written appointment.

ALMYROS

MONASTERY OF THE PANAGIA XENIA
Almyros (near)
Gold-embroideries, church plate, wood-carvings and bound gospels.
Enquire locally at Metropolis of Dimitrias (at Volos).

MUSEUM
Office of Orthrys Antiquaries' Society, Almyros
Prehistoric finds. Greek and early Christian sculpture and pottery.
Daily ex. M. 8-1, 3-6; Su. and holidays 10-1, 3-6. Winter: Daily ex. M. 9-1, 3-5; Su. and holidays 9-1, 3-5.

AMBELAKIA

THE G. SCHWARZ MANSION
Ambelakia
Built 1797-98. Considered to be the most typical example of a Greek mansion with an admixture of elements of western influence. Also interesting for its interior decoration. Wood-carvings, metalwork, various folk art items and old documents.
On application to the caretaker.

AMFISSA

EXHIBITION OF CONTEMPORARY GREEK PAINTERS
Town Hall (ground floor), Amfissa
Paintings by Greek artists and local painters.
Variable.

AMORGOS

CHOZOVIOTISSA MONASTERY
Amorgos (near)
The sacristy contains icons, vestments, church plate (some

Byzantine, the majority post-Byzantine) and illuminated manuscripts.
Enquire locally at Metropolis of Thira.

AMPHIARAION

SITE MUSEUM
Amphiaraion
Sculpture. Inscriptions. Early Herm. Torsoes. Reassembled architectural parts of temple and stoa.
Summer: Daily 8-1, 3-6; Su. and holidays 10-1, 3-6. Winter: Daily 9-1, 3-5; Su. and holidays 9-1, 3-5. Closed Jan. 1, Mar. 25, Good F. (until noon), Easter Su. and Christmas Day. Closed M.

ANAFI

ARCHAEOLOGICAL COLLECTION
Primary School, Anafi
Roman sculptures.
During school hours, on request.

ANDRITSAINA

ARCHAEOLOGICAL COLLECTION
Library, Andritsaina
Chance finds, mainly pottery and bronzes.
During library hours.

ANDROS

ARCHAEOLOGICAL COLLECTION
Primary School, Andros
Some archaic, classical and Hellenistic sculptures; geometric pottery.
During school hours, on request.

ANO KARDAMYLA

KARDAMYLA CULTURAL CENTRE OF MICHAEL AND STAMATIA XYLAS
Ano Kardamyla, Chios
Icons, wood-carvings, and woven materials.
Daily 10-12, 5-7.

ANO MERA

MONASTERY OF THE PANAGIA TOURLIANI
Ano Mera, Mykonos
Wood-carvings, church plate, sacred embroideries and vestments.
Enquire locally at Metropolis of Syros, Tinos, Andros, Kea and Milos (at Ermoupolis).

ANTISSA

MONASTERY OF ST. JOHN THE DIVINE, YPSILOU
Antissa, Lesvos
Icons, ecclesiastical plate and embroideries, some wood-carvings, manuscripts.
Enquire locally at Metropolis of Mytilini, Eressos and Plomarion (at Mytilini).

APEIRANTHOS

ARCHAEOLOGICAL COLLECTION
Apeiranthos, Naxos
Prehistoric vases and figurines of stone and terracotta. Stone plaques of the first Cycladic period. Daggers. A few Roman reliefs.
Summer: Daily 8-1, 3-6; Su. and holidays 10-1, 3-6. Winter: Daily 9-1, 2.30-5; Su. and holidays 10-1, 2.30-5. Closed Jan. 1, Mar. 25, Good F. (until noon), Easter Su. and Christmas Day.

APOIKIA

MONASTERY OF AGIOS NIKOLAOS
Apoikia, Andros (near)
Church plate and embroidery.
Enquire locally at Metropolis of Syros, Tinos, Andros, Kea and Milos (see at Ermoupolis).

ARGOS

ARCHAEOLOGICAL MUSEUM
Vassilissis Olgas Street, Argos
Finds from the excavations at Lerna, mainly early and late Neolithic, Early Helladic, Middle Helladic and Mycenean pottery, Mycenean vases, statuettes and small finds. Protogeometric, Geometric, early Corinthian, Corinthian, black-figure and red-figure vases. Jewellery, breastplates, weapons, spits, statuettes and other items from the Geometric and archaic periods. Roman sculpture and, in the courtyard, a large mosaic floor representing the seasons and the months.
Summer: Daily 8-1, 3-6; Su. and holidays 10-1, 3-6. Winter: Daily 9-1, 2.30-5; Su. and holidays 10-1, 2.30-5. Closed Jan. 1, Mar. 25, Good F. (until noon), Easter Su. and Christmas Day. Closed M.

ARGOSTOLION

ARCHAEOLOGICAL MUSEUM
Argostolion, Kefallinia
Mycenean and sub-Mycenean pottery, bronze weapons and small finds. Geometric and archaic pottery. Hellenistic sculpture and pottery. Roman bronze head.
Summer: Daily 8.30-1, 4-6; Su. and holidays 10-1. Winter: Daily 9-1, 2.30-5; Su. and holidays 10-1, 2.30-5. Closed Jan. 1, Mar. 25, Good F. (until noon), Easter Su. and Christmas Day. Closed M.

E. BASSIAS HISTORICAL AND FOLKLORE MUSEUM
Koryaleneios Library, Argostolion, Kefallinia
Icons of the 17th-19th centuries; vestments; Venetian sculpture. Woven materials, wood-carvings, metalwork. Lithographs, maps and photographs.
On request.

COLLECTION OF THE MTROPOLIS OF KEFALLINIA
Bishop's Palace, Argostolion, Kefallinia
Post-Byzantine icons and vestments.
Summer: Daily 8-1, 3-6; Su. and holidays 10-1, 3-6. Winter: Daily 9-1, 2.30-5; Su. and holidays 10-1, 2.30-5. Closed Jan. 1, Mar. 25, Good F. (until noon), Easter Su. and Christmas Day.

ARTA

ARCHAEOLOGICAL COLLECTION
Trapeza tis Parigoritissas, Arta
Housed in the most important monument in Arta, 13th century. Classical and Hellenistic sculpture, pottery, statuettes and inscriptions from ancient Ambracia. Byzantine sculpture, some icons and small objets d'art.
Summer: Daily 8-1, 3-6; Su. and holidays 10-1. Winter: Daily 9-1, 2-5; Su. and holidays 10-1. Closed Jan. 1, Mar. 25, Good F. (until noon), Easter Su. and Christmas Day. Closed M.

ASTROS

ARCHAEOLOGICAL COLLECTION
Astros
In a building belonging to the local Council, near the primary school. Some sculpture, pottery and small finds of various periods.
Daily ex. M. 9-4.

ATHENS

ACROPOLIS MUSEUM
on the Acropolis, Athens
Sculpture of the archaic and classical periods, which used to form the architectural decoration of the temples or elsewhere erected as votive offerings in the sanctuary of the Acropolis. Poros pediments from archaic temples, still painted in their original colours, mostly depicting ancient myths; slabs from the frieze, some metopes and sculptures from the pediments of the Parthenon (448 B.C.). Frieze slabs depicting Victories from the parapet round the temple of Athena Nike (Wingless Victory) (410 B.C.). Figures from the frieze of the Erechtheion (409-405 B.C.). Korai, the 'Moschophoros', horsemen, statues of youths, Hellenistic and Roman sculpture. Vases and terracotta plaques from the Geometric to the classical period.
Daily ex. Tu. 9-5. (9-4 in winter); Su. and holidays 10-2.

AGORA MUSEUM
Stoa of Attalos II, Athens
Finds from the excavations of the American School of Classical Studies in the Agora, on the south slope of the Acropolis and on the Pnyx. Neolithic, Early Helladic, Middle Helladic and Mycenean pottery, bronze and gold jewellery and ivory articles. Geometric vases, statuettes, weapons, jewellery. Grave groups. Sculptures of the archaic, classical, Hellenistic and Roman periods. Archaic pottery and statuettes. Vases including black-figure, Hellenistic and Roman. Bronze and terra-cotta statuettes of all periods. Amphorae, household utensils and lamps of all periods. Articles used in public life. Inscriptions. Mosaic floor of 4th century A.D. Byzantine pottery.
Mar. 16-Oct. 14, Daily ex. M. 9-5; Su. and holidays 10-2. Oct. 15-Mar. 15, Daily ex. M. 9-4; Su. and holidays 10-2.

R. ANDREADIS PRIVATE COLLECTION
11 Vas. Georgiou II Avenue, Athens
Ancient pottery. Icons.
By written appointment.

F. ANOYANAKIS PRIVATE COLLECTION
4 Sevastias Street, Athens
Three hundred traditional folk musical instruments from the 18th to 20th centuries, arranged according to the Hornbostel-Sachs system.
By written appointment.

ANTHROPOLOGICAL AND ETHNOLOGICAL MUSEUM
University of Athens, Papadiamandopoulou Street, Goudi, Athens
Ethnographical collections from all over the world, including costumes, domestic items, arms and objects in everyday use. Exhibits relating to anatomy and biology of various cultures, going back to prehistoric man.
M., W. and F. 9-12. Closed Su. and holidays.

D. ARTEMIS PRIVATE COLLECTION
42 Panayi Kyriakou Street, Athens
Cycladic figurines and vases. Ancient coins.
By written appointment.

ATHENS EPIGRAPHICAL COLLECTION
National Archaeological Museum, 1 Tositsa Street, Athens
Contains more than 13,000 inscriptions from the 6th century B.C. up to 300 A.D. On display are the most important inscriptions of historical or religious significance or great literary merit, and statue bases bearing the names of great artists.
Daily ex. Su. 8-1.30. Winter: 8-2.

ATHENS NUMISMATIC COLLECTION
National Archaeological Museum (first floor), 1 Tositsa Street, Athens
Coins from the 7th century B.C. up to the present day (ancient Greek issued by the various city-states, Roman, Byzantine, medieval, later and modern Greek, and examples from other European countries). Lead seals. Ancient tokens of copper and lead. Ancient and Byzantine weights. Collection of carved stones.
Daily ex. Su. 7.30-1.30. Winter: Daily ex. Su. 8-2.30.

BENAKI MUSEUM
1 Koumbari Street, Athens
Greek art from prehistoric times to the present day. Ancient pottery, bronze items, especially jewellery. Byzantine and post-Byzantine icons, manuscripts, outstanding church plate, vestments and embroideries, jewellery and wood-carvings. Ecclesiastical reliefs brought by refugees in the exchange of populations from Asia Minor, Pontus and E. Thrace. Traditional local costumes, embroideries, jewellery, pottery, metal-work, wood-carvings. Weapons, relics and historic mementoes from the 1821 War of Independence up to the present. Eleftherios Venizelos room, with personal possessions, manuscripts and photographs. 18th-19th century paintings and engravings on Greek subjects. Coptic, Islamic and Turkish objets d'art. Chinese porcelain from Neolithic times to the 19th century.
Daily ex. Tu. and p.m. Su., 9.30-1.30, 4.30-7.30; Su. and holidays 9.30-1.30. Winter: Daily ex. Tu. 9.30-2; Su. and holidays 9.30-2.

L. BENAKIS PRIVATE COLLECTION
4 Neofytou Vamva Street, Athens
Classical and Hellenistic sculpture and vases. Hellenistic terracotta statuettes, 'caricatures'.
By written appointment.

BOTANICAL MUSEUM
Athens University, University Town, Ilissia, Athens
Specimens of dried plants. Fungi, seaweed and bryophyta. Greek and foreign flora.
M.-Sa. 8-1; closed Su. and holidays.

BYZANTINE MUSEUM
22 Vassilissis Sofias Avenue, Athens
Housed in the Duchess of Plaisance's mansion, built by S. Cleanthis (1848) in the style of a Florentine palace. Byzantine art. Early Christian, Byzantine and Frankish sculptures and architectural fragments. Byzantine and post-Byzantine icons; frescoes, Byzantine manuscripts. Embroidered vestments, church plate and jewellery. Wood-carvings, pottery and sundry other small articles. In the courtyard, early Christian mosaic floors, early Christian and Byzantine sculptures and skylights from village houses in the Cyclades.
Daily ex. M. 8-1, 3-6; Su. 10-2. Winter: Daily ex. M. 9-4; Su. and holidays 10-2.

COLLECTION OF THE LIKION TON ELLINIDON (LYCEUM CLUB OF GREEK WOMEN)
14 Dimokritou Street, Athens
Local costumes and embroideries.
By appointment.

M. DAPERGOLAS PRIVATE COLLECTION
Exoni, Ano Voula, Athens
Ancient pottery, post-Byzantine icons.
By written appointment.

D. ECONOMIDIS PRIVATE COLLECTION
27 Navarchou Nikodimou Street, Athens
Ancient and Byzantine pottery. Icons. Greek, Roman and Byzantine coins. Lead seals.
By written appointment.

R. EVELPIDIS PRIVATE COLLECTION
6 Vas. Sofios Avenue, Athens
Coins.
By written appointment.

GEOLOGICAL AND PALAEONTOLOGICAL MUSEUM
University of Athens, 46 Acadimias Street, Athens
Fossils of vertebrae found in Greece, including elephants, rhinoceri, hippopotami, oxen, stags.
M.-Sa. 9-12. Closed Su. and holidays.

GOULANDRI BOTANICAL MUSEUM
5 Levidou Street, Kifissia, Athens
Plants of Greece.
Summer: Daily 8-1, 3-6; Su. and holidays, 10-1, 3-6. Winter: Daily 9-1, 2.30-5; Su. and holidays, 10-1, 2.30-5. Closed Jan. 1, Mar. 25, Good F. (until noon), Easter Su. and Christmas Day.

A. GOULANDRIS PRIVATE COLLECTION
4 Vas. Georgiou II Avenue, Athens
Cycladic figurines and vases. Some Greek sculpture and pottery.
By written appointment.

GREEK FOLKLORE SOCIETY MUSEUM COLLECTION
12 Didotou Street, Athens
Woven materials. Embroideries. Wood-carvings. Local costumes.
By appointment.

A. HADJIDIMOU PRIVATE COLLECTION
12 Vas. Sofias Avenue, Athens
Vases and statuettes.
By written appointment.

HISTORICAL AND ETHNOLOGICAL MUSEUM
Odos Patission 42, Athens
Codices, pictures and relics from the time of the Turkish dominion.
Summer: Daily 8-1, 3-6; Su. and holidays 10-1, 3-6. Winter: Daily 9-1, 2.30-5; Su. and holidays 10-1, 2.30-5. Closed Jan. 1, Mar. 25, Good F. (until noon), Easter Su. and Christmas Day.

A. IOLAS PRIVATE COLLECTION
Paradissos, Ayia Paraskevi, Athens
Greek sculpture, pottery, bronzes, jewellery and glass vases. Icons.
By written appointment.

P. KANELLOPOULOS PRIVATE COLLECTION
5 Irodou tou Attikou Street, Athens
Greek sculpture, bronzes, vases, statuettes, jewellery and coins. Byzantine and post-Byzantine icons, church plate, metal-work, jewellery and coins.
By written appointment.

KERAMEIKOS MUSEUM
148 Ermou Street, Athens
Contains mainly the finds of the German Archaeological Institute's excavations in the Kerameikos cemetery. Grave sculptures of the archaic and classical periods. Pottery from the sub-Mycenean to the Roman period. Statuettes, bronzes and other grave material.
Daily 8-1, 3-6; Su. and holidays 10-6; M. 12-6. Winter: Daily 8-5; Su. and holidays 10-5; M. 12-6.

I. KONSTANDOGLOU PRIVATE COLLECTION
13 Xenokratous Street, Athens
Ecclesiastical and secular plate. Wood-carvings.
By written appointment.

E. KOUTLIDIS PRIVATE COLLECTION
27 Vas. Sofias Avenue, Athens
Paintings by Greek artists.
By written appointment.

A. KYROU PRIVATE COLLECTION
29 Yperidou Street, Athens
Coins.
By written appointment.

LOVERDO MUSEUM
58A Academy Street, Athens
Collection of Byzantine icons, ancient wood-carvings and rare embroideries.
Daily 9-4: check locally.

A. MELAS PRIVATE COLLECTION
36 Emm. Benaki Street, Kifissia, Athens
Icons and wood-carvings.
By written appointment.

MUSEUM OF GREEK POPULAR ART
1 Areos Street, Plateia Monastiriou, Athens
Housed in an 18th century mosque. Comprehensive collection of traditional costumes, woven materials, embroideries of all kinds, lace, jewellery, metalwork, wood-carvings and pottery.
Daily ex. Tu. 9-1, Winter, Daily ex. Tu. 9-2.

MUSEUM OF SACRED ICONS OF THE ARCHBISHOPRIC OF ATHENS
Archbishop's Palace, 21 Ayias Filotheis Street, Athens
Post-Byzantine icons, vestments and church plate. Ecclesiastical documents.
Open only to specialists, tel. 237-654.

NATIONAL ARCHAEOLOGICAL MUSEUM
Odos Patission 44, Athens
Ancient Greek art. Sculpture, bronzes, pottery and jewellery from the Geometric to the Hellenistic period, from nearly all parts of Greece.
Daily ex. M. 8-1, 3-6; Su. and holidays 10-2. Winter: Daily ex. M. 9-4; Su. and holidays 10-2.

NATIONAL HISTORICAL MUSEUM
Stadiou Street, Athens
Most of the exhibits are relics and mementoes of the wars and revolts thatbrought about the emergence of the Greek nation, together with paintings, engravings and sculptures connected with them. Documents, seals and personal possessions of historic figures from the time of the preparations leading up to the 1821 Revolution to the first World War. Military relics from the periods of the Byzantine Empire and the Turkish occupation. Local costumes, embroideries, wood-carvings, pottery, metal-work and other folk art.
Daily ex. M. 9-4.

NATIONAL PICTURE GALLERY AND ALEXANDROS SOUTSOS MUSEUM
Vasilissis Sophias, Athens
Works by Greek painters from the late 18th century to the present day. Four El Grecos. Paintings of the Italian School (Veneziano Palmezzano, Tiepolo, L. Giordano, Selaco); the Flemish (Jordaens De Voss, Jan Brueghel II) and the Dutch School (De Heens, Van Mieris). Drawings by Rembrandt, Van Dyck, Watteau, and engravings by foreign masters from Dürer and Brueghel to Braque and Picasso. Engravings by Greek artists from the early 19th century to the present day.
Daily ex. Tu. and Su. afternoon, 9-1, 5-8.

I. PAPANDONIOU PRIVATE COLLECTION
3 Plateia Victorias, Athens
Traditional local costumes, woven materials, embroideries and jewellery.
By written appointment.

I. AND D. PASSAS MUSEUM OF EUROPEAN AND ORIENTAL ART
2 Evelpidou Street, Athens
Chinese objets d'art. Paintings.
By written appointment.

RESEARCH CENTRE OF GREEK FOLKLORE
Academy of Athens, 14 Anagnostopoulou Street, Athens
Woven materials. Embroideries. Lace. Pottery. Traditional musical instruments. Metal-work. Wood-carvings.
By appointment.

THEATRICAL MUSEUM
Society of Greek Theatrical Writers, 19 Kavalloti Street, Athens
Models of stage sets, costumes and photographs of theatrical productions. Letters and mementoes of well-known figures in contemporary Greek theatre.
W. and F. 6-8.30.

Z. VAOS PRIVATE COLLECTION
27 Polymnias Street, Holargos, Athens
Prehistoric obsidian weapons and tools.
By written appointment.

WAR MUSEUM
Military Academy Polygonon, Athens
Arms and uniforms from 5th century B.C. to the present day.
By appointment, daily. Su. 10-12.

I. YEROULANOS PRIVATE COLLECTION
Trahones, Athens
Finds from the Trahones area, dating from the Early Helladic period to the Middle Ages. Particularly noteworthy are the exhibits of the Geometric period.
By written appointment.

ZOOLOGICAL MUSEUM
Zoological Laboratories, University of Athens, University Town, Ilissia, Athens
Zoological collections from all over the world.
Temporarily closed.

AVLON

ZYGOMALA MUSEUM
Avlon
Notable embroideries and gold-embroideries.
Su. 10-12. Weekdays by arrangement with the curator.

AXIOKASTRON

ARCHAEOLOGICAL COLLECTION
Primary School, Axiokastron
Pottery and bronze jewellery of the early Iron Age.
During school hours on request.

BATSI

MONASTERY OF THE ZOODOCHOS PIGI OR AGIA
Batsi (near), Andros
Sacristy contains icons, vestments, church plate, reliquaries, manuscript codices.
Enquire locally at Metropolis of Syros, Tinos, Andros, Kea and Milos (see at Ermoupolis).

CAVALA

ARCHAEOLOGICAL MUSEUM
Cavala
Finds from Eastern Macedonia and Thrace, including jewellery from Amphipolis and sculptures of the Roman period from Philippi.
Daily ex. M. 8-1, 3-6; Su. and holidays 10-1, 3-6. Winter: Daily ex. M. 9-1, 2.30-5; Su. and holidays 10-1, 2.30-5.

CHAIRONEIA

ARCHAEOLOGICAL MUSEUM
Chaironeia
Pottery of the Neolithic, Early and Middle Helladic and Mycenean periods. Classical and Roman vases, sculpture and inscriptions. Weapons and ornaments.
Summer: Daily 8-1, 3-6; Su. and holidays 10-1, 3-7. Winter: Daily 9-1, 2.30-5; Su. and holidays 10-1, 2.30-5. Closed Jan. 1, Mar. 25, Good F. (until noon), Easter Su. and Christmas Day.

CHALKIS

ARCHAEOLOGICAL MUSEUM
21 El. Venizelou Avenue, Chalkis, Euboea
Contains the sculptures from the temple of Apollo Daphnephoros at Eretria and Hellenistic and Roman sculpture. Prehistoric and Geometric pottery. Inscriptions.
Summer: Daily 8-1, 3-6; Su. and holidays 10-1, 3-6. Winter: Daily 9-1, 2.30-5; Su. and holidays 10-1, 2.30-5. Closed Jan. 1, Mar. 25, Good F. (until noon), Easter Su. and Christmas Day. Closed M.

BYZANTINE COLLECTION
Mosque, Chalkis, Euboea
Mosaic floors, sculpture and pottery of the early Christian and Byzantine periods. Venetian coats of arms and Turkish reliefs.
Summer: Daily 8-1, 3-6; Su. and holidays 10-1, 3-6. Winter: Daily 9-1, 2.30-5; Su. and holidays 10-1, 2.30-5. Closed Jan. 1, Mar. 25, Good F. (until noon), Easter Su. and Christmas Day.

CHANIA

ARCHAEOLOGICAL MUSEUM
Monastery of St. Francis, Chania, Crete
Neolithic pottery. Minoan terracotta, stone and bronze vases, terracotta idols and weapons. Greek and Roman sculpture. Vases and statuettes from the Geometric to the Roman period. Lamps and glass vases. Weapons and gold

plaques. Roman mosaic floor. Inscriptions and coins.
Summer: Daily 8-1, 3-6; Su. and holidays 10-1, 3-6. Winter: Daily 9-1, 2.30-5; Su. and holidays 10-1, 2.30-5. Closed Jan. 1, Mar. 25, Good F. (until noon), Easter Su. and Christmas Day. Closed M.

HISTORICAL MUSEUM AND CRETAN CORNER
20 I. Sfakianaki Street, Chania, Crete
Relics and other objects, photographs and documents relating to the political and military history of Crete, chiefly from the 19th century up to the second World War. Room devoted to Eleftherios Venizelos, containing his personal possessions and documents. The Folklore Collection contains mainly woven materials, embroideries and other local handicraft products.
Summer: Daily 8-1, 3-6; Su. and holidays 10-1, 3-6. Winter: Daily 9-1, 2.30-5; Su. and holidays 10-1, 2.30-5. Closed Jan. 1, Mar. 25, Good F. (until noon), Easter Su. and Christmas Day.

CHIOS

ADAMANTIOS KORAIS LIBRARY
Korai Street, Chios
Collection of mementoes of A. Korais and other well-known Chian men of letters.
Summer: Daily 8-1, 3-6; Su. and holidays 10-1, 3-6. Winter: Daily 9-1, 2.30-5; Su. and holidays 10-1, 2.30-5. Closed Jan. 1, Mar. 25, Good F. (until noon), Easter Su. and Christmas Day.

ARCHAEOLOGICAL MUSEUM
Mosque, Chios
Neolithic and early Helladic finds (vases and tools), mainly from the excavations at Emborion. Archaic, classical, Hellenistic and Roman sculpture and pottery. Byzantine sculpture and vases. Frankish sculpture. Coins.
Summer: Daily 8-1, 3-6; Su. and holidays 10-1, 3-6. Winter: Daily 9-1, 2.30-5; Su. and holidays 10-1, 2.30-5. Closed Jan. 1, Mar. 25, Good F. (until noon), Easter Su. and Christmas Day. Closed M.

BOYS' GYMNASIUM
Secondary School, Chios
Collection of folk handicrafts.
During school hours, on request.

ETHNOLOGICAL AND FOLKLORE MUSEUM OF THE A. KORAIS LIBRARY
Korai Street, Chios
Local costumes, woven materials from Chios and elsewhere, embroideries, wood-carvings.
Summer: Daily 8-1, 3-6; Su. and holidays 10-1, 3-6. Winter: Daily 9-1, 2.30-5; Su. and holidays 10-1, 2.30-5. Closed Jan. 1, Mar. 25, Good F. (until noon), Easter Su. and Christmas Day.

NEA MONI MONASTERY
Chios
11th century mosaics, including a Dormition of the Virgin, the Descent into Hell and the Raising of Lazarus. Post-Byzantine sacred embroideries (including 'pefki' gold embroidery). Church plate.
Enquire locally.

CHORA

ARCHAEOLOGICAL COLLECTION
Gymnasium (secondary school), Chora, Amorgos
Prehistoric pottery; sculpture, archaic 'anthemia' and inscriptions.
During school hours, on request.

ARCHAEOLOGICAL COLLECTION
Chora, Astypalaia
Hellenistic and Roman sculpture and inscriptions. Post-Byzantine icons.
Summer: Daily 8-1, 3-6; Su. and holidays 10-1, 3-6. Winter: Daily 9-1, 2.30-5; Su. and holidays 10-1, 2.30-5. Closed Jan. 1, Mar. 25, Good F. (until noon), Easter Su. and Christmas Day.

ARCHAEOLOGICAL COLLECTION
Village Hall, Chora, Kea
Sculpture and inscriptions from the archaic to the Hellenistic period.
Daily 7.30-sunset; Su. and holidays 10-1, 3-7. Winter: Daily 9-sunset; Su. and holidays 10-1, 2.30-5.

ARCHAEOLOGICAL MUSEUM
Council Offices, Chora, Kythira
Large collection of Middle Minoan earthenware and steatite vases from the excavations of the Minoan colony at Kastri. Mycenean pottery. Head from 4th century statue.
During office hours on request.

MONASTERY OF ST. JOHN THE DIVINE
Chora, Patmos
Byzantine and post-Byzantine icons, including a mosaic icon. Vestments, sacred embroideries, church plate. Illuminated Byzantine manuscripts. Early printed books.
Enquire locally.

CHORA TRIFYLIAS

ARCHAEOLOGICAL MUSEUM
Chora Trifylias
Finds from the excavation of the Palace of Nestor (at Ano Englianos). Fragments of frescoes, pottery, gold jewellery, tablets inscribed with Linear B script. Also Mycenean pottery, gold articles and jewellery from the excavations at Volimidia.
Summer: Daily 8-1, 3-6; Su. and holidays 10-1, 3-6. Winter: Daily 9-1, 2.30-5; Su. and holidays 10-1, 2.30-5. Closed Jan. 1, Mar. 25, Good F. (until noon), Easter Su. and Christmas Day.

COMOTINI

ARCHAEOLOGICAL MUSEUM
Comotini
Sculpture, vases and small objects from Rodope and Evros.
Daily ex. M. 8-1, 3-6; Su. and holidays 10-1, 3-6. Winter: Daily ex. M. 9-1, 2.30-5; Su. and holidays 10-1, 2.30-5.

CORFU

ARCHAEOLOGICAL MUSEUM
3 Vraila Street, Garitsa, Corfu
Gorgon pediment and lion from the funerary mound of Menekrates, both archaic. Archaic terracotta architectural fragments, Protocorinthian and Corinthian vases, statuettes and bronzes. Roman sculpture. Coins.
M.-Sa. 8.30-1, 4-6; Su. 10-1. Closed Sa. afternoon and M. Winter: Daily ex. M. 9-1, 3-5; Su. 10-1. Closed Jan. 1, Mar. 25, Good F. (until noon), Easter Su. and Christmas Day.

BYZANTINE COLLECTION
Royal Palace, Corfu
Frescoes of the 11th and 13th centuries. Byzantine and post-Byzantine icons. Mosaic floors from the basilica of Palaeopolis and some sculpture.
Summer: Daily 8-1, 3-6; Su. and holidays 10-1, 3-6. Winter: Daily 9-1, 2.30-5; Su. and holidays 10-1, 2.30-5. Closed Jan. 1, Mar. 25, Good F. (until noon), Easter Su. and Christmas Day.

ECCLESIASTICAL MUSEUM
Church of the Pantocrator, Corfu
Icons belonging to the Metropolis (Cathedral).
By appointment.

R. EVELPIDIS PRIVATE COLLECTION
1 Nafsikas Street, Corfu
Ancient pottery and statuettes. Coins.
By written appointment.

HISTORICAL MUSEUM
Corfu
Historic relics. Folk art products. Paintings of the 17th-19th centuries.
By appointment.

SINO-JAPANESE MUSEUM
Royal Palace (second floor), Corfu
Chinese and Japanese art from the Neolithic period to the 19th century. Stone, bronze and terracotta objects and porcelain. Miniatures, paintings, theatrical masks, weapons.
M.-Sa. 8.30-1, 4-6; Su. 10-1. Closed Sa. afternoon and M. Winter: Daily ex. M. 9-1, 3-5; Su. 10-1.

SOLOMOS MUSEUM
Mourayio, Corfu
Museum contains mementoes of the poet and is on the site of the poet's house (destroyed in 1940).
Summer: Daily 8-1, 3-6; Su. and holidays 10-1, 3-6. Winter: Daily 9-1, 2.30-5; Su. and holidays 10-1, 2.30-5. Closed Jan. 1, Mar. 25, Good F. (until noon), Easter Su. and Christmas Day.

CORINTH

ANCIENT CORINTH MUSEUM
Corinth
Archaeological site of the ancient city of Corinth. Collections illustrate the rise of Corinth from a small settlement to an important manufacturing city state. Roman exhibits include statues, fragmentary sarcophagus of Hadrian's day. Medieval and modern coins. Bronze weight in the likeness of the Emperor Constantine. Protomajolica ware.
Summer: Daily 8-1, 3-6; Su. and holidays 10-1, 2.30-5. Winter: Daily 9-1, 2.30-5; Su. and holidays 10-1, 2.30-5. Closed Jan. 1, Mar. 25, Good F. (until noon), Easter Su. and Christmas Day. Closed M.

DELOS

ARCHAEOLOGICAL MUSEUM
Delos
Among the ruins of the ancient city, the museum contains a collection of sculptures (archaic, classical, Hellenistic and Roman) and architectural fragments. Prehistoric, Geometric, archaic, classical and Hellenistic pottery. Terracotta and bronze statuettes and figurines of various periods. Ivory reliefs, gold and bronze jewellery. Remains of frescoes of the 2nd-1st century B.C. Small finds and household utensils.
Summer: Daily 8-1, 3-6; Su. and holidays 10-1, 3-6. Winter: Daily 9-1, 2.30-5; Su. and holidays 10-1, 2.30-5. Closed Jan. 1, Mar. 25, Good F. (until noon), Easter Su. and Christmas Day. Closed M.

DELPHI

ARCHAEOLOGICAL MUSEUM
Delphi
Next to the archaeological site containing the ruins of the sanctuary and oracle of Apollo. Contains many of the outstanding examples of Greek sculpture: the late archaic sculptures from the Sicyonian, Siphnian and Athenian treasuries and the temple of Apollo, 'kouroi', the Naxian Sphinx. Bronze Charioteer. Classical, Hellenistic and Roman sculptures. Inscriptions (one with musical notation). Pottery, statuettes, bronze weapons, tools, bronze votive tripods and small finds from prehistoric to Roman times. In the front courtyard, an early Christian mosaic floor.
Daily 8-1, 3-6; Su. and holidays 10-1, 3-6; M. 11.30-1, 2.30-5. Winter: Daily 9-1, 2.30-5; Su. and holidays 10-1, 2.30-5; M. 11.30-1, 2.30-5. Closed Jan. 1, Mar. 25, Good F. (until noon), Easter Su. and Christmas Day.

DIDYMOTEICHON

ARCHAEOLOGICAL COLLECTION
Gymnasium (secondary school), Didymoteichon
Prehistoric sherds. Roman reliefs and inscriptions.
During school hours on request.

DIMITSANA

ARCHAEOLOGICAL COLLECTION
Library, Dimitsana
Mycenean pottery. Archaic sculptures. Terracotta and bronze statuettes. Hellenistic and Roman sculpture and pottery.
Summer: Daily 8-1, 3-6; Su. and holidays 10-1, 3-6. Winter: Daily 9-1, 2.30-5; Su. and holidays 10-1, 2.30-5. Closed Jan. 1, Mar. 25, Good F. (until noon), Easter Su. and Christmas Day.

GREEK FOLK MUSEUM
Library, Dimitsana
Woven materials, looms, metalwork, and other examples of folk art.
Summer: Daily 8-1, 3-6; Su. and holidays 10-1, 3-6. Winter: Daily 9-1, 2.30-5; Su. and holidays 10-1, 2.30-5. Closed Jan. 1, Mar. 25, Good F. (until noon), Easter Su. and Christmas Day.

DION

ARCHAEOLOGICAL MUSEUM
Dion
Hellenistic, Roman and early Christian sculpture from the excavations at the sacred city of the ancient Macedonians.
Summer: Daily 8-1, 3-6; Su. and holidays 10-1, 3-6. Winter: Daily 9-1, 2.30-5; Su. and holidays 10-1, 2.30-5. Closed Jan. 1, Mar. 25, Good F. (until noon), Easter Su. and Christmas Day.

DIROS

CAVES OF DIROS
Diros
Prehistoric human skulls and bones. Stone tools, pottery, marble and clay figurines. Rock drawings.
Tu.-Su. 9-5. Closed public holidays.

DISPILION, KASTORIA

ARCHAEOLOGICAL COLLECTION
Primary School, Dispilion, Kastoria
Contains the Neolithic finds (mainly tools) from the lakeside settlement nearby.
During school hours on request.

DRAMA

ARCHAEOLOGICAL COLLECTION
Cathedral, Drama
Roman and early Christian sculpture.
Summer: Daily 8-1, 3-6; Su. and holidays 10-1, 3-6. Winter: Daily 9-1, 2.30-5; Su. and holidays 10-1, 2.30-5. Closed Jan. 1, Mar. 25, Good F. (until noon), Easter Su. and Christmas Day.

DRYOPIS

ARCHAEOLOGICAL COLLECTION
Primary School, Dryopis, Kythnos
Sculptures and inscriptions.
During school hours on request.

EDESSA

ARCHAEOLOGICAL COLLECTION
Mosque, Edessa
Mainly Hellenistic and Roman reliefs and inscriptions.
Summer: Daily 8-1, 3-6; Su. and holidays 10-1, 3-6. Winter: Daily 9-1, 2.30-5; Su. and holidays 10-1, 2.30-5. Closed Jan. 1, Mar. 25, Good F. (until noon), Easter Su. and Christmas Day. Closed M.

ELASSON

AGIA TRIADA MONASTERY
Sparmos, Elasson
The sacristy contains post-Byzantine icons.
Enquire locally at the Metropolis of Elasson.

ARCHAEOLOGICAL COLLECTION
Mosque, Elasson
Architectural fragments. Hellenistic and Roman inscriptions.
Summer: Daily 8-1, 3-6; Su. and holidays 10-1, 3-6. Winter: Daily 9-1, 2.30-5; Su. and holidays 10-1, 2.30-5. Closed Jan. 1, Mar. 25, Good F. (until noon), Easter Su. and Christmas Day.

OLYMPIOTISSA MONASTERY
Elasson
The sacristy contains Byzantine and post-Byzantine icons, wood-carvings (including the door of the monastery church, dating from 1296 or 1305). Gold-embroideries; church plate; architectural fragments of the Byzantine period.
Enquire locally at the Metropolis of Elasson.

ELEFSIS

ARCHAEOLOGICAL MUSEUM
Elefsis
Within the site of the sanctuary of Demeter. Archaic, classical, Hellenistic and Roman sculpture. Prehistoric pottery, weapons, bronze and gold jewellery. Vases and votive offerings from the Geometric, archaic (large amphora depicting scenes from mythology), classical, Hellenistic and Roman periods. Grave groups.
Summer: Daily 8-1, 3-6; Su. and holidays 10-1, 3-6. Winter: Daily 9-1, 2.30-5; Su. and holidays, 10-1, 2.30-5. Closed Jan. 1, Mar. 25, Good F. (until noon), Easter Su. and Christmas Day.

ELEUSIS

ELEUSIS MUSEUM
Archaeological Site, Eleusis
Mycenean and classical sculpture and vases. Marble stele. Cast of Eleusinian relief. Amphora of c.610 B.C. from Megara. Inhumation burials.
Summer: Daily 8-1, 3-6; Su. and holidays 10-1, 3-6. Winter: Daily 9-1, 2.30-5; Su. and holidays 10-1, 2.30-5. Closed Jan. 1, Mar. 25, Good F. (until noon), Easter Su. and Christmas Day.

EPIDAVROS

ARCHAEOLOGICAL MUSEUM
Epidavros
Within the site of the sanctuary of Asclepios. Architectural fragments; the famous Corinthian capital by the younger Polycleitos; terracotta architectural ornaments; reconstructions of buildings in the sanctuary of Asclepios (4th century B.C.). Important inscriptions. Some classical, Hellenistic and Roman sculpture and casts of statues now in the National Archaeological Museum in Athens. Statuettes, bronze articles and surgical instruments, mainly of the Roman period.
Summer: Daily 8-1, 3-6; Su. and holidays 10-1, 3-6. Winter: Daily 9-1, 2.30-5; Su. and holidays 10-1, 2.30-5. Closed Jan. 1, Mar. 25, Good F. (until noon), Easter Su. and Christmas Day. Closed M.

ERESSOS

ARCHAEOLOGICAL MUSEUM
Eressos, Lesvos
Hellenistic and Roman sculpture. 4th century and later pottery and statuettes. Early Christian sculpture and mosaic floors.
Summer: Daily 8-1, 3-6; Su. and holidays 10-1, 3-6. Winter: Daily 9-1, 2.30-5; Su. and holidays 10-1, 2.30-5. Closed Jan. 1, Mar. 25, Good F. (until noon), Easter Su. and Christmas Day. Closed M.

ERETRIA

ARCHAEOLOGICAL MUSEUM
Eretria, Euboea
Pottery: prehistoric (from Lefkandi) and also archaic, classical and Hellenistic (note especially the Panathenaic amphorae). Classical and Hellenistic sculpture. Inscribed tombstones.
Summer: Daily 8-1, 3-6; Su. and holidays 10-1, 3-6. Winter: Daily 9-1, 2.30-5; Su. and holidays 10-1, 2.30-5. Closed Jan. 1, Mar. 25, Good F. (until noon), Easter Su. and Christmas Day. Closed M.

MONASTERY OF ST. GEORGE OF ILIA
Eretria, Euboea
Sacristy contains church plate, relics, vestments.
Enquire locally at Metropolis of Chalkis.

ERMOUPOLIS

ARCHAEOLOGICAL COLLECTION
Town Hall, Ermoupolis, Syros
Prehistoric marble and earthenware vases. Hellenistic and Roman sculpture and inscriptions.
Summer: Daily 8-1, 3-6; Su. and holidays 10-1, 3-6. Winter: Daily 9-1, 2.30-5; Su. and holidays 10-1, 2.30-5. Closed Jan. 1, Mar. 25, Good F. (until noon), Easter Su. and Christmas Day.

FALIKA

PANACHRANTOS MONASTERY
Falika (near), Andros
Collection of church plate, vestments, embroideries and wood-carvings.
Enquire locally at Metropolis of Syros, Tinos, Andros, Kea and Milos (see at Ermoupolis).

FARSALA

ARCHAEOLOGICAL COLLECTION
Farsala
Hellenistic and Roman architectural fragments and inscriptions.
Summer: Daily 8-1, 3-6; Su. and holidays 10-1, 3-6. Winter: Daily 9-1, 2.30-5; Su. and holidays 10-1, 2.30-5. Closed Jan. 1, Mar. 25, Good F., Easter Su. and Christmas Day.

FENEOS

ARCHAEOLOGICAL COLLECTION
Primary School, Feneos
Hellenistic architectural fragments (2nd century B.C.).
During school hours, on request.

FERRAI

ARCHAEOLOGICAL COLLECTION
Precinct of Byzantine Church of the Pantanassa, Ferrai
Roman sarcophagus and Byzantine architectural fragments.
On application to the sacristan.

FILIATRA

ARCHAEOLOGICAL COLLECTION
Town Hall, Filiatra
Icons collected from churches in the neighbourhood and early Christian sculpture.
On application to the caretaker.

FILIPPI

ARCHAEOLOGICAL MUSEUM
Filippi
Prehistoric vases and stone tools from the excavations at the Dikili-Tash. Roman and early Christian sculpture and architectural fragments. Classical, Hellenistic and Roman small finds. Inscriptions. Coins.
Summer: Daily 8-1, 3-6; Su. and holidays 10-1, 3-6. Winter: Daily 9-1, 2.30-5; Su. and holidays 10-1, 2.30-5. Closed Jan. 1, Mar. 25, Good F. (until noon), Easter Su. and Christmas Day.

FLORINA

ARCHAEOLOGICAL MUSEUM
Florina
Hellenistic and Roman pottery, weapons and coins. Reliefs from the end of the Roman period. Byzantine sculpture and post-Byzantine icons.
Summer: Daily 8-1, 3-6; Su. and holidays 10-1, 3-6. Winter: Daily 9-1, 2.30-5; Su. and holidays 10-1, 2.30-5. Closed Jan. 1, Mar. 25, Good F., Easter Su. and Christmas Day.

FOLEGANDROS

ARCHAEOLOGICAL COLLECTION
Village Hall and Primary School, Folegandros
Fragments of Roman sculpture and inscriptions.
During school hours, on request.

GALAXIDI

ARCHAEOLOGICAL COLLECTION
Village Hall, Galaxidi
Pottery from prehistoric to Roman times. Some sculptures and coins.
On application to the caretaker.

NAUTICAL MUSEUM
rear of Council Offices, Galaxidi
Paintings of ships, folk art seascapes. Sailing gear, charts, figureheads and models of ships.
On application to the caretaker.

GERAKI

ARCHAEOLOGICAL COLLECTION
'Ralleion' building, Geraki
Hellenistic and Roman architectural fragments.
On application to the caretaker.

GREVENA

ARCHAEOLOGICAL COLLECTION
Gymnasium (secondary school), Grevena
Weapons of the late Mycenean period. Roman reliefs.
During school hours, on request.

GYTHION

ARCHAEOLOGICAL COLLECTION
Town Hall, Gythion
Archaic Laconian reliefs. Greek, Roman and Byzantine sculpture. Inscriptions.
On application to the caretaker.

HORA

ARCHAEOLOGICAL MUSEUM
Hora
Finds from the surrounding district. Traditional local handicrafts.
Summer: Daily 8-1, 3-6; Su. and holidays 10-1, 3-6. Winter: Daily 9-1, 2.30-5; Su. and holidays 10-1, 2.30-5. Closed Jan. 1, Mar. 25, Good F. (until noon), Easter Su. and Christmas Day.

HYDRA

HISTORICAL ARCHIVES OF HYDRA
Hydra
Historic documents of the 1821 Revolution. Portraits and personal possessions of heroes of the Revolution, and various relics.
Daily ex. Sa. 8-12.

IERAPETRA

ARCHAEOLOGICAL COLLECTION
Old Town Hall, Ierapetra, Crete
Mainly vases and interesting painted terracotta sarcophagi of the late Mycenean period. A little red-figure pottery. Hellenistic statuettes and Roman sculpture and inscriptions.
On application to the caretaker.

IOANNINA

FOLKLORE MUSEUM AND ARCHIVES OF THE IOANNINA FACULTY OF PHILOSOPHY
University, Ioannina
Woven materials, embroideries, silverware, wood-carvings, pottery, metalwork, musical instruments and ritual objects.
During workshop hours.

MUNICIPAL MUSEUM
Asian Pasha Mosque, Castle, Ioannina
Collections of woven materials, embroideries, gold-embroideries, silverware, woodcarvings and weapons.
Daily 8-1, 4-7.

MUSEUM
Ano Plateia, Ioannina
Palaeolithic tools of stone and bone, and Neolithic pottery. Bronze Age pottery, both local and Mycenean, weapons and jewellery. Bronze utensils, statuettes and weapons, mostly from the sanctuary of Dodoni, from the Geometric to the Roman period. Classical, Hellenistic and Roman sculpture and architectural fragments. Classical and Hellenistic pottery. Jewellery and small finds. Inscriptions. Coins. Early Christian and Byzantine sculpture. 13th century miniatures. Icons. Post-Byzantine metalwork and silverware. Art gallery containing 19th-20th century Greek paintings and 20th century sculpture.
On request.

NISI MUSEUM OF THE PREREVOLUTIONARY PERIOD
Monastery of St. Panteleimon, Ioannina
Woven materials, documents, lithographs and photographs, housed in two cells of the monastery where Ali Pasha was killed.
Daily 8-1, 3-6; Su. and holidays 10-1, 3-6. Winter: Daily 8-1, 2.30-5; Su. and holidays 10-1, 2.30-5. Closed M.

IOS

ARCHAEOLOGICAL COLLECTION
Primary School, Ios
Pottery of the first Cycladic and Roman periods. Roman reliefs and inscriptions. Egyptian statuettes.
During school hours, on request.

IRAKLION

ARCHAEOLOGICAL MUSEUM
Xanthoudidou Street, Iraklion, Crete
The collection give a comprehensive picture of the Minoan civilisation (2500-1400 B.C.). Finds from excavations (Greek, English, French and Italian) at the palaces and villas of Knossos, Phaistos, Malia, Tylissos and Zakro, and at the centres of worship and tombs of prehistoric Crete. Examples of frescoes, vases of earthenware, stone and alabaster, terracotta and bronze idols and figurines, terracotta sarcophagi, weapons, jewellery, plaques and other articles of faience and ivory. Seal-stones made of semi-precious stones, ritual objects and articles of household use. Tablets and fragments bearing hieroglyphic script (Mycenean A and Mycenean B). Archaic, classical, Hellenistic and Roman sculpture, pottery and bronzes. Coins.
Tu.-Sa. 8-1, 4-6; Su. and M. 10-1.

HISTORICAL MUSEUM OF CRETE
Mansion of A. and M. Kalokerinos, Lyssimachou Kalokerinou Street, Iraklion, Crete
Presents a picture of Cretan civilisation from the early Christian period to the present day. Collection of sculpture and inscriptions with examples of early Christian, Byzantine, Venetian and Turkish work. Byzantine Medieval collection, containing frescoes, post-Byzantine icons, wood-carvings, vestments, church plate and 17th century pottery. Folklore collection, including a replica of a Cretan home and a mass of folk art products (woven materials, embroideries, lace, local costumes, jewellery, wood-carvings). Weapons, flags, documents and relics of Cretan revolts. Rooms dedicated to the memory of N. Kazantzakis and E. Tsouderos.
Tu.-Sa. 8-1, 4-6.30; Closed Su. and holidays.

K. KAFATOS PRIVATE COLLECTION
21 Dedalou Street, Iraklion, Crete
Cretan 'petsetes'.
By written appointment.

E. KASTRINOYANNIS PRIVATE COLLECTION
23 Idomeneos Street, Iraklion, Crete
Cretan woven materials and a few white embroideries.
By written application.

N. METAXES PRIVATE COLLECTION
4 Plateia Analipseos, Iraklion, Crete
Stone and earthenware vases, figurines and statuettes, bronzes and seal-stones of the Minoan period. Greek and Roman vases, statuettes, bronzes and jewellery. Coins from the Arab occupation of Crete.
By written appointment.

MONASTERY OF ST. GEORGE EPANOSIFIS
Iraklion (near), Crete
The sacristy contains church plate, reliquaries, vestments, gold-embroideries, bound gospels and an illuminated manuscript gospel.
Enquire locally at the offices of the Archbishopric of Crete, at Iraklion.

ISTHMIA

ARCHAEOLOGICAL COLLECTION
Isthmia
On the archaeological site, the museum contains finds from the excavations at Kenchreai and Isthmia. Pottery and small finds of all periods. Roman mosaic floors from Kenchreai.
On application to the caretaker.

ISTIAIA

ARCHAEOLOGICAL COLLECTION
Town Hall, Istiaia, Euboea
Hellenistic pottery. Roman sculpture and architectural fragments.
On application to the caretaker.

KALAMATA

ARCHAEOLOGICAL MUSEUM
Benakis Mansion, Benaki Street, Kalamata
Stone tools and Neolithic pottery from the excavations at Malthi. Mycenean, Protogeometric and Geometric pottery and a few Mycenean figurines from the excavations at Karpophora. Archaic and Hellenistic pottery. Late classical, Hellenistic and Roman sculpture. Mosaic floor of the Roman period. Post-Byzantine icons, folk embroidery and relics of the 1821 Revolt.
Summer: Daily 8-1, 3-6; Su. and holidays 10-1, 3-6. Winter: Daily 9-1, 2.30-5; Su. and holidays 10-1, 2.30-5. Closed Jan. 1, Mar. 25, Good F., Easter Su. and Christmas Day. Closed M.

HISTORICAL AND FOLKLORE MUSEUM
Corner of Kyriakou and Ayiou Ioannou Streets, Kalamata
Folk art products (household utentils). Weapons and a few contemporary paintings (mostly by E. Drakos) on subjects taken from the 1821 revolt.
By appointment only.

MUSEUM OF THE METROPOLIS OF MESSINIA
Frangolimnis Square, Kalamata
Small collection of icons, church plate, bound gospels and vestments.
On application to the caretaker.

KALAMOS

ARCHAEOLOGICAL MUSEUM
Amphiareion, Kalamos
Classical, Hellenistic and Roman sculpture, architectural fragments and inscriptions.
Not open to visitors at present.

KALAVRYTA

AGIA LAVRA MONASTERY
Kalavryta (near)
The sacristy of the monastery has been laid out as a small museum, containing icons, Byzantine illuminated manuscripts (11th and 14th century), ecclesiastical gold embroideries, vestments, church plate, carved wooden crosses framed with precious materials and reliquaries. Patriarchal bulls, Venetian and Turkish documents.
Enquire locally at Metropolis of Kalavryta and Aigialeia (at Aigion).

MEGA SPILEON MONASTERY
Kalavryta (near)
Icons, a few illuminated manuscripts, church plate and embroideries, vestments, silverware, and wood-carvings.
Enquire locally at Metropolis of Kalavryta and Aigialeia (at Aigion).

KALLONI

MONASTERY OF ST. IGNATIOS, LIMONOS
Kalloni (near), Lesvos
Collections of icons, church plate, reliquaries, gold-embroideries, folk art embroideries and wood-carvings. Manuscripts, printed papers, Greek and Turkish documents.
Enquire locally at Metropolis of Mithymna (at Kalloni). Women not admitted.

KALYMNOS

ARCHAEOLOGICAL MUSEUM
Palio Tapitouryion, Kalymnos
Housed in an old carpet-making workshop, the museum contains Neolithic and classical pottery, classical and Roman sculpture. Inscriptions.
Summer: Daily 8-1, 3-8; Su. and holidays 10-1, 3-6. Winter: Daily 9-1, 2.30-5; Su. and holidays 10-1, 2.30-5. Closed Jan. 1, Mar. 25, Good F. (until noon), Easter Su. and Christmas Day.

THE VOUVALINA MANSION
Kalymnos
A typical mansion of the period around the turn of this century, containing household furniture and copies of well-known paintings by Kalymnian painters of the 19th and 20th centuries.
Enquire locally.

KALYVIA ILIDOS

ARCHAEOLOGICAL COLLECTION
Kalyvia Ilidos
On the archaeological site of ancient Elis. Some classical and many Hellenistic and Roman sculptures. Pottery of the same periods.
Summer: Daily 8-1, 3-8; Su. and holidays 10-1, 3-6. Winter: Daily 9-1, 2.30-5; Su. and holidays 10-1, 2.30-5. Closed Jan. 1, Mar. 25, Good F. (until noon), Easter Su. and Christmas Day.

KAMMENA VOURLA

KARANASSOS PRIVATE COLLECTION
Kammena Vourla
Archaic and classical pottery and bronzes. Coins.
By written appointment.

KAMPOS

ARCHAEOLOGICAL MUSEUM
Kampos, Ikaria
Classical and Hellenistic sculpture. Archaic, classical and Hellenistic pottery and statuettes.
Summer: Daily 8-1, 3-6; Su. and holidays 10-1, 3-6. Winter: Daily 9-1, 2.30-5; Su. and holidays 10-1, 2.30-5. Closed Jan. 1, Mar. 25, Good F. (until noon), Easter Su. and Christmas Day.

KARDAMYLI, MESSINIA

ARCHAEOLOGICAL COLLECTION
Mourdzinos Tower, Kardamyli, Messinia
Archaic capitals and architectural fragments of the classical period. Some prehistoric and Hellenistic pottery. Folk art products, mostly wood-carvings.
Summer: Daily 8-1, 3-6; Su. and holidays 10-1, 3-6. Winter: Daily 9-1, 2.30-5; Su. and holidays, 10-1, 2.30-5. Closed Jan. 1, Mar. 25, Good F. (until noon), Easter Su. and Christmas Day.

KARDITSA

COLLECTION OF THE KARDITSA FOLKLORE SOCIETY
Town Hall, Karditsa
Local costumes, woven materials, embroideries, wood-carvings and other folk art products.
By appointment.

KORONI MONASTERY
Karditsa
Post-Byzantine icons, wood-carvings, reliquaries and manuscripts.
Enquire locally at Metropolis of Thessaliotis and Fanariofarsala (at Karditsa).

RENDINA MONASTERY
Karditsa
Post-Byzantine icons kept in the Abbot's lodgings.
Enquire locally at Metropolis of Thessaliotis and Fanariofarsala (at Karditsa).

KARPENISSION

PROUSSOU MONASTERY
Karpenission (near)
The treasury is housed in two cells in the east building of the monastery and contains icons, vestments, silverware, crosses and gospel bindings. Manuscript codices, bulls and firmans.
Enquire locally at Metropolis of Nafpaktia and Evrytania (at Nafpaktos).

TATARNA MONASTERY
Karpenission (near)
The sacristy contains icons (particularly a 13th century mosaic icon), gold-embroideries, some church plate and wood-carvings. Manuscripts and printed documents.
Enquire locally at Metropolis of Nafpaktia and Evrytania (at Nafpaktos).

KARYSTOS

ARCHAEOLOGICAL MUSEUM
Yiokaleion Foundation, Karystos, Euboea
Hellenistic and Roman reliefs and pottery.
By written application.

KASTELLI KISAMOU

ARCHAEOLOGICAL COLLECTION
Main Square, Kastelli Kisamou, Crete
Sculpture and architectural fragments, pottery, spears and coins from Greek and Roman times. Early Christian inscriptions.
Summer: Daily 8-1, 3-6; Su. and holidays 10-1, 3-6. Winter: Daily 9-1, 2.30-5; Su. and holidays 10-1, 2.30-5. Closed Jan. 1, Mar. 25, Good F. (until noon), Easter Su. and Christmas Day.

KASTELLORIZON

ARCHAEOLOGICAL MUSEUM
Mosque, Kastellorizon
Hellenistic and Roman sculpture, pottery and inscriptions. Local costumes, woven materials and embroideries.
Summer: Daily 8-1, 3-6; Su. and holidays 10-1, 3-6. Winter: Daily 9-1, 2.30-5; Su. and holidays, 10-1, 2.30-5. Closed Jan. 1, Mar. 25, Good F. (until noon), Easter Su. and Christmas Day.

KASTORIA

ARCHAEOLOGICAL COLLECTION
Chapel of Girls' Orphanage, Kastoria
Prehistoric vases and Roman reliefs. Byzantine and post-Byzantine icons and wood-carvings.
By arrangement with the Directrice.

KASTRO

ARCHAEOLOGICAL COLLECTION
Kastro, Kos
Classical sculptures and others of the early Christian period. Hellenistic, Roman, early Christian and Byzantine inscriptions.
Summer: Daily 8-1, 3-6; Su. and holidays 10-1, 3-6. Winter: Daily 9-1, 2.30-5; Su. and holidays 10-1, 2.30-5. Closed Jan. 1, Mar. 25, Good F. (until noon), Easter Su. and Christmas Day.

KASTRON AGIOU GEORGIOU

CHURCH OF THE EVANGELISTRIA
Kastron Agiou Georgiou, Kefallinia
Collection of post-Byzantine icons from local churches.
On application to the sacristan.

KATAPOLA

ARCHAEOLOGICAL COLLECTION
Primary School, Katapola, Amorgos
Classical, Hellenistic and Roman sculpture and inscriptions.
During school hours, on request.

KATERINI

ARCHAEOLOGICAL COLLECTION
Primary School, Katerini
Classical, Hellenistic and Roman sculpture and pottery.
During school hours, on request.

KAVALA

COLLECTION OF THE KAVALA METROPOLIS
Bishop's Palace, Kavala
Collection of post-Byzantine icons.
On application to the caretaker.

ARCHAEOLOGICAL MUSEUM
Kavala
Exhibits from the cities of Thrace; Neapolis (the ancient Kavala), Amphipolis, Abdera. Late Neolithic and Bronze Age pottery and figurines. Architectural fragments (mostly from the 5th century B.C. Temple of the Parthenos at Neapolis) conventionally restored, and classical Hellenistic and Roman sculpture. Collection of pottery, statuettes and half-figures or busts from the archaic to the Roman period, from various workshops. Archaic terracotta architectural fragments. Part of a 3rd century tomb from Amphipolis with wall-paintings and a painted grave stele of the same period. Collection of gold jewellery and wreaths, Hellenistic gilded and painted terracotta ornaments, mostly from tombs at Amphipolis. Hellenistic and Roman bronze utensils and vases. Coins and inscriptions. Mosaic floors.
Summer: Daily 8-1, 3-6; Su. and holidays 10-1, 3-6. Winter: Daily 9-1, 2.30-5; Su. and holidays 10-1, 2.30-5.

KILKIS

ARCHAEOLOGICAL MUSEUM
Kilkis
An archaic 'kouros' and reliefs, portraits, inscriptions and small finds, mainly of the Roman period.
Daily ex. M. 8-1, 3-6; Su. and holidays 10-1, 3-6. Winter: Daily ex. M. 9-1, 2.30-5; Su. and holidays 10-1, 2.30-5.

KIMOLOS

ARCHAEOLOGICAL COLLECTION
Yirokomeion, Kimolos
Housed in the basement of the old people's home, the collection consists of Geometric, Hellenistic and Roman pottery.
By arrangement with the Director.

KISSOS, PILION

CHURCH OF AGIA MARINA
Kissos, Pilion
A collection of post-Byzantine icons, church plate and books from small churches in the area.
On application to the sacristan.

KOLYMVARI

MONASTERY OF THE ODIGITRIA, CHANIA
Kolymvari, Crete
Exhibition of vestments and church plate. In the monastery church, post-Byzantine icons. Post-Byzantine documents and manuscripts.
Enquire locally at Metropolis of Kisamos and Selinos (at Kastelli).

KOMOTINI

ARCHAEOLOGICAL MUSEUM
Komotini
Prehistoric vases and tools. Sculpture from the archaic to the early Christian period. Gold head of the Roman Emperor Marcus Aurelius. Inscriptions of all periods.
Summer: Daily 8-1, 3-6; Su. and holidays 10-1, 3-6. Winter: Daily 9-1, 2.30-5; Su. and holidays 10-1, 2.30-5. Closed Jan. 1, Mar. 25, Good F. (until noon), Easter Su. and Christmas Day.

ECCLESIASTICAL MUSEUM
Ioakeimideion Boys' Orphanage, Mitropolitou Anthimou Street, Komotini
Collection includes Icons, a gold-embroidered 'epitaphios', other embroideries, some wood-carvings, pottery and silverware of the post-Byzantine period.
By arrangement with the Director.

FOLKLORE MUSEUM OF THRACE
8 Kouloglou Street, Komotini
Local costumes, silverware, some wood-carvings, ecclesiastical embroideries and bronze utensils.
On application to the caretaker.

KOS

ARCHAEOLOGICAL MUSEUM
Kos
Prehistoric pottery and figurines. Classical, Hellenistic and Roman sculpture. Pottery. Hellenistic mosaic floor. Inscriptions. Coins. Ceramics.
Daily ex. M. 9-1.

CASA ROMANA
Kos
Restored 3rd century Roman dwelling, with mosaics.
Daily 8-1, 3-6; Su. and holidays 10-1, 3-6. Winter: Daily 9-1, 2.30-5; Su. and holidays 10-1, 2.30-5.

FOLK ART MUSEUM OF THE METROPOLIS OF KOS
Bishop's Palace, Kos
Post-Byzantine icons and gold-embroideries. Woven materials, embroideries. Wood-carvings and pottery.
Daily ex. M. 9-1.

KOSMITI, XANTHI

ARCHAEOLOGICAL COLLECTION
Kosmiti, Xanthi
Roman sculpture.
Summer: Daily 8-1, 3-6; Su. and holidays 10-1, 3-6. Winter: Daily 9-1, 2.30-5; Su. and holidays 10-1, 2.30-5. Closed Jan. 1, Mar. 25, Good F. (until noon), Easter Su. and Christmas Day.

KOZANI

ARCHAEOLOGICAL COLLECTION
Public Library, Main Square, Kozani
Bronze Age, Iron Age, classical, Hellenistic and Roman pottery. Iron Age and classical weapons. Hellenistic and Roman reliefs. Coins. Roman inscriptions. Fragments of frescoes from the basilica at Voskochorio and part of an early Christian mosaic floor. Post-Byzantine icons, silverware and inscriptions. Wood-carvings from mansions in the town. Documents, letters of Ali Pasha and old maps.
Summer: Daily 8-1, 3-6; Su. and holidays 10-1, 3-6. Winter: Daily 9-1, 2.30-5; Su. and holidays 10-1, 2.30-5. Closed Jan. 1, Mar. 25, Good F. (until noon), Easter Su. and Christmas Day.

LACHANAS

MUSEUM
Lachanas
Local costumes. Weapons and relics of the Balkan wars.
On application to the caretaker.

LAMIA

ARCHAEOLOGICAL COLLECTION
Offices of the Prefecture, Municipal library, Lamia
Pottery, from Mycenean to Roman period. Late 4th century sculptures from Echinos. Classical, Hellenistic and Roman inscriptions.
During library hours, on request.

A. KOUNOUPIS PRIVATE COLLECTION
17 Myronos Street, Lamia
Ancient pottery and sculpture. Folk art. Jewellery. Weapons.
By written appointment.

G. PLATIS PRIVATE COLLECTION
5 Diovouniotou Street, Lamia
Classical pottery.
By written appointment.

LARISSA

ARCHAEOLOGICAL MUSEUM
Mosque, 2 Triakostis Protis Avgoustou Street, Larissa
Palaeolithic and pre-pottery neolithic finds from the German Archaeological Institute's excavations. Neolithic pottery. Menhirs. Archaic and classical grave stelae.
Summer: Daily 8-1, 3-6; Su. and holidays 10-1, 3-6. Winter: Daily 9-1, 2.30-5; Su. and holidays 10-1, 2.30-5. Closed Jan. 1, Mar. 25, Good F. (until noon), Easter Su. and Christmas Day. Closed M.

G. GOURYOTIS PRIVATE COLLECTION
22 Triakostis Protis Avgoustou Street, Larissa
Objects of mother-of-pearl. Miniatures.
By written appointment.

G. KATSIGRAS PRIVATE COLLECTION
Plateia Riga Fereou, Larissa
Paintings by Greek artists.
By written appointment.

D. TLOUPAS PRIVATE COLLECTION
28 Volou Street, Larissa
Neolithic figurines and tools.
By written appointment.

LEFKAS

ARCHAEOLOGICAL COLLECTION
Municipal Library, Kefkas
Early Helladic finds (mostly pottery) from excavations at Nydri. Classical, Hellenistic and Roman sculpture. Classical and Hellenistic vases, statuettes and relief terracotta plaques.
Daily ex. M.

COLLECTION OF ECCLESIASTICAL PAINTINGS AND RELICS OF ORTHODOXY
Municipal Library, Lefkas
Icons, church plate, sacred relics, gospels (two in manuscript).
Daily ex. M.

LEMNOS

LEMNOS ISLAND MUSEUM
Lemnos
Prehistoric finds from Hephaisteia and Poliokhni.
Summer: Daily 8-1, 3-8; Su. and holidays 10-1, 3-6. Winter: Daily 9-1, 2.30-5; Su. and holidays 10-1, 2.30-5. Closed Jan. 1, Mar. 25, Good F. (until noon), Easter Su. and Christmas Day.

LIKNADES, KOZANI

ARCHAEOLOGICAL COLLECTION
Primary School, Liknades, Kozani
Prehistoric tools and sherds. Classical, Hellenistic and Roman pottery. Coins.
During school hours, on request.

LIMENARIA

I. PAPAGEORGIOU PRIVATE COLLECTION
Papageorgiou Hotel, Limenaria, Thassos
Statuettes. Vases. Greek and Roman metalwork and coins. Samples of local weaving and embroidery.
By written appointment.

LINDOS

ARCHAEOLOGICAL COLLECTION
Papakonstandinou Mansion, Lindos, Rhodes
Housed in an old sea-captain's house with decorative reliefs on the façade and painted ceilings. Classical and Hellenistic sculpture and inscriptions.
Summer: Daily 8-1, 3-6; Su. and holidays 10-1, 3-6. Winter: Daily 9-1, 2.30-5; Su. and holidays 10-1, 2.30-5. Closed Jan. 1, Mar. 25, Good F. (until noon), Easter Su. and Christmas Day.

H. GEORGIOU PRIVATE COLLECTION
Lindos, Rhodes
Traditional pottery.
By written appointment.

P. IOANNIDIS PRIVATE COLLECTION
Lindos, Rhodes
Ornamental plates.
By written appointment.

E. KASKINES PRIVATE COLLECTION
Lindos, Rhodes
Traditional pottery.
By written appointment.

LIXOURI

ARCHAEOLOGICAL COLLECTION
Iakovateious Public Library, Lixouri, Kefallinia
Classical and Hellenistic pottery. Icons.
During library hours, on request.

LOUTRA AIDIPSOU

ARCHAEOLOGICAL COLLECTION
Town Hall (Basement), Loutra Aidipsou, Euboea
Roman sculpture and inscriptions.
During office hours, on request.

LYKOSOURA

ARCHAEOLOGICAL MUSEUM
Lykosoura
In ruins of sanctuary of Despoina, 15 km. from Megalopolis. Fragments from statue group of Despoina and Demeter by Damophon (2nd century B.C.). Architectural sculpture and inscriptions.
Summer: Daily 8-1, 3-6; Su. and holidays 10-1, 3-6. Winter: Daily 9-1, 2.30-5; Su. and holidays 10-1, 2.30-5. Closed Jan. 1, Mar. 25, Good F. (until noon), Easter Su. and Christmas Day.

MAKRYNITSA

D. MAVROS PRIVATE COLLECTION
Makrynitsa
Collection of plates, wood-carvings, metalwork and old loom accessories.
By written appointment.

MANDRAKI

ARCHAEOLOGICAL COLLECTION
Town Hall and Primary School, Mandraki, Nissyros
Hellenistic and Roman sculpture and pottery. Inscriptions. Post-Byzantine icons of the 18th-19th centuries.
During working hours, on request.

MARONEIA

ARCHAEOLOGICAL COLLECTION
Primary School, Maroneia
Prehistoric finds from the cave of Maroneia. Neolithic and early Helladic vases, tools and small finds. Classical, Hellenistic and Roman sculpture and inscriptions.
During school hours, on request.

MAVRADZEI

MONASTERY OF THE TIMIOS STAVROS
Mavradzei, Samos (near)
Church plate, reliquaries, manuscripts and rare books.
Enquire locally at Metropolis of Samos and Ikaria (at Samos).

MAVROMATION, MESSINIA

ARCHAEOLOGICAL COLLECTION
Custodian's Hut, Archaeological Site, Mavromation, Messinia
Finds from excavations at ancient Messene: sculpture, architectural fragments and inscriptions of the Hellenistic and Roman periods.
Summer: Daily 8-1, 3-6; Su. and holidays 10-1, 3-6. Winter: Daily 9-1, 2.30-5; Su. and holidays 10-1, 2.30-5. Closed Jan. 1, Mar. 25, Good F. (until noon), Easter Su. and Christmas Day.

MAVROPIGI, KOZANI

ARCHAEOLOGICAL COLLECTION
Primary School, Mavropigi, Kozani
Hellenistic and Roman vases and coins.
During school hours, on request.

MEGARA

ARCHAEOLOGICAL COLLECTION
Gymnasium (secondary school), Megara
Classical and Roman sculptures. Pottery of all periods.
During school hours, on request.

MELOS (MILOS)

MELOS MUSEUM
Melos, Plaka
Mycenean and cycladic vases. Archaeological site. Catacombs.
Summer: Daily 8-1, 3-6; Su. and holidays 10-1, 3-6. Winter: Daily 9-1, 2.30-5; Su. and holidays 10-1, 2.30-5. Closed Jan. 1, Mar. 25, Good F. (until noon), Easter Su. and Christmas Day. Closed M.

MESOLONGION

ART GALLERY OF THE MUNICIPALITY AND TOWN OF MESOLONGION
Town Hall, Mesolongion
Paintings by Greek and foreign artists of 19th and 20th centuries. Lithographs.
On application to the caretaker.

METEORA

MONASTERY OF AGION PANTON (VARLAAM)
Meteora
The refectory houses the monastery's treasures: icons, manuscripts, church plate, sacred embroideries, reliquaries and wood-carvings.
Enquire locally at Metropolis of Trikki and Stagoi (at Trikala).

MONASTERY OF AGIOS STEPHANOS
Meteora
Icons. Church plate. Sacred embroideries. Reliquaries. Wood-carvings.
Enquire locally at Metropolis of Trikki and Stagoi (at Trikala).

MONASTERY OF THE METAMORPHOSIS SOTIROS (METEORON)
Meteora
Byzantine and post-Byzantine icons, notably the 'Doubting Thomas', the icon of Maria Paleologina (1367-84) and the diptych of Christ and the Virgin, the 'Supreme Humiliation' (end of 14th century). Manuscripts, church plate, sacred embroideries, reliquaries and wood-carvings.
Enquire locally at Metropolis of Trikki and Stagoi (at Trikala).

METSOVON

MUSEUM OF EPIROT FOLK ART
Metsovon
Restored old mansion containing icons, furniture, wood-carvings, woven materials, copperware, utensils and weapons.
On application to the caretaker.

MISTRA

MISTRA MUSEUM
Mistra
Material from Byzantine churches. Murals. Marble relief of Christ.
Summer: Daily 8-1, 3-6; Su. and holidays 10-1, 3-6. Winter: Daily 9-1, 2.30-5; Su. and holidays 10-1, 2.30-5. Closed Jan. 1, Mar. 25, Good F. (until noon), Easter Su. and Christmas Day.

MOLYVOS

ARCHAEOLOGICAL COLLECTION
Mayor's Residence, Molyvos, Lesvos
Hellenistic sculpture and Roman sculpture and pottery. Coins.
Summer: Daily 8-1, 3-6; Su. and holidays 10-1, 3-6. Winter: Daily 9-1, 2.30-5; Su. and holidays 10-1, 2.30-5. Closed Jan. 1, Mar. 25, Good F. (until noon), Easter Su. and Christmas Day.

MONEMVASSIA

ARCHAEOLOGICAL COLLECTION
Mosque, Monemvassia
Byzantine and Frankish sculptures.
On application to the caretaker.

MYKONOS

ARCHAEOLOGICAL MUSEUM
Mykonos
Protogeometric, Geometric, archaic and classical pottery. Statuettes of various periods. Hellenistic and Roman sculpture. Bronze vessels and utensils. Inscriptions.
Summer: Daily 8-1, 3-6; Su. and holidays 10-1, 3-6. Winter: Daily 9-1, 2.30-5; Su. and holidays 10-1, 2.30-5. Closed Jan. 1, Mar. 25, Good F. (until noon), Easter Su. and Christmas Day.

FOLKLORE COLLECTION
Mykonos
Old Mykonos woven and knitted materials. Embroideries, lace, pottery from all over the Aegean. Sculptures. Lamps. Weights and measures. Replicas of stamps used for decorating bread. Samples of basket-weaving. Archives of the naval history of Mykonos.
Summer: Daily 8-1, 3-6; Su. and holidays 10-1, 3-6. Winter: Daily 9-1, 2.30-5; Su. and holidays 10-1, 2.30-5. Closed Jan. 1, Mar. 25, Good F. (until noon), Easter Su. and Christmas Day.

MYRINA

ARCHAEOLOGICAL MUSEUM
Myrina, Limnos
Prehistoric finds from the excavations of the Italian School of Archaeology at Polyochni (pottery, effigies, tools). Figurines, pictorial plaques and Etruscan vases. Roman sculpture. Bronze cauldron handles. Inscriptions.
Summer: Daily 8-1, 3-6; Su. and holidays 10-1, 3-6. Winter: Daily 9-1, 2.30-5; Su. and holidays 10-1, 2.30-5. Closed Jan. 1, Mar. 25, Good F. (until noon), Easter Su. and Christmas Day.

MYSTRAS

MUSEUM
North Cloister of Church of St. Dimitrios, Mystras
Fragments of frescoes from chapels in Mystras. Sculpture fragments. Pottery, jewellery and metalwork. Coins and inscriptions, mostly from late Byzantine (Palaeologue) period.
On application to the sacristan.

MYTILINI (MYTILENE)

ARCHAEOLOGICAL COLLECTION
Corner of Eftalioti and Ogdois Noemvriou Streets, Mytilini (Mytilene), Lesvos
Early Helladic, archaic and classical pottery. Aeolic capitals, classical, Hellenistic and Roman sculpture. Roman mosaic floor illustrating comedies by Menander. Important inscriptions. Byzantine icons and pottery. Hand-carved chests.
Daily ex. M. 8-1, 3-6; Su. and holidays 10-1, 3-6. Winter: Daily ex. M. 9-1, 2.30-5; Su. and holidays 10-1, 2.30-5.

H. BINOS PRIVATE COLLECTION
2 Harilaou Trikoupi Street, Mytilini (Mytilene), Lesvos
Hand-carved chests. 'Tchevredes' (embroidered kerchiefs).
By written appointment.

NATIONAL FOLK MUSEUM OF LESVOS
2nd Boys' Gymnasium (secondary school), Mytilini (Mytilene), Lesvos
Pottery. Embroideries. Lace. Wood-carvings. Metalwork. Library containing Byzantine and post-Byzantine manuscripts and old documents.
During school hours, on request.

M. NIKOU PRIVATE COLLECTION
19 Vyronos Street, Mytilini (Mytilene), Lesvos
Hand carved chests.
By written appointment.

M. VLACHOS PRIVATE COLLECTION
6 Mitropoleos Street, Mytilini (Mytilene), Lesvos
Collection of hand-carved chests, woven materials, 'tchevredes' and metalwork.
By written appointment.

NAFPAKTOS

ARCHAEOLOGICAL COLLECTION
Library, Nafpaktos
Architectural sculpture and inscriptions of the classical and Roman periods.
Daily ex. M. 9-4.

NAFPLION

ARCHAEOLOGICAL MUSEUM
Plateia Syntagmatos, Nafplion
Housed in a naval storehouse (1686-1715), the collection consists of finds from Tiryns, Mycenae, Asine, Midea, Dendra. Early, Middle and Late Helladic pottery. Menhirs from Midea. Fragments of frescoes and tablets with Linear B script from the palace at Mycenae. Part of the cornice of the Treasury of Atreus. Bronze breastplate and helmet from Dendra. Bronze tools and weapons. Mycenean idols, stone jars and jewellery. Geometric pottery, statuettes, black-figure and red-figure pottery and small finds of various periods.
Summer: Daily 8-1, 3-6; Su. and holidays 10-1, 3-6. Winter: Daily 9-1, 2.30-5; Su. and holidays 10-1, 2.30-5. Closed Jan. 1, Mar. 25, Good F. (until noon), Easter Su. and Christmas Day.

NAOUSSA

ECCLESIASTICAL COLLECTION
Church of St. Nicholas, Naoussa, Paros
Post-Byzantine icons, wood-carvings and small articles.
On application to the sacristan.

NAXOS

ARCHAEOLOGICAL MUSEUM
Gymnasium (secondary school), Naxos
Prehistoric marble figurines and pottery. Mycenean daggers, swords, jewellery and ivory objects. Sculpture from the archaic to the Roman period. Geometric and archaic pottery. Byzantine icons.
Daily ex. M. 8-1, 3-6; Su. and holidays 10-1, 3-6. Winter: Daily ex. M. 9-1, 2.30-5; Su. and holidays 10-1, 2.30-5.

NEA ANCHIALOS

ARCHAEOLOGICAL COLLECTION
Nea Anchialos
Architectural fragments. Sculptures and pottery of the early Christian period. Roman gold, jewellery.
Summer: Daily 8-1, 3-6; Su. and holidays 10-1, 3-6. Winter: Daily 9-1, 2.30-5; Su. and holidays 10-1, 2.30-5. Closed Jan. 1, Mar. 25, Good F. (until noon), Easter Su. and Christmas Day.

NEAPOLIS

ARCHAEOLOGICAL COLLECTION
Kosti Adosidi Pasha Street, Neapolis, Crete
Prehistoric and earthenware vessels. Figurines. Roman sculpture. Inscriptions and coins of various periods. Byzantine and Venetian sculpture, a Byzantine manuscript gospel.
Summer: Daily 8-1, 3-6; Su. and holidays 10-1, 3-6. Winter: Daily 9-1, 2.30-5; Su. and holidays 10-1, 2.30-5. Closed Jan. 1, Mar. 25, Good F. (until noon), Easter Su. and Christmas Day.

NEAPOLIS, VOION

ARCHAEOLOGICAL COLLECTION
Town Hall, Neapolis, Voion
Hellenistic and Roman sculpture.
Daily ex. Su. 9-4.

NEMEA

ARCHAEOLOGICAL COLLECTION
Archaeological Site, Nemea
Housed in a Roman bathhouse built on the site of the palaestra. Sculptures, architectural fragments and inscriptions from the sanctuary of Zeus.
Summer: Daily 8-1, 3-6; Su. and holidays 10-1, 3-6. Winter: Daily 9-1, 2.30-5; Su. and holidays 10-1, 2.30-5. Closed Jan. 1, Mar. 25, Good F. (until noon), Easter Su. and Christmas Day.

NEOS SKOPOS, SERRAI

ARCHAEOLOGICAL COLLECTION
Primary School, Neos Skopos, Serrai
Hellenistic and Roman vases and statuettes.
During school hours, on request.

NESTORION, KASTORIA

ARCHAEOLOGICAL COLLECTION
Gymnasium (secondary school), Nestorion, Kastoria
Roman reliefs and inscriptions.
During school hours, on request.

NIKOPOLIS

ARCHAEOLOGICAL COLLECTION
Archaeological Site, Nikopolis
Roman sculpture, architectural fragments and inscriptions.
Summer: Daily 8-1, 3-6; Su. and holidays 10-1, 3-6. Winter: Daily 9-1, 2.30-5; Su. and holidays 10-1, 2.30-5. Closed Jan. 1, Mar. 25, Good F. (until noon), Easter Su. and Christmas Day.

OINOUSSAI

NAUTICAL MUSEUM
Oinoussai
Paintings of ships, mostly by the Chian artist, Aristidis Glykas (1906).
Enquire locally.

OLYMPIA

ARCHAEOLOGICAL MUSEUM
Olympia
Mycenean pottery and bronzes. Bronze votive offerings, chiefly of the Geometric and archaic periods (statuettes, tripods, tripod-handles and griffins, decorated shields, breast-plates, helmets and greaves). Statues from the pediments of the temple of Zeus. Metopes from the same temple depicting the Labours of Hercules. The Victory of Paionios (425-421 B.C.) and the Hermes of Praxiteles. Architectural fragments from the Heraion and the temple of Zeus. Terracotta figures of the pre-classical period. Roman sculpture.
M.-Sa. 7.30-sunset; Su. 10-1, 3-6. Winter: Daily 9-1, 2.30-5; Su. and holidays 10-1, 2.30-5. Closed Jan. 1, Mar. 25, Good F. (until noon), Easter Su. and Christmas Day.

OLYMPIC GAMES MUSEUM
Olympia
Relics and souvenirs of the revived Games. Postage stamps issued by various countries commemorating the Olympics.
Summer: Daily 8-1, 3-6; Su. and holidays 10-1, 3-6. Winter: Daily 9-1, 2.30-5; Su. and holidays 10-1, 2.30-5. Closed Jan. 1, Mar. 25, Good F. (until noon), Easter Su. and Christmas Day.

OLYMPOS

ARCHAEOLOGICAL COLLECTION
Olympos, Karpathos
Classical and early Christian sculpture and lamps.
Summer: Daily 8-1, 3-6; Su. and holidays 10-1, 3-6. Winter: Daily 9-1, 2.30-5; Su. and holidays 10-1, 2.30-5. Closed Jan. 1, Mar. 25, Good F. (until noon), Easter Su. and Christmas Day.

OREOI

ARCHAEOLOGICAL COLLECTION
Village Hall, Oreoi, Euboea
Statue of a bull of the classical period. Classical and Hellenistic pottery.
On application to the caretaker.

PALAIA KORINTHOS

ARCHAEOLOGICAL MUSEUM
Palaia Korinthos
Neolithic pottery. Early and Middle Helladic and Mycenean vases. Figurines. Tools. Gold jewellery. Protogeometric, Geometric, Protocorinthian and Corinthian vases and figurines. Classical, Hellenistic and Roman pottery, statuettes, lamps, gold jewellery and articles of household use. Sculpture. Roman statues. Classical and Roman mosaic floors. Early Christian and Byzantine sculpture. Byzantine pottery. Coins and inscriptions.
Summer: Daily 8-1, 3-6; Su. and holidays 10-1, 3-6. Winter: Daily 9-1, 2.30-5; Su. and holidays 10-1, 2.30-5. Closed Jan. 1, Mar. 25, Good F. (until noon), Easter Su. and Christmas Day.

PANAGITSA PELLIS

CHURCH OF THE KOIMISSIS TIS THEOTOKOU
Panagitsa Pellis
Post-Byzantine icons, sacred embroideries and church plate brought over by the Greeks of Pontus in the 1922 exchange of populations.
On application to the sacristan.

PARAMYTHIA

ARCHAEOLOGICAL COLLECTION
Paramythia
Roman architectural fragments and important inscriptions. Classical and Roman small finds.
Summer: Daily 8-1, 3-6; Su. and holidays 10-1, 3-6. Winter: Daily 9-1, 2.30-5; Su. and holidays 10-1, 2.30-5. Closed Jan. 1, Mar. 25, Good F. (until noon), Easter Su. and Christmas Day.

PARGA

CHURCH OF THE HOLY APOSTLES
Parga
Relics of the history of Parga. Icons. Manuscripts. Church plate. 17th-18th century vestments. An 'epitaphios' (17th century), and bound gospels.
On application to the sacristan.

PAROS

ARCHAEOLOGICAL MUSEUM
Paros
Neolithic and Cycladic vases and figurines. Archaic, classical and Roman sculpture. Pottery and statuettes of the Geometric, archaic and classical periods. Inscriptions. Roman mosaic floors from Katapoliani.
Summer: Daily 8-1, 3-6; Su. and holidays 10-1, 3-6. Closed M. Winter: Daily 9-1, 2.30-5; Su. and holidays 10-1, 2.30-5. Closed Jan. 1, Mar. 25, Good F. (until noon), Easter Su. and Christmas Day.

BYZANTINE COLLECTION OF KATAPOLIANI
Church, Paros
Post-Byzantine icons, vestments, church plate. Byzantine sculpture.
On application to the sacristan.

PATMOS

MONASTERY OF ST. JOHN
Treasury Library, Patmos
Embroidered stoles (15th-18th centuries). Icons, notably a miniature mosaic framed in silver of St. Nicholas (11th century). Church furniture, including a chalice of 1679, a crozier (1677) with gold relief decoration and pale blue enamel work, ornamented with diamonds. Benediction crosses in wooden filigree. Pendant model ships (16th century) in enamelled silver set with precious stones, worn by the wives of rich ship-owners.
Winter: Daily 8.30-12, 2-4; Su. 8-12. Summer: Daily 8-12, 3-6.

PATRAI

ARCHAEOLOGICAL MUSEUM
42 Mezonos Street, Patrai
Early and Middle Helladic and Mycenean pottery, bronze vessels, weapons and jewellery. Archaic, classical, Roman sculpture. Geometric, Hellenistic and Roman pottery. Lamps and statuettes of various periods. Bronze vases, statuettes and helmets. Bronze and gold jewellery. Roman mosaic floor. Coins. Byzantine sculpture.
Summer: Daily 8-1, 3-6; Su. and holidays, 10-1, 3-6. Winter: Daily 9-1, 2.30-5; Su. and holidays 10-1, 2.30-5. Closed Jan. 1, Mar. 25, Good F. (until noon), Easter Su. and Christmas Day.

PELLA

ARCHAEOLOGICAL COLLECTION
Archaeological Site, Pella
Finds from the excavations of Pella (capital of ancient Macedonia). Classical and Hellenistic sculpture. Architectural fragments. Pottery. Jewellery. Various small finds. Mosaic floors.
Summer: Daily 8-1, 3-6; Su. and holidays 10-1, 3-6. Winter: Daily 9-1, 2.30-5; Su. and holidays 10-1, 2.30-5. Closed Jan. 1, Mar. 25, Good F. (until noon), Easter Su. and Christmas Day.

PERACHORA

ARCHAEOLOGICAL COLLECTION
Perachora
Corinthian pottery and some bronzes (griffins) from the excavation of the Heraion.
Summer: Daily 8-1, 3-6; Su. and holidays, 10-1, 3-6. Winter: Daily 9-1, 2.30-5; Su. and holidays, 10-1, 2.30-5. Closed Jan. 1, Mar. 25, Good F. (until noon), Easter Su. and Christmas Day.

PERATATA

MONASTERY OF AGIOS ANDREAS
Peratata, Kefallinia
Frescoes, icons, wood-carvings, vestments and ecclesias-

tical embroideries of the post-Byzantine period, collected from churches destroyed in the 1953 earthquake.
Not open to visitors.

PETRA

T. ELEFTHERIADIS PRIVATE COLLECTION
Petra, Lesvos
Paintings by the folk artist, Theophilos Hadjimichail. Some folk art pottery and metalwork.
By written application.

PIRAEUS

ARCHAEOLOGICAL MUSEUM
38 Filellinon Street, Piraeus
Funerary and votive reliefs of the 5th and 4th centuries B.C. Hellenistic and Roman sculpture. Pottery of the classical period, bronze statuettes and coins.
Daily 8-1, 3-6; Su. and holidays 10-1, 3-6. Winter: Daily 9-1, 2.30-5; Su. and holidays 10-1, 2.30-5. Closed Jan. 1, Mar. 25, Good F. (until noon), Easter Su. and Christmas Day.

MARITIME MUSEUM
Ereatis, Akti Themistocleous, Piraeus
Ship models dating from ancient Greek period onwards. Busts of warriors. Paintings of naval battles. Uniforms and souvenirs. Historic documents, books and photographs.
Summer: Daily 9-1, W-Sa. also 6-9; Su. and holidays 10-1, 6-8. Winter: Daily 9-1; W.-Sa. also 5-7; Su. and holidays 10-1, 5-8.

PLAKA

ARCHAEOLOGICAL MUSEUM
Plaka, Milos
Cycladic vases, figurines and obsidian blades. Greek and Roman sculpture, pottery and inscriptions.
Summer: Daily 8-1, 3-6; Su. and holidays 10-1, 3-6. Winter: Daily 9-1, 2.30-5; Su. and holidays 10-1, 2.30-5. Closed Jan. 1, Mar. 25, Good F. (until noon), Easter Su. and Christmas Day.

PLATANOS

ARCHAEOLOGICAL COLLECTION
Municipal Library, Platanos, Leros
Hellenistic sculpture. Hellenistic and Roman pottery. Inscriptions.
On application.

POLYGYROS

ARCHAEOLOGICAL MUSEUM
Polygyros
Classical and Hellenistic sculpture and vases.
Summer: Daily 8-1, 3-6; Su. and holidays, 10-1, 3-6. Winter: Daily 9-1, 2.30-5; Su. and holidays, 10-1, 2.30-5. Closed Jan. 1, Mar. 25, Good F. (until noon), Easter Su. and Christmas Day. Closed M.

I. LAMBROPOULOS PRIVATE COLLECTION
Polygyros
Vases, bronzes and various small finds of the Hellenistic and Roman periods.
By written appointment.

PYLOS

ANTONOPOULEION ARCHAEOLOGICAL MUSEUM
Pylos
Collection includes pottery, an earthenware bath, gold vases, jewellery and other finds of the Mycenean period (chiefly from excavations at Peristeria). Hellenistic pottery and glassware from excavations at Tsopani Rakhi and Yalova. Two Roman bronze statues. Engravings collected by the Frenchman, René Pyaux.
Summer: Daily 8-1, 3-6; Su. and holidays 10-1, 3-6. Winter: Daily 9-1, 2.30-5; Su. and holidays 10-1, 2.30-5. Closed Jan. 1, Mar. 25, Good F. (until noon), Easter Su. and Christmas Day. Closed M.

PYRGOS

KARDAMITSIS PRIVATE COLLECTION
Pyrgos, Tinos
Skylights from houses on the island.
By written appointment.

MONASTERY OF PROFITIS ILIAS
Pyrgos (near), Thira
Collection of post-Byzantine icons, church plate, carved wooden crosses, vestments, bound gospels, firmans and books.
Enquire locally at Metropolis of Thira, Amorgos and islands (at Thira).

P. NOMIKOS PRIVATE COLLECTION
Pyrgos, Thira
19th century woven materials, embroideries, gold-embroideries and metalwork from mansions on the island. Paintings and porcelain.
By written application.

MONASTERY OF THE KOIMISSIS TIS THEOTOKOU, KECHROVOUNI
Pyrgos, Tinos
Post-Byzantine icons.
Enquire locally at Metropolis of Syros, Tinos, Andros, Kea and Milos (at Ermoupolis).

PYTHAGOREION

ARCHAEOLOGICAL COLLECTION
Village Hall, Pythagoreion, Samos
Archaic and Roman sculpture, architectural fragments and inscriptions.
On application to the caretaker.

RETHYMNON

ARCHAEOLOGICAL MUSEUM
Venetian Officers' Club, Corner of Arkadiou and Konstantinou Paleologou Streets, Rethymnon, Crete
Sub-Neolithic and Mycenean vases. Minoan figurines, sarcophagi, seal-stones, amulets. Egyptian scarabs and Minoan double-headed axes. Greek and Roman sculpture. Red-figure and Hellenistic pottery, votive plaques, bronze statuettes, mirrors, glass vessels, seal-stones. Byzantine and Venetian reliefs. Coins. Inscriptions.
Summer: Daily 8-1, 3-6; Su. and holidays, 10-1, 3-6. Winter: Daily 9-1, 2.30-5; Su. and holidays, 10-1, 2.30-5. Closed Jan. 1, Mar. 25, Good F. (until noon), Easter Su. and Christmas Day. Closed M.

ARKADI MONASTERY
Rethymnon, Crete
Fragments of the old marble decoration of the monastery. Post-Byzantine icons. Church plate. Weapons. wood-carvings. Gold embroideries. Room containing portraits of Cretan resistance fighters and relics of revolts.
Enquire locally at Metropolis of Rethymnon and Mylopotamos (at Rethymnon).

COLLECTION OF THE LIKION TON ELLINIDON
Rethymnon Branch, Prokymea El. Venizelou (on the quay), Rethymnon, Crete
Embroideries from Rethymnon (originals and copies). Folk art pottery.
On application to the caretaker.

MONASTERY OF AGIOS IOANNIS PREVELIS
Rethymnon (near), Crete
Post-Byzantine icons, church plate, vestments. Some weapons and jewellery.
Enquire locally at Metropolis of Lambi and Sfakia (at Spili, Rethymnon).

RHODES

ARCHAEOLOGICAL MUSEUM
Street of the Knights, Rhodes
Neolithic pottery and tools. Vases, gold and ivory jewellery from Mycenean tombs, mostly from Ialyssos. Geometric, archaic and classical pottery, statuettes and terracotta sarcophagi from tombs at Ialyssos and Kamiros. Bronze votive offerings. Archaic, classical, Hellenistic and Roman sculpture. Early Christian mosaic floors. Coins. Coats of arms and tombstones of the Knights.
Daily ex. M. 8-1, 3-7; Su. and holidays 10-1, 3-7. Winter: Daily ex. M. 9-1, 2.30-5; Su. and holidays 10-1, 2.30-5.

DECORATIVE ARTS COLLECTION OF THE MUSEUM OF RHODES
Plateia Arghyrokastrou, Rhodes
Carved chests and other wood-carvings. Embroideries. Symi pottery. Glassware.
M., W. and F., 9-1.

PALACE OF THE GRAND MASTERS (KASTELLO)
Street of the Knights, Rhodes
16th-17th century western European furniture and tapestries. Roman and early Christian mosaic floors from Kos and Karpathos. Early Christian sculpture.
Daily ex. M. 9.30-1, 3.30-7; Su. and holidays 10-1, 2.30-5. Closed Jan. 1, Mar. 25, Good F. (until noon), Easter Su. and Christmas Day.

SALAMIS

ARCHAEOLOGICAL MUSEUM
Salamis
Classical grave reliefs. Mycenean pottery, statuettes, grave groups. Inscriptions.
Summer: Daily 8-1, 3-6; Su. and holidays 10-1, 3-6. Winter: Daily 9-1, 2.30-5; Su. and holidays 10-1, 2.30-5. Closed Jan. 1, Mar. 25, Good F. (until noon), Easter Su. and Christmas Day.

SAMARINA, GREVENA

CHURCH OF THE PANAGIA
Samarina, Grevena
Icons. Fragments of carved wooden altar-screens. Church plate. Vestments.
On application to the sacristan.

SAMOS

ARCHAEOLOGICAL MUSEUM
Samos
Archaic, classical and Roman sculpture. Geometric, archaic (from local, Rhodian and Laconian workshops) and classical pottery. Cypriot statuettes and vases. Egyptian and Assyrian statuettes and utensils. Bronze, ivory and wooden figurines and utensils of the Geometric and archaic periods.
Summer: Daily 8-1, 3-6; Su. and holidays 10-1, 3-6. Winter: Daily 9-1, 2.30-5; Su. and holidays 10-1, 2.30-5. Closed Jan. 1, Mar. 25, Good F. (until noon), Easter Su. and Christmas Day.

BYZANTINE MUSEUM OF THE METROPOLIS OF SAMOS AND IKARIA
Bishop's Palace, Samos
Collection of post-Byzantine icons, vestments, church plate, reliquaries and old books.
On application to the caretaker.

SAMOTHRAKI

ARCHAEOLOGICAL MUSEUM
Archaeological Site, Samothraki
Archaic, classical and Hellenistic sculpture, architectural fragments and reconstructions of representative sections of the main buildings in the sanctuary. Fragments of bronze statues. Pottery of the Bronze Age, and of the classical and Hellenistic periods. Votive offerings, utensils, ornaments and small finds. Hellenistic and Roman grave goods. Coins and inscriptions. Bronzes and pottery of the Byzantine period.
Summer: Daily 8-1, 3-6; Su. and holidays 10-1, 3-6. Winter: Daily 9-1, 2.30-5; Su. and holidays 10-1, 2.30-5. Closed Jan. 1, Mar. 25, Good F. (until noon), Easter Su. and Christmas Day.

SERIFOS

ARCHAEOLOGICAL COLLECTION
Village Hall, Serifos, Schimatari
Roman sculpture.
On application to the caretaker.

SERRAI

ARCHAEOLOGICAL COLLECTION
Bezesteni (covered market), Serrai
Hellenistic and Roman sculpture, housed in a Turkish building of the 15th-16th centuries.
On application to the caretaker.

SIATISTA

ARCHAEOLOGICAL COLLECTION
Gymnasium (secondary school), Siatista
Pottery, stone tools, weapons, bronze and iron ornaments from prehistoric to Roman times.
During school hours, on request.

SIFNOS

ARCHAEOLOGICAL COLLECTION
Church of St. Antony at Kastro, Sifnos
Hellenistic and Roman sculpture. Archaic statuettes and vases.
On application to the sacristan.

SIKINOS

ARCHAEOLOGICAL COLLECTION
Primary School, Sikinos
Reliefs and inscriptions.
During school hours, on request.

SIKYON

ARCHAEOLOGICAL MUSEUM
Roman bathhouse, Sikyon
Archaic sculpture. Terracotta architectural fragments from the temple of Artemis. Pottery and statuettes of all periods. Mosaic floor of the 4th century B.C. Early Christian and Byzantine sculpture.
Summer: Daily 8-1, 3-6; Su. and holidays 10-1, 3-6. Winter: Daily 9-1, 2.30-5; Su. and holidays, 10-1, 2.30-5. Closed Jan. 1, Mar. 25, Good F. (until noon), Easter Su. and Christmas Day. Closed M.

SKIATHOS

MONASTERY OF THE EVANGELISMOS TIS THEOTOKOU
Skiathos
At Agallianos, at the top of Mt. Karafildzanakas. Post-Byzantine icons, church plate, glassware and porcelain, books, documents, bulls and firmans.
Enquire locally at the Metropolis of Chalkis.

SKOPELOS

MONASTERY OF THE EVANGELISTRIA
Skopelos
Post-Byzantine icons, church plate and embroideries.
Enquire locally at the Metropolis of Chalkis.

SKYROS

ARCHAEOLOGICAL MUSEUM
Skyros
Early Helladic and Mycenean pottery. Protogeometric vases. Sculpture. Roman and Byzantine reliefs and inscriptions. Replica of the interior of a Skyros house.
Summer: Daily 8-1, 3-6; Su. and holidays, 10-1, 3-6. Winter: Daily 9-1, 2.30-5; Su. and holidays, 10-1, 2.30-5. Closed Jan. 1, Mar. 25, Good F. (until noon), Easter Su. and Christmas Day.

SOLOMOS

SOLOMOS AND EMINENT ZANTIANS MUSEUM
off Arseniou Street, Solomos
Byzantine art, mainly from ruined churches. Local carving of various iconostases. Sculptured relief by Thorvaldsen from a monument (1820) to Maitland.
Summer: Daily 8-1, 3-6; Su. and holidays 10-1, 3-6. Winter: Daily 9-1, 2.30-5; Su. and holidays 10-1, 2.30-5. Closed Jan. 1, Mar. 25, Good F. (until noon), Easter Su. and Christmas Day. Closed M.

SOULI

PRIMARY SCHOOL
Souli
Small collection of weapons and cannonballs.
During school hours, on request.

SPARTI

ARCHAEOLOGICAL MUSEUM
Sparti
Neolithic pottery, tools and jewellery from the cave of Alepotrypa and Pyrgos tou Dirou. Vases, weapons and other finds from the Menelaion and from Mycenean tombs. Sculpture of the archaic and classical periods. Hellenistic and Roman sculpture. Geometric and archaic pottery from local workshops. Terracotta reliefs and relief pithoi of the archaic period. Terracotta architectural fragments. Bronze, lead and terracotta votive offerings from the sanctuaries of Artemis Orthia and Athena Chalkioikos, the Menelaion, the Amyklaion and elsewhere. Archaic terracotta votive masks.
Summer: Daily 8-1, 3-6; Su. and holidays, 10-1, 3-6. Winter: Daily 9-1, 2.30-5; Su. and holidays, 10-1, 2.30-5. Closed Jan. 1, Mar. 25, Good F. (until noon), Easter Su. and Christmas Day.

COLLECTION OF THE METROPOLIS OF MONEMVASSIA AND SPARTI
Bishop's Palace, Sparti
Post-Byzantine icons and carved wooden crosses.
On application to the caretaker.

MONASTERY OF AGII SARANDA
Sparti
Icons, church plate, vestments and bulls of the post-Byzantine period.
Enquire locally at Metropolis of Movemvassia and Sparti.

SPETSAI

MUSEUM
Mansion of Hadjiyannis Mexis, Spetsai
Relics of the naval history of Spetsai. Flag of the 1821 Revolution, figureheads, drawings and paintings of Spetsai's ships, books and documents, the bones of Bouboulina, weapons and mementoes of leading families. Archaeological collection with local costumes and other folk art products. Pottery.
Not open to visitors.

SPILAION, GREVENA

ARCHAEOLOGICAL COLLECTION
Primary School, Spilaion, Grevena
Iron Age weapons. Hellenistic and Roman pottery.
During school hours, on request.

STAVROS

ARCHAEOLOGICAL MUSEUM
Stavros, Ithaki
Early Helladic, Mycenean, Geometric and Corinthian pottery. Fragments of bronze tripods.
Not open to visitors.

STEIRI

MONASTERY OF OSSIOS LOUKAS
Steiri (near)
11th century mosaics and frescoes. Icons. Vestments. Church plate.
Not open to visitors.

SYMI

ARCHAEOLOGICAL COLLECTION
Symi
Hellanistic and Roman sculpture and inscriptions. Byzantine and post-Byzantine sculpture and icons. Folk art. Wood-carvings. Woven materials. Metalwork. Silverware. Pottery.
Summer: Daily 8-1, 3-6; Su. and holidays 10-1, 3-6. Winter: Daily 9-1, 2.30-5; Su. and holidays, 10-1, 2.30-5. Closed Jan. 1, Mar. 25, Good F. (until noon), Easter Su. and Christmas Day.

MONASTERY OF THE ARCHANGEL MICHAEL PANORMITIS
Symi
Vestments and silverware.
Enquire locally at the Metropolis of Rhodes.

TANAGRA

ARCHAEOLOGICAL COLLECTION
Tanagra
Sculpture, architectural fragments, inscriptions and pottery from the archaic to the Byzantine period.
Summer: Daily 8-1, 3-6; Su. and holidays 10-1, 3-6. Winter: Daily 9-1, 2.30-5; Su. and holidays, 10-1, 2.30-5. Closed Jan. 1, Mar. 25, Good F. (until noon), Easter Su. and Christmas Day.

TEGEA

ARCHAEOLOGICAL MUSEUM
Tegea
Prehistoric pottery from Asea and Ayiorghitika. Sculpture, chiefly fragments from the decoration of the temple of Alea Athena. Classical pottery, Hellenistic statuettes and small bronze votive offerings.
Summer: Daily 8-1, 3-6; Su. and holidays 10-1, 3-6. Winter: Daily 9-1, 2.30-5; Su. and holidays 10-1, 2.30-5. Closed Jan. 1, Mar. 25, Good F. (until noon), Easter Su. and Christmas Day. Closed M.

THASSOS

ARCHAEOLOGICAL MUSEUM
Thassos
Sculptures of the archaic, classical, Hellenistic and Roman periods. Bronze and terracotta statuettes. Collection of archaic and classical pottery and lamps. Archaic terracotta architectural reliefs. Jewellery. Coins. Inscriptions. Early Christian sculpture.
Summer: Daily 8-1, 3-6; Su. and holidays 10-1, 3-6. Winter: Daily 9-1, 2.30-5; Su. and holidays 10-1, 2.30-5. Closed Jan. 1, Mar. 25, Good F. (until noon), Easter Su. and Christmas Day.

THEBES

THEBES MUSEUM
Pindharou, Thebes
Archaic and funerary stelae from Akraiphion. Marble torsoes and relief. Pottery and vases. Cylinder seals of lapis lazuli. Granulated jewellery. Worked ivory. Terracotta statuettes. Inscriptions.
Daily 8-1, 3-6. Closed M. morning. Su. and holidays 10-1, 3-6. Winter: Daily 9-1, 2.30-5. Closed M. morning. Su. and holidays 10-1, 2.30-5 or 3-6.

THERA

THERA MUSEUM
Thera, Santorin
Vases of the Geometric period. Finds from archaeological excavations.
Summer: Daily 8-1, 3-6; Su. and holidays 10-1, 3-6. Winter: Daily 9-1, 2.30-5; Su. and holidays 10-1, 2.30-5. Closed Jan. 1, Mar. 25, Good F. (until noon), Easter Su. and Christmas Day. Closed M.

THERMON

ARCHAEOLOGICAL MUSEUM
Thermon
Painted terracotta metopes from the archaic temple of Apollo, and other terracotta architectural fragments and tiles from the same temple. Mycenean, archaic and Hellenistic pottery. Inscriptions.
Summer: Daily 8-1, 3-6; Su. and holidays 10-1, 3-6. Winter: Daily 9-1, 2.30-5; Su. and holidays, 10-1, 2.30-5. Closed Jan. 1, Mar. 25, Good F. (until noon), Easter Su. and Christmas Day. Closed M.

THESPIAI

ARCHAEOLOGICAL COLLECTION
Village Hall, Thespiai
Sculpture, architectural fragments and inscriptions from the archaic to the Roman period.
Any time.

THESSALONIKI

ARCHAEOLOGICAL COLLECTION
Faculty of Philosophy, University of Thessaloniki, Thessaloniki
Pottery and statuettes of various periods.
By written appointment.

ARCHAEOLOGICAL MUSEUM
Thessaloniki
Pottery, weapons and jewellery from the Neolithic to the Iron Age. Archaic, classical, Hellenistic and Roman sculpture. Architectural fragments, vases, statuettes (from Olynthos) and bronzes. Gold jewellery and bronze krater from Derveni. Roman mosaic floors and glass utensils. Preserved portion of the mosaics from the war-damaged Cathedral of Serrai and a pair of enamelled bracelets of the mid-Byzantine period. Coin collection.
Summer: Daily 8-1, 3-6; Su. and holidays 10-1, 3-6. Winter: Daily 9-1, 2.30-5; Su. and holidays 10-1, 2.30-5. Closed Jan. 1, Mar. 25, Good F. (until noon), Easter Su. and Christmas Day. Closed M.

BYZANTINE MUSEUM OF THE ROTUNDA OF ST. GEORGE
Thessaloniki
This monument, built by Galerious c.300 A.D., was converted into a Christian church at the end of the 4th century. 5th century mosaics. Roman and early Christian sculpture and architectural fragments.
Summer: Daily 8-1, 3-6; Su. and holidays, 10-1. Winter: Daily 9-1, 2.30-5; Su. and holidays, 10-2. Closed Jan. 1, Mar. 25, Good F. (until noon), Easter Su. and Christmas Day. Closed M.

FOLKLORE MUSEUM AND ARCHIVES
Faculty of Philosophy, University of Thessaloniki, Thessaloniki
Wood-carvings. Woven material. Embroideries. Metalwork. Pottery.
Daily 8-1.30.

FOLKLORE MUSEUM OF NORTHERN GREECE
51 Vassileos Konstantinou Avenue, Thessaloniki
Woven materials. Local costumes. Embroideries. Wood-carvings. Metalwork. Silverware.
Daily ex. Sa. and Su. afternoons, 9-1, 4-7.

V. KYRIAZOPOULOS PRIVATE COLLECTION
11 Vassileos Konstantinou Avenue, Thessaloniki
Contemporary Greek folk pottery, chiefly the work of Minas Avramidis.
By written appointment.

I. PAPAILIAKIS PRIVATE COLLECTION
14 Venizelou Street, Thessaloniki
Ancient sculpture, pottery and jewellery.
By written appointment.

G. PARALIS PRIVATE COLLECTION
near the American College, Thessaloniki
Contemporary Greek folk pottery.
By written appointment.

G. PHILIPPOU PRIVATE COLLECTION
11 Vassileos Konstantinou Avenue, Thessaloniki
Ancient Greek and Roman pottery. Coins.
By written appointment.

I. VASSILIOU PRIVATE COLLECTION
6 Paraskevopoulou Street, Thessaloniki
Ancient pottery, bronzes, coins and jewellery. Icons.
By written appointment.

THIRA

ARCHAEOLOGICAL MUSEUM
Thira
Prehistoric pottery and figurines. Archaic, classical, Hellenistic and Roman sculpture. Geometric, archaic and classical pottery and archaic statuettes. Roman glassware. Lamps. Inscriptions.
Summer: Daily 8-1, 3-6; Su. and holidays 10-1, 3-6. Winter: Daily 9-1, 2.30-5; Su. and holidays 10-1, 2.30-5. Closed Jan. 1, Mar. 25, Good F. (until noon), Easter Su. and Christmas Day.

THIRA ECCLESIASTICAL MUSEUM
Bishop's Palace, Thira
Icons. Carved wooden crosses.
On application to the caretaker.

THIVAI

ARCHAEOLOGICAL MUSEUM
1 Threpsiadi Street, Thivai
Early, middle and late Helladic pottery and clay sarcophagi. Mycenean finds from the Cadmeia: vases, bronze articles, weapons, ivory relief plaques and fragments of a throne, jewellery made from gold, agate. Cylinder-seals from the East, tablets with text in Linear B script. Sculptures of the archaic, classical, Hellenistic and Roman periods. Engraved funerary stelae. Geometric, archaic and classical pottery. Terracotta and bronze statuettes of all periods. Inscriptions. Early Christian and Byzantine sculpture. Mosaic floor.
Summer: Daily 8-1, 3-6; Su. and holidays 10-1, 3-6. Winter: Daily 9-1, 2.30-5; Su. and holidays 10-1, 2.30-5. Closed Jan. 1, Mar. 25, Good F. (until noon), Easter Su. and Christmas Day.

THYRREION

ARCHAEOLOGICAL MUSEUM
Thyrreion
Classical, Hellenistic and Roman sculpture, architectural fragments and inscriptions. Roman mosaic floor.
Summer: Daily 8-1, 3-6; Su. and holidays, 10-1, 3-6. Winter: Daily 9-1, 2.30-5; Su. and holidays, 10-1, 2.30-5. Closed Jan. 1, Mar. 25, Good F. (until noon), Easter Su. and Christmas Day.

TILOS

ARCHAEOLOGICAL COLLECTION
Village Hall, Tilos
Classical and Hellenistic sculpture. Inscriptions.
On application to the caretaker.

TINOS

ARCHAEOLOGICAL MUSEUM
Tinos
Archaic and classical sculpture. Geometric pottery and archaic relief pithoi. Inscriptions.
Summer: Daily 8-1, 3-6; Su. and holidays 10-1, 3-6. Winter: Daily 9-1, 2.30-5; Su. and holidays 10-1, 2.30-5. Closed Jan. 1, Mar. 25, Good F. (until noon), Easter Su. and Christmas Day. Closed M.

BYZANTINE MUSEUM
Tinos
Post-Byzantine icons.
On application to the caretaker.

CHURCH OF THE PANAGIA EVANGELISTRIA
Tinos
The sacristy contains post-Byzantine icons, vestments, church plate, wood-carvings, precious articles and votive offerings.
On application to the sacristan.

MUSEUM OF A. SOHOS
Tinos
Sculptures by A. Sohos, donated by the artist.
On application to the caretaker.

MUSEUM OF TINIAN ARTISTS
Tinos
Works by N. Ghyzis, N. Lytras, G. Halepas, D. Filippotis and others.
On application to the caretaker.

I. PAPADOPOULOS PICTURE GALLERY
Tinos
Works by modern Greek artists (including K. Volanakis and K. Parthenis); copies of Renaissance paintings.
Enquire locally.

'THEOMITORIKI' EXHIBITION
Tinos
Representations of the Blessed Virgin from all over the world.
On application to the caretaker.

TRAIANOUPOLIS (LOUTROS)

ARCHAEOLOGICAL COLLECTION
Traianoupolis (Loutros)
Roman reliefs and inscriptions. Byzantine architectural fragments. Medieval reliefs.
Summer: Daily 8-1, 3-6; Su. and holidays 10-1, 3-6. Winter: Daily 9-1, 2.30-5; Su. and holidays 10-1, 2.30-5. Closed Jan. 1, Mar. 25, Good F. (until noon), Easter Su. and Christmas Day.

TRIKALA

ARCHAEOLOGICAL COLLECTION
Opposite Phaneromeni Church, Trikala
Classical and Hellenistic sculpture (grave stelae) and statuettes. Pottery of the late Byzantine and early post-Byzantine periods.
Summer: Daily 8-1, 3-6; Su. and holidays 10-1, 3-6. Winter: Daily 9-1, 2.30-5; Su. and holidays 10-1, 2.30-5. Closed Jan. 1, Mar. 25, Good F. (until noon), Easter Su. and Christmas Day.

ECCESIASTICAL MUSEUM OF THE METROPOLIS OF TRIKKI AND STAGOI
Bishop's Palace, Trikala
Icons of 16th-18th centuries. Sacred embroideries. Church plate. Reliquaries and wood-carvings collected from churches and chapels in the area.
On application to the caretaker.

MONASTERY OF AGIOS VISSARION (DOUSSIKOU)
Trikala
Post-Byzantine icons. Church plate. Sacred gold-embroideries, reliquaries. Gospel bindings. Manuscripts and documents.
Enquire locally at Metropolis of Trikki and Stagoi (at Trikala). Women not admitted.

TSOTYLI

ARCHAEOLOGICAL COLLECTION
Boys' Gymnasium (secondary school), Tsotyli
Hellenistic and Roman pottery and sculpture.
During school hours, on request.

VAREIA

THEOPHILOS MUSEUM
Vareia, Lesvos
Works by Theophilos Hadjimichail. (Tériade bequest).
On application to the caretaker.

VATHY

ARCHAEOLOGICAL MUSEUM
Vathy, Ithaki
Protocorinthian and Corinthian pottery and small bronze articles from the excavations on Mt. Aetos.
By appointment.

VEROIA

ARCHAEOLOGICAL MUSEUM
47 Anixeos Street, Veroia
Early neolithic and Bronze Age vases and figurines. Iron Age weapons and jewellery from the excavations at Vergina. Geometric, Hellenistic and Roman pottery. Hellenistic and Roman sculpture. Architectural fragments. Inscriptions. Coins. Byzantine icons, sculptures. Manuscripts and documents.
Daily 8-1, 3-6; Su. and holidays 10-1, 3-6. Winter: Daily 9-1, 2.30-5; Su. and holidays 10-1, 2.30-5.

VOLOS

ATHANASSAKEION ARCHAEOLOGICAL MUSEUM
1 Athanassaki Street, Volos
Neolithic and Bronze Age pottery, figurines, tools and other items of bone and stone. Archaic, classical, Hellenistic and Roman sculpture. Painted grave stelae from Dimitrias (3rd-2nd century B.C.). Geometric and classical pottery. Gold jewellery and weapons from the graves of the Geometric and classical periods. Glass vases. Coin collection.
Summer: Daily 8-1, 3-6; Su. and holidays 10-1, 3-6. Winter: Daily 9-1, 2.30-5; Su. and holidays 10-1, 2.30-5. Closed Jan. 1, Mar. 25, Good F. (until noon), Easter Su. and Christmas Day.

A. BASTIS PRIVATE COLLECTION
112 Gallias Street, Volos
Neolithic figurines, tools and jewellery.
By written appointment.

K. A. MAKRIS PRIVATE COLLECTION
22 Afendouli Street, Volos
Folk art murals, mostly the work of Athanassios and Yannis Pagonis. Paintings by Theophilos Hadjimichail and N. Christopoulos. Wood-carvings, woven materials, jewellery, various utensils and miniatures typical of the folk art of Mount Pilion.
By written appointment.

MUNICIPAL ART GALLERY
Ogl and Orpheos Streets, Volos
Works by modern Greek artists.
On application to the caretaker.

SEFEL PRIVATE COLLECTION
Pefkakia, Volos
Vases and bronze statuettes, mainly of the Geometric period.
By written appointment.

VRAVRON

ARCHAEOLOGICAL MUSEUM
next to the Sanctuary of Artemis, Vravron
From the Sanctuary itself, classical sculptures, alabaster vases, jewellery, mirrors, vases, terracotta plaques and other votive offerings. From the Mesoyia district, prehistoric, Geometric, archaic and classical pottery, statuettes and tomb sculpture.
Summer: Daily 8-1, 3-6; Su. and holidays 10-1, 3-6. Winter: Daily 9-1, 3-5; Su. and holidays 10-1, 2.30-5. Closed Jan. 1, Mar. 25, Good F. (until noon), Easter Su. and Christmas Day. Closed M.

VRONTADOS

MUSEUM OF THE VRONTADOS SOCIETY FOR PROGRESS
Xeniion Girls' School, Vrontados, Chios
Wood-carvings and embroideries. Pictures of ships by local artists. Nautical gear. Historic relics of the liberation of Chios.
During school hours, on request.

XANTHI

COLLECTION OF THE METROPOLIS OF XANTHI
Bishop's Palace, Xanthi
Icons. Manuscripts.
On application to the caretaker.

FOLKLORE MUSEUM
Xanthi
Local costumes and embroideries.
Open only during local festivals.

YPATI

AGATHONOS MONASTERY
Ypati (near)
Icons, vestments, church plate, carved wooden crosses and reliquaries of the post-Byzantine period. Religious books of the 18th-19th centuries.
Enquire locally at Metropolis of Phthiotis (at Lamia).

ZAKYNTHOS

BYZANTINE MUSEUM
Solomou Square, Zakynthos
Frescoes, including one of 12th century, and many post-Byzantine examples. Post-Byzantine icons and paintings of the Heptanesian school. Wood-carvings (notably the screens from the churches of the Pantocrator and Agios Dimitrios tou Kolla). Hellenistic and Byzantine sculpture. Coats of arms of noble families.
Summer: Daily 8-1, 3-6; Su. and holidays 10-1, 3-6. Winter: Daily 9-1, 2.30-5; Su. and holidays 10-1, 2.30-5. Closed Jan. 1, Mar. 25, Good F. (until noon), Easter Su. and Christmas Day. Closed M.

MUSEUM OF SOMOMOS AND OTHER ILLUSTRIOUS ZAKYNTHIANS
Eleftherias Square, Zakynthos
Manuscripts of Solomos and mementoes of famous Zakynthians of the 19th century. Local costumes and weapons.
On application to the caretaker.

ZANTE

POST-BYZANTINE MUSEUM
Zante
Portable icons of the post-Byzantine era.
Summer: Daily 8-1, 3-6; Su. and holidays 10-1, 3-6. Winter: Daily 9-1, 2.30-5; Su. and holidays 10-1, 2.30-5. Closed Jan. 1, Mar. 25, Good F. (until noon), Easter Su. and Christmas Day.

ZAVORDA

MONASTERY OF OSSIOS NIKANOR
Zavorda
Icons. Vestments. Gold-embroideries. Embroideries. Church plate. Reliquaries. Wood-carvings. Manuscripts.
Enquire locally at Metropolis of Grevena. Women not admitted.

ZERBITSA

MONASTERY OF THE KOIMISSIS TIS THEOTOKOU
Zerbitsa
Post-Byzantine icons. Ecclesiastical gold-embroideries (notably the 'epitaphios' dating from 1539 and the monastery's banner dating from 1639). Wood-carvings. Plate. Documents.
Enquire locally at Metropolis of Monemvassia and Sparti (at Sparti).

Guadeloupe

Guadeloupe is rum, sugar and banana territory and has been for a long time past. Its museum, however, prefers to see the basic activity of producing these goods in terms of what the natives do in their spare time and how they live, rather than how they behave when they are at work - which does no harm so long as one realises that there is another side to the picture.

POINTE-A-PITRE

SCHOELCHER MUSEUM
24 rue Peynier, Pointe-a-Pitre
China. Engravings. Documents relating to the First World War.
Daily ex. M. 9-12, 3-6.

Guatemala

Given the necessary funds, which at present do not exist in this hard-pressed country, it would be possible to set up a number of exceedingly interesting specialist museums devoted to, for example, coffee, mahogany and chewing gum (Guatemala is the second-largest producer in the world of the gum used for chewing gum manufacture). A museum of chewing gum has immense possibilities and could be a major tourist attraction. This is not yet to be found, however, and what we have instead, all in Guatemala City, are the normal South American collections of archaeology, ethnography and folk art.

GUATEMALA CITY

ARCHAEOLOGICAL MUSEUM
Finca La Aurora, Zona 13, Guatemala City
Archaeology. Mayan art. Ethnography of Guatemala.
By appointment.

MUSEUM OF HISTORY AND FINE ARTS
Finca La Aurora, Zona 13, Guatemala City
Paintings. Engravings. Sculpture. Furniture. Numismatics. Artists represented include Rafael Rodriguez Padilla, Alfredo Suarez, Humberto Garavito, Arturo Martinez, Rodolfo Torres, Carlos Velenti, Roberto Ossaye, Max Saravia Gual.
Tu.-F. 10-5.30; Sa. and Su. 10-12, 3-5.30; closed M.

MUSEUM OF NATURAL HISTORY
Finca La Aurora, Zona 13, Guatemala City
Botanical and zoological collection, including animals from several continents. Geology.
Tu.-F. 10-5.30; Sa. and Su. 10-12, 3-5.30; closed M.

NATIONAL MUSEUM OF ART AND HANDICRAFTS
10 Avenida, 10-72, Zona 1, Guatemala City
Metal and wooden objects belonging to indigenous races. Ceramics. Masks. Costumes.
Tu.-F. 9-5.30; Sa. and Su. 10-12, 3-5.30; closed M.

Guinea

The Western view of Guinea as a country entirely inhabited by head-hunters and cannibals is encouraged to some extent by the contents of its museums, which understandably make great play with the splendid fetishes, masks and tattooing instruments which visitors have found so appealing for a century or more. The task of presenting these picturesque items in their correct ethnographical and social context is being energetically tackled by the museum authorities, but at present the situation is almost that of an embarrassment caused by riches.

BEYLA

BEYLA REGIONAL MUSEUM
Institut National de Recherches et de Documentation de la Guinée, Beyla
Ethnography. Prehistory. Paintings. Sculpture.
Daily 7.30-3.

CONAKRY

CONAKRY NATIONAL MUSEUM
B.P. 561, Conakry
Ethnography. Prehistory. Fetishes; masks of the 'Sacred Forest'. Paintings.
Daily 7.30-3.

KISSIDOUGOU

KISSIDOUGOU MUSEUM
Kissidougou
Prehistory, ethnography and art. Masks and fetishes.
Daily 7.30-3.

KOUNDARA

FEDERAL MUSEUM
Annexe de Koundara, Koundara
Ethnographic collections of the Coniagui and Bassare tribes.
Daily 7.30-3.

N'ZEREKORE

LOCAL MUSEUM
B.P. 114, N'Zerekore
Ethnography, botany and zoology. Tattooing instruments. Pipes carved out of stone.
Daily 7.30-3.

YOUKOUNKOUN

YOUKOUNKOUN MUSEUM
Youkounkoun
Prehistory, ethnography and art.
Daily 7.30-3.

Guyana

Guyana is sugar, gold, diamonds and bauxite. Its museum details mainly the natural history, folklore and handicrafts of the country, with some sideways glances at its history under first the Dutch and then the British.

GEORGETOWN

GUYANA MUSEUM
Cultural Centre, North Street, Georgetown
Industry. Art. History. Anthropology. Zoology.
Daily ex. M. 9-12, 3-6.

Haiti

This is a poor agricultural country, and few nations would feel inclined to establish museums to document their poverty and general backwardness. In the circumstances, two museums, one general and one of art, must seem a very creditable and reasonable performance.

PORT-AU-PRINCE

ARTS CENTRE
Rue de la Révolution, Port-au-Prince
Exhibitions of Haitian art in the Americas and Western Europe.
Daily ex. M. 9-12, 2-5.

NATIONAL MUSEUM
Turgeau, C.S., Port-au-Prince
Numismatics; paper money. Documents. Paintings. Stones. Utensils. Arms.
Daily ex. M. 9-12, 2-5.

Honduras

Honduras, like several other South American countries, has the great blessing of Maya relics, with which a museum can hardly go wrong. This apart, perhaps the chief point to make is that in 1958 the country suffered the great disaster of having its National Museum destroyed by fire, after which the exhibits had to be put into store. The place chosen for the store was, most prudently, the Central Bank.

COMAYAGUA

MUSEUM OF RELIGIOUS ART
Comayagua
Religious and colonial relics.
M.-Sa. 8-12, 2-5; Su. 10-12, 4-5.

REGIONAL MUSEUM OF ARCHAEOLOGY AND COLONIAL EXHIBITS OF THE COMAYAGUA VALLEY
Comayagua
Archaeological and colonial material discovered in and around Comayagua.
M.-Sa. 8-12, 2-5; Su. 10-12, 2-5.

COPÁN

REGIONAL MUSEUM OF MAYAN ARCHAEOLOGY
Copán Ruins
Relics of the Mayan civilisation.
M.-Sa. 8-12, 2-5; Su. 10-12, 2-5.

OMOA

CASTILLO DE SAN FERNANDO DE OMOA
Omoa
Old Spanish fortress, now being restored. Colonial and historical items.
M.-Sa. 8-12, 2-5; Su. 10-12, 2-5.

QUIMISTÁN

MIGUEL PAZ BARAONA HISTORICAL MUSEUM
Aldea de Pinalejo, Município de Quimistán
Archaeological, colonial and contemporary art of the region.
M.-Sa. 8-12, 2-5; Su. 10-12, 2-5.

Hong Kong

For all the extensive and profitable links that Hong Kong has with the West, its museums remain unswervingly Chinese, a fact which may surprise the outside world but which seems completely right within the atmosphere of Hong Kong itself.

HONG KONG

CITY MUSEUM AND ART GALLERY
City Hall, Edinburgh Place, Hong Kong
Chinese antiquities. Archaeology. Paintings, prints and drawings of Hong Kong, Macao and China. Contemporary works by local artists. Early bronzes, pottery, porcelain. Lacquerwork.
Daily ex. Th. 10-6; Su. and public holidays 1-6.

FUNG PING SHAN MUSEUM
University of Hong Kong, Bonham Road, Hong Kong
Chinese art and antiquities. Pottery, bronzes, porcelain and paintings. Archaeology.
M.-Sa. 10-6.

KOWLOON

LEI CHENG UK TOMB SITE MUSEUM
Lei Cheng Uk, Kowloon
Actual Han tomb site and the articles excavated from it.
Daily ex. Tu. 12-7.

SHA TIN

ART GALLERY OF THE INSTITUTE OF CHINESE STUDIES
Chinese University of Hong Kong, Sha Tin, New Territories, Hong Kong
Chinese art and antiquities.
M.-F. 10-4.30; Sa. 10-12.30.

Hungary

Up to 1914, Hungarian museums, such as existed, were heavily concentrated in the capital. The policy of the Austro-Hungarian empire had been to confine industry and the appurtenances of civilisation largely to an area in and around Budapest, which was regarded as a convenient and pleasant extension of Vienna, and to keep the remainder of Hungary rural and benighted, a convenient and profitable area for producing grain, cattle and horses, and for hunting and shooting.

During the 1920s and 1930s, something, but not much, was done to bring the rest of Hungary into the twentieth century. A number of provincial museums were established or developed, but the effort was half-hearted and the funds quite inadequate. In 1939, when the Germans moved in to control the country, Hungary was still very backward, poor, and apart from one or two pockets, hardly industrialised at all. When the war ended, the real process of industrialisation and modernisation began, a process which is well reflected in the nation-wide network of museums which the country now has.

The war and later upheavals caused great damage to Hungarian museums, especially in Budapest where, to take only one example, the Agricultural Museum lost most of its collections. On the other hand, the nationalisation of the estates, castles and mansions of the old aristocracy, landowners and industrialists brought splendid private collections into the public field, and these have provided the basis of a number of new museums.

The present position is that Hungary now has a large, well-organised and well-balanced museum system, which does its best - a very good best - to meet the needs of the country as a whole, and to integrate the national traditions with a rapidly expanding industrial economy. In the development of its museums, Hungary has encouraged one particularly welcome feature, the small, intimate house-museum devoted to a single person. The proportion of such museums is exceptionally and refreshingly high. They are cheap to establish, cheap to maintain and, providentially, they are in line with a growing and well-founded international belief that the public is very fond of small museums.

ABONY

LAJOS ABONYI VILLAGE MUSEUM
Zalka Máté utca 16, Abony, Pest megye
Lajos Abonyi memorial collection. Archaeology. Ethnography.
Su. 10-12.

ÁBRAHÁMHEGY

ORNITHOLOGICAL COLLECTION
Ábrahámhegy, Veszprén megye
Birds of the Lake Balaton area.
Daily, ex. public holidays, 10-6.

AGÁRD

GÉZA GÁRDONYI MEMORIAL MUSEUM
Gárdonyi Géza utca, Agárd, Fejer megye
Life and work of Géza Gárdonyi.
Tu.-Su. 10-1, 3-6.

ÁLMOSD

KÖLCSEY HOUSE MUSEUM
Álmosd, Hajdu-Bihar megye
Life and work of the Álmosd poet, Kölcsey.
On request.

ASZÓD

PETŐFI MUSEUM
Szontágh lépcsö 2, Aszód, Pest megye
Archaeology. Ethnography.
Tu., W., 9-12. Th., F., Sa. 3-6; Su. 10-5.

ÁTA

MUSEUM ROOM
Községi Kultúrotthon, Áta, Baranya megye
Furniture. Household equipment. Costumes.
During opening hours of the Cultural Centre.

BADACSONY

IRODALMI MUSEUM
Badacsony, Veszprém megye
18th century house, formerly home of the poet, Kisfaludy, with his furniture and manuscripts. Implements used in vineyard cultivation.
Tu.-Su. 10-6.

BAJA

ISTVÁN TÜRR MUSEUM
Deák Ferenc utca 1, Baja, Bács-Kiskun megye
Archaeology. Ethnography. 19th-20th century paintings by Hungarian artists.
Tu., Th., F. 3-7; W., Sa. 10-2; Su. 11-1, 5-7. Closed public holidays.

BAKONSZEG

GYÖRGY BESSENYEI HOUSE MUSEUM
Bakonszeg, Hajdu-Bihar megye
Home of the writer, György Bessenyei (d.1811). Collections illustrating his life and work.
On request.

BALASSAGYARMAT

PALÓC MUSEUM
Palóc liget 1, Balassagyarmat, Nógrád megye
Natural history. Archaeology. Roman material. Folk art, expecially by shepherds. Nógrád costumes. Toys. Musical instruments.
M., Tu., W. 10-2; Th., F. 2-6; Su. 10-12, 2-4.

BALATONFÜRED

JÓKAI MEMORIAL MUSEUM
Jókai utca 1, Balatonfüred, Veszprém megye
Manuscripts, books and personal possessions of the novelist, Mór Jókai.
May-Oct., daily 10-6. Nov.-Apr., daily 10-6; closed public holidays.

BALATONSZÁRSZÓ

ATTILA JÓZSEF MEMORIAL MUSEUM
József Attila utca 7, Balatonszárszó, Somogy megye
Life and work of the poet, Attila József (d.1937), who committed suicide by throwing himself in front of a train.
Dec.-Feb., daily 11-12. Mar.-May and Sept. 16- Nov. 30, daily 9-1. June 1- Sept. 15, daily 9-1, 3-7. Closed public holidays.

BALATONSZEMES

POSTAL MUSEUM
Balatonszemes, Somogy megye
History of the postal service and of postage stamps.
June-Sept., daily 9-1, 3-7.

BÉKÉS

BÉKÉS MUSEUM
Széchenyi utca 6, Békés, Békés megye
Local history.
Tu., F., Su. 10-12.

BÉKÉSCSABA

MIHÁLY MUNKÁCSY MUSEUM
Széchenyi utca 9, Békéscsaba, Békés megye
Regional archaeology and ethnology. 19th-20th century Hungarian paintings.
Tu.-Su. 9-5.

BONYHÁD

LOCAL HISTORY COLLECTION
Bonyhád, Tolna megye
Ethnography. Local history.
By appointment.

BORJÁD

PETŐFI MEMORIAL APIARY
Borjád, Tolna megye
History and techniques of bee-keeping.
Su. 9-5.

BUDAPEST

GÜL BABA'S TOMB
Mecset utca 20, Budapest II
Tomb (1543-48) of the Islamic preacher, Gül Baba. Place of pilgrimage during Turkish occupation of Hungary.
Daily 11-6.

GIZI BAJOR MEMORIAL MUSEUM
Stromfeld Aurel utca 16, Budapest XII
Collection illustrating life and career of Gizi Bajor, in his former home.
Tu., Th., Sa. 3-7; Su. 10-6.

CASTLE VAULTS
Uri utca 9, Budapest I
Medieval storage cellars. History of the Castle.
Sa. 3-6; Su. 10-6.

CHINESE MUSEUM
Gorkij fasor 12, Budapest VI
Chinese porcelain, textiles, lacquer-ware, calligraphy, sculpture.
Tu.-Sa. 9-5; Su. 9-6.

ANDOR GÁBOR MEMORIAL MUSEUM
Zichy Géza utca 8, Budapest XVI
Life and work of Andor Gábor.
W., F., Su. 10-2.

HERCULES VILLA
Meggyfa utca 19-21, Budapest II
Excavated remains of Roman villa. Mosaics, including representations of Hercules.
Tu.-Sa. 10-1; Su. 10-6.

FERENC HOPP MUSEUM OF ORIENTAL ART
Nepköztárraság útca 103, Budapest VI
Chinese silk-tapestry. Chinese silk-damask book-covers. Japanese priests' vestments. Vietnamese embroidered textiles. Chinese, Japanese, Vietnamese porcelain. Chinese, Korean lacquer-ware. Indian, Burmese, Mongolian, Cambodian art.
Tu.-Sa. 8.45-4.45; Su. 9.45-5.45.

HUNGARIAN AGRICULTURAL MUSEUM
Városliget, Budapest XIV
Cattle and horse-breeding. Crops. Machinery. Tractors. Wine-production. Fishing and fish-farming. Forestry. Hunting.
Tu.-Sa. 10-5; Su. 10-6.

HUNGARIAN HOTEL AND CATERING MUSEUM
Fortuna utca 4, Budapest I
Collections illustrating 18th-20th century history of hotel and restaurant-keeping and of the tourist trade in Hungary. Equipment. Furniture. Table-settings. Financial aspects of catering and tourism.
Tu.-Su. 10-6.

HUNGARIAN NATIONAL GALLERY
Kossuth Lajos tér 12, Budapest V
19th-20th century Hungarian art, reflecting struggle for national independence. Paintings. Sculpture. Graphics.
Tu.-Su. 11-7.

HUNGARIAN NATIONAL MUSEUM
Múzeum körút 14-16, Budapest VIII
Prehistory - Palaeolithic, Neolithic, Copper Age, Bronze Age, Iron Age. Early history - Roman, period of migration - of Hungary. Medieval - 19th century history. Historical portraits. Weapons. Coins. Crown of the Byzantine emperor, Constantinum Monomachus. Furniture. Ceramics.
Tu.-Su. 10-6.

HUNGARIAN TRANSPORT MUSEUM
Városligeti körút 11, Budapest XIV
Models and originals illustrating development of road, rail and air transport. Old vehicles. Nautical and aeronautical collections. Road- and bridge-building.
Tu.-Th., Sa., Su. 10-6.

JEWISH HISTORY COLLECTIONS
Dohány utca 2, Budapest VII
Jewish history and traditions. History of the Jewish Community in Budapest. Liturgical objects.
M., Tu.-F. 11-1.

JÓKAI MEMORIAL ROOM
Költö utca 21, Budapest XII
Summer residence of the novelist, Maurice Jókai. Furniture. Decorative arts.
W., F., Sa., Su. 10-6.

ATTILA JÓZSEF MEMORIAL ROOM
Gát utca 3, Budapest IX
Collections illustrating life and work of the poet, Attila József.
Tu.-Su. 10-6.

JÓZSEF TOWN LOCAL MUSEUM
Bródy Sandor utca 23B, Budapest VIII
Local history.
Tu.-Su. 11-7.

MIHÁLY KÁROLYI MEMORIAL MUSEUM
Károlyi Mihály utca 16, Budapest V
Life and work of Mihály Károlyi (1875-1955), President of the Republic of Hungary.
Tu.-Su. 10-6.

MAGDALEN TOWER
Kapistrán tér, Budapest 1
13th century church tower. Local and religious history.
Su. 10-6.

MATTHIAS CHURCH ECCLESIASTICAL COLLECTION
Szentháromság tér 3, Budapest I
Religious art. Liturgical objects.
Daily 9-7.

MEDIEVAL JEWISH PRAYER HOUSE
Tancsics utca 26, Budapest I
Collection of medieval relics of the Budapest Jews.
Su. 10-6.

MUSEUM OF APPLIED ARTS
Üllöi út 33-7, Budapest IX
14th-20th century European furniture, especially Italian Renaissance, French, Austrian, German, Baroque, French rococo, 18th - early 19th century English. Furnished Hungarian interiors, including Köszeg Pharmacy and Sümeg Library. 17th-18th century woodcarvings. Musical instruments. European porcelain, faience, stoneware, pottery, tiles. Glass. Goldsmiths' work, especially German. Ivories. Wrought iron. Carpets. Tapestry. Lace. Costumes.
Tu.-Su. 10-6.

MUSEUM OF ETHNOGRAPHY
Könyves Kálman körút 40, Budapest VIII
European peasant cultures. African (especially Nigerian), Far Eastern (especially Siberian, Japanese), N. and S. American, New Guinea collections. World-wide collection of folk-music recordings.
Tu.-Su. 10-6.

MUSEUM OF FINE ART
Dózsa György út 41, Budapest XIV
13th-19th century Italian, Dutch, Spanish (especially El Greco), German, French, English paintings. 19th-20th century paintings, especially French, Austrian. 4th-20th century European sculpture. European graphics, especially 19th-20th century. Greek and Roman antiquities, especially Greek sculpture, vases. Egyptian sculpture, mummies. Early Hungarian art. Venetian fountains.
Tu.-Su. 10-6.

MUSEUM OF FIRE-FIGHTING
Martinovics tér 12, Budapest X
History of fire-fighting, especially in Budapest. Fire-fighting equipment. Photographs. Prints. Uniforms worn by members of fire-brigade.
W., F., Su. 10-2.

MUSEUM OF THE HISTORY OF BUDAPEST: DEPARTMENT OF MODERN HISTORY
Kiscelli utca 108, Budapest III
Also known as Kiscell Museum. In former monastery

(1738-47). History of Budapest in the post-medieval period. Paintings, drawings, prints illustrating history of Budapest. Maps. Porcelain. Glass. Silver. Sculpture. Wrought iron. Guild chests. Shop signs. Medals. Late 19th century electric motors. Correspondence and personal possessions of Adam Clark. Early 19th century furniture. Equipment of pharmacy. MSS of music by Bartók and Kodály.
Tu.-Su. 10-6.

MUSEUM OF THE HISTORY OF BUDAPEST: DEPARTMENT OF PREHISTORY AND ANTIQUITY
Szentendrei út 139, Budapest III
Also known as Aquincum Museum. Collections illustrating history of Budapest in prehistoric and early historical times. Roman material from excavations on site of Aquincum. Roman air-blown organ. Glass. Mosaics. Pottery. Sculpture.
Tu.-Su. 10-6.

MUSEUM OF THE HISTORY OF BUDAPEST: MEDIEVAL DEPARTMENT
Szentgyörgy tér 2, Budapest I
Collections illustrating history of Hungary in the Medieval and Renaissance periods. Sculpture. Pottery. Tiles. Glass. Woodcarving. Furniture.
Tu.-Su. 10-6.

MUSEUM OF THE HISTORY OF BUDAPEST: PALACE MUSEUM
Szent György utca 2, Budapest I
In former royal palace. Relics of the thousand-year-old capital and medieval royal palace.
Tu.-Su. 10-6.

MUSEUM OF THE HISTORY OF THE HUNGARIAN COMMUNIST PARTY
Visegrádi utca 15, Budapest XIII
History of the Hungarian Communist Party, with memorabilia of its leading members.
Tu.-Su. 10-6.

MUSEUM OF MILITARY HISTORY
Tóth Árpád sétány 40, Budapest I
History of the Hungarian army, 1849-1918. Contribution of Hungarian volunteers in Spanish Civil War. Hungarian forces of liberation in World War II. Development of military technology.
Tu.-Su. 9-5.

MUSEUM OF POSTAGE STAMPS
Dob út 75-81, Budapest VII
Postage stamps of the world.
W. 9-3.30; Sa. 9-2.30; Su. 9-1.

MUSEUM OF THE WORKERS' MOVEMENT
Szentháromság tér 2, Budapest I
Collections illustrating history of the Hungarian Workers' Movement, 1849-1945.
Tu.-Sa. 10-6.

NAGYTÉTÉNY PALACE MUSEUM
Csókási utca 9, Budapest XXII
18th century palace. 15th-16th century European furniture, decorative arts. 18th century Hungarian furniture. 19th century upholstered furniture. Stove ceramics and stoves. Roman castrum and stones.
W., Sa., Su. 10-6.

NATIONAL THEATRE MUSEUM
Krisztina körút 57, Budapest I
History of the Hungarian theatre. Portraits of actors, actresses, directors. Scenic designs. Posters. Programmes. Tickets. Press notices.
Tu., Th., Sa. 2-6; Su. 10-6.

NATURAL HISTORY MUSEUM
Baross utca 13 and Múzeum körút 14-16, Budapest VIII
Geology. Mineralogy, including crystals, meteorites. Evolution of life and history of the Earth, including footprints of prehistoric animals. Flora and fauna of Hungary. Origin of man. Prehistoric man.
Tu.-Su. 10-6.

PASTOR JÁNOS MEMORIAL MUSEUM
Szüret utca 15, Budapest XV
Life and work of Pastor János.
By appointment.

PESTERZSÉBETI MÚZEUM
Kossuth Lajos utca 39, Budapest XX
History of Pest and of the workers' movement.
Tu.-Su. 11-9.

PETŐFI MUSEUM OF LITERATURE
Károlyi Mihály utca 16, Budapest V
Hungarian literary MSS, especially 19th-20th century. Portraits and memorabilia of Hungarian writers.
Tu.-Su. 10-6.

POSTAL MUSEUM
Varfók utca 24, Budapest XI
History of the Hungarian postal and telecommunications services. Equipment. Uniforms. Technical displays.
W.-Su. 9-2.

ROMAN BATH
Flórián tér 3-7, Budapest III
Excavated ruins of Roman bath.
Tu.-Su. 10-6.

ROMAN FORTRESS MUSEUM
Március 15 tér, Budapest V
Excavated ruins of the Roman fortress.
Tu.-Su. 10-6.

SEMMELWEIS MUSEUM OF THE HISTORY OF MEDICINE
Apród utca 1-3, Budapest I
History of medical treatment and pharmacy since medieval times. Outstanding figures in Hungarian medicine.
Tu.-Su. 10.30-6.

TABORVAROS MUSEUM OF RUINS
Korvin Ottó utca 3-4, Budapest III
Excavated ruins of Roman buildings, with objects found in them.
Tu.-Sa. 10-1; Su. 10-6.

CECE

ISTVÁN CSÓK MUSEUM
Cece, Fejér megye
Life and work of István Csók.
Tu.-Su. 10-1, 3-6.

CEGLÉD

KOSSUTH MUSEUM
1 Marx utca 5, Cegléd, Somogy megye
Memorabilia and personal possessions of Lajos Kossuth, including his sword, pistol, death mask and relics of his exile in Turin. Archaeology. Ethnography. History of Cegléd.
May-Sept., daily 10-6. Oct.-Apr., daily 10-4. Closed public holidays.

CSÁKVÁR

LOCAL HISTORY MUSEUM
Csákvár, Fejér megye
Archaeology. Local history.
Tu.-Su. 10-1, 3-6.

CSESZTVE

IMRE MADÁCH MEMORIAL MUSEUM
Kossuth utca 75, Csesztve, Nógrad megye
Life and work of Imre Madách.
On request.

CSONGRÁD

CSONGRÁD MUSEUM
Iskola utca 2, Csongrád, Csongrád megye
Archaeology. Local history.
Tu. 8.30-10.30; W. 8-12; Th. 3-7; F. 9.30-12.30; Su. 10-12.

DEBRECEN

DÉRI MUSEUM
Déri tér 1, Debrecen, Hajdú-Bihar megye
Chinese, Japanese, Indian and Persian art. Archaeology. Local history. Ethnography. Folk art. Coins. Medals. Paintings, including Munkácsy's 'Ecce Homo', and sculpture by Hungarian artists.
Tu.-Su. 10-6.

DÖMSÖD

PETŐFI MEMORIAL MUSEUM
Bajcsy-Zsilinszky utca 6, Dömsöd, Pest megye
Memorabilia of the writer and patriot Petőfi. Local history.
Tu., Th., Su. 9-12, 2-5.

DUNAPATAJ

LOCAL HISTORY COLLECTION
Jókai utca 8, Dunapataj, Bács megye
Furniture. Household equipment. Ethnography. Folk art.
On request.

DUNAÚJVÁROS

DUNAÚJVÁROS MUSEUM
Ady Endre utca 5, Dunaújváros, Fejér megye
Prehistory. Roman and medieval collections. Regional history.
Tu.-Su. 10-1, 3-6.

DUNAVECSE

PETŐFI REGIONAL MUSEUM
Petőfi tér 1, Dunavecse, Bács-Kiskun megye
Ethnology. Local history.
Tu.-F. 10-12; Sa. 3-5; Su. 10-12, 2-4.

EGER

ISTVÁN DOBÓ CASTLE MUSEUM
Vár 1, Eger, Heves megye
In 14th-15th century bishop's palace. History of the Castle. Folklore.
May-Sept., daily 8-6. Oct.-Apr., daily 9-5.

GÉZA GÁRDONYI MEMORIAL MUSEUM
Gárdonyi utca 28, Eger, Heves megye
Former home of the writer, Géza Gárdonyi, Books, furniture, and personal possessions.
Daily 9-5.

EGERÁG

VILLAGE MUSEUM
Kossuth Lajos utca 31, Egerág, Baranya megye
Local history. Ethnography.
On request.

EGYHÁZASHETYE

DÁNIEL BERZSENYI MEMORIAL MUSEUM
Egyházashetye, Vas megye
Collections illustrating life and work of Berzsenyi, in his native village.
Tu.-Su. 10-6.

ESZTERGOM

MIHÁLY BABITS MEMORIAL MUSEUM
Babits Mihály utca 13, Esztergom, Komárom megye
Collections illustrating life and work of the poet, Mihály Babits (d.1941), in his former country house.
Tu.-Su. 11-5.

BÁLINT BALASSI MUSEUM
Bajcsi-Zsilinszky utca 28, Esztergom, Komárom megye
In Cathedral library. Commemorates 16th century poet and warrior, Bálint Balassi, killed during a siege of Esztergom. Prehistoric archaeology. Local history, especially period of Turkish occupation. Coins. Porcelain, especially Meissen, Bécs.
Tu.-Su. 9-5.

CASTLE MUSEUM
Vár, Esztergom, Komárom megye
History of the castle. Local history, Roman period-Renaissance.
Daily 9-5.

MUSEUM OF CHRISTIANITY
Berényi Zsigmond utca 2, Esztergom, Komárom megye
13th-16th century European art, especially Dutch, German, Italian, French paintings. Gold- and silversmiths' works. Delftware. Ivories. Pewter. Tapestries.
Tu.-Su. 9.30-5.

TREASURY OF ESZTERGOM CATHEDRAL
Bazilika, Szt. István tér 1, Esztergom, Komárom megye
Medieval and Renaissance gold- and silversmith's work, vestments, altar-cloths. Cross of the Coronation Oath (13th century). 12th century Byzantine Kiss of Peace tablet.
Daily 9-4.

FERTÖD

CHÂTEAU MUSEUM
Fertöd, Győr-Sopron megye
Fine and applied arts.
Tu.-Su. 10-4.

GYOMA

IMRE KNER MUSEUM
Gyoma
In former home of Kner family. Development of Kner Printing Works, 1907-present day, and of Andor Tevan printing and publishing company. Foot-operated Liberty platen-press. Books produced by Kner.
Tu.-Su. 10-6.

GYÖNGYÖS

MÁTRA MUSEUM
Kossuth Lajos utca 40, Gyöngyös, Heves megye
History of Gyöngyös. Peasant furniture, costumes. Folk art. Vineyard-cultivation.
Daily 9-5.

GYŐR

JÁNOS XÁNTUS MUSEUM
Széchenyi tér 5, Győr, Győr-Sopron megye
History of Győr and its region from prehistoric times. Roman lapidarium. Anthropology. Natural science. Paintings.
Tu.-Su. 10-6.

GYULA

FERENC ERKEL MUSEUM
Kossuth Lajos utca 15, Gyula, Békés megye
Archaeology. Local history. Ethnography. Paintings. Applied art.
Mar.-Oct., Tu.-Su. 9-7. Nov.-Apr., Tu.-Su. 9-5.

HAJDÚBÖSZÖRMÉNY

HAJDÚ MUSEUM
Hajdú-Székhaz, Hajdúböszörmény, Hajdú-Bihar megye
Archaeology. History of the town. Ethnography. Paintings. Sculpture.
Tu.-Su. 10-6.

HAJDÚRZOBOSZLÓ

BOCSAY MUSEUM
Hajdúrzoboszló, Hajdú-Bihar megye
Local history. Ethnography.
Daily 10-6.

HEJÖKERESZTÚR

LOCAL HISTORY MUSEUM
Hejökeresztúr, Borsod megye
Local history.
Daily, except public holidays, 10-12, 2-4.

HEREND

PORCELAIN FACTORY MUSEUM
Herend, Verzprém megye
History and manufacture of local porcelain.
Tu.-Su. 10-6.

HÓDMEZÖVÁSARHELY

JÁNOS TORNYAI MUSEUM
Szántó Kovács János utca 16-18, Hódmezövásarhely, Csongrád megye
Archaeology. Ethnography. Folk art. Paintings by János Tornyai. Medgyessy sculpture. Memorabilia of János Tornyai.
Tu.-Su. 11-7.

HOLLÓKŐ

VILLAGE MUSEUM
Kossuth Lajos utca 85, Hollókő, Nógrád megye
Three rooms, furnished in early 19th century vernacular style.
On request.

HORPÁCS

KÁLMÁN MIKSZÁTH MEMORIAL MUSEUM
Horpács, Nógrád megye
Life and work of Kálmán Mikszáth.
On request.

ISASZEG

ISASZEG VILLAGE MUSEUM
Madách Imre utca 15, Isaszeg, Pest megye
Local history.
M.-Sa. 2-5. Closed public holidays.

JÁSZBERÉNY

JÁSZ MUSEUM
Tánsics Mihály utca 5, Jászberény, Szolnok megye
Prehistory collections. Ethnography. Local history. Collections include the 11th century Byzantine Horn of Lehel.
Tu.-F. 9-12, 4-6; Su. 10-3. 3-6.

KALOCSA

KÁROLY VISKI MUSEUM
Hunyadi János utca 27, Kalocsa, Bács-Kistun megye
Costumes. Crafts.
Tu., Th. 2-3; Su., public holidays, 10-12.

KÁPOLNÁSNYÉK

MIHÁLY VÖRÖSMARTY MEMORIAL MUSEUM
Kápolnásnyék, Fejér megye
Collection illustrating life and work of Mihály Vörösmarty.
Tu.-Sa. 10-1, 3-6.

KAPOSVÁR

SÁNDOR LATINKA MEMORIAL MUSEUM
Kaposvár, Somogy megye
Life and work of Sándor Letinka (d.1919), leader of the Hungarian workers' movement.
Apr.-June, M.-Su. 8-4, June-Aug., M.-Su. 10-2, Sept.-Dec., Tu.-Su. 8-4.

RIPPL-RÓNAI MUSEUM
Rippl-Ronai tér 1, Kaposvár, Somogy megye
Archaeology. Ethnography. Paintings by Rippl-Rónai and other regional artists. Carvings from 12th century Benedictine monastery.
Nov.-Apr., Tu., Th., Sa. 2-6; W., F., Su. 10-2. May-Oct., Tu.-Su. 10-6.

KAPUVÁR

RÁBAKÖZI MUSEUM
Fö tér 1, Kapuvár, Győr-Sopron megye
Local history. Costumes.
Tu.-Sa. 10-12, 4-6; Su. 9-1.

KARCAG

ISTVÁN GYÖRFFY MUSEUM
Kálvin utca 4-7, Karcag, Szolnok megye
Archaeology. Local history. Ethnography. Folk art.
On request.

KECSKEMET

JÓZSEF KATONA MUSEUM
Bethlen város 75, Kecskemét, Bács-Kiskun megye
Archaeology. Ethnography. Paintings. Drawings. Sculpture.
Tu.-Su. 10-6.

KELEMÉR

MIHÁLY TOMPA MEMORIAL MUSEUM
Kelemér, Borsod megye
Life and work of Mihály Tompa.
Daily 10-12, 2-4.

KESZTHELY

BALATON MUSEUM
Múzeum utca 2, Keszthely, Veszprém megye
Prehistory and history of Lake Balaton area. Folklore. Paintings.
Daily 10-6. Nov.-Apr., closed public holidays.

KISKÖRÖS

PETŐFI MEMORIAL MUSEUM
Petőfi tér 1, Kiskörös, Bács-Kiskún megye
House (1790), birthplace of Petőfi. Collection illustrating Petőfi's life and work.
Tu.-Su. 8-1, 3-6.

KISKUNFÉLEGYHÁZA

KISKUN MUSEUM
Vöröshadsereg utca 9, Kiskunfélegyháza, Bács-Kiskun megye
Ethnography. Archaeology. Penology.
Tu.-Su. 9-1, 3-7.

KISKUNHALAS

JÁNOS THORMA MUSEUM
Köztársaság utca 2, Kiskunhalas, Bács-Kiskun megye
Lace, made in Kiskunhalas.
Tu.-Sa. 10-1; Su. 10-1, 3-7.

KISNÁNA

KISNÁNA CASTLE COLLECTIONS
Kisnána, Heves megye
Archaeology. Local history.
Daily 9-5.

KISVÁRDA

CASTLE MUSEUM
Vár utca 30, Kisvárda, Szaboles-Szatmár megye
Archaeology. History of the Kisvárda castle.
Tu.-Su. 9-5.

KOMÁROM

GYÖRGY KLAMPKA MUSEUM
Igmándi eröd, Komárom, Komárom megye
Archaeology.
Tu., Th., F., 10-2; Su. 10-4.

KOMLÓ

KOMLÓ MUSEUM
Kossuth Lajos utca 117, Komló, Baranya megye
History of Komló and its mining industry.
Tu., Su. 9-12; W., Sa. 4-7.

KÖRMEND

RÁBA LOCAL COLLECTIONS
Várudvar, Körmend, Vas megye
Biology. Local history. Ethnography.
Daily 10-6. Closed public holidays.

KŐSZEG

MIKLÓS JURISICH MUSEUM
Vár és Hősök tornya, Kőszeg, Vas megye
History of Kőszeg, from its foundation to the liberation from the Turks.
Vár: May-Oct., daily 9-1, 2-6. Nov.-Apr., closed public holidays.
Hözök: Tu.-Su. 10-1, 2-5.

KÖVÁGÓŐRS-PÁLKOVE

BAJCSY-ZSILINSKY MEMORIAL MUSEUM
Kövágóőrs-Pálkove, Veszprém megye
Documents and other material illustrating life and work of Endre Bajcsy.
Apr.-Oct., Tu.-Su. 10-6.

MAKÓ

ATTILA JÓZSEF MUSEUM
Felszabirlár utca 4, Makó, Crongrád megye
Local history.
W., F., Su. 10-4.

MARTONVÁSÁR

BEETHOVEN MUSEUM
Martonvásár, Fejér megye
Beethoven memorabilia.
Apr. 15-Oct. 15, Su. 8-12, 3-5. Oct. 16-Apr. 14, Su. 10-12, 3-5.

MÁTÉSZALKA

SZATMÁR ETHNOLOGICAL COLLECTION
Mátészalka, Szabolcs-Szatmár megye
Regional ethnology.
Tu.-Su. 10-4.

MEZŐKÖVESD

MATYÓ MUSEUM
Mezőkövesd, Borsod megye
Matyó peasant handicrafts. Costumes. Embroidery.
Daily 10-12, 2-4.

MISKOLC

HERMAN OTTÓ MUSEUM
Papszer utca 1, Miskolc, Borsod-Abaúj-Zemplén megye
Regional archaeology, ethnography. Paintings. Sculpture. Applied art.
Tu.-Su. 10-6.

MISKOLC-DIÓSGYÖR

DIÓSGYÖR CASTLE MUSEUM
Vár, Miskolc-Diósgyör, Borsod-Abaúj-Zemplén megye
Museum containing historical material from excavations at the 13th-15th century castle.
Sept.-May, Tu.-Su. 8-4. June-Aug., 8-6.

MISKOLC-HÁMOR

CENTRAL MUSEUM OF METALLURGY
Miskolc-Hámor, Borsod megye
Mineralogical collections. Displays illustrating metallurgical techniques.
By appointment.

MISKOLC-LILLAFÜRED

HERMAN OTTÓ MEMORIAL MUSEUM
Erzébet sétány, Miskolc-Lillafüred, Borsod megye
Life and work of the naturalist, Herman Ottó.
Daily 10-6.

MOHÁCS

DOROTHYA KANIZSAI MUSEUM
Szerb utca 2, Mohács, Baranya megye
Ethnography. Folk art.
Tu.-Su. 9-12, 3-6.

MONOK

KOSSUTH MEMORIAL MUSEUM
Monok, Borsod-Abaúj-Zemplén megye
Collection illustrating Lajos Kossuth's life and work, especially 1848-49.
On request.

MOSONMAGYARÓVAR

HANSÁG MUSEUM
Lenin utca 101, Mosonmagyaróvar, Győr-Sopron megye
Archaeology. History. 17th-18th century furniture, decorative arts.
Tu.-Sa. 2-6; Su. 10-6.

NAGYGERESD

LOCAL HISTORY COLLECTION
Petőfi utca 54, Nagygeresd, Vas megye
Ethnography. Local history.
On request.

NAGYHORTOBÁGY

SHEPHERDS' MUSEUM
Nagyhortobágy, Hajdú-Bihar megye
Ethnography.
Tu.-Su. 10-6.

NAGYKANIZSA

GYÖRGY THURY MUSEUM
Szabad tér 11 és Lenin utca 5-7, Nagykanizsa, Zala megye
Archaeology. Local history. Coins.
Tu., Th., Sa. 3-7; W., F., Su. 9-1.

NAGYKEREKI

BOCKSAY PALACE MUSEUM
Nagykereki, Hajdú-Bihar megye
Historical collections.
On request.

NAGYKŐRÖS

JÁNOS ARANY MEMORIAL MUSEUM
X Hösök tér 8, Nagykőrös, Pest magye
Life and work of the poet János Arany.
M.-Sa. 10-1.

JÁNOS ARANY MUSEUM
X Ceglédi utca 19, Nagykörös, Pest megye
Life and work of the poet, János Arany. Local archaeology, history, folklore.
Tu., W., Th., Sa. 3-6; Su. 10-12, 3-6.

NAGYTARCSA

VILLAGE MUSEUM
Múzeumkert 4, Nagytarcsa, Pest megye
Local history. Folklore.
Su. 3-5.

NAGYVÁZSONY

KINIZSI CASTLE
Nagyvázsony, Veszprém megye
Restored castle, with period rooms.
Daily 7-7.

OPEN-AIR MUSEUM OF ETHNOLOGY
Nagyvázsony, Veszprém megye
In timber farmhouse and out-buildings (c.1825). Agricultural implements. Craftsmen's tools, equipment. Furniture.
Apr.-Oct., daily 10-6.

NIKLA

DÁNIEL BERZENYI MEMORIAL MUSEUM
Nikla, Somogy megye
Life and work of the poet, Dániel Berzenyi, with special emphasis on his local activities.
Daily 10-4.

NOVA

FERENC PLANDER MEMORIAL MUSEUM
Nova, Zala megye
Local history. Folklore.
M.-Sa. 6-10; Su. 10-6.

NYÍRBÁTOR

ISTVÁN BÁTHORI MUSEUM
Károlyi utca 11, Nyírbátor, Szabolcs-Szatmár megye
Archaeology. Local history.
Tu.-Su. 10-6.

NYÍREGYHÁZA

ANDRÁS JÓSA MUSEUM
Egyház utca 15, Nyíregyháza, Szabolcs-Szatmár megye
Archaeology. Ethnography. Local history, especially material from the age of the Great Migrations. Paintings and sculpture by Hungarian artists.
Tu.-Su. 10-6.

OROSHÁZA

KOVÁCS SZÁNTÓ MUSEUM
Dózsa utca 9, Orosháza, Békés megye
Archaeology. Local history. Folklore.
Tu.-Su. 10-12.

OZORA

CASTLE MUSEUM
Var, Ozora, Tolna megye
Local history. Folklore.
By appointment.

ŐRISZENPÉTER

LOCAL HISTORY COLLECTIONS
Müvelődési ház, Őriszenpéter, Vas megye
Local history.
Tu.-Su. 9-5.

PANNONHALMA

ECCLESIASTICAL MUSEUM
Apátság, Pannonhalma, Győr-Sopron megye
Hungarian religious history. Archaeology. Paintings by Flemish, Dutch, Spanish, French and Italian artists. Ornaments. Liturgical objects.
Daily 8.30-5.

PÁPA

LOCAL HISTORY MUSEUM
Várkastély, Pápa, Veszprém megye
Archaeology. Local history. Applied art. History of the workers' movement. Ethnography.
Tu.-Su. 10-6.

MUSEUM OF INDIGO-DYEING
Kluge-ház, Pápa, Veszprém megye
Early 19th century dyeing works, with original equipment.
Daily 10-1, 2-6.

PARÁD

PÁLOC HOUSE
Sziget utca 10, Parád, Heves megye
Folklore.
Daily 9-5.

PÉCS

JANUS PANNONIUS MUSEUM
Széchenyi tér 12, Pécs, Baronya megye
Local history. Archaeology. Folk art. 19th-20th century Hungarian paintings, sculpture. Natural sciences.
Tu.-Su. 9-12, 3-6.

PÉCSVÁRAD

CASTLE MUSEUM
Vár, Pécsvárad Baranya megye
Archaeology. Collection illustrating history of the Castle.
Tu.-Su. 10-6.

PENC

VILLAGE MUSEUM
Rácóczi utca 25, Penc, Pest megye
Archaeology.
Su. 3-5.

PÜSPÖKLADÉNY

FERENC KARACS MUSEUM
Gimnázium, Püspökladény, Hajdú-Bihar megye
Local history. Folklore.
On request.

RÁBATAMÁSI

MARI JÁSZAI MEMORIAL ROOM
Rábatamási, Győr-Sopron megye
Life and work of Mari Jászai.
Daily 10-4.

RÁCKEVE

ÁRPÁD MUSEUM
Kossuth Lajos utca 95, Ráckeve, Pest megye
Furniture. Local history.
M., Tu., Th. 9.30-1.30; Su. 10-2.

RUDABÁNYA

ORE AND MINERAL MINING MUSEUM
Rudabánya, Borsod-Abánj-Zemptén megye
History of ore and mineral mining. Miners' life.
Daily 8-4.

RUM

SÁNDOR FÜRST MEMORIAL HOUSE
Rum, Vas megye
Life and work of Sándor Fürst.
Tu.-Su. 10-6.

SALGÓRTARJÁN

MUSEUM OF UNDERGROUND MINING
Bajcsy-Zsilinsky utca 3, Salgótarján, Nógrád megye
History of coal-mining.
Guided tours, as announced locally.

SÁROSPATAK

MUSEUM OF THE REFORMED CHURCH
Rákóczi utca 1, Sárospatak, Borsod-Abaúj-Zemplén megye
History of the Rákóczi family. Folk art. Early scientific apparatus used at the College. Comenius collection.
M. 9-4; Su. 11-1.

RÁKOCZI MUSEUM
Vár, Sárospatak, Borsod-Abaúj-Zemplén megye
In 13th-16th century castle. Guard room, kitchen, chapel and council chamber, with furniture, weapons, implements and utensils of the periods of the castle's occupation.
May-Sept., daily 9-5. Oct.-Apr., daily 9-12, 2-5.

SÁRVÁR

FERENC NADASDY CASTLE MUSEUM
Vár, Sárvár, Vas megye
16th century castle. History of the castle. Frescoes. Wrought-ironwork. 16th-17th century weapons.
Tu.-Su. 10-12, 1-5.

SELLYE

GÉZA KISS MUSEUM
Fő tér 3, Sellye, Baranya megye
Folklore.
Daily 8-12.

SIKLÓS

CASTLE MUSEUM
Vár, Siklós, Baranya megye
12th century castle. History of the castle. Furniture. Military history. 20th century Hungarian ceramics.
Tu.-Su. daily 8-6.

SIÓFOK

JÓZSEF BESZÉDES MUSEUM
Sió utca 2, Siófok, Somogy megye
History of Balaton shipping. Folk art.
Dec.-Feb., daily 11-12. Mar.-May and Sept. 16-Nov. 30, daily 9-1. June 1-Sept. 15, daily 9-1, 3-7. Closed public holidays.

SOMOGYTÚR

KUNFFY GALLERY
Somogytúr, Somogy megye
Collection of paintings from the bequest of Lajos Kunffy.
Nov.-Apr., daily 10-12. May-Oct., daily 10-12, 3-5.

SOPRON

CENTRAL MINING MUSEUM
Templum utca 2, Sopron, Győr-Sopron megye
Mining history. Mining tools, equipment, clothing. Mine-models.
Daily 10-2.

FERENC LISZT MUSEUM
Majus 1, tér 1, Sopron, Győr-Sopron megye
Memorabilia and personal possessions of Liszt. Folk art. Archaeology. Local Baroque art.
Tu.-Su. 10-6.

MINERS' MEMORIAL MUSEUM AT THE BRENNBERG MINE
Sopron, Győr-Sopron megye
Miner's living room. Exhibits illustrating life and work in a mining community.
Tu.-Su. 10-12.

SUKORÓ

SUKORÓ FOLKLORE MUSEUM
Szilvás sor 7, Sukoró, Fejér megye
Furnished peasant house.
Tu.-Su. 10-1, 3-6.

SÜMEG

KISFALUDY MEMORIAL MUSEUM
Kisfaludy utca, Sümeg, Veszprém megye
Literary history. Documents relating to the 19th century writers, Sándor and Károly Kisfaludy. Historical geology of Bakony.
Daily 10-6. Closed public holidays.

SZADA

BERTALAN SZÉKELY MEMORIAL MUSEUM
Székely Bertalan utca 22, Szada, Pest megye
Memorabilia of Bertalan Székely. Paintings by Árpád Székely.
May-Oct., Su. 10-6.

SZATMÁRCSEKE

FERENC KÖLCSEY MEMORIAL ROOM
Táncsics utca 72, Szatmárcseke, Szabolcs-Szatmár megye
Life and work of Ferenc Kölcsey.
On request.

SZEGED

FERENC MÓRA MUZEUM
Roosewelt tér 1-3, Szeged, Csongrád megye
Regional natural history. Archaeology. Ethnography, especially embroidery, weaving and other cottage industries. Regional history. Manuscripts of works by leading Hungarian writers. Paintings. Sculpture.
Tu.-Su. 10-6.

SZEGVÁR

VILLAGE MUSEUM
11 Hunyadi János utca 13, Szegvár, Csongrád megye
Local history.
W.-Sa. 3-7; Su. 8-12.

SZÉKESFEHÉRVÁR

ISTVÁN CSÓK GALLERY
Bartók Béla tér 1, Székesfehérvár, Fejér megye
20th century Hungarian paintings.
M., W., F. 11-6; Tu., Th., Sa. 1-6; Su. 10-6.

GARDEN OF RUINS
Szabadság tér, Székesfehérvár, Fejér megye
Excavated site of former 11th century cathedral and Royal Palace.
Apr. 15-Oct. 15, Tu.-Su. 9-1, 3-5. Oct. 16-Apr. 14, Tu.-Su. 9-3.

KING ISTVÁN MUSEUM
Gagarin Tér, Székesfehérvár, Fejér megye
Prehistory. Roman and medieval archaeology. Regional ethnography. Anthropology. Zoology. Paintings. Sculpture. Music.
Tu.-Su. 10-1, 3-6.

YBL COLLECTION AND BUDENZ HOUSE
Arany János utca 12, Székesfehérvár, Fejér megye
House (1781). Applied and industrial art.
Tu., W., F.-Su. 10-1, 3-6.

SZEKSZÁRD

BABITS MEMORIAL HOUSE
Babits Mihály utca 13, Szekszárd, Tolna megye
Memorabilia of the poet, Mihály Babits (d.1941).
Tu.-Su. 9-1.

ADÁM BALOGH MUSEUM
Mártírok tér 26, Szekszárd, Tolna megye
Archaeology. Folk art. Folklore.
Tu. 9-1, 2-6.

SZENDRŐ

SZENDRŐ DYE-HOUSE
Szendrő, Borsod megye
History of the Szendrő indigo-dyeing industry.
Daily 10-12, 2-4.

SZENTENDRE

COLLECTION OF SERBIAN CHURCH HISTORY
Engels utca 6, Szentendre, Somogy megye
Icons and other 15th-18th century items of Serb religious art.
Tu.-Su. 11-4.

KÁROLY FERENCZY MUSEUM
Marx tér 6, Szentendre, Pest megye
House (1794). Archaeology. Prehistory. Ethnography. Local history. Paintings by local artists, including members of the Ferenczy family.
Tu.-Su. 9-5.

OPEN-AIR MUSEUM
Angyal utca, Szentendre, Pest megye
Houses and other buildings from 23 regions of Hungary.
Tu.-Su. 9-5.

SCULPTURE GARDEN
Bartók Béla utca 6, Szentendre, Pest megye
18th-20th century sculpture by Hungarian artists.
May-Sept., Tu.-Su. 10-6.

SZENTES

JÓZSEF KOSZTA MUSEUM
Széchenyi liget Alsórét 187 és József Attila utca 19, Szentes, Csongrád megye
Archaeology. Ethnography. Paintings by Koszta (d.1948).
Tu.-Sa. 2-6; Su. 10-6.

SZÉPHALOM

KAZINCZY MEMORIAL MUSEUM
Széphalom, Borsod-Abánj-Zemplén megye
Life and work of Kazinczy.
Daily 10-12, 2-4.

SZERENCS

PICTURE-POSTCARD MUSEUM
Vár, Szerencs, Borsod-Abaúj-Zemplén megye
19th and 20th century picture postcards, especially Hungarian.
Tu.-Su. 10-12, 2-4.

SZIGETVÁR

MIKLÓS ZRÍNYI MUSEUM
Vár, Szigetvár, Baranya megye
Local history, especially of the period of Turkish occupation (16th-17th century).
Tu.-Su. 8-6.

SZOB

BÖRZSÖNY MUSEUM
Hámán Kató utca 14, Szob, Pest megye
Local history.
Tu.-Su. 9-5.

SZOLNOK

JÁNOS DAMJANICH MUSEUM
Kossuth tér 4, Szolnok, Szolnok megye
Archaeology. Palaeontology. Local history. Applied art. Paintings and sculpture by Szolnok artists.
Tu.-Su. 11-1, 3-7.

SZOMBATHELY

GYULA DERKOVITS MEMORIAL MUSEUM
Vorosilov utca 4, Szombathely, Vas megye
Life and work of the painter, Gyula Derkovits. Personal possessions. Household and painting equipment.
Daily 10-5.

RUINS OF ISTVÁN PAULOVICS VILLA
Alkotmańy utca 1, Szombathely, Vas megye
Excavated site of Roman villa. Mosaics.
Apr.-Sept., daily 8-6. Oct.-Mar., daily 8-4.

RUINS OF TEMPLE OF ISIS
Zrinyi Ilona utca 9, Szombathely, Vas megye
Excavated and partly restored Roman temple.
Daily 10-2, 3-6.

SAVARIA MUSEUM
Kisfaludy Sándor utca 9, Szombathely, Vas megye
Archaeology. Natural sciences. Ethnography. Roman sculpture, inscriptions.
Daily 9-1, 4-6.

TÁC

GORSIUM MUSEUM
Tác, Fejér megye
Excavated Roman site at Gorsium.
At any time.

TÁPIÓSZELLE

BLASKOVICH MUSEUM
Múzeum utca 13, Tápiószelle, Pest megye
Local history. Archaeology.
May-Sept., daily 10-12, 2-5. Oct.-Apr., Tu., F., Sa., public holidays, 10-12, 2-4.

TATA

DOMOKOS KUNY MUSEUM
Öregvár, Tata, Komárom megye
Archaeology. Prehistory. Applied art. Memorabilia of Samuel Mikoviny (d.1749).
Tu.-F. 10-5; Sa. 10-2; Su. 10-6.

TIHANY

MUSEUM AND EXHIBITIONS
Batthyány utca (Apátság), Tihany, Veszprém megye
History of the Balaton highland region. Shipping. Guild materials.
Oct.-Feb., Tu.-Su. 10-4. Mar.-Apr., Tu.-Su. 10-6. May-June, Tu.-Su. 10-6. July-Aug., daily 9-7.

OPEN-AIR FOLKLORE MUSEUM
Pisky sétány, Tihany, Veszprém megye
Peasant houses, with furnishings and domestic equipment. Craftsmen's tools. Agricultural implements.
May-June, Sept.-Oct., daily 10-6. July-Aug. daily 9-7.

TISZACSÉCSE

ZSIGMOND MÓRICZ HOUSE-MEMORIAL
Kossuth utca 29, Tiszacsécse, Szabolcs-Szatmár megye
Collection illustrating life and work of Zsigmond Moricz, in his former home.
Tu.-Su. 10-12, 2-5.

TISZACSEGE

VILLAGE HOUSE
Tiszacsege, Hajdú-Bihar megye
Furnished peasant house.
On request.

TISZAFÖLDVÁR

TISZAZUG GEOGRAPHICAL MUSEUM
Tiszaföldvar, Szolnok megye
Geology and geography of the region.
Tu.-Su. 10-6.

TISZAFÜRED

PÁL KISS MUSEUM
Tiszafüred, Szolnok megye
Archaeology. Local history. Folklore.
Tu., Th., Su. 10-12.

TISZAVASVÁRI

PÁL VASVÁRI MUSEUM
Tiszavasvári, Szabolcs-Szatmár megye
Local prehistory and history.
Tu.-Su. 10-2.

TOKAJ

LOCAL HISTORY MUSEUM
Tokaj, Borsod-Abaúj-Zemplén megye
In former 18th century church. History of Tokaj Castle. Past and present of grape-growing. Implements and utensils for grape harvesting and wine-making. 18th century winepress belonging to Rácózy family.
Apr.-Oct., daily 10-6.

TORMÁS

VILLAGE MUSEUM
Fő utca 1, Tormás, Baranya megye
Local history. Folklore.
On request.

TÖRÖKSZENTMIKLÓS

LOCAL HISTORY MUSEUM
Törökszentmiklós, Szolnok megye
Local history.
W., F., Sa., Su. 1-6.

TUNYEGMATOLCS

MÁTÉ ZALKA MEMORIAL ROOM
Racóczi utca 118, Tunyogmatolcs, Szabolcs-Szatmár megye
Collection illustrating life and work of Mate Zalka.
On request.

TURKEVE

FINTA MUSEUM
Attila utca 1, Turkeve, Szolnok megye
Agricultural history. Ethnography. Local history.
M., Th., Su. 10-12, 3-6.

TÜSKEVÁR

LOCAL HISTORY COLLECTION
Tüskevár, Veszprém megye
Archaeology. Local history. History of the workers' movement.
M., Su. 10-6.

VÁC

VAK BOTTYÁN MUSEUM
Múzeum utca 4, Vác, Somogy megye
Prehistory. Roman and medieval material from local site.
Tu.-Su. 10-12, 1-5.

VAJA

ADAM VAY MUSEUM
Damjanich utca 75, Vaja, Szabolcs-Szatmár megye
Period rooms.
Tu.-Su. 10-6.

VÁL

JÁNOS VAJDA MEMORIAL MUSEUM
Vál, Fejér megye
Memorabilia of János Vajda.
Tu.-Su. 10-1, 3-6.

VÁRPALOTA

LOCAL HISTORY COLLECTION
"Jószerencsét", Művelődési Ház, Várpalota, Veszprém megye
Archaeology. Local history.
M., Su. 10-5.

VÁSÁROSNAMÉNY

VÁSÁROSNAMÉNY REGIONAL MUSEUM
Rákóczi utca 6, Vásárosnamény, Szabolcs-Szatmár megye
Ethnology collections.
Tu.-Su. 2-4.

VASVÁR

DISTRICT MUSEUM
Bartók Béla utca 3, Vasvár, Vas megye
Local history. Folklore.
W., F., Su. 9-12.

VERPELÉT

BLACKSMITH'S SHOP
Kossuth Lajos utca 54, Verpelét, Heves megye
Blacksmith's shop, with tools and equipment.
Daily 9-5.

VÉRTES

JÁNOS IRINYI MEMORIAL ROOM
Vértes, Hajdú-Bihar megye
Memorial collection to Irinyi, the inventor of the match.
On request.

VÉRTESSZŐLLŐS

VÉRTESSZŐLLŐS EXHIBITION
Vértesszőllősi Östelep, Vértesszőllős, Komárom megye
Collections illustrating prehistoric life in the area.
Apr. 15- Oct. 3, Tu.-Su. 10-3.

VESZPRÉM

BAKONY MUSEUM
Lenin liget 5, Veszprém, Veszprém megye
Natural history. Ethnographical, archaeological and historical collections from the Bakony mountains.
Daily 10-6. Closed public holidays.

CASTLE MUSEUM
Vár, Veszprém, Veszprém megye
History of the castle. 13th-15th century religious history. Frescoes.
Apr.-Oct., daily 9-5.

VISEGRÁD

KING MÁTYÁS MUSEUM
Fö utca 41, Visegrád, Somogy megye
18th century mansions, formerly royal hunting-lodge. Plans, drawings, models illustrating history of Visegrád. Material from excavations in 15th century palace.
Tu.-Su. 10-12, 1-5.

ZALA

MIHÁLY ZICHY MEMORIAL MUSEUM
Zala, Somogy megye
Life of Mihály Zichy. Paintings, drawings.
Tu.-Su. 10-2.

ZALAEGERSZEG

GÖCSEJ MUSEUM
Marx tér 1, Zalaegerszeg, Zala megye
Regional ethnography. Folk art.
Mar.-Sept., Tu., F., Su. 9-1, 3-7. Oct.-Feb., Tu., F., Su. 9-1, 3-6.

GÖCSEJ VILLAGE MUSEUM
Megközelithebö az 1, Zalaegerszeg, Zala megye
Open-air museum. Rural houses. Agricultural implements. Household utensils. Furniture.
Apr. 1- Oct. 15, Tu.-Su. 10-6. Nov.-Dec., Su. 10-6.

ZALASZENTGRÓT

JENŐ HAMBURGER MEMORIAL MUSEUM
Zalaszentgrót, Zala megye
Life and achievements of Hamburger, prominent in the Hungarian workers' movement.
On request.

ZALAVÁR

LOCAL HISTORY COLLECTIONS
Zalavár, Veszprém megye
Local history.
Tu.-Su. 1-4.

ZEBEGÉNY

ISTVÁN SZŐNYI MUSEUM
Bartóky utca 7, Zebegény, Somogy megye
In former studio of the neo-Impressionist painter, István Szőnyi. Works by Szőnyi and other local artists. Memorabilia of Szőnyi.
Tu.-Su. 10-6.

ZIRC

ANTAL REGULY MUSEUM
Apátsági épulet, Zirc, Veszprém megye
Popular art. Wildlife.
M., public holidays, 10-6.

Iceland

The Icelandic museums present a fair picture of the country's early history, especially during the period of settlement and dependence on Denmark. The spectacular natural history of the island is also well represented, together with the fast-disappearing evidence of the old folk cultures. It is somewhat curious, however, to find so little attention given to the highly important Icelandic activities of fishing, shipping and air transport. One might have thought, too, that the Americanisation of this once very self-contained and provincial community during the past thirty years would have been worthy of some form of museum display, but no doubt this will come when the situation is less sensitive than it is at the moment.

REYKJAVIK

ARBOER FOLK MUSEUM
Arboer, Reykjavik
Housed in old Icelandic farmhouse. Local history. Outdoor collection of old houses, furniture, domestic equipment.
Daily ex. M. 2-6.

GALLERY OF ÁSGRÍMUR JÓNSSON'S PAINTINGS
v/Njarðargötu, Reykjavik
Paintings by Ásgrímur Jónsson, on view in his home.
July-Aug., daily ex. Sa. 1.30-4. Other months, Su., Tu., Th. 1.30-4.

ICELANDIC STUFFED ANIMALS COLLECTION
v/Skólavörðustíg, Reykjavik
Collection of stuffed and mounted Icelandic animals.
Summer: daily 10-10. Winter: daily 1-6.

EINAR JONSSON ART MUSEUM
v/Freyjugötu, Reykjavik
Mainly sculptural works by the Icelandic artists, Einar Jonsson.
Summer: daily 1.30-4.

MUSEUM OF NATURAL HISTORY
Hverfisgata 116, Reykjavik
Botany. Geology. Geography. Zoology.
Su., Tu., Th. and Sa., 2.30-4.

NATIONAL ART GALLERY
v/Suðurgötu, Reykjavik
Collections of paintings and sculptures, both ancient and contemporary.
Summer: daily 1.30-4. Rest of year, Su., Tu., Th. and Sa., 1.30-4.

NATIONAL LIBRARY AND ARCHIVES
v/Hverfisgötu, Reykjavik
Old manuscripts and literature written by Icelanders, both in Icelandic and other languages. Foreign department.
Daily 9-7. Summer: closed at 12, Sa.

NATIONAL MUSEUM OF ANTIQUITIES
v/Suðurgötu, Reykjavik
Archaeological objects and antiquities. Ethnography. Portraits. Folklore. Numismatics.
Summer: daily 1.30-4. Rest of year, Su., Tu., Th., and Sa., 1.30-4.

India

India's museums are of four main types - those attached to colleges and universities, those based on local temples or shrines, those which commemorate someone who was locally or nationally distinguished, and those which aim at instructing a large number of people in simple, practical matters. There are a few large and important museums which belong to city authorities, as in Delhi and Bombay. These museums were established during the period of British rule and, although they may benefit the national prestige abroad, they are expensive to run and they may not serve the best needs of India as a whole. Their number is certainly most unlikely to grow and the next twenty years may well see a considerable measure of decentralisation, with more travelling and temporary exhibitions, drawing on the material held by the great museums and more use of television as a means of bringing museums to the masses of the people.

As the situation is at present, however, one can distinguish certain landmarks - excellent and well-presented collections of archaeology, religious sculpture, handicrafts, and private and public health. The museums of hygiene attack very basic problems - sanitation, contraception, common diseases - and they present their themes in the simple, direct form of "models showing a sanitary village in contrast to an insanitary village". Such displays are well suited to being taken on tour. It is no more than a matter of practical convenience that they should be found within a city museum at any given time. The insanitary village-dwellers, not the insanitary city-dwellers, need to be shown models of a sanitary village, and, for this kind of material, the urban museum building is no more than a depot and publicity centre.

It is not easy to be fully up-to-date with one's information in the case of such a huge land-mass as India, but we have not so far come across an example of the village-type open-air museum. This is somewhat curious, since the climate and the circumstances of India would appear to be very favourable to museums of this type.

Two kinds of Indian museum do, however, call for special mention. One is the museum devoted to forestry, of which there are several excellent examples, and the second is the group of Gandhi museums, usually and appropriately small, but arranged without the gross and ludicrous idolatry which characterises so many of the Lenin museums in the Communist world. The departed glories of the British Raj, incidentally, are documented more fully in British than in Indian museums, which is possibly to be expected.

AGRA

ST. JOHN'S COLLEGE MUSEUM
Agra, Uttar Pradesh
Zoology: land and sea animals; fossils and models of prehistoric animals; evolution of man. Collection of insects of North India. Botany: plant fossils, plant life, flowers, and seeds; economic plant products. Commercial and industrial products of the country. Schools of Indian painting. Classical Western paintings.
During college hours on all working days.

TAJ MUSEUM
Agra, Uttar Pradesh
Archaeological collections.
By appointment.

AHAR

ARCHAEOLOGICAL MUSEUM
Ahar, Rajasthan
Excavated material from the Chalcolithic site (1800 B.C. onwards) of Ahar. Sculptures and bronzes.
Daily ex. F. and gazetted holidays, 7.30-10.30, 3.30-6 (winter: 10-5).

AHMEDABAD

B. J. MEDICAL COLLEGE MUSEUMS
B. J. Medical College, Ahmedabad, Gujarat
Collections illustrating Anatomy, Pathology, Pharmacology, Hygiene and Forensic Medicine.
During working hours of the college.

CALICO MUSEUM OF TEXTILES
Ahmedabad, Gujarat
Textiles and Indian costumes. Economic and technological conditions in India. Machine-looms. Raw materials: cotton, wool, linen, silk, nylon. Stages of evolution in the method from that adopted by primitive man to the latest mode of spinning and weaving and the machine loom.
Daily ex. M. 5-6 p.m.

GANDHI MEMORIAL MUSEUM
Ahmedabad, Gujarat
Personal possessions, portraits and Gandhian literature. Exhibits include a shirt sewn by Gandhi, a desk table used by him and his *charkha.*
Daily 8-7.

GUJARAT MUSEUM SOCIETY
Culture Centre, Kocharab, Ahmedabad 6, Gujarat
Archaeology. Anthropology. Ethnography. Costumes. Paintings, including the N.C. Mehta Collection of miniatures. Science.
Daily ex. M. 8-11, 4-8.

TRIBAL RESEARCH AND TRAINING INSTITUTE
Gujarat Vidyapith, Ahmedabad 14, Gujarat
Anthropology.
Daily ex. Su. 11-6.

AHMEDNAGAR

HISTORY MUSEUM
Ahmednagar College, Ahmednagar, Maharashtra
Archaeology. Paintings.
Daily ex. Su. 9-12, 3-7.

AJMER

RAJPUTANA MUSEUM
Ajmer, Rajasthan
Sculptures. Inscriptions. Coins. Paintings. Weapons and armour of Rajasthan.
Daily ex. F. 7-10, 3.30-6. July-Apr. 10-5.

ALAMPUR

ARCHAEOLOGICAL SITE MUSEUM
Alampur, Andhra Pradesh
Sculptures, inscriptions and architectural fragments from excavations in the area.
Daily 9-1, 2-5.

ALIGARH

MUSEUM OF SCIENCE AND CULTURE
General Education Centre, Aligarh Muslim University, Aligarh, Uttar Pradesh
Science. History. Literature.
Daily ex. Su. and holidays, 9.30-1, 3-5; F. 9-11.

ALLAHABAD

ALLAHABAD MUSEUM
Alfred Park, Allahabad, Uttar Pradesh
Stone and bronze sculptures. Terracottas. Miniatures. Modern Indian paintings. Gifts of Pandit Jawahar Lal Nehru. Musical instruments. Images from Kharjuraho, Nagor and Kaushambi.
Daily 7-10.30, 4-4.30 (Aug. 15-Mar. 31, 11-5).

UNIVERSITY MUSEUMS
University of Allahabad, Allahabad, Uttar Pradesh
Zoology. Botany. Archaeology and antiquities. Inscriptions, seals, terracotta figurines and sculptures, coins, beads, bangles, iron implements, stylus and antimony rods, all from excavations at Kausambi.
10-4 on working days.

ALWAR

GOVERNMENT MUSEUM
Alwar, Rajasthan
Sculptures. Inscriptions. Arms. Miniatures. Decorative arts. Illuminated manuscripts.
Daily ex. F. and gazetted holidays, 7.30-10.30, 3.30-6 (winter: 10-5).

AMARAVATI

ARCHAEOLOGICAL MUSEUM
Amaravati, Andhra Pradesh
Finds from the site of the Amaravati stupa. Slabs, uprights, cross-bars, coping pieces, figures of Buddha. Inscriptions.
Daily 9-5.30.

AMBER

ARCHAEOLOGICAL MUSEUM
Amber, Rajasthan
Sculptures and excavated material from Bairat, Sambhar, Rairh and Nagar in Jaipur region.
Daily ex. F. and gazetted holidays, 7.30-10.30, 3.30-6 (winter: 10-5).

AMRELI

SHRI GIRDHARBHAI CHILDREN'S MUSEUM
Amreli, Amerli District, Gujarat
All aspects of local history, art and archaeology, ethnology, natural history, transport, science, "in a form easily assimilated by children". Models and working parts.
Daily ex. W. 9-12, 3.30-6.30.

AMRITSAR

CENTRAL SIKH MUSEUM
Darshan Deori, Clock Tower, Amritsar, Punjab
Weapons and armour. Paintings illustrating Sikh history. Sacred letters of the Gurus. Old manuscripts in Gurmukhi. Coins. Musical instruments. Memorabilia of Guru Gobind Singh and Maharaja Ranjit Singh.
Daily ex. M. 8-11.30, 4.30-7 (winter: 9-12, 3-6).

MUSEUM OF THE BOTANY DEPARTMENT
Punjab University, Amritsar, Punjab
Botanical specimens.
Daily ex. Su. and gazetted holidays, 7.30-1.30 (winter: 10-5).

ANNAMALAINAGAR

ZOOLOGY MUSEUM
Annamalai University, Annamalainagar, Madras
Fossil collections from Arialur and Vridhachalam beds. Fresh water and marine fish of South India. Amphibians, reptiles, invertebrates and osteological specimens. Dissected specimens illustrating comparative anatomy.
Daily ex. Su. 10-5.

AUNDH

SRI BHAVANI MUSEUM
Aundh, Gujarat
Indian and European schools of painting. European masters dating from 15th-20th centuries. Kangra school. Sculptures. Bronze images (Indian, European, Asian copies and originals). Inscriptions. Ancient gold coins. Objects of sandal-wood and ivory. Persian, Arabic, Marathi and Sanskrit manuscripts.
Daily ex. Tu. 12-5.30.

BANGALORE

CENTRAL COLLEGE MUSEUMS
Central College, Bangalore, Mysore
Geology: rocks, minerals, fossils, crystals and models to show structural features. Botanical specimens. Zoological specimens of invertebrates and vertebrates, especially mammals.
11.30-6 on college working days.

MYSORE GOVERNMENT MUSEUM
Kasturba Road, Bangalore 1, Mysore
General collections, including relics of the Chandravalli excavations (Neolithic period), and old jewellery. Natural history. Botany. Zoology.
Daily ex. W. and gazetted holidays, 8-5.

VISVESVARAYA INDUSTRIAL AND TECHNOLOGICAL MUSEUM
Kasturba Road, Bangalore 1, Mysore
The history of science and technology: the latest developments are illustrated by working models and exhibits.
Daily ex. M. 10-1, 2-5.

BARIPADA

BARIPADA MUSEUM
Baripada, Orissa
Archaeology: Palaeolithic and Neolithic implements and copper axe heads. Historical documents. Gold, silver and copper coins. Beads and terracottas. Stone inscriptions. Paper sanads. Painted palm-leaf manuscripts. Seals.
Daily ex. Su. and Government holidays, 10.30-4.30.

BARODA

HEALTH MUSEUM
Sayaji Bag, Baroda, Gujarat
Health and hygiene. Models showing a sanitary village in contrast to an insanitary village. Model of modern sewage works. Model illustrating the water supply for Baroda city. Models and charts illustrating midwifery, maternity, human anatomy, the functions of the heart, eye and ear. Control of disease. Famous bio-chemists, surgeons, physicians and bacteriologists.
Daily ex. Su. 11-6; Sa. 2-6.

MEDICAL COLLEGE MUSEUMS
Baroda, Gujarat
Exhibits related to Anatomy, Pharmacology-Toxicology, Pathology and Preventive Medicine.
Daily ex. Su. and public holidays 9-5; Sa. 9-1.

MUSEUM OF THE DEPARTMENT OF ARCHAEOLOGY
University of Baroda, Baroda, Gujarat
Archaeological objects from Gujarat and Narmada valley. Material from the Australian Institute of Archaeology, Melbourne.
Daily 11-5.

MUSEUM AND PICTURE GALLERY
Sayaji Park, Baroda 5, Gujarat
Indian archaeology: prehistoric, protohistoric and historic. Ancient, medieval and modern Indian art. Numismatics. Paintings. Asiatic and Egyptian collection. Greek, Roman, European civilisations and art. Ethnography. Geology. Zoology.
Daily ex. Th. 9.30-5; Th. 10-5. Closed five gazetted holidays.

BELKHANDI

BELKHANDI MUSEUM
Belkhandi, Orissa
Open-air museum with displays of stone sculptures discovered on the site during excavations.
Daily 10-5.

BENARES

MUSEUM OF INDIAN ARTS AND ARCHAEOLOGY
Benares Hindu University, Benares, Uttar Pradesh
Gold and other coins of the Gupta period. Arts, crafts and sculpture. Indian pictorial art.
Daily 7-11.30 a.m.

SARNATH MUSEUM
nr. Benares, Uttar Pradesh
Finds from the excavations, dating from 3rd century B.C. to 12th century A.D. Images, stucco figures, reliefs, inscriptions, domestic objects of stone and terracotta, pottery. Architectural pieces belonging to the Maurya, Sunga, Andhra, Kuahan, Gupta and medieval periods. The Lion Capital of Asoka, adopted as the crest of the Republic of India, and the statue of the preaching Buddha of the Gupta period.
Daily ex. F. and gazetted holidays, 7.30-10.30, 3.30-6 (winter: 10-5).

BHARATPUR

STATE MUSEUM
Bharatpur, Rajasthan
Excavated material from Noh (1000 B.C. and onwards). Sculptures. Inscriptions. Coins. Weapons.
Daily ex. F. and gazetted holidays, 7.30-10.30, 3.30-6 (winter: 10-5).

BHAWANAGAR

GANDHI SMRITI MUSEUMS
Arts and Crafts Museum, Gandhi Smriti, Bhawanagar, Gujarat
Embroidery and bead work from Saurastra. Costumes. Ornaments. Woodwork. Clay objects. Antiquities from Valabin. Coins and fossils from Piram Island.
Daily ex. M. and public holidays, 8.30-12, 3-7 (winter: 8.30-12, 2.30-6.30).

GANDHI SMRITI MUSEUMS
Barton Museum, Gandhi Smriti, Bhawanagar, Gujarat
Fossils. Archaeology: sculpture, coins, stones and inscriptions. Copper plates. Manuscripts. Copies of Shilrot Wall paintings. Musical instruments. Brass utensils. Old locks. Artistic nutcrackers. Weapons.
Daily ex. M. and public holidays, 8.30-12, 3-7 (winter: 8.30-12, 2.30-6.30).

GANDHI SMRITI MUSEUMS
Children's Museum, Gandhi Smriti, Bhawanagar, Gujarat
Relief map of Bhavanagar. Aquarium. Toys. Philatelic collection. Stuffed birds, reptiles and amphibians.
Daily ex. M. and public holidays, 8.30-12, 3-7 (winter: 8.30-12, 2.30-6.30).

GANDHI SMRITI MUSEUMS
Gandhi Museum, Gandhi Smriti, Bhawanagar, Gujarat
Photographs, collections of documents and personal relics. Audio-visual material on Gandhi.
Daily ex. M. and public holidays, 8.30-12, 3-7 (winter: 8.30-12, 2.30-6.30).

BHOPAL

CENTRAL MUSEUM
Bhopal, Madhya Pradesh
Paintings. Coins. Porcelain. Toys of metal and ivory. Woodwork. Needlework.
Daily ex. Su. and Government holidays, 10.30-5.

BHUBANESHWAR

ORISSA STATE MUSEUM
Bhubaneshwar 6, Puri District, Orissa
Archaeology. Paintings. Costumes. Ethnography. Anthropology. Science. Manuscripts.
Daily ex. M. and gazetted holidays, 11-5.

BHUJ

KUTCH MUSEUM
Bhuj, Gujarat
Silver-ware. Embroideries. Enamel-ware. Weapons peculiar to the region. Minerals. Kutch sculptures, coins and other articles.
Daily ex. Sa. afternoon, Su. and holidays, 11-6.

BIJAPUR

ARCHAEOLOGICAL MUSEUM
Bijapur, Mysore
Stone sculptures. Inscriptions. Manuscripts. Weapons. China. Wood-carvings. Carpets.
Daily 9-5.30.

BIKANER

GANGA GOLDEN JUBILEE MUSEUM
Bikaner, Rajasthan
Sculptures. Terracottas. Miniatures. Textiles. Arms. Decorative arts. 13th century marble goddess Saraswati.
Daily ex. F. and gazetted holidays, 7.30-10.30, 3.30-6 (winter: 10-5).

BODHGAYA

ARCHAEOLOGICAL MUSEUM
Bodhgaya, Gaya District, Bihar
Archaeology: stone and bronze sculpture.
Daily 9-5.

BOMBAY

GRANT MEDICAL COLLEGE MUSEUMS
Bombay, Maharashtra
Pathology: sections on pathology, forensic medicine, hygiene and public health. *Anatomy*: specimens illustrating normal and abnormal anatomies, human embryology and comparative anatomy. *Preventive and Social Medicine.*
Pathology and Anatomy: on working days, 9-5; Sa. 9-1. Preventive and Social Medicine: 10.30-5.30.

HERAS INSTITUTE OF INDIAN HISTORY AND CULTURE
St. Xavier's College, Bombay 1, Maharashtra
Archaeology. Paintings. Sculpture. Iconography. Manuscripts and rare books.
By appointment only (not Su.).

JEHANGIR ART GALLERY
Fort Bombay, Bombay 1, Maharashtra
Contemporary works of art.
On request.

MANI BHAVAN SANGRAHALAYA
19 Laburnum Road, Gamdevi, Bombay 7, Maharashtra
Memorabilia and documents relating to Gandhi.
Daily ex. Su. 10-5.

MUSEUM OF THE INDIAN HISTORICAL RESEARCH INSTITUTE
St. Xavier's College, Bombay, Maharashtra
Indian sculpture, including metal images, Brahmanical, Buddhist and Jain. Coin cabinet. Manuscripts.
8-5 on working days.

NATURAL HISTORY MUSEUM
St. Xavier's College, Bombay, Maharashtra
Zoological section has a fairly complete collection of birds from Bombay, Salsette islands and other parts of India. Herbarium or collection of dried plants from many parts of Bombay State.
8-5 on working days.

PRINCE OF WALES MUSEUM OF WESTERN INDIA
Fort Bombay, Bombay 1, Maharashtra
Archaeology. Paintings. Costumes. Bronzes; ivories; porcelain; jade. Natural history, with dioramas. Exhibits from the Maratha period.
Daily ex. M. 10-6.30. July-Sept. 10-6. Oct.-Feb. 10-5.30.

SETH GORDHANDAS SUNDERDAS MEDICAL COLLEGE MUSEUM
Bombay, Maharashtra
Specimens of anatomical interest. Pathology. Embryology.
8-5 on working days.

VICTORIA AND ALBERT MUSEUM
Victoria Gardens, Byculla, Bombay, Maharashtra
Natural history. Geology. Agriculture. Miscellaneous art objects. Most of the exhibits relate to Bombay and Western India.
Daily ex. M. 10-5.

BUDDH GAYA

ARCHAEOLOGICAL MUSEUM
Buddh Gaya, Bihar
Stone and metal images, mostly of the Pala period. Stone Yakshis of the 1st century B.C.
Daily 9-5.

CALCUTTA

ART IN INDUSTRY MUSEUM
15 Park Street, Calcutta 16, West Bengal
Indian arts and crafts in leather and clay. Contemporary Indian paintings and sculptures.
Daily 10-5.

ASIATIC SOCIETY OF BENGAL MUSEUM
1 Park Street, Calcutta 16, West Bengal
Western paintings. Coins. Miniatures (Pala, Arabic and Persian). Copper Plates. Manuscripts.
Daily 12-7, by appointment only.

ASUTOSH MUSEUM OF INDIAN ART
Centenary Building, University of Calcutta, Calcutta 12, West Bengal
Archaeology. Art. Bengal folk art. Paintings and textiles.
During University term, weekdays 10.30-5.30; Sa. 10.30-2.

BIRLA ACADEMY OF ART AND CULTURE
108-109 Southern Avenue, Calcutta 29, West Bengal
Archaeology. Paintings. Costumes. Anthropology.
Daily ex. Tu. 4-8; Sa. and Su. 12-8.

BIRLA INDUSTRIAL AND TECHNOLOGICAL MUSEUM
19a Gurusaday Road, Calcutta 19, West Bengal
History of science and technology.
M.-F. 1.30-8; Sa. 1.30-9.30; Su. and public holidays 10.30-9.30.

BIRLA PLANETARIUM AND ASTRONOMICAL RESEARCH CENTRE
96 Chowranghee, Calcutta 16, West Bengal
Educational activities. Research problems. Popularisation of astronomy and allied fields. Metallurgy. Petroleum. Electricity. Nuclear Physics. Electronics. Television. Optics.
M.-F. 1.30-8; Sa. 1.30-9.30; Su. and public holidays 10.30-9.30.

CRAFTS MUSEUM
Artistry House (1st floor), Calcutta, West Bengal
Dolls and toys. Paintings. Textiles. Stone and ivory pieces. Wood and metal objects. Paintings representing traditional schools from Rajasthan and folk schools from Bengal and Orissa.
Daily ex. Sa. and Su. 10-4.

CULTURAL RESEARCH INSTITUTE MUSEUM
Scheduled Castes & Tribes Welfare Department, New Secretariat Buildings, 1st floor, Block B, 1 Hastings Street, Calcutta 1, West Bengal
Ethnography and anthropology.
Daily ex. Su. and Government holidays, 10.30-5.30; Sa. 10.30-2.

GOVERNMENT INDUSTRIAL AND COMMERCIAL MUSEUM
45 Ganesh Chandra Avenue, Calcutta 13, West Bengal
Industry and commerce. Folk art and handicrafts.
Daily ex. Su. 10.30-5.30; Sa. 10.30-2.

GURUSADAY MUSEUM
Thakurpukur, Joka Paraganas, Calcutta, West Bengal
Scrolls. Paintings. Terracottas. Sculptures. Old earthenware utensils. Toys. Stone figures and architectural fragments.
Daily ex. Th. 12-4.

INDIAN MUSEUM
Chowringhee, Calcutta 13, West Bengal
Antiquities illustrating the cultural history of India from prehistoric times to the present day. Indian coins. Gems and jewellery. Indian textiles, carpets, wood and lacquer-work. Objects in ivory, metal and horn, stone and glass, and pottery. Persian and Indian paintings. Tibetan banners. Life and habits of the primitive tribes of India. Geological section.
Daily ex. M. 10-5 (Dec.-Feb. 10-4.30).

R. G. KAR MEDICAL COLLEGE (PATHOLOGY) MUSEUM
R. G. Kar Medical College, Calcutta, West Bengal
History of medicine, ancient and modern, by means of charts, maps, photographs and descriptive notes. "Palaeopathology".
Daily ex. Su. and holidays, 12-4.

MEDICAL COLLEGE MUSEUMS
Medical College, Calcutta, West Bengal
Anatomy: dissected specimens and models of different parts of the human body - neuro-anatomical and embryological.
Pathology: morbid specimens, models, drawings and diagrams.
Daily ex. Su. and government holidays, 10-4, Sa. 10-2.

MUNICIPAL MUSEUM
Calcutta, West Bengal
Pictures, diagrams, charts and models on public health, social and personal hygiene, civic knowledge and consciousness, maternity and child welfare, epidemic diseases and activities of the Calcutta Corporation.
Daily ex. Su. and holidays, 1-6.

MUSEUM OF THE BANGIYA SAHITYA PARISHAD
Ramesh Bhavan, Calcutta, West Bengal
Manuscripts. Valuable sculptures of the Pala school. Bronzes. Articles used by celebrated poets and writers.
Daily ex. Th. and public holidays, 1-7.

MUSEUM
School of Tropical Medicine, Calcutta, West Bengal
Preserved biological specimens of different categories. Dissected specimens. Plaster models representing tropical diseases. Wax casts of sections of the human body, showing effects of leprosy, smallpox, etc. Charts and pictures on distribution of tropical diseases and outlining methods of prevention. Medical plants and drugs.
Daily ex. Su. and holidays 10-5.

STATE ARCHAEOLOGICAL GALLERY
33 Chittaranjan Avenue, Calcutta 13, West Bengal
Prehistoric and protohistoric excavated material. Terracottas. Pala stone sculptures. Bronzes. Wood-carvings. Textiles.
Daily ex. public holidays, 11-5.30.

VICTORIA MEMORIAL HALL
1 Queensway, Calcutta 16, West Bengal
Museum of modern Indian history. Historical paintings: water-colours, late Mughal paintings. Statues of famous people. Archival material. Manuscripts. Weapons and armour.
Daily ex. M. 10-5 (winter: 10-4).

CHAMBA

BHURI SINGH MUSEUM
Chamba, Himachal Pradesh
Archaeology. Anthropology. Costumes. Ethnography. Miniature paintings.
Daily ex. M. 10-5.

CHANDIGARH

GOVERNMENT MUSEUM AND ART GALLERY
Sector 10-C, Chandigarh, Punjab
Paintings, including miniatures. Modern art. Sculptures (including Gandhara sculptures).
Daily ex. M. and some holidays, 10-1, 2-5.

CHHATARPUR

STATE MUSEUM
Dhubela, Chhatarpur, Madhya Pradesh
Archaeology. Paintings. Costumes.
Daily ex. M. and gazetted holidays, 10.30-5.30.

CHHINDWARA

TRIBAL RESEARCH INSTITUTE MUSEUM
Tribal Research Institute, Chhindwara, Madhya Pradesh
Ethnographic material relating to the tribes of Madhya Pradesh. Paintings and models showing the life of the people.
Open on the working days of the Madhya Pradesh Government, 11-5.

CHITRADURGA

LOCAL ANTIQUITIES MUSEUM
Chitradurga, Mysore
History and archaeology of the district. Coins, pottery, inscriptions.
Daily ex. M., Sa. afternoon and Government holidays, 8-10.30, 2.30-5.

COIMBATORE

AGRICULTURAL COLLEGE MUSEUM
Coimbatore, Madras
Agricultural and allied sciences. Seeds and products of cereals, pulses, oilseeds and fibres. Minerals and rocks. Insect pests and fungus diseases. Models of implements and tools. Stuffed birds, snakes, poultry and small animals.
Daily ex. Su. 8-11, 2-5.

SOUTHERN FOREST RANGERS COLLEGE AND RESEARCH CENTRE
Gass Forest Museum, R. S. Puram, Coimbatore 2, Madras
Museum of forestry, and allied subjects. Utilisation: timber, minor forest produce. Botany. Mycology. Zoology. Geology. Pedalogical collections. Ethnography. Shikar specimens.
Daily ex. Su. and Government holidays, 9-1, 2-4.30.

DARBHANGA

STATE CHANDRADHARI MUSEUM
Darbhanga, Bihar
General collections: art objects, manuscripts, coins, arms, paintings. Numismatics. Geology. Folk art. Textiles. Archaeology. Natural history.
Daily ex. M. and some holidays.

DARJEELING

NATURAL HISTORY MUSEUM
Darjeeling, West Bengal
Mammals, birds, reptiles, fishes, birds' eggs, insects and other invertebrates. Specimens from Darjeeling, Jalpaiguri and Sikkim State.
Daily ex. Su. and Sa. afternoon, 9-1, 3-5.

DEHRA DUN

GEODETIC BRANCH MUSEUM (SURVEY OF INDIA)
Dehra Dun, Uttar Pradesh
Photographs of founders of the "Great Trigonometrical Survey". Ancient and modern theodolites. Astronomical instruments. Pendulums. Early maps. Magnetometer. Tide gauge.
Daily ex. Sa. afternoons, Su. and gazetted holidays, 9.30-4.30.

MUSEUMS OF THE FOREST RESEARCH INSTITUTE AND COLLEGES
Dehra Dun, Uttar Pradesh
Timber Museum: Indian timbers. Demonstration models of wood seasoning, wood preserving and timber testing installation. Uses of Indian timber.
Minor Forest Products Museum: Products other than timber. Drugs, spices, perfumery materials, dyes, tans, fibres, flosses, gums, resins and methods of their extraction and utilisation.
Silviculture Museum: Silviculture practices. Soil erosion. Implements used in forestry. Planned land use. Rock samples. Sections of important species of trees. Maps and posters.
Daily ex. Sa. afternoon, Su. and gazetted holidays, 9.30-11, 1.30-4.30.

DHAR

DHAR DISTRICT MUSEUM
12 Ootavad Darwaja, Dhar, Madhya Pradesh
Archaeological finds from the district: sculptures and stone inscriptions. Coins. Terracotta. Figurines. Bricks. Beads, glass, conch and bangles. Historical drawings.
Daily ex. M. and gazetted holidays, 10-5.30.

DHARAMPUR

LADY WILSON MUSEUM
Dharampur, Bulsar District, Gujarat
Anthropology. Industrial art. Natural history.
Daily ex. M. 10.30-5.30.

DHARWAR

MUSEUM OF ART AND ARCHAEOLOGY
Kannada Research Institute, Karnatak University, Dharwar 3, Mysore
Archaeology. Epigraphy. Manuscripts. Sculptures. Numismatics. Paintings.
Daily ex. Su. 11-6.

DHULIA

I.V.K. RAJWADE SANSHODHAN MANDAL MUSEUM
Dhulia, Gujarat
Moghul and Rajput paintings. Coins. Copper-plates. Stone sculptures. Metal images. Manuscripts and documents. Stone implements and pottery. Pictures with historical themes.
Daily ex. Tu. morning and some holidays, 8.30-11, 4.30-8.

ERNAKULAM

ZOOLOGY AND BOTANY MUSEUM
Maharaja's College, Ernakulam, Kerala
Zoology. Botany.
During college working hours, 10-4.

GAUHATI

ASSAM FOREST MUSEUM
Gauhati, Assam
Specimens of timbers, bamboos, canes and forest products. Ivory works. Lacquer works. Cane and bamboo carving. Resin. Turpentine. Agarwood. Medicinal herbs. Photographs of forests, rhino catching, elephant catching, with charts and maps. Plywood and composite wood. Models of bridges. Tusks and horns.
Daily ex. Sa. afternoon, Su. and Government holidays, 10-4.30.

ASSAM STATE MUSEUM
Gauhati 1, Assam
Archaeology. Stone sculptures. Inscriptions. Paintings. Costumes. Ethnography. Coins, including punch-marked coins and Padma tankas. Assamese coins. Manuscripts.
Daily ex. M. 10-4; Sa. 10-1.30; Su. 8-11.

COMMERCIAL MUSEUM
Gauhati University, Jalukabari, Gauhati, Assam
Economic development of India. Commercial products: minerals and rocks, forest products, specimens of handicrafts, industrial and chemical products, agricultural implements, office appliances and labour-saving devices. Documents, pictures and models, coins.
M.-Sa. 12.30-6.30.

COTTAGE INDUSTRIES MUSEUM
Gauhati, Assam
Arts and crafts from various districts.
Daily ex. Sa. afternoon, Su. and Government holidays, 10-4.

GAUHATI MEDICAL COLLEGE
Gauhati 5, Assam
Science. Medicine. Anatomy.
Daily ex. Su. and Gazetted Holidays, 10-4.

MUSEUM OF ANIMAL HUSBANDRY AND VETERINARY SCIENCE
Assam Veterinary College, Gauhati 22, Assam
Veterinary science.
Daily ex. Su. 9-4.30.

GAYA

GAYA MUSEUM
Gaya, Bihar
Archaeology. Paintings. Costumes. Ethnography. Textiles. Manuscripts. Paintings on paper and ivory. Silver coins.
Daily ex. M. 6.30-11.30 a.m. (winter 10.30-4.30).

GUNTUR

ARCHAEOLOGICAL MUSEUM
Amaravati, Guntur, Andhra Pradesh
Stupa slabs and other fragments. Inscriptions.
Daily 9-5.30.

MEDICAL COLLEGE MUSEUMS
Guntur, Andhra Pradesh
Anatomy: Embryological models. Circulatory systems graphically presented. *Pathology*: morbid and anatomical specimens. *Pharmacology*: crude drugs; herbs and leaves from which drugs are prepared. *Forensic Medicine*: morbid and anatomical specimens illustrating causes of death in cases like snake-bite, stabbing, food poisoning, gunshot wounds. *Social and Preventive Medicine*: charts and models related to public health and infectious diseases.
On working days during college hours.

GURUKUL JHAJJAR

HARYANA PRANTIYA PURATATVA SANGRAHALAYA
Gurukul Jhajjar, Rohtak District, Haryana
Archaeology. Paintings. Costumes. Anthropology. Science. Geology. Numismatics. Sculptures. Crafts. Manuscripts.
Daily ex. Su. 8-11, 2-4.

GWALIOR

CENTRAL ARCHAEOLOGICAL MUSEUM
Gujari Mahal, Fort, Gwalior, Madhya Pradesh
Stone sculptures. Terracottas. Bronzes. Miniatures. Coins. Paintings, including copies of frescoes from the Bagh caves.
Daily ex. M. and gazetted holidays, 10-5.30.

STATE MUSEUM
Jamna Bagh, Gwalior, Madhya Pradesh
Natural history. Armoury. Art. Coins. Ivory and wood carvings. Brass. Forest products. Corals. Geology.
Daily ex. M. and holidays, 7-11 a.m. (winter: 2-6).

HALEBID

ARCHAEOLOGICAL MUSEUM
Halebid, Mysore
Stone sculpture. Architectural pieces of the Hoysala period.
Daily 9-5.30.

HAMPI

ARCHAEOLOGICAL MUSEUM
Hampi, Mysore
Sculptures and architectural pieces of the Vijayanagar period. Palm-leaf manuscripts. Coins. Beads and gold ornaments.
Daily 9-5.

HARDWAR

GURUKULA MUSEUM
Gurukula Kangri, Hardwar, Uttar Pradesh
Archaeological finds from the district. Terracottas of different periods. Coins. Paintings of the Kangra school. Frescoes of Kankhal of the early 19th century. Inscriptions. Manuscripts. Science. Local industries and crafts, with some examples of Kashmir and Burmese industries.
Daily 7-12, 4-7 (winter: 8-12, 1-5).

HOSHIARPUR

MUSEUM OF THE ZOOLOGY DEPARTMENT
Punjab University, Hoshiarpur, Punjab
Zoological collections.
Daily ex. Su. and gazetted holidays, 7.30-1.30 (winter: 10-5).

HYDERABAD

AJANTA PAVILION
Public Gardens, Hyderabad, Andhra Pradesh
Plastercasts and reproductions of wall paintings from the caves which, before Independence, were part of Hyderabad State.
Daily ex. F. 10.30-5.

CHOW MAHALLA PALACE
Hyderabad, Andhra Pradesh
One of the Nizam's palaces. Furniture. Decorative arts.
On request.

HEALTH MUSEUM
Public Gardens, Hyderabad, Andhra Pradesh
Information on health. Sections dealing with environmental sanitation, epidemic diseases, fevers, physiology and anatomy, school hygiene, maternity and child welfare, nutrition, family planning, insects, worms, snakes and scorpions, rural medical aid, statistics, rules of health, industrial hygiene and history of medicine. Discoveries in medical science with portraits of eminent medical men.
Daily ex. Th. and public holidays, 9-12, 3.30-6.30.

SALARJUNG MUSEUM
Hyderabad 2, Andhra Pradesh
Western Indian paintings. Textiles. Porcelain. Jade. Carpets. Manuscripts. Antique furniture. Ivory, glass, clocks, bronze, silver, Bidriware. Toys in Children's Section. Chinese and Japanese objets d'art. French furniture.
Daily ex. F. 10.30-5. Closed some holidays, including Salar Jung death anniversary (Mar. 2).

STATE ARCHAEOLOGICAL MUSEUM
Public Gardens, Hyderabad 4, Andhra Pradesh
Archaeology. Stone sculptures. Coins. Paintings and costumes. China. Weapons. Textiles. Illuminated manuscripts in Arabic and Persian.
Daily ex. F. and government holidays, 9-12, 2-5.

YELLESHWARAM MUSEUM
Gunfoundry, Hyderabad, Andhra Pradesh
Archaeology.
Daily ex. Su. 10.30-5.

IMPHAL

MANIPUR STATE MUSEUM
Polo Ground, Imphal, Manipur
Anthropology. Archaeology. Ethnography. Costumes. Paintings. Geology. Zoology.
Daily ex. Su. 9.30-4.30.

INDORE

CENTRAL MUSEUM
Bombay Agra Road, Indore 1, Madhya Pradesh
Archaeology. Paintings. Brahmnical and Jain images of stone and metal. Architectural fragments. Pottery. Coins. Ancient manuscripts and historical documents.
Daily ex. M. 10-5.

JAIPUR

CENTRAL MUSEUM
Ramniwas Gardens, Jaipur 4, Rajasthan
Sculptures. Miniature paintings. Ethnography. Anthropology. 16th century Persian garden carpet. Damascene work in gold and brassware. Enamel work mainly of Indian origin. Zoology and botany.
Daily ex. F. and gazetted holidays, 7.30-10.30, 3.30-6.

THE MAHARAJA OF JAIPUR MUSEUM
City Palace, Jaipur 2, Rajasthan
Miniatures. Costumes. Weapons. Armour. Textiles, including Moghul carpets. Indian paintings of different schools, notably the large paintings of the dancing Radha and Krishna.
Daily 10.30-3. Closed all day Vijaya Dashami and Dhoolandi. Open 8-1 Teej Mela, Mela Amber, Deepmalika, Holi and Gangore (both days).

JAMMU

DOGRA ART GALLERY
Jammu, Jammu and Kashmir
Miniature paintings, especially by Pahari. Historic weapons. Textiles. Manuscripts. Sculptures. Musical instruments. Rocks and fossils found in the Siwaliks.
Daily ex. Su. and gazetted holidays, 7-11.30, 5-7 (Winter: 10-4).

JAMNAGAR

JAMNAGAR MUSEUM OF ANTIQUITIES, LAKHOTE BUILDING
Jamnagar, Gujarat
Sculptures from sites in the old Nawanagar State. Epigraphy: stone inscriptions and copper-plates. Kshatrapa, Gupta, and local coins as well as seals of the Kshatrapa period. Rajput paintings. Manuscripts dating from 16th century. Excavated potsherds, terracottas, beads, conch, bangles, polished red ware and black and red and buff ware. Natural history. Folk art. Children's section contains toys and stuffed animals.
Daily ex. Su. and Sa. afternoon, 9.30-12.30, 2-6.

JHALAWAR

ARCHAEOLOGICAL MUSEUM
Jhalawar, Rajasthan
Sculptures. Inscriptions. Coins. Miniature paintings and manuscripts.
Daily ex. F. and gazetted holidays, 7.30-10.30, 3.30-6 (winter: 10-5).

JODHPUR

SARDAR MUSEUM
Jodhpur, Rajasthan
Indian paintings, mainly of the Rajasthani school. Archaeology. Coins. Historical records. Arts and crafts of Jodhpur.
Daily ex. F. 10-5.

STATE MUSEUM
Mandore, Jodhpur, Rajasthan
Science. Natural history. Paintings.
Daily ex. F. and gazetted holidays, 10-5.

JOYSAGAR

SIBSAGAR COLLEGE MUSEUM
Sibsagar College, Joysagar, Assam
Archaeology. Costumes. Ethnography. Science.
Daily ex. Su. and holidays 9-4.

JUNAGADH

DARBAR HALL MUSEUM
Shilekhana Sakkar Bagh, Junagadh, Gujarat
Archaeology. Paintings. Costumes. Inscriptions in Brahmi, Sanskrit and Persian. Coins. Sculptures.
Daily ex. Su. and State holidays, 9-12, 3-6.

KALPI

MAHATMA GANDHI HINDI SANGRAHALAYA
Hindi Bhawan, Kalpi, Uttar Pradesh
Antiquities dating from the beginning of the Christian era to the 17th century. Sculpture. Paintings. Terracottas. Metal images. Inscriptions. Coins and manuscripts. Early mould for minting coins.
Daily 7-11, 4-9.

KANTHALPARA

RISHI BANKIM MUSEUM AND LIBRARY
Kanthalpara, West Bengal
Housed in the writer's former home, the collection consists of objects used by Shri Bankim Chandra: his turban, shawl, lamp, box. Letters written by Chandra. Documents.
Daily ex. Th. and Government holidays, 12-6.

KHAJURAHO

ARCHAEOLOGICAL MUSEUM
Khajuraho, Madhya Pradesh
Archaeology: stone sculpture from Khajuraho and vicinity.
Daily 9-5.30.

KHICHING

KHICHING MUSEUM
Khiching, Orissa
Archaeology: Stone sculpture, stone implements, beads, pottery, copper-plates and sanads.
Daily 7-11, 2-5.

KONARAK

ARCHAEOLOGICAL MUSEUM
Konarak, Puri District, Orissa
Stone sculpture.
Daily 9-5.

KOLHAPUR

KOLHAPUR MUSEUM
Kolhapur, Gujarat
Objects from local excavations, 2nd century B.C. - 13th century A.D. Paintings. Industrial art. Weapons of the Nasik and Kagel. Local artists' work. Coins. Sculpture.
Daily ex. M. and gazetted holidays, 11-6; Sa. 3-6.

KONDAPUR

ARCHAEOLOGICAL MUSEUM
Kondapur, Andhra Pradesh
Architectural fragments of Stupa. Slabs. Sculpture. Antiquities of the Satavahana period: pottery, figurines, terracottas, beads, bangles, coins, iron objects.
Daily 9-5.30.

KOTAH

MUSEUM AND SARASWATI BHANDAR
Garh, Kotah, Rajasthan
Paintings. Costumes. Weapons. Manuscripts.
Daily ex. F. and gazetted holidays, 7.30-10.30, 3.30-6 (winter: 10-5).

LUCKNOW

MOTILAL NEHRU BAL SANGRAHALAYA
Motilal Nehru Marg, Charbagh, Lucknow, Uttar Pradesh
Children's museum. Health: causes and effects of various kinds of disease, their prevention and cure. Mechanical toys, models and dolls of various countries. Educative play materials. Natural history: flora and fauna.
Daily ex. Su. 10-7; Sa. 10-5.

PROVINCIAL HYGIENE INSTITUTE MUSEUM
Lucknow, Uttar Pradesh
Environmental hygiene and social medicine. Models, charts and slides relating to nutrition, diseases and disease-carriers.
Daily ex. Su. and gazetted holidays, 10-4.

STATE MUSEUM
Banarasibagh, Lucknow, Uttar Pradesh
Archaeology. Stone sculpture. Bronzes. Terracottas. Inscriptions. Anthropology. Paintings. Costumes. Ethnography. Natural history. Coins from Kushan, Gupta and of Moghul origins.
Daily ex. W. and some holidays, 10.30-4.30.

UNIVERSITY OF LUCKNOW MUSEUMS
Lucknow, Uttar Pradesh
Anatomy: General embryology, special senses, regional anatomy, comparative embryology.
Pathology. Pharmacology. Forensic Medicine. Public Health.
Zoology: Fishes, amphibia, reptiles, birds, mammals and invertebrates.
Anthropology: Pre- and protohistoric implements from India and abroad. Pottery and other antiquities. Material culture from contemporary primitive society: canoes, costumes, ornaments, fishing-tackle, baskets, musical instruments, weapons.
Daily 9-5 during college hours. Closed holidays.

MADRAS

CENTRAL INDUSTRIAL MUSEUM
Madras Industries Association, Madras
Exhibits representing small scale cottage and co-operative industries. Mineral and agricultural wealth of the State.
Daily ex. Su. and Government holidays, 10-5.

FORT ST. GEORGE MUSEUM
Madras
Paintings and prints. Coins. Medals. Textiles. Porcelain. Manuscripts of early Indo-British history.
Daily 9-5.

THE GOVERNMENT MUSEUM AND NATIONAL ART GALLERY
Egmore, Madras 8
Archaeology. Stone and bronze sculpture. Art. Anthropology. Numismatics. Zoology. Botany. Geology. Children's section. Philately. Ancient paintings of all schools. Modern art. Metal sculpture.
Daily ex. F. 7-5.

MEDICAL COLLEGE MUSEUMS
Madras Medical College, Madras
Diseased organs removed from patients after operation or death. Hygiene and preventive medicine. Human anatomy. Comparative embryology.
10-4 on working days.

MUSEUM OF THE COLLEGE OF ENGINEERING
Guindy, Madras
Civil and mechanical engineering models. Extensions to Madras harbour. Working model of a canal with lock gates. Howrah bridge.
Daily 10-4 on College working days.

STANLEY MEDICAL COLLEGE MUSEUM
Stanley Medical College, Madras
Pathology and its related subjects. Specimens are arranged on a regional basis. Dissected parts of the human body. Comparative anatomy. Embryology. Hygiene and preventive medicine. Pharmacology: crude drugs, toxicology, pharmaco-dynamics.
8.30-8 on working days.

VICTORIA TECHNICAL INSTITUTE
Madras
Wooden carvings, ivory figures, cane work, sandalwood carvings, leather work, red and lightwood carvings. Ivory fretwork. Carpets, lace and embroidery. Tanjore and Quilandy brass, silver and copper-work. Grass mats, toys, pottery.
Daily 9-1, 2-5.30; Sa. 9-1.

MADURAI

GANDHI SMARAK SANGRAHALAYA
Tamukkam, Madurai 13, Madras
Souvenirs and relics of Gandhi. Photographs, manuscripts. Library. Arts and crafts of South India.
Daily ex. W. 9.30-1, 2-5.30.

MADANAPALLE

MADANAPALLE COLLEGE MUSEUM
Madanapalle, Andhra Pradesh
Sculptures from the area, including bas-reliefs and portraits. Copies of Ajanta frescoes and wall paintings from an old palace in Cochin State.
During college hours.

MALDA

B. R. SEN MUSEUM
Malda, West Bengal
Images of the Brahmanical Pantheon. Copper-plate inscriptions. Coins. Books and manuscripts.
Daily 7-9, 6-9. Saturdays are "exclusively for ladies".

MANDAPAM CAMP

CENTRAL MARINE FISHERIES RESEARCH STATION REFERENCE MUSEUM
Mandapam Camp, Madras
Reference collection of marine fishes. Models of fishing gear and equipment used in different parts of India. Seaweeds and seaweed products.
On application to the Chief Research Officer.

MANGALORE

GOVERNMENT MUSEUM
Shrimanthi Bhavan, Bijai, Mangalore, Mysore
Art objects from all over the world. Local history.
Daily 10-5.

MAHATMA GANDHI MUSEUM
Canara High School, Mangalore, Mysore
Zoology. Anthropology. Art. Silver and gold coins. Palm-leaf manuscripts.
M.-Sa. 9.30-12.30, 2-5.30.

MATHURA

ARCHAEOLOGICAL MUSEUM
Dampier Park, Mathura, Uttar Pradesh
Stone sculptures, particularly of Kushana and Gupta periods of Mathura school. Terracottas. Bronzes. Indian art.
Daily ex. W. and main holidays, 10.30-4.

MYSORE

MEDICAL COLLEGE MUSEUMS
Medical College, Mysore
Anatomical dissections and bone preparations. Embryology. Animal skulls. Comparative anatomy. Pathology and histo-pathological sections. Pharmacology: drugs; paintings of plants; charts. Preventive and social medicine.
By appointment.

SRI CHAMRAJENDRA ART GALLERY
Jaganmohan Palace, Mysore City
Paintings of local, Rajput and Moghul schools.
Daily ex. Th. 8-11.30, 3-5.

NAGARJUNKONDA

ARCHAEOLOGICAL MUSEUM
Nagarjunkonda, Andhra Pradesh
Satavahana period antiquities: stone sculptures, pottery, terracotta, beads, bangles, coins and iron objects.
Daily 9-5.30.

NAGPUR

CENTRAL MUSEUM
Nagpur, Maharashtra
Archaeology. Anthropology. Paintings. Geology. Natural history. Copper Age implements and silver bulls. Antiquities from megalithic sites. Inscriptions.
Daily ex. M. 9-5.30.

NALANDA

ARCHAEOLOGICAL MUSEUM
Nalanda, Patna District, Bihar
Archaeology: stone and bronze sculptures. Pottery, coins, seals, iron objects. Buddhist and Brahmanical iconography.
Daily 9-5.30.

NEW DELHI

ANTHROPOLOGY DEPARTMENT MUSEUM
Department of Anthropology, University of Delhi, New Delhi 7
Cultural and physical anthropology. Articles used by aborigines. Fetishes and cult objects. Exhibits from Arabia, Tibet, China, Fiji. Costumes. Basketry. Prehistory. Comparative anatomy.
Daily ex. Su. and University holidays, 10-5.

ARCHAEOLOGICAL MUSEUM
Red Fort, New Delhi
Historical collections of the Moghul period: costumes, arms, coins, jades. Astronomical instruments. Miniatures. Documents and seals.
Daily 9-5.

BHARTIYA ADIM JATI SEVAK SANGH MUSEUM
Dr. Ambedkar Road, New Delhi
History of government. Costumes. Tribal handicrafts.
Daily ex. Su. and gazetted holidays, 10-5.

CRAFTS MUSEUM
Thapar House, 124 Janpath, New Delhi 1
Archaeology. Paintings. Costumes. Ethnography. Anthropology. Crafts. Dolls and toys. Textiles. Stone and ivory carvings. Jewellery. Pottery and terracottas. Basketry and leather work.
Daily ex. Su. and Government holidays, 9.30-4.30.

ENGINEERING MUSEUM
New Delhi
National development in the sphere of irrigation and power development in India, with the help of models, charts and maps. Engineering structures of other countries.
Daily ex. M. and public holidays, 10-5.

GANDHI MEMORIAL MUSEUM AND LIBRARY
Rajghat, New Delhi 1
Photographs; relics; paintings; sculptures. Mementoes include one of the bullets that killed Gandhi and his blood-stained clothes.
Daily ex. M. and some holidays, 9-6.

INDIAN WAR MEMORIAL MUSEUM
Red Fort, New Delhi
War trophies. Arms and ammunition and photographs relating to the first World War. Trophies from Mesopotamia, East Africa and the North-West Frontier. Coins and currency notes. Regimental badges.
Daily 8-11, 4-7 (winter: 10-1, 3-6).

INTERNATIONAL DOLLS MUSEUM
Nehru House, Bahadurshah Zafar Marg, New Delhi 1
Dolls from all over the world.
Daily ex. M. 10-6.

LADY HARDINGE MEDICAL COLLEGE MUSEUMS
New Delhi
Pathological and surgical specimens. Specimens and models of human and comparative anatomy and embryology.
M.-Sa. 9-4.

NATIONAL CHILDREN'S MUSEUM
Bal Bhavan, Kotla Road, New Delhi
Dolls. Paintings and photographs.
Daily ex. Th. 10-5.

NATIONAL GALLERY OF MODERN ART
Jaipur House, New Delhi 11
Contemporary paintings (1857 onwards). Sculptures. Graphic arts. Paintings of Ravindra Nath Tagore and Amrita Shergil.
Daily ex. M. and national holidays, 9.30-1, 1.30-4.30.

NATIONAL MUSEUM OF INDIA
Janpath, New Delhi 11
Prehistory. Protohistory. Sculpture; bronzes; copper plates; coins. Miniatures. Arms. Pre-Columbian arts. Anthropology. Central Asian collections, including mural paintings from Buddhist shrines, silk painting and sculptures.
Daily ex. M. 10-5.

NATIONAL PHILATELIC MUSEUM
Dak Tar Bhavan, Sardar Square, Parliament Street, New Delhi 1
Philately.
M. and W. 11-4 by prior appointment with Philatelic Officer (tel. 380230). F. and Sa. 2-5.

NEHRU MEMORIAL MUSEUM
Teen Murti Marg, New Delhi
Personal possessions of Pandit Nehru, including his library.
Daily ex. M. 9.30-1, 2-5.

RABINDRA BHAVAN ART GALLERY
35 Ferozeshah Road, New Delhi
Gallery of the National Academy of Fine Arts and venue of the National Exhibition of Art.
Daily, except public holidays, 10-5.

SCIENCE MUSEUM
National Physical Laboratory, New Delhi
Development of the physical sciences. Working models showing the principles of science. Among subjects covered are: time measurement through the ages; development of electronics; glass technology; development of incandescent electric lamps; optical experiments; development of microscopes and binoculars; economic minerals and ores; crystallography; weather and climate; electricity; vacuum pumps.
Daily ex. Sa. afternoon, Su. and public holidays, 10-5.

TIBET HOUSE MUSEUM
16 Jor Bagh, New Delhi
Tibetan sculptures. Paintings (Thankas). Ritual objects. Carpets.
Daily ex. M. 10-1, 2-5.

WAR MEMORIAL MUSEUM
Red Fort, Delhi
Trophies of the first World War. Regimental relics.
Daily ex. M. 9-5.30.

NOWGONG

STATE MUSEUM
Dhubela Palace, Nowgong, Madhya Pradesh
Sculpture, including a series of Jain images of Tirthankaras. Stone records of the Kushana and Gupta periods. Medieval stone inscriptions of the Kalachuris. Coins. Paintings. Heirlooms of the Maharajas of Rewa. Wood and ivory work.
Daily ex. Su. and gazetted holidays, 10.30-4.30.

PADMANABHAPURAM

MUSEUM OF ANTIQUITIES
Palace, Padmanabhapuram, Madras
Inscriptions. Coins. Stone images illustrating the early history of Travancore. The Palace is the ancient seat of the royal family of Travancore and has furniture, household and religious articles, mural paintings and weapons. Woodcarvings.
Daily ex. M. 9.30-1.30, 2.30-5.30.

PARGANAS

GANDHI SMARAK SANGRAHALAYA
14 Riverside Road, Barrackpore, 24 Parganas, West Bengal
Souvenirs of Gandhi: relics, manuscripts, replicas, photographs and library.
Daily ex. W. and gazetted holidays, 12-6.

PATIALA

STATE MUSEUM
Patiala, Punjab
Archaeology. Anthropology. Costumes. Paintings. Ethnography. Geology. Science.
Daily ex. W. 9-5.

PATNA

GANDHI MEMORIAL MUSEUM
North West Gandhi Ground, Patna 1, Bihar
Souvenirs and documents relating to Gandhi.
Daily 7-11, 5-7.

PATNA MUSEUM
Patna-Gaya Road, Buddha Marg, Patna 1, Bihar
Archaeology. Stone and bronze sculpture. Coins. Inscriptions. Art. Weapons. Tibetan and Nepalese ethnography. Natural history. Geology.
Daily ex. M. 10-5 (10.30-5 Sept.-Mar.). Closed Dashehra, Holi, Republic Day and Independence Day.

PILANI

CENTRAL MUSEUM
Institute of Technology and Science, Pilani, Rajasthan
Paintings. Science and technology. Major Indian industries. Engineering and transport. Models of railways and hydro-electric power plant. Dioramas of industries and people at work in them.
Daily ex. M. 8-12.30, 3.30-5. (winter: 9-1, 3-5).

POONA

BHARTIYA ITIHASA SAMSHODHAKA MANDALA MUSEUM
Poona, Maharashtra
Marathi, Sanskrit, Persian, Hindi and Kannada documents. Manuscripts on palm-leaf and paper. Coins. Paintings. Copper-plates and stone inscriptions. Sculptures. Arms. Maps. Playing cards. Costumes.
Daily ex. F. and holidays, 8-10, 4-8.

B.J. MEDICAL COLLEGE MUSEUM
Poona, Maharashtra
Pathology. Parasitology. Bacteriology. Human diseases. Hygiene and public health. Medical jurisprudence. Pharmacology.
M.-F. 9-5; Sa. 9-1.

DECCAN COLLEGE MUSEUM
Poona, Maharashtra
Excavated materials from Nevasa, Jorwe, Nasik. Maratha period objects. English autograph letters written by persons connected with the British in India. Art objects and armour from the Rajah of Jamkhandi: swords, daggers, spears, chinaware, sandalwood and ivory carvings, lamps, metalware and coins.
Daily ex. Su. and public holidays, 11-5; Sa. 11-2.

LORD REAY MAHARASHTRA INDUSTRIAL MUSEUM
Poona, Maharashtra
Agriculture. Forestry. Education. Science and industry.
Daily ex. W. 9-6. Closed Republic Day, Independence Day, Anant Chaturdashi and Dhooli Vandan.

MAHATMA PHULE VASTU SANGRAHALAYA
Ghole Road, Poona, Maharashtra
Archaeology. Agriculture. Anthropology. Costumes. Ethnography. Forestry. Industry. Paintings. Science.
Daily ex. W. 9-6. Closed Jan. 26, Aug. 15, Anant Chaturdashi and Dhooli Vanden Day.

RAJA KELKAR MUSEUM
1378 Shukrawar peth Natu Bag, Raja Kelkar Street, Poona, Maharashtra
Archaeology. Anthropology. Ethnography. Costumes. Paintings.
Daily ex. Tu. 11-6.

PRABHAS PATAN

PRABHAS PATAN MUSEUM
Prabhas Patan, Gujarat
Inscriptions in Sanskrit and Persian. Coins. Sculptures.
Daily ex. Sa. afternoon, Su. and gazetted holidays, 8-12, 3-6.

PUDDUKKOTTAI

GOVERNMENT MUSEUM
T.S. No. 6169, Big Street, Tirugokarnam, Puddukkottai 2, Trichy District, Madras
Archaeology. Paintings. Costumes. Ethnography. Anthropology. Geology. Zoology. Botany.
Daily ex. M. and public holidays, 8-11.30, 2-5.

RAIPUR

MAHANT GHASI DASS MEMORIAL MUSEUM
Raipur, Madhya Pradesh
Archaeology. Paintings. Costumes. Anthropology. Natural history. Arts and crafts.
Daily ex. M. and gazetted holidays, 10-5.30.

RAJAMUNDRY

ANDHRA KESARI YUVAJANA SAMITI MUSEUM
Rajamundry 2, East Godavari, Andhra Pradesh
Paintings and photographs. Art. Archaeology. Numismatics. History. Literature. Anthropology. Historical maps. Old palm-leaf manuscripts.
Daily 8-10, 3-9.

RAJKOT

WATSON MUSEUM
Jubilee Bagh, Rajkot, Gujarat
Archaeology. Anthropology. Costumes. Ethnography. Science. Geology. Natural history.
Daily ex. 2nd and 4th Sa. in month, Su. and Government holidays, 9-11.45, 3-5.45.

RANCHI

BIHAR TRIBAL WELFARE RESEARCH INSTITUTE
Morabadi Road, Ranchi 8, Bihar
Ethnography: culture of the tribes of Bihar.
Daily ex. Su. and gazetted holidays 10.30-5.

SANCHI

ARCHAEOLOGICAL MUSEUM
Sanchi, Raisen District, Madhya Pradesh
Stone sculptures, terracottas and other finds, including relic caskets, fragments of gateways, and pottery.
Daily 7.30-1, 3-6 (Nov.-Feb. 9-5.30).

SANGARIA

SIR CHOTURAM MUSEUM
Sarasvati Mandir, Sangaria, Rajasthan
Sculptures and terracottas from Rajghat. Tibetan banners. Paintings of the Rajasthani school. Embossed metal panels from Rajasthan. Metal images from Ceylon and Nepal. Wooden and porcelain work from China. Coins. Armour.
Daily ex. M. and gazetted holidays, 10-5.

SANTINIKETAN

KALA BHAVAN
Visva Bharati University, Santiniketan, West Bengal
Fine arts and handicrafts.
In University term, on working days, 7-11, 2-4.

TAGORE MEMORIAL MUSEUM
Santiniketan, West Bengal
Material connected with the life and works of Rabindranath Tagore: manuscripts, paintings, photographs, records, costumes, books and journals.
Daily ex. W. and University holidays, 6.30-11, 2.30-5 (winter: 7-11.30, 2-4.30). Closed Tu. afternoon.

SARNATH

SARNATH MUSEUM
Sarnath, Uttar Pradesh
Antiquities ranging from 3rd century B.C. to 12th century A.D., including images, bas-reliefs, architectural fragments, inscribed slabs, objects of stone and metal, seals, beads, toys, terracotta figures and pottery.
Daily 9-5.

SATNA

TULSI SANGRAHALAYA
Ramban, Satna, Madhya Pradesh
Local archaeological finds. Stone sculpture.
Daily 7-5.

SERAMPORE

SERAMPORE COLLEGE MUSEUM
Serampore, West Bengal
Rare books and manuscripts. Furniture used by missionaries in the 19th century. Miniature steam engine of the same period, in working order.
Daily ex. Su. and gazetted holidays, 10-4.30; Sa. 10-1.

SERINGAPATAM

TIPU SULTAN PALACE
Summer Palace, Dariya-Doulat-Bagh, Seringapatam, Madras
Objects connected with the history of Haidar Ali and Tipu Sultan and their contemporary history.
Daily 9-5.30.

SEVAGRAM

GANDHI MEMORIAL MUSEUM
Sevagram, Maharashtra
Personal relics of Gandhi, portraits and Gandhian literature.
Daily 10-5.

SHILLONG

CENTRAL MUSEUM
Lachmmiera, Shillong 1, North-East Frontier Agency
Archaeology. Anthropology. Ethnography. Costumes.
Daily ex. Su. 10-4.30; Sa. 10-1.

SHIVPURI

FOREST SCHOOL
Shivpuri, Madhya Pradesh
Forestry and forest products. Ethnography.
Daily ex. Su. 8-11, 2-5.

SHIVPURI DISTRICT MUSEUM
Ban Ganga Road, Shivpuri, Madhya Pradesh
30 stone images (Jain Tirthankars). Exhibits on Harappan culture.
Daily ex. M. and Government holidays, 10-5.30.

SIKAR

SIKAR MUSEUM
Sikar, Rajasthan
Archaeology. Arts and crafts of the Shekhawati. Weapons. Armour.
Daily 7-11, 4-7 (winter: 8-11, 4-6).

SIROHI

STATE MUSEUM
Mount Abu, Sirohi District, Rajasthan
Science. Paintings. Handicrafts.
Daily ex. F. and gazetted holidays, 10-5.

SONAGIR

DIGAMBER JAIN MUSEUM
Sonagir, Madhya Pradesh
Archaeological material, mostly Jain sculptures.
Daily 7-4.

SRINAGAR

S.P.S. MUSEUM
Lalmandi, Srinagar, Jammu and Kashmir
Archaeology. Paintings. Costumes. Anthropology. Arts and crafts. Minerals. Numismatics. Natural history. Finds from Harwan, a Buddhist site of the 3rd century. Carpets and textiles.
Daily ex. Th. and gazetted holidays, 11-5 (winter: 11-4.30).

SRIRANGAM

DEVASTHANAMS MUSEUM
Srirangam, Madras
Ivory carvings of the time of the Nayaks of Madura, representing contemporary portraits of Kings and nobles in various attitudes in their harems. Bronzes. Copper-plate grants. Coins. Silver images. Iron locks. Arms and armour. Wood-work.
Daily ex. Su. and Government holidays, 10-1, 3-6.

SURAT

SARDAR V. PATEL MUSEUM
Sonifalia, Surat, Gujarat
Archaeology. Paintings. Costumes. Manuscripts on paper and palm-leaf. Weapons. Zoology.
Daily ex. W. 11.45-2, 2.45-6; Th. and F. 2.45-6.

TAL. KHATAV

SHRI BHAVANI MUSEUM AND LIBRARY
Aundh (Satara), Tal. Khatav, Satara District, Maharashtra
Archaeology. Paintings. Stone and bronze statues. Sandalwood carvings and some textiles.
Daily ex. W. and public holidays, 11-5.30.

TAMBARAM

ZOOLOGICAL MUSEUM
Madras Christian College, Tambaram, Madras
Zoological and botanical specimens. Fossils. Models and charts.
Mainly intended for students' use. By appointment.

TAMLUK

HAMILTON HIGH SCHOOL MUSEUM
Tamluk, West Bengal
Antiquities, including terracottas and uninscribed cast coins of the 2nd century B.C. Sculpture and carved pillars. Earthenware jars and pottery. Fossils, rocks and minerals from the district. Zoological specimens. Shawl and walking stick belonging to Pandit Iswar Chandra Vidyasagar.
During school hours.

TANJORE

THE TANJORE ART GALLERY
Palace Buildings, Tanjore, Madras
Early Chola sculpture and bronzes.
Daily 8.30-12, 3-6. Closed Pongal, Tamil New Year's Day, Ayudha Pooja Day and Deepavali.

TIRUCHIRAPALLI

NATURAL HISTORY MUSEUM
St. Joseph's College, Tiruchirapalli, Madras
Insects, birds, mammals, snakes and geological specimens. Weapons.
9-5 on 275 days of the year.

TIRUPATI

SRI VENKATESWARA MUSEUM
Tirupati, Andhra Pradesh
Stone and metal images. Coins. Weapons. Wooden, stone and metal articles. Paintings.
Daily ex. public holidays 10-4.

TRICHUR

ARCHAEOLOGICAL MUSEUM AND PICTURE GALLERY
Trichur, Kerala
Antiquities from Mohenjodaro, Harappa and Taxila. Pottery, beads of quartz and glass from megalithic and urn burial sites of Cochin and mid-Kerala regions. Silver coins. Decorated potsherds, pottery, iron and copper objects from excavations at Cranganur (Muziris). Wood-carvings. Metal images. Reproductions of mural paintings from the Mattancheri Palace and other places. Early Malayalam stone records from 15th-18th centuries.
Daily 11-5.

STATE MUSEUM
Trichur, Kerala
Arts and crafts. Wood carvings. Natural history. Geology. Gold coins. Industry of the area.
Daily ex. F. and some holidays, 7-11.30, 3-6.

TRIVANDRUM

ART MUSEUM
Trivandrum, Kerala
Sculpture of metal and wood. Ivory work. Lamps. Musical instruments. Numismatics. Handicrafts. Paintings.
Daily ex. M. and some holidays, 8-6.

NATURAL HISTORY MUSEUM
Department of Museums and Zoos, Trivandrum, Kerala
Geology. Ethnography. Zoology.
Daily ex. M. and five holidays, 8-6.

SRI CHITRA LAYAM ART GALLERY
Gallery of Asian Paintings, Trivandrum 1, Kerala
Indian fine art. Rajput, Moghul, and Persian, Tanjore, Tibetan, Chinese, Japanese, Balinese, Indo-European (water and oil paintings), etchings and woodcuts. Modern Indian paintings, murals.
Daily ex M. and some holidays, 8-6

SRI MOOLAM SHASTYABDAPURTI MEMORIAL INSTITUTE MUSEUM
Trivandrum, Kerala
Cottage industry products: articles of ivory, wood, screw-pine, rattan, cutlery, bell metal, kuft gari, palmyra leaves, coconut shell, coir, lacework.
Daily ex. Su. and public holidays, 10-5.

UDAIPUR

RANA PRATAP MUSEUM
nr. Pichhola Lake, Udaipur, Rajasthan
Sculpture. Inscriptions. Coins. Paintings and local crafts.
Daily ex. F. and gazetted holidays, 7.30-10.30, 3.30-6 (winter: 10-5).

VICTORIA HALL MUSEUM
Udaipur, Rajasthan
Archaeological exhibits from different parts of Mewar, dating from 3rd century B.C. Ethnography. Arts and crafts. Weapons.
Daily ex. F. and gazetted holidays, 7.30-10.30, 3.30-6 (winter: 10-5).

VAISALI

VAISALI MUSEUM
Vaisali, Bihar
Antiquities from the Vaisali region, covering about 100 villages.
Daily 8-5.

VALLABH VIDYANAGAR

MUSEUM OF ART AND ARCHAEOLOGY
Vallabh Vidyanagar, Gujarat
Sculpture. Thoothi collection of bronzes. Coins. Epigraphy. Antiquities and fossils. Maps. Wood-carvings.
Daily ex. Su. and gazetted holidays, 9-12, 2.30-5.30.

VARANASI

ARCHAEOLOGICAL MUSEUM
Sarnath, Varanasi, Uttar Pradesh
Stone and bronze sculpture. Seals. Beads. Toys. Terracottas. Pottery.
Daily 9-5.30.

BHARAT KALA BHAVAN
Benaras Hindu University, Varanasi 5, Uttar Pradesh
Souvenirs of Gandhi. Philately. Architecture. Bronzes. Glassware. Arms. Roorich paintings. Jades and gems. Ornaments. Modern art. Textiles. Coins. Miniatures. Terracottas. Sculpture. Sections on Nepal and Tibet.
Daily ex. Su. 11-4.30.

MAHARAJA BANARAS MUSEUM
Fort Ram Nagar, Varanasi, Uttar Pradesh
Stone sculpture. Textiles, including Benaras brocades. Arms. Manuscripts. Paintings and decorative arts. Palanquins and howdas.
Daily 9-5.30.

VIDISHA

DISTRICT ARCHAEOLOGICAL MUSEUM
Vidisha, Madhya Pradesh
Archaeology. Terracotta objects. Coins. Harrappan Art.
Daily ex. M. and gazetted holidays, 10-5.30.

VIJAYAWADA

VICTORIA JUBILEE MUSEUM
Vijayawada, Andhra Pradesh
Archaeology. Images. Architectural fragments. Stone inscriptions. Natural history. Painted gesso work. Examples of local village industries.
Daily ex. M. 8-11, 2-5.

VISAKHAPATNAM

ANDHRA MEDICAL COLLEGE MUSEUMS
Department of Anatomy, Andhra Medical College, Visakhapatnam 1, Andhra Pradesh
Anthropology. Anatomy. Pathology. Preventive and social medicine.
Working days 8-4. Holidays 8-12.

WARDHA

MAGAN SANGRAHAYALA
Maganwadi, Wardha, Maharashtra
Khadi and village industries.
Daily ex. Su. 8.30-11.30, 1.30-5.

Indonesia

Indonesia's museums show life as it was before machinery, motorcars and tourists arrived to undermine, transform and, as some would say, corrupt the old world. They are, in brief, museums of the Indonesia that enthusiastic travel writers used to write about, with the collections of the art, handicrafts and theatrical equipment of a people who once took the making of beautiful things for granted.

BANDUNG

GEOLOGICAL MUSEUM
Bandung
Geological collections.
Tu.-Su. 8-1.

ZOOLOGICAL MUSEUM
Bandung
Zoological collections.
Tu.-Su. 8-1.

BOGOR

BOGOR ZOOLOGICAL MUSEUM
Lembaga Biologi Nasional, Djalan Ir. H. Djuanda 3, Bogor, Java
Tropical fauna, molluscs to man, particularly S.E. Asia. Departments of malacology, entomology, acarology, ichthyology, herpetology, ornithology and mammalogy.
Daily 8-12. Holidays 8-3.

BUKIT TINGGI

MUNICIPAL MUSEUM
Bukit Tinggi, Sumatra
Local history and culture.
Tu.-Su. 8-1.

DENPASAR

BALI MUSEUM
Denpasar, Bali
Archaeology. Local arts, crafts and folk arts, including a collection of masks. Theatrical arts section.
Tu.-Su. 8-5.

DJAKARTA

MUSEUM OF INDONESIAN CULTURE
Djl. Medan Merdeka Barat 12, Djakarta
Ceramics. Ethnography. Prehistory. Archaeology. Anthropology.
Daily ex. M. 8-1.

SEDJARAH MUSEUM
Djalan Pintu Besar Utara 27, Djakarta-Kota
History of Indonesia. Ethnography: furniture; sculptures; Inscriptions of the East Indian Company (17th-18th centuries); costumes; puppets (barongan) used in traditional ceremonies; coins; Dutch silver work; weapons; portraits; gravestones.
Daily ex. M. 8-1.

GIANJAR

MUSEUM GEDONG ARTJA
d/a Lembaga Purbakala, Bedaulu, Gianjar, Bali
Palaeolithic implements (chopping tools, flat-iron choppers, proto hand-axes); Mesolithic implements (bone and shell implements); Neolithic implements. Stone sarcophagi. Pottery and earthenware from excavations at Gilimanuk Bay (West Bali). Axes. Jewellery. Hindu statues and relics. Copperplate inscriptions from Central Java (885 and 903 A.D.).
By appointment.

JOGJAKARTA

MUSEUM SANA BUDOJA
Jogjakarta, Central Java
Archaeology. History. Art. Ethnography.
Daily ex. M. 8-1.

PALACE MUSEUM
Jogjakarta, Central Java
Art. Historical objects. Regalia.
Daily ex. M. 8-1.

KEDIRI

MUNICIPAL MUSEUM
Kediri, East Java
Local history and archaeology.
Daily ex. M. 8-1.

MEDAN

MUNICIPAL MUSEUM
Medan, North Sumatra
Local history. Ethnography.
Daily ex. M. 8-1.

MODJOKERTO

MUNICIPAL MUSEUM
Modjokerto, Java
Local history. Ethnography.
Daily ex. M. 8-1.

PALEMBANG

MUNICIPAL MUSEUM
Palembang, Sumatra
Local history and culture.
Daily ex. M. 8-1.

SANUR

MEMORIAL MUSEUM
Sanur, Bali
Collections illustrating the life and work of the Belgian painter, Le Mayeur.
Daily ex. M. 8-1.

SURAKARTA

ART MUSEUM
Palace, Surakarta, Central Java
Collection of Indonesian art.
Daily ex. M. 8-5.

MUSEUM RADYA PUSTAKA
Surakarta, Central Java
Arts. Decorative arts.
Daily ex. M. 8-5.

PALACE MUSEUM
Surakarta, Central Java
Art. Historical objects. Regalia.
Daily ex. M. 8-5.

UBUD

MUSEUM PURI LUKISAN RATNAWARTHA
Ubud, Bali
Collections of modern Balinese paintings and some sculptures.
Daily ex. M. 8-12, 1-5.

Iran

The museums of Iran have a strongly royal or sometimes ex-royal flavour about them. Some are housed in palaces and one, as our list shows, is in a former pleasure pavilion, used for the king's entertainment. There are two museums entirely stocked with gifts made to the Royal Family by foreign monarchs and another contains the Crown Jewels. Iran, under its former name of Persia, was famous for its carpets and rugs, and many examples of this national speciality are to be found in museum collections, together with brocades, national costumes, and the ornaments to go with them. A number of museums also possess notable early copies of the Koran, reminding us of the great skill of the Persians in calligraphy.

ABADAN

ABADAN MUSEUM
Abadan
Local history.
Weekdays: 8.30-12, 4-7.

BANDAR ABBAS

MOHITSHENASI MUSEUM
Bandar Abbas
Collection of costumes. Gold and silver ornaments.
Weekdays: 8.30-12, 4-7.

GORGAN

GORGAN MUSEUM
Gorgan
Local history.
Weekdays: 8.30-12, 4-7.

ISFAHAN

CHEHEL SOTOUN MUSEUM
Isfahan
In former pleasure pavilion used for the king's entertainments. Local history. Ethnography. Historical frescoes. Paintings. Persian china.
Weekdays: 8.30-12, 4-7.

KARAJ

ZOOLOGICAL MUSEUM
Agricultural College, Karaj
Zoological collections.
Weekdays: 8.30-12, 4-7.

KASHAN

KASHAN MUSEUM
Kashan
Historical objects from prehistoric times to the present day. Local costumes.
Weekdays: 8.30-12, 4-7.

KERMAN

GANJALI-KHAN BATH-HOUSE MUSEUM
Kerman
Local history.
Weekdays: 8.30-12, 4-7.

KHOY

KHOY MUSEUM
Khoy
Local history.
Weekdays: 8.30-12, 4-7.

KHUZESTAN

SHUSH MUSEUM
Susa, Khuzestan
Local history. Archaeological fragments.
Weekdays: 8.30-12, 4-7.

MASHHAD

ASTANE QODS MUSEUM
Mashhad
Brocades and rugs of the Safavid period.
Weekdays: 8.30-12, 4-7.

PERSEPOLIS

TAKHT-I-JAMSHID MUSEUM
Persepolis
Historical and ethnographical objects from Fars Province.
Weekdays: 8.30-12, 4-7.

QAZVIN

QAZVIN MUSEUM
Qazvin
Objects belonging to the Safavid period. Coins issued in Qazvin.
Weekdays: 8.30-12, 4-7.

QOM

ASTANEH MUSEUM
Qom
Rugs, tiles and kincobs from the Safavid period. Early Korans.
Weekdays: 8.30-12, 4-7.

HAZRAT MASOUMEH SHRINE
Qom
Souvenirs and gifts presented by ruling monarchs of different religions and countries.
Weekdays: 8.30-12, 4-7.

RASHT

RASHT MUSEUM
P.O. Box 105, Rasht
Anthropology: the way of life of the people of Guilan. Archaeological exhibits from the area and from Iran in general.
Daily ex. Sa. 9-1, 2-7.

REZAIYEH

REZAH SHAH THE GREAT MUSEUM
Rezaiyeh
Local history.
Weekdays: 8.30-12, 4-7.

SHIRAZ

PARS MUSEUM
Zand Street, Shiraz
Objects dating from prehistoric times to the present day. Local history. Manuscripts. Earthenware. Ancient coins.
Weekdays: 8.30-12, 4-7.

TABRIZ

EAST AZARBAYJAN MUSEUM
National Library, Tabriz
Archaeology. Anthropology. Relics of the Constitutional Revolution.
Weekdays: 8.30-12, 4-7.

TEHERAN

ARCHAEOLOGICAL MUSEUM
Sepah Avenue at Ghavam Saltaneh Avenue, Teheran
Antiquities from the Palaeolithic era to the 19th century. Pre-Islamic material. Arts of the Islamic period. Sculpture, including a Parthian bronze male figure found at Shami.
Daily ex. M. 8.30-12, 4-7; F. 9-12.

CADET COLLEGE MUSEUM
Sepah Street, Teheran
History of the College.
Weekdays: 8.30-12, 4-7.

CRIMINOLOGICAL MUSEUM
Forughi Street, Teheran
History of crime in Iran and methods of combatting it. Weapons. Uniforms. Documents.
Weekdays: 8.30-12, 4-7.

GOLESTAN PALACE
Maidan Ark, Teheran
Court souvenirs. Gifts from visiting monarchs, displayed in a rich royal dwellings, a 19th century period house. Porcelain. Miniatures. Ivories. Enamelled tableware. The Peacock Throne.
Weekdays: 8.30-12, 4-6. Closed F.

MILITARY ACADEMY MUSEUM
Teheran
Weapons and armaments.
Weekdays: 8.30-12, 4-7.

MUSEUM OF DECORATIVE ARTS
227 Amir Kabir Avenue, Teheran
Decorative arts, principally of late 18th and 19th centuries, including weapons, rugs, other textiles, jewellery, woodwork, metal work, costumes, calligraphy.
Weekdays: 8-12, 4-7; F. 8-12. Closed Tu.

MUSEUM OF ETHNOLOGY
Maidan Ark, (Golestan Palace), Teheran
Ethnography of Iran, illustrating the costumes, crafts and customs of people in various parts of the country, using paintings, miniature dioramas and, especially, life-size wax manikins of ethnic types in costume, in natural settings of village, town or farm.
Weekdays: 8.30-12, 4-6. Closed F.

NATIONAL ARTS MUSEUM
Maldan Baharestan, Kamalolmolk Street, Teheran
Cabinet-work. Wood carving. Inlay. Ivories. Metalwork. Pottery. Paintings, especially Persian miniatures of the 16th and 17th centuries.
Weekdays: 8.30-12.30, 3-6; F. 8-1. Closed Th.

PAHLAVI MUSEUM
Marble Palace, Teheran
21 period rooms. Architecture, mirror-decoration, inlaid-work and decorations of Reza Shah the Great era.
Weekdays: 8.30-12, 4-7.

SHAHYAD MUSEUM
Maidan Shahyad, Eisenhower Avenue, Teheran
History, ethnography.
Weekdays: 9-12, 4-7; F. 9-1. Closed Sa.

TREASURY OF THE CROWN JEWELS
Bank Markazi Iran, Ferdowsi Avenue, Teheran
The Crown Jewels of Iran, including the Nadir Throne (late 18th century, containing 26,733 gems) and the Kiani Crown (early 19th century, set with pearls and other gems). Jewellery; flasks and decanters; candlesticks; objets d'art; swords; robes; gold coins and commemorative medals; foreign insignias and decorations; crowns and tiaras. The outstanding item is the Darya-i-Nur or Sea of Light diamond, the largest pink diamond in the world, weighing 182 carats.
Mid. May-mid. Sept., 4.30-7. Mid. Sept.-mid. May 3.30-6. Closed F. and holidays. Hours subject to change without prior notice.

Iraq

A country which is in a position to establish a museum in the middle of the ruins of Babylon would appear to have certain natural advantages, and archaeology is certainly Iraq's strongest card in the museum game. The modern age does, even so, receive a good deal of attention, with collections of, for example, the personal possessions of Faisal I and Faisal II, and documents and mementoes of the Al-Baath Socialist party. But, oddly, there is nothing about petroleum, without which Iraq would have found some difficulty in balancing the national budget for some time past.

AQER QUF

LOCAL MUSEUM
Aqer Quf
Objects from Aqer Quf excavations. The two rooms of the museum are the original and actual rooms of part of the big Temple of the Heaven god, Enlil. Pottery jars, bricks and stone door sockets with cuneiform inscriptions.
Daily except Th. and public holidays. Apr.-Sept. 8.30-12.30, Oct.-Mar. 9.30-1.30.

ARBIL

ARBIL MUSEUM
Arbil
Objects from Iraqi history up to the Arabic-Islamic period.
Daily ex. Th. and public holidays: Apr.-Sept. 8.30-12.30, Oct.-Mar., 9.30-1.30.

BAB-AL-SHARQUI

PICTURE GALLERY
Bab-al-Sharqui
Paintings mainly by Iraqi artists.
Daily except Th. and public holidays. Apr.-Sept. 8.30-12.30, Oct.-Mar. 9.30-1.30.

MEMORIAL MUSEUM OF HIS MAJESTY THE LATE KING OF IRAQ, FAISAL I
Bab-al-Sharqui
Personal effects of His Majesty, the late King Faisal I are exhibited in a special room attached to the Museum of Ethnography as well as pictures showing the various periods in His Majesty's life.
Daily except Th. and public holidays. Apr.-Sept. 8.30-12.30. Oct.-Mar. 9.30-1.30.

BABYLON

LOCAL MUSEUM
Babylon
Built in the centre of the ruins of Babylon, the museum houses models, pictures and paintings of the main remains to be found in the city, together with antiquities.
Daily except Th. and public holidays. Apr.-Sept. 8.30-12.30, Oct.-Mar. 9.30-1.30.

BAGHDAD

THE ABBASID PALACE MUSEUM
Baghdad
Exhibited in the rooms of this Palace are features of Islamic architecture, such as mural ornaments in gypsum and bricks; a group of Mihrabs (Niches) removed from ancient mosques; glazed tiles and models of ancient Islamic buildings, with plans and photographs.
Daily except Th. and public holidays. Apr.-Sept. 8.30-12.30, Oct.-Mar. 9.30-1.30.

AL-BAATH SOCIALIST PARTY MUSEUM
c/o Directorate General of Antiquities, Baghdad
History of the Al-Baath Socialist party. Documents, photographs.
Daily 9-5.

AL-MADA'IN MUSEUM
al-Mada'in, Baghdad
Pottery, oil lamps and coins from Parthian, Selucid Sassanian periods, from excavations in the area.
Daily ex. Th. and public holidays. Apr.-Sept., 8.30-12.30. Oct.-Mar., 9.30-1.30.

AL-MUSTANSIRIYIA SCHOOL MUSEUM
nr. al-Shuhada' bridge, Baghdad
Early Islamic college, restored to its original condition. Mosque. Study rooms. Dining rooms. Bookstore. Hospital. Pharmacy. Clock. Bathroom. Garden. Arabic calligraphy and the stages of its development. Historical cartography.
Daily ex. Th. and public holidays. Apr.-Sept. 8.30-12.30. Oct.-Mar. 9.30-1.30.

THE ARAB MUSEUM
Banks Street, Baghdad
Islamic antiquities. Collection of decorated gypsum plaques from Samarra. Pottery and other objects from Wasit and Samarra. Copper vessels. Wooden sarcophagus with inscriptions and decorations. Doors ornamented and inlaid with gold and shell. Collection of Korans, manuscripts.
Daily except Th. and public holidays. Apr.-Sept. 8.30-12.30, Oct.-Mar. 9.30-1.30.

BAGHDAD GOVERNORATE MUSEUM OF COSTUMES AND ETHNOGRAPHY
Al-Rashid Street, Baghdad
Ethnography of Iraq. Weaving and knitting from the regions. Styles of houses. Architecture. Sumerian, Babylonian, Akkadian, Assyrian, Hatrene and Islamic costumes.
Daily ex. Th. and public holidays. Apr.-Sept. 8.30-12.30. Oct.-Mar. 9.30-1.30.

BAGHDADI MUSEUM
Maamoon Street, Baghdad
Life-sized statues of tradesmen and workers, e.g. the weaver, the water-carrier, the woodcarver, the saddle-maker, with costumes and authentic backgrounds. Paintings of Iraqi street scenes. Books dealing with ancient and modern Baghdad.
Apr.-Aug., daily 9-8. Sept.-Mar., daily 9-6.

THE IRAQ MUSEUM
Karkh, Museum Square, Baghdad
Prehistory. Coins. Collections on the Sumerian, Akkadian and Old Babylonian, Assyrian and Neo Babylonian, Parthian (Hatra) Roman and Islamic periods.
Daily 9-5.

IRAQI MILITARY MUSEUM
Bab al Muatham, Baghdad
Arms, ammunition and various Army sections' uniforms, from the period of the Abbasid rule to the present day. Gifts from different armies to the Iraqi Army and rulers of Iraq, including three large cannon and other arms from the Ottoman rule.
Daily ex. Sa. 8.30-12.30.

IRAQ NATURAL HISTORY MUSEUM
Waziriya, Baghdad
Zoology. Botany. Geology.
Daily ex. Th. and public holidays, Apr.-Sept. 8.30-12.30, Oct.-Mar. 9.30-1.30.

MUSEUM OF ARAB ANTIQUITIES
Samawal Street, Baghdad
Restored building of 14th century A.D. Arab antiquities, illustrating different Islamic cultural periods in Iraq. Exhibits mainly from Wasit, Samaria and Kufa.
Daily ex. Th. and public holidays. Apr.-Sept. 8.30-12.30. Oct.-Mar. 9.30-1.30.

MUSEUM OF ARMS
Shaikh Omar District, Baghdad
Various types of medieval and post-medieval arms: swords, daggers, rifles, cannons, iron breastplates and helmets. Models of ancient Baghdad and Talisman Gate with plans and photographs.
Daily except Th. and public holidays. Apr.-Sept. 8.30-12.30, Oct.-Mar. 9.30-1.30.

MUSEUM OF ETHNOGRAPHY
Bab-al-Shargi, Baghdad
Costumes and other ethnographical items dating from the early twentieth century to the present time. Royal relics of King Faisal I. Picture gallery.
Daily except Th. and public holidays. Apr. - Sept. 8.30-12.30, Oct.-Mar. 9.30-1.30.

NATIONAL MUSEUM OF MODERN ART
Kifah Street, Baghdad
Modern art collections, from Iraq and foreign countries.
Daily ex. Th. and public holidays, Apr.-Sept. 8.30-12.30. Oct.-Mar. 9.30-1.30.

ERBIL

ERBIL MUSEUM
Erbil
Prehistory and history up to the Islamic periods. Exhibits are mostly from the surrounding district. Bronzes.
Daily ex. Th. and public holidays. Apr.-Sept. 8.30-12.30. Oct.-Mar. 9.30-1.30.

KIRKUK

KIRKUK MUSEUM
Kirkuk
Prehistoric stone objects. Antiquities from the ancient Sumerian, neo-Sumerian, ancient Babylon, Assyrian, Hatrene and Islamic periods.
Daily ex. Th. and public holidays. Apr.-Sept., 8.30-12.30. Oct.-Mar. 9.30-1.30.

MOSUL

BAB NERGAL MUSEUM
Mosul
Gypsum casts of royal Assyrian sculptures. Material on the reigns of the Royal Assyrian kings.
Daily 9-5.

LOCAL MUSEUM
Dawassa, Mosul
Assyrian antiquities of 9th and 8th centuries B.C., found at Nimrud. Objects from the ruins of Hatra dating back to 2nd century B.C. and 2nd century A.D. Agricultural tools and pottery vessels from the 5th and 4th millennia B.C. Photographs of excavated buildings at Tepe Gawra. Maps of the Assyrian Empire, Nimrud and Hatra. Prehistoric and Islamic exhibits.
Daily except Th. and public holidays. Apr.-Sept. 8.30-12.30, Oct.-Mar. 9.30-1.30.

NASIRRIYA

AL-NASIRRIYA MUSEUM
Nasirriya
Sumerian and other archaeological objects.
Daily ex. Th. and public holidays. Apr.-Sept. 8.30-12.30. Oct.-Mar. 9.30-1.30.

SAMARRA

LOCAL MUSEUM
Samarra
Housed in an old gate of the modern city, the museum contains samples of material excavated from the ruins of Samarra.
Daily except Th. and public holidays. Apr.-Sept. 8.30-12.30, Oct.-Mar. 9.30-1.30.

SULAIMANIYA

AL-SULAIMANIYA MUSEUM
Sulaimaniya
Prehistory. Sumerian antiquities. Exhibits from Babylon. Islamic material, including Humuraby stelae.
Daily 8.30-1.30.

Ireland

Ireland is not short of folk-heroes, and they are adequately, possibly more than adequately, represented in the Republic's museums. One comes across, for instance, the Parnell museums, the cottage in which the rebels Michael Dwyer and Samuel MacAllister were trapped in 1799, Kilmainham Jail, in which so many of Ireland's leaders were at one time incarcerated and which is now a museum of Irish rebellions and revolutions. The literary heroes are reasonably well looked after, with museums to both James Joyce and W. B. Yeats; and the famous tenor, Count John McCormack, also receives proper attention.

Porter, the national drink, is well documented in the excellent new Guinness Museum, decently situated within the precincts of the brewery, but no other industry has a museum to itself, not even such adequate and professional treatment within a general museum. South of the border, there is no equivalent of the splendid industrial and transport collections at the Royal Ulster Museum in Belfast. Nor, strangely enough, is there a museum devoted to either agriculture or to the agriculture-based industries, which have always been of outstanding importance to Ireland. Here, too, one might reasonably expect to find a really imaginative and comprehensive Museum of the Potato, but there is nothing. Nor, although Ireland is surrounded by sea and dependent on ports and shipping, is there a Maritime Museum. A Museum of Emigration would also seem called for. There is, however, an interesting open-air folk museum, or folk-park as the Irish prefer to call it, at Bunratty, with peasant cottages brought from various parts of the region.

A number of eighteenth- and nineteenth-century country houses open to the public have fine collections of Irish and English furniture and silver, and one still retains, complete with equipment, the Victorian kitchen and laundry.

Irish monasteries and churches, although numerous and, in a few cases, rich and old established, are not distinguished by the works of art in their possession, although some of the finest early treasures of Christian art are preserved in the national museums and libraries. The ecclesiastical museum most worth a visit is at the great seminary of Maynooth, where, in addition to some good items of the conventional kind, there are the scientific relics of the inventive Victorian priest, Rev. Dr. Nicholas Callan, including his pioneering 1000-volt battery.

ADARE

ADARE MANOR
Adare, County Limerick
House (1720-30, remodelled 1830s). Flemish cupboards, book-presses. 18th century lacquered furniture. Early Vic-

torian furniture. Quin family portraits. Dutch, Flemish, German paintings. Racing pictures.
May-Sept., M.-F. 10-5.30; Su. 2-5.30.

ASHFORD

MOUNT USHER MUSEUM
Ashford, County Wicklow
House (1860). Historic carriages made by coachbuilders in Dublin, Gorey, Newtownards and London.
May-Sept. M.-Sa. 10-6; Su. 2.30-5.30. Oct.-Apr., M.-Sa. 10-5.

ATHLONE

OLD ATHLONE SOCIETY MUSEUM
Adamson Castle, Athlone, County Westmeath
History and antiquities of Athlone. Domestic equipment. Farm tools. Sections devoted to famous local people, including Count John McCormack.
June-Sept. 2.30-5.30, 7.30-8.30.

AVONDALE

PARNELL MUSEUM
Avondale, County Wicklow
Photographs, documents, personal items and furniture relating to Parnell.
By appointment (with Forestry Division, 22 Upper Merrion Street, Dublin 2).

BANTRY

BANTRY HOUSE
Bantry, County Cork
18th century house, remodelled in 19th century. 17th-19th century European furnishings, including Gobelins, Flemish and Aubusson tapestries. Savonnerie and Aubusson carpets. 18th century French and English furniture. Venetian glass. Italian paintings.
Apr. 1 - Oct. 15, M.-F. 10-12.30, 2-6; Su. 2.30-6.

BUNRATTY

BUNRATTY CASTLE AND FOLK PARK
Bunratty Castle, Bunratty, County Clare
15th century, the Castle contains a collection of 14th-17th century furniture and furnishings. The adjoining Folk Park has a number of farm and fishermen's houses of different regional types, with furnishings and agricultural tools.
Daily 9.30-5.30.

CASTLEPOLLARD

TULLYNALLY CASTLE
Castlepollard, County Westmeath
16th century castle, remodelled in 18th and 19th centuries. Contains first central heating system (1766) to be installed in private house in Great Britain or Ireland. 18th-19th century furnishings, including completely equipped Victorian laundries, kitchens.
May-Sept., Sa., Su., public holidays 2-6.

CASTLEREA

CLONALIS HOUSE
Castlerea, County Roscommon
Mid 19th century house, home of O'Conor Don, descendant of last High Kings of Ireland. Collections illustrating family history. Library, with early Irish manuscripts. 18th-19th century furniture. Victorian costumes.
May-June, Sa., Su., M. 2-6. July-Aug., Th.-M. 2-6. Sept. 1-15, Sa.-M. 2-6.

CELBRIDGE

CASTLETOWN HOUSE
Celbridge, Co. Kildare, Ireland
Built 1722. Venetian chandeliers. Print Room. Irish 18th century furniture and pictures.
Apr.-Sept. W.-M. 2-6.

CELBRIDGE MOTOR MUSEUM
Temple Mills House, Celbridge, County Kildare
Vintage motor-cars and motor-cycles. Steam engine models.
By appointment.

CLONFERT

CLONFERT MUSEUM
nr. Cathedral, Clonfert, County Galway
In restored gate tower of the medieval walled town of Loughrea. 12th-17th century carved wooden figures from Irish churches. Neolithic axes. Coins. Ecclesiological material associated with Diocese of Clonfert.
By appointment.

CORK

CORK PUBLIC MUSEUM
Fitzgerald Park, Cork
Neolithic, Bronze Age and medieval archaeology. History of Cork City since 1782. 1916-21 historical collection, including material relating to Terence McSweeney and Thomas McCurtain. Coins and trade tokens. Albino birds.
May-Sept. M.-F. 11-1, 2.15-6. Oct.-Apr. M.-F. 11-1, 2.15-5. Sa. and Su. all year 11.30-1.

CURRAGH CAMP

CURRAGH CAMP MILITARY MUSEUM
Curragh Camp, County Kildare
Mainly weapons, but some documents.
By appointment.

DERRYNAMUCK

DWYER-MACALLISTER COTTAGE
Derrynamuck, County Wicklow
Cottage in which the rebels, Michael Dwyer and Samuel MacAllister, were trapped in 1799. Period furniture and domestic utensils.
Key on request from adjoining farm.

DUBLIN

DUBLIN CIVIC MUSEUM
City Assembly House, South William Street, Dublin, County Dublin
History of Dublin. Paintings, prints, maps, coins, newspapers.
Daily 10-6; Su. 11-2. Closed M.

EGESTORFF COLLECTION
25 Wellington Place, Dublin 4, County Dublin
History of science and technology, including mathematical and astronomical instruments of the 18th and 19th centuries, several signed by the well-known Dublin and London makers. Collections of lathes and vintage motor cars.
1st W. of each month, 7-9 p.m. and by appointment.

GUINNESS MUSEUM
Arthur Guinness Son & Co. (Dublin) Ltd., St. James's Gate, Dublin 8
Brewing equipment and machinery. Coopers' tools. Transport used in the industry. Advertising material. Brewing in Ireland.
Sept.-May, M.-F. 11-12.45, 2-4.15. June-Aug. M.-F. 11-4.15.

KILMAINHAM JAIL MUSEUM
Kilmainham, Dublin
In former jail where William Smith O'Brien and Charles Stewart Parnell were imprisoned. Documents, guns, uniforms used in connection with rebellions and revolutions in Ireland in 19th and 20th centuries. Museum commemorates those shot in the courtyard of the jail in 1916.
Su. 3-5. At other times parties should contact Kilmainham Jail Restoration Society.

MUNICIPAL GALLERY OF MODERN ART
Parnell Square North, Dublin, County Dublin
Sir Hugh Lane collection. European painting and sculpture, especially Corot, Rodin, Epstein. Sculptures by Andrew O'Connor.
Tu.-Sa. 10-6; Su. 11-2. Closed M.

NATIONAL GALLERY OF IRELAND
Merrion Square West, Dublin 2, County Dublin
Paintings of the Italian, Dutch, Flemish, French, Spanish and English Schools. Works by Irish painters, including J. W. Yeats. 18th-20th century portraits.
Weekdays 10-6; Th. also until 9; Su. 2-5.

NATIONAL MUSEUM OF IRELAND
Kildare Street and Merrion Street, Dublin 2, County Dublin
Irish antiquities, from Stone Age to medieval times. Gold ornamanets. Tara Brooch. Adagh Chalice. Cross of Cong. Shrines. Irish industry and handicrafts. History, including notable 1916-21 section. Botany and vegetable products. Zoology.
Tu.-Sa. 10-5; Su. 2-5. Closed M., Good Friday and Christmas Day.

STATE APARTMENTS
Dublin Castle, Dublin, County Dublin
Mainly 18th century buildings. 18th-19th century furnishings. 18th century plaster-work. Heraldry collection.
M.-F. 10-12.15, 2-5; Sa., Su. 2-5.

EDGEWORTHSTOWN

EDGEWORTH SOCIETY MUSEUM
Old School House, Edgeworthstown, County Longford
Material relating to Maria Edgeworth. First editions. Letters.
Daily 10-6.

ENNISCORTHY

CASTLE MUSEUM
Enniscorthy, County Wexford
Local history, especially of Wexford and Enniscorthy. Ecclesiastical room. Rooms commemorating the Rebellions of 1798 and 1916. Regional crafts. Rush lights. Ships' figureheads.
May-Sept. 10-9. Oct.-Apr. 2.30-5.30.

GLANMIRE

RIVERSTOWN HOUSE
Glanmire, County Cork
Rebuilt by Bishop of Cork, 1734. Period furnishings. Plasterwork by Francini brothers.
May-Sept., M.-F. 2-6.

GLENCOLUMBKILLE

AN CLACHAN
Glencolumbkille, County Donegal
Open air museum. 3 reconstructed cottages (c.1700). Household and farm equipment. Querns. Spinning wheels. Milking utensils.
May-Sept. 10-9.

GORT

LOUGH CUTRA CASTLE
Gort, County Galway
Castle, designed by John Nash (1811). 17th-19th century furnishings.
Easter-Sept., Su., M. 2-5.30. Other times by appointment.

THOOR BALLYLEE
Gort, County Galway
16th century tower house, summer home of the poet, W. B. Yeats, 1917-29. Yeats' furnishings, first editions.
Apr.-June, Sept.-Oct., daily 10-6. July-Aug., daily 10-7.

KILKENNY

ROTHE HOUSE MUSEUM
Parliament Street, Kilkenny, County Kilkenny
In restored 17th century merchant's house. Local archaeology and history. 17th-19th century furniture. Pewter. Costumes. Folk museum of the district.
May-Sept. 10.30-12.30, 3-5. Oct.-Apr. Tu., F., Sa., Su., 3-5.

KILLARNEY

MUCKROSS HOUSE
near Killarney, County Kerry
In mid.-19th century mansion. Period rooms. Cultural history of County Kerry. Prints and maps of Killarney. Natural history. Geology. Botany. Zoology. Irish crafts and workshops.
Easter- June 30, Sept.-Oct., daily 10-7. July-Aug., daily 9-9.

KINSALE

KINSALE REGIONAL MUSEUM
Old Town Hall, Kinsale, County Cork
Local history. Town charters. Municipal records from 1652. Scale model of HMS 'Kinsale' (1700). Fire engine (1852). Ship-smith's forge. Cooper's tools.
Weekdays 11-1. Su. 3-5.30.

LIMERICK

LIMERICK CITY MUSEUM
Perry Square, Limerick, County Limerick
Stone and Bronze Age antiquities from Lough Gur, Bruff and Kildare. Gold ornaments. Medieval bronze, iron and bone items. Anglo-Saxon coins and silver ingots. Bell of Cashel (9th century). Singland bell (10th century). 16th-19th century maps of Limerick. Natural history.
M.-F. 10-1, 2.30-7. Sa. 10-1.

LISSADELL

LISSADELL HOUSE
Lissadell, County Sligo
House (1830-36), home of the Gore-Booth family. 18th-19th century furnishings. Bedroom where W. B. Yeats slept when he visited Lissadell.
May-Sept., M.-Sa. 2.30-5.30.

LOUGHREA

CLONFERT DIOCESAN MUSEUM
beside Cathedral, Loughrea, County Galway
Housed in medieval tower which formed part of the old town wall. Medieval statuary, including wooden statues from abroad.
On request.

MALLOW

MALLOW CASTLE MUSEUM
Mallow, County Cork
Items connected with the Jephson family. Local history. Armour.
Weekdays 12-6; Su. 2-5.

MAYNOOTH

CARTON
Maynooth, County Kildare
House (1739-47, with early 19th century additions). Period furnishings. Ceilings by Francini brothers. 17th-19th century paintings. Mid 18th century Chinese wallpaper.
Easter-Sept., Sa., Su., public holidays 2-6.

MUSEUM OF ECCLESIOLOGY AND PHYSICS
St. Patrick's College, Maynooth, County Kildare
Early electrical machines associated with Rev. Dr. Nicholas Callan (d.1864), including his 577 cell cast-iron battery, capable of delivering 1000 volts. Chalices, vestments, rosaries, crosses of the 17th-early 20th centuries. Papal medals from the 16th century onwards.
Mid. June-mid. Sept. M.-F. 10-1, 2-5. Sa., Su. 2-6.

MOUNTRATH

ROUNDWOOD
Mountrath, Co. Leix
Display of Irish dolls' houses.
Apr.-Sept., W., Sa., Su. and Bank Holiday M. 2-6.

MULLINGAR

MUSEUM OF THE 4TH ARTILLERY REGIMENT
Columb Barracks, Mullingar, County Westmeath
History of the regiment since 1922. Irish military relics from the 17th century onwards, including mementoes of the Irish involvement with the U.N. peace-keeping force. Part of Alcock and Browne's transatlantic plane, 1919.
Daily 10-6.

NEWGRANGE

NEWGRANGE TOURIST OFFICE
Newgrange, County Meath
Material connected with the Tumulus of Newgrange, Ireland's best-known prehistoric monument. Casts of prehistoric engraved stones. Details of passage-graves. Photographs of local antinquities.
May-Oct. 10-7. Nov.-Apr. 10-6.

QUIN

KNAPPOGUE CASTLE
Quin, County Clare
15th century castle, with 19th century additions. 17th-19th century furnishings. Smithy and other workshops.
Daily 10-5.

ROSMUCK

PEARSE'S COTTAGE
Rosmuck, County Galway
Cottage used by Padraig Pearse (1879-1916) as his summer residence.
May-Sept. Daily 9.30-5.30. At other times on request.

ROSSNOWLAGH

MUSEUM OF THE COUNTY DONEGAL HISTORICAL SOCIETY
Franciscan Friary, Rossnowlagh, County Donegal
Local history, especially of the 18th century and 1916-21. Archaeology. Firearms. Uniforms. Prison diaries.
Daily 9-9.

SANDYCOVE

JAMES JOYCE MUSEUM
Sandycove, County Dublin
Personal mementoes of the writer, James Joyce, including editions of his books, photographs, manuscripts and his death mask. Collections are housed in a tower, (1804), which is the setting for the opening scene of 'Ulysses'.
May-Sept., Weekdays 10-1, 2.15-5.15; Su. 2.30-6.

SLIGO

COUNTY SLIGO MUSEUM
Stephen Street, Sligo, County Sligo
Local archaeology and history. Ethnography. Coins. Paintings by Jack B. Yeats and George Russell. W. B. Yeats room, commemorating Yeats and his contemporaries in the Irish Literary Renaissance. Collection of material dealing with the War of Independence.
Daily 10-5.

STRADBALLY

STRADBALLY STEAM MUSEUM
Stradbally, County Laois
Steam engines and steam engine models. Many of the full-sized items are of Irish manufacture, including a narrow gauge locomotive (1855), built for a garden railway. Early steam-powered farm implements. Steam rollers.
May-Sept. 2-8. Oct.-Apr. 2-5.

THOOR BALLYLEE

YEATS MUSEUM
Thoor Ballylee, County Galway
A 16th century four-storey tower. Together with the adjoining cottage, it was repaired and lived in by the poet, W. B. Yeats, in the 1920s. Restored in 1965 as a Yeats' museum and now contains a collection of first editions of his works.
May-mid. Oct. daily 9.30-5.30.

TUAM

MILL MUSEUM
Shop Street, Tuam, County Galway
300-year-old corn mill with exhibits illustrating the entire oatmeal milling operation. Various aspects of milling, and the importance of the industry through the ages. The mechanics of milling.
M.-Sa. 10.30-12.30, 3-6; Su. 3-6.

WATERFORD

REGINALD'S TOWER MUSEUM
The Quay, Waterford, County Waterford
13th century tower, used at different times as a mint and a prison. Local history and archaeology. Waterford Regalia.
May-Sept. M.-Sa. 9-9: Su. 2-8. Oct.-Apr. M.-F. 9-5.30. Closed Sa. and Su.

WESTPORT

WESTPORT HOUSE
Westport, Co. Mayo
House (1730, with later additions). Furniture. Waterford glass. Irish silver.
Apr.-mid. Oct., Daily 2-6 (early July-early Sept. 10.30-6.30).

WEXFORD

MARITIME MUSEUM
aboard the lightship 'Guillemot', Wexford Harbour, Wexford, County Wexford
Maritime history of Wexford. 19th century logbooks of Wexford schooners. Documents relating to vessels trading between Wexford and St. John, New Brunswick. Ships' models.
Daily 10.30-9.

YOUGHAL

CLOCK TOWER MUSEUM
Main Street, Youghal, County Cork
History and archaeology of the Youghal area. Town charters. Silverware. Local crafts and industries.
May-Sept. 10-8.

Israel

The museum authorities in Israel could hardly complain that they are short of raw material. The area's long period of civilisation, its many cultures, and its repeated political upheavals have provided a richer variety of museums than one can find anywhere close in the Middle East. The Romans, the Crusaders and the Israelites of the Old Testament rub shoulders with nineteenth-century Turks and the members of Haganah. One museum, of Arab and Druze folklore, is in an old Turkish bath-house and another contains the prison cell once occupied by Ze'ev Jabotensky, who organised the Jewish resistance movement between the two World Wars. Considerable use is made of synagogues and Christian churches no longer needed for their original purpose but often interesting and attractive settings for museums of art and archaeology.

While the emphasis is certainly on Jewish history and culture, considerable pains have been taken to reflect the cultures of the different races which have lived at one time and another in the territory which now forms the state of Israel. The art and ethnography of the Muslim peoples form an important part of the national museum collections and the important maritime exhibits, showing the development of navigation in the Middle East, also pay proper attention to the Arab contribution.

Many of the local museums in Israel are simple in both form and concept, often being attached to kibbutzim, with the aim both of documenting the story of the settlement and of placing it within its historical context. That context is, of course, both national and international and, in the city and the kibbutz museums, the European persecution and suffering of the Jews is fully remembered. So, too, is the achievement of the outstanding Zionists, such as Chaim Weizmann, who helped to establish the Jewish National Home in Israel and to develop its economy and technology on a modern basis.

The most attractively developed Israeli museum is probably at Haifa, devoted to the somewhat unpromising subject of the history of grain-handling in Israel and situated in the modern office block of a huge grain-storage and milling complex. The museum which most effectively and most sympathetically links the present-day Israelis to their Old Testament forebears is the National Museum of Taxation.

ABU-GHOSH

LOCAL MUSEUM
Lazarite Monastery, Church of the Resurrection, Abu-Ghosh
Religious art.
On request.

AKKO (ACRE)

AKKO MUNICIPAL MUSEUM
Akko, Old City
Housed in old Turkish bath-house. Collections of local antiquities. Medieval and modern Arab and Druze folklore. Oriental jewellery. Crusader excavations. Ethnography. Ceramics. Coins. Domestic articles. Weapons.
M.-Sa. 10-1, 2-5; Su. 2-5.

MUSEUM HAGEVURA
Akko Citadel, Akko
Resistance museum, housed in former mental hospital. Contains cell occupied by Ze'ev Jabotinsky, who organised the Jewish Resistance Movement between the two World Wars.
M.-Sa. 10-1, 2-5; Su. 2-5.

ASHDOT YA'AKOV

MUSEUM OF ART
Kibbutz, Ashdot Ya'akov
Art collections.
M.-F. 10-1, 2-5; Su. 2-5.

ASHKELON

LOCAL MUSEUM
Ashkelon
Roman archaeological remains.
On request.

AVEDAT

LOCAL MUSEUM
Avedat
Nabataean and Byzantine exhibits.
On request.

AVIHAIL

ARMY MUSEUM
Avihail, Nathanya
Military history.
M.-F. 10-1, 2-5; Su. 2-5.

AYELET HASHAHAR

HAZOR MUSEUM
Ayelet Hashahar, Upper Galilee
Local history. Finds from excavations in the area.
On request.

BAR'AM

LOCAL MUSEUM
Bar'am
Ancient synagogue.
On request.

BAT-YAM

BAT-YAM MUSEUM
Ramat Joseph, Hadadi Street, Bat-Yam
Art collections.
M.-F. 10-1, 2-5; Su. 2-5.

BEERSHEBA

NEGEV MUSEUM
Beersheba
Exhibits from regional excavations, mainly from the Chalcolithic, Israelite, Roman and Byzantine periods. Bedouin folklore. Modern Israeli art.
Daily ex. Sa. 10-1, 2-5; Sa. 10-1.

BEIT ALPHA

LOCAL MUSEUM
Beit Alpha
Ancient synagogue.
On request.

BEIT SHEARIM

LOCAL MUSEUM
Beit Shearim
Ancient synagogue and necropolis.
On request.

BETH SHE'AN

BETH SHE'AN MUSEUM
Beth She'an
Prehistoric flints, pottery, bronzes. Roman and Byzantine mosaics. Remains of Roman theatre, Canaanite and Israelite culture. Scythopolis and Decapolos coins.
Su.-F. 10-1, 2-5; Sa. 10-1.

CAESAREA

LOCAL MUSEUM
Caesarea
Relics from the Roman and Crusader periods.
On request.

DAN

USSISHKIN HOUSE
Institute for Natural History of Huleh Valley, Dan, Kibbutz, Upper Galilee
Natural history. Archaeology. Local history. Geology.
On request.

DEGANIA

A. D. GORDON MUSEUM
Kibbutz Degania, nr. Tiberias
Natural history collections, especially of Israel.
Su.-F. 10-1, 2-5; Sa. 10-1.

EILAT

RED SEA MARITIME MUSEUM
P.O. Box 25, Eilat
Marine specimens. Flora and fauna of the sea.
Su.-F. 10-1, 2-5; Sa. 10-1.

MUSEUM OF MODERN ART
Eilat
Modern art.
Su.-F. 10-1, 2-5; Sa. 10-1.

EIN-HAROD

MUSEUM OF ART
Kibbutz, Ein-Harod, Gilboa District
Art collections. Paintings and sculptures of Israelis from Europe and Israel. Folklore.
Su.-F. 10-1, 2-5; Sa. 10-1.

BETH STURMAN MUSEUM AND INSTITUTE FOR NATURE, HISTORY AND ECONOMICS OF GILBOA DISTRICT
Ein-Harod, Kibbutz, Gilboa District
Archaeology. History. Economy. Natural history. Defence. Stuffed birds and animals.
Su.-F. 10-1, 2-5; Sa. 10-1.

GVULOT

LOCAL MUSEUM
Gvulot, Neger
Prehistoric flints. Objects of the Israelite period.
On request.

HAIFA

DAGON COLLECTION
Dagon Silos, Plumer Square, Haifa
The history of grain handling in Israel. Cereals. Reconstructed silo from the times of the Kings of Judah.
By appointment: guided tours, Su.-Th. at 10.30 a.m.

ETHNOLOGICAL MUSEUM AND FOLKLORE ARCHIVES
19 Arlosoroff Street, Haifa
Ethnographical material from all countries, with special emphasis on Israel. Collection of folk tales from Israel. Religious objects. Ceramics. Jewellery. Domestic equipment.
Daily 10-1, 4-7.

IMMIGRATION AND MARINE MUSEUM
204 Allenby Road, Haifa
Development of navigation in the Middle East from prehistoric times. Ship models. Carved figures. Maps, globes, prints. Anchors, chains, sextants.
Daily 10-1, 4-7.

MUSEUM OF ANCIENT ART
Municipality Building, Haifa
Greek and Roman sculpture, terracottas. Archaeological finds from Shikmona (Haifa) from the Bronze Age to the Byzantine period. Biblical terracottas; Greek coins from Palestine; Coptic textiles. Collections up to 6th century A.D.
M.-Th. 10-1, 4-7; F.-Sa. 10-1. Closed Su.

MUSEUM OF MODERN ART
Townhall, 4 Bialik Street, Haifa
Israeli and world contemporary art, prints, art posters, arts and crafts. 19th-20th century prints.
M.-Th. 10-1, 4-7; F.-Sa. 10-1. Closed Su.

MUSEUM OF NATURAL HISTORY AND PREHISTORY
124 Hatishbi Street, Haifa
Prehistory. Natural history. Zoology.
Daily 10-1, 4-7.

MUSIC MUSEUM
23 Arlosoroff Street, Haifa
Musical instruments, especially from Israel.
Daily 10-1, 4-7.

NATIONAL MARITIME MUSEUM
2 Hanamal Street, Haifa
Large collection of ship models illustrating 5,000 years of navigation and shipbuilding. Old maps. Undersea archaeology. Ancient coins connected with seafaring. Marine ethnology.
Daily 10-1, 4-7.

TIKOTIN MUSEUM OF JAPANESE ART
89 Hanassi Avenue, Haifa
Paintings, prints, drawings. Textiles. Netsuke. Lacquer work. Ceramics. Metalwork. Woodblock prints of old masters. Japanese crafts, including kimonos.
Daily 10-1, 4-7.

HANITA

LOCAL MUSEUM
Hanita
Byzantine church, with collection of ecclesiastical art.
On request.

HAZOR

LOCAL MUSEUM
Hazor
Canaanite and Israelite material.
On request.

HAZOREA

WILFRID ISRAEL HOUSE FOR ORIENTAL ART AND STUDIES
Kibbutz, Hazorea
Oriental art. Finds from local excavations.
On request.

HERZLIYA

ART MUSEUM
15 Bar Ilan Street, Herzliya
Paintings. Sculpture.
Su.-F. 10-1, 2-5; Sa. 10-1.

JERUSALEM

ALEXANDER MONASTERY MUSEUM
Russian Orthodox Mission, Muristan, Jerusalem
Roman antiquities.
On request.

BEIT HA'OMANIM
(Jerusalem Artists' House), 12 Shmuel Hanagid Street, Jerusalem
Works by Jerusalem artists.
Su.-F. 10-1, 2-5; Sa. 10-1.

BEZALEL NATIONAL ART MUSEUM
P.O. Box 1299, The Israel Museum, Jerusalem
Collection of Jewish ceremonial art, ethnographical objects, paintings, sculptures, drawings, prints.
Daily ex. F. and Sa. afternoons, 10-6.

BILLY ROSE ART GARDEN
The Israel Museum, Jerusalem
Part of Israel Museum. Modern European and Israeli sculpture. Reuven Lipchitz collection of Jacques Lipchitz's bronze sketches.
Daily 10-6; F., S. 10-2.

BRONFMAN BIBLICAL AND ARCHAEOLOGICAL MUSEUM
Israel Museum, Jerusalem
Archaeology of Israel from earliest times to Islamic and Crusader periods. Cultures of Iran, Italy.
Su., M., W., Th. 10-6; Tu. 10-10; F., Sa. 10-2.

COLLECTION OF THE PONTIFICAL BIBLICAL INSTITUTE
3 Paul E. Botta Street, Jerusalem
Archaeology.
By arrangement.

DOMINUS FLEVIT MUSEUM
Mount of Olives, Jerusalem
Jewish tombs. Byzantine church.
On request.

HAREM ESH SHERIF MUSEUM
Dome of the Rock, El Aqsa Mosque, Jerusalem
Local history. Turkish collection.
On request.

HERZL MUSEUM
Har Herzl, Jerusalem
Printed, written and photographic material relating to the six million Jews exterminated by the Nazis.
Daily 9-1, 3-5. Closed afternoons of W., F. and Sa.

JERUSALEM MODEL
Holy Land Hotel, Jerusalem
Model of the city as it was, 1st century A.D.
On request.

L. A. MAYER MEMORIAL INSTITUTE FOR ISLAMIC ART
2 Palmach Street, Jerusalem
Collection of Islamic art.
Su.-F. 10-1, 2-5; Sa. 10-1.

MUSEUM DOR VADOR
Hechal Shlomo, 58 King George Street, Jerusalem
Jewish religious art and folklore. Textiles. Manuscripts.
Weekdays 9.30-1.30; F. 9.30-12.

MUSEUM OF MUSICAL INSTRUMENTS
Rubin Academy of Music, 7 Peretz Smolenskin Street, Jerusalem
Collection of folk instruments.
Weekdays 10-1.

MUSEUM OF NATURAL HISTORY
6 Mohilever Street, Jerusalem
Natural history of Israel.
Daily 10-1, 4-6; Sa. 10-1. Closed F.

MUSEUM OF PREHISTORY
Department of Archaeology, The Hebrew University, Mr. Scopus Campus, Jerusalem
Objects from prehistoric sites in Israel.
By appointment.

MUSEUM OF THE STUDIUM BIBLICUM FRANCISCANUM
P.O. Box 19424, Convent of the Flagellation, Via Dolorosa, Jerusalem
Roman antiquities.
On request.

MUSEUM OF TAXES
32 G. Agron Street, Jerusalem
History of taxation.
Su., Tu., Th. 1-4.

MUSEUM YAD VASHEM
Har Hazikaron, P.O. Box 84, Jerusalem
Memorial museum of martyrs and heroes.
Weekdays 9-5; F. 9-2.

POLOMBO MUSEUM
Mount Zion, P.O. Box 8110, Jerusalem
Paintings. Sculpture. Applied art.
Su.-F. 10-1, 2-5; Sa. 10-1.

ROCKEFELLER ARCHAEOLOGICAL MUSEUM
Rockefeller Building, East Jerusalem
Formerly Palestine Archaeology Museum. Archaeology of Israel from earliest times up to the end of Islamic period. Pottery and tools from Acre and Galilee.
Daily 10-6; F., Sa. 10-2.

ST. ANNE'S MUSEUM
Monastery of the White Fathers, Via Dolorosa, Jerusalem
Material from the Hellenistic and Crusader periods.
On request.

ST. ETIENNE'S MUSEUM
Shechem Road, Jerusalem
Byzantine collection.
On request.

ST. JAMES' MUSEUM
Armenian Patriarchate, Jerusalem
Material from the Crusader period and later.
On request.

SHRINE OF THE BOOK
D. Samuel and Heanne H. Gottesman Center for Biblical MSS, Israel Museum, Jerusalem
Houses the Dead Sea Scrolls (discovered in Qumran) and manuscripts from adjacent sites on western shore of the Dead Sea (Masada and Hahan Hever).
Su., M., W., Th. 10-6; Tu. 10-10; F., Sa. 10-2.

I. WOLFSON MUSEUM
28 King George Road, Jerusalem
Jewish ceremonial art. Manuscripts.
Su.-F. 10-1, 2-5; Sa. 10-1.

Y.M.C.A. "HERBERT E. CLARK" COLLECTION OF NEAR EASTERN ANTIQUITIES
Y.M.C.A. Building, 26 David Hamelech Street, Jerusalem
Collections of flint implements, pottery, glass, jewellery, cylinder seals, cuneiform tablets, scarabs, terracotta and bronze figurines.
On request.

KEFAR MENAHEM

LOCAL MUSEUM
Kibbutz, Kefar Menahem, Shephela
Archaeology. Art.
On request.

KEFAR MONASH

LOCAL MUSEUM
Midreshet Ruppin, Kefar Monash, Emeq Hefer
Archaeology. History. Natural history.
On request.

KEFAR NAHUM

LOCAL MUSEUM
Franciscan Friary, Kefar Nahum
Ancient synagogue.
On request.

KISSUFIM

LOCAL MUSEUM
Kissufim, Neger
Finds from the Palaeolithic, Chalcolithic and Byzantine periods.
On request.

KFAR MENAHEM

REGIONAL MUSEUM
Kfar Menahem
Archaeology. Epigraphy.
Su.-F. 10-1, 2-5; Sa. 10-1.

KOKHAV-HA-YARDEN

LOCAL MUSEUM
Kokhav-ha-Yarden
Material from the Crusader period.
On request.

LOHAME-HAGETA'OT

BEIT KATZNELSON MUSEUM
Lohame-Hageta'ot
Collections illustrating the life and work of the poet Katznelson, murdered at Auschwitz.
On request.

GHETTO FIGHTERS' MEMORIAL MUSEUM
Lohame-Hageta'ot
Archives and documents relating to the various deportation camps of 1940-44. Paintings. Art objects. Kibbutz founded on the anniversary of the uprising in the Warsaw Ghetto, by refugees from the various ghettos of Central Europe.
On request.

MAABAROT

LOCAL MUSEUM
Kibbutz, Maabarot
Local history.
On request.

MA'AYAN BARUCH

MA'AYAN BARUCH PREHISTORIC MUSEUM OF THE HULEH VALLEY
Ma'ayan Baruch, Upper Galilee
Regional antiquities, including implements from all prehistoric periods and exhibits from Middle Bronze Age tombs and from Roman and Byzantine periods.
On request.

MASSADA

LOCAL MUSEUM
Massada
Herodian and Byzantine material.
On request.

MEGIDDO

SITE MUSEUM
Megiddo
Canaanite and Israelite archaeology.
On request.

NAHARIYA

MUSEUM OF ARCHAEOLOGY, HISTORY AND ART
The Municipality, Nahariya
Archaeology. History. Art. Prehistoric objects. Mosaics. Sculpture.
Su.-F. 10-1, 2-5; Sa. 10-1.

NAZARETH

TERRA SANCTA MUSEUM
Terra Sancta Monastery, P.O. Box 23, Nazareth
Byzantine (and later) remains. Coins. Roman and Byzantine glass. Antiquities from excavations in the monastery compound.
On request.

NIR-DAVID

MUSEUM OF MEDITERRANEAN ARCHAEOLOGY
National Park, Gan Hashlosha, Nir-David
Mediterranean archaeology. Etruscan and Roman art. Art of Palestine, Syria and Persia.
Su.-F. 10-1, 2-5; Sa. 10-1.

NIRIM

LOCAL MUSEUM
Kibbutz, Nirim
Ancient synagogue. Jewish antiquities. Mosaic floor.
On request.

PALMAHIM

LOCAL MUSEUM
Kibbutz, Palmahim
Local history. Material from excavations in the area.
On request.

PETAH-TIQVA

MUSEUM OF THE HUMAN BODY
14 Anderson Street, Petah-Tiqva
Anatomy. Hygiene.
On request.

YAD-LEBANIM MEMORIAL CENTRE
30 Arlosoroff Street, Petah-Tiqva
Archaeology. History. Ethnography. Military history.
Su.-F. 10-1, 2-5; Sa. 10-1.

POST EMEK SOREK

SHEPHELA REGIONAL MUSEUM
Kibbutz Kefar Menahem, Post Emek Sorek
Regional antiquities. Mineralogy. Petrology. Israeli paintings, sculpture.
Su.-F. 10-1, 2-5; Sa. 10-1.

RAMAT-GAN

MUSEUM BEIT IMMANUEL
18 Hibbat-Zion, Ramat-Gan
Art collections.
Su.-F. 10-1, 2-5; Sa. 10-1.

REHOVOT

WEIZMANN ARCHIVES
Exhibition Hall, P.O. Box 26, Rehovot
Material relating to Chaim Weizmann, Israel's first president (d. 1952), scientist and discoverer of acetone. Author of works on chemistry of colouring matter, explosives, ferments, biological chemistry and bacteriology.
Su.-F. 10-1, 2-5; Sa. 10-1.

YAD LEBANIM MEMORIAL CENTRE
Habanim Street, Rehovot
Art collections.
Su.-F. 10-1, 2-5; Sa. 10-1.

SAFED

GILCENSTEIN MUSEUM
Safed
Paintings and sculptures of the artist, Hanoch Glicenstein.
Su.-F. 10-1, 2-5; Sa. 10-1.

MUSEUM OF THE PRINTING ARTS
Kiriat Ha Omanim, P.O. Box 1016, Safed
History and techniques of printing.
Su.-F. 10-1, 2-5; Sa. 10-1.

SASA

LOCAL MUSEUM
Kibbutz, Sasa
Local history. Material from excavations in the area.
On request.

S'DOM

LOCAL MUSEUM
S'dom, Nevei Zohar
Dead Sea studies. Technology. History.
On request.

SEDOT YAM

CAESAREA MUSEUM
Kibbutz, Sedot Yam
Collection of antiquities from the region of ancient Caesarea. Ceramics, glassware. Jewellery. Coins.
On request.

SH'AR HA-GOLAN

MUSEUM OF PREHISTORY
Sh'ar Ha-golan, Jordan Valley
Exhibits from the Neolithic Yarmukian culture excavated in the region.
On request.

SHIVTA

LOCAL MUSEUM
Shivta
Nabataean and Byzantine antiquities.
On request.

STELLA MARIS

CARMELITE MONASTERY MUSEUM
Stella Maris Street, Stella Maris, Haifa
Local history.
On request.

TABGHA

LOCAL MUSEUM
Church of the Bread and Fish, P.O. Box 52, Tiberias
Byzantine church. Collection of ecclesiatical art.
On request.

TEL-ADASHIM

SARA MEMORIAL HOUSE
Tel-Adashim, Emeq Yezreel
Archaeology. History. Art.
On request.

TEL-AVIV

ALPHABET MUSEUM
Museum Centre, Ramat Aviv, P.O. Box 17068, Tel-Aviv
Documentary exhibition on the development of writing all over the world, showing the emergence of our present alphabet. Casts of stone and marble inscriptions, relevant archaeological finds, original inscribed scrolls, papyri.
Su., M., Tu., Th. 10-5; W. 10-8; F. 10-1; Sa. and holidays 10-2.

CERAMICS MUSEUM
Museum Centre, Ramat Aviv, P.O. Box 17068, Tel-Aviv
Pottery in the service of man. The significance of pottery in the study of human history. Reconstructed biblical house. Contemporary pottery.
Su., M., Tu., Th., 10-5; W. 10-8; F. 10-1; Sa. and holidays 10-2.

GLASS MUSEUM
Museum Centre, Ramat Aviv, P.O. Box 17068, Tel-Aviv
Ancient glass dating from c.1500 B.C. to the Middle Ages (15th century A.D.).
Su., M., Tu., Th. 10-5; W. 10-8; F. 10-1; Sa. and holidays 10-2.

HAGANAH MUSEUM
23 Rothschild Boulevard, Tel-Aviv
History of Israel's army from the 1930s to the present day. Immigrant-smuggling. 1948 war. Sinai campaign. Six-Day War.
Weekdays 10-5; F. 10-1.

HISTORICAL FOLK MUSEUM OF THE LAND OF ISRAEL
14 Beeri Street, Tel-Aviv
Folk art and traditions of Israel.
Daily ex. Tu. 10-1, 4-8.

HISTORICAL MUSEUM OF TEL-AVIV
26 Bialik Street, Tel-Aviv
Documents, letters, notes and photographs relating to the city's foundation. Maps. Models.
Daily 9-2; W. 9-1, 4-7; F. 9-1; Sa. and holidays closed.

JABOTINSKY MUSEUM
King George Street, Tel-Aviv
Exhibits and photographs relating to the life and activities of V. Jabotinsky; the Jewish Legion in World War I; disturbances in Jerusalem (1920); struggle for free immigration to Palestine under the Mandatory Regime, and the work of various organisations. Material on the Ghetto Fighters and Partisans under German-occupied Europe in World War II.
Su., Tu., Th. 10-3; M., W. 10-3, 6-8; F. 10-1.

KADMAN NUMISMATIC MUSEUM
Museum Centre, Ramat Aviv, P.O. Box 17068, Tel-Aviv
History of coinage from its beginnings to the present day, supplemented by casts of ancient sculptures, maps, documents and transparencies.
Su., M., Tu., Th. 10-5; W. 10-8; F. 10-1; Sa. and holidays 10-2.

MUSEUM "ADAM VA'AMALO"
14 Be'eri Street, Tel-Aviv
History of tools and installations in Israel.
M., Tu., Th. 11-1; Su., W. 11-1, 6-8.

MUSEUM OF THE ANTIQUITIES OF TEL-AVIV-YAFO
10 Mifratz Shlomo Street, Tel-Aviv
History of Tel-Aviv-Yafo from the earliest human settlement there. Inscriptions. Photographs. Models.
Su., M., Tu., Th. 10-5; W. 10-8; F. 10-1; Sa. and holidays 10-2.

MUSEUM OF ETHNOGRAPHY AND FOLKLORE
Museum Centre, Ramat Aviv, P.O. Box 17068, Tel-Aviv
Exhibitions of Jewish popular art and costumes. Religious and secular art. Ceremonial objects arranged in order of Jewish festivals. Scenes from the life of the communities, with traditional costumes, jewellery and household utensils.
Su., M., Tu., Th. 10-5; W. 10-8; F. 10-1; Sa. and holidays 10-2.

MUSEUM OF SCIENCE AND TECHNOLOGY
Museum Centre, Ramat Aviv, P.O. Box 17068, Tel-Aviv
Applied mathematics. Physics. Aeronautics. Energy. Planetarium. History of transportation. Mathematical dioramas.
Su., M., Tu., Th. 10-5; W. 10-8; F. 10-1; Sa. and holidays 10-2.

MUSEUM OF TEL-QUASILA EXCAVATIONS
nr. Ramat Aviv, P.O. Box 17068, Tel-Aviv
Finds from excavations of Israelite city, ranging from period of Monarchy to Islamic period.
Su., M., Tu., Th. 10-5; W. 10-8; F. 10-1; Sa. and holidays 10-2.

TEL-AVIV MUSEUM
Helena Rubinstein Pavilion, 6 Tarsat Street and 27-29 Sd. Shaul Hamelech, Tel-Aviv
Also at Dizengoff House, 16 Rothschild Boulevard. Paintings of 18th-20th centuries. Modern paintings. Graphic art and sculptures, including works by Israeli artists. Prints, especially by German Expressionists, and works by Marc Chagall, Whistler, Zorn and contemporary American engravers.
Su., M., W., Th. 10-1, 4-7; Tu. 10-1, 4-10; F. 10-2; Sa. 7 p.m. - 11 p.m.

ZOOLOGICAL MUSEUM
Tel-Aviv University, 155 Herzl Street, Tel-Aviv
Zoology, especially of the Middle East and Israel.
By appointment only, Su., Tu. 9-2.

TEL-HAI

THE TEL-HAI COURTYARD
Kefar Giladi, Tel-Hai
Reconstruction of 1920 settlement.
On request.

TIBERIAS

LOCAL MUSEUM
Hot Springs, Tiberias
Ancient synagogue.
On request.

MUNICIPAL MUSEUM OF ANTIQUITIES
P.O. Box 283, Tiberias
Antiquities from Tiberias and region, mainly of the Roman, Byzantine and Arab periods.
Su.-F. 10-1, 2-5; Sa. 10-1.

YEHI'AM

LOCAL MUSEUM
Yehi'am
Roman and Crusader material.
On request.

Italy

The guidebooks know where they are with Italian museums. It would hardly be an exaggeration, in fact, to say that the writers of guidebooks learnt their trade by discovering how to produce saleable, upper-class copy about the museums and galleries of Italy. Here, it is possible to turn out such throwaway lines as "other rooms contain paintings by Tintoretto, Titian and Veronese", and to say of a remote monastery that it contains the bed of St Francis and terracottas by Andrea Della Robbia. Even after two centuries of warfare, intensive looting and selling abroad, Italy is still extremely rich in great works of art and in the archaeological remains of the peoples who lived within her boundaries. It would have to be a poor system of museums that failed to make something of such advantages, and of the benefit of having had an exceedingly wealthy and artistically-minded church, aristocracy and merchant class for so many centuries.

A rough estimate shows that of every ten museums in Italy, six are mainly concerned with the fine or applied arts, three with what might be loosely termed archaeology and one with all the other subjects which form the collections of museums - science, technology, modern history, transport, ethnography and the rest. The proportion changes very slowly, partly because one cannot very well throw away the Filippo Lippis and the

Botticellis - they are a respectable and extremely valuable national investment, which are quite rightly expected to yield a dividend in the shape of visitors' entrance fees - and partly because most Italians are only half-convinced that culture is made up of more than paintings, sculpture, literature and music. This is curious, in view of the great Italian contributions to science, medicine and technology, and of the highly developed nature of its manufacturing industries.

In this connexion, one should perhaps record with great regret the fact that Italian industrialists have shown themselves only fractionally more public-spirited, posterity-conscious and museum-minded than their French equivalents. There are very few company museums in Italy and those which do exist are usually designed, at least in part, as a fairly dynamic promotional exercise on behalf of the company's product.

ABBAZIA DI CASAMARI

ABBEY MUSEUM
Abbazia di Casamari
Religious art. Liturgical items. Manuscripts.
Tu.-Su. 10-12, 3-6.

ACIREALE

ARCHAEOLOGICAL MUSEUM
Via San Giuliano 15, Acireale, Sicily
Archaeological material from excavations in the area.
Tu.-Su. 9.30-12.30, 3-6.

ART GALLERY
Accademia Zelantea, Via Marchese di San Giuliano 17, Acireale, Sicily
Local history. Archaeology. 17th-18th century Sicilian paintings.
Daily 9-1.

MUSEUM OF THE RISORGIMENTO
Via San Giuliano 15, Acireale, Sicily
Documents and other material illustrating Italy's struggle for independence.
Tu.-Su. 9.30-12.30, 3-6.

ACQUASPARTA

MUNICIPAL MUSEUM
Palazzo del Municipio, Acquasparta
Local history, paintings. Jewellery. Wood sculpture (15th century).
Daily 9-1.

ADRANO

ARCHAEOLOGICAL MUSEUM
Piazza Umberto I, Adrano, Sicily
Prehistoric material from Neolithic to Iron Age. Archaic and classical exhibits.
Summer: M.-Sa. 9-1, 3-6; Su. and holidays 9.30-1.30. Winter: M.-Sa. 9.30-4; Su. and holidays 9.30-1.30.

ADRIA

ARCHAEOLOGICAL MUSEUM
Corso del Popolo 35, Adria
Greco-Etruscan bronzes, vases, jewellery (6th-2nd century BC). Iron chariot of a Gaulish chieftain (4th century BC), found with skeletons of its two horses. Ceramics.
Daily ex. M. 9-12, 1-4 or 3-6; Su. and holidays 9-1. Winter: 9-12, 1-4.

MUNICIPAL MUSEUM
Corso Vittorio Emanuele II 35, Adria
Local history. Prints. Medieval and modern art. 14th century terracottas.
Tu.-Sa. 9-12, 3-6; Su. and holidays 9-1. Winter: 9-12, 1-4.

AGLIE

DUCAL CASTLE
Aglie
In 17th century castle. Furniture and furnishings. Archaeological finds from the district.
Tu.-Su. 9-12, 3-6.

AGRIGENTO

ANTIQUARIUM
Villa Aurea, Agrigento, Sicily
Archaeological material, from prehistoric times to 4th century B.C.
Daily before noon, on request.

BIRTHPLACE OF PIRANDELLO
Villa Seta, Caos, Agrigento, Sicily
Memorabilia of Pirandello, in the house where he was born.
Tu.-Su. 9.30-1.

DIOCESAN MUSEUM
Town Hall, Via Atenea, Agrigento, Sicily
Roman sarcophagus depicting the story of Phaedra, which was admired by Goethe. Two caskets in 12th century Limoges enamelware. 17th-18th century pavements.
Apr.-Sept. M.-Sa. 9-5; Su. and holidays 9-1. Oct.-Mar. M.-Sa. 9.30-4; Su. and holidays 9-1. Closed Jan. 1, May 1, Aug. 15, Easter and Christmas.

MUNCIPAL MUSEUM
Via Atenea, Agrigento, Sicily
Medieval and modern art, including Sicilian landscapes. Local history.
Daily 9-12, 4-6 (winter: 9-12, 2-4). Closed Su. and holiday afternoons.

NATIONAL ARCHAEOLOGICAL MUSEUM
Piazza del Municipio 316, Agrigento, Sicily
Archaeological finds from local excavations. Coins. Greek vases. The Agrigento Ephebus. Head of the god Telamon from the Temple of Jupiter.
Apr.-Sept. M.-Sa. 9-5; Su. and holidays 9-1. Oct.-Mar. 9.30-4; Su. and holidays 9-1. Closed Jan. 1, May 1, Aug. 15, Easter and Christmas.

ALASSIO

DON BOSCO NATURAL HISTORY MUSEUM
Via San Giovanni 5, Alassio
Natural history, including fossils and animals of the Ligurian Sea, ornithology and petrography. Japanese and African weapons.
Tu.-Su. 9-12, 3-6.

ALATRI

MUNICIPAL MUSEUM
Corso Vittorio Emanuele, Alatri
Local history and folk art. Roman and medieval tombstones. Modern paintings, sculpture.
Tu.-Su. 9-12.30, 2.30-5.30.

ALBA

EUSEBIO ARCHAEOLOGICAL MUSEUM
Via Paruzza 1, Alba
Archaeological finds from the area. Roman sculptures, architectural fragments, ceramics, tombs.
Tu.-Su. 9.30-12.30, 2.30-5.30.

ALBENGA

MUNICIPAL MUSEUM
Peloso-Cipolla Palace, Piazza San Michele 12, Albenga
Archaeological finds from the area. Sculptures. Tombstones.
Daily 10-11.30, 3-5.30.

ROMAN MARITIME MUSEUM
Peloso-Cipolla Palace, Piazza San Michele 12, Albenga
Roman exhibits. Amphorae and other art objects recovered from the sea. Documents on ancient ships.
Daily 9-11.30, 2-5.30.

ALBISOLA SUPERIORE

VILLA GAVOTTI
Albisola Superiore
17th-18th century mansion formerly belonging to the Della Roveres family, the family of Popes Julius II and Sixtus IV. Local ceramics. 18th century Lombard School stucco.
Daily 10-12, 3-6; Su. 10-12. Closed Sept.

ALESSANDRIA

MUNICIPAL MUSEUM AND ART GALLERY
Via Tripoli 8, Alessandria
Local history. Napoleonic and Renaissance history. Religious art. Coins.
Tu.-Su. 9.30-12.30, 2.30-5.30.

ALFADENA

AUFIDENATE MUNICIPAL MUSEUM
Alfadena
Local history, archaeology. Folklore. Natural history.
Tu.-Su. 9.30-12.30, 3-6.

ALTAMURA

MUNICIPAL MUSEUM
Piazza Zanardelli, Altamura
Local history, archaeology. Paintings.
Tu.-Su. 9.30-12.30, 3-6.

ALTINO

ARCHAEOLOGICAL MUSEUM
Altino
Archaeological finds from the area. Sculptures. Mosaics. Coins. Jewellery.
Daily ex. M. 9-12, 3-6.

AMALFI

MUNICIPAL MUSEUM
Amalfi
Local history, archaeology. Natural history. Folklore.
Tu.-Su. 9.30-12.30, 3-6.

AMELIA

ARCHAEOLOGICAL COLLECTION
Palazzo Comunale, Amelia
Archaeological finds from the area. Sculptures.
Tu.-Sa. 9.30-12.30, 2.30-5.30.

ANACAPRI

DELLA TORRE MUSEUM
Main Street, Anacapri, Isle of Capri
Collection of old weapons and armour.
Tu.-Su. 9-12, 3-6.

VILLA SAN MICHELE
Via San Michele, Anacapri, Isle of Capri
Built 80 years ago for the Swedish doctor-writer Axel Munthe (d.1949), who described the island in his *Story of San Michele*. 17th century furniture.
Daily 10-sunset.

ANAGNI

CATHEDRAL TREASURY
Anagni
13th century vestments, notably Boniface VIII's cope of embroidered red silk. Religious art. Jewellery.
On application.

ANCONA

ARCHAEOLOGICAL MUSEUM
Palazzo Ferretti, Monte Guasco, Ancona
Antique remains and sculptures. 14th century sarcophagus by T. Giulio Gorgonio.
Tu.-Su. 9.30-12.30, 3-6 (winter 10-4).

DIOCESAN MUSEUM OF SACRED ART
Vecchio Episcopio, Ancona
Religious art. Architecture.
Tu.-Su. 9.30-12.30, 3-6 (Winter 10-4).

NATIONAL MUSEUM OF THE MARCHES
Palazzo Ferretti, Via Ferretti, Ancona
In 16th century palazzo built by Tibaldi. Prehistory and archaeology. Attic urns from the cemetery of Numana. 1st century Roman gilt bronzes and *orificerie* from the Gallic cemeteries. Golden crowns from Montefortino.
Apr. 16- Sept. 13, daily ex. M. 9-1, 3-6. Oct. 1- Apr. 15, daily ex. M. 10-4. Closed Jan. 1, May 1, June 2, Aug. 15, Easter Su., Christmas Day, and Su. and holiday afternoons.

PODESTI PICTURE GALLERY
Palace of the Ancients, Piazza Stracca, Ancona
Paintings include a *Madonna* by Crivelli, and two *Saints* by Titian. Works by Andrea del Sarto, Lotto, Maratti.
Apr.-Sept., Tu.-Su. 9-1, 3-6. Oct.-Mar., Tu.-Su. 9.30-12.30, 2-5. Closed Su. afternoons, and afternoons of Jan 6, Mar. 19, Easter M., Apr. 25, May 19, June 9, 29, Nov. 1,

4, Dec. 8, 26. Closed all day Jan. 1, May 1, June 2, Aug. 15, Christmas and Easter.

SCIENTIFIC COLLECTION OF THE TECHNICAL INSTITUTE
Ancona
Mineralogy. Palaeontology. Ornithology. Herbarium.
By appointment.

ANGERA

THE ROCCA
Angera, Lake Maggiore
14th century Gothic castle, with apartments showing life of the aristocracy in the Middle Ages. Period furniture and furnishings. Paintings. Frescoes depicting castle's history.
June Sept., daily 9-12, 1.30-6. Oct.-May, daily 10-12, 2-4.

ANTICOLI CORRADO

COMMUNAL GALLERY OF MODERN ART
Casa Conti, Anticoli Corrado
19-20th century paintings, sculpture, graphics, especially by Italian artists.
Tu.-Su. 10-12, 3-6.

AOSTA

ARCHAEOLOGICAL MUSEUM
Via San Orso 10, Aosta
Archaeological finds from the area. Coins. Inscriptions.
Tu.-Su. 9-11.30, 2-6 (winter 2-5).

CATHEDRAL TREASURY
Aosta
Religious art and vestments. Ivory diptych of 406 A.D. and 15th century chalice of St. Gratto.
Apply to Canon Edoardo Brunod, 2 Piazza Giovanni XXIII.

TREASURY OF THE COLLEGIATE CHURCH OF SAN ORSO
Aosta
Ecclesiastical art.
On request.

AQUILEIA

ARCHAEOLOGICAL MUSEUM
Via Roma 1, Aquileia
Archaeological finds from the area. Sculptures. Statues. Semi-precious stones, cameos and intaglios. Amber. Finds from tombs. Metalwork. Ceramics. Glass. Coins.
Daily 8.30-12, 3-6 (Winter 1-4).

PALEOCHRISTIAN MUSEUM
Via Roma 1, Aquileia
Archaeological finds from the area. Christian inscriptions, objects. Mosaics.
Daily 8.30-12, 3-6 (winter 1-4).

AQUINO

CATHEDRAL TREASURY
Aquino
Religious art. Liturgical items. Sacred vessels.
Tu.-Su. 10-12, 3-6.

AREZZO

ARCHAEOLOGICAL MUSEUM
Via Aretino, Arezzo
Aretian vases of the Roman period. Etruscan bronze statuettes, 6th-5th century B.C.
Daily ex. W. 9-4; Su. and holidays 9-12.

DIOCESAN MUSEUM OF SACRED ART
Piazza del Duomo, Arezzo
Religious art.
Tu.-Su. 9.30-1.

PICTURE GALLERY AND MUSEUM OF MEDIEVAL AND MODERN ART
Palazzo della Dogana, Via San Lorentino 8, Arezzo
Works by Jacopo del Sellaio, Margaritone, Luca Signorelli, Salvator Rosa, Lodovico Carracci and Magnasco. Coins. Bronzes. Sculptures. Ceramics of the Renaissance period. Ivories. Enamels.
Tu.-Su. 9.30-4. Closed Jan. 1, May 1, June 2, Aug. 15, Easter, Christmas, Su. and holiday afternoons.

VASARI'S HOUSE
Via Venti Settembre 55, Arezzo
Frescoes, paintings and letters of Giorgios Vasari (1511-1574). Memorabilia of Tuscan painters.
Tu.-Sa. 9-12, 3-6; Su. 9-1.

ARQUA PETRARCA

PETRARCH'S HOUSE
Arqua Petrarca
Souvenirs of Petrarch (1304-1374), in his former home. These include the chair in which the poet died, and a visitors' book containing the signatures of Mozart and Byron.
Mar. 16- Oct. 15, Tu.-Su. 9-12.30, 2-7.30. Rest of year 9.30-12.30, 1.30-4.30. Closed Jan. 1, Easter and Christmas.

ASCIANO

ETRUSCAN MUSEUM
Corso Matteotti, Asciano
Finds from Etruscan tombs.
Tu.-Su. 9.30-12.30, 3-6.

MUSEUM OF SACRED ART
Via Collegiata 1, Asciano
Wooden statues. Religious art (mainly 15th century).
Tu.-Su. 9.30-12.30, 3-6.

ASCOLI PICENO

DIOCESAN MUSEUM
Piazza dell'Arringo, Ascoli Piceno
Religious art. Liturgical items.
Tu.-Su. 9.30-1.

PICTURE GALLERY
Palazzo Comunale, Piazza dell'Aringo, Ascoli Piceno
Works by Pietro Alemano (late 15th century), Cola dell'Amatrice. Portraits by Carlo Naratti (17th century) and Van Dyck. A Titian, *St. Francis receiving the Stigmata.* Watercolours by Guardi, and paintings by Strozzi and Magnasco.
Apr.-Oct. M.-Sa. 10-1, 4.30-6.30; Su. and holidays 10-12. Nov.-Mar. M.-Sa. 8-1; Su. and holidays 10-12.

ASCOLI SATRIANO

MUNICIPAL MUSEUM
Largo Gioia 2, Ascoli Satriano
Local history. Inscriptions. Finds from tombs. Icons.
Tu.-Su. 9.30-12.30, 3-6.

ASOLO

MUNICIPAL MUSEUM
Via Regina Cornaro, Asolo
Finds from local excavations. Roman sculptures, paintings, decorative art. Memorabilia of the poets Robert Browning (1812-1889) and Gabriele d'Annunzio (1863-1938), and of the actress Eleonora Duse (1859-1924).
Tu.-Su. 9.30-12.30, 3-6.

ASSISI

CAPITOLARE MUSEUM
Piazza San Rufino, Assisi
Ecclesiastical art. Goldsmiths' work.
Daily 8-1, 1.30 until the Angelus. Closed during services. Apply to the Sacristan.

GALLERY OF CONTEMPORARY SACRED ART
Cittadella Cristiana, Assisi
Paintings, drawings. Sculptures. Mosaics. Enamels. Ceramics. African and Asian art.
Tu.-Su. 9-12.30, 3-6.

MUNICIPAL ART GALLERY
Palazzo del Comune, Assisi
13th-17th century Umbrian paintings.
Tu.-Su. 9.30-12.30, 3-6.

MUNICIPAL MUSEUM
Via Portica 2, Assisi
Local history. Paintings. Sculpture. Roman and Etruscan urns.
Tu.-Su. 9.30-12.30, 3-6.

MUSEUM OF THE BASILICA OF SANTA MARIA DEGLI ANGELI
Annesso alla Basilica, Assisi
Religious paintings, portraits of St. Francis. Goldsmiths' work. Numismatics. Archaeological exhibits. Ethnography.
Tu.-Su. 9.30-12.30, 3-6.

TREASURY OF THE CONVENTO DI SAN FRANCESCO
Annesso alla Basilica, Assisi
Religious art. 12th-14th century relics. Goldsmiths work.
Tu.-Su. 9.30-12.30, 3-6.

ASTI

ALFIERI MUSEUM
Corso Alfieri 375, Asti
Birthplace of the poet, Vittorio Alfieri (d.1803), with collections and study rooms devoted to his work.
Tu.-Su. 9.30-12.30, 3-6.

ARCHAEOLOGICAL MUSEUM
Palazzo di Bellino, Corso Alfieri 375, Asti
Egyptian, Etruscan and Roman antiquities.
Tu.-Su. 9.30-12.30, 3-6.

CHURCH OF SAN PIETRO IN CONSAVIA MUSEUM
Corso Alfieri, Asti
Lapidary collection.
Tu.-Su. 10-12, 4-7.

MUNICIPAL ART GALLERY
Palazzo de Bellino, Corso Alfieri 357, Asti
19th-20th century paintings. Local views.
Tu.-Su. 10-12, 3-7.

MUSEUM OF THE RISORGIMENTO
Corso Alfieri 357, Asti
Documents and other material illustrating the country's struggle for independence.
Tu.-Su. 9.30-12.30, 3-6.

ATRI

CAPITOLARE MUSEUM
Via Luca d'Atri, Atri
Local history.
Tu.-Su. 9-12, 2.30-5.30.

CATHEDRAL MUSEUM
Cathedral Annexe, Atri
Religious art. Ancient manuscripts.
Tu.-Su. 9-12, 2.30-5.30.

AVELLINO

IRPINO REGIONAL MUSEUM
Palazzo della Cultura, Avellino
Local archaeological finds.
On request.

BACOLI

PISCINA MIRABILE
Bacoli
Cistern designed to supply water to the Roman fleet in the port of Miseno - 75 yards long, 28 yards wide and nearly 50 feet high (70 x 25 x 15 metres). It is divided into five sections, whose roofs are supported by 48 pillars.
Apply to the keeper at Via Carannante 9.

BAGHERIA

HISTORICAL MUSEUM
Corso Umberto I, Bagheria
Regional history.
Tu.-Su. 9.30-12.30, 3-6.

BAIA

ROMAN BATHS
Baia
Recently excavated Roman baths.
F.-W. 9- 1 hour before sunset. Closed Jan. 1, May 1, June 2, Aug. 15, Easter and Christmas.

BARANELLO

MUNICIPAL MUSEUM
Palazzo Comunale, Via Santa Maria 11, Baranello
Local history, archaeology, decorative arts. Paintings. Coins.
Tu.-Su. 9-12, 3-6.

BARI

ARCHAEOLOGICAL MUSEUM
Piazza Umberto I, Bari
Greco-Roman collections from the region, including Corinthian vases, bronzes, jewellery and medals. *Tu.-Su. 9-2.*

COLLECTION OF THE BOTANICAL INSTITUTE
Bari
Natural history. Botany. Herbarium.
By appointment.

COLLECTIONS OF THE CAVOUR TECHNICAL AND COMMERICAL INSTITUTE
Bari
Zoological collections.
By appointment.

COLLECTIONS OF THE INSTITUTE OF COMPARATIVE ANATOMY
Palazzo Ateneo, Bari
Natural history. Mammals. Reptiles. Amphibians.
By appointment.

COLLECTIONS OF THE INSTITUTE OF GEOLOGY AND PALAEONTOLOGY
Bari
Geology and palaeontology of Italy.
By appointment.

COLLECTIONS OF THE INSTITUTE OF PETROGRAPHY AND MINERALOGY
Bari
Petrography. Mineralogy.
By appointment.

GIPSOTECA (PLASTER-CAST MUSEUM)
Castello, Piazza Federico II di Svezia, Bari
In 13th century castle. Plaster sculptures and architecture of the Romanesque period in Apulia.
Tu.-Sa. 8-1; Su. and holidays 9-1.

HISTORICAL MUSEUM
Largo Urbano II 2, Bari
Local history. Relics of World War I.
Tu.-Su. 9-1.

MUSEUM OF THE BASILICA OF SAN NICOLA
Bari
Religious art.
Tu.-Su. 9-2.

REGIONAL ART GALLERY
Palazzo della Provincia, Lungomare Nazario Sauro, Bari
Paintings include a *San Rocco* by Tintoretto, *St. Peter the Martyr* by Giovanni Bellini, a *Madonna and Saints* by Veronese, and figures from an 18th century Neapolitan presepio.
Su. 10-1.

BARLETTA

MUSEUM AND PICTURE GALLERY
Via Cavour 8, Barletta
Local history. Paintings, including works by the local artist, Guis. de Nittis (1846-84). Sculpture. Weapons.
May-Sept., M.-Sa. 9-1, 5-7. Oct.-Apr., M.-Sa. 9-1, 4-6. Su. 9-12.

BASSANO DEL GRAPPA

MUNICIPAL MUSEUM AND PICTURE GALLERY
Convent of San Francesco, Piazza Garibaldi, Bassano del Grappa
History of the area. Paintings, including works by the Venetian artists, Jacopo da Ponte, *St. Valentine baptising St. Lucia*; Guariento and Vivarini. *Monks burying one of their Brethren* by Magnasco. Sculptures by Canova. Engravings.
Daily ex. M. and Su. afternoon, 10-12.30, 3.30-6.30 (winter 3-6).

BAZZANO

MUNICIPAL ARCHAEOLOGICAL MUSEUM
Palazzo Comunale, Via Contessa Matilde 1, Bazzano
Finds from excavations in the area. Roman objects, bronzes, decorated vases.
Tu.-Su. 9.30-12.30, 3-6.

BEDONIA

MUSEUM OF THE SEMINARY
Via San Stefano Raffi, Bedonia
Local archaeological material.
Tu.-Su. 9-1.

BELLUNO

MUNICIPAL MUSEUM
Piazza del Duomo 16, Belluno
Paintings by Bartolomeo Montagna, Solario, Longhi and local painters, Marco and Sebastiano Ricci. Archaeology. Numismatics. Documents on the Risorgimento. Local history.
Apr.-Oct. Tu.-Su. 9-12, 3-6. Closed holiday afternoons.

BENE VAGIENNA

MUNICIPAL MUSEUM
Palazzo delle Scuole, Via Roma, Bene Vagienna
Local history, archaeology. Architectural fragments. Bronzes. Glass. Ceramics. Paintings. Material on the Risorgimento.
Tu.-Su. 9.30-12.30, 3-6.

BENEVENTO

SANNIO MUSEUM
Piazza S. Sofia, Benevento
Ornaments from the Cathedral. Vestments. Golden rose. Bronze coffer (11th-12th century). Local history. Numismatics. Medieval and modern art.
On request.

BERGAMO

DONIZETTI MUSEUM
Via Arena 9, Bergamo
Memorabilia of Donizetti.
Tu.-Su. 9.30-12.30, 3-6.

GALLERY OF CARRARA ACADEMY
Piazza Giacomo Carrara 82, Bergamo
Paintings by Cariani and Moroni (16th century) and Fra. Galgario (18th century). Works of the Venetian School, notably by Lorenzo Lotto (1480-1556), who worked at Bergamo. Works by Botticelli and Pisanno, Bellini and Mantegna. Portraits by Moroni and works by Dürer and Clouet. Still lifes of musical instruments by Baschenis (1617-1677). Flemish-Dutch collection.
Daily 9-12, 2-5. Closed Jan. 1, Easter Su. and Christmas Day.

MUSEUM
Istituto Musicale Donizetti, Via dell'Arena 9, Bergamo
Small collection of musical souvenirs.
On request.

MUSEUM OF ARCHAEOLOGY AND NATURAL HISTORY
Piazza Cittadella 13, Via dell'Arena, Bergamo
Archaeology, including epigraphs, statues and reliefs. Natural history: ornithology, fossils, butterflies.
Daily ex. Tu. 9-12, 3-5 or 6. Closed Th. and F. also in winter.

MUSEUM OF THE RISORGIMENTO
Parco Rimembrenze, Bergamo
Collections illustrating the "Five days of Bergamo" (18th-22nd March 1848), and on Garibaldi's action in the town.
Daily 9-1, 2-5.

BESOZZO

BRUNELLA GEOLOGICAL MUSEUM
Besozzo
Natural history. Geology. Fossils.
Tu.-Su. 9-1, 3-6.

BETTONA

MUNICIPAL MUSEUM AND ART GALLERY
Piazza Cavour, Bettona
Local history, archaeology. Decorative arts. Paintings of the Umbrian School.
Tu.-Su. 9-1, 3-6.

BEVAGNA

ANTIQUARIUM
Via Porta Guelfa, Bevagna
Roman antiquities, architecture. Mosaic pavement. Epigraphs.
Tu.-Su. 9-1, 3-6.

MUNICIPAL ART GALLERY
Corso Matteotti, Bevagna
Works of the Umbrian School. Material on the entomologist, Filippo Silvestri. Archaeology.
Tu.-Su. 9.30-12.30, 2-5.

BIELLA

COLLECTIONS OF THE BIELLA SEMINARY
Biella
Herbarium. Entomology. Flora of Italy and Northern Europe.
By appointment.

COLLECTIONS OF THE ITALIAN ALPINE CLUB
Biella
Minerals, rocks and fossils of the district.
By appointment.

MUNICIPAL MUSEUM
Via Pietro Micca 38, Biella
Local history, archaeology. Modern art. Ceramics. Egyptian antiquities.
Tu.-Su. 9.30-12.30, 3-6.

QUINTINO SELLA INSTITUTE COLLECTIONS
Biella
Minerals and rocks of the district.
By appointment.

BITONTO

EPISCOPAL ART GALLERY
Episcopio, Bitonto
Religious art.
Tu.-Su. 9.30-1.

MUNICIPAL MUSEUM
Piazzo Gramsci 2, Bitonto
Local archaeology, history. Natural history. Folklore.
Tu.-Su. 9.30-12.30, 3-6.

BOBBIO

MUSEUM OF THE BASILICA OF SAN COLOMBANO
Piazza Santa Fara, Bobbio
Archaeological material. Sculpture. Antiques.
Tu.-Su. 9-12, 3-6.

BOLOGNA

CAPELLINI MUSEUM
Institute of Geology and Palaeontology, Via Zamboni 65, Bologna
Geology, palaeontology, fossils and stones from Europe, Africa, America and Asia.
By appointment.

CAPUCIN FRIARS MUSEUM AND ART GALLERY
Via Bellinzona 6, Bologna
Historical material relating to the Capucin Friars. Religious art.
Tu.-Su. 9.30-12.30, 3-5.

CARDUCCI HOUSE AND LIBRARY
Piazza Carducci 5, Bologna
Former home of the poet Carducci (1835-1907). Portraits. Family relics. Early editions of his works. Collection of Carducci manuscripts.
M.-Sa. 9-12, 3-5; Su. and holidays 9-1.

COLLECTION OF ANCIENT MAPS
Via Zamboni 33, Bologna
Geographical maps (17th century). Navigation maps. Ships' models.
Tu.-Su. 9.30-12.30, 3-6.

COLLECTION OF THE INSTITUTE OF HUMAN ANATOMY
Via Irnerio 48, Bologna
Anatomy. Skulls.
By appointment.

COLLECTION OF THE ORTHOPAEDIC CLINIC
Istituto Ortopedico Rizzoli, Bologna
History of orthopaedics. Surgical instruments. Early books, paintings.
By appointment.

COMMUNAL ART COLLECTIONS
Palazzo del Comune, Piazza Maggiore, Bologna
Paintings of the Bolognese school. Glass; majolica; goldsmiths' and silversmiths' work. Miniatures.
M.-Sa. 9-2; Su. and holidays 9-12.30. Closed Tu.

DAVIA BARGELLINI ART GALLERY AND MUSEUM OF INDUSTRIAL ART
Via Maggiore 44, Bologna
Furniture, ornaments and minor arts from 16th-18th centuries. *Madonna* painted in 1345 by Vitale da Bologna.
M.-Sa. 9-2; Su. and holidays 9-12.30. Closed Tu.

GALLERY OF MODERN ART
Via Saragozza 228-230, Bologna
Painting and sculpture from 19th century to the present day.
M.-Sa. 9-2; Su. and holidays 9-12.30. Closed Tu.

GOZZADINI MUSEUM
Archiginnasio, Portico del Pavaglione, Bologna
Umbrian and other antiquities.
Daily ex. M. 9-12, 3-6.

HISTORICAL MUSEUM
University of Bologna, Via Zamboni 33, Bologna
History of life at the University of Bologna from medieval times to the 19th century.
By appointment.

MARITIME MUSEUM
Via Zamboni 33, Bologna
Maritime history. Ships' models.
Tu.-Su. 9.30-12.30, 3-6.

MARSILIANA MUSEUM
Via Zamboni 35, Bologna
Memorabilia of the author L. F. Marsili (d.1394).
Tu.-Su. 9.30-12.30, 3-6.

MUNICIPAL ARCHAEOLOGICAL MUSEUM
Via dell'Archiginnasio 2, Bologna
Archaeological and prehistoric collections: Iron Age, Etruscan, Roman. Egyptian antiquities, including head of the Pharoah Amenophis IV and bas-reliefs from the tomb of Harembab. Greek and Roman collections. Stelae and vases.
Tu.-Sa. 9-2; Su. and holidays 9-12.30. Closed M.

MUNICIPAL MUSEUM OF MUSICAL BIBLIOGRAPHY
Piazza Rossini 2, Bologna
Collection of historical musical manuscripts and other documents.
Tu.-Su. 9.30-12.30, 3-6.

MUSEUM OF THE INSTITUTE OF ANTHROPOLOGY
Bologna
Palaentology. Anthropology: skeletons, skulls.
By appointment.

MUSEUM OF THE INSTITUTE OF ASTRONOMY
The University, Via Zamboni 33, Bologna
Historic globes. 16th century quadrants, lenses.
By appointment.

MUSEUM OF THE INSTITUTE OF COMPARATIVE ANATOMY
Via Belmeloro, Bologna
Anatomical specimens and preparations.
By appointment.

MUSEUM OF THE INSTITUTE OF MINERALOGY AND PETROGRAPHY
Piazza San Donato 1, Bologna
Mineralogy. Petrography.
By appointment.

MUSEUM OF OBSTETRICS
Istituto di Clinica Ostetrica, Bologna
Obstetrics.
By appointment.

MUSEUM OF THE RISORGIMENTO
Portici del Pavaglione 2, Bologna
Material relating to the Italian struggle for independence.
Tu.-Su. 9.30-12.30, 3-6.

MUSEUM OF SAN DOMENICO
adjoining Basilica, Piazza San Domenico 13, Bologna
Paintings. Frescoes. Terracottas. Reliquaries. Inlaid work. Vestments.
Daily 6.30-12, 3-7.

MUSEUM OF SAN PETRONIO
Piazza Galvani 5, Bologna
Material on the history of the Basilica. Plans of the church. Ancient vestments. Jewellery.
Daily 10-12, 4-6. Closed Tu. and Sa. afternoon.

MUSEUM OF SANTO STEFANO
adjoining Basilica, Via Santo Stefano 24, Bologna
Paintings, mainly by Bologna artists. Roman and Byzantine inscriptions.
Daily 9-12, 3-6.

MUSEUM OF THE ZOOLOGICAL INSTITUTE
Via San Giacomo 9, Bologna
Zoology of Mozambique. Birds from Italy and elsewhere. Corals. Fish of Brazil.
By appointment.

NATIONAL HISTORIC AND EDUCATIONAL MUSEUM OF UPHOLSTERY AND FURNISHING TEXTILES
Palazzo Salina, Via Barberia 13, Bologna
Brocades, velvets and other fabrics from Europe and the Middle East.
M.-Sa. 10-12, 4.30-7; Su. and holidays 10.30-12, 4.30-7.30.

NATIONAL PICTURE GALLERY
Via Belle Arti 56, Bologna
Works, mainly of the Emilian school, from 14th-18th centuries: Vitale da Bologna, Francia, the Caraccis, Reni and Guercino. Foreign schools.
Tu.-Sa. 9.30-3.30; Su. and holidays 9.30-12.30. Closed M.

POMPEO ARIA ETRUSCAN MUSEUM
Via Porrettana Sud 13, Bologna
Fragments of architecture. Bronzes. Ceramics. Inscriptions.
Daily 9- 1 hour before sunset.

VETERINARY MUSEUM
University Institute of Anatomy, Bologna
History of veterinary techniques.
By appointment.

ZOOLOGICAL COLLECTIONS
Via Osservanza 22, Bologna
Zoology.
Tu.-Su. 9.30-12.30, 3-6.

BOLSENA

MUNICIPAL ANTIQUARIUM
Palazzo del Municipio, Bolsena
Local archaeology and architecture.
Tu.-Su. 9-1.

BOLZANO

MUNICIPAL MUSEUM
Via del Museo, Bolzano
Local antiquities and bygones. Regional ethnography. Local wood carving (13th-16th century). 15th-18th century paintings.
Daily ex. M. morning, 10-12, 3-5.

BORDIGHERA

BICKNELL MUSEUM
Istituto Internazionale di Studi Liguri, Via Romana 17, Bordighera
Natural history collections. Prehistoric and Roman archaeology.
Weekdays 10-12, 3.30-5.30.

GARIBALDI ORNITHOLOGICAL COLLECTION
Villa delle Palme, Bordighera
Birds and mammals of Italy.
Tu.-Su. 9-1.

BORGO

ARTURO TOSCANINI'S BIRTHPLACE
Via Tanzi, Borgo
Memorabilia of Toscanini, in the house where he was born.
Tu.-Su. 9.30-12.30, 3-6.

BORGO GROTTA GIGANTE

MUSEUM OF SPELEOLOGY AND GROTTOS
Borgo Grotta Gigante
History of the caves in the district.
Tu.-Su. 9.30-12.30, 3-6.

BORMIO

MUNICIPAL MUSEUM
Castello De Simoni, Bormio
Local history, archaeology. Natural history. Paintings.
Tu.-Su. 9.30-12.30, 3-6.

BRA

CRAVERI MUSEUM AND MUSEUM OF THE HISTORY OF ART
Via Craveri 15, Bra
Local history. Natural history. Archaeology. Local paintings and sculpture.
Tu.-Su. 9-12, 3-6.

NATURAL HISTORY COLLECTIONS OF THE CRAVERI MUSEUM
Via Craveri 15, Bra
Natural history. Botany. Zoology. Fossils. Ethnography.
Tu.-Su. 9-12, 3-6.

BRACCIANO

CASTLE
Bracciano
15th century castle where Charles VIII, King of France, lived during the Italian Wars (1495). Apartments are furnished and decorated with stucco and frescoes.
Apr.-Sept., Th. Sa. and Su. 9-12, 3-6. Oct.-Mar. Th., Sa. and Su. 10-12, 3-5.

BRENO

CAMUNO MUSEUM
Palazzo Comunale, Via Garibaldi 6, Breno
Local history. Folklore.
Tu.-Su. 9-12, 3-5.

BRESCELLO

ANTIQUARIUM
Brescello
Roman inscriptions and sculptures from local excavations.
Tu.-Su. 9.30-12.30, 3-6.

BRESCIA

CAVELLINI COLLECTION OF MODERN ART
Via Bonomelli 16, Brescia
Modern art.
By appointment.

GALLERY OF MODERN ART
Via dei Musei 81, Brescia
Works ranging from Canova's bust of Eleanora d'Este, and F. Hayez, to painters of the modern avant-garde.
Tu.-Su. 9-12, 2-5 or 3-6.

MUSEUM OF CHRISTIAN ART
Church of the Monastery of Santa Giulia, Via dei Musei, Brescia
Pre-Romanesque and Renaissance art. Cameos, gems and engraved designs ('intaglii') ornamenting 8th century cross of Desiderio. 4th century ivory casket. Medals by Pisanello (15th century). 16th century Martinengo tomb.
Daily ex. M. 9-12, 3-6 (Oct.-Apr. 2-5).

MUSEUM OF THE RISORGIMENTO
Castello, Colle Cidneo, Brescia
Exhibits relating to the history of Brescia, and the struggle for Italian independence.
Daily ex. M. 9-30-12.30, 3-6 (Winter: 10-4).

MUSEUM OF ROMAN ANTIQUITIES
Via dei Musei 57, Brescia
Roman remains, including a Winged Victory and bronze busts. Inscriptions. Mosaics. Bronzes. Ceramics. Glass. Statues.
Tu.-Su. 9-12, 3-6 (Oct.-Apr. 2-5).

RAGAZZONI NATURAL HISTORY MUSEUM
Via dei Musei 81/A, Brescia
Natural history. Geology. Mineralogy. Palaeontology. Entomology. Ornithology.
Tu.-Su. 9.30-12.30, 3-6 (winter: 10-4).

TOSIO MARTINENGO PICTURE GALLERY
Via Martinengo da Barco 1, Brescia
Works by artists of the Brescian school, including Moretto, Moroni and Romanino. *Portrait of Henri III* by Clouet; a *Nun* by the Master of Utrecht (early 16th century); *Christ Giving His Blessing* and an *Angel* by Raphael. *Nativities* by Salvodo, Moretto and Lorenzo Lotto.
Tu.-Su. 9-12, 3-6 (Oct.-Apr. 2-5).

BRESSANONE

LIBRARY AND PICTURE GALLERY
Convent of Novacella, nr. Bressanone
On the Pusteria road, 4 km. from Bressanone. Manuscripts. Paintings of the local 15th century school.
On request.

DIOCESAN MUSEUM
Via Alboino 2, Bressanone
Treasury of the Cathedral. Locally carved Presepi, or Cribs.
Daily ex. M. 9-12, 2-5.

BRINDISI

FRANCESCO RIBEZZO REGIONAL MUSEUM
Piazza del Duomo, Brindisi
Messapian, Greek and Roman inscriptions, coins and sculptures.
M.-Sa. 8.30-12.30; Su. 10-12.

BUDRIO

INZAGHI MUNICIPAL ART GALLERY
Via Mentana 9, Budrio
Paintings, prints, drawings of the Bologna school (14th-15th century).
Tu.-Su. 9.30-12.30, 3-6.

BUIA

MARANGOLI ORNITHOLOGICAL COLLECTION
Presso la Scuola Media, Buia
Ornithology.
Tu.-Su. 9-1.

BUONCONVENTO

ART MUSEUM
Annexe of the Church of Saints Peter and Paul, Buonconvento
Regional paintings. Sculpture. Goldsmiths' work.
Tu.-Su. 9.30-12.30, 3-6.

BUSSETO

MUNICIPAL MUSEUM
Villa Pallavicino, Via Provesi 41, Busseto
16th century house with Baroque additions. Furniture. Paintings.
Tu.-Su. 9.30-12.30, 3-6.

CADENABBIA

VILLA CARLOTTA
Cadenabbia
Villa (1747). Sculpture, including Thorvaldsen's frieze of the *Triumphal Entry of Alexander into Babylon*, cast in plaster for Napoleon in 1811-12. Works by Canova.
Daily 8-8.

CAGLIARI

COLLECTION OF THE BOTANICAL INSTITUTE
Cagliari, Sardinia
Botany. Plants. Herbarium.
By appointment.

MUNICIPAL ART GALLERY
Viale Regina Elena, Cagliari, Sardinia
17th-20th century Sardinian paintings. Oriental decorative arts. Folk art of Sardinia. Ethnography.
Tu.-Su. 9-1, 4-6.

MUSEUM OF THE INSTITUTE OF GEOLOGY AND PALAEONTOLOGY
Via Sa Duchessa, Cagliari, Sardinia
Geology and palaeontology of the region.
By appointment.

MUSEUM OF MINERALOGY AND PETROGRAPHY
Cagliari, Sardinia
Mineralogy and petrography of the area.
By appointment.

NATIONAL ARCHAEOLOGICAL MUSEUM
Piazza Indipendenza 7, Cagliari, Sardinia
Weapons. Pottery. Sculptures of the earliest period of Sardinian history. Punic, Greek and Roman art. Paintings of the Sardinian school, 13th-15th centuries.
Daily ex. M. 9-1, 4-6. Winter: M.-Sa. 8.30-2.30; Su. and holidays 9-1.

SARDO MUSEUM OF ANTHROPOLOGY AND ETHNOGRAPHY
Via G. T. Porcelli 2, Cagliari, Sardinia
Sardinian anthropology and ethnography. Skulls.
Tu.-Su. 9-1, 3-6.

ZOOLOGICAL MUSEUM
University Institute of Zoology, Viale San Bartolomeo 1, Cagliari, Sardinia
Zoological speciments.
By appointment, weekdays 8-12.

CALASCIBETTA

MUNICIPAL MUSEUM
Palazzo Comunale, Calascibetta, Sicily
Local history, archaeology. Paintings. Folklore.
Tu.-Su. 9.30-12.30, 3-6.

CALTAGIRONE

MUNICIPAL MUSEUM
Corte Capitaniale, Via del Duomo, Caltagirone, Sicily
Pre-Hellenic antiquities, Greek vases. Majolica of local design.
Daily 9-1.

MUSEUM OF CERAMICS
Via Roma 10, Caltagirone, Sicily
Historical development of Sicilian ceramics.
Tu.-Su. 9-1, 3-6.

CALTANISSETTA

MUNICIPAL MUSEUM
Via Colajanni, Caltanissetta, Sicily
Local history, archaeology. Natural history. Paintings.
Tu.-Su. 9-30-12.30, 3-6.

MUSEUM OF FOLKLORE
Via Pisani, Caltanissetta, Sicily
Sicilian folklore and customs. Costumes. Domestic utensils. Paintings.
Tu.-Su. 9.30-12.30, 3-6.

MUSEUM OF MINERALOGY AND PALAEONTOLOGY
Istituto Tecnico Industriale ad Indirizzo Minerario, Via Berengario Gaetani 42, Caltanissetta, Sicily
Mineralogy. Palaeontology. Fossils.
By appointment.

CAMAIORE

MUSEUM OF SACRED ART
Piazza Diaz, Camaiore
Religious art. Tapestries. Goldsmiths' work.
Tu.-Su. 9-1.

CAMERINO

ARCHAEOLOGICAL MUSEUM
Via San Francesco, Camerino
Archaeological finds from the district. Roman coins and inscriptions.
Tu.-Su. 9-30-12.30, 3-6.

COLLECTION OF FOSSILS, MINERALS AND ROCKS
Istituto di Mineralogia e Geologia, Via Venanzi, Camerino
Fossils, minerals and rocks of the region.
By appointment.

MUNICIPAL MUSEUM AND ART GALLERY
Via San Francesco, Camerino
Local history. Paintings by local masters. Ceramics. 13th-14th century frescoes.
Tu.-Su. 9.30-12.30, 3-6.

MUSEUM OF AUTOPSY
Istituto di Medicina Legale, Camerino
Preserved specimens from autopsies.
By appointment.

MUSEUM OF COMPARATIVE ANATOMY
Istituto di Anatomia degli Animali Domestici, Camerino
Comparative anatomy.
By appointment.

ZOOLOGICAL MUSEUM
Istituto di Zoologia, Camerino
Mammals. Birds. Invertebrates.
By appointment.

CAMPOBASSO

SANNITIC MUSEUM
Via Vittorio Veneto 21, Campobasso
Sannitic weapons, decorative arts, numismatics.
Tu.-Su. 9-12, 3-6.

CANNE DELLA BATTAGLIA

ANTIQUARIUM
Canne della Battaglia
Regional archaeology from the prehistoric to the medieval period. Grave goods (6th-3rd centuries B.C.). Relics of the Battle of Cannae, 216 B.C.
Tu.-Su. 9-sunset.

CANOSA DI PUGLIA

MUNICIPAL MUSEUM
Palazzo del Comune, Piazza Martiri 23, Canosa di Puglia
Local history. Archaeological material, 3rd-2nd centuries B.C. Ceramics. Bronzes. Roman epigraphs and sculptures.
Tu.-Su. 9.30-12.30, 3-6.

CANOSSA

CAMPANINI MUSEUM
Castello, Canossa
Finds from excavations in the area. Decorative arts. Roman architecture.
Tu.-Su. 9-12, 2-5.

CAPRERA

CASA BIANCA
Island of Caprera, off Sardinia
Home of Giuseppe Garibaldi (1807-88) from 1856 until his death. Memorabilia of Garibaldi. Bust by Bistolfi.
Enquire locally.

CAPRESE

MICHELANGELO MUSEUM
Via del Castello 3, Caprese
Memorabilia of Michelangelo, in house where he was born. Antique furniture.
Tu.-Su., 10-12, 2-5.

CAPUA

CAMPANO MUSEUM
Palazzo Antignano, Via Roma 68, Capua
Archaeology, including Greek vases and Roman statues and mosaics. Medieval sculpture. Southern Italian art of the 15th-18th century.
Daily ex. M. and holidays, 8-2; Su. 8-1.

CARAMINA

ANTIQUARIUM
Casa Pace, Caramina, Sicily
Archaeological material from excavations in the area.
Tu.-Su. 9.30-sunset.

CARPI

GIULIO FERRARI MUNICIPAL MUSEUM
Castello dei Pio, Piazza dei Martiri, Carpi
In 14th century castle. Local history, paintings. History of the Risorgimento. Italian xylography.
Tu.-Su. 9.30-12.30, 3-6.

CARRARA

MARMO MUSEUM
Accademia di Belle Arti, Carrara
Sculptures of the medieval period.
Tu.-Su. 9-1.

CASALE MONFERRATO

MUNICIPAL MUSEUM
Via Mameli 29, Casale Monferrato
Local history. Archaeology. Paintings.
Tu.-Su. 10-12, 3-6.

CASAMARI

MONASTERY MUSEUM
Casamari Abbey, Casamari
Ecclesiastical collections. Sculpture. Ceramics. Coins. Archaeological finds.
Summer: daily 9-12, 3.15-7. Winter: daily 2.15-6.30.

CASERTA

PALAZZO REALE
Parco della Reggia, Caserta, Campania
Building 1752-1774. Royal apartments, with Empire style furnishings. Apartments of the Bourbon King Ferdinand IV (1780) including library and an 18th century Neapolitan crib. The bedroom of Joachim Murat, King of Naples (1767-1815) contains an Empire bed decorated with pikes and warlike emblems.
M.-Sa. 10-4; Su. and holidays 10-1.30.

CASOLA VALSENIO

SCIENTIFIC COLLECTIONS
Scuola Media Statale "A. Oriani", Casola Valsenio
Natural history. Herbs.
By appointment.

CASTEL DISANGRO

MUNICIPAL COLLECTION
Biblioteca Civica, Castel Disangro
Local history, antiquities.
Tu.-Su. 9-12, 3-6.

CASTELFIORENTINO

ART GALLERY
Annexe of the Church of S. Verdiana, Castelfiorentino
Paintings of the Florentine school.
Tu.-Su. 9-1.

CASTELFRANCO VENETO

MUNICIPAL MUSEUM
Castelfranco Veneto
Local history, archaeology. Paintings. Engravings. Furniture.
Tu.-Su. 9.30-12.30, 2-5.

CASTELLAMMARE DI STABIA

ANTIQUARIUM
Cathedral Annexe, Castellammare di Stabia
Archaeological finds from the classical and medieval periods.
Tu.-Su. 9.30-12.30, 3-6.

STABIAN ANTIQUARIUM
Via Marco Mario 22, Castellammare di Stabia
Local archaeological finds. Bas-reliefs. Ceramics. Decorative arts of pre-Roman period.
Tu.-Su. 9.30-12.30, 3-6.

CASTELL'ARQUATA

FOSSIL COLLECTION OF THE PIACENZA DISTRICT
Torrione Farnese, Castell'Arquata
Geology, palaeontology and fossils of the region.
Tu.-Su. 9-12, 3-6.

CASTELL'ARQUATO

MUSEUM
Castell'Arquato
In 14th century cloister. Paintings. Goldsmiths' work. Sculpture.
Tu.-Su. 9-1.

CASTELLI

MUSEUM OF CERAMICS
Palazzo Comunale, Castelli
Ceramics, especially Italian.
Tu.-Su. 9.30-4.30.

CASTELLO

VILLA DI CASTELLO
Castello, nr. Florence
Villa of 1477, restored in 18th century. Period furnishings. 16th century terraced garden with fountain by Tribolo.
Sept.-Oct. Daily 9-6. Rest of year 9-12. Afternoons, 2-5, in March; 2-6 Apr.; 3-7 May 2-Aug. 31; 1-4 Nov. 1-Feb. 28. Closed Jan. 1, May 1, June 2, Aug. 15, Easter Su. and Christmas Day.

CASTEL SANT'ELIA

MUSEUM OF SACRED ART
Santuario Maria S. S. ad Rupes, Castel Sant'Elia
Religious art, vestments, ornaments. 12th century mitres.
Tu.-Su. 9-1.

CASTELVETRANO

SELINUNTINO MUSEUM
Piazza Garibaldi, Castelvetrano, Sicily
Local history. 6th-4th century B.C. ceramics.
Tu.-Su. 9.30-12.30, 3-6.

CASTIGLIONCELLO

NATIONAL ARCHAEOLOGICAL MUSEUM
Via del Museo, Castiglioncello
Archaeological exhibits, 3rd-1st century B.C.
Tu.-Su. 9.30-12.30, 3-6.

CASTIGLIONE DELLA STIVIERE

INTERNATIONAL MUSEUM OF THE RED CROSS
Via Garibaldi 46, Castiglione della Stiviere
History of the Red Cross
Tu.-Su. 9.30-12.30, 3-6.

CASTIGLIONE FIORENTINO

MUNICIPAL ART GALLERY
Piazza del Municipio 12, Castiglione Fiorentino
Paintings. Goldsmiths' work.
Tu.-Su. 9.30-12.30, 3-6.

CASTROVILLARI

MUNICIPAL MUSEUM
Via Bertani 2, Castrovillari
Local history, archaeology. Natural history. Folklore.
Tu.-Su. 9.30-12.30, 3-6.

CATANIA

BELLINI MUSEUM
Piazza San Francesco d'Assisi 3, Catania, Sicily
Memorabilia of the composer, Vincenzo Bellini (1801-1835), in the house where he was born.
Daily 9-2; Su. and holidays 9-1.

CATHEDRAL AND TREASURY
Piazza del Duomo, Catania, Sicily
Ecclesiastical art.
Treasury can be seen "on festivals of the saint".

COLLECTIONS OF THE INSTITUTE OF GEOLOGY
Corso Italia 21, Catania, Sicily
Palaeolithic geology.
By appointment.

MUNICIPAL MUSEUM AND PICTURE GALLERY
Ursino Castle, Piazza Federico di Svevia, Catania, Sicily
Archaeology: Ephebus' head (5th century B.C.). Pre-Corinthian vases. Terracottas of the archaic period. Italic bronzes. 16th-17th century classical bronzes. Ivory caskets. Paintings, including works by Antonello de Saliba, Giordano, Morales, Novelli, Fontanesi, Caprile and Gandolfo. Engravings relating to Catania and the eruptions of Etna.
Daily 9-2; Su. and holidays 9-1.

MUSEUM OF ZOOLOGY AND COMPARATIVE ANATOMY
Via Androne, Catania, Sicily
Local and European fauna. Maritime fauna of the Mediterranean.
Tu.-Su. 9-1.

STUDY MUSEUM
Palazzo dell'Università, Catania, Sicily
History of the university. Medals. Diplomas.
By appointment.

CATANZARO

ENTOMOLOGICAL COLLECTION
Istituto Tecnico Agrario, Catanzaro
Natural history. Butterflies. Entomology.
By appointment.

MINERALOGICAL AND PALAEONTOLOGICAL COLLECTIONS
Liceo Scientificio, Catanzaro
Mineralogy. Palaeontology.
By appointment.

REGIONAL MUSEUM
Villa Trieste, Catanzaro
Bronze objects, including a Greek helmet from Tiriolo, coins and a marble head from Strógnoli. Paintings include a *Madonna and Child*, by Antonello de Saliba (1508).
Daily 10-1, 4-7.

CAVA DEI TERRENI

DELLA BADIA MUSEUM
Via Morcaldi 6, Cava dei Terreni
Religious art. Greek and Roman coins, antiquities. 15th-18th century paintings.
M.-Sa. 9.30-12.30; Su. and holidays 9-11.

CAVALESE

ART GALLERY
Palazzo della Communita, Cavalese
Local history. Paintings, including works by Unterperger.
Tu.-Su. 9-12, 3-6.

CEFALÙ

MENDRALISCA MUSEUM
Via Mendralisca 15, Cefalù, Sicily
Local history. Paintings, including *Portrait of a Man* by Antonello da Messina (1470). Ancient Sicilian coins.
Daily 9.30-12, 3.30-6. Closed Su. and holiday afternoons.

CENTO

MUNICIPAL ART GALLERY
Via Matteotti, Cento
Paintings, drawings, especially by Aroldo Bonzagni. Modern art.
Tu.-Su. 9.30-12.30, 3-6.

CENTURIPE

ANTIQUARIUM
Centuripe, Sicily
Local archaeological finds. Greek statues, terracottas, vases, architecture.
Tu.-Su. 9-1.

CERTALDO

MUSEUM OF BOCCACCIO
Upper Town, Certaldo
In former home of Boccaccio, which was largely destroyed in the war and has been rebuilt. Mementoes and souvenirs of the writer. Furniture and domestic utensils.
Summer: Daily 8-7. Winter: Daily 8-6. On application to Signora Branchi at the neighbouring grocer's.

CERVETERI

CERITE NATIONAL MUSEUM
Cerveteri
Archaeological finds from excavations in the area. Items from graves, 7th-1st centuries B.C.
Summer: daily 9-7. Winter: daily 9-4.

CESENA

MALATESTIANA LIBRARY
Castle of the Malatestas, Via Bufalini 2, Cesena
Manuscripts, including some from the School of Miniaturists at Ferrara. Missorium. (6th century).
June 21-Sept. 30, M. 3-5.30; Tu.-Sa. 8.30-12. Oct. 1-June 20, M. 3-5.30; Tu.-Sa. 9.30-12, 3-5.30. Closed Su. and holidays.

MUNICIPAL ART GALLERY
Piazza Bufalini, Cesena
Paintings, especially by local artists.
Tu.-Su. 9.30-12.30, 3-6.

CHERASCO

ADRIANI MUSEUM
Via Ospedale 40, Cherasco
Local history, archaeology. Numismatics. Paintings, engravings.
Tu.-Su. 9.30-12.30, 3-6.

CHIANCIANO TERME

ANCIENT ART COLLECTION
Via Solferino 38, Chianciano Terme
Paintings of the Siennese and Florentine schools.
Tu.-Su. 9-1.

CHIARI

REPOSSI ART GALLERY
Via Bernardino Varisco 9, Chiari
Paintings, prints. Statues.
Tu.-Su. 9.30-12.30, 3-6.

CHIAVENNA

TREASURY
Collegiate Church of San Lorenzo, Chiavenna
Ecclesiastical collections, including a Rhenish lectern-cover (12th century).
Daily 8-11, 3-5.

CHIESA VALMALENCO

PIETRO SIGISMUND MINERALOGICAL COLLECTION
Chiesa Valmalenco
Rocks, minerals of the district.
Tu.-Su. 9-1.

CHIETI

ART GALLERY
Palazzo della Provincia, Corso Marrucino, Chieti
Modern and contemporary art.
Tu.-Su. 9-12, 3-6.

DIOCESAN MUSEUM
Piazza Vico, Chieti
Religious art. Local paintings. Sculptures.
Tu.-Su. 9-12, 3-6.

MUNICIPAL ART GALLERY
Piazza Vittorio Emanuele II, Chieti
15th century paintings. 17th-18th century paintings, bronzes. Original manuscript by D'Annunzio (1863-1938).
Tu.-Su. 9-12, 3-6.

NATIONAL MUSEUM OF ANTIQUITIES
Villa Comunale, Chieti
Sarcophagi and other objects from the burial grounds in the area. *Canopae* (cremation urns) in human form, adorned with griffins to frighten away evil spirits. Bronze vase for offerings to Charon. Jewels and *cippi* (rounded tombstones).
Apr. 1-Oct. 15, M.-Sa. 8.30-12, 3-6; Su. and holidays

10-1. Oct. 16-Mar. 31, M.-Sa. 9-12, 2.30-5; Su. and holidays 10-1.

CHIOGGIA

NATURAL HISTORY COLLECTION
Seminario Vescovile, Chioggia
Natural history. Crustaceans. Algae.
Tu.-Su. 9-1.

CHIUSI

ETRUSCAN MUSEUM
Piazza della Cattedrale, Chiusi
Collection of Etruscan sarcophagi, including an alabaster example depicting the deceased, Lars Sentinatis.
Tu.-Su. 8.30-12.30, 3-6.

CHIAVARI

SCIENTIFIC COLLECTION
Seminario Vescovile, Piazza N. S. dell'Orto, Chiavari
Mineralogy. Geology. Fossils. Zoology. Anatomy. Metereology. Seismography.
By appointment.

CIANO D'ENZA

MUSEUM AND CASTLE OF CANOSSA (OR CAMPANINI)
Ciano d'Enza
Material from excavations of the Castle.
Summer: M.-Sa. 9-1, 3.30-6.30; Su. and holidays 10-1, 2-4. Winter: M.-Sa. 9.30-4; Su. and holidays 9.30-1.30.

CITTÀ DI CASTELLO

CHAPTER HOUSE MUSEUM
Cathedral annexe, Città di Castello
12th century goldsmiths' work. Collection of early silver church utensils.
Apply at the sacristy.

MUNICIPAL ART GALLERY
Via della Cannoniera 22, Città di Castello
15th century paintings. Works by Luca Signorelli and a standard painted by Raphael at the age of 16 (1499). *Head of Christ* by Just de Grand. Della Robbia terracottas.
If closed, apply to the Casa del'Azione Cattolica, Piazza Gabriotti 4.

CIVIDALE DEL FRIULI

CHAPTER MUSEUM
Cathedral, Cividale del Friuli
Baptismal font of the Patriarch Callisto, redesigned in 15th century with some 8th century features. 8th century 'altar' of Duke Ratchis in marble with carved sides depicting the Assumption, the Epiphany and the Visitation.
Daily 9-sunset.

NATIONAL ARCHAEOLOGICAL MUSEUM
Piazza del Duomo 5, Cividale del Friuli
Roman and medieval sculptures. Gold and silver, including Lombard art (7th century) and a gold cross by Gisulfo. Silver and gold plate of the Middle Ages. 13th century St. Elizabeth psalter, ornamented with miniatures.
Apr.-Sept., Tu.-Su. 9-12.30, 3-6; Su. and holidays closed at 5. Oct.-Mar., Tu.-Su. 9-12.30, 2-4.30. Closed Jan. 1, Apr. 25, May 1, June 2, Aug. 22, Easter Su. and Christmas Day.

CIVITACASTELLANA

ANTIQUARIUM
Nella Rocca, Civitacastellana
Etruscan archaeological material, especially ceramics from the necropolis at Falerii.
Tu.-Su. 9-12, 3-6.

CIVITANOVA ALTA

MORETTI GALLERY OF MODERN ART
Piazza Liberta, Civitanova Alta
19-20th century paintings, sculptures.
Tu.-Su. 9.30-12.30, 3-6.

CIVITAVECCHIA

MUNICIPAL MUSEUM
Largo Plebiscito, Civitavecchia
Collection of local archaeological finds.
Daily ex. M. 9-12, 3-6.

COL DI RODI

RAMBALDI ART GALLERY
Piazza San Sebastiano 15, Col di Rodi
16th-17th century Tuscan paintings. Works by Bolognese and Neapolitan artists.
Tu.-Su. 9.30-12.30, 2-5.

COLLEGNO

ANTIQUARIUM
Church of San Massimo, Collegno
Finds from excavations in the area.
Tu.-Su. 9.30-1.

COLLE VAL D'ELSA

MUNICIPAL MUSEUM
Via del Castello, Colle val d'Elsa
Local history, archaeology. Folklore. Natural history.
Tu.-Su. 9.30-12.30, 3-6.

COLLODI

CHÂTEAU
Collodi, nr. Montecatini Terme
18th century and Empire furniture. In the kitchen of the Château Carlo Lorenzini, alias Collodi, began to relate the adventures of the famous puppet, Pinocchio.
Variable: enquire locally.

COLOGNA VENETA

MUNICIPAL MUSEUM
Piazza Mazzini, Cologna Veneta
Local history, archaeology. Roman and Venetian coins. Relics of the Risorgimento and World War I.
Tu.-Su. 9.30-12.30, 3-6.

COLORNO

LOMBARDI MUSEUM
Via Aurelio Saffi, Colorno
History. Paintings. Material illustrating life in 18th and 19th centuries.
Tu.-Su. 9.30-12.30, 3-6.

COMO

BARI ENTOMOLOGICAL COLLECTION
Via Zezio 35, Como
Butterflies. Beetles.
By appointment.

GARIBALDI MUSEUM
Piazza Medaglie d'Oro 1, Como
Historical material on the Risorgimento and World War I.
Tu.-Su. 9-12, 2-4.

MUNICIPAL MUSEUM
Piazza Medaglie d'Oro, Como
Prehistoric archaeology. Roman and Romanesque marbles. Numismatics. History of the Cathedral of Como. Prints. Decorative arts. 18th-19th century paintings.
Daily 10-12, 2-4.

NATURAL HISTORY COLLECTION
Liceo Scientifico Paulo Giovio, Como
Palaeontology. Ornithology. Zoology. Botany. Anatomy.
Tu.-Su. 9.30-12.30, 3-6.

POZZI MONTANDON ENTOMOLOGICAL COLLECTION
Via Diaz 98, Como
Butterflies. Beetles.
By appointment.

SILK MUSEUM
Scuola di Setificio, Como
European and oriental silks.
By appointment.

VOLTA MUSEUM
Viale Marconi, Como
Memorabilia of Alexander Volta (1745-1827). Inventions and designs by Volta.
Tu.-Su. 9.30-12.30, 3-6.

CONEGLIANO

MUNICIPAL MUSEUM
Castello, Piazzale di Castelvecchio, Conegliano
15th century bronzes, fescoes. Local history. Numismatics.
Tu.-Su. 9-1.

COPPARO

GALLERY OF MODERN ART
Palazzo Comunale, Copparo
Modern art collections.
Tu.-Su. 9.30-12.30, 3-6.

CORBETTA

PISANI-DOSSI ARCHAEOLOGICAL COLLECTION
Corbetta
Pre-Roman and Roman archaeology, vases. Pre-Columbian finds.
Tu.-Su. 9-1.

CORFINIO

CORFINIO MUSEUM
Via Basilica di S. Pelino, Corfinio
Local history, archaeology.
Tu.-Su. 9.30-12.30, 2-5.

CORI

ARCHAEOLOGICAL MUSEUM
Cori
Finds from archaeological excavations in the area.
Summer: daily 9-12, 3-6. Winter: daily 9-12, 3-5.

CORREGGIO

MUNICIPAL MUSEUM
Palazzo dei Principe, Correggio
In 16th century palace. Paintings include works by Mantegna and Flemish masters.
Tu.-Su. 9.30-12.30, 2-5.

CORRIDONIA

ARCHAEOLOGICAL COLLECTION
Corridonia
Prehistoric and Roman archaeology.
Tu.-Su. 9-1.

ART GALLERY
Via Cavour 52, Corridonia
Paintings, including works by local artists.
Tu.-Su. 9.30-12.30, 3-6.

CORTONA

DIOCESAN MUSEUM
Gesu Church, Piazza del Duomo, Cortona
Paintings by Signorelli, including a *Communion of the Apostles* and a *Descent from the Cross.* Works by other Italian artists, including Crespi of Bologna (1665-1747). Gold plate. Vagnucci reliquary (15th century) by Justus of Florence.
Daily 7-8 p.m.

MUSEUM OF EGYPTIAN AND ETRUSCAN ANTIQUITIES
Praetorian Palace, Piazza Signorelli, Cortona
Etruscan works, including a 5th century B.C. bronze oil lamp. Greco-Roman exhibits. Paintings, notably *Miracle of St. Benedict* (17th century Spanish school). Egyptian antiquities.
Daily ex. M. 9-12, 3.30-6 (3-5 in winter).

MUSEUM OF NATURAL SCIENCE
Monastero die Padri Redentoristi, Cortona
Natural history. Fossils. Minerals.
Tu.-Su. 9-12, 3.30-6.

COSENZA

MUNICIPAL MUSEUM
Piazza XV Marzo 7, Cosenza
Bronze objects from necropolis at Torre Mordilo (9th-7th century B.C.).
M.-Sa. 9-1; Su. 10-12.

COVIGNANO

MISSIONARY MUSEUM OF ART AND ETHNOGRAPHY
Le Grazie, Covignano
Ethnographical material collected by missionaries in Far East, Africa, South and Central America.
Tu.-Su. 9.30-12.30, 3-6.

CREMNA

MUNICIPAL MUSEUM
Via Dante 49, Cremna
Local history, archaeology. Natural history. Folklore. Paintings.
Tu.-Su. 9.30-12.30, 3-6.

CREMONA

CATHEDRAL
Cremona
17th century Brussels tapestries. Inlaid stalls (1490). Frescoes. Illuminated antiphonaries (1476-96). Sacristy cupboard with 29 intarsia-work doors by G. M. Platina (1477).
Treasury: Daily ex. M. and Su. afternoon, 9-12, 2-5.

MUNICIPAL MUSEUM AND PICTURE GALLERY
Palazzo Affaitati, Via Ugolani Dati 2, Cremona
Paintings by artists from Cremona, including works by Bembo (15th century), the Campi family (16th Century) and Boccaccino (d. 1525). Other artists include Salvator Rosa, Elsheimer, Nuvolone. Foreign schools: Provost, Breughel and Magnasco.
Daily 9-12, 3-6 (2-5 in winter).

MUSEUM OF NATURAL HISTORY
Palazzo dell'Arte, Piazza Marconi, Cremona
Mineralogy. Zoology. Ornithology. Entomology.
Tu.-Su. 9-12, 2-5.

ST. AUGUSTINE'S CHURCH
Cremona
Portraits of Francesco Sforza and Bianca Visconti by Bembo. 14th century bas-relief. Madonna (1494) by Perugino.
Usually closed 12-3.

STRADIVARIUS MUSEUM
Palazzo dell'Arte, Cremona
Memorabilia of the violin makers of Cremona.
Daily 9-12, 3-6 (2-5 in winter).

CROTONE

MUNICIPAL MUSEUM
Via Risorgimento, Crotone
Local history. Collection of coins of local mint showing a representation of the Delphic tripod.
Daily 10-1.

CUGGIONO

STUCCHI BOTANICAL COLLECTION
Cuggiono
Botanical collections.
By appointment.

CUNEO

MUNICIPAL MUSEUM OF HISTORY
Via Cacciatori delle Alpi 9, Cuneo
In 17th century palace. Local history. Folk art. Paintings. Archaeology. Religious art.
Tu.-Su. 9.30-12.30, 3-6.

DERUTA

MUNICIPAL ART GALLERY
Piazza dei Consoli, Deruta
Paintings. Local majolica (13th century onwards).
Tu.-Su. 9.30-12.30, 3-6.

DESIO

MARIANI SCIENTIFIC COLLECTION
Via XX Settembre 41, Desio
Natural history. Mineralogy. Geology. Fossils.
Tu.-Su. 9.30-12.30, 2-5.

MUNICIPAL MUSEUM OF NATURAL HISTORY
Preso il Municipio, Desio
Natural history. Mineralogy. Fossils.
Tu.-Su. 9.30-12.30, 2-5.

DOMODOSSOLA

GALLETTI MUSEUM
Piazza Convenzione 5, Domodossola
Mineralogy. Natural history. Numismatics. Paintings.
Tu.-Su. 9-12, 2-5.

NATURAL HISTORY COLLECTION
Collegio Rosmini, Domodossola
Mineralogy. Botany. Zoology.
By appointment.

SILVA MUSEUM
Palazzo Silva, Via del Museo 1, Domodossola
Antiquities from local excavations. Decorative arts. Paintings. Numismatics.
Tu.-Su. 9.30-12.30, 3-6; Su. 10-1.

SIMPLON MUSEUM
Collegio Mellerio Rosmini, Via Rosmini, Domodossola
Collections illustrating the construction of the Simplon Tunnel.
Daily ex. M. 9.30-12.30, 3-6; Su. 10-1.

EMPOLI

ART GALLERY
Collegiata di Sant'Andrea, Empoli
14th-17th century Tuscan painting, sculpture, miniatures.
By appointment.

ENNA

ALESSI MUSEUM
Casa Canonica, Piazza Duomo, Enna, Sicily
Material from the Cathedral treasury. Sicilian, Greek and Roman coins. Missiles (glandes). Bronzes. Pottery.
Daily 9-1.

ERACLEA MINOA

ANTIQUARIUM AND ARCHAEOLOGICAL SITE
Eraclea Minoa, Sicily
Archaeological material from excavations in the area.
Tu.-Su. 9.30-sunset.

ERBA

MUNICIPAL ARCHAEOLOGICAL MUSEUM
Villa Majnoni, Erba
Finds from excavations in the area. Sculpture. Inscriptions.
Tu.-Su. 9.30-12.30, 3-6.

ERICE

CORDICI CATALDO MUSEUM
Piazza Municipio, Erice, Sicily
Fragments from the Temple of Venus. Paintings include an *Annunciation* by Antonello Gagini (1525).
M.-Sa. 8.30-2.30; Su. 9-1 (also 4-6 in summer).

ESINO LARIO

GRIGNA MUSEUM
Via Adamello, Esino Lario
Gallo-Roman archaeology. Palaeontology. Folklore.
Tu.-Su. 9.30-12.30, 2-5.

ESTE

ATESTINO NATIONAL MUSEUM
Palazzo Mocenigo, Via Negri, Este
Archaeological collections: Venetian antiquities, including engraved bronze vases and statuettes. Roman mosaics and coins.
Daily ex. M. 9-12, 3-6 (Oct.-Mar. 1-3). Closed Jan. 1, May 1, June 2, Aug. 15, Easter Su. and Christmas Day.

FABRIANO

CANAVARI MUSEUM OF MINERALOGY
Viale Gramsci, Fabriano
Mineralogy, especially of Italy
Tu.-Su. 9-12, 2-5.

MUNICIPAL ART GALLERY AND ARAZZI MUSEUM
Piazza Umberto di Savoia 3, Fabriano
Local history. Paintings. 17th century rugs. Flemish tapestries.
Tu.-Su. 9.30-12.30, 3-6.

ORNITHOLOGICAL COLLECTION
Seminario Vescovile, Via Gioberti 2, Fabriano
Ornithology.
By appointment.

FAENZA

GALLERY OF MODERN ART
Corso Matteotti, Faenza
19-20th century paintings, sculpture, graphics, especially by Italian artists.
Tu.-Su. 9.30-12.30, 3-6.

DIOCESAN ART GALLERY
Palazzo Vascovile, Faenza
Religious art. Miniatures.
Tu.-Su. 9.30-1.

INTERNATIONAL CERAMICS MUSEUM
Viale Baccarini, Faenza
Italian and foreign ceramics. Majolica of the Italian Renaissance from Urbino, Castello and Liguria. Modern pottery by Matisse, Picasso, Chagall, Léger and Lurçat.
Daily ex. Su. afternoon, 9-1, 3-6. Nov. 1 - June 15, 2.30-5.30.

MUNICIPAL MUSEUM AND PICTURE GALLERY
Town Hall, Piazza del Popolo, Via S. Maria dell'Angelo 2, Faenza
Paintings and statues, including a *Byzantine Madonna* by Giovanni da Rimini, a wooden statue of St. Jerome the Hermit, attributed to Donatello, pictures of the Ferrara school (1484) and a bust of St. John the Baptist as a child by Antonio Rossellino. Other works include *The Lovers* by Vouet, and a portrait of King Charles I of England by Franz Pourbus the Younger.
Daily ex. Sa. and Su. afternoons, 9.30-12.30, 2.30-4.30.

MUSEUM OF THE RISORGIMENTO
Via Manfredi 14, Faenza
Documents and other material illustrating Italy's struggle for independence.
Tu.-Su. 9.30-12.30, 3-6.

THEATRE MUSEUM
Via Manfredi 14, Faenza
History of the theatre. Costumes. Stage sets. Posters. Programmes.
Tu.-Su. 9.30-12.30, 3-6.

TORRICELLI MUSEUM
Via Manfredi 14, Faenza
Collections illustrating the life and work of the physicist, E. Torricelli (1608-1647).
Tu.-Su. 9-1, 3-6.

TORRICELLI MUSEUM OF NATURAL SCIENCES
Liceo Ginnasio Statale, Faenza
Natural history. Zoology. Grottos.
By appointment.

ZOOLOGICAL MUSEUM
Giardino Zoologico, Faenza
Zoology.
Tu.-Su. 9.30-12.30, 3-6.

FALCONARA MARITTIMA

CUPPARI MUSEUM
Istituto Tecnico Commerciale e per Geometri, Falconara Marittima
Geo-mineralogy. Natural history. Botany.
By appointment.

MORODER ENTOMOLOGICAL COLLECTION
Villa Moroder, Falconara Alta, Falconara Marittima
Entomology.
Tu.-Su. 9.30-12.30, 3-6.

FALERONE

MUNICIPAL MUSEUM
Palazzo Comunale, Falerone
Local history. Roman archaeology. Remains of Roman theatre. Paintings. Urns.
Tu.-Su. 9.30-12.30, 3-6.

FANO

FEDERICIANA LIBRARY
Fano
Library Museum. Globes of Colonnelli.
During library hours.

MALATESTIANO MUSEUM
Piazza XX Settembre, Fano
Local history. Paintings. Ceramics. Coins.
Tu.-Su. 9-1, 3-6.

NATURAL HISTORY COLLECTIONS
Malatestiano Museum, Piazza XX Settembre, Fano
Natural history.
Tu.-Su. 9-1, 3-6.

FAVARA

BARONE ANTONIO MENDOLA MUNICIPAL MUSEUM AND LIBRARY
Piazza Cavour 56, Favara, Sicily
Local history. Minerals. Volcanic stones. Natural history.
Tu.-Su. 9.30-12.30, 3-6.

FELTRE

ART MUSEUM
Via Lorenzo Luzzo, nr. the Porta Oria, Feltre
Paintings, including a portrait by Bellini, a Virgin by Cima da Congegliano and a landscape attributed to Jan Metzys.
Daily 8-12, 2-6.

MUNICIPAL MUSEUM
Via Lorenzo Lauro, Feltre
Roman and Etruscan remains. Paintings by Morto da Feltre. Local history.
Daily 8-12, 2-6.

RIZZARDA MUSEUM
Via del Paradiso, Feltre
Wrought-iron work. Gallery of modern art.
Daily 8-12, 2-6.

FÈNIS

THE FORTRESS
Fènis, Valle d'Aosta
Frescoes. Carved furniture in the style of the Valle d'Aosta.
Daily ex. M. 9-12, 2-6 (2-5 in winter).

FERENTINO

MUNICIPAL COLLECTION
Viale XX Settembre 4, Ferentino
Local history, archaeology. Medieval reliefs.
Tu.-Su. 9.30-12.30, 3-6.

FERMO

ARCHAEOLOGICAL MUSEUM
Piazza Calzecchi, Fermo
Archaeological finds from sites in the district.
Tu.-Su. 9-1, 3-6.

MUNICIPAL ART GALLERY
Palazzo del Comune, Fermo
Paintings, especially by local artists.
Tu.-Su. 9-1, 3-6.

FERRARA

ARIOSTO'S HOUSE
Via Ariosto 67, Ferrara
Former home of Ariosto. Memorabilia of the poet.
Tu.-Su. 9.30-12.30. 3-6.

CASA ROMEI MUSEUM
Via Savonarola 30, Ferrara
In 15th century 'Casa Romei'. Original decorations, frescoes. Medieval and Renaissance sculptures.
Tu.-Su. 8.30-12, 2-6 (winter 8.30-12, 2-5).

CATHEDRAL MUSEUM
Cathedral, Piazza Cattedrale, Ferrara
Bas-reliefs of the late 12th century representing the months of the year, taken from the south door. Two early 15th century statues by Jacopo della Quercia. 16th century tapestries portraying St. George and St. Maurillo, patron saints of Ferrara, and two works by Cosimo Tura, and *Annunciation* and a *St. George slaying the Dragon.*
Daily ex. Su. and holiday afternoons, 10-12, 3-5.

ESTE CASTLE
Ferrara
Public rooms painted with 16th century mythological and allegorical frescoes. Chapel of Princess Renée of France, decorated with porphyry and marble. Cell in which Parisina and Hugo were murdered in 1425.
Daily 9-12, 3-6 (Oct.-Mar. 2-5). Closed Jan. 1, June 2, Nov. 4, Easter Su. and Christmas Day.

LAPIDARY MUSEUM
Palace of Diamonds, Corso Ercole d'Este 2, Ferrara
Lapidary collections. Inscriptions. Roman epitaphs.
Daily ex. M., Su. and holiday afternoons, 9-1, 3-6 (Nov.-May 9-4).

MUNICIPAL MUSEUM
Schifanoia Palace, Via Scandiana 23, Ferrara
Collection of missals and antiphonaries illuminated with miniatures. Medals. Room of the Months is decorated with frescoes (1467-1470) by Francesco Cossa and Ercole dei Roberti, among others.
May-Aug. Daily ex. Tu., Su. and holiday afternoons, 9-12, 3-6. Sept.-Apr. 10-12, 2-5.

MUNICIPAL MUSEUM OF NATURAL HISTORY
Via Previati 24, Ferrara
Mineralogy. Geology. Palaeontology. Zoology. Botany. Lithology.
Tu.-Su. 9-12, 3-6.

MUSEUM OF THE RISORGIMENTO
Palace of Diamonds, Corso Ercole d'Este 19, Ferrara
History of the area. The struggle for Italian independence. Documents. Weapons. Uniforms. Medals.
Daily ex. M., Su. and holiday afternoons, 9-1, 3-6 (Nov.-May 9-4).

PALAZZINA MARFISA D'ESTE
Corso Giovecca, Ferrara
House (1559) frequented by friends of the Marfisa d'Este, subject of poems by Tasso. Painted ceilings. 16th century furniture. Outdoor theatre with frescoes of a trellis perched on by flocks of birds.
Daily ex. M. 9-12, 3-6 (Oct.-Mar. 10-12.30, 2-5). Closed from 12.30 on Su. and holidays.

PICTURE GALLERY
Palace of Diamonds, Corso Ercole d'Este 21, Ferrara
Paintings of the Ferrara school, including a *St. Jerome* attributed to Ercole dei Roberti, and two medallions; the *Capture* and *Martyrdom of St. Maurillo* by Cosima Tura; *Death of a Virgin* by Carpaccio. Altarpieces and a fresco of the Last Supper by Garofalo. *Madonna between Saints* by Dosso Dossi in chiaroscuro. Modern art gallery.
Daily ex. M., Su. and holiday afternoons, 9-1, 3-6 (Nov.-May 9-4).

SPINA NATIONAL ARCHAEOLOGICAL MUSEUM
Palace of Ludovic the Moor, Via XX Settembre 124, Ferrara
Finds from excavations of the Etruscan city of Spina. Ceramics brought from Greece (5th and 4th century B.C.) and found in tombs at Spina. Gold ornaments. Etruscan, Greek statuettes, bronzes.
Daily ex. Tu., Su. and holiday afternoons, 9-1, 3-6 (Oct.-Apr. 9.30-4).

FIDENZA

MUSEUM OF THE RISORGIMENTO
Piazza Garibaldi, Fidenza
Material illustrating Italy's struggle for independence.
Tu.-Su. 9.30-12.30, 3-6.

FIESOLE

BANDINI MUSEUM
Via Giovanni Dupré, Fiesole
15th century paintings, including work by Jacopo del Sellaio. Terracottas by Della Robbia. Paintings by Nicolo Pisano.
Daily 9-12, 3-8. (winter: daily 10-12, 2-5).

MISSIONARY MUSEUM
Franciscan Friary, Via San Francesco 13, Fiesole
Collections of Far Eastern objets d'art.
On application.

MUSEUM OF STONES AND FOSSILS
Roman Theatre, Fiesole
Collections of stones and fossils from the area. Archaeological exhibits. Stelae and urns. Sculpture. Early Christian and medieval antiquities. The Roman Theatre was built at the time of Sulla.
Summer: Daily 9-12, 3-8. Winter: Daily 10-12, 2-5.

FINALE LIGURE

MUNICIPAL MUSEUM
Via Ghiglieri 1, Finale Ligure
Local history. Archaeological finds from caves in the district.
Tu.-Su. 9.30-12.30, 3-6; winter 10-4.

FLORENCE

"A. DELLA RAGIONE" MODERN ART COLLECTIONS
Piazza Signoria 5, Florence
Paintings by contemporary Italian artists.
Daily 9-4; Tu. 9-12.

ANTHROPOLOGICAL AND ETHNOGRAPHICAL MUSEUM
Via del Proconsolo 12, Florence
Anthropology and ethnography, including objects from America, Africa, Asia and New Guinea. Bones and skulls.
On request, Su. and holidays 9.30-12.30.

ARCHAEOLOGICAL MUSEUM
Via della Colonna, Florence
Etruscan, Egyptian and Greco-Roman art. Statues, pottery, sarcophagi, mummies, coins. Precious stones. Ceramics from Cyprus, Crete, Rhodes and Greece. Vases and terracottas. Etruscan plaster-casts and paintings.
Summer: M.-Sa. 9-1, 3-6. Winter: M.-Sa. 9.30-4. Su. 9-1. Holidays 10-1.

BARDINI MUSEUM AND CORSI GALLERY
Piazza de'Mozzi, Florence
Paintings. Sculptures. Antique furniture. Terracottas. Stuccos. Weapons. Persian carpets. Paintings by Della Robbia, Tiepolo, Piazzetta, Guercino, Paolo Ucello. 16th-20th century paintings.
M.-Sa. 9-4; Su., W. and holidays 9-12.

BOBOLI GARDENS
Piazza Pitti, Florence
Antique and Renaissance statues in terraced gardens (1550).
Summer: M.-Sa. 9-6.30. Winter: M.-Sa. 9-4.30.

BOTANICAL MUSEUM
Via Lamarmora 4, Florence
Botanical specimens from Italy and elsewhere.
M., W., F. 9-12.

CARTOGRAPHY AND INSTRUMENTS MUSEUM
Istituto Geografico Militare, Florence
Astronomy. Geodesy. Topography. Historic instruments. 16th-19th century maps.
By appointment.

CHURCH OF THE HOLY CROSS MUSEUM
Piazza S. Croce 16, Florence
Museum of religious art.
M.-Sa. 9-12, 3-6; Su. and holidays 10-12.

CLOISTERS OF SANTA MARIA NOVELLA
Palazza Santa Maria Novella, Florence
Cloisters decorated with frescoes by 14th-17th century Tuscan masters. 14th century religious frescoes.
Tu.-Su. 9.30-12.30, 3-6.

COLLECTION OF CARRIAGES
Palazzo Pitti, Piazza Pitti, Florence
Carriages, or berlines, formerly in use in the Courts of Tuscany, Modena and the Two Sicilies, and dating from 17th-18th centuries.
On application

COLLECTIONS OF THE GALILEO ISTITUTO TECNICO COMMERCIALE E GEOMETRI
Florence
Physics. Chemistry. Topography. Commerce. Agriculture. Ceramics. Palaeontology.
By appointment.

CORSINI GALLERY
Palazgo Corsini, Via Parione 11, Florence
Paintings by Italian and foreign artists, including Sustermans, Rigaud and Van Dyck. Italian artists include Botticelli, Filippino Lippi, Luca Signorelli, Andrea del Castagno, Caravaggio, Salvator Rosa, Fra. Bartolomeo and Luca Giordano.
Sa. 12-1.

DUPRÉ MUSEUM
Via degli Artisti 12, Florence
Sculptures, terracottas and marbles by Giovanni Dupré.
Tu.-Su. 9.30-12.30, 3-6.

"FLORENCE AS IT WAS"
Via dell'Oriuolo 24, Florence
History of the city of Florence, especially between 1800 and 1900. Water-colours, drawings, paintings by Callot, Zocchi, Signorini, Rosai, illustrating the city.
Daily ex. Th. 9-4; Th. 9-12.

FOLIGNO SALON AND FERONI GALLERY
Via Faenza 42, Florence
15th-18th century paintings.
Tu.-Sa. 10-4; Su. and holidays 10-1.

GALLERY OF THE ACADEMY
Via Ricácoli 52, Florence
Florentine primitives and works by Michaelangelo, including the original of *David.*
Summer: Tu.-Sa. 9.30-4.30. Winter: Tu.-Sa. 9.30-4. Su. 9-1.

GALLERY OF THE OSPEDALE DEGLI INNOCENTI
Piazza Santissima Annunziata 12, Florence
15th century portico by Brunelleschi, with corners decorated with medallions of children (1463) by Andrea Della Robbia. Gallery contains an *Adoration of the Magi* (1488) by Ghirlandaio, a terracotta *Virgin and Child* by Luca Della Robbia, and works by Filippo Lippi and Piero di Cosimo (15th century).
Tu.-Sa. 9.30-1, 2-4.30, Holidays 9-1. Closed M.

GHIRLANDAIO COLLECTION
Borgo Ognissanti 38, Florence
Collection of paintings by Ghirlandaio, including his *Last Supper* (1480).
Tu.-Su. 9.30-1.

HOUSE OF MICHELANGELO BUONARROTI
Via Ghibellina 70, Florence
Works by Michelangelo. *Madonna* in marble. *Battle of the Centaurs and the Lapithae.* Sketches. Works by other artists, illustrating Michelangelo's life and the history of his family.
Summer: M.-Sa. 10-4.30. Winter: M.-Sa. 10-4. Su. and holidays 9-1. Closed Tu.

LA SPECOLA MUSEUM OF ZOOLOGY
University of Florence, Via Romana 17, Florence
Zoology. 18th-19th century anatomical preparations.
Winter: Tu. 9-12.30; Sa. 2-5. Summer: Tu. 9-12.30; Sa. 3-7; Su. 9-12.30.

LOGGIA DELLA SIGNORIA
Piazza degli Uffizi, Florence
Building (1376-81). Sculptures: *Rape of the Sabines*, by Giambologna (1583); *Perseus*, by Benevenuto Cellini; *Hercules and the Centaur*, by Giambologna; *Rape of Polyxena*, by Pio Fedi (1866).
Daily ex. M. 9-12, 3-6.

MEDICI CHAPELS
Piazza Madonna degli Aldobrandini, Florence
Princes' Chapel, containing tombs of the Medicis, Grand Dukes of Tuscany, in 17th-18th centuries. The architecture and sculptures in the New Sacristy are by Michelangelo - the tombs designed so that Giuliano de'Medici (d.1516) appears as Action, Lorenzo II de'Medici (d.1519) as a Thinker.
Summer: M.-Sa. 9-5. Winter: M.-Sa. 9-4. Su. and holidays, 9.30-12.30.

MEDICI MUSEUM
Medici-Riccardi Palace, Via Cavour 1, Florence
On ground floor of Renaissance palace. Exhibits include a *Virgin and Child* by Filippo Lippi; death mask of Lorenzo the Magnificent; portrait of Catherine de'Medici by Clouet and a series of portraits of the Medicis by Bronzino. A chapel on the first floor of the palace contains frescoes by Benozzo Gozzoli (1459).
M-Sa. 9-1, 3-5.30; Su. and holidays 9-12.

MODERN ART GALLERY
Palazzo Pitti, Piazza Pitti, Florence
Paintings and sculptures of 19th-20th centuries, mainly works by Tuscan artists: Fattori, Signorini, Lega, Sernesi, Fontanesi, Toma, Morelli. Sculptors include Gemito, Rosso, Dupré and Libero Andreotti.
Summer: M.-Sa. 9.30-4.30; Su. 9-1. Winter: M.-Sa. 9.30-4; Su. 9-1. Closed Tu.

MONASTERY OF SANTA APOLLONIA
Via XXVII Aprile 1, Florence
Refectory contains *Last Supper* (1430) by Andrea del Castagno, and portraits of Dante, Petrarch, Boccaccio and others, by the same artist.
Daily 9-11.30, 2-3.30. Closed Jan. 1, May 1, June 2, Aug. 15, Dec. 25 and Su. and holiday afternoons.

MOSAICS WORKSHOPS
Via Alfani 78, Florence
Collection of mosaics and of materials used in their manufacture.
M.-F. 9.30-4.30; Sa., Su. and holidays, 9.30-12.30.

MUSEUM OF THE CATHEDRAL DI SANTA MARIA DEL FIORE
Piazza Duomo 9, Florence
Statues from former façade of the Cathedral. Manuscripts and gold plate. Statues by Donatello of the prophets Jeremiah and Habakkuk. *Cantorie* (choiristers' tribunes) from the cathedral, by Luca Della Robbia and Donatello.
Apr.-Sept. M.-Sa. 9.30-1, 2.30-5.30. Oct.-Mar. M.-Sa. 9.30-4; Su. and holidays 10-12.30. Closed Jan. 1, May 1, June 2, Easter and Christmas.

MUSEUM OF THE CENACOLO DI SANTO SPIRITO
Piazza Santo Spirito, Florence
In refectory. Frescoes. Sculptures. Stuccoes. Marbles.
Tu.-Su. 9.30-12.30, 3-6.

MUSEUM OF GEOLOGY AND PALAEONTOLOGY
University of Florence, Via Lamarmora 4, Florence
Geology. Palaeontology.
M. 2-5.30; Th., Sa. 10-1. Closed holidays, also July 15-Aug. 31.

MUSEUM OF THE HORNE FOUNDATION
Via dei Benci 6, Florence
Furniture. Drawings by Giotto. Works by Benozzo Gozzoli, Lorenzetti, S. Martini. Sculpture by Des. da Settignano and Ben. da Rovezzano.
M. and Th. 10-1, 3-5. Closed Aug.

MUSEUM OF MINERALOGY
University of Florence, Via Lamarmora 4, Florence
Mineralogical specimens.
M.-Sa. 9-12.

MUSEUM OF MUSICAL INSTRUMENTS
Via degli Alfani 84, Florence
Instruments made by Stradivarius, Amati, Ruggieri and Guarneri del Gesù, and others.
M.-Sa. 10-12.

MUSEUM OF THE OLD FLORENTINE HOUSE
Palazzo Davanzati, Piazza Davanzati, Florence
14th century palazzo, displaying furnishings and fittings of a Florentine house of 15th-17th centuries. Wall-paintings and frescoes.
Summer: Tu.-Sa. 9.30-4.30. Winter, 9.30-4. Su. 9-1. Closed M.

MUSEUM OF PREHISTORY
Via Sant'Egidio 21, Florence
Prehistoric finds from all parts of the world.
Tu.-Su. 9.30-12.30, 3-6.

MUSEUM OF SAN MARCO
Piazzo San Marco, Florence
Collection of paintings by Fra. Angelico, Fra. Bartolomeo and Ghirlandaio. Monks' cells decorated by Fra. Angelico and his associates. Savonarola's cell, containing souvenirs and his portrait by Fra. Bartolomeo. Library contains illuminated choir-books and psalters (15th-16th century).
Summer: Tu.-Sa. 9.30-4.30. Winter: Tu.-Sa. 9.30-4; Su. 9-1.

NATIONAL MUSEUM
Palazzo del Bargello, Via del Proconsolo 4, Florence
Paintings by Dontatello, Michelangelo. Terracottas by Della Robbia. Works by Cellini. Renaissance sculptures by Sansovino, Antonio Pollavolo and Verrocchio (statue of David). Medals. Bronzes.
Summer: M.-Sa. 9.30-4.30. Winter: 9.30-4. Su. 9-1. Closed Tu., also Jan. 1, May 1, June 2, Aug. 15, Christmas Day.

NATIONAL MUSEUM OF DECORATIVE ARTS
Piazza della Libertà 1, Florence
Decorative arts.
Tu.-Su. 9.30-12.30, 3-6.

NATIONAL MUSEUM FOR THE HISTORY OF SCIENCE
Piazza dei Giudici 1, Florence
Instruments illustrating the progress of science from ancient times. Optical, mathematical and electrical instruments. Pacinotti's electromagnetic apparatus. Edison's first phonograph. Italian, French and English barometers. Original instruments of Galileo. Old works dealing with seaports, old maps, and rare atlases.
M.-Sa. 10-1, 2-4. Closed public holidays.

ORSANMICHELE (TABERNACOLO)
Via Arte della Lana 1, Florence
Originally a granary, and rebuilt 1337-1404 as an oratory for the craftsmen and guilds of Florence. Statues of the patrons of the corporations, fine examples of 14th-16th century Florentine sculpture. 14th century Gothic tabernacle by Orcagna.
M.-Sa. 9-12, 3-6. Holidays 9-12.

PALATINE GALLERY
Palazzo Pitti, Piazza Pitti, Florence
Eleven Raphaëls, including *Madonna of the Chair* and the *Grand Duke's Madonna.* Other paintings include works by Filippo Lippi, Andrea del Sarto, Titian, Tintoretto, Rubens, Veronese, Van Dyck and Breughel.
Summer: M.-Sa. 9.30-4.30; Su. 9-1; holidays 9-4. Winter: M.-Sa. 9.30-4; Su. 9-1; Closed Tu.

PALAZZO VECCHIO AND MONUMENTAL APARTMENTS
Piazza Signoria, Florence
Paintings and sculptures, including works by Vasari and Benedetto da Maiano. The Sala dei Cinquecento contains frescoes by Vasari and others, and a group carved by Michelangelo. 16th century Florentine tapestries.
Apr.-Sept. M.-F. 9-6. Oct.-Mar. M.-F. 9-4. Sa., Su. and holidays 9-12.

PERUGINO COLLECTION
Via della Colonna 11, Florence
Collection of paintings by Perugino.
Tu.-Su. 9.30-1.

SAN SALVI MONASTERY
Via Andrea del Sarto 16, Florence
Former refectory of the abbey contains a *Last Supper* (1526-27) by Andrea del Sarto.
M.-Sa. 9.30-4; Su. and holidays 9-1. Closed Jan. 1, June 2, Aug. 15, Easter Su. and Christmas Day.

SCALZO CLOISTER MUSEUM
Via Camillo Cavour 69, Florence
In 16th century cloister. 16th century frescoes.
Tu.-Su. 9.30-12.30, 3-6.

SCIENTIFIC COLLECTIONS
Istituto Italiano di Paleontologia Umana, Via del Proconsolo 12, Florence
Human palaeontology, osteology.
By appointment.

SEMI-PRECIOUS STONE WORKSHOP MUSEUM
Via degli Alfani 82, Florence
Uncut stones, prepared stones and part of the material for the Medici Chapel.
Tu.-Sa. 8-2; Su. and holidays 9.30-12.30.

SILVER MUSEUM
Palazzo Pitti, Piazza Pitti, Florence
Collection of silversmiths' work. Carvings. Porcelain. Ivory. Tapestries. Limoges enamels. The Medici gems include cameo portraits of famous Florentines and others.
Summer: M.-Sa. 9.30-4.30; Su. 9-1. Winter: M.-Sa. 9.30-4; Su. 9-1. Closed Tu.

STIBBERT MUSEUM
Via Stibbert 26, Florence
Weapons (including some from China, Japan and other oriental countries). Terracottas. Decorative objects. Bronzes. Medals. Porcelain. Paintings.
M.-Sa. 9-4; Su. and holidays 9-12. Closed Th.

UFFIZI GALLERY
Loggiato degli Uffizi 6, Florence
16th century tapestries. Classical Greek sculpture, notably the *Medici Venus.* Florentine and Tuscan Paintings (14th-16th centuries). Paintings of the Italian and foreign schools of the 15th and 16th centuries. Works by Montegna, Bellini, Dürer, Holbein, Cranach and Correggio. 15th-19th century miniatures. Italian paintings of 16th-18th centuries, including works by Titian, Veronese and Tintoretto. 17th century Flemish school: Rubens and Van Dyck. 17th-18th century French school.
Tu.-Sa. 9.30-4; Su. and holidays 9-1. Closed M., and Jan. 1, May 1, June 2, Aug. 15 and Dec. 25.

FOGGIA

MUNICIPAL MUSEUM
Piazza Nigri 1, Foggia
Local archaeological material. Bygones. Gallery of modern paintings.
M.-Sa. 9-1.

PEDONE ORNITHOLOGICAL COLLECTION
Presso Museo Comunale, Convento di San Domenico, Foggia
Ornithology. Prehistoric finds. Applied arts.
Tu.-Su. 9-1.

FOLIGNO

ARCHAEOLOGICAL MUSEUM AND PICTURE GALLERY
Palazzo Trinci, Foligno
Paintings and historical exhibits in rooms decorated with 15th century frescoes.
May-Sept. Daily 9-12, 4-6.30. Oct.-Apr. Daily 9-12, 2-4.30. Closed Su. afternoon.

FONDI

ANTIQUARIUM
Cloister of the Convento di San Francesco, Fondi
Epigraphs. Local historic architecture. Sculpture.
Tu.-Su. 9-1.

FONTANELLATO

MUSEUM OF THE ROCCA DEI SANVITALE
Piazza Matteotti 1, Fontanellato
Frescoes by Parmigianino. 17th-18th century furniture and furnishings.
Tu.-Su. 9.30-12.30, 3-6.

FORIO D'ISCHIA

GIOVANNI MALTESE MUNICIPAL MUSEUM
Forio d'Ischia
Sculpture by local master Giovanni Maltese (d.1913).
Tu.-Su. 9.30-12.30, 3-6.

FORLI

ETHNOGRAPHICAL MUSEUM
Corso Vittorio Emanuele 32, Forli
Furniture. Folk art. Costumes. Domestic interiors. Applied arts.
Tu.-Su. 9-12.30, 3.30-6.

MUSEUM OF CERAMICS
Corso della Repubblica 72, Forli
Ceramics, especially Italian.
Tu.-Su. 9.30-12.30, 3-6.

MUSEUM AND PICTURE GALLERY
Corso della Repubblica 72, Forli
In former hospital (1772). Finds from prehistoric sites, and Roman material from the province. Art. Flemish tapestries. Works by Rossellino, Fra Angelico. Ethnographical section. Ceramics. Weapons. Armour.
Daily 9-12.30, 3.30-6; Sa. 9-12.

MUSEUM OF THE RISORGIMENTO
Corso Garibaldi 96, Forli
History of the Risorgimento and memorabilia of local participants.
Tu.-Su. 9.30-12.30, 3-6.

MUSEUM OF THE TEATRO ROMAGNOLO
Corso Garibaldi 26, Forli
History of the Teatro Romagnolo. Memorabilia of local authors, actors, musicians.
Tu.-Su. 9.30-12.30, 3-6.

FORLIMPOPOLI

MUNICIPAL MUSEUM
Nella Rocca Sforzesca, Forlimpopoli
Local Roman archaeology.
Tu.-Su. 9-1.

FORMIA

ANTIQUARIUM
Piazza della Vittoria, Formia
Epigraphs. Bronzes. Medieval coins. Architecture. Military history.
Tu.-Su. 9.30-12.30, 3-6.

FOSSOMBRONE

VERNARECCI MUNICIPAL MUSEUM
Via Cortile Emilia Pia 3, Fossombrone
History. Archaeology. Numismatics. Sculpture. Paintings, drawings, engravings. Ceramics.
Tu.-Su. 9.30-12.30, 3-6.

FRANCAVILLA AL MARE

MUNICIPAL ART GALLERY
Palazzo Comunale, Francavilla al Mare
Paintings, especially by local artists.
Tu.-Su. 9.30-4.

FRASCATI

ETHIOPIAN MUSEUM
Convento dei Cappuccini, Via Massaia 26, Frascati
Ethnographical collections, including manuscripts and other material from Ethiopia.
Tu.-Su. 9.30-12.30, 3-6.

TUSCANY MUSEUM
Piazza Paolo III, Frascati
Prehistoric - Roman archaeology, sculpture and decorative arts.
Tu.-Su. 9.30-12.30, 3-6.

FUCECCHIO

LENSI ORNITHOLOGICAL COLLECTION
Piazza San Giovanni 12, Fucecchio
Birds of the Fucecchio area. Migrant birds. Birds of prey.
Tu.-Su. 9-1.

GAETA

DIOCESAN MUSEUM
Piazza del Duomo, Gaeta
Religious art. 12th-17th century paintings, sculpture.
Tu.-Su. 9.30-12.30, 3-6.

GAIOLI IN CHIANTI

MALACOLOGICAL COLLECTION
Villa Spaltenna, Gaioli in Chianti
Zoology. Invertebrates.
Tu.-Su. 9.30-12.30, 3-6.

GALATINA

PIETRO CAVOTI MUSEUM OF ART
Via Umberto I 36, Galatina
Decorative arts. Local paintings. Ethnography of Abyssinia.
Tu.-Su. 9.30-12.30, 3-6.

GALEATA

MAMBRINI MUSEUM
Via Ferdinando Zannetti 14, Galeata
Iron Age and Roman archaeological finds. Roman sculpture, armaments.
Tu.-Su. 9-1.

GALLARATE

MUSEUM OF THE GALLARATE SOCIETY FOR NATIONAL STUDIES
Via Borgo Antico 4, Gallarate
Prehistoric and Roman finds. Local history. Material on the Risorgimento.
Tu.-Su. 9.30-12.30, 3-6.

GALLIPOLI

MUNICIPAL MUSEUM
Via Antonietta de Pace 108, Gallipoli
Local history. Natural history. Ethnography. Archaeology. Paintings.
Tu.-Su. 9.20-12.30, 3-6.

GANDINO

CATHEDRAL MUSEUM
Gandino
Local history. Ancient textiles. Folklore. Goldsmiths' work.
On request.

GARDONE DI SOPRA

MUSEUM
Vittoriale degli Italiani, Gardone di Sopra
Collections illustrating the life and work of Gabriele d'Annunzio (1863-1938).
Daily ex. M. 8-6.30.

GARDONE RIVIERA

VITTORIALE ESTATE
Gardone Riviera, Lake Garda
Villa belonging to Gabriele d'Annunzio (1863-1938), who is buried here. Mementoes of d'Annunzio.
Daily 8-6. Oct.-Apr. closed 12-2.

GAVARDO

MUNICIPAL MUSEUM
Via Mulino 44, Gavardo
Local prehistory, history. Archaeology. Palaeontology.
Tu.-Su. 9.30-12.30, 3-6.

GELA

NATIONAL MUSEUM
Corso Vittorio Emanuele, Gela
Archaeology. Pottery. Vases. Medals.
Apr.-Sept. Daily 9-1, 3-5. Oct.-Mar. Daily 9-2.

GEMONA DEL FRIULI

TREASURY
Cathedral, Gemona del Friuli
Ecclesiastical paintings, liturgical items, including a Gothic reliquary.
May-Sept. Daily 8-12, 3-7. Oct.-Apr. 9-12, 2-5. Apply to the sacristan.

GENOA

ART GALLERY
Palazzo Bianco, Via Garibaldi 11, Genoa
Flemish and Dutch paintings, including works by Provost, Van der Goes, Gerard David, Van Dyck and Rubens. Exhibits by artists of the local school. Sculpture. Tapestries. Paganini's violin. Letters of Columbus.
Tu.-Sa. 10-12, 2-6; Su. 10-12. Closed afternoons of Feb. 11, Sept. 28, Oct. 4, Nov. 2, Dec. 24 and 31, and all day holidays. Closed M.

ART GALLERY
Palazzo Rosso, Via Garibaldi 18, Genoa
Works by local artists. Paintings by Veronese, Tintoretto, Caravaggio, Il Guercino and Dürer. Collection of Van Dyck portraits. Sculpture. Ceramics. Medals.
M.-Sa. 10-12, 2-6; Su. 10-12. Closed Tu. and holidays. Closed afternoons of Feb. 11, Sept. 28, Oct. 4, Nov. 2, Dec. 24 and 31.

CATALDI PALACE
Via Garibaldi 4, Genoa
Frescoes and decorations by G. B. Castello. Gilded gallery, painted by Lorenzo de Ferrari.
M.-Sa. 9-12, 3-7; Su. 9-12. Apply to the Chamber of Commerce.

CHIOSSONE MUSEUM
Palace of the Accademia Lugistica di Belle Arti, Piazza de Ferraris 5, Genoa
Japanese painting and engraving. Fabrics. Armour. Enamels. Statues. Ceramics.
Daily ex. M. 9.30-12.30, 3-6 (winter: 10-4). Closed public holidays.

COLLECTIONS OF THE HAMBURY BOTANICAL INSTITUTE
Corso Dogali 1/C, Genoa
Botany. Flora of Europe. Herbarium.
Tu.-Su. 9-1.

COLLECTION OF THE INSTITUTE OF COMPARATIVE ANATOMY
Via Balbi 5, Genoa
Comparative anatomy.
By appointment.

COLLECTIONS OF THE INSTITUTE OF GEOLOGY
Via Balbi 5, Genoa
Geology. Palaeontology.
By appointment.

COLLECTIONS OF THE ISTITUTO NAVALE DELLA FACOLTA DI INGEGNERIA
Genoa
Ships' models. Models of steamers, submarines, sailing ships.
By appointment.

COLLECTIONS OF THE INSTITUTE OF ZOOLOGY
Via Balbi 5, Genoa
Zoology.
By appointment.

COLLECTIONS OF NATURAL HISTORY
The University, Genoa
Zoology. Botany. Anatomy. Mineralogy. Geology.
By appointment.

COLLECTIONS OF THE UNIVERSITY INSTITUTE OF MINERALOGY
Via Leon Battista Alberti 4, Genoa
Mineralogy. Stones.
By appointment.

DORIA TURSI PALACE (NOW PALAZZO MUNICIPALE)
Via Garibaldi, Genoa
Bronze table dating from before 117 B.C. Violin of Paganini, who was Genoese. Historical material on the city. Fragments of the skeleton of Christopher Columbus, found at San Domingo (1877).
M.-F. 8-12, 3-6.30; Sa. 8-12. Closed Su. and holidays. Apply to the porter.

FRANCISCAN MISSIONARY MUSEUM
Church of N. S. Sul Monte, Genoa
Religious art. Historical material relating to the Franciscan missionaries.
Tu.-Su. 9-1.

HOSPITAL MUSEUM
Ospedale di San Martino, Viale Benedetto XV, Genoa
Ancient apothecary jars. Ceramics from Faenza, Urbino, Castelli and Caltagirone.
Tu.-Su. 9-1.

LIGURIAN MUSEUM OF ARCHITECTURE AND SCULPTURE
Church of Sant-Agostino, Piazza Negri 8, Genoa
Statues; Frescoes (11th-18th centuries). Monument in memory of Marguerite de Brabant by Pisano. Lapidary collection in cloister.
Daily ex. M. 9.30-12.30, 3-6 (winter: 10-4). Closed public holidays.

LUNARDI AMERICAN MUSEUM
Piazzale Kennedy, Genoa
History of the United States and of its leading personalities. Americana.
Tu.-Su. 9.30-12.30, 3-6.

MARITIME MUSEUM
Cristoforo Bonavino, Genoa-Pegli
Ships' models. Maritime relics. Nautical instruments. Navigation maps.
Tu.-Su. 9.30-12.30, 3-6.

MAZZINI HOUSE
Via San Luca 13, Genoa
Birthplace of Giuseppe Mazzini (d.1872). Memorabilia of Mazzini.
Daily ex. W. 10-12, 3-6. Su. 10-12.

MUNICIPAL ETHNOGRAPHICAL MUSEUM
Castello D'Albertis, Corso Dogali 18, Genoa
Pre-Columbian ethnography and art of Middle and South America, Pacific Islands.
Tu.-Su. 10-12, 2-6.

MUSEUM OF THE INSTITUTE OF HUMAN ANATOMY
The University, Genoa
Human anatomy. Skulls. Skeletons.
By appointment.

MUSEUM OF THE INSTITUTE OF MEDICINE
The University, Genoa
Human anatomy.
By appointment.

MUSEUM OF MODERN ART
Villa Serra, Via Capolungo 3, Genoa
19th-20th century Ligurian art.
Tu.-Su. 9.30-12.30, 3-6.

MUSEUM OF THE RISORGIMENTO
Via Lomellini 11, Genoa
History of the Risorgimento period, in house of the revolutionary, Giuseppe Mazzini (1805-1872). Military history, 1915-1945.
Tu.-Su. 9.30-12.30, 3-6.

MUSEUM OF SANTA MARIA DI CASTELLO
Church of Santa Maria di Castello, Genoa
Religious art.
Tu.-Su. 9.30-1, 3-6.

NATURAL HISTORY MUSEUM
Via Brigata Liguria 9, Genoa
Zoology. Botany. Mammals, birds and insects.
Th. and Sa. 2.30-5.30; Su. 10-12, 2.30-5.30. Closed July and Aug.

PETROGRAPHIC MUSEUM
Institute of Geography, The University, Genoa
Geology. Petrography. Maps.
By appointment.

ROYAL PALACE (NOW BALBI-DURAZZO PALACE)
Via Balbi 10, Genoa
Antique furniture. Van Dyck Room. Greek and Roman statues. Frescoes by Parodi. Works by Bolognese artists. Brussels tapestries.
Tu., Th. and Su. 9-12.

SPINOLA PALACE GALLERY
Piazza di Pellicceria 1, Genoa
Paintings of the Italian and Flemish Renaissance (Messina, Joos Van Cleve), of the Flemish 17th century (Van Dyck) and the Italian 17th century - mainly Genoese. Contemporary furniture.
May 2- Sept. 30, Daily ex. M. 10-12.30, 3.30-5.30. Oct.-Apr. 10-1.30; Su. and holidays 9.30-12.30. Closed Jan. 1, May 1, Aug. 15, Easter Su. and Christmas Day.

TREASURY
St. Lawrence's Cathedral, Archiepiscopal Palace, Genoa
Religious art and ecclesiastical exhibits, including the *Sacro Catino*, a cup given to Solomon by the Queen of Sheba, from which Christ is said to have drunk at the Last Supper.
M., W., F. and Su. 10-12, 3-6. Closed afternoons of Feb. 11, Sept. 28, Oct. 4, Nov. 2, December 24, and all day on holidays.

UNIVERSITY MEDICAL MUSEUM
The University, Genoa
Collections illustrating the nervous system.
By appointment.

GIGNESE (STRESA)

MUSEUM OF UMBRELLAS AND PARASOLS
Palazzo della Scuole, Gignese (Stresa)
History of umbrellas and parasols.
Tu.-Su. 9.30-12.30, 3-6.

GIOIA DEL COLLE

ARCHAEOLOGICAL MUSEUM
c/o Public Library, Gioia del Colle
Archaeological material from local excavations.
Tu.-Su. 9.30-12.30, 3-6.

GIULIANOVA

BINDI MUNICIPAL GALLERY OF ART
Corso Garibaldi, Giulianova
19th century Neapolitan paintings.
Tu.-Su. 10-12, 2-5.

GORIZIA

ART GALLERY
Piazza Edmondo De Amicis 2, Gorizia
16th century paintings by local masters. Documents and other material on the Risorgimento and World War I.
Tu.-Su. 9.30-12.30, 3-6.

MUSEUM OF HISTORY AND ART
Borgo Castello 15, Gorizia
Religious art. Decorative art. Furniture. Coins. Archaeology.
Tu.-Su. 9.30-12.30, 3-6.

GORLA MINORA

MUSEUM OF NATURAL HISTORY
Presso il Collegio Rotondi, Gorla Minora
Mineralogy. Fossils. Molluscs. African animals.
Tu.-Su. 9.30-12.30, 3-6.

GRADARA

THE ROCCA
Gradara
Furniture. Frescoes. Terracottas by Andrea Della Robbia.
Daily 9-11.30, 3-5.30.

GROPELLO CAIROLI

ANCONA ANTIQUARIUM
Aula dell'Edificio Scolastico, Gropello Cairoli
Finds from regional excavations. History of the pre-Roman and Roman period.
Tu.-Su. 9-1.

GROSSETO

ARCHAEOLOGICAL MUSEUM
Via Mazzini 28, Grosseto
Prehistoric, Etruscan and Roman finds.
Tu.-Su. 9.30-12.30, 3-6.

DIOCESAN MUSEUM OF SACRED ART
Piazetta del Campanile, Grosseto
Religious art. 13th-17th century Sienese paintings. Ivories.
Tu.-Su. 9.30-12.30, 3-6.

MUSEUM OF NATURAL HISTORY
Grosseto
Natural history. Regional minerals, fossils.
Tu.-Su. 9.30-12.30, 3-6.

NATURAL HISTORY COLLECTIONS
Scuole Magistrale, Grosseto
Natural history. Ornithology. Zoology.
By appointment.

GROTTAFERRATA

BADIA GRECA MUSEUM
Corso del Popolo 128, Grottaferrata
Sculpture. Architectural remains.
On application.

GUALDO TADINO

MUNICIPAL ART GALLERY
Corso Italia, Gualdo Tadino
Paintings, especially by local artists.
Tu.-Su. 9-1, 3-6.

GUARDIAGRELE

MUNICIPAL MUSEUM
Convento Michettiano, Guardiagrele
Roman, Gothic remains and sculpture from cathedral. Local history.
Tu.-Su. 9.30-12.30, 3-6.

GUASTALLA

MUSEUM
Maldotti Library, Corso Garibaldi 4, Guastalla
Local history. Sculpture. Paintings. Coins. Medals.
During library hours.

GUBBIO

DUCAL PALACE
Gubbio
Built 1476 onwards for Federigo da Montefeltro, Duke of Urbino, to plans of Francesco di Giorgio Martini. Frescoes. Carved chimney pieces.
Daily ex. M. and Su. afternoon, 9-12.30, 3-6 (Oct.-May 3-sunset). Apply to the porter.

FRANCISCAN MUSEUM
Convent of San Francesco, Gubbio
Religious art. Documents.
Tu.-Su. 9.30-1.

MUSEUM AND PICTURE GALLERY
Palazzo dei Consoli, Piazza della Signoria, Gubbio
Paintings. Bronze *Tavole Eugubine*, a series of tablets recording the ancient Umbrian language. Coins. Pottery by Maestro Giorgio.
Daily 9-12.30, 3-sunset.

HERCULANEUM

Founded, according to tradition, by Hercules, this Roman town on the seashore was overwhelmed during the eruption of Vesuvius in A.D. 79.
Excavations have taken place since 1828. Public and private houses can be seen, including a dyer's shop, bakery; the Casa del Bicentenario (in which a small cross is visible in a stucco panel, the oldest evidence of the Christian religion in the Roman Empire); House with the Wooden Cupboard; House of the Stags; a Theatre with accommodation for 2,000 spectators. Mosaics. Frescoes. Public baths.
Jan. 16- Oct. 15, Daily 9-1 hour before sunset. Oct. 16-Jan. 15, Daily 9-4. Closed Jan. 1, May 1, June 2, Aug. 15, Easter Su. and Christmas Day. The chief houses are enclosed behind gates which are opened on request.

IESI

MUSEUM AND ART GALLERY
Palazzo della Signoria, Iesi
Building (1486-98). Local history. The art gallery contains five paintings by Lorenzo Lotto.
Daily ex. M. 9-12, 3-6.

IGLESIAS

MUSEUM OF THE TECHNICAL INSTITUTE
Via Roma 14, Iglesias, Sardinia
Minerals, stones and fossils of Sardinia and other areas.
By appointment.

IMOLA

ARCHAEOLOGICAL MUSEUM
Via Emilia 80, Imola
Prehistoric, Roman archaeology. Natural history. Numismatics. Ceramics. Ethnography.
Tu.-Su. 9-12.30, 3-6.

MUSEUM AND PICTURE GALLERY
former Convent of San Francesco, Via Emilia, Imola
Local history. Folklore. Paintings include a *Madonna* by Innocenzo Francucci (d.1550).
Daily 9-12.30, 3-6. Closed Sa. afternoon.

MUSEUM OF THE RISORGIMENTO
Via Emilia 80, Imola
Local history. Portraits. Medals.
Tu.-Su. 9-12.30, 3-6.

IMPERIA

IL RONDO MUNICIPAL ART GALLERY
Piazza Dante and Piazza del Duomo, Imperia
Paintings, especially by local artists.
Tu.-Su. 9.30-12.30, 3-6.

MUNICIPAL MUSEUM
Piazza Pagliari, Imperia
Local history. Prehistoric finds. Ligurian paintings. Prints, drawings.
Tu.-Su. 9.30-12.30, 3-6.

ISCHIA

ISLAND MUSEUM
Via Roma 125, Ischia
History of Ischia. Natural history. Folklore.
Tu.-Su. 9.30-12.30, 3-6.

PIETROLOTTI ANTIQUARIUM
Palazzo Comunale, Ischia
Finds from archaeological excavations in the district.
Tu.-Su. 9.30-12.30, 3-6.

ISCHIA DI CASTRO

ANTIQUARIUM
Palazzo Comunale, Ischia di Castro
Local archaeological material.
Tu.-Su. 10-12, 3-6.

ISERNIA

MUNICIPAL MUSEUM
Piazza Santa Maria 8, Isernia
Local history. Antiquities. Sculpture.
Tu.-Su. 9.30-12.30, 2-5.

ISOLA BELLA

PALACE
Isola Bella
Furniture. Tapestries. Weapons. Picture gallery contains *Portrait of a Lady* by Boltraffio, other Lombard paintings, and landscapes by Tempesta.
Daily ex. M. 9.30-12.30, 3-6; Su. 10-1. Winter: 10-4.

ISOLA MAGGIORE

ARMY MUSEUM
Castello Guglielmi, Isola Maggiore
Military collections. Uniforms. Medals. Weapons.
Tu.-Su. 9.30-12.30, 3-6.

IVREA

GARDA MUSEUM AND ARCHAEOLOGICAL MUSEUM
Palazzo degli Studi, Ivrea
Archaeology, mainly of the Roman period. Chinese and Japanese art and armaments.
Tu.-Su. 9.30-12.30, 3-6.

MUNICIPAL MUSEUM
Piazza a di Città, Ivrea
Local history. Natural history. Ethnography of Japan, China.
Tu.-Su. 9.30-12.30, 3-6.

JESI

PICTURE GALLERY
Palazzo della Signoria, Jesi
Paintings by the Venetian, Lorenzo Lotto (1480-1556), including one of his best-known works, a *Study of Santa Lucia*.
M.-Sa. 9-12, 4-7. Winter: 9.30-12, 3-6.30. 1st and 3rd Su. in month, 10-12.

LA FAVORITA

PITRÉ MUSEUM OF SICILIAN ETHNOGRAPHY
Parco della Favorita, La Favorita, nr. Palermo, Sicily
Sicilian life illustrated by customs, costumes, popular arts (painted carts, ex-votos, etc.), musical instruments, implements and domestic articles.
Daily ex. Su. afternoon, 9-1, 3-6.

LANUVIO

MUNICIPAL MUSEUM
Via della Maddelena 1, Lanuvio
Local archaeological finds. Local history.
Tu.-Su. 9-1.

L'AQUILA

ABBRUZZO NATIONAL MUSEUM
Castle, L'Aquila
Roman archaeology. Palaeontology. Medieval art, including 13th century coloured wooden statue and frescoes of the same period. Gothic statues. Polyptych by Iacobello del Fiore (1370-1438). Goldsmiths' work. Renaissance art. Abruzzi pottery.
May 2- Oct. 31, Tu.-Su. 9-1, 3.30-6.30; Su. and holidays 10-1, 4-8. Nov.-Apr., Tu.-Su. 9-4; Su. and holidays 9-1. Closed Jan 1, 6, May 1, June 2, Aug. 15, Easter and Christmas.

DIOCESAN MUSEUM
Piazza San Giuseppe, L'Aquila
Religious objects, sculptures. Religious art. Paintings by local and Neapolitan masters.
Tu.-Su. 9.30-12.30, 3-6.

INTERNATIONAL MUSEUM OF PUPPETS AND MARIONETTES
Via Sassa 15, L'Aquila
Puppets and marionettes from all over the world.
Tu.-Su. 9.30-12.30, 3-6.

PALAEONTOLOGICAL MUSEUM
Castle, L'Aquila
Palaeontology. Skeletons. Fossils.
May 2- Oct. 31, Tu.-Su. 9-1, 3.30-6.30; Su. and holidays 10-1, 4-8. Nov.-Apr., Tu.-Su. 9-4; Su. and holidays 9-1. Closed Jan. 1, 6, May 1, June 2, Aug. 15, Easter and Christmas.

LA SPEZIA

MUNICIPAL AND ARCHAEOLOGICAL MUSEUM
Corso Cavour 251, La Spezia
Local history. Palaeontology. Archaeology. Roman and medieval antiquities. Natural history. Modern art.
Tu.-Su. 9.30-12.30, 3-6.

MUSEUM OF NATURAL HISTORY AND ETHNOGRAPHY
Corso Cavour 39, La Spezia
Palaeontology. Natural history. Zoology. Ornithology. Ethnography.
Tu.-Su. 9.30-12.30, 3-6.

NAVAL MUSEUM
Piazza Chiodo, La Spezia
Naval history. Ships' models. Maps and other documents.
Tu.-Su. 9.30-12.30, 3-6.

LATINA

ANTIQUARIUM
Public Library, Latina
Local history, archaeology.
During library hours.

LAVELLO

MUNICIPAL MUSEUM
Castello Svevo, Lavello
Archaeology. Vases. Bronze and iron objects. Epigraphs. Local history.
Tu.-Su. 9-1.

LA VERNA

MONASTERY OF LA VERNA
nr. Arezzo
The bed of St. Francis. Terracottas by Andrea Della Robbia, including a pair representing the *Annunciation* and the *Nativity*.
May-Sept. Daily 9-12, 2-7. Oct.-Apr. Daily 10-12, 2-5.

LECCE

CASTROMEDIANO MUSEUM
Palazzo della Prefettura, Lecce
Statues from the Roman theatre. Messapian and Attic vases. Polyptych by Paolo Veneziano.
Su., M., W. and F., 10-1.

NATURAL SCIENCE COLLECTIONS
Istituto Tecnico Statale Commerciale e per Geometri O. G. Costa, Lecce
Geology. Palaeontology. Botany. Zoology.
Tu.-Su. 9-1.

LECCO

CIVIC MUSEUM
Palazzo Belgioioso, Lecco
Archaeology. Natural history. Maritime collections.
Tu.-Su. 9.30-12.30, 3-6.

HISTORICAL MUSEUM
Piazza XX Settembre, Lecco
In 15th century castle tower. Local history. Memorabilia of Garibaldi and Mazzini.
Tu.-Su. 9.30-12.30, 3-6.

MUNICIPAL MUSEUM
Via Matteotti 32, Lecco
Local history. Prehistory. Archaeology. Natural history.
Tu.-Su. 9.30-12.30, 3-6.

VILLA DI ALESSANDRO MANZONI
Lecco
Memorabilia of the writer, Manzoni. Local history.
Tu.-Su. 9.30-12.30, 3-6.

LEGNAGO

COLLECTIONS OF THE ISTITUTO TECNICO STATALE COMMERCIALE E PER GEOMETRO CARLO DELL'ACQUA
Legnago
Physics. Chemistry. Zoology.
By appointment.

MUSEUM
Via Matteotti 39, Legnago
Local history, Bronze Age to present day.
Tu.-Su. 9-1.

LEGNANO

MUNICIPAL MUSEUM
Via Mazzini 2, Legnano
Regional archaeology. 15th-16th century frescoes. Paintings by Previati.
Tu.-Su. 9-12, 2-5.

LENTINI

ARCHAEOLOGICAL MUSEUM
Via Piave, Lentini, Sicily
Archaeological finds from the district, including grave goods from the necropolis of ancient Leontini.
Tu.-Su. 9-1.

LE RONCOLE-VERDI

HOUSE OF GIUSEPPE VERDI
Le Roncole-Verdi
Former home of Verdi. Furniture, manuscripts and other memorabilia of the composer.
Tu.-Su. 9.30-12.30, 3-6.

LEVANZO

GENOVESE GROTTO COLLECTION
Levanzo
Palaeolithic and Neolithic art. Carved animals and human figures.
Tu.-Su. 9- one hour before sunset.

LIPARI

ARCHAEOLOGICAL MUSEUM
Via del Castello, Lipari, Sicily
Neolithic and Iron Age exhibits and items from the Greek and Roman necropoli at Lipari (late 4th century - 2nd century B.C.).
Summer: M.-Sa. 9-1, 3-6; Su. and holidays 9.30-1.30. Winter: M.-Sa. 9.30-4; Su. and holidays 9.30-1.30.

LIVORNO

MUNICIPAL MUSEUM
Villa Fabbricotti, Piazza Matteotti 19, Livorno
Local history. Archaeology. Medieval and modern art.
M.-Sa. 10-12.30; Th. also 3.30-6.30; Su. 10-1.

MUNICIPAL MUSEUM OF NATURAL HISTORY
Piazzale Mascagni 1, Livorno
Natural history. Ornithology. Malacology. Entomology. Palaeontology.
Tu.-Su. 10-12.30, 3-6.

LOCRI

ARCHAEOLOGICAL MUSEUM
Viale Regina Margherita, Locri
Finds from the ancient city. Numismatics.
M.-Sa. 9-1; Su. 10-12.

LODI

GORINI COLLECTION
Ospedale Maggiore, Corso Umberto, Lodi
Anatomical preparations. Mummification.
By appointment.

MUNICIPAL MUSEUM
Corso Umberto I 63, Lodi
Local history, archaeology, art. 14th-18th century paint-

ings. 16th-19th century ceramics. 14th century wooden altar by Lupi brothers.
Tu.-Su. 9.30-12.30, 3-6.

SCIENTIFIC COLLECTIONS
Collegio San Francesco, Via San Francesco 23, Lodi
Physics. Mineralogy. Zoology.
Tu.-Su. 9-1.

LONATO

UGO DA COMO FOUNDATION
Via da Como 2, Lonato
Regional history. Furniture. Drawings. Prints. Material from the Brescia region.
Tu.-Su. 9-12, 2-5.

LORETO

APOSTOLIC PALACE
Piazza della Madonna, Loreto
16th century Brussels tapestries after Raphaël. Paintings, including a *Last Supper* by Simon Vouet (17th century) and works by Lorenzo Lotto, a Venetian who died at Loreto.
Apply in advance to the Amministrazione Pontificia delle Santa Casa, Loreto.

TREASURY
Sanctuary of the Holy House, Loreto
Urbino faience vessels. 13th century Madonna of Limousin workmanship.
Daily ex. Su. 9-12, 3-6.30 (until 5 Oct.-Apr.). Closed holiday afternoons.

LORETO APRUTINO

MUSEUM OF ANCIENT ABRUZZI CERAMICS
Palazzo del Barone Giacomo Acerbo, Via del Baio, Loreto Aprutino
History of the production of Abruzzi ceramics, 15th-18th centuries.
Tu.-Su. 9.30-12.30, 3-6.

LOVERE

TADINI MUSEUM
Piazza Garibaldi 1, Lovere, Lake Iseo
Paintings by Bellini and Il Parmigianino. Sculptures by Canova. Porcelain. Weapons.
Apr.-Sept. Daily 9.30-12, 2.30-8. Oct.-Mar. Daily 2.30-5.

LUCCA

CIVIC MUSEUM
Villa Guinigi, Piazza San Francesco, Lucca
Sculpture of the Pisan school, including bas-reliefs of the Annunciation attributed to Civitali (15th century). Paintings, notably a triptych by a local artist, Puccinelli (14th century) and works by Filippino Lippi. Works by Luccan and modern painters.
Tu.-Sa. 9.30-4; Su. and holidays 9-4. Closed M.

MASSAGLI ORNITHOLOGICAL COLLECTION
Palazzo Bongi, Via Filungo 74, Lucca
Ornithology, especially Italian.
Tu.-Su. 9.30-12.30, 3-6.

NATURAL HISTORY MUSEUM
Machiavelli Liceo Classico, Lucca
Mineralogy. Geology. Botany. Zoology. Egyptian mummies, sarcophagi.
Tu.-Su. 9-1.

PICTURE GALLERY OF THE PALAZZO DUCALE
Piazza Napoleone, Lucca
Paintings, including works by Fra. Bartolomeo and an *Ecstasy of St. Catherine* by Pompeo Batoni. 13th-15th century sculptures of the Pisan school.
Tu.-Sa. 9.30-4; Su. and holidays 9-1. Closed M.

PUCCINELLI MUSEUM AND HERBARIUM
Presso l'Orto Botanico, Lucca
Botanical collections. Herbarium of the Lucca area.
Tu.-Su. 9.30-12.30, 3-6.

LUCERA

FIORELLI MUSEUM
Via de Nicastri, Lucera
Roman Venus. Mosaic pavement (1st century). Terracottas (3rd century B.C.). Ceramics of the Saracen and Angevin periods.
M.-Sa. 9-1.

LUCIGNANO

MUNICIPAL MUSEUM
Piazza Tribunale, Lucignano
Local history, paintings, decorative arts. Goldsmiths' work, 14th century.
Tu.-Su. 9-12, 3-6.

LUCUS FERONIAE

CAPENATE ARCHAEOLOGICAL MUSEUM
Lucus Feroniae
Finds from archaeological sites in the district.
Tu.-Su. 10-12, 3-6.

LUGANO

HISTORICAL MUSEUM
Mansion, Parco Civico, Lugano
Local history.
Daily ex. M. 9.30-12.30, 3-6; Su. 10-1.

PICTURE GALLERY
Villa Favorita, Castagnola, Lugano
Flemish and German paintings, including works by Dürer, Cranach, Hans Baldung, Holbein, Van Eyck, Patinir, Rubens and Van Dyck. Italian art is represented by Uccello, Fra. Angelico, Ghirlandaio, Raphaël, Titian, Carpaccho, Caraveggio and Correggio. *Portrait of a Women* by Fragonard.
Apr.-Oct. F. and Sa. 10-12, 2-5; Su. and holidays 2-5.

LUGO

FRANCESCO BARACCA MUSEUM
Nella Rocca, Lugo
In medieval castle. Memorabilia of local hero, Francesco Baracca.
Tu.-Su. 9-12, 3-6.

LUGO VICENTINO

ANDREA PIOVENE MUSEUM OF PREHISTORY
Villa Godi Valmarana, Lugo Vicentino
Archaeology. Prehistory. Palaeontology. Fossils.
Tu.-Su. 9.30-12.30, 3-6.

LUNI

ANTIQUARIUM
Luni
Finds from local excavations. Ceramics. Coins. Epigraphs. Glassware.
Tu.-Su. 9.30-12.30, 3-6.

MACERATA

MUNICIPAL MUSEUM AND ART GALLERY
Piazza Vittorio Veneto 6, Macerata
Local history. 15th-19th century paintings.
Tu.-Su. 9.12, 2-5.

SPADONI MUSEUM OF THE RISORGIMENTO
Piazza Vittorio Veneto 6, Macerata
Documents and other material illustrating Italy's struggle for independence.
Tu.-Su. 9.30-12.30, 3-6.

MAGLIE

PREHISTORIC MUSEUM
Via Umberto I 3, Maglie
Finds from local excavations.
Tu.-Su. 9-12, 3-6.

MAIOLATI SPONTINI

SPONTINI MUSEUM
Via Spontini, Maiolati Spontini
Local history.
Tu.-Su. 9-12, 3-6.

MALCESINE

MUSEUM
Castle of the Scaligers, Malcesine
Collections of local history and folklore, in 13th-14th century castle.
Apr.-Oct., daily 9-6 or 7.

MANDURIA

MUNICIPAL ANTIQUARIUM
Piazza Garibaldi, Manduria
Archaeological material from local excavations.
Tu.-Su. 9.30-12.30, 3-6.

MANTUA

CATHEDRAL
Piazza Sordello, Mantua
Paintings by Alberti, Ghisi, Andreini, Feti, Mazzola, Cignaroli, Farinati and Balestra. Statues by Giambattista Scuttori. Sacristy contains fabrics, ornaments, baldaquins, silver and illuminated missals.
Sacristy: on application.

CAVRIANI PALACE
Via Trento, Mantua
18th century Venetian-style rooms. Paintings by Brazzani. Manuscripts. Medals. Bronzes.
Daily ex. M. 9-12, 2-4 or 6.

DUCAL PALACE
Castello dei Gonzaga, Piazza Sordello 40, Mantua
16th and 18th century furniture and furnishings. Medieval and Renaissance statues. Greco-Roman sculptures. Paintings by Rubens, Morone, Tintoretto, Feti and others. Brussels tapestries after Raphaël. Frescoes of the Bridal Chamber by Mantegna.
Mar., Apr. and Oct. M.-Sa. 9-12, 1-5. May 2- Sept. 30, M.-Sa. 9-12.30, 2.30-6. Nov.-Feb. M.-Sa. 9-4. Su. and holidays all the year, 9-1. Closed Jan. 1, May 1, June 2, Aug. 15, Dec. 25.

MUNICIPAL MUSEUM
Palazzo degli Studi, Piazza S.Teresa, Mantua
Local history. Archaeological material. Folklore.
Daily ex. M. 9-12, 3-6.

REGGIA DEI GONZAGA
Piazza Sordello, Mantua
13th century fortress-palace, rebuilt 17th-18th centuries. Medallions. Paintings of the Mantegna school. Frescoes. Busts. Tombs and inscriptions. The marriage chamber (Camera degli Sposi) contains series of frescoes by Mategna (1464-74). Series of minature apartments and stairs built for the dwarfs of Duke Vincenzo. Music room and study of Isabella d'Este.
Guided tours only. Summer: daily 9-12, 2.30-6. Winter: M.-Sa. 9-4; Su. and holidays, 9-1.30.

MUSEUM OF MEDIEVAL AND MODERN ART
Via dell'Accademia 47, Mantua
Medieval and modern art collections.
Tu.-Su. 9-12, 2.30-6.

MUSEUM OF THE RISORGIMENTO AND NATURAL HISTORY MUSEUM
Palazzo d'Arco, Mantua
Collections illustrating Italy's struggle for independence. Natural history. Botany. Zoology. Mammals. Birds. Reptiles.
Tu.-Su. 9.30-12.30, 3-6.

MARENGO

MUSEUM OF THE BATTLE OF MARENGO
Via Genova 7/A, Marengo
Relics of the Battle of Marengo. Documents. Weapons.
Tu.-Su. 9.30-12.30, 3-6.

MARSALA

MUNICIPAL MUSEUM
Via Cavour, Marsala, Sicily
Local history. Ethnography.
Daily 9-1.

MARZABOTTO

POMPEO ARIA ETRUSCAN MUSEUM
Via Porrettana, Marzabotto
Archaeological finds from excavations at Misa.
Tu.-Su. 9-one hour before sunset.

MASER

CAR MUSEUM
nr. Villa Maser, Maser
Collection of vintage motor-cars.
Tu., Sa. and Su. 3-6 (2-5 in winter).

VILLA BARBARO (or VILLA MASER)
Maser
Built by Palladio for Marcantonio and Daniele Barbaro. Decorations by Veronese. Frescoes, including the group of Venus and Apollo, Bacchus, the gods on Mount Olympus, and the Seasons.
Tu., Sa. and Su. 3-6 (2-5 in winter).

MASERADA SUL PIAVE

MINERALOGICAL COLLECTION
Maserada sul Piave
Mineralogy.
Tu.-Su. 9-1.

MASSA CARRARA

PELLEGRINI BOTANICAL AND MINERALOGICAL COLLECTION
Via Pellegrini, Massa Carrara
Natural history. Italian flora. Fossils. Mussels.
Tu.-Su. 9.30-12.30, 3-6.

MASSA MARITIMA

MINERALOGICAL COLLECTION
Istituto Minerario, Piazza Matteotti, Massa Maritima
Mineralogy.
By appointment.

MUNICIPAL MUSEUM
Piazza Matteotti, Massa Maritima
Local history. Paintings.
Tu.-Su. 9.30-12.30, 3-6.

MATÉLICA

PICTURE GALLERY
Palazzo Piersanti, Via Umberto I 11, Matélica
Paintings especially from Italy.
Daily ex. M. 9-12, 3-6.

MATERA

RIDOLA NATIONAL MUSEUM
Via Ridola 24, Matera
Prehistoric collection. Regional divinities. Mineralogy. Palaeontology.
Tu.-Sa. 9-2; Su. and holidays 9-1. Closed M., Jan. 1, May 1, June 2, Aug. 15, Easter Su. and Christmas Day.

MAZARA DEL VALLO

MUSEUM
Palace of the Knights of Malta, Mazara del Vallo, Sicily
Roman antiquities.
Daily 9-1.

MUNICIPAL MUSEUM
Via del Carmine 21, Mazara del Vallo, Sicily
Local history, archaeology. Natural history. Paintings.
Tu.-Su. 9.30-12.30, 3-6.

MEDICINA

MUNICIPAL MUSEUM
Edificio Scolastico, Medicina
Local history, archaeology. Numismatics.
Tu.-Su. 9.30-12.30, 3-6.

MEGARA HYBLAEA

ANTIQUARIUM
Megara Hyblaea
Material from excavations in the area. Sculpture. Architecture.
Tu.-Su. 9-12, 3-6.

MELFI

ANTIQUARIUM COMUNALE
Palazzo Comunale, Melfi
Finds from excavations in the area.
Tu.-Su. 9-sunset.

MENTANA

GARIBALDI MUSEUM
Ara dei Caduti, Mentana
Memorabilia of Garibaldi and of the Risorgimento.
Tu.-Su. 9.30-12.30, 3-6.

MERANO

MUSEUM
Via Galilei 55, Merano
Local history. Folklore.
Daily ex. M. 10-12, 4-6.

PRINCIPESCO CASTLE
Via dei Portici, Merano
Castle built 1445-80 by Archduke Sigismund, containing contemporary furnishings.
Daily ex. Su. 9-12, 3-6.

MESAGNE

ARCHAEOLOGICAL COLLECTION
Palazzo Comunale, Via di Riordinamento, Mesagne
Local history. Archaeological material from excavations in the district. Sculpture.
Tu.-Su. 9.30-12.30, 3-6.

MUSEUM
Via de Rinaldi 6, Mesagne
Local history. Vases.
Tu.-Su. 9-1.

MESSINA

COLLECTIONS OF THE INSTITUTE OF BOTANY
Via Pietro Castelli 2, Messina
Botanical collections.
Tu.-Su. 9-12, 2-5.

MUSEUM OF THE INSTITUTE OF ZOOLOGY
Via dei Verdi 56, Messina, Sicily
Zoology. Italian fauna. African fauna. Vertebrates.
Tu.-Su. 9-12, 3-6.

NATIONAL MUSEUM
Viale della Liberta 465, Messina, Sicily
Paintings, sculptures. Polyptych by Antonello da Messina (1473): Works by Caravaggio. 13th century Crucifix and a bronze pelican. 16th century sculpture of Scylla by Montorsoli. A *St. Catherine* by A. Gagini (16th century). *Descent from the Cross* by a Flemish painter, Colin van Cote (early 16th century).
Daily ex. M. 9-4; Su. and holidays 9-1; Closed Jan. 1, May 1, Aug. 15, Easter Su. and Christmas Day.

METAPONTO

ANTIQUARIUM
Strada Nazionale Taranto-Reggio Calabria, Metaponto
Archaeological material from excavations in the area. Numismatics.
Tu.-Su. 9-12, 3-6.

MILAN

AMBROSIAN GALLERY
Piazza Pio XI 2, Milan
14th-19th century paintings. Works include the cartoon by Raphaël for the Vatican fresco of the School of Athens, the *Atlantic Codex* by Leonardo da Vinci and the *Fruit Basket* by Caravaggio.
Daily 9.30-4.30. Closed all day Jan. 1, Easter Su. and M., Apr. 25, May 1, June 2, Aug. 15, Dec. 25-26, and afternoons of Jan. 6, Mar. 14 and 19, Ascension Day, June 29, Nov. 1, 2 and 4, Dec. 7, 8, 24 and 31.

ARCHAEOLOGICAL MUSEUM
Corso Magenta 15, Milan
Greek vases. Works of art from the Roman period. Bronzes of 1800 B.C. Exhibits of the Neolithic period. History of Milan.
Daily ex. M. 9.30-12.30, 3-6 (winter 10-4). Closed public holidays.

ART COLLECTION
Ospedale Maggiore, Via Francesco Sforza 28, Milan
Drawings, 15th century - present day.
By appointment.

ACHILLE BERTARELLI COLLECTION
Castello Sforzesco, Milan
15th century - present day drawings. Iconography.
Tu.-Su. 9-5.

BRERA PICTURE GALLERY
Via Brera 28, Milan
Paintings of Venetian and Lombard schools, as well as other Italian schools. Works by Lorenzo Lotto, Veronese, Titian, Mantegna, Gozzoli, Raphaël, Caravaggo, as well as Rubens, Van Dyck and Rembrandt.
Daily ex. M. 9.30-4. F. also 9-11 p.m. Closed Jan. 1, Apr. 25, May 1, June 2, Aug. 15, Easter Su. and Christmas Day.

CATHEDRAL MUSEUM
Piazza del Duomo 14, Milan
Religious paintings, sculptures, relics and documents. Liturgical items.
Daily 9.30-12.30, 2.30-5.30. Closed M. except when a holiday, and on Su. afternoons.

CIVIC MUSEUM OF NATURAL HISTORY
Corso Venezia 55, Milan
Animals and birds. Insects. Minerals. Rocks and fossils.
Daily ex. M. 9.30-12.30, 2.30-5.30.

COLLECTION OF THE INSTITUTE OF ENTOMOLOGY
Milan
Entomology.
By appointment.

COLLECTIONS OF THE INSTITUTE OF GEOLOGY
Via Botticelli, Milan
Geology. Rocks. Fossils.
By appointment.

COLLECTION OF THE INSTITUTE OF MICROBIOLOGY
Via Mangiagalli 31, Milan
Bacteriology. Microbiology.
By appointment.

COLLECTION OF THE INSTITUTE OF MINERALOGY, PETROGRAPHY AND GEOCHEMISTRY
Via Botticelli 23, Milan
Mineralogy. Geology. Petrography. Geochemistry.
By appointment.

COLLECTIONS OF THE INSTITUTE OF ZOOLOGY
Via Celoria 10, Milan
Zoological collections. Anthropology.
Tu.-Su. 9.30-12.30, 3-6.

COLLECTION OF PHYSICS APPARATUS
Liceo Parini, Milan
Physics apparatus.
By appointment.

CONVENT REFECTORY
Piazza Santa Maria delle Grazie, Milan
Leonardo's *Last Supper.*
Summer: daily 9.30-12.30, 2.30-5.30. Winter: daily 9.30-12.30, 1.30-4.30. Su. and holidays 9.30-12.30.

GALLERY OF CONTEMPORARY SACRED ART
Via Giovanni Terruggia 14, Milan
Religious art. Sculpture.
Tu.-Su. 9.30-12.30, 3-5.

GALLERY OF MODERN ART
Villa Communale, Via Palestro 16, Milan
19th-20th century Lombard painting. Canvases by Bianchi, Segantini, Previati, Lega, Signorini, Fontanesi, Morelli and Mancini.
Daily ex. Tu. 9.30-12.30, 2.30-5.30. Closed Jan. 1, May 1, Aug. 15, Easter Su. and Christmas Day.

INSTITUTE OF BOTANY HERBARIUM
The University, Milan
Botanical collections. Herbarium.
By appointment.

LEONARDO DA VINCI MUSEUM OF SCIENCE AND TECHNOLOGY
Via S. Vittore 21, Milan
Evolution of the sciences and their application since the time of Leonardo da Vinci. Metallurgy. Motors. Aeronautics. Land transport. Oil research. Telecommunications. Physics. Navigation.
Daily ex. M. 10-12.30, 3-7.

LUZZATTO HERBARIUM
Via Canova 7, Milan
Botany. Herbarium.
Tu.-Su. 9-4.30.

THE MILAN MUSEUM
Via St. Andrea 6, Milan
Collections illustrating historical events in the city, its development, the transformation of building, and life in the city in the past.
Daily ex. M. 9.30-12.30, 2.30-5.30.

MUNICIPAL MUSEUM OF NATURAL HISTORY
Corso Venezia 55, Milan
Palaeontology. Mineralogy. Zoology. Entomology. Ornithology.
Tu.-Su. 9.30-12.30, 3-6.

MUNICIPAL NUMISMATIC COLLECTION
Castello Sforzesco, Milan
Coins and medals of all periods, especially Roman and Milanese.
Tu.-Sa. 9.30-12.30, 2.30-5.30.

MUSEUM OF ANCIENT MUSICAL INSTRUMENTS
Castello Sforzesco, Piazza Castello, Milan
The evolution of musical instruments.
Tu.-Su. 9.30-12.30, 2.30-5.30.

MUSEUM OF ANCIENT WEAPONS
Via Carducci 41, Milan
Arms and armour, especially of 16th and 17th centuries. 15th century harness for quadrupeds, arquebus, sabres, muskets.
Daily ex. M. 10-12.30, 3-6.

MUSEUM OF ANCIENT ART
Castello Sforzesco, Piazza Castello, Milan
Sculpture, including 14th century tomb of Barnabo Visconti, a *Pietà* by Michelangelo and the reclining figure of Gaston de Foix, who was killed at Ravenna in 1512. Paintings, including works by Foppa, Boltraffio, Lotto, Bellini, Correggio and Magnesco. Foreign schools are represented by Van Dyck, Rigaud and Teniers. 16th-17th century weapons. Ethnography. Chinese and Japanese art, with exhibits from 3rd century B.C. to the present day.
Daily ex. M. 9.30-12.30, 2.30-5.30. Closed Jan. 1, May 1, Aug. 15, Easter Su. and Christmas Day.

MUSEUM OF THE BASILICA OF SANT-AMBROGIO
Piazza Sant-Ambrogio 15, Milan
Vestments of St. Ambrose, and art treasures of the Basilica. Reliquaries. Monastrances.
Daily ex. M. 9.30-12.30, 2.30-5.30.

MUSEUM OF CONTEMPORARY HISTORY
Via St. Andrea 6, Milan
Collection of material on the two World Wars.
Daily ex. M. 9.30-12.30, 2.30-5.30.

MUSEUM OF FAR EASTERN ART AND ETHNOGRAPHY
Via Monterosa 81, Milan
Material from China, India and Burma, including drawings, sculpture, coins.
Tu.-Su. 9.30-12.30, 3-6.

MUSEUM OF THE NATIONAL RISORGIMENTO
Via Borgo Nuovo 23, Milan
Relics, flags, painting and manifestoes of the period between the middle of the 18th century and the first World War. Cloak, crown and sceptre used for the Coronation of Napoleon I as King of Italy. Historic collection of the Commune of Milan.
Daily ex. M. 9.30-12.30, 2.30-5.30.

NATIONAL CENTRE OF MANZONI STUDIES
Via Morone 1, Milan
Relics, portraits and books in house which formerly belonged to the writer Alessandro Manzoni.
Enquire locally.

NAVAL MUSEUM
Via S. Vittore 21, Milan
Machinery, models and various exhibits relating to the merchant marine and the navy.
Daily ex. M. 10-12.30, 3-10.

POLDI-PEZZOLI MUSEUM
Via Manzoni 12, Milan
Greek ceramics. Roman bronzes. Byzantine and Renaissance gold and silver work.
Murano glass. Books and parchments. Collection of arms. Paintings, including works by Pollaiolo, Botticelli, Cranach, Mantegna, Signorelli, Bellini, Guardi, Van der Meer and Breughel. Tapestries.
Daily 9.30-12.30, 2.30-5.30. (Oct.-Mar. 10-1, 2-5). Th. also 9-11 p.m.

THE SCALA THEATRE MUSEUM
Piazza della Scala 2, Milan
Collection of objects and relics relating to the history of the Scala Theatre. Theatrical art from classical antiquity to the present day.
Daily 9-12.30, 2-6. Closed Easter and Christmas.

SCIENCE COLLECTION
Liceo Beccaria, Milan
Physics. Mineralogy. Zoology.
By appointment.

VINCIANO COLLECTION
Piazza Santa Maria delle Grazie 2, Milan
Religious art. Drawings.
Tu.-Su. 9.30-4.30.

ZOOLOGICAL MUSEUM
Giardino Zoologico, Milan
Zoological collections.
Tu.-Su. 9.30-12.30, 3-6.

MINTURNO

NATIONAL ANTIQUARIUM AND ARCHAEOLOGICAL SITE OF THE FORMER MINTURNAE
Via Appia, km 156, Minturno
Finds from archaeological excavations on the site of the former Minturnae.
Tu.-Su. 9-1, 3-6. (winter: 9.30-4).

MIRANDOLA

MUNICIPAL MUSEUM
Public Library, Via Verdi 12, Mirandola
Local history, archaeology. Natural history.
Tu.-Su. 9.30-5.

MODENA

BOTANICAL COLLECTION AND HERBARIUM
Istituto di Botanica, Modena
Botany. Herbarium.
By appointment.

CAMPORI GALLERY
Palazzo dei Musei, Piazza San Agostino 309, Modena
Paintings, including works by Veronese, Goya, Sebastiano del Piombo, and Correggio.
May-Sept. daily 9.30-1, 3-6. Oct.-Apr. daily 9.30-4. Closed Su. afternoons and holidays.

CATHEDRAL LAPIDARY MUSEUM
Via Lanfranco 6, Modena
12th century metopes, bas-reliefs formerly surmounting Cathedral buttresses.
On application to the sacristan.

CITY MUSEUM
Palazzo dei Musei, Largo di Porta 48, Modena
Palaeontology. Local paintings, sculptures. Pottery. Weapons. Musical instruments. Italian and oriental fabrics. Philately. Maps. Historic physics instruments. Lace. Ethnography of Asia, Africa, America.
May-Sept. Daily 9.30-1, 3-6. Oct.-Apr. Daily 9.30-4. Closed Su. afternoons and holidays.

ESTE GALLERY
Palazzo dei Musei, Largo di Porta 48, Modena
Emilian and Tuscan Primitives. Works by Barnaba da Modena (14th century), Tomaso da Modena, Giovanni di Paolo. Venetian 16th century paintings by Veronese, Bassano, Tintoretto, El Greco and artists of the Emilian school, including Correggio, Il Parmigianino, Dossi and Niccolo dell'Abbate. 18th century paintings. French, German and Flemish paintings. Portrait of Francesco I d'Este by Velasquez. Medieval, Classical and Renaissance sculpture.
May-Sept. Daily 9.30-1, 3-6. Oct.-Apr. Daily 9.30-4. Closed Su. afternoons and holidays.

LAPIDARY MUSEUM
Palazzo dei Musei, Largo di Porta 48, Modena
Medieval and modern Greek and Roman sculptures.
May-Sept. Daily 9.30-1, 3-6. Oct.-Apr. Daily 9.30-4. Closed Su. afternoons and holidays.

MEDAL CABINET
Palazzo dei Musei, Largo di Porta 5, Modena
Coins.
May.-Sept. Daily 9.30-1, 3-6. Oct.-Apr. Daily 9.30-4. Closed Su. afternoons and holidays.

MUSEUM OF THE INSTITUTE OF HUMAN ANATOMY
Via Berengario 16, Modena
Anatomic preparations. Skeletons. Brains.
By appointment.

MUSEUM OF THE INSTITUTE OF MINERALOGY
Via Università 4, Modena
Mineralogy of Emilia, Sicily, Val di Fassa and Vesuvius.
By appointment.

MUSEUM OF THE INSTITUTE OF PALAEONTOLOGY
Via Università 4, Modena
Palaeozoology. Palaeobotany. Geology. Fossils.
By appointment.

MUSEUM OF THE INSTITUTE OF TROPICAL MEDICINE
University, Modena
Tropical diseases. Contagious diseases. Serology.
By appointment.

MUSEUM OF THE INSTITUTE OF ZOOLOGY
Via Università 4, Modena
Zoology of the Modena district. Vertebrates from Europe and elsewhere.
By appointment.

MUSEUM OF THE RISORGIMENTO
Palazzo dei Musei, Largo di Porta 48, Modena
History of the struggle for Italian independence.
May-Sept. Daily 9.30-1, 3-6. Oct.-Apr. Daily 9.30-4. Closed Su. afternoons and holidays.

POLETTI GALLERY
Palazzo dei Musei, Largo di Porta 48, Modena
Modern paintings, sculpture, graphics, by Italian and foreign artists.
May-Sept. Daily 9.30-1, 3-6. Oct.-Apr. Daily 9.30-4. Closed Su. afternoons and holidays.

MODIGLIANA

DON GIOVANNI VERITA MUSEUM
Via Garibaldi 29, Modigliana
Local history, archaeology. Documents on the Risorgimento.
Tu.-Su. 9-1.

MOLFETTA

ARCHAEOLOGICAL COLLECTION
Seminario Maggiore Appulo, Molfetta
Finds from excavations in the district.
Tu.-Su. 9.30-1.

MONDAVIO

MUNICIPAL MUSEUM
Via Matteotti, Mondavio
Local archaeology, history. Paintings. Natural history.
Tu.-Su. 9.30-5.

MONFORTE D'ALBA

ORNITHOLOGICAL AND MALACOLOGICAL COLLECTION
Scuola di Agricultura, Col. Paolo Domenico Martina, Monforte d'Alba
Natural history. Ornithology. Invertebrates.
By appointment.

MONSELICE

ART COLLECTION
Castello Ezzelini da Romano, Via del Duomo, Monselice
Collection of paintings. Armaments.
By application only. Apply to the office of Count Vittorio Cini S. Vio, Palazzo Loredan, Venice.

MUNICIPAL MUSEUM
Via Garibaldi 74, Monselice
Local history. Sculptures. Amphorae.
Tu.-Su. 9.30-12.30, 3-6.

MONTALCINO

DIOCESAN MUSEUM
Annesso al Seminario, Montalcino
Religious art. 14th century sculpture. Paintings of the 14th and 15th centuries.
Tu.-Su. 9-4.30.

MUNICIPAL MUSEUM
Piazza Cavour 13, Montalcino
Paintings, including fine *Coronation of the Virgin* by Bartolo di Fredi.
Daily ex. M. 9.30-12.30, 2.30-5.30.

MONTE BERICO

MUSEUM OF THE RISORGIMENTO
Monte Berico
Documents and other material relating to Italy's struggle for independence.
Tu.-Su. 9.30-12.30, 3-6.

MONTECATINI VALDINIEVOLE

PREPOSITURA MUSEUM
Montecatini Valdinievole
14th-15th century paintings, frescoes.
Tu.-Su. 9.30-12.30, 3-6.

MONTEFALCO

MUNICIPAL ART GALLERY
Church of St. Francis, Via Ringhiera Umbra, Montefalco
Eccesiastical art including 15th century frescoes by the Florentine painter, Benozzo Gozzoli, and by Melanzio and Berugino of the Umbrian school.
Daily 9-1, 3-6.30. Apply to the caretaker.

MONTEFORTINO

MUNICIPAL ART GALLERY
Via Roma, Montefortino
17th century paintings.
Tu.-Su. 9.30-4.

MONTEPULCIANO

MUNICIPAL MUSEUM
Via Ricci 15, Montepulciano
Paintings of the Tuscan and Umbrian schools.
Daily ex. M. 9-12, 3-6.

MONTERUBBIANO

MUNICIPAL MUSEUM
Via Trento e Trieste 2, Monterubbiano
Local history, ethnography. Archaeology. Folklore.
Tu.-Su. 9.30-12.30, 2-5.

MONTEVARCHI

PALAEONTOLOGICAL MUSEUM
Via Poggio Bracciolini 38, Montevarchi
Fossils, mostly from the Valdarno Superiore area.
Tu.-Su. 9.30-5.

MONTEVERGINE

MUSEUM OF THE SANCTUARY
Montevergine
Religious art.
Tu.-Su. 9.30-1.

MONZA

CATHEDRAL AND TREASURY
Piazza Rana, Monza
15th century frescoes depicting scenes from the life of Queen Theodolinda. Facsimile of the Iron Crown of the Kings of Lombardy, so called because it contained an iron band said to have been forged from a nail of the Holy Cross. Treasury contains gold plate and objects of historic interest.
Treasury: Daily ex. M. 9-12, 2-6.

COLONIAL MUSEUM
Villa Reale, Monza
Ethiopian paintings, armaments, zoology.
Tu.-Su. 9-12, 2-6.

HISTORICAL MUSEUM
Villa Reale, Monza
Local history. Finds from excavations in the area.
Tu.-Su. 9-12, 2-6.

MUNICIPAL ART GALLERY
Villa Reale, Monza
14th-17th century paintings. Modern art.
Tu.-Su. 9-12, 2-6.

MUNICIPAL MUSEUM
Arengario, Monza
Local history, archaeology. Natural history. Folklore. Paintings.
Tu.-Su. 9.30-12.30, 3-6.

MOTYA

ARCHAEOLOGICAL MUSEUM
Motya, Sicily
Antiquities excavated in the area, including a Mycenean group of two lions attacking a bull.
Daily 9-1.

MURANO

MUSEUM OF GLASSWARE
Palazzo Giustinian, Murano, Venetian Lagoon
Glass from the oldest Egyptian to the present day. Specimens of 15th-16th century Murano ware, Spanish and Bohemian glass. Products of the modern factories at Murano.
Summer: M.-Sa. 9-12.30, 2.30-6.30. Su. 9-12.30. Winter: M.-Sa. 9-5; Su. 9-12.30.

NAPLES

COLLECTION OF NAPLES ZOOLOGICAL STATION
Villa Comunale, Naples
Maritime exhibits found in the Gulf of Naples, including fish, shells, fossils, plant life.
By appointment.

ETHNOGRAPHICAL COLLECTION
Istituto Orientale di Napoli, University, Naples
Material from former Italian colonies, including medical and surgical items, apothecary jars.
By appointment.

FILANGERI MUSEUM
Cuomo Palace, Via del Duomo 288, Naples
Late 15th century palace. Paintings by Mattia Preti and Ribera. *Head of a Youth* by Giovanni Della Robbia. Roman exhibits. Personal possessions of Filangeri. Greek vases and majolica. Weapons.
Daily 10-4; Su. and holidays 10-1.

GALLERY OF THE ACADEMY OF FINE ART
Via Bellini 37, Naples
19th-20th paintings, sculpture.
Tu.-Su. 9.30-12.30, 3-6.

MUSEUM OF ANTHROPOLOGY
Via Mezzocannone 8, Naples
Anthropology. Skulls. Skeletons. Heads of Egyptian and Peruanic mummies. Heads from catacombs in Naples.
Tu.-Su. 9.30-12.30, 3-6.

MUSEUM OF THE CARTHUSIAN MONASTERY OF ST. MARTIN
Naples
Historical section, including bust of Murat by Castex and portrait of François Gerard. Neapolitan crib. Monks' chancel contains marbles, stucco, statues and paintings. Communion table. Refectory has 18th century carved furniture and contemporary fresco of the Wedding at Cana.
Tu.-Sa. 9.30-4; Su. and holidays 9.30-1. Closed M.

MUSEUM OF GEOLOGY AND PALAEONTOLOGY
Largo S. Marcellino 10, Naples
Italian and European geology and palaeontology.
Tu.-Su. 9.30-12.30, 3-6.

MUSEUM OF THE STATE ARCHIVES
Via del Grande Archivo, Naples
Documents relating to the history of the Kingdom of Naples, and to the subsequent development of the Province.
Tu.-Su. 9.30-12.30, 3-6.

MUSEUM OF THE STATE INSTITUTE OF ART
Piazzetta Salazar 6, Naples
Art, especially ceramics.
Tu.-Su. 9.30-12.30, 3-6.

MUSIC MUSEUM
Conservatory of Music, Via S. Pietro a Majella, Naples
Manuscripts by Paisiello, Scarlatti, Mercadante, Cimarosa, Donizetti, Rossini and Verdi.
By appointment.

NATIONAL CERAMICS MUSEUM
Villa Floridiana, Via Cimarosa 77, Naples
Enamels, ivories. China and porcelain, both Italian and foreign. Neapolitan paintings of the 17th and 18th centuries. Goldsmiths' work.
Daily ex. M. 9-4.

NATIONAL GALLERY OF NAPLES
Capodimonte Palace, Parco di Capodimonte (Porta Piccola), Naples
Porcelain salons. 7 Brussels tapestries (1531) after Van Orley, depicting episodes of the Battle of Pavia. Paintings of foreign schools, with works by Cranach, Breughel the Elder. Florence: Bernardo Daddi, Masolino. Venetian school: works of the Vivarinis and portraits by Mantegna and Lorenzo Lotto, Bellini, Titian. Bust of Ferdinand I of Aragon by Guido Mazzoni. *The Drinkers* by Velasquez (17th century). Portraits by El Greco. Paintings of the Neapolitan and Genoese schools. Furniture, faience, glassware, porcelain and enamels. Renaissance bronzes. 19th century Italian sculpture, paintings.
Daily ex. M. 9.30-3; Su. and holidays 9.30-1.

NATIONAL ARCHAEOLOGICAL MUSEUM
Piazza Museo, Naples
In 16th century palace. Greco-Roman sculpture. Roman portraits. Bust of the blind Homer. Mosaics. Bronzes from excavations at Herculaneum and Pompeii. Small bronzes. Paintings.
Daily ex. W. 9.30-3.30; Su. and holidays 9.30-1. Closed Jan. 1, May 1, June 2, Aug. 15, Easter Su. and Christmas Day.

NATIONAL MUSEUM OF SAN MARTINO
Certosa di San Martino, Via Torrione, Naples
History, art and life of Naples from 16th century to the present day. Paintings of 19th century Neapolitan school. Neapolitan crib by Cuciniello.
Daily ex. M. 9.30-12.30, 2.30-5.30.

PAGLIARA ART COLLECTION
Corso Vittorio Emanuele Cariati, Naples
16th-19th century drawings, prints. Ceramics.
Tu.-Su. 9.30-5.

PRINCIPE DIEGO ARAGONA PIGNATELLI CORTES MUSEUM
Riviera di Chaia 200, Naples
18th century wall paintings. Porcelain.
Tu.-Su. 9.30-12.30, 3-6.

ROYAL PALACE
Piazza del Plebiscito 1, Naples
Palace built in 17th century. Beauvais tapestries in honour of Louis XIV, signed by La Tour. Paintings of the French school, including works by Grimou and Doyen. Work-table cased in Sèvres porcelain, by Parisian cabinet-maker Carlin and given by Marie Antoinette to her sister, Marie Caroline.
Daily ex. Tu. 9.30-4; Su. 9.30-1.

ZOOLOGICAL MUSEUM
Giardino Zoologico, Viale Kennedy, Naples
Zoology.
Tu.-Su. 9.30-12.30, 3-6.

ZOOLOGICAL MUSEUM
Via Mezzocannone 8, Naples
Zoology. Entomology. Elmintology.
Tu.-Su. 9.30-12.30, 3-6.

NARNI

MUNICIPAL ART GALLERY
Palazzo Comunale, Narni
Paintings. Marble carvings.
Tu.-Su. 9.30-12.30, 3-6.

MELI PALAEONTOLOGICAL COLLECTION
Narni
Palaeontology.
Tu.-Su. 9.30-12.30, 2-5.

NEMI

MUSEUM OF THE SHIPS OF NEMI
Nemi
Hulls of ancient Roman ships recovered from the bed of Lake Nemi.
Tu.-Su. 9.30-12.30, 3-6.

NERVI

GALLERY OF MODERN ART
Villa Serra, Piazza Pittaluga, Nervi, nr. Genoa
Paintings by 19th and 20th century Ligurian artists. Sculpture. Etchings. Sketches.
Daily ex. M. 10-12, 2-5; Su. 10-12.

GIANNETTINO LUXORO MUNICIPAL MUSEUM
Villa Luxoro, Nervi, nr. Genoa
Antiquities. Crib figurines. 19th century Genoese furniture, furnishings. Majolica. 17th-18th century clocks.
Daily ex. M. 10-12, 2-5; Su. 10-12.

NOCERA UMBRA

ART GALLERY
Piazza Caprera, Nocera Umbra
Paintings. Frescoes. Archaeology.
Tu.-Su. 9-1.

NOLA

ANTIQUARIUM
Via Seminario Vescovile, Nola
Archaeology. Wall paintings.
Tu.-Su. 9.30-12.30, 3-6.

NONANTOLA

TREASURY
Abbey Church of San Silvestro, Nonantola, nr. Modena
Miniatures. Gold plate.
May-Sept. Daily 8.30-12, 2-6. Oct.-Apr. Daily 9-12, 2-4.

NORCIA

MUNICIPAL COLLECTION
Piazza San Benedetto, Norcia
Paintings. Sculpture. Local history.
Tu.-Su. 9-1.

NOTO

MUNICIPAL MUSEUM
Corso Vittorio Emanuele 134, Noto, Sicily
Local history, archaeology. Folklore.
Tu.-Su. 9.30-12.30, 3-6.

NOVARA

ARCHAEOLOGICAL MUSEUM
Palazzo del Broletto, Corso Rosselli, Novara
Local archaeological finds. Numismatics.
Daily ex. Tu. 9.30-12.30, 2.30-5.30.

FARAGGIANA MUSEUM OF NATURAL HISTORY AND ETHNOGRAPHY AND FERRANDI ETHNOGRAPHICAL MUSEUM
Palazzo Faraggiana, Via G. Ferrari 13, Novara
Ethnography, including collections from East Africa. Natural science.
Daily ex. Tu. 9.30-12.30, 2.30-5.30.

GIANNONI GALLERY
Palazzo del Broletto, Corso Rosselli, Novara
Modern and contemporary art collections.
Daily ex. Tu. 9.30-12.30, 2.30-5.30.

MUNICIPAL MUSEUM
Palazzo Faraggiana, Corso Rosselli, Novara
Natural history. Ethnography.
Daily ex. Tu., 9.30-12.30, 2.30-5.30.

ZOOLOGICAL MUSEUM
Novara
Zoology.
Daily ex. Tu. 9.30-12.30, 2.30-5.30.

NOVELLARA

MUNICIPAL MUSEUM
Piazzale Marconi 1, Novellara
Local history, archaeology. Folklore. Domestic equipment.

NUORO

REGIONAL MUSEUM OF COSTUME AND POPULAR TRADITIONS
Viale Sant'Onofrio, Nuoro, Sardinia
Local history, ethnography. Costumes of Sardinia. Folklore. Domestic utensils.
Tu.-Su. 9.30-12.30, 3-6.

ODERZO

MUNICIPAL MUSEUM
Via Garibaldi 18, Oderzo
Archaeology, especially mosaics.
Tu.-Su. 9.30-12.30, 2-5.

MUSEUM OF NATURAL HISTORY
Collegio Brandolini Rota, Oderzo
Natural history. Zoology. Ornithology. Entomology. Ichthyology. Mineralogy.
By appointment.

OFFIDA

ALLEVI MUNICIPAL MUSEUM
Nelle Scuole Comunali, Offida
Finds from excavations in the area.
Tu.-Su. 9.30-1.

ONEGLIA

MUSEUM OF THE HISTORY OF SPAGHETTI
Agnese Spaghetti Factory, Oneglia
Origins, development and types of spaghetti. Old and modern manufacturing techniques.
By appointment.

ORBETELLO

MUNICIPAL ANTIQUARIUM
Via Ricasoli 137, Orbetello
Archaeology. Etruscan graves, vases. Numismatics.
Tu.-Su. 9.30-12.30, 3-5.

ORIA

MILIZIA MUNICIPAL MUSEUM
Via Astore, Oria
Local history, archaeology. Paintings. Natural history.
Tu.-Su. 9.30-12.30, 3-6.

ORISTANO

ANTIQUARIUM
Via Vittorio Emanuele 10, Oristano, Sardinia
Sardinian culture.
Tu.-Su. 9.30-12.30, 3-6.

OROPA

NATURAL HISTORY COLLECTION
Santuario d'Oropa, Oropa
Minerals of the district. Entomology.
Tu.-Su. 9-1, 3-6.

ORTE

MUSEUM OF SACRED ART
Chiesa di San Silvestro, Orte
Religious art, including, Madonna in mosaic (8th century, restored) from the old basilica of St. Peter in Rome; A Madonna by Taddeo di Bartolo; 13th century panel of St. Francis; 4 panels depicting the life of St. Egidio; reliquary cross by Vannuccio di Vivo da Siena (1352).
On request.

ORTONOVO

NATIONAL ARCHAEOLOGICAL MUSEUM
Corso Cavour, Ortonovo
Roman material from excavations in the area.
Summer: M.-Sa. 9-1, 3-6; Su. and holidays 9-4. Winter: M.-Sa. 9-12, 2-5; Su. and holidays 9-1.

ORVIETO

CATHEDRAL MUSEUM
Papal Palace, Piazza del Duomo 29, Orvieto
Madonna by Simone Martini. Sculptures by Arnolfo di Cambio, Maitani and the Pisanos.
Apr.-Nov. Daily 9-1, 3-6. Dec., Mar. 9-1, 2.30-4.30.

CLAUDIO FAINA MUSEUM
Piazza Duomo 29, Orvieto
Archaeological collections, including Etruscan graves. Greek vases. Ceramics.
Daily 9-1, 3-6.

OSOPPO

HISTORICAL MUSEUM
Nella Fortezza, Osoppo
Manuscripts and documents on the Risorgimento.
Tu.-Su. 9-1.

OSTIA ANTICA

DELLA ROCCA CASTLE AND MUSEUM
Ostia Antica
Bas-reliefs. Sarcophagi. Statues and busts of Imperial families. Paintings from the cemetery at Ostia, including a fresco of a lion devouring a bull.
Daily ex. M. 9-1 hour before sunset. Closed Jan. 1, May 1, June 2, Aug. 15, Easter Su. and Christmas Day.

OSTIA

OLD TOWN
Ostia
Founded 4th century B.C. and became chief trading port of Rome and a naval base. The city was depopulated by malaria and silting up of the harbour. Excavations began at the beginning of 20th century: Roman building methods can be seen, and their use of mosaic and mural painting. Firemen's barracks; Baths; Shops; Public fountain; Warehouses; Forum; Temples.
Any time.

PADUA

BASILICA OF SANT'ANTONIO
Piazza del Santo, Padua
Treasury chapel contains relics of St. Anthony and gold plate. Sculptures. Wall paintings.
Closed 12-3.

MEDICAL MUSEUM
The University, Padua
Obstetrics. Gynaecology.
By appointment.

MUNICIPAL MUSEUM
Monastery of St. Anthony, Piazza del Santo 10, Padua
Paintings, including a Crucifixion by Tintoretto, a Crucifix by Giotto, and works by Piazzetta, Longhi and Guariento. 15th century Arras tapestry illustrating the "Chanson de Geste" of Jourdain de Blaye. Lapidary collection. Archaeology. Museum of the Risorgimento.
May 16-Sept. 15, Daily ex. M. 9-12.30, 3.30-6. Rest of year 9-12.30; Su. and holidays 9.30-1.

MUSEUM OF ARCHAEOLOGY AND ART
Liviano, Padua
Archaeological exhibits include a headless Athena (4th century B.C.), a wax mould of Donatello and plaster statuettes by Ammannati. Paintings.
Weekdays, on request.

MUSEUM OF THE INSTITUTE OF ANTHROPOLOGY
The University, Padua
Anthropology. Ethnography. Skulls. Skeletons.
By appointment.

MUSEUM OF THE INSTITUTE OF GEOLOGY
Via Giotto 20, Padua
Geology. Palaeobotony. Fossils.
Tu.-Su. 9-12, 3-6.

MUSEUM OF THE INSTITUTE OF PETROGRAPHY AND MINERALOGY
Corso del Popolo 9, Padua
Mineralogy, petrography of the Adamello area. Crystals. Gems.
By appointment.

MUSEUM OF THE INSTITUTE OF ZOOLOGY, COMPARATIVE ANATOMY AND GENETICS
The University, Padua
Entomology. Ornithology. Ichthyology. Parasitology.
By appointment.

MUSEUM OF THE SCUOLA DEL CARMINE
Piazza Petrarca 1, Padua
Religious art. 15th century frescoes.
Tu.-Su. 9.30-12.30, 2-5.

MUSEUM OF THE SCUOLA DI SAN ROCCO
Via Santa Lucia, Padua
Religious art. Wall-paintings.
Tu.-Su. 9.30-12.30, 2-5.

MUSEUM OF THE SCUOLO DEL SANTO
Piazza del Santo, Padua
Religious art. Wall-paintings.
Tu.-Su. 9.30-12.30, 2-5.

PALAZZO DELLA RAGIONE MUSEUM
Piazza delle Erbe, Padua
Art collection. Frescoes.
Tu.-Su. 9.30-12.30, 3-6.

UNIVERSITY MUSEUM
Palazzo dell'Universita, Via 8 Febbraio, Padua
Collections include Galileo's chair, and the first anatomical theatre in Europe (1594) where Fabrizio di Acquapendente and Giovan Battista Morgagni taught.
Weekdays, on application.

PADULA

ARCHAEOLOGICAL MUSEUM OF WESTERN LUCANIA
Certosa di San Lorenzo, Padula
Finds from excavations in the area of tombs in the Tanagro Valley (8th-2nd centuries B.C.).
Tu.-Su. 9.30-12.

PAESTUM

NATIONAL MUSEUM
nr. Temple of Ceres, Paestum
Finds from excavations of this ancient Greek colony founded in the 6th century by Achaeans from Sybaris. 34 metopes (bas-reliefs in Doric style of 6th century B.C.) from the base of the Temple of Hera near mouth of the Sele river. Bronze vases from Underground Temple. Prehistory.
Daily 9-4.

PALAZZO ACREIDE

ANTIQUARIUM
Palazzo Acreide, Sicily
Archaeological material from excavations in the area.
Tu.-Su. 9.30-sunset.

PALERMO

ARCHAEOLOGICAL MUSEUM
Mormino Foundation, Via Roma 185, Palermo, Sicily
Archaeological finds from the island.
On request.

BORZI BOTANICAL MUSEUM
Via Lincoln, Palermo, Sicily
Botany. Exotic flora.
Tu.-Su. 9.30-12.30, 2.30-5.30.

BOTANICAL COLLECTION
Via Lincoln, Palermo, Sicily
Botany. Tropical and subtropical plants.
Tu.-Su. 9-1.

CASINA CINESE
Parco della Favorita, Palermo, Sicily
In palace. Furniture and furnishings. Chinese art objects.
Tu.-Su. 9.30-12.30, 2.30-5.30.

DIOCESAN MUSEUM
Palazzo Vescovile, Via Bonello 2, Palermo, Sicily
Fragments from the old cathedral and other churches. Sculptures by Gagini and his school. Works by Velasquez. 17th-18th century Sicilian paintings. 12th-16th century Italian paintings.
Daily ex. M. 9.30-12.30, 2.30-5.30.

GALLERY OF MODERN ART
Via Filippo Turati 10, Palermo, Sicily
19th-20th century art. Paintings of the Sicilian scene by local artists.
Daily ex. M. 9.30-12.30, 2.30-5.30.

MUSEUM OF ANATOMY AND PATHOLOGY
Institute of Anatomy, The University, Palermo, Sicily
Anatomy. Pathology.
By appointment.

MUSEUM OF THE INSTITUTE OF HUMAN ANATOMY
Via Feliciuzza, Palermo, Sicily
Human anatomy.
By appointment.

MUSEUM OF MINERALOGY
Via Archirafi 36, Palermo, Sicily
Mineralogy and fossils of the area.
Tu.-Su. 9.30-12.30, 3-6.

MUSEUM OF PALAEONTOLOGY AND GEOLOGY
Via Maqueda, Palermo, Sicily
Palaeontology. Geology. Fossils from Sicily and elsewhere.
Tu.-Su. 9.30-12.30, 3-6.

MUSEUM OF THE RISORGIMENTO
Piazza San Domenico, Palermo, Sicily
Documents and other material on the Risorgimento.
Tu.-Su. 9.20-12.30, 3-6.

NATIONAL ARCHAEOLOGICAL MUSEUM
Piazza Olivella, Palermo, Sicily
Material from excavations in Sicily. Metopes and bas-reliefs of 5th century B.C. from Selinus. Ram from Syracuse. Hercules slaying a Stag, found at Pompeii. Mosaic floors, masks and lions' muzzles from the Temple of Imera. Etruscan funeral urns. Arabic vases. Metal objects, sculptures and inlaid work. Greek terracottas. Coloured figurines from Selinonte. Greek and Attic vases.
Daily ex. M. 9-3; Su. and holidays 9-1. Closed Jan. 1, May 1, June 2, Aug. 15, Easter Su. and Christmas Day.

NATIONAL GALLERY OF SICILY
Palazzo Abbatellis, Via Alloro 6, Palermo, Sicily
Paintings include a 15th century fresco of Death Triumphant. 15th century bust of Eleanor of Aragon by Francesco Laurana. *Annunciation* by Antonello da Messina. Medieval paintings, sculptures.
Daily ex. F. 9.30-4; Su. and holidays 9.30-1. Closed Jan. 1, May 1, Aug. 15, Easter Su. and Christmas Day.

PITRÉ ETHNOGRAPHICAL MUSEUM
Parco della Favorita, Palermo, Sicily
Sicilian folklore and culture. Tools. Domestic equipment. Ceramics. Sculpture. Musical instruments.
Tu.-Su. 9.30-12.30, 3-6.

ZOOLOGICAL MUSEUM
Via Archirafi 18, Palermo, Sicily
Zoology. Anatomy. Osteology. Fish of the Mediterranean.
Tu.-Su. 9.30-12.30, 3-6.

PALESTRINA

NATIONAL ARCHAEOLOGICAL MUSEUM
Palazzo Barberini, Piazza della Cortina, Palestrina
Exhibits from the medieval city. Local history.
Tu.-Su. 9.30-12.30, 2.30-5.30; Su. 10-12.

PALINURO

ANTIQUARIUM
Palinuro
Material from local excavations.
Tu.-Su. 9-5.

PALLANZA

LOCAL MUSEUM
Palazzo Dugnani, Via Cavour 40, Pallanza
Local history. Paintings. Folklore.
Daily ex. M. 10-12, 2-4 or 5.

PALMI

ARCHAEOLOGICAL MUSEUM
Nel Municipio, Palmi
Finds from Taurianum. Ceramics. Wood.
Tu.-Su. 9.30-12.30, 3-6.

CALABRESE MUSEUM OF ETHNOGRAPHY AND FOLKLORE
Palazzo Comunale, Palmi
Local history, folklore. Masks. Ceramics. Religious art. Agricultural tools. Wood sculptures.
Tu.-Su. 9.30-12.30, 3-6.

PARMA

ART MUSEUM
Camera di San Paolo, Via Melloni, Parma
Paintings. Frescoes by Araldi (1514).
Tu.-Su. 9-1.

"VITTORIO BOTTEGO" ERYTHREAN ZOOLOGICAL MUSEUM
University of Parma, Via Cavestro 7, Parma
Exhibits collected by the explorer, Vittorio Bottego.
During University term, on application.

COLLECTION OF THE INSTITUTE OF HUMAN ANATOMY
Presso l'Ospedale Maggiore, Parma
Anatomical preparations. Skulls.
By appointment.

COLLECTIONS OF THE INSTITUTE OF MINERALOGY
Via dell'Università, Parma
Mineralogy of the region and elsewhere.
By appointment.

GENERAL COLLECTIONS
Institute of Zoology, Parma
Zoology. Vertebrates. Invertebrates. Skeletons. Preparation of embryos.
By appointment.

LOMBARDI MUSEUM
Viale Mariotti, Parma
Collections devoted to mementoes of Marie-Louise, former Empress who became Duchess of Parma. Jewels. Ducal coat and metal embroidered train in which the Duchess posed for her portrait by Robert Lefèvre. Napoleon's wedding present. Travelling medicine chest. Letters. Water-colours, signed by Marie-Louise. Souvenirs of the King of Rome and the Emperor. Water-colour by Isabey showing Marie-Louise at the Tuileries after the birth of the King of Rome.
Apr.-Sept. Daily ex. M. 9.30-12.30, 3.30-6.30. Rest of year, 9.30-12.30, 3-6. Su. 9.30-1.

MUSEUM OF CHINESE ART
Via Mamalo 2, Parma
Chinese bronzes, porcelain, ceramics, paintings, coins.
Tu.-Su. 9.30-12.30, 3-6.

MUSEUM OF CHINESE ETHNOGRAPHY
Via San Martino 8, Parma
Chinese, Japanese and African art, ethnography.
Tu.-Su. 9.30-12.30, 3-6.

MUSEUM OF PALAEONTOLOGY
Via Massimo d'Azeglio 85, Parma
Palaeontology. Fossils. Stones.
Tu.-Su. 9-1.

MUSEUM OF THE RISORGIMENTO
Via della Repubblica 41, Parma
Material illustrating Italy's struggle for independence.
Tu.-Su. 9.30-12.30, 3-6.

NATIONAL GALLERY
Palazzo della Pilotta, Via della Pilotta 4, Parma
Tuscan, Emilian and Venetian painters of 14th-16th centuries, including Dosso Dossi, Francia, Fra. Angelico, Cima da Conegliano, Bassano, El Greco *(Cure of the Blind Man)*, Il Parmigianino. Works by Correggio, including *The Virgin with St. Jerome, Madonna with a Bowl* and *Coronation of the Virgin.* Monochrome painted *Head of an Adolescent* by Leonardo da Vinci. 17th and 18th century works by Neapolitan, Genoese, Venetian and Flemish painters. 18th century French paintings.
May-Sept. Daily ex. M. 9.30-1, 3-6. Rest of year 9-1, 2-4.30. Su. and holidays 9-1.

NATIONAL MUSEUM OF ANTIQUITIES
Palazzo della Pilotta, Via della Pilotta 4, Parma
Finds from excavations at Velleia, west of Parma. Pottery and statues. A Food Table, reminder of a foundation started in the reign of Trajan for the benefit of 300 poor children. Medals and coins.
May-Sept. Daily ex. M. 9-1, 3-6. Oct.-Apr. Daily ex. M. 9.30-4; Su. and holidays 9-1. Closed Jan. 1, May 1, June 2, Aug. 15, Easter Su. and Christmas Day.

PALATINE GALLERY
Palazzo della Pilotta, Via della Pilotta 4, Parma
Former dining room of the Abbess of the Convent of St. Paul, with a ceiling decorated by Correggio in 1519 with a secular theme, including the Triumphs of Diana, Adonis, *putti* (love scenes), the Three Graces and the Three Fates.
May-Sept. Daily ex. M. 9.30-1, 3-6. Rest of year 9-1, 2-4.30. Su. and holidays 9-1.

PIOLA CONGOLESE COLLECTION
Institute of Zoology, Parma
Ethnography and zoology of the Congo.
By appointment.

SAN GIOVANNI EVANGELISTA HISTORICAL COLLECTION
Via Borgo Pipa 1, Parma
15th century furniture. 15th-18th century ceramics, vases. 16th century frescoes. Household articles.
Tu.-Su. 9.30-12.30, 3-6.

STUARD ART GALLERY
Via Cavestro 14, Parma
Paintings, notably Tuscan primitives.
May-Sept. Daily ex. M. 9.30-1, 3-6. Rest of year 9-1, 2-4.30. Su. and holidays 9-1.

PATIGLIANO

MUNICIPAL MUSEUM
Viale Manin, Patigliano
Local history, archaeology. Folklore. Natural history. Paintings.
Tu.-Su. 9.30-12.30, 3-6.

PAVIA

ARCHAEOLOGICAL MUSEUM
Institute of Archaeology and Numismatics, The University, Pavia
Archaeological finds from the area. Coins.
By appointment.

CARTHUSIAN MONASTERY MUSEUM
Pavia
In monastery founded 1396. Angels by Bergognone; bronze candelabra by Fontana (1580) and reclining figures of Ludovico il Moro and Beatrice d'Este by Cristoforo Solari (1499). Door with 7 portraits of the Dukes of Milan by Amadeo and Briosco, and a tryptych made from hippopotamus teeth (1409), Renaissance fountain. Door by Amadeo has 7 portraits of Duchesses of Milan; frescoes by Luini. Bas-reliefs depicting life of Gian Galeazzo. 17th century carved wardrobes. Works by Bergognone, including a Crucifixion and altarpiece.
Mornings, 9.30-12.30 throughout the year. Afternoons, Jan., Feb., Nov. and Dec. 1.30-4.30; Mar., Apr., Sept. and Oct. 2-5; May. June, July and Aug. 2-6. Closed M. except when these are holidays, also Jan. 1, May 1, June 2, Aug. 15, Easter Su. and Christmas Day.

CERTOSA MUSEUM
Palazzo Ducale, Pavia
15th century drawings. Sculpture. A *Pala* by Mantegna and bas-reliefs by Mantegazza.
Tu.-Su. 9.30-12.30, 3-6.

GALLERY OF MODERN ART
Castle of the Viscontis, Piazza Castello, Pavia
Modern art, especially Italian.
Apr.-Sept. Daily ex. M. 10-12, 3-5. Rest of year 10-12, 2-4. Closed Jan. 1, Nov. 1 and 4, Easter Su. and Christmas Day.

HISTORICAL COLLECTION
Istituto di Farmacologia e Terapia Sperimentale, Pavia
Early pharmacy, with original equipment.
By appointment.

HISTORICAL MUSEUM
University, Pavia
History of the University.
By appointment.

MALASPINA ART GALLERY
Piazza Petrarca 2, Pavia
Paintings, including works by Correggio, Ambr. Bergognone, Carlo Crivelli and Antonello da Messina. Collection of engravings and prints.
Daily ex. M. and holidays, 10-12, 2-4 or 3-5.

MEDICAL MUSEUM
Istituto di Obstetricia, Pavia
Obstetrics. Gynaecology.
By appointment.

MUNICIPAL MUSEUM
Castle of the Viscontis, Piazza Castello, Pavia
Fragments from Roman Pavia as well as sculptures from Lombard royal tombs. Medieval mosaics, sculpture and reconstructed portals from destroyed 11th-12th century churches. Wooden model of Cathedral by Fugazza (1497-1519). Paintings include works by Correggio, Bergognone, Carlo Crivelli, Antonello da Messina.
Apr.-Sept. Daily ex. M. 10-12, 3-5. Rest of the year 10-12, 2-4. Closed Jan. 1, Nov. 1 and 4, Easter Su. and Christmas Day.

MUSEUM OF THE INSTITUTE OF COMPARATIVE ANATOMY
Piazza Botta 10, Pavia
Comparative anatomy. Osteology. Skulls. Skeletons. Embryology.
By appointment.

MUSEUM OF THE INSTITUTE OF GEOLOGY
Strada Nuova 65, Pavia
Palaeontology. Mineralogy. Geology. Fossils.
By appointment.

MUSEUM OF THE INSTITUTE OF HUMAN ANATOMY
Via Forlanini 8, Pavia
Histology. Human anatomy.
By appointment.

MUSEUM OF THE INSTITUTE OF MINERALOGY AND PETROGRAPHY
University, Pavia
Mineralogy. Petrography.
By appointment.

MUSEUM OF NATURAL HISTORY
Bordoni Technical Institute, Pavia
Natural history. Mineralogy. Zoology.
By appointment.

MUSEUM OF THE RISORGIMENTO
Castle of the Viscontis, Piazza Castello, Pavia
Material on the struggle for the independence of Italy. Relics of the Cairioli brothers.
Apr.-Sept. Daily ex. M. 10-12, 3-5. Rest of year 10-12, 2-4. Closed Jan. 1, Nov. 1 and 4, Easter Su. and Christmas Day.

NATURAL HISTORY COLLECTION
Liceo 'U. Foscolo', Pavia
Mammals, birds of the region.
By appointment.

PEGLI

ARCHAEOLOGICAL MUSEUM OF LIGURIA
Villa Durazzo Pallavicini, Pegli, nr. Genoa
Ligurian prehistory. The ancient necropolis of Genoa. Roman Liguria, including objects found at Labarna and Tortona.
Daily ex. F. 10-12, 2-5; Su. 2-6.

ARCHAEOLOGICAL AND ETHNOGRAPHICAL MUSEUM OF AMERICA
Villa Durazzo Pallavicini, Pegli, nr. Genoa
Peruvian culture. Exhibits from Peru. Finds from Ligurian cave dwellings.
Daily ex. F. 10-12, 2-5; Su. 2-6.

MARITIME MUSEUM
Villa Doria, Pegli, nr. Genoa
Collections belonging to the municipality, and those presented by the engineer, Fabio Garelli. 16th-17th century maps and globes. Ship-models. Maritime prints and paintings.
Tu.-Sa. 10-12, 2-5; Su. 10-12.

PENNABILI

BERGAMASCHI DIOCESAN MUSEUM
Via Seminario, Feretrano, Pennabili
Religious art. Liturgical items.
Tu.-Su. 9.30-1.

PERGOLA

PICCININI FOSSIL COLLECTION
Pergola
Fossils. Palaeontology.
By appointment.

PERTICARTA

MUSEUM OF THE HISTORY OF MINERALS
Via Decio Raggi, Perticarta
History of minerals in the area. Fossils. Geology.
Tu.-Su. 9.30-12.30, 3-6.

PERUGIA

ART MUSEUM
Nobile Collegio del Cambio, Corso Vannucci, Perugia
15th century frescoes.
Tu.-Su. 9-1.

CHAPTERHOUSE MUSEUM
Cathedral, Piazza IV Novembre, Perugia
Ecclesiastical paintings and objects, including a Madonna (1484) by Luca Signorelli. Illuminated manuscripts (breviaries, missals, graduals and antiphonals); gold and silver reliquaries.
Daily 9-12, 3-6. Apply to the sacristan.

COLLECTION OF THE INSTITUTE OF BIOLOGY
Perugia
Biology. Zoology.
By appointment.

COLLECTIONS OF THE INSTITUTE OF BOTANY
Perugia
Botany. Herbarium.
By appointment.

HYPOGEUM OF THE VOLUMNI
Ponte San Giovanni, Perugia
Funeral urns and grave goods from the Necropolis of Palazzone.
Summer: Tu.-Su. 9-1, 3-5.30. Winter: Tu.-Sa. 9-1, 2-4; Su. and holidays 9-1.

MUSEUM OF NATURAL HISTORY
Seminario Arcivescovile, Perugia
Palaeontology. Botany. Mineralogy. Zoology.
Tu.-Su. 9-1.

MUSEUM OF PREHISTORY OF CENTRAL ITALY
Perugia
Finds from excavations in the region.
Tu.-Su. 9.30-12.30, 3-6.

NATIONAL ARCHAEOLOGICAL MUSEUM OF UMBRIA
Convento di San Domenico, Corso Cavour, Perugia
Etruscan urns and sarcophagi. Roman antiquities. Prehistory. Inscriptions. Bronzes, vases and terracottas. Models of cave dwellings in the Iron Age. Objects made of flint. Pottery. Vases, bone implements, household equipment.
Tu.-Su. 9-1.

NATIONAL GALLERY OF UMBRIA
Palazzo dei Priori, Corso Vannucci, Perugia
14th century frescoes from churches in Perugia. 13th century wood carving of a Dead Christ. Umbrian and Sienese primitives. Marble statuettes by Nicolo and Giovanni Pisano and Arnolfo di Cambo (14th century). Panel by Francesco da Rimini. Tuscan paintings, including works by Fra. Angelico and Pierro della Francesca. Bronze bas-relief by Francesco di Giorgio. Works by Boccati (15th century). Umbrian paintings by Pintoricchio. French enamels and ivories of 13th-14th centuries. Sculptures by Agostino di Duccio.
May-Oct. Daily ex. M. 9-1, 3-5.30. Nov.-Apr. Daily ex. M. 9-1, 2-4. Closed Su. and holiday afternoons.

NATURAL HISTORY COLLECTION
Istituti della Facolta di Scienze Agrarie, Borgo XX Giugno 74, Perugia
Botany. Microbiology. Entomology. Geology. Mineralogy.
By appointment.

NATURAL HISTORY COLLECTION
Liceo Scientifico 'Galeazzo Alessi', Perugia
Minerals. Fossils. Herbarium. Zoology.
By appointment.

TOPOGRAPHICAL AND HISTORICAL MUSEUM OF THE CITY AND TERRITORY OF PERUGIA
Convent of San Domenico, Corso Cavour, Perugia
Documents of city life through the centuries.
Tu.-Su. 9-1.

PESARO

MUNICIPAL MUSEUM
Palazzo Toschi-Mosca, Via Mazzolari, Pesaro
Paintings, mainly primitives, including the *Pala di Pesaro* by Giovanni Bellini and other works by the same artist.
Apr.-Sept. 10-12, 4-6. Oct.-Mar. 10-12, 2-4.

MUSEUM OF MAJOLICA
Palazzo Toschi-Mosca, Via Mazzolari, Pesaro
Umbrian pottery. Items from Castel Durante, Urbina and Pesaro. Works by Maestro Giorgio Andreoli, the inventor of metal lustre, and Nicolo Pellipario. Medallion of a *condottiere* by Andrea Della Robbia.
Apr.-Sept. 10-12, 4-6. Oct.-Mar. 10-12, 2-4.

OLIVERI ARCHAEOLOGICAL MUSEUM
Palazzo Almerici, Via Mazzi 97, Pesaro
Etruscan monuments, bronzes and inscriptions. Roman sculptures.
M.-Sa. 4-7; Su. 10-12.

ROSSINI'S HOUSE
Via Rossini 34, Pesaro
House where the composer lived. Memorabilia of Rossini (1792-1868).
Daily ex. M. 9-12, 3-6.

PESCARA

HOUSE OF GABRIELE D'ANNUNZIO
Corso Manthoné, Pescara
Memorabilia of the poet, Gabriele d'Annunzio (1863-1938), in the house where he was born.
Tu.-Su. 9.30-12.30, 3-6.

PESCASSEROLI

MUSEUM OF THE ABRUZZO NATIONAL PARK
Via Santa Lucia, Pescasseroli
History of the National Park. Botany. Ecology. Maps and drawings.
Tu.-Su. 9.30-12.30, 3-6.

PESCIA

BOTANICAL COLLECTION
Istituto Tecnico Agrario Statale, Pescia
Herbarium. Italian flora.
By appointment.

MUNICIPAL MUSEUM
Piazza S. Stefano, Pescia
Tuscan paintings of the 14th-16th centuries. Local history and folklore.
Daily ex. M. 9.30-12.30, 3-6.

PIACENZA

ALBERONI GALLERY
Via Emilia 77, Piacenza
17th and 18th century German, Flemish and Italian tapes-

tries. Paintings, including *Christ of the Column* (1473) by Antonello da Messina and a *Holy Family* by Raphaël and his pupils. *Su. 3-6; Su. mornings and other times apply to the Gallery Director (tel: 21 633).*

CHAPTERHOUSE MUSEUM
Piazza del Duomo, Piacenza
Religious art. Vestments. Ornaments.
Tu.-Su. 9.30-1.

GIUSEPPE RICCI ODDI GALLERY OF MODERN ART
Via San Siro 13, Piacenza
Italian and foreign paintings (19th-20th centuries), designs and sculptures.
Tu.-Su. 10-12, 3-6.

MUNICIPAL MUSEUM
Via Gazzola, Piacenza
Archaeological exhibits, including the Piacenza Liver, and Etruscan bronze covered with inscriptions which enabled diviners to interpret the entrails of sacrificial victims. 17th and 18th century paintings. *Virgin* by Botticelli.
Su. 10-12. Other times apply to the Instituto Gazzola, 9 Via Gazzola.

MUSEUM OF THE RISORGIMENTO
Via Sopramuro 60, Piacenza
Material illustrating Italy's struggle for independence.
Tu.-Su. 9.30-12.30, 3-6.

MUSEUM OF SANT' ANTONIO
Annesso alla Basilica, Via Chiostro San Antonino 6, Piacenza
Religious art. Miniatures.
Tu.-Su. 9.30-12.30, 3-6.

THEATRE MUSEUM
Via Verdi 41, Piacenza
History of the theatre.
Tu.-Su. 9-1.

PIADENA

PLATINA ANTIQUARIUM
Palazzo Municipale, Piadena
Archaeological material from local excavations.
Tu.-Su. 9.30-12, 2-5.

PIAZZA ARMERINA

IMPERIAL VILLA
nr. Piazza Armerina, Sicily
Country mansion of Diocletian's co-Emperor Maximian (Maximianus Herculeus), late 3rd century. Mosiacs of the Roman-African school of A.D. 297-300. Thermae. Peristyle. Private apartments.
Daily 9-1, 3-6. Closed holiday afternoons.

MUNICIPAL MUSEUM
Piazza Armerina, Sicily
Local history, archaeology. Natural history.
Tu.-Su. 9.30-4.

PIEDIMONTE D'ALIFE

ALIFE MUSEUM
Via Sorgente 4, Piedimonte d'Alife
Local archaeology. Graves. Vases. Ceramics. Numismatics.
Tu.-Su. 9.30-12.30, 3-6.

PIENZA

MUSEUM
Via del Castello 1, Pienza
Paintings of 14th and 15th century Sienese school. Flemish tapestries of 15th and 16th centuries. 14th century cope made in England and presented to the Cathedral by Pius II.
Daily 10-1, 3-6.

PIEVE BOVIGLIANA

PIEVE MUSEUM
Via Napoleone 62, Pieve Bovigliana
Local history, folklore. Epigraphs.
Tu.-Su. 9-12, 3-6.

PIEVE DI CADORE

MUSEUM
Titian's Birthplace, Pieve di Cadore
Home of the painter Titian (1490-1576), with collections illustrating his life and work.
June-Sept. Daily 9-12, 3-7. Other times apply to Signor Giacobbi (tel: 3123).

MUSEUM OF THE RISORGIMENTO
Palazzo Communita, Pieve di Cadore
Documents on the Italian struggle for independence.
Tu.-Su. 9-1, 3-6.

PINEROLO

MUNICIPAL MUSEUM
Via Trieste 8, Pinerolo, Sardinia
History of Sardinia.
Tu.-Su. 9.30-12.30, 3-6.

PISA

ANATOMY MUSEUM
Faculty of Veterinary Medicine, University, Pisa
Anatomy of domestic animals.
By appointment.

CEMETERY
Piazza del Duomo, Pisa
12th century burial ground surrounded by ossuaries. 14th and 15th century frescoes in the galleries. Greco-Roman sarcophagi. Tombs and sculptures.
Daily Jan. 9-4.30 (4.45 holidays); Feb. 9-5; Mar. 8.30-6; Apr. 8-6.30; May 1-Aug. 15, 8-7.30; Aug. 16-31 8-7; Sept. 8.30-6.30; Oct. 9-5.30; Nov. and Dec. 9-4.30. Check these times locally.

COLLECTION OF THE INSTITUTE OF BOTANY
University, Pisa
Botany. Plants of Italy and Europe.
By appointment.

DOMUS GALILEIANA
Via Santa Maria 26, Pisa
Memorabilia of Galileo, in his former home.
Tu.-Su. 9.30-12, 3-5.30.

DOMUS MAZZINIANA
Via Mazzini 71, Pisa
Memorabilia of Mazzini (1805-1872), in house where he was nursed by Rosselli Nathan.
Tu.-Su. 9.30-12.30, 3-6.

MUSEUM OF GEOLOGY AND PALAEONTOLOGY
Via Santa Maria 53, Pisa
Geology. Palaeontology.
Tu.-Su. 9.30-12.30, 3-6.

MUSEUM OF THE INSTITUTE OF HUMAN ANATOMY
University, Pisa
Anatomical collections.
By appointment.

NATIONAL MUSEUM OF SAN MATTEO
Monastery of St. Matthew, Piazza S. Matteo, Pisa
Medieval sculpture of the Pisan school, including a room devoted to Giovanni Pisano. Polyptych by Masaccio and wooden statue of the Virgin of the Annunciation by Andrea Pisano. Paintings. Crucifixes of the Pisan school. *Nursing Madonna* by Nino Pisano. Polyptych by Simone Martini.
Daily ex. M. 9.30-4; Su. and holidays 9-1.

PISTOIA

CATHEDRAL MUSEUM
Via Puccini, Pistoia
Religious art. Miniatures. Roman sculpture. Paintings (14th century).
Tu.-Su. 9.30-12.30, 2.30-5.30.

CIVIC MUSEUM
Via Curtatone e Montanara, Pistoia
Paintings, including works by Berlinghieri, Mariotto di Nardo, Lorenzo di Nicolo Gerini, Lorenzetti, Fiamberti, Lorenzo di Credi, Fra. Paolino, Ghirlandaio. Wooden statues. Pottery.
Daily ex. M. 9.30-12.30, 2-30.5-30.

PITIGLIANO

MUNICIPAL MUSEUM
Vicolo Manin, Pitigliano
Finds from local excavations. Etruscan ceramics.
Tu.-Su. 9-12, 3-6.

PIZZIGHETTONE

MUNICIPAL MUSEUM
Torre de Francesco I, Pizzighettone
Local archaeology. Paintings. Etruscan ceramics.
Tu.-Su. 9.30-12.30, 3-6.

POGGIO A CAIANO

VILLA MEDICEA
Poggio a Caiano, nr. Florence
Built 1485 by Sangello for Lorenzo the Magnificent. It is said that Francesco I de'Medici and Bianca Capello were poisoned here in 1587. Drawing room has coffered ceiling and frescoes by Andrea del Sarto, Alessandro Allori and Pontormo. The ceiling of the loggia and façade were decorated by the Della Robbias.
Sept.-Oct. Daily 9-6. Rest of the year 9-12. Afternoon, 2-5 in Mar.; 2-6 Apr.; 2-7 May 2-Aug. 31; 1-4 Nov. 1-Feb. 28. Closed Jan. 1, May 1, June 2, Aug. 15, Easter Su. and Christmas Day.

POLICORO

SIRTIDE ANTIQUARIUM AND ZONA ARCHEOLOGICA OF THE HERACLEA CHURCH OF SANTA MARIA D'ANGLONA
Policoro, nr. Tursi
Finds from excavations in the area.
Tu.-Su. 9.30-12.30, 3-6.

POMPEI

Founded in the 5th century B.C. In A.D. 79 the eruption of Vesuvius covered the town with molten lava and cinders. Systematic excavations began in 1748, and two-thirds of the city are visible.
Typical luxurious Pompeiian villas can be seen. The Antiquarium contains historical relics, objects in daily use and reconstructions of mills and dye-works. Petrified humans and animals in the attitudes in which they died. Also to be seen are the Forum, Great Theatre, the Fullonica Stephani (laundry and dyeworks), Amphitheatre, the Stabian Baths (the most complete in Pompei), the Forno (baker's oven and flour mills) and the Casa dei Vettii, the best decorated house in the town, which remains as it was found in 1894.
Daily 9-1 hour before sunset. Closed Jan. 1, May 1, June 2, Aug. 15, Easter Su. and Christmas Day. Mid-June-Sep. also Sa. 8-11 p.m., when the buildings are floodlit.

HALL OF THE TREASURY
Santuario della Madonna del Rosario, Santuario della Madonna del Rosario, Pompei
Finds from the Sanctuary.
Daily 8.30-sunset.

VESUVIAN MUSEUM
Istituto Maschile Bartolo Longo, Via Sacra, Pompei
Pieces of lava, mineral and volcanic curiosities from Vesuvius.
Daily 9.30-12.30.

PONTEDASSIO

MUSEUM OF THE HISTORY OF SPAGHETTI
Via Garibaldi 96, Pontedassio
Origins, development and type of spaghetti. Old and modern manufacturing techniques.
Tu.-Su. 9.30-12.30, 3-6.

PONZANO VENETO

BURLINI COLLECTION
Ponzano Veneto
Entomology. Italian fauna.
By appointment.

POPULONIA

ETRUSCAN MUSEUM
Villa della Società Populonia Italica, Populonia
Archaeology. Topographical maps of the region. Graves.
By appointment.

PORDENONE

ART GALLERY
Palazzo del Commune, Pordenone
Paintings, including works by Pordenone and Bassano.
On request.

PORTICI

FILIPPO SILVESTRI MUSEUM
Istituto di Entomologia Agraria, Facolta di Agraria della Università, Portici
Entomological collection.
By appointment.

PORTO D'ISCHIA

MUSEUM OF THE ISLAND OF ISCHIA
Via Roma 125, Porto d'Ischia
Prehistoric finds from excavations in the area.
Tu.-Su. 9.30-12.30, 3-6.

PORTOFERRAIO

FORESIANA GALLERY OF ART
Piazza Hutre, Portoferraio
Paintings, especially of the 19th century.
Tu.-Su. 9-1, 3-6.

NAPOLEONIC MUSEUM
Mill Villa, Portoferraio, Isle of Elba
House sometimes occupied by Napoleon I and containing souvenirs and his personal library.
Weekdays 9-1, 3-6 (Oct.-Apr. 9.30-4); Su. and holidays 9-1. Closed M. (Oct.-Apr.), also Jan. 1, Apr. 29, May 1, June 2, Aug. 15, Easter and Christmas Day.

PORTOGRUARO

ARCHAEOLOGICAL MUSEUM
Via del Seminario 10, Portogruaro
Objects from the excavations of the Roman colony of *Concordia Sagittaria*, a mile to the south. Sarcophagi inscriptions.
Daily ex. M. 9.30-12.30, 2.30-5.30.

FAVERO ORNITHOLOGICAL COLLECTION
Via Zapetti 2, Portogruaro
Ornithology. Rare birds of Italy.
By appointment.

GAMBARINI BOTANICAL COLLECTION
Villa Gambarini, Portogruaro
Botanical collection.
By appointment.

POSSAGNO

CANOVA MUSEUM
Via Canova, Possagno
Memorabilia of the sculptor, Antonio Canova (1757-1822), in the house where he was born.
Tu.-Su. 9.30-12.30, 3-6.

POTENZA

LUCANO REGIONAL MUSEUM
Via Malta, Potenza
Objects from Metaponto and other Lucanian excavations, notably local antique ceramic ware, archaic bronze statuettes, terracottas, and a bronze helmet from Vaglio.
M.-Sa. 9-1; Su. 10-12.

POZZUOLI

ANTIQUARIUM
Pozzuoli
Archaeology. Roman sculpture.
On request.

PRATICA DI MARE

ANTIQUARIUM
Pratica di Mare
Finds from excavations in the district.
Tu.-Su. 9.30-12.30, 3-6.

PRATO

DIOCESAN MUSEUM
Piazza del Duomo 49, Prato
Religious art. 16th century paintings. Frescoes.
Tu.-Sa. 9.30-12, 3.30-6.

GALLERY OF MODERN ART
Piazza del Comune, Prato
19-20th century paintings, sculpture, graphics, especially by Italian artists.
Tu.-Su. 9.30-1.

MUNICIPAL GALLERY
Palazzo Pretorio, Piazza del Commune, Prato
Paintings, including a 15th century predella telling the story of the Holy Girdle, and works by Lorenzo Monaco, Filippo Lippi and Filippino Lippi. Baroque statue of Bacchus as a child by Tacea. Medallion portrait of Cardinal Nocolo da Prato.
Apr.-Sept. M.-Sa. 9.30-12, 3.30-6. Oct.-Mar. M.-Sa. 9.30-12, 2-4.30. Su. and holidays 9-12. Closed Jan. 1, May 1, June 2, Aug. 15, Easter Su. and Christmas Day.

QUARTO D'ALTINO

ALTINO MUSEUM
Quarto D'Altino
Local history. Folklore. Paintings.
Tu.-Su. 9.30-12.30, 3-6.

RAGUSA

ARCHAEOLOGICAL MUSEUM
Via Natalelli, Ragusa
Archaeological finds from excavations in the area.
Tu.-Su. 9-12, 3-6.

RICCA ORNITHOLOGICAL COLLECTION
Piazza Vescovo Ferdinando Ricca, Ragusa
Ornithology.
By appointment.

RAVENNA

ARCHAEOLOGICAL MUSEUM
Piazza dell'Arcivescovado 1, Ravenna
5th-6th century sculpture and inscriptions.
Tu.-Su. 9-1, 3-6.

BASILICA OF SANT'APOLLINARE IN CLASSE
Ravenna
Ravenna mosaics.
Daily 8-12, 2-6.

CHURCH OF SAN VITALE AND MAUSOLEUM OF GALLA PLACIDA
Ravenna
Ravenna mosaics.
Summer: daily 8.30-12, 2-6. Winter: daily 8.30-12, 2-5.

DANTE MUSEUM
Via Guido da Polenta, Ravenna
Memorabilia of Dante's stay in Ravenna.
Tu.-Su. 9-12, 3-6.

GALLERY OF THE ACADEMY OF FINE ART
Via Roma, Ravenna
16th-17th century paintings of the Tuscan, Venetian and Emilian schools.
Tu.-Su. 9.30-12.30, 3-6.

MUSEUM AND TOMB OF DANTE
Via Dante, Ravenna
Memorabilia of Dante.
Tu.-Su. 9.30-12.30, 3-6.

NATIONAL MUSEUM OF ANTIQUITIES
Via San Vitale 11, Ravenna
Roman sculpture and tombstones. Oriental fabrics. Byzantine bas-reliefs. Panels painted in the Veneto-Cretan period. Ivories. The Diptych of Murano. Head carved by Tullio Lombardo (16th century), attributed to Gaston de Foix.
Tu.-Su. 9.30-12, 2-5 (2-4 Oct.-Apr.); Su. 9.30-1. Closed Jan. 1, May 1, Aug. 15, Easter and Christmas.

RECANATI

DIOCESAN MUSEUM
Recanati
Ecclesiastical art. Vestments. Church plate. Manuscripts.
Apply to sacristan of the Cathedral.

CIGLI MUSEUM
Palazzo Comunale, Recanati
Memorabilia of the singer, Beniamino Gigli (1890-1957).
Tu.-Su. 9-12, 3-6.

LEOPARDI PALACE
Recanati, nr. Loreto
Mementoes of the poet Leopardi (1798-1837), who was born in the town.
On request.

MUNICIPAL ART GALLERY
Palazzo Comunale, Recanati
Paintings by local artists.
Tu.-Su. 9.30-12.30, 3-6.

REGGIO CALABRIA

NATIONAL MUSEUM
Piazza Nava 26, Reggio Calabria
Collections include an equestrian group in terracotta from the Temple of Locri, as well as other groups. Votive tablets illustrating the legend of Persephone (5th century B.C.). Works by Antonello da Messina.
June-Aug. Daily ex. M. 9-1, 3.30-6; closed Su. afternoons. Sept.-May daily ex. M. 9.30-4 (until 1.30 Su.).

ORNITHOLOGICAL COLLECTION
Societa di Tiro a Volo, Reggio Calabria
Ornithology.
By appointment.

REGGIO EMILIA

CIVIC MUSEUM
Piazza Cavour, Reggio Emilia
Natural history. Palaeontology. Paintings. Finds from local excavations. Weapons.
Daily ex. Su. 9-1; Su. 10-12.

MUSEUM OF THE RISORGIMENTO
Via Emilia a San Pietro, Reggio Emilia
Material illustrating Italy's struggle for independence.
Tu.-Su. 9.30-12.30, 3-6.

PARMEGGIANI GALLERY
Via Mazzoni, Reggio Emilia
15th-17th century gold plate and velvets. Paintings, sculptures, and furniture. Works by Tiepolo, Veronese, Van Eyck and El Greco. Room devoted to the Spanish school.
M.-Sa. 9-12, 3-5.30; Su. 10-12.30, 3-6.

LAZZARO SPALLANZANI MUSEUM OF NATURAL HISTORY
Via L. Spallanzani 1A, Reggio Emilia
Mineralogy. Geology. Palaeontology. Zoology. Botany. Anatomy.
Tu.-Su. 9.30-12.30, 3-6.

RIESE PIO X

S. PIO X HOUSE AND MUSEUM
Via Sarto, Riese Pio X
Memorabilia of Pope Pio X, in his former home.
Tu.-Su. 9.30-12.30, 3-6.

RIETI

MUNICIPAL MUSEUM
Palazzo Communale, Piazza Vittorio Emanuele II, Rieti
Classical and medieval sculpture. 17th century paintings. Jewellery.
Summer: daily 10-1, 4-6. Winter: daily 4-6.

RIMELLA

MUNICIPAL MUSEUM
Rimella
Local history. Armaments. Numismatics. Paintings.
Tu.-Su. 9-12, 3-6.

RIMINI

FRANCESCAN MISSIONARY MUSEUM
Via San Lorenzo Monte 75, Rimini
Collections of ethnography and folk art gathered by missionaries.
Tu.-Su. 9-12, 3-6.

MUNICIPAL MUSEUM AND ART GALLERY
Biblioteca Gambalunghiana, Via Gambalunga 27, Rimini
Roman mosaics and sculpture. Etruscan tomb-furniture of the Villanovan period, with an axe-mould. Coinage of Ariminum. Paintings include works by Ghirlandaio, Giovanni Bellini and Perin del Vaga.
July-Sept., daily 8-12.30. Oct.-June, daily 9-12.30, 3.30-6.30.

RIPATRANSONE

MUNICIPAL MUSEUM AND ART GALLERY
Palazzo Comunale, Ripatransone
Archaeological material from excavations in the area. Local history. Paintings.
Tu.-Su. 9.30-12.30, 3-6.

RIVA DEL GARDA

CIVIC MUSEUM
Rocca, Piazza 3 Novembre, Riva del Garda
Local history. Prehistoric exhibits. Armour. Locally printed books, including a Talmud of 1558.
Daily ex. M. 9.30-12.30, 2.30-5.30.

ROME

ACADEMY OF SAN LUCA
Palazzo Carpegna, Piazza dell'Accademia di San Luca 77, Rome
17th-19th century paintings. Artists include Raphaël, Jacopo da Bassano, Guercino, Rubens and Canova. Terracottas. Sculpture.
M., W., F. 10-1. Closed holidays and Aug.

AFRICAN MUSEUM
Via Ulisse Aldovrandi 16A, Rome
African art and ethnography
Daily ex. M. 9-1, 4-7; Su. 9-12.

ANTIQUARIUM
Piazzale Caffarelli 4, Rome
Epigraphy. Bronzes. Vases. Glass.
Tu.-Su. 9-1, 3-6.

ANTIQUARIUM OF THE FORUM
Piazza Santa Maria Nova 53, Rome
Archaeological material found in the forum.
On request.

ANTIQUARIUM OF THE PALATINE
Piazza Santa Maria Nova 53, Rome
Collection of works found on the Palatine since 1870.
On request.

ART MUSEUM
Quadreria della Cassa Depositi e Prestiti, Piazza Almonte di Pietà, Rome
17th century paintings.
Tu.-Su. 9-1.

ASTRONOMICAL AND COPERNICUS MUSEUM
Via Trionfale 204, Rome
Ancient astronomical instruments. Maps. Memorabilia of Copernicus.
Tu.-Su. 9.30-12.30, 3-6.

AURORA PALLAVICINI GALLERY
Via XXIV Maggio 43, Rome
Paintings by Signorelli, Lotto, Rubens. Botticelli's *Derelitta.*
1st of each month, 10-12, 3-5.

BARRACCO MUSEUM
Piccola Farnesina, Corso Vittorio Emanuele 168, Rome
Egyptian and Greek sculpture. Greek and archaic Etruscan tombstones. Assyrian and Phoenician art.
Tu. and Th. 9-2; Th. also 5-8; Su. 9-1.

BASILICA OF S. PAOLO FUORI LE MURA
Via Ostiense, Rome
5th century mosaics. 13th century Gothic tabernacle by Arnolfo di Cambio. Paschal candelabrum of 1180. Medallions with portraits of the Popes. 12th century frescoes.
Usually closed 12-3.

BORGHESE GALLERY
Villa Borghese, Porta Pinciana, Via Veneto, Rome
Palace (1613) to house collections belonging to Cardinal Scipione Borghese. Paintings by Bernini and Canova ('Paolina'). Paintings by Raphaël, Antonello da Messina, Il Sodoma, Bronzino, and Cranach. Room devoted to works by Caravaggio. Titian's *Sacred and Profane Love.* Works by French, Spanish, German, Dutch and Flemish artists.
Daily ex. M. 9-4; holidays 9-1.

BRACCIO NUOVO MUSEUM (VATICAN MUSEUMS)
Vatican City, Rome
Portrait of the Emperor Augustus. Portrait of Demosthenes. The Nile. Doryphorus, from the original by Polycleitus.
Daily ex. Su. 9-2. Closed religious feast days.

BURCARDO MUSEUM
Via del Sudario 44, Rome
Nordic style house (1503). Material on the history of the theatre. Puppet collection.
Daily ex. Su. 9-1. Closed Aug.

CANONICA MUSEUM
Nella 'Fortezzuola' di Villa Borghese, Rome
Memorabilia of Pietro Canonica.
Tu.-Su. 9.30-1.

CAPITOLINO MUSEUM
Piazzo del Campidoglio, Rome
Housed in Palaces built by Michelangelo. Paintings and sculptures, including the *Capitolene Venus*, the *Dying Gladiator*, the *Etruscan She-Wolf with the Twins* by Pollaiolo. Roman remains. Coins and medals.
Daily ex. M. 9-2; Tu. also 5-8.

CAPRONI DI TALIEDO AERONAUTICAL MUSEUM
Via Azuni 13e, Rome
History of aeroplanes. Models.
Tu.-Su. 9.30-12.30, 3-6.

CENTRAL MUSEUM OF THE RISORGIMENTO
Monument to King Victor Emmanuel II, Vittoriano, Piazza Venezia, Rome
Exhibits illustrating Italy's struggle for independence. Section devoted to the first World War.
Daily ex. holidays 9-2.

CHIARAMONTE MUSEUM (VATICAN MUSEUMS)
Vatican City, Rome
Roman portrait busts; including those of Cicero, Augustus. Sculptures. Bas-reliefs. Fragments of Greek and Roman art.
Daily 9-2. Closed Su. and religious feast days.

COLLECTION OF THE ASTRONOMICAL OBSERVATORY
Monte Mario, Rome
Historic astronomical and meteorological instruments. Globes.
Tu.-Su. 9.30-12.30, 3-6.

COLLECTIONS OF THE INSTITUTE OF BOTANY
Città Universitaria e Parco di Villa Corsini, Rome
Botany. Herbaria.
By appointment.

COLLECTION OF THE INSTITUTE OF CLINICAL NEURO-PSYCHIATRY
Policlinico Umberto I, Viale Regina Elena, Rome
Neuropsychiatry. Diseases of the nervous system.
By appointment.

COLLECTION OF THE INSTITUTE OF COMPARATIVE ANATOMY
Via Borelli 50, Rome
Comparative anatomy. Osteology. Neurology. Embryology.
By appointment.

COLLECTION OF THE INSTITUTE OF GEOGRAPHY
The University, Rome
Facsimiles of historic geographic maps.
By appointment.

COLLECTION OF THE INSTITUTE OF MEDICAL RADIOLOGY
Ospedale di San Spirito, Rome
Historical apparatus and instruments relating to medical radiology.
By appointment.

COLLECTION OF THE INSTITUTE OF MERCEOLOGY
Piazza Borghese 9, Rome
History of commerce and trade.
By appointment.

COLLECTION OF THE INSTITUTE OF PARASITOLOGY
University, Rome
Parasites on human and animal pathology. Ticks.
By appointment.

COLLECTION OF THE INSTITUTE OF PATHOLOGICAL ANATOMY
Policlinico Umberto I, Viale Regina Elena 324, Rome
Pathology, anatomy of the human heart.
By appointment.

COLLECTION OF THE INSTITUTE OF TROPICAL DISEASES
Policlinico Umberto I, Viale Regina Elena 324, Rome
Tropical and subtropical diseases.
By appointment.

COLLECTION OF THE INSTITUTE OF UROLOGY
Policlinico Umberto I, Viale Regina Elena 324, Rome
Urological preparations.
By appointment.

COLLECTIONS OF THE INSTITUTE OF ZOOLOGY
Viale Regina Elena 324, Rome
Zoology. Entomology.
By appointment.

COLLECTION OF THE ITALIAN GEOGRAPHICAL SOCIETY
Villa Celimontana, Via della Navicella 12, Rome
Maps, busts, pictures of conquerors and explorers. Arms. Material from Africa, Burma, Indonesia, China and Thailand.
On request.

COLLECTIONS OF THE ITALIAN INSTITUTE OF HUMAN PALAEONTOLOGY
Via Ulisse Aldrovandi, Rome
Prehistoric finds from all over Italy.
By appointment.

COLLECTIONS OF THE ITALIAN INSTITUTE OF NUMISMATICS
Palazzo Barberini, Via Quattro Fontane 13, Rome
Coins. Medals.
Tu.-Su. 9-4.

COLLECTION OF THE NATIONAL INSTITUTE OF ENTOMOLOGY
Via Catone 34, Rome
Insects. Herbarium.
By appointment.

COLONNA GALLERY
Via della Pilotta 17, Rome
Paintings by Italian and foreign artists dating from the Renaissance onwards. Works by Melozzo da Forli, Vivarini, Veronese, Palma the Elder, Tintoretto, Bronzino, Guercino and Salvator Rosa.
Daily 9-1. Closed Aug.

CRIMINOLOGY MUSEUM
Via Giulia 52, Rome
Historical documentation of crime and preventive measures.
Su. 9-12. Admission granted by the Ministry of Grace and Justice.

CRISTIANO MUSEUM (VATICAN MUSEUMS)
Vatican City, Rome
Religious paintings, enamels and ivories.
Daily ex. Su. 9-2. Closed religious feast days.

DORIA PAMPHILJ GALLERY
Palazzo Doria, Corso Umberto I 1A, Rome
16th-17th century paintings, including works by Titian, Tintoretto, Correggio, Raphaël, Lo Spagnoletto, Guercino, Bellini, Parmigianino, Breughel the Younger, Rubens, Velasquez, Bernini. Private apartments contain 15th-16th century Brussels tapestries; triptych; polyptych of 15th century Tuscan school. Memorabilia of Andrea Doria. Collection of Trapani corals, ambers and ivories. 18th century cradle in carved and gilded wood. 17th century marble altar in chapel. Frescoes. Paintings. Sculpture.
Su., Tu., F., Sa. 10-1.

EGIZIANO MUSEUM (VATICAN MUSEUMS)
Vatican City, Rome
Sarcophagi. Basalt and granite statues. Mummies. Papyri.
M.-Sa. 9-2. Closed religious feast days.

ETRUSCAN MUSEUM (VATICAN MUSEUMS)
Vatican City, Rome
Bronze statues. Mirrors. Vases of Etruscan and Attic art.
M.-Sa. 9-2. Closed religious feast days.

FRANCESCAN MUSEUM
Via Buoncompagni 71, Rome
Embroidery. Ivory carvings. Medals. Majolica. Pharmaceutical jars and ceramics.
Tu.-Su. 9.30-12.30, 3-6.

FRANCISCAN MUSEUM OF THE CAPUCIN BROTHERS
G.R.A. at km. 68,800, Rome
History of the Order.
On request.

GENIO MUSEUM
Piazzale Maresciallo Giardino, Rome
Italian military transport, bridge building and communications. Military aircraft of 1909. Models of historical fortifications. Armoury from Roman times to the present day.
Su. 9-1.

HISTORICAL MUSEUM OF BANKING
Piazza Armellini 20, Rome
History of banking houses in Italy.
Tu.-Su. 9-1.

HISTORICAL MUSEUM OF THE CARABINIERI
Piazza del Risorgimento 46, Rome
History of the Caribinieri. Documents. Photographs. Arms. Sculptures.
Tu.-Su. 9.30-12.30, 3-6.

HISTORICAL MUSEUM OF THE ITALIAN INFANTRY
Porta Pia, Rome
Military collections illustrating history of the Italian infantry. Arms. Medals. Documents. Uniforms.
Tu.-Su. 9.30-12.30, 3-6.

HISTORICAL MUSEUM OF MILITARY MOTORISATION
Viale dell'Esercito 86, Rome
Collection illustrating history of mechanised transport and fighting vehicles in the Italian army.
Tu.-Su. 9.30-12.30, 3-6.

HISTORICAL MUSEUM OF THE SARDINIAN GRENADIERS
Piazza Santa Croce in Gerusalemme 7, Rome
History of the Sardinian Grenadiers. Uniforms. Weapons.
Tu.-Su. 9.30-1.

HISTORY MUSEUM OF THE BROTHERHOOD OF SAN GIOVANNI DECOLLATO
Via di San Giovanni Decollato, Rome
History of the Brotherhood and its activities.
Tu.-Su. 9.30-12.30, 3-6.

JOHN KEATS' HOUSE
Scalinata della Trinita dei Monti, Piazza di Spagna 26, Rome
House in which the poet died (1821), now containing relics of Keats, Shelley, Byron and Leigh Hunt.
Daily ex. Sa. and Su. p.m., 9-12, 3-5. June-Sept. 9-12, 4-6.

LATERAN MISSIONARY MUSEUM OF ETHNOGRAPHY (VATICAN MUSEUMS)
Vatican City, Rome
Ethnographical material from the Far East, Africa, and South America, collected by missionaries.
Tu.-Su. 9-2. Closed religious feast days.

LITTLE MUSEUM OF THE SOULS IN PURGATORY
Chiesa del S. Cuore, Lungotevere Prati 12, Rome
Religious paintings, sculpture.
Tu.-Su. 9.30-1.

MAP GALLERY AND CANDELABRA GALLERY (VATICAN MUSEUMS)
Vatican City, Rome
16th century maps and antiques. Candelabra.
M.-Sa. 9-2. Closed religious feast days.

MEDIEVAL MUSEUM
Palazzo Delle Scienze, Viale Lincoln 1, Rome
Italian material from the fall of the Roman Empire to 10th century A.D. Sculpture. Gold. Jewellery. Glass. 7th-10th century church reliefs and friezes. 7th-9th century pottery from Roman Forum.
Tu.-F. 9-2; Sa. 9-1.

MUNICIPAL GALLERY OF MODERN ART
Exhibition Palace (2nd floor), Via Milano, Rome
Paintings by Pietro Tenerani, Bartolomeo Pinelli and Roesler-Franz.
W. and Sa. 9-2.

MUSEUM OF ANTHROPOLOGY
Istituto di Antropologia 'Giuseppe Sergi', The University, Rome
Skeletons and skulls of all races and periods. Pathology. Morphology. Histology. Neanderthal finds.
By appointment.

MUSEUM OF THE CATACOMBS OF SAN SEBASTIANO
Via Appia Antica 134, Rome
Archaeology. Sarcophagi.
Tu.-Su. 9.30-12.30, 3-6.

MUSEUM OF ETRUSCAN AND ITALIC ANTIQUITY
Faculty of Letters, The University, Rome
Etruscan and Italic art, archaeology.
By appointment.

MUSEUM OF THE GEOLOGICAL SERVICE
Ufficio Geologico, Largo Santa Susanna 13, Rome
Geological collection.
M., W. and F. 9-12.

MUSEUM OF HISTORICAL APPARATUS FOR THE REPRODUCTION OF SOUND
Via Michelangelo Caetani 32, Rome
History of instruments for the reproduction of sound and music.
Tu.-Su. 9-1.

MUSEUM OF THE INSTITUTE OF HEALTH
Viale Regina Margherita 293, Rome
Pathology. Anatomy. Models of fungi. Italian herbs.
By appointment.

MUSEUM OF THE INSTITUTE OF THE HISTORY OF MEDICINE
Viale dell'Università 34a, Rome
History of medical instruments.
By appointment.

MUSEUM OF THE INSTITUTE OF MINERALOGY
The University, Rome
Minerals. Meteorites.
By appointment.

MUSEUM OF THE LIBERATION OF ROME
Via Tasso 145, Rome
History of Rome during the German occupation, 1943-44.
Tu.-Su. 9.30-12.30, 3-6.

MUSEUM OF MUSICAL INSTRUMENTS
Caserma dei Granatieri (Sessorium), Piazza Santa Croce, Rome
European musical instruments.
Tu.-Su. 9-12.

MUSEUM OF THE PALAZZO DEI CONSERVATORI
Piazza Senatorio, Rome
Picture gallery. Sculpture, including statue of Charles of Anjou, attributed to Arnolfo di Cambio (late 13th century); the Etruscan Wolf, and the emblem of Rome.
Daily 9-2; Tu. and Th. also 5-8; Sa. also 9-11 p.m. Closed after 1 p.m. on Su., Jan. 6, Feb. 11, Shrove Tu., Mar. 19, Maundy Th., Easter M., Apr. 25, Ascension Day, Corpus Christi, Sept. 28, Oct. 4, Nov. 1, 2 and 4, Dec. 8, 24, 26 and 31. Closed all day Jan. 1, Apr. 25, Easter Su., May 1, June 2 and 29, Aug. 15, Dec. 25.

MUSEUM OF THE PALAZZO VENEZIA
Piazza Venezia 3, Rome
Decorative arts. Sculpture. Tapestry. Small Renaissance bronzes by Bernini and the school of Giambologna. Woodcarvings. Goldsmith's work. Paintings by Gazzoli, Filippino Lippi, Veronese, Giorgione, Martini, Romano and Lotto, as well as by German and Flemish artists.
May-Sept. Daily 9-1. 3.30-6. Oct.-Apr. Daily 9.30-4. Closed Jan. 1, May 1, June 2, Aug. 15, Easter Su. and Christmas Day, also Su. and holiday afternoons.

MUSEUM OF THE PONTIFICAL BIBLICAL INSTITUTE
Piazza della Pilotta 33, Rome
Biblical codices, manuscripts. Early printed bibles.
Tu.-Su. 9-2.

MUSEUM OF POSTAL HISTORY AND TELECOMMUNICATIONS
Via Andreoli 11, Rome
Casket of 1300 used by the Pontifical P.O. of Urbino and 17th century letter-boxes, including a 'bocca di leone'. Pioneer air-mail flights. Ethiopian military cancellers. History of the telephone and telegraph, including apparatus used by Marconi in his 1901 experiments between Cornwall and Newfoundland.
Tu., Su. 9-1.

MUSEUM OF PREHISTORY AND ARCHAEOLOGY
Facolta di Lettere dell'Università, Rome
Finds from Etruscan and Italian excavations.
By appointment.

MUSEUM OF THE ROAD TO OSTIA
Porta San Paolo, Piazza della Porta San Paolo, Rome
History of the road to Ostia, including milestones, tomb paintings and reliefs, together with models of Ostia and its port in Imperial times.
Daily ex. M. 9-1.30.

MUSEUM OF ROMAN CIVILISATION
Piazza Agnelli, Rome
Plaster casts of famous statues and monuments, and reconstructions of buildings which illustrate the history of Rome and the influence of Roman civilisation throughout the world.
Weekdays ex. M. 9-2; Su. 9-1. Tu. and Th. also 5-8.

MUSEUM OF ROME
Palazzo Braschi, Piazza di San Pantaleo 10, Rome
Documents and works on the historical development of Rome. Paintings by 19th-20th century Roman artists.
Daily ex. M. 9-2; Tu. and Th. also 5-8.

MUSEUM OF SAN PANCRAZIO
Annesso alla Basilica di San Pancrazio, Rome
Religious art. Sculptures. Inscriptions.
Tu.-Su. 9-1.

MUSEUM OF THE SOVEREIGN MILITARY ORDER OF THE KNIGHTS OF MALTA
Piazza dei Cavaliera di Malta 3, Rome
Collections illustrating history of the Order.
Tu.-Su. 9.30-1.

MUSEUM OF TRANSPORTATION
Stazione di Roma Termini, Rome
Transportation. Signals. Telecommunications. Models of railway stations, viaducts, bridges. Model of first Italian railway.
Tu.-Su. 9.30-12.30, 3-6.

NAPOLEONIC MUSEUM
Via Zandardelli 1, Rome
Napoleonic objects donated by Count Primoli, descendant of Carlotta Bonaparte. Mementoes of Napoleon I and the Bonaparte family.
Daily ex. M. 9-2; Tu. and Th. also 5-8; closed Aug.

NATIONAL GALLERY OF ANCIENT ART
Barbarini Palace, Via Quattro Fontane 13, Rome
Renaissance and Baroque pictures. 13th and 18th century Italian, Flemish, Spanish and French Schools. Works by Raphaël, Caravaggio, Holbein, Simone Martini, Lotto, Metzys, El Greco, Van Dyck, Rubens and Bronzino. Italian decorative arts.
Daily ex. M. 9-4; holidays 9-1 (June-Oct. 9-1, 3.30-6; W. 9-11.30 p.m.).

NATIONAL GALLERY OF ANCIENT ART
Palazzo Corsini, Via della Lungara 10, Rome
17th century paintings by Italian masters. Works by Flemish and Dutch artists.
Summer: M.-Sa; 9-12. 3-6; Su. and holidays 9-1. Winter: 9.30-4. Closed Tu.

NATIONAL GALLERY OF MODERN ART
Viale delle Belle Arti 131, Rome
Italian art from 19th century to the present day. Artists include Faruffini, Palizzi, Morelli, Lega, Fattoria, Toma, Ciardi, Fontanesi, Boldini, Gignous, Gola, Pasini, Gioli D'Orsi, Previati, Segantini, Pellizza, Morbelli, Mancini, Spadini and Medaro Rosso.
Daily ex. M. 9-2; holidays 9-1.

NATIONAL MILITARY MUSEUM
Piazza Santa Croce in Gerusalemme 8, Rome
Collection of Italian soldiers' uniforms.
Tu.-Su. 9.30-12.30, 3-6.

NATIONAL MUSEUM OF ARTS AND POPULAR TRADITIONS
Piazza Marconi 8, Rome
Life and popular customs in Italy. The home. Agriculture. Seafaring. Town life. Songs, music and dancing. Costumes. Religion.
Daily ex. M. 9-2; Su. 9-1.

NATIONAL MUSEUM OF CASTEL SANT'ANGELO
Lungotevere Castello, Rome
Collection of weapons and armour, dating from Palaeolithic flints to Renaissance arms. Historic relics. Paintings. Sculpture. Hunting equipment. Military uniforms. Cinerary urns of the Imperial family.
Daily ex. M. 9-2; holidays 9.30-1.

NATIONAL MUSEUM OF ENGRAVINGS
Via della Stamperia, Rome
Copper-plate engravings. It contains all the engravings of G. B. Piranesi (1432 plates) and examples of the work of Marcantonio Raimondi, Rossini, Pinelli and others.
Weekdays 9-1.30.

NATIONAL MUSEUM OF THE HISTORY OF MEDICINE
Arciospedale di Santo Spirito, Borgo Santo Spirito, Rome
History of medicine, and of medical instruments. 16th century pharmacy. Ceramics. Mortars. Jars.
M., W. and F. 10-12.

NATIONAL MUSEUM OF MUSICAL INSTRUMENTS
Palazzo Venezia, Via del Plebiscito, Rome
International collection of historic musical instruments.
May-Sept. daily 9-1, 3.30-6. Oct.-Apr., daily 9.30-4. Closed Jan. 1, May 1, June 2, Aug. 15, Easter Su. and Christmas Day, also Su. and holiday afternoons.

NATIONAL MUSEUM OF ORIENTAL ART
Via Merulana 248, Rome
Prehistoric ceramics from Iran. Luristan bronzes, weapons and horse-bits. 9th-15th century glazed pottery. Sculpture from Afghanistan. Chinese, Japanese and Korean bronzes, ceramics and Buddhas. 18th century paintings on vellum from Tibet. Oriental coins.
Daily ex. Tu. 9-1; holidays 10-1.

NATIONAL MUSEUM OF VILLA GIULIA
Piazza di Villa Giulia 9, Viale delle Belle Arti, Rome
Archaeological finds from Southern Etruria, including the Apollo from Vejo, the Cista Ficoroni, the warrior from Capestrano. Etruscan and Italian art.
Daily ex. M. 9-3; holidays 10-1. Closed Jan. 1, May 1, June 2, Aug. 15, Easter Su. and Christmas Day.

NATIONAL STAMP COLLECTION
Via della Lungara, Rome
World-wide stamp collection.
Tu.-Su. 9.30-12.30, 3-6.

NUMISMATIC MUSEUM OF THE ZECCA
Via XX Settembre 97, Rome
Numismatics. Papal collection from 1417 to the present day. Collection of wax seals by Benedetto Pistrucci, who designed the St. George and dragon on the English sovereign.
M.-Sa. 9-12. Visit granted following prior request.

ODESCALCHI COLLECTION OF WEAPONS
Palazzo Corsini, Via della Lungara 10, Rome
Ancient weapons.
Summer: M.-Sa. 9-12, 3-6; Su. and holidays 9-1. Winter: 9.30-4. Closed Tu.

PAOLINO MUSEUM (VATICAN MUSEUM)
Viale Vaticano, Rome
Roman and neo-Attic sculpture. Mosaics. Early Christian sculpture. Inscriptions from public monuments connected with Christian worship. Inscriptions from cemeteries (2nd-6th centuries). 2nd-5th century Christian sarcophagi. Crafts, ways of life and religious customs in countries penetrated by missionaries. Cultures of Balkan States, Africa, America, Australia, India, Middle and Far East. Adaptations of European sacred art, especially in Indo-China. Section devoted to martyrs, including instruments of torture, relics and Japanese persecution lists.
M., W. and F. 9-2. Closed Su., Jan. 1, Mar. 19, May 1, June 29, Aug. 14-15, Nov. 1-2, Dec. 8, 24, 25, 26, Ash W., Good F., Ascension Day, Corpus Domini, anniversary of the death of Pope John XXIII, anniversary of the Pope's coronation, and whenever special reasons make it necessary.

PICTURE GALLERY (VATICAN MUSEUMS)
Vatican City, Rome
Primitives, including works by Giotto, Alegretto Nuzi and Bernardo Daddi. Frescoes by Melozzo da Forli. Copy of *Last Supper* by Leonardo da Vinci (Flanders, late 16th century). 16th century schools of Ferrara and Venice. Raphaël room, including his tapestries woven in Brussels by Pieter Coecke van Aelst. 17th century paintings, including works by Guercino and Caravaggio. 19th and 20th century artists, including Rodin, Rouault, Utrillo.
M.-Sa. 9-2. Closed religious feast days.

LUIGI PIGORINI MUSEUM OF PREHISTORY AND ETHNOGRAPHY
Collegio Romano, Piazza del Collegio Romana 26, Rome
Ethnography of Brazil, Argentina, the Amazon region, Polynesia, the Arctic Circle. American Indian material from North America, Central and S. America. Material from New Guinea, Borneo, Solomon Islands, Australia, Indonesia, Africa, Mexico, Ethiopia (including jewellery and ceremonial dress given by King Victor Emmanuel III). Prehistoric material from Palidoro (nr. Rome) of the Early Iron Age and from Polada (Brescia) of the Bronze Age.
Weekdays 9-2. Su. 9-1. Closed M.

PIO-CLEMENTINO MUSEUM (VATICAN MUSEUMS)
Vatican City, Rome
Greco-Roman antiques collected by the popes. Mosaic of Greeks and Centaurs, Nereids and Tritons. Statue of Ariadne Asleep (3rd century B.C.). Eros, attributed to Cephisodotus. The cabinet of masks contains the Venus of Cnidus, a copy of Praxiteles, and the Crouching Venus, copied from 3rd century B.C. Greek original. Torso of the Belvedere.
M.-Sa. 9-2. Closed religious feast days.

PIRANDELLO'S HOUSE
Via Bosio 15, Rome
Memorabilia of the writer, Luigi Pirandello, in his former home.
Tu.-Su. 9- one hour before sunset.

PROFANO MUSEUM (VATICAN MUSEUMS)
Vatican City, Rome
Etruscan, Roman and Greek vases, ivories, cameos, mosaics, mirrors and bronzes.
Daily ex. Su. 9-2. Closed religious feast days.

RAPHAËL ROOMS (VATICAN MUSEUMS)
Vatican City, Rome
Frescoes and paintings by Raphaël, including the *Burning of the Borgo, Dispute of the Holy Sacrament, the Celestial Zone and Terrestrial Zone, Assembly of Wise Men and Philosophers of Antiquity.* In his *Parnassus,* Raphaël depicts the great Greek, Roman and Italian poets grouped round Apollo and the Muses. One room is devoted to the glorification of Pope Julius II.
M.-Sa. 9-2. Closed religious feast days.

ROMAN NATIONAL MUSEUM
(Museum of the Thermae), Viale delle Terme, Rome
Built from design attributed to Michelangelo, in halls of ancient Thermae of Diocletian. Works found in ancient Rome: Venus of Cyrene, Ludovisi Throne, Girl from Antium. Full-length portrait of the Emperor Augustus. 2000-year-old mummy of a young girl.
Daily ex. M. 9.30-3. Holidays 9-1.

SACRED MUSEUM OF THE FLAGS OF THE NAVY
Monumento a Vittorio Emanuele II, Rome
Historic Italian naval flags, pennants.
Tu.-Su. 9.30-12.30, 3-6.

ST. PETER'S BASILICA, SACRISTY AND TREASURY
Rome
Religious art. Vestments. Liturgical items.
Any time.

SISTINE CHAPEL (VATICAN MUSEUM)
Viale del Vaticano, Rome
Built 1473 by Giovanni de'Dolci. Decorations by painters of the Tuscan or Umbrian Quattrocento (1481-83) and Michelangelo (1508-12, 1534-41). Works by Pinturicchio, Botticelli, Cosimo Rosselli, Signorelli. *The Last Judgment* by Michelangelo. Tapestries after cartoons by Raphaël.
M.-Sa. 9-2. Closed religious holidays.

SPADA GALLERY
Palazzo Spada, Piazza Capo di Ferro 3
Paintings, including works by Titian, Andrea del Sarto, Rubens and Niccolo dell'Abate.
Daily ex. M. 9-2; holidays 9-1.

TAPESTRY GALLERY (VATICAN MUSEUMS)
Vatican City, Rome
Tapestries, including scenes from the Passion. the Credo (Tournai, 15th century) and tapestries after Raphaël, woven in Brussels in the 16th century.
M.-Sa. 9-2. Closed religious feast days.

TASSIANO MUSEUM
Monastery, Piazzale di Sant'Onofrio 2, Rome
Memorabilia of the epic poet, Torquato Tasso (1544-95) who died here, including his death-mask, armchair, crucifix, inkstand, mirro and manuscripts, editions and translations of his works.
M.-Sa. 10-12, 1-4 (Apr.-Oct. 4-7); Su. 9-1.

TORLONIA MUSEUM
Vicolo Corsini 5, Rome
Finds from excavations in the city. Sculptures, including the *Giustiniani Hestia,* attributed to Kalamis (5th century B.C.) and a bas-relief of Heracles liberating Theseus and Peirithôos (school of Pheidas, 4th century B.C.). Roman copies of works by Greek sculptors. Iconography. Etruscan paintings.
Visit subject to Administration's permit.

VATICAN LIBRARY
Vatican City, Rome
Manuscripts, illuminated missals and famous signatures. The original manuscript of the *Divine Comedy,* illustrated by Botticelli.
M.-Sa. 9-2. Closed religious feast days.

VILLA ALBANI MUSEUM
Via Salaria, corner Via di Villa Albani, Rome
Paintings by Roman and Greek artists.
Visit subject to Administrator's permit.

VILLA DELLA FARNESINA
Via della Lungara, Rome
Paintings by Peruzzi, Sebastiano del Piombo and others. Frescoes by Raphaël and Il Sodoma.
Daily 10-1. Closed holidays.

ZOOLOGICAL MUSEUM
Viale del Giardino Zoologico, Villa Boghese, Rome
Zoology.
Tu.-Su. 9.30-12.30, 3-6.

ZOOLOGICAL MUSEUM
Via Ulisse Aldovrandi 18, Rome
Zoology. Mammals, birds, fish. Geology. Mineralogy.
Daily 9.30-sunset.

RORA

VALDESE HISTORICAL MUSEUM
Rora
Local history.
Tu.-Su. 9-1, 2-5.

ROSSANO

DIOCESAN MUSEUM
Rossano, Sila Massif
Paintings. Gold and silverware. Manuscripts, including 6th century Greek Gospel.
Daily 9-6.

ROSARNO

MUNICIPAL ANTIQUARIUM
Rosarno
Finds from excavations in the area.
Tu.-Su. 9.30-5.

ROVERETO

MUNICIPAL MUSEUM
Via Calcinari 18, Rovereto
Local history, archaeology. Folklore. Numismatics. Science.
Tu.-Su. 8-12, 2-5.

MUSEUM OF THE HISTORY OF THE WAR
Via Castelbarco 7, Rovereto
History of the First World War.
Tu.-Su. 8-12, 2-5 or 7.

ROVETTA

FANTONI MUSEUM
Via Andrea Fantoni 1, Rovetta
Paintings collected by the Fantoni family.
Tu.-Su. 9-1.

ROVIGO

ART GALLERY OF THE CONCORDI ACADEMY
Piazza Vittorio Emanuele 14, Rovigo
Paintings of the Venetian School.
Tu.-Su. 9.30-12.30, 3-6.

SEMINARY MUSEUM
Via Tre Martiri 49, Rovigo
Finds from local archaeological excavations. 17th-19th century paintings.
Tu.-Su. 9.30-12.30, 3-6.

RUVO

JATTA MUSEUM
Piazza Bovio 35, Ruvo
Finds from local excavations and tombs.
Tu.-Su. 9-1.

SAGRADO

SAN MICHELE MUSEUM
Piazzale Cima 3, Sagrado
Memorabilia of World War I.
Tu.-Su. 9-1.

SALEMI

CASTLE MUSEUM AND MUSEUM OF THE RISORGIMENTO
Piazza Alicea, Salemi, Sicily
Local history. Ethnography. Paintings. Documents and other material on the Risorgimento.
Tu.-Su. 9.30-12.30, 3-6.

SALERNO

CATHEDRAL MUSEUM
Via Nicola Monterisi 2, Salerno
Treasury includes 12th century Salerno ivories illustrating scenes from the Old and New Testaments.
Daily 10-1.

PROVINCIAL ARCHAEOLOGICAL MUSEUM
Via San Benedetto, Salerno
Etruscan and Greek finds from local excavations.
Tu.-Su. 10-1.

SALÒ

ADOLFO BATTISTI MUSEUM
Lungolago Zanardelli 53, Salò
Military collection.
Tu.-Su. 9-1.

SALUZZO

CAVASSA HOUSE
Via San Giovanni 5, Saluzzo
Renaissance buildings. Period furniture, furnishings.
Tu.-Su. 9.30-12.30, 3-6.

SAN GIMIGNANO

ART GALLERY
Palazzo del Popolo, Piazza del Duomo, San Gimignano
Building (1288-1323), badly damaged in the war. Paintings, including works by Benozzo Gozzoli; Filippino Lippi (1483); Pinturicchio; Taddeo di Bartolo; Coppo di Marcovaldo.
Daily ex. M. 9-1, 3-5 or 7.

MUSEUM OF SACRED ART
Piazza Pecori 1, San Gimignano
Ecclesiastical works of art, notably 13th-15th century sculpture, vestments, jewels, and illuminated choir-books.
Daily 9-12, 3-6.

SAN GINESIO

SCIPIONE GENTILI MUSEUM
Via Matteotti 5, San Ginesio
Paintings by Italian artists.
Tu.-Su. 9-1.

SAN GIOVANNI IN COMPITO

ANTIQUARIUM
San Giovanni in Compito
Roman finds from local excavations.
On request.

SAN GIOVANNI VALDARNO

MUSEUM OF THE BASILICA OF SANTA MARIA DELLE GRAZIE
Piazza Masaccio 9, San Giovanni Valdarno
15th-19th century paintings of the Florentine school.
Tu.-Su. 10-1.

SAN LORENZO IN CAMPO

ANTIQUARIUM
Palazzo Comunale, San Lorenzo in Campo
Archaeological material from excavations in the area.
Tu.-Su. 9.30-12, 2-5.

MUSEUM OF AFRICAN ETHNOGRAPHY
Palazzo Comunale, San Lorenzo in Campo
African ethnography.
Tu.-Su. 9.30-12.30, 3-6.

SAN MARTINO DELLA BATTAGLIA

MILITARY MUSEUM
San Martino della Battaglia
Military collection, including uniforms, arms, flags, documents.
Tu.-Su. 9.30-12.30, 3-6.

SAN MARTINO IN RIO

COLLECTION OF VINTAGE CARS
San Martino in Rio
Vintage cars from Italy and elsewhere.
Tu.-Su. 9.30-12.30, 3-6.

SAN MAURO PASCOLI

BIRTHPLACE OF G. PASCOLI
Via Pascoli, San Mauro Pascoli
Memorabilia of the poet, Giovanni Pascoli, in the house where he was born.
Tu.-Su. 9.30-5.

SAN MINIATO

DIOCESAN MUSEUM OF SACRED ART
Piazza del Duomo, San Miniato
Religious art. Miniatures.
Tu.-Su. 9.30-12.30, 3-5.30.

NATURAL HISTORY COLLECTIONS
Carducci Institute, San Miniato
Mineralogy. Botany. Mammals.
By appointment.

PALAEONTOLOGICAL COLLECTION
Il Seminario, San Miniato
Mineralogy. Palaeontology.
Tu.-Su. 9-1.

SAN PANCRAZIO DI RUSSI

ORNITHOLOGICAL MUSEUM
San Pancrazio di Russi
General ornithological collections. Rare birds of Romagna.
Tu.-Su. 9.30-12.30, 3-6.

SAN PLACIDO CALONERO

NATURAL HISTORY COLLECTION
Istituto Tecnico Agrario, San Placido Calonero
Ornithology. Petrography. Botany. Ceramics. Frescoes by Piero della Francesca.
Tu.-Su. 9.30-12.30, 3-6.

SANSEPOLCRO

PICTURE GALLERY
Old Town Hall, Via Matteotti 6, Sansepolcro
Paintings, including two works by Piero della Francesco, a *Virgin of Pity* and a *Resurrection. Crucifix* by Luca Signorelli; *Virgin and Child* by Andrea Della Robbia. *Nativity* by Giovanni Della Robbia.
M.-Sa. 9-1, 3-6; Su. and holidays 10-1.

SAN SEVERINO MARCHE

MUNICIPAL ART GALLERY
Piazza del Popolo, San Severino Marche
Paintings by local artists.
Tu.-Su. 9-1.

SANTA MARIA CAPUA VETERE

ANTIQUARIUM
Piazza 1 Ottobre 1860, Santa Maria Capua Vetere
Finds from local excavations. Sculptures.
On request.

MUSEUM OF THE RISORGIMENTO
Corso Garibaldi, Santa Maria Capua Vetere
History of the battle of Volturno.
Tu.-Su. 9.30-12.30, 3-6.

SANT'ANGELO LODIGIANO

GABRINIANO DELLA PACE AND MORANDO MUSEUMS
Sant'Angelo Lodigiano
14th century castle interiors. Furnishings.
Tu.-Su. 9.30-12.30, 3-6.

SANTENA

CAVOUR MUSEUM
Castello Cavour, Santena
Memorabilia of Cavour and of the Risorgimento.
Tu.-Su. 9-12, 3-6.

SAN TROVASO DI PREGANZIOL

FRANCHETTI ZOOLOGICAL COLLECTION
San Trovaso di Preganziol
Zoology.
By appointment.

SARNANO

MUNICIPAL ART GALLERY
Palazzo Comunale, Sarnano
Paintings of the Renaissance period. Local scenes.
Tu.-Su. 9.30-12.30, 3-6.

SARZINA

DIOCESAN MUSEUM
Palazzo Episcopale, Via Curia Vescovile, Sarzina
Finds from local excavations. Sculptures. Epigraphy.
Tu.-Su. 9.30-12.30, 3-6.

SARZINA ARCHAEOLOGICAL MUSEUM
Via Cesio Sabino 7, Sarzina
Prehistoric sculptures and bronzes.
Tu.-Su. 9.30-12.30, 3-6.

SASSARI

COLLECTION OF THE INSTITUTE OF BIOLOGY AND ZOOLOGY
Sassari, Sardinia
Biology. Zoology. Invertebrates. Mammals. Birds.
By appointment.

COLLECTION OF THE INSTITUTE OF BOTANY
Sassari, Sardinia
Herbarium. Botany. Herbs of Sardinia and Italy.
By appointment.

COLLECTION OF THE INSTITUTE OF MINERALOGY
Sassari, Sardinia
Minerals, stones of Sardinia and Europe.
By appointment.

SANNA NATIONAL MUSEUM
Via Roma 64, Sassari, Sardinia
Paintings of the Flemish school. *Madonna* (1473) by Bartolomeo Vivarini. Archaeology. Sardinian ethnography.
Daily 10-4. Winter: 10-1, 4-6.

SCIENTIFIC COLLECTIONS
Istituto di Entomologia Agraria, Piazza Conte di Moriana 8, Sassari, Sardinia
Biology, Entomology of Sardinia and elsewhere.
By appointment.

SASSOCORVARO

MUNICIPAL MUSEUM
Via della Rocca, Sassocorvaro
Local history. Art. Majolica.
Tu.-Su. 9-12.30, 3-6.

ZOOLOGICAL COLLECTION
Istituto Massaioli, Sassocorvaro
Natural history. Zoology. Mammals. Birds. Lichens.
By appointment.

SASSOFERRATO

MUNICIPAL GALLERY OF MODERN AND CONTEMPORARY ART
Piazza Matteotti, Sassoferrato
Modern and contemporary paintings, sculptures, graphics from Italy and elsewhere.
Tu.-Su. 9.30-12.30, 3-6.

MUNICIPAL MUSEUM
Piazza Matteotti, Sassoferrato
Local history, archaeology. Natural history. Paintings. Folklore.
Tu.-Su. 9.30-12.30, 3-6.

SAVIGLIANO

MUNICIPAL MUSEUM
Corso Roma 32, Savigliano
Local archaeological finds. Paintings by local artists.
Tu.-Su. 9.30-12.30, 3-6.

SAVIGNANO SUL RUBICONE

ROMAN-GALLIC-ETRUSCAN MUSEUM
Via Emilia, Savignano sul Rubicone
Roman, Gallic and Etruscan finds from excavations in the district.
Tu.-Su. 9.30-12.30, 3-6.

SAVONA

CIVIC ART GALLERY
Palazzo Pozzobenello, Via Quarda Superiore 7, Savona
Paintings include a *Calvary* by Dontato de' Bardi and a polyptych by Vinc. Foppa.
W.-Su. 3-6.

MUNICIPAL MUSEUM OF NATURAL HISTORY
Savona
Mineralogy. Palaeontology. Archaeology. Ornithology. Botany. Maritime animals.
Tu.-Su. 9.30-12.30, 3-6.

MUSEUM OF THE SANTUARIO DI NOSTRA SIGNORA MISERICORDIA
Piazza Santuario 6, Savona
Religious art. Vestments. Sacred vessels.
W.-Su. 3-6.

SCALDASOLE

ANTIQUARIUM
Scaldasole
Archaeological material from local excavations.
Tu.-Su. 9.30- one hour before sunset.

SCORRANO

CAGGIUOLA ETHNOGRAPHICAL COLLECTION
Scorrano
Ethnography, mainly of the Congo.
By appointment.

SELINUNTE

ANTIQUARIUM AND ARCHAEOLOGICAL SITE
Marinella, Selinunte, Sicily
Archaeological material from local excavations.
Tu.-Su. 9.30- one hour before sunset.

SENIGALLIA

BOIDI COLLECTION
Via Camposanto Vecchio 3, Senigallia
Natural history. Ornithology. Entomology.
By appointment.

BOTANICAL MUSEUM
Senigallia
Botany. Algae.
Tu.-Su. 9-1.

MUSEUM OF THE HISTORY OF THE MARCHES
Rocca Roveresca, Senigallia
Regional history. Paintings.
Tu.-Su. 9.30-12.30, 3-5.

SERMONETA

ARCHAEOLOGICAL MUSEUM
Sermoneta
Finds from excavations in the district.
Tu.-Su. 9.30-1.

SESTINO

ANTIQUARIUM
Presso la Pieve, Sestino
Finds from local excavations. Sculpture. Coins.
Tu.-Su. 9-1.

SESTO CALENDE

CESARE MUSEUM
Palazzo Comunale, Sesto Calende
Roman finds from excavations in the district.
Tu.-Su. 9-12, 3-6.

SESTO FIORENTINO

VILLA STIBBERT
Via Federico Stibbert 15, Sesto Fiorentino, nr. Florence
Building (14th-15th centuries). Etruscan and medieval armour, notably an equestrian figure of a Condottiere, with 15th century armour; a cavalcade of 14 fully-armed knights of the 16th century; five rooms of Asiatic armour.
M.-Sa. 9-4; Su. and holidays 9-12.

SESTRI LEVANTE

RIZZI ART GALLERY
Via dei Cappuccini 8, Sestri Levante
Paintings of the Venetian school.
Tu.-Su. 9-1.

SIBARI-STAZIONE

SIBARITIDE ANTIQUARIUM
Via Taranto, Sibari-Stazione
Archaeological material from local excavations.
Tu.-Su. 9.30-4.

SIENA

ANDREUCCI COLLECTION
Istituto di Biologia e Zoologia, Siena
Zoology. Ornithology. Entomology.
By appointment.

ART COLLECTION
Tavolette di Biccherna, Via Banchi di Sotto 52, Siena
17th century paintings.
Tu.-Su. 9-1.

ART MUSEUM
Societa di Esecutori di Pie Disposizioni, Via Roma 71, Siena
Paintings of the Sienese school.
By appointment.

BOTANICAL MUSEUM
Via P. A. Mattioli 4, Siena
Plants of Italy. Herbs. Drugs.
Tu.-Su. 9-1.

AURELIO CASTELLI MUSEUM
Via dell'Osservanza 7, Siena
15th-16th century paintings, sculptures. Incunabula. Miniatures.
Tu.-Su. 9.30-12.30, 3-6.

CATHEDRAL MUSEUM
Via del Capitano, Siena
The Three Graces, a copy of Praxiteles. Statues of prophets and sibyls by Giovanni Pisano. Ecclesiastical gold plate. Fragments of cathedral paving. *Maestà* by Duccio. Sienese primitives.
May-Aug. Daily 9-1, 2.30-6. Sept.-Apr. Daily 9-12.30, 2.30-5. Closed Jan. 1 and 6, Easter and Christmas.

ETRUSCAN ARCHAEOLOGICAL MUSEUM
Via della Sapienza 3, Siena
Etruscan and Roman antiquities.
M.-Sa. 9.30-4; Su. 10-1.

GALLERY OF TUSCAN PAINTING
Chigi-Saracini Palace, Via di Citta 89, Siena
Paintings by Tuscan artists including works by Sassetta and Botticelli. Historical musical items.
Apply in person to Count Guido Chigi Saracini.

GEO-MINERALOGICAL MUSEUM
Via Matteoli, Siena
Minerals. Fossils.
Tu.-Su. 9.30-12.30, 3-6.

MUNICIPAL MUSEUM AND APARTMENTS
Palazzo Pubblico, Piazza del Campo, Siena
Apartments in which governors and members of the council lived. Paintings include *Maestà* (1315) by Simone Martini, and portrait of the Sienese general, Guidoriccio da Fogliano, by the same artist. Frescoes (1337-1343) depicting *Effects of Good and Bad Government*, by Ambrogio Lorenzetti. Chapel contains frescoes by Taddeo di Bartolo (1408), chancel railing (1444) and a painting by Il Sodoma. Coins. Ceramics. Local history.
Daily 9.30-12.30, 2-5.

MUSEUM OF ANATOMY
Via del Laterino 8, Siena
Anatomy. Osteology. Craniology.
Tu.-Su. 9-1.

PICCOLOMINI LIBRARY
Piazza del Duomo, Siena
Renaissance building (1495). Frescoes by Pinturicchio and his pupils (1502-9). Choir books of the cathedral and the Scala hospital, illuminated by Liberale da Verona, Girol. da Cremona, Sano di Pietro, and others.
Daily 9-1, 2.30-5 or 7; festivals 9-1.

PICTURE GALLERY
Palazzo Buonsignori, Via S. Pietro 29, Siena
13th-16th century Sienese paintings. 12th-13th century painted crucifixes. Works by Duccio, Segna di Bonaventura, Luca Thome, Ambrogio and Pietro Lorenzetti. Primitives, including works by Taddeo di Bartolo, Giovanni di Paolo, Matteo di Giovanni and Sano di Pietro.
May 2- Sept. 30, Daily ex. M. 9-1, 2.30-5.30. (9-4 Oct.-Apr.). Closed Jan. 1, May 1, June 2, Aug. 15, Easter, Christmas and afternoons of other holidays and Su.

PUBLIC LIBRARY
Via della Sapienza, Siena
Illuminated missals, breviaries and books of hours. St. Catherine's letters. 7th century papyrus from Ravenna. Drawings by Peruzzi and Beccafumi. A Dante, with illuminations by Botticelli. Bookbinding.
M.-Sa. 9.30-12, 3.30 or 4.30-8.

SIRMIONE

ANTIQUARIUM OF THE GROTTOS OF CATULLUS
Sirmione
Material from Roman excavations in the area.
Summer: daily 8-8. Winter: daily 9-5.

SOLFERINO

MUSEUM OF THE 1859 WAR
Via Correale 48, Solferino
Documents and memorabilia of the war of 1859.
Tu.-Su. 9.30-12.30, 3-6.

SOLUNTO

ANTIQUARIUM
Solunto, Sicily
Finds from local excavations.
Daily 9- one hour before sunset.

SORRENTO

CORREALE MUSEUM
Palazzo Correale, Via Correale 48, Sorrento
Campanian decorative arts, 15th-18th centuries. Archaeological finds from the Sorrentine peninsula. Medieval sculpture. 17th-18th century furniture. Dresden china. Paintings, including the *Sleeping Shepherd* by Palizzi. Works by Giacinto Gigante.
Daily ex. Tu. and Su. afternoon, 9.30-12.30, 5-7 (3-5 Oct. and Dec.-May). Closed holiday afternoons and Nov.

SPELLO

ANTONELLI COLLECTION
Spello
Mineralogy.
By appointment.

MUSEUM OF THE CHURCH OF SANTA MARIA MAGGIORE
Via Cavour, Spello
Renaissance frescoes, sculpture.
Tu.-Su. 9-1.

SPERLONGA

ARCHAEOLOGICAL MUSEUM
Via Flacca, Sperlonga
Statues of 4th, 3rd and 2nd centuries B.C. Theatrical masks.
Apr.-Sept. Daily ex. M. 10-5; Su. and holidays 9.30-1.30. Oct.-Mar. 9.30-4; Su. 9-1.

SPÉZIA

ARCHAEOLOGICAL MUSEUM
Corso Cavour, Spézia
Ligurian statue-stelae (Bronze and Iron Age) and Roman remains from Luni.
M.-Sa. 10-12, 4-6; Su. 10-12.

MARITIME MUSEUM
Piazza Chiodo, Spézia
Models and relics collected since 1571 illustrate the maritime history of Savoy and Italy.
Daily 8-12.30, 3-6.

SPOLETO

COLLECTION OF THE LICEO SCIENTIFICO
Spoleto
Geology. Palaeontology.
By appointment.

MUNICIPAL GALLERY OF MODERN ART
Palazzo Collicola, Piazza Liberta, Spoleto
Paintings, graphics, sculpture particularly since 1953.
Tu.-Su. 9.30-12.30, 3-6.

MUNICIPAL MUSEUM
Via del Duomo 31, Spoleto
Roman sculptures, vases and coins.
Tu.-Su. 9.30-12.30, 3-6.

PICTURE GALLERY
Palazzo Communale, Via del Municipio, Spoleto
Paintings include a triptych by Foligno, and a *Madonna* by Antonello da Saliba (1494). Frescoes and paintings by La Spagna. *Mary Magdalene* by Guercino.
On application.

THEATRE MUSEUM
Via Filitteria 1, Spoleto
History of the theatre. Photographs. Costumes. Posters. Programmes.
Tu.-Su. 10-12, 3-6.

STIA

ORNITHOLOGICAL MUSEUM
Stia
Ornithology. Local birds.
Tu.-Su. 9-1.

STRA

VILLA NAZIONALE
Stra, nr. Padua
Formerly Villa Pisani, and 18th century villa with large rooms furnished in period style. *Apotheosis of the Pisani Family* by Tiepolo.
Apr.-Sept. M.-Sa. 9-12.30, 3-6; Su. and holidays 9-1. Oct.-Mar. M.-Sa. 9-12.30, 2-5; Su. and holidays 9-1.

STRESA

BOTANICAL MUSEUM
Gardino Alpinia, Stresa
Botany. Alpine flowers and plants.
Tu.-Su. 9.30-12.30, 3-6.

BOTANICAL MUSEUM
Isola Madre and Isola Bella, Palazzo Borromeo, Stresa
Botany.
Tu.-Su. 9-1.

PALAZZO BORROMEO MUSEUM
Stresa
Furniture. Furnishings. Lombard architecture and paintings.
Tu.-Su. 9.30-12.30, 3-6.

STUPINIGI

PALAZZINA DI STUPINIGI
Stupinigi, nr. Turin
Hunting lodge (early 18th century) built by Juvara for Victor Amedeus II of Savoy. The apartments are decorated with stucco and paintings by Cignaroli and Van Loo. Furniture. Objets d'art.
Daily ex. M. and F. 10-12.30, 3-6. (2-5 mid. Oct.-mid. Apr.). Closed Jan. 1, Nov. 1, Easter Su. and Christmas Day.

SULMONA

CATHEDRAL MUSEUM
Annesso alla Cattedrale, Sulmona
Religious art. Wall paintings. 14th century decorations.
Tu.-Su. 9.30-12.30, 3-6.

MUNICIPAL MUSEUM
Piazza dell'Annunziata, Sulmona
Local history. Renaissance sculpture. 14th-17th century sculptures in wood and stone.
Tu.-Su. 9.30-12.30, 3-6.

SUSA

MUNICIPAL MUSEUM
Via Palazzo di Città 38, Susa
Local history, archaeology.
Tu.-Su. 9.30-12.30, 3-6.

NATURAL HISTORY COLLECTION
Palazzo Municipale, Susa
Mineralogy. Zoology. Archaeology.
Tu.-Su. 9.30-12.30, 3-6.

SUTRI

ANTIQUARIUM
Municipio, Sutri
Collection of Etruscan antiquities, mainly sculpture and inscriptions.
On request.

SYRACUSE

ANTIQUARIUM
Castello Eurialo, Syracuse, Sicily
History of the castle. Furniture. Furnishings.
Summer: daily 9-1, 3.30-sunset. Winter: daily 9-1, 2-sunset.

MUSEUM OF ANCIENT AND MODERN ART
Palazzo Bellomo, Via Giuseppe Capodieci 16, Syracuse, Sicily
Sculpture. 17th and 18th century carriages. Paintings include an *Annunciation* by Antonello da Messina (1474). Two polyptychs in the Sicilian-Catalan style.
Daily 9-2.

NATIONAL ARCHAEOLOGICAL MUSEUM
Foro Italico, Piazza del Duomo 14, Syracuse, Sicily
Greek civilisation in Sicily. Outstanding are the *Venus Anadyomene*, a Roman copy of an original Greek statue, and a small Heracles (4th century). Reconstruction of the temple roofs. Early Christian sarcophagus of Valerius and Adelpha (4th century).
Daily 9-4; Su. and holidays 9.30-1.30. Closed Jan. 1, May 1, June 2, Aug. 15, Easter and Christmas.

TAGGIA

DOMINICAN ART COLLECTION
Taggia
Paintings, including local scenes.
On request.

TAORMINA

ANTIQUARIUM
Greco-Roman Theatre, Via Teatro Antico, Taormina, Sicily
Greek, Roman and Christian objects from local excavations, including inscriptions relating to athletics and financial matters.
Summer: daily 9-1, 4-7.30. Winter: daily 9-1, 2- one hour before sunset.

TARANTO

NATIONAL MUSEUM
Corso Umberto 54, Taranto
Greek pottery dating from 7th century B.C. to Roman period. Amphorae and terracotta statuettes. Archaeological exhibits illustrating the period of Magna Graecia, when Taranto belonged to the Spartans. Antique jewellery. Prehistory.
Daily ex. M. 9-2. Closed Jan. 1, May 1, June 2, Aug. 15, Easter Su. and Christmas Day.

NATURAL HISTORY COLLECTION
Istituto Sperimentale Talassografico, Taranto
Flora and fauna of the Ionic Sea.
On request.

TARQUINIA

NATIONAL MUSEUM
Palazzo Vitelleschi, Tarquinia
Sarcophagi (6th-5th century B.C.) with effigies of priests and magistrates. Ancient, Oriental and Greek pottery. Attic bowls and amphora (6th century). Winged horses from fronton of temple at Tarquinia.
Tu.-Su. 9-4; M. 9-1. Closed Jan. 1, May 1, June 2, Aug. 15, Easter Su. and Christmas Day.

NECROPOLIS
nr. Tarquinia
Thousands of tombs dating from 6th-1st century B.C. Paintings on walls of the burial chambers depict the life and religion of the Etruscans: festivals and dances, hunting and fishing, horse races, games and plays, gods, funeral rites and religious symbols.
Tu.-Sa. 9-3; Su. 9-4; M. 9-1. Closed Jan. 1, May 1, June 2, Aug. 15, Easter Su. and Christmas Day.

TEGGIANO

MUNICIPAL MUSEUM
Church of San Pietro, Teggiano
Local history. Natural history.
Tu.-Su. 9.30-1.

TEMPIO PAUSANIA

STAZZA COLLECTION
Piazza San Pietro, Tempio Pausania
Birds of Sardinia and Eritrea.
By appointment.

TERAMO

MUNICIPAL MUSEUM AND ART GALLERY
Villa Comunale, Viale Bovio 1, Teramo
16th-17th century paintings of the Roman school. Finds from archaeological excavations and from sepulchres. Coins. Bronzes.
Tu.-Su. 9.30-12.30, 3-6.

TERLIZZI

'DE NAPOLI' ART GALLERY
Corso Garibaldi 9, Terlizzi
Paintings by Michele de Napoli.
Tu.-Su. 9-1.

TERMINI IMERESE

MUNICIPAL MUSEUM
Via del Museo Civico, Termini Imerese, Sicily
Prehistory. Fragments of Roman buildings. Statuary. Vases. Sicilian paintings.
Tu.-Su. 9.30-12.30, 3-6.

NATURAL HISTORY COLLECTION
Via Gregorio Ugualina 5, Termini Imerese, Sicily
Mineralogy. Fossils. Volcanic stones from Ferdinandea Island. Entomology. Semi-precious stones.
Tu.-Su. 9.30-12.30, 3-6.

TERNI

MUSEUM AND ART GALLERY
Via Manassi 6, Terni
Local prehistory, history. Roman architecture, statuary. Paintings of the Umbrian school. Modern art.
Tu.-Su. 9.30-12.30, 3-6.

TERRACINA

ANTIQUARIUM
Piazza Municipio, Terracina
Sculpture. Paintings. Epigraphy
Tu.-Su. 9-1.

TINDARI

ANTIQUARIUM
Tindari, Sicily
Finds from archaeological excavations in the area.
Summer: daily 9-1, 3.30- one hour before sunset. Winter: daily 9-1, 2- one hour before sunset.

TIVOLI

ANTIQUARIUM
Villa Adriana, Tivoli
Archaeological finds from the region.
Tu.-Su. 9-1.

ART MUSEUM
Villa d'Este, Tivoli
16th century paintings by local artists.
Tu.-Su. 9.30-12.30, 3-6.

MENSA PONDERARIA
Via del Duomo, Tivoli
Site of the ancient public scales. Two weighing platforms, with measures of capacity.
Th. 9-4 (winter 9.30-4).

MUNICIPAL MUSEUM
Tivoli
Local history. 17th century paintings.
Tu.-Su. 9.30-12.30, 3-6.

TODI

FRANCESCAN MISSIONARY MUSEUM
Piazza Vittorio Emanuele II, Todi
Religious art. Ethnography. Photographs and other illustrations of the missionary life.
Tu.-Su. 9-1.

MUNICIPAL MUSEUM AND ART GALLERY
Palazzo del Popolo, Piazza Vittorio Emanuele II, Todi
Local history, prehistory. Etruscan and Roman finds from the district. Ceramics. Paintings, including works by dello Spagna.
Tu.-Su. 9.30-12.30, 3-6.

TOLENTINO

ETHNOGRAPHICAL MUSEUM
Basilica di S. Nicola, Tolentino
Regional ethnography. Costumes. Domestic equipment.
Tu.-Su. 9.30-12.30, 3-6.

INTERNATIONAL MUSEUM OF CARICATURES
Palazzo Parisani-Bezzi, Tolentino
Caricatures from many periods and countries.
Tu.-Su. 9.30-12.30, 3-6.

MUNICIPAL MUSEUM
nr. Basilica of San Nicola, Piazza Silveri 2, Tolentino
Local history. Objects from Umbrian necropolis. Collection of majolica.
Daily ex. M. 9-12, 3-6.

TOLFA

MUNICIPAL MUSEUM
Piazza Vittorio Emanuele, Tolfa
Local history, archaeology. Folklore. Paintings.
Tu.-Su. 9.30-12.30, 3-6.

TOLMEZZO

CARNICO MUSEUM OF ARTS AND POPULAR TRADITIONS
Piazza Garibaldi 2, Tolmezzo
Local history, ethnography. Costumes. Embroidery.
Tu.-Su. 9.30-12.30, 3-6.

TORCELLO

MUSEO DELL'ESTUARIO
Gothic Palaces of the Archives and Council, Torcello, Venetian Lagoon
Greco-Roman finds from Altinum. Remains of silver altarpiece from the Cathedral (10th century). Embroidered banner of Santa Fosca (1366) and painted organ panels attributed to Veronese.
Daily ex. M. 9-6.

TORRE DEL GRECO

CORALLO MUSEUM
Piazza L. Palomba 6, Torre del Greco
Sculpture.
Tu.-Su. 9-1.

TORRE DE'PASSERI

MUSEUM OF SAN CLEMENTE A CASAURIA
Annesso all'Abbazia, Torre de'Passeri
Finds from excavations in the region.
Tu.-Su. 9.30-12.30, 3-6.

TORRE PELLICE

HISTORICAL MUSEUM
Via Roberto d'Azeglio 2, Torre Pellice
Local history. Agriculture. Military items.
Tu.-Su. 9-1.

TORTONA

MUNICPAL MUSEUM
Palazzo Guidobono, Via Mirabello, Tortona
Archaeology. Sculpture. Sarcophagi.
Tu.-Su. 9.30-12.30, 3-6.

ROMAN MUSEUM
Piazza Arzano 2, Tortona
Finds from excavations in the area.
Tu.-Su. 10-12, 3-6.

TRAPANI

PEPOLI MUSEUM
Conventual Buildings, Via Pepoli 196, Trapani, Sicily
Picture gallery containing a polyptych by 15th century Sienese school, and *St. Francis receiving the Stigmata* by Titian. Local crafts, including coral work. Sculpture. Pottery from Erice, Selinunte, Motya and Lilibeo.
Daily ex. M. 9.30-4; holidays 9.30-1. Closed Jan. 1, May 1, Aug. 15, Easter and Christmas.

TREBISACCE

ETHNOGRAPHICAL COLLECTION
Via Lutri, Trebisacce
Ethnography from different parts of the world. Animals. Plants. Food. Tools. Models. Bengali house.
Tu.-Su. 9.30-12.30, 3-6.

TREMEZZO

VILLA CARLOTTA
Tremezzo, Lake Como
18th century villa. 19th century marble statues, including *Love and Psyche* by Canova and figures by the Danish sculptor, Thorvaldsen.
Mar.-Oct. Daily 8-6. Nov.-Feb. Daily 8-12, 1-5.

TRENT

DIOCESAN MUSEUM
Palazzo dei Pretorio, Piazza dei Duomo, Trent
Objects from the Cathedral. Paintings of the Council of Trent. Renaissance tapestries by Peter van Aelst.
Daily 9-12, 2-6. Closed Su. morning and W. afternoon.

MUSEUM OF THE RISORGIMENTO
Castello del Buon Consiglio, Trent
Documents and other material relating to the Risorgimento.
Tu.-Su. 9.30-12.30, 3-6.

NATIONAL MUSEUM
Castello del Buon Consiglio, Piazza della Mostra, Trent
Frescoes, including portraits of the prince-bishops, in whose apartments are housed collections of archaeology, ethnography and paintings. Renaissance bronzes. Faenza ceramics. Meissen statuettes. Frescoes in the Loggia by Romanino da Brescia (1531).
Daily 9-12, 2-6 (2-5 Oct.-May). Closed Jan. 1, May 1, Aug. 15, Easter, Christmas, and Su. and holiday afternoons, Oct.-May.

TREVI

MUNICIPAL ART GALLERY
Piazza Mazzini, Trevi
Paintings of the Piedmontese school.
Tu.-Su. 9-1.

TREVIGNANO ROMANO

ANTIQUARIUM
Trevignano Romano
Archaeological material from local excavations.
Daily 9.30-4.

TREVISO

BAILO MUSEUM
Via Cavour 22, Treviso
Frescoes by Tommaso da Modena on the life of St. Ursula. Paintings by Cima, Giovanni Bellini, Girolamo da Treviso, Guardi and Jacopo Bassano. Portrait of Domitian by Lotto. Works by Paris Bordone. *St. John the Baptist Preaching*, by Tiepolo. Archaeological objects found in the bed of the Sile. Astronomic and geodetic instruments.
Tu.-Sa. 9-12, 2-6 (2-4 Oct.-Apr.); Su. and holidays 10-12. Closed M.

DIOCESAN MUSEUM
Piazza Duomo, Treviso
Religious art. Vestments. Sacred vessels.
Tu.-Su. 9.30-12.30, 3-6.

MUSEUM OF THE TREVIGLIANA HOUSE
Via Canova 40, Treviso
Local history. Musical instruments. Ceramics. Sculptures in marble and wood.
Tu.-Su. 9.30-12.30, 3-6.

NATURAL HISTORY COLLECTION
Riccati Istituto Tecnico, Treviso
Mineralogy. Natural history.
By appointment.

SCARPA ZOOLOGICAL MUSEUM
Presso il Seminario Vescovile, Treviso
Zoology. European fauna. Vertebrates. Birds. Amphibia.
Tu.-Su. 9.30-12.30, 3-6.

TRIESTE

GALLERY OF ANCIENT ART
Castello di Miramare, Trieste
16th-18th century paintings.
Tu.-Su. 9.30-12.30, 3-6.

HISTORICAL INSURANCE DISPLAY OF THE RIUNIONE ADRIATICA DI SICURTA COMPANY
Via Dante 1, Trieste
History of insurance in Italy. Documents.
On request.

HISTORICAL MUSEUM
Miramare Castle, Trieste
Furniture, weapons and paintings from the former Royal Palace in the Castle.
Summer: M.-Sa. 9-1, 2-5; Su. and holidays 9-1.30. Winter: M-Sa. 9.30-4; Su. and holidays 9.30-1.30.

MARITIME MUSEUM
Via di Campo Marzio 1, Trieste
Fishing. Navigation. Harbours. Nautical instruments. Models of fishing boats. Sketches.
Daily ex. M. 9-12, 3-6.

MERCANTILE MUSEUM
Faculty of Economics, University, Trieste
History of trade and commerce in Italy.
By appointment.

MORPURGO MUNICIPAL MUSEUM
Piazza Cattedrale 3, Trieste
Paintings. Majolica.
Tu.-Su. 10-4.

MORPURGO MUSEUM OF NATIONAL HISTORY AND THE STAVROPULOS ART COLLECTIONS
Via Matteo Renato Imbriani 5, Trieste
History of Trieste. Paintings.
Tu.-Su. 9.30-12.30, 3-6.

MUSEUM OF HISTORY AND ART
Piazza della Cattedrale 1, Trieste
Roman altars, stelae, inscriptions. Roman antiquities from Tergeste and its neighbourhood. 14th century Venetian triptych. A *Last Supper* in Limoges enamel. Paintings include works by Magnasco and Tiepolo.
Daily ex. M. 9-1, 4-6. Open at 10 on holidays.

MUSEUM OF MINERALOGY
Piazzale Europa, Trieste
Mineralogy. Petrography. Italian marble.
Tu.-Su. 9.30-12.30, 3-6.

MUSEUM OF RELIGIOUS ART
Piazza della Cattedrale 15, Trieste
Religious art. Architecture. Sculptures.
Tu.-Su. 9-1.

MUSEUM OF THE RISORGIMENTO
Viale XXIV Maggio 4, Trieste
History of Trieste, and the town's struggle for independence from the Risorgimento until 1918.
Tu.-Su. 9-1, 4-6.

NATURAL HISTORY MUSEUM
Piazza Hortis 4, Trieste
Zoology. Botany. Mammals, birds and insects. Palaeontology. Geology.
Daily ex. M. 10-1.

NATIONAL MUSEUM OF APPLIED ART
Viale Miramare 345, Trieste
Applied art, especially wrought iron work.
Daily ex. M. 9-12, 3-6.

REVOLTELLA MUSEUM
Via Diaz 27, Trieste
Contemporary Italian and foreign art. Works by painters from Trieste. Sculptures. Graphic art.
Daily ex. M. 9.30-12.30, 2.30-5.30.

SARTORIO MUSEUM
Largo Giovanni XXIII, Trieste
Collections of the minor arts.
Daily ex. M. 10-1, 4-6.

SAULI ENTOMOLOGICAL COLLECTION
Via dell'Agro 6/2, Trieste
Entomology.
By appointment.

TEATRO VERDI MUSEUM
Piazza dell'Unita d'Italia, Trieste
Theatre history.
Daily 10-1.

TECHNICAL MUSEUM
Via Valerio, Trieste
Industrial raw materials. Technology.
Tu.-Su. 9-1.

TRIORA

REGIONAL MUSEUM
Biblioteca Ferraioni, Triora
Local history, archaeology. Geology.
Tu.-Su. 9-1.

TROIA

CATHEDRAL TREASURY
Troia
Collection of vestments, chalices, reliquaries. Manuscripts.
On request.

TRULLI

CASTELLANA CAVES
Trulli District
Caves, and richly coloured stalactites and stalagmites. Many have greenish-yellow tints caused by sulphur deposits.
Apr. 15 - Sept. 30: Short tours at 9, 10, 11, 12, 2.30, 3.30, 4.30 and 6. Complete tours at 11, 3 and 5. Oct. 1 - Apr. 14; Short tours at 10.30, 12, 3.30 and 4.30. Complete tours at 11 and 3.30.

TUORO SUL TRASIMENO

ANTIQUARIUM
Palazzo Civico, Tuoro sul Trasimeno
Local history, including finds from the battle of 217 B.C.
Tu.-Su. 9-1.

TURIN

ABRUZZI MUSEUM
Monte dei Cappuccini, Turin
Memorabilia and documents relating to the Duke of Abruzzi.
Tu.-Su. 9.30-12.30, 3-6.

ALBERTINA GALLERY
Accademia Albertina di Belle Arti, Via dell'Accademia Albertina 6, Turin
Works include drawings by Gaud. Ferrari and Lanino, and paintings by Piedmontese artists.
Daily ex. Su. and holidays, 10-12. Apply to the Segretaria.

ARTILLERY MUSEUM
Cittadella, Corso Galileo Ferraris, Turin
Firearms, wrought-iron and cast-iron, bronze and leather equipment from 14th century to the present day. Prehistoric and ancient objects in stone, bronze and iron from all over Italy. Flags of regiments of the Sardinian army. Hand weapons. Bronze cannons.
Daily ex. M. and F. 9.30-11, 3-5.30. Holidays 9.30-11.50. Closed Jan. 1, May 1, June 2, Aug. 15, Easter Su. and Christmas Day.

CARLO BISCARETTI DI RUFFIA MOTOR MUSEUM
Corso Unità d'Italia 40, Turin
History of the motor car, with cars, chassis, engines, motorcycles and bicycles on display.
Daily ex. M. 10-12.30, 3-5.30. Closed Jan. 1, May 1, June 2, Aug. 15, Nov. 1, Easter Su. and Christmas Day.

CIVIC MUSEUM OF ART
Palazzo dell'Accademia di Belle Arti, Piazza Castello, Turin
Important collection of works by Italian painters. Local archaeological finds.
Daily ex. M. and holidays (not Su.), 9.30-12, 3-6. Closed Jan. 1, Easter Su., May 1, June 2, Aug. 15 and Christmas Day.

DUCAL CASTLE
Agliè, Turin
Pictures. Frescoes. Collection of Roman sarcophagi and statues excavated at Veii.
Tu.-Sa. 9-12, 2-4; Su. 9-12.30. Closed M. and Jan. 1, May 1, June 2, Aug. 15, Nov. 1, Easter Su. and Christmas Day.

EGYPTIAN MUSEUM
Accademia delle Scienze, Via Accademia delle Scienze 6, Turin
Egyptian exhibits, including statues of Rameses II and Thotmes II. The "Regio" papyrus, which lists the Pharoahs to the XVII Dynasty.
Tu.-Sa. 9-4; Su. 9.30-12.30, 3.30-5. Other holidays 9.30-12.30. Closed M. and Jan. 1, Easter Su., May 1, June 2, Aug. 15 and Christmas Day.

HISTORICAL MUSEUM
Ospedale di San Giovanni Battista e della Città di Torino, Turin
Historic pharmacy, with original equipment.
Tu.-Su. 9-1.

MARTINI MUSEUM OF HISTORY AND ETHNOGRAPHY
Pessione, Turin
History of the region. Ethnography. Costumes.
M.-Sa. and holidays, 9-12, 2.30-6.

MUNICIPAL GALLERY OF MODERN ART
Via Magenta 31, Turin
Paintings, especially by Piedmontese artists. Sculpture, drawings and engravings of 19th and 20th centuries. Oriental department with Buddhist sculpture, Islamic glass and Assyrian bas-reliefs dating from the reign of Sargo II.
Daily ex. M. and holidays (not Su.), 9.30-12, 3-6. Closed Jan. 1, Easter Su., May 1, June 2, Aug. 15 and Christmas Day.

MUSEUM OF ANCIENT ART
Palazzo Madama, Piazza Castello, Turin
Gothic carvings from 15th century stalls of the Abbey of Stafforda. Paintings include a *Madonna* by Barnabeo da Modena, a *Trinity* of the 15th century French school, a *Portrait of a Man* by Antonello da Messina (15th century) and pictures by Piedmontese artists.
18th century Venetian state barge which belonged to the King of Sicily. 17th-18th century paintings by Italian and Flemish artists. 18th century apartments with furniture and paintings of the period. Faience. Porcelain. Ivory. Glass. Enamels. Bronzes. Leatherwork. Ironwork. Fabrics. Bookbindings.
Daily ex. M. 9.30-12.30, 3-6. Closed weekday holidays.

MUSEUM OF ANTHROPOLOGY AND ETHNOLOGY
Via Accademia Albertina 17, Turin
Anthropological and ethnological collections.
Su. and Th. 9-12.

MUSEUM OF ANTIQUITIES
Palazzo dell'Accademia delle Scienze, Via Accademia delle Scienze 6, Turin
Objects from Piedmont and Liguria. Etruscan and Greek vases. Roman glass bottles and cups. Late Mycenean ceramics (1200-1000 B.C.). Palaeolithic instruments. Bronze Age swords, Iron Age helmets. Etruscan cinerary urns. Sculptures. Mosaics. Roman and barbarian goldsmiths' work.
Daily ex. Tu. 9-12, 2.30-5.

MUSEUM OF FORENSIC SCIENCE
Corso Galileo Galilei 22, Turin
Forensic medicine. Skulls. Anthropology.
Tu.-Su. 9.30-12.30, 3-6.

MUSEUM OF GEOLOGY AND PALAEONTOLOGY
Palazzo Carignanao, Turin
Geology. Mineralogy. Fossils.
Tu.-Su. 9.30-12.30, 3-6.

MUSEUM OF HUMAN ANATOMY
Corso Massimo d'Azeglio 52, Turin
Human anatomy.
By appointment.

MUSEUM OF NATURAL SCIENCE
The University, Turin
Natural science collections.
By appointment.

NATIONAL CAVALRY MUSEUM
Pinerolo, Turin
Collections illustrating history of the Italian cavalry equipment.
Tu.-Sa. 9-11, 3.15-5.15. Holidays 9-11.15. Closed Jan. 1, May 1, June 2, Aug. 15, Nov. 1, Easter Su. and Christmas Day.

NATIONAL MOUNTAIN MUSEUM
Monte dei Cappuccini, Turin
Collection of material connected with mountain life and climbing.
Daily ex. F. 9-12, 3-6. Closed Jan. 1, May 1, June 2, Aug. 15, Nov. 1, Easter Su. and Christmas Day.

NATIONAL MUSEUM OF THE CINEMA
Piazza San Giovanni 2, Turin
History of films and of the cinema.
Tu.-Su. 9.30-12.30, 3-6.

NATIONAL MUSEUM OF THE ITALIAN RISORGIMENTO
Palazzo Carignano, Via Accademia della Scienze 5, Turin
History of the struggle for Italian independence. Documents. Uniforms. Weapons. Medals.
Tu.-Sa. 9-11, 3-5.30; Su. and holidays 9-11.30. Closed M. and Jan. 1, May 1, June 2, Aug. 15, Nov. 1, Easter Su. and Christmas Day.

PIETRO MICCA MUSEUM
Via Guicciardini 7, Turin
Relics of the 1706 siege in which Pietro Micca was killed.
Tu.-Su. 9.30-12.30, 3-6. Closed M. and holidays (not Su.). Also Jan. 1, May 1, June 2, Aug. 15, Nov. 1, Easter Su. and Christmas Day.

ROYAL ARMOURY
Palazzo Reale, Piazza Castello 191, Turin
Collection of weapons belonging to the Savoy princes. Military souvenirs, Particularly of the time of Napoleon. Examples of inlay, embossing and engraving.
M.-Sa. 9-12.30, 2.30-5; Su. and holidays 9-12.30. Closed F., Jan. 1, May 1, June 2, Aug. 15, Nov. 1, Easter Su. and Christmas Day.

ROYAL PALACE
Piazza Castello, Turin
State apartments furnished in 18th century style. Historical paintings. Chinese porcelain. Statues of the Savoy princes.
Daily ex. M. 9-12 or 12.30, 2-4 or 3-5.30.

SABAUDA GALLERY
Palazzo dell'Accademia delle Scienze, Via Accademia delle Scienze 6, Turin
Primitive paintings, including *St. Francis receiving the Stigmata* by Van Eyck; the *Passion* by Memling; the *Visitation* by Roger van der Weyden, and a *Virgin and Child* by Barnabeo da Modena. Renaissance art is represented by Montegna, Pollaivolo, Bronzino and François Clouet. 17th century Flemish paintings include Van Dyck's *Children of Charles I of England.* Dutch school: work by the young Rembrandt. The Gualino Collection: gold and silver; 15th and 16th century Florentine furnishings and paintings, including works by Matteo di Giovanni, Bartolomeo Montagna, Francesco Guardi. Sculptures.
Tu.-Sa. 9-12, 2-5; Su. 9.30-12.30, 3-5; holidays not Su. 9.30-12.30. Closed M., Jan. 1, May 1, June 2, Aug. 15, Nov. 1, Easter Su. and Christmas Day.

SCIENTIFIC COLLECTIONS OF THE MUNICIPAL MUSEUM
Via Magenta 31, Turin
Weapons and tools from Africa and America. Palaeontology.
Tu.-Su. 9.30-12.30, 3-6.

ZOOLOGICAL MUSEUM
Parco Michelotti, Turin
Zoology.
Tu.-Su. 9-1.

ZOOLOGICAL MUSEUM
Via Giolitti 32, Turin
Natural history. Mammals. Birds. Fish. Reptiles. Amphibians. Insects.
Tu.-Su. 9.30-12.30, 3-6.

TUSCANIA

BISHOP'S PALACE
Tuscania
Small collection of Etruscan finds.
Daily ex. M. 9-12, 3-6.

MUNICIPAL MUSEUM
Church of San Pietro, Tuscania
Local history, archaeology. Paintings.
Tu.-Su. 9.30-12.30, 3-6.

UDINE

CASTLE MUSEUM AND PICTURE GALLERY
Castle, Vicolo Sottomonte, Udine
Numismatics. Paintings by Tiepolo and Carpaccio, and other painters of the Venetian school. Prints and drawings. Exhibits on the Italian Risorgimento. Bronzes. Medals. Coins. Stones. Jewels. Pottery.
Daily ex. M. 9.30-12.30, 3-6 (2-4 Oct. 15 - Mar. 31). Closed Su. and holiday afternoons in winter.

FOSSIL COLLECTION
Stazione Chimico-Agraria Sperimentale, Via Marangoni 97, Udine
Palaeontology. Fossils.
By appointment.

FRUILANO MUSEUM OF NATURAL HISTORY
Largo Ospedale Vecchio, Udine
Natural history. Mammals. Amphibians. Fossils.
Tu.-Su. 9.30-12.30, 3-6.

FRIULANO MUSEUM OF POPULAR ARTS AND TRADITIONS
Via Viola 3, Udine
Popular art of the region. Local customs. Costumes. Domestic equipment.
Tu.-Su. 9.30-12.30, 3-6.

NATURAL HISTORY COLLECTION
Seminario Arcivescovile, Udine
Palaeontology. Petrography. Botany. Zoology.
Tu.-Su. 9-1.

ORNITHOLOGY MUSEUM
Federazione Italiana della Caccia - Sezione Provinciale, Viale Duodo 42, Udine
Ornithology. Birds of the district.
By appointment.

ZOOLOGICAL COLLECTION
Comitato Provinciale della Caccid di Udine, Piazza Patriarcato 3, Udine
Zoology. Birds of the region.
By appointment.

ZOOLOGICAL COLLECTION
Liceo 'Jacopo Stellini', Udine
Zoology. Palaeontology. Botany.
By appointment.

UGENTO

ARCHAEOLOGICAL MUSEUM
Via Zecca, Ugento
Archaeological material from excavations in the area. Sculptures.
Tu.-Su. 9.30-12.30, 3-6.

URBANIA

MUNICIPAL MUSEUM
Palazzo Ducale, Urbania
Furniture. Furnishings. Baroque drawings.
Tu.-Su. 9-1.

URBINO

BOTANICAL COLLECTION
Orto Botanico, Presso la Facoltà di Farmacia, Urbino
Botany. Herbarium.
Tu.-Su. 9-1, 3-6.

DIOCESAN MUSEUM AND MUSEUM ALBANI
Basilica, Urbino
Religious art. Local history. Paintings.
Tu.-Su. 9.30-12.30, 3-6.

NATIONAL GALLERY OF THE MARCHES
Ducal Palace, Urbino
17th century Gobelins tapestries. Polyptych by Vivarini. Paintings of 15th century Venetian school. Duke's apartments contain a *Madonna* by Verrocchio; a predella of the *Profanation of the Host* (1468) by Paulo Uccello, the *Communion of the Apostles* by Just van Grand; the *Flagellation* and the *Madonna of Senigallia* by Piero della Francesca; *The Mute* by Raphaël. The Duke's study is furnished with inlays, probably after Botticelli, surmounted with panels representing famous men, painted by Just van Grand and Pedro Berruguete.
Apr. 15- Sept. 30, M.-Sa. 9-1, 3-6 (9.30-4 rest of year). Su. and holidays 10-1.

RAPHAËL'S HOUSE
Via Raffaello Sanzio 57, Urbino
Raphaël lived here until he was 14. In the room where he was born is a fresco of the Madonna, his first work. The Virgin is a portrait of Raphaël's mother, and the Child one of Raphaël himself. The stone on which the boy ground his colours is shown in the courtyard.
Apr. 16- Sept. 30, Daily 9-1, 3-7. Oct. 1- Apr. 15, Daily 10-12.30.

URBISAGLIA

NAPOLEONIC ROOM
Palazzo Barisani-Bezzi, Urbisaglia
Memorabilia of Napoleon.
Tu.-Su. 9.30-12.30, 3-6.

VADO LIGURE

DON CESARE QUEIROLO ART GALLERY
Palazzo Comunale, Vado Ligure
Paintings by local artists.
Tu.-Su. 9.30-12.30, 3-6.

MUNICIPAL MUSEUM
Piazza San Giovanni Battista 1, Vado Ligure
Local history, archaeology. Sculptures. Coins. Sepulchres.
Tu.-Su. 9.30-12.30, 3-6.

VALDAGNO

PALAEONTOLOGICAL COLLECTION
Scuole Elementari, Valdagno
Palaeontology.
On request.

VALDOTTAVO

FLORA LUCENSIS HERBARIUM
Villa Mezzetti, Valdottavo
Botany. 19th century herbarium.
Tu.-Su. 9.30-12.30, 3-6.

VARALLO SESIA

ART GALLERY
Via Sacro Monte, Varallo Sesia
Paintings and drawings of the region.
Tu.-Su. 9.30-12.30, 3-6.

CALDERINI MUNICIPAL MUSEUM
Via Sacro Monte, Varallo Sesia
Geology. Zoology. Entomology. Local history. Armaments. Medals. Coins.
Tu.-Su. 9.30-12.30, 3-6.

MUSEUM OF ZOOLOGY
Giardino Zoologico, Varallo Sesia
Zoology.
Tu.-Su. 9.30-12.30, 3-6.

VARENNA

ORNITHOLOGICAL MUSEUM
Via Venini, Varenna
Ornithology. Local birds.
Tu.-Su. 9.30-12.30, 3-6.

SCANAGATTA COLLECTION
Varenna
Zoology. Invertebrates of the region.
By appointment.

VARESE

AERONAUTICAL MUSEUM
Villa Caproni di Taliedo, Venegono Superiore, Varese
Aeronautics. Historic models.
Tu.-Su. 9.30-12.30, 3-6.

BAROFFIO MUSEUM
Annesso al Santuario di Santa Maria del Monte, Varese
History of the region. 17th-19th century documents.
Tu.-Su. 10-12, 3-6.

MUNICIPAL MUSEUM
Villa Mirabello, Piazza delle Motte, Varese
Prehistoric finds. Local history. Palaeontology. Geology. Mineralogy. Zoology. Entomology.
Daily ex. Tu. 10-12, 3-5.30 or 6.

SAVERI COLLECTION
Via Brambilla 6, Varese
Butterfly collection.
By appointment.

SCIENCE COLLECTIONS
Istituto Magistrale Statale 'A. Manzoni', Varese
Mineralogy. Zoology. Physics. Scientific apparatus.
By appointment.

VASTO

MUNICIPAL MUSEUM AND ART GALLERY
I. Spaventa, Vasto
Finds from local excavations. Paintings.
Tu.-Su. 9.30-12.30, 3-6.

VELLEIA

ANTIQUARIUM
Velleia
Finds from archaeological excavations in the area. Architectural fragments.
Tu.-Su. 9- 1 hour before sunset.

VELLETRI

CHAPTERHOUSE MUSEUM
Via Fabio Filzi 4, Velletri
Religious art. Drawings. Miniatures.
Tu.-Su. 9.30-12.30, 3-6.

MUNICIPAL MUSEUM
Palazzo Comunale, Velletri
Local history. Finds from local excavations. Architectural ornaments.
Tu.-Su. 9.30-12.30, 3-6.

VENEGAZZÙ DI VOLPAGO DEL MONTELLO

GASPERINI COLLECTIONS
Venegazzù di Volpago del Montello
African ethnography, zoology.
By appointment.

VENEGONO SUPERIORE

CAPRONI DI TALIEDO AERONAUTICAL MUSEUM
Villa Caproni di Taliedo, Venegono Superiore
History of aeronautics. Models of aeroplanes. Diagrams. Charts.
Tu.-Su. 9.30-12.30, 3-6.

VENICE

ACADEMY OF FINE ARTS
former Convent and Church of St. Mary of Charity, Venice
Painting, mainly Venetian. Works by Giovanni Bellini, Carpaccio, Giorgione's *Tempest* (c. 1505). Tintoretto's *Virgin of the Treasurers*; Lorenzo Lotto; Veronese, *Meal in the House of Levi.* Series of 9 pictures (1490-96) by Carpaccio, the *Legend of St. Ursula.* Titian's *Presentation of the Virgin at the Temple. Portrait of a Young Man* by Hans Memling.
Apr. 15- Sept. 14, Tu.-Sa. 9-1, 3-6 (rest of year 9-4); Su. and holidays 9.30-1. Closed M.

ARCHAEOLOGICAL MUSEUM
Libreria Vecchia, Piazza San Marco, Venice
Greco-Roman sculpture. Roman portraits. Coins, bronzes and vases. Copies of Greek and Hellenistic works of art.
Summer: Daily 10-12. Winter: on request. Apply to the library caretaker at No. 7 San Marco.

ARMENIAN MONASTERY
Island of San Lazzaro, Venice
Manuscripts and books in Armenian. Printing shop equipped with the type required for printing in 36 languages. Oriental, Venetian and Roman art. Paintings by Cima, Moretto. Salvator Rosa, Guercino, Garofalo, Canaletto, Reni and Crespi.
Daily 3-5.

ART COLLECTION
Scuola Dalmata die SS Giogio e Trifone, Calle dei Furlani, Sant'Antonin, Venice
Paintings, including works by Carpaccio.
Tu.-Su. 9-1.

ART COLLECTION
Scuola Grande Arciconfraternita di Santa Maria del Carmelo, Campo Santa Margherita, Venice
Paintings, including works by Tiepolo.
Tu.-Su. 9-1.

ART COLLECTION
Scuola Grande di San Giovanni Evangelista, Campo della Salute, Venice
Paintings by Carpaccio, Gentile Bellini and Tintoretto.
Tu.-Su. 9-1.

CADAMURO MORGANTE COLLECTION
S. Elena, Colle Oslavia 10, Venice
Collection of Italian beetles.
By appointment.

CASA GOLDONI
Palazzo Contarini, Via San Tomà 2794, Venice
Memorabilia of the dramatist Carlo Goldoni (1707-1793), in his former home (15th century).
Tu.-Su. 9.30-12.30, 3-6.

CORRER MUSEUM
Fabbrica Nuova, Portico dell'Ascensione, Piazza San Marco, Venice
Historical and artistic collections of the city. Paintings include the portrait of Doge Mocenigo by Gentile Bellini; a *Pietà, Madonna* and *Crucifixion* by Giovanni Bellini; the *Courtesans* by Carpaccio; a *Madonna* by Thierry Bouts; a *Crucifixion* by Van der Goes. Bronzes. Medals. Ivories. Embossed leather. Enamels. Italian and Oriental pottery. Lace. Sculpture. 16th-17th century engravings. Models. Designs of Venetian boats and gondolas. Vignettes of Venetian festivals.
Apr. 15- Oct. 31, M.-Sa. 9-12, 2.30-6 (9-5 rest of year). Closed Su. afternoons and holidays.

DIPINTI MUSEUM OF SACRED BYZANTINE ART
Ponte dei Greci, Venice
Byzantine art.
Tu.-Su. 9.30-12.30, 3-6.

DOGES' PALACE
Piazza San Marco, Venice
The doges' apartments include the room of the Scarlatti and those of the Ducat, Grimani, Erizzo and others, with works by Bosch, Bellini and Tiepolo, and the originals of Rizzo's Adam and Eve. Other rooms contain paintings by Tintoretto, Titian and Veronese. The Grand Council Chamber's walls are decorated with paintings illustrating Venetian history. Over the Doges' throne Tintoretto painted his *Paradise*, at the age of 70. On the ceiling, near the throne, is the *Apotheosis of Venice* by Veronese. The cornice bears the portraits of the 72 doges.
Mar. 16- May 15, Daily 9.30-5. May 16- Sept. 15, Daily 9-6. Sept. 16- Mar. 15, Daily 10-4. Closed Jan. 1 and 6, Apr. 18, May 1, June 2, Nov. 1 and 4, Dec. 8 and 25, and afternoons of Mar. 19, Apr. 16 and 25, May 27, June 17, Nov. 2 and 21, Dec. 24, 26 and 31.

ENTOMOLOGY COLLECTION
S. Marco 1757, Venice
Italian, Mediterranean beetles.
By appointment.

THE FRANCHETTI GALLERY
Calle della d'Oro, Strada Nuova, Venice
Tapestries. Sculptures. Paintings, including a *St. Sebastian* by Mantegna. Works by Carpaccio, Guardi, Filippino Lippi and Bordone. *Venus with a Looking Glass* by Titian.
M.-Sa. 9-4 (winter 9.30-4). Su. 9-1. Closed holidays.

GALLERY OF MODERN ART
Palazzo Pesaro, Calle Longo, Venice
Works by 19th century and contemporary Venetian and foreign painters.
Apr. 15- Sept. 15, M.-Sa. 9.30-12.30, 3-6; Su. 9-1. Rest of year M.-Sa. 9-5; Su. 9-12.30. Closed holidays.

PEGGY GUGGENHEIM COLLECTION
Palazzo Venier dei Leoni, Venice
Modern art (after 1910). Among artists represented are Picasso, Brancusi, Marc Chagall, Max Ernst, Paul Klee, Salvador Dali, and Henry Moore.
Apr.-Oct., Tu. and F. 3-6.

LEONARDI COLLECTION
S. Stin, Calle Soranzo 2521, Venice
Palaeontology. Mineralogy. Fossils.
By appointment.

LEVRINI COLLECTION
Corte Bertoloni 543, Giudecca, Venice
Butterfly collection.
By appointment.

MANFREDIANA PICTURE GALLERY
Seminario Patriarcale, Zattere ai Salone, Venice
Italian paintings by Cima da Conegliano, Filippino Lippi, Albertinelli, Vivarini, Veronese. Foreign artists include Wouweman, Lesueur, Hackert and Teniers. Terracottas by Vittoria. Busts by Canova and Rinaldo Rinaldi. Lapidary collection on ground floor.
Daily 10-12.

MARCELLO BOTANICAL COLLECTION
S. Fantin 3666, Venice
Botany. Venetian flora. Herbarium.
By appointment.

MARCIANA LIBRARY
Libreria Vecchia, Piazza San Marco, Venice
The Sansovino Room has a ceiling decorated by Veronese, Strozzi and others, and contains miniatures and also the Grimani Breviary (Flemish school, 15th-16th century).
Summer: daily 10-12. Winter: on request only. Apply to the library caretaker at No. 7 San Marco.

MARITIME MUSEUM
Arsenal, Calle del Pestrin, Venice
Maritime exhibits, including a model of one of the doges' Bucentaurs (state barges). Story of Venice's maritime history and Italian maritime power. Documents relating to the battle of Lepanto.
Daily ex. Tu. 9.30-12.30, 4.30-6.30. Sept. 16- Apr. 30, 9.30-12.30, 2.30-4.30. Closed Su. afternoons and holidays.

MEGGIOLARO COLLECTION
S. Croce 121A, Venice
Collection of beetles.
By appointment.

MUSEUM OF THE CONVENTO DEI MINORI CAPPUCCINI
SS Redentore Giudecca 194, Venice
In monastery. 16th century pharmacy. 17th-18th century ceramic jars.
Tu.-Su. 9-1.

MUSEUM OF THE ISRAELITE COMMUNITY
Campo del Ghetto Nuovo, Venice
History of the Israelite community in Venice.
Tu.-Su. 9-1.

MUSEUM OF NATURAL HISTORY
Fondaco dei Turchi 1730, Ponte della Stazione, Venice
Natural history and lapidary collections. Fish of the Adriatic. Birds.
Summer: Daily 9-12, 4-6. Winter: daily 9-12. Closed M.

MUSEUM OF NATURAL HISTORY
Seminario Patriarcale, Campo della Salute, Venice
Natural history, especially of the Venetian Lagoon.
Tu.-Su. 9-1.

MUSEUM OF ORIENTAL ART
Palazzo Pesaro, Calle Longo, Venice
Oriental art and curios. Lacquer work and bronzes.
Apr. 15- Sept. 15, M.-Sa. 9.30-12.30, 3-6; Su. 9-1. Rest of year, M.-Sa. 9-5; Su. 9-12.30. Closed holidays.

MUSEUM OF THE RISORGIMENTO
Palazzo Reale, Piazza San Marco, Venice
Documents and other items relating to events from the fall of the Venetian Republic to the present day. Models. Portraits. Flags. Uniforms. Weapons. Water-colours. Engravings.
Daily ex. M. 9.30-12.30, 2.30-5.30.

PERALE COLLECTION
Campo dei Biri, Cannaregio, S. Casciano 5394b, Venice
Ornithology.
By appointment.

PICTURE GALLERY
Palazzo Querini-Stampalia, Via S. Zaccarin 4778, Venice
Paintings illustrating Venetian life in the 17th and 18th centuries. Works by Lorenzo di Credi, Giovanni Bellini, Palma il Vecchio, Tiepolo and Pietro Longhi.
Apr. 15- Nov. 14, M.-Sa. 9.30-12.30, 2.30-6.30; Su. 10-12; holidays 10-4. Nov. 15- Apr. 14, M.-Sa. 9-5; Su. 10-12; holidays 10-4.

PICTURE GALLERY
Seminary, nr. Piazza San Gregorio, Venice
Paintings by Italian, especially Venetian artists.
Daily 10-12; closed Su. and 15-30 Sept.

SCUOLA GRANDE DI SAN ROCCO
Calle della Chiesa, Venice
Paintings by Tintoretto, including an *Annunciation*, a *Jesus before Pilate* and a *Crucifixion. Annunciation* by Titian. Statues by Campagna. Woodcarvings by Francesco Pianta.
Mar. 16- Oct. 31, Daily 9-1, 3.30-6.30. Rest of year, 10-1. Open mornings only on Su. and holidays. Closed May 1, Nov. 1 and 4, Easter Su. and Christmas Day.

SETTECENTO MUSEUM
Left Bank, Grand Canal, Venice
Porcelain and majolica. 18th century costumes. Venetian baroque furniture, black and gold and heavily coloured. Frescoes by Gian-Battista Tiepolo. Pastels by Rosalba Carriera. Paintings by Guardi and Longhi, and sketches by Gian-Domenico Tiepolo.
Apr. 15- Oct. 31, Daily 9-12, 2.30-6 (rest of year 9-5). Closed Su. and holiday afternoons.

TOLOTTI COLLECTION
S. Angelo 3814, Venice
Ornithology. Rare species. Wading birds of the Venetian Lagoon.
By appointment.

TREASURY OF THE BASILICA SAN MARCO
Piazza San Marco, Venice
The treasury was partly formed in the 13th century from booty from the pillage of Constantinople by the Crusaders in 1204. Byzantine gold work and enamels. The Pulpit of St. Mark. Reliquaries. A Thorn of the Crown. A Nail of the Cross.
M.-Sa. 10-12.30, 2-5.30; Su. and holidays 2-4.30.

ZOOLOGICAL COLLECTION
Stazione Idrobiologica del C.N.R., Venice
Fauna and flora of the Venetian Lagoon.
On request.

VENOSA

BRISCESE COLLECTION
Corso Vittorio Emanuele II 125, Venosa
Archaeology. Iron Age ceramics.
Tu.-Su. 9.30-12.30, 3-6.

VENTIMIGLIA

BARMA GRANDE MUSEUM
Balzi Rossi, Ventimiglia
Archaeological finds from the region.
Tu.-Su. 10-12, 3-6.

BOTANICAL COLLECTION
Giardino Hambury a La Martola, Ventimiglia
Botanical collection.
Tu.-Su. 10-12, 3-6.

GIROLAMO ROSSI MUNICIPAL MUSEUM OF ARCHAEOLOGY
Palazzo Comunale, Ventimiglia
Finds from Ligurian *Albium Intemelium*, later Albintimilium on the Roman Via Aurelia, where Agricola spent his boyhood.
M.-Sa. 10-12, 3-6; Su. 10-12.

VENTOTENE

ANTIQUARIUM
Ventotene
Archaeological material from local excavations.
Daily 9.30-4.

VERBANIA

NATURAL HISTORY COLLECTION
Istituto Italiano di Idrobiologia, Verbania
Hydrobiology.
On request.

PAESAGGIO MUSEUM
Viale Umberto I, Verbania
Regional history. Paintings. Maps.
Tu.-Su. 10-12, 3-6.

VILLA TARANTO
Verbania
Botanical collection.
Tu.-Su. 10-12, 3-6.

VERBANIA-PALLANZA

HISTORICAL MUSEUM AND ART GALLERY
Via Cavour 40, Verbania-Pallanza
Local history. Paintings, especially by local artists.
Tu.-Su. 9.30-12.30, 3-6.

VERCELLI

BORGOGNA MUSEUM
Via Antonio Borgogna 10, Vercelli
Paintings by Italian and foreign artists. Works by Titian, Palma the Elder, Ferrari, Sodoma and Lanino.
Tu.-Su. 9.30-12.30, 2.30-5.30.

CATHEDRAL MUSEUM
Piazza San Eusebio, Vercelli
Religious art. Miniatures. Relics. Vestments.
Tu.-Su. 9.30-12.30, 3-6.

GALLERY OF MODERN ART
Via Sereno 7, Vercelli
Modern art, from Italy and elsewhere.
Tu.-Su. 9.30-12.30, 3-6.

LEONE MUSEUM
House of the Alciati, Via Verdi 7, Vercelli
Objects d'art. Local history. Engravings. Pottery. Glass. Jewellery.
Daily ex. M. 9.30-12.30, 2.30-5.30.

VEROLI

ABBEY OF CASAMARI
Veroli
Small carvings. Coins. Inscriptions. Pottery.
Summer: Tu.-Su. 8.30-12, 4-sunset. Winter: Tu.-Su. 8.30-12, 2.30-sunset.

VERONA

ARCHAEOLOGICAL MUSEUM
Via Rigaste Redentore, Verona
Local archaeology. Etruscan, Greek and Roman finds, sculpture, glass, bronzes.
Summer; 9-12.30, 3-6.30. Winter: 9-12.30, 2-5.30.

CASTELVECCHIO MUSEUM
Corso Cavour, Verona
Veronese statues and carvings of 10th-15th centuries. 12th-16th century frescoes by local artists. Paintings by Pisanello; Stefano da Verona; Giambono; Iacopo, Gentile and Giovanni Bellini; Mantegna; Buonsignori and Carpaccio. The Veronese school is represented by Morone, Cavazzola, Girolamo dai Libri and Veronese. Venetian school: Tintoretto, Titian, Lotto, Guardi and Tiepolo.
Summer: 9-12.30, 2-6.30. Winter: 9-12.30, 2-5.30.

ERIZZO MUSEUM
Via San Mammaso 2, Verona
Material from local excavations. Sculpture. Bronzes. Paintings of the Venetian school.
Tu.-Su. 9.30-12.30, 3-6.

MAFFEIANO MUSEUM
Piazza Bra, Verona
Greek, Etruscan and Roman finds. 18th century documents.
Tu.-Su. 9.30-12.30, 3-6.

MODERN ART GALLERY
Palazzo Forti, Via Emilei 1, Verona
Collections of modern art, from Italy and other countries.
Summer: 9-12.30, 3-6.30. Winter: 9-12.30, 2-5.30.

MUSEUM OF ART
Castelvecchio, Corso Cavour, Verona
Italian and foreign paintings including works by Titian, Veronese, Tiepolo, Guardi, Carpaccio, Mantegna, Vivarini, Moretto, Iacopo Bellini, Giovanni Bellini, Crivelli and Rubens.
Daily ex. M. 9-12.30, 3-6.

MUSEUM OF THE CHAPTER LIBRARY
Piazza del Duomo 13, Verona
Early religious books, manuscripts.
By appointment.

MUSEUM OF NATURAL HISTORY
Palazzo Pompei, Lungo Adige Porta Vittoria 9, Verona
Palaeontology. Mineralogy. Zoology. Botany.
Tu.-Su. 9.30-12.30, 3-6.

RISORGIMENTO MUSEUM
Palazzo Forti, Via Emilei 1, Verona
Collection illustrating Italy's struggle for independence. Documents. Uniforms. Weapons. Medals.
Summer: 9-12.30, 3-6.30. Winter: 9-12.30, 2-5.30.

VERRÈS

CASTLE OF ISSOGNE
Verrès, Val d'Ayas
Late medieval residence, rebuilt 1497-98, containing frescoes and local furniture and furnishings.
Daily 9-12, 2-5 or 6.

VERRUCHIO

COMMUNAL GALLERY OF MODERN ART
Piazza Malatesta, Verruchio
19th-20th century paintings, sculptures, graphics.
Tu.-Su. 9.30-12.30, 3-6.

PREHISTORIC AND LAPIDARY MUSEUM
Via della Rocca, Verruchio
Finds from local excavations. Inscriptions. Epigraphs.
Tu.-Su. 9.30-12.30, 3-6.

VESTENANUOVA

FOSSIL MUSEUM
Bolca di Vestenanuova, Vestenanuova
Palaeontology. Fossils of the region.
Tu.-Su. 10-12, 3-6.

VETULONIA

ARCHAEOLOGICAL MUSEUM
Casa del Popolo, Vetulonia
Archaeological finds. Architectural fragments. Bronzes. Sculpture. Ceramics.
Tu.-Su. 10-12, 3-6.

VIADANA

PARAZZI MUNICIPAL MUSEUM
Via Ludovico Grossi 28, Viadana
Local history, paintings. Frescoes. Majolica. Coins.
Tu.-Su. 10-12, 3-6.

VIBO VALENTIA

MUSEUM
Palazzo Cordopatri, Vibo Valentia
Greek antiquities.
By appointment.

NATIONAL ARCHAEOLOGICAL MUSEUM
Palazzo Gagliardi, Vibo Valentia
Archaeological finds from excavations in the area. Sculpture.
Tu.-Su. 9.30-12.30, 3-6.

VICENZA

MUNICIPAL MUSEUM
Palazzo Chiericati, Piazza Matteoti, Vicenza
Venetian primitives. *Crucifixion* attributed to Memling. Paintings by Bartolomeo Montagna, Mantegna, Carpaccio, Buonconsiglio, Lotto, Veronese, Bassano, Piazzetta, Tintoretto and Tiepolo. *Madonna* by Jan Breughel and *The Ages of Man* by Van Dyck.
Daily ex. M. and holidays 9-12.30, 2.30-5.30.

MUSEUM OF THE RISORGIMENTO
Villa Guiccioli, Vicenza
Documents, coins, medals and journals relating to the Risorgimento.
Tu.-Su. 9.30-12.30, 3-6.

NATURAL HISTORY MUSEUM
Piazza Matteotti, Vicenza
Palaeontology. Natural history of the region. Fossils.
Tu.-Su. 9-12.30, 2.30-5.30

PALAEONTOLOGICAL COLLECTION
Seminario Classico 'Pigafetta', Vicenza
Palaeontology. Fossils of the area.
On request.

PALAEONTOLOGICAL COLLECTION
Seminario Vescovile, Vicenza
Palaeontology. Fossils of the area.
On request.

VILLA VALMARANA
nr. Vicenza
17th century villa with frescoes by Viovanni Battista Tiepolo and his son, Domenico (1735).
Daily ex. Su. and holiday afternoons, 9.30-12, 4-7 (6 in winter).

VIGEVANO

ARCHAEOLOGICAL MUSEUM
Palazzo Crespi, Corso Cavour, Vigevano
Archaeological finds from the area.
Tu.-Su. 10-12, 3-6.

VINCI

VINCIANO MUSEUM
Castle, Vinci
Town where Leonardo da Vinci was born (1452). The museum contains machines made from his models. Library.
June 21-Sept. 21, M.-Sa. 8-11.30, 4-6.30; Su. and holidays 10-11.30, 4-6.30. Dec. 21-Mar. 21, 2-4.30; Mar. 22-June 20, and Sept. 22-Dec. 20, 3-5.30. Closed Jan. 1, May 1, Aug. 15, Easter Su. and Christmas Day.

VIPITENO (STERZING)

MÜLTSCHER MUSEUM
Piazza Mitra 112, Vipiteno (Sterzing)
Exhibits include four panels painted by Hans Mültscher for the parish church altarpiece and sculpture which formed part of the same altarpiece.
Daily ex. M. 9.30-12.30, 2.30-5.30.

MUNICIPAL MUSEUM
Palazzo Comunale, Vipiteno (Sterzing)
Local history, archaeology.
Tu.-Su. 9.30-12.30, 2.30-5.30.

VITERBO

MUNICIPAL MUSEUM
Piazza Crispi 2, Viterbo
Etruscan exhibits. Paintings include Sebastiano del Piombo's *Dead Christ*, the design of which is attributed to Michelangelo, Sebastiano's teacher.
Daily ex. M. 9-4.

VITTORIO VENETO

CENEDESE MUSEUM
Piazza Marcantonio Flaminio, Vittorio Veneto
Archaeology. Wall paintings. Frescoes.
Tu.-Su. 10-12, 3-6.

MUSEUM OF THE BATTLE
Piazza della Cattedrale, Vittorio Veneto
Material on World War I.
Tu.-Su. 10-12, 3-6.

VOLTERRA

ETRUSCAN MUSEUM
Via Don Minzoni 15, Volterra
Ceramics. Over 400 funeral urns - some carved with reclining figures and domestic scenes. Mosaics from Roman baths.
Apr.-Sept. Daily 9-1, 3-6. Oct.-Mar. Daily 9.30-12.30, 2.30-4. Closed Jan. 1, Easter Su., Christmas Day and Su. and holiday afternoons.

MUSEUM OF SACRED ART
Palazzo della Prepositura, Via Roma 13, Volterra
Works by Benedetto da Maiano, Giuliano da Maiano, Mainardi and Tamagni.
Daily ex. M. 9-1, 3-6.

PICTURE GALLERY
Palazzo dei Priori, Piazza del Priori, Volterra
Works by Tuscan artists. Altarpiece and predella by Taddeo di Bartolo and Benedetto di Giovanni. *Annunciation* (1491) by Luca Signorelli. *Descent from the Cross* by Il Rosso.
Daily 9-1, 3-7.

VULCI

ARCHAEOLOGICAL SITE AND ANTIQUARIUM
Castello dell'Abbazia, Vulci
Finds from local excavations.
Tu.-Su. 9.30-4.30.

IVORY COAST

With a population of a little over four million, divided into a large number of tribal and ethnic groups, and an economy based almost entirely on coffee, cocoa, timber and bananas, it would seem proper for the Ivory Coast to concentrate its museum resources on collecting ethnographical material, and this is exactly what has happened.

ABIDJAN

MUSEUM OF THE CENTRE DES SCIENCES HUMAINES
(IFAN), B.P. 1600, Abidjan
Ethnography. Masks. Statues. Ritual requisites. Musical instruments.
Daily ex. M. 9-12, 2.30-5.30.

JAMAICA

The history of Jamaica, as has been pointed out often enough, is largely the history of slavery, sugar and the British navy, and all three are generously, if not always entirely objectively, documented in the island's museums. So, too, are local natural history and the folksier aspects of native culture, completing the list of flavour-items tourists want to have brought to their attention. Topics such as recent social, political and economic history, which are of great interest to black Jamaicans but unpopular with the travel agencies, are not, as more than one outspoken non-white has emphasised recently, illustrated or discussed by museums.

HALF-WAY TREE

AFRICAN MUSEUM
Devon House, nr. Half-Way Tree
African art and crafts.
M.-Sa. 10-5.

DEVON HOUSE
nr. Half-Way Tree
19th century residence. 17th-19th century paintings and historical relics. Master bedroom furnished with period antiques.
M.-Sa. 10-6.

KINGSTON

EXHIBITION GALLERY
Institute of Jamaica, Tower and West Streets, Kingston
Works by Jamaican artists.
M.-F. 9.30-5; Sa. 9.30-4.

NATURAL HISTORY MUSEUM
Institute of Jamaica, Tower and West Streets, Kingston
Plants and animals, mostly Jamaican. Herbarium contains specimens from the Caribbean and a fine collection of Jamaican fern flora. Birds, reptiles, amphibia, marine invertebrates. Insects. Molluscs. Fossils.
M.-F. 9.30-5; Sa. 9.30-4.

WEST INDIA REFERENCE LIBRARY HISTORICAL GALLERY
West India Reference Library, East Street, Kingston
Jamaican cartography. Water-colours, engravings and aquatints of Jamaica and other West Indian territories. History of Jamaica: the discovery by Columbus; development of the sugar industry and the slave trade; Emancipation movement to freedom in 1838; post Emancipation problems. 17th century tortoise shell work. Documents. Philately. 1st century Roman altarpiece recovered from Kingston Harbour.
M.-Sa. 9.30-5.

SPANISH TOWN

FOLK MUSEUM
Old King's House, Spanish Town Square, Spanish Town
In stables and outbuildings of Old King's House (c.1760). History of Jamaica up to 1872. Folk exhibits include a wattle and thatched cottage and kitchen, a small country shop, and equipment relating to agriculture, carpentry, fishing.
Daily 10-5.

WHITE MARL

ARAWAK MUSEUM
White Marl
Located on Kingston/Spanish Town road, and on the site of the largest known Indian Village, occupied from c.900-1400 A.D. Displays on the early inhabitants of Jamaica. Material from excavations.
Daily 10-5. Closed Christmas Day, Good F. and Easter Su.

PORT ROYAL

PORT ROYAL MUSEUM
Fort Charles, Port Royal
History of Port Royal, particularly during 18th century when most of Britain's famous Admirals served at the Port Royal Station.
The Naval Hospital (1817) is also being restored.
Provisionally M.-Sa. 9.30-5.

ST. ANN

SEVILLE MUSEUM
Seville, St. Ann
House (1745). Relics from the Castle of the first Spanish Governors.
Provisionally: M.-Sa. 9.30-5.

UP PARK CAMP

FORCES MUSEUM
Up Park Camp
Approach from Camp Road through Curphey Gate. Military history. Relics of the Jamaica Militia and the West India Regiment. Relics from World War I.
M.-F. 10-5.

Japan

The number of Japanese museums is growing at a rate equalled only in the United States, a fact which can no doubt be attributed both to the prosperity and to the steady Americanisation of the country. Twenty-five years ago it would hardly have been possible to visit a public art gallery which consisted, on the best American model, of the collections made by Shoyiro Ishibashi, founder of the Bridgestone Tyre Co., or to enjoy the Natural History Museum of the Toyohashi Railway Company; but such evidence of enlightened and public-spirited capitalism is now becoming more common each year, especially as more and more rich people make their collections available to the public at large. It still remains true, however, that, except in large cities, the typically Japanese museum is the Treasure Hall of a shrine or temple, rather than the more didactic and secular type of museum to which Western countries are accustomed.

The Japanese undoubtedly have a flair for museums, and the national tradition makes for a more selective kind of display than one usually finds elsewhere. In art museums especially, the individual object is more important than the collection as a whole. Curators have no scruples about moving even the most precious items back into store after a period on public show. The goods do not all have to be in the shop window at the same time, and the window will, at any given moment, appear sparsely arranged to anyone who has grown up with the bazaar method of presentation which has become traditional in the West. Instead of a wall of paintings or several well-filled cases of porcelain, one is more likely to find ''Vase with wisteria flowers, by Ninsei'', or ''Red and White Plum screen, by Ogala Korin''.

Certain national preferences and peculiarities will be obvious from our list - a fondness for volcano museums and insect museums, for instance. We are aware of no other country which can boast of an Insectarium. And only in Japan have we discovered a museum which is open ''daily, except on rainy days'' or one which announces that there is ''no admittance for minors''. There are tea-cult museums, gold-mining museums, museums devoted to pearl-culture, a baseball museum, a snow museum, a children's Buddhist museum and many excellent museums of natural history, archaeology and the physical sciences. Japan has, too, a pair of museums which it would certainly prefer to have been without - those commemorating the American atomic bombs dropped on Hiroshima and Nagasaki.

One turns away with nostalgia and relief to the museum which contains ''relics of Miss Okichi, loved by T. Harris, the first American consul-general to Japan''.

ABASHIRI-SHI

ABASHIRI MUNICIPAL MUSEUM
Katsuracho, Abashiri-shi, Hokkaido 093
Local industries and social history of the region. Archaeology and ethnology, especially collections from the Moyoro

shell mounds in the suburbs of Abashiri, and articles pertaining to the native tribes of Ainu and Giliak.
Apr.-Sept. Daily 9-5. Oct.-Mar. Daily 9-4. Closed M. and national holidays.

AIKAWA-MACHI

AIKAWA LOCAL MUSEUM
Kitazawa, Oaza, Aikawa-machi, Sado-gun, Niigata-ken 952-15
Collection relating to the Sado Gold Mine: models of deposits, minerals and ores. Documents, maps. Ceramics. Local, social and economic history.
Apr.-Oct. 8.30-5. Nov.-Mar. 9-5. Closed M.

AIZUWAKAMATSU-SHI

BYAKKOTAI MEMORIAL COLLECTION
412 Sekihataotsu, Hachimanaza, Minomachi Oaza, Aizuwakamatsu-shi, Fukushima-ken 965
Material on the Aizu Civil War and Byakkotai, including panoramas and pamphlets, collected in memory of a group of youths, 'Byakkotai', all under 17, who fought and died in the Meiji Restoration of 1868.
Apr.-Nov. Daily 8.30-5. Dec.-Mar. Daily 9-4.

AKAHO-SHI

UNE ARCHAEOLOGICAL COLLECTION
Une, Narahara, Akaho-shi, Okayama-ken
Stone implements. Earthen-ware. Bronze halberds. Tiles. Coffins.
Daily 9-4.

AKASHI-SHI

AKASHI CITY PLANETARIUM & SCIENCE HALL
2-6 Hitomaru-cho, Akashi-shi, Hyogo-ken 673
Planetarium. Science. Industry.
Daily ex. Sa. 9.30-5.30. Aug. Sa. also, 9.30-9. Closed Dec. 26-Jan. 1.

MEMORIAL HALL OF THE EMPEROR MEIJI'S TEMPORARY HEADQUARTERS AT AKASHI
Kajiya-machi, Akashi-shi, Hyogo-ken
Treasures and possessions of the Emperor Meiji.
On request.

AKITA-SHI

AKITA CITY MUSEUM OF ART
Senshu Park, Akita-shi, Akita-ken 010
Built to commemorate Japan's entry into the United Nations. Folklore. Handicrafts. Popular art.
Daily ex. M. 9-4. Closed Dec. 24-Jan. 3.

MUSEUM OF AKITA UNIVERSITY, FACULTY OF MINING
28-2 Ozawa, Tegata-aza, Akita-shi, Akita-ken 010
Minerals. Rocks. Fossils. Jewels. Models of mines.
Apr. 30-Nov. 1, Daily ex. Su. 9-4. Nov. 15-Apr. 15, M.-F. 9-4; Sa. 9-12. Closed Dec. 28-Jan. 4.

AKKESHI-MACHI

AKKESHI MUSEUM OF HOKKAIDO UNIVERSITY
Akkeshi-machi, Kushirokoku-shicho, Hokkaido
Specimens of mammals, birds, plants, aquatic animals and plants, minerals and fossils.
May-Oct. Daily 8.30-5. Closed winter.

AKO-MACHI

NATIONAL PEARL RESEARCH INSTITUTE EXHIBITION ROOM
Kashikojima, Ako-machi, Shima-gun, Mie-ken 571-05
Materials illustrating the cultivating, processing, utilisation, construction and history of pearl culture.
Daily 9-3. Closed Sa. afternoon, Su., national holidays and Dec. 28-Jan. 3.

ARITA-MACHI

ARITA CHINA-WARE ART MUSEUM
1356 Arita-cho, Nishimatsu-ura gun, Saga-ken 844
Porcelain of Imari, Kakiemon and Nabeshima schools. History of porcelain in Hizen (Saga) district.
Daily ex. M. 9-5. Closed Dec. 28-Jan. 3.

ASAHIKAWA-SHI

ASAHIKAWA LOCAL MUSEUM
1 chome, 1 jo, 4-Ku Asahikawa-shi, Hokkaido 070
Local products. Specimens of fish, birds, insects, mammals and plants from Mt. Daisetsu. Ainu folk art objects.
Daily 9.30-4.30. Closed M. and national holidays. also closed Dec. 28-Jan. 3

ASAHI-MACHI

MIYAZAKI OPEN-AIR MUSEUM
Miyashiko, Asahi-machi, Shimoni'ikawa-gun, Toyama-ken 939-07
Specimens of birds, fossils and rocks. The open-air section includes Kashima Natural Forest, Tomari and Sasagawa Stratum (where fossils may be found) and ruins of Miyazaki Castle.
Daily except M. 8-5.

ATAMI-SHI

ATAMI ART MUSEUM
26-1 Momoyamacho, Atami-shi, Shizuoka-ken
Japanese, Chinese and Korean art. Sculptures. Calligraphy. Paintings, Handicrafts. Screens, including 'Red and White Plum' by Ogata Korin. Porcelain, including vase with wisteria flowers by Ninsei.
Daily ex. Th. 9-4. Closed Dec. 24-Jan. 3.

BEPPU-SHI

ANCIENT CULTURE MUSEUM, BEPPU UNIVERSITY
c/o Beppu-Daigaku, 82 Kita ishigaki, Beppu-shi, Oita-ken 874
Fine arts. Objects relating to the ancient culture of Japan.
Daily 8-5.

BEPPU MUNICIPAL MUSEUM OF ART
Beppu, Beppu-shi, Oita-ken 874
Modern Japanese paintings.
Apr.-Oct. 8.30-5 daily. Nov.-Mar. Daily 9-5. Closed M., National Holidays and New Year season.

KINSUIEN ART MUSEUM
1,006-1 Matogahama-kaigan, Beppu-shi, Ojta-ken 874
Armour, weapons, handicrafts, sculptures, paintings, gourds collected by the owner of the Hotel Kinsuien.
Many ukiyoe prints and documents on sexual themes are not generally accessible.
Daily 9-10 p.m. No admittance for minors.

CHIKUFUJIMA

TREASURE HOUSE ON SHIKUFUJIMA ISLANDS
Chikufujima, Higashi-Asai-gun, Shiga-ken 526-01
Attached to the temple, the collection includes part of the Sutra of the lotus, portraits of 16 of Buddha's disciples, a painting of the coming down of Amita Buddha to welcome the spirit of his believer; paintings of Avalokitesvara with Cintama on silk canvas; swords and sutras.
Daily 9-5.

CHINO-SHI

TOGARI'ISHI ARCHAEOLOGICAL MUSEUM
Minamioshio, Chino-shi, Nagano-ken 391-02
Large collection of findings from the ruins of Togari'ishi in the foothills of Yatsugadake.
Daily 9-5. Closed Dec. 29-Jan. 3.

CHIYODA-MACHI

GEIHOKU ETHNOGRAPHICAL MUSEUM
650-1 Oaza-arita, Chiyoda-machi, Yamagata-gun, Hiroshima-ken 731-15
Folk art material.
Daily on request.

DAZAIFU-MACHI

TREASURE HOUSE OF THE DAZAIFU-TENMANGU SHRINE
1114 Daizaifu Oaza, Dazaifu-machi, Tsukushi-gun, Fukuoka-ken 818-01
Books, writings, pictures, artistic crafts, swords and other religious items.
Daily 8.30-5.

EBINA-MACHI

EBINA ARCHAEOLOGICAL COLLECTION
1931 Kokubu, Ebina-machi, Koza-gun, Kanagawa-ken 243
Relics of local archaeological interest.
Apr.-Dec. 25, Daily 10-4. Closed Su., National Holidays.

ENGARU-MACHI

KATEI-GAKKO MUSEUM OF LOCAL HISTORY
34 Tomeokaaza, Engaru-machi, Monbetsu-gun, Hokkaido 099-04
Stone implements. Earthenware. Animals and plants.
Daily 8-6.

FUEDA

ART GALLERY OF THE TOKIWAYAMA FOUNDATION
Fueda, Kamakura, Fueda
Japanese and Chinese sculpture, painting, handicrafts and calligraphy.
Weekends only.

FUKAE-SHI

GOSHA SHRINE HISTORICAL COLLECTION
Kamiotsu-machi, Fukae-shi, Nagasaki-ken 853
Earthenware. Mirrors. Manuscripts. Documents.
On request.

FUKUI-SHI

FUKUI HISTORY HALL
1-8-16 Asuwa, Fukui-shi, Fukui-ken 910
Local archaeology, history and folk art. Documents and records on native people of the Fukui Prefecture.

FUKUI MUNICIPAL NATURAL HISTORY MUSEUM
147 Ashibakami-machi, Fukui-shi, Fukui-ken 910
Local zoology, botany and physical geography.
Apr.-Oct. Daily ex. M. 9-5. Nov.-Mar. Daily ex. Su. and national holidays, 9-4.

FUKUI PREFECTURAL OKAJIMA MEMORIAL ART HALL
3-11-13 Hoei, Fukui-shi, Fukui-ken 910
Bronze Buddhist sculpture. Coins. Handicrafts. Musical instruments.
Apr.-Sept. 9-4.30 daily. Oct.-Mar. Daily 9.30-4.30. Closed M., New Year Season and National Holidays.

FUKUOKA-SHI

TREASURE HOUSE OF THE HAKOZAKI SHRINE
Hakozaki-machi, Fukuoka-ku, Fukuoka-shi, Fukuoka-ken 812
Historical documents, calligraphy and swords, housed in a 16th century building.
Daily 9-4.

FUTTSU

FUTTSU OCEANOGRAPHIC MUSEUM OF CHIBA PREFECTURE
2280 Futtsu, Futtsu-cho, Kimitsu-gun, Chiba-ken 299-13
Models and photographs of ships, fishing equipment, the belongings of fisher-women. Specimens of shells, fishes and plants. Palaeontology. Zoology. Oceanography.
Daily 9-4. Closed Sa. afternoon, Su., national holidays and Dec. 28-Jan. 3.

GIFU-SHI

GIFU CHILDREN'S SCIENCE HALL
251 Ochiya, Gifu-shi, Gifu-ken 500
Material showing the principles of electric power generation, power transmission, electric supply, communication, motive power, transport and water service.
Daily 9.30-5.30. Closed M., day after national holidays and Dec. 29-Jan. 3.

LOCAL MUSEUM OF GIFU UNIVERSITY
1466 Jonouchi, Nagarajo, Gifu-shi, Gifu-ken 500
Materials on the history, archaeology and documentation of the region.
Daily 9-5.

NAWA INSECT MUSEUM
Gifu-koen, 2 Omiya-machi, Gifu-shi, Gifu-ken 500
Collection of insect specimens.
Apr.-Oct. Daily 9-5.30. Nov.-Mar. Daily 9-4.

HAGI-SHI

HAGI LOCAL MUSEUM
525-4 Eko, Oaza, Hagi-shi, Yamuguchi-ken 758
Zoology. Botany. Geology. Mineralogy. Meteorology. Astronomy. Local history. Fine art.
Mar.-Oct. Daily 8.30-5. Nov.-Feb. Daily 8.30-4.30. Closed M. and national holidays, also Dec. 28-Jan. 3.

HAGURO-MACHI

TREASURE HOUSE OF THE DEWA-SANZAN SHRINE
33 Haguroyama, Temuki-aza, Haguromachi-oaza, Higashi-tagawa-gun, Yamagata-ken 997-02
Treasures of the Shrines of Gassan, Yudonosan and Dewa. Mirrors. Mountaineering exhibits.
Mar.-Sept. Daily 8-5. Oct.-Dec. Daily 9-5. Closed Jan. 1-Mar. 19.

HAKODATE-SHI

HAKODATE MUNICIPAL MUSEUM
Aoyagi-cho, Hakodate-shi, Hokkaido 040
Oldest local museum in Japan. Archaeology. Anthropology. Ethnography, including articles of the Ainu, Giliak and other native tribes. Natural science of Hokkaido. Botany. Zoology. Geology. Palaeontology. Collections left by foreigners, including Horace Capron, Walter Whitman, Edward Morris, who lived in Japan in the early days of Hokkaido.
Apr.-Sept. daily 9-4.30. Oct.-Mar. daily 9-4. Closed M. and end of each month, also national holidays.

HAKONE-MACHI

GORA PARK HAKONE NATURAL HISTORY MUSEUM
1300 Gora, Hakone-machi, Ashigara-shimo-gun, Kanagawa-ken 250-04
Model of Hakone volcanoes. Diorama showing animals and plants of the district.
Sept.-July 19, Daily 9-5. July 20 - Aug. Daily 9-9.

HAKONE MUSEUM
79 Hakone, Hakone-machi, Ashigara-shimo-gun, Kanagawa-ken 250-05
Historical material on the Hakone Sekisho (Hakone barrier-guard).
Daily 9-4. Closed Dec. 16 - Mar. 15.

HAKONE ART MUSEUM
1,300 Gora, Hakone-machi, Ashigara-shimo-gun, Kanagawa-ken 250-04
Modern and ancient Japanese paintings. Chinese paintings. Calligraphy. Ceramics. China. Metalwork. Wooden and stone sculptures.
Daily ex. Th. 9-4. Closed Dec. 1 - Mar. 31.

OPEN AIR MUSEUM
Hakone-machi, Ashigara-shimo-gun, Kanagawa-ken 250-04
Sculptures.
Daily ex. Th. 9-4. Closed Dec. 24 - Jan. 3.

TREASURE HOUSE OF THE HAKONE SHRINE
Motohakone, Hakone-machi, Kanagawa-ken 250-04
Exhibits include a picture scroll "Incarnation of Buddha to Hakone", image of Saint Mangan and other artistic items and historical documents.
Daily 8-5.

HAMAMATSU-SHI

HAMAMATSU CITY MUSEUM
49-2 Motoshiro-machi, Hamamatsu-shi, Shizuoka-ken 430
Exhibits from Shijimizuka-kaizuka (Shijimizuka shell mounds) and the ruins of Iba.
Apr.-Oct. Daily 8-5.30. Nov.- Mar. Daily 9-4. Closed M. and the day after national holidays, also Dec. 29 - Jan. 4.

HANAMAKI-SHI

TIBETAN COLLECTION ATTACHED TO THE KOTOKUJI TEMPLE
95 Minamigawa-machi, Hanamaki-shi, Iwate-ken 025
Buddhist statues, pictures, Sutras. Altar fittings from Tibet and articles concerning the Dalai Lama.
On demand.

HATANO-SHI

KOAN COLLECTION
1,393 Tsurumaki, Hatano-shi, Kanagawa-ken
Folk art objects.
Daily 10-4.

HIKONE-SHI

ECONOMIC DOCUMENT COLLECTION
Faculty of Economics, Shiga University, 1-1-1 Baba, Hikone-shi, Shiga-ken 522
Material on the social and economic history of modern Japan.
Daily 9-4.30. Closed Su. and National Holidays.

HIKONE CASTLE COLLECTION
Kinkame-cho, Hikone-shi, Shiga-ken 522
Weapons and furniture of the I'I family, former lords of Hikone Castle.
Daily 8.30-5.

I'I ART MUSEUM
Hikonejo-nai, 1 Kinki, Hikone-shi, Shiga-ken
Paintings. China. Weapons. Lacquer ware. Noh masks. Musical instruments.
Daily 9-5. Closed M.

PRIME MINISTER I'I MEMORIAL COLLECTION
515 Matsubara-cho, Hikone-shi, Shiga-ken
Personal relics and writings of Naosuke I'I, the prime minister at the end of the Tokugawa régime.
Daily 9-5. Closed M.

HIRADO-SHI

MATSURA HISTORICAL MUSEUM
12 Kagami kawa-machi, Hirado-shi, Nagasaki-ken 889-51
Items relating to the history of Hirado. Relics and furniture of the Matsura clan, former feudal lords. Objects regarding Japan-Netherlands Treaty in the post-Edo era.
Apr.-Nov. Daily 8.30-5. Dec.-Mar. Daily 9-4. Closed Dec. 29 - Jan. 1.

HIRAIDE

HIRAIDE KOKOHAKUBUTSUKAN
Soga-ku, Shiojiri-shi, Hiraide
Historic site.
On request.

HIRAIZUMI-MACHI

TREASURE HOUSE OF THE CHUSONJI TEMPLE
48 Iseki, Hiraizumi-aza, Hiraizumi-machi, Nishiban-i-gun, Iwate-ken 029-41
Buddhist statues, pictures and altar fittings, including statues of Ichijikonrinbutsu, Amithava, Shaka and Yakushi. Konjikido ("glittering hall"). Treasures mostly date from the late period of Heian (801-1185).
Daily 8.30-4.30.

HIRATA-SHI

TREASURE HOUSE OF THE WANIBUCHIJI TEMPLE
Bessho-machi, Hirata-shi, Shimane-ken 691
The temple was founded in the 8th century, reconstructed in the Edo era. The treasure house contains many articles of great value.
Daily except rainy days and rainy season.

HIROSHIMA-SHI

HIROSHIMA PEACE MEMORIAL MUSEUM
Zaimoku-cho, Hiroshima-shi
Manuscripts, documents and photographs on the destruction and suffering caused by the A-bomb. Data on atomic energy for peaceful purposes.
Daily 9-4.30. Closed New Year Season.

HIWA-MACHI

HIWA MUSEUM OF NATURAL HISTORY
Hiwa Oaza, Hiwa-machi, Hiba-gun, Hiroshima-ken 727-03
Mammals. Plants. Minerals.
Apr.-Dec. Daily 9-5. Jan.-Mar. Daily 9.30-5. Closed Su.

HOJO-SHI

KASHIMA MUSEUM
1596-1, Hojo-shi, Ehime-ken 779-24
Marine shells and fish. Minerals. Fossils. Weapons. Pottery from local excavations.
Daily 8.30-5.

HON-YABEKEI-MACHI

YABAKEI MEMORIAL COLLECTION
Shosui-en, Hon-yabekei-machi, Oita-ken 871-02
Local history of the Yabakei valley.
Daily 9-5.

HORAI-MACHI

NATURAL HISTORY MUSEUM OF TOYOHASHI RAILWAY COMPANY
16 Horai-machi, Minamishidara-gun, Aichi-ken
Collection of animals, plants and minerals.
Daily 8-4.

HOROBETSU-MACHI

NOBORIBETSU HOT SPRING MUSEUM
Noboribetsu, Horobetsu-machi, Hokkaido-ken
Material showing the relationship between volcanoes and hot springs, faults and hot springs, medical effects of hot springs and geysers.
June-Oct. Daily 8-8. Nov.-May Daily 8-5.

IBURI-SHICHO

FOREST MUSEUM OF TOYA NATIONAL PARK
Sobetsu-mura, Usu-gun, Iburi-shicho, Hokkaido-ken
The collection includes statistical tables and charts, diorama, panorama showing forestry and forest, mounted forest animals.
Daily 9-5 May-Oct.

THE VOLCANO MUSEUM
Sobetsu-mura, Usu-gun, Iburi-shicho, Hokkaido-ken
Material illustrating the eruptions of Showa Shinzan and its characteristic volcanic activities; models; data.
Apr. 20 - Nov. Daily 7-6.

ICHINOMIYA-SHI

MAMIZUKA ARCHAEOLOGICAL COLLECTION
Mamizuka, Ichinomiya-shi, Aichi-ken 491
Finds from the ruins of Mamizuka, especially coffins.
Daily 9-5.

IKARUGA-MACHI

TREASURE HOUSE OF THE HORYUJI TEMPLE
Horyuji, Ikaruga-machi, Ikegome-gun, Nara-ken 636-01
Horyuji is among the most important temples, consisting of two groups, the East and West temples, regarded generally as the oldest wooden structures in the world. Founded by Prince Shotoku in 607, and contains many treasures of great value.
Mar. 11 - Nov. 19, Daily 8-5. Nov. 20 - Mar. 10, Daily 8-4.30.

IKOMASAN

ASTRONOMICAL MUSEUM
2006 Toyoura-cho, Hiraoka-shi, Ikomasan
Planetarium. Astronomy.
Daily ex. M. 9-4. Closed Dec. 24 - Jan. 3.

INAWASHIO-MACHI

DR. HIDEYO NOGUCHI MEMORIAL MUSEUM
Mitsushirogata, Inawashio-machi, Yaba-gun, Fukishima-ken 969-32
Exhibits relating to Dr. Hideyo Noguchi.
Apr.-Oct. Daily 8-5. Nov.-Mar. Daily 8-4. Closed Jan. 1-3.

ISE-SHI

JINGU HISTORICAL AND AGRICULTURAL MUSEUM
1728 Kushimotocho, Kanda, Ise-shi, Mie-ken 516
Treasures of the Ise Grand Shrine (Naigu Shrine and Gegu Shrine), objects of historical interest including paintings, drawings, sculptures and old documents. Items connected with agriculture, forestry, fishing and gardening. Over 40 species of shark.
Mar.-Nov. Daily 8.30-4.30. Dec.-Feb. Daily 8.30-4. Closed Dec. 28 - 31.

ISHAZAKI-SHI

AIKAWA ARCHAEOLOGICAL COLLECTION
6-10 Sanko-cho, Ishizaki-shi, Gunma-ken 372
Relics of prehistoric and proto-historic age. Old documents. Armour. Weapons.
1st, 3rd and 4th Su. in month; also Sa. afternoons.

ISHIKAWA-GUN

ABUKUMA ARCHAEOLOGICAL COLLECTION
Tamagawa-mura, Ishikawa-gun, Fukushima-ken
Archaeological relics excavated from north-east Japan.
Daytime.

ISHIMAKI-SHI

MARUTOSHI ART MUSEUM
2-8-1 Chuo, Ishimaki-shi, Miyagi-ken 986
A part of Kankeimaru Department Store which is used as a museum to exhibit Japanese china and pottery.
Daily 9-6. Closed 1st and 3rd Th. in month.

ISHINOMAKI-SHI

ENDO-MORI ARCHAEOLOGICAL COLLECTION OF ISHINOMAKI
1-8-29 Sumiyoshi-cho, Ishinomaki-shi, Miyagi-ken 986
Stone Age tools, Haniwa (terra-cotta tomb figure). Industrial art of Tumli period.
Any time by appointment.

ITOIGAWA-SHI

GYOFU SOMA MEMORIAL COLLECTION
52-1 Omachi Oaza, Itoigawa-shi, Ni'igata-ken 941
Folk art. Archaeological exhibits.
Daily 9-4. Closed Sa. afternoon, Su., national holidays.

IWAKI-SHI

NAKASO ART MUSEUM
60 Iritabane, Sekiden, Nakoso-cho, Iwaki-shi, Fukushima-ken 979-01
Earthenware. Armour. Weapons. Calligraphy and paintings. Buddhist sculptures and handicrafts.
Daily 9-5.

IWAKUNI-SHI

IWAKUNI MUNICIPAL MUSEUM
2-7-19 Yokoyama, Iwakuni-shi, Yamaguchi-ken 741
Historical material on the old Iwakuni clan, and possessions of the former feudal lord.
Daily 9-4.30. Closed M. and day after national holidays, also Dec. 28 - Jan. 5. Tu. 1-4.30.

IWATA-SHI

IWATA LOCAL MUSEUM
245-2 Mitsuke, Iwata-shi, Shizuoka-ken 424
Folk art. Archaeological collection, especially historical relics found at the site of Kokubunji.
Daily 9-5. Closed M. and day after national holidays, also Dec. 28 - Jan. 5.

IZUMOZAKI-MACHI

RYOKAN MEMORIAL COLLECTION
Komeda Oaza, Izumozaki-machi, Santo-gun, Nigata-ken 949-43
Relics of the priest, Ryokan, a famous poet and calligrapher in the Edo period.
Daily 9-4.

KAGOSHIMA-SHI

KAGOSHIMA MUNICIPAL MUSEUM OF ART
4-36 Shiroyame-cho, Kagoshima-shi, Kagoshima-ken 892
Paintings and sculptures, especially those by Seiki Kuroda, forerunner of oil painting in Japan.
Daily 9-4.30. Closed M., National Holidays and New Year season.

KAGOSHIMA PREFECTURAL MUSEUM
1-5 Shiroyamacho, Kagoshima-shi, Kagoshima-ken 892
Natural science. Archaeology. Ethnology. Objects relating to the explosion of Mt. Sakura-jima.
Daily 9-5. Closed M., every 15th of month, National Holidays, also Nov. 10-25 and Dec. 28-Jan. 3.

SHOKO SHUSEI-KAN MEMORIAL COLLECTION
Yoshino-machi Iso, Kagoshima-shi, Kagoshima-ken 892
Exhibits relating to the Meiji Restoration and the Shimazu family.
Mar. 16 - Nov. 30, Daily 8.30-5.30. Dec. 1 - Mar. 15, Daily 8.30-5.

KAKUDATE-MACHI

PUBLIC LIFE EXHIBITION HALL
Iwase, Kakudate-machi, Senboku-gun, Akita-ken
Archaeological material, earthenware, stone implements. Ethnography. Agricultural implements. Fishing tackle for river fish. Hunting implements. Toys. Lighting equipment.
Daily 8.30-4. Closed Su. and National Holidays.

KAMAKURA-SHI

KAMAKURA NATIONAL TREASURE HOUSE
2-1-1 Yukinoshita, Kamakura-shi, Kanagawa-ken 248
Sculptures, paintings, handicrafts and documents concerning Kamakura city and other places in the prefecture are stored at the Treasure House "to protect them from natural disasters". Japanese works produced in the Kamakura and Muromachi periods. Chinese items of the Sung and Yuan periods.
Jan.-Dec. 27, Daily 9-5. Closed M. and national holidays.

MODERN ART MUSEUM OF KANAGAWA PREFECTURE
1,051 Yukinoshita, Kamakura-shi, Kanagawa-ken 248
Modern art, from Japan and other countries.
Daily 9-4. Open until 4.30 Sa. and Su. Closed M. also Dec. 28 - Jan. 3.

TOKIWAYAMA COLLECTION
1933 Fueta, Kamakura-shi, Kanagawa-ken 248
Collection of paintings, sculpture, handicrafts, calligraphy. Documents on shrines.
Su. and National Holidays 10-4; Sa. 1-4.

TREASURE HALL OF THE KAMAKURAGU SHRINE
154 Nikaido, Kamakura-shi, Kanagawa-ken 248
Articles relating to the Imperial Prince Yoshinaga, the enshrined Deity.
Daily 8-5.

TREASURE HOUSE OF THE TSURUGAOKA-HACHIMAN SHRINE
2-1-31 Yukinoshita, Kamakura-shi, Kanagawa-ken 248
Historic relics. Masks for court dances and music. Weapons. Crafts.
Apr.-Sept. Daily 8-5. Oct.-Mar. Daily 9-4. Closed Sept. 15.

KAMEYAMA-SHI

KAMEYAMA HISTORICAL COLLECTION
545 Nishimaru-cho, Kameyama-shi, Mie-ken 519-01
Samurai Estate at the end of the Edo period. Weapons and furnishings from the feudal period.
Daily 9-4. Closed M. and the day after National holidays.

KAMINOYAMA-SHI

KAISENDO MUSEUM
Taka-machi, Kaminoyama-shi
Lacquer-ware. Swords.
Daily ex. M. 9-4. Closed Dec. 24 - Jan. 3.

KAMIYAMA-SHI

KANISENDO MUSEUM
277 Tanaka, Tokamachi aza, Kamiyama-shi, Yamagata-ken 999-31
Swords. Armour. Lacquer-ware, including especially Chinese items.
Apr.-Nov. 9-5. Dec.-Mar. 9-4 daily. Closed F. and Dec. 25 - Jan. 10.

KAMO-GUN

CHOHACHI MEMORIAL COLLECTION
c/o Jokanji, Matsuzaki-cho, Kamo-gun, Shizuoka-ken 410-36
Works by Chohachi Irie, a famous plasterer from the end of the Edo Period to the early years of Meiji.
Daily 8-5.

KANAZAWA-MACHI

KANAZAWA BUNKO MUSEUM
217 Kanazawa-machi, Yokohama-shi, Kanagawa-ken 236
Fine arts exhibits. Paintings. Documents. Sculpture designated as national treasures, including images of Buddha.
Daily ex. M. 9-4.30. Closed national holidays and Dec. 28 - Jan. 4.

KANAZAWA-SHI

SEISONKAKU
1-2 Eirokucho, Kanazawa-shi, Ishikawa-ken 920
Building built 1863 by Mariyasu Maeda, former lord of the castle, as a retreat for his mother, and now containing articles handed down in the Maeda family.
Daily 8.30-4.30. Closed 1st and 3rd M. in month, also Dec. 29 - Jan. 2.

KARATSU-SHI

OGASAWARA MEMORIAL HALL
Nishidera-machi, Karatsu-shi, Saga-ken
Articles belonging to the Ogasawara family, former feudal lords.
Apr.-Sept. Daily 9-6. Oct.-Mar. Daily 9-5.

KARIHA-GUN

TEA CULT MUSEUM
Okano-cho, Takayanagi-cho, Kariha-gun, Ni'igata-ken
Housed in wooden building converted from a warehouse of the feudal period. 17th-19th century fine arts, documents, china, vases, pitchers relating to the tea cult.
10 May - 20 Oct. Daily 9-5. Closed M. and when wind and rain are strong.

KASAI-SHI

TREASURE HOUSE OF THE ICHIJOJI TEMPLE
Sakomoto, Kasai-shi, Hyogo-ken 675-22
Art objects, including picture of the Imperial Prince Shotoku and high priests (national treasure), picture of Amithava and statue of Amithava.
Sa. and Su. 11-5.

KASAMA-SHI

KASAMA MUNICIPAL MUSEUM OF ART
Sahakukoen, Kasama-shi, Ibaraki-ken 309-16
Many Buddhist images are kept at temples around Kasama City and reproductions of these have been made in case they are destroyed by disaster. These reproductions are exhibited in the Museum of Art.
By appointment.

KASAMATSU-MACHI

KASAMATSU JUNIOR HIGH SCHOOL SCIENCE MUSEUM
Kasamatsu Middle School, Kasamatsu-machi, Hashima-gun, Gifu-ken 501-61
Materials prepared for teaching purposes on natural science, mostly collected by pupils, including zoology, botany, geology, astronomy, meteorology, physics, chemistry, food, clothing and housing.
During school hours.

KASHIMA-MACHI

TREASURE HALL OF THE KASHIMA SHRINE
2403 Guchu, Kashima-machi, Kashima-gun, Ibaraki-ken 314
Statues. Weapons. Altar fittings.
Daily 9-4.

KASHIMA-SHI

YUTOKU MUSEUM
1686 Otsu Furueda, Kashima-shi, Saga-ken 849-15
Shrine treasures. Feudal daimyo's everyday articles. Archaeological relics.
Daily 8-5.

KASHIWARA-SHI

YAMATO HISTORICAL MUSEUM
Unebi-machi, Kashiwara-shi, Nara-ken
Findings from the site of ancient dwellings.
Jan. 6 - Dec. 25, Daily 9-4.30. Closed Tu., National Holidays and M. afternoons.

KAWAGUCHIKO-MACHI

FUJI MUSEUM
Funatsu, Kawaguchiko-machi, Minamitsuru-gun, Yamanashi-ken 410-03
Local collections. Archaeological relics. Domestic utensils. Specimens of animals and plants.
Daily ex. Tu. 8-5. Closed Jan. 1-3.

KAWANISHI-CHO

KIKUSUI HANDICRAFT MUSEUM
2,911 Nakakomatsu, Kawanishi-cho, Tochishi-gun, Yamagata-ken 999-01
Bronze-ware. Wooden Buddhist images and armour from Japan, Korea and China.
Daily 9-4. Closed Dec. 1 - Apr. 15.

KAWANISHI-MURA

IZUMIDA LOCAL MUSEUM
Dainichidokyonai, Koizumi, Kawanishi-mura, Nagano-ken 386-11
Finds from the Tumuli period. Archaeological relics.
By appointment.

KESEN'NUMA-SHI

KESEN'NUMA MUSEUM OF MARINE PRODUCTS
167 Ikkeijima, Kesen'numa-shi, Miyagi-ken
Occupies two room of the Fisheries High School building. The collection includes models of nets, fishing-boats. Specimens of fish.
Daily 9-4.

KIBI-GUN

KIBI ARCHAEOLOGICAL COLLECTION
Jitokatayama Oaza, Yamate-mura, Shinbi-cho, Kibi-gun, Okayama-ken 701-03
Jomon and Yayoi pottery. Stone implements.
On request.

KIKUCHI-SHI

TREASURE HOUSE OF THE KIKUCHI SHRINE
Kikuchijinjanai, 1257 Waifu, Kikuchi-shi, Kumamoto-ken 861-13
Pictures. Sculpture. Crafts. Historical documents.
Apr.-Oct. Daily 8-5. Nov.-Mar. Daily 9-4.

KISARAZU-SHI

EXCAVATED COLLECTION OF KINREIZUKA
361 Ota, Kisarazu-shi, Chiba-ken 292
Finds from the Kinrezuka burial mounds of Zenpo-Koen-Fun.
Daily 9-4.30. Closed M. afternoon and Tu., also Dec. 28-Jan. 3.

KISO-GUN

TOSON SHIMAZAKI MEMORIAL HALL
4256-1 Kamisaka, Yamaguchi-mura aza, Kiso-gun, Nagano-ken 399-52
Manuscripts and mementoes of the novelist Toson Shimazaki.
Daily 8-5. Closed Dec. 28-31.

KITAKYU-SHU-SHI

YAHATA MUNICIPAL ART AND HANDICRAFT MUSEUM
2-6-4 Okura, Yahata-ku, Kitakyu-shu-shi, Fukuoka-ken 805
Japanese art, handicrafts.
Daily ex. M. 10-6. Closed national holidays and Dec. 29-Jan. 3.

KOBE-SHI

HAKUTSURU ART MUSEUM
1545 Ochiai, Sumujoshi-cho, Higashinada-ku, Kobe-shi, Hyogo-ken 658
Chinese bronze vessels of Shang and Chou dynasties. T'ang mirrors and silverware. T'ang, Sung and Ming ceramics. Works by Nara craftsmen. Paintings, Handicrafts. Archaeology.
Daily ex. M. Apr.-May 10-5. Aug. 15-Nov. 14, 10-4.

KOBE MUNICIPAL MUSEUM OF ART
1-35 Kumanai-cho, Fukiai-ku, Kobe-shi, Hyogo-ken 651
Collection of Nanban paintings and prints, calligraphy and documents relating to General Masashige Kusunoki. Armour. Religious and commercial history of the Nanban arts, includings Christian relics, paintings, wood-cuts, copper-plate prints (19th century) and handicrafts. Early Japanese paintings in Western style.
Daily ex. M. 9-4.30. Closed from 25th of each month, also Dec. 21-Jan. 4 and Aug. 1-31.

INTERNATIONAL PORTS AND HARBOURS MUSEUM
Naka-Tottai, Ikuta-ku, Kobe-shi, Hyogo-ken 651
History of shipping and of ports.
By appointment.

KOCHI-SHI

KAITOKUKAN HISTORICAL COLLECTION
1, Marunouchi, Kochi-shi, Kochi-ken 780
The Kochi Castle Tower and the palace of the lord of the Kochi clan, built in the Edo period. Archaeology. Folk art. Animals. Plants.
Daily 8-30-5. Closed from 16th to end of month.

KOCHI-NAGANO-SHI

TREASURE HOUSE OF THE KANSHINJI TEMPLE
Kanshinji Kyonai, Teramoto, Kochi-nagano-shi, Osaka-fu 586
Material concerning the Kusunokis, Gozoku of this province in 14th century. Buddhist statues. Sutras. Altar fittings. Weapons.
Daily 9.30-5.

KOJIMA-SHI

GORYU BUDDHISTIC MUSEUM
952 Hayashi, Kojima-shi, Okayama-ken 710-01
Collections illustrating the monastery life of Buddhist monks.
On request.

KOKUBUNJI

KOKUBUNKI-MACHI BUNKAZARI HOZONKAI
1631 Kokubunji, Kitatala-gun
Historic site.
Daily ex. M. 9-4. Closed Dec. 24-Jan. 3.

KOMAGANE-SHI

AKAHO MUSEUM
2423-6 Akaho, Komagane-shi, Nagano-ken 399-41
Botany. History. Archaeology. Alpine flora of Mt. Komagatake. Relics and earthenware excavated from tomb near Komagane. Regional history.
Daily 10-6. Closed M. and end of month, also national holidays. Closed Dec. 28-Jan. 3.

KOMATSU-SHI

KOMATSU MUNICIPAL MUSEUM
Ashiki Park, Komatsu-shi, Ishikawa-ken 923
Natural history. Botany. Minerals. Rocks. History. Archaeology.
Apr.-Oct. Daily 9-5. Nov.-Mar. Daily 9-6. Closed M. and national holidays. Closed Dec. 29-Jan. 3.

TREASURE HOUSE OF THE NAYAJI TEMPLE
Naya-machi, Komatsu-shi, Ishikawa-ken
The main hall, three-storied pagoda, Homa Hall and belfry of the Temple are all designated artistic monuments.
Daily 8-5.

KORIYAMA-SHI

WATANABE SHINPO MEMORIAL HALL
Minami-cho, Koriyama-shi, Fukushima-ken
Collections of calligraphy and paintings of Japan and China belonging to Mr. Watanabe (1867-1938) and of his own works of art.
On request.

KOTOHIRA-MACHI

KOTOHIRA MUSEUM
892 Kotohira-machi, Nakatado-gun, Kagawa-ken 766
Shrine treasures, including armour and Buddhist images. Sculpture. Paintings.
Apr.-Sept. Daily 8-4. Oct.-Mar. Daily 9-4.

KOYA-SAN

TREASURE HOUSE OF THE TEMPLES ON MT. KOYA
on Mt. Koya, Koya-san, Ito-gun, Wakayama-ken
Exhibit rooms in Azekura style of architecture, housing Buddhist statues, pictures, Sutras and altar fittings. Centre of Buddhism in Japan.
Feb.-Apr. Daily 9-4. May-Sept. Daily 8-5. Closed Dec. 28-Jan. 31.

KUMAMOTO-SHI

KUMAMOTO MUSEUM
7-17 Hanabatake-cho, Kumamoto-shi, Kumamoto-ken 860
Archaeology. Folklore. Botany. Mineralogy. Technology, especially in Kumamoto prefecture. Historical collections relating to Mt. Aso.
Daily 9-5. Closed M. and national holidays, also Nov. 11-15, Dec. 26-Jan. 5.

TREASURE HOUSE OF THE HONMYOJI TEMPLE
6 Hanazono-machi, Kumamoto-shi, Kumamoto-ken 860
Articles related to the founder of the Temple, Kiyomasa Kato. Armour and weapons. Pictures. Calligraphy. Furnishings. Buddhist statues.
Daily 9-5 (until 4 Nov.-Mar.) Closed M., Dec. 28-31.

KURASHIKI-SHI

KURASHIKI ARCHAEOLOGICAL MUSEUM
1,015 Maegami-cho, Kurashiki-shi, Okayama-ken 710
Local archaeological discoveries.
Daily 9-4. Closed M., also Su. of Spring and Autumn Festival, Emperor's Birthday, and Dec. 30-Jan. 3.

KURASHIKI HANDICRAFT MUSEUM
Maegami-cho, Kurashiki-shi, Okayama-ken 710
Old warehouse of the Edo period converted into a museum for displaying handicrafts from Japan and other countries.
Daily 9-4. Closed M., Emperor's birthday (29 April), spring and autumnal equinox days, New Year season.

KURASHIKI HISTORICAL MUSEUM
Honmachi, Kurashiki-shi, Okayama-ken 710
Armour and furniture of the feudal period.
Daily 9-5. Closed M.

OHARA ART MUSEUM
312 Shinkawa-cho, Kurashiki-shi, Okayama-ken 710
Western sculpture and paintings, including "The Annunciation" by El Greco and works by Renoir, Monet and Gaugin. Paintings by Japanese artists, Chinese archaeological relics and works by Kojima. Ceramics and sculpture from Persia, Turkey. Arts and crafts.
Daily 9-4. Closed M., and Dec. 29-Jan. 4.

KURUME-SHI

ISHIBASHI ART MUSEUM
c/o Ishibashi Cultural Centre, Nonaka-cho, Kurume-shi, Fukuoka-ken 830
Exhibitions of Japanese and Western art.
Daily 9-5. July-Aug. 9-6. Closed Dec. 28-Jan. 1.

KUSHIRO-SHI

KUSHIRO MUNICIPAL MUSEUM
3 Tsurugatake, Kushiro-shi, Hokkaido 085
Local history. Natural history. Pottery. Minerals. Local crafts and industries, including Ainu folk arts.
Daily 9-5. Closed M. and national holidays, also Dec. 29-Jan. 3.

KYOTO

ARCHAEOLOGICAL & HISTORICAL COLLECTION
Faculty of Letters, Kyoto University, c/o Kyoto University, Yoshida-Honmachi, Sakyo-ku, Kyoto-shi, Kyoto-fu 606
Archaeological relics of Japan, the Orient and Western countries. Documents and records on the history of Japan. Collection on geography and local customs. Reference material on Egypt.
Any time by arrangement.

KUWANA-SHI

RAKUO MEMORIAL COLLECTION
3421-6 Yoshinomaru, Kuwana-shi, Mie-ken 511
Various articles relating to the Matsudaira family, former feudal lords.
Daily 9-4.

KYOTO

CHILDREN'S BUDDHIST MUSEUM
Maruyama Park, Higashiyama-ku, Kyoto 605
Objects of interest in the study of Buddhism. History. Geography. Science. Fine arts. Ancient customs.
Tu.-Su. 9-4.30.

DAITOKU-YI
Kyoto
Zen sect temple. Calligraphy. Painting.
On request.

FUJI'I COLLECTION
44 Enshoji-machi, Okazaki, Sakyo-ku, Kyoto-shi, Kyoto 606
Chinese classic art. Bronze vessels. Inscribed stone. Paintings. Calligraphy. Ceramics. Lacquerware. Sculpture. Seals.
1st and 3rd Su. of each month, 1-4.

GENERAL NOGI MEMORIAL COLLECTION
32 Itakurashubo, Momoyama-cho, Fushimi-ku, Kyoto-shi, Kyoto-fu 612
Clothes, furniture, writings and swords belonging to General Nogi, hero of the Russo-Japanese War.
Daily 7-6.

HALL OF 33 SPACES
Kyoto
Building is 1251. 1001 wooden images of Kaqnon. Sculpture of the Kamakura period (1185-1333).
On request.

HISTORICAL MUSEUM
Sanjo Takakura, Kyoto-shi, Kyoto-fu
Japanese and Kyoto history.
Daily 9-4.30.

IKENO TAIGA ART MUSEUM
57 Matsuobankoku-cho, Ukyo-ku, Kyoto-shi, Kyoto-fu 615
Works by the Japanese painter Ikeno Taiga (1723-1776).
Daily 9-5.

KYOTO BOARD OF EDUCATION SCIENCE ROOM
14 Yoshidakawara-machi, Sakyo-ku, Kyoto
Instruments for scientific experiments and for the study of astronomy. Practical training machinery for automobile engineering.
Daily 9-5. Closed Su., National Holidays and school holidays.

KYOTO MUNICIPAL MUSEUM OF ART
124 Enkatsujicho, Okazaki Park, Sakyo-ku, Kyoto-shi, Kyoto-fu 606
Japanese and Western paintings. Sculpture. Calligraphy. Handicrafts. Decorative arts.
Daily ex. M. 9-5. Closed Dec. 28-Jan. 3.

KYOTO NATIONAL MUSEUM
Shichyo-agaru, Yamato-oji, Higashiyama-ku, Kyoto 605
Japanese art since the Heian period, especially paintings, calligraphy, crafts. Historical items from Asia, chiefly of

Japan. Industrial art. Archaeology. Important art objects from temples and shrines in and around Kyoto.
Daily ex. M. 9-4.

KYOTO PREFECTURAL LIBRARY
Hagi-cho, Shimogamo, Kyoto-shi, Kyoto-fu
Exhibition of arts, crafts and industries.
Daily ex. M. 9-4.30.

KYOTO SCIENCE AND ENGINEERING INSTITUTE
14 Yoshidakawara-cho, Sakyo-ku, Kyoto
Exhibits to promote industries and develop the level of scientific technology, including machines, experimental apparatus and models of machinery.
Daily 8.30-5. Closed Su., National Holidays and New Year season.

MT. HIEI NATURAL HISTORY MUSEUM AND ROCK GARDEN
Hieisancho, Sankyo-ku, Kyoto-shi, Kyoto-fu 601-12
Exhibits include birds, insects, plants and fresh-water shells. The garden contains shrubs, trees, herbs, Alpine plants and local plants.
Jan. - July 20, Daily 8.30-4.30. July 21 - Dec. 31, Daily 8-9.

MUSEUM OF THE HISTORY OF THE RESTORATION
1 Ryozen-cho, Seikanji, Higashiyama-ku, Kyoto 605
History of the Meiji Restoration and Japan's entry into the modern world.
Daily 9-5.

NATIONAL MUSEUM OF MODERN ART
Enshoji-cho, Okazaki, Sakyo-ku, Kyoto
Modern handicrafts, paintings, sculptures.
Daily ex. M. 10-5.

NI'IJIMA MEMORIAL ROOM
c/o Doshisha University, Genbu-machi, Chogan Toniju, Idekawadoni, Kamikyo-ku, Kyoto-shi, Kyoto-fu 602
Letters, paintings, text-books and photographs belonging to Jo Ni'ijima, founder of Doshisha University.
Any time by arrangement.

RYOANJI TEMPLE
Ryoanji goryo-shita-machi, Ukyo-ku, Kyoto-shi, Kyoto-fu 616
Ancient literature, including "Thaihei-ki". Garden. Gold pavilion.
Daily 8-5.

THE SILVER TEMPLE
Ginkakuji-cho, Sakyo-ku, Kyoto
Temple (1483) by Soami, a Shogun of Ashikaga, arranged as 12 separate buildings in the grounds of his villa. Now only the Silver Hall and the Togudo are left.
Daily 8-5.

SUMITOMO COLLECTION
25 Shimo-Mujanomae-cho, Shishigatani, Sakyo-ku, Kyoto
Private collection of Chinese Shang and Chon bronzes.
By appointment.

TAIGAKU BUNKO, PROVINCIAL IWAKURA MEMORIAL
100 Kamikura-machi, Iwakura, Sakyo-ku, Kyoto-shi, Kyoto-fu 606
Mementoes of Tomomi Iwakura, "who distinguished himself in the Meiji Restoration".
Daily 9-4.

TEXTILE MUSEUM
Imadegawa Omiya, Kyoto-shi, Kyoto-fu
Collection of Nishijin textile products.
Daily 9-4. Closed 1st and 3rd Su. of month.

TO-JI
Kyoto
9th century temple. Sculpture from the Heian period (796-1185). The 56 m. (183 ft.) high five-storey pagoda is the tallest of its kind in Japan.
Daily 8-5.

TREASURE HALL OF THE CHISHAKUIN TEMPLE
Higashi-Kawaramachi, Higashiyama-ku, Kyoto
Buddhist equipment and utensils, old documents, paintings, calligraphy, sutras. Books in Japanese and Chinese.
Daily 8-5.

TREASURE HALL OF THE DAIGOJI TEMPLE
22 Daigo-Higashi-oji-machi, Fushimi-ku, Kyoto-shi, Kyoto-fu 601-13
Buddhist statues, pictures, artistic crafts, sutras and historical documents, amounting to 120,000 items.
Apr., May, Oct. 8-4 daily. Closed June-Sept., Nov.-Mar.

TREASURE HOUSE OF THE KITANO TENMANGU SHRINE
Bakuro-cho, Kamikyo-ku, Kyoto-shi, Kyoto-fu 602
Scrolls of Kitano Tenjin and other paintings. Historical documents. Swords.
10-9 on 25th of every month.

TREASURE HOUSE OF THE KORYUJI TEMPLE
36 Futohata-hachigaoka-machi, Ukyo-ku, Kyoto-shi, Kyoto-fu 616
A wooden statue, Miroku Bosatsu, the oldest sculpture in Kyoto, dates from 7th century. Buddhist statues, pictures, altar fittings and historical documents.
Daily 9-5.

TREASURE HOUSE OF THE MYOHOIN TEMPLE
Daibutsu Myohoinmae-machi, Higashiyama-ku, Kyoto
Possessions of Toyotomi-Hideyoshi, and other national treasures.
Daily 8-5.

TREASURE HOUSE OF THE NISHI HONGANJI TEMPLE
Kyoto-shi, Kyoto-fu
Founded 1272, moved to present site in 1591. National treasures, including Hiunkaku Pavilion.
Daily 9-4.

TREASURE HOUSE OF THE NINNAJI TEMPLE
Ouchi Mimuro, Sakyo-ku, Kyoto-shi, Kyoto-fu 606
Buddhist statues, pictures, artistic crafts and historical objects.
Daily 9-4.

TREASURE HALL OF THE RENGEOIN TEMPLE
Daibutsu Myohoinmae-machi, Higashiyama-ku, Kyoto
"One Thousand Images" and many other Buddhist images.
Daily 9-4.

TREASURE HOUSE OF THE SHOREN-IN TEMPLE
Sanjobo-machi, Awadaguchi, Higashiyama-ku, Kyoto
Rare books. Manuscripts. Paintings.
Daily 9-4.

TREASURE HOUSE OF THE TOYOKUNI SHRINE
530 Shomenchaya-machi, Yamato-oji, Higashiyama-ku, Kyoto-shi, Kyoto-fu 605
Armour and artistic crafts, clothes, pictures, historical documents, swords belonging to Toyotomi-Hideyoshi. Painted screens.
Daily 9-5.

UJI BYODOIN
Kyoto
Temple (1052). Sculpture, including Jocho's 'Amida Nyorai'.
By appointment.

YOGEN'IN TEMPLE
Sanjusangendo Enmachi, Higashiyama-ku, Kyoto-shi, Kyoto-fu
Collection of Shohekiga (pictures on the wall or sliding door) painted in the early years of the Edo period.
10 Mar. - Nov. Daily 8-5. Dec. - 9 Mar. Daily 8-4. Closed 21 Jan., May and Sept. and 28-31 Dec.

YURINKAN COLLECTION
44 Okazaki-Enshoji-machi, Sakyo-ku, Kyoto
Chinese fine art, including bronze and jade ware, porcelain, seals, Buddhist images, pictures and calligraphy. The collection is privately owned by the Fuju family.
By appointment, 1st and 3rd Su. in month, 12-3.

THE ZOOLOGICAL SPECIMEN GALLERY OF DOSHISHA HIGH SCHOOL
Osagi-machi, Iwakura, Sakyo-ku, Kyoto
Specimens of mammals, birds and invertebrates.
On request only.

MAMIZUKA

MAMIZUKA SHUTSUDOHIN CHINRETSUKAN
Mamizukagonai, Ichinomuja-shi, Aichi-ken
Historic site.
Daily 9-4.

MATSUE-SHI

LAFCADIO HEARN MEMORIAL HALL
322 Okuyama-cho, Matsue-shi, Shimane-ken 690
Domestic articles and manuscripts belonging to Lafcadio Hearn, who spent half his life as a teacher of English in Japan.
Apr.-Sept. Daily 8.30-6. Oct.-Mar. Daily 8.30-5.

MATSUE CASTLE TOWER
1, Tonomachi, Matsue-shi, Shimane-ken 690
Armour of Naomasa Matsudaira, former feudal lord. Models of the tower.
Apr.-Sept. Daily 8.30-6. Oct.-Mar. Daily 8.30-5.

SHIMANE PREFECTURAL MUSEUM
1 Tonomachi, Matsue-shi, Shimane-ken 690
Former Tokugawa Collection of court music instruments and old arts of the prefecture where ancient mythological Japan began.
Apr.-Sept. Daily 8.30-5. Oct.-Mar. Daily 9-5. Closed M., National Holidays. Dec. 28 - Jan. 4.

MATSUMOTO-SHI

MATSUMOTO MUNICIPAL MUSEUM
4-1 Marunouchi, Matsumoto-shi, Nagano-ken 390
Natural science. History. Archaeology. Mountaineering. Agriculture. Ethnology, articles for everyday use and religious objects of the Matsumoto region. Weapons.
Daily 9-4.30. Closed Dec. 29 - Jan. 3.

MATSUSHIMA-MACHI

MATSUSHIMA MUSEUM, KANRANTEI
56 Uchi Azamachi, Matsushima-machi, Miyagi-gun, Miyagi-ken 981-02
In the Kanrantei, Japanese-style garden, with a section of the building of the Hushimi Momoyama-jo Castle.
Furniture. Weapons used by the Date family. Animals, plants, marine shells from Matsushima Bay.
Daytime.

TREASURE HOUSE OF THE KANRANTEI
Matsushima, Matsushima-machi, Miyagi-gun, Miyagi-ken 981-02
Kanrantei is said to have replaced a part of the famous Fushimi Momoyama Castle by Tadamune Date, the Daimyo (feudal lord) of this province, and is now preserved as an historic monument. Weapons and artistic crafts connected with the Date families.
Daily 9-7.

ZUIGANJI MUSEUM
91 Matsushima Azamachinai, Matsushima-machi, Miyagi-gun, Miyagi-ken 981-02
Situated in the precincts of the Zuiganji Temple on one of the beautiful pine-clad islands of Matsushima, and containing Buddhist statues and altar fittings.
Daily 7.30-4.

MATSUYAMA-SHI

MUSEUM OF EHIME PREFECTURAL LIBRARY
4-7-1-bancho, Matsuyama-shi, Ehime-ken 790
Specimens of plants, animals, rocks and minerals.
Daily 9-4.30. Closed Su. and National holidays, also Dec. 28 - Jan. 4.

MIMA-GUN

MIMA LOCAL MUSEUM
8 Ganshoji, Mima-cho, Mima-gun, Tokushima-ken 771-21
Local historical items. Fine arts.
Daily 8-5.

MINAMIARIMA-MACHI

HARA CASTLE MEMORIAL HALL
Minamiarima-machi, Minamihara-gun, Nagasaki-ken 859-24
Historical material relating to the Amakusa Shimabara civil war.
M., W. and F. 9-4. Closed New Year season.

MINAMIAZUMI-GUN

ROKUZAN ART MUSEUM
5095-1 Hotaka-oaza, Hotaka-cho, Minamiazumi-gun, Nagano-ken 399-83
Works by Rokuzan Ogiwara, forerunner of modern sculpture in Japan. Bronzes. Paintings.
Apr.-Oct. Daily 9-5. Nov.-Mar. Daily 9-4.30. Closed M., and Dec. 21 - Jan. 9.

MINOBU-MACHI

TREASURE HOUSE OF THE KUONJI TEMPLE
3567 Minobu Oaza, Minobu-machi, Minami Kyoma-gun, Yamanashi-ken 409-25
Books. Calligraphy. Buddhist statues. Paintings. Handicrafts.
Daily 8-5.

THE YAMANASHI PREFECTURAL MUSEUM OF FUJI NATIONAL PARK
Minobu-machi, Minamikyoma-gun, Yamanashi-ken
The collection includes birds, fish, insects, fresh-water shells, plants, minerals, rocks, fossils and archaeological materials from the Fuji National Park.
Daily 9-5. Closed New Year season.

MINO'O-SHI

MINO'O PARK ENTOMOLOGICAL MUSEUM
Mino'o-koen, Mino'o-shi, Osaka-fu 562
Specimens of insects.
Daily 9-5.

MISHIMA-SHI

TAMAZAWA TREASURE HOUSE
Myohogeji Tamazawa, Mishima-shi, Shizuoka-ken
Collections concerning Saint Nichiren.
On demand.

TREASURE HOUSE OF THE HYOHOGEJI TEMPLE
1 Tamasawa, Mishima-shi, Shizuoka-ken 411
Portrait of Saint Nichiren on silk canvas; coloured painting of Mandala; scrolls written by Saint Nichiren and Nissho.
Open when the weather is good.

MITO-SHI

IBARAKI PREFECTURAL MUSEUM OF ART
697 Higashi kubo, Sennami-cho, Mito-shi, Ibaraki-ken
Japanese and Western-style paintings. Sculptures. Handicrafts. Archaeological material.
Daily 9.30-5. Closed Dec. 27- Jan. 4.

IBARAKI PREFECTURAL MUSEUM OF ATOMIC ENERGY
1 Kita-sannomaru, Mito-shi, Ibaraki-ken
Displays of models, apparatus, machinery and photographs, designed "to popularise atomic power as one kind of energy and its peaceful use for industry".
Daily 9-4.

MITSUKUNI TOKUGAWA AND NARIAKI TOKUGAWA MEMORIAL COLLECTION
1-3-1 Tokiwa-cho, Mito-shi, Ibaraki-ken 310
Treasures and property of Pitsukuni Tokugawa and Nariaki Tokugawa.
Daily 8.30-4. Closed Dec. 30-31.

MIYAJIMA-CHO

TREASURE HALL OF THE ITSUKUSHIMA SHRINE
Miyajima-cho, Saeki-gun, Hiroshima-ken
Paintings. Calligraphy. Sutras. Swords and other ancient weapons.
Daily 9-4.

MIYAKO-SHI

FISHERIES MUSEUM OF MIYAKO FISHERIES HIGH SCHOOL
163 Hotokezawa, Sokei, Miyako-shi, Iwate-ken 027-02
Marine biology. Ship-models. Fishing equipment.
Daily 9-5.

MIYAZAKI-SHI

AGRICULTURAL MUSEUM OF MIYAZAKI UNIVERSITY
Faculty of Agriculture, 100 Funatsuka-machi, Miyazaki-shi, Miyazaki-ken 880
Specimens of animals, plants and minerals. Agricultural implements. Fibres. Agricultural products.
Daily 9-5. Closed Su., National holidays.

HISTORICAL MUSEUM IN THE MIYAZAKI SHRINE
Miyazaki Shrine, Jingu-machi, Miyazaki-shi, Miyazaki-ken
Objects of historical and archaeological interest.
Daily 9-4.

MORIOKA-SHI

MORIOKA MUNICIPAL MUSEUM
14-1 Atago-cho, Morioka-shi, Iwate-ken 021
Regional culture and history. Botany. Natural history. Science.
Daily 9-4.30. Closed M., end of month, National Holidays.

NAGANO-SHI

DAIHONGAN TREASURE HOUSE OF THE JODO SECT OF ZENKOJI TEMPLE
Motoyoshi-cho, Nagano-shi, Nagano-ken 380
Buddhist pictures, altar fittings, Sutras and historical documents.
Sunrise onwards.

DAIKANJIN TREASURE HOUSE OF THE TENDAI SECT OF ZENKOJI TEMPLE
492 Motoyoshi-cho, Nagano-shi, Nagano-ken 380
Buddhist paintings, statues, altar fittings and archives.
Sunrise onwards.

NAGAOKA-SHI

NAGAOKA MUNICIPAL MUSEUM OF NATURAL SCIENCE
Yukyusan Park, 96 Oyama-cho, Nagaoka-shi, Niigata-ken 940
Zoology. Botany. Entomology. Archaeology, especially material of the Tumuli period.
Daily 9-5. Closed Su. from Dec.-Mar. Also Closed Dec. 28- Jan. 3.

NYOZEZO COLLECTION
3 chome, Tai-machi, Nagaoka-shi, Nigata-ken 940
Local historical items. Material on well-known local people.
Daily 9-4.

SNOW MUSEUM
Gakko-machi, Nagaoka-shi, Ni'igata-ken
Material relating to snow-precipitation, snow removal. Transport. Agriculture. Forestry. Local customs.
Daily 9-4.

NAGASAKI-SHI

ATOMIC BOMB MEMORIAL ROOM
Hamaguchi-cho, Nagasaki-shi, Nagasaki-ken
Collection of the materials and survivals from A-bomb dropped 9th August 1945.
Daily 9-5.

NAGASAKI MUNICIPAL CHILDREN'S SCIENCE HALL
6 Tokiwamachi, Nagasaki-shi, Nagasaki-ken 850
Specimens of animals, plants, aquatic life. Astronomy.
Daily 9-5. Closed M., and Dec. 28- Jan. 4.

NAGASAKI MUNICIPAL MUSEUM
International House of Culture, 7-8 Hirano-cho, Nagasaki-shi, Nagasaki-ken 853
Material illustrating history of trade with the West, and of early Christianity in Japan. Japanese art.
Daily 9-5.

NAGOYA

MUNICIPAL SCIENCE MUSEUM
17-22 Sakae, 2-chome, Maka-ku, Nagoya 460, Aichi-ken
Physical sciences. Planetarium. Transport.
Daily ex. M. 9.15-5.30.

NAGOYA CASTLE COLLECTION
1-1 Motomaru, Naka-ku, Nagoya 460, Aichi-ken
Shohekiga (paintings on a sliding-door) painted by the Kano school in the early Edo period. Art gallery.
Daily 9-4.30. Closed on rainy days and in New Year season.

TOKUGAWA ART GALLEY
27 2-chome, Tokugawacho, Higashi-ku, Nagoya, Aichi-ken 461
Culture of the Tokugawas of Bishu Province (now Aishu), including the Genji Monogatari Eman. Armour. Swords. Scrolls. Buddhist sutras. Handicrafts. Noh roles. Domestic utensils.
Daily 9-4. Closed Dec. 26- Jan. 3.

TOKUGAWA ART MUSEUM
2-27 Tokugawa-cho, Higashi-ku, Nagoya-shi, Aichi-ken 461
Armour. Swords. Scrolls. Buddhist sutras. Poetry. Manuscripts. Handicrafts. Noh roles. Utensils.
Daily 9-4. Closed Su. and Dec. 25- Jan. 1.

NAKA-GUN

SANNOMUJA ARCHAEOLOGICAL MUSEUM
Hibita, Isehara-cho, Naka-gun, Kanagawa-ken 259-11
Archaeological collection, including ceramics and documents.
Nov.-Mar. Daily 9-5. Apr.-Oct. Daily 9-6.

NAKA KOMATSU

KIKUSUI KOGEIKAN
Kawanishi-machi, Yamaguta, Naka Komatsu
Japanese, Chinese and Korean ceramics.
Apr.-Oct. Daily 9-5.

NAKATSU-SHI

FUKUZAWA MEMORIAL HALL
Rusuicho, Nakatsu-shi, Oita-ken 871
Founded in memory of Yukichi Fukuzawa, pioneer of the Meiji Restoration, and located near his old house. Domestic tools and collections left by him.
Daily except National Holidays, 9-4.

NARA-SHI

THE AYAMEIKE MUSEUM OF NATURAL HISTORY
1,355-12 Nishi-Otera-machi, Nara-shi, Nara-ken 631
Natural history collections, dioramas and panoramas. Fossils.
Daily 9-5.

CHUGUJI TEMPLE
Nunnery, Toin of Horyuji, Nara-shi, Nara-ken 630
Nyoirin Goddess Kannon, a wooden Buddhist image (7th century). Tenjukoku Mandala, an embroidery showing the Paradise of Buddhism (also 7th century).
Daily 9-4 on request.

HOKKE-JI TEMPLE
Nara-shi, Nara-ken 631
Temple established 742. Wooden sculpture, especially the standing image of the Eleven-faced Kannon.
On request.

HORYUJI TEMPLE
Nara-shi, Nara-ken 630
Founded 607, and consists of about 40 buildings, all of which are registered as National Treasures. Architecture. Sculpture. Art objects.
Daily 9-4.

KOFUKU-JI TEMPLE
Nara Park, Nara-shi, Nara-ken 630
Temple (710). Sculpture of the Nara, Fujiwara and Kamakura periods.
On request.

MURO-JI
Nara-shi, Nara-ken 630
Temple established 681. 9th century sculpture.
On request.

NARA NATIONAL MUSEUM
50 Noborioji-cho, Nara-shi, Nara-ken 630
Japanese art, paintings, sculptures, handicrafts, calligraphy. Archaeology. Architure. Buddhist art items dating from 7th century deposited in the museum by shrines and temples in the area.
Mar.-Oct. Daily 9-4.30. Nov.-Feb. Daily 9-4. Closed M. and Dec. 26- Jan. 3.

NARA PREFECTURE CULTURE HALL
Noborioji Street, Nara-shi, Nara-ken 630
Exhibitions of historical, cultural and artistic material.
Daily ex. W. 9-6.

NEIRAKU ART MUSEUM
74 Suimon-cho, Nara-shi, Nara-ken 630
China, bronzes, Chinese mirrors and seals. Korean pottery. The garden was constructed in the Edo period (17th century).
Daily 10-4. Closed Tu. and Dec. 29- Jan. 5.

ORIENTAL FOLK MUSEUM
Ayameike-machi, Nara-shi, Nara-ken 630
Collection of folk art objects.
Daily 9-6.

SAIDAIJI TEMPLE
Saidaiji, Nara-shi, Nara-ken 630
One of the seven great temples of Nara. Buddhist sculpture.
Daily 9-4.

SHIN-YAKUSHIJI TEMPLE
Nishinokyo, Nara-shi, Nara-ken 631
8th century temple. Wooden standing images of Buddha.
Daily 9-4.

SHOSOIN TREASURE HOUSE
Zoshimachi, Nara-shi, Nara-ken
Collection of artistic crafts, treasures and historical archives and documents dating from the Tempyo Period (710-794). Jewels. Silverware. Glass. Musical instruments. Masks of the Gigaku dance.
Restricted permission in November.

TOSHODAIJI TEMPLE
Nishinokyo Station, Nara-shi, Nara-ken 630
8th century building. Dry-lacquer statue of Vairocana, 3.3m. (11 ft.) high.
Daily 9-4.

TREASURE HOUSE OF THE KASUGA SHRINE
160 Kasugano-machi, Nara-shi, Nara-ken 630
National treasures and art objects, including wooden masks of Bugaku dances, drums, swords, mirrors and armour. Lanterns.
Apr.-Oct. Daily 8.30-5. July-Aug. Daily 8.30-4.30. Nov.-Mar. Daily 9-4.30.

TREASURE HALL OF THE TODAIJI TEMPLE
406 Zoshi-cho, Nara-shi, Nara-ken 630
The Great Image of Buddha, Two Deva Kings, and many other treasures and ancient documents. Adjoining buildings contain images of Buddha, as well as treasures and personal belongings of Emperor Shomu.
Daily 9-4.

UNIVERSITY MUSEUM
Tenri University, 1 Furu, Tenri-shi, Nara-ken
Archaeology. Ethnography. Transport. Tourism.
By appointment.

YAKUSHIJI TEMPLE
Nishi-no-Kyo-machi, Nara-shi, Nara-ken 630
Bronze images of the Yakushi Trinity. 1,300 year-old pagoda.
Daily 9-4.

YAMATO CULTURAL HOUSE
1-11-6 Gakuen Minami, Nara-shi, Nara-ken 631
Paintings. Sculptures. Calligraphy. China. Metal-work. Textile dyeing of Japan, Korea, China, Middle East and Near East. Lacquerwork. Weaving.
Daily ex. M. 10-5. Closed Dec. 28 - Jan. 3.

NARITA-SHI

NARITASAN REIKO MUSEUM
Narita Park, Narita-shi, Chiba-ken 286
Historical articles, folk art related to the faith of the Naritasan. Archaeological finds from the region.
Daily 8.30-4. Closed M., national holidays, July 7-9, Jan. 13-15. Dec. 26-30.

SOGO MEMORIAL HALL
558 Shimokata, Narita-shi, Chiba-ken 286
Articles left by Sogo Kiuchi, "who sacrificed himself for the peasants' uprising". Local history.
Apr.-Sept. Daily 8-5. Oct.-Mar. Daily 9-4.

NATORI-GUN

HORSEMANSHIP MUSEUM OF TAKEKOMA SHRINE
1 Minami, Azamachi, Iwanuma-cho, Natori-gun, Miyagi-ken 989-24
Items relating to the history of the horse and of harness.
On request.

NICHINAN-SHI

THE HATTORI BOTANICAL LABORATORY
3,888 Obi, Nichinan-shi, Miyazaki-ken
Specimens of mosses.
On request.

NI'IGATA-SHI

NI'IGATA SCIENCE AND TECHNOLOGY MUSEUM
5923 Ichibanbori-dori, Ni'igata-shi, Ni'igata-ken
Specimens of botany and zoology. Models and photographs explaining the features of industries and agriculture in the district. Machinery and experimental apparatus.
Daily except Su. 8.30-5. Sa. 8.30-noon.

NI'IHAMA-SHI

NI'IHAMA LOCAL MUSEUM
2-2 Ojimachi, Ni'ihama-shi, Ehime-ken 792
Anthropology, Local industries. Civil engineering.
Daily 9-5. Closed M. and national holidays, also Dec. 28 - Jan. 3.

NIKKO-SHI

NIKKO MUSEUM OF NATURAL HISTORY
Tamozawa, Nikko-shi, Tochigi-ken 321-4
Panorama of natural history of Nikko National Park, including insects, birds, mammals, fish and geological materials.
Daily 8.30-5.

NIKKO TREASURE HOUSE
Zannai, Nikko-shi, Tochigi-ken 321-14
Local crafts, including Noh dance-dresses, armour and garments used by the Tokugawa.
Apr.-Oct. Daily 8-5. Nov.-Mar. Daily 8-4.

OKUNIKKO MUSEUM OF NATURAL HISTORY
Chuzenjikohan, Chuzenji, Nikko-shi, Tochigi-ken
Exhibits include mammals, birds, fresh-water fish, insects and alpine plants.
July-mid. Sept. Daily 6-6.

TREASURE HOUSE OF THE CHUZENJI TEMPLE
at lakeside of Chuzenjiko, Nakaguji, Nikko-shi, Tochigi-ken 321-14
The temple is reputed to have been founded by Saint Shodo, the developer of Nikko and preserves many valuable materials concerning the mountain ascetics (Shuegndo).
Daily 7-5.

TREASURE HOUSE OF THE JOKODO, RINNOJI TEMPLE
Sannai, Nikko-shi, Tochigi-ken 321-14
Hanging lanterns. Masks. Buddhist statues, picture, Sutras. Swords. Historical documents, including material on Nikko before the Tokugawa Era.
Apr.-Oct. Daily 8-5. Nov.-Mar. Daily 8-4.

NODA-SHI

NODA CITY MUSEUM
370 Noda, Noda-shi, Chiba-ken 278
Collection of objects relatings to Soy. Distilling. Provincial history and archaeology.
Daily 9-4. Closed M. and day after National Holidays.

NOGAMI-MACHI

CHICHIBU MUSEUM OF NATURAL HISTORY
1417 Nagatoro, Nogami-machi Oaza, Chichibu-gun, Saitama-ken 369-13
Exhibits include mammals, birds, reptiles, fish, insects, seed-plants and mosses of the area. Minerals, rocks and fossils.
Apr.-Sep. Daily 8-5. Oct.-Mar. Daily 8.30-4.30. Closed New Year season.

NAGATORO KYUKOKAN ARCHAEOLOGICAL COLLECTION
4241 Kitabou, Nogami-machi, Chichibu-gun, Saitama-ken 369-13
Local history and archaeology.
Daily 9-4. Closed M.

NO'O-MACHI

NO'O MARINE AND MARITIME MUSEUM
No'o-machi, Nishikubiki-gun, Ni'igata-ken
Exhibits include aquatic animals and plants, fishing implements, model vessels and meteorological instruments.
Daily 8-5.

NUMAZU-SHI

MITO PEARL MUSEUM
46 Uchuira Mito, Numazu-shi, Shizuoka-ken
Collections illustrating pearl culture.
Daily 8-5.

OARI-MACHI

JOYO MEMORIAL MUSEUM OF MEIJI THE GREAT
8231 Jsohama, Oari-machi, Higashi'ibaraki-gun, Ibaraki-ken 311-13
Treasures and personal possessions of Emperor Meiji. Drawings and paintings left by patriots of the Meiji restoration.
Apr.-Oct. Daily 8-5. Nov.-Mar. Daily 9-4. Closed Dec. 29 - Jan. 3.

OARAI-MACHI

OARAI MARINE MUSEUM
6870 Isohama, Oarari-machi, Higashi-gun, Ibaraki-ken 311-13
Models of fishing nets and fishing boats. Specimens of shell in the Arafura Sea.
Apr.-Sept. Daily 8-5. Oct.-Mar. Daily 9-4.

OBAMA-MACHI

TREASURE HOUSE OF THE ICHIJOJI TEMPLE
320 Onzen, Minamikorai-gun, Nagasaki-ken 850
Sutras. Buddhist statues. Mirrors.
Daily 7-7.

ODAWARA-SHI

MATSUNAGA MEMORIAL HALL
517 Itabashi, Odawara-shi, Kanagawa-ken 250
Japanese art.
Daily 10-4 Nov. 24-30 only.

ODAWARA LOCAL MUSEUM
3-22 Jonai, Odawara-shi, Kanagawa-ken 250
Archaeological relics. Paintings. Panoramas. Industrial arts.
Daily 9-5. Closed M. and the day after holidays, also Dec. 20, Dec. 28-Jan. 4.

TREASURE HOUSE OF THE HOTOKU NINOMIYA SHRINE
Jonai, Odawara-shi, Kanagawa-ken 250
Manuscripts and articles belonging to Sontoku Ninomiya, "to honour his meritorious services to agriculture".
Daily 9-4.

OJIKA-MACHI

MUSEUM OF WHALING
1 Kiyozaki, Ayukawahama, Ojika-machi, Ojika-gun, Miyagi-ken 986-25
Materials illustrating the history of whaling.
Daily 9-4. Closed Jan. 1-2.

OKANO

MEISHO TEIKAN-EN HURETSU CHADO BIJUTSU-KAN
Tokayanagi-machi, Kariwa, Niigata, Okano
Arts of the tea-ceremony.
2 months in the summer.

OKAYA-SHI

OKAYA SILK-THREAD MEMORIAL COLLECTION
4-1-39 Motomachi, Okaya-shi, Nagano-ken 392
Material on the history of the silk industry.
Daily 8.30-5. Closed Su., national holidays, Dec. 29 - Jan. 3.

OKU-MACHI

OKU ARCHAEOLOGICAL COLLECTION
Yamate, Oku-machi, Oku-gun, Okayama-ken
Local archaeology.
Afternoons, 2-4.30.

OMACHI-SHI

OMACHI ALPINE MUSEUM
Shineicho, Oaza Omachi, Omachi-shi, Nagano-ken 398
Mountaineering in the Japanese Alps. History. Folklore. Geology. Meteorology. Botany. Zoology. Equipment and tools for mountain-climbing, Articles for every use by people living in snowy districts.
Apr.-Sept. 8.30-5 daily. Oct.-Mar. daily 9-4.

OMISHIMA-MACHI

TREASURE HOUSE OF THE OYAMAZUMI SHRINE
Miyaura, Omishima-machi, Ochi-gun, Ehime-ken 794-13
Collection of armour and weapons. Mirross.
Apr.-Sept. Daily 8-5. Oct.-Mar. Daily 9-4.

ONO-MACHI

OGAWA ARCHAEOLOGICAL COLLECTION
Oibi, Ono-machi, Ibi-gun, Gifu-ken 501-05
Archaeological finds, mostly pottery, excavated in the region.
Daily 9-4.

OSAKA

ELECTRIC SCIENCE MUSEUM
5 Nishinagabori Kitadori, 1-chome, Nishi-ku, Osaka
Planetarium. Atomic power. Electric wave exhibits. Communications. Television. Domestic applicances.
Daily ex. M. 9-5.

FUJITA ART MUSEUM
2 Higashinoda-cho, Miyakoyima-ku, Osaka-shi, Osaka 534
Former residence of Baron Fujita. Art collection. Tea ceremony utensils. Sculpture. Calligraphy. Handicrafts. Ceramics. Lacquerware. Chinese bronze vessels. The 'Illustrated Diary' of Murusaki Shikibu, author of the 'Tales of Genji'.
Daily ex. M. 10-4. Closed at certain times in spring and autumn.

IKOMASAN ASTRONOMICAL MUSEUM
2006 Toyoura-cho, Hiraoka-shi, Osaka
Collection of astronomical items, including models, graphs, panels, photographs and telescopes. Planetarium.
Daily 10-4 except in July and Aug. July and Aug. Weekdays 9-7; Sa. and Su. 9 a.m. - 10 p.m.

ITSUO ART MUSEUM
7-17 Tateishi-cho, Ikeda-shi, Osaka-fu 563
Japan and Oriental paintings. Calligraphy. Sculpture. Handicrafts.
Daily 10-4. Closed M. and Dec. 25 - Jan. 5.

JAPAN HANDICRAFT MUSEUM
3-619 Shinkawa, Naniwa-ku, Osaka-shi, Osaka-fu 556
Japanese handicrafts.
Daily 10-5. Closed M. and Dec. 25 - Jan. 6.

MUNICIPAL ART MUSEUM
121 Chausuyama-cho, Tennoji-ku, Osaka
Japanese sculpture and painting from the earliest times. Chinese Ming and Ch'ing paintings.
Daily 9-5. Closed Dec. 29 - Jan. 5.

MUNICIPAL MUSEUM
Osaka Castle, Baba-machi, Higashi-ku, Osaka-shi, Osaka-fu 540
Archaeology, art, history, economy and culture of the Osaka area. Folk crafts, mainly of the Momoyama period.
Daily 9-5.

MUSEUM OF INSECTS
Ikue-machi, Asahi-ku, Osaka
Exhibits include insects found in the district as well as those from Formosa, South Asia and South America.
Apr.-Sept. Daily 10-4. Oct.-Mar. Daily 10-3. Closed New Year season.

MUSEUM OF JAPANESE FARMHOUSES
Hattori Ryokuchi, Toyonaka, Osaka
12 different and representative farmhouses from various regions of Japan have been reassembled, together with articles in daily use from the mountain village of Shirakawa in Gifu Prefecture.
Daily ex. M. 9.30-4.30.

NATURAL SCIENCE MUSEUM
2-chome, Utsubo, Nishi-ku, Osaka-fu 550
Plants, animals, insects. Minerals. Fossils. Shells. Fish. Mosses and lichens. Whale skeleton.
Daily ex. M., holidays and the last day of the month, 9-5.

OSHAYA-MACHI

TREASURE HOUSE OF THE IZUMO O'OYASHIRO
195 Kizuki, Oshaya-machi, Hikawa-gun, Shimane-ken 699-07
Ancient and modern art. History. Archaeology. Documents.
Daily 8-4.

OTA

KINRETZUKA IBUTSU HOZONKAN
Otayama Park, Ota
Historic site.
Daily 9-4.

OTARU-SHI

OTARU CITY MUSEUM
3-7-8 Shikinai, Otaru-shi, Hokkaido 047
Oceanography. History and archaeology. Zoology. Botany. Otaru bay shipping. Ainu folk art. Works by artists from Otaru.
Daily 9-4. Closed M. and national holidays, also Dec. 29 - Jan. 3.

OTSU

SHIGA PREFECTURAL MUSEUM
Prefecture, Higashiura, Ichibancho, Otsu
Archaeology. Ethnograph. Folk art. Paintings. Works by local artists. Industrial arts.
Daily ex. M. 9-4.

RIKUZENTAKADA-SHI

RIKUZENTAKADA MUNICIPAL MUSEUM
Kesen-machi, Rikuzentakada-shi, Iwate-ken 029-22
History. Natural science. Lacquer-ware. Ceramics. Archaeology.
Apr.-Sept. 8-4 daily. Oct.-Mar. 9-4 daily. Closed M.

SAGA-SHI

SAGA CULTURAL MUSEUM
Matsubara-cho, Saga-shi, Saga-ken
Ceramics. Natural history. Marine shells. Objects from old tombs near Saga City. Industrial art.
Daily 9-5. Closed Su. and National holidays.

TAIKO MEMORIAL HALL
1-11-11 Mizugae, Saga-shi, Saga-ken 840
Mementoes of Hideyoshi Toyotomi, Taiko (Grand Minister of State in the 16th century).
Daily ex. M. 9-5. Closed day after national holidays, also Dec. 29 - Jan. 3.

SAGAMIKO-MACHI

SAGAMIKO ELECTRIC SCIENCE MUSEUM
283 Yose, Sagamiko-machi, Tsukui-gun, Kanagawa-ken 199-01
Electrical engineering apparatus, models and machinery, including a model of power generation plant and atomic power generation plant.
Daily except Tu. 9-4. Closed Dec. 28 - Jan. 4.

SAGAWA-MACHI-KO

SEIZAN BUNKO HISTORICAL COLLECTION
Sagawa-machi-ko, Takaoka-gun, Kochi-ken 789-12
Exhibits relating to local history, fine arts, the Meiji Restoration and the Imperial Household.
Daily 8.30-5. Closed the day after National Holidays.

SAIJO-SHI

SAIJO LOCAL MUSEUM
237-1 Akeyashiki, Saijo-shi, Ehime-ken 793
Natural science. Animals and plant specimens. Marine shells, minerals and mineral ores. Rocks gathered from the Ichinokawa Mine.
Ceramics. Archaeology.
Daily 9-5. Closed M. and National Holidays. Also closed Dec. 29 - Jan. 3.

SAITO-SHI

SAITO MUNICIPAL MUSEUM
54-1 Tsuma Oaza, Saito-shi, Miyazaki-ken 881
Excavated objects from the Saitobara tombs.
Daily 9-5. Closed M.

SAKAIDE-MACHI

KAMATA LOCAL MUSEUM
1-1-24 Motomachi, Sakaide-machi Sakaide-shi, Kagawa-ken 762
Natural and human science. Antiquities. Regional social history. Photographs of temples and shrines. Fine arts. Animals. Plant specimens. Minerals and rocks.
Daily 9-4. Closed M. and national holidays. Su. 9-2. Closed Dec. 31 - Jan. 3.

SAKATA-SHI

HONMA ART MUSEUM
7-7 Onarimachi, Sakata-shi, Yamagata-ken 998
Housed in wooden building (1813) which was formerly a villa of the Homma family, and containing their private collection of Oriental paintings, calligraphy, china-ware, lacquer-ware, swords, metal work, armour, modern paintings, children's drawings.
Apr.-Oct. Daily ex. M. 9-5. Nov.-Mar. Daily ex. M. 9-4. Closed Dec. 27 - Jan. 7.

SAPPORO-SHI

AINU MUSEUM
Botanical Gardens, Sapporo-shi, Hokkaido 060
Ainu and Gilyak costumes, canoes, harpoons and other objects used by the northern races.
Daily ex. M. 9-4.30.

NATURAL HISTORY MUSEUM OF HOKKAIDO UNIVERSITY
c/o Hokudai Shokubutsuen-nai, Nishi 8-chome, Kita-sanjo, Sapporo-shi, Hokkaido 060
Animals. Plants. Minerals.
Apr.-Sept. Daily 9.4-30. Oct.-Nov. Daily 9-4. Closed Nov. 4 - Apr. 28.

SAPPORO COLLECTION OF LOCAL HISTORY
Imai Department Store, Sapporo-shi, Hokkaido 060
Material of interest in the study of the Ainus. Militia and colonisation projects in Hokkaido.
Daily 10-5. Closed M.

SASEHO-SHI

SASEHO CULTURAL MUSEUM
140-1 Shimase-machi, Saseho-shi, Nagasaki-ken 857
Products of local industries.
Daily ex. M. 8.30-5.

SAWADA-MACHI

SADO MUSEUM
2041 Yatiata Oaza, Sawada-machi, Sado-gun, Ni'igata-ken 952-13
Geology. Zoology. Botany. Archaeology. History. Folklore. Art. Technology. Industry.
Apr.-Oct. 8-5. Nov.-Mar. 9-4. Closed New Year season, Dec. 29 - Jan. 5.

SEKIGAHARA-MACHI

SEKIGAHARA PUBLIC MUSEUM
Sekigahara-machi, Fuwa-gun, Gifu-ken 503-15
Local history. Historical material on the Sekigahara Battle (16th century).
Daily 9-4. Closed Su., national holidays, Dec. 28 - Jan. 3.

SENDAI-SHI

ARCHAEOLOGICAL COLLECTION OF TOHOKU UNIVERSITY
Katahira-cho, Sendai-shi, Miyagi-ken 980
Local archaeological material, with other items from Hokkai-cho, Saghalien, and Korea.
Any time on request.

KAWAGUCHI TIBETAN COLLECTION OF TOHUKU UNIVERSITY
Tohoku University Japanese Art History Study Centre, Katahira-2 chome, Sendai-shi, Miyagi-ken 980
Sculpture of Tibet, India, Burma and Nepal. Buddhist statues.
Any time on request, 10-5. Closed Su. and University holidays.

MASAOKA MEMORIAL COLLECTION
Higashikyuban-cho, Sendai-shi, Miyagi-ken 980
Articles left by Hatsuko Misawa, "popularly known as a model of Masaoka in the Kabuki repertory called Sendai-hagi".
Daily 9-4.

SAITO HO'ONKAI MUSEUM
2-20-1 Honcho, Sendai-shi, Miyagi-ken 980
Zoology. Botany. Geology. Archaeology. History of the north-eastern district of Japan.
Daily 9-4. Closed M. and July 25. Also Dec. 25 - Jan. 10

THE SCIENCE ROOM, LEISURE CENTRE OF SENDAI
62 Higashi-sanbancho, Sendai-shi, Miyagi-ken
Physical sciences.
M.-F. 2-4.30 or by request.

SHIBAYAMA-CHO

SHIBAYAMA HANIWA MUSEUM
298 Shibayama, Shibayama-cho, Sanbu-gun, Chiba-ken 289-16
Haniwa (terra-cotta tomb figure); offerings and other items from Tonozuka tumulus and Himezuka tumulus.
Daily 9-5. Closed M.

SHIBI-MURA

TREASURE HOUSE OF THE EIHEIJI TEMPLE
5-15 Shibi, Eeiheiji cho, Yoshida-gun, Fukui-ken 910-12
Wooden treasure house containing art treasures of local and national importance.
Daily 9-4.

SHIDO-MACHI

TREASURE HOUSE OF THE SHIDO TEMPLE
Shido-machi, Okawa-gun, Kagawa-ken 769-21
Picture of eleven-faced Avalokitesvara on silk canvas; pic-

ture scroll entitled "The History of Shidoji Temple".
Daily 9-5.

SHIMADA-SHI

TREASURE HOUSE OF THE CHIMANJI TEMPLE
Chiba, Shimada-shi, Shizuoka-ken 427
The treasure house is made of wood and contains a thousand-handed Avalokitesvara as well as other Buddhist statues, paintings and writings, swords and altar fittings.
On request.

SHIMIZU-SHI

JIROCHO MEMORIAL COLLECTION
3-8 Minamiokacho, Shimizu-shi, Shizuoka-ken 424
Weapons, writings and every-day possessions of Jirocho Shimizu, kyokaku ("a man of chivalrous spirit") and his followers.
Mar.-Nov. Daily 8-5. Dec.-Feb. Daily 8-9.

TREASURE HOUSE OF THE MIHO SHRINE
1073 Miho, Shimizu-shi, Shizuoka-ken 424
Swords, old mirrors, lances, match-locks left by the Ota families, feudal lords of the province.
On request.

SHIMODA-MACHI

CHORAKUJI COLLECTION
Shichiken-cho, Shimoda-machi, Kamo-gun, Shizuoka-ken 415
Temple treasures, including images of Buddha.
Daily 9-4.

GYOKUSENJI COLLECTION
Kakizaki, Shimoda-machi, Kamo-gun, Shizuoka-ken 415
Articles relating to the first U.S. Consulate in Japan, and to T. Harris, the first consul-general.
By arrangement.

OKICHI MEMORIAL HALL
1-18-26 Shimoda-machi, Kamo-gun, Shizuoka-ken 415
Relics of Miss Okichi, "loved by T. Harris, the first American consul-general to Japan".
Daily 8-5.

RYOSENJI COLLECTION
3-12-12 Shimoda-machi, Kamo-gun, Shizuoka-ken 415
Historical material on the opening of Japan to foreign trade at the end of the Tokugawa regime.
Daily 8 a.m. - 10 p.m.

SHIMODA MEMORIAL COLLECTION OF OPENING JAPAN TO COMMERCE
2732-7 Shirakama, Shimoda-machi, Kamo-gun, Shizuoka-ken 415
Collections on the history of the period when T. Harris and M. C. Perry visited Japan.
Daily 8-5.

SHIMOGATA-GUN

TSUSHIMA LOCAL MUSEUM
668 Imayashiki, Itsukushima-machi, Shimogata-gun, Nagasaki-ken 817
Relics of the middle Jomon, Yayoi and Tumli periods; materials on Japanese-Korean relations.
Daily ex. M. 9-5. Closed Dec. 29 - Jan. 3.

SHIMONOSEKI-SHI

CHOFU MUSEUM
2,162 Kawabatacho, Chofu, Shimonoseki-shi, Yamaguchi-ken 752
Historical material on the Meiji Restoration, and on clan politics preceding the feudal age. Archaeological relics from the Shimonoseki area.
Daily ex. M. 9-5. Closed day after national holidays and Dec. 29 - Jan. 3.

JAPAN-CHINA PEACE NEGOTIATIONS MEMORIAL HALL
43 Amidaji-machi, Shimonoseki-shi, Yamaguchi-ken 751
Memorial chairs, lamps, ink-case stone, busts of Munemitsu Mutsu and Hirobumi Ito.
Daily 9-5.

TREASURE HOUSE OF THE INOMIYA SHRINE
Miyanouchi, Chofu-machi, Shimonoseki-shi, Yamaguchi-ken 752
Historical documents, pictures, weapons, altar fittings from the Meiji period and later.
Daily 9-5.

TREASURE HOUSE OF THE SUMIYOSHI SHRINE
Ichinomiya-machi, Shimonoseki-shi, Yamaguchi-ken 750-01
Karakura (saddle); writings of the Emperor Goyozei (16th-17th century) and the Emperor Reigen (17th century).
Daily 9-4.

SHIMOSUWA-MACHI

SHIMOSUWA PUBLIC MUSEUM
3580 Shimosuwa-machi, Suwa-gun, Nagano-ken 393
Findings from tumuli, especially armour.
Daily 9-5.

SHINGU-SHI

TREASURE HOUSE OF THE KUMANO SHINGU SHRINE
1 Shingu, Shingu-shi, Wakayama-ken 647
Articles ranging from the Kamakura Era to the Muromachi Era, including art objects.
Mar.-Sept. Daily 8-5. Oct.-Feb. Daily 9-4.

SHINOHARA-MACHI

BUSO ARCHAEOLOGICAL COLLECTION
Busodai, Shinohara-machi, Kohoku-ku, Yokohama
Materials of archaeological and historical interest found in the Sagami and Musashino districts. Folk art.
Daily 9-4. Closed M. and National Holidays.

SHIOBARA-MACHI

MUSEUM OF FOSSILISED LEAVES
472 Nakashiobara Oaza, Shiobara-machi, Shioya-gun, Tochigi-ken 329-29
Collection of fossilised leaves.
Daily 8-5.

SHIOJIRI-SHI

HIRAIDE SITE ARCHAEOLOGICAL MUSEUM
1011-3 Hiraide, Soga-Oaza, Shiojiri-shi, Nagano-ken 399-64
Finds from the ruins of Hiraide. Straw pattern pottery. Stone implements. Farmer's house from the Nara period.
Mar. - Nov. Daily ex. M. 8.30-5. Dec.-Feb. Daily ex. M. 8.30-4. Closed Dec. 29 - Jan. 3.

SHIOKI-MACHI

TREASURE HALL OF THE CHOSHOJI TEMPLE
Shioki, Shioki-machi, Ikukata-gun, Ibaraki-ken 311-24
The temple was established in 1185 by Shogun Minamoto Yoritomo. Historical pictures, documents.
Daily 9-2.

SHIZUOKA-SHI

SHIZUOKA ARCHAEOLOGICAL MUSEUM
410 Takamatsu, Shizuoka-shi, Shizuoka-ken 420
Objects from the ruins of Toro.
Daily 9-4.30. Closed M. and the day after National Holidays, also Dec. 26 - Jan. 5.

SHUHO-MACHI

AKIYOSHIDAI MUSEUM OF NATURAL HISTORY
Akiyoshi Oaza, Shuho-cho, Mine-gun, Yamaguchi-ken 754-05
Zoology. Geology. Palaeontology. Archaeology. Industry.
Apr.-Nov. Daily 9-4.30. Dec.-Mar. Daily 9-4. Closed Dec. 28 - Jan. 4.

SUWA-SHI

KATAKURA MEMORIAL COLLECTION
Nakahama-cho, Kamisuwa, Suwa-shi, Nagano-ken
Local archaeology. Industry. History of the silk industry.
Any time by appointment.

SUWA MUNICIPAL MUSEUM OF ART
4-1-14 Kogishi dori, Suwa-shi, Nagano-ken 392
Painting. Sculpture. Handicrafts by Japanese artists.
Daily 9-5. Closed M. and day after national holidays, also Dec. 28 - Jan. 3.

TAJIMI-SHI

TAJIMI MUNICIPAL OLD CHINA-WARE EXHIBITION HALL
c/o Tajimi Citizens Centre, 1-18 Shinmachi, Tajima-shi, Gifu-ken 507
China excavated from the site of old kilns at Tajimi, covering the period from 13th to 19th century.
Daily 8.30-5. Closed Dec. 29 - 31.

TAJIRI-MACHI

MISAWA COLLECTION
31 Kitano-sawa, Osawa-aza, Tajiri-machi, Onda-gun, Miyagi-ken 989-43
Stone implements. Pottery. Paintings.
Any time by arrangement.

TAHARA-MACHI

TAHARA LOCAL MUSEUM
12-1 Taharahako Oaza, Tahara-machi, Atsumi-gun, Aichi-ken 441-34
Mementoes of Kazan Watanabe, a scholar of European studies during the Edo period. Local history.
Daily 9-4. Closed M., the day after national holidays, and Dec. 28 - Jan. 5.

TAISHA-MACHI

TAISHA ARCHAEOLOGICAL COLLECTION
1236 Kinezukiminami, Taisha-machi, Hinokawa-gun, Shimane-ken 699-07
Earthenware, stone implements and other items from the Izumo area.
Daily 9-5. Closed M. and F. afternoons.

TAKAMATSU-SHI

TAKAMATSU MUNICIPAL MUSEUM OF ART
1-20-17 Ritsurin-machi, Takamatsu-shi, Kagawa-ken 760
Works by local artists.
Daily ex. M. 9-4.30. Closed Dec. 29 - Jan. 3.

TAKANOSU-MACHI

AGRICULTURAL MUSEUM OF TAKANOSU PREFECTURAL AGRICULTURAL AND FORESTRY HIGH SCHOOL
Takanosu-machi, Kita'akita-gun, Akita-ken
Collection relating to agriculture, forestry and biology.
Daily except Su. 8-5. Closed National Holidays, the last 10 days of July and New Year season.

TAKAOKA-SHI

TAKAOKA MUNICIPAL MUSEUM OF ART
1-5 Kojo, Takaoka-shi, Oyoma-ken 933
Chiefly works by local artists, including paintings, calligraphy, sculpture and handicrafts. Industrial arts.
Daily 9-5. Closed Dec. 28 - Jan. 3.

TAKAYAMA-SHI

TAKAYAMA LOCAL MUSEUM
75 Ichino-machi, Takayama-shi, Gifu-ken 506
Items collected from the Hida area.
Daily 9-5. Closed Dec. 29 - Jan. 1.

TAKEDA-SHI

HISOKA MAEJIMA MEMORIAL COLLECTION
1299 Jinmeigae, Shimoikebe-aza, Oaza, Takeda-shi, Niigata-ken 943-01
Relics, manuscripts and photographs relating to the life and achievements of Hisoka Maejima, the founder of the modern Japanese postal service.
Daily 9-4. Closed Dec. 29 - Jan. 3.

TAMANO-SHI

TAMANO MARINE MUSEUM
250 Shibukawa, Tamano-shi, Okayama-ken 706
Aquatic animals and plants. Fossils. Earthenware. Salt-industry. Fishing industry.
Daily 8.30-5.

TENRI-SHI

TENRI MUSEUM
1 Furu-machi, Tenri-shi, Nara-ken 632
Relics of ancient civilisation. Folk art.
Daily 9-4. Closed Su. and National Holidays, also Dec. 28 - Jan. 4.

TESHIKAGA-MACHI

AKAN WAGOTO MUSEUM
Wagoto, Teshikaga-machi, Kawakami-gun, Hokkaido 088-33
Articles relating to the Ainu tribe. Specimens of insects, fish, mammals and birds, plants, antiquities from the Akan National Park area.
May-Oct. 8-6. Closed in winter.

TOKONAME-SHI

TOKONAME CHINA-WARE HALL
45 Okegake aza, Tokoname-shi, Aichi-ken 479
Modern pottery, porcelain from local factories.
Daily ex. M. 9-4. Closed national holidays and Dec. 28-Jan. 4.

TOKUSHIMA-SHI

ATTACHED SCIENCE ROOM FOR CHILDREN OF TOKUSHIMA LIBRARY
1 Shironouchi, Tokushima-shi, Tokushima-ken
The main exhibits are models and machinery connected with electrical engineering.
Daily from 8.30 a.m. Closed Tu. and National holidays.

TOKUSHIMA MUSEUM
1-1 Nishiyamate-machi, Tokushima-shi, Tokushima-ken 770
Art. Industry. Civil engineering. Biology. Geology. Archaeology of Tokushima district.
Daily 9.30-4.30. Closed M. and National Holidays. Also closed 3rd Th. of each month, and Dec. 28-Jan. 4.

TOKYO

ARCHAEOLOGICAL COLLECTION
Faculty of Letters, Tokyo University, 1 Motofuji-cho, Tokyo
Archaeology of Japan, Asia and Europe.
Daily 9-4.

ARCHAEOLOGICAL COLLECTION OF KOKUBUNJI
1-13-16 Nishi-moto-machi, Kokobunji-shi, Tokyo 185
Tiles from the site at Kokubunji. Stone implements and earthenware from the region.
Daily 8-5.

ARCHAEOLOGICAL COLLECTION OF KOKUGAKUIN UNIVERSITY
4-10-28 Higashi, Shibuya-ku, Tokyo 150
Archaeology of Japan, the Orient and America. Articles associated with the Festival of Matsuri.
Daily ex. Su. 9-4.30. Closed national holidays and other days decided by the University.

ARCHAEOLOGICAL COLLECTION OF MEIJI UNIVERSITY
1-1 Surugadai, Kanda, Chiyoda-ku, Tokyo 101
Archaeological material. Relics of Pre-Jomon, Jomon and Yayoi periods.
Daily 10-5. Closed Su. and national holidays.

BASEBALL HALL OF FAME AND MUSEUM
3-61 1-chome, Koraku, Bunkyo-ku, Tokyo 112
History of baseball in Japan. Memorabilia of the game's leading personalities. Sport medicine. Photographs.
Daily 10-5. Closed Feb. 1-7, Dec. 28-31.

BRIDGESTONE MUSEUM OF ART
1-1 Kyobashi, Chuo-ku, Tokyo
Collection made by Shojiro Ishibashi, founder of Bridgestone Tyre Co. European paintings, sculptures and objets d'art from 25th century B.C. to present day. Japanese Western style paintings from Meiji period to present day. Porcelain.
Daily 10-5.30. Closed Su. in July and Aug., and on M. rest of year.

BROADCASTING MUSEUM
1-10 Shiba-aitomachi, Minato-ku, Tokyo 105
Collection of equipment, models and photographs illustrating history of radio and televison.
Daily 9.30-4.30. Closed M. and Dec. 26-Jan. 4.

THE CICADA MUSEUM OF THE KATO INSTITUTE FOR ENTOMOLOGY
2-1,800 Kamashakujii, Nerima-ku
The collection includes insect speciments, toys made of cicada and toys of cicada pattern.
Apr.-Sept. Daily 8-4. Oct.-Mar. Daily 9-4. Closed New Year season.

COLLECTION OF FIRE-FIGHTING EQUIPMENT
20 Nagata-cho, Chiyoda-ku, Tokyo
Large collection of fire-fighting equipment, including items used in the Edo period.
Daily 9-4. Closed M. and National Holidays.

COMMUNICATIONS AND POSTAL SERVICE MUSEUM
2-3-1 Otemachi, Chiyoda-ku, Tokyo 100
History of the postal service in Japan. Postage stamps.
Daily except M. 9-4.30. Closed Dec. 29-Jan. 3.

CORRECTIONAL MUSEUM
2-8 Harumicho, Fuchu, Tokyo
Criminology. Methods of dealing with criminals and delinquents.
Daily 9-4.30 by appointment.

COSTUME MUSEUM
6-13, 4-chome, Kami-osaki, Shinagawi-ku, Tokyo
European and Asiatic costumes.
Daily 10-4.

CRIMINAL MUSEUM OF MEIJI UNIVERSITY
1-1 Surugadai, Kanda, Chiyoda-ku, Tokyo 101
Collection illustrating history of the law and law enforcement.
Daily 10-4. Closed Su. and National Holidays.

DOCUMENTARY COLLECTION OF THE MINISTRY OF EDUCATION
16-10 1-Chome, Yutakacho, Shinagawa-ku, Tokyo
Historical records relating to education in Japan. Folklore materials.
M.-F. 9.30-4.30; Sa. 9.30-11.30.

EDOGAWA-KU LOCAL MUSEUM
1-38 1-chome, Matsushima, Edogawa-ku, Tokyo
Archaeology. Agriculture. Fishing. Ethnology.
Daily 9-4.30.

ELECTRICAL SCIENCE MUSEUM OF TOKYO METROPOLITAN ELECTROTECHNICAL LABORATORY
3-5 Yuraku-cho, Chiyoda-ku, Tokyo
Models, panels, experimental apparatus and machinery explaining fundamental principles and applications of electricity.
Daily 9-4.30. Closed Su., National Holidays and New Year season.

ETHNOGRAPHICAL MUSEUM OF HOYA
Shimohoya, Hoya-machi, Kitatama-gun, Tokyo
Clothing, eating utensils, dwellings, religious objects of Japan's early inhabitants.
Jan. 5-Dec. 27, Daily 10-4. Closed M. and the day after National Holidays.

EXHIBITION HALL OF TOKYO UNIVERSITY OF ARTS LIBRARY AND MASAKI MEMORIAL HALL
Ueno-koen, Daito-ku, Tokyo 110
Paintings. Sculpture. Metalwork.
During term-time, daily 10-4. Closed Sa., Su. and national holidays.

FIBRE MUSEUM
Faculty of Technology, Tokyo University of Agriculture and Technology, 24-16 2-chome, Nagamachi, Koganei-shi, Tokyo
Exhibits of natural and synthetic fibres.
M.-F. 9-4; Sa. 9-12.

FOLK ART MUSEUM
3-33 4-chome, Komaba, Meguro-ku, Tokyo
Folk arts and crafts of various countries, including Japan.
Daily 10-4.

FOLKLORE COLLECTION OF IGUSA HACHIMAN-GU SHRINE
33-1 1-chome, Zenpukuji, Tokyo
Domestic equipment. Agricultural implements.
Daily: winter 10-3. summer 9-5.

FOLK MUSEUM OF SETAGAYA
29-18 1-chome, Setagaya, Setagaya-ku, Tokyo
Decorative arts. Handicrafts.
Daily 9-4.30.

FUCHU MUNICIPAL FOLK MUSEUM
3-1 Mujamachi, Fuchu-shi, Tokyo
Local history and archaeology.
Daily 9-5.

GAS MUSEUM
2-590 Onumacho, Kodaira-shi, Tokyo
In former sales office (1909) of the Gas Company. History of the use of gas for lighting and heating.
Daily 10-4.

GOTO ART MUSEUM
111 Kaminoge, Tamagawa, Setagaya-ku, Tokyo 158
Calligraphy. Paintings. Lacquerware. China. Mirrors. Sculptures. Tea utensils. Oriental art, including picture scroll of the Tales of Genji. Archaeological relics. Early Chinese jades. Korean ceramics.
Daily ex. M. 10-4.

GOTOH PLANETARIUM AND ASTRONOMICAL MUSEUM
2-21-12 Shibuya, Shibuya-ku, Tokyo 150
Exhibits include Coelostat Telescope; model of solar and lunar eclipse; model of moon rocket (Lunik). Planetarium.
Apr.-Sept. Daily 9-8. Oct.-Mar. Daily ex. M. 9-6.30. Closed Dec. 28-Jan. 1.

GYOKUDO ART MUSEUM
75 Mitake, Ome-shi, Tokyo
Works of the painter, Gyokudo Kawai.
Daily 9-4.

HACHIOJI CITY MUSEUM
70 Ueno-machi, Hachioji City, Tokyo
Local textile industry. Archaeology. Architectural history.
Daily 9-4.30.

HATAKEYAMA COLLECTION
20-12 2-chome, Shiroganedai, Shiba, Minato-ku, Tokyo
History. Ethnography. Tea ceremony room. Tea garden. Japanese painting and sculpture.
Daily 10-4.

HIDEYO NOGUCHI MUSEUM
26 Daikyomachi, Shinjuku-ku, Tokyo
Life, achievements and personal possessions of the physician, Dr. Hideyo Noguchi.
Daily 9-4.

ICHI-YO MEMORIAL MUSEUM
18-4 2-chome, Ryusen, Daito-ku, Tokyo
Life and work of the writer, Ichi-Yo.
Daily 9-4.30.

IDEMITSU ART GALLERY
12 1-chome, Marunouchi, Chujoda-ku, 9th floor of Teigeki Kaikan, Tokyo
Private collection of Japanese oil magnate.
Pottery from old kiln sites in Japan, China, Korea, Middle and Near East. Collections of Karatsu-ware and Sengai paintings. *Ukiyo-e* prints and screens.
Daily ex. M. 10-5.

INDUSTRIAL SAFETY MUSEUM
1-4-6 Ume-en, Kiyosemachi, Kitatama-gun, Tokyo 180-04
Safety devices for machinery. Panels describing instructive data and safety in factories and schools.
M.-F. 9.30-4.30; Sa. 9.30-12. Closed Su., national holidays and Dec. 28-Jan. 4.

JAPANESE FOLK CRAFT MUSEUM
861 Komaba, Meguro-ku, Tokyo 152
Japanese handicrafts, including wood, pottery and straw. Basketry. Textiles. Lacquer-ware.
Daily 10-5. Closed M., also Dec. 27-Feb. 28.

JAPANESE FOUNDATION FOR THE PROMOTION OF MARITIME SCIENCE
35 Shibakotohiracho, Minato-ku, Tokyo
Ship models. Techniques of shipbuilding.
Daily 9-4.30.

JAPANESE SWORD MUSEUM
25-10 4-chome, Yoyogi, Shibuya-ku, Tokyo
Swords and fittings.
Daily 9-4.

KOMABA HIGH SCHOOL MUSEUM
18-11 2-chome, Ohashi, Megoru-ku, Tokyo
Founded in memory of the painter, Torao Makino (d. 1946). Paintings, including works by Makino. Casts of European sculpture.
Daily 9-4.

THE LABOUR MUSEUM OF LABOUR SCIENCE INSTITUTE
2-1, 226 Soshigaya, Setagaya-ku, Tokyo
Material illustrating pathology, physiology, of working conditions and fatigue. Protective and measuring equipment.
Daily 9-4. Closed Sa., Su., National Holidays and Jan.

LOCAL HISTORY MUSEUM
16-10 1-chome, Yutakacho, Shinagawa-ju, Tokyo
Local history.
Daily ex. M. 9-4.

MEGURO PARASITOLOGICAL MUSEUM
4-1-1 Shimo-Meguro, Meguro-ku, Tokyo 153
Collection illustrating parasitology.
Daily 11-4. Closed M. and National Holidays, also Dec. 28-Jan. 4.

MEIJI THE GREAT MEMORIAL GALLERY
9 Kasumigaoka, Shinjuku-ku, Tokyo 160
Eighty paintings of the life story of Emperor Meiji.
Daily 9-4. Closed Dec. 31.

MEIJI THE GREAT MEMORIAL HALL OF TAMA
2198 Renko-ji, Tama-machi, Minamitama-gun, Tokyo 192-02
Possessions and paintings of Emperor Meiji and the Meiji warriors.
Daily 9-5.

MEIJI MEMORIAL MUSEUM
2184 Renkoji, Tamamachi, Minamitama-gun, Tokyo
Manuscripts, letters and personal possessions of leading figures in the Meiji Restoration.
Daily 9-5.

MEIJI SHRINE TREASURE MUSEUM
Yoyogi, Shibuya-ku, Tokyo
Treasures and possessions of Emperor Meiji and Empress Shoken. Picture gallery.
Daily ex. M. 9-4.

MEIJI UNIVERSITY MUSEUM OF CRIMINOLOGY
1-1 Kanda-Surugadai, Chujoda-ku, Tokyo
History of punishment of criminals. Police equipment. Records of criminal cases.
Daily 10-5.

MEIJI UNIVERSITY MUSEUM OF TRADE AND COMMERCE
1-1 Kanda-Surugadai, Chujoda-ku, Tokyo
Collections illustrating commercial methods and techniques, together with the principal products involved.
M.-F. 10-5; Sa. 10-1.

MEMORIAL HALL OF THE RECONSTRUCTION OF TOKYO
3-25 2-chome, Yokoami, Sumida-ku, Tokyo 130
Material illustrating damage done to Tokyo by the Great Earthquake. Replanning of Tokyo.
Daily 9-4 on the following dates: Mar. 9, 10, 20, 21, 22; July 14-16; Aug. 31; Sept. 1, 23-25.

THE MEMORIAL SPORT MUSEUM OF PRINCE CHICHIBU
c/o National Sports Arena, 10 Kasumigaoka, Shinjuku-ku, Tokyo 160
Personal effects of the late Prince Chichibu, including mementoes and materials for the Olympic Games, Asian Games, medals, cups and trophies of various athletic meetings, films and records.
Daily ex. M. 9.30-5. Closed Apr. 1, Dec. 28-Jan. 3, and two weeks in spring and autumn.

METROPOLITAN KOMABA HIGH SCHOOL ART MUSEUM
2-18-11 Ohashi, Meguro-ku, Tokyo 153
Works of Torao Makino. Copies of European paintings.
Daily ex. Su. 9-4.

MIAGEIKAN MUSEUM OF MODERN ART
801 Komaba-cho, Meguro-ku, Tokyo
Ethnology. Folklore. Folk-art. Paintings.
Daily ex. M. 9-4.

MUSASHINO LOCAL MUSEUM
Koganei Park, Koganei-shi, Tokyo 184
Archaeology. Historical. Folk art.
Daily 9-4.30. Closed Dec. 29-31.

MUSEUM OF ART AND HISTORY OF THE UNIVERSITY OF TOKYO
8-1 3-chome, Komaba, Megoro-ku, Tokyo
Art, history, anthropology and geography of the Far East.
Summer: Daily 10-4. Winter: Daily 10-12.30.

MUSEUM OF CALLIGRAPHY
2-10-4 Negishi, Daito-ku, Tokyo 110
Collection of Japanese and Chinese calligraphy. Old manuscripts. Coins.
Daily 10-4. Closed M. and Dec. 25-Jan. 10.

MUSEUM OF MODERN JAPANESE LITERATURE
3-55 4-chome, Komaba, Meguro-ku, Tokyo
Literary manuscripts. Books and background material relating to modern Japanese literature.
Daily 9.30-4.30.

MUSEUM OF MUSICAL INSTRUMENTS
1-13 Hanezawa, Nerima-ku, Tokyo
Musical instruments from Europe and the Far East.
Daily 10-3.

MUSEUM OF THE NATIONAL RESEARCH LABORATORY OF METROLOGY
10-4, 1-chome, Itabashi-ku, Tokyo
Japanese weights and measures.
M.-F. 10-4; Sa. 10-12.

MUSEUM OF THE PATENT OFFICE
1 Sannencho, Chujoda-ku, Tokyo
Patents. Models.
Apr.-Oct. Daily ex. Su. and public holidays 8-7. Nov.-Mar. 9-6. Closed Dec. 26-Jan. 4, the last week in Sept. and the 3rd week in Oct.

MUSEUM OF TRANSPORT
1-25 Suda-cho, Chiyoda-ku, Tokyo 101
Collections illustrating railway history and the fundamental principles of traffic engineering. Exhibits include vehicles, equipment, models of railways, automobiles, ships and aircraft. Among them is the oldest locomotive in Japan.
Daily 9.30-5. Closed M. and Dec. 29-Jan. 3.

NAKANO WARD HISTORY MUSEUM
Tokyo
Local history, archaeology and folklore.
Daily 9-4.30.

NATIONAL MUSEUM
1 Ueno Park, Daito-ku, Tokyo
Formerly the Museum of the Imperial Family. Archaeology. Antiquities. Painting. Sculpture. Decorative arts. A 17th century ceremonial tea house has been reconstructed in the Museum gardens. Calligraphy. Stone Buddhist images. Ceramics. Lacquerware.
Daily ex. M. Mar.-Oct. 9-4.30. Nov.-Feb. 9-4. Closed Dec. 26-Jan. 3.

NATIONAL MUSEUM OF ANTIQUES
Hotel Okura, Akasaka Aoi-cho, Tokyo
European artifacts. Ancient Japanese *magatama*, the early symbols of the prehistoric people here.
Daily ex. M. and national holidays, 10-4.

NATIONAL MUSEUM OF MODERN ART
3 Kita no Marunouchi Park, Chiyodaku, Tokyo 102
Sculpture, paintings, handicrafts and calligraphy, from Japan and Europe. Decorative arts. Prints. Crafts.
Daily 10-5. Closed M. and Dec. 28-Jan. 4.

NATIONAL MUSEUM OF WESTERN ART
7-7 Ueno-koen, Daito-ku, Tokyo
Museum building is by Le Corbusier. Mainly French painting and sculpture, especially by Rodin ('The Citizen of Calais' and 'The Gate of Hell'), from the early 19th century to 1914. The works in the Museum come from the Matsukata collection, built up in France before 1939. Works by Matisse and Picasso.
Daily 9-5. Closed M.

NATIONAL SCIENCE MUSEUM
7 Ueno Park, Daito-ku, Tokyo
Physical sciences. Natural history. Technology. Models of the flora of Japan in wax and other materials. Engineering. Experimental apparatus. Machinery.
Daily 9-4.30. Closed M.

NEZU ART MUSEUM
6-5-36 Aoyama Minamicho, Minato-ku, Tokyo 107
Paintings. Calligraphy. China and lacquer-ware. Metalwork. Utensils for tea ceremony. Buddhist sculptures and satras as well as paintings including Korin's painting on byobu. Chinese bronzes. Scrolls. Archaeology.
Daily 9-4.30. Closed M., the day after National Holidays, July-Aug., and Dec. 25-Jan. 5.

N.H.K. MUSEUM OF BROADCASTING
10 1-chome, Atagocho, Shiba, Minato-ku, Tokyo
History of broadcasting.
Daily 9.30-4.30.

OBUNSHA CENTER OF PUBLISHING CULTURE
55 Yokoteramachi, Shinjuku-ku, Tokyo
History of printing and publishing. Ceramics. Glass. Coins.
Daily 9-5; Sa. 9-12.

ODAWARA CARCINOLOGICAL MUSEUM
11-4 3-chome, Azabujuban, Minato-ku, Tokyo
Carcinology.
By appointment.

OKURA MUSEUM
3 Aoi-cho, Akasaka-Aoicho, Minato-ku, Tokyo
Japanese and Oriental classic art. Archaeology.
Daily ex. M. and public holidays, 10-4. Closed Dec. 29-Jan. 4.

OKURA MUSEUM
Aoi-cho, Akasaka, Minato-ku, Tokyo 170
Japanese and Oriental art. Archaeological relics.
Daily ex. M. 10-4. Closed Dec. 29-Jan. 4.

OME RAILWAY PARK
155 Katsunuma, Ome, Tokyo
Locomotives and rolling stock formerly in use on Japanese railways.
Daily: Summer 9-5; winter 9-4.

PENTAX GALLERY
202 Kasumicho Corpo, 21-30 3-chome, Nishiazabu, Tokyo
Cameras from various countries.
Daily 10-5.

PAPER MUSEUM
1-1-8 Funabozi, Kita-ku, Tokyo 114
Large collection of samples of domestic and European papers. Paper goods. Machines and tools for making paper. History of paper-making.
Mar.-Oct. Daily 9-5. Nov.-Feb. Daily 9.30-4.30. Closed Su., national holidays and Dec. 29-Jan. 4.

PRINCE CHICHIBU MEMORIAL SPORTS MUSEUM
National Stadium, 10 Kasumigaoka, Shinjuku-ku, Tokyo
History and personalities of sport in Japan.
Daily 9-4.30.

PROFESSOR AIZU MEMORIAL EXHIBITION ROOM OF ORIENTAL ARTS
c/o Waseda University, Totsuka-cho, Shinjuku-ku, Tokyo 160
Mirrors of Japan and China. Tiles of Japan, China and Korea. Calligraphy. Buddhist sculpture. Coins.
Tu., Th. and Sa. 9-4. Closed during University vacations.

PUBLICATION CENTRE OF OBUNSHA COMPANY
Yokodera-cho, Shinjuki-ku, Tokyo 162
Japanese and foreign books, magazines. Techniques and history of book production.
Daily 9-5; Sa. 9-12. Closed Sa. afternoons and Su.

RED CROSS MUSEUM
5-gochi, Shiba-koen, Minato-ku, Tokyo
History of the Red Cross. Relationship between health and clothes, food, water and parasites. Health of mother and baby. Epidemics. Models of dissected human body. Charts for health.
Daily 9-4. Closed M. and New Year season.

RYUSHI KAWABABA MUSEUM
2-1 4-chome, Chuo, Ota-ku, Tokyo
Paintings by Ryushi.
Daily 9-4.

SCIENCE MUSEUM
2-1 Kitanamoru Park, Chiyoda-ku, Tokyo
Machinery. Scientific equipment. Models.
Daily 9.30-5.

SUGINO GAKUEN COSTUME MUSEUM
4-6-13 Kamiosaki, Shinagawa-ku, Tokyo 141
Collection of costumes and materials, showing history of costumes in Japan, Belgium, Italy and Hungary.
Daily ex. Su. 10-4. Closed Dec. 29-Jan. 4.

SUMO MUSEUM
2-1-9 Kuramae, Daito-ku, Tokyo 111
Materials on the history of Sumo, a traditional sport similar to wrestling.
Daily 9-5. Closed Su. and National Holidays, also Dec. 31-Jan. 4.

SUNTORY ART GALLERY
10 1-chome, Marounouchi, Chujoda-ku, Tokyo
"Classical art objects close to the daily life of the Japanese people." *Edo* and *Muromachi* articles connected with the households of that period.
Daily ex. M. and public holidays, 10-5.

TENRI GALLERY
1-9 Kanda-Nishikicho, Chiyoda-ku, Tokyo
Archaeology, from excavations in China and Japan. Decorative arts. Toys. Ethnography and folk art from various parts of the world, including pre-Columbian, African and Oceanic work.
Daily 9-5; Sa. 9-3.

TAKANAWA ART MUSEUM
10-30 4-chome, Takanawa, Minato-ku, Tokyo
Images of Buddha. Japanese paintings. Lacquer work.
Daily 9-4.

TEXTILE MUSEUM
Faculty of Textile Industry, Tokyo University of Agriculture and Technology, 2-24-16 Naka-machi, Koganei-shi, Tokyo 184
Textile raw materials. Specimens of finished textiles.
M.-F. 9-4. Sa. Closed Su., National Holidays and Dec. 28-Jan. 4.

TOKYO DENRYOKU IKEBUKURO SERVICE CENTRE WITH HISTORICAL MATERIALS OF ELECTRIC ENTERPRISE
8-9 1-chome, Higashi, Ikebukoro, Tochima-ku, Tokyo
Old Japanese electrical equipment.
Daily 10-6.

TOKYO METROPOLITAN ART GALLERY
8-51 Ueno Park, Daito-ku, Tokyo
Contemporary paintings, sculpture.
Daily 9-5.

TOKYO-TO TAKAO MUSEUM OF NATURAL HISTORY
2463 Takaomachi, Hachioji-shi, Tokyo
Natural history.
Daily 9-4.

TOSHIMAEN INSECTARIUM
25-1 3-chome, Mukoyama, Nerima-ku, Tokyo
Mounted and living land and water insects.
Daily 9-5.

TRANSPORT MUSEUM
25, 1-chome, Kanda-Sudacho, Chiyoda-ku, Tokyo
Working train models. Miniature (16.5 mm.) trains of Japanese National Railways. Actual examples, or models, of ships, motorcars, aeroplanes.
Daily 9.30-5.

TREASURE HOUSE OF THE MEIJI SHRINE
1-1 Kamizonomachi, Yoyogi, Shibuya-ku, Tokyo
Mementoes of the Emperor Meiji and his consort.
Apr.-Sept. Daily 8.30-4. Oct.-Mar. Daily 9.30-4.30.

TREASURE HOUSE OF THE YASUKUNI SHRINE
1-1 3-chome, Kudankita, Chujoda-ku, Tokyo
Personal mementoes of those killed in battle since the time of the Meiji Restoration. Paintings. Swords and other weapons. Helmets.
Summer: Daily 9.30-4. Winter: Daily 8.30-4.

TSUBOUCHI MEMORIAL MUSEUM OF WASEDA UNIVERSITY
1-647 Tozuka-cho, Sinju-ku, Tokyo 160
The building is a replica of the Elizabethan Fortune Theatre in London, built in memory of Dr. Tsubouchi, a distinguished scholar who translated the complete works of Shakespeare. Objects connected with Japanese drama. Books, drawings, costumes, properties, other equipment used on the stage. Colour prints. Programmes. Wood blocks.
Daily 9-4. Closed M. and the day following National Holidays.

UMEZAWA MUSEUM
4th floor, Nihon Iji-Shinpo Building, 9 2-chome, Kanda-Surugadai, Chujoda-ku, Tokyo
Japanese and Chinese ceramics. Painting. Calligraphy. Tea ceremony utensils.
Daily 10-5.

VISCOUNT KURODA MEMORIAL ROOM
c/o National Institute of Cultural Properties, Uenokoen, Daito-ku, Tokyo 110
Established by the will of Viscount Seiki Kuroda, a painter and statesman, for the basic study of arts and to exhibit his works. Oils, sketch books and designs.
Th. afternoons 1-4.

YAMASHINA INSTITUTE OF ORNITHOLOGY
49 Nanpeidaimachi, Shibuya-ku, Tokyo
Skins of birds from all over the world.
Daily 9.30-4.

YAMATANE MUSEUM OF ART
30 2-chome, Kabutocho, Nihonbashi, Chuo-ku, Tokyo
Paintings and decorative arts, mainly modern Japanese.
Daily 11-5.

TOMIOKA-SHI

GUNMA PREFECTURAL MUSEUM
1,353 Ichinomiya, Tomioka-shi, Gunma-ken 370-24
Archaeological relics. Folk art. Local history.
Daily 9-4.30. Closed M. and National Holidays, also Dec. 28-Jan. 5.

TOSAYAMADA-MACHI

THE RYUGADO MUSEUM
1340 Sakagawa, Tosayamada-machi, Kami-gun, Kochi-ken 782
Archaeology. Material from lime-stone caves, including stalactites. Specimens of lime-stone flora, minerals and rocks.
Daily 8-6.

TOTTORI-SHI

TOTTORI HANDICRAFT MUSEUM
653 Sakacho, Tottori-shi, Tottori-ken 680
Handicrafts, especially china.
Daily 10-5. Closed M. and Dec. 30-Jan. 4.

TOTTORI PREFECTURAL SCIENCE MUSEUM
2-121 Higashi-cho, Tottori-shi, Tottori-ken 680
Zoology. Botany. Physical geography. Experimental apparatus related to physics and chemistry.
Daily 9-4.30. Closed M., National Holidays and Dec. 29-Jan. 3, also Su. and Sa. afternoon in winter.

TOWADA-MACHI

TOWADA MUSEUM OF NATURAL HISTORY
16 Towada, Okuseaza, Towada-machi Oaza, Kamikita-gun, Aomori-ken 034-03
Topographical and zoological collections.
May-Nov. 19, Daily 8-6. Apr.-Nov. 20, Daily 8-5.

TOYAMA-SHI

TOYAMA LOCAL MUSEUM
1-62 Motomaku, Toyama-shi, Toyama-ken 930
Natural science. Paintings. Drawings. Ceramics, stuffed birds and mammals from Toyama district. Regional social history.
Daily 9-5. Closed M. and also Dec. 29-Jan. 3.

TOYONAKA-SHI

THE MUSEUM OF JAPANESE FOLK DWELLINGS
1203 Chokoji Oaza, Toyonaka-shi, Osaka-fu 560
Exhibits showing Japanese folk dwellings: Gassho-zukuri; Takakura; Suiyo; Shirakawamura-house, with original furnishings.
Daily ex. M. 9.30-4.30. Closed National Holidays (except in Oct. and Nov.), also Dec. 29-Jan. 3.

TOYOTA-GUN

KOZOJI TEMPLE MUSEUM
553-2 Setoda, Oaza, Setodacho, Toyota-gun, Hiroshima-ken 722-24
Built by a merchant, with its buildings modelled on famous examples of architecture in Japanese history. Buddhist arts including sculptures and utensils. Calligraphy. Mirrors. Handicrafts. Modern paintings and sculpture.
Daily 8-5.

TSUDAKA-MACHI

SAKANO MEMORIAL HALL ATTACHED COMMUNICATION MUSEUM
463 Yoshimune Oaza, Tsudaka-machi, Mitsu-gun, Okayama-ken 701-11
In memory of Tetsujiro Sakano, "who devoted himself to the Japanese postal service". Exhibits relating to him and to the postal service.
Daily 9-4. Closed M. and Dec. 28-Jan. 4.

TSUGU-MACHI

TSUGU LOCAL COLLECTION
33-22 Midehara, Tsugu-mura aza, Kitashidara-gun, Aichi-ken 441-26
Collection of items, illustrating local history of the Okumikawa area.
Daily Nov.-Apr. 9.30-4. May-Oct. 9-4. Closed Su., Sa. afternoon, and national holidays.

TSUKUBA-MACHI

TREASURE HOUSE OF THE TSUKUBASAN SHRINE
Tsukubasan Chufuku, Tsukuba-machi, Tsukuba-gun, Ibaraki-ken 300-43
Articles bequeathed to the Shrine.
On request.

TSUKUI-MACHI

GAKUDO OZAKI MEMORIAL HALL
Nakano, Tsukui-machi, Tsukui-gun, Kanagawa-ken 220-02
Relics of Gakudo Ozaki, one of the great forerunners of modern democracy in Japanese politics.
Daily 9-4.

TSURUGA-SHI

TSURUGA PROVINCIAL MUSEUM
1-3-3 Mishima-cho, Tsuruga-shi, Fukui-ken 914
"Provincial materials for the education of humanities and natural sciences".
Apr.-Oct. Daily 9-4. Nov.-Mar. Daily 9-3.

TSURUOKA-SHI

CHIDO MUSEUM
10-18 Yanaka-shin-machi, Tsuruoka-shi, Yamagata-ken 997
Stone implements, pottery-images, earthenware dating from the Stone Age. Domestic articles. Material related to the Chidokan School.
Daily 9-5. Closed Dec. 29-Jan. 3.

TSU-SHI

MIE PREFECTURAL MUSEUM
147 Komei-cho, Tsu-shi, Mie-ken 514
Local history. Archaeology. Art. Natural science. Industry.
Daily 9-4.30. Closed M., end of month, also Dec. 28-Jan. 3.

TSUWANO-MACHI

TSUWANO LOCAL COLLECTION
127 Mori-mura Ro, Tsuwano-machi Oaza, Katari-gun, Shimane-ken 699-56
Historical material on the Tsuwano clan; documents and records of well-known people from the region.
Daily 9-5.

TSUYAMA-SHI

TSUYAMA HISTORICAL HALL
26 Minamishinza, Tsuyama-shi, Okayama-ken 708
Local history. Manuscripts. Coffins.
Daily 9-4. Closed M. and National Holidays, also Dec. 29-Jan. 1.

TSUYAMA SCIENCE AND INDUSTRY MUSEUM
973 Yamashita, Tsuyama-shi, Okayama-ken 708
Collections of plants, mammals, birds, fish, shells, insects, fossils and minerals. Industry.
Daily 9-4.

UEDA-SHI

UEDA MUNICIPAL MUSEUM
3-3 Ni-no-maku, Ueda-shi, Nagano-ken 386
Archaeology. History. Natural history. Weapons. Documents. Excavated objects of Jomon and Yayoi periods. Domestic articles. Specimens of animals and plants, minerals and rocks.
Daily 8.30-5. Closed W. and national holidays, also Dec. 27-Jan. 4.

UENO-SHI

BASHO MEMORIAL HALL
117-13 Marunouchi, Ueno-shi, Mie-ken
Autographs and manuscripts by Basho Matsuo, a haiku master (famous haiku verse reader in Edo Period).
Daily 9-4. Closed M. and Th. afternoon. Also day after national holidays and Dec. 29-Jan. 3.

IGA ART AND INDUSTRY INSTITUTE
6 1-Marunouchi, Ueno, Ueno-shi, Mie-ken
Collections illustrating local art and industry.
By appointment.

UJI'IEKAMI-MACHI

KINUGAWA LOCAL MUSEUM
Uji'iekami-machi, Shioya-gun, Tochigi-ken
Archaeological, historical and geological collections.
Any time by arrangement.

UME-MACHI

UME LOCAL MUSEUM
341 Kozan, Oaza, Ume-machi, Minamiamabe-gun, Oita-ken 879-32
Minerals. Mineral ores. Rocks from Kiura tin mine. Tools and equipment used by miners.
Daily 8-5.

UOZU-SHI

UOZU BURIED FOREST MUSEUM
814 Shakado-machi, Uozu-shi, Toyama-ken 937
Fossils from the buried forest, mostly of 200-800 year old cedars, and rocks.
Daily 8.30-5.

URAWA-SHI

SAITAMA PREFECTURAL MUSEUM OF ART
Bessho, Urawa-shi, Saitama-ken 336
Works by local artists.
Daily 9-4.

YAHIKO-MURA

TREASURE HOUSE OF THE YAHIKO SHRINE
2898 Yahiko, Yahiko-mura, Nishikambara-gun, Niigata-ken 959
Swords. Japanese old gold coins. Art collection.
Daily 9-4.

YAMAGATA-SHI

LOCAL MUSEUM OF YAMAGATA UNIVERSITY
1-4-12 Koshira Kamamachi, Yamagata-shi, Yamagata-ken 990
Stone implements. Earthenware. Documents.
Daily 9-5. Closed National holidays, Su. and Dec. 29 - Jan. 3.

YAMAGUCHI-SHI

YAMAGUCHI PREFECTURAL MUSEUM
8-2 Kasugacho, Yamaguchi-shi, Yamaguchi-ken 753
Natural science. Geology. Mineralogy. Local history. Industry. Electricity. Specimens of animals, plants, minerals, fossils, marine shells. Documents. Weapons. Outdoor exhibits include stone coffins, canoes and petrified trees.
Daily ex. M. 9-4. Closed Dec. 28-31, Jan. 2-4.

YAMATO-MURA

TREASURE HALL OF THE RAKUHOJI TEMPLE
Motoki, Yamato-mura, Makabe-gun, Ibaraki-ken 309-12
The statue of Buddha, the principal image, and the ones of two other avalokitesvara are designated as national art treasures.
Daily 9-4.

YASUKI-SHI

WAKO MEMORIAL HALL
881 Yasuki-machi, Yasuki-shi, Shimane-ken 692
Ancient Japanese metallurgy. Literature on Japanese swords.
Daily 8.30-4. Closed Su. and National Holidays.

YOKOGOSHIMURA

HOPPO BUNKA MUSEUM
Soumi Oaza, Yokogoshimura, Nakakanbara-gun, Niigata-ken 950-02
Fine art of Japan, China, Korea, India, Egypt and Greece. Folk art objects. Domestic articles. Tea-ceremony room.
Daily 8-5.

YOKOHAMA-SHI

KANAGAWA PREFECTURAL MUSEUM
Nikaido Kamakura-shi, Yokohama-shi, Kanagawa-ken 222
Botany. Natural history. Far Eastern art and archaeology.
Daily 9-4.

KUMANO LOCAL MUSEUM
Shioka-machi, Kohoku-ku, Yokohama-shi, Kanagawa-ken 222
Local history and archaeology.
Daily 8-5.

YOKOHAMA

SILK MUSEUM
1 Yamashita-cho, Naka-ku, Yokohama-shi, Kanagawa-ken 231
Samples of silk fabrics. Specimens of silk cocoons and silk-yarns.
Daily 9-4.30. Closed M., the day after national holidays, and Dec. 29 - Jan. 3.

YOKOSUKA-SHI

KANNONZAKI NATURAL HISTORY MUSEUM
4 Kamoi, Yokosuka-shi, Kanagawa-ken 239
Models of the Miura Peninsula, and a lighthouse. Whaling. Models of fishing vessels.
Daily 8.30-5.

YOKOSUKA CITY MUSEUM
6-14-1 Kurihama, Yokosuka-shi, Kanagawa-ken 213
Local history. Archaeology. Natural science. Mammal and bird specimens of the Miura area. Marine shells. Insects and crustaceans. Reptiles, amphibians of the Miura area. Decorative arts. Paintings. Woodcuts.
Daily 9-4.30. Closed M. and National Holidays, also Foundation Day of the city, and Dec. 29 - Jan. 3.

YONAGO-SHI

SAN'IN HISTORICAL COLLECTION
127 Kume-machi, Yonago-shi, Tottori-ken 683
Archaeological relics from the San'in district. Armour of feudal times.
Daily 9-5. Closed M.

YONEZAWA-SHI

TREASURE HOUSE OF THE UESUGI SHRINE
1-4-13 Marunouchi, Yonezawa-shi, Yamagata-ken 992
Historical documents. Paintings, including coloured Vaisaravans painted on silk canvas, Prajna-paramita-sutra written by Gonara Emperor. Swords and lances made by famous swordsmiths.
On demand, 9-4.

YONEZAWA LOCAL MUSEUM
Minamihoribata-cho, Yonezawa-shi, Yamagata-ken
Manuscripts. Folk art. Ceramics. Sculpture.
Daily 9-4. Closed M. and National Holidays.

YOSHINO-MACHI

TREASURE HOUSE OF THE NYOIRINJI TEMPLE
1024 Yoshinoyama, Yoshino-machi, Yoshino-gun, Nara-ken 639
Buddhist statues and pictures. Wooden statue of Zao-Gongen and of Emperor Daigo. Armour, saddle and helmet of 14th century loyalist Masatsura Kusunoki.
Mar.-Nov. Daily 7-6. Dec.-Feb. Daily 7-5.

ZENTSUJI-SHI

TREASURE HOUSE OF THE ZENTSUJI TEMPLE
Zentsuji-machi, Zentsuji-shi, Kagawa-ken 765
Buddhist statues, pictures, portraits, sutras and historical documents.
Daily 8-5.

ZINGU-MACHI

MIYAZAKI PUBLIC MUSEUM
Zingu-machi, Miyazaki-ken 880
Local archaeology, history. Fine art.
Daily 9-4.30. Closed M. and first day of each month, also national holidays (except Bunka Day and Children's Day) and Dec. 28 - Jan. 3.

Jordan

Jordan is a far from rich country, with acute political problems, and its museums look safely and inexpensively backwards, with archaeology as the main theme and a number of famous classical ruins, such as Petra, to add glamour to the scene.

AMMAN

JORDAN ARCHAEOLOGICAL MUSEUM
Department of Antiquities, P.O. Box 88, Amman
Objects from all periods of the country's history, from upper Palaeolithic to Medieval Arab times.
Daily 8-6; F. 10-4.

IRBID

IRBID MUSEUM
Irbid
Local history. Objects from excavations in the area.
Daily 8-6; F. 10-4.

KERAK

KERAK MUSEUM
Kerak
Local history. Objects from excavations in the area.
Daily 8-6; F. 10-4.

MADABA

MADABA MUSEUM
Madaba
Local history. Objects from excavations in the area.
Daily 8-6; F. 10-4.

PETRA

PETRA MUSEUM
Petra
Local history. Objects from excavations in the area.
Daily 8-6; F. 10-4.

Kenya

Making the most of Kenya's natural advantages, the museum authorities have emphasised the country's abundance of interesting wildlife, and its prehistoric archaeology. The native arts and ethnography have not, however, been neglected and some of these exhibits are not easily paralleled elsewhere. A good example of this individual quality is provided by the banana-fibre collage mentioned below, which forms part of a collection of art produced by Kenyans.

GEDI

NATIONAL MUSEUM
P.O. Malindi, Gedi
Historical ruins of abandoned Arabic city.
Daily 8-6.

KITALE

STONEHAM MUSEUM AND RESEARCH CENTRE
P.O. Box Kitale, Kitale
Art. Local history. Archaeology. Ethnography. Natural science. Mammals. Ornithology. Anthropology. Entomology.
Daily 10-6.

LAMU

NATIONAL MUSEUM
P.O. Box 48, Lamu
Collections of historical material. Archaeology and ethnography.
Daily 8-6.

MOMBASA

NATIONAL MUSEUM
Fort Jesus, P.O. Box 82412, Mombasa
Historical archaeology of the East African coast, housed in a 15th century Portuguese building. Chinese porcelain. Islamic earthenware. Musical horns.
Daily 8-6.

NAIROBI

NATIONAL MUSEUM
P.O. Box 40658, Nairobi
Collections of mammals, entomology, ornithology, herpetology, archaeology, ethnography, palaeontology, anthropology, and osteology.
The Museum administers the prehistoric sites at Olorgesaillie, Kariandusi, Fort Ternan, Songhor and Hyrax Hill.
Daily 9.30-6.

NEW STANLEY ART GALLERY
New Stanley Hotel, P.O. Box 75, Kimathi Street, Nairobi
Pictorial Batik: Banana fibre collage. Kenyan scenes and wildlife subjects. Sculptures of local people and wildlife.
Daily except Sa. 9-5.

PAA-YA-PAA ART GALLERY
Sadler House, P.O. Box 9646, Sadler Lane, off Koinauge Street, Nairobi
Paintings, sculptures by Kenyan artists.
Daily except Su. 8.30-12.30. Also 2-6 except Sa.

Khmer Republic

This ex-French territory, with a population of nearly seven million, supports itself mainly by agriculture, forestry and fishing. Industry is developing slowly and, in recent years, much of the country's wealth and manpower has been devoted to military purposes. The museums are concerned only with archaeology, history and art and, so far, little has been done to relate them to the requirements of a developing nation.

BATTAMBANG

POVÉAL MUSEUM
Battambang
Archaeological fragments and sculptures. Local history. Religious history and art.
By appointment.

KAMPON THOM

ARCHAEOLOGICAL MUSEUM
Kampong Thom
Archaeological material from the area. Inscriptions. Architectural fragments. Sculpture.
Tu.-Su. 10-12, 3-6.

PHNOM-PENH

NATIONAL MUSEUM
Phnom-Penh
Khmer art, 5th-13th centuries. Sculptures. Bronzes. Architectural fragments. Terracotta. Ceramics. Inscriptions. Material from excavations throughout the country. Ethnography. Traditional religious paintings. Decorative arts.
Tu.-Su. 10-12, 3-6.

Korea, Democratic People's Republic of

Since 1945, the main effort of the Democratic People's Republic of Korea within the museum field has been to develop regional centres which would provide instruction in the historical development of the country and the area. These collections are summarised in our list by the bare words 'local history'. This phrase should be interpreted in the national terminology, as 'history of economic development of the struggle for national liberation, especially against the Japanese, and of the workers' and revolutionary movements'. These regional museums aim at building up an awareness of history, of technology and of the political situation among the whole mass of the people.

BOCHUN COUNTY

STATE HISTORICAL MUSEUM
Bochun County
Local history.
Daily 8-5.

CHUNGJIN STATE HISTORICAL MUSEUM
Chungjin
Local history.
Daily 8-5.

HAEJU STATE HISTORICAL MUSEUM
Haeju
Local history.
Daily 8-5.

HAMHEUNG STATE HISTORICAL MUSEUM
Hamheung
Local history
Daily 8-5.

HESAN STATE HISTORICAL MUSEUM
Hesan
Local history.
Daily 8-5.

KAESONG STATE HISTORICAL MUSEUM
Kaesong
Local history.
Daily 8-5.

KANGGE STATE HISTORICAL MUSEUM
Kangge
Local history.
Daily 8-5.

MYOHYANG MT. STATE HISTORICAL MUSEUM
Myohyang Mt.
Local history.
Daily 8-5.

PYONGYANG KOREAN REVOLUTIONARY MUSEUM
Pyongyang
Historical exhibits from the second half of the 19th century.
Daily 8-5.

STATE CENTRAL ETHNOGRAPHIC MUSEUM
Pyongyang
Ethnography of Korea and of other countries.
Daily 8-5.

STATE CENTRAL FINE ARTS MUSEUM
Pyongyang
Fine arts. Paintings, drawings, sculpture by Korean artists.
Daily 8-5.

STATE CENTRAL HISTORICAL MUSEUM
Pyongyang
Exhibits from the prehistoric period to the early 20th century (the end of the Li dynasty).
Daily 8-5.

STATE CENTRAL LIBERATION STRUGGLE MUSEUM
Pyongyang
Historical material from the latter half of the 19th century to the present day, including exhibits from the armed struggle against Japan in the 1930s and the more recent Korea war.
Daily 8-5.

SARIWON STATE HISTORICAL MUSEUM
Sariwon
Local history.
Daily 8-5.

SHINCHUN COUNTY STATE HISTORICAL MUSEUM
Shinchun County
Local history.
Daily 8-5.

SHINUIJU

STATE HISTORICAL MUSEUM
Shinuiju
Local history.
Daily 8-5.

WONSAN STATE HISTORICAL MUSEUM
Wonsan
Local history.
Daily 8-5.

Korea, Republic of

The museums of North Korea go for the history of the revolutionary movement and the development of industry and friendship with the Soviet Union. South Korea, on the other side of the political fence, emphasises ethnography and period rooms. Neither, of course, conveys the whole story of what life in its respective part of Korea is all about.

KYONGJ CITY

NATIONAL MUSEUM
Kyongju City, North Kyongsang Province
Kyongju was former capital of the Silla dynasty. Monuments and mound tombs from the period of Great Silla (668-935 A.D.). Material from the various sites, and funeral offerings from some of the mound tombs.
Tu.-Su. 9-5.

PUSAN

NATONAL UNIVERSITY MUSEUM
Pusan
Cultural relics. Art objects. Antiques. Historical remains of Kyongsang-Namdo province.
By appointment.

PUYO

NATIONAL MUSEUM
Puyo
Exhibits from the Packche Dynasty (18 B.C. - 660 A.D.).
Tu.-Su. 9-5.

SEOUL

MUSEUM
Ehwa Women's University, Seoul
Prehistory, including Silla pottery and gold. Paintings. Calligraphy. Decorative arts. Pottery and porcelain.
By appointment.

MUSEUM OF CHANG-DUK PALACE
Chang-Duk Palace, Seoul
Regalia, costumes, utensils, arms, seals, manuscripts and documents of the Yi dynasty. Rooms furnished in period style, as they were when occupied by the Yi family.
Tu.-Su. 9-5.

MUSEUM OF KOREAN FOLKLORE
Kyong-Bok Palace, Seoul
Room-settings. Items belonging to traditional life in Korea, in their natural settings.
Tu.-Su. 9-5.

NATIONAL MUSEUM
Duksoo Palace, 5 Chongdong Sodaemun-ku, Seoul
Archaeology, including gold crowns, jewellery and pottery of the Old Silla dynasty (5th-6th centuries A.D.). The adjoining building houses fine arts. Antiquities of the Buddhist periods, including fine Buddha images of 6th-7th centuries. Ceramics. Paintings. Korean pottery and porcelain of the Koryo dynasty (10th-14th centuries). Chinese, Jāpanese and Central Asian archaeology.
Tu.-Su. 9-5. Closed the day after public holidays.

NATIONAL SCIENCE MUSEUM
2 Waryong-dong, Chongno-ku, Seoul
Natural history.
Daily ex. M. 9-4. Closed public holidays.

UNIVERSITY MUSEUM
Korea University, Seoul
Archaeology. Ethnography.
By appointment.

UNIVERSITY MUSEUM
Seoul National University, Seoul
Paintings. Calligraphy. Archaeology. Ethnography, including rural and traditional cultures and also Shamanism.
By appointment.

TAEGU

UNIVERSITY MUSEUM
Kyong-Buk University, Taegu
Archaeology. Art. History.
By appointment.

Kuwait

Kuwait finds itself in the curious position of having a great deal of public money, derived from its oil royalties, but as yet only one large institution which is a museum in the strict sense. This is, however, comprehensive, and well furnished with the necessary technical facilities, and presents an excellent picture of the history and life of the country. By contrast, the old Kuwaiti house, with its pre-oil bonanza furnishings, shows what the situation would almost certainly have been for the museum field if Allah, in the shape of oil, had not been good.

FAILAKA ISLAND

FAILAKA ARCHAEOLOGICAL MUSEUM
Failaka Island
Copies of material found during excavations on Failaka Island. The originals are to be found in the Kuwait Museum.
Tu.-Su. 9-5.

FAILAKA ETHNOGRAPHICAL MUSEUM
Failaka Island
In old Kuwaiti house, furnished as it was before oil was found in the country.
Tu.-Su. 9-1, 3-6.

KUWAIT

BAIT AL-BADER
Arabian Gulf Street, Kuwait
Typical Kuwaiti house of the 19th century. Living accommodation. Stable. Farm buildings.
Tu.-Su. 9-12, 3-6.

KUWAIT MUSEUM
Kuwait
Finds from excavations on Failaka island, dating back to Bronze age and Hellenistic period. Models of Kuwaiti ships. Local birds and migratory species. The old system of education in Kuwait. Paintings by local artists. Musical instruments. Furniture. Bedouins' way of life. Jewellery. Coins. Carved doors. National costumes. Fish of the Arabian Gulf. Ancient and modern methods of transporting water.
Tu.-Su. 9-12, 3-6.

KUWAIT NATURAL HISTORY MUSEUM
Kuwait
Animals and birds of the Arabian Gulf.
Tu.-Su. 9-12, 3-6.

Lebanon

The Lebanon, so far as its museums are concerned, relies heavily on the country's archaeological remains and on the material which as been excavated from them and at them. Little is said about the agricultural and industrial development of the country, which has been very interesting for many years, nor about the political history of the area, in which the Lebanon has played no small part.

BEIRUT

ARCHAEOLOGICAL MUSEUM
American University, Beirut
Stone Age flint implements. Bronze tools and implements from Early Bronze Age to Byzantine period. Pottery from various periods. Arabic pottery from 8th-16th centuries. Phoenician glass-ware. Egyptian artifacts from Neolithic to Dynastic periods. Pottery from the Neolithic period of Mesopotamia. Cylinder seals and cuneiform tablets from Sumer and Akkad. Numismatics of the countries in the eastern basin of the Mediterranean.
By appointment.

GEOLOGICAL MUSEUM
American University, Beirut
Geology of the Lebanon.
By appointment.

NATIONAL MUSEUM OF LEBANON
Rue de Damas, Beirut
Archaeological finds from the Lebanon. Royal jewellery, arms and statues of the Phoenician epoch. Sarcophagus of King Ahiram (13th century B.C.) with first known alphabetical inscriptions. Sarcophagi of the Greek and Hellenistic periods. Terracotta statues of the Hellenistic period. Roman and Byzantine mosaics. Ceramics.
Daily 9-12, 3-6 (winter 2-5).

PREHISTORIC MUSEUM
Université St. Joseph, Beirut
Collection of flints from various periods and sites in the Lebanon.
By appointment.

SURSOCK MUSEUM
Beirut
Paintings, icons and oriental carpets of recent origin.
Daily 9-12, 3-6 (winter 2-5).

BEIT-ED-DINE

LEBANESE MUSEUM
Beit-ed-Dine
Historical collections of the 16th-19th centuries.
Daily 9-12, 3-6 (winter 2-5).

Lesotho

The museums of Lesotho have so far confined their attention to recording and preserving the relics of the country's culture as it was in the nineteenth century. The documentation of missionary activities and of the old tribal culture is regarded as the most urgent task at a time when this type of material is all too liable to disappear.

MASITISE

MISSION CAFE HOUSE
Masitise
First mission house in this part of the country. Wildlife.
On request.

MORIJA

MUSEUM OF MORIJA
P.O. Box 4, Morija
Collections started by the missionaries of the Paris Evangelical Missionary Society. Dinosaur bones. Fossils. Stone Age flint stones. Ethnography of Lesotho, including weapons, decorations, divining bones of the medicine man, the Basotho shield.
M., W., F. and Sa. afternoons. Other times by arrangement.

Liberia

The two museums of Liberia have very little to say about the interesting conditions which brought the country to birth, and place their emphasis on the more traditional African matters of devil-masks and ankle-rings.

MONROVIA

NATIONAL MUSEUM OF LIBERIA
Capitol Hill, Monrovia
Liberian cultural and historical objects, including ceremonial masks and musical instruments.
Daily 10-3.30.

ROBERTSPORT

TUBMAN CENTRE OF AFRICAN CULTURES
Robertsport, Cape Mount
Art gallery. Collections of devil masks, drums, ankle-rings and agricultural implements.
Daily 8-12, 2-4.

Libyan Arab Republic

Nearly all the museums in the Republic are archaeological museums, presenting to the public the remains of the civilisations of Greece, Rome, Byzantium, Islam and Phoenicia.

APOLLONIA

SUSA MUSEUM
Apollonia
Greek, Roman and Byzantine statues, inscriptions, pottery and mosaics.
Daily 9-12, 3-6.

CYRENE

SITE MUSEUM
Cyrene
Sculpture, pottery, coins, mosaics and inscriptions from the Greek, Roman, Byzantine and Islamic periods.
Daily 9-12, 3-6.

GASR LEBIA

SITE MUSEUM
Gasr Lebia
Established on the site of ancient Theodorias, the museum contains a rich collection of Byzantine mosaics.
Daily 9-12, 3-6.

GERMA

GERMA MUSEUM
Germa
Archaeological material from excavations in the area. Local history.
Daily ex. M. 8-8.

LEPCIS MAGNA

SITE MUSEUM
Lepcis Magna
The collection includes pieces of sculpture and pottery from the Roman period.
Daily 9-12, 3-6.

PTOLEMAIS

MUSEUM OF TOLMEITA
Ptolemais
Pieces of sculpture, pottery, mosaics and inscriptions from the Greek and Roman periods.
Daily 9-12, 3-6.

SABRATHA

SABRATHA MUSEUM
Sabratha
Statues, inscriptions, mosaics, pottery and glass, mostly related to the Punic, Roman and Byzantine periods.
Daily 9-12, 3-6.

SEBHA

SEBHA MUSEUM
Sebha
Archaeological material from excavations in the area. Local history.
Tu.-Su. 8-8.

TOCRA

SITE MUSEUM
Tocra
Greek archaeology of the sixth, fifth and fourth centuries B.C., including pottery with Greek inscriptions.
Daily 9-12, 3-6.

TOLMEITA

TOLMEITA MUSEUM
Tolmeita
Classical antiquities.
Daily 9-12, 3-6.

TRIPOLI

ARCHAEOLOGICAL MUSEUM
The Castle, Tripoli
Ancient Libyan, Punic, Roman and Byzantine antiquities, including sculpture, pottery, glass, frescoes, mosaics and coins.
Daily 9-12, 3-6.

EPIGRAPHIC MUSEUM
The Castle, Tripoli
The collection consists of Latin, Arabic and Turkish inscriptions.
Daily 9-12, 3-6.

ETHNOGRAPHICAL MUSEUM
The Castle, Tripoli
Collection depicting life in various parts of the Libyan Arab Republic.
Daily 9-12, 3-6.

MUSEUM OF THE LIBYAN NATIONAL RESISTANCE
The Castle, Tripoli
Collections illustrating the Libyan National resistance against the Italians, including clothes, arms and other objects belonging to the Libyan fighters in the period 1911-1932.
Daily 9-12, 3-6.

MUSEUM OF PREHISTORY
The Castle, Tripoli
Objects from prehistoric times from various parts of the country.
Daily 9-12, 3-6.

NATURAL HISTORY MUSEUM
The Castle, Tripoli
Collection of resident, migratory and winter visitor birds. Mammals, reptiles, amphibians. Marine life section. Embryology, geology and fossils. Botany and insects.
Daily 9-12, 3-6.

Liechtenstein

Museums to Liechtenstein mean primarily the frills and elegance of life - paintings and postage stamps - and since this fits very well into the slightly feudal atmosphere of this little state, nobody is likely to be greatly bothered.

TRIESENBERG

REGIONAL MUSEUM
Triesenberg
Handicrafts, especially weaving. Weights and measures. Furniture. Household equipment. Popular religious art. Ethnography.
By appointment.

VADUZ

LIECHTENSTEIN PROVINCIAL MUSEUM
Vaduz
Prehistory. History. Religious sculpture. Weapons. Ethnography. Coins.
Daily 10-12. 2-5.

POSTAL MUSEUM
Vaduz
Liechtenstein stamps. Displays illustrating design and printing of stamps. Work of World Postal Union.
Daily 10-12, 2-5.

STATE ART COLLECTION
Vaduz
19th-20th century drawings, prints.
Daily 10-12, 2-5.

Luxembourg

One of the most interesting museums in Luxembourg is also the least characteristic, the house in which Victor Hugo lived during one of his numerous periods of not exactly uncomfortable exile abroad. But the five museums, considered as a group, cover a very good range of material.

ESCH-SUR-ALZETTE

RESISTANCE MUSEUM
Hôtel de Ville, Esch-sur-Alzette
Material illustrating local Resistance movement.
On request.

LUXEMBOURG

STATE MUSEUM
Marché-aux-Poissons, Luxembourg
Gallo-Roman archaeology: inscriptions, objects in pottery, bronze and iron, coins. Merovingian and Middle Ages exhibits. Collection of arms and armour. Uniforms. Paintings and sculpture. Contemporary art. History of the fort-

ress of Luxembourg. Folklore. Natural history. Prehistoric exhibits. Zoology. Planetarium.
Daily ex. M. 10-12, 2-6. Nov. - Mar. 15, closed Su. mornings.

JEAN-PIERRE PESCATORE MUSEUM
Villa Vauban, Avenue de l'Arsenal, Luxembourg
17th century Flemish and Dutch paintings. Works ascribed to Canaletto (18th century). Dutch paintings of 18th and 19th centuries. 19th century French paintings include works by Delacroix, Isabey and Courbet. 19th century Belgian paintings. Sculpture.
Whitsun - Oct. 1, Daily ex. M. 2.30-6.30. Oct. 1 - Whitsun, Sa. 2.30-6.30; Su. 10.30-12.30.

VIANDEN

VICTOR HUGO MUSEUM
Vianden
Home of the poet during his stay in Luxembourg. Memorabilia. Documents. Manuscripts.
May-Sept., Daily 10-12, 2-6.

MUSEUM OF RURAL ARTS
Vianden
In old bourgeois house. Furniture, domestic equipment and other items relating to life in earlier times.
May-Sept. daily 10-12, 2-6.

Malagasy Republic

After a fairly lengthy interregnum during which it was under the control of France, Malagasy (Madagascar) became independent once more in 1960. Its eighteen ethnic groups provide a paradise for ethnologists, and the island's museums have taken full advantage of this, which is probably as well since the alternative subjects for museum collections are butter beans, raffia and bananas.

TANANARIVE

MUSEUM OF ART AND ARCHAEOLOGY
University of Madagascar, P.O. Box 564, Isoraka, Tananarive
Archaeological material from all over Madagascar, including sculptures from West Sakalava and Mahafaly and pottery from the Highlands. Ethnographical exhibits, including domestic equipment. Aboriginal and Chinese pottery from excavations in Chinese and Arab sites in the north-west and north-east of the country.
Tu.-Th. 3-5.30.

MUSEUM OF ART AND ARCHAEOLOGY
18 rue Dr. Villette, Tananarive
Archaeological exhibits. Paintings, sculpture.
Th., Su. 8-12, 2-5.

MUSEUM OF FINE ART AND HISTORY
Palais de la Reine, Manjakaniadana, Tananarive
Furniture. Jewellery. History of Madagascar.
Th., Su. and public holidays, 8-12, 2-5; Sa. 2-5.

MUSEUM OF FOLKLORE, ARCHAEOLOGY AND PALAEONTOLOGY
ORSTOM (Office de la Recherche Scientifique et Technique Outre-Mer), Parc de Tsimbazaza, Tananarive
Art, archaeology, palaeontology, zoology, fauna of Madagascar. Folklore. Pottery.
Th., Su. and public holidays, 8-12, 2-5; Sa. 2-5.

Malawi

As the list given below makes clear, Malawi has shown considerable ingenuity and breadth of imagination in selecting items and sites for its museums. In addition to the ethnographical material which, like most other recently liberated African countries, it has wisely presented and featured in its collections, one notices with enthusiasm such exhibits as the Victorian steamers which have sailed on Lake Malawi for generations and, an equally good touch, the Postal Museum in the rest-hut once used by the letter-carriers who took the mail around on foot.

BLANTYRE

MUSEUM OF MALAWI
Chichiri, Blantyre
Collections covering wide aspects of Malawi archaeology, history, ethnography, natural history and local crafts. In the museum are three early steam engines.
Daily except M. 10-4.

MANGOCHE

LAKE MALAWI MUSEUM
Mangoche
Situated at the southern end of Lake Malawi, the museum contains open displays featuring traditional lakeshore life, fishing and the various steamers that have sailed on the lake since Livingstone's time, as well as cases showing lakeshore artifacts from the Stone Age onwards.
Daily 9-5. Closed Good F. and Martyr's Day.

NAMAKA

MTENGATENGA POSTAL MUSEUM
Namaka
A small wayside museum on the main road between Blantyre and Zomba, built originally in 1906 as a rest-hut for carriers (mtengatenga) taking mail on foot between the two towns, 40 miles apart. The museum, which is also a rural post office with its own cancellation frank, features items relating to the postal and telegraph history of Malawi.
Th.-M. 8.30-5. Closed Tu. and W.

Malaysia

Malaysia has one museum for roughly every million-and-a-half of its population, which can hardly be deemed excessive. This is, however, an essentially non-urban country, three-quarters of it being covered by forests, and to arrange satisfactory museum provision for even a majority of the population would be something of a problem. The museums which do exist, however, are good, a great deal of trouble having been taken to present the everyday life of ordinary people in an interesting and sensible way, often with the help of dioramas.

ALOR STAR

MUSEUM NEGERI KEDAH
Bakar Bata, Alor Star
Social history section includes a replica of gold and silver flowers presented by the Sultan of Kedah as tributes when the state of Kedah was under the suzerainty of the Siamese Kingdom. Natural history. Industry. Archaeology section, including a diorama of an Indian temple believed to be 1,200 years old. Local pottery.
Daily ex. M. 10-5.

KOTA KINABALU

SABAH MUSEUM
Kota Kinabalu
Archaeology. History. Anthropology. Natural history.
Daily ex. M. 9-5.30.

KUALA LUMPUR

NATIONAL MUSEUM
Damansara Road, Kuala Lumpur
Ceremonial and cultural exhibits include tableaux and dioramas of a 19th century Malay Royal Wedding, traditional dance drama, Chinese traditional theatre scenes, a Malacca Chinese Baba house, and displays of shadow play figures from Malaysia, India, Indonesia, Thailand, Cambodia and China. Silat (Malay art of self-defence). History of Malaysia from the early Stone Age to the present day: crafts and weapons, and an aboriginal section. Indian sculptures. Malaysian industry and technology. Natural history, mainly zoology, including dioramas, Malayan shells and sea coral, insects and animals. Displays of a sub-montane deep forest, a bear diorama and a mangrove swamp life scene.
Daily 9.30-6. Closed F. 12-2.

MALACCA

MALACCA MUSEUM
7 Jalan Kota, Malacca
Weapons, including Malay daggers and knives and Dutch and Portuguese items. Chinese porcelain, furniture and costumes. Malay wedding costumes and brassware dating back to 14th century. Musical instruments. Wooden carvings. Dutch furniture, including Almeirahs. Photographs and drawings of the old port of Malacca, and also of the Fort of Malacca during the Portuguese (1511) and Dutch (1640) eras.
Daily 9-5.30.

PENANG

PENANG MUSEUM AND ART GALLERY
Jalan Farquhar, Pulau Pinang
Documents, artifacts, pictures and models illustrating life in Penang through the ages. Chinese room includes an ornate bridal chamber and examples of the performing arts. Farming, fishing and mining activities. Embroidery. Jewellery. Coins and currency. Transport. War relics. Natural history. Weapons. Foreign and local awards made to Tunku Abdul Rahman, the first Prime Minister of independent Malaya, and then Malaysia. The art gallery contains examples of local artists' work.
Daily 10-6.30. Closed F. 12-2, also on Hari Raya Puasa and Hari Raya Haji (Malay New Year).

PERAK

TAIPING MUSEUM
Taiping, Perak
Ethnography and antiquities of the Malay States. Zoology. Malay weapons and silverware.
Daily 9.30-5.30. Closed F. 12-2.

SARAWAK

SARAWAK MUSEUM
Kuching, Sarawak
Bornean ethnographical, archaeological, zoological and historical collections. Chinese ceramics of the Tang/Sung and Ming/Ching Dynasties.
Tu.-F. 9.15-5.30; Sa. and Su. 9.15-6. Closed M.

SEREMBAN

NEGERI SEMBILAN MUSEUM
Seremban
Local history. Ethnography. Natural history.
Daily ex. M. 10-5.

Maldives, Republic of

These coral islands with a population of no more than 100,000 sustain an interesting little museum which reflects the living conditions and customs of a people whose livelihood depends almost entirely on the sea and fishing.

MALÉ

MALÉ MUSEUM
"Darul Aasaaru", Malé
Collections illustrating the history of the Republic.
By appointment.

Malta

Malta, with its long history and highly developed tourist trade, is a natural field for museums and there are in fact a number of interesting collections here. One might emphasise particularly the archaeological material which includes certain picturesque items not easily found elsewhere, such as prehistoric steatopygous figurines. The armour formerly used by the Knights of St John is also a prized island possession and a well-known tourist attraction, as is the George Cross awarded to Malta as a result of its wartime fortitude.

BIRZEBBUGA

GHAR DALAM CAVE AND MUSEUM
Bir-id-Deheb Road, Birzebbuga
Earliest known habitat of man in Malta. Animal fossils found in the cave, including bones of deer, hippopotami, wild bears and dwarf elephant.
Oct. 1-June 15, daily 8.30-1, 2-4.30. June 16-Sept. 30, M.-F. 8.30-1.30, 2-5; Sa. and Su. 8.30-1.30.

MDINA

CATHEDRAL MUSEUM
The Cathedral, Mdina
Drawings include one by Luca Cambiaso (1581). Woodcuts by Dürer and engravings from them by Marcantonio Raimondi. Engravings by Goya. Panels from 14th century polyptych, and inlaid panels from choir stalls from the Cathedral. Vestments, including specimens of ancient Maltese lace. MSS include an early antiphonal. Portable altar decorated with Byzantine enamel work. Ceremonial cross (c.1099).
June 16-Sept. 30, daily 9.30-1.30. Oct. 1-June 15, daily 8.30-1, 2-4.30. Closed public holidays.

MUSEUM OF NATURAL HISTORY AND FOLKLORE
Magesterial Palace, St. Publius Square, Mdina
Natural history, especially flora and fauna of Malta and Gozo.
June 16-Sept. 30, daily 8.30-1.30. Oct. 1-June 15, daily 8.30-1, 2-4.30. Closed public holidays.

THE NORMAN HOUSE
Palazzo Falzon, Villegaignon Street, Mdina
Building in the Siculo-Norman style (c.1495), said to be the house occupied by de L'Isle Adam after his first arrival in Malta.
On request.

MGARR

TA' HAGRAT NEOLITHIC TEMPLES
Mgarr
Temples of the Tarxien-period, with grey and red pottery.
Oct. 1-June 15, daily 8.30-1. 2-4.30. June 16-Sept. 30, M.-F. 8.30-1.30, 2-5; Sa. and Su. 8.30-1.30.

NAXXAR

BIRD MUSEUM
Naxxar
Private collection of more than 600 birds.
Daily 9-12, 3-6.

PAOLA

HAL SAFLIENI HYPOGEUM
Paola
Labyrinthine subterranean sanctuary, c. 2450 B.C. Objects found during excavations.
Oct. 1-June 15, daily 8.30-1, 2-4.30. June 16-Sept. 30, M.-F. 8.30-1.30, 2-5; Sa. and Su. 8.30-1.30.

QRENDI

HAGAR QIM AND MNAJDRA NEOLITHIC TEMPLES
Qrendi
Prehistoric temples. Many steatopygous figurines (fat divinities) were found here (now in National Museum, Valletta).
Oct. 1-June 15, daily 8.30-1, 2-4.30. June 16-Sept. 30, M.-F. 8.30-1.30, 2-5; Sa. and Su. and Su. 8.30-1.30.

RABAT

ROMAN HOUSE AND MUSEUM OF ANTIQUITIES
Museum Road, Rabat
Punic remains in Malta. Roman statues, inscriptions, mosaics, ornaments, lamps, household articles, jars and vases. Arabic jars and lamps. The Majmuns stone. Sarcophagi.
Oct. 1-June 15, daily 8.30-1, 2-4.30. June 16-Sept. 30, M.-F. 8.30-1.30, 2-5; Sa. and Su. 8.30-1.30.

THE ST. AGATHA CATACOMBS
Rabat
Passages and alcoves used as burial place in 4th-5th centuries, and dedicated to a young girl who fled here from the persecutions of the Emperor Decius in Catania.
Daily 8-6.

ST. PAUL'S CATACOMBS
Rabat
An extensive system of passages and alcoves used as a burial place in 4th-5th centuries.
Oct. 1-June 15, daily 8.30-1, 2-4.30. June 16-Sept. 30, M.-F. 8.30-1.30, 2-5; Sa. and Su. 8.30-1.30.

ST. PAUL'S GROTTO
Rabat
Giovanni Beneguas, who came from Cordova to join the Knights, lived here instead as a hermit, a cave now beneath the church. This is venerated as either the 'dwelling' or 'prison' of St. Paul, and credited with a miraculous propensity for staying the same size however much stone is removed from it.
Daily 8.30-12, 1.30-6.

TARXIEN

NEOLITHIC TEMPLES
Tarxien
Megalithic temples. Replicas of features such as altars found during excavations (originals in National Museum, Valletta).
Oct. 1-June 15, daily 8.30-1, 2-4.30. June 16-Sept. 30, M.-F. 8.30-1.30, 2-5; Sa. and Su. 8.30-1.30.

VALLETTA

MANOEL THEATRE
Old Theatre Street, Valletta
Building (1731), claimed to be the oldest theatre in the Commonwealth. Interior restored in 1960.
Summer: daily 10-12. Winter: daily 10-12, 3-4.40.

NATIONAL MUSEUM
Kingsway, Valletta
Stone Age, Phoenician, Roman and Arab remains from different sites on the island. Picture Gallery. Maltese coins. Vestments, portraits of Grand Masters. Silver from hospital of the Santo Spirito. Historical views of Malta. Iron anchors from galleys of the Knights. Tarxian sculpture.
Oct. 1-June 15, daily 8.30-1, 2-4.30. June 16-Sept. 30, M.-F. 8.30-1.30, 2-5; Sa. and Su. 8.30-1.30.

PALACE ARMOURY
Palace of the Grand Masters, Valletta
Armour, coats of mail and weapons used by the Knights of St. John. Ceremonial suits made for La Vallette and Wignacourt (Milanese, inlaid with gold). Turkish shields. Souvenirs of second siege, including George Cross and Fragment of 'Faith', one of 3 Gladiator fighters.
Oct. 1-June 15, daily 8.30-1, 2-4.30. June 16-Sept. 30, M.-F. 8.30-1.30, 2-5; Sa. and Su. 8.30-1.30.

ST. JOHN'S MUSEUM AND CATHEDRAL
Co-Cathedral of St. John, St. John's Square, Valletta
Flemish tapestries by Judocus de Voz (1697), based on paintings by Rubens and Poussin. Bronze lecterns (1557). Silver screen and gates (1752). 15th century crucifix. Vestments. Silver vessels.
Weekdays, 9-1, 3-5.30.

VICTORIA (GOZO)

THE GOZO MUSEUM
The Citadel, Castle Hill, Victoria
Punic remains in Malta. Relics (anchors, amphora) of Roman ships sunk around Malta's coast. Agricultural implements and Roman remains from Gozo. Prehistoric finds from Ggantija, including objects connected with fertility rites, stone rollers and pottery.
Oct. 1-June 15, daily 8.30-12, 2-4.30. June 16-Sept. 30, daily 8.30-1.30. Closed public holidays.

VITTORIOSA

INQUISITOR'S PALACE
Main Gate Street, Vittoriosa
Building late 16th century. Furnishings and furniture. Coats-of-arms of Inquisitors.
June 16-Sept. 30, daily 8.30-1.30. Oct. 1-June 15, daily 8.30-1, 2-4.30. Closed public holidays.

XAGHRA (GOZO)

GGANTIJA NEOLITHIC TEMPLES
Xaghra
Copper Age temples, with large perimeter wall constructed of header and stretcher stones of gigantic size.
Oct. 1-June 15, daily 8.30-12, 2-4.30. June 16-Sept. 30, daily 8.30-1.30. Closed public holidays.

ZABBAR

ZABBAR CHURCH MUSEUM
Zabbar
Religious art.
On request.

Martinique

French since 1635 and heavily dependent on sugar and the things made from sugar, Martinique has introduced a welcome variety into its museum collections by developing a section dealing with volcanoes, which are always popular.

FORT-DE-FRANCE

FORT SAINT-LOUIS MUSEUM
Fort-De-France
Documents, engravings and arms concerning the military history of the Petites Antilles during the last three centuries.
Daily ex. M. 10-12, 2-5.

SAINT-PIERRE

VOLCANIC MUSEUM
Saint-Pierre
Mineralogy and geology. Exhibits illustrating local volcanoes.
Daily ex. M. 10-12, 2-5.

Mauritius

As will be seen from the brief list that follows, little money has so far been made available for the development of museum activities in Mauritius, and it is consequently somewhat ironical that prominent among the museums that do exist there should be a Police Museum. This does, however, have certain interesting links with at least the agriculture of the Island, in the form of exhibits of the special type of cannabis so eagerly and skilfully produced by local inhabitants.

MAHEBOURG

HISTORICAL MUSEUM
Mahebourg
The collection includes a set of maps, lithographs and objects showing aspects of the history of Mauritius. Naval relics.
Daily except Tu., F. and public holidays, 9-4.

PORT LOUIS

MUSEUM OF THE MAURITIUS POLICE
Police Headquarters, Line Barracks, Port Louis
Records of police enquiries into famous murder cases. Collection of old rifles, revolvers, daggers, swords and other weapons, some of which were used in crimes and others handed to the police. Samples of cannabis Sativa unlawfully cultivated in the country and known as 'gandia'; specimens of articles used for the smoking of gandia and opium. Counterfeit coins and bank notes and the machinery used to make them. Reminders of the 'good old days' of the Force.
By appointment only. M.-F. 9-3.30; Sa. 9-12.

NATURAL HISTORY MUSEUM
Mauritius Institute, Port Louis
Mainly exhibits of the fauna of Mauritius, with some botany, geology and meteorology.
M.-Th. 9-4. Closed F.-Su.

SOUILLAC

R. E. HART MUSEUM
Souillac
Souvenirs of the life and work of the Mauritian poet, Robert Edward Hart, housed in the bungalow where he spent his last years.
Daily except Tu., F. and public holidays, 9-4.

Mexico

Mexico is the fortunate possessor of modern museum buildings which are among the architecturally most distinguished in the world, and which add greatly to the nation's cultural prestige. They range from the homes of major public collections, especially in Mexico City itself, to the building created by the painter, Diego Rivera, in the form of a Mayan tomb, to display his private collection of pre-Hispanic sculpture and ceramics.

The Aztec monuments and the great sculptures of the Maya and Olmec cultures are almost, one might say, Mexico's trademark and they lend themselves wonderfully well to dramatic museum displays. The smaller and later artifacts, the baskets, textiles and pottery, with their strong colours and wild shapes, also make superb exhibits, especially in the kind of interior lighting that the Mexican climate makes possible. One natural history museum has incorporated the national climate, or rather climates, into its exhibits, by allowing the visitor to experience all Mexico's five climates as he passes from room to room and from floor to floor, and to shiver and sweat in turn.

The religious history of Mexico is well illustrated in its museums, and there are a number of good collections of the paintings, wood-carvings, silver, furniture and other secular art and applied art of the colonial period.

One of the most imaginative ideas, in a country where museums have attracted a refreshingly high proportion of the national money and talent, is a museum, strategically and sensibly placed on the border between the United States and Mexico, to present tourists as they arrive with a foretaste of what they can expect to find during their travels. It is a good but slightly wicked mental exercise to wonder what a corresponding United States museum on the other side of the frontier would contain.

Mexico's museums do their best to carry out the difficult double task of reflecting the country's present economy and at the same time making their contribution to creating the approved historical atmosphere which North American tourists expect to find. A notable symbol of this willingness to bring old and new into the same focus is to be found in one convent's collection of religious art and early motor cars.

ACAPULCO

REGIONAL MUSEUM
Fuerte de San Diego, Acapulco
Regional history.
Tu.-Sa. 9-1, 3-7; Su. 9-1.

ACOLMAN

ACOLMAN MUSEUM OF THE COLONIAL PERIOD
Acolman, Edo de Mexico
In former convent (1554). Paintings and furniture of the colonial period. Pre-Hispanic material from the surrounding district.
Daily 9-2, 4-6.

ACTOPAN

ACTOPAN MUSEUM OF THE COLONIAL PERIOD
Former Convento de San Nicolas, Actopan, Hidalgo
Building of 1560. Otomian handicrafts, especially basket making and textiles.
Daily ex. Su. 9.30-2, 2.30-6.

CAMPECHE

CAMPECHE ARCHAEOLOGICAL MUSEUM
Baluarte de la Soledad, Campeche
Maya culture. Objects from the Central Plateau and from the Gulf Coast.
Tu.-Sa. 9-2, 3-8; Su. 9-1.

LOCAL MUSEUM
Calle 8, Campeche
Local history.
Tu.-Sa. 9-12, 3-8; Su. 9-1.

NAVAL AND MILITARY MUSEUM
Castillo de San Miguel, Campeche
In San Carlos bastion of the 18th century castle. Naval history. Ships' models. Military relics.
Tu.-Sa. 9-12, 3-8; Su. 9-1.

CARMEN

REGIONAL MUSEUM
Carmen
Regional history.
Tu.-Sa. 9-1, 3-7; Su. 9-1.

CHIAPAS

CHIAPAS REGIONAL MUSEUM
Palacio de la Cultura, Avenida Central, Chiapas
Maya and Olmeca cultures. History of the Province of Chiapas.
Daily 8.30-2; Sa. 8.30-1.

CHIAPA DE CORZO

MUSEUM OF LACQUER-WARE
Plaza Angel Albino Corzo, Chiapa de Corzo
Antique and modern lacquer-ware.
Daily ex. M. 9-3.30, 4-6.

CHIHUAHUA

CHIHUAHUA REGIONAL MUSEUM
Paseo Bolwar 404, Chihuahua
Prehispanic art of the Tula, Aztec and Mixtec cultures from the Antiplano archaeological collection from Casas Grandes. Mexican costumes and folk-art of the 19th century.
Daily ex. Su. and public holidays 9-1, 3-6.

CHOLULA

CHOLULA MUSEUM OF ARCHAEOLOGY
Cholula, Puebla
Pottery. Model of the Cholula pyramid, showing the different periods of its construction.
M.-Sa. 9-1, 4-6.

CHURUBUSCO

HISTORICAL MUSEUM
Churubusco
Regional history, ethnography.
Tu.-Sa. 9-12, 3-8; Su. 9-1.

CIUDAD GUZMAN

REGIONAL MUSEUM
Ciudad Guzman
Regional history, ethnography, folk art.
M.-Sa. 9-1, 4-6.

COLIMA

COLIMA REGIONAL MUSEUM
Calle 27 de septiembre, Colima
Regional archaeology, history, ethnography.
M.-Sa. 9-1, 4-6.

CUAUTLA

MORELOS HOUSE
Calle Morelos, Cuautla
House occupied by the patriot, Father Morelos, during the siege of Cuautla. Flags and other items connected with the War of Independence. Replicas of furniture of the time.
Daily 10-1.30, 2.30-6.

CULIACAN

SINALOA REGIONAL MUSEUM
Centro Cívico Constitución, Calle Rafael Buelna, Culiacan, Sinaloa
16th-19th century weapons, including a ballista. Prehispanic sculpture and pottery. Portraits of State governors.
Daily ex. Su. and public holidays, 9-1, 4-6.

DOLORES HIDALGO

CASA DE HIDALGO
Calle Morelos 1, Dolores Hidalgo, Chihuahua
Building of 1779. At one time the home of Miguel Hidalgo y Castulo. Contains his personal effects and furniture of the late 18th and 19th centuries. Regional pottery of the 18th-19th centuries.
M.-Sa. 10-5.

DURANGO

REGIONAL MUSEUM
Durango
Regional history, folk art.
Tu.-Sa. 9-1, 3-7; Su. 9-12.

DZIBILCHALTUN

DZIBILCHALTUN REGIONAL ARCHAEOLOGICAL MUSEUM
Dzibilchaltun, Yucatan
Maya pottery.
Daily ex. Su. 6-6.

GUADALAJARA

GUADALAJARA REGIONAL MUSEUM
Avenida Alcalde, Guadalajara, Jalisco
In former monastery. Archaeology of Western Mexico. Local history from Colonial times onwards. Folk art. Gallery of works by local painters.
Daily 10-1.30, 2.30-6.

JOSÉ CLEMENTE OROZCO STUDIO MUSEUM
Aurelio Aceves 27, Guadalajara, Jalisco
Works by Orozco. Drawings, lithographs, engravings, paintings. Studio equipment and tools. Furniture and personal possessions of the artist (d. 1949).
Tu.-Sa. 10-5; Su. 10-2.

REGIONAL MUSEUM OF ANTHROPOLOGY AND HISTORY
Guadalajara
Ethnography, anthropology and history of the region. Paintings, sculpture of the colonial period.
Daily 10-1.30, 2.30-6.

GUADALUPE

GUADALUPE REGIONAL MUSEUM
Former Convento de Guadalupe, Jardín Juárez Otte, Guadalupe, Zacatecas
18th century religious pictures, images and furniture belonging to the Convent. Guadalupe and peasant pottery of the 18th-19th centuries.
M.-Sa. 10-1, 2-5.

GUANAJUATO

ALFREDO DUGES MUSEUM
Universidad, Guanajuato
Geology. Mineralogy. Biology. Zoology.
By appointment.

GUANAJUATO REGIONAL MUSEUM
Calle 5 de mayo, Guanjuato
Stone and ceramic sculpture of several cultures, especially that of Chupícuaro. Carved wooden images. Religious paintings. Portraits. Furniture and ornaments of the 19th century. Folk art.
M.-Sa. 8-2, 4-6; Su. 10-2.

HERMOSILLO

SONORA MUSEUM AND PUBLIC LIBRARY
Hermosillo, Sonora
Regional history. Prehispanic pottery and sculpture from Central America. Prehistoric items from the State of Sonora.
Daily ex. Su. 9-1; Sa. 9-12.

HUEJOTZINGO

MUSEUM
Monastery, Huejotzingo
Collections housed in monastery of 1529. History, ethnography of the region.
By appointment.

JALAPA

ARCHAEOLOGICAL MUSEUM
Jalapa
Archaeological material of the Olmec, Totonac and Huastec coastal cultures of ancient Mexico. The colossal heads, dating from 2nd-5th centuries A.D., and displayed in the open air, are Olmec.
M.-Sa. 10-1, 2-5.

MADERO

MUSEUM OF THE HUASTECA CULTURE
Instituto Technológico, Madero, Tamps
Collections illustrating the prehispanic Huasteca culture.
Daily ex. Tu. 9.30-12, 4-7.

MATAMOROS

MEXICAN MUSEUM
Matamoros, Tamaulipas
Mexican art, archaeology and history, designed to present prospective tourists with a foretaste of what can be expected in Mexico.
M.-Sa. 10-1, 2-5.

MERIDA

ARCHAEOLOGICAL MUSEUM
Palacio Cantón, Paseo de Montejo, Merida, Yucatan
Archaeological exhibits from the region.
Daily 8-2.

YUCATAN MUSEUM OF ANTHROPOLOGY
Palacio Cantón, Paseo Montejo, Calle 56A 485, Merida, Yucatan
Material belonging to the prehispanic cultures. Items in stone, pottery, shell, bone, copper, gold, wood, jade, turquoise and quartz.
Daily 9-7; Su. 9-2.

MEXICO CITY

CARMEL MUSEUM OF COLONIAL HISTORY
Plaza del Carmen 4 and 6, Mexico City
18th century Mexican painting and furniture. 18th century glazed tiles. Statue of the Virgin del Carmen. Carved and painted images.
Daily ex. M. 10-6.

CHAPULTEPEC GALLERY
Insurgentes Sur 11, Mexico City
Paintings. Drawings. Sculpture.
M.-Sa. 9-1, 3-7.

CONVENT OF SANTA MARIA DE LOS ANGELES
Calle del Jardín del Convento, Mexico City
Religious paintings, 17th-18th centuries. Carved and painted wooden images. Stone figures. Glazed tiles. 19th century ornaments. 18th-19th century carriages. Early 19th century motorcars. Peasant pottery. Flags and lithographs relating to the Spanish-American war.
M.-Sa. ex. F. 8-2.30; Su. 9-2, 3-5.

DIEGO RIVERA MUSEUM OF ANAHUACALLI
San Pablo Tepetlapa, Coyoacán, Mexico City
Building designed by the painter, Diego Rivera, to display his collection of Pre-hispanic sculpture and ceramics. The building takes the form of a pseudo Mayan tomb.
Daily 3-6; Su. 10-2.

ETHNOGRAPHICAL MUSEUM
Guatemala y Seminario, Mexico City
Wax sculptures representing native dances and Mexican scenes and costumes. Idols. Model of the area of the Templo Mayor.
M. 10-7, Tu.-Sa. 10-6; Su. 10-3.

ISIDRO FABELA MUSEUM
Plaza de San Jacinto 15, Mexico City
Local history. Paintings. Folk art.
Tu.-Sa. 9-1, 3-6; Su. 9-1.

GALLERY OF ANCIENT AND MODERN ART
Genova 2-105, Mexico City
Mexican paintings. 19th century Spanish paintings.
Tu.-Sa. 9-1, 3-7; Su. 9-1.

GALLERY OF THE FRANCES INSTITUTE OF LATIN AMERICA
Rio Nazas 43, Mexico City
Paintings, sculpture, graphics by Latin-American artists.
Daily 9-1, 3-7.

GALLERY OF THE NATIONAL SCHOOL OF PLASTIC ARTS
Academia 22, Mexico City
Sculpture.
By appointment.

GALLERY OF THE PALACE OF FINE ART
Angela Peraeta y Avenida Juárez, Mexico City
Paintings by Mexican artists, mainly 19th century. Murals by Diego Rivera.
Daily 9-6.

GEOLOGICAL MUSEUM
Cipres 176, Mexico City
Geology of Mexico and South America.
Tu.-Sa. 9-1, 3-6; Su. 9-1.

BENITO JUÁREZ MEMORIAL MUSEUM
Palacio Nacional, Mexico City
Collection illustrating career of the revolutionary, Benito Juárez.
Daily 9-1, 4-7.

FRIDA KAHLO MUSEUM
Calle Allende, Mexico City
Home and studio of the mural artist, Diego Rivera, whose wife was Frida Kahlo. Works by Rivera, with his personal possessions.
Daily 3-6; Su. 10-2.

MUNICIPAL SCULPTURE GALLERY
Pergolas de la Alameda Central, Mexico City
Sculpture, mainly 19th-20th century.
Tu.-Sa. 9-1, 3-6; Su. 9-1.

MUSEUM OF THE CITY OF MEXICO
Casa de los Condes de Santiago de Calimaya, Mexico City
Local history.
Tu.-Su. 10-6.

MUSEUM OF HYGIENE
Doncleles 39, Mexico City
Collections illustrating history and techniques of public health.
Daily 9-5.

MUSEUM OF THE MEXICO-NORTH AMERICAN INSTITUTE OF CULTURAL RELATIONS
Hamburgo 115, Mexico City
Paintings, sculpture, graphics by Mexican and North American artists.
M.-Sa. 10-5.

MUSEUM OF NATURAL HISTORY
Chapultepec Park, Mexico City
Natural history of Mexico.
Daily 9.30-6.30; Su. 10-5.30.

MUSEUM OF RURAL LIFE (CHARRERIA)
Casa Chata, Mexico City
18th-19th century religious paintings. 19th-20th century peasant furniture, costumes, ornaments and utensils.
Daily ex. public holidays 10-2, 3-5.

MUSEUM OF RELIGIOUS ART
Guatemala 17, Mexico City
Items from Mexican churches. Paintings and sculptures from Europe and Asia.
Tu.-Sa. 9-5; Su. 9-1.

MUSEUM OF THE SCHOOL OF FINE ARTS
Corner of Academia and Calle Moneda, Mexico City
Mexican Colonial paintings. European paintings by Geertgentot Sint Jans, Titian (3), Tintoretto (3), Ingres, Poussin, Daumier, Pisarro, Delacroix, El Greco (2), Goya, Zurburan, Ribera, the 14th century Catalan Luis Borrasa, Rubens, Breughel, and Lawrence and Opie of the English school.
Daily 10-1.

MUSEUM OF WESTERN MEXICAN CULTURE
Calle Dr. Angel González 21, Mexico City
Prehispanic pottery. Colonial paintings and coins. 15 drawings by the Mexican painter, José Clemente Orozco, with one of his easels.
Daily ex. public holidays 10-2, 3-5.

MUSEUM OF WORLD CULTURES
Moneda 13, Mexico City
World anthropology, prehistory and ethnography.
M.-Sa. ex. F. 10-6; Su. 10-4.

NATIONAL ANTHROPOLOGICAL MUSEUM
Avenida Reforma y la Milla, Mexico City
Mexican archaeology, physical anthropology and ethnography. Story of Mexico from prehistoric to modern times. Giant Aztec monuments, including 22 ton calendar stone and 137 ton figure of Tlaloc, God of Rain. Folk costumes.
Tu.-Su. ex. F. 10-6; F. 10-8. Closed M.

NATIONAL HISTORICAL MUSEUM
Castillo de Chapultepec, Mexico City
Paintings; miniatures; photographs. Decorative arts. Flags. Documents and other material illustrating the history of Mexico. Maps, plans. Coins and medals. Costumes.
Daily ex. Tu. 9-6.

NATIONAL HISTORICAL MUSEUM
'The Struggle of the Mexican People for its Liberty', Bosque de Chapultepec, Mexico City
Dioramas and models illustrating the movements for independence and reform. Unfinished mural by Siqueiros and a notable mural by O'Gorman on the theme of Independence.
Daily 10-6.30; Su. 10-5.30.

NATIONAL MUSEUM OF ARTS AND CRAFTS
Avenida Juárez 44, Mexico City
18th century building, originally convent Chapel. Examples of Mexican folk art from the late 18th century to the present day. Collection of photographs, slides and recorded music.
Daily 10-6, ex. W. Sa. 10-8.

NATIONAL MUSEUM OF EDUCATION
Calle Presidente Masaryk 526, Mexico City
History of Education in Mexico.
M.-Sa. 9-1, 3-6.

NATIONAL MUSEUM OF FLORA AND FAUNA
Mexico City
Flora and fauna of Mexico.
Tu.-Sa. 9-6; Su. 9-1.

NATIONAL MUSEUM OF MODERN ART
Palacio de Bellas Artes, Bosque de Chapultepec, Mexico City
Engravings and vignettes by José Gpe. Posada; 19th century folk art. Paintings by José Ma. Velasco and Francisco Gostia, and by contemporary artists. Engravings. Sculpture.
Daily 10-5.

NATURAL HISTORY MUSEUM
Calle Chopo 10, Santa Maria, Mexico City
Natural history of Mexico.
M.-F. 10-1, 3-5.

PALACE OF FINE ARTS
Alameda, Mexico City
Paintings. Sculpture. Prints. Includes oils and water-colours by Rivera and frescoes by Orozco, Tamaya, Siguerros and Rivera. The fresco by Rivera is a copy of the original rubbed out with disapproval at Radio City, New York.
Daily 10-5.30; Su. 10-2.

POSTAL MUSEUM
Edificio de la Central de Correos, Mexico City
History of the Mexican postal service. Stamps.
M.-Sa. 9-6.

SAGRANO METROPOLITANO
Calle Guatemala, Mexico City
Church (1769). Museum of religious relics.
M.-Sa. 9.30-7; Su. 10-3.

SAN CARLOS MUSEUM
Calle Academia 22, Mexico City
European paintings of the 14th-early 20th centuries. Flemish, Italian, Spanish, French, English and Belgian schools.
Daily ex. M. 10-5.

SAN DIEGO MUSEUM OF MEXICAN (COLONIAL) PAINTING
Calle Dr. Mora 7, Mexico City
Paintings, mainly religious subjects, but with a few portraits of nuns, priests and viceroys. Three landscapes, probably second half of the 18th century.
Tu.-Su. 10-5.

UNIVERSITY MUSEUM OF SCIENCE AND ART
Cuidad Universitaria, Mexico City
Science and art collections.
M.-Sa. 10-2, 4-7; Su. 11-2.

V. CARRANZA HOUSE AND MUSEUM OF THE REVOLUTION
Calle Lerma 35, Mexico City
Reproduction of the house inhabited by Venustiano Carranza. Collections illustrating his life and work.
M.-F. 10-1.

MITLA

SITE MUSEUM
Mitla
Finds from excavations in the area. Local history.
M.-Sa. 10-1, 2-5.

MONTE ALBAN

MUSEUM
Colonial House, Monte Alban, nr. Oaxaca
Local history, ethnography.
M.-Sa. 10-1, 2-5.

MONTERREY

GALLERY OF PLASTIC ARTS
Aramberri 504 Pte., Monterrey, Nuevo León
Sculpture.
Tu.-Sa. 10-1, 3-6; Su. 10-4.

MONTERREY REGIONAL MUSEUM
Former Archbishopric, Monterrey, Nuevo León
Late 18th century building. Mexican archaeology. Colonial and modern history of Nuevo León.
Tu.-Sa. 10-1, 3-6; Su. 10-4.

MORELIA

CASA DE MORELOS
Morelia, Michoacán
Local history, ethnography.
M.-Sa. 10-1, 2-5.

MICHOACAN REGIONAL MUSEUM
Calle Allende 305, Morelia, Michoacan
Regional archaeology, ethnography. Armchairs, benches, tables, wardrobes of the 18th-early 19th centuries. Personal possessions of Generalismo José Ma. Morelos y Pavón, hero of the struggle for national independence.
M.-Sa. 9-1, 3-6; Su. 9-1, 6-9.

NAYARIT

REGIONAL MUSEUM
Palacio del Goierno, Nayarit
Regional archaeology, history, ethnography.
Tu.-Sa. 9-1, 3-6; Su. 9-1.

OAXACA

JUÁREZ HOUSE
Calle de Garcia Vigil 43, Oaxaca
House in which Benita Juárez was taught his first letters. Glass objects which belonged to Juarez. Paintings on canvas and wood, first half of 19th century. Early 19th century furniture.
Daily ex. Sa. 9-1, 4-6.

OAXACA REGIONAL MUSEUM
Calle Independencia 33, Oaxaca
In former colonial mansion. Prehispanic items from Yagul, Monte Albán and other sites. These include the jewels from excavations at the ruins of the nearby Zatopec city of Monte Albán.
Daily ex. Sa. 9-1, 4-6.

OAXTEPEC

COLONIAL MUSEUM
Oaxtepec
History of the district in the colonial period.
M.-Sa. 10-5.

PALENQUE

ARCHAEOLOGICAL MUSEUM OF THE PALENQUE REGION
Palenque, Chiapas
Site museum of memorial stones, pottery and other objects discovered in the ruins of this ancient Mayan centre. The buildings include a palace, temples and pyramids.
Daily 9-1.30, 4-7.

PATZUCARO

MUSEUM OF FOLK ARTS AND CRAFTS
Enseñanza y Alcantarida, Patzucaro, Michoacan
In College of San Nicolás Obispo. Lacquerware, 17th century to present day. 18th century armchairs, benches, chairs. Paintings on wood and canvas, 18th-19th centuries.
M.-F. 9-1, 3-5.

PATZCUARO

REGIONAL MUSEUM
Patzcuaro, Michoacan
Regional archaeology, history.
M.-F. 9-1, 3-5.

PUEBLA

MUSEUM OF THE ACADEMY OF FINE ART
Puebla
Exhibition of Mexican colonial paintings.
M.-Sa. 10-1, 2-5.

JOSÉ LUIS BEELO Y GONZALEZ MUSEUM
Poniente 302, Puebla
Wrought ironwork. European and Mexican paintings. Ivories. Furniture. Chinese, Japanese, French and German porcelain.
Daily ex. Tu. 10-5.

MUSEUM OF HANDICRAFTS
Unidad Cívica 5, Mayo Puebla, Puebla
Handicrafts and industries during the colonial period. Pottery. Textiles. Leather. Evolution of maize.
Daily ex. M. 10-6.

MUSEUM OF NON-INTERVENTION
Fuente de Loreto, Puebla
Weapons. Paintings. Coins and medals. Documents. Murals, models, dioramas, with recorded commentary.
Daily ex. Su. 9.30-5.

PLAZA DE LAS AMERICAS
Puebla
Local history.
M.-Sa. 10-1, 2-5.

PUEBLA REGIONAL MUSEUM
Casa del Alfeñique, Avenida 4 de Oriente 416, Puebla
Colonial period building, originally designed to house important visitors. Paintings. Sculptures. Local history. Religious art.
Daily ex. Tu. 10-5.

REGIONAL MUSEUM OF THE REVOLUTION
Casa Aquiles Serdán, Calle 6 Oriente 206, Puebla
Weapons. Portraits. Furniture, books and personal possessions of the Serdán family.
Daily 10-5.

SANTA MONICA COLONIAL MUSEUM
18 Poniente 103, Puebla
17th-19th century paintings. Sculpture of the colonial period. 19th century furniture and ornaments.
Daily ex. Sa. 10-4.30; Sa. 10-3.

QUERETARO

PIO MARIANO MUSEUM
Plaza Obregon, Queretaro
History and archaeology of Mexico. Paintings, manuscripts.
M.-Sa. 10-1, 2-5.

QUERETARO REGIONAL MUSEUM
Former Convento de San Francisco, Queretaro
Building is late 16th century. Paintings by the Mexican artist, Juan Rodríguez, depicting the life of St. Francis of Assisi and St. Antony of Padua. Mexican romantic painting of the second half of the 19th century. Prehispanic regional items. 16th-19th century books.
Daily ex. M. 10-2, 4-6.

SAN CRISTOBAL DE LAS CASAS

LOCAL MUSEUM
San Cristobal de las Casas, Chiapas
Archaeology. Local history.
M.-Sa. 10-1, 2-5.

SAN CRISTOBAL ECATEPEC

CASA DE MORELOS
23 km. from Mexico City on the Laredo road, San Cristobal Ecatepec, Edo de Mexico
Built as resting point for the Viceroys, before their arrival at Mexico City. Armchairs, tables, wardrobes and other 18th century furniture. Portraits of Viceroys.
Daily 9-1, 3-4.

SAN LUIS POTOSI

SAN LUIS POTOSI REGIONAL MUSEUM
Calle Galeana 450-470, San Luis Potosi
Franciscan convent, 18th century. Prehispanic items, mostly belonging to the Huasteca culture. Regional handicrafts. Wrought iron. Maps. Embroidery. Textiles.
Daily ex. Th. 10-1, 3-6.

SAN MIGUEL DE ALLENDE

ITZCUINAPAN REGIONAL ARCHAEOLOGICAL MUSEUM
Calle Mesones 81, San Miguel de Allende
Regional archaeology.
M.-Sa. 10-5; Su. 10-1.

IGNACIO RAMIREZ CULTURAL CENTRE
Hernandez Macias 71, San Miguel de Allende
Regional archaeology, history, folklore, folk art.
M.-Sa. 10-5; Su. 10-1.

SANTIAGO TUXTLA

REGIONAL MUSEUM
Santiago Tuxtla
Regional history, archaeology, folklore.
Tu.-Sa. 9-1, 3-6; Su. 10-1.

TAXIO

LOCAL MUSEUM
Taxio
Collection of Prehispanic sculptures formed by William Spratling.
On request.

TENAYUCA

TENAYUCA ARCHAEOLOGICAL MUSEUM
Tenayuca, Edo de Mexico
Pottery. Sculpture. Drawings showing local architecture.
Tu.-Su. 9.30-6.

TEOTIHUACAN

TEOTIHUACAN MUSEUM
30 miles north-east of Mexico City, Teotihuacan, Edo de Mexico
Archaeological material from excavations at Teotihuacan and neighbouring sites. Pyramids and temples. History of the colonial period. Regional handicrafts.
Tu.-Su. 9.30-6.

TEPEXPAN

PREHISTORIC MUSEUM OF THE VALLE DE MEXICO
On Laredo Road, Tepexpan, Edo de Mexico
On site where the remains of the prehistoric man were discovered. Stone implements. Drawings and paintings of life as it was at the time of prehistoric man.
Tu.-Su. 9-30-6.

TEPIC

NAYARIT REGIONAL MUSEUM
Avenida Mexico 91 Norte, Tepic, Nayarit
Archaeology. Ethnography. Sculpture.
Daily 8.30-2; 3.30-7.

TEPOZOTLAN

COLONIAL ART MUSEUM
Jesuit Abbey, Tepozotlan
Colonial art collections. Paintings.
Daily ex. M. 10-1, 2-5.

TLALPAN

CHARRERIA MUSEUM
Tlalpan, nr. Mexico City
Collections devoted to *Charreria*, the national horse-riding sport.
M.-Sa. 10-1, 2-5.

TLAQUEPAQUE

REGIONAL CERAMICS MUSEUM
Calle Independencia 237, Tlaquepaque, Jalisco
Pottery and tiles from Tonalá, Santa Cruz, Tatepozco and Maquepaque. Dining-room and kitchen decorated in the Mexican style.
Daily ex. Su. 10-5.

TOLUCA

MUSEUM OF NATURAL HISTORY AND ARCHAEOLOGY
Santos Delgollado 102, Toluca, Edo de Mexico
Colonial sculpture and furniture. Sala de Chaireriá. Armour and flags of the Napoleonic period.
Daily 10-2, 4-7.

NATIONAL MUSEUM OF FOLK ART
Avenida Hidalgo Oriente, Toluca, Edo de Mexico
Pottery. Wool textiles. Woven rushes. Carved bone. Furniture. Toys. Clothing.
Daily ex. M. 10-2, 4-7.

TULA

ARCHAEOLOGICAL SITE MUSEUM
Tula, Hidalgo
Monoliths, monuments, pottery and other material from local excavations. Immense human figures in black basalt around a pyramid and temple, with friezes of jaguars and eagles.
Daily 7-6.

TUXTLA GUTIERREZ

STATE ARCHAEOLOGICAL MUSEUM
Tuxtla Gutierrez, Chiapas
Finds from excavations in the area. Pottery.
Daily 10-1, 2-5.

TZINZUNTZAN

MUSEUM OF ETHNOGRAPHY AND ARCHAEOLOGY
Tzinzuntzan
Regional archaeology, ethnography.
M. S. 9-1, 3-7; Su. 10-1.

UNIVERSITY CITY

NATURAL HISTORY MUSEUM
University of Mexico, University City
The museum enables the visitor to experience Mexico's five climates as he passes through the building. Temperatures are so regulated that he shivers or sweats by turn.
M.-Sa. 10-1, 2-5.

URUAPAN

REGIONAL MUSEUM OF MEXICAN ART
Huatápera, Uruapan
Mexican folk art. Regional history.
Tu.-Sa. 9-1, 3-6; Su. 9-1.

VERACRUZ

VERACRUZ REGIONAL MUSEUM
Baluarte de Santiago, Callejón de los Hornos, Veracruz
Building forms part of the 17th century city wall. Copies of 16th-18th century maps. 19th century weapons. Flags and banners.
Daily 10-1, 4-6.

VILLAHERMOSA

PARK MUSEUM
Anexo Parque de Tabasco, Villahermosa, Tabasco
Altars, olmec stone heads, stelae and monolithic figures dug from a swamp 30 miles south-east of the city, and arranged here in a parkland and lake setting.
Daily 8-12, 3-6.

TABASCO REGIONAL MUSEUM
Vicente Guerrero 12, Villahermosa, Tabasco
Archaeology. 7 very large stone sculptures. Collection of axes. Maya material. Reproduction of Prehispanic paintings.
Daily 10-1, 5.30-8.

VILLA OBREGON

COLONIAL MUSEUM
Villa Obregon
History and art of the colonial period.
Daily 9-1, 3-6.

XALAPA

VERACRUZ MUSEUM OF ANTHROPOLOGY
In western suburb of Xalapa, 4 km. from city centre, Veracruz
Archaeology of the Olmeca, Totonaco and Huasteca cultures, 15th century B.C. to 16th century A.D. Costumes. Folk art. Originals and copies of 16th century MSS.
Daily ex. Su. 10-1, 2-5.

YURIRIA

COLONIAL MUSEUM
Convento de Agustinos, Yuriria
Art and history of the colonial period. Religious art.
On request.

Monaco

Monaco is a wealthy princedom, with a prosperous casino and a fashionable holiday and relaxation industry. It has the appropriate museums.

MONACO

OCEANOGRAPHIC MUSEUM
Monaco Ville, Monaco
Aquarium. Collections of marine zoology, physical and applied oceanography.
Daily 9.30-7.

ROYAL PALACE
Monaco
Built 13th-17th centuries. Rooms with paintings by Van der Meulen, Holbein, Brueghel, Vanloo, Largillière, Rigaud.
July-Sept. Daily 9-5.30.

MONTE CARLO

MUSEUM OF PREHISTORIC ANTHROPOLOGY
Près du Jardin exotique, Monte Carlo
Bones of men and of prehistoric animals; tools from the paleolithic and neolithic periods. Objects made of gold.
Daily 9-12, 2.30-6.30. In winter 2 until nightfall.

NATIONAL FINE ARTS MUSEUM
Rue des Genêts, Monte Carlo
Paintings, drawings, prints, engravings and sculpture by European artists.
Daily 9-12, 2.30-6.30

VILLA ISPAHAN
Boulevard du Jardin-Exotique, Monte Carlo
Iranian art. Sculptures, paintings, objets d'art, furniture, costumes.
Daily 10-12, 3-7.

Morocco

For museum buildings, Morocco makes good use of a number of its surplus royal palaces. These provide an extra attraction for visitors and are well suited to displaying the collections of furniture, handicrafts and costumes which Morocco has in abundance and which form the bulk of what the Museums have to show.

FEZ

BATHA MUSEUM
Place du Batha, Fez
In former Batha Palace. Handicrafts. Decorative arts. Workshops of bookbinder, illumination and marquetry craftsman. Moroccan kitchen. Costumes.
Oct.-Apr. Daily 8.30-12, 2.30-6. May-Sept. Daily 8-12, 3-5.

BORDJ NORD MUSEUM OF WEAPONS
Rue de Batha, Fez
In the Bordj Nord (fortress, 1582). Development of weapons and military equipment from prehistoric times to present day.
May-Sept. Daily 8-12.30, 3-6.30. Oct.-Apr. 8.30-12, 2-6.

MARRAKESH

DAR SI SAID MUSEUM
Rue de la Bahia-Riad, Zitoun-Kdem, Marrakesh
In former Si Said Palace (1900). Furniture. Pottery. Carpets. Embroidery. Weapons. Tapestry.
Sept. 16-July 14, Daily 10-1, 2.30-6. July 15-Sept. 15 Daily 10-1, 4-7.

MUSEUM OF THE MENARA
Marrakesh
Decorative arts.
Daily 10-1, 2.30-5.30.

MEKMES

DAR JAMAÏ MUSEUM
Sebbaghini 1, Mekmes
In former Jamaï Palace. Local handicrafts and decorative arts. Furniture. Domestic equipment. Pottery, especially vases. Embroidery. Ironwork. Woodwork. Brassware. Agricultural implements.
Daily 9-7.

RABAT

MUSEUM OF THE CHÉRIF SCIENTIFIC INSTITUTE
Avenue Moulay Chérif, Rabat
Botanical collections.
Daily 8.30-12, 2-6.

MUSEUM OF ANTIQUITIES
(Louis Chatelain Museum), 23 rue Pierre Parent, Rabat
Archaeological material, especially from sites at Volubilis, Banasa, Themusida and Chellah. Rock-paintings and engravings. Tablets. Pottery. History of the Roman settlement. Judaism and early Christianity.
Daily 8.30-12, 2.30-6.

MUSEUM OF THE OUDAIAS
Kasbah des Oudaia, Rabat
In former 18th century palace. Carpets. Musical instruments. Jewellery. Reconstruction of Moroccan house interior. Koran manuscripts.
Daily 9-12, 2.30-6.

TANGIER

MUSEUM OF ANTIQUITIES
(Micheaux-Bellaine Museum), Kasbah Palace, Tangier
Prehistory. Greek and Roman antiquities.
Daily ex. M., Th. 9-12, 2.30-6.

KASBAH MUSEUM
Tangier
In former palace (18th century). Moroccan handicrafts. Woodwork. Embroidery. Ironwork. Carpets. Pottery. Jewellery.
Daily 10-1, 2.30-5.30.

TETOUAN

TETOUAN ARCHAEOLOGICAL MUSEUM
2 rue Bouhçein, Tetouan
Material from excavations in the Tetouan area. Bronze and stone sculpture. Pottery. Jewellery. Glass. Weapons.
Daily 10-1, 2.30-5.30.

TETOUAN MUSEUM
Bab al-Ugla, Tetouan
In former fortress (1813). Collections illustrating the life and culture of Andalusia, and its influence on Morocco. Handicrafts. Weapons. Musical instruments. Costumes. Domestic equipment. Reconstruction of interiors.
Daily 10-1, 2.30-5.30.

Mozambique

It is a curious fact that the museums of an island producing mainly bananas, sugar and rum should be concerned to such a remarkable extent with geology and military history. This is, however, the case; and we can only note that a Museum of Posts and Railways and a Municipal Art Gallery are planned for the very near future.

BEIRA

MUNICIPAL MUSEUM
Rua Correia de Brito, Box 1702, Beira
Archaeology. History. Ethnography. Palaeontology. Mineralogy. Numismatics. Conchology.
Daily ex. Su. and public holidays, 7.30-11.30, 3-7.

BOANE

MILITARY MUSEUM
Boane
Military relics and documents. Uniforms. Weapons.
Daily 9-12, 3-5.

INHACA ISLAND

MUSEUM OF MARINE BIOLOGY
Inhaca Island
Marine biology exhibits.
By appointment.

LOURENÇO MARQUES

DR. ALVARO DE CASTRO PROVINCIAL MUSEUM
Largo do Padrao das Descobertas, Lourenço Marques
Natural history. Palaeontology. Ethnography, especially silver from the Tete area.
Daily 9-11.30.

FREIRE DE ANDRADE MUSEUM
Direccao das Servicos de Geologia e Minas, Avenida Infante de Sagres 2, Lourenço Marques
Mineralogy, geology and palaeontology of Mozambique. Prehistory. Specimens of turmaline and Columbo tantelites.
Apr.-Oct. W. and Sa. 2-5. Nov.-Mar. W. and Sa. 2.30-5. Open to research workers any time, except Su.

HISTORICAL MUSEUM
Praça 7 de Marco, Lourenço Marques
Historical collections: arms, coins, decorations and medals, tombstones, furniture and art objects. Religious paintings and Malhöa pictures.
Daily 9-11.30, 2-5. Su. and public holidays, 9-12.

MUNICIPAL MUSEUM
Town Hall, Praça Mouzinho de Albuquerque, Lourenço Marques
History of Lourenço Marques.
Enquire locally.

MUSEUM OF MILITARY HISTORY
Fortress of Our Lady of Conception, Lourenço Marques
Historical collections, including arms, uniforms, medals. Paintings and drawings.
Daily 9-11.30.

MANICA

MOSTRUÁRO DE MANICA MUSEUM
Vila Manica, Manica
Mineralogy and petrology. Zoology (mammals).
Daily ex. Sa. and W. morning, 8-11.30, 2-5.

Nepal

The museums of Nepal are essentially preservation museums. They exist to care for the arts and crafts of the peoples within its territory and have no deliberate educational or propaganda function. The important forestry industry is not represented, and one might have expected to discover some display devoted to one of Asia's most exotic exports, medicinal herbs, which is responsible for a large part of the foreign revenue of Nepal.

BHAKTAPUR

PICTURE GALLERY
Lal Baithak Palace, Bhaktapur
Paintings. Illustrated manuscripts. Thankas (Buddhist and Hindu religious hanging scrolls). Murals. Stone sculptures.
Daily ex. M. 9-12, 2-5.

WOODWORK MUSEUM
Palace of Fifty-Five Windows, Bhaktapur
Examples of woodwork from all parts of Nepal.
Daily ex. M. 9-12, 2-5.

KATHMANDU

NATIONAL MUSEUM OF NEPAL
Chhauni, Kathmandu
Arms. Historic portraits. Decorative art objects. Items lent by the present King. Ethnography. Natural history. Sculpture. Paintings. Miniatures. Oils and water-colours.
Daily ex. M. 9-12, 2-5.

NUMISMATIC MUSEUM
First Floor, Hanuman Dhoka Palace, Kathmandu
Numismatic collections.
Daily ex. M. 9-12, 2-5.

Netherlands

Most people associate the Netherlands with seafaring, painting, windmills, gin, canals and bulb-growing, and there are museums devoted to all these national specialities, and to a good many more besides, including clog-making, cheese, printing and land drainage. The Dutch, with their strong instincts for tourism and business and their small-country need to maintain morale, are not given to hiding their light under a bushel.

The art galleries are prodigiously well stocked, especially with paintings by artists reared in what are now the Netherlands and Belgium. One thinks immediately of the great collections of Rembrandts in Amsterdam and the Hague, but institutions in other countries would be equally envious of the Dutch gallery which possesses no fewer than 260 works by Van Gogh. A considerable proportion of the nation's works of art are still, as our list indicates, in private hands. One of the more remarkable characteristics of Dutch art collections is, in fact, the number which are still owned by rich men who give visitors very similar rights of admission to those offered by public museums. In the Netherlands, the transformation of a private museum into a public one can be hardly noticed.

The history of the Netherlands and its former empire is well documented in museums. The period of Spanish occupation and the rule of the House of Orange-Nassau are both generously illustrated, especially by portraits and documents. The German neighbours, too, have a sizeable, if not always honoured, place in Dutch museums. The last Emperor, Wilhelm II, is particularly well represented, which is as it should be, since he spent his last years in the Netherlands. The former overseas territories are remembered in a variety of museums, with collections ranging from tropical medicine to the history of the East and West India Companies.

Windmills are excellently cared for and promoted, both individually and in groups. So too are the polders, the creation of which has been one of the greatest and most prudent achievements in Dutch history. The open-air museums of rural buildings are good and agriculture and horticulture are well served but - an extraordinary fact in view of the way the Netherlands has to earn a living - there is no national museum of industry or technology. Individual museums, however, have their own specialised and often excellent museums in different parts of the country.

Reference to our list will show that a surprisingly large number of Dutch museums are accommodated in former weigh-houses, illustrating the long-established Dutch passion for weighing and measuring things. One of these weigh-houses still has the special scales for weighing witches, a sign that the Dutch have not always been as sober and rational as they are today.

With such a wealth of interesting museums as the Netherlands has to offer, everyone must be permitted his own favourite. Ours, we are not ashamed to admit, is the Museum of Taxation, which includes a special collection of jokes about taxes and tax-collectors.

AALTEN

AALTEN MUSEUM OF ANTIQUITIES
Markt 14, Aalten, Gelderland
Geology. Prehistory. Local history. Period rooms, including peasant kitchen. Loom. Weapons. Costumes. Coins.
July-Aug., M.-F. 10-12, 3-5.

AARDENBURG

DISTRICT MUSEUM
Gemeentehuis, Markstrasse 18, Aardenburg, Zeeland
Geology. Palaeontology. Archaeology. Stone-Age material from local excavations. Medieval (especially French, English, Flemish) pottery, bronzes, architectural features, coins.
Daily 10-5.

ALKMAAR

MUNICIPAL MUSEUM
Doelenstrasse 3, Alkmaar, Noord Holland
Prehistory and history of the Alkmaar area. Architectural items. Paintings. Portraits, especially of members of the van Foreest family. Costumes. Toys.
M.-F. 10-12, 2-5; Sa. 10-12. Closed public holidays.

ALPHEN

REGIONAL MUSEUM OF ANTIQUITIES
Baarleseweg 1, Alphen, Noord Brabant
Archaeological material, including ornaments, urns, from Frankish burial site near Alphen.
M.-F. 2-4.

ALPHEN AAN DEN RIJN

OLD ALPHEN MUSEUM
Rijnkade 11, Alphen aan den Rijn, Zuid Holland
Roman, medieval, 17th century pottery. 18th century period rooms. 18th-19th century tools. Coins. Medals. Paintings, prints with local views.
F. 7 p.m.-9; Sa. 2-5. Other times on request.

ALMEN

A. BONGER COLLECTION
Groot Have, Almen, Gelderland
Paintings by Bernard, Cézanne, Van Gogh. Paintings, drawings, lithographs by Odilon Redon.
M.-Sa., on request.

AMERONGEN

COLLECTION OF THE HEIRS OF COUNT VAN ALDENBURG BENTINCK
Kasteel Amerongen, Amerongen, Utrecht
Paintings. Decorative arts. 17th-18th century furniture.
Tu., W., Th., 10-12. Closed public holidays, Jan. 1, Queen's Birthday.

AMERSFOORT

MUSEUM FLEHITE
Westringel 50, Amersfoort, Utrecht
Geology. Prehistory. Topographical prints. Pottery. Porcelain. Guild history. Memorabilia of Johan van Oldenbarneveldt and Everard Meyster, Jacob van Campen. Period rooms. Toys. Lace. Coins. Seals.
Tu.-Sa. 10-12, 2-5; Su., public holidays 2-5.

AMSTELVEEN

AEMSTELLE
Amsterdamseweg 511, Amstelveen, Noord Holland
Local history. Amstel porcelain. Peat-cutters' tools.
M.-Sa. 2-5; Su. 12-5. F. also 7.30 p.m.-10.

AMSTERDAM

ALLARD PIERSON MUSEUM
Archaeological Museum of the University of Amsterdam, Sarphatistrant 129-131, Amsterdam, Noord Holland
Greek and Roman antiquities. Near-Eastern and Egyptian vases, bronzes, terra cotta.
Mar.-Sept., M., W., F.-Su. 1-5. Oct.-Feb., M., W., F.-Su. 1-4.

BILDERDIJK MUSEUM
Buitenveldert, de Boelelaan 1081, Amsterdam, Noord Holland
Life and work of the poet, W. Bilderdijk. Personal possessions. Portraits. Manuscripts.
W. 10-5. Other times on request.

LUCAS BOLS MUSEUM
Rozengracht 103, Amsterdam, Noord Holland
In restored distillery (1575). History of distilling in the Netherlands, especially the career and achievements of Erven Lucas Bols.
M.-F., conducted tour 10.30.

BOTANICAL MUSEUM
Plantage Middenlaan 2A, Amsterdam, Noord Holland
Pressed and preserved botanical specimens. 17th-19th century water-colour drawings of hothouse plants.
By appointment.

CITROEN COLLECTION
Kalverstraat 1, Amsterdam, Noord Holland
Decorative and applied arts, 1830-1940, especially gold, silver.
On request.

CITY MUSEUM
Paulus Potterstraat 13, Amsterdam, Noord Holland
20th century paintings, especially Van Gogh, Chagall, Malewitch, Mondriaan, Cobra. European and American sculpture, drawings, prints, since 1945. 19th-20th century applied art, industrial art. Dutch coins. 17th-19th century period rooms. Prints. Drawings. Medals.
M.-Sa. 9.30-5; Su. 1-5.

COLLECTION OF BARON VAN HEECKEREN VAN WALIEN
Princes Margrietstraat 24, Amsterdam, Noord Holland
Early Chinese bronzes and tomb sculptures. Chinese lacquer work. Dutch porcelain, especially Weesp, Loosdrecht. Family portraits.
Tu., Th., Sa. 10-12.

COLLECTION OF THE NETHERLANDS TYPE-FOUNDRY AND PRINTING MACHINERY COMPANY
Bilderdijkstraat 163, Amsterdam, Noord Holland
Typography. Graphics.
M.-F. 9-5.

FREDERIK VAN EEDEN MUSEUM
Singel 423, Amsterdam, Noord Holland
Life and work of the poet and physician, F. van Eeden. Personal possessions. Portraits. Manuscripts. Books.
By appointment.

FAN MUSEUM
Prinsengracht 1083, Amsterdam, Noord Holland
History of fans, especially Chinese, Japanese. Period rooms. Paintings.
On request.

GEOLOGICAL INSTITUTE OF THE UNIVERSITY OF AMSTERDAM
Nieuwe Prinsengracht 130, Amsterdam, Noord Holland
Geology. Mineralogy. Precious and semi-precious stones. Fossils. Ores.
W. 2-5.

GUILD HOUSE OF THE WINE COOPERS
Kolstraat 10-12, Amsterdam, Noord Holland
Items connected with the wine-trade. Paintings. Glass.
M.-W., F., Sa. 10-5; Su. 1-5.

HERENGRACHT 524
Amsterdam, Noord Holland
Room (1771), with period furnishings and original wall-paintings by Jurriaan Andriessen.
By appointment.

HISTORICAL COLLECTION OF THE UNIVERSITY OF AMSTERDAM
Voorburgwal 231, Amsterdam, Noord Holland
History of the University and of student life. Paintings. Portraits. Prints. Medals.
M.-F. 8.30-12.30, 1.30-5.

E. A. KLATTE COLLECTION
Amsteldijk 285, Amsterdam, Noord Holland
Delft pottery, Chinese porcelain. 15th-17th century Dutch, Flemish paintings. Impressionist paintings by Dutch artists.
M., W., F. 10-12.

MULTATULI MUSEUM
Korsjerpoortsteeg 20, Amsterdam, Noord Holland
Birthplace of the writer, Multatuli (E. D. Dekker). Life and work of Multatuli. Portraits. Manuscripts. Medals. Books. Personal possessions.
By appointment.

MUSEUM AMSTELKRING
Voorburgwal 40, Amsterdam, Noord Holland
In 18th century church and adjoining house (1613). 17th-18th century period rooms. Paintings. Sculpture. Silver and other liturgical items. Prints of Amsterdam churches.
M.-Sa. 10-5; Su. 1-5. Closed Jan. 1, Dec. 25.

MUSEUM OF BIBLICAL ANTIQUITIES
Hemonylaan 19, Amsterdam, Noord Holland
Antiquities from Palestine, Egypt. Sumerian clay-tablets, pottery, lamps. Models of the Tabernacle, Herod's Temple and Jerusalem in Roman times. Flowers, prints and animals of Palestine. Daily life in Biblical times.
M.-W., F., Sa. 10-12, 2-5.

MUSEUM OF CULINARY HISTORY
Wibautstraat 220-2, Amsterdam, Noord Holland
In Confectionery School. Old bakery and baker's shop. Confectioner's equipment. Prints. Menus.
W. 2-5, except during school holidays. Other times on request.

MUSEUM FODOR
Keizersgracht 609, Amsterdam, Noord Holland
Exhibition of porcelain, 18th-19th century paintings, 16th-19th century prints, drawings, from permanent collections, based on bequest of C. J. Fodor (d.1860).
M.-Sa. 9.30-5; Su. 1-5.

MUSEUM OF THE HISTORY OF AMSTERDAM
Kalverstraat 93, Amsterdam, Noord Holland
Collections illustrating history of Amsterdam.
M.-Sa. 9.30-5; Su. 1-5.

MUSEUM OF THE HISTORY OF MEDICINE AND PHARMACY
Koestraat 10-12, Amsterdam, Noord Holland
History of pharmacy and of the art of healing. Reconstruction of 18th century apothecary's shop. Medical instruments.
M.-W., F., Sa. 10-5; Su. 1-5.

MUSEUM OF THE INSTITUTE OF SAFETY
Hobbemastraat 22, Amsterdam, Noord Holland
Fire precautions. Testing systems. Protection against radioactivity. Safety in use of woodworking and metalworking machinery. Danger from explosives.
M.-F. 8.30-12, 1-4.30.

MUSEUM OF JEWISH HISTORY
Waagebouw, Nieuwemarkt, Amsterdam, Noord Holland
Collection illustrating history of the Jews in the Netherlands. Liturgical items. Religious art.
M.-Sa. 9.30-5; Su. 1-5.

MUSEUM OF THE TROPICS
Linnaeusstraat 2, Amsterdam, Noord Holland
Life in tropical and sub-tropical countries. Housing. Clothing. Agriculture. Cattle-rearing. Religion. Popular art. Medicine and health. Timbers. Minerals. Textiles.
Mar.-Oct., M.-Sa. 10-5. Nov.-Feb., M.-Sa. 10-4, Su., public holidays, 12-5. Closed Jan. 1 and Queen's birthday.

MUSEUM OF THE WERKSPOOR COMPANY
Oostenburgergracht 79, Amsterdam, Noord Holland
Collections illustrating the history of the East India Company, from its foundation at Oostenburg in 1663 to the beginning of the 19th century, and the history of the Werkspoor Company from 1827.
W. 12-4.

MUSEUM WILLET-HOLTHUYSEN
Herengracht 605, Amsterdam, Noord Holland
17th-18th century furniture, paintings, porcelain, glass. Paintings, drawings, objets d'art connected with the Backer family, early 17th century - present day.
M.-Sa. 9.30-5; Su. 1-5.

NATIONAL MUSEUM: DEPARTMENT OF DUTCH HISTORY
Stadhouderskade 42, Amsterdam, Noord Holland
Collections illustrating history of the Netherlands. Portraits. Paintings of battles and of subjects illustrating seafaring and colonial expansion. Ship models. History of E. and W. India Companies. Costumes. Uniforms. Weapons. Medals. Glass. Ceramics. Silver.
Daily 10-5; Public holidays 1-5. Closed Jan. 1.

NATIONAL MUSEUM: DEPARTMENT OF FAR-EASTERN ART
Hobbemastraat 19, Amsterdam, Noord Holland
Art of India, Indonesia, Burma, Thailand, Indo-China, Nepal, Tibet, China, Japan, Korea. Special collections include Javanese stone sculpture, Chinese bronzes, Chinese and Japanese wooden sculpture, Tibetan and Japanese paintings, Chinese and Japanese porcelain.
Daily 10-5; public holidays 1-5. Closed Jan. 1.

NATIONAL MUSEUM: DEPARTMENT OF PAINTINGS
Stadhouderskade 42, Amsterdam, Noord Holland
15th-19th century Dutch paintings, especially before 1700. European paintings, especially Flemish, Italian, Spanish, French. Pastels. Water colours. Miniatures.
Daily 10-5; public holidays 1-5. Closed Jan. 1.

NATIONAL MUSEUM: DEPARTMENT OF SCULPTURE AND INDUSTRIAL ART
Stadhouderskade 42, Amsterdam, Noord Holland
Dutch sculpture 1150-1850. 15th-16th century portrait sculpture, especially bronzes of Italy and S. Netherlands. Dutch, Italian, French furniture. European, Chinese, Islamic ceramics. Works in precious and non-precious metals. Italian, Dutch, German glass. Tapestries. Lace. Carpets. Textiles.
Daily 10-5; public holidays 1-5. Closed Jan. 1.

NATIONAL MUSEUM: NATIONAL CABINET OF PRINTS AND DRAWINGS
Stadhouderskade 42, Amsterdam, Noord Holland
International collection of prints and drawings, 15th century to present day. Special collections of Dutch historical prints, Dutch, Italian, French drawings, prints by Rembrandt, Dürer and their contemporaries, Japanese and Chinese prints, posters, prints for children.
Daily 10-5; public holidays 1-5. Closed Jan. 1.

NATURAL HISTORY COLLECTION
Koenenkade, A'dam Z2, Amsterdam, Noord Holland
Plants and wildlife of the Amsterdam Bos. Maps. Models.
Daily 10-4.30.

NETHERLANDS FILM MUSEUM
Paulus Potterstraat 13, Amsterdam, Noord Holland
Cinema posters. Stills advertising films. Sheet-music, for accompaniment to silent films. Library of Dutch and foreign films.
By appointment.

NETHERLANDS INSTITUTE OF SCIENCE AND TECHNOLOGY
Rozengracht 224, Amsterdam, Noord Holland
Displays and equipment illustrating scientific principles and industrial processes.
M.-F. 10-4; Sa. 1-4. Oct.-Apr. also Su. 1-4. Closed public holidays.

NETHERLANDS MARITIME MUSEUM
Cornelius Schuystraat 57, Amsterdam, Noord Holland
Maritime history of the Netherlands, since 16th century. Ship models. Paintings. Drawings. Prints. Charts. Globes. Atlases. Navigation instruments. Ship-building.
M.-Sa. 10-4; Su., public holidays 1-5. Closed Jan. 1 and Queen's birthday.

NETHERLANDS MUSEUM OF THE PRESS
Oude Turfmarkt 151, Amsterdam, Noord Holland
Collection of newspapers and periodicals published in the Netherlands since the early 17th century. Material illustrating the history of the Press and the notabilities.
M.-F. 10-5.

NIEMEYER DUTCH TOBACCO MUSEUM
Amstel 57, Amsterdam, Noord Holland
History of tobacco and of the use of tobacco in the Netherlands. Pipes. Tobacco and snuff boxes. Tobacconist's shop. Herbals.
M.-Sa. 1-5.

FERDINAND DOMELA NIEUWENHUIS MUSEUM
Herengracht 262-6, Amsterdam, Noord Holland
In former bookshop of F. D. Nieuwenhuis (d.1919). Personal possessions. Portraits. Drawings. Furniture. Books.
M.-F. 9.30-4.30.

OCCO HOUSE
Nieuwe Keizersgracht 94, Amsterdam, Noord Holland
16th-18th century portraits of the Occo family.
Daily 10-4, by appointment.

E. PROEHL COLLECTION
Koningslaan 17, Amsterdam, Noord Holland
Dutch, French, Italian and early Flemish paintings. 17th-18th century French, Italian furniture. Italian silver, bronzes, porcelain.
M.-F. 11-4.

REMBRANDT HOUSE
Jodenbreestraat 4-6, Amsterdam, Noord Holland
Nearly complete collection of Rembrandt etchings. Material associated with life of Rembrandt.
Mar.-Sept., 10-5; Oct.-Feb., 10-4; public holidays 1-4.

ROOTHAAN MUSEUM
Pastorie 'de Krijtberg', Singel 448, Amsterdam, Noord Holland
Life and work of J. F. Roothaan (b. Amsterdam 1785), General of the Jesuit Order. Writings. Personal possessions.
On request.

A. SCHWARTZ COLLECTION
Apollolaan 135, Amsterdam, Noord Holland
Benin bronzes, ivories. Chinese porcelain. 17th-20th century drawings, prints. engravings. 17th-19th century paintings.
M., W., F. 3-5.

SIX COLLECTION
Amstel 218, Amsterdam, Noord Holland
Dutch paintings, drawings, etchings. Furniture. Objets d'art. Delft pottery. Chinese porcelain. Roman, Italian, Dutch glass.
May-Oct., M.-F. 10-12, 2-4. Nov.-Apr., M.-F. 10-12.

DR. B. SLINGENBERG'S COLLECTION
Keizersgracht 414, Amsterdam, Noord Holland
17th-18th century Delft pottery. European, Chinese porcelain. Clocks. 17th-18th century stained glass. Paintings. Pewter. Copper. Period rooms.
M., W., Th., 10-12.

THEATRE MUSEUM
Herengracht 168, Amsterdam, Noord Holland
History of the theatre, especially in the Netherlands. Prints. Drawings. Portraits. Posters. Programmes. Manuscripts. Memorabilia of actors, producers.
M.-Sa. 10-5; Su. 1-5.

VONDEL MUSEUM
Singel 423, Amsterdam, Noord Holland
Collection illustrating the life and work of the poet, J. van

den Vondel, and his friends and contemporaries. Manuscripts. Drawings. Prints. Portraits. Medals. Books. Personal possessions.
By appointment.

ZOOLOGICAL MUSEUM OF THE UNIVERSITY OF AMSTERDAM
Plantage Middelaan 53 and Zeeburgerdijk 21, Amsterdam, Noord Holland
Dioramas and study collections of insects, reptiles, amphibians, mammals, molluscs, crustacea, birds, snakes.
M.-Sa. 8.30-5; Su., public holidays 1-5.

ANGERLO

VAN WEEDE COLLECTION
Kasteel Bingerden, Angerlo, Gelderland
Paintings. Furniture. Porcelain.
Tu., W., Th., 10-12.

APELDOORN

MOERMAN HISTORICAL MUSEUM
Loolaan 44A, Apeldoorn, Gelderland
Local history. Prehistoric material from local excavations. Architectural items. Paper industry. Prints illustrating Het Loo Palace. Portraits of members of the House of Orange. Coins. Medals.
Tu.-Sa. 10-5.

APPELSCHA

NATURAL HISTORY MUSEUM
Boerestreek 1, Appelscha, Friesland
Mounted specimens of animals. Geology.
May 1 - Sept. 15, daily 9-8.

APPINGEDAM

REGIONAL HISTORICAL MUSEUM
Kerkstraat, Appingedam, Groningen
History of the former province of Fivelingo. Tools. Household equipment. Agricultural implements. Costumes. Prints. Documents. Photographs.
M.-F. 3-5. Other times on request.

ARNEMUIDEN

TOWN HALL
Langstraat 35, Arnemuiden, Zeeland
History of Arnemuiden and district. Town archives, 1500-1852. Maps. Views. Portraits. Silver.
M.-F. 9-12, 2-4.

BRONBEEK MUSEUM
Velperweg 147, Arnhem, Gelderland
In Royal Veterans Home. Military history of the former Netherlands East Indies. Ethnographical collections from the Royal Palaces of Noordeinde and Huis ten Bosch.
Daily 9-5.

ARNHEM

LOCAL MUSEUM
Utrechtseweg 87, Arnhem, Gelderland
16th-20th century paintings, especially from lower Rhine area. Chinese porcelain. Delft, Arnhem pottery. 20th century ceramics. 17th-20th century glass, silver. Alexander Verhuell memorial room. Prints. History of Gelderland. Prehistoric material from local excavations. Engravings. Coins. Medals. Portraits. Sculpture.
M.-Sa. 10-5. Good Friday, Ascension Day, Easter Day, 1-5. Closed Jan. 1 and Queen's Birthday.

MUSEUM OF THE HISTORY OF THE GRENADIERS AND JAGERS
Onder de Linden 101, Arnhem, Gelderland
History of the Grenadier and Jager regiments. Uniforms. Weapons. Equipment. Portraits of officers since 1829. Documents. Flags. Insignia.
M.-F. 9-5 on request.

NATIONAL MUSEUM OF ETHNOLOGY: NETHERLANDS OPEN-AIR MUSEUM
Hoeferlaan, Arnhem, Gelderland
Characteristic rural buildings from the whole of the Netherlands, with furnishings and equipment. Costumes. Tools. Agricultural implements. Paintings of village life.
Apr. - Oct., M.-Sa. 9-6; Su. 11-8.

VAN SIMMEREN VAN DER WEERD COLLECTION
Van Heemstralaan 102, Arnhem, Gelderland
17th-19th century paintings. 16th-19th century furniture, drawings, prints. Spanish, Italian, Delft pottery. Pewter and copper, especially 17th-18th century.
M., Tu., F. 2-4.

ASSELT

ASSELT MUSEUM OF FOLKLORE
Pastoor Pinckersstraat, Asselt, Limburg
In former bakery (18th century) and coachhouse (19th century). Prehistory. Fossils. Ceramics. Religious art. Portraits. Copper and pewter ware. Coins. Weapons. Textile printing blocks.
On request.

ASSEN

DRENTHE PROVINCIAL MUSEUM
Brink 4-5, Assen, Drenthe
Prehistory and history of Drenthe. Popular art. Costumes. Period rooms.
May-Sept., M.-Sa. 9.30-5. Oct.-Apr., M.-Sa. 9.30-4. Closed public holidays.

ASTEN

BELL AND CARILLON MUSEUM
Raadhuis, Asten, Noord Brabant
International collection of bells. Bell-founding. Mechanical toys.
Sa. 9-12, Other times on request.

AXEL

AXEL MUSEUM OF RURAL LIFE
Kanaalkade 9, Axel, Zeeland
Costumes, ornaments, tools, household equipment of the Axel district. 19th century period rooms.
Daily, on request, 9-12, 1-5.

BAKKUM

WAYSIDE MUSEUM
Zeeweg, Bakkum, Noord Holland
Natural history, especially birds, eggs, butterflies. Local history.
Apr. 1 - Sept. 15, daily 10-12, 2-5. July 1 - Aug. 15 also M., W., F. 7 p.m.-9.

BARNEVELD

NAIRAC MUSEUM OF THE VELUW
Nieuwstraat 31, Barneveld, Gelderland
Prehistory, archaeology and history of the Barneveld district. Sculpture. Glass. Coins.
M.-F. 9-12, 2-5.

BENNEKOM

BOEKELO MUSEUM OF LOCAL HISTORY
Achterstraat 11, Bennekom, Gelderland
Items illustrating history of the Bennekom district.
May-Sept., M.-Sa. 9-12, 2-5. Other times on request.

BEERS

GATEHOUSE OF BEERS STINZENMUSEUM
Beers, Friesland
Local history, especially material relating to Stinzen. Pictures of surviving gateways of old Stinzen. Coats of arms. Items connected with swan-shooting.
M.-Sa. 10-12, 2-5.

BEETSTERZWAAG

VAN HARINXMA THOE SLOETEN FOUNDATION
Harinxma State, Beetsterzwaag, Friesland
17th-19th century furniture. Family portraits.
Sept.-June, M., Tu., W. 2-4.

BERGEN

STERKEN HOUSE, DISTRICT MUSEUM
Oude Prinsweg 21, Bergen, Noord Holland
In 17th century house. Local history. Costumes. Period rooms. Maps. Paintings and prints of local subjects.
May-Sept., 10-12, 2-4. July-Aug., also M., W., F., 8 p.m.-10.

BERGEN OP ZOOM

DISTRICT MUSEUM
Het Markiezenhof, Steenbergsestraat 6, Bergen op Zoom, Noord Brabant
Local history. Pottery. Pewter. Copper. Guild history. Toys. Architectural items. Prints. 16th century tapestry. 15th-18th century paintings. 15th-16th century wood sculpture. 17th-18th century furniture, period rooms.
May-Sept., M.-F. 10-12, 2-5; Sa., Su., public holidays, 2-5. Oct.-Apr., W.-Su. 2-5. Closed Easter, Whitsun, Jan. 1, Queen's Birthday.

BERLICUM

VAN RIJCKEVORSEL COLLECTION
De Wamberg, Berlicum, Noord Brabant
17th-1th century furniture. Chinese porcelain. English pottery. Family portraits.
M., Sa. 10-12; Th. 2-4.

BEVERWIJK

KENNEMER MUSEUM OF LOCAL HISTORY
Velserweg 2, Beverwijk, Noord Holland
History of Beverwijk region. Paintings. Prints. Material from local excavations. 17th century coats of arms.
June-Aug., Tu., Th. 2-4.30, 7.30-9.30; F. 2-4.30. Remainder of year, M., Tu., Th. 7.30 p.m.-9.30.

BOLSWARD

BOLSWARD LOCAL HISTORY MUSEUM
Jongemastraat 2, Bolsward, Friesland
Items related to history of Bolsward. Furniture. Porcelain. Pottery. Coins. Silver.
M.-Sa. 9-12, 2-5. June 15 - Sept. 1 also 7 p.m.-10.

BORCULO

FIREFIGHTING MUSEUM
Korte Wal 11 and Burg Bloemerstraat 40, Borculo, Gelderland
Fire-fighting equipment, 1648-present day. Medals. Uniforms.
June 15 - Sept. 15 10-12, 2-5.

DE LEBBENBRUUGE FARM
Lebbenbruggedijk D.82, Borculo, Gelderland
Farmhouse and inn (1850) with household equipment, agricultural tools. Period kitchen. Weaving room. Granary. Baking oven. Barns.
June 15 - Aug. 30, Tu.-Sa. 10-12, 2-5; Su. 2-5. Other times on request.

STORM-DISASTER MUSEUM
Burg Bloemerstraat 40, Borculo, Gelderland
Mementoes of the cyclone which devastated Borculo in 1925. History of the rebuilding of the town.
June 15 - Sept. 15, 10-12, 2-5.

BORGER

FARM MUSEUM
Hoofdstraat 3, Borger, Drenthe
In farmhouse (1619). Local history. Furniture. Tools. Household equipment. Paintings.
Apr.-Oct., Tu.-Sa. 10-12, 2-5.

BORNE

BUSSEMAKER HOUSE
Ennekerdijk 11, Borne, Overijssel
18th-19th century furniture.
W., Sa. 10-12, 2-4.

BRAKEL

LOEVESTEIN CASTLE
Brakel, Gelderland
Castle (1357-68, with later additions). Local history.
Apr.-Oct., 9-5. Nov.-Mar., 10-4.

BREDA

DIOCESAN MUSEUM
Grote Markt 19, Breda, Noord Brabant
Religious art, mainly from diocese of Breda. Paintings. Wood sculpture. Ornaments. Liturgical objects.
10-12.30, 1.45-5.30; Su. 2-5.30. Closed Jan. 1, Dec. 25.

JUSTINUS VAN NASSAU MUSEUM OF ETHNOLOGY
Kastellplein 13, Breda, Noord Brabant
Collections illustrating non-Western cultures, Indian, Indonesia, New Guinea, South Pacific, S.E. Asia, China, Japan. Australia, America, Africa.
M.-Sa. 10-5; Su., public holidays 1-5. Closed Jan. 1, Dec. 25, Nov. 1.

MUNICIPAL MUSEUM
Grote Markt 19, Breda, Noord Brabant
Local history. Paintings. Coins. Weapons. Breda silver. Fire-fighting equipment. Coins. Guild history.
M.-Sa. 10-12.30, 1.45-5.30; Su. 2-5.30. Closed Jan. 1, Dec. 25.

BREUKELEN

GUNTERSTEIN RESIDENCE
Zandpad 48, Breukelen, Utrecht
Tapestries. Family portraits. Furniture. Autograph letters of Johan van Oldenbarneveldt and King Louis Napoleon. Travel diaries. Letters of credit. Prints. Coins.
On request.

DEN BRIEL

TROMP MUSEUM
Venkelstrad 4, Den Briel, Zuid Holland
In former weigh-house and prison (1623). Local history and folk-lore. Costumes. Tiles. Furniture. Architectural items. Weapons.
June-Aug., Tu.-Su. 10-5. Sept,-May, Tu.-Sa., 10-5.

BRUINISSE

LOCAL HISTORY MUSEUM
Oudestraat 27, Bruinisse, Zuid Holland
In 17th century house. 18th-19th century furniture, household equipment. Costumes. Equipment relating to crab and mussel industries.
June-Sept., Sa. 3-5.

BUREN

THE FARM WAGGON
Culemborgse Poort, Buren, Gelderland
Farm carts and waggons from Gelderland. Waggon building, including complete workshop. Carving. Blacksmith's work.
May-Sept., Tu.-Su. 1.30-5.30.

BUSSUM

E. A. VELTMAN COLLECTION
Koningslaan 37, Bussum, Noord Holland
Paintings and watercolours of the Hague and Amsterdam Schools. 17th century furniture. Chinese porcelain. Delft pottery. Egyptian and Greek objets d'art. Clocks. Sculpture. Wood-carving.
M., W., F. 10-12.

CADIER EN KEER

CADIER EN KEER AFRICA CENTRE
Rijksweg 3, Cadier en Keer, Limburg
Art and ethnology of West Africa, Sudan, Guinea Coast.
M.-Sa. 9-12, 2-5; Su. 2-5. Closed Jan. 1, Dec. 24-5.

COTTEN

BARON VAN HARDENBROEK COLLECTION
Kasteel Hardenbroek, Cotten, Utrecht
17th-19th century furniture. 17th-18th century condolence cards. Chinese porcelain. Family portraits.
By appointment.

CULEMBORG

CULEMBORG AND DISTRICT MUSEUM OF LOCAL HISTORY
Elisabeth Weeshuis, Heerenstraat 29, Culemborg, Gelderland
Local history. 16th-18th century portraits of Culemborg notabilities. 16th century religious paintings. Items relating to local administration. Prints. Coins. Guild plate. Architectural items.
M.-F. 9-12, 2-5.

DALFSEN

VON MARTELS DANKERN AND RÖELL VAN HAZERWOUDE COLLECTION
Huize De Horte C.67, Dalfsen, Overijssel
Dutch paintings. Chinese porcelain. Glass. Silver. 17th-18th century furniture.
By appointment.

VAN RECHTEREN LIMPURG COLLECTION
Casteel Rechteren, Dalfsen, Overijssel
17th century paintings, 17th-18th century furniture. Chinese porcelain. 18th century silver.
M., Th., F. 9.30-11.30, by appointment.

DEN BURG

LOCAL HISTORY MUSEUM
Kogerstraat 1, Den Burg, Noord Holland
History of Texel. Prints. Costumes. Tools. Household equipment. Furnished room. Folklore.
May 15- Sept. 15, M.-Sa. 9-12, 2-5.

TEXELS MUSEUM
Gerritslanderdijk, De Dennen, Den Burg, Noord Holland
Local geology, natural history, archaeology.
Easter- Sept. 30, daily 9-6. Oct. 1- Easter, M.-F. 9-6.

DELFSHAVEN

THE ZAKKENDRAGEN HOUSE
Voorstraat 13-15, Delfshaven, Zuid Holland
Pewter foundry. Bronze moulds, mainly 17th-18th century. Tools. Pewterer's stamps. Memorabilia of Piet Heyn (born here) and of the Pilgrim Fathers.
M.-Sa. 10-5; Su. 11-5. Closed Jan. 1.

DELFT

ELECTRO-TECHNOLOGY STUDY COLLECTION
T. H. Delft, Afd. Elektrotechnick, Mekelweg 4, Delft, Zuid Holland
Collection illustrating development of electricity, telecommunications, radio, radar, measuring techniques.
On request.

PAUL TETAR VAN ELVEN MUSEUM
Koornmarkt 67, Delft, Zuid Holland
18th century house. Furniture. Paintings. 18th-19th century Chinese and Japanese porcelain. Delft pottery. 18th century costumes. 19th century period rooms.
M.-F. 11-4; Su. 1-3.

ETHNOGRAPHICAL MUSEUM
Agathaplein 4, Delft, Zuid Holland
Ethnography, mainly of Indonesia and the West Indies. Ship-models. Textiles. Weapons. Silver. Copper. Pottery. Wicker and canework. Ornaments.
M.-Sa. 10-5; Su., public holidays 1-5. Closed Jan. 1.

VAN GRATIE ALMSHOUSE
Van der Mastenstraat, Delft, Zuid Holland
Building (1660, remodelled in 19th century). Portraits and other paintings. Furniture. Ceramics.
W., Sa., guided tour at 12 noon. Other times by appointment.

HET PRINSENHOF MUNICIPAL MUSEUM
Agathaplein 1, Delft, Zuid Holland
In former Convzt of St. Agatha (c.1400). Memorabilia of Prince William I and of the struggle against Spain. Paintings. Prints. Ceramics. Silver. Coins.
M.-Sa. 10-5; Su., public holidays 1-5. Closed Jan. 1.

MUSEUM OF THE HOUSE OF ORANGE-NASSAU
Agatha 1, Delft, Zuid Holland
Portraits, prints, and other material relating to the House of Orange-Nassau. Ceramics. Medals.
M.-Sa. 10-5; Su., public holidays 1-5. Closed Jan. 1.

NATIONAL MUSEUM: LAMBERT VAN MEERTEN HOUSE
Oude Delft 199, Delft, Zuid Holland
Architectural items. Furniture. Ceramics, especially from North Holland. Delft pottery and silver. Italian and Spanish tiles.
On request.

STUDY COLLECTION OF THE GENERAL HOEFER MILITARY MUSEUM
Korte Geer 1, Delft, Zuid Holland
History of weapons and military equipment. Items used by the Netherlands, British, French, German, American and Russian armies.
By appointment.

DELFZIJL

MUSEUM IN THE ADAM MILL
Molenberg 9, Delfzijl, Groningen
In former Adam grist-mill (c.1875). Natural history. History of the Delfzijl area. Shipping. Models of sailing, steam and motor ships.
May 15- Sept. 15, 9-12, 2-5.

DENEKAMP

'NATURE TEACHER' MUSEUM
Oldenzaalsestraat 27-9, Denekamp, Overijssel
Geology. Fossils. Mammals. Birds. Insects. Shells.
Apr.-Aug., M.-Sa. 10-1, 2-5. Oct.-Mar., W., Sa., Su. 2-5. Other times by appointment.

SINGRAVEN
Denekamp, Overijssel
17th century paintings. French and English prints. 17th-18th century furniture. Tapestry. Delft pottery.
Apr. 15- June 30, Sept. 1- Apr. 14, M., W., F., guided tours at 10, 11, 2, 3.30. July-Aug., guided tours, M., W., F., Sa., 10, 11, 2, 3.30.

DE STEEG

MIDDACHTEN CASTLE
Rentambt Middachten, De Steeg, Gelderland
17th-18th century furniture. Family portraits. Pottery. Porcelain.
On request.

DEURNE

DEURNE COURTHOUSE MUSEUM
Haageind 39, Deurne, Noord Brabant
In 17th century courthouse. Paintings. Gouaches. Silver. Coins. Terra cotta. Bronze and wood sculpture.
Daily 12-5. Closed religious festivals. Other times on request.

DEVENTER

MUSEUM OF TROPICAL AGRICULTURE AND ETHNOLOGY
Brinkgreverweg 184, Deventer, Overijssel
Agricultural products, implements, techniques of tropical countries, especially Indonesia. Ethnology.
On request.

THE THREE HERRINGS
Brink 55, Deventer, Overijssel
Building (1575). Toys. Children's books. Miniature furniture. Period rooms. Architectural items. Costumes.
On request.

WEIGH HOUSE MUSEUM
Brink 57, Deventer, Overijssel
Former Weighhouse and House of the Watch (1528). Prehistory, history and folklore of the Deventer area. Architectural items. Ceramics. Coins. Medals. Paintings. Prints. Tools. Household equipment. 17th century period rooms.
M.-Sa. 10-12.30, 2-5; Su. 2-5. Closed Jan. 1, Ascension Day, Queen's Birthday.

DIEVER

SCHULTE HOUSE
Brink 6, Diever, Drenthe
Furniture, porcelain, 1600-onwards.
Tu.-Sa. 9-12, 3-5.

DOESBURG

DOESBURG MUSEUM OF LOCAL HISTORY
Roggestraat 2, Doesburg, Gelderland
Prehistory, history of Doesburg area. Drawings. Coins.
Daily 9-12. Other times by appointment.

DOETINCHEM

DE KELDER MUSEUM
Kelderlaan, Doetinchem, Gelderland
In restored 15th century hunting lodge. History of Doetinchem area. Furniture. Tools. Household equipment. Weapons.
May 15- Sept. 15, Tu.-Sa. 10- 12, 2-5.30; Su. 2-5.30.

DOKKUM

'ADMIRALTY HOUSE' DISTRICT MUSEUM
Schoolsteg 1, Dokkum, Friesland
Prehistory, archaeology and history of Dokkum area. Ceramics. Tools. Household equipment. Dokkum silver. Toys. Costumes.
Apr.-Sept., Tu.-Sa. 10-12, 2-5; M. 2-5. Oct.-Mar., M., W.-Sa. 2-5.

MASTER S. E. WENDELAAR BONGA MUSEUM
Kereweer 5, Dokkum, Friesland
Natural history. Dioramas. Geology. Birds. Shells.
Sa. 2-5. Other times by appointment.

DOORN

DOORN HOUSE
Langbrockerweg, Doorn, Utrecht
Possessions of the former German Emperor, Wilhelm II. Furniture. Paintings. Porcelain. Silver. Gold.
June-Aug., M.-Sa. 9-5.30; Su. 1-5.30. Mar. 15- May 31, Sept.-Oct., 10-12, 2-5.

MAARTEN MAARTENS HOUSE
De Zonheuvel, Doorn, Utrecht
Collections of the writer, J. M. W. van der Poorten Schwarz (Maarten Maartens). Furniture. Books. Decorative arts.
On request.

DOORNENBURG

DOORNENBURG CASTLE
Doornenburg, Gelderland
16th century Dutch and German furniture. Household utensils. Paintings of the castle. Engravings of castles in Gelderland and Cleves. Maps.
May-Sept., Tu.-Sa. 10-12, 2-5; Su. 2-5. Rest of year, Su. 2-5, M. on request.

DORDRECHT

BILDERBEEK-LAMAISON NATIONAL MUSEUM
Dordrecht, Zuid Holland
19th-20th century paintings, including works by Dutch Impressionists. Dordrecht pottery.
M.-Sa. 10-5; Su. 1-5. Closed Jan. 1.

DORDRECHTS MUSEUM
Museumstraat 42, Dordrecht, Zuid Holland
17th-20th century paintings, especially by artists of the Dordrecht School and by Dutch Impressionists. Paintings, drawings, prints, sculpture by Ary Scheffer.
M.-Sa. 10-5; Su. 1-5. Closed Jan. 1.

SIMON VAN GIJN MUSEUM
Nieuwe Haven 29, Dordrecht, Zuid Holland
Period rooms, including Louis XIV room, with mid-18th century Brussels tapestries. Dordrecht guild silver. Prints of historical subjects. Ship-models and paintings. Costumes. Toys. Furniture. Glass. Pottery. Porcelain. Coins. Seals.
Apr.-Sept., M.-Sa. 10-5; Su. 1-5. Oct.-Mar., M.-Su. 10-4. Closed Jan. 1.

MUSEUM OF LIPS' SAFE AND LOCK COMPANY
Merwederstraat 48, Dordrecht, Zuid Holland
Locks. Keys. Safes.
On request.

DRACHTEN

THE BLEACH HOUSE
Moleneind ZZ.11, Drachten, Friesland
House (c.1800). Local prehistory, history, folklore. Paintings by local artists, especially Theo van Doesburg, Pier Pander, Ids Wiersma.
W., Sa. 2-4. Other times on request.

ECHT

ECHT AND DISTRICT MUSEUM OF LOCAL HISTORY
Gemeentehuis, Platz 1, Echt, Limburg
Geology. Fossils. Prehistory. History of the Echt area. Weapons. Silver. Tools. Coins. Model of mine.
2nd and 4th Su. in month (not Oct., Nov.) 10-12, 2-6.

EDAM

EDAM'S MUSEUM
Damplein 6, Edam, Noord Holland
16th century house. History of the Edam area. Furnished rooms, including kitchen and cellar.
Apr.-Sept., daily 10-12, 2-5.

NIEUWENKAMP MUSEUM
Voorhaven 137, Edam, Noord Holland
Drawings, prints, paintings, made by W. O. J. Nieuwenkamp in the Netherlands, Italy and the Far East. Ethnographical material from the Far East.
May-Sept., daily 9-5.

EDE

OLD EDE
Driehoek 32, Ede, Gelderland
Furniture and equipment of an Ede farmhouse and bakery. Agricultural implements. Local history, illustrated by drawings, photographs. Clog-making.
June 15- Sept. 15, daily 9-12, 2-5. Other times on request.

EERNEWOUDE

JAN EN SJUT'S COOK-SHOP
Flietsteech 16, Eernewoude, Friesland
18th century house. Period rooms, including one with Biblical figures carved in peat and painted.
June-Aug., daily 10-11, 3-5, 8-9.

EERSEL

LOCAL HISTORY MUSEUM
Gemeentehuis Markt 28, Eersel, Noord Brabant
Furnished interior of farmhouse. Agricultural implements.
On request.

EGMOND AAN ZEE

MUSEUM EGMOND AAN ZEE
Zuiderstraat 7, Egmond aan Zee, Noord Holland
History of Egmond. Drawings. Prints. Household objects. Period rooms. Natural history, especially birds, fish.
July-Aug., M.-Sa. 3-5.

EGMOND-BINNEN

MUSEUM OF THE ABBEY OF EGMOND
Vannewatersweg 25, Egmond-Binnen, Noord Holland
In Abbey Chapter House. Archaeological material from the Abbey site and the surrounding area. Prehistoric and Roman items. Medieval and later pottery.
By appointment.

EINDHOVEN

EVOLUON
Noordbrabantlaan 1A, Eindhoven, Noord Brabant
Displays illustrating influence of science and technology on the evolution of society.
M.-Sa. 10-6; Su., public holidays 1-6.

KEMPENLAND MUSEUM
Paradijslaan, Waagstraat, Eindhoven, Noord Brabant
History of Eindhoven region. Farmhouse living room (c.1900). Weapons. Costumes. Guild history. Weaving. Clog-making. Paintings.
W. 7 p.m.-9; Su. 2-5.

VAN ABBE MUNICIPAL MUSEUM
Bilderdijklaan 10, Eindhoven, Noord Brabant
20th century sculpture.
M.-Sa. 10-5; Su., public holidays 2-6.

ELBURG

ELBURG LOCAL MUSEUM
Jufferenstraat 6, Elburg, Gelderland
Local history. Guild silver. Execution equipment. Tools. Coins. Medals. Prints. Weapons. Navigation instruments.
M.-F. 9-12, 2-5.

'SEEING IS KNOWING' NATURAL HISTORY MUSEUM
Havenkade 3B, Elburg, Gelderland
Local birds and mammals. Dioramas.
M.-Sa. 9 a.m.-10 p.m.; Su. 1-6.

ELSLOO

SHIPPING EXCHANGE REGIONAL MUSEUM
Gemeentehuis, Op den Berg 4-5, Elsloo, Limburg
Fossil skull of Homo Sapiens L. Neolithic, Roman and Gallo-Roman material. Agricultural implements. Household utensils and equipment.
May-Sept., Tu.-Th. 4-6; Su. 4-7. Other times by appointment.

ELST

MUSEUM UNDER THE N.H. CHURCH
Grote Molen Straat 2, Elst, Gelderland
Remains of Gallo-Roman temple, with archaeological material from excavations.
On request.

EMMEN

DE HONDSRUG MUSEUM OF ANTIQUITIES
Marktplein 17, Emmen, Drenthe
Local prehistory, history. Costume.
M.-Sa. 9-12, 2-5.

ENKHUIZEN

NATIONAL ZUIDERZEE MUSEUM
Wierdijk 13, Enkhuizen, Noord Holland
In former warehouse (1625) of United East India Company. History of the former Zuiderzee area. Shipping. Fishing. Ships and ship-models. Costumes. Painted furniture. Prints. Paintings. Maps. Tiles. Farmhouse equipment. Agricultural implements.
M.-Sa. 10-5; Su., public holidays 12-5.

TOWN HALL MUSEUM
Breedstraat 53, Enkhuizen, Noord Holland
Local history. Paintings. Drawings. Maps. Dies from the West Frisian mint. Weapons. Ceramics. Grocer's and baker's shops.
M.-F., guided tours, 10.15, 11.15, 2.30, 3.45.

WEIGH-HOUSE AND SURGEON'S ROOM
Kaasmarkt 8, Enkhuizen, Noord Holland
Old weighing equipment, cheese-presses, weights. Medical instruments. Herbals. Medical books.
May 15- Sept. 15, M.-Sa. 10-12.30, 1.30-6.

ENSCHEDE

NATURAL HISTORY MUSEUM
De Ruyterlaan 2, Enschede, Overijssel
Geology, mineralogy, botany, zoology of the Enschede region. Molluscs. Fish. Insects. Amphibians. Mammals.
Tu.-Sa. 10-12, 2-5; Su. 2-5. Closed Easter, Whitsun, Christmas.

TWENTE AND GELDER TEXTILE MUSEUM
Espoortstraat 182, Enschede, Overijssel
Historical development of local textile industry. Flax processing. Spinning. Weaving. Social and economic influence of textile manufacturing.
Tu.-Sa. 10-12, 2-5; Su. 2-5. Closed Dec. 25, Ascension Day, Jan. 1.

TWENTE MUSEUM OF LOCAL HISTORY
Lasondersingel 129, Enschede, Overijssel
Prehistory of Twente area. Coins. Medals.
Tu.-Sa. 9-1, 2-5.30; Su., public holidays 2-5.30.

TWENTE NATIONAL MUSEUM
Lasondersingel 129, Enschede, Overijssel
Medieval religious manuscripts, sculpture, paintings. 17th century tapestries. 17th-19th century Dutch portraits, landscapes, still-life paintings. 17th-19th century animal paintings. French Impressionist paintings. 17th-19th century Delft pottery. Silver. Gold and silver ornaments. Clocks.
Tu.-Sa. 9-1, 2-5.30; Su., public holidays 2-5.30.

ETTEN-LEUR

JAN OUTEN HOUTE MUSEUM OF LOCAL HISTORY AND FOLKLORE
Paulushofje, Markt 55, Etten-Leur, Noord Brabant
Furnished farmhouse interior. Costumes. Coffee-house. Shop. Furniture maker's, potter's and clog-maker's workshops. Agricultural implements. Prints.
M.-Sa. 2-4; 1st Su. in month 3-5. Other times by appointment.

FRANEKER

DR. COOPMAN'S HOUSE MUNICIPAL MUSEUM
Voorstraat 49, Franeker, Friesland
Van Schlumbach's botanical collection, given to the Franeker Academy by King Louis Napoleon (c.1809). Memorabilia of Anna Maria van Schurman and her family, given to Academy in 1783, and including self-portraits, miniatures, manuscripts. Silver. Dutch, Chinese, Japanese ceramics. 17th century model of Franeker. Old Frisian kitchen.
May-Sept., M.-Sa. 9-12, 2-6. Oct.-Apr., 10-12, 2-5.

EISE EISINGA PLANETARIUM
Eise Eisingastraat 3, Franeker, Friesland
House (1769). Planetarium. Astronomical instruments. Manuscripts of Eise Eisinga.
M.-Sa. 9-12, 2-6.

FREDERIKSVORD

MIRAMAR MUSEUM OF THE SEA
Vledderweg 25, Frederiksvord, Drenthe
Shells. Coral. Starfish. Sea-urchins. Fossils. Beach and water birds. Dioramas.
Easter-Sept. 15, M.-Th. 10-12, 1.30-6.

GEERTRIUDENBERG

MUNICIPAL MUSEUM OF LOCAL HISTORY
Markt 46, Geertriudenberg, Noord Brabant
Local history. Documents. Costumes. Household utensils and equipment.
Apr.-Oct., W.-Sa. 2-5.

GEERVLIET

GEERVLIET LOCAL HISTORY MUSEUM
Kaaistraat 2, Geervliet, Zuid Holland
Local history. Household utensils and equipment. Tools.
On request.

GELDROP

LOCAL HISTORY MUSEUM
Heuvel 5, Geldrop, Noord Brabant
Local history and archaeology. Household equipment. Furniture. Coins. Medals. Old photographs illustrating economics, social and cultural life of Geldrop. Craftsmen's tools.
M.-F. 1-5.

GELEEN

GELEEN SCHOOL MUSEUM
Jubileumplein 3, Geleen, Limburg
Natural history, especially geology. Prehistoric and Roman antiquities. Local history.
M.-Sa. 3-6; Tu., Th., Sa. also 10.30-12.30.

GOES

SOUTH AND NORTH BEVELAND MUSEUM
Singelstraat 13, Goes, Zeeland
Costumes. Prints showing development of Goes region. Guild silver. Coins. Antiquities illustrating history of Goes. Weapons.
Apr.-Sept., Tu.-Sa. 10-12, 2-5.

GOIRLE

HET SMISKE MUSEUM OF LOCAL HISTORY
Nieuwe Rielseweg 8, Goirle, Noord Brabant
In 18th century weaver's house. Local history. Household utensils and equipment. Weaving equipment. Clothing.
May-Sept., Su. 3-5. Other times by appointment.

GORINCHEM

HOUSE IN BETHLEHEM MUSEUM
Gasthuisstraat 25, Gorinchem, Zuid Holland
House (1566). Local history. Paintings. Prints. Coins.
May-Sept., M.-F. 9.5; Sa. 10-4. Oct.-Apr. M., W., Sa. 2-4.

GORREDIJK

'DE ZUID OSTHOCK' MUSEUM OF LOCAL HISTORY AND NATURAL HISTORY
Hoofdstraat 59, Gooredijk, Friesland
Local handicrafts. Carpenters' tools. Agricultural implements. Textiles. Silver. Copper. Apothecary's shop. Palaeolithic material. Paintings.
May-Oct., F. 7 p.m.-9; Sa. 3-6. Other times by appointment.

GOUDA

CATHARINA INN MUNICIPAL MUSEUM
Oosthaven 10, Gouda, Zuid Holland
16th-20th century paintings. Ceramics, especially from Gouda. Painted glass. Period rooms, including room of the Surgeons' Guild (1699), with old medical instruments. Inn kitchen. Apothecary's shop. Toys.
M.-Sa. 10-5; Su. 2-5.

GOUDA STAINED GLASS
St. Janskerk, Gouda, Zuid Holland
Stained glass windows, including 10 by Wouter Crabeth (d.1571).
M.-Sa. 9-5.

DE MORIAAN PIPE AND POTTERY MUSEUM
Westhaven 29, Gouda, Zuid Holland
Tobacconist's shop equipment. Pipes. Tiles. Gouda pottery. Material relating to history of pipe-making and pottery-making guilds.
M.-Sa. 10-12.30, 1.30-5; Su. 2-5.

GRAMSBERGEN

TOWN HISTORICAL MUSEUM
Gemeentehuis, Esch 1, Gramsbergen, Overijssel
Material illustrating history and prehistory of Gramsbergen and its area. Household utensils and equipment.
M.-F. 9-12, 1.30-5.30.

'S GRAVELAND

H. L. HOUTHOFF COLLECTION
'de Trompenburgh', Zuid 403, 's Graveland, Noord Holland
17th-19th century furniture. Clocks and clockwork.
M., Tu., Th. 10-12.

'S GRAVENHAGE

D. H. G. BOLTEN COLLECTION
Statenlaan 4, 's Gravenhage, Zuid Holland
Delft pottery. Hague silver. 17th-18th century furniture, paintings.
On request.

BREDIUS MUSEUM
Prinsegracht 6, 's Gravenhage, Zuid Holland
Paintings, especially 17th century Dutch. Industrial art.
M.-Sa. 10-5; Su. 1-5; W. also 8 p.m.-10.

EDUCATIONAL MUSEUM
Hemsterhuisstraat 2E, 's Gravenhage, Zuid Holland
Physics. Biology. Ethnology. Prehistory. History.
M.-Sa. 10-4; Su., public holidays 1.30-4.

'IN DER SCHULP' SHELL MUSEUM
Marien Biologisch Centrum, Zuidhollandlaan 5, 's Gravenhage, Zuid Holland
World-collection of shells. Fossil shells.
Sa. 2-5. Other times on request.

INTERNATIONAL PRESS MUSEUM
Javastraat 32, 's Gravenhage, Zuid Holland
Collections illustrating history of the press. Newspapers. Periodicals. Memorabilia of journalists.
M.-F. 9.30-12, 2.30-4.30.

HENDRIK WILLEM MESDAG NATIONAL MUSEUM
Laan van Meerdevoort 7, 's Gravenhage, Zuid Holland
19th century French paintings, drawings, etchings. Italian, Hungarian, Dutch (especially Hague School) paintings. Applied art. Pottery from the Oud-Rozenburg factory.
M.-Sa. 10-5; Su., public holidays 1-5.

MESDAG PANORAMA
Zeestraat 65B, 's Gravenhage, Zuid Holland
Panorama of Scheveningen in 1880. Paintings, watercolours, sketches by H. W. Mesdag and his wife.
May-Sept., 10-5; Su., public holidays 12-5. Oct.-Nov., Mar.-Apr., 10-4; Su., public holidays 12-4. Dec.-Feb., 10-3; Su., public holidays 12-3.

MUNICIPAL MUSEUM
Stadhouderslaan 41, 's Gravenhage, Zuid Holland
History of The Hague. Historical and topographical paintings, portraits, drawings and prints, 16th century onwards. 19th-20th century sculpture. Pewter. Bronze. Furniture. Period rooms. Musical instruments. Coins. Ceramics, including Chinese, Japanese, Spanish, Italian, Dutch. Glass. Silver.
M.-F. 10-5.

MUSEUM OF THE CHANCERY OF THE ORDERS OF THE NETHERLANDS
Javastraat 50, 's Gravenhage, Zuid Holland
Collections of Dutch and foreign orders and honours. Decorations. Uniforms. Paintings.
Tu., Th., Sa. 2-5. Other times on request.

MUSEUM OF THE DEPARTMENT OF WEIGHTS AND MEASURES
Stadhouderslaan 140, 's Gravenhage, Zuid Holland
Historical weights and measures. Weighing and measuring equipment.
M.-F., on request.

MUSEUM OF SCOUTING
Zeestraat 76, 's Gravenhage, Zuid Holland
History of scouting in the Netherlands. Equipment. Photographs. Books. Periodicals.
M.-F. 10-12, 2-5.

NATIONAL MEERMAN AND WESTREENEN MUSEUM
Prinsessegracht 30, 's Gravenhage, Zuid Holland
In 18th century house, former home of Baron van Westreenen. Manuscripts. Incunabula. Prehistory. Greek, Roman, Egyptian antiquities. Modern typography.
M.-Sa. 1-5.

NATIONAL PRISON MUSEUM
Buitenhof 33, 's Gravenhage, Zuid Holland
Exhibits illustrating administration of law in former days. Paintings, prints and other memorabilia of people imprisoned here.
Apr.-Sept., M.-Sa. 10-4; Su., public holidays 1-4. Oct.-Mar., M.-F. 10-4; Sa. 10-12. Dec. 15-31, Su., public holidays 1-4. Closed Jan. 1.

NETHERLANDS COSTUME MUSEUM: CABINET OF FASHION AND TASTE
Lange Vijverberg 14, 's Gravenhage, Zuid Holland
Dutch fashions since 1750.
M.-Sa. 10-5; Su. 1-5; W. also 8 p.m.-10.

NETHERLANDS MUSEUM OF LITERATURE
Juffrouw Idastraat 11, 's Gravenhage, Zuid Holland
Manuscripts. Letters. Proofs. Newspapers. Periodicals. Recordings. Films. Portraits of Dutch literary personalities.
M.-F. 1-5. Closed public holidays.

NETHERLANDS POSTAL MUSEUM
Zeestraat 82, 's Gravenhage, Zuid Holland
History and present operations of the postal, telegraph and telephone services. Models. Equipment. Stamps.
M.-Sa. 10-5; Su., public holidays 1-5. Closed Jan. 1.

POLICE MUSEUM
Hoofdbureau van politie, Burg de Monchyplein 19, 's Gravenhage, Zuid Holland
Displays illustrating work of police and activities of criminals.
On request.

ROYAL ARCHIVE
Noordeinde 74, 's Gravenhage, Zuid Holland
Historical material relating to House of Orange-Nassau. Paintings. Prints. Miniatures. Coins. Medals. Manuscripts.
By appointment.

ROYAL CABINET OF COINS, MEDALS AND CARVED STONES
Zeestraat 71B, 's Gravenhage, Zuid Holland
Greek, Roman, Dutch coins. 15th-20th century Dutch and foreign coins. Cameos. Intaglios. Seals. Tile stamps.
M.-Sa. 10-1, 2-5.

ROYAL GALLERY OF PAINTINGS: MAURITSHUIS
Plein 29, 's Gravenhage, Zuid Holland
15th-17th century Flemish paintings. 16th-18th century Dutch paintings. 16th-18th century portrait miniatures, mainly English. Special collection of works by Holbein, Cranach and their contemporaries. Sculpture.
Apr.-Sept., 10-5; F. also 8 p.m.-10; Su., public holidays 11-5. Oct.-Mar., 10-5; Su., public holidays 1-5. Closed Jan. 1.

H. H. F. SALOMON COLLECTION
Noordeinde 80, 's Gravenhage, Zuid Holland
17th-18th century furniture, decorative arts.
M., W., F. 2-4.

THURKOW COLLECTION
Plein 1813 No. 1, 's Gravenhage, Zuid Holland
16th-19th century Dutch, French, Italian, Spanish paintings. 18th century tapestries, panelling. 17th-18th century furniture.
On request.

GROENLO

GROLSCH MUSEUM
Notenboomstraat 15, Groenlo, Gelderland
In farmhouse (c.1620). Pottery. Weapons. Craftsmen's tools. Household equipment. Fire-fighting apparatus. Stations of the Cross.
May-Sept., Tu., Th. 3-4. Other times on request.

GRONINGEN

GRONINGEN MUSEUM OF NATURAL HISTORY
Agricolastraat 9, Groningen, Province of Groningen
Wildlife of the Netherlands. Geology. Fossils.
M.-Sa. 9-12.30, 2-5.30.

MUSEUM OF THE GRONINGEN REGION
Praediniussingel 59, Groningen, Province of Groningen
Archaeology. History of the town and province of Groningen. Industrial art. Groningen silver. Oriental ceramics. 16th-20th century paintings, drawings.
Tu.-Sa. 10-5.

NATIONAL UNIVERSITY: INSTITUTE OF BIOLOGY AND ARCHAEOLOGY
Poststraat 6, Groningen, Province of Groningen
Prehistory. Osteology. Anthropology. Prehistoric animal remains.
W. 2-5. Other times on request.

NIEMEYER'S NETHERLANDS MUSEUM OF TOBACCO
Porterswoldseweg 43, Groningen, Province of Groningen
History of tobacco and use of tobacco in the Netherlands, 16th century - present day. Pipes. Tobacco and snuff boxes. Tobacconist's shop (c.1800). Prints. 17th-19th century writings about tobacco.
M.-F. 9-12, 2-4. Closed public holidays.

NORTHERN INSTITUTE OF EDUCATION AND INSTRUCTION
Verzetsstrijderslaan 2, Groningen, Province of Groningen
Permanent exhibition of educational equipment, methods and teaching aids.
M., W., F. 2-6; Tu., Th. 2-8.

NORTHERN MUSEUM OF SHIPS AND NAVIGATION
St. Walburgstraat 9, Groningen, Province of Groningen
History of shipping, especially in the nothern provinces. Ship-models. Navigational instruments. Ships' logs. Atlases. Charts. Paintings.
Sept.-June, daily 2-5. July-Aug., 10-5; Su. 2-5. Closed Mar. 1-31, Aug. 28.

UNIVERSITY MUSEUM
Academiegebouw, Broerstraat, Groningen, Province of Groningen
History of the University, of its buildings, and of student life. Scientific instruments.
M.-F. 9-12, 2-4.

GROUW

LOCAL MUSEUM
Gemeentehuis, Stationsweg 15, Grouw, Friesland
Material illustrating history of Grouw and its region. Household equipment. Costumes. Ornaments. Porcelain. Natural history.
July-Aug., 7.30-9. Other times on request.

HAARLEM

DIOCESAN MUSEUM OF RELIGIOUS ART
Jansstraat 79, Haarlem, Noord Holland
Religious art, especially from the northern provinces of the Netherlands. Medieval and baroque sculpture. Ornaments. Lace. Paintings. Prints. Manuscripts. Book-binding. Medals.
Tu-Sa. 10-12.30, 2-5; Su., public holidays 2-5.

ENSCHEDÉ MUSEUM
Klokhuisplein 5, Haarlem, Noord Holland
History of printing and type-founding in the Netherlands, especially by the firm of Joh. Enschedé and Sons. File of the *Haarlemsche Courant* since 1656. 17th century atlases.
M.-F. 10-12, 2-4.

FRANS HALS MUSEUM
Groot Heiligland 62, Haarlem, Noord Holland
16th-20th century paintings, especially by Haarlem artists. Group portraits, including works by Frans Hals. Drawings. Development of printing. Period rooms. Apothecary's shop. Furniture. Silver. Copper. Pewter. Pottery. Porcelain. Glass. Coins. Medals. Sculpture. Applied art. Silhouette portraits.
M.-Sa. 10-5; Su., 1-5. Apr.-May, also 8.30 p.m.-10.30. July-Sept., also Sa. 8.30 p.m.-10.30. Closed Jan. 1.

TEYLER'S MUSEUM
Spaarne 16, Haarlem, Noord Holland
19th-20th century paintings. 16th-19th century French, Italian, Dutch drawings. Geology. Mineralogy. Palaeontology. Scientific instruments, including Van Marum's electricity machine (1785). Coins. Medals.
Mar.-Sept., Tu.-Sa. 10-5. Oct.-Feb., 10-4. 1st Su. in month, Mar.-Sept., 1-5; Oct.-Feb., 1-4. Ascension Day 1-5.

TOWN HALL
Grote Markt, Haarlem, Noord Holland
Mid. 14th century building. 16th-17th century religious art. 16th century portraits of the Counts of Holland. Tapestries. Painted ceilings.
On request.

HAARZUILENS

VAN ZUYLEN VAN NIJVELT VAN DE HAAN COLLECTION
Kasteel de Haar, Post Vleuten, Haarzuilens, Utrecht
Paintings. Family portraits. French tapestries. Persian rugs. Dutch, English, French, Italian furniture.
Feb. 15- Aug. 15, Oct. 15- Nov. 15, M.-W., F. 9-12, 1.30-4.45.

HAASTRECHT

MUSEUM OF THE BISDOM VAN VLIET FOUNDATION
Hoogstr. 166, Haastrecht, Zuid Holland
Late 19th century house, originally home of Bisdom van Vliet family, with original furnishings and equipment. History of Haastrecht and its area.
Apr. 15- Oct. 15, Tu.-Th., Sa. 10-4; Su. 2-5.

HAELEN

VISITOR CENTRE AT THE ST. URSULA MILL, LEUDAL
Haelen, Limburg
In former oil-mill. History of the Leudal region and of the St. Ursula legend. History and operating techniques of watermills.
June 15- Aug. 31, M.-F. 1-6; Sa., Su. 2-6.

HARDEWIJK

MUSEUM OF THE HISTORY OF THE VELUWE
Donkestraat 4, Hardewijk, Gelderland
Geology and archaeology of the Veluwe. History of Hardewijk. Material illustrating history of University of Hardewijk. Town mint. Coins. Medals. Costumes. Silver. Fishing industry. 19th century furniture.
M.-F. 9-12, 2-5.

HARLINGEN

HANNEMA HOUSE LOCAL MUSEUM
Voorstraat 56, Harlingen, Friesland
18th century house. Material illustrating history of Harlingen. Paintings. Prints. Tiles. Shipmodels.
Apr. 1- Sept. 30, W., F., Sa. 3-5, 7-9; M., Tu., Th., 10-12, 3-5. Oct. 1- Mar. 31, W., Sa. 3-5, 7-9.

HASSELT

TOWN HALL
Markt 1, Hasselt, Overijssel
15th-16th century Town Hall. 17th century paintings. Weapons.
M.-F. 8.30-12, 2-5.

HATTEN

DIJKPOORT MUSEUM
Kruisstraat 1, Hatten, Gelderland
Material illustrating history of Hatten area. Guild items. Pewter. Prints. Ceramics. Household utensils, equipment.
June-Sept., 9-12.30, 2-6. Other times on request.

HEEMSE

HARDENBERG MUSEUM
Voorstraat 34, Heemse, Overijssel
Local prehistory and history. Fossils. Agricultural implements. Household utensils, equipment. Coins.
On request.

HEEMSTEDE

DE RAAF BRAND VAN STRAATER COLLECTION
De Sphinx, Bronsteeweg 1, Heemstede, Noord Holland
Prehistory, early history. Roman and medieval archaeology. Furniture. Pottery. Tiles. Majolica. Wood-sculpture. Pewter. Bronze. Copper. Oriental carpets. Bells.
M., Tu., W. 10-12.

'S HEERENBERG

BERGH HOUSE
Hof van Berg 12, 's Heerenberg, Gelderland
14th-18th century Dutch, German, Italian paintings. Furniture. Sculpture. Woodcarvings. Ivories. Book-binding. Manuscripts. Incunabula. Enamels. Wrought-iron. Weapons. Coins. Heraldry. Regional topography. Geology.
On request.

HEERENVEEN

BATAVUS MUSEUM
Industrieweg 2, Heerenveen-Zuid, Friesland
Bicycles. Tricycles. Motorcycles. Motor-cars. Motoring accessories. Advertisements, books, prints relating to bicycles.
May-Sept., 2-5.

HEERENVEEN LOCAL MUSEUM
Vleesmankt 9, Heerenveen, Friesland
Peat-digging equipment. Prehistory. Agricultural implements. Furniture. 18th century living room. Paintings. Porcelain. Gold. Silver. Coins.
Tu.-Sa. 10-12, 1.30-5; F. also 7.30 p.m.-9.30. Other times on request. New Year, Easter, Christmas, 2-5.

HEERLEN

LOCAL HISTORY MUSEUM
Orpheusstraat 2, Heerlen, Limburg
Material illustrating Roman and medieval settlement in South Limburg. Prints. Sculpture. Household equipment.
M.-F. 9-12.30, 2-4.30; Sa. 10-12.

SOUTH LIMBURG GEOLOGICAL MUSEUM
Akerstraat 88, Heerlen, Limburg
Coal-fossils. Models, maps, relief maps showing geology of the area. Minerals.
M.-F. 9-12, 2-5. Other times on request.

HEEZE

VAN TUYLL VAN SEROOSKERKEN VAN HEEZE EN LEENDE COLLECTION
Kasteel Heeze, Heeze, Noord Brabant
17th-18th century furniture. Family portraits. 17th-18th century paintings. Tapestries from cartoons by Rubens and Charles Lebrun.
Tu., W., Th., 10-12. Closed Aug.

HEINENOORD

HOEKSCHE WARD DISTRICT MUSEUM
Hoflaan 13, Heinenoord, Zuid Holland
Building (1767). Local history. Costumes. Topography. Craftsmen's tools, equipment. Agricultural implements. Wallpaper illustrating Greek War of Independence (1830).
Sa. 10-12; Tu., W., Sa. 2-5; F. 7 p.m.-9.

HEINO

HANNEMA-DE STUERS FOUNDATION
Kasteel het Nyenhuis, Heino, Overijssel
17th century Dutch, French, Italian paintings. 16th-20th century drawings, sculpture. 20th century paintings. Chinese ceramics. 17th-20th century furniture.
On request.

DEN HELDER

HELDER NAVAL MUSEUM
Het Torentje, Hoofdgracht, Den Helder, Hoord Holland
History of the Dutch Navy (1813 - present day). Models. Charts. Uniforms. Decorations. Weapons. Portraits. Paintings of ships. Flags.
Tu.-Sa. 10-5.

HELLENDOORN

LOCAL HISTORY MUSEUM
Reggeweg 1, Hellendoorn, Overijssel
Craftsmen's tools, equipment. Spinning. Weaving. Tanning. Butter-making. Wood-turning. Clog-making. Peat-digging.
May-Sept., M.-F. 10-11, 2-4; W., also 7 p.m.-8.

HELLEVOETSLUIS

NATIONAL FIRE-FIGHTING MUSEUM
Industriehaven 8, Hellevoetsluis, Zuid Holland
Fire-fighting equipment (1650 - present day). Coins. Medals. Uniforms.
Daily 10-4. Evenings on request.

HELMOND

LOCAL MUSEUM
Kasteel Roadhuis, Helmond, Noord Brabant
Prehistory and history of Helmond area. Paintings. Drawings. Photographs. Household equipment. Tools.
M.-F. 8.30-12.30, 2-5.45. Sa., Su. by appointment.

HELVERSUM

DE VAART MUSEUM OF ART
Waartweg 163, Helversum, Noord Holland
Geology and archaeology. Local history. Loosdrecht and Amstel porcelain.
M.-Sa. 10-5; Su. 2-5.

'S HERTOGENBOSCH

BROTHERHOOD OF OUR BLESSED LADY
Zwanenbroedershuis, Hinthamerstraat 94, 's Hertogenbosch, Noord Brabant
Parts of altar (1477). 15th-16th century antiphons. 16th-17th century wine-containers. Medals. Liturgical vessels.
F. 11-3.

NORTH BRABANT MUSEUM
Bethaniëstraat 4, 's Hertogenbosch, Noord Brabant
Prehistoric and Roman material. Local history. Guild items. Pewter. Silver. Copper. Coins. Seals. Religious art.
M.-F. 10-5.

HEUSDEN

HEUSDEN DISTRICT MUSEUM
Gemeentehuis, Heusden, Noord Brabant
Local history. Prints. Maps. Archaeological material. Coopering. Clog-making. Coins.
Daily 2-4.

HILVARENBEEK

MUSEUM OF LOCAL HISTORY AND ANTIQUITIES
Gemeentehuis, Vorijthof, Hilvarenbeek, Noord Brabant
Prehistory and history of the Hilvarenbeek area. Prehistoric, Roman, medieval pottery. Craftsmen's tools. Maps.
M.-F. 9-12, 2-5.

HINDERLOOPEN

HIDDE NIJLAND FOUNDATION
Kerkstraat 2, Hinderloopen, Friesland
In former Town Hall and weigh-house (17th century). Local history. Shipping. Paintings. Period room. Household equipment. Costumes.
Mar. 15 - Nov. 15, 9-12, 1.30-5; Su. 1.30-5.

HOLTEN

'PIET BOS' MUSEUM OF NATURAL HISTORY
Holterberg 45, Bolten, Overijssel
Birds and animals of the Netherlands. Dioramas.
May-Sept., 8.30-6.

HOORN

DE VISSER COLLECTION
Binnenluiendijk 3, Hoorn, Noord Holland
In 17th century house. 17th-18th century furniture. Lace.
Tu., Th., Sa. 10-12, 2-4.

WEST FRISIAN MUSEUM
Rode Steen 1, Hoorn, Noord Holland
Building (1591). Art and applied art relating to Hoorn and Westfriesland. Local history. Material illustrating guilds, trade, industry, shipping. Costumes. Agricultural implements. Weigh-house, with weighing equipment.
Apr.-Sept., 10-5; Su., public holidays 12-5. Oct.-Mar., M.-F. 10-12, 2-5. Oct., Mar., Su. 2-5.

HULST

'DE VIER AMBACHTEN' LOCAL HISTORY MUSEUM
Grote Markt, Hulst, Zeeland
Local history. Maps. Prints. Agricultural implements. Craftsmen's tools. Costumes. Guild material.
M.-F. on request, 9-12, 2-5.

IJMUIDEN

PIETER VERMEULEN MUSEUM
Moerbergplantsoen 22, Ijmuiden, Noord Holland
Natural history. Model of Ijmuiden harbour. Ship-models.
M.-Sa. 9.30-12, 2-4.30. Closed public holidays.

IJSSELSTEIN

CASTLE IJSSELSTEIN MUSEUM OF ANTIQUITIES
Kronenburgplantsoen 9, Ijsselstein, Utrecht
Local prehistory, history. Household equipment.
May-Sept., W., F. 2-5.

JANUM

CHURCH MUSEUM
Janum, Friesland
Sculpture. Paintings.
Daily 9-5.

KAMPEN

BROEDERPOORT MUNICIPAL MUSEUM
2E Ebbingestraat 50, Kampen, Overijssel
Local history. Town and guild silver. Costumes. Ceramics. Paintings. Prints.
May-Oct., M.-Sa. 9-12.30, 2-5.

OLD TOWN HALL
Oudestraat 133, Kampen, Overijssel
16th century Council Room, with carved seating (1545). 16th century paintings. Execution equipment. Coins. Coin-stamps.
M.-F. 8.30-12.30, 1.30-5.30.

KAMPERZEEDIJK

MASTENBROEK STEAM-ENGINE
Kamperzeedijk, Overijssel
Marine steam engine (1856), with paddle wheels.
M.-Sa. 9-5.

KETELHAVEN

IJESSELMEERPOLDER MUSEUM OF MARINE ARCHAEOLOGY
Ketelhaven, Noord Holland
Salvaged ships. Ship-building tools. Items from ships in the Zuiderzee area (prehistoric times - present day).
M.-Sa. 8-5, Su., public holidays 10-6. Closed Jan. 1.

KOOG AAN DE ZAAN

HET PINK OIL-MILL
Pinkstraat 12, Koog aan de Zaan, Noord Holland
Machinery and equipment from old oil-mills. Blue-making. Model-looms.
Apr.-Oct., daily 12-2. 1st Su. in month 2.30-5.

ZAAN MILL MUSEUM
Museumlaan 18, Koog aan de Zaan, Noord Holland
In 18th century house. Exhibits illustrating history and working of the Zaan mills. Painting. Prints. Models. Milling machinery and equipment. Milling techniques.
Daily 2-5.

KRIMPEN AAN DEN IJSSEL

CRIMPENERHOF DISTRICT MUSEUM
Ijsseldijk 314, Krimpen aan den Ijssel, Zuid Holland
Tools and implements used in agriculture, shipbuilding, brick and tile making. Furniture, household equipment from farmhouses. Folk pottery.
On request.

LAREN

VERWOLDE HOUSE
Laren, Gelderland
17th-18th century furniture. 18th century Chinese porcelain. 18th century family silver. Family portraits.
Tu.-Th. 2-4.

SINGER MUSEUM
Oude Drift 1, Laren, Noord Holland
European paintings, especially Dutch.
Mar.-Sept., M.-Sa. 10-5. Oct.-Feb., M.-Sa. 10-4. Su., public holidays 1-5. Closed Jan. 1, Queen's Birthday.

LEEK

NATIONAL CARRIAGE MUSEUM
Nienoold, Leek, Groningen
18th-20th century carriages. 17th-20th century sleighs. Harness. Paintings. Prints. Drawings.
Apr.-Sept., 9-6.

LEENS

OMMELAND MUSEUM OF AGRICULTURE AND HISTORY
Borg Verhildersum, Wierde 40, Leens, Groningen
Castle (c.1514). Local history. Period rooms (c.1850). Kitchen and equipment. Agricultural implements. Craftmen's tools.
Mar. 23 - Oct. 15, Tu.-Su., 11-6.

LEERDAM

GATEHOUSE MUSEUM
Kerkstraat 91, Leerdam, Zuid Holland
History of Leerdam and district. Prints. Craftsmen's tools and equipment.
May-Oct., 10-11.30, 2-5. Other months on request.

LEERDAM NATIONAL GLASS MUSEUM
Lingedijk 28, Leerdam, Zuid Holland
Roman - 19th century glass. Modern European glass, especially from Netherlands. Bottles.
Oct.-Apr., M.-F. 10-5. May-Sept., M.-Sa. 10-5, Su. 1-5.

LEEUWARDEN

FRISIAN MUSEUM
Turfmarkt 24, Leeuwarden, Friesland
Frisian prehistory, history. Paintings by Frisian artists. Portraits. 16th-18th century Frisian silver. Chinese and Japanese porcelain. Frisian pottery. Period rooms. Popular art. Costumes. Prints. Maps. Coins. Medals.
Nov.-Feb., M.-Sa. 9-12.30, 2-4. Mar.-Oct., M.-Sa. 9-12.30, 2-5. July 17 - Aug. 20, also Su. 2-5. Easter, Ascension Day, Whitsun, 2-5. Closed Jan. 1, Queen's Birthday.

FRISIAN MUSEUM OF NATURAL HISTORY
Heerestraat 13, Leeuwarden, Friesland
Geology, flora and fauna of Friesland. Herbarium. Dioramas of Frisian landscapes.
M.-Sa. 2-5. Other times on request.

MUSEUM OF FRISIAN LITERATURE
Grotekerkstraat 20, Leeuwarden, Friesland
History of literature in Friesland. Manuscripts. Letters. Paintings. Portraits. Memorabilia of writers. Printing works. Press cuttings.
M.-F. 9-12, 2-5.

FRIESLAND SCHOOL MUSEUM
St. Anthonystraat 4, Leeuwarden, Friesland
Teaching equipment, aids.
W. 2-4.

PIER PANDER MUSEUM
Prinsentuin, Leeuwarden, Friesland
House (c.1820). Sculpture by Pier Pander (d.1919).
M.-Sa. 9-5. F. also 7 p.m.-9. Mar.-Sept., also Su. 2-5. Public holidays 2-5.

PIER PANDER TEMPLE
Noorderplantage, Leeuwarden, Friesland
Sculpture by Pier Pander (d.1919).
M.-F. 10-12, 2-5; Sa. 2-5.

HET PRINCESSEHOF LOCAL MUSEUM
Grote Kerkstraat 11, Leeuwarden, Friesland
House (1630). European and Oriental ceramics and applied art. 18th century period room. Tiles. Dutch paintings, drawings, prints since 1900.
M.-Sa. 9-12, 2-5. Su., public holidays 2-5.

LEIDEN

COIN AND MEDAL CABINET OF THE NATIONAL UNIVERSITY
Kloksteeg 25, Leiden, Zuid Holland
Coins and medals, especially of Portugal and Brazil. French medals commemorating the Revolution of 1848.
On request.

DUTCH ARMY AND WEAPONS MUSEUM
Pesthuislaan 7, Leiden, Zuid Holland
History of the Dutch army and of the military arts. 17th-20th century paintings. Prints. Flags. Decorations. Uniforms. Weapons (Bronze Age - onwards). East India Company cannon. Firearms (15th century - onwards). Commemorative medals.
M.-F. 10-5; Su. 1-4. Closed Jan. 1, Oct. 3.

HISTORICAL MUSEUM OF THE NATIONAL UNIVERSITY
Rapenburg 73, Leiden, Zuid Holland
In former convent chapel (16th century). History of the University and of the academic staff and student body.
Tu.-F. 2-5. Other times on request.

LAKENHAL MUNICIPAL MUSEUM
Oude Singel 28-30, Leiden, Zuid Holland
History of Leiden and district. Dutch paintings (16th century - present day). Sculpture. Silver. Glass. Ceramics. Guild items. Tapestries. Period rooms. Costumes.
Apr.-Oct., M.-Sa. 10-5; Su. 1-5. Nov.-Mar., M.-Sa. 10-4; Su. 1-4. Oct. 3, 10-12.

MEERMANSBURG
Oude Vest 159, Leiden, Zuid Holland
Portraits of members of the Meerman family.
Daily 9-4.

NATIONAL HERBARIUM
Schelpenkade 6, Leiden, Zuid Holland
Plants of the whole world, especially Holland, Malaysia.
M.-F. 10-5.

NATIONAL MUSEUM OF ANTIQUITIES
Rapenburg 28, Leiden, Zuid Holland
Egyptian sculpture, crafts, mummies. Near-Eastern archaeology, art and antiquities. Art and antiquities of Greece, Rome, Etruria, Cyprus. Prehistory and early history of the Netherlands.
M.-Sa. 10-5; Su., public holidays 1-5. Closed Jan. 1, Oct. 3.

NATIONAL MUSEUM OF ETHNOLOGY
Steenstraat 1, Leiden, Zuid Holland
Indonesian prehistory, stone-sculptures, bronzes. Ethnographical material from New Guinea, South Pacific (especially Melanesia), Tibet, Siberia. Japanese Buddhist art. Chinese ceramics, drums, wooden sculpture. Near-Eastern miniatures. African and Islamic collection. N. American Indian and Eskimo artifacts. Material illustrating pre-Columbian cultures of Mexico, Peru.
M.-Sa. 10-5; Su., public holidays 1-5. Closed Jan. 1, Oct. 3.

NATIONAL MUSEUM OF GEOLOGY AND MINERALOGY
Hooglandse Kerkgracht 17, Leiden, Zuid Holland
Regional geology of the Netherlands. Palaeontology. Petrography. Mineralogy. Meteorites. Textiles. Gemstones. Economic geology.
M.-F. 10-12, 2-4. Closed Jan. 1, Oct. 3, public holidays.

NATIONAL MUSEUM OF THE HISTORY OF THE NATURAL SCIENCES
Steenstraat 1A, Leiden, Zuid Holland
History of natural sciences. Scientific instruments and equipment, especially microscopes. Weights and measures. 16th century alchemist's laboratory. Portraits. Prints. Medals. Documents.
M.-Sa. 10-4; Su. 1-4.

NATIONAL MUSEUM OF NATURAL HISTORY
Raamsteg 2, Leiden, Zuid Holland
Pleistocene fossils from former Netherlands Indies. Insects. Birds. Fish. Mammals. Molluscs. Reptiles. Amphibians.
By appointment.

PILGRIM FATHERS HOUSE
Boisokade 2A, Leiden, Zuid Holland
Originals and photographs of documents relating to Pilgrim Fathers. Views of Leiden (c.1610-20).
M.-F. 9-12, 2-4.

PRINT CABINET OF THE NATIONAL UNIVERSITY
Kloksteeg 25, Leiden, Zuid Holland
Prints and drawings, especially Dutch, Flemish, 1500-present day. Book-illustrating. Collection illustrating history of photography.
M.-F. 2-5. Closed public holidays, Feb. 8, Oct. 3.

DE VALK MILL MUSEUM
2E Binnenvestgracht 1, Leiden, Zuid Holland
Miller's house. Milling equipment. Smithy. Display showing different types of mill.
Apr. 1-Sept. 15, Tu.-Sa. 10-5; Su. 1-5.

LEIDSCHENDAM

NATIONAL AUTOMOBILE MUSEUM
Veursestraatweg 280, Leidschendam, Zuid Holland
Cars. Motorcycles. Bicycles. Sleighs. Fire-fighting equipment. Tractors. Agricultural implements.
Daily 9-6.

LELYSTAD

LELYSTAD HARBOUR EXHIBITION BUILDING
Oostelijk Flevoland, Lelystad, Noord Holland
History of the development of the Zuiderzee polders. Geology. Archaeology. Drainage and dyke-making techniques. Colonisation. Agriculture.
Daily 10-5. Closed Christmas, Jan. 1.

LIEVELDE

KOTS OPEN-AIR MUSEUM
Eimersweg 4, Lievelde, Gelderland
Household equipment. Tools. Archaeology, especially Egyptian.
Daily 10-6.

LIMMEN

MUSEUM OF BULB GROWING
Schoolweg 5, Limmen, Noord Holland
Displays illustrating history and techniques of bulb growing. Tools and equipment. Cultivation. Catalogues.
On request.

LOENEN

F. DUYVENZ COLLECTION
Huize Bijdorp, Oud-Over 8, Loenen, Utrecht
17th-19th century period rooms.
On request.

LOOSDRECHT

SYPESTEYN CASTLE MUSEUM
Nieuw-Loosdrechtsedijk 150, Loosdrecht, Utrecht
16th-18th century Dutch paintings, including Van Sypesteyn family portraits. Furniture. Weapons. Clocks. Chinese and Dutch porcelain. Pottery. Wood sculpture. Glass. Silver.
May 1-Sept. 15, Tu.-Sa. 10-12.30, 1.30-5; Su., public holidays, 1.30-5.

MAASSLUIS

MAASSLUIS LOCAL MUSEUM
Zuiddijk 16, Maassluis, Zuid Holland
Local history.
Tu.-Su. 2-5. Tu. also 7 p.m.-9.

MAASTRICHT

BONNEFANTEN MUSEUM
Bonnefantenstraat 4, Maastricht, Limburg
Prehistory and history of Maastricht area. Roman, Frankish, Carolingian archaeology. Roman, medieval sculpture. Medieval-18th century ceramics. Paintings. Furniture. Maastricht silver, glass. Religious art. Liturgical items.
M.-F. 10-12, 2-5; Sa., Su., public holidays 2-5. Closed Christmas, Jan. 1, Carnival day.

T. J. BOTKE COLLECTION
Bredestraat 5, Maastricht, Limburg
Furniture. Decorative arts. 18th century paintings. Paintings by Pike Koch.
M., W., F. 10-12.

NATURAL HISTORY MUSEUM
De Bosquetplein 7, Maastricht, Limburg
Geology, palaeontology, botany, wildlife, especially of Limburg and its region.
M.-F. 9-12, 2-5; Sa. 9-12; Su. 2-4.30.

TREASURY OF THE BASILICA OF OUR LADY
O. L. Vrouweplein 8, Maastricht, Limburg
18th-19th century religious art. Reliquaries. Chalices. Ornaments. Paintings.
June 1-Sept. 15, 10.30-5.30. Other times by appointment.

TREASURY OF ST. SERVAAS CHURCH
Keizer Karelplein 6, Maastricht, Limburg
Religious art. Reliquaries. Ornaments. Fabrics. Copper. Ivory. Paintings. Furniture.
May 13-Sept. 30, M.-Sa. 10.30-5.30; Su. 3-5.

MAKKUM

FRISIAN POTTERY MUSEUM IN THE WEIGH HOUSE
Pothuis, Turfmarkt, Makkum, Friesland
In former Weigh House (1695). Frisian majolica, faience, tiles, pottery. Local history.
May-Sept., daily 10-5.

MARSSUM

HERINGA STATE
Poptaslot, Marssum, Friesland
17th century paintings, furniture. Material illustrating history of Heringa State.
M.-Sa. 9-12, 2-5.

MEDEMBLIK

MEDEMBLIK LOCAL HISTORY MUSEUM
Kaasmarkt 2, Medemblik, Noord Holland
In former 17th century weigh-house. Local history.
July-Aug., M.-Sa. 9-12, 1.30-6.

ST. MICHIELSGESTEL

NATURAL HISTORY MUSEUM OF THE ROMAN CATHOLIC SCHOOL AND SEMINARY 'BEEKOLIET'
Beekkant 1, St. Michielsgestel, Noord Brabant
Botany and zoology of the Netherlands. Fossils. Herbarium. Dioramas showing birds and mammals.
On request.

MIDDELBURG

ZEALAND MUSEUM
Wagenaarstraat 1, Middelburg, Zeeland
House (c.1730). Maps. Fossils. Prehistoric and medieval material from local excavations. Paintings. Portraits. Coins. Medals. Folklore. Costumes.
M.-Sa. 10-12.30, 1.30-5.

MIDDELSTUM

MENDEL BAKERY MUSEUM
Kerkstraat 3, Middelstum, Groningen
In former bakery. Baker's shop (c.1829), with fittings and equipment.
On request.

MIDDEN-BEEMSTER

BETJE WOLFF HOUSE
Middenweg 178, Midden-Beemster, Noord Holland
Local history. Folk art. Reconstruction of Betje Wolff's workroom. 18th-19th century period rooms.
Apr.-Nov., M.-Sa. 10-12, 2-5; Su., public holidays 2-4. Other times on request.

MODDERGAT

THE FISHERMAN'S HOUSE
Moddergat, Friesland
Fisherman's house (c.1800). Old fishing equipment.
May 15-Sept. 15, Tu.-Sa. 2-5.

MONNIKENDAM

'T HAVENLAND' GOUWZEE MUSEUM
Havenstraat 20, Monnikendam, Noord Holland
Fisherman's house. Exhibits illustrating sailmaking, coopering, Shot-making. Clog-maker's Workshop. Eel-pond. Fish-lodge. Pond with Gouwzee fish.
Apr.-Sept., daily 10-6.

THE WEIGH-HOUSE
Middendam 7, Monnikendam, Noord Holland
Weigh-House (c.1660). Dutch tiles, majolica.
On request.

MONTFOORT

LOCAL HISTORY MUSEUM
Gemeentehuis, Hoogstraat 36, Montfoort, Utrecht
History of Montfoort. Paintings. Prints. Topography. Household utensils, equipment. Weapons. Coins. Architectural items. Woodcarving.
M.-F. 9-12, 2-4.

MOORDRECHT

THE OLD CRAFTSMAN'S HOUSE
Dorpstraat 60, Moordrecht, Zuid Holland
Collections illustrating history of Moordrecht.
On request.

MUIDEN

MUIDEN CASTLE NATIONAL MUSEUM
Muiden, Noord Holland
Castle (originally 1280). 17th century interior. Furniture. Carpets. Copper. Pewter. Pottery. Hearth-backs. Household equipment. Weapons. Paintings.
May-Sept., Tu.-Sa. 10-5; Su. 1-5. Oct.-Apr., Tu.-Sa. 10-12.30, 1.30-4; Su., public holidays 1-4. Closed Jan. 1.

NAALDWIJK

WESTLAND DISTRICT MUSEUM
Heilige Geest Hofje 7, Naaldwijk, Zuid Holland
In 17th century chapel. Neolithic, Roman, medieval material from local excavations. Views of Naaldwijk and other Westland villages. Paintings. Portraits.
M.-F. 9.30-12, 1.30-5.

NAARDEN

NETHERLANDS COMENIUS MUSEUM
Turfspoorstraat 27, Naarden, Noord Holland
House (1615). Writings and memorabilia of Jan Amos Comenius (d.1670).
Daily 2-5. Other times on request.

VESTING MUSEUM
Westwalstraat, Naarden, Noord Holland
Local history. Weapons. Uniforms. Models. Dioramas. Paintings. Watercolours. Documents. Maps. Fire-fighting equipment.
May 15-Sept. 30, M.-Sa. 10-4.30; Su. 1.30-5.

NIEUW-VOSSEMEER

ASSUMBURG MILL MUSEUM
Veerweg 1, Nieuw-Vossemeer, Noord Brabant
Models, photographs, technical descriptions of the different types of Dutch windmill.
May-Sept., Sa., Su., public holidays 2-5.

A. M. DE JONG MUSEUM
Voorstraat 42, Nieuw-Vossemeer, Noord Brabant
Books, manuscripts, personal possessions of the writer, A. M. de Jong, born here.
Daily 2-5.

NOORDWIJK AAN ZEE

OLD NOORDWIJK FARMHOUSE MUSEUM
Jan Kroonsweg 23, Noordwijk aan Zee, Zuid Holland
Farmhouse and contents (1880). Costumes. Models of fishing-boats. Shells. Coins. Photographs showing development of town.
July-Aug., M.-Sa. 2-5, 8-10. Closed public holidays.

NUNSPEET

VELUWE DIORAMA
Marktstraat 17-19, Nunspeet, Gelderland
Mounted specimens of birds, deer, wild pigs.
May-Aug., M.-Sa. 9-12, 2-5.30. Other times on request.

NIJ BEETS

DAMHÛS PEAT MUSEUM
Domela Nieuwenhuisweg, Nij Beets, Friesland
Peat-cutting tools, equipment.
May-Sept., daily 9-5.

NIJMEGEN

AFRICA MUSEUM
Berg en Dal, Nijmegen, Gelderland
African art. African village. Film illustrating African life. Recordings of African music.
May-Aug., daily 9-5. Sept.-Apr., daily 9-12.30, 1.30-5.

BIBLICAL OPEN-AIR MUSEUM
Heilig-land, Nijmegen, Gelderland
Reconstruction of Palestinian monuments, peasant houses. Domestic utensils, craftsmen's tools, agricultural equipment from the Holy Land.
Easter-July 15, Aug. 20-Oct. 31, guided tours daily 10-5.30.

G. M. KAM NATIONAL MUSEUM
Museum Kamstraat 45, Nijmegen, Gelderland
Prehistory, early history of the Nijmegen area, especially Roman material from local excavations, including pottery, bronze, glass, silver, gold, amber.
Daily 10-5; Su., public holidays 1-5. Closed Jan. 1.

LOCAL HISTORY MUSEUM
Mariënburg 26, Nijmegen, Gelderland
In former 15th century church. Local history. Guild pewter. Coins. Medals. Maps. Nijmegen silver. 15th-18th century pottery.
Daily 10-5. Closed Christmas, New Year, Queen's Birthday.

OENKERK

STANIA STATE AGRICULTURAL MUSEUM
Rengersweg 98, Oenkerk, Friesland
History of Frisian agriculture. Models of farmhouses and mills. Drawings. Carts and waggons. Sleighs. Implements. Dairying equipment.
Apr.-Sept., 9-12, 2-6. Oct.-Mar., 9-4.

DEN OEVER

WIERING FARM MUSEUM
Hofstraat 36, Den Oever, Noord Holland
In old West Frisian farm buildings. Agricultural implements, equipment.
May-Sept., Tu.-Su., 10-2. Oct.-Apr., Sa., Su., 10-2. Other times on request.

ZUIDERZEE WORKS INFORMATION CENTRE
Sluiskolkkade 2, Den Oever, Noord Holland
Models, maps, photographs, illustrating drainage of Zuiderzee and development of polders. Prehistoric material from the Zuiderzee area.
M.-F. 9-5. Closed public holidays.

OLDENZAAL

PALTHE HOUSE HISTORICAL MUSEUM
Marktstraat 13, Oldenzaal, Overijssel
Archaeology, prehistory, history of Oldenzaal. Town and country kitchens. 19th century doctor's pharmacy and library. Weapons. Spectacles. Pipes. Astrolabes.
Tu.-F. 10-12, 2-5; Sa., Su. 2-5. Closed Jan. 1 and 1st day of two-day public holidays.

TREASURY OF THE BASILICA OF ST. PLECHELMUS
St. Plechelmusplein, Oldenzaal, Overijssel
Reliquaries. Monstrances. Ornaments.
Daily 8-5, except during church services.

OMMEN

OMMEN LOCAL HISTORY MUSEUM
Den Oordt 7, Ommen, Overijssel
Geology, prehistory, history of Ommen district. Costumes. Ornaments. Restored mills.
June-Sept., M.-F. 10-12, 2-5; Sa. 2-5. Closed public holidays.

OOSTBURG

CADANZE ROOM
Raadhuisplein 1, Oostburg, Zeeland
Farmhouse room (c.1900), with furnishings, household equipment. Women's costumes.
M.-F. 9-12, 2-5.

OPHEMERT

OPHEMERT CASTLE
Dreef 2, Ophemert, Gelderland
Louis XV, Louis XVI, Queen Anne, Biedermeier furniture. Family portraits. Silver. European porcelain. Chinese, Japanese porcelain, lacquerware.
Tu., W., Th. 10-12, by appointment.

OSPEL

MIJL OP ZEVEN VISITOR CENTRE
Moostdijk 8, Ospel, Limburg
History and techniques of local peat-industry.
Apr. 15-Sept. 15, 9-6.

OSS

JAN CUNEN MUSEUM
Molenstraat 65A, Oss, Noord Brabant
Geology, prehistory, history of Oss and North Brabant. Sculpture. Costumes. Household equipment.
On request.

OTTERLOO

'IT NOFLIK STÉ' TILE MUSEUM
Elkenzoom 10, Otterloo, Gelderland
Dutch tiles and other ceramics, 1300-present day. Stove-tiles. Foreign tiles.
Apr.-Oct., Tu.-Sa. 2-5; Su. 2-4. Other times by appointment.

KROLLER-MULLER NATIONAL MUSEUM
Nationaal Park, De Hoge Veluwe, Otterloo, Gelderland
16th-18th century Italian, German, Dutch paintings. European paintings, sculpture since 1860, including 270 works by Van Gogh. Dutch, Italian, French, Belgian drawings, prints. Delft, Egyptian, Chinese, Greek, French ceramics. Chinese jade, bronzes, ivories. Furniture.
M.-Sa. 10-5; Su., public holidays 1-5. (Apr.-Oct., Su. 11-5).

OUD-ZUILEN

ZUYLEN CASTLE
Tournooiveld 1, Port Maarssen, Oud-Zuilen, Utrecht
Furniture. 17th century Delft tapestries. 16th-18th century glass, porcelain, pottery. Portraits. Letters from William of Orange, Duke of Aloa. Royal charters. Memorabilia of Belle van Zuylen, afterwards Madame de Chavrière.
Mar. 15-Nov. 15, Tu.-Sa. 9-12.30, 1.30-5.

OUDEMIRDUM

KLIF EN GAAST DISTRICT MUSEUM OF NATURAL HISTORY
Star Numansivei, Oudemirdum, Friesland
Flora and fauna of the region.
May 15-Sept. 15, M.-Sa. 9.30-12, 1.30-5.30.

OUDEWATER

WITCHES WEIGH-HOUSE
Markt, Oudewater, Zuid Holland
In former Weigh-House (1595). Local history. Paintings. Weapons. Coins. Scales on which witches were weighed.
May-Aug., M.-F. 9-12, 2-5. Other times on request.

OVERLOON

NETHERLANDS NATIONAL MUSEUM OF WAR AND THE RESISTANCE MOVEMENT
Museumpark 1, Overloon, Noord Brabant
German and Allied weapons used in World War II. Tanks. Aircraft. Amphibian vehicles. Booby-traps.
May-Sept., daily 9-7. Oct.-Nov., Mar.-Apr., 9-5. Closed Dec. 1-Feb. 28.

OVERWEEN

KLATTE-DE WAAL COLLECTION
Huize Beladano, Ruysdaelweg 2, Overween, Noord Holland
Chinese, Delft, English, German pottery and porcelain.
M., W., Sa. 10-12.

PURMEREND

PURMEREND'S MUSEUM
Stadhuis, Purmerend, Noord Holland
Local history. Agricultural implements. Whaling. Sleighs. Music. Paintings. Prints.
May-Sept., Tu. 2-4; Th. 7.30 p.m.-9.

RENKUM

AIRBORNE MUSEUM
Kastel Doorwerth, Renkum, Gelderland
Material illustrating battle fought by airborne troops, 1944. Model of Battle of Arnhem.
May-Sept., M.-Sa. 9-6; Oct.-Apr., M.-Sa. 9-5. All year, Su. 1-6.

RHENEN

RHENEN DISTRICT MUSEUM
Molenstraat 25, Rhenen, Utrecht
Local prehistory, history. Merovingian ornaments, utensils. Medieval pottery. Tiles. Guild-silver. Drawings. Prints.
M., Tu., Th.-Sa., 11-12.30, 2-5.

RIJNSBURG

SPINOZA HOUSE
Spinozalaan 2, Rijnsburg, Zuid Holland
Reconstruction of house (c.1660) in which Spinoza lived. Books by and about Spinoza. Portraits. Facsimiles of documents. Old instruments for grinding lenses.
M.-Sa. 10-4; Su., public holidays 2-4. Closed Jan. 1.

DE RIJP

'IN THE WOODEN HOUSE' MUSEUM OF DE RIJP
Jan Boonplein 2, De Rijp, Noord Holland
Local history. Charts and documents relating to whaling and the herring-fishery. 17th century material concerning the Seamen's guild. 17th-18th century pottery, majolica, architecture items.
Apr. 15-Oct. 31, M.-Sa. 10-12, 2-5; Su., public holidays 2-5.

RIJSSEN

MUSEUM OF ANTIQUITIES
Haarstraat 2, Rijssen, Overijssel
History of Rijssen area. Household utensils, equipment. Photographs. Paintings.
On request.

RIJSWIJK

RIJSWIJK MUSEUM
Herenstraat 67, Rijswijk, Zuid Holland
History of Rijswijk area. Ceramics. Prints. Photographs. Household utensils, equipment.
W., Sa. 2-5.

ROERMOND

LOCAL MUSEUM
Andersonweg 8, Roermond, Limburg
Prehistory, early history (especially Roman) and history of Roermond and district. Paintings. Drawings. Furniture. Oriental weapons.
Tu.-Sa. 10-12, 2-5; Su. 2-5.

ROSENDAAL

MUSEUM OF THE GOLDEN ROSE
Oud Raadhuis, Markt 1, Rosendaal, Noord Brabant
Local history. Costumes. Household utensils, equipment. Agricultural implements. Craftsmen's tools. Weapons. Toys. 16th-19th century paintings. 17th century Delftware. 16th century Antwerp majolica. Guild beakers. 13th-17th century German and Dutch stoneware. 17th-18th century cutlery. Drawings, watercolours by Alfred Ost.
1st Su. in month, 2-5. May-Sept., W., F., 9-12, 2-5. Oct.-Apr., W. 9-12, 2-5. Other times on request.

ROTTERDAM

ATLAS VAN STOCK FOUNDATION
Groene Wetering 11, Rotterdam, Zuid Holland
Dutch historical, allegorical prints. Caricatures. Portraits. Drawings.
On request, M., Tu., Th., F., 10-12, 2-4. W. 10-12.

BOYMANS AND VAN BEUNIGEN MUSEUM
Mathenesserlaan 18-20, Rotterdam, Zuid Holland
15th-19th century Italian, French paintings. Dutch paintings, Van Eyck to Van Gogh. 15th-16th century German paintings. 19th-20th century European paintings. 15th-20th century European drawings, prints. Medieval and modern sculpture. Pottery. Porcelain. Glass. Pewter. Silver. Furniture.
M.-Sa. 10-5; Su., public holidays 11-5; W. also 7.30 p.m.-10.

CABINET OF MEDALS RELATING TO THE DUTCH ECONOMY
Pieter de Hoochweg 122, Rotterdam, Zuid Holland
Medals reflecting the economic life of the Netherlands.
On request.

CHABOT MUSEUM
Oude Raadhuislaan 4, Hillegersberg, Rotterdam, Zuid Holland
War paintings (1940-5) by Hendrik Chabot.
Tu., W., Th. 3-5.

DIORAMA BUILDING OF THE NATURAL HISTORY MUSEUM
Van Aerssenlaan 49, Rotterdam, Zuid Holland
Dioramas of mammals and birds. Pleistocene animals. Landscapes. Photographs.
Daily 10-5.

ERASMUS ROOM
Nieuwe Markt 1, Rotterdam, Zuid Holland
Manuscripts, books, prints, medals relating to Erasmus.
1st Sa. in month, 2-5. Other times on request.

FIRE-FIGHTING MUSEUM OF THE CITY OF ROTTERDAM
Kleinpolderplein 3-5, Rotterdam, Zuid Holland
Fire-fighting equipment. Steam fire-engines. Photographs.
M.-Sa. 8-6. Closed public holidays.

FOUNDATION OF THE HISTORICAL MUSEUM OF THE ROYAL MOUNTED POLICE
Westersingel 12, Rotterdam, Zuid Holland
Paintings. Watercolours. Drawings. Photographs. Uniforms. Weapons. Equipment.
Tu.-Th., 2-5. Other times on request.

HISTORICAL MUSEUM
Korte Hoogstraat 31, Rotterdam, Zuid Holland
History of Rotterdam. Models. Maps. Paintings. Drawings. Engravings. Prints. Documents. Portraits. Woodcarving. Guild items. Glass. Pottery. Tiles. Coins. Silver. Porcelain. Clocks. Costumes. Period rooms. Pewter foundry.
M.-Sa. 10-5; Su. 11-5.

MUSEUM OF ETHNOLOGY
Willemskade 25, Rotterdam, Zuid Holland
Worldwide ethnological collections. African woodsculpture, masks, bronzes, pottery, weapons, musical instruments. Jades and pre-Columbian artifacts from Central America. Eskimo and American Indian material. Chinese and Tibetan bronzes. Collections from Indonesia, South Pacific, New Guinea.
M.-Sa. 10-5; Su. 11-5. Closed Jan. 1, Queen's Birthday.

MUSEUM OF THE NATIONAL TECHNICAL INSTITUTE OF SHIPPING AND AVIATION
Burg s'Jacobplein 10, Rotterdam, Zuid Holland
Collections illustrating modern shipping, navigation and aviation. Models. Machinery. Tools. Equipment. Harbour installations. Aerodynamics. Fishing techniques. Lifesaving equipment. Tugs and towing.
M.-Sa. 10-5; Su., public holidays 2-5. Closed Jan. 1, Queen's Birthday.

NATURAL HISTORY MUSEUM
Kastanjesingel 107, Rotterdam, Zuid Holland
Geology and fauna of the Netherlands. Tropical butterflies.
M.-Sa. 10-5; Su., public holidays 11-5. Closed Jan. 1.

PROF. DR. VAN DEN POEL MUSEUM OF TAXATION, DUTY AND EXCISE
Parklaan 14 and 16, Rotterdam, Zuid Holland
Weights and measures. Hallmarked gold and silver. Regulations. Pamphlets. Seals. Coins. Playing cards. Contraband. Paintings. Engravings. History of Benelux. Mementoes of the 1940-45 War. Collection of jokes about taxes and tax-collectors.
M.-F. 9.30-4.30.

PRINCE HENDRIK MARITIME MUSEUM
Burg s'Jacobplein 8, Rotterdam, Zuid Holland
Models of 15th-20th century ships. Half-models. Shipbuilding tools. Globes. Atlases. Charts. Navigation instruments. Paintings. Drawings. Prints.
M.-Sa. 10-5; Dec. 24, 11-5. Closed Jan. 1, Queen's Birthday.

H. REMKES COLLECTION
Schietbaanstraat 54A, Rotterdam, Zuid Holland
Paintings, books, prints, maps relating to Rotterdam. Coins. Medals. Gramophone records c.1900.
May-Aug., Nov.-Mar., W., F. 2-6.

WILLEM VAN DER VORM FOUNDATION
Westersingel 66, Rotterdam, Zuid Holland
17th century Dutch paintings. 19th century French, Dutch paintings. 17th-18th century Delft ware.
Su., W., F. 2-5; Tu., Th. 11-3. Closed Dec. 24, Easter, Whitsun, Jan. 1.

ST. GEERTRUD

SAVELSBOS VISITOR CENTRE
Moerslag 14, St. Geertrud, Limburg
Mounted specimens of animals. Marl-digging. Archaeological material from local excavations.
Apr.-Aug., Sa., Su. 11-5.

ST. MICHIELSGESTEL

LOCAL HISTORY MUSEUM
Instituut von Doven, St. Michielsgestel, Noord Brabant
Roman material from local excavations, including pottery, coins, glass, bronzes. Reconstruction of double-walled Roman well.
W.-Sa., Su. a.m., on request.

SANTPOORT

BREDERODE RUINS
Velserenderlaan 2, Santpoort, Noord Holland
Castle (c.990, largely rebuilt late 15th century). Material found during site-excavations. Tiles. Domestic utensils. Weights. Keys. Glass. Coins. Pottery.
Apr.-May, daily 9-6. June-July, 9-8. Aug.-Sept., 9-6. Oct.-Mar., M., Tu., F., Sa. 9-4; W., Th., Su. 1-5.

SCHEVENINGEN

H. M. KNIGHT COLLECTION
Zeekant 100E, Scheveningen, Zuid Holland
Chinese pottery, porcelain. Lacquerware. Cloisonné enamels. Ivories. Bronzes.
M., W., F. 10-12.

LOCAL HISTORY AND FISHERY MUSEUM
Badhuisstraat 262, Scheveningen, Zuid Holland
History of shipping and fishing. Ship-models. Instruments. Ships' logs. Costumes. Paintings. Prints.
May 15 - Sept. 30, M.-Sa. 10-5.

SCHIEDAM

LIQUEUR MUSEUM, WITH B. J. DE JONGH'S COLLECTION
Lange Haven 74, Schiedam, Zuid Holland
Miniature bottles of liqueurs and spirits from 60 countries.
M.-F. 10-12, 2-4. Closed public holidays.

NATIONAL MUSEUM OF DISTILLED LIQUOR
Hoogstraat 112, Schiedam, Zuid Holland
Collection illustrating history of local gin industry. Paintings. Equipment. Bottles.
M.-Sa. 10-5; F. also 8 p.m.-10; Su., public holidays 12.30-5. Closed Jan. 1.

MUNICIPAL MUSEUM
Hoogstraat 112, Schiedam, Zuid Holland
History of Schiedam. Architectural items. Guild material. 16th-20th century paintings, sculpture, applied art. Schiedam pottery.
M.-Sa. 10-5; F. also 8 p.m.-10. Su., public holidays 12.30-5. Closed Jan. 1.

SCHIERMONNIKOOG

NATURAL HISTORY MUSEUM
Middenstreek 25, Schiermonnikoog, Friesland
Birds. Mammals. Insects. Shells. Diorama of sand dunes.
May-Sept., M.-F. 7.30 p.m.-9. Other times on request.

SCHIPHOL-CENTRUM

AVIODROME
Luchthaven Schiphol, Noord Holland
History of aviation and space-flight. Operating techniques at Schiphol Airport.
Daily 9-5.

SCHIPLIUDEN

H. JUNGELING COLLECTION
Vlaardingsekade 57, Schipliuden, Zuid Holland
17th century paintings. Paintings and drawings by J. Taven Gaat (d.1881) and J. A. Zandleven (d.1923).
On request.

SCHOKLAND

IJSSELMEER POLDER MUSEUM
Middelbuurt, Schokland, Overijssel
Geology, archaeology, history and wildlife of the Ijsselmeer area.
M.-Sa. 8-5; Su., public holidays 10-6. Closed Jan. 1.

SCHOONHAVEN

MUNICIPAL COLLECTIONS OF ANTIQUITIES
Standhuis Haven 41, Schoonhaven, Zuid Holland
History of Schoonhaven area. Furniture. Household equipment. Paintings. Engravings. Portraits of members of the House of Orange.
May-Oct., M.-F. 10.30-11.30, 2.30-3.30.

SCHOONOORD

THE SEVEN MARKS
Transtraat 73, Schoonoord, Drenthe
Farmhouse. Turf-huts. Geology. Fossils. Social and working-life c.1900.
Easter-Sept. 30, 9-6.

SITTARD

SITTARD DISTRICT MUSEUM
Plakstraat 32, Sittard, Limburg
History and culture of the Sittard region. Prehistoric, Roman, Frankish, and medieval material. Drawings. Architectural fragments.
On request.

SLIEDRECHT

SLIEDRECHT MUSEUM
Kerkbuurt 99, Sliedrecht, Zuid Holland
History of Sliedrecht, and especially dredging industry, dyke and drainage works.
W., Sa. 2-5. Other times by appointment.

SLOTEN

SLOTEN LOCAL HISTORY COLLECTION
Heerenwal 48, Sloten, Friesland
History of Sloten. Paintings. Prints. Household equipment. Craftsmen's tools. Weapons. Flags.
May-Sept., M.-Sa. 9-12, 1-6. Oct.-Apr., M.-Sa. 9-12, 1-5.

SLUIS

TOWN LOCAL HISTORY COLLECTION
Gemeentehuis, Grote Markt 1, Sluis, Zeeland
16th-17th century paintings. 17th century tapestry. Wrought-ironwork (1744). Views of the town. Collection illustrating history of Sluis.
June-Sept., 10-12, 2-5; Su., public holidays 2-7.

SNEEK

FRISIAN SHIPPING MUSEUM AND SNEEK LOCAL HISTORY MUSEUM
Kleinzand 12-14, Sneek, Friesland
History of Frisian shipping. Ship-models. Charts. Navigation instruments. Frisian trade tokens. Paintings. Prints. History of Sneek area. Archaeology. 18th century woodwork. Sneek silver.
Apr. 15 - Oct. 15, M.-Sa. 9-12.30, 1.30-5.

SOMEREN

SOMEREN LOCAL HISTORY MUSEUM
Gemeentehuis, Wilhelminaplein 1, Someren, Noord Brabant
Prehistoric urns from local sites. Tools, household equipment from Someren area. Coins.
M.-F. 9-12, 2-5. Other times on request.

SOMMELSDIJK

GOEREE AND OVERFLAKEE DISTRICT MUSEUM
Kerkstraat, Sommelsdijk, Zuid Holland
Roman material from local excavations. Ship-models. Local shipping and fishing industries. Costumes. Period rooms.
Apr.-Sept., Tu.-Sa. 2-5. Other times on request.

SPANKEREN

J. G. WURFBAIN COLLECTION
De Geldersche Toren, Spankeren, Gelderland
Chinese porcelain. Delft pottery. 17th-18th century furniture. Maps.
M., W., F. 2-4, on request.

STAPHORST

OLD STAPHORST FARMHOUSE
Muldersweg 4, Staphorst, Utrecht
Farmhouse, with complete furnishings and household equipment, c.1900.
Daily 8-6. Closed Christmas, Easter, Whitsun.

STEIN

ARCHAEOLOGICAL RESERVE
Schepersgat 6, Stein, Limburg
Museum on site of gallery-graves (c.2850 B.C.). Prehistory, history of Stein area, including Roman, Merovingian-Frankish material.
May-Sept., 4 p.m.-6. Oct.-Apr., Sa., Su. 4-6.

STEYL

STEYL MISSION MUSEUM
Missiehuis St. Michaël, St. Michaëlstraat 7, Steyl, Limburg
Items collected by missionaries. Ethnology. Mammals, insects, butterflies.
M.-Sa. 10-12, 2-6; Su., public holidays 11-12, 2-6.

ROZENDAAL

MUSEUM OF THE INTERNATIONAL CASTLES INSTITUTE
Kastel Rosendael, Rozendaal, Gelderland
History and study of castles in the Netherlands and abroad. Models. Photographs. Weapons.
May 24 - Sept. 30, M.-Sa. 10-6; Su. 11-6.

RUINERWOLD

RUINERWOLD FARM MUSEUM
Dr. Larijweg 21, Ruinerwold, Drenthe
18th century farmhouse. Mill. Agricultural implements. Household equipment. Most rooms contain tile-pictures illustrating Bible stories.
May-Sept., 8-6. Oct.-Apr., 9-4. Closed Jan. 1, Queen's Birthday.

TEGELEN

TEGELEN LOCAL HISTORY MUSEUM
Roermondseweg 60, Tegelen, Limburg
North Limburg pottery. Tobacco jars. Ornamental boxes. Mementoes.
On request.

TER APEL

TER APEL MONASTERY
Boslaan 3, Ter Apel, Groningen
16th century church and monastery, with furnishings, glass.
Tu.-Sa. 9-12, 1-7; Su. 1-7. Closed Dec. 25, Jan. 1.

THORN

MONASTERY CHURCH MUSEUM
Gemeentehuis, Thorn, Limburg
In 15th century chapter house of church. 16th-18th century religious art. Liturgical items. Murals. Paintings. Engravings. Coins.
Maundy Thursday - Oct. 16, 9-6. Other times on request.

TIEL

TIEL AND DISTRICT LOCAL HISTORY MUSEUM
St. Agnietenstraat 28, Tiel, Gelderland
Roman material from local excavations. Pottery. Wall-tiles. Pewter and pewter-making equipment. Glass and glass-blowing equipment. Painting. Prints. Maps. Model of Tiel (c.1650). Weapons. Coins.
Apr.-Sept., Sa., Su. 3-5. Oct.-Mar., Su. 3-5.

TILBURG

NATURAL HISTORY MUSEUM
Kloosterstraat 26, Tilburg, Noord Brabant
Plants, animals, rocks, minerals of the Netherlands. Collections relating to forestry, mining, fishing, bee-keeping.
M.-F. 2-6.

NETHERLANDS MUSEUM OF ETHNOLOGY
Kloosterstraat 24, Tilburg, Noord Brabant
Ethnological material, tools. Household equipment from Central and S. America, China, Japan, Indonesia, Philippines, New Guinea, Africa.
M.-F. 9-12, 2-5; Su. 2-5.

NETHERLANDS TEXTILE MUSEUM
Gasthuisring 23, Tilburg, Noord Brabant
Persian, Peruvian, Oriental textiles. European damasks, brocades. Costumes, especially from N. Brabant. Tools and equipment formerly used in the textile industry.
M.-F. 10-12, 2-5; Sa., Su. 2-5. M. also 7.30 p.m.-12. Closed Christmas, New Year.

TYPEWRITING AND WRITING MUSEUM
Gasthuisring 54, Tilburg, Noord Brabant
Typewriters. Duplicators. Calculating machines. Inkpots. Pens. Letter-openers. Writing manuals and copybooks. Blotters.
1st Sa. in month, 2-5.

UITHUIZEN

MENKEMA CASTLE MUSEUM
Mankemaborgweg 2, Uithuizen, Groningen
In castle (15th-16th century). 17th-19th century furnishings. Portraits of former occupants of the Castle.
Oct.-Apr., 10-12, 1-4. May-Sept., 10-12, 1-5. Closed Jan. 1-31.

UTRECHT

ARCHAEOLOGICAL INSTITUTE
Domplein 24, Utrecht, Utrecht
Egyptian, Greek, Etrurian, Roman antiquities.
W. 2-5. Other times by appointment.

VAN BAAREN MUSEUM
Oude Gracht 317, Utrecht, Utrecht
19th-20th century French, Dutch paintings. 20th century Dutch sculpture. 18th century Dutch silver.
On request.

CABINET OF COINS AND MEDALS OF THE ROYAL MINT
Leidseweg 90, Utrecht, Utrecht
Coins of the Netherlands and the overseas territories, 800 - present day. Foreign coins, medals and tokens.
Tu., F. 9-12, 2-4, by appointment.

CENTRAL MUSEUM
Agnietenstraat 1, Utrecht, Utrecht
15th-19th century paintings, sculpture, drawings, prints, especially by Utrecht artists. Period rooms. Furniture. Dolls' house (c.1680). Pottery. Porcelain. Silver. Coins. Medals. 18th-20th century costumes and accessories. Religious art. History of Utrecht. Guild material.
M.-Sa. 10-5; Su., public holidays 2-5.

CENTRAL MUSEUM
Maliebaan 42, Utrecht, Utrecht
Works by 19th-20th century Dutch artists. Paintings. Sculpture. Drawings. Engravings. Prints. Ceramics. Enamels. Furnishings.
M.-Sa. 10-5; Su., public holidays 2-5.

DIOCESAN MUSEUM
Agnietenstraat 1, Utrecht, Utrecht
In 16th century chapel of St. Agnes convent. Religious art, especially medieval and including works by 13th-15th century Italian artists. 15th-16th century Dutch paintings. 7th century Merovingian reliquary. Early 11th century Byzantine reliefs. Medieval sculpture. Miniatures. Ornaments. Early printed books. Book bindings.
M.-Sa. 11-5; Su. 1-5. Closed Jan. 1.

MUSEUM OF MODERN RELIGIOUS ART
Lange Nieuwstraat 38, Utrecht, Utrecht
20th century Dutch religious art. Paintings. Sculpture. Glass.
Daily 2-5. Closed Dec. 25, Jan. 1.

MUSEUM OF PIPES, COFFEE AND TEA
Douwe Egberts Koninklyke Tabaksfabrick, Keulsekade 143, Utrecht, Utrecht
History of smoking and of coffee and tea preparation and drinking.
M.-F. 9-5, on request.

MUSEUM OF THE UTRECHT STUDENT CORPS
Janskerkhof 14, Utrecht, Utrecht
Collections illustrating student life in Utrecht since 1636. Paintings. Drawings. Prints. Photographs. Almanacks. Student newspapers. Costumes. Banners. Medals.
On request.

MUSEUM OF UTRECHT UNIVERSITY
Trans 8, Utrecht, Utrecht
History of the University. Instruments, lenses and clock as used by Christiaan Huygens. Microscopes owned by Van Leeuwenloek and Musschenbroek. Weights and measures used by Van Swinden. Zoological specimens. Physiological instruments. Portraits. Coins. Music. Documents.
M.-F. 2-5.

MUSEUM OF UTRECHT UNIVERSITY: DEPARTMENT OF DENTISTRY
Jutfaseweg 7, Utrecht, Utrecht
History of dentistry, 16th century-onwards. Instruments. Materials. X-rays. Photographs.
W., F. 9.30-12, 2-5. Other times, including University vacations, by appointment.

MUSEUM OF UTRECHT UNIVERSITY: VETERINARY DEPARTMENT
Bildstraat 172, Utrecht, Utrecht
Collections illustrating development of veterinary science, especially in Netherlands.
On request.

NETHERLANDS GOLD, SILVER AND CLOCK MUSEUM
Lange Nieuwstraat 38, Utrecht, Utrecht
17th-19th century Dutch gold and silver, including religious art. Gold- and silversmiths' tools, equipment. Sundials. Hour-glasses. Clocks and clock-work. Clock-making tools. Navigation instruments.
M.-Sa. 10-12, 2-5; Su., public holidays 2-5. Closed Jan. 1, Easter Sunday, Whitsunday, Dec. 25.

NETHERLANDS RAILWAY MUSEUM
Joan van Oldenbarneveltlaan 6, Utrecht, Utrecht
In railway station (1874). Collections illustrating history of Dutch railways and tramways. Original locomotives, carriages, equipment. Models. Paintings. Drawings. Prints. Photographs. Medals.
Apr.-Oct., Tu.-Sa. 10-5; Su., public holidays 1-5. Nov.-Mar., Tu.-Sa. 10-4; Su., public holidays 1-4. Closed Jan. 1, Dec. 25, Easter Sunday, Whitsun.

OLD CATHOLIC MUSEUM
Mariahoek 9, Utrecht, Utrecht
Collections illustrating history of old Catholic Church in Netherlands. Manuscripts. Liturgical items. Prints. Ornaments. Material from Abbey of Port Royal, Paris.
Apr. 15 - Oct. 14, M.-Th., Sa. 10-12, 2-5; Su., public holidays 2-5. Oct. 15 - Apr. 14, W., Sa., Su. 2-5.

PIEREMENT MUSICAL BOX MUSEUM
Lange Nieuwstraat 38, Utrecht, Utrecht
Automatic musical instruments.
W., Sa., Su., 2-5.

PROVINCIAL MUSEUM OF ANTIQUITIES
Agnietenstraat 1, Utrecht, Utrecht
Prehistorical, Roman and early medieval material, mainly from Province of Utrecht and including items from excavations at Vechten.
M.-Sa. 10-5; Su., public holidays 2-5.

VAASSEN

CANNENBURCH CASTLE
Vaassen, Gelderland
Castle (14th century, reconstructed 1661, 1751). Portraits of members of Gelderland families. Furniture. 16th-19th century ceramics.
May 15 - Oct. 15, M.-Sa. 9-6; Su. 1-6.

VALKENBURG-HOUTHEM

FALKENBURG DISTRICT MUSEUM
Grotestraat 31, Valkenburg-Houthem, Limburg
Geology, prehistory and history of the Falkenburg area. Fossils. Maps. Prints. Early books. Portraits of the De Guasco family.
Easter-Sept. 30, 10-12, 2-6, 7-9.

MUSEUM OF THE CATACOMBS FOUNDATION
Plenkerstraat 55, Valkenburg-Houthem, Limburg
Christian religious artifacts from catacombs in Rome and Egypt.
June-Aug., 9-6; Sa. 10-5. Su. 10-6.

VEENDAM

PEAT SETTLEMENT MUSEUM
Kerkstraat 18, Veendam, Groningen
Documents, paintings, books and equipment relating to the Groningen peat-marsh settlement.
M. 2-6; Tu.-F. 9-12.30, 2-6; Sa. 9-12.30.

VEENKLOSTER

FOGELSANGH STATE
Veenkloster, Friesland
17th century manor house, remodelled in 18th, 19th century. Copper-beater's workshop, 19th century kitchen and equipment. Furniture. Portraits. Hunting collection. Toys. Carriages. Sleighs.
May-Sept., M.-Sa. 10-12, 2-5. July-Sept., also Su. 2-4.

VEENWOUDEN

DANTUMADEEL MUSEUM OF ANTIQUITIES
Hoofdstraat 1, Veenwouden, Friesland
Weapons, mainly Napoleonic period.
Tu.-Sa. 9-12, 2-5. Closed public holidays.

VEERE

THE SCOTS HOUSES
Kade 25-7, Veere, Zeeland
History of Veere. Early paintings of Town Hall. Furniture. Decorative arts. Costumes. Ornaments. Porcelain. Fishing industry.
Mar. 1- Sept. 15, M.-Sa. 10-12, 2-5. Other times on request.

STADHUIS
Markt 5, Veere, Zeeland
Building (1586). History of Veere. Administration of justice. Guild items. Paintings. Tapestries.
May-Aug., M.-Sa. 10.30-12, 2-5.

VENLO

GOLTZIUS MUSEUM
Goltziusstraat 21, Venlo, Limburg
Archaeology of Venlo and N. Limburg. History of Venlo. Maps. Paintings. Prints. Pottery. Porcelain. Glass. Pewter. Weapons. Coins. Medals. Venlo silver. Period rooms.
Tu.-F., 10-12, 2-5; Sa., Su. 2-5.

MUSEUM OF THE LIMBURG JAGER REGIMENT
Goltziusstraat 21, Venlo, Limburg
History of Limburg. Jager Regiment. Paintings. Prints. Documents. Uniforms. Weapons.
Tu.-F. 10-12, 2-5; Sa., Su. 2-5.

VENRAY

LOCAL HISTORY MUSEUM
Gemeentehuis, Venray, Limburg
Burial urns (800-400 B.C.). Prehistoric stone implements. Coins. Roman utensils.
M.-F. 9-12, 2-5.30. Sa., Su. on request.

VIANEN

TOWN HALL MUSEUM
Voorstraat 30, Vianen, Zuid Holland
Renaissance furniture, paintings. Pewter. Bronze. Silver. Gold. Ivory. Coins. Medals. Pottery, especially Delft. Cut-glass. Porcelain.
M.-F. 9-5. Other times on request.

VIJFHUIZEN

CRUQUIUS MUSEUM
Cruquiusdijk 32, Vijfhuizen, Noord Holland
Original steam-engine used for draining Haarlemmermeer. Models of polders and water-mills. Maps.
Apr.-Oct., daily 9-12.30, 2-5.

VLAARDINGEN

MUSEUM OF THE NETHERLANDS FISHING INDUSTRY
Westhavenkade 45, Vlaardingen, Zuid Holland
Techniques and equipment of Dutch fishing industry. Whaling. Navigation.
M.-Sa. 10-5; Su. 2-5.

TOWN HALL
Markt 11, Vlaardingen, Zuid Holland
Old coats of arms of Amsterdam, Bergen op Zoom, Dordrecht, Gouda, 's-Gravenzande, Maasland, Rotterdam, Schiedam, Vlaardingen.
M.-F. 8.30-12.30, 1.30-5.45.

VLIELAND

NATURAL HISTORY MUSEUM
Kerkplein, Vlieland, Friesland
Plants and wildlife of the Netherlands. Plants. Birds. Butterflies. Shells. Seals.
May-Aug., 10-12, 2-5. Tu., F., also 8 p.m.-9.

TROMP HOUSE
Dorpstraat 99, Vlieland, Friesland
17th century house. Wall-paintings. Lapland artifacts. Norwegian popular art. Paintings by B. R. Akersloot-Berg.
May-Sept., M.-F. 10-12, 2-5; Tu., F., also 8 p.m.-9.

VLISSINGEN

HAIRDRESSING MUSEUM
Badhuisstraat 64, Vlissingen, Zeeland
History of men's and women's hairdressing, and of perfumes.
M.-F. 9-12.

MUNICIPAL MUSEUM
Bellamypark 19, Vlissingen, Zeeland
History of Vlissingen (Flushing). Paintings. Municipal and guild silver. Wood-sculpture. Tiles. House-fronts. Coins. Pewter. Ship-models. 18th century room, with furnishings.
Tu.-Sa. 10-12, 2-5; Su., M., 2-5.

VOORBURG

HOFWIJK HUYGENS MUSEUM
Westeinde 2, Voorburg, Zuid Holland
House (1639-41). Memorabilia and possessions of the Huygens family. Portraits. Drawings. Sculpture. Letters.
Daily 1-4. July-Aug., 11-5.

SWAENSTEYN MUSEUM
Herenstraat 101, Voorburg, Zuid Holland
Local history. Works by contemporary Voorburg artists.
Tu., Th., Sa. 1-4.

VOORSCHOTEN

DUIVENSVOORDE CASTLE
Voorschoten, Zuid Holland
17th-19th century period rooms. Porcelain. Family portraits.
Mar. 15- Oct. 15, Tu., Th., Sa. 10-5.

VORDEN

VICTOR DE STUERS COLLECTION
De Wiersse E 127, Vorden, Gelderland
16th-18th century furniture. Dutch and foreign ceramics. 17th century paintings. Drawings.
M., W., F. 10-12.

VRIES

CHURCH MUSEUM AND BELL-FOUNDRY
Brink 3, Vries, Drenthe
Model of 1917 bell-foundry. 12th century sarcophagi.
M.-Sa. 9-6; Su., public holidays 2-6.

VRIEZENVEEN

VRIEZENVEEN MUSEUM OF ANTIQUITIES
Westeinde 65, Vriezenveen, Utrecht
Archaeological material from local excavations. Medieval pottery. Russian household equipment. Photographs of Russian life. Mementoes of trade with Czarist Russia. Farmhouse kitchen, with utensils, equipment.
May-Sept., Th., F. 2-5; W. 7 p.m.-9. Other times on request.

WAALWIJK

NETHERLANDS MUSEUM OF SHOES, LEATHER AND LEATHER GOODS
Grotestraat 148, Wallwijk, Noord Brabant
International collection of footwear. Shoemaking tools, equipment. Paintings, prints showing shoemaking. Guild silver.
Apr.-Sept., M.-Sa. 10-12, 2-5.

WARFFUM

HET HOGELAND MUSEUM
Schoolstraat 2-4, Warffum, Groningen
Local history. 18th-19th century agricultural history. Period rooms. Educational history.
Tu.-F. 10-12, 3-5.30. Other times on request.

WEERT

LOCAL MUSEUM
Maasstraat 10, Weert, Limburg
Prehistory and history of Weert area. Folklore. Craftsmen's tools. Prints. Coins. Natural history.
W.-Su. 2-5.

NETHERLANDS TRAM MUSEUM
Kruisstraat 6, Weert, Limburg
Tramcars and tramway equipment. Photographs and documents illustrating history of Dutch tramways.
Apr. 1- Nov. 15, Sa. 2-6; Su. 2-7. Other times by appointment.

WEESP

LOCAL MUSEUM
Nieuwstraat 41, Weesp, Noord Holland
History of Weesp. Paintings. Maps. Gravestones. 18th century Weesp porcelain. Weapons. Guild history.
M.-F. 9-12, 2-5; Sa. on request.

WESTERBORK

NETHERLANDS MUSEUM OF PAPER-CUTTING
Westeind 6, Westerbork, Drenthe
Silhouettes and other examples of the art of paper-cutting.
M., Sa. 9-6. Other times on request.

WEST-TERSCHELLING

BRANDARIS MUSEUM OF BIRDS
West-Terschelling, Friesland
Mounted specimens of birds.
June 15- Sept. 15, M.-Sa. 10.30-12.

DISTRICT MUSEUM OF NATURAL HISTORY
Burg Redekerstraat 11, West-Terschelling, Friesland
Flora, fauna, birds of Terschelling.
Mar.-Oct., M.-Sa. 9-12, 2-5.30. Nov.-Feb., W. 10-12, 2-5.

LOCAL MUSEUM
Commandeurstraat 30-2, West-Terschelling, Friesland
Local history. Furnishings. Household equipment. Craftsmen's tools., equipment. Popular art. Ship-models. Shipping. Pilotage. Fishing industry. Whaling.
June-Aug., 9-12, 2-5. Sept.-Nov., Mar.-May, M.-Sa. 10-12, 2-4.

WIJCHEN

FRANS BLOEMEN MUSEUM OF ANTIQUITIES
Koetshuis, Wijchen, Gelderland
Prehistoric and Roman material from local excavations.
M.-F. 10-12, 3-5. Other times on request.

WIJK BIJ DUURSTEDE

MUNICIPAL AND CANTONAL MUSEUM OF ANTIQUITIES
Kasteel Duurstede, Wijk bij Duurstede, Utrecht
Prehistory, history of the Wijk bij Duurstede area. Coins. Model of the castle.
Apr.-Sept., 9.30-6.

WINTERSWIJK

MUSEUM
Satinkplas, Winterswijk, Gelderland
Geology. Natural history. Local history and folklore.
Su. 3-5. June-Sept., also M.-F. 7 p.m.-9.

WITTEM

CARDINAL VAN ROSSUM MUSEUM
Redemptoristenklooster, Wittem, Limburg
Life and work of Cardinal van Rossum.
Daily 8.30-7.30.

WOERDEN

LOCAL MUSEUM
Kerkplein 6, Woerden, Zuid Holland
Local history, archaeology. Paintings by Woerden artists.
May 15- Sept. 30, M.-Sa. 10-5. Closed public holidays.

WOLVEGA

WESTELLINGWERF MUSEUM OF LOCAL HISTORY
Molen Windlust, Hoofdstraat, Wolvega, Friesland
In windmill (1888). Local history. Portraits. Photographs. Costumes. Weapons. Maps. Views.
May-Sept., F. 7 p.m.-9; Sa. 3-5.

WORKUM

WARKUM'S ERFSKIP MUSEUM OF ANTIQUITIES
Waaggebouw op de Merk, Workum, Friesland
In former Weigh House (1650). Pottery. Tiles. Silver. Tools. Models of mills and ships. Engravings of Workum.
June-Aug., M.-Sa. 9.30-12, 2.30-5.30.

WOUBRUGGE

LOCAL MUSEUM
Dokter Lothlaan 1, Woubrugge, Zuid Holland
Local history. Paintings. Prints. Maps. Manuscripts. School equipment.
May-Nov., Sa. 2-4.

ZAANDAM

CZAR PETER'S COTTAGE
Krump 23, Zaandam, Noord Holland
Collection relating to Peter the Great and his residence in Zaandam. Paintings. Prints. Furniture. Memorabilia.
M.-F. 10-1, 2-6. Closed Jan. 1.

ZAANDIJK

ZAANLAND MUSEUM OF LOCAL HISTORY
Lagedijk 80, Zaandijk, Noord Holland
History of Zaandijk, with special emphasis on domestic life. Costumes. Ship-models. Toys.
Tu.-Sa. 10-12, 2-4. Su. 2-4.

ZALTBOMMEL

MAARTEN VAN ROSSUM MUSEUM
Nonnenstraat 7, Zaltbommel, Gelderland
Local history. Paintings. Drawings. Prints. Photographs. Manuscripts. Copper. Pewter. Weapons. Coins. Architectural items. Furniture. Porcelain. Glass. Pottery.
Sept.-Apr., W., Sa. 2-4. May-June, Su.-F. 2-4; Sa. 10-12, 2-4. July-Aug., M.-Sa. 10-12, 2-4; Su. 2-4.

ZEELST

OLD CASTLE MUSEUM
Hemelrijken 14, Zeelst, Noord Brabant
Local history, prehistory. 16th century material from excavations on castle site. 16th-18th century tools, household equipment, pottery. Coins. Venetian glass.
Apr. 5- Nov. 30, Sa., Su. 1-5; W. 7 p.m.-10.

ZEIST

VAN DE POLL FOUNDATION
Krullelaan 28, Zeist, Utrecht
Local history.
May-Aug., on request.

ZEVENBERGEN

WILLEM VAN STRIJEN LOCAL HISTORY MUSEUM
Burg Vranckenstraat 4, Zevenbergen, Noord Brabant
Local history. Agricultural implements. Craftsmen's tools. Pottery. Porcelain. Silver. Cut-glass. Maps. Period rooms.
2nd Sa. in month, 2.30-4.30.

ZIERIKZEE

LOCAL MUSEUM
Stadhuis, Meelstraat 8, Zierikzee, Zeeland
History of Zierikzee. Trade. Industry. Fishing. Prints. Drawings. Silver. Porcelain. Pottery. Agricultural implements. Madder-growing and processing equipment. Ship-models.
Apr.-May., Sept.-Oct., M.-F. 10-12, 1.30-4. June-Aug., M.-Sa. 10-12, 2-4. Closed Queen's Birthday.

MUNICIPAL ORPHANAGE
Poststraat 45, Zierikzee, Zeeland
House (1531). Louis XV furniture. Paintings. Pewter.
Daily 9-5.

ZOELEN

SOELEN CASTLE
Zoelen, Gelderland
17th-18th century French, Dutch furniture, Chinese porcelain. Delftware. 18th century silver. 17th-19th century paintings.
Aug. 20 - June 9, M., W., F. 10-12, by written application.

ZUTPHEN

LIBRARY OF ST. WALBURG'S CHURCH
Kerkelijk Bureau der Herv. Gemeente, Lange Hofstraat 7, Zutphen, Gelderland
Library room (1564). Manuscripts. Incunabulae.
M.-F., guided tours, 10-4.

MUNICIPAL MUSEUM
Rozengracht 3, Zutphen, Gelderland
History of Zutphen area. Archaeology. Architectural items. Maps. Prints. Silver. Glass. Tiles. Coins. Medals. Costumes. 19th century period rooms, apothecary's shop. Toys.
Tu.-Sa. 10-12.30, 2-5; Su. 3-5. Closed Sa. p.m. Nov.-Mar., Good Friday, Jan. 1, Queen's Birthday.

ZWARTSLUIS

SCHOONEWELLE NATURAL HISTORY MUSEUM
Zomerdijk 13, Zwartsluis, Overijssel
Wildlife of the region. Birds. Mammals. Butterflies. Eggs.
M.-Sa. 9-12, 2-5.30.

ZWOLLE

OVERIJSSEL PROVINCIAL MUSEUM
Melkmarkt 41, Zwolle, Overijssel
Prehistory and history of Overijssel. Topography. Manuscripts. 16th-20th century paintings by Overijssel artists. Silver. Furniture. Porcelain. Glass. Costumes. Coins. Medals. 17th-19th century period rooms.
M.-Sa. 10-5; Su. 2-5. Closed Jan. 1 and the first day of two-day public holidays.

PASSION FLOWER MILL
Vondelkade, Zwolle, Overijssel
Operating windmill (1776). Local crafts and trades.
May-Sept., M.-Sa. 10-5.

NETHERLANDS ANTILLES

The group of islands known as the Netherlands Antilles exists almost entirely on the income obtained from tourists and from oil refining. The one museum in Curaçao has nothing to suggest either of these two sources of revenue, and confines itself to paintings and to history.

CURAÇAO

CURAÇAO MUSEUM
Curaçao
Paintings. Historical collections.
Daily ex. M. 9-12, 2-5.

NEW ZEALAND

Until comparatively recently, the major provincial museums in New Zealand were mostly restricted to Polynesian and Maori collections, natural history and some Greek and Roman material. The opening of the Canterbury Colonists Galleries in the Canterbury Museum, Christchurch, in 1959, marked the beginning of a new and more professional interest in the recent past. Between 1958 and 1966 the number of art galleries and museums nearly doubled. Most of this increase was in small local history collections, several in the former gold-field areas, and often first got together to celebrate a centenary.

New Zealand, like Australia, is characterised by what could be not unfairly or unkindly described as all-sorts museums, museums containing, often cheek by jowl, early telephones, Bishop Selwyn's folding bed, a bicycle made by a local blacksmith, relics of Chinese miners, a 19th century printing-press and once-venerated pieces of Victorian china- the fascinating raw material amassed by a country in the process of discovering its identity and forming its own distinctive national culture. There is a great deal of Europe in its museums, from English and Italian paintings and musical instruments to the largest collection of Dumas manuscripts outside the Bibliothèque Nationale in Paris, looking a little strange and far away from home in the midst of gold-mining relics, early missionary equipment and carved Kauri-gum.

At present, one cannot say that New Zealand's museums provide anything like a complete picture of the country's development, or of the economic basis of its life. There are several excellent geological museums, the early settlement is reasonably well covered, gold-mining even better, and Maori culture is not neglected, but there is no museum or collection which does anything like justice to maritime history or to the exceedingly important agricultural and horticultural industries, although one can learn much and in great detail about the damage done to agriculture and horticulture by rabbits, deer, goats, birds and opossums, and about climate and soils.

Apart from Captain Cook, New Zealand seems to be short of great men to celebrate in its museums. One has the impression of a remarkably even-textured society, with few notabilities large or important enough even to qualify for museum attention. This is, no doubt, one of the unexpected problems which a thorough-going democracy has to face.

AKAROA

LANGLOIS-ETEVENEAUX HOUSE
Corner Rue Lavaud and Rue Balguerie, Akaroa, Canterbury Province
Known as 'Canterbury's Oldest House'. French furnishings, household goods and costumes of the 1840s, agricultural implements and equipment, colonial kitchen alcove, European uniforms and weapons, china, silver. Maori ethnological relics.
Summer: M.-Su. 1.15-5. Winter: M.-Su. 1.30-4; or by appointment.

ALEXANDRA

ALEXANDRA MUSEUM
Walton Street, Alexandra, Otago Province
Relics of the pioneering and gold mining periods. Photographs.
M.-F. 2-4; F. also 7-9.

ARROWTOWN

LAKES DISTRICT CENTENNIAL MUSEUM
Buckingham Street, Arrowtown, Otago Province
Gold and mineral specimens. Goldminers' tools and implements. Relics of the Chinese miners. Household articles. Local history from 1862 onwards. Agricultural implements. Vehicles.
Daily 9-12.30, 1.30-5. Closed Su. morning June-July.

ARTHUR'S PASS

ARTHUR'S PASS NATIONAL PARK MUSEUM
Arthur's Pass, Canterbury Province
Natural history of the Park. Historical exhibits related to the district.
Daily 8-5.

AUCKLAND

AUCKLAND CENTRAL PUBLIC LIBRARY
Wellesley Street East, Auckland 1
Medieval manuscripts. Books printed by Caxton. Shakespeare first folio of 1623. Alexander Dumas manuscripts. Musical scores and literature. Manuscripts in Maori dealing with tribal genealogies.
M.-F. 9.30-9; Sa. 9.30-8; Su. 2-6.

AUCKLAND CITY ART GALLERY
Wellesley Street East, Auckland 1
16th-17th century European drawings and prints; 19th and 20th century European paintings, prints and sculpture; 19th and 20th century British drawings. The New Zealand section contains paintings, drawings, prints and sculpture from the time of Captain Cook's voyages to the present day. Contemporary American drawings and prints. 20th century Japanese prints.
M. 12-4.30; Tu.-Th. 10-4.30; F. 10-8.30; Sa. 10-4.30; Su. 2-4.30.

AUCKLAND WAR MEMORIAL MUSEUM
The Domain, Auckland 1
Maori and general ethnology. Geology. Botany. Zoology, with emphasis on New Zealand and adjacent Pacific region. Applied arts. Maritime Hall. History of weapons and the Armed Services. Centennial Street of 1866.
Summer: M.-Sa. 10-5. Winter: M.-Sa. 10-4.15. Su. all the year 11-5.

EWELME COTTAGE
14 Ayr Street, Parnell, Auckland 1
Built in 1864 by the Rev. Vicesimus Lush and lived in by his descendants until 1968. Now restored with original furniture and effects, including William Morris wallpaper.
Daily 10.30-12.30, 1.30-4.30.

FENCIBLE COTTAGE
Garden of Memories, Unxbridge Road, Howick, Auckland
Part of the cottage is furnished in the style of 1848, the other in later Victorian style.
Su. 2.30-4.30.

'JOURNEY'S END' COTTAGE AND MUSEUM
Jellicoe Park, Onehunga, Auckland 6
Erected from plans dated 1847, the cottage has been reerected in Jellicoe Park. The kitchen, parlour and two bedrooms are furnished with authentic period items, and there is a display of photographs, maps and information about the early history of the district.
Opening times uncertain: enquire locally.

MELANESIAN MISSION MUSEUM
Tamaki Drive, Mission Bay, Auckland 5
Melanesian weapons and other artefacts from the British Solomon Islands. Relics of Bishop Patterson, martyred in 1871.
Tu. and Th. 2-4.30; Sa. 10.30-12; Su. 2-4.30. Other times by arrangement.

MUSEUM OF TRANSPORT AND TECHNOLOGY
Great North Road and Meola Road, Western Springs, Auckland 3
Established in 1964 around the nucleus of a pumping-station built in 1876 for the city water supply. Industrial and domestic technology, engineering and physical science associated with the history of New Zealand since European settlement. Sections include road transport, rail and tramway, aviation, communications, general engineering, agriculture, photographic, printing and graphic arts, business and office equipment. Colonial village.
Daily 9-5.

PLANT DISEASES DIVISION
Department of Scientific and Industrial Research, 120 Mount Albert Road, Auckland 3
Mycological (fungal) herbarium specialising in plant-pathogenic fungi: New Zealand rusts, smuts, Gasteromycetes, Polyporaceae, Thelephoraceae and Hypocreales.
M.-F. 8-4.35.

THE TREATY HOUSE
179 Green Lane West, Green Lane, Auckland 5
Historical material relating to early 19th century New Zealand. Copy of the Treaty of Waitangi. Military relics. Letter of indent signed by Captain James Cook. European and Oriental brass.
Daily 11-4.30.

AVARUA (RAROTONGA)

COOK ISLANDS LIBRARY AND MUSEUM
near Church, Avarua, Rarotonga, Cook Islands
Cook Islands artifacts. Shells and natural history exhibits. Photographic collection of the Islands' history. Historical printing machinery and stamps.
M.-F. 10-5; Tu., Th. also 7-8.30 p.m.; Sa. 9-12 noon.

BLENHEIM

RENWICK MUSEUM
High Street, Renwick, Blenheim, Marlborough Province
Relics of early New Zealand pioneers. The exhibits include the first bicycle made locally by a blacksmith (J. Borbeck).
Daily 8-5.

RIVERLANDS COB COTTAGE
P.O. Box 308, Blenheim, Marlborough Province
Restored cottage of 1865 furnished in the style of 1860-1880.
Daily during daylight hours.

BURNHAM

MEDICAL CORPS MUSEUM
Medical Corps Depot, Burnham Camp, nr. Christchurch, Canterbury Province
History of the Medical Corps.
By arrangement.

CAMBRIDGE

MUSEUM OF THE CAMBRIDGE HISTORICAL SOCIETY
Town Hall, Leamington, Cambridge, Auckland Province
Maori artifacts of local history, including a scale model of Je Totara Pah, which Captain James Cook mentioned in his log book on his journey round New Zealand. Souvenirs of early settlers in the district.
Su. afternoons and F. evenings. By arrangement for parties.

CHRISTCHURCH

BOTANY DIVISION
Department of Scientific and Industrial Research, Lincoln, nr. Christchurch, Canterbury Province
Native, adventive and cultivated plants of New Zealand. Phanerogams and cryptogams excluding fungi. Seed herbarium. Pollen and spore collections.
M.-F. 8.30-4.30.

CANTERBURY MUSEUM
Rolleston Avenue, Christchurch, Canterbury Province
World collections in geology (mineralogy and palaeontology), zoology (notably birds and mammals) and ethnology (from Somalia to Brazil). Archaeology collections, notably Wairau Bar Moa-hunter material. Maori and Polynesian ethnology and archaeology. Melanesian ethnology. Domestic relics of the British settlement of Canterbury. Furniture and domestic fine arts of Britain to the Stuart period. Relics of pioneer Antarctic exploration. Local shipping and whaling exhibits. Firearms. New Zealand stamps, coins and tokens.
M.-Sa. 10-4.30; Su. 2-4.30.

CANTERBURY PUBLIC LIBRARY
Corner Cambridge Terrace and Hereford Street, Christchurch, Canterbury Province
Mainly mid-20th century New Zealand paintings and lithographs. British and German mid-20th century lithographs. Commercially published prints.
M.-F. 10-9; Su. 2-5, 7-9; Sa. 9.30-11.30.

THE FERRYMEAD TRUST
P.O. Box 81, Christchurch, Canterbury Province
Applied arts and science exhibits, including restored examples of transport and technology such as a steam tram and a full-sized replica of a Lunar Landing Module. Operating tramway and railway. Working examples of restored vehicles, machinery and scientific equipment.
Weekends, or by special arrangement during week.

ROBERT MCDOUGALL ART GALLERY
Botanic Gardens, Rolleston Avenue, Christchurch, Canterbury Province
British late 19th and early 20th century paintings and watercolours, 20th century British etchings. Early and contemporary New Zealand paintings, watercolours and drawings, including a number by Sydney L. Thompson; Maori paintings by C. F. Goldie; Works by Petrus van der Velden, Graphics. Miniatures. Sculpture. Pottery.
M.-Sa. 10-4.30; Su. 2-4.30.

UNIVERSITY OF CANTERBURY
James Logie Memorial Collection, Hereford Street, Christchurch, Canterbury Province
Collection of Greek pottery and related material, maintained for teaching purposes.
By prior telephone appointment.

DEPARTMENTS OF BOTANY, GEOLOGY AND ZOOLOGY
University of Canterbury, Christchurch, Canterbury Province
Teaching collections of botany, geology and zoology.
By application to the Professors of the Departments.

CLYDE

VINCENT COUNTY AND DUNSTAN GOLDFIELDS MUSEUM
Clyde, Otago Province
Former second Court House (1864). Dock leg irons, gaol door and other relics. Pioneer household goods and clothing. Books on mining. Mineral specimens including nuggets and goldsand. Photograph room.
Daily except M. 2-4; or by prior arrangement for tours and students of history.

COROMANDEL

SCHOOL OF MINES MUSEUM
Kapanga Road, Coromandel, Auckland Province
Material on history of gold mining. Photographs of mines. Relics of Kauri timber, when it was worked on the peninsula. Old mining books, plans and newspapers.
Christmas-Easter, Daily 2-4. Easter-Labour Weekend, Sa. and Su. 2-4. Labour Weekend, Daily 2-4. Labour Weekend-Christmas, Sa. and Su. 2-4.

DARGAVILLE

DARGAVILLE MUSEUM
Normanby Street, Dargaville, Auckland Province
Maori artifacts. Kauri gum. Local historical photographs. Pioneer and early shipping relics.
Daily 2-4.

DUNEDIN

DUNEDIN PUBLIC ART GALLERY
Logan place, Dunedin, Otago Province
British and European drawings, paintings, landscapes and portraits (16th-19th century). Works by Frances Hodgkins; 18th and 19th century British watercolours. New Zealand paintings and watercolours. Ceramics. Textiles. Furniture. Prints. Contemporary graphics.
M.-Th. 10-4.30; Sa. 10-5; Su. 2-5. Public holidays 10-5.

DUNEDIN PUBLIC LIBRARY
Moray Place, Dunedin, Otago Province
Japanese and Chinese prints. Illuminated manuscripts. Reproductions of old and modern masters.
M.-F. 9.30-9.30; Sa. 9.30-12.

HOCKEN LIBRARY
University of Otago, Hocken Wing, Otago Museum, Great King Street, Dunedin, Otago Province
Early books, newspapers, maps, manuscripts and pictures relating to New Zealand and the Pacific. New Zealand paintings, prints and sketch-books from 1779. Post 1930 New Zealand paintings.
M.-F. 9-5; Sa. 9-12.

OTAGO EARLY SETTLERS' ASSOCIATION (INC)
Museum and Portrait Gallery, Lower High Street, Dunedin, Otago Province
Displays on early settlement in Otago. Early printing press and lithographic press. Model pioneer cottage. Paintings and lithographs of early Dunedin. Portrait collection of pre-1869 settlers. Transport (locomotives).
M.-F. 9-4.30; Sa. 10-4.

OTAGO MUSEUM
Great King Street, Dunedin, Otago Province
Zoology. Geology. Botany. Physical anthropology. Archaeology. Ethnology. Technology. Numismatics. Maori war canoe and meeting house. Hawaiian royal feather cape. Japanese and Korean ceramics. Egyptian, classical and West European antiquities. West European furniture.
Sept.-Apr. M.-Sa. 10-5. May-Aug. M.-Sa. 10-4.30; Su. all year 2-4.

THE THEOMIN GALLERY (OLVESTON)
42 Royal Terrace, Dunedin, Otago Province
Four-storeyed Jacobean style house designed by Sir Ernest George (1904-6). Rooms furnished in original style, and

include oak, mahogany and satinwood furniture, paintings, sculpture, china, ceramics, bronzes, brassware, weapons, Persian rugs. Kitchenware from Edwardian times.
M.-F. 10.40-4; Sa. 10.30-4; Su. 2-4.

UNIVERSITY OF OTAGO
Great King Street, Dunedin, Otago Province
Botany, Geology and Zoology teaching and reference collections.
On written application.

GISBORNE

ART GALLERY AND MUSEUM
18 Stout Street, Gisborne, Auckland Province
Paintings by New Zealand artists. Prints of European paintings. Maori artifacts. Local relics of early European settlement. Early photographs. Natural history.
Daily 2-4.30.

GREYMOUTH

GREYMOUTH RETURNED SERVICES ASSOCIATION WAR MUSEUM
187 Tainui Street, Greymouth, Westland Province
Weapons, uniforms, medals, badges, photographs and war relics.
By appointment.

HAMILTON

WAIKATO GALLERY
Grantham Street, Hamilton, Auckland Province
European and New Zealand paintings and sculpture. Collection of drawings by English artists.
M.-Th. 11-4.30; F. 11-8.30; Su. 2-4.30.

WAIKATO MUSEUM
Barton Street, Hamilton, Auckland Province
Maori artifacts. Kauri gum. Mineral specimens. Shells. Coins. Hunting trophies. Local history.
M.-F. 11-3.30; Su. 2-5.

HAVELOCK

HAVELOCK MILLING MUSEUM
Lions Club, Havelock
Local history. Milling. Home distilling. Mining. Farming. Early home life. Working engines and machines, including 1912 Hornby engine, petrol-driven.
Daily 9-5.

HOKITIKA

WEST COAST HISTORICAL MUSEUM
Public Library Building, Hamilton Street, Hokitika, Westland Province
Mining and mineral displays; documents, drawings, photographs and maps. Timber and wild life of the area.
M.-F. 10-12, 2-5; F. also 7-9. Other times by arrangement.

INVERCARGILL

INVERCARGILL PUBLIC ART GALLERY
Anderson Park, Invercargill, Otago Province
New Zealand paintings of the last 25 years; 19th and 20th century watercolours of Invercargill and South. European paintings.
Tu., Th., Sa., Su. and public holidays, 2-4.30.

SOUTHLAND MUSEUM
Victoria Avenue, Invercargill, Otago Province
Southland's natural history. Ethnography. Pioneering relics. Maori section. Paintings and reproductions.
M.-Sa. 10-4.30. W. evening 6.30-8.30; Su. 2-4.30.

KAIKOURA

KAIKOURA MUSEUM
Kaikoura
In old wooden church. Relics of whaling days. Domestic equipment.
Open 2 p.m. on certain days. Enquire locally.

KAITAIA

FAR NORTH REGIONAL MUSEUM
Centennial Buildings, South Road, Kaitaia, Auckland Province
Early district history, especially Maori. Early missionary and Dalmatian settlements. Industry.
M.-Sa. 11-4.30.

LOWER HUTT

ANIMAL ECOLOGY DIVISION
Department of Scientific and Industrial Research, N.I.M.U. Building, Laings Road, Lower Hutt, Wellington Province
Ecology and behaviour of rabbits and hares. Bird damage to agriculture and horticulture; ecology and movement of red deer; ecology of goats, opposums, rodents and birds. Mammal skins.
M.-F. 8.30-5.

THE DOWSE ART GALLERY
P.O. Box 30396, Lower Hutt, Wellington Province
New Zealand painting, sculpture, prints and ceramics. New Zealand pottery.
Daily except M. 10-4.30. Weekend 1-4.30. Closed Christmas Day.

NEW ZEALAND GEOLOGICAL SURVEY
Department of Scientific and Industrial Research, State Insurance Building, Andrews Avenue, Lower Hutt, Wellington Province
New Zealand and foreign rock types, including comprehensive range of samples from Antarctica, the Sub-Antarctic Islands and outlying island areas in the Pacific. Marine fossil invertebrates from New Zealand. Fossil and recent foreign molluscs. Fossil plant collection.
M.-F. 8-4.30.

MASTERTON

WAIRARAPA ARTS CENTRE
Bruce Street, Masterton
Painting by MacDiarmid, prints by John Drawbridge, Gary Tricker and Barry Cleavin and drawings by M. T. Woolaston. Work in copper by Barbara Hepworth, "Galliard" - Forms in Movement. Aquatint by Georges Roualt, "Hoani Rangitakaiwaho" by Gottfried Lindauer and "Pot" by Takeichi Kawai.
M.-F. 1-5; Sa. and Su. 2-4.30.

MATAKOHE

OTAMATEA KAURI AND PIONEER MUSEUM
between Maungaturoto and Dargaville, State Highway 12, Matakohe, Auckland Province
Kauri gum. Colour enlargements showing the 'Story of the Kauri' and a display of kauri, rimu and other native timbers in panel form. Large artifacts of the kauri timber industry. Rooms furnished with kauri furniture.
Daily 10-4. Closed Christmas Day.

MURCHISON

MURCHISON MUSEUM
Murchison, Nelson-Marlborough
History of the district. Gold-mining. Mementoes of the earthquake (1929).
On request.

NAPIER

HAWKE'S BAY ART GALLERY AND MUSEUM
Herschel Street, Napier, Hawke's Bay Province
Local history. Maori and Polynesian artifacts. Early Hawke's Bay home and farm equipment. Natural history exhibits. Maori and European painting and sculpture. Early New Zealand books. Native flower paintings. Furniture. Porcelain. Silver, and Moa Hunter artifacts collection.
M.-F. 12.30-4.30; Sa., Su. and public holidays, 2.30-4.

NASEBY

MANIOTOTO EARLY SETTLERS' MUSEUM
Leven Street and Earwe Street, Naseby, Otago Province
Specimens from the School of Mines which was in Naseby until 1902. Gold, implements for collecting and weighing gold. Household articles of the gold-mining days.
Daily 2-4.

NELSON

BISHOP SUTER ART GALLERY
Queen's Gardens, Bridge Street, Nelson
Water-colour drawings by John Gully (1819-1888) and J. C. Richmond (1827-1898). Modern English and European paintings, drawings.
Dec.-Feb. Daily 10-4. Mar.-Nov. Daily 12-4.

CAWTHRON INSTITUTE MUSEUM
170 Milton Street, Nelson
Exhibitions cover climate, soils, Maori agriculture, native and exotic vegetation, local crops, animal husbandry, local geology, rocks and commercial minerals.
Tu., Th., F. 2-5; Su. and all public holidays 2-4.30.

ENTOMOLOGY DIVISION
Department of Scientific and Industrial Research, 108 Halifax Street, Nelson
Collection of diptera, lepidoptera, coleoptera and other insect orders. Aphid Collection.
M.-F. 8.30-12, 1-5.

ISEL HOUSE
Isel Park, Stoke, Nelson
Display of the pioneering, civic and mineral development of Nelson. Silver and Sheffield ware. Ceramics. Furniture.
Sa. and Su. 2-4.

NELSON PROVINCIAL MUSEUM
Hardy Street, Nelson
Maori and pioneer relics of the Province, including Bishop Selwyn's folding bed and Lord Rutherford's cot. Mineral collection. Foreign molluscs.
M.-F. 9.30-5. Closed Sa., Su. and public holidays.

NEW PLYMOUTH

THE GABLES
(Old Colonial Hospital), Brooklands Drive, New Plymouth, Taranaki Province
The Dispensary contains local history exhibits from 1849 onwards. Jewellery.
Tu., Th., Sa. and Su. 2-4.

GOVETT-BREWSTER ART GALLERY
Queen Street, P.O. Box 647, New Plymouth, Taranaki Province
Contemporary paintings, sculpture, drawings, prints and other items from countries bordering and in the Pacific. At present, New Zealand, Australia and America are well represented.
Tu.-Th. 10-5; F. 10-5 and 6-9; Sa. 10-12, 1-5; Su. 1-5.

RICHMOND COTTAGE
Corner Brougham and Ariki Streets, New Plymouth, Taranaki Province
A stone cottage of three rooms with a roof of wooden tiles, built in 1853-4 and furnished with relics of that period, as well as the complete library of William Devenish who arrived in New Zealand in 1842.
M.-F. 2-4; Su. 2-4.

TARANAKI MUSEUM
War Memorial Building, Brougham Street, New Plymouth, Taranaki Province
Maori artifacts including large woodcarvings. Household relics, weapons, tools and other items of the early settlers. Natural history exhibits of the area.
M.-F. 1-4; School holidays 11-4; Su. 2-4.

NORSEWOOD

NORSEWOOD PIONEER MUSEUM
North Norsewood, Norsewood, Hawke's Bay Province
The display illustrates the early settlers' household, farming and milling equipment, and the history of the Scandinavian settlement.
Daily 9-5.

OAMARU

NORTH OTAGO PIONEER GALLERY
64 Thames Street, Oamaru, Otago Province
Collection of pioneer and early settlers' relics, domestic and industrial. The Thomas Forester Laboratory Equipment for research into the district's datomaceaous deposits (1886-1890). New Zealand Post Office Collection of early telephones. Historical photographs and records.
F. 2-4; or by appointment.

OBAN

RAKIURA MUSEUM
Ayr Street, Halfmoon Bay, Oban, Stewart Island
Display on the early whaling period; tools, harpoons, bombguns, ambergris, whales' teeth and scrimshaw. Samples of tin and gold from Port Pegasus. Miners' tools. Relics of early saw-mills. Personal relics of Capt. J. B. Greig and the Rev. J. H. Wohlers. Maori artifacts. Photographs and paintings of early settlers, whaling ships, ferry boats, and of Stewart Island.
Hours dependent on Bluff-Stewart Island ferry timetable. Mar.-Dec. every Tu. and F., more frequently in summer.

ONGAONGA

ONGAONGA OLD SCHOOL MUSEUM
Highway 50, Ongaonga, Hawke's Bay Province
Half the museum is set up as a classroom furnished in the period 1875 to 1886, the rest exhibits relics of pioneering

days, including firearms from the Maori Wars, kitchen utensils, sewing machines, historic sword, bound copies of the *New Zealand Times* of 1879, a phonograph and photographs.
Su. afternoon or by request at local store or Post Office.

PAIHIA

TREATY HOUSE
Waitangi National Reserve, Paihia, Bay of Islands
Portraits of people of both races significant in the development of New Zealand from 1830 onwards. Paintings, drawings and prints of Maori chiefs and scenes of Maori life as well as documents and relics relating to this period.
Daily 10-5.

PALMERSTON NORTH

PALMERSTON NORTH ART GALLERY
Corner Grey and Carroll Streets, Palmerston North, Wellington Province
Painting and water-colours by New Zealand artists. Prints. Bronzes. Wood sculptures.
M.-F. 12-5; F. evening 7.30-9; Su. 2-5.

PICTON

RAI VALLEY PIONEER HOUSE
Tennyson Inlet Road, Picton, Marlborough Province
Pioneer house with period furnishings.
Continuously.

SMITH MEMORIAL MUSEUM
Foreshore, Picton, Marlborough Province
Maori artifacts. Whaling relics. Early colonial household effects. Maps and old photographs of the district.
Nov.-Mar. M.-Sa. 10.30-4.30; Apr.-Oct. Su. only 2-4.

PUKEKOHE

PIONEER MEMORIAL COTTAGE
Roulston Park, Pukekohe, Auckland Province
The cottage contains colonial furniture and relics of early local settlements.
Sa., Su. and public holidays (except Good Friday and Christmas Day), 2-4. Other times by appointment.

QUEENSTOWN

THE OLD HOUSE
Beach Street, Queenstown, Otago Province
A privately owned house furnished in mid-Victorian style. Pioneer household relics and clothing. Gold miners' relics and equipment. Collection of kerosene lamps.
Dec.-Mar. Daily 10.30-9. Apr.-Dec. M.-Sa. 1.30-4; or by appointment.

RANGIORA

RANGIORA AND DISTRICT EARLY RECORDS SOCIETY MUSEUM
60 Ayers Street, Rangiora, Canterbury Province
Local history.
W. and Su. 2-4.30; or by special request for parties.

REEFTON

BLACK'S POINT MUSEUM
Black's Point, Reefton, Nelson Province
Gold mining equipment.
Daily 2-4 or by arrangement.

ROTORUA

MAORI PA
Whakarewarewa Village, Rotorua, Auckland Province
Work produced by the Maori Arts and Crafts Institute.
Daily 8.30-5.30. These hours may vary in winter.

ROTORUA CITY MUSEUM
Tudor Towers Building, P.O. Box 627, Rotorua, Auckland Province
Maori culture. Colonial cottage. Photographs. Watercolours. Geology and forestry of the Volcanic Plateau. Wildlife.
M.-F. 9-4.45; Sa. and Su. 10-4.

TE AMORANGI MUSEUM
35 Robinsons Avenue, Holdens Bay, Rotorua, Auckland Province
Housed in the Dutch Colonial-style house built for Major Hannah, after whom Hannah's Bay was named. The collection includes Maori artifacts. Missionary, armed constabulary and pioneer material. Whaling relics, including ships' logs.
By appointment.

RUSSELL

CAPTAIN COOK MEMORIAL MUSEUM
incorporating Russell Centennial Museum, York Street, Russell, Bay of Islands
Relics of Captain Cook. Local relics of early European settlement. Maori culture and war relics. Whaling gear. Bushman's tools. Scrimshaw. Household articles.
Boxing Day to first M. in June, M.-Sa. 10-12, 2-4; Su. 2-4. From 1st M. in June to Christmas Eve, open on request. Closed Christmas Day and Good Friday.

POMPALLIER HOUSE
The Strand, Russell, Bay of Islands
Relics of French missions. Catholic Mission printing. Whaling exhibits. Furniture.
Daily 10-12.30, 2-5.

TAURANGA

THE ELMS OR THE MISSION HOUSE
Middion Street, Tauranga, Auckland Province
Collection of buildings dating from 1838, including the Mission House, the Library and the Belfry. Mission equipment and records. Household and personal items.
Daily except Su. at 2 p.m. for conducted tour (1 hr.). Gardens open during daylight hours M.-Sa.

TE AWAMUTU

GAVIN GIFFORD MEMORIAL MUSEUM
Teasdale Street, Te Awamutu, Auckland Province
Maori collections. Local and missionary history. Waikato war relics.
M.-F. 1.30-3.30; Su. 2-4.

THAMES

THAMES MINERALOGICAL MUSEUM
Corner Cochrane and Brown Streets, Thames, Auckland Province
Specimens of ores, minerals, metals. Fossils. Semi-precious stones. Carved Kauri gum. Models of mining machinery. Tools, photographs and relics of local gold mining days. Exhibits from the Broken Hill and Mount Morgan mines in Australia.
M.-Sa. 2-4. 26 Dec. - 3 Jan. also 10-12.

TIMARU

AIGANTIGHE ART GALLERY
49 Wai-iti Road, Timaru, Canterbury Province
New Zealand paintings from 1910 to the present day. Prints. Drawings. Sculpture. New Zealand pottery.
Tu., W., Th., Sa. and Su. 2-4.30.

SOUTH CANTERBURY CENTENNIAL MUSEUM
4 Perth Street, Timaru, Canterbury Province
Early settlers' domestic equipment. Furniture. Costumes. China. Paintings. Maps. Sporting and agricultural trophies. Maori artifacts. Development of the port of Timaru.
Tu., W., F. and Su. 2-4.30.

WAIHI

WAIHI ARTS CENTRE AND MUSEUM
Kenny Street, Waihi, Auckland Province
Local mining relics and records, 1875 to 1955. Maps and plans of the workings. Geological specimens from the former Waihi School of Mines. Paintings, drawings, photographs and records of the Ohinemuri district. Radio equipment.
Labour Day-Easter, M.-F. 10.30-4; Su. 1.30-4. Easter-Labour Day Tu.-F. 1-4; Su. 1.30-4. Closed Good Fri. and Christmas Day.

WAIMATE

THE CUDDY
Gorge Road, Waimate, Canterbury Province
The first European home in the Waimate district. It is constructed of totara slabs and cob, thatched with snowgrass, with a sod chimney.
A cob building 30 miles from Waimate is a further museum project.
During daytime: no fixed hours.

WAIMATE HISTORICAL MUSEUM
Harris Street, Waimate, Canterbury Province
Pioneer household and farm implements. Machinery. Farm vehicles. Relics from gold-digging times. Firearms. 1914-18 war relics. Maori artifacts. Local history.
Su. 2-4, or by appointment.

WAIMATE NORTH

WAIMATE MISSION HOUSE
Te Ahuahu Road, Waimate North, Bay of Islands
The Mission House was first occupied in 1832 and is the second oldest house in New Zealand. It has been completely restored and furnished in period style.
Daily 10-12.30, 2-5. Closed Christmas Day and Good Friday.

WAIOURU

ARMY MUSEUM
Signposted on Desert Road section of the Auckland-Wellington Main Highway, Waiouru, Wellington Province
Military uniforms, weapons, equipment, badges, medals, documents and photographs.
By appointment.

WAIPU

PIONEERS' MEMORIAL MUSEUM
Main State Highway 1, Waipu, Auckland Province
Local pioneering relics. Maori artifacts. Polished Kauri gum. War relics. Genealogies of original clans who settled in Waipu. Documents. Photographs.
M.-Sa. 10-12, 1-4.

WAIUKU

WAIUKU MUSEUM
King Street, Waiuku, Auckland Province
Household and farm articles of the pioneering period. Firearms used in the Maori wars. Photographs.
Sa and Su. 1.30-4. Other days by arrangement.

WANGANUI

SARJEANT ART GALLERY
Queen's Park, Wanganui, Wellington Province
New Zealand paintings, watercolours and prints of the 19th and 20th century. British paintings, watercolours, prints and cartoons of 19th and 20th century. European paintings, drawings.
M.-F. 10-4; Sa. 10-12.30; Su. 2-4.

WANGANUI PUBLIC MUSEUM
Queen's Park, Wanganui, Wellington Province
Maori and Polynesian artifacts and a War Canoe. New Zealand and overseas birds. Moa and whale skeletons. Fish. Shells. Minerals. Entomological specimens. Firearms. Medals. Coins. Early Colonial relics. South Pacific, Eastern and early civilisation exhibits. Paintings by Gottfried Lindauer. Drawings. Photographs.
M.-F. 10-5; Sa. and Su. 1-5. Closed Christmas Day and Good Friday.

WELLINGTON

ALEXANDER TURNBULL LIBRARY
Bowen Street, Wellington
Pacific Collection of history, ethnology, literature and early voyaging, with particular emphasis on New Zealand. Paintings and prints of historical and topographical significance.
M.-Th. 9-8; F. 9-5; Sa. 9-12. Closed Su. and public holidays.

DOMINION MUSEUM
Buckle Street, Wellington
Geology and palaeontology. Herbarium. Entomology. Molluscs. Crustacea. Fish. Birds. Marine mammals (skeletons). Oceanic and New Zealand ethnography from 1769. European life in New Zealand up to 1900.
M.-Sa. 10-5; Su. 1-5.

NATIONAL ART GALLERY
Buckle Street, Wellington
New Zealand, Australian, British and foreign 19th and 20th century paintings, drawings and sculpture. Etchings and engravings. British watercolours of 18th-19th centuries. New Zealand watercolours, paintings and drawings.
M.-Sa. 10-5; Su. 1-5.

NEW ZEALAND OCEANOGRAPHIC INSTITUTE
Department of Scientific and Industrial Research, 177 Thorndon Quay, Wellington
Research collection comprising samples gathered in the course of work on benthic ecology and sedimentation from the New Zealand Shelf and Slope, New Zealand Plateau, Macquarie Ridge, Ross Sea and tropical Pacific.
M.-F. 8.30-5.

VICTORIA UNIVERSITY OF WELLINGTON
Kelburn Parade and Salamanca Road, Wellington
Teaching collections in the Departments of Botany, Geology and Zoology.
By written appointment only.

THE ZILLAH AND RONALD CASTLE COLLECTION OF EARLY AND UNIQUE INSTRUMENTS AND MUSIC
27 Colombo Street, Newtown, Wellington
Over 300 keyboard, string, wind, percussion and folk instruments from all over the world, including an 18th century Kirkmann harpsichord, a 17th century Stanesby tenor recorder, hurdy-gurdy. Clementi square piano, dulcimers, as well as Asian and European folk instruments.
By appointment.

WELLSFORD

ALBERTLAND CENTENNIAL MEMORIAL MUSEUM
Port Albert Domain, Wellsford, Auckland Province
The collection includes domestic relics, firearms, farm implements, tools, Maori artifacts, printing press and photographs from the pioneering period.
Daily.

WHANGAREI

CLAPHAM CLOCK COLLECTION MUSEUM
Cafler Avenue, Whangarei, Auckland Province
Collection of clocks from all parts of the world.
M.-F. 10-12.30, 1.30-4.30; Sa. and Su. 10-12, 1.30-3.

WHANGAREI CITY COUNCIL MUSEUM
Cafler Avenue, Whangarei, Auckland Province
Tools gathered by the pre-World War I Kauri Bushmen's Association. Pioneer relics. Flora and fauna of Northland and the off-shore islands.
Dec.-Feb. M.-F. 10-4. Mar.-Nov. W., Th., F. 10-4.

Nicaragua

Before the earthquake of December 1972, Nicaragua had nine museums which were open to the public as of right, and thirty-seven private and institutional collections which could be occasionally visited by special permission. In due course and under the pressure of taxation, most of these private collections will no doubt pass into some form of public ownership, but meanwhile we do not feel able to classify them as museums according to the criteria we have been using. In this special case, we have decided to mention the names of the owners of these collections, in case visitors to these towns should feel inclined to make a personal approach.

It should be emphasised that the earthquake destruction in Managua, the capital, was very severe, and at the time of going to press it is still not possible to establish how many museums and private collections were damaged or obliterated, or how many are once again functioning. So far as Managua is concerned, the details which follow should therefore be treated with caution. The information was, however, correct in October 1972.

Mr Paco Guerra Morice *Chinandega*
Mr Montealegre *Granada*
Mr Enrique Fernandez
Dr Lorenzo Guerrero
Mr Enrique Marin
Dr Carlos Cuadra Pasos
Dr Manuel Vélez *Juigalpa*
Intellectual Society *Léon*
Ruben Dario Cultural Club
National University
Hermano Alvarado Sarria *Managua*
Mr D. R. Ballantynes
Mr Mario Belli
Mr Alfredo Bequillard
Don Francisco Bunge
Mr Juan Caligaris
Mr Pablo Antonio Cuadra
Mr Endekre
Dr Fernando Fuentes
Dr Julio Gómez
Mrs Melita Heinz
Hermano Hildeberto Maria
Mr Mauricio Marragou
Mr José Mateu
Ministry of Public Education
Don Fritz Morlock
National Tourist Board
Dr Navarro
Mr Gerardo O. Nissen
Mr Enrique Pallais
Col. Lazlo Pataky
Mr Ivan Osorio Peters
Mr Ubaldo Rios
Dr Ramiro Sánchez
Dr Samuel Santos
Sengelman Company
Mr Roberto Spislinger *Rivas*

The museums proper, mostly belonging to religious organisations, are as follows.

DIRIAMBA

MUSEUM OF THE INSTITUTE OF EDUCATION
Diriamba
In College of the La Salle Brothers. Natural sciences. Historical collections.
By appointment.

GRANADA

ARCHAEOLOGICAL MUSEUM
Colegio Centro América, Granada
In Jesuit College. Archaeology of Nicaragua, especially the Department of Granada.
By appointment.

LEÓN

MUSEUM OF THE COLLEGE OF THE BLESSED SALAMÓN
León
Religious art, history. Archaeology.
By appointment.

MANAGUA

JUAN FRANCISCO AGUERRI MUSEUM
Managua
Paintings. Sculpture. Archaeology. Handicrafts.
By appointment.

MUSEUM OF NATURAL SCIENCE
Colegio Centro América, Managua
In Jesuit College. Geology. Mineralogy. Botany. Zoology.
By appointment.

MUSEUM OF THE VARONES INSTITUTE OF EDUCATION
Varones, Managua
In Institute of the La Salle Brothers. Local history. Religious and folk art. Natural history.
By appointment.

NATIONAL MUSEUM OF NICARAGUA
4a Avenida No. 606, Managua
Archaeology. Ceramics. Zoology. Botany. Numismatics.
Tu.-Su. 8-12, 3-6.

NUMISMATICS COLLECTION
Banco Nacional de Nicaragua, Managua
Historical collection of the coins and currency notes of Nicaragua.
M.-F. 8-3.

NINDIRÍ

ARCHAEOLOGICAL MUSEUM
Nindirí
Regional archaeology. Handicrafts.
By appointment.

Niger

It is not easy to imagine an exciting museum created from exhibits of millet, beans, groundnuts, salt and gum arabic, but no doubt an imaginative and determined curator would manage more than one might expect with these staple products of the Republic of the Niger. Uranium is, however, another matter, and one would certainly reckon that within the next few years the exploitation of the enormous deposits of this popular metallic ore will have modified the attitudes and amenities of the country to a considerable extent. At the moment, however, the National Museum offers only the traditional crafts, houses, costumes and peasant way of life.

NIAMEY

NATIONAL MUSEUM OF NIGER
P.O. Box 248, Niamey
Prehistory. Archaeology. History. Ethnography. Representative collection of tribal costumes. Crafts. Tribal houses.
Daily ex. M. 9-12, 2-5.

Nigeria

The museums of Nigeria raise considerable problems of both indexing and integrity. They contain collections of some of the finest, most praised and, from a Western point of view, most influential African sculpture, including the celebrated Benin bronzes. Are these items to be considered art or folk art? Are they the creations of artists or of folk artists?

ARGUNGU

KANTA'S MUSEUM
Argungu, North Western State
Historical relics of Kanta, including drums, swords and armour. The inner courtyard contains graves of former emirs.
Daily 9-7.

BENIN CITY

BENIN MUSEUM
Benin City, Mid-Western State
Finds from local excavations, including bronzes.
Daily 9-7.

ESIE

ESIE MUSEUM
Esie, Kwara State
The museum was built to house the largest known group of stone figures in Africa - about a thousand human figures, half-life size. They may be of Yoruba or Nupe origin, and are still revered by the local population.
Daily 9-7.

IFE

IFE MUSEUM
Ile-Ife, Western State
Houses the bronze and terra-cotta heads and stone sculptures of Ife, the ancient sacred city of the Yorubas. Yoruba culture.
Daily 9-7.

JOS

JOS MUSEUM
Jos, Benue Plateau State
Archaeological exhibits, including 2,000-year-old terracottas of the Nok culture, earliest known plastic art in Africa south of the Sahara. The grounds contain the beginnings of an open-air museum of traditional architecture.
Daily 9-7.

KADUNA

GEOLOGICAL SURVEY MUSEUM
Kaduna, North Central State
Collections of rocks, fossils and minerals of Nigeria.
Daily 9-7.

KANO

MAKAMA'S HOUSE
Kano Museum, Kano State
The town house of the Makama of Kano, one of the oldest houses in the town. Antiquities and arts and crafts typical of the Hausa and Fulani of the Kano area.
Daily 9-7.

LAGOS

NIGERIAN MUSEUM
Department of Antiquities, Onikan, Lagos
Ethnography and archaeology, including Nok and Ife terracottas and bronzes and Benin bronzes. Nigerian art. Ogboni brasswork. Egungun costumes. House posts and utensils. Ibo and Ibibio facemasks. Beads. Wooden door panels.
Daily 9-7.

ORON

ORON MUSEUM
Oron, South Eastern State
Collection of hardwood figure carvings depicting the ancestors of the Oron clan of the Ibibio tribe.
Daily 9-7.

OWO

OWO MUSEUM
Owo, Western State
Arts and crafts of the Eastern districts of Yorubaland.
Daily 9-7.

Norway

Norwegian museums, as a group, have a distinctly outdoor flavour about them. In addition to the normal Scandinavian type of open-air museum, with the normal Scandinavian array of wooden houses, churches and farm-buildings, there are excellent museums of fishing, hunting and seafaring, reflecting the importance of these activities in the national life since Viking times. It might usefully be pointed out, perhaps, that the traditional wooden buildings, well coated with tar, are exceedingly inflammable and that very few Norwegian towns and villages have escaped disastrous fires during the past two centuries. Moving the old buildings to open-air museums, where they are usually well distributed over the site and where the potential sources of fire are limited, is consequently a prudent fire-precaution, as well as a means of preserving historic buildings from developers, modernisers and vandals, of which Norway, despite the myths about civilised Scandinavia, has her fair share.

Apart from the traditional pursuits of fishing, hunting and going to sea, the industries and handicrafts best represented in Norwegian museums are those connected with wood and, to a lesser degree, iron. Local museums have good, but not always well displayed, collections of costumes, folk art and rural crafts, and Grieg, Ibsen and other figures on the not very extensive list of national heroes are well commemorated in museums. Prehistoric Norway and the Vikings are to be found everywhere.

One of the most agreeable and, in its off-beat way, characteristic Norwegian museum collections is devoted to what are pleasantly described as witchcraft accessories. And in Oslo there is one of the best, most dignified and certainly most sophisticated of the many European museums which tell the dreadful story of the German occupations. This is the more impressive because it contains one of the very few collections of military material to be found in Norway.

AALESUND

AALESUND MUSEUM
Rasmus Rønnebergsgate 16, Aalesund 6000
Local history and culture of the town and immediate surroundings. Natural history. Archaeology. Hunting and fishing, including old fishing methods and arctic hunting.
M.-Sa. 11-3; Su. 12-3.

SUNNMØRE MUSEUM
Borgundgavlen, N-6000 Aalesund
History of the main occupations in the area, farming and fishing. Boats, craftsmen's tools, textiles. Archaeology. Marine biology. Old dairy equipment. Farming tools and vehicles. Open-air museum includes two farm houses, a gate saw, a boat-builder's house and a grinding mill.
May-Sept. M.-Sa. 11-3; Su. 1-5.

AKERSHUS FYLKE

EIDSVOLL WORKS
Akershus Fylke
Almost unchanged since it was the home of Carsten Anker, owner of the Eidsvoll iron foundry, and furnished to look as it did when the Constituent Assembly met to sign the free constitution of Norway in 1814. 18th and early 19th century furniture.
M.-Sa. 11-3; Su. 12-3.

OTTO AND TILLA VALSTAD'S COLLECTION
Akershus Fylke
Collections of the folk history of Asker.
May 1 - Sept. 30, daily 10-6.

SKEDSMO MUSEUM OF BUILDINGS
Akershus Fylke
Open-air museum. Collection of wooden houses and outer buildings, moved to site.
May 1 - Sept. 30, daily 10-6.

ÅL

AL MUSEUM OF BUILDINGS
Ål 3570
Wooden house, workshops and other buildings brought to the museum site.
May 1 - Sept. 30, daily 10-6.

AMLA

THE HEIBERG COLLECTIONS
Amla, Sogn
Open-air grouping of old farm buildings, including the Gjeithus building from Arnefjord (1596), the storehouse from Råstad (1589), a cooking-house from Fossen in Vadheim, an old inn, and the rectory from Vik. Collection of old tools and implements. Boat gallery.
Summer: daily 10-6.

ANDRE STASJONER

HADELAND FOLK MUSEUM
Halvdanshaugen pa Jaren, Gran, Andre Stasjoner
Folk-art. Costumes. Handicrafts.
M.-Sa. 10-5.

HEIBERG COLLECTION
Sogndal Sogn, Andre Stasjoner
Collection illustrating local industries and commerce.
On request.

STENBERG MUSEUM
Beverbru, Andre Stasjoner
Local history.
On request.

ARENDAL

AUST AGDER MUSEUM
Parkveien 16, Arendal 4800
Prehistory. Social history. Coins and medals. Ethnography. Natural history. Maritime section.
M.-Sa. 10-3; Su. 12-3.

MERDÖ HOUSE
Tromøy, Arendal 4800
18th century house formerly belonging to a sea-captain and containing period furnishings and curiosities which had been brought home from distant parts. Next door is to be found a sailmaker's workshop to show how large sails of the period were made.
M.-Sa. 10-3; Su. 12-3.

ASKIM

ASKIM HISTORICAL MUSEUM
Askim 1800, Østfold
A hamlet or "bygdetun" arranged to illustrate styles and techniques of wooden building, during the 17th-19th centuries.
Summer: daily 10-6.

BAGN

ISLANDMOEN FARM
Bagn 2930, Oppland
Open-air collection of buildings, mainly agricultural and including barns, cowsheds, farm-houses.
Summer: daily 10-6.

BERG

KRAGERØ MUSEUM
Berg, Telemark
Manor house in miniature, restored with period furnishings.
May-Sept., daily 9-8. Oct.-Apr., daily 10-6.

BERGEN

BERGEN AQUARIUM
Nordnes, Bergen 5000
Marine and fresh water fish. Lower marine fauna.
May-Sept. Daily 9-8. Oct.-Apr. Daily 10-6.

BERGEN ART ASSOCIATION
Lars Hilles gate 6, Bergen 5000
Contemporary paintings, sculpture mainly by Norwegian artists.
Tu.-Su. 12-3.

BERGEN MARITIME MUSEUM
Sydneshaugen, 5010 Bergen
Development of Norwegian shipping from ancient times to the present day. Models of Viking ships and sailing ships. Original objects from these vessels. Figureheads. Exhibits illustrating the sailor's day on board. Shipbuilding section, including models, tools and careening equipment. Clinker-building. Steamships. Tankers, tramp-ships, liners and passenger ships. Engine-building.
Sept.-Apr. M.-Sa. 11-2; Su. 11-3. May-Aug. Daily 11-3.

FISHERY MUSEUM
Permanenten, Bergen 5000
History of the fishing industry. Evolution of the boat. Life histories of different fish. Fishing grounds. Finds from Bronze Age. Modern methods of fishing and of preserving fish.
May 15- Aug. 31, M.-Sa. 10-3; Su. 12-3.

GAMLE BERGEN (OLD BERGEN)
Elsesro Estate, Sandviken, Bergen 5000
Houses from the 18th and 19th centuries, complete with cobbled streets, market place and shops, and furnished in period style, with craftsmen's tools and equipment in original workshops transferred to the museum site.
May 1- Sept. 15, Daily 10-7.

GEOLOGICAL MUSEUM
University of Bergen, Joachim Frielesgate 1, Bergen 5000
Minerals, rocks and fossils, especially from Western Norway, Spitzbergen and Jan Meyen. Material from quaternary deposits throughout Norway.
Daily ex. F. 11-2.

HANSEATIC MUSEUM
Finnegården, Bryggen, Bergen 5000
In one of the oldest and best preserved houses on the Quay, furnished and equipped to show what the counting house and living-quarters of one of the merchants was like c.1700.
Summer: daily 10-4. May and Sept. 11-2. Rest of year, Su., M. and F., 11-2.

HISTORICAL MUSEUM
University of Bergen, Sydneshaugen, 5010 Bergen
Medieval and post-Reformation ecclesiastical art. Architecture and furniture from Bergen. Rural exhibits. Prehistory. Viking exhibits. Ethnographical material from all over the world, including collection of Javanese shadow puppets. Coins. 19th century watercolours, gouaches, oil paintings and lithographs. Folk art. Wood carvings. National costumes. Textiles.
Daily ex. F. 11-2.

HORDALAND AGRICULTURAL MUSEUM
pa Garnes, Bergen 5000
Agricultural tools and implements. Old boats. Old farm buildings.
May 23- Aug. 31, M.-Sa. 11-2; Su. 12-2. Other times by appointment.

LEPROSY MUSEUM
St. George's Hospital, 59 Kong Oscargate, Bergen 5000
18th century buildings on site of a leper hospital in the Middle Ages. Exhibits showing the Norwegian contribution to the research into leprosy.
mid. May- Aug. daily 12-3.

MUNICIPAL ART MUSEUM
Permanenten, Bergen 5000
Paintings, sculpture, drawings and engravings. Works by Norwegian artists from Johan Christian Dahl (1788-1857) to modern times. Dutch and Italian paintings. Russian icons. Modern works by Braque, Derain, Lhote, Le Parc, Picasso, Rivera and Utrillo. Furniture. Room interiors. Rococo interior with wall and ceiling decorations by Mathias Blumenthal.
May 16- Aug. 31, M.-Sa. 10-3; Su. 12-3. Sept. 1- May 15, Daily ex. M. 12-3.

MUSEUM OF NATURAL HISTORY
Sydneshaugen, Bergen 5000
Botanical collections from Norway and other Scandinavian countries, as well as from other parts of the world. Geology. Zoology.
Daily ex. Th. 11-2.

SCHØSSTUENE
50 Øvregaten, Bergen 5000
Four old assembly rooms illustrating social life in Bergen, mainly during the 19th century.
Summer: daily 10-4. Rest of year, Su., Tu., Th. and Sa., 11-2.

HILL FARM MUSEUM
Fanafjell, Nr. Bergen
Collection illustrating characteristic features of Norwegian farming in former days. Agricultural implements. Domestic and dairying equipment.
Enquire locally. Museum is normally open only during summer months.

"TROLDHAUGEN"
nr. Bergen
Edvard Grieg's country home. Souvenirs and personal possessions of the composer. Burial place of Grieg and his wife, Nina.
May 2- Oct. 1, daily 11-2, 3-6. During Festival period, only open 3-6. Park open all the year.

WESTERN NORWAY MUSEUM OF APPLIED ART
Permanenten, Bergen 5000
Norwegian and European furniture, glass, porcelain, silver and textiles from the Renaissance to the present day. Collection of Chinese art.
May 15- Aug. 31, M.-Sa. 10-3; Su. 12-3. Sept. 1- May 14, Daily ex. M. 12-3.

ZOOLOGICAL MUSEUM
University of Bergen, Muséplatz 3, 5000 Bergen
Zoological collections, including sections on vertebrates, invertebrates, osteology and entomology.
Daily ex. Th. 11-2.

BODØ

NORDLAND FOLK MUSEUM
Prinsensgate 116, Bodø 8001
Life in the county of Nordland. Fisheries. Agriculture. Trades. Archaeology. Numismatics. Birds and fishes.
M.-F. 8.30-3; Sa. 8.30-2; Su. 12-3.

BÖVERBRU

TOTEN MUSEUM
Stenberg Farm, 2846 Böverbru
Former home of Laurits Weidemann (1775-1856). Period furniture. Local history.
May 15- Sept. 15, Daily 12-6.

BRYNE

ROGALAND FOLK MUSEUM
Kolbeinstveit, Bryne 4340
40 buildings of historic interest, including three hill farm-houses, a mill-house, a drying-house and a smithy.
June 15- Aug. 15, Daily 12-4.

DAGALI

DAGALI MUSEUM
Dagali 3588
Open-air museum illustrating the old farming culture of the district. Houses, farmhouses, barn, cowshed, stable and a school.
July 1- Aug. 10, Daily 11-4.

DRAMMEN

ART GALLERY
Drammen 3000, Buskerud
Norwegian paintings.
Summer: daily 10-6.

DRAMMENS MUSEUM
Strømsø, Drammen 3000, Buskerud
History of the area. Ecclesiastical exhibits. Period interiors. Agriculture. Forestry. Hunting. Fishing. Stoves. Farmyard from Hallingdal. Transport.
May-Oct. Daily 12-6.

MARIENLYST MANOR AND MARITIME MUSEUM
Drammen 3000, Buskerud
The manor house has period furniture and houses the maritime museum in one wing.
May-Oct., daily 12-6.

EGERSUND

DALANE FOLK MUSEUM
Slettebø Gård, Egersund 4370, Rogaland
One-time residence of a district judge. Period furniture. Maritime exhibits. Crafts. Agricultural implements. Local history.
May-Oct., daily 10-6.

ELVERUM

GLOMDAL MUSEUM
Elverum 2400, Hedmark
Open-air museum consisting of about 70 old buildings, grouped round their respective courtyards. Particularly noteworthy are the Tynset farm, with seven separate buildings, and farms from Alvdal and Folldal. Medieval Stemsrud House.
Summer: daily 10-6.

NORWEGIAN FORESTRY MUSEUM
Norsk Skogbruksmuseum, Prestøya, Elverum 2400
History of forestry in Norway. Specimens of timber.
Summer: daily 10-6.

FAGERNES

VALDRE FOLK MUSEUM
Fagernes 2900, Oppland
Old buildings from Valdres, including the Hande loft. Hunting. Animal traps.
May-Oct., daily 10-6.

FARSUND

FARSUND MUSEUM
Farsund 4550, Vest-Agder
Sea-captain's house, with period furnishings and souvenirs of travels.
Summer: daily 10-6.

FLEKKEFJORD

FLEKKEFJORD DISTRICT MUSEUM
Flekkefjord 4400, Vest-Agder
Open-air museum. Collection of buildings brought to museum site.
May-Sept., Daily 10-6.

FLEKKEFJORD TOWN MUSEUM
Flekkefjord 4400, Vest-Agder
18th century house. Furniture. Porcelain. Textiles. Silver.
Summer: M.-Sa. 10-3; Su. 12-3.

FOLKENBORG

EIDSBERG AND MYSEN HISTORICAL MUSEUM
Folkenborg, Østfold
Local history.
M.-Sa. 10-4.

FØRDE

SUNNIFJORD FOLK MUSEUM
Moskog, Førde
Wooden buildings moved to site. Period furniture, household equipment.
Summer: daily 10-6.

GAUSDAL

AULESTAD
Gausdal, nr. Lillehammer
Home of Karoline and Bjønstjerne Bjørnson, with memorabilia and examples of stories, poetry and plays.
May-Sept., M.-Sa. 10-3; Su. 12-3.

GRIMSTAD

IBSEN HOUSE AND GRIMSTAD MUSEUM
Henrik Ibsens gate, Grimstad 4890
House where Ibsen began his career by writing 'Catilina'. Souvenirs of Ibsen, including his handwritten poems, letters and manuscripts. First edition of 'Catilina'. Oils and watercolours painted by Ibsen. Pharmacy equipment. History of the town from 1700. Models of sailing ships, tools from the ship-yards and equipment from the sailing-ship period.
June-Aug. M.-Sa. 10-3; Su. 12-3. Other times by arrangement.

GRUE FINNSKOG

FINNISH VILLAGE
Grue Finnskog 2256, Hedmark
Culture of the Finns living in the forests near the Swedish border.
May-Sept., M.-Sa. 10-3; Su. 12-3.

HALDEN

MEMORIES OF HALDEN MUSEUM
Fortress of Fredriksten, Halden 1750, Østfold
Collections illustrating life in the old border town of Halden, which owes its character to the many disputes between Norway and Sweden.
May-Sept., M.-Sa. 10-3; Su. 12-3.

HALLINGDAL

HALLINGDAL FOLK MUSEUM
Nesbyen, Hallingdal, Buskerud
Life and folk art of Hallingdal. Old buildings, including the medieval loft from Stave, Kolsrudstuen from Flå, and Villandsstuen (18th century).
Summer: daily 10-6.

LOCAL MUSEUM
Al, Hallingdal, Buskerud
Local history. Ethnography. Costumes.
Summer: daily 10-3.

LOCAL MUSEUM
Hol, Hallingdal, Buskerud
Local history. Folklore. Costumes.
Summer: M.-Sa. 10-3; Su. 12-3.

HAMAR

HEDMARK MUSEUM
Hamar 2300
Converted 18th century stone barn. Site of the ruins of medieval cathedral and bishop's castle. Medieval and post-Reformation material recovered from the site and surrounding area.
May 15-June 15, Daily 10-4. June 16-Aug. 15, Daily 10-6. Aug. 16-Sept. 15, Daily 10-4.

OPEN-AIR MUSEUM
Hamar 2300
Folk museum. 25 17th and 18th century farm buildings from the surrounding district.
May 15-June 15, Daily 10-4. June 16-Aug. 15, Daily 10-6. Aug. 16-Sept. 15, Daily 10-4.

RAILWAY MUSEUM
Lake Mjøsa, Hamar 2300
Old station buildings, permanent way and rolling stock, including narrow gauge Royal Carriage, open 4th class waggon without seats, and old ambulance carriage. Models, uniforms, posters and documents relating to Norway's railway history.
May-Sept. M.-Sa. 10-4; Su. 12-3. Oct.-Apr. M.-Sa. 10-4. Closed Su. and public holidays.

HAUGESUND

HAUGESUND GALLERY
Erl Skjalgssonsgate 4, Haugesund 5500
Paintings, especially by Norwegian artists.
M.-Sa. 10-3; Su. 12-3.

HAUGESUND ART ASSOCIATION MUSEUM
Erl Skjalgssonsgate 4, Haugesund 5500
Prehistory. Social history. Maritime section.
M.-Sa. 10-3; Su. 12-3.

HAUGESUND MUSEUM
Rådhusgate 66, Haugesund 5500
Local history, particularly the shipping industry. Folklore.
M.-Sa. 10-3; Su. 12-3.

HJERTØYA

FISHERY MUSEUM
Hjertoya, Romsdal
History of fishing in the area. Ships' models. Charts.
Summer: M.-Sa. 10-3; Su. 12-3.

HOLMESTRAND

TOWN MUSEUM
Holmestrand 3080
House dating from 1756, containing local history collection.
Summer: M.-Sa. 10-3; Su. 12-3. Winter: on request.

HORNINDAL

THE ANDERS SVOR MUSEUM
Hornindal 6790, Sogn
Representative collection of the works of the sculptor, Anders Svor (1864-1929).
Summer: M.-Sa. 10-3; Su. 12-3.

HORTEN

NAVAL MUSEUM
Carl Johans Vaern, Horten 3190
Housed at the naval base built by King Carl XIV Johan of Sweden and Norway. History of the Norwegian Navy from the middle of the 19th century up to the second World War. Curiosities collected by naval officers on expeditions.
M.-Sa. 10-3; Su. 12-3.

HØVIKODDEN

SONJA HENIE AND NIELS ONSTAD FOUNDATION
The Art Centre, Høvikodden, Baerum
20th century art. Works by Munch, Bonnard, Juan Gris, Villon, Picasso and Miro. French abstract and expressionist paintings. Room devoted to the skating trophies and medals of Sonja Henie.
Daily 11-10.

INDRØY

INDRØY MUSEUM
nr. Sakshaug Church, Indrøy 5997, Nord-Trøndelag
Dwelling house. Store-house. Stable.
Summer: daily 10-6.

KABELVÅG

MUSEUM OF FISHERIES AND THE LOFOTEN ISLANDS
8310 Kabelvåg
Collections illustrating the fisheries, the fishermen's life at sea, and their houses on shore. Boats and model crafts, instruments and tools used in and around the Lofoten Islands. Aquarium.
May 15-Sept. 15, Daily 12-3. Other times by arrangement.

KARASJOK

LOCAL MUSEUM
9730 Karasjok
Culture, ecology and history of Finnmark. Economic, scientific and artistic aspects of Lapp life.
M.-F. 8.30-3.30.

KAUPANGER

HEIBERG COLLECTION
Kaupanger 5880
Domestic arts and crafts. Peasant costumes, bridal crowns, needlework, kitchen and dining-room utensils and weapons. Interiors from Sogn churches. Silver and pewter. Witchcraft accessories. Heiberg family paintings, watercolours and pastels, and collection of books written by members of the family or dealing with its history. Sogn picture gallery, with paintings, lithographs, etchings and woodcuts by Sogn artists. Agricultural implements. Utensils used for fishing, hunting, brewing, distilling, carpentry, weaving, spinning and dyeing. Boats and boat-building equipment. Open-air museum includes 18 buildings, among them old farm buildings, grain-stores, hearth-houses and an old inn, all furnished in period style.
May-Sept. M.-Sa. 9-6; Su. 11-5.

KONGSBERG

LAGDAL MUSEUM
3600 Kongsberg
Open-air collection of 20 wooden farm buildings dating from 1600-1800. Implements and tools representing urban and rural cultures.
Apr. 1-Oct. 1, Daily 10-6.

SILVER MINE MUSEUM
Sølvverket Kongsberg, Hytteg. 3, Kongsberg 3600
History of the silver-mines from the 17th century to the present day, with equipment, photographs and other exhibits.
May-Sept., M.-Sa. 10-3; Su. 12-3.

KRAGERØ

BERG-KRAGERØ MUSEUM
Kragerø 3770
Country house (1800). Furniture. Silver. Delft ware. China. Glass. Paintings dating from 1650-1850.
May 15-Oct. 1, Su. 12.30-7; M. 5-7; W. 12-2; F. 5-7.

KRISTIANSAND

KRISTIANSAND MARITIME MUSEUM
Gyldenløves g. 14, Kristiansand 4600, Vest-Agder
Collections illustrating the importance of sailing ships and the sea to Norway.
Summer: M.-Sa. 10-3; Su. 12-3.

VEST-AGDER FOLK MUSEUM
Kongsgaard, Kristiansand 4600, Vest-Agder
27 buildings illustrating life in the district. 19th century houses. Workshops of cabinet-maker, turner, shoe-maker and gunsmith. Maritime collection. Corporation chests and journeymen's test pieces. Norwegian farm-yard. Groups of houses ranging from 1650-1850 and 1859-1875. Small country schoolhouse.
June 20-Aug. 15, M.-Sa. 11-6.30; Su. 12-6.30.

KRISTIANSUND

KRISTIANSUND MUSEUM
Knudtzondalen, Kristiansund N-6500, Nordmøre
Farm houses of the district, containing examples of local folk art.
Summer: daily 10-6.

KVERNES

LOCAL MUSEUM
Kvernes 6540, Nordmøre
Local history and industries.
Summer: M.-Sa. 10-3; Su. 12-3.

LANDE

DOKKA MUSEUM
Lande 8954, Oppland
Collection of old wooden buildings from the Lande area.
Summer: daily 10-6.

LÅRDAL

LOCAL MUSEUM
Lårdal, Telemark
Collection of buildings preserved on their original sites.
Summer: daily 10-6.

LARVIK

LARVIK MUSEUM
Herrengården, Larvik 3250
In 17th century restored manor house. Period furniture and furnishings. Local history. Folklore.
Summer: M.-Sa. 10-3; Su. 12-3.

LEIRVIK

SUNNHORDLAND FOLK MUSEUM
Leirvik 5940, Stord Island, Hordaland
Old houses, including a medieval house from Ådland and another from Stolmen (both of the "Røkstue" type, heated by a smoke-oven).
Summer: daily 10-6.

LILLEHAMMER

DE SANDVIGSKE SAMLINGER
Lillehammer 2600
Open-air museum with three complete farms and a variety of buildings from the Gudbrandsdal valley. Handicraft section, with old workshops from all parts of Norway.
May-Sept. Daily 10-7. Oct.-Apr. Daily 10-3. Open-air section closed in winter.

LILLEHAMMER MUNICIPAL ART GALLERY
Kirkegaten 69, Lillehammer 2600
Norwegian paintings, sculpture and graphic art. Works by Henrik Sørensen, Thorvald Erichsen, Einar Sandberg.
Summer: M.-Sa. 10-3; Su. 12-3.

LOM

OPEN-AIR MUSEUM
Lom 2686, Oppland
Old buildings from the surrounding district.
Summer: daily 10-6.

MANDAL

MANDAL MUSEUM
Andorsengården, Mandal 4500, Vest-Agder
Local history collections. Municipal art collection.
M.-Sa. 10-3; Su. 12-3.

MANDAL AND DISTRICT FOLK MUSEUM
Øyslebo, Mandal 4500, Vest-Agder
Three old buildings from Mjåland in Åseral, furnished in period style.
Summer: daily 10-6.

MELBU

VESTERAL COLLECTION OF BUILDINGS
Melbu 8490, Nordland
Collection of furniture, folk-art, books, implements, in typical old Nordland houses.
Summer: M.-Sa. 10-3; Su. 12-3.

MELDAL

MELDAL MUSEUM OF BUILDINGS
nr. Meldal Church, Bergslia 7390
Open-air museum. Buildings include a storehouse, a dwelling-house with an open fireplace, another large house from Munan, and a house of the "smoke-oven" type from Månesetra.
Summer: daily 10-6.

MO I RANA

MO AND NORTH-RANA MUSEUM OF BUILDINGS
Mo i Rana, Nord-Helgeland
Open-air museum. History of the district. Lapp culture.
Summer: M.-Sa. 10-3; Su. 12-3.

MOLDE

HJERTØYA FISHERIES MUSEUM
Molde 6400
History of Romsdal coast. Boats, nets and fishing gear. Houses. Domestic life. Kettle and pans for producing cod liver oil.
June 25 - Aug. 15, Daily 10-4.

ROMSDAL MUSEUM
Molde 6400
20 old houses from the district showing the development of rural culture from early times to the end of the 19th century. 15th century cottage shows how people lived here from the Viking period onwards. Farmstead. Chapel. Church art.
May 25 - June 15, M.-Su. 10-2, Su. 12-3. June 16 - Aug. 20, M.-Sa. 10-7; Su. 12-6. Aug. 21 - Sept. 10, M.-Sa. 10-2; Su. 12-3.

MOSJØEN

VEFSN LOCAL COLLECTION
nr. Mosjøen 8650, Nordland
Group of old buildings, with collections of furniture and domestic equipment in one of them.
Summer: daily 10-6.

MOSS

MOSS AND DISTRICT MUSEUM
Rabek Manor, Moss 1500, Østfold
Manor-house museum. Local history. Furnishings.
Summer: M.-Sa. 10-3; Su. 12-3.

MOSTUN

ROGALAND FOLK MUSEUM
Mostun, Rogaland
Local history. Folklore. Costumes. Local traditions.
Summer: M.-Sa. 10-3; Su. 12-3.

NAMSOS

NAMDAL MUSEUM
Namsos 7800
Old-buildings re-erected around a courtyard. Lapp culture. Collections illustrating rural life in the district. Tools and implements.
June 20 - Aug. 20, Daily 12-4.

NES

OLD HVAM
Akershus Agricultural School, Nes 3524
17th century farm building with store-houses and massive out-houses in heavy timbers, furnished as if they were still in use.
Summer: daily 10-6.

NESBYEN

HALLINGDAL FOLK MUSEUM
Nessameiet, Rukkedal Hill, Nesbyen 3540
Buildings illustrating the cultural and architectural history of the valley, including a Staveloft dating from 1349. Wood-carving. Costumes. Bedclothes. Hand-woven tapestries. Set of church accounts on calfskin (1675) and articles used by Norwegian Resistance Movement during Second World War.
June 24 - Sept. 1, Daily 11-5. Other times by arrangement.

NOTODDEN

HEDDAL AND NOTODDEN MUSEUM
Notodden 3670, Telemark
Group of six old buildings arranged round a courtyard.
Summer: daily 10-6.

ØRSTA

THE AASEN FARM
Ørsta, Møre og Romsdal
Books and personal possessions of the author, Ivar Aasen (1813-1896).
Summer: M.-Sa. 10-3; Su. 12-3.

OSLO

AKERSHUS PALACE AND FORTRESS
Kirkegate and Rådhusgate, Oslo 1
Built by King Håkon V Magnusson in 1300 A.D., rebuilt by King Christian IV c.1600 and subsequently restored and redecorated.
Apr. 15 - May 16, Su. 12.30-2.45. May 18 - Sept. 15, M.-Sa. 11-2.45; Su. 12.30-2.45. Closed in winter.

"AMUNDSEN"
Ingierstrandveien, Bålerud, Oslo
Home of the Polar explorer, Roald Amundsen, which remains as he left it on his death in 1928.
May 16 - Sept. 15, Daily 11-5.

ARMY MUSEUM
Akershus, Oslo MIL, Oslo 1
Military equipment from late Middle Ages to 1945. Weapons, Artillery, cavalry, engineering and signalling equipment. Armour. Quartermaster's equipment.
Apr. 15 - May 16, Su. 12.30-2.45. May 18 - Sept. 15, M.-Sa. 11-2.45, Su. 12.30-2.45.

BOGSTAD MANOR
Sørkedalen, Oslo
Manor (c.1750), with art collection. At one time home of Prime Minister, Peder Anker.
May 15 - Sept. 15, Su. 12-7. July 1 - Aug. 15, W., tours at 5 and 6.

BOTANICAL MUSEUM OF THE UNIVERSITY
Trondheimsveien 23B, Oslo 5
Lichen collection. Chinese vascular plants. Uredineae. Vascular plants from Canary Islands. Bryophytes and fungi from Scandinavia. Arctic plants and lichens.
By written appointment.

CABINET OF COINS AND MEDALS
University of Oslo, Frederiks gate 2, Oslo 1
Numismatics. Ancient, medieval European, modern European and overseas, Mohammedan, Indian and Far East coins. Tokens. Banknotes. Medals and jetons; orders and decorations.
June-Aug. Daily 11-3. Sept.-May Daily 12-3.

CITY MUSEUM
Frogner Hovedgård, Frognerveien 67, Oslo 2
In Frogner Manor (1790). Pictures. Models of old buildings. Period furniture. Exhibits illustrate the cultural history and topography of the old town.
May-Sept. M.-F. 11-5; Sa. 11-4; Su. 12-5.

COLLECTION OF ANTIQUITIES
University of Oslo, Frederiks gate 2, Oslo 1
Utensils, weapons, ornaments and trinkets from the Stone, Bronze and Iron Ages. Medieval ecclesiastical art. Gold and silver. Medieval art prior to 1530.
Sept. 1 - May 31, Daily 12-3. June-Aug. Daily 11-3. Closed Good F., Easter Su., Ascension, Whit. Sa., May 1, 17, Sept. 2.

ETHNOGRAPHICAL MUSEUM
University of Oslo, Frederiksgate 2, Oslo 1
Clothing, tools, utensils and idols, together with the ethnographical collection assembled by the explorer, Roald Amundsen. Material from the Arctic and Antarctic, America, Africa, Asia. Oceanography.
Sept.-May Daily 12-3. June-Aug. Daily 11-3. Closed Good F., Easter Su., Ascension, Whit. Sa., May 1, 17, Sept. 2.

FRAM
Bygdöynes, Oslo 2
Polar exploration vessel used by Nansen, Amundsen and Sverdrup on expeditions.
Apr. 15-30, Daily 12-3. May 2-14, Daily 11-5. May 15 - Aug. 31, Daily 10-6. Sept., Daily 11-5. Oct., Daily 11-4. Nov., Su. 12-3. Whit. Sa. 10-3. Midsummers's Eve 10-1.

HISTORICAL MUSEUM
Frederiksgate 2, Oslo 1
University collection of antiquities, with emphasis on the Viking age, and medieval ecclesiastical art. Ethnography. Numismatic collection.
Summer: Daily 12-3.

KON-TIKI MUSEUM
Bygdøynes, Oslo 2
Museum built specially to house the balsawood raft, 'Kon-Tiki', on which Thor Heyerdahl and his five companions drifted 5000 miles across the Pacific in 1947. Cast of 31 ft. high Easter Island statue. Underwater display, featuring sharks. Prehistoric craft from the Pacific.
Apr. 16 - May 14, Daily 11-5. May 15 - Aug. 31, Daily 10-6. Sept. Daily 11-5. Oct. 1 - Apr. 15, Daily 11-4. Closed Good F., Easter Su. and May 17.

MUSEUM OF CRIME AND CRIMINALS
Møllergatan 17, Oslo 1
History of crime, and methods of combatting it. Weapons. Documents.
By written application.

MINERALOGICAL-GEOLOGICAL MUSEUM
University of Oslo, Sarsgate 1, Tøyen, Oslo 5
Rocks and minerals. Geological processes, including volcanic eruptions, earthquakes and ice and water erosion. Norway's geological history. Relief model of the Oslo area. Minerals, including gold from Bleka in Telemark, silver from Kongsbert and uranium-bearing Norwegian minerals. Norwegian mining and quarrying industries.
Sept. 16 - May 14, Su. 12-4; Tu. and Th. 12-3; Sa. 12-2. May 15 - Sept. 15, Tu.-Su. 12-3. Closed M. Closed Good F., Easter Su., Whit. Su., May 1, 17.

MUNCH MUSEUM
Tøyengate 53, Oslo 5
Works by Edvard Munch. Paintings. Drawings. Watercolours. Graphic works. Sculptures. Books, letters and other documents.
Daily ex. M. 11-7; Su. 12-7. Maundy Th., Easter M., Dec. 26, 12-4. Closed Good F., Easter Su., Whit. Su., May 1, 17.

MUSEUM OF APPLIED ARTS
St. Olavsgate 1, Oslo 1
Domestic art from the Middle Ages to the present day. The Baldishol Tapestry (c.1180). European applied arts from the Renaissance onwards. Interiors from old city mansions. 18th century glass and faience from Nöstetangen and Herreböe.
Tu.-Sa. 11-3; Su. 12-3; closed M. Also closed Good F., Easter Su., Whit. Sa. and Su., May 1, 17.

NATIONAL GALLERY
Universitetsgaten 13, Oslo 1
Norwegian paintings and sculpture. 16th-18th century European paintings. Modern French, Danish and Swedish art. Prints and engravings. Greek and Roman sculpture. Casts.
Summer: M.-F. 10-4; Sa. 10-3; Su. 12-3; W. and F. also 6-8. Sept. 16 - May 15, M.-Sa. 11-3; Su. 12-3; W. also 6-8. Closed Good F., Easter Su., Whit. Su., May 1, 17.

NORGES BANK MUSEUM COLLECTION
Bankplassen 4, Oslo 1
Items connected with banking, from 1816 onwards, including printing plates for different issues of banknotes, forged notes and equipment for transporting notes and documents in the early days. Relics from the German occupation, 1940-45.
M.-Sa. 9-3 on request.

NORWAY'S RESISTANCE MUSEUM
Akershus, Oslo 1
The museum attempts to give a true picture of major events in Norway, from the German attack in 1940 until the day of liberation in 1945.
Apr. 15 - Sept. 30, M.-Sa. 10-4; Su. 11-4. Oct. 1 - Apr. 14, M.-Sa. 10-3; Su. 11-4. Closed Good F., Easter Su., Whit. Su., May 1, 17.

NORWEGIAN CUSTOMS MUSEUM
5th floor, Schweigaardsgate 15, Oslo 6
The collection consists of original exhibits, models, photographs and historical archives illustrating the work of the Customs authorities.
Tu.-F. 12-3. Closed Good F., May 1, 17.

NORWEGIAN FOLK MUSEUM
Museumsveien 10, Bygdøy, Oslo 2
Indoor and open-air sections. Rural culture (including display of weaving). Church history; Henrik Ibsen's study. Lapp collection. Open-air museum consists of 140 old buildings (including a 12th century stave church); examples of different farms; relics from all over Norway arranged as an old town quarter.
Sept. 1 - May 14, M.-Sa. 11-4; Su. 12-3. May 15 - Aug. 31, M.-Sa. 10-6; Su. 12-6. Closed Good F., Easter Su., May 17.

NORWEGIAN MARITIME MUSEUM
Bygdøynes, Oslo 2
Representative selection of the boats in use along the Norwegian coast, together with models of sailing ships, the yards in which they were built, and fishing villages.
Oct. 15 - May 14, Su. 12-3. May 15 - Aug. 31, Daily 10-6. Sept. Daily 11-5. Oct. 1-14, Daily 11-4. Closed Good F., Easter Su., May 1, 17.

NORWEGIAN SCIENCE AND INDUSTRY MUSEUM
Fyrstikkalléen 1, Etterstad, Oslo 6
The advances in science and technology are illustrated in sections on steam and gas propulsion, hydraulic machinery, communications, aviation, electricity, X-rays, telegraphy, telephony and radio. Working model of an atomic power plant. The aircraft used in 1914 by Tryggve Gran to cross the North Sea. Large model railway. Exhibition of old mechanical musical instruments.
M.-Sa. 10-4; Su. 10-5. Oct. 1 - Mar. 31 also Tu. 6-9 p.m. Easter Sa., Whit. Sa. 10-3. Closed Good F., Easter Su., Whit. Su., May 1, 17.

MUSEUM OF CITY PLANNING AUTHORITY
Trondheimsveien 5, Oslo 1
Models showing individual buildings. Development plans.
By appointment.

PALAEONTOLOGY MUSEUM
University of Oslo, Sarsgate 1, Oslo 5
Collections of prehistoric plants and animals. Evolution and genealogy. Plaster casts and specimens of prehistoric reptiles. Evolution of man. Reproductions of ancient cave paintings.
Oct. 15 - May 14, Su. 12-3. May 15 - Aug. 31, Daily 10-6. Sept. Daily 11-5. Oct. 1-14, Daily 11-4. Closed Good F., Easter Su., May 1, 17.

POST OFFICE MUSEUM
Central Post Office (3rd floor), Dronningens gate 15, Oslo 1
Postal history of Norway depicted through equipment and pictures. Models of ships, mail coaches, postillions. Models of post offices. Collection of "message sticks", Stamps. Postmarks, proofs and errors.
Tu., Th. and F. 10-3; Su. 12-3.

SKI MUSEUM
Holmenkollen, Oslo
Situated at the top of the Olympic ski-jump, the museum contains large collections of old skis, equipment and pictures. Skis and equipment used by the Norwegian polar expeditions (Roald Amundsen, South Pole, 1911) and skis used by Captain R. F. Scott (South Pole, 1912). Skis found in bogs, believed to be 2,500 years old.
March 15 - May 15 and Oct.-Nov., Sa. and Su. 10-4. May 18 - Sept. 30, Daily 10-6 (July 10-10).

VIGELAND SCULPTURE PARK AND MUSEUM
Frogner Park and Nobelsgate 32, Oslo 2
The 80-acre park comprises 150 sculpture groups, culminating in a 60-ft. granite monolith.
The Museum, at Nobelsgate 32, in Gustav Vigeland's former studio, contains many of his original works, as well as sketches and woodcuts.
Museum: Daily ex. M. 1-7. Maundy Th., Easter Sa., Easter M. 1-4. Closed Good F., Easter Su., Whit. Su., May 1, 17.

VIKING SHIPS MUSEUM
Huk Aveny 35, Bygdøy, Oslo 2
The Oseberg, Gokstad and Tune Viking ships, found near the Oslo fjord. Household articles found in the ships.
May 2 - Aug. 31. Daily 10-6. Sept. Daily 11-5. Oct.-Apr. Daily 11-3.

ZOOLOGICAL MUSEUM
Sarsgate 1, Oslo 5
Norwegian vertebrates and invertebrates. Arctic, Antarctic and exotic, particularly Australian, collections.
Summer: Su., Tu., F. 12-3; W. evenings 6-8.

ØYSLEBØ

MANDAL AND OPPLANDS FOLK MUSEUM
Øyslebø 4532, Vest-Agder
Houses and other wooden buildings, brought to site.
May 1 - Sept. 30, daily 10-5.

ØYSTESE

INGEBRIGT VIK MUSEUM
Øystese 5610, Hordaland
Works by the sculptor, Ingebrigt Vik (1867-1927).
Summer: daily 10-6.

KVAM MUSEUM OF BUILDINGS
Øystese 5610, Hordaland
Buildings include the Torstein house (dating from 1661), as well as a boat house from Fikse with a boat used for rowing to church.
Summer: daily 10-6.

PRESTFOSS

SIGDAL AND EGGEDAL MUSEUM
Prestfoss 3350, Buskerud
Local history.
M.-Sa., 10-4.

RAKKESTAD

RAKKESTAD OPEN-AIR MUSEUM
Rakkestad 1890, Østfold
Different types of buildings from the surrounding area. Furniture and furnishings.
Summer: daily 10-6.

RINGERIKE

RINGERIKE MUSEUM
Norderhov, Ringerike, Buskerud
Section devoted to Jørgen Moe (1813-1882), one of the earliest collectors of folk tales in Norway. Local history. Folklore.
Summer: M.-Sa. 10-3; Su. 12-3.

RISØYHAMN

ANDØY MUSEUM
Risøyhamn 9490, Nordland
Local history. Maritime history. Fishing.
Tu.-Sa. 10-5.

RJUKAN

TINN MUSEUM
Bjørkhaug, Rjukan 3660, Telemark
Folk museum with groups of old buildings arranged around two courtyards.
Summer: daily 10-6.

RØROS

MINING MUSEUM
Røros 7460
Tools, machinery and equipment used in the copper works since it was established in 1650.
By appointment.

RØROS MUSEUM
7460 Røros
Folklore. Local handicrafts. Costume collection. Furniture. Lapp culture. Church furnishings. The museum owns five old cottages in Slegg-Veien, which have been restored and furnished in period style.
June-Aug. Daily 11-3.

SANDANE

NORDFJORD FOLK MUSEUM
Sandane 6860
17th-19th century houses and farm buildings, collected from all over Nordfjord. The houses are furnished in period style and contain tools and other equipment. Nearby is a local type of sailing-ship, the 'Nordfjord-jekt', built here in 1881.
July 1 - Aug. 15, Daily 11-1, 4-6. Other times by appointment.

SANDEFJORD

COMMANDER CHR. CHRISTENSEN'S WHALING MUSEUM
Radhusgatan 4, Sandefjord 3200
History of Norwegian whaling. Ethnography, geology, geography and zoology of the Antarctic.
May-Sept. M.-Sa. 12-5; Su. 12-6. Oct.-Apr., Su. 12-4.

SANDEFJORD MARITIME MUSEUM
Prinsensgate 18, Sandefjord 3200
Maritime history from its early days. Sandefjord as a maritime centre for over a thousand years. Collection relating to Roald Amundsen, gathered together by Helmer Hanssen, his mate and captain on his Arctic and Antarctic expeditions.
June-Sept. M.-Sa. 12-5; Su. 12-6. Oct.-May Su. 12-4.

TOWN MUSEUM
Pukkestad Gård, Sandefjord 3200
In house (1800), restored and furnished to give the impression of a prosperous home of the period. Folk art and local history.
June-Sept., M.-Sa. 12-5; Su. 12-6. Oct.-May, Su. 12-4.

SARPSBORG

FOLK MUSEUM FOR ØSTFOLD
Kont. fylkeskonservator lektor, Vaktmest, Sarpsborg 1700
Groups of old buildings illustrating the life lived by the farming community and rich families of the district. Magistrate's house from Snekkenes; rectory from Øymark; ferry stage from Sollisundet; old Østfold farm with sawmill and tenants' cottages. The museum has a prehistoric section and ethnographical collections from Østfold.
Summer: daily 10-6.

SETESDAL

SETESDAL MUSEUM
Farm of Rygnestad in Valle, Setesdale, Aust-Agder
Medieval farm, housing historical and ethnographical collections.
Summer: M.-Sa. 10-3; Su. 12-3.

SKIEN

TELEMARK AND GRENLAND FOLK MUSEUM
Søndre Brekke, Skien 3700
Peasant art-carvings, rose-paintings, embroidery and costumes from the Telemark valleys. Old houses from the parishes of Telemark and Grenland. Main building is furnished with items from the Renaissance and Baroque periods, to the mid 19th century. Henrik Ibsen's reading room, blue drawing-room and bedroom from Arbien Street, Oslo.
May 15 - Sept. 15, M.-Sa. 10-7; Su. 12-6.

VENSTØP FARM
Skien 3700
The farm where Ibsen spent his childhood. The main building, out-houses and store-houses have been completely preserved as they were at the beginning of the 19th century. Puppet theatre.
May 15 - Sept. 15, Daily 12-6.

STAVANGER

ART GALLERY
Stavanger 4000
Norwegian paintings over the last hundred years. Works by artists of the Stavanger School, especially Hertervig, the Jaeren painter.
Summer: M.-Sa. 10-3; Su. 12-3.

MANOR HOUSE
Ledaal, Stavanger 4000
Furnished in style of 1800. Members of the royal family stay here when visiting Stavanger.
Summer: M.-Sa. 10-3; Su. 12-3.

MARITIME MUSEUM
Museg 16, 4000 Stavanger
Ship paintings, figureheads, models of ships and shipyards. Model of Stavanger harbour in 1890. Ship-building tools. Captain's cabin from sailing-ship period, and first-class passenger lounge from passenger steamer (1914). Model of oil-drilling rig. Navigational instruments. Models in bottles. Sea chests.
June-Aug. Daily 10-2. Sept.-May, Su. 10-2.

STAVANGER MUSEUM
Museg 16, Stavanger 4000
Nordic prehistory. Zoology. Urban and rural items from the county of Rogaland, illustrating the cultural history of the area. Ethnographic collection.
June-Aug., Su.-F. 10-2; Sa. 10-1. Sept.-May, Su. 10-2.

WEST NORWEGIAN SCHOOL MUSEUM
Stavanger 4000
19th-20th century educational history of West Norway.
M.-Sa., daily 10-5.

STAVERN

THE BLOCK HOUSE
Stavern 3290
Building of 1788, housing military and naval material and relics from the period c.1800.
M.-Sa. 10-3; Su. 12-3.

STORHAMARLÅVEN

LOCAL MUSEUM
Storhamarlåven
Local history. Folklore.
Summer: M.-Sa. 10-3; Su. 12-3.

SUNNDAL

LEIKVIN MUSEUM OF BUILDINGS
Sunndal, Nørdmore
Housed in an old Sunndal farm with additions, including a chapel. The museum collections give a picture of the significance of the English salmon-fishers to villages in the West of Norway in the second half of the 19th century.
Summer: M.-Sa. 10-3; Su. 12-3.

TINGELSTAD

HADELAND FOLK MUSEUM
Tingelstad, Oppland
Old farm buildings from the surrounding districts, many of them grouped round a Hadeland farmyard, and including a dwelling house from Ulven in Lunner. Agricultural machinery. Ethnographical collections.
Summer: M.-Sa. 10-3; Su. 12-3.

TØNSBERG

VESTFOLD FOLK MUSEUM
Farmannsveien 30, Tønsberg, Vestfold
Archaeology. Maritime history. Whaling. History of agriculture. Urban history.
May-Sept. Daily 10-7. Oct.-Apr. Daily 10-3. Open-air section closed in winter.

TOTEN

TOTEN MUSEUM
Stenberg gård, Toten, Oppland
Former residence of the County Governor. Furniture and furnishings of the early 19th century. Agricultural machinery.
Summer: M.-Sa. 10-3; Su. 12-3.

TRØGSTAD

TRØGSTAD OPEN-AIR MUSEUM
Trøgstad, Østfold
Different types of buildings from the district. Furniture and furnishings.
Summer: daily 10-6.

TROMSÖ

TROMSÖ MUSEUM
Folkeparken, Tromsö 9000
Scientific and anthropological investigations in northern Norway and the Arctic regions. Natural history. Archaeology, including slate implements from the Stone Age, and finds in silver from the Viking Period and early Middle Ages. Church art: examples of late medieval workmanship of Hanseatic origins as well as specimens from the baroque period. Folk art. Urban culture. Lapp collection.
M.-Sa. 10-3; Su. 12-3.

TRONDHEIM

HOME FRONT MUSEUM
Erkebispegården, Trondheim 7000
Uniforms, weapons and personal possessions of the Norwegian resistance groups, World War II.
June-Sept., Daily 10-3.

MARITIME MUSEUM
Fjordgaten 6, Trondheim 7000
Models of sailing vessels. Paintings. Ships' equipment.
June 1 - Oct. 1, daily 11-3. Su. all year round, 12-3.

MILITARY MUSEUM
The Armoury, Archbishop's Palace, Trondheim 7000
Old uniforms, weapons, paintings and effects from wartime in Scandinavia, dating from Middle Ages to World War II.
June-Aug. M.-Sa. 9-2; Su. 11-2.

MUSEUM OF THE ROYAL NORWEGIAN SOCIETY OF SCIENCES AND LETTERS
University of Trondheim, Erling Skakkesgate 47, N-7000 Trondheim
Zoological collection, including mammals (particularly Nordic animals), birds and fishes. Herbarium. Minerals and rock samples. Antiquities from Nordmøre, Romsdale, Trøndelag and S. Nordland. Archaeological finds from Stone Age to the Vikings. Ecclesiastical art. Coin collection. Lapp and Eskimo cultures. Collection illustrating everyday life in Trondheim from the Reformation to the 19th century.
May 2-31, M.-Sa. 12-3; June 1 - Sept. 30, M.-Sa. 11-3. Oct.-Apr. Su. 12-3.

NORTH NORWAY MUSEUM OF APPLIED ARTS
Munkegt. 5, Trondheim 7000
Norwegian and foreign applied art. 20th century collections beginning with the art-nouveau movement (Van de Velde). Furniture, textiles, glass, ceramics. Metalwork from the Renaissance to the present day.
May 19 - Sept. 15, M.-F. 10-4; Sa. 10-3; Su. 12-4.

RINGVE MUSICAL HISTORY MUSEUM
Ringve, Trondheim 7000
2,000 musical instruments, music boxes and barrel organs from all over the world, kept, as far as possible, in playable condition. Rooms named after composers and furnished in different styles. Letters, signed photographs and other mementoes of famous composers, singers and musicians.
May 1 - Nov. 1 Daily 9.30-6.

STONEWORK COLLECTION
Nidaros Cathedral, 7000 Trondheim
Medieval sculpture from the cathedral.
June 1-15, M.-F. 11-3; Sa. 11-2; Su. 1.30-3. June 16 - Sept. 1, M.-F. 10-6; Sa. 10-2; Su. 1.30-4. Sept. 1 - June 1, M.-F. 12-2; Sa. 12-2; Su. 1.30-3.

TORDENSKIOLD MUSEUM
Ringve Manor Farm, Trondheim 7000
Farm where Tordenskiold spent his childhood, preserved in late 17th century style. Memorabilia of Tordenskiold.
May 1 - June 20, conducted tours at 11.30 and 1.00 daily. Aug. 20 - Nov. 1, conducted tours daily at 11.30 and 1.

TRONDHEIM ART ASSOCIATION GALLERY
Bispegaten 7, 7000 Trondheim
Norwegian art and paintings, from J. C. Dahl to present day. Paintings from Trøndelag. Danish and French paintings. Negro sculptures. Grecian art.
Tu.-Sa. 12-3, 6-8; Su. 12-4.

TRONDHEIM AND TRØNDELAG FOLK MUSEUM
Svalbergpl., Sverresborg, Trondheim 7000
Ethnographical collections from central Norway. Naturally-grouped buildings and systematically-arranged collections of objects showing daily life, handicrafts and folk art. Remnants of castle built by King Sverre of Norway (1182-83).
May 15 - Sept. 14, conducted tours every hour from 11-6 (last tour at 5). Sept. 15-30, conducted tours 11-3.

UTNE

HARDANGER MUSEUM OF BUILDINGS
Utne 5797, Hordaland
Buildings include "smoke-oven" houses from Utne, a sea-shed, a boathouse and a smithy. Works by the sculptor Lars Utne (1862-1923).
Summer: daily 10-6.

VÅGÖ

OPEN-AIR MUSEUM
Vågå, Oppland
Farm-house and outer wooden buildings brought to the museum site.
Summer: daily 10-6.

VALDRES

FOLK MUSEUM
Valdres
Local history. Folklore. Costumes.
Summer: M.-Sa. 10-3; su. 12-3.

VANSE

LISTA MUSEUM
Midthasselhuset, Vanse 4560, Vest-Agder
Typical sea-captain's home, with maritime and prehistoric exhibits and a collection of the works of the sculptor Mathias Skeibrok (1851-1896).
Summer; M.-Sa. 10-3; Su. 12-3.

VARDAL OG SNERTINGDAL

OPEN-AIR MUSEUM
Vardal og Snertingdal 2810, Oppland
Old buildings from the surrounding area, brought to the museum site.
Summer: daily 10-6.

VARDØ

VARDØ MUSEUM
Vardohus, Vardø 9950, Finnmark
Local history. Weapons.
Summer: M.-Sa. 10-3; Su. 12-3.

VERDAL

VERDAL MUSEUM
nr. Stiklestad Church, Verdal 7650, Nord-Trondelag
Farm buildings set out around a dwelling house from Mo. The house is partly furnished.
Summer: daily 10-6.

VOLDA

VOLDA MUSEUM OF BUILDINGS
Volda 6100, Møre og Romsdal
Collection of old farm buildings, brought to the museum site.
Daily 10-6 (summer).

VOSS

VOSS FOLK MUSEUM
Mølster, Voss 5700, Hordaland
Exhibits are housed at the old farm of Mølster. Most of the buildings are 18th century, but there is a barn dating from 1680 and two medieval lofts.
Summer: daily 10-6.

Pakistan, West

Nearly everything that we have said about the museums of India applies with equal force to the museums of West Pakistan, and there is no point in repeating it here. The museums which exist today are for the most part the museums that were there when the British left a quarter of a century ago. Their emphasis continues to be archaeological and artistic, and the few collections dealing with scientific and technical subjects form part of universities or research institutions.

BAHAWALPUR

VETERINARY MUSEUM
Bahawalpur
Biological, anatomical and pathological collections, used in the training of veterinary students.
By appointment.

BANBHORE

ARCHAEOLOGICAL MUSEUM
Banbhore, Thatta District, Sind
Site museum. Material from local excavations. 8th-13th century remains of wall and structures thought to have been the first Muslim settlement in the country.
Sa.-Th. 9-4.

HARAPPA

ARCHAEOLOGICAL MUSEUM
Harappa, Dist. Montgomery
Site museum, containing material from excavations in the area.
Sa.-Th. 9-4.

KARACHI

AIWEN-E-RIFAF MUSEUM AND ART GALLERY
Karachi
Paintings. Handicrafts. Applied arts.
Sa.-Th. 9-4; F. 9-12.30.

NATIONAL MUSEUM OF PAKISTAN
Burns Garden, Karachi
Palaeolithic implements from the Soan Valley. Antiquities from Kot-Diji, Mohenjodaro, Harappa, Chanhudaro and Jhukar (2,500-1,500 B.C.). Gandhara and Indo-Afghan sculptures (1st-6th centuries A.D.). Items from Taxila and Paharpur. Hindu sculptures. Coins. Paintings on paper and ivory. Documents. Ethnography.
Sa.-Th. 9-5, F. 9-12.30.

QUAID-I-AZAM BIRTHPLACE AND MUSEUM
Karachi 2
House in which Quaid-i-Azam was born. Original furnishings. Collections illustrating his life and work.
On request.

ARCHAEOLOGICAL MUSEUM
University of Karachi, Karachi
Archaeological collections illustrating cultural history of Pakistan.
By appointment.

LAHORE

INDUSTRIAL AND COMMERCIAL MUSEUM
Bank Square, Lahore
Up-to-date collection of the raw material resources, handicrafts, art-ware and manufactured products of West Pakistan.
Daily ex. F. 9-4; F. 9-12.30; Su. closed.

LAHORE MUSEUM
Lahore
Graeco-Buddhist sculpture. Indian coins. Paintings of the Mughal, Rajput and Kangra schools. Gandhara collection, including a Fasting Buddha.
Winter: daily 9-4. Summer: daily 9-5.

LAHORE FORT MUSEUM
Lahore
Arms and armour. Mughal gallery. Mughal paintings, coins, calligraphy. Sikh gallery. Paintings and art of the Sikh period.
Winter: daily 9-4. Summer: daily 9-5.

PUNJAB GOVERNMENT RECORD OFFICE MUSEUM
Punjab Government Central Record Office, Lahore
Documents illustrating history of the Punjab.
Sa., M.-Th. 9-4.

ZOOLOGICAL MUSEUM
Lahore
Collections illustrating zoology of Pakistan.
Daily 9-4.

MOENJODARO

ARCHAEOLOGICAL MUSEUM
Moenjodaro, Larkana, Sind
Antiquities unearthed from the 5,000-year-old prehistoric site, the largest of the excavated Indus Valley culture cities.
Daily, 9-4.

PESHAWAR

ARCHAEOLOGICAL MUSEUM
University of Peshawar, Peshawar
Archaeological material from excavations and sites in Pakistan, especially the Peshawar region.
By appointment.

ARCHIVAL MUSEUM
Central Record Office, Peshawar
Documents illustrating history of Peshawar and its region.
Sa.-Th. 10-4.

FOREST MUSEUM
Pakistan Forestry Institute, Peshawar University, Peshawar
Forestry and allied subjects.
By appointment.

PESHAWAR MUSEUM
Peshawar
Sculptures of the Gandhara School: images of Buddha, the Bodhisattvas, Buddhist deities, reliefs illustrating the life of Buddha and Jataka stories. Architectural pieces and minor antiquities excavated at Charsadda, Sahri-Bahlol, Shaji-ki-Dheri, Takht-i-Bahi and Jamal Garhi. Art gallery. Industrial and mineral products. Forestry. Effigies of Red Kafirs.
Daily 10-4.

QUETTA

GEOLOGICAL SURVEY OF PAKISTAN MUSEUM
Quetta
Petrology. Mineralogy. Palaeontology.
By appointment.

RAWALPINDI

ARMY MUSEUM
Rawalpindi
Weapons. Military equipment. History of the Pakistan army.
Daily, 9-4.

RAWALPINDI GALLERY OF MODERN ART
Rawalpindi
Works by 20th century Pakistani artists.
Daily, 10-5.

TAXILA

ARCHAEOLOGICAL MUSEUM
Taxila, Rawalpindi
Gandhara sculptures in stone and stucco. Gold and silver ornaments. Household utensils, pottery. Antiquities from sites of Taxila and monastic area (6th century B.C. - 5th century A.D.).
Daily, 9-4.

Panama

This is a banana, rice and mahogany economy, with tourists thrown in for good measure. None of the country's four museums has anything to say about such important matters, but does very well with folk art, ceramics and such antidotes to the sordid business of earning a living.

GUARARE

MANUEL F. ZARATE MUSEUM
Guarare, Los Santos
Folk art, ethnography of Panama.
Tu.-Sa. 9-12, 2-5; Su. 2-6. Closed public holidays.

LAS TABLAS

BELISARIO PORRAS MUSEUM
Las Tablas, Los Santos
Collections illustrating life and work of the political leader, Belisario Porras.
Tu.-Sa. 9-12, 2-5; Su. 2-6. Closed public holidays.

PANAMA

NATIONAL MUSEUM
Avenida Cuba, Calles 29-30, Aptdo 662, Panama 1
Archaeology. Ethnography. History of Panama. Fauna of Panama and other countries.
Tu.-Sa. 9-12, 2-5; Su. 2-6. Closed public holidays.

PENONOMÉ

PENONOMÉ MUSEUM
Penonomé
Collection of ceramics, formerly the possessions of the Conte family.
By appointment.

Panama Canal Zone

The building of the Panama Canal early in the present century was one of the most important civil engineering achievements in the world, and it is pleasant to be able to record the existence of a museum to celebrate and document the enormous effort and skill that went into this task, and the successful struggle against disease and other natural hazards that it represents. The Canal, 50 miles long and used by commercial shipping since 1914, was essentially a United States triumph but, as the presence of an American military museum within the Canal Zone reminds us, the Canal was not built for fun.

BALBOA HEIGHTS

CANAL ZONE LIBRARY-MUSEUM
Balboa Heights
History of the Panama Canal; the French canal effort; the building of the Panama Railroad. Models of equipment used in construction of the Canal; tools; household and office items of the period. Handicrafts and pre-Columbian pottery

from the Republic of Panama. Paintings of the Canal and adjacent areas by E. J. Read (1913-14). Japanese art. Sculpture by local artists.
M.-Sa. 9.30-9.

FORT AMADOR

MILITARY MUSEUM
Headquarters, United States Army Forces Southern Command, Fort Amador
Local U.S. military history.
By appointment.

Papua and New Guinea, Territory of

This museum contains everything that an avid reader of travel books and adventure stories could hope to find.

PORT MORESBY

PAPUA AND NEW GUINEA PUBLIC MUSEUM
House of Assembly Building, McGregor Street, Port Moresby, Papua
Anthropology and archaeology of Papua and New Guinea. Natural history. Arts and crafts of the country. Exhibits include wooden cult-crocodile from the Karawari River, East Sepik District (25 feet, 8 inches long); unique larger-than-life wooden sculpture of a human figure representing a hunting spirit from the Yuat River; large carved housepost from the spirit house at Kanganamum.
Daily 9-5. Closed Good F., Easter Su. and Christmas Day.

Paraguay

This is a timber-producing, cattle-raising, agricultural country, with about two million people and a high rate of adult illiteracy. Its museums illustrate the lives of the poor (ethnography) and of the well-to-do (period furnishings and household equipment), with religious art and contemporary paintings to some extent bridging the gap between the two.

ASUNCION

MONSEÑOR SINFORIANO BAGARIN MUSEUM
Avenida Kubistchek y Cerro Corá, Asuncion
Collection of religious art, formed by the former Archbishop, Monseñor Sinforiano Bagarin.
Tu.-Su. 10-1, 2-5.

ETHNOGRAPHICAL COLLECTION
Calle Don Bosco 323, Asuncion
Collections illustrating the native cultures of Paraguay.
Tu.-Su. 10-1, 2-5.

ETHNOGRAPHICAL MUSEUM
España 395 esquina Mompox, Asuncion
Archaeological and ethnographical collections illustrating the native cultures of Paraguay.
Tu.-Su. 10-1, 2-5.

EXHIBITION OF NATIONAL PRODUCTS
Avenida España 477, Asuncion
Permanent exhibition of the industrial and agricultural products of Paraguay.
Tu.-Su. 10-1, 2-5.

JULIAN DE LA HERRERIA MUSEUM
Estados Unidos esquina República de Colombia, Asuncion
Collections illustrating life and work of the artist, Julian de la Herreria.
Tu.-Su. 10-1, 2-5.

MUSEUM OF FINE ARTS AND ANTIQUITIES
Calle Mariscal Estigarribia esquina Iturbe, Asuncion
Paintings, sculpture by Paraguayan and foreign artists.
Tu.-Su. 10-1, 2-5.

MUSEUM OF THE HOUSE WHERE INDEPENDENCE WAS BORN
Calle 14 de Mayo esquina Presidente Franco, Asuncion
House (1772), in which the campaign to obtain Paraguay's independence began (1871). Furniture and other material of the period.
Tu.-Su. 10-1, 2-5.

MUSEUM OF MILITARY HISTORY
Calle Vice Presidente Sánchez esquina Av. Mariscal López, Asuncion
Collection relating to the War of the Triple Alliance (1864-70) and the Chaco War (1932-35).
Tu.-Su. 10-1, 2-5.

MUSEUM OF NATURAL HISTORY
Avenida Artigas y Primer Presidente - Stma. Trinidad, Asuncion
Collections illustrating the botany, zoology, ethnography and archaeology of Paraguay.
Tu.-Su. 10-1, 2-5.

MUSEUM OF POSTAL HISTORY
Calle Alberdi entre las de Benjamin Constant y el Paraguayo Independiente, Asuncion
Postage stamps of Paraguay and foreign countries.
Tu.-Su. 10-1, 2-5.

NATURAL SCIENCE MUSEUM OF THE INTERNATIONAL COLLEGE
Calle Rio de Janeiro esquina Mayor Fleitas, Asuncion
Geology. Zoology. Botany.
M.-F. 10-1, 2-5; Sa. 10-1.

NUMISMATIC COLLECTION OF THE CENTRAL BANK OF PARAGUAY
Calle Independencia Nacional entre 25 de Mayo y Cerro Corá, Asuncion
Coins and currency notes of Paraguay.
Tu.-Su. 10-1, 2-5.

CARLOS ALBERTO PUSINERI SCALA COLLECTION
Hernandarias 1313, Asuncion
Collections illustrating the archaeology and history of Paraguay. Colonial art. Military trophies. Coins. Medals.
Tu.-Su. 10-1, 2-5.

ITAUGUÁ

MUSEUM OF ICONOGRAPHY
Itauguá
Regional history. Religious art.
Tu.-Su. 10-1, 2-5.

LUQUE

GENERAL ELIZARDO AQUINO MUSEUM
Luque
Local history.
Tu.-Su. 10-1, 2-5.

PILAR

CABILDO MUSEUM
Pilar
In restored Cabildo building. Local history.
Tu.-Su. 10-1, 2-5.

YAGUARÓN

DOCTOR FRANCIA MUSEUM
Yaguarón
Late 18th century house, with period furnishings and equipment.
Tu.-Su. 10-1, 2-5.

Peru

The great glory of the museums of Peru is, of course, the archaeology material and sculpture from the cities of the Incas, and from other pre-colonial cultures. There are, however, a number of excellent collections of art and handicrafts from the colonial period, including remarkable work by gold and silversmiths - one complete museum is devoted to gold - and much ethnographical material. The nineteenth-century struggles to achieve national independence are documented in several museums, with some surprising relics, including an admiral's shinbone. Among the more exotic exhibits are the remains of the Blériot aeroplane in which a Peruvian pilot made the first crossing of the French Alps. There are two museums of bull-fighting, as good as any to be found in Spain.

ANCASH

ARCHAEOLOGICAL MUSEUM
Ancash
Exhibits include 400 stone carvings and megalithic statues from Huarás.
M.-F. 9-6; Sa. 9-2.

AREQUIPA

CATALINA CONVENT
Arequipa
Colonial streets, shops and residences. Period furniture. Kitchen utensils. Paintings.
M.-F. 9-6; Sa. 9-2.

STATE MUSEUM
Arequipa
Archaeology. Ethnography. History.
M.-F. 9-6; Sa. 9-2.

ATE

PURUCHUCO SITE MUSEUM
Central Highway, Ate
Ruins of pre-Inca chief's lodgings, used as administrative centre by the Incas in the 15th century. Museum contains objects found in tombs: pottery, textiles, anthropological material.
Tu.-Su. 9-5.

AYACUCHO

REGIONAL HISTORICAL MUSEUM OF AYACUCHO
Ayacucho
Archaeology. Anthropology. History. Popular crafts.
Tu.-Su. 9-5.

CALLAO

PERUVIAN NAVAL MUSEUM
121 Jorge Chavez Avenue, Callao
Prow-guards, uniforms and swords. Memorabilia of Admiral Miguel Grau, hero of the war with Chile, including a piece of his shin-bone. Ships' models. Historical documents. Map collection.
Summer: daily 10-12. Winter: daily 10-12, 3-5.

CUZCO

MUSEUM AND ARCHAEOLOGICAL INSTITUTE
National University of Cuzco, Cuzco
Archaeological exhibits excavated from sites in the area.
By appointment.

REGIONAL HISTORICAL MUSEUM
Calle Heladeros, Cuzco
Peruvian colonial art. Local history.
Tu.-Su. 9-5.

HUANCAYO

ARCHAEOLOGICAL MUSEUM
Huancas 251, Apdo. 189, Huancayo
Archaeological specimens from Nazca and other Peruvian cultures. Examples of weaving, gold and bronze ornaments. Fossils.
Tu.-Su. 9-5.

ICA

ARCHAEOLOGICAL MUSEUM
Ica
Material excavated from sites in the region.
Tu.-Su. 9-6.

IQUITOS

MUSEUM
Ramirez Hurtado No. 622, Iquitos
Large collection of stuffed Amazonian fauna.
M.-F. 9-5; Sa. 9-2.

LAMBAYEQUE

"BRUNING" ARCHAEOLOGICAL MUSEUM
Calle 2 de Mayo 48, Lambayeque
Gold, silver, textiles, ceramics, wood and stone objects. Two unique blue and black granite mortars incised with mythological figures in "Chavin" style.
Tu.-Su. 9-5.

LIMA

ARCHAEOLOGICAL MUSEUM
Puruchuco, Lima
11 km. from Lima on the Central Transandine Highway. Ceramics, textiles and other items from the lower Rimac or Lima Valley.
Tu.-Su. 9-11.30, 2.30-5. Closed M.

ARCHAEOLOGY MUSEUM
Catholic University, 459 Camana, Lima
Archaeological exhibits.
Tu. 4-7; Th. 10-7.

GEOLOGICAL MUSEUM OF THE NATIONAL UNIVERSITY OF ENGINEERING
Camino Ancon, Lima
Geological and mineralogical collections of Peru.
By appointment.

RAFAEL LARCO HERRERA MUSEUM
Avenida Bolivar 16th block, Lima
This is the Chiclin Museum, transplanted from Trujillo. Exhibits from the Mochica period, (400-800 A.D.). The Cupisnique period, dating back to 1,000 B.C., as well as exhibits from the Nazca, Chimu and Inca periods, are also well represented. Pottery. Textiles.
M.-Sa. 9-1, 3-6. Closed Su. and holidays.

MUNICIPAL ART GALLERY
Municipal Building, Plaza de Armas, Lima
Collections of paintings by Peruvian artists, including works by Ignacio Merino (1817-1876).
Daily 9-1, 3-6; Jan.-Mar. 9-1.

MUSEUM OF ART
Paseo Colon 125, Parque de la Exposicion, Lima
1,000-year-old mantles from Paracas. Paintings by Bernardo Bitti and Diego Quispe Tito. Water-colours by Pancho Fierro. Paintings by Francisco Lazo and José Sabogal. Cultural history of Peru from pre-Hispanic period to the present day. Sculpture. Ceramics. Textiles. Gold and silver work. Furniture. Tapestries. Costumes. Miniatures.
Winter: daily 10-12, 3-7. closed M. F. 10-12, 3-10. Summer: daily ex. M. 9-12, 4-8; F. 9-12, 4-10.

MUSEUM OF THE BULLFIGHTING ART
Jr. Conde de Superunda 341, Lima
History of bullfighting seen through art. Paintings, engravings, posters, plates and fans. Bullfight posters from the Colonial period to the present day. Prints by Gustavo Doré.
By appointment.

MUSEUM OF THE CONGRESS
Inquisicion Square, (Junin 5th Block), Lima
Historical documents and manuscripts relating to the political history of the Republic. The innaugural record of Peru's first constitutional Assembly. Autographed copy of the Constitution of the Republic of April 9, 1933.
M.-Sa. 10-6; Su. and holidays closed.

MUSEUM OF ITALIAN ART
Paseo de la Republica, 2nd block, Parque Neptuno, Lima
Italian paintings (mostly reproductions). Originals by Impressionists such as Mancini, Spadini, Gola, Tito Michetti. Sculptures by Gemito, Riualta, Bistolfi, Canonica, Tofamari. Engravings by Guilani Giovanni, Sartorio, Fratino, Grazioni. Pottery. Facade of the building is decorated with mosaics by Buffa.
Tu.-Sa. 10-12, 4-7; Su. and holidays, 4-7.

MUSEUM OF MILITARY HISTORY
Real Felipe Fortress, Callao, Lima
Cannons; the Spanish flag that flew during the last Spanish stand in the fortress. Portraits of General Rodil and of Lord Cochrane. Remains of small Blériot plane in which the Peruvian pilot, Jorge Chavez, made the first crossing of the Alps from Switzerland to Italy. Weapons. Decorations. Medals. Sculptures. Paintings. Trophies and relics.
Winter: Tu.-Su. 9-12, 3-5. Summer: Tu., Th., Sa. and Su., 8-12, 3-5.

MUSEUM OF THE PRE-HISPANIC ANTHROPOLOGY AND AGRICULTURE INSTITUTE
Agrarian University, Camilo Carrillo 300A, Lima
Agricultural techniques, costumes, arts, customs and traditions of the ancient Peruvians. Views of pre-Hispanic towns and villages. 10,000 year-old mummies.
M.-F. 9-12.30, 3-6.

MUSEUM OF REPLICAS
San Marcos University, Basement of National Library, Abancay Avenue, Lima
Copies of paintings ranging from the Roman-Gothic period, through the Renaissance, to the Spanish, German and French schools of the 16th and 17th centuries, and up to Impressionism and Post-Impressionism.
Winter: M.-Sa. 9-12, 4.30-6.30. Summer: M.-Sa. 9-1, 5-8. Closed Su. and holidays.

MUSEUM OF SAN FRANCISCO THE GREAT
San Francisco Square, Lima
In monastery. Architectural, historic and cultural collections of four centuries. Paintings by Francisco Zurbaran (received c.1626). Embroidery hall, with pieces of ecclesiastical robes embroidered in gold and silk, a gift of Emperor Carlos V. Paintings by José de la Rivera. Silversmith work from Lima and Cuzco.
Daily 10-11.30, 3-5.30.

MUSEUM OF THE SUMMER LINGUISTIC INSTITUTE
Ministry of Education, Lima
Ethnography of ten Amazonian tribes: ceremonial ornaments, domestic equipment. Photographs of work done by the Institute in the Peruvian jungle.
M.-F. 9-12.

MUSEUM OF THE VICEROYALTY
Quinta de Presa, Lima
Colonial portraits, furniture, dresses, candelabra. One of the Viceroy's carriages.
Daily ex. Sa. 9-12, 3-6. Jan.-Mar. 9-1.

NATIONAL MUSEUM OF ANTHROPOLOGY AND ARCHAEOLOGY
Bolivar Square, (22nd block of Brasil Avenue), Pueblo Libre, Lima
Archaeological specimens in stone, bone, wood, shell, gold, silver and bronze. Textiles from Paracas. Basketwork and other objects from burial grounds along coast and inland. Primitive surgical instruments. Collection of trepanned skulls. Art and history of the aboriginal races of Peru. Ceramics of the Chimu, Nasca and Pachacamac cultures.
Daily 10-7.

NATIONAL MUSEUM OF HISTORY
Plaza Bolivar, Pueblo Libre, Lima
Colonial material: the first crosses erected by the Spanish conquerors (16th century). Baptismal font, religious and decorative objects of the time. Weapons. Independence period: dedicated to San Martin and Bolivár, with pictures, furniture and personal belongings, including San Martin's poncho, sword and horse harness. Paintings of the Oath of Independence; the execution of Maria Parado de Bellido; the Conference of Punchauca. Portraits of Luna Pizarro and other celebrities of the time.
M.-F. 9-6; Su. and holidays 9-12, 3-6. Closed Sa.

NATIONAL MUSEUM OF PERUVIAN CULTURE
Avenida Alfonso Ugarte 650, Lima
Costumes worn by Indians in various parts of Peru. Jewellery. Silverwork. Pottery. Textiles. Handicrafts. Amazonic ethnography.
M.-F. 8.30-12.30, 3-6; Sa. 9-12.

NUMISMATIC MUSEUM
National Mint, Junin 791, Lima
Official currency of Colonial and Republican epochs. Private coins, bills, wedges, minting machinery, medals and Peruvian decorations. Fake coins. Banknotes issued by the Bank since 1822. Complete collection of medals by Armando Pareja. Medals of gold and silver, inlaid with precious stones.
M., W., F. 10-1. Closed holidays.

THE PERUVIAN GOLD MUSEUM
Prolongación Primavera, Hda. de San Antonio, Surco
Underground museum. Weapons. Gold objects from Mochica and Chimu civilisations to the end of the Inca Empire, 1532; tunics, necklaces, idols, funeral masks, litters, sceptres.
M.-F. 3-7; Sa. 9-1.

PHILATELIC MUSEUM
First Floor, Post Office Passage, Lima
History of the postal and communications service in Peru. Postage stamps.
M.-F. 8-6.

POPULAR ART COLLECTION
199 Hernán Velarde Park, Lima
Popular art.
By appointment, afternoons only.

JAVIER PRADO NATURAL HISTORY MUSEUM
Avenida Arenales 1256, Lima
Peruvian flora, birds, mammals, butterflies, reptiles, fish and insects. Dioramas of Peru's mineral wealth. Shells. Botanical collection of Antonio Raimondi. Specimen of a Sun fish (only one outside Japan).
M.-F. 8.30-6.30; Sa., Su. 8.30-12.

PACHACAMAC

PACHACAMAC MUSEUM
Lurin, Pachacamac
31 km. from Lima, on the South Panamerican Highway. Site museum. Former sacred city and then the centre of pre-Inca civilisations. City and temple dedicated to Pachacamac, creator of the world. Exhibits include the idol that the Spanish conquerors in Pachacamac discovered in the 16th century.
Tu.-F. 9-5; Sa. and Su. 8.30-5.30. Closed M.

RIMAC

COLONIAL MUSEUM
"Quinta de Presa", 3rd block of Francisco Pizarro Avenue, Rimac
Colonial mansion (1763), named after the aunt of Don Pedro Carrillo de Albornoz, a Knight of the Order of Montesa and Colonel of the Royal Armies of Spain. Furniture, candelabra, costumes, paintings. Portraits of Ferdinand VII

and Viceroy Amat. Works of the Peruvian artist, Teofilo Castillo. Some of the objects belonged to Micaela Villegas, "La Perricholi", mistress of Viceroy Amat.
M.-F. 9-6; Su. and holidays 9-12, 3-6. Summer 2-6. Closed Sa.

MESON BULLFIGHTING MUSEUM
Hualgayoc 334, Rimac
Paintings, sculptures, objects of historic and artistic value, photographs and books on the art of bullfighting. Reproductions of bulls found in caves of Altamira, in Asturias, Spain. Bullfighting costume worn by "El Cordobes". Engravings by Antonio Carnicero and Fictor Adam. Reproduction of Goya's "Tauromaquia". Drawings. Prints. Costumes. Swords. Capes.
M.-F. 9-6; Sa. 9-2. Closed Su. and holidays.

SACSAYHUAMAN

ARCHAEOLOGICAL MUSEUM
Sacsayhuaman
Spanish paintings of Inca royalty dating from shortly after the Conquest.
M.-F. 9-5.

SAN ISIDRO

HUALLAMARCA SITE MUSEUM
Nicolas de Rivera 201, San Isidro
On site of a huaca (pre-Columbian burial ground), made of mud bricks shaped like corn cobs and placed forming a pyramid. Pottery, textiles from the tombs.
Tu.-Su. 10-12, 3-6. Closed M.

TRUJILLO

ARCHAEOLOGICAL MUSEUM
Diego de Almagro, 3rd block, Plaza de Armas, Trujillo
Archaeological exhibits from sites in the area. Inscriptions. Pottery.
Daily 8-12, 3-6. Jan.-Mar. 8-1.

Philippines

Two types of museum stand out in the Philippines list - those devoted to archaeology and to the late nineteenth-century struggle for national independence. The two great national heroes, Apolinario Mabini, the 'sublime paralytic', and José Rizal, are commemorated by two museums each, the Rizal collections being particularly distinguished by a life-size figure of Rizal in his prison cell and (probably without parallel elsewhere) by part of his backbone, removed after his execution and now displayed in a cut-glass jar.

Today's people and occupations are hardly represented at all, but there are good collections of local birds, animals and plants.

BAGUIO CITY

ST. LOUIS UNIVERSITY MUSEUM
Baguio City
Natural history.
M.-Sa. 9-12, 2-5. Closed during university vacations.

BATANGAS

LEON APACIBLE MUSEUM AND LIBRARY
Taal, Batangas
18th century house containing the private law library of Don Leon Apacible, his personal possessions and other historical material. He was one of the signatories of the Malolos Constitution.
Daily 8-5.

JOSÉ P. LAUREL MEMORIAL MUSEUM
Tanauan, Batangas
Personal possessions and documents of José P. Laurel, statesman, legislator and jurist.
Daily 8-5.

TALAGA MABINI SHRINE
Barrio Talaga, Tanauan, Batangas
Birthplace of Apolinario Mabini, the "Sublime Paralytic". Replica of his house, made of nipa, wood and bamboo. His coffin, paintings depicting his life during the Revolution, furniture and documents.
Daily, including holidays, 8-5.

CAGAYAN DE ORE CITY

XAVIER FOLKLIFE MUSEUM
Xavier University, Cagayan de Ore City
Philippine folklife and folklore. Ethnography of the Mindanao region.
M.-Sa. 9-5. Closed during university vacations.

CALAMBA

RIZAL SHRINE
Rizal Street, Calamba, Laguna
Memorabilia of Dr. José Rizal, in the house where he was born. Replicas of the furniture of the time. Books and manuscripts.
Daily, including holidays, 8-5.

CALBAYOG CITY

REV. FR. BASILIO ROSALES PRIVATE COLLECTION
Calbayog City
Religious objects. Archaeological finds.
By appointment.

CAVITE

AGUINALDO SHRINE
Kawit, Cavite
Historic mansion where Philippine Independence was proclaimed in 1898, and now housing the memorabilia of General Emilio Aguinaldo, first President of the Republic. Historical relics of the Museum of the Revolution. Documents on the Philippine Revolution. Tomb of the General.
Daily, including holidays, 8-5.

CEBU CITY

ST. THERESA'S COLLEGE MUSEUM
St. Theresa's College, Elizabeth Pond Street, Cebu City
Filipino folk life and folklore collections. Religious objects. Exhibits on pagan minorities.
By appointment.

UNIVERSITY MUSEUM
University of San Carlos, Cebu City
Archaeology. Anthropology. Biology. Geology.
M.-Sa. 9-5. Closed during university vacations.

DAPITAN

RIZAL SHRINE
Talisay, Dapitan, Zamboanga
Personal possessions and other souvenirs of Dr. José Rizal, during his exile in Dapitan (1892-6) before his execution at Bagumbayan in 1896. Replicas of original square house, octagonal house, hexagonal house and small hospital-houses, all made of nipa, wood and bamboo.
Daily, including holidays, 8-5.

DUMAGUETE CITY

SILLIMAN UNIVERSITY CULTURAL RESEARCH CENTRE
Silliman University, Dumaguete City
Archaeology. Anthropology. Ethnography.
M.-Sa. 9-5. Closed during university vacations.

MANILA

THE BEYER COLLECTION
1610 Laurel Street (2nd floor), Manila
Archaeology. Ethnography. Filipiniana library.
Daily 8-5.

MUSEUM OF ARTS AND SCIENCES
University of Santo Tomas, Espana Street, Sampaloc, Manila
Philippine natural history, ethnography and art. Cultural collections of the Far East. Coins, medals and stamps from all over the world. Chinese ceramics.
M.-Sa. 9-12, 2-5.

MUSEUM OF THE CITY OF MANILA
Arroceros Street, Manila
History of the city of Manila.
Daily 8-5.

NATIONAL MUSEUM OF THE PHILIPPINES
Taft Avenue, Herran Street, Manila
Archaeology, ethnography, entomology, conchology, ichthyology, ornithology, mammalogy, geology and palaeontology of the Philippines.
M.-F. 8-12, 1-5; Sa., Su. and holidays 9-12, 2-5. Closed Nov. 1, Dec. 25, Jan. 1 and Good F.

PANDACAN MABINI SHRINE
Otis Street, Pandacan, Manila
Replica of house where Apolinario Mabini, the "Sublime Paralytic" and brain of the Revolution, spent his last days. Replica of furniture used in Mabini's time.
Daily, including holidays, 8-5.

PRESIDENTIAL MUSEUM
Malacañang, Manila
Mementoes of the Presidents of the Republic of the Philippines.
Daily 8-5.

QUEZONIANA
National Library Building, T. M. Kalaw Street, Manila
Works and memorabilia of the late President, Manuel Luis Quezon.
Daily 8-5.

RIZAL SHRINE
Fort Santiago, Intramuros, Manila
Memorabilia of Dr. José Rizal. Works of art and publications by and about the national hero, including a wax figure of Rizal in his prison cell. Clothes. Furniture. Portion of Rizal's vertebra in a crystal container.
Daily, including holidays, 8-8.

SANTA ANA ARCHAEOLOGICAL SITE AND LITURGICAL ARTS MUSEUM
Plaza Felipe Calderon, Santa Ana Church, Manila
Archaeological finds from 13th century Filipino graveyard in the church patio. Colonial liturgical art objects,
Daily 8-5.

MARAWI CITY

AGA KHAN MUSEUM OF MUSLIM ARTS
Mindanao State University, Marawi City
Relics and artifacts from Mindanao, Sulu and Palawan. Philippine fauna, especially from the island of Mindanao. Brassware. Musical instruments. Weapons. Ornaments. Woven materials. Ceremonial porcelain and stoneware jars. Coins, a result of trade between the Philippines and other parts of the world for many centuries.
M.-Sa. 8-12, 1-5; Su. and holidays, open only during visit by dignitaries or on other special occasions.

NAGA CITY

UNIVERSITY MUSEUM
University of Nueva Caceres, Naga City
Archaeological finds from the Bicol region. Anthropology. Ornithology.
Daily 8-5.

NUEVA VIZCAYA

DALTON FIELD STATION
Dalton, Nueva Vizcaya
Stuffed birds caught in the area by the National Museum Bird-Ringing team.
By appointment.

PALAWAN ISLAND

TABON FIELD STATION
Quezon, Palawan Island
Archaeological finds from the Tabon Caves and other habitation and burial sites on Palawan Island.
On request.

PANGASINAN

BOLINAO FIELD STATION
Bolinao, Pangasinan
Archaeological finds from grave sites of Bolinao, housed near the church in the residence of Mr. Qu. Caasi.
By appointment.

PASAY CITY

CLARO M. RECTO MEMORIAL FOUNDATION
1750 Leveriza Street, Pasay City
Memorabilia of the late Senator Recto, politician, writer and jurist.
M.-F. 9-12, 2-5; Sa. 9-12.

LOPEZ MEMORIAL MUSEUM
10 Lancaster, Pasay City
Paintings by Filipino painters, Juan Luna and Felix Resurreccion Hidalgo. Letters and papers belonging to Dr. José Rizal.
Daily 8-5.

PILA

PILA MUSEUM
Pila, Laguna
Archaeological finds from the area.
Daily 8-5.

QUEZON CITY

ATENEO ART GALLERY
Ateneo de Manila University, Loyola Heights, Quezon City
Philippine paintings, sculpture, prints and drawings.
Daily 8-5.

MUSEUM OF ANTHROPOLOGY
College of Arts and Sciences, University of the Philippines, Diliman, Quezon City D-505
Ethnographical, archaeological and prehistoric collections. Porcelain. Early Filipino archaeology, including human remains, stones, jars, body adornments and utensils.
M.-F. 8-5. Closed Sa., Su. and holidays.

RIZAL

GENERAL CARLOS P. ROMULO'S MEMORABILIA AND LIBRARY
74 McKinley Road, Forbes Park, Mataki, Rizal
Mementoes of General Romulo, journalist, diplomat, writer, and President of the United Nations Assembly, Secretary of Foreign Affairs, Secretary of Education and President of the University of the Philippines.
Daily 8-5.

MUSEUM OF PHILIPPINE HISTORY AND ICONOGRAPHIC ARCHIVE
5th Floor, Insular Life Building, Ayala Avenue, Makati, Rizal
Philippine history. Iconography.
Daily 8-5.

SAN PABLO CITY

ESCUDERO PRIVATE MUSEUM
Villa Escudero, San Pablo City
Local history. Paintings.
By appointment.

TACLOBAN CITY

LEYTE-SAMAR MUSEUM
Tacloban City, Leyte
Novenas. Statues of saints. Clothes of heroes. Carvings and other items found around the Lyete-Samar Eastern Visayas area.
Daily 8-5.

Poland

The great national museums of Poland were not founded until the country was liberated from control by the Russians in 1918. They had, in consequence, only twenty years in which to build up their collections and organisation before war broke out once again in 1939. During the six years which followed, the Germans treated Poland with exceptional savagery, imprisoning and killing large numbers of her intellectuals, destroying many buildings - Warsaw suffered particularly severely in this way - and, in general, doing everything possible to extinguish the concept of Poland as a nation with an identity and culture of its own. There was extensive pillaging of both public and private collections of works of art.

After the war, there were three urgent problems which had to be faced in connexion with museums:

(*a*) the restoration of surviving museum buildings, at least to a point where their contents would not be further damaged by exposure to the weather;

(*b*) the location and return of material which had been taken to Germany and the Soviet Union;

(*c*) carrying out a nationwide survey to discover what material existed, especially in the ethnographical and technical fields, that might be included in future museum collections.

There were also the political and cultural problems involved in absorbing the collections of the former German territories which were now to become part of Poland. A master-plan for the reorganisation of Polish museums was drawn up, based on a policy which laid down that museums were to 'associate their work with the life of the nation and with the social and cultural requirements of each region'. The plan was a thoroughgoing one, based on a system of major museums controlling those of lesser importance. It also became possible for a large specialised museum, such as the National Technical Museum in Warsaw, to have attached to it buildings and sites of historical importance throughout the country, on a kind of extramural basis.

What has been built up during the past twenty-five years would have seemed unbelievable in 1945. Poland now has what could be justly claimed to be one of the most successful networks of museums to be found anywhere in the world. The collections are, with few exceptions, arranged according to the best modern practice - there are some very good open-air museums - the staff are well trained, and every attempt has been made both to interest local people in their museums and to make sure that the national tourist organisation is properly briefed about those museums which are likely to be of particular interest to visitors from other countries.

ANDRYCHOW

TEXTILES MUSEUM
Andrychow
History of local textile industry. 18th-19th century textiles.
Tu.-Su. 10-5.

ANTONIN

CHOPIN MEMORIAL MUSEUM
Antonin
Collections illustrating life and times of Chopin.
Tu.-Su. 10-5.

AUGUSTÓW

REGIONAL MUSEUM
Ul. 1 Maja 60, Augustów
Regional history, ethnography. Agriculture. History of Augustów Canal.
Tu.-Su. 10-4.

BABIMOST

REGIONAL MUSEUM
Lubuskiego Towarzystwa Kultury, Babimost
Regional history, ethnography. Peasant costumes, musical instruments. Material illustrating 1939-45 war.
Tu.-Su. 10-5.

BARANÓW

LOCAL MUSEUM
Baranów
Local history, especially period of German occupation.
On request.

BARANÓW SANDOMIERSKI

PALACE MUSEUM
Zamek, Baranów Sandomierski
In 16th-19th century palace. History of the palace. Regional archaeology, history, ethnography.
Tu.-Sa. 9-3; Su. 10-4.

BARCZEWO

FELIX NOWOWIEJSKI MUSEUM
Ul. Mickiewicza 13, Barczewo
Collections illustrating life and work of the composer, F. Nowowiejski (d.1946).
Tu.-Su. 10-5.

BARTNE

UKRAINIAN COLLECTIONS
Bartne
Paintings. Decorative arts. Ethnography.
Tu.-Su. 10-5.

BĘDZIN

LOCAL MUSEUM
Zamek, Ul. Zamkowa, Będzin
Local archaeology, history, ethnography. Handicrafts. Coins. Natural history.
Tu., Th.-Su. 9-2; W. 12-5.

BÉNDOMIN

JOSEF WYBICKI MUSEUM
Béndomin
Collections illustrating life and work of the political writer, J. Wybicki (d.1822).
On request.

BIAŁOWIEŹA

NATURAL HISTORY MUSEUM
Parku Narodowego, Białowieźa
In National Park. Collections illustrating geology, geography, botany, zoology, entomology, ornithology and history of the region.
Tu.-Su. 8-3.

BIAŁY DUNAJEC

LENIN HOUSE MUSEUM
Ul. Lenina 6, Biały Dunajec
Collections illustrating life and work of Lenin and his wife, in the house where he stayed during 1913 and 1914.
Tu.-Sa. 8-4.

BIAŁYSTOK

DISTRICT MUSEUM
Rynek Kościuszki, Białystok
Archaeology. 16th-19th century history. Ethnography. 18th-19th century Polish paintings. Weapons.
Tu.-Su. 11-5.

MUSEUM OF THE HISTORY OF THE REVOLUTIONARY MOVEMENT
Ul. Kilińskiego 6, Białystok
In 18th century palace. History of the Polish workers' and revolutionary movements in the 19th and 20th centuries. History of the Nazi occupation.
Tu.-Su. 10-4.

TEXTILES MUSEUM
Białystok
History and products of local textile industry.
Tu.-Su. 11-5.

BIECZ

REGIONAL MUSEUM
Ul. Kromera 2, Biecz
Regional archaeology, history. Incunabula. Numismatics. Religious art.
M.-Sa. 9-1.

BIELINY

MUSEUM OF ETHNOGRAPHY
Bieliny
Forester's cottage (1789). 19th century furniture, household equipment. Folk art.
By appointment.

BIELSKO-BIAŁA

REGIONAL MUSEUM
Ul. Wzgórze 16A, Bielsko-Biała
Regional ethnography, handicrafts. Paintings.
W., F. 9-3; Th.-Sa. 9-5; Su. 10-4.

BIELSK PODLASKI

SCHOOL MUSEUM
Liceum, Bielsk Podlaski
Local history. Folk art.
On request.

BIERUTOWICE

LOCAL MUSEUM
Bierutowice
Local history.
On request.

BIŁGORAJ

LOCAL MUSEUM
Biłgoraj
Regional costumes, handicrafts, history.
Tu.-Su. 10-4.

BISKUPIN

LOCAL MUSEUM
Biskupin
Site museum, 12 km from Biskupin, containing archaeological material from excavations at this prehistoric fortified settlement.
Apr. 15-Nov. 30, daily 10-5.

BLIZNE

LOCAL MUSEUM
Blizne
Local history (19th century). Folk art.
On request.

BŁONIL

LOCAL MUSEUM
Błonil
Archaeology.
Tu.-Su. 10-5.

BÓBRKA

LOCAL MUSEUM
Bóbrka
On site of natural source of naptha. Models illustrating exploitation of the naptha and the dangers involved.
Daily 9-4.

BOCHNIA

REGIONAL MUSEUM
Rynek 20, Bochnia
Regional history, ethnography. Oriental art. Peasant art, handicrafts.
Tu.-Su. 10-3.

BOCHOTNICA

MEMORIAL ROOM
Bochotnica
Local history. Life under the German occupation.
On request.

BOGUSZÓW

REGIONAL MUSEUM
Ul. M. Fornalskiej 39, Boguszów
Mineralogy. Archaeology. 18th century mining, textiles in Silesia. Regional history.
Tu.-Su. 10-4.

BOLISTAWIEC

LOCAL MUSEUM
Ul. Mickiewicza 13, Bolistawiec
17th-19th century Polish ceramics.
Tu.-Su. 10-3.

BOLKÓW

CASTLE MUSEUM
Bolków
In 14th century castle remodelled in 18th century. History of the castle. Ethnography. 18th century furniture, paintings.
Tu.-Su. 10-4.

BRZEG

PRASTÓW SILESIAN MUSEUM
pl. Zamkowy 1, Brzeg
History, ethnography of Silesia. Paintings. Portraits. Handicrafts. Graphics. Costumes.
Tu., F. 12-7; W., Th., Sa. 9-3; Su., public holidays 10-2.

BRZOZÓW

LOCAL MUSEUM
Brzozów
Local history.
On request.

BYDGOSZCZ

ADAM GRZYMALA-SIEDLECKI MEMORIAL MUSEUM
Bydgoszcz
Collection illustrating life and work of Siedlecki (d.1967). Theatrical history.
Tu.-Sa. 10-4; Su. 10-2.

LEON WYCZÓŁKOWSKI MEMORIAL MUSEUM
Al. 1 Maja 4, Bydgoszcz
Local archaeology, history. Life under the Nazi occupation. Coins. Paintings, graphics, sculpture by Leon Wyczółkowski. 19th century Polish paintings, graphics, sculpture.
Tu., Th., Sa. 10-4; W., F. 12-7; Su., public holidays 10-2.

BYSTRZYCA KŁODZKIA

MUSEUM OF LIGHTING
Mały Rynek 1, Bystrzyca Kłodzkia
History of lighting from oil-lamps to electricity.
Oct.-Apr., Su. 10-3. May-Sept., Tu.-Su. 10-3.

BYTOM

MUSEUM OF UPPER SILESIA
pl. E. Thälmanna 2, Bytom
Geology. Petrography. Mineralogy. Palaeontology. Zoology. Botany. Archaeological collection from excavations in Silesia. History of the region. Polish furniture, textiles, ceramics. Rural handicrafts. Costumes. 16th-20th century Italian, French, English, Scottish, German, Dutch paintings. 18th century Polish paintings. European graphics.
Tu., Th., Sa., Su. 10-3; W. 2-7; F. 10-6.

BYTÓW

REGIONAL MUSEUM
Zamek, Bytów
Regional ethnography.
Daily 9-3.

CEDYNIA

LOCAL MUSEUM
Rynek, Cedynia
Ruins of castle (972). Exhibits illustrating history of castle.
Daily 10-4.

CHEŁM

REGIONAL MUSEUM
Ul. Lubelska 55, Chełm
Geology. Mineralogy. Climatology. Anthropology. Regional archaeology, history, ethnography. Portraits. Graphics. Porcelain. Folk art.
Tu.-Su. 10-3.

CHLEWISKA

FOUNDRY MUSEUM
Chlewiska
In 18th century foundry. Museum illustrating iron-foundry techniques.
Tu.-Su. 10-5.

CHOCHOŁÓW

LOCAL MUSEUM
Chochołów
Collection illustrating rural life.
On request.

CHOJNICE

REGIONAL HISTORICAL COLLECTIONS
Albina Makowskiego, Ul. Drzymały 5, Chojnice
Regional archaeology, history, art. History of Stutthof concentration camp and of the German occupation.
W., Sa., Su. 9-3.

REGIONAL MUSEUM
Brama Człuchowska, Ul. 31 Stycznia, Chojnice
Regional archaeology, history, ethnography. Paintings by regional artists. History of sport.
W., Sa., Su. 9-3.

CHOJNÓW

REGIONAL MUSEUM
Zamek Piastowski, pl. Zamkovy 2, Chojnów
Regional prehistory, history, ethnography. Applied and decorative arts.
Tu.-Su. 10-3.

CHORZÓW

CHORZÓW MUSEUM
Ul. Powstańców 25, Chorzów
History and ethnography of Silesia. Coins. Polish paintings, graphics, with the themes of industry and labour.
Tu., Th.-Su., W. 12-6.

CHRZENÓW

REGIONAL MUSEUM
Ul. Mickiewicza 13, Chrzenów
Regional geology, zoology, ethnography, history. Prints. Drawings. Photographs.
Tu., Th., Sa. 9-1; W., F. 4-7; Su. 11-2.

CIECHANOWIEC

REGIONAL MUSEUM OF AGRICULTURE
Ul. Kósciuszki 15, Ciechanowiec
Local and regional history. Farm implements. Farm-house equipment. Memorial collection to Jan Krzysztof Kluk.
Th. 11-4; Su. 11-6.

CIEPLICE ŚLĄSKIE ZDRÓJ

REGIONAL MUSEUM OF NATURAL HISTORY
Ul. Kościelna 5-7, Cieplice Śląskie Zdrój
Geology, zoology and botany of the region.
Tu.-Su. 10-5.

CIESZYN

REGIONAL MUSEUM
Ul. Regera 6, Cieszyn
Regional archaeology, history, ethnography, art. Geology.
Tu.-Sa. 9-3; Su., public holidays 10-1.

CZARNCA

MEMORIAL MUSEUM
Czarnca
Memorial collection to the hetman, Stefan Czarniecki.
On request.

CZARNOLAS

JAN KOCHANOWSKI MUSEUM
Czarnolas, Zwoleń
Life, work and times of the Polish poet, Jan Kochanowski.
Tu., Th.-Sa., 8-3; W., Su. 12-6.

CZĘSTOCHOWA

ARCHAEOLOGICAL SITE MUSEUM
Ul. Pokoju, Częstochowa
Museum of archaeological material discovered on Lusatian site.
Tu., Th.-Su. 10-3; W. 1-6.

MUNICIPAL MUSEUM
Ratusz pl. Biegańskiego 45, Częstochowa
Religious art. Archaeology. History, including that of the workers' movement. Natural history. Ethnography. Paintings, sculpture and graphics by Polish artists.
Tu., Th.-Su. 10-3; W. 1-6.

TREASURY
klasztor Paulinów, Ul. Kordeckiego 2, Częstochowa
Religious art. Portraits. Weapons (including Turkish). Textiles. 17th-19th century musical instruments.
M.-F. 11-1, 3-5.

CZŁUCHÓW

REGIONAL MUSEUM
Zamek, Człuchów
Regional archaeology, history, ethnography.
Daily 10-2.

CZORSZTYN

REGIONAL MUSEUM
Czorsztyn
Regional history. Peasant art.
Daily 10-3.

DĄBROWA GÓRNICZA

REGIONAL MUSEUM OF GEOLOGY
Dąbrowa Górnicza
Regional geology, history. Mammoth tusks.
Tu.-Su. 10-5.

ALEKANDR ZAWADZKI MUSEUM
Pałacu Kultury Zagtębia, Pl. Wolności, Dąbrowa Górnicza
Collection illustrating life and work of Zawadzki.
Daily 10-1.

DĄBRÓWKA WIELKOPOLSKA

LOCAL MUSEUM
Dąbrówka Wielkopolska
Collections illustrating rural life. Material relating to the 1939-45 war.
On request.

DARŁOWO

REGIONAL MUSEUM
Ul. Zamkowa 4, Darłowo
Geology. Natural history. Archaeology. Local and regional history. Local and Gdańsk furniture. Ethnography, especially fishing. Religious sculpture.
Tu.-Su. 10-4.

DĘBICA

REGIONAL MUSEUM
Dębica
Regional history.
Tu.-Su. 10-4.

DĘBNO

LOCAL MUSEUM
Zamek, Dębno
Local archaeology, history.
On request.

DOBCZYCE

REGIONAL MUSEUM
Zamek, Dobczyce
Regional archaeology, history, ethnography. Coins. Ceramics. Weapons.
Apr. 15-Oct. 31, Su., public holidays 9.30-12.30, 2-7.

DOBRA

PAROCHIAL MUSEUM
Dobra
Religious art. Historical documents.
Daily 10-3.

DOBRA SZLACHECKA

LOCAL MUSEUM
Dobra Szlachecka
In 15th century bell-tower. Local history, ethnography.
On request.

DUBIECKO

IGNAZ KRASICKI MUSEUM
Dubiecko
Memorial collection to the poet, I. Krasicki (d.1801).
On request.

DUKLA

LOCAL MUSEUM
Dukla
In 17th century palace. 18th century decorative arts, furniture. Military history.
Tu.-Su. 10-5.

DUSZNIKI ZDRÓJ

MUSEUM OF PAPER-MAKING
Duszniki Zdrój
In water-powered paper mill, c.1605. Exhibits showing manufacture of hand-made paper in Poland.
Tu.-Su. 10-4.

DYNÓW

LOCAL MUSEUM
Dynów
Local history, ethnography.
On request.

ELBLAG

REGIONAL MUSEUM
Ul. Wigilijna 11-12, Elblag
Local history, archaeology. Industrial art.
Tu.-Sa. 10-5; Su. 10-3.

EŁK

REGIONAL MUSEUM
Ul. Wojska Polskiego 107, Ełk
Memorial collection to the poet, Michal Kajka, in his former home. Regional ethnography.
M.-Sa. 9-4.

SCHOOL MUSEUM
Ełk
Local and regional history.
On request.

FROMBORK

MIKOŁAJA KOPERNIKA (COPERNICUS) MUSEUM
Ul. Katedralna 12, Frombork
Collections illustrating life and scientific work of Copernicus, with a reconstruction of his observatory. Astronomical instruments. Paintings. Drawings. Books.
June 15-Aug. 31, Tu.-Su. 10-6; Sept. 1-June 14, Tu.-Su. 10-4.

GAĆ

LOCAL MUSEUM
Gać
Local history. Natural history.
On request.

GDAŃSK

ARCHAEOLOGICAL MUSEUM
Ul. Mariacka 25-6, Gdańsk
Prehistoric and medieval material from archaeological sites in Pomerania.
Tu., F. 12-6; W., Th., Sa. 10-3.

MARITIME MUSEUM
Ul. Szeroka 67, Gdańsk
History of shipping and navigation in Gdańsk.
Tu., W., F.-Sa. 10-4; Su. 12-6.

MUSEUM OF THE HISTORY OF GDAŃSK
Ul. Długa, Gdańsk
Collections illustrating history of the city of Gdańsk from earliest times.
Tu.-F. 10-3; Su. 12-5.

MUSEUM OF SHIPBUILDING
Gdańsk-Stoeznia, Gdańsk
History and technology of shipbuilding in Gdańsk.
Tu.-Sa. 10-3; Su. 12-5.

POMERANIAN MUSEUM
Ul. Rzeźnicka 25, Gdańsk
Regional history, archaeology, ethnography. Medieval sculpture. Decorative arts. Faience. Porcelain. Textiles. Paintings by Polish artists. European paintings, especially Dutch, Flemish, French, German. Prints. Drawings.
Tu., Th.-Sa. 10-3; W., Su. 10-6.

GDYNIA

'BURZA' NAVAL MUSEUM
Gdynia
In the former Polish destroyer, 'Burza'. Naval history.
May 1-Oct. 15, Tu.-Su. 10-5.

MUSEUM OF THE CITY OF GDYNIA
Ul. Starowiejska 30, Gdynia
History of the city. Memorial collection to the rising of 1945 and to Anton Abraham.
Tu.-Su. 10-5.

NAVAL MUSEUM
Bulivar Szwedzki, Gdynia
History of the Polish navy. Models of 16th-19th century Polish and foreign warships. Guns. Naval equipment.
Tu.-Su. 10-5.

OCEANOGRAPHICAL MUSEUM
Ul. Zjednoczenia 1, Gdynia
Aquarium. Museum of marine biology.
Tu.-Su. 10-5.

GIECZ

MUSEUM OF ARCHAEOLOGY
Giecz
Open-air museum. Archaeological material from regional sites.
Daily 9-5.

GIERŁOŻ

LOCAL MUSEUM
Gierłoż
Reconstruction of bunker in which Hitler died in Berlin, 1945.
On request.

GLIWICE

GLIWICE MUSEUM
Ul. Dolnych Wałow 89 and Pod Murami 2, Gliwice
Regional archaeology, history, ethnography. Handicrafts. 18th-20th century Silesian and W. European ceramics, graphics, sculpture. 18th-20th century artistic iron-work from Gliwice.
Tu. 9-2; W. 12-6; Th.-Sa. 9-2; Su. 10-3.

GŁOGOW

REGIONAL MUSEUM
Zamek, Głogow
Collections illustrating history and techniques of the local iron and steel industry.
Tu.-Su. 10-5.

GŁUCHA PUSZCZA

REGIONAL MUSEUM
Głucha Puszcza
Regional archaeology, history, ethnography. Numismatics.
Tu.-Su. 10-4.

GNIÉZNO

ARCHAEOLOGICAL MUSEUM
Ul. Św Jana 9, Gniézno
Regional archaeology, history.
Tu., Th., Sa. 9-3; W., F. 1-7; Su., public holidays 10-2.

GOŁOTCZYZNA

LOCAL MUSEUM
Gołotczyzna
Collections illustrating life and work of the writer, Aleksander Świetochowski (d.1938).
On request.

GOŁUB-DOBRZYN

DOBRZYN REGIONAL MUSEUM
Gołub-Dobrzyn
In 14th century town hall. Local archaeology, history. Coins.
Tu.-Su. 10-5.

GOŁUCHÓW

GOŁUCHÓW MUSEUM
Gołuchów
In restored 16th-17th century palace. European paintings, sculpture. Brussels tapestries. European and Oriental porcelain. Chinese bronzes.
Tu.-Su. 10-4.

GORLICE

REGIONAL MUSEUM
Ul. Waska 11, Gorlice
History of the town and region. Ethnography.
Tu. 10-12; W., Th. 9-1; F. 10-2; Su. 10-12.

GORZEŃ GÓRNY

EMIL ZEGADŁOWICZ MUSEUM
Gorzeń Górny
Collections illustrating life and work of the writer, Zegadłowicz (d.1941), in his former home.
On request.

GORZOW WIELKOPOLSKI

REGIONAL MUSEUM
Ul. Warzawska 35, Gorzow Wielkopolski
Oceanography. Geology. Mineralogy. Archaeology. History.
Tu., W. 10-5; Th., F., Sa. 9-4; Su. 10-4.

GOSTYŃ

REGIONAL MUSEUM
Gostyń
Regional history. Paintings.
Tu.-Sa. 9-4; Su. 10-4.

GOZDOWICE

MUSEUM OF THE POLISH CORPS OF ENGINEERS
Gozdowice
History of the Corps. Equipment. Models.
Daily 10-4.

GRABOWIEC

LOCAL MUSEUM
Grabowiec
Local history. Peasant furniture, art, handicrafts.
On request.

GRABÓWNO

MICHAL DRZYMAL MEMORIAL MUSEUM
Grabówno
Collections illustrating life and work of Drzymal, in his former home.
On request.

GRANICA

MUSEUM OF THE KAMPINOS NATIONAL PARK
Granica
Museum illustrating military history of the National Park area. Documents. Weapons.
Daily 8-3.

GRODZISK MAZOWIECKI

PTTK MUSEUM
Ul. Parkowa 1, Grodzisk Mazowielcki
Local history, ethnography.
Tu., W., F. 10-2; Th. 3-7; Su. 10-1.

GRODZISK WIELKOPOLSKI

LOCAL MUSEUM
Grodzisk Wielkopolski
Collection illustrating local life and history.
On request.

GRUDZIĄDZ

MUNICIPAL MUSEUM
Ul. Wodna 3-5, Grudziądz
Archaeology. Local history. Natural history. Fishing. 19th-20th century Polish paintings. Coins.
Su. 10-2; Tu. 10-6; W.-F. 9-3.

GUBIN

WILHELM PIECK MUSEUM
Ul. Wilhelma Piecka 5, Gubin
Collection illustrating life and work of Pieck (d.1960), President of the GDR, 1949-60.
Tu., F. 1-7; W., Th., Sa. 9-3.

HACZÓW

CHURCH MUSEUM
Haczów
15th century polychrome mural painting.
Daily 9-5.

HEL

MUSEUM OF FISHING
Ul. Portowa, Hel
History of the local fishing industry. Paintings, photographs, models of fishing boats. Navigational and fishing equipment.
Tu.-Su. 8-6.

HRUBIESZÓW

HRUBIESZÓW REGIONAL MUSEUM
Ul. Dzierzyńskeigo 7a, Hrubieszów
Local archaeology, history, ethnography. Peasant art, handicrafts. Ceramics.
W., F. 11-6; Su. 10-4.

INOWROCŁAW

JAN KASPROWICZ MUNICIPAL MUSEUM
Plac. Obrońców Pokujuz, Inowrocław
Paintings. Local history. Memorial collection to the humanist, Jan z Ludziska, the writers Gustaw Zieliński, Jan Kasprowicz, and Stanisław Przybyszewski, the historian H. F. Hayer and the scientist, Jakub Jasinski.
Tu.-Sa. 11-6; Su. 2.30-6.

ISTEBNA

REGIONAL MUSEUM
Istebna
Ethnography. Folk art. Handicrafts. Musical instruments.
Tu. Sa. 9-4; Su. 10-5.

ISTEBNA NA KUBALONCE

MUSEUM OF RELIGIOUS ART
Istebna na Kubalonce
Regional religious art.
Daily 9-5.

JAGNIĄTKÓW

GERHARDT HAUPTMANN HOUSE-MUSEUM
Jagniątków
Memorial collection to the German writer, Gerhardt Hauptmann, in his former home.
On request.

JANÓW PODLASKI

LOCAL HISTORY MUSEUM
Liceum, Janów Podlaski
Costumes. Early books. Coins.
On request.

JAROCIN

REGIONAL MUSEUM OF ETHNOGRAPHY
Jarocin
Regional archaeology, history, ethnography. Coins.
Daily 11-1, 4-6.

JAROSŁAW

REGIONAL MUSEUM
Ul. Tribunalska 1, Jarosław
Archaeology. Ethnography. History. Decorative arts. Paintings.
Tu.-Th., Sa., Su. 10-2; F. 10-1, 4-7.

JASŁO

REGIONAL MUSEUM
Jasło
Local and regional history. Collections illustrating regional village life.
Tu.-Su. 9-3.

JAWOR

REGIONAL MUSEUM
Ul. Armii Radziechiej 18, Jawor
In former Franciscan monastery. Regional history, archaeology, ethnography. Natural history. Handicrafts. Costumes.
Tu.-Su. 10-5.

JAWORZYNKA ŚLĄSKA

REGIONAL MUSEUM
Jaworzynka Śląska
Ethnography.
Daily 9-5.

JĘDRZEJOW

PRYZPKOWSKICH NATIONAL MUSEUM
Rynek 7-8, Jędrzejow
History. Astronomy. Industry. Pharmacy. Gastronomy.
Tu.-Su. 10-5.

JELENIA GÓRA

REGIONAL MUSEUM
Ul. Matejki 28, Jelenia Góra
Regional ethnography. Industry, especially glass-making. Paintings by regional artists or on regional subjects.
Tu., W., F., Sa. 9-2.30; Th. 11-5; Su. 10-5.

KALISZ

MUNICIPAL MUSEUM
Ul. Kościuzki, Kalisz
Natural history. Ethnography. Local and regional history. Handicrafts. Costumes. Coins. Paintings. Graphics.
Tu., Th., Sa., Su. 10-3; W., F. 12-6.

KAMIENNA GÓRA

MUNICIPAL MUSEUM
Pl. Wolności 24, Kamienna Góra
Ethnography. Natural history, especially geology. History of textile industries.
Tu.-Sa. 9-2; Su. 9-12, 2-5.

KAMIEŃ POMORSKI

CATHEDRAL MUSEUM
Kamień Pomorski
Religious art. Archaeology.
When Cathedral is open.

KARCZMISKA

LOCAL MUSEUM
Karczmiska
Local prehistory. 20th century history. Costumes. Coins.
Tu.-Sa. 9-2; Su. 9-5.

KARPACZ

MUSEUM OF RURAL MEDICINE
Karpacz
Collections illustrating history and practice of medicine in rural areas.
Tu.-Su. 10-4.

KARTUZY

KASUBIAN MUSEUM
Ul. Kościerska 1, Kartuzy
Regional archaeology, history. Agricultural implements. Paintings on glass. Ceramics. Musical instruments.
Tu.-Su. 9-3.

KASIMIERZ DOLNY

REGIONAL MUSEUM
Ul. Senatorska 11, Kasimierz Dolny
Regional ethnography. Local history. Paintings, drawings, graphics with regional themes.
Tu.-Su. 10-3.

KATOWICE-JANÓW ŚLĄSKI

JÓZEF WIECZORKI MUSEUM
Ul. Szopienicka 1, Katowice-Janów Śląski
Memorial collection to the Silesian Communist party

leader, Józef Wieczorki. History of the Silesian Communist party.
W., F. 6.30-8.

KCYNIA

LOCAL MUSEUM
Miejska Rada Narodowa, Rynek 7, Kcynia
Ethnography.
Tu.-Su. 10-5.

KĘPNO

REGIONAL MUSEUM
Kępno
Regional archaeology, history, ethnography. Paintings. Sculpture.
Tu. 11-2; Sa. 11-1.

KĘTRZYN

KĘTRZYN MUSEUM
Ul. Powstańców Warzawy 1, Kętrzyn
Natural history, especially geology. Archaeology of the Neolithic period. 15th-17th century religious art. Local history. Coins.
Tu.-Su. daily 10-2 (July-Sept. 10-4).

KIELCE

MUSEUM OF THE HOLY CROSS
Pl. Partyzantów 2-4, Kielce
Regional ethnography and history. Geology. Mineralogy. Prehistoric archaeology. 18th-20th century Polish paintings.
Tu.-F. 9-4; Sa. 10-4; Su. 10-5.

ŚWIĘTOKRZYKIE MUSEUM
Pl. Partyzantów, Kielce
18th-20th century Polish paintings, sculpture. Archaeology. Natural history. Architecture. Folk art.
Tu.-F. 9-4; Sa. 10-4; Su. 10-5.

STEFAN ZEROMSKI MEMORIAL MUSEUM
Ul. Swierczewskiego 25, Kielce
Collections illustrating the early life of the writer, Stefan Zeromski, in his former school.
Daily 9-3.

KŁODZKO

REGIONAL MUSEUM
Pl. Bolesława Chrobiego 22, Kłodzko
In 18th century palace. Regional archaeology, history, ethnography. Religious art. Paintings, sculpture by local artists.
Tu.-Su. 10-3.

KLUCZBORK

KLUCZBORK MUSEUM
Ul. 15 Grudnia 12, Kluczbork
Archaeology. Bee-keeping.
Tu.-F. 10-3; Su. 10-1.

KLUKI

FARM MUSEUM
Smoldzino 38, Kluki
Open-air museum. Farm buildings. Collections illustrating rural life, agriculture, handicrafts.
May-Sept., daily 10-5.

KOLBUSZOWA

LASOWIAKOW REGIONAL MUSEUM
Ul. Piekarska, Kolbuszowa
Regional archaeology, ethnography. Peasant arts and crafts. Ceramics. Costumes. Musical instruments. Local furniture.
W., F., Su. 10-1.

KOŁOBRZEG

MUSEUM OF THE LIBERATION OF CENTRAL POMERANIA
Kołobrzeg
History of the Polish Army and of the liberation of Central Pomerania from the Germans in 1945.
On request.

REGIONAL MUSEUM
Ul. Emilii Gierczak 5, Kołobrzeg
Regional archaeology, history, natural history. Paintings, sculpture by regional artists.
Tu.-Su. 10-4.

KONARZEWO

ADAM MICKIEWICZ MUSEUM
Palac, Konarzewo
Collection illustrating period spent by Mickiewicz in the region. Ethnographical material.
Tu.-Su. 10-4.

KONIAKÓW

LACE MUSEUM
Koniaków
Collection of Polish lace.
Daily 9-3.

KONIECPOL

REGIONAL MUSEUM
Koniecpol
Regional archaeology, history. Handicrafts.
Tu.-Su. 10-4.

KONIN

REGIONAL MUSEUM
Ul. Słowackiego 8, Konin
Regional prehistory, history, ethnography. Handicrafts. Coins. Military history.
M.-Sa. 5-7.

KÓRNIK

KÓRNIK MUSEUM
Zamek, Kórnik
In 15th century palace. 16th-19th century European and Polish furniture, paintings, portraits. Porcelain.
Apr. 1-Oct. 15, Tu.-F. 9-5; Sa. 9-2. Oct. 16-Mar. 31, Tu.-F. 9-3; Sa. 9-2; Su. 10-2.

KORYZNÓWKA

JAN MATEJKI MUSEUM
Koryznówka
Collection illustrating life and work of Matejki.
Tu.-Su. 9-3.

KOSZALIN

MUSEUM OF ARCHAEOLOGY
Ul. Armii Czerwonej 53, Koszalin
Prehistory, ethnography, natural history, and applied arts of Central Pomerania.
Tu.-Su. 10-4.

KOSZUTY

LOCAL MUSEUM
Koszuty
In 18th century mansion. Regional archaeology, ethnography. Decorative arts.
On request.

KOTACZKOWO

REGIONAL MUSEUM
Kotaczkowo
Literary manuscripts. Memorabilia of Polish authors.
Tu.-Su. 10-3.

KRAKÓW

ARCHAEOLOGICAL MUSEUM
Ul. Senacka 3, Kraków
Prehistoric and medieval archaeology of Poland.
M., Tu., F., Sa. 10-2; F. 3-7; Su. 10-1.

AVIATION MUSEUM
Rakowicach, Kraków
History of aviation, especially in Poland.
Tu.-Su. 10-4.

CLOTH-HALL MUSEUM
Rynek Glówny, Kraków
18th-19th century Polish paintings.
M., W., F., Sa. 10-3.45; Th. 12-6; Su., public holidays 10-3.45.

CZAPSKI MUSEUM
Ul. Manifestú Lipcowego 12, Kraków
Maps, atlases. Coins. Medals. Bank notes. Polish watercolours. 17th-19th century furniture. Porcelain. Faience. Glass. Musical instruments. Chinese, Japanese, Korean art. Icons. Polish literary manuscripts. Military relics. Paintings, prints of Kraków.
Tu. 1-5.45; Th. 10-1.45.

CZARTORYSKI MUSEUM
Ul. Pijarsha 15, Kraków
16th-18th century European glass, porcelain, furniture, tapestries. Oriental porcelain. 13th-18th century European paintings. Polish military history. Religious art. Prints. Drawings.
M., Tu., F., Sa. 10-2.45; Th. 12-6; Su., public holidays 9-2.45.

ETHNOGRAPHICAL MUSEUM
pl. Wolnica 1, Kraków
Covers whole of Poland, Slav countries, Africa, America.
Daily 11-3.

GEOLOGICAL MUSEUM
Ul. Senacka 3, Kraków
Geology of Poland.
By appointment.

GRAPHICS COLLECTION OF THE POLISH ACADEMY OF SCIENCES
Ul. Sławkowska 17, Kraków
15th-19th century European drawings, engravings, especially Italian, French, Dutch, English, German.
M.-Sa. 9-2. Closed public holidays.

LENIN MUSEUM
Ul. Topolowa 5, Kraków
Collections illustrating life and work of Lenin, especially his visits to Poland. History of the workers' movement in the Kraków region.
Tu., Th., Sa. 9-4; W., F. 9-6.

JAN MATEJKO HOUSE MUSEUM
Ul. Floriańska 41, Kraków
Professor Matejko's collection of paintings, portraits, furniture, photographs, in his former home.
M.-Th., Sa., Su., public holidays 10-2.45; F. 1-6.

MUSEUM OF THE HISTORY OF THE KRAKÓW THEATRE
Ul. Szpitalna 4, Kraków
Collections illustrating history of the theatre in Kraków. Portraits. Paintings. Drawings. Stage and costume designs. Programmes. Posters.
M., Tu., Th., Sa. 9-3; W. 11-6; Su., public holidays 10-2.

MUSEUM OF THE IRON AND STEEL INDUSTRY
Al. Miekiewicza 30, Kraków
Geology and other sciences related to mining and metallurgy. Models, pictures illustrating history and development of the local iron and steel industry. Equipment used in the industry.
M.-Sa. 10-1. Closed public holidays.

MUSEUM OF THE JAGELLONIAN LIBRARY
Al. Mickiewicza 22, Kraków
18th century Polish drawings, engravings. 16th-19th century scientific illustrations. Architectural drawings. Maps. Illuminated manuscripts.
M.-Sa. 8-3.

MUSEUM OF JEWISH CULTURE
Ul. Szeróka 24, Kraków
History of the Jewish community in Poland, especially in Kraków.
M., Tu., Th., Sa. 9-3; W. 11-6; Su., public holidays 10-2.

MUSEUM OF KRAKÓW
Rynek Główny 35, Kraków
Collections illustrating history of Kraków from earliest times.
Tu., Th., Sa. 9-3; W. 11-6; Su., public holidays 10-2.

MUSEUM OF NATURAL HISTORY
Ul. Slowackiego 17, Kraków
Zoology. Marine biology. Palaeontology.
Tu.-Su. 10-1.

MUSEUM OF PHARMACY
Ul. Basztowa 3, Kraków
History of pharmacy in Poland. Paintings, prints illustrating apothecaries' and pharmacists' premises. 17th-19th century apothecaries' shops, with original equipment. 13th-19th century pharmaceutical vessels, equipment, materials.
M.-Sa. 10-1. Closed public holidays.

NATIONAL ART COLLECTIONS
Wawel 5, Kraków
In Castle. History of the Castle. 15th-19th century European painting, sculpture. French, Flemish tapestries. Illuminated manuscripts. 16th-19th century European furni-

ture, ceramics, enamels. Religious art. Polish royal regalia. European weapons, armour. Oriental art, antiquities.
Tu.-Th., Sa., Su. 9-3; F. 12-6.

NEW BUILDING
Al. Trzeciego Maja 1, Kraków
20th century Polish paintings, drawings.
Tu., Th.-Sa. 10-2.45; W. 12-6; Su., public holidays 10-3.45.

SZOŁAYSKI HOUSE
pl. Szezepański 9, Kraków
14th-18th century Polish paintings.
M., W.-Sa. 10-2.45; Su., public holidays 10-3.45.

UNIVERSITY MUSEUM OF ANTHROPOLOGY
Ul. Krupnicza 50, Kraków
Anthropology of Poland and Asia.
By appointment.

UNIVERSITY MUSEUM OF FINE ART
Ul. Św. Anny 8, Kraków
Painting. Graphics. Egyptian, Greek, Roman antiquities. History of science. Science. Collection of 16th-17th century globes. Coins. 16th-18th century portraits of University worthies. 15th century religious art. Ceramics. Glass. Early scientific instruments.
M.-Sa. 12-2. Closed public holidays.

UNIVERSITY MUSEUM OF NATURAL HISTORY
Ul. Krupnicza 50, Kraków
World-wide zoological collections.
By appointment.

KRASNYSTAW

REGIONAL MUSEUM
Ul. Nocznickiego 3, Krasnystaw
Art. Archaeology and antiquities. Natural history. Ethnography. History.
M.-Sa. 10-3; Su. 10-6.

KRÓSCIENKO

PIENIN MUSEUM
Parku Narodowego, Króscienko
Regional geology, botany, zoology.
Tu.-Sa. 8-2; Su., public holidays 10-1.

KROŚNIEWICE

COLLECTIONS OF JERZY DUNIN-BORKOWSKI
Pl. Wolności 1, Krośniewice
Polish literary manuscripts. Incunabula. Coins. Paintings. Portraits. Miniatures. Furniture. Glass. Porcelain.
Tu.-Su. 10-3.

KROSNO

REGIONAL MUSEUM
Ul. Marcelego Nowotki 16, Krosno
Regional archaeology, history. 19th-20th century history of the workers' and revolutionary movements. Life under the Nazi occupation. Local history. Works by regional painters.
Tu., W., F., Sa. 10-3; Th. 10-6; Su., public holidays 9.30-1.30.

KROSNO ODRZÁNSKIE

LOCAL MUSEUM
Zamek, Krosno Odrzánskie
13th-16th century mansion. Regional history, archaeology.
W., Th., Sa., Su. 9-3; Tu., F. 1-5.

KROTOSZYN

REGIONAL MUSEUM
Ul. Koźmińska 36, Krotoszyn
Regional geology, archaeology, history, ethnography. Rural arts and crafts.
M., Th. 5-6; Su., public holidays 10-12.

KRYNICA

NATURAL HISTORY MUSEUM
Ul. Świerczewskiego 11, Krynica
Ornithology.
Tu.-Su. 10-4.

KRZEMIONKI OPATOWSKIE

ARCHAEOLOGICAL SITE MUSEUM
Krzemionki Opatowskie
12 k.m. from Krzemionki Opatowskie. Prehistoric site. Museum of archaeological material discovered during excavations.
Daily 10-dusk.

KRZESŁAWICE

JAN MATEJKO MUSEUM
Krzesławice
Mansion and gardens, formerly home of J. Matejko. Furnishings. Decorative arts.
Tu.-Su. 10-3.

KUTNO

COMMEMORATIVE MUSEUM OF THE BATTLE ON THE BZURA
Kutno
Models, relics and other material illustrating the Battle.
Tu.-Su. 10-4.

KWIDZYN

REGIONAL MUSEUM
Zamek, Ul. Katedralna 1, Kwidzyn
Regional archaeology, history, ethnography. Handicrafts. Textile printing. Garnet industry. Agricultural implements.
Tu.-Su. 10-3.

ŁAMBINOWICE

MUSEUM OF THE MARTYROLOGY OF PRISONERS OF WAR
Ul. Obozowa 1, Łambinowice
Memorial museum to the prisoners of war of eight nations who died in the German prisoner-of-war camp, Stalag VIII B, Lamsdorf.
Tu.-Su. 10-5.

ŁAŃCUT

CARRIAGE MUSEUM
Zamek, Ul. Zamkowa 1, Łańcut
Coaches, carriages by Polish and English makers.
Tu.-Sa. 9-3; June-Sept., Su., public holidays 10-7.

JEWISH MUSEUM
Łańcut
In former synagogue. Collections illustrating Jewish life and culture.
On request.

REGIONAL MUSEUM
Zamek, Ul. Zamkowa 1, Łańcut
In 17th century palace. Polish paintings, portraits. Sculpture. Graphic arts. Greek and Roman antiquities. Local history. Furniture, especially French. English clocks. Chinese porcelain.
Tu.-Sa. 9-3; June-Sept., Su., public holidays 10-7.

REGIONAL MUSEUM
Ul. Tkacka 5, Łańcut
Regional history, ethnography.
Daily 9-3.

LĘBORK

LOCAL MUSEUM
Ul. Mlynarska 14-5, Lębork
Regional archaeology, history, mineralogy.
Tu.-Sa. 9-4; Su., public holidays 9-6.

ŁĘCZNA

REGIONAL MUSEUM
Łęczna
In former synagogue. Rural life and culture in the region.
Tu.-Su. 10-4.

ŁĘCZYCA

REGIONAL MUSEUM
Zamek, Łęczyca
Natural history. Ethnography. Local history.
Tu.-Su. 10-5.

LEGNICA

REGIONAL MUSEUM
Ul. Sw. Jana 1, Legnica
Regional archaeology, history. History, development and products of local industries. 19th-20th century Polish paintings.
Tu., W., F., Sa. 10-3; Th., Su. 10-5.

LEGNICKIE POLE

MUSEUM OF THE BATTLE OF LEGNICKIE
Legnickie Pole
Display illustrating battle of Legnickie (1241).
Tu.-Sa. 10-3; Su. 10-6.

LESKO

LOCAL MUSEUM
Lesko
In former synagogue. Collections of local flora, wildlife.
M.-F., Su. 10-4.

LEŚNICA

MUSEUM OF THE UPRISING
Ul. Powstańców Śląskich 1, Leśnica
Collections commemorating the local struggle and revolt against the Nazi occupation.
Tu.-Sa. 10-3; Su. 10-5.

LEŻAJSK

REGIONAL MUSEUM
Rynek 15, Leżajsk
Regional archaeology, history.
Tu.-Sa. 10-3; Su., public holidays 10-5.

LEZNO

REGIONAL MUSEUM
Plac dra Metziga 17, Lezno
Regional archaeology, history. Ethnography. Portraits. Material relating to J. A. Komenski (Comenius). Peasant art, handicrafts, furniture, musical instruments.
Tu., Th. 2-7; W., F., Sa. 9-2; Su., public holidays 10-2.

LIDZBARK WARMIŃSKI

LOCAL MUSEUM
Zamek, Lidzbark Warmiński
Ceramics. Glass.
May 15-Sept. 5, Tu.-Su. 9-7. Sept. 6-May 14, Tu.-Su. 10-3.

LIW

REGIONAL MUSEUM
Zamek, Liw
Regional history, ethnography. Weapons.
Tu.-Su. 9-4.

ŁOBŹENICA

LOCAL MUSEUM
Łobźenica
Collections illustrating rural life.
On request.

ŁÓDŹ

ARCHAEOLOGICAL AND ETHNOGRAPHICAL MUSEUM
plac. Wolności 13-14, Łódź
Covers whole of Poland. Prehistory. Coins. Costumes. Ornaments. Jewellery. Architecture. Crafts.
Tu.-Th., Sa. 10-4; F. 12-6; Su., public holidays 11-5.

MUSEUM OF ARCHAEOLOGY AND ETHNOGRAPHY
Plac. Wolności 13-4, Łódź
Regional archaeology, ethnography. Furniture. Costumes. Folk art. Pottery. Agricultural implements. Coins.
Tu.-Th., Sa. 10-4; F. 12-6; Su. 11-5.

MUSEUM OF FINE ART
Ul. dra Stanisława Więckowskiego 36, Łódź
15th-18th century European paintings, especially Italian, Dutch, French. 17th-19th century Polish paintings. 19th century Russian paintings. 20th century European paintings.
Tu., Th. 11-7; W., F., Sa. 9-3; Su. 10-4.

MUSEUM OF THE HISTORY OF THE RUSSIAN REVOLUTION
Ul. Gdańska 13, Łódź
History and organisation of the Russian Revolution. History of the Polish Communist Party and Workers' Movement. Collections illustrating Poland under the German occupation, 1939-45.
Tu. 11-6; W., F., Su. 10-5; Th. 11-7.30; Sa. 10-3.

MUSEUM OF THE HISTORY OF TEXTILES
Ul. Petrowska 28, Łódź
Collections illustrating history and techniques of textile-manufacturing, especially in Poland. Machinery. Models. Pattern-books.
M.-Sa. 10-5; Su. 11-4.

MUSEUM OF MUSIC
Palac. Schiebler, Pl. Zwycięstwa, Łódź
Musical manuscripts. Correspondence and memorabilia of musicians. Portraits. Paintings.
Tu.-Sa. 10-5; Su. 10-2.

MUSEUM OF PHARMACY
Łódź
History of pharmacy, in apothecary's shop of 1783.
Tu.-Sa. 10-5; Su. 10-2.

JULIAN TUWIM MEMORIAL MUSEUM
Palac. Młodzierzi, Łódź
Collections illustrating life and work of the poet, J. Tuwim.
Tu.-Sa. 10-5; Su. 10-2.

UNIVERSITY OF ŁÓDŹ MUSEUM OF EVOLUTION
Park Sienkiewicza, Łódź
Zoology. Ethnography.
Tu.-Sa. 10-5; Su., public holidays 10-2.

ŁOMŹA

REGIONAL MUSEUM
U. Sadowa 10, Łomźa
Regional natural history, ethnography, history. Coins.
Tu., W., F., Sa. 8-3; Th. 10-5; Su. 1-5.

LUBLIN

JOZEF CZECHOWICZ MUSEUM
Ul. Narułowieza 10, Lublin
In 17th century monastery building. Collections illustrating 20th century Polish literature, especially poetry.
Tu.-Su. 10-3.

ŁOPUSZNA

MUSEUM OF THE HISTORY OF MOUNTAINEERING
Łopuszna
Collections illustrating history of mountaineering, especially in the Tatra.
Tu.-Su. 10-5.

ŁOWICZ

REGIONAL MUSEUM
Rynek Kościuszki 4, Łowicz
Prehistory and history of the Łowicz area. Documents. Early printed books. Portraits. Models. Maps. Relics of the German occupation, 1939-45. Ethnography, including housing, furniture, costumes, folk art.
M.-F. 10-4; Sa. 10-4; Su., public holidays 10-6.

LUBACZÓW

REGIONAL MUSEUM
Ul. Mickiewicza 9, Lubaczów
Regional archaeology, history, ethnography. Ceramics. Coins.
Tu.-Su. 10-4.

LUBARTÓW

REGIONAL MUSEUM
Lubartów
Local ceramics manufacture (1840-50).
Tu.-Sa. 10-3; Su. 10-5.

LUBLIN

MEMORIAL MUSEUM OF THE MAJDAN CONCENTRATION CAMP
Lublin
In buildings of the former Nazi concentration camp. Exhibits showing how the camp was organized, daily life of the prisoners.
Tu.-Su. 8-3.

NATIONAL MUSEUM
Zamek, Ul. Zamkowc 9, Lublin
Prehistoric archaeology. 18th-20th century collections illustrating regional life and culture. 15th-20th century Polish paintings, graphics. 14th-19th century Polish ceramics, furniture, metalwork. Coins.
M.-Sa. 10-3; Su. 10-6.

UNIVERSITY ZOOLOGICAL MUSEUM
Ul. Królewska 6, Lublin
Evolution. Vertebrates. Invertebrates.
Tu. 10-11; W.-Sa. 4-8; Su. 10-2.

ŁUKOW

REGIONAL MUSEUM
Ul. Świerczewskiego 23, Łukow
Regional archaeology, history, ethnography. Handicrafts, especially weaving.
Tu.-Su. 10-4.

MALBORK

CASTLE MUSEUM
Malbork
Local history, archaeology. Paintings. Sculpture. Collection of amber. Specimens of different kinds of amber. Objects made from amber.
May-Sept., daily 7.30-7.30. Oct.-Apr., M.-F. 10-4; Sa., Su. 10-7.

MALENIEC

HISTORIC IRON-WORKS
Maleniec
Iron-foundry and forge (1784). Display illustrating history of the works.
Tu.-Su. 10-4.

MARKOWE SZCZAWINY

MUSEUM OF MOUNTAIN TOURISM
Markowe Szczawiny
Exhibition illustrating scenery, amenities and natural resources of the Babiej Góry region.
Daily 9-5.

MIECHÓW

MIECHÓW MUSEUM
Ul. Racławicka 23, Miechów
History of Miechów and its region. Geology. Prehistory. Coins.
M.-Sa. 10-2.

MIĘDZYRZECZ WIELKOPOLSKI

MIĘDZYRZECZ REGIONAL MUSEUM
Ul. Podzamczi 1-3, Międzyrzecz Wielkopolski
Prehistory. Archaeology. Ethnography. History. Natural history. Decorative arts.
M.-Sa. 10-2.

MIĘDZYZDROJ

NATURAL HISTORY MUSEUM
Ul. Niepodległości 3, Międzyzdroj
Geology. Plants and wildlife of the Baltic.
May 15- Sept. 15, M.-Sa. 9-1, 2-8; Su. 9-3. Sept. 16- May 14, M.-Sa. 9-3.

MŁAWA

REGIONAL MUSEUM
Ul. Obrońców Stalingradu 5, Mława
Art. Regional archaeology, history, ethnography.
Tu., Sa. 10-12, 4-6; Su. 11-3.

MORĄG

JOHANN GOTTFRIED HERDER MUSEUM
Plac. Wolności-Ratusz, Morąg
Collections illustrating life and work of the German philosopher, Herder, who was born at Morąg (1744). Exhibits showing local life as it was in Herder's time.
Tu., Th., Sa. 8-3; W., F. 3-5; Su. 10-1.

MUSZYNA

REGIONAL MUSEUM
Ul Kity 16, Muszyna
Collections illustrating rural life and customs. Folk art.
Tu., Th. 4-6; Su. 9-1.

MYŚLENICE

REGIONAL MUSEUM
Ul. 3 Maja 1A, Myślenice
Paintings, drawings, sculpture by regional artists. Regional archaeology, history.
Daily 10-12.

MYSŁOWICE

MARTYRS' MEMORIAL MUSEUM
Mysłowice
Collection illustrating life and suffering in the district under German occupation.
On request.

NAKŁO

REGIONAL MUSEUM
Nakło
Regional archaeology, history. Life in the region under German occupation.
Tu.-Sa. 9-5; Su. 11-2.

NAŁĘCZÓW

MUSEUM OF THE POLISH SYNDICATIST MOVEMENT
Technikum Sztuk Plastycznych, Nałęczów
Collections illustrating history of the Syndicatist Movement.
M.-F. 10-5.

NAŁECZOW

BOLESŁAW PRUS MUSEUM
Palac Małachowskich, Nałeczow
Collections illustrating life and work of the writer, Bolesław Prus (d.1912). Manuscripts of other local writers.
M.-Sa. 10-3; Su., public holidays 10-2, 3-6.

STEFAN ŹEROMSKI MUSEUM
Ul. Stefana Batorego 2, Nałęczow
Collections illustrating life and work of Źeromski, in his former home. Furniture. Portraits. Paintings.
M.-Sa. 10-3; Su., public holidays 10-2, 3-6.

NAMYSŁOW

LOCAL MUSEUM
Namysłow
Displays illustrating local life and history.
Tu.-Su. 10-3.

NIDZICA

REGIONAL MUSEUM
Nidzica
In 13th-14th century castle. 17th-19th century portraits, furniture.
Apr.-Oct., daily 8-1, 3-6.

NIEBORÓW I ARKADIA

NIEBORÓW PALACE
Nieborów i Arkadia
Late 17th century palace. Portraits. Polish, French, English furniture. 17th century globes, maps.
Tu.-F. 9-4; Sa. 9-2.

NOWA HUTA

NOWA HUTA ARCHAEOLOGICAL MUSEUM
Os. Zielone 7, Nowa Huta
Prehistoric site. Museum displays material from excavations.
May-Sept., daily 10-4.

NOWA SÓL

REGIONAL MUSEUM
Ul. Swierczewskiego 20, Nowa Sól
In 19th century palace. Regional natural history, archaeology, history, ethnography, military history. Coins.
Daily 10-4.

NOWE MIASTO

REGIONAL MUSEUM
Nowe Miasto
Regional history, ethnography.
May-Sept., daily 10-5. Oct.-Apr., daily 4-6.

NOWE MIASTO LUBAWSKIE

REGIONAL MUSEUM
Nowe Miasto Lubawskie
Regional archaeology, history, ethnography. Handicrafts. Looms.
Tu.-Su. 10-5.

NOWY JASIENIC

AGRICULTURAL MUSEUM
Nowy Jasienic
Agricultural implements, equipment. Collections illustrating crops, livestock, cultivation techniques.
Tu.-Su. 10-4.

NOWY SĄCZ

REGIONAL MUSEUM
Ul. Lwowska 3, Nowy Sącz
Regional ethnography, history, archaeology and antiquities. Natural history. Polish paintings.
Tu.-Su. 10-4.

NOWY TARG

REGIONAL MUSEUM
Ul. Szaflarksa 1, Nowy Targ
Ethnography.
M.-Sa. 10-3.

NYSA

REGIONAL MUSEUM
Ul. Marcinkowskiego 1, Nysa
Regional geology, archaeology, ethnography. 16th-20th century European paintings.
M.-Sa. 10-3.

OBLĘGOREK

HENRYK SIENKIEWICZ MUSEUM
Oblęgorek
Collections illustrating life and work of the writer and Nobel Prize winner, Henryk Sienkiewicz.
Tu.-Sa. 9-5; Su., public holidays 9-1, 2-5.

ODOLANÓW

REGIONAL MUSEUM
Odolanów
Regional archaeology, ethnography. Costumes. Folk art. Agricultural implements. Craftsmen's tools.
Tu.-Su. 9-3.

OGRÓDEK

MICHAŁA KAJKI MUSEUM
Ogródek
Collections illustrating the life and work of Kajki.
Tu.-Su. 10-4.

OJCÓW

NATURAL HISTORY MUSEUM
People's Park, Ojcówski Park Narodowy, Ojców
Local zoology, botany.
Tu.-Su. 10-5.

OLESŃICA

ARCHAEOLOGICAL MUSEUM
Olesńica
Archaeological material from regional sites.
Tu.-Su. 10-4.

OLESŃICA MUSEUM
Olesńica
Local history, ethnography.
Tu.-Sa. 10-5; Su. 11-5.

OLESNO

REGIONAL MUSEUM
Ul. Pieloka 18, Olesno
Archaeology. Ethnography, including furnished peasant cottage. 19th-20th century history.
Tu., W., Th. 10-5.

OLIWA

FORGE MUSEUM
Oliwa
18th century forge, with exhibits illustrating its working and history.
May-Sept., daily 9-5.

REGIONAL MUSEUM OF ETHNOGRAPHY
Ul. Cystersów 15, Oliwa
Collections illustrating traditional peasant life and culture. Furniture. Ceramics. Musical instruments. Agricultural implements, equipment.
On request.

OLKUSZ

REGIONAL MUSEUM
Plac Grudnia 15, Olkusz
Regional prehistory, archaeology.
Tu., W., F., Sa. 4-6.

OLSZTYN

MAZURIAN MUSEUM
Ul. Zamkowa 2, Olsztyn
Regional ethnography, science, natural history. 16th-19th century European paintings, drawings.
May 15-Oct. 15, Tu.-Su. 9-7; Oct. 16-May 14, Tu.-Su. 10-3.

OLSZTYNEK

MUSEUM OF RURAL BUILDINGS
Olsztynek
Cottages, mills, farm buildings from the region, re-erected on museum site.
Oct.-Apr., daily 10-3. May-Sept., daily 10-6.

OLSZTYN

OPEN-AIR MUSEUM
Ul. Sportowa 5, Olsztyn
Rural buildings from the region. Furniture. Folk art. Handicrafts.
May 15-Oct. 15, Tu.-Su. 9-7. Oct. 16-May 14, Tu.-Su. 10-3.

OPINOGÓRA

MUSEUM OF ROMANTICISM
Zamek, Opinogóra
Collections aimed at recapturing the atmosphere of the Romantic period. Memorial collection to the Polish Romantic poet, Zygmunt Krasiński.
Tu.-Su. 11-2, 3-6.

OPOCZNO

REGIONAL MUSEUM
Zamek, Opoczno
Regional ethnography, folk art.
Tu.-Su. 10-4.

OPOLE

SILESIAN MUSEUM
Mały Rynek 7, Opole
Regional archaeology, history, ethnography. Natural history. Coins. 19th-20th century Polish paintings, applied art.
Tu., F. 10-5; M., W., Th.-Su. 10-3.

OPOLE-BIERKOWICE

OPEN-AIR MUSEUM
Opole-Bierkowice
Rural buildings from Silesia, re-erected on museum site. Furniture. Handicrafts.
Tu.-Su. 10-3.

OPORÓW

REGIONAL MUSEUM
Zamek, Oporów
Furniture. Paintings. Local history.
Tu., W., F. 10-5; Th., Sa. 10-4; Su., public holidays 11-3.

OSTROWIEC ŚWIĘLKRZYSKI

REGIONAL MUSEUM
Ul. Parkowa 2, Ostrowiec Święlkrzyski
In 19th century palace. Collections illustrating the history of Kielce iron-industry, and of the local manufacture of porcelain and faience.
Tu.-Sa. 10-3; Su. 10-5.

OSTRÓW LEDNICKI

LOCAL MUSEUM
Ostrów Lednicki
Local archaeology (8th-11th centuries). Peasant houses and other rural buildings.
Tu.-Su. 9-4.

OSTRÓW LUBELSKI

LOCAL MUSEUM
Ostrów Lubelski
Collections illustrating life in the district under the German occupation.
On request.

OŚWIĘCIM

MUSEUM OF THE MARTYRS
Oświęcim
In buildings of the former German concentration and extermination camp, Auschwitz. Exhibits showing the working, methods and life of the camp.
Tu.-Su. 8-3.

PABIANICE

REGIONAL MUSEUM
Plac Obrónców, Stalingradu 1, Pabianice
Regional natural history, archaeology, history, ethnography.
Tu.-Th. 10-3; F. 10-6; Sa. 10-2; Su. 10-1.

PARLEZA WIELKA

LOCAL MUSEUM
Parleza Wielka
Local history.
On request.

PASYM

REGIONAL MUSEUM
Pasym
Collections illustrating traditional rural life and culture.
Tu.-Su. 10-4.

PELPIN

DIOCESAN MUSEUM
Pelpin
Furniture. Polish paintings, sculpture. Religious art.
Tu.-Sa. 10-5.

PIESKOWA SKAŁA

CASTLE MUSEUM
Zamek, Pieskowa Skała
In 14th century castle, remodelled 17th century. Exhibits showing history of the castle.
Tu.-Su. 10-5.

PIŁA

STANISŁAW STASZIC MUSEUM
Ul. Browarna 18, Piła
Collections illustrating life and work of the writer, Staszic, in his former home. Geology of Poland. Local archaeology, history, ethnography.
Tu.-Su. 11-4.

PIŃCZOW

REGIONAL MUSEUM
Pińczow
Local history. Collections illustrating local life during 1939-45 war and activities of local partisans.
Tu.-Su. 10-5.

PIOTRKÓW TRIBUNALSKI

NATIONAL MUSEUM
Plac. Zamkowy 4, Piotrków Tribunalski
Regional prehistory, ethnography, history. Paintings. Sculpture.
Tu.-Su. 10-4.

PŁOCK

DIOCESAN MUSEUM
Ul. Tumska 3A, Płock
Gothic sculpture. Folk art. Coins. Medals. Portraits. Flemish, French, Spanish, Dutch, German paintings.
M., W.-Sa. 10-1; 3-5; Su. 12-1, 3-5.

MAZOVIAN MUSEUM
Plac. Naturowicza 8, Płock
Regional natural history, prehistory, ethnography, history. Polish paintings, coins, medals. Collection illustrating local petro-chemical industry.
Tu., F. 2-7; W., Th., Sa., Su. 9-3.

PODDĘBICE

REGIONAL MUSEUM
Poddębice
In early 17th century palace, restored in 19th century. Paintings. Furniture. Decorative arts.
Daily 2-4.

PODEGRODZIE

REGIONAL MUSEUM
Podegrodzie
Collections illustrating traditional rural life and culture. Folk art. Agricultural implements.
Tu.-Su. 10-5.

POLICE

CAMP MEMORIAL
Police
In hut of former S.S. punishment camp. Display showing methods in use at the camp, which had prisoners from many European countries.
Daily 10-4.

POLICHNO

MUSEUM OF THE RESISTANCE
Polichno
Collections illustrating activities of the local Resistance Movement, 1939-45.
Daily 9-4.

PORĘBA WIELKA

WŁADYSŁAW ORKAN MUSEUM
Poręba Wielka
Collection illustrating life and work of the poet, Orkan (d.1930).
On request.

PORONIN

LENIN MUSEUM
Ul. Lenina 160, Poronin
Collections illustrating the achievements of Lenin and the history of the workers' movement.
Tu.-Su. 8-4.

POZNAŃ

ARCHAEOLOGICAL MUSEUM
Mielżyńskiego 27-29, Poznań
Prehistoric material from excavations in Poland. Greek, Roman and Medieval antiquities.
Tu., Th., Sa. 9-3; W., F. 1-7; Su. 10-2.

H. CEGIELSKI FACTORY MUSEUM
Poznań
History and products of this engineering and metallurgical factory. History of the local workers' movement.
By appointment.

DIOCESAN MUSEUM
Ul. Lubranskiego 1, Poznań
14th-18th century paintings, mainly by Polish artists. Sculpture. Ceramics. Fabrics. Decorative arts. Coins. Medals.
Daily 9-1.

MUSEUM OF DECORATIVE ARTS
Góra Przemysława 1, Poznań
Oriental and European ceramics. Glass. Tapestries. Furniture, especially 18th century. Coins. 17th-18th century portraits.
Tu.-Su. 10-3.

MUSEUM OF THE HISTORY OF THE WORKERS' MOVEMENT
Stary Rynek 3, Poznań
History of the Polish Workers' Movement, illustrated by documents, posters, photographs, paintings, newspapers and relics.
Tu.-Sa. 10-6; Su. 10-3.

MUSEUM OF THE LIBERATION
Cytadel, Poznań
Collection illustrating the successful struggle to liberate the Poznań region from Prussian and German rule.
May-Sept., daily 11-4. Oct.-Apr., daily 12-4.

MUSEUM OF THE MARTYRS
Ul. Polska, Poznań
Memorial museum to those killed during the Nazi occupation of the Poznań region.
Tu.-Su. 2-5.

MUSEUM OF MUSICAL INSTRUMENTS
Stary Rynek 45, Poznań
European musical instruments, especially Polish, 11th century onwards. Collection of non-European instruments.
M.-Sa. 9-3; Su. 10-3.

MUSEUM OF RURAL CULTURE AND HANDICRAFTS
Ul. Grobla 25, Poznań
Covers whole of Poland, with emphasis on the Greater Poland and the Territory of Lubusk. Collections include material from Mexico, Africa, New Guinea.
Tu.-Sa. 9-3; Su. 10-1.

NATURAL HISTORY MUSEUM OF THE INSTITUTE OF ZOOLOGY
Ul. Świerczewskiego 19, Poznań
Collections covering the whole of Poland. Geology. Mineralogy. Palaeontology. Zoology. Botany.
Tu., Th., Sa., Su. 9-4; W., F. 11-6.

POLISH MILITARY MUSEUM
Stary Rynek, Poznań
Polish military history since the 11th century.
M., Th.-Sa. 9-3; W. 12-6; Su. 10-3.

POZNAŃ NATIONAL MUSEUM
Ul. Marcinskowskiego 9, Poznań
Antiquities. Polish and foreign paintings and sculpture. Decorative arts. Drawings and engravings. Coins. Popular culture and art. Posters.
Tu.-Sa. 9-3; Su. 10-3.

POZNAŃ HISTORICAL MUSEUM
Stary Ratusz, Stary Rynek 1, Poznań
History of Poznań since medieval times. European paintings, especially Spanish, Flemish, Dutch. Folk art.
M., Tu., Th., F. 9-3; W. 12-6; Su. 10-3.

PRANIE

K. I. GAŁCZYŃSKI MUSEUM
Pranie
Collection illustrating life and work of the poet, K. I. Gałczyński (d.1953).
On request.

PRUDNIK

SILESIAN MUSEUM
Ul. Chrobrego 11, Prudnik
Regional ethnography, history.
Tu.-Su. 8-2. W. also 3-7.

PRZEMYŚL

DIOCESAN MUSEUM
pl. Czackiego 10, Przemyśl
Paintings. Sculpture. Vestments. Coins. Medals. Gobelins tapestries.
Tu., W. 10-12; Su. 3-5.

REGIONAL MUSEUM
Plac. Tadeusza Czackiego 3, Przemyśl
Regional archaeology, history, ethnography. Handicrafts.
Tu.-Su. 10-2; F. also 5-7.

PRZEWORSK

MUNICIPAL MUSEUM
Rynek 1, Przeworsk
In 15th century town hall. Local archaeology, ethnography, history. Costumes. Handicrafts.
Su. 10-2. Other days by appointment.

PRZYBSŁAWICE

MUSEUM OF RURAL LIFE
Przybsławice
Local ethnography, history. Years of Nazi occupation.
M.-Su. 11-3.

PSZCZEW

REGIONAL MUSEUM
Pszczew
Regional archaeology, history.
Tu.-Su. 10-4.

PSZCZYNA

PALACE MUSEUM
Pszczyna
In 18th century palace. Furniture. Tapestries. Ceramics. Paintings. Graphics. Coins. Portraits.
Tu.-Sa. 9-2.30; Su., public holidays 10-2.30.

PUŁAWY

REGIONAL MUSEUM
Puławy
Regional archaeology, history, ethnography. European and Polish paintings, graphics.
Daily 9-6.

PUŁKOWO WIELKIE

REGIONAL MUSEUM
Pułkowo Wielkie
Rural building from the Dobrzyń region. Peasant art, handicrafts.
Tu.-Su. 10-4.

PUŁTUSK

REGIONAL MUSEUM
Rynek, Pułtusk
Regional archaeology, history, ethnography. 18th century portraits.
Tu., F., Sa. 3-6; Su. 11-1, 3-6.

PUSZCZYKOWO

NATURAL HISTORY MUSEUM
Wielkopolskiego Parku Narodowego, Puszczykowo
Zoology and botany of the region.
Tu.-F., Su. 10-4.

PYRZYCE

LOCAL MUSEUM
w budynku Gminnej Spółdzielni, Pyrzyce
Local history.
On request.

PYZDRY

REGIONAL MUSEUM
pl. Wolnosci 17, Pyzdry
Regional history, ethnography. Costumes. Ceramics. Coins.
Su., public holidays 10-2.

RABKA ZDROJ

REGIONAL MUSEUM 'WŁADYSŁAW ORKAN'
Ul. Krakowska 34, Rabka Zdroj
Collections illustrating rural culture of the region. Agriculture. Paintings on glass. Handicrafts.
W.-M. 9-4.

RACIBÓRZ

MUNICIPAL MUSEUM
Ul. Chopina 12, Racibórz
Archaeology. Natural history. Ethnography. Costumes. Military history. 14th-18th century Silesian paintings.
Tu., Th., F. 10-3; W. 11-6; Su., public holidays 10-2.

RADOM

MUNICIPAL MUSEUM
Ul. Marcelogo Nowotki 12, Radom
Regional collection of history, archaeology, decorative arts, art, ethnography. Costumes. 19th-20th century Polish paintings.
Tu., F. 11-6; W., Th., Sa. 8-3; Su. 10-5.

RADZYN CHEŁMIŃSKI

REGIONAL MUSEUM
Radzyn Chełmiński
In 13th-14th century castle. Paintings. Furnishings.
Tu.-Su. 8-3; Su. 10-5.

RAKÓW

REGIONAL MUSEUM
Raków
Regional archaeology, ethnography.
Tu.-Su. 10-5.

RAWA MAZOWIECKA

REGIONAL MUSEUM
Baszta Zamkowa, Rawa Mazowiecka
Regional archaeology, ethnography, history. Coins. Costumes.
Tu., Th., Su. 10-2.

ROGALIN

LOCAL MUSEUM
Rogalin
In early 19th century palace. 16th-18th century Italian, Dutch, Polish furniture. Mortlake tapestries. Porcelain, especially Delft. Paintings. Portraits. In annexe: 19th-20th century European paintings.
Tu.-Sa. 9-3; Su., public holidays 10-4.

ROMANÓW

JÓZEF IGNACZ KRASZEWSKI MUSEUM
Romanów
Collections made by Kraszewski (d.1887). Manuscripts. Paintings. Drawings.
Tu. 2-7; W.-Sa. 10-3.

ROPCZYCE

MUNICIPAL MUSEUM
Ul. J. Kochanowskiego 15, Ropczyce
Regional archaeology, history, ethnography. Costumes. Paintings.
Tu., W., F.-Su. 11-1.

ROZEWIE

MUSEUM OF LIGHTHOUSES
Latarni Morskiej, Rozewie
Lighthouse mechanism and operation. Navigational instruments.
May-Sept., daily 8-6. Nov.-Apr., daily 9-3.

RYBNIK

RYBNIK-WODZISŁAW MUSEUM
Rynek 17, Rybnik
Art. Archaeology. Ethnography. History.
Tu., F., Su. 10-3.

RZESZOW

REGIONAL MUSEUM
Ul. 3 Maja 17, Rzeszow
Religious art. Archaeology. Ethnography. Folk art. Pottery. Polish furniture. Handicrafts. Paintings.
M., W., Th., Sa. 10-2; Tu., F. 10-6.

SAMSANÓW

EARLY BLAST-FURNACE
Samsanów
Restored early 19th century blast-furnace, with exhibition illustrating smelting techniques.
Daily 9-5.

SANDOMIERZ

DIOCESAN MUSEUM
Ul. Długosza 9, Sandomierz
In 15th century house. 15th-19th century paintings. Sculpture. Glass. Porcelain. Prehistoric archaeology. Coins. Medals. Folk art.
Daily 10-4.

REGIONAL MUSEUM
Ul. Rynek 10, Sandomierz
Archaeology. Collections illustrating 19th-20th century rural life and culture. Coins.
Tu., Th., F., Sa. 10-3; W. 10-6; Su., public holidays 10-5.

SANOK

OPEN-AIR MUSEUM
Ul. Traugutta 3 and Olchowce, Sanok
18th-19th century peasant houses, and other rural buildings, with furniture, handicrafts and other material illustrating rural life.
Tu.-Su. 9-2.

SANOK MUSEUM
Ul. Zamkowa 5, Sanok
Ethnography. Local history. 14th-19th century Polish paintings, graphics. Glass. Porcelain. Textiles. Furniture. Weapons.
Tu.-Su. 9-2.

SĄSIADKA

LOCAL MUSEUM
Sąsiadka
Local archaeology, history.
On request.

SIEDLICE

MUSEUM OF THE PODLASKI REGION
Siedlice
Regional history, ethnography, handicrafts, folk art.
Tu.-Su. 10-5.

SIEDLISKO

LOCAL MUSEUM
Siedlisko
In Renaissance town hall. Handicrafts. Lapidarium.
Tu.-Sa. 11-3.

SIEDLISZCZE

LOCAL MUSEUM
Siedliszcze
Local archaeology, history. Mementoes and history of the German occupation.
On request.

SIELPIA WIELKA

OLD LAKE MUSEUM
Sielpia Wielka
In 18th century rolling-mill, with machinery still in working order.
Daily 9-4.

SIERADZ

SIERADZ MUSEUM
Ul. Dominiskańska 2, Sieradz
Palaeontology. Archaeology. Ethnography. Ceramics. Musical instruments. 19th-20th century Polish paintings. Graphics. Coins.
Tu. 10-6; W., Th. 10-3; F. 10-4; Sa. 10-1; Su. 10-4.

SIOŁKOWICE

JAKUB KANIA MUSEUM
Siołkowice
Collection illustrating life and work of the Silesian poet, Jakub Kania (d.1957).
Tu.-Su. 10-3.

SKOCZOW

GUSTAW MORCINEK MUSEUM
Ul. Leśna 2, Skoczow
Memorial collection to Gustaw Morcinek (d.1963). Collection illustrating organisation and methods of the Nazi concentration camps.
Tu.-Sa. 10-3; Su., public holidays 10-12.

SKÓRCZ

MUSEUM OF ARCHAEOLOGY
Skórcz
Archaeological material from local excavations.
On request.

SKLARSKA PORĘBA

MUSEUM OF CUT GLASS
Sklarska Poręba
Cut glass from local factories.
Daily 9-5.

SŁAKÓW BOROWY

ŁOWICK MUSEUM OF ART
Słaków Borowy
In former home of Justyn Gregory. Peasant arts and crafts.
Tu.-Su. 10-5.

SŁUPIA NOWA

ANCIENT FOUNDRIES MUSEUM
Słupia Nowa
Nearly 2,000-year-old furnaces discovered in area. Exhibition of items discovered during excavations.
Tu.-Su. 9-4.

SŁUPSK

REGIONAL MUSEUM OF ETHNOGRAPHY
Plac. Zwycięstwa 'Nowa Brama', Słupsk
In old mill. Ethnography. Costumes. Local history. Paintings. Sculpture. Handicrafts.
Tu.-Su. 10-5.

SŁUŹEWO

LOCAL MUSEUM
Sluźewo
Memorial collection to Fryderyk Chopin.
On request.

ŚMIEŁOW

REGIONAL MUSEUM
Śmiełow
In late 18th century palace. Local history. Collections illustrating work of Adam Mickiewicz and Henryk Svenkiewicz.
Tu.-Su. 9-3.

ŚMIGIEL

MUNICIPAL MUSEUM
pl. Rozstrzelanch 26, Śmigiel
Local archaeology, history. Coins.
Tu.-Su. 10-4.

SMOLNIK

OPEN-AIR MUSEUM
Smolnik
Rural buildings brought to museum site. Horse-drawn vehicles. Agricultural implements. Religious art. Ethnography.
May-Sept., daily 9-5.

SOBIESZÓW

KARKONOSKI PARK MUSEUM
Ul. Chałubiński 23, Sobieszów
Geology. Botany. Zoology.
Tu.-Sa. 10-3; Su., public holidays 10-1.

SOBÓTKA

MUSEUM OF THE ŚLĘZAŃSKI REGION
Ul. Czerwonej Armii 19, Sobótka
Art. Archaeology. Natural history. Ethnography. Handicrafts.
Tu., W., F., Sa. 10-3; Th. 12-6; Su. 10-6.

SOSNOWIEC

MINING MUSEUM
Ul. Tomasza Bando 10, Sosnowiec
Geology. Collections illustrating local mining industry.
Tu.-Sa. 8-3; Su. 10-2.30.

ŚRODA SLĄSKA

MUNICIPAL MUSEUM
Ratusz Rynek, Środa Sląska
Local history. 16th-17th century furniture.
Tu., F., Su. 11-3.

STARACHOWICE

REGIONAL MUSEUM
Starachowice
Regional archaeology, history, ethnography.
Tu.-Su. 10-5.

STARA ŚWIĘTA

OPEN-AIR MUSEUM
Stara Święta
Peasant cottages and other rural buildings moved to museum site.
May-Oct., daily 9-5.

STARGARD SZCZECIŃSKI

REGIONAL MUSEUM
Rynek Staromiejski 14, Stargard Szczeciński
Paintings. Graphics. Archaeology. Military history. Handicrafts.
Daily 11-5.

STARY SĄCZ

ART MUSEUM
Rynek 6, Stary Sącz
18th-19th century peasant handicrafts, art. Ceramics.
Tu.-Su. 10-4.

STĘBARK

GRUNWALD MUSEUM
Pole Bitwy 28, Stębark
Military history.
May-Sept., daily 10-6. Other times by appointment.

STRZELIN

REGIONAL MUSEUM
Strzelin
In 12th-15th century church. Local and religious history.
Daily 9-5.

STRZEZÓW

JULIAN PUVOWARSKI COLLECTION
Strzezów
Private collection of Polish coins and medals, 12th century onwards.
On request.

STRZYZÓW

LOCAL MUSEUM
Ul. Mieckiewicza 10, Strzyzów
Local and regional history.
On request.

SULEJÓW

REGIONAL MUSEUM
Sulejów
Local history. Paintings. Ceramics. Costumes. Handicrafts. Ethnography. Collection illustrating life and work of the writer, Lucjan Rudnicki.
Tu.-Su. 10-4.

SULMIERZYCI

REGIONAL MUSEUM
Stary Ratusz, Sulmierzyci
Archaeology. Ethnography. Local history. Weapons. Costumes.
Daily 8-6.

SURAŹ

REGIONAL MUSEUM
Suraź
Archaeological material from local 11th century site.
Daily 10-3.

SUWAŁKI

REGIONAL MUSEUM
Ul. Kościuszki 81, Suwałki
Natural history. Ethnography. Local history.
Tu.-Th., 8-3; F.-Su. 10-5.

SWIDNICA

MUSEUM OF TRADE
Swidnica
Collections illustrating history of Silesian internal and external trade and commerce.
Tu.-Su. 10-4.

ŚWIĘTNO

LOCAL MUSEUM
Świętno
Collections illustrating local life and history.
On request.

ŚWIĘTY KRZYŹ

NATIONAL PARK MUSEUM
Święty Krzyź
Natural history, archaeology, history of the National Park area.
May-Sept., daily 9-6. Other months by appointment.

ŚWINOCYŚCIE

LOCAL MUSEUM
Świnocyście
Local archaeology, history. Shipping. Fishing. Model boats. Local flora, wildlife.
Daily 10-4.

SZAFARNIA

MEMORIAL ROOM
Szafarnia
Memorabilia of Fryderyk Chopin.
On request.

SZAMOTUŁY

REGIONAL MUSEUM
Baszta Halozki, Szamotuły
Archaeology. Ethnography. History. Handicrafts. Coins.
Tu., Th., Sa., Su. 10-3; W., F. 12-6.

SZCZECIN

MARINE MUSEUM OF THE BALTIC INSTITUTE
Ul. Wały Chrobrego 3, Szczecin
Fishing. Oceanography. Commerce. Natural history.
Su., public holidays, 10-4; Tu., Th. 11-5; W., F., Sa. 9-3.

MEMORIAL MUSEUM
Szczecin
History of the workers' movement and of the Nazi concentration camps.
Daily 9-5.

NATIONAL MUSEUM
Ul. Staromłyńska 27, Szczecin
Western Pomeranian collections. Archaeology and antiquities. Natural history. Maritime history. Paintings. Graphics. Sculpture.
Tu., Th. 11-5; W., F., Sa. 9-3; Su. 10-4.

SZCZECINEK

REGIONAL MUSEUM
Ul. Elzbiety 6, Szczecinek
Regional archaeology, history. Paintings by regional artists.
Tu.-Sa. 10-3; Su. 11-1.

SZCZEKOCINY

REGIONAL MUSEUM
Szczekociny
Furniture. Ceramics. Weapons. Local history.
Tu.-Sa. 10-3; Su. 11-1.

SZCZYRZYC

LOCAL MUSEUM
Szczyrzyc
In 16th-19th century Cistercian monastery. Religious art. Incunabula. Manuscripts. Handicrafts. Weapons.
Tu.-Su. 9-5.

SZCZYTNO

LOCAL MUSEUM
Ul. Sienkiewicza 1, Szczytno
Local history, ethnography.
Tu.-Su. 10-4.

SZRENIAWA

AGRICULTURAL MUSEUM
Szreniawa
Agricultural history. Re-organisation of Polish agriculture after 1945. Agricultural implements. Displays illustrating products, livestock, techniques.
Tu.-Sa. 10-5; Su. 11-3.

SZTUM

REGIONAL MUSEUM
Zamek, Sztum
Regional history. Rural life and handicrafts.
On request.

SZTUTOWO

STUTTHOF MUSEUM
Ul. Mariacka 25-26, Sztutowo
On site of the former Nazi concentration and extermination camp. Exhibits illustrating camp life and methods.
Daily 8-5.

SZYDŁOW

REGIONAL MUSEUM
Szydłow
Natural history. Archaeology. Local and military history. Ceramics.
Tu.-Su. 8-3.

SZYMBARK

REGIONAL MUSEUM
Szymbark
In Renaissance manor-house. Furniture. Paintings. Local history.
Tu.-Su. 10-4.

TARNOGRÓD

RURAL MUSEUM ROOM
Dom Kultury, Tarnogród
Local history. History of the German occupation.
On request.

TARNÓW

DIOCESAN MUSEUM
pl. Katedralny 5, Tarnów
Gothic paintings. Paintings on glass. Vestments. Sculpture. Folk art.
M.-Sa. 10-1; Su. 10-3.

TARNOW

MUNICIPAL MUSEUM
Ul. Kniewskiego 24, Tarnow
Ethnography. Local history. 17th-18th century Polish paintings. 17th-19th century Italian, Dutch, German, French paintings. 16th-19th century French, German, English, Italian drawings, engravings. Handicrafts. European ceramics, furniture.
Tu.-F. 9-6; Sa. 9-3; Su. 10-1.

TARNOWSKIE GÓRY

SILVER-MINE MUSEUM
Rynek 1, Tarnowskie Góry
Reconstruction of 18th century silver-mine. Local history, ethnography.
Tu., Th., Sa., Su. 10-3; W. 12-4; F. 12-7.

TATARY POD KADZIDŁEM

KURPIE MUSEUM
dom Czesławy Konopkowny, Tatary pod Kadzidłem
Natural history. Spiders. Handicrafts, including cut-paper peasant wall-coverings (with occasional demonstrations of the technique). Cake-making.
Tu.-Su. 9-5.

TOMASZÓW LUBELSKI

REGIONAL MUSEUM
Szpital Miejski, Tomaszów Lubelski
Regional archaeology, history, ethnography.
Th., Su. 8-4.

TOMASZÓW MAZOWIECKI

REGIONAL MUSEUM
Ul. Armii Ludowej 15, Tomaszów Mazowiecki
Archaeology. Natural history. Ethnography. History. Handicrafts.
Tu., Th.-Sa. 10-5; W. 10-7; Su., public holidays 10-4.

TORUŃ

HALL OF THE TEUTONIC KNIGHTS
ul. Przedzamcze 3, Toruń
14th century building. History of the hall, and of the Teutonic Knights. Ceramics. Furniture.
Apr. 15- Oct. 15, Tu., W., F. 10-4; Th. 11-5; Sa., Su. 10-3.

MIKOŁAJ KOPERNIKI (COPERNICUS) MUSEUM
Ul. Kopernicka 17, Toruń
Collections illustrating life and scientific work of Copernicus, in his former home. Documents. Models. Astronomical instruments.
Tu., W. 10-4; Th. 11-5; F. 10-6; Sa., Su 10-3.

MUSEUM OF ART
Rynek Staromiejski 35, Toruń
Art of the Far East. Paintings. Graphics. Sculpture. Furniture. Porcelain. Textiles.
W., F. 10-4; Th. 11-5; Sa., Su. 10-3.

REGIONAL MUSEUM
Rynek Staromiejski 1, Ratusz, Toruń
Regional ethnography, prehistory, history. Military history. Coins. 16th-20th century Polish paintings. Drawings. Engravings. European glass. Polish ceramics, furniture, faience.
W., F. 10-4; Th. 11-5; Sa., Su. 10-3.

SCULPTURE GALLERY
Nowy Rynek 17, Toruń
Sculpture by Polish artists.
Daily 9-7.

TORUŃ ETHNOGRAPHICAL MUSEUM
Waly Gen. Sikorskiego 13, Toruń
Collections illustrating traditional culture of the whole of Poland. Folk art, handicrafts, costumes. Open-air section.
Tu., F. 11-7; M., W., Th., Sa. 10-4; Su. 10-3.

TOSZEK

REGIONAL MUSEUM
Zamek, Toszek
In 15th century town hall. Local history. Furniture.
Tu.-Su. 10-5.

TRZCIANKA

REGIONAL MUSEUM
Ul. Mochnackiego 3, Trzcianka
Regional archaeology, history.
M.-Sa. 10-1.

TUROBIN

MEMORIAL ROOM
Turobin
Collections illustrating the German occupation and partisan activities.
On request.

TYCHNOWY

LOCAL MUSEUM
Tychnowy
Local history. History of the German occupation.
Tu.-Su. 9-12, 2-5.

ULUCZ

ECCLESIASTICAL MUSEUM
Ulucz
In former Orthodox church (1510). 16th-17th century paintings, murals.
Daily 9-5.

URSUS

INDUSTRIAL MUSEUM
Ursus
Factory museum. Engineering history.
On request.

USTKA

LOCAL MUSEUM
Ul. Marynarki Polskiej 10, Ustka
Local history, ethnography.
May-Nov., daily 11-5.

WAŁBRZYCH

REGIONAL MUSEUM
Ul. Maja 9, Wałbrzych
Art. Archaeology. Natural history. Ethnography. Local history. Mining history. Local porcelain.
Tu.-Sa. 10-1; Su. 3-6.

WARKA-WINIARY

WARKA MUSEUM
Kasimierza Pułaskiego, Warka-Winiary
In house where Kasimierz Pułaski was born. Local history. 19th century emigration to America.
May 1 - July 22, daily 10-2, 3-5.

WARSAW

ŁADISLAUS BRONIEWSKI MUSEUM
Ul. Jarosława Dąbrowskiego 51, Warsaw
Works by Broniewski, in the house where the poet lived, 1953-62. Manuscripts. Letters. Personal possessions.
Tu., Th. 12-6; W., F. 10-3; Su. 12-5.

CABINET OF PRINTS AND ENGRAVINGS OF THE UNIVERSITY OF WARSAW
Krakowskie Przedmiescie 26-28, Warsaw
16th-20th century prints and engravings, drawings, especially German, Dutch, Flemish, Italian, Polish. Architectural plans, drawings.
Su. 11-3; Tu.-F. 11-5.

FRYDERYK CHOPIN MUSEUM
Ul. Okólnik 1, Zamek Ostrogskich, Warsaw
Collection illustrating life and work of Chopin. Musical manuscripts. Portraits. Concert programmes. Letters. Documents. The composer's last piano.
M.-Sa. 10-2.

WARREN XAVIER DUNIKOWSKI MUSEUM
Ul. Puławska 113A, Warsaw
In 18th century palace, known as the Warren. Sculpture, drawings, paintings, models by Dunikowski. Sketches made in Oświęcim concentration camp. Mementoes, tools, correspondence of the sculptor.
Tu.-Th., Sa., Su. 10-4; F. 10-6.

HENRYKA MARII FUKIERA MUSEUM OF WINE
Ul. Privna 44, Warsaw
Collection of equipment, paintings, photographs, documents illustrating history and techniques of the production of wine.
Tu.-Su. 10-3.

GRAPHICS COLLECTION OF THE NATIONAL LIBRARY
pałac Krasińskich, pl. Krasińskich 5, Warsaw
18th-19th century Polish drawings, water-colours, engravings, architectural drawings. 17th-18th century Flemish, French, English drawings, mezzotints.
Daily 9.30-8.30.

HUNTING MUSEUM
Ul. Nowy Świat 35, Warsaw
Hunting weapons, equipment. Trophies. Paintings, sculpture illustrating hunting scenes.
M., W., F. 3-7; Su. 10-2.

KROLIKARNI PALACE MUSEUM
Puławska 113, Warsaw
Sculpture. Paintings. Memorial collection to the victims of Oświęcim concentration camp.
Tu.-Su. 10-4.

ŁAZIENKACH MUSEUM
Ul. Agrykoli 6, Warsaw
In former Łazienki Palace. Furniture. Paintings. Decorative arts.
Tu.-Su. 10-4.

LENIN MUSEUM
Al. Swierczewskiego 62, Warsaw
Collections illustrating life and achievements of Lenin and the history of the Russian Revolution.
Tu.-Sa. 10-5; W., Th., F. 11-6; Su., public holidays 10-4.

MARIE-SKŁODOWSKA CURIE MUSEUM
Ul. Freta 16, Warsaw
Collections illustrating life and work of Marie Curie. Scientific instruments. Diplomas. Prizes.
Tu.-Sa. 10-5; Su. 10-3.

MARTYRS' MUSEUM
Ul. 1 Armii Wojska Polskiego 25, Warsaw
Memorial museum in Gestapo headquarters to the Poles imprisoned, tortured and executed by the Germans, 1939-44.
M., W., F. 9-4; Tu., Th. 11-6; Su., public holidays, 10-4.

MEDICAL MUSEUM
Ul. Chocimska 22, Warsaw
History of medicine in Poland. Paintings, prints on medical subjects. Instruments. Manuscripts and documents.
Tu.-F. 10-5.

METEOROLOGICAL MUSEUM (MIAR MUSEUM)
Ul. Elektoralna 2, Warsaw
Exhibits showing techniques for observing and forecasting the weather. Instruments and equipment.
M.-Sa. 9-2.

ADAM MICKIEWICZ MUSEUM
Rynek Starego Miasta 18-20, Warsaw
Collections illustrating life and work of Mickiewicz. Manuscripts. Correspondence. Manuscripts and portraits of 18th-20th century Polish writers.
W., Th. 12-7; Tu., F., Sa. 10-3; Su. 11-5.

MUSEUM OF APPLIED ARTS
Ul. Podwale 11, Warsaw
Polish handicrafts, applied and decorative arts.
Tu., Th. 8.30-10.

MUSEUM OF ARCHITECTURE
Ul. Górnośląska 31, Warsaw
In Warsaw School of Architecture. Architectural history and techniques, illustrated by architectural fragments, models, drawings, photographs.
On request.

MUSEUM OF ARTISTIC AND PRECISION HANDICRAFTS
Ul. Piekarska 20, Warsaw
18th-20th century clocks, watches. Optical items. Spectacles. Brass and inlaid work.
Tu.-Su. 10-4.

MUSEUM OF EARTH SCIENCES
Al. Na Skarpie 20-26, Warsaw
Geology. Palaeontology. Palaeobotany. History of geology. Amber.
M., Tu., W., F. 9-3; Th. 9-6; Su. 10-5.

MUSEUM OF THE GEOLOGICAL INSTITUTE
Ul. Rakowiecka 4, Warsaw
Collections illustrating the geology and mineralogy of Poland.
M.-F. 9-3; Sa. 9-3; Su. 10-2.

MUSEUM OF THE HISTORY OF THE CITY OF WARSAW
Rynek Starego Miasta 28, Warsaw
Collections illustrating history and culture of Warsaw from earliest times. Nazi occupation and 1944 insurrection. Paintings. Drawings. Furniture. Architectural items. Ceramics.
Tu.-Th. 12.30-7; W., F., Sa. 10-3.30; Su. 11-4.30.

MUSEUM OF THE HISTORY OF THE REVOLUTIONARY MOVEMENT
Plac. Dzierżyńskiego, Warsaw
Displays illustrating revolutionary and socialist movements in Poland. Mementoes. Pictures. Documents.
Tu.-Th. 11-6. M., W., F. 10-5. Su., public holidays 10-4.

MUSEUM OF THE INSTITUTE OF JEWISH HISTORY
Al. Świerczewskiego 79, Warsaw
Collections illustrating history and culture of the Jews in Poland.
M.-F. 9-4. Sa. 9-12.

MUSEUM OF PHYSICAL CULTURE AND TOURISM
Ul. Wawelska 5, Warsaw
Sports equipment, trophies. History of sport and tourism, especially in Poland. Paintings, sculpture, photographs, music and literature relating to physical culture, tourism and outdoor exercise.
Tu., W., F.-Su. 11-4; Th. 11-6.

MUSEUM OF THE POLISH ARMY
Al. Jerozolimskie 3, Warsaw
History of the Polish army, 10th century - present day. Weapons. Armour. Equipment. Uniforms. Paintings. Prints.
M., Tu., Sa. 12-5; Th. 1-7; F. 10-3; Su. 10.30-5.

MUSEUM IN THE X PAVILION OF THE WARSAW CITADEL
Ul. Skazańców 25, Warsaw
Collections illustrating part played by the Citadel in the movements for national liberation and against Nazi oppression. Reconstructed cells.
M., W., F., 9-4; Tu., Th. 11-6; Su., public holidays 10-4.

MUSEUM OF THE WARSAW MUSICAL ASSOCIATION
Ul. Zakroczymska 2, Warsaw
Musical manuscripts by Polish composers, including a number by Chopin.
Daily 8-3.

NATIONAL ETHNOGRAPHICAL MUSEUM
Ul. Mazowiecka 13, Warsaw
Collections illustrating traditional Polish culture. Hunting. Fishing. Handicrafts. Costumes. Folk art. Ethnography of other countries, especially Africa, Oceania, Australia.
Tu., Th. 12-6; Su. 10-5; W., F., Sa. 10-4.

NATIONAL MUSEUM
Al. Jerozolimskie 3, Warsaw
Italian, Flemish, Dutch, German, Russian paintings. Polish paintings, religious art, portraits. European furniture, ceramics. Decorative arts. Coins. History. Drawings. Posters. Art. Archaeology of the Middle East, Greece, Rome and Medieval Europe.
W., F., Sa. 10-4; Tu., Th. 12-6; Su., public holidays 10-5.

NATIONAL MUSEUM OF ARCHAEOLOGY
Ul. Długa 52, Warsaw
Prehistoric and classical archaeology of Poland.
M. 1-7; Tu.-F. 10-4; Su. 11-5.

NUMISMATICS MUSEUM
Ul. Pereca 21, Warsaw
18th century Warsaw coins, medals, stamps.
M.-Sa. 9-2.30; Su. 9-12.30.

'PARVIAK' PRISON MUSEUM
Ul. Dzielna 24-26, Warsaw
Prison established by the Tsar for political offenders and used by the Nazis during the 1939-45 occupation. Museum illustrating its history.
M.-F. 9-4; Su., public holidays 10-4.

PEDAGOGICAL MUSEUM
Ul. Hipoteczna 8, Warsaw
Geology. Botany. Medical sciences. Pedagogy.
M.-Sa. 10-5.

POSTER MUSEUM
Wilanów Palac, Warsaw
In former palace of Jan III Sobieski. Historical collection of posters, especially Polish and Japanese.
Daily 10-4.

RAILWAY MUSEUM
Ul. Szczęśliwicka 56, Warsaw
In College of Railway Technology. Models, photographs, paintings and other material illustrating Polish railway history.
On request.

TECHNICAL MUSEUM
Palace of Culture and Science, Warsaw
Collections showing development of science and technology, with special reference to Poland. Physical sciences. Mechanisation of agriculture. Power. Mining. Iron and steel. Communications. Aviation and astronautics. Electronics.
Tu., W., F., Sa. 9-4; Th. 12-7; Su. 10-5.

THEATRE MUSEUM
Grand Theatre, Pl. Teatralny, Warsaw
History of the Polish theatre since the 18th century and of the Grand Theatre in particular. Paintings. Photographs. Stage and costume design. Portraits. Posters.
Tu., F., Su. 11-2.

WATER-SUPPLY MUSEUM
Ul. Filtrowej, Warsaw
At central waterworks. Paintings, drawings, photographs and other material illustrating the history of Warsaw's water-supply.
Tu.-Sa. 10-2.

WILANÓW MUSEUM
Wilanów Pałac, Warsaw
In former palace of Jan III Sobieski. 18th-19th century furniture, especially English. Aubusson tapestries. Faience. Japanese, Chinese, German porcelain. Polish ceramics. Limoges enamels.
Tu.-Su. 10-4.

ZOOLOGICAL MUSEUM OF THE POLISH ACADEMY OF SCIENCES
Ul. Wilcza 64, Warsaw
Zoology. Entomology.
Tu.-Sa. 9-5; Su. 10-2.

WDZYDZE KISZEWSKIE

OPEN-AIR MUSEUM
Wdzydze Kiszewskie
Rural buildings, including peasant houses. Ethnography.
May-Sept., Tu.-Su. 10-5.

WEJHEROWO

MUSEUM OF MUSIC
Ul. 12 Marca 1951, Wejherowo
Musical instruments. Memorabilia of Polish musicians.
Tu.-Su. 10-4.

WIELICZKA

ROCK-SALT MUSEUM
Zup Krakowskich, Wieliczka
In 17th century rock-salt mine. History of Polish mining technology. Tools. Machinery. Mineral and geological specimens. Documents. Prints showing the life of miners.
Daily 9-7; public holidays 9-9.

WIELUŃ

REGIONAL MUSEUM
Wieluń
Local archaeology, history.
Tu.-Su. 10-4.

WILKOŁAZ

MEMORIAL MUSEUM
Wilkołaz
Costumes. Agricultural implements. Collections illustrating the German occupation.
Tu.-Su. 10-3.

WISŁA-ZDRÓJ

BESKIDZKI MUSEUM
Wisła-Zdrój
Culture of the mountain-dwellers of the Beskides. Handicrafts. Folk art.
Tu.-Su. 10-4.

WIŚLICA

REGIONAL MUSEUM
Wiślica
Regional history, ethnography.
Tu.-Su. 10-4.

WŁOCŁAWEK

JOZEF ARENTOWICZ COLLECTION OF MEASURING INSTRUMENTS
Ul. Swierczewskiego 29, Włocławek
Historical collection of all types of measuring instruments and vessels.
Daily 10-6.

WŁVEŁAWEK

KUJAWSKI MUSEUM
Ul. Słowackiego 1A, Wlvelawek
Geology. Regional archaeology, history, ethnography. Agricultural implements. Handicrafts. Costumes.
Tu., W., F. 12-3; Th. 3-6; Su. 10-2.

WOLA GUŁOWSKA

LOCAL MUSEUM
Wola Gułowska
In Podstawow school. Collections illustrating the military command of General Kleeberg in October, 1939.
On request.

WOLA OKRZEJSKA

HENRYK SIENKIEWICZ MUSEUM
Wola Okrzejska
Collections illustrating life and work of the writer, in his former house.
Tu.-Su. 10-5.

WOLSZTYN

ROBERT KOCH MUSEUM
Wolsztyn
Collections illustrating life and work of Koch.
Daily 9-4.

MARCIN ROZKI MUSEUM
Wolsztyn
Paintings, photographs and personal possessions illustrating the German occupation. Life and work of Rozki.
Daily 9-4.

WROCŁAW

ANTHROPOLOGICAL MUSEUM OF THE UNIVERSITY OF WROCŁAW
Wrocław
Prehistory. Archaeology. Anthropology.
By appointment.

ARCHAEOLOGICAL MUSEUM
Ul. Kazimieza Wielkiego 34, Wrocław
Prehistory of Silesia. Medieval archaeology.
May-Oct., Tu.-Su. 11-6; Nov. Apr., Tu.-Su. 10-3.

ARCHIDIOCESAN MUSEUM
Ul. Kanoniczna 12, Wrocław
Gothic paintings, sculpture. Textiles. Silver. Altars. Religious art. Prehistory.
Tu.-Su. 10-3.

CABINET OF PRINTS AND DRAWINGS
Ul. Szewska 37, Wrocław
16th-20th century European prints, drawings, especially English, German, French, Polish. Miniatures. Photographs, drawings, documents illustrating history of theatre in Wrocław.
M.-F. 8-2; Sa. 8-1.

COIN COLLECTION
Ul. Szewska 37, Wrocław
Polish coins, paper money, 10th-19th centuries.
Daily 10-2.

COLLECTIONS OF THE ACADEMY OF PLASTIC ARTS
Ul. Traugutta 19-21, Wrocław
Decorative and architectural ceramics. Industrial and electrical ceramics.
Daily 9-2.

ETHNOGRAPHICAL MUSEUM
Ul. Kasimierza Wielkiego 33, Wrocław
Collections illustrating traditional culture of Polish Silesia, 17th-19th centuries. Folk art. Handicrafts. Costumes. Paintings on glass.
M.-W., F., Sa. 10-3; Su. 11-6.

MUSEUM OF AGRICULTURE
Ul. Bartla 6, Wrocław
History of agriculture in Polish Silesia. Implements. Paintings. Photographs. Crops. Livestock.
M.-Sa. 8-3; Su. 11-2.30.

MUSEUM OF ARCHITECTURE AND RECONSTRUCTION
Ul. Bernardyńska 5, Wrocław
In restored 15th century Cistercian convent and church. Architectural fragments and elements from historic Wrocław buildings destroyed, 1939-45. Models and plans of historic and new buildings. Documents. Photographs.
Tu., W., F., Sa. 10-3; Th., Su. 11-7.

MUSEUM OF MEDALS
Stary Ratusz, Rynek, Wrocław
16th-20th century Polish medals and decorations. Dies.
Tu., W., F., Sa. 10-3; Th.-Su. 11-7.

MUSEUM OF POSTS AND TELECOMMUNICATIONS
Ul. Krasińskiego 1, Wrocław
Paintings. Portraits. Drawings. Documents. Photographs. Original equipment and models illustrating history of telephone and telegraph services. Postage stamps.
M.-Sa. 8-3; Su. 11-2.30.

NATIONAL MUSEUM
Pl. Powstańców Warszawy 5, Wrocław
Paintings by Dutch, Flemish, German, Polish artists. Sculpture. Ceramics. Folk art. Medieval antiquities. Graphics. Glass. Handicrafts. History of Silesia, and of Poland.
Tu., W., F., Sa. 10-4; Th., Su. 11-6.

SEALS AND NUMISMATICS COLLECTION OF THE NATIONAL BIBLIOGRAPHICAL INSTITUTE
ul. Szewska 37, Wrocław
Polish coins, medals, paper-money. Polish seals, heraldry.
Tu.-F. 8-2; Sa. 8-1.

UNIVERSITY MUSEUM OF ZOOLOGY
Ul. Sienkiewicza 21, Wrocław
Zoology, especially osteology.
By appointment.

WRZÉSMA

REGIONAL MUSEUM
ul. Dzieci Wrzesińskich 13, Wrzésma
Regional history. Paintings.
Daily 10.30-1.

WSCHOWA

REGIONAL MUSEUM
Pl. Jedności Robotniczej 2, Wschowa
In late 17th century house. Local history. Portraits. Paintings. Furniture. Military relics.
Tu., Th., Sa., Su. 9-3; W., F. 1-5.

WZDÓW

MUSEUM OF RURAL LIFE
w budynku Universytelu Ludowego 2MW, Wzdów
Regional history and ethnography.
On request.

ZABRZE

MINING MUSEUM
Zabrze
History and technology of the local mining industry.
W., F.-Su. 10-2; Tu.-Th. 10-6.

REGIONAL MUSEUM
pl. Krakowski 9, Zabrze
Regional archaeology, history. Collections illustrating history of local coal and iron industries. Mineralogy. Paintings. Folk art.
W., F.-Su. 10-2; Tu., Th. 10-6.

ZACHEŁMIE

LUDOMIR ROZYCKI HOUSE-MUSEUM
Villa 'Pan Twardowski', Zachelmie
Collections illustrating life and work of the composer, Ludomir Rozycki (d.1953).
Tu.-Su. 10-5.

ZAGAŃ

MARTYRS' MUSEUM
Zagań
On site of the German prisoner-of-war camp, Stalag VIII. Exhibits illustrating history and organisation of the camp, and fate of its inmates.
Tu.-Su. 9-4.

ZAGÓRZ

LOCAL MUSEUM
Zagórz
Local history, ethnography.
On request.

ZAGÓRZE ŚLĄSKIE

REGIONAL MUSEUM
Zamek Grodno, Zagórze Śląskie
History of the Zamek (Château) and of local peasant revolts.
Daily 10-5.

ZAKOPANE

CHATA 'TEA' (TEA COTTAGE)
Ul. Slowackiego 39, Zakopane
18th century cottage, with regional ethnographical collections.
Tu., F., Su. 10-12, 4-6.

JAN KASPROWICZ MEMORIAL MUSEUM
Harenda 129, Zakopane
Collections illustrating life and work of the poet, Jan Kasprowicz (d.1926), in his former home.
Tu.-Su. 10-1, 3-6.

K. MAKUSZYŃSKI MEMORIAL MUSEUM
Ul. Tetmajera 15, Zakopane
Collections illustrating life and work of the writer, Kornelow Makuszyński, in his former home. Correspondence. Paintings. Drawings. Handicrafts.
Tu.-Su. 10-1, 3-6.

TATRA MUSEUM AND T. CHAŁUBIŃSKI MEMORIAL
Ul. Krupówki 10, Zakopane
Open-air museum. Regional collections of ethnography, natural history, popular art. Musical instruments. Costumes. Rural buildings brought to site. Furniture. Handicrafts.
Tu.-Su. 9-2.45.

ZAMOŚĆ

ROSA LUXEMBURG MUSEUM
Ul. Staszica 33, Zamość
Collections illustrating life and work of the German Communist leader, Rosa Luxemburg.
Tu.-Su. 10-3.

MARTYRS' MUSEUM
Rotunda, Zamość
History of the German occupation, and memorial to Poles who were killed.
Tu.-Su. 10-3.

REGIONAL MUSEUM
Ul. Ormiańska 26, Zamość
Regional archaeology, history, ethnography. Portraits. Furniture. Coins. Weapons. Pottery. Textiles. Folk art.
Tu.-Su. 10-3.

ŻARNOWIEC

MARIA KONOPNICKI MUSEUM
Żarnowiec
Collections illustrating the life and work of the poet, Maria Konopnicki (d.1910).
M.-Sa. 10-2; Su. 10-1.

ZAWOJA

BABIEJ GÓRY NATIONAL PARK MUSEUM
Dolina Basáncowa, Zawoja
Regional natural history. Geology. Botany. Zoology.
May-Sept., daily 9-3.

ZBĄSZIN

REGIONAL MUSEUM
Zamek, Zbąszin
In restored 13th century manor house. Regional history. Folk art, handicrafts, musical instruments.
Tu.-Su. 10-4.

ŻELAZOWA WOLA

FRYDERYK CHOPIN MUSEUM
Żelazowa Wola
Chopin's birthplace. Relics of the composer and his family.
May-Sept., daily 9-6. Oct.-Apr., daily 9-4.

ZIEBICE

ZIEBICE MUSEUM
Ul. Przemystawa 10, Ziebice, Silesia
Art. Decorative arts. Natural history. Ethnography. History.
Tu.-Su. 10-3.

ZIELONA GÓRA

ZIELONA GÓRA MUSEUM
Al. Niepodleglosci 15, Zielona Góra
Regional archaeology, ethnography. Handicrafts. Folk art. Applied art. History of vineyard culture and production of wine, especially in Zielona Góra and Lower Silesia. Implements and equipment, including casks, wine-presses. Wine cups and glasses. Reconstruction of medieval wine shop.
Tu.-Su. 9-3.

ZŁOTÓW

ETHNOGRAPHICAL PARK
Złotów
Rural buildings re-erected on museum site. Exhibits of agricultural implements, folk art, handicrafts.
Tu.-Sa. 10-3; Su., public holidays 1-4.

ZŁOTOW

REGIONAL MUSEUM
Ul. Wojska Polskiego 2A, Złotow
Regional archaeology, history, ethnography.
M.-Sa. 10-3; Su. (May-Sept.) 1-4.

ZŁOTY STOK

LOCAL MUSEUM
Złoty Stok
Collections illustrating ancient gold-mining in the area of Złoty Stok.
Tu.-Su. 10-4.

ZNIN

PAŁUK REGIONAL MUSEUM
Plac Wolnosci 8, Znin
Archaeology, history and ethnography of the river-basin of the Notec and Wełna.
Tu.-Sa. 4-6; Su. 11-1.

ZOFIPOLE

ARCHAEOLOGICAL SITE MUSEUM
Zofipole
Collection of material discovered during excavations on this prehistoric site.
On request.

ŻORAWINA

MUSEUM OF MANNERISM
Żorawina
Restored 16th-17th century church, with polychrome decorations and other decorative arts of the period.
By appointment.

ZUBRZYCA GORNA

OPEN-AIR MUSEUM
Orawski Park, Zubrzyca Gorna
Rural buildings from the region. Peasant houses. Cowbarns, sheep-folds and other farm buildings.
May-Sept., Tu.-Su. 10-6.

ŻYRARDÓW

HISTORICAL MUSEUM OF THE WORKERS' MOVEMENT
Ul. Malinowskiego 1, Żyrardów
Collections illustrating the German occupation of the district, 1939-45, the local workers' movement and the establishment of socialism.
W., Sa., Su. 10-6.

ZYWIEC

REGIONAL MUSEUM
Ul. Kościuszki, Zywiec
Archaeology. Natural history. Ethnography. History. Local religious art, especially 15th century.
Tu.-Su. 10-3.

Portugal

Portuguese museums are mainly concerned, as one might have supposed, with the country's distinguished past, from Roman times to the early nineteenth century. As one of the great Catholic nations, it has very properly spent a good deal of money on the preservation of its ecclesiastical treasures, some of which are of an unconventional kind. There is, for instance, a sixteenth century Franciscan chapel faced with the bones and skulls of 5000 brothers, the aim and hope of the creator of such an architectural oddity being that it would "induce meditation in his fellow men". Elsewhere, there is the Gothic tomb of the Count of Viarra, killed by the Moors in Africa. It contains all it ever contained, one of the Count's teeth.

There are several good museums of maritime history, and comprehensive collections of folk art and weapons. Bullfighting has its museums and so do the Moors, but, very strangely in such an overwhelmingly rural country, there is no museum of agriculture and, greatest neglect of all, no museum devoted to port wine. There is, however, a seaplane which crossed the South Atlantic in 1922 and the piano on which Liszt played when he gave concerts in Lisbon.

Portugal also has, in one of its museums, a piece of equipment not readily available elsewhere. It is a phenakistoscope, one of the early predecessors of the cinema. This praiseworthy and enterprising piece of preservation should not, however, give the impression that Portugal is rich in museums of science and technology. Absolutely the opposite is the case. One phenakistoscope does not, regrettably, make a summer.

ALPIARÇA

MUSEUM
Casa dos Patudos, Alpiarça, nr. Santarém
17th-19th century tapestries and carpets. Arraiolos carpets with silk embroidery. Indo-Portuguese silk carpets. Castelo Branco coverlets. Aubusson tapestries. China and porcelain from France, Portugal, Germany and the Far East. Primitive paintings. Portuguese paintings by Josefa de Obidos, Silva Porto and Malhoa. Sculpture by Soares dos Reis, Teixeira Lopes and Machado de Castro. 18th century *azulejos* illustrating the life of St. Francis of Assisi.
Th., Su. and holidays, 2-6. Other days on request.

AMARANTE

MUSEUM
Amarante
Modern paintings, including works by the Cubist painter, Amadeu de Souza Cardoso, born near Amarante.
Daily ex. Su. 9-12.30, 2-5.

AVEIRO

REGIONAL MUSEUM
Rua Santa Joana, Aveiro
In former Convent of Jesus. Baroque sacred art. 18th century paintings on copper foil. Sculpture of 16th century Coimbra school. Primitive paintings, including a 15th century portrait on wood of Princess Joana, attributed to Nuno Gonçalves. Church gallery contains a 14th century Crucifixion in which Christ's expression changes according to the angle from which it is viewed.
Daily ex. M. and holidays, 10-12.30, 2-5.

BARCELOS

MUNICIPAL ARCHAEOLOGICAL MUSEUM
Barcelos
In former palace of the Ducal Counts of Barcelos. Archaeological finds from the area. 14th century monument to the legendary Barcelos Cock. Ceramics.
Daily ex. M. 10-12, 2-7.

BATALHA

UNKNOWN SOLDIER'S MUSEUM
Batalha
In former monastery. Displays commemorating the victorious Battle of Aljubarrota, which gave Portugal two centuries of independence.
Daily ex. M. 10-12, 2-7.

BEJA

REGIONAL MUSEUM
Beja
In former Convent of the Conception. Wood-carvings. Inscriptions. Christmas crib figures and Visigoth sculp-

tures. Paintings, including a 17th century portrait of St. Jerome by Ribera and a 15th century *Ecce Homo*. Alentejo costumes. Reconstruction of cell window through which Sister Mariana Alcoforado is said to have talked with Count de Chamilly. Tombs.
Daily ex. Tu. and holidays, 9.30-1, 1.30-5.

BRAGA

MUSEUM OF RELIGIOUS ART
Cathedral, Braga
Hispano-Arab *azulejos*. Old engravings. Tombs, including lid of tomb of St. Ovidio. Iron crucifix (15th century). Alabaster Virgin (17th century). Sacerdotal ornaments. Vestments. Moorish casket of carved ivory. Crosses and cruxifixes.
Daily ex. M. 10-5.

TREASURY
Cathedral, Braga
Ecclesiastical plate, including a 10th century Mozarabic chest made of ivory. Vestments. Statues. 18th century gilded wooden choir stalls. Statue of St. Crispin, patron saint of shoemakers.
Guided tours daily.

BUÇACO

MILITARY MUSEUM
outside Town Wall, Buçaco
Features the battle of Buçaco and the campaigns of 1810.
Daily 9-12, 1-6 (winter 10-12, 1-5).

CALDAS DA RAINHA

MALHOA MUSEUM
Caldas da Rainha
Paintings, including works by José Malhoa (1855-1933) and Columbano (1857-1929), the "Master of Half Light". Sculptures by Leopoldo de Almeida and Francisco Franco.
Daily ex. M. and holidays, 10-15.

CARAMULO

ART MUSEUM
Caramulo
Flemish tapestries depicting the arrival of the Portuguese in India. 15th century Portuguese statues. Paintings by contemporary artists, including Picasso, Lurçat and Fernand Léger.
June-Sept. Daily 10-6. Oct.-May Daily ex. M. 10-5.

CAR MUSEUM
Caramulo
Collection of motor-cars in working order, including a 1902 Darracq and a 1906 De Dion Bouton.
June-Sept. Daily 10-6. Oct.-May Daily ex. M. 10-5.

COIMBRA

MACHADO DE CASTRO MUSEUM
Coimbra
In former Bishop's Palace. Gothic wood-carvings. Sculpture, including 14th century equestrian statue of a medieval knight. Porcelain. 16th century red clay vases. Ecclesiastical plate. Stained glass from Royal Palace of Leiria. Paintings. Mementoes of Queen Saint Isabel, including jewellery. Sculptures of the Coimbra school, notably an anonymous altarpiece of the Life of the Virgin. Boxes and chests. Carpets. Alabaster. Door mirrors. Musical instruments. Chinese bronzes, porcelain, fabrics and paintings.
Daily ex. M. and holidays, 10-5.

OLD CATHEDRAL
Coimbra
Gothic altarpiece in gilded wood. Paintings.
Daily.

CONIMBRIGA

MUSEU MONOGRÁFICO
Conimbriga
Mosaics. Ceramics. Marble busts.
Daily 9-8. Mar., Apr. and Oct. 9-6. Nov.-Feb. 9-5.

ELVAS

REGIONAL MUSEUM
Largo de Vasco da Gama, Elvas
Roman mosaics. 14th and 16th century statues. Roman stones and pottery. Estremoz pottery (1889-1950). Hispano-Moorish *azulejos*. Jewellery. Articles in wood, wrought iron and pewter. Sacerdotal ornaments. Reliquaries, chalices and missals. Paintings.
Daily ex. M. 11-5.

ESTREMOZ

REGIONAL MUSEUM
62b Rossio, Estremoz
Collections illustrating life of the people of Alentejo. Costumes. Local crafts.
M.-Sa. 9.30-12.30, 2-5. Su. on request to the Casa do Povo de Santa Maria.

ÉVORA

MUSEUM OF ANCIENT ART
former Episcopal Palace, Évora
Roman, medieval, Manueline and Luso-Moorish sculpture. Primitive paintings. 16th century paintings, including works by Frei Carlos and Gregorio Lopes. Limoges triptych, enamel on copper, early 16th century. 18th century banner of the Inquisition.
Daily ex. M. and holidays, 9.30-11.30.

OSSUARY CHAPEL
Church of St. Francis, Évora
Erected in 16th century by a Franciscan, "to induce meditation in his fellow men". The chapel walls and pillars are faced with the bones and skulls of 5,000 brothers.
Daily 7-1, 2.30-8.

TREASURY
Cathedral, Évora
Church plate, including a 13th century French ornamental opening Virgin in ivory and a 17th century reliquary in silver gilt and multi-coloured enamel.
Daily 9-12.30, 2-6.30 on application to the sacristan.

FARO

MARITIME MUSEUM
Faro
Housed in former office of the captain of the port, the museum contains ships' models and miniatures of different kinds of fishing vessels (sardine, tunny, etc.).
Daily ex. Su. and holidays, 9.30-12.30, 2-5.30; Sa. 9.30-1.

FUNCHAL

THE CROSSES' QUINTA
Funchal, Madeira
Villa housing 16th century Portuguese furniture from private houses in Funchal. 17th century India Company china. Limoges enamels. Triptych in cedar wood. English and French furniture of 17th and 18th centuries. Ivories.
Tu.-Sa. 2-5; Su. 12-5. Closed M.

FIREMEN'S MUSEUM
Rua Pedro Jose de Ornelas, Funchal, Madeira
Old fire engines mounted on sledge-runners for pulling by hand. Evolution of fire-fighting techniques since the late 19th century and the different catastrophes which befell the firemen of Funchal are depicted in a series of engravings.
Tu. and Th. 7-9 p.m. Su. 9-1, 6-9.

MUNICIPAL MUSEUM
Rua da Mouraria, Funchal, Madeira
Natural history collections.
M.-Sa. 9.30-5; Su. 12-5.

MUSEUM OF RELIGIOUS ART
21 Rua do Bispo, Funchal, Madeira
Paintings on wood of 15th and 16th century Portuguese and Flemish schools. Gold and silver plate, including 16th century Gothic Manueline silver cross. Church ornaments. Low reliefs in gilded wood.
Daily ex. M. 10-12, 2-5; Su. 3-5.

GUIMARÃES

ALBERTO SAMPAIO MUSEUM
Guimarães
In Church of Our Lady of the Olive Tree. Statues and paintings. Ceramics. Church plate, including Gothic silver chalice with enamel embossing. Silver Manueline Cross depicting scenes from the Passion. Silver gilt triptych said to have been given to the Church by João I.
Daily ex. M. and holidays, 10-12.30, 2-5.

MARTINS SARMENTO MUSEUM
Guimarães
In Cloister of Church of St. Dominic. Archaeological finds from the pre-Roman cities of Sabroso and Briteiros. Inscriptions. Stone sarcophagus. Pottery from the serra da Penha.
Tu.-Th. 1-6. June-Sept. also Su. 10-12, 2-4.

PALACE OF THE DUKES OF BRAGANCA
Guimarães
Gobelins, Aubusson and Flanders tapestries. 17th century Persian carpets. 17th century Portuguese furniture. Paintings by Josefa de Obidos.
Daily 9.30-6 (5 in winter). Closed Christmas Day.

ILHAVO

CERAMICS MUSEUM
Ilhavo
In Vista Alegre Ceramics factory. Development of the manufacture of china and glass.
M.-F. 2.30-6. Closed holidays.

LOCAL MUSEUM
Ilhavo, nr. Aveiro
History of the sea and of the fishing industry. Vista Alegre ceramics.
Daily 10-12, 2-5.

LAMEGO

REGIONAL MUSEUM
former Episcopal Palace, Lamego
16th-18th century *azulejos*. Two Baroque chapels of carved and gilded wood. Ornate 15th century cross. Early 16th and 17th century Brussels tapestries. 16th century paintings by Vasco Fernandes. Reredos from the Cathedral attributed to a Dutch painter. Religious vestments. Religious articles in chased gold and enamel.
Daily ex. M. and holidays, 10-12.30, 2-5.

LISBON

ARCHAEOLOGICAL MUSEUM
Rua de Carmo, Lisbon
In Carmo Church. Bronze Age pottery. Marble low reliefs. Romanesque and Gothic tombs. Spanish Arabic *azulejos*. Mosaics. Wooden sculptures. Sarcophagus of King Ferdinand I (14th century).
Daily ex. M. and holidays, 10-5. 11-5 in winter.

ARCHAEOLOGICAL MUSEUM
Lisbon
Iberian antiquities, in 19th century wing of St. Mary's church.
Daily ex. M. and holidays, 10-5.

CALOUSTE GULBENKIAN MUSEUM
Avenida Antonio Augusto de Aguiar, Lisbon
Artistic collections of Calouste Sarkis Gulbenkian, given to Portugal in 1953. Contemporary Portuguese paintings. Egyptian, Greco-Roman and Mesopotamian exhibits. Chinese vases. Japanese lacquerwork. European works of art, including oils by Guardi (1712-1793). French Impressionist paintings. Sculpture by Carpeaux, Rodin and Houdon. 18th century furniture.
Daily ex. M. and holidays 10-5. 10-8 W. and Sa.

FOLK ART MUSEUM
Avenida Brasilia, Belém, Lisbon
Handicrafts from every Portuguese province.
Daily ex. M. and public holidays, 10-5.

GEOLOGICAL AND MINERALOGICAL MUSEUM
Academiadas Ciências, Rua da Academia das Ciências, Lisbon
Tertiary epoch mammals. Fossilised plants. Stratigraphic and palaeontological collections. Anthropology and prehistoric archaeology: human and animal bones, neolithic pottery, prehistoric jewellery. Minerals and building materials. Portuguese and Portuguese African mineralogical and rock specimens.
M.-Sa. 9-12, 2-5.

MARITIME MUSEUM
West Wing, Hieronymite Monastery, Lisbon
Galleys and models of Portuguese ships from 15th century to the present day. Royal galleys, charts, nautical instruments, uniforms. Seaplane used in 1922 South Atlantic crossing.
Daily ex. M. and public holidays, 10-5.30.

MILITARY MUSEUM
Arsenal do Exército, Largo do Museu de Artilharia, Lisbon
Arms and armour. Paintings by contemporary artists. Uniforms. Medals. Flags and pennants. Cannons, ordnance, culverins, bombards and basilisks.
Daily ex. M. and holidays, 2-5.

MUNICIPAL MUSEUM
Palácio da Mitra, Avenida Infante, Lisbon
Material illustrating Lisbon's development and growth. Documents. Paintings, including Malhoa's *The Fado*.
Daily 9-5.

MUSEUM
Galveias Palace, Praça de Touros, Lisbon
Collection of paintings and furniture.
Daily ex. M. 10-5.

MUSEUM OF BULLFIGHTING
Camp Pequeno, Lisbon
Costumes of bullfighters, together with mementoes and portraits.
Daily ex. M. 10-5.

MUSEUM OF CONTEMPORARY ART
Rua Serpa Pinto, Lisbon
Paintings by Columbano (1857-1929), José Malhoa (1855-1933) and João Reis. Sculpture by Teixeira Lopes, *The Widow.* Works by naturalist painters, including Silva Porto, Sousa Pinto, Salgado, F. Santos and J. da Silva.
Daily ex. M. and holidays, 10-5.

MUSEUM OF DECORATIVE ART
former Palace of the Counts of Azurara, Lisbon
17th and 18th century Portuguese and Indo-Portuguese furniture. Silver. Carpets. 18th century Venetian chandelier.
Daily ex. M. and holidays, 10-5.

MUSEUM OF THE NATIONAL CONSERVATORY OF MUSIC
R. dos Caetanos, Lisbon
Ancient musical instruments. Piano at which Liszt gave concerts at São Carlos Theatre, Lisbon.
Daily ex. Su. and holidays, 9-12, 2-5.30.

MUSEUM OF POPULAR ART
Praĉo do Império, Lisbon
Art and folklore traditions of the various provinces of Portugal. Crafts. Articles associated with local fetes. Utensils made of wicker, glass and iron. Models of bullock carts and fishing boats. Blankets of patchwork and dogs' skin. musical instruments. Costumes. Linen. Lace. Embroidery.
Daily ex. M. and holidays, 10-5.

MUSEUM OF ROYAL COACHES
Paĉo de Belém, Praĉa Afonso de Albuquerque, Lisbon
16th-19th century royal coaches and old four-wheelers, in former riding school. Gobelins tapestry. Sedan chairs. 18th century stage coach of the Infanta Donã Antonia. Coach with writing table. Picadors' saddles. Uniforms, liveries, buttons, boot buckles and festival harness.
Daily ex. M. and holidays, 10-5.

MUSEUM OF RELIGIOUS ART
Church of St. Rock, Lisbon
16th century Portuguese paintings. Furnishings. Church plate and ornaments with Baroque decoration. Canopied altar in chased silver. Silk chasubles and altar furnishings embroidered in gold and silver thread. 16th century oriental chasuble. 14th century Virgin and Child. Silver-gilt sculpture of Rhineland School.
Daily ex. M. and holidays, 10-5.

NATIONAL MUSEUM OF ANCIENT ART
Rocha do Conde de Obidós, Lisbon
15th and 16th century Portuguese primitives, including the polyptych of the Adoration of St. Vincent (c.1460) by Nuno Gonçalves. Foreign schools of painting, including *Temptation of St. Anthony* by Hieronymus Bosch, *St. Jerome* by Dürer and works by Hans Holbein and Zurbaran. Gold and silver plate. 16th century Indo-Portuguese caskets. Altar curtain from the Belém monastery (1506). Carpets. Ceramics.
Daily ex. M. and holidays, 10-5.

NATIONAL MUSEUM OF ARCHAEOLOGY AND ETHNOLOGY
Praça do Império, Lisbon
Palaeolithic and neolithic material. Domestic articles from medieval period. Statues and steles. Roman mosaics. Inscriptions in Iberian characters. Roman boundary stones. Egyptian mummies from acropolis at Akhmin. African section: stone instruments, arms, fetishes, yokes. Portuguese and Hispano-Arabian glazed tiles of 16th-18th centuries. Local modern pottery from Algarve and Alentejo.
Daily ex. M. 11-5.

MUSEUM OF OVERSEAS AGRICULTURE
Palace of the Pátio das Vacas, Calçada do Galvão, Lisbon
Products of agriculture and of the forests of Portuguese overseas possessions.
Daily ex. M. 11.30-4.30.

MUSEUM OF THE VETERANS' ASSOCIATION
Rua João Pereira da Rosa 18, Lisbon
Souvenirs of Portuguese campaigns in France and overseas.
M.-F. 10-1, 3-6.30; Sa. 10-1. Closed Sa. afternoons, Su. and holidays.

OVERSEAS ETHNOGRAPHY MUSEUM
R. Portas de St. Antão, Lisbon
Objects relating to the history and art of the overseas provinces.
M.-F. 3-6. Closed Sa., Su. and holidays.

PORTUGUESE NUMISMATIC MUSEUM
Avenida Dr. António José de Almeida, Lisbon
Coins from 5th century B.C.
W. 9-12, 2-5.30; Sa. 9-12.30.

POST OFFICE MUSEUM
R. Dona Estefânia, Lisbon
Documents and objects illustrating the history of the postal and telephone services.
Daily ex. M. and public holidays, 10-5.

RAFAEL BORDALO PINHEIRO MUSEUM
Campo Grande, Lisbon
Memorial room of Rafael Bordalo Pinheiro. Ceramics. Drawings, water-colours and reproductions.
Daily ex. M. 10-5.

SACRISTY
Cathedral, Lisbon
Baroque room containing religious art objects, including a 16th century enamel monstrance and an oriental casket in mother-of-pearl containing relics of St. Vincent. Baroque statuettes.
Daily ex. M. 10-5.

ZOOLOGICAL AND ANTHROPOLOGICAL MUSEUM
R. Escola Politécnica, Lisbon
Zoological collections. Anthropology.
Th. 10-12, 2-4.

MAFRA

PALACE MUSEUM
Mafra
Religious art.
Daily 9.30-6. Closed Christmas Day.

OPORTO

ETHNOGRAPHICAL MUSEUM
Rua da Victoria, Oporto
Objects concerned with the folklore of the province of Douro Litoral.
Daily ex. M. and public holidays, 10-5.

GUERRA JUNQUEIRO MUSEUM
Oporto
Arts objects collected by the poet, Guerra Junqueiro, including 15th and 16th century Hispano-Arabic pottery. Portuguese furniture and 16th century Flemish tapestries.
Daily ex. M. 11-4.30.

SOARES DOS REIS MUSEUM
Carrancas Palace, Oporto
Local 18th-19th century pottery. Portuguese primitive paintings, including works by Gaspar Vaz, Vasco Fernandes and Cristóvão de Figuiredo. Sculptures by Soares dos Reis (1847-1889), Teixeira Lopes, Silva Porto and Pousão. Portraits of Marguerite de Valois and Henry II of France by François Clouet, 16th century. Religious art. 16th century Limoges enamels.
Daily ex. M. and holidays, 10-5.

ROMEU

MUSEUM OF CURIOSITIES
Romeu, nr. Mirandela
Dutch ovens. Sewing machines. Phenakistoscope (predecessor of the cinema). Collection of musical boxes in various forms. Vintage cars.
On request.

SANTARÉM

ARCHAEOLOGICAL MUSEUM
Santarém
In Church of São João de Alporão. Arab and Romanesque pottery. *Azulejos.* Coins. Chinaware. Sculpture, including funerary steles and coats of arms. Gothic tomb of Duarte de Meneses, Count of Viaria, containing only a tooth (he was killed by the Moors in Africa).
Daily ex. F. 9-12, 2-5; Su. 9-12, 2-6.

SETUBAL

MUNICIPAL MUSEUM
Cloister of Church of Jesus, Setubal
15th and 16th century Portuguese Primitives. 16th century *azulejos* with geometric motifs.
Daily ex. M. and holidays, 10-12, 2-5.

SINTRA

ROYAL PALACE
Sintra
16th and 17th century *azulejos* in Arabic Hall, the Chapel and the Sirens' Hall.
Daily 9.30-6. Closed Dec. 25.

VIANA DO CASTELO

MUNICIPAL MUSEUM
Viana do Castelo
In Palace of Barbosa Macieis. *Azulejos* painted in 1721 by Pilicarpo de Oliveira Bernardes, representing hunting and fishing scenes, receptions, and distant lands. Indo-Portuguese and Spanish-Arabic furniture and furnishings.
Daily ex. M. and holidays, 10-5.

VILA DO BISPO

MUSEUM
Vila Do Bispo, nr. Sabugal
Art objects, including ivory crucifixes.
On request.

VILA REAL DE SANTO ANTONIO

ARCHAEOLOGICAL MUSEUM
Castle, Vila Real de Santo Antonio
Archaeological finds from the district.
Daily 9-7.

DUCAL PALACE
Vila Real de Santo Antonio
17th century enamels. Brussels and Aubusson tapestries and Arraiolos carpets. Paintings. 16th century triptych. 17th and 18th century coaches. Armoury.
Daily 9-7 (6 in winter).

VISEU

GRÃO VASCO MUSEUM
Viseu
Tres Escalões Palace. 13th-18th century sculpture, including part of a 14th century throne of Grace and 13th century Pièta. 16th century Spanish-Arabic enamels. Spanish paintings and works by modern and contemporary Portuguese painters. Primitives of the Viseu school. Watercolours and drawings. Religious art.
Daily ex. M. and holidays, 10-5.

Portuguese Guinea

Discovered by the Portuguese in 1446 and held by them ever since. The economy which the museum collections illustrate is a simple and basic one, centred on palm-oil, groundnuts and other tropical products.

BISSAU

MUSEUM OF PORTUGUESE GUINEA
Praça do Império, Bissau
Ethnography. History. Natural science. Collections illustrating economy of Portuguese Guinea.
Daily 8-12, 3-5.

Réunion

Réunion has belonged to France since 1642. It produces a great deal of rum and, possibly for this reason, has excellent air services. Its museums reflect both the long and close links with France and the remarkable wildlife which has existed in the area at one time or another.

SAINT-DENIS

LÉON DIERX FINE ARTS MUSEUM
Rue Sainte Marie et Rue de Paris, Saint-Denis
Local history. Paintings, especially French Impressionists. Casts of Roman and Gothic sculptures. East India Company. Drawings. Engravings.
Daily ex. F. 10-12, 1-7.

MUSEUM OF NATURAL HISTORY
Jardin de l'Est, Saint-Denis
Geology. Zoology, including skeleton of a dodo and the crest of a *Bourbon Fregilupus varius*, a bird from the Mascareignes which has not been seen since the 18th century. Other rare birds, including the kiwi and species from Madagascar. Small collection of large exotic butterflies.
Tu. 8-12, 2-6; Su. 8-12, 2-6; Sa. 2-6.

Rhodesia

The museums of Rhodesia tell the story of black men, rocks, animals and plants that have been there for a very long time, and of white men who have been there for a very short time. The white men receive most space and attention, the natural history comes next, and the black men third, an order of priorities which is not particularly surprising. For the whites (250, 000) we have Cecil Rhodes and David Livingstone, railways, mining machinery, military weapons and equipment and contemporary European art, and for the blacks and browns (14,500,000), rock paintings, pottery, carvings and a reconstructed village.

BULAWAYO

KHAMI RUINS SITE MUSEUM
Bulawayo
Archaeological finds from Khami Ruins complex (dwellings of lesser Matabele rulers). Early, middle and late Stone Age relics of the area. Rock paintings. Early Iron Age material.
Daily except Good F. and Christmas Day, 10-4.30.

NATIONAL MUSEUM OF RHODESIA
Centenary Park, Bulawayo
Cultural history of Rhodesia. History of Rhodesia since the European occupation. Personal relics of Cecil Rhodes. Natural history. Geology. Insects.
M.-Sa. 9-5; Su. 2.30-5.

RHODESIA RAILWAYS MUSEUM
Prospect Avenue and First Street, Raylton, Bulawayo
Archives and relics of Rhodesia Railways, including early locomotives in steaming condition, and a mobile 'museum coach'.
Daily 8.30-5.

RHODESIAN MINING ANTIQUARIA
National Museum of Rhodesia, Centenary Park, Bulawayo
Historic items of mining machinery used in Rhodesia from the beginning of European settlement.
Daily 8.30-5.

FORT VICTORIA

ZIMBABWE RUINS SITE MUSEUM
Private Bag 9158, Fort Victoria
Pottery, carvings, ornaments found in ruins of city of Zimbabwe (1450-1833). Reconstructed 19th century Karanga village. Replicas of Zimbabwe bird's heads.
Daily 10-4.30. Closed Good F. and Christmas Day.

GWELO

ARMY MUSEUM
School of Infantry, P.O. Box 734, Gwelo
Machine guns, arms and equipment of various countries. Weapons dating back to pioneer days in Rhodesia. Well-preserved Brown Bess Musket and a Maxim Machine Gun which was used in the Boer War, as well as East European arms and equipment.
On request.

INYANGA

NYAHOKWE RUINS SITE MUSEUM
Inyanga
Iron-age site. Locally-found relics of the Ziwi culture. Stone Age material from nearby site.
Daily 9-4.30. Closed Christmas Day and Good F.

MARANDELLOS

CHILDREN'S MUSEUM
c/o Children's Library, The Green, Marandellos
Man and his implements from early Stone Age to pioneering days. Rocks and minerals. Local ornithology.
Tu.-F. 9-1, 2-5; Sa. 9-1, 2-4.

SALISBURY

GEOLOGICAL SURVEY MUSEUM
Maufe Building, Corner 4th Street/Selous Avenue, Salisbury
Rocks and minerals, with special emphasis on those found in Rhodesia.
M.-F. 7.45-1, 2-4.45.

NATIONAL ARCHIVES
Archives Building, Borrowdale Road, Private Bag 729, Causeway, Salisbury
The history of Rhodesia since the arrival of the Europeans. Paintings by early travellers. Relics of David Livingstone.
M.-F. 8-4.30; Sa. 8-12.

QUEEN VICTORIA MUSEUM
Rotten Row, P.O. Box 8006, Causeway, Salisbury
Prehistoric art. Pioneer history. Series of tableaux on the story of man, from the earliest bushmen to the pioneers. The later exhibits in this section feature original furniture and clothing. Natural history, especially birds, mammals, reptiles and fossils of Mashonaland.
M.-Sa. 9-5; Su. 2.30-5.

RHODES NATIONAL GALLERY
Kings Crescent, Salisbury
Contemporary European art, but with some earlier European paintings. Traditional and contemporary West African art.
Daily ex. M. 9-5.

UMTALI

UMTALI MUSEUM
Victory Avenue, Umtali
Natural history, with collections of reptiles, amphibia, lepidoptera, shells. Regional historical and ethnographical material. Reconstructions of early settler's house and blacksmith's shop. Weapons. Two early locomotives.
Weekdays 9-5; Su. 2-5. Closed Good F. and Christmas Day.

Romania

If the ratio of museums to population is of any significance, Romanian museums are in a flourishing condition. More important, however, is the distribution of the museums, and the balance within the subject-matter of their collections. Romania does well on both counts. Bucharest does not overwhelm the rest of the country. Museums in provincial cities have been allocated a high proportion of the national resources and prestige and the tendency to remove the finest material to the capital has not been as marked in Romania as it has elsewhere. There are, in consequence, no huge museums in Bucharest. The texture of the Romanian museum-pattern is remarkably even and there are a number of instances of important specialist museums in comparatively minor towns.

Romania is particularly strong in museums which illustrate rural life and handicrafts. There are two excellent open-air museums, containing wooden buildings moved to the site from different parts of the country, and many good collections of costumes, peasant furniture and folk art. Prehistoric, Greek and Roman archaeology is also well represented. The important Romanian oil industry has a museum to itself and there are others dealing with the development of the chemical industry and with industry and technology in general. As our list makes clear, much attention has been given to establishing house-museums devoted to leading Romanian writers of the nineteenth and twentieth centuries. There are a surprisingly large number of these, largely, perhaps, because a high proportion of the writers of the pre-1939 period were closely identified with the struggle to achieve, first, national independence and then a more twentieth-century type of economy and government. In the Romanian context, to commemorate one's leading writers is to document what is generally known in Communist countries as either the workers' or the revolutionary movement. One does, even so, find one or two Romanian examples of the conventional museum of political history, with such stirring and copy-book titles as 'Museum of the Trial of the Railwaymen and Petroleum Workers, June-July 1934'.

The Romanians are not, to judge by their museums, much interested in military history, a fact which makes them exceptional among the Communist countries.

ADY ENDRE

ADY ENDRE MUSEUM
Ady Endre
In birthplace of the poet, Ady Endre (d.1919). Collection illustrating life and work of Endre.
On request.

AGAPIA

ALEXANDRU VLAHUŢĂ HOUSE-MUSEUM
Agapia
Life and work of the writer, Alexandru Vlahută, in his former home.
On request.

AGNITA

AGNITA MUSEUM
Strada Găriu 2, Agnita
Prehistory and history, especially medieval, of the Hirtibaciu Valley. Local blue and white pottery. Guild history.
Tu.-Su. 10-1, 3-5.

AIUD

AIUD HISTORICAL MUSEUM
Piaţa Republicii 24, Aiud
In 14th century house. Prehistory. Classical archaeology. Regional history since medieval times.
Tu.-Su. 11-7.

NATURAL HISTORY MUSEUM
Strada 11 Iunie, Aiud
Natural history of the region. Geology. Mineralogy. Palaeontology. Birds. Insects.
Tu.-Su. 10-5.

ALBA IULIA

ALBA IULIA MUSEUM
Strada 13 Decembrie 5, Alba Iulia
Roman archaeology. Medieval collections, including goldsmith's work, coins. History of the Romanian struggle for independence. Ethnography.
Tu.-Su. 10-7.

ALBEŞTI

SANDOR PETŐFI MUSEUM
Albeşti
At site of the battle where the Hungarian poet and revolutionary was killed (1849). Collection illustrating life and work of Petőfi.
On request.

ALEXANDRIA

ALEXANDRIA MUSEUM
Alexandria
Local prehistory, history.
Daily 10-1.

ARAD

ARAD MUSEUM
Piaţa Enescu 1, Arad
Prehistoric and medieval archaeology. Ethnography. History and relics of the Revolution of 1848-49 in Transylvania. Paintings by Romanian and Hungarian artists. 17th-20th century European paintings. Decorative arts.
Tu.-Su. 10-1, 5-7.

AUREL VLAICU

AUREL VLAICU MUSEUM
Aurel Vlaicu
In birthplace of the aviation pioneer, Aurel Vlaicu (d.1913). Vlaicu's life and work. Tools used in building his aeroplanes.
By appointment.

AVRAM IANCU

AVRAM IANCU MUSEUM
Avram Iancu
In birthplace of the revolutionary, Avram Iancu (d.1872). Weapons used by the peasants. Personal possessions of Iancu, including his sabre. Folklore.
On request.

BABADAG

LOCAL MUSEUM
Babadag
Paintings, graphics, sculpture by contemporary Romanian artists.
On request.

BACĂU

BACĂU HISTORICAL MUSEUM
Strada Karl Marx 14, Bacău
Prehistoric and early historical material from local excavations. Local history.
Tu.-Su. 10-1, 3-7.

MUSEUM OF ART
Strada Mărăşeşti 42, Bacău
Paintings by Romanian artists.
Tu.-Su. 10-1, 3-7.

NATURAL HISTORY MUSEUM
Strada Karl Marx 2, Bacău
Historical geography. Palaeontology. Evolution.
Tu.-Su. 10-1, 3-7.

BAIA MARE

MARAMUREŞ DISTRICT MUSEUM
Strada 1 Maia 8, Baia Mare
Local prehistory and history. Development of mining and commerce. 19th-20th century paintings by Romanian artists, especially from the Baia Mare area.
Tu.-Su. 10-5.

BEIUŞ

FOLKLORE MUSEUM
Strada 23 August 1, Beiuş
Local history and folklore.
On request.

BEREVOIEŞTI

BEREVOIEŞTI MUSEUM
Berevoieşti
19th-20th century Romanian paintings, sculpture.
On request.

BICAZ

BICAZ MUSEUM
Bicaz
Early historical material from local excavations. Models, diagrams and other documents illustrating the V.I. Lenin hydraulic power station.
Tu.-Su. 10-1, 3-5.

BÎRLAD

GHEORGHE GHEORGHIU DEJ MUSEUM
Strada Trotuş 52, Bîrlad
Life and political work of G. G. Dej.
Daily 10-5.

VASILE PÂRVAN MUSEUM
Strada Sterian Dumbravă 1, Bîrlad
Local history and folklore.
Daily 10-5.

BISTRIŢA

BISTRIŢA MUSEUM
Piaţa Unirii 10, Bistriţa
Archaeology. Natural history. Folklore. Local history.
Tu.-Su. 11-7.

BOTOŞANI

BOTOŞANI MUSEUM
Calea Naţională 162, 251, Botoşani
Prehistoric material from local excavations. History of Botoşani and its region, up to c.1850. Natural history. Paintings.
Tu.-Su. 10-5.

BRAD

GOLD MUSEUM
Brad
History of gold-mining in Romania. Mining tools and equipment.
Daily 9-5.

BRĂILA

ART GALLERY
Strada Galaţi 1, Brăila
19th-20th century paintings by Romanian artists.
Tu.-Su. 9-12, 2-5.

LOCAL HISTORY MUSEUM
Piaţa Lenin 3, Brăila
Archaeological material from local excavations. Local history and ethnography. Memorial-room to the Bulgarian poet and revolutionary, Christo Botew, who lived in Brăila.
On request.

BRAN

BRAN CASTLE MUSEUM
Strada Principală 460, Bran
In 14th century castle. History of the castle. Furniture. Weapons. Armour. Tools. Open-air museum of ethnography.
Tu.-Su. 10-5.

BRAŞOV

BRAŞOV MUSEUM
Piaţa 23 August 30, Braşov
In 15th century Town Hall. Prehistory and history of Transylvania. Paintings by Romanian artists, and by foreign artists living in Romania. Greek manuscripts.
M.-Sa. 9-5; Su. 10-1.

FORTRESS MUSEUM
Strada Castelului 2, Braşov
History of Braşov. Craftsmen's tools. Weapons. Armour. Coins. Guild material. Models, plans, documents illustrating development of Braşov.
M.-Sa. 9-5; Su. 10-1.

ST. NICOLAE SCHOOL MUSEUM
Piaţa Unirii 1, Braşov
Medieval and religious paintings, sculpture. Early printed books. Romanian, Slavonic, Greek manuscripts.
M.-Sa. 9-5; Su. 10-1.

BUCHAREST

THEODOR AMAN MUSEUM
Strada C. A. Rossetti 8, Bucharest
Former home and studio of Theodor Aman (d.1891). Furniture, woodcarvings, paintings, watercolours, drawings, engravings by Aman, with his studio equipment.
Tu.-Su. 2-8.

ART MUSEUM
Strada Stirbei Vodă 1, Bucharest
Development of Romanian art since medieval times. Gold and silver embroidery. Book-binding. Wood-carvings. 16th century mural paintings. Icons. Illuminated manuscripts. 13th-20th century European paintings, drawings, engravings. 19th-20th century portraits. Oriental and Near-Eastern paintings, miniatures, bronzes, ivories, porcelain, rugs and carpets.
Tu.-Su. 11-7.

PROF. DR. VICTOR BABEŞ MEMORIAL MUSEUM
Strada Andrei Mureşanu 14A, Bucharest
Life and work of Prof. Babeş (d.1926), a pioneer of medical science in Romania. History of medicine in Romania.
Tu., Th., Su. 10-1, 4-7.

'BUCHAREST AS SEEN BY ARTISTS'
Strada Biserica Amzei 5-7, Bucharest
19th-20th century paintings, drawings illustrating the city and life of Bucharest.
Tu.-Su. 2-8.

CABINET OF PRINTS AND ENGRAVINGS
Calea Victoriei 125, Bucharest
Works by Romanian and European artists. Japanese engravings.
Daily 9-3.

I. L. CARAGIALE MUSEUM OF THE NATIONAL THEATRE
Calea Victoriei 42, Pasajul Majestic, Bucharest
History, especially 15th-20th century, of the Romanian theatre. Stage design. Posters. Portraits. Costumes. Letters. Photographs.
Tu.-Su. 10-1, 7-9.

CENTRAL MILITARY MUSEUM
Strada Izvor 137, Bucharest
History of fortifications and weapons in Romania. Paintings. Photographs. Documents. Uniforms. Flags.
W.-M. 10-6.

COIN CABINET OF THE ACADEMY LIBRARY
Calea Victoriei 125, Bucharest
Romanian coins and medals. Cameos.
Tu.-Su. 9-3.

COIN COLLECTION
Calea Victoriei 151, Bucharest
History of coinage and currency in Romania. Weights and measures. Medals.
Tu.-Su. 11-6.

COLLECTION OF THE GEOLOGY COMMITTEE
Şoseaua Kisseleff 2, Bucharest
Geological, mineralogical and fossil collections.
M.-Sa. 9-5.

ELENA AND DR. I. N. DONA COLLECTION
Strada General Dona 12-14, Bucharest
Paintings, sculpture, ceramics, rugs, mostly by Romanian artists and craftsmen. Wooden and silver icons.
Tu., Th., Su. 10-1, 4-7.

GEORGE ENESCU MUSEUM
Calea Victoriei 141, Bucharest
In former home of the composer, George Enescu. Collection illustrating his life and work. Portraits. His piano and violin. Scores. Letters.
Tu.-Su. 10-1, 5-7.

GRIGORE ANTIPA MUSEUM OF NATURAL HISTORY
Şoseaua Kisseleff 1, Bucharest
World-wide collections of rocks, minerals, mammals, birds, insects, especially butterflies, moths. Skeleton of *Dinotherium gigantinimum.* Wild-life dioramas.
Tu.-Su. 10-2, 4-7.

I. ISER COLLECTION OF PAINTINGS
Bulevardul N. Bălescu 9, Bucharest
Works by the artist, Iosif Iser (d. 1958), in his former home and studio. Paintings. Drawings. Engravings. Sketches. Photographs, documents, personal possessions.
Th. 4.30-7.30; Su. 10-30-1.

KARADJA COLLECTION
Strada Gr. Mora 31, Bucharest
In former home of the historian, Constantin Karadja (d. 1950). Romanian folk art, handicrafts.
Th. 10-1.

ING. D. LEONIDA MUSEUM OF THE CENTRE FOR TECHNICAL DOCUMENTATION
Parcul Libertătii 5, Bucharest
History of technology in Romania. Original machines and equipment. Models. Photographs.
Th. 7-5; Su. 9-8.

PROF. DR. GH. MARINESCU MUSEUM
Strada Julius Fučik 27, Bucharest
In former home of Prof. Marinescu (d. 1938), pioneer of neurology in Romania. Collections illustrating his life and work.
Tu., Th., Su. 10-1, 4-7.

CORNEL MEDREA MUSEUM
Strada General Budişteanu 16, Bucharest
Sculpture by Cornel Medrea (d. 1964).
Tu.-Su. 2-8.

DR. N. MINOVICI MUSEUM OF FOLK ART
Strada Dr. N. Minovici 1, Bucharest
Furniture. Rugs. Woodcarvings. Ceramics. Musical instruments. Glass icons. Painted Easter eggs. Memorabilia of Dr. Minovici.
Tu.-Su. 10-1, 4-6.

ING. MINOVICI MUSEUM OF MEDIEVAL ART
Strada Dr. N. Minovici 3, Budapest
Furniture. Tapestries. Ceramics. Paintings. Sculpture. Oriental carpets. Manuscripts and early printed books.
Tu.-Sa. 10-1, 5-7. M., Su. 10-1.

ION MINULESCU COLLECTION
Bulevardul Gh. Marinescu 19, Bucharest
In former home of the poet, Ion Minulescu (d. 1944). Romanian paintings. Applied art. Glass icons. Ceramics.
Su. 11-1.

MOGOŞOAIA MUSEUM OF THE ART OF THE BRÂNCOVEANU PERIOD
Mogoşoaia, Strada Donca Simo 18, Bucharest
In former Mogoşoaia Palace (1702). Decorative arts. Silversmith's work. Wood-carving. Gold and silver embroidery. Paintings. Sculpture. Religious art.
Tu., W., F.-Su. 10-7.

MUSEUM OF ANATOMY
Bulevardul Dr. Petru Groza 2, Bucharest
Human anatomy.
M.-Sa. 9-3.

MUSEUM OF ANTHROPOLOGY
Boulevardul Dr. Petru Groza 2, Bucharest
World-wide collections of skulls and embryology.
M.-Sa. 9-3.

MUSEUM OF FIRE-FIGHTING
Bulevardul Gh. Dimitrov 33, Bucharest
History of fire-protection and fire-fighting in Romania.
Tu.-Su. 10-1, 5-7.

MUSEUM OF FOLK ART
Calea Victoriei 107, Bucharest
Peasant rooms, with furnishings. Costume. Ornaments. Handicrafts, especially wood. Pottery. Household equipment. Engravings. Photographs.
Tu.-Su. 11-7.

MUSEUM OF THE HISTORY OF BUCHAREST
Bulevardul 1848 2, Bucharest
In former Suţu Palace. History of Bucharest since prehistoric times. Documents, plans, maps, illustrating development of the city. Material illustrating history of the workers' and revolutionary movements in Bucharest.
Tu.-Su. 11-8.

MUSEUM OF THE HISTORY OF THE ROMANIAN COMMUNIST PARTY AND OF THE REVOLUTIONARY AND DEMOCRATIC MOVEMENT
Şoseaua Kisseleff 3, Bucharest
Material illustrating the history of socialism in Romania. Documents. Pamphlets. Drawings. Prints. Models. Photographs.
Tu., Th. 10-2, 4-8; W., F. 4-8; Su. 10-2.

MUSEUM OF ROMANIAN LITERATURE
Strada Fundatiei 4, Bucharest
Collections illustrating life and work of the leading Romanian writers. Manuscripts. First editions. Book-illustrations. Portraits. Personal possessions.
Tu., Th., Sa., Su. 10-6; W., F. 2-6.

NATIONAL MUSEUM OF ANTIQUITIES
Strada I. C. Frimu 11, Bucharest
Stone and Bronze Age archaeology. Roman bronzes, coins. Greek amphorae. Antiquities of the Middle East. Gold ornaments. Pottery. Medieval weapons, armour. Roman lapidarium. Pietroasa gold treasure.
Tu.-Su. 10-3.

NATIONAL MUSEUM OF THE HISTORY OF THE ROMANIAN PEOPLE
Calea Victorei 12, Bucharest
History of the Romanian people since early medieval times.
Tu.-Su. 10-3.

NATIONAL OBSERVATORY AND MUSEUM OF EXPERIMENTAL SCIENCE
Boulevardul Ana Ipătescu 21, Bucharest
Astronomical instruments. Astronomical techniques. Exhibits illustrating space-travel and satellites. Portraits of astronomers.
W.-Su. 10-1, 6-9.

C. I. AND C. C. NOTTARA MUSEUM
Bulevardul Dacia 51, Bucharest
Memorial collections, illustrating the life and work of the producer, Constantin Nottara (d. 1935), and the musician, C. C. Nottara. (d. 1957).
Tu., Th., Su. 10-1, 4-7.

G. OPRESCU COLLECTION
Strada Dr. Clunet 16, Bucharest
Paintings. Drawings. Engravings. Incunabula. Early printed books. Rugs. Ceramics.
Su. 3-5.

RAILWAY MUSEUM
Calea Griviţei 193B, Bucharest
Documents, photographs, paintings, prints, models, illustrating development of transport in Romania, from the cart to the diesel train. First railway engine built in Romania (1873).
Tu.-Sa. 9-2; Su. 9-1.

MARIA AND DR. G. SEVEREANU COLLECTION
Strada I. C. Frimu 26, Bucharest
Prehistory and early history of Bucharest. Tools. Weapons. Ornaments. Ceramics. Coins. Documents. Engravings. Medieval reliquaries.
Tu.-Su. 11-6.

ANASTASE SIMU ART MUSEUM
Strada Biserica Amzei 9, Bucharest
19th-20th century Romanian paintings, sculpture. 16th-19th century European paintings.
Tu.-Su. 2-8.

SLATINEANU COLLECTION
Strada Obedenaru 3, Bucharest
Romanian and European furniture, ceramics, textiles, weapons, glass icons.
Tu., Th. 9-1; F., Sa. 3-8; Su. 10-6.

STATE ARCHIVES MUSEUM
Strada Arhivelor 2, Bucharest
11th-20th century documents. Seals. Engravings.
Tu., Th., Su. 10-6.

TOMA STELIAN MUSEUM
Şoseaua Kisseleff 8, Bucharest
Paintings, drawings, sculpture by Romanian artists.
Tu.-Su. 10-1, 3-5.

CECILIA AND FREDERIC STORCK MUSEUM
Strada Vasile Alecsandri 16, Bucharest
19th-20th century paintings, sculpture by members of the Storck family.
Tu., Th., Su. 10-1, 4-7.

G. L. TATTARESCU MEMORIAL MUSEUM
Strada Domniţa Anastasia 7, Bucharest
Home and studio of the painter, Gheorghe Tattarescu (d. 1894). Paintings, especially portraits, by Tattarescu. Studio equipment, library and personal possessions of the artist.
Tu., F., Su. 10-1; Th. 3-6.

VILLAGE MUSEUM
Şoseaua Kissileff 20, Bucharest
18th-19th century houses, mills, workshops and other rural buildings from different parts of Romania. Workshops. Windmills. Watermills. Agricultural implements. Collection of textiles, furniture, household equipment, painted Easter eggs, musical instruments.
Tu.-Su. 10-6.

MOISE M. WEINBURG COLLECTION
Strada Alexandru Sahia 36, Bucharest
Paintings, drawings, prints by Romanian artists, especially by Iosif Iser. Objets d'art. Carpets. Bohemian crystal.
Th., Su. 4-6.

ZAMBACCIAN MUSEUM
Strada Muzuel 21A, Bucharest
Romanian paintings, sculpture. 19th-20th century French paintings.
Tu.-Su. 11-6.

BUZĂU

MUSEUM OF THE HISTORY OF BUZĂU
Strada Unirü 145, Buzău
Local archaeology and history, including material from Bronze Age settlement at Sărata-Monteoru.
Tu.-Su. 10-1, 3-5.

CĂLĂRAŞI

CĂLĂRAŞI MUSEUM
Strada Progresului 72, Călăraşi
Local archaeology and history.
Tu.-Sa., 10-5; Su. 10-1.

CARACAL

CARACAL MUSEUM
Strada Negru Vodă 1, Caracal
Local archaeology and history. Lapidarium. Ethnography. Iancu Jianu (d. 1842) memorial collection. Japanese woodcuts.
Tu.-Su. 10-6.

CAREI

CAREI MUSEUM
Carei
Local history. Natural history.
On request.

CERNEŢI

TUDOR VLADIMIRESCU HOUSE-MUSEUM
Cerneţi
Former home of Tudor Vladimirescu, leader of the 1821 Rebellion. Collection illustrating his life and work.
On request.

CÎMPINA

NICOLAE GRIGORESCU MUSEUM
Strada 23 August 170, Cîmpina
Former home and studio of the painter, Nicolae Grigorescu (d.1907). Paintings. Furniture. Personal possessions.
On request.

HASCLEU MUSEUM
Strada 23 August 199, Cîmpina
In former home of the historian, Prof. Bogdan Petriceicu Hascleu (d.1907). Collection illustrating his life and work.
On request.

CÎMPULUNG

CÎMPULUNG-MUSCEL MUSEUM
Strada Republicii 5, Cîmpulung
Local history, ethnography, natural history. Lapidarium. Pottery. 19th-20th century Romanian paintings.
M.-Sa. 9-6; Su. 9-1.

CÎMPULUNG-MOLDOVENESC

MOLDOVENIAN MUSEUM
Strada Pictor Grigorescu 1, Cîmpulung-Moldovenesc
History and ethnography of the region. Costumes. Tools. Armour. Natural history. Forestry. Ornamental wooden objects.
M.-Sa. 9-6; Su. 9-1.

CIUCEA

OCTAVIAN GOGA MEMORIAL MUSEUM
Ciucea
In castle. Life and work of Goga. Ethnography.
On request.

CLUJ

ARDELEAN MUSEUM
Strada Kogelniceanu 8, Cluj
Mineralogy. Botany. Zoology. Archaeology.
Tu.-Su. 10-6.

ART MUSEUM
Piaţa Libertăţii 30, Cluj
In 18th century palace. Paintings, sculpture by Romanian artists. Italian, Flemish, Dutch, German and Hungarian paintings. Religious art. Guild chests. Pewter. Ornaments. Rugs and carpets. 16th century painted altar.
Tu.-Su. 10-6.

BOTANICAL GARDEN AND HERBARIUM
Strada Republicii 42, Cluj
Herbarium, with world-wide collections.
Tu.-Su. 10-6.

HISTORY MUSEUM
Strada Emil Isac 2, Cluj
Prehistory and early history of the Cluj region. Pottery. Utensils. Ornaments. Roman, Egyptian, medieval antiquities. Mosaics. Roofing-tiles. History of Cluj in the feudal period. Coins. History of pharmacy.
Tu.-Su. 10-6.

EMIL ISAC MUSEUM
Strada 1 Mai 23, Cluj
Memorial museum devoted to the later years of the poet, Emil Isac (d.1954). Manuscripts. Correspondence. Personal possessions. Library.
On request.

OPEN-AIR MUSEUM
Hoia, Cluj
Farmhouses, workshops, mills and other rural buildings from different parts of Transylvania, with furnishings, tools, equipment.
Daily 10-5.

TRANSYLVANIAN MUSEUM OF ETHNOGRAPHY
Strada 30 Decembrie 21, Cluj
History and ethnography of the Transylvanian peoples. Fishing. Agriculture. Housing. Crafts. Furniture. Household equipment. Tools. Pottery. Textiles. Costumes.
Tu.-Su. 10-6.

ZOOLOGICAL MUSEUM
Babeş-Bolya University, Calea Mico 5-7, Cluj
World-wide zoology collections.
Tu.-Su. 10-6.

CONSTANŢA

ARCHAEOLOGICAL MUSEUM OF THE DOBRUDSCHA
Strada Muzeelor 23, Constanţa
Prehistory and early history of the region. Neolithic, Bronze Age and Iron Age tools, ornaments, utensils. Greek and Roman amphorae, coins, sculpture. Architectural fragments. Lapidarium.
M.-Sa. 10-5; Su. 11-1.

DUBROGEA MUSEUM OF ART
Strada Muzeelor 12, Constanţa
19th-20th century paintings, drawings, prints, sculpture by Romanian artists.
M.-Sa. 10-5; Su. 11-1.

CORABIA

CORABIA MUSEUM
Strada Cuza Vodă 64, Corabia
Local archaeology and history. Natural history. Folklore.
M.-Sa. 9-1, 3-5; Su. 10-1.

COŞBUC

GEORGE COŞBUC MUSEUM
Coşbuc
House was birthplace of the poet and patriot, George Coşbuc (d.1918). Life and work of Coşbuc, illustrated by photographs, books, manuscripts, documents, newspapers.
On request.

CRAIOVA

ART MUSEUM
Calea Lenin Unirii 15, Craiova
19th-20th century paintings, sculpture by Romanian artists, especially Brancusi, Aman. Italian, French, Flemish and Dutch (especially 17th century) paintings. Icons. Liturgical objects.
Tu.-Su. 10-5.

DISTRICT MUSEUM
Strada Maxim Gorki 58, Craiova
History and natural history of the Craiova region.
Tu.-Su. 10-5.

OLTENIEI MUSEUM
Strada Maxim Gorki 44, Craiova
Natural history, history and ethnographical collections. Agricultural implements. Craftsmen's tools. Household equipment. Pottery. Wood carvings. Costumes. Ornaments. Rugs.
Tu.-Su. 10-5.

TRAIAN DEMETRESCU MUSEUM
Strada Silozului 41, Craiova
Memorial museum to the poet and workers' leader, Traian Demetrescu (d.1896). Documents. Manuscripts. Personal possessions.
On request.

TRIAL OF THE RAILWAYMEN AND PETROLEUM WORKERS, JUNE-JULY 1934, MUSEUM
Strada Unirii 9, Craiova
In former Military Tribunal building. Exhibits illustrating the trial of leaders of the workers who went on strike in 1933.
M.-Sa. 9-5; Su. 10-1.

CRISTURUL

CRISTURUL MUSEUM
Strada Libertătii 115, Cristurul
Natural history. Local history. Ethnography. Material from excavations at Dacian, Roman and 7th century sites. Roman coins.
M.-Sa. 9-5; Su. 10-1.

DEJ

DEJ MUSEUM
Strada 1 May 2, Dej
Local natural history, ethnography. Roman material from excavations at the military and administrative centre of Căşeui.
On request.

DEVA

DEVA MUSEUM
Piaţa Dr. Petru Groza 4, Deva
Local prehistory and history. Dacian and Roman material. Craftsmen's tools and equipment. Development of the guilds. Gold-mining. Ethnography. Geology. Birds.
Tu.-Sa. 9-1, 2-5; Su. 10-1.

DOFTANA

DOFTANA MUSEUM
Doftana
In former prison, in which workers' leaders were imprisoned during 1930s and 1940s. Instruments of torture. Police documents. Examples of the underground press.
Daily 9-5.

DOROHOI

DOROHOI MUSEUM
Strada Alexandrii Sahia 3, Dorohoi
Natural history. Local history.
On request.

GEORGE ENESCU MEMORIAL MUSEUM
Strada Republicii 81, Dorohoi
Life and work of the composer and conductor, George Enescu (d.1955).
Tu.-Sa. 10-5.

DRAGOSLOVENI

ALEXANDRU VLAHUŢĂ MUSEUM
Dragosloveni
Life and work of the writer, Alexandru Vlahuţa.
On request.

DURĂU

DURĂU MUSEUM
Durău
Ethnographical collections.
Daily 10-4.

EFORIE SUD

ARCHAEOLOGICAL MUSEUM
Bulevardul Republicii, Eforie Sud
Neolithic, Greek and Roman material from local excavations. Sculpture. Architectural fragments. Amphorae. Lamps. Ornaments.
Tu.-Sa. 10-5; Su. 10-1.

FĂGĂRAŞ

FĂGĂRAŞ MUSEUM
Piaţa Republicii 22, Făgăraş
Local history and folklore.
On request.

FĂLTICENI

FĂLTICENI MUSEUM
Strada Republicii 294, Fălticeni
Regional prehistory and archaeology. History. Work of the writers, I. Creangăs and M. Sadoveanus. Paintings by Romanian artists. Plants and wildlife of the region.
Tu.-Su. 10-12, 2-5.

FILIAŞI

BRANCUSI MUSEUM
Filiaşi
Open-air museum of sculpture by Constantin Brancusi.
At all times.

FOCŞANI

HISTORY MUSEUM
Bulevardul Karl Marx 3, Focşani
History of the area. Weapons. Pottery. Coins. Engravings. Seals.
Tu.-Sa. 9-6; Su. 10-1.

MUSEUM OF ETHNOGRAPHY
Bulevardul Karl Marx 8, Focşani
Ethnography of the Galaţi area. Agriculture. Hunting. Fishing. 12 completely equipped peasant living-rooms.
Tu.-Sa. 9-6; Su. 10-1.

NATURAL HISTORY MUSEUM
Strada Republicii 79, Focşani
Insects. Birds. Mammals. Invertebrates. Herbaria.
Tu.-Sa. 9-6; Su. 10-1.

GALAŢI

HISTORY MUSEUM
Strada Al. I. Cuza 80, Galaţi
History of the Galaţi region since prehistoric times. Ethnography.
Tu.-Su. 10-1, 3-6.

MUSEUM OF MODERN AND CONTEMPORARY ROMANIAN ART
Bulevardul Republicii 141, Galaţi
In former Bishop's Palace. 19th-20th century paintings, graphics, sculpture, ceramics by Romanian artists.
Tu.-Su. 10-1, 3-6.

NATURAL HISTORY MUSEUM
Strada Avîntului 9, Galaţi
Dioramas of local wildlife. Botany.
Tu.-Su. 10-12, 3-6.

GEORGE ENESCU

GEORGE ENESCU MUSEUM
George Enescu
Birthplace of Enescu (1881-1955). Collections illustrating the life and work of the conductor.
On request.

GHEORGHE GHEORGHIU-DEJ

MUNICIPAL MUSEUM
Bulevardul Republicii 4, Gheorghe Gheorghiu-Dej
Archaeological material of the Gethian-Dacian period from local excavations. Development of the Romanian chemical industry.
Tu.-Sa. 9-1, 3-6; Su. 10-1.

GHERLA

HISTORY MUSEUM
Strada Avram Iancu 7, Gherla
Collections illustrating early history of Gherla (especially Roman period). Development of the guilds. Archaeology. Ethnography.
M.-Sa. 10-1, 2-5; Su. 10-1.

GIURGIU

GIURGIU MUSEUM
Strada Dorobanţilor 16, Giurgiu
Natural history. Local archaeology and history.
On request.

GOLEŞTI

MUSEUM OF HISTORY AND ETHNOGRAPHY
Goleşti
House (1640). Collections illustrating the uprisings of 1821 and 1841, and the beginnings of national education. Peasant handicrafts. Folk art. 4 completely equipped peasant living-rooms. Historical development of the Romanian wine and fruit industries. Fishing.
Daily 10-5.

GURA HUMORULUI

GURA HUMORULUI MUSEUM
Strada Mihail Kogălniceanu 1, Gura Humorolui
Local history and folklore.
On request.

HUMULEŞTI

ION CREANGĂ MUSEUM
Humuleşti
Life and work of the writer, Ion Creangă, who spent his childhood here. Manuscripts. Works of Creangă in Romanian and translations.
On request.

HUŞI

DIMITRIE CANTEMIR MUSEUM
Strada M. Kogălniceanu 17, Huşi
Natural history. Local history and folklore. Paintings.
Daily 9-12, 2-4.

IAŞI

ION CREANGĂS HOUSE-MEMORIAL
Strada Simon Bărnuţiu 4, Iaşi
Peasant cottage in which the writer, Ion Creangăs, spent the last years of his life. Memorabilia of Creangăs.
On request.

MOLDAVIAN MUSEUM OF ETHNOLOGY
Strada Palatului 1, Iaşi
In the Palace of Culture. Craftsmen's tools. Hand-mills. Wine-presses. Potter's and smith's workshops. Costumes. Old musical instruments.
Tu.-Su. 10-6.

MOLDAVIAN MUSEUM OF HISTORY
Strada Palatului 1, Iaşi
In the Palace of Culture. Archaeological material from local excavations. Underground museum, showing parts of the city wall and with collections of weapons, tools, ceramics and coins.
Tu.-Su. 10-6.

MUSEUM OF ART
Strada Palatului 1, Iaşi
In the Palace of Culture. Paintings by Romanian and European artists, including works by Cranach, Caravaggio, Veronese, Tintoretto, Murillo, Poussin.
Tu.-Su. 10-6.

MUSEUM OF THE UNIFICATION OF ROMANIA
Strada Lăpuşneanu 14, Iaşi
Former residence of Prince Alexandru Ioan Cuza. Documents and objects illustrating the struggle of Cuza and others to obtain the unification of the territories of the Romanian princes. Paintings. Sculpture.
Tu.-Su. 10-6.

NATURAL HISTORY MUSEUM
Strada Gh. Dimitrov 72, Iaşi
Geology. Palaeontology. Botany. Zoology.
Tu.-Su. 10-6.

ILIE PINTILIE MUSEUM
Ciurea 28, Şoseaua Iaşi, Iaşi
Former home of the Communist leader, Ilie Pintilie (d.1941). History of the workers' movement in the Iaşi area.
On request.

POLYTECHNIC MUSEUM
Strada Palatului 1, Iaşi
In the Palace of Culture. History of technology and of the industrial development of Romania.
Tu.-Su. 10-6.

IPOTEŞTI

MIHAIL EMINESCU MUSEUM
Ipoteşti
Former home of the poet, Mihail Eminescu (d.1889). Paintings, manuscripts, papers and other material illustrating his life and work.
On request.

LENAUHEIM

LENAU MUSEUM
Lenauheim
House-memorial to the poet, Nikolaus Lenau, who was born here. Collection illustrating his life and work.
On request.

LIMANU

LOCAL MUSEUM
Limanu
Contemporary Romanian art.
Daily 9-4.

LIPOVA

LIPOVA MUSEUM
Strada Nicolae Bălescu 2, Lipova
Archaeology and ethnography of the area.
Tu.-Su. 10-5.

LIVIU REBREANU

LIVIU REBREANU MUSEUM
Liviu Rebreanu
In former family home of the writer, Liviu Rebreanu (d.1944). Collections illustrating life and work of Rebreanu.
On request.

LUGOJ

LUGOJ MUSEUM
Strada Gării 8, Lugoj
History and ethnography of the area.
Tu.-Sa. 10-1, 3-5; Su. 10-1.

LUPŞA

VILLAGE MUSEUM
Calea Turzü 1, Lupşa
Peasant handicrafts. Mining. Weaving. Costumes. Wood-carvings.
M.-Sa. 10-12, 2-4; Su. 10-12.

MANGALIA

ARCHAEOLOGICAL MUSEUM
Strada Izvorului 1, Mangalia
Greek and Roman material from the Mangalia area. Sculpture. Pottery. Glass. Ornaments. Architectural fragments.
Tu.-Su. 10-4.

MEDGIDIA

LOCAL MUSEUM
Medgidia
Contemporary Romanian art.
M.-Sa. 10-1, 3-5.

MEDIAŞ

MEDIAŞ MUSEUM
Strada 23 August 3, Mediaş
Local archaeology, ethnography. Natural history.
Tu.-Sa. 10-1, 3-5; Su. 10-1.

MIERCUREA CIUC

MIERCUREA CIUC MUSEUM
Strada Florilor 8, Miercurea Ciuc
Natural history, Local history and ethnography. Silver goblets, bracelets, brooches.
Daily 10-4.

MIRCEŞTI

VASILE ALECSANDRI MUSEUM
Mirceşti
In former home of the poet, Vasile Alecsandri (d.1890), with his furniture, books, manuscripts, letters and personal possessions.
On request.

NĂMĂEŞTI

G. TOPÎRCEANU MUSEUM
Nămĕşti
Life and work of the poet, George Topîrceanu (d.1937). Family portraits. Manuscripts. Personal possessions.
On request.

NĂSĂUD

NĂSĂUD MUSEUM
Bulevardul Republicii 25, Năsăud
Local plants, wildlife, history, ethnography. Pottery. Weapons. Costumes. Woodcarving.
Tu.-Su. 10-5.

NEAMŢ

NEAMŢ MONASTERY
Neamţ
Collection of religious paintings, sculpture, vestments, liturgical objects.
On request.

NEGREŞTI

OPEN-AIR MUSEUM
Negreşti
Houses and other village buildings brought to museum site. Peasant handicrafts, pottery, furniture, painted glass.
Tu.-Su. 10-5.

ODORHEI

ODORHEI MUSEUM
Strada Lenin 13, Odorhei
Local plants, archaeology, ethnography. Embroidered peasant costumes.
Tu.-Sa. 10-1, 3-5; Su. 10-1.

OLTENIŢA

OLTENIŢA MUSEUM
Olteniţa
Archaeological material, especially pottery, from local excavations.
On request.

ORADEA

TĂRII CRIŞURILOR MUSEUM
Strada Stadionului 2, Oradea
Local history. Natural history. Paintings.
Tu.-Su. 10-5.

ADY ENDRE MUSEUM
Oradea
Memorial museum to the Hungarian poet, Ady Endre, who lived in Oradea, 1900-10.
On request.

ORIŞANA MUSEUM
Strada Muzeului 4, Oradea
Natural history. History of settlement in the area from the beginnings to feudal times. Paintings, drawings, engravings, including engravings by Dürer, whose father was born near Oradea.
Tu.-Su. 10-5.

IOSIF VULCAN MUSEUM
Strada Iosif Vulcan 4, Oradea
Memorial museum to the writer, Iosif Vulcan (d.1907), who was born in Oradea.
On request.

ORĂŞTIE

ORĂŞTIE MUSEUM
Piata Aurel Vlaicu, Orăştie
Local ethnography and folk art.
M.-Sa. 10-12, 2-5; Su. 10-12.

ORLEA

LOCAL MUSEUM
Orlea
Natural history. Pottery and coins from local excavations.
On request.

PÂULEŞTI

LOCAL MUSEUM
Pâuleşti
Local history, ethnography.
On request.

PETROŞENI

MUSEUM OF THE INSTITUTE OF MINING
Strada Institutului 20, Petroşeni
History of the coal-mining industry in the Jiu valley.
By appointment.

PIATRA NEAMŢ

CALISTRAT HOGAŞ MUSEUM
Strada Avîntul 1, Piatra Neamţ
House-memorial to the writer, Calistrat Hogaş (d.1917). Furniture. Books. Personal possessions.
On request.

MUSEUM OF ARCHAEOLOGY
Piaţa Libertatii 1, Piatra Neamţ
Archaeological material from local excavations. Contemporary Romanian paintings, graphics.
Tu.-Su. 10-6.

NATURAL HISTORY MUSEUM
Strada V. I. Lenin 26, Piatra Neamţ
Flora and fauna of the Romanian Carpathians. Minerals. Fossils. Mounted specimens of birds, mammals. Herbarium. Butterflies and insects.
Tu.-Su. 10-6.

PITEŞTI

ARGES DISTRICT MUSEUM
Strada Horia, Cloşca si Crişan 44, Piteşti
Geology. Zoology. Local history. 19th-20th century Romanian paintings, sculpture.
M.-Sa. 9-5; Su. 10-1.

PITEŞTI MUSEUM
Bulevardul Republicii 60, Piteşti
Local prehistory, history, natural history. 19th-20th century paintings by Romanian artists.
M.-Sa. 9-5; Su. 10-1.

PLOIEŞTI

I. L. CARAGIALE MUSEUM
Strada C. T. Grigorescu 1, Ploieşti
Memorial collection illustrating the life and work of the writer, Ion Luca Caragiale (d.1912).
On request.

HISTORY MUSEUM
Strada Nicuale Bâlcescu 25, Ploieşti
Regional archaeology, especially Roman. Industry. Commerce. Guilds. Coins. Ethnography. Folk art. History of the workers' movement.
Tu.-Su. 10-5.

MUSEUM OF ART
Palace of Culture, Ploieşti
19th-20th century paintings and sculpture by Russian artists.
Tu.-Su. 10-5.

MUSEUM OF CLOCKS
Palace of Culture, Ploieşti
European clocks and watches.
M.-Sa. 9-2; Su. 9-1.

HAGI PRODAN HOUSE
Strada Democraţiei 2, Ploieşti
18th century house. Furniture. Carpets. Paintings. Folk art. Local history.
Tu.-Sa. 9-12, 2-5; Su. 9-12.

PROVINCIAL PETROLEUM MUSEUM
Strada Dr. Bagdazar 8, Ploieşti
History of the extraction and use of petroleum. Modern techniques of prospecting, boring, transporting and refining petroleum. Romanian petro-chemical industry.
M.-Su. 10-5.

POIANA SIBIULUI

LOCAL MUSEUM
Poiana Sibiului
Ethnography. Social history. Folk art, especially shepherds' paintings.
On request.

PUTNA

MUSEUM OF PUTNA MONASTERY
Putna
Manuscripts. Incunabula. Embroidered vestments, altar-cloths.
On request.

RĂDĂUŢI

RĂDĂUŢI MUSEUM OF ETHNOGRAPHY
Strada Bogden Voda 2, Rădăuţi
Peasant crafts. Agriculture. Costumes. Furniture. Household equipment.
M.-Sa. 9-12, 2-4.

RĂŞINARI

LOCAL MUSEUM
Răşinari
Local history. Folk art.
On request.

REGHIN

REGHIN MUSEUM
Strada Karl Marx 51, Reghin
Ethnography. Open-air museum, with peasant houses, furniture, agricultural equipment.
Tu.-Su. 10-5.

REŞIŢA

LOCAL MUSEUM
Strada 7 Noiembrie 50, Reşiţa
Mineralogy. Local prehistory, history. History of the workers' movement. Development of local iron-foundry and iron-forging.
M.-Sa. 9-12, 2-5; Su. 10-12.

RETEAG

ION POP RETEGANUL MUSEUM
Reteag
Memorial Museum to the ethnographer, teacher and journalist, I. P. Reteganul, in the house where he was born.
On request.

RIMETEA

LOCAL MUSEUM
Rimetea
Local mining and iron industries. Pottery. Weaving. Costumes. Furnished farmhouse living-room.
M.-Sa. 10-6; Su. 10-1.

RIMNICU SARAT

RIMNICU SARAT MUSEUM
Strada Suvorov 62, Rimnicu Sarat
Local industries. Textiles. Forestry. Costumes. Paintings by contemporary Romanian artists.
M.-Sa. 9-5; Su. 9-12.

RÎMNICU VILCEA

ANTON PANN MEMORIAL HOUSE
Strada Stirbei Vodă 18, Rîmnicu Vilcea
Memorial museum to the writer, Anton Pann (d.1854), in his former home.
On request.

RÎMNICU VILCEA MUSEUM
Strada Arges 35, Rîmnicu Vilcea
Roman material from local excavations. Local history. Ethnography. Paintings of local scenes.
Tu.-Su. 9-5.

ROMAN

NATURAL HISTORY MUSEUM
Strada Proletariatlui 4, Roman
Wildlife of the region.
M.-Sa. 10-6; Su. 10-1.

ROMAN MUSEUM
Strada Cuza Vodă 33, Roman
Archaeological material of the Dacian period. Local history. Paintings, especially by local artists.
M.-Sa. 10-6; Su. 10-1.

ROŞIORII DE VEDE

RĂSCOALA DIN 1907 MUSEUM
Roşiorii de Vede
History of the peasant uprising of 1907.
Daily 10-5.

SĂCELE

MUSEUM OF THE SEVEN VILLAGES
Săcele
In 14th century tithe house, the 'domus dominorum'. History of the new township of Săcele, formed by the amalgamation of seven villages.
Tu.-Su. 10-5.

SALONTA

JÁNOS ARANY MUSEUM
Piaţa Libertăţii, Salonta
Life and work of the Hungarian poet, János Arany.
On request.

SARMIZEGETUSA

MUSEUM OF HISTORY AND ARCHAEOLOGY
7 ud. Hunedoara, Sarmizegetusa
Archaeological material from the Roman town of Ulpia Traiana. Ruins of the amphitheatre, forum and other public buildings. Pottery. Marble and bronze statuettes. Weapons. Ornaments. Coins.
Daily 9-5.

SATU MARE

SATU MARE MUSEUM
Piaţa Libertăţii, Satu Mare
Archaeology and history of Transylvania. Folklore. Folk art. Paintings by Aurel Poffs.
M.-Sa. 10-1, 3-6; Su. 10-1.

SEBEŞ

SEBEŞ MUSEUM
Parcul 8 Mai, Sebeş
In 15th century house. Natural history. Local history and folklore.
M.-Sa. 9-5; Su. 10-1.

SECUENI

LOCAL MUSEUM
Strada Ady Endre 3, Secueni
Local history and folklore.
On request.

SFÎNTU GHEORGHE

SFÎNTU GHEORGHE MUSEUM
Strada 16 Februarie 10, Sfîntu Gheorghe
Prehistoric and Roman material from local sites. Local history. Mementoes of the Revolution of 1848. Natural history. Ethnography. Paintings by Romanian artists.
Daily 10-5.

SIBIU

BRUKENTHAL MUSEUM
Piata Republicii 4, Sibiu
In 18th century palace. Paintings and sculpture by Romanian artists. 15th-18th century Flemish, Dutch, German,

Austrian, French, Italian paintings. Prehistoric and Roman archaeology. Local history, geology, botany. Weapons. Armour. Coins. Guild history. Ceramics. Textiles. Furniture. Costumes. Manuscripts. Early printed books.
Tu.-Su. 10-5.

NATURAL HISTORY MUSEUM
Strada Kossuth 1, Sibiu
Palaeontology. Zoology. Entomology. Ornithology.
Tu.-Su. 2-5.

OPEN-AIR MUSEUM OF PRE-INDUSTRIAL TECHNOLOGY
Dumbrava Sibiului, Sibiu
Wind and watermills. Oil and wine-presses. Stills. Sawmills. Craftsmen's workshops. Collections of peasant handicrafts.
Daily 10-5.

SIGHET

SIGHET MUSEUM
Strada Bogdan Vodă 1, Sighet
Zoology. Ethnographical collections, arranged according to occupations, e.g. fishing, hunting, shepherding. Costumes. Carpets. Glass icons. Woodcarving.
M.-Sa. 10-5; Su. 10-1.

SIGHIŞOARA

SIGHIŞOARA MUSEUM
Piaţa Maior Isakov 1, Sighişoara
History of Sighişoara region since medieval times. Tools. Weapons. Coins. Guild history. Commerce.
M.-Sa. 10-12, 2-5; Su. 10-12.

SINAIA

PELEŞ MUSEUM
Strada Peleş 1, Sinaia
In former Royal palace (1873-83). Oriental carpets. 16th-17th century Swiss painted glass. Paintings. Sculpture. 15th-16th century weapons.
Tu.-Su. 10-5.

SIRIA

ION SLAVICI MUSEUM
Siria
Life and work of the writer, Ion Slavici (d.1925).
On request.

SLATINA

LOCAL MUSEUM
Strada Ioneşcu 81, Slatina
Prehistoric and Roman material from local sites. Coins. Weapons. Early printed books.
Daily 10-1, 3-6.

SUCEAVA

SUCEAVA MUSEUM
Strada Ciprian Porumbescu 2, Suceava
Prehistory and history of the district. Stone-, Bronze- and Iron Age tools, weapons, pottery, ornaments. Medieval chain-mail. Natural history. Memorial collection to the composer, Ciprian Porumbescu (d.1883).
M.-Sa. 10-5; Su. 10-1.

TECUCI

TECUCI MUSEUM
Strada 23 August 36, Tecuci
Geology. Local prehistory, history, folklore.
On request.

TIMIŞOARA

BANAT MUSEUM
Piaţa Huniadi 1, Timişoara
In restored 14th century castle. Prehistory and history of the Banat. Natural history, especially birds. Ethnographical collections showing the development of the Romanian people. Furnished rooms. Pottery. Costumes. Handicrafts. Paintings, sculpture, graphics by Romanian artists. Italian, Dutch, Flemish, German, French paintings.
Tu.-Su. 10-6.

TINCA

NATURAL HISTORY MUSEUM
Strada Avram Iancu 55, Tinca
Geology. Palaeontology. Zoology.
Daily 9-12, 2-5.

TÎRGOVIŞTE

DÎMBOVITA DISTRICT MUSEUM
Strada Muzeului 4, Tîrgovişte
Local prehistory, history. Medieval archaeology.
Tu.-Su. 10-5.

TÎRGAVISTE

MUSEUM OF PRINTING AND EARLY PRINTED BOOKS
Strada Justiţiei 3-5, Tîrgaviste
History of printing in Romania.
Tu.-Su. 10-5.

TÎRGOVISTE

MUSEUM OF TÎRGOVISTE WRITERS
Strada Justiţiei 3-5, Tîrgoviste
Books, manuscripts, portraits, memorabilia of writers who have lived in Tîrgoviste.
Tu.-Su. 10-5.

TÎRGU JIU

TIRGU JIU MUSEUM
Strada Tudor Vladimirescu 73, Tîrgu Jiu
Local history and ethnography. Housing. Wood-carving. Costumes. Religious art.
Daily 9-5.

TÎRGU MUREŞ

MUSEUM OF ART
Strada Enescu 2, Tîrgu Mureş
In Palace of Culture. Paintings, sculpture by 19th-20th century Romanian artists.
Tu.-Su. 10-6.

REGIONAL MUSEUM
Strada Horia 24 and Piaţa Trandafirilor 11, Tîrgu Mureş
Prehistoric, Dacian, Roman material from local excavations. History of the guilds. Ethnography. Natural history.
Tu.-Su. 10-6.

TÎRGU NEAMŢ

ŞTEFAN CEL MARE MUSEUM
Strada V. I. Lenin 173, Tîrgu Neamţ
Local history and ethnography.
M.-Sa. 9-1, 3-5; Su. 10-1.

MONASTERY MUSEUM
Tîrgu Neamţ
Early printed books. Icons. Embroidered vestments, altar-cloths.
Daily 10-5.

TOPALU

LOCAL MUSEUM
Topalu
19th-20th century Romanian paintings, graphics, sculpture.
On request.

TULCEA

MUSEUM OF THE DANUBE DELTA
Strada Progresului 52, Tulcea
Natural history and history of the region of the Danube delta. Geology. Plants. Wildlife. Fishing equipment. Agricultural implements. Archaeology. Ethnology, including open-air section. Coins.
Daily 10-5.

TURDA

TURDA MUSEUM
Strada B. P. Hasdeu 2, Turda
Greek, Roman and medieval material from local excavations. Local history.
Daily 9-5.

TURNU SEVERIN

IRON GATE (PORŢILE DE FIER) MUSEUM
Strada Indepentenţei 2, Turnu Severin
Neolithic, Bronze Age, Dacian and Roman material from local excavations. Religious art. Weapons. Coins. Ethnography. Handicrafts. Geology. Plants. Wildlife.
Tu.-Su. 10-5.

URLAŢI

MUSEUM OF ETHNOGRAPHY
Strada Orzoaia de Sus 12, Urlaţi
Furniture. Carpets and rugs. Sculpture. Handicrafts. Household equipment, tools. Paintings.
M.-Sa. 9-12, 2-5; Su. 9-12.

VĂLENII DE MUNTE

NICOLAE IORGA MUSEUM
Strada George Enescu 3, Vălenii de Munte
In former country home of the historian, Nicolae Iorga (d.1940). Furniture. Carpets and rugs. Prints. Iorga's library.
Daily 10-1, 3-5.

VATRA DORNEI

VATRA DORNEI MUSEUM
Strada 7 Noiembrie 17, Vatra Dornei
Natural history. Ethnography.
On request.

VÎNĂTORI

MIHAIL SADOVEANU MUSEUM
Vînători
Former home of the writer, Mihail Sadoveanu (d. 1961). Manuscripts. Copies of his works. Furniture. Personal possessions.
On request.

VLADIMIR

TUDOR VLADIMIRESCU MUSEUM
Vladimir
Birthplace of Vladimirescu, leader of the 1821 rebellion. Collection illustrating his life and work.
On request.

ZALĂU

ZALĂU MUSEUM
Strada Pietii 9, Zalău
Archaeological material from the Dacian and Roman settlement of Porolissum. Ethnography. Contemporary Romanian paintings, sculpture.
M.-Sa. 10-5; Su. 10-1.

Rwanda

Rwanda, under Belgian control until 1961, is the most densely populated country in Africa outside the Nile delta. These three-and-a-half million Rwandais share four museums between them, one specialising in geology and mineralogy, two in native handicrafts and housing, and the fourth in sculpture by students at the School of Fine Arts. It is difficult to see how a poor agricultural country could have achieved a great deal more so far.

BUTARE

RWANDA NATIONAL MUSEUM
Astrida, P.O. Box 80, Butare
Archaeology. Geology. Botany. Ethnology: basket-work, carvings and handicrafts. Metallurgy. Fully-equipped traditional hut.
Daily ex. Tu. 8-12.30, 2-4.30; Su. 10-12, 2-4.30.

KABGAYI

KABGAYI MUSEUM
Archevêché de Kabgayi, Kigali
Mineralogy. Historical documents. Pottery and basketwork. Rwandais objets d'art. Local craftsmanship. Musical instruments.
By appointment.

NYUNDO/GISENYI

NYUNDO SCHOOL OF ART
P.O. Box 177, Nyundo/Gisenyi
Sculptures by students of the School of Fine Arts. Statuettes. Triptych.
Any time.

RUHENGERI

MUSEUM OF PETROGRAPHY AND MINERALOGY
Ruhengeri
Mineralogical collections, including specimens of ferberite, wolframite, anthoinite, cassiterite, colombo-tantalite and beryl.
M.-F. 7.30-12, 2-4.30; Sa. and Su. 7.30-12.

St Helena

The St Helena administrative group of islands - Ascension, Tristan da Cunha and St Helena itself - has only one museum, on Ascension. This has interesting collections relating to all three units of the group, with particular emphasis on geology and wildlife, and on the strategic importance of the area as a naval and communications centre.

GEORGETOWN

FORT HAYES MUSEUM
Ascension Historical Society, Georgetown, Ascension
Books, maps and publications relating to Ascension, St Helena and Tristan da Cunha. Royal Marine and Navy relics. Artifacts, c.1815-1922, excavated and found locally amongst old military structures. Natural history: geology of the island covers every aspect of volcanic action. Biology. Plants and animal life of Ascension. Communications equipment c.1890-1968; submarine cable and wireless equipment, including latest earth satellite triangulation equipment. 1873 fire wagon drawn by eight horses. 1800 carriage. Stamp and coin collection of Ascension.
Th. only, 5-7. Other times on request.

San Marino, Republic of

Few people visiting the museums of San Marino would suspect that they were not in Italy, but for political reasons it would be entirely improper to list the Republic's three museums with those of its very large and powerful neighbour.

SAN MARINO

GOVERNMENT MUSEUM AND PICTURE-GALLERY
San Marino
Etruscan, Greek, Roman and Chinese antiquities, as well as those from San Marino. Fossils. Coins and medals. Memorabilia of Garibaldi. Paintings by Ribera, Batoni, Strozzi, Ghirlandaio and Guercino. Flemish School (16th century). Venetian Armenian School. Tuscan School (16th century).
Tu.-Su. 10-1, 2-5.

SAN FRANCESCO ART GALLERY
Convent of San Francesco, San Marino
Building (14th century). Paintings include works by Girolamo Marchesi da Cotignola, Bernardino di Mariotto, Guercino, Timoteo Viti and Nicolo l'Alunno. Parts of frescoes of the Rimini style, 14th century. Inscriptions and low-reliefs.
Tu.-Su. 10-1, 2-5.

STATE ARMS MUSEUM
Il Torre, San Marino
Large collection of weapons and armour from all periods.
Tu.-Su. 10-1, 2-5.

Senegal

This is a fertiliser and cement country, with a large export trade in both, and it is therefore very appropriate that the museums should contain such comprehensive geological and mineralogical collections. It has not, however, been overlooked that there are people as well as rocks in Senegal and there are several excellent collections devoted to the ethnography of the area.

DAKAR

ETHNOGRAPHICAL MUSEUM
Institut Fondamental d'Afrique Noire, Place Tacher, P.O. Box 206, Dakar
Ethnographical collections, including masks of Baoulé.
Daily 9-12, 3-7. Closed M. and also W. morning.

HISTORICAL MUSEUM OF GORÉE
Université de Dakar, Institut Fondamental d'Afrique Noire, P.O. Box 206, Dakar
History of the Isle of Gorée, with documents and material showing traces of European occupation. African and Senegalese prehistory. History of West Africa.
Daily 9-12, 3-7. Closed M. and also W. morning.

MUSEUM OF AFRICAN GEOLOGY
Direction des Mines et de la Géologie, P.O. Box 1238, Dakar
Rocks and minerals to be found in Guinea, the Ivory Coast, Togo, Dahomey, the Upper Volta, Mauritania, Senegal, Mali and Niger. Displays of minerals with details of their characteristics and use. Geology. Fossils.
Daily 8-12, 2.30-6. Closed Sa. afternoon.

ILE DE GORÉE

HISTORICAL MUSEUM OF WEST AFRICA AT GORÉE
Rue Malavois, Ile de Gorée, Dakar
Prehistory and archaeology of West Africa.
Daily ex. M. 9-12, 3-7.

MARITIME MUSEUM
Castle of Gorée, Ile de Gorée, Dakar
Natural science, especially oceanography.
Daily ex. M. and F. 9-12, 3-7.

SAINT-LOUIS

MICHEL ADANSON MUSEUM
Centre de Recherches et de Documentation du Sénégal, P.O. Box 382, Saint-Louis
Historical material, especially relating to Senegal. Prehistory. Way of life of the people of the area. The "Bassari". African art.
Daily ex. Tu. and W. morning, 9-12, 2-6.30.

Seychelles

It should perhaps be pointed out that the flora referred to in the museum contents below include several highly profitable agricultural crops, some of which have been exploited by the French since the eighteenth century. They include cinnamon, vanilla and patchouli. There is, in fact, a direct link between the spices of the Seychelles and the French Stone of Possession, also in the museum.

MAHÉ

SEYCHELLES MUSEUM OF HISTORICAL AND NATURAL HISTORY
Victoria, Mahé
Shells. Coral. Flora. Fauna. Portraits of Governors. Handicrafts. Paintings. The Stone of Possession put up by the French on 1st November 1756. Weapons.
M.-F. 8-12; Sa. 8-12.

Sierra Leone

Sierra Leone is fortunately rich in minerals, including diamonds and bauxite, but these have not yet been developed to a point at which they qualify for museum coverage. The National Museum is consequently able to concentrate with a good conscience on the traditional village industries and on fishing. The word 'history' which begins the list of contents conceals the interesting fact that Sierra Leone was at one time used as a settlement for Africans who had been rescued from slave ships.

FREETOWN

SIERRA LEONE NATIONAL MUSEUM
(Cotton Tree), P.O. Box 908, Freetown
History. Archaeology. Ethnography. Original Charter (1799) by which the Settlement became an Independent Colony. Statue of the late Temne Warrior Chief, Bai Bureh. Devil-masks of secret societies. Chieftains' crowns. Ceremonial carvings.
M.-F. 8.30-4; Sa. 8.30-1.30; Su. 2-5. Closed holidays.

Singapore

Singapore has been for many generations one of the great cultural meeting points of South-East Asia and the collections in its museums reflect this, in their large collections of art and ethnographical material from many countries in the area. Singapore's main industries nowadays, tourism and military bases, are more difficult to illustrate in museums and for the time being they have quite reasonably been left alone.

SINGAPORE

ART MUSEUM AND EXHIBITION GALLERY
University of Singapore, Singapore 10
Asian art, including classical Chinese ceramics, painting and sculpture, Chinese export wares, Islamic pottery, classical Indian sculpture, Indian Mughal miniature paintings, Indian historical and traditional textiles. Thai, Khmer and Annamese ceramics. Khmer sculpture. Contemporary Indian painting. Contemporary Malaysian and Indonesian painting. Traditional textiles.
M.-F. 9-4.30; Sa. 9-1. Closed Su.

NATIONAL MUSEUM
Stamford Road, Singapore 6
Anthropology of Malaya and the neighbouring regions. Archaeology. Silver and brassware of Malaya, Indonesia and Thailand. Aboriginal artifacts from Malaya and Borneo. Textiles, costumes, woodcarving, Weapons and earthenware from Malaya and Indonesia. Chinese pottery and bronzes. Maps and prints of Singapore and South-east Asia.
Daily 9-5.30.

Solomon Islands

The museum at Honiara justifies the belief that a museum is possible anywhere, even in those cases, as here, where the people have a subsistence economy and where nothing changes very much from one generation to the next.

HONIARA

SOLOMON ISLANDS MUSEUM
Honiara
Material from the Solomon Islands. History. Folklore. Costumes.
Daily 9-5.

Somali Democratic Republic

This 1960 merger of the former British and Italian territories has one museum for its four-and-a-half million people. Its comprehensive collections of Somali handicrafts are supplemented by other material illustrating living conditions and occupations of its still almost entirely agricultural country.

MOGADISHU

NATIONAL MUSEUM OF SOMALIA
Corso Repubblica, Mogadishu
History of Somalia. Ethnography. Traditional Somali handicrafts. Arab metal work, weapons and jewellery. Somali historic documents. Early Somali books.
Daily 7-2.

South Africa, Republic of

The museums of South Africa are the museums of white South Africa. The non-white majority is represented, not in the planning and organisation of museums, but in ethnographical collections and exhibits - the European section of the population is, for some reason, not considered suitable material for ethnography - in Bushman dioramas, in recordings of speech, folk-tales and music, and in displays of "facial casts of African peoples". An interesting attempt to reflect both the native and the European contributions to South African history, although hardly on the same footing, is to be found in the Museum of the History of Medicine in Johannesburg, where the development of Western medicine is shown side by side with the traditions of the Bantu herbalists and witch-doctors. There is no museum in the whole of the Republic which is devoted to native cultures in their own right. History is invariably presented from the point of view of the white man and there is at least one major institution where black and white visitors are admitted at different times.

Within these scientific and philosophical limitations, South Africa has some professionally noteworthy museums. Most of them illustrate, in one way or another, what is often referred to as "Our Heritage", by which is meant the European background of white South Africans and the conquest and settlement of South Africa by the British and the Dutch. There are excellent public collections of European paintings, porcelain and furniture, early farm implements, Voortrekker belongings and military relics. Plants, wildlife and the mining industry are well covered - gold mining much better than diamond mining - but agriculture and horticulture receive surprisingly little attention. One might well have expected to find at least sections of museums devoted to such important South African specialities as fruit-growing and wine-production, but such collections, if they exist, do not seek the limelight.

The very strong and long-established Jewish contribution to the economy of South Africa is reflected in two special museums and in several lesser collections. Some, but by no means all, of the major figures in nineteenth- and twentieth-century South African history are commemorated by museums set up in their former homes. Three former Prime Ministers, Smuts, Malan and Bolan, are generously served in this way.

ADELAIDE

"OUR HERITAGE" MUSEUM
Queen Street, Adelaide, Cape Province
Parsonage house of 1855. Rooms furnished in mid-19th century style. Voortrekker furniture. Comprehensive collection of porcelain, china and glass. Costumes. Waggons, carts, dairy and farm implements.
Daily 9-12.30, 2.30-5. W. and Sa. mornings only. Open Su. by arrangement only.

ALICE

E. S. MALAN ETHNOGRAPHICAL MUSEUM
Fort Hare, Alice, Cape Province
Ethnographical museum, covering Cape Nguni, Zulu and Sotho cultures. Works of art by contemporary African artists.
M.-F. 8.30-4.30; Sa. 8.30-11. Closed public holidays.

BARBERTON

BARBERTON MUSEUM
P.O. Box 33, Pilgrim Street, Barberton, Transvaal
Collections illustrating Lowveld goldrush in 1880s.
Weekdays 10-1, 2.30-6. W. 2.30-6 only. Sa. 10-1 only.

BEAUFORT WEST

BEAUFORT WEST MUSEUM
P.O. Box 9, Old Town Hall, Beaufort West, Cape Province
Fire arms. Domestic implements. Photographs showing early settlement of Beaufort West. Silver and glassware used by Napoleon on St. Helena.
M.-F. 10-1, 2.30-5.30; Sa. 9.30-12.30.

BETHULIE

VAN RIEBEECK CENTENARY MUSEUM
P.O. Box 42, Springfontein, Bethulie, Orange Free State
In old Pellissier house. Local history. Clothing, utensils, documents, old photographs.
W. 2.30-5; F. 11-12, or by special arrangement.

BLOEMFONTEIN

NATIONAL MUSEUM
P.O. Box 266, Aliwal Street, Bloemfontein, Orange Free State
Archaeology, including the Florisbad skull. Heads and horns of extinct giant buffalo. Customs and material culture of the Bushmen. Costumes. Period rooms. Local history.
Weekdays 9.30-5; Su. and public holidays 2-5.

WAR MUSEUM
P.O. Box 704, Monument Road, Bloemfontein, Orange Free State
Relics of the two South African wars, and of the intervening period, 1880-1902. Material relating to prisoners-of-war and concentration camps. Paintings and drawings of Boer generals and leaders, and of war scenes.
M.-Sa. 8.30-5; Su. and public holidays 2-5.

BREDASDORP

BREDASDORP MUSEUM
6 Independence Street, Bredasdorp, Cape Province
House with rooms furnished in different period styles, 1838-1910. Old Independent Church has collections on history and relics of numerous shipwrecks on the coast, 1650 to the present day. Merino woolgrowing industry. Farm implements.
Not yet decided: probably M.-F. 10-1, 2-5.30; Sa. 10-1.

BURGERSDORP

BURGERSDORP CULTURAL HISTORY MUSEUM
P.O. Box 156, Burgersdorp
Articles relating to the Border of the Cape Colony in 19th century, its culture and surroundings, including implements, clothing and furniture.
M.-F. 9-12, 2-5.

CAPE TOWN

CASTLE OF GOOD HOPE
Grand Parade, P.O. Box 1, Cape Town, Cape Province
17th century building. Military museum illustrating South African military history since 1652. William Fehr collection of Delft, Chinese and Japanese porcelain. Cape and Dutch East Indian furniture. Cape-made brass, silver, copper and glass.
M.-F. 10-4; mid. Dec.-mid. Jan. also Sa. 10-4.

COMPTON HERBARIUM
Kirstenborch Botanic Garden, Newlands, nr. Cape Town, Cape Province
National Botanic Gardens. Herbarium collections of South African Museum.
Daily 9-5.

GROOT CONSTANTIA MANOR HOUSE
Constantia, Cape Town, Cape Province
Farm house (1685), subsequently enlarged and restored. Cape furniture. Dutch paintings. Delft and Chinese porcelain. 18th century swimming bath. Agricultural museum.
Daily 10-5 (Apr.-Sept.); 10-5.30 (Oct.-Mar.).

JEWISH MUSEUM
Old Synagogue, Government Avenue, Old Hatfield Street, Cape Town, Cape Province
Housed in South Africa's first synagogue (1862). Jewish ceremonial art. Archives of local Jewish community.
Tu. and Th. 2-5; Su. 10-12.30.

KOOPMANS DE WET HOUSE
35 Strand Street, Cape Town, Cape Province
Late 18th century patrician's house. Collection of 18th century Cape furniture. Silver. Glass. China. Paintings. Material illustrating domestic conditions in South Africa in 18th and 19th centuries.
Daily 10-4.45.

MICHAELIS COLLECTION
Greenmarket Square, Cape Town, Cape Province
In the old Town House (1755). 17th century Dutch paintings. Dutch and Flemish graphic art, including etchings by Rembrandt.
M.-F. 10-5.30; Sa. 10-1; Su. 10-5.

RUST EN VREUGD
76 Buitenkant Street, Cape Town, Cape Province
House (1777). William Fehr collection of maps and pictures of South Africa.
M.-F. 10-1, 2-4. Mid-Dec. - late Jan. also Sa. and Su.

SOUTH AFRICAN MUSEUM
P.O. Box 61, Queen Victoria Street, Cape Town, Cape Province
Natural history. Archaeology. Ethnography (including Bushman groups). History of printing. Planetarium. Geology. Palaeontology.
M.-Sa. 10-5; Su. 2-5.

SOUTH AFRICAN CULTURAL HISTORY MUSEUM
P.O. Box 645, 49 Adderley Street, Cape Town, Cape Province
Cultural history of South Africa. Egyptian and Roman archaeology. Greek, Chinese and Japanese art. Arms and armour, especially Indian and Tibetan. Maritime collection. Postage stamps, coins.
M.-Sa. 10-5; Su. 2-5.

SOUTH AFRICAN NATIONAL GALLERY
Government Avenue, Cape Town, Cape Province
16th-20th century European painting and sculpture. Works by South African artists.
M.-Sa. 10-5.30; Su. 10-5.

MUSEUMS OF THE UNIVERSITY OF CAPE TOWN
Anthropological Museum in School of African Studies
M. R. Drennan Anatomical Museum, in Department of Anatomy, Medical School, Mowbray
P. A. Wagner Museum, in Department of Geology
By special arrangement.

COLESBERG

KEMPER MUSEUM
Town Hall, P.O. Box 39, Colesberg, Cape Province
Relics of early settlers in the area, and of 1899-1902 war.
On application, M.-F. only.

CRADOCK

ZEBRA NATIONAL PARKS MUSEUM
Cradock, Cape Province
Farm homestead (1830). 19th century furniture, domestic implements. Dairy room. Waggon house, with carriages, waggons. Harvesting equipment.
Daily 9-5, on application.

DUNDEE

DEPARTMENT OF MINES MUSEUM
P.O. Box 93, Dundee, Natal
Geological and metallurgical material connected with local mining. Fossils. Stone-Age tools. History of local mining.
On application.

DURBAN

DURBAN MUSEUM AND ART GALLERY
City Hall, South Street, Durban, Natal
Natural history. Ethnography. Geology. Archaeology. European painting. Modern European graphic art. European and Eastern applied art.
W. 9.30-2. Other weekdays 9.30-5.

MUSEUM OF LOCAL HISTORY
Old Court House, Aliwal Street, Durban, Natal
Development of Natal, especially Durban, since colonial times. Life of early settler families. Collection of period costumes.
Daily 9.30-5; W. 9.30-2; Su. 2.30-5. Public holidays 9.30-5.

NATAL HERBARIUM
Botanic Gardens Road, Durban, Natal
Foreign and African specimens, with emphasis on flora of Natal and Zululand.
Weekdays 8-12.45, by appointment only.

THE OLD HOUSE
31 St. Andrew's Street, Durban, Natal
Mid-19th century house, with period furniture and domestic equipment.
Daily 9.30-5; W. 9.30-2; Su. 2.30-5. Public holidays 9.30-5.

WILLIAM CAMPBELL MUSEUM
Muckleneuk, 220 Marriott Road, Durban, Natal
Home of Campbell family. Cape and European furniture. Early pictures of African scenes. Mashu Museum of African arts and crafts. Paintings of African costumes by Barbara Tyrrell.
By arrangement.

EAST LONDON

ANN BRYANT ART GALLERY
9 St. Mark's Road, c/o Town Clerk, P.O. Box 134, East London, Cape Province
English paintings. Contemporary South African art.
M.-F. except Tu., 10-12.30, 3-5.30; Sa. and Su. 2.30-5.30 (Oct.-Mar. 6.30).

EAST LONDON MUSEUM
Upper Oxford Street, East London, Cape Province
Natural history. The first Coelacanth to be discovered in 1938. Geology. Archaeology. Ethnography, especially Xhosa and Fingo ornaments and implements. Objects relating to Kaffir Wars and to the British settlers of 1820 and the German settlers of 1856-58.
M.-F. 9.30-12.30, 2-5; Sa. 9.30-12; Su. 9.30-12.30, 2.30-4.30.

GATELY HOUSE
East London, Cape Province
The house (1875) was the home of John Gately, the first mayor of East London. Original contents, practically unaltered.
Tu.-Sa. 9.30-12.30, 3-5; Su. 3-5. Closed M.

ESHOWE

ZULULAND HISTORICAL MUSEUM
Fort Nongqai, c/o Town Clerk, Box 37, Eshowe, Natal
History of Zululand. Personal items, furniture and regalia formerly belonging to Bishop Schreuder of Zululand. Zulu ethnography.
Daily, except M., 10-5.

FORT BEAUFORT

FORT BEAUFORT (HISTORICAL) MUSEUM
P.O. Box 94, 30 Durban Street, Fort Beaufort, Cape Province
History of the Fort Beaufort area, in former Officers' Mess House. The original kitchen range bears the monogram of George IV. Collection of old guns, swords, spears, small cannon and other implements of war. Collection of photographs of the town dating back to 1835.
M., W., F. and Sa. 9-1; Th. 2-6.

FRANSCHHOEK

HUGUENOT MEMORIAL MUSEUM
P.O. Box 37, Lambrechts Street, Franschhoek, Cape Province
Documents and photographic material relating to the history of the Cape Huguenots. Antique Cape furniture. Genealogical matter relating to the descendants of the Cape Huguenots.
Weekdays 8-5; Su. 2-5.

GEORGE

GEORGE MUSEUM
P.O. Box 19, Market Street, George, Cape Province
History of George, especially local timber industry. Over 30 old mechanical musical instruments, including gramophones, musical boxes. Early cameras, telephones, typewriters. Complete collection of all South African buck horns. Semi-precious stones from South-West Africa and Northern Cape.
M., Tu., Th., F. 11-1, 3-5; W. 11-1, 7.45-8.45. Closed Su.

GRAAFF-REINET

GRAAFF-REINET MUSEUM
Parsonage Street, P.O. Box 104, Graaff-Reinet, Cape Province
Parsonage house (1812). Garden has what is claimed to be the largest vine stem in the world. Period rooms with 18th and early 19th century Cape furniture made of yellow wood and stinkwood. Wooden agricultural implements.
Daily 9-12, 3-5. Closed Good F. and Christmas Day. Closed Sa. afternoon and Su.

HESTER RUPERT ART MUSEUM
Church Street, Graaff-Reinet, Cape Province
In Mission Church (1821). Contemporary South African art.
Weekdays 10-12, 3-5 (3.30-5.30 in winter).

GRAHAMSTOWN

ALBANY MUSEUM
Somerset Street, Grahamstown, Cape Province
Natural history. Herbarium. Bantu woodcarvings, ornaments, clothing, utensils. African masks, musical instruments, dolls. Archaeology of Africa, Scandinavia, Egypt. Incorporates the municipal art collection and the *1820 Settlers Memorial Museum* which has relics of 150 Settler families, including household utensils and agricultural implements. Costumes. Weapons. Works by South African artists. Sculptures by Ivan Mitford-Barberton. Cape Dutch cultural history.
M.-F. 8.30-1, 2-5; Sa. 8.30-1; Su. 2.30-5. Closed Good F. and Christmas Day.

GREYTOWN

UMVOTI MUSEUM
Municipal Library, Pine Street, Greytown, Natal
History of Greytown, relics of pioneer families, of the Umvoti Mounted Rifles and of the 1906 rebellion. Zulu exhibits.
M.-F. 10-12, 4-5.30; Sa. 9-12.

GRIQUATOWN

MARY MOFFAT MUSEUM
Main Street, Griquatown, Natal
In old mission building, in which Mary Moffat, daughter of the missionary Dr. Robert Moffat and wife of David Livingstone, was born. Relics of Moffat, Livingstone and Waterboer.
Weekdays 9-5; Sa. 8-1.

HARRISMITH

BURNS-THOMPSON MEMORIAL MUSEUM
Town Hall, Harrismith
South African birds. Geology. War relics.
On request.

HARTENBOS

HARTENBOS MUSEUM
Atkv-Strandoord, Posbus 3, Hartenbos, Cape Province
Clothes, old Dutch family Bibles, rifles, crockery, etc. used during and after the "Great Trek" in 1838 by the "Voortrekkers", Afrikaans-speaking pioneers who moved to the uncivilised interior because of the policy at the Cape at that time.
Daily except Su. and public holidays 9-4.30.

IRENE

GENERAL SMUTS MUSEUM
Doornkloof, Irene, Transvaal
The farm which was the home of General Jan Christian Smuts for over forty years, and originally the officers' mess at Kitchener's headquarters at Middleburg in the Transvaal. Smuts bought it from the British and transported it to Irene. Mrs. Smuts' bedroom contains the original furniture and there are other original items in the house, which has been restored as far as possible to its condition during the time it was occupied by the Smuts family.
M.-F. 9-12, 2-4.30; Sa., Su. and public holidays 9-12, 2-5.

JOHANNESBURG

AFRICANA MUSEUM
Public Library, Market Square, Johannesburg, Transvaal
Cultural, historical and ethnographical museum, illustrating contribution made by English, Dutch and Africans to the development of South Africa. History of Johannesburg. Zeederberg mail and stage coach. Pre-20th century paintings, prints, drawings made in South Africa.
Daily 9-6; Su. and public holidays 2-6.

ARCHAEOLOGICAL MUSEUM
University of the Witwatersrand, Jan Smuts Avenue, Johannesburg, Transvaal
African pre-history, especially prehistoric technology. Comparative material from other continents. Rock engravings and paintings.
M.-F. 9-5.

BERNARD PRICE INSTITUTE FOR PALAEONTOLOGICAL RESEARCH
Douglas Smith University of the Witwatersrand, Jan Smuts Avenue, Johannesburg, Transvaal
Vertebrate specimens from the Karoo beds. Mammalian fossils from Makapansgat excavations.
By arrangement.

BLELOCH MUSEUM
Department of Geology, University of the Witwatersrand, Jan Smuts Avenue, Johannesburg, Transvaal
Geological material, with emphasis on economic ore deposits and minerals of South Africa. Collection of banket from Witwatersrand goldfield. Gold specimens and gemstones.
Weekdays 8.30-5.

ETHNOLOGICAL MUSEUM OF THE DEPARTMENT OF SOCIAL ANTHROPOLOGY
University of the Witwatersrand, Jan Smuts Avenue, Johannesburg, Transvaal
Material culture of the peoples of Africa, especially the Bushman, Ovambo and Pedi. Some exhibits from Pacific. Collection of recorded music and language.
M.-F. 8-5; Sa. 8-12.

GEOLOGICAL MUSEUM
Public Library, Market Square, Johannesburg, Transvaal
History of the Earth. South African minerals and gemstones. Stone implements.
Daily 9-6; Su. and public holidays 2-6.

JAMES HALL MUSEUM OF TRANSPORT
Pioneers' Park, Rosettenville Road, La Rochelle, Johannesburg, Transvaal
Different means of public transport used in Johannesburg over the years. Includes Cape carts and other horse and ox-drawn vehicles.
Daily 9-6.

JEWISH MUSEUM
4th floor, Sheffield House, corner of Main and Kruis Street, P.O. Box 11180, Johannesburg, Transvaal
Jewish religious art; history of Jewish community in South Africa. Judaica from European synagogues and private collections.
By appointment.

JOHANNESBURG ART GALLERY
Jonbert Park, Johannesburg, Transvaal
19th and 20th century paintings by English, French and Dutch schools. Graphics, including works by Dürer, Rembrandt and 19th century French artists. Modern European sculpture. Chinese ceramics. Cape furniture. Works by South African artists.
Daily except M. 10-5. Oct.-May also W. and Su. 8-10.

MOSS HERBARIUM
Department of Botany, University of the Witwatersrand, Jan Smuts Avenue, Johannesburg, Transvaal
Flora of the Witwatersrand.
M.-F. 9-12, 2-5.

MUSEUM OF THE HISTORY OF MEDICINE
South African Institute for Medical Research, Hospital Street, P.O. Box 1038, Johannesburg, Transvaal
In the old Director's House of the Institute. Medical and surgical instruments and equipment. Stamp Collection, 'medicine in philately'. Medical traditions of the Bantu herbalists and witch doctors.
Weekdays 10-2 and by appointment.

MUSEUM OF MAN AND SCIENCE
111 Central Street, Houghton, P.O. Box 1049, Johannesburg, Transvaal
Archaeology. Ethnography. Cultural anthropology. Dart collection of facial casts of African peoples.
M.-F. 9-5.30 or by appointment.

MUSEUMS OF THE UNIVERSITY OF THE WITWATERSRAND
These specialist museums are intended primarily for the use of staff and students. They are open to the public by arrangement only.
Hunterian Museum, Department of Anatomy, Medical School:
contains more than 2000 human skeletons.
Museum of the Oral and Dental Hospital:
Dentition of vertebrates. Palaeontological and fossil remains. Dental historical and dental surgical section. Casts of dentitions of various racial groups in South Africa.
By appointment.

PHOTOGRAPHIC MUSEUM
17 Empire Road, Parkdown, Johannesburg, Transvaal
Development of photography in general and in South Africa in particular. Old cameras and other equipment. Photographic prints of historical interest.
Weekdays 9-1, 2-5; Su. and public holidays 2-6.

SOUTH AFRICAN NATIONAL WAR MUSEUM
Erlswold Way, Saxonwold, Johannesburg, Transvaal
Aircraft, including Mosquito and Spitfire; tanks, guns; small arms dating back to 1750. South African built armoured cars. Medals, uniforms. 1939-45 paintings by official war artists.
Daily 9.30-5, except M. Non-whites Th., Sa. 1-5.

SOUTH AFRICAN RAILWAY MUSEUM
Under Johann Rissik Bridge, Johannesburg Station, Johannesburg, Transvaal
Scale models of railway rolling stock, ships, aircraft and road vehicles. Dioramas of harbours. Actual locomotives and rolling stock temporarily in store elsewhere.
M.-F. 9-4; Sa. 9-3. Closed Su. and religious holidays.

KENHARDT

KENHARDT MUSEUM
Division Council, Private Bag 3, Kenhardt, Cape Province
Local history. Collection of prehistoric stone implements.
9-5.30.

KIMBERLEY

ALEXANDER MCGREGOR MEMORIAL MUSEUM
Chapel Street, P.O. Box 316, Kimberley, Orange Free State
Local natural history, archaeology and anthropology. Rock art. Herbarium. Kimberley Regiment. Reconstructed chemist's shop and Victorian room interior. The museum owns two historic buildings - the Kimberley Sanatorium and the house of C. D. Rudd - and also the site of the Battle of Magersfontein, where a field museum is under construction.
Under review.

DUGGAN-CRONIN BANTU GALLERY
Egerton Road, Kimberley, Orange Free State
Photographs of Bantu life. Ethnographical collections. Bechuana hut and other tribal dwellings. Recordings of Bantu music.
M.-F. 10-5; Sa. 10-1; Su. 2-5.

KIMBERLEY MINE MUSEUM
De Beers Consolidated Mines Ltd., P.O. Box 616, Kimberley, Orange Free State
Open-air museum, with original buildings and other material associated with the early days of Kimberley diamond mines. Barnsy Barnato's Boxing Academy. Sir David Harris's ballroom. J. N. de Beer's farm. Cecil Rhodes Board Room.
Daily 8.15-6 (gates close 5.45). Closed Good F. and Dec. 16 (Day of the Covenant).

WILLIAM HUMPHREYS ART GALLERY
Civic Centre, P.O. Box 885, Kimberley, Orange Free State
Flemish and Dutch paintings of the 16th and 17th centuries. 18th and 19th century English paintings. Works by South African artists. European and Cape furniture. Ceramics.
M.-Sa. 10.30-1, 2.30-6; Su. 2.30-6.

KING WILLIAM'S TOWN

THE KAFFRARIAN MUSEUM
3 Albert Road, King William's Town, Cape Province
Natural history, including collection of 19,000 South African mammal skins (many mounted). Huberta, the wandering hippo. Local and military history. Weapons. Uniforms. Victorian and Edwardian costumes and utensils.
M.-F. 8-5; Sa. 8-1; Su. 2-5. Closed Good F., Ascension Day, Day of the Covenant and Christmas Day.

LADYSMITH

LADYSMITH MUSEUM
adjoining Town Hall, P.O. Box 29, Ladysmith, Natal
Items relating to early history of Ladysmith and particularly to siege period during Boer War.
M.-F. 9-5.30.

LYDENBURG

VOORTREKKER CHURCH AND SCHOOL
Lydenburg
Museum is in old Dutch Reformed Church (1851) and in the Transvaal's first school (1851). Voortrekker relics. Gold mining. Early school books, writing implements, furniture.
By appointment.

MODDERFONTEIN

MODDERFONTEIN DYNAMITE FACTORY MUSEUM
P.O. Northrand, Modderfontein
History of the district and the Dynamite Factory. Victorian manager's house, with original furnishings. Documents and other objects illustrate the factory's close association with the history of the old Transvaal Republic and its occupation by British troops under General Baden-Powell.
By appointment only (Johannesburg 608-1211).

MOORREESBURG

WHEAT INDUSTRY MUSEUM
P.O. Box 134, Moorreesburg, Cape Province
Every kind of implement used in the wheat industry, from the earliest days to the present time.
By appointment.

MOSSEL BAY

MOSSEL BAY MUSEUM
P.O. Box 25, Bland Street, Mossel Bay, Cape Province
Maritime history of the Bay. Maps. Photographs. Utensils. Outstanding collection of rare shells from all over the world.
M., Tu., Th. and F. 9-12, 2.30-4.45. W. and Sa. 9-12.

MOLTENO

MOLTENO MUSEUM
Smith Street, Molteno, Cape Province
Local history. Early European settlement. Costumes. Utensils. Bantu culture.
M. and F. 10-11.45; Tu. 4-6; W. 11-12.30, 5.30-7; Th. 4-6.

OUDTSHOORN

CANGO CAVES MUSEUM
Cango Caves, 18 miles north of Oudtshoorn, Cape Province
Fossils. Minerals. History of the Caves. Bushman dioramas, showing day-to-day occupations.
Europeans: Jan., Feb., Apr. and Dec. Every hour, on the hour, from 8-6. All other months at 9, 11, 1 and 3.
Non-Europeans: Every day, including Su. and public holidays, at 9.30, 11.30 and 2.30.

C.P. NEL MUSEUM
P.O. Box 453, Oudtshoorn, Cape Province
Local history. Special displays relating to the early pioneers, the ostrich trade and the tobacco industry. Fire-arms. Collection of old vehicles includes an ox-waggon (1837) and a chain-driven motor car (1898).
M.-Sa. 8.30-12.30, 2-5. Su. 2.30-5. Closed Ascension Day and Christmas.

PAARL

OLD PARSONAGE MUSEUM
Main Street, Paarl, Cape Province
In old parsonage house (1787). Antiques and relics related to the history of Paarl and of the Cape. Cape-made stinkwood furniture and silver. Kitchen equipment. Handicrafts. Press on which the first Afrikaans newspapers and periodicals were printed. Vehicles. Agricultural implements.
M.-Sa. 10-12, 3-5. Closed Su. and public holidays.

PIETERMARITZBURG

MINES DEPARTMENT MUSEUM
Department of Mines, Pietermaritzburg, Natal
Geology. Archaeology. Safety in mines and quarries.
M.-F. 9-5.30.

NATAL MUSEUM
237 Loop Street, Pietermaritzburg, Natal
African fauna. Local and cultural history. Ethnography, especially Zulu material. Reconstruction of early Pietermaritzburg street scene, with original buildings.
Daily 9-4.30. Su. 2-5.

TATHAM ART GALLERY
City Hall, Pietermaritzburg, Natal
European art, especially British, 1880-1920, and French landscapes of the Barbizon school. Oriental rugs. Chinese, Dutch, German and French ceramics.
Weekdays 10-5.

VOORTREKKER MUSEUM
Church Street, P.O. Box 998, Pietermaritzburg, Natal
In Church of the Vow (1838). Voortrekker history and material culture. Furniture. Household utensils. Fire-arms. Costumes. The original pulpit is now a national monument.
M.-F. 9-1, 2-4.30; Sa. 9-12.30.

PORT ELIZABETH

KING GEORGE VI ART GALLERY
1 Park Drive, Port Elizabeth, Cape Province
Paintings, mainly British and South African. Indian and Persian miniatures. Japanese woodcuts. European graphics, including works of Rembrandt, Goya, Whistler and Picasso. Chinese ceramics.
M. 2-6. Tu.-Sa. 10-12.45, 2-6. Su. 2.30-5.30. Public holidays 10.30-12.30, 2.30-5.30.

NO. 7 CASTLE HILL
Port Elizabeth, Cape Province
House (1830). Period rooms contain Port Elizabeth antiques. Folk art.
Daily 9-1, 2-5. Closed Good F. and Christmas Day.

PORT ELIZABETH MUSEUM
Snake Park and Early Settler House, Humewood, Port Elizabeth, Cape Province
Geology. Archaeology, including Boskoop Skull. Marine biology. Dioramas of local birds. Local history.
Daily 9-1, 2-5. Closed Good F. and Christmas Day.

POTGIETERSRUS

AREND DIEPERINK MUSEUM
98 Ruiter Road, P.O. Box 582, Potgietersrus, Transvaal
History of Northern, North-western and Eastern Transvaal. Personal relics of the Voortrekker leader, Piet Potgieter.
M.-F. 9-5.30.

POTCHEFSROOM

MUNICIPAL MUSEUM
Potgieter Street, Potchefsroom, Transvaal
Cultural and historical background of Potchefsroom and its surrounding district. Voortrekker utensils, furniture, wagons, weapons. Hut of Bantu witchdoctor. Dioramas of 1881 siege of the British fortress. Paintings and drawings by Otto van Landsberg.
M.-F. 9-5; Sa. 9-12.45; Su. 2.30-5.

PRETORIA

ANTHROPOLOGICAL MUSEUM OF THE UNIVERSITY OF SOUTH AFRICA
Skinner Street, Pretoria, Transvaal
Anthropology. Archaeology. Stone Age artifacts from the Pretoria district and Eastern Transvaal. Prehistoric rock art.
By appointment.

ENGELENBURG HOUSE ART COLLECTION
Corner of Hamilton and Ziervogel Street, Pretoria, Transvaal
Cape, English and Dutch furniture. Oriental and European ceramics.
By appointment.

FORT KLAPPERKOP
Defence Headquarters, Pretoria, near Pretoria, Transvaal
Fortress (1898). Military history of the Transvaal Republic. Arms and military vehicles, 1914-18 and 1939-45.
M.-F. 10-4; Sa., Su. and public holidays 10-6.

KRUGER HOUSE MUSEUM
Church Street West, Pretoria, Transvaal
In former residence of President Kruger. Interior substantially as in Kruger's time. Documents and books associated with Kruger and the South African War. Kruger's horse-carriage and rail-coach.
Weekdays 10-5; Su. and public holidays 2-5.

MELROSE HOUSE
Jacob Maré Street, Pretoria, Transvaal
Victorian town house where the peace treaty at the close of the 1899-1902 war was signed. Period furnishings.
Tu.-Sa. 10-5; Su. 1-6.

MUSEUM OF THE GEOLOGICAL SURVEY
223 Visagie Street, Pretoria, Transvaal
Geology, crystallography, mineralogy and palaeontology. Precious and semi-precious stones. Industrial minerals, with models showing mining and processing.
M.-F. 9-4; Sa. 9-5; Su. 2-5.

MUSEUM OF SCIENCE AND INDUSTRY
P.O. Box 1758, Pretoria
Art. Education. Science. History. Biography. Travel.
Weekdays 10.30-5; Su. 2-5.

MUSEUM OF THE SOUTH AFRICAN MINT
Visagie Street, P.O. Box 464, Pretoria, Transvaal
History of the Mint. Reference collection of coins, tokens, medals, plaques, badges from all over the world.
Temporarily closed, during rebuilding of Mint.

NATIONAL CULTURAL HISTORY AND OPEN-AIR MUSEUM
Boom Street, P.O. Box 3300, Pretoria, Transvaal
Prehistory, including large collection of rock engravings. Ethnography, concentrating on Transvaal tribes. Cultural history of the European population. Cape furniture and silver. Voortrekker furniture. Costumes. History of old Transvaal Republic.
Weekdays 10-30-5; Su. 2-5.

PRETORIA ART MUSEUM
Arcadia Park, Schoeman Street, Pretoria, Transvaal
Specialises in works by South African artists. 17th century Dutch paintings. Dutch Impressionists.
Tu.-Sa. 10-3; Su. 1-6. Closed M.

SOUTH AFRICAN POLICE MUSEUM
Pretorius Street, Pretoria, Transvaal
History of the South African Police. Uniforms. Weapons. Documents.
M.-F. 7.30-4; Sa. 8-12.

TRANSVAAL MUSEUM
Paul Kruger Street, P.O. Box 413, Pretoria, Transvaal
Natural history. Palaeontology. Anthropology.
Weekdays 9-4. Su. and public holidays 2-5.

VOORTREKKER MONUMENT MUSEUM
Voortrekker Monument, P.O. Box 3300, near Pretoria, Transvaal
History and material culture of the Voortrekkers. Tapestries showing various stages of the Great Trek. Transvaal pioneer's cottage. Period rooms. Reconstructed camping scene.
Weekdays 9-5; Su. 2-5.

QUEENSTOWN

QUEENSTOWN AND FRONTIER MUSEUM
13 Shepstone Street, P.O. Box 296, Queenstown, Cape Province
History of Queenstown and surrounding area. Maritime gallery, including ships' Figureheads. Dolls and toys. Natural history, including major collections of butterflies. Shells.
M.-F. 9.30-12.45, 2-5; Sa. 9-12.45; Su. and public holidays 2.30-5; Tu. and Th. also 7.30-9.

RIVERSDALE

JULIUS GORDON AFRICANA CENTRE
Versveld House, Long Street, Riversdale, Cape Province
South African paintings. Furniture, including early Cape stinkwood chairs. Clocks. Domestic utensils.
M. 7.30-9 p.m.; W., F. 10-12, 3-5.

ROODEPORT

ROODEPORT MUNICIPAL MUSEUM
Municipal Offices, P.O. Box 217, Roodeport, Transvaal
Local and Voortrekker history. Semi-precious stones.
Weekdays 9.30-5.

SKUKUZA

STEVENSON-HAMILTON MEMORIAL LIBRARY
P.O. Box 3, Skukuza, Transvaal
Library contains museum dealing with history, fauna, flora and geology of the Kruger National Park. Some ethnographical exhibits.
Daily 10-12.30, 2-4, 7.30-9.

STELLENBOSCH

THE BURGERHUIS
Die Braak, Stellenbosch, Cape Province
In house of 1797. Cape antiques, including glass, silver and stinkwood armoires. European porcelain. Kitchen equipment.
M.-F. 8.30-1, 2-5.

D. F. MALAN MUSEUM
Carnegie Library, Andringa Street, Stellenbosch, Cape Province
Personal relics of Dr. D. F. Malan, with documents and photographs illustrating his life and times.
Weekdays 9-5.30.

STELLENBOSCH MUSEUM
Grosvenor House, Drostdy Street, Stellenbosch, Cape Province
In house of 1781 (enlarged 1803). Local history. Period rooms, with Cape-made furniture and utensils. Cape silver, handicrafts, coins and banknotes. Farming history. Early fire-engines. Weapons, guns.
M.-Sa. 9-5; Su. and religious holidays 2-5. Closed Christmas Day and Good Friday.

SWELLENDAM

DROSTDY MUSEUM
Swellengrebel Street, Swellendam, Cape Province
Historic buildings of 1746 and 1865. Regional history. Period rooms. Domestic and agricultural implements. Kakebeen wagons. Crafts and workshops.
M.-Sa. 8-1, 2-5. Closed Su., Good F. and Christmas Day.

TULBAGH

OUDEKERK VOLKSMUSEUM
Church Street, Tulbagh, Cape Province
Building is church of 1743. Cape cultural history. Cape stinkwood furniture. Musical instruments. Costumes. First edition of Voltaire's works and a Lutheran Bible (1545).
M.-Sa. 8-1, 2-5. Closed Su.

UITENHAGE

UITENHAGE AFRICANA MUSEUM
Town Hall, P.O. Box 45, Uitenhage, Cape Province
Pioneer life in Uitenhage district. Costumes. Furniture. Household utensils.
M. 9.30-11.30; Tu.-F. 2.30-5.

UPINGTON

MUNICIPAL LIBRARY MUSEUM
Municipal Library, Private Bag 981, Upington, Transvaal
Local history. Bushman implements and weapons. Semi-precious stones.
Weekdays 10-12.30, 3-6, 7.30-8.30.

VENTERSDORP

VENTERSDORP MUSEUM
Municipal Offices, P.O. Box 15, Ventersdorp, Transvaal
Local history.
By appointment.

VICTORIA WEST

VICTORIA WEST MUSEUM
Church Street, Victoria West, Cape Province
Local history and prehistory, including books, documents, photographs, clothes, tools, weapons, newspapers, copperware, glassware, porcelain and furniture. Fish fossils and stone implements of the early Stone Age.
M.-F. 8.45-1.30, 3-5.30; Sa. 10.30-12.30.

VEREENIGING

VEREENIGING MUSEUM
P.O. Box 136, Vereeniging, Transvaal
Local history. Palaeontology, specially fossilised plants from coal measures. Archaeology.
M.-F. 10-1, 2-5; Sa. 9-12.30.

VRYBURG

VRYBURG MUSEUM
Library, P.O. Box 49, Vryburg, Transvaal
Historical relics of the town and district, including flag of the one-time republic of Stellaland.
W., Sa. 10.30-12.30. Other weekdays 10.30-12.30, 3-5.30.

VRYHEID

NIEUWE REPUBLIEK MUSEUM
119 Landdros Street, Vryheid, Natal
Articles relating to the New Republic (1884-8) and to the succeeding period (1888-99) when the area was part of the Zuid-Afrikaansche Republiek. Official weights and measures. Furniture. Documents. Coins. Banknotes.
M., W., Th. 10-12, 3-4.

WEENEN

WEENEN MUSEUM
P.O. Box 13, Weenen, Natal
Historical items from Weenen area, including grinding mill with waterwheel originally belonging to the Voortrekker leader, Andries Pretorius.
M.-F. 8.30-1, 2-4; Sa. 8.30-12.

WORCESTER

WORCESTER MUSEUM
Corner of Baring and Church Street, Worcester, Cape Province
Old Cape furniture, brass, domestic utensils, fire-arms.
W., Sa. 10-12. Other weekdays 10-12, 2.30-5.

South-West Africa (Namibia)

Two open-air museums of buildings moved to museum sites, the oldest animal fossils in South Africa, diamond mining, relics of the German colonial period, missionaries and bushmen - the museums of South-West Africa take a great slicing cut through the history and life of the area and produce some interesting and well presented collections in the process.

FISCHFLUSS CANYON

OPEN-AIR MUSEUM
Fischfluss Canyon
Buildings moved to site. Ethnography.
Daily 8.30-5.30.

FORT NAMUNTONI

HISTORICAL MUSEUM
Fort Namuntoni
History of the region.
M.-F. 8-12.45, 2-5; Sa., Su. and public holidays 3-6.

LÜDERITZ

LÜDERITZ MUSEUM
P.O. Box 512, Diaz Street, Lüderitz
Archaeology, ethnography, history and natural science. Oldest fossils in South Africa: Pteridinum simplex from Aar; fossilised footprints of big game from the Namib; skeleton of a rhinoceros (approx. 10,000 years old). Diamond mining. Whales. Bushman arts and crafts.
W., Th. and Sa. 4-6.

MUKEROB

OPEN-AIR MUSEUM
Mukerob
Buildings moved to the site from different regions of South-West Africa.
Daily 8.30-5.30.

OKAUKUEJO

EDUCATIONAL MUSEUM
Okaukuejo
Regional history, ethnography.
M.-F. 8.45-12, 2-5; Sa., Su., public holidays 3-6.

SWAKOPMUND

SWAKOPMUND MUSEUM
Roonstra., P.O. Box 56, Swakopmund
Near public park on the beach. History of Portuguese era, German colonial period. Development of postal services, railways and transport. Bushmen. Mineralogy. Marine life.
Daily 10.30-12.30, 4-6. Sa. also 8-9 p.m.

WINDHOEK

ALTE FESTE
Leutwein Street, Windhoek
Fortress (1890). Historical museum, covering early pioneers and missionaries, German administrators and period as a South African protectorate.
M.-F. 8-12.45, 2-5; Sa., Su. and public holidays 3-6.

ART GALLERY
John Meinert/Leutwein Street, P.O. Box 994, Windhoek
Paintings, drawings, sculpture by South-West African artists.
Daily 9-1, 3-5.30; Sa. 9-12.

STATE MUSEUM
Leutwein Street, P.O. Box 1203, Windhoek
Zoology; Geology. Ethnography of the Nama, Bushman, Damara, Herero, Ovambo and smaller groups in the Kavango and Kaoko areas. Stone Age cultures.
M.-F. 8-12.45, 2-5; Sa., Su. and public holidays 2-5.

Spain

Even a casual glance through our list will show where the strengths and weaknesses of Spanish museums lie. There are many remarkable collections of paintings, sculpture and archaeology, but very few covering the sciences, technology or industry, a situation which reflects Spain's long period as a Roman province, the power and wealth of its church and monarchy during the fifteenth, sixteenth and seventeenth centuries, and its dwindling away to become a European backwater during the nineteenth and twentieth centuries.

For much of Spain, as of Italy, it is hardly an exaggeration to say that one has only to scratch the soil to find something Roman. The museums are consequently well stocked with Roman material and with mementoes of the occupation by North African Arabs. Palaces and churches as well as museums are full of works of art commissioned and acquired by the Court, by the aristocracy and by the Church. A major difficulty in drawing up a list of Spanish museums is to decide when a church can reasonably be called a museum, since so many Spanish churches are, in effect, museums of religious art. The criterion is whether or not the paintings or vestments or gold plate are part of the equipment or atmosphere of a building which is still in use for religious purposes. If they are, we are not dealing with a museum. It is possible, of course, to establish a true museum in a special section of the church or cathedral, and where we are satisfied that this is the case, the museum appears in our list.

Spain is a country which depends a great deal on tourists for its livelihood, and the assumption, probably correct, has been that tourists are not greatly interested in anything which feels too modern. This may partly explain the paucity of museums which aim to show something of Spain's more recent past. There is also the consideration, however, that by turning the attention of visitors well back over their shoulders, awkward and sensitive political issues can be avoided. To play up old history and old art is, nevertheless, to ignore the cultural and educational needs of the Spaniards of the 1970s, people who have to be equipped, practically and philosophically, to earn a living in the world of today and tomorrow.

AGREDA

MUSEUM OF SISTER MARIA DE JESUS DE AGREDA
Convento de la Concepción, Agreda, Soria
Books, correspondence and personal possessions of Maria Coronel y de Arana (1602-65), a Franciscan nun, secretary and adviser of Philip IV.
Daily 10-12, 1-3, 4-6.

AGUILAR DE CAMPOO

FONTANEDA COLLECTION
Casa Fontaneda, Aguilar de Campoo, Oviedo
Former palace of the Marquises of Aguilar. Prehistoric and classical archaeology. Medieval art.
By appointment.

ALBACETE

PROVINCIAL ARCHAEOLOGICAL MUSEUM
Avda José Antonio 2, Albacete
Prehistory and archaeology of the Romans, Visigoths, Arabs and Goths.
Daily 10-1.30, ex. during Aug. and on Su. and public holidays.

ALBARRACIN

CATHEDRAL
Calle de la Catedral, Albarracin, Teruel
Material in Sacristy, Capula de San Juan, Treasury and Upper Cloister. 16th century Brussels tapestries. Church plate (gold). Paintings, including works by Goya and El Greco. Sculpture. 'Custodia' (1524) by Enrique de Arfe, with 260 silver-gilt statuettes. 18th century Gigantones, giant processional figures.
Daily May-Sept., M.-Sa. 11-2, 4.30-7. Public holidays 12.30-2, 5.30-8. Oct.-Apr. by appointment.

ALBOCACER

PAROCHIAL MUSEUM
Plaza de la Iglesia, Albocacer, Castellon de la Plana
Religious art, from disused churches and private collections in the district. Paintings. Sculpture. Goldsmiths' work.
May-Sept. Daily 11-2, 5-7. Oct.-Apr. Daily 11-2, 3-6.

ALCALA DE HENARES

BIRTHPLACE OF CERVANTES
Calle Mayor 48, Alcala de Henares, Madrid
Present house (1955) is built on the site where Miguel Cervantes was born 1547, now furnished in the style of the 16th century. Other rooms contain books and documents relating to Cervantes.
Daily 10-2, 4-8.

MUSEUM OF THE HISTORY OF PUBLIC ADMINISTRATION IN SPAIN
Antigua Universidad, Alcala de Henares, Madrid
Material illustrating the history of the public service.
Daily ex. July 15, Sept. 1, May 1-Sept. 30, 9-2, 5-7. Oct.-Apr. 9-2, 4-6.

ALCANTARILLA

MUNICIPAL MUSEUM OF ETHNOLOGY
Acequia Barreras, Alcantarilla, Murcia
Regional ethnology. Agriculture. Local industries. Furniture and household utensils. Handicrafts. Village inn, serving typical Murcia dishes.
Daily 9-2, 5-9.

ALCAZAR DE SAN JUAN

FRAY JUAN COBO ARCHAEOLOGICAL MUSEUM
Capilla de Palacio, Calle don Quijote 16, Alcazar de San Juan, Ciudad Real
Ethnography of the Alcazar district. Roman mosaics.
Daily, by appointment.

ALCOY

MUNICIPAL ARCHAEOLOGICAL MUSEUM
'Camilo Visedo Molto', Calle San Miguel 29, Alcoy, Alicante
Local prehistory and archaeology. Coins. Natural sciences.
Daily 10-1.

ALCUDIA

MUNICIPAL ARCHAEOLOGICAL MUSEUM
Calle Goded 7, Alcudia, Mallorca, Balearic Islands
Local archaeology of the Roman period.
May-Sept. Daily ex. M. and F. 9-1. Oct.-Apr. Daily ex. M. and F. 10-12.

ALICANTE

PROVINCIAL ARCHAEOLOGICAL MUSEUM
Alicante
Prehistory. Archaeology. Medieval ceramics.
Daily 9-1.30.

ALMERIA

CATHEDRAL MUSEUM
Cathedral, Almeria
Religious paintings. Vestments.
Daily 11-7.30.

LUIS SIRET PROVINCIAL ARCHAEOLOGICAL MUSEUM
Calle Javier Sanz 14, Almeria
Prehistory and archaeology.
Daily ex. Su. and public holidays, 11-1.30.

ALQUEZAR

PAROCHIAL MUSEUM
Antiqua Colegiata, Alquezar, Huesca
Religious art.
Daily 10-1, 3-6.

AMBRONA

MUSEUM OF THE EXCAVATIONS AT TORRALBA
Ambrona, Soria
Site Museum. Palaeontology, including fossilised remains of prehistoric mammals. Palaeolithic archaeology.
By appointment.

AMPOSTA

MUNICIPAL MUSEUM
Ayuntamiento, Plaza de España, Amposta, Tarragona
Local archaeology.
M.-Sa. 4-8.

AMPUDIA

FONTANEDA COLLECTION
Castillo de Ampudia, Ampudia, Palencia
Prehistoric and Roman collections. Medieval art.
By appointment.

AMPURIAS

LA ESCALA
nr. Ampurias, Gerona
Site museum. Items from the excavations of Greek and Roman sites.
Daily 9-dusk.

ANTEQUERA

MUNICIPAL MUSEUM
Palacio de Nájera, Plaza Guerrero Muñoz, Antequera, Malaga
Local ethnography and history. Archaeology, mainly Roman.
Daily 10-1, 5-8.

ARACENA

MUSEUM OF FOLK ARTS AND CUSTOMS
Aracena, Huelva
Cultural history and ethnography of the Sierra Morena.
By appointment.

ARANJUEZ

CASA DE MARINOS
Rio Tajo (facing Castillo), Aranjuez, Madrid
House in which the 18th century Kings of Spain prepared themselves for their journeys by sea. Royal gigs.
Daily May-Sept. 10-1, 3-30-7. Oct.-Apr. 10-1, 3-5.30. Closed all day Jan. 1, Good F., July 18, Dec. 25. Closed p.m. May 30, Sept. 4, 5.

REAL CASA DEL LABRADOR
Calle de la Reina, Jardin del Principe, Aranjuez, Madrid
Royal Palace (1803). Decorative and applied arts. Paintings. Furniture.
Daily May-Sept. 10-1, 3.30-7. Oct.-Apr. 10-1, 3-5.30. Closed all day Jan. 1, Good F., July 18, Dec. 25. Closed p.m. May 30, Sept. 4, 5.

ROYAL PALACE
Jardin de la Isla, Aranjuez, Madrid
Paintings, including works by Luca Giordano and Raphael Mengs. Sumptuary art.
Daily May-Sept. 10-1, 3.30-7. Oct.-Apr. 10-1, 3-5.30. Closed all day Jan. 1, Good F., July 18, Dec. 25. Closed p.m. May 30, Sept. 4, 5.

ARCOS DE LA FRONTERA

PARISH MUSEUM AND TREASURY
Plaza de España, Arcos de la Frontera, Cadiz
In 16th century church. Religious art. Murals. Sculpture. Goldsmiths' work. Vestments. Choir-books.
Su., public holidays, 1-3, 4-6. M.-Sa. by appointment.

ARENAS DE SAN PEDRO

MUSEUM OF THE ROYAL CHAPEL
Convent of San Pedro de Alcántara, Arenas de San Pedro, Avila
Religious art. Tomb of San Pedro de Alcántara.
Daily 10-12.30, 3.30-8.

ARENYS DE MAR

FIDEL FITA MUNICIPAL MUSEUM
Plaza de la Villa 2, Arenys de Mar, Barcelona
Local archaeology. Folk-art. Navigation.
Daily 11-1. May-Sept. 6-9. Oct.-Apr. 5-8.

AROCHE

MUSEUM OF THE HOLY ROSARY
Calle Alférez Lobo 7, Aroche, Huelva
Religious art and history.
By appointment.

MUNICIPAL MUSEUM
Ayuntamiento (archaeology) **and Grupo Escolar Municipal** (natural sciences), **Aroche, Huelva**
Prehistory. Roman and Arab archaeology. Mineralogy. Fauna.
By appointment.

ARTA

REGIONAL MUSEUM
Calle Rafael Blanes 8, Arta, Mallorca, Balearic Islands
Natural history. Ethnography. Prehistory and archaeology. The megalothic village, Talayot de Ses Pahisses, is under the custodianship of the Museum.
By appointment.

ASTORGA

DIOCESAN AND CATHEDRAL MUSEUM
Cathedral, Avenida del Dr. Mérida, Astorga, León
Paintings. Carvings. Gold. Ceramics. These include 11th-13th century statues of the Virgin. Wooden chest from Carrizo, with all the Apostles painted on the front, and a 10th century chest.
Daily 9-1, 4-7.

MUSEUM OF JOURNEYS (DE LOS CAMINOS)
Calle Santa Maria, Astorga, León
Art and history of pilgrimages to Santiago de Compostella. Roman and medieval archaeology. Regional ethnography.
Daily May-Sept. 10-2, 4-8. Oct.-Apr. 11-2, 3-6.

AVILA

BIRTHPLACE OF ST. TERESA DE JESUS
Carmelite Convent, Plaza de la Santa 4, Avila
House in which St. Teresa was born (1515). The museum, documenting and illustrating her life, is in what was her bedroom.
Daily 9.30-1.30, 3-8.

CATHEDRAL MUSEUM
Cathedral, Avila
Religious paintings. Vestments. 15th century choir books.
Daily 10-1.30. May-Sept. 3-6.30. Oct.-Apr. 3-5.30.

MUSEUM OF ORIENTAL ART
Dominican Convent, Bajada de Santo Tomás, Avila
Decorative art from the Philippines, China, Japan and Vietnam.
Daily 9.30-12.30, 3.30-8.30.

PROVINCIAL MUSEUM
Casa de los Deanes, Plaza Nalvillos 5, Avila
Archaeology. Paintings. Ceramics. Folk art. Handicrafts.
Daily 10.30-1.30, 3.30-8.

VIRGEN DE LA PORTERÍA MUSEUM
Convent of San Antonio, Paseo de San Antonio 5, Avila
Religious art. Sculpture. Embroidery. Reliquaries.
Daily 10.30-12.30. May-Sept. 4-7.30. Oct.-Apr. 4-6.

AVILES

MUSEUM OF THE NATURAL SCIENCES
Calle Dr. Graiño 25, Aviles, Oviedo
Fauna, mainly regional. Mineralogy.
By appointment.

AYLLON

MUNICIPAL MUSEUM
Edificio del Ayuntamiento, Calle Mayor 29, Ayllon, Segovia
Contemporary painting and sculpture.
Daily 11-1, 5-7.

AZPEITIA

GÁRATE HOUSE-MUSEUM
Caserio de 'Errecarte', Azpeitia, Guipuzcoa
Birthplace of Francisco Gárate (d.1929). Collections illustrating his life and work.
Daily 10-12.30, 3.30-8.

BADAJOZ

ARCHAEOLOGICAL MUSEUM
La Galera, Plazotela de Reloj, Badajoz
Prehistory. Roman, Visigoth, Arab and Moorish archaeology.
May-Sept. Daily 10-1, 4-7, Ex. Su. afternoon, public holidays and M. morning.

DIOCESAN AND CATHEDRAL MUSEUM
Cathedral, Badajoz
Religious art. Paintings. Sculpture. Goldsmiths' work.
Daily 11-1.

PROVINCIAL MUSEUM OF FINE ART
Palacio de la Diputación, Calle Felipe Checa, Badajoz
19th-20th century paintings and sculptures by local artists.
Daily 10-2.

BADALONA

MUNICIPAL MUSEUM
Plaza del Obispo Irurita, Badalona, Barcelona
Roman archaeology. Local history. Folk art. Observatory.
M.-Sa. 4-9. Public holidays, 10-2, 5-9.

BALSARENY

COLLECTION OF PAINTING AND HISTORY
Castillo, Balsareny, Barcelona
Paintings. Furniture. Manuscripts. Books and documents.
Daily 10-7.

BAÑOLAS

DARDER MUNICIPAL MUSEUM
Plaza Estudios, Bañolas, Gerona
Palaeontology. Mineralogy. Zoology. Anthropology.
Daily 11-1, 4-8.

DISTRICT ARCHAEOLOGICAL MUSEUM
Pia Almoina, Plaza de la Fuente 10, Bañolas, Gerona
Prehistory. Ibero-Roman and medieval archaeology. Coins. 14th-18th century ceramics.
Public holidays 11-1.30. Other days by appointment.

BARBASTRO

DIOCESAN AND CATHEDRAL MUSEUM
Cathedral, Barbastro, Huesca
Religious art.
Daily 10-4.

BARCELONA

AMATLLER INSTITUTE OF SPANISH ART
Paseo de Gracia 41, Barcelona
Medieval paintings. Italian and Spanish glass of the 16th-18th centuries.
Daily 10-1, 4-7. Closed Aug.

ARCHAEOLOGICAL MUSEUM
Parque de Montjuich, Calle de Lérida, Barcelona
Exhibits dating from prehistoric times to the 8th century. Archaeological discoveries from Ampurias and the Balearic Islands. Roman mosaics.
Daily 10-4. Holidays 10-1.

BOTANICAL INSTITUTE
Avenida de Montañans, Barcelona
Botanical collections.
Daily 9-2.

CAMBÓ COLLECTION AND MUSEUM OF DECORATIVE ART
Palacio de la Virreina, Rambla de las Flores 99, Barcelona
House of 1772-8. Paintings, bequeathed to City of Barcelona by Francisco Cambó, of the Italian, Spanish, Flemish, Dutch and French Schools. Furniture, tapestries, ceramics, glass, textiles, enamels, ivories. Gold and silversmith's work.
Daily 10-4, 6-9.

CATHEDRAL MUSEUM
Calle Obispo Irurita, Barcelona
Religious art. Paintings. Vestments. Goldsmiths' work. Paintings and retables of the Catalan Gothic School, including the 'Piedad del Arcediano Desplá' by Bartolomé Bermejo.
Daily 10-1. Closed on 1st and 15th of each month.

CLARÁ MUSEUM
Calle Dr. Carulla 22, Barcelona
Studio of Jose Clará (1878-1958), with his collection of sculpture.
Daily 10-2.

COIN CABINET OF CATALONIA
Palacio del Museo de Arte Moderno, Parque de la Ciudadela, Barcelona
Coins and medals.
Daily 10-2.

DIOCESAN MUSEUM
Seminario Conciliar, Calle Disputación 231, Barcelona
Religious art. Painting. Sculpture. Goldsmiths' work.
By appointment.

FEDERICO MARES MUSEUM
Calle Condes de Barcelona 8, Barcelona
Sculpture ranging from the Greek to the Roman and paleo-Christian periods, and from 12th-18th centuries. Medieval religious statuary. Decorative and sumptuary arts. Costumes.
M.-Sa. 9-1.45, 4-7. Holidays 11-4.

GAUDI HOUSE MUSEUM
Parque Güell, Barcelona
Furniture designed by Gaudi. His studio. Material illustrating his work and that of his close collaborators.
M.-Sa. by appointment. Su. 11-2, 5-7.

GEOLOGICAL MUSEUM OF THE SEMINARY
Seminario Conciliar, Calle Diputación 231, Barcelona
Geology. Fossils, mainly tertiary.
By appointment.

MANUEL ROCAMORA MUSEUM OF COSTUMES
Palacio Marqués de Lió, Calle Montecada 12, Barcelona
Costumes of the 16th-20th centuries.
Daily 10-2. Closed Jan. 1, Mar. 19, May 1, June 24, July 18, Nov. 1, Dec. 8, 25, 26, Easter M., Whit. M.

MARITIME MUSEUM
Puerta de la Paz 1, Barcelona
Naval history and archaeology. Maps. Ships' models. Folk art. Fishing. Coins. Pottery bearing maritime designs. Reproduction of the ship 'Santa Maria'.
Daily ex. M. and Su. p.m. 10-2, 4-6. 'Santa Maria', 9-dusk.

MIGUEL SOLDEIRA MUSEUM
Escuela Massana, Calle Hospital 156, Barcelona
Works by the enameller, Soldeira, who was Director of the Escuela Massana.
Daily 10-1, 4-8.

MILITARY MUSEUM OF THE CASTLE OF MONTJUICH
Castillo de Montjuich, Barcelona
Armour. Weapons. Military history.
May-Sept. Daily 10-2, 4-8. Oct.-Apr. Daily 10-2, 4-7.

MONASTERY OF SANTA MARIA DE PEDRALBES
Plaza del Monasterio, Barcelona
Monastery of 14th century. Religious art, including murals of 1346. Paintings. Sculpture. Ceramics.
Su. 12-2.

MUNICIPAL INSTITUTE OF NATURAL SCIENCE
Parque de la Ciudadela, Barcelona
Collections of stuffed animals. Flora and fauna of the region.
Daily 10-1.

MUNICIPAL MUSEUM OF MUSIC
Calle Bruch 110, Barcelona
Musical instruments. Orchestral and popular instruments, Spanish and foreign. Scores and mementoes of great musicians.
Daily ex. Su. and public holidays, 10-2.

MUSEUM OF BULL-FIGHTING
Plaza de Toros Monumental, Barcelona
Photographs. Documents. Bullfighters' costumes, 1726-present day. Posters. Bulls' heads. Cattle-brands.
Daily 10-1, 4-7. Closed p.m. on days when bull-fighting takes place.

MUSEUM OF CATALONIAN ART
Palacio Nacional, Parque de Montjuich, Barcelona
Roman and Gothic murals. Spanish paintings of the 16th-18th centuries, including works by El Greco, Velásquez, Zurbarán and Ribera. Sculpture. Enamels.
Daily 10-2.

MUSEUM OF CERAMICS
Palacio Nacional, Parque de Montjuich, Barcelona
Spanish ceramics from the Middle Ages onwards.
Daily 10-2.

MUSEUM OF CRIME
Facultad de Derecho, Avenida Generalismo Franco, Barcelona
History of crime and criminology.
By appointment.

MUSEUM OF DECORATIVE ARTS
Palacio de la Virreina, Rambla de las Flores 99, Barcelona
Sumptuary and decorative art. Furniture of 18th-20th centuries. Bargueños of the 15th-18th centuries. Clocks, watches, enamels and glass of the 16th-19th centuries. Fans of the 18th-20th centuries.
Daily 10-2, 6-9, ex. Su. p.m.

MUSEUM OF ETHNOLOGY
Parque de Montjuich, Barcelona
Ethnography and Folk Arts of Spain, Africa, America, Asia and the Pacific. Indian and Japanese religious art. Graphic Arts.
Daily 10-1, 4-7. Holidays 10-2.

MUSEUM OF GEOLOGY (MARTORELL MUSEUM)
Parque de la Ciudadela, Barcelona
Petrology. Mineralogy. Palaeontology. Stratigraphy.
Daily ex. M. 10-2.

MUSEUM OF THE HISTORY OF THE CITY OF BARCELONA
Plaza del Rey, Barcelona
Local history (institutions, customs, famous characters, stages of urban growth). Documents. Paintings. Sculpture. Ceramics.
M.-Sa. 9-2, 5-8. Public holidays 11-12. Closed Su.

MUSEUM OF INDUSTRY AND POPULAR ARTS
Pueblo de Montjuich, Barcelona
Christmas cribs. Engravings. Arts and crafts. Folklore.
Daily 9-8.

MUSEUM OF THE INSTITUTE OF THEATRE
Conde del Asalto 3, Barcelona
Exhibits showing the evolution of the theatre, its scenery, fashions, costumes, posters, personal mementoes.
Daily ex. M. and p.m. public holidays, 11-2, 5-7.

MUSEUM OF MODERN ART
Parque de la Ciudadela, Barcelona
Painting and sculpture of the 19th and 20th centuries. Paintings by Fortuny, Rusiñol, Casas, Nonell, Regoyos, Zuloaga, Sunyer, Sotomayor and Solana. "Harlequin" and other paintings by Picasso. Sculptures by Llemona, Gargallo, Hugué, Clara, Casanovas and Rebull.
Daily 10-2.

MUSEUM OF ZOOLOGY
Parque de la Ciudadela, Barcelona
Fauna, especially of Europe and Africa. Shells of land and sea creatures. Insects of the Mediterranean region.
Daily ex. M. 10-2.

PALACIO DE PEDRALBES
Avenida Generalismo Franco, Barcelona
Former royal palace, given to the City by Alfonso XIII in 1925. Paintings. Furniture. Decorative arts.
M.-Sa. 10-1, 3.30-5.30. Public holidays 10-2.

PICASSO MUSEUM
Calle Montcada 15, Barcelona
House mainly 15th century. Paintings, drawings, engravings and ceramics by Pablo Ruiz Picasso.
Daily 10-2.

POSTAL MUSEUM
Palacio de la Virreina, Rambla de las Flores 99, Barcelona
History of the postal service in Spain. Collection of the world's stamps, 1840-1940.
Daily 10-2, 6-9.

TECHNICAL MUSEUM
Escuela de Ingenieros Industriales, Avenida Generalismo Franco 999, Barcelona
Industrial machinery and equipment.
By appointment.

TEXTILE MUSEUM
Calle Hospital 56, Barcelona
Textiles. Textile manufacturing techniques, equipment.
Daily 10-1.

VERDAGUER MUSEUM
Villa Joana, Vallvidrera, Barcelona
Collections illustrating life and work of the poet, Jacinto Verdaguer.
Su. and public holidays, 10-2.

BARCO DE AVILA

PAROCHIAL MUSEUM
Church of Our Lady of the Assumption, Plaza de la Igleria, Barco de Avila, Avila
Religious art. Paintings. Sculpture. 15th century goldsmiths' work.
By appointment.

BEJAR

MUNICIPAL MUSEUM
Palacio Ducal, Plaza Mayor 29, Bejar, Salamanca
Spanish, Flemish and Dutch painting. Sculpture. Handicrafts. Far East ethnography, folk-art.
Th., Sa. p.m. Oct.-Apr. 6-9. May-Sept. 7-10; Su. 9-2.

BELMONTE

PAROCHIAL MUSEUM
Colegiata Parroquia de San Bartolomé, Belmonte, Cuenca
Religious art. Sculpture. Painting. Goldsmiths' work. Vestments.
By appointment.

BENALMADENA

MUNICIPAL ARCHAEOLOGICAL MUSEUM
Avenida de Juan Luis Peralta, Benalmadena, Málaga
Local and Mexican archaeology.
Daily 10-1, 4-8.

BERGA

MUNICIPAL MUSEUM
Calle Angeles 7, Berga, Barcelona
Local archaeology and history.
Daily 10-2.

BESALU

MUNICIPAL ARCHAEOLOGICAL COLLECTION
Plaza de San Pedro 11, Besalu, Gerona
Local archaeology. Paintings.
By appointment.

BILBAO

MUSEUM OF FINE ART
Parque de Da. Casilda Iturriza 3, Bilbao, Vizcaya
Paintings of the 13th-19th centuries, including works by Tiepolo, El Greco, Ribalta, Ribera, Velásquez and Goya. Sculpture. Ceramics.
Daily ex. M. a.m., May-Sept. 10:30-1.30, 4-7. Oct.-Apr. 10.30-1.30, 3.30-6.

MUSEUM OF MODERN ART
Parque de Da. Casilda Iturriza 3, Bilbao, Vizcaya
Paintings of the 19th-20th centuries.
Daily ex. M. a.m. May-Sept. 10.30-1.30, 4-7. Oct.-Apr. 10.30-1.30, 3.30-6.

MUSEUM OF REPRODUCTIONS OF WORKS OF ART
Calle Conde de Mirasol 2, Bilbao, Vizcaya
Casts of sculpture and architectural features.
Daily ex. Su. and p.m. public holidays, 9-1, 4-7.

VIZCAYA HISTORICAL MUSEUM
Calle Cruz 4, Bilbao, Vizcaya
Archaeology. Ethnography. Local history.
Daily 9.30-1.30, 3.30-6.

BOCAIRENTE

PAROCHIAL MUSEUM
Calle Abadía, Bocairente, Valencia
Paintings. Sculpture. Vestments. Church plate (gold).
By appointment.

BUEU

MASSÓ NAVAL MUSEUM
Industrias Massó, S.A., Bueu, Pontevedra
Early books and other material relating to seafaring and navigation.
By appointment.

BURGO DE OSMA

CATHEDRAL MUSEUM
Plaza de la Catedral, Burgo de Osma, Soria
Illuminated books. Church plate (gold). Painting. Sculpture.
Daily May-Sept. 9-1.30, 4-8. Oct.-Apr. 10-1.30, 3.30-7.

BURGOS

DIOCESAN AND CATHEDRAL MUSEUM
Cathedral, Burgos
Tapestries. Vestments. Goldsmiths' work. Paintings.
Daily 8-1, 3-8.

ISLA PALACE
Paseo de la Isla, Burgos
House and headquarters of General Franco, 1936-39. Exhibitions showing how the General planned and carried out Civil War campaigns.
By appointment.

MARCELIANO SANTA MARIA MUSEUM
Claustro Antiquo Monasterio de San Juan, Burgos
Material relating to the life and work of the painter, Marceliano Santa Maria. Paintings and sculpture of the 16th and 17th centuries. Furniture.
May-Sept. Daily 10-2, 5-8. Oct.-Apr. Daily 10-2.

PROVINCIAL ARCHAEOLOGICAL MUSEUM
Casa Miranda, Calles Calera 25, Burgos
Prehistory. Archaeology. 15th-19th century painting. Sculpture. Enamels. Medieval ivories. Coins and medals. 10th century Arabic ivory case from the workshop of Medina Azahara.
Daily 10-1, 5-7. Closed public holidays and evenings before public holidays.

ROYAL CONVENT OF LAS HUELGAS
Prolongación de la Castellona, Burgos
Pantheon of the Kings of Castilla and Leon. Collections of medieval dresses, fabrics and jewellery taken from the royal tombs. Banner, the Pendón de las Navas, captured from the Moors at the Battle of Las Navas de Tolosa (1212).
Daily 11-2, 4-6.

SEMINARY MUSEUM
Calle Fernàn González, Burgos
Natural sciences.
9-1, 4-7, by appointment.

BURRIANA

MUNICIPAL HISTORICAL MUSEUM
Ayuntamiento, Burriana, Castellon de la Plana
Local archaeology and ethnography.
M.-Sa. 2-4, 8-10.

CÁCERES

CASA DEL MONO
Cáceres
15th century house. Religious art.
May-Oct., Daily 10-1, 4-6. Nov.-Apr., daily 10-1, 5-7. Closed public holidays.

PROVINCIAL MUSEUM
Plaza Veletas 1, Cáceres
Provincial prehistory and archaeology. Coins. Ethnography.
May-Sept. Daily 10-1, 5-7. Oct.-Apr. 10-1, 4-6. Closed p.m. public holidays.

CADIZ

ARCHAEOLOGICAL MUSEUM
Plaza Generalismo Franco, Cadiz
Archaeology. Jewellery. 18th century carving. Punic money. South American ethnography.
M.-Sa. 10.30-1.30, 3.30-5.30; Su. 11-1 Closed public holidays.

CATHEDRAL MUSEUM
Plaza de Pio XII, Cadiz
Religious art. Paintings. Sculpture. Goldsmiths' work. Ornaments.
May-Sept. Daily 9-1, 4-7. Oct.-Apr. Daily 9-1, 4-6.

MUNICIPAL HISTORICAL MUSEUM
Calle Santa Inés, Cadiz
Art and local history.
May-Sept. Daily 9.30-1.30, 5-9. Oct.-Apr. Daily 9.30-1.30, 3-6. Su. and public holidays 9-2.

PROVINCIAL MUSEUM OF FINE ART
Plaza de Mina, Cadiz
Paintings of the 15th-20th centuries, including works by Murillo, Bernadino Luini, Rubens, Alonso Cono, Zurbarán. Sculpture. Tapestries. Archaeology, including material from the Phoenician necropolis of Cadiz.
M.-Sa. 10.30-1.30, 3.30-5.30; Su. 11-1. Closed public holidays.

CALAHORRA

CATHEDRAL AND DIOCESAN MUSEUM AND TREASURY
Calahorra, Logroño
Religious art from the Cathedral and churches in the diocese. Material from excavations of Roman sites. 12th century illuminated manuscripts.
By appointment.

GUTIERREZ ACHUTEGUI COLLECTION
Biblioteca Pública Municipal, Calahorra, Logroño
Local archaeology.
Daily ex. public holidays, May-Sept. 12-1, 7-9. Oct.-Apr. 12-1, 6.30-8.30.

CALATAYUD

BILBILITANO MUSEUM
Casa de la Cultura, Calatayud, Zaragoza
Local history and archaeology.
By appointment.

CALDAS DE MONTBUY

ARCHAEOLOGICAL MUSEUM
Calle José Antonio 98, Caldas de Montbuy, Barcelona
Local history and archaeology. Roman baths.
Su., public holidays, 11-2. Roman baths: daily, sunrise to sunset.

MOSÉN DALGER MUSEUM
Calle Joaquin Dalger, Caldas de Montbuy, Barcelona
Collection of paintings, sculpture, applied arts, formerly in the possession of Mosén Dalger.
Su. and public holidays, 11-2.

CANDUELA

VALLES DE CAMPOO ETHNOGRAPHICAL MUSEUM
La Torrona, Canduela, Oviedo
18th century manor house. The outbuildings have been restored and now exhibit agricultural implements, carts and wagons and rural handicrafts.
By appointment.

CAPDEPERA

TORRE DE CANYAMEL
Capdepera, Mallorca, Balearic Islands
In 14th century house. Ethnography of Mallorca.
Daily 3-6 and by appointment.

CAPELLADES

AMADOR ROMANI ARCHAEOLOGICAL MUSEUM
Moli de la Vila, Calle Immaculade Concepción, Capellades, Barcelona
Material from excavations at Abrigo Romani. Local prehistory and geology.
Su., public holidays 12-2.

PAPERMILL MUSEUM
Moli de la Vila, Calle Immaculada Concepción, Capellades, Barcelona
In mid-19th century papermill. History of hand-made paper. Equipment and tools. Techniques of paper-making.
Su. and public holidays, 12-2.

CARDEDEU

BALVEY MUSEUM AND ARCHIVES
Plaza San Juan 1, Cardedeu, Barcelona
Archaeology. Former Balvey pharmacy. Popular art. Costumes. Manuscripts concerning local history of the 11th-19th centuries.
By appointment.

CARMONA

MUSEUM OF THE ROMAN NECROPOLIS
Calle Jorge Bonsor, Carmona, Sevilla
Site museum. Material from the Roman cemetery.
Daily 10-6.

CARTAGENA

MUNICIPAL MUSEUM OF ARCHAEOLOGY
Calle Baños del Carmen, Cartagena, Murcia
Iberian and classical archaeology. Architecture. Sculpture. Mining. Underwater archaeology. 19th century handicrafts.
Daily ex. M. and p.m. public holidays, 10-1, 4-6.

CASTELLO DE AMPURIAS

PAROCHIAL MUSEUM
Plaza Jacinto Verdaguer, Castello de Ampurias, Gerona
Religious art.
May-Sept. Daily. Oct.-Apr. by appointment.

CASTELLON

PROVINCIAL MUSEUM OF FINE ART
Diputación, Plaza de las Aulas, Castellon, Castellon de la Plana
Paintings. Archaeology. Textiles. 15th century coats of arms.
Daily 9-2.

CAZORLA

MUSEUM OF FOLK ART AND CUSTOMS
Cazorla, Jaen
History and ethnology of the Upper Guadalquivir region.
Oct.-Apr., daily 10-2, 3-6. Mar.-Sept., daily 10-1, 5-8.

CELANOVA

PAROCHIAL MUSEUM
Antiguo Monasterio de San Salvador, Celanova, Orense
Religious art.
By appointment.

CERVERA

DURAN Y SANPERE DISTRICT MUSEUM
Centro Comarcal de Cultura, Calle Mayor 15, Cervera, Lerida
Local history and art.
Daily ex. M. 12-2, 6-8.

EDUARDO CAMPS CAVA MUNICIPAL MUSEUM
Calle Eduardo Camps 1, Cervera, Lerida
Local history and archaeology.
Public holidays 12-1.

MUSEUM DEL BLAT Y DE LA PAGESIA
Antigua Universidad, Calle Vidal de Montpalan 45, Cervera, Lerida
Rural life. Agriculture. Ethnography.
Daily ex. Su. 10-1, 3-7.

CHILLON

PAROCHIAL MUSEUM
Plaza del Caudillo, Chillon, Ciudad Real
Religious sculpture and gold plate. Paintings. Murals.
By appointment.

CHIPIONA

MUSEO MISIONAL DE NUESTRA SEÑORA DE REGLA
Colegio de Misioneros Franciscanos, Chipiona, Cadiz
Early Roman Christian relics. Egyptian, North African art, archaeology. Coins.
On request.

CIUDADELA

DIOCESAN ARCHAEOLOGICAL MUSEUM
Calle Obispo Villa 9, Ciudadela, Minorca, Balearic Islands
Local archaeology and religious art.
By appointment.

CIUDAD REAL

ARCHAEOLOGICAL COLLECTION
Casa de la Cultura, Calle Prado 7, Ciudad Real
Local archaeology.
Daily 10-1.30, 4-8.

CATHEDRAL MUSEUM
Calle del Prado, Ciudad Real
Vestments. Material relating to the Second Vatican Council.
Daily 11-1.30, 5-9.

COLLECTIONS OF ART AND NATURAL SCIENCES
Palacio de la Diputación, Ciudad Real
Paintings and sculpture by local artists. Coleopteri.
Daily 10-8.

CLUNIA

MUSEUM OF THE EXCAVATIONS
Peñalba de Castro, Clunia, Burgos
Material from the site of the Roman colony of Clunia Sulpicia.
Dawn-dusk.

COLMENAR DE OREJA

CHECA MUNICIPAL MUSEUM
Calle Costanilla de los Silleros 1, Colmenar de Oreja, Madrid
Works by the local painter, Ulpiano Checa.
Daily 10-1, 3-5.

COLMENAR VIEJO

PAROCHIAL MUSEUM
Parroquia de la Asunción, Calle del Cura, Colmenar Viejo, Madrid
Religious art. Goldsmiths' work. Service books. Vestments.
By appointment.

CONSUEGRA

MUNICIPAL MUSEUM
Consuegra, Toledo
Local archaeology.
Su. 12-2.

CORDOBA

ALCAZAR OF THE CHRISTIAN KINGS
Campo Santo de los Mártires, Cordoba
In 15th century mansion, for more than 300 years the headquarters of the Inquisition in Cordoba. Roman archaeology.
May-Sept. Daily 9.30-1.30, 5-8. Oct.-Apr. Daily 9.30-1.30, 4-7.

CATHEDRAL MUSEUM AND TREASURY
Cathedral, Cordoba
Paintings. Sculpture. Tapestries. Vestments. Goldsmiths' work. Illuminated books.
Daily 10-1.30. May-Aug. 4.30-8.30. Nov.-Feb. 3.30-6. Remaining months 3.30-7.

CITY HISTORICAL MUSEUM
Torre de la Calaberra, Cordoba
In former Moorish fortress. Local history.
Daily 9.30-1.30, 5-8.

JULIO ROMERO DE TORRES MUSEUM
Plaza del Potro 2, Cordoba
Life and work of the Cordoban painter, Julio Romero de Torres.
Nov.-Feb. Daily 10-1, 3-5. Apr.-Sept. Daily 10-1, 4-7. Mar. and Oct. Daily 10-1, 3-6. Public holidays 10-2.

MEZQUITA COLLECTION
Calle de Velázquez Bosco, Cordoba
Architectural details of Mezquita Cathedral not used in the restoration of the Cathedral.
By appointment.

MUNICIPAL MUSEUM OF ART AND BULLFIGHTING
Plaza Marmónides 5, Cordoba
Local handicrafts. Silversmiths' work. Leatherwork. Old weights and measures. History of bullfighting in Cordoba, with mementoes of local matadors and collections of trophies, suits, posters and programmes.
May-Sept. Daily 9.30-1.30, 5-8. Oct.-Apr. Daily 9.30-1.30, 4-7.

MUSEUM OF THE EXCAVATIONS OF MEDINA AZ-ZAHARA
nr. Cordoba
Architectural and other material discovered on the site of the palace (936) of Abd al-Rahman. Pottery, wrought iron and jewellery.
Daily 9.30-1.30. May 15-Sept. 15, 3.30-7. Sept. 16-May 15, 3-5.30.

PALACE OF THE MARQUISES OF VIANA
Reja de Don Gome 2, Cordoba
Paintings. Furniture. Tapestries. Spanish and embossed leather.
By appointment.

PROVINCIAL ARCHAEOLOGICAL MUSEUM
Plaza Jerónimo Páez, Cordoba
Local prehistory and archaeology. Art of the Iberian, Roman, Visigoth, Moslem, Medieval and Renaissance periods.
Daily ex. Su., public holidays, July and Aug. p.m. May-Sept. 10-1.30, 5-7. Oct.-Apr. 10-1.30, 4-6.

PROVINCIAL MUSEUM OF FINE ART
Plaza del Potro 2, Cordoba
Religious art, mainly from local monasteries. Paintings, including works by Valdés Leal, Zurburán, Morales, Ribera, Murillo and Goya, and by Antonio del Castillo y Soavedra (d. 1668), a native of Cordoba. Sculpture, with one room devoted to works of the Cordoban, Mateo Inurria. Drawings. Engravings.
Nov.-Feb. Daily 10-1, 3-5. Apr.-Sept. Daily 10-1, 4-7. Mar. and Oct. Daily 10-1, 3-6. Public holidays, 10-2.

LA CORUÑA

CLOCK MUSEUM
Palacio Municipal, Plaza de Maria Pita 1, La Coruña
English, French, German, Dutch and Spanish clocks.
Daily 8-10 p.m.

HISTORICAL AND ARCHAEOLOGICAL MUSEUM
Castillo de San Antón, La Coruña
Archaeology and history of the City. Heraldry. Celtic treasure from Elvina. Material recalling Drake's siege of La Coruña.
Daily ex. M. May-Sept. 10-1, 4-6. Oct.-Apr. 9-2.

PROVINCIAL MUSEUM OF FINE ART
Plaza Pintor Sotomayor, La Coruña
Paintings. Sculpture. Drawings. Engravings. Musical scores. Ceramics. Coins.
May-Sept. Daily 10-2, 4-6. Oct.-Apr. Daily 10-2.

COVADONGA

MUSEUM AND TREASURY OF THE SANTINA
Calle Santuario, Covadonga, Oviedo
Church plate (gold) and vestments.
Oct.-Apr. by appointment. May-Sept. Daily 9-8.

COVARRUBIAS

PAROCHIAL MUSEUM
Calle Chindasvinto 10, Covarrubias, Burgos
Contains material from Arlanza monastery and from other ruined churches in the area. Painting and sculpture of the 14th-16th centuries. Goldsmiths' work. 15th-18th century vestments. Tombs of the early Counts of Castille and Infantas of Covarrubias.
May-Sept. Daily 10-1, 3-8. Oct.-Apr. Daily 10-1, 3-6.

CREVILLENTE

MUNICIPAL MUSEUM
'Mariano Benlliure', Calle de San Cayetano, Crevillente, Alicante
In annexe to Church of Our Lady of Belén. Benlliure collection of works of art and of sketches and models of sculptures.
By appointment with the Guardia Municipal.

CUENCA

CASA COLGADAS
Cuenca
Spanish abstract painting and sculpture.
M.-F. ex. Tu. 11-6; Sa. 4-12. Closed Oct.-Mar.

DIOCESAN AND CATHEDRAL MUSEUM
Palacio Episcopal, Cuenca
Paintings. Sculpture. Vestments.
Daily 10.30-1, 5-7.

PROVINCIAL MUSEUM
Calle Pósito 2, Cuenca
Iberian and Roman archaeology, especially statuary from Segóbriga and Valeria.
Daily ex. M. 10-2, 4-7.

DAROCA

MUSEUM OF THE HOLY MYSTERY
Colegiata de Santa Maria, Plaza de España, Daroca, Zaragoza
Painting. Sculpture. Church plate (gold). Vestments.
Daily ex. public holidays, 10-12, 4-6.

DENIA

MUNICIPAL ARCHAEOLOGICAL MUSEUM
Calle Castillo, Denia, Alicante
Local archaeology.
Daily 10-12, 4-7. Closed Su. afternoon.

DEYA

ARCHAEOLOGICAL MUSEUM
Calle Torrente, Deya, Mallorca, Balearic Islands
Local archaeology.
Daily 10-1, 5-7.

SON MARROIG
Deya, Mallorca, Balearic Islands
Furniture. Ceramics.
Daily May-Sept. 9-5. Oct.-Apr. 9-7.

ECIJA

PAROCHIAL MUSEUM
Plaza de Santa Maria, Ecija, Sevilla
Roman and Arab archaeology.
Daily 9-1, 4-8.

ELCHE

MUNICIPAL MUSEUM
Parque Municipal, Elche, Alicante
Local prehistory and archaeology.
Daily 9-1, 4-7. Closed M.

LA ESCALA

MUSEO MONOGRAFICO DE AMPURIAS
La Escala, Gerona
Collection of excavations of the Greco-Roman city.
Daily 9-dusk.

EL ESCORIAL

MONASTERY OF SAN LORENZO DE EL ESCORIAL
El Escorial
Contains many works by international artists of the 16th century and 18th century from Royal residences.
Apr. 1-Oct. 15, daily 10-1, 3-7. Oct. 16-Mar. 31, daily 10-1, 3-6. Closed Jan., Good F., July 18, Dec. 15, Feb. 28 (p.m.), Aug. 10 (p.m.).

EL PARDO

HOUSE OF THE PRINCE
(Casa del Principe), El Pardo, Madrid
18th century furnishings. Lamps.
Daily 10.30-1.30, 3.30-6. Closed Jan. 1, Good F., July 18, Dec. 25.

EL TOBOSO

HOUSE OF DULCINEA
El Toboso, Toledo
Copies of *Don Quixote* in various languages. Material illustrating life in Spain at the time of Cervantes.
By appointment.

EPILA

COLLECTION OF THE HOUSE OF ALBA
Palacio de los Condes de Aranda, Epila, Zaragoza
Royal costumes for the Feast of the Magi, worn by Alfonso XII and XIII.
By appointment.

ESPLUGA DE FRANCOLI

TOWN MUSEUM
Espluga de Francoli, Tarragona
Local history and archaeology. Arts and crafts.
By appointment.

ESTELLA

GUSTAVO DE MAEZTU MUSEUM
Palacio de los Reyes de Navarra, San Nicolas 2, Estella, Navarra
Late 12th century building. Material relating to the life and work of the artist, Gustavo de Maeztu (d.1947).
May-Sept. Daily 4-7. Public holidays Daily 11-1, 4.30-7.30. Oct.-Apr. Daily 4-6. Public holidays 11-1.

FALSET

MUSEUM AND ARCHIVES OF FALSET AND DISTRICT
Calle Calvo Sotelo 1, Falset, Tarragona
Local history and archaeology. Geology and mineralogy. Botany. Fine art. Local crafts and industries, especially the production of wine.
Daily ex. M. May-Sept. 12-1, 8-10. Oct.-Apr. 7-9.

FIGUERAS

MUSEUM OF THE AMPURDÁN
Rambla 2, Figueras, Gerona
Regional art and history. Paintings and watercolours. Las Sardanas Room. Monturiol Room. Models of the Ampurdán as it used to be.
Daily 7-9 p.m.

FUENDETODOS

BIRTHPLACE OF GOYA
Plaza Goya-Zuloaga, Fuendetodos, Zaragoza
Personal possessions and memorabilia of Goya.
By appointment.

GANDESA

MUSEUM OF THE ARCHPRIESTS
Plaza de la Iglesia, Gandesa, Tarragona
Church plate (gold). Coins. Archaeology.
By appointment.

GANDIA

MUNICIPAL MUSEUM OF PREHISTORY
Plaza del Rey D. Jaime, Gandia, Valencia
Local prehistory.
By appointment.

PALACIO DUCAL
Plaza San Francisco de Borja, Gandia, Valencia
Birthplace of San Francisco de Borja (d.1572), Duke of Gandia. Furniture. Paintings.
Daily 9-12.30, 4-7.30.

GASCUEÑA

PAROCHIEL MUSEUM
Adjoining Church, Gascueña, Cuenca
Religious art.
By appointment.

GERENA

BULL-FIGHTING COLLECTION
Calle Millán Astray 19, Gerena
Posters. Mementoes. Branding irons.
By appointment.

GERONA

CATHEDRAL MUSEUM AND TREASURY
Cathedral, Gerona
Tapestries. Textiles. Gold. Painting. Sculpture. Handicrafts. Illuminated books.
May-Sept. Daily 9-1.30, 3-7. Closed Oct.-Apr. except public holidays.

DIOCESAN MUSEUM
Plaza de España 2, Gerona
Archaeological discoveries from Ampurias. Ceramics. Glass. Coins. Illuminated codices. Textiles. Goldsmiths' work. Sculpture. Paintings.
Daily 9-1, 3-5.

PAROCHIAL MUSEUM
Subida de San Felix, Gerona
Religious painting, sculpture, textiles. Goldsmiths' work.
By appointment.

PROVINCIAL ARCHAEOLOGICAL MUSEUM
San Pedro de Galligans, Subida Santa Lucia, Gerona
Provincial prehistory and archaeology. Painting. Sculpture. Architectural items from demolished and reconstructed buildings. Folk art and handicrafts. Coins.
May-Sept. Daily 10-1, 3-5. Oct.-Apr. Daily 10-1, 4-7.

TOWN HISTORICAL MUSEUM
Calle Forsa 13, Gerona
Material relating to the siege of Gerona, 1808-9.
May-Sept. Daily 10-2, 4-8. Oct.-Apr. Daily 10-1, 4-5. Closed public holidays.

GIJON

JOVELLANOS MUSEUM
Calle de Jovellanos, Gijon, Oviedo
Paintings given by G. M. de Jovellanos. Material relating to his life and work.
Daily 11.30-1.30, 5.30-9.30.

NATIONAL GUITAR MUSEUM
Antigua Instituto de Jovellanos, Plaza Generalismo 8, Gijon, Oviedo
Old and modern guitars from Spain (especially Galicia, the Asturias and Mallorca) and from other countries. Guitar workshop.
Daily May-Sept. 8.30-1, 5-9. Oct.-Apr. 9-2.

GRANADA

ART COLLECTION
Carmen Rodriguez Acosta, Torre Bermeja, Granada
Contemporary Spanish painting. Oriental art.
p.m. only, by appointment.

BASILICA OF SAN JUAN DE DIOS
Calle de San Juan de Dios, Granada
Religious painting, including works by Bocanegra and Sánchez Sararabla.
Daily 10-1, 4-7.

CASA DE LOS TIROS
Calle Paveneras 19, Granada
Local history. Decorative arts. Costumes.
Daily ex. Su. and p.m. public holidays, 10-1, 4-7.

CATHEDRAL MUSEUM
Plaza de Alonso Cano, Granada
Religious paintings and sculptures. Gold. Vestments. 16th century tapestries. Illuminated service books.
May-Sept. Daily 11-1, 3.30-7.30. Oct.-Apr. Daily 11-1, 3.30-6.30.

CHARTERHOUSE OF THE ASSUMPTION
Paseo de la Cartuja, Granada
Painting and sculpture, including works by Vicente Carducho and Fray Juan Sánchez Cotán.
May-Sept. Daily 10-1, 4-7. Oct.-Apr. Daily 10-1, 3-6.

LA ALHAMBRA
Granada
In Moorish buildings - fortress and palace - of the 9th-14th centuries. Illustrates the art and architecture of the period.
Jan., Nov., Dec. Daily 10-6. Feb.-Mar. Daily 10-6.30. Apr., Oct. Daily 9.30-7. May Daily 9-7. June-July Daily 9-8.30. Aug. Daily 9-8. Sept. Daily 9.30-7.30.

MANUEL DE FALLA HOUSE-MUSEUM
Granada
Material relating to the life and work of the composer, Manuel de Falla.
May-Sept. Daily ex. public holidays, 10-1, 5-8. Oct.-Apr. 10-1, 4-6.

MUNICIPAL COLLECTION
Ayuntamiento, Plaza del Carmen, Granada
Art. Local history.
Municipal office hours.

MUSEUM OF THE CATHOLIC KINGS
Capilla Real, Calle de Oficios, Granada
Marble tombs of the Catholic Kings, Ferdinand (d.1516), Isabella (d.1504), Philip the Handsome (d.1506), Joanna the Mad (d.1555). Sculpture. Painting, including Flemish panels by Rogier van der Weyden and Memling, among others. Ornaments. Illuminated books. Flags and ensigns.
May-Sept. Daily 10-1, 4-7. Oct.-Apr. Daily 11-1, 4-7.

MUSEUM OF SACROMONTE ABBEY
Camino del Sacromonte, Granada
Paintings. Sculpture. Religious ornaments. Goldsmiths' work. Tapestries. Arabic manuscripts.
May-Oct., daily 11-1, 4-7. Nov.-Apr., daily 10-1, 4-7.

NATIONAL MUSEUM OF SPANISH-MOSLEM ART
Casa Real de la Alhambra, Granada
In Palace of Charles V (1526 onwards), adjoining Alhambra Palace. Ceramics, items of architecture, glass and inscriptions brought from the Alhambra, including the Alhambra Vase (1320).
Daily ex. M. and public holidays p.m. Jan., Nov., Dec. 10-6. Feb., Mar. 10-6.30. Apr., Oct. 9.30-7. May 9-7. June, July 9-8.30. Aug. 9-8. Sept. 9.30-7.30.

PROVINCIAL ARCHAEOLOGICAL MUSEUM
Carrera del Darro 43, Granada
Art and archaeology of all the cultural periods of the Iberian peninsula - prehistoric, Punic, Greek, Roman, Iberian, Celtic, Visigoth, Moslem, Gothic, Mudéja, Moorish. Inscriptions. Coins. Ceramics from Manises and Fajalauza. Castril glass. Weapons.
Daily ex. Su. p.m. May-Sept. 10-2, 4-7. Oct.-Apr. 10-2, 4-6.

PROVINCIAL MUSEUM OF FINE ART
Palacio de Carlos V, Alhambra, Granada
15th-20th century sculpture. Paintings. Enamels. Stained glass, especially of the Granada School.
Daily ex. p.m. Su., M. Mar. 15- July 14, and Nov. 1 - Mar. 14, 10-1.30, 4-6. July 15- Aug. 31 10-2. Closed Jan. 1, 2, 6, Feb. 1, Mar. 19, Good F., May 1, Corpus Christi, July 18, Aug. 15, Oct. 12, Nov. 1, 8, 25.

GRANOLLERS

MUNICIPAL MUSEUM
Granollers, Barcelona
Archaeology. Prehistory. Paintings. Medieval ceramics. Natural sciences.
Daily 11-1, 4-6.

GUADALUPE

MONASTERY OF OUR LADY OF GUADALUPE
Plaza Generalismo Franco, Guadalupe, Caceres
Paintings. Vestments. Illuminated choir-books.
Daily 9.30-1.30, 3.30-7.

GUADIX

CATHEDRAL MUSEUM
Cathedral, Guadix, Granada
Religious art.
Daily 10-11, 5-6.

LA GUARDIA

MUSEUM OF THE CITANIA OF SANTA TECLA
Monte de Santa Tecla, La Guardia, Pontevedra
Archaeological material from the Citania excavations.
Daily 10-2, 3-8.

GUERNICA Y LUNO

ARCHIVAL MUSEUM
Casa de Juntas, Calle Allendesalazar, Guernica y Luno, Vizcaya
Documents illustrating the history of the Seignory of Vizcaya.
Daily 10-6. Closed p.m. Jan. 1, 6. Th. in Easter Week, Aug. 16. Closed all day on Good F.

GUISONA

EDUARDO CAMPS CAVA MUNICIPAL MUSEUM
Calle Eduardo Camps 1, Guisona, Lérida
Local archaeology and history.
Public holidays, 12-1.

GUMIEL DE HIZAN

MUSEO DE GOMELLANO
Church of Our Lady of the Assumption, Plaza Mayor, Gumiel de Hizan, Burgos
Paintings. Reliquaries and Romanesque sculpture from the former Monastery of San Pedro de Gomellano.
By appointment.

HUELVA

PROVINCIAL MUSEUM
Avenida Montenegro, Huelva
Prehistory and local archaeology.
By appointment.

HUESCA

PROVINCIAL MUSEUM
Universidad Sertoriana, Plaza de la Universidad 4, Huesca
Prehistory. Archaeology. Sculpture. Paintings. Drawings. Engravings.
May-Sept. Daily 10-1.30, 5-7. Oct.-Apr. Daily 10-1.30, 4-6.

IBIZA

ARCHAEOLOGICAL MUSEUM
Plaza Catedral, Ibiza, Balearic Islands
Local archaeology, ethnology, art and handicrafts.
Daily 9-1, 4-6.30. Closed Sa. p.m., Su.

CATHEDRAL MUSEUM
Cathedral, Ibiza, Balearic Islands
Religious art.
Oct.-Apr. by appointment. May-Sept. 11-1.

MONOGRAPHIC MUSEUM AND PUNIC NECROPOLIS OF PUIG DES MOLINS
Calle Romana, Ibiza, Balearic Islands
Punic and Roman material from local excavations.
Daily 9-2, 4-7.

IGUALADA

MUSEUM OF LEATHER
Carretera de Manresa, Igualada, Barcelona
Preparation and uses of leather.
Daily 9-12, 4-7.

TOWN AND DISTRICT MUSEUM
Carretera de Manresa, Igualada, Barcelona
Religious and popular art. Textiles. History of the area. Fossils.
Daily 9-12, 4-7.

ILLESCAS

HOSPITAL AND SANCTUARY OF OUR LADY OF CHARITY
Calle Cardenal Cisneros 2, Illescas, Toledo
Paintings, including five by El Greco. Reliquaries from Flanders and Italy. Church plate (gold). Vestments.
By appointment.

ISLA PLANA O NUEVA TABARCA

SOLEDAD ALVAREZ ESTERADA ARCHAEOLOGICAL COLLECTION
Isla Plana o Nueva Tabarca, Alicante
Local archaeology, with special emphasis on Roman pottery.
By appointment.

JACA

DIOCESAN MUSEUM
Cathedral, Jaca, Huesca
Religious art, mainly 11th-13th century frescoes brought from seven churches in the diocese.
Daily 11-2, 4-6.

JAÉN

CATHEDRAL MUSEUM
Cathedral, Plaza Santa Maria, Jaén
Religious art.
Daily 8-2, 4-8.

PROVINCIAL MUSEUM
Avenida del Generalismo 27, Jaén
Prehistory and archaeology. Sculpture. Paintings. Spanish-Moslem items.
Mar.-Sept. Daily 10-1, 5-8. Oct.-Feb. Daily 10-2, 3-6.

JATIVA

MUNICIPAL MUSEUM
Calle José Carchano, Jativa, Valencia
Local archaeology. Paintings.
M.-Sa. by appointment. Public holidays 12-2.

JAVIER

CASTILLO
Javier, Navarra
Birthplace of San Francisco Javier (d.1552). Collection of paintings.
Daily 9-1, 4-8.

JEREZ DE LA FRONTERA

FLAMENCO MUSEUM
Caledra de Flamencoloqia, Jerez de la Frontera, Cadiz
Musical instruments. Gramophone records of folk-music. Costumes. Folk art.

MUNICIPAL ARCHAEOLOGICAL MUSEUM
Plaza Asunción 1, Jerez de la Frontera, Cadiz
Local prehistory and archaeology.
May-Sept. Daily 10-1, 6-9. Oct.-Apr. Daily 10-1, 5-8.

JERICA

MUNICIPAL MUSEUM
Ayuntamiento, Jerica, Castellon de la Plana
Local history. Works of art from the Jerica district.
May-Sept. Daily 11-1, 4-6. Oct.-Apr. Daily 11-1, 6-8.

JUMILLA

MUNICIPAL MUSEUM
Calle General Moscardó, Jumilla, Murcia
Local Bronze Age, Iberian and Roman archaeology.
Daily May-Sept. 9-1, 5-8. Oct.-Apr. 10-1, 4-7.

JUNQUERA DE AMBIA

PAROCHIAL MUSEUM
Antigua Colegiata, Junquera de Ambia, Orense
Religious art, especially gold liturgical objects.
By appointment.

LAGUARDIA

MUSEUM OF THE FRIENDS OF LAGUARDIA SOCIETY
Calle Mayor, Laguardia, Alava
Local history and ethnography. Sculpture. Ceramics. Mementoes of the Carlist Wars.
Daily 11-7.

LAS PALMAS

COLUMBUS HOUSE-MUSEUM
Calle Colón 1, Las Palmas, Canary Islands
Life and achievements of Columbus. Spanish and Italian paintings of the 16th-20th centuries.
Daily ex. Tu. 9-1, 4-6.

DIOCESAN MUSEUM OF RELIGIOUS ART
Calle Doctor Chil 31, Las Palmas
Paintings. Sculpture. Furniture. Tapestries. Ornaments. Early printed books.
Daily 9-1, 4-7.

MUSEUM OF THE CANARY ISLANDS
Calle Dr. Chil 33, Las Palmas, Canary Islands
Material illustrating the volcanic origin of the Islands, their population, history and their conversion to Christianity.
Daily ex. p.m. public holidays, 10-1, 3-6.

NESTOR MUSEUM
Pueblo Canario, Parque de Doramas, Las Palmas, Canary Islands
Local history, folklore.
M.-Sa. 4-8; Su. and public holidays 11-2, 5-8.

PÉREZ GALDOS HOUSE-MUSEUM
Calle Cano 33, Las Palmas, Canary Islands
Home of the writer, Benito Pérez Galdós (d.1920). His living apartments and library. Engravings and drawings illustrating his work.
M. 3-6; Tu.-Sa. 9-1, 3-6; Su. and public holidays 9-12.

PROVINCIAL MUSEUM OF FINE ART
Plaza Pilar Nuevo 1, Las Palmas, Canary Islands
Paintings and sculpture by local artists, 18th-20th centuries.
Daily 9-1, 4-6.

LEÓN

CATHEDRAL MUSEUM
Calle Cardenal Landazuri 2, León
Material from the restoration of the Cathedral (1901). Paintings, 16th century painted panels. 13th-16th century sculpture. Ivories. 13th century Moslem cupboards. Goldsmiths' work. Codices.
Daily 9-1, 4-7.

DIOCESAN MUSEUM OF RELIGIOUS ART
Seminario Mayor, León
Religious art of the 10th-18th centuries, from churches in the diocese.
May-Sept. Daily 10-1, 4-8. Oct.-Apr. Daily 10-1, 4-6.

PROVINCIAL ARCHAEOLOGICAL MUSEUM
Plaza de San Marcos, León
Regional prehistory and archaeology. Sculpture. Paintings. Ivories. Architectural items from local buildings. Gold and ornaments.
Daily 10-2, 5-7.

ROYAL COLLEGE OF SAN ISIDORO
Plaza de San Isidoro, León
12th century frescoes. Liturgical objects. 11th-12th century Persian and Arabian textiles. Royal tombs. Service books. Illuminated codices.
May-Sept. Daily 9-2.30, 4-7.30. Oct.-Apr. Daily 10-1.30, 4-7.

LERIDA

ARCHAEOLOGICAL MUSEUM OF THE INSTITUTE OF ILERDIAN STUDIES
Antiguo Hospital de Santa Maria, Avenida Blondel 62, Lerida
Local prehistory and archaeology, with an emphasis on material from the former pais ilergeti.
M.-Sa. 12.30-2, 7.30-9. Su. 11.30-1.30. Public holidays 11.30-1.30.

CATHEDRAL MUSEUM
Plaza de la Catedral, Lerida
Tapestries. Paintings. Vestments. Goldsmiths' work. Illuminated manuscripts.
By appointment.

DIOCESAN MUSEUM
Calle Jaime Conquistador 67, Lerida
Local archaeology. Medieval painting and sculpture. Incunabuli. Textiles. Coins and medals.
By appointment.

JAIME MORERA MUSEUM OF MODERN ART
Antiguo Hospital de Santa Maria, Avenida Blondel 62, Lerida
Paintings, drawings and engravings of the 19th-20th centuries. 20th century sculpture. Emphasis on works by local artists, especially Jaime Morera.
Tu.-Sa. 10.30-1.30, 6.30-8.30. Public holidays 11.30-1.30.

MUSEUM OF THE PAHERIA OF THE CITY OF LERIDA
Plaza de la Paheria, Lerida
Local history. Heraldry. Seals. Engravings.
Daily 10-2, 4-7.

LINARES

ARCHAEOLOGICAL MUSEUM
Calle Pontón 49, Linares, Jaén
Local history and archaeology.
Su. 11-2.

LLIVIA

PHARMACY MUSEUM
Ayuntamiento, Plaza Mayor, Llivia, Gerona
History of pharmacy, 15th-19th centuries. 15th century pharmacy, believed to be the oldest in Europe. Painted jars, with portraits of distinguished people in the world of medicine.
May-Sept. Daily 8-7. Oct.-Apr. Daily 10-6.

LLUCH

LLUCH TREASURY AND MUSEUM
Monastery of Our Lady of Lluch, Lluch, Mallorca, Balearic Islands
Local prehistory and archaeology. Religious art. Vestments of the 16th-18th centuries. Mallorca furniture. Goldsmiths' work. Coins. Mallorca Folk Art.
Daily May-Sept. 9-1, 2-7.30. Oct.-Apr. 9-1, 2-6.

LOARRE

CASTLE
nr. Loarre, Huesca
11th century castle and palace, on site of earlier buildings. Archaeology.
By appointment.

LOS BARRIOS DE SALAS

YEBRA MUSEUM
Villar de Barrios, Calle Mayor 1, Los Barrios de Salas, Leon
Paintings. Sculpture. Popular art and handicrafts. Weapons. Ceramics from Sargadelos.
Daily ex. Su. and public holidays. May-Sept. 10-8. Oct.-Apr.

LOGROÑO

PROVINCIAL MUSEUM
Palacio de Espartero, Calle San Agustin, Logroño
Architecture. Sculpture. Local archaeology. Casts of classical and Renaissance sculpture. 14th century shrine doors from San Millan de la Cogolla. 16th century paintings. 17th-20th century Spanish paintings, including 'Arrogance' by Baldomero Gili Roig.
Daily ex. M. 10-1.30.

LOYOLA

BIRTHPLACE OF SAN IGNACIO
Avenida de Loyola, Loyola, Guipuzcoa
15th century house in which Ignacio Lopez de Loyola was born in 1491.
Daily 10-12.30, 4-7.

LUANCO

MARITIME MUSEUM OF THE ASTURIAS
Calle del Conde del Real Agrado, Luanco, Oviedo
History of ships and navigation. Charts and maps. Instruments. Ships' models.
Daily 10-1, 4-6.

LUGO

CATHEDRAL MUSEUM AND TREASURY
Cathedral, Lugo
Religious art, including medieval and Renaissance items.
By appointment.

DIOCESAN MUSEUM
Seminario, Lugo
Religious art.
By appointment.

PROVINCIAL MUSEUM
Plaza de la Soledad 6, Lugo
Archaeology. Painting and sculpture. Popular art and crafts. Coins.
M.-Sa. 11-2; public holidays 12-2.

MADRID

ABBEY OF SAN ANTONIO
Colegio de San Antón, Hortaleza 63, Madrid
Paintings, especially by Goya.
Daily 10-7.30.

AFRICAN MUSEUM
Paseo de la Castellana 5, Madrid
Prehistory and ethnography of Morocco, the Sahara, Fernando Po and the Rio Muni.
Daily ex. Su., public holidays, 10-1.

AMERICAN MUSEUM
Avenida Reyes Católicos, Ciudad Universitaria, Madrid
History of South America. Civilisation of the Pueblos Indians, before and after the conquest. Colonisation. Work of the missions.
Daily ex. M. and Aug. 10-2.

ANATOMY COLLECTION
Faculty of Medicine, Ciudad Universitaria, Madrid
Anatomical specimens.
Open on days when the University is in session. Room 1, 12-2. Room 2, 11-1.

ARMY MUSEUM
Calle Méndez Núñez 1, Madrid
Military history. Uniforms and badges of the Infantry, Engineers, Artillery, Cavalry, Ordnance, Civil Guard and Medical Service. Models of guns.
Daily ex. M. 10-2.

BOTANICAL GARDEN
Plaza de Murillo 2, Madrid
Established 1781. Herbarium.
Su. 11-1. M.-Sa. Nov.-Mar. 9-1, 4-6. Apr.-Oct. 9-1, 4-7.30.

BULLFIGHTING MUSEUM
Plaza Monumental de las Ventas, Patio de Caballos, Madrid
History of bullfighting. Paintings and engravings with bullfighting as theme. Models.
Daily 10-1.30, 3.30-6 ex. public holidays. Open until 7 in summer.

CABINET OF ANTIQUITIES
Royal Academy of History, Calle del León 21, Madrid
Classical and early Christian archaeology. 15th-19th century painting. Textiles. Coins.
Daily ex. Su., public holidays, 10.30-12.30.

CAJAL MUSEUM
Calle Velásquez 144, Madrid
Life and work of the histologist, Santiago Ramón y Cajal (d.1934), winner of the Nobel Prize for Medicine in 1906.
Daily 9-1, 5-8. Closed Aug. and public holidays. Closed p.m. Sa. and in July and Sept.

CERRALBO MUSEUM
Calle Ventura Rodriguez 17, Madrid
Paintings. Drawings. Armour. Tapestry. Furniture. Porcelain. Weapons. Works by El Greco, Ribera, Titian, Van Dyck and Tintoretto.
Daily 9-2. Closed Mar., Aug., Jan. 1, Good F., May 1, Nov. 1, Dec. 8-25. Closed Tu.

COLLECTION OF AMERICAN ARCHAEOLOGY AND ETHNOGRAPHY
Department of American History, Faculty of Philosophy and Letters, Ciudad Universitaria, Madrid
Material relating to the history and cultures of Spanish America.
During term-time, M., W., F. 10-2.

COLLECTION OF THE BANCO EXTERIOR
Carrera de San Jerónimo 36, Madrid
Paintings, displayed in various departments of the Bank building.
By appointment.

COLLECTION OF THE BANK OF SPAIN
Alcalá 50, Madrid
Paintings. Tapestries.
By appointment.

COLLECTION OF THE FACULTY OF PHILOSOPHY AND LETTERS
Ciudad Universitaria, Madrid
Spanish painting, including works by Sorolla, Benuete, Inza and Sala. Phoenician and Roman archaeology.
During University term, by appointment.

COLLECTION OF THE HOUSE OF ALBA
Palacio de Liria, Princesa 20, Madrid
Collection begun by the 1st Duke of Alba and continued by his successors. Paintings. Weapons. Tapestries. Furniture. Sculpture. Porcelain. Codices. Documents.
By appointment.

COLLECTION OF THE LIBRARY OF MUSIC
Calle Imperial 8, Madrid
Musical instruments and scores. Photographs.
Daily ex. Aug. and public holidays, 10.30-1.30, 5.30-7.30.

COLLECTION OF THE NATIONAL OBSERVATORY
Alfonso XII, 3, Madrid
Instruments used at the Observatory since its foundation in 1851. Telescopes. Chronographs. Signal-recorders.
Daily ex. public holidays, 9-2.

COLLECTION OF PAINTINGS
Fernando el Santo 14, Madrid
Collection formed by the Marquis of Casa-Torres (d.1907). Paintings, especially 17th-19th century works by Spanish artists.
By appointment.

COLLECTION OF THE URQUIJO BANK
Casa de las Siete Chimineas, Placa del Rey, Madrid
Paintings. Furniture.
By appointment.

CONVENT OF THE INCARNATION
Plaza de la Encarnación 1, Madrid
Paintings. Furniture. Reliquaries.
Daily ex. Jan. 1, 10.30-1.30, 4-6.

CONVENT OF LAS DESCALZAS REALES
Plaza de las Descalzas Reales 3, Madrid
16th century building. Collections of paintings, sculpture and tapestries. Goldsmith's work.
M.-Th. 10-1, 4-6; F.-Su. 10-1.

GALLERY OF SCULPTURE AND MUSEUM OF REPRODUCTIONS
Museo de América, Ciudad Universitaria, Madrid
Reproductions of Oriental, Greek, Roman works of art. Hispano-Roman, medieval and Renaissance statues.
M.-F. 10-4; Sa. 10-1. Closed Aug. 1-31.

HOUSE OF LOPE DE VEGA
Calle Cervantes 11, Madrid
House (1587) in which Lope de Vega lived 1610-35. Has inscription by Lope, 'Parva propria magna aliena parva' - a small possession of one's own is great, a great possession of another is small. Furnished as it was in his lifetime.
Daily ex. M. and from July 15 - Sept. 15, 11-2.

INSTITUTO DE VALENCIA DE DON JUAN
Calle Fortuny 43, Madrid
Ceramics. Textiles. Jet ornaments. Weapons. Paintings. Coins and medals.
Daily 5-7. Closed Aug. 1 - Sept. 15.

LAZARO GALDIANO MUSEUM
Calle Serrano 122, Madrid
Spanish, early Flemish, Italian, French and English paintings. Drawings. Jewels. Pottery. Enamel work. Coins. Medals. Gold and silver work. Ivory. Sculpture. Furniture. Weapons. Textiles.
Daily 9.15-1.45. Closed Jan. 1, Good F., July 18, Nov. 1, Dec. 25.

MESONERO ROMANOS MUSEUM
Plaza de la Villa 3, Madrid
House (14th-15th century). Contains the study of the writer, Ramón Mesonero Romanos (d.1882).
Th. 9-1.30.

MUNICIPAL COLLECTION
Ayuntamiento and Casa de Cisneros, Plaza de la Villa, Madrid
Paintings. Goldsmiths' work. Tapestries. Town maps.
M.-Sa. 4-7; Su. 10-1.

MUNICIPAL MUSEUM
Calle Fuencarral 78, Madrid
History of Madrid, 16th-20th centuries. Paintings. Sculptures. Coins from the local mint. Popular arts and handicrafts. Photographic prints. Medals. Insignia.
Closed for reorganisation: enquire locally.

MUSEUM OF AERONAUTICS AND ASTRONAUTICS
Ministerio del Aire and Hangar de Cuatro Vientos, Madrid
Plans and models showing the development of aviation and astronautics.
By appointment.

MUSEUM OF ANCIENT HISTORY
Calle Jorge Juan 51, Madrid
Early history, especially Roman, of the Iberian peninsula.
Daily 10-2, 4-6.30.

MUSEUM OF CARRIAGES
Palacio Nacional, Campo del Moro, Ribera del Manzanares, Madrid
Litters. Royal coaches and carriages of the 16th-18th centuries. Harnesses.
Summer: Daily 10-12.45, 4-6.15. Winter: 10-12.45, 3.30-5.45. Su. and holidays 10-1.30.

MUSEUM OF DR. OLAVIDE
Hospital de San Juan de Dios, Calle Doctor Esquerdo 46, Madrid
Established at end of 19th century by Dr. José Olavide, dermatologist. Consists of wax reproductions of deep and superficial lesions, for the study of dermatology.
By appointment.

MUSEUM OF THE GENERAL POLICE SCHOOL
Calle Miguel Angel 5, Madrid
History of the police. Photographs. Anthropometry. Weapons. Instruments and equipment used by criminals.
9-2, by appointment.

MUSEUM OF ICONOGRAPHY
Plaza Santa Catalina de los Donados 2, Madrid
10th-20th century art. Paintings on wood, canvas, copper. Enamels. Byzantine crucifixes. Miniatures. Embroidery.
By appointment.

MUSEUM OF THE MINT AND STAMP PRINTING WORKS
Calle Dr. Esquerdo 38, Madrid
History of coins and medals. Coins from Europe and Spanish America. Engravings. Punches and dies. Machines.
Daily ex. Su. p.m., M., Aug., 10-2, 4-7.

MUSEUM OF THE MUNICIPAL ARCHAEOLOGICAL INSTITUTE
Calle Enrique D'Almonte 1, Madrid
Archaeology and palaeontology of Madrid and the surrounding district.
Tu.-Sa. 11 1, 4 8. Su. 10 2. Closed Aug.

MUSEUM OF REPRODUCTIONS OF WORKS OF ART
Cuidad Universitaria, Madrid
Reproductions of Oriental, Greek, Roman and Hispano-Roman statuary, medieval and Renaissance art, classical and medieval decorative arts.
M.-F. 10-4; Sa. 10-1.30.

MUSEUM OF THE ROMANTIC PERIOD
Calle San Mateo 13, Madrid
Paintings and furniture, 1820-68. Books. Engravings.
Su., public holidays, 10-2. Closed Aug. 1 - Sept. 15. Weekdays 11-6.

MUSEUM OF THE SCHOOL OF MINES
Calle Rios Rosas 21, Madrid
Mineralogy. Fossils. Models of machinery, furnaces and kilns.
Daily ex. Sa. p.m., Su. 10-1, 5-7.

MUSEUM OF SCIENCE AND TECHNOLOGY
Ciudad Universitaria, Madrid
Science. Technology.
By appointment.

MUSEUM OF SPANISH BOOKS
Biblioteca Nacional, Paseo de Recoletos 20, Madrid
Manuscripts. Rare books. Bindings. Musical manuscripts and scores.
Daily ex. Su., public holidays, 9-2.30, 3.30-10 (Sa. 3.30-7).

MUSEUM OF SPANISH FOLKLORE
Plaza de la Marina Espanola, Madrid
Waxworks, showing regional costumes and other material illustrating the traditional life of Spain.
May-Oct., daily 9-2, 4-7.30. Nov.-Apr., daily 9-2, 4-5.

MUSEUM OF SPANISH PHARMACY
Faculty of Pharmacy, Ciudad Universitaria, Madrid
Pharmacopoeia. Ceramic, porcelain and glass vessels of the 16th-19th centuries.
Daily 10-1.30 ex. Su., Aug., Jan. 1, Mar. 19, Th., F. in Easter week, May 1-15, Ascension Day, Corpus Christi, July 18-25, Oct. 12, Nov. 1, Dec. 8-25.

MUSEUM OF THE SPANISH VILLAGE
Plaza de la Marine Española 9, Madrid
Spanish regional costumes. Furniture. Handicrafts. Textiles. Lace. Embroidery. Ceramics. Transport. Agriculture. Cattle-raising. Music. Popular literature and customs. Historical costumes.
Daily 9-2.

NATIONAL ARCHAEOLOGICAL MUSEUM
Calle Serrano 13, Madrid
Iberian, Celtic, Punic, Greek, Roman, Early Christian and Visigoth archaeology. Painting. Sculpture. Medieval and modern handicrafts. Coins. Also contains the *American Museum*, illustrating the ancient cultures of Mexico, Central and South America.
Daily 9.30-1.30. Closed Jan. 1, May 1, July 18. Cueva de Altamira also open M.-Sa. 4-8.

NATIONAL ENGRAVING WORKS
Calle Alcalá 13, Madrid
18th-20th century plates and engravings. Printing workshops.
Daily ex. Su. and public holidays, 10-2.

NATIONAL MUSEUM OF ANTHROPOLOGY AND ETHNOLOGY
Paseo de Atocha, Madrid
Anthropology. Ethnography of Spain, Africa, Oceania, America and the Philippines. Mummies from the Andes. Dioramas representing life among the Amazon tribes, the Eskimos, and in Tierra del Fuego.
Daily ex. M., Aug., 10-1.30.

NATIONAL MUSEUM OF ARCHITECTURE
Architectural High School, Ciudad Universitaria, Madrid
Plans. Models. Drawings. Engravings. Architectural details.
May-Oct., daily 9-2, 4-7.30. Nov.-Apr., daily 9-2, 4-5.

NATIONAL MUSEUM OF CONTEMPORARY ENGRAVING
Teatro Real, Felipe V, Madrid
20th century engravings.
By appointment.

NATIONAL MUSEUM OF DECORATIVE ART
Calle Montalbán 12, Madrid
Sumptuary and popular art, mostly of Spain. Furniture. Ceramics. Far Eastern section.
Daily ex. M., Aug., 10-1.30.

NATIONAL MUSEUM OF GEOLOGY
Calle Ríos Rosas 23, Madrid
Mineralogy. Palaeontology. Petrology.
Daily ex. Su., public holidays, 9-2.

NATIONAL MUSEUM OF NATURAL SCIENCE
Paseo de la Castellana 84, Madrid
Geology. Palaeontology. Zoology. Entomology.
Daily, May-Sept. 10-2, 5-7.30. Oct.-Apr. 10-2, 4-6.30. Su. and public holidays a.m. only. Closed Jan. 1-16, May 1, Nov. 1, Dec. 25.

NATIONAL MUSEUM OF PAINTING AND SCULPTURE
Museo del Prado, Paseo del Prado, Madrid
Paintings of the Spanish School, 12th-19th centuries; of the Italian, 14th-18th centuries; and of the Flemish, Dutch, French, German and English. Sculpture, chiefly Greek and Roman. Drawings. Engravings. Treasury of the Delfin. Coins.
Daily Nov.-Jan. 10-5. Feb.-May and Sept. 21 - Oct. 31, 10-5.30. June-Sept. 20, 10-6. Su. all year 10-2. Closed Jan. 1, Good F., Nov. 1, Dec. 25. Closed p.m. only, Mar. 19, 28, Apr. 19, May 2, 15, Th. in Easter Week, Ascension Day, Corpus Christi, June 29, July 18, 25, Oct. 1, 12, Nov. 20, Dec. 8.

NATURAL SCIENCE MUSEUM
Paseo de la Castellana 84, Madrid
Zoological, geological, palaeontological and entomological collections.
Daily 10-2, 5-7.30; Su. and holidays 10-2.

NAVAL MUSEUM
Calle Montalbán 2, Madrid
History of Nautical Sciences and of the Spanish Navy. Model ships. Navigation charts, including the map used by Juan de la Cosa. Nautical instruments.
Daily 10.30-1.30, ex. M., Aug. and rainy days.

PALACIO DE LA MONCLOA
Ciudad Universitaria, Madrid
Paintings. Furnishings. Tapestries. Lamps. Clocks and watches.
Daily ex. Su. 10-1, 4-6. Closed public holidays p.m., all day on Jan. 1, Good F., July 18, Dec. 25, and "whenever a guest of the Spanish Government is in residence".

PALACIO DE ORIENTE
Calle Bailén, Madrid
Painting. Tapestries. Sculpture. Furnishings. Porcelain. Glass. Clocks and watches. Miniatures. Lamps. Armour and clothes of the royal Infantes.
Daily 10-1.30, 3-30-6.30. Closed Su. and public holidays p.m. and all day on Jan. 1, Good F., July 18, Dec. 25, and the afternoon before and the morning of "credentials day".

PANTEON DE GOYA
Ermit de San Antonio de la Florida, Paseo de la Florida, Madrid
Frescoes by Francisco de Goya (d.1828). Engravings, drawings, and paintings connected with the life of the artist. Goya's tomb.
Summer: Daily ex. W. 10-1, 4-7; Su. 10-1.30. Winter: Daily ex. W. 11-1.30, 3-6.

PENITENTIARY MUSEUM
Escuela de Estudios Penitenciarios, Avenida de los Poblados, Madrid
Prison architecture. Work carried out by prisoners. Curiosities. Utensils.
By appointment.

PHARMACEUTICAL COLLECTION
Hospital Provincial, Santa Isabel 52, Madrid
Established in the 18th century. Includes apothecaries' jars of that period.
Daily 10-2.

RAILWAY MUSEUM
Calle de San Cosme y San Domián 1, Madrid
History and equipment of the Spanish railway system.
Daily 10-1.30.

ROYAL ARMOURY
Palacio Nacional, Calle Bailén, Madrid
Royal weapons and armour. Historic jewels.
Daily ex. p.m. Su., public holidays, 10-1.30, 3.30-6.30.

ROYAL CARPET FACTORY
Calle Fuenterrabía 2, Madrid
Contains collection of 18th century tapestries, drawings and carpets.
Daily May-Sept. 10-2. Oct.-Apr. 10-1, 4-6. Closed p.m. public holidays, Sa.

ROYAL LIBRARY
Palacio Nacional, Calle Bailén, Madrid
Manuscripts. Incunabuli. 15th century Book of Hours. Unique copies of 16th-20th century books. Engravings. Musical manuscripts. Medal cabinet of the Bourbons.
Daily 10-1.30, 3.30-6.30.

ROYAL PALACE
Plaza de Oriente, Madrid
Paintings. Tapestries. Furniture. Porcelain. Armour. Coach museum.
May-Sept. M.-Sa. 10-12.45, 4-6.15. Oct.-Apr. 10-12.45, 3.30-5.45. Su., public holidays 10-1.30.

ROYAL PHARMACY (OFICINA DE FARMACIA)
Palacio Nacional, Calle Bailén, Madrid
Material from the Royal Pharmacy, founded 1594 by Felipe II and continued by his successors. Includes late 18th century apothecary's jars from the Royal Porcelain Factory at Buen Retiro and the Royal Glass Factory at San Ildefonso.
Daily 10-1.30, 3.30-6.30. Closed p.m. Su., public holidays.

SAN FERNANDO FINE ARTS ACADEMY MUSEUM
Calle de Alcala 13, Madrid
Spanish paintings from 8th to 19th centuries.
M.-Sa. 10-1.30, 4-6.30. Su. and holidays 10-1.30.

SOROLLA MUSEUM
Calle Martínez Campos 37, Madrid
In house built (1912) by the painter, Joaquín Sorolla (d.1923) as a residence and studio. Paintings and sketches by Sorolla.
Daily, ex. M. 10-2.

SPANISH MUSEUM OF CONTEMPORARY ART
Avenida Calvo Sotelo 20, Madrid
Paintings, sculpture, drawings and engravings of the 19th-20th centuries.
Daily 10.30-2.

SPANISH THEATRE MUSEUM
Calle de la Beneficencia 16, Madrid
Waxworks collection representing famous actors and actresses, as well as old scenery and costumes.
By appointment.

ZULOAGA'S STUDIO
Plaza de Gabriel Miró 7, Madrid
Furniture and household equipment belonging to the painter, Zuloaga, with some of his last paintings and sketches.
Daily ex. Tu., public holidays and Aug. 1 - Oct. 1, 10-2.

MADRIGAL DE LAS ALTAS TORRES

BIRTHPLACE OF ISABEL LA CATOLICA
Placio de Juan II, Plaza del Cristo, Madrigal de las Altas Torres, Avila
15th century house in which Isabel la Catolica was born in 1451. Paintings, sculpture and tapestries of the 15th-17th centuries.
Daily 9.30-12.30. Oct.-Mar. 4-6. Apr.-Sept. 4-8.

MAHON

PROVINCIAL MUSEUM OF FINE ART
Plaza de la Conquista 8, Mahon, Minorca, Balearic Islands
Prehistory. Archaeology. Local and Aztec ethnography. Coins and ceramics.
Daily ex. Su. 10-1.

MALAGA

CATHEDRAL MUSEUM
Plaza de la Catedral, Malaga
Paintings. Textiles. Manuscripts.
M.-Sa. 10.30-1, 3.30-7. Public holidays 4-6.

MUSEUM AND TREASURY OF THE COFRADIA OF THE EXPIRACION
Plaza de San Pedro, Malaga
Religious art.
Daily 10.30-1.30, 3.30-7.30. Closed p.m. Su., public holidays.

PROVINCIAL ARCHAEOLOGICAL MUSEUM
Alcazaba, Malaga
Arab, early Christian and Roman archaeology. Hispano-Arab ceramics and other items discovered during excavations on the Alcazaba site.
Daily May-Sept. 11-1, 5-9. Oct.-Apr. 11-1, 5-8.

PROVINCIAL MUSEUM OF FINE ART
Calle San Agustin 6, Malaga
16th-20th century painting. Sculpture. Roman archaeology.
Daily May-Sept. 10-1.30, 5-8. Oct.-Apr. 4-7.

MANACOR

MUNICIPAL ARCHAEOLOGICAL MUSEUM
Plaza Rector Rubí, Manacor, Mallorca, Balearic Islands
Roman and early Christian archaeology. Basilica of Son Peretó.
Daily ex. Sa. May-Sept. 3-7. Oct.-Apr. 3.30-6.

MANISES

CASANOVA DALFO-SANCHIS CAUSA MUNICIPAL MUSEUM
Calle Sagrario 28, Manises, Valencia
Manises ceramics of the 15th-20th centuries. Ceramics by José Jimeno Martínez (d.1967). Local history.
Daily 4-8.

MARCHENA

PAROCHIAL MUSEUM
Iglesia de San Juan Bautista, Calle Cristóbal de Morales, Marchena, Sevilla
15th century church. 16th century Flemish paintings. Choir-stalls carved in cedar by Juan de Valencia. Church plate (gold). Vestments. Illuminated books.
By appointment.

MARRATXI

VERI COLLECTION
Son Veri, La Cabaneta, Marratxi, Mallorca, Balearic Islands
Paintings and handicrafts.
By appointment.

MARTIN MUÑOZ DE LAS POSADAS

CARDINAL ESPINOSA MUSEUM
Martin Muñoz de las Posadas, Segovia
Local ethnography. 'Calvary' by El Greco.
On request.

MARTORELL

L'ENREJOLADA SANTACANA PROVINCIAL MUSEUM
Calle Francisco Santacana 15, Martorell, Barcelona
Architectural features from demolished buildings. Art and ceramics of Catalonia.
Tu.-Sa. 3-6. Public holidays 11-2.

VICENTE ROS MUNICIPAL MUSEUM
Calle Capuchinos, Martorell, Barcelona
Local archaeology. Paintings. Ceramics of the 14th-18th centuries.
Tu.-Sa. 10-1. Public holidays 11-2.

MASNOU

MUNICIPAL MUSEUM
Calle Anselmo Clavé, Masnou, Barcelona
Naval history. Local history and archaeology.
Sa. 2-5.30. Su. and public holidays, 10-5.30.

MUSEUM OF THE HISTORY OF PHARMACY AND MEDICINE
Laboratorio del Norte de España, Masnou, Barcelona
18th century pharmacy of the Monastery of Santa Maria la Real, Nájera. Engravings of medical subjects. Mortars of the 15th-19th centuries.
By appointment.

MATARO

MUNICIPAL MUSEUM
Calle Enrique Granados 17, Mataro, Barcelona
16th century house. Archaeology, including material from excavations at the Roman villa, Can Llauder. Industrial art. Modern painting.
M.-Sa. 7-9 p.m. Public holidays, 11.30-1.30, 7-9.

MUSEUM AND HISTORICAL ARCHIVE OF THE ARCHPRIESTS
Parroquia de Santa Maria, Plaza Dr. Sansó, Mataro, Barcelona
Works by local artists. Local history.
Daily 1-3. Other times by appointment.

MEDINACELI

MUSEUM OF THE COLLEGIATE CHURCH
Plaza de la Colegiata, Medinaceli, Sevilla
Paintings. Sculpture. Church plate (gold). Choir-books.
Daily 9-1, 3-6.

MEDINA DE POMAR

MONASTERY MUSEUM
Calle Santa Clara, Medina de Pomar, Burgos
In the former residence of the Constables of Castille, now the Monastery of Santa Clara. Religious art, including the Renaissance tomb of the Duke of Frías.
Daily 9-12, 4-7.

MEDINA DE RIOSECO

INTERPAROCHIAL MUSEUM AND TREASURY
Santa Maria de Medinvilla, Calle de Santa Maria, Medina de Rioseco, Valladolid
Church plate (gold).
By appointment.

MELILLA

MUNICIPAL MUSEUM
Baluarte de la Concepción, Melilla
In the 16th century Torre de la Concepción. Local history and art.
Daily ex. M. 10-1.

MENDOZA

CASTILLO
nr. Mendoza, Alava
11 k.m. from Mendoza, on the Irun-Madrid road. Castle (14th century) of the Mendozas. Heraldry of Alva.
Daily 10-6.

MERIDA

ARCHAEOLOGICAL MUSEUM
Plaza de Santa Clara 5, Merida, Badajoz
Art of the Romans and Visigoths.
Daily 10-1. Oct.-Apr. 3-6. May-Sept. 4-7. Closed Su., public holidays in afternoon, M. morning.

MOGUER

ZENOBIA-JUAN RAMÓN HOUSE-MUSEUM
Calle Juan-Ramón Jiménez 10, Moguer, Huelva
Life and work of the poet and Nobel prize-winner (1956), Juan Ramón Jiménez. Also commemorates his wife, Zenobia.
Daily 9-1, 4-8.

MONOVAR

AZORIN HOUSE MUSEUM
Calle Calvo Solelo 10, Monovar, Alicante
House of José Martinez Ruiz Azorin. Books, furniture and other possessions of the writer.
By appointment.

MANRESA

HISTORICAL MUSEUM OF THE CATHEDRAL CHURCH
Basilica de Santa Maria del Alba, Bajada de la Seo, Manresa, Barcelona
Religious art. Paintings. Sculpture. Textiles. Goldsmiths' work. Historical items relating to the Church.
Public holidays, 11-2, 4-6.

MANRESA MUSEUM
Calle Villardordis 1, Manresa, Barcelona
Prehistory. Archaeology. Local modern painting. Industrial and popular art.
M.-Sa. by appointment; Su. 11-1.

MOLINS DE REY

MOLINS DE REY MUSEUM
Calle F. Samaranch 11, Molins de Rey, Barcelona
Prehistory. Archaeology. Painting. Sculpture. Folk art. Handicrafts.
M.-Sa. by appointment. Public holidays 12-2.

MONTBLANC

MUSEUM AND ARCHIVE OF MONTBLANC AND DISTRICT
Calle Josa 6, Montblanc, Tarragona
Local history and archaeology. Palaeontology.
Public holidays 11-2.

MONTSERRAT

MUSEUM
Abadia de Montserrat, Montserrat, Barcelona
In Monastery of Santa Maria. Bibles, including material brought from Middle East by Benedictine missionaries. Art gallery of works by Italian, Spanish and French painters, from the 15th century onwards. Natural history. Arts and crafts.
May-Sept. 10-6. Oct.-Apr. 10-1, 3-5.

MORELLA

ETHNOLOGICAL MUSEUM OF MORELLA AND THE MAESTRAZGO
Real Convento de San Francisco, Plaza de San Francisco, Morella, Castellon de la Plana
15th-19th century textiles. Folk art. Handicrafts. Agricultural implements. Archaeology. Painting, sculpture and goldsmiths' work by local artists.
May-Sept. Daily 9-2, 3-8. Oct.-Apr. Daily 9-1, 3-6.

MUSEUM OF THE ARCHPRIESTS
Basilica de Santa Mariá la Mayor, Plaza de la Arciprestal-Basilica, Castellon, Morella
Religious art. Medieval manuscripts. Early printed books.
June-Sept., daily 9-2, 3-8. Oct.-May, by appointment.

MOTRIL

EXOTICUARIUM
Calle González Espinosa II, Motril, Granada
Marine and river fauna of the Mediterranean, Siam, Indochina, India and the Amazon.
Daily 10-6.

MOYA

DISTRICT MUSEUM
Calle Casenovas, Moya, Barcelona
Art and history, especially of the Moya area.
Daily 11-1, 4-6.

MURCIA

CATHEDRAL MUSEUM
Cathedral, Calle Salzillo 2, Murcia
Roman archaeology. Sculpture. Painting. Goldsmiths' work. Vestments.
Daily 9-1, 4-7.

MUSEUM OF THE ARAB WALL
Plaza de Santa Eulalia, Murcia
Site museum, showing pottery and other material from the 12th-15th century Moslem fortifications and cemetery.
Daily ex. M. and p.m. public holidays.

PROVINCIAL MUSEUM OF ARCHAEOLOGY
Calle Alfonso X 5, Murcia
Bronze Age, Iberian, Roman, Arab and medieval Christian periods. Medieval and modern handicrafts. Inscriptions. Coins. Heraldry of the 16th-18th centuries.
Daily ex. M. and p.m. public holidays, 10-2, 6-7.30.

PROVINCIAL MUSEUM OF FINE ART
Calle Obispo Frutos 12, Murcia
17th-20th century paintings. Engravings. Drawings. Sculpture.
Daily ex. p.m. public holidays, May-Sept. 9-1, 5-7. Oct.-Apr. 10-2, 4-7.

SALZILLO MUSEUM
Calle San Andrés 1, Murcia
Sculptures and cartoons by Francisco Salzillo (1707-1783).
Daily ex. Good F. and p.m. public holidays, May-Sept. 9.30-1, 4-7. Oct.-Apr. 9.30-1, 3-6.

MURIEDAS

ETHNOGRAPHICAL MUSEUM OF CANTABRIA
Casa de Velarde, Muriedas, Santander
In 17th century house, which was birthplace of Pedro Velarde (1779-1808). Material relating to the life of Velarde. Regional ethnology. Agricultural implements.
Daily 10-2, 4-7.

NAJERA

MONASTERY OF SANTA MARIA LA REAL
Calle del Rey Don Garcia, Najera, Logroño
Buildings of the 11th-16th centuries. Contains mausoleum of the kings of Navarre, Castille and León.
Daily 9.30-12.30, 4.30-8.30.

NERJA

ARCHAEOLOGICAL MUSEUM
Cueva, Anejo de Maro, nr. Nerja, Malaga
Local archaeology.
Daily 9-1, 4-8.

OLOT

ARCHAEOLOGICAL MUSEUM
Calle Hospicio 4, Olot, Gerona
Local archaeology. Popular arts and handicrafts. Coins. Weapons.
May-Sept. Daily 11-1, 6-8. Oct.-Apr. Daily 11-1, 4-6.

MUSEUM OF MODERN ART
Parque de la Ciudad, Olot, Gerona
Paintings, sculpture, drawings and engravings by local artists.
May-Sept. Daily 11-1, 6-8. Oct.-Apr. Daily 11-1, 4-6.

PAROCHIAL MUSEUM AND TREASURY
Church of San Esteban, Olot, Gerona
Paintings, including El Greco's "Christ on the Cross" Carvings. Gold. Vestments.
Dawn-dusk.

ONCALA

MUSEUM OF TAPESTRIES
Iglesia de San Millán, Oncala, Sevilla
17th century Flemish tapestries. 18th century vestments.
By appointment.

ONDA

MUNICIPAL MUSEUM
Calle Cervantes 4, Onda, Castellon de la Plana
Local history. Art, especially ceramics.
Public holidays 12-2. Other days by appointment.

MUSEUM OF THE NATURAL SCIENCES
Tales Road, nr. Onda, Castellon de la Plana
Zoology. Biology. Entomology. Anatomy. Botany. Geology. Palaeontology. Phytopathology. Ethnography. Anthropology. Subsidiary section devoted to coins, medals and archaeology.
Daily 9-8.

ORENSE

DIOCESAN AND CATHEDRAL MUSEUM
Cathedral, Orense
Cathedral treasury and works of art from other parishes in the diocese.
By appointment.

PROVINCIAL MUSEUM OF ARCHAEOLOGY
Antiguo Palacio Episcopal, Calle Obispo Carrascosa, Orense
Roman archaeology. Art - Mozarabic, Visigoth, Romanesque, Gothic and modern.
Daily 10-1, 5-7.

ORIHUELA

DIOCESAN MUSEUM OF RELIGIOUS ART
Cathedral, Orihuela, Alicante
Paintings. Sculpture. Goldsmiths' work.
Daily 11-2.

JOSÉ MA. SOLER PROVINCIAL ARCHAEOLOGICAL MUSEUM
Edificio del Ayuntamiento, Plaza de Santiago 2, Orihuela, Alicante
Local prehistory and archaeology. Pre-Roman goldsmiths' work (Villena and Cabeza Redondo treasures). Medieval pottery.
Daily 11-7.

TOWN MUSEUM
Fernando de Loazes Library, Calle Alfonso XIII, Orihuela, Alicante
Local archaeology. Paintings.
Daily 12.30-2, 5-9. Closed Aug.

TREASURY OF THE PARISH OF SANTIAGO
Plaza de Santiago 3, Orihuela, Alicante
Sculpture. Church plate, mostly gold.
Daily 11-2, 5-8.

OSUNA

MONASTERY OF THE INCARNATION
Descalzas, Osuna, Sevilla
18th century ceramic *socle*, with scenes of hunting and of life in Seville. Paintings. Church plate (gold). Sculpture.
Daily 10-1, 4-6.

MUSEUM OF ARCHAEOLOGY
Torre del Agua, Cuesta de San Antón, Osuna, Sevilla
Archaeological material from the Iberian and Roman towns of Osuna.
Oct.-Apr., daily 10-1.30, 3.30-6. May-Sept., daily 10-1.30, 3.30-7.

MUSEUM OF RELIGIOUS ART
Iglesia Colegial, Osuna, Sevilla
Paintings. Sculpture. 15th-19th century goldsmiths' work. Liturgical objects.
Oct.-Apr., daily 10-1.30, 3.30-6. May-Sept., daily 10-1.30, 3.30-7.

OVIEDO

CÁMARA SANTA
Cathedral, Oviedo
The Treasury of the earlier Cathedral, mainly gold liturgical objects (6th-14th centuries), including the 9th century Cruz de los Angeles and Cruz de la Victoria.
Daily 9.30-1, 4-8.

PROVINCIAL MUSEUM
Calle San Vicente 3, Oviedo
Archaeology. Pre-Roman, Roman and Gothic art. Coins. Inscriptions.
Daily ex. M., public holidays, 9-2, 4-6.30.

PADRON

PADRON MUSEUM OF RELIGIOUS ART
Casa Restoral, Calle Santa Maria, Padron, La Coruña
Gold and ornaments of the 15th-18th centuries.
By appointment.

ROSALIÁ DE CASTRO HOUSE-MUSEUM
Lugar de 'La Matanza', Iria Flavia, Padron, La Coruña
Former home of the poet, Rosaliá de Castro (d.1885). Collections illustrating her life and work.
By appointment.

PALAMOS

CAU DE LA COSTA BRAVA MUSEUM
Plaza del Horno 4, Palamos, Cordoba
Local prehistory and archaeology. Coins. 20th century paintings.
May-Sept. Daily 10-1, 5-9. Oct.-Apr. Daily 6-9 p.m. Closed public holidays p.m.

PALENCIA

CATHEDRAL MUSEUM
Cathedral, Plaza de la Immaculada, Palencia
Paintings. Sculpture. Tapestries. Church plate (gold). Vestments.
Daily 9-1, 4-6.

PROVINCIAL ARCHAEOLOGICAL MUSEUM
Palacio de la Diputación, Calle Burgos 1, Palencia
Archaeology. Medieval tombs. 14th century retables. Coins.
By appointment.

PALMA DE MALLORCA

CASTILLO BELLVER MUSEUM
Castillo Bellver Museum, Palma de Mallorca (near), Balearic Islands
Local archaeology, history and art. Copies of 16th century Roman statues. Cell in which Jovellanos was imprisoned, 1802-8.
Daily, sunrise to sunset.

CATHEDRAL MUSEUM
Cathedral, Plaza Almoina, Palma de Mallorca, Balearic Islands
In the 13th century Sacristy and Chapter House. Religious art. Paintings. Goldsmiths' work. Tapestries. Vestments. Books and manuscripts.
Daily 10.30-12.30, 4-7.

DIOCESAN MUSEUM
Palacio Episcopal, Calle Mirador, Palma de Mallorca, Balearic Islands
Prehistory and archaeology of Mallorca. Painting and sculpture of the 14th-18th centuries. Ceramics. Vestments. Antiphonaries.
Daily ex. Su. May-Sept. 10-1.30, 4-7. Oct.-Apr. 10-1.30, 4-6.

KREKOVIC COLLECTION
Son Fusturet, Camino Viejo de Buñola, Palma de Mallorca, Balearic Islands
Works of the Peruvian painter, Kristian Krekovic. South American art and ethnology.
Daily Apr.-Oct. 11-1, 4-8. Nov.-Mar. 11-1.

MALLORCA MUSEUM
(a) Archaeological Section: Casa de la Cultura
(b) Fine Art Department: Antigua Lonja, Paseo Sagrera
(c) Ethnological Section: Calle Major 15, Muro
Palma de Mallorca, Balearic Islands
Archaeology. Roman material from excavations on Mallorca. Gothic painting. Ethnography. Folk art. Handicrafts. Old Noceras Pharmacy.
May-Sept. Daily 9-1, 5-8.30. Oct.-Apr. Daily 9-1, 4-7.30.

MARITIME MUSEUM OF THE BALEARICS
Consulado del Mar, Paseo Sagrera, Palma de Mallorca, Balearic Islands
In 17th century house, built for the College (Collegro) of Commerce. Pictures and objects relating to seafaring and trade.
Daily May-Sept. 10-1, 5-8. Oct.-Apr. 10-1, 4-7.

PALACIO MORELL
San Cayetano 22, Palma de Mallorca, Balearic Islands
18th century house belonging to the Morell family. Period rooms and furniture. Paintings.
Daily 10-1.30, 4-6.

PALACIO RESIDENTIAL DE LA ALMUDIANA
Plaza Almoina, Palma de Mallorca, Balearic Islands
History and art of Palma de Mallorca.
Daily 10-1, 3-6.

SARIDAKIS MUSEUM OF ART
Calle de Calvo Sotelo, Palma de Mallorca (near), Balearic Islands
Material from excavation of old city. Domestic utensils. Tools. Glazed tiles. Iron-work.
Oct.-Apr. Sa. 4-6; Su. 11-1. May-Sept. Th., Sa. 4-6; Su. 11-1.

VIVOT COLLECTION
Calle Zavellá 2, Palma de Mallorca, Balearic Islands
House (early 18th century) of the Marqués de Vivot. Contemporary furnishings and decoration. Paintings. Sculpture. Library.
Daily 10-1, 4-7.

PAMPLONA

DIOCESAN MUSEUM
Cathedral, Calle Dormitaleria, Pamplona, Navarra
Medieval frescoes. Goldsmiths' work. Vestments. Statuary.
Daily Easter-Oct. 11-1, 4-7. Remainder of year, 11-1.

ETHNOLOGICAL MUSEUM
Calle de Santo Domingo, Pamplona, Navarra
Life and customs of the Pyrenees.
By appointment.

HISTORICAL MUSEUM
Calle Mercado 7, Pamplona, Navarra
Material relating to the Carlist wars.
By appointment.

NAVARRA MUSEUM
Calle Santo Domingo, Pamplona, Navarra
Regional archaeology and architecture. 13th-16th century frescoes from Olite, Artajona, Pamplona, Oriz and Gallipienzo. 11th century capitals from the first Cathedral at Pamplona.
M.-Sa. 10-1.30; public holidays 11-1.30.

SARASATE MUSEUM
Conservatorio de Musica, Calle Aoiz, Pamplona, Navarra
Material relating to the life and work of the local violinist and composer, Pablo Martin Sarasate de Navascués (d.1908).
Daily 10-12, 4-6.

PARADAS

PAROCHIAL MUSEUM
Parroquia de San Eutropia, Calle Pedro Basea 33, Paradas, Sevilla
Paintings, including El Greco's 'La Magdalena'. Church plate (gold). Vestments.
By appointment.

PAREDES DE NAVA

MUSEUM OF THE PARISH OF SANTA EULALIA
Plaza de España, Paredes de Nava, Oviedo
Religious painting and sculpture. Church plate (gold) and furniture. Vestments.
Daily 10-2, 4-8.

PASTRANA

PAROCHIAL MUSEUM
Church of Our Lady of the Assumption, Plaza de los Caidos, Pasrana, Guadalajara
15th century French tapestries given to the Church by the Dukes of Pastrana. 16th century tombs of the Dukes of Pastrana. Gold.
M.-Sa. 10-1, 5-7. Su. and public holidays, 10-2, 4-8.

PEÑARANDA DE DUERO

PHARMACEUTICAL MUSEUM
Calle José Grijalba 13, Peñaranda de Duero, Burgos
18th century pharmacy and laboratory. Talavera pots. Medicaments. Furniture and fittings. Garden of medicinal plants.
Daily 10-2, 4-8.

PEÑISCOLA

EL MACHO CASTLE
Calle del Castillo, Peñiscola, Castellon de la Plana
13th century fortress, built by the Templars. Art. History.
Daily 10-2, 4-7.

PERELADA

MATEU COLLECTION
Castillo-Palacio de Perelada, Calle del Castillo, Perelada, Gerona
Coins. Glass. Ceramics. Paintings. Carvings. Sculpture.
By appointment. The collections of paintings and carvings are available only to students.

PIEDRAFITA DE EL CEBRERO

MUSEUM OF FOLK ARTS AND CUSTOMS
'Pallozas', Piedrafita de el Cebrero, Lugo
In 4 restored Celtic dwellings. Ethnography of the Galician mountain region. Furniture. Utensils. Handicrafts. Religious art.
May-Oct., daily 10-1, 4-8. Nov.-Apr., daily 10-1, 4-6.

PLASENCIA

MUSEUM AND TREASURY OF THE CATHEDRAL
Cathedral, Plasencia, Cáceres
Religious art. Vestments. Paintings. Goldsmiths' work.
Daily 10-12, 4-6.

POBLET

ROYAL MONASTERY OF SANTA MARIA
Poblet, Tarragona
Cistercian monastery of 1150, enlarged in 18th century. The museum contains architectural elements of the old monastery, not used in the 1925-40 restoration. Local archaeology.
Daily 10-1, 3-6.

POLLENSA

HOUSE AND STUDIO OF THE PAINTER, HERMENE ANGLADA CAMARASA
Pasada Anglada Camarasa 87, Pollensa, Mallorca, Balearic Islands
Works by Camarasa. Chinese sumptuary art of the 16th-18th centuries.
Daily ex. W. p.m. Apr.-Oct. 10.30-8. Nov.-Mar. 10.30-2, 3.30-6.

MUSEUM OF COSTA Y LLOBERA COLLEGE
Calle Guillermo Cyre 13, Pollensa, Mallorca, Balearic Islands
Fossils and fauna of Mallorca.
M.-Sa. by appointment. Closed Su. and public holidays.

PONTEVEDRA

NATURAL HISTORY COLLECTION
Instituto, Calle Montero Ríos, Pontevedra
Fauna. Minerals.
Daily 9-1.

PONTEVEDRA MUSEUM
Plaza de la Leña, Calle de Pasantería, Pontevedra
Local archaeology. 19th-20th century paintings. Prehistoric and medieval goldsmiths' work. Jet ornaments. Folk art and handicrafts.
Daily 11-1, 5-8.

PUERTO REAL

MUNICIPAL MUSEUM
Calle Marqués de Comillas, Puerto Real, Cadiz
Local archaeology.
Daily 6-9.

PUIG DE SANTA MARIA

ROYAL MONASTERY OF SANTA MARIA DEL PUIG
Puig de Santa Maria, Valencia
Paintings. Vestments. Church plate (gold). Ceramics. Ironwork. Coins.
By appointment.

QUEJANA

DOMINICAN MONASTERY
Quejana, Ayala
On Amurrio-Valmaseda road. Fortified monastery of the 14th century. Collections of paintings and goldsmiths' work.
9-1, 4-7, by previous arrangement with monastery.

QUESADA

ZABALETA MUSEUM
Plaza Coronación 10, Quesada, Jaén
Paintings, watercolours and drawings by Rafael Zabaleta (1907-60).
Daily 10-1.

LA RABIDA

MONASTERIO DE SANTA MARIA
Palos de la Frontera, La Rabida, Huelva
Monastery buildings of 13th-18th centuries. Material relating to the discovery and conquest of South America. Frescoes (1930) by Vásquez Díaz.
Daily May-Sept. 10-1, 4-8. Oct.-Apr. 10-1, 3-6.30.

REUS

MUNICIPAL MUSEUM
Avenida Martires 13, Reus, Tarragona
Art and history of the Reus district. Folk arts. Handicrafts.
Daily ex. W. 11-1, 3-5.

REQUENA

REQUENA AND DISTRICT HISTORICAL MUSEUM
Calle del Castillo, Requena, Valencia
Archaeology. Ethnology. Local history. Historic books and documents.
By appointment.

REUS

PRIM-RULL MUSEUM
Calle San Juan 27, Reus, Tarragona
Art and historical collection of Pedro Ruel Trula.
By appointment.

LA RIBA

JOSÉ SERRA FARRÉ LIBRARY AND MUSEUM
Ayuntamiento, La Riba, Tarragona
18th-19th century weapons. Glazed tiles.
By appointment.

RIBADAVIA

MUSEUM OF FOLK ART AND CUSTOMS
Casa de Martin Vazquez, Ribadavia, Orense
In 17th century house. Ethnography of the Galician Valley, especially the Ribeiro district.
By appointment.

RIOFRIO

NATIONAL HUNTING MUSEUM
Palacio Real, Riofrio, Segovia
Dioramas of animals and birds hunted in Spain. Spanish and foreign hunting trophies. Weapons and equipment. Art with hunting as a theme, including 'Head of a Stag' by Velasquez.
Daily 10-1, 3-7.

RIPOLL

PAROCHIAL MUSEUM AND ARCHIVE OF FOLKLORE
Former Church of San Pedro, Plaza del Abad Oliva, Ripoll, Gerona
Ethnography. Guns made in Ripoll, 15th-19th centuries. Coins. Costumes.
May-Sept. Daily 9-1, 3-8. Oct.-Apr. Daily 10-1, 3-6.

RODA DE ISABENA

PAROCHIAL MUSEUM
Sala Capitular, Antigua Catedral, Roda de Isabena, Huesca
15th-16th century paintings. Sculpture. Liturgical objects. Ornaments. Furniture. Medieval textiles.
Daily 8-6.

RONCESVALLES

MUSEUM OF ART
Real Colegiata, Roncesvalles, Navarra
Paintings. Goldsmiths' work. Vestments. Mausoleum of Sancho el Fuente, King of Navarre, and his wife.
Daily 11.30-1, 4.30-7.

RUBI

LOCAL MUSEUM
Biblioteca Municipal, Calle Calvo Sotelo, Rubi, Barcelona
Art and local history collections.
Su., public holidays, 11-2.

SABADELL

FINE ARTS MUSEUM
Calle Tres Cruces, Sabadell, Barcelona
Spanish paintings, sculpture, applied arts.
Su., public holidays 11.30-1.30.

MUSEUM OF HISTORY
Calle San Antonio 13, Sabadell, Barcelona
Prehistory. Archaeology. Mineralogy. Palaeontology. History of Sabadell. Textiles. Coins. Furniture. Folk art. Works by local artists.
Su., public holidays, 11.30-1.30.

PROVINCIAL INSTITUTE AND MUSEUM OF PALAEONTOLOGY
Calle Escuela Industrial 23, Sabadell, Barcelona
Palaeontology collections, with special reference to Spain. Postage stamps with palaeontology as a theme.
Sa. 5-8. Public holidays 11-2.

SAGUNTO

ARCHAEOLOGICAL MUSEUM
Calle Castillo, Sagunto, Valencia
Material, mostly Roman, from local excavations. Mosaics from Prado Villa and other sites. 13th and 15th century frescoes. Ivories. Bronzes.
Daily May-Sept. 9-8. Oct.-Apr. 9-6.

SAHAGUN

MONASTERY OF THE HOLY CROSS
Calle Alfonso VI, Sahagun, León
Religious art. Textiles. Tombs of Alfonso VI, his wife and other important figures in the history of Castille and León.
Daily 10-1, 4-7.

SALAMANCA

DIOCESAN MUSEUM
Catedral Vieja, Salamanca
15th-16th century paintings. 14th-18th century sculpture. Church plate (gold). Textiles.
Daily May-Sept. 10.30-1.30, 3.30-7.30. Oct.-May 10.30-1, 3-6.

MUSEUM OF THE CONVENT OF ST. URSULA
Calle de las Ursulas, Salamanca
14th-16th century paintings. Sculpture.
Daily 9-12, 4.30-7.30.

PROVINCIAL MUSEUM OF FINE ART
Calle Fray Luis de León 1, Salamanca
Local archaeology. 15th-19th century paintings.
Daily May-Sept. 9-1, 4.30-8.30. Oct.-Apr. 10-3.

UNAMUNO HOUSE-MUSEUM
Antigua Rectoral, Libreros 7, Salamanca
In former home of the writer, Miguel de Unamuno y Jugo (d.1936), Rector of the University of Salamanca. Unamuno's furniture, personal possessions, correspondence.
By appointment.

SALLENT

BIRTHPLACE OF SAN ANTONIO MARIA CLARET
Iglesia de San Antonio, Plaza de la Paz, Sallent, Barcelona
Material relating to the life of the Saint (canonised 1950).
By appointment.

SAN CUGAT DEL VALLES

MONASTERIO DE SAN CUGAT
Plaza Octaviano, San Cugat del Valles, Barcelona
Architectural items from buildings of the district. Paintings. Material relating to the history of the Monastery.
Daily ex. M. 10-1, 3-7.

SAN FELIU DE GUIXOLS

MUNICIPAL MUSEUM
Plaza Monasterio, San Feliu de Guixols, Gerona
Archaeology. 18th-19th century ceramics from Catalonia and Valencia. 15th-18th century missals.
May-Sept. Daily 11-1, 4-6. Oct.-Apr. 1st Su. in month, 12-2.

SAN GINES DE VILASAR

MUNICIPAL ARCHAEOLOGICAL MUSEUM
Plaza del Caudillo 7, San Gines de Vilasar, Barcelona
Local history. Archaeological material from the excavations in the area. Art.
By appointment.

SAN ILDEFONSO O LA GRANJA

ROYAL PALACE
San Ildefonso o la Granja, Segovia
Palace (1721-23). Furniture. Tapestries. Lamps.
Daily 10-1, 2-6.

SAN JUAN DE LAS ABADESAS

ARCHIVE AND MUSEUM OF THE MONASTERY
Former Monastery, now parish church of St. John, San Juan de las Abadesas, Gerona
Vestments. Service books. Sculpture.
By appointment.

SAN JUAN DE LA PEÑA

ROYAL MONASTERY DE SAN JUAN DE LA PEÑA
Botaya, San Juan de la Peña, Huesca
Buildings of 9th-12th centuries. Architectural and sculptural items from the former Royal Monastery (11th-15th centuries).
Daily 10-6.

SAN JUAN DE VILASAR

MONJÓ GALLERY
Camino Real 36, San Juan de Vilasar, Barcelona
Collection of sculptures presented by Enrique Monjó.
Daily 12-2. May-Oct. also 6-8.

SAN LORENZO DE EL ESCORIAL

MONASTERY OF SAN LORENZO
San Lorenzo de El Escorial, Madrid
Buildings of 16th-18th centuries. Paintings. Furnishings. Tapestries. Lamps. Goldsmiths' work. Vestments.
Daily Apr. 15-Oct. 15, 10-1, 3-7. Oct. 16-Apr. 14, 10-1, 3-6. Closed all day, Jan. 1, Good F., July 18, Dec. 25. Closed a.m. Feb. 28; closed p.m. Aug. 10.

SAN LORENZO DE MORUNYS

MUSEUM OF THE PATRONATO OF VALL DE LORD
Nuestra Señora dels Collis 1, San Lorenzo de Morunys, Lerida
Archaeology. Paintings. Coins. Popular arts and crafts. Geology.
By appointment.

SAN MATEO

PAROCHIAL MUSEUM
Church of San Mateo, Plaza Generalismo, San Mateo, Castellon de la Plana
Liturgical vessels. Medieval sculpture.
By appointment.

SAN MILLAN DE LA COGOLLA

MONASTERY OF SAN MILLAN DE SUSO
San Millan de la Cogolla (near), Logroño
Buildings of 10th-11th centuries. Tombs of the seven Infantes de Lara and their tutor, Nuño Salido.
Daily 9-dusk.

MONASTERY OF SAN MILLAN DE YUSO
San Millan de la Cogolla, Logroño
Painting. Sculpture. Ivories of the 11th century. Smithy.
May-Sept. Daily 9-12, 4-8. Oct.-Apr. Daily 9-12, 4-7.

SAN PEDRO DE CARDEÑA

MONASTERY OF SAN PEDRO
Castrillo del Val, San Pedro de Cardeña, Burgos
Contains chapel (1736) built to house the remains of El Cid and Doña Jimena. Religious art and history.
May-Sept. 10-1, 4-7. Oct.-Apr. Daily 10-1, 2-5.

SAN ROQUE

HISTORICAL MUSEUM
Ayuntamiento, San Roque, Cadiz
Documents on Gibraltar. Material from Carteyan excavations.
By appointment.

SAN SADURNI DE NOYA

MUSEUM OF THE ORDER OF LOS HOMENAJES A LA VEJEZ
(Veneration for Old Age), Calle Francisco Moragas 1, San Sadurni de Noya, Barcelona
Material relating to the foundation of the Order and to its subsequent expansion over the world.
By appointment.

SAN SEBASTIAN

CASA DE UQUENDO
Barrio de Gros, San Sebastian, Guipuzcoa
16th-17th century paintings and furniture.
Daily ex. Su. p.m., M. a.m. May-Sept. 10-1.30, 3.30-7. Oct.-Apr. 10-1.30, 3.30-6.

MUNICIPAL MUSEUM OF SAN TELMO
Plaza Ignacio Zuloaga, San Sebastian, Guipuzcoa
15th-20th century paintings. Basque ethnography. Weapons. Prehistory. Archaeology. Anthropology. Ancient chapel decorated with 11 murals by José María Sert. Works by Goya, El Greco.
Daily ex. Su. p.m., M. a.m. May-Sept. 10-1.30, 3.30-7. Oct.-Apr. 10-1.30, 3.30-5.30.

MUSEUM OF MILITARY HISTORY
Monte Urgull, San Sebastian, Guipuzcoa
Weapons. Military history.
Daily ex. M. a.m. May-Sept. 10-1, 3.30-7. Oct.-Apr. 10-1, 3.30-6.

NAVAL MUSEUM
Sociedad de Oceanografia de Guipuzcoa, San Sebastian, Guipuzcoa
Models of famous ships, portraits of navigators. Equipment used by local fishermen. Oceanography.
Daily ex. M. a.m.; May-Sept. 10-1, 3.30-7. Oct.-Apr. 10-1, 3.30-6.

SANTA COLUMBA DE QUERALT

MUSEUM OF THE TOWN ARCHAEOLOGICAL SOCIETY
Patio de Armas del Castilo, Santa Columba de Queralt, Tarragona
Material relating to the history of the district.
May-Sept. Daily 10.30-2.30, 6-8. Oct.-Apr. 9-2.

SANTA CRUZ

MUSEUM OF ETHNOGRAPHY AND NATURAL HISTORY
Wandevalle, Santa Cruz, Isla de la Palma, Santa Cruz de Tenerife, Canary Islands
Local ethnography.
Daily 9-1, 3-6.

PROVINCIAL MUSEUM OF FINE ART
Casa de la Cultura, Santa Cruz, Isla de la Palma, Santa Cruz de Tenerife, Canary Islands
19th century Spanish paintings.
Daily 9-1, 3-6.

SANTA CRUZ DE TENERIFE

ARCHAEOLOGICAL MUSEUM
Calle Bravo Murillo, Santa Cruz de Tenerife, Canary Islands
Archaeology and anthropology of the Canary Islands.
Daily 9-1, 5-7.

MUNICIPAL MUSEUM
Antiguo Convento de San Francisco, Calle J. Murphy 6, Santa Cruz de Tenerife, Canary Islands
Ethnology. Paintings. Sculpture. Weapons.
Daily May-Sept. 9-1. Oct.-Apr. 9-1, 6-8.

SANTA EULALIA DEL RIO

BARRAU MUSEUM
Church of Puig de Missa, Santa Eulalia del Rio, Ibiza, Balearic Islands
In 16th century fortified church. Collection relating to the life and work of the painter Laureano Barrau y Buñol (d.1957).
May-Sept. 5-8.

SANTA GADEA DEL CID

PAROCHIAL MUSEUM
Church of St. Peter the Apostle, Plaza de la Fuente, Santa Gadea del Cid, Burgos
Religious art. Ornaments. Sculpture. Illuminated song-books. Medieval manuscripts.
Dawn-dusk, except during service times.

SANTA MARIA DEL CAMPO

PAROCHIAL MUSEUM
Parroquia de la Asunción, Plaza Mayor, Santa Maria del Campo, Burgos
Church of 1527. Religious paintings (4 by Pedro de Berraguete) and goldsmiths' work. Brussels tapestries.
By appointment.

SANTANDER

MENÉNDEZ PELAYO HOUSE-MUSEUM
Calle Gravina 4, Santander
House of the writer, Marcelino Menéndez y Pelayo (1856-1912), preserved as it was at the time of his death.
Daily 9-1, 4-7.

MUNICIPAL MUSEUM OF FINE ART
Biblioteca Ménendez Pelayo, Calle Rubio 6, Santander
Painting and sculpture, mainly regional. Contains study of Marcelino Ménendez y Pelayo, in which he wrote his *History of Aesthetic Ideas in Spain.*
Daily ex. public holidays, 10-1, 4-8.

PROVINCIAL MUSEUM OF PREHISTORY AND ARCHAEOLOGY
Diputación Provincial, Calle de Juan de la Cosa 1, Santander
Chiefly prehistoric material from the excavations at Cuevas del Castillo and El Pendo. Celtic stelae connected with sun worship. Roman collection. Prehistoric art.
Daily May-Sept. 10-1, 5-7. Oct.-Apr. 10-1.

SANTIAGO DE COMPOSTELA

CATHEDRAL MUSEUM
Piaterias, Santiago de Compostela, La Coruña
Tapestries. Sculpture. Goldsmiths' work. Vestments. Archaeology and archaeological items from the earlier Romanesque Cathedral. Illuminated manuscripts.
May-Sept. Daily 9.30-1.30, 4-7.30. Oct.-Apr. Daily 10-1.30, 4-6.

LUIS IGLESIAS MUSEUM OF NATURAL HISTORY
Facultad de Ciencias, Avenida de las Ciencias 1, Santiago de Compostela, La Coruña
Mineralogy and zoology, especially of the region.
By appointment.

MUNICIPAL MUSEUM
Convento de Santo Domingo, Santiago de Compostela, La Coruña
Art. Local history.
Daily 10-7.

MUSEUM OF PILGRIMAGES
Calle San Miguel 4, Santiago de Compostela, La Coruña
Material relating to pilgrimages made to the shrine of St. James of Compostela.
May-Sept. Daily 10-2, 5-8. Oct.-Apr. Daily 10-2.

SANTILLANA DEL MAR

ALTAMIRA CAVES
Santillana del Mar, Santander
Palaeolithic rock-paintings. Prehistoric material from local excavations.
Daily 10-3, 4-8.

DIOCESAN MUSEUM
Monasterio de Regina Coeli, Santillana del Mar, Santander
Religious art from churches in the diocese. Furniture. Photographic exhibition of Romanesque art and architecture in the Province of Santander.
Daily June 15-Sept. 30, 10-8. Remainder of year by appointment.

MUSEUM OF THE COLLEGIATE CHURCH OF SANTA JULIANA
Claustro Románico, Santillana del Mar, Santander
Architectural and artistic items of the Church.
When church is open, except during services.

SANTIPONCE

ITALICA ARCHAEOLOGICAL MUSEUM
Santiponce, Sevilla
Material from the Roman city of Italica.
Mar.-Oct. Daily 9-7.30. Nov.-Feb. Daily 9-5.30.

SANTO DOMINGO DE SITOS

MUSEUM OF ARCHAEOLOGY AND NATURAL HISTORY
Monastery of Santo Domingo, Santo Domingo de Sitos, Burgos
Pottery from local excavations. Coins. Roman art. Manuscripts. Geology. Natural history. 17th century pharmacy.
Daily 9-2, 4-7.

SEGORBE

DIOCESAN AND CATHEDRAL MUSEUM
Calle de Santa Maria, Segorbe, Castellon de la Plana
Paintings, sculptures, ornaments and other works of art belonging to the Cathedral.
May-Sept. Daily 11-1.30, 5-7. Oct.-Apr. Daily 11-1.30, 5-7.

SEGOVIA

ALCAZÁR
Plaza del Alcazár, Segovia
Palace (1076, restored) contains weapons and furniture.
Daily May-Sept. 9-sunset. Oct.-Apr. 10-sunset.

ANTONIO MACHADO HOUSE-MUSEUM
Calle de Los Desamparados, Segovia
Home of the poet, 1919-33, with his books, furniture and personal possessions, including signed pen and ink drawing by Picasso, as a token of esteem to Machado from Spanish artists.
Daily 9-6.

ARCHAEOLOGICAL MUSEUM
San Agustin 8, Segovia
Local archaeology.
Daily May-Sept. 10.30-1.30, 3.30-7. Oct.-Apr. 10.30-1.30, 3.30-6. Closed Good F. and p.m. June 29, July 18.

CATHEDRAL MUSEUM
Cathedral, Plaza Mayor, Segovia
Religious paintings and sculpture. Church plate (gold). Tapestries. Vestments.
Daily May-Sept. 9-6. Oct.-Apr. 9-1, 3-6.

LA VERA CRUZ
Barrio de San Marcos, Segovia
Early 13th century church, built by the Knights Templar. Frescoes of the 13th century.
Daily ex. M. 10-1.30, 4-sunset.

MONASTERY OF SAN ANTONIO EL REAL
Calle de San Antonio el Real 4, Segovia
Paintings. Sculpture. Furniture. Vestments. 15th century panelled ceilings. Choir-books.
Daily 10-1, 3-7.

PALACIO DE LA GRANJA DE SAN ILDEFONSO
Segovia
Gardens and fountains in imitation of Versailles. Tapestry museum.
May-Oct., daily 10-1, 2.30-6. Nov.-Apr., daily 10-1, 3-7. Closed July 18.

PALACIO DE RIOFRIO
Segovia
Furniture and paintings of the Spanish romantic movement.
May-Oct., daily 10-1, 2.30-6. Nov.-Apr., daily 10-1, 3-7. Closed July 18.

PROVINCIAL MUSEUM OF FINE ART
Casa del Hidalgo, San Agustin 8, Segovia
Paintings. Sculpture. Ceramics. La Granja cut glass. Wrought ironwork.
Daily May-Sept. 10.30-1.30, 3.30-7. Oct.-Apr. 10.30-1.30, 3.30-6. Closed Good F. and p.m. June 29, July 18.

ZULOAGA MUSEUM
Church of San Juan de los Caballeros, Segovia
Ceramics by Daniel Zuloaga (d.1921). Paintings.
Daily 9-2, 4-7.

SEO DE URGEL

DIOCESAN MUSEUM
Cathedral and Church of the Pienad, Seo de Urgel, Lerida
Religious art from churches in the diocese. 13th century textiles. Illuminated codices and service books.
May-Sept. Daily 9-6. Oct.-Apr. Public holidays only, 10-2.

SEVILLE

ALCAZAR
Plaza del Triunfo, Seville
Palace of various periods, 12th century onwards. Tapestries. Paintings. Mosaics. 'Virgin of the Navigators' by Alejo Fernández, the first European work of religious art connected with the discovery of the Indies.
Daily May-Sept. 9-12.45, 4-6.45. Oct.-Apr. 9-12.45, 3-5.

CASA DE PILATOS
Plaza de Pilatos 1, Seville
16th century palace. Roman antiquities, mostly from Italy. Paintings. Tiles.
Daily May-Sept. 9-1, 3-9. Oct.-Apr. 10-1, 3-9.

CATHEDRAL MUSEUM
Avenida Queipo de Llano, Seville
15th century Cathedral contains the tomb and library of Columbus. Painting. Sculpture, including the statue of Faith carrying the banner of Constantine, which revolves as a weathervane. Church plate. Vestments. Objects of historical interest, 15th-20th centuries.
Daily May-Sept. 10.30-1, 4-6.30. Oct.-Apr. 10.30-1, 3-5.30.

HOLY WEEK MUSEUM
Hospicio de Venerables Sacerdotes, Plaza Venerables 8, Seville
Collection of religious art belonging to the Confraternities of Seville. Church plate. Statuary. Gold and silver embroidery.
Daily ex. Su. p.m. 10-2, 4-8.

HOSPITAL DE LA SANTA CARIDAD
Iglesia de San Jorge, Calle Temprado 3, Seville
Painting. Sculpture.
Daily 9-5.

HOUSE OF THE COUNTESS OF LEBRIJA
Calle Cuna 18, Seville
Archaeological collections formed by the Countess of Lebrija in the early 19th century. Mostly Roman, from excavations in Italy, but with some medieval (Spanish Moslem) items.
Daily 11-1, 3-5.

HOUSE OF THE DUEÑAS
Calle de las Dueñas 5, Seville
15th century palace. Paintings. Sculpture.
By appointment.

MUSEUM OF CONTEMPORARY ART
Antiqua iglesia de San Hermenegildo, Seville
20th century European art.
Daily 10-2, 5-7.

MUSEUM OF THE GOLDEN TOWER
(Torre del Oro), Paseo de Cristóbal Colón, Seville
13th century watch tower, now a maritime museum. Contains collection of old nautical instruments.
Tu.-Sa. 10-2. Public holidays 10-1.

MUSEUM AND TREASURY OF THE BASILICA OF THE MACARENA
Calle Bécquer 1, Seville
19th-20th century embroidery. Church plate (gold). Vestments. Processional images.
Daily 9-1, 5-9.

MUSEUM AND TREASURY OF THE TEMPLO DEL GRAN PODER
Plaza de San Lorenzo, Seville
Church plate (gold). Vestments.
Daily 10-12, 4-6.

OSUNA COLLECTION
Calle Alfonso XII 48, Seville
Paintings. Furniture. Tapestries. Porcelain. Fans.
By appointment.

PAROCHIAL MUSEUM
Plaza de Santa Maria, Seville
Roman and Arab material from local excavations. Includes a bust of Germanicus.
Daily 9-1, 4-8.

PROVINCIAL ARCHAEOLOGICAL MUSEUM
Plaza de América, Seville
Classical and medieval archaeology, including material from the Roman ruins at Italica. Imperial busts. Tartessian collection from El Carambolo.
Daily ex. M., public holidays, May-Sept. 9-2, 5-7. Oct.-Apr. 9-2, 4-6.

PROVINCIAL MUSEUM OF FINE ART
Plaza Museo 8, Seville
In former friary. Spain's second most important picture gallery. 15th-20th century paintings, including works by Zurbarán, Murillo and Valdés Leal, and by Seville artists. Sculpture. Drawings. Ceramics. Furniture. Weapons.
Daily ex. public holidays 10-2.

SIERRA DE YEGUAS

MUSEO DEL COMPO
Sierra de Yeguas, Malaga
Local ethnography.
By appointment.

SIGÜENZA

CATHEDRAL MUSEUM
Cathedral, Sigüenza, Guadalajara
Sculpture. Paintings. Tapestries.
Daily 11.30-1.30, 4.30-7.

DIOCESAN MUSEUM OF ANCIENT ART
Antigua Casa de los Barrenas, Plaza del Obispo D. Bernardo, Sigüenza, Guadalajara
Archaeological material from local sites. Religious art. Paintings. Sculpture. Goldsmiths' work. 12th-18th century architectural features.
Daily 9-2, 4-8.

SITGES

MARICEL DE MAR MUSEUM
Sitges, Barcelona
Jewels. Mosaics. Ceramics. Glass. Modern paintings.
Tu.-Su. 10-1.30, 4-6.

MUSEUM OF CAU FERRAT
Sitges, Barcelona
Artistic ironwork in Europe. Ceramics and paintings, including works by El Greco, Zuluago, Utrillo and Rusinol. Sculpture. Furniture. Glass.
Daily 9-1, 3-7.

PROVINCIAL MUSEUM OF THE ROMANTIC PERIOD
Casa Llopis, Sitges, Barcelona
Furniture and decoration, late 18th-19th centuries. 17th-19th century dolls.
Daily ex. M. 10-1.30, 4-7.

SOLSONA

DISTRICT MUSEUM OF ETHNOGRAPHY
Calle Castillo 20, Solsona, Lerida
History, art and ethnology of the Solsona area. Cutler's workshop.
Daily 10-1, 4.30-7.30.

DIOCESAN ARCHAEOLOGICAL MUSEUM
Palacio Episcopal, Solsona, Lerida
Religious art from churches in the diocese. Paintings of the 10th-15th centuries. Medieval and Renaissance sculpture.
Daily 10-1.

SORIA

CELTIBERIAN MUSEUM
Calle Caballeros 17, Soria
Local archaeology.
Daily 10-1.

NUMANCIA MUSEUM
Calle General Yagüe 8, Soria
Material discovered during excavations at Numancia.
Daily ex. p.m. public holidays, May-Sept. 10-1, 3-7. Oct.-Apr. 10-1, 3-6.

SAN JUAN EPIGRAPHIC MUSEUM
Antiguo Monasterio de San Juan, Soria
In former monastery buildings of the 12th-13th centuries. Roman inscriptions and mosaics.
Daily 10-5.

TALAVERA DE LA REINA

RUIZ DE LUNA MUSEUM OF CERAMICS
Plaza General Primo de Rivera 5, Talavera de la Reina, Toledo
Collection of local ceramics made by the Ruiz de Luna family. Old pottery factory.
Daily 10.30-2, 3.30-7.

TARRAGONA

CITY MUSEUM
Plaza Pallol 1, Tarragona
Prints and maps showing development of Tarragona. Iberian and Roman ceramics. Glass. Heraldry. Inscriptions. Coins.
Daily ex. public holidays and Su. p.m., May 1 - Sept. 30, 9-1, 3-7. Oct.-Apr. 9-1, 3-5.

DIOCESAN MUSEUM
Cathedral, Tarragona
14th-18th century paintings, especially the collection of primitives. 14th-18th century sculpture. Tapestries. Church plate. Vestments. Handicrafts. 18th-19th century medals. Coins. Local archaeology, including finds from Escornalbou.
Daily May-Sept. 10-1, 3.30-6. Oct.-Apr. 10.30-12.30, 3.30-5.

MOLAS COLLECTION
Llano de la Catedral 6, Tarragona
Collection of works of art, formed by Juan Molas Sabaté. Coins.
By appointment.

MUSEUM OF EARLY CHRISTIANITY
Carretera de Alcolea, Tarragona
Material from early Christian cemetery. 4th-6th century lead and marble sarcophagi. Tombstones. Mosaics. Ivory doll from 4th century child's grave.
Daily 10-1, 3-6.

MUSEUM OF FOLK ART AND CUSTOMS
Plaza Pallol 1, Tarragona
Prints and drawings of Tarragona. Pottery. Heraldry. Glass. Coins. Ethnography.
May-Oct., M.-Sa. 9-1, 3-7; Su. 9-1. Nov.-Apr., M.-Sa. 9-1, 3-5. Closed public holidays.

MUSEUM OF THE ROMANTIC PERIOD
Palacio Castellarnau, Calle Caballeros, Tarragona
Local history. Decorative arts of the 18th-19th centuries.
By appointment.

PROVINCIAL ARCHAEOLOGICAL MUSEUM
Plaza del Rey 1, Tarragona
Roman and medieval archaeology. 14th-16th century paintings. 15th century ceramics from Manises and Paterna.
Daily 10-1.30, 4-7.

TARRASA

BIOSCA TEXTILE MUSEUM
Calle General Sanjurjo, Tarrasa, Barcelona
Textiles from Spain and from medieval and Renaissance Europe, Near and Far East and South America. Spanish lace. Costumes. Religious ornaments. French and Spanish prints and engravings of the 18th-19th centuries. Handicrafts.
Daily ex. M. 11-1.30. Closed Holy Week and second half of July.

IGLESIAS DE EGARA
Plaza de Nector Horns, Tarrasa, Barcelona
Complex of three 11th-12th century churches, containing frescoes, retables and other paintings of the 13th-15th centuries.
Daily, dawn to dusk.

MUNICIPAL MUSEUM OF ART
Castillo-Cartuja Vallparadis, Calle General Sarjurjo 24, Tarrasa, Barcelona
Archaeology. Decorative arts. Paintings. Sculpture. Architectural details from local buildings. Coins.
Daily ex. M. and public holidays p.m., 10-2, 4-7.

TARREGA

MUNICIPAL MUSEUM
Plaza Mayor 1, Tarrega, Lerida
Local archaeology and palaeontology.
By appointment.

TELDE

LEON Y CASTILLO HOUSE MUSEUM
Biblioteca Pública Municipal, Telde, Las Palmas, Canary Islands
Library and other possessions of the politician, Fernando de León y Castillo.
By appointment.

TERUEL

DIOCESAN MUSEUM OF RELIGIOUS ART
Palacio Episcopal, Plaza del Venerable Francés de Aranda, Teruel
Works of art and liturgical objects from churches in the diocese.
By appointment.

PROVINCIAL ARCHAEOLOGICAL MUSEUM
Plaza de Pérez Prado, Teruel
Archaeology. Teruel pottery from the 13th century to the present day.
Daily 11.30-2.

TOLEDO

EL GRECO MUSEUM
Travesia del Transito, Toledo
Furniture and other objects of the period of El Greco. Paintings by El Greco and by other artists of the 15th-17th centuries. Photographs of all known works by El Greco. The adjoining El Greco House is a restored part of the 16th century palace where El Greco lived 1585-6 and 1604-13. It contains paintings by him, and by Murillo, Velasquez and others.
Daily May-Sept. 10-1.30, 3.30-7. Oct.-Apr. 10-1.30, 3.30-6.

MUSEUM OF THE COUNCILS AND OF VISIGOTH CULTURE
Antiquo Templo de San Román, Plaza de San Román, Toledo
Architectural features from the Church of Santa Leocadia, principal meeting place of the Councils of Toledo. Archaeology of the Visigoths.
Daily 10-2, 3.30-7.

MUSEUM OF THE DUKE OF LERMA'S FOUNDATION
Hospital Tavera, Toledo
Pharmacy of the Hospital (16th century). Paintings. Furniture. 17th century period rooms. Sumptuary art.
Daily May-Sept. 10-1, 4-7. Oct.-Apr. 10-1, 3-6.

MUSEUM OF THE PARISH OF SANTO TOME
Calle de Santo Tome, Toledo
Paintings, including one by El Greco (1596).
May-Sept. M.-Sa. 10-1.30, 3-7; Su. 10-10.45, 1-7. Oct.-Apr. M.-Sa. 10-1.30, 3-6; Su. 10-10.45, 1-6.30.

MUSEUM OF THE SANTA HERMANDAD
Calle Hermandad 4, Toledo
History and organisation of the Santa Hermandad, a 15th century rural police force and judiciary.
Daily 10-1, 3-6.

MUSEUM OF THE SIEGE
Alcázar, Calle General Moscardó 4, Toledo
Material documenting the siege of the Alcázar in 1936.
Daily Oct. 15-Feb. 14, 9.30-6. Feb. 15-Apr. 14, 9.30-6.30. Apr. 15-Oct. 14, 9.15-7.45.

MUSEUM AND TREASURY OF THE CATHEDRAL
Cathedral, Plaza Generalismo, Toledo
Paintings. Church plate (gold). Vestments. Illuminated books.
M.-Sa. 10.30-1, 3.30-7. Public holidays 10.30-1.30, 3.30-7.

PALACE OF FUENSALIDA
Plaza del Conde 4, Toledo
In 19th century palace. Collections illustrating the history and art of this century, the Golden Century.
Daily 10-2, 3.30-7.

SANTA CRUZ MUSEUM
Calle Cervantes, Toledo
Archaeology of the Roman, Visigoth, Arab and Moslem periods. Fine Arts, especially 16th-17th century paintings by artists belonging to or associated with Toledo, including El Greco, Ribera, Murillo. Ceramics. Glass. Textiles. Wrought iron. Goldsmiths' work.
Daily May-Sept. 10-2, 3.30-7.30. Oct.-Apr. 10-2, 3.30-7.

SEPHARDIC MUSEUM
Samuel-Ha-Levi Synagogue, Travesia del Tránsito, Toledo
Jewish history and art. Tombstones. Liturgical lamps. Documents. 14th century Synagogue of the Tránsito.
Oct.-Mar. Daily 10-2, 3.30-6. Apr.-Sept. Daily 10-2, 3.30-7. Closed Good F. all day, and the afternoon of Christmas Day.

TALLER DEL MORO (MOORISH WORKSHOP)
Plaza Generalismo, Toledo
Moorish archaeology. Industrial arts.
Daily 10-2, 3.30-7.

VICTORIO MACHO HOUSE MUSEUM
Roca Tarpeya, Calle Santa Ana 1, Toledo
Sculpture and drawings by Macho (d.1966), in the house where he lived and worked.
Daily ex. M. May-Sept 10-2, 3.30-7. Oct.-Apr. 10-2, 3.30-6.30.

TOMELLOSO

MUSEUM OF HORSE-DRAWN TRANSPORT AND AGRICULTURE
Tomelloso, Ciudad Real
On outskirts of village, on road to Pedro Muñoz. Local ethnography. Transport. Agriculture.
On request.

TORDESILLAS

ROYAL MONASTERY OF SANTA CLARA
Tordesillas, Valladolid
Paintings. Sculpture. Textiles. Furniture. Choir-books.
May-Sept. Daily 9.30-1, 3-6. Oct.-Apr. Daily 9.30-1, 3-6.

TORTOSA

CATHEDRAL MUSEUM
Cathedral, Plaza de la Olivera, Tortosa, Tarragona
Tapestries. Church plate (gold). Enamels.
By appointment.

MUNICIPAL MUSEUM AND ARCHIVE
Calle Santo Domingo, Tortosa, Tarragona
Local art and history. Roman inscriptions.
Daily May-Sept. 9-2, 6-8. Oct.-Apr. 9-2.

TOSSA

MUNICIPAL MUSEUM
Villa Vella, Tossa, Gerona
Items from Roman villa excavations. Modern painting and sculpture, especially by Catalan artists.
May-Sept. Daily 10-1, 4-8. Oct.-Apr. Daily 10-1, 3-7.

TRAIGUERA

MUSEUM PARROQUIAL DE LA ASUNCIÓN
Calle Mayor, Traiguera, Castellon de la Plana
Religious ornaments and liturgical goldsmiths' work.
By appointment.

TUDELA

DIOCESAN MUSEUM
Cathedral, Plaza de Santa Maria, Tudela, Navarra
Religious paintings and sculpture. Archaeology. Vestments.
By appointment.

TUY

CATHEDRAL MUSEUM
Cathedral, Tuy, Pontevedra
Religious art. Archaeology. Stone inscriptions.
By appointment.

ULLASTRET

MUSEUM OF THE EXCAVATIONS
Acropolis del Puig de Sant Andreu, Ullastret, Gerona
Items from excavations on 1st-2nd century site.
Daily, dawn-dusk.

VALDEPEÑAS

GREGORIO PRIETO MILL-MUSEUM
Calle Gregorio Prieto, Valdepeñas, Ciudad Real
On three floors of the largest mill in Spain. Paintings and drawings by Gregorio Prieto.
By appointment.

VALENCIA

BENLLIURE HOUSE-MUSEUM
Calle Blanquerías 23, Valencia
House and studio of the painter Jose Benlliure Gil (d.1937). Paintings by him, his son and other contemporary painters.
By appointment.

BIRTHPLACE OF SAN VICENTE FERRER
Calle Pociet de Sant Vincent, Valencia
House in which Vicente Ferrer y Miguel (d.1419), canonised 1455, was born. Material illustrating the life of the saint.
M.-Sa. 9-1, 4-8.30; Su. 9-1.

CITY HISTORICAL MUSEUM
Ayuntamiento, Plaza Candillo 1, Valencia
Material illustrating the history of Valencia.
Daily 9-1.

COLLECTION OF THE SAVINGS BANK
Caja de Ahorros, General Tovar 3, Valencia
Paintings and sculpture in different parts of the Savings Bank (Caja de Ahorros) building.
By appointment.

DIOCESAN AND CATHEDRAL MUSEUM
Plaza Almoyna, Valencia
Paintings, including works by Goya and Jacomart. Goldsmiths' work, including items by Cellini. Chalice, said to be the Holy Grail used by Christ at the Last Supper. Enamels. Vestments. Rare books.
Daily ex. Su. and public holidays p.m., May-Sept. 9-1, 4-7. Oct.-Apr. 9-1, 3-6.

GONZALEZ MARTI NATIONAL MUSEUM OF CERAMICS
Rinconada Garcia Sanchez, Valencia
Collection formed by Manuel Gonzalez Marti. Prehistoric, Greek, Roman, medieval and modern ceramics from Aragon, Catalonia, Valencia, Talavera, Seville and Toledo, and from Italy. Valencia silks. 18th century fans.
Daily ex. Th., Good F., May-Sept. 11-2, 6-9. Oct.-Apr. 11-2, 5-8.

MUNICIPAL MUSEUM OF PALAEONTOLOGY
Almudin, Calle del Almudin, Valencia
In medieval granary. Fossils of South American fauna. Anthropology.
Daily 10-2, ex. public holidays and 'one day a week' (not specified).

MUSEUM OF BULL-FIGHTING
Plaza de Toros, Pasaje Dr. Serra, Valencia
History and art of bull-fighting.
Daily 10-2, 4-8.

MUSEUM OF THE PATRIARCH
Colegio Corpus Christi, Calle de la Nave 1, Valencia
15th-16th century Brussels tapestries. Paintings, chiefly Spanish and Flemish. Church plate (gold). Furniture.
Daily 11-1, 5-7. Women not admitted.

MUSEUM OF PREHISTORY
Palacio de la Bailía, Plaza Manises 2, Valencia
Prehistory and archaeology of the Valencia region.
Daily ex. Su. 9-1.

MUSEUM OF THE UNIVERSITY LIBRARY
Universidad, Calle de la Nave, Valencia
Early printed books. Manuscripts. Illuminated manuscripts. Coins and medals. Paintings.
Daily 10-2.

MUSEUM OF THE VALENCIA SILK INDUSTRY
Calle Hospital 7, Valencia
Products and manufacturing processes of the local silk industry.
By appointment.

PROVINCIAL MUSEUM OF FINE ART
Calle San Pio V, 9, Valencia
Paintings, including works by Hieronymus Bosch, Ribalta, Ribera, Van Dyck, Goya and a self-portrait of Velasquez. Gothic reredoses. Sculpture. Archaeology. Engravings. 18th-19th century woodcarvings. Drawings. Industrial arts.
M.-Sa. 10-2. Public holidays 9-2.

VALLADOLID

HOUSE OF CERVANTES
Calle del Rastro 10-16, Valladolid
House in which Cervantes lived (1603-6) and in which he probably wrote the first part of *Don Quixote*. Material illustrating history of the house and the life and work of Cervantes. Contemporary furnishings.
Daily ex. Su. and public holidays p.m., 10-1.30, 4-7.

HOUSE-MUSEUM OF COLUMBUS
Calle Colón, Valladolid
Documents and maps illustrating the achievements of Columbus. Colonisation of America.
By appointment.

HOUSE OF ZORRILLA
Calle Fray Luis de Granada 1, Valladolid
Furniture and other possessions of the poet, José de Zorrila (d.1893). Manuscripts of his work.
Daily 10-1, 4-6.

MUSEUM OF THE CONVENT OF SANTA ANA
Monastereo de San Joaquín y Santa Ana, Plaza de Santa Ana, Valladolid
Painting. Sculpture. Liturgical ornaments.
M.-Sa. 11-1.30, 4-6. Public holidays 4-6.

MUSEUM OF THE DIOCESE AND CATHEDRAL
Cathedral, Calle Arribas 1, Valladolid
Religious art from the Cathedral and from churches in the

diocese. Images. Jewellery. Wooden reredos of St. John the Baptist. Silver monstrance by Juan de Arfe, of Toledo.
Apr.-Oct. Daily 9.30-1, 4-7. Nov.-Mar., Su., public holidays, 9.30-2.

MUSEUM OF THE MISSIONS
Paseo de Filipinos 7, Valladolid
Collections from the Spanish missions in China, S. America and the Phillipines. Archaeology. Paintings. Porcelain. Bronzes. Coins.
By appointment.

MUSEUM OF PAINTINGS
Iglesia de la Pasión, Calle de la Pasión, Valladolid
Paintings of the 14th-18th centuries.
Daily ex. Su. and p.m. public holidays, 10-1.30, 4-10.

NATIONAL MUSEUM OF SCULPTURE
Calle Cadenas de San Gregorio 1, Valladolid
Castilian, especially religious, sculptures of the 13th-18th centuries, including works by Alonso Berruguete and Gregorio Fernandez.
May-Sept. 10-1.30, 4.30-7; Su., public holidays, 10-3. Oct.-Apr. 10-1.30; Su., public holidays, 10-1.

PROVINCIAL MUSEUM OF ARCHAEOLOGY
Palacio de Fabio Nelli, Plaza de Fabio Nelli, Valladolid
Archaeology. Medieval and modern art.
Daily 9-2, 3.30-6. Closed Aug.

VALLDEMOSA

ROYAL CHARTERHOUSE
Plaza Cartuja, Valldemosa, Mallorca, Balearic Islands
17th century apothecary's shop. Museum of Chopin and George Sand. Collection of books and engravings from the House of Guasp. Material associated with Archduke Luis Salvador. Paintings, sculpture.
Daily ex. Su. p.m. May-Sept. 9.30-1.30, 3-7. Oct.-Apr. 9.30-1.30, 3-6.

VALLS

TOWN MUSEUM
Plaza Mártires 10, Valls, Tarragona
Local history. Paintings and sculpture by contemporary artists.
M.-Sa. by appointment. Su., public holidays, 12-2.

VENDRELL

MUNICIPAL MUSEUM
Calle Calvo Sotelo 14, Vendrell, Tarragona
Archaeology. Regional ethnography. Contemporary art.
Su., public holidays, 12-2. Th., Sa. 6-8.

VERDU

PAROCHIAL MUSEUM AND TREASURY
Church of Santa Maria, Plaza Obispo Cornella 6, Verdu, Lerida
Gold liturgical objects.
By appointment.

SANCTUARY OF SAN PEDRO CLAVES
Calle San Pedro Claves 30, Verdu, Lerida
Material relating to the life of the Jesuit, Pedro Claves (d.1654), who was born in the district and is known as the Apostle to the Negroes.
By appointment.

VERUELA

MONASTERY OF SANTA MARIA
Veruela, Zaragoza
Local history. Iberian archaeology.
By appointment.

VICH

BALMES MUSEUM
Casa de la Cultura, Plaza de don Miguel de Clariana, Vich, Barcelona
Books, furniture and other personal possessions of Jaime Balmes (1810-48).
By appointment.

EPISCOPAL MUSEUM OF ART AND ARCHAEOLOGY
Antiquo Colegio de San José, nr. Cathedral, Vich, Barcelona
Sculpture. Paintings and liturgical objects of the 11th-15th centuries. Archaeology. Coins. Medals. Decorative art. Handicrafts.
May-Sept. Daily 10-1, 4-7. Public holidays a.m.

VIGO

QUIÑONES DE LEÓN MUNICIPAL PAZO MUSEUM
Parque de Quiñones de León, Vigo, Pontevedra
In pazo of 1670. Paintings. Sculpture. Miniatures.
Tu.-Sa. 11-1, 4-6. Public holidays 11-2.

VILAFRANCA DEL PANADES

VILAFRANCA MUSEUM
Palacio de los Reyes de Aragon, Plaza de Jaime 1, Vilafranca del Panades, Barcelona
Collections illustrating the art of vine-growing and the techniques of wine-making in the Iberian peninsula and elsewhere. Exhibits include paintings, wine-glasses, gourds and containers, corks and cork-making equipment, barrels, vats and bottles, wine labels. Paintings by regional artists and records of the wine-festivals over the years.
Daily ex. M. 10-2, 4-6. May-Sept. 10-2, 4-8.

VILAJUIGA

GEOLOGICAL MUSEUM
Calle San Sebastián, Vilajuiga, Gerona
Mineralogy. Folk arts and handicrafts. Weapons.
Daily 10-1, 4-7.

VILEÑA

MUSEUM OF THE MONASTERY OF SANTA MARIA LA REAL
Calle Alta, Vileña, Burgos
Sarcophagi of 13th-14th centuries. Medieval sculpture. Liturgical objects.
Daily 9-12, 3-6.

VILLAGARCIA DE CAMPOS

MUSEUM OF THE COLLEGIATE CHURCH
Avenida Generalismo, Villagarcia de Campos, Valladolid
Painting. Sculpture. Church plate (gold). Presses of the Villagarcia printing establishment and copies of books produced there.
By appointment.

VILLANUEVA Y GELTRU

PROVINCIAL MUSEUM OF THE ROMANTIC PERIOD
Casa Papiol, Calle Mayor 30-32, Villanueva y Geltru, Barcelona
Furniture and decoration of the 18th-19th centuries.
Daily ex. M. 10-1.30, 4-7.

VICTOR BALAGUER MUSEUM
Plaza Estación, Villanueva y Geltru, Barcelona
House of the poet and politician, Victor Balaguer (1826-1901). Prehistory. Archaeology. 12th-17th century sculpture. 16th-20th century paintings. Decorative arts. Handicrafts.
Daily ex. M. 10-1, 4-7.

VILLANUEVA DE LORENZANA

MUSEUM OF RELIGIOUS ART
Church of Santa Maria de Valdeflores, Villanueva de Lorenzana, Lugo
Religious art.
By appointment.

VILLENA

JOSE MARIA SOLER MUNICIPAL MUSEUM OF ARCHAEOLOGY
Edifico del Ayuntamiento, Plaza de Santiago 2, Villena, Alicante
Local prehistory, archaeology. Villena and Cabezo Redondo gold treasures. Medieval pottery.
Daily 9-6.

VISO DEL MARQUES

DON ALVARO DE BAZÁN MUSEUM AND ARCHIVES
Antiquo Palacio de Don Alvaro de Bazán, Viso del Marques, Ciudad Real
In 16th century house of Don Alvara, Captain-General of the Navy. Material relating to his career and to the Spanish Navy in his time.
Dawn to dusk.

VITORIA

ALAVA PROVINCIAL MUSEUM
Paseo Fray Francisco 8, Vitoria, Alava
Prehistory and archaeology. Painting and sculpture of the 15th-20th centuries. Weapons and armour.
Daily 11-2, 5-7. Closed p.m. M., public holidays.

CASA DEL CORDON
Calle Cuchillería 24, Vitoria, Alava
15th century house, residence of Cardinal Adrian of Utrecht, in which he received the news of his election to the Papacy, as Adrian VI. Memorabilia of the Cardinal and the event.
Daily 11-2, 5-7. Closed p.m. M., public holidays.

MUSEUM OF THE BATTLE OF VITORIA
El Portalón, Calle Correria 151, Vitoria, Alava
Material relating to the Battle of Vitoria (1813).
Daily 11-2, 5-7. Closed p.m. M., public holidays.

MUSEUM OF BULLFIGHTING
El Portalón, Calle Correria 151, Vitoria, Alava
History of bull-fighting. Paintings of bull-fighting.
Daily 11-2, 5-7. Closed p.m. M., public holidays.

MUSEUM OF PLAYING-CARDS
Calle Heraclio Fournier, Vitoria, Alavo
Collection of playing-cards, made by Heraclio Fournier and his descendants since the establishment of their playing-card factory here in 1870.
By appointment.

YECLA

ARCHAEOLOGICAL COLLECTION
Casa de la Cultura, Yecla, Murcia
Local archaeology.
Daily 11-2.

YUSTE

MUSEUM OF HISTORY AND ART
Monastery of San Jeronimo de Yuste, Yuste, Cáceres
Religious history and art.
May-Sept. Daily 9-1, 3.30-7. Oct.-Apr. Daily 9-1, 2-6.

ZAFRA

CONVENT OF SANTA CLARA
Calle Sevilla, Zafra, Badajoz
Paintings. Sculpture. Goldsmiths' work. Religious ornaments of the 16th-18th centuries.
Daily 10-7.

ZAMORA

CATHEDRAL MUSEUM
Cathedral, Zamora
14th-16th century French-Flemish tapestries. Sculpture. Paintings. Church plate (gold).
Daily 11-1, 4-7.

MUSEUM OF HOLY WEEK
Plaza Santa Maria la Nueva, Zamora
Easter images and processional sculptures.
Daily 9-9.

PROVINCIAL MUSEUM OF FINE ART
Iglesia de la Gota de Sangre, Calle Santa Clara 17, Zamora
Paintings. Sculpture. Drawings. Engravings. Archaeology. Heraldry. Coins.
Daily ex. Th. 10-2.

ZARAGOZA

ARAGON MUSEUM OF ETHNOLOGY AND NATURAL SCIENCES
Parque Primo de Rivera, Zaragoza
Regional flora and fauna. Costumes.
Daily 10-1.30, 3-6.

BASILICA OF NOSTRA SEÑORA DEL PILAR
Plaza de las Catedrales, Zaragoza
Sculpture. Paintings, including frescoes by Goya. Church plate (gold).
Daily 10-12, 3-4.

CATHEDRAL MUSEUM
Cathedral, Plaza de la Seo, Zaragoza
Tapestries, some of them 15th century. Religious paintings and gold plate.
Apr.-Oct. 9-1, 4-7. Nov.-Mar. 9-1, 4-6.

PROVINCIAL MUSEUM OF FINE ART
Plaza de Jose Antonio 6, Zaragoza
Paintings, from the Aragon primitives to the 20th century. Drawings. Engravings. Ceramics from Teruel and Muel. Medals.
Daily May-Sept. 10-1, 4-6. Oct.-Apr. 10-2, 3-5. Closed National Holidays.

ZUMARRAGA

LEGAZPI HOUSE MUSEUM
Avenida Padre Urdaneta, Zumarraga, Guipuzcoa
Birthplace of Miguel López de Legaspi, conqueror of the Philippines (d. Manila 1572). Collections illustrating his life and achievements.
Daily 10-1.30, 3.30-7.

Sri Lanka, Republic of

The museums of Sri Lanka draw most of their material from the sixteenth to the nineteenth century, the last period of the Sinhala Kings. There are rich collections of jewellery, furniture and weapons, and a great deal of religious sculpture for which the Republic, in its days as Ceylon, was formerly famous. About the modern world there is remarkably little.

ANURADHAPURA

FOLK MUSEUM
Old Town, Anuradhapura, North Central Province
Folk art objects of the North Central Province. Archaeology of the area. Amaravati, Gupta, Medieval and Hindu sculptures. 6th-12th century iron objects. Coins. Stone inscriptions, 4th-12th centuries. Pottery.
Daily ex. F. 9-5.

COLOMBO

NATIONAL MUSEUM
Sir Marcus Fernando Mawatha, Colombo 7
Geology. Zoology. Entomology. Anthropology. Prehistory. Ethnography. Archaeology. Ancient and modern art. Crown and throne of the last Kings of Kandy. Arms and armour. Textiles. Coins and currency.
Daily ex. F. 9-5.

DEDIGAMA

ARCHAEOLOGICAL MUSEUM
Dedigama, Sabaragamuva Province
Archaeology. Material from excavations in the Province. Gold images of Buddha. Coins.
Daily ex. F. 9-5.

KANDY

NATIONAL MUSEUM
Dharmapala Mawatha, Kandy
Housed in part of palace of the last King of Kandy. Ethnographical collections illustrating the past three centuries of the rule of the Sinhala Kings, with Kandy as their capital city. Lamps, statuettes, jewellery, ivory combs, arms and weapons, pottery, brassware, lacquered objects.
Daily ex. F. 9-5.

RATNAPURA

NATIONAL MUSEUM
Main Road, Godigamuva, Ratnapura, Sabaragamuva Province
Geology, zoology, palaeontology, prehistory and ethnography of the Sabaragamuva Province. 17th-18th century antiques from the Province of Sabaragamuva. Jewellery, statuettes, brassware. Animal fossils from Ratnapura and Balangoda districts.
Daily ex. F. 9-5.

Sudan

The Sudan has not forgotten General Gordon, although it celebrates him in a way which would possibly not be in order in the country where he was born, by featuring both his medals and his chains. Apart from Gordon, military history bulks fairly large in the museums of the Sudan, although not to the extent of overwhelming other types of material. The archaeological collections in particular are full of interesting items.

EL OBEID

SHIEKAN MUSEUM
El Obeid
Archaeology. Ethnography. Weapons from famous Shiekan battles - guns, swords, spears and one machine gun of Haksi Pasha.
Daily ex. M. 8.30-2.

KHARTOUM

ETHNOGRAPHICAL MUSEUM
University Avenue, P.O. Box 178, Khartoum
Ethnographical collections.
Daily ex. M. 8.30-7.

GEOLOGICAL SURVEY MUSEUM
P.O. Box 410, Sharia Abu Sin, Geological Survey Department, Khartoum
Geology and mineralogy. Specimens of rocks and fossils. Meteorites.
Daily ex. M. 8-2.

GRAPHIC MUSEUM
Ministry of Health, P.O. Box 2046, Khartoum
Health education.
Daily ex. M. 8.30-7.

NATURAL HISTORY MUSEUM
University of Khartoum, P.O. Box 321, Gama Avenue, Khartoum
Natural sciences: birds and wild game of Sudan.
Daily ex. F. 8.30-7.

SUDAN ARCHAEOLOGICAL MUSEUM
P.O. Box 178, Nile Avenue, Khartoum
History and archaeology. Fossils, skulls. Statues of ancient kings. Seals. Golden ornamental objects.
Daily ex. M. 8-7.

MEROWE

MEROWE MUSEUM
Merowe
Archaeology and ethnography of Sudan. Huge granite statues of Napatan Kings. Large granite coffin and lid of Onalamni. Gun belonging to Sultan Ali Dinar. Prayer mat.
Daily ex. M. 8.30-2.

OMDURMAN

KHALIFA'S HOUSE MUSEUM
Omdurman
Objects relating to the Mahodie period, an important phase in Sudan's history. Weapons; Gordon's medals and chains. Documents.
Daily ex. M. 8.30-7.

Surinam

This former Dutch and British colony has a very mixed population and five widely-spoken languages, of which two are European. The State Museum illustrates the results of this complex mixing of cultures and contains collections which give an impression of the natural history of the country and of its prosperous timber and mining industries.

PARAMARIBO

SURINAM STATE MUSEUM
P.O. Box 2306, 8 and 9 Mededelingen, Paramaribo
History and culture of Surinam. Natural history.
Daily 8-1. 3 days a week also 4-7.

Sweden

By comparison with their fellows in the rest of capitalist Europe, Swedish industrialists appear to have an exceptionally well developed interest in history, and an equally praiseworthy and public-spirited wish to set up company museums of one kind and another. This is particularly true of the paper, mining and metal-working industries, where there are a number of excellent privately financed museums and preservation schemes. Brewing, too, has been elaborately, if somewhat flamboyantly, provided for in the Stockholm brewery museum, Pripporama. Other leading Swedish industries, relatively less prosperous, have not done so well in the fields of conservation and preservation. The early years of textiles, glass and shipbuilding are, for instance, much less well documented than iron or copper.

The care devoted to one great museum-piece of the shipbuilder's art does, however, go beyond anything else the world can show. The enormously expensive and enormously successful project to raise, preserve and restore the monumental wooden battleship *Wasa* and its contents has been a technical and financial exercise of the first importance, and an impressive proof of the old commercial theory that in order to make money one must first spend money. As a dividend yielding museum investment, the *Wasa* seems likely to leave a Picasso or a Rembrandt a long way behind.

By comparison with the *Wasa* the wooden structures at the open-air museum at Skansen, the revered mother of all open-air museums, were acquired and set out for display very cheaply. Skansen has stood the test of time and the weather very well and it now has, besides a tunnel-escalator, what must surely be the only museum souvenir-shop in the world to contain no kitsch.

Swedish museums, as a whole, are strong in ethnography, handicrafts, costumes, folk art and what can be broadly termed local history, but weak in painting, largely, one fears, because nineteenth-century Scandinavian painting in oils was a rather regrettable affair. The portraits, drawings and watercolours are fortunately more pleasing and stimulating.

There are, inevitably, surprises. Sweden has, one is glad to discover, the largest collection of Chinese Stone Age ceramics outside China and, a major irony in such a liquor-fearing country, a museum entirely devoted to the history of the Swedish wine and spirit trade since medieval times.

ALVASTRA

STRAND
Hästholmen, Alvastra
Home of Ellen Key.
May-Sept. 10-5, by arrangement. Telephone Hästholmen 330 30.

ÄLVDALEN

ROTS SKANS FORT AND HOMESTEAD MUSEUM
Älvdalen, Dalarna
An entrenchment of 1676 made of timbers, rocks and gravel, intended as protection against attacks which it was thought might come from the former Norwegian provinces of Jämtland and Härjedalen during Charles XI's Danish war. Now forms the basis of a homestead museum and inside the walls are 25 timber-block houses (the oldest 1610). Furniture and domestic equipment.
May 15- Aug. 15, M.-Sa. 10-6; Su. 1-6.

ARBOGA

ARBOGA MUSEUM
Arboga
Local history and archaeology.
May-Sept. M.-Sa. 1.30-4.30; Su. 1-5. Oct.-Apr. Su. 1-3.

ARVIKA

ARVIKA MUSEUM
Arvika
Archaeology. Ethnology. Open-air museum of rural buildings.
May-Sept. Daily 12-5. Oct.-Apr. 1-3.

ASKERSUND

STJERNSUND CASTLE
Askersund
Neo-classical style castle, built 1798-1803 and refurnished c.1850. Furniture and portraits from the late 18th century.
May-Sept. Daily 10-5.

BORÅS

BORÅS MUSEUM
Ramnaparken, Borås
Archaeology. Ethnography. History of local textile industry. Open-air museum of rural buildings.
May-Sept. 10-4; Su. 12-4. Oct.-Apr. 12-3; Su. 12-4.

BORÅS MUSEUM OF ART
12-14 St. Brogatan, Borås
Swedish painting and sculpture.
May-Sept. daily 12-5; Oct. daily 1-4 and 6-8.

BUNGE

BUNGE MUSEUM
Fårösund, Gotland
Open-air museum. Farm buildings. Workshops. Mills. Fishermen's cottages and boats. 8th century picture stone.
June-Aug. 10-6.

ESKILSTUNA

DJURGÅRDEN MUSEUM
Djurgården, Eskilstuna
Open-air museum. Workshops and houses from early 17th century onwards, including the 20 Rademacher smithies (c.1650) from which the modern Eskilstuna steel and cutlery industry developed.
Daily 10-4. June-Aug. also 7-9.

ESKILSTUNA MUSEUM OF ART
Kyrkogatan 9, Eskilstuna
Sculpture, paintings, drawings, photographs, mostly Scandinavian.
Daily 1-4; Tu. and Th. also 7-9.

FALKENBERG

FALKENBERG MUSEUM
8 St. Lars Kyrkogata, Falkenberg
Archaeology. Ethnography. Local history.
June-Aug. Tu.-F. and Su. 2-6. Sept.-May W. and Su. 2-5.

FALKÖPING

FALBYGDENS MUSEUM
St. Olofsgatan 33, Falköping
Archaeology of Stone, Bronze and Iron Ages. Medieval material from local sites. Collections illustrating peasant life. Domestic interiors. Country shop.
M.-F. 11-4; Sa., Su. 1-4.

FALSTERBO

FALSTERBO MUSEUM
Falsterbo
Archaeology. Ethnography. Maritime history.
June-Aug. 9-9.

FALUN

DALARNAS MUSEUM
Stiggatan 2-4, Falun
Provincial museum of archaeology, art and ethnography. Peasant paintings. Painted peasant furniture.
Mid. May-mid. Sept. M.-Sa. 11-5; Su. 1-5. Mid. Sept.-mid. May M.-F. 1-4, 6-8; Sa. and Su. 1-5.

MINING MUSEUM
Stora Kopparbergs, Bergslags AB, Falun
History of mining, especially of the Falun copper-mine. Includes models of mining inventions made by Christopher Polhem (1661-1751). 18th century mineral cabinet. Company charter of 1347.
June-Aug. M.-Sa. 12.30-4.30; Tu. also 6-8; Su. 1-5. Sept.-May W., Sa., Su. 1-5.

SELMA LAGERLÖFS HOUSE
Falun
Former home of Selma Lagerlöf, furnished in period style.
May-Sept. M.-Sa. 12-5.30; Su. 1-5.30.

GÄVLE

GÄVLE MUSEUM
20 S. Strandgatan, Gävle
Art and handicrafts. Archaeological and ethnographical collections from province of Gästrikland. Maritime history.
Tu.-F. 11-3; Sa. 1-6; Su. 1-4. Sept.-Apr. Th. also 7-9.

GÖTEBORG

ARCHAEOLOGICAL MUSEUM
12 Norra Hamngatan, Göteborg
In 18th century premises of the Swedish East India Company. Collections illustrating archaeology of West Sweden. Rock carvings.
Weekdays 10-4; Su. 12-4.

ETHNOGRAPHICAL MUSEUM
12 Norra Hamngatan, Göteborg
Main collections relate to Africa, South America, South-East Asia, Lappland. Early Peruvian textiles.
Weekdays 10-4; Su. 12-4.

GÖTEBORG ART GALLERY
Götaplatsen, Göteborg
European painting, (including works by Rembrandt and French Impressionists), sculpture, engravings, drawings and photographs. Collections of Scandinavian art.
Weekdays 10-4; Su. 12-4.

HISTORICAL MUSEUM
12 Norra Hamngatan, Göteborg
Life and culture of Western Sweden, especially of Göteborg. Furniture. Household utensils. Clothing. Room interiors. Collection of Chinese porcelain and art. Armorial china. Coins.
Weekdays 10-4; Su. 12-4.

MARITIME MUSEUM
Gamla Varvsparken, Göteborg
Original items, models and paintings showing development of shipping, fishing, air transport, harbour installations, shipbuilding, naval defence and oceanography. Aquarium.
May-mid. Sept. Weekdays 10-6; Su. 11-4. Mid.Sept.-Apr. Weekdays 10-4; Su. 11-4.

MUSEUM FOR THE HISTORY OF INDUSTRY
2-4 Ekmansgatan, Göteborg
History of industry and handicrafts in Göteborg and West Sweden. Complete workshops.
Weekdays 10-4.

NATURAL HISTORY MUSEUM
Slottskogen, Göteborg
Mammals, birds, lower vertebrates, invertebrates. Dioramas. Whales and whale skeletons. Mineralogical department.
Mid.May-mid.Sept., Weekdays 11-5; Su. 12-5. Mid.Sept.-mid.May, Weekdays 10-4; Su. 12-4.

RÖHSS MUSEUM OF ARTS AND CRAFTS
37-9 Vasagatan, Göteborg
Swedish furniture, pottery, textiles, pewter, ironwork, bookbindings, silver, glass. Interiors to show changes in style. Oriental collections, mainly from China and Japan.
Weekdays mid.May-mid.Sept. 12-5; Su. 12-4. Mid.Sept.-mid.May Weekdays 11-4; Su. 12-4; Tu. also 7-9.

SCHOOL MUSEUM
6 Hvitfeldspatsen, Göteborg
History of school buildings, equipment and educational methods in Sweden.
Th. 5-7.

SKANSEN KRONAN MILITARY MUSEUM
Kronan Fortress, Göteborg
Fortress containing almost complete collection of Swedish army uniforms. Weapons.
W. 7-9; Sa. 1-3; Su. 12-3.

THEATRE MUSEUM
Götaplatsen, Lorensberg, Göteborg
Original objects, models, pictures, illustrating theatre history in Göteborg.
Weekdays 12-3. Oct.-Mar. also Su. 1-4.

GRÄNNA

ANDRÉE MUSEUM
Brahegatan 38, Gränna
Memorial collection of the polar explorer, Andrée (1854-97) and his ill-fated balloon expedition to the Arctic.
May-Sept. 10-6.

VÄTTER MUSEUM
Gränna
Local history and ethnography.
May-Sept. 10-6.

HALMSTAD

HALLANDS MUSEUM
Tollsgatan, Halmstad
Swedish peasant life (collection of painted wall hangings). Maritime history. Room interiors. Church art. Archaeology.
Daily 1-5; W. also 7-9.

HALLANDSGÅRDEN MUSEUM
Galgberget, Halmstad
Open-air museum, consisting of 12 buildings of different character from the country settlements of the past. It

includes Hörsåsstugan, which illustrates the oldest dwelling conditions in Sweden, and also the old school house from Eldsberga, a half-timbered building which contains a school museum.
May-Sept. Daily 1-6.

HÄLSINGBORG

FREDRIKSDAL OPEN-AIR MUSEUM
Hälsingborg
Open-air museum with a botanical garden, containing Scandinavian plants and wild flower collections.
Summer: Daily 11-6.

TOWN MUSEUM
31S. Storgatan, Hälsingborg
Exhibitions of bourgeois culture, applied art, archaeology and local history. Handicrafts design.
Summer: Daily 11-6. Winter: Daily 10-4.

VIKINGSBERG ART MUSEUM
Hälsingborg
Former private residence, in classical style, with collections of paintings, sculpture, furniture, ranging from 17th century to the present day.
Summer: Daily 11-6. Winter: Daily 10-4.

HAMMARBY

LINNAEUS MUSEUM
Hammarby, nr. Uppsala
Wooden house built by Linnaeus in 1762, with much of the original furniture and fittings. Stone building erected by Linnaeus to house his natural history collections (these have now been transferred elsewhere).
May-Aug. 10-12, 1-6.

HÄRNÖSAND

MUSEUM OF CULTURAL HISTORY
Härnösand, Norrland
History and culture of the province. Handicrafts. Collection of religious art, especially sculpture and textiles. Open-air museum with 80 buildings, including schools, fishing sheds and the old Town Hall of Härnösand.
M.-Sa. 10-4; Su. 1-4.

HÄSSLEHOLM

MUSEUM OF ETHNOGRAPHY
1 Parkgatan, Hässleholm
Local history and archaeology. Ethnography.
May-Sept. 12-4. Oct.-Apr. 1-3.

HEDEMORA

MUSEUM OF LOCAL HISTORY AND ARCHAEOLOGY
nr. Lake Hönsam, Hedemora
Local history. Folklore. Archaeology.
Summer: Tu.-Su. 10-5.

HÖGANÄS

HÖGANÄS MUSEUM
Höganäs
Local history. Ceramics.
May-Aug. Tu.-Su. 1-5. Sept.-Apr. Tu.-F. 6-8; Su. 2-5.

HUDIKSVALL

HÄLSINGLANDS MUSEUM
Storgatan 31, Hudiksvall
Cultural history of Hudiksvall and province of Hälsingland, especially fishing, agriculture, folk art, ecclesiastical art, pewter, silver. Paintings by John Sten (1879-1922).
Mid.June - mid.Aug. Daily 10-9. Mid.Aug. - mid.June 1-4.

HUSKVARNA

HUSKVARNA MUSEUM
Grännavägen, Huskvarna
Archaeology. Ethnology. Local history. History of technology.
May-Sept. Su. 3-5.

JOKKMOKK

JOKKMOKK MUSEUM
Jokkmokk
Lapp life and culture. Exhibits include silver spoons and cups, a magic drum, log houses and a goatti (nomadic family's tent). Modern Lapp (or Same) handicrafts. The museum is the focus for an annual fair which has been held for the past 367 years without a break.
Summer: Daily ex. Su. 9-9; Su. 12-9. Winter: W.-F. 6-7 p.m.; Sa. and Su. 1-4.

JÖNKÖPING

JÖNKÖPING MUSEUM
1 Stadsparken, Jönköping
Ironmaking. Missionary activities abroad. Medieval and later crafts. Art Collection.
Tu.-Sa. 11-4; Th. and F. also 7-9; Su. 1-5.

MUNICIPAL PARK OPEN-AIR MUSEUM
Stadsparken, Jönköping
Ethnography. Peasant culture. Local industries. Rural buildings.
June-Aug. Tu.-Su. 11-5.

JULITA

JULITA MANOR
Julita gård, Julita
Manor-house with period furnishings.
May-Sept. M.-Sa. 11.30-6; Su. 12-6.

OPEN-AIR MUSEUM
Julita
Old local cottages. Collections of historic furniture and household utensils.
May-Sept., M.-Sa. 11.30-6; Su. 12-6.

KALMAR

KALMAR MUSEUM
Kalmar Castle, 38100 Kalmar
Archaeology. Ethnography. Local history. Maritime and military history.
May-Sept. Weekdays 9-4; Su. 1-4. Oct.-Nov. and Mar.-Apr. Weekdays 12-2; Su. 1-3. Dec.-Feb. Su. 1-3.

KRUSENTIERN MANSION
St. Dammgatan 11, Kalmar
House, park and interiors of 18th-19th centuries.
June-Aug. M.-Sa. 10-4; Su. 1-5. Sept. M.-Sa. 11-1; Su. 1-3.

MUSEUM OF FINE ARTS
Slottsvägen 1, 38100 Kalmar
19th-20th century Swedish paintings, drawings, sculpture.
Summer (June 15 - Aug. 15) Daily 1-7. Winter: M.-F. 1-5, 7-9; Sa. and Su. 1-5.

KARLSHAMN

KARLSHAMN MUSEUM
85 Drottninggatan, Karlshamn
Local history and archaeology. Maritime history.
June-Aug. Daily 1-3. Sept.-May M. and F. 2-3.

SKOTTSBERG HOUSE
Karlshamn
Local history.
June-Aug. Su. 3-5. Sept.-May M. and F. 3-4.

KARLSKRONA

BELKINGE MUSEUM
27 Amiralitetstorget, Karlskrona
Archaeology. Ethnology. Local History. Local textiles.
M.-F. 10-12, 1-4; Sa. 10-1; Su. 12-3.

NAVAL DOCKYARD MUSEUM
Amiralitetstorget, Karlskrona
Ship models. Tools. Items from ships now broken up. Trophies. 18th century collection of Chinese model boats. Ships' figureheads (1781-1828) by Johan Törnström.
July: M.-F. 10-8; Sa. and Su. 10-4. Aug.-June M.-Sa. 10-4; Su. 11-4.

VÄMÖ PARK
Karlskrona
Open-air museum. Ethnography.
Mid.June-Aug. 10-6.

KARLSTAD

MARIEBERGSSKOGEN
Karlstad, Värmland
Open-air museum. Ethnography. Old Värmland buildings.
May-Sept. 12-4.

VÄRMLAND MUSEUM
Box 335, Karlstad 1
Collections of art and cultural history, especially from the province of Värmland. One section deals with the Finnish immigrants and their lives, and another is devoted to the revivalist and free church movements. Exhibition on the history of photography.
Winter: Weekdays 12-4; W. 12-9; Su. 1-5. Summer: Weekdays 11-4; W. 11-9; Su. 1-5.

KIRUNA

JUKKASJÄRVI ETHNOGRAPHICAL MUSEUM
Kiruna
Ethnography. Lapp collection.
May-Sept. 9-9.

KÖPING

KÖPING MUSEUM
28 Karlbergsgatan, Köping
Archaeology. Local history.
Su. 2-4.

KRISTIANSTAD

KRISTIANSTAD MUSEUM
Kristianstad
In armoury of 1610. Local history. Military history. Peasant culture.
Summer: 1-5 and 7-9. Winter: Tu.-Su. 1-5; W. and F. also 7-9.

KRISTINEHAMN

KRISTINEHAMN MUSEUM
Nämndhuset, Kristinehamn
Archaeology. Local history.
M.-F. 10-4.

KUNGSÖR

KUNGSÖR MUSEUM
Kungsudden, Kungsör
Local history.
May-Sept. Su. 3-5.

LAHOLM

SOUTH HALLAND MUSEUM OF HISTORY AND ETHNOGRAPHY
19 Östertullsgatan, Laholm
Local archaeology and history. Ethnography. Art collection.
May-Sept. 10-4.

LANDSKRONA

LANDSKRONA MUSEUM
Landskrona
Local history, trades and handicrafts. Section devoted to Sweden's first aircraft factory, begun at Landskrona in 1914 by Enoch Thulin.
Mid.May - mid.Sept. 12-4. Mid.Sept. - mid.May 1-4; Th. also 7-9.

LINKÖPING

LINKÖPING MUSEUM
16 Vasavägen, Linköping
Archaeology. Ethnography. Local history. Medieval religious art, ceremonial objects and vestments. Costume collection. 18th and 19th century Swedish paintings.
Tu.-F. 12-4; Sa. 12-3; Th. also 7-8; Su. 1-4.

UNCLE ADAMS HOUSE
Linköping
Local history collection.
Mid.May - mid.Sept., W., Sa. and Su. 1-3.

LÖFSTAD

LÖFSTAD PALACE
Löfstad
18th century nobleman's residence. Preserved complete with original furnishings, including servants' rooms.
Mid.May-Sept. Tu.-Su. 1.30-5.

LULEÅ

NORBOTTEN MUSEUM
Gültzau-udden, Luleå
Lapp culture. Handicrafts. Costumes. Tools.
M.-F. 8-8; Sa. 12-3; Su. 1-5. Summer 10-3.

UDDEN OPEN-AIR MUSEUM
Luleå
Houses and workshops from Luleå area. Peasant furniture.
By arrangement with Norbottens Museum.

LUND

ARCHIVES OF DECORATIVE ART
University of Lund, Lund
Preparatory material used in creation of sculptures and monuments. Preliminary sketches, outlines, full-scale models, experiments in techniques.
Daily 1-4.

MUSEUM OF CULTURAL HISTORY
Kulturen, Lund
Open-air museum, showing development of civilisation of southern Sweden. Town and country houses representing different social classes. Ceramics. Glass. Textiles. Medieval archaeology.
Beginning to middle of May: Weekdays 11-4; Su. 12-5. Mid.May-Sept. Weekdays 10-5; Su. 12-6. Oct.-Apr. Weekdays 11-3; Su. 12-4.

UNIVERSITY ART GALLERY
Lunds Universitet, Institute of Art History, Box 1135, Lund
Collection of Swedish paintings and Dutch works of the 17th century. Prints. Sculptures.
No display at present.

UNIVERSITY OF LUND HISTORICAL MUSEUM
Krafts Torg, Lund
Archaeological collections and medieval church art, from Skåne. Knutsdorp curved sword. Brågarp bronze lure. Coins and medals.
Tu.-F. 11-1; Su. 1-3.

ZOOLOGICAL MUSEUM
nr. University Library, Lund
Zoology. Mammals. Birds, especially of Scandinavia.
M.-F. 9-12, 1-3; Sa. 9-12.

MALMÖ

MALMÖ MUSEUM
Malmöhusvägen, Malmö
In 16th century castle. Natural history. Local history. Fine and applied art. Special collections of art from the Baltic and from Skåne.
Weekdays 12-4; Su. 11-4. W. also 7-9 p.m.

CARRIAGE MUSEUM
Drottningtorget, Malmö
Horse-drawn vehicles.
Su. 11-4.

MÅRBACKA

THE MANOR HOUSE
Mårbacka
House where Selma Lagerlöf was born in 1858 and where she lived until she went to Stockholm in 1882 to teach. The house passed out of the family, but she bought it in 1907 and lived here every summer. The house was rebuilt and she died here in 1940. Everything is left as at the time of her death, and many of her books were written at Mårbacka.
May 15-Sept. 15, Daily 10-7.

MARIEFRED

GRIPSHOLM CASTLE
Mariefred
Buildings are of 16th and 17th centuries. Contains most of the National Portrait Gallery, the remainder, portraits from 1804, being at Gripsholm Folk High School, with a few paintings in public buildings throughout Sweden. Furniture. Tapestries. Late 18th century theatre.
Mid.May-mid.Sept. Weekdays 10-5; Su. 12-5. Mid.Oct. and Mar.-Apr. Weekdays 10-4; Su. 12-4. Nov.-mid.Dec. and mid.Jan.-Feb. Weekdays 10-3; Su. 12-3. Closed mid-Dec. to mid.Jan.

MARIESTAD

VADSBO MUSEUM
Marieholm, Mariestad
Archaeology. Ethnology. Local history.
Su. 1-3.30. May-Sept. also W. 6-8.

MÖLNDAL

GUNNEBO
Mölndal, nr. Göteborg
Gunnebo manor house (late 18th century). Building, grounds, interior decoration, furniture and tiled stoves all by the same architect, C. W. Carlberg.
Apr.-Oct. M.-F. 1-2; Sa. 3-4; Su. 12-3. Nov.-Mar. W. and Su. 1-2.

MORA

ZORN HOUSE-MUSEUM
Vasagatan, Mora
Home of the painter Anders Zorn, with original contents and with part of his collection of peasant art and textiles.
Mid.June-mid.Aug. M.-Sa. 11-6; Su. 1-6. Mid.Aug.-mid.June M.-Sa. 12-5; Su. 1-5.

ZORN MUSEUM OF OLD BUILDINGS
Skeriol, Vinäsvägen, Mora
Open-air museum. Buildings collected by Anders Zorn from the province of Dalarna.
June-Aug. Weekdays 11-5; Su. 1-5.

NORBERG

NORBERGS MUSEUM OF VERNACULAR BUILDINGS
Karlberg, Norberg
Open-air museum. Ethnography. Rural buildings.
Daily 1-3.

NORRKÖPING

FÄRGAR HOUSE
3 St. Persgatan, Norrköping
History of science and technology.
M.-Sa. 1-3; 1st and last Su. of each month 1-3.

NORRKÖPING MUSEUM
Kristinaplatsen, Norrköping
Swedish art from late 18th century to present day. Coins. Prints. Drawings. History of Norrköping. Ethnographical material from South Seas.
June-Aug. 12-5; Sept.-May 1-4 and 7-9; Sa. only 1-4.

NYKÖPING

SÖDERMANLAND COUNTY MUSEUM
Nyköpingshus, Nyköping
In Nyköpingshus, a 16th century fortress. Models of fortifications. Finds from excavations. 19th century paintings of national historical subjects. In 18th century building, once the Governor's residence, a museum of cultural history, with 18th century interiors. Art gallery devoted mainly to Swedish art.
Daily mid.May-mid.Sept. 11-5. Mid.Sept.-mid.May 1-4.

ÖREBRO

ÖREBRO MUSEUM
Slottsparken, Örebro
History, crafts, industries of the town and province. Ecclesiastical art. Coins. Medals. Art gallery, with collection of contemporary paintings, sculpture.
Mid.May-mid.Sept. M.-F. 12-4; Sa. and Su. 1-5; Th. also 7-9.

ÖRNSKÖLDSVIK

ÖRNSKÖLDSVIK MUSEUM
3 Skyttegatan, Örnsköldsvik
Open-air museum. Collections include Stone Age tools found in the area; bins, cupboards and furniture from 1660-1800; a furnished country kitchen; tools of shoemaker, joiner, watchmaker, dentist. Agricultural implements. Weaving and flax-making tools. Coin collection. Sleighs and harnesses.
M.-F. 12-3; Su. 1-4. Closed Sa.

ÖSTERSUND

JÄMTLAND MUSEUM
Östersund
Peasant life and handicrafts, especially objects carved in wood. Överhogdal tapestry (12th century). Art section devoted mainly to works from Jämtland and Norway.
M.-F. 10-4; Sa. 12-3; Su. 1-4.

JAMTLI MUSEUM
Östersund
Open-air museum. Buildings include 15th century pilgrim's hut.
May-Sept. 12-5.

MUNICIPAL MUSEUM AND OLOF AHLBERGS GALLERY
Rådhusplanen, Östersund
Paintings and sculptures by local artists. Local history.
Mid.June-mid.Aug. 1-4; May-mid.June and mid.Aug.-Oct., Su. 1-4.

RANSÄTER

GEIJERS HOUSE-MUSEUM
Ransäter
Home of Erik Gustaf Geijer, Professor of History at the University of Uppsala, born here, 1783, and spent his childhood and youth here. The collection reflects Geijer's activities as a historian, philosopher, poet, composer and politician. F. A. Dahlgren (1816-1895), author of "Värmlänningarna" - a Romeo and Juliet drama from Värmland - also grew up in the manor house. He is also known for his humorous dialectal poems.
May 15-Sept. 15, Daily 9-1, 2-7. From June 15-Aug. 15 also 1-2. Other times of the year, on request.

ROTHNEROS

ROTHNEROS PARK
Rothneros
Open-air museum of Swedish sculpture.
Mid.May-June and Aug.-Sept. 8.30-7; July 8-8.

SÄTER

ÅSGÅRD MUSEUM
Säter
Open-air museum, consisting of more than 20 houses moved from their original sites. These include an 18th century pottery, blacksmith's shop and a chapel. Collections of domestic and other equipment.
May-Sept. Daily 1-5. Other times, on request.

SIMRISHAMN

ÖSTERLEN MUSEUM
Simrishamn
Peasant furniture. History of fishing, agriculture and maritime commerce.
Summer: Daily 10-4. Winter: W., Sa. and Su. 1-4.

SKARA

WEST GÖTLAND MUSEUM
Stadsträdgården, Skara
Archaeology. Ethnography. Local social history. Medieval religious sculptures in wood and stone. Medieval textiles and metal work.
M.-F. 10-4; Sa. and Su. 1-3.

SKELLEFTEÅ

SKELLEFTEÅ MUSEUM
Nyborg, Skellefteå
Archaeology. Ecclesiastical art. Ethnography. Open-air museum.
June-Aug. 1-3.

SKOKLOSTER

SKOKLOSTER CASTLE
Skokloster
Castle is mid. 17th century. Period rooms. Tapestries. Collection of pictures (mainly Swedish and Dutch). Bookbindings. Silver. Glass. Ceramics. Ivory. Tools. Household equipment. Weapons.
June-Aug. Tu.-Su. 11-4.

SKÖVDE

SKÖVDE MUSEUM
Skövde
Archaeology. Ethnography. Local history.
W. and Sa. 11-2; Su. 1-4.

SÖDERHAMN

SÖDERHAMN MUSEUM
5 Oxtorgsgatan, Söderhamn
Development of local industry and handicrafts.
June-Sept. M.-F. 1-5; Sa. and Su. 1-3.

STJÄRNSUND

STJÄRNSUND CASTLE
Stjärnsund
Building of 1798. Interiors mainly 1823-60. Relics of royal family.
May-Sept., M.-Sa. 10-5; Su. 12-5.

STOCKHOLM

BANK MUSEUM
Sturegatan 38, Stockholm
Exhibits connected with history of banking in Sweden.
M.-F. 11-3.30.

BIOLOGICAL MUSEUM
Djurgården, Stockholm
Natural history of Scandinavia.
Daily 10-5. During winter, at dusk.

BREWERY MUSEUM
"Pripporama", Voltvägen 29, Bromma, Stockholm
History and traditions of the brewing industry. Presentation based on films and electronic techniques.
By arrangement. Guided tours only.

CHINESE PAVILION
Kina, Drottningholm Palace, nr. Stockholm
Rococo building (1763-9) of, despite the name, mainly European character. The Chinese elements are in the Yellow and Red Anterooms.
May-Aug. Weekdays 11-5; Su. 1-5. Apr. and Sept.-Nov. Su. 1-3.

CITY MUSEUM
Södermalmstorg, Stockholm
In the old City Hall (1660-80). Exhibits showing development of Stockholm over the centuries. The Loheskatten treasure. Special section devoted to Carl Michael Bellman (1740-95).
M.-F. 11-9; Sa. 11-5; Su. 12-5.

DANCE MUSEUM
Filmhuset, Borgvägen, Stockholm
Based on collections of Rolf de Maré. Far Eastern section contains large collections from India, Sri Lanka, Indonesia, Siam, China, Japan. European ballet décor and costume designs.
Daily, hours as advertised in press.

DROTTNINGHOLM COURT THEATRE AND MUSEUM
nr. Stockholm
Theatre of 1764-6, intact with original stage machinery and 30 sets of scenery of 1766. Exhibits showing development of theatrical art in Europe from 1585 to 1800.
Guided tours every hour. May-Aug. Weekdays 11-4; Su. 1-4. Apr., Sept. and Oct. 1-3.

DROTTNINGHOLM PALACE
nr. Stockholm
Built 1662-86 by Nicodemus Tessin the elder and his son. Extra storey added 1746-60. Many rooms still in original baroque style. Collection of royal portraits, tapestries, furniture and objets d'art.
Guided tours every hour. May-Aug. Weekdays 11-4; Su. 1-4. Apr., Sept. and Oct. 1-3.

ELDH'S STUDIO-MUSEUM
Lögebodavägen 10, Bellevue Park, Stockholm
Collected works of the sculptor, Carl Eldh.
Daily except M., May-Sept. 12-4.

GUSTAV III'S COLLECTION OF ANTIQUITIES
Royal Palace, Stockholm
Collection of antique sculpture formed by Gustav III (d.1792).
Weekdays 12-4; Su. 1-4.

GUSTAV III'S PAVILION
Haga Park, nr. Brunnsviken, nr. Stockholm
The pavilion (1787-92) preserves the state rooms and some of the bedrooms in their original condition.
May-Oct. Weekdays 12-4; Su. 1-4.

HALLWYL MUSEUM
Hamngatan 4, Stockholm
Residence (1893-1898) of Wilhelmina von Hallwyl, with original furniture and household equipment, and other family possessions, including collections of arms, silver, Chinese ceramics and bronzes, oriental carpets, Dutch paintings, carriages.
Guided tours: Tu.-F. at noon and one; Su. at 1, 2, 3.

HOUSE OF THE NOBLES
Riddarhustorget, Stockholm
17th century palace, designed by J. and S. de la Vallée. Furnishings. Paintings.
Guided tour M.-F. 11.30. Closed Sa., Su.

KARL-JOHAN'S MUSEUM
Villa Rosendal, Djurgården, Stockholm
Villa (1823-27) built for Karl Johan XIV. Early 19th century furnishings. Royal collection of paintings.
Mid.May-Sept., Tu.-Sa. 11-4.

MILLES MUSEUM
Lidingö, nr. Stockholm
In Millesgården, the house of the sculptor, Carl Milles (1875-1955). Contains most of Milles' works, in the original or as replicas, with his personal collection of medieval sculpture, European painting, Chinese statuettes and Greco-Roman antiquities.
May-Oct. 11-5; June-July Tu. and F. 7-9.

MUSEUM OF FAR EASTERN ANTIQUITIES
41 Storgatan, Stockholm
Chinese Stone Age ceramics (largest collection outside China). Ceramics and jade from Hang to Sung periods. Bronzes.
Tu.-Su. 12-4. Tu. also 7-9.30. Closed M.

MUSEUM OF MEDICAL HISTORY
Asögatan 146, Stockholm
Instruments. Pictures. Documents. Pharmaceutical collections.
Th. and F. 1-4. Other days and times by appointment. Closed July.

MUSEUM OF MEDITERRANEAN AND NEAR EASTERN ANTIQUITIES
Järntorget 84, Stockholm
Egyptian exhibition in 17th century building, originally Bank of Sweden. Prehistoric pottery. Sculptures, mummy-cases and other items from Dynastic Egypt. Botanical collection illustrating Egyptian agriculture in prehistoric and dynastic times.
Tu.-Sa. 12-3; Su. 1-4.

MUSEUM OF MODERN ART
Skeppsholmen, Stockholm
Painting and sculpture since 1910. Important works by Picasso, Matisse, Gris, Kandinsky and Munch. Modern Scandinavian art is strongly represented.
Daily 12-10.

MUSEUM OF NATIONAL ANTIQUITIES AND ROYAL COIN CABINET
17 Narvavägen, Stockholm
Greek, Etruscan, Roman and Near Eastern Antiquities. Material from Swedish excavations in Cyprus. Luristan bronzes. Mycenaean and archaic Greek pottery, Attic vases, Greek terracotta figurines. Roman sigillata and portraits. Medieval textiles. History of Swedish coins and banknotes.
Tu.-F. and Su. 1-4; Sa. 11-4; Th. also 7-9.

MUSEUM OF TELECOMMUNICATIONS
Karlaplan 2, Stockholm
Development of telecommunications from 18th century optical telegraph to present-day techniques.
Su. 1-3. Other times by appointment.

MUSIC MUSEUM
Slottsbacken 6, Stockholm
2700 musical instruments, including a virginal of 1642, a Kirkman harpsichord of 1763 and early 19th century grand pianofortes.
Daily 12-3.

NATIONAL MARITIME MUSEUM
Djurgårdsbrunnsvägen, Stockholm
Development of Royal Swedish Navy and Swedish Mercantile Marine. 18th and 19th century models from Royal dockyards. Ship-building techniques. Harbours. Nautical instruments.
Daily 11-4.

NATIONAL MUSEUM
Södra Blasieholmshamnen, Stockholm
The principal national art collection, with an emphasis on Swedish art, 1650-1900. Ten works by Rembrandt, including *The Oath of the Batavians* and *Simon with the Christ Child* and several by Chardin, Boucher and Watteau. German and French porcelain. Products of Swedish potteries and glass works.
Tu.-Sa. 11-4; Su. 1-4. (Sept.-May). June-Aug. daily 10-4 also Tu. 7-10.

NATIONAL MUSEUM OF ETHNOGRAPHY
Norra Djurgården, Stockholm
Permanent exhibitions of Asian ethnography and archaeology. Temporary exhibitions from different parts of the world. Exceptional collections from China, Tibet, Central Asia, Japan and the South Pacific. Chinese musical instruments.
Tu.-Sa. 12-3; Su. 1-4.

NATURAL HISTORY MUSEUM
Frescati, Stockholm
Botany. Entomology. Invertebrates. Mineralogy. Palaeontology. Paleozoology. Vertebrates. Complete herbarium of Scandinavian plants. Sjögren mineral collection. Hall of whales.
Weekdays 10-4; Su. 11-5.

NORDIC MUSEUM
Djurgården, Stockholm
Swedish folk-lore and culture. Lapp exhibition. Life and work of farmers, hunters, fishermen. Period rooms. Eating habits and utensils. Costumes.
Tu.-Sa. 10-4; Su. 12-5; closed M.

POSTAL MUSEUM
Lilla Nygatan 6, Stockholm
History of Swedish Postal Service. Collection of postage stamps.
M.-F. 1-3; Su. 1-4; Th. also 7-9.

PRINCE EUGEN'S HOUSE
Waldemarsudde, Djurgården, Stockholm
Residence (1903-5) of Prince Eugen. Reception rooms in original state. Picture gallery (1914) with collection of paintings by Prince Eugen and other, mainly Swedish, artists. Sculptures in grounds.
Tu.-Sa. 11-4; Su. 11-5. Closed M.

RAILWAY MUSEUM
19 Torsgatan and Tomteboda, Stockholm
Models illustrating history of Swedish railways.
M.-F. 11-4; Sa. 11-2; Su. 1-4. Engine-hall at Tomteboda May-Oct. Su. and W. 1-3.

ROYAL ARMOURY
Djurgården, Stockholm
Costumes and armour worn by members of the Swedish Royal Family, from the 16th century to the present day. Gifts from foreign rulers and ambassadors. Complete armouries from Tidö, Tureholm and Bergshammar.
Tu.-Sa. 10-4; Su. 12-5; closed M.

ROYAL ARMY MUSEUM
Riddargatan 13, Stockholm
In former Artillery depot (1767-9). History of the Swedish Army from the Middle Ages to the present day. Weapons. Uniforms. Maps.
Daily 1-4.

ROYAL PALACE
State, Bernadotte and Guest Apartments, Stockholm
Built 1697-1754 to the designs of Nicodemus Tessin the younger. Charles XI's Gallery, the Throne Room and the Royal Chapel are still largely Tessin's Tapestries. 18th century furniture, Meissen and Sèvres porcelain. The Treasury contains the Swedish regalia.
May-mid.Sept. Weekdays 10-2.30; Su. 1-2.30. Mid.Sept.-Apr. Weekdays 11-1.30; Su. 1-2.30. Throne Room and Chapel: *Mid.May-mid.Sept. Weekdays 12-3; Su. 12-3. Mid.Sept.-Oct. Sa. and M. 12-3; Su. 1-3.* Treasury: *Early May-Sept. Weekdays 10-4; Su. 12-4. Oct.-Apr. M., W., F., Sa. 12-3; Tu., Th. 6-9; Su. 12.30-4.* Palace Museum: *May-Aug. Weekdays 10-3; Su. 1-3. Sept.-Apr. Weekdays 11-2; Su. 1-3.*

SKANSEN
Djurgården, Stockholm
Pioneering open-air museum. Houses, workshops, farm buildings, from all over Sweden. Wooden church from Seglora. Old Stockholm is represented by burghers' houses and workshops.
Park open daily 8 a.m. - 11.30 p.m. Buildings open in summer 11-5 (closed 12-1). Some buildings open in winter 11-3.

STRINDBERG MUSEUM
The Blue Tower, Drottninggatan 85, Stockholm
Manuscripts, furniture and other relics concerning August Strindberg.
Tu. and F. 6-8. Sa. and Su. 1-4.

STUREHOV MANOR
Botkyrka, Lake Mälaren, nr. Stockholm
Manor house (1778-81). Restored and furnished in original style. Decorated faience stoves from Marieberg factory.
Su. 1-4. Other times by arrangement.

SVINDERSVIK MANOR
Nacka, nr. Stockholm
Manor house of c.1740. Original 18th century furniture and decorations, including hand-painted Chinese wallpaper. Separate kitchen wing has original equipment.
M.-F. 5-8; Sa., Su. 1-5.

SWEDISH MUSEUM OF ARCHITECTURE
Skeppsholmen, Stockholm
Archives of photographs and drawings. Exhibitions of architecture and planning.
M.-F. 9-5; Sa. 12-4. Occasional Su. as advertised in press.

TECHNICAL MUSEUM
N. Djurgården, Museivägen 7, Stockholm
Collections illustrating history of science and technology. Original machines. Natural-size drift of iron-ore mine. Royal Model Chamber, containing original 18th century models of machinery.
M.-F. 10-4; Sa. and Su. 12-4.

THIEL ART GALLERY
Djurgården, Stockholm
Collection formed by Ernest Thiel, c.1900 in specially designed house and gallery. Mainly Swedish art, 1890-1905. Original Thiel household furniture.
Weekdays 11-3; Su. 1-4.

TOBACCO MUSEUM
Gubhyllan, Skansen, Djurgården, Stockholm
History of tobacco. Manufacture of cigarettes and cigars on old machines.
Weekdays 11-3. Su. 1-4. Summer Su. only for demonstrations.

TRAMWAY MUSEUM
8 Tulegatan, Stockholm
Stockholm public transport yesterday and today. Vehicles from horse-drawn days onwards.
Weekdays 10-5; Su. 1-5.

WASA DOCKYARD
Djurgården, Stockholm
Warship *Wasa*, lost 1628, raised in 1961. The ship itself, with special exhibition illustrating life on board. Lightship Finngrundet, built 1903.
Daily: Summer 10-8; Winter 10-5.

WINE AND SPIRIT MUSEUM
AB Vin and Spritcentralen, St. Eriksgatan 121, Stockholm
History of wine and spirit trade. Swedish legislation concerning alcoholic beverages since the Middle Ages.
Tu. and F. 10-12. Evenings (groups only) by appointment.

STRÄNGNÄS

ROGGEBORGEN
Strängnäs
Local history. Ecclesiastical art.
Daily 10-5.

SUNDBORN

CARL LARSSON HOUSE-MUSEUM
S-79015 Sundborn
Home of the artist, Carl Larsson, containing his workshop and studio. Antique objects and curiosities collected by Larsson during his lifetime. Etchings by Anders Zorn. Miner's room brought from a village near Falun by Larsson, in order to preserve some of the peasant art of the 1700s.
May-Sept. M.-Sa. 10-4.30; Su. 1-4.30.

SUNDSVALL

MEDELPAD MUSEUM
Sundsvall
History and ethnography of Sweden. Includes open-air museum.
May-Sept. M.-Sa. 11-4; Su. 12-4.

SUNDSVALL MUSEUM OF HANDICRAFTS
Sundsvall
Arts and crafts from Sundsvall district.
May-Sept. M.-Sa. 11-4; Su. 12-4.

SUNDSVALL MUSEUM
29 Storgatan, Sundsvall
Technical and social development of forest industries. Archaeology, especially 6th century finds from mount of Högom.
M.-F. 10-4, 7-9; Sa. 10-4; Su. 1-4.

SUNNE

MÅRBACKA MANOR
Sunne
Home of Selma Lagerlöf.
Mid.May- mid.Sept. daily 10-7.

SVEG

MUSEUM OF OLD BUILDINGS
Sveg
Open-air museum of rural buildings.
May-Sept. 12-5.

TRELLEBORG

EBBES ART GALLERY
1 Hesekillegatan, Trelleborg
Paintings and sculpture, mostly Swedish.
May-Sept. 12-5; Oct.-Apr. 1-5.

TRELLEBORG MUSEUM
58 Östergatan, Trelleborg
Local history and archaeology. Ethnography.
Tu.-F. 3-6; Sa. 1-3; Su. 2-4.

TYRESÖ

TYRESÖ CASTLE
Tyresö, nr. Stockholm
Castle of 1620-3, much altered. 18th and 19th century interiors. Items associated with Marie Antoinette.
F.-Su. 12-6. May-Sept. only.

UDDEVALLA

UDDEVALLA MUSEUM
30 Kungsgatan and, Kungstorget, Uddevalla
History and archaeology of coastal and border regions of Bohuslän province, with special emphasis on fishing. Art collection. Weapons.
30 Kungsgatan: Tu.-Su. 10-1.30; Su. 12-1.30.
Kungstorget: Tu.-Sa. 2-3.30; Su. 2-4.

UMEÅ

VÄSTERBOTTEN MUSEUM
Umeå
Local and Lapp ethnography. Open-air museum, including mill-owner's mansion and wooden church (1802). Art gallery.
Late June- mid.Aug. M.-F. 9-7; Sa. and Su. 1-7. Mid.Aug. - late June, M.-F. 9-5; Sa. and Su. 1-5.

UPPSALA

LINNAEUS MUSEUM
27 Svartbäcksgatan, Uppsala
Relics and other exhibits illustrating life and achievements of the botanist, Carl Linnaeus.
Mar.-May and Sept. 1-3; June-Aug. 1-4.

OPEN-AIR MUSEUM
Gamla Uppsala, 755 90 Uppsala
Open air museum with 22 buildings from 16th-18th centuries, including a central Swedish farm. One building contains wall-paintings by the local painter, Erik Wikström (early 19th century). Weekend demonstrations of different tasks on a local farm during the 19th century.
May-Sept. Daily guided tours.

UNIVERSITY COIN CABINET
Uppsala
Coins and medals.
Sept. - mid.Dec. and mid.Jan. - June. Th. 6-7.

UNIVERSITY MUSEUM OF NATIONAL ANTIQUITIES
Universitetshuset, Uppsala
Archaeology of Uppland, including finds from tribal burial place at Valsgärde (7th-12th centuries).
Sept. - mid.Dec. and mid.Jan. - June, W. 6.30-7.30. June-Aug. M.-F. 12-3; Sa. 11-1. Sept.-May, Sa. 1-2.

UPPLAND MUSEUM
St. Eriks Torg 10, 752 20 Uppsala
Housed in 18th century mill, the collections include a number of rare provincial 'rya' rugs, and a large number of carved wooden folk art pieces. Life and culture of the province since medieval times.
M.-Sa. 12-4; Su. 1-5. W. also 7-9.

VICTORIA MUSEUM
Gustavianum, Uppsala
Egyptian archaeology, including stelae, fragments of reliefs, stone and wooden chests, bronze, wood and faience statues and statuettes, stone vessels, pottery, furniture, funeral objects, human and animal mummies, tomb models, ivories. Egyptian and Coptic textiles, Fajum-portraits, sandcore glass, coins and jewellery. 1,500 ostraca, mainly with demotic and coptic inscriptions. Objects received as gifts from the Egyptian government during the 1880s by Queen Victoria of Sweden (1862-1930), to whom the museum owes its name.
By appointment.

ZOOLOGICAL MUSEUM
9 Villavägen, Uppsala
Natural history.
Sept.-May 1st and 3rd Su. of month, 12-1.30.

VÄNERSBORG

VÄNERSBORG MUSEUM
Vänersborg
Characteristic Victorian collections of archaeology, ethnography, coins, art history, natural history, in building erected for the purpose in 1887. Collection of African birds.
June-Aug. Tu.-F. 11-1; Su. 1-3. Sept.-May Tu., W. and F. 11-1; Su. 1-3.

VARBERG

VARBERG MUSEUM
Varberg Castle, Varberg
Peasant culture. Local history. 14th century clothing (Bocksten Man). Archive of local building methods. Folk traditions and dialect.
Mid.June - mid.Aug. 10-7. Mid.Aug. - mid.June M.-F. 10-4; Sa. 10-1; Su. 1-4.

VÄSTERÅS

VALLBY OPEN-AIR MUSEUM
Västerås, Västmanland
45 buildings from Västmanland, including a farmyard, 17th century manor house from Bergslagen (a mining district), and an open-air theatre. One group illustrates wooden architecture in the smaller towns. Each house is furnished with contemporary furniture.
Daily 8-8. May-Oct. 2, guided tours twice a day.

ALMÄNNA SVENSKA ELEKTRISKA AKTIEBOLAGET (ASEA)
Vasa Park, Västerås
Works museum, illustrating history of one of the largest factories for electrical machinery in Sweden.
By appointment.

VÄSTERÅS ART GALLERY
Stadhuset, Västerås
Art collections, mostly Swedish.
M.-F. 12-4; Sa. and Su. 1-4; W. also 6-8.

VÄSTMANLAND MUSEUM
Västerås Palace, Västerås
Local history and archaeology. Ethnography. Ecclesiastical art.
May-Sept. M.-Sa. 11-4; Su. 1-4. Oct.-Apr. Tu.-Su. 1-4; W. and F. also 6-8.

VÄSTERVIK

TJUSTBYDENS MUSEUM OF CULTURAL HISTORY
Kulbacken, Västervik
Local history. Maritime history.
Apr.-mid.Oct. M.-Sa. 10-4; Su. 1-5. Mid.Oct.-Mar. Su. 1-4.

VÄXJÖ

SMÅLAND MUSEUM
2 S. Järnvägsgatan, Växjö
Archaeology. Ethnography. Church art. Glass and glassmaking. Forest industries.
June-Sept. M.-F. 9-4; Sa. 9-1; Su. 1-4. Oct.-May M.-F. 9-4; Sa. 9-3; Su. 1-5.

VETLANDA

OPEN-AIR MUSEUM
Vetlanda
Open-air museum of rural buildings.
May-Aug. Sa. 5-7; Su. 3-7.

VISBY

GOTLAND HISTORICAL MUSEUM
12-14 Strandgatan or 19 Mellangatan, Visby
Picture stones of 5th-8th centuries. Medieval sculpture and stained glass. Weapons and armour of the 14th century. Viking treasures. Social history.
June-Aug. M.-Sa. 11-5; Su. 1-5. Sept.-May M.-F. 1-3.

YSTAD

ART MUSEUM
St. Knuts Torg, Ystad
Paintings, sculpture, prints on loan from the National Museum in Stockholm, covering the period from the 16th century to the present day. Collection of Danish 19th century art.
Summer: M.-F. 10-12, 1-4; Tu. and Th. also 5-7; Sa. 11-2; Su. 1-4. Winter: M.-F. 1-4; Tu. and Th. also 5-7; Su. 1-4; closed Sa.

CHARLOTTE BERLIN MUSEUM
Dammgatan 23, Ystad
Donated to the city by Charlotte Berlin (1841-1916). Example of a prosperous 19th century home, with furniture, decorations and bric-brac still in place and unchanged.
Summer: M.-F. 10-12, 1-4; Tu. and Th. also 5-7; Sa. 11-2; Su. 1-4. Winter: M.-F. 1-4; Tu. and Th. also 5-7. Su. 1-4. Closed Sa.

FRIARY WITH ST. PETER'S CHURCH
Ystad
Town history including finds from excavations and documents from restored buildings from the Middle Ages, as well as workshops of different crafts from the last two centuries.
Summer: M.-F. 10-12, 1-4; Tu. and Th. also 5-7; Sa. 11-2; Su. 1-4. Winter: M.-F. 1-4; Tu. and Th. also 5-7; Su. 1-4. Closed Sa.

DRAGOON MUSEUM
St. Knuts Torg, Ystad
Collections belonging to the Royal Skåne Regiment of Dragoons, no longer in service. Portraits of all the regimental commanders and the gigantic paintings, "The Skåne Dragoons ride to bathe" (1906) by Danish artist, Oscar Mathiesen (1861-1959).
Summer: M.-F. 10-12, 1-4; Tu. and Th. also 5-7; Sa. 11-2; Su. 1-4. Winter: M.-F. 1-4; Tu. and Th. also 5-7; Su. 1-4. Closed Sa.

Switzerland

The average quality of Swiss museums is almost certainly higher than in any other country in the world. One can only speculate on the possible reasons for this - freedom from wars, long and unbroken cultural traditions, considerable respect for education, a highly developed tourist economy and a willingness to spend public money on public amenities. The rubbishy, ill-arranged museum is comparatively rare in Switzerland. It does not fit the distinctly house-proud national style, which is based on the assumption that everything has to be available for critical public inspection at any moment.

Switzerland's history and specialities are well reflected in her museums. There are, predictably, collections devoted to such national institutions as William Tell, Pestalozzi, goat-keeping, cheese, watch and clock-making, Voltaire, Rousseau and winter sports. One can also notice the Confederation's cultural heritage illustrated in more general ways, and in both large and small museums - the collections of Roman and prehistoric archaeology, of folk art, of weapons and armour, of costumes, of coins, of hunting and Alpine farming.

There are, inevitably, a number of surprises. Switzerland has the best of all Sherlock Holmes museums, based on the material bequeathed by Sir Arthur Conan Doyle and his son, and including an admirable reconstruction of the famous drawing room in Baker Street. Wine museums are remarkably abundant - there are more of them in Switzerland than in France, Italy or Germany. No one, unfortunately, has established a museum dedicated to that great national export, Gruyère cheese, but, another major export, people - especially skilled people - is documented, sadly but efficiently, in a type of museum we have not come across elsewhere, "a museum relating to emigration".

AARAU

AARGAU ART MUSEUM
Rathausplatz, Aarau, Aargau
Works by Swiss artists, 1750 - present day. Paintings. Drawings. Prints. Sculpture. French paintings, including works by Corot, Gauguin, Courbet, Utrillo.
Th.-Sa. 10-12, 2-5; Su. 10-12.

MUSEUM OF NATURAL HISTORY AND LOCAL LIFE
Feerstrasse 17, Aarau, Aargau
Geology. Palaeontology. Animals, birds, fish, insects of the Aargau. Hunting. Fishing. Forestry. Conservation.
Th.-Su. 10-12, 2-5.

OLD AARAU MUSEUM
Schlossplatz 12, Aarau, Aargau
History of Aarau. 16th-19th century period rooms. Weapons. Trade archives. Memorabilia of General Herzog and other Aaraú notabilities.
Sa. 2-5; Su. 10-12. Other times by appointment.

AARBURG

REGIONAL MUSEUM
im Städtli, Aarburg, Aargau
Local history. Prints and drawings of the town. Furnishings and household equipment. Tools. Weapons.
2nd and 4th Su. in month, 10.30-12.

AARWANGEN

HISTORICAL COLLECTION
Altes Schützenhaus, Aarwangen
Local and regional history.
Tu.-Su. 10-12, 2-5.

AESCH BEI BIRMENSDORF

VILLAGE MUSEUM
Aesch bei Birmensdorf, Zurich
In former blacksmith's shop. Peasant furnishings, household equipment. Agricultural implements. Tradesmen's tools.
By appointment.

AGNO

TOWN MUSEUM
Agno, Ticino
Roman archaeology. Sarcophagi. Funeral objects. Inscriptions. Coins.
May-Sept. Su. 11-12.

AIGLE

WINE MUSEUM
Schloss Aigle, Aigle, Vaud
History of the vineyards of Aigle and Yvorne. Vine-growing. Processing techniques. Equipment.
On request.

ALLSCHWIL

REGIONAL MUSEUM
Baslerstrasse 48, Allschwil, Basel-Land
Local history. Weapons. Costumes. Archaeological material from local excavations.
Th., Su. 10-12, 2-5.

ALTDORF

URI HISTORICAL MUSEUM
Gotthardstrasse, Altdorf, Uri
Material relating to the history of Uri Canton. 15th-18th century ecclesiastical art, especially wood carvings and sculpture. Peasant costumes. Furniture. Pewter. Clocks. Uniforms. Flags. Portraits.
M.-Sa. 9-11, 2-4; Su. 11-4.

ALTSTÄTTEN

HISTORICAL MUSEUM
Zur Prestegg, Rabengasse, Altstätten, St. Gallen
Local history. Furniture. Household equipment. Pewter. Weapons. Coins.
Apr.-Oct. Su. 2-5.

AMRISWIL

ROBERT SALLMANN CARRIAGE COLLECTION
Weinfelderstrasse 15, Amriswil, Thurgau
18th-19th century horsedrawn vehicles. Carriages. Carts. Sleighs. Harness.
By appointment.

APPENZELL

REGIONAL MUSEUM
Rathaus, Hauptgasse, Appenzell, Appenzell-Innerrhoden
Archaeological material from Wildkirchli and Burg Clanx. 18th-19th century agricultural tools, implements. Furniture. Peasant costumes and paintings. Ecclesiastical art, mainly 16th-19th century. European embroidery, especially from the Appenzell area.
July 1 - Sept. 15, Daily 1.30-4.30.

ARBON

HISTORICAL MUSEUM
Schloss Arbon, Arbon, Thurgau
Archaeological material from local Neolithic, Bronze Age and Roman sites. Handicraft tools and equipment. Weapons.
1st Su. in month, 10-12. Other times by appointment.

AROSA

SCHANFIGGER REGIONAL MUSEUM
Postsyrasse, Arosa, Graubünden
Local minerals and flora. Material relating to ironmining. Agricultural tools, implements. Furniture. Household equipment. Documents illustrating history of winter sports.
July-Sept. M., F. 2.30-4.30. Jan.-Mar. F. 2-4.

ARTH

AVALANCHE MUSEUM
Goldau, Arth, Schwyz
Material relating to the avalanche of 1806 and to the history of Goldau.
May-Oct. Daily 9.30-11.30, 2-6.

ASCONA

MARIANNE WEREFKIN MUSEUM
Casa Don Pietro Pancaldi, Via Borgo, Ascona, Ticino
Life and work of the painter, Marianne Werefkin, in the house where she lived, 1918-38.
Apr.-Oct. Tu., Th., Sa. 3-6.

ATTISWIL

REGIONAL MUSEUM
Dorfstrasse, Attiswil, Bern
In 18th century 'Heidenstock'. Roman archaeology. Local history. Peasant household equipment. Craftsmen's tools.
Su. 2-5.

AUBONNE

MUSEUM OF THE CHÂTEAU OF AUBONNE
Aubonne, nr. Geneva
Regional history.
On request.

AUGST

ROMAN HOUSE AND MUSEUM
Rheinsprung 20, Augst, Basel-Land
Reconstruction of merchant's house in the Roman town of Augusta Raurica, with replicas of furniture and household equipment. The Museum contains plans and models of Augusta Raurica and archaeological material from excavations, including 4th century silver.
Apr.-Oct. Th.-Su. 10-12, 1.30-6; M. 1.30-6. Nov.-Mar. 1.30-5.

AVENCHES

ROMAN MUSEUM
Avenches, Vaud
Material from the Roman town of Aventicum. Sculpture. Pottery. Gold. Mosaics. Displays illustrating Roman art and religion and daily life in Aventicum.
Mar.-Oct. Daily 9-12, 1-6.

BADEN

HISTORICAL MUSEUM
Landvogtelschloss, Baden, Aargau
Prehistoric and Roman archaeology from the Baden area. Ecclesiastical art. Altar (1564). Wooden sculpture. Bells. Local history. Painted glass. Coins and medals. Gemstones. Prints and drawings.
Apr.-Oct. Tu.-Su. 10-12, 2-5.

BALSTHAL

REGIONAL MUSEUM OF OLD FALKENSTEIN
Schloss Alt-Falkenstein, Balsthal, Solothurn
Local history. Peasant furniture, domestic equipment. Aedermannsdorf and Matzendorf ceramics. Medieval archaeology. Coins. Weapons.
Apr. 15-Oct. 10, Tu.-Su. 9-12, 2-5. Mar. 1-Apr. 14, Oct. 11-Nov. 30, 10-12, 2-4.

BASEL

ANATOMICAL MUSEUM
Pestalozzistrasse 20, Basel
Anatomy. Prepared skeletons, including one by Andreas Vesalius (1543), the oldest surviving prepared anatomical specimen in the world. Embryology, including late 16th century embryological models by Wilhelm His.
Su. 10.30-12.

ART GALLERY
Steinenberg 7, Basel
Exhibition of works drawn from the permanent collection of paintings and sculpture by Swiss artists, mainly 19th-20th centuries.
During exhibitions, daily 10-12.15, 2-5; Tu., Th. also 8-10 p.m.

CITY AND MINSTER MUSEUM IN THE LITTLE KLINGENTAL
Unterer Rheinweg 26, Basel
In restored buildings of the former Klingental Convent. Displays illustrating architectural history of Basel. Models. Plans. Drawings. Sculptures and engravings, carvings, both original and casts from the Minster.
Tu.-Sa. 2-5; Su. 10-12.30, 2-5.

COLLECTION OF OLD MUSICAL INSTRUMENTS
Leonhardstrasse 8, Basel
16th-19th century musical instruments. Models of organs and pianos. Displays showing development of principal instruments. Recordings of instruments in the collection. 15th-16th century music.
Su. 10-12.30, 2-5.

EXHIBITION OF BASEL MISSION
Missionsstrasse 21, Basel
Ethnographical material collected in Borneo, Java, Ghana and the Cameroons by the Basel Evangelical Mission Society.
M.-F. 9-12, 2-6.

HISTORICAL MUSEUM
Barfüsserkirche, Basel
Art and cultural history of the Basel and Upper Rhine area. Archaeological material from Gallic, Roman and Alemannic sites. Medieval sculpture in stone and wood. Medieval religious art, furniture and painted glass. 16th-17th century period rooms. 17th-18th century Basel guild silver. 16th-17th century painted glass, including items by Holbein the Younger. Erasmus collection. 16th-17th century goldsmith's work. Weapons. Flags. Uniforms. Coins.
Daily 10-12.30, 2-5; W. also 8-10 p.m.

KIRSCHGARTEN
Elisabethenstrasse 27, Basel
In Haus zum Kirschgarten (1777-80). 18th-19th century period rooms. 16th-19th century clocks, watches, hourglasses, sundials from Switzerland, Germany, France, England. Faience. Porcelain. Wrought-iron. 17th-18th century casks. Sleighs. Toys.
Daily 10-12.30, 2-5. W. also 8-10 p.m.

MUSEUM OF APPLIED ARTS
Spalenvorstadt 2, Basel
Exhibitions from material in the permanent collections. Furniture. Textiles, including Coptic and Peruvian items. Ceramics, especially Persian. Glass. Metalwork. Printing. Bookbinding. 14th-18th century architectural drawings, books.
During exhibitions, 10-12, 2-5; W. also 8-10.

MUSEUM OF ETHNOLOGY
Augustinergasse 2, Basel
Art of Oceania, especially wood sculpture from Melanesia. Pre-Columbian art of S. and Central America. Boats from many areas of the world. Extensive study collections, not usually displayed, of material from all continents, and notably Melanesia, S. America, New Guinea. Important textile collections. Films, photography. Recordings.
Daily 10-12.30, 2-5. W. also 8-10 p.m.

MUSEUM OF GREEK AND ROMAN ART
St. Albangraben 5, Basel
Greek art, 2500-100 B.C., including Pythos relief with earliest representation of story of Theseus and the Minotaur. Attic vases. Tomb reliefs. Italic and Roman bronzes, terracottas and vases, including Roman copies of lost Greek original sculpture.
Daily 10-12.30, 2-5; W. also 8-10.

MUSEUM OF THE HISTORY OF PHARMACY
Tötengässlein 3, Basel
Medicaments from Europe and other countries. Reconstructions of pharmaceutical laboratories of the 16th-19th centuries. 18th-19th century apothecaries' shops. Pharmaceutical vessels and instruments.
M.-F. 9-11, 2-5.

MUSEUM OF SWISS FOLKLORE
Augustinergasse 2, Basel
Popular culture of Europe, especially Switzerland, Poland and the Balkans. Agricultural implements, equipment and techniques. Household equipment. Pottery. Costumes. Christmas cribs. Religious art. Easter eggs. Toys. Peasant art.
Daily 10-12.30, 2-5. W. also 8-10 p.m.

NATURAL HISTORY MUSEUM
Augustinergasse 2, Basel
Geology. Mineralogy. Zoology. Osteology. Anthropology.
Daily 10-12.30, 2-5. W. also 8-10 p.m.

PAPER MUSEUM
Augustinergasse 2, Basel
History of hand-made paper. Operational medieval papermill. Reconstruction of old papermills from Europe and other parts of the world. Paper samples.
Daily 10-12.30, 2-5. W. also 8-10 p.m.

PUBLIC ART COLLECTION
St. Albangraben 16, Basel
Paintings by 15th-16th century Swiss and Upper Rhine artists, including Konrad Witz, Holbein the Younger, Cranach, Grünewald. 16th-17th century Flemish and Dutch paintings. 18th century Swiss paintings. 19th century Swiss and German paintings. 19th-20th century French paintings, especially the Impressionists. 20th century European and American paintings, especially Cubists. 15th-20th century Swiss and S. German drawings, printing. 17th-20th century European drawings and engravings, especially by the German Romantics and French post-Impressionists.
Picture Gallery: Oct.-May 10-12.30, 2-5; W. also 8-10 p.m. June-Sept. Daily 10-5; W. also 8-10 p.m. Graphics Cabinet: Th.-Sa. 9-12.30, 2-6.

RHINE NAVIGATION MUSEUM, 'OUR WAY TO THE SEA'
Rheinhafen Basel-Kleinhüningen, Basel
History of Rhine shipping and navigation. Ships' models. Photographs. Documents.
M.-F. 9-12, 1-6; Sa., Su. 9-12, 2-6.

SCULPTURE GALLERY
Mittlere Strasse 17, Basel
Casts of Greek, Roman, Medieval and Renaissance sculpture.
Daily 10-12.30, 2-5; W. also 8-10 p.m.

SWISS JEWISH MUSEUM
Kornhausgasse 8, Basel
History of the Jewish Community in Basel. Jewish teaching, festivals and daily life.
M., W. 2-5; Su. 10-12.

SWISS MUSEUM OF FIREFIGHTING
Kornhausgasse 18, Basel
History and technical development of fire-fighting, with particular reference to Basel.
Su. 2-5.

SWISS MUSEUM OF GYMNASTICS AND SPORT
Missionsstrasse 28, Basel
History of physical exercise, mainly in Switzerland. Development of equipment and apparatus. Posters. Paintings, prints, photographs. Documents.
M.-Sa. 2-5; Su. 10-12, 2-5.

BAULMES

MUSEUM OF OLD BAULMES
Rue du Thé, Baulmes, Vaud
Local history. Prehistoric material from excavations at Baulmes. Furniture. Drawings. Prints.
On request.

BEINWIL AM SEE

PFAHLBAUSAMMLUNG
Schulhaus, Beinwil am See, Luzern
Collections illustrating lake-dwellings and settlements.
Tu.-Su. 10-12, 2-5.

BELLINZONA

MUNICIPAL MUSEUM
Castello di Montebello, Bellinzona, Ticino
Regional history and archaeology. Material from Bronze Age, Iron Age and Roman sites. 15th-19th century weapons.
Daily 9-12, 2-5.

MUSEUM OF COSTUMES OF THE TICINO
Castello di Sasso Corbaro, Bellinzona, Ticino
Prints and other documents illustrating regional costumes. Peasant paintings. Pictures showing history of Bellinzona and its region.
Mar.-Oct. Daily 9-12, 2-6.

BERINGEN

REGIONAL MUSEUM
Mitteldorf, Beringen, Schaffhausen
Local history collection.
By appointment.

BERN

ART MUSEUM
Hodlerstrasse 12, Bern
15th-20th century Swiss paintings, with emphasis on Bern artists. Italian painting, especially Trecento. 19th-20th century European painting, and sculpture. Paul Klee collection. 16th-19th century Swiss prints, drawings.
M. 2-5; Tu. 10-12, 2-5, 8-10; W.-Su. 10-12, 2-5. Graphics collection: M.-F. 10-12.

BERN HISTORICAL MUSEUM
Helvetiaplatz 5, Bern
Prehistoric material, mainly from local sites. Palaeolithic, Mesolithic, Neolithic, Bronze Age, Hallstatt, La Tène. Migration period. Celtic. Roman bronzes. History of the City and Canton of Bern, from medieval period to 19th century. Textiles. Wrought iron. Ecclesiastical art. Faience. Porcelain. Furniture. 16th-18th century period rooms. Musical instruments. Costumes. Folklore. Art of Africa, S. America, India, China, Japan, Oceania. Coins and medals, especially of the Roman Republic, Switzerland and the Far East.
M. 2-5; Tu.-Sa. 9-12, 2-5; Su. 10-12, 2-5.

CANTONAL MUSEUM OF APPLIED ART
Zeughausgasse 2, Bern
Exhibitions of material from permanent collection. Ceramics. Textiles, especially lace. Metalwork. Wood. Glass. Prints. Posters.
During special exhibition. Times announced locally.

NATURAL HISTORY MUSEUM
Bernastrasse 15, Bern
Geology. Mineralogy. Palaeontology. Invertebrates and vertebrates. Zoolpgy. Dioramas. Anthropology.
M. 2-5; Tu.-Sa. 9-12, 2-5; Su. 10-12, 2-5.

SWISS ALPINE MUSEUM
Helvetiaplatz 4, Bern
History and techniques of Alpine climbing. Equipment. Rescue methods. Maps and map-making. Geology. Glaciology. Meteorology. Zoology. Botany. Costumes and customs of the Alpine peasants.
M. 2-5 (Oct.-Mar. 2-4); Tu.-Sa. 9-12, 2-5 (Oct.-Mar. 2-4); Su. 10.30-12, 2-5.

SWISS MUSEUM OF SHOOTING
Bernastrasse 5, Bern
19th-20th century firearms, mainly Swiss. Hunting trophies.
Tu.-Sa. 9-12, 2-4 (Apr.-Sept. 2-5); Su. 10.30-12, 2-4.

SWISS POSTAL, TELEPHONE AND TELEGRAPH MUSEUM
Helvetiaplatz 4, Bern
Postal services from Roman times to present day. Models.

Pictures. Equipment. Development of electrical communications. Postage stamps.
M. 2-5; Tu.-Sa. 9-12, 2-5; Su. 10-12, 2-5.

SWISS TECHNICAL MUSEUM OF BOOKBINDING
Zeughausgasse 2, Bern
History of bookbinding and printing. Tools. Machines. Materials. Historic books.
Th.-Sa. 10-12, 2-5.

SWISS THEATRE COLLECTION
Landesbibliothek, Hallwylstrasse 15, Bern
Stage and costume designs. Masks. Marionettes. Costumes. Theatre history in Switzerland and abroad, illustrated by posters, photographs, portraits, recordings, press cuttings, manuscripts.
M.-F. 9.30-12, 2.30-4.30.

BEROMÜNSTER

CHURCH TREASURY OF THE CHORAL FOUNDATION
Stiftskirche, Beromünster, Luzern
Ritual objects from 7th century to present day, especially of the medieval and Renaissance periods.
M.-F. 10-5.30; Sa. 10-2.30; Su. 10.30-2.30, 3.15-7.

REGIONAL MUSEUM
Schloss, Beromünster, Luzern
Tower in which Helias Helye produced the first dated Swiss book (1470). Replica of his printing press. Books printed by Helye and by Ulrich Gering. Prehistoric material from local excavations. Pictures and documents illustrating traditions and handicrafts of Beromünster area.
Su. 2-5, by appointment.

BIEL

SCHWAB MUSEUM
Seevorstadt 50, Biel, Bern
Collection of prehistoric material from the Bielersee area. Neolithic. Bronze Age. Hallstatt. Items from La Tène and Petinesca sites.
Tu.-Sa. 8-12, 2-6; Su. 10-12, 2-5.

BISCHOFSZELL

LOCAL MUSEUM
Schloss, Bischofszell, Thurgau
Local history.
May-Oct., 1st Su. in month, 11-12, 2-4.

BISSONE

TENCALLA HOUSE
Via Tencalla, Bissone, Ticino
16th century patrician house. Rooms furnished in 17th-19th century regionsl style.
Daily 10-12, 2.30-5.

BOSCO-GURIN

GURIN HOUSE OF THE WAISERS
Bosco-Gurin, Ticino
History of the German-speaking community of the Waisers. Furniture. Costumes. Tools, implements, household equipment.
By appointment.

BOUDRY

L'AREUSE MUSEUM
Avenue du Collège 18, Boudry, Neuchâtel
Prehistoric material from sites at Cortaillod and Auvernier. Regional history and folklore. Birds and animals of the area. Ethnographical collection from Gabon.
Tu., Th., Sa. 1-5; Su. 11-12, 1-5.

MUSEUM OF WINE AND THE VINE
Château de Boudry, Boudry, Neuchâtel
Cultivation of the vine. Wine-press. Cellar equipment. Bottling machinery. Glassware. Documents illustrating the history of wine.
Th.-Tu. 10-6.

BOURG-SAINT-PIERRE

MUSEUM OF THE GREAT ST. BERNARD SHELTER FOR TRAVELLERS
Bourg-Saint-Pierre, Valais
History of the area and the Hospice. Ecclesiastical gold plate and ornaments. Roman material from the St. Bernard Pass. Statues, votive tablets, coins. Minerals and insects of the St. Bernard region.
June-Oct. Daily 9-12, 1-5.

BRIEG

CASTLE OF THE STOCKALPERS
Brieg, Valais
Material illustrating the history of Brieg, Canton Valais, the Stockalper family and the Bishops of Sitten. Portraits. Furniture. Coins and medals. Documents. Popular culture of Valais.
Easter-Oct. 31, guided tours daily at 9, 11, 2, 3, 4.

BRISSAGO

CANTONAL BOTANICAL GARDEN AND MUSEUM OF AFRICAN ETHNOGRAPHY
Isole di Brissago, Ticino
Plants of the Mediterranean, S. America, Africa, China, Japan, and New Zealand. Weapons and domestic utensils from Upper Egypt, the Sudan and the Congo.
Daily 8-6.

BRUGG

REGIONAL MUSEUM
Untere Hofstatt, Brugg, Aargau
Local history.
Apr.-Oct. 1st Su. in month, 10-11.30.

STÄBLIS MUSEUM
Zeughaus, Brugg, Aargau
Works by the Brugg painter, Adolf Stäbli, and by 19th-20th century artists from Canton Aargau.
1st Su. in month, 10-12.

VINDONISSA MUSEUM
Museumstrasse 1, Brugg, Aargau
Material from the Roman Legionary Camp at Vindonissa. Weapons. Tools. Pottery. Glass. Leather. Coins. Architectural items. Inscriptions. Prehistoric, Roman and medieval material from Canton Aargau is in store at the museum.
Tu.-Su. 10-12, 2-4 (May-Sept. 2-5.30).

BUBIKON

MUSEUM OF THE ORDER OF THE JOHANNITER
Ritterhaus, Bubikon, Zurich
History of the Knightly Orders, especially the Johanniter. Paintings. Engravings. Coins. Medals. Seals. Insignia. Weapons. Material relating to the historian, Johannes Stumpf (1500-78).
Apr.-Oct. Sa.-Th. 9-11, 2-6.

BULLE

MUSEUM OF THE GRUYÈRE DISTRICT
Rue Victor Tissot, Bulle, Fribourg
Regional history, art, folklore. 15th-19th century furnishings. Religious paintings, sculpture. Paintings by local artists. Memorabilia of Victor Tissot and Abbé Joseph Bovet. Costumes. Tools. Utensils. Musical instruments. Popular cult objects. Diorama of regional wildlife.
Tu.-Sa. 9-12, 2-6; Su. 2-5.

BURGDORF

ETHNOGRAPHICAL COLLECTION
Am Kirchbühl, Burgdorf, Bern
Material from Indonesia, Melanesia and the Amazon. Smaller collections from Africa, N. America, Asia and Australia.
1st and 3rd Su. in month, 10-12. Other times by appointment.

HISTORICAL MUSEUM OF THE BURGDORF HALL OF THE KNIGHTS SOCIETY
Schloss Burgdorf, Burgdorf, Bern
Local history and archaeology. 19th century costumes. Pottery. Glass. Agricultural tools and equipment. Beekeeping. Milk-processing and cheesemaking. Weapons. Musical instruments. Memorabilia of Pestalozzi, the Schnell brothers and Jeremias Gotthelf. 18th-20th century self-portraits by painters from the Burgdorf area. Reconstruction of the Landschreiberei (1764).
Apr.-Oct. Th.-F. 1-6; Sa., Su. 10-12, 1-5.

BÜRGLEN

TELL MUSEUM
Tellenturm, Bürglen, Uri
Material relating to Wilhelm Tell. Engravings. Paintings. Sculpture. Chronicles. Coins. Medals.
June-Oct. Daily 9.30-12, 2-5.30.

CASTAGNOLA

SCHLOSS ROHONCZ COLLECTION
Villa Favorita, Castagnola, Ticino
Works by Italian painters, including Veronese, Titian, Tintoretto, Tiepolo, Fra. Angelico. Flemish and Dutch paintings, including works by Memling, Bosch, Rembrandt, Rubens. 16th-18th century French paintings. Spanish paintings, including group by El Greco. 14th-16th century German paintings, including works by Cranach, Dürer, Holbein. 12th-16th century Italian sculpture.
Mar.-Oct. F., Sa., 10-12, 2-5.

CASTANEDA

PREHISTORIC COLLECTION
Scuola Elementare, Castaneda, Grigioni
Objects from Iron Age necropolis at Castaneda.
On request.

CEVIO

MUSEUM OF THE VALLEMAGGIA
Cevio, Ticino
Agricultural implements. Tradesmen's tools. Popular art of the Vallemaggia area. Collections relating to emigration.
May-Sept. Sa., Su., 10-12, 2-5.

CHÂTEAU D'OEX

MUSEUM OF THE FORMER PAYS D'ENHAUT AND OF THE AUGUST COTTIER FOUNDATION
Château d'Oex, Vaud
History and art of the region. Charters. Engravings. Drawings. Sculpture. Replicas of mountain-dwelling interiors, 16th-19th centuries, including cheese-making rooms. Handicrafts tools. Agricultural implements. Stained glass.
Tu., Th., F. 10-12, 2-4.30; Su. 11.15-12, 2-4.30.

LA CHAUX-DE-FONDS

MUSEUM OF FINE ART AND MUSEUM OF ETHNOGRAPHY
33 rue de l'Envers, La Chaux-de-Fonds, Neuchâtel
Works by artists from La Chaux-de-Fonds. 19th-20th century paintings by Swiss and Neuchâtel artists. Contemporary European paintings. Ethnographical material from Angola, the Congo, Australia and Oceania.
Tu.-Su. 10-12, 2-5.

MUSEUM OF HISTORY, COINS AND MEDALS
11 rue de la Loge, La Chaux-de-Fonds, Neuchâtel
16th-18th century Neuchâtel interiors. Furniture. Pewter. Glass. Portraits. Engravings. Neuchâtel coins, medals. Weapons, mainly 19th century.
Sa. 2-5; Su. 10-12, 2-5 (Nov.-Mar. 2-4).

MUSEUM OF NATURAL HISTORY
Avenue Léopold Robert 63, La Chaux-de-Fonds, Neuchâtel
Regional geology. Zoological collections from Angola, Portuguese Guinea, the Cameroons, Switzerland and Canton of Neuchâtel.
Tu.-Sa. 2-4.30; Su. 10-12, 2-5.

WATCH AND CLOCK MUSEUM
Rue du Progrès 40, La Chaux-de-Fonds, Neuchâtel
Historical collection of Swiss, French and English clocks, watches and clockwork automata. Marine chronometers.
May-June, Oct. Daily 2-5. July-Sept. Daily 10-12, 2-5. Nov.-Apr. Su. 10-12, 2-5.

CHUR

ART COLLECTION
Postplatz and Grabenstrasse, Chur, Graubünden
18th-20th century Graubünden paintings, sculpture. 19th-20th century Swiss paintings. Swiss drawings, engravings, prints.
Tu.-Sa. 9-12, 2-5; Su. 10-12, 2-4.

BÜNDER NATURAL HISTORY AND NATURAL PARK MUSEUM
Grabenstrasse 31 and Masanserstrasse 3, Chur, Graubünden
Geology, mineralogy, petrography, zoology and botany of Canton Graubünden. Small teaching collection of natural history material at Masanserstrasse.
Grabenstrasse: Tu.-Sa. 9-12, 2-5; Su. 10-12, 2-4.
Masanserstrasse, W. 2-5; Su. 10-12.

CATHEDRAL TREASURY AND MUSEUM
Hof 18, Chur, Graubünden
Religious art and ritual objects, 8th-19th centuries. Reliquaries. Crosses. Monstrances. Wood sculpture, carvings. Textiles.
M.-Sa. 9-12, 3-5; Su. 3-5.

MUNICIPAL MUSEUM
Hofstrasse 1, Chur, Graubünden
Prehistoric material from sites in the Canton. Roman and medieval archaeology. Religious art. Portraits. Drawings.

Engravings. Painted glass. Metalwork. Textiles. Pottery. Weapons. Flags. Furniture. Household equipment. Agricultural implements. Handicraft tools. Costumes. Horsedrawn vehicles. Sleighs.
M.-Sa. 9-12, 2-5 (Nov.-Mar. 2-4).

COFFRANE

AGRICULTURAL MUSEUM
Coffrane, Neuchâtel
Museum collections arranged at old farm. Agricultural implements, household equipment and handicraft tools from the Val de Ruz. Tools used in flax growing, harvesting, processing.
On request.

COLOMBIER

MILITARY MUSEUM AND MUSEUM OF PAINTED BLINDS
Château de Colombier, Neuchâtel
Swiss and foreign weapons. Armour. Uniforms. Flags and banners, especially 17th-19th century Neuchâtel flags. Relics of the Meuron regiment. History of Neuchâtel painted blinds. Memorabilia of Claude Bovet, founder of the factory for the blind at Boudry.
Guided tours 2.30-3.30, Mar.-Oct., Tu.-F. and 1st Su. in month.

COPPET

CHÂTEAU COPPET AND MUSEUM OF THE SWISS WHO SERVED ABROAD
Coppet, Vaud
Château (1784) built by Jacques Necker. 18th-19th century French furniture. Memorabilia of Necker and his daughter, Madame de Staël. Portraits. Miniatures. Porcelain. Objets d'art. 17th-19th century material illustrating Swiss in military and civilian service abroad. Uniforms. Weapons. Portraits. Flags. Documents.
Mar.-Oct. Tu.-Su. 10-12, 2-4.

VIEUX-COPPET REGIONAL MUSEUM
Grand-Rue, Coppet, Vaud
In 16th century house. Local history.
May-Sept. Th. 2-4.

CULLY

VIEUX-LIVAUX MUSEUM
Rue Davel 124, Cully, Vaud
Local history.
July-Sept. Daily 2.30-5.30.

DAVOS

ERNST LUDWIG KIRCHNER HOUSE
Frauenkirch, Wildboden, Davos, Graubünden
Home of the painter E. L. Kirchner, 1923-38. Memorabilia and works of Kirchner.
Aug. 2-31, Daily 2-4.

REGIONAL MUSEUM
Altes Pfrundhaus, Davos, Graubünden
Regional history. Furnished interiors of peasant and patrician houses. Household equipment. Agricultural implements.
May-Oct. Su. 2-6.

DELÉMONT

JURA MUSEUM
Grand-Rue, Delémont, Bern
Archaeological material from local caves, from Lake Bienne and from Roman sites. Medieval religious art. Baroque sculpture. Documents. Charters. Costumes. Examples of local watch and clockmaking. Paintings, drawings and prints from the Jura. 19th century period room.
May-Sept. Sa., Su. 2-5. Oct.-Apr. Sa. 2-5.

DIESSENHOFEN

LOCAL MUSEUM
Oberes Amtshaus, Diessenhofen, Thurgau
19th century fabric printing in Thurgau and adjoining areas. Paintings by Carl Roesch.
May-Sept., Sa., Su. 2-5. Oct.-Apr. Su. 2-5.

DIETIKON

LOCAL MUSEUM
Obere Reppischstrasse 17, Dietikon, Zurich
Prehistoric archaeology from local excavations. Medieval material from Burg Glanzenberg and Burg Schönenwerd. Handicrafts, tools and equipment, especially for straw, hemp, flax. Pictures and documents illustrating history of the Limmatal.
By appointment.

DISENTIS

COLLECTION OF THE BENEDICTINE ABBEY
Disentis, Graubünden
Church textiles, especially lace. Religious sculpture. Peasant costumes. Agricultural implements. Cheese-making equipment.
May-Sept. by written application for appointment.

DORNACH

REGIONAL MUSEUM OF SCHWAZBUBENLAND
Hauptstrasse, Oberdornach, Solothurn
In old Mauritius Church. Local archaeological material. Religious art. Historical material relating to Battle of Dornach (1499). Craftsmen's tools. Agricultural implements, equipment. Works of the geologist, Amanz Gressley.
Su. 11-12, 3-5.

EBIKON

WILDLIFE PANORAMA
Luzernerstrasse 63, Ebikon, Luzern
Dioramas of wildlife from Switzerland and abroad. Paintings of birds and animals by W. Linsenmaier. Collections of birds of paradise and insects.
Mar.-Oct. M.-Sa. 1.30-5; Su. 10-12, 1.30-5. Nov.-Feb. Su. 10-12, 1.30-5.

EBNAT-KAPPEL

ALBERT EDELMANN FOUNDATION
Ebnat-Kappel, St. Gallen
Furniture, musical instruments (including house-organs) and peasant art from the Toggenburg area. Paintings by Edelmann, Brühlmann and Hofer.
M.-F. 10-12, 2-5. 2nd and 4th Su. in month, 10-12, 2-5.

EGLISAU

LOCAL MUSEUM
Gemeindehaus, Eglisau, Zurich
History of the town. Models. Prints. Drawings. Paintings. Craftsmen's tools.
1st Su. in month, 1.30-5.

EINSIEDELN

GREAT HALL OF THE BENEDICTINE ABBEY
Einsiedeln, Schwyz
Wall paintings. Portraits. 17th century Turkish carpet. Sculptures, by the Einsiedeln artist, Curigen.
Daily 9-11, 1.30-6.

ELGG

REGIONAL MUSEUM
Gasthaus Krone, Elgg, Zurich
Local history. Peasant furnishings, household equipment. Craftsmen's tools.
On request.

ENGELBERG

ANTIQUITIES COLLECTION OF THE BENEDICTINE ABBEY
Engelberg
Scriptorium. 12th-17th century church plate. Ornaments. 12th century sculpture.
By appointment.

ESTAVAYER-LE-LAC

MUSEUM
86 rue de Chavannes, Estavayer-le-Lac, Fribourg
Neolithic and Bronze Age material from local collections. Local craftsmen's tools. Furniture. Household equipment. Pottery. Weapons. Local wildlife.
May-Sept. Daily 9-12, 2-5. Oct.-Apr. Daily 9-12, 2-4.

EVOLÈNE

FOLKLORE MUSEUM
Les Haudènes, Evolène, Valais
Furniture, costumes, tools from the Evolène valley. Paintings by Joseph Georges.
Daily 8-8.

FLEURIER

MUSEUM
Fleurier, Neuchâtel
Zoology. Mineralogy. Palaeontology. Prehistory. Ethnography. Costumes. Reconstruction of kitchen, bedroom and clockmaker's workshop. Weapons. Horse-drawn vehicles.
May-Oct., 1st and 3rd Sa. in month, 2-4.

FLUMS

SARGANSERLAND REGIONAL MUSEUM
Flums, Schwyz
Local and regional history.
On request.

FRAUENFELD

CANTON THURGAU MUSEUM
Luzernerhaus, Freiestrasse 24, Frauenfeld, Thurgau
Geology, botany, zoology and anthropology of Canton Thurgau.
Tu.-Sa. 2-5; Su. 10.30-12, 2-5.

CANTON THURGAU MUSEUM
Schloss, Frauenfeld, Thurgau
Prehistoric and Roman material from sites in Thurgau. Weapons. 17th-19th century furnished room interiors. Coins. Clocks and watches. Astronomical instruments. Pewter. Painted glass. Ceramics. 16th-18th century religious art.
Tu.-Sa. 2-5; Su. 10.30-12, 2-5.

PUBLIC ART COLLECTION
Bernerhaus, Frauenfeld, Thurgau
Works by 19th-20th century Thurgau artists.
Su. 10.30-12, 4-6.

FREIENBACH

REGIONAL MUSEUM
Freienbach
Regional history.
Tu.-Su. 10-12, 2-5.

FRIBOURG

ETHNOGRAPHICAL COLLECTION
University, Bâtiment du Séminaire, Fribourg
Ethnographical material from N. America, N. and W. Africa, New Guinea and Central India.
M.-F. 8-7.

FINE ART GALLERY
Université, Fribourg
Sculptures from the Cathedral and other Fribourg buildings. 17th-18th century tapestries. 19th-20th century Swiss paintings.
When University is open.

MUSEUM OF ART AND HISTORY
Rue Pierre-Aeby 227, Fribourg
Prehistoric and Roman archaeology. 10th-18th century Fribourg paintings and sculpture. 15th-19th century furnishings. Pewter. Faience. Porcelain. Gold. Tapestry. 15th-18th century stained glass. 18th-19th century Fribourg drawings. Coins. Medals.
Tu.-Su. 10-12, 2-5.

MUSEUM OF THE INSTITUTE OF ANATOMY
Rue Albert Gockel 1, Fribourg
Anatomy. Embryology. Osteological material from excavations in Fribourg Canton.
M.-F. 8-12.

MUSEUM OF NATURAL HISTORY
Pérolles, Bâtiment de la Faculté des Sciences, Fribourg
Maps. Minerals of the Vallée de Binn. Regional geology, palaeontology and zoology.
M.-F. 9-12, 2-5 (Nov.-Mar. 2-4).

PRINT COLLECTION
Bibliothèque Cantonale et Universitaire, rue St. Michel 16, Fribourg
Prints illustrating the history of Fribourg Canton.
M.-F. 10-12, 2-5.

SWISS PEDAGOGICAL MUSEUM
16 rue St. Michel, Fribourg
History and theory of teaching methods.
M.-F. 10-12, 2-5.

GANDRIA

CUSTOMS MUSEUM
Cantine di Gandria, Ticino
Objects and documents relating to contraband and smuggling. Uniforms. Weapons. Ticino folklore.
June-Sept., Th., Su. 2-5.

GELFINGEN

HEIDEGG CASTLE
Gelfingen, Luzern
17th-18th century furniture, stoves, paintings. Hunting weapons. Falconry collection.
Apr.-Oct. Daily 8.30-12, 2-5.

GENEVA

ARIANA MUSEUM
Avenue de la Paix 10, Geneva
Porcelain and faience: 18th-19th century European, Chinese, Japanese and Islamic. 15th-19th century European furniture. 16th-18th century Swiss stained glass windows. 17th century Flemish tapestries. 18th-19th century paintings.
Apr.-Oct. Tu.-Su. 10-12, 2-5.

BAUR COLLECTION
Rue Munier-Romilly 8, Geneva
17th-19th century Chinese and Japanese art. Chinese ceramics and jades. Japanese ceramics, lacquer-work, netsuke, sabre ornaments, prints.
Tu., Th., Sa. 2-4; Su. 10-12, 2-4.

COLLECTION OF PRINTS AND ENGRAVINGS
Promenade du Pin 5, Geneva
Prints by Italian, German, Dutch, French, English and Spanish artists. 18th-19th century Swiss prints.
Tu.-Su. 10-12, 2-6; M. 2-6.

HISTORY OF EDUCATION
Palais Wilson, Quai Wilson 51, Geneva
Collections illustrating educational problems and methods in 48 countries. Teaching material. Children's work. Photography and models of buildings.
Daily 9-12, 2-4.

MUSEUM OF ART AND HISTORY
Rue Charles Galland 2, Geneva
Greek, Etruscan and Roman antiquities, especially Greek vases and Roman sculpture. Egyptian pottery, statues, bas-reliefs. Cuneiform tablets. Mesopotamian seals. Cypriot vases, figurines and statuettes. 15th-20th century Swiss paintings. Italian, German, Flemish primitive paintings. 18th-20th century French paintings. Sculpture, especially by Rodin. 16th-20th century Limoges and Geneva miniatures. 16th-19th century clocks, watches. Medieval art. Weapons. Armour. Musical instruments. Jewels. Models and documents illustrating old Geneva. Coins and medals. Byzantine weights.
Tu.-Su. 10-12, 2-6; M. 2-6.

MUSEUM OF THE ATHENEUM
2 rue de l'Athénée, Geneva
19th-20th century European paintings.
M.-Sa. 10-12, 2-6; Su. 10-12.

MUSEUM OF THE HISTORY OF THE REFORMATION
Bibliothèque Publique et Universitaire, Promenade des Bastions, Geneva
Material illustrating history of the Reformation.
Th. 2-4; Su. 11-12, 2-4.

MUSEUM OF THE HISTORY OF SCIENCE
Villa Bartholoni, Rue de Lausanne 128, Geneva
History of science in Geneva. Astronomical instruments, 1772-1836. Apparatus used by 18th-19th century physicists. Microscopes. Biology. Medicine. Geology. Clocks and clockwork mechanisms.
M.-Sa. 2-6; Su. 10-12, 2-6.

MUSEUM AND INSTITUTE OF ETHNOGRAPHY
Boulevard Carl Vogt 65-7, Geneva
World-wide ethnography, especially of Australia, Nepal, Pre- and Post-Columbian America (including silver of the colonial period), Africa. Special collections of musical instruments and domestic pottery.
Tu.-Su. 10-12, 2-5; F. also 8-10 p.m.

MUSEUM OF OLD MUSICAL INSTRUMENTS
Rue Lefort 23, Geneva
Musical instruments, mainly European.
Tu. 3-7; Th. 10-12; F. 8-10 p.m.

NATURAL HISTORY MUSEUM
Route de Malagnou, Geneva
Zoology. Comparative anatomy. Palaeontology, especially from Argentine pampas. Geology. Stratigraphy. Mineralogy. Precious stones. Wildlife of the Geneva region.
Tu.-Su. 10-12, 2-5.

PETIT PALAIS
Terrasse Saint-Victor 2, Geneva
French paintings, 1880-1930, especially by lesser-known artists.
M.-Th. 10-22, 2-4; F. 10-12, 2-6, 8.30-10; Sa., Su. 10-6.

JEAN-JACQUES ROUSSEAU MUSEUM
Bibliothèque Publique et Universitaire, Promenade des Bastions, Geneva
Works and manuscripts of Rousseau. Memorabilia. Paintings, engravings and sculptures representing Rousseau or inspired by his work.
Th. 2-4; Su. 11-12, 2-4.

TAVEL HOUSE
Rue du Puits-St. Pierre 6, Geneva
14th century merchant's house. Local history.
Tu.-Sa. 2-7; Su. 10-12, 2-6.

VOLTAIRE INSTITUTE AND MUSEUM
Rue des Délices 25, Geneva
Collections relating to Voltaire and his times.
Tu.-Sa. 2-5; Su. 10-12, 2-5.

GLARUS

ART GALLERY
Museumstrasse, Glarus
19th-20th century paintings, sculpture by Swiss artists. European drawings, prints. Autographed manuscripts of famous musicians. Iconography of Canton Glarus.
Su. 10-12, 2-5 (Nov.-Mar. 2-4).

NATURAL SCIENCE COLLECTIONS OF CANTON GLARUS
Museumstrasse, Glarus
Regional zoology, especially fauna of Canton Glarus. Geology. Mineralogy. Palaeontology.
Su. 10-12, 2-5 (Nov.-Mar. 2-4).

GOSSAU

OBERBERG MUSEUM
Schloss Oberberg, Gossau, St. Gallen
Local and regional history. Court-room. Torture-chamber.
Su. 11-5.

GRANDSON

CHÂTEAU
Place du Château, Grandson, Vaud
13th-18th century furnishings. Documents relating to the Grandson family and to the château. Weapons. Armour. Models and plans of Swiss and foreign castles. Old cars.
Easter-Nov. Daily 9-6. Dec.-Easter Su. 9-4.

GRANDVAUX

BUTTIN-DE LOËS HOUSE
Grandvaux, Vaud
18th-19th century furnishings and domestic equipment.
Mar.-Nov. Daily 3-6.

GRANDVILLARD

BANNERET HOUSE
Grandvillard, Fribourg
17th century house, with period furnishings. Local and regionsl history.
M.-Sa. 9-12, 2-6; Su. 2-6.

GRENCHEN

MUSEUM SOCIETY'S COLLECTION
Mühlestrasse, Grenchen, Bern
Palaeontology. Ethnography. Local and regional history.
On request.

GRINDELWALD

REGIONAL MUSEUM
Talhaus, Grindelwald, Bern
Local history. Furniture. Craftsmen's tools. Alpine farming. Winter sports. Alpine climbing.
June 15-Sept. 15, Tu., Th., Sa. 3-5.30; Su. 10.30-12, 3-5.30.

GRÜNINGEN

MUSEUM
Schloss, Grüningen, Zurich
Local history. Models. Prints. Drawings. Peasant tools and domestic equipment.
Apr.-Oct. Su. 2-5.

GRUYÈRES

CHÂTEAU
Gruyères, Fribourg
Living accommodation of the Counts of Gruyères. Furniture. Tapestries. Stained glass windows. Weapons. Flags. Salon decorated by, among others, Corot. Works and memorabilia of the sculptor and medallist, A. Bovy, and the painter, A. Baud-Bovy.
Daily 8-12, 1-6.

GUGGISBERG

REGIONAL MUSEUM
Guggisberg
Local and regional history.
Tu.-Su. 10-12, 2-5.

HALLAU

REGIONAL MUSEUM
Kirschulhaus, Hallau, Schaffhausen
Prehistoric archaeology. Local history. Coins. Weapons. Costumes. Household equipment. Craftsmen's tools.
By appointment.

HALTEN

HALTEN TOWER
Halten, Solothurm
Local history. Furnishings, household equipment from the Kriegstetten district. Costumes and ornaments. Agricultural implements.
May-Nov. Su. 2-5.

HEIDEN

MUSEUM
Postgebäude, Heiden, Appenzell-Ausserrhoden
Local history. Peasant furnishings, household equipment. Weapons. Uniforms. Memorabilia of the Swiss philanthropist, Henri Dunant. Minerals, animals and birds of the Appenzell district. Ethnography.
June-Sept. Tu., Th., Su. 10-12.

HERISAU

MUSEUM
Altes Rathaus, Herisau, Appenzell-Ausserrhoden
Local history. Archaeological material from excavations at Rosenberg and Rosenburg. Peasant paintings and handicrafts. Weapons, including some from Persia. Uniforms. Flags. Glass-paintings.
Su. 10.30-12.

HERZOGENBUCHSEE

LOCAL MUSEUM
Gast- und Gemeindehaus zum Kreuz, Kirchgasse, Herzogenbuchsee, Bern
Local history. Archaeological material from Stone Age sites on the Burgäschisee.
Daily 8 a.m. - 10 p.m.

HILTERFINGEN

SCHLOSS HÜNEGG
Hilterfingen, Bern
Castle (1861-3). Art Nouveau furnishings.
June-Sept., M.-Sa. 2-5; Su. 10-12, 2-5.

HINWIL

LOCAL MUSEUM
Oberdorfstrasse 11, Hinwil, Zurich
In 18th century farmhouse. Furnished rooms. Craftsmen's tools. Agricultural implements. Weapons. Musical instruments. Local history.
Apr.-Nov. 1st Su. in month, 1.30-5.

HITZKIRCH

PREHISTORIC COLLECTION
Lehrerseminar, Hitzkirch, Luzern
Prehistoric material, mainly Neolithic and Bronze Age, from sites in the Seetal and on the shores of the Boldeggersee.
By appointment.

HORGEN

LOCAL MUSEUM
Alte Sust, Horgen, Zurich
Prehistoric material from the Lake Settlement at Horgen. Local history. Transport. Textile industry. Coal mining. Local handicrafts. 18th-20th century weapons.
Su. 10.30-12, 2-4.

HUTTWIL

REGIONAL MUSEUM
Altes Schulhaus, Huttwil, Bern
Local history. Craftsmen's tools. Costumes. Uniforms. Weapons.
Su. 10-12, 2-5.

ISÉRABLES

MUSEUM
Station de Teleferique Riddes-Isérables, Valais
Craftsmen's tools. Agricultural implements and equipment.
Daily 1.30-4.

JEGENSTORF

SCHLOSS JEGENSTORF
Jegenstorf, Bern
Renaissance-19th century, especially 18th century, period rooms. Furniture. Clocks. Portraits. Stoves. Memorabilia of the architect, Heinrich von Fischer, and the writer, Rudolf von Tavel.
May 15- Oct. 15, Tu.-Su. 10-12, 1.30-5.

KILCHBERG

LOCAL HISTORY COLLECTION
Alte Landstrasse 170, Kilchberg, Zurich
In former home of the poet, C. F. Meyer. Meyer's study. 18th century Zürich porcelain, 19th century faience and stoneware from local potteries. Fishing and navigation on the Zürichsee.
Tu.-Sa. 2-5 (Nov.-Mar. 2-4); Su. 10.30-12.

KLOSTERS

NUTLI-HÜSLI REGIONAL MUSEUM
Monbielerstrasse, Klosters, Graubünden
Peasant house (1564) with 18th-early 19th century furniture, household utensils and equipment. Mineral collection.
May-Oct., M., Th. 2-4.

KÖLLIKEN

ICON COLLECTION
Haus Klostermatt, Kölliken, Aargau
Icons from Russia and the Middle East.
On request.

PREHISTORIC AND HISTORICAL COLLECTION
Altes Schulhaus, Richtergasse, Kölliken, Aargau
Prehistoric material from regional sites. Local and regional history.
On request.

KREUZLINGEN

REGIONAL MUSEUM
Roseneggschulhaus, Bärenstrasse, Kreuzlingen, Thurgau
Local history. Weapons. Craftsmen's tools and equipment.
May-Oct., 1st Su. in month, 2-4.

KÜSSNACHT AM RIGI

REGIONAL MUSEUM
Spritzenhaus, Küssnacht am Rigi, Schwyz
Local prehistory and history. Religious art, including reliquary, 1489.
Whitsun-Oct. 31, Su. 10.30-11.30, 4-5.30.

KYBURG

CASTLE
Kyburg, Zurich
Local history. Furnished rooms. 15th-18th century Swiss weapons.
Tu.-Su. 9-12, 1-5 (Nov.-Mar. 1-4).

KYBURG-BUCHEGG

BUCHEGGBERGISCHES REGIONAL MUSEUM
Schloss Buchegg, Kyburg-Buchegg, Solothurn
Local history and archaeology. Furnishings. Craftsmen's tools and equipment, particularly for flax and linen.
Apr.-Oct. Su. 10-12, 2-4.

LE LANDERON

MUSEUM
Hôtel de Ville, Le Landeron, Neuchâtel
Prehistoric and Roman material from local sites. Documents illustrating history of Landeron. 15th-18th century goldsmith's work. Weapons. Uniforms. Furnished interiors. Birds of the region.
On request.

LANGENTHAL

REGIONAL MUSEUM
Bahnhofstrasse 11, Langenthal, Bern
Palaeontology. Oberaargau textile industry. Late 18th century country apothecary's shop. Prints, engravings, illustrating 19th century history of the Oberaargau.
By appointment.

LANGNAU IM EMMENTAL

REGIONAL MUSEUM
Bärenplatz 2A, Langnau im Emmental, Bern
Langnau ceramics. Flüeli glass and Schliffglass. Reconstruction of potter's workshop. Craftsmen's tools, equipment, especially weaving. History of local agriculture and milk industry. Memorabilia of the miracle-working doctor, Micheli Schüppach, 'Mechanikus' Christian, 'Physikus' Ulrich Schenk and Carl Schenk.
Tu.-Su. 9-11.30, 1.30-6.

LAUFEN

LAUFENTAL REGIONAL MUSEUM
Rathaus, Laufen, Bern
History of Laufen and of Laufental. Furniture. Craftsmen's tools. Prehistoric and medieval archaeology. Memorabilia of the Laufen printer, Helias Helye. Reconstruction of prison cell.
3rd Su. in month, 10-12, 2-4.

LAUSANNE

CANTON BOTANICAL MUSEUM
Palais de Rumine, Place de la Riponne, Lausanne, Vaud
Herbaria. Paintings by Rosalie de Constan of botanical subjects.
By appointment.

CANTONAL CABINET OF COINS AND MEDALS
Palais de Rumine, Place de la Riponne, Lausanne, Vaud
Greek, Roman and Gaulish coins. Coins and medals from the archbishopric of Lausanne, from Canton Vaud, and from the surrounding area.
Daily 10-12, 2-5.

CANTONAL GEOLOGICAL MUSEUM
Palais de Rumine, Place de la Riponne, Lausanne, Vaud
Palaeontology. Petrography. Mineralogy.
Daily 10-12, 2-5.

CANTONAL MUSEUM OF ART AND HISTORY
Palais de Rumine, Place de la Riponne, Lausanne, Vaud
Neolithic, Bronze Age, Iron Age and Roman material from excavations in Vaud. Gold bust of Marcus Aurelius. Objects from Burgundian tombs.
Daily 10-12, 2-5.

CANTONAL MUSEUM OF FINE ART
Palais de Rumine, Place de la Riponne, Lausanne, Vaud
18th-20th century paintings by Vaud artists. 17th-18th century Dutch paintings. 17th-19th century French paintings. Contemporary paintings, sculpture. Gothic sculpture. Oriental art. Egyptian sculpture.
W.-M. 10-12, 2-5; Tu. 2-5.

CANTONAL ZOOLOGICAL MUSEUM
Palais de Rumine, Place de la Riponne, Lausanne, Vaud
Birds and animals of the whole world. Almost complete collection of Swiss vertebrates. Comparative anatomy. Osteology.
Daily 10-12, 2-5.

CATHEDRAL MUSEUM
Cathédrale, Lausanne, Vaud
Sculpture. Fragments of stained glass. Photographs and documents illustrating history of cathedral.
Daily 9-12, 2-5, except during services.

COLLECTIONS OF THE INTERNATIONAL CENTRE OF ANCIENT AND MODERN TAPESTRIES
Avenue Villamont 4, Lausanne, Vaud
European tapestries.
Daily 8-12, 2-6.

HISTORICAL MUSEUM OF THE OLD BISHOPRIC
Place de la Cathédrale 2, Lausanne, Vaud
Prehistoric, Roman and medieval archaeology. 17th-19th century furnished interiors. Furniture. Pewter. 18th-19th century Lausanne silver. Paintings, drawings, prints connected with Lausanne. Medieval jewellery.
June-Aug. Daily 10-12, 2-5; Th. also 8-10 p.m. Sept.-May W., Sa. 2-4; Su. 10-12, 2-4.

MON REPOS MUSEUM
Parc de Mon Repos, Lausanne, Vaud
Reception rooms of the City, with 18th-19th century furniture, tapestries, paintings, engravings. Benoist collection of 18th-19th century furniture, porcelain, tapestry. Juge collection of 17th-19th century faience, porcelain.
Tu.-F. 9-12, 2-5.

MUSEUM OF DECORATIVE ARTS
Avenue Villamont 4, Lausanne, Vaud
Ceramics. Fabrics. European and Oriental graphics.
During exhibitions: M.-Sa. 1-7; Su. 10-12, 2-6.

VIDY ROMAN MUSEUM
Chemin du Bois de Vaux, Vidy, Lausanne, Vaud
Roman material from excavations at Vidy. Pottery. Mural painting. Coins. Bronze objects. Inscriptions.
W., Sa. 2-4; Su. 10-12, 2-4.

LENZBURG

CANTONAL HISTORICAL COLLECTION
Schloss Lenzburg, Lenzburg, Aargau
16th-18th century furnished interiors. Medieval and baroque sculpture. Painted glass. Pewter. Ceramics. Weapons.
Apr.-Oct. Th.-Su. 9.30-12, 1.30-5.

REGIONAL MUSEUM
Aavorstadt 18, Lenzburg, Aargau
Late Bronze Age and Roman archaeology from local sites. Weapons. Craftsmen's tools. Lenzburg faience. Paintings and drawings by Lenzburg artists.
Apr.-Oct. Su. 10.30-11.45.

LICHTENSTEIG

TOGGENBURG REGIONAL MUSEUM
Rathaus, Lichtensteig, St. Gallen
Regional history. Alpine farming. Goat-keeping. Peasant furniture, musical instruments, art and costumes. Weapons. Glass painting. Prehistoric material from local sites.
Tu.-Sa. 9-11, 1-6; Su. (ex. 1st Su. in month) 9-11, 1-5.

LIESTAL

BASEL-LAND CANTONAL MUSEUM
Regierungsgebäude, Liestal, Basel-Land
Geology. Palaeontology. Mineralogy. Zoology. Palaeolithic material from French sites. Neolithic, Bronze Age, Hallstatt and La Tène material from local sites. Roman, Alemannic and medieval archaeology. Agricultural implements. Furniture. Costumes. Coins. Ethnography. Paintings. Drawings. Prints.
M.-Sa. 8-12, 2-6; Su. 9-12, 2-5.

MUNZACH ROMAN VILLA
Bintalstrasse, Liestal, Basel-Land
Site museum. Foundations of villa. Mosaics. Archaeological material from excavations.
Sa. 1-6; Su. 2-6.

POETS' MUSEUM
Gemeinderathaus, Liestal, Basel-Land
Letters, drawings by Georg Herwegh. Memorabilia of J. V. Widmann and Carl Spitteler.
1st Su. in month, 2-5.

LIGORNETTO

VELA MUSEUM
Ligornetto, Ticino
Sculptures and models by Vincenzo Vela. Books, sketches, documents and memorabilia of the artist. Drawings and paintings by Spartaco Vela. Drawings and sculpture by Lorenzo Vela. 16th-19th century paintings by Lombardy and Ticino artists, collected by Vincenzo Vela.
Feb.-Nov. Daily 9-12, 2-5.

LOCARNO

MUNICIPAL MUSEUM
Castello, Locarno, Ticino
Prehistoric material from Bronze and Iron Age sites. Roman sculpture, pottery, terracotta statuettes, glass, jewels. Coins. Carolingian bas-reliefs. Furniture, portraits, wood sculpture from the Locarno area. Weapons. Mineralogy. Palaeontology. Ornithology.
Apr.-Oct. Tu.-Su. 9-12, 2-4.

LE LOCLE

FINE ART MUSEUM
Rue Marie Anne Calame 6, Le Locle, Neuchâtel
Works by Swiss artists, especially K. E. Girardet.
W. 2-4; Su. 11-12, 2-4.

ALEXANDRE GIROD MUSEUM
Les Petits Monts, Le Locle, Neuchâtel
Works and memorabilia of the painter, Alexandre Girod.
Su. 2-5.

MUSEUM OF HISTORY AND CLOCKMAKING
Château des Monts, Monts 65, Le Locle, Neuchâtel
Original documents illustrating history of Le Locle. History of time-measurement from its beginnings to our own times.

Clocks. Watches. Clock-makers' tools. Astronomical instruments. 16th-19th century automata.
Apr. 30- Oct. 31, Tu.-F. 2-5. Nov. 1- Mar. 31, Su. 2-5.

LOCO

MUSEUM OF THE ONSERNONE VALLEY
Loco, Ticino
Agricultural implements. Women's costumes from the Onsernone Valley. Flags and rifles of the Loco militia. Paintings by Carlo Agostino Meletta.
Daily 9-12, 1.30-6.30.

LUCENS

CONAN DOYLE FOUNDATION
Château de Lucens, Lucens, Vaud
Reconstruction of Sherlock Holmes' drawing room. Personal possessions of Sir Arthur Conan Doyle and his son. Furnishings of the Château.
By appointment.

LUGANO

MUSEUM OF FINE ART, CACCIA FOUNDATION
Villa Ciani, Parco Civico, Lugano, Ticino
Paintings by 17th-20th century Swiss artists, especially from the Ticino. Portraits. 19th-20th century French paintings. Prize-winning works at the Lugano International Exhibition.
Tu.-Su. 9-12, 2-6.

MUSEUM OF HISTORY AND ARCHAEOLOGY
Villa Saroli, Viale Stefano Franscini, Lugano, Ticino
Material from Bronze Age and Iron Age sites in Ticino. Stones with N. Etruscan inscriptions. Roman material, especially inscriptions, mosaics, sculpture. Gothic and Renaissance sculpture. 16th-19th century furniture, household equipment. Ticino costumes, uniforms. Portraits, documents and other material illustrating history of Ticino. 18th-19th century architects' design, sculpture and decorative arts from Ticino.
Mar.-Nov. Tu.-Su. 9-12, 2-6.

LÜTZELFLÜH

GOTTHELF ROOM
Pfarrhaus, Lützelflüh, Bern
Memorabilia of Jeremias Gotthelf. Portraits. Documents.
May-Oct. Daily 10.15-11.15, 2-5.

LUZERN

ART MUSEUM
Robert Zünd Strasse 1, Luzern
Medieval, Renaissance and Baroque paintings from Central Switzerland. 15th-20th century Swiss paintings. Contemporary European paintings. 16th-20th century drawings, prints by artists from Central Switzerland.
Tu.-Su. 10-12, 2-5.

GLACIER GARDEN AND GLACIER MUSEUM
Denkmalstrasse 4, Luzern
Open-air museum of geological and palaeontological specimens. Molluscs, palms and other material found in glaciers. Prehistoric collection. Local fauna. 17th-19th century Luzern furnished interiors. Costumes. History of Luzern.
Mar.-Apr. and Oct.-Nov. Daily 8-12, 1.30-6.

HISTORICAL MUSEUM
Rathaus, Kornmarkt, Luzern
Prehistoric and Roman material from sites in the Canton. Early bricks. Costumes. Textiles. Church ornaments. 15th-17th century glass paintings. Coins and coin-dies. Medals.
May-Oct. M.-Sa. 9-12, 2-6; Su. 10-12, 2-5.

NATURAL HISTORY MUSEUM
Kasernenplatz 6, Luzern
Material from excavations at Neolithic lake-dwellings. Local birds and mammals. Molluscs. Butterflies. Geology. Mineralogy. Herbarium.
May-Nov. M.-F. 2-5.

SWISS MUSEUM OF BREAD AND CAKES
Bäckerfaschule Richemont, Rigistrasse 28, Luzern
Bread and cake-making equipment. Displays illustrating history and techniques of baking.
During exhibitions, M., W., F. 2-5.

SWISS MUSEUM OF COSTUMES AND REGIONAL LIFE
Utenberg, Luzern
Swiss local costumes still in use, with some foreign examples. Needlework. Ornaments.
Easter- All Saints' Day (Nov. 1) 9-12, 2-6.

SWISS MUSEUM OF TRANSPORT
Lidostrasse 5, Luzern
History of transport by road, rail, ship and air. Space travel. Horse-drawn vehicles. Locomotives. Bicycles and motor cycles. Sleighs. Ships. Cars. Aeroplanes. Displays showing development of telephone, telegraph, radio, television. Planetarium.
Mar. 16- Nov. 15, Daily 9-6. Nov. 16- Mar. 15, Tu., Th., Sa. 1.30-5.30; Su. 10-6.

TREASURY OF ST. LEODEGAR'S FOUNDATION
Hofkirche, Luzern
13th-20th century church goldsmiths' work and textiles.
Sa. 2-3, by appointment.

RICHARD WAGNER MUSEUM
Tribschen, Luzern
House in which Wagner lived, 1866-72. Scores. Portraits of Wagner. Books by and about Wagner. Musical instruments from Africa, China, Egypt. European musical instruments, including Swiss collection of instruments for peasant and military bands.
Apr. 16- Sept. 14, M.-Sa. 9-12, 2-6; Su. 10.20-12, 2-5. Sept. 15- Apr. 15, M., W., F. 9-12, 2-6; Su. 10.30-12, 2-5.

MELLEN

LOCAL MUSEUM
Kirchgasse, Mellen, Zurich
History of Mellen and Lake Zurich.
Su. 10.30-12.

MEIRINGEN

MUSEUM OF HASLI COUNTY
Meiringen, Bern
Agricultural tools, implements. Local furniture. Material illustrating history of Hasli valley. Minerals of Upper Hasli.
By appointment.

MELLINGEN

HISTORICAL COLLECTION
Zeitturm, Mellingen, Aargau
Local history.
By appointment.

MONTHEY

OLD MONTHEY MUSEUM
Château, Monthey, Valais
Local history. Furniture. Pictures showing development of Monthey. Industry and handicrafts.
1st and 3rd Su. in month, 2-4.

MONTREUX-VEYTAUX

CHÂTEAU DE CHILLON
Montreux-Veytaux, Vaud
Material from excavations at the Château. Furniture. Weapons.
July-Aug. M-Sa. 9-7; Su. 9-6. Apr.-June, Sept., Daily 9-12, 1.30-6. Mar. Daily 10-12, 12.30-5. Oct. Daily 10-12, 12.30-5. Jan.-Feb. and Nov.-Dec. Daily 10-12, 1.30-4.

MUSEUM OF OLD MONTREUX
Rue de la Gare 40, Montreux-Veytaux, Vaud
Local history.
Tu.-Sa. 9-11, 3-6.

MÖRIKEN

WILDEGG CASTLE
Möriken, Aargau
16th-19th century furnished interiors. Possessions, 1484-1912, of the Effinger von Wildegg family. Furniture. Domestic equipment. Portraits. Weapons.
Daily 9-12, 1.30-5.30.

MORGES

ALEXIS FOREL MUSEUM
Grand-Rue 54, Morges, Vaud
House (16th century) was home of the engraver, Alexis Forel, and contains his private collection. 15th-19th century furniture, 16th-18th century tapestries, 16th-19th century prints, engravings, especially works by Dürer, Rembrandt, Forel. Chinese and Nyon porcelain. Glass. 18th-19th century dolls and toys.
Tu.-Su. 2-6.

VAUD MILITARY MUSEUM
Château, Morges, Vaud
15th-20th century military material, with emphasis on 19th century, on local military units and on Swiss regiments in the service of France and the Kingdom of Naples. Weapons. Armour. Uniforms. Flags. Models.
Apr. 15- Oct. 15, Sa., Su. 1.30-6.

MÔTIERS

JEAN-JACQUES ROUSSEAU MUSEUM
Rue Jean-Jacques Rousseau, Môtiers, Neuchâtel
Rooms occupied by Rousseau 1762-65. Works of Rousseau. Material illustrating his life and achievements.
On request.

MOUDON

EUGÈNE BURNAND MUSEUM
Bourg, Moudon, Vaud
Paintings, drawings, engravings by Eugène Burnand. Ethnograph of Afghanistan. Pottery. Jewels. Weapons. Coins.
May-Oct. Su. 2-6.

MUSEUM OF OLD MOUDON
Château de Rochefort, Moudon, Vaud
Material from prehistoric, Roman and medieval sites. 16th-19th century furnished interiors. Craftsmen's tools. Agricultural implements. Weapons, including carbines made at Moudon. Prints and documents illustrating history of the region. Paintings by Burnand and Cerjat.
Mar. 15- Oct. 15, Su. 2-5.

MOUTIER

MUSEUM OF FINE ART
Rue Centrale 53, Moutier, Bern
Paintings by contemporary Swiss artists, especially from the Jura.
Daily 8-10 p.m. W.-Sa. also 2-6 and Su. 10.30-12, 2-6.

MURTEN (MORAT)

MURTEN HISTORICAL MUSEUM
Murten (Morat), Bern
Local and regional history.
By appointment.

MÜSTAIR

MUSEUM OF THE MONASTERY
Benediktinerinnenkloster St. Johann, Müstair, Graubünden
History of the monastery. Carolingian sculptures. Romanesque wall-paintings. Gothic and Baroque woodcarving and painting. 16th-17th century furniture, furnished interiors.
M.-Sa. 9-11, 2-5; Su. 10.30-11, 3-5.

NÄFELS

MUSEUM OF GLARUS CANTON
Freulerpalast, Näfels, Glarus
Prehistoric and Roman material from local excavations. 16th-19th century weapons, uniforms, flags. Material relating to Colonel Caspar Freuler, Commander of the Regiment of Swiss Guards in the French Army, and builder of the Palace at Näfels. Biographic material concerning Glarus notabilities in science and the arts. History of Glarus cotton industry.
Apr.-Oct. Tu.-Su. 8-11.30, 1-5.

NEUCHÂTEL

CANTONAL MUSEUM OF ARCHAEOLOGY
Avenue Du Peyrore 7, Neuchâtel
Material from archaeological sites in the Canton, especially lake villages, Cotencher caves, La Tène. Roman and Burgundian items. European history.
Tu.-Su. 2-5.

MUSEUM OF ART AND HISTORY
Quai Leopold Robert, Neuchâtel
Works by Swiss artists, especially from Neuchâtel. Paintings. Drawings. Sculpture. Prints. 18th-20th century French paintings. Neuchâtel watch and clock industry. Automata by Jaquet-Droz. Coins. Ceramics. Glass. Goldsmith's work. Weapons, especially of Napoleonic period. Portraits. Documents and other material illustrating history of Neuchâtel.
Tu.-Su. 10-12, 2-5.

MUSEUM OF ETHNOGRAPHY AND INSTITUTE OF ETHNOLOGY
St. Nicholas 4, Neuchâtel
Ethnographical material from Angola, S. Africa, N. Africa, especially Mauretania, Pacific, Iles Marquises, Far East, N. and S. America. Egyptian archaeology. Collection of wind instruments.
Tu.-Su. 10-12, 2-6.

MUSEUM OF NATURAL HISTORY
Place Numa-Droz 3, Neuchâtel
Dioramas showing Swiss mammals, birds, butterflies.
Tu., W., F. 8-12, 2-5; Th. 2-5; Sa., Su. 10-12, 2-5.

NEUNKIRCH

LOCAL MUSEUM
Oberhof, Neunkirch, Schaffhausen
Local history. Furniture. Craftsmen's tools. Household equipment.
1st Su. in month, 2-5.

LA NEUVEVILLE

HISTORICAL MUSEUM
Hôtel de Ville, La Neuveville, Bern
Prehistoric material, including canoe, from sites on Lake Bienne, 15th century cannons. 14th-15th century banners of La Neuveville. 17th-18th century furnished interiors. Landolt stoves. Local history collection. Items relating to the Winegrowers' Association. Memorabilia of General Samuel Gross. Weapons.
Apr.-Oct. 1st and 3rd Su. in month, 9.30-11, 3-5.

NYON

HISTORICAL MUSEUM
Château, Nyon, Vaud
Prehistoric material from regional sites. Roman antiquities from Nyon. Burgundian funeral items. Medieval pottery. Costumes. Local historical collection. Pharmacists' pots. Porcelain and faience from the Nyon factory. 17th-18th century furniture.
Feb.-Dec. Tu.-Sa. 9-11, 2-5. Su. 2-5.

LAKE LÉMAN MUSEUM
8 quai Bonnard, Nyon, Vaud
Collections relating to Lake Leman. Geography. Meteorology. Fishing. Shipping. Flora. Fauna. Art.
Good F. - Sept. 30, Tu.-Sa. 9-11, 2-5; Su. 2-5.

OBERDORF

HISTORICAL COLLECTION OF THE TEACHER TRAINING COLLEGE
Realschule, Oberdorf, Basel-Land
Neolithic, Roman and medieval material from local sites. Agricultural implements. Household equipment.
During college terms, 8-12, 1-5.

OBERHOFEN AM THUNERSEE

CASTLE
Oberhofen am Thunersee
Regional domestic life. 15th-19th century furnished interiors. Peasant faience. Alpine agriculture. Dairying. 16th-18th century weapons. 15th century wall paintings.
May 15- Oct. 15, Daily 10-12, 2-5.

OBERRIET

MONTLINGEN MUSEUM
Schulhaus, Oberriet, St. Gallen
Prehistoric, Roman and medieval archaeology from regional sites.
By appointment.

OBERUZWIL

MUSEUM OF LOCAL LIFE AND CUSTOMS
Primarschulhaus, Oberuzwil, St. Gallen
Local history.
By appointment.

OBERWENIGEN

LOCAL MUSEUM
Speicher, Oberwenigen, Zurich
Local life and history. Costumes. Furniture. Agricultural implements. Household equipment.
By appointment.

OLIVONE

SAN MARTINO MUSEUM
Piazza della Chiesa, Olivone, Ticino
Furniture and other items illustrating the daily life and traditions of the Val Bienio. Religious art from local churches.
On request.

OLTEN

HISTORICAL MUSEUM
Konradstrasse 7, Olten, Solothurn
Archaeological material from prehistoric, Roman, Alemannic and medieval sites in the region. Costumes and ornaments. Matzendorf and Aedermannsdorf faience. 18th-19th century European porcelain. Peasant furniture, household equipment. Pewter. Clocks. Weapons. 19th century Swiss uniforms. Coins and medals. Seals. 17th-18th century goblets. Religious art. Bells. Farm and craftsmen's tools. Lighting equipment.
Tu.-Sa. 9-12, 2-5; Su. 10-12, 2-5.

MUSEUM OF ART
Kirchgasse 8, Olten, Solothurn
Paintings, drawings, prints by the Olten artist, Martin Disteli and his pupils. Material illustrating life of Disteli. 19th-20th century Swiss paintings and engravings, especially by Solothurn artists. Portraits. Sculpture by Jakob Probst and Karl Geiser.
Tu.-Sa. 9-12, 2-5; Su. 10-12, 2-5.

MUSEUM OF NATURAL HISTORY
Kirchgasse 10, Olten, Solothurn
Mineralogy. Palaeontology. Fossils. Mammoth skull. Animals of the region.
Tu.-Sa. 9-12, 2-5; Su. 10-12, 2-5.

ORBE

MUSEUM OF OLD ORBE
Rue Centrale, Orbe, Vaud
Local history. Furniture. Engravings. Local fauna. 7 Roman mosaics, preserved on their original site at Boscéaz, are in the care of the museum.
1st Su. in month, 11-12.

ORON-LE-CHÂTEL

CHÂTEAU
Oron-le-Châtel, Vaud
17th-18th century furnishings and paintings.
Tu.-Su. 9-12, 2-6.

PAYERNE

MUSEUM
Place du Tribunal, Payerne, Vaud
Prehistoric material, especially from Burgundian cemetery at Pramay. Weapons. Armour. 14th century jousting saddle. Memorabilia of General Jomini. Paintings by Aimée Rapin.
By appointment.

PFÄFFIKON

LOCAL MUSEUM
Kehrstrasse, Pfäffikon, Zurich
Prehistoric material from local sites. Peasant household equipment. Agricultural implements.
May-Oct. 1st and 3rd Su. in month, 2-5.

PFYN

LOCAL MUSEUM
Schulhaus, Pfyn, Thurgau
Neolithic material from excavations at Breitenloo.
By appointment.

POSCHIAVO

VALLIGIANO POSCHIAVINO MUSEUM
Piazza Comunale, Poschiavo, Graubünden
Local history. Domestic equipment. Agricultural implements. Textile-making equipment.
May-Sept. Tu.-F. 10-12, 3-5.

PULLY

MUSEUM
Chemin Davel 2, Pully, Vaud
Modern paintings by artists, especially René Auberjonois, connected with Pully. Books, manuscripts and other memorabilia of C. F. Ramuz. Portraits of General Guisan.
Sa. 2-4; Su. 11-12.

RATZ

LOCAL MUSEUM
Dorfstrasse 412, Ratz, Zurich
Peasant furnishings and household equipment. Craftsmen's tools. Agricultural implements.
Apr.-Nov. 1, 2nd Su. in month, 2-5.

RANCATE

GIOVANNI ZÜST CANTONAL ART GALLERY
Rancate, Ticino
19th-20th century paintings, drawings by Ticino artists.
Mar.-Nov. Tu.-Su. 9.30-12, 2-5.

RAPPERSWIL

MUSEUM OF THE SWISS CASTLE ASSOCIATION
Schloss, Rapperswil, St. Gallen
Displays illustrating Swiss castles and the Orders of Knighthood. Weapons. Armour. Equipment. Collection of Polish material.
Mar.-Nov. Th.-Su. 9.30-5.

REGIONAL MUSEUM
Am Herrenberg, Brenyhaus, Rapperswil, St. Gallen
Roman material, including potters' kilns. Items illustrating history of Rapperswil. Weapons. Furniture. Glass paintings. 15th-19th century local pottery. Goldsmith's work. 16th century religious art.
Easter-Oct., Sa.-Th. 2-5.30.

REGENSBERG

LOCAL MUSEUM
Regensberg, Zurich
Local history.
By appointment.

REIGOLDSWIL

LOCAL HISTORY COLLECTION
Realschule, Reigoldswil, Basel-Land
Prehistoric and medieval material from local sites. Local history. Craftsmen's tools. Household equipment.
By appointment.

REINACH

COLLECTION OF PREHISTORY AND EARLY HISTORY
Bezirksschulhaus, Reinach, Basel-Land
Prehistoric and early historical material from local sites.
On request.

REGIONAL MUSEUM
Gemeindehaus, Reinach, Basel-Land
Local and regional history. Furniture. Household equipment. Agricultural implements. Displays illustrating techniques of vine-growing, basket-making, brewing.
Oct.-Mar., 2nd and 4th Su. in month, 2-5.

RHEINFELDEN

FIRCKTALER MUSEUM
Marktgasse 12, Rheinfelden, Aargau
Geology. Archaeological material from local Bronze Age, Roman, Hallstatt and Alermannic sites. Architectural history of Rheinfelden. Guild history. Handicrafts. Shipping. Salmon fishing. Timber-floating. Religious arts. Furniture. Furnished room (1700). Weapons.
May-Sept. Tu., Th., Sa. 3-5; Su. 10-12.

RICKENBACH BEI WINTERTHUR

HANNSELI GRANARY
Alte Dorfstrasse, Rickenbach bei Winterthur, Zurich
Agricultural implements. Craftsmen's tools and equipment. Reconstructions of a 17th-18th century living room and an 18th-19th century kitchen.
May-Sept. 1st Su. in month, 2-5.

RIGGISBERG

MUSEUM OF THE ABEGG FOUNDATION, BERN
Riggisberg, Bern
Textiles, sculpture and carving, wall-paintings, applied arts from Europe and Far East. European religious art. Iranian, Coptic, Byzantine and Renaissance collections.
May-Sept. Daily 2-5.

ROMAINMÔTIER

ROMAINMÔTIER PRIORY
Romainmôtier, Vaud
11th century Cluniac Priory and Church. Murals. Sculptures. 7th-13th century frescoes. Tombs.
Apr. 15- Oct. 15, Daily 8-7. Oct. 16- Apr. 14, daily 10-4.

RORSCHACH

REGIONAL MUSEUM
Kornhaus, am Hafen, Rorschach, St. Gallen
Prehistoric material from sites in Lake Constance area. Reconstructions of Neolithic and Bronze Age huts, with their contents. Paintings, models, prints and photographs illustrating history of Rorschach. 15th-18th century furnished interiors. Development of embroidery since 1830. Geography and natural history of the region. Contemporary paintings.
Apr. 15- Oct. 15, Tu.-Su. 10-12, 2-5.

RÜEGGISBERG

MUSEUM OF STONES
Pfarrant, Rüeggisberg, Bern
Material from local excavations. Paving stones. Architectural carvings. Ceramics.
Daily 10-5.

RÜSCHLIKON

LOCAL MUSEUM
Bodengasse 1, Rüschlikon, Zurich
Local and regional history.
By appointment.

SAINTE-CROIX

MUSEUM
Avenue des Alpes 10, Sainte-Croix, Vaud
Zoology, especially exotic birds. Mineralogy. Palaeontology. Ethnography, mainly of Gaboon. Prehistoric archaeology. Greek vases. Tanagra statuettes. Roman coins. Displays illustrating local industry. Lace. Watch and clock making. Musical boxes. Gramophones. Cameras. Typewriters.
1st and 3rd Su. in month, 10-12.

MUSEUM OF OLD MECHANICAL MUSICAL INSTRUMENTS
L'Auberson, Sainte-Croix, Vaud
All types of mechanical instruments, including Barbary organs and orchestrions.
May-Oct. Su. 9-12, 2-6. July 20-Aug. 31 also M.-F., guided tour, 3. Nov.-Apr., 1st and 3rd Su. in month, 9-12, 2-6.

ST. GALLEN

MUSEUM OF INDUSTRIAL AND APPLIED ARTS
Vadianstrasse 2, St. Gallen
Swiss and European lace and embroidery.
M.-Sa. 10-12, 2-5.

NEW MUSEUM
Museumstrasse 50, St. Gallen
Prehistoric archaeology. History of the town of St. Gallen. Guild history. Coins. Seals. Locksmiths' work. Pewter. Linen-weaving. 14th-18th century Church art. Glass paintings. 15th-19th century furnished interiors. Costumes. Textiles. Folk art. Faience. Porcelain. Weapons. Flags. World ethnography, especially of India, Indonesia, Nepal, Japan, Africa, Greenland, Peru.
Apr.-Oct. Tu.-Sa. 10-12, 2-5.

OLD MUSEUM
Museumstrasse 32, St. Gallen
19th-20th century Swiss, especially East Swiss, paintings. 19th century French and German paintings. Drawings. Prints. Mineralogy. Petrography. Zoology. Birds' eggs. Dioramas of local animals.
Apr.-Oct. Tu.-Sa. 10-12, 2-5; Su. 10-12, 2-4. Nov.-Mar. Tu.-Sa. 10-12, 2-4.

REGIONAL MUSEUM
Museumstrasse 27, St. Gallen
Herbarium of regional plants. Insects. Mineralogy, petrography and palaeontology of the Alps. Palaeolithic material from Alpine cave-dwellings.
Apr.-Oct. Tu.-Sa. 10-12, 2-5; Su. 10-12, 2-4. Nov.-Mar. Tu.-Su. 10-12, 2-4.

SAINT-MAURICE

ABBEY TREASURY
Saint-Maurice, Valais
Medieval goldsmiths' work. 13th-15th century crosses, ciboria, reliquaries, candle-holders, monstrances, caskets. 16th-20th century liturgical items. Vestments. Fabrics. Sculpture.
July-Aug. guided tours at 9.30, 10.30, 11.15, 2, 3, 4, 5.30.

ST. MORITZ

ENGADINE MUSEUM
Badstrasse, St. Moritz, Graubünden
16th-19th century furnished interiors. Furniture. Household equipment. Needlework. Costumes. Neolithic, Bronze Age and Roman material from excavations in the Engadine.
June-Sept. M.-Sa. 9.30-12, 2-5; Su. 10-12.

SEGANTINI MUSEUM
Suvrettastrasse, St. Moritz, Graubünden
Works by the painter, Giovanni Segantini.
M.-Sa. 9.30-12, 2-5 (Nov.-Mar. 2-4).

SALENSTEIN

NAPOLEON MUSEUM
Schloss Arenenberg, Salenstein, Thurgau
Castle was home of Empress Hortense and her son, Prince Louis Napoleon. History of 1st and 2nd Empires. 19th century furnishings. Paintings. Sculpture.
May-Sept. Tu.-Sa. 9-12, 1.30-6. Apr. and Oct. 10-12, 1.30-5. Nov.-Mar. Tu.-Su. 10-12, 1.30-4.

SAN VITTORE

MOESANO MUSEUM
Palazzo Viscardi, San Vittore, Grigioni
Local history. Religious art, especially goldsmiths' work and wood-sculptures. Agricultural tools and implements, including wine-press and flax-processing equipment. Furniture. Household equipment.
By appointment.

SARGANS

CASTLE
Sargans, St. Gallen
Weapons. Hunting trophies. Furniture. Regional history.
Apr.-Oct. M.-F. 9-12, 1.30-4.

SARNEN

REGIONAL MUSEUM
Brünigstrasse, Sarnen, Obwalden
Prehistoric and Roman material from regional sites. 15th-19th century weapons, uniforms, flags. 14th-18th century religious art. Reconstruction of Alpine hut. Furnishing. Agricultural implements. Costumes. Coins. 17th-20th century paintings, sculpture by local artists. Geology, geography and zoology of the region.
Apr. 15-Oct. 15, Su.-F. 10-11, 2-5.

LA SARRAZ

CHÂTEAU
La Sarraz, Vaud
15th-19th century furniture, mainly French and Swiss. Portraits. Porcelain. Clocks. Book of Hours, (1421). 13th-16th century stained glass windows. Costumes. Paintings by regional artists. Tomb of François I (d.1363).
Apr.-Oct. 9-12, 2-6.

SAXON

MUSEUM OF OLD SAXON
Rue du Collège, Saxon, Valais
Local history. Reconstruction of 19th century schoolroom, with period furnishings and equipment. Displays illustrating bread, cheese and wine making. Forestry. 19th century weapons.
Su. 10-12.

SCHAFFHAUSEN

ALL SAINTS' MUSEUM
Klosterplatz 1, Schaffhausen
Palaeolithic, Michelsberg, Hallstatt, Roman and Alemannic material from regional sites. Medieval manuscripts. Incunabula. Romanesque sculpture. Goldsmiths' work. Craftsmen's tools. Pottery and porcelain. Glass. Pewter. 16th-17th century glass paintings. 15th-19th century period rooms. Guild history. Costumes. Weapons. Uniforms. Flags. Displays illustrating industrial development of Schaffhausen. Paintings and engravings by local artists. In restored monastery.
Nov.-Mar. Tu.-Su. 10-12, 1.30-4.30. Apr.-Oct. Tu.-Su. 9-12, 1.30-5.

MUSEUM STEMMLER
Sporengasse 7, Schaffhausen
Zoological and ornithological specimens. European mammals and birds. Ammonites.
Su. 2-5.

SCHINZNACH-DORF

REGIONAL MUSEUM
Schinznach-Dorf, Aargau
Regional life and history. Agriculture. Wine. Straw plaiting and weaving. Stoves. Peasant pottery.
1st and 3rd Su. in month, 2-6.

SCHLIEREN

LOCAL MUSEUM
Schulhaus Hofacker, Schlieren, Zurich
Local history. Prehistoric and medieval material from local excavations. Agricultural implements. Craftsmen's tools, equipment.
Jan.-Apr. and Dec., 1st Su. in month, 10-12.

SCHLEITHEIM

GYPSUM MUSEUM
Schleitheim, Schaffhausen
History of local gypsum industry. Machinery and equipment, including mill (1810).
Apr.-Oct., 1st Su. in month, 2-5.

SCHÖNENWERD

BALLY MUSEUM FOUNDATION
Oltenerstrasse 80, Schönenwerd, Solothurn
Geology. Mineralogy. Meteorlogy. Fossils. Art and applied art from the Far East, especially China, Japan. Prehistoric material. Local history.
Feb.-May, and Sept.-Nov., Su. 2-5. June-Aug., 1st and 3rd Su. in month, 2-5.

SHOE MUSEUM
Ausstellung Felsgarten, Schönenwerd, Solothurn
Museum of the Bally company. History of shoes, with examples from all over the world. Displays illustrating production of shoes. Tools. Machines.
1st Sa. in month, 2-5.

SCHÖTZ

WIGGERTAL REGIONAL MUSEUM
Schötz, Luzern
Local history, 16th-19th century. Prehistoric material from lake village sites.
By appointment.

SCHWYZ

DIOCESAN MUSEUM
Schwyz
Sculpture of the late Romanesque, Gothic and Renaissance periods.
By appointment.

FEDERAL ARCHIVES
Bahnhofstrasse, Schwyz
Collections illustrating foundation and development of Swiss Federation. 13th-18th century Swiss flags and banners.
May-Sept. Daily 10-11.30, 2-5. Oct.-Apr. Daily 10-11.30, 2-4.

TOWER MUSEUM
Archivgasse, Schwyz
Museum of Cantonal life and history. Geology. Uniforms. Weapons. Flags. Religious art. Portraits. Memorabilia of Aloys von Reding. Medals. Coins. Seals. Swiss ethnography, especially costumes, masks.
May-Sept. Daily 9-12, 1.30-6. Apr. and Oct. 10-12, 1.30-4.

SCUOL-SCHULS

LOWER ENGADINE MUSEUM
Plaz 66, Scuol-Schuls, Graubünden
History of Lower Engadine. Furniture. Household equipment. Agricultural implements. Natural history. Prehistory.
May 1-Oct. 15, Sa. 4-5.30. June-Aug. also Tu., Th. 10-11.30, 3-5.

SEEDORF

À PRO CASTLE
Seedorf, Uri
Castle (1556-58) built for Jakob à Pro. Works by Canton Uri artists.
May-Sept. Su. 11-5; Th., Sa. 1-4. Oct.-Apr. Sa. 1-4; 2nd Su. in month, 1-4.

SEENGEN

HALLWIL CASTLE
Seengen, Aargau
History of the Castle and its inhabitants. Neolithic material from local sites. Models illustrating Neolithic technology. Local history. Displays showing straw-plaiting industry. 17th-18th century domestic life.
Apr.-Oct. Daily 8-12, 1-6.

SEMPACH

TOWN HALL MUSEUM
Sempach, Basel-Land
Local history. Ornithological collection of the Schweizer Vogelwarte (Swiss bird-watching station).
Daily 8-11.30, 2-5.30 (5 in winter).

SIERRE-SIDERS

VILLA MANOR
Rue du Château, Sierre-Siders, Valais
Wine and vineyard museum. Weapons. Hunting trophies. Memorabilia of R. M. Rilke.
Daily 2-6.

SION

CANTONAL MUSEUM OF FINE ART
Place de la Majorie, Sion, Valais
Paintings, drawings, prints by Valais artists.
May-Oct. Daily 8-7. Nov.-Apr. Tu.-Su. 9-5.

CANTONAL MUSEUM OF NATURAL HISTORY
Collège, Avenue de la Gare 40, Sion, Valais
Regional geology, mineralogy, botany, zoology.
Sept.-June, Sa., Su. 2-6. July-Aug. Tu.-Su. 2-6.

VALÈRE CANTONAL MUSEUM
Valère, Sion, Valais
Prehistoric and Roman material from regional excavations. 4th-11th century religious art. Romanesque and Gothic wood sculpture. Furniture. Goldsmith's work. Pewter. Weapons. Costumes. Folklore. Coins.
May-Oct. Daily 8-7. Nov.-Apr. Tu.-Su. 9-5.

SISSACH

REGIONAL MUSEUM
Zunzgerstrasse, Sissach, Basel-Land
Local history. Furniture. Agricultural implements. Costumes. Medieval archaeology.
Mar.-Dec., 1st Su. in month, 10-12, 2-4.

SOLOTHURN

CASTLE BLUMENSTEIN HISTORICAL MUSEUM
Blumensteinweg, Solothurn
Regional history. 18th century furnishings, household equipment. Gold and silversmiths' work. Pewter. Pottery. Porcelain. Textiles. Glass paintings. Drawings. Prints. Portraits. Coins. 18th century 'Ambassadora' crib.
Tu.-Sa. 2-5; Su. 10-12, 2-5.

CATHEDRAL TREASURY
St. Ursen Kathedrale, Solothurn
15th-19th century goldsmiths' work. Textiles. Coins. Medals.
M.-Sa. 11-12, except during services.

KOSCIUSZKO MUSEUM
Gurzelngasse 12, Solothurn
Memorabilia of Field-marshal Tadeusz Kosciuszko, who lived in this house, 1815-17. Furniture. Portraits. Documents.
Daily 9-12, 2-5.

SOLOTHURN MUNICIPAL MUSEUM
Werkhofstrasse 30, Solothurn
15th-18th century European paintings. 19th-20th century Swiss paintings. Natural history, especially Swiss. Geology. Mineralogy. Palaeontology, including fossilised tortoises. Zoology. Anthropology. Neolithic, Roman and medieval material from local sites.
Tu.-Sa. 9-12, 2-5; Su. 10-12, 2-4.

WEAPON AND UNIFORM COLLECTION
Altes Zeughaus, Riedholzplatz 1, Solothurn
Weapons, uniforms, flags, from late medieval period onwards, including trophies from Burgundian and Swabian wars.
Su. 10-12, 1-4. Oct.-Mar. Tu.-Sa. 9-12, 1-5. Apr.-Sept. Tu.-Sa. 8-12, 1-5.

SPIEZ

CASTLE
Schlossstrasse, Spiez, Bern
13th-18th century period rooms.
Easter-mid.Oct. Tu.-Su. 9.30-12, 2-6; M. 2-6.

STÄFA

LOCAL MUSEUM
Zur Farb, Stäfa, Zurich
Local history. Furniture. Household equipment. Period rooms.
Sa. and 1st Su. in month, 2-5.

STAMPA

CIÄSE GRANDA
Stampa, Grigioni
Natural history of the Val Bregaglia. Paintings by Giovanni and Augusto Giacometti. Local history.
May-Sept. Daily 2-5.

PALAZZO CASTELMUR
Coltura, Stampa, Grigioni
Patrician house (1723) and mid-19th century palazzo of the Castelmur family. Original 19th century furnishings. Rooms with furniture from the Val Bregaglia.
May-Oct. Daily 9-11.30, 2-6.

STANS

HISTORICAL MUSEUM
Stansstaderstrasse, Stans, Nidwalden
In former salt and grain warehouse (1700). Prehistoric material. Weapons. Flags. Uniforms. 18th-19th century costumes. Reconstruction of Nidwald peasant room. 16th-19th century regional religious art. Paintings and sculptures by local artists. Ethnographical collection of material from Borneo and Bali.
Daily 8-12, 1-7.

STECKBORN

MUSEUM OF SEWING MACHINES
Gegauf Bernina-Nähmaschinenfabrik, Steckborn, Thurgau
History of the sewing machine. Original machines. Models. Pictorial displays.
W. 10-12.

UNTERSEE REGIONAL MUSEUM
Turmhof, Steckborn, Thurgau
Neolithic, Roman and Alemannic material from regional sites. 17th-19th century furnishings. Craftsmen's tools, equipment, mostly 18th-19th century. Smithy. Turner's workshop.
May 1-Oct. 15, Tu.-Sa. 2-5.

STEIN AM RHEIN

MUSEUM OF ST. GEORGEN MONASTERY
Stein am Rhein, Schaffhausen
In Benedictine monastery (1525). 15th-16th century furnishings, many of them original. 15th-16th century church furniture, woodcarvings. Prehistoric and medieval archaeology. Craftsmen's tools. Household equipment.
Feb.-Nov. Daily 9-12, 1.30-5.

SUHR

REGIONAL MUSEUM
Tramstrasse 279, Suhr, Aargau
History of the Suhrental. Furniture. Household equipment. Craftsmen's tools. 15th-18th century furniture, fittings and door-knockers. Dolls' houses.
1st Su. in month, 2-5.

SURSEE

CHURCH TREASURY
Katholische Pfarrkirche, Sursee, Luzern
15th-19th century liturgical objects, ornaments and sculpture.
By appointment.

MUSEUM OF THE SWISS PROVINCE OF CAPUCHINS
Kapuzinerkloster, Sursee, Luzern
History and work of the Capuchin Order in Switzerland. Paintings. Sculpture and carvings. Prints. Manuscripts. Books.
Mar.-Nov. Tu., Th., Su., guided tours at 1.30 and 4.

TARASP

CASTLE
Tarasp, Graubünden
16th-18th century furniture, period rooms from Graubünden and the Tirol. Pewter. 16th-17th century Swiss glass paintings. Weapons.
Guided tours only, June 1-30, M.-Sa. 4.15. July 15-Aug. 31, M.-Sa. 2.45, 4.15. Sept. 1-20, M.-Sa. 2.45.

THUN

ART COLLECTION OF THUN
Thunerhof, Hofstettenstrasse, Thun, Bern
20th century Swiss, especially Bern, paintings, sculpture. 16th-19th century drawings, prints.
Tu.-Su. 10-12, 2-5. M. 2-5. W., F. also 8-9.30 p.m. during special exhibitions.

HISTORICAL MUSEUM
Schloss, Thun, Bern
Material of prehistoric and early historical periods from regional excavations. Medieval weapons, flags, textiles. Ceramics, especially Heimberg. Glass. Pottery kilns. Peasant furniture. Costumes. Craftsmen's tools. 18th-19th century Swiss weapons, uniforms.
Apr.-May and Oct. 10-5. June-Sept. 9-6.

SCHADAU GALLERY
Thun, Bern
19th-20th century paintings, sculpture, drawings by Swiss artists.
Apr.-June and Sept. Daily 10-12, 1.30-5. July-Aug. M. 1.30-7; Tu.-Su. 10-5.

TRUN/TRUNS

SURSILVAN MUSEUM
Cuort Ligia Grischa, Trun/Truns, Graubünden
Furnished interiors, including Alpine hut. Household equipment. Craftsmen's tools. History of the Bündner Oberland.
May-Oct. Daily 9-12, 2-6. Nov.-Apr. Daily 9-11, 2-4.

TWAN (DOUANNE)

VINEYARD MUSEUM
Twann (Douanne), Basel-Land
Local vine-growing. Preparation of wine. Equipment.
On request.

UNTERSTAMMHEIM

STAMMHEIMERTAL REGIONAL MUSEUM
Gemeindehaus, Unterstammheim, Zurich
Peasant furnishings. Agricultural implements. Craftsmen's tools, equipment. Material illustrating regional history.
May-Oct., 1st Su. in month, 2-5.

URDORF

LOCAL MUSEUM
Schulstrasse, Urdorf, Zurich
Local history.
M. 6.30-8 p.m.

UTZENSTORF

LANDSHUT CASTLE
Utzentorf, Bern
17th century furnishings, household equipment. Hunting and shooting collections. Weapons. Trophies. Agricultural implements. 18th century sleighs.
June 15-Oct. 15, Tu.-Su. 10-12, 2-5.

UZNACH

MUSEUM OF LOCAL LIFE AND HISTORY
Tönierhaus, Uznach, St. Gallen
Hallstatt material from local excavations. Local history. Views. Portraits. Furniture. Silversmiths' work. Household equipment. Tools.
By appointment.

VALANGIN

MUSEUM
Château, Valangin, Neuchâtel
16th-19th century furniture. Stoves. Household equipment. Engravings of local and historical subjects. Blinds. Lace. Weapons. Material from excavations at Château.
Tu.-Su. 9-12, 2-6.

VALS

GANDA HOUSE
Vals, Graubünden
Furniture. Household equipment. Tools.
By appointment.

VEVEY

JENISCH MUSEUM
Avenue de la Gare 2, Vevey, Vaud
19th-20th century Swiss paintings. Works by European painters, especially Courbet. Mineralogy. Palaeontology. Zoology, especially regional fauna.
May-Oct. Tu.-Sa. 10-12, 2-4; Su. 10-12, 2-5. Nov.-Apr. Tu.-Sa. 2-4; Su. 11-12, 2-4.

MUSEUM OF THE FRATERNITY OF WINE PRODUCERS
Rue d'Italie, Vevey, Vaud
Models, documents, costumes relating to the Vevey wine-festivals, dating from 1797.
Tu.-Sa. 10-12, 2-5; Su. 11-12, 2-5.

MUSEUM OF OLD VEVEY
Rue d'Italie, Vevey, Vaud
Material from local prehistoric and Roman sites. Egyptian, Greek, Roman antiquities. Costumes. Furniture. Paintings. Prints. Printing works of the *Messager Boiteux*. Pewter workshop. 15th-18th century French and Italian ironwork. 19th century weapons and uniforms of Swiss and Vaud soldiers in French service.
Tu.-Sa. 10-12, 2-5; Su. 11-12, 2-5.

WÄDENSWIL

LOCAL MUSEUM
Florhofstrasse 6, Wädenswil, Zurich
Local history. Peasant handicrafts and household equipment. Geography.
Su. 10.30-12, 2-4; W. 3-5.

WALD

REGIONAL MUSEUM
Wald, Zurich
Local history.
By appointment.

WALTENSBURG/VUORZ

ARCUN DA TRADIZIUN
Waltensburg/Vuorz, Graubünden
Local history. Craftsmen's tools. Agricultural implements.
May-Oct. Su. 4-6.

WANGEN AN DER AARE

LOCAL COLLECTION
Gemeindehaus, Wangen an der Aare, Bern
Local history. Stove ceramics (1820-70) from the Anderegg pottery.
By appointment.

WEIACH

LOCAL MUSEUM
Oberdorf 297, Weiach
Local history.
Tu.-Su. 10-12, 2-5.

WETTINGEN

COLLECTIONS OF WETTINGEN MONASTERY
Wettingen, Aargau
Religious art. Historical material relating to the former Cistercian monastery.
Daily 2-5.

WETZIKON

LOCAL MUSEUM
Farbstrasse 1, Wetzikon, Zurich
Lake village archaeology. Peasant furnishings, household equipment. Agricultural implements. Memorabilia of the composer, H. G. Nägeli.
Oct.-Mar. 1st Su. in month, 10.30-12, 2-5.

WIEDLISBACH

HISTORICAL MUSEUM
Kornhaus, Hauptstrasse, Wiedlisbach, Bern
Ceramics from local and Swiss potteries. Swiss glass. Pewter. Local history. Agricultural implements.
By appointment.

WIESENDANGEN

LOCAL MUSEUM
Dorfstrasse, Wiesendangen, Zurich
Local history. Peasant household equipment. Agricultural implements. Costumes.
1st Su. in month, 2-5. Other times by appointment.

WIL

MUNICIPAL MUSEUM
Im Hof, Wil, St. Gallen
Prehistoric and medieval material from regional sites. 16th-18th century stoves. Baroque portraits. Religious paintings and sculpture. Liturgical objects. Local history.
Daily 9-11.30, 2-5.

WINTERTHUR

JAKOB BRYNER AND KONRAD KELLENBERGER COLLECTION
Rathaus, Winterthur, Zurich
17th-19th century clocks, watches.
On request.

INDUSTRIAL SAFETY EXHIBITION OF THE FEDERAL LABOUR INSPECTORATE
Ackeretstrasse 17, Winterthur, Zurich
Displays illustrating problems and techniques of industrial safety. Machines. Models. Drawings. Photographs.
W. 2-5; Sa. 9-12. Other times by appointment.

LINDENGUT REGIONAL MUSEUM
Römerstrasse 8, Winterthur, Zurich
History of Winterthur from Roman times to 19th century. 18th century furnished interiors. Textiles. Winterthur applied arts, especially 16th-17th century ceramics, glass-paintings, clocks.
Tu.-Th., Sa. 2-5. Su. 10-12, 2-5.

MUSEUM OF APPLIED ART
Kirchplatz 14, Winterthur, Zurich
Temporary exhibitions from the Museum's permanent collections of wrought iron-work, ceramics, glass, textiles.
M.-F. 2-6; Tu., Th. also 8-10 p.m. Sa., Su. 10-12, 2-5.

MUSEUM OF ART
Museumstrasse 52, Winterthur, Zurich
16th century paintings by Swiss and S. German artists. 17th-18th century paintings by Winterthur and Zurich artists. 19th-20th century Swiss paintings. Post-Impressionist French paintings. 19th-20th century German paintings. 20th century Italian paintings. 19th-20th century Swiss, French, Italian sculpture. Prints. Drawings.
Tu.-Su. 10-12, 2-5; M. 2-5.

NATURAL SCIENCE COLLECTION OF THE TOWN OF WINTERTHUR
Museumstrasse 52, Winterthur, Zurich
Palaeontology, especially Mastodon. Mineralogy. Petrography. Zoology, especially local birds and animals. Coral. Relief maps showing types of Swiss landscape. Ethnographical material from Central Africa, East Asia, Far East.
Tu.-Su. 10-12, 2-5; M. 2-5.

OSKAR REINHART COLLECTION
Haldenstrasse 95, Winterthur, Zurich
European paintings, especially by 19th century French artists.
Tu.-Su. 10-4.

OSKAR REINHART FOUNDATION
Stadthausstrasse 6, Winterthur, Zurich
18th-19th century Swiss, German, Austrian paintings, sculpture, drawings, prints.
Tu.-Su. 10-12, 2-5; M. 2-5. 1st Th. in month also 8-10 p.m.

SWISS TECHNORAMA
Palmstrasse 16/11 and Frauenfelderstrasse, Winterthur, Zurich
History of technology, especially 19th-20th century. Apparatus and equipment. Models. Photographs. Plans.
By appointment.

WINTERTHUR MUNICIPAL COLLECTION OF COINS AND MEDALS
Museumstrasse 52, Winterthur, Zurich
Greek and Roman coins. Swiss coins, medals. Small Greek and Roman artistic objects.
Sa. 2-5; Su. 10-12, 2-5.

WINTERTHUR-HEGI

HEGI CASTLE
Winterthur-Hegi, Zurich
Regional history. 15th-18th century furnished interiors. 19th century weapons.
Mar.-Oct. Tu., W., Sa. 2-5; Su. 10-12, 2-5. Nov.-Feb. Su. 10-12, 2-5.

WINTERTHUR-MÖRSBURG

MÖRSBURG CASTLE
Stadel, Winterthur-Mörsburg, Zurich
Rural life. Household equipment. Ceramics. Clocks. 17th-19th century weapons.
Apr.-Nov. Tu.-Su. 10-12, 1.30-5. Dec.-Mar. Su. 10-12, 1.30-5.

WITTENBACH

LOCAL MUSEUM
Alter Schulhaus, St. Ulrichsberg, Wittenbach, St. Gallen
Local history. Rural furniture and musical instruments. Craftsmen's tools.
1st Su. in month, 2-4.

WOHLEN

COLLECTION OF THE FREIAMT HISTORICAL SOCIETY
Bezirksschulhaus, Bremgartenstrasse, Wohlen, Aargau
Prehistoric material from local Halstatt and La Tène graves.
By appointment.

WOHLENSCHWIL

PEASANT MUSEUM
Alte Dorfkirche, Wohlenschwil, Aargau
Models, pictures illustrating typography and development of the Swiss peasant house. Straw-plaiting and weaving.
W., Sa., Su. 1-6.

YVERDON

MUSEUM OF OLD YVERDON
Château, Hôtel de Ville, Yverdon, Vaud
Archaeological material from local sites of the Neolithic, Bronze, La Tène, Roman and Burgundian periods. Medieval weapons, pottery. Egyptian antiquities. Oriental art and handicrafts. Local history. Pestalozzi Room. Dioramas showing animals of the region. Geology. Mineralogy.
Apr.-Oct. M.-Sa. 9-12, 2-5; Su. 11-12.

ZERMATT

ALPINE MUSEUM
Zermatt, Valais
Minerals, animals and plants of the Swiss Alps. Memorabilia of famous guides and climbers. Maps. Peasant life.
Daily 9-12, 2-6.

ZOFINGEN

MUSEUM
General Guisan Strasse 18, Zofingen, Aargau
Material of the prehistoric and early historical periods from local sites. 13th-18th century weapons. Glass paintings. Tiles. Furniture. History of Zofingen. Coins. Geology. Mineralogy. Zoology.
Su. 10-12. Oct.-Mar., 1st and 3rd Su. in month also 2-4.

ZOLLIKON

LOCAL HISTORY COLLECTION
Zollikerstrasse 91, Zollikon, Zurich
Local history.
Tu., F. 6.30-9 p.m.; Sa. 2-6.

ZUG

CANTONAL MUSEUM FOR PREHISTORY
Aegerisstrasse 56, Zug
Material from excavations in the Canton: Mesolithic, Neolithic, Late Bronze Age, Roman.
W., Sa. 2-5.

COLLECTION OF THE GERMAN-SWISS BEE-KEEPERS ASSOCIATION
Gasthaus Rosenberg, Zug
Anatomy and life of bees. Beekeeping. Products obtained from beeswax.
During months when the hotel is open.

FISHERY MUSEUM
Untergasse, Zug
Fish and birds of the Zugersee. Fishing boats and equipment.
By appointment.

ZURICH

BOTANICAL GARDEN AND MUSEUM
Pelikanstrasse 40, Zurich
World-herbarium, with emphasis on plants of S. and S.W. Africa and New Caledonia. Swiss herbarium.
May-Oct., M.-Sa. 7-7; Sa. 8-6. Nov.-Apr. 8-5.

CENTRAL LIBRARY
Zähringerplatz 6, Zurich
Permanent exhibition, with displays illustrating life and work of Ulrich Zwingli, Gottfried Keller and Conrad Ferdinand Meyer.
W., Sa. 2-4.

CERAMICS COLLECTION
Zunfthaus zur Meisen, Münsterhof 20, Zurich
18th century Swiss porcelain and faience.
Tu.-Su. 10-12, 2-5.

COLLECTION OF THE E. G. BÜHRLE FOUNDATION
Zollikerstrasse 172, Zurich
Medieval, especially 15th century, wood sculpture. Dutch and Flemish paintings. 18th century Italian paintings. 19th-20th century French paintings.
Tu., F. 2-5.

COLLECTION OF THE CULTURE OF THE NORTH AMERICAN INDIANS
Schulhaus, Feldstrasse 89, Zurich
North American Indian culture.
Sa. 2-5. Closed school vacations.

LE CORBUSIER-HEIDI WEBER CENTRE
Bellivestrasse and Höschgasse 8, Zurich
In last building (1966) designed by Le Corbusier. Works by Le Corbusier. Paintings. Drawings. Tapestries. Sculpture. Furniture. Exhibitions related to Le Corbusier and to his work.
Tu.-Su. 10-6; May-Oct. also Tu., F. 8-10 p.m.

ETHNOLOGICAL COLLECTION OF THE UNIVERSITY OF ZURICH
Universität, Rämistrasse 71, Zurich
Ethnographical material from Africa, Oceania, Indonesia, Tibet, India, Ceylon, Thailand, China, Japan, Polar regions, North, Central and S. America.
M.-F. 10-12, 2-5; last Su. in month, 10-12.

GEOLOGICAL AND MINERALOGICAL-PETROGRAPHICAL COLLECTIONS OF THE FEDERAL TECHNICAL UNIVERSITY
E.T.H., Sonneggstrasse 5, Zurich
Geology, mineralogy and petrography of Switzerland and neighbouring area. Phytopalaeontological collection. Regional geology and mineralogy. Minerals and ores. Geotechnical exhibits.
M.-Sa. 10-12, 2-5.

GRAPHICS COLLECTION OF THE FEDERAL TECHNICAL UNIVERSITY
E.T.H., Hauptgebäude, Zurich
15th-20th century European drawings, engravings, prints, including works by Dürer, Rembrandt, Goya, and with special emphasis on Italian Renaissance. Greek vases.
M.-Sa. 10-12, 2-5.

HERMANN HALLER'S STUDIO
Höschgasse-Bellerivestrasse, Zurich
Works by the sculptor, Hermann Haller, and by contemporary Swiss sculptors.
May-Oct., as announced locally.

THOMAS MANN COLLECTION
Schönerggasse 15, Zurich
Memorabilia, books and manuscripts of Thomas Mann.
W., Sa. 2-4.

MURALTENGUT HOUSE
Seestrasse 203, Zurich
18th century country house. Carpets from Central Asia, Caucasus, Persia, Turkmenia, Samarkand. Japanese woodcuts.
1st Su. in month, 10-12, 2-6.

MUSEUM BELLERIVE
Höschgasse 3, Zurich
Applied art.
Tu.-Sa. 10-12, 2-5; Su. 2-5.

MUSEUM OF APPLIED ART
Ausstellungstrasse 60, Zurich
European and non-European applied art. Industrial design. Popular art. Musical instruments. Graphics, especially posters.
Tu.-F. 10-12, 2-6; Th. also 6-9 p.m. Sa., Su. 10-12, 2-5.

MUSEUM OF ART
Heimplatz 1, Zurich
Greek and Roman sculpture. Medieval, especially German, wood and stone sculpture. Italian, German, Dutch medieval paintings. Paintings on wood by Zurich and Bern artists. Portraits by Hans Asper. 17th century Dutch paintings. 17th-18th century paintings by Zurich artists, especially J. H. Füssli. Modern European paintings and sculpture. Sculpture, drawings, paintings by Giaconetti. 19th-20th century European drawings.
M. 2-5; Tu.-Su. 10-5; Tu.-F. also 8-10 p.m.

MUSEUM RIETBERG
Gablerstrasse 15, Zurich
Indian sculpture. Tibetan temple-pictures and bronzes. Chinese sculpture, calligraphy, wood-carving, parasols, calligraphy. Primitive art from Africa and the Pacific. Eskimo and N.W. American Indian masks, carvings. Pre-Columbian art.
Tu.-F. 10-12, 2-6; Sa., Su. 10-12, 2-5; W. also 8-10 p.m.

PESTALOZZI COLLECTION
Beckenhofstrasse 31-7, Zurich
Pestalozzi memorabilia. Furniture. Portraits. Books and manuscripts.
Tu.-F. 9-11.30, 2-6; Sa. 9-11.30, 2-5.

SWISS NATIONAL MUSEUM
Museumstrasse 2, Zurich
Prehistoric and early history. Palaeolithic. Mesolithic. Neolithic. Middle and Late Bronze Age. La Tène. Roman archaeology from Cantons Zurich and Aargau. Alamannic, Burgundian, Lombard grave material. Medieval religious art. Goldsmiths' work. Glass paintings. Ceramics, especially Winterthur faience. Paintings, sculpture, 1530-1850. Furniture, furnished interiors. Textiles. Glass. Pewter. Clocks. Costumes. Weapons. Uniforms. Flags. Coins. Medals. Banknotes. Seals. Swiss drawings, prints, 15th-19th centuries.
Tu.-Su. 10-12, 2-5.

UNIVERSITY ARCHAEOLOGICAL COLLECTION
Rämistrasse 73, Zurich
Egyptian art, especially amulets. Roman-Egyptian terracotta figures and mummy-portraits. Assyrian reliefs. Greek vases and terra-cottas. Casts of Greek and Roman sculpture.
M., W. 2-5; F. 8-10 p.m.

UNIVERSITY MUSEUM OF ZOOLOGY AND PALAEONTOLOGY
Künstlergasse 16, Zurich
Non-European vertebrates. Mammoths. Mammal fossils from Argentina. Fish.
Tu.-Su. 2-5; Su. also 10-12; F. also 8-10 p.m.

ZURICH UNIVERSITY COLLECTION OF THE HISTORY OF MEDICINE
Universität, Rämistrasse 71, Zurich
History of medicine and public health, especially in Switzerland. Primitive medicine. Medieval medicine. 17th-19th century anatomical models. Medical and surgical instruments. Reconstructions of old apothecary's shop and sickroom. Portraits and careers of famous Swiss doctors.
W. 2-5.

ZURICH-ALBISRIEDEN

LOCAL MUSEUM
Ginterstrasse, Zurich-Albisrieden
History of the village of Albisrieden.
Oct.-Apr., 1st Su. in month, 10-12.

ZURICH-ALTSTETTEN

LOCAL MUSEUM
Dachslernstrasse 6, Zurich-Altstetten
History of the village of Altstetten. Roman and Alemannic material.
Oct.-May, 1st Su. in month, 10-12.

ZURICH-HÖNGG

MUSEUM OF LOCAL HISTORY
Ackersteinstrasse 190, Zurich-Höngg
Local history. Craftsmen's tools. Wine production.
Sept.-June, 1st Su. in month, 10-12.

ZURZACH

FAIR AND DISTRICT MUSEUM
Im Höfli, Zurzach, Aargau
Prehistoric and early history. History of Zurzach fair. Agricultural implements.
Apr.-Oct., Th. 2-4; Su. 10-11.

Syrian Arab Republic

There is no more agreeable museum in the Middle East than the National Museum in Damascus, a solid reminder of how much Syria owes to the French. Most of the museum collections in Syria are concerned with archaeology, but there are two interesting and successful attempts, both in Damascus, to bring past and present into the same focus. The theme of one is agriculture and of the other military operations, with collections ranging from prehistoric items to the twentieth century.

ALEPPO

ALEPPO NATIONAL MUSEUM
Rue Al-Maarri, Aleppo
Archaeology of the different civilisations which have existed in Syria. Sculpture. Tablets. Coins. Jewellery. Pottery. Glass. Utensils.
Daily ex. Tu. Apr.-Sept. 8-1, 4-7; Oct.-Mar. 8-1, 2-4.

BOSRA

BOSRA MUSEUM
Bosra
In one of the towers of the Citadel. Archaeological material from local excavations. Sculptures. Mosaics. Inscriptions. Jewellery. Glass.
Daily ex. Tu. Apr.-Sept. 8-1, 4-7; Oct.-Mar. 8-1, 2-4.

CHAHBA

MOSAICS MUSEUM
Chahba
Mosaic pavements discovered at Chahba, the former Philippolis.
Daily ex. Tu. Apr.-Sept. 8-1, 4-7; Oct.-Mar. 8-1, 2-4.

DAMASCUS

DAMASCUS AGRICULTURAL MUSEUM
Rue Halbouni, Damascus
History of food and agriculture in Syria. Implements. Fossilised and carbonised foodstuffs. Manuscripts relating to agriculture. Olive press of the 1st century A.D.
Daily ex. Tu. Apr.-Sept. 8-1, 4-7; Oct.-Mar. 8-1, 2-4.

DAMASCUS MILITARY MUSEUM
Rue Rida Saïd, Damascus
Material relating to the history of warfare in Syria from prehistoric times onwards. Sculpture. Paintings. Tablets. Weapons. Models of siege equipment.
Daily ex. Tu. Apr.-Sept. 8-1, 4-7; Oct.-Mar. 8-1, 2-4.

DAMASCUS NATIONAL MUSEUM
Rue Rida Saïd, Damascus
Archaeology of the different civilisations which have existed in Syria. Reconstructed buildings. Sculpture. Mosaics. Tools. Textiles. Goldsmiths' work. Glass. Pottery. Astrolabes and other scientific instruments.
Daily ex. Tu. Apr.-Sept. 8-1, 4-7; Oct.-Mar. 8-1, 2-4.

MUSEUM OF ARAB CALLIGRAPHY
Bab Brid, Damascus
Manuscripts and inscriptions illustrating the development of Arabic writing. Writing equipment.
Daily ex. Tu. Apr.-Sept. 8-1, 4-7; Oct.-Mar. 8-1, 2-4.

MUSEUM OF POPULAR ARTS AND TRADITIONS
Rue Bzourich, Palais Azem, Damascus
Swords, pistols, daggers, guns, made at Damascus. Musical instruments. Costumes. Carpets. Curtains. Jewellery. Glass. Furniture. Domestic equipment. Watches.
Daily ex. Tu. Apr.-Sept. 8-1, 4-7; Oct.-Mar. 8-1, 2-4.

HAMA

HAMA MUSEUM
Rue Abul-Fida, Hama
Archaeological material from local excavations. Sculpture. Mosaics. Ceramics, including faience. Glass. Coins. Goldsmiths' work.
Daily ex. Tu. Apr.-Sept. 8-1, 4-7; Oct.-Mar. 8-1, 2-4.

PALMYRA

PALMYRA MUSEUM
Palmyra
Archaeological material from excavations at Palmyra. Sculpture. Mosaics. Coins. Textiles. Glass. Pottery.
Daily ex. Tu. Apr.-Sept. 8-1, 4-7; Oct.-Mar. 8-1, 2-4.

SOUEIDA

SOUEIDA MUSEUM
Palais du Gouvernement, Soueida
Archaeological material from sites in the region of the Museum. Sculpture. Mosaics.
Daily ex. Tu. Apr.-Sept. 8-1, 4-7; Oct.-Mar. 8-1, 2-4.

TARTOUS

TARTOUS MUSEUM
Tartous
Archaeological material from local excavations. Sculptures. Frescoes. Mosaics. Jewellery. Glass. 19th century Oriental ceramics. Ship models. Tools and utensils.
Daily ex. Tu. Apr.-Sept. 8-1, 4-7; Oct.-Mar. 8-1, 2-4.

Tanzania

It may be seen from the list that follows that the museums of Tanzania are concerned very little with the country's attempts to develop its economy and particularly to increase the numbers of scientifically-educated people. Even so, the range of museums is good, including a village museum, a National Parks museum, collections illustrating the slave trade and anthropological material of the first importance from the Olduvai Gorge.

ARUSHA

NATIONAL PARKS MUSEUM
P.O. Box 3134, Arusha
Collections include mounted animals and birds and archaeological objects.
Open throughout the day.

BAGAMOYO

BAGAMOYO MUSEUM
P.O. Box 71, Bagamoyo
Historical collections with a section on the slave trade. Natural history.
On request.

BWERANYANGE

BWERENYANGE MUSEUM
Bweranyange
Collection of metal objects and drums belonging to the Karagwe Kingdom which flourished in 18th and 19th centuries. Royal regalia.
Daily 7.30-6.

DAR ES SALAAM

NATIONAL MUSEUM OF TANZANIA
P.O. Box 511, Dar es Salaam
Archaeology and palaeontology from the Stone Age onwards, including Olduvai Gorge materials. History. Ethnographic collection of objects belonging to the present day inhabitants of Tanzania.
M.-Sa. 9.30-7; Su. and Christmas Day, 1-7; public holidays 10-7.

VILLAGE MUSEUM
Branch of National Museum, Dar es Salaam
8 km. north of Dar es Salaam. Houses belonging to the different ethnic groups of the population of Tanzania, depicting the varied traditional architecture. Domestic utensils. Wood carvers and weavers demonstrate their skills.
M.-Sa. 9.30-7; Su. and Christmas Day, 1-7; public holidays 10-7.

DODOMA

GEOLOGICAL MUSEUM
P.O. Box 903, Dodoma
Collection of Tanzania minerals and rocks.
M.-F. 7.30-2.30; Sa. 7.30-12.30.

MBEYA

GAME MUSEUM
P.O. Box 63, Mbeya
Animals and birds of Tanzania.
M.-F. 7.30-2.30; Sa. 7.30-12.30.

MOROGORO

NATIONAL PARKS MUSEUM
P.O. Box 462, Morogoro
Situated in Mikumi park. Collections include mounted game and birds, and archaeological objects.
Open throughout the day.

MWANZA

BUJORA MUSEUM
P.O. Box 76, Mwanza
Collection of Sukuma traditional objects with special emphasis on Sukuma royal regalia.
Open throughout the day.

GAME MUSEUM
P.O. Box 851, Mwanza
Animals and birds of Tanzania.
M.-F. 7.30-2.30; Sa. 7.30-12.30.

MWEKA

NATURAL HISTORY MUSEUM
College of African Wildlife Management, P.O. Box 3031, Moshi, Mweka
African mammals. Heads of European and North American large mammals. African birds, reptiles, fish and amphibians. Marine animals. Tanzanian minerals and rocks. Herbarium.
Open throughout the day.

Thailand

Thailand earns its living from the production of timber, especially teak, rice and minerals. Its museums tell us a good deal about minerals, something about rice and nothing at all about forestry. As a substitute, however, we have some very good archaeological and ethnographical collections, with the Thai drama well represented.

AYUDHYA

AYUDHYA MUSEUM
Chandrakasem Palace, Ayudhya
Objects from local excavations, including gold ornaments. Archaeology. Ethnography.
Tu.-F., Su. 9-4.30.

CHAO SAM PHYA NATIONAL MUSEUM
Ayudhya
Finds from excavations in the area, especially Buddha-images. Gold ornaments and ceramics. Large sculptures of the Dvaravati period.
Su.-F. 9-4.

BANGKOK

HILL TRIBE MUSEUM
Border Patrol Police, Police Headquarters, Bangkok
Ethnography of the Hill Tribes, including costumes and jewellery.
By appointment.

KAMTHIENG HOUSE MUSEUM
Siam Society, 131 Asoka Road (Lane 21), Bangkok
19th century northern Thai dwelling of traditional wooden structure, furnished in period style, with utensils and implements. An adjacent traditional rice granary contains a collection of traditional tools, farming implements, fishing gear. *M.-Sa. 9-12.*

MUSEUM OF MINERALOGY
Department of Natural Resources, Bangkok
Geology, mineralogy of Thailand.
By appointment.

MUSEUM OF MOUNTED ANIMALS
Bangkok
Zoological specimens, some in habitat groups in dioramas, others mounted individually. Emphasis is given to fauna of Thailand, but there are specimens from Africa and elsewhere.
Tu.-F., Su. 9-4.30.

NATIONAL MUSEUM
Naphrathatu Road, Bangkok
Prehistoric artifacts. Bronze and stone sculptures. Costumes. Ceramics. Textiles. Royal chairs and seats. Theatrical masks and dresses. Pali manuscripts and illustrated books. Shadow play figures. Musical instruments. Cremation chariots. Khmer statues. Thai art from Chieng Saen to Bangkok period.
Tu.-F., Su. 9-4.30.

SUAN PAKKAD PALACE
352 Sri Ayudhya Road, Bangkok
Buildings include 18th century monastery library building. Thai archaeological and art objects. Contemporary paintings.
Tu., Th., Sa., Su. 9-12, 2-4.

JIM THOMPSON HOUSE
Rama I Road, Bangkok
Private residence made by assembling and joining several traditional Thai houses. Thai archaeology and arts, arranged as in the decoration of a home. Thai paintings. Sawankalok pottery (13th-14th century). Benjarong porcelain. Khmer statuary. Burmese and Thai Buddha statues.
M. and Th. 9-12.

CHIENGMAI

MUSEUM OF THE TRIBAL INSTITUTE
Chiengmai University Campus, Chiengmai
Traditional huts of six of the Hill Tribes. Ethnography.
By appointment.

NATIONAL MUSEUM
Chiengmai
Regional archaeology, history, ethnography.
Tu.-F., Su. 9-4.30.

CHIENG-SAEN

CHIENG-SAEN MUSEUM
Chieng-Saen, Chiengrai Province
Regional archaeology, history, ethnography.
Tu.-F., Su. 9-4.30.

KAMPHAENGPHET

NATIONAL MUSEUM
Kamphaengphet
Archaeological finds from the area. Ethnography.
Su.-F. 9-4.30.

KHON-KAEN

NATIONAL MUSEUM
Khon-Kaen
Regional archaeology, history, ethnography.
Tu.-Su. 9-4.30.

LOPBURI

LOPBURI MUSEUM
Narai Ratcha Nivet Palace, Lopburi
Fine arts. Finds from excavations in the area.
W.-Su. 8.30-4.30. Closed M., Tu., holidays.

NAKHOM PATHOM

PHRA PATHOM CHEDI NATIONAL MUSEUM
Nakhom Pathom
Regional archaeology, history, ethnography.
Tu.-F., Su. 9-4.30.

PHRA BOROMADHAT

MONASTERY MUSEUM
Phra Boromadhat, Chainat Province
Local history. Religious art.
Tu.-F., Su. 9-4.30.

SUKHOTHAI

RAMKHAMHAENG NATIONAL MUSEUM
Sukhothai
Finds from local excavations. Art of the Sukhothai Kingdom.
W.-Su. 9-12, 1-4. Closed M., Tu., holidays.

U-THONG

U-THONG NATIONAL MUSEUM
U-Thong, Suphanburi Province
Archaeological material from the Dvaravati period, 5th-11th centuries, excavated in the region.
W.-Su. 9-12, 1-4.

Togo

Togo's one museum owes its existence to the enterprise of a private citizen who has devoted much time and attention to bringing together collections illustrating the history of this former German colony, together with such examples of its art and handicrafts as have not found their way into collections abroad.

LOMÉ

KPONTON COLLECTION
15 rue Kwassi Bruce, Lomé
Historical and art collections, including historical photographs and memorabilia of the German colonial period.
By appointment in writing.

Trinidad and Tobago

This important source of oil and asphalt does not appear to have spent a great deal on its cultural amenities. The single museum, however, does contain a range of collections which covers most of the islands' activities and presents a somewhat conventional picture of the history of the area.

PORT-OF-SPAIN

NATIONAL MUSEUM AND ART GALLERY
117 Frederick Street, Port-of-Spain
History of Trinidad and Tobago. Natural science. Ethnography. Traditional crafts. Paintings, sculpture.
Tu.-Su. 10-1, 2-5.

Tunisia

The museums of Tunisia deal, if the word is permitted, in four cultures, Phoenician, Roman, Islamic and French, and the collections are consequently very rich and very varied. They range from souvenirs of the unpleasant religious rites of the Phoenicians, such as urns containing the bones of children sacrificed to Ba'al Hammon, to the sculpture and mosaics of the Romans and the antique fez-cupboards of the Moslems. There are several very good ethnographical collections, especially strong on fishing and handicrafts, an abundance of archaeology and a fine display of coins and banknotes in the former Mint. One will look in vain, however, for either a museum or section of a museum devoted to that cornerstone of the Tunisian economy for so many years, the date.

CARTHAGE

ANTIQUARIUM
Carthage
In a Roman villa of the late 2nd century. Roman and Phoenician glass, lamps, statues, terracotta, mosaics and stelae.
Apr.-Sept. Daily 9-12, 3-6.30. Oct.-Mar. Daily 9-12, 2-5.30.

BATHS OF ANTONIUS
Carthage
Area surrounding the Baths of Antonius. Sculpture, pottery and other material discovered on the site.
Apr.-Sept. Daily 9-12, 3-6.30. Oct.-Mar. Daily 9-12, 2-5.30.

NATIONAL MUSEUM OF CARTHAGE
Colline de Byrsa, Carthage
Phoenician, Roman and early Christian art and architecture.
Apr.-Sept. Daily ex. M. 9-12, 3-6.30. Oct.-Mar. Daily ex. M. 9-12, 2-5.30. Closed public holidays.

OCEANOGRAPHIC MUSEUM
Carthage
Stuffed fish and birds. Models of ancient and modern craft. Plaster models of seashore fauna.
Oct. 15- Mar., daily ex. M. 2-5. Apr.-June, 3-6. July- Oct. 14, 4-7; also Su. 9-11.

TOPHET OF SALAMBÔ
Carthage
Open-air museum containing the remains of the temple (tophet) dedicated to Tanit and to Ba'al Hammon.
Apr.-Sept. Daily 9-12, 3-6.30. Oct.-Mar. Daily 9-12, 2-5.30.

EL JEM (THYSDRUS)

EL-JEM MUSEUM
El Jem
Collections from the Roman town of Thysdrus. Mosaics. Statues and bronze objects of the Phoenician, Roman and early Christian periods.
Apr.-Sept. Daily ex. M. 9-12, 3-6.30. Oct.-Mar. Daily ex. M. 9-12, 2-5.30. Closed public holidays.

ENFIDAVILLE

ENFIDA MUSEUM
Enfidaville
In former church. Mosaics and inscriptions of the Christian period.
Apr.-Sept. Daily ex. M. 9-12, 3-6.30. Oct.-Mar. Daily ex. M. 9-12, 2-5.30. Closed public holidays.

JERBA

JERBA MUSEUM
Jerba
Costumes. Jewellery. Pottery. Potter's workshop. Furniture, including fez-cupboards. Reconstruction of kitchen, with utensils and equipment. Weaver's shop. Peasant hut. Fishing boat and equipment. Local superstitions.
Apr.-Sept. Daily ex. M. 9-12, 3-6.30. Oct.-Mar. Daily ex. M. 9-12, 2-5.30. Closed public holidays.

KAIROUAN

KAIROUAN MUSEUM
Kairouan
Material from the Moslem sites of Kairouan, Sabra, Mansowrya and Rakkada. Parchment manuscripts of the Koran. 9th century Moslem bindings. Pottery and glass. Islamic headstones.
Apr.-Sept. Daily ex. M. 9-12, 3-6.30. Oct.-Mar. Daily ex. M. 9-12, 2-5.30. Closed public holidays.

MACTAR

MACTAR MUSEUM
Mactar
Material from excavations at the adjoining Phoenician city of Mactaris. Stelae to Ba'al Hammon and Saturn. Marble and bronze sculptures.
Apr.-Sept. Daily ex. M. 9-12, 3-6.30. Oct.-Mar. Daily ex. M. 9-12, 2-5.30. Closed public holidays.

MAHDIA

MAHDIA MUSEUM
Mahdia
In house decorated in the Turkish style. Carved and painted woodwork. Costumes. Jewellery. Furniture.
Apr.-Sept. Daily ex. M. 9-12, 3-6.30. Oct.-Mar. Daily ex. M. 9-12, 2-5.30. Closed public holidays.

MATMATA

LOCAL MUSEUM
Matmata
Rugs. Silver goblets. Pictures of Mecca. Local history. Costumes.
Apr.-Sept., daily 9-12, 3-6.30. Oct.-Mar., daily 9-12, 2-5.30.

METLAOUI

CHOUMOVITCH MUSEUM
Metlaoui
Fossils. Stuffed birds. Pickled reptiles. Birds' eggs. Butterflies.
On request.

MOKNINE

MOKNINE MUSEUM
Moknine
In an old marabout (14th century). Agricultural implements. Irrigation equipment. Costumes, especially wedding costumes. Weaver's workshop. Jewellery. Material excavated at local Roman sites.
Apr.-Sept. Daily ex. M. 9-12, 3-6.30. Oct.-Mar. Daily ex. M. 9-12, 2-5.30. Closed public holidays.

MONASTIR

ALI BOURGUIBA MUSEUM
Ribat Fortress, Monastir
In coastal fortress (796). Islamic art. Manuscripts of the Koran. Jewellery. Glass. Miniatures. Pottery. Textiles.
Apr.-Sept. Daily ex. M. 9-12, 3-6.30. Oct.-Mar. Daily ex. M. 9-12, 2-5.30.

SALAMBO

MUSEUM AND AQUARIUM
Institut National Scientifique et Technique d'Océanographie, Salambo
Aquarium. Sea creatures preserved in formaline or perspex. Models of fishing gear. Tunisian birds.
Apr.-Sept. Daily ex. M. 3.30-6.30; Su. 10-12, 3.30-6.30. Oct.-Mar. Daily ex. M. 2-5; Su. 10-12, 2-5. Closed feasts of Aïd Seghir, Aïd Kébir and Mouled.

SFAX

MUSEUM OF ANTIQUITIES
Sfax
Material from excavations at Thenae, Skhira and Acholla. Roman mosaics, sculpture, lamps, glass and bronze objects. Moslem manuscripts and bindings. Stelae. Prehistoric artifacts.
Apr.-Sept. Daily ex. M. 9-12, 3-6.30. Oct.-Mar. Daily ex. M. 9-12, 2-5.30. Closed public holidays.

MUSEUM OF POPULAR ARTS AND TRADITIONS (JELLOULI MUSEUM)
5 rue Sidi Ali Nouri, Sfax
In house, Dar Jallouli, with painted wooden ceilings and sculpture. Faience. Costumes from the Sfax area. Jewellery. Painted woodwork, especially beds and chests.
Apr.-Sept. Daily ex. M. 9-12, 3-6.30. Oct.-Mar. Daily ex. M. 9-12, 2-5.30. Closed public holidays.

SOUSSE

ARCHAEOLOGICAL MUSEUM
Casbah, Sousse
Phoenician monuments from the Tophet of Hadrumète (7th-1st centuries B.C.). Stelae. Urns containing bones of children and lambs sacrificed to Tanit and Ba'al Hammon. Roman monuments. Mosaics. Lamps. Bas reliefs.
Apr.-Sept. Daily ex. M. 9-12, 3-6.30. Oct.-Mar. Daily ex. M. 9-12, 2-5.30. Closed public holidays.

TABARKA

REGIONAL MUSEUM
Tabarka
Housed in former church. Local history. Ethnography. Local coral-work.
Apr.-Sept., daily 9-12, 3-6.30. Oct.-Mar. daily 9-12, 2-5.30.

TUNIS

ARAB MUSEUM
Palace of Le Bardo, nr. Tunis
Adjoining Le Bardo National Museum. Copperware. Inlaid Damascus-work. Musical instruments. Weapons. Costumes.
Apr.-Sept., daily ex. M. 9-12, 3-6.30. Oct.-Mar. daily ex. M. 9-12, 2-5.30. Closed public holidays.

LE BARDO NATIONAL MUSEUM
(formerly Alaoui Museum), Palace of Le Bardo, nr. Tunis
Palace (1855-82), housing Phoenician, Roman, Christian and Moslem art and architecture. Greek marble and bronze statues from Mahdia. Tunisian prehistory. Mosaics. Treasure from sunken ship (c. 81 B.C.).
Apr.-Sept. Daily ex. M. 9-12, 3-6.30. Oct.-Mar. Daily ex. M. 9-12, 2-5.30. Closed public holidays.

MUSELMAN DE SIDI-BOU-KRISSAN LAPIDARY MUSEUM
12b rue B. Mahmoud, Tunis
Tombstone-inscriptions showing almost every style of Arabic calligraphy.
Apr.-Sept. Daily ex. M. 9-12, 3-6.30. Oct.-Apr. Daily ex. M. 9-12, 2-5.30. Other times by arrangement.

MUSEUM OF THE CONSERVATOIRE
16 avenue Mohamed V, Tunis
Collections illustrating musical history. Manuscripts. Memorabilia of composers, performers. Musical instruments.
Apr.-Sept., daily ex. M. 9-12, 3-6.30. Oct.-Mar., daily ex. M. 9-12, 2-5.30. Closed public holidays.

MUSEUM OF ISLAMIC ART
National Institute of Archaeology and Arts, Dar Hussein, Rue du Dey, Tunis
Arts and handicrafts from Tunisia and other Moslem countries, especially Egypt, Iraq, Persia and Turkey. Hafsite money. Papyri and parchments. Illuminated Korans. Arabic weapons, wooden implements, phials, bowls and toilet articles. Coptic cloth, silks and fragments of mosque pulpits (minbars). Islamic ceramics. Pottery.
Apr.-Sept., daily ex. M. 9-12, 2.30-6. Oct.-Mar., daily ex. M. 9-12, 2-5.30. Closed public holidays.

MUSEUM OF THE MINT
Rue de Rome, Tunis
History of money in Tunisia from Carthaginian times to 1968. Foreign notes. Old Tunisian gold and silver from Roman times onward.
Daily 10-12, 3-6. Closed public holidays.

MUSEUM OF MOSLEM ART
Ribat Fortress, Tunis
In coastal fortress (820). Pottery. Glass. Jewellery. Textiles. Miniatures. Manuscripts of the Koran.
Apr.-Sept. Daily ex. M. 9-12, 3-6.30. Oct.-Mar. Daily ex. M. 9-12, 2-5.30. Closed public holidays.

NATIONAL MUSEUM OF POSTS AND TELECOMMUNICATIONS
29b rue Es-Sadikia, Tunis
Tunisian postage stamps. Telephone equipment used in Tunisia. Old postal equipment. Photographs illustrating the history of the postal service in Tunisia.
Apr.-Sept. Daily ex. M. 9-12, 3-6.30. Oct.-Mar. Daily ex. M. 9-12, 2-5.30. Closed public holidays.

UTICA

UTICA MUSEUM
Utica
Roman and Phoenician antiquities. Mosaics. Sculptures. Pottery. Terracotta. Tomb furniture. Coins. Amphorae. Oil lamps.
Apr.-Sept. Daily ex. M. 9-12, 3-6.30. Oct.-Mar. Daily ex. M. 9-12, 2-5.30. Closed public holidays.

Turkey

A fair general comment on the museums of Turkey would be that they reflect the ancient world reasonably well and the modern world very inadequately. A number of the palaces of the old Ottoman Empire have been converted into museums, with considerable effect and a minimum of expense; the relics of the Greeks, Trojans and Romans are suitably looked after, with the interests of the expanding tourist industry particularly in mind; and some attempt has been made, notably in the Museum of Mosaics in Istanbul, to recreate the spirit and the details of daily life in ancient times. Despite the wholesale removal of classical and Byzantine material to the West during the nineteenth century, much still remains in Turkey and there are some good archaeological collections, often, as in the case of Bergama (the former Pergamon), on or close to the site where the items were discovered.

The traditional life of the rural areas is well documented in a few of the larger museums and Turkey's long maritime history also receives its fair share of attention. Collections covering nineteenth- and twentieth-century political history are to be found almost entirely in the major cities. Very few modern notabilities have been thought worthy of memorial collections. The museum limelight has been reserved for the founder of modern Turkey, Kemal Atatürk. His house in Istanbul has been preserved as it was when he lived in it and another place of pilgrimage for visitors to the capital is the building where he made his momentous speech announcing the abolition of the fez.

ADANA

ADANA MUSEUM
Adana, Seyhan Province
Archaeology. Neolithic, Chalcolithic, Hittite material from excavations at Yümüktepe and Gözlükule.
Tu.-Su. 9-12, 1.30-5.30.

AFYON

ARCHAEOLOGICAL MUSEUM
Afyon
Items found at excavations in Kütahya, Isparta, Burdur and Uşak, some dating back to the Bronze Age.
Tu.-Su. 9-12, 1.30-5.30.

AHLAT

ARCHAEOLOGICAL MUSEUM
Ahlat
Finds from excavations in the area. Local history.
Tu.-Su. 9-12, 1.30-5.30.

AKŞEHIR

ARCHAEOLOGICAL MUSEUM
Akşehir
Finds from excavations in the area. Material relating to Nasreddin Hoca, one of the first great names in Turkish literature (14th century), born at Akşehir.
Tu.-Su. 9-12, 1.30-5.30.

ALACAHÖYÜK

ARCHAEOLOGICAL MUSEUM
Alacahöyük
Finds from excavations in the area, including objects from the third millenium B.C., Hittite bas-reliefs, and Roman and Byzantine tombstones.
Tu.-Su. 9-12, 1.30-5.30.

ALANYA

ARCHAEOLOGICAL MUSEUM
Alanya
Finds from excavations in the area. Local history.
Tu.-Su. 9-12, 1.30-5.30.

AMASRA

ARCHAEOLOGICAL MUSEUM
Amasra
Finds from local excavations. Statues. Architectural fragments.
Tu.-Su. 9-12, 1.30-5.30.

AMASYA

ARCHAEOLOGICAL MUSEUM
Amasya
Material from excavations in the area. Local history.
Tu.-Su. 9-12, 1.30-5.30.

ANKARA

ANIT KABIR MUSEUM
Atatürk Mausoleum, Ankara
Mementoes of the War of Independence and Atatürk, including his personal possessions.
Tu.-Su. 9-12, 1.30-5.30.

ARCHAEOLOGICAL MUSEUM
Outer rampart of Citadel, Ankara
Material from the Palaeolithic, Neolithic, Chalcolithic, Early Bronze Age, Hittite, Phrygian and Urartian periods. Hittite reliefs from Alaca, Carchemish, Sakcagözü and Aslantepe. Objects from excavations throughout Turkey. Cuneiform tablets. Coins.
Tu.-Su. 9-12, 1.30-5.30.

ETHNOGRAPHICAL MUSEUM
Talat Paşa Boulevard, Ankara
Turkish and Islamic art. Islamic numismatics. Musical instruments. Weapons. Tools. Household objects. Costumes. Carpets. Tiles. Religious objects.
Tu.-Su. 9-12, 1.30-5.30.

MUSEUM OF THE NATIONAL ASSEMBLY
Cumhuriyet Boulevard, Ankara
Turkish history, in building used for the first meetings of the Turkish Parliament.
Tu.-Su. 9-12, 1.30-5.30.

ANTALYA

ARCHAEOLOGICAL MUSEUM
Yivli Minare Cami, Antalya
Mosaics from Xanthos, depicting the infant Achilles being dangled by one heel as his mother dips him into the River Styx. Greek ceramics. Figurines, including one of Apollo dating from 3rd century B.C. Sarcophagi.
Tu.-Su. 9-12, 1.30-5.30.

AYDIN

ARCHAEOLOGICAL MUSEUM
Aydin
Material from excavations in the area. Local history.
Tu.-Su. 9-12, 1.30-5.30.

BERGAMA

ETHNOGRAPHICAL MUSEUM
Bergama
Ethnography. Domestic equipment. Costumes. Models.
Tu.-Su. 9-12, 1.30-5.30.

PERGAMON MUSEUM
Bergama
Historical relics from excavations at Pergamon, the modern Bergama. Statues, bas-reliefs, mosaics.
Tu.-Su. 9-12, 1.30-5.30.

BODRUM

ARCHAEOLOGICAL MUSEUM
Bodrum
Statues and amphora recovered from the sea. History of the city (formerly Halicarnassus).
Tu.-Su. 9-12, 1.30-5.30.

BURDUR

ARCHAEOLOGICAL MUSEUM
Burdur
Objects from excavations in the area including, notably, items from the earliest Neolithic age. Some exhibits from the nine levels unearthed at Hacilar, 15 m. south-west of Burdur.
Tu.-Su. 9-12, 1.30-5.30.

BURSA

ARCHAEOLOGICAL MUSEUM
Bursa
In former theological school. Bythinian, Hellenistic and Roman finds. Hand-written copies of the Koran.
Tu.-Su. 9-12, 1.30-5.30.

ÇANAKKALE

ARCHAEOLOGICAL MUSEUM
Çanakkale
Material from excavations in the area. Trojan exhibits.
Tu.-Su. 9-12, 1.30-5.30.

ÇEŞME

ARCHAEOLOGICAL MUSEUM
Çeşme
Finds from excavations in the area.
Tu.-Su. 9-12, 1.30-5.30.

ÇORUM

BOĞAZKÖY MUSEUM
Çorum
Finds from excavations in the area, especially from the Ottoman period.
Tu.-Su. 9-12, 1.30-5.30.

DENIZLI

ARCHAEOLOGICAL MUSEUM
Denizli
Finds from excavations in the area.
Tu.-Su. 9-12, 1.30-5.30.

DIYARBAKIR

ARCHAEOLOGICAL MUSEUM
Zincirli, Diyarbakir
Finds from local excavations, covering a period of some 4,000 years.
Tu.-Su. 9-12, 1.30-5.30.

EDIRNE

ETHNOGRAPHICAL MUSEUM
Medrese (school), Edirne
Ethnography of the area. Domestic utensils. Costumes. Local history.
Tu.-Su. 9-12, 1.30-5.30.

EFES

ARCHAEOLOGICAL MUSEUM
Efes
Finds from excavations in the area. Local history.
Tu.-Su. 9-12, 1.30-5.30.

ELÂZIĞ

ARCHAEOLOGICAL MUSEUM
Elâziğ
Finds from excavations in the area.
Tu.-Su. 9-12, 1.30-5.30.

ERDEMLI

ARCHAEOLOGICAL MUSEUM
Erdemli
Finds from excavations in the area.
Tu.-Su. 9-12, 1.30-5.30.

EREGLI

ARCHAEOLOGICAL MUSEUM
Eregli
Finds from excavations in the area.
Tu.-Su. 9-12, 1.30-5.30.

ERZURUM

ARCHAEOLOGICAL MUSEUM
Koranic College, Erzurum
Finds from excavations in the area. Local history.
Tu.-Su. 9-12, 1.30-5.30.

ESKIŞEHIR

ARCHAEOLOGICAL MUSEUM
Eskişehir
Finds from excavations in the area. Local history.
Tu.-Su. 9-12, 1.30-5.30.

FETHIYE

ARCHAEOLOGICAL MUSEUM
Fethiye
Finds from excavations in the area.
Tu.-Su. 9-12, 1.30-5.30.

GAZIANTEP

ARCHAEOLOGICAL MUSEUM
Seljuk Medrese (school), Gaziantep
Objects from the sites of Zincirli, Sakçagözü and Kargamis. Collection of Hittite seals.
Tu.-Su. 9-12, 1.30-5.30.

GÖREME

ARCHAEOLOGICAL MUSEUM
Göreme
Finds from excavations in the area, particularly from rock churches and grottos. Frescoes.
Tu.-Su. 9-12, 1.30-5.30.

HACIBEKTAŞ

ARCHAEOLOGICAL MUSEUM
Hacibektaş
Finds from excavations in the area. Material relating to the religious sect founded here by Haci Baktaş Veli in early 16th century.
Tu.-Su. 9-12, 1.30-5.30.

HATAY

HATAY MUSEUM
Gündüz Cad. No. 1, Antakya, Hatay
Mosaics from Roman Antioch. Finds from Al-Mina, Atchana, Catal Hüyük, Judeidah and Tainat excavations.
Tu.-Su. 9-12, 1.30-5.30.

ISTANBUL

ARCHAEOLOGICAL MUSEUM OF ISTANBUL
Sultanahmet, Istanbul
Archaeological material. Sumerian, Akkadian, Hittite, Assyrian, Egyptian, Urartu, Greek, Roman and Byzantine works of art. Coins.
Tu.-Su. 9-12, 1.30-5.30.

ATATÜRK MUSEUM
Halâskârgazi Caddesi, Istanbul
Kemal Atatürk's house, unchanged, with memorabilia and documents dating from the birth of the Turkish Republic.
Daily ex. M. 10-12, 2-5.

CHURCH OF THE HOLY SAVIOUR IN CHORA
Kariye Mosque, Edirne Gate, Istanbul
Byzantine era. Mosaics and frescoes.
Daily ex. Tu. 9.30-5.

DOLMABAHÇE SARAYI
Istanbul
19th century imperial residence. 19th-20th century paintings.
Daily ex. M. and Tu., 9-11, 1.30-4.

MARITIME MUSEUM
Barbaros parki yani Besiktas, Istanbul
Maritime history since ancient times. Ships' models. Instruments. Charts. Dioramas.
Tu.-Su. 9-12, 1.30-5.30.

MUNICIPAL MUSEUM
Sarachanebasi Fatih, Bayezit Square, Istanbul
History of Istanbul, especially during the 19th century. Costumes.
Tu.-Su. 9-12, 1.30-5.30.

MUSEUM OF THE FORTRESS OF RUMELI
Rumeli Hisari, Bogazici, Istanbul
Three fortresses (15th century). Weapons. Guns.
Tu.-Su. 9-12, 1.30-5.30.

MUSEUM OF THE JANISSARIES
Harbiye, Istanbul
Military uniforms, weapons and trophies, dating from early times.
Tu.-Su. 9-12, 1.30-5.30.

MUSEUM OF MOSAICS
Palace of Constantine, Istanbul
In 4th century palace. Mosaic pictures, architectural designs, illustrating daily life in ancient times.
Tu.-Su. 9-12, 1.30-5.30.

MUSEUM OF ORIENTAL ANTIQUITIES
Gülhane Park, Istanbul
Mesopotamian, Anatolian and Egyptian antiquities.
Tu.-Su. 9-12, 1.30-5.30.

MUSEUM OF PAINTING AND SCULPTURE
Dolmabahçe Cad., Istanbul
19th century works in traditional European style. Paintings by contemporary European artists. 19th-20th century works by Turkish artists.
Tu.-Su. 9-12, 1.30-5.30.

MUSEUM OF TURKISH AND ISLAMIC ART
Süleymaniye, Istanbul
Turkish and Islamic rugs, illuminated manuscripts, sculpture in stone and stucco. Woodcarvings. Metalwork. Ceramics. Miniatures. Turkish manuscripts. Prayer mats.
Tu.-Su. 9-12, 1.30-5.30.

SAINT SOPHIA MUSEUM
Ayasofya Meydani Cad. No. 3, Sultan Ahmet, Istanbul
Housed in Byzantine basilica (537 A.D.). Byzantine and Turkish antiquities.
Tu.-Su. 9-12, 1.30-5.30.

TANZIMAT MUSEUM
Cadir Köskü Besiktas, Istanbul
Paintings and inscriptions of the Tanzimat period (19th century).
Tu.-Su. 9-12, 1.30-5.30.

TOPKAPI PALACE MUSEUM
Istanbul
Palace built by Muhammad II. Turkish armour, cloth, embroidery, tiles, glass and porcelain, copper- and silverware, treasure, paintings, miniatures, illuminated manuscripts. Royal coaches. Sèvres and Bohemian crystal and porcelain. Clocks. Chinese and Japanese porcelain amassed by the Sultans. Islamic relics. Seals of the Sultans. Manuscripts. Ottoman tent. Restored building of the harem.
Daily ex. Tu. 9-12, 1.30-5.30.

IZMIR

ARCHAEOLOGICAL MUSEUM
Kulturpark, Izmir
Classical and prehistoric exhibits from the Aegean coast, including a bronze statue of Demeter, fished from the sea at Bodrum.
Tu.-Su. 9-12, 1.30-5.30.

IZMIT

ARCHAEOLOGICAL MUSEUM
Izmit
Finds from excavations in the area. Local history.
Tu.-Su. 9-12, 1.30-5.30.

IZNIK

ARCHAEOLOGICAL MUSEUM
Iznik
Finds from excavations in the area. Roman, Ottoman and Turkish material.
Tu.-Su. 9-12, 1.30-5.30.

KARAIN

ARCHAEOLOGICAL MUSEUM
Karain
Finds from local excavations. Local history.
Tu.-Su. 9-12, 1.30-5.30.

KARAKASU

APHRODISIAS ARCHAEOLOGICAL MUSEUM
Karakasu
Site of the Greco-Roman settlement of Aphrodisias. Statues. Carved stones. Capitals. Bas-reliefs. Sarcophagi.
Tu.-Su. 9-12, 1.30-5.30.

KARAMAN

ARCHAEOLOGICAL MUSEUM
Karaman
Finds from excavations in the area.
Tu.-Su. 9-12, 1.30-5.30.

KARATEPE

ARCHAEOLOGICAL MUSEUM
Karatepe
Finds from excavations in the area. Bilingual inscriptions, in both Phoenician and Hittite.
Tu.-Su. 9-12, 1.30-5.30.

KARS

ARCHAEOLOGICAL MUSEUM
Kars
Finds from excavations in the area. Local history.
Tu.-Su. 9-12, 1.30-5.30.

KASTAMONU

ARCHAEOLOGICAL MUSEUM
Kastamonu
In building where Atatürk announced, in 1926, the abolition of the fez. Finds from local excavations. Local history.
Tu.-Su. 9-12, 1.30-5.30.

KAYSERI

ARCHAEOLOGICAL MUSEUM
Kayseri
Finds from excavations in the area. Local history.
Tu.-Su. 9-12, 1.30-5.30.

KONYA

ATATÜRK MUSEUM
Konya
Documents and objects connected with Atatürk, Typical Konya clothing. Ethnography.
Tu.-Su. 9-12, 1.30-5.30.

CLASSICAL MUSEUM
Konya
Neolithic, Hittite, Phrygian, Greek, Roman and Byzantine monuments.
Tu.-Su. 9-12, 1.30-5.30.

MEVLÂNA MUSEUM
Konya
Seljuk, Ottoman and Turkish collections. Clothing. Carpets. Weapons. Coins. Oil lamps. Manuscripts.
Tu.-Su. 9-12, 1.30-5.30.

SELJUK MUSEUM
Ince Minareli Medresse, Konya
Stone and wooden artifacts of the Seljuk period. Art.
Tu.-Su. 9-12, 1.30-5.30.

SIRCALI MEDRESSEH MUSEUM
Konya
Sarcophagus and inscriptions. Collections of the Seljuk and Ottoman periods.
Tu.-Su. 9-12, 1.30-5.30.

TURKISH CERAMICS MUSEUM
Karatay Medresse, Konya
Ceramics of 13th - 18th centuries.
Tu.-Su. 9-12, 1.30-5.30.

KÜLTEPE

ARCHAEOLOGICAL MUSEUM
Kültepe
Finds from excavations in the area. Bronze Age material. Tablets. Seals. Ceramics. Idols. Other material from the area is in the Kayseri Regional Museum and the Ankara Archaeology Museum.
Tu.-Su. 9-12, 1.30-5.30.

KÜTAHYA

ARCHAEOLOGICAL MUSEUM
Kütahya
Finds from local excavations. History of the local tile-making industry.
Tu.-Su. 9-12, 1.30-5.30.

LETOON

ARCHAEOLOGICAL MUSEUM
Letoon
Finds from local excavations.
Tu.-Su. 9-12, 1.30-5.30.

MALATYA

ARCHAEOLOGICAL MUSEUM
Malatya
Objects from excavations at Arslantepe, including bas-reliefs and material from ancient Hittite settlements.
Tu.-Su. 9-12, 1.30-5.30.

MANISA

ARCHAEOLOGICAL MUSEUM
Manisa
Finds from excavations in the area. Local history.
Tu.-Su. 9-12, 1.30-5.30.

MARAS

ARCHAEOLOGICAL MUSEUM
Maras
Material from local excavations. Hittite treasures. Maras claims to have the densest concentration of mosques in Turkey per square mile.
Tu.-Su. 9-12, 1.30-5.30.

MARDIN

ARCHAEOLOGICAL MUSEUM
Mardin
Finds from local excavations.
Tu.-Su. 9-12, 1.30-5.30.

MERSIN

ARCHAEOLOGICAL MUSEUM
Mersin
Material from the Stone Age, Bronze Age and the Hittite area. Pottery.
Tu.-Su. 9-12, 1.30-5.30.

MILET

ARCHAEOLOGICAL MUSEUM
Milet
Finds from excavations in the area. Local history.
Tu.-Su. 9-12, 1.30-5.30.

MUDANYA

ARCHAEOLOGICAL MUSEUM
Mudanya
Finds from excavations in the area.
Tu.-Su. 9-12, 1.30-5.30.

NEVŞEHIR

ARCHAEOLOGICAL MUSEUM
Nevşehir
Finds from excavations in the area. Local history.
Tu.-Su. 9-12, 1.30-5.30.

NIĞDE

ARCHAEOLOGICAL MUSEUM
Niğde
Housed in white medrese (Akmedrese, 1409). Regional history. Material from local excavations.
Tu.-Su. 9-12, 1.30-5.30.

PERGAMUM

ARCHAEOLOGICAL MUSEUM
Pergamum
Works of art found in the ruins of Pergamum, including sculptures of the Hellenistic period, Roman statues and bronzes, and figurines in Myrina earthenware.
Tu.-Su. 9-12, 1.30-5.30.

ETHNOGRAPHY MUSEUM
Pergamum
Ethnography of the area. Costumes. Local customs and traditions. Trades.
Tu.-Su. 9-12, 1.30-5.30.

POLATLI

ALAGÖZ MUSEUM
Polatli
Finds from excavations in the area. Local history.
Tu.-Su. 9-12, 1.30-5.30.

SAMSUN

REGIONAL MUSEUM
Samsun
Hotel in which Mustafa Kemal stayed after the Turkish Republic was founded in Samsun, 19th May 1919 Archaeological finds from the area, notably from Duhdar. Ethnography.
Tu.-Su. 9-12, 1.30-5.30.

SIDE

ARCHAEOLOGICAL MUSEUM
Side
In old Roman Baths. Statues. Sarcophagi. Capitals. Bas reliefs.
Tu.-Su. 9-12, 1.30-5.30.

SILIFKE

ARCHAEOLOGICAL MUSEUM
Silifke
Archaeological finds from the area, including Roman and Byzantine material.
Tu.-Su. 9-12, 1.30-5.30.

SINOP

ARCHAEOLOGICAL MUSEUM
Alaiye Medrese, Sinop
Building (1262). Local history. Material from excavations in the area.
Tu.-Su. 9-12, 1.30-5.30.

SIVAS

INKILÂP MUSEUM
Meeting Hall, Sivas
Revolutionary material, in the place where Atatürk stayed when the congress was convened by him in 1919 which decided the liberation of Turkey, then still partly occupied. Memorabilia of Atatürk.
Tu.-Su. 9-12, 1.30-5.30.

TARSUS

ARCHAEOLOGICAL MUSEUM
Tarsus
Birthplace of St. Paul. Finds from excavations in the area.
Tu.-Su. 9-12, 1.30-5.30.

TEKIRDAĞ

ARCHAEOLOGICAL MUSEUM
Tekirdağ
Finds from the ancient town of Rhodestos. Local history.
Tu.-Su. 9-12, 1.30-5.30.

TIRE

REGIONAL MUSEUM
Tire
Housed in mosque of Yahşi Bey. Regional history. Material from excavations in the area. Costumes.
Tu.-Su. 9-12, 1.30-5.30.

TOKAT

ARCHAEOLOGICAL MUSEUM
Gök Medrese, Tokat
Material from local excavations. Tiles. Byzantine frescoes, and geometrical designs.
Tu.-Su. 9-12, 1.30-5.30.

TRABZON

ARCHAEOLOGICAL MUSEUM
Church of St. Sophia, Trabzon
Formerly Trapezos and Trebizond. Finds from local excavations, including magnificent frescoes.
Tu.-Su. 9-12, 1.30-5.30.

TRUVA

ARCHAEOLOGICAL MUSEUM
Truva
Site of the ancient city of Troy. Greek pottery of the classical period. Finds from excavations.
Tu.-Su. 9-12, 1.30-5.30.

URFA

ARCHAEOLOGICAL MUSEUM
Urfa
Finds from excavations in the area. Local history.
Tu.-Su. 9-12, 1.30-5.30.

ÜRGÜP

ARCHAEOLOGICAL MUSEUM
Ürgüp
Finds from the excavations in the area, including frescoes.
Tu.-Su. 9-12, 1.30-5.30.

UŞAK

ARCHAEOLOGICAL MUSEUM
Uşak
Material from excavations in the area. Material relating to the War of Independence.
Tu.-Su. 9-12, 1.30-5.30.

VAN

ARCHAEOLOGICAL MUSEUM
Van
Finds from local excavations, including material from the Toprakkale mound, where remains of a Urartean city have been found.
Tu.-Su. 9-12, 1.30-5.30.

YALVAC

ARCHAEOLOGICAL MUSEUM
Yalvac
Finds from local excavations. Local history.
Tu.-Su. 9-12, 1.30-5.30.

YASSIHÜYÜK

GORDION MUSEUM
Yassihüyük
Finds from excavations in the area and the former town of Gordion, the source of the expression 'severing the Gordian knot'.
Tu.-Su. 9-12, 1.30-5.30.

Uganda

Uganda has a number of well-organised museums. Their subject-matter ranges from the Uganda Rifles to elephants and they combine, perhaps more effectively than any other recently-independent African country, the two tasks of illustrating the country's traditional culture and of providing the kind of collections needed by a country attempting to develop and modernise itself on modern lines. The National Museum, with its collections of Ugandan ethnography, art, musical instruments, technology and industry, is the focal point of this all-front attempt to show the nation to itself. There are good agricultural and forestry collections, two National Park Museums and a medical museum which is open to the public, "if they can stomach the look of the specimens".

ENTEBBE

GEOLOGICAL MUSEUM
above Entebbe Pier, P.O. Box 9, Entebbe
Rocks and minerals of Uganda.
Daily 10-1, 2-6.

JINJA

THE UGANDA RIFLES MUSEUM
Jinja
History of the Uganda Rifles. Weapons. Uniforms. Flags. Documents.
On request.

KAMPALA

ART MUSEUM
School of Art, Makerere Hill, Kampala
African sculpture.
On request.

FOREST DEPARTMENT UTILISATION DIVISION AND MUSEUM
P.O. Box 1752, Kampala
Uganda timbers. Entomology. Preservation, seasoning and woodworking tests. Logging and milling research.
By appointment.

KAWANDA AGRICULTURAL RESEARCH STATION
Herbarium and Insect Collection, P.O. Box 265, Kampala
Herbarium. Insects.
By appointment.

MEDICAL SCHOOL MUSEUM
P.O. Box 7072, Kampala
Pathological and surgical specimens, combined with displays of some specific diseases (Burkitt's Lymphoma, Rheumatic Heart Disease, Endomyo-cardial Fibrosis, Buruli and Tropical Ulcers, Malignant Melanoma).
Open to the public "if they can stomach the look of the specimens and wax models". M.-F. 8-12.30, 2-5; Sa. 8-12. Closed Su. and public holidays.

NOMMO GALLERY
52 Kampala Road, P.O. Box 16132, Kampala
National collection of Ugandan art.
Daily 10-12.30, 2-5; Su. 11-1, 3-6.

UGANDA MUSEUM
Kira Road, P.O. Box 365, Kampala
Ethnography. Ethnomusicology. Natural history. Science and industry. African musical instruments. Archaeology.
Daily 10-1, 2-6; Su. 3-7.

ZOOLOGICAL MUSEUM
Makerere University College, P.O. Box 262, Kampala
Zoological collections, including animals of Uganda; fossils; birds; butterflies; the African elephant; insects; coral and sponges; evolution of fish; reptiles and amphibia; termites and fungi; evolutionary history of skulls; shells.
Daily ex. Su. 8-12.30, 2-4; Sa. 8-12.30.

MBARARA

FOLK MUSEUM
Mbarara
Ethnographical material relating to the Banyankole peoples.
Daily 10-1, 2-6.

MWEYA

QUEEN ELIZABETH NATIONAL PARK MUSEUM
Queen Elizabeth National Park, Mweya
Fauna, birds, animals, snakes and mammals which are found in the park.
Daily 7.30-6.30.

PARAA

MURCHISON FALLS NATIONAL PARK MUSEUM
Murchison Falls National Park, Paraa
Park fauna; bird collection of the park; animals, snakes and mammals.
Daily 7.30-6.30.

SOROTI

ITESO MUSEUM
P.O. Box 63, Soroti
Ethnographical material relating to the Iteso people.
Daily 10-1, 2-6.

U.S.S.R.

Before the Revolution, what is now the U.S.S.R. had very few museums which were regularly open to the general public.

There were great collections of paintings and other works of art in the palaces and mansions of the royal family and the aristocracy, but these were to be found almost entirely in the western part of the country, especially in the Moscow and Leningrad areas. What might be described as public art was to be seen largely in churches, many of which, as in Vladimir, are now designated as museums.

With the overthrow of Tsarism, the situation completely changed. All private collections became the property of the state, and during the early 1920s a far-reaching programme was worked out to integrate museums into the educational system. The essential features of the new policy, which has since become deeply embedded in Soviet policy and organisation, may be summarised as follows: (*a*) Museums were to have a basically "cultural", that is, didactic purpose. Collections were to be presented in such a way as to make them meaningful to the average citizen and to show their significance within the general context of scientific and historical development. They were, and still are, to be visited in a spirit of serious inquiry. (*b*) All parts of the Soviet Union were to be provided with an adequate museum service. Central Asia and Siberia were no less deserving than Moscow or the Ukraine. (*c*) The collections belonging to the various scientific institutes would, of course, be assembled and arranged primarily for the purposes of teaching and research. Wherever possible, however, they should be made accessible to the general public as well. (*d*) All provincial museums should be entitled to the expert advice and help of the great central museums and research institutions. It would be unrealistic to suppose the programme has as yet been carried out in its entirity throughout the Soviet Union. The citizens of Vladivostok do not, even now enjoy facilities as good as those which are available in Moscow. They are, however, vastly better served now than they were fifty years ago.

Soviet museums suffered great damage and heavy losses during the 1939-45 war, especially in the territories south and west of Moscow. The destruction and pillage was probably equalled only in Western Poland. After the war, a high priority was given to rebuilding, restoring and restocking museums and the situation, both in quantity and quality, is now better than it was in 1939. In view of these achievements, it is remarkable that, alone among the Eastern European countries, the Soviet Union has still not published a comprehensive catalogue of its museums and their collections.

ABOVYAN

TCHAVTCHAVADZÉ HOUSE-MUSEUM
Abovyan, Armenian S.S.R.
Collections illustrating life and work of the Armenian writer, Tchavtchavadzé.
On request.

ABRAMTSEVO

AKSAKOV HOUSE-MUSEUM
Abramtsevo, R.S.F.S.R.
Collections illustrating life and work of the writer, Aksakov.
On request.

ALMA-ATA

CENTRAL STATE MUSEUM OF THE KAZAKH SSR
Park imeni 28, Panfilovtsev, Alma-Ata, Kazakh S.S.R.
Geology, geography, climate, vegetation, wildlife, history of Kazakhstan.
Tu.-Su. 9-5.

T. G. SHEVCHENKO ART GALLERY
Ul. Sovietskaya 22, Alma-Ata, Kazakh S.S.R.
19th-20th century Kazakh, Soviet and foreign paintings, sculpture, graphics.
Tu.-Su. 9-5.

ALTAI

NATIONAL PARK MUSEUM
Altai, Siberia
Park Museum, illustrating geology, animals, birds, plants of the region.
May-Sept., daily 9-6.

ALTAN-BULAG

D. SUHE-BATOR HOUSE MUSEUM
Altan-Bulag, Mongolian People's Republic
Collections illustrating life and revolutionary activities of Suhe-Bator, in his former home.
Daily 10-4.

ALUPKA

PALACE MUSEUM
Alupka, Ukrainian S.S.R.
Paintings. Furniture. Sculpture.
Tu.-Su. 10-5.

ALUSHTA

C. N. SERGEEV-TSENSKY HOUSE-MUSEUM
Ul. Sergeeva-Tsenkogo 15, Alushta, Ukrainian S.S.R.
Collections illustrating life and work of the novelist, in his former home.
On request.

ARBYOMOVSK

GEOLOGICAL MUSEUM
Lenin ul. and Profinterna ul., Arbyomovsk
Regional geological, mineralogical collections.
Tu.-Su. 10-5.

ARCHANGEL

MANOR-HOUSE MUSEUM
Archangel, R.S.F.S.R.
Open-air museum in grounds of former country house. Rural buildings from the region, brought to museum site. In house: furniture, decorative arts, paintings.
May-Sept., daily 9-6.

ARMAVIR

LOCAL MUSEUM
Lenin ul. 92, Armavir, Armenian S.S.R.
Archaeological material illustrating history of former capital of Armenia. Folk art. Industrial and agricultural development of the area.
Su.-M. 10-5.

ASHAGA-STAL

SULEIMAN STAL HOUSE-MUSEUM
Ashaga-Stal, Daghestan S.S.R.
Home of Suleiman Stal, former Moslem ruler of the area. Furnishings. Memorabilia of Suleiman.
On request.

ASHDAM

REGIONAL MUSEUM
Ashdam
Regional history, archaeology, folklore.
Tu.-Su. 9-5.

ASHKHABAD

REGIONAL MUSEUM
Ul. Engelsa 20, Ashkhabad, Turkmenian S.S.R.
Collections illustrating history and traditions of the region. Handicrafts. Musical instruments. Furniture. Paintings. Household equipment. Agriculture.
Daily 9-4.

STATE FINE ART MUSEUM OF THE REPUBLIC OF TURKMENISTAN
Pr. Svobody 84, Ashkhabad, Turkmenian S.S.R.
Paintings, sculpture, drawings by Soviet and W. European artists. Turkmenian carpets.
Daily 9-4.

ASKANIA-NOVA

NATURAL HISTORY MUSEUM
Askania-Nova, Ukrainian S.S.R.
Regional geology, wildlife, botany.
Daily 8-4.

ASTRAKHAN

MUSEUM OF THE NATIONAL PARK OF ASTRAKHAN
Astrakhan, R.S.F.S.R.
Geology, botany and wildlife of the Volga delta, in which the National Park is situated.
May-Sept., daily 8-5.

BAKHCHISARAI

MUSEUM OF HISTORY AND ARCHAEOLOGY
Krymskaya Oblast, Bakhchisarai, Crimea
Regional archaeology and history, including material from cave dwellings. Paintings.
Daily 10-5.

BAKU

ARCHITECTURAL MUSEUM
Baku, Azerbaijan S.S.R.
In former palace of the kings of Shirvai. Photographs, paintings, models illustrating the architecture of Azerbaidjan. Decorative arts.
Tu.-Su. 10-5.

V. I. LENIN MUSEUM
Baku, Azerbaijan S.S.R.
Collections illustrating life and work of Lenin.
Tu.-Su. 9-5.

MUSEUM OF ETHNOGRAPHY
Baku, Azerbaijan S.S.R.
Collections illustrating the traditional life of Azerbaijan region. Furniture. Household equipment. Folk art. Costumes. Tools. Handicrafts.
Tu.-Su. 10-5.

MUSEUM OF THE HISTORY OF AZERBAIJAN
Ulitsa Malygina 4, Baku, Azerbaijan S.S.R.
History of the Azerbaijan peoples. Archaeology. Costumes. Handicrafts.
Tu.-Su. 10-5.

MUSEUM OF THE PETROLEUM INDUSTRY AND OF INDUSTRIAL SAFETY
Baku, Azerbaijan S.S.R.
Collections illustrating history and technical development of the Baku petroleum industry. Models. Photographs. Paintings. Drawings. Display showing methods of ensuring safety at work.
Tu.-Su. 9-5.

R. MUSTAFAEV STATE ART MUSEUM
Ul. Chkalova 9, Baku, Azerbaijan S.S.R.
Paintings, sculpture, applied art by Azerbaijan and Soviet artists.
Tu.-Su. 10-5.

NATIONAL MUSEUM OF THE DZABARLY THEATRE
Ul. Miasnikov 4, Baku, Azerbaijan S.S.R.
Collections illustrating the history of the theatre in Azerbaijan. Paintings. Photographs. Programmes. Stage and costume designs.
Daily 2-8.

STATE MUSEUM OF AZERBAIJAN LITERATURE
Ul. Kommunistcheskaya 33, Baku, Azerbaijan S.S.R.
Manuscripts and early editions of works by Azerbaijan writers. Portraits, memorabilia and personal possessions of writers.
Tu.-Su. 9-5.

BARAGKHAN

VILLAGE MUSEUM
Baragkhan
Open-air museum. Houses, farm-buildings, brought to museum site. Furniture. Household equipment. Tools and implements.
Apr.-Oct., daily 9-5.

BAROVICHI

LOCAL MUSEUM
Barovichi
Local history. Industrial and agricultural development. Handicrafts. Paintings.
M.-Su. 10-5.

BATUM

MUSEUM OF THE REVOLUTION
Batum, Georgian S.S.R.
History of the pre-revolutionary workers' movement and of the part played by Batum in the establishment of socialism in the USSR.
Daily 10-5.

STATE MUSEUM OF THE REVOLUTION
Batum, Georgian S.S.R.
History of the workers' and revolutionary movements in Georgia, especially in Batum.
W.-Su. 9-5.

BELAYA TSERKOV

LOCAL MUSEUM
Zamkowskaya ul. 15, Belaya Tserkov, Ukrainian S.S.R.
Natural history. Local history. Relics of Ukrainian-Polish battles (1648-54).
Th.-Tu. 10-6.

BELGOROD

LOCAL MUSEUM
Frunze ul. 42, Belgorod, R.S.F.S.R.
History and industrial development of Belgorod.
W.-Su. 10-6.

BELINSKIY

V. G. BELINSKIY MUSEUM
Ul. Belinskogo 11, Belinskiy
Collections illustrating life and work of the writer and revolutionary, V. G. Belinskiy (d.1848).
Daily 9-6.

V. G. LERMONTOV MUSEUM
Belinskiy
Collections commemorating the work of Lermontov, in the town where he was born and lived.
On request.

BENDERY

LOCAL MUSEUM
Dzerzhinsky ul., Bendery, Moldavian S.S.R.
Social, political and industrial history of the city and its region, with particular reference to its textile industry.
Tu.-Su. 10-5.

BERDICHEV

LOCAL MUSEUM
Komsomolskaya ul. 23, Berdichev, Ukrainian S.S.R.
Local history. Paintings. Folk art. Handicrafts.
Daily 9-4.

BIRZAI

LOCAL MUSEUM
Birzai, Lithuanian S.S.R.
History of the Birzai area. Paintings. Religious art. Agriculture. Costumes.
W.-M. 10-5.

BOKHARA

HISTORICAL AND ETHNOGRAPHICAL MUSEUM OF BOKHARA
Bokhara, Uzbekistan S.S.R.
Collections illustrating life and history of the Bokhara region. Textiles. Gold and silversmiths' work. Furniture. Costumes.
Daily 10-5.

BORISOV

MUSEUM OF HISTORY AND ETHNOGRAPHY
Borisov, Byelorussian S.S.R.
History of the district, including exhibits illustrating defeat of Napoleon (1812). Local customs, occupations, handicrafts.
Tu.-Su. 10-6.

BREST-LITOVSK

LOCAL MUSEUM
Ul. Lenina 34, Brest-Litovsk, Byelorussian S.S.R.
Political and social history of the city and its region. Life during the 1940-45 war. Reconstruction of the city.
W.-M. 10-5.

FORTRESS DEFENCE MUSEUM
Ul. Geroyev Brestkoy Kreposti, Brest-Litovsk, Byelorussian S.S.R.
Fortress (1836-42). Collections illustrating history of Brest, and the Fortress, and the battles of the 1940-45 war.
Tu.-Su. 10-5.

REGIONAL MUSEUM
Ul. Lenina 34, Brest-Litovsk, Byelorussian S.S.R.
History of the region. Workers' and revolutionary movements. Military history, especially 1940-45.
W.-Su. 11-5.

REGIONAL MUSEUM OF FOLK ART
Komsomolskaya ul. 1, Brest-Litovsk, Byelorussian S.S.R.
Traditional handicrafts of the region. Costumes. Paintings. Religious art.
Tu.-Su. 9-5.

BYELOVEZHSKAYA PUSCHA

BYELOVEZHSKAYA PUSCHA MUSEUM
Byelovezhskaya Puscha Natural Park, Brestskaya District, Byelorussian S.S.R.
Regional natural history.
May-Sept., daily 8-6. Rest of year, daily 9-5.

CESIS

REGIONAL MUSEUM
Cesis, Latvian S.S.R.
Local history. Paintings. Applied arts. Costumes.
Tu.-Su. 10-6.

CHERNIGOV

MUSEUM OF MUSICAL INSTRUMENTS
Chernigov, Ukrainian S.S.R.
In factory of musical instruments. Early and historic musical instruments.
W.-M. 10-5.

CHERNOVTSY

FEDKOVICH LITERARY MUSEUM
Kotsubinskaya ul. 2, Chernovtsy, Ukrainian S.S.R.
Life and work of the Ukrainian writer, Yuri Fedkovich, in his former home.
W.-M. 10-5.

INDUSTRIAL MUSEUM
Chernovtsy, Ukrainian S.S.R.
Collections illustrating industrial development of the region, with particular reference to the history and technology of the textile, engineering and chemical industries.
Th.-Tu. 10-5.

KOBILYANSKA MUSEUM OF LITERATURE
Dmitrov ul. 5, Chernovtsy, Ukrainian S.S.R.
House in which the Ukrainian writer, Olga Chernovtsy (d.1942) lived for more than 50 years. Collections illustrating her life and work.
W.-M. 10-4.

MUSEUM OF UKRAINIAN FOLKLORE
Chernovtsy, Ukrainian S.S.R.
Handicrafts. Costumes. Folk art. Household equipment.
Th.-Tu. 10-5.

REGIONAL MUSEUM
Kobilyanka ul. 28, Chernovtsy, Ukrainian S.S.R.
History of the region. Life during the German occupation. Partisan activities. Agricultural development. Folklore.
Th.-Tu. 10-5.

CHUGUYEV

REPIN MUSEUM
Ploshchad Krasnikh Bortsov, Chuguyev, Ukrainian S.S.R.
Chuguyev was birthplace of the realist painter, Ilya Repin. Collections illustrating his life and work. Reproductions of his paintings.
Tu.-Su. 10-5.

DNEPROPETROVSK (formerly JEKATERINOSLAV)

MUSEUM OF ART
Dnepropetrovsk, Ukrainian S.S.R.
Regional folk art, handicrafts. Soviet and W. European paintings, sculpture, applied art.
Tu.-Su. 10-5.

DRUSKININKAJ

M. K. CHIURLENISA MEMORIAL MUSEUM
Druskininkaj, Lithuanian S.S.R.
Collections illustrating life and work of Chiurlenisa, in his former home.
On request.

DUSHANBE (formerly STALINABAD)

MUSEUM OF THE REPUBLIC OF TADZHIKISTAN
Ul. Lenina 56, Dushanbe, Tadzhik S.S.R.
History and ethnography of the Tadzhik peoples. Costumes. Furniture. Tools and implements. Folk art. 19th-20th century paintings.
Daily 11-6.

REGIONAL HISTORICAL MUSEUM
Dushanbe, Tadzhik S.S.R.
History and archaeology of the Tadzhik Republic. Folklore. Literature. Music.
W.-M. 10-5.

EREVAN

ARIN-BERD MUSEUM
Erevan, Armenian S.S.R.
Historic site, with exhibition of archaeological material discovered during excavations of the ancient citadel, forerunner of the present city.
Apr.-Oct., daily 9-5.

ARMENIAN MUSEUM OF THE THEATRE
Erevan, Armenian S.S.R.
Collections illustrating the history of the theatre and popular drama in Armenia. Paintings. Photographs. Documents. Posters. Programmes.
Tu.-Su. 11-6.

MUSEUM OF ETHNOGRAPHY
Erevan, Armenian S.S.R.
Ethnographical collections, illustrating traditional culture of Armenia. Costumes. Agricultural implements. Folk art. Handicrafts.
Tu.-Su. 9-4.

MUSEUM OF LITERATURE AND ART OF THE ACADEMY OF SCIENCES
Erevan, Armenian S.S.R.
Paintings, drawings, sculpture by Armenian artists. Manuscripts of Armenian literature. Early editions of Armenian books. Portraits and memorabilia of authors.
Tu.-Su. 9-5.

STATE HISTORICAL MUSEUM
Pl. Lenina, Erevan, Armenian S.S.R.
History and archaeology of Armenia. Architecture. Rural and urban social life. Religious art.
Tu.-Su. 10-5.

STATE PICTURE GALLERY OF THE ARMENIAN S.S.R.
Ul. Aboviana 2, Erevan, Armenian S.S.R.
19th-20th century paintings, sculpture, drawings by Soviet and W. European artists.
Tu.-Su. 9-5.

FEODOSIJA

J. K. AJVAZOVSKOGO ART GALLERY
Galerejnaja 2, Feodosija, Crimea
Russian paintings of the 19th and 20th centuries, including views of the Crimea.
Daily 10-5.

FRUNZE

STATE HISTORICAL MUSEUM OF THE KIRGHIZ S.S.R.
Krasnooktyabrskaya ul. 236, Frunze, Kirghiz S.S.R.
History of Kirghisia from prehistoric times to present day.
Tu.-Su. 10-6.

G. GAGARIN (formerly GZHATSK)

YURI GAGARIN MEMORIAL MUSEUM
Ul. Gagarin, G. Gagarin, Smolensk Region, R.S.F.S.R.
Collections illustrating the career and achievements of the cosmonaut, Yuri Gagarin.
Daily 10-5.

GHELENDZHIK

LOCAL MUSEUM
Lenina ul. 23, Ghelendzhik
Local history. Natural history. Handicrafts. Industrial development.
Tu.-Su. 8-1, 2-5.

GORI

MUSEUM OF HISTORY AND ETHNOGRAPHY
Gori, Georgian S.S.R.
In former fortress. Political and social history of Georgia. Folklore. Handicrafts. Development of local industries.
Tu.-Su. 10-5.

STALIN MUSEUM
Stalin ul., Gori, Georgian S.S.R.
Contains hut in which Stalin was born. Life and work of Stalin. Georgian rôle in the Bolshevik Revolution.
W.-Su. 9-6.

GORKI

GORKI STATE MUSEUM OF ART
Nab. im Zhdanova 3, Gorki, R.S.F.S.R.
19th-20th century paintings, graphics, sculpture by Russian and W. European artists.
Tu.-Su. 10-5.

KASHIRIK MUSEUM
Gorki, R.S.F.S.R.
Home of Gorki's grandfather. Original and period furnishings. Family possessions.
On request.

MUSEUM OF TRANSPORT
Gorki, R.S.F.S.R.
Collections illustrating development of road, rail and inland water transport. Models. Original vehicles. Paintings. Prints. Photographs. Documents.
Tu.-Su. 10-5.

STATE LITERARY MUSEUM A. M. GORKI
Ul. Lenina 26, Gorki, R.S.F.S.R.
Life and work of A. M. Gorki. Includes cottage which was Gorki's boyhood home, with original furnishings.
Tu.-Su. 10-5.

GRODNO

MUSEUM OF HISTORY AND ARCHAEOLOGY
Grodno, Byelorussian S.S.R.
History of the Grodno region, especially 1939-45. Post-war reconstruction. Paintings. Religious art. Applied arts. Archaeological material from regional excavations.
Tu.-Su. 10-5.

GRORNYI

REGIONAL MUSEUM
Grornyi
Regional history, ethnography. Paintings. Handicrafts.
W.-M. 10-6.

ILYICHOVO

LENIN HOUSE-MUSEUM
Ilyichovo
Wooden house in which Lenin lived (1917). Restored to show Lenin's room as it originally was.
Tu.-Su. 10-5.

IRKUTSK

MUSEUM OF ART
Ul. Karla Marksa 23, Irkutsk, R.S.F.S.R.
19th-20th century Russian paintings, drawings, prints.
Tu.-Su. 10-5.

IVANOVO

REGIONAL MUSEUM
Ivanovo, R.S.F.S.R.
Collections illustrating history and political and economic development of the region, particularly its iron, chemical and textile industries. Paintings. Costumes.
Daily 9-5.

IVANOVSK

MUSEUM OF PALEKH ART
Ul. Bakanova 50, Ivanovsk
Paintings, handicrafts of the Palekh region.
Tu.-Su. 10-5.

IZYUM

LOCAL MUSEUM
Sverdlov ul. 12, Izyum, Ukrainian S.S.R.
Local history, ethnography. Collection of idols worshipped by nomads.
W.-M. 10-6.

JAROSLAVL

MUSEUM OF FINE ART
Ploshchad Chelyuskinsko 2, Jaroslavl
Paintings, drawings, sculpture by Russian artists.
W.-M. 10-5.

REGIONAL MUSEUM
Pl. Sovietskaya 19/-, Jaroslavl
Local and regional history, ethnography.
M.-Su. 10-5.

KAKHOVA

LOCAL MUSEUM
Lenin ul. 12, Kakhova, Ukrainian S.S.R.
Local history. Exhibits illustrating attack on Perekop (1920), preceding taking of Crimea by the Red Army.
Tu., Th., Sa. 10-7.

KALININ

LOCAL MUSEUM
Sovietskaya ul. 3, Kalinin, R. S.F.S.R.
History of Kalinin. Religious art. Paintings. Folk art. Handicrafts.
W.-M. 10-5.

MUSEUM OF FINE ART
Kalinin, R.S.F.S.R.
In former Church of the Ascension (1813). Religious art. Paintings. Sculpture. Gold and silversmiths' work.
Tu.-Su. 10-6.

KALUGA

K. E. TSIOLKOVSKI MUSEUM
Ul. Korolieva, Kaluga, R.S.F.S.R.
Space-science and space exploration. Work of the scientist, Konstantin E. Tsiolkovski.
Tu.-Su. 10-4.

KAMENETS-PODOLSK

REGIONAL MUSEUM
Ul. K. Marxa 20, Kamenets-Podolsk, Ukrainian S.S.R.
Regional history, ethnography. Natural history.
W.-M. 10-5.

KAMENSK URALSK

A. S. PUSHKIN MEMORIAL MUSEUM
Kamensk Uralsk, R.S.F.S.R.
Life and literary work of Pushkin.
Tu.-Su. 10-5.

KANEV

T. G. SHEVCHENKO MUSEUM
Kanev, Ukrainian S.S.R.
Collections illustrating life and work of Shevchenko.
W.-M. 10-5.

KAUNAS

M. K. CHIURLENIS STATE ART MUSEUM
Ul. Salonei Neris 45, Kaunas, Lithuanian S.S.R.
Paintings, drawings, sculpture by Lithuanian, Russian, French and Italian artists.
Tu.-Su. 10-5.

MILITARY MUSEUM
Kaunas, Lithuanian S.S.R.
History of the Red Army, and of military operations in Lithuania since medieval times. Weapons. Military equipment. Paintings. Documents.
Tu.-F. 10-5.

PRINCE VYTANSAS MUSEUM
Kaunas, Lithuanian S.S.R.
In former Vytansas palace. Original furnishings, paintings, porcelain. Portraits.
Daily 10-6.

STATE MUSEUM
Ul. Donelaichio 64, Kaunas, Lithuanian S.S.R.
Archaeology and history of Lithuania, especially Kaunas. Rural and urban furnishings, household equipment. Paintings. Engravings. Applied arts. Industrial development of the region. Weapons. Coins.
Tu.-Su. 10-5.

KAUPEDAS

MUNICIPAL MUSEUM
Kaupedas
Local history. Paintings. Folk art. Applied art.
W.-M. 10-5.

KAZAN

STATE MUSEUM OF THE TARTAR REPUBLIC
Ul. Lenina 2, Kazan, Tartar ASSR
History, art and natural resources of the Tartar ASSR.
Tu.-Su. 10-5.

KAZBEGI

LOCAL MUSEUM
Ploshchad, Kazbegi, Georgian S.S.R.
In former home of the Georgian writer, Kazbegi. Collections illustrating his life and work. Weapons. Costumes.
Daily 9-5.

KEIDAINIAI

MUNICIPAL MUSEUM
Keidainiai, Lithuanian S.S.R.
Political and social history of the area. Furniture. Household equipment. Paintings. Applied art. Folk art.
Tu.-Su. 10-5.

KERCH

KERCH STATE MUSEUM OF HISTORY AND ARCHAEOLOGY
Ul. Sverdlova 22, Kerch, Ukrainian S.S.R.
Prehistory. History of Kerch from medieval times to present day.
W.-M. 10-5.

KHARKOV

HOUSE OF TECHNOLOGY
Kharkov, Ukrainian S.S.R.
Collections illustrating 19th-20th century development of technology, with particular reference to the industries of the Kharkov region.
W.-M. 10-6.

KHARKOV STATE ART MUSEUM
Sovnarkomovskaya ul. 11, Kharkov, Ukrainian S.S.R.
Pre-revolutionary works by Ukrainian and Russian artists. 16th-19th century icons of the Novgorod, Pskov and other schools. Soviet art.
Sa.-Th. 11-7.

KHARKOV STATE HISTORICAL MUSEUM
Universitetskaya ul. 10, Kharkov, Ukrainian S.S.R.
History of the Ukrainian people from prehistoric times to the present day. History of Kharkov and of the revolutionary movement. Weapons. Armour.
W.-M. 10-6.

KHERSON

YURI GAGARIN PLANETARIUM
Suvorov ul. 28, Kherson, Ukrainian S.S.R.
Planetarium. Exhibits illustrating space-travel and astronomical techniques, instruments.
Tu.-Su. 10-5.

HISTORICAL AND ARCHAEOLOGICAL MUSEUM
Ushakov Prospekt 16, Kherson, Ukrainian S.S.R.
Scythian and Sarmalian material from the Greek colony at Olvia.
Th.-Tu. 10-5.

NATURAL HISTORY MUSEUM
Gorky ul. 5, Kherson, Ukrainian S.S.R.
Botany. Zoology. Geology.
Th.-Tu. 10-5.

KIEV

KIEV NATIONAL MUSEUM OF WESTERN AND ORIENTAL ART
Ul. Repina 15, Kiev, Ukrainian S.S.R.
European and Oriental paintings, sculpture, applied art. Collections include works by Rubens, Hals, Velasquez.
Sa.-Th. 10-5.

V. I. LENIN MUSEUM
Vladimirskaya ul. 57, Kiev, Ukrainian S.S.R.
Political career and achievements of Lenin.
Tu.-Su. 10-7.

SHEVCHENKO HOUSE-MUSEUM
Shevchenko Pereulok 8A, Kiev, Ukrainian S.S.R.
Collections illustrating the life and work of T. G. Shevchenko, in house where the poet lived in 1846.
Sa.-Th. 10-5.30.

T. G. SHEVCHENKO STATE MUSEUM
Boulvard Shevchenko 12, Kiev, Ukrainian S.S.R.
Life and work of the Ukrainian poet, artist and revolutionary, T. G. Shevchenko.
W.-M. 10-5.

STATE HISTORICAL MUSEUM
Vladmirskaya ul. 2, Kiev, Ukrainian S.S.R.
History of the Ukraine, from prehistoric times to the present day.
Th.-Tu. 10-6.

STATE MUSEUM OF POPULAR AND DECORATIVE ART
Ul. Yanvarskogo Vosstaniya 21, Kiev, Ukrainian S.S.R.
In former monastery. 17th-20th century textiles. 16th-19th century handicrafts. Painted eggs. Costumes.
Tu.-Su. 10.30-6.

STATE MUSEUM OF RUSSIAN ART
Ul. Repina 9, Kiev, Ukrainian S.S.R.
Russian paintings, sculpture, carvings from the medieval period to the present day. 18th-20th century porcelain, glass.
Sa.-Th. 10-6.

STATE MUSEUM OF UKRAINIAN ART
Ul. Kirova 29, Kiev, Ukrainian S.S.R.
15th-20th century Ukrainian art. Icons. Portraits. Paintings. Woodcarving.
Sa.-Th. 10-5.

UKRAINIAN GEOLOGICAL MUSEUM OF THE ACADEMY OF SCIENCES
Vladmirskaya 2, Kiev, Ukrainian S.S.R.
Geology and mineralogy of the Ukraine.
By appointment.

UKRAINIAN STATE MUSEUM OF THEATRICAL, MUSICAL AND CINEMA ART
Sichnevoho Povstanya ul. 21/6, Kiev, Ukrainian S.S.R.
History of the theatre, cinema and music, especially in the Ukraine.
Tu.-Su. 10.30-5.

ZOOLOGICAL MUSEUM OF THE ACADEMY OF SCIENCES
Vladimirskaya ul. 55, Kiev, Ukrainian S.S.R.
Zoological collections, Europe and U.S.S.R.
M.-F. 10-5.

ZOOLOGICAL MUSEUM OF THE STATE UNIVERSITY OF THE UKRAINE
Korolenkova ul. 52, Kiev, Ukrainian S.S.R.
Zoology. Entomology. Palaeontology.
By appointment.

KIROV

GORKI PROVINCIAL MUSEUM
Kirov, R.S.F.S.R.
History of Kirov and its region. Ethnography. Handicrafts.
Tu.-Su. 10-4.

KIROVSK

HOUSE OF TECHNOLOGY
Kirovsk, R.S.F.S.R.
History and technology of local industries, especially mining, chemicals. Modern developments in engineering, communications.
Daily 11-6.

KISHINEV

ISKRA MUSEUM
Podolskaya ul. 39, Kishinev, Moldavian S.S.R.
House in which the illegal newspaper 'Iskra' was produced (1901-2). Exhibits illustrating the importance, production and distribution of the paper.
Th.-Tu. 11-6.

KOTOVSKY AND SERGEI LAZO MUSEUM
Komsoholskaya ul. 31, Kishinev, Moldavian S.S.R.
Exhibits illustrating the life of the two heroes of the Civil War, born in Moldavia.
W.-M. 11-6.

LOCAL MUSEUM
Pirogrova ul. 82, Kishinev, Moldavian S.S.R.
Local history. Handicrafts. National costumes. Carpets.
Th.-Tu. 12-7.

MOLDAVIAN MUSEUM
Kishinev, Moldavian S.S.R.
Ethnographical collections illustrating traditions, handicrafts, rural life of Moldavia.
Tu.-Su. 10-5.

MUSEUM OF FINE ART
Lenin Prospekt 115, Kishinev, Moldavian S.S.R.
16th-17th century Flemish, Dutch, German paintings, drawings. 18th-20th century Russian paintings, sculpture.
W.-M. 11-6.

MUSEUM OF THE HEROES OF CULTURE
Kishinev, Moldavian S.S.R.
Memorabilia, portraits and other illustrative material relating to outstanding local writers, artists and teachers.
Tu.-Su. 10-5.

PUSHKIN HOUSE-MUSEUM
Antonovskaya ul., Kishinev, Moldavian S.S.R.
House in which Pushkin lived (1820-23) and in which he began to write *Eugene Onegin*. Memorabilia of Pushkin.
Tu.-Su. 11-6.

REGIONAL MUSEUM OF THE REPUBLIC OF MOLDAVIA
Kishinev, Moldavian S.S.R.
Regional history, archaeology. Agriculture. Rural handicrafts, furniture, household equipment. Paintings.
Tu.-Su. 10-5.

KISLOVODSK

SERGO ORDZHONIKIDZE MUSEUM
Kislovodsk, R.S.F.S.R.
In Sergo Ordzhonikidze sanatorium. Collections illustrating the writer's life and work.
On request.

YAROSHENKO MUSEUM
Yaroshenko alleya 3, Kislovodsk, R.S.F.S.R.
Life and work of the painter, Nikola Yaroshenko (d.1898).
W.-M. 11-6.

KIZHI

OPEN-AIR MUSEUM
Kizhi, R.S.F.S.R.
Wooden buildings from Karelia, including houses, granaries, mills, bath-house, barns, chapel. Collections of handicrafts, ornaments, tools, agricultural implements. Household utensils.
May-Sept., daily 9-6.

KJAHTA

REGIONAL MUSEUM
Kjahta
Local history. Paintings. Furniture. Household equipment.
Tu.-Su. 10-5.

KLIN

P. J. TCHAIKOVSKY MEMORIAL MUSEUM
Ul. Cajkovskogo 48, Klin, R.S.F.S.R.
Collections illustrating life and work of Tchaikovsky, in house where he once lived.
Tu.-Su. 11-4.

KOBRIN

SUVOROV MUSEUM OF MILITARY HISTORY
Suvorov ul. 16, Kobrin, Byelorussian S.S.R.
Exhibits illustrating Russian military history, in house where General Suvorov lived, 1797-1800.
Tu.-Su. 10-4.

KOKČETOV

V. V. KUIBYSHEV MEMORIAL MUSEUM
Kokčetov, Khazakhstan
Collections illustrating life and work of Kuibyshev, in his former home.
On request.

KOLONNA

MUSEUM OF POPULAR ART OF THE GOUTZOULES
Teatralnaya ul. 25, Kolonna, Ukrainian S.S.R.
Paintings. Religious art. Furniture. Textiles. Woodcarvings.
Tu.-Su. 10-5.

KONCHANSKOYE-SUVOROVSKOYE

A. V. SUVOROV MEMORIAL MUSEUM
Konchanskoye-Suvorovskoye
Collections illustrating life and work of the military leader, Alexander Suvorov.
Daily 11-5.

KORSUN

HERSONES MUSEUM
Korsun, Ukrainian S.S.R.
Archaeological material from excavations on the site of the former Greek town of Hersones. Coins.
Tu.-Su. 10-5.

KOTOVSKOYE

KOTOVSKY MUSEUM
Kotovskoye, Moldavian S.S.R.
Local history, especially 20th century. Special collections illustrating the life and political work of the Civil War hero, Kotovsky.
Tu.-Su. 9-4.

KRASNODAR

MUSEUM OF HISTORY, FOLKLORE AND ART
Kommunisticheskaya ul. 53, Krasnodar, R.S.F.S.R.
Local and regional history. Paintings by Russian, especially regional, artists. Ethnography. Handicraf ts.
Tu.-Su. 11-6.

A. V. LUNACHARSKY KRASNODAR REGIONAL ART MUSEUM
Krasnaya ul. 11, Krasnodar, R.S.F.S.R.
19th-20th century Russian paintings. 18th-19th century miniatures.
Su., M. 11-6.

MUSEUM OF THE HEROES OF THE YOUNG GUARD
Krasnodar, R.S.F.S.R.
Regional history of the workers' and revolutionary movements, and of the 1940-45 war.
Tu.-Su. 9-5.

KRASNOYARSK

V. I. SURIKOV MEMORIAL MUSEUM
Krasnoyarsk, Krasnoyarsk Province
Collections illustrating life and work of the writer, V. I. Surikov.
Tu.-Su. 10-5.

KROTOSK

KROTOSK NATIONAL PARK MUSEUM
Krotosk, Kamchatka S.S.R.
Park museum, with collections illustrating geology, mineralogy, botany and wildlife of the area.
May-Sept., daily 9-6.

KUIBYSHEV

LENIN MUSEUM
Kuibyshev, R.S.F.S.R.
Collections illustrating Lenin's life and political achievements.
M.-Su. 10-6.

MUSEUM OF FINE ART
Kuibyshev, R.S.F.S.R.
19th-20th century paintings, drawings, graphics, sculpture by Russian and Soviet artists.
Tu.-Su. 10-5.

REGIONAL ETHNOGRAPHICAL MUSEUM
Kuibyshev, R.S.F.S.R.
Social and cultural history of Kuibyshev and its region. Handicrafts. Costumes. Housing. Furniture. Folklore.
M.-Su. 10-6.

KURSK

MUSEUM OF FINE ART
Sovietskaya ul. 3, Kursk, R.S.F.S.R.
19th-20th century Russian paintings, drawings.
Tu.-Su. 10-5.

REGIONAL MUSEUM
Ul. Lunacharskogo 6, Kursk, R.S.F.S.R.
History of the city since medieval times. Exhibits illustrating agricultural, commercial and industrial importance of Kursk. Planetarium.
W.-M. 10-5.

UFIMTSEV MUSEUM
Semenovskaya ul. 31, Kursk, R.S.F.S.R.
Life and work of the inventor and aero-engine designer, Anatoli Ufimtsev (d.1936), who was born in Kursk.
Tu.-Su. 10-5.

KUSKOVO

NATIONAL CERAMIC MUSEUM
Kuskovo
In 18th century manor-house of Kuskovo, with period furnishings, decorations. European and Russian ceramics.
W.-Su. 10-6.

KUTAISI

MUSEUM OF HISTORY AND ETHNOGRAPHY
Ul. Tbilisi 1, Kutaisi, Georgian S.S.R.
10th-13th century icons. 11th-19th century religious manuscripts. Armour. Musical instruments.
Su.-Tu. 10-6.

TSULUKIDZE MUSEUM
Tsilukidzaya ul. 21, Kutaisi, Georgian S.S.R.
Collections illustrating life and work of Alexander Tsulukidze (d.1905), Georgian revolutionary, in his birthplace and former home.
Tu.-Su. 10-6.

LENINGRAD

ACADEMICIAN F. N. CHERNYSCHEV CENTRAL SCIENTIFIC GEOLOGICAL AND PROSPECTING MUSEUM
Sredny Prospekt 72B, Leningrad V-26
Geological, palaeontological and petrographical collections covering the whole Soviet Union.
Tu.-F., Su. 11-5.

ACADEMICIAN I. P. PAVLOV MUSEUM
Ul. Akademika Pavlova 12, Leningrad
In Institute of Experimental Medicine, where the physiologist, Pavlov, lived, 1890-1936. Collection illustrating his life and work, in his former study.
M.-F. 10-5.

BOTANICAL MUSEUM OF THE V. L. KOMAROV BOTANICAL INSTITUTE
Ul. Prof. Popova 2, Leningrad
Botanical collections covering the whole Soviet Union.
Daily 10-5.

BRODSKY MUSEUM
Pl. Iskusstv 3, Leningrad
Former house (1924-39) of the painter, Isaak Brodsky. Works by Brodsky, with his private collection of 19th-20th century paintings, drawings.
F.-Tu. 11-5.30; W. 11-3.30.

CENTRAL NAVAL MUSEUM
Pl. Pushkinskaya 4, Leningrad B-164
History of the Tsarist and Soviet Navy. Founded (1709) by Peter the Great, who ordered ships' models to be kept here. Includes Peter the Great's boat, from which the Russian navy began.
M.-W., Su. 11-6; Th. 1-6; F. 11-4.

CRUISER 'AURORA'
Leningrad
Ship (1903), taken over by the crew during the October Revolution and used in attack on Winter Palace. Includes radio room from which Lenin's manifesto announcing victory of Revolution was transmitted.
Su.-Tu., Th., F. 11-5. Groups only, by previous appointment.

V. V. DOKUCHAYEV CENTRAL MUSEUM OF SOIL SCIENCE
Birzhevoi Provezd 6, Leningrad
Geology. Flora. Fauna. Agricultural aspects of the soil.
Tu., Th., F. 10-6; Su. 11-4.

GEOLOGICAL MUSEUM, A. P. KARPINSKY
Nab. Makarova, Leningrad
Geological and mineralogical collections, especially relating to the U.S.S.R.
Tu.-F., Su. 11-5.

HERMITAGE MUSEUM
M. Dvortsovaya naberezhnaya 34, Leningrad
In the Old Hermitage (1775-84), the New Hermitage (1839-50) and the Hermitage Theatre (1787). There are 7 departments: Western European Art; Primitive Culture of the area of the U.S.S.R.; Art and Culture of the Ancient World; Art and Culture of the Near and Far East; Art and Culture of the Soviet Far East; History of Russian Culture; Coins.
Oct.-Apr., F.-W. 11-6. May-Sept., F.-W. 10-9.

HOUSE-MUSEUM OF ACADEMICIAN I. P. PAVLOV
Sedmaya Liniya 2, Leningrad
Collections illustrating life and work of the biologist, I. P. Pavlov, in his former home.
Tu.-Su. 11-5.

HOUSE OF SCIENTIFIC AND TECHNICAL PROPAGANDA
Nevsky Prospekt 58, Leningrad
Machine-building and instrument manufacturing industries of Leningrad.
F.-M., W. 11-8.

S. M. KIROV MUSEUM
Kirovsky Prospekt 26-28, Leningrad
Kirov's home, 1926-34. Collections illustrating his life and work.
F.-Tu. 11-5; Th. 12-7.

KIROV THEATRE MUSEUM
Teatralnaya pl., Leningrad
History of the Theatre and its productions, with special section devoted to the singer, Fyodor Chaliapin.
Open during performances.

LENINGRAD PLANETARIUM
Park Lenina 4, Leningrad
Exhibition illustrating the theme, 'Man Conquers Space'. Foucault pendulum.
M., Tu., Th.-Sa. 3-8; Su. 12-8.

LENIN MEMORIAL APARTMENTS
Pereulok Kyicha 7/4; Ul. Lenina 8; Desyataya Sovietskaya ul. 17A; Sendobolskaya ul. 1/92; Naberezhnaya reki Karpovki 32; Khersonskaya ul. 5/7, Leningrad
Apartments in which Lenin stayed or worked in Leningrad at various times. Mementoes of Lenin, and of people associated with him.
Th.-M. 11-6; Tu. 11-4.

V. I. LENIN MUSEUM
Ul. Khalturina 5/1, Leningrad
Collections illustrating Lenin's life and work. Mementoes and relics. Paintings. Drawings. Photographs. First editions of his works. Armoured car from which Lenin spoke on his final return from exile, April 1917.
M., Th.-Su. 11-6; Tu. 11-4.

LESGAFT MUSEUM OF HUMAN MORPHOLOGY
Prospekt Maklina 32, Leningrad
Comparative anatomy.
M.-F. 10-4.30; Sa. 10-3.

M. V. LOMONOSOV MUSEUM
Universitetskaya Nab., Leningrad
Documents and relics illustrating Lomonosov's life and work in science, history, philosophy, literature. The first Russian chemical laboratory, set up by him. His instruments for research in optics and atmospheric electricity.
Su.-Th. 11-5.

D. I. MENDELEYEV HOUSE-MUSEUM
Universitetskaya Naberezhnaya 7-9, Leningrad
Collections illustrating life and work of Mendeleyev, in his former home.
M., W., F. 12-5.

D. I. MENDELEYEV MUSEUM
Prospekt J. V. Stalina 19, Leningrad
In Mendeleyev Metrological Research Institute. Museum illustrating Mendeleyev's scientific achievements, in his former study.
M.-Sa. 10-5.

MUSEUM OF ANTHROPOLOGY AND ETHNOLOGY
Universitetskaya Nab. 3, Leningrad B-164
In the former Kunstkammer (1718-34), where the Academy of Sciences first began its work. Includes collections made by Peter the Great for the first natural science museum in Russia. Early anatomical preparations.
Th., Su. 11-4. May-Sept., also Tu. 11-4.

MUSEUM OF THE ARCTIC AND THE ANTARCTIC
Ul. Marata 24A, Leningrad
Documents and equipment of the Soviet expeditions to the Arctic and Antarctic.
M. 12-4; W.-Sa. 12-6; Su. 11-5.

MUSEUM OF THE ARTILLERY, SIGNAL CORPS AND CORPS OF ENGINEERS
Park Lenina 7, Leningrad
History of the Artillery, the Signal Corps and the Corps of Engineers in the Tsarist and Soviet periods. Development of Russian weapons. Uniforms.
Su. 10.30-6; M. 11-3; W.-Sa. 11.30-6.

MUSEUM OF THE COLLEGE OF DECORATIVE ARTS
Solyanoi Pereulok 13, Leningrad
18th-20th century European and Russian decorative arts.
M.-F. 11-5.30; Sa. 11-2.30.

MUSEUM OF THE EVOLUTION OF THE NERVOUS SYSTEM
Ul. Mayakovskogo 12, Leningrad
At A. L. Polenov Research Institute for Neuro-surgery. Research and study collections illustrating evolution of the nervous system in animals and man.
By appointment.

MUSEUM OF THE GORKI THEATRE
Nab. reki Fontanki 65, Leningrad
Collections illustrating history of the Gorki Theatre. Portraits. Documents. Photographs. Stage and costume designs. Posters. Programmes.
Open during performances.

MUSEUM OF THE GREAT OCTOBER SOCIALIST REVOLUTION
Ul. Kuibysheva 4, Leningrad
Collections documenting the October Revolution. History of Socialism and the Civil War. History of World War II.
Tu.-Su. 10-6.

MUSEUM OF THE HISTORY OF RELIGION AND ATHEISM
Kazanskaye pl. 2, Leningrad
In former Kazan Cathedral (1801-11). Displays illustrating religion, sects, denominations. Church plate. Religious art. Origins of Christianity. History of the struggle against religion.
M. 1-7; Tu. 12-4; Th., F., Sa. 12-6; Su. 11-6.

MUSEUM OF HYGIENE
Ul. Rakova 25, Leningrad
History of hygiene.
Tu.-Su. 11-6.

MUSEUM OF THE INSTITUTE OF RUSSIAN LITERATURE
Nab. Makarova 4, Leningrad
Manuscripts, archives, letters of prominent 18th-19th century writers. Permanent exhibitions devoted to Radishchev, Lermontov, Gogol, Dostoyevsky, Turgenev and other Russian writers. Early editions of Russian printed books.

Memorabilia of famous writers, including Gogol's chair, boots made by Tolstoy, Dostoyevsky's spectacles.
W.-F., Su., M. 11-5; Sa. 11-4.

MUSEUM OF THE MALY OPERA THEATRE
Pl. Iskusstv 1, Leningrad
History of the theatre and its performances.
Open during performances.

MUSEUM OF MILITARY MEDICINE
Lazaretnu per. 2, Leningrad F-180
Collections illustrating history of the organisation and techniques of the Russian and Soviet army medical services.
M.-F. 11-6; Su. 11-5.

MUSEUM OF MUSICAL INSTRUMENTS
Isaakievskaya pl. 5, Leningrad
Instruments made by Russian and foreign craftsmen, including items in the possession of Glinka, Borodin, Rimsky-Korsakov and other Russian composers.
W.-M. 12-6.

MUSEUM OF THE OCTOBER REVOLUTION
Ul. Kuibysheva 4, Leningrad
In former Kshesinskaya Palace (1902). Documents, photographs and other exhibits illustrating political and economic background of the Revolution, the Civil War and the Second World War. Development of socialism in the U.S.S.R.
M.-F. 12-8; Tu., Sa., Su. 11-7; W. 11-5.

MUSEUM OF THE G. V. PLEKHANOV MINING INSTITUTE
21 Liniya, Leningrad
History of the evolution of the earth and of mining techniques. Crystals, gem-stones, especially diamonds.
M.-F. 10-5; Sa. 10-2.

MUSEUM OF PORCELAIN
Prospekt Obuchovské Obrany 151-2, Leningrad
18th-20th century European and Russian porcelain, including examples from the Leningrad factories.
M.-F. 11-5.30; Sa. 11-2.30.

MUSEUM OF RAILWAY HISTORY
Ul. Sadovaya 50, Leningrad
History of railway transport in Russia. Models of locomotives and carriages.
W.-Su. 12-6; M. 12-3.

MUSEUM OF ST. ISAAC'S CATHEDRAL
Isaakijevskaya Ploschchad, Leningrad
Cathedral (1819-59). Early 19th century paintings, sculpture.
W.-Su. 11-6; M. 11-4.

MUSEUM OF SCIENTIFIC RESEARCH
Universitetskaya Naberezhnaya 17, Leningrad
Collections illustrating history of Russian scientific research.
W.-Su. 11-6; M. 11-4.

MUSEUM OF URBAN SCULPTURE
Pl. Alexandra Nevskovo 1, Leningrad
In former Alexander Nevsky monastery. Original models of many of the works of art which decorate the city.
May-Sept., M., Tu., F. 11-8; W. 11-4. Oct.-Apr., M., Tu., F. 11-6; W. 11-4.

NATIONAL MUSEUM OF ETHNOGRAPHY OF THE PEOPLES OF THE U.S.S.R.
Inzhenernaya ul. 4/1, Leningrad
Ethnography and decorative arts of the peoples of the U.S.S.R., 19th-early 20th centuries.
W.-Su. 11-6; M. 11-4.

NATIONAL MUSEUM OF THE HISTORY OF LENINGRAD
Nab. Krasnoya Flota 44, Leningrad
Architecture and history of Leningrad. Models and dioramas, including Nevsky Prospekt c.1750, transporting of the great rock for the Bronze Horseman and an early 18th century firework display in St. Petersburg. Special exhibit illustrating defence of Leningrad during World War II.
M., Th., Sa., Su. 11-7; Tu.-F. 1-9.

NATIONAL PUSHKIN MUSEUM
Dvortsovaya Naberezhnaya 34, Leningrad
In the Winter Palace. Collections illustrating Pushkin's life and work.
F.-Tu. 11-6; W. 11-4.

NATIONAL RUSSIAN MUSEUM
Inzhenernaya ul. 4, Leningrad
Russian sculpture, paintings, drawings, popular art. Children's drawings. Coins.
W.-Su. 11-6; M. 11-4.

N. A. NEKRASOV HOUSE-MUSEUM
Liteiny prospekt 36, Leningrad
Collections illustrating life and work of Nekrasov, in his former home.
Su., W., F. 11-6; Th., Sa. 1-8.

PERMANENT EXHIBITION OF LENINGRAD ARTISTS
Nevski prospekt 8, Leningrad
Paintings, drawings, prints, sculpture by artists living in Leningrad.
M.-Sa. 11-7.

PETER AND PAUL FORTRESS
Pl. Revolutsii, Leningrad
Building begun 1712. Tsars' tombs. Dungeons and cells in which 19th-20th century revolutionaries were imprisoned.
Th.-M. 11-6; Tu. 11-4.

PETER THE GREAT'S COTTAGE
Petrovskaya Naberezhnaya 5, Leningrad
Log cabin (1703), painted to resemble bricks, used by Peter the Great as summer cottage. Collections illustrating Russia's victory in the Northern War and the early years of St. Petersburg.
M. 12-7; W.-F. 12-8; Sa., Su. 12-5.

G. V. PLEKHANOV MUSEUM
Krasnoarmeiskaya ul. 32, Leningrad
Collections illustrating life and work of the philosopher and writer, G. V. Plekhanov. Personal possessions. Replica of his study in Geneva.
M.-F. 10-5; Sa. 10-2.

A. S. POPOV CENTRAL MUSEUM OF COMMUNICATIONS
Per. Podbelskovo 4, Leningrad
History of postal services and telecommunications in the U.S.S.R. State postage stamp collection. Memorial museum to Alexander Popov, first director of the institute, in his former study.
W., F.-M. 12-6; Th. 1-8.

A. S. PUSHKIN HOUSE-MUSEUM
Nab. reki Moiki 12, Leningrad
Apartment where Pushkin lived, 1836-37, restored to its original appearance, with a number of his personal possessions. Exhibits illustrating the last period of his life and work.
Su., W., F. 11-6; Th., Sa. 1-8; M. 11-4.

I. R. REPIN HOUSE-MUSEUM
Repino, Leningrad
Collections illustrating life and work of the painter, Repin, in his former home, "Penaty".
W.-Su. 11-6.

SHED AND BARN MUSEUMS
Razliv, Leningrad
Museums in former hayfield and in barn loft, illustrating months spent by Lenin (1917) in Razliv, living and working in a shed, disguised as seasonal haymaker.
Th.-M. 11-6; Tu. 11-4.

STATE CIRCUS MUSEUM
Nab. reki Fontanki 3, Leningrad
Collections illustrating history of the European circus. Paintings. Plans. Sketches.
M.-Sa. 12-5, by appointment.

SUMMER PALACE MUSEUM
Letny Sad, Leningrad
In Peter the Great's Summer Palace (1710-14). Tiled stoves. Furnishings. Decorative arts.
May-Nov., W.-M. 12-8.

A. V. SUVOROV MUSEUM
Ul. Saltykova - Shchedrina 41B, Leningrad
Personal possessions of the 18th century general. Documents. Trophies captured by the Russian army during his campaigns.
Th.-Tu. 11-7.

THEATRE MUSEUM
Pl. Ostrovskovo 6, Leningrad
History of the theatre in Russia, especially in Leningrad. Paintings. Portraits. Costumes and stage designs. Posters. Programmes.
M. 12-5; W.-Su. 12-7.

ZOOLOGICAL MUSEUM OF THE ACADEMY OF SCIENCES
Universitetskaya, Naberezhnaya 1, Leningrad
Collections illustrating origins and evolution of the animal world.
W., F., Sa., Su. 11-5.

LENKORAN

REGIONAL MUSEUM
Lenkoran, Azerbaydzhan S.S.R.
History and archaeology of the region. 19th-20th century paintings. Costumes. Agriculture. Handicrafts.
Tu.-Su. 10-5.

LERMONTOVO

M. Y. LERMONTOV MUSEUM
Penzenskaya ob., Lermontovo, R.S.F.S.R.
In the château-type former principal house of Lermontovo. 18th-19th century furniture, paintings, silver, porcelain.
W.-Su. 11-5.

LOMONOSOV (formerly ORANIENBAUM)

FINE ART MUSEUM
Lomonosov, R.S.F.S.R.
European paintings, sculpture, applied arts.
W.-Su. 11-5.

LUDZA

REGIONAL MUSEUM
Ludza, Latvian S.S.R.
Regional history, art, literature, ethnography. Paintings. Applied art.
Tu.-Su. 10-5.

LVOV

ART GALLERY
Ul. Stefanika 3, Lvov, Ukrainian S.S.R.
Russian and European paintings, including works by Rubens, Titian, Goya, Tintoretto.
Tu.-Su. 12-7.

IVAN FRANKO MUSEUM
Franko ul. 152, Lvov, Ukrainian S.S.R.
Life and work of the writer, Ivan Franko.
W.-M. 10-7.

YAROSLAV GALAN MUSEUM
Gvarderskaya ul. 18, Lvov, Ukrainian S.S.R.
Collections illustrating life and work of the Ukrainian political writer, Y. Galan.
Su.-Tu., Th. 10-4.

V. I. LENIN MUSEUM
Prospekt Lenina 20, Lvov, Ukrainian S.S.R.
Life and work of Lenin.
Tu.-Su. 10-7.

LVOV HISTORICAL MUSEUM
Pl. Rynok 4-6, Lvov, Ukrainian S.S.R.
History of the Western Ukraine. Exhibits showing industries and industrial products of the region.
M., Tu., Th.-Sa. 11-7.

MUSEUM OF ETHNOGRAPHY AND INDUSTRIAL ARTS
Prospekt Lenina 15, Lvov, Ukrainian S.S.R.
Ethnography and handicrafts of the Western Ukraine. Costumes.
Tu.-Su. 11-6.

MUSEUM OF UKRAINIAN ART
Dragomanov ul. 3, Lvov, Ukrainian S.S.R.
14th-18th century paintings by Ukrainian artists. Icons.
Tu.-Su. 12-7.

NATURAL HISTORY MUSEUM
Teatralnaya ul. 18, Lvov, Ukrainian S.S.R.
Regional geology, botany, zoology.
Tu.-Su. 11-5.

LYALA RATUSHNAYA

LOCAL MUSEUM
Lyala Ratushnaya
Collections illustrating life of the young local partisan, Lyala Ratushnaya, killed in World War II.
Daily 10-4.

MALOYAROSLAVETS

MUSEUM OF THE MILITARY HISTORY OF 1812
Moskovskaya ul. 13, Maloyaroslavets, R.S.F.S.R.
Regional history. Relics of campaign in 1812.
Daily 10-5.

MAZEIKAI

LOCAL MUSEUM
Mazeikai, Lithuanian S.S.R.
Local history. Paintings. Handicrafts.
W.-M. 9-5.

MELIKHOVASKYA

HOUSE MUSEUM OF A. P. CHEKHOV
Melikhovaskya
On the former Chekhov family estate. Life and work of Chekhov.
On request.

MELITOPOL

LOCAL MUSEUM
Dzerzhinskaya ul. 25, Melitopol, Ukrainian S.S.R.
Local history. Agricultural development, expecially fruit-growing.
Daily 8-5.

MIASS

MUSEUM OF THE ILMEN MINERAL PARK
Miass 1, Chelyabinsk Region, R.S.F.S.R.
Collection of minerals found in the Park.
Tu.-Su. 9-6.

MINSK

BYELORUSSIAN MUSEUM OF ART
Ul. Lenina 40, Minsk, Byelorussian S.S.R.
Paintings, sculpture, graphics, applied art, by Byelorussian, Soviet and foreign artists.
Tu.-Su. 10-5.

BYELORUSSIAN MUSEUM OF THE GREAT PATRIOTIC WAR
Pl. Svobody 23, Minsk, Byelorussian S.S.R.
Collections illustrating military operations and guerilla activities in Byelorussia during the second World War. Weapons. Banners of partisan detachments. Personal belongings of soldiers and partisans. Portraits.
Tu.-Su. 10-5.

GEOLOGICAL-MINERALOGICAL MUSEUM OF THE BYELORUSSIAN ACADEMY OF SCIENCES
Minsk, Byelorussian S.S.R.
Geology and mineralogy of the USSR, especially of the Minsk and adjoining regions.
By appointment.

YAKUB KOLAS MUSEUM
Leninsky Prospekt 66A, Minsk, Byelorussian S.S.R.
Collections illustrating life and work of the poet, Yakub Kolas.
Su.-F. 9.30-3.30.

YANKO KUPALA MUSEUM
Ul. Yanki Kupaly 27, Minsk, Byelorussian S.S.R.
Collections illustrating life and work of the folk poet, Yanko Kupala.
Sa.-Th. 10-5.

MUSEUM OF THE FIRST CONGRESS OF THE RUSSIAN SOCIAL DEMOCRATIC PARTY
Leninsky Prospekt 31A, Minsk, Byelorussian S.S.R.
Replica of house in which the Social Democrats met in 1898. Exhibits illustrating history, activities and importance of the Party.
Sa.-Th. 11-6.

MUSEUM OF LOCAL HISTORY AND FOLKLORE
Revolyutionnaya ul., Minsk, Byelorussian S.S.R.
History of Minsk and its area. Regional folk art, handicrafts. Minsk in the 1940-45 war.
W.-M. 10-5.

STATE GALLERY OF BYELORUSSIA
Ul. Lenina 20, Minsk, Byelorussian S.S.R.
Russian, Byelorussian and W. European paintings.
F.-W. 11-7.

STATE MUSEUM OF THE BYELORUSSIAN S.S.R.
Ul. Marxa 12-k, Minsk, Byelorussian S.S.R.
History of Byelorussia, from prehistoric times to the present day.
Tu.-Su. 10-5.

UNIVERSITY MUSEUM OF ZOOLOGY
Minsk, Byelorussian S.S.R.
Zoological collections representing the USSR, especially the Ukraine and the surrounding areas.
By appointment.

MOSCOW

D. N. ANUCHIN ANTHROPOLOGICAL INSTITUTE AND MUSEUM
Prospekt Marxa 18, Moscow
Prehistoric anthropology and archaeology. African material brought back by Soviet explorers.
Tu.-Su. 11-6.

APARTMENT-MUSEUM OF F. M. DOSTOIEVSKI
Ul. Dostoievskogo 2, Moscow
In the apartment where Dostoievski lived (1823-28). Exhibits illustrating his life and work.
M. 10-4; W., F. 2-9; Th., Sa., Su. 11-6. Closed Tu. and last day of each month.

APARTMENT-MUSEUM OF V. I. NEMIROVICH-DANCHENKO
Ul. Nemirovich-Danchenko 5-7, Moscow
Apartment of the producer and writer who, with Stanislavski, founded the Gorki Theatre. The three rooms are left as they were in his lifetime. Exhibits illustrating his life and work.
W., Su. 12-6.

APARTMENT-MUSEUM OF N. A. OSTROVSKI
Ul. Grokogo 14, Moscow
Home of the writer, Nikolai Ostrovski, during the last years of his life. Exhibits illustrating his life and work.
Tu., Th., Sa., Su. 10-6; W., F. 12-8. Closed M.

ARCHITECTURAL MUSEUM
Donskoj Monastyr, Donskaia pl. 1, Moscow
In the former Konskoi monastery (1591). History and achievements of leading Russian architects. Drawings. Models.
Daily 11-6, ex. M. and last day of each month.

ARKHANGELSKOYE ESTATE MUSEUM
Arkhangelskoye, near Moscow
Contains former palace of Prince Yusupov. Paintings, including works by Van Dyck, Boucher, Tiepolo. Furniture. China. Glass. Early 19th century serf theatre, with collection illustrating the history of the theatre.
Tu.-Su. 10-5.

BOLSHOI THEATRE MUSEUM
Pl. Sverdlova 1/6, Moscow
History of the Russian theatre and of the work of the Bolshoi.
Tu.-Su. 11-6.

CATHEDRAL OF THE INTERCESSION
(Pokrovsky Sobor), Red Square, Moscow
Also known as St. Basil's Cathedral (Sobor Vassiliya Blazhennogo). Cathedral (1555-60), now a museum. Religious art. History of the original construction and subsequent history of the cathedral.
W.-Su. 10.30-7; M. (except 1st in month) 10.30-2.30.

CENTRAL MUSEUM OF MUSICAL CULTURE, 'M. J. GLINKA'
Ul. Herzen 13, Moscow
In former Boyar Troyekurov Mansion. History of Russian music. Documents, photographs, scores, books, notes, manuscripts, disc and tape recordings and personal effects recalling the life and musical careers of Glinka and other leading Russian composers.
Daily ex. Su. 9-4; Sa. 9-3.

CENTRAL MUSEUM OF THE SOVIET ARMY
Ul. Sovetskoi Armii 2, Moscow
History of the Army of the U.S.S.R., from its beginnings to the present day. Dioramas. Paintings. Photographs. Documents. Weapons. War trophies.
Su., W., F. 10-5; M., Tu., Th. 12-7. Closed Sa. and the last F. in each month.

CENTRAL THEATRE MUSEUM OF THE A. A. BAKHRUSIN THEATRE
Ul. Bakhrushina 31/12, Moscow
History of the national theatre before the Revolution and during the Soviet period. Manuscripts, models, portraits, drawings and sketches, scenic design, costumes and accessories.
Su., M., Th., Sa. 12-7; W., F. 2-9. Closed Tu. and last day of each month.

A. P. CHEKHOV HOUSE-MUSEUM
Sadovaya-Kundrinskaya 6, Moscow
Chekhov's home, 1886-90. Apartment and its contents have been preserved as they were in Chekhov's lifetime.
M. 10-4; Th., Sa., Su. 11-6; W., F. 2-9. Closed Tu. and last day of each month.

18TH CENTURY KUSKOVO ESTATE AND CERAMICS MUSEUM
Moscow
Furniture. Decorative arts. Paintings. Russian and European porcelain.
Oct.-Apr., W.-M. 10-4. May-Sept., 4-6. Closed last M. in month.

EXHIBITION GALLERY OF THE PAINTERS OF THE RUSSIAN FEDERATION
Ul. Gorki 46b, Moscow
20th century paintings by artists working in the Russian Federal Republic.
Daily ex. M. 12-7.

EXHIBITION OF SOVIET ECONOMIC ACHIEVEMENT
Mira prospekt, Moscow
Soviet economic planning in action. Sections devoted to agriculture, industries, construction, transport and communication, science, education and welfare.
Daily 9.30 a.m. - 10 p.m. (until 11 p.m. Sa., Su.).

M. V. FRUNZE CENTRAL MUSEUM OF AVIATION AND ASTRONAUTICS
Ul. Krasnoarmeiskaya 14, Moscow
History of Russian aviation. Exhibits include Kostovich's model of an airship and engine (1883-4) and aeroplane built by Mozhaisky (1882).
Tu.-Su. 11-6.

HOUSE-MUSEUM OF K. S. STANISLAVSKI
Ul. Stanislavskogo, dom 6, Moscow
Home of the Soviet actor and producer, now converted into a museum to illustrate his life and achievements.
Su. 12-7; Tu., Th. 3-9.

KOLOMENSKOYE ESTATE MUSEUM
nr. Moscow
The former country estate of the Tsars. The museum includes Peter the Great's house from Arkhangelsk and an exhibition of Russian applied art.
W.-Su. 10-5.

KRASNAYA PRESNYA MUSEUM
Bolshevistskaya ul. 4, Moscow
Timber house where the Presnya District Revolutionary Committee met in October 1917. One of the headquarters of the armed uprising.
Tu.-Su. 10-6.

KUTUZOV HUT
Kutuzovski prospekt 38, Filacti, Moscow
Peasant hut in which Kutuzov held his Council of War before the Battle of Borodino (1812). Museum with relics of the battle.
Tu.-Su. 10-6.

V. I. LENIN CENTRAL MUSEUM
Pl. Revolucii 2, Moscow
Objects illustrating the life and achievements of Lenin. Replica of Lenin's study in the Kremlin.
Tu.-Su. 11-7.

MAXIM GORKI MUSEUM
Ul. Vorovskogo 25a, Moscow
Life and literary activity of Gorki.
Tu., F. 1-8; Su., W., Th. 10-5; Sa. 10.30-4. Closed M.

MEMORIAL MUSEUM IN THE FLAT OF THE ACTRESS, M. N. ERMOLOVA
(Branch of National Theatre Museum), Bahrusin q.v., Moscow
Exhibits illustrating life and theatrical career of Ermolova.
Tu.-Su. 10-5.

MINERALOGICAL MUSEUM
Pr. Marxa 18, Moscow
Minerals, crystals, gemstones of the U.S.S.R. and of foreign countries.
Tu.-Su. 11-6.

MOSCOW STATE UNIVERSITY ZOOLOGICAL MUSEUM
Ul. Herzena 6, Moscow
World-wide collections of mammals, birds, amphibians, reptiles.
Tu.-Su. 11-6.

MUSEUM OF ANTHROPOLOGY
Marx Prospekt 18, Moscow
Fossil remains of primitive man. Exhibits illustrating the history of man and development of the human race.
Tu.-Su. 11-6.

MUSEUM OF THE BATTLE OF BORODINO
Kutuzovski Prospekt 38, Moscow
Panorama of the battle, 115 m. long, 15 m. high, painted by Franz Rubo in 1912, but not shown to the public until 1972.
Daily 10-5.

MUSEUM OF DECORATIVE ARTS
Ul. Razin 18/2, Moscow
In former Mansion of the Boyars Romanov (1565-67), birthplace of Mikhail Fyodorovich, first Tsar of the Romanov dynasty. Collection of 17th-19th century Russian art, decorative art, furnishings.
F.-W. 9.30-12.30, 1.30-5.30.

MUSEUM OF EARTH SCIENCES
Leninskie Gory, Moscow
Geology. Climate. Natural resources and their conservation. Geography. Flora. Fauna. Biology.
M.-Sa. 10-5.

MUSEUM OF FOLK ART
Ul. Stanislavskogo 7, Moscow
In Naryshkin Palace of the monastery of Vysoko-Petrovski. Toys, trays, embroidery, jewellery and other examples of handicrafts and industrial art, especially from the more important centres, such as Mstéra, Fédoskino, Khokhloma, Jestovo. Furniture.
Daily 11-5, ex. Su. and the last day of each month.

MUSEUM OF THE HISTORY OF MICROSCOPY
Leninsky prospekt 86, Moscow
Collections illustrating the history, construction and use of microscopes.
M.-Sa. 9-5.

MUSEUM OF HISTORY AND OF THE RECONSTRUCTION OF MOSCOW
Novaya pl. 12, Moscow
Two divisions - before and after the October Revolution - showing the history and development of Moscow from ancient times to the present day. Post-1945 housing, science, transport and education.
Su., Th., Sa. 10-6; W., F. 2-9; M. 10-4.

MUSEUM OF HYGIENE
Velka Pirogovská, Moscow
History and techniques of public health and hygiene.
Tu.-Su. 10-5.

MUSEUM OF INDUSTRIAL SAFETY
Leninsky prospekt 10, Moscow
Permanent exhibition, showing techniques and regulations for achieving safety at work.
M.-F. 9-5; Sa. 9-3.

MUSEUM OF KARL MARX AND FRIEDRICH ENGELS
Ul. Marksa-Engelsa 5, Moscow
Collections and exhibits illustrating the work of Marx and Engels in the context of the world Communist and labour movements. 1st editions. Personal possessions.
Su., Th., Sa. 11-5; W., F. 3-7; M. 1-5.

MUSEUM OF ORIENTAL ART
Ul. Obukha 16, Moscow
Art of Soviet Central Asia and the Caucasus, India, Iran, Turkey, China, Japan, Vietnam, Korea and Mongolia from ancient times to present day.
W., F. 2-9; Tu., Th., Su. 11-6.

MUSEUM OF THE STATE ACADEMIC MALY THEATRE
Sverdlov pl. 1-6, Moscow
History of the Maly Theatre.
Tu.-Su. 11-6.

MUSEUM OF THE ARTS THEATRE OF THE U.S.S.R., 'M. GORKI'
Pr. Khudozhestvennogo teatra, 3a, Moscow
History of the Gorki Theatre. Photographs. Posters. Programmes. Designs.
Daily 10-5.

NATIONAL ARMOURY
Palata Moskovskogo Kremlia, Moscow
The oldest Russian museum (1814). Weapons, armour. Gold and silverware. Crown Jewels. Costumes and fabrics. Utensils. Royal ceremonial carriages. Gifts to the Tsars from foreign States. Clothes worn by Tsars and Tsarinas.
Sa.-Th. 9-4.30.

NATIONAL HISTORICAL MUSEUM
Pl. Krasnaja 1-2, Moscow
The main collections illustrate the social, economic and cultural history of the U.S.S.R. from primitive times to the 1917 Revolution.
M., Th., Su. 10.30-5.30; W., F., Sa. 12-7. Closed Tu. and last day of each month.

NATIONAL M. J. KALININ MUSEUM
Markxa prospekt 21, Moscow
Life and political achievements of Kalinin, Chairman of the Central Committee of the Communist Party for 27 years and then President of the Supreme Soviet.
Tu., Th., Sa., Su. 10-6; W., Sa. 12-7. Closed M.

NATIONAL MUSEUM OF LITERATURE
Ul. Dimitrova 38, Moscow
Documents related to the history of Russia and Soviet literature. First editions. Portraits. Manuscripts. Recordings of the voices of Tolstoy, Yesenin, Mayakovski and other writers.
M. 11-4; W., F. 2-9; Th., Sa., Su. 11-6. Closed Tu. and last day of each month.

NATIONAL MUSEUM OF THE REVOLUTION
Ul. Grokogo 21, Moscow
In former palace (1812), which once housed the English Club. Material illustrating the origins and development of the proletarian Revolution and the formation and growth of Soviet society. Books, underground literature and newspapers, photographs, documents, letters, personal possessions of revolutionary leaders. Secret printing shop, used by Workers' party 1905-6.
M., W., F. 12-8; Tu., Th., Su. 10-6; Closed Sa.

NOVODEVICHY MONASTERY
Bolshaya pirogovskaya 2, Frunzenky obvod, Moscow
Convent building of 1524. Branch of National History Museum. Ecclesiastical art, gold and silver ware, vestments of the 16th-20th centuries.
Daily ex. Tu. and last day of each month. May-Oct., 11-5 (M. 11-3). Nov.-Apr., 11-4.30 (M. 11-2.30).

NOVODEVICHY CONVENT
Pl. Novodevichy, Moscow
Early 17th century building. Many of the country's leading actors, painters, writers, military leaders are buried in the cemetery.
W.-M. 11-4.30. Closed first M. in month.

OSTAKINO MUSEUM OF SERF ART
Ul. Pervaya Ostankinskaya 5, Moscow
18th century timber palace, built by the serf craftsmen of Count Sheremetev. Furniture. Carvings. Decorated stoves, fireplaces. Theatre, convertible into ballroom.
May-Sept., daily 11-5. Oct.-Apr., daily 10-3.

PALAEONTOLOGICAL MUSEUM OF THE ACADEMY OF SCIENCE
Leninski prospekt 16, Moscow
Fossil specimens of fish, amphibians, reptiles, mammals.
Tu.-Su. 10-6.

PARK OF ETHNOGRAPHY (ETHNOPARK)
nr. Moscow
On shores of Lake Kliazma. Wooden buildings from all parts of Russia, including houses, farm-buildings, churches, workshops.
May-Sept., daily 9-6.

PAVLOV MUSEUM OF GEOLOGY AND PALAEONTOLOGY
Pr. Marxa 18, Moscow
Geology. Palaeontology. Palaeobotany.
M.-Sa. 10-6.

PERMANENT EXHIBITION OF THE SOVIET CONSTRUCTION INDUSTRY
30 náb. Frunzenskaia, Moscow
History, techniques, materials of building and civil engineering.
Daily 10-6, except last day of each month.

PHARMACEUTICAL MUSEUM OF THE CENTRAL DRUG RESEARCH INSTITUTE
Krassikova ul. 20, Moscow
Collections illustrating history of pharmacy in the U.S.S.R.
M.-F. 9-5.

PLANETARIUM
Ul. Sadovaya-Kudriskaja 5, Moscow
Astronomy. Physics. Astronautics. Geography.
M.-Sa. 12-7; Su. 11-7.

POLYTECHNICAL MUSEUM
Novaya pl. 3, Moscow
History and contemporary achievements of Soviet science and technology.
Tu., Th., Sa. 1-8; W., F., Su. 10-5. Closed M. and last day of each month.

PUPPET MUSEUM
Ul. Gorki 32A, Moscow
In Sergei Obraztrov's Central Puppet Theatre. Old and modern theatrical puppets from 30 countries, including the U.S.S.R.
W.-M. 10-5.

ALEXANDER PUSHKIN MUSEUM
Ul. Kropotkina 12/24, Moscow
Pushkin and his times. Contemporary literature. Portraits. Water-colours and engravings of Moscow and St. Petersburg.
Su., M., 11-3.30; W., Th., F. 1-7.30; Sa. 10-5. Closed Tu. and last day of each month.

ANDREI RUBIEV MUSEUM OF ANCIENT RUSSIAN ART
Pl. Pryamikov 10, Moscow
In former Andronikov Monastery. Works of the 15th-17th century Russian artists, including Andrei Rubylov.
Tu.-Su. 10-4.30.

A. N. SCRIABIN MUSEUM
Vakhtangova ul. 11, Moscow
In apartment where the composer, Alexander Scriabin, lived and died. Manuscripts. Letters. Scriabin's personal library.
W.-M. 10-7.

B. V. SHCHUKIN MEMORIAL MUSEUM
Ul. Shchukina 8, Moscow
Collection illustrating life and work of the actor, B. Shchukin.
On request.

A. V. SHCHUSEV NATIONAL MUSEUM OF RUSSIAN ARCHITECTURE
Kalinski prospekt 5, Moscow
Early Russian architecture (Novgorod, Vladimir, churches, the Kremlin). Architecture of the 17th-19th centuries. Plans. Models. Photographs. Details of construction and materials.
Daily ex. Tu. M., Th., Sa., Su. 10-6; W., F. 12-8.

STATE V. V. MAYAKOVSKI LIBRARY AND MUSEUM
Pereuluk Majakovskogo 13-15, Moscow
The museum is in the house where the poet lived. It displays memorabilia and documents concerning Mayakovski and his influence.
M., Tu., F. 12-8; W., Sa., Su. 10-6. Closed Th.

STATE MUSEUM OF DARWINISM
Malaja Pirogovskaya ul. 1, Moscow
Darwinism and the theory of evolution. Materialist teaching in the origins of life.
Tu.-Su. 11-6.

STATE PUSHKIN MUSEUM OF THE FINE ARTS
Ul. Volkhonka 12, Moscow
Egyptian antiquities. Greek and Roman art, including statuettes from Tanagra, Roman portraits and works of art discovered during excavations on the Black Sea coast. Western European art, especially French paintings and sculpture of the 18th-20th centuries.
Daily ex. Tu. and last day of each month, 10.30-8.

STATE MUSEUM OF THE WRITER, N. A. OSTROVSKI
Ul. Gorkogo 14, Moscow
Exhibits illustrating Ostrovski's life and work, in his former home.
Tu.-Su. 10-5.

TCHAIKOVSKI MUSEUM
Mayakovski pl. 20, Moscow
Collection and work of the composer, Peter Tchaikovski.
Tu.-Su. 10-5.

K. A. TIMIRYAZEV HOUSE-MUSEUM
Ul. Granovskogo 2, Moscow
Collections illustrating life and work of the scientist, K. Timiryazev, in the apartment where he lived.
On request.

TIMIRYAZEV STATE BIOLOGICAL MUSEUM
Malaya Gruzinskaya 15, Moscow
Origins and evolution of life.
Tu.-Su. 10-5.

LEO TOLSTOY HOUSE MUSEUM
Ul. Lev Tolstogo 21, Moscow
House in which Tolstoy and his family lived. The interior is preserved as it was during his lifetime. Portraits, photographs, autograph letters and personal effects of Tolstoy.
M. 10-3; W.-Su. 10-5. Closed Tu., and the last day of each month.

L. N. TOLSTOY MUSEUM
Kropothinskaya nabereznaya 11, Moscow
Material illustrating the life and work of Tolstoy. Manuscripts, books, documents. Portraits, sculpture, drawings.
M. 10-3; W., F. 2-8; Th., Sa., Su. 11-5. Closed Tu.

TRETJAKOV NATIONAL GALLERY
Lavrushenski per. 10, Moscow
Six principal sections: early Russian art; art of the 18th century; art of the first half of the 19th century; art of the second half of the 19th century; art of the end of the 19th century and beginning of the 20th century; Soviet art.
Daily ex. M. 10-8.

UNDERGROUND PRESS OF THE C. C. R.S.D.L.P. (B) 1905-6
Lesnaya ul. 55, Moscow
Underground premises where the revolutionary newspaper, *Rabochi*, was printed.
Tu.-Su. 11-7.

E. B. VAKHTANGOV MUSEUM
Ul. Arbat 26, Moscow
Collection illustrating life and work of Vakhtangov, in his former home.
W.-M. 10-5.

VAKHTANGOV THEATRE MUSEUM
Vakhtangov Theatre, Moscow
Collections illustrating history of the Vakhtangov Theatre.
M.-Sa. 10-6.

VICTOR VASNETSOV HOUSE-MUSEUM
Pereuluk Vasnetsova 13, Moscow
Former home and studio of the artist, Victor Vasnetsov. Works by Vasnetsov. Studio equipment and personal possessions.
Tu.-Su. 10-5.

N. E. ZHUKOVKSKI MEMORIAL MUSEUM
ul. Radio 17, Moscow
Achievements of the aviation pioneer, Zhukovski, in his former home. Development of Soviet aviation and space exploration.
Daily ex. Sa. 11-7; Su. 11-5.

MOZHAISK

BORODINO MUSEUM
Mozhaisk
Site museum commemorating Battle of Borodino (1812). Paintings. French and Russian weapons, equipment, uniforms. Sketches of the battle, by Frantz Rubo. Field-carriage and personal effects of General Kutozov.
Tu.-Su. 10-5.

MSTERA

MUSEUM OF HANDICRAFTS
Mstera, R.S.F.S.R.
Regional handicrafts, folk art, costumes.
Tu.-Su. 10-5.

NAKHICHEVAN

REGIONAL MUSEUM
Nakhichevan, Azerbaijan Province
Regional history, ethnography, archaeology.
W.-M. 10-5.

NALCHIK

LOCAL MUSEUM
Lenin Prospekt, Nalchik, R.S.F.S.R.
Collections illustrating life and achievements of Lenin, and his place within the workers' and revolutionary movements.
Su.-F. 11-6.

MUSEUM OF FINE ARTS
Lenin Prospekt 35, Nalchik, R.S.F.S.R.
19th-20th century paintings, drawings, sculpture by Russian artists.
Su.-F. 11-6.

NEZHIN

REGIONAL MUSEUM
Nezhin, Ukrainian S.S.R.
Regional history, ethnography. Paintings. Furniture. Handicrafts. Industrial development.
Tu.-Su. 10-5.

NIKOLAYEV

NATURAL HISTORY MUSEUM
Nikolayev, Ukrainian S.S.R.
Geology, botany and zoology of the Nikolayev area.
Tu.-Su. 9-5.

NOGINSK

MUSEUM OF HISTORY AND GEOGRAPHY
Nam. Bugrova 2, Noginsk, R.S.F.S.R.
Social and political history of the area. Natural resources. Local industries.
Tu.-Su. 10-6.

NOVGOROD

GRANOVITAYA PALACE MUSEUM
Kreml, Novgorod, R.S.F.S.R.
Icons and other religious art.
Tu.-Su. 10-5.

HISTORICAL MUSEUM
Kreml, Novgorod, R.S.F.S.R.
In former kremlin. Russian history. History of Russian architecture. 11th-15th century letters on birchbark.
Tu.-Su. 10-5.

NOVOCHERKASSK

GREKHOV MUSEUM
Grekhov ul. 124, Novocherkassk, R.S.F.S.R.
In former home of Mitrofan Grekhov (d.1934), painter of military subjects.
Tu., Th.-Su. 11-5.

MUSEUM OF THE HISTORY OF THE DON COSSACKS
Sovietskaya ul. 38, Novocherkassk, R.S.F.S.R.
Relics of campaigns in which the Don Cossacks took part. English sword, given to General Count Matvei Platov (d.1818) for his leadership against Napoleon. Gold items from Sarmat burial mounds (2nd century B.C.). Memorabilia of peasant revolutionary, Stefan Razin.
W.-M. 10-5.

NOVOGRUDOK

ADAM MICKIEWICZ MEMORIAL MUSEUM
Novogrudok, Byelorussian S.S.R.
Collections illustrating life and work of the Polish poet and patriot, Adam Mickiewicz, in the town where he lived as a youth.
On request.

NOVOROSSISK

LOCAL MUSEUM
Soviettovaya ul. 58, Novorossisk, R.S.F.S.R.
History and archaeology of the town and area. Maritime collections. Natural history. Industrial development, especially cement.
Tu.-Su. 10-5.

NOVOKUZNETZK (formerly STALINSK)

TECHNICAL MUSEUM OF THE METALLURGICAL INDUSTRY
Novokuznetzk, R.S.F.S.R.
Exhibits showing development of technology, especially relating to the coal, iron, steel, aluminium and engineering industries.
Daily 9-5.

NOVYE PETROVCY

MEMORIAL MUSEUM OF THE RED ARMY
Novye Petrovcy
Relics, documents, photographs illustrating history of the Red Army, especially during 1940-45.
Daily 9-5.

NUKHA

REGIONAL MUSEUM
Nukha, Azerbaijan Province
Local history. Folk art. Handicrafts.
Tu.-Su. 11-5.

ODESSA

ARCHAEOLOGICAL MUSEUM
Ul. Lastochkina 4, Odessa, Ukrainian S.S.R.
Egyptian art. Roman and Greek material from excavations on Black Sea coast. History of communities on n. shore of Black Sea.
Th.-Tu. 10-8.

MARITIME MUSEUM
Ul. Lastockkina 6, Odessa, Ukrainian S.S.R.
History of Russian and Soviet shipping in the Black Sea. Navigation. Whaling industry. Naval history.
Th.-Tu. 10-6.

MUSEUM OF THE SIEGE OF ODESSA
Odessa, Ukrainian S.S.R.
Photographs, relics, documents, illustrating the German siege of Odessa, 1941-44.
Tu.-Su. 10-5.

MUSEUM OF WESTERN AND EASTERN ART
Pushkinskaya ul. 9, Odessa, Ukrainian S.S.R.
Western European art, including works by Rubens, Rembrandt, Véronese, Murillo. Persian miniatures. Handicrafts from China, India, Japan. Greek and Roman sculpture (mostly casts).
Th.-Tu. 11-5.30.

NATIONAL ART GALLERY
Ul. Korolenko 5, Odessa, Ukrainian S.S.R.
18th-20th century Russian and Ukrainian art. Soviet paintings, graphics.
Th.-Tu. 11-4.

REGIONAL MUSEUM
Ul. Lastochkina 24, Odessa, Ukrainian S.S.R.
Natural resources, flora and fauna of the region.
Su.-F. 9-5.

REGIONAL MUSEUM OF HISTORY AND ETHNOLOGY
Khalturin ul. 4, Odessa, Ukrainian S.S.R.
Regional history. Partisan life and activity, 1941-45. Industrial development. Ethnology.
Su.-F. 9-5.

OLVIA

ARCHAEOLOGICAL MUSEUM
Olvia
Greek and Roman material from excavations at Olvia.
Tu.-Su. 9-5.

OMSK

DISTRICT MUSEUM
Omsk, W. Siberia, R.S.F.S.R.
Collections illustrating local history, traditions and customs. Omsk in its former days as caravan centre. Religious art. Industrial development.
Daily 9-5.

ORSHA

KONSTANTIN ZASLONOV MUSEUM
Orsha, Byelorussian S.S.R.
Collections illustrating life and work of Zaslonov, in his former home.
Tu.-Su. 10-5.

ORDZHONIKIDZE

KIROV AND ORDZHONIKIDZE MUSEUM
Kirov ul. 20, Ordzhonikidze, Caucasia, R.S.F.S.R.
History of the Bolshevik revolutions.
Th.-Tu. 9-5.

KOSTA KHETAGUROV MUSEUM
Voikov ul. 20, Ordzhonikidze, Caucasia, R.S.F.S.R.
In 19th century Osselian church. Collections illustrating development of literature in the Osselian language, in which Kosta Khetagurov wrote.
F.-W. 10-6.

MUSEUM OF ART
Mir Prospekt 12, Ordzhonikidze, Caucasia, R.S.F.S.R.
Paintings, sculpture by Russian artists, especially of the Realist school.
Th.-Tu. 10-6.

ORDZHONIKIDZE MUSEUM: HISTORY COLLECTIONS
Muzeinyi Pereulok 5, Ordzhonikidze, Caucasia, R.S.F.S.R.
Regional history, archaeology, ethnography.
Su.-M. 10-6.30.

ORDZHONIKIDZE MUSEUM: NATURAL HISTORY COLLECTIONS
Katsayev ul. 64, Ordzhonikidze, Caucasia, R.S.F.S.R.
In former morgue. Regional geology, palaeontology, botany, zoology.
Su.-M. 10-6.30.

OREL

MUSEUM OF LOCAL WRITERS
Ul. Sedmogo Noyabrya 24, Orel, R.S.F.S.R.
Memorabilia of Leskov, Bunin, Andrev and other famous Russian writers who lived near Orel.
Sa.-Th. 10.30-6.

REGIONAL MUSEUM
Moskovskaya ul 1/3, Orel, R.S.F.S.R.
Geography, history of the Orel region. 17th-19th century furniture, costumes. Paintings. Exhibits showing part played by the Orel area in the 1940-45 war.
W.-M. 9-5.

I. G. TURGENEV MUSEUM
Turgenevskaya ul. 11, Orel, R.S.F.S.R.
Rooms reconstructed to give impression of Turgenev's life at the former family estate of Spasskoye, near Orel.
Sa.-Th. 10.30-6.

OSTANKINO

ART GALLERY
Ostankino
Belonged formerly to the Counts Cheremetrev. European paintings, graphics, sculpture, furniture, mainly 18th-19th century.
W.-Su. 11-5.

OSTROG

REGIONAL MUSEUM
Ostrog, Ukrainian S.S.R.
Regional history, ethnography. Paintings, drawings, mostly by Ukrainian artists, or of Ukrainian subjects.
Tu.-Su. 9-5.

PAKHOMOVKA

RURAL MUSEUM
Pakhomovka
Popular traditions. Household equipment. Agricultural history.
Daily, on request.

PALEKH

MUSEUM OF HANDICRAFTS
Palekh
Local handicrafts. Pottery. Woodcarving. Costumes.
Tu.-Su. 10-4.

PANERCZYR

LOCAL MUSEUM
Panerczyr
Local, political and economic history. Agricultural development. Handicrafts. Paintings.
W.-M. 10-4.

PANTIKAPEL

ARCHAEOLOGICAL MUSEUM
Pantikapel
Site museum, containing material from excavations of buildings dating from the former kingdom of the Bosphorus, 6th century B.C. and 5th century A.D.
May-Sept., daily 9-5.

PARKHOMOVKA

REGIONAL MUSEUM
Parkhomovka
Natural history and ethnography of the region.
W.-Su. 9-5.

PAVLOVSK

MUSEUM OF FINE ARTS
Leningradski obl., Pavlovsk, Leningrad
In former palace. 18th-19th century European paintings, furniture, silver, porcelain.
Tu.-Su. 10-5.

PEREYASLAV-KHMEL'NITSKIY

HISTORICAL MUSEUM
Pereyaslav-Khmel'nitskiy, Ukrainian S.S.R.
Open-air museum of ethnography, with rural buildings moved to museum site. Houses. Farm-buildings. Church. Mill. Workshops.
Apr.-Sept., daily 10-6.

PERESLAYL-ZALESSKIY

GORITSKI MONASTERY
Kardovskaya ul., Pereslayl-Zalesskiy, R.S.F.S.R.
Falconnet's model for his 'Bronze Horseman'. Plaster mask of Peter the Great. Icons. Paintings by Dmitri Kardovsk (d.1943).
W.-M. 10-4.

PERM (formerly MOLOTOV)

GALLERY OF FINE ART
Komsomotsky prospekt 2, Perm, R.S.F.S.R.
19th-20th century paintings, drawings, graphics, sculpture by Russian artists. Gold and silversmiths' work. Ceramics.
Tu.-Su. 10-5.

PETROVORETZ (formerly PETERHOF)

MUSEUM OF FINE ART
Petrovoretz
16th-20th century European paintings, drawings, sculpture. Furniture.
Tu.-Su. 10-5.

PETROZAVODSK

MUSEUM OF REGIONAL HISTORY
Zavodskaya pl. 1, Petrozavodsk, R.S.F.S.R.
Social, economic and natural history of the region.
Daily 10-6.

NATIONAL HISTORICAL MUSEUM
Ul. Zavodskaya 14, Petrozavodsk, R.S.F.S.R.
Regional history, archaeology. Furniture. Applied arts. Folklore. Collections illustrating industrial development of the area.
Tu.-Su. 10-5.

PIATIGORSK

LERMONTOV MUSEUM
Lermontovskaya ul. 1, Piatigorsk, R.S.F.S.R.
Collection illustrating the exile in the Caucasus of the poet and novelist, M. Y. Lermontov.
Tu.-Su. 10-5.

LOCAL MUSEUM
Sacco a Vancetti ul. 2, Piatigorsk, R.S.F.S.R.
Natural history. Local history. Paintings by Russian artists.
W.-M. 10-4.30.

PITSUNDA

CATHEDRAL OF ST. SOPHIA
Pitsunda, Georgian S.S.R.
6th century cathedral, now museum of religious art.
Daily 8-5.

PODOLSK

V. I. LENIN HOUSE-MUSEUM
Podolsk, R.S.F.S.R.
Collections illustrating life and work of Lenin, in house where he once lived.
Daily 10-4.

LENIN MUSEUM
Moskovskaya ul., Podolsk, R.S.F.S.R.
House where Lenin's family lived during 1890s. Collections illustrating life of Lenin.
On request.

POLENOVO

V. D. POLENOV NATIONAL HOUSE-MUSEUM
Polenovo
Collections illustrating life and work of the writer, V. D. Polenov, in his former home.
On request.

POLTAVA

BATTLE OF POLTAVA MUSEUM
Poltava, Ukrainian S.S.R.
Exhibits illustrating Battle of Poltava (1709), at which the Russians defeated Charles XII of Sweden.
Daily 10-5.

KOROLENKO MUSEUM OF LITERATURE
Korolenko ul., Poltava, Ukrainian S.S.R.
Manuscripts, early editions, portraits, memorabilia relating to Ukrainian writers.
Tu.-Su. 10-5.

PANAS MIRNYI MUSEUM
Mirnyi ul. 56, Poltava, Ukrainian S.S.R.
Collections illustrating life and work of Mirnyi.
Daily 10-5.

MUSEUM OF FINE ART
Dzerzhinski ul. 11, Poltava, Ukrainian S.S.R.
18th-20th century European (mostly Russian) paintings, drawings, graphics, sculpture.
Sa.-Th. 10-5.

REGIONAL MUSEUM AND KOTLYAREVSKY LITERARY MUSEUM
Ul. Lenin, Poltava, Ukrainian S.S.R.
Regional history, customs, art, handicrafts. Memorabilia of writers who lived in the area, or were associated with it.
Th., Tu. 10-5.

PUSHKIN

ALL-UNION PUSHKIN MUSEUM
Komsomolskaya ul. 1, Pushkin, R.S.F.S.R.
Collections illustrating life and work of Alexander Pushkin.
Tu.-Su. 9-5.

LYCÉE IN PUSHKIN
Komsomolskaya Ploschchad 1, Pushkin, R.S.F.S.R.
Collections illustrating Pushkin's schooldays and his later creative work.
M. 11-4; W.-Su. 11-6.

PUSHKINO

MUSEUM OF FINE ART
Pushkino, Saratov, R.S.F.S.R.
19th-20th century European and Russian paintings.
Tu.-Su. 10-6.

YEKATERINSKI PALACE
Pushkino, Saratov, R.S.F.S.R.
Restored and furnished rooms in former palace of Peter the Great.
Daily 11-6.

PUSHKINSKIYE GORY

PUSHKIN ESTATE
Pskovskaya obl., Pushkinskiye Gory
Former estate, with buildings, of the poet, Alexander Pushkin, including the church with his grave.
Daily, on request.

RIGA

LATVIAN HISTORICAL MUSEUM
Pl. Pionerov 3, Riga, Latvian S.S.R.
History, archaeology of Latvia, and of Riga. Maritime history. Paintings. Furniture. Historical documents.
Tu.-Su. 10-5.

J. RAINU MUSEUM OF LITERATURE
Piohierulauk 3, Riga, Latvian S.S.R.
Collections illustrating the history of literature in the Latvian language and by writers living in Latvia. Manuscripts, early editions. Portraits. Memorabilia.
Tu.-Su. 10-6.

P. STRADIN MUSEUM OF THE HISTORY OF MEDICINE
L. Paegles ul. 1, Riga, Latvian S.S.R.
History of medicine and pharmacy in Latvia since medieval times.
Tu.-Su. 10-6.

MUSEUM OF THE REVOLUTION
Ul. Smilshu 20, Riga, Latvian S.S.R.
History of the workers' and revolutionary movements in Latvia, especially Riga. Reconstruction and development since 1945.
Daily 9-5.

NATIONAL MUSEUM OF FINE ARTS
Pl. Pioneroi 3, Riga, Latvian S.S.R.
Paintings, drawings, graphics, sculpture by European artists. Religious art. Applied art.
Tu.-Su. 10-5.

NATIONAL MUSEUM OF LATVIAN AND RUSSIAN ART
Gorkogo ul. 10, Riga, Latvian S.S.R.
19th-20th century paintings, drawings, graphics, sculpture by Latvian and Russian artists. Religious art.
Tu.-Su. 10-6.

OPEN-AIR MUSEUM OF ETHNOGRAPHY
Riga, Latvian S.S.R.
Houses, farm-buildings, mills, workshops from different regions of Latvia. Implements. Craftsmen's tools. Household equipment.
Apr.-Sept., daily 10-5.

ROSLAVL

LOCAL MUSEUM
Roslavl, R.S.F.S.R.
Local history. Religious art.
W.-M. 10-6.

ROSTOV-ON-DON

FINE ARTS MUSEUM
Pushkinskaya ul. 115, Rostov-on-Don, R.S.F.S.R.
19th-20th century paintings by Russian artists.
Tu.-Su. 10-6.

MUSEUM OF HISTORY
Engelskaya ul. 79, Rostov-on-Don, R.S.F.S.R.
Archaeology and history of the Rostov area. Ethnography. Collection of 11th-12th century stone idols, worshipped by nomads. Planetarium.
Tu.-Su. 10-6.

MUSEUM OF THE REVOLUTIONARY PAST AND THE GLORY OF LABOUR
Gusev ul. 2, Rostov-on-Don, R.S.F.S.R.
Regional history of the workers' and revolutionary movements.
Tu.-Su. 10-6.

ROSTOV VELIKI

LOCAL MUSEUM
Rostov Veliki, R.S.F.S.R.
In former monastery. 16th-20th century icons. Porcelain. Woodcarving. Collection of gifts made to the monastery by members of the Imperial family.
Th.-Tu. 9-5.

ROVNO

LOCAL MUSEUM
Krasnoarmeiskaya ul. 32, Rovno, Ukrainian S.S.R.
Collections illustrating life of the local partisan, Nikolai Kuznetsov.
Daily 10-5.

RYAZAN

PAVLOV MUSEUM
Ryazan, R.S.F.S.R.
Collection illustrating work of the physiologist, I. P. Pavlov.
Tu.-Su. 10-4.

REGIONAL MUSEUM OF ART
Kreml 11, Ryazan, R.S.F.S.R.
Russian paintings, applied art, mostly 19th-20th century.
Daily 9-5.

SAMARKAND

NATIONAL MUSEUM
Sovetskaya ul. 51, Samarkand, Uzbekh S.S.R.
History, ethnography and art of Uzbekistan.
Daily 9-5.

SARATOV

P. S. CHERNICHEVSKI MEMORIAL MUSEUM
Saratov, R.S.F.S.R.
Collections illustrating life and work of the writer, P. S. Chernichevski, in his former home.
On request.

A. N. RADISHCHEV NATIONAL MUSEUM OF ART
Pl. Radisceva 39, Saratov, R.S.F.S.R.
19th-20th century paintings, drawings, graphics by Russian artists. Religious art.
Tu.-Su. 2-5.

A. S. SERAFIMOVICH HOUSE-MUSEUM
Saratov, R.S.F.S.R.
Collections illustrating life and work of the writer, A. S. Serafimovich, in his former house.
On request.

SERPUKHOV

MUSEUM OF FINE ART
Serpukhov, R.S.F.S.R.
Paintings, graphics, mostly 19th-20th century, by Russian artists.
Tu.-Su. 10-6.

MUSEUM OF HISTORY AND ART
Chekhov ul. 87, Serpukhov, R.S.F.S.R.
West European works of art, formerly in possession of local landowners. Icons.
Tu.-Su. 10-5.

MUSEUM OF HISTORY AND GEOGRAPHY
Ul. Chechova 87, Serpukhov, R.S.F.S.R.
Natural history of the Serpukhov region. Collections illustrating social and political history of the region. Industrial development, especially engineering, textiles.
Tu.-Su. 10-6.

SEVASTOPOL

KHERSONES MUSEUM OF HISTORY AND ARCHAEOLOGY
Sevastopol, Ukrainian S.S.R.
Material from local excavations.
Daily 10-5.

MUSEUM OF THE BATTLE FOR THE DEFENCE OF SEVASTOPOL, 1941-44
Sevastopol, Ukrainian S.S.R.
Collections illustrating the fighting at Sevastopol during the German War. Photographs. Military relics. Mementoes.
M.-Su. 12-6.

MUSEUM OF THE BLACK SEA FLEET
Lenina ul. 11, Sevastopol, Ukrainian S.S.R.
History of the Russian and Soviet Black Sea Fleet. Models. Paintings. Documents. Portraits. Relics and mementoes of ships and engagements.
Tu.-Su. 10-5.

MUSEUM OF FINE ART
Nakhimov Prospekt 9, Sevastopol, Ukrainian S.S.R.
19th-20th century Russian paintings. 14th-17th century Italian, Dutch, Flemish paintings.
M.-Su. 12-6.

MUSEUM OF KOVALEVSKI BIOLOGICAL STATION
Primorski Prospekt, Sevastopol, Ukrainian S.S.R.
Marine biology.
Tu.-Su. 10-4.

SAPUN-GORA MUSEUM
Sevastopol, Ukrainian S.S.R.
Site museum, containing archaeological material from excavations at the early settlement of Sapun-Gora
Daily 9-5.

SEVASTOPOL PANORAMA
Istoricheski Prospekt, Sevastopol, Ukrainian S.S.R.
Painting, 115 m. by 14 m., showing storming of Sevastopol (1855).
Tu.-Su. 9-8.

SHEVCHENKO

T. G. SHEVCHENKO MUSEUM
Shevchenko, Kazakhstan
Collections illustrating life and work of Shevchenko.
On request.

SHUSHENSKOYE

V. I. LENIN MUSEUM
Shushenskoye, R.S.F.S.R.
House in which Lenin lived during his exile, (1877). Collections illustrating Lenin's life and political achievements.
Daily 9-5.

SIAULIAI

AUSZA MUSEUM
Siauliai, Lithuanian S.S.R.
Local history.
On request.

SIKHOTE-ALINE

MUSEUM OF THE NATIONAL PARK OF SIKHOTE-ALINE
Sikhote-Aline, Eastern Siberia
Park museum, with collections illustrating geology, botany and wildlife of the Park region of Manchuria and Eastern Siberia.
May-Sept., daily 9-6.

SIMFEROPOL

LOCAL MUSEUM
Ul. Pushkinska 18, Simferopol, Ukrainian S.S.R.
Local prehistory, history. Collections include material from Neapolis excavations.
Th.-Tu. 10-3.

MUSEUM OF FINE ART
Karla Liebknechta ul. 35, Simferopol, Ukrainian S.S.R.
18th-20th century Russian paintings, sculpture, especially works by Repin and other realist painters.
W.-M. 10-4.

MUSEUM OF NATURAL HISTORY
Simferopol, Ukrainian S.S.R.
Geology, mineralogy, botany and zoology of the Ukraine. Ecology.
Th.-Tu. 10-3.

SMOLENSK

MUSEUM OF ART
Krupskaya ul. 7, Smolensk, R.S.F.S.R.
15th-17th century Italian paintings. 16th-17th century Dutch, Flemish paintings. 18th-20th century French, German, Russian paintings.
Sa.-Th. 10-7.

MUSEUM OF HISTORY
Leninskaya ul. 9, Smolensk, R.S.F.S.R.
Local history and archaeology, 10th century onwards. Exhibits relating to prominent personalities of the region. History of the revolutionary movement and of the 1941-45 war. Collection devoted to the cosmonaut, Yuri Gagarin.
Sa.-Th. 11-7.

NATURAL HISTORY MUSEUM
Sobornyi Dvor 7, Smolensk, R.S.F.S.R.
Natural resources of the Smolensk region and their economic utilisation.
Sa.-Th. 10-7.

SOCHI

N. A. OSTROVSKI MUSEUM
Ostrovskova Alleya 4, Sochi, R.S.F.S.R.
Part of museum is in the former home of the novelist Nikolai Ostrovski (d. 1936). Life and work of Ostrovski.
Th.-Tu. 10-10.

SOCHI MUSEUM
Ordzhonikidze ul. 29, Sochi, R.S.F.S.R.
Natural history of Black Sea and Caucasus. Ethnography. Local history.
Su.-M. 10-6.

SPASSKOYE-LUTOVINOVO

TURGENEV ESTATE-MUSEUM
Spasskoye-Lutovinovo
Former Turgenev family home and estate. Surviving parts restored to their 1881 appearance, when Turgenev last lived here. Turgenev's hunting equipment.
Tu.-Su. 9-5.

STEPANAVAN

STEPAN SHAUMYAN MUSEUM
Stepanavan, Armenian S.S.R.
House-museum of the revolutionary, Shaumyan, with his furniture, personal possessions and other material illustrating his life and work.
On request.

SUJA

N. B. FRUNZE MUSEUM
Suja
Collections illustrating life of the military historian and technician, N. B. Frunze.
Tu.-Su. 10-5.

SUKHUMI

DMITRI GULUYA STATE MUSEUM
Ul. Lenina 20, Sukhumi, Abkhasian S.S.R.
Named after Dmitri Guluya, the Abkhazian poet. Regional natural history. Ethnography. Agriculture. History of the Abkhazian people. Archaeology of the former Greek city of Dioscuria.
Daily 9-5.

LOCAL MUSEUM
Lenin ul. 20, Sukhumi, Abkhasian S.S.R.
Local history. Natural history.
Daily 9-5.

MUSEUM OF THE ABKHASIAN S.S.R.
Ul. Lenina 22, Sukhumi, Abkhasian S.S.R.
Regional history.
Tu.-Su. 9-5.

MUSEUM OF SCIENCE
Sukhumi, Abkhasian S.S.R.
Regional geology, natural history. Exhibits showing developments in physics, engineering, chemistry.
Daily 9-5.

SUMY

SUMY ART MUSEUM
Ul. Lenina 67, Sumy, Ukrainian S.S.R.
Paintings, sculpture, graphics, especially by Ukrainian artists.
Tu.-Su. 10-5.

SVERDLOVSK

BAZHOV LITERARY MUSEUM
Pushkinskaya ul. 27, Sverdlovsk, R.S.F.S.R.
Collections illustrating life and work of the regional writers Mamin-Sibiriak and Bazhov.
Daily 9-6.

HOUSE OF TECHNOLOGY
Sverdlovsk, R.S.F.S.R.
Collections illustrating principles and development of science and technology, with particular reference to the steel, coal, chemical and engineering industries of the Sverdlovsk region.
Tu.-Su. 10-6.

REGIONAL MUSEUM
Sverdlovsk, R.S.F.S.R.
Cultural, social, political and industrial history of Sverdlovsk and its region. Paintings. Handicrafts. Furnishings. Domestic equipment. Natural history.
W.-M. 10-5.

SVERDLOVSK ART GALLERY
Ul. Vajneia 11, Sverdlovsk, R.S.F.S.R.
Paintings, graphics, sculpture by 19th-20th century Russian and Soviet artists.
Tu.-Su. 10-6.

V. V. VAKHRUSEHV GEOLOGICAL MUSEUM
Ul. Kuibysheva 30, Sverdlovsk, R.S.F.S.R.
Geology of the Urals.
Daily 10-5.

TAGANROG

A. P. CHEKHOV HOUSE-MUSEUM
Ul. Lenina 72, Taganrog, R.S.F.S.R.
Chekhov's birthplace. Collections illustrating his life and work, including manuscripts, documents, photographs.
Tu.-Su. 10-5.

TAGANROG SCHOOL MUSEUM
Taganrog, R.S.F.S.R.
School attended by Chekhov. 19th century school furnishings, equipment. Material illustrating Chekhov's school-days.
Tu.-Su. 10-5.

TALASHKINO

LOCAL MUSEUM
Talashkino
In 2-storey wooden tower, on the former estate of Maria Tenisheva, contains studios in which famous Russian artists worked in the late 19th century. Local folk art, especially paintings, embroideries, lace, carvings.
Tu.-Su. 10-5.

TALLINN

CITY MUSEUM
Ul. Vene 17, Tallinn, Estonian S.S.R.
History of Tallinn, 1700 - present day.
W.-M. 11-6.

ESTONIAN MUSEUM OF FINE ART
Kadriorg Palast, Weizenbergi 18, Tallinn, Estonian S.S.R.
History of art in Estonia, early 19th century - present day. Paintings, sculpture by West European artists.
W.-M. 12-7.

ESTONIAN STATE PARK MUSEUM
Rocca al Mare, Tallinn, Estonian S.S.R.
Open air museum, containing 18th-19th century wooden buildings from all over Estonia. Farm buildings. Mills. Bath-house. Smithy. Wooden church.
Daily 10-6.

MARITIME MUSEUM
Ul. Pikk 70, Tallinn, Estonian S.S.R.
History of Estonian shipping and navigation.
Daily 10.30-6.

MUSEUM OF HISTORY
Ul. Pikk 17, Tallinn, Estonian S.S.R.
Archaeology, history, ethnography of Estonia. Weapons. Armour. Coins and medals. Paintings. Portraits.
Th.-Tu. 11-6.

MUSEUM OF MUSIC AND THE THEATRE
Muurivahe 12, Tallinn, Estonian S.S.R.
History of music and the theatre in Estonia. Musical instruments. Early gramophones. Musical manuscripts. Letters. Photographs. Posters. Costumes. Sketches.
Tu.-Su. 10-5.

MUSEUM OF NATURAL HISTORY
Ul. Lai 29, Tallinn, Estonian S.S.R.
Earth's geological structure. Evolution of life at various geological periods. The most important minerals and natural resources and their place in the national economy. World zoology.
W.-M. 11-7.

PETER THE GREAT'S COTTAGE
Kadriorg, Tallinn, Estonian S.S.R.
Cottage where Peter the Great lived while Kadriorg Palace was being built. Original furnishings. Personal effects of Peter the Great.
On request.

EDUARD VILDE MEMORIAL MUSEUM
Kadriorg, Tallinn, Estonian S.S.R.
Collections illustrating the career and work of the Estonian writer, Eduard Vilde, in the house where he spent the last years of his life.
W.-F., Su., M. 11-6; Sa. 11-4.

TARTU

OSKAR LUTKA HOUSE MUSEUM
Ul. Riia 38, Tartu, Estonian S.S.R.
Collections illustrating the life and work of the historian, Oskar Lutka.
Daily 1-6.

MUSEUM OF THE CITY OF TARTU
Ul. Oru 2, Tartu, Estonian S.S.R.
History of Tartu. Paintings. Furniture. Craftsmen's tools, equipment.
Daily 11-6.

MUSEUM OF ETHNOGRAPHY
Ul. 1 Burdenko 32, Tartu, Estonian S.S.R.
Ethnography of Estonia. Folk art. Household equipment. Handicrafts. Agricultural implements.
M.-F. 11-5; Sa. 11-3; Su. 11-6.

MUSEUM OF FINE ART
Ul. Vallikraavi 14, Tartu, Estonian S.S.R.
European paintings, drawings, graphics, mainly 19th-20th century. Paintings, sculpture by contemporary Lithuanian artists.
May-Aug., daily 12-7. Sept.-Apr., daily 11-7.

TARTU STATE UNIVERSITY MUSEUM OF CLASSICAL ARCHAEOLOGY
Ulikooli 18, Tartu, Estonian S.S.R.
Greek and Roman archaeology, originals and reproductions. 19th-20th century European graphics.
M.-F. 10-5.

ZOOLOGICAL MUSEUM
Ul. Vanemuizhe 43, Tartu, Estonian S.S.R.
Zoology of Estonia.
M.-Sa. 10-4.

TASHKENT

CENTRAL REGIONAL MUSEUM
Tashkent, Uzbek S.S.R.
Geology, zoology, botany of the region. Ethnography. Folk art. Handicrafts.
Tu.-Su. 10-5.

HISTORICAL MUSEUM
Ul. Kuibysheva 8, Tashkent, Uzbek S.S.R.
History of Uzbekistan. Industrial development, especially silk manufacturing. Literature and music of the Republic.
Tu.-Su. 10-5.

MUSEUM OF APPLIED ART
Ul. Spulvkova 11, Tashkent, Uzbek S.S.R.
Handicrafts of Uzbekistan. Silver. Leather. Woodcarving. Ironwork. Textiles.
Tu.-Su. 10-5.

MUSEUM OF SCIENTIFIC PROPAGANDA
Tashkent, Uzbek S.S.R.
Scientific collections arranged to illustrate methods and development of science. Physical and natural sciences. Engineering.
Daily 10-6.

NATIONAL ART MUSEUM OF UZBEKISTAN
Ul. Gogolya 1M, Tashkent, Uzbek S.S.R.
19th-20th century paintings, graphics, sculpture by Russian artists. Handicrafts, especially of Uzbekistan.
Tu.-Su. 10-5.

NATURAL HISTORY MUSEUM OF THE ACADEMY OF SCIENCES
Ul. Sarban 12, Tashkent, Uzbek S.S.R.
Collections illustrating geology, botany, zoology of the region.
By appointment.

TBILISI

CHAVCHAVADZE HOUSE-MUSEUM
Ordzhonikidze ul. 22, Tbilisi, Georgian S.S.R.
Collections illustrating the life and work of the poet, Alexander Chavchavadze (d.1846), in his former home.
Tu.-Su. 10-2.

DZHANASHIYA GEORGIAN MUSEUM
Rustaveli Prospekt 3, Tbilisi, Georgian S.S.R.
Mineralogy, zoology. Prehistory and history of Georgia. Manuscripts. Coins. Ceramics. Household equipment. Costumes. Reconstruction of peasant's house. Agriculture.
Tu.-Su. 10-4.

GEORGIAN ART MUSEUM
Ketskhoveli ul. 1, Tbilisi, Georgian S.S.R.
In former seminary where Stalin studied. Paintings by Georgian artists. Icons. Porcelain.
W.-M. 11-5.

V. I. LENIN MUSEUM
Rustaveli Prospekt 29, Tbilisi, Georgian S.S.R.
In building of Marxism-Leninism Institute. Life and work of Lenin. History of the revolutionary movement.
Tu.-Su. 10-5.

LITERARY MUSEUM OF GEORGIA
Georgiashvili Street 8, Tbilisi, Georgian S.S.R.
Manuscripts, portraits, memorabilia of Georgian writers. First editions.
Tu.-Su. 10-5.

MUSEUM OF HISTORY AND ETHNOGRAPHY
Komsomolskaya Alleya 11, Tbilisi, Georgian S.S.R.
History of Tbilisi and its region. Regional ethnography, handicrafts. Models showing development of city. Documents. Paintings. Photographs.
Tu.-Su. 10-5.

MUSEUM OF TOYS
Rustaveli Prospekt 6, Tbilisi, Georgian S.S.R.
Georgian toys, mainly 19th century.
Tu.-Su. 10-4.

NATURAL HISTORY MUSEUM OF GEORGIA
Pl. Lenina, Tbilisi, Georgian S.S.R.
Geology. Palaeontology. Mineralogy. Botany. Zoology.
Tu.-Su. 10-5.

NATIONAL MUSEUM OF ART OF GEORGIA
Rustaveli Prospekt 13, Tbilisi, Georgian S.S.R.
Building (1880s) to commemorate victories of Russian Army in the Caucasus. 19th-20th century paintings, sculpture by Georgian artists.
Daily 11-9.

TELSHIAI

'ALKA' MUSEUM
Telshiai, Lithuanian S.S.R.
Local history.
Tu.-Su. 10-5.

TIKHVIN

RIMSKY-KORSAKOV HOUSE-MUSEUM
Tikhvin, R.S.F.S.R.
Collections illustrating life and work of the composer, Nikolai A. Rimsky-Korsakov, in his former house.
On request.

TIRASPOL

LOCAL MUSEUM
25 Oktyabr ul., Tiraspol, Moldavian S.S.R.
Collections illustrating the political, social and cultural history of the area, with particular reference to its agricultural development, and to its milling and tobacco industries.
Daily 10-6.

TOGLIATTI (formerly STAVROPOL)

REGIONAL MUSEUM
Togliatti, R.S.F.S.R.
Regional history, natural history, ethnography. Industrial development of the area, especially engineering. 19th-20th century Russian paintings.
Tu.-Su. 10-6.

TORZHOK

LOCAL MUSEUM
Lunacharsky ul., Torzhok, R.S.F.S.R.
Natural history. Local history. Handicrafts.
On request.

MUSEUM OF HISTORY AND ART
Museum ul., Torzhok, R.S.F.S.R.
Regional history, ethnography. Paintings. Natural history.
Tu.-Su. 10-5.

TOS

PEAT MUSEUM
Tos
History and techniques of the peat industry of the USSR.
Daily 9-5.

TRAKAI

HISTORICAL MUSEUM
Trakai, Lithuanian S.S.R.
Cultural and economic history of Trakai and its region.
Tu.-Su. 10-5.

TUAPSE

LOCAL MUSEUM
Politayeva ul. 8, Tuapse, R.S.F.S.R.
Technology and history of local oil-refinery. History of local workers' movement. Natural history.
Su.-M. 10-6.

TULA

LOCAL MUSEUM
Sovietskaya ul. 68, Tula, R.S.F.S.R.
Political, industrial and social history of the Tula region, with particular reference to its agricultural, iron and steel, and engineering industries.
Th.-Tu. 11-6.

MUSEUM OF HISTORY OF WEAPONS
Leninsky Prospekt, Tula, R.S.F.S.R.
Russian and foreign weapons from prehistoric times.
Tu.-Su. 11-3.

POLENEV HOUSE-MUSEUM
Tula, R.S.F.S.R.
Collections illustrating life and work of Polenev, in his former home.
Tu.-Su. 10-5.

REGIONAL MUSEUM OF ART
Lenin Prospekt 44, Tula, R.S.F.S.R.
19th-20th century paintings, sculpture, graphics by Russian artists.
F.-W. 11-6.

UFA

V. I. LENIN HOUSE-MUSEUM
Ufa, Bashkir Province, R.S.F.S.R.
Collections illustrating period spent by Lenin at Ufa.
On request.

ULAN-BATOR

FINE ARTS MUSEUM
Ulan-Bator, Mongolian People's Republic
Pre-revolution and contemporary paintings, sculpture, woodcarving. Prehistoric rock paintings.
Daily 10-4.

V. I. LENIN MUSEUM
Ulan-Bator, Mongolian People's Republic
Life and work of the founder of the Soviet Union. Models. Copies of manuscripts. Photographs.
Daily 10-4.

MUSEUM-TEMPLE OF THE CHOYZHUN-LAMA
Ulan-Bator, Mongolian People's Republic
In former temple, erected (1903-5) in honour of younger brother of Bogd-Khan. Religious sculpture, statues, masks.
Daily 10-4.

NATSAGDORZH MUSEUM
Ulan-Bator, Mongolian People's Republic
Life and work of the author and poet, Dashdorjiyn Natsagdorzh (1906-37), founder of contemporary Mongolian literature and a leading figure in its development.
Daily 10-4.

PALACE MUSEUM
Ulan-Bator, Mongolian People's Republic
Palace of the former Bogd-Khan, Head of the Buddhist Church in Mongolia and Head of State, 1911-24, and neighbouring lamasery. Sculpture. Paintings. Tapestries. Personal possessions of Bogd-Khahn. Stuffed rare animals.
Daily 10-4.

REVOLUTIONARY MUSEUM
Ulan-Bator, Mongolian People's Republic
Material illustrating the history and achievements of Mongolia since 1921.
Daily 10-4.

STATE CENTRAL MUSEUM
Ulan-Bator, Mongolian People's Republic
Natural history of Mongolia. History. Art. Archaeology. Gobi desert dinosaur eggs and skeletons. Meteorites. Soils. Plants. Animals.
Daily 10-4.

SÜHBAATAR AND CHOYBALSAN MUSEUM
Ulan-Bator, Mongolian People's Republic
Collections illustrating the lifes and activities of the two revolutionary leaders after whom the museum is named.
Daily 10-4.

ULAN-BATOR MUSEUM
Ulan-Bator, Mongolian People's Republic
History of the town and its reconstruction.
Daily 10-4.

ULYANOVSK

V. I. LENIN HOUSE-MUSEUM
Ul. Lenin 58, Ulyanovsk, R.S.F.S.R.
Collections illustrating life and political achievements of Lenin, in the house where he was born. Family portraits, furniture, books, Mementoes of Lenin's schooldays.
Daily, on request.

MUSEUM OF FINE ART
Ulyanovsk, R.S.F.S.R.
19th-20th century paintings, drawings, sculpture by Russian artists.
W.-Su. 11-5.

UMAN

LOCAL MUSEUM
Oktyabrskaya ul. 33, Uman, Ukrainian S.S.R.
Local history, ethnography.
Th.-Tu. 10-5.

UZHGOROD

LOCAL MUSEUM
Kremlovskaya ul. 27, Uzhgorod, Ukrainian S.S.R.
Natural history. Local handicrafts.
Th.-Tu. 11-7.

MUSEUM OF ART
Kremlovskaya ul. 27, Uzhgorod, Ukrainian S.S.R.
19th-20th century paintings by Russian and Ukrainian artists.
Tu.-Su. 11-7.

REGIONAL MUSEUM
Uzhgorod, Ukrainian S.S.R.
Regional history. History of the 1940-45 war and of the German occupation. Folklore. Development of agriculture and the food-processing industry.
Tu.-Su. 11-5.

VENTSPILS

LOCAL MUSEUM
Ventspils, Latvian S.S.R.
Local history. Folklore. Handicrafts. Agriculture. Local industries.
Tu.-Su. 10-4.

VESKOVO

BOTIK MUSEUM
Veskovo
Part of the former Botik estate, where Peter the Great built his first boats. Naval guns and other relics of his fleet, including one of his ships, the 'Fortune'.
Tu.-Su. 10-5.

VIBORG

FORTRESS MUSEUM
Viborg, R.S.F.S.R.
Cultural and military history of Viborg. Furniture. Portraits. Weapons.
Tu.-Su. 9-4.

VILNIUS (formerly WILNO)

HISTORICAL AND ETHNOGRAPHICAL MUSEUM OF THE LITHUANIAN REPUBLIC
Ul. Vrublevskio 1, Vilnius, Lithuanian S.S.R.
History and archaeology of Lithuania. Architecture. Postwar reconstruction. Agriculture. Fishing. Maritime collections. Handicrafts. Household equipment. Costumes. Religious art.
Tu.-Su. 10-5.

MANOR-HOUSE MUSEUM
Vilnius, Lithuanian S.S.R.
Early 19th century chateau-type residence. 18th-19th century furniture, paintings, silver. Portraits.
Tu.-Su. 10-5.

MUSEUM OF MUSIC AND THE THEATRE
Vilnius, Lithuanian S.S.R.
Collections illustrating history of music and the theatre in Lithuania, especially in Vilnius. Manuscripts. Concert and theatre programmes. Memorabilia and portraits of writers and musicians.
Tu.-Su. 10-5.

NATIONAL MUSEUM OF FINE ART
Ul. Gorkogo 55, Vilnius, Lithuanian S.S.R.
European paintings, drawings, mainly 18th-19th century. 19th-20th century Russian paintings. Paintings, drawings, graphics, sculpture by Lithuanian artists.
Tu.-Su. 10-5.

VINNITSA

LOCAL MUSEUM
Volodarsky ul. 6, Vinnitsa, Ukrainian S.S.R.
Contains Kremlin made of sugar. Handicrafts. Local history. Agriculture. Industrial development of the city and area. Paintings.
Tu.-Su. 10-5.

PIROGOV HOUSE-MUSEUM
Vinnitsa, Ukrainian S.S.R.
Collections illustrating life and work of Pirogov, in his former home.
On request.

A. V. SUVOROV MUSEUM
Vinnitsa, Ukrainian S.S.R.
Collections illustrating the life and work of A. V. Suvorov.
Tu.-Su. 9-5.

VLADIVOSTOK

MUSEUM OF THE INSTITUTE OF THE PACIFIC
Leninskaya ul. 20, Vladivostok, Siberia
Oceanography. Marine biology. Maritime history. History of the local fishing industry.
Tu.-Su. 11-4.

VOLGOGRAD (formerly STALINGRAD)

MUSEUM OF THE SIEGE OF STALINGRAD
Ul. Gogolya 10, Volgograd, R.S.F.S.R.
Exhibits illustrating siege of Stalingrad, Sept.-Nov. 1942.
Daily 10-5.

STALIN MEMORIAL MUSEUM
Volgograd, R.S.F.S.R.
Collections illustrating life and work of Joseph Stalin.
On request.

VOTKINSK

TCHAIKOVSKY MEMORIAL MUSEUM
Votkinsk, R.S.F.S.R.
Memorabilia of Tchaikovsky, in house in which he once lived.
On request.

VOYKOVO

METEOROLOGICAL MUSEUM OF THE CENTRAL GEOPHYSICAL OBSERVATORY
Voykovo, Ukrainian S.S.R.
Collection illustrating the study of meteorology.
M.-F. 10-5.

YAKUTSK

MUSEUM OF FINE ART
Ul. Maxima Ammosova 14, Yakutsk, R.S.F.S.R.
17th-20th century paintings, sculpture, applied art from Russia and W. Europe. Folk art.
Tu.-Su. 9-6.

YALTA

ALUPKA PALACE MUSEUM
Yalta, Ukrainian S.S.R.
Former palace (1830-48) of the Vorontsovs. Original decorations, furnishings, paintings, sculpture, objets d'art.
Tu.-Su. 10-4.

A. P. CHEKHOV MUSEUM
Ul. Kirova 112, Yalta, Ukrainian S.S.R.
House in which Chekhov lived, 1898-1904, preserved as it was in his lifetime, with his furniture, including writing table, and personal possessions.
W.-M. 10-4.

MUSEUM OF HISTORY AND ARCHAEOLOGY
Zagorodnaya ul. 3, Yalta, Ukrainian S.S.R.
Collections illustrating history of Yalta and its region since classical times.
Th.-Tu. 10-5.

MUSEUM OF LITERATURE
Pavlenko Proyezd 10, Yalta, Ukrainian S.S.R.
Manuscripts, early editions, portraits, memorabilia of writers who lived or stayed at Yalta.
Th., Sa., Su. 10-5.

REGIONAL MUSEUM
Ul. Pushkina 21, Yalta, Ukrainian S.S.R.
Pre- and post-revolution history of the Crimean south coast. Handicrafts. Folk art.
Th.-Tu. 10-4.

YASNAYA POLYANA

TOLSTOY MUSEUM
Yasnaya Polyana, Primor'ye
House and estate of L. N. Tolstoy. Museum illustrating his life and work. Furniture. Personal possessions. Portraits. Library, with books marked by Tolstoy during his reading.
Th.-Tu. 9-6.

WRITERS' MUSEUM
Yasnaya Polyana, Primor'ye
In former village school. Literature, paintings and other material illustrating the period of Tolstoy. Photographs of Tolstoy's manuscripts.
Th.-Tu. 9-6.

YEKABPILS

OPEN-AIR MUSEUM
Yekabpils, Latvian S.S.R.
Houses, farm-buildings and other rural structures. Agricultural implements. Household equipment. Handicrafts.
Apr.-Sept., daily 9-5.

ZAGORSK

METROPOLITAN'S HOUSE MUSEUM
Zagorsk, R.S.F.S.R.
In former Trinity Monastery of St. Sergius. Ecclesiastical paintings, sculpture. 17th-19th century furniture, pottery, porcelain, glass. 14th-18th century French, Italian fabrics. 17th century Persian, Syrian, Turkish fabrics. Russian handicrafts.
Sa.-Th. 10-5.

NATIONAL MUSEUM-PARK OF THE HISTORY OF ART
Zagorsk, R.S.F.S.R.
Open-air museum of sculpture.
May-Sept., daily 9-6.

TOY MUSEUM
Krasnaya Armiya Prospekt 136, Zagorsk, R.S.F.S.R.
Toys, Bronze Age - present day.
Tu.-Su. 10-5.

ZAPOROZHE (formerly DNEPRASTROY)

LOCAL MUSEUM
Lenin Prospekt 59, Zaporozhe, Ukrainian S.S.R.
Collections illustrating political, social and industrial history of the area. Hydro-electric power. Metal industries. Chemical industry.
Tu.-Su. 10-6.

REGIONAL MUSEUM
Ul. Budennogo 42, Zaporozhe, Ukrainian S.S.R.
Collections illustrating history of the city and its region. Industrial development, especially iron and steel, chemicals, engineering. Post-war reconstruction.
Tu.-Su. 10-6.

ZUGDIDI

LOCAL MUSEUM
Oktyabrskaya ul. 2, Zugdidi, Georgian S.S.R.
Local history. Ethnography. Folk art.
Tu.-Su. 10.30-4.30.

ZVENIGOROD

MUSEUM OF HISTORY AND ETHNOGRAPHY
Zvenigorod, R.S.F.S.R.
In former Sauvino-Storozhevsky monastery. Religious art. Paintings. Local folklore. Handicrafts.
Daily 10-5.

United States

The United States has always seen its museums as fundamentally educational institutions, with an important part to play in the life of the community. In taking this view, it has done no more than continue a tradition already established in colonial New England, where culture was regarded as the concern of the people as a whole and where élitism, in education as in all other fields, was regarded with great suspicion. In recent years, this established principle, that the community should control the way its museum is run, has been bringing considerable problems to administrators, since many citizens have been demanding, sometimes violently, a complete transformation of a local museum. The demand has usually been for a greater degree of public involvement and for an end to the old notion of a museum as a storehouse of treasures and a centre of scholarly research. Such a reaction has been particularly marked among the young and the blacks, who, not unnaturally, favour museums which reflect their own attitudes to life and to the world.

The next few years will undoubtedly bring changes to both the character and the location of American museums, not least because many of the oldest and most famous of the existing museums now find themselves in serious financial difficulties, even to the extent of being forced to sell off items from their collections. This problem, caused partly, as in Europe, by monumental and obsolete buildings, is not in itself of any great consequence, because most of these paintings and other works of art will be sold to wealthy American private collectors, who will eventually die and bequeath their collections to public museums and art galleries once again, a process which has been going on for several generations and is part of the national economy. It also appears inevitable that the concept of American museums as privately endowed, self-financing institutions will have to be abandoned and that both Federal and State money will have to be made available on a scale which is normal in many other countries, but which may well be labelled as dangerous socialism by Americans of the old school.

Meanwhile, it is only fair and just to report that most of the United States' 6000-odd museums appear to be solvent, if not always as prosperous as they might wish, and that no country in the world is experimenting more or more fruitfully with new methods of presentation, promotion and public involvement and with new types of museum - living museums, historic houses, visitor centres, orientation centres, electronic help-yourself guiding systems, area preservation projects, museums in poor areas, mobile museums. Despite all its problems, the United States remains the greatest museological laboratory in the world.

ABERCROMBIE

FORT ABERCROMBIE STATE PARK MUSEUM
Abercrombie, North Dakota 58001
Restored stockade and blockhouses of fort (1857). Local and military history. Agriculture. Pioneer life. Indian material.
M.-Sa. 9-9; Su. 10-9. Closed Nov. 1 - Apr. 30.

ABERDEEN

DACOTAH PRAIRIE MUSEUM
21 S. Main Street, Aberdeen, South Dakota 57401
In former bank (1886). Natural history. Local history. Furniture. Tools. Indian crafts, artifacts.
M.-F. 9-5; Sa., Su. 1-4.

ABERDEEN PROVING GROUND

U.S. ARMY ORDNANCE MUSEUM
Aberdeen Proving Ground, Maryland 21040
Military history. Rifles, 16th century to present day. Artillery. Tanks. Military transport. Armour.
Tu.-F. 12-4; Sa., Su. 12-5. Closed national holidays.

ABILENE

DICKINSON COUNTY HISTORICAL SOCIETY MUSEUM
412 S. Campbell Street, Abilene, Kansas 67410
Local history. Agriculture. Memorabilia of cattle drives.
M.-Sa. 10-4.30; Su. 1-5. Closed Dec. 1 - Mar. 31, Thanksgiving.

DWIGHT D. EISENHOWER CENTER
Abilene, Kansas 67410
Library containing papers, books and other material relating to President Eisenhower. Museum has murals depicting Eisenhower's life and career, with items associated with him and his family. Eisenhower family home, with original furnishings, was occupied by member of the family from 1898-1946.
Daily 9-4.45. Closed New Year, Thanksgiving, Christmas.

WESTERN MUSEUM
201 S.E. 6th Street, Abilene, Kansas 67410
Pioneer history of the American West. Log jail (1859), log church (1860), schoolhouse (1873), log house (1878) are in the care of the museum.
June 1 - Aug. 31, daily 7.30-9.30. Sept. 1 - May 31, 8-5. Closed New Year, Thanksgiving, Christmas.

ABILENE FINE ARTS MUSEUM
S. 7th and Barrow Streets, Abilene, Texas 79605
Paintings and prints by 20th century American artists.
Tu.-F. 10-12, 1-5; Sa., Su., public holidays 1-5. Closed Thanksgiving, Christmas.

HARDIN-SIMMONS UNIVERSITY ART GALLERY
Department of Art, Ambler Avenue, Abilene, Texas 79601
Works by contemporary American artists. Paintings. Sculpture. Prints. Photographs.
M.-F. 8-5. Alternate Sundays 1-5.

HERITAGE MUSEUM
P.O. Box 2775, Abilene, Texas 79604
Early ranch life. Miscellaneous 19th century material from local building site and dump excavations.
May 1 - Sept. 30, daily 8-10. Oct. 1 - Apr. 30, daily 9-7.

ABINGDON

MUSEUM OF HISTORICAL SOCIETY OF VIRGINIA
Washington County Court House, Abingdon, Virginia 24210
County history. Law office (c.1860) of the historian, L. P. Summers, is in the care of the Society.
By appointment.

ABINGTON

MUSEUM OF DYER MEMORIAL LIBRARY
Centre Avenue, Abington, Massachusetts 02351
History of Plymouth County. Pottery. Glass. Agriculture.
M., Tu., Th., F. 2.30-5, 6.30-8.30; Sa. 2.30-5. Closed public holidays.

ABIQUIU

GHOST RANCH MUSEUM
Route 84, Abiquiu, New Mexico 87510
Beaver exhibit. Conservation dioramas. Natural resources of Natural Forests.
Sept. 1 - Apr. 30, daily 8-5. May 1-31, daily 8-6. June 1 - Aug. 31, daily 8-8.

ACADEMIA

TUSCARORA ACADEMY MUSEUM
Academia, Pennsylvania 17059
Academy building (1849 conversion of church of 1816). Period furnishings and equipment, some original. History of Academy and of Juniata County. Household equipment. Farm tools. Indian artifacts.
May 1 - Sept. 30, Tu.-F. 11-5; Sa. 10-6; Su. 1-6. Oct. 1 - Apr. 30, Tu.-F. 8-2; Sa. 8-4; Su. 12-5. Closed public holidays.

ACCOKEEK

NATIONAL COLONIAL FARM
Route 1, Box 697, Accokeek, Maryland 20607
Open-air museum of crops and farming techniques in the Colonial period. Folklore. Indian artifacts.
July 16 - Labour Day, daily 10-5.

ACTON

ACTON HISTORICAL SOCIETY MUSEUM
Box 389, Acton, Massachusetts 01720
Local history.
By appointment.

HISTORICAL MUSEUM OF THE NORTH AND SOUTH
15 Thoreau Road, Acton, Massachusetts 01720
Civil War material.
M.-Sa. by appointment.

IRON WORK FARM IN ACTON
Acton, Massachusetts 01720
Local history. Industry. Decorative arts. Faulkner Homestead (1773) and Jones Tavern (1818) are in the care of the same organization.
Public holidays 1-5.

ADA

NORMAN COUNTY MUSEUM
West Main Street, Ada, Minnesota 56510
Pioneer life. Pioneer village, with reconstructed buildings, furnishings and artifacts.
Tu., Sa. 2-5; F. 7 p.m. - 10 p.m.

EAST CENTRAL STATE COLLEGE MUSEUM
College Library, Ada, Oklahoma 74820
Geology. Palaeontology. Ethnology. Anthropology. Natural history. Local history. Indian material. Archaeology. Transport. Aviation. Paintings, drawings, sculpture by local artists. American furniture. Anasazi artifacts.
M.-F. 8-5.30; Sa., Su. by appointment. Closed college vacations.

ADRIAN

GOVERNOR CROSWELL'S HOME
228 N. Broad Street, Adrian, Michigan 49221
House (1841). Period furnishings.
By appointment.

LENAWEE HISTORICAL SOCIETY MUSEUM
4380 Evergreen Drive, Adrian, Michigan 49221
Local history. Agriculture. Flags. Township Hall (1826-7) and Country school (1875) are in the care of the Society.
Tu.-Sa. 1-5.

LITTLE GALLERY
Studio Angelico, Siena Heights College, 1257 Siena Heights Drive, Adrian, Michigan 49221
Paintings. Graphics. Sculpture. Decorative arts. Archaeology.
Tu.-Th. 1-5, 7-9; Sa., Su. 1-5. Closed Easter, Christmas, college vacations.

AINSWORTH

SELLOR'S MEMORIAL MUSEUM
312 N. Elm Street, Ainsworth N.E., Nebraska 69210
Local history. Industry. Furniture. Tools. Indian artifacts. Stuffed birds. Eggs.
June 1 - Labour Day: M.-Sa. 11-4; Su., public holidays, 12.30-5.

AKRON

AKRON ART INSTITUTE
69 E. Market Street, Akron, Ohio 44308
Chinese, Tahitian, Siamese paintings. European, Oriental, pre-Columbian Indian decorative arts. American and European paintings, sculpture, prints.
M.-F. 12-5; W., Th. 7 p.m. - 10. Sa. 10-5, Su. 12-5. Closed national holidays.

AKRON MUSEUM OF NATURAL HISTORY
500 Edgewood Avenue, Akron, Ohio 44307
Children's museum of natural history.
Daily 10-7.

THE JOHN BROWN HOME
514 Diagonal Road, Akron, Ohio 44320
House (c.1830). Local history.
Tu.-Su. 1-5. Closed national holidays.

GOODYEAR RUBBER EXHIBIT
1144 E. Market Street, Akron, Ohio 44316
History of rubber manufacture. Development of processes. Rubber products. Memorabilia of Charles Goodyear.
M.-F. 8.30-4.30. Closed public holidays.

MUSEUM OF SUMMIT COUNTY HISTORICAL SOCIETY
550 Copley Road, Akron, Ohio 44320
In Perkins Mansion (1837). Early Americana. Pottery. Costumes. Transport.
John Brown House (1825), Bronson Church (1839) and schoolhouse (1840) are in the care of the Society.
Tu.-Su. 1-5. Closed public holidays.

STAN HYWET HALL
714 N. Portage Path, Akron, Ohio 44303
House (1911-15), built for Frank A. Seiberling, founder of Goodyear Co. 16th-17th century furnishings, paintings, sculpture, tapestries. Musical instruments.
Tu.-Sa. 10-4.15; Su. 1-5.

ALAMAGORDO

MUSEUM OF TULAROSA BASIN HISTORICAL SOCIETY
Alamagordo, New Mexico 88310
Pioneer life. Artifacts of south-west Indians.
M.-Sa. 10-4; Su. 1-4.

WHITE SANDS NATIONAL MONUMENT VISITOR CENTER
U.S. Highway 70, Alamagordo, New Mexico 88310
Panel and diorama exhibits on natural history of the White Sands. History of the Tularosa Basin. Works by local artists on subjects connected with White Sands and Tularosa Basin.
Daily, Jan. 1 - Mar. 1, 8-5. Mar. 12 - Apr. 21, 8-6. Apr. 22 - May 26, 8-7. May 27 - Sept. 4, 8-8. Sept. 5 - Oct. 22, 8-7. Oct. 23 - Dec. 31, 8-6.

ALAMO

LIVE STEAM MUSEUM
Route 1, Box 11A, Alamo, Texas 78516
Steam engines and pumps, all operating. Industry. Collection includes cotton gin and oil field steam engines. Aeronautics.
Daily 9-5. Engines operated Su. Nov. 15 - Apr. 14. Closed public holidays.

ALAMOSA

ADAMS STATE COLLEGE MUSEUM
ES Building, Alamosa, Colorado 81101
Local history. Archaeology. Anthropology. Ethnology. Indian artifacts.
M.-F., 8-5.

GREAT SAND DUNES NATIONAL MONUMENT
P.O. Box 60, Alamosa, Colorado 81101
Geology. Natural history. Herbarium. Archaeology. Anthropology. Indian artifacts.
May 1 - Sept. 30, daily 7 a.m.-8 p.m. Oct. 1 - Apr. 30, daily 8-5.

ALBANY

ALBANY AREA MUSEUM
516 Flint Avenue, Albany, Georgia 31701
Geology. Natural history. Local history. Industry. Indian artifacts. Costumes. The first brick house (1860) built in Albany is in the care of the Museum.
M.-F. 9-12, 2-5. Closed Aug. 1-31, Thanksgiving, Christmas, New Year.

ALBANY COUNTY HISTORICAL ASSOCIATION MUSEUM
9 Ten Broeck Place, Albany, New York 12210
In former home (1798) of General Ten Broeck. Federal period furniture. Paintings.
Tu.-Su. 3-4. Closed public holidays.

ALBANY INSTITUTE OF HISTORY AND ART
125 Washington Avenue, Albany, New York 12210
18th century paintings of the Albany-Hudson-Mohawk area. 18th-20th century American and European paintings. 18th century Dutch and English period rooms. Albany-made furniture, silver, pewter. Netsukes. Greco-Roman artifacts. European porcelain figurines.
Tu.-Sa. 10-4.45; Su. 2-6.

HISTORIC CHERRY HILL
S. Pearl Street, Albany, New York 12202
House (1768). Original furniture, silver, china. Portraits.
Tu.-Sa. 10-4; Su. 1-4. Closed public holidays in winter.

NEW YORK STATE MUSEUM
History Collection, 31 Washington Avenue, Albany, New York 12210
Weapons. Agricultural implements. Costumes. Uniforms. Country store. New York furniture, silver, pewter, glass. Photographic and medical equipment.
Daily 9-4.30. Closed New Year, Thanksgiving, Christmas.

NEW YORK STATE MUSEUM
Science Collection, State Education Building, Albany, New York 12210
Geology. Fossils. Entomology. Natural history. Reconstructed mastodon. Iroquois Indian groups. Indian artifacts.
Daily 9-4.30.

SCHUYLER MANSION
Clinton and Catharine Streets, Albany, New York 12202
House (1762), where Gen. Burgoyne was imprisoned after Battle of Saratoga. Alexander Hamilton married Gen. Schuyler's daughter here (1780). Period furnishings, including many original Schuyler family pieces.
Tu.-Sa. 9-5; Su. 12-5.

STATE CAPITOL
Albany, New York 12202
Military museum.
May 31 - Sept. 6, daily 9-4. Rest of year, M.-F. 10-3; Sa. 10-12.

UNIVERSITY ART GALLERY
State University of New York, 1400 Washington Avenue, Albany, New York 12222
20th century graphics.
M.-F. 9-5; Sa., Su. 1-5. Closed university vacations.

LEDBETTER PICKET HOUSE MUSEUM
1010 Railroad Street, Albany, Texas 76430
Restored ranch house (c.1870). Period furnishings. Relics of Ledbetter Salt Works.
Daily 8-5.

ALBEMARLE

MUSEUM OF MORROW MOUNTAIN STATE PARK
Route 2, Box 204, Albemarle, North Carolina 28001
Geology, botany and natural history of area. Indian culture. Pioneer artifacts.
June 1 - Labour Day, daily 9-6. Rest of year: Sa., Su. 8-5. Weekdays by appointment.

STANLY HISTORICAL KITCHEN MUSEUM
813 W. Main Street, Albemarle, North Carolina 28001
Early kitchen equipment. Lighting. Weaving. Local history.
By appointment.

ALBERT LEA

MUSEUM OF FREEBORN COUNTY HISTORICAL SOCIETY
Bridge Avenue, Box 105, Albert Lea, Minnesota 56007
Local history. Pioneer life. Log cabin (1853), and several later log houses (c.1860), Lutheran Church (1878) and County Schoolhouse (1882) are in the care of the Society.
Apr. 1 - June 30, Sept. 1 - Nov. 30: W., Su. 2-5. June 1 - Aug. 31; Tu.-Th., Su. 2-5.

ALBION

ALBION COLLEGE ART MUSEUM
Albion, Michigan 49224
15th-20th century European and American paintings, sculpture, prints. Decorative arts. Folk arts. Glass.
Sept. 8 - June 7: M.-W., F. 9-5; Th. 9-5, 7-9; Sa. 9-12; Su. 2-5. Closed College vacations.

BRUECKNER MUSEUM OF STARR COMMONWEALTH FOR BOYS
26 Mile Road, Albion, Michigan 49224
Paintings. Sculpture. Graphics. Furniture.
Sept. 1 - May 31: M.-F. 1-3. Other times by appointment.

GARDNER HOUSE MUSEUM
606 Linden Lane and 509 S. Superior Street, Albion, Michigan 49224
House (1869). 5 rooms arranged and furnished to represent typical mid-west dwelling of the 1869-1900 period. Local history, illustrated by artifacts, pictures, documents.
Apr. 15 - Nov. 15: Sa., Su. 2-5.

COBBLESTONE SOCIETY MUSEUM
Route 1, Ridge Road, Albion, New York 14411
Cobblestone architecture. Agriculture. Folklore. Children's museum. Cobblestone church (1834) and school (1849) are in the care of the museum.
Tu.-Sa. 11-5; Su. 1-5. Closed Labour Day - Memorial Day.

ALBUQUERQUE

THE CLASSICAL SCHOOL GALLERY
2460 6th Street N.W., Albuquerque, New Mexico 87107
15th-17th century Italian paintings.
Daily 10-12, 3-5.

JONSON GALLERY, UNIVERSITY OF NEW MEXICO
1909 Los Lomas Road N.E., Albuquerque, New Mexico 87106
Paintings, mainly by American artists. Objets d'art.
Tu.-Su. 12-6.

MAXWELL MUSEUM OF ANTHROPOLOGY
Roma and University Streets N.E., Albuquerque, New Mexico 87106
Pueblo ethnology and archaeology. N.W. Coast anthropology. Archaeology of the Andes region. Navajo silver, rugs. Musical instruments.
M.-F. 9-4; Sa. 10-4. Closed University holidays. Christmas.

ALBERT K. MITCHELL COLLECTION OF WESTERN ART
5200 Gibson Boulevard S.E., Albuquerque, New Mexico 87108
Paintings. Sculpture. Graphics.
M.-F. 8-5; Sa. 8-12. Closed public holidays.

MUSEUM OF ALBUQUERQUE
Yale Boulevard S.E., P.O. Box 1293, Albuquerque, New Mexico 87103
Local history. Decorative arts. Costumes. Photography.
Tu.-F. 10-5; Sa., Su. 1-5. Closed New Year, Washington's Birthday, July 4, Thanksgiving, Christmas.

MUSEUM OF GEOLOGY
University of New Mexico, Albuquerque, New Mexico 87106
Geology. Palaeontology. Fossil animals and plants. New Mexico metallic and non-metallic ores. Fluorescence-phosphorescence exhibit. Gem-stones. Meteorites. Seismic recorder.
M.-F. 9-4; Sa. 1-4. Closed New Year, Thanksgiving, Christmas.

MUSEUM OF UNIVERSITY OF NEW MEXICO BIOLOGY DEPARTMENT
Albuquerque, New Mexico 87106
Palaeontology. Herbarium. Herpetology. Birds. Mammals.
By appointment.

NEW MEXICO ART LEAGUE OLD TOWN GALLERY
400 Romero, N.W., Albuquerque, New Mexico 87107
Historical collections of the Armijo family. Paintings, sculpture, decorative arts by contemporary New Mexico artists.
Tu.-F., Su. 2-4.

ERNIE PYLE MEMORIAL
900 Girard Boulevard S.E., Albuquerque, New Mexico 87106
In Ernie Pyle's former home (1943). Collections of his work.
Tu., Th. 12.30-8; W., F. 12.30-5.30; Sa. 9-5.30. Closed public holidays.

SANDIA ATOMIC MUSEUM
Kirkland Air Force Base, Albuquerque, New Mexico 87115
Nuclear weapons.
Daily 9-5; Closed New Year, Thanksgiving, Christmas.

SANDIA LABORATORIES EXHIBIT CENTER
12th and F Streets, Albuquerque, New Mexico 87115
Testing, research and development of nuclear weapons and atomic energy projects.
M.-F. by appointment. Closed public holidays.

TELEPHONE PIONEER MUSEUM
625 Silver Street S.W., Room 306, Albuquerque, New Mexico 87103
History of telephone communications, especially in New Mexico.
M.-F. 8-5. Closed public holidays.

UNIVERSITY ART MUSEUM
University of New Mexico, Fine Arts Center, Albuquerque, New Mexico 87106
Contemporary American paintings, prints, with emphasis on artists who have worked in New Mexico. 16th-18th century European prints. 19th-20th century lithographs. Santos and Spanish Colonial silver.
Tu.-F. 10-5; Su. 1-5. Closed Aug. 1-31, national holidays.

ALCOVA

SUN MUSEUM
Alcova, Wyoming 82620
In ranch house (1877). Geology. Mineralogy. Local history. Indian artifacts. Costumes.
Apr. 1 - Nov. 30, daily 9-5.

ALDEN

ALDEN HISTORICAL SOCIETY MUSEUM
13213 Broadway, Alden, New York 14004
Building (1859). Local history. Tools. Domestic equipment.
By appointment.

ALDIE

OAK HILL
Aldie, Virginia 22001
House (1821), home of President Monroe. Period furnishings. Geology. Palaeontology. Local history.
By appointment, except during Virginia Garden Week.

ALEXANDRIA

CARLYLE HOUSE
121 North Fairfax Street, Alexandria, Virginia 22314
House (1752). Period furnishings. Gen. Braddock's headquarters in 1755.
May 1 - Sept. 30, daily 10-6. Oct. 1 - Apr. 30, daily 10-dusk. Closed Christmas.

FORT WARD MUSEUM
4301 West Braddock Road, Alexandria, Virginia 22304
Fort (1861-5) was built to protect Washington in Civil War. Restored North West Bastion and reconstructed officers' hut contain Civil W relics.
M.-Sa. 9-5; Su. 12-5. Closed Thanksgiving, Christmas.

GADSBY'S TAVERN
Cameron and N. Royal Streets, Alexandria, Virginia 22313
Building (1752). Local history. Paintings. Drawings. Prints. Decorative arts.
M.-Sa. 10-4.30; Su. 12-5.

ROBERT E. LEE'S BOYHOOD HOME
607 Oronoco Street, Alexandria, Virginia 22314
House (1795). Early 19th century furnishings. Memorabilia of Gen. Lee.
Daily 9-5.

MUSEUM OF HISTORIC ALEXANDRIA FOUNDATION
1007 King Street, Alexandria, Virginia 22314
Local history. Lloyd House (1792), boyhood home of Robert E. Lee (1795) and the Lyceum (1839) are in the care of the Foundation.
By appointment.

STABLER-LEADBEATER APOTHECARY MUSEUM
107 S. Fairfax Street, Alexandria, Virginia 22314
Drugstore building (1791-2). Early pharmaceutical equipment.
M.-Sa. 10-5.

GEORGE WASHINGTON NATIONAL MASONIC MEMORIAL
Alexandria, Virginia 23301
Masonic history, especially associated with Washington. Reproduction of lodge room. Portraits of Lord Fairfax by Reynolds and of George Washington by Williams.
Daily 9-5. Closed Thanksgiving, Christmas, New Year.

ALEXANDRIA BAY

BOLDT CASTLE
Heart Island, Alexandria Bay, New York 13607
Building (1897). Period furnishings.
Daily 8-6.

ALLAIRE

ALLAIRE STATE PARK
Route 524, Allaire, New Jersey 07727
Contains Howell Works (1830), a restored ironworks, and Allaire village, self-contained ironworking community.
M.-Sa., public holidays 10-12, 1-5; Su. 12-5. Closed New Year, Thanksgiving, Christmas, M., Oct. 1 - Mar. 31.

ALLEGAN

ALLEGAN COUNTY HISTORICAL MUSEUM
113 Walnut Street, Allegan, Michigan 49010
In former County jail (1906). Regional history.
May 1 - Sept. 30: F.-Su., public holidays, 2-5.

ALLEN

MUSEUM OF DIXON COUNTY HISTORICAL SOCIETY
Allen, Nebraska 68710
Local history. Agriculture. Costumes. Children's museum.
May 1 - Sept. 30, Su. 1-4.

ALLENTOWN

ALLENTOWN ART MUSEUM
5th and Court Streets, Allentown, Pennsylvania 18105
Italian, Dutch, Flemish, German, Austrian paintings, 1350-1760. 19th-20th century American paintings. American etchings.
M.-Sa. 10-5; Su. 2-5. Closed national holidays.

ALLEY SPRING

THE OLD RED MILL
Alley Spring State Park, Alley Spring, Missouri 65431
Water-powered grist mill, with original machinery.
Daily 8-5.

ALLIANCE

ALLIANCE KNIGHT MUSEUM
908 Yellowstone Street, Alliance, Nebraska 69301
Mineralogy. Pioneer life. Indian artifacts.
May 1 - Oct. 31: M.-Sa. 9-5; Su. 1-5.

MABEL HARTZELL MUSEUM
840 N. Park Street, Alliance, Ohio 44601
Local history. Haines House (1860) and Mathew Early House (1867) are in the care of the Museum.
June 1 - Oct. 31: M.-F. by appointment; Su. 1-5.

ALLISON

BUTLER COUNTY HISTORICAL SOCIETY MUSEUM
303 6th Street, Allison, Indiana 50602
In former schoolhouse (1870). Local history. Agriculture.
Th. 2-4.

ALMA

MILL CREEK MUSEUM AND CAMP GROUND
Rural Route 1, Alma, Kansas 66401
Household equipment of the 1850s. Early agricultural implements.
May 1 - Sept. 30, Tu.-Su. 24 hours. Oct. 1 - Apr. 30, Sa., Su. 24 hours. Closed New Year, Christmas.

WABAUNSEE COUNTY HISTORICAL MUSEUM
Missouri and 3rd Streets, Alma, Kansas 66401
Local history. Costumes. Indian artifacts.
Tu.-Sa. 10-12, 1-4; Su., public holidays 1-4. Closed New Year, Christmas.

ALPENA

JESSE BESSER MUSEUM
491 Johnson Street, Alpena, Michigan 49707
Geology. Mineralogy. Planetarium. Local history. Archaeology. Indian material. Agriculture. Lumbering. 19th century shop interiors.
M.-F. 9-5; Tu., Th. also 7-9; Su. 1-5. Closed public holidays.

ALPINE

MUSEUM OF THE BIG BEND
Sul Ross State University Campus, Alpine, Texas 79830
Local history. Archaeology. Period rooms. Blacksmith's shop. General store. Stage coach.
Tu.-Sa. 1-5; Su. 2-6.

ALTENBURG

MUSEUM OF PERRY COUNTY LUTHERAN HISTORICAL SOCIETY
Main Street, Altenburg, Missouri 63732
Local history. Lutheran church history. Concordia Log Cabin College (1839) and Big School (1845) are in the care of the Society.
By appointment.

ALTOONA

BLAIR COUNTY HISTORICAL SOCIETY
Allegheny Furnace, Altoona, Pennsylvania 16602
County history. Furniture.
May-Oct., Sa. 1.30-4.30. Other times by appointment.

ALTUS

MUSEUM OF THE WESTERN PRAIRIE
1100 N. Hightower, Altus, Oklahoma 73521
Local history. Indian artifacts. Agricultural implements.
Tu.-F. 10-5; Sa. 1-5; Su. 2-5. Closed public holidays.

ALVA

NORTHWESTERN STATE COLLEGE MUSEUM
Jesse Dunn Hall, Alva, Oklahoma 73717
Geology. Mineralogy. Palaeontology. Botany. Biology. Natural history. Anthropology. Indian artifacts.
M.-F. 9-5. Closed college vacations, Sa., Su.

AMADOR CITY

GOLD RUSH MUSEUM
Fleeheart and Main Streets, Amador City, California 95601
Relics of the Sierra Nevada Gold Rush. Mining equipment. Wells Fargo office.
F.-Su., 10-5. Closed Jan. 1 - Feb. 28.

AMAGANSETT

AMAGANSETT HISTORICAL SOCIETY MUSEUM
Main Street, Amagansett, New York 11930
Local history, especially photography. Miss Amelia Cottage Museum (1725) is in the care of the Society.
June 1 - Oct. 1: Tu.-Su. 1-4.

EAST HAMPTON TOWN MARINE MUSEUM
Bluff Road, Amagansett, New York 11930
Natural history. Maritime history. Fishing. Whaling. Folklore. Children's museum.
June 1 - Sept. 30, daily 1.30-5.

AMARILLO

JULIAN BIVINS MUSEUM
Old Tascosa Courthouse, Amarillo, Texas 79101
History of Texas Panhandle area, and of Col. Farley's Boys Ranch.
June 1 - Labour Day, daily 1-5. Labour Day - May 3, Sa., Su. 1-5. Other times by appointment.

NIELSEN MEMORIAL MUSEUM
Police Department, 609 Pierce Street, Amarillo, Texas 79101
Weapons. Pioneer furniture. Personal belongings of Nielsen family.
M.-F. 8-5.

AMBRIDGE

OLD ECONOMY VILLAGE
14 and Church Streets, Ambridge, Pennsylvania 15003
17 restored buildings of village built by German Harmonists (1825-31). History of community. Handicrafts. Furnishings.
M.-Sa. 8.30-5; Su. 1-5. Closed Christmas, New Year, Thanksgiving, Good Friday, Easter.

AMERICAN FALLS

MASSACRE ROCKS STATE PARK MUSEUM
American Falls, Idaho 83211
Palaeontology. Indian artifacts.
May 15 - Sept. 15, M.-F. 8-6; Sa., Su. 9-6.

AMERICAN FORK

TIMPANEGOS CAVE NATIONAL MONUMENT
Route 1, Box 200, American Fork, Utah 84003
Palaeontology. Archaeology. Natural history.
Daily 8-4.30.

AMERICUS

GEORGIA SOUTHWESTERN COLLEGE
Art Department, Americus, Georgia 31709
Indian art of the S.E. Contemporary American prints.
M.-F. 8-5.

AMES

PAINT 'N PALETTE CLUB
R.R.3, Ames, Iowa 55205
In former Antioch School, attended by Grant Wood. Local history. Lithography by Grant Wood. Paintings by May Amelia Rumple.
June 1 - Oct. 15, Su. 2-5. Other times by appointment.

AMESBURY

JOHN GREENLEAF WHITTIER HOME
86 Friend Street, Amesbury, Massachusetts 01913
House (1820). Furnishings. Manuscripts and personal possessions of Whittier.
Tu.-Sa. 10-5. Closed Thanksgiving, Christmas.

ROCKY HILL MEETING-HOUSE
Portsmouth Road, Amesbury, Massachusetts 01913
Building (1785), with original box-pews, pulpit and other furnishings.
June-Oct., W.-Sa. 1-5.

AMHERST

AMHERST HISTORICAL SOCIETY MUSEUM
Amity Street, Amherst, Massachusetts 01002
In Nehemiah Strong House (1744). Amherst history. Furniture. Portraits. Clothing.
July 1 - Aug. 31: M.-F. 2-5. Closed July 4.

JONES LIBRARY
43 Amity Street, Amherst, Massachusetts 01002
Paintings by American artists, especially Ruth Payne Burgess. Local history.
M., F. 10-5.30. Tu., W., Th. 10-9.30; Sa. 10-5.30.

MEAD ART BUILDING
Amherst College, Amherst, Massachusetts 01002
American paintings, drawings, prints. 18th century French furniture. Textiles. Coins.
M.-Sa. 9-5; Su. 11.30-5. Closed New Year, July 4, Aug. 1-31. Christmas.

MUSEUM OF ZOOLOGY
Department of Zoology, Amherst, Massachusetts 01002
Zoology. Anatomy. Ecology.
M.-F. 7 a.m. - 11 p.m.; Sa. 7-5; Su. 12-10. Closed public holidays.

UNIVERSITY OF MASSACHUSETTS ART COLLECTION
Art Department, Bartlett Hall, Amherst, Massachusetts 01002
Contemporary American paintings, drawings, sculpture.
M.-F. 10-5; Sa., Su. 1-5.

AMSTERDAM

WALTER ELWOOD MUSEUM
300 Guy Park Avenue, Amsterdam, New York 12010
Natural history. Mohawk Valley Indian relics. Early Americana. Costumes. Children's and junior museum.
M.-F. 8-4.30.

GUY PARK HOUSE
366 W. Main Street, Amsterdam, New York 12010
House (1766, with 19th century additions). Period furnishings. Local history.
Tu.-Sa., Memorial Day, Labour Day, July 4, 9-5. Su. 1-5. Closed other public holidays.

ANADARKO

ANADARKO MUSEUM
City Hall, Anadarko, Oklahoma 73005
Local history. Indian artifacts. Photographs of pioneer life and of Anadarko Indians.
M.-F. 1-5. Closed Thanksgiving, Christmas.

INDIAN CITY, U.S.A.
State Highway 8, Anadarko, Oklahoma 73005
Reconstructions of villages, representing cultures of Navajo, Chiricahua Apache, Wichita, Caddo, Pawnee and Pueblo Indians. Indian arts and crafts.
May 1 - Oct. 31, daily 9-6. Nov. 1 - Apr. 30, 9-5.

NATIONAL HALL OF FAME FOR FAMOUS INDIANS
Highway 62, P.O. Box 808, Anadarko, Oklahoma 73005
Bronze busts of famous American Indians. Indian artifacts.
Daily, 24 hours.

SOUTHERN PLAINS INDIAN MUSEUM AND CRAFTS CENTER
Highway 62E, P.O. Box 749, Anadarko, Oklahoma 73005
Art and handicrafts of 19th century Southern Plains Indians. Contemporary Indian paintings, sculpture, graphics.
June 1 - Sept. 30; Tu.-Sa. 9-5; Su., public holidays: 1-5. Oct. 1 - May 31: Tu.-Sa. 9-5. Su., public holidays, 1-5. Closed New Year, Thanksgiving, Christmas.

ANCHORAGE

ANCHORAGE HISTORICAL AND FINE ARTS MUSEUM
121 West 7th Avenue, Anchorage, Alaska 99501
Geology. Archaeology. Ethnology. American Indian, Eskimo, and Aleutian artifacts.
June 1 - Aug. 31: Tu.-Sa., 9-9; Su. 1-5. Sept. 1 - May 31: Tu.-Sa., 9-5; Su., public holidays, 1-5. Closed national holidays.

ANCHORAGE LOG CABIN MUSEUM
700 Fifth Avenue, Anchorage, Alaska 99501
Natural history. Preserved specimens of animals of the American North, including a world-record walrus, weighing 2000 pounds.
June 1 - Aug. 31, 8-8. Rest of year, 9-6.

COOK INLET HISTORICAL SOCIETY MUSEUM
121 Seventh Avenue, Anchorage, Alaska 99501
Archaeology and history of Alaska.
June 1 - Aug. 31, 9-9; Sept. 1 - May 31, M., Th., Sa., 9-5, W. 11-9, Su., public holidays, 1-5. Closed Christmas, New Year.

U.S. FOREST SERVICE
Visitor Center and Natural History Museum, 6927 Forest Highway, Anchorage, Alaska 99502
Local and natural history.
Memorial Day - Labour Day, daily 9-6.

MUSEUM OF LOUISVILLE SCHOOL OF ART
100 Park Road, Anchorage, Kentucky 40223
Paintings. Graphic arts, especially by American artists.
M.-F. 9-4; Sa., 9-12. Su. 2-5. Closed public holidays and Kentucky Derby Day.

ANDERSON

ALFORD HOUSE AND ANDERSON FINE ARTS CENTER
226 West 8th Street, Anderson, Indiana 46016
In Alford House (1870). Paintings. Sculpture. Graphics. Theatre history. Music. Special collection of Hoosier art.
Tu. 10-5, 7-9; W.-Sa. 10-5; Su. 2-5. Closed public holidays, Aug. 1-31.

ANDERSON COLLEGE MUSEUM OF BIBLE AND NEAR EASTERN STUDIES
Charles E. Wilson Library, 1100 E. 3rd Street, Anderson College, Anderson, Indiana 46011
Biblical and Near Eastern archaeology.
By appointment.

STEINHAGEN LOG CABIN
S.H. 90, Anderson, Texas 77830
Cabin (c.1858). Pioneer furnishings. Tools. Farm implements.
By appointment.

ANDOVER

ANDOVER HISTORICAL SOCIETY MUSEUM
5th and Mulberry Streets, Andover, Illinois 61233
House (1867). Period furniture. Household equipment, utensils. Clothing.
May 29 - Sept. 4, daily 9-4.

ANDOVER MUSEUM
Andover, Illinois 61233
Local history. Furniture and furnishings of 1860-1900.
June 1 - Oct. 31, Su. 1-5. Public holidays 11-5.

MUSEUM OF COMMUNICATIONS SATELLITE CORPORATION
Andover, Maine 04216
Displays and presentations illustrating communication by satellite.
May 1 - Oct. 31, daily 9-5. Other months by appointment.

ADDISON GALLERY OF AMERICAN ART
Phillips Academy, Andover, Massachusetts 01810
American paintings, sculpture, prints, drawings. Glass. Furniture. Ship models.
M.-Sa. 10-5; Su. 2.30-5.

ANDOVER HISTORICAL SOCIETY MUSEUM
97 Main Street, Andover, Massachusetts 01810
In Deacon Amos Blanchard House (1818-19). Local history. Agricultural implements. Household equipment. Furniture.
Oct. 1 - Apr. 30: M., W., F. 2-4; 1st Su. each month 2-5. Closed public holidays.

JOHN-ESTHER ART GALLERY
Abbot Academy, Andover, Massachusetts 01810
19th century American paintings. Prints. Photographs.
Sept. 1 - May 31: M.-F. 9-5; Sa., Su. 2-5.

ROBERT S. PEABODY FOUNDATION FOR ARCHAEOLOGY
Phillips and Main Streets, Andover, Massachusetts 01810
N. American, especially New England, archaeology and ethnology.
M.-Sa. 9-4.30; Su. 2-5.

ANDREWS

ANDREWS COUNTY MUSEUM
212 N.W. 2nd Street, Andrews, Texas 79714
History of Adams County. Early photographs. Pioneer tool collection. Indian artifacts. Geology. Anthropology.
M.-W. 1-5. Closed national holidays.

ANNAPOLIS

CHASE-LLOYD HOUSE
22 Maryland Avenue, Annapolis, Maryland 21401
House (begun 1769) of Samuel Chase, who signed Declaration of Independence. 18th-19th century furnishings.
M.-F. 10-12, 2-4.

HALL OF RECORDS COMMISSION
P.O. Box 828, Annapolis, Maryland 21404
Maryland history. Folklore.
M.-Sa. 8.30-4.30. Closed public holidays.

HAMMOND-HARWOOD HOUSE
19 Maryland Avenue, Annapolis, Maryland 21401
House (1774). Period furniture, paintings, decorative arts.
May 1 - Sept. 30: Tu.-Sa. 10-5; Su. 2-5. Oct. 1 - Apr. 30: Tu.-Sa. 10-4; Su. 1-4. Closed Christmas.

HISTORIC ANNAPOLIS
18 Pinkney Street, Annapolis, Maryland 21401
Local architecture, based on 3 historic houses: Slicer Shiplap House (1723), Paca House (1765) and Hancock's Resolution (c.1670), with period furniture.
M.-F. 9-5. Closed public holidays.

MARYLAND STATE HOUSE
State Circle, Annapolis, Maryland 21401
State House (1779) is oldest state capitol still in legislative use. Original Senate Chamber. Historic flags. Portraits of Washington, Lafayette and important Marylanders.
Daily 9-5. Closed Thanksgiving, Christmas.

OLD TREASURY BUILDING
Annapolis, Maryland 21404
Building (1735). Exhibits of 18th century banknotes, coins, bills of credit.
May 1 - Oct. 31: 9.30-4.30. Nov. 1 - Apr. 30: M.-F. 9.30-4.30. Closed public holidays.

U.S. NAVAL ACADEMY MUSEUM
U.S. Naval Academy, Annapolis, Maryland 21402
History of U.S. Navy. Local maritime history. Paintings. Coins. Flags. Uniforms and costumes. Instruments.
M.-Sa. 9-5; Su., public holidays, 11-5. Closed New Year, Thanksgiving, Christmas.

ANN ARBOR

ARGUS PLANETARIUM
601 W. Stadium Boulevard, Ann Arbor, Michigan 48104
Planetarium. Astronomy.
Daily, by appointment.

THE EXHIBIT MUSEUM
University of Michigan, 1109 Washtenaw and N. University Avenues, Ann Arbor, Michigan 48104
Geology. Mineralogy. Palaeontology. Astronomy. Planetarium. Botany. Natural history. Anthropology. Anatomy. Indian artifacts. Primitive technology.
M.-Sa. 9-5; Su. 1.30-5.30. Closed public holidays.

HERBARIUM OF THE UNIVERSITY OF MICHIGAN
North University Building, Ann Arbor, Michigan 48104
Herbarium. Botany.
M.-F. 9-5. Closed New Year, July 4, Labour Day, Christmas.

HISTORICAL SOCIETY OF MICHIGAN MUSEUM
2117 Washtenaw, Ann Arbor, Michigan 48104
Local history. Victorian period room.
M.-F. 9-5. Closed public holidays.

KELSEY MUSEUM OF ANCIENT AND MEDIEVAL ARCHAEOLOGY
434 South State Street, Ann Arbour, Michigan 48104
Greek, Roman and Near Eastern archaeology, especially Coptic Egyptian. Greek and Roman inscriptions.
By arrangement with University. Closed public holidays.

MATTHAEI BOTANICAL GARDENS
University of Michigan, 1800 North Dixboro Road, Ann Arbor, Michigan 48105
Herbarium. Anatomy. Natural history.
M.-F. 8-5; Sa., Su., public holidays 9-5.

MUSEUM OF ANTHROPOLOGY
University of Michigan, Ann Arbor, Michigan 48104
Archaeology. Anthropology. Ethnology.
By appointment.

MUSEUM OF ART
University of Michigan, Alumni Memorial Hall, State Street and S. University, Ann Arbor, Michigan 48104
6th-19th century European art. 20th century European, American paintings, sculpture, drawings, prints. Islamic, Near Eastern and Far Eastern art. Ceramics, manuscripts from India, China, Korea, Japan.
M.-Sa. 9-5; Su. 2-5. Closed national holidays.

MUSEUM OF PALAEONTOLOGY
University of Michigan, Washtenaw and N. University Avenues, Ann Arbor, Michigan 48104
Palaeontology. Micropalaeontology. Palaeobotony.
M.-F. 8-5.

MUSEUM OF ZOOLOGY
University of Michigan, 1109 Washtenaw, Ann Arbor, Michigan 48104
Zoology.
By appointment.

STEARNS COLLECTION OF MUSICAL INSTRUMENTS
School of Music, University of Michigan, Ann Arbor, Michigan 48104
History of Western musical instruments. Ethnology.
Tu., F. 3-4.

ANNISTON

REGAR MEMORIAL MUSEUM OF NATURAL HISTORY
1411 Gurnee Avenue, Aniston, Alabama 36201
Archaeology. Anthropology. Astronomy. Geology. Mineralogy. Palaeontology. Entomology. Herpetology. Natural habitat groups.
Tu.-Sa. 10-5; Su. 2-5. Closed M., New Year, July 4, Thanksgiving, Christmas.

ANOKA

MUSEUM OF ANOKA COUNTY HISTORICAL SOCIETY
Court House, Anoka, Minnesota 55303
In Locke House, Fridley (1847). Period furniture.
By appointment.

ANSONIA

MANSFIELD HOUSE
22 Jewett Street, Ansonia, Connecticut 06401
17th-19th century American furniture and household equipment. Samplers. Local portraits.
By appointment.

ANSTED

HAWK'S NEST MUSEUM
Hawk's Nest State Park, U.S. Highway 60, Ansted, West Virginia 25812
Civil War history. Pioneer relics.
Apr.-Nov. daily 8-8.

MUSEUM OF FAYETTE COUNTY HISTORICAL SOCIETY
Midland Trail, Ansted, West Virginia 25812
Building (1830), includes restored schoolhouse and house with period furnishings. Indian artifacts. Tools, untensils of pioneers.
June 1 - Sept. 30: Tu.-Sa. 10-5; Su. 1-5. May 1-31, Su. 1-5.

ANTIGO

LANGLADE COUNTY HISTORICAL SOCIETY MUSEUM
1208 Clermont Street, Antigo, Wisconsin 54409
Local history. Pioneer farm implements and domestic equipment. Furnishings. Logging tools.
Tu.-F. 2-5. Closed public holidays.

ANTWERP

OTTO E. EHRHART AND PAULDING COUNTRY HISTORICAL SOCIETY MUSEUM
City Hall, N. Main Street, Antwerp, Ohio 45813
Geology. Archaeology. Ethnology. Local history. Postage stamps.
June 1 - Oct. 31: W.-F. 2-4. Nov. 1 - May 31: W.-Th. 3-5.

APALACHICOLA

GORRIE STATE MUSEUM
Gorrie Square, Apalachicola, Florida 32320
Local history. Memorabilia of Dr. John Gorrie, inventor of first ice machine (1845).
M.-Sa. 8-6; Su. and holidays 1.30-5.30.

APPLETON

DARD HUNTER PAPER MUSEUM
1043 E. South River Street, Appleton, Wisconsin 54911
History of paper-making by hand. Paper-mills. Moulds. Watermarks.
M.-F. 8.30-4.30. Closed public holidays.

APPOMATOX

MUSEUM OF APPOMATOX COURT HOUSE NATIONAL HISTORIC PARK
Appomatox, Virginia 24522
Military history. Exhibits relating to surrender of Gen. Lee to Gen. Grant. Park consists of restoration of village of Appomatox Court House. Buildings (1819-50) include tavern, general store, law office.
Daily 8.30-5. Closed Christmas.

ARABI

CHALMETTE NATIONAL HISTORICAL PARK
P.O. Box 429, Arabi, Louisiana 70032
Military history. Rene Beauregard House (1832) is in the care of the Park.
Sept. 1 - May 30: daily 8-5. June 1 - Aug. 31: daily 8-6. Closed Mardi Gras, Christmas.

ARAPAHOE

FURNAS COUNTY MUSEUM
Arapahoe, Nebraska 68922
Local history.
Sa., Su. 1-5. Other times by appointment.

ARCADE

ARCADE AND ATTICA RAILROAD MUSEUM
Arcade, New York 14009
Grover Cleveland private coach. Railway equipment.
May 31 - Oct. 31: Sa., Su., public holidays 12.30-5. July 1 - Aug. 31, also W. 2-4.30.

WYOMING HISTORICAL PIONEER ASSOCIATION MUSEUM
18 E. Main Street, Arcade, New York 14009
Replica of 1877 log cabin. Early 19th century pioneer items.
By appointment.

ARCADIA

LOS ANGELES STATE AND COUNTY ARBORETUM
301 North Baldwin Avenue, Arcadia, California 91106
Botany. Decorative arts. Local history. Indian culture. Transport. Children's Museum. Four historic buildings (1839-1890) are in the care of the Arboretum. They include the Santa Anita Railroad Depot (1890).
M.-F., 8-5; Sa., Su., public holidays, 8-5.30. Closed Christmas.

ARCHER CITY

ARCHER COUNTY HISTORICAL MUSEUM
County Courthouse, Main Square, Archer City, Texas 76351
Local history. Pioneer items.
M.-F. 8-5.

ARCO

CRATERS OF THE MOON NATIONAL MONUMENT
Arco, Idaho 83213
Geology. Botany. Natural history. Local history.
May 1 - Sept. 30, daily 8-8. Oct. 1 - Apr. 30, daily 8-5.

ARCOLA

PRAIRIE HERITAGE MUSEUM
Route 133, Arcola, Illinois 61910
Pioneer and later local history. Ewing House (1872), with period furnishings, is in the care of the Museum.
Tu.-Sa. 10-5; Su. 1-5.

ARDMORE

TUCKER TOWER MUSEUM
Lake Murray State Park, P.O. Box 1649, Ardmore, Oklahoma 73401
Meteorites. Fossils. Minerals. Restored Indian dwellings. Indian arts and crafts.
Tu.-Su. 8-4.30. Closed Christmas.

ARGONIA

ARGONIA AND WESTERN SUMNER COUNTY HISTORICAL SOCIETY MUSEUM
Argonia, Kansas 67004
In Salter House (1884), home of first woman mayor in USA. 19th century furnishings. 18th century household equipment.
May-Sept. daily 1-5. Other times by appointment.

ARKADELPHIA

HENDERSON STATE COLLEGE MUSEUM
Arkadelphia, Arkansas 71923
Mineralogy. Natural history. Indian artifacts from S.W. Arkansas. Replicas of famous diamonds. Coins. Weapons, especially 19th century guns.
Su. 1-5; M., W. 2-5.

ARKANSAS CITY

ARKANSAS CITY MUSEUM
Kate Adams Avenue, Arkansas City, Arkansas 71630
Local history. Agriculture. Indian artifacts. Costumes.
M.-Sa., by appointment. Su., 2-5.

CHEROKEE STRIP LIVING MUSEUM
South Summit Street Road, Arkansas City, Kansas 67005
Local history, especially of the Cherokee Strip. Agriculture. Hardy Oklahoma Jail (1800) is in the care of the Museum.
May 15 - Sept. 15, M.-Sa. 11-5; Su. 1-5. Closed Christmas.

ARLINGTON

ARLINGTON HISTORICAL SOCIETY MUSEUM
7 Jason Street, Arlington, Massachusetts 02174
In Jason Russell House (1670). 17th and 18th century furnishings.
Apr. 1 - Nov. 30: Tu.-Sa. 2-5.

CURTIS-LEE MANSION, ROBERT E. LEE MEMORIAL
Arlington National Cemetery, Arlington, Virginia 22211
House (1802-18), restored to 1861 condition. Home of Robert E. Lee. 18th-19th century furnishings. Lee memorabilia and personal possessions.
Apr. 1 - Sept. 30, daily 9.30-6. Oct. 1 - Mar. 31, 9.30-4.30. Closed Christmas.

HUME SCHOOL HISTORICAL MUSEUM
1805 S. Arlington Ridge Road, Arlington, Virginia 22202
In former school (1893). Local history, from Civil War to early 1900s. Civil War weapons, uniforms. Desk used by Jefferson Davis. Late 19th century furnished schoolroom and parlour. Farm tools, equipment. Kitchen utensils. Victorian fashions. Indian material including trade beads. Toys.
Su. 2-4. M.-Sa. by appointment.

ARLINGTON HEIGHTS

HISTORICAL SOCIETY AND MUSEUM OF ARLINGTON HEIGHTS
500 North Vail Avenue, Arlington Heights, Illinois 60004
Museum building (1882). Local history.
W. 2-4; Sa. 1-4; Su. 2-5. Other days by appointment. Closed public holidays.

ARMOUR

DOUGLAS COUNTY HISTORY MUSEUM
Courthouse Grounds, Armour, South Dakota 57313
Local history. Furniture. Domestic equipment.
By appointment.

ARROW ROCK

ARROW ROCK STATE PARK
Arrow Rock, Missouri 65320
Restored village, at beginning of Santa Fé Trail.
June 1 - Aug. 31, daily 8-5.

GEORGE CALEB BINGHAM HOME
Arrow Rock State Park, Arrow Rock, Missouri 65320
House (1837) was formerly home of artist, G. C. Bingham. Period furnishings.
June 1 - Aug. 31, daily 9-11, 1-3.

DR. MATTHEW HALL HOUSE
Arrow Rock State Park, Arrow Rock, Missouri 65320
House (1847) was formerly home of village doctor. Period furnishings.
June 1 - Aug. 31, daily 9-11, 1-3.

MUSEUM OF FRIENDS OF ARROW ROCK
Main Street, Arrow Rock, Missouri 65320
Local history. Theatre history. Old Courthouse (1830), George Caleb Bingham house (1837), John P. Sites house (c.1837), John P. Sites gun shop (1846), I.O.O.F. Hall (1868) and former Baptist Church (1872) are in the care of the Museum.
Apr. 1 - May 31, Sept. 1 - Oct. 31, by appointment.

OLD COURT HOUSE
Arrow Rock, Missouri 65320
Court House (c.1839). Period furnishings.
June-Aug., daily 9-11, 1-3.

OLD TAVERN MUSEUM
Arrow Rock, Missouri 65320
Building (1834). Americana. Indian artifacts.
Tu.-Su. 10-8. Closed Christmas, Jan. 1-31.

JOHN SITES GUNSHOP
Arrow Rock, Missouri 65320
Gunsmith's tools of the mid-19th century.
Apr. 1 - Aug. 31, daily 10-3.

ARTESIA

ARTESIA HISTORICAL MUSEUM AND ART CENTER
505 W. Richardson Street, Artesia, New Mexico 88210
Geology. Local history. Archaeology. Indian artifacts. Agriculture. Folklore.
Tu.-Su. 2-5.

ARTHUR

ARTHUR COUNTY HISTORICAL SOCIETY MUSEUM
Court House Square, Arthur, Nebraska 69121
In Court House (1913). Pioneer history. Baled Hay Church (1920) is in the care of the Society.
M.-Sa. 8-5.

ASHAWAY

TOMAQUAG INDIAN MEMORIAL MUSEUM
Burdickville-Old Hopkinton Roads, Ashaway, Rhode Island 02804
Displays showing Indian life in southern New England. Archaeology. Ethnology. Wildlife.
May 15- Oct. 15, daily 10-7. Oct. 16- May 14, daily 2-4. Other times by appointment.

ASHBURNHAM

ASHBURNHAM HISTORICAL SOCIETY MUSEUM
77 Main Street, Ashburnham, Massachusetts 01430
Natural history. Local history. Industry. Transport. Costumes. Paintings. Textiles. Maps.
June 1- Aug. 31, Sa. 2-5.

ASHEBORO

MUSEUM OF RANDOLPH COUNTY HISTORICAL SOCIETY
Public Library, 201 Worth Street, Asheboro, North Carolina 27203
Local history. The Female Academy (1836) is in the care of the Society.
M., W., F., Sa. 9-6; Tu., Th. 9-8. Closed Sa., May 1- Sept. 30, public holidays, Dec. 24-6.

ASHEVILLE

ASHEVILLE ART MUSEUM
152 Pearson Drive, Asheville, North Carolina 28801
Contemporary paintings, prints, sculpture by European and American artists. Pottery.
Tu.-F. 10-5; Sa. 1-5; Su. 2-5. Closed Dec. 25- Jan. 1, July 4, Thanksgiving.

BILTMORE HOUSE
Asheville, North Carolina 28803
House (1891-95) with 250 rooms, built for George W. Vanderbilt. Furniture. Carpets. Paintings. Sculpture. Prints.
Feb. 1- Dec. 15, daily 9-6. Closed Thanksgiving.

COLBURN MEMORIAL MINERAL MUSEUM
170 Coxe Avenue, Asheville, North Carolina 28801
Gems, minerals, mainly from Asheville area.
M.-F. 11-5. Closed Dec. 15- Jan. 2.

CRAGGY GARDENS VISITOR CENTER
Blue Ridge Parkway, Asheville, North Carolina 28801
Natural history of the S. Appalachian region, especially high mountain flora and fauna.
May 1- Oct. 31, daily 9-5.

THOMAS WOLFE MEMORIAL
48 Spruce Street, Asheville, North Carolina 28801
Boyhood home of the writer, Thomas Wolfe, furnished as early 20th century boarding house.
May-Oct., M.-Sa. 10-12.30, 2-5.30; Su. 2-6.

ASHLAND

PIONEER MUSEUM
Highway 160, Ashland, Kansas 67831
History of pioneer life in the district.
May 1- Sept. 30, daily 10.30-6. Oct. 1- Apr. 30, 12.30-4.30. Closed Christmas.

SANTA FE MUSEUM
Grant Street and Highway 160, Ashland, Kansas 67831
History of Santa Fe Railway. Santa Fe Depot (1911) is in the care of the museum.
By appointment.

ASHLAND LOGGING MUSEUM
Box 87, Ashland, Maine 04732
Reproduction of early logging camp. Tools. Machinery. Equipment.
May-Oct., by appointment.

ASHLAND HISTORICAL SOCIETY MUSEUM
Town Hall, Main Street, Ashland, Massachusetts 01721
In Town Hall (1854). Local history. Paintings.
By appointment.

SOUTHERN OREGON COLLEGE MUSEUM OF VERTEBRATE NATURAL HISTORY
1250 Siskujon Boulevard, Ashland, Oregon 97520
Bird and mammal skins. Fish. Reptiles. Amphibians.
By appointment.

SCOTCHTOWN
107 Stebbins Street, Ashland, Virginia 23005
House (1719), home of Patrick Henry. Period furnishings.
Apr. 1- Oct. 31: M.-Sa. 10-5; Su. 2-5. Other times by appointment.

ASHLAND MUSEUM
500 W. 2nd Street, Ashland, Wisconsin 54806
Local history. Indian relics. Costumes.
M.-F. 1-4.30. Closed public holidays.

ASHLEY FALLS

COLONEL ASHLEY HOUSE
Cooper Hill Road, Ashley Falls, Massachusetts 01222
House (1735). Colonial furnishings. Pottery.
June 1- Oct. 15, W.-Su. 1-5.

ASHTABULA

ASHTABULA ARTS CENTER
4134 Lake Avenue, Ashtabula, Ohio 44004
Contemporary American paintings, graphics.
M., W. 9-5, 7-9; Tu., Th., Sa. 9-5. Closed public holidays.

ASKOV

PINE COUNTY HISTORICAL SOCIETY MUSEUM
Askov, Minnesota 55704
Local history. Agriculture. Folklore. Great Northern railway depot (1900) is in the care of the Society.
May 1- Aug. 31: Tu.-Su. 1-4.

ASPEN

ASPEN HISTORICAL SOCIETY MUSEUM
620 West Bleeker, Aspen, Colorado 81611
In Stallard House (1890). Local history, expecially mining. Household equipment, tools and other material illustrating life in a mountain mining town.
June 15- Sept. 30, Dec. 1- Apr. 15, Tu.-Su., 1-4. Closed Christmas.

ASTORIA

CLATSOP COUNTY HISTORICAL CENTER
441 8th Street, Astoria, Oregon 97103
In Flavel House (1883). Flavel family and period furnishings. Relics of shipwrecks on northwest coast. Victorian musical instruments. History of Clatsop County.
May 1- Sept. 30, daily 10-5. Oct. 1- Apr. 30, Tu.-Su. 12-5.

COLUMBIA RIVER MARITIME MUSEUM
16th and Exchange Streets, Astoria, Oregon 97103
Maritime history of Northwest. Ship models. Shipbuilding equipment. Lightship 'Columbia' is in the care of the Museum.
May 1- Sept. 30, daily, 10.30-5. Oct. 1- Apr. 30, Tu.-Su. 10.30-5. Closed Christmas.

FORT CLATSOP NATIONAL MEMORIAL
Route 3, Box 604 FC, Astoria, Oregon 97103
House is replica of winter quarters (1805-6) of Lewis and Clark expedition. History of the expedition.
Daily, June 15- Sept. 1, 8-8; Sept. 2- June 14, 8-5. Closed Christmas.

ATASCADERO

TREASURE OF EL CAMINO REAL
6500 Palma Avenue, Atascadero, California 93422
Local history. Indian artifacts. Costumes. Decorative arts. Palaeontology. Natural history. Museum House (1917) is in the care of the Society.
M.-F., 1-4. Closed public holidays.

ATCHISON

BENEDICTINE COLLEGE MUSEUM
Department of Biology, North Campus, Atchison, Kansas 66002
Geology. Botany. Zoology. Ethnology. Archaeology.
By appointment. Closed school vacations.

ATHENS

GEORGIA MUSEUM OF ART, UNIVERSITY OF GEORGIA
Jackson Street, North Campus, Athens, Georgia 30601
American paintings, watercolours, prints, sculpture, decorative arts. European paintings, prints, drawings. Pre-Columbian and American Indian art. Japanese prints. African and Pacific crafts.
M.-F. 8-5; Sa. 9-12; Su. 2-5. Closed University vacations, public holidays, Aug. 20- Labour Day.

TIOGA POINT MUSEUM
724 S. Main Street, Athens, Pennsylvania 18810
Natural history. Local history. Canals and railways. Indian culture. Stephen Foster collection.
M. 7-9; W., Sa. 2-5. Other times by appointment.

MCMINN COUNTY CHAPER HISTORICAL SOCIETY MUSEUM
Court House, Athens, Tennessee 37303
History of McMinn County. Indian artifacts.
By appointment.

ATHOL

ATHOL HISTORICAL SOCIETY MUSEUM
1307 Main Street, Athol, Massachusetts 01331
History of Athol. Mementoes of Civil and Spanish-American Wars. Glass.
May 1- 3rd W. in Oct., W. 2-5.

HOME ON THE RANGE CABIN
Athol, Kansas 66932
House (1872). Period furnishings.
Daily on request.

ATLANTA

ATLANTA HISTORICAL SOCIETY MUSEUM
3099 Andrews Drive N.W., P.O. Box 12423, Atlanta, Georgia 30305
Local history. Civil War relics. Decorative arts. Tullie Smith House (c.1835) and Swan House (1927-8) are in the care of the Society.
M.-F. 9-5; Su. 1.30-3.30. Closed public holidays.

ATLANTA MUSEUM
537-9 Peachtree Street N.E., Atlanta, Georgia 30308
National and local history. Furniture. Decorative arts. Original Eli Whitney cotton gin. Whitney gun collection. Horse-drawn vehicles. Indian artifacts. Coca Cola history. Cinema history. Indian Chief William McIntosh Home (1800-21) is in the care of the Museum.
M.-F. 9-4.30. Closed New Year, July 4, Labour Day, Thanksgiving, Christmas.

CYCLORAMA
Boulevard at Cherokee, Atlanta, Georgia 30308
Local history. Painting, 50 ft by 400 ft, depicting Battle of Atlanta.
Daily 9-5. Closed Christmas.

EMORY UNIVERSITY MUSEUM
Arkwright Drive, Emory University, Atlanta, Georgia 30322
Geology. Archaeology. Zoology. Entomology. Ethnology.
M.-F. 10-12, 2-4; Sa. 10-12. Closed university vacations.

FERNBANK SCIENCE CENTER
136 Heaton Park Drive N.E., Atlanta, Georgia 30307
Mineralogy. Palaeontology. Herpetology. Observatory. Herbarium.
M., Sa. 8.30-5; Tu.-F. 8.30-10; Su. 1.30-5. Closed public holidays.

GEORGIA STATE MUSEUM OF SCIENCE AND INDUSTRY
Room 431, State Capitol, Atlanta, Georgia 30334
Geology. Zoology. Herpetology. Maritime and military history. Industry.
M.-F. 8.30-4.30; Sa. 9.30-3. Closed public holidays.

HIGH MUSEUM OF ART
1280 Peachtree Street N.E., Atlanta, Georgia 30309
14th-18th century European paintings, sculpture, graphics. 19th-20th century European and American prints. Oriental, Pre-Columbian, European, American decorative arts.
M.-W., F., Sa. 10-5. Th. 10-10; Su. 12-5. Closed public holidays.

ATTICA

ATTICA HISTORICAL SOCIETY MUSEUM
Main Street, Attica, New York 14011
History of New York State, and of America. Local industries. Pioneer books. Indian artifacts.
W., Su. 3-6.

ATTLEBORO

ATTLEBORO MUSEUM
Capron Park, Attleboro, Massachusetts 02703
Paintings by 20th century American artists. Products of local jewellery industry.
Sept.-July, Tu-Su. 2-5. Closed public holidays.

BRONSON MUSEUM
8 N. Main Street, Attleboro, Massachusetts 02703
Palaeolithic and Neolithic archaeology in New England.
May 1 - Sept. 30: M., W. 9-4; Oct. 1 - Apr. 30: M.-Th. 9-4.

ATWOOD

MUSEUM OF RAWLINS COUNTY HISTORICAL SOCIETY
700 Vine Street, Atwood, Kansas 67730
In Stevens Chapel (1890). Mineralogy. Local history. Furnished rooms of the 1890s. Country store.
Tu.-Sa. 2-5.

AUBURN

PLACER COUNTY MUSEUM
Fair Grounds, High Street, Auburn, California 95603
Mining equipment and other relics of pioneer days. Rooms illustrating life of pioneers.
By appointment. Closed Christmas, Thanksgiving, July 4, Labour Day.

MUSEUM OF ANDROSCOGGIN HISTORICAL SOCIETY
2 Turner Street, Auburn, Maine 04210
Local history.
M.-F., by appointment. Closed public holidays.

CAYUGA MUSEUM OF HISTORY AND ART
203 Genesee Street, Auburn, New York 13021
Museum building (1840). Mineralogy. Local history. Indian artifacts. Paintings. Sculpture. Fillmore Memorial Log Cabin (1791), Hallcock House (1824) and Owaco stockaded Indian village are in the care of the Museum.
Tu.-F. 1-5; Sa. 9-12, 1-5; Su. 2-5. Closed New Year, Labour Day, Thanksgiving, Christmas.

SEWARD HOUSE
33 South Street, Auburn, New York 13021
House (1816) was home of W. H. Seward, Secretary of State largely responsible for purchase of Alaska (1867). Civil War relics. Victorian furniture. Paintings. Lincoln letters.
Mar.-Dec., M.-Sa. 1-5. Closed public holidays.

OWASCO STOCKADED INDIAN VILLAGE
Emerson Park, Auburn, New York 13021
Indian history and artifacts.
Su.-F. 1-5; Sa. 9-12, 1-5.

WHITE RIVER VALLEY HISTORICAL SOCIETY MUSEUM
19 H. Street S.E., Auburn, Washington 98002
Local history. Indian artifacts. Photographs.
Th., Su. 2-4.30.

AUGUSTA

AUGUSTA RICHMOND COUNTY MUSEUM
540 Telfair Street, Augusta, Georgia 30901
Geology. Mineralogy. Natural history. Anthropology. Archaeology. Ethnography. Local history. Civil War relics. Paintings. Sculpture. Graphics. Costumes. Brahe House (1850) is in the care of the Museum.
Tu.-Sa. 2-6; Su. 2-5. Closed Labour Day, Dec. 20 - Jan. 2.

GERTRUDE HERBERT MEMORIAL INSTITUTE OF ART
506 Telfair Street, Augusta, Georgia 30901
16th-20th century European paintings, sculpture, graphics. Ware's Folly House (1818) is in the care of the Institute.
M.-F. 10-12, 2-5; Sa., Su. 3-5. Closed Christmas, to New Year.

MACKAY HOUSE
1822 Broad Street, Augusta, Georgia 30904
House (c.1760). 18th century furnishings. Exhibits illustrating pre-Revolution Indian trade and Southern theatre of operations during the Revolution.
Oct.-Apr., Tu.-Sa. 10-5; Su. 2-5. May-Sept., Tu.-Sa. 10-5.30; Su. 2-5.30. Closed Thanksgiving, Christmas.

MEADOW GARDEN
1320 Nelson Street, Augusta, Georgia 30904
Residence (1780-1804) of George Walters, signatory of Declaration of Independence. Walton family furnishings and personal possessions.
Daily 10-4.

WHITE HOUSE
1822 Broad Street, Augusta, Georgia 30904
House (c.1805). Period furnishings.
May 1 - Sept. 30, M.-Sa. 9-5; Su. 2-5. Oct. 1 - Apr. 30, M.-Sa. 9-6; Su. 2-6.

AUGUSTA HISTORICAL MUSEUM
305 State Street, Augusta, Kansas 67010
Local history.
May 15 - Sept. 15, daily 1-5.

FORT WESTERN MUSEUM
Bowman Street, Augusta, Maine 04330
In buildings of Fort Western (1754 onwards). Period rooms. Military history. Indian artifacts.
May 15 - Aug. 31, M.-Sa. 10-5; Su. 1-5.

BLAINE HOUSE
State Street, Augusta, Maine 04330
Former State Governor's residence (1832-5). Period furnishings. Silver from battleship 'Maine' (1895-8, 1905-22).
M.-F. 2-4. Closed public holidays.

MAINE STATE MUSEUM
State House, Augusta, Maine 04330
Geology. Mineralogy. Science. Natural history. Anthropology. Ethnology. Technology. Marine biology.
Daily 10-5. Closed New Year, Thanksgiving, Christmas.

KENNEBEC HISTORICAL SOCIETY MUSEUM
Lithgow Library Building, Augusta, Maine 04330
Local history.
By appointment.

AURIESVILLE

KATERI MUSEUM
Route 5S, Auriesville, New York 12016
Mohawk Indian culture. Site of martyrdom of Father Isaac Jogues (1642). Paintings. Anthropology. Archaeology.
M.-F. 9-5; Sa., Su., public holidays 8-8. Closed last Su. in Oct - 1st Su. in May.

AURORA

AURORA HISTORICAL MUSEUM
304 Oak Avenue, Aurora, Illinois 60506
Museum building (1856). Palaeontology. Bones and tusks. Indian material. Costumes. Vehicles.
W., Su. 2.30-5; Tu.-F. by appointment.

HILLFOREST HISTORICAL FOUNDATION
213 5th Street, Aurora, Indiana 47001
In Hillforest Mansion (1852-6). Household equipment. Furniture. Local history.
Apr. 1 - Dec. 31, Tu.-Su. 1-5.

AURORA HISTORICAL SOCIETY MUSEUM
5 S. Grove Avenue, Aurora, New York 14052
Local history.
W. 1-4. Other times by appointment.

AURORA HISTORICAL SOCIETY MUSEUM
115 Aurora Road E., Aurora, Ohio 44202
Local history. Agriculture, especially cheese making. Furniture.
M.-Sa. 9-5. Closed New Year, Washington's Birthday, Memorial Day, July 4, Labour Day, Christmas.

CHAMPOEG STATE PARK MUSEUM
Route 1, Aurora, Oregon 97002
Natural history. Local history, especially of State Park area. Indian artifacts. Decorative arts. Transport.
May 1 - Sept. 30, daily 11-5. Oct. 1 - Apr. 30, F.-Su. 11-4.

AUSABLE CHASM

AUSABLE CHASM ANTIQUE CAR MUSEUM
Route 9, Ausable Chasm, New York 12911
Early American cars.
June 15 - Sept. 15, daily 10-6. May - June 14, Sept. 16 - Oct. 30, Su. 10-5.30.

AUSTIN

MOWER COUNTY PIONEER AND HISTORICAL CENTER
Fairgrounds, Austin, Minnesota 55912
Civil War relics. Horse-drawn vehicles. Caboose. Steam locomotive. Sherman tank.
June 1 - Aug. 31, Su. 1-5. Also by appointment.

AUSTIN NATURAL SCIENCE CENTER
401 Deep Eddy Avenue, Austin, Texas 78703
Geology. Palaeontology. Botany. Entomology. Herpetology. Mammalogy. Junior museum.
Daily 2-5. Closed public holidays, Thanksgiving, Christmas.

DAUGHTERS OF THE REPUBLIC OF TEXAS MUSEUM
21000 Hartford Road, Austin, Texas 78701
Exhibits illustrating lives and achievements of famous Texans. Indian artifacts.
Tu.-Sa. 9-12, 1-5. Closed public holidays.

ELISABET NEY MUSEUM
304 E. 44th Street, Austin, Texas 78751
In former studio (1892) of sculptress, Elisabet Ney. Works by her. Memorabilia.
M.-F. 3-5, 10-12; Sa., Su. 2-5. Closed public holidays.

FRENCH LEGATION
802 San Marcos Street, Austin, Texas 78702
Former residence of French Chargé d'Affaires in 1840s. French and Creole kitchen utensils, equipment. Life in Republic of Texas 1836-46.
Tu.-Su. 1-5. Closed public holidays.

LAGUNA GLORIA ART MUSEUM
3809 W. 35th Street, Austin, Texas 78703
Paintings, graphics, sculpture, especially by Texas artists.
Tu.-F. 9-5; Sa. 10-5; Su. 2-5. Closed public holidays.

MEMORIAL MUSEUM
24th and Trinity Streets, Austin, Texas 78705
Geology. Palaeontology. Mineralogy. Plants and animals of Texas. Human evolution. Culture of American Indians. Texas history.
M.-Sa. 9-5; Su. 2-5. Closed public holidays.

NEILL-COCHRAN MUSEUM HOUSE
2310 San Gabriel Street, Austin, Texas 78705
House (c.1855). Period furnishings.
Tu. 10-12; Sa., Su. 3-5. Other times by appointment.

O HENRY MUSEUM
409 E. 5th Street, Austin, Texas 78701
Furniture, personal possessions, letters, photographs of O Henry (William Sydney Potter) and his family, in the writer's former home (1888).
Tu.-F. 9.30-11.30, 1.30-4.30; Sa.-M. 1.30-4.30. Closed public holidays.

OLD BAKERY
1006 Congress Street, Austin, Texas 78710
Bakery (1876). Oven and early bakery equipment.
M.-F. 9-3. Closed public holidays and school vacations.

SWEDISH PIONEER CABIN
2220 Barton Springs Road, Austin, Texas 78705
Pioneer home (c.1840), moved to present site. Swedish memorabilia. Pioneer household items.
Tu.-Su. 10-4.30. Closed Christmas, New Year.

STATE LIBRARY
State Capitol, 1201 Brazos Street, Austin, Texas 78711
Texas archives. Pease Room, with furniture of Governor Pease period (1853-69).
M.-F. 8-5. Closed public holidays.

TEXAS CONFEDERATE MUSEUM
112 E. 11th Street, Austin, Texas 78701
Museum of Confederate and Southern History. Uniforms. Texas regimental flags.
Tu.-Sa. 9-12, 1-5. Closed public holidays.

UNIVERSITY OF TEXAS ART MUSEUM
23rd Street and San Jacinto Boulevard, Austin, Texas 78705
Paintings, graphics, drawings by 20th century American artists.
M.-F. 10-6; Sa. 9-1; Su. 1-5.

UNIVERSITY OF TEXAS
Eugene C. Barker Texas History Center, Austin, Texas 78712
Texas history. Paintings by Frank Reaugh of ranching and other Texas scenes.
By appointment.

AU TRAIN

PAULSON HOUSE
U.S. Forest Service Road 2278, Au Train, Michigan 49806
Early 19th century cedar loghouse. Period furniture. Household equipment.
By appointment.

AVA

GALE'S PIONEER MUSEUM
R.R. 2, Ava, Illinois 62907
Pioneer relics. Indian artifacts.
Daily, by appointment.

AVALON

CATALINA ISLAND MUSEUM
Box 366, Avalon, California 90704
Natural history. Archaeology. Indian artifacts from Catalina Island.
June 15 - Sept. 14, daily 1-4, 8-10. Sept. 15 - June 14, Sa., Su. 1-3.

AZTEC

AZTEC RUINS NATIONAL MONUMENT
Route 1, Box 101, Aztec, New Mexico 87410
Archaeology and artifacts of Southwest and Pueblo Indians.
June 1 - Aug. 31, 7-6.30. Sept. 1 - May 31, 8-5.

BACONE

BACONE COLLEGE MUSEUM
Bacone, Oklahoma 74420
Indian artifacts.
M.-Th. 8-5; F. 8-4.30; Sa., Su. by appointment. Closed public holidays.

BAGLEY

MUSEUM OF CLEARWATER COUNTY HISTORICAL SOCIETY
Bagley, Minnesota 56621
Local history. Agriculture. Lumber industry.
F. 12-5; Sa. 1-4.

BAILEY

COUNTRY DOCTOR MUSEUM
Box 34, Bailey, North Carolina 27807
Apothecary and medical history. 19th century medical instruments, pharmacy jars and bottles. 2 doctors' surgeries (1857 and 1890) are in the care of the Museum.
W. 10-5; Su. 2-5.

BAIRD

CALLAHAN COUNTY PIONEER MUSEUM
County Courthouse, Market and W. 4th Streets, Baird, Texas 79504
Pioneer life in Callahan County.
M.-F. 9-5. Closed public holidays.

BAKER

O'FALLON HISTORICAL SOCIETY MUSEUM
P.O. Box 528, Baker, Montana 59313
Local history. Early 19th century household and agricultural equipment.
Memorial Day - Labour Day, Sa., Su., W., Th. 2-8. Labour Day - Memorial Day, Su. 2-5.

LEHMAN CAVES NATIONAL MONUMENT
Baker, Nevada 89311
Geology. Mineralogy. Cave formations. Herbarium. Entomology.
Daily 8-4.30.

BAKER COUNTY HISTORICAL SOCIETY MUSEUM
1655 1st Street, City Hall, Baker, Oregon 97814
History of Baker County.
By appointment.

BAKERSFIELD

CUNNINGHAM MEMORIAL ART GALLERY
1930 R Street, Bakersfield, California 93301
Paintings. Sculpture. Graphics. Decorative arts.
Tu.-Su., 1.30-4.30. Closed New Year, Christmas, Aug.

KERN COUNTY MUSEUM
3801 Chester Avenue, Bakersfield, California 93301
Natural history. Flora and fauna of California. Mineralogy. Palaeontology. Indian artifacts. Outdoor museum. Pioneer village, with narrow gauge railway, shops, houses, jail, church. Californian primitive paintings.
M.-F. 8-5; Sa., Su., public holidays, 12-5. May 1 - Sept. 30, daily 12-7.

BALBOA

NEWPORT HARBOUR ART MUSEUM
400 Main Street, Balboa, California 92661
Paintings. Sculpture. Graphics. Decorative arts.
M., 6-9; W.-Su., 1-5. Closed public holidays.

BALDWIN CITY

OLD CASTLE MUSEUM
5th and Dearborn Streets, Baldwin City, Kansas 66006
In former Santa Fe Trail Post Office (1858). Local history. Replica of Kibbee Cabin (1853).
Tu.-Su. 2-5.

BALDWYN

BRICE'S CROSSROADS MUSEUM
Highway 45 N, Baldwyn, Mississippi 38824
In replica of pioneer home. Early American history. Civil War items. Indian artifacts. Archaeology.
M.-F. 10-6; Sa. 9-6; Su. and public holidays 1-6.

BALLSTON SPA

SARATOGA COUNTY HISTORICAL SOCIETY MUSEUM
Brookside, Charlton Street and Fairground Avenue, Ballston Spa, New York 12020
Local history. Industry. Agriculture. Indian artifacts. Costumes. Junior museum.
June 15 - Sept. 30, Sa., Su. 2-5. Other times by appointment.

BALSAM LAKE

POLK COUNTY HISTORICAL MUSEUM
14 Polk County Center Building, Balsam Lake, Wisconsin 54810
In school building (1860). Local history. Farm tools, implements. Indian artifacts.
M.-F. 8-5. Closed public holidays.

BALTIMORE

BALTIMORE AND OHIO TRANSPORTATION MUSEUM
Pratt and Poppleton Streets, Baltimore, Maryland 21223
Dioramas illustrating railway history. Railway equipment. Mount Clare Station (1830) and passenger coach roundhouse (1881) are in the care of the Museum.
W.-Su. 10-4. Closed public holidays.

BALTIMORE FIREMAN'S MUSEUM
423 N. Gay Street, Baltimore, Maryland 21202
History of Baltimore City Fire Department.
M. 7-10. Other times by appointment.

BALTIMORE MUSEUM OF ART
Art Museum Drive, Baltimore, Maryland 21218
19th-20th century French paintings, sculpture, drawings, especially by Matisse. 15th-20th century European paintings, sculpture, prints, drawings. 18th-20th century American paintings. Aubusson tapestries. Maryland silver. Antioch mosaics. Oriental art. Pre-Columbian, African, Oceanic art.
Tu.-F. 11-5; Sa. 10.30-5; Su. 1-5. Closed New Year, Good F., July 4, Thanksgiving, Christmas.

CARROLL MANSION
Lombard and Front Streets, Baltimore, Maryland 21202
Restored as Baltimore townhouse of 1810-40, with decorative arts, paintings and furnishings of the period.
W.-F. 10.30-4.30; Sa., Su. 1-5. Closed public holidays.

CYLBURN MANSION
4915 Greenspring Avenue, Baltimore, Maryland 21209
Children's and junior museum. Geology, minerals and natural history.
M.-F. 8-4; Sa. 8-11.30 during school terms. Su. p.m. as announced. Other times by appointment.

'DRAGONFISH' SUBMARINE MUSEUM
Pier 4, Pratt Street, Baltimore, Maryland 21202
Pictures and plans of submarines, 1779-1972. Battle flags. Captured weapons.
Daily 10-5. Closed Christmas, New Year, Good F.

EVERGREEN HOUSE
4545 N. Charles Street, Baltimore, Maryland 21210
House (1850-60). Former home of Ambassador John W. Garrett with his paintings, library, furniture. Coins. French Impressionist and post-Impressionist paintings.
M.-F. 2-5.

FORT McHENRY NATIONAL MONUMENT AND HISTORIC SHRINE
Baltimore, Maryland 21230
Site of bombardment (1814) which inspired The Star-Spangled Banner. Military history.
Labour Day - June 30, daily 9-5. July 1 - Labour Day, 8-8. Closed Christmas.

GALLERY OF ART
Morgan State College, Murphy Fine Arts Center, Coldspring Lane and Hillen Road, Baltimore, Maryland 21212
Contemporary American paintings, sculpture, graphics. Archaeology.
M.-F. 10-5; Sa., Su., college vacations by appointment. Closed Easter, Thanksgiving, Christmas.

JOHNS HOPKINS UNIVERSITY ART GALLERY
Library, Homewood Campus, Charles and 33rd Streets, Baltimore, Maryland 21218
French Impressionist and Post-Impressionist paintings, drawings, sculpture.
By appointment.

JOHNS HOPKINS UNIVERSITY, MUSEUM OF CLASSICAL ART
Gilman Hall, Homewood, Charles and 34th Streets, Baltimore, Maryland 21218
Greek, Roman and Egyptian art.
W. 1-5.

SAMUEL KIRK MUSEUM
225 Holiday Street, Baltimore, Maryland 21218
Silverware, 1815 onwards.
Tu.-F. 10.30-4.30; Sa., Su. 1-5. Closed public holidays.

LLOYD STREET SYNAGOGUE
Lloyd and Lombard Streets, Baltimore, Maryland 21202
Synagogue (1845), with original furnishings. Liturgical items.
Weekdays.

LOVELY LANE MUSEUM
2200 St. Paul Street, Baltimore, Maryland 21218
In John Evans House (1764). History of Methodism. Paintings. Documents. Costumes.
M.-F. 9.30-4. Closed public holidays.

MARYLAND HOUSE
Druid Hill Park, Baltimore, Maryland 21217
Natural history of Maryland. Indian artifacts.
May-Oct., daily 9-5.

MARYLAND INSTITUTE COLLEGE OF ART
1300 Mount Royal Avenue, Baltimore, Maryland 21217
Chinese ceramics. Barye bronzes. 17th-20th century European and American paintings, sculpture, drawings, prints.
M.-F. 10-5; Sa., Su. 1-5.

MASONIC MUSEUM
225 N. Charles Street, Baltimore, Maryland 21201
Masonic history.
M.-F. 9 a.m. - 10 p.m.; Sa. by appointment. July 1 - Aug. 31, daily 9-4. Closed public holidays.

McCORMICK AND COMPANY'S TEA HOUSE AND MUSEUM
414 Light Street, Baltimore, Maryland 21202
Replicas of English houses of 16th-18th centuries. History and culture of tea. Tea-making equipment.
M.-F. 9-5.

MOTHER SETON HOUSE
600 N. Paca Street, Baltimore, Maryland 21201
House (1807-8). Furnishings of federal period.
By appointment.

MOUNT CLARE MANSION
Carroll Park, Baltimore, Maryland 21230
House (1754). Furnishings of Colonial period. Portraits by Charles Willson Peale.
Apr. 1 - Oct. 31: Tu.-Sa. 11-4.30; Su. 2-4.30. Nov. 1 - Mar. 31: Tu.-Sa. 11-4; Su. 2-4.

MOUNT CLARE RAILROAD STATION AND TRANSPORTATION MUSEUM
Pratt and Poppleton Streets, Baltimore, Maryland 21202
1st railway station in America (1830). Round House museum contains locomotives, rolling stock, model systems, dioramas, railway relics.
W.-Su. 10-4.

MOUNT VERNON MUSEUM OF INCANDESCENT LIGHTING
717 Washington Place, Baltimore, Maryland 21201
History of the electric light bulb.
M.-F. 9-5; Sa. 9-1; Su. by appointment. Closed Easter, Labour Day, Christmas.

MUSEUM OF AUGUSTINE HERMAN CZECH AMERICAN HISTORICAL SOCIETY
700 N. Collington Avenue, Baltimore, Maryland 21205
History of Czech immigration. Costumes. Documents.
By appointment.

MUSEUM OF MARYLAND ACADEMY OF SCIENCES
7 W. Mulberry Street, Baltimore, Maryland 21201
Geology. Palaeontology. Astronomy. Natural history. Ethnology. Science. Technology. Behavioural sciences.
M.-F. 9-4.30; Labour Day-Memorial Day also Sa. 9-4. Closed public holidays.

MUSEUM OF MARYLAND HISTORICAL SOCIETY
201 Monument Street, Baltimore, Maryland 21201
Portraits. Landscapes. Furniture. Silver. Glass. Ceramics. Textiles. Chesapeake Bay maritime collection. Original draft of *Star Spangled Banner*.
Tu.-Sa. 11-4; Su. 1-4.

THE MUSEUM OF NATURAL HISTORY
Maryland House, Druid Hill Park, Baltimore, Maryland 21217
Natural history of Maryland. Geology. Mineralogy. Fossils. Mammals. Amphibians. Reptiles. Birds. Ecology. Indian culture.
Tu., W., F., Sa. 10-4; Su. 1-5. Closed New Year, Thanksgiving, Christmas.

MUSEUM OF UNITED METHODIST HISTORICAL SOCIETY OF THE BALTIMORE CONFERENCE
2200 St. Paul Street, Baltimore, Maryland 21218
Methodist history. Costumes. Paintings. John Evans House (1764) is in the care of the Society.
M.-F. 9-4. Closed public holidays.

PATHOLOGY MUSEUM
University of Maryland Medical School, 660 W. Redwood Street, Baltimore, Maryland 21201
Pathology teaching collections.
M.-F. 8.30-10; Sa., Su. 10-10. Closed public holidays.

PEALE MUSEUM
225 Holliday Street, Baltimore, Maryland 21202
Museum building (1814). Baltimore history shown in maps, engravings, lithographs, photographs, paintings and artifacts. Paintings by Baltimore artists, including Rembrandt Peale and Charles Wilson Peale. Victorial furniture. Mastodon bones. Early gas-making equipment. Kirk collection of silver, 1815 to present day.
Tu.-F. 10.30-4.30; Sa., Su. 1-5. Closed New Year, Easter, Memorial Day, July 4, Labour Day, Thanksgiving, Christmas.

EDGAR ALLAN POE HOUSE
203 N. Amity Street, Baltimore, Maryland 21223
House (c.1830). Period furnishings. Lamps. Candlesticks.
Sa. 1-4.

STAR-SPANGLED BANNER FLAG HOUSE AND MUSEUM
844 E. Pratt Street, Baltimore, Maryland 21202
House (1793) where the original Star-Spangled Banner was made by Mary Young Pickersgill. Furnishings and personal possessions of Mary Pickersgill. History of the War of 1812 and Battle of Baltimore. Maps. Weapons. Uniforms. Prints. Ship's models.
Tu.-Sa. 10-4; Su. 2-4.30. Closed New Year, Easter, Thanksgiving, Dec. 24-5.

U.S. FRIGATE 'CONSTELLATION'
Constellation Dock Pier, 1 Pratt Street, Baltimore, Maryland 21202
Ship (1797), in commission (1798-1955). Naval and maritime history.
Labour Day-June 19: M.-Sa. 10-4; Su. 12-5. June 20-Labour Day: M.-Sa. 10-6; Su. 12-6. Closed New Year, Christmas.

UNIVERSITY OF MARYLAND DENTAL SCHOOL MUSEUM
666 W. Baltimore Street, Baltimore, Maryland 21201
History of dentistry, 1800 onwards. Equipment. Paintings. George Washington's dentures.
M.-F. 9-5. Closed Thanksgiving, Christmas.

WALTERS ART GALLERY
Charles and Center Streets, Baltimore, Maryland 21201
European and Near-Eastern Art from Egyptian times to present day. Roman sculpture. Etruscan, Byzantine, medieval art. Sèvres porcelain. Jewellery. Weapons. Armour. Decorative arts.
M. 1-5; Tu.-Sa. 11-5; Su. 2-5. Closed public holidays.

WELCH LIBRARY
Johns Hopkins Medical School, 1900 E. Monument Street, Baltimore, Maryland 21205
Paintings, prints of medical subjects. Portraits of doctors.
By appointment.

BANDERA

FRONTIER TIMES MUSEUM
2 blocks N. of Courthouse, Bandera, Texas 78003
Pioneer tools and implements. Paintings of the Old West.
Tu.-Sa. 10-12, 1-4.30; Su. 1-4.30.

BANGOR

BANGOR HISTORICAL SOCIETY MUSEUM
159 Union Street, Bangor, Maine 04401
Marine biology. Local history. Civil War relics. Indian artifacts.
May 1-Sept. 30, Tu.-Sa. 10-4. Rest of year, M.-F. 10-4. Closed public holidays.

PENOBSCOT HERITAGE MUSEUM
City Hall, Harlow Street, Bangor, Maine 04401
Local history. Indian artifacts. History of logging and lumbering industry.
M.-F. 9-4.30.

BANNING

MALKI MUSEUM
Marongo Indian Reservation, 11-795 Fields Road, Banning, California 92220
Natural history. Material illustrating the culture of the Indians of Southern California, especially the Cahuilla tribe.
Tu.-Su., 10-5.

BARABOO

CIRCUS WORLD MUSEUM
426 Water Street, Baraboo, Wisconsin 53913
Historic material relating to circuses throughout the world. Winter quarters (1900) of Ringling Bros. Circus. Elephant barn (1895). Performing horse barn (1900). Camel barn (1902).
May 15-Sept. 15, daily 9-5.30.

SAUK COUNTY HISTORICAL MUSEUM
531 4th Avenue, Baraboo, Wisconsin 53913
Geology. County history, especially railway and circus exhibits. Indian artifacts.
May 15-Sept. 15, Su. and public holidays 2-5.

BARBOURSVILLE

DAR TOLL HOUSE MUSEUM
Barboursville, West Virginia 25504
A James River and Kanawha Turnpike way station, built 1837 and restored. History of Cabell County.
Tours by arrangement.

BARBOURVILLE

DR. THOMAS WALKER STATE PARK MUSEUM
State 459, Barbourville, Kentucky 40906
One-room log-cabin, replica of first settler's house in Kentucky, built 1750 by Dr. Thomas Walker. Period furniture.
Daily 9-5.

BARDSTOWN

BARTON MUSEUM OF WHISKEY HISTORY
Barton Road, Bardstown, Kentucky 40004
History of the domestic whisky industry.
Daily 8-12, 1-4.30.

MY OLD KENTUCKY HOME STATE PARK
U.S. Highway 150, Bardstown, Kentucky 40004
House (1795-1800) was Rowan family home. Visited 1852 by Stephen Foster, whose song, 'My Old Kentucky Home', relates to it. Original furnishings. Mementoes of Stephen Foster.
Dec. 1-Feb. 28: Tu.-Su. 9-5. Mar. 1-June 14: daily 9-5.30. June 15-Labour Day: daily 9-7.30. Labour Day-Nov. 30: daily 9-5.

WICKLAND
U.S. Highway 62 and Bloomfield Road, Bardstown, Kentucky 40004
House (1813-17), home of 3 Kentucky Governors. Antique furniture and furnishings.
Daily 9-dusk. Closed Easter, Thanksgiving, Christmas.

BAR HARBOR

ROBERT ABBE MUSEUM OF STONE AGE ANTIQUITIES
Bar Harbor, Maine 04609
Prehistoric archaeology. Ethnology.
June 1-Sept. 30, daily 9-5.

BAR HARBOR HISTORICAL SOCIETY MUSEUM
34 Mount Desert Street, Bar Harbor, Maine 04609
Local history.
June 16-Labour Day, Tu., Th., Sa. 3-6.

ISLEFORD MUSEUM
Acadia National Park, Route 1, Box 1, Bar Harbor, Maine 04646
History of French and English colonisation of Maine. Maritime history.
June 15-Sept. 15, daily 10-4.

MUSEUM OF RUGGLES HOUSE SOCIETY
Bar Harbor, Maine 04609
Ruggles House (1818). Carved woodwork. Period furniture.
June 1-Oct. 15: M.-Sa. 8.30-4.30; Su. 10-4.

SONOGEE MANSION
Route 3, Bar Harbor, Maine 04609
Mansion and estate formerly owned by Vandervelt and Atwater Kent. Collection of Atwater Kent radios.
Memorial Day-Sept. 30, daily 9-5. July 1-Aug. 31, 9-8.

BARNEGAT LIGHT

BARNEGAT LIGHT HISTORICAL SOCIETY MUSEUM
5th and Central Avenues, Barnegat Light, New Jersey 08006
Lens from original Barnegat Lighthouse (1858). Long Beach Island history, late 1800s-early 1900s.
June 1-30, Sept. 1-30: Sa., Su. 2-5. July 1-Aug. 31, daily 2-5.

BARNESVILLE

GAY NINETIES MANSION MUSEUM
532 N. Chestnut Street, Barnesville, Ohio 43713
House (1802-77). Agriculture. Industry. Transport. Furniture. Indian artifacts. Costumes. Paintings. Glass.
May 1-Sept. 30: Th., Su. 1-5.

BARNSTABLE

CROCKER HOUSE
Main Street, Barnstable, Massachusetts 02630
House (c.1754). 18th-19th century furniture from Essex County.
June-Oct., Tu., Th., Sa. 1-5.

STURGES LIBRARY
Main Street, Barnstable, Massachusetts 02630
In Rev. Lottrop House (1644). Cape Cod history.
M. 7-9 p.m.; Tu., Th. 2-5, 7-9; Sa. 2-5. Closed public holidays.

DONALD G. TRAYSER MEMORIAL MUSEUM
Main Street, Barnstable, Massachusetts 02630
In old Customs House (1856). Local and maritime history. Ship models. Indian artifacts.
July 1-Sept. 15: Tu.-Sa. 1-5; Sept. 15-Oct. 31: Sa. 1-5. Closed public holidays.

BARRANQUITOS

LUIS MUÑOZ RIVERA LIBRARY AND MUSEUM
Calle Luis Muñoz Rivera, Barranquitos, Puerto Rico 00618
In house where Rivera was born (1859). Furniture. Books. Maps. Personal possessions. His motor-car, 'Pierce Arrow'.
M.-F. 8-5; Sa. 10-12; Su. 2-4; public holidays 10-12. Closed New Year, Three Kings Day, Good Friday, Christmas.

BARRE

BARRE HISTORICAL SOCIETY MUSEUM
Common Street, Barre, Massachusetts 01005
House (1836). Local history. Costumes.
May-Sept., Th.-Su. 2-5.

BARRE HISTORICAL SOCIETY MUSEUM
Elm and Washington Streets, Barre, Vermont 05641
Local history.
Th. 2.30-4.30. Other times by appointment.

BARRINGTON

BARRINGTON HISTORICAL SOCIETY MUSEUM
111 W. Station Street, Barrington, Illinois 60010
In former Wickmann blacksmith's shop. Blacksmith's tools. Agricultural tools, equipment. Local history.
Sept.-May, Su., public holidays 2-4. June-Aug., F. 7-9; Su., public holidays 2-4. Closed Jan. 1-31.

BARRON

MUSEUM OF BARRON COUNTY HISTORICAL SOCIETY
Highway 8, Barron, Wisconsin 54812
Local history. Agricultural tools, implements. Indian artifacts.
June 1 - Labour Day, Sa., Su. 1-5.

BARTLESVILLE

PHILLIPS PETROLEUM EXHIBIT HALL
Bartlesville, Oklahoma 74003
Photographic collection showing development of Oklahoma oil industry. Displays of oil workings.
M.-F. 9-5.30; Sa., Su. 9-4.30.

WOOLAROC MUSEUM
State Highway 123, Bartlesville, Oklahoma 74003
Art and culture of American Indians, with emphasis on Southwest.
Daily 10-5.

BASSETT

MUSEUM OF HENRY COUNTY HISTORICAL SOCIETY
Bassett, Virginia 24055
Local history.
M.-F. 10-5; Sa. 9-12. Closed public holidays.

BASTROP

BASTROP COUNTY HISTORICAL SOCIETY MUSEUM
704 Main Street, Bastrop, Texas 78602
In Cornelson-Fehr House (1850-4). Local history. Pioneer life.
Sa. 9-12, 1-6; Su. 1-6. Closed Jan. 1 - Feb. 28.

BATAVIA

BATAVIA HISTORICAL SOCIETY MUSEUM
11 North Batavia Avenue, Batavia, Illinois 60510
Local history. Tools. Handicrafts. Transport, especially railways. Clothing. Burlington railway depot (1850) is in the care of the Society.
By appointment.

HOLLAND LAND OFFICE MUSEUM
131 W. Main Street, Batavia, New York 14020
Building (1815). Pioneer settlement of Western New York. Indian artifacts. Agriculture.
M.-Sa. 10-5; Su. 2-5. Closed public holidays.

MUSEUM OF CLERMONT COUNTY HISTORICAL SOCIETY
Batavia, Ohio 45103
Local history.
By appointment.

BATH

BATH MARINE MUSEUM
963 Washington Street (mansion) and 263 Washington Street (shipyard), Bath, Maine 04530
32 room mansion. Local history. Maritime history. Tools. Paintings. Sculpture. Decorative arts. Percy and Small Shipyard. 19th century shipbuilding tools, machinery.
May 1 - Oct. 14, daily 10-5. Shipyard closed Labour Day.

BONNER HOUSE
Bath, North Carolina 27808
House (1825), with period furnishings.
Tu.-Sa. 10-5; Su., public holidays 2-5. Closed Thanksgiving, Christmas.

HISTORIC BATH STATE HISTORIC SITE, VISITOR CENTER
Bath, North Carolina 27807
History of Bath.
Tu.-Sa. 9-5; Su. 1-5. Closed Thanksgiving, Dec. 24-6.

PALMER-MARSH HOUSE
Bath, North Carolina 27808
House (1744), with period furnishings.
Tu.-Sa. 10-5; Su., public holidays 2-5. Closed Thanksgiving, Christmas.

HALE FARM AND WESTERN RESERVE VILLAGE
2686 Oak Hill Road, Bath, Ohio 44210
6 early 19th century houses, preserved as a group, with period furnishings. Agriculture.
May-Oct., Tu.-Sa. 10-5; Su. 1-5.

BATON ROUGE

ANGLO-AMERICAN ART MUSEUM
Memorial Tower, Louisiana State University, Baton Rouge, Louisiana 70803
Collections illustrating impact of English culture on America. Paintings. Graphics. Sculpture. Decorative arts.
M.-F. 9-4; Sa., Su. 9-12, 1-4.30.

LOUISIANA ART COMMISSION
100 North Boulevard, Old State Capitol, Baton Rouge, Louisiana 70801
Contemporary Louisiana paintings, graphics, sculpture, photography.
M.-F. 10-4.30; Sa., Su. 1-5. Closed public holidays.

LOUISIANA ARTS AND SCIENCE CENTER
502 N. Boulevard, Baton Rouge, Louisiana 70802
Planetarium. Children's museum. Paintings. Sculpture. Graphics.
Tu.-Sa. 10-5; Su. 1-5. Closed Mardi Gras, public holidays.

LOUISIANA STATE UNIVERSITY HERBARIUM
Baton Rouge, Louisiana 70803
Herbarium of flowering plants and ferns, especially of Louisiana.
Sept. 10 - Aug. 10, M.-F. 7.30-4.30.

MUSEUM OF GEOSCIENCE
Louisiana State University, Baton Rouge, Louisiana 70803
Geology. Palaeontology. Archaeology. Anthropology.
Daily 8-5. Closed Christmas.

MUSEUM OF NATURAL SCIENCE
Louisiana State University, Baton Rouge, Louisiana 70803
Mammalogy. Icthyology. Ornithology. Herpetology.
M.-F. 8-5; Sa. 8-12; Su. 2-5. Closed New Year, Christmas.

OLD ARSENAL MUSEUM
State Capitol Grounds, Baton Rouge, Louisiana 70804
History of Louisiana. Flags. Dioramas of scenes in State history. Civil War material. Portraits.
Tu.-Su. 10-5.

RURAL LIFE MUSEUM
Louisiana State University, Burden Research Plantation, Baton Rouge, Louisiana 70800
Overseer's house, slave cabins, smithy, farm houses and other rural buildings moved to site from elsewhere in Louisiana. 19th century furnishings, domestic and agricultural equipment. Cane crusher. Sugar-boiler.
By appointment with Office of Public Relations, Louisiana State University.

BATTLE CREEK

BATTLE CREEK CIVIC ART CENTER
265 Emmett Street, Battle Creek, Michigan 49017
Paintings and graphics by contemporary American artists.
M.-F. 9.30-12, 1-4.30; Su. 1-4. Closed Aug., public holidays.

KIMBALL HOUSE MUSEUM
196 Capital Avenue N.E., Battle Creek, Michigan 49017
House (1886), with period furnishings. Local history. 19th century medical instruments.
Tu., Th., Su. 1-4.30.

KINGMAN MUSEUM OF NATURAL HISTORY
Leila Arboretum, Battle Creek, Michigan 49017
Geology. Mineralogy. Palaeontology. Natural history. Aquarium. Human biology. Anthropology. Early American history. Pioneer life. Geography. Children's Museum.
M.-Sa. 9-5; Su. 2-5. Closed school holidays.

BATTLESHIP COVE

MARINE MUSEUM AT FALL RIVER
70 Water Street, Battleship Cove, Massachusetts 02722
Maritime history. Models. Paintings. Prints. Documents.
M.-Sa. 9-5; Su. 12.30-5. Closed New Year, Thanksgiving, Christmas.

BAYAMÓN

JOSE CELSO BARBOSA MUSEUM
Bayamón, Puerto Rico 00619
In birthplace of Dr. Barbosa, with furniture, documents and personal possessions. The house is arranged to show typical 19th century Puerto Rican country house.
M.-Sa. 10-5.

BAY CITY

JENNISON TRAILSIDE MUSEUM
Bay City State Park, Bay City, Michigan 48706
Geology. Natural science. Botany. Natural history.
May 1 - Sept. 30, daily 12-5; F.-Su., also 7.30 p.m.-9. Remainder of year by appointment.

MUSEUM OF THE GREAT LAKES
1700 Center Avenue, Bay City, Michigan 48706
Archaeology. History of Michigan and Great Lakes.
M.-F. 1-5; Sa., Su. 2-5. Closed public holidays.

MATAGORDA COUNTY MUSEUM
1024 6th Street, Bay City, Texas 77414
History of Matagorda County. Story of early pioneers.
Tu.-Su. 2-5.

BAYFIELD

GEM VILLAGE MUSEUM
Bayfield, Colorado 81122
Geology. Mineralogy. Archaeology. Indian artifacts.
By appointment.

BAY SHORE

BUCKLAND MUSEUM OF WITCHCRAFT AND MAGICK
6 1st Avenue, Bay Shore, New York 11706
Witchcraft. Voodoo. Satanism. Folklore.
Apr.-Nov., M., Tu., Th., Su. 10-6. Dec.-Mar., Sa., Su. 12-5.

BAY VILLAGE

LAKE ERIE JUNIOR NATURE AND SCIENCE CENTER
28728 Wolf Road, Bay Village, Ohio 44140
Geology. Astronomy. Botany. Herbarium. Physical sciences. Agriculture. Maritime history. Indian material.
May 1 - Oct. 31, M.-Tu., Th.-Su. 1-5. Nov. 1 - Apr. 30: M.-Sa. 1-5. Closed Dec. 24-6, 31, Jan. 1-2, Easter.

BEACH HAVEN

SCHOONER 'LUCY EVELYN'
325 9th Street, Beach Haven, New Jersey 08008
Schooner (1917). Shells. Scrimshaw. Coins.
May 1 - Sept. 30, daily 10-10. Oct. 1 - Apr. 30: M., W.-Su. 10-5. Closed New Year, Thanksgiving, Christmas.

BEACON

MADAM BRETT HOMESTEAD
50 Van Nydeck Avenue, Beacon, New York 12508
House (1709). 18th century furniture, china, glass.
Apr.-Nov. M.-F. 2-4.30. Other times by appointment.

BEAR MOUNTAIN

BEAR MOUNTAIN TRAILSIDE MUSEUMS
Bear Mountain State Park, Bear Mountain, New York 10911
Geology. Mineralogy. Botany. Herbarium. Natural history. Local history. Indian history.
Daily 9-5.

BEATRICE

HOMESTEAD NATIONAL MONUMENT
R.R.3, Beatrice, Nebraska 68310
Exhibits illustrating the homestead period in America. Palmer-Epard cabin homestead (1867). Agricultural implements.
Daily 8-5. Closed New Year, Thanksgiving, Christmas.

BEAUFORT

ALPHONSO WHALING MUSEUM
Front Street, Beaufort, North Carolina 28516
History of local boat-building, fishing and whaling industries. Tools. Relics.
June 1 - Labour Day: M.-Sa. 9-6; Su. 2-6.

JOSEPH BELL HOUSE
Turner Street, Beaufort, North Carolina 28516
House (c.1767), formerly home of the plantation owner, Col. Joseph Black. Period furnishings.
June-Aug. Tu.-Sa. 10-5; Su. 2-5.

JOSIAH BELL HOUSE
Turner Street, Beaufort, North Carolina 28516
House (c.1820). Period furnishings.
June-Aug., Tu.-Sa. 10-5; Su. 2-5.

HAMPTON MARINE MUSEUM
120 Turner Street, North Carolina 28516
Marine biology. Snakes. Shells. Birds. Ship models.
Oct. 1 - Mar. 31: Tu.-Th., Sa. 9-12; Su. 2-5. Apr. 1 - Sept. 30: Tu.-Sa. 10-5, Su. 2-6.

BANK OF BEAUFORT HOUSE MUSEUM
Bay and Charles Streets, Beaufort, South Carolina 29902
House (c.1840). Period furnishings.
M.-Sa. 11-3.

BEAUFORT MUSEUM
Craven Street, Beaufort, South Carolina 29902
Natural history. Local history. Indian artifacts.
M.-F. 9-4; Sa., Su. 1-4.30. Closed public holidays.

JOHN MARK VERDIER HOUSE (LAFAYETTE HOUSE)
801 Bay Street, Beaufort, South Carolina 29902
House (1791). Period furnishings.
Daily 9-12.

BEAUMONT

FRENCH TRADING POST MUSEUM
2995 French Road, Beaumont, Texas 77704
House (1845), built by John Jay French. Period furnishings. History of French's tannery and trading post.
May 1 - Sept. 30: Tu.-Sa. 9-1; Su. 2-5. Rest of year, Sa., Su. 2-5.

BEAUMONT ART MUSEUM
1111 9th Street, Beaumont, Texas 77703
Works by 20th century American artists.
Tu.-F. 10-5; Sa., Su. 2-5. Closed public holidays.

SPINDLETOP MUSEUM
8866 College Street, Beaumont, Texas 77700
Open-air museum, illustrating history of Texas oil industry, on site of first oilwell gusher (1901). Replica of early wooden derrick. 1901 wooden storage tank.
Su. 2-5. Other times by appointment.

TEMPLE OF THE BRAVE
Millard Park, Sabine Pass and Riverside Avenue, Beaumont, Texas 77651
Memorial chapel. Military memorabilia, including Civil War material.
Memorial Day, Veteran's Day, July 4, Flag Day, 8-5.

BEAVER

BEAVER MUSEUM
Main Street, Beaver, Oklahoma 73932
Local history. Pioneer life. Farm implements. Household equipment. Bead room.
M.-Sa. 11-5; Su. 2-5.

BEAVER DAM

DODGE COUNTY HISTORICAL SOCIETY MUSEUM
127 Spring Street, Beaver Dam, Wisconsin 53916
Local history. Indian relics.
M.-Sa., 2nd Su. in month, 2-5.

BECKLEY

BECKLEY EXHIBITION MINE
Beckley, West Virginia 25801
Coal mine. Mining exhibits.
May-Sept., daily 10-6.

BEDFORD

LAWRENCE COUNTY HISTORICAL MUSEUM
Court House, Bedford, Indiana 47421
Local history.
M., Tu., Th.-Sa. 9-12, 1-4.

BEDFORD HISTORICAL SOCIETY MUSEUM
15 Great Road, Bedford, Massachusetts 01730
History of Bedford. Documents. Furniture. Pewter. Glass.
By appointment.

MUSEUM OF BEDFORD HISTORICAL SOCIETY
Route 22, Bedford, New York 10506
Local history. Costumes. Historical Hall (1806), general store (1838), Court House (1787) and schoolhouse (1829) are in the care of the Society.
W.-Su. 2-5.

BEDFORD HISTORICAL SOCIETY MUSEUM
30 S. Park Street, Bedford, Ohio 44146
Ohio history. Indian artifacts. Archaeology. Coins. Glass. Bedford Township Hall (1874) is in the care of the Society.
M.-W. 7.30 p.m. - 10 p.m.; 2nd Su. in month 2-5. Closed Aug. 1-31.

FORT BEDFORD MUSEUM
Fort Bedford Drive, Bedford, Pennsylvania 15522
Model of original fort and displays showing early settler life are in blockhouse. Indian artifacts.
Apr. 1 - Oct. 31, daily 10-9. Nov. 1 - Mar. 31, Sa., Su. 10-9.

PEAKS OF OTTER VISITOR CENTER
Blue Ridge Parkway, Bedford, Virginia 24523
Herbarium. Natural history. Entomology. Archaeology. Pioneer history.
June 15 - Labour Day, daily 8-7. Apr. 1 - June 15, Labour Day - Nov. 30: Sa., Su. 9-6.

BEL AIR

HISTORICAL SOCIETY OF HARFORD COUNTY
324 Kenmore Avenue, Bel Air, Maryland 21210
County history. Hays House (1711) in the care of the Society.
By appointment.

BELCHERTOWN

BELCHERTOWN HISTORICAL ASSOCIATION MUSEUM
Maple Street, Belchertown, Massachusetts 01007
In Stone House (1827). Local history.
May 15 - Oct. 15: W., Sa. 2-5.

BELHAVEN

BELHAVEN MEMORIAL MUSEUM
P.O. Box 141, Belhaven, North Carolina 27810
History of coastal Carolina. Indian artifacts. Maritime history.
Daily 1-5. Other times by appointment.

FANNIE MEBANE RALPH LIBRARY AND GALLERY
Belhaven, North Carolina 27810
16th-19th century European prints. Miniatures. 19th-20th century American paintings, serigraphs, portraits, woodcuts.
M., W., F. 2-5.

BELLEFONTAINE

LOGAN COUNTY HISTORICAL MUSEUM
W. Chillocothe Avenue and Seymour Street, Bellefontaine, Ohio 43311
Geology. Local history. Household equipment. Indian artifacts. Costumes.
M.-Sa. by appointment; Su. 2-4.30.

BELLEFONTE

CENTRE COUNTY LIBRARY AND HISTORICAL MUSEUM
203 N. Allegheny Street, Bellefonte, Pennsylvania 16823
In Humes House (1816-17). Period furniture. Local history.
Tu.-F. 11-8; Sa. 9-5.

BELLEVILLE

ST. CLAIR COUNTY HISTORICAL SOCIETY MUSEUM
701 East Washington Street, Belleville, Illinois 62221
House (1866) with period furnishings.
Su. 2-4. Closed public holidays.

BELLINGHAM

WHATCOM MUSEUM OF HISTORY AND ART
121 Prospect Street, Bellingham, Washington 98225
Geology. Mineralogy. Local history. Forestry and forest products. Anthropology. Costumes. Indian art, especially N.W. coast. Pioneer artifacts. 19th century furniture. Contemporary American art. City Hall (1892) is in the care of the Museum.
Tu.-Sa. 12-5; Su. 1-5. Closed New Year, Christmas.

BELLOWS FALLS

ADAMS OLD STONE GRIST MILL MUSEUM
Mill Street, Bellows Falls, Vermont 05101
Mill site (1831). Natural history. Local history and archaeology. Agricultural implements. Industry. Transport. Costumes.
June 1 - Oct. 31: M.-F. 9 a.m.-10 p.m., by appointment. Sa., Su. 2-4.

MUSEUM OF ROCKINGHAM FREE PUBLIC LIBRARY
65 Westminster Street, Bellows Falls, Vermont 05101
Local history.
M.-F. 2-4. Closed public holidays.

STEAMTOWN U.S.A.
Route 5, Bellows Falls, Vermont 05101
20 mile operating railway. Steam locomotives and equipment. Coaches include President Franklin D. Roosevelt's dining car, 'The Mountaineer'.
May 1 - Aug. 31: daily 9.30-5.30. Sept. 1 - Oct. 31: Sa., Su. 9.30-5.30.

BELLPORT

BELLPORT-BROOKHAVEN HISTORICAL SOCIETY MUSEUM
Bellport Lane, Bellport, New York 11713
House (1832). Local history.
By appointment.

BELMONT

BELMONT HISTORICAL SOCIETY MUSEUM
Belmont Memorial Library, Concord Avenue, Belmont, Massachusetts 02178
Local history. Agriculture. Transport.
M.-Sa. 10-4.30. Closed public holidays.

MILLION DOLLAR SHOW
Route 106, Belmont, New Hampshire 03220
Medieval armour, weapons. 16th-18th century French, Spanish, Italian furniture. 17th-18th century flags, heraldic plaques.
Apr. 1 - Oct. 31, daily 8-sundown.

BELOIT

LITTLE RED SCHOOL HOUSE
123 N. Mill Street, Beloit, Kansas 67420
Building (1907). Old schoolbooks and maps. Costumes. Indian artifacts.
May 1 - Aug. 31, daily 1-7.

BARTLETT MEMORIAL HISTORICAL MUSEUM
2149 St. Lawrence Avenue, Beloit, Wisconsin 53511
Local history. Civil War and Spanish American War items. Handicrafts. Farm implements. Costumes. Bartlett farm buildings (1850).
Apr. 1 - Nov. 31: Tu.-F., Su. 1-4. Closed public holidays.

LOGAN MUSEUM OF ANTHROPOLOGY
Beloit College, Beloit, Wisconsin 53511
European and North African palaeolithic exhibits. North American and Indian archaeology, ethnology. North African ethnology.
M.-F. 9-4.30; Sa. 9-12; Su. 1.30-4.30. Closed public holidays, Dec. 20 - Jan. 2, Apr. 15 - May 2, Aug. 14 - Sept. 2.

THEODORE LYMON WRIGHT ART CENTER
Beloit College, Beloit, Wisconsin 53511
16th-19th century European furniture, paintings, prints, drawings, sculpture. Chinese and Japanese decorative arts. Korean ceramics.
M.-F. 9-12, 1-5, 7-9; Sa. 9-12, 1-5; Su. 2-5. Closed college vacations.

BELVEDERE-TIBURON

BELVEDERE-TIBURON LANDMARKS SOCIETY MUSEUM
P.O. Box 134, Belvedere-Tiburon, California 94920
In Old St. Hilary's Church (1888). Botany. Indian artifacts. Victorian kitchen utensils, equipment.
Apr.-Sept., W., Su., public holidays 1-4.

BELVIDERE

THAYER COUNTY MUSEUM
Belvidere N.E., Nebraska 68315
Natural history. Local history and folklore. Indian artifacts. Archaeology. Agriculture. Industry. Textiles. Transport. Reconstructed shops.
June 1 - Aug. 31, daily 2-5. Sept. 1 - May 31, W., Su. 2-5.

BEMIDJI

MUSEUM OF BELTRAMI COUNTY HISTORICAL SOCIETY
3rd Street and Bemidji Avenue, Bemidji, Minnesota 56601
Local history. Indian material. Log house (1896), log school (1903), with original furnishings, and school (1912) are in the care of the Society.
May 15 - Labour Day, daily 9-9.

BENICIA

BENICIA CAPITOL STATE HISTORIC MONUMENT
1st and G Streets, Benicia, California 94510
Seat of California's government (1853-4). Original building restored with period furnishings and exhibits.
Daily 10-5. Closed New Year, Thanksgiving, Christmas.

BENJAMIN

KNOX COUNTY MUSEUM
Courthouse, U.S. 82 and S.H. 283, Benjamin, Texas 79505
History of Knox County. Early pioneer life.
M.-F. 8-5.

BENKELMAN

MUSEUM OF DUNDY COUNTY HISTORICAL SOCIETY
Benkelman, Nebraska 69021
History of homestead and open-range period. Indian relics. Cattle brands. Early rural school material.
May 1 - Sept. 30: Th. 1-5; Su. 2-5.

BENNINGTON

BENNINGTON BATTLE MONUMENT
Monument Circle, Bennington, Vermont 05201
Site of Revolutionary War Battle. Diorama showing battle. Relics of war and battle include General Burgoyne's camp kettle.
Mar. 21 - Nov. 30, daily 9-6.

BENNINGTON MUSEUM
W. Main Street, Bennington, Vermont 05201
Regional history. Revolutionary and Civil War collection. Uniforms. Costumes. Flags. Bennington pottery. Early American glass. 17th-19th century American furniture. Dolls. Toys. 17th-18th century European paintings. Works by contemporary Vermont painters. Silver. Grandma Moses gallery, with 80 of her paintings. 19th-20th century European and American sculpture.
May 1 - Sept. 30, daily 9-6. Oct. 1 - Apr. 30, daily 9.30-4.30. Closed Dec. 1 - Feb. 28, Thanksgiving.

BENSON

SWIFT COUNTY HISTORICAL SOCIETY MUSEUM
Public Library, 1415 Kansas Avenue, Benson, Minnesota 56215
Local history.
M.-F. 9-12, 1-5. Closed Memorial Day, July 4, Labour Day.

BENTON

OLD FORT MARR
Benton, Tennessee 37307
Fort (1814). Local and mititary history. Indian artifacts.
Daily 9-5.

BEREA

BEREA COLLEGE MUSEUMS
Berea, Kentucky 40403
Collections illustrating folk cultures of the Appalachian region. Geology. Botany. Natural history. Local history. Open-air museum. Renaissance paintings. Prints. Sculpture. Textiles. Decorative arts.
May 1 - Sept. 30, M.-Sa. 9-9; Oct. 1 - Apr. 30, M.-Sa. 9-6, Su. 1-6. Closed New Year, Christmas.

WALLACE NUTTING MUSEUM
Log House, Berea, Kentucky 40403
Life and work of the woodworker, Wallace Nutting, with his collection of furniture.
Daily 7.30-7.

BERGEN

BERGEN MUSEUM OF LOCAL HISTORY
7547 Lake Road, Bergen, New York 14416
In former schoolhouse (1843). Local history. Archaeology. Costumes. Glass. Pottery. Decorative arts. Folklore. Paintings.
Apr. 1 - Oct. 31, Su. 2-5.

BERKELEY

BERKELEY ART CENTER
1275 Walnut Street, Berkeley, California 94709
Paintings. Sculpture. "Environments".
Tu.-Su., 11-5. Closed public holidays.

ENTOMOLOGICAL COLLECTIONS
Department of Entomology, 313 Wellman Hall, University of California, Berkeley, California 94720
Terrestrial anthropods.
M.-F. 8-5. Closed University administrative holidays.

LAWRENCE HALL OF SCIENCE
North Canyon Road, Berkeley, California 94720
Collections related to science education.
M.-F. 9.30-4.30; Sa., Su. 10-5. Closed public and university holidays.

ROBERT H. LOWRIE MUSEUM OF ANTHROPOLOGY
103 Kroeber Hall, University of California, Berkeley, California 94720
Anthropology, ethnology and archaeology of the Americas, Oceania, Europe, Asia and Africa.
M.-F. 10-4, Sa., Su. 12-4. Closed New Year, Easter Sunday, Thanksgiving, Christmas.

JUDAH L. MAGNES MEMORIAL MUSEUM
2911 Russell Street, Berkeley, California 94705
Jewish history. Religious art. Liturgical items.
Su.-F. 10-4. Closed Jewish holidays.

MUSEUM OF PALAEONTOLOGY
Earth Sciences Building, University of California, Berkeley, California 94720
Vertebrate and invertebrate palaeontology. Palaeobotany.
M.-F. 8-5. Closed public holidays.

MUSEUM OF VERTEBRATE ZOOLOGY
University of California, Berkeley, California 94720
Natural history. Anatomy.
By appointment.

NATURE CENTER
East Bay Regional Park District, Tilden Regional Park, Berkeley, California 94708
Geology, botany and wildlife of the Park area.
Daily 8-5.

PALESTINE INSTITUTE MUSEUM
Pacific School of Religion, 1758 Scenic Avenue, Berkeley, California 94709
Biblical archaeology. Material from Israel, especially Tel-en-Nasbeh, Eygpt, Syria, Cyprus, Greece, Rome.
M.-F. 9-5; Sa., Su. by appointment.

UNIVERSITY ART MUSEUM
2626 Bancroft Way, Berkeley, California 94720
Renaissance and Baroque paintings, sculpture. Chinese paintings. 20th century European paintings. 20th century American paintings, sculpture.
W.-Su., public holidays 11-5. Closed New Year, Christmas.

UNIVERSITY OF CALIFORNIA HERBARIUM
2010 Life Sciences Building, Berkeley, California 94720
Herbarium, specialising in North and South America and the Pacific.
M.-F., 8-12, 1-5. Closed University vacations.

BERLIN

BERLIN ART AND HISTORICAL COLLECTION
Berlin, Massachusetts 01503
Local history. Folklore. Costumes. Powder House (1814) and the Town Hall (1870) are in the care of the same authority.
Memorial Day 10-5. Other times by appointment.

CLARK SCHOOL MUSEUM
Riverside Park and Water Street, Berlin, Wisconsin 54923
In mid-19th century Clark School. Period school furnishings and equipment. History of Berlin area.
Last Su. in May - Sept. 30, Su. 2-4.

BERNANILLO

CORONADO STATE MONUMENT
Bernanillo, New Mexico 87005
Ruins of Pueblo Indian houses (c.A.D.1300). Museum illustrates Pueblo Indian culture and Spanish colonial period.
May 1 - Sept. 30: daily 9-5; public holidays 2-5. Oct. 1 - Apr. 30: Tu.-Su. 9-5; public holidays 2-5. Closed Thanksgiving, Christmas.

BERRIER SPRINGS

BERRIER SPRINGS COURTHOUSE
U.S. 31, Berrier Springs, Michigan 49103
In restored courthouse (1839). Pioneer artifacts. Local history.
Sa. 10-5; Su. 1-6.

BERRYVILLE

MUSEUM OF CARROLL COUNTY HISTORICAL SOCIETY
Court House, Berryville, Arkansas 72616
Local history. Photographs of railway building c.1900. Domestic equipment. Early radios and telephones. Illegal stills. Rural post-office, c.1900. Early store equipment. Tape recordings of memories of early pioneers.
By appointment.

SAUNDERS MEMORIAL MUSEUM
113-115 Madison Street, Berryville, Arkansas 72616
Gun-making. Pistols and revolvers (Col. Saunders collection). Personal possessions of Chief Sitting Bull and Geronimo. Furniture. Paintings. Silver. China.
M.-Sa., 9-5; Su., 1-5. Closed Dec. 15 - Mar. 15.

BERWICK

MUSEUM OF BERWICK HISTORICAL SOCIETY
535 E. 2nd Street, Berwick, Pennsylvania 18603
Local history.
Tu. 3-5.

BETHANY

HARRISON COUNTY HISTORICAL MUSEUM
City Hall, N. 16th Street, Bethany, Missouri 64424
Local history.
By appointment.

BETHEL

BETHEL MUSEUM
Bethel, Alaska 99559
Eskimo history. Artifacts of the Eskimos and American Indians.
Tu.-F. 1-6; Sa. 9-6; Su. by appointment.

BETHLEHEM

BETHLEHEM HISTORICAL MUSEUM
50 West Church Street, Bethlehem, Pennsylvania 18015
In Piston's House (1744). 18th century Moravian artifacts.
4th M. of every month. Other times by appointment.

HISTORIC BETHLEHEM INCORPORATED
Main and Church Streets, Bethlehem, Pennsylvania 18018
History of Moravian community in Bethlehem. Buildings used by Moravians. Brethren's House (1748), grist-mill (1745), miller's house (1763), tannery (1761), water-works (1762) and Goundie house (1810) are in the care of the Museum.
M.-F. 1-4.

ANNIE S. KEMERER MUSEUM
427 N. New Street, Bethlehem, Pennsylvania 18018
18th-19th century American furniture, china, glass. 19th century American landscapes.
M.-F. 1-4. 1st Su. each month 2-4.

LEHIGH UNIVERSITY COLLECTIONS
Bethlehem, Pennsylvania 18015
Natural history. Archaeology. Chinese prints, porcelain. 17th-20th century American, English, French paintings. American and European prints, water-colours.
M.-F. 9-5; Sa. 9-12; Su. 2-5. Closed public holidays.

MORAVIAN MUSEUM
66 W. Church Street, Bethlehem, Pennsylvania 18018
In Moravian church (1741). Collections illustrating life of early Moravian settlers. Furnishings. Kitchen equipment. Musical instruments. Tools. Needlework.
Tu.-Sa. 1-4. Closed public holidays.

BETHUNE

MUSEUM OF LYNCHES RIVER HISTORICAL SOCIETY
Bethune, South Carolina 29009
Agriculture. Indian artifacts. Household equipment.
1st Su. in month, 3-5.

BEVERLY

JOHN BALCH HOUSE
448 Cabot Street, Beverly, Massachusetts 01915
House (1636). 17th-18th century furniture, household equipment. Weaving and spinning equipment.
June 15 - Sept. 15, M.-Sa. 10-4.

BEVERLY HISTORICAL SOCIETY MUSEUM
117 Cabot Street, Beverly, Massachusetts 01915
In Cabot House (1781). Local history. Maritime history. Ship models. Navigation instruments. Paintings of ships. Portraits by Gilbert Stuart of early merchants and ship-captains. Glass. Porcelain. Pewter. Embroidery. Documents of the Colonial and Revolutionary periods.
Sept. 1 - June 30, M., W., F.-Sa. 10-4. July 1 - Aug. 31, M.-Sa. 10-4.

REV. JOHN HALE HOUSE
39 Hale Street, Beverly, Massachusetts 01915
House (1694), formerly home of John Hale, first minister of Beverly. 17th-18th century furnishings, household equipment.
June 15 - Oct. 15, Tu.-Sa. 10.30-4.

BEVERLY HILLS

FRANCIS E. FOWLER, JR., FOUNDATION MUSEUM
9215 Wilshire Boulevard, Beverly Hills, California 90210
American and European silver. Porcelain. Glass. Carved ivory. Ship models. French paperweights. Weapons. Russian paintings. Oriental art.
M.-Sa. 1-5. Closed public holidays.

BIG BASIN

MUSEUM OF BIG BASIN REDWOODS
State Park, Big Basin, California 95006
Flora and fauna of the area. Entomology. Local history.
Daily, May 1 - Sept. 30, 8-10; Oct. 1 - Apr. 30, 8-5.

BIG BEN NATIONAL PARK

BIG BEND NATIONAL PARK MUSEUM
Big Bend National Park, Texas 79834
Herbarium. History of Big Bend Park. Birds. Mammals.
Daily 8-6.

BIGFOOT

BIGFOOT WALLACE MUSEUM
Main Street, Bigfoot, Texas 78005
Log-cabin, with front room as replica of home of Bigfoot Wallace, hero of Texas War of Independence. Memorabilia of Wallace. Tools. Farm implements.
Tu.-Su. 9-6.

BIG HORN

BRADFORD BRINTON MEMORIAL MUSEUM
Big Horn, Wyoming 82833
In Quarter Circle A ranchhouse (1892). History of the American West. Drawings. Prints. Indian arts and crafts. Paintings and sculpture by Western artists.
May 15 - Sept. 15, daily 9-5. Other days by appointment.

BIG POOL

MUSEUM OF FORT FREDERICK STATE PARK
Big Pool, Maryland 21711
Domestic equipment. Agricultural implements. Firearms. Indian relics.
Apr. 15 - Nov. 1, daily 10-9.

BIG RAPIDS

MECOSTA COUNTY HISTORICAL MUSEUM
Elm and Stewart Streets, Big Rapids, Michigan 49307
Local history. Agriculture. Logging and lumbering. Indian artifacts. Costumes. Folklore. Coins. Children's Museum.
June 1 - Sept. 30: F. 2-5, 7-9. Oct. 1 - May 31: F. 2-5, 7-9. Closed F. following Christmas and New Year.

BIG STONE GAP

SOUTH-WEST VIRGINIA MUSEUM
10 W. 1st Street N., Big Stone Gap, Virginia 24219
In Ayers Mansion (1888-95). Natural history. Pioneer period in southwest Virginia. Indian artifacts.
Tu.-Sa. 9.30-5; Su. 2-5. Closed New Year, Thanksgiving.

BILLERICA

BILLERICA HISTORICAL SOCIETY
36 Concord Road, Billerica, Massachusetts 01821
In late 18th century house, with period furniture.
By appointment.

MIDDLESEX CANAL MUSEUM
37 Concord Road, Billerica, Massachusetts 01821
History of Middlesex Canal.
May 1 - Sept. 30, Su. 2-4.

BILLINGS

YELLOWSTONE COUNTY FINE ARTS CENTER
401 N 27th Street, Billings, Montana 59101
Contemporary European and American paintings, graphics, ceramics. Western Americana. African sculpture.
Tu.-Su. 12-5; Th., F. also 7-9 p.m.

YELLOWSTONE COUNTY MUSEUM
Longan Field, Billings, Montana 59103
Dinosaur bones. Cowboy and pioneer life. Chuck waggon, sheep wagon and other horse-drawn vehicles. Indian artifacts.
Tu.-Sa. 10.30-12, 1-5; Su. 2-5. Closed Thanksgiving, Christmas.

BILOXI

JEFFERSON DAVIS SHRINE
West Beach, Biloxi, Mississippi 39531
Beauvoir (1848), former home of Jefferson Davis. Furniture. Paintings. Clothing. Confederate money. Firearms.
Daily 9-4.30.

BINGHAMPTON

MUSEUM OF BROOME COUNTY HISTORICAL SOCIETY
30 Front Street, Binghampton, New York 13905
In Roberson Mansion (1905-6). Local history. Archaeology. Costumes.
M.-F. 9-5; Sa., Su. 12-5. Closed public holidays.

ROBERSON CENTER FOR THE ARTS AND SCIENCES
30 Front Street, Binghampton, New York 13905
Local history. Natural history. Science. Paintings. Sculpture. Porcelain, especially Meissen, Royal Worcester. Indian artifacts. Planetarium.
M.-F. 9-5; Sa., Su. 12-5. Closed public holidays.

UNIVERSITY ART GALLERY
State University of New York, Binghampton, New York 13901
Paintings. Sculpture. Graphics. Decorative arts. Archaeology.
M.-F. 9-5; Sa. 11-5; Su. 1-5. Closed university vacations.

BIRDSBORO

DANIEL BOONE HOMESTEAD
Daniel Boone Road, Birdsboro, Pennsylvania 19508
House (1760-1803), with outbuildings and workshops. Water-powered sawmill (1750). House, on site of Boone family home, restored and furnished to create picture of country life in 18th century Pennsylvania.
May-Sept., M.-Sa. 8.30-5; Su. 1-5. Oct.-Apr., M.-Sa. 9-4.30; Su. 1-4.30. Closed public holidays.

BIRMINGHAM

ARLINGTON ANTEBELLUM HOME AND GARDENS
331 Cotton Avenue South West, Birmingham, Alabama 35211
House (1822). Period furnishings.
Tu.-Sa. 9-5; Su. 1-6. Closed Christmas.

BIRMINGHAM MUSEUM OF ART
Oscar Wells Memorial Building, 8th Avenue and 20th Street N, Birmingham, Alabama 35203
Roman, Greek, Near-Eastern and Oriental antiquities. American Indian and pre-Columbian artifacts. American and European paintings and sculpture. European silver, glass and porcelain. New Guinea primitive art.
M.-W., Sa. 10-5; Th. 10-9; Su. 2-6. Closed New Year, Christmas.

BIRMINGHAM PUBLIC LIBRARY
2020 Seventh Avenue N, Birmingham, Alabama 35203
Art gallery forming part of Library. Contains American and European paintings, drawings and prints. Mexican pottery.
M.-F. 9-9; Sa. 9-6; Su. 3-6. Closed New Year, Easter, July 4, Labour Day, Thanksgiving, Christmas.

BISBEE

BISBEE MEMORIAL MUSEUM
21 Main Street, Bisbee, Arizona 85603
Minerals. Early mining tools. Women's clothes, accessories, jewellery, c.1900. Photographs of Bisbee, 1879-1909.
M.-Sa. 9-5. Closed May 30, labour Day, Christmas, New Year.

BISHOP HILL

BISHOP HILL STATE MEMORIAL
Bishop Hill, Illinois 61419
Preserved buildings (1846-51) of Swedish colony. Church (1848), used as living accommodation. Original furnishings. Artifacts and tools. Paintings by Olaf Krans (1838-1916), a record of life on the prairie in the 1850s.
Daily 9-5. Closed Thanksgiving, Christmas, New Year.

MUSEUM OF BISHOP HILL HERITAGE ASSOCIATION
Bishop Hill, Illinois 61419
In Steeple Building (1853). Local history. A blacksmith's shop (1851), and Colony Store (1853) are in the care of the Association.
Daily 10-5.

BISMARCK

CAMP HANCOCK MUSEUM
First and Main Streets, Bismarck, North Dakota 58501
Local history. Material relating to early settlement of North Dakota.
June-Sept., M.-F. 9-12, 1.30-5; Sa. 9-4. Closed holidays.

STATE HISTORICAL SOCIETY MUSEUM
Liberty Memorial Building, Bismarck, North Dakota 58501
Archaeology and ethnology of the Plains Indians. Local history. Firearms. Folk art. Early dentist's surgery. Costumes. Dioramas and mounted specimens of North Dakota wildlife.
M.-F. 9-5; Sa. 9-4. June-Aug., Su. 1-5.

BLACK RIVER FALLS

JACKSON COUNTY HISTORICAL SOCIETY MUSEUM
Main Street, Black River Falls, Wisconsin 54615
County history. Photographs of Winnebago Indians.
By appointment.

BLACKSBURG

SMITHFIELD PLANTATION
U.S. Route 460 Bypass and South Gate Road, Blacksburg, Virginia 24060
House (1773) built by William Preston. Home of 3 Governors of Virginia. Period rooms of Colonial and Federal periods. Local history.
Apr. 15 - Nov. 15: W., Sa., Su. 1-5.

BLAIRSDEN

PLUMAS EUREKA STATE PARK MUSEUM
Johnsville State Route, Blairsden, California 96103
On site of Hardrock Mining (1870-90). Stamp mill. Blacksmith's shop, boarding house (1872). Geology. Indian artifacts.
Daily 8-5. Closed Thanksgiving, Christmas, New Year.

BLAKELY

KOLOMOKI MOUNDS MUSEUM
Route 1, Blakely, Georgia 31723
Site museum at 13th century Indian burial mound and village.
Apr. 1 - Sept. 30, Tu.-Su. 10-6. Oct. 1 - Mar. 31, Sa., Su. 10-6.

BLANDING

NATURAL BRIDGES NATIONAL MONUMENT MUSEUM
Star Route, Blanding, Utah 84511
Geology. Natural history. Archaeology.
Apr. 1 - Nov. 30, daily 8-5. Dec. 1 - Mar. 31, Sa., Su. 8-4.30.

BLISS

FRONTIER GHOST TOWN
Bliss, Idaho 83314
Local history.
Daily 8 a.m. - 9 p.m.

BLOCK ISLAND

BLOCK ISLAND HISTORICAL MUSEUM
Block Island, Rhode Island 02807
Local history and handicrafts.
June-Aug., M., W., Sa. 11-4. Other times by appointment.

BLOOMFIELD

HISTORICAL MUSEUM OF ACADEMY OF MEDICINE OF NEW JERSEY
317 Belleville Avenue, Bloomfield, New Jersey 07003
History of medicine.
By appointment.

MUSEUM OF HISTORICAL SOCIETY OF BLOOMFIELD, NEW JERSEY
90 Broad Street, Bloomfield, New Jersey 07003
Local history. Costumes.
W. 1.30-4.

CHACO CANYON NATIONAL MONUMENT
Star Route, Bloomfield, New Mexico 87413
Indian habitation sites. Museum includes geology, herbarium, zoology, herpetology, ethnology, archaeology.
June 1 - Sept. 30, daily 7.30 a.m.-9.30 p.m. Oct. 1 - May 31, daily 8-5.

BLOOMFIELD HILLS

CRANBROOK INSTITUTE OF SCIENCE
500 Lone Pine Road, Bloomfield Hills, Michigan 48013
Mineralogy. Botany. Herbarium. Zoology. Anthropology.
M.-F. 10-5; Sa., Su. 1-5. Closed public holidays.

GALLERIES OF CRANBROOK ACADEMY OF ART
500 Lone Pine Road, Bloomfield Hills, Michigan 48013
Egyptian antiquities. Pre-Columbian art. Oriental ceramics, painting, bronze. Italian and Flemish paintings. Sculpture by Carl Mille.
Tu.-Su. 1-5. Closed public holidays.

BLOOMINGTON

DAVID DAVIS MANSION (CLOVER LAWN)
Davis Street and Monroe Drive, Bloomington, Illinois 61701
House (1872). Period furnishings.
Tu.-Su. 1-5. Closed Thanksgiving, Christmas and New Year.

SAN BERNADINO COUNTY MUSEUM
18860 Orange Avenue, Bloomington, California 92316
Earth sciences. Ornithology. North American mammals. Local history. Horse-drawn vehicles. Railway locomotives and rolling stock. Logging. Mining. Indian material. Assistencia de San Gabriel (1830), Sepulveda Adobe (1842) and Agua Mansa Cemetery (1840) are in the care of the Museum.
Daily 1-5.

SAN BERNADINO COUNTY HISTORICAL SOCIETY MUSEUM
10039 Lilac Avenue, Bloomington, California 92316
Local history.
Tu.-Su. 10-5; M. 1-5.

DAVID DAVIS MANSION
Bloomington, Illinois 61701
Mansion (1872), with original furnishings.
Tu.-Su. 1-5. Closed New Year, Thanksgiving, Christmas.

MCLEAN COUNTY HISTORICAL SOCIETY MUSEUM
201 East Grove Street, Bloomington, Illinois 61701
Local history. Pioneer tools and equipment. Indian artifacts. Stamps.
Tu.-Sa. 9.30-11.30, 2.30-4.30. 1st Su. each month 2-5. Closed public holidays.

MUSEUM OF BLOOMINGTON NORMAL ART ASSOCIATION
202 East Washington Street, Withers Public Library, Bloomington, Illinois 61761
Paintings, sculptures, graphics, by local artists.
Sa. 10-6; Su. 2-5.

INDIANA UNIVERSITY ART MUSEUM
Fine Arts Building, Bloomington, Indiana 47401
Egyptian, Greek, Roman, Oriental art. European paintings and sculpture. 16th-20th century prints and drawings. Decorative arts. Glass. Coins. African, Pre-Columbian, Oceanic art.
M.-Sa. 9-5; Su. 1-5. Closed public holidays.

INDIANA UNIVERSITY MUSEUM
Student Building 107, Bloomington, Indiana 47401
Archaeology, enthnology and history of the Great Lakes and Ohio Valley region. Historical collections from N. America, Latin America, W. Africa.
M.-Sa. 9-12, 1-5. Su. 1-5. Closed public holidays.

BLOOMINGTON HISTORICAL SOCIETY MUSEUM
10200 Penn Avenue S., Bloomington, Minnesota 55431
In old Town Hall (1892). Local history. Indian artifacts.
Oct. 1 - May 31, Su. 2-5.

BLOOMSBURG

BERWICK HISTORICAL SOCIETY MUSEUM
Bloomsburg State College, Bloomsburg, Pennsylvania 17815
Local history.
M.-F. 8-10 a.m. Other times by appointment.

MAGEE TRANSPORTATION MUSEUM
Millville Road, P.O. Box 150, Bloomsburg, Pennsylvania 17815
Horse-drawn vehicles. Agricultural implements. Replica of general store of 1864.
May 1 - 29; Labour Day - Nov. 1, Sa., Su. 12-7. Memorial Day - Labour Day, Tu.-F. 10-4; Sa., Su. 12-7.

MAGEE MUSEUM
698 W. Main Street, Bloomsburg, Pennsylvania 17815
Local history. Transport. Aviation. Silver. Textiles. Glass. China. Costumes.
Sa., Su., public holidays 1-8. Closed Dec. 1 - Jan. 31.

MUSEUM OF COLUMBIA COUNTY HISTORICAL SOCIETY
Bloomsburg State College, E. Main and Penn Streets, Bloomsburg, Pennsylvania 17815
History of Columbia County. Agricultural implements. Indian artifacts.
M.-F. 9-4.30; Sa. 9-12; Su., public holidays by appointment.

BLUE EARTH

FARIBAULT COUNTY HISTORICAL SOCIETY
405 East Sixth Street, Blue Earth, Minnesota 56013
In Wakefield House (1880). Period furnishings. Local history.
Tu.-Su. 2-5. Closed holidays.

BLUE HILL

PARSON FISHER HOUSE
Blue Hill, Maine 04614
House (1814), former home of Rev. Jonathan Fisher. Paintings, books, clock belonging to Fisher. Furniture made by him.
July-mid. Sept., Tu., F. 2-5.

BLUE MOUNDS

LITTLE NORWAY
Route 1, Blue Mounds, Wisconsin 53517
Log buildings (1856) constructed by first settlers, restored and decorated in 19th century Norwegian style. Farm and household equipment of the Norwegian pioneers.
May 1 - June 30, Sept. 1 - Oct. 31, daily 9-5. July 1 - Aug. 31, daily 9-7.

BLUE MOUNTAIN LAKE

ADIRONDACK MUSEUM
Routes 28N and 30, Blue Mountain Lake, New York 12812
Indoor and outdoor museum, showing history of Adirondacks. Dioramas. Folk art. Railway locomotive and coach. Horse-drawn vehicles, including stage-coach. Boats. Tools. Lumbering.
June 15 - Oct. 15, daily 10-5.

BLUE RIDGE PARKWAY

HUMPBACK ROCKS VISITOR CENTER AND MUSEUM
Blue Ridge Parkway, Virginia 24064
Local history. Reconstruction of pioneer mountain farm.
June 15 - Labour Day, daily 9-5.

BLUE SPRINGS

MISSOURI TOWN 1855
Blue Springs, Missouri 64015
15 houses (1820-60) from western Missouri, moved here and reassembled in village setting. Agriculture. Costumes. Decorative arts. Indian relics.
Daily 9-5. Closed New Year, Thanksgiving, Christmas.

BLUFFTON

WELLS COUNTY HISTORICAL MUSEUM
211 West Washington Street, Bluffton, Indiana 46714
Local history. Pioneer log cabin (c.1800) is in the care of the Museum.
Apr. 1 - Sept. 30, Su. 1-4. Other times by appointment.

BLUNT

MENTOR GRAHAM MUSEUM
Blunt, South Dakota 57522
Formerly home of Abraham Lincoln's tutor, Mentor Graham. Original furnishings.
By appointment.

BOALSBURG

BOAL MANSION AND MUSEUM, CHRISTOPHER COLUMBUS FAMILY CHAPEL
Route 322, Boalsburg, Pennsylvania 16827
House (1789). Interior of 16th century chapel brought from Spain in 1919. Local history. Spanish, Italian, Flemish, French, American paintings.
May 1-31, Labour Day - Oct. 31, daily 2-5. June 1 - Labour Day 10-5.

PENNSYLVANIA MILITARY MUSEUM
P.O. Box 148, Boalsburg, Pennsylvania 16827
Military history of Pennsylvania. Naval history. Aviation. Exhibits illustrating history and achievements of 28th Division.
Tu.-Sa. 9-4.30; Su. 1-5. Closed public holidays.

BOISE

BOISE GALLERY OF ART
Julia Davis Park, P.O. Box 1505, Boise, Idaho 83701
Paintings, sculpture, decorative arts by American, European, Oriental artists.
Tu., Th.-Su. 12-5; W. 12-9. Closed New Year, Thanksgiving, Christmas.

IDAHO STATE HISTORICAL MUSEUM
610 N. Julia Davis Drive, Boise, Idaho 83706
History of Idaho and Pacific North-West. Indian material. Children's museum.
Tu.-F. 9-5; Sa., Su. 1-5. Closed New Year, Easter, Christmas.

BOLTON

BOLTON HISTORICAL SOCIETY MUSEUM
Main Street, Bolton, Massachusetts 01740
In Sawyer House (1810). Local history. Household equipment. Crafts. Industries.
By appointment.

BOLTON LANDING

MARCELLA SEMBRICK MEMORIAL STUDIO
Route 9N, Lake George Park, Bolton Landing, New York 12814
Mementoes of the singer, Marcella Sembrich and her musical colleagues.
July 1 - Sept. 6, daily 10-12.30, 2-5.30.

BONHAM

SAM RAYBURN LIBRARY
W. Sam Rayburn Drive, Bonham, Texas 75418
Historical material and displays illustrating career of Sam Rayburn, Speaker of Congress. Replica of Rayburn's office in Washington.
M.-F. 10-5; Sa. 1-5.

BONNER SPRINGS

AGRICULTURAL HALL OF FAME AND NATIONAL CENTER
County Park, Bonner Springs, Kansas 66012
Horse-drawn carriages. Furnished log-cabin. Butter churn collection. Blacksmith's shop. Farm machinery. Old cars. One room schoolhouse.
M.-Su. 9-5.

WYANDOTTE COUNTY MUSEUM
Wyandotte County Park, Bonner Springs, Kansas 66109
Local history. Indian material. Household equipment.
Tu.-Su. 1-5. Closed Thanksgiving, Christmas.

BOONSBORO

WASHINGTON MONUMENT STATE PARK MUSEUM
Boonsboro, Maryland 21713
Building (1827). Civil War relics. Firearms. Indian artifacts.
Daily.

BOOTHBAY

BOOTHBAY PLAYHOUSE THEATRE MUSEUM
Boothbay, Maine 04537
Theatre history. Costumes. Play bills. Portraits. Prints. Photographs. Music.
June 30 - Sept. 1: M.-Sa. 10-11.

BOOTHBAY RAILWAY MUSEUM
Route 27, Boothbay, Maine 04537
Railway history and relics. Old cars. Thorndike and Freeport Stations are in the care of the Museum.
Daily 10-5.30. Closed Labour Day - Memorial Day.

BOOTHBAY HARBOR

MUSEUM OF BOOTHBAY REGION HISTORICAL SOCIETY
Boothbay Harbor, Maine 04538
Local history. Shipbuilding. Fishing.
June 15 - Labour Day: daily 1-5. Labour Day - June 14: Sa. 1-5.

BORDENTOWN

GILDER HOUSE
Crosswicks Street, Bordentown, New Jersey 08505
House (c.1760), with furnishings of pre-revolutionary period.
Su. 1-3. Other times by appointment.

OLD CLARA BARTON SCHOOL
Crosswicks and Burlington Streets, Bordentown, New Jersey 08505
School (1852), with original furnishings. Paintings. Documents and records.
By appointment.

BOSTON

BOSTON ATHENAEUM
101-2 Beacon Street, Boston, Massachusetts 02108
Building (1847-9). Paintings. Sculpture. Topographical prints and photographs of New England.
M.-F. 9-5.30; Oct. 1 - May 31, Sa. 9-4. Closed public holidays.

BOSTON PUBLIC LIBRARY
Copley Square, Boston, Massachusetts 02117
Building (1888). Murals. Sculpture. Prints. Dioramas illustrating famous books and printmakers at work.
M.-F. 9-9; Sa. 9-6; Oct. 1 - May 31, Su. 2-6. Print collection: M.-F. 9-5. Closed public holidays.

BUNKER HILL MONUMENT
20 Somerset Street, Charlestown, Boston, Massachusetts 02108
Material relating to Battle of Bunker Hill and Revolutionary War.
Daily 9-3.30.

CHILDREN'S ART CENTER
36 Rutland Street, Boston, Massachusetts 02118
Paintings. Sculpture.
M.-F. 9-5; Sa. 9-12. Closed public holidays.

CHILDREN'S MUSEUM
Jamaicaway, Boston, Massachusetts 02130
Natural history. Shells. Electronics. American history. Indian material.
Oct. 1 - June, Tu.-F. 2-5; Sa., Su., public holidays, school vacations, 10-5. June 21 - Aug. 31, M.-F. 11-5, Sa., Su. 10-5. Closed New Year, July 4, Thanksgiving, Sept., Christmas.

GIBSON HOUSE MUSEUM
137 Beacon Street, Boston, Massachusetts 02167
House (c.1856). Victorian furniture. Decorative arts. Paintings. Sculpture. Costumes.
Tu.-Su. 2-5.

HARRISON GRAY OTIS HOUSE
141 Cambridge Street, Boston, Massachusetts 02100
House (1796). Furnished and decorated to illustrate changing taste in Boston from late 1790s to 1820. Collections of glass, pottery, silver, pewter, painted ware, ships' models.
M.-F. 10-4.

INSTITUTE OF CONTEMPORARY ART
1175 Soldiers Field Road, Boston, Massachusetts 02134
Contemporary paintings, sculpture, by local artists.
M.-F. 9-6; Sa. 2-5.

MASSACHUSETTS HISTORICAL SOCIETY MUSEUM
1154 Boylston Street, Boston, Massachusetts 02215
American and New England history. Paintings. Sculpture. American prints and portraits.
M.-F. 9-4.45. Closed 3rd M. in Feb., Apr., last M. in May, public holidays.

MOSES PIERCE-HICHBORN HOUSE
29 North Square, Boston, Massachusetts 02100
House (c.1711). 18th century furnishings.
May 15 - Oct. 15, Su.-F. 10-4.

MUSEUM OF ANCIENT AND HONORABLE ARTILLERY COMPANY OF MASSACHUSETTS
Faneuil Hall, Boston, Massachusetts 02109
Military history. Paintings on military subjects. Portraits.
M.-F. 10-4. Closed public holidays, 2 weeks in Oct.

MUSEUM OF FINE ARTS
Huntington Avenue, Boston, Massachusetts 02115
Greek, Roman, Egyptian and Oriental art. 14th-20th century European paintings, especially French impressionists and Post-Impressionists. French and Flemish tapestries. Peruvian and Coptic textiles. European and Near-Eastern printed fabrics, embroideries, lace. American and European furniture. 18th-19th century American paintings, watercolours, drawings. Costumes. Colonial silver. Ancient musical instruments. Ship models. Chinese export porcelain. Archaeology.
Tu. 10-9; W.-Su. 10-5. Closed New Year, July 4, Thanksgiving, Christmas.

MUSEUM OF SCIENCE
Science Park, Boston, Massachusetts 02114
Geology. Mineralogy. Palaeontology. Natural history. Medical science. Talking transparent woman. Models of space rockets, satellites. Planetarium.
M.-Th., Sa. 10-5; F. 10-10; Su. 11-5. Closed public holidays.

OLD SOUTH MEETING HOUSE
Milk and Washington Streets, Boston, Massachusetts 02108
Built (1729) as Congregational Church. Used for Town Meetings before American Revolution. Exhibits on Boston Massacre, Boston Tea Party, Battle of Bunker Hill.
Oct. 1 - May 31, M.-Sa. 9-4. June 1 - Sept. 30, M.-F. 9-5; Sa., public holidays, 9-4. Closed Jan. 1, Thanksgiving, Dec. 25.

OLD STATE HOUSE
206 Washington Street, Boston, Massachusetts 02109
House (1713). History of Boston. Maritime history. Transport.
M.-Sa., public holidays 9-4. Closed New Year, Thanksgiving, Christmas.

PAUL REVERE HOUSE
19 North Square, Boston, Massachusetts 02113
House (1680) was home of Paul Revere. Period furnishings.
M.-Sa. 10-4. Closed national holidays.

ST. BOTOLPH CLUB
115 Commonwealth Avenue, Boston, Massachusetts 02216
Works by local artists.
Daily 2-5.

STATE ARCHIVES MUSEUM
State House, Beacon Street, Boston, Massachusetts 02133
Official documents, 1630 onwards.
M.-F. 8.45-5. Closed public holidays.

ISABELLA STEWART GARDNER MUSEUM
2 Palace Road, Boston, Massachusetts 02115
In replica of 15th century Venetian palace. 14th-20th century European paintings, especially Italian, Dutch, Flemish. Greek, Roman, Romanesque, Gothic, Renaissance sculpture. 18th-20th century American paintings. 15th-18th century European textiles. Furniture. Wrought-iron. Ceramics. Oriental art.
Tu. 1-9.30; W.-Su. 1-5.30. July 1 - Aug. 31 closed Tu. evening and Su. Closed public holidays.

U.S.S. CONSTITUTION
Boston Naval Shipyard, Boston, Massachusetts 02129
Frigate 'Old Ironsides' (1797). Uniforms. Cannon. Material relating to 1812 war.
Daily 9.30-4.

WOMEN'S CITY CLUB OF BOSTON
40 Beacon Street, Boston, Massachusetts 02108
In 2 adjoining houses (1818). Original French wallpaper. Adam and Salem mirrors. Furniture of Federal period.
W. 10-4.

BOTTINEAU

NORTH DAKOTA SCHOOL OF FORESTRY
Bottineau, North Dakota 58518
Herbarium.
School hours.

BOULDER

PIONEER MUSEUM
1655 Broadway at Arapahoe, Boulder, Colorado 80302
Pioneer life in the Boulder district. Mining relics. Transport. Clothing. Musical instruments. Domestic equipment. Tools.
May 1 - Sept. 30, daily 2-5; Oct. 1 - Apr. 30, Sa., Su., 2-5.

UNIVERSITY OF COLORADO MUSEUM
Broadway, between 15th and 16th Streets, Boulder, Colorado 80302
Geology. Palaeontology. Mineralogy. Natural history. Botany. Archaeology. Ethnology. Indian artifacts. Textiles. Paintings. Sculpture. Decorative arts.
M.-F. 9-5; Sa. 9-4; Su., public holidays, 2-5. Closed Christmas.

BOULDER CITY

LAKE MEAD NATIONAL RECREATION AREA
Park Museum, 601 Nevada Highway, Boulder City, Nevada 89005
Natural history of the area. Herbarium.
M.-F. 8-12, 1-5.

BOURNE

APTUXCET TRADING POST
24 Aptuxcet Road, Bourne, Monument Beach, Massachusetts 02553
Replica (1930) of original Pilgrim, Dutch and Indian Trading Post, built 1627. Historical relics from Pilgrim period. Working replica of salt works. Indian village.
Apr. 1 - May 31, Sept. 1 - Oct. 31, Tu.-Sa. 10-5, Su. 1-5. June 1 - Aug. 31, M.-Sa. 10-5.

BOWLING GREEN

KENTUCKY MUSEUM
Western Kentucky University, Bowling Green, Kentucky 42101
Palaeontology. Mastodon bones. Natural history. Local history. Furniture. Pioneer cabin, tools, equipment. Indian artifacts. Dolls. China. Glass. Prints. Miniatures. Paintings from S. Europe.
M.-F. 9-5; Sa. 9-4; Su. 2-4. Closed university vacations.

WESTERN KENTUCKY UNIVERSITY ART GALLERY
Room 1, Cherry Hall, Bowling Green, Kentucky 42101
Paintings, prints by American artists.
M.-F. 8-5.

MUSEUM OF WOOD COUNTY HISTORICAL SOCIETY
301 Sand Ridge Road, Bowling Green, Ohio 43402
County history. Railroad Depot (1859) is in the care of the Society.
M.-Sa. 8-5; Su. 1-5. Closed public holidays.

CAROLINE HISTORICAL SOCIETY MUSEUM
Box 324, Bowling Green, Virginia 22427
Geology. Natural history. Local history and archaeology. Glass.
By appointment. Closed New Year, Easter, July 4, Christmas.

BOXFORD

BOXFORD HISTORICAL SOCIETY MUSEUM
Lawrence Road, Boxford, Massachusetts 01921
In Holyoke French House (1760). Farm implements. Furniture. Indian artifacts. Costumes.
May 30 - Oct. 12, Su. 3-5.

BOYERTOWN

BOYERTOWN MUSEUM OF HISTORIC VEHICLES
Warwick Street, Boyertown, Pennsylvania 19512
Vehicles manufactured in Berks. County, 1763 onwards.
M.-F. 8-4; Sa., Su. by appointment. Closed public holidays, weeks containing July 4 and Labour Day.

BOYS RANCH

JULIAN BIVINS MUSEUM
Boys Ranch, Texas 79010
In old Tascasa Courthouse (1884). Local history. Indian artifacts.
May-Aug., daily 1-5. Sept.-Apr., Su. 1-5. Other times by appointment. Closed Christmas, New Year.

BOZEMAN

MONTANA STATE UNIVERSITY HERBARIUM
Lewis Hall, Montana State University Campus, Bozeman, Montana 59715
Plants of Montana.
M.-F. 1-5.

GALLATIN PIONEERS MUSEUM
Bozeman, Montana 59715
Local history. Pioneer life. Indian material.
M.-F. 8-5.

MUSEUM OF THE ROCKIES
Montana State University, Bozeman, Montana 59715
Mineralogy. Palaeontology. Anthropology. Local history. Technology.
M.-F. 8-9; Sa., Su. 1-5. Closed New Year, Thanksgiving, Christmas.

BRACKETTVILLE

ALAMO VILLAGE
Farm Road 674, Brackettville, Texas 78832
Replica of a San Antonio street in 1836.
Daily 9-dusk.

JOHN FRITTER MEMORIAL MUSEUM
El Paso Street, Brackettville, Texas 78832
In restored stage coach stand (c.1870). Early life in Brackettville and Fort Clark.
By appointment.

BRADENTON

CONQUISTADOR HISTORICAL FOUNDATION
809 14th Street West, Bradenton, Florida 33505
Spanish-American history, artifacts.
M.-F., 9-5. Closed public holidays.

DE SOTO NATIONAL MEMORIAL
P.O. Box 1377, Bradenton, Florida 33505
Natural history. Local history.
Daily 8-5. Closed Christmas.

SOUTH FLORIDA MUSEUM AND BISHOP PLANETARIUM
201 10th Street, Bradenton, Florida 33505
Geology. Palaeontology. Astronomy. Planetarium. Natural history. Aquarium. Ethnology. Anatomy. Archaeology. Local history. Indian artifacts. Costumes. Coins.
Tu.-F. 10-5; Sa. 10-5, 7-9; Su., public holidays 1-5.

BRAINERD

LUMBERTOWN USA
Box 387, Route 6, Brainerd, Minnesota 56401
Replica of 1870 lumber-town. 30 buildings. Indian art. Agriculture.
Sept. 1 - May 29, daily 10-7. May 30 - Labour Day, daily 10-5.

MUSEUM OF CROW WING COUNTY HISTORICAL SOCIETY
Court House, Brainerd, Minnesota 56401
Local history. Archaeology. Natural history. Industry. Indian artifacts. Costumes. Paintings.
June 1 - day preceding Labour Day: Tu.-F. 1-5. Labour Day - May 31: Tu., F. 1-5.

BRAINTREE

GENERAL SYLVANUS BIRTHPLACE
786 Washington Street, Braintree, Massachusetts 02185
House (1720). Local history. Costumes.
May 1 - Sept. 30: Tu.-F., Su. 1.30-4; Sa. 10-4. Oct. 1 - Apr. 30: M. 9-1; Tu., Th., Sa. 1.30-4.

BRAINTREE HISTORICAL SOCIETY MUSEUM
Braintree, Vermont 05646
In restored birthplace of Gen. Sylvanus Thayer (c.1720). Early Americana with local associations.
May 1 - Sept. 30: Tu.-F., Su. 1.30-4; Sa. 10-4. Oct. 1 - Apr. 30: M. 9-1; Tu.-Th., Sa. 1.30-4. Closed New Year, Easter, Christmas.

BRANSON

SHEPHERD OF THE HILLS FARM
Memorial Museum, Highway 76, Branson, Missouri 65616
Museum at place made famous by Harold Bell Wright's book, *The Shepherd of the Hills*. Ozark handicrafts.
Apr. 1 - Oct. 31, daily 8-6.

BRECKENRIDGE

WILKINS COUNTY HISTORICAL SOCIETY MUSEUM
St. Francis Home, Breckenridge, Minnesota 56520
Local history. Furniture. Pioneer life.
By appointment.

BRECKSVILLE

BRECKSVILLE HISTORICAL ASSOCIATION
9367 Brecksville Road (41), Brecksville, Ohio 44141
In Squire Rich house (1845). Period furnishings. Agricultural implements.
Su. 2-5. Other times by appointment.

BREEZEWOOD

CRAWFORD'S MUSEUM
U.S. Highway 30, Breezewood, Pennsylvania 15533
Mounted specimens of animals.
M., Tu., Th.-Sa. 10-10; W. 10-6; Su. 1-6.

BREMERTON

KITSAP COUNTY HISTORICAL SOCIETY
837 4th Street, Bremerton, Washington 98310
In Telephone Building (1910). History of Kitsap County. 19th century furniture.
Tu.-Sa. 1-4. Closed Christmas, New Year, Memorial Day, Thanksgiving.

NAVAL SHIPYARD MUSEUM
Washington State Ferry Terminal Building, Bremerton, Washington 98310
U.S. naval history. History of Puget Sound Naval Shipyard.
M.-Sa. 9.30-4; Su. 12.30-4. Closed public holidays.

BRENTWOOD

BUCKLAND MUSEUM OF WITCHCRAFT AND MAGICK
111 Timberline Drive, Brentwood, New York 11717
Religio-magical artifacts. Witchcraft. Folklore.
May 1 - Oct. 31, by appointment.

BREWERTON

FORT BREWERTON MUSEUM
5439 Railroad Street, Brewerton, New York 13029
Local history. Archaeology. Indian artifacts. Transport. Costumes. Glass.
July 1 - Aug. 31: W.-M. 10-5. May 1 - June 30, Sept. 1-30: Sa., Su. 2-5.

BREWSTER

CAPE COD MUSEUM OF NATURAL HISTORY
Route 6A, Brewster, Massachusetts 02631
Flora and natural history of Cape Cod. Aquarium. Archaeology.
Labour Day - June 15: Tu., Th., Sa. 9.30-4.30; Su. 1.30-4.30. June 15 - Labour Day: M.-Sa. 10-5. Closed Thanksgiving - Christmas.

DRUMMER BOY MUSEUM
Route 6A, Brewster, Massachusetts 02631
History of American Revolution, with dioramas of Boston Tea Party, Capture of Paul Revere and other events.
May 15 - Oct. 12, daily 9.30-6.

DINOSAUR LAND
Route 2, Brewster, New York 10509
Dinosaur tracks and life-size models. Mineral grotto. Replica of mine.
May 28 - June 13, Sept. 11-25: Sa., Su. 10-5. June 18 - Sept. 6, daily 10-5.

SOUTHEAST MUSEUM ASSOCIATION MUSEUM
Main Street, Brewster, New York 10509
Mineralogy. Local history.
Apr. 1 - Nov. 15: W., Sa. 2-5. July 1 - Aug. 31: Tu., W., F., Sa. 2-5. Closed July 4, Labour Day.

FORT OKANOGAN HISTORICAL MUSEUM
Brewster, Washington 98812
Archaeology. Pioneer life. Indian artifacts. Costumes. Decorative arts. Transport.
May 1 - Sept. 30, daily 8-6.

BRIDGE HAMPTON

CORWITH HOMESTEAD
Montauk Highway, Bridge Hampton, New York 11932
Local history. Indian artifacts. Agriculture. Costumes. Old internal-combustion engines. Wheelwright's shop (1872), with tools.
June 15 - Sept. 15: Th.-M. 10-4.

BRIDGEPORT

BODIE STATE HISTORIC PARK
Bodie Road, Bridgeport, California 93517
Gold Rush ghost town (c.1860-1880), preserved "in a state of arrested decay".
Always open.

BARNUM MUSEUM
820 Main Street, Bridgeport, Connecticut 06604
Furniture and other personal possessions of P. T. Barnum. Clothes worn by Tom Thumb and his wife. Circus material. Paintings. Mementoes of Jenny Lind. Replica of 19th century Swiss village.
Tu.-Sa., 12-5; Su., 2-5. Closed New Year, Feb. 12, 22, Good Friday, July 4, Thanksgiving, Christmas.

CAPTAIN BROOKS HOUSE
199 Pembroke Street, Bridgeport, Connecticut 06608
House (1788). Period furnishings.
By appointment.

HOUSATONIC MUSEUM OF ART
Housatonic Community College, Bridgeport, Connecticut 06601
Paintings, prints, sculpture by contemporary American artists.
Daily 9-6.

MUSEUM OF ART, SCIENCE AND INDUSTRY
4450 Park Avenue, Bridgeport, Connecticut 06604
Paintings by American and European artists. Planetarium. Artifacts by Connecticut Indians. Circus memorabilia. Industry and technology. 18th century furniture from Captain John Brooks House (1788), which is in the care of the Museum.
Tu.-Su. 2-5. Closed public holidays.

RUSSELL CAVE NATIONAL MONUMENT
Box 175, Route 1, Bridgeport, Alabama 35740
Geology. Archaeology. Culture of the Woodland Indians. Antiquities and ethnology of the South-Eastern States.
Labour Day - Memorial Day, daily 8-5; Rest of year 8-6.

BRIDGEWATER

UPSTATE ANTIQUE AUTO MUSEUM
Route 20, Bridgewater, New York 13313
Petrol, steam and electric vehicles. Bicycles and motorcycles.
June 1 - Sept. 30, daily 9-6. May 1-31, Oct. 1-31, Su. only 9-6.

BRIGHAM CITY

BEAR RIVER MIGRATORY BIRD REFUGE
Brigham City, Utah 84302
Natural history.
Daily 8-4.30. Jan. 1 - Feb. 28, closed Sa., Su.

BRISTOL

AMERICAN CLOCK AND WATCH MUSEUM
100 Maple Street, Bristol, Connecticut 06010
In Miles Lewis House (1801). History of clocks and watches from c.1700 to present day.
Tu.-Su. 1-5. Closed Nov. 1 - Mar. 31.

THE GREGORY HOUSE
Torreya State Park, Florida Highway 12, Bristol, Florida 32321
House (c.1830), moved across river to present site in 1935. 1850-60 period furnishings.
M.-F. 10-12, 2-4; Sa., Su., public holidays 10-5.

ELKHART COUNTY HISTORICAL SOCIETY MUSEUM
Bristol, Indiana 46507
Local history. Agriculture. Children's museum.
Sa. 1-4; Su. 1-5. Closed New Year, Thanksgiving, Christmas.

BRISTOL HISTORICAL SOCIETY MUSEUM
48 Court Street, Bristol, Rhode Island 02809
18th century furnishings. Local history. Indian artifacts. Costumes. Former Bristol County Jail (1828) is in the care of the Society.
Apr. 1 - Dec. 31, W. 2.30-5.

HAFFENREFFER MUSEUM OF ANTHROPOLOGY
Brown University, Mount Hope Street, Bristol, Rhode Island 02809
Culture of Pacific, Africa, Eskimo and American Indians. Anthropology. Ethnology. Archaeology.
Sept. 1 - May 30: Sa. 10-4; Su. 1-4. June 1 - Aug. 30: Tu.-Su. 1-4. Closed Feb. 1-28, public holidays.

BROADUS

MUSEUM OF NATURAL HISTORY
P.O. Box 466, Broadus, Montana 59317
Mineralogy. Conchology. Indian relics. Coins. Stamps.
On request.

BROCKFORT

WESTERN NEW YORK HISTORICAL SOCIETY MUSEUM
151 Main Street, Brockfort, New York 14420
Morgan Manning House (c.1860). Victorian furnishings.
Su. 2-4; Th. 12-2. Other times by appointment.

BROCKTON

BROCKTON ART CENTER
Fuller Memorial, Oak Street, Brockton, Massachusetts 02401
S.E. New England contemporary paintings, sculpture, graphics. Massachusetts 19th-20th century paintings, sculpture, decorative arts, folk art.
Tu., W., F., Su. 1-5; Th. 1-10. Closed July 4, Labour Day, Thanksgiving, Christmas.

BROCKTON PUBLIC LIBRARY AND ART GALLERY
304 Main Street, Brockton, Massachusetts 02401
Paintings by New England artists, c.1880-c.1920.
M.-Sa. 9-9.

BROCKVILLE

E. M. PARKER INDIAN MUSEUM
Route 322, Brockville, Pennsylvania 15825
Indian archaeology and artifacts from Pennsylvania, E. Ohio and New York. Early American tools and furniture. Coins.
By appointment.

BROKEN BOW

CUSTER COUNTY MUSEUM
345 S. 9th Avenue, Broken Bow, Nebraska 68822
Natural history. Local history. Archaeology. Guns. Clothing. Tools.
M.-Sa. 8-5. Closed July 1 - Aug. 31, public holidays.

MEMORIAL INDIAN MUSEUM
2nd and Allen Streets, Broken Bow, Oklahoma 74728
Mineralogy. Local history. Indian artifacts, prehistoric-modern times. Glass.
M.-Sa. 8-5; Su. 1-5.

BRONX

BRONX MUSEUM OF THE ARTS
851 Grand Concourse, Bronx, New York 10451
Roman sculpture. Murals.
M.-F. 10-4.30. Closed public holidays.

NEW YORK BOTANICAL GARDEN
200th Street and Southern Boulevard, Bronx, New York 10458
Herbarium. Natural history. Science and technology. Lorillard Snuff Mill building (1800) is in the care of the Garden.
May 31 - Sept., daily 10-6. Oct.-May 30, daily 10-dusk.

VALENTINE-VARIAN HOUSE MUSEUM OF BRONX HISTORY
3266 Bainbridge Avenue, Bronx, New York 10467
House (1756). Paintings, prints, photographs illustrating history of the Bronx. Natural history. Indian artifacts.
Su. 1-5.

BROOKFIELD

BROOKFIELD HISTORICAL SOCIETY MUSEUM
3140 Pilgrim Road, Brookfield, Wisconsin 53005
Local history. Children's museum.
By appointment.

BROOKFIELD CENTER

MUSEUM OF HISTORICAL SOCIETY OF BROOKFIELD
Brookfield Center, Vermont 05036
In Marvin Newton house (1835). 19th century furnishings.
July 1 - Aug. 31, Su. 2.30-5.

BROOKHAVEN

MANOR OF ST. GEORGE
Smith's Point, Mastic Beach, Brookhaven, New York 11719
Third Manor House on site (c.1780). Material connected with Col. William Tangier Smith (d.1705) and his descendants. Period furnishings.
May 1 - Oct. 31: W.-Su. 10-5.

BROOKINGS

MUSEUM AND HERITAGE CENTER OF SOUTH DAKOTA STATE UNIVERSITY
Agricultural Engineering Department, Brookings, South Dakota 57006
Geology. Botany. Natural history. Archaeology. Agriculture. Indian artifacts. Children's museum.
Su. 1.30-4.30.

SOUTH DAKOTA MEMORIAL ART CENTER
Medary Avenue and 10th Street, Brookings, South Dakota 57006
Paintings. Graphic arts. Sculpture. Decorative arts.
Tu.-F. 8-5, 7-9; Sa. 10-5; Su. 1-5. Closed Easter, Thanksgiving, Christmas, New Year.

BROOKLINE

MUSEUM OF TRANSPORTATION
Larz Anderson Park, 15 Newton Street, Brookline, Massachusetts 02146
In former coachhouse and stable of the Anderson estate. 19th century carriages, sleighs. Early bicycles. Automobiles from early 'horseless carriage' to 1950s.
Tu. 10-9; W.-Su. 10-5. Closed Jan. 1, July 4, Thanksgiving, Dec. 25.

EDWARD DEVOTION HOUSE
347 Harvard Street (46), Brookline, Massachusetts 02146
House (1740). Period furnishings. Portraits.
W. 2-4, and by appointment.

MARY BAKER EDDY MUSEUM
120 Seaver Street, Brookline, Massachusetts 02146
Material relating to Mary Baker Eddy and the Christian Science Church. 5 houses associated with Mary Baker Eddy are in the care of the Society.
Tu. 10-9, W.-Su. 10-5. Closed Jan. 1, July 4, Thanksgiving, Christmas.

JOHN F. KENNEDY NATIONAL HISTORIC SITE
83 Beals Street, Brookline, Massachusetts 02146
House (1909), birthplace of John F. Kennedy. Furnished as on May 29, 1917.
Daily 9-5.

BROOKLYN

MUSEUM OF BROOKLYN AREA HISTORICAL SOCIETY
Brooklyn, Michigan 49230
In Town Hall (1840). Local history.
By appointment.

BROOKNEAL

RED HILL
Brookneal, Virginia 24528
House (c.1750), home and burial place of Patrick Henry. Period furnishings. Henry's personal possessions.
Apr. 1 - Oct. 31, daily 9-5. Nov. 1 - Mar. 31, daily 9-4. Closed Christmas.

BROOKS AIR FORCE BASE

EDWARD H. WHITE MEMORIAL MUSEUM
Hangar 9, Brooks Air Force Base, Texas 78235
In 1918 hangars. Aviation history. Space travel. Aviation medicine.
M.-F. 8-4.30. Closed public holidays.

BROOKVILLE

FRANKLIN COUNTY SEMINARY AND MUSEUM
5th and Mill Street, Brookville, Indiana 47012
In Franklin County Seminary (1828-31). County and State history. Little Cedar Grove Baptist Church (1812), Old Brick Church (1820-1), are in the care of the Museum.
By appointment.

BROOMALL

THOMAS MASSEY HOUSE
Marple Township, Broomall, Pennsylvania 19008
House (1696, with later additions). Period furnishings. Massey family history.
May 1 - Sept. 15, Su. 2-5. Other times by appointment.

BROWNING

MUSEUM OF THE PLAINS INDIAN
Browning, Montana 59417
19th-20th century Plains Indian handicrafts and art. Quillwork. Skin paintings. Beadwork. Featherwork. Carvings. Costumes. Blackfoot Agency records.
June 1-14, daily 8-5. June 15 - Sept. 15, daily 8-8. Sept. 16-30, daily 8-5. Oct. 1 - May 31, M.-F. 9-5. Closed public holidays.

SCRIVER MUSEUM OF MONTANA WILDLIFE
P.O. Box 172, Browning, Montana 59417
Dioramas and mounted specimens of birds, animals and fishes of Montana. Game animals.
Easter - Thanksgiving, daily 7-8.

BROWNINGTON

OLD STONE HOUSE
Brownington, Vermont 05860
House (1836). Period furnishings. Agricultural implements. Household equipment.
May 15 - Oct. 15, daily 9-5.

BROWNS VALLEY

SAM BROWN LOG HOUSE
Browns Valley, Minnesota 56219
House (1863). Indian artifacts. Dugout canoe. Furniture and equipment used by Brown family. Guns. Indian skulls.
Memorial Day - Sept. 14, daily 1-9.

BROWNSVILLE

FLINT RIDGE MUSEUM
Interstate 70, Licking County, Brownsville, Ohio 43721
Geology. Prehistoric Indian artifacts.
Mar. 1 - Nov. 30: Tu.-Su. 9.30-5. Dec. 1 - Feb. 28, Su. 9.30-5.

LINN COUNTY PIONEER MUSEUM
Spaulding Street, Brownsville, Oregon 97327
In Moyer House (1881). Local history. Pioneer items.
Tu.-Su. 2-5.

STILLMAN HOUSE MUSEUM
1305 E. Washington, Brownsville, Texas 78520
House (1850). Local history. Furniture. Paintings.
Sept. 1 - June 30, M.-F. 9-12, 2-5.

BROWNVILLE

BROWNVILLE HISTORICAL SOCIETY ANTIQUES MUSEUM
3rd and Main Streets, Brownville, Nebraska 68321
In Carson House (1860), formerly home of banker and financier John L. Carson. Period rooms and furniture. Brownville history.
June 1 - Aug. 31, daily 2-5. May 1-31, Sept. 1 - Oct. 31, Su. 2-5.

BROWNVILLE HISTORICAL SOCIETY GENERAL MUSEUM
Main Street, between 4th and 5th, Brownville, Nebraska 68321
In Captain Bailey House (1877). Local history. Agriculture. Glass. Indian artifacts. Costumes.
June 1 - Aug. 31, daily 2-5. May 1 - Oct. 31, Su. 2-5.

MUIR HOUSE
2nd and Atlanta Streets, Brownville, Nebraska 68321
House (1868), with period furniture. American paintings, sculpture, decorative arts. 19th century salesmen's samples.
June 1 - Oct. 31, by appointment.

BROWN MANSION
Brown Boulevard, Brownville, New York 13615
House (c.1820), home of Jacob Brown, hero of War of 1812. Portraits. Personal possessions of Brown.
W. 2-5.30; Sa. 10-5.30.

BROWNVILLE RAILROAD MUSEUM
Brownville, New York 13615
Restored NYCRR depot. Railway history.
May 21 - Nov. 19, F. 7.30-9.

BRUNSWICK

BOWDOIN MUSEUM OF ART
Brunswick, Maine 04011
In Walker Art Building (1894). Mesopotamian sculpture. Greek and Roman antiquities. 16th-18th century European paintings, drawings. 18th-19th century American paintings.

European and American silver. Chinese and Japanese ceramics, jades.
July 1 - Labour Day: M.-Sa. 10-5, 7.30-9; Su. 2-5. Rest of year: M.-F. 10-4; Sa. 10-5; Su. 2-5. Closed public holidays.

MUSEUM OF PEJEPSCOT HISTORICAL SOCIETY
12 School Street, Brunswick, Maine 04011
Local history. Agriculture. Industry. Shipping. Costumes. Decorative arts. Portraits.
June 1 - Aug. 31, M.-F. 1-5.

BRYAN

JUNIOR MUSEUM OF NATURAL HISTORY
Rec Building, Municipal Golf Course, Bryan, Texas 77801
Geology. Astronomy. Botany. Natural history. Ecology.
During school hours and by appointment.

BRYCE CANYON

BRYCE CANYON NATIONAL PARK, VISITOR CENTER
Bryce Canyon, Utah 84717
Geology. Palaeontology. Botany. Herbarium. Natural history. Entomology. Indian artifacts. Archaeology. Local history.
May 1 - Sept. 30, daily 8-9. Oct. 1 - Apr. 30, M.-F. 8-5.

BUCKEYE

BUCKEYE HISTORICAL AND ARCHAEOLOGICAL MUSEUM
City Park, Buckeye, Arizona 85326
Local history and archaeology. Indian artifacts.
Tu.-Su. 1-5.

BUCKLAND

BUCKLAND HISTORICAL SOCIETY MUSEUM
Buckland, Massachusetts 01803
History of Buckland area.
July 1 - Aug. 31, W. 2-5.

BUCKNER

FORT OSAGE
Buckner, Missouri 64016
Reconstruction of fort (1808-27). Officer's quarters. Soldiers' huts. Fur trading post.
Daily 9-5. Closed New Year, Thanksgiving, Christmas.

BUCKSPORT

BUCKSPORT HISTORICAL SOCIETY MUSEUM
Main Street, Bucksport, Maine 04416
Local history. Shipping. Naval and military history. Old Maine Central Railway Station (1874), with historical collection, is in the care of the Museum.
July 1 Aug. 31: Th.-Sa. 2-5. May, Sept., Oct. by appointment.

BUENA PARK

BOXING MUSEUM
Knott's Berry Farm, Buena Park, California 90620
Collection, formed by Al Nelson, illustrating history of boxing.
Daily 9-5. Closed Christmas.

BUENA PARK HISTORICAL SOCIETY MUSEUM
Manchester and Whitaker Streets, Buena Park, California 90620
Whitaker-Jaynes House (1887), with period furnishings.
By appointment.

WESTERN TRAILS MUSEUM
Knott's Berry Farm, Buena Park, California 90620
Collection illustrating development of American West, formed 1889-1956 by Marion Speer. Guns. Tools. Indian artifacts. Mission history. Minerals. Buttons.
Daily 9-5. Closed Christmas.

BUFFALO

ALBRIGHT-KNOX ART GALLERY
1285 Elmwood Avenue, Buffalo, New York 14222
Sculpture 3000 B.C. to present day. 18th century English paintings. 19th-20th century American and European paintings.
Su., public holidays 12-5; Tu.-Sa. 10-5. Closed New Year, Thanksgiving, Christmas.

BUFFALO MUSEUM OF SCIENCE
Humboldt Park, Buffalo, New York 14211
Geology. Astronomy. Botany. Local flora and fauna. Anthropology. Egyptian collection. Herbarium.
May 1 - Sept. 30, M.-Sa. 10-5; Su., public holidays, 1.30-5.30. Oct. 1 - Apr. 30, F. 10-10. Closed Christmas.

MUSEUM OF BUFFALO AND ERIE COUNTY HISTORICAL SOCIETY
25 Nottingham Court, Buffalo, New York 14216
In remaining building of Pan American Exposition (1901). Archaeology. Agriculture. Industry. Military history. Transport. Maritime history.
M.-F. 10-5; Su., public holidays 2-5. Closed July 4, Labour Day, Thanksgiving, Christmas, New Year.

THEODORE ROOSEVELT INAUGURATION NATIONAL HISTORIC SITE
641 Delaware Avenue, Buffalo, New York 14202
In Pointsett Barracks (1838), where President Roosevelt was inaugurated (1901). Memorabilia of his inauguration.
M.-Sa. 10-5; Su. 12-6. Closed July 4, Labour Day, Thanksgiving, Christmas, New Year.

JOHNSON COUNTY, JIM GATCHELL MEMORIAL MUSEUM
10 Fort Street, Buffalo, Wyoming 82834
Mineralogy. Pioneer and Indian history in Wyoming and the West. Paintings. Indian artifacts. Horse-drawn vehicles.
June 1 - Labour Day, daily 9-9. Closed July 4.

BUFFALO GAP

ERNIE WILSON MUSEUM
Buffalo Gap, Texas 79508
Pioneer history. Guns. Tools. Riding equipment. Indian artifacts.
May-Sept., Sa., Su., holidays, 2-6. Rest of year, 2-5.

BUNNELL

BULOW PLANTATION STATE HISTORIC SITE
P.O. Box 655, Florida State Highway 5, Bunnell, Florida 32010
Museum illustrating history of the Bulow sugar, cotton and indigo plantation. Implements. Machinery. Ruins of sugar-mill and slave quarters.
Daily 8-dusk.

BURKITTSVILLE

GATHLAND STATE PARK MUSEUM
Burkittsville, Maryland 21718
In Gath Hall (1885), designed by G. A. Townsend. Civil War relics. Firearms. Indian artifacts.
Daily.

BURLINGTON

STEWART M. LORD MEMORIAL HISTORICAL SOCIETY MUSEUM
Burlington, Maine 04417
In former general store (1850). Local history. Lumbering. Household equipment.
May 29 - Sept. 30, F.-Su., public holidays 2-4.

MUSEUM OF BURLINGTON HISTORICAL SOCIETY
Bedford Street, Burlington, Massachusetts 01803
Agriculture. School equipment. Costumes.
By appointment.

LAWRENCE HOUSE
459 High Street, Burlington, New Jersey 08016
House (1742) was birthplace of Capt. James Lawrence. Period furnishings. Mementoes of Capt. Lawrence and of the Navy.
Tu.-Sa. 10-12, 1-5; Su., public holidays 2-5. Closed New Year, Thanksgiving, Christmas.

MUSEUM OF COLONIAL BURLINGTON FOUNDATION
Wood Street, Burlington, New Jersey 08016
In Thomas Revel house (1685). Period furnishings. Local history.
By appointment.

ALAMANCE BATTLEGROUND STATE HISTORIC SITE
Route 1, Burlington, North Carolina 27215
Visitor Centre has exhibits showing 18th century history of the area. The site includes Allen House (1782), log-cabin, with original furnishings.
Tu.-Sa. 9-5; Su. 1-5. Closed Thanksgiving, Dec. 24-6.

BURLINGTON HISTORICAL SOCIETY MUSEUM
P.O. Box 411, Burlington, North Carolina 27215
Local history.
Daily 9-5.

MCDADE WILDLIFE MUSEUM
1333 Overbrook Road, Burlington, North Carolina 27215
Geology. Mineralogy. Archaeology. Mounted specimens of birds and animals from N. and S. America, India, Africa, Australia.
M.-F. 8-5; Su. 2-4. Closed holidays.

ROBERT HULL FLEMING MUSEUM
University of Vermont, Colchester Avenue, Burlington, Vermont 05401
Arts of primitive cultures. Works from N., S., and Central America, Africa, Asia, and S. Pacific. European medieval and Renaissance art. 19th-20th century European and American paintings, sculpture, graphics. Anthropology. Archaeology. Costumes.
M.-F. 9-5; Sa. 9-3; Su. 2-5.

PRINGLE HERBARIUM
601 Main Street, Burlington, Vermont 05401
Collections of botanical specimens from U.S. and Mexico.
M.-F. 8-12, 1-5. Closed public holidays.

BURLINGTON HISTORICAL SOCIETY MUSEUM
232 N. Perkins Boulevard, Burlington, Wisconsin 53105
Local history. Indian artifacts. Costumes. Dolls. Toys.
Memorial Day - Labour Day, Su. 1-4.

BURNET

FORT CROGHAN MUSEUM
S.H.29 W., Burnet, Texas 78611
Restoration of fort (1848). Includes powder house, stage coach station, blacksmith's shop. Furniture, guns and other pioneer relics.
June 1 - Sept. 15, W.-Sa. 10-6; Su. 1-6.

BURNS

BENSON MEMORIAL MUSEUM
Malheur National Wildlife Refuge, Burns, Oregon 97720
Specimens of birds and mammals found in the Refuge.
Daily, 24 hours a day.

HARNEY COUNTY MUSEUM
330 N. Broadway, Burns, Oregon 97720
Geology. Mineralogy. Natural history. Local history and archaeology. Indian artifacts. Round Barn (1887) is in the care of the Museum.
June 1 - Sept. 30: Tu.-Sa. 9-12, 1-5.30.

CUMBERLAND PRESBYTERIAN HISTORIC SHRINE
Montgomery Bell State Park, Burns, Tennessee 37029
Building (1810). Original furniture.
Daily 8-6.

BURTON

GEAUGA COUNTY HISTORICAL SOCIETY
14653 E. Park Street, Burton, Ohio 44021
Local history. Agriculture. Indian artifacts. 7 local buildings (1825-89) are in the care of the Society.
Mar. 1 - Dec. 31: Tu.-Sa., July 4, 10-5; Su. 1-5. Closed Memorial Day.

BURWELL

GARFIELD COUNTY HISTORICAL MUSEUM
737 H Street, Burwell, Nebraska 68823
Local history. Indian artifacts.
Tu., F., Su. 1-4.30.

BUSHNELL

DADE BATTLEFIELD HISTORIC MONUMENT
U.S. Highway 301, Bushnell, Florida 33513
Site of battle (1835) with Seminole Indians. Interpretative exhibits of battle.
Daily 8-12, 1-5.

BUTLER

BATES COUNTY HISTORICAL SOCIETY MUSEUM
620 W. Harrison, Butler, Missouri 64730
In Old Bates County Jail (1894). Pioneer furnishings. Household utensils. Guns. Indian relics. Minerals.
May 1 - Nov. 30, daily 1-5.

BUTTE

MINERAL MUSEUM
W. Park Street, Butte, Montana 59701
Worldwide collection of minerals and fossils.
May 1 - Sept. 30, daily 8-5. Oct. 1 - Apr. 30, M.-F. 8-5.

WORLD MUSEUM OF MINING
Butte, Montana 59701
Mineralogy. Local history. Mining. Paintings of Montana subjects. Open-air museum of 19th century buildings.
June 1 - Labour Day, daily 9-9. Labour Day - June 1, Tu.-Su. 9-5.

BUXTON

CAPE HATTERAS NATIONAL SEASHORE
Bodie Island Visitor Center, Buxton, North Carolina 27920
Formerly Bodie Island Lighthouse Keeper's house. Exhibits telling natural history story of the seashore.
June 20 - Aug. 31, daily 9-6.

BYRDSTOWN

CORDELL HULL BIRTHPLACE MEMORIAL
Byrdstown, Tennessee 38549
Birthplace of Secretary of State Cordell Hull. Hull memorabilia.
By appointment.

BYRON

BYRON HISTORICAL MUSEUM
E. Main Street, Byron, New York 14422
Local history.
June 1 - Sept. 30, W. 2-5.

CABOOL

OZARKS HILLBILLY VILLAGE
Junction Highway 60-63, Cabool, Missouri 64730
Mineralogy. Local history. Agriculture. Folklore. Indian material. Transport. Medical history.
Apr. 1 - Nov. 31: M.-Sa. 8-5; Su. 1-6.

CABOT

CABOT HISTORICAL SOCIETY MUSEUM
Main Street, Cabot, Vermont 05647
Local history. Costume.
July 4 and by appointment.

CAHOKIA

CAHOKIA COURT HOUSE
214 West First Street, Cahokia, Illinois 62206
Local history.
Daily 9-5. Closed New Year, Thanksgiving, Christmas.

CAIRO

MAGNOLIA MANOR
2700 Washington Avenue, Cairo, Illinois 62914
House (1869). Civil War history. Local history. 19th century furnishings.
Daily 9-5. Closed Christmas, New Year.

CALAIS

KENT MUSEUM
Calais, Vermont 05648
Former stage coach tavern (1837). Period furnishings. Tools and implements. Country store. Gallery of miniature rooms.
July 1 - Aug. 31, daily 1-5.

MUSEUM OF ST. CROIX HISTORICAL SOCIETY
241 Main Street, Calais, Maine 04619
Local history. Indian relics.
July 1 - Aug. 31, M.-F. 1-5.

CALDWELL

JEWETT EXHIBITION CENTER
College of Idaho, Caldwell, Idaho 83605
Prints by American and European artists.
M.-F. 8-6. Closed college vacations.

ODDFELLOWS HISTORICAL BUILDING
920 Grant Street, Caldwell, Idaho 83605
Oddfellows' history. Local history.
M.-F. 9-5. Closed public holidays.

VAN SLYKE MUSEUM
Caldwell Memorial Park, Caldwell, Idaho 83605
Agricultural history. McKenzie Log Cabin (1861) and Johnson Brothers Log Cabin (1864) are in the care of the Museum.
By appointment.

GROVER CLEVELAND BIRTHPLACE
207 Bloomfield Avenue, Caldwell, New Jersey 07006
House (1832) was originally Presbyterian Manse. Cleveland born here 1837. Period furnishings and mementoes of Grover Cleveland. Portraits of him and of his family and friends. Letters. Documents.
Tu.-Sa. 10-12, 1-5; Su., public holidays 2-5. Closed Thanksgiving, Christmas, New Year.

BURLESON COUNTY HISTORICAL MUSEUM
County Courthouse, Caldwell, Texas 78836
Pioneer life. Mexican artifacts. 19th century furniture.
M.-F. 8-5. Closed public holidays.

CALEDONIA

HOUSTON COUNTY HISTORICAL MUSEUM
Caledonia, Minnesota 55921
Local history. Agriculture. Indian artifacts. Brownsville Church (c.1875) and Eitzen store (1890) are in the care of the Museum.
By appointment.

BIG SPRINGS MUSEUM
Main Street, Caledonia, New York 14423
Domestic equipment, furniture from homes of Scottish pioneers. Agricultural implements. Indian life. Costumes. Portraits.
May 1 - June 30, F. 1-4. July 1 - Sept. 1, F. 7-9. Sept. 2 - Nov. 30, F. 1-4. Dec. 1 - Apr. 30, Su. 2-5. Closed Easter, Memorial Day, July 4, Christmas.

STEVENS BLACKSMITH'S SHOP
Caledonia, Pennsylvania 17201
Reconstruction of blacksmith's shop owned by Thaddeus Stevens (d.1868), crusader for negroes' rights.
May-Oct., by appointment.

CALHOUN

NEW ECHOTA
Route 3, Calhoun, Georgia 30701
Group of buildings illustrating local history. Indian capital of Cherokee nation (1825). Samuel Worcester's Mission (1827). Vann Tavern (1830s). Courthouse (c.1830). Printing house (1828), where newspaper, *Cherokee Phoenix*, was printed in Cherokee and English.
Oct. 1 - Apr. 30: Tu.-Sa. 9-5; Su. 2-5. May 1-Sept. 30: Tu.-Sa. 9-5.30; Su. 2-5.30. Closed Thanksgiving, Christmas.

CAMBRIDGE

HENRY COUNTY HISTORICAL SOCIETY MUSEUM
Steeple Building, Bishop Hill, Cambridge, Illinois 61238
House (1853). Local history. History of medicine. Contains doctor's surgery (1880).
May 15 - Oct. 30: M.-Sa. 9-5; Su. 12-5.

THE DORCHESTER COUNTY HISTORICAL SOCIETY
Cambridge, Maryland 21613
In Meredeith House (c.1770). County history.
Weekends, by appointment.

BOTANICAL MUSEUM OF HARVARD UNIVERSITY
Oxford Street, Cambridge, Massachusetts 02138
Economic botany. Narcotic plants. Palaeontology. Palaeobotany. Glass models of plants.
M.-Sa. 9-4.30; Su. 1-4.30. Closed public holidays.

BUSCH-REISINGER MUSEUM
29 Kirkland Street, Cambridge, Massachusetts 02138
German, Austrian, Swiss, Scandinavian art from the Middle Ages to the present day. Bauhaus material. Papers and drawings of Lyonel Feininger. Paintings. Sculpture.
M.-Sa. (Oct. 1 - Apr. 30, M.-F.) 9-5. Closed public holidays.

CAMBRIDGE HISTORICAL SOCIETY MUSEUM
159 Brattle Street (38), Cambridge, Massachusetts 02138
In Lee-Nichols House (c.1660). Period furnishings. Local history.
Th. 3-5.

COOPER-FROST-AUSTIN HOUSE
21 Linnaean Street, Cambridge, Massachusetts 02138
House (c.1657). Period furniture.
Tu. 2-4; Th. 2-4, 7-9.

FOGG ART MUSEUM
Harvard University, 32 Quincy Street, Cambridge, Massachusetts 02138
Egyptian antiquities. Greek sculpture, vases. Roman coins. Chinese sculpture, bronzes, jade, crystal, paintings, prints. Japanese prints. Cambodian sculpture. Romanesque and Gothic sculpture. Italian, Spanish, Flemish, French paintings. French sculpture. American paintings. English and American water-colours, silver. 18th-19th century English paintings. European and American drawings, prints. Wedgwood china. Pre-Columbian art.
M.-Sa. 9-5; Su. 2-5. Closed public holidays and July 1 - Labour Day, Sa., Su.

GEOLOGICAL MUSEUM
Harvard University, 24 Oxford Street (38), Cambridge, Massachusetts 02138
Town and area models, including one of Greater Boston. Rocks. Building stones.
M.-Sa. and holidays 9-4.30; Su. 1-4.30. Closed July 4 and Christmas.

GRAY HERBARIUM
22 Divinity Avenue, Cambridge, Massachusetts 02138
Herbarium, especially of N. America.
By appointment.

HAYDEN GALLERY
14W-11 Massachusetts Institute of Technology, Cambridge, Massachusetts 02139
20th century paintings, sculpture, drawings, graphics. Photographs. Decorative arts.
M.-Sa. 10-5; Closed New Year, Thanksgiving, Christmas.

THE LONGFELLOW HOUSE
105 Brattle Street, Cambridge, Massachusetts 02138
House (1759). Washington's headquarters.
May-Oct. M.-F. 10-5; Sa. 12-5; Su. 1-5. Nov.-Apr. M.-F. 10-4; Sa., Su. 2-4.

MINERALOGICAL MUSEUM OF HARVARD UNIVERSITY
Oxford Street, Cambridge, Massachusetts 02138
Minerals. Meteorites. Gemstones. Economic geology.
M.-Sa. 9-4.30; Su., public holidays 1-4.30. Closed July 4, Christmas.

MUSEUM OF COMPARATIVE ZOOLOGY
Oxford Street, Cambridge, Massachusetts 02138
Palaeontology. Comparative anatomy. Mammalogy. Ornithology. Marine zoology. Icthyology. Malacology. Arachnology. Herpetology.
M.-Sa. 9-4.30; Su. 1-4.30. Closed New Year, July 4, Thanksgiving, Christmas.

PEABODY MUSEUM OF ARCHAEOLOGY AND ETHNOLOGY
11 Divinity Avenue, Cambridge, Massachusetts 02138
Ethnology. Human osteology. Ethnology.
M.-Sa. 9-4.30; Su. 1-4.30. Closed New Year, July 4, Thanksgiving, Christmas.

FRANCIS RUSSELL HART NAUTICAL MUSEUM
Massachusetts Institute of Technology, 77 Massachusetts Avenue, Cambridge, Massachusetts 02139
Ship models and half-models. Whaling and marine prints.
By appointment.

SEMITIC MUSEUM
Divinity Avenue, Cambridge, Massachusetts 02138
Archaeological material from the Near East, chiefly Palestine, Syria, Mesopotamia, Egypt.
By appointment.

GUERNSEY COUNTY MUSEUM
218 N. 8th Street, Cambridge, Ohio 43727
Geology. Local history. Costumes.
Sa., Su., public holidays 2-5.

CAMDEN

CHIDESTER HOUSE
926 Washington, Camden, Arkansas 71701
House (1848) and period furniture.
M.-F., 9-5.

CONWAY HOUSE
Conway Road, Camden, Maine 04843
Restored farmhouse and barn (c.1768). Period furnishings.
June 15 - Labour Day, Tu.-Su. 11-5.

MUSEUM OF CAMDEN-ROCKPORT HISTORICAL SOCIETY
Camden, Maine 04843
Local history. Folklore. Costumes. Paintings. Photographs. 8 historic buildings, including Old Conway House (late 18th century), are in the care of the Society.
July 1 - Labour Day, Tu.-Su., public holidays 1-5.

CAMDEN DISTRICT HERITAGE FOUNDATION
P.O. Box 710, Camden, New Jersey 29020
In Cornwallis House (1777). 18th century local history. Weapons. Indian artifacts.
Craven House (1786), Bradley Log House (1800) and Drakeford Log House (1812) are in the care of the Foundation.
Oct.-Apr., M.-F. 10-4; Sa. 10-5; Su., public holidays 1-5. May-Sept., M.-Sa. 10-7; Su., public holidays 1-7.

CAMPBELL MUSEUM
Campbell Place, Camden, New Jersey 01801
Soup bowls and tureens, 500 B.C. onwards.
M.-F. 9-5. Closed public holidays.

MUSEUM OF CAMDEN COUNTY HISTORICAL SOCIETY
Park Boulevard and Euclid Avenue, Camden, New Jersey 08103
In Pomona Hall (1726). Local history. Agriculture. Glass. Costumes. Maps.
Tu.-F. 9.30-4.30; Su. 12.30-4.30. Closed public holidays, Dec. 16-31.

WALT WHITMAN HOUSE
330 Mickle Street, Camden, New Jersey 08103
House lived in by Whitman, 1884-92. Furnishings, books and other mementoes of Whitman.
M.-Sa. 10-12, 1-5; Su. 2-5. Closed Thanksgiving, Christmas, New Year.

CAMDENTON

KELSEY'S ANTIQUE AUTOMOBILES
U.S. Highway 54, Camdenton, Missouri 65020
Old cars, all in working condition. Mechanical music makers and instrument players.
Daily 8-8.

CAMERON

BARRON COUNTY HISTORICAL SOCIETY MUSEUM
Highway 8, Cameron, Wisconsin 54822
Agriculture. Logging. Household equipment. Indian artifacts.
June 1 - Labour Day, Sa., Su. 1-5.

CAMP VERDE

FORT VERDE STATE HISTORIC PARK
P.O. Box 397, Camp Verde, Arizona 86322
Fort (1871). Museum recalling conflict between U.S. Army and Apache Indians in the 1870s. Military and pioneer history. Indian artifacts.
Daily 8-5.30. Closed p.m. Thanksgiving, and Christmas.

MONTEZUMA CASTLE NATIONAL MONUMENT
Box 219, Camp Verde, Arizona 86322
Natural history. Herpetology. Archaeology. Indian history and artifacts.
Daily 8-5.

CANAAN

CANAAN HISTORICAL SOCIETY
Warner's Crossing Road, Canaan, New York 12029
In former Meeting House (1829). Local history. Furniture.
July 1 - Aug. 31, Sa. 2-5.

CANADIAN

HEMPHILL COUNTY PIONEER MUSEUM
Old Moody Hotel, 122 Main Street, Canadian, Texas 79014
Building (1904). Pioneer history. Bank. Dentist's surgery. Barber's shop. Country store.
M.-Sa. 9-5; Su. 1-5.

CANAJOHARIE

CANAJOHARIE ART GALLERY
Library, Canajoharie, New York 13317
Paintings by American artists.
M.-F. 10-5.15; F. also 7-9 p.m.; Sa. 10-2.

CANANDAIGUA

BRISTOL HISTORICAL SOCIETY MUSEUM
R.D.3, Canandaigua, New York 14424
Local history.
By appointment.

GRANGER HOMESTEAD AND CARRIAGE MUSEUM
Main and Granger Streets, Canandaigua, New York 14424
House (1814), was home of Gideon Granger, postmaster in Jefferson and Madison cabinets. Original furniture, with additional period furnishings. Collection of horse-drawn vehicles.
Tu.-Su. 10-5. Carriage Museum, July 1 - Aug. 31 only, Tu.-Su. 10-5.

ONTARIO COUNTY HISTORICAL MUSEUM
55 N. Main Street, Canandaigua, New York 14424
Local history. 6 Nations copy of Pickering Treaty (1794), allowing pioneers to settle in Western New York. Period rooms. Indian relics.
Tu.-Sa. 1-5. Closed public holidays.

CANASTOTA

CANAL TOWN MUSEUM
Canal Street, Canastota, New York 13032
History of Erie Canal.
May 1 - Oct. 31, daily 9-5.

CANON CITY

CANON CITY MUNICIPAL MUSEUM
612 River Street, Canon City, Colorado 81212
Mineralogy. Fossils. Natural history, including habitat groups of dinosaurs and buffaloes. Colorado paintings.
May 1 - Sept. 30, daily 9-5; Oct. 1 - Apr. 30, daily 1-5. Closed New Year, Thanksgiving, Christmas.

CANTERBURY

PRUDENCE CRANDALL MEMORIAL MUSEUM
Canterbury Green, Canterbury, Connecticut 06331
Afro-American culture. Prudence Crandall homestead (c.1800) is in the care of the Museum.
By appointment.

CANTON

CANTON HISTORICAL SOCIETY MUSEUM
1400 Washington Street, Canton, Massachusetts 02021
Material relating to the Colonial period and Civil War. Guns. Indian relics. Maps. Documents.
By appointment.

HISTORY CENTER OF ST. LAWRENCE COUNTY
Courthouse, P.O. Box 43, Canton, New York 13617
Geology. Mineralogy. Local history. Indian artifacts. Folklore. Costumes. Glass. Transport.
M., Th. 9-4. Other times by appointment. Closed public holidays.

ST. LAWRENCE COUNTY HISTORICAL ASSOCIATION MUSEUM
Canton, New York 13617
Local history. Folklore. Tools. Costumes. Former Baptist Church, Richville (1855), is in the care of the Association.
July 1 - Aug. 31, by appointment.

CANTON ART INSTITUTE
1001 Market Avenue N., Canton, Ohio 44702
18th-19th century English and American portraits. 16th-20th century Italian, Spanish, American paintings. 20th century paintings by Ohio artists. Sculpture. Graphics. Decorative arts. Children's museum.
Tu.-Th. 9-5, 7-9. Closed Christmas, Thanksgiving, New Year.

STARK COUNTY HISTORICAL SOCIETY MUSEUM
749 Hazlett Avenue N.W., Canton, Ohio 44701
Local history. Indian relics. Glass. Transport. Astronomy. Children's museum.
M.-F. 10-5; Sa. 12-5; Su. 1.30-5. Closed New Year, Easter, Labour Day, Thanksgiving, Christmas.

EARL BOYCE MUSEUM
221 E. 4th Street, Canton, South Dakota 57013
Exhibits illustrating life in Canton and Lincoln County during late 1800s and early 1900s.
By appointment, M.-F. 3-9; Sa. 10-5.

CANYON

PANHANDLE-PLAINS HISTORICAL MUSEUM
2401 4th Avenue, Canyon, Texas 79015
Geology. Palaeontology. Natural history. Anthropology. Local history. Cattle industry. Paintings by Texan and South-Western artists. Prints.
M.-Sa. 9-5; Su. 2-6. Closed Dec. 24-5.

CANYON CITY

HERMAN AND ELIZA OLIVER MUSEUM
101 S. Canyon City Boulevard, Canyon City, Oregon 97820
Natural history. History of 1862 gold rush. Indian artifacts. Joaquin Miller House (c.1864) and Greenhorn Jail (1910) are in the care of the Museum.
Apr. 1 - Oct. 31: Tu.-Sa. 9-5; Su. 1-5.

CAPARRA

MUSEUM OF CONQUEST AND COLONISATION OF PUERTO RICO
Route 2, Caparra, Puerto Rico 00922
Near Guaynabo intersection, on site of Ponce de Léon's Settlement of 1508. Artifacts and historical display of the period.
Daily 9-12, 1-5.

CAPE GIRARDEAU

CAPE GIRARDEAU HISTORICAL SOCIETY MUSEUM
1124 William Street, Cape Girardeau, Missouri 63701
Local history. Agriculture. Medicine. Stamps. Children's museum.
Sa., Su. 1-5.

CAPE MAY

CAPE MAY COUNTY HISTORICAL MUSEUM
Court House, Main Street, Cape May, New Jersey 08210
Rooms of Colonial period. Furniture. South Jersey glass. China. Needlework. Indian artifacts. Military history.
M.-Sa. 9-12, 1-4. Closed public holidays.

VICTORIAN VILLAGE MUSEUM
653 Washington Street, Cape May, New Jersey 08204
Hughes Estate (1870). Period furnishings.
May 15 - Sept. 30, M.-Sa. 10-12, 1-4; Su. by appointment.

CAPE VINCENT

CAPE VINCENT HISTORICAL ROOMS
Community House, Market Street, Cape Vincent, New York 13618
Local history. Costumes.
W. 10-4, 7-9. Other times by appointment.

CAPULIN

CAPULIN MOUNTING NATIONAL MONUMENT
Capulin, New Mexico 88414
Museum exhibits cover geology, botany, entomology of the area.
May 1 - Sept. 30, daily 7-dusk. Oct. 1 - Apr. 30, M.-F. 8-4.30.

CARBONDALE

UNIVERSITY GALLERIES
Southern Illinois University, Carbondale, Illinois 62901
Paintings, sculptures, graphics, by contemporary American artists.
M.-F. 10-4.30. Closed Sept., university vacations, public holidays.

UNIVERSITY MUSEUM
Southern Illinois University, Carbondale, Illinois 62901
Geology. Mineralogy. Archaeology, especially of Mexico and Mid-West. Anthropology. Regional history. Ethnology and folklore. Indian culture. Music.
M.-F. 9-12, 1-4. Closed public holidays.

CARIBOU

NYLANDER MUSEUM
Caribou, Maine 04736
Geology and mineralogy of Maine. Marine life. Herbarium. Indian artifacts.
Apr. 1 - Nov. 30: M.-F. 1-5. Oct. 1 - Mar. 31: M.-F. 1-4. Closed public holidays.

CARLISLE

CUMBERLAND COUNTY HISTORICAL SOCIETY MUSEUM
21 N. Pitt Street, Carlisle, Pennsylvania 17013
History of Cumberland County. Indian artifacts.
M.-Tu. 7-9; W.-F. 2-5. Closed public holidays.

HESSIAN GUARDHOUSE MUSEUM
Carlisle Barracks, Carlisle, Pennsylvania 17013
In Guardhouse (1777), built by prisoners-of-war from Hesse. Military history.
May 1 - Sept. 30, Sa.-Su. 1-4.30. Other times by appointment.

CARLSBAD

CARLSBAD CAVERNS NATIONAL PARK
P.O. Box 1598, Carlsbad, New Mexico 88220
Geology. Palaeontology. History of Carlsbad Caverns. Botany. Herpetology. Entomology. Archaeology.
May 1 - Sept. 30, daily 6 a.m.-9 p.m. Oct. 1 - Apr. 30, daily 7.30-5.

CARLSBAD MUNICIPAL MUSEUM
Halagueno Park, 101 S. Halagueno Street, Carlsbad, New Mexico 88220
Mineralogy. Ethnology. Archaeology. Indian artifacts.
M.-Sa. 1-7.30. Closed Memorial Day, July 4, Thanksgiving, Christmas.

CARLTON

MUSEUM OF CARLTON COUNTY HISTORICAL SOCIETY
315 Court House, Carlton, Minnesota 55718
Local history. Agriculture. Indian material.
M.-F. 12-4.

CARLYLE

FUNSTON MEMORIAL HOME
Carlyle, Kansas 66718
Boyhood home of General Fred Funston, a military figure in the Spanish-American war. Memorabilia of General Funston.
M.-Sa. 10-5; Su. 1.30-5.

CARMEL

CARMEL MISSION
3080 Rio Road, Carmel, California 93921
Indian artifacts. Textiles.
M.-Sa., 9.30-5; Su., public holidays, 10.30-5. Closed Christmas, Thanksgiving.

CARMI

WHITE COUNTY HISTORICAL SOCIETY MUSEUM
216 E. Main Street, Carmi, Illinois 62821
Local history. Letters written by Illinois pioneers. Robinson-Stewart house (1814) and Ratcliff Inn (1828) are in the care of the Society.
M.-F., Su. 1-4; Sa. 10-12, 1-4. Closed public holidays.

CARPENTERSVILLE

MUSEUM OF DUNDEE TOWNSHIP HISTORICAL SOCIETY
21 Washington Street, Carpentersville, Illinois 60110
Local history.
F. 9.30-2; Sa. 2-4. Closed public holidays.

CAROLINA BEACH

BLOCKDALE RUNNER MUSEUM
Carolina Beach, North Carolina 28428
Local and maritime history. Confederate naval history.
May 1 - Sept. 30, daily 9-6. Oct. 1 - Apr. 30, daily 10-5. Closed Dec. 24-6.

CARPENTER

HOMESTEAD MUSEUM
Carpenter, Wyoming 82054
Local history and archaeology. Agricultural tools and implements.
By appointment.

CARROLLTON

GREENE COUNTY HISTORICAL SOCIETY MUSEUM
Sixth Street, Carrollton, Illinois 62016
Local history.
M.-F. 9-5.

GENERAL BUTLER STATE PARK MUSEUM
Carrollton, Kentucky 41008
History and wildlife of Ohio River. Butler Mansion, with period furnishings.
May-Oct. daily 9-5.

CARROLL COUNTY HISTORICAL MUSEUM
Highway 65 N, Carrollton, Missouri 64633
History of Carroll County.
Daily 2-5.

CARROLL COUNTY HISTORICAL SOCIETY MUSEUM
Public Square, Carrollton, Ohio 44615
Local and military history. Medical instruments.
May 30 - Sept. 15: W.-Su., public holidays 10-5.

MCCOOK HOUSE STATE MEMORIAL
Public Square, Carrollton, Ohio 44615
Home (1837) of Major Danial McCook, Civil War officer. Civil War history.
June 1 - Sept. 30: W.-Su. 10-5.

CARROLTON

OLD JAIL MUSEUM
Carrolton, Mississippi 38917
In former jail (1836). Local history. Indian artifacts. Folklore. Agriculture. Costumes. Archaeology.
By appointment.

CARSON CITY

BOWERS MANSION
U.S. Highway 395, Carson City, Nevada 89701
House (1865), with European and American Victorian furnishings. Billiard table with cast-iron crouching lion legs.
May 15 - Oct. 31, daily 11-4.30.

NEVADA STATE MUSEUM
N. Carson Street, Carson City, Nevada 89701
In former U.S. Mint (1869). Nevada history. Mineralogy. Palaeontology. Natural history. Entomology. Ethnology. Indian artifacts. Coins. Costumes.
Daily 8.30-4.30. Closed New Year, Memorial Day, Thanksgiving, Christmas.

CARTERSVILLE

ETOWAH MOUNDS ARCHAEOLOGICAL AREA
Route 1, Cartersville, Georgia 30120
Site Museum. Archaeology of prehistoric Indian centre, of political and religious life in Etowah Valley.
May 1 - Oct. 31, 9-5.30. Nov. 1 - Apr. 30, 9-5. Closed Thanksgiving, Christmas, New Year.

CARTHAGE

CARTHAGE MUSEUM
Courthouse, Garthage, Missouri 64836
Geology. Archaeology. Civil War material.
Daily 8-5. Closed public holidays.

HOUSE IN THE HORSESHOE
State Highway 1644, Carthage, North Carolina 28327
House (1770), later occupied by Governor Benjamin Williams (d.1814). Period furnishings.
Tu.-Sa. 9-5; Su. 1-5.

CASA GRANDE

CASA GRANDE VALLEY HISTORICAL SOCIETY MUSEUM
404 North Marshall Street, Casa Grande, Arizona 85222
Local history.
W., F., Su. 2-5.

CASHMERE

WILLIS CAREY HISTORICAL MUSEUM
E. Sunset Highway, Cashmere, Washington 98815
History of Central Washington. Indian artifacts. Pioneer village of 19th century buildings moved to site, all with period furnishings.
May 1 - Oct. 31: M.-Sa. 10-5; Su. 1-5.

CASPER

FORT CASPAR HISTORIC SITE AND MUSEUM
14 Fort Caspar Road, Casper, Wyoming 82601
In reconstructed 1863 old Fort Caspar. Military history. Relics of early forts on Fort Caspar Site. History of Oregon and Mormon Trails.
May 15 - June 1, Sept. 1-15: Tu.-Su. 9-5. June 1 - Aug. 31, daily 9-9.

NATRONA COUNTY PIONEER MUSEUM
Casper, Wyoming 82601
In former St. Mark's Episcopal Church (1891). Local history. Indian artifacts.
May 1 - Labour Day: M., W.-Su. 9.30-5.

CASPIAN

IRON COUNTY MUSEUM
Highway 424, Caspian, Michigan 49915
In former Engine House of old Caspian Mine (1903-37). Exhibits showing history of lumbering and mining industries. Models. Replicas of underground mining stope. Pioneer life.
June 1 - Sept. 30, daily 9-5; Su. 1-5.

CASS

CIVIL WAR MUSEUM
Cass, West Virginia 24927
Situated near Cass railroad station. Steam-powered Shay locomotive, which runs through Monongahela National Forest.
Daily, 9-6 (May 30 - Oct. 31).

CASSOPOLIS

PIONEER LOG CABIN
406 S. Broadway, Cassopolis, Michigan 49031
Pioneer history.
June 1 - Aug. 31: W.-Su. 10-4.

CASSVILLE

BARRY COUNTY HISTORICAL SOCIETY MUSEUM
516 Central Avenue, Cassville, Missouri 65625
Local history.
Daily 8-4.30.

STONEFIELD
Nelson Dewey State Park, Cassville, Wisconsin 53806
Wisconsin village (c.1890), with period furnishings. Craftsmen's workshops. In Nelson Dewey Homestead (1865), with outbuildings.
May 1 - Nov. 30, daily 9-5.

CASTILE

CASTILE HISTORICAL SOCIETY MUSEUM
17 E. Park Road, Castile, New York 14427
Regional history. Seneca Indian relics. Farm implements.
M.-Sa. 2-5. Su. by appointment.

LETCHWORTH STATE PARK MUSEUM
Letchworth State Park, Castile, New York 14427
Local history. Ethnology. Indian material. Council House (c.1760) and Nancy Jemison's cabin (1800) are in the care of the museum.
May 15 - Nov 1: Tu.-Su. 10-5.

CASTINE

FORT GEORGE STATE MEMORIAL
Castine, Maine 04421
Preserved and interpreted ruins of British fort (1779).
May 15 - Sept. 15, daily 8 a.m.-9 p.m.

WILSON MUSEUM
Perkins Street, Castine, Maine 04421
Geology. Local history. Tools. Indian material from North and Central America. Anthropology. European Stone, Bronze and Iron Age material. John Perkins House (1770) is in the care of the Museum.
May 27 - Sept. 15: Tu.-Su. 2-5.

CASTLETON

CASTLETON HISTORICAL SOCIETY MUSEUM
Main Street, Castleton, Vermont 05735
Local history. Paintings. Documents.
By appointment.

CASTROVILLE

LANDMARK INN
Florence and Florella Streets, Castroville, Texas 78009
In Mond-Vance House (1848-54). Period furnishings. Costumes. Paintings. Mill (1854).
M.-Sa. 9.30-11.30, 1-5. Su. by appointment. Closed public holidays.

CATALINA ISLAND

CATALINA MUSEUM SOCIETY
Casino Building, Avalon, Catalina Island, California 90704
Local history and archaeology.
June 15 - Sept. 15, daily 2-4, 8-10; Sept. 16 - June 14, Sa., Su., 2-4.

CATHARAUGUS

CATHARAUGUS AREA HISTORICAL CENTER
23 Main Street, Catharaugus, New York 14719
Indian artifacts. Agriculture. Industry. Costume. Military relics.
Otto Congregational Church (1862) is in the care of the Center.
May 1 - Sept. 30, Sa. 3-5.

CATHEDRAL CITY

MUSEUM OF ANTIQUITIES AND ART
Plumby Place, Hotel Arner Grounds, Cathedral City, California 92234
Mineralogy. Palaeontology. Pre-Colombian artifacts. Middle East and Far East collections.
Daily 2.30-5, 7.30-9.

CATHLAMET

MUSEUM OF WAHKIAKUM COUNTY HISTORICAL SOCIETY
City Center, Cathlamet, Washington 98612
History of Pacific North West. Indian artifacts. Pioneer life, especially on lower Columbia River. Logging industry.
June 1 - Aug. 31: M., W.-Su. 11-4. Sept. 1 - May 31: Th.-Sa. 11-4. Closed New Year, Christmas.

CATTARAUGUS

CATTARAUGUS AREA HISTORICAL CENTER
23 Main Street, Cattaraugus, New York 14719
Local history. Agriculture. Industry. Costumes.
May-Sept., Sa. 3-5.

CAZENOVIA

LORENZO
Ledyard Avenue, Cazenovia, New York 13035
In 1807-1809 mansion, with theatre and smokehouse. 19th-20th century American furnishings, decorative arts.
By appointment.

CEDARBURG

OZAUKEE COUNTY HISTORICAL SOCIETY MUSEUM
543 Mequon Street, Cedarburg, Wisconsin 53012
Open-air museum, with 11 buildings (1848-90). Agricultural equipment. Folklore.
1st Su. in June - 2nd Su. in Oct., W.-Su. 12-5.30.

CEDAR CITY

CEDAR BREAKS NATIONAL MONUMENT, VISITOR CENTER
P.O. Box 749, Cedar City, Utah 84720
Geology. Flora of area. Mounted animal specimens.
May 25 - Sept. 15, daily 8-6.

MUSEUM OF NATURAL HISTORY
College of Southern Utah, Cedar City, Utah 84721
Geology. Botany. Zoology. Biology. Anthropology. Archaeology.
May-Sept., daily 9-5.

PIUTE INDIAN MUSEUM
75 N. Street, Cedar City, Utah 84720
Indian history, artifacts.
May-Sept., daily 9-5.

CEDAR FALLS

CEDAR FALLS HISTORICAL SOCIETY
303 Clay Street, Cedar Falls, Iowa 50613
Museum building (1862). Local history. Costumes.
W.-Sa. 2-4; Su., holidays, 2-5. Closed New Year, Thanksgiving, Christmas.

UNIVERSITY OF NORTHERN IOWA MUSEUM
31st Street and Hudson Road, Cedar Falls, Iowa 50613
Geology. Mineralogy. Palaeontology. Anthropology. Zoology. Local history. Indian artifacts.
M.-F. 1-4.30. Summer session 9-12. 1st and 3rd Sundays in month 2-4.30. Closed University vacations.

CEDAR KEY

ST. CLAIR WHITMAN MUSEUM
Florida Highway 24, Cedar Key, Florida 32625
History of Cedar Key area. Lumber Industries. Shells. Natural history.
Daily 9-5.

CEDAR RAPIDS

CEDAR RAPIDS ART CENTER
324 3rd Street S.E., Cedar Rapids, Iowa 52401
20th century paintings, especially by regional artists. Prints. Photographs. Decorative arts.
Tu.-W., F.-Sa., 10-5; Th. 10-8.30; Su. 2-5. Closed public holidays.

COE COLLEGE ART GALLERIES
Coe College, Cedar Rapids, Iowa 52402
19th-20th century paintings, prints, drawings by American artists.
M.-F. 7-9; Sa. 10-12; Su. 2-4.

COE COLLEGE, THOMAS W. SINCLAIR MEMORIAL ART GALLERY
Cedar Rapids, Iowa 52402
Chinese jades. Paintings. Sculpture.
M.-F. 3-4.30; Sa. 9-12; Su. 2-4.30.

CELINA

MERCER COUNTY HISTORICAL SOCIETY, INC.
126 S. Main Street, Celina, Ohio 45822
Local history. Indian relics. Agricultural implements.
Tu., F., Su. 1-5.

CENTER

SHELBY COUNTY MUSEUM
Shelbyville and Riggs Streets, Center, Texas 75935
Local history.
W. 1-4; Su. 2-5.

CENTERPORT

VANDERBILT MUSEUM AND PLANETARIUM
Little Neck Road, Centerport, New York 11721
On estate of William K. Vanderbilt. Natural history. Habitat animal groups from Africa and India. Furniture. Paintings. Astronomy.
May 1 - Oct. 31: Tu.-Sa. 10-4; Su., public holidays 12-5.

CENTER SANDWICH

MUSEUM OF SANDWICH HISTORICAL SOCIETY
Maple Street, Center Sandwich, New Hampshire 03227
House (c.1850). Furniture. Domestic equipment. Replica of country store. Crafts.
M.-Sa. 2-5. Closed Labour Day - July 1.

CENTERVILLE

CAPE COD MUSEUM OF HISTORY AND ART
South Main Street, Centerville, Massachusetts 02632
Local history. Paintings by Cape Cod artists. Decorative arts.
Tu.-Su. 10-4.30.

CENTRAL CITY

CENTRAL CITY OPERA HOUSE ASSOCIATION THEATER MUSEUM
Chain O'Mines Hotel, Central City, Colorado 80427
Models of sets. Stage and costume designs. Costumes.
June 15 - Labour Day, 2-8.

CENTRAL GOLD MINE AND MUSEUM
126 Spring Street, Central City, Colorado 80427
In Mason M. Seavy Block (1868). History of gold mining. Mine machinery and equipment. Old City Jail (1860), Henry E. Newcomb Block (1863), Hawley Warehouse (1875), and Miller Block (1881) are in the care of the Museum.
May 1 - Sept. 30, daily 9-5. Other times by appointment.

TELLER HOUSE
Central City, Colorado 80427
House (1872), Housed miners during the Gold Rush. Period furnishings.
May 25 - Labour Day, daily 10-6.

MERRICK COUNTY HISTORICAL MUSEUM
822 C. Avenue, Central City, Nebraska 68826
Local history, archaeology, folklore. Anthropology. Indian material. Costumes.
Su. 2-5. Other times by appointment.

CENTRAL MINE

YESTERYEAR HOUSE
Central Mine, Michigan 49113
House (1860), belonging to mine. Period Furnishings. Family and local history.
July 1 - Labour Day, M.-Sa. 10-5.

CENTREVILLE

MUSEUM OF QUEEN ANNE'S COUNTY HISTORICAL SOCIETY
Box 296, S. Commerce Street, Centreville, Maryland 21617
In 18th century plantation house. 18th century American furniture. Wright's Chance (1744) and Tucker House (c.1795) are in the care of the Society.
May 1 - Oct. 31: F. 11-4. Other times by appointment.

CHADDS FORD

BRANDYWINE BATTLEFIELD PARK
U.S. Route 1, Chadds Ford, Pennsylvania 19317
Site of Revolutionary War battle with Washington's and Lafayette's headquarters. Museum of local and military history, costumes and agricultural tools and implements.
Memorial Day - Labour Day, daily 10-5. Rest of year, Sa., Su. 10-5.

CHADRON

CHADRON STATE COLLEGE MUSEUM
Main Street, Chadron, Nebraska 69337
Geology. Mineralogy. Palaeontology. Natural history. Anthropology.
M.-F. 8-5. Closed college vacations.

MUSEUM OF THE FUR TRADE
Route 2, Box 18, Chadron, Nebraska 69337
History of N. American fur trade, 17th-19th centuries. Trade goods. Trapper's equipment. American Indian material. Botanical exhibit of Plains Indian food crops. Restored James Bordeaux trading post (1846-72).
June 1 - Sept. 1, daily 8-6. Other times by appointment.

CHAMBERSBURG

OLD BROWN'S MILL SCHOOL
R.D.6, Chambersburg, Pennsylvania 17201
Schoolhouse (c.1830). Early school furnishings and equipment.
Tu.-Su. by appointment. Closed New Year, Good Friday, Easter, Thanksgiving, Christmas.

CHAMPAIGN

KRANNERT ART MUSEUM
500 Peabody Drive, University of Illinois, Champaign, Illinois 61820
European paintings, 15th-17th century. 20th century European and American paintings, sculpture, prints, drawings. Malayan textiles and artifacts. Early American furniture. Pre-Columbian art.
M.-Sa. 9-5; Su. 2-5. Closed public holidays.

CHAMPION

CHASE COUNTY HISTORICAL SOCIETY MUSEUM
Champion, Nebraska 69023
Local history. Indian artifacts. Barbed wire.
May 10 - Sept. 13, su. 1.30-5.

CHANDLER

CHANDLER HISTORICAL SOCIETY MUSEUM
West Chicago Street, P.O. Box 926, Chandler, Arizona 85224
Local history. Indian artifacts.
By appointment.

LINCOLN COUNTY HISTORICAL MUSEUM
717 Manuel Avenue, Chandler, Oklahoma 74834
Early American furniture. Clothing. China. Spanish-American War clothing, guns. Indian artifacts. Drug-store fixtures. Doctor's instruments.
Tu.-Sa. 1.30-4.30. Closed public holidays.

CHANUTE

MARTIN AND OSA JOHNSON SAFARI MUSEUM
16 S. Grant Street, Chanute, Kansas 66720
Hunting trophies, photographs and other material brought back by the Johnsons from their expeditions to Africa and the Pacific Islands.
M.-Sa. 10-5.30; Su. 12-5.30. Public holidays 12-5.30. Closed Christmas.

CHAPEL HILL

WILLIAM HAYES ACKLAND MEMORIAL ART CENTER
S. Columbia Street, Chapel Hill, North Carolina 27514
European and American art. 15th-20th century prints. 16th-20th century paintings, sculpture, drawings. Archaeology. Decorative arts.
Tu.-Sa. 10-5; Su. 2-6. Closed public holidays, 3rd week of August.

MOREHEAD PLANETARIUM
E. Franklin Street, Chapel Hill, North Carolina 27514
Astronomy. Planetarium. Orrery. Sundial. Art collection.
M.-F. 2-5, 7.30-10; Sa. 10-5, 7.30-10; Su. 1-5, 7.30-10. Closed Dec. 24-5.

MUSEUM OF RESEARCH LABORATORIES OF ANTHROPOLOGY
Person Hall, University of Carolina, Chapel Hill, North Carolina 27514
Fossils. Archaeology. Bones. Pottery. Anthropology. Ethnology.
M.-F. 9-5. Closed public holidays.

CHAPPAQUA

CHAPPAQUA HISTORICAL SOCIETY MUSEUM
101 King Street, Chappaqua, New York 10514
Local history. Horace Greeley material. Quaker history.
Sept. 1 - May 31, W. 1.30-4.

CHAPPELL HILL

CHAPPELL HILL HISTORICAL SOCIETY MUSEUM
Old Schoolhouse, Cedar Street, Chappell Hill, Texas 77426
Local history. Furniture. Farm implements. Blacksmiths shop.
W., Su. 1.30-5. Other times by appointment.

CHARLES CITY

IOWA COUNTY HISTORICAL SOCIETY AND MUSEUM
400 Ferguson Street, Charles City, Iowa 50616
Geology. Archaeology. Local history. Agriculture. Industry. Transport.
Mutchlar cabin (1850) and pioneer legal drugstore building are in the care of the Society.
May 1 - Sept. 3: Th.-Su., public holidays, 1.30-4. Other times by appointment.

BERKELEY PLANTATION
Harrison's Landing, Route 2, Charles City, Virginia 23030
House (1726), family home of Presidents William Henry Harrison and Benjamin Harrison. 18th - early 19th century furniture. Civil War relics. Indian material.
Daily 8.30-5.

SHERWOOD FOREST
Route 5, Charles City, Virginia 23030
House (1740, enlarged 1840), home of President John Tyler. Period furniture.
M.-Sa. 9-5.

SHIRLEY PLANTATION
Route 2, Charles City, Virginia 23030
House (1723), home of General Lee's mother, Anne Hill Carter. Hill Carter family furnishings, portraits, silver.
Daily 9-5. Closed Christmas.

CHARLESTON

MISSISSIPPI COUNTY HISTORICAL SOCIETY MUSEUM
200 E. Commercial Street, Charleston, Missouri 63834
Local history. Archaeology. Costumes.
Daily 1-5. Closed Christmas.

CITADEL MUSEUM
The Citadel, Charleston, South Carolina 29409
Military history. Uniforms. Weapons. Documents. Photographs. Medals.
M.-F., Su. 2-5; Sa. 9-5. Closed Christmas, New Year.

CHARLESTON MUSEUM
Rutledge Avenue and Calhoun Street, Charleston, South Carolina 29400
Oldest museum in U.S.A. (1773). History of Charleston. Period furnishings. Anthropology. Natural history. Herbarium.
M.-Sa. 10-5; Su., public holidays 2-5.

CONFEDERATE MUSEUM
188 Meeting Street, Charleston, South Carolina 29401
In former Market Hall (1841). Civil War mementoes.
Mar. 15 - Oct. 15, Tu.-F. 12-3.

THOMAS ELFE WORKSHOP
54 Queen Street, Charleston, South Carolina 29400
House (c.1760), home and workshop of the cabinet-maker, Thomas Elfe. 18th century Charleston furniture.
Tu.-F. 10-5. May-Sept., Sa. 10-5.

FORT SUMTER
Charleston, South Carolina 29400
Fort where first shot of Civil War was fired (1861). Museum illustrates history of Civil War.
Guided tours only. Daily, Jan. 2 - Mar. 14, 2.30. Mar. 15 - June 14, 9.30-2.30. June 15 - Labour Day, 9.30-4. Day following Labour Day - Oct. 15, 9.30-2.30. Oct. 16 - Dec. 24, 2.30 only. Dec. 24 - Jan. 1, 9.30-2.30.

GIBBS ART GALLERY
135 Meeting Street, Charleston, South Carolina 29401
Works by American, especially South Carolina artists. Paintings. Sculpture. Prints. Miniatures. Decorative arts.
M.-Sa. 10-5; Su. 3-6.

HEYWARD-WASHINGTON HOUSE
97 Church Street, Charleston, South Carolina 29401
House (c.1770). Charleston furniture.
Jan.-June, M.-Sa. 10-5. July-Dec. M.-Sa. 10-2. Closed national holidays.

HISTORIC CHARLESTON FOUNDATION
51 Meeting Street, Charleston, South Carolina 29401
In Nathaniel Russell House (c.1809). Period furnishings. Local history.
M.-Sa. 10-1, 2-5; Su., holidays 2-5. Closed Christmas.

HUNLEY MUSEUM
50 Broad Street, Charleston, South Carolina 29400
In bank building (1758). Replica of Confederate submarine 'Hunley', sunk 1864.
M.-Sa. 9-5.

THE MANIGAULT HOUSE
350 Meeting Street, Charleston, South Carolina 29403
House (c.1803). Period furnishings.
Tu.-Su. 10-5. Closed national holidays.

OLD SLAVE MART MUSEUM
6 Chalmers Street, Charleston, South Carolina 29401
Cultural history of American negro. Handicrafts. Paintings.
Tu.-Sa. 10-5; Su., M. 2-5. Closed Jan. 1-31, Christmas, Thanksgiving.

POWDER MAGAZINE
79 Cumberland Street, Charleston, South Carolina 29401
Military history.
Oct.-Aug., M.-F. 9.30-4.

THE PROVOST DUNGEON
Exchange Building, East End of Broad Street, Charleston, South Carolina 29400
Underground prison (1780). 17th-18th century artifacts discovered during excavation of sea-wall. Story of Stede Bonnet and his pirates.
Daily 10-5.

CHARLESTON ART GALLERY OF SUNRISE
755 Myrtle Road, Charleston, West Virginia 25314
Works by contemporary American artists. Paintings. Drawings. Sculpture. Ceramics.
Tu.-Sa. 10-5; Su. 2-5. Closed public holidays.

CHILDREN'S MUSEUM AND PLANETARIUM OF SUNRISE
746 Myrtle Road, Charleston, West Virginia 25314
Geology. Natural history. Science. Planetarium. American and local history.
Tu.-Sa. 10-5; Su. 2-5. Closed public holidays, Sept. 1-6.

MUSEUM OF FORT SCAMMON HISTORICAL ASSOCIATION
411 Ohio Avenue, Charleston, West Virginia 25302
Civil War history and relics.
Daily, by appointment.

MUSEUM OF WEST VIRGINIA DEPARTMENT OF ARCHIVES AND HISTORY
400 E. State Capitol, Charleston, West Virginia 23505
History of West Virginia. Geology. Archaeology. Palaeontology. Firearms and tools of early settlers. Pioneer kitchen. Daniel Boone collection. Civil War flags. Animals and birds of W. Virginia. Development of natural resources and industry.
M.-Sa. 9-5; Su. 1-5. Closed New Year, Christmas.

CHARLES TOWN

BUNKER HILL MONUMENT
Monument Square, Charles Town, Massachusetts 02633
Local history.
Daily 9-3.30. Closed Thanksgiving, Christmas.

JEFFERSON COUNTY HISTORICAL SOCIETY MUSEUM
Box 485, Charles Town, West Virginia 25414
Local history.
Apr. 1 - Oct. 31: M.-Sa. 10-4; Su. 1-4. Closed public holidays.

CHARLESTOWN

OLD FORT NUMBER 4 ASSOCIATES MUSEUM
Route 4, Charlestown, New Hampshire 03603
Local history. Furnishings, tools of the colonial period. Weapons. Indian artifacts. Reconstruction of 1745 fort buildings.
June 13 - Labour Day, daily 11-5. May 13 - June 12, Labour Day - Oct. 22, Sa.-Su. 11-5.

CHARLOTTE

EATON COUNTY HISTORICAL MUSEUM
404 South Sheldon Street, Charlotte, Michigan 48813
In Froebel School (1874). Geology. Local history. Glass.
By appointment.

CHARLOTTE NATURE MUSEUM
1658 Sterling Road, Charlotte, North Carolina 28200
Geology. Rock and mineral collections. Fossils. Biology. Ethnological collections from Africa and Alaska. Planetarium.
M.-Sa. 9-5; Su. 2-5. Closed Jan. 1, July 4, Labour Day, Thanksgiving, Christmas.

HEZEKIAH ALEXANDER HOME
3420 Shamrock Drive, Charlotte, North Carolina 28211
House (1774), with period furnishings.
By appointment.

MINT MUSEUM OF ART
501 Hempstead Place, Charlotte, North Carolina 28207
16th-20th century European, 18th-20th century American art. Paintings, prints. Decorative arts, especially ceramics. Coins.
M.-F. 10-5; Sa., Su. 2-5. Closed public holidays.

CHARLOTTE COUNTY

PATRICK HENRY MEMORIAL FOUNDATION
Charlotte County, Virginia 24528
In Henry's last house, Red Hill, with his personal possessions.
Apr.-Oct., daily 9-5. Nov.-Mar., daily 9-4. Closed Christmas.

CHARLOTTESVILLE

ASH LAWN
State Route 53, Charlottesville, Virginia 22903
House (1799), was home of President Monroe. Original and period furnishings. Memorabilia personal possessions of Monroe.
Daily 7-7.

MICHIE TAVERN MUSEUM
R.R.6, Charlottesville, Virginia 22901
Building (1735). English and American tavern furnishings.
Daily 8.30-5. Closed New Year, Christmas.

MONTICELLO
P.O. Box 316, Charlottesville, Virginia 22902
Plantation house (1768-1809), home of Thomas Jefferson. Original and period furnishings. Personal possessions and inventions. Outbuildings include kitchen, with utensils, laundry, smoke-house and weaving house. Memorabilia of Jefferson.
Mar. 1 - Oct. 31, daily 8-5. Nov. 1 - Feb. 28, daily 9-4.30.

CHATHAM

CHATHAM HISTORICAL SOCIETY MUSEUM
Chatham, Massachusetts 02633
Railway history. Models. Local history. Atwood House (1752) is in the care of the Society.
M., W., F. 2-5. Closed July 4, Labour Day, Sept. 20 - June 20.

CHATHAM RAILROAD MUSEUM
Depot Road, Chatham, Massachusetts 02633
Railway history. Models. Documents. Equipment. Chatham railway station (1887) is in the care of the Museum.
June 15 - Sept. 15, M.-F. 2-5.

CHATTANOOGA

CHATTANOOGA AUDUBON SOCIETY MUSEUM
N. Sanctuary Road, Chattanooga, Tennessee 37403
In cabin (1704), built by Cherokee Indians. Indian artifacts.
Daily, 6 a.m. onwards.

HOUSTON ANTIQUE MUSEUM
201 High Street, Chattanooga, Tennessee 37403
French, English and American glass. 18th-19th century American furniture. Pewter. Porcelain. Collection of pitchers.
M.-F. 10-4.30; Su. 2-4.30. Closed public holidays.

GEORGE THOMAS HUNTER GALLERY OF ART
10 Bluff View, Chattanooga, Tennessee 37403
Oriental and American paintings, drawings, woodcuts, prints, decorative arts. English paintings, decorative arts.
M.-Sa. 10-5; Su. 1-4. Closed public holidays.

HARRIS SWIFT MUSEUM OF RELIGIOUS AND CEREMONIAL ARTS
526 Vine Street, Chattanooga, Tennessee 37403
Paintings, sculpture, utensils, decorative arts of all religions.
M.-F. 9-5. Closed public holidays.

TENNESSEE VALLEY RAILROAD MUSEUM, INC.
Cumberland and Cleveland Avenues, Chattanooga, Tennessee 37401
Steam locomotives and railway equipment, 1900-1950.
By appointment.

UNIVERSITY GALLERY
University of Tennessee, Baldwin Street, Chattanooga, Tennessee 37401
20th Century American paintings, graphics.
M.-F. 9-4. Closed university vacations.

CHAZY

ALICE T. MINER COLONIAL COLLECTION
Box 334, Chazy, New York 12921
House (1824). 19th century furnishings. Indian artifacts. Glass. Decorative arts. Paintings. Music.
Tu.-Sa. 11-5.

CHEHALIS

LEWIS COUNTY HISTORICAL MUSEUM
1070 Washington Street, Chehalis, Washington 98532
County history. Anthropology. Indian artifacts. Costumes. Claquato Church (1853) is in the care of the Museum.
Th., Su. 1-4. Closed New Year, Thanksgiving, Christmas.

CHELMSFORD

CHELMSFORD HISTORICAL SOCIETY MUSEUM
40 Byam Road, Chelmsford, Massachusetts 01824
In Barrett-Byam Homestead (c.1660). Local history. Indian material.
M.-F. by appointment. Sun. 2-4.

OLD CHELMSFORD GARRISON HOUSE
Chelmsford, Massachusetts 01824
House (1690). Period furnishings. Local history. Indian material.
June-Oct. 15, Su. 2-5.

CHELSEA

GOVERNOR BELLINGHAM CARY HOUSE
34 Parker Street, Chelsea, Massachusetts 02150
House (1659), with period furnishings. Local history.
Apr. 1 - Nov. 30, Th. 2-5.

CHENEY

TILICUM WOMEN'S CLUB HISTORICAL MUSEUM
1104 2nd Street, Cheney, Washington 99004
Furniture. Pioneer history. Spinning wheels. Musical instruments.
By appointment.

CHEROKEE

SANFORD MUSEUM AND PLANETARIUM
17 E. Willow Street, Cherokee, Iowa 51012
Geology. Palaeontology. Zoology. Ethnology. Local history. Planetarium.
M.-F. 9-12, 1-5; Sa. 9-12; Su. 2-5. Closed public holidays.

MUSEUM OF THE CHEROKEE INDIAN
U.S.441, Cherokee, North Carolina 28719
Cherokee Indian artifacts.
Apr. 1 - June 30, Sept. 1 - Oct. 31, daily 9-5. July 1 - Aug. 31, 8-7.

OCONALUFTEE INDIAN VILLAGE
Great Smoky Mountains National Park, Cherokee, North Carolina 28719
Reproduction of Cherokee Indian Village. Exhibits showing Indian customs, crafts, daily life.
Labour Day - June 14, daily 8-4.30. June 15 - Labour day, daily 8-8. Closed Dec. 25.

CHERRYVALE

BENDER MUSEUM
120 S. Neosho Street, Cherryvale, Kansas 67335
Material relating to the Benders. Replica of Bender house.
May 1 - Sept. 30, M.-Sa. 10-5; Su. 1-5.

CHERRYVALE MUSEUM
215 E. 4th Street, Cherryvale, Kansas 67335
Local history. Costumes. Toys. Glass. Children's museum.
Daily 2-5. Closed Christmas.

CHERRY VALLEY

EDWARD DEAN MUSEUM OF DECORATIVE ARTS
Riverside County Art and Cultural Center, 9401 Oak Glen Road, Cherry Valley, California 92223
Paintings. Sculpture. Furniture.
Tu.-Su., 1-5. Closed public holidays and for 2 weeks following Labour Day.

CHERRY VALLEY MUSEUM
49 Main Street, Cherry Valley, New York 13320
House (1834). Local history. Farm and village life since c.1780.
May 30 - Oct. 1, daily 9-6.

CHESAPEAKE

CHESAPEAKE PLANETARIUM
300 Cedar Road, Chesapeake, Virginia 23320
Astronomy. Scale model of solar system. Space exploration.
M.-W., F. 10.30-4.30; Th. 10.30-4.30. Closed Christmas.

CHESTER

PIERRE MENARD HOUSE
N. of Chester, Illinois 62221
Restored house (1802) of Menard, first Lieutenant-Governor of Illinois. Period furniture and room settings.
Daily 9-5. Closed Thanksgiving, Christmas, New Year.

LIBERTY COUNTY MUSEUM
Chester, Montana 59522
Local history. Agriculture. Indian artifacts. Costumes. Open-air museum.
June 1 - Aug. 31, daily 2-5, 7-9.

CHESTER HISTORICAL SOCIETY MUSEUM
Gibson Hill Road, Chester, New York 10918
Local history.
By appointment.

DESHONG MEMORIAL ART GALLERY
11th and Edgemont Avenue, Chester, Pennsylvania 19013
Late 19th century European paintings, drawings, prints. Ivories.
By appointment.

KIRBY MEMORIAL CHAPEL
F.M.2097, Chester, Texas 75936
Chapel (1912) built by J. H. Kirby. Former Indian trading post. Memorabilia of Tyler County.
Mar. 1 - Oct. 31: F.-Su. 1-5.

CHESTERFIELD

CHESTERFIELD HISTORICAL SOCIETY MUSEUM
Main Road, Chesterfield, Massachusetts 01012
Local history. Agriculture.
May 1 - Sept. 30, Sa. 2-4.

CHESTERTOWN

MUSEUM OF HISTORICAL SOCIETY OF KENT COUNTY
101 Church Alley, Chestertown, Maryland 21620
In house of c.1750. Local history. Indian artifacts.
On special occasions and by appointment.

MUSEUM OF LOCAL HISTORY
Town Hall, Main Canada Drive, Chestertown, New York 12817
Agriculture. Indian artifacts. Archaeology. Costumes. Industry.
Apr. 1 - June 30, Sept. 1 - Nov. 30, Sa. 10-12, 1-3. July 1 - Aug. 31, M.-Sa. 10-12. Other times by appointment. Closed public holidays.

CHETOPA

CHETOPA HISTORICAL MUSEUM
5th and Maple Streets, Chetopa, Kansas 67336
Local history.
June 1 - Oct. 15, M.-Sa. 1-5.

CHEYENNE

BLACK KETTLE MUSEUM
Highway 283, Cheyenne, Oklahoma 73628
Indian arts and handicrafts, 1860-80. Pioneer life. Relics of U.S. Cavalry.
Tu.-Sa. 9-5; Su. 2-5. Closed Thanksgiving, Christmas.

FORT BRIDGER STATE MUSEUM
Cheyenne, Wyoming 82001
In 15 buildings (1842) of Fort Bridger. Pioneer history. Industry. Indian exhibits. Transport. Military history.
Apr.-May, daily 9-5. June 1 - Sept. 15, daily 8-8. Sept. 16 - Dec. 15, Sa., Su. 9-5. Closed Thanksgiving.

FORT FETTERMAN STATE MUSEUM
Cheyenne, Wyoming 82001
In former Officers' Quarters (1879). Military history.
May-Sept., M.-Sa. 9-5; Su. 12-6. Closed Thanksgiving.

MUSEUM OF WYOMING STATE ARCHIVES AND HISTORICAL DEPARTMENT
22nd Street, between Warren and Central Avenues, Cheyenne, Wyoming 82001
Maps, paintings, prints, drawings, archives documenting history of State.
M.-Sa. 9-5; May 1 - Sept. 30 also Su. 9-8. Closed Sa., Christmas, Easter, Thanksgiving.

WARREN MILITARY MUSEUM
Building 211, Frances E. Warren Air Force Base, Cheyenne, Wyoming 82001
In former Military Post Office (1900). Uniforms. Equipment. Aeroplane models. Missiles.
Su., public holidays 1-5. Other days by appointment.

WYOMING STATE ART GALLERY
22nd Street, between Warren and Central Avenues, Cheyenne, Wyoming 82001
Works by 19th-20th Century American artists. Paintings. Sculpture. Prints.
M.-Sa. 9-5, Memorial Day, Labour Day also Su. 12-5. Closed Christmas.

WYOMING STATE MUSEUM
State Office Building, 22nd and Warren Streets, Cheyenne, Wyoming 82001
History of Wyoming and the American West. Pioneer life. Indian material. Saddles. Branding irons. Mineralogy. Gemstones. Stage-coach relics.
May 1 - Sept. 30, M.-F. 9-5; Sa., Su. 9-8. Oct. 1 - Apr. 30, M.-Sa. 9-5. Closed Christmas, Thanksgiving.

CHICAGO

ADLER PLANETARIUM
1300 S. Lake Shore Drive, Chicago, Illinois 60605
Astronomy. Collections illustrating the development of astronomical, mathematical and navigation instruments.
June 1 - Aug. 31, M. 9.30-4.30; Tu.-Su. 9.30-9.30; Sa. 9.30-5. Sept. 1 - May 31, Tu. 9.30-9.30; M., W., Th. 9.30-4.30; F. 9.30-9.30. Sa., Su., public holidays, 9.30-5.

AMERICAN INSTITUTE OF RADIOLOGY
20 North Wacker Drive, Chicago, Illinois 60606
History and techniques of radiology.
M.-F. 9-4. Closed public holidays.

ART INSTITUTE OF CHICAGO
Michigan Avenue at Adams Street, Chicago, Illinois 60603
15th-20th century European paintings, especially French. 15th-20th century European prints, drawings. Chinese sculpture, painting, jade, lacquer, textiles, ceramics, bronzes, furniture. Japanese sculpture, painting, prints, illustrated books. Indian sculpture and miniatures. Turkish and Greek Island embroideries. English pottery, porcelain. English and American furniture, silver. French silver. African, Oceanic, Peruvian art.
M.-W., F., Sa., 10-5; Th. 10-8.30; Su., public holidays 1-6. Closed Christmas.

BALZEKAS MUSEUM OF LITHUANIAN CULTURE
4021 S. Archer Avenue, Chicago, Illinois 60632
History, ethnology, and folklore of Lithuania. Costumes. Coins. Textiles. Music.
Daily 1-4.30. Closed Christmas.

CHICAGO ACADEMY OF SCIENCES
2001 North Clark Street, Chicago, Illinois 60614
Geology, palaeontology, botany, ecology and natural history of Chicago region.
Daily 10-5. Closed Christmas.

CHICAGO PUBLIC LIBRARY MEMORIAL HALL
78 E. Washington Street, Chicago, Illinois 60602
Exhibits and relics illustrating Civil War.
M.-Sa. 9-5. Closed Su. and holidays.

DUSABLE MUSEUM OF AFRICAN AMERICAN HISTORY
3806 S. Michigan Avenue, Chicago, Illinois 60653
Afro-American cultural history. Documents. Sculpture. Prints.
Tu.-F. 10-5; Sa., Su. 1-5. Closed public holidays, mid-Aug. to Labour Day.

FIELD MUSEUM OF NATURAL HISTORY
Roosevelt Road at Lake Shore Drive, Chicago, Illinois 60605
Geology. Mineralogy. Palaeontology. Botany. Herbarium. Natural history. Archaeology. Anthropology. Ethnology. Costumes.
Nov. 1 - Feb. 28: M.-F. 9-4; Sa., Su., 9-5. Mar. 1 - Apr. 30, Sept. 1 - Oct. 31: daily 9-5. May 1 - Aug. 31, daily 9-6. Mid-June - Labour Day: W., F., Sa., Su. 9-8. Closed New Year, Christmas.

GLESSNER HOUSE
1800 S. Prairie Avenue, Chicago, Illinois 60616
House (1886). Original Isaac Scott furniture. Frank Lloyd Wright furniture. Photographs and drawings of Chicago buildings.
Tu., Th., Sa. 10-5; Su. 1-5. Other times by appointment.

GEORGE F. HARDING MUSEUM
86 E. Randolph Street, Chicago, Illinois 60601
Weapons. Armour. Ship models and figureheads. Antique keyboard instruments. Paintings. Sculpture.
By appointment.

ILLINOIS BELL PIONEER HISTORICAL MUSEUM
225 West Randolph Street, Chicago, Illinois 60606
History of telecommunications.
M.-F. 9-4.30. Closed public holidays.

ILLINOIS FUNERAL SERVICE FOUNDATION MUSEUM
515 N. Dearborn Street, Chicago, Illinois 60616
History of funerals and mortuary science.
M.-F. 9-12. Closed college vacations.

MUSEUM OF CHICAGO HISTORICAL SOCIETY
North Avenue and Clark Street, Chicago, Illinois 60614
History of Chicago. Dioramas. Period rooms. Lincoln collection. Civil War material. Portraits. Maps. Costumes. Prints. Photographs. Decorative arts. Transport.
M.-Sa. 9.30-4.30; Su. 12.30-5.30. Closed New Year, Thanksgiving, Christmas.

MUSEUM OF CHICAGO SCHOOL OF ARCHITECTURE FOUNDATION
1800 South Prairie Avenue, Chicago, Illinois 60616
Drawings. Photographs. Architectural items. Glessner House (1886) is in the care of the Foundation.
1st Sunday of month 2-5. Other times by appointment.

MUSEUM OF CONTEMPORARY ART
237 E. Ontario Street, Chicago, Illinois 60611
Paintings. Sculpture. Graphic art.
M.-W., F., Sa. 10-5: Th. 10-8; Su. 12-5. Closed New Year, Christmas.

MUSEUM OF SCIENCE AND INDUSTRY
57th Street and S. Lake Shore Drive, Chicago, Illinois 60637
Science and technology exhibits, sponsored by major U.S. industrial corporations. Transport, especially automobiles. Agriculture. Mining. Medicine. Aeronautics. Telecommunications. Glass. Aviation. Astronautics. Circus history.
May 1 - Sept. 30: M.-Sa. 9.30-5.30; Su. 10-6. Oct. 1 - Apr. 30: M.-Sa. 9.30-4; Su., public holidays 10-6. Closed Christmas.

NATIONAL HISTORICAL FIRE FOUNDATION MUSEUM
400 North Michigan Avenue, Suite 711, Chicago, Illinois 60611
History of fire-fighting.
May 29 - day after Labour Day, M.-Su. 10-5.

ORIENTAL INSTITUTE MUSEUM
University of Chicago, 1155 E. 58th Street, Chicago, Illinois 60637
Art and archaeology of the Near East. Sculpture. Decorative arts. Handicrafts.
Tu.-Su. 10-5. Closed public holidays.

THE POLISH MUSEUM OF AMERICA
984 N. Milwaukee Avenue, Chicago, Illinois 60622
Polish and Polish-American paintings and sculpture. Polish folk art. Domestic equipment. Uniforms. Paderewski collection of furniture, manuscripts and personal possessions. Kosciuszko collection. Helena Modrzejewska collection.
Tu.-Th., Sa. Su., public holidays 1-4.

RENAISSANCE SOCIETY AT THE UNIVERSITY OF CHICAGO
1010 E. 59th Street, Chicago, Illinois 60637
Paintings. Sculpture. Graphics. Decorative arts.
Tu.-Sa. 10-5. Closed Jul. 1 - Sept. 30, public holidays.

MAURICE SPERTUS MUSEUM OF JUDAICA
72 E. 11th Street, Chicago, Illinois 60605
Jewish ceremonial and decorative arts. Archaeology. Ethnology.
M.-Th. 10-4; Su. 10-3. Closed all Jewish holidays, Easter, Christmas.

SWEDISH PIONEER HISTORICAL SOCIETY
5125 N. Spaulding Avenue, Chicago, Illinois 60625
History of Swedish immigration, and Swedish-American life.
M.-Sa. 9.30-12. Closed public holidays.

LORADO TAFT MIDWAY STUDIOS
6016 Ingleside Avenue, Chicago, Illinois 60637
Building (1900) was formerly studios of Lorado Taft and of sculptors associated with him. Works by Taft and Louis Sullivan.
M.-F. 9-5; Sa., Su. 12-5. Closed public holidays.

CHICO

BIDWELL MANSION
525 Esplanade, Chico, California 95926
House (1845-68) was home of General John Bidwell. Period decorations and furnishings.
Daily 10-5. Closed New Year, Thanksgiving, Christmas.

CHILLICOTHE

ADENA STATE MEMORIAL
Allen Avenue, Chillicothe, Ohio 45601
House (1802-7), formerly residence of Governor. 18th-early 19th century furniture.
Apr. 1 - Oct. 31: Tu.-Su. 9.30-4.30.

MOUND CITY GROUP NATIONAL MONUMENT
State Route 104, P.O. Box 327, Chillicothe, Ohio 45601
Archaeological site, Hopewell Indian culture. Prehistoric burial mounds. Site museum with exhibits of prehistoric Indian culture.
Labour Day - Memorial Day, daily 8-5. Rest of year, daily 8-8. Closed Dec. 25 - Jan. 1.

MUSEUM OF CHILLICOTHE RESTORATION FOUNDATION
Chillicothe, Ohio 45601
House (1823). Botany. Herbarium. Natural history. Medical history. Costumes. Decorative arts.
By appointment.

ROSS COUNTY HISTORICAL SOCIETY MUSEUM
45 W. 5th Street, Chillicothe, Ohio 45601
Early state and local history. Prehistoric artifacts. Pioneer life. Furnishings and domestic equipment. Toys. Costumes. Naval paintings.
McClintick House (1838) and McCandless Library (1838) are in the care of the Society.
Feb. 1 - Nov. 30, Tu.-Su., W., 1-5.

CHILTON

MUSEUM OF CALUMET COUNTY HISTORICAL SOCIETY
509 S. State Street, Chilton, Wisconsin 53014
County history. Farm implements, tools, household equipment and school items used by early settlers.
June 1 - Aug. 31: Sa., Su. 1.30-4.30.

CHINA

ALBERT CHURCH BROWN LIBRARY
China, Maine 04926
In early 19th century house. Local history collection.
May 1 - Sept. 30: Tu. 2-5, 7-9; Th. 2-5; Sa. 10-12. Oct. 1 - Apr. 30: Tu. 10-12, 2-5: Th. 2-5; Sa. 10-12.

CHINA LAKE

MATURANGO MUSEUM OF INDIAN WELLS VALLEY
P.O. Box 5514, China Lake, California 93555
Geology. Palaeontology. Natural history. Botany. Indian history. Mining tools and equipment.
M.-F., by appointment; Sa., Su., public holidays, 2-5. Closed Christmas.

CHINCOTEAGUE

OYSTER MUSEUM
403 S. Main Street, Chincoteague, Virginia 23336
Exhibits showing old and new methods of oyster farming and processing.
Apr. 1 - Oct. 31, daily 9-5.

CHINLE

CANYON DE CHELLY NATIONAL MONUMENT
Box 588, Chinle, Arizona 86503
Archaeology. Anthropology.
A number of ruins and prehistoric sites are in the care of the Monument.
May 1 - Sept. 30, daily 8-6; Oct. 1 - Apr. 30, 8-5. Closed New Year, Christmas.

CHINOOK

D.A.R. HOUSE MUSEUM
Fort Columbia State Park, Chinook, Washington 98614
Commanding officer's house (1902), with contemporary furniture, equipment.
June 1 - Aug. 31, daily 10-5.

FORT COLUMBIA STATE PARK HISTORICAL MUSEUM
P.O. Box 172, Chinook, Washington 98614
Local history. Pioneer tools, furnishings. Indian artifacts. Maps. Paintings. Prints. Ship relics.
June-Sept., Tu.-Su. 10-5.

CHIRENO

HALF-WAY HOUSE
S.H.21, Chireno, Texas 75937
Restored stage coach inn (c.1840). Period furnishings.
Daily 9-5.

CHISHOLM

MINNESOTA MUSEUM OF MINING
West Lake Street, Chisholm, Minnesota 55719
Geology. Mineralogy. Mining history and techniques.
Memorial Day - Labour Day, daily 8.30-6.

CHOTEAU

TETON TRAIL MUSEUM
Choteau, Montana 59422
Local and Indian history
June 10 - Labour Day, daily 10-9.

CIMARRON

OLD MILL MUSEUM
Cimarron, New Mexico 87714
In grist mill (1864). History of American S.W., especially N.E. New Mexico.
Daily 8-5.

ERNEST THOMPSON SETON MEMORIAL LIBRARY AND MUSEUM
Philmont Scout Ranch and Explorer Base, Cimarron, New Mexico 87114
Local history. Ethnology. Archaeology. Paintings by local artists.
The Museum is responsible for Kit Carson home (c.1849), Cyphers Mine Cabin (c.1880) and French Henry Mine Cabin (c.1890).
June 1 - Aug. 31, daily 8-5. Sept. 1 - May 31, M.-F. 8-5. Oct. 1 - Apr. 30, Kit Carson home, Cyphers Mine and French Henry Mine, by appointment only.

CINCINNATI

CINCINNATI ART MUSEUM
Eden Park, Cincinnati, Ohio 45202
Mediterranean and Near Eastern Art. Oriental sculpture, paintings, ceramics, textiles. 19th-20th century European and American paintings, sculpture, prints, drawings, decorative arts. Primitive art of America, Africa, S. Pacific. Musical instruments. Playing cards. Ethnology. Indian, Persian miniatures. 17th-19th century English, French, American period rooms. Early American glass.
M., W.-Sa. 10-5; Tu. 10-9.30; Su. 1-5. Closed Thanksgiving, Christmas.

CINCINNATI MUSEUM OF NATURAL HISTORY
1720 Gilbert Avenue, Cincinnati, Ohio 45202
Geology. Mineralogy. Palaeontology. Botany. Astronomy. Planetarium. Natural history. Anthropology. Ethnology. Indian material. Archaeology.
Tu.-Sa. 9-4.30; Su. 1-5. Closed public holidays.

CINCINNATI SCIENCE CENTER
Union Terminal, Cincinnati, Ohio 45203
Physical sciences.
Tu.-Sa. 10-5; Su. 1-5. Closed New Year, Thanksgiving, Christmas.

CONTEMPORARY ARTS CENTER
115 E. 5th Street, Cincinnati, Ohio 45202
Science. Technology. Music. Textiles. Transport.
Tu.-Sa. 10-5; Su. 1-5. Closed public holidays.

HEBREW UNION COLLEGE MUSEUM
3101 Clifton Avenue, Cincinnati, Ohio 45220
Archaeology of Palestine. Jewish ceremonial art, illuminated manuscripts. Works by Jewish artists. Coins. Textiles.
M.-F. 9-5. Closed Jewish and public holidays.

KEMPER LOG CABIN
3400 Vine Street, Cincinnati, Ohio 45220
House (1804). Pioneer furnishings, tools.
Apr. 1 - Nov. 30, daily 9-5.

MIAMI PURCHASE ASSOCIATION
812 Dayton Street, Cincinnati, Ohio 45214
In John Hanck House (1870). Local history. Decorative arts. 19th century furnishings.
Gorham Worth House (1819) and Elk Lick House (1865) are in the care of the Association.
M.-W., F. by appointment. Th. 10-3. Closed Thanksgiving, Christmas.

MUSEUM OF CINCINNATI HISTORICAL SOCIETY
Eden Park, Cincinnati, Ohio 45202
History of Ohio and Cincinnati. Botany.
M.-F. 8.30-4.30; Sa., day following Labour Day - May 31, 9-4. Closed public holidays.

ALFRED K. NIPPERT NATURE MUSEUM
10245 Winton Road, Cincinnati, Ohio 45231
Geology. Mineralogy. Palaeontology. Natural history. Anthropology. Archaeology.
Daily 8-4.

HARRIET B. STOWE HOUSE STATE MEMORIAL
2950 Gilbert Avenue, Cincinnati, Ohio 45200
History of the negroes in Ohio.
June 1 - Sept. 15, Sa., Su., public holidays 10-5.

TAFT MUSEUM
316 Pike Street, Cincinnati, Ohio 45202
17th-19th Century English, Dutch, French, Spanish paintings. Chinese porcelain. Limoges enamels. Italian Majolica and engraved rock crystals. 17th-18th century watches. 18th - early 19th century French, English textiles, especially satins. Duncan Phyfe furniture.
M.-Sa. 10-5; Su., public holidays 2-5. Closed Thanksgiving, Christmas.

WILLIAM HOWARD TAFT NATIONAL HISTORIC SITE
P.O. Box 19072, 2038 Auburn Avenue, Cincinnati, Ohio 45219
House (c.1840), birthplace and boyhood home of President Taft. Family papers, furnishings. Memorabilia of the President.
Daily 8-5.

UNIVERSITY OF CINCINNATI GEOLOGY MUSEUM
Department of Geology, University of Cincinnati, Cincinnati, Ohio 45221
Geology. Mineralogy. Palaeontology. Petrology. Natural history. Archaeology. Anthropology. Indian artifacts.
M.-F. 9-5; Sa., Su., public holidays by appointment. Closed university vacations.

CIRCLE

McCONE COUNTY MUSEUM
Main Street, Circle, Montana 59215
Local history.
June 1 - Sept. 30: Tu., Th., Sa. 2-5. Other days by appointment.

CLAREMONT

HUMANITIES MUSEUM
Scripps College, Claremont, California 91711
Local history, ethnology, archaeology. Oriental art. Paintings by American artists.
M.-F., 9-12, 1-5. Closed public holidays, school vacations.

MONTGOMERY ART CENTER
College and Bonita Streets, Claremont, California 91711
Archaeology. Paintings. Sculpture, especially Yoruba. Graphics. Decorative arts.
M.-F., 10-5; Sa., Su., 1-5. Closed public holidays and College summer vacation.

MUSEUM OF RANCHO SANTA ANA BOTANIC GARDENS
1500 North College Avenue, Claremont, California 91711
Herbarium. Anatomy.
Daily, 8-5. Closed New Year, July 4, Thanksgiving, Christmas.

MUSEUM OF CLAREMONT HISTORICAL SOCIETY
165 Broad Street, Claremont, New Hampshire 03743
Local history. Archaeology.
Jul. 1 - Oct. 31: Th. 1-5, 7-9.

CLAREMORE

J. M. DAVIS GUN COLLECTION
Mason Hotel, 5th Street and Highway 66, Claremore, Oklahoma 74017
Guns. Indian artifacts. Saddles. Swords and knives.
Sept. 1 - May 31, M.-Sa. 8.30-5, Su. 1-5. June 1 - Aug. 31, M.-Sa. 8.30-7, Su. 1-7. Closed Christmas.

LONG'S WAX AND HISTORICAL MUSEUM
1002 W. Will Rogers Highway, Claremore, Oklahoma 74017
Wax figures of famous Americans. Guns. Early farm and domestic equipment. Indian relics.
Apr. 1 - Labour Day, 9-9. Rest of year 9-5.

LYNN RIGGS MEMORIAL
121 N. Weenonah Street, Claremore, Oklahoma 74017
Memorabilia of the author, Lynn Riggs. Manuscripts. Photographs.
M.-Sa. 9-5.

WILL ROGERS MEMORIAL
P.O. Box 157, State Highway 88, Claremore, Oklahoma 74017
Rogers' memorabilia. Saddles. Paintings. Dioramas.
Daily 8-5.

CLARENCE

MUSEUM OF THE HISTORICAL SOCIETY OF THE TOWN OF CLARENCE
Main Street, Clarence, New York 14032
Local history and archaeology. Indian artifacts.
July-Aug., W. 10-3; Su. 2-5.

CLARINDA

PAGE COUNTY HISTORICAL SOCIETY
620 S. 16th Street, Clarinda, Iowa 51632
In Goldenrod schoolhouse (1873), Local history.
Su. 1-5, by appointment.

CLARION

4-H HISTORICAL BUILDING
Central West, Highway 3, Clarion, Iowa 50525
In rural school (1908). School books. Local history. Agriculture. History of early 4-H.
June 1 - Aug. 31, by appointment.

CLARION COUNTY HISTORICAL SOCIETY MUSEUM
Court House, Clarion, Pennsylvania 16214
Local history. Indian artifacts. Early industry. Pioneer life.
F. 2-4. Other times by appointment.

CLARKDALE

TUZIGOOT NATIONAL MONUMENT
P.O. Box 68, Clarkdale, Arizona 86324
Excavated site of Indian village, abandoned in 14th century. Site museum contains beads, shell bracelets, pottery and other grave offerings.
May 1 - Sept 30, daily 7-7. Oct. 1 - Apr. 30, daily 7-7.

CLARKSON

CLARKSON HISTORICAL MUSEUM
Clarkson, Nebraska 68629
History of early settlement of Clarkson. Domestic equipment. Musical instruments. Handicrafts.
Daily 9-5. Public holidays by appointment.

CLARKSTON

VALLEY ART CENTER
842 6th Street, Clarkston, Washington 99403
Graphics. Sculpture. Indian art.
Tu.-F. 1-4; Su. 2-5. Closed Dec. 10 - Jan. 1.

CLARKSVILLE

ROANOKE RIVER MUSEUM
Prestwould Foundation, P.O. Box 872, Clarksville, Virginia 23927
In Prestwould House (1795). Local history. Costumes. Archaeology.
Sept.-May. W., Su. 2-5. Other times by appointment.

CLAY CITY

MUSEUM OF RED RIVER HISTORICAL SOCIETY
Box 195, Clay City, Kentucky 40312
Geology. Mineralogy. Palaeontology. Zoology. Science. Local history and archaeology.
Mar. 1 - Nov. 30, Su. 12-6.

CLAYTON

CUSTER MUSEUM
Clayton Ranger Station, Clayton, Idaho 83227
Goldrush history 1870-1900. Mining equipment. Pioneer history.
Custer Schoolhouse (1870) and former saloon (1870) are in the care of the Museum.
June 15 - Sept. 5, daily 10-7.

GENERAL DANIEL BISSELL HOME AND JEFFERSON BARRACKS HISTORICAL PARK
7900 Forsythe Street, Clayton, Missouri 63105
House (1812). Furnishings of 1812-80. Barracks contains uniforms, weapons.
W.-Sa. 8-5; Su., public holidays 1-5. Closed Christmas, New Year.

ST. LOUIS COUNTY MUSEUM
7922 Bonhomme, Clayton, Missouri 63105
Local history. Archaeology. Costumes. Indian material
General Daniel Bissell House (1815) and Jefferson Barracks (1851-7) are in the care of the Museum.
W.-Sa. 8-5; Su. 1-5. Closed New Year, Christmas.

MUSEUM OF NORTHERN NEW YORK AGRICULTURAL HISTORICAL SOCIETY
R.D.1, Clayton, New York 13624
In former church (1837). Agricultural tools, machinery, equipment. Household equipment.
June-Oct., M., W.-Su. 1-4.

THOUSAND ISLANDS MUSEUM
Old Town Hall, 401 Riverside Drive, Clayton, New York 13624
Shipbuilding. Boats. Indian life and artifacts. History of St. Lawrence River. Costumes. Children's museum. Duck decoys.
Daily 9-9.

CLEARFIELD

MUSEUM OF CLEARFIELD COUNTY HISTORICAL SOCIETY
104 E. Pine Street, Clearfield, Pennsylvania 16830
Lumbering. Carpenter's tools. Indian flints. Glass.
Su. 1-5. Other times by appointment.

CLEARWATER

FLORIDA GULF COAST ART CENTER
111 Manatee Road, Clearwater, Florida 33516
European and American paintings. Ceramics. Sculpture. Graphics.
M.-Sa. 10-4; Su. 3-5.

PINELLAS COUNTY HISTORICAL COMMISSION
315 Haven Street, Courthouse, Clearwater, Florida 33516
Local history. Costumes.
M.-F. 9-5. Closed public holidays.

CLEBURNE

LAYLAND MUSEUM
Public Library, 201 N. Caddo Street, Cleburne, Texas 76031
History of Johnson County. Tools.
M., F. 3-5; Sa. 9-12. Closed public holidays.

CLE ELREM

CLE ELREM HISTORICAL MUSEUM
301 E. 2nd Street, Cle Elrem, Washington 98922
In former Bell Telephone building. History of the telephone.
Memorial Day - Oct. 31, Tu.-Su. 1.30-4.30.

CLEMSON

FORT HILL
University Campus, Clemson, South Carolina 29631
House (1803), was home of John C. Calhoun, founder of the University. Original furnishings. Flemish and family portraits.
Tu.-Sa. 10-12, 1-5.30; Su. 2-6.

HANOVER HOUSE
University Campus, Clemson, South Carolina 29631
House (c.1780), moved to present site. Originally a residence and fortress, with gun-slots in basement.
Tu.-Sa. 10-12, 1-5.30; Su. 2-6.

RUDOLPH LEE GALLERY
College of Architecture, Clemson University, Clemson, South Carolina 29631
17th-18th Century Dutch, Flemish paintings. Contemporary American paintings, graphics.
M.-F. 9-4.30; Sa. Su. 2-6. Closed Dec. 24 - Jan. 2, public holidays.

CLEVELAND

WHITE COUNTY HISTORICAL SOCIETY MUSEUM
P.O. Box 281, Cleveland, Georgia 30528
In Courthouse (1859-60). Local history. Civil War documents.
By appointment.

ART GALLERY OF CLEVELAND PUBLIC LIBRARY
325 Superior Avenue, Cleveland, Ohio 44114
19th-20th century paintings, drawings, sculpture by American, especially Ohio, artists.
M.-F. 9-8.30; Sa. 9-6. Closed public holidays.

CLEVELAND HEALTH MUSEUM AND EDUCATION CENTER
8911 Euclid Avenue, Cleveland, Ohio 44106
Anatomy. Physiology. Human reproduction. Environmental health.
M.-Sa. 9-5; Su. 1-5. Closed Thanksgiving, Christmas.

CLEVELAND METROPOLITAN PARK DISTRICT TRAILSIDE MUSEUM
2000 Standard Building, Cleveland, Ohio 44113
Park museum. Geology. Natural history. Indian materials.
M.-Sa. 9-5; Su. 11-7; public holidays 10-7. Closed Christmas, Easter.

CLEVELAND MUSEUM OF ART
11150 East Boulevard, Cleveland, Ohio 44106
Primitive art. Oriental painting, sculpture, carvings, drawings. Mediterranean and Near Eastern art. 14th-20th century European paintings, sculpture, graphic arts, decorative arts. 17th-20th Century American art. Music. Coins.
Tu., Th., F. 10-6; W. 10-10; Sa. 9-5; Su. 1-6. Closed New Year, July 4, Thanksgiving, Christmas.

CLEVELAND MUSEUM OF NATURAL HISTORY
Wade Oval, University Circle, Cleveland, Ohio 44106
Formation and history of the earth. Geology. Mineralogy. Palaeontology. Fossils, including mastodons. Astronomy. Planetarium. Birds and insects of Ohio. Anthropology. Ethnology. Medical history.
M.-Sa. 10-5; Su. 1-5.30. Closed public holidays.

SALVADOR DALI MUSEUM
24050 Commerce Park Road, Cleveland, Ohio 44122
Paintings and graphics by Dali, including 'Hallucinogenic Toreador'.
Tu.-Sa. 10-4, by appointment. Closed public holidays.

HOWARD DITTRICK MUSEUM OF HISTORICAL MEDICINE
11000 Euclid Avenue, Cleveland, Ohio 44106
History of medicine, dentistry, pharmacy and nursing. Roman surgical instruments. 18th-19th century microscopes. Doctor's surgery (1880).
M.-F. 9-5; Sa. 1-5. Closed Sa., public holidays, Jul. 1 - Aug. 31.

DUNHAM TAVERN MUSEUM
6709 Euclid Avenue, Cleveland, Ohio 44103
Building (1824). Shaker rooms. Ohio room. Early American furniture. Pewter. Lustre ware. Mocha ware. Glass. Textiles. Folklore.
Tu.-Su., public holidays 12.30-4.30. Closed New Year, Thanksgiving, Christmas.

FRANKLIN COUNTY HISTORICAL SOCIETY AND MUSEUM
280 E. Broad Street (15), Cleveland, Ohio 43215
Early history of Franklin County.
M. 1-9; Tu.-Sa. 10-4.30; Su. 1-5.30. Closed Christmas, New Year.

GREAT LAKES HISTORICAL SOCIETY MUSEUM
320 Republic Building (15), Cleveland, Ohio 44115
Local history.
Daily 10.30-5.

GUND COLLECTION OF WESTERN ART
1 Erieview Plaza, Cleveland, Ohio 44114
19th-20th century American paintings, graphics, sculpture.
By appointment.

THE SHAKER HISTORICAL SOCIETY MUSEUM
Moreland School, Lee Road and Van Aken Boulevard (20), Cleveland, Ohio 44101
Local history. Pioneer tools, household equipment. Shaker furniture, handicrafts.
School days 1-3; Th. 9-4 (winter). Th. 9-4 (summer).

TEMPLE MUSEUM OF JEWISH RELIGIOUS ART AND MUSIC
University Circle and Silver Park, Cleveland, Ohio 44106
Jewish ceremonial and decorative arts. Archaeology. Paintings. Silver. Sculpture.
M.-F. 9-5; Su. 10-12. Closed public holidays, Jewish holidays, May 1 - Sept. 30 Sa., Su.

WESTERN RESERVE HISTORICAL SOCIETY AND FREDERICK C. CRAWFORD AUTO-AVIATION MUSEUM
10825 E. Boulevard, Cleveland, Ohio 44106
Ohio history and archaeology. Shaker and Amish exhibits. Pioneer life. Military history. Memorabilia of Lincoln and Washington. Furniture. Paintings, sculpture, graphics, decorative arts by Ohio artists. Crawford collection of old cars, early aeroplane engines and aircraft models. 1919 Curtis aeroplane.
Tu.-Sa. 10-5; Su. 2-5. Crawford collection: daily 1-6. Closed public holidays.

CLIFTON

BOSQUE MEMORIAL MUSEUM
South Avenue Q, Clifton, Texas 76634
Local pioneer history. Texas rock and fossil collection.
Su. 2-5. Other times by appointment.

CLINTON

STANTON HOUSE
63 East Main Street, Clinton, Connecticut 06413
House (1789). 18th-19th century American furniture, china, glass.
May 1 - June 30, Sept. 1 - Oct. 31: Tu.-Su. 2-5; July 1 - Aug. 31, 11-5. Other months by appointment.

FINE ARTS CENTRE OF CLINTON
119 West Macon Street, Clinton, Illinois 61727
Contemporary American paintings, photographs.
Sept. 1 - July 30: M.-F. 10-12, 1-5; Sa. 10-12. 1st Sunday of month, 3-5. Closed Christmas, Easter, Thanksgiving, Lincoln's birthday.

HOMESTEAD MUSEUM
219 E. Woodlawn Street, Clinton, Illinois 61727
In John W. Bishop House (1863 and 1876). Furnishings. Clothing. Agriculture. Railway history. Guns.
Tu.-Su. 1-5.

SHOWBOAT 'RHODODENDRON' HISTORICAL MUSEUM
Riverfront, Clinton, Iowa 52732
In sternwheel riverboat 'Rhododendron'. Local history.
June 1 - Sept. 30, daily 9-5.

CLINTON HISTORICAL SOCIETY MUSEUM
210 Church Street, Clinton, Massachusetts 01510
Local history.
Open on days of meetings only.

MUSEUM OF MISSISSIPPI BAPTIST HISTORICAL COMMISSION
Mississippi College Library, 101 Monroe Street, Clinton, Mississippi 39056
Baptist history.
M.-F. 8-4. Closed College vacations.

HENRY COUNTY HISTORICAL MUSEUM
Courthouse, Clinton, Missouri 64735
Local history. Costumes. Jewellery. Arrowheads.
2nd and 4th Tu. in month, 12-4.

CLINTON HISTORICAL MUSEUM
Main Street, Clinton, New Jersey 08809
Early American industries. Agriculture. Handicrafts. Oil-mill (1800). Lime kilns (1840). Colonial shops and period rooms.
Apr. 1 - Oct. 31: Tu.-F. 1-5; Sa., Su. 10-5.

HUNTERDON ART CENTER
7 Center Street, Clinton, New Jersey 08809
In 18th century mill. Paintings. Sculpture. Prints.
Tu.-Su. 1-5. Closed public holidays.

WESTERN TRAILS MUSEUM
2229 Gary Freeway, Clinton, Oklahoma 73601
Western Oklahoma Indian relics. Pioneer life. Early farm tools, implements.
Daily 9-5.

CLINTONVILLE

MUSEUM OF FOUR WHEEL DRIVE FOUNDATION
105 E. 12th Street, Clintonville, Wisconsin 54929
In Zachow-Besserdick Machine Shop (1906). History of motor transport and of F.W.D. Corporation.
May 1 - Oct. 31: M.-F. 10-12, 1.30-4.30. Other times by appointment.

COALTON

COALTON HISTORICAL SOCIETY
Coalton, Ohio 45621
Building was birthplace of Governor James Rhodes. Memorabilia of the Governor.
By appointment.

COCHRANE

PRAIRIE MOON MUSEUM
Cochrane, Wisconsin 54622
Geology. Mineralogy. Botany. Local history. Indian artifacts. Farm implements. Sculpture.
May 1 - Nov. 30, 8-6.

COCKEYSVILLE

BALTIMORE COUNTY HISTORICAL SOCIETY MUSEUM
9811 Van Buren Lane, Cockeysville, Maryland 21030
County history. Agriculture. Indian artifacts. Household equipment. Furniture.
By appointment.

CODY

BUFFALO BILL HISTORICAL CENTER
Box 1020, Cody, Wyoming 82414
House (1840), Buffalo Bill's boyhood home, moved to site. Memorabilia of Buffalo Bill and of Wild West Show period. Plains Indian material. Early waggons.
May 1-31, Sept. 1-30, daily 8-5. June 1 - Aug. 31, daily 7 a.m.-10 p.m.

COFFEYVILLE

DALTON MUSEUM
113 E. 8th Street, Coffeyville, Kansas 67337
Local history. Indian artifacts.
Daily 8-8.

COHASSET

COHASSET HISTORIC HOUSE
Elm Street, Cohasset, Massachusetts 02025
House (1805). Period furnishings. Lincoln and Civil War items. Indian material. Early Americana.
June 15 - Labour Day: Tu.-Sa. 1.30-4.30. Closed July 4.

COHASSET MARITIME MUSEUM
Elm Street, Cohasset, Massachusetts 02025
House (c.1760). Mineralogy. Local and maritime history. Indian artifacts.
June 15 - Labour Day: Tu.-Sa. 1.30-4.30. Closed July 4.

INDEPENDENCE GOWN MUSEUM
S. Main Street, Cohasset, Massachusetts 02025
House (1848). Local history. Folklore. Costumes.
June 15 - Labour Day: Tu.-Sa. 1.30-4.30. Closed July 4.

COHOES

VAN SCHAICK MANSION
Van Schaick Avenue, Cohoes, New York 12047
House (1737), military headquarters in Revolution, French and Indian Wars and War of 1812. Period furnishings. Military history.
By appointment.

COKATO

H. C. BULL MEMORIAL LIBRARY AND MUSEUM
W. Fifth Street, Cokato, Minnesota 55321
Pioneer handicrafts, tools, agricultural implements.
School year, daily 8.30-4.

COLBY

SOD TOWN PRAIRIE PIONEER MUSEUM
U.S. Highway 24 E, Colby, Kansas 67701
Replicas of sod buildings used in settlement of the prairie regions, with 1870-1930 furnishings. Indian artifacts.
Mar. 15 - Nov. 15, daily 8-8. Other times by appointment.

COLD SPRING

BOSCOBEL
Route 9D, Cold Spring, New York 10516
18th century house. Period rooms. Carriage house.
Mar. 1 - Dec. 31: W.-M. 9.30-5. Jan. 1 - Feb. 28, 9.30-4.30.

FOUNDRY SCHOOL MUSEUM
63 Chestnut Street, Cold Spring, New York 10516
Schoolhouse (1825). Exhibits relating to local gun factory, the West Point Foundry. Hudson River material. 19th century paintings.
W. 9.30-4; Su. 2-5.

COLDSPRING

SAN JACINTO COUNTY HISTORICAL MUSEUM
City Park, Coldspring, Texas 77331
History of early settlement of San Jacinto County. Documents. Family papers.
June 1 - Aug. 31: M.-F. 8-5; Su. 2-6.

COLD SPRING HARBOR

WHALING MUSEUM
Main Street, Cold Spring Harbor, New York 11724
History and techniques of whaling. Diorama of Cold Spring in 1840s, at zenith of whaling period. Ship-models. Whaling equipment. Prints. Maps. Photographs. Navigation instruments. Ships' figureheads. Scrimshaw. Sailors' knots.
Apr. 15 - June 14, Sept. 15 - Oct. 15: Sa., Su., public holidays 1-5. June 15 - Sept. 14: Th.-Su., public holidays 1-5.

COLDWATER

COMANCHE COUNTY HISTORICAL SOCIETY MUSEUM
Coldwater, Kansas 67029
Geology. Mineralogy. Palaeontology. Local history. Agriculture. Indian artifacts.
Sa., Su. 2-5. Other times by appointment.

COLEBROOK

COLEBROOK HISTORICAL SOCIETY MUSEUM
P.O. Box 85, Colebrook, Connecticut 06021
Local history.
May 30 - Oct. 12, Sa., Su., public holidays, 2-4.

COLEMAN

COLEMAN COUNTY MUSEUM
City Park, Coleman, Texas 76834
In replica of Camp Colorado. Early history of Coleman County.
June 1 - Aug. 31, daily, except Th., 1-6. Rest of year, Sa., Su. 1-6.

COLLEGE

UNIVERSITY OF ALASKA MUSEUM
College, Alaska 99701
Archaeology and history of Alaska.
May 1 - Sept. 30, Daily 9-5; Oct. 1 - Apr. 30, 1-5. Closed Christmas.

COLLEGE PARK

ART GALLERY OF UNIVERSITY OF MARYLAND
Department of Art, J. Millard Tawes Fine Arts Center, College Park, Maryland 20742
20th century American paintings, sculpture, prints.
M.-Sa. 9-5; Su. 1-5. Closed public holidays and university summer vacation.

COLLEGE POINT

POPPENHUSEN INSTITUTE
College Point, New York 11356
Collections illustrating growth and development of College Point. Pictures. Maps. Documents. Memorabilia.
By appointment.

COLLEGEVILLE

MUSEUM OF THE HISTORICAL SOCIETY OF TRAPPE
Main Street, Trappe, Collegeville, Pennsylvania 19426
In Dewees Tavern (1795). Local history.
By appointment.

COLOMA

JAMES W. MARSHALL GOLD DISCOVERY MUSEUM
P.O. Box 265, Coloma, California 95613
Site of first discovery of gold in California by James Marshall. Museum building (1850), illustrating history of gold rush, was former Chinese store. Several other mid-19th century buildings are preserved. Operating replica of 1847 sawmill.
Sept. 1 - Apr. 30, daily 10-5. May 1 - Aug. 31, daily 10-6. Closed New Year, Thanksgiving, Christmas.

COLONIAL HEIGHTS

VIOLET BANK MUSEUM
Colonial Heights, Virginia 23834
House (1775). Civil War relics.
May 1 - Sept. 30: M.-Sa., public holidays 10-4; Su. 1-5.

COLORADO CITY

COLORADO CITY HISTORICAL MUSEUM
175 W. 3rd Street, Colorado City, Texas 79512
Palaeontology. Pioneer life. Portraits. Horse-drawn hearse.
June 1 - Aug. 31, daily 9-5. Sept. 1 - May 31, Tu.-Su. 2-5.

COLORADO SPRINGS

CARRIAGE HOUSE MUSEUM
Broadmoor, Colorado Springs, Colorado 80901
Horse-drawn carriages. Covered wagons. Stage coaches.
Tu.-Su., 10-12, 1-5. Closed New Year, Thanksgiving, Christmas.

COLORADO SPRINGS FINE ARTS CENTER
30 West Dale Street, Colorado Springs, Colorado 80901
South-western U.S. primitive folk art. American Indian art. American and European paintings. Latin American arts and crafts.
M.-Sa., 9-5; Su., 1.30-5. Closed public holidays.

HALL OF PRESIDENTS
1056 South 21st Street, Colorado Springs, Colorado 80904
Local history. Decorative arts.
June 1 - Sept. 15, daily 8 a.m.-10 p.m. Sept. 16 - May 31, daily 9-6. Closed Christmas.

MAY NATURAL HISTORY MUSEUM
Lytle Star Route, Colorado Springs, Colorado 80903
Natural history, expecially entomology.
June 15 - Labour Day, daily 8 a.m.-9 p.m. May 1 - June 15, Sept., daily 8-6. Closed Oct. 1 - May 1.

MCALLISTER HOUSE MUSEUM
423 North Cascade Avenue, Colorado Springs, Colorado 80902
House (1873) with period furnishings.
June 1 - Sept. 14, Tu.-Sa., 10-5, Su., 2-5. Rest of year, by appointment.

MUSEUM OF THE AMERICAN NUMISMATIC ASSOCIATION
818 North Cascade, Colorado Springs, Colorado 80903
Coins. Banknotes. Tokens. Medals.
M.-F., 8-5. Public holidays, by appointment.

PIKES PEAK GHOST TOWN
Highway 24 West at 21st Street, Colorado Springs, Colorado 80901
Colorado Pioneer history. Mining relics.
Tu.-Sa., 10-5; Su., 2-5. Closed public holidays.

PIONEERS' MUSEUM
25 W. Kiowa Street, Colorado Springs, Colorado 80902
Mineralogy. Indian artifacts. Coins. Paintings. New England antiques. 3 rooms of Helen Hunt Jackson home rebuilt in Museum. World-wide collection of pipes.
Tu.-Sa., 10-5; Su., 2-5. Closed public holidays.

WESTERN MUSEUM OF MINING AND INDUSTRY
1025 Northgate Road, Colorado Springs, Colorado 80901
Mining machinery. Steam engines. Electrical equipment. Mineralogy.
Daily 10-5.

COLUMBIA

MUSEUM OF COLUMBIA STATE HISTORIC PARK
P.O. Box 151, Columbia, California 95310
History of Gold Rush. Indian history. Several historic buildings (1854-60), including a saloon, schoolhouse and Wells Fargo bank, are in the care of the Museum.
Daily, 8-5. Closed Thanksgiving, Christmas.

MISSOURI SCHOOL OF RELIGION MUSEUM
9th and Lowry Streets, Columbia, Missouri 65201
History of religion. Archaeology. Coins.
M.-Th. 8-5. Closed public holidays.

MUSEUM OF ANTHROPOLOGY
University of Missouri, 100 Swallow Hall, Columbia, Missouri 65201
Ethnographical and archaeological material from the United States, Mexico, Africa.
M.-F. 9-5; Sa. 1-5. Closed Aug. 1-31, University Christmas vacation.

MUSEUM OF ART AND ARCHAEOLOGY
University of Missouri, Library 4D11, Columbia, Missouri 65201
Ethnology of Oceania, Africa, Central and S. America. Archaeology of Near East and Mediterranean. Art of S.E. Asia. European and American paintings, sculpture, graphics.
Daily 2-5. Closed Thanksgiving, Christmas, New Year.

MUSEUM OF DEPARTMENT OF GEOLOGY
University of Missouri, Columbia, Missouri 65201
Geology. Mineralogy. Palaeontology.
M.-F. 8-5; Sa. 8-12. Closed public holidays.

MUSEUM OF STATE HISTORICAL SOCIETY OF MISSOURI
University Library Building, Hitt and Lowry Streets, Columbia, Missouri 65201
Paintings, engravings, etchings, lithographs by American and European artists. American cartoons.
M.-F. 8-4.30. Closed public holidays.

UNIVERSITY OF MISSOURI MUSEUM
Columbia, Missouri 65201
Mineralogy. Botany. Zoology. Herpetology. Entomology. Anthropology.
Daily 8-5.

COLUMBIA MUSEUM OF HOROLOGICAL ANTIQUITIES
333 N. 3rd Street, Columbia, Pennsylvania 17512
International collection of clocks, watches.
By appointment.

COLUMBIA MUSEUM OF ART
Senate and Bull Streets, Columbia, South Carolina 29201
Spanish Colonial art. 13th-19th century European and American painting, sculpture, graphics. Paintings by South Carolina artists. Colonial decorative arts.
Tu.-Sa. 10-5; Su. 2-6.

COLUMBIA SCIENCE MUSEUM
1519 Senate Street, Columbia, South Carolina 29201
Natural history of South Carolina, with mounted and living specimens. Planetarium.
Tu.-Sa. 10-5; Su. 2-6.

HAMPTON-PRESTON HOUSE
Blanding Street, Columbia, South Carolina 29200
House (c.1818). Period furnishings.
M.-Sa. 10-5; Su. 1-6.

HISTORIC COLUMBIA FOUNDATION, INC.
Columbia Museum of Art and Science, 1527 Senate Street, Columbia, South Carolina 29201
In former Ainsley Hall Mansion (1823), now Robert Mills Historic House and Park, as memorial to architect of Washington Monument and U.S. Treasury. Period furnishings. Displays illustrating life and work of Robert Mills.
Tu.-Sa. 10-1, 2-4. Su. 2-5.

SOUTH CAROLINA CONFEDERATE RELIC ROOM AND MUSEUM
World War Memorial Building, Sumter and Pendleton Streets, Columbia, South Carolina 29201
South Carolina history. Costumes and uniforms. Military relics.
M.-F. 9-5; Sa. by appointment. Closed public holidays, and certain other days by local announcement.

SOUTH CAROLINA GOVERNOR'S MANSION
800 Richland Street, Columbia, South Carolina 29200
Remaining part of military school, burned in 1865. Furnishings, paintings and other personal possessions of former Governors. Silver mess-service of the battleship, 'South Carolina'.
M.-F. 9-5, by appointment.

SOUTH CAROLINA STATE HISTORICAL MUSEUM
Midlands Exposition Park, 1615 Blanding Street, Columbia, South Carolina 29201
On site containing Hampton-Preston House (1823) with original Hampton family furnishings. New Museum in West Dome has artifacts on display showing life in 17th-19th century South Carolina. Civil War collections.
Daily 9-5.

THE STATE HOUSE
Gervais Street, Columbia, South Carolina 29201
Building (begun 1855, completed 1905). Museum of relics of Confederate Period.
M.-F. 9-12.30, 2-5.

UNIVERSITY MUSEUM
University of South Carolina, War Memorial Building, Columbia, South Carolina 29208
Silver. Gemstones. Mineralogy.
M.-F. 9-5. Closed public holidays.

WOODROW WILSON HOME
1705 Hampton Street, Columbia, South Carolina 29200
House in which President Wilson lived as a boy (1871-74) when his father was professor at Columbia Theological Seminary. Contains bed in which the President was born and the desk he used as Governor of New Jersey.
Tu.-Sa. 10-1, 2-4; Su. 2-5.

JAMES K. POLK ANCESTRAL HOME
301 W. 7th Street, Columbia, Tennessee 38401
House (1816) was home of President Polk. Furniture, china, personal possessions of Polk family.
M.-Sa., public holidays, 9-5; Su. 1-5. Closed Christmas.

COLUMBIA CITY

WHITLEY COUNTY HISTORICAL MUSEUM
108 West Jefferson Street, Columbia City, Indiana 46725
In Marshall House (1875, remodelled 1895). Local history.
Su. 2-5.

COLUMBIA FALLS

RUGGLES HOUSE
Main Street, Columbia Falls, Maine 04623
House (1818). Wood carving. Period furnishings.
June 1 - Oct. 15, daily 10-5.

COLUMBUS

COLUMBUS MUSEUM OF ARTS AND CRAFTS
1251 Wynton Road, Columbus, Georgia 31906
English, Flemish, Dutch, Italian paintings. Sculpture. Prints. American paintings, drawings, especially by Georgia artists. American and foreign guns, dolls. African sculpture. American Indian material. Oriental ivories, porcelain. Needlework. Jewellery. Persian rugs.
Tu.-Sa. 10-5; Su. 2-5. Closed New Year, July 4, Thanksgiving, Christmas.

CONFEDERATE NAVAL MUSEUM
202 Fourth Street, Columbus, Georgia 31901
Local and naval history. Models of Confederate gunboats. Remains of the Confederate gunboats 'Muscogee' and 'Chattahoochee'.
Oct. 1 - Apr. 30: Tu.-Sa. 9-5; Su. 2-5. May 1 - Sept. 30: Tu.-Sa. 9-5.30; Closed Thanksgiving, Christmas.

BARTHOLOMEW COUNTY HISTORICAL SOCIETY
524 Third Street, Columbus, Indiana 47201
In McEwan House (1865). Local history.
By appointment.

MERLE EVANS CIRCUS MUSEUM
217 E. Walnut Street, Columbus, Kansas 66725
Circus history. Costumes. Posters. Photographs.
By appointment.

MUSEUM OF COLUMBUS BELMONT BATTLEFIELD STATE PARK
State Highway 80, Columbus, Kentucky 42032
Civil War relics.
May 1 - Labour Day, daily 10-5.

MISSISSIPPI STATE COLLEGE FOR WOMEN
Art Gallery and Museum, Fine Arts Building, Columbus, Mississippi 39701
American paintings, drawings, prints, especially by Mississippi artists.
M.-F. 8-5.

STILLWATER COUNTY HISTORICAL SOCIETY MUSEUM
Columbus, Montana 59019
Photographs, paintings, prints, drawings illustrating history of Stillwater County.
M.-F. 8-12, 1-5; Sa., Su., public holidays on request.

PANCHO VILLA MUSEUM
Lima Street, Columbus, New Mexico 88029
Pancho Villa photographs, guns, mementoes. Civil War uniforms. Aviation.
M.-Sa. 9-5. Closed New Year, Easter, Thanksgiving, Christmas.

CENTER OF SCIENCE AND INDUSTRY
280 E. Broad Street, Columbus, Ohio 43215
Science. Planetarium. Weather station. Industry. Reproduction of Main Street buildings, 1840-1910. Dioramas showing Columbus life in 1850. Dolls. Doctor's surgery of Civil War period.
M.-Sa. 10-4.30. Su. 1-5.30. Closed Independence Day, Thanksgiving, Christmas, New Year.

COLUMBUS GALLERY OF FINE ARTS
480 E. Broad Street, Columbus, Ohio 43215
Primitive art of S. Pacific. Indian artifacts. 16th-19th century European paintings. 19th-20th century French and American paintings. Paintings and lithographs by George Bellows.
Daily 12-5. Closed New Year, July 4, Thanksgiving, Christmas.

DURELL FARM MUSEUM
c/o Union Fork and Hoe Company, 500 Dublin Avenue, Columbus, Ohio 43216
Early American farm and garden books and household equipment. Craftsmen's tools. Lighting fitments.
M.-F. 9-4, by appointment. Closed public holidays.

DR. JOHN HARRIS DENTAL MUSEUM
40 S. 3rd Street, Columbus, Ohio 43215
Building (1827), formerly surgery of Dr. Harris. History of dentistry.
Apr. 1 - Oct. 31: Tu.-Su. 9-5.

OHIO HISTORICAL CENTER
Interstate 71 and 17th Avenue, Columbus, Ohio 43211
Mineralogy. Natural history. Prehistoric archaeology of Mid-West. Local and military history. Industry. Handicrafts. Paintings. Drawings. Prints. Decorative arts.
M.-Sa. 9-5. Su., Public holidays 1-5. Closed Christmas, New Year.

ORTON MUSEUM
155 S. Oval Drive, Columbus, Ohio 43210
Geology. Mineralogy. Palaeontology.
M.-F. 9-5.

CONFEDERATE MEMORIAL MUSEUM
Milam and Walnut Streets, Columbus, Texas 78934
In former Water tower (1883). Social history of Colorado County. Life in Texas Republic. Civil War material.
By appointment.

COMANCHE

BURKS MUSEUM
Highway 16 N., Comanche, Texas 76442
In old log courthouse (1855). Early farm implements. Transport. Indian artifacts.
Su. 2-5. Other times by appointment.

COMFORT

COMFORT HISTORICAL MUSEUM
High and 8th Streets, Comfort, Texas 78013
Photographs and relics of pioneer settlement. Early household equipment. Agriculture. Indian artifacts. Glass.
Sa. 1-5. Other times by appointment.

CONCORD

CONCORD ANTIQUARIAN SOCIETY MUSEUM
200 Lexington Road, Concord, Massachusetts 01742
Period rooms. Emerson study. Thoreau room. Revolutionary War relics. Cincinnati china.
Feb. 1 - Nov. 3, M.-Sa. 10-4.30; Su. 2-4.30.

MINUTE MAN NATIONAL HISTORICAL PARK MUSEUM
Concord, P.O. Box 160, Massachusetts 01742
Local history. Furniture.
The Wayside (1717) and Ephraim Hartwell Tavern (1732) are in the care of the Park Authority.
Oct. 1 - May 31: M.-F. 8-5. June 1 - Sept. 30: Sa., Su. 9-6. Closed New Year, Christmas.

MUSEUM OF CONCORD ART ASSOCIATION
15 Lexington Road, Concord, Massachusetts 01742
House (1720). Early American portraits. American paintings, sculpture, graphics.
Apr. 1 - Oct. 31: Tu.-Sa. 11-4.30; Su. 2-4.30.

THE OLD MANSE
Monument Street, Concord, Massachusetts 01742
House (1769) was home of the Emerson, Ripley and Hawthorne families. Period furnishings. Memorabilia of the three families who lived here.
Apr. 19 - May 31, Oct. 16 - Nov. 11, weekends and holidays 10-4.30. June 1 - Oct. 15, Tu.-Sa. 10-4.30; Su. 1-4.30.

ORCHARD HOUSE
399 Lexington Road, Concord, Massachusetts 01742
18th century house, at one time a school of philosophy. Memorabilia of Louisa May Alcott and her family.
Apr. 20 - Nov. 10: M.-Sa. 10-5; Su. 2-6.

RALPH WALDO EMERSON MEMORIAL MUSEUM
28 Cambridge Turnpike, Concord, Massachusetts 01742
House (1828), occupied by Emerson, 1835-82. Original furnishings. Emerson's personal possessions.
Apr. 19 - Oct. 1: Tu.-Sa., public holidays 10-11.30, 1.30-5.30; Su. 2.30-5.30.

MANN HOUSE
Hanover Street, Concord, Michigan 49237
House (1883). Victorian furnishings. Family photographs. Carriage house, with horse-drawn vehicles, farm-implements, household equipment.
Tu.-F. 10-5; Sa., Su., public holidays 1-5.

NEW HAMPSHIRE HISTORICAL SOCIETY MUSEUM
30 Park Street, Concord, New Hampshire 03301
History of New Hampshire. 17th-18th century period rooms. Paintings. Silver. Concord coach.
M.-Sa. 9-4. Closed public holidays, 3rd M. in April, 1st Sa. in May.

FRANKLIN PIERCE HOUSE
52 S. Main Street, Concord, New Hampshire 03301
House (1856), home of President Pierce, 1857-69. Period furnishings. Material relating to President Pierce.
Apr. 1 - Dec. 15, by appointment.

CONCORDIA

CLOUD COUNTY HISTORICAL MUSEUM
County Courthouse, Concordia, Kansas 66901
County history.
M.-F. 2-5.

CONNEAUT

CONNEAUT RAILROAD HISTORICAL MUSEUM
Depot Station, P.O. Box 643, Conneaut, Ohio 44030
In former New York Central depot (1900). Local railway history. Locomotives. Rolling stock. Equipment.
Memorial Day - Labour Day, daily 10-6.

CONNERSVILLE

HENRY H. BLOMMEL HISTORIC AUTOMOTIVE DATA COLLECTION
Route 5, Connersville, Indiana 47331
History of automobile industry and transport by automobile.
By appointment.

CONRAD

BANKA'S SHELL MUSEUM
403 S. Delaware Street, Conrad, Montana 59425
Geology. Molluscs. Indian artifacts from Mexico and Central America.
By appointment.

CONSTABLEVILLE

CONSTABLE HALL
Constableville, New York 13325
House (1810-19), built as copy of ancestral home in Dublin. Some original furnishings.
June 10 - Nov. 1: Tu.-Sa. 10-5; Su. 1-5.

CONSTANTINE

JOHN S. BARRY HOUSE
Constantine, Michigan 49042
House (1835-36), former home of Governor Barry. Local history collection. 19th century furniture.
By appointment.

CONWAY

FAULKNER COUNTY HISTORICAL SOCIETY MUSEUM
Box 731, Conway, Arkansas 72032
In log-cabin, Greathouse Home (c.1830). Local history.
Apr. 1 - Oct. 31, M.-F. 2.30-5.

LORD HOUSE
Main Street, Conway, New Hampshire 03818
House (1810). Local history. Agriculture. Transport. Costumes. Glass. Textiles.
June 1 - Oct. 31, W. 1-5. July 1 - Sept. 30, Sa. 1-5.

COOLIDGE

CASA GRANDE RUINS NATIONAL MONUMENT
Box 518, Coolidge, Arizona 85228
Natural history. Botany. Herbarium. Herpetology. Archaeology. Ethnology of the Pima and Papago Indians. Burial and cremation sites. Artifacts of the Pueblo and Hohokan Indians.
House, Casa Grande (1350-1450) and a number of pre-Columbian village sites are in the care of the Monument.
Daily 7-6.

COOPERSTOWN

BASEBALL HALL OF FAME AND MUSEUM
Main Street, Cooperstown, New York 13326
Plaques commemorating leading players. Trophies. Pictures. Equipment.
May 1 - Oct. 31, daily 9-9. Nov. 1 - Apr. 30, 9-5.

CARRIAGE AND HARNESS MUSEUM
Elk Street, Cooperstown, New York 13326
Horse-drawn vehicles. Harness and equipment.
May 1 - Labour Day, daily 9-12, 1-5. Labour Day - Apr. 30, M.-F. 9-12, 1-5; Sa. 9-12. Closed New Year, Thanksgiving, Christmas.

FARMERS MUSEUM
Lake Road, Cooperstown, New York 13326
Agricultural history. Farm vehicles, implements. Reconstruction of village crossroads (1790-1860).
May 1 - Oct. 31, daily 9-6. Nov. 1 - Apr. 30, Tu.-Sa. 9-5; Su. 2-5.

MUSEUM OF NEW YORK STATE HISTORICAL ASSOCIATION
Fenimore House, Lake Road, Cooperstown, New York 13326
American folk art. Life Masks. Portraits and landscapes relating to New York State. Memorabilia of James Fenimore Cooper. Costumes. Sculpture. Indian artifacts.
May 1 - June 30, Sept. 1 - Oct. 31, daily 9-6. July 1 - Aug. 31, daily 9-9. Nov. 1 - Apr. 30, daily 9-5. Closed New Year, Thanksgiving, Christmas.

INDIAN MUSEUM
1 Pioneer Street, Cooperstown, New York 13326
Indian life. Dioramas. Artifacts.
Labour Day - Oct. 15, May 1 - June 30, daily 1-5. Rest of year, daily 10-8.

MUSEUM OF HISTORICAL SOCIETY OF EARLY AMERICAN DECORATION
Cooperstown, New York 13326
Decorative arts, especially furniture, mirrors, clocks. Decorated tin and papier-mâché.
Nov. 1 - Apr. 30, Tu.-Sa., public holidays 9-5. Su. 1-5. May 1 - Oct. 31, daily 9-6. Closed New Year, Thanksgiving, Christmas.

COOS BAY

COOS ART MUSEUM
515 Market Avenue, Coos Bay, Oregon 97420
Works by contemporary local artists. Paintings. Sculpture. Graphics.
Tu.-Su. 1-4. Closed Dec. 25 - Jan. 2.

COPPER HARBOR

FORT WILKINS STATE PARK
Copper Harbor, Michigan 49918
Fort (1844), built to give military protection to copper miners. 13 restored buildings within stockade. Historical museum and period furnishings in one of officers' quarters.
May 15 - Oct. 15, daily 8.00 a.m.-8.00 p.m.

COQUILLE

COQUILLE VALLEY ART ASSOCIATION GALLERY
Box 625, Fairview Route, Coquille, Oregon 97423
Works by Oregon artists. Paintings. Textiles.
Tu., Th.-Su. 1-4; W. 9 a.m.-10 p.m. Closed public holidays.

CORAL GABLES

LOWE ART MUSEUM
University of Miami, 1301 Miller Drive, Coral Gables, Florida 33146
Archaeology. 15th-18th Century European painting. American Indian and Oriental art. Contemporary European and American paintings, sculpture, graphics.
M.-F. 12-5; Sa. 10-5; Su. 2-5. Closed New Year, Thanksgiving, Christmas.

CORDELE

WORLD WAR I AND II MUSEUM
Veterans Memorial State Park, Cordele, Georgia 31015
Material relating to both wars. Documents. Photographs. Uniforms. Equipment.
Tu.-Su. 10-6.

CORINNE

RAILROAD MUSEUM
Corinne, Utah 84307
Early steam locomotives. Railway coaches. Replica of Pony Express building. Section house, with Chinese laundry. Blacksmith's shop. Railway station.
May 1 - Sept. 30: M. by appointment; Tu.-Sa. 9-5; Su. 2-5.

CORNING

CORNING MUSEUM OF GLASS AND CORNING GLASS CENTER
Centerway - Houghton Park, Corning, New York 14830
History of glass-making. 200 inch telescope disc, duplicate of one cast for Palomar Observatory. Modern uses of glass.
June 1-30, Sept. 1 - Oct. 31, daily 9.30-5. July 1 - Aug. 31, 8.30-5. Rest of year, Tu.-Su. 9.30-5. Closed New Year, Thanksgiving, Christmas.

HORNBY MUSEUM
Hornby Forks, R.D.3, Corning, New York 14830
Domestic equipment. Farm implements and tools.
July 1 - Aug. 31, W.-F. 1-5. Other times by appointment.

ROCKWELL GALLERY
Rockwell's Department Store, Corning, New York 14830
Paintings, bronzes by Remington, Russell, Sharp and other Western American artists. Carder Steuben glass. Guns. Toys.
M.-Sa. 10-5.30 (F. 10-9).

CORNISH

SAINT-GAUDENS NATIONAL HISTORICAL SITE
Saint-Gaudens Road, Cornish, New Hampshire 03746
Studio (1800) of sculptor, Augustus Saint-Gaudens, (1848-1907). Works by Saint-Gaudens.
Aspet (1790), home of Saint-Gaudens, is under the same administration.
May 25 - Oct. 15, daily 8.30-5.

CORNWALL

CORNWALL HISTORICAL SOCIETY MUSEUM
Cornwall, Connecticut 06753
Local history.
May 1 - Oct. 31, by appointment.

CORNWALL FURNACE
Cornwall, Pennsylvania 17016
Charcoal iron furnace (1742, remodelled 1856-7), which made weapons and munitions during Revolutionary War. Charcoal store. Tools and equipment of early iron-making. Local mineral samples.
May 1 - Sept. 30: M.-Sa. 8.30-5; Su. 1-5. Oct. 1 - Apr. 30: M.-Sa. 9-4.30; Su. 1-4.30. Closed public holidays.

CORNWALL-ON-HUDSON

MUSEUM OF THE HUDSON HIGHLANDS
The Boulevard, Cornwall-on-Hudson, New York 12520
Natural history, history and paintings of the Hudson Highlands. Botany. Indian artifacts. Children's museum.
Sa.-Th., public holidays 2-5. Closed New Year, Easter, July 4, Thanksgiving, Christmas.

CORPUS CHRISTI

CORPUS CHRISTI MUSEUM
1919 N. Water Street, Corpus Christi, Texas 78401
Natural history. Gulf Coast shells, fossils. Local history and archaeology.
Tu.-Sa. 10-5. Su. 2-5.

CORRY

MUSEUM OF CORRY AREA HISTORICAL SOCIETY
Box 107, Mead Avenue, Corry, Pennsylvania 16407
History of Corry area. Agriculture. Transport. Industry. Costumes. Music.
June 1 - Sept. 30: Sa., Su., public holidays 2-8. Other times by appointment.

CORSICANA

PETROLEUM INDUSTRY PARK
401 S. 12th Street, Corsicana, Texas 75110
Early history and development of local, state and national oil industry.
Daily, never closed.

PIONEER VILLAGE
901 W. Park, Corsicana, Texas 75110
Museum of pioneer life in 7 log buildings (1838-65) moved to site, including Indian trading post, slave cabin, general store, blacksmith's shop.
M.-Sa. 9-5; Su. 1-5.

CORTEZ

FOUR CORNERS MUSEUM
700 E. Montezuma Street, Cortez, Colorado 81321
Local history. Pueblo Indian artifacts, including pottery, arrowheads.
M.-F. 10-8; Sa., 2-6. Closed public holidays.

CORTLAND

MUSEUM OF CORTLAND COUNTY HISTORICAL SOCIETY
25 Homer Avenue, Cortland, New York 13045
In Suggett House (c.1870). History of Cortland County. Indian artifacts. Pioneer tools and implements. Paintings.
M., W., F. 1-5. Closed public holidays.

SCIENCE MUSEUM
State University College, Science Building, Bowers Hall, Cortland, New York 13045
Geology. Gemstones. Fossils. Planetarium. Natural history. Botany. Anatomy. Aquarium. Biology. Physics.
M.-F. 7 a.m.-10 p.m.; Sa. 7-4, 5-10; University vacations, M.-F. 8-5. Closed public holidays.

CORVALLIS

HORNER MUSEUM
Coliseum, Oregon State University, Corvallis, Oregon 92331
Mineralogy. Palaeontology. Fossils. Natural history. Local history. Indian artifacts. Costumes. Coins. Glass. Decorative arts, especially Oriental.
M.-F. 9-5; Su. 2-5. Closed public holidays.

OREGON STATE UNIVERSITY NATURAL HISTORY MUSEUM
Corvallis, Oregon 97331
Natural history. Zoology.
Oct. 1-June 14, M.-F. 8-5. Sa. 8-12.

OREGON STATE UNIVERSITY MEMORIAL UNION BUILDING
Oregon State University, Corvallis, Oregon 97331
American paintings, sculpture.
M.-Th. 7-11; F., Sa. 7-1; Su. 7-11. Closed New Year, Thanksgiving, Christmas.

CORYDON

CORYDON CAPITOL STATE MEMORIAL
Corydon, Indiana 47112
Building (1816), with original furnishings.
Daily 8-12, 1-5.

WAYNE COUNTY HISTORICAL SOCIETY MUSEUM
Corydon, Iowa 50060
Natural history. Agriculture. Indian artifacts.
May-Nov., Tu.-Su., public holidays 1-5.

COSHOCTON

JOHNSON-HUMRICKHOUSE MEMORIAL MUSEUM
3rd and Sycamore Streets, Coshocton, Ohio 43812
In former school (1853). Furniture, domestic equipment, guns, used by pioneer Ohio families. Indian, Eskimo, Mexican artifacts. Chinese, Indian and Japanese art and handicrafts. European porcelain, pewter, glass.
Tu.-Sa. 1-4.30; Su. 2-5. Closed public holidays, except Memorial Day, Independence Day, Labour Day.

COTTONWOOD

ST. GERTRUDE'S MUSEUM
College of St. Gertrude, Cottonwood, Idaho 83522
Geology. Botany. Herbarium. Natural history. Postage stamps. Coins. Manuscripts. Indian material.
By appointment.

COTTONWOOD FALLS

RONIGER MEMORIAL MUSEUM
Cottonwood Falls, Kansas 66845
Local history. Indian artifacts. Natural history.
Daily 2-5.

COTUIT

HISTORICAL SOCIETY OF SANTUIT AND COTUIT
Main Street, Cotuit, Massachusetts 02635
House (1800-50). Period furnishings.
June 20-Sept. 30: Tu. 3-5; Su. 4-6.

COUDERSPORT

MUSEUM OF POTTER COUNTY HISTORICAL SOCIETY
308 N. Main Street, Coudersport, Pennsylvania 16915
Pioneer history.
M.-F. 2-4.

COULEE DAM

FORT SPOKANE MUSEUM
Box 37, Coulee Dam, Washington 99122
Local and military history. Exhibits of the Army period, 1880-99, and the Colville Indian Agency period, 1900-29. Buildings include guardhouse (1892), quartermaster stable (1884), powder magazine (1888) and reservoir house (1889).
Sept. 1-June 30, daily 8-5. July 1-Aug. 31, daily 8-8.

COUPEVILLE

ISLAND COUNTY HISTORICAL SOCIETY MUSEUM
Alexander Street, Coupeville, Washington 98239
Local history. Indian artifacts.
May 1-Sept. 30, W.-Su. 1.30-4.30.

COURTLAND

WALTER C. RAWLS MUSEUM
Courtland, Virginia 23837
Paintings, prints, sculpture by contemporary Virginia artists.
M.-F. 9-5; Sa. 9-12.30. Closed public holidays.

COVE FORT

OLD COVE FORT MUSEUM
Cove Fort, Utah 84713
Restored fort (1867). Pioneer relics. Guns. Indian artifacts.
Daily 7-8.

COVENTRY

NATHAN HALE HOMESTEAD
South Street, Coventry, Connecticut 06238
House (1776). Period furniture and furnishings, many original to the house. Hale family memorabilia.
Daily, May 15-Oct. 15, 1-5.

GENERAL NATHANAEL GREENE HOMESTEAD
50 Taft Street, Coventry, Rhode Island 02816
House (1770). Colonial furniture, from 1670.
Mar. 1-Nov. 30: W., Sa., Su. 2-5. Closed public holidays.

WESTERN RHODE ISLAND CIVIC HISTORICAL SOCIETY MUSEUM
Coventry, Rhode Island 02816
In Paine House. 18th-19th century furnishings. Local history.
By appointment.

COVINGTON

FOUNTAIN COUNTY HISTORICAL SOCIETY MUSEUM
Court House, Covington, Indiana 47932
Local history.
M.-F. 8-12, 1-4.30; Sa. 8-12. Closed public holidays.

BEHRINGER-CRAWFORD MEMORIAL MUSEUM OF NATURAL HISTORY
Devou Park, Covington, Kentucky 41011
Mineralogy. Palaeontology. Archaeology. Zoology. Local history.
Tu.-Sa., public holidays 9-5; Su. 1-5. Closed Christmas, Easter.

COXSACKIE

BRONCK HOUSE MUSEUM
Route 9W, Coxsackie, New York 12051
Museum based on group of houses and barns (1663-1738). Agricultural implements. Domestic equipment. Furniture.
June 15-Sept. 30: Tu.-Sa. 10-5; Su. 2-6.

CRAIG

MOFFAT COUNTY MUSEUM
Court House, Craig, Colorado 81625
Local history. Indian artifacts.
M.-F., 7-5. Sa., Su., public holidays, by appointment.

CRANFORD

CRANFORD HISTORICAL SOCIETY MUSEUM
124 N. Union Avenue, Cranford, New Jersey 07016
Building (1840). Local history.
Sa. 10-12; Su. 3-5.

CRANSTON

CRANSTON HISTORICAL SOCIETY MUSEUM
1351 Cranston Street, Cranston, Rhode Island 02910
Local history.
Joy Homestead (1750) and Governor Sprague Mansion (1790) are in the care of the Society.
July 4-Sept. 15, Tu., Su. 2-4.

CRATER LAKE

CRATER LAKE NATIONAL PARK VISITOR CENTER
Crater Lake, Oregon 97604
Geology. Mineralogy. Botany. Herbarium. Natural history. Local history.
June 15-Sept. 10, daily 8.15-7.

CRAWFORD

FORT ROBINSON MUSEUM
Box 304, Crawford, Nebraska 69339
Museum of military and Indian history, based on Fort buildings (1874-1905). These include blacksmith's and wheelwright's shop, harness repair shop and stable.
Apr. 1-Nov. 14: M.-Sa. 8-5; Su. 1-5. Rest of year by appointment.

CRAWFORDSVILLE

CONFEDERATE MUSEUM
Alexander J. Stephens State Park, Crawfordsville, Georgia 30631
Local, especially Confederate, history.
Liberty Hall (c.1780), with the slave quarters, is in the care of the Museum.
Tu.-Sa. 9-5; Su. 1-5. Closed New Year, Thanksgiving, Christmas.

GENERAL LEW WALLACE STUDY
East Pike Street, Crawfordsville, Indiana 47933
Lew Wallace's house (1896), with study of author of Ben Hur, contains his furniture and personal effects.
Apr. 10-Nov. 30: M., W.-Sa. 10.30-12, 1.30-5; Su. 1.30-5. Closed public holidays.

CREEDE

CREEDE MUSEUM
Creede, Colorado 81130
Local history.
July 1-Aug. 31, daily 1-5.

CRESCENT CITY

MUSEUM OF DEL NORTE COUNTY HISTORICAL SOCIETY
710 H Street, Crescent City, California 95531
Museum building (1926) was originally jail. Archaeology. Local history, especially of the lumber industry.
Battery Point Lighthouse (1856) and McNulty Pioneer Memorial Home (1926) are in the care of the Society.
Museum: Tu.-Sa. 1-4. Pioneer Home, Tu.-Sa. 10-12. Lighthouse: Sa.-Th. "daylight to dusk, when tide is favourable for crossing". Closed public holidays.

CRESSON

ALLEGHENY POSTAGE RAILROAD NATIONAL HISTORIC SITE
P.O. Box 247, Cresson, Pennsylvania 16630
In Stone House Tavern (1836). Railway, river and canal transport.
June-Sept., daily 9-8. Oct.-May, M.-F. 9-5; Sa., Su., public holidays 9-6.

HAL S. SMITH FARM MACHINERY MUSEUM
Box 88, Highway 377, Cresson, Texas 76035
Early steam tractors and other pioneer farm equipment. Syrup mill.
By appointment.

CRESTLINE

CRESTLINE SHUNK MUSEUM
211 Thoman Street, Crestline, Ohio 44827
Building (1860). Local history. Paintings. Farm tools and implements. Furniture. Domestic equipment. Railway history. Paintings.
Th., Sa. 1-5. Closed Jan. 1 - Feb. 28.

CRESTWOOD

THOMAS SAPPINGTON HOUSE
1015 S. Sappington Road, Crestwood, Missouri 63126
House (1808). Period furnishings. Decorative arts.
Tu.; Sa. 10-4; Su. 12-4. Closed New Year, Easter, July 4, Thanksgiving, Christmas.

CRESWELL

SOMERSET PLACE STATE HISTORIC SITE
Box 215, Creswell, North Carolina 27928
Restoration of former plantation. Plantation history. Includes Colony House (c.1829) and Collins Mansion House (c.1830), with bath house, wash-house, icehouse and other estate buildings.
Tu.-Sa. 9-5; Su. 1-5. Closed Thanksgiving, Dec. 24-6.

CRIPPLE CREEK

CRIPPLE CREEK DISTRICT MUSEUM
East Bennett Avenue, Cripple Creek, Colorado 80813
In former railroad depot (1896). Local history. Transport. Gold-mining. Cattle brands. Victorian furnishings.
May 31 - Sept. 30, daily 9.30-5.30. Oct. 1 - May 30, Sa., Su., 10-5. Closed New Year, Thanksgiving, Christmas.

CROOKSTON

POLK COUNTY HISTORICAL MUSEUM
N. Washington and Lowell Streets, Crookston, Minnesota 56716
In former McKinley School (1900). History of Polk County. Old store. Barber shop. Evolution of washing machine. Costumes. Indian artifacts. Agriculture. Railway history. Largest oxcart in world.
May 30 - Oct. 1, M.-Sa. 9-12, 1-6; Su. 12-6. Evenings by appointment.

CROSBY

DIVIDE COUNTY MUSEUM
Crosby, North Dakota 58730
Local history. Pioneer life.
June 1 - Aug. 31, daily 2-9.

CROSBYTON

CROSBYTON COUNTY PIONEER MEMORIAL MUSEUM
101 W. Main Street, Crosbyton, Texas 79322
In replica of Hank Smith house, first pioneer home in County (1876-7). Period rooms. Pioneer life. Early agricultural implements. Guns, saddles. Cowboy equipment.
Tu.-Sa. 9-12, 2-5; Su., public holidays 2-4.

CROSS RIVER

TRAILSIDE NATURE MUSEUM
Ward Pound Ridge Reservation, Cross River, New York 10518
Geology. Natural history. Entomology. Indian material.
W.-Su. 9-5.

CROSS VILLAGE

GREAT LAKES INDIAN MUSEUM
Cross Village, Michigan 49723
Indian artifacts. Ethnology.
June 15 - Labour Day, daily 9-6.

CROW AGENCY

CUSTER BATTLEFIELD NATIONAL MONUMENT
Crow Agency, Montana 59022
Material associated with Gen. George A. Custer and the Sioux War, especially Battle of the Little Bighorn.
May 1-31, 8-5. June 1 - Labour Day, 7 a.m.-8 p.m. Labour Day - Oct. 31, 8-5. Nov. 1 - Apr. 30, 8-4.30. Closed New Year, Thanksgiving, Christmas.

CROWELL

FOARD COUNTY MUSEUM
Box 608, McAdams Ranch, F.R.654, Crowell, Texas 79227
Ranch house (1918), with original furnishings. Family mementoes. Ranching memorabilia. Indian relics.
Su. 2-6. Other times by appointment.

CROWN POINT

OLD HOMESTEAD
227 South Court Street, Crown Point, Indiana 46307
House (1847), with period furnishings.
By appointment.

CROWN POINT RESERVATION
Route 8, Crown Point, New York 12928
Ruins of Fort St. Frederic (1731. French) and Fort Crown Point (1759. British). Museum of local and military history.
May 30 - Sept. 15, 8-4.30.

CRYSTAL FALLS

CRYSTAL FALLS IRON MINE
Crystal Falls, Michigan 49920
Mine was operational 1882-1907. Pumped out in 1960 and opened to public.
Daily 9-5.

CRYSTAL RIVER

CRYSTAL RIVER HISTORIC MEMORIAL
P.O. Box 85, Crystal River, Florida 32629
Natural history. Archaeology. Indian artifacts. Indian temple, burial and refuse mounds.
Daily 8-5.

CUERO

DEWITT COUNTY HISTORICAL MUSEUM
207 E. Main Street, Cuero, Texas 77954
Early history of County. Spanish American War and Civil War exhibits. Indian artifacts.
M.-F. 12-5. Closed public holidays.

CULBERTSON

MUSEUM OF NORTHEASTERN MONTANA THRESHERS AND ANTIQUE ASSOCIATION
Culbertson, Montana 59218
Old agricultural equipment and implements. Pioneer house.
Daily dawn-dusk.

CUMBERLAND

MUSEUM OF ALLEGANY COUNTY HISTORICAL SOCIETY
218 Washington Street, Cumberland, Maryland 21502
House (1856) with period kitchen, dining room and schoolroom. Local history. Costumes. Glass. History of medicine.
May 1 - Oct. 31: Su. 1.30-4.30.

GEORGE WASHINGTON'S HEADQUARTERS
Greene Street, Cumberland, Maryland 21502
Log Cabin (1755), used by Washington in 1794. Early history of Allegany County. French and Indian war relics.
By appointment.

CUMMINGTON

WILLIAM CULLEN BRYANT HOMESTEAD
Cummington, Massachusetts 01026
House (1794) was home of the poet, W. C. Bryant. Bryant memorabilia.
June 15 - Sept. 15, M., W., F. 2.30-5.

CURRIE

MOORES CREEK NATIONAL MILITARY PARK MUSEUM
Currie, North Carolina 28435
On site of Battle of Moore's Creek. Material illustrating Revolutionary War period in North Carolina.
Daily 8-5. Closed Christmas.

CUSTER

CUSTER STATE PARK
Historical Museum, Custer, South Dakota 57730
Local history. Geology. Forestry.
May 15 - Sept. 30, daily.

WIEHE'S FRONTIER MUSEUM
25 N. 5th Street, Custer, South Dakota 57730
Frontier and Indian history.
June 15 - Aug. 30, M.-Sa. 8-8; Su. 9-9.

CUTCHOGUE

OLD HOUSE
Main Road, Cutchogue, New York 11935
House (c.1649). Furnishings of Colonial period.
July 1 - Aug. 31, daily 2-5. June 1-30, Sept. 1-30: Sa., Su. 1-5.

CUYAHOGA FALLS

RAILWAYS OF AMERICA
3656 Akron-Cleve Road, Cuyahoga Falls, Ohio 44221
In railway station (1900). Railway history, including rolling stock. Circus history.
Daily 11-8.

CUYAMACA

CUYAMACA STATE PARK MUSEUM
Cuyamaca, California 93214
History and culture of the Diegueno Indians. Indian artifacts.
Daily.

DADE CITY

PIONEER FLORIDA MUSEUM
1 mile W. of Dade City, Florida 33525
History of settlement of Florida. Agriculture.
Su. 2-5.

DAHLONEGA

DAHLONEGA COURTHOUSE GOLD MUSEUM
P.O. Box 478, Dahlonega, Georgia 30533
Courthouse building (1836). Local history.
Oct. 1 - Apr. 30: Tu.-Sa. 9-5; Su. 2-5. May 1 - Sept. 30: Tu.-Sa. 9-5.30; Su. 2-5.30.

GOLD HILLS OF OLD DAHLONEGA
Highway 60, Dahlonega, Georgia 30533
In former Lumpkin County Courthouse (1836). Gold specimens. Photographs illustrating history of local gold-mining industry, 1828-61. Miner's workshop building (1850).
Apr. 1 - May 31, Sa., Su. 10-7. June 1 - Oct. 31, Tu.-Su. 10-7.

DALLAS

'AGE OF STEAM' RAILROAD MUSEUM
Fair Park, Washington Avenue, Dallas, Texas 75225
Locomotives, coaches and equipment of the steam railway years. Buildings include first Dallas station (1872).
June 1 - Aug. 31, daily 10-5. Sept. 1 - May 31, Su. 11-5. During State Fair in Aug., daily 10-7.

BAYLOR DENTAL MUSEUM
800 Hall Street, Dallas, Texas 75226
Early dental equipment, instruments and materials.
By appointment.

DALLAS HISTORICAL SOCIETY
Hall of State, Fair Park, Dallas, Texas 75226
Texas history.
M.-Sa. 9-5; Su., public holidays 2-6. Closed Easter, Christmas, 2 weeks before Texas State Fair.

DALLAS MUSEUM OF FASHION
2300 Stemmons Freeway, Dallas, Texas 75207
Exhibits on 19th-20th century fashion, including accessories.
Tu.-F. 10.30-3.30.

DALLAS MUSEUM OF FINE ARTS
Fair Park, 2nd Avenue, Dallas, Texas 75226
African art. Pre-Columbian art. Contemporary European paintings, sculpture. 18th-20th century American paintings. French impressionist paintings. Texas folk art. 16th-19th century European paintings, prints, drawings, sculpture. Egyptian, Etruscan, Greek, Near-Eastern antiquities.
Tu.-Sa. 10-5; Su., public holidays 12-6.

DALLAS HEALTH AND SCIENCE MUSEUM
1st and Forest Avenue, Fair Park, Dallas, Texas 75226
Science. Planetarium. Anatomy and physiology. Story of Life gallery (human reproduction). Exhibits on good health and human disease.
M.-Sa. 9-5; Su., public holidays 2-6. Closed fortnight before State Fair.

DALLAS MUSEUM OF NATURAL HISTORY
Box 26193, Fair Park, Dallas, Texas 75226
Natural history of Texas. Dioramas of mammals, birds. Porcelain.
M.-Sa. 8-5; Su. 12-6. Closed Christmas.

McCORD THEATER MUSEUM AND LIBRARY
Easterwood Building, 500 N. Akard Street, Dallas, Texas 75201
Theatre history. Playbooks. Scripts. Photographs. Engravings. Designs. Costumes. Memorabilia of theatre and cinema personalities.
Tu., F. 10-4; other times by appointment.

MEADOWS MUSEUM AND SCULPTURE COURT
Owen Fine Arts Center, Southern Methodist University, Dallas, Texas 75222
15th-20th century Spanish paintings. 19th-20th century sculpture.
M.-Sa. 10-5; Su. 1-5. Closed Christmas, New Year.

MILLERMORE MUSEUM
1400 E. Ervay Street, Dallas, Texas 72505
House (c.1860). Period rooms, 1840-70.
Tu.-F. 10.30-1.30; 1st, 3rd Su. each month 1.30-4.30. Closed Sept. 1-30 and 3rd Su. in Dec.

POLLOCK GALLERIES
Owen Arts Center, Southern Methodist University, Dallas, Texas 75222
Works by contemporary Texas artists.
M.-Sa. 9-5; Su. 1-5.

TEXAS SPORTS HALL OF FAME
Varied Exhibits Building, State Fair of Texas, Dallas, Texas 75221
Memorabilia of Texans noted in field of sport. Equipment. Photographs.
M.-F. 10-6; Sa. 10-9; Su. 2-9. Closed Christmas.

DALTON

CRANE MUSEUM
Housatonic Street, Dalton, Massachusetts 01226
In Old Stone Mill (1844). History of Crane and Co., papermakers. U.S. Currency paper.
June 1 - Sept. 30: M.-F., except public holidays, 2-5.

DAMARISCOTTA

CHAPMAN-HALL HOUSE PRESERVATION SOCIETY
Main Street, Damariscotta, Maine 04543
House (1754). 18th-19th century furniture, and furnishings. Local and maritime history. Handicrafts.
June 15 - Sept. 15, Tu.-Su. 1-5.

DANBURY

DANBURY SCOTT-FANTON MUSEUM
43-45 Main Street, Danbury, Connecticut 06810
In 3 historic buildings, moved to Museum site. David Taylor house (c.1750) contains Chinese export porcelain, Lowestoft and Canton china, Connecticut furniture, children's clothing and toys, dresses, needlework, uniforms. The Dodd house and hat shop (1770) - by appointment only - shows history of local hatting industry. The Charles Ives house (c.1780), home of the composer, contains Ives family furniture and memorabilia.
W.-F. 2-5; Sa. 10-5; Su. 1-5.

DANSVILLE

DANSVILLE AREA HISTORICAL MUSEUM
Church and W. Liberty Streets, Dansville, New York 14437
Local history.
By appointment.

DANVERS

DANVERS HISTORICAL SOCIETY MUSEUM
Memorial Hall, 13 Page Street, Danvers, Massachusetts 01923
Local history. Handicrafts. 17th-18th century furnishings. Paintings. Costumes. Uniforms. Guns. Coins. Indian artifacts.
July-Aug., W. 2-4. Other times by appointment.

JEREMIAH PAGE HOUSE
11 Page Street, Danvers, Massachusetts 01923
House (1754). Period furnishings.
July-Aug., W. 2-4. Other times by appointment.

REBECCA NOURSE HOUSE
149 Pine Street, Danvers, Massachusetts 01923
House (1650), owned by Francis Nourse, whose wife was hanged as a witch. Material relating to history of Massachusetts 1650-1700.
Tu., Th., Su. 1-5.

DANVERS PORT

SAMUEL FOWLER HOUSE
166 High Street, Danvers Port, Massachusetts 01923
House (1810). Original wallpapers. Family furniture of Federal and Empire periods.
June-Sept., Tu., Th., Sa. 1-5.

DANVILLE

VERMILION COUNTY MUSEUM SOCIETY
116 N. Gilbert Street, Danville, Illinois 61832
Natural history. Botany. Herbarium. Local history. Paintings. Sculpture. Graphics. Decorative arts.
Mann's Chapel (1857) and Dr. Fithian Home (1857) are in the care of the Society.
Tu.-Sa. 10-5; Su. 1-5. Closed Thanksgiving, Christmas.

CONSTITUTION SQUARE STATE PARK MUSEUM
U.S. Highways 150 and 127, Danville, Kentucky 40422
Museum based on Post Office (1792), and replicas of the late 18th-early 19th century jail, courthouse, meeting house.
Daily 9-5.

MCDOWELL HOUSE AND APOTHECARY SHOP
125-127 S. 2nd Street, Danville, Kentucky 40422
Buildings of 1800 and 1795. Botany. Herbarium. Paintings. Local history. History of pharmacy and medicine.
M.-Sa. 10-4; Su. 2-4.

MONTOUR COUNTY HISTORICAL SOCIETY MUSEUM
1 Bloom Street, Danville, Pennsylvania 17821
Local history.
Summer: W. 1.30-4.30.

NATIONAL TOBACCO AND TEXTILE MUSEUM
614 Lynn Street, Danville, Virginia 24541
In former tobacco factory (1880). History of tobacco and textile industries.
By appointment.

DARIEN

BATES-SCOFIELD HOMESTEAD
45 Old King's Highway North, Darien, Connecticut 06820
House (c.1730). Folklore. Costumes.
W. 10-4; Su. 2.30-4.30. Closed Christmas.

MILESTONE VILLAGE MUSEUM
1844 Boston Post Road, Darien, Connecticut 06820
Village museum. Restored houses, stores, workshops, theatre. Costumes. Textiles.
By appointment.

FORT KING GEORGE
P.O. Box 711, Darien, Georgia 31305
Material illustrating history of Fort King George; (1721), oldest fort in Georgia, subsequently sawmilling centre.
Oct. 1 - Apr. 30: Tu.-Sa. 9-5; Su. 2-5. May 1 - Sept. 30: Tu.-Sa. 9-5.30; Su. 2-5.30. Closed Thanksgiving, Christmas.

DARTMOUTH

CHILDREN'S MUSEUM
Russell Mills Road, Dartmouth, Massachusetts 02714
Natural history. Local history.
Tu.-F. 11-4; Sa., Su. 2-4. Closed Christmas - Washington's birthday, Easter, July 4, Thanksgiving.

DAVENPORT

DAVENPORT MUNICIPAL ART GALLERY
1737 W. 12th Street, Davenport, Iowa 52804
Haiti primitive art. European, American, Spanish-American and Mexican Colonial paintings. American sculpture, folk art. Japanese prints. Cameos and intaglios.
Tu.-Sa. 10-4.30; Su. 1-4.30. Closed public holidays.

DAVENPORT MUSEUM
1717 W. 12th Street, Davenport, Iowa 52804
Palaeontology. Botany. Natural history. Anthropology. Ethnology. Archaeology. Primitive art. Prints. Drawings. English water-colours. Chinese and Japanese art. History of the Mississippi Valley.
M.-Sa. 9-5; Su. 1-5. Closed public holidays.

LINCOLN COUNTY HISTORICAL MUSEUM
P.O. Box 585, Davenport, Washington 99122
County history. Agricultural implements. Costumes. Furniture. Guns. Indian artifacts.
By appointment.

DAVIDSON

CUNNINGHAM FINE ARTS CENTER
Davidson College, Davidson, North Carolina 28036
Contemporary European and American drawings, lithographs.
M.-Sa. 9-9.

DAVIS

MEMORIAL UNION ART GALLERY
University of California, Davis, California 95616
19th-20th century European prints, drawings. Contemporary American paintings, sculpture, prints, photographs.
M.-F., 8-5; Sa., Su., 1-4. Closed school vacations.

MUSEUM OF ENTOMOLOGY
Department of Entomology, University of California, Davis, California 95616
Arthropod specimens. Insectology.
M.-F. 8-5. Closed public holidays.

DAVISTON

HORSESHOE BEND NATIONAL MILITARY PARK
Route 1, Box 63, Daviston, Alabama 36256
Site of final battle in Creek Indian War (1814). Military equipment. Indian artifacts.
M.-F., 8-4.30; Sa., Su. 8-5.30. Closed Christmas.

DAYTON

AULLWOOD AUDUBON CENTER
1000 Aullwood Road, Dayton, Ohio 45414
Herbarium. Natural history.
Nov. 1 - Mar. 31, M.-Sa. 9-5. Apr. 1 - Oct. 31, M.-Sa. 7 a.m.-8 p.m. Closed public holidays.

AULLWOOD AUDUBON FARM
9101 Frederick Road, Dayton, Ohio 45414
Agricultural history.
M.-Sa. 9-5; Su. 1-5. Closed public holidays.

DAYTON ART INSTITUTE
Forest and Riverview Avenues, Dayton, Ohio 45401
Primitive and pre-Columbian art. Mediterranean, Near Eastern and Oriental art. 16th-20th century European and American paintings, sculpture, prints, ceramics, decorative arts. Archaeology.
Tu.-F. 12-5; Sa. 9-5; Su. 12-5. Closed public holidays.

DAYTON MUSEUM OF NATURAL HISTORY
2629 Ridge Avenue, Dayton, Ohio 45414
Geology. Palaeontology. Astronomy. Planetarium. Botany. Herbarium. Natural history. Anthropology. Ethnology. Indian material.
M., W., Th., Sa. 9-6; Tu., F. 9-9; Su. 2-6. Closed public holidays.

DAYTON POWER AND LIGHT COMPANY MUSEUM
25 N. Main Street, Dayton, Ohio 45401
History of gas and electricity as local public utilities.
M.-F. 8-5. Evenings by appointment.

DEEDS CARILLON AND CELESTRON
2001 S. Patterson Street, Dayton, Ohio 45409
Open-air museum. History of transport. Wright Brothers aeroplane (1905). Concord coach. Conestoga waggon. Railway coach (1903). Grasshopper locomotive. Tram (1903). Early cars. Lock of Miami and Erie Canal.
Newcom Tavern (1798) and pioneer house (1815) are in the care of the Museum.
May 1 - Oct. 31: Tu.-Sa. 10-8.30; Su. 1-8.30.

PAUL L. DUNBAR HOUSE
219 Summit Street, Dayton, Ohio 45407
Home of black poet, Paul Lawrence Dunbar. Memorabilia of Dunbar.
June 1 - Sept. 15: Sa., Su., public holidays 10-5.

MUSEUM OF MONTGOMERY COUNTY HISTORICAL SOCIETY
Old Court House, Dayton, Ohio 45402
In old Court House (1847-50). History of Montgomery County. Pioneer life.
M.-F. 8.30-4.30. Closed public holidays.

U.S. AIR FORCE MUSEUM
Wright-Patterson Air Force Base, Dayton, Ohio 45433
History of aviation and of U.S. Air Force.
M.-F. 9-5; Sa., Su. 10-6. Closed Christmas.

DAYTONA BEACH

HALIFAX HISTORICAL SOCIETY MUSEUM
224 1/2 S. Beach Street, Daytona Beach, Florida 32018
Natural history. Archaeology. Planetarium. Indian artifacts. Paintings.
Cuban Art Museum (c.1925), former home of Batista, is in the care of the Society.
Daily 9-12, 2-5. Closed public holidays.

MUSEUM OF ART AND SCIENCES
1040 Museum Boulevard, Daytona Beach, Florida 32014
18th-20th century Cuban paintings. Caribbean, Central American, United States paintings, sculpture, drawings, decorative art. Planetarium.
M.-Sa. 9-5; Su. 1-5. Closed public holidays.

DEADWOOD

ADAMS MEMORIAL HALL MUSEUM
54 Sherman, Deadwood, South Dakota 57732
Geology. Pioneer history. Costumes. Indian artifacts.
Oct.-Apr., M.-Sa. 9-12, 1-5; Su. 2-5. May-Sept., Daily 8-8. Closed Christmas, New Year.

DEANSBORO

MUSICAL MUSEUM
Route 12B, Deansboro, New York 13328
Old musical instruments. Melodeons. Phonograph. Musical boxes. Orchestreons. Nickolodeons. Early pipe organs. Street organs.
Daily 10-5. Closed Thanksgiving, Christmas.

DEARBORN

COMMANDANT'S QUARTERS
21950 Michigan Avenue, Dearborn, Michigan 48124
The most important remaining structure of the Detroit Arsenal. House (1833). Military and pioneer history. 19th century furniture, costumes.
Tu.-F. 10.30-6.30; Sa. 9-5; Su. 2-5. Closed national holidays.

DEARBORN HISTORICAL MUSEUM
915 Brady Street, Dearborn, Michigan 48124
In McFadden-Ross House (1839). Local history. Archaeology. Industry. Indian artifacts. Transport. Agriculture. Textiles. Costumes. Paintings.
Commandant's Quarters (1833) are in the care of the Museum.
Tu.-F. 10.30-5.30; Sa. 9-5; Su. 2-5. Closed public holidays.

GREENFIELD VILLAGE AND HENRY FORD MUSEUM
Oakwood Boulevard, Dearborn, Michigan 41121
Mechanical arts hall, covering agriculture, handicrafts, industrial machinery, power, communications, lighting, transport. Decorative arts galleries. Street of early American shops. Material associated with Washington, Lincoln, Edison, McCormick, Byrd, Lindbergh. 100 historical buildings have been re-assembled around village green. They include parts of factories, workshops, Edison's Menlo Park laboratory and homes of famous Americans.
May 1 - Sept. 30, daily 9-6. Oct. 1 - Apr. 30, M.-F. 9-5. Closed New Year, Thanksgiving, Christmas.

DEARBORN HEIGHTS

DEARBORN HEIGHTS HISTORICAL MUSEUM
6045 Fenton Avenue, Dearborn Heights, Michigan 48127
In former schoolhouse (1876). Local history. Indian artifacts.
Tu., Th. 2-5.

DEATH VALLEY

DEATH VALLEY MUSEUM
Death Valley National Monument, Death Valley, California 92328
Geology. Archaeology. Natural history. Herbarium. Anthropology. Local history.
Harmony borax works (1883) and a group of charcoal kilns (1876) are in the care of the Museum.
Apr. 1 - Oct. 31, 8-5; Nov. 1 - Mar. 31, 8-9.

DEATH VALLEY SCOTTY'S CASTLE
Death Valley, California 92328
Castle in Spanish-Moorish style, built by Death Valley Scotty. Spanish leather hangings, tiles, carved beams, paintings.
Daily 9-5.

DE BARY

DE BARY HALL STATE MUSEUM
210 Sunrise Boulevard, De Bary, Florida 32713
Mansion (1871), built by Baron Frederick de Bary, with every comfort available at the time, including indoor plumbing, life and ice-house. 19th century furnishings. Original coal and wood stove and 7 ft. ice-boxes in kitchen. De Bary's collection of hermetically sealed rare birds. Paintings. Sculpture. Drawings.
Tu.-Su. 1-5.

DECATUR

DEKALB HISTORICAL SOCIETY MUSEUM
215 Sycamore Street, Decatur, Georgia 30030
Early County history.
M.-Sa. 10-6.

KIRKLAND FINE ARTS CENTER
Millikin University, Decatur, Illinois 62522
19th-20th century American paintings, sculpture, decorative arts.
M.-Th. 12-9; F.-Su. 12-6. Closed University vacations.

OLD STONE PRISON
103 E. Pecan Street, Decatur, Texas 76234
Basement of house was first County jail. Pre-1900 furnishings.
By appointment.

WISE COUNTY HERITAGE MUSEUM
1602 S. College Street, Decatur, Texas 76234
County history.
By appointment.

DECORAH

NORWEGIAN-AMERICAN MUSEUM
502 W. Water Street, Decorah, Iowa 52101
History of Norwegian immigration and settlement. Agriculture. Industry. Costumes. Domestic life. Paintings.
4 early buildings (1851-60) are in the care of the Museum.
May 1 - June 30, Sept 1., Oct. 31, daily 10-4. July 1 - Aug. 31, daily 9-5.

DEDHAM

DEDHAM HISTORICAL SOCIETY MUSEUM
612 High Street, Dedham, Massachusetts 02026
History of Dedham. Industry. Portraits. Paintings. Furniture. Pottery. Indian material.
Powder house (1776) is in the care of the Society.
Sept. 1 - June 30, M.-Sa. 2-5. July 1 - Aug. 31, M.-F. 2-5. Closed public holidays.

FAIRBANKS HOUSE
511 East Street, Dedham, Massachusetts 02026
Frame house (1636). Period furnishings.
Tu.-Su., public holidays. 9-5.

DEERFIELD

HELEN GEIER FLYNT FABRIC HALL
The Street, Deerfield, Massachusetts 01342
Costumes. Textiles. Decorative arts.
May 1 - Oct. 31: M.-Sa. 9.30-4.30; Su. 1.30-4.30. Nov. 1 - Apr. 30: M.-Sa. 10-3.30; Su. 1.30-3.30. Closed Thanksgiving, Dec. 15 - Jan. 5.

HISTORIC DEERFIELD
The Street, Deerfield, Massachusetts 01342
Local history. Folklore. Furniture. Costumes. Paintings Glass. Pottery.
8 houses (1717-1824) are in the care of the Foundation.
May 1 - Oct. 31: M.-Sa. 9.30-4.30; Su. 1.30-4.30. Nov. 1 - Apr. 30: M.-Sa. 10-3.30; Su. 1.30-3.30. Closed Thanksgiving, Dec. 15 - Jan. 5.

HILSON GALLERY
Deerfield Academy, Deerfield, Massachusetts 01342
Paintings, sculpture, graphics, decorative arts by contemporary regional artists.
Nov. 1 - Apr. 30: Sa., Su. 2-5.

INDIAN HOUSE MEMORIAL
Main Street, Deerfield, Massachusetts 01342
Indian history.
May 1 - Oct. 15: M., W.-Sa. 9.30-12, 1-5; Su. 1-5; public holidays 9-12, 1-5.

MEMORIAL HALL COLONIAL MUSEUM
Deerfield, Massachusetts 01342
In first building of Deerfield Academy (1798). Indian relics. Period rooms. 18th-19th century furniture. Agricultural implements. Inn signs. Paintings. Musical instruments.
Apr.-Nov., M.-Sa. 9.30-5; Su. 1.30-5.

PARKER AND RUSSELL SILVER SHOP
The Street, Deerfield, Massachusetts 01342
In former silver shop (1844). Early American silver. Local history.
May 1 - Oct. 31: M.-Sa. 9.30-4.30; Su. 1.30-4.30. Nov. 1 - Apr. 30: M.-Sa. 10-3.30; Su. 1.30-3.30. Closed Thanksgiving, Dec. 15 - Jan. 5.

WILSON PRINTING HOUSE
The Street, Deerfield, Massachusetts 01342
Building (1816). 19th century printing equipment. Books printed in the building.
May 1 - Oct. 31: M.-Sa. 9.30-12, 1-4.30; Su. 1.30-4.30. Nov. 1 - Apr. 30: M.-Sa. 10-3.30; Su. 1.30-3.30. Closed Thanksgiving, Dec. 15 - Jan. 5.

DEER ISLE

DEER ISLE-STONINGTON HISTORICAL SOCIETY MUSEUM
Deer Isle, Maine 04627
In Salome Sellers House (1830). Local history. Agriculture. Indian artifacts. Costumes. Maritime history.
July 1 - Sept. 15: W. 2-5; Sa., Su. 2-5.

DEER LODGE

POWELL COUNTY MUSEUM AND ARTS FOUNDATION
City Hall, Deer Lodge, Montana 59722
Local history.
By appointment.

DEER PARK

SAN JACINTO MUSEUM OF HISTORY
P.O. Box 758, Deer Park, Texas 77536
History of the region and of Texas.
June 1 - Labour Day, M.-Sa. 9.30-5.30; Su. 10-6. Rest of year, closed M. Closed Dec. 24-25.

DEFIANCE

DANIEL BOONE HOME
Highway F, Defiance, Missouri 63341
House (1803-10), designed and lived in by Daniel Boone. Furniture and tools belonging to Boone family.
Daily 8.30-dusk. Closed Christmas.

DEKALB

ANTHROPOLOGY MUSEUM
Northern Illinois University, DeKalb, Illinois 60115
Ethnography of N., S. and Central America, S.E. Asia, Pacific Islands, Africa, Greece. North American archaeology.
M.-Sa. 8 a.m. - 9 p.m. Closed university vacations.

ELLWOOD HOUSE MUSEUM
509 North First Street, DeKalb, Illinois 60115
House (1879). Local history. Costumes. Barbed wire collection.
Apr. 1 - Dec. 15: W., Su. 2-4.30.

DELAFIELD

HAWKS INN
428 Wells Street, Delafield, Wisconsin 53018
Building (1846), restored stage coach inn. Period furniture.
May 28 - Sept. 30, Su. 1-4. June 1 - Aug. 31, W. 1-4. Other times by appointment.

DE LAND

DE LAND MUSEUM
449 E. New York Avenue, De Land, Florida 32720
In former home of Henry De Land. Geology. Mineralogy. Natural history. Indian material. Costumes.
M.-F. 1-5; Sa. 10-12. 1st Sa. in month 3-5. Closed public holidays.

GILLESPIE MUSEUM OF MINERALS
Stetson University, De Land, Florida 32720
Mineralogy.
M.-F. 9-4.30. Closed public holidays.

L. L. RICE PLANETARIUM AND MONROE HEATH MUSEUM
Stetson University, De Land, Florida 32720
Planetarium. Geology. Anthropology. Zoology. Archaeology.
By appointment.

STETSON UNIVERSITY GALLERY OF ART
De Land, Florida 32720
19th-20th century American paintings, sculpture, graphics.
M.-F. 9-4; Sa., Su. 2-4. Closed public holidays.

DELANO

DELANO HERITAGE PARK MUSEUM
Lexington and Garces Streets, Delano, California 92328
Local, including agricultural, history.
Heritage House (1890) and Hasmine School (1916) are in the care of the Museum.
By appointment.

DELAWARE

MUSEUM OF DELAWARE COUNTY HISTORICAL SOCIETY
157 E. Williams Street, Delaware, Ohio 43015
History of early settlement of Delaware County.
W., Su. 2-4.30.

OHIO WESLEYAN UNIVERSITY
Department of Fine Arts, Lyon Art Hall, Delaware, Ohio 43015
Persian, Peruvian, Mayan pottery. Chinese, Japanese porcelain. Paintings. Sculpture. Prints.
Daily 9 a.m. - 10 p.m.

DELAWARE CITY

FORT DELAWARE
Pea Patch Island, Delaware City, Delaware 19706
On site of Fort Delaware (1848-59). Local history, especially material relating to Delaware's part in the Civil War.
Sa., Su., public holidays, June 1 - Oct. 31, 12-7.

DE LEON

TEXAS CENTRAL RAILROAD MUSEUM
De Leon Railroad Station, De Leon, Texas 76446
Railway rolling stock and equipment. Photographs.
May 30 - Sept. 1: Sa., Su. 8-5.

DELHI

FRISBEE HOUSE MUSEUM
Route 10, Delhi, New York 13753
House (1804), headquarters of Delaware County Historical Association. Period furnishings. Farm kitchen. Bathroom of 1890s. Laundry shed, with collection of old washing machines. Dairy room. Serving room. Nursery. Farm tools. The Museum also contains the Crow Hill schoolhouse, Amos Wood gun shop and a toll-gate house.
Memorial Day - Labour day: Sa., Su. 2-4. Other times by appointment.

DEL RIO

WHITEHEAD MEMORIAL MUSEUM
1308 S. Main Street, Del Rio, Texas 78840
In old Perry Mercantile Establishment. Life of early settlers. Costumes.
M.-F. 9-11, 3-5.

DELTA

DELTA COUNTY HISTORICAL SOCIETY MUSEUM
Box 125, Delta, Colorado 81416
Natural history. Local history. Indian history. Industry. Agriculture. Transport.
June 1 - Sept. 30, M.-Th., 1.30-4.30. All year, F. 1.30-4.30.

DELTON

BERNARD HISTORICAL SOCIETY MUSEUM
Rural Route 1, Delton, Michigan 49046
Local history.
In one-room schoolhouse (1873). Local history.
May 1 - June 30, Su. 1-5. July 1 - Aug. 31, daily 1-5. Sept. 1 - Oct. 31, Su. 1-5.

DEMING

LUNA COUNTY MUSEUM
300 S. Nickel Avenue, Deming, New Mexico 88030
Geology. Minerals. Local history. Folklore. Indian artifacts. Paintings.
Tu., Th. 11-5; Sa. 10-5.

DEMOPOLIS

MARENGO COUNTY HISTORICAL SOCIETY MUSEUM
North Commissioners Avenue, Demopolis, Alabama 36732
Regional history. Costumes.
Bluff Hall (1832-50) is in the care of the Society.
Su. 2-5. Closed Thanksgiving, Christmas.

DENISON

EISENHOWER BIRTHPLACE STATE PARK
208 E. Day Street, Denison, Texas 75020
Restored house (1883), in which President Eisenhower was born. Period furnishings. Personal possessions of the President.
Daily 10-12, 1-5.

DENTON

NTSU STATE HISTORICAL COLLECTION
W. Mulberry Street and Avenue A, North Texas State University Campus, Denton, Texas 76203
Life of early settlers. Ranching industry. Firearms. Dolls.
M.-Sa. 2-5. Closed university vacations.

STATE MUSEUM OF THE D.A.R.
1103 Bell Avenue, Two Campus, Household Arts and Sciences Building, Denton, Texas 76204
Furnishings. Costumes. Inaugural gowns of the wives of Presidents and Governors of Texas.
M.-F. 9-12, 1.30-5; Sa. 9-12.

TEXAS WOMEN'S UNIVERSITY ART GALLERIES
1 Circle Drive, Denton, Texas 76204
Primitive art. African masks, figurines. N.W. Coast Indian wood carvings. Eskimo carvings.
M.-F. 8-5; Sa. 8-12.

DENVER

CHIEF IRON SHELL MUSEUM
12 West Irvington Street, Denver, Colorado 80203
Indian history. Artifacts. Glass beads.
M.-Th., Sa., 9-11, 1-4; F., 9-11, 1-4, 7-9. Closed New Year, Memorial Day, July 4, Thanksgiving, Christmas.

COLORADO STATE MUSEUM
200 14th Avenue, Denver, Colorado 80203
Mineralogy. Mesa Verde archaeology. Colorado history. Culture of Ute Indians. Late 19th century furnishings.
M.-F., 9-5; Sa., Su., public holidays, 10-5. Closed Christmas.

COLORADO TRANSPORTATION MUSEUM
15th and Platte Street, Denver, Colorado 80202
In former theatre (1871). Transport. Aeronautics. Power Station (1901) is in the care of the Museum.
Daily 11-6.

DENVER ART MUSEUM
100 West 14th Avenue, Parkway, Denver, Colorado 80204
South American, African and Oriental art. 18th-20th Century American paintings. European, North African, Near Eastern paintings and sculpture. Costumes. Textiles. Period rooms.
Tu.-Sa., 9-5; W. 6 p.m. - 9; Su., 1-5. Closed public holidays.

DENVER BOTANIC GARDENS
909 York Street, Denver, Colorado 80206
Herbarium.
M.-Th., 9-5; F., 9-5. 7-9; Sa., Su., 10-5. Closed Christmas, public holidays.

DENVER MUSEUM OF NATURAL HISTORY
City Park, Denver, Colorado 80205
Palaeontology. Mineralogy. Archaeology. Natural history. Big-game mammals of Colorado. Habitat fossils of bears and sea-mammals. Special collections from Australasia and South America. Ecology.
May 1 - Sept. 30, M.-Sa., 9-5; Su., public holidays, 12-5. Oct. 1 - Apr. 30, M.-Sa., 9-4.30; Su., public holidays, 12-5. Closed New Year, Thanksgiving, Christmas.

FORNEY TRANSPORTATION MUSEUM
1416 Platte Street, Denver, Colorado 80202
History of transport, agriculture, industry. Costumes.
May 1 - Sept. 30, M.-Sa., 10-7; Su., 1-7. Oct. 1 - Apr. 30, M.-Sa., 10-5; Su., 1-7. Closed Christmas.

MUSEUM OF THE STATE HISTORICAL SOCIETY OF COLORADO
200 14th Avenue, Denver, Colorado 80203
Local history and archaeology. Anthropology. Ethnology. Indian history. Coins. Paintings. Textiles.
10 historic buildings are in the care of the Society. They include an ore processing mill (1875) at Georgetown and the railroad station (1880) at Silver Plume.
M.-F., 9-5; Sa., Su., Holidays, 10-5. Closed Christmas.

VETERAN CAR MUSEUM
2030 South Cherokee, Denver, Colorado 80223
Old cars. Motoring clothes. Photographs, prints, illustrating history of motoring. Old watches, costume jewellery. Indian handicrafts.
M.-F., 9-5; Sa., 9-12.30.

DE PERE

HERITAGE HALL
366 Main Avenue, De Pere, Wisconsin 54115
In former Piller's Bank (1836). Local history. Junior museum.
M.-F. 2-5. Closed public holidays.

DESERT HOT SPRINGS

CABOT YERXA OLD INDIAN PUEBLO MUSEUM
67-616 Desert View Avenue, Desert Hot Springs, California 92240
Mineralogy. Local history. Indian history and pottery. Paintings.
Daily, except Tu., 9-5.

DES MOINES

DEPARTMENT OF HISTORY AND ARCHIVES MUSEUM
E. 12th and Grand Avenue, Des Moines, Iowa 50319
Geology, palaeontology and natural history of Iowa. Local history. Indian culture.
Daily 8-4.

DES MOINES ART CENTER
Greenwood Park, Des Moines, Iowa 50312
17th-20th century European and American paintings, sculpture. Medieval and Romanesque sculpture and religious art. Graphics.
Tu.-Sa. 11-5; Su., public holidays 1-6.

DES MOINES CENTER OF SCIENCE AND INDUSTRY
4500 Grand Avenue, Des Moines, Iowa 50312
Science and technology. Planetarium.
Daily 11-5. Closed Christmas, New Year.

IOWA STATE CONSERVATION COMMISSION
State Office Building, 300 4th Street, Des Moines, Iowa 50319
3 historic buildings, with period furnishings and equipment, Fort Atkinson (1840), Plum Grove (1844), and Wildcat Den grist mill (1850).
Fort Atkinson: May 16 - Oct. 30 by appointment.
Plum Grove: Apr. 15 - Nov. 15.
Wildcat Den: Su. 1-5.

POLK COUNTY HISTORICAL SOCIETY MUSEUM
317 S.W. 42nd Street, Des Moines, Iowa 50312
In Des Moines Birthplace Cabin (1843-46). Local history.
By appointment.

SALISBURY HOUSE
4025 Tonawanda Drive, Des Moines, Iowa 50312
15th-17th century European furnishings, tapestries, paintings.
M.-F. 8-4.30. Labour Day - Memorial Day, also Sa. 9-12. Closed Good F., Memorial Day, July 4, Labour Day, Veterans' Day, Thanksgiving, Christmas, New Year.

DE SOTO

WASHINGTON STATE PARK MUSEUM
De Soto, Missouri 63020
Indian artifacts, including stone carvings. Local plants, animals, insects, rocks and minerals.
June 1 - Aug. 31, daily 8-5.

DES PLAINES

MUSEUM OF DES PLAINES HISTORICAL SOCIETY
777 Lee Street, Des Plaines, Illinois 60016
House (1906). County and state history. Agriculture. Folklore. Children's museum.
W., Sa., Su. 2-4. Closed public holidays.

DETROIT

CHILDREN'S MUSEUM
67 E. Kirby Avenue, Detroit, Michigan 48202
Geology. Planetarium. Science. Natural history. Ethnology. Anthropology. Indian artifacts. Archaeology. Folklore. History. Costumes. Textiles. Decorative arts. Writing, printing. Music.
M.-F. 8.15-4.30. Oct. 1 - May 31, Sa. 9-4. Closed public holidays.

DETROIT HISTORICAL MUSEUM
5401 Woodward Avenue, Detroit, Michigan 48202
Detroit history. Furniture. Arts and crafts. Industry. Tools. History of automobile industry.

U. S. Grant House (1849) and Palmer Log Cabin (1885) are in the care of the Museum.
Tu.-Sa. 10-5.45. Su. 1-5. Closed New Year, Memorial Day, Thanksgiving, Christmas.

DETROIT INSTITUTE OF ARTS
5200 Woodward Avenue, Detroit, Michigan 48202
European paintings, sculpture, graphic arts, decorative arts. American paintings. Oriental and Near-Eastern art. French-Canadian paintings, graphic arts. Textiles. Theatre designs. Costumes. Period rooms. Indian artifacts. Archaeology. Weapons. Armour. Flemish tapestries. American furniture, decorative arts. French silver.
Tu.-Su. 9.30-5.30. Closed public holidays.

DOSSIN GREAT LAKES MUSEUM
Belle Isle, Detroit, Michigan 48207
History of Great Lakes. Paintings. Ship models. Photographs. Smoking lounge of the steamer 'City of Detroit III' (1912).
W.-Su. 10-5.45. Closed public holidays.

FORT WAYNE MILITARY MUSEUM
6053 West Jefferson Avenue, Detroit, Michigan 48209
Site of Fort Wayne (1843-9). Military and Indian history. Civil War barracks room restoration, with uniformed figures, bunks, utensils. Indian habitat setting, with reconstructed wigwam and furnishings.
W.-Su. 10-5.30. Closed public holidays.

INDIAN VALLEY HISTORIC DISTRICT
Mack, Burns and Seminole Avenues, Detroit, Michigan 48200
347 houses, 1811-1840, preserved and restored to illustrate architectural history of the period.
On request.

INTERNATIONAL INSTITUTE OF METROPOLITAN DETROIT
111 East Kirby Street, Detroit, Michigan 48202
European folk art and handicrafts.
M. 12-6; Tu.-F. 10-6; Su. 2-6. M.-F. evenings, 6-9. Closed weekends July-Aug. Closed national holidays.

MCGREGOR MEMORIAL
Community Arts Gallery, Wayne State University, 450 W. Kirby Street, Detroit, Michigan 48202
American and European paintings, sculpture, graphics.
M.-F. 9-9; Sa., Su. 1-5.

MUSEUM OF ANTHROPOLOGY
Merrick and Anthony Wayne Drives, Detroit, Michigan 48202
Ethnography. Prehistoric Michigan Indian material. Ceramics.
By appointment.

NATIONAL BANK OF DETROIT MONEY MUSEUM
611 Woodward Avenue, Detroit, Michigan 48232
Coins. Primitive tokens of exchange.
M.-Th. 9.30-4.30; F. 9.30-5.30. Closed when banks are closed.

U. S. GRANT HOUSE
Michigan State Fair Grounds, Detroit, Michigan 48202
House (c.1840), originally in E. Fort Street, rented by Gen. Ullysses Simpson Grant 1849-51. Period rooms.
Daily 10-5, during Michigan Fair week.

WAYNE STATE UNIVERSITY MUSEUM OF ANTHROPOLOGY
Merrick Street and Anthony Wayne Drive, Detroit, Michigan 48202
Local history. Archaeology. Ethnology. Indian artifacts. Ceramics. Glass.
By appointment.

DETROIT LAKES

MUSEUM OF BECKER COUNTY HISTORICAL SOCIETY
Courthouse, 915 Lake Avenue, Detroit Lakes, Minnesota 56501
Natural history. Pioneer life. Indian artifacts.
M.-F. 2-5. Closed public holidays.

DEVIL'S TOWER

DEVIL'S TOWER VISITOR CENTER
Devil's Tower, Wyoming 82714
Geology. Botany. Natural history. Indian artifacts.
May 1-31, Sept. 1 - Oct. 31, daily 8-5. June 1 - Aug. 31, daily 8-8.

DEWEY

TOM MIX MUSEUM
721 N. Delaware Street, Dewey, Oklahoma 74029
Career and personal possessions of Tom Mix. Saddles. Trophies. Clothing. Photographs.
Tu.-Su. 10-5.

DEXTER

DEXTER HISTORICAL SOCIETY MUSEUM
Grist Mill Museum, Main Street, Dexter, Maine 04930
In former grist mill (1853). Local history. Agriculture.
June 15 - Sept. 15, M.-Sa. 1-5.

DIAMOND

GEORGE WASHINGTON CARVER NATIONAL MONUMENT
Diamond, Missouri 64840
House (1880). Local history. Material relating to Carver's life and career. Herbarium.
Daily 8.30-5. Closed Christmas.

DIGHTON

LANE COUNTY HISTORICAL SOCIETY MUSEUM
Dighton, Kansas 67839
County history. Furnishings, clothing of the pioneer period. Maps. Paintings.
Summer: Su. 2-5. Weekends, by appointment.

DILLON

BEAVERHEAD COUNTY MUSEUM
15 S. Montana, Dillon, Montana 59725
County history. Porcelain. Silver. Coins. Minerals, birds, mammals of the region.
M.-Sa. 9.30-12, 1-5 (all year); Su. 1-5; Evenings 7-9 (June 15 - Sept. 15). Closed New Year, Feb. 22, May 30, Thanksgiving, Christmas.

DILWORTHTOWN

1704 BRINTON HOUSE
Dilworthtown, Pennsylvania
House (1704). Furnishings of 1751. Agricultural implements. Horse-drawn vehicles.
Apr.-Nov., Tu., Th., Sa. 2-5. Other times by appointment. Closed national holidays.

DINOSAUR

DINOSAUR QUARRY VISITOR CENTER
P.O. Box 101, Dinosaur, Colorado 81610
Palaeontology. Geology.
May 1 - Sept. 30, daily 7-9; Oct. 1 - Apr. 30, daily 8-5.

DIXON

MUSEUM OF LEE COUNTY HISTORICAL SOCIETY
Dixon, Illinois 61021
In Old Settler's Memorial Log Cabin (1894). Local history.
May 27 - Sept. 30: M.-F. by appointment; Sa., Su. 2-4. Public holidays 2-5. July 1, 1-6, July 2, 4-8, July 3-4, 2-8.

DODGE CENTER

MUSEUM OF DODGE COUNTY OLD SETTLERS AND HISTORICAL SOCIETY
Dodge Center, Minnesota 55927
In former Episcopal Church (1869). Local history. Agriculture. Costumes. Paintings.
Civil War recruiting station (c.1860) and 2 schoolhouses (c.1865 and 1870) are in the care of the Society.
Su. 1-6. Other times by appointment.

DODGE CITY

BEESON MUSEUM
Old Front Street, Dodge City, Kansas 67801
History of Dodge City. Frontier doctor's instruments. 19th century bank, general store, apothecary shop, doctor's and dentist's surgeries, barber shop, marshal's office. Doll collection.
May 1 - Sept. 30, 7.30 a.m.-10 p.m. Oct. 1 - Apr. 30, 8-6.

BOOT HILL MUSEUM
500 W. Wyatt Earp Street, Dodge City, Kansas 67801
Local natural history. Music machines, playing popular tunes of the 1870s. Cowboy equipment and tools. Indian artifacts. Gun collection. Old Fort Dodge Jail.
May 1 - Sept. 30, 7.30 a.m.-10 p.m. Oct. 1 - Apr. 30, 8-6.

HOME OF STONE
112 E. Vine Street, Dodge City, Kansas 67801
Home of Stone (1880). Local history. Glass.
June 1 - Aug. 31, daily 9-8.

HARDESTY HOUSE
Boot Hill and Old Front Street, Dodge City, Kansas 67801
House of Col. R. J. Hardesty, cattle baron of the 1870s. Original furnishings.
May 1 - Sept. 30, 7.30 a.m.-10 p.m. Oct. 1 - Apr. 30, 8-6.

HISTORIC OLD FRONT STREET
Dodge City, Kansas 67801
Replica of Old Front Street as it was in the 1870s. Long Branch Saloon contains portraits of famous Dodge City citizens. Long Branch Gambling Room, with 19th century gambling devices.
May 1 - Sept. 30, 7.30 a.m.-10 p.m. Oct. 1 - Apr. 30, 8-6.

DORAN

WILKIN COUNTY HISTORICAL SOCIETY MUSEUM
Doran, Minnesota 56530
Local history.
By appointment.

DORCHESTER

BLAKE HOUSE
Edward Everett Square, Dorchester, Massachusetts 02122
House (c.1848), with metal-framed casements. Period furnishings.
2nd Sa. of each month, 2-4. By appointment at other times.

DORCHESTER HISTORICAL SOCIETY MUSEUM
195 Boston Street, Dorchester, Massachusetts 02125
Local history, based on 3 houses (1636-1805).
2nd Sa. in month, 1-5.

MUSEUM OF THE NATIONAL CENTER OF AFRO-AMERICAN ARTISTS
122 Elm Hill Avenue, Dorchester, Massachusetts 02121
African sculpture. Drawings and paintings by black American artists.
M.-F 12-9; Sa. 12-4; Su. 2-5. Closed public holidays.

MUSEUM OF SALINE COUNTY HISTORICAL SOCIETY
Dorchester, Nebraska 68343
Local history. Agriculture.
Rural school (1873), railway depot (1871) and post office (1896) are in the care of the Society.
Su. 1-5.

DOUGLAS

FORT FETTERMAN STATE MUSEUM
Route 3, Douglas, Wyoming 82633
Restored officers' quarters (1879). Military and local history.
May 1 - Sept. 30: M.-Sa. 8.30-12, 1-5; Su. 1-6.

WYOMING PIONEER ASSOCIATION MUSEUM
P.O. Box 235, Douglas, Wyoming 82633
Wyoming pioneer life. Costumes. Indian artifacts. Farm tools, implements.
Schoolhouse (1890) and log cabin (1896) are in the care of the Association.
Apr. 15 - Oct. 15: Tu.-F. 9-5; June 1 - Aug. 31: Sa., Su. 1-5. Closed July 4.

DOUGLASS

DOUGLASS MUSEUM
314-316 South Forest Street, Douglass, Kansas 67039
Local and pioneer history. Tools. Domestic equipment. Costumes. Indian artifacts.
M.-F. 1-5; Sa. 9-12. Closed Jan. 1-31.

DOUGLASSVILLE

MARY MERRITT DOLL MUSEUM
Route 422, Douglassville, Pennsylvania 19518
18th-19th century dolls.
By appointment.

DOVER

DELAWARE STATE MUSEUM
316 S. Governors Avenue, Dover, Delaware 19901
In old Presbyterian Church (c.1790). Botany. Natural history. Indian artifacts. Furniture. Agricultural implements. Craftsmen's workshops and tools. Delaware silver. Music. Costumes. Maritime history. Transport.

John Dickenson house (c.1740), Allee House (1750), are in the care of the Museum.
Tu.-Sa., 10-5; Su., 1-5. Closed Easter, Thanksgiving, Christmas.

BENJAMIN CARYL HOUSE
Dedham Street, Dover, Massachusetts 02030
House (1777). Period furnishings.
Sa. 10-5.

SAWIN MEMORIAL BUILDING
Dedham Street, Dover, Massachusetts 02030
Natural history.
Sa. 1-5. Closed July 1 - Aug. 31, public holidays.

ANNIE E. WOODMAN INSTITUTE
182-192 Central Avenue, Dover, New Hampshire 03820
In old Garrison House (1682), Hale House (1813) and Woodman House (1818). Geology. Mineralogy. Natural history. Local, military and maritime history. Archaeology. Indian artifacts.
Tu.-Su. 2-5. Closed New Year, Thanksgiving, Christmas.

DOVER HISTORICAL SOCIETY MUSEUM
410 N. Wooster Avenue, Dover, Ohio 44622
Geology. Mineralogy. Local history and archaeology. Agriculture. Costumes. Paintings. Glass. Music.
By appointment.

WARTHER MUSEUM
331 Karl Avenue, Dover, Ohio 44622
Models illustrating development of steam power. Wooden models of locomotives. Working model of Dover steam plant. Indian material.
Daily 8 a.m.-9 p.m.

FORT DONELSON NATIONAL MILITARY PARK
Highway 79, Dover, Tennessee 37058
In Dover Hotel (1853). Civil War relics.
Daily 8-4.30. Closed Christmas.

DOVER-FOXCROFT

BLACKSMITH SHOP MUSEUM
88 Lincoln Street, Dover-Foxcroft, Maine 04426
Blacksmith's shop (1863).
May 1 - Oct. 31, daily 8-8.

DOWNEY

DOWNEY MUSEUM OF ART
10419 S. Rives Avenue, Downey, California 90241
Contemporary paintings, sculpture, graphics, photography by Californian artists.
Tu.-Su., public holidays 1-5. Closed New Year, Easter, Christmas.

DOWNIEVILLE

SIERRA COUNTY MUSEUM
P.P. Box 147, Downieville, California 95936
Local history, including replica of gold stamp mill.
House (mid-19th century), of shale rock, is in the care of the Museum.
M., W., Su., 10-5. Closed Nov. 1 - Apr. 30.

DOYLESTOWN

MERCER MUSEUM
Pine and Ashland Streets, Doylestown, Pennsylvania 18901
Pre-industrial tools and artifacts. Indian material. Pennsylvania Dutch handicrafts, folk art. China and pottery. Paintings by Edward Hicks.
Tu.-Sa. 10-5. Apr. 1 - Oct. 31, also Su. 1-5. Closed Jan. 1 - Feb. 28, public holidays.

DRAGON

AMERIND FOUNDATION MUSEUM
Dragon, Arizona 85609
Archaeology and ethnology of Mexico, the Southwest, the Great Plains, California and the Arctic.
Sa., Su., by appointment. Closed public holidays.

DRESDEN

POWNALBOROUGH COURT HOUSE
Dresden, Maine 04342
Court House (1761). Local history. Paintings.
July 1 - Aug. 31, daily 10-5. Rest of year by appointment.

INGERSOLL MEMORIAL HOUSE
Routes 14 and 54, Dresden, New York 14441
Birthplace of Robert G. Ingersoll. Mementoes and personal possessions of Ingersoll. Paintings. Photographs. Letters. Manuscripts.
May 1 - Sept. 30, daily 10-4.

DRUMMOND ISLAND

DRUMMOND ISLAND HISTORICAL MUSEUM
Drummond Island, Michigan 49726
Geology. Local history. Indian artifacts.
June 1 - Sept. 9: M.-Sa. 1-6; Su. 1-5.

DRUMRIGHT

DRUMRIGHT COMMUNITY HISTORICAL MUSEUM
Broadway and State Highways 33 and 99, Drumright, Oklahoma 74030
In former Sante Fe railway depot (1915). Local history. Oilfields history and exploration equipment.
Su., F. 1-5.

DUBUQUE

HAM HOUSE MUSEUM
1769 University Avenue, Dubuque, Iowa 52001
In 1840 mansion. Geology. Mineralogy. Anthropology. Local history. Indian artifacts. Costumes.
One-room school (1883) and CBQ caboose (1906) are in the care of the Museum.
Memorial Day - Labour Day, Tu.-Su. 12.30-5. Other times by appointment. Closed public holidays.

MUSEUM OF DUBUQUE ART ASSOCIATION
596 W. 11th Street, Dubuque, Iowa 52001
American paintings, sculpture, graphics.
M.-Sa. 3-5, 7-9.

DULUTH

A. M. CHISHOLM MUSEUM
1832 E. 2nd Street, Duluth, Minnesota 55812
Geology. Natural history. Anthropology. Industry. Transport. Indian life. American history.
M.-F. 9-5; Sa. 9-12; 1st Su. in month 2.30-5. Closed public holidays.

MUSEUM OF NORTHERN BIBLE SOCIETY
715 W. Superior Street, Duluth, Minnesota 55802
Bibles. Scrolls of Torah and Koran. Religious artifacts.
Apr. 1 - Sept. 30: M.-F. 8.30-4. Closed public holidays.

MUSEUM OF ST. LOUIS COUNTY HISTORICAL SOCIETY
2228 E. Superior Street, Duluth, Minnesota 55812
Building (1901). Local history. Paintings and drawings of Chippewa Indians. Industry.
M.-F. 9-5; 1st Su. in month 2.30-5. June 1 - Aug. 31, Sa., Su. 1-5. Closed public holidays.

TWEED MUSEUM OF ART
2400 Oakland Avenue, University of Minnesota, Duluth, Minnesota 55812
16th-19th century European and American paintings, especially 18th century French portraits, 18th-early 19th century American portraits, 19th century landscapes. Sculpture. Graphics. Decorative arts.
M.-F. 8-4.30; Sa., Su. 2-5. Closed public holidays.

DUNDEE

DUNDEE TOWNSHIP HISTORICAL SOCIETY MUSEUM
Dundee, Illinois 60118
Local history.
By appointment.

DURAND

SHIAWASSEE COUNTY HISTORICAL SOCIETY MUSEUM
Box 2, Durand, Michigan 48429
Local history.
Comstock Cabin (1836) is in the care of the Society.
By appointment.

DURANGO

MUSEUM OF THE FOUR CORNERS MUSEUM ASSOCIATION
1828 Forest Avenue, Durango, Colorado 81301
Local history. Indian history.
Joy Cabin (1884) is in the care of the Association.
June 1 - Sept. 30, daily 3-9.30.

DURANT

OKLAHOMA HISTORICAL SOCIETY MUSEUM
Fort Washita, Durant, Oklahoma 74701
Museum of military and local history. Includes barracks (1842).
Tu.-F. 9-5; Sa., Su. 2-5. Closed public holidays.

DURHAM

DURHAM HISTORIC ASSOCIATION MUSEUM
P.O. Box 73, Durham, New Hampshire 03824
In former Town Hall (c.1825). Local history. Costumes. Indian artifacts.
July-Aug., Tu.-Sa. 1-4.

SCUDDER GALLERY
University of New Hampshire, Paul Creative Arts Center, Durham, New Hampshire 03824
19th-20th century paintings, drawings, prints, sculpture by European and American artists.
M.-F. 9-4, Sa. 10-4, Su. 1-4.

BENNETT PLACE STATE HISTORIC SITE
Durham, North Carolina 27701
Reconstructed early 19th century farmhouse. Period furnishings. Site of North Carolina surrender, 1865.
June-Aug., Tu.-Sa. 9-5; Su. 1-5. Sept.-May, Sa. 9-5; Su. 1-5. Other times by appointment. Closed Thanksgiving, Dec. 24-26.

DUKE HOMESTEAD
Duke Homestead Road, Durham, North Carolina 27701
House (1851), birthplace of James B. Duke, pioneer of tobacco industry and founder of Duke University. Period furnishings. Memorabilia of Duke family.
Apr.-Sept., Su. 2.30-5.30. Other times by appointment.

DUKE UNIVERSITY MUSEUM OF ART
Box 6877, Durham, North Carolina 27708
Medieval and Renaissance sculpture, decorative arts. Greek and Roman sculpture. European, American graphics.
Tu.-F. 9-5; Sa., Su. 2-5. Closed public holidays, July 3-21.

DURHAM CHILDREN'S MUSEUM
433 Murray Avenue, Durham, North Carolina 27704
Geology. Mineralogy. Palaeontology. Anthropology. Natural history. Life-size models of large animals and dinosaurs. Transport.
Tu.-Sa. 10-5; Su. 2-5. Closed Dec. 24-25.

NORTH CAROLINA MUSEUM OF LIFE AND SCIENCE
433 Murray Avenue, Durham, North Carolina 27704
Geology. Palaeontology. Aerospace.
Tu.-Sa. 10-5; Su. 2-5.

TRENT COLLECTION IN THE HISTORY OF MEDICINES
Duke University Medical Center Library, Durham, North Carolina 27706
Medical portraits, drawings, prints. Instruments. History of medicine and biology.
M.-F. 8.30-5.30. Sa. by appointment.

DUTCH JOHN

FLAMING GORGE DAM VISITOR CENTER
Dutch John, Utah 84023
Exhibits showing building of dam. Natural history.
May 1-31: Sa., Su. 11-4; public holidays 9-7. June 1 - Aug. 31: daily 9-7. Sept. 1-30: daily 11-4; public holidays 9-7.

RED CANYON VISITOR CENTER
Dutch John, Utah 84023
Geology. Botany. Natural history. Local history. Indian artifacts.
May 1-31: Sa., Su. 11-4; public holidays 9-7. June 1 - Aug. 31: daily 9-7. Sept. 1-30, daily 11-4; public holidays 9-7.

DUXBURY

JOHN ALDEN HOUSE
105 Alden Street, Duxbury, Massachusetts 02332
House (1653). Antique furnishings.
June 24 - Labour Day, daily 9.30-5.

DUXBURY RURAL AND HISTORICAL SOCIETY MUSEUM
St. George Street, Duxbury, Massachusetts 02332
House (1825). Local history. Furniture. Portraits. Civil War material. Ship models. Ship's logs.
June-Sept., Tu.-Su. 2-6. Closed national holidays.

EAGLE

EAGLE HISTORICAL SOCIETY MUSEUM
Eagle, Alaska 99738
Local history museum based on Court House (1900), U.S. Army Mule Barn (1858), U.S. Army Post, Fort Egbert (1900-11). Furniture. Horse-drawn vehicles. Tools.
June-Sept., daily 11-5.

EAGLE BAY

OLD TRADING POST
Eagle Bay, New York 13331
Mounted animals, birds and fish. Paintings. War relics.
Daily 8 a.m.-midnight.

EAGLE BRIDGE

GRANDMA MOSES SCHOOLHOUSE
Eagle Bridge, New York 12057
Mementoes of the primitive painter, Grandma Moses.
June 1 - Oct. 31, daily 1-5.

EAST AURORA

AURORA HISTORICAL SOCIETY MUSEUM
5 S. Grove Street, East Aurora, New York 14052
Local history.
W. 1-4.

ELBERT HUBBARD LIBRARY MUSEUM
Village Hall, 571 Main Street, East Aurora, New York 14052
Crafts from the Roycraft Shops, founded 1897 by Elbert Hubbard. Furniture. Leather. Copper. Brass.
June 1 - Oct. 31: W., Sa., Su., 2.30-4.30. Other times by appointment.

EASTCHESTER

MUSEUM OF EASTCHESTER HISTORICAL SOCIETY
1217 California Road, Eastchester, New York 10709
In Marble schoolhouse (1835). Period furnishings. Costumes. Educational history. Local history.
By appointment.

EAST DURHAM

BUTTERFLY ART MUSEUM
Wright Street, East Durham, New York 12423
Butterflies. Moths. Spiders. Beetles. Sea shells. Paintings.
June - Sept., daily 9-11, 2-5.

DURHAM CENTER MUSEUM
Route 145, East Durham, New York 12423
Minerals and fossils. Indian artifacts. Pioneer farming tools. Railway relics. Military history.
May 30 - Sept. 6: Sa., Su. 9-5.

EAST GRANBY

OLD NEW-GATE PRISON AND COPPER MINE
Newgate Road, East Granby, Connecticut 06026
Used as prison 1773-1827, on site of old copper mine, which prisoners worked for a time. Underground cells. History of prison and mine.
Memorial Day - Oct. 31, Tu.-Sa. 10-4.30.

EAST GREENWHICH

VARNUM HOUSE
57 Pierce Street, East Greenwich, Rhode Island 02818
House (1773), formerly home of Brig.-Gen. James Mitchell Varnum. 18th century furnishings. Indian artifacts.
June 1 - Labour day: Su., W. 3-5.

EAST GREENWICH

VARNUM MILITARY AND NAVAL MUSEUM
6 Main Street, East Greenwich, Rhode Island 02818
Firearms, 1675 onwards. Colonial period uniforms.
By appointment.

EAST HADDAN

GILLETTE CASTLE
Gillette Castle State Park, East Haddan, Connecticut 06423
Home (1919-37) of the actor, William Gillette. Furnishings, art collection, and personal possessions. Mementoes of Gillette's houseboat, 'The Aunt Polly'.
Memorial Day - Oct. 12, daily 11-5.

EASTHAM

EASTHAM HISTORICAL SOCIETY MUSEUM
Locust and Saltpond Road, Eastham, Massachusetts 02642
In former schoolhouse (1869). Education history. Indian artifacts. Household and farm equipment.
M., W., F., Sa., 2-5. Closed Oct. 1 - May 31, July 4, Labour day.

EAST HAMPTON

EAST HAMPTON HISTORICAL SOCIETY MUSEUM
Main Street, East Hampton, New York 11937
In Clinton Academy (1784). Local history. Furniture. Tools. Household equipment. Costumes. Indian relics.
July 1 - Sept. 6: daily 1-5.

EAST HAMPTON MARINE MUSEUM
Hither Lane, East Hampton, New York 11937
Natural history. Folklore. Maritime history. Archaeology.
July 1 - Labour Day, daily 1.30-5.

'HOME, SWEET HOME' HOUSE
14 James Lane, East Hampton, New York 11937
House (1660), boyhood home of John Howard Payne, composer of 'Home, Sweet Home'. Payne memorabilia. Staffordshire and Wedgwood china. Waterford crystal. Pewter. Quilts and coverlets.
M.-W., Sa. 10-4; Su. 2-4. Closed New Year, Thanksgiving, Christmas.

GUILD HALL
158 Main Street, East Hampton, New York 11937
Early American architecture. Paintings and sculpture by regional artists.
June 1 - Sept. 30: M.-Sa. 10-5; Su. 2-5. Rest of year, closed Tu. Closed New Year, Easter, Thanksgiving, Christmas.

HOOK MILL
East Hampton, New York 11937
Wind-powered grist mill (1806).
June 28 - Sept. 6, daily 10-5, Su. 2-5.

MULFORD HOUSE
E. Main Street, East Hampton, New York 11937
House (c.1700). Local history. Period furnishings.
June 22 - Sept. 6, daily 1.30-5.

EAST HAVEN

BRANFORD TROLLEY MUSEUM
17 River Street, East Haven, Connecticut 06512
Electric railway and tramway cars and equipment. Models. Visitors can ride in some of the trams, which run over a special museum track.
July, Aug., M.-F. 10-5, Sa., Su. 11-6. June, Sept., Sa. 1-5. Apr., May, Sept.-Nov., Su. 1-5. Memorial Day, July 4, Labour Day, 11-6. Closed weekdays Labour Day - June; Sa., Oct.-May; Su., Dec.-Mar.

EAST HUBBARDTON

HUBBARDTON BATTLEFIELD AND MUSEUM
East Hubbardton, Vermont 05749
Site of Revolutionary War battle (1777). Displays showing significance of battle.
May 25 - Oct. 15, daily 9-6.

EAST LANSING

ABRAMS PLANETARIUM
Michigan State University, East Lansing, Michigan 48823
Astronomy. Meteorites. Planetarium.
M.-F. 9-12, 1-4.30. Closed New Year, Christmas.

BEAL-DARLINGTON HERBARIUM
Department of Botany, Michigan State University, East Lansing, Michigan 48823
Plants of Michigan, Alpine areas of N. America, S. America, W. Indies, Mexico.
M.-F. 8-5. Closed public holidays.

KRESGE ART CENTER GALLERY
Michigan State University, East Lansing, Michigan 48823
Contemporary American paintings, graphic arts. Archaeology.
M.-F. 9-12, 1-5; Tu. also 7-9; Sa., Su. 2-5. Closed Dec. 25 - Jan. 1, public holidays.

MICHIGAN STATE UNIVERSITY MUSEUM
West Circle Drive, East Lansing, Michigan 48823
Geology. Palaeontology. Natural history. Anthropology. Ethnology. Local history. Agriculture. Indian material.
M.-F. 9-5; Sa., Su., public holidays 1-5. Closed New Year, Thanksgiving, Easter Sunday, Christmas.

EAST LIVERPOOL

EAST LIVERPOOL HISTORICAL SOCIETY MUSEUM
Carnegie Public Library, E. 4th Street and Broadway, East Liverpool, Ohio 43920
Local history and archaeology. Eastern Ohio pottery.
M.-Sa. 9-8; Su. by appointment. Closed public holidays.

EAST LYME

LITTLE BOSTON SCHOOLHOUSE
Shore Road, East Lyme, Connecticut 06357
19th century schoolhouse, with original and period furnishings, equipment.
June-Sept. Tu.-Su. 12-5.

EAST MEADOW

NASSAU COUNTY HISTORICAL MUSEUM
Eisenhower Park, Old Country Road and Hempstead Turnpike, East Meadow, New York 11554
History of Nassau County. Indian artifacts. Agricultural implements. Domestic equipment. Transport. Toys and games.
Daily 9-5, by appointment.

EAST NORTHFIELD

NORTHFIELD HISTORICAL SOCIETY MUSEUM
Pine Street, East Northfield, Massachusetts 01360
Local history.
By appointment.

EASTON

ACADEMY OF THE ARTS
Harrison and S. Streets, Easton, Maryland 21601
Paintings and sculpture by Maryland artists.
M.-F. 10-5. Closed public holidays.

MUSEUM OF HISTORICAL SOCIETY OF TALBOT COUNTY
29 S. Washington Street, Easton, Maryland 21601
Building (1755-1802). Furniture. China. Costumes.
May 1 - Sept. 30: Tu., F., Sa. 10-4; Su. 1-4. Oct. 1 - Apr. 30: Tu., F. 10-4. Closed New Year, Dec. 24-25.

GEORGE TAYLOR HOME
4th and Ferry Streets, Easton, Pennsylvania 18042
House (1757) was home of George Taylor, who signed Declaration of Independence. Period furnishings.
By appointment.

MUSEUM OF NORTHAMPTON COUNTY HISTORICAL SOCIETY
101 S. 4th Street, Easton, Pennsylvania 18042
In Meisell House (1832). Local history and folklore. Costumes. Indian material.
Sa. 1.30-3.30. Other times by appointment.

EAST ORANGE

EAST ORANGE HISTORICAL SOCIETY MUSEUM
10 Oraton Parkway, East Orange, New Jersey 07017
Local history.
By appointment.

EASTPORT

BORDER HISTORICAL SOCIETY MUSEUM
168 Water Street, Eastport, Maine 04631
In 1810-15 Fort Sullivan barracks. Local history. Indian artifacts. Local war relics.
June 15 - Aug. 31: M.-Sa. 10-12, 1-5.

EAST POULTNEY

POULTNEY HISTORICAL SOCIETY MUSEUM
The Green, East Poultney, Vermont 05741
Local history. Horace Greeley collection. Farm implements. Civil War weapons. Melodians. Paintings.
Blacksmith's shop (1800), later Melodian factory, is in the care of the Society. It contains collections of early household equipment and farm implements.
June 1 - Sept. 30, Su. 1-5.

EAST PRAIRIE

TOWOSAHGY
State Historical Site, East Prairie, Missouri 63845
Archaeology. Indian artifacts.
June-Aug., during excavations.

EAST PRINCETON

PRINCETON HISTORICAL SOCIETY MUSEUM
Goodnow Library, East Princeton, Massachusetts 01517
Local history. Paintings. Prints. Decorative arts.
By appointment.

EAST ROCKAWAY

OLD GRIST MILL MUSEUM
Memorial Park, East Rockway, New York 11518
Reconstructed mill (1688). Local history exhibits.
May 30 - Sept. 1: Sa., Su. 1-5.

EAST SETAUKET

SHERWOOD-JAYNE HOUSE
Old Post Road, East Setauket, New York 11733
House (partly 1730). Antique furniture.
May 1 - Oct. 31: W.-M. 1-5.

EASTSOUND

ORCAS ISLAND HISTORICAL MUSEUM
Eastsound, Washington 98245
In 6 homestead cabins (1885-1902). Local history. Indian artifacts. Pioneer furnishings, domestic equipment.
June 1 - Labour Day, daily 1-4. Other times by appointment.

EAST SPRINGFIELD

HYDE HALL
Glimmerglass State Park, East Springfield, New York 13333
Building (1819-33). Local history.
By appointment.

EAST WEYMOUTH

ABIGAIL ADAMS HISTORICAL SOCIETY MUSEUM
Norton and North Streets, East Weymouth, Massachusetts 02189
In Abigail Adams House (1685). Period furniture.
July 1 - Aug. 31: Tu.-Sa. 1-4.

EAST WINDSOR

CONNECTICUT ELECTRIC RAILWAY ASSOCIATION MUSEUM
58 N. Road, East Windsor, Connecticut 06088
Electric tram and railway equipment, 1880-1947.
Su., public holidays 12-5. Apr.-Dec., also Sa. 1-5. Closed Jan. 1 - Mar. 31, Christmas.

EAU CLAIRE

PAUL BUNYAN CAMP
Carson Park, Eau Claire, Wisconsin 54701
Restored logging camp. Bunkhouse. Dining hall. Blacksmith's shop.
May 1 - Oct. 31: M., Th.-Su. 10-6.

CHIPPEWA VALLEY HISTORICAL MUSEUM
129 Chippewa Street, Eau Claire, Wisconsin 54701
Local history. Indian artifacts. Clothing. Household equipment.
W., Th. 2-5. Other times by appointment.

EBENSBURG

CAMBRIA COUNTY HISTORICAL SOCIETY
201 W. Sample Street, Ebensburg, Pennsylvania 15931
Local history. 19th century agriculture and industry. Indian artifacts. Coins.
Tu., Th. 1.30-4.30.

EDEN

EDEN HISTORICAL SOCIETY MUSEUM
8584 S. Main Street, Eden, New York 14057
Local history.
By appointment.

EDENTON

JAMES IREDELL HOUSE
107 E. Church Street, Edenton, North Carolina 27932
House (1776), home of James Iredell, appointed Associate Justice of U.S. Supreme Court in 1790. Period furnishings. Kitchen-museum. Carriage house. Schoolhouse moved to site from Brandon Plantation.
Tu.-Sa. 10-4.30; Su. 2-5.

MUSEUM OF HISTORIC EDENTON
S. Broad Street, Edenton, North Carolina 27932
18th-19th century artifacts relating to Colonial period of area. Drawings. Maps.
4 houses (1725-59) and St. Paul's Episcopal Church (1736) are in the care of the same authority.
Tu.-Sa. 10-4.30. Closed Thanksgiving, Christmas, New Year, Easter.

EDGARTOWN

THOMAS COOKE HOUSE
Edgartown, Massachusetts 02539
Indian material. Whaling relics. Furniture. Tower with Fresnel lens from Gay Head lighthouse (1856).
June-Sept., Tu.-Su. 10-4.30; Su. 2-4.30. Oct.-May, Tu.-W. 1-4.

DUKES COUNTY HISTORICAL SOCIETY MUSEUM
School and Cooke Streets, Edgartown, Massachusetts 02539
In Thomas Cooke House (1756). Local history and archaeology. Industry. Whaling. Naval and maritime history. Indian material. Herbarium.
Tu.-Sa. 10-4.30; Su. 2-4.30.

EDGEFIELD

EDGEFIELD COUNTY HISTORICAL SOCIETY
320 Norris Street, Edgefield, South Carolina 29824
In Magnolia Dale (1810). Local history, Indian artifacts. Costumes. Early American furniture.
By appointment.

EDGEMONT

COLGAN'S OLD GENERAL STORE MUSEUM
P.O. Box 66, Edgemont, South Dakota 57735
Store (1900). Colgan family possessions. Tools. Early bank and doctor's surgery.
July-Aug., M.-Sa. 10-5.

EDGERTON

LANESFIELD HISTORICAL SOCIETY MUSEUM
Route 1, Edgerton, Kansas 66021
In Old Rock Schoolhouse (1869). Local history. Agriculture. Folklore. Open-air museum.
M.-F. 9-2; Su. 1-5. Other times by appointment. Closed Thanksgiving, Christmas.

ALBION ACADEMY HISTORICAL SOCIETY MUSEUM
Academy Drive, Edgerton, Wisconsin 53534
In Kumlien Hall (1868). History of Albion Academy. Paintings. Portraits.
May-Oct., Sa., Su. 1-6, and by appointment.

EDGEWOOD ARSENAL

EDGEWOOD ARSENAL MUSEUM
Edgewood Arsenal, Maryland 21010
History of chemical, biological and radiological warfare.
M.-F. 8-4.30. Closed public holidays.

EDINBURG

HIDALGO COUNTY HISTORICAL MUSEUM
Box 482, 121 McIntyre Street, Edinburg, Texas 78539
In restored Hidalgo County jail. Early life in Hidalgo County and the Rio Grande Valley.
W., Sa., Su. 2-5.

EDINA

KNOX COUNTY HISTORICAL MUSEUM
Edina, Missouri 63537
Local history.
M., F. 1-4.

EDMOND

CENTRAL STATE COLLEGE
The Laboratory of History, Evans Hall, 400 E. Hurd Street, Edmond, Oklahoma 73034
Local, state and American history. Civil War, 1st and 2nd World War relics. Portraits.
Academic year: daily 9-12, 1-5. Summer session: 1-5 or by appointment.

EDWARDSVILLE

MADISON COUNTY HISTORICAL MUSEUM
715 North Main, Edwardsville, Illinois 62025
House (1836). Natural history. Local history. Indian artifacts.
W., 1-5; Sa. 1-5; Su. 2-5. Closed public holidays.

EFFINGHAM

EFFINGHAM HISTORICAL SOCIETY MUSEUM
Route 153, Effingham, New Hampshire 03814
In former store (c.1810). Local history. Farm and craftsmen's tools. Costumes. Quilts.
By appointment.

EGYPT

NORTHINGTON-HEARD MEMORIAL MUSEUM
Box 35, Egypt, Texas 77436
Wharton County history 1800-1900. Pioneer life. Furniture. Photographs.
M.-Sa. 8-5.

EKALAKA

CARTER COUNTY MUSEUM
Ekalaka, Montana 59324
Geology. Mineralogy. Palaeontology. Fossils of prehistoric animals. Local history and archaeology.
Tu.-Su. 1-4. Closed New Year, Easter, Christmas.

ELBOW LAKE

GRANT COUNTY HISTORICAL SOCIETY MUSEUM
Elbow Lake, Minnesota 56531
Prehistory of the area. Early Indian artifacts. Pioneer life. Restored log cabin, with period furnishings. Schoolhouse, with furnishings and equipment.
May 1 - Sept. 30, daily 10-5. Rest of year by appointment.

EL CAMPO

EL CAMPO MUSEUM
203 Monsarette Street, El Campo, Texas 77437
Pioneer memorabilia of Wharton Cou nty. Needlework. Early toys.
Sa., Su. 2.30-5. Other times by appointment.

EL DORADO

BUTLER COUNTY HISTORICAL SOCIETY MUSEUM
P.O. Box 11, El Dorado, Kansas 67042
Local history. Indian artifacts.
Log cabin (1858), formerly courthouse and post-office, is in the care of the Society.
M.-F. 1-5. Other times by appointment.

ELGIN

AUDUBON MUSEUM
Lord's Park, Elgin, Illinois 60120
Mounted birds and animals. Shells.
May-Sept., Tu.-Su. 12-4.

MUCHOW'S ANTIQUE RADIO MUSEUM
819 Forest Avenue, Elgin, Illinois 60120
Wireless equipment, Marconi - present day. Transmitter. Receivers. Loudspeakers. Components.
By appointment.

ELIZABETH

BOXWOOD HALL
1073 E. Jersey Street, Elizabeth, New Jersey 07204
House (c.1750). Furnishings of Colonial and Federal periods. Household equipment. Clothing.
Tu.-Sa. 10-12, 1-5; Su., public holidays 2-5. Closed New Year, Thanksgiving, Christmas.

ELIZABETH CITY

MUSEUM OF THE ALBEMARLE
Route 3, Elizabeth City, North Carolina 27909
Social history of the Albemarle Sound area. Indian artifacts. Colonial history. Household equipment. Agriculture. Lumbering.
Tu.-Sa. 10-5; Su. 2-5. Closed New Year, July 4, Thanksgiving, Christmas.

ELIZABETHTOWN

ADIRONDACK CENTER MUSEUM
Court Street, Elizabethtown, New York 12932
History of Essex County iron mining and lumbering. Pioneer life. Trapping. Costumes. Horse-drawn vehicles.
May 15 - Oct. 14: M.-Sa. 9-5; Su., public holidays 1-5.

ELK CITY

OLD TOWN MUSEUM
U.S. Highway 66 and Pioneer Road, Elk City, Oklahoma 73644
Museum building (1912). History of Western Oklahoma. Indian material. Medicine. Costumes. Glass. Schoolroom.
Tu.-Sa. 8-5; Su. 2-5. Closed New Year, Thanksgiving, Christmas.

ELKHORN

WEBSTER HOUSE MUSEUM
Rockwell and Washington Streets, Elkhorn, Wisconsin 53121
House (c.1840). Local history. Farm implements. Indian material. Costumes. Musical instruments. Children's museum.
Schoolhouse (1889) and Sharon Town Hall (1892) are in the care of the Museum.
May 1 - Oct. 31: Tu.-Sa. 11-12, 1-5; Su., public holidays 1-5.

ELKO

NORTH-EASTERN NEVADA MUSEUM
1515 Idaho Street, Elko, Nevada 89801
In Ruby Valley Pony Express Station. Natural history. Anthropology. Local history. Indian material.
M.-Sa. 9-5; Su. 1-5. Closed New Year, Thanksgiving, Christmas.

ELK RIVER

OLIVER H. KELLY FARM
Elk River, Minnesota 55330
House (c.1880). Period furnishings.
May 1 - Sept. 30, daily 10-4. Oct. 1-31, Sa., Su. 10-4.

ELKTON

MUSEUM OF HISTORICAL SOCIETY OF CECIL COUNTY
Cecil County Library Building, Elkton, Maryland 21921
Local history. Indian artifacts.
3 historic buildings, including school (1799) and store (1855) are in the care of the Society.
Th., Sa. 1-5.

ELLENDALE

WHITESTONE BATTLEFIELD HISTORIC PARK
Ellendale, North Dakota 58436
Site of battle with Sioux Indians (1862). Relics of battle, including guns, tomahawks, flint arrows, cooking utensils.
May 1 - Oct. 15, daily 8-5.

ELLENTON

GAMBLE MANSION HISTORIC MEMORIAL
U.S. 301, Manatee River, Ellenton, Florida 33532
House (c.1840). Civil War material. Pre-Civil War furnishings, including some of the original furniture of the house and Jefferson Davis' wedding bed.
Tu.-Sa. 9-5.

ELLENVILLE

HARRY RESNICK MOTOR MUSEUM AND DOLL HOUSE
Canal and Hickory Streets, Ellenville, New York 12428
Old cars. Model racing cars. Dolls.
Apr. 1 - Oct. 30, daily 10-5.

ELLICOTT CITY

HOWARD COUNTY HISTORICAL SOCIETY, INC.
53 Court Avenue, Ellicott City, Maryland 21043
County History.
Open only at meetings.

ELLIS

BOYHOOD HOME OF WALTER P. CHRYSLER
Ellis, Kansas 67687
House (c.1880). Parlor and kitchen, with original furnishings, and domestic equipment. Pump organ.
May 1 - Aug. 31, 9-5.

ELLIS GROVE

PIERRE MENARD HOME MEMORIAL
Rural Route 1, Ellis Grove, Illinois 62241
House (1802), former home of first Lt.-Governor of Illinois. Period furnishings.
Daily 9-5. Closed New Year, Thanksgiving, Christmas.

ELLSWORTH

HOGDEN HOUSE MUSEUM
104 West Main Street, Ellsworth, Kansas 67439
Hogden House (c.1870). Local history. Archaeology. Agriculture. Costumes. Indian artifacts.
Tu.-Sa. 10-12, 1-5; Su. 1-5. Closed New Year, Thanksgiving, Christmas.

STANWOOD HOMESTEAD
Route 3, Ellsworth, Maine 04605
House (1850), birthplace of ornithologist, Cordelia J. Stanwood. Ornithology. Material relating to Cordelia Stanwood.
June 15 - Oct. 15, daily 10-4.

COLONEL BLACK MANSION
W. Main Street, Ellsworth, Maine 04605
House (1827), home of the Black family. Original furniture. China. Glass. Carriages.
June 1 - Oct. 15: M.-Sa. 10-5.

ELMHURST

ELMHURST HISTORICAL MUSEUM
Elmhurst Public Library, Wilder Park, Elmhurst, Illinois 60126
Local history.
Tu., Sa. 2-5; Th. 2-5, 7-9. Closed public holidays.

LIZZADRO MUSEUM OF LAPIDARY ART
220 Cottage Hill Avenue, Elmhurst, Illinois 60126
Geology. Mineralogy. Palaeontology. Precious and semiprecious gemstone carvings. Jade. Ivory.
Tu.-F. 1-5; Sa. 10-5; Su. 1-5. Closed public holidays.

ELMIRA

ARNOT ART MUSEUM
235 Lake Street, Elmira, New York 14901
Building (1833). American paintings. Northern Baroque paintings. 19th century French paintings. Oriental art. Sculpture. Graphics. Decorative arts.
Tu.-F. 12-5; Sa., Su. 2-5. Closed public holidays, Aug. 1-31.

CHEMUNG COUNTY HISTORICAL CENTER
304 William Street, Elmira, New York 14901
Local history. Mark Twain collection. Indian and Eskimo artifacts. Civil War material. Agriculture. Industry. Transport.
Tu., W., F. 1-4.30; Su. 2-5. Closed public holidays.

NATIONAL SOARING MUSEUM
Harris Hall, Elmira, New York 14901
History of gliding.
June 19 - Sept. 6, daily 11-5. May 28 - June 13, Sept. 11 - Nov. 28: Sa., Su. 11-5.

EL MONTE

EL MONTE HISTORICAL MUSEUM
3100 Tyler Avenue, El Monte, California 91731
Local history. Furnishings. Clothes. Farm implements. Natural history.
The first El Monte jail (1880) is in the care of the Society.
M. 1-4; Tu.-F. 10-4. Closed public holidays and August.

ELMWOOD

LORADO TAFT MUSEUM
North Magnolia, Elmwood, Illinois 61529
Local history.
By appointment.

EL PASO

CHAMIZAL NATIONAL MEMORIAL
620 South West Center, 300 E. Main Drive, El Paso, Texas 79901
Regional history, ethnography, art.
Daily 8 a.m. - midnight.

EL PASO CENTENNIAL MUSEUM
University of Texas, University Avenue and Wiggens Road, El Paso, Texas 79999
Regional natural history. Geology. Botany. Archaeology. Ethnology.
M.-F. 10-5; Sa., Su., public holidays 1-5.

EL PASO MUSEUM OF ART
1211 Montana Street, El Paso, Texas 79902
Pre-Columbian art. Mexican Colonial and 19th-20th century paintings, sculpture. European Renaissance and Baroque art. 19th-20th century American paintings, sculpture, drawings. Contemporary European and American graphics. Decorative arts.
Tu.-Sa. 10-5; Su. 1-5.

EL RENO

CANADIAN COUNTY HISTORICAL SOCIETY MUSEUM
Citizens National Bank Building, El Reno, Oklahoma 73036
In former Rock Island Railway Station (1906). Railway history. Horse-drawn vehicles. Local history. Agriculture. Household equipment.
Tu.-F. 10-5; Su. 1-5. Closed public holidays.

ELSAH

SCHOOL OF NATIONS MUSEUM
Principia College, Elsah, Illinois 62028
Oriental art. American Indian handicrafts. House and boat models. Dolls. Costumes. Textiles. Pottery. Cameos. Ivory. Jade. Weapons. Japanese Imari collection.
Sept. 10 - June 4: M.-F. 9-4.30; Sa., Su. by appointment. Closed Christmas, college vacations.

ELVERSON

HOPEWELL VILLAGE
R.D.1, Elverson, Pennsylvania 19520
Restored buildings of early 19th century iron-making community. Brooke manor house (c.1835) with original furnishings. Furnaces. Working waterwheel. Records and exhibits illustrating history of the works and of charcoal iron industry.
Mar 1 - Oct. 31, daily 9-6. Nov. 1 - Feb. 28, daily 9-5. Closed Christmas, New Year.

ELY

WHITE PINE PUBLIC MUSEUM, INC.
2200 Aultman, Ely, Nevada 89301
Local and pioneer history. Minerals and mining. Furniture. Musical instruments. Railway coaches. Fire engines. Pony Express exhibits. Slot machines.
M.-Sa. 9-5; Su. 1-6. Closed national holidays.

ELYRIA

INDIAN RIDGE MUSEUM
8714 W. Ridge Road, Elyria, Ohio 44035
Log cabins (1760-1865). Pioneer life. Weapons. Furnishings. Clothing. Indian artifacts and archaeology.
Tu.-Su. 1-5.

LORAIN COUNTY HISTORICAL SOCIETY MUSEUM
331 5th Street, Elyria, Ohio 44035
Local history. Agriculture. Clothing. Indian material. Children's museum.
Tu.-Sa. 2-5.

ELYSIAN

LE SUEUR COUNTY HISTORICAL SOCIETY MUSEUM
Elysian, Minnesota 56028
Local history. Archaeology. Agriculture. Costumes. Ottawa Methodist Church (1858) is in the care of the Society.
June 1 - Aug. 31: W.-F. 1.30-5.30. May 1 - Aug. 31 also Sa., Su. 1.30-5.30.

EMMAUS

MUSEUM OF SHELTER HOUSE SOCIETY
S. 4th Street Extension, Emmaus, Pennsylvania 18049
In Shelter House (1734-41). Local history.
Sa., Su., public holidays 10-5.

EMPIRE

RED MEN HALL MUSEUM
U.S. Highway 40, Empire, Colorado 80438
Local history. Mineralogy.
June 1 - Sept. 30, daily 3-5.

EMPORIA

BIOLOGY DEPARTMENT MUSEUM
Kansas State Teachers College, 1200 Commercial Street, Emporia, Kansas 66801
Natural history.
M.-F. 8-5; Sa. 8-12. Closed college vacations.

LYON COUNTY HISTORICAL SOCIETY MUSEUM
Civic Auditorium, E. 6th Avenue, Emporia, Kansas 66801
Local history and archaeology. Costumes. Indian artifacts.
By appointment.

ENCAMPMENT

GRAND ENCAMPMENT MUSEUM
Encampment, Wyoming 82325
Geology. Local history. Indian material. Costumes.
May 1 - Aug. 31, daily 1-5. Sept. 1 - Oct. 31: Sa., Su. 1-5.

ENCINO

MUSEUM OF LOS ENCINOS STATE HISTORICAL PARK
16756 Moorpark Street, P.O. Box 184, Encino, California 91316
Early Californian rancho. Near first recorded discovery of California oil, at La Brea Tar pits. Exhibits showing early ranch life. Local, including Indian, history. Costumes. Several historic buildings, including adobe (1849) and blacksmith's shop (1872) are in the care of the Museum.
Daily 1-4.30. Closed New Year, Thanksgiving, Christmas.

ENFIELD

LOCKEHAVEN SCHOOLHOUSE MUSEUM
Enfield, New Hampshire 03748
Schoolhouse (1864). Material relating to history of school.
June 1 - Oct. 15, Su. 2-5.

ENID

CHEROKEE STRIP MUSEUM
Phillips University, Enid, Oklahoma 73701
Local history.
Tu.-F. 10-5; Sa., Su. 2-5. Closed public holidays.

GRACE PHILLIPS JOHNSON ART GALLERY
Phillips University, Enid, Oklahoma 73701
European and American paintings, sculpture, graphics, decorative arts.
Tu.-F. 10-5; Sa., Su. 2-5. Closed public holidays.

EPHRATA

EPHRATA CLOISTER
632 W. Main Street, Ephrata, Pennsylvania 17522
Restored buildings (c.1740) of Communal Society of Seventh Day German Baptists. Furnishings, domestic equipment, workshops, tools, documents and other material illustrating history of the Society.
M.-Sa. 9-4.30; Su. 1-4.30. Closed public holidays.

MUSEUM OF HISTORICAL SOCIETY OF THE COCALICO VALLEY
249 W. Main Street, Ephrata, Pennsylvania 17522
In former Connell Mansion (1860). Furnishings. Local history.
June 1 - Sept. 1: M.-Sa. 11-4; Su. 1-4. Rest of year, by appointment.

GRANT COUNTY HISTORICAL SOCIETY MUSEUM
742 Basin Street N.W., Ephrata, Washington 98823
Mineralogy. Indian artifacts. Decorative arts. Glass. Costumes. Toys.
May 1 - Sept. 15: Th.-Tu. 1-4.30.

WANAPUM DAM TOUR CENTER
Box 878, Ephrata, Washington 98823
Mining history. Archaeology. Indian artifacts.
May-Sept., daily 10-8.

EPPING

BUFFALO TRAILS MUSEUM
Epping, North Dakota 58843
In former general store (1906) and harness and hardware store (1906). Geology. Mineralogy. Natural history. Archaeology. Local history. Indian artifacts.
July-Aug., M-Sa. 9-5; Su. 1.30-5.30. Other times by appointment.

ERIE

ERIE ART CENTER
338 W. 6th Street, Erie, Pennsylvania 16507
American paintings, graphics, sculpture.
Tu.-F. 1-9; Sa., Su. 1-5.

ERIE PUBLIC MUSEUM AND PLANETARIUM
356 W. 6th Street, Erie, Pennsylvania 16507
Local history. Pioneer life. Indian handicrafts. Planetarium. Paintings by Eugene Ivens.
Curtze Mansion (1895) is in the care of the Museum.
Tu.-Sa. 10-5; Su. 2-5. Closed public holidays, Dec. 25 - Jan. 1.

FLAGSHIP 'NIAGARA'
State Street, Erie, Pennsylvania 16507
Reconstruction of Commodore Perry's ship at Battle of Lake Erie (1813).
May 1 - Sept. 30: M.-Sa. 8.30-5; Su. 1-5. Oct. 1 - Apr. 30: M.-Sa. 9-4.30; Su. 1-4.30. Closed public holidays.

COMMODORE PERRY MEMORIAL HOUSE AND DICKSON TAVERN
201 French Street, Erie, Pennsylvania 16507
House (1809). Early 19th century furnishings.
Sa. and Su. 1-4. June 15 - Sept. 15, daily 1-4.

MUSEUM OF ERIE COUNTY HISTORICAL SOCIETY
407 State Street, Erie, Pennsylvania 16501
Local and military history. 18th - early 19th century furnishings. Tools.
Old Customs House (1839) and Cashier's house (c.1839) are in the care of the Society.
May 1 - Oct. 31: Tu.-F. 1-4.30; Sa. 9-12.

ESCANABA

MUSEUM OF DELTA COUNTY HISTORICAL SOCIETY FOUNDATION
Ludington Park, Escanaba, Michigan 49829
Local history. Anthropology. Indian artifacts. Agriculture. Aviation.
July 1 - Sept. 1, daily 1-9. May 20 - July 1, Sa., Su. 1-5.

ESHERVILLE

MUSEUM OF EMMET COUNTY HISTORICAL SOCIETY
107 S. 6th Street, Esherville, Iowa 51334
In restored country school. Local history.
May 1 - Oct. 31: Th., Su. 2-5; other day s by appointment. Dec. 1 - Mar. 31: by appointment.

ESPERANCE

ESPERANCE HISTORICAL MUSEUM
Esperance, New York 12066
Rural school equipment. Old farm tools and implements.
May 29 - Sept. 5: Sa., Su. 11-5.

ESSEX

ESSEX HISTORICAL SOCIETY MUSEUM
Prospect Street, Essex, Connecticut 06426
Local history. Industry in Essex County.
Apr.-June, Sept.-Nov., 3rd Th. each month.

PRATT HOUSE
20 W. Avenue, Essex, Connecticut 06426
House (c.1750). Contains Griswold collection of American furniture and furnishings.
By appointment.

ESSINGTON

GOVERNOR PRINTZ PARK
2nd Street, Essington, Pennsylvania 19029
Reconstruction of house built (1643) by the Swedish Royal Governor, Johan Printz. Indian relics.
Dawn-dusk.

ESTES PARK

ROCKY MOUNTAIN NATIONAL PARK MUSEUM
Estes Park, Colorado 80517
Geology. Botany. Natural history.
June 1 - Sept. 15, daily 8-5.

EUGENE

LANE COUNTY PIONEER MUSEUM
740 W. 13th Avenue, Eugene, Oregon 97402
In Lane County Clerk's Building (1853). Local history. Tools. Clothing. Horse-drawn vehicles.
M.-W. 9-5; Sa., Su. 1-5. Closed public holidays.

MUSEUM OF ART
University of Oregon, Eugene, Oregon 97403
Oriental art. Russian ikons. Works by European and American, especially contemporary Northwest, artists. Syrian glass. Persian miniatures.
Tu.-Su. 12-5. Closed Aug. 18 - Sept. 18, New Year, July 4, Thanksgiving, Christmas.

MUSEUM OF NATURAL HISTORY
University of Oregon, Eugene, Oregon 97403
Geology. Palaeontology. Botany. Herbarium. Anthropology. Ethnology.
M.-F. 8-4.30; Sa., Su. 1-4.30. Closed July 4, Thanksgiving, Christmas, New Year.

WAGON MUSEUM
University of Oregon, Eugene, Oregon 97403
Scale reproductions of American horse-drawn vehicles.
M.-Sa. 9-5; Su. 1-6.

EUREKA

CLARKE MEMORIAL MUSEUM
240 E. Street, Eureka, California 95501
Mineralogy. Natural history. Local history. Transport. Indian artifacts. Archaeology. Anthropology. Paintings. Decorative arts.
Tu.-Sa., 10-4.

FORT HUMBOLDT STATE HISTORIC PARK
3431 Fort Avenue, Eureka, California 95501
Military post of the 1850s. Exhibits showing early military and logging life in the area.
Daily, dawn to dusk. Closed New Year, Thanksgiving, Christmas.

HISTORICAL SOCIETY MUSEUM
Society of Humboldt County Pioneers, 2309 B Street, Eureka, California 95501
Local history.
Tu.-Su. 10-4.

LOG CABIN MUSEUM
Eureka, Montana 59917
Log cabin (1897). Period furnishings.
June 1 - Aug. 31, daily 9-9.

EUREKA SPRINGS

HATCHET HALL MUSEUM
Steele Street, Eureka Springs, Arkansas 72632
Home (1908) of Carry Nation, the prohibitionist, who became famous for chopping up saloons with her hatchet. Also contains paintings illustrating early settler life in the district.
May 1 - Sept. 30, M.-Sa. 9.30-5.30.

EVANSTON

EVANSTON HISTORICAL SOCIETY MUSEUM
225 Greenwood Avenue, Evanston, Illinois 60201
Local history. Exhibits relating to Revolutionary, Civil, Spanish-American, 1914-18, 1939-45 Wars. Memorabilia of General Charles Gates Dawes. Early history of Northwestern University.
M., Tu., Th., F. 1-5; Sa. 9-12. Closed New Year, Thanksgiving, Christmas.

LEVERE MEMORIAL FOUNDATION
1856 Sheridan Road, Evanston, Illinois 60204
History of Sigma Alpha Epsilon fraternity.
M.-F. 8.30-5; Sa. 10-12; Su. 3-5. Closed public holidays.

FRANCES E. WILLARD HOUSE
1730 Chicago Avenue, Evanston, Illinois 60201
Items collected during world journeys by Frances Willard and her fellow-workers in the Woman's Christian Temperance Union.
M.-F. 9-4.30. Sa., Su. by appointment.

EVANSVILLE

EVANSVILLE MUSEUM OF ARTS AND SCIENCES
411 S.E. Riverside Drive, Evansville, Indiana 47713
Geology. Planetarium. Natural history dioramas, specimens. Indian artifacts. Pioneer life. Period rooms. Medical and dental history. Weapons. Armour. Oriental art. 16th-19th century European sculpture, paintings, graphics. 20th century American paintings. Transport, including steam locomotive, railway station, cars.
Tu.-Sa. 10-5; Su. 12-5. Closed New Year, Christmas.

RESHAW EXHIBIT
439 3rd Street, Evansville, Wyoming 82636
Pioneer life. Indian material.
M.-F. 9-5.30; Sa. 9-12. Closed public holidays.

EVERETT

SNOHOMISH COUNTY MUSEUM
Legion Park, Everett, Washington 89201
County history. Indian material. Industry. Photographs of logging. Costumes.
Shannahan Cabin (1885) is in the care of the Museum.
Su. 2-5. Other times by appointment. Closed Christmas week, New Year's week.

EVERGREEN

BELLS OF GRANITE GLEN MUSEUM
Granite Glen, Evergreen, Colorado 80439
History and manufacture of bells. World-wide bell collection.
Tu.-Su., public holidays 10-5.

EXETER

CINCINNATI MEMORIAL HALL
Water and Governor Streets, Exeter, New Hampshire 03833
In Ladd-Gilman House (1721). Late 18th century furnishings. Personal possessions of Washington family.
Mid.-Apr. - mid.-Oct., Th. 2-4.

GILMAN GARRISON HOUSE
12 Water Street, Exeter, New Hampshire 03833
Late 18th century log-house, with 18th century additions. 17th-18th century furnishings.
By appointment.

THE LAMONT ART GALLERY OF THE PHILLIPS EXETER ACADEMY
Alumni Hall, Front Street and Tan Lane, Exeter, New Hampshire 03833
Contemporary European and American paintings, prints.
During School Year: Tu.-Sa. 9-5, Su. 2-5.

EXIRA

AUDUBON COUNTY HISTORICAL SOCIETY MUSEUM
Exira, Iowa 50076
Indian history.
May 30 - Oct. 1, Su. 1.30-4.30.

EXTON

THOMAS NEWCOMEN MEMORIAL LIBRARY AND MUSEUM
412 E. North Ship Road, Exton, Pennsylvania 19341
History of steam engines. Working models of Newcomen and other important engines.
M.-F. 9.30-4. Closed public holidays.

FABIUS

PIONEER'S MUSEUM
Highland Forest, Fabius, New York 13063
Pioneer relics. Indian artifacts. Agriculture. Archaeology. Children's museum.
May 1 - Nov. 30: M.-F. 1-4; Sa., Su. 10-6. Rest of year by appointment.

FAIRBANKS

PIONEER MUSEUM
Pioneer Building, Alaskaland, Fairbanks, Alaska 99701
History of early settlement of Alaska.
May 25 to Labor Day, daily 12-8. Other times by appointment.

UNIVERSITY OF ALASKA MUSEUM
Fairbanks, Alaska 99701
Geology. Palaeontology. Botany. Natural history. Archaeology. Ethnology. Anthropology.
May-Sept., daily 9-5. Oct.-Apr., daily 1-5. Closed Christmas.

FAIRBURY

JEFFERSON COUNTY MUSEUM
612 Fourth Street, Fairbury, Nebraska 68352
Prehistoric artifacts. Local history. Indian relics. Material relating to Oregon Trail and Pony Express Stations.
Th. and Sa. 2-5. Memorial Day-Thanksgiving, holidays, 2-5. Closed Easter, Christmas, New Year.

FAIRFAX

FAIRFAX HISTORICAL SOCIETY MUSEUM
Route 104, Fairfax, Vermont 05454
Local history.
June 1 - Nov. 12: Su., public holidays 2-4. Other days by appointment.

FAIRFAX COUNTY

WOOD LAWN PLANTATION
9000 Richmond Highway, Fairfax County, Virginia 22309
House (1800). Period furniture owned by Lewis family.
Daily 9.30-4.30. Closed Christmas.

FAIRFIELD

AUDUBON SOCIETY OF THE STATE OF CONNECTICUT
2325 Burr Street, Fairfield, Connecticut 06430
Natural history.
Tu.-Sa., 10-5; Su., 12-5. Closed New Year, Easter, Thanksgiving, Christmas.

BIRDCRAFT MUSEUM
314 Unquowa Road, Fairfield, Connecticut 06431
Mounted mammals and birds. African animal room. Decoy collections.
Tu., Th., Su., 2-5.

FAIRFIELD HISTORICAL SOCIETY MUSEUM
636 Old Post Road, Fairfield, Connecticut 06430
Local paintings, glassware, lustreware, from Colonial period onwards. Connecticut furniture, clocks, portraits.
M.-F., 9.30-4.30. Closed public holidays.

FAIRFIELD PUBLIC LIBRARY MUSEUM
Court and Washington Streets, Fairfield, Iowa 52556
Geology. Natural history. Pioneer history.
M.-F. 1-6; Sa. 10-6. Closed public holidays.

FREESTONE COUNTY HISTORICAL MUSEUM
302 E. Main Street, Fairfield, Texas 75840
In old County Jail (1857). Early history of Freestone and adjoining counties. Pre-Civil War period rooms. 2 restored log cabins, with furnishings and pioneer memorabilia.
W., Sa., 9.30-5.30; Su. 1.30-5.30.

MOODY-BRADLEY HOUSE
318 Moody Street, Fairfield, Texas 75840
House (1860), birthplace of W. L. Moody founder of Moody Foundation. Original and period furnishings.
Su. 1-5. Other times by appointment.

STAGE COACH INN
State Highway 73, Fairfield, Utah 84013
In Camp Floyd, U.S. largest army encampment in 1850s. Museum is in former army commissary building (1858). Military and local history. Stage Coach Inn has been reconstructed on original site.
Mar. 16 - Nov. 15, daily 9-5.

PRESIDENT CHESTER A. ARTHUR BIRTHPLACE
Routes 36 and 108, Fairfield, Vermont 05455
Replica of house in which President Arthur was born, 1830. Period furnishings.
June-Sept. daily 10-5.

FAIRHOPE

PERCY H. WHITING ART CENTER
401 Oak Street, Fairhope, Alabama 36532
19th-20th century American paintings.
M.-Sa. 10-12, 2-5. Closed Thanksgiving, Christmas, New Year.

FAIRLEE

WALKER MUSEUM
Route 3, Fairlee, Vermont 05045
Botany. Local history and archaeology. Civil War relics. Craftsmen's tools. Farm tools, implements, vehicles. Furniture. Sculpture. Drawings. 18th-19th century American paintings. Costumes. Household equipment.
May 25 - Oct. 15, daily 10-5.

FAIRMONT

MUSEUM OF MARTIN COUNTY HISTORICAL SOCIETY
304 E. Blue Earth Avenue, Fairmont, Minnesota 56031
History of Martin County.
May 1 - Sept. 30: Tu.-F. 1.30-4.30.

FAIRPORT

PERINTON HISTORICAL SOCIETY MUSEUM
42 E. Avenue, Fairport, New York 14450
Local history.
Tu., W. 1-4.

FAIRPORT HARBOR

FAIRPORT MARINE MUSEUM
129 2nd Street, Fairport Harbor, Ohio 44077
In Fairport Lighthouse (1871) and keeper's house. Maritime history of Great Lakes. Ship models. Navigation instruments. Anchors. Lanterns. Paintings. Charts. Indian relics.
June 1 - Sept. 15: Sa., Su. 1-6.

FAIRVIEW

JEFFERSON DAVIS MONUMENT STATE PARK
Fairview, Kentucky 42221
Local history.
Mar. 1 - Nov. 30, daily 9-5.30. Dec. 1 - Feb. 28, Sa., Su. 9-5.30.

FAIRVIEW MUSEUM OF HISTORY AND ART
85 N. 100 Street E., Fairview, Utah 84629
Geology. Mineralogy. Anthropology. Farm tools, implements. Local history. Indian artifacts. Paintings. Sculpture.
M.-Sa. 9-7; Su., public holidays 2-7.

FALFURRIAS

TEXAS RANGER MUSEUM
124 N. St. Mary's Street, Falfurrias, Texas 78355
History of Texas Rangers. Guns. Equipment. Photographs. Personal papers.
M.-F. 9-5; Sa. 9-12.

FALLON

CHURCHILL COUNTY MUSEUM
S. Main Street, Fallon, Nevada 89406
Geology. Mineralogy. Natural history. Anthropology. Archaeology. Decorative arts. Indian artifacts.
M.-F. 9-5; Sa., Su., public holidays 12-5.

FALL RIVER

MARINE MUSEUM
Battleship Cove, Fall River, Massachusetts 02721
In battleship 'Massachusetts'. Ship models. Maritime relics. Marine steam engines. History of Fall River Line of side-wheel paddle-steamers. Indian material.
Daily 9-5. Closed Thanksgiving, Dec. 25.

FALL RIVER PUBLIC LIBRARY
104 N. Main Street, Fall River, Massachusetts 02720
Mineral collection.
M.-F. 9-9; Sa. 9-5. Closed Sa. July 1 - Aug. 31, public holidays.

GREAT FALL RIVER ART ASSOCIATION
80 Belmont Street, Fall River, Massachusetts 02720
20th century American graphics, ceramics.
Sept. 1 - June 30, daily 1-4.

MUSEUM OF FALL RIVER HISTORICAL SOCIETY
451 Rock Street, Fall River, Massachusetts 02720
Local and maritime history. Costumes. Furniture. China. Glass. Paintings.
Tu.-F. 9-4.30; Sa. 9-12; Su. 2-4. Closed public holidays.

FALL RIVER MILLS

FORT CROOK HISTORICAL MUSEUM
Fall River Mills, California 96028
Local history. Agriculture. Industry. Transport. Indian artifacts.
Apr. 1 - Oct. 31 daily, 1-4. Other times by appointment.

FALLS CITY

RICHARDSON COUNTY HISTORICAL SOCIETY
Falls City, Nebraska 68355
Local history.
By appointment.

FALLSINGTON

HISTORIC FALLSINGTON
4 Yardley Avenue, Fallsington, Pennsylvania 19054
Restoration of village. Buildings open to public include Burges-Lippincott House (1780) and stage-coach tavern (c.1770).
Mar. 15 - Nov. 15: W.-Su. 1-5.

FALLS VILLAGE

FALLS VILLAGE - CANAAN HISTORICAL SOCIETY MUSEUM
Main Street, Falls Village, Connecticut 06031
Local history. Costumes.
F. 2-5.

FALMOUTH

FALMOUTH HISTORICAL SOCIETY MUSEUM
Palmer Avenue, P.O. Box 174, Falmouth, Massachusetts 02541
In Dr. Francis Wicks House (1790). 18th century wallpaper. Furniture. Ceramics. Glass. Portraits. Local history. Whaling collection.
June 15 - Sept. 15, daily 2-5.

FARGO

CASS COUNTY HISTORICAL MUSEUM
Minard Hall, North Dakota State University, Fargo, North Dakota 58102
Mineralogy. Agriculture. Pioneer life. Handicrafts. Indian artifacts. Reproduction of pioneer village.
Tu.-F. 1-5. Closed university vacations.

FORSBERG HOUSE
815 3rd Avenue S., Fargo, North Dakota 58102
House (1903), formerly home of Anna Marie Forsberg. Furnishings of 1700-1850. Americana. Folk art. Paintings by local artists.
By appointment.

FARIBAULT

MUSEUM OF RICE COUNTY HISTORICAL SOCIETY
12 N.E. 1st Avenue, Faribault, Minnesota 55021
Local history.
By appointment.

FARMINGTON

FARMINGTON MUSEUM
37 High Street, Farmington, Connecticut 06032
House (c.1660). Local history. 17th-18th century American furniture, glass, silver, pewter. Musical instruments.
Apr. 1 - Nov. 30, Tu.-Sa. 10-12, 2-5; Su. 2-5. Dec. 1 - Mar. 31, F., Sa. 10-12, 2-5; Su. 2-5. Closed Good Friday, Thanksgiving, Christmas.

HILL-STEAD MUSEUM
671 Farmington Avenue, Farmington, Connecticut 06032
Impressionist paintings; works by Manet, Monet, Dégas, Whistler and others. Decorative arts. Sculpture. Graphics. English, French, American furniture, mainly 18th century. English, French clocks. Chinese porcelain. Japanese prints.
W.-Su., 2-5. Closed Thanksgiving, Christmas.

NORDICA HOMESTEAD
Farmington, Maine 04938
House (c.1840), formerly home of Lillian Nordica, opera singer. Furniture. Photographs. Jewellery. China. Costumes.
June 1 - Labour Day, Tu.-Su. 10-5. Sept. 1 - Oct. 31, by appointment.

VILLAGE OF ST. FRANÇOIS
Farmington, Missouri 63640
19th century log structures, moved and reassembled to form village. Indian artifacts. Transport. Dolls. Toys.
June 1 - Oct. 31: Tu.-Sa. 10-5; Su. 10-6.

FORT NECESSITY NATIONAL BATTLEFIELD
R.D.1, Farmington, Pennsylvania 15437
Site museum of local and military history. Mount Washington Tavern (1828). Reconstructed Fort Necessity stockade.
M.-Sa. 9-5; Su. 10-6. Closed New Year, Thanksgiving, Christmas.

FAYETTE

FAYETTE ART MUSEUM
Fayette, Alabama 35555
Paintings, graphics by American artists.
M.-F. 8-12, 1-5.

FAYETTE STATE PARK
Fayette, Michigan 49830
Preserved remains of industrial town (1867-92), centred on charcoal-fired smelting operations of the Jackson Iron Company. Restored charcoal kiln.
Memorial Day - Labour Day, daily 8-8.

FAYETTEVILLE

ARTS CENTER GALLERY
University of Arkansas, Garland Street, Fayetteville, Arkansas 72701
Paintings. Sculpture. Drawings. Prints.
M.-Sa. 8 a.m. - 11 p.m.

UNIVERSITY OF ARKANSAS MUSEUM
University of Arkansas, University Hall, Fayetteville, Arkansas 72701
Geology. Palaeontology. Mineralogy, including collection of quartz crystals. Archaeology. Glass. Ethnology, including Arkansas Indian material. Albert Pike schoolhouse (1820) is in the care of the Museum.
M.-Sa., 9-5; Su., 1-5. Closed Christmas.

WASHINGTON COUNTY HISTORICAL SOCIETY MUSEUM
118 E. Dickson Street, Fayetteville, Arkansas 72701
Headquarters House (1852). Local history.
June 1 - Oct. 31, Tu.-Su., 2-4.

FERGUS FALLS

OTTER TAIL COUNTY HISTORICAL SOCIETY MUSEUM
Court House, Fergus Falls, Minnesota 56537
Local history.
M.-F. 1.30-5. Closed public holidays.

FERNANDINA BEACH

FORT CLINCH MUSEUM
P.O. Box 524, Fernandina Beach, Florida 32034
History of Amelia Island. Handicrafts. Confederate paper money. Local minerals, insects, fish, amphibians, reptiles, mammals.
Daily 9-5.

FERRISBURG

ROKEBY
U.S. Route 7, Ferrisburg, Vermont 05456
House (1784), former home of Rowland Evans Robinson. Family possessions of the Robinson family. Vermont history.
May 16 - Oct. 14, daily 9-5.

FESSENDEN

MUSEUM OF WELLS COUNTY HISTORICAL SOCIETY
Fessenden, North Dakota 58438
History of Wells County. Pioneer and Indian artifacts.
Su. 2-5. Other days by appointment.

FILER

MUSEUM OF TWIN FALLS COUNTY HISTORICAL SOCIETY
Route 2, Filer, Idaho 83328
Local history. Agriculture. Mining. Indian material.
M.-F. 10-5; Su. 2-5. Closed public holidays.

FILLMORE

TERRITORIAL STATEHOUSE
50 W. Capitol Avenue, Fillmore, Utah 84631
Building (1851-5) was Utah's first Capitol. Pioneer life. Furniture. Handicrafts. Tools. Farm implements. Indian artifacts. Cotton-growing. Costumes. Paintings. Sculpture. Decorative arts.
Apr. 1 - May 31: M.-Sa. 8-5. June 1 - Aug. 31: M.-Sa. 8-9. Other times by appointment.

FISHERS

GHOST TOWN OF VALENTOWN MUSEUM
Valentown Square, Fishers, New York 14453
Manor House (1830). Community Center (1870). Indian artifacts. Military history. Science.
Mar. 1 - Nov. 30, daily 1-5.

FISHKILL

HENDRICK KIP HOUSE
Fishkill, New York 12524
House (1720, with later additions). Decorative arts. Indian artifacts. Folk art. Glass.
June 1 - Aug. 31: M., Tu., Th., F. by appointment. Closed public holidays.

VAN WYCK HOMESTEAD MUSEUM
Fishkill, New York 12524
In Van Wyck House (1735). Local history. Revolutionary War material. Agriculture. Technology.
M.-F. by appointment; Sa., Su. 9-5.

FITCHBURG

FITCHBURG ART MUSEUM
Merriam Parkway, Fitchburg, Massachusetts 01420
Paintings. Sculpture. Graphic arts. French provincial furniture. Decorative arts, especially American and English silver.
Sept. 1 - June 30: Tu., Th.-Sa. 9-5; W. 9-9; Su. 2-5. Closed New Year, Thanskgiving, Christmas.

MUSEUM OF FITCHBURG HISTORICAL SOCIETY
50 Grove Street, Fitchburg, Massachusetts 01420
Local history. Portraits by American artists.
Sept. 15 - June 15: Th., Sa. 2-4. Other times by appointment.

FLAGSTAFF

GREAT METEOR CRATER MUSEUM OF ASTROGEOLOGY
U.S. 66, East of Flagstaff, Flagstaff, Arizona 86047
Astrogeological material.
Daily 8 a.m. - sunset.

LOWELL OBSERVATORY RESEARCH MUSEUM
P.O. Box 1269, Flagstaff, Arizona 86001
Astronomy photographs.
M.-F. 1.30-2.30. Alternate Fridays June 1 - Aug. 31, 8-10. Closed Sa., Su., national holidays.

MUSEUM OF NORTHERN ARIZONA
Fort Valley Road, Flagstaff, Arizona 86001
Geology. Botany. Zoology. Prehistory. Indian arts and crafts, especially Hopi, Navajo, Havasupai.
M.-Sa. 9-5; Su. 1.30-5; closed Dec. 23 - Feb. 28.

NORTHERN ARIZONA PIONEER HISTORICAL SOCIETY MUSEUM
Fort Valley Road, Flagstaff, Arizona 86001
Material relating to the settlement of Northern Arizona, 1888-1920. Kolb film and photographic collection.
M.-Sa., 9-5; Su., 1.30-5. Closed Oct. 1 - Apr. 15.

NORTHERN ARIZONA UNIVERSITY ART GALLERY
Box 5801, Flagstaff, Arizona 86001
20th century American, European prints. American paintings of the South-West.
M.-F., 9-4; Sa., Su., by appointment. Closed university and public holidays.

WALNUT CANYON NATIONAL MONUMENT
Route 1, Box 790, Flagstaff, Arizona 86001
On site of ruined prehistoric village of Sinaqua Indians. Indian artifacts. Botany. Zoology.
Labour Day - Memorial Day, M.-Sa. 8-5. Rest of year M.-Sa. 7-7. Closed Su., Christmas, New Year.

WUPATKI NATIONAL MONUMENT
Tuba Star Route, Flagstaff, Arizona 86001
Archaeology.
May 1 - Sept. 30, 8-7; Oct. 1 - Apr. 30, 8-5. Closed Thanksgiving, Christmas.

FLAMINGO

EVERGLADES NATIONAL PARK
Flamingo Visitor Center, Flamingo, Florida 33030
Wall displays and dioramas showing plume hunting period. Flamingo and Cape Sable history, hurricane ecology, geology, wildlife.
Daily 8-5.

FLANDREAU

MOODY COUNTY MUSEUM
E. Pipestone Avenue, Flandreau, South Dakota 57028
Local history. 19th century furnishings, household equipment. Horse-drawn vehicles. Early cars. Rural schoolhouse.
Memorial Day - Labour Day, Su., public holidays 2-5. Other times by appointment.

FLEMINGTON

DORIC HOUSE
114 Main Street, Flemington, New Jersey 08822
Doric House (1845). 18th-19th century furnishings. Agriculture. Indian artifacts.
Holcombe House (1711) is in the care of the Museum.
Th., Sa. 1-3. Closed public holidays.

FLINT

FLINT INSTITUTE OF ARTS
De Waters Art Center, 1120 E. Kearsley Street, Flint, Michigan 48503
19th-20th century European and American paintings and sculpture. 16th-18th century European decorative arts. 18th-19th century European glass. French and American paperweights. Japanese and Chinese art. Tapestries. Prints, drawings.
M.-Sa. 10-5; Tu., Th. 7-9; Su. 12-5. Closed public holidays, p.m. May 1 - Sept. 30.

ROBERT T. LONGWAY PLANETARIUM
1310 E. Kearsley Street, Flint, Michigan 48503
Astronomy. Planetarium.
Sa., Su. 2-8.

SLOAN MUSEUM
1221 Kearsley Street, Flint, Michigan 48503
Local history. Historical dioramas. Horse-drawn vehicles. Old automobiles.
Tu.-F. 10-5; Sa., Su. 12-5. Closed public holidays.

SLOAN PANORAMA OF TRANSPORTATION
303 Walnut Street, Flint, Michigan 48503
Horse-drawn carriages, especially those made in Flint. Flint-manufactured automobiles. Local history. Miniature figures of American historic personalities.
Tu.-F. 10-5; Sa., Su. 12-5. Closed public holidays.

FLORENCE

MUSEUM OF PINAL COUNTY HISTORICAL SOCIETY
2201 S. Main Street, Florence, Arizona 85232
Local history, from pre-Columbian times onwards. Ranching. Mining. Indian exhibition. Collection showing history of barbed wire. Domestic equipment. Dr. Brockman's dental chair.
W.-Su. 1-5. Closed Aug.

FLORENCE PIONEER MUSEUM
Pikes Peak Avenue and Front Street, Florence, Colorado 81226
Museum building (1894). Mineralogy. Local history. Industry. Indian artifacts.
The old city jail (1875) is in the care of the Society.
June 1 - Sept. 30, daily 1-4. Other months by appointment.

FLORENCE MUSEUM
Spruce and Graham Streets, Florence, South Carolina 29501
Local history. Natural history. S. Carolina and S.W. Indian collections. American, European paintings. American sculpture. Pueblo pottery, jewellery. Furniture. Minerals.
Tu.-Sa. 10-5; Su. 2.30-5. June 1 - Aug. 31, by appointment only.

FLORIDA

FRIENDS OF FLORIDA MUSEUM
Rural Route 2, Florida, via Stoutsville, Missouri 65283
Local history.
Stage-coach Inn (1836) is in the care of the Friends.
Su. 11-5. Other days by appointment.

FLORISANT

COLORADO PETRIFIED FOREST
Florisant, Colorado 80816
Material from petrified forest and fossil beds. Entomology.
Apr. 1 - Oct. 31, M.-F., 8-6; Sa., Su., 8-7.

FLORISSANT

FLORISSANT VALLEY HISTORICAL SOCIETY MUSEUM
Florissant, Missouri 63032
In Taille de Noyer house (original 1790, with later additions). Local history. Period furnishings.
W.-Sa. 1-4; Su. 12-5. Closed New Year, Christmas, Thanksgiving.

FLUSHING

BOWNE HOUSE
37-01 Bowne Street, Flushing, New York 11354
House (1661), built by John Bowne, who allowed Quakers to meet there. 17th-18th century furnishings. Pewter.
Tu., Sa., Su. 2.30-4.30. Closed New Year, Easter, Christmas.

HALL OF SCIENCE OF THE CITY OF NEW YORK
P.O. Box 1032, Flushing, New York 11352
Technology. Physical sciences. Aeronautics. Communications. Nuclear energy. Space science.
Tu.-Sa. 10-5; Su. 1-5. Closed Thanksgiving, Christmas, New Year.

QUEEN'S COLLEGE ART COLLECTION
Paul Kalpper Library, Flushing, New York 11367
Near Eastern, Oriental, European and American art. Paintings. Graphics. Sculpture.
M.-F. 9-9; Sa. 10-2. Closed Thanksgiving, Christmas, New Year, Human Rights Day.

FOLSOM

FOLSOM POWERHOUSE
Riley Street and Greenback Lane, Folsom, California 95630
Powerhouse from which electricity was sent more than 5 miles for the first time in 1895.
May 1 - Sept. 30, Sa., Su. 10-5. Other times by appointment.

FONDA

MOHAWK-CAUGHNAWAGO MUSEUM
Takakwitha Friary, R.D. 1, Box 6, Fonda, New York 12068
Mohawk village site museum. Mohawk artifacts. N. and S. American Indian artifacts.
June - Sept.: M.-Sa. 10-11.30, 1.30-4.30; Su. 1.30-4.30.

FOND DU LAC

GALLOWAY HOUSE AND VILLAGE
336 E. Pioneer Road, Fond du Lac, Wisconsin 54935
Farmhouse (1880). 19th century village buildings furnished as if in use. Farm implements, vehicles. Clothing. Transport.
June 1 - Sept. 30: Tu.-Su., public holidays 1-5.

FOREST GROVE

PACIFIC UNIVERSITY MUSEUM
Forest Grove, Oregon 97116
In old College Hall (1850). History of the University and of Forest Grove. Northwest Indian artifacts.
Chinese items.
Th. 2-5. Other times by appointment.

FORKED RIVER

LACEY TOWNSHIP OLD SCHOOLHOUSE MUSEUM
Route 9, Forked River, New Jersey 08734
Schoolhouse (1860). Local history.
July 1 - Aug. 31: M., W., F. 1-3; Sa. 10-12. Other times by appointment.

FORSYTH

ROSEBUD COUNTY PIONEER MUSEUM
Forsyth, Montana 59327
Local history.
May 1 - Sept. 15: Tu.-Su., public holidays 9-9.

FORT ASHBY

FORT ASHBY
Fort Ashby, West Virginia 26719
Fort (1755), built to protect settlers from Indians. Military and Indian history.
June 1 - Aug. 31, Th. 11-4.

FORT ATKINSON

HOARD HISTORICAL MUSEUM
409 Merchant Avenue, Fort Atkinson, Wisconsin 53538
House (1865). Local history. Jefferson County Indian artifacts. Farm implements. Household equipment. Photographs. Costumes. Toys.
Foster House (1841) and May House (1863) are in the care of the Museum.
Tu., Th., F. 11-3; W., Sa. 8.30-5; 1st Su. in month 1-5. Closed public holidays.

FORT BELVOIR

U.S. ARMY CORPS OF ENGINEERS MUSEUM
21st and Flagler Road, Fort Belvoir, Virginia 22060
History of U.S. military engineering. Paintings. Photographs. Documents. Maps. Uniforms.
M.-F. 8-5. Closed public holidays.

FORT BENNING

U.S. ARMY INFANTRY MUSEUM
U.S. Army Infantry Center, Fort Benning, Georgia 31905
History of U.S. and foreign infantry, including Russian, Chinese, Japanese and Vietcong material. Weapons, equipment, uniforms.
Tu.-F. 10-4.30; Sa., Su. 12.30-4.30. Closed New Year, Christmas.

FORT BENTON

FORT BENTON MUSEUM
1801 Front Street, Fort Benton, Montana 59442
Near ruins of Fort Benton (1846). Local history illustrated by means of models, maps, paintings, prints and dioramas. Early trade routes. Indian artifacts.
June 1 - Aug. 31, May 1-5, 10-31, Sept. 1-30, daily 10-12, 1.30-5; Su., public holidays 10-7.

FORT BLISS

FORT BLISS REPLICA MUSEUM
Sheridan and Pleasanton Roads, Fort Bliss, Texas 79916
Local and military history, in 4 adobe buildings. 19th century household equipment. Weapons. Uniforms. Maps. Paintings. Prints.
Daily 9-4.45. Closed New Year, Easter, Thanksgiving, Christmas.

FORT BRAGG

BOISE CASCADE CORPORATION MUSEUM
90 Redwood Avenue, Fort Bragg, California 95437
History of local logging and lumbering industry. Tools. Machinery. Equipment.
M.-F., 8-5.

82nd AIRBORNE DIVISION WAR MEMORIAL
Ardennes Road, Gela Street, Fort Bragg, North Carolina 28307
History of the Division.
Tu.-Su. 11.30-4. Closed Dec. 24-6, Dec. 31, Jan. 1.

FORT BRIDGER

FORT BRIDGER STATE MUSEUM
Fort Bridger State Historic Site, Fort Bridger, Wyoming 82933
Restored fort buildings. Local history and archaeology. Indian material. Pioneer life. Horse-drawn vehicles.
Apr. 1 - Sept. 14, daily 8-7. Sept. 15 - Dec. 15, Sa., Su. 9-5. Closed Dec. 16 - Mar. 31.

FORT BUFORD

FORT BUFORD HISTORIC SITE MUSEUM
Fort Buford, North Dakota 58837
Indian clothing and artifacts. Pioneer furniture and tools. Military history.
May 1 - Sept. 15, 9-7.

FORT CALHOUN

WASHINGTON COUNTY HISTORICAL MUSEUM
14th and Monroe Streets, Fort Calhoun, Nebraska 68023
Indian artifacts and archaeology. Pioneer settlement. Farm implements. Weapons. Furniture. Musical instruments. Toys. History of Fort Atkinson.
Apr. 1 - Nov. 31: W., Sa., Su. 1.30-4.30. Rest of year by appointment.

FORT CAMPBELL

FORT CAMPBELL MUSEUM
Don F. Pratt Memorial Hall, Fort Campbell, Kentucky 42223
Military history. American and foreign uniforms. Equipment and documents relating to World War 2 and the Korean war, especially history of 101st Airborne Division.
Tu.-Su., public holidays 1-4.30. Closed New Year, Christmas.

FORT CARSON

FORT CARSON MUSEUM
849 Oconnel Boulevard, Fort Carson, Colorado 80913
Displays illustrating U.S. involvement in wars from the Revolutionary War to the present day. Mountain and dog training equipment. Weapons used by foreign armies. Kit Carson material.
Daily 9-5. Closed New Year, Easter, Thanksgiving, Christmas.

FORT CLINCH

FORT CLINCH STATE PARK
Florida A1A, Fort Clinch, Florida
Fort, 1847. Exhibits illustrating history of its fort and the area.
Daily 9-5.

FORT COLLINS

FORT COLLINS PIONEER MUSEUM
219 Peterson Street, Fort Collins, Colorado 80521
Pioneer and Indian history.
Antoine Janis trapper's cabin (1864) and Auntie Stone Cabin (1844) are in the care of the Museum.
M.-Sa., 1-5. Closed public holidays.

FORT DAVIS

DAVIS MOUNTAINS STATE PARK, INTERPRETIVE CENTER
Fort Davis, Texas 79734
Geology. Botany. Herbarium. Natural history.
June 1 - Aug. 30: M.-F. 1-5; Sa., Su. 8-5.

FORT DAVIS NATIONAL HISTORIC SITE
Box 785, Fort Davis, Texas 79734
Restoration of frontier fort (1854). Military history of period 1854-91. 19th century military music.
June 1 - Aug. 31, daily 8-8. Sept. 1 - May 31, daily 8.30-5.30.

NEILL MUSEUM
Fort Davis, Texas 79734
In Truehart House (1899). Period furnishings. Dolls. Texas-made toys. Children's museum.
May 15 - Sept. 15, daily 10-6. Other times by appointment.

FORT DODGE

BLANDEN ART GALLERY
920 3rd Avenue S., Fort Dodge, Iowa 50501
Archaeology. 17th-19th century European, American, African and Oriental art. Contemporary European and American paintings, sculpture. Decorative arts. Contemporary Japanese prints.
Tu.-F. 1.30-4.30; Sa. 9-12, 1-4; Su. 1.30-5.

FORT DODGE HISTORICAL MUSEUM
Museum Road, Fort Dodge, Iowa 50501
In schoolhouse (1855). History of Fort Dodge. Indian artifacts. Costumes.
May 11 - Oct. 31, 9-8.

FORT EDWARD

FORT EDWARD HISTORICAL SOCIETY MUSEUM
29 Broadway, Fort Edward, New York 12828
In Old Fort House (1755). Local history. Dioramas. Furniture.
July 1 - Aug. 31, daily 1-5.

WASHINGTON COUNTY HISTORICAL SOCIETY
County Building, Fort Edward, New York 12828
Local history.
W. 9-5.

FORT EUSTIS

U.S. ARMY TRANSPORTATION MUSEUM
Fort Eustis, Virginia 23604
History of U.S. military transport.
M.-F. 8-5; Sa., Su. 1-5. Closed public holidays.

FORT FISHER

FORT FISHER STATE HISTORIC SITE
Fort Fisher, North Carolina
Civil War fort, named in honour of Col. Charles F. Fisher. Visitor centre and museum tells story of Fort Fisher and includes items recovered from sunken blockade-runners.
Tu.-Sa. 9-5; Su. 1-5.

FORT GARLAND

OLD FORT GARLAND
P.O. Box 208, Fort Garland, Colorado 81133
Restored army post (1858-83). Dioramas. Historical exhibits.
May 1 - Oct. 31, daily 8-5.

FORT GIBSON

FORT GIBSON STOCKADE
State Highway 80, Fort Gibson, Oklahoma 74434
Reconstructed log fort (1824). Civil War relics.
Daily 9-5. Closed Christmas.

FORT HANCOCK

HUDSPETH VALLEY WOMEN'S CLUB MUSEUM
Highway 80, Fort Hancock, Texas 79841
Early settlement of Hudspeth county. It ems from old Fort Hancock. Scale model of Fort.
2nd, 4th W. each month 8-12. Other times by appointment.

FORT HUACHUCA

FORT HUACHUCA HISTORICAL MUSEUM
P.O. Box 766, Fort Huachuca, Arizona 85613
History and settlement of South-East Arizona.
M.-F., 9-4; Sa., Su., 1-4. Closed public holidays.

FORT HUNTER

SCHOHARIE CROSSING
Fort Hunter, New York 12069
Local history. Indian artifacts. Transport. Science. Technology. Maritime history.
By appointment.

FORT JOHNSON

FORT JOHNSON
Fort Johnson, New York 12070
House (1749). Local history. Indian collections.
May 1 - June 30, Sept. 1 - Oct. 31, daily 1-5. July 1 - Aug. 31, daily 10-5.

MUSEUM OF MONTGOMERY COUNTY HISTORICAL SOCIETY
Routes 5 and 67, Fort Johnson, New York 12070
In former home (1749) of Sir William Johnson. Indian and Civil War material. 17th-19th century Mohawk Valley artifacts.
Miller's House (1743) in the care of the Society.
May 1 - June 30, Sept. 1 - Oct. 31, daily 1-5. July 1 - Aug. 31, daily 10-5.

FORT KENT

FORT KENT STATE MEMORIAL
Fort Kent, Maine 04743
Museum in blockhouse (1839), built during frontier disagreements between Maine and New Brunswick.
May 15 - Sept. 15, daily 8 a.m.-9 p.m.

FORT KNOX

PATTON MUSEUM OF CAVALRY AND ARMOR
Old Ironsides Avenue, Fort Knox, Kentucky 40121
Weapons. Armoured vehicles. Medals. Paintings. Memorabilia of Gen. Patton.
Daily 9-4.30. Closed Dec. 24, 25, 31, Jan. 1.

FORT LARAMIE

FORT LARAMIE NATIONAL HISTORIC SITE
Fort Laramie, Wyoming 82212
Restored and furnished fort buildings (1849-85). Museum of local and military history in former Commissary. Trade beads. Weapons.
June 15 - Labour Day, 7-7. Rest of year, 8-4.30. Closed Christmas, New Year.

FORT LAUDERDALE

FORT LAUDERDALE MUSEUM OF THE ARTS
426 E. Las Olas Boulevard, Fort Lauderdale, Florida 33301
American Indian pottery, baskets. Japanese Inro and Netsuke. American and European paintings, sculpture, graphics from late 19th century to present day.
M.-F. 10-4.30; Sa. 10-5; Su. 12-5. Closed New Year, July 4, Thanksgiving, Christmas.

MUSEUM OF FORT LAUDERDALE HISTORICAL SOCIETY
850 N.E. 12th Avenue Extended, Fort Lauderdale, Florida 33304
Local and Florida history. Furniture with historic Fort Lauderdale associations. Domestic equipment, including flat irons. Dolls. Clothing of c.1900. Models and paintings showing development of city. Sewing machine (1893), used for instructing Indians.
M.-Th. 8-4; F. 8-noon.

UNIVERSITY GALLERY
University of Florida, Fort Lauderdale, Florida 32601
Oriental, European, American art.
M.-F. 9-5; Su. 1-5. Closed public holidays.

FORT LEAVENWORTH

FORT LEAVENWORTH MUSEUM
Andrews Hall, Reynolds and Gibbon Avenues, Fort Leavenworth, Kansas 66027
Horse-drawn vehicles, including waggons, coaches, family carriages, military transport. Military miniatures, 'Regiments of the World 1880-1914'. Uniforms. Artillery.
M.-Sa. 10-4; Su., public holidays 12-4. Closed New Year, Easter, Thanksgiving, Christmas.

FORT LEE

U.S. ARMY QUARTERMASTER CORPS MUSEUM
22nd Street and Avenue A, Fort Lee, Virginia 23801
History of Corps. Dioramas. Uniforms. Flags. Equipment. Paintings.
M.-F. 8-5; Sa., Su. 1-5. Closed Christmas.

FORT LEWIS

FORT LEWIS MILITARY MUSEUM
Building T 2257, Fort Lewis, Washington 98433
Military history of the N.W. Weapons. Uniforms. Equipment. Photographs.
Tu.-Su. 12-4. Closed Jan. 1-2, Dec. 24-25.

FORT LYON

KIT CARSON MEMORIAL CHAPEL
Veterans Administration Hospital, Fort Lyon, Colorado 81038
Building in which Kit Carson died. Pictures illustrating his life.
By appointment.

FORT MADISON

NORTH LEE COUNTY HISTORICAL SOCIETY
Fort Madison, Iowa 52627
County schoolroom (1870). Schoolbooks. Diplomas. Merit certificates.
By appointment.

FORT MCCLELLAN

EDITH NOURSE ROGERS MUSEUM
U.S. Women's Army Corps Center, Fort McClellan, Alabama 36201
History of Women's Army Corps. Uniforms. Photographs, books and documents. Flags. Music.
M.-F. 7.30-4.30. Closed national holidays.

FORT GEORGE G. MEADE

FIRST U.S. ARMY MUSEUM
Building T, 4674 Griffin Avenue, Fort George G. Meade, Maryland 20755
Military history. Paintings. Documents. Training manuals.
W.-F. 1-4.30; Sa. 11-4; Su. 1-4. Closed public holidays.

FORT MONMOUTH

U.S. ARMY SIGNAL CORPS MUSEUM
Myer Hall, Avenue of Memories, Fort Monmouth, New Jersey 07703
Foreign and American military communications, from 1850 onwards.
M.-F. 8-4. Closed public holidays.

FORT MONROE

FORT MONROE CASEMATE MUSEUM
Box 341, Fort Monroe, Virginia 23351
Fort Monroe and the Civil War. Paintings. Prints. Relics. Cell where Jefferson Davis was imprisoned, 1865.
Daily 8-5.

FORT MYERS

EDISON HOME MUSEUM
2341 McGregor Boulevard, Fort Myers, Florida 33901
Pre-fabricated house (1884), built in Maine and shipped to Florida. Inventions of Thomas Edison.
M.-Sa. 9-4; Su. 12.30-4.30. Closed Christmas.

FLORIDA MARINE MUSEUM
U.S. Highway 41, Fort Myers, Florida 33901
Shells.
Daily 9-5. Closed Christmas and Easter.

MUSEUM OF SOUTH-WEST FLORIDA HISTORICAL SOCIETY
2312 1st Street, Fort Myers, Florida 33902
Local history.
Tu. 9-12. Other times by appointment.

FORT OGLETHORPE

CHICKAMAUGA-CHATTANOOGA NATIONAL MILITARY PARK
Fort Oglethorpe, Georgia 30741
Civil War material. Rifles.
Daily 8-5. Closed Christmas.

FORT PECK

FORT PECK MUSEUM
Powerhouse No. 1, Fort Peck, Montana 59223
Geology, palaeontology, archaeology and history of the Fort Peck area.
May 30 - Labour Day: 9.30-5.30.

FORT PECK PROJECT
Fort Peck Theatre, Fort Peck, Montana 59223
Palaeontology. Bones of dinosaurs and other prehistoric animals. Fossils of marine creatures.
On request.

FORT PIERCE

ST. LUCIE COUNTY MUSEUM
414 Seaway Drive, Fort Pierce, Florida 33450
Local history. Mineralogy. Agriculture. Indian artifacts. Paintings. Glass. Music. Seminole Wars. Shipwrecks.
M.-F. 10-4.30, Su. 1-4.30. Closed New Year, Easter, Thanksgiving, Christmas, Aug. 1-31.

FORT PLAIN

FORT KLOCK HISTORIC RESTORATION
Fort Klock, Route 5, Fort Plain, New York 13339
Farmhouse (1750), fortified during War of Independence. Local history. Period furnishings. Restored schoolhouse (1825).
June 1 - Labour Day, Tu.-Su. 9-5.

FORT PLAIN MUSEUM
Canal Street, Fort Plain, New York 13339
Site of Revolutionary War fort. Local history. Colonial and Indian artifacts.
June 1 - Sept. 15: Daily 10-5.

TRYON COUNTY MUZZLE LOADERS, INC.
Fort K Lock, Fort Plain, New York 13339
In Revolutionary war fort. Local history. Handicrafts. Costumes.
By appointment.

FORT RALEIGH

FORT RALEIGH NATIONAL HISTORIC SITE
Fort Raleigh, Roanoke Island, North Carolina 27870
Exhibits illustrating first British attempts at colonisation.
July-Aug., daily 9-6. Sept.-June, daily 8.30-5.

FORT RANSOM

FORT RANSOM HISTORICAL SOCI ETY MUSEUM
Fort Ransom, North Dakota 58033
Indian artifacts. Material illustrating European, and especially Norwegian, settlement of area, 1878-1900. Household equipment. Military relics. Open-air museum, with burial mounds. Inscribed stones. Mooring stones.
May 1 - Sept. 30, daily 9-5.

FORT RECOVERY

FORT RECOVERY HISTORICAL SOCIETY, INC.
Fort Street, Fort Recovery, Ohio 45846
Indian material. Relics of battlefield where St. Clair was defeated (2792).
Tu.-Su. 9-Z.

FORT RILEY

U.S. CAVALRY MUSEUM
Fort Riley, Kansas 66442
In building of 1855 fort. History of the Fort and of the U.S. Cavalry. Local history. Indian artifacts.
Daily 1-4. Closed New Year, Thanksgiving, Christmas.

FORT SILL

FORT SILL MUSEUM
U.S. Highways 277 and 281, Fort Sill, Oklahoma 73503
In Fort Sill (1870-3). History of U.S. Field Artillery. Weapons. Uniforms and equipment. Horse-drawn vehicles. Indian exhibits. Graves of Geronimo and other Indian chiefs.
Daily 8-4.30. Closed Christmas, New Year.

FORT SMITH

FORT SMITH ART CENTER
423 N. 6th Street, Fort Smith, Arkansas 72901
In Fort Smith building (1857). Works by contemporary American artists. Paintings. Sculpture. Graphics. Decorative arts.
Tu.-Sa., 10-4; Su., 2-5. Closed New Year, July 4, Labour Day, Thanksgiving, Christmas.

FORT SMITH NATIONAL HISTORIC SITE
P.O. Box 1406, Fort Smith, Arkansas 72901
Barracks, commisary (1839-71). Local and military history exhibition.
Daily 8.30-5. Closed New Year, Christmas.

FORT STOCKTON

ANNIE RIGGS MEMORIAL MUSEUM
301 S. Main Street, Fort Stockton, Texas 79735
In former Riggs Hotel (1899). Life in Fort Stockton area c.1900. Pioneer life. Cowboy room. Kitchen. Mineral exhibit. Cattle paintings, 1895-1910.
M.-Sa., except W., 9.30-11.30; Su. 3-6.

FORT TOTTEN

FORT TOTTEN HISTORIC SITE MUSEUM
Fort Totten, North Dakota 58335
Military post (1867), with restored quarters, barracks, hospital. Pioneer history. Indian artifacts.
May 1 - Sept. 30, daily 9-5.

FORT WAINWRIGHT

JONATHAN WAINWRIGHT MUSEUM AND NATURAL RESOURCE CENTER
Building 1020, APO Seattle, Fort Wainwright, Alaska 98731
Botany. Natural history.
M.-F. 7.30-4.30; Sa. 8-12. Closed Sunday and national holidays.

FORT WALTON BEACH

HISTORICAL SOCIETY MUSEUM
732 Revere Avenue, Fort Walton Beach, Florida 32548
Social and industrial history of the district.
M., W., F., Sa. 10-4; Su. 2.30-4.30. Closed public holidays.

TEMPLE MOUND MUSEUM
139 Miracle Strip Parkway S.E., Walton Beach, Florida 32548
Local history. Anthropology. Archaeology. Natural history. Indian artifacts. Children's museum.
Tu.-W., F. Sa. 11-4. Th. 11-4, 6-8. Su. 1-4. Closed New Year, Christmas M.-F., Labour Day- Memorial Day by appointment.

FORT WASHINGTON

HOPE LODGE
Old Bethlehem Pike, Fort Washington, Pennsylvania 19034
House (c.1750). 18th - early 19th century furnishings.
May 1 - Sept. 30: Tu.-Sa. 8.30-5; Su. 1-5. Oct. 1 - Apr. 30: Tu.-Sa. 9-4.30; Su. 1-4.30. Closed public holidays.

FORT WAYNE

ALLEN COUNTY AND FORT WAYNE HISTORICAL SOCIETY MUSEUM
1424 West Jefferson, Fort Wayne, Indiana 46804
Museum building (1844). Local history.
Tu.-F. 10-12, 1-5; Sa., Su. 1-5.

FORT WAYNE MUSEUM OF ART
1202 W. Wayne Street, Fort Wayne, Indiana 46804
Paintings. Sculpture. Graphics.
M.-F., Su. 1-5; Sa. 10-5. Closed New Year, Independence Day, Memorial Day, Labour Day, Thanksgiving, Christmas.

LINCOLN NATIONAL LIFE FOUNDATION
1301 S. Harrison Street, Fort Wayne, Indiana 46802
Material relating to Abraham Lincoln and the Civil War.
M.-F. 8-4.30. Closed public holidays.

FORT WORTH

AMON CARTER MUSEUM OF WESTERN ART
3501 Camp Bowie Boulevard, Fort Worth, Texas 76101
Paintings, drawings, prints, sculpture by artists associated with the frontier West in the late 19th century.
M.-Sa. 10-5; Su., public holidays 1-5.30. Closed Christmas and M., Sept. 1 - May 31.

FORT WORTH ART CENTER MUSE UM
1309 Montgomery Street, Fort Worth, Texas 76107
19th and 20th century American and Eu ropean paintings, drawings, prints.
Tu.-Sa. 10-5; Su. 1-5.

FORT WORTH MUSEUM OF SCIENCE AND HISTORY
1501 Montgomery Street, Fort Worth, Texas 76107
Texas pioneer history. Earth sciences. Planetarium. Medical science. Texas mammals and birds. Indian artifacts. Anthropology. Botany.
M.-Sa. 9-5; Su. 2-5. (June 1 - Aug. 31, 2-6). Closed Dec. 24-25, New Year, Labour Day, Thanksgiving.

HERITAGE HALL
604 Main Street, Fort Worth, Texas 76102
Living museum of the Old West. Fort Worth history, 1841-76, shown by displays, sound effects and recorded dialogue.
M.-Sa. 10-5; Su. 1-5.

KIMBELL ART MUSEUM
Will Rogers Road W., Fort Worth, Texas 76107
European art from classical times to early 20th century. Oriental, African and pre-Colombian American art.
Tu.-Sa. 10-5; Su. 12-6. Closed Christmas.

LOG CABIN VILLAGE
2121 Colonial Parkway, Fort Worth, Texas 76107
7 restored log cabins (1848-70) with period furnishings.
M.-Sa. 9-5; Su. 1-4. Closed New Year, Thanksgiving, Christmas.

NATURAL HISTORY MUSEUM
Texas Christian University, University Drive (29), Fort Worth, Texas 76129
Geology. Zoology.
M.-Sa. 8 a.m. - 10 p.m.

PATE MUSEUM OF TRANSPORTATION
Highway 3775, Fort Worth, Texas 76101
Railway coaches, locomotives, equipment. Aeroplanes. Cars. Boats.
Tu.-Sa., public holidays 9-5. Su. 12-5. Closed Christmas.

FOSSIL

CITY OF FOSSIL MUSEUM
1st Street, Fossil, Oregon 97830
Local history. Transport. Indian artifacts.
Daily 10-5.

FOSTORIA

EMERINE COLLECTION
First National Bank, Fostoria, Ohio 44830
Early mechanical coin banks. Mechanical toys.
During banking hours or by appointment.

FOSTORIA MUSEUM
Tiffin and Wood Streets, Fostoria, Ohio 44830
Indian artifacts. Weapons. Musical instruments.
By appointment.

FRAMINGHAM

MUSEUM OF FRAMINGHAM HISTORICAL AND NATURAL HISTORY SOCIETY
Vernon Street, Framingham, Massachusetts 01701
Local history. Agriculture. Costumes.
Old Framingham Academy (1837) and Edgell Memorial Art and Education Center are in the care of the Society.
2nd Su. in month 2.30-5, and by appointment.

FRANCESTOWN

THE FRANCESTOWN VILLAGE IMPROVEMENT SOCIETY MUSEUM
Francestown, New Hampshire 03043
Local history. Soapstone industry.
W., Sa. afternoon; Sa. evening.

FRANKFORT

LIBERTY HALL MUSEUM
218 Wilkinson Street, Frankfort, Kentucky 40601
House (1796-1801). Family portraits. 18th century furniture, silver, porcelain.
Tu.-Sa. 10-5; Su. 2-5. Closed public holidays.

MUSEUM OF EXPERIMENTAL GAME FARM
Route 2, Frankfort, Kentucky 40601
Mounted birds and animals, illustrating Kentucky natural history.
Daily 8 a.m. - 8.30.

OLD GOVERNOR'S MANSION
High Street, Frankfort, Kentucky 40601
Lieutenant Governor's house (1798). Period furnishings.
M.-F. 11-4.

OLD STATE HOUSE
Broadway, Frankfort, Kentucky 40601
Building (1830). Documents, books, maps relating to history of Kentucky. Confederate and Civil War history. Indian artifacts. Cannon, rifles. Portraits of Kentucky governors. Silver service from battleship 'Kentucky'.
M.-Sa. 9-4.30; Su., public holidays, 9-4.30.

ORLANDO BROWN HOUSE
202 Wilkinson Street, Frankfort, Kentucky 40601
House (1835-6), with original and period furniture and furnishings.
Tu.-Sa. 10-5. Su. 2-5. Closed New Year, July 4, Christmas.

FRANKLIN

JOHNSON COUNTY HISTORICAL MUSEUM
150 West Madison Street, Franklin, Indiana 46131
Local history. Civil War material. Indian artifacts. Costumes. Furniture. Domestic equipment. Agricultural implements.
By appointment.

FRANKLIN COUNTY HISTORICAL SOCIETY MUSEUM
Franklin, Nebraska 68939
Local history.
June-Sept., Su. 1-5.

FRANKLIN AREA HISTORICAL SOCIETY MUSEUM
Franklin, Ohio 45005
Local history. Costumes.
Tu.-Sa. 2-5.

HARDING MUSEUM
P.O. Box 121, Franklin, Ohio 45005
War relics and personal possessions of Maj.-Gen. E. Forrest Harding.
Sa., Su., public holidays 1-5.

VENANGO COUNTY HISTORICAL SOCIETY MUSEUM
Franklin Public Library, 415 12th Street, Franklin, Pennsylvania 16323
History of Venango County and Northwest Pennsylvania.
Apr. 1 - Nov. 30, Tu.-Sa. 1-5; Su. 2-5. Closed holidays.

CARTER HOUSE
1140 Columbia Avenue, Franklin, Tennessee 37064
House (1830), was Federal Headquarters at Battle of Frankfurt. Civil War relics. Uniforms. Guns. Paintings. Drawings. Photographs.
M.-Sa. 9-4; Su. 2-4; public holidays 9-4. Closed Christmas.

EXPERIMENTAL AIRCRAFT ASSOCIATION
Air Education Museum, 11311 W. Forest Home Avenue, Franklin, Wisconsin 53132
Aviation history. Aircraft. Engines. Equipment. Air show posters.
M.-F. 8.30-5; Sa. 9-5; Su. 1-5. Closed public holidays.

FRANKLIN CENTER

GALLERY OF GREAT AMERICANS
c/o Franklin Mint, Franklin Center, Pennsylvania 19063
Personal possessions and memorabilia of the Greatest Americans.
Daily 9-5.

FRANKLINVILLE

ISCHUA VALLEY HISTORICAL SOCIETY
R.D.1, Franklinville, New York 14737
House (1814). Local history. Agriculture. Costumes. Open-air museum.
May 1 - Oct. 31, Sa. 2-5. Other times by appointment.

FRANKVILLE

FRANKVILLE MUSEUM
Frankville, Iowa 52101
Local history. Agriculture. Indian material. Costumes.
May 1 - Sept. 30, M.-Sa. by appointment, public holidays 1-4.

FREDERICK

MUSEUM OF HISTORICAL SOCIETY OF FREDERICK COUNTY
24 E. Church Street, Frederick, Maryland 21701
House (1835). 18th-19th century furniture, silver, glass. Lustre ware. Paintings by American artists. Civil War relics.
By appointment.

ROGER BROOK TANEY HOME AND MUSEUM
121 S. Bentz Street, Frederick, Maryland 21701
House (1799), with period furnishings and personal possessions of Taney.
Apr. 15- Sept. 1, daily 10-3.

BARBARA FRITCHIE MUSEUM
154 W. Patrick Street, Frederick, Maryland 21701
House is restored home of Barbara Fritchie. Personal possessions. Furniture.
Daily 9-5. Closed Christmas, Easter, Thanksgiving.

FREDERICKSBURG

ADMIRAL NIMITZ CENTER
340 E. Main Street, Fredericksburg, Texas 78624
In restored Charles H. Nimitz Hotel. Life and career of Admiral Nimitz. History of U.S. naval engagement in Pacific.
M.-Sa. 8-5. Closed New Year, Thanksgiving, Christmas.

PIONEER MEMORIAL MUSEUM
309 W. Main Street, Fredericksburg, Texas 78624
History of German community in Central Texas. Items brought from Germany or made locally in early days of settlement.
Kammlah House (1847) is in the care of the Museum.
June 1 - Aug. 31, M.-Sa. 10-5. Sept. 1 - May 31: Sa. 10-5; Su. 1-5. Other times by appointment.

FREDERICKSBURG NATIONAL MILITARY PARK
1300 Lafayette Boulevard, Fredericksburg, Virginia 22401
Civil War history and relics. House (1828) where General Stonewall Jackson died.
Museum: daily 8.30-6. Jackson House: May 1 - Sept. 30, daily 9-5. Rest of year: F.-Tu. 9-5. Closed Christmas.

KENMORE
1201 Washington Avenue, Fredericksburg, Virginia 22401
House (1752-6). 18th century furniture. Plantation office and kitchen. Portraits and manuscripts of Fielding Lewis family.
Mar. 1 - Nov. 14, daily 9-5. Nov. 15 - Feb. 28, daily 9-4.30. Closed Dec. 25-6, Jan. 1-2.

HUGH MERCER APOTHECARY SHOP
1020 Caroline Street, Fredericksburg, Virginia 22401
Shop (1761). Pharmaceutical and medical equipment.
Daily 9-5. Closed New Year, Christmas.

JAMES MONROE MUSEUM AND MEMORIAL LIBRARY
908 Charles Street, Fredericksburg, Virginia 22401
Building (1758) where President Monroe began practising law. Monroe family possessions. Portraits. Costumes. 18th century French furniture. Sculptures. China. Silver. Monroe's library.
Daily 9-5. Closed Christmas.

RISING SUN TAVERN
1306 Caroline Street, Fredericksburg, Virginia 23401
House (1760), house of Charles, brother of George Washington. 18th century furnishings, musical instruments and music. American and English pewter.
Mar. 1 - Nov. 15, daily 9-5. Nov. 16 - Feb. 28, daily 9-4.30.

STONER'S STORE
1202 Prince Edward Street, Fredericksburg, Virginia 22401
Local history. Agriculture. Industry. Medicine. Prints. Drawings.
Daily 9-5. Closed Dec. 24 - Jan. 1.

MARY WASHINGTON HOUSE
1200 Charles Street, Fredericksburg, Virginia 22401
House (1770), home of George Washington's mother. Period furnishings.
Mar. 16 - Nov. 14, daily 9-5. Nov. 15 - Mar. 15, daily 9-4.30. Closed Jan. 1-2, Dec. 25-6.

FREDONIA

MUSEUM OF WILSON COUNTY HISTORICAL SOCIETY
Courthouse, Fredonia, Kansas 66736
Settlement and subsequent history of Wilson County and Kansas. Agriculture. Indian artifacts. Costumes. Folklore. Children's books and clothing. Toys.
M.-F. 1-5. Closed public holidays.

MICHAEL C. ROCKEFELLER ARTS CENTER
State University College, Fredonia, New York 14063
Contemporary paintings, drawings, sculpture, prints, ceramics.
M.-Tu., Th.-Sa. 11-5; W. 11-5, 7-9; Su. 1-5.

FREEHOLD

MUSEUM OF MONMOUTH COUNTY HISTORICAL ASSOCIATION
70 Court Street, Freehold, New Jersey 07728
Local history. Indian artifacts. Folklore. Costumes. Glass. Paintings. Decorative arts. Children's and junior museums. 17th-19th century furnishings.
Marlpit Hall (1684-1725), Hendrickson House (c.1717), Clinton's Headquarters (c.1706) and Allen House (c.1700) are in the care of the Association.
Tu.-Sa. 11-5; Su. 2-5.

FREEMAN

FREEMAN JUNIOR COLLEGE MUSEUM
Freeman, South Dakota 57029
Indian artifacts. Transport.
Sept.-May, F. 1-4.30.

FREEPORT

MUSEUM OF STEPHENSON COUNTY HISTORICAL SOCIETY
1440 South Carroll Avenue, Freeport, Illinois 61032
House (1857). Local history. Letters and personal possessions of Jane Addams. Industrial, agricultural history. Material relating to Lincoln-Douglas debate 1858. Farm implements.
Sa., Su. 1.30-4. Closed public holidays.

RAWLEIGH MUSEUM
223 E. Main Street, Freeport, Illinois 61032
Paintings. Sculpture. Mosaics. Indian and Mexican artifacts.
M.-F. 7.30-4.30.

FREEPORT HISTORICAL MUSEUM
350 S. Main Street, Freeport, New York 11520
Early history of Freeport. Fishing. Schools. Home entertainment. Communications. Photography.
Mar. 14 - July 4, Su. 2-5. July 8 - Dec. 31, Su. 2-5.

FREMONT

MISSION SAN JOSE DE GUADALUPE
Fremont, California 94536
Mission building (1797). History and artifacts of Mission period.
Daily 10-5.

WINDMILL GARDENS
Luce Avenue, Fremont, Michigan 49412
Windmills, including the 100 ft. Ensley Tower mill. Mill machinery. Model village.
Daily 9-5.

LOUIS E. MAY MUSEUM
1643 E. Nye Street, Fremont, Nebraska 68025
House (1874). Local history. Dolls.
W., Su. 1.30-4.30. Closed Dec. 15 - Feb. 28.

GOVERNOR CHARLES B. AYCOCK BIRTHPLACE
Box 207, Fremont, North Carolina 27830
House (1840). Exhibits related to Aycock's life and to his work as Governor. Restored schoolhouse (1870) forms part of Museum, devoted to the career and work of North Carolina's 'Education Governor' (1900-1904).
Tu.-Sa. 9-5; Su. 1-5. Closed Thanksgiving, Dec. 24-6.

RUTHERFORD B. HAYES LIBRARY AND MUSEUM
1337 Hayes Avenue, Fremont, Ohio 43420
House (1859) was home of President Hayes. Memorabilia of the President. American history.
Dillon House (1873) is in the care of the Museum.
M.-Sa. 9-5; Su., public holidays 1.30-5. Closed New Year, Thanksgiving, Christmas.

FRENCH CAMP

FRENCH CAMP ACADEMY MUSEUM
French Camp, Mississippi 39745
Local history. Archaeology. Indian artifacts.
M.-F. 8-11.30, 3-4.30; Sa. 8-11.30, 12.30-1.30, 2.30-4; Su. 1-4. Closed school vacations.

FRESNO

HISTORICAL SOCIETY
Academy of California Church History, 1530 N. Fresno Street, Fresno, California 93703
Material, mainly books and manuscripts, relating to Spanish period in history of California.
By appointment.

MUSEUM OF FRESNO COUNTY HISTORICAL SOCIETY
7160 West Kearney Boulevard, Fresno, California 93706
Local history. Agriculture. Industry. Transport. Anthropology. Ethnology. Costumes. Paintings. Sculpture. Decorative arts. Indian culture.
Four historic buildings, including Tarpey railroad station (1881), are in the care of the Museum.
Mar. 1 - Dec. 31: W.-Su., public holidays, 2-5. Rest of year by appointment. Closed New Year, Christmas.

FRESNO ARTS CENTER
3033 E. Yale Avenue, Fresno, California 93703
Pre-Columbian and later Mexican art. Oriental paintings, sculpture, prints. Contemporary American paintings, graphics.
Tu.-Su. 12-4; W. also 7.30-10 p.m. Closed New Year, Easter, Thanksgiving, Christmas, Aug. 1-31.

FRESNO MUSEUM OF NATURAL HISTORY AND JUNIOR MUSEUM
1944 N. Winery Avenue, Fresno, California 93703
Geology. Botany. Natural history. Local history. Astronomy. Anthropology.
M.-Sa., 9-5; Su., public holidays 12-5. Closed New Year, July 4, Thanksgiving, Christmas.

FRIDAY HARBOR

MUSEUM OF SAN JUAN HISTORICAL SOCIETY
P.O. Box 441, Friday Harbor, Washington 98250
Local history. Furniture. Household equipment. Tools.
Sa. 2-4.

SAN JUAN ISLAND NATIONAL HISTORICAL PARK
P.O. Box 549, Friday Harbor, Washington 98250
Relics of the Pig War (1859-72). Restored barracks, blockhouse, commisary.
Daily 8-4.30. Closed Christmas, New Year.

FRIENDSHIP

FRIENDSHIP MUSEUM
Friendship, Maine 04547
Building (c.1820) was formerly schoolhouse. Local history.
June 23 - Labour Day: M.-Sa. 10-5; Su., public holidays 2-5.

FRUITA

COLORADO NATIONAL MONUMENT
Box 438, Fruita, Colorado 81521
Local geology, history, natural history and ethnology. Casts and photographs of dinosaur fossils. Wild-life dioramas. Indian culture.
Labour Day - June 13, Daily 8-5. June 14 - Labour Day, daily 8-8. Closed New Year, Christmas.

FULTON

WINSTON CHURCHILL MEMORIAL
7th Street and Westminster Avenue, Fulton, Missouri 65251
Material documenting life and career of Sir Winston Churchill. Reconstructed Wren church of St. Mary the Virgin, Aldermanbury, London.
Dec. 1 - Mar. 31: M.-Sa. 10-4; Su. 11-4.45. Apr. 1 - Nov. 30: M.-Sa. 9-4.45; Su. 10-4.45. Closed New Year, Thanksgiving, Christmas.

FUQUAY-VARINA

JOHNSON GOURD MUSEUM
U.S. Highway 55, Fuquay-Varina, North Carolina 27526
Gourd artifacts, including Indian musical instruments.
Daily 7 a.m. - 9 p.m.

GAIL

BORDEN COUNTY HISTORICAL MUSEUM
Courthouse, Gail, Texas 79738
Geology. Natural history. Pioneer life in Borden County. Memorabilia of early families. Indian artifacts. Medicine. Doward Drug Store (1900) is in the care of the Museum.
M., Th., Su. 2-5. Closed Christmas.

GAINESVILLE

FLORIDA STATE MUSEUM
University of Florida, Gainesville, Florida 32601
Geology. Palaeontology. Natural history. Archaeology. Anthropology. Local history.
M.-Sa. 9-5; Su., public holidays 1-5. Closed Christmas.

MARJORIE KINNAN RAWLINGS STATE MUSEUM
Cross Creek, Gainesville, Florida 32601
Home of the novelist and Pulitzer Prize winner, Marjorie Rawlings (d.1953). Original Furnishings. Personal possessions of Mrs. Rawlings.
Daily 9-5.

UNIVERSITY OF FLORIDA PLANETARIUM
University Classroom Building, Gainesville, Florida 32601
Astronomy. Planetarium.
By appointment.

UNIVERSITY GALLERY
Gainesville, Florida 32601
Indian art and handicrafts. Paintings. Sculpture. Graphic art.
M.-F. 9-5; Su. 1-5. Closed Sept., public holidays.

MORTON MUSEUM OF COOKE COUNTY
Dixon and Pecan Streets, Gainesville, Texas 76240
In old Fire Station (1884). History of Cooke County.
F., Su. 2-5. Closed Christmas.

GALENA

JOHN DOWLING HOUSE
Diagonal and Perry Streets, Galena, Illinois 61036
House (1826). Furnished as merchant's house and trading post of the period.
Apr. 1 - Nov. 30, daily 9-5.

'GALENA GAZETTE' MUSEUM
213 S. Main Street, Galena, Illinois 61036
Hand and foot-operated presses. Wooden type. Early issues of the 'Gazette'.
M.-F. 10-5.

GALENA HISTORICAL SOCIETY MUSEUM
221 S. Bench Street, Galena, Illinois 61036
Local history. Agriculture. Domestic equipment. Civil War murals. Mining room.
May 1 - Oct. 30, 10-5.

GALENA MARKET HOUSE STATE MEMORIAL
Water Street, Galena, Illinois 61036
Market House (1845). Contains exhibition of Illinois architecture.
Daily 9-5. Closed New Year, Thanksgiving, Christmas.

J. R. GRANT LEATHER STORE
Main Street, Galena, Illinois 61036
Replica of mid-19th century store.
Daily 10-5.

ULYSSES S. GRANT HOME STATE MEMORIAL
Bruthillier Street, Galena, Illinois 61036
House (1859). Grant family furniture, and personal possessions.
Daily 10-5.

OLD FIREHOUSE
Washington and Bench Streets, Galena, Illinois 61036
Old fire-fighting equipment, including rope-hauled Fire Masheen of 1855.
Daily 10-5.

OLD GENERAL STORE
Main Street at Green Street, Galena, Illinois 61036
Reproduction of 19th century store.
M.-Sa. 10-5.

OLD STOCKADE
Main and Perry Streets, Galena, Illinois 61036
Built (1832) for protection of settlers. Log-house. Indian relics.
Daily 10-5.

VINEGAR HILL LEAD MINE
U.S. Highway 20, Galena, Illinois 61036
Working lead mine.
Apr. 1 - Nov. 30, 10-5.

GALESBURG

CARL SANDBURG BIRTHPLACE
331 East Third Street, Galesburg, Illinois 61401
House (1870). Mementoes of Sandburg, biographer of Lincoln, and Lincoln. Period furnishings.
M.-Sa. 9-12, 1-5; Su. 1-5. Closed New Year, Thanksgiving, Christmas and a.m. Feb.

GALETON

PENNSYLVANIA LUMBER MUSEUM
Galeton, Pennsylvania 16922
Botany. Natural history. History of lumber industry. Reconstructed logging camp. Ecology.
M.-Sa., public holidays 9-5; Su. 1-5.

GALION

LOUIS BROMFIELD MALABAR FARM FOUNDATION
Route 2, Box 72, Galion, Ohio 44833
In The Big House, former home of Louis Bromfield. Original furnishings.
M.-Sa. 9-5; Su. 10-5. Closed Thanksgiving, Christmas.

HERITAGE COTTAGE
Heritage Lane, Galion, Ohio 44833
Regional history and archaeology. Indian artifacts.
M.-Sa. by appointment. 1st Su. in month 2-4.

GALLATIN

CRAGFONT
State Highway 25, Gallatin, Tennessee 37066
House (1802), was home of General James Winchester. Original and period furnishings. Farm tools and implements.
Apr. 15 - Nov. 1: Tu.-Sa. 10-5; Su. 1-6. Other times by appointment.

GALLATIN GATEWAY

LORENE'S ANTIQUE MANSION
Gallatin Gateway, Montana 59730
Furniture. Guns. Glass. Transport.
May 1-31, Sept. 1-30, daily 1-5. June 1 - Aug. 31, daily 8-12, 1-5.

GALLIPOLIS

OUR HOUSE STATE MEMORIAL
434 1st Avenue, Gallipolis, Ohio 45631
Restored tavern (1819). Period furnishings.
Apr. 1 - Oct. 31: Tu.-Su. 9.30-5.

GALLUP

GALLUP MUSEUM OF INDIAN ARTS AND CRAFTS
103 W. 66 Avenue, Gallup, New Mexico 87301
Arts and crafts of S.W. Indians.
June 1 - Aug. 31: M.-Sa. 7-9. Sept. 1 - May 31: M.-F. 9-12, 1-5; Sa. 9-12. Closed public holidays.

GALVESTON

BISHOP'S PALACE
1402 Broadway, Galveston, Texas 77550
House (1886), built by Col. Walter Gresham from materials and components gathered around the world.
May 31 - Labour Day, daily, except Tu., 10-5; Su. 1-5. Rest of year, daily, except Tu., 1-5.

CENTRE ON THE STRAND
2127 Strand, Galveston, Texas 77550
Natural history. History of Galveston Island and Galveston Bay.
Tu.-Sa. 10-5; Su. 2-5. Closed Christmas, New Year, Memorial Day, Thanksgiving.

GALVESTON HISTORICAL FOUNDATION, INC.
3601 Avenue P, Galveston, Texas 77550
In Samuel May Williams House (1838). Furniture. Local history.
June-Aug. daily 1-5.

KARANKAWA INDIAN MUSEUM
Bob Smith Drive, Jamaica Beach, Galveston, Texas 77552
Indian life and artifacts. Burials. Teepees. Canvas.
Daily, 9-6.

POWHATAN HOUSE
3427 Avenue O, Galveston, Texas 77550
House (c.1847). Period furnishings.
June 1 - Sept. 8, daily 1-5. Other times by appointment.

ROSENBERG LIBRARY
2310 Sealy Avenue, Galveston, Texas 77550
Paintings. Graphics. Sculpture. Decorative arts. Archaeology. Ethnography.
M.-Th. 9-9; F.-Sa. 9-6. Closed April 21, public holidays.

TIMEWEALTH CORPORATION KARANKAWA INDIAN MUSEUM
Jamaica Beach, Galveston, Texas 77550
Indian archaeology, artifacts.
Daily 9-6.

TRUBE HOUSE
1627 Sealy Avenue, Galveston, Texas 77556
House (1890), built on pattern of Danish castle. Period furnishings. Glass.
By appointment.

SAMUEL MAY WILLIAMS HOUSE
3601 Avenue P, Galveston, Texas 77550
House (1837-40), home of Austin Colony land agent, Samuel Williams. Period furnishings. Willia ms family memorabilia. Pioneer relics.
June 1 - Labour Day, daily 10-5.

GANADO

HUBBELL TRADING POST NATIONAL HISTORIC SITE
Box 298, Ganado, Arizona 86505
Buildings, 1880-1930, belonging to former Hubbell trading post. Local archaeology, ethnology and history. Agriculture. Paintings. Sculpture. Graphics.
May 1- Sept. 30, daily 8-6; Oct. 1- Sept. 30, daily 8-5. Closed New Year, Thanksgiving, Christmas.

GARBERVILLE

RICHARDSON GROV E STATE PARK
Garberville, California 95440
Exhibits on redwood forests and forest wildlife.
May-Sept., daily 8 a.m. - 10 p.m. Oct.-Apr., daily 8-5. Closed Thanksgiving, Christmas, Jan. 1.

GARDEN CITY

MUSEUM OF FINNE Y COUNTY HISTORICAL SOCIETY
Finney Park, S. 4th Street, Garden City, Kansas 67846
Local history.
May 15 - Sept. 30: daily 2-7. Oct. 1 - May 14: Sa., Su. 2-5.

NANKIN MILLS NATURE CENTER
33175 Ann Arbor Trail, Garden City, Michigan 48135
Early 19th century grist mill, restored by Henry Ford, Preserving millrace and turbine. Now natural history museum.
Daily 9-5. Closed public holidays.

NASSAU COUNTY HISTORICAL SOCIETY
Garden City, New York 11530
Local history.
Daily 9-5.

GARDEN GROVE

STANLEY HOUSE MUSEUM
12174 The Euclid Heritage Park, Garden Grove, California 52640
Local history. Agriculture. Furniture.
Sa., Su. 2-4.

GARNAVILLO

GARNAVILLO HISTORICAL MUSEUM
Garnavillo, Iowa 52049
In former church (1866). Anthropology. Archaeology. Local history. Indian artifacts.
May 15 - Oct. 15, Sa., Su., public holidays 1-5, 7-10.

GARNETT

ANDERSON COUNTY HISTORICAL MUSEUM
Court House, Garnett, Kansas 66032
History of early settlement of Anderson County. Guns. Indian artifacts.
M.-F. 1.30-4.

BRIDGET WALKER ART COLLECTION
Garnett Public Library, 125 W. 4th Avenue, Garnett, Kansas 66032
Paintings, watercolours, drawings by 19th-20th century American artists.
M.-Sa. 2-5, 7-9. Closed July 4, Labour Day, Thanksgiving. Christmas.

GARRISON-ON-HUDSON

BOSCOBEL RESTORATION
Route 9-D, Garrison-on-Hudson, New York 10524
House (1804-6). 18th-19th century furnishings, decorative arts.
Apr. 1 - Oct. 31: W.-M. 9.30-5. Nov. 1 - Dec. 31, Mar., W.-M. 9.30-4. Closed Thanksgiving, Christmas.

GASTONIA

SCHIELE MUSEUM OF NATURAL HISTORY AND PLANETARIUM
1500 E. Garrison Boulevard, Gastonia, North Carolina 28052
Geology. Mineralogy. Palaeontology. Botany. Herbarium. Natural history. Zoology. Anthropology. Indian artifacts and culture.
Tu.-F. 9-5; Sa., Su., public holidays 2-5.

GATES MILLS

GATES MILLS HISTORICAL SOCIETY
Old Mill Road, Gates Mills, Ohio 44040
Local history since c.1850. Furnishings. Domestic equipment.
M., W., F. 1-9; Tu., Sa. 9-1.

GATLINBURG

CADES COVE OPEN AIR MUSEUM
Great Smoky Mountains National Park, Gatlinburg, Tennessee 37738
Village museum, illustrating pioneer life.
Daily, dawn-dusk.

HOMESPUN VALLEY MOUNTAINEER VILLAGE
8 Airport Road, Gatlinburg, Tennessee 37738
Mountain pioneer village. Log Cabin. Blacksmith's shop. Grist mill. Whisky still. Museum illustrating pioneer life.
June 1 - Oct. 15: M.-Sa., public holidays 7.30-11.

OCONALUFTEE VISITOR CENTER
Great Smoky Mountains National Park, Gatlinburg, Tennessee 37738
18th - 19th century life in the Southern Highlands. Pioneer artifacts. Reconstructed homestead.
May 1 - Sept. 30, daily 8-9. Oct. 1 - Apr. 30, daily 8-4.30.

SUGARLANDS VISITOR CENTER
Great Smoky Mountains National Park, Gatlinburg, Tennessee 37738
Natural history. Flora of the National Park.
May 1 - Oct. 31, daily 8-9. Nov. 1 - Apr. 30, daily 8-4.30.

GAUTIER

GAUTIER'S PLANTATION HOUSE
Highway 90, Gautier, Mississippi 39553
Plantation House (1856), with original, mostly French, furniture. Meissen, Sèvres, Dresden, French Bisque China. Clocks. Glass. Indian artifacts. Costumes. Log house (1767).
M.-Sa. 9-5; Su. 12-5. Closed Dec. 15 - Jan. 1, Easter.

GAYLORD

CALL OF THE WILD MUSEUM
850 S. Wisconsin Avenue, Gaylord, Michigan 49735
Natural history of N. America.
May 1- Sept. 30, 8-9. Oct. 1 - Apr. 30, 8.30-6. Closed Christmas.

GEM VALLEY

GEM VALLEY MUSEUM
Gem Valley, Colorado 88112
Geology. Local history and archaeology. Anthropology.
By appointment.

GENESEO

GENESEO MUSEUM
P.O. Box 461, Geneseo, Kansas 67444
House (1926). Period furnishings.
By appointment.

FINE ARTS GALLERY
State University of New York, Fine Arts Building, Geneseo, New York 14454
Paintings. Sculpture. Graphics. Ceramics. Furniture.
By local announcement.

LIVINGSTON COUNTY HISTORICAL MUSEUM
30 Center Street, Geneseo, New York 14454
In former school (1838). Local history. Agriculture. Indian artifacts. Pioneer life. Civil War exhibits. Concord coach. Toys.
May 1 - Oct. 31: Tu., Th. 2-5. Other times by appointment.

GENEVA

LIMBERLOST STATE MEMORIAL
Sixth and Williams Streets, Geneva, Indiana 46740
In Limberlost Cabin (1895), home of novelist, Gene Stratton Porter. Memorabilia and personal possessions of Porter family.
Daily 9-12, 1-5.

GENEVA HISTORICAL MUSEUM
453 S. Main Street, Geneva, New York 14456
In Prouty-Chew House (1825). Local and Indian history. Costumes. China. Glass. Dolls. Toys. Items from local glass factory.
Rose Hill Mansion (1839) is in the care of the Museum.
Tu.-Sa. 1.30-4.30. Closed public holidays.

ROSE HILL MANSION
Route 96A, Geneva, New York 14456
House (1839) with original furnishings.
May 1 - Oct. 31: M.-Sa. 10-4; Su. 1-4.

HOBART AND WILLIAM SMITH COLLEGE MUSEUM
Geneva, New York 14456
Geology. Mineralogy. Palaeontology. Botany. Herbarium. Natural history.
M.-Sa. 9-5. Closed college vacations.

GENOA

MORMON STATION STATE HISTORICAL MONUMENT
Genoa, Nevada 89411
Restored log fort and trading station (1851). Local history before 1880.
May 1 - Sept. 30, daily 9-7.

GEORGETOWN

HAMILL HOUSE
Argentine and Third Streets, Georgetown, Colorado 80444
House (1867) with camel-hair wallpaper, gold chandeliers and door-knob, onyx and marble fireplaces. Mining memorabilia. Costumes. Office building (1875).
June 1 - Sept. 30, daily 9.30-6.

HOTEL DE PARIS
Georgetown, Colorado 80444
Building (c.1874). Original hotel furnishings.
June 15 - Sept. 15, daily 9-5.30.

CAPTAIN SAMUEL BROCKLEBANK MUSEUM
108 E. Main Street, Georgetown, Massachusetts 01830
House (1660). Local history. Paintings. Furniture. Indian artifacts.
Memorial Day - Labour Day, W. 2-5; Sa., Su. 1.30-5.30. Labour Day - Oct. 12, Su. 1.30-5.30.

GRANT SCHOOLHOUSE
South Water Street, Georgetown, Ohio 45121
Building (1804). Material relating to General Grant and the Civil War.
Tu.-Su. 12-5.

HOPSEWEE PLANTATION
U.S. Highway 17, Georgetown, South Carolina 29440
House (1735-40). Period furnishings.
Tu.-F. 10-5.

PYATT-DOYLE HOUSE
630 Highmarket Street, Georgetown, South Carolina 29440
House (1790). 18th - early 19th century furnishings.
M., Tu., Th., F. 9-2, 4-6; closed public holidays.

THE RICE MUSEUM
Front and Screven Streets, Georgetown, South Carolina 29440
History of rice culture in Georgetown County. Maps. Dioramas. Tools and equipment. Paintings, drawings.
M.-Sa. 9-5; Su. 2-5.

WEDGEFIELD PLANTATION
S.C. Highway 701, Georgetown, South Carolina 29440
House (1762). Period furnishings.
Tu.-Th., Sa., Su. 10-3.

GEORGE WEST

LIVE OAK COUNTY MUSEUM
Courthouse, George West, Texas 78022
Historical relics and documents illustrating early settlement of Live Oak County.
M.-Sa. 8-5.

GERING

MUSEUM OF NORTH PLATTE VALLEY HISTORICAL ASSOCIATION
1349 10th Street, Gering, Nebraska 69341
Local history. Handicrafts. Musical instruments.
Tu.-Th. 1-5, Su., public holidays 2-5.

OREGON TRAIL MUSEUM
Scotts Bluff National Monument, Gering, Nebraska 69341
Palaeontology. Archaeology. Paintings, including works by W. H. Jackson, illustrating migration over Oregon, California and Mormon Trails.
June 1 - Aug. 31, daily 7 a.m. - 8 p.m. Sept. 1 - May 31, daily 8-4.30. Closed Christmas.

GERMANTOWN

CLERMONT
R.R. 1, County Road 6, Germantown, New York 12526
Livingston family mansion (1730, 1778). Family portraits. 19th century furnishings.
By appointment.

GETTYSBURG

GETTYSBURG NATIONAL MILITARY PARK
Gettysburg, Box 70, Pennsylvania 1732 5
Site of Battle of Gettysburg 1863, with key points indicated. Visitor Centre contains battle relics and cyclorama of events.
Daily, May 1 - Oct. 31, 8-9; Nov. 1 - Apr. 30, 8-5. Closed New Year, Christmas.

GETTYSBURG NATIONAL MUSEUM
R.D.1, Gettysburg, Pennsylvania 17325
Civil War history and relics.
Jan. 1 - Mar. 31, daily 9-5. Apr. 1 - May 31, Sept. 1 - Oct. 31, daily 8-7.30. June 1 - Aug. 31, daily 8-9. Closed Christmas.

LINCOLN MUSEUM
Lincoln Square, Gettysburg, Pennsylvania 17325
Lincoln memorabilia, especially relating to his visit to Gettysburg.
Mar.-Oct. daily 9-9.

LINCOLN TRAIN MUSEUM
Steinwehr Avenue, Gettysburg, Pennsylvania 17325
Railway history.
Easter - Oct. 31, daily 9-10.

MUSEUM OF ADAMS COUNTY HISTORICAL SOCIETY
Lutheran Seminary Campus, Gettysburg, Pennsylvania 17325
Building (1832). Local history. Indian artifacts.
W. 1-5; Sa. 9-5. Closed public holidays.

GIDDINGS

LEE COUNTY MUSEUM
P.O. Box 424, City Hall, Hempstead and Main Streets, Giddings, Texas 78942
Lee County history. Material from Wendish colony, established 1854. Farm implements. Household equipment and utensils. Clothing. Photographs.
Sa. 3-5.

GILA HOT SPRINGS

GILA CLIFF DWELLINGS NATIONAL MONUMENT
Visitor Gallery, Gila Hot Springs, New Mexico 88061
Indian history. Pottery. Ethnology. Botany.
Oct.-May, daily 8-5. June-Sept., daily 8-7. Closed New Year, Christmas.

GILLETT

ARKANSAS COUNTY MUSEUM
Gillett, Arkansas 72055
Local history. Agriculture. Transport. Archaeology. Costumes. Textiles. Music. Glass.
Refeld-Hinman house (1877) is in the care of the Museum.
M.-Sa., 9-5; Su., 1-5. Closed New Year, Thanksgiving, Dec. 24-26.

ARKANSAS POST NATIONAL MEMORIAL
Gillett, Arkansas 72055
Local history. Indian artifacts.
Daily 8-5. Closed Christmas.

WELTNER WONDER MUSEUM
Highway 59, Gillett, Wisconsin 54124
Old cars. Guns. Indian artifacts.
May 1 - Nov. 31, daily 9-9. Jan. 1 - Mar. 31 by appointment.

GLASTONBURY

HISTORICAL SOCIETY MUSEUM
1944 Main Street, Glastonbury, Connecticut 06033
Local history.
Welles-Shipman House (1755) is in the care of the Society.
By appointment.

GLENCOE

MUSEUM OF WABASH, FRISCO AND PACIFIC ASSOCIATION
General office, Glencoe, Missouri 63038
Operates narrow-gauge steam railway. Collection of scale-model locomotives and rolling-stock.
May 1 - Sept. 30: Su., public holidays 12-3.30.

GLEN COVE

NASSAU MUSEUM OF NATURAL HISTORY
Garvies' Point Divinity Library, Barry Drive, Glen Cove, New York 11542
Geology and archaeology of coastal New York.
M.-Sa. 10-5; Su., public holidays 1-5.

GLENDALE

CALIFORNIA NATIONAL WATER COLOR SOCIETY
1323 Columbia Drive, Glendale, Califo rnia 91205
Water-color paintings.
By appointment.

CASA ADOBE DE SAN RAFAEL
1330 Dorothy Drive, Glendale, California 91202
House (1864). Early Californian furniture and domestic equipment.
By appointment.

FOREST LAWN MUSEUM
1712 South Glendale Avenue, Glendale, California 91209
American history. Weapons and armour. Indian ivory painting. Coins. Room interiors.
Daily, 10-6.

GLENDIVE

FRONTIER GATEWAY MUSEUM
Frontage Road, Glendive, Montana 59330
History of early settlement of eastern Montana and western N. Dakota. Prehistoric and historic Indian artifacts. Transport.
May 1-31, Sept. 1-30, daily 1-5. June 1 - Aug. 31, daily 8-12, 1-5.

GLENDORA

GLENDORA HISTORICAL SOCIETY MUSEUM
304 N. Glendora Avenue, Glendora, California 91740
Local history. Indian artifacts.
3rd Saturday every month, except July 1 - Aug. 31, Dec. 1-31.

GLEN ECHO

CLARA BARTON HOUSE
5801 Oxford Road, Glen Echo, Maryland 20768
House (1892), with period furnishings. Former house of Clara Barton, founder of American Red Cross.
Tu.-Su. 1-5. Closed public holidays.

GLEN ELLEN

JACK LONDON STATE HISTORIC PARK
London Ranch Road, P.O. Box 358, Glen Ellen, California 95442
Ruins of London's Wolf House Mansion (1813). House of the Happy Walls (1919), home of Charmian London, with London's South Sea collection, personal possessions and furniture. Horse-drawn vehicles, harness.
Daily 10-5. Closed New Year, Thanksgiving, Christmas.

GLEN ROSE

SOMERWELL COUNTY MUSEUM
Elm and Vernon Streets, Glen Rose, Texas 76043
Rocks and minerals. Fossils. Pioneer life. Indian artifacts. Furnishings. Tools.
June 1 - Labour Day, M.-Sa. 10-5. Su. 12.30-5. Labour Day - May 31, M.-F., by appointment; Sa.-Su. 12.30-5.

GLENS FALLS

HYDE COLLECTION
161 Warren Street, Glens Falls, New York 12801
European and American paintings, including works by Rembrandt, Rubens, Raphael, Dégas, Renoir, Picasso. Furniture. European decorative arts, drawings, tapestries, sculpture. American and European furniture.
Tu., W., F., Su. 2-5. Closed public holidays.

MUSEUM OF GLENS FALLS HISTORICAL SOCIETY
2 Bacon Street, Glens Falls, New York 12801
In Zopher Isaac DeLong House (1860). Industrial, commerical, transport, military and social history of the Adirondack region.
M. 7 p.m.-9 p.m. Tu., Th. 2-5. Other time by appointment. Closed public holidays.

GLENWOOD

MILLS COUNTY HISTORICAL SOCIETY AND MUSEUM
P.O. Box 170, Glenwood, Iowa 51534
Furniture. Glass. China. Indian artifacts. Dolls. Guns. Machinery.
May 1 - Sept. 30, M.-Sa. by appointment; Su., public holidays 1.30-5.30.

MUSEUM OF POPE COUNTY HISTORICAL SOCIETY
S. Highway 104, Glenwood, Minnesota 56334
Local history. Indian artifacts. Paintings. Decorative arts. Dolls.
M.-F. 9-12, 1-5; public holidays 1-5. May 1 - Sept. 30 Sa., Su. 1-5.

MUSEUM OF OREGON ELECTRIC RAILWAY HISTORICAL SOCIETY
Star Route, Box 1318, Glenwood, Oregon 97120
Electric railway coaches, some operating, and equipment.
Memorial Day - July 4: Sa., Su. 11-du sk. July 4 - Labour Day: Tu.-Su. 11-dusk. Labour Day - Thanksgiving: Sa., Su. 11-dusk.

GLOUCESTER

BABSON HISTORICAL ASSOCIATION
58 Middle Street, Gloucester, Massachusetts 01930
In former cooper's workshop (1658). Early American tools. Cooper's equipment.
July - Labour Day, Tu.-Su. 2-5.

BEAUPORT
Eastern Point Boulevard, Gloucester, Massachusetts 01930
House created during first quarter of this century by Henry Sleeper, from rooms, mostly pre-Revolution, brought from other Massachusetts houses. Each room furnished in accordance with Mr. Sleeper's sense of the period.
June-Sept., M.-F., guided tours only at 2.30, 3.30, 4.30

CAPTAIN ELIAS DAVIS HOUSE AND MUSEUM
27 Pleasant Street, Gloucester, Massachusetts 01930
Paintings, drawings by the American marine painter, Fitz Hugh Lane. 18th-19th century furniture. Silver. Fishing boat models. Fishing gear.
Tu.-Sa. 11-4.

HAMMOND MUSEUM
Hesperus Avenue, Gloucester, Massachusetts 01930
Medieval European architecture.
June 1 - Sept. 15: M.-Sa. 10-3. Apr. 1 - Oct. 31: Su. 2-4. Closed New Year, Thanksgiving, Christmas.

MUSEUM OF CAPE ANN HISTORICAL ASSOCIATION
27 Pleasant Street, Gloucester, Massachusetts 01930
In Federal House (c.1800). Period furniture. Silver. China. Glass. Local history. Paintings by Fitz Hugh Lane. White-Ellery House (c.1700) is also in the care of the Association.
Tu.-Sa. 11-4. Closed New Year, Thanksgiving, Christmas.

OPEN-CHURCH FOUNDATION BIBLE MUSEUM
62 Middle Street, Gloucester, Massachusetts 01930
Bibles. Illuminated manuscripts.
Daily 9-5. Closed national holidays.

SARGENT-MURRAY-GILMAN-HOUGH HOUSE
49 Middle Street, Gloucester, Massachusetts 01930
House (1768), with furniture and paintings of the families who have lived there.
June-Sept., Tu.-Sa. 11-5.

GNADENHUTTEN

MUSEUM OF GNADENHUTTEN HISTORICAL SOCIETY
State Park County Route 10, Gnadenhutten, Ohio 44629
History of village and missions. Indian artifacts.
May 1 - Sept. 30, daily public holidays 1-5.

GOLDEN

BUFFALO BILL MEMORIAL MUSEUM
Route 5, P.O. Box 950, Golden, Colorado 80401
Personal possessions of William F. Cody (Buffalo Bill), including saddle, guns, show costumes. Posters, programmes, photographs, paintings and other Buffalo Bill Wild West show material. Indian artifacts, especially Sioux beadwork and quillwork.
Oct. 1 - Apr. 30, daily 10-5. May 1 - Sept. 30, daily 9-7.

COLORADO RAILROAD MUSEUM
17155 West 44 Avenue, Golden, Colorado 80401
History of Colorado railways.
Daily 9-5. Closed Christmas.

PIONEER MUSEUM
911 Tenth Street, Golden, Colorado 80401
Local history. Minerals. Silver. Textiles.
M.-F. 2-5.

GOLDENDALE

KLICKITAT COUNTY HISTORICAL SOCIETY MUSEUM
127 W. Broadway, Goldendale, Washington 98620
In Presby House (1903). County history. Agriculture. Costumes.
May 1 - Oct. 20, daily 10-5.

GOLIAD

GOLIAD STATE PARK MUSEUM
Franklin and Market Streets, Goliad, Texas 77963
Relics and memorabilia of Texas Revolutionary War (1835-6). Spanish and Indian artifacts.
Daily 8-5.

PRESIDIO LA BAHIA
Refugio Highway, Goliad, Texas 77963
Restored Spanish mission fort (1749). Indian, pre-Colonial, Colonial and Republican cultures and periods.
Daily 9-5. Closed Good Friday, Christmas.

MISSION ESPIRITU SANTO DE ZUNIGA
Goliad, Texas 77963
Restored Mission buildings. Chapel. Living quarters. Granary.
By appointment.

OLD MARKET HOUSE MUSEUM
Goliad, Texas 77963
In Market House (c.1871). History of Goliad and adjacent counties. Paintings by local artists.
Tu.-Su. 10-12, 1-5.

GONZALES

GONZALES HISTORICAL MUSEUM
E. St. Lawrence Street, Gonzales, Texas 78629
Southwestern and Civil War history. Photographic collection of portraits of leading citizens of Gonzales, 1820s onwards.
W.-Su. public holidays 1-5.

GOOCHLAND

GOOCHLAND COUNTY HISTORICAL MUSEUM
County Courthouse, Goochland, Virginia 23063
Local history and archaeology. Folklore.
M.-F. 9-4. Closed public holidays.

GOODWELL

NO MAN'S LAND HISTORICAL MUSEUM
Sewell Street, Goodwell, Oklahoma 73939
Geology. Mineralogy. Palaeontology. Natural history. Anthropology. Local history. Indian artifacts. Archaeology. Agriculture.
Sept. 1 - July 31, M.-F., Su. 1-5. Other times by appointment.

GORDON

MARI SANDOZ MUSEUM
Gordon, Nebraska 69343
Pioneer life.
By appointment.

GORHAM

ART GALLERY OF UNIVERSITY OF MAINE
Gorham Campus, Gorham, Maine 04038
Paintings. Sculpture. Graphics.
M.-Sa. 10-5; Su., public holidays 2-5.

BAXTER MUSEUM
South Street, Gorham, Maine 04038
In Baxter House (c.1800). Period furniture. Local history.
July 1 - Aug. 31, W., Sa. 2-5.

MUSEUM OF MARCUS WHITMAN HISTORICAL SOCIETY
Gorham, New York 14461
Local history. Tools, domestic equipment used in Gorham area, 1789-1910. Photographs. Documents. Indian artifacts.
May 30 - Oct. 1, Sa. 2-5. Other times by appointment.

GOSHEN

GOSHEN HISTORICAL SOCIETY MUSEUM
Old Middle Road, Goshen, Connecticut 06756
Geology. Conchology. Natural history. Local history. Indian material. Textiles.
July 1 - Aug., F., 2-5. Sa. 2-4. Sept. 1-30, F. 2-5. Oct. - June, by appointment.

HALL OF FAME OF THE TROTTER
240 Main Street, Goshen, New York 10924
Trotting racing. Equipment used in trotting. Paintings, prints, lithographs. Dioramas of horses.
M.-Sa. 10-5; Su. 1.30-5. Closed New York, Thanksgiving, Christmas.

ORANGE COUNTY COMMUNITY OF MUSEUMS AND GALLERIES
240 Main Street, Goshen, New York 10924
History of Orange County. Paintings. Decorative arts. Staffordshire ware. History of Delaware and Hudson Canal.
M.-F. 9-5. Closed public holidays.

GOTHENBURG

PONY EXPRESS STATION
Ehmen Park, Gothenburg, Nebraska 69138
Pony Express Station (1854). History of Pony Express.
May 1-31, Sept. 11 - 30, daily 8-5.30. June 1 - Sept. 10, daily 7.30-9.

GRAFTON

WILLARD HOUSE AND CLOCK SHOP
Willard Street, Grafton, Massachusetts 01519
Local history. Willard clocks. 18th century furniture.
Tu.-Sa. 10-12, 1-4. Su. 1-5. Public holidays 10-12, 1-5.

GRAFTON HISTORICAL SOCIETY MUSEUM
Robin Lawn, Grafton, Vermont 05146
Local history. Tools. Clothing.
June 1 - Oct. 12: Sa., Su. 2.30-4.30. Other times by appointment.

GRAHAM

SIMPSON COLLEGE MUSEUM
Graham, Missouri 64455
Local history.
May-Sept., Su. 2-4.

GRANBY

SALMON BROOK HISTORICAL SOCIETY MUSEUM
208 Salmon Brook Street, Granby, Connecticut 06035
In Abijah Rowe House (c.1750). Local history.
May 1 - Nov. 30, Su. 2-4. Other days by appointment.

GRAND CANYON

GRAND CANYON NATIONAL PARK
Visitor Center, Box 129, Grand Canyon, Arizona 86023
Geology. Natural history. Herbarium. Archaeology. Ruins of prehistoric Indian settlement.
May 1 - Sept. 30, daily 7-9; Oct. 1 - Apr. 30, daily 8-5.

TUSAYAN MUSEUM
Grand Canyon, Arizona 86023
Archaeology. Indian village sites.
May 1 - Sept. 30, daily 8-9.

YAVAPAI MUSEUM
Grand Canyon, Arizona 86023
Geology. Palaeontology. Zoology.
May 1 - Sept. 30, daily; Oct. 1 - Apr. 30, daily 8-5.

GRAND FORKS

UNIVERSITY OF NORTH DAKOTA ZOOLOGY MUSEUM
Grand Forks, North Dakota 58201
Natural history. Fauna of N. Dakota.
M.-F. 9-6; Sa. 9-5. Closed public holidays.

GRAND HAVEN

TRI-CITIES HISTORICAL SOCIETY MUSEUM
2281-2 Washington Street, Grand Haven, Michigan 49417
In former railway depot (1870). Local history. Agriculture. Lumbering. Texiles. Costumes. Indian artifacts.
May 1 - Sept. 30, M.-Sa. 2-4, 7-8. Rest of year by appointment.

GRAND ISLAND

MUSEUM OF HALL COUNTY HISTORICAL SOCIETY
721 W. Koenig Street, Grand Island, Nebraska 68801
Local history.
By appointment.

STUHR MUSEUM OF THE PRAIRIE PIONEER
Highway 281 and R.R.2, Grand Island, Nebraska 68801
Central Nebraska pioneer history. Local history, 1850-1930. Indian artifacts. Reconstructed 19th century pioneer town. Agricultural machinery.
M.-Sa. 9-5; Su. 1-5. Closed New Year, Christmas.

GRAND ISLE

HYDE LOG CABIN
Route U.S.2, Grand Isle, Vermont 05458
Log-house (1783), built by Jedediah Hyde. Period furnishings.
Memorial Day - Labour Day, daily 8-5.

GRAND JUNCTION

HISTORICAL MUSEUM AND INSTITUTE OF WESTERN COLORADO
4th and Ute Streets, Grand Junction, Colorado 81501
Geology. Mineralogy. Palaeontology. Local history and archaeology. Ethnology. Weapons. Indian artifacts. Costumes.
Mar. 15 - May 31, Sept. 1 - Nov. 30, Tu.-Sa., 10-6; Su., 2-5. June 1 - Aug. 31, Tu.-Sa. 9-7, Su. 2-5.

GRAND MARAIS

GRANT PORTAGE NATIONAL MONUMENT
Grand Marais, Minnesota 55604
History of fur trade. Restored fur trading post. Ojibway Indian artifacts.
May 25 - Oct. 15: daily 8-6.

MUSEUM OF COOK COUNTY HISTORICAL SOCIETY
Broadway, Grand Marais, Minnesota 55604
In lighthouse keeper's residence (1890). Geology. Local history. Agriculture. Industry. Indian artifacts. Folklore. Junior museum.
June 1 - Sept. 30; M.-Sa., public holidays 1-8.

GRAND PRAIRIE

TEXAN SPORTS HALL OF FAME
501 E. Safari Parkway, Grand Prairie, Texas 75050
Sports mementoes.
Daily 9-5.

GRAND RAPIDS

GRAND RAPIDS ART MUSEUM
230 E. Fulton Street, Grand Rapids, Michigan 49502
18th-19th century French paintings. German expressionist paintings. 19th-20th century American paintings. Renaissance paintings. American and European sculpture, graphic arts, decorative arts.
M.-Sa. 9-5, Su. 2-5. Closed public holidays, M. June 1 - Aug. 31.

GRAND RAPIDS PUBLIC MUSEUM
54 Jefferson Avenue S.E., Grand Rapids, Michigan 49502
Geology. Palaeontology. Planetarium. Archaeology, especially Norton Indian mounds. Indian artifacts. Ethnology. Costumes. Decorative arts. Local history.
M.-F. 10-5; Sa., Su. 2-5. Museum closed Christmas. Planetarium closed Aug. 1-31.

GRANDVIEW

RAY E. POWELL MUSEUM
313 Division, Grandview, Washington 98930
Furniture. Guns. Indian artifacts. Toys. Dolls.
Tu.-Su. 9-5. Closed Easter, Thanksgiving, Christmas.

GRANGEVILLE

IDAHO COUNTY HISTORICAL SOCIETY
Grangeville, Idaho 83530
Local history.
Gold Stamp Mill is in the care of the Society.
By appointment.

GRANITE FALLS

YELLOW MEDICINE COUNTY HISTORICAL MUSEUM
Rural Route 2, Granite Falls, Minnesota 56241
Local history. Indian artifacts.
2 pioneer homes (1870, 1877) are in the care of the Museum.
May 1 - Oct. 30: Tu.-Sa. 1-5; public holidays, Su. 1-8.

GRANITE QUARRY

OLD STONE HOUSE
Granite Quarry, North Carolina 28072
Also known as Michael Braun House (1758-66). Period furnishings.
By appointment.

GRANT

MUSEUM OF PERKINS COUNTY HISTORICAL SOCIETY
Box 174, Grant, Nebraska 69140
Building (1910). Local history. Agriculture. Education. Costumes.
Schoolhouse (1890) is in the care of the Society.
June 1 - Aug. 31, Su. 2-5. Other times by appointment.

GRANTS

GRANTS AND WEST VALENCIA COUNTY CHAMBER OF COMMERCE MUSEUM
500 W. Santa Fe Street, Grants, New Mexico 87020
Uranium ore. Radioactive dinosaur bones. Indian artifacts, especially pottery.
M.-F. 8-5. Closed public holidays.

GRANTSBURG

BURNETT COUNTY HISTORICAL SOCIETY MUSEUM
Grantsburg, Wisconsin 54840
Local history.
Daily 9-5.

GRANVILLE

DENISON UNIVERSITY GALLERY
Granville, Ohio 43023
Local history and archaeology. Early 19th century tools. Furniture. Domestic equipment. Costumes. Paintings. Prints. Drawings. Cuna Indian, African and American Indian art.
M.-F. 9-4. Closed public holidays.

GRANVILLE HISTORICAL MUSEUM
Broadway, Granville, Ohio 43023
Building (1816) was formerly Alexandrian Bank. Geology. Local history and archaeology. Agriculture. Carpenter's tools. Industry. Decorative arts. Costumes.
Sa., Su. 2-5: other times by appointment.

GRAYLING

HARTWICK PINES STATE PARK
Star Route 1, Grayling, Michigan 49738
Natural history. History of Michigan logging industry.
May 1 - Oct. 31, daily 8-8.

GREAT BEND

ORLIN BAKER ART GALLERY
2323 Broadway, Great Bend, Kansas 67530
House (1876). Geology. Fossils. Navajo rugs. Furniture.
Tu., F., Su. 2-5. Closed July 1 - Labour Day.

GREAT FALLS

C. H. RUSSELL MUSEUM
1201 4th Avenue N., Great Falls, Montana 59401
In Russell's studio (1830). Paintings and sculpture by C. H. Russell, the cowboy artists. Letters.
M.-Sa. 10-5; Su. 1-5. Closed M., Sept 15 - May 15, and public holidays, except July 4.

GREELEY

GREELEY MUNICIPAL MUSEUM
919 7th Street, Greeley, Colorado 80631
History of Greeley P. Weld Company. Local history. Indian artifacts. Costumes.
M.-F., 9-12, 1-5. Closed public holidays.

MEEKER MEMORIAL MUSEUM
1324 9th Avenue, Greeley, Colorado 80631
House (1870), home of Nathan Meeker, founder of Greeley. Material illustrating his life.
Daily, 9-12, 1-5. Closed public holidays.

GREEN BAY

BROWN COUNTY HISTORICAL SOCIETY MUSEUM
3319 Delahaut Street, Green Bay, Wisconsin 54301
In Cotton House (c.1845). Period furnishings.
Baird House (1836) is in the care of the Society.
May 1 - Oct. 31: Tu.-Sa. 10-5; Su. 2-5. Other times by appointment. Closed public holidays.

COTTON HOUSE
2632 S. Webster Avenue, Green Bay, Wisconsin 54301
House (1840). 18th-19th century furniture. Costumes. Local history.
May-Oct., Tu.-Sa. 10-5; Su. 12-5. M. by appointment.

NATIONAL RAILROAD MUSEUM
205 E. Walnut Street, Green Bay, Wisconsin 54301
14 steam locomotives. Rolling stock and operational equipment. Railway relics.
May 1 - Sept. 30, daily 9-5.

NEVILLE PUBLIC MUSEUM
129 S. Jefferson Street, Green Bay, Wisconsin 54301
Local history and archaeology. Costumes. Coins. Geology. Natural history. Anthropology. Ethnology. Paintings. Sculpture. Prints. Drawings. Decorative arts. Glass. Musical instruments.
M.-Sa. 9-5; Su. 2-5. Closed public holidays.

OLD FORT HOWARD HOSPITAL
402 N. Chestnut Street, Green Bay, Wisconsin 54303
Hospital and ward (1826-28). Officers' quarters (1816). Furnishings.
M.-Sa. 9-5; Su. 2-5.

ROI-PORLIER-TANK COTTAGE
860 5th Street, Green Bay, Wisconsin 54304
Wattle house (1776), built by French fur-trader. Local history. Dutch marquetry furniture.
May 1 - Oct. 31: Tu.-Sa. 10-12, 1-5; Su. 2-5.

GREENBUSH

OLD WADE HOUSE
Old Wade House State Park, Greenbush, Wisconsin 53026
Restored stage-coach inn (1849-51). Period furnishings. Smokehouse. Blacksmith's shop. Maple-sugaring cabin.
May 1 - Oct. 31, daily 9-5.

JUNG CARRIAGE MUSEUM
Greenbush, Wisconsin 53026
19th-early 20th century horse and hand-drawn vehicles.
May 1 - Oct. 31, daily 9-5.

GREENEVILLE

ANDREW JOHNSON NATIONAL HISTORIC SITE
127-31 Depot Street, Greeneville, Tennessee 37743
Houses (1827 and 1849), which were homes of Andrew Johnson. Period furnishings. Visitor Center, with exhibits illustrating Johnson's life, contains the Andrew Johnson tailor's shop (c.1820).
June 1 - Sept. 15, daily 9-5. Closed Christmas.

GREENFIELD

OLD LOG JAIL MUSEUM
Route 40 and North A Streets, Greenfield, Indiana 46140
Indiana history. Material relating to the Hancock Company.
May 15 - Oct. 15: Sa., Su. 1-4. Other times by appointment.

JAMES WHITCOMB RILEY OLD HOME
250 West Main Street, Greenfield, Indiana 46140
House (1850-3), home of James Whitcomb Riley, containing his furniture, pictures and personal possessions.
May 1 - Oct. 31: M.-Sa. 10-5; Su. 1-5.

MUSEUM OF HISTORICAL SOCIETY OF GREENFIELD
Church Street, Greenfield, Massachusetts 01301
House (1852). Local history.
By appointment.

GREENFIELD HISTORICAL SOCIETY MUSEUM
11313 W. Coldspring Road, Greenfield, Wisconsin 53228
In reconstructed log-cabin (1832). Period furnishings. Tools. Local history.
May 1 - Oct. 31, Su. 1-3.30.

GREENFIELD PARK

GREENFIELD SCHOOL
Greenfield Park, New York 12435
Local history.
May 30 - Labour Day, Tu.-Su., public holidays 1-5.

GREENLAND

MUSEUM OF GREENLAND HISTORICAL SOCIETY
189 Post Road, Greenland, New Hampshire 03840
Local history.
By appointment.

GREEN LANE

GOSCHENHOPPEN FOLKLIFE LIBRARY AND MUSEUM
Box 476, Green Lane, Pennsylvania 18054
Herbarium. Agriculture. Local history. Costumes.
Su. 1.30-4. M.-Sa. by appointment. Closed Dec. 15 - Jan. 15.

GREEN RIVER

HUTTON'S LITTLE MUSEUM
185 E. 2nd Street N., Green River, Wyoming 82935
Geology. Mineralogy. Archaeology. Indian artifacts.
By appointment.

SWEETWATER COUNTY MUSEUM
50 W. Flaming Gorge Way, Green River, Wyoming 82935
History of S.W. Wyoming. Industry. Ranching. Indian artifacts. Pioneer life.
M.-F. 10-4.30; Su. 2-4.30; July 4, 10-4.30. Closed Su., June, Aug., Dec., public holidays except July 4.

GREENSBORO

MAGNOLIA GROVE HOBSON MEMORIAL SHRINE
1002 Hobson Street, Greensboro, Alabama 36744
House (1835-8) was family home of Admiral Richard Pearson Hobson. Original furnishings.
M.-F. 9-12, 2-5; Su. 2-5.

GREENSBORO HISTORICAL MUSEUM
130 Summit Avenue, Greensboro, North Carolina 27401
Building (1895). History of founding and development of Guildford County. Natural history. Dolly Madison Room. Period furniture rooms. China. Glass. Industry. 18th-19th century vehicles. O'Henry collection. Full-size replicas of early Greensboro buildings, with original furnishings and equipment.
Francis McNairey House (1762) is in the care of the Museum.
Tu.-Sa. 10-5; Su. 2-5. Closed New Year, Easter, Thanksgiving, Christmas.

GREENSBORO MASONIC MUSEUM
426 W. Market Street, Greensboro, North Carolina 27401
Masonic history. Books. Aprons. Jewels. Medals. Badges. Stamps. Seals. Coins.
M.-Sa. by appointment.

GUILFORD COURTHOUSE NATIONAL MILITARY PARK
New Garden Road and Old Battleground Road, Greensboro, North Carolina 27408
History of Revolutionary War in North Carolina. Weapons. Equipment.
Sept. 1 - June 14, daily 8.30-5. June 15 - Aug. 31, daily 8.30-6. Closed Christmas, New Year.

NATURAL SCIENCE CENTER
4301 Lawndale Drive, Greensboro, North Carolina 27408
Children's Museum. Geology. Mineralogy. Botany. Her-

barium. Astronomy. Natural history. Archaeology. Anthropology. Indian artifacts.
Tu.-Sa. 9-5; Su. 2-5. Closed New Year, Easter, Christmas.

WEATHERSPOON ART GALLERY
University of North Carolina, Walker Avenue and McIver Street, Greensboro, North Carolina 27412
19th-20th century European and American paintings, sculpture, graphics, textiles.
M.-F. 10-5; Su. 2-5. Closed university vacations.

GREENSBURG

OLD COURT HOUSE MUSEUM
Greensburg, Kentucky 42742
Local history.
M.-Sa. 1-3. Closed public holidays.

WESTMORELAND COUNTY MUSEUM OF ART
221 N. Main Street, Greensburg, Pennsylvania 15601
19th century American period rooms. English 18th century period rooms, paintings, silver. American paintings, sculpture, drawings, prints, decorative arts. Pennsylvania folk art.
Tu. 1-9; W.-Sa. 10-5; Su. 2-6. Closed public holidays.

GREENVILLE

DELAWARE MUSEUM OF NATURAL HISTORY
Kennett Pike, Route 52, Box 3937, Greenville, Delaware 19807
Mammals. Birds and eggs. Molluscs.
W.-Sa. 9-4; Su. 1-5. Closed public holidays.

MUSEUM OF BOND COUNTY HISTORICAL SOCIETY
211 East Vine Street, Greenville, Illinois 62246
History of Bond County.
By appointment.

WINTERVILLE INDIAN MOUNDS MUSEUM AND STATE PARK
Route 3, Box 600, Greenville, Mississippi 38701
Archaeology. Indian artifacts.
Tu.-Sa. 9-12, 1-6; Su. 1-6. Closed Dec. 24-5.

GREENVILLE ART CENTER
802 Evans Street, Greenville, North Carolina 27834
Works by 20th century American artists. Paintings. Sculpture. Graphics. Ceramics.
M.-F. 9-12, 2-5; Sa. 9.30-12.30. Closed public holidays.

GARST MUSEUM
205 N. Broadway, Greenville, Ohio 45331
In Garst House (1852). History of Darke County. Relics of Indian Wars. Indian artifacts. Worldwide doll collection.
Tu., F., Su. 1-5. Closed New Year, Good Friday, Christmas.

GREENVILLE COUNTY MUSEUM OF ART
106 Dupont Drive, Greenville, South Carolina 29607
American (especially contemporary) paintings, sculpture, prints.
M.-F. 9-5; Sa. 9-1; Su. 2-6. Closed New Year, July 4, Labour Day, Thanksgiving, Christmas.

BOB JONES UNIVERSITY COLLECTION OF SACRED ART
Greenville, South Carolina 29614
Antiquities from the Holy Land. European religious paintings. Paintings on revealed religion by Benjamin West.
Sept. 1-May 31, Tu.-Sa. 12-5; Su. 1.30-6. June 1-Dec. 24, Tu.-Su. 2-4. Closed New Year, Christmas.

ENDE-GAILLARD HOUSE
Graham Park, P.O. Box 448, Greenville, Texas 75401
House (1859). Original furniture. Personal possessions of Ende and Gaillard families.
June 1-Sept. 30, Su. 2-5. Other times by appointment.

GREENWICH

BRUCE MUSEUM
Steamboat Road, Greenwich, Connecticut 06830
Regional ecology and natural history, especially in dioramas. Animal heads and horns. Astronomy. Space science. Volcanoes. 17th-19th century European paintings. Near Eastern pottery. Chinese porcelain. Ivories from China, Japan, India. Etruscan bronzes.
M.-F., 10-5; Su., 2-5. Closed public holidays.

PUTNAM COTTAGE
243 E. Putnam Avenue, Greenwich, Connecticut 06830
House (c.1690) used by General Israel Putnam during the American Revolution. Personal possessions of Gen. Putnam. Early Americana. 18th century furnishings.
M., Th., Sa., 1-5. Closed public holidays, except Washington's Birthday and July 4th.

CUMBERLAND COUNTY HISTORICAL SOCIETY
YeGreate Street, Greenwich, New Jersey 08323
In Gibbon House (1730), with period rooms. Local history. Indian artifacts. Costumes. Civil War material. Agriculture.
Apr. 1-Oct. 31, M.-F. 9-4. Sa., Su. 2-5. Nov. 1-Mar. 31, M.-F. 9-4. Closed New Year, Thanksgiving, Christmas.

GREENWOOD

OLD JAIL HISTORICAL MUSEUM
Greenwood, Arkansas 72936
In former prison building (1893). Local history. Farm equipment, tools, utensils.
M.-Sa., 9-5; Su., 1-5; public holidays, 9-5. Closed Oct. 1-Mar. 31.

THE MUSEUM
Phoenix Street, Greenwood, South Carolina 29646
Geology. Fossils. Zoology. Local history. Indian artifacts.
M.-F. 9-1; Sa. 9-12; Su. 2-5. Other times by appointment. Closed Easter, Thanksgiving, Christmas.

GRENADA

GRENADA HISTORICAL MUSEUM
Poplar Street, Grenada, Mississippi 38901
Local history. Archaeology. Indian artifacts.
Sa., Su. 2-5. Closed Dec. 18-Jan. 8.

GREYBULL

GREYBULL MUSEUM
Greybull Avenue, Greybull, Wyoming 82426
Geology. Mineralogy. Fossils. Indian artifacts. Local history.
Sept. 1-May 30: M.-Sa. 1-5. June 1-Aug. 31: M.-Sa. 8-9; Su. 1-9.

GROSSE ILE

GROSSE ILE HISTORICAL MUSEUM
E. River Drive and Parkway, Grosse Ile, Michigan 48138
In railway station (1904). Local history. Maritime history. Transport.
Lighthouse (1894) is in the care of the Museum.
Th. 10-2; Su. 1-4. Other days by appointment. Closed public holidays.

GROTON

MONUMENT HOUSE
Park Avenue, Groton, Connecticut 06430
Local history and archaeology. Whaling relics. Indian artifacts. Paintings. Furniture, china, prints, glass. Costumes. Children's museum.
June 1-Labour Day, Tu.-Sa. 1-4. Su., public holidays 1-5.

SUBMARINE FORCE LIBRARY AND MUSEUM
Naval Submarine Base New London, Groton, Connecticut 06340
History and development of U.S. and foreign submarines. Models. Photographs. Diaries and other documents. Films. Mementoes of submariners.
M., W., Th., F. 9-4; Tu. 9-8; Sa., public holidays 10-4; Su. 12-4. Closed New Year, Thanksgiving, Christmas.

GROTON HISTORICAL SOCIETY MUSEUM
Main Street, Groton, Massachusetts 01450
In Governor Bontwell House (1852). Local history.
May 1-Sept. 30: Sa. 3-5.

GUERNSEY

FREDERICK MUSEUM
Box 332, Guernsey, Wyoming 82214
Local history and archaeology. Indian material.
By appointment.

GUERNSEY STATE MUSEUM
Guernsey State Park, Guernsey, Wyoming 82214
Natural history. Botany. Anthropology. Ethnology. Local history. Industry. Transport.
May 15-Labour Day, M., Tu., Th.-Sa. 10-5; Su. 8-6.30.

GUILFORD

HENRY WHITFIELD MUSEUM
Whitfield Street, Guilford, Connecticut 06437
Henry Whitfield House (1639). 17th century American furniture, textiles, furnishings. Indian material. Firearms.
Apr. 1-Oct. 30, W.-Su., 11-5; Nov. 1-Mar. 31, 11-4. Closed Dec. 15-Jan. 15.

HYLAND HOUSE
84 Boston Street, Guilford, Connecticut 06437
House (1660). Period furnishings and domestic equipment.
June 15-Sept. 30 10-5.

THOMAS GRISWOLD HOUSE
171 Boston Street, Guilford, Connecticut 06437
Saltbox type house (1735). Kitchen with period furniture and equipment. Dining room with Victorian furnishings. One upstairs room as museum of costumes, 1840-1940. Barn has collection of agricultural implements.
Apr. 1-Nov. 30 11-5.

GUNNISON

GUNNISON COUNTY PIONEER AND HISTORICAL SOCIETY MUSEUM
S. Adams Street, Highway 50 E., Gunnison, Colorado 81230
Geology. Mineralogy. Local history. Agriculture. Transport. Costumes.
The Paragon schoolhouse (1904) is in the care of the society.
May 30-Labour Day, daily 1.30-5.

CLARENCE T. HURST MUSEUM
Western State College, Gunnison, Colorado 81230
Archaeology.
Tu., 2-4; W., 1.30-3.30. Closed college vacations.

HACKETTSTOWN

WARREN COUNTY HISTORICAL SOCIETY
52 Main Street, Hackettstown, New Jersey 07840
Local history.
Sa., Su. 1-5.

HADDONFIELD

INDIAN KING TAVERN
233 E. King's Highway, Haddonfield, New Jersey 08033
House (c.1750). Period furnishings.
Tu.-Sa. 10-12, 1-5; Su., public holidays 2-5. Closed New Year, Thanksgiving, Christmas.

MUSEUM OF HISTORICAL SOCIETY OF HADDONFIELD
343 King's Highway E., Haddonfield, New Jersey 08033
Personal possessions of Elizabeth Haddon, Haddonfield's first settler (1713). Local and Quaker history. Costumes. Geology. Botany. Music. Industry. Transport.
Greenfield Hall (1747-1841) and Hip Roof House (1708) are in the care of the Society.
Sept. 1-June 30, Tu., Th. 2-5.

HADLEY

MOUNT HOLYOKE SUMMIT HOUSE
Skinner State Park, Hadley, Massachusetts 01035
In Prospect House (1851). Furniture. Pictures. Maps.
Apr. 15-Oct. 15, daily 10-half an hour after sunset.

MUSEUM OF HADLEY FARM MUSEUM ASSOCIATION
Russell Street, Hadley, Massachusetts 01635
In barn (1782). Farm implements. Sleighs. Stage coach.
May 1-Oct. 15: Tu.-Sa. 10-12, 1-4.30; Su. 1.30-4.30.

PORTER-PHELPS-HUNTINGTON FOUNDATION
130 River Drive, Hadley, Massachusetts 01305
House (Forty Acres 1752). Period furnishings.
May 15-Oct. 15: daily 1-4.30.

HAGERSTOWN

HAGER HOUSE MUSEUM
19 Key Street, Hagerstown, Maryland 21740
House (1740). Period furnishings. Coins. Glass. China.
Apr. 1-Oct. 31: Tu.-Sa. 10-5; Su. 1-5.

MUSEUM OF WASHINGTON COUNTY HISTORICAL SOCIETY
135 W. Washington Street, Hagerstown, Maryland 21740
In Miller House (1820-25). Local history.
3 historic houses (1739-1910) are in the care of the Society They include Mansion House (1840).
Su. 2-5.

WASHINGTON COUNTY MUSEUM OF FINE ARTS
City Park, Box 423, Hagerstown, Maryland 21740
16th-19th century European paintings. 19th-20th century American paintings. Oriental paintings, jades. Tibetan banners. Italian furniture, tapestry.
Tu.-Sa. 10-5; Su., public holidays 1-6. Closed New Year, Christmas.

HAILEY

BLAINE COUNTY HISTORICAL MUSEUM
Main Street, Hailey, Idaho 83333
Local history. Political buttons. Arrow-heads.
Tu.-Su. 10-5. Closed Sept. 15-June 15, Labour Day, Memorial Day, July 4.

HAINES

ALASKA INDIAN ARTS
Port Chilkoot, Haines, Alaska 99827
Indian ethnology and crafts. Tlinget Indian costumes.
Totem village (1962) and Fort William H. Seward (1904) are in the care of the Museum.
M.-F. 10-4. Closed national holidays.

SHELDON'S MUSEUM
Box 236, Haines, Alaska 99827
Indian and Eskimo art. Pictures and relics of the pioneer period.
May 16-Sept. 14, daily 2-4; Sept. 15-May 15, by appointment.

EASTERN OREGON MUSEUM
Route 1, Box 109, Haines, Oregon 97833
Horsedrawn vehicles. Agriculture. Blacksmith's shop. Musical instruments. Uniforms. Guns.
May-Oct., daily 9-5.

HALIFAX

CONSTITUTION HOUSE
Halifax, North Carolina 27839
House (c.1770), with period furnishings. Reputed to be building in which first State Constitution was drafted. Moved to present site in 1920.
Tu.-Sa. 9-5; Su. 1-5.

OWENS HOUSE
Halifax, North Carolina 27839
Merchant's house (c.1760). Pre-Revolutionary period furnishings.
Tu.-Sa. 9-5; Su. 1-5.

HALSTEAD

KANSAS HEALTH MUSEUM
309 Main Street, Halstead, Kansas 67056
Health and Health Education.
M.-F., public holidays, 10-4; Su. 1-5. Closed Labour Day, Thanksgiving, Christmas, New Year, Independence Day.

HAMDEN

HAMDEN HISTORICAL SOCIETY MUSEUM
Mount Carmel Avenue, Hamden, Connecticut 06518
In Jonathan Dickerman house (1770). Period furnishings. Local history. Herbarium.
June-Aug., Sa., Su., 2-5.

HAMILTON

RICKETTS MEMORIAL MUSEUM
Hamilton, Montana 59840
Historical and medical material connected with spotted fever and other zoonotic diseases. Natural history. Archaeology. Paintings.
June 1-Sept. 30, M.-F. 10-5.

PICKER GALLERY
Dana Creative Arts Center, Colgate University, Hamilton, New York 13346
Pre-Columbian art. Paintings. Sculpture. Graphics. Archaeology.
M.-F. 9-4.30; Sa., Su., public holidays 1-5. Closed university vacations.

HAMILTON COUNTY MUSEUM
County Courthouse, Hamilton, Texas 76531
History of County. Pioneer relics.
M.-Sa. 8-5.

HAMMOND

HAMMOND HISTORICAL SOCIETY MUSEUM
564 State Street, Hammond, Indiana 46320
Local history.
By appointment.

HAMMONDSPORT

GLEN H. CURTISS MUSEUM
Lake and Main Streets, Hammondsport, New York 14840
Early aviation material connected with Glenn H. Curtiss and other pioneer aviators. History of Glenn Curtiss aircraft. Local history.
May 15-Oct. 31: M.-Sa. 10-4.

GREYTON H. TAYLOR WINE MUSEUM
Bully Hill Road, Hammondsport, New York 14840
Wine history, especially in U.S. Viticulture. Paintings. Wine-making equipment. Bottles. Labels. Cooperage.
May 1-Oct. 31: M.-Sa. 9-4.30; Su. 1-4.30.

HAMMONTON

BATSO VILLAGE
Batso R.D.1, Hammonton, New Jersey 08037
Restored 18th-early 19th century iron and glass-making village. Workers' houses. Saw mill. Gristmill. Blacksmith's shop.
M.-F. 9-5; Sa., Su., public holidays 10-6. Closed New Year, Thanksgiving, Christmas.

HAMPTON

MEETING HOUSE GREEN MEMORIAL AND HISTORICAL ASSOCIATION MUSEUM
40 Park Avenue, Hampton, New Hampshire 03842
Local history, based on 4 preserved buildings. General store. Law office. Blacksmith's shop. Printing shop.
July 1-Aug. 31, daily 1-4.

COLLEGE MUSEUM
Hampton Institute, Hampton, Virginia 23368
Anthropology. African, American Indian, Oceanic and pre-Columbian artifacts. Paintings. Drawings. Prints.
M.-F. 1-5. Other times by appointment.

MUSEUM OF HAMPTON ASSOCIATION FOR THE ARTS AND HUMANITIES
123 E. Queen Street, Hampton, Virginia 23369
Local history and archaeology. Paintings. Sculpture. Photographs.
May 1-Sept. 30: M.-Sa. 10-9. Oct. 1-Apr. 30: M.-F. 1-6; Sa. 10-12. Closed school vacations.

KENNETH E. RICE MEMORIAL MUSEUM
29 Harris Creek Road, Hampton, Virginia 23369
Fossils. Shells. Coral.
M.-Sa. 9.30-5.30; Su. 2-6.

SYMS-EATON MUSEUM
418 W. Mercury Boulevard, Hampton, Virginia 23369
History of Hampton, and of first free school in the U.S.
Daily 8-5. Sa., Su., public holidays 1-5. Closed Christmas, New Year.

HANALEI KAUAI

HANALEI MUSEUM
Box 91, Hanalei Kauai, Hawaii 96714
House (1880). Agriculture. Furniture. Local history.
Tu.-F. 10-5; Sa., Su. 10-6.

HANCOCK

HANCOCK SHAKER VILLAGE
Route 20, Pittsfield, Hancock, Massachusetts 01201
22 buildings (1780 onwards). Shaker furniture, agricultural implements, domestic equipment, handicrafts. Paintings.
Daily 9.30-5. Closed Oct. 15-June 1.

HANCOCK HISTORICAL SOCIETY MUSEUM
Main Street, Hancock, New Hampshire 03449
Local history. Indian artifacts.
May 1-Sept. 15, Sa. 2-5. Closed July 4, Labour Day.

HANCOCK'S BRIDGE

HANCOCK HOUSE
Hancock's Bridge, New Jersey 08038
House (1734), site of massacre by British in Revolutionary War, 1778. Antique furnishings. Local history.
Tu.-Sa. 10-12, 1-5; Su., public holidays 2-5. Closed New Year, Thanksgiving, Christmas.

HANNIBAL

MOLLY BROWN HOUSE
Butler and 7th Streets, Hannibal, Missouri 63401
History of Marion County.
May-Sept., daily 1-5.

JOHN N. CLEMENS LAW OFFICE
Hannibal, Missouri 63401
House where John Clemens, Mark Twain's father, held Justice of Peace court.
Sept. 1-May 31, daily 8-5. June 1-Aug. 31, 8-8. Closed New Year, Thanksgiving, Christmas.

PILASTER HOUSE
Hannibal, Missouri 63401
House of Clemens family, where John Clemens, father of Mark Twain, died. Period furnishings.
Sept. 1-May 31, daily 8-5. June 1-Aug. 31, 8-8. Closed New Year, Thanksgiving, Christmas.

MARK TWAIN BOYHOOD HOME
208 Hill Street, Hannibal, Missouri 63401
House (1844). Restoration of Mark Twain's parlour, kitchen and bedrooms. Personal possessions of the author.
Sept. 1-May 31, daily 8-5. June 1-Aug. 31, 8-8. Closed New Year, Thanksgiving, Christmas.

MARK TWAIN HOME BOARD MUSEUM
208 Hill Street, Hannibal, Missouri 63401
Items relating to Mark Twain and his period. Furniture. Paintings. Letters. 1st editions.
Sept. 1-May 31, daily 8-5. June 1-Aug. 31, 8-8. Closed New Year, Thanksgiving, Christmas.

HANOVER

BRADLEY-CAMPBELL GEOLOGICAL MUSEUM
Goodrich Hall, Hanover College, Hanover, Indiana 47243
Orduvisian, Silurian, Devonian fossils from the Ohio valley. Rocks and minerals.
M.-F. 7-5 during College terms. Other times by appointment.

WASHINGTON COUNTY OREGON TRAIL ASSOCIATION
Hanover, Kansas 66945
County history.
M.-Th., Sa. 9-5; F., Su. 1-5.

DARTMOUTH COLLEGE MUSEUM
E. Wheelock Street, Hanover, New Hampshire 03755
Geology. Palaeontology. Zoology. Entomology. Anthropology, especially American Indian, African and Oceanic artifacts. History.
M.-Sa. 9-5; Su. 2-5. Closed New Year, July 4, Labour Day, Thanksgiving, Christmas.

HOPKINS CENTER ART GALLERIES
E. Wheelock Street, Hanover, New Hampshire 03755
Chinese art. European and American painting, sculpture, drawings, prints. Greek, Russian icons. Indian sculpture. Early Massachusetts silver.
Oct. 1-Apr. 30: M.-Sa. 12-5, 7-10; Su., public holidays, 2-5, May 1-Sept. 30, 7-10.

HANOVER HISTORICAL SOCIETY MUSEUM
Hanover, Virginia 23069
In former County Jail (1835). Local history.
Daily 9-5. Closed Christmas, New Year.

HARBOR SPRINGS

CHIEF ANDREW J. BLACKBIRD MUSEUM
349 E. Main Street, Harbor Springs, Michigan 49740
House (c.1855) was formerly home of Chief Blackbird. Indian material. Arts and crafts, tools, utensils, clothing of the American Indians.
June 1-Labour Day, daily 10-12, 1-5.

HARDIN

WELTNER'S MUSEUM
13 W. 8th Street, Hardin, Montana 59034
In former County Jail (1913). Guns. Mounted animals. Furniture. Indian artifacts.
June 1-Aug. 31, daily 9-5.

HARDWICK

MUSEUM OF HARDWICK HISTORICAL SOCIETY
Hardwick Common, Hardwick, Massachusetts 01037
Building (1840). Costumes. Tools. Indian material. China.
Th. 1-4. Other days by appointment.

HARDY

WASHINGTON T. BOOKER NATIONAL MONUMENT
Route 1, Box 195, Hardy, Virginia 24101
In replica of slave cabin where Booker was born. Story of

Booker's life and achievements. Plantation equipment. Blacksmith's tools.
Apr. 1 - May 31, Labour Day - Oct. 31: M.-F. 8-4.30; Sa., Su. 9.30-6. June 1 - Labour Day: M.-F. 8-6; Sa., 9.30-6; Su. 9.30-8. Nov. 1 - Mar. 31, daily 8-4.30. Closed Christmas.

HARLAN

SHELBY COUNTY HISTORICAL SOCIETY
1003 7th Street, Harlan, Iowa 51537
In early log cabin. Local history.
Oct. 1 - 31, by appointment.

HARLINGEN

CONFEDERATE AIR FORCE FLYING MUSEUM
Rebel Field, Harlingen, Texas 78550
22 American combat aeroplanes from World War II, in flying condition.
M.-F. 9-5; Sa., 9-6; Su. 1-6.

LOWER RIO GRANDE VALLEY MUSEUM
Harlingen Air Park, Harlingen, Texas 78550
Geography and history of Lower Valley area. Pioneer Artifacts. Guns. Medallions.
W., Su. 3-5. Other times by appointment.

HARPER

HARPER ART ASSOCIATION
105 W. Main Street, Downtown Gallery, Harper, Kansas 67058
Painting, sculpture, graphics by deceased Harper artists.
Sa., Su. 2-5. Closed Thanksgiving, Christmas.

OLD RUNNYMEDE CHURCH
11th and Pine Streets, Harper, Kansas 67058
Building (1889). Original furnishings.
Summer: Su. 12-5 (During County Fair).

HARPERS FERRY

HARPERS FERRY NATIONAL HISTORICAL PARK
Harpers Ferry, West Virginia 25425
40 restored buildings (1782-1865). Local history, especially relating to Civil War. Excavated remains of Civil War gun-factory.
May 1 - Sept. 30, daily 8-8. Rest of year, daily 8-5.

HARPURSVILLE

ST. LUKE'S EPISCOPAL CHURCH MUSEUM
Harpursville, New York 13787
Church (1828). Local history. Agriculture. Folklore. Early industries. Craft tools.
June 1 - Sept. 30: Sa., Su. 10-5. Other days by appointment.

HARRISBURG

SALINE COUNTY HISTORICAL SOCIETY MUSEUM
Harrisburg, Illinois 62946
Local history.
By appointment.

MUSEUM OF BANNER COUNTY HISTORICAL SOCIETY
Harrisburg, Nebraska 69345
Local history. Indian artifacts. Agriculture.
Su. 9-5.

FORT HUNTER MUSEUM
5300 N. Front Street, Harrisburg, Pennsylvania 16507
House (1789). 19th century dolls, pottery, costumes.
Tu.-Su. 10-5.

MUSEUM OF HISTORICAL SOCIETY OF DAUPHIN COUNTY
219 S. Front Street, Harrisburg, Pennsylvania 17104
In John Harris Mansion (1766). 18th-early 19th century furnishings. Indian material.
Jan. 1 - June 30, Sept. 1 - Dec. 31: M.-F. 1-4.30; Sa. 1-4; July 1 - Aug. 15. M.-F. 1-4.30. Closed Aug. 1-14.

WILLIAM PENN MEMORIAL MUSEUM
3rd and N. Streets, Box 1026, Harrisburg, Pennsylvania 17108
Geology. Mineralogy. Botany. Natural history. Pennsylvania history, art and handicrafts. Transport. Industry. Period rooms. Decorative arts. Folk art. Planetarium.
M.-Sa., public holidays 9-5; Su. 1-5. Closed New Year, Christmas.

HARRIS COUNTY

SAN JACINTO MUSEUM OF HISTORY
P.O. Box 758, Deer Park, Harris County, Texas 77536
History of the region and of Texas.
June 1 - Labour Day, M.-Sa. 9.30-5.30. Rest of year, Tu.-Sa. 9.30-5.30; Su. 10-6. Closed Dec. 24-25.

HARRISON

AGATE FOSSIL BEDS NATIONAL MONUMENT
Rural Route, Harrison, Nebraska 69346
Palaeontology. Indian artifacts.
June 1 - Aug. 31, daily 8.30-5.30. Sept. 1 - May 31: M.-F. by appointment; Sa., Su. 8-5.

HARRISONBURG

M. T. BRACKBILL PLANETARIUM
Park Road, Harrisonburg, Virginia 22801
Astronomy. Planetarium.
M.-F. by appointment; Sa., 4-5; Su. 2.30-3.30. Closed Christmas.

EASTERN MENNONITE COLLEGE MUSEUM
Harrisonburg, Virginia 22801
Geology. Mineralogy. Palaeontology. Botany. Zoology. Anthropology.
By appointment.

D. RALPH HOSTETTER MUSEUM OF NATURAL HISTORY
Harrisonburg, Virginia 22801
Geology. Palaeontology. Botany. Mineralogy. Zoology. Anthropology.
By appointment.

MADISON COLLEGE PLANETARIUM
Harrisonburg, Virginia 22801
Astronomy. Planetarium.
By appointment.

ROCKINGHAM COUNTY HISTORICAL SOCIETY MUSEUM
345 S. Main Street, Harrisonburg, Virginia 22801
Local history. Indian artifacts. Folklore.
June 1 - Aug. 31, daily 10-4.

HARRODSBURG

OLD FORT HARROD MANSION MUSEUM
Old Fort Harrod State Park, Harrodsburg, Kentucky 40330
Mansion (1831). Local archaeology and history. Indian artifacts. Costumes. Decorative arts.
Mar. 1 - Nov. 30, daily 9-5. Dec. 1 - Feb. 28, Sa., Su. 9-5.

SHAKERTOWN
Pleasant Hill, Route 4, Harrodsburg, Kentucky 40330
Restored early 19th century Shaker village. Exhibits illustrating Shaker life. Operational weaving and cabinetmaking workshops.
Daily 9-5. Closed Christmas.

HARROGATE

LINCOLN MEMORIAL UNIVERSITY MUSEUM
Duke Hall, Harrogate, Tennessee 37752
Material relating to Civil War and Abraham Lincoln.
M., W., F. 8-12, 1-5; Sa. 8-12; Su. 2-5. Closed New Year, Thanksgiving, Christmas, Aug. 15 - Sept. 15.

HARTFORD

CONNECTICUT HISTORICAL SOCIETY
1 Elizabeth Street, Hartford, Connecticut 06105
Local history. Indian material. Portraits. Prints. Furniture, glass, silver, china. Costumes. Weapons.
Hartford State House (1796) is in the care of the Society.
Museum: M.-Sa., 9.30-5.30. Old State House: Tu.-Sa., 12-4. Closed public holidays.

CONNECTICUT STATE CAPITOL BUILDING
Capitol Hill, Hartford, Connecticut 06103
State history. Paintings. Statues. Historical relics, including Lafayette's camp bed. Civil War flags of Connecticut regiments.
M.-F. 8.30-4; guided tours, 8.30-3.30.

CONNECTICUT STATE LIBRARY MUSEUM
231 Capitol Avenue, Hartford, Connecticut 06115
Local history. Indian material. State Governors' portraits. Clocks. Coins. Buttons. Colt firearms. Military relics. Posters of World War I.
M.-F., 8.30-5; Sa., 9-1. Closed public holidays.

PRUDENCE CRANDALL MEMORIAL MUSEUM
59 S. Prospect Street, Hartford, Connecticut 06106
Afro-American history.
By appointment.

HARTFORD STATE HOUSE
800 Main Street, Hartford, Connecticut 06103
Building (1776). Local history collections.
Tu.-Sa. 12-4.

MUSEUM OF THE ANTIQUARIAN AND LANDMARKS SOCIETY OF CONNECTICUT
394 Main Street, Hartford, Connecticut 06103
Decorative arts. Furniture.
6 houses (1692-1816) are in the care of the Society.
May 15 - Oct. 15, daily 1-5.

OLD NEWGATE PRISON AND COPPER MINE
59 S. Prospect Street, Hartford, Connecticut 06106
Mining history. History and mementoes of the prison, closed 1827.
Memorial Day - Oct. 31, Tu.-Su. 10-4.30.

SLOANE-STANLEY MUSEUM AND KENT FURNACE
59 S. Prospect Street, Hartford, Connecticut 06106
On site of Kent Iron Furnace. Early American iron industry. Tools.
May 29 - Oct. 31, W.-Su., public holidays 10-4.30.

STOWE-DAY FOUNDATION
77 Forest Street, Hartford, Connecticut 06105
Decorative arts. Documents.
Harriet Beecher Stowe House (1871) is in the care of the Foundation.
Mar. 1 - June 15, Sept. 1 - Dec. 31, Tu.-Sa., 10-5; Su., 2-5. Jan.-Feb., W.-Sa. 10-5, Su. 2-5. Closed New Year, Memorial Day, Labour Day, Thanksgiving, Christmas.

MARK TWAIN MEMORIAL
351 Farmington Avenue, Hartford, Connecticut 06105
Mark Twain house (1874), the S. façade resembling a Mississippi steamboat. Books, pictures and other material illustrating the life and work of Mark Twain.
Mar. 1 - June 30, Sept. 1 - Dec. 31, Tu.-Sa., 10-5; Su., 2-5. Jan. 1 - Feb. 28, W.-Sa. 10-5, Su. 2-5. Closed public holidays.

WADSWORTH ATHENEUM
600 Main Street, Hartford, Connecticut 06103
European and American paintings, drawings, prints. Central and South American art. European tapestries, arms and armour, porcelain, silver. Early American furniture. Costumes. 18th-19th century period rooms. Oriental art. Ballet design and costumes. Ship models.
Tu.-Sa., 11-4; Su., 1-5. Closed New Year, July 4, Thanksgiving, Christmas.

HARTLAND

FLORENCE B. DEARING MUSEUM
3688 N. Hartland Road, Hartland, Michigan 48029
Local history. Agriculture. Household equipment.
M., W., F., Sa. 9-5; Tu., Th. 9-8.30. Closed public holidays.

HARVARD

FRUITLANDS MUSEUMS
Prospect Hill, Harvard, Massachusetts 01451
Fruitlands Museums group include: 1. *Fruitlands*, early 18th century farmhouse where Bronson Alcott and leaders of the Transcendental Movement attempted a new social order (1843). It contains a restored colonial kitchen, 18th-19th century furnishings, Louisa May Alcott material. 2. *Old Shaker House*, with Shaker furniture, handicrafts. 3. *American Indian Museum*, with prehistoric implements, burial items, dioramas and N. American Indian arts and industries. 4. *Picture Gallery*, with portraits by 18th-19th century itinerant artists, Hudson River School landscapes.
June 1 - Sept. 30, Tu.-Su. 1-5.

MUSEUM OF HARVARD HISTORICAL SOCIETY
Harvard, Massachusetts 01451
Local history. Costumes.
Still River Baptist Church (1832) is in the care of the Society.
July 1 - Sept. 30: Sa., Su. 1-5. Other days by appointment.

HARWOOD

TEXAS INDIAN MUSEUM
R.R. 1,78632, Harwood, Texas 78632
Indian material from central Texas. Pre-Columbian Mexican artifacts.
Sept.-May, daily 6-8. June-Aug., daily 6-10.

HASKELL

HASKELL RAILROAD MUSEUM
S. 6th Street and Avenue C., Haskell, Texas 79521
In old Haskell Railroad Station (1912). Railway history.
Daily 9-5.

HASTINGS

CHARLTON PARK VILLAGE AND MUSEUM
Rural Route 1, Charlton Park Road, Hastings, Michigan 49058
Mineralogy. Local history. Agriculture. Folklore. Indian artifacts. Transport.
June 1 - Oct. 31, daily 1-5. Rest of year M.-F. 9-5.

HASTINGS MUSEUM, HOUSE OF YESTERYEAR
1330 N. Burlington Street, Hastings, Nebraska 68901
Geology. Mineralogy. Astronomy. Planetarium. Natural history. Habitat groups. Local history. Plains Indian artifacts. Coins.
Sept. 1 - May 31, M.-Sa. 8-5; Su. 1-5; June 1 - Aug. 31, M.-Sa. 8-8; public holidays 2-5. Closed New Year, Christmas.

HATBORO

GRAEME PARK
County Line Road, Hatboro, Pennsylvania 19040
House (1721). 18th - early 19th century furnishings.
May 1 - Sept. 30: 8.30-5; Su. 1-5. Oct. 1 - Apr. 30: Tu.-Sa. 9-4.30; Su. 1-4.30. Closed public holidays.

HATFIELD

VI TEEPLES THUNDERBIRD MUSEUM
Hatfield, Wisconsin 54754
Mineralogy. Natural history. Local history and archaeology. Indian artifacts. Medicine.
May 1 - Sept. 30: Tu.-Su. 10-5.

HATTERAS ISLAND

CAPE HATTERAS NATIONAL SEASHORE MUSEUM OF THE SEA
Cape Hatteras, Hatteras Island, North Carolina 27943
Maritime collections.
June 15 - Aug. 31, daily 8-6. Sept.-June 1, daily 8-4.30.

HAVERFORD

HAVERFORD TOWNSHIP HISTORICAL SOCIETY MUSEUM
Karakung Drive, Powder Mill Park, Haverford, Pennsylvania 19083
In Lawrence Cabin (c.1710), with period furnishings. Local history. Railway history. Locomotives.
May 1 - Oct. 31: Su. 2-4. Other times by appointment.

QUAKER COLLECTION
Haverford College Library, Haverford, Pennsylvania 19041
Early Quaker books and pamphlets. Maps of Pennsylvania. Paintings, photographs, drawings, silhouettes of Quakers. Manuscript journals. Autograph letters.
By appointment.

HAVERHILL

THE BRITTONWOODS
240 Water Street, Haverhill, Massachusetts 01830
House (1814). 18th-19th century furnishings. Indian relics. Memorabilia of Hannah Dustin and Justice William H. Moody.
Sept. 15 - June 1, Tu., Th., Sa. 2-5. June 2 - Sept. 14, Tu.-Sa. 1-5.

HAVERHILL PUBLIC LIBRARY
99 Main Street, Haverhill, Massachusetts 01830
20th century American paintings.
M.-F. 9-9; Sa. 9-5.30.

MUSEUM OF HAVERHILL HISTORICAL SOCIETY
240 Water Street, Haverhill, Massachusetts 01830
Archaeology. Indian artifacts. Colonial furniture. Portraits. Lamps and lighting. Glass. China.
John Ward House (1641), White family house (1815) and former shoe shop (1870) are in the care of the Society.
May 1 - Sept. 30: M.-Sa. 1-5. Oct. 1 - Apr. 30: Tu., Th., Sa. 2-5.

THE JOHN WARD HOUSE
Haverhill, Massachusetts 01830
House (1641), built by settlers for their first pastor. Complete 17th century furnishings.
Sept. 15 - June 1, Tu., Th., Sa. 2-5. June 2 - Sept. 14, Tu.-Sa. 1-5.

JOHN GREENLEAF WHITTIER HOMESTEAD
305 Whittier Road, Haverhill, Massachusetts 01830
Whittier family house (1688), birthplace of John Greenleaf Whittier. Original furnishings.
Tu.-Sa. 10-6; Su. 1-6.

HAVRE

H. EARL CLACK MUSEUM
612 17th Street, Havre, Montana 59501
Archaeology. Local history. History of Chippewa-Cree Indians. Indian artifacts.
Memorial Day - Labour Day: M.-Sa. 9-9; Su. 12-9. Other times by appointment.

NORTHERN MONTANA COLLEGE COLLECTIONS
Northern Montana College, Havre, Montana 59501
Geology. Fossils. Botany. Chippewa and Cree Indian artifacts, clothing.
M.-F. 9-5. Closed college vacations.

HAWAII VOLCANOES NATIONAL PARK

THOMAS A. JAGGAR MEMORIAL MUSEUM
Hawaii Volcanoes National Park, Hawaii 96718
Geology. Natural history. Anthropology. Ethnography. Archaeology.
M.-F. 7.30-5; Sa., Su. 9-5.

HAWK'S STATE PARK

HAWK'S NEST MUSEUM
U.S. 60, Hawk's State Park, West Virginia
Displays depicting the settlement and development of West Virginia.
Daily 10-12, 2-5.

HAYS

STERNBERG MEMORIAL MUSEUM
Fort Hays Kansas State College, Hays, Kansas 67601
Geology. Palaeontology. Natural history. Archaeology.
M.-F. 8-5; Sa., Su. 2-5. During College vacations, daily 2-5.

HAYWARD

SULPHUR CREEK PARK NATURE CENTER
1801 D Street, Hayward, California 94541
Natural history of California. Junior museum.
M.-F., 1-5; Sa., 10-5. Su. 12-5. Closed public holidays.

HISTORYLAND
Hayward, Wisconsin 54843
Restored logging camp. Logging. Fur trade. Ojibwa Indian material.
June 25 - Labour Day, daily 10-6.

HAZELWOOD

LITTLE RED SCHOOLHOUSE
450 Brookes Lane, Hazelwood, Missouri 63042
In restored 1-roomed schoolhouse (1852). 19th century school books, equipment.
By appointment.

HEAVENER

PETER CONSER HOUSE
Heavener, Oklahoma 74937
House (1894), formerly home of Peter Conser, Choctaw Indian leader. Life of Conser. Indian history.
M.-Sa. 9-5; Su. 1-5. Closed public holidays.

CLEM HAMILTON HEAVENER RUNESTONE STATE PARK
Heavener, Oklahoma 74939
Runestone inscription, date 1012.
Daily 9-5.

HELENA

ARCHIE BRAY FOUNDATION
Route 2, Helena, Montana 59601
Contemporary American ceramics.
M.-Sa. 9-5.

MUSEUM OF LAST CHANCE GULCH RESTORATION ASSOCIATION
212 S. Park Avenue, Helena, Montana 59601
Pioneer cabin (1864-5). Furnishings of period of Montana Gold Rush, 1864-80.
May 1 - Labour Day, daily 12-4.

MUSEUM OF MONTANA HISTORICAL SOCIETY
225 N. Roberts Street, Helena, Montana 59601
Local history and archaeology. Pioneer life. Paintings by C. M. Russell. Sculpture. Anthropology.
Labour Day - Memorial Day: M.-F. 8-5; Sa., Su., public holidays 12-5. Rest of year: daily 8-8; public holidays 12-5. Closed New Year, Thanksgiving, Christmas.

HELLERTOWN

GILMAN MUSEUM
Durham Street, Hellertown, Pennsylvania 18055
Geology. Mineralogy. Botany. Animal specimens from N. and S. America, Africa. Agriculture. Indian artifacts. Guns.
Daily 9-9.

HEMPSTEAD

EMILY LOWE GALLERY
Hofstra University, Hempstead, New York 11550
Pre-Colombian art. Indian sculpture. 16th-17th century European, especially Italian, paintings. 20th century American, European, paintings, sculpture. Currier and Ives prints.
May-Sept., M.-F. 10-1. ct.vpr., M., Tu., F. 10-5; W., Th. 10-5, 6-9; Sa., Su. 1-5. Closed public holidays, university vacations.

HENDERSON

JOHN JAMES AUDUBON MUSEUM
Audubon State Park, Henderson, Kentucky 42420
Exhibits illustrating Audubon's life and work in Kentucky. Personal possessions. Natural history. Paintings. Costumes.
Apr. 1 - May 31, Sept. 1 - Oct. 31: Tu.-Su. 9-5. June 1 - Aug. 31: M. 9-5.

MUSEUM OF SIBLEY COUNTY HISTORICAL SOCIETY
Henderson, Minnesota 56044
House (1884). Local history. Agriculture. Industry.
Log cabin (1860) is in the care of the Society.
Last Su. in May - last Su. in Oct.: Su. 2-5. Other times by appointment.

SOUTHERN NEVADA MUSEUM
240 Water Street, Henderson, Nevada 89015
Geology. Mineralogy. Palaeontology. Archaeology. Indian artifacts.
M.-Sa. 9-5; Su. 1-5. Closed New Year, Christmas.

HOWARD-DICKINSON HOUSE
501 S. Main Street, Henderson, Texas 75652
House (1855). Furnishings of 1860-1900. Rusk County memorabilia.
May 1 - Sept. 30, Tu.-Su. 1-5. Oct. 1 - Apr. 30, Su. 1-5.

HEPPNER

MORROW COUNTY MUSEUM
Main Street, Heppner, Oregon 97836
Local history.
Sa. 10-5; Su. 1-5. Other times by appointment.

HEREFORD

CORONADO NATIONAL MEMORIAL
Star Route, Hereford, Arizona 85615
Natural history. 16th century Spanish costumes, weapons.
Daily 8-5.

DEAF SMITH COUNTY MUSEUM
400 Sampson Street, Hereford, Texas 79045
County history. Pioneer life. Farming. Ranching. Windmill. Photographs. Pre-pioneer paintings. Santa Fe Railroad collection. Reconstructed half-dugout.
W., Sa., Su. 2-5.

HERKIMER

MUSEUM OF HERKIMER COUNTY HISTORICAL SOCIETY
400 N. Main Street, Herkimer, New York 13350
Regional history.
July 1 - Aug. 31, M.-Sa. 1-5.

HERMANN

GENTNER HOUSE
108 Market Street, Hermann, Missouri 65041
House (1850), with original furnishings.
Apr.-Oct., 1st Su. in month.

HISTORIC HERMANN MUSEUM
4th and Schiller Streets, Hermann, Missouri 65041
In former German School building (1871). History of local German settlement. Indian artifacts. Missouri river navigation.
Old Stone Hill (1869) and Rotunda (1870).
M.-Sa. 10-5; Su., public holidays 1-5.

HERMITAGE

MUSEUM OF HICKORY COUNTY HISTORICAL SOCIETY
Courthouse, Hermitage, Missouri 65668
Archaeology. Local history. Furniture. Costumes.
M.-F. 8-4.

LADIES HERMITAGE ASSOCIATION
Route 4, Hermitage, Tennessee 37076
In The Hermitage (1819), home of President Andrew Jackson. Family furniture, personal possessions, documents. Costumes. Agriculture.
Tulip Grove (1836) and Old Hermitage Church (1823) are also in the care of the Association.
Daily 9-5.

TULIP GROVE
Route 1, Hermitage, Tennessee 37076
House (1836). Donelson family portraits. Original and period furnishings.
Daily 9-5. Closed Christmas.

HERMOSA

CUSTER STATE PARK MUSEUM
Custer State Park, Hermosa, South Dakota 57744
Pioneer relics. Military history.
May 15- Sept. 30, daily 8-5.

HERSHEY

HERSHEY MUSEUM
Park Avenue and Derry Road, Hershey, Pennsylvania 17033
Pennsylvania Dutch artifacts. Clocks. Stiegel glass. Early Americana. Indian material.
Daily 10-5. Closed Christmas, New Year.

HERTFORD

MUSEUM OF PERQUIMANS COUNTY HISTORICAL SOCIETY
Box 285, Hertford, North Carolina 27944
Local history, archaeology.
By appointment.

HICKORY

HICKORY MUSEUM OF ART
3rd Street and 1st Avenue N.W., Hickory, North Carolina 28601
American and European paintings. Sculpture. Guns. Coins. Chinese porcelain.
M.-F. 10-5; Su., public holidays 3-5. Closed Aug. 1-31.

HICKSVILLE

GREGORY MUSEUM
207 Cottage Boulevard, Hicksville, New York 11801
Mineralogy. Entomology.
M.-F. 9-5.

HIGHLANDS

TWIN LIGHT MUSEUM
Highlands, New Jersey 07732
Material relating to history of U.S. Life Saving Service. Jersey shore fishing industry. Artifacts of the Lenni-Lennape Indians. Shipping beacon, 1828.
Memorial Day- Labour Day, Tu.-Su. 10-12, 1-5.

HIGH POINT

JOHN HALEY HOUSE
1805 E. Lexington Avenue, High Point, North Carolina 27261
House (1786). Period furnishings. Operating blacksmith's shop.
Tu.-Su. 9.30-4.30.

HIGH POINT HISTORICAL SOCIETY MUSEUM
1805 E. Lexington Avenue, High Point, North Carolina 27261
Local history. Archaeology. Indian artifacts. History of local furniture and hosiery industries.
John Haley House (1786), Mendenhall Plantation (1812) and Jamestown Friends Meeting House (1820) are in the care of the museum.
Tu.-F. 9.30-4.30; Sa.-Su. 2-5. Closed public holidays.

SPRINGFIELD MUSEUM OF OLD DOMESTIC ARTS
508 Hayworth Circle, High Point, North Carolina 27261
In former Meeting House (1854). Local history. Agriculture. Tools and implements used by early settlers. Domestic life.
By appointment.

HILL CITY

OIL MUSEUM
U.S. Highway 24, Hill City, Kansas 67642
Working model of drilling rig. Display showing oil exploration, extraction, processing.
Daily 9.30-5. Evenings by request.

BLACK HILLS CENTRAL RAILROAD
Hill City, South Dakota 57745
19th century locomotives, coaches. 10 miles of operating railway.
M.-Sa., railroad trips at 9, 10.30, 12.30, 2, 3.30; Su. 2, 2.30.

HILLIARD

TRAINS OF YESTERDAY MUSEUM
P.O. Box 455, Hilliard, Florida 32046
Railway history. Models. Equipment. Paintings of railway subjects. Documents.
3 historic buildings, including the former Longwood railway station (1903) are in the care of the Museum.
Daily 9-7.

HILLSBORO

HILLSBORO ADOBE MUSEUM
116 E. Grand Street, Hillsboro, Kansas 67063
In adobe house (1876). Pioneer history. Folklore. Agriculture.
M.-F. 9-12, 2-5; Sa., Su., public holidays 2-5.

FOX STATE FOREST MUSEUM
Center Road, Hillsboro, New Hampshire 03244
Botany. Herbarium. Natural history. Entomology. Forestry and forest products. Forest diseases. Fire prevention.
By appointment.

FRANKLIN PIERCE HOMESTEAD
Hillsboro, New Hampshire 03244
House (1804), formerly home of President Pierce. Period furnishings.
June 9- Labour Day, daily. Labour Day- Oct. 15, Sa., Su.

TRAILL COUNTY HISTORICAL SOCIETY MUSEUM
Hillsboro, North Dakota 58045
Local history. Agriculture. Indian material.
Memorial Day- Sept. 30, Su. 2-5. Other times by appointment.

FORT HILL MUSEUM
State Route 41, Hillsboro, Ohio 45133
Natural science. Hopewell Indian artifacts.
Mar. 1- Nov. 30: Tu.-Su. 9.30-5.

MUSEUM OF HIGHLAND COUNTY HISTORICAL SOCIETY
E. Main Street, Hillsboro, Ohio 45133
In Highland House (1842). History of Highland County.
May 1- Sept. 30, Su. 2-5.

WASHINGTON COUNTY HISTORICAL SOCIETY AND MUSEUM
Hillsboro, Oregon 97123
Local history.
M., W., F. 1-5. Closed national holidays.

CONFEDERATE RESEARCH CENTER AND GUN MUSEUM
Hill Junior College, Coricana Road, Hillsboro, Texas 76645
Artifacts and records of Hood's Texas Brigade. Confederate and Texas firearms.
M.-F. 8-5. Closed school vacations.

MUSEUM OF HILLSBORO AREA HISTORICAL SOCIETY
Albert Field Memorial Park, Hillsboro, Wisconsin 54634
Restored log cabin (1853). Period furnishings. Local history.
June 1- Aug. 31: Su., public holidays 2-4.

HILLSBOROUGH

ORANGE COUNTY HISTORICAL MUSEUM
East King Street, Hillsborough, North Carolina 27278
In old Orange County Courthouse (1844). Local history of the Colonial period. Local silver. Domestic utensils. Royal weights and measures. Firearms. Diorama of Occoneechee Indian village.
Tu.-Su. 1.30-4.30. Closed Christmas.

HILO

LYMAN HOUSE MEMORIAL MUSEUM
276 Haili Street, Hilo, Hawaii 96720
House (1839). Geology. Mineralogy. Lava specimens. Shells and coral. Local history. Handicrafts. Missionary relics. Costumes. Chinese teak furniture.
M.-Sa. 10-4; Su. 1-4. Closed New Year, July 4, Thanksgiving, Christmas.

HILTON HEAD ISLAND

HARBOUR TOWN MUSEUM
Harbour Town, Hilton Head Island, South Carolina 29928
History of exploration of S.E. coast. Maps, charts. Navigation instruments. Early European maps.
Daily 9-5.

HINGHAM

OLD ORDINARY
21 Lincoln Street, Hingham, Massachusetts 02043
Building, Old Ordinary (1683). 18th century furnishings.
June 1- Sept. 15: Tu.-Sa. 11.30-4.30.

HINSDALE

HINSDALE HEALTH MUSEUM
40 S. Clay Street, Hinsdale, Illinois 60521
Human biology, physiology, growth and development.
M.-Sa. 9-5; Su. 1-5. Closed public holidays.

THE OLD GRAUE MILL AND MUSEUM
York Road, Oak Brook, Hinsdale, Illinois 60521
Restored and operating water-mill (1852). Farm equipment. Early American sitting-room and kitchen. Horse-drawn vehicles.
May 6- Oct. 31, daily 11-6.

HODGENVILLE

ABRAHAM LINCOLN BIRTHPLACE NATIONAL HISTORIC SITE
Route 1, Hodgenville, Kentucky 42748
On Sinking Spring Farm, birthplace of Abraham Lincoln. Pioneer history. Lincoln family bible.
Sept.-May, daily 8-4.45. June-Aug., daily 8-6.45. Closed Christmas.

HOGANSBURG

AKWESASNE MOHAWK INDIAN VILLAGE
St. Regis Reservation, Hogansburg, New York 13655
Iroquois long houses. Dwellings of other Indian tribes. Arts and crafts.
June 27- Sept. 6: M.-Sa. 10-10; Su. 12-10. Sept. 7- Oct. 31: Sa., Su. and by appointment, 12-10.

HOHENWALD

MERIWETHER LEWIS NATIONAL MONUMENT, VISITOR CENTER
Natchez Trace Parkway, Hohenwald, Tennessee 38462
Exhibits illustrating life of Meriwether Lewis (1774-1809), explorer of the American West and Governor of Louisiana.
Daily, 24 hours.

HOLBROOK

RAINBOW FOREST MUSEUM
Petrified Forest National Park, Holbrook, Arizona 86025
History and natural history of the Park area. Herbarium. Palaeontology. Minerals. Zoology. Archaeology. Ethnology.
Daily during daylight hours.

HOLCOMB

ANTIQUE WIRELESS ASSOCIATION MUSEUM
Main Street, Holcomb, New York 14469
History of radio communications.
May 1- Oct. 31: M.-F. 7-10 p.m., by appointment.

HOLDREGE

MUSEUM OF PHELPS COUNTY HISTORICAL SOCIETY
512 E. Avenue, Holdrege, Nebraska 68949
Local history. Agriculture. Indian artifacts.
M.-W. 2-5; Th. 7-9; F.-Su. 2-5. Closed public holidays.

HOLLAND

BAKER FURNITURE MUSEUM
E. 6th Street, Holland, Michigan 49423
17th-19th century European and Oriental furniture. Decorative arts.
M.-Sa. 10-5; Su. 1-5.

NETHERLANDS MUSEUM
8 E. 12th Street, Holland, Michigan 49423
Netherlands history and culture. Replicas of Dutch kitchens.
May 1 - Sept. 15, daily 11.30-5. Sept. 16 - Apr. 30, M.-Sa. 9-5. Closed Dec. 31, Thanksgiving, Christmas.

POLL MUSEUM
U.S. Highway 31 and New Holland Street, Holland, Michigan 49423
Vintage cars. Early fire-fighting equipment. Model ships and trains.
May 1 - Oct. 31, M.-Sa. 8.30-5.30.

HOLLIDAYSBURG

BAKER MANSION MUSEUM
Hollidaysburg, Pennsylvania 16648
House (1846). 30 furnished rooms. Furniture includes Belgian suite (c.1850). History of Blair County. Tools. Papers of Baker family. Records of Allegheny Portage Railroad. Models of Portage rolling stock and of boats used on Pennsylvania Canal.
By appointment.

HOLLISTON

MUSEUM OF HOLLISTON HISTORICAL SOCIETY
547 Washington Street, Holliston, Massachusetts 01746
In Asa Whiting House (1812). Local history. Costumes.
By appointment.

HOLLY SPRINGS

KATE FREEMAN CLARK ART GALLERY
College, Holly Springs, Mississippi 38635
Paintings by Kate Freeman Clark, local artist of early 1900s.
Daily 10-5, on request.

HOLLYWOOD

SOTTERLEY MANSION
Box 67, Hollywood, Maryland 20636
House (1710). Furniture and furnishings, 1710-50. Warehouse. Smoke house. Slave cabin.
Apr. 1 - Nov. 30, daily 11-5.

HOLTSVILLE

SACHEN HISTORICAL SOCIETY
1057 Waverly Avenue, Holtsville, New York 11742
Local history.
By appointment.

HOLYOKE

HOLYOKE MUSEUM - WISTARIAHURST
238 Cabot Street, Holyoke, Massachusetts 01040
Geology. Natural history. Ethnology. Archaeology. Indian material. Local history, including dioramas. 18th century furniture. Egyptian art. Paintings. Sculpture. Graphics. Period rooms.
M.-Sa. 1-5; Su. 2-5. Closed July, public holidays.

HOMER

HOMER MUSEUM
Bartlett Street, Homer, Alaska 99603
History, archaeology, anthropology and ethnology of the Kenai Peninsula. Mineralogy. Natural history. Coins. Paintings.
Memorial Day to Labour Day, 10-5. At other times by appointment.

HERBERT S. FORD MEMORIAL MUSEUM
502 N. 2nd Street, Homer, Louisiana 71040
Local history. Indian artifacts. Medical history.
Original City Hall (1900) is in the care of the Museum.
May 1 - Sept. 30, M., Tu., Th., F. 8-12, 1-4.30. W. 8-12. Closed public holidays.

HOMESTEAD

EVERGLADES NATIONAL PARK
P.O. Box 279, Homestead, Florida 33030
History of Indians and of Fort Jefferson. Natural history of the National Park area. Herbarium.
Daily 8-5.

HOMOSASSA

YULEE SUGAR MILL
Florida State Highway 490, Homosassa, Florida 32646
Restored mill (1851) of former sugar plantation.
Daily 8-dusk.

HONAUNAU

CITY OF REFUGE NATIONAL HISTORIC PARK
P.O. Box 128, Honaunau, Hawaii 96726
Local history and archaeology.
Hale-o-Keawe house (1650) is in the care of the Park.
Daily 7.30-5.

HONESDALE

WAYNE COUNTY HISTORICAL SOCIETY MUSEUM
810 Main Street, Honesdale, Pennsylvania 18431
In Delaware and Hudson Canal Building (1860). Local history. Indian artifacts. Farm implements. Costumes. Paintings. Glass.
Delaware and Hudson Canal Lock (1825) and Stourbridge Lion Building (1929), with replica of 'Stourbridge Lion', first locomotive to run in U.S., are in the care of the Society.
June 1 - Sept. 30: M.-Sa. 10-12, 1-4; Oct. 1 - May 31: Tu., W., F., Sa. 10-12, 1-4. Closed New Year, Thanksgiving, Christmas.

HONEOYE FALLS

MUSEUM OF TOWN OF MENDON HISTORICAL SOCIETY
N. Main Street, Honeoye Falls, New York 14472
Local history. Farm tools and implements. Clothing. Furniture. Photographs.
Su. 2-5. Other times by appointment.

HONOLULU

BERNICE PAUAHI BISHOP MUSEUM
1355 Kalihi Street, Honolulu, Hawaii 96817
Geology. Natural history. Botany. Ethnology. Local history. Hawaiian stamps. Maritime museum in the ship 'Falls of Clyde' (1878).
M.-Sa. 9-5; Su. 12-5. Closed New Year, Easter, Thanksgiving, Christmas.

CHILDREN'S MUSEUM OF NATURAL HISTORY
Ala Moana Park, Honolulu, Hawaii 96814
Geology. Natural history.
Daily 9-5. Closed New Year, Christmas.

HAWAIAN WAX MUSEUM
2340 Kalakua Avenue, Honolulu, Hawaii 96815
History of Hawaii from arrival of early Polynesian settlers to annexation by U.S. in 1898, in figures by Katherine Stubergh Keller.
Daily 9.30 a.m. - 10.30 p.m.

HONOLULU ACADEMY OF ARTS
900 S. Beretania Street, Honolulu, Hawaii 96814
Chinese and Japanese painting, sculpture, decorative arts. Korean and Islamic ceramics. Early Mediterranean and medieval Christian art. European and American paintings, sculpture, prints, decorative arts. Pacific Islands art.
Tu.-Sa. 10-4.30; Su. 2-5. Closed New Year, July 4, Labour Day, Thanksgiving, Christmas.

MISSION HOUSES MUSEUM
553 South King Street, Honolulu, Hawaii 96813
Based on 3 historic houses (1821, 1831, 1840). Natural history. Agriculture. Printing. Mission history. Costumes. Music.
Tu.-Su. 10-5. Closed New Year, Thanksgiving, Christmas.

QUEEN EMMA SUMMER PALACE
2913 Pali Highway, Honolulu, Hawaii 96817
Palace (c.1847). Household effects and personal belongings of Queen Emma and Kamehameka IV.
M.-F. 9-4; Sa., Dec. 24 and 31, 9-12. Closed public holidays.

TENNENT ART FOUNDATION GALLERY
203 Prospect Street, Honolulu, Hawaii 96813
Paintings, drawings by Madge Tennent.
Tu.-Sa. 10-12; Su. 2-4.

HOOD RIVER

HOOD RIVER COUNTY MUSEUM
Court House, State Street, Hood River, Oregon 97123
County history. Indian artifacts. Social life. Tools. Clothing.
M.-F. 8-5. Closed public holidays.

HOPE

HOPE HISTORICAL SOCIETY MUSEUM
High Street, P.O. Box 168, Hope, New Jersey 07844
Local history. Handicrafts. Moravian exhibits.
May 1 - Sept. 30: Sa., Su. 2-5.

STEELE COUNTY HISTORICAL SOCIETY MUSEUM
Hope, North Dakota 58046
Local history. Agriculture.
Su. 2-5.30.

HOPEDALE

LITTLE RED SHOP
Hopedale Street, Hopedale, Massachusetts 01747
Textile museum of the Draper Company. Models of early Draper looms. Weaving equipment. Textiles.
By appointment.

HOPEWELL

HOPEWELL MUSEUM
28 E. Broad Street, Hopewell, New Jersey 08525
Local history, Colonial period - 1900. Furnishings. Domestic equipment. Agriculture. Indian artifacts.
M., W., Sa. 2-5. Closed public holidays.

HOPKINTON

NEW HAMPSHIRE ANTIQUARIAN SOCIETY MUSEUM
Main Street, Hopkinton, New Hampshire 03301
Local history. Indian artifacts, including dug-out canoe. Agriculture. Household equipment. Early music books. Books and pamphlets published in New Hampshire.
July 1 - Aug. 31, F. 2-5.

HORSEHEADS

ERIN HISTORICAL SOCIETY
R.D.3, Horseheads, New York 14845
In Town Hall (1871). Local history.
F., Sa., public holidays, by appointment.

HOT SPRINGS

HOT SPRINGS NATIONAL PARK MUSEUM
Reserve and Central Avenues, Hot Springs, Arkansas 71901
Geology. Natural history. Herbarium. Local history. Indian artifacts.
Daily 8-5. Closed Christmas.

NATURAL SCIENCE MUSEUM
I.Q. Zoo, 380 Whittington Street, Hot Springs, Arkansas 71901
Exhibits of psychologically conditioned animal behaviour.
May-Sept. daily 9-5. Oct.-Apr. daily 10.30-4.30.

QUARTZ CRYSTAL CAVE AND MUSEUM
435 Whittington Avenue, Hot Springs, Arkansas 71901
Crystals from the Hot Springs area and the south-west.
Daily 8-6.

WIND CAVE NATIONAL PARK MUSEUM
Hot Springs, South Dakota 57747
Natural history. Archaeology. Indian artifacts.
Daily 8-5.

HOTSVILLE

SACHEM HISTORICAL SOCIETY MUSEUM
1057 Waverly Avenue, Hotsville, New York 11742
Local history.
By appointment.

HOUGHTON

A. E. SEAMAN MINERALOGICAL MUSEUM
College Avenue, Houghton, Michigan 49931
Geology. Michigan copper and iron.
M.-F. 9-4.30; Sa. 9-12. Closed New Year, July 4, Thanksgiving, Christmas.

HOULTON

AROOSTOOK HISTORICAL AND ART MUSEUM OF HOULTON
109 Main Street, Houlton, Maine 04730
Natural history. Local history. Pioneer tools and equipment. Indian relics.
Tu., Sa. 1-5. Closed public holidays.

HOUSTON

BATTLESHIP 'TEXAS'
3901 Westheimer Street, Houston, Texas 77027
U.S.S. 'Texas', which saw service in World Wars I and II.
May 1 - Aug. 31, daily 12-6.

BAYOU BEND COLLECTION
1 Westcott Street, Houston, Texas 77007
Antique collection of Ima Hogg. 17th-19th century American furniture, paintings, decorative arts, porcelain, crystal.
Tu. 1.15-4.30; W.-F. 10-4.30; Sa. 10-1.30. 2nd Su. in each month, except Mar., 1-5. Closed Aug. 1-31, New Year, Labour Day, Thanksgiving, Christmas.

CLASSIC CAR SHOWCASE
3009 S. Post Oak Road, Houston, Texas 77027
Classic cars of the 1930s.
M.-Sa. 10-6; Su. 12-6.

CONTEMPORARY ARTS MUSEUM
5216 Montrose Street, Houston, Texas 77006
Contemporary American paintings, sculpture.
Tu.-Sa. 10-5; Su. 12-6. Closed Thanksgiving, Christmas, New Year.

HARRIS COUNTY HERITAGE SOCIETY MUSEUM
1100 Bagby Street, Houston, Texas 77000
5 restored and furnished houses (1840-68). Reconstructed Long Row (1837), containing 19th century general store, barber's shop, circulating library.
M.-F. 10-4; Sa. 11-3; Su. 2-5.

HOUSTON MUSEUM OF NATURAL SCIENCE
5800 Caroline Street, Hermann Park, Houston, Texas 77004
Geology. Space science. Planetarium. Natural history. Archaeology.
Su., M. 12-5; Tu.-Sa. 9-5; F., Sa. also 7.30-9.

INSTITUTE FOR THE ARTS
Rice University, Houston, Texas 77000
Paintings. Prints. Pottery. Photographs. Sculpture.
F.-W. 10-6; Th. 10-10.

MUSEUM OF AMERICAN ARCHITECTURE AND DECORATIVE ARTS
Houston Baptist College, Houston, Texas 77036
American architecture and decorative arts. Period rooms. Furniture. China. Pewter. Glass. Dolls. Miniature furniture.
Tu.-Th. 10-4. Other times by appointment. Closed first 3 weeks of Aug., Easter and Christmas vacations.

MUSEUM OF FINE ARTS
1001 Bissonet Street, Houston, Texas 77005
Art of Egypt, Greece, Rome. Primitive art of Africa, Oceania, N. and S. America. Renaissance and Baroque European paintings. 20th century American paintings and decorative arts, including works by Frederic Remington. Near and Far Eastern textiles. European lace. Spanish furniture. S.W. American Indian art. Pre-Columbian artifacts.
Tu.-Sa. 9.30-5; Su. 12-6. Oct.-May, 1st W. in month, 9.30-9. Closed public holidays.

MUSEUM OF MEDICAL SCIENCE
Caroline Street, Hermann Park, Houston, Texas 77005
Human anatomy and physiology. Health education.
Su., M. 12-5; Tu.-Sa. 9-5; F., Sa. also 7.30-9 p.m. Closed Thanksgiving, New Year, Christmas.

MUSEUM OF TEXAS GULF COAST HISTORICAL ASSOCIATION
University of Houston, Houston, Texas 77004
Collections illustrating commercial and industrial development of the Texas Gulf Coast.
M.-F. 9-5. Closed university vacations.

MUSEUM OF UNIVERSITY OF HOUSTON
Department of Geology, 3801 Cullen Boulevard, Houston, Texas 77004
Geology. Mineralogy. Palaeontology. Petrology.
M.-F. 9-6. Closed Labour Day, Thanksgiving, Christmas, New Year.

WEATHERBY ARMS MUSEUM
2510 Westridge, Houston, Texas 77025
Weapons. Armour. Instruments of torture. Pirate and sunken treasure section.
Tu.-Su. 10-6. Closed Christmas, New Year.

HUBBARDTON

HUBBARDTON BATTLEFIELD MUSEUM
Hubbardton, Vermont 05749
Site museum. Military history.
Memorial Day - Oct. 15, daily 9-6.

HUDSON

AMERICAN MUSEUM OF FIRE-FIGHTING
Firemen's Home, Harry Howard Avenue, Hudson, New York 12534
History of the Volunteer Fire Service, 1731 to present day. Apparatus. Banners. Prints. Portraits.
Daily 9-5.

OLANA
Routes 9G and 23, Hudson, New York 12534
House (1870-2) was home of Frederic E. Church, 19th century landscape artist. Paintings by Church and other artists.
Apr. 1 - Nov. 30, daily 9-5.

HUDSON LIBRARY AND HISTORICAL SOCIETY MUSEUM
22 Aurora Street, Hudson, Ohio 44236
In Frederick Baldwin House (1833). History of town of Hudson.
M., Tu., Th.-Sa. 10-5.

ST. CROIX COUNTY HISTORICAL SOCIETY MUSEUM
Public Library Basement, 304 Locust, Hudson, Wisconsin 54016
County history. Furnishings. Household equipment.
M.-F. 10-5. Closed national holidays.

HUGOTON

STEVENS COUNTY GAS AND HISTORICAL MUSEUM
711 Van Buren Street, Hugoton, Kansas 67951
Early gas industry equipment. Indian artifacts.
Daily 1-5. Closed Thanksgiving, Christmas, New Year.

HUMBOLDT

MUSEUM OF HUMBOLDT COUNTY HISTORICAL ASSOCIATION
Humboldt, Iowa 50548
Local history. Indian material.
Mill farmhouse (1879) and Norway No. 6 District School (1883) are in the care of the Association.
Oct. 1 - Apr. 30, 1st and 3rd Su. each month, 10-4. May 1 - Sept. 30, 1st and 3rd Su. each month, Th.-F. 10-4.

HUNTINGDON

SWIGART MUSEUM
Box 214, Museum Park, Huntingdon, Pennsylvania 16652
Old American cars, engines and accessories.
July 1 - Aug. 31, daily 9-9. June 1-30, 9-5. May 1-31, Sept. 1 - Oct. 31: Sa., Su. 9-5.

HUNTINGTON

HUNTINGTON COUNTY HISTORICAL SOCIETY MUSEUM
Huntington County Court House, Huntington, Indiana 46750
Local history.
Tu.-F. 1-4.

HECKSCHER MUSEUM
Prime Avenue, Huntington, New York 11743
16th-20th century paintings by European (especially English, French) artists. 18th-20th century American paintings.
Tu.-Sa. 10-5; Su. 2-5; public holidays 2-5.

MUSEUM OF HUNTINGTON HISTORICAL SOCIETY
County Court House, 2 High Street, Huntington, New York 11746
In Conklin farmhouse (1750). Local history. Period rooms.
Tu.-F. 1-4; Su. 2-5.

QUAKER THOMAS POWELL HOUSE
434 Park Avenue, Huntington, New York 11746
House (1663). Indian material. Costumes. Huntington pottery. Long Island paintings.
W., Th. 1-4.30.

WALT WHITMAN HOUSE
246 Walt Whitman Road, Huntington, New York 11743
Farmhouse (1810), Whitman's birthplace and boyhood home. Whitman manuscripts, pictures, books.
Daily 10-4.

HUNTINGTON GALLERIES
2033 McCoy Road, Huntington, West Virginia 25701
19th-20th century English paintings. American paintings, sculpture. 18th-19th century English silver. Turkish prayer rugs.
Tu.-Sa. 10-4; Su. 1-5. Closed Christmas, New Year.

GEOLOGY MUSEUM, MARSHALL UNIVERSITY
15th Street, Huntington, West Virginia 25701
Geology. Mineralogy.
M.-F. 8-4.30. Closed university vacations.

HUNTSVILLE

SAM HOUSTON MEMORIAL MUSEUM
Sam Houston Avenue, Huntsville, Texas 77340
Mementoes of Texas Revolution. Personal possessions of Sam Houston.
Houston's house (1847), his law office (1847) and Steamboat House (1858) are in the care of the Museum.
Daily 9-5. Closed Thanksgiving, Christmas.

HURON

SOUTH DAKOTA STATE FAIR PIONEER MUSEUM
State Fair Grounds, Huron, South Dakota 57350
Local history. Pioneer life. Indian artifacts.
May 30 - Labour Day, M.-F. 6-9; Sa., Su. 1-9.

HURON CITY

PIONEER HURON CITY
U.S. Highway 25, Huron City, Michigan 48226
Restored buildings showing the logging town as it was in the 19th century. Log cabin. Inn. School. Chapel. Store.
At all times.

WILLIAM LYON PHELPS MUSEUM
Huron City, Michigan 48226
Paintings of local lumbering industry. Costumes.
July-Aug., Tu.-Su. 3-5.

HYANNIS

TALES OF CAPE COD
47 Cherry Street, Hyannis, Massachusetts 02601
Local history and archaeology. Indian artifacts. Folklore.
M.-Sa. 9-9.

MUSEUM OF GRANT COUNTY HISTORICAL SOCIETY
Court House, Hyannis, Nebraska 69350
Local history.
Th. 2-4. Other times by appointment.

HYDE PARK

FRANKLIN D. ROOSEVELT LIBRARY AND MUSEUM
Route 9, Hyde Park, New York 12538
The President's books, papers, photographs, ship-models, personal possessions. 19th century naval paintings and prints. Coins. Stamps.
Daily 9-5. Closed Christmas.

FRANKLIN D. ROOSEVELT NATIONAL HISTORIC SITE
Route 9, Hyde Park, New York 12538
House (c.1865). Birthplace of President Roosevelt, where he and his wife are buried. Furniture. Family portraits. Naval prints.
Apr. 1 - Nov. 30, daily 9-5. Dec. 1 - Mar. 31, W.-Su. 9-5. Closed New Year, Christmas.

VANDERBILT MANSION NATIONAL HISTORIC SITE
Route 9, Hyde Park, New York 12538
House (1896-8) was home of F. W. Vanderbilt. Italian and French furnishings. European tapestries, paintings, sculpture, objects d'art.
Apr. 1 - Nov. 30, W.-Su. 9-5. Closed New Year, Christmas.

IDAHO CITY

BOISE BASIN MUSEUM
Box 4065, Idaho City, Idaho 83631
Local history. Costumes. Glass.
May 31 - Oct. 1, Tu. 2-4; Sa. 1-6.

IDAHO FALLS

SPORTSMAN'S PARK MUSEUM
Idaho Falls, Idaho 83401
Mounted birds and animals.
Daily 9-dusk.

ILION

REMINGTON GUN MUSEUM
Hoefler Avenue, Ilion, New York 13357
History of firearms made by Remington Arms Co., 1840, onwards.
Daily 9-9.

IMPERIAL

IMPERIAL COUNTY PIONEER MUSEUM
P.O. Box 308, Imperial, California 92251
Geology. Minerals. Handicrafts. Costumes. Paintings. Sculpture. Prints. Drawings.
Sa., Su. 10-12.

INDEPENDENCE

EASTERN CALIFORNIA MUSEUM
155 Grant Street, Independence, California 93526
Mineralogy. Palaeontology. Natural history. Botany. Transport. Indian artifacts.
Commander's House (1872) is in the care of the Museum.
Daily, 10-5. Closed New Year, Christmas.

INDEPENDENCE MUSEUM
123 N. 8th Street, Independence, Kansas 67301
Local history. Paintings. Indian artifacts.
W., Sa. 1-5; Su. 2-5. Closed July 4, Christmas.

COURTHOUSE
107 W. Kansas Avenue, Independence, Missouri 64050
Building (1827). Original furnishings.
M.-Sa. 9-4. Closed holidays.

HERITAGE HALL
The Auditorium, Independence, Missouri 64051
History of Reorganised Church of Jesus, Latter Day Saints. 6 churches and houses (1803-81) are in the care of the Church.
M.-Sa. 9-12, 1-5; Su., public holidays 1-5. Closed New Year, Easter, Thanksgiving, Christmas.

HARRY S. TRUMAN LIBRARY AND MUSEUM
U.S. Highway 24 and Delaware Street, Independence, Missouri 64050
Career of Harry S. Truman. History of U.S. Presidency. History of 35th Division, U.S. Army. Paintings. Sculpture. Graphics. Coins. Stamps.
May 16- Sept. 15: M.-Sa. 9-5; Su. 10-5. Sept. 16- May 15: M.-Sa. 9-5; Su. 2-5. Closed New Year, Thanksgiving, Christmas.

JACKSON COUNTY HISTORICAL SOCIETY MUSEUM
217 N. Main Street, Independence, Missouri 64050
In former jail (1859). History of Jackson County. 19th century furnishings.
M.-Sa. 9-5; Su., public holidays 1-5. Closed New Year, Thanksgiving, Christmas.

TEXAS BAPTIST HISTORICAL CENTER MUSEUM
Highways 50 and 390, Independence, Texas
In old Independence Baptist Church (1839), where Sam Houston was baptised. History of contribution made by Independence to educational and cultural development of Texas.
Tu.-Sa. 9-5; Su. 1-5.

INDIANA

MUSEUM OF HISTORICAL AND GENEALOGICAL SOCIETY OF INDIANA COUNTY
S. 6th Street and Wayne Avenue, Indiana, Pennsylvania 15701
Building is log house (c.1840, reconstructed 1961). Local history.
Croyland (1872) is in the care of the Society.
Tu., Th. 1.30-4, 6.30-9.

INDIANAPOLIS

CHILDREN'S MUSEUM OF INDIANAPOLIS
3010 North Meridian Street, Indianapolis, Indiana 46208
Geology. Palaeontology. Natural history. Ethnology. Indian material. Transport. Costumes. Folklore. Decorative arts.
Tu.-Sa. 9-5; Su. 2-5. Closed public holidays.

CLOWES FUND COLLECTION
3744 Spring Hollow Road, Indianapolis, Indiana 46208
15th-17th century Italian paintings. 16th-18th century Spanish paintings. 17th-18th century Dutch, French, Flemish paintings. 18th-19th century English paintings.
Sept.-July, Th., Su. 2-6.

ELI LILLY AND CO.
Archives and Company Museum, Lilly Center, 893 South Delaware, Indianapolis, Indiana 46206
History of Eli Lilly Company, and of the pharmaceutical industry. Replica of original laboratory (1876).
M.-F. 9-4. Closed public holidays.

HOOSIER SALON
15 E. Washington Street, Indianapolis, Indiana 46204
Paintings, sculptures, prints, mostly by American artists.
M.-F. 9-4.30. Closed July, Aug.

INDIANAPOLIS MOTOR SPEEDWAY MUSEUM
4790 W. 16th Street, Indianapolis, Indiana 46222
Cars raced at Indianapolis, 1903 onwards. Photographs. Trophies.
Daily 9-5.

INDIANAPOLIS MUSEUM OF ART
1200 W. 38 Street, Indianapolis, Indiana 46208
Oriental art, especially jade, porcelain, bronzes, textiles. 16th-18th century European paintings, particularly Dutch and Flemish. 19th-20th century French and American Impressionist paintings. Contemporary American art. Egyptian, African, Pre-Columbian art. 18th century decorative arts. Furniture.
Krannert and Clowes Pavilions: Tu. 10-9; W.-F. 10-5; Sa., Su. 12-6.
Lilly Pavilion (18th century furniture): Tu.-Su. 1-4.

INDIANA STATE MUSEUM
202 N. Alabama Street, Indianapolis, Indiana 46204
Indiana natural history, history, geology, palaeontology. 18th century European graphics, decorative arts. 19th century American paintings, sculpture.
Oldfields (1912), former home of J. K. Lilly, is in the care of the Museum.
Sept. 1- May 31, M.-Sa. 9-5, Su. 2-5. Closed New Year, Thanksgiving, Christmas.

LOCKERBIE STREET HOME OF JAMES WHITCOMB RILEY
528 Lockerbie Street, Indianapolis, Indiana 46206
House (1872) was home of the poet, James Whitcomb Riley. Furnishings, library, personal possessions.
Tu.-Sa. 10-4; Su. 12-4. Closed Thanksgiving, Christmas.

MORRIS-BUTLER MUSEUM OF THE HIGH VICTORIAN DECORATIVE ARTS
1204 N. Park Avenue, Indianapolis, Indiana 46202
House (C.1861). Furniture. Decorative arts. Victorian sculpture. Flint glass collection. Paintings by early Indiana artists.
Th., Su. 1-5. Closed Aug., public holidays.

MUSEUM OF INDIAN HERITAGE
6040 De Long Road, Indianapolis, Indiana 46254
Archaeology, history and ethnology of American Indians.
Tu.-Su. 10-5. Closed Christmas.

MUSEUM OF ROSCOE TURNER AVIATION FOUNDATION
Weir Cook Airport, Indianapolis, Indiana 46241
History of aviation.
Tu.-Su. 12-5. Closed public holidays.

PARK AVENUE VICTORIAN COTTAGE
324 N. Park Avenue, Indianapolis, Indiana 46202
Cottage (c.1865). Period furnishings, sculpture.
By appointment.

PRESIDENT BENJAMIN HARRISON MEMORIAL HOME
1230 North Delaware Street, Indianapolis, Indiana 46202
House (1872-4) was home of President Harrison. Original furniture. Personal possessions. Campaign banners and badges.
M.-Sa. 10-4; Su., public holidays 12.30-4. Closed Dec. 25- Jan. 1.

JOSEPH STAUB HOUSE
342 North College Avenue, Indianapolis, Indiana 46202
House (1859). Furniture. Decorative arts.
M.-F. 9-3, by appointment. Closed public holidays.

INDIAN SPRINGS

INDIAN CHIEF WILLIAM MCINTOSH HOME
U.S. Highway 23, Indian Springs, Georgia 30231
House (1821), formerly home of Chief McIntosh. Period furnishings. Indian artifacts.
Mar.-Oct. daily 9-5.

INDIAN CREEK MUSEUM
Indian Springs State Park, Georgia 30231
Indian material.
May 1- Sept. 1, Tu.-Su. 10-6.

INTERNATIONAL FALLS

KOOCHICHING COUNTY HISTORICAL SOCIETY MUSEUM
214 6th Street, International Falls, Minnesota 56649
Local history.
Memorial Day- Labour Day: M.-Sa. 10-7; Su. 2-5; public holidays 10-7.

INTERIOR

BADLANDS NATIONAL MONUMENT
U.S. 16A, Box 72, Interior, South Dakota 57750
Palaeontology. Natural history. Sioux Indian collection.
Oct. 1- May 7, daily 8-5. June 1- Sept. 7, daily 7-8. May 8-31, Sept. 8-30, daily 8-6. Closed Christmas, New Year.

IOLA

ALLEN COUNTY HISTORICAL SOCIETY MUSEUM
Courthouse, Iola, Kansas 66749
County history. Household equipment. Clothing. Agricultural tools, implements.
Old Allen County Jail (1869) is in the care of the Society.
May-Sept., M.-Sa.

IOWA CITY

MUSEUM OF NATURAL HISTORY
University of Iowa, Iowa City, Iowa 52240
North American birds, mammals, marine invertebrates. Habitat groups. Archaeology.
M.-Sa. 8-5; Su. 1-4.30. Closed public holidays.

ROBERT LUCAS PLUM GROVE HOME
727 Switzer Avenue, Iowa City, Iowa 52240
House (1844), home of first Governor of Iowa. Period furnishings.
Apr. 16- Nov. 15, Tu.-Su. 1-5.

UNIVERSITY OF IOWA MUSEUM OF ART
Riverside Drive, Iowa City, Iowa 52240
Early 20th century American, European paintings. 17th-18th century European prints. 17th-19th century English silver.
M.-F. 10.30-5; Sa. 10-5; Su. 2-5. Closed public holidays.

IPSWICH

HOWARD HOUSE
Turkey Shore Road, Ipswich, Massachusetts 01938
House (c.1648). 17th-18th century furnishings.
June-Oct., Tu., Th., Su. 1-5. Other times by appointment.

IPSWICH HISTORICAL SOCIETY
53 South Main Street, Ipswich, Massachusetts 01938
House (1640). 17th-18th century furnishings. American lace.
By appointment.

LAKEMAN-JOHNSON HOUSE
16 East Street, Ipswich, Massachusetts 01938
House (1837). Lakeman family furniture. Oriental objets d'art.
June-Oct., Tu., Th., Su. 1-5.

PLATT-BRADSTREET HOUSE
Main Street, Rowley, Ipswich, Massachusetts 01938
House (1670). Period furnishings. Shoemaker's shop.
By appointment.

WATERS MEMORIAL (JOHN HEARD HOUSE)
Ipswich, Massachusetts 01938
House (1795). Period furnishings. China. Guns.
By appointment.

JOHN WHIPPLE HOUSE
52 Main Street, Ipswich, Massachusetts 01938
House (1640, 1670). 17th-18th century furnishings.
Apr.-Nov., Tu.-Sa. 10-5; Su. 1-5.

EDMUNDS COUNTY MUSEUM
Ipswich, South Dakota 57451
Local history. Clocks.
June-Aug., W.-Sa. 2.30-5. Closed public holidays.

IRAAN

IRAAN ARCHAEOLOGICAL MUSEUM
Alley Oop Park, Highway 29, Iraan, Texas 79744
Geology and minerals of Iraan area and West Texas. Tools

and artifacts of early man from excavations in Pecos River Valley.
Apr. 1 - Nov. 30, W.-F. 2-7, Sa. 10-12, 2-7. Su. 2-6.

IRON MOUNTAIN

HOUSE OF YESTERYEAR
U.S.2 at 141 Jct., Iron Mountain, Michigan 49801
Geology. Mineralogy. Agriculture. Industry, including foot-powered broom machine. Domestic life. Transport. Old cars. Guns and pistols.
May 1 - Oct. 31: M.-Sa. 8-8.

IRON MOUNTAIN IRON MINE
U.S. Highway 2, Iron Mountain, Michigan 49801
19th century iron-mine. Underground drifts and tunnels open to public.
M.-Sa. 9-5.

IRON RIVER

IRON COUNTY MUSEUM
Route 3, Box 334A, Iron River, Michigan 49935
Lumbering. Mining.
June 15 - Aug. 31, M.-Sa. 9-5; Su. 1-5.

IRONVILLE

PENFIELD HOMESTEAD MUSEUM
Ironville, New York
House (1828) was home of Allen Penfield, iron manufacturer, whose use of electromagnet to separate ores was the first industrial application of electricity. Replica of original magnet. Period furnishings. Civil War material.
May 15 - Oct. 15: Tu.-Su. 10-5.

IRVINE

MUSEUM OF SYSTEMATIC BIOLOGY
University of California, Irvine, California 92664
Herbarium. Vertebrate zoology. Conchology. Entomology. Herpetology.
M.-F. 8-5. Closed university administrative vacations.

IRWINVILLE

JEFFERSON DAVIS MUSEUM
Jefferson Davis Memorial State Park, Irwinville, Georgia 31760
Local history. Relics of Confederate period.
Tu.-Su. 9-6. Closed national holidays.

ISHPEMING

NATIONAL SKI HALL OF FAME
Ishpeming, Michigan 49849
Evolution of the ski. Trophies. Displays relating to outstanding world skiers.
Sept. 1 - June 15: W.-Su. 1-4. June 16 - Labour Day, 10-4.

ISLAND POND

ISLAND POND HISTORICAL SOCIETY MUSEUM
Island Pond, Vermont 05846
Local history. Railways. Lumbering.
By appointment.

ISLEBORO

SAILORS MEMORIAL MUSEUM
Grindle Point Lighthouse, Isleboro, Maine 04848
In keeper's house (1850). Local and maritime history.
June 20 - Labour Day: Tu.-Su., public holidays 10-4.

ISLE DE LA MOTTE

MUSEUM OF ISLE DE LA MOTTE HISTORICAL SOCIETY
Isle de la Motte, Vermont 05254
In 19th century blacksmith's shop. 18th-19th century furniture, domestic equipment, tools. Indian material.
July 1 - Aug. 31, Sa. 2-5.

ISLEFORD

ISLEFORD MUSEUM
Little Cranberry Island, Isleford, Maine 04646
History of settlement of Maine. Tools.
June 21 - Aug. 30: W.-Su., public holidays 8-4.30.

ITHACA

L. H. BAILEY HORTORIUM
Cornell University, A. R. Mann Library, Ithaca, New York 14850
Herbarium. Vascular plants. Natural history.
M.-F. 8-5. Closed public holidays, except by appointment.

DEWITT HISTORICAL SOCIETY MUSEUM
121 E. Court Street, Ithaca, New York 14850
Indian relics. Costumes. Glass. Paintings. Lithographs. Domestic equipment. Tools.
Schoolhouse (1827) and Courthouse (1854) are in the care of the Society.
Tu.-F. 12-5; Su. 2-5. Closed public holidays.

ITHACA COLLEGE MUSEUM OF ART
120 E. Buffalo Street, Ithaca, New York 14850
Primitive art, especially from S. Pacific. 18th-19th century American paintings. Sculpture. Graphics. Decorative art. Contemporary American crafts, paintings.
Sept. 1 - May 31: Tu.-Sa. 10.30-5; Su. 2-5. June 1 - Aug. 31: Tu.-Sa. 10.30-4.

HERBERT F. JOHNSON MUSEUM OF ART
Cornell University, Ithaca, New York 14850
Asian art. Primitive art. European and American paintings. Sculpture. Graphics.
Tu.-Sa. 11-5; Su. 1-5. Closed New Year, Memorial Day, July 4, Labour Day, Christmas.

PALAEONTOLOGICAL RESEARCH INSTITUTION
1259 Trumansburg Road, Ithaca, New York 14850
Geology. Palaeontology. Natural history.
M.-F. 9-4.30. Sa. 2-4.30. Su. by appointment. Closed public holidays.

MARTHA VAN RENSSELAER ART GALLERY
Cornell University, Ithaca, New York 14850
Paintings, drawings, prints, sculpture by American and European artists.
M.-F. 12-5.

WILLARD STRAIGHT HALL
Cornell University, Central Avenue, Ithaca, New York 14850
Paintings, drawings, prints, sculpture by American and European artists.
Daily 7.30 a.m. - 11 p.m. Closed Christmas.

JACKSON

AMADOR COUNTY MUSEUM
225 Church Street, Jackson, California 95642
House (1859). Local history. Indian artifacts.
Daily, except Tu., 12-4. Closed New Year, Easter, Thanksgiving.

MUSEUM OF JACKSON COUNTY HISTORICAL SOCIETY
1113 1st Street, Jackson, Michigan 49203
History of Jackson County, 1833 onwards.
By appointment with Society, at 1113 First Street, Jackson.

ELLA SHARP MUSEUM
3225 4th Street, Jackson, Michigan 49203
In Merriman-Sharp farm house (c.1857). Pioneer and Victorian furniture. Tools. Costumes. Decorative arts.
Schoolhouse (1870), and log-house (c.1860) are in the care of the Museum.
Tu.-F. 10-4.30; Sa., Su. 12.30-4.30 (Jan. 1-31, Su., M. only).

MUSEUM OF FORT BELMONT COMPANY
Highway 16, Jackson, Minnesota 56143
Local history. Pioneer life. Indian artifacts. Old cars.
Log House (1860) and log chapel (1861) are in the care of the Museum.
Memorial Day - Labour Day: M.-Sa. 9-8; Su. 10.30-8.

MISSISSIPPI ART ASSOCIATION
846 N. President Street, Jackson, Mississippi 39205
Contemporary American paintings, drawings, prints.
Tu.-Sa. 9-5; Su. 2-5. Closed New Year, Christmas.

MISSISSIPPI MUSEUM OF NATURAL SCIENCE
111 N. Jefferson Street, Jackson, Mississippi 39202
Mississippi natural history. Paintings of wild flowers.
M.-F., public holidays 8-4.30; Sa. 8-12. Closed Thanksgiving, Christmas.

MISSISSIPPI STATE HISTORICAL MUSEUM
Capitol and N. State Streets, Jackson, Mississippi 39205
In old Capitol (1839). History of Mississippi. Dioramas. Governor's office, with period furnishings. Archaeology.
Tu.-Sa. 9.30-4.30. Nov. 1 - Apr. 30, Su. 12.30-4.30; May 1 - Oct. 31, Su. 1-5. Closed public holidays.

MUNICIPAL ART GALLERY
839 N. State Street, Jackson, Mississippi 39201
Paintings, prints, sculpture by contemporary American artists.
Th., Su. afternoons; Th. evening by appointment.

OAKS
823 N. Jefferson Street, Jackson, Mississippi 39202
Local history.
M.-Sa. 10-5.

BUCKEYE FURNACE
State Route 124, Jackson, Ohio 45640
Restored furnace of the Hanging Rock iron region.
Daily, dawn-dusk.

CASEY JONES' HOME AND RAILROAD MUSEUM
211 W. Chester Street, Jackson, Tennessee 38301
House (1880). Personal possessions of Casey Jones' family. Railway history and relics.
May 1 - Oct. 31: M.-Sa. 9-8. Nov. 1 - Apr. 30: M.-F. 9-4; Su. 1-4. Closed public holidays.

JACKSON HOLE MUSEUM
101 N. Glenwood Street, Jackson, Wyoming 83001
Relics and photographs of early trappers and settlers. Indian artifacts.
May 15 - Sept. 15, daily 9-9.

JACKSON COUNTY

WATERLOO AREA FARM MUSEUM
9998 Waterloo-Munith Road, Jackson County, Michigan 49201
Michigan pioneer history. Windmills. Ice-house.
Memorial Day - Labour Day, Tu.-Su. 1-4. 2nd Su. in Oct., 12-5.

JACKSONPORT

JACKSONPORT COURTHOUSE MUSEUM
Jacksonport State Park, Jacksonport, Arkansas 72075
In former Courthouse building (1869). Period rooms. Furniture. Local history, including agriculture. Uniforms. Costumes. Textiles. Indian artifacts. Household utensils. Tools. Surgical and medical instruments.
Tu.-Su., 2-6. Closed New Year, Christmas.

JACKSONVILLE

CUMNER GALLERY OF ART
829 Riverside Avenue, Jacksonville, Florida 32204
European and American paintings, sculpture, prints. Furniture. Tapestries. Early Meissen porcelain.
Tu.-Sa. 10-5; Su. 2-5. Closed public holidays.

FORT CAROLINE NATIONAL MEMORIAL
12713 Fort Caroline Road, Jacksonville, Florida 32225
Local history. Material relating to 16th century French colonists. Indian artifacts.
Daily 8-5. Closed Christmas.

JACKSONVILLE ART MUSEUM
4160 Boulevard Center Drive, Jacksonville, Florida 32207
20th century paintings. Sculpture. Archaeology. Pre-Columbian ceramics. Oriental porcelain.
M.-W. 10-5; 8-10; 10-5; Sa., Su. 2-5. Closed public holidays.

JACKSONVILLE CHILDREN'S MUSEUM
1025 Gulf Life Drive, Jacksonville, Florida 32207
Minerals. Shells. Fossils. Palaeontology. Florida natural history. Anthropology. Ethnology of Japan, India, Africa and American Indians. Astronomy. Planetarium.
Sept. 1 - July 31, Tu.-Sa. 9-5; Su. 2-5. Closed Aug., public holidays.

KINGSLEY PLANTATION HISTORIC MEMORIAL
Fort George Island, Florida 32226
Local history. Natural history.
Anna Jai's house (c.1792), Kingsley House (1817), carriage house (1736-83), Army-Navy Club House (1936) and slave cabins (1817) are in the care of the Memorial.
Daily 8-5.

DAVID STRAWN ART GALLERY
331 W. College Avenue, Jacksonville, Illinois 62650
House (1890) was home of Dr. David Strawn. Pre-Columbian pottery.
Sept. 1 - May 31: Tu.-Th. 2-5; F. 2-5, 7-9; Sa., Su. 2-5. Closed Christmas.

BEEKMAN BANK
Jacksonville, Oregon 97530
Building (1857). Period furnishings. Local history.
By appointment.

JACKSONVILLE MUSEUM
Jacksonville, Oregon 97530
In old Jackson County Court House (1883). History of Southern Oregon. Minerals. Mining display. Early photo-

graphs and photographic equipment. Indian artifacts. Transport. Costumes. Furniture.
Methodist Church (1854), Beekman Bank (1856), U.S. Hotel (1880), Beekman House (c.1880), Parish House (1861) and Rogue River Valley Railroad Depot (c.1890) are in the care of the Museum.
M.-Sa. 9-5; Su. 12-5. Closed New Year, Thanksgiving, Christmas.

MCCULLY HOUSE DOLL MUSEUM
240 California Street, Jackson, Oregon 97530
House (1860). Period furnishings. Dolls.
Mar. 1 - Dec. 31, daily 10-5. Closed Thanksgiving, Christmas.

VANISHING TEXANA MUSEUM
Jacksonville Public Library, 310 S. Bolton Street, Jacksonville, Texas 75766
Local history. Pioneer tools, household equipment.
May 1 - Oct. 31: M.-Sa. 9-2.

JAMAICA

KING MANOR HOUSE
King Park, Jamaica, New York 11400
House (c.1730, with later additions). Home of Rufus King, Senator and Ambassador to Great Britain. Period furnishings. Memorabilia of King.
By appointment.

STORE FRONT MUSEUM
162 Liberty Avenue, Jamaica, New York 11433
Paintings, drawings, sculpture by black artists.
M.-F. 10.30-5; Sa., Su. 12-3.

JAMAICA PLAIN

LORING-GREENOUGH HOUSE
12 South Street (30), Jamaica Plain, Massachusetts 02130
House (1760). Collection of visiting-card cases.
By appointment.

JAMESPORT

FRED J. CALL ROCK MUSEUM
Jamesport, Missouri 64648
Mineralogy. Indian archaeology and artifacts.
Daily 8-5, by appointment.

JAMESTOWN

MUSEUM OF FENTON HISTORICAL SOCIETY
68 S. Main Street, Jamestown, New York 14701
In Fenton mansion (1864). Local history. Industry. Transport.
M.-Sa. 1-5. Closed public holidays.

JAMES PRENDERGAST LIBRARY ASSOCIATION ART GALLERY
509 Cherry Street, Jamestown, New York 14701
Paintings, by local and European artists, especially 1870-90.
M.-F. 9-9; Sa., May 1 - Oct. 31, 9-5, Nov. 1 - Apr. 30, 9-6; Su., Oct. 1 - May 30, 2-5. Closed public holidays.

MUSEUM OF FORT SEWARD HISTORICAL SOCIETY
321 3rd Avenue S.E., Jamestown, North Dakota 58401
Local history. Agricultural tools and implements. Domestic equipment. Dolls. Indian artifacts.
June 1 - Sept. 30: W., Su. 2-5, 7-9.

STUTSMAN COUNTY MEMORIAL MUSEUM
321 3rd Avenue S.E., Jamestown, North Dakota 58401
Military history. Medicine. Music. Indian artifacts. Children's museum.
June 1 - Oct. 31: W.-Su. 2-9. Other times by appointment.

JAMESTOWN MUSEUM
Jamestown, Rhode Island 02835
Local history. History of Jamestown ferries. Operating windmill (1787) is in the care of the Museum.
May-Oct., Sa., Su. 2-5.

JAMESTOWN FESTIVAL PARK
Jamestown, Virginia 23081
Outdoor museum on site of first permanent English settlement in America (1607). Reconstruction of James Fort, Powhatan's Indian Lodge and 3 ships. Exhibits telling story of Jamestown. Virginia Indian and British settler artifacts.
Daily 9-5. Closed Christmas, New Year.

JAMESTOWN MUSEUM
Jamestown, Virginia 23081
Local history. 17th century artifacts. Glass.
Daily 8-5. Closed Christmas.

JANESVILLE

MUSEUM OF ROCK COUNTY HISTORICAL SOCIETY
440 N. Jackson St., Janesville, Wisconsin 53545
Museum in 4 restored houses - Tallman House (1855-7), Carriage House (1855-7), Stone House (1842), Schoolhouse (1853). Period furnishings. Local history and archaeology. Pioneer life. Indian relics. Firearms.
1st Su. in May - last Su. in Oct.: Tu.-F. 1-4; Sa., Su. 11-4. May, Sept., Oct., Sa., Su. only.

JASPER

JASPER COUNTY MUSEUM
Jasper, Texas 75951
Early settlement of E. Texas. Local industries, especially lumbering. Documents. Photographs.
M.-F. 9-5.

JEANNETTE

BUSHY RUN BATTLEFIELD MUSEUM
Bushy Run Road, Jeannette, Pennsylvania 15644
Military history. Campaign of 1763. Paintings of fort sites and battle episodes. Indian artifacts.
May 1 - Sept. 30: Tu.-Sa. 8.30-5; Su. 1-5. Oct. 1 - Apr. 30: Tu.-Sa. 9-4.30; Su. 1-4.30. Closed public holidays.

JEFFERSON

CRAWFORD W. LONG MEDICAL MUSEUM
U.S. Highway 129, Jefferson, Georgia 30549
Medical history, especially history of anaesthetics. Site of first operation, by Crawford W. Long, using ether. Diorama of Dr. Long performing operation. Long Memorabilia, personal possessions, documents on early use of ether.
May 1 - Sept. 30: Tu.-Sa. 9-5.30; Su. 2-5.30. Oct. 1 - Apr. 30: Tu.-Sa. 9-5; Su. 2-5. Closed Thanksgiving, Christmas.

JENNIE MUNGER GREGORY MEMORIAL MUSEUM
P.O. Box. 193, Jefferson, Ohio 44047
Building (1823). Local history.
May 15 - Sept. 30: Th.-Su. 1-5.

EXCELSIOR HOUSE
Austin Street, Jefferson, Texas 75657
House (1850). Period furnishings.
Su.-F. 9-5.

JEFFERSON HISTORICAL SOCIETY MUSEUM
223 Austin Street, Jefferson, Texas 75657
History of E. Texas area. Period rooms. Household items. Farm implements and tools. Paintings.
Daily 9.30-5.

JAY GOULD PRIVATE RAILROAD CAR
Excelsior Hotel, Austin Street, Jefferson, Texas 75657
88 ft., 4-stateroom railway coach, used by Jay Gould on his travels through Texas.
Daily 9-5.

AZTALAN MUSEUM
R.R.2, Jefferson, Wisconsin 53549
Local history and archaeology. Aztalan Indian artifacts. Aztalan Baptist Church (1852), Percy Cabin (1843), Loom house (1849) and Zickert House (1867) are in the care of the Museum.
May 1 - Oct. 31: M.-Sa. 9-6; Su., public holidays 1-6.

JEFFERSON CITY

COLE COUNTY HISTORICAL MUSEUM
109 Madison Street, Jefferson City, Missouri 65101
Building (1871) was former home of Governor Brown. Period furnishings. Inaugural gowns of Governors' wives.
Tu.-Sa. 1-5. Closed New Year, Decoration Day, July 4, Thanksgiving, Dec. 17-31.

GRAHAM CAVE STATE PARK
Box 176, Jefferson City, Missouri 65101
Outdoor museum of archaeology and Indian artifacts.
Daily 8-5.

MISSOURI STATE MUSEUM
State Capitol, Jefferson City, Missouri 65101
Geology. Mineralogy. Palaeontology. Natural history. Botany. Anthropology. Archaeology. Architecture. Costumes. Industry. Transport. Indian material. Murals by local artists.
Daily 8-5. Closed New Year, Thanksgiving, Christmas.

JEKYLL ISLAND

JEKYLL ISLAND MUSEUM (ROCKEFELLER COTTAGE)
329 Riverview Drive, Jekyll Island, Georgia 31520
Formerly winter home of William Rockefeller, with original furnishings. Tiffany stained-glass window.
Daily 9-7.

JENKINTOWN

MUSEUM OF OLD YORK ROAD HISTORICAL SOCIETY
Abington Library, Old York Road, Jenkintown, Pennsylvania 19046
History of Old York Road area.
Lyceum Building (1839) is in the care of the Society.
By appointment. Closed public holidays.

JENNER

FORT ROSS STATE HISTORIC PARK
19005 Coast Highway, Jenner, California 95450
Historic fort. Museum in former Commander's house has collection illustrating military and local history. Exhibits illustrating history of Russian settlement at Fort Ross and of Russian-American Fur Company.
Daily 9-6. Closed New Year, Thanksgiving, Christmas.

JEROME

JEROME STATE HISTORIC PARK
P.O. Box D, Jerome, Arizona 86331
Museum was home of James Douglas family and tells the story of this former copper-mining town.
Daily, except Christmas, 8-5.30.

VERDE VALLEY ARTIST
Main Street, P.O. Box 1017, Jerome, Arizona 86331
Paintings. Sculpture. Graphics. Decorative arts.
Tu.-Su., 1-5. Closed Jan. 1 - Feb. 28.

JETMORE

HAUN MUSEUM
Jetmore, Kansas 67854
Local history. Indian artifacts.
M.-Sa. 2-5. Closed July 4 and 2nd Saturday Oct. to 2nd Monday May.

JIM THORPE

ASA PACKER MANSION
Packer Road, Jim Thorpe, Pennsylvania 18229
House (c.1860). Personal possessions of Packer family. Period furnishings.
May 16 - Oct. 31, Tu.-Su. 1-5.

JOHNSON CITY

CARROLL REECE MUSEUM
E. Tennessee State University, Johnson City, Tennessee 37601
Tennessee history. Folklore. Costumes. Handicrafts. Costumes. Music. Paintings. Graphics.
M.-F. 12.45-4.45; Sa., Su. 1-5.

ELIZABETH SLOCUMB GALLERY
Department of Art, East Tennessee State University, Johnson City, Tennessee 37601
Paintings. Sculpture. Graphics. Decorative arts.
M.-F. 8.30-5. Closed university vacations.

TIPTON-HAYNES LIVING HISTORICAL FARM
Erwin Highway, Johnson City, Tennessee 37601
Local history. Agricultural tools, implements. Tipton-Haynes House (1784), with outbuildings, including slave quarters. Haynes law office (c.1850).
M.-Sa. 10-5. Closed public holidays.

LYNDON B. JOHNSON NATIONAL HISTORIC SITE
Johnson City, Texas 78636
House (1886) lived in by President Johnson, 1914-34. Scene of his first political rally, 1937. Johnson family furniture and memorabilia.
Daily 9-5. Closed Christmas.

JOHNSTOWN

JOHNSON HALL
Johnstown, New York 12095
House (1763), was home of Sir William Johnson, Superintendent of Indian Affairs. 18th century furniture. Personal possessions of Sir William.
Tu.-Sa. 9-5; Su. 1-5.

JOHNSTOWN HISTORICAL SOCIETY MUSEUM
17 N. William Street, Johnstown, New York 12095
History of Johnstown. Indian artifacts. Industry. Costumes.
M.-Sa. 10-5; Su. by appointment. Closed public holidays.

ALLEGHENY PORTAGE RAILROAD
National Historic Site Museum, U.S. 22 E, Cresson, Johnstown, Pennsylvania 15907
In Lemon House (1830-4). History of the Portage Railroad.
May 1 - Sept. 30, daily 10-8. Oct. 1 - Apr. 30, 9-4.30.

JOLON

SAN ANTONIO MISSION
Jolon, California 93928
In restored Mission buildings, with workshops, mill and wine-press of Spanish colonial period.
M.-Sa., 9-4.30; Su., 11-5. Public holidays, 9-4.30.

JONESBORO

ARKANSAS STATE UNIVERSITY ART GALLERY
Fine Arts Center, State University, Jonesboro, Arkansas 72467
19th-20th century European prints. Contemporary prints, paintings, drawings, sculpture by American artists.
M.-F. 9-5.

ARKANSAS STATE UNIVERSITY MUSEUM
State University, Jonesboro, Arkansas 72467
Local history. Archaeology and anthropology. Palaeontology. Natural history. Indian artifacts from the south-west. Pressed glass.
M.-F. 9-12, 1-5; Su. 1-5. Closed public holidays.

JOPLIN

SCHIFFERDECKER MINERAL MUSEUM
Schifferdecker Park, Joplin, Missouri 64801
Mineralogy.
Tu.-Sa. 9.30-5; Su. 1-5.

SPIVA ART CENTER
Newman and Duquesne Roads, Joplin, Missouri 64801
19th century American paintings. New Guinea sculpture. Mary Gregory room.
M.-F. 9-4; Sa. 9-12; Su. 2-4. Closed Aug. 1-31 and 1st Sa., Su., M. in each month.

TRI-STATE MINERAL MUSEUM
Fourth Street and Schifferdecker Avenue, Joplin, Missouri 64801
Local minerals. Models illustrating lead mining techniques, equipment.
Tu.-Sa. 10-5; Su. 1-5.

JULESBURG

JULESBURG HISTORICAL MUSEUM
320 Cedar Street, Julesburg, Colorado 80737
Natural history. Local history. Archaeology. Transport. Union Pacific and Pony Express exhibits. Indian artifacts.
June 1 - Aug. 30, M.-Sa., 9-5; Su., 2-5. Rest of year, Tu.-Su., 2-5.

JULIAN

CUYAMACA RANCHO STATE PARK
Julian, California 92036
Indian life. Natural and cultural history of the area.
May-Sept., daily 8 a.m. - 10 p.m. Oct.-Apr., daily 8-5. Closed Thanksgiving, Christmas, Jan. 1.

JULIAETTA

ARROW MUSEUM
Route 1, Box 44, Juliaetta, Idaho 83535
Local history. Indian artifacts.
Daily 8-6.

JUNCTION

KIMBLE COUNTY HISTORICAL MUSEUM
College and 4th Streets, Junction, Texas 76849
History of Kimble County. Pioneer tools. Household items. Photographs.
Su. 2-5. Other times by appointment.

JUNEAU

ALASKA STATE MUSEUM
Juneau, Alaska 99801
Natural history. Herbarium. Anthropology. Ethnology. Indian artifacts. Aeronautics.
June 1 - Aug. 31, daily 8-4.30, 7-10; Sept. 1 - May 31, M.-F. 8-4.30, Sa., Su., 12-4.30. Closed Christmas.

KAHULUI

HALEAKALA NATIONAL PARK MUSEUM
Kahului, Hawaii 96732
Geology. Botany. Herbarium. Natural history.
Daily 7.30-4.

KAILUA-KONA

HULIHEE PALACE
Alii Drive, Kailua-Kona, Hawaii 96740
In palace (1838), occupied by Royal Family until 1916. Collections of material relating to Kalakaua dynasty.
M.-F. 9-4; Sa., Dec. 24 and 31, 9-12. Closed public holidays.

KALAMAZOO

GENEVIEVE AND DONALD GILMORE ART CENTER
314 S. Park Street, Kalamazoo, Michigan 49006
20th century American paintings, graphics. Sculpture.
July 5 - Labour Day: Tu.-Sa. 10-4. Rest of year: Tu.-F. 11-4.30; Sa. 9-4; Su. 1.30-4.30. Closed Aug. 17-31, public holidays.

KALAMAZOO NATURE CENTER
7000 N. Westnedge Avenue, Kalamazoo, Michigan 49001
Botany. Natural history. Geology. Children's museum.
June 1 - Aug. 31: M.-Sa. 9-5. Sept. 1 - May 31: Tu.-Sa. 9-5; Su., Memorial Day, July 4, Labour Day, 1-5.

KALAMAZOO PUBLIC MUSEUM
315 S. Rose Street, Kalamazoo, Michigan 49006
Egyptian artifacts, mummies and re-created tomb. Babylonian clay tablets. American Indian artifacts. Japanese musical instruments. Costumes. Glass.
M.-Sa. 9-5.30.

KALISPELL

HOCKADAY CENTER FOR THE ARTS
2nd Avenue E. and 3rd Street, Kalispell, Montana 59901
20th century American painting, sculpture, graphics.
M.-Sa. 12-5. Closed Thanksgiving, Christmas.

KANAB

KANAB CHAMBER OF COMMERCE MUSEUM AND INFORMATION CENTER
Kanab, Utah 84741
Pioneer history. Furnishings, costumes, pictures, recalling early days in Kane County.
May-Oct., daily 9-6.

KANE

MUSEUM OF LOBO WOLF PARK
R.D.1, Kane, Pennsylvania 16735
Zoology. Natural history, particularly wolves, lobos.
May 1 - Nov. 30, daily 10-dusk. Other months by appointment.

KANEOHE

ULU MAU VILLAGE
46 - 465 Kamehamena Highway, Kaneohe, Hawaii 96744
Reconstructed Hawaiian Chief Village. Archaeology. Anthropology. Decorative arts.
Daily, 9.30-4.30. Closed public holidays.

KANKAKEE

MUSEUM OF KANKAKEE COUNTY HISTORICAL SOCIETY
8th Avenue and Water Street, Kankakee, Illinois 60901
History of Kankakee County. Household equipment. Clothing. Photographs. Toys. Civil War material. Indian artifacts.
M.-F. by appointment; Sa., Su. 2-5.

KANOPOLIS

FORT HARKER MUSEUM
Kanopolis, Kansas 67454
Military mementoes of 1870s. Uniforms. Indian artifacts. Guardhouse (1867).
Oct. 1 - Apr. 30: Sa. 10-12, 1-5; Su. 1-5. May 1 - Sept. 30: Tu.-Sa. 10-12, 1-5; Su. 1-5. Closed New Year, Thanksgiving, Christmas.

KANSAS CITY

GRINTER PLACE MUSEUM
1420 S. 78th Street, Kansas City, Kansas 66111
House (1857). Period furnishings.
Tu.-Sa. 10-5. Su. 1.30-5.

ART RESEARCH CENTER
1609 Washington Street, Kansas City, Missouri 64108
Contemporary paintings, drawings, modular sculpture by local artists. Computer drawings.
M.-F. 2-6.

CHARLOTTE CROSBY KEMPER GALLERY
4415 Warwick Boulevard (11), Kansas City, Missouri 64111
19th-20th century paintings, drawings, prints by American artists.
M.-F. 9-5; Su. 2-5. Closed national holidays.

DAUGHTERS OF OLD WESTPORT MUSEUM
937 W. 42nd Street, Kansas City, Missouri 64111
Local history.
By appointment.

FOLGER COFFEE COMPANY MUSEUM
330 W. 8th Street, Kansas City, Missouri 64105
English silver coffee pots and coffee sets.
M.-F. 8-4. Closed public holidays.

KANSAS CITY MUSEUM OF HISTORY AND SCIENCE
3218 Gladstone Boulevard, Kansas City, Missouri 64123
Building (1909-11) was former R. A. Long mansion. Geology. Palaeontology. Planetarium. Natural History. Indian history and archaeology. Local history. Costumes.
M.-Sa., public holidays 9-5; Su. 12-5. Closed New Year, Thanksgiving, Christmas.

LIBERTY MEMORIAL
100 W. 26th Street, Kansas City, Missouri 64106
Military history. World War I relics.
Tu.-Su. 9.30-4.30. Closed New Year, Thanksgiving, Christmas.

WILLIAM ROCKHILL NELSON GALLERY AND ATKINS MUSEUM OF FINE ARTS
4525 Oak Street, Kansas City, Missouri 64111
Primitive art. Greek, Roman and Egyptian sculpture, painting. Oriental, especially Chinese, art. European and American painting, sculpture, prints, drawings. Period rooms. English pottery. European and American portrait miniatures. Pre-Columbian and American Indian art.
Tu.-Sa. 10-5; Su. 2-6. Closed New Year, Memorial Day, July 4, Thanksgiving, Christmas.

KASKASIA

KASKASIA STATE MEMORIAL
Kaskasia, Illinois
Postal address: Route 1, St. Mary's, Minnesota 63673.
Local history.
Daily 9-5.

KATAHDIN

KATAHDIN IRON WORKS
T.6 and R.9, Katahdin, Maine 04043
Restored blast furnace and charcoal kiln (1843).
Daily 10-5.

KATMAI

KATMAI NATIONAL MONUMENT
King Salmon, Alaska 99613
Site museum. Pithouse of Eskimo village (c.1300).
Daily 8-5.

KATONAH

JOHN JAY HOUSE
Jay Street, Katonah, New York 10536
House (c.1800) was home of John Jay, 1st Chief Justice of Supreme Court. Period furnishings. Portraits.
W.-Su. 9-5. Closed New Year, Easter, Thanksgiving, Christmas.

KATONAH GALLERY
Katonah, New York 10536
Contemporary American, European art. Coptic, pre-Columbian and American Indian collections.
Sept. 15 - July 31, Tu.-Sa. 10-5. Closed national holidays.

KAUKANA

GRIGNON HOME
Augustine Street, Kaukana, Wisconsin 54130
House (1836). Paintings. Decorative arts. Indian material.
May 30 - Labour Day: Tu.-Su., public holidays 11-5.

KEARNEY

FORT KEARNEY MUSEUM
311 S. Central Avenue, Kearney, Nebraska 68847
Geology. Mineralogy. Natural history. Anthropology. Local history and archaeology. Indian and pioneer history. Tools. Weapons. Egyptian, Oriental and African artifacts. Costumes. Glass. American paintings, sculpture, graphics. Circus history.
May 1 - 31, daily 9-5. June 1 - Labour Day, daily 9-9.

FORT KEARNEY STATE HISTORICAL PARK MUSEUM
Rural Route 1, Kearney, Nebraska 68847
History of Fort Kearney, 1848-71. History of Oregon Trail.
Memorial Day - Labour Day, daily 8 a.m. - 9 p.m. Labour day - Oct. 31, daily 9-5. Nov. 1 - May 15, Sa., Su. 1-4. May 15 - Memorial Day, daily 9-5.

KEENE

WYMAN TAVERN
339 Main Street, Keene, New Hampshire 03431
Tavern (1762). Local history collections. History of Cheshire County. Furnishings. Locally printed books. Portraits. Firearms.
June 1 - Sept. 30: W.-Su. 2-5.

KEKAHA

HUI O LAKA
Box 518, Kokee Park, Kekaha, Hawaii 96752
Geology. Mineralogy. Natural history. Botany. Archaeology.
Spring, summer, autumn, daily 10-4. Winter, daily 11-3.

KELSO

COWLITZ COUNTY HISTORICAL MUSEUM
Courthouse Annex, Church and 4th Streets, Kelso, Washington 98626
Indian artifacts. Reproductions of 19th century shops and rooms, including 1880 kitchen. Civil and Spanish American War relics. Costumes. Dolls.
Tu.-Sa. 10.30-4.30; Su. 2-5. Closed public holidays.

KEMMERER

KEMMERER CITY MUSEUM
Triangle Park, Kemmerer, Wyoming 83101
Geology. Mineralogy. Relics of pioneer period.
June 1 - Aug. 31: M.-Sa. 9-9.

KENNEBUNK

BRICK STORE MUSEUM
117 Main Street, Kennebunk, Maine 04043
Building (1825). Local history. Portraits. Maritime history. Ship models. Costumes. Early Americana. 18th-19th century American paintings, prints.
Apr. 1 - Oct. 14: Tu.-Sa. 10-4.30. Closed public holidays.

KENNEBUNKPORT

MUSEUM OF KENNEBUNKPORT HISTORICAL SOCIETY
N. Street, Kennebunkport, Maine 04046
Local History. Costumes.
District School House (1900) is in the care of the Society.
May 1 - Sept. 30: Tu.-F. 2-4.30.

SEASHORE TROLLEY MUSEUM
Log Cabin Road, Kennebunkport, Maine 04046
90 trams, 1873-1940. Vehicles from Japan, Australia, New Zealand, Italy, Germany, Britain, Canada and 19 states of the USA. Operating tracks.
May 30 - June 14, Labour Day - Apr. 30, Sa., Su. 12-5. June 15 - Labour Day, daily 10-6.

KENNETT SQUARE

LONGWOOD GARDENS
Kennett Square, Pennsylvania 19348
Botany. Herbarium. Local history.
Joshua Peirce House (1730), Red Lion Inn (1789) and Longwood Meeting House (1850) are within the area of the Gardens.
Daily 8-dusk.

KENNESAW

BIG SHANTY MUSEUM
P.O. Box 418, Kennesaw, Georgia 30144
Industry. Railway history. Operating cotton gin.
Daily 9.30-6.

KENOSHA

KENOSHA PUBLIC MUSEUM
5608 10th Avenue, Kenosha, Wisconsin 53140
Geology. Mineralogy. Palaeontology. Indian artifacts. Paintings. Sculpture. Prints. Drawings. Coins. Ivories. Glass. Wisconsin pottery. New Guinea carvings. Wildlife. Lorado Toft dioramas.
M.-F. 8-9; Sa., 8-12; Su., 2-4. Closed public holidays.

MUSEUM OF KENOSHA COUNTY HISTORICAL SOCIETY
6300 3rd Avenue, Kenosha, Wisconsin 53140
County history. Indian artifacts. Americana. Costumes. Medicine.
Tu., Th., Sa., Su. 2-4.30.

KENT

BRIMFIELD MEMORIAL HOUSE ASSOCIATION MUSEUM
4158 State Route 43, Kent, Ohio 44240
In William R. Kelso House (1833). Period furnishings. Local history.
Sylvester B. Jones House (c.1870) is under the same authority.
June 1 - Nov. 30, Su. 2-5. Other times by appointment.

SCHOOL OF ART GALLERY
Kent State University, Kent, Ohio 44240
20th century American paintings, prints, sculpture.
M.-F. 8-5; Sa. 8-12. Closed university vacations.

KENTLAND

MUSEUM OF NEWTON COUNTY HISTORICAL SOCIETY
Kentland, Indiana 47951
In George Ade House (1904). Furnishings. Local history.
By appointment.

KENTON

HARDIN COUNTY RELIC ROOM
Hardin County Courthouse, Kenton, Ohio 43326
Local history. Indian artifacts.
M.-Th. by appointment; F. 3-5. Closed public holidays.

KEOKUK

KEOKUK RIVER MUSEUM
Johnson Street, Keokuk, Iowa 52632
In Mississippi River steamboat (1927). History of river transport.
Apr. 15 - Nov. 1, M.-Sa. 9-5; Su. 10-6.

KEOSAUQUA

VAN BUREN COUNTY HISTORICAL SOCIETY MUSEUM
Keosauqua, Iowa 52565
Museum based on Pearson House (1845). Local history.
May 1 - Sept. 30; Su. 1-4. Other times by appointment.

KERBY

KERBYVILLE MUSEUM
24195 Redwood Highway, Kerby, Oregon 97531
In old Naucke Residence (1871). County history. Tools. Domestic equipment. Indian artifacts. Musical instruments. Country store. American Express office. Mining. Agriculture. Logging.
May 1 - Oct. 31, daily 10-5.

KERMIT

COMANCHE TRAILS MUSEUM
Haley Brothers Ranch, Highway 302, P.O. Box 839, Kermit, Texas 79745
Indian artifacts. Guns. Early ranch furniture. Part of ranch corrals, (1898).
Daily 9-7.

JAYCEE PARK MUSEUM
Kermit, Texas 79745
Moseley House (1910), moved to park, with furnishings of 1900-10 period. Homesteader's one-room shack. Cable tool derrick with walking beam.
Daily 9-6.

KETCHIKAN

TONGASS HISTORICAL SOCIETY MUSEUM
P.O. Box 674, 629 Dock Street, Ketchikan, Alaska 99901
Geology. Archaeology. Anthropology. Ethnology. Indian artifacts. Local history. Exploring. Trading. Mining. Fishing. Logging. Maritime history.
June 1 - Aug. 31, M.-F. 11-5, Sa., Su., 1-4; Sept. 1 - May 31, Tu.-F. 1-5, Sa., Su. 1-4.

KEWEENAW PENINSULA

OFFICERS' QUARTERS AT FORT WILKINS
Keweenaw Peninsula, Michigan 49020
Building (1844). Local history.
Summer only.

KEY BISCAYNE

CAPE FLORIDA STATE PARK MUSEUM
1200 South Crandon Boulevard, Key Biscayne, Florida 33149
Natural history. Local history. History of Seminole Indians. Cape Florida Lighthouse (1864), with keeper's house, is in the care of the State Park.
Daily 9-5.

KEYSTONE

MOUNT RUSHMORE NATIONAL MEMORIAL
Keystone, South Dakota 57751
Tools used in construction of the Memorial.
Sept.-May, daily 9-5. June-Aug., daily 6 a.m. - 10 p.m.

KEYTESVILLE

GENERAL STERLING PRICE MUSEUM
Keytesville, Missouri 65261
Memorabilia of the Confederate General, Sterling Price, who lived in Keytesville. Civil War history. Costumes. Silver. China. Glass.
May-Oct., Tu.-Su. 2-5.

KEY WEST

AUDUBON HOUSE AND GARDENS
205 Whitehead Street, Key West, Florida 33040
In Geiger House (1832). Natural history. Local history. Antique furniture and furnishings. 4 volume Audubon folio.
Daily 9-12, 1-5.

FORT JEFFERSON NATIONAL MONUMENT
Park Museum, U.S. Coast Guard Base, Key West, Florida 33040
Fort (1847). Display describing history of fort.
Daily 8-5. Closed national holidays.

HEMINGWAY HOME AND MUSEUM
907 Whitehead Street, Key West, Florida 33040
House (1851) was home of Ernest Hemingway from 1931 to 1961. Original furnishings. Personal possessions of Hemingway. Hunting trophies.
Daily 9-5.

LIGHTHOUSE MILITARY MUSEUM
Whitehead at Truman, Key West, Florida 33040
In former lighthouse keeper's home (1846). Local and naval history. Documents. Paintings of nautical subjects.
Daily 9.30-5. Closed Christmas.

MARTELLO GALLERY AND MUSEUM
S. Roosevelt Boulevard, Key West, Florida 33040
Local history. Paintings and woodcarvings by Florida artists. Naval history. Steam-driven torpedoes.
Daily 9.30-5.

OLD COFFEE MILL MUSEUM AND FLORIDA RAILROAD MUSEUM
512 Green Street, Key West, Florida 33040
Local history. Mineralogy. Agriculture. Aquarium. Aeronautics. Florida railway history.
4 historic buildings, including 2 Florida East Coast Railway buildings (1900, 1925) and the Cuban Coffee Mill (1899) are in the care of the Museum.
M.-Sa. 9-5; Su. 12-5. Closed Labour Day - Nov. 1

KEZAR FALLS

MUSEUM OF PARSONFIELD-PORTER HISTORICAL SOCIETY
Main Street, Kezar Falls, Maine 04047
Local history.
May 1 - Christmas, by appointment.

KIMBALL

PLAINS HISTORICAL SOCIETY MUSEUM
Kimball, Nebraska 69145
Natural history. Local history. Agriculture. Indian artifacts. Paintings, drawings by local artists.
W., Sa. 10-5.

KINDERHOOK

COLUMBIA COUNTY HISTORICAL SOCIETY MUSEUM
16 Broad Street, Kinderhook, New York 12106
House (1810). Furnishings (1790-1845) from Hudson River area. Van Buren memorabilia. Agricultural tools and equipment. Folklore.
Van Allen House (1737) is in the care of the Society.
May 30 - Sept. 30: M.-Sa. 10.30-4.30; Su. 1.30-4.30.

VAN ALLEN HOUSE
Kinderhook, New York 12106
Dutch farmhouse (1737). President Van Buren memorabilia.
Tu.-Sa. 10.30-4.30; Su. 1.30-4.30.

KING

CARL L. BROSIUS MILITARY MUSEUM
Grand Army Home for Veterans, King, Wisconsin 54946
Local and military history. Indian artifacts.
Daily 9-11, 1-4.

KING AND QUEEN

MUSEUM OF KING AND QUEEN COUNTY HISTORICAL SOCIETY MUSEUM
Courthouse, King and Queen, Virginia 23085
In Clerk's Building (c.1868). Local history, mainly documents.
By appointment.

KINGFISHER

CHISHOLM TRAIL MUSEUM
605 Zellers Avenue, Kingfisher, Oklahoma 73750
Local history and archaeology. Agriculture. Indian material.
Daily 9-5. Closed Thanksgiving, Christmas.

SEAY MUSEUM
Overstreet, Kingfisher, Oklahoma 73750
House (1892) was home of Governor Seay. Period furnishings.
Tu.-Su. 8-5.

KINGMAN

MOHAVE MUSEUM OF HISTORY AND ARTS
400 West Beale Street, Kingman, Arizona 86401
Archaeology. Anthropology. Local history. Indian artifacts. Open-air museum.
M.-F. 10-12, 1-5; Sa., Su. 1-5. Closed New Year, Thanksgiving, Christmas.

KINGMAN COUNTY MUSEUM
242 Avenue A West, Kingman, Kansas 67068
Geology. Archaeology. Local history. Costumes. Indian artifacts. Salt mine. Agriculture.
Tu.-Su. 2-5. Closed New Year, Christmas.

KINGS CREEK

KINGS MOUNTAIN NATIONAL MILITARY PARK
Kings Creek, South Carolina 29719
Relics of Revolutionary War.
M.-Sa. 8.30-5; Su. 9.30-5.30.

KINGS MOUNTAIN

MUSEUM OF KINGS MOUNTAIN NATIONAL MILITARY PARK
Kings Mountain, North Carolina 28086
Pioneer life. Weapons, including replica of Ferguson long rifle. Exhibits telling story of Battle of Kings Mountain.
Memorial Day-Labour Day, daily 8.30-6.; Sun., public holidays, 9- dusk. Rest of year: M.-Sa. 8.30-5; Su., public holidays 9-6. Closed Christmas.

KINGSPORT

ANDREW JACKSON SCHOOL CHILDREN'S MUSEUM
Jackson Street, Kingsport, Tennessee 37660
Natural history. Science.
By local announcement.

MUSEUM OF NETHERLAND INN ASSOCIATION
Netherland Inn Road, Kingsport, Tennessee 37600
In Netherland Inn (1803) with outbuildings. Period furnishings. Local history and archaeology. Indian artifacts. Folklore. Transport. Paintings.
M.-Sa. 10-5; Su. 1-5. Closed public holidays.

KINGSTON

MAJOR JOHN BRADFORD HOUSE
Maple Street and Landing Road, Kingston, Massachusetts 02364
House (1674); 18th - early 19th century furnishings. Doll collection.
July 1 - Aug. 31: M.-Sa. 10-5; Su. 1-5.

SENATE HOUSE
312 Fair Street, Kingston, New York 12401
Colonial furnishings, portraits and autographs of New York Governors, in Senate House (1676). Senate House Museum has paintings by local artist, John Vanderlyn (1775-1852). Pottery. Glass. Steamboat relics.
W.-Sa. 9-5; Su. 1-5. Closed New Year, Easter, Thanksgiving, Christmas.

SUDAN HOUSE
Main and Wall Street, Kingston, New York 12401
House (1795). Period furnishings.
M.-Sa. 10-5.

HELME HOUSE
1319 Kingstown Road, Kingston, Rhode Island 02881
House (1802). Rhode Island furniture, c.1750-1800.
Tu.-Su. 2-5, as notified locally.

PETTAQUAMSCUTT HISTORICAL SOCIETY MUSEUM
1348 Kingstown Road, Kingston, Rhode Island 02881
In former Washington County Jail (1790). 18th century furniture. Civil War collection.
July-Sept., Sa. 1-4; Su. 1-5. Other times by appointment.

SOUTH COUNTY ART ASSOCIATION
1319 Kingstown Road, Kingston, Rhode Island 02881
In Helme House (1802). Period furnishings. Paintings, drawings, prints.
Daily 3.30-5.30.

UNIVERSITY OF RHODE ISLAND
Department of Zoology Museum, Kingston, Rhode Island 02881
Marine zoology of Narragansett Bay. Birds and mammals of Rhode Island. Insects of New England. Worldwide collection of characae.
M.-F. 8-5; Sa. 8-12.

KINGSVILLE

JOHN E. CONNER MUSEUM
Texas A and I University, Kingsville, Texas 78863
Geology. Farms and ranch equipment of c.1890. Branding irons and cattle brands. Barbed wire. Weapons. 19th century furnishings. Indian artifacts. Coins. Walling knives.
M.-F. 10-12, 1-5; Sa. 9-12; 2nd Su. each month 2.30-5.

KINGSLEY

EDWARDS COUNTY HISTORICAL MUSEUM
Half Way Park, Kingsley, Kansas 67547
Local history. Agriculture. Indian artifacts. Costumes. Sod house replicas.
June 1 - Aug. 31: M.-Sa. 10-6; Su. 1-6. May, Sept.: daily 12-6. Oct. 1 - Apr. 30 by appointment.

KINSTON

CASWELL-NEUSE STATE HISTORIC SITE, VISITOR CENTER
Box 3043, Kinston, North Carolina 28501
Objects from Confederate naval vessel 'Neuse', sunk in 1865, refloated and restored 1963-4. Memorabilia of Governor Caswell.
Tu.-Sa. 9-5; Su. 1-5. Closed Thanksgiving, Dec. 24-26.

GOVERNOR RICHARD CASWELL MEMORIAL, VISITOR CENTER
Kinston, North Carolina 28501
Memorabilia of Richard Caswell (d.1798), Governor of North Carolina.
Tu.-Sa. 9-5; Su. 1-5. Closed Thanksgiving, Dec. 24-6.

KIRKSVILLE

E. M. VIOLETTE MUSEUM
N. E. Missouri State College, Kirksville, Missouri 63901
Local history. Agriculture. Indian artifacts.
M.-F. 1-4. Closed college vacations.

KIRKWOOD

HISTORY HOUSE
249 E. Argonne Drive, Kirkwood, Missouri 63122
Local history.
Daily 10-3.

KIT CARSON

KIT CARSON HISTORICAL SOCIETY MUSEUM
Kit Carson, Colorado 80825
Natural history. Local history. Indian artifacts. Union Pacific depot (1907) is in the care of the Museum.
May 15 - Sept. 15, daily 10-8.

KITTERY POINT

FORT MCCLARY STATE MEMORIAL
Kittery Point, Maine 03905
Blockhouse (1844). Rifleman's House. Powder House. Display illustrating history of Fort.
By appointment.

LADY PEPPERELL HOUSE
Kittery Point, Maine 03905
House (1760), with period furniture and furnishings.
June 15 - Sept. 15: Tu.-Sa. 11-4.

KLAMATH FALLS

COLLIER STATE PARK LOGGING MUSEUM
P.O. Box 428, Klamath Falls, Oregon 97601
Logging equipment. Pioneer log houses (1860-1910). Indian artifacts.
Daily, 24 hours a day.

FAVELL MUSEUM OF WESTERN ART AND ARTIFACTS
125 W. Main Street, Klamath Falls, Oregon 97601
Pioneer relics. Indian artifacts.
Oct.-Apr., Tu.-Sa. 9.30-5.30; Su. 1-5. May-Sept., Tu.-Sa. 9.30-9; Su. 1-9.

KLAMATH COUNTY MUSEUM
1451 Main Street, Klamath Falls, Oregon 97601
Natural history. Botany. Herbarium. Local history and archaeology.
Tu.-Sa. 9-5; Su. 1-5. Closed New Year, July 4, Thanksgiving, Christmas.

KNOXVILLE

KNOX COUNTY MUSEUM
Public Square, Knoxville, Illinois 61448
History of Knox County
May 1 - Oct. 31, Su. 2-5.30.

MUSEUM OF KNOXVILLE PUBLIC LIBRARY
Knoxville, Pennsylvania 16928
Local history.
W., F. 6.30-8.30; Sa. 1-4.

CONFEDERATE MEMORIAL HALL 'BLEAK HOUSE'
3148 Kingston Pike, Knoxville, Tennessee 37919
House (1850). Civil War period relics, furniture. Confederate history. Costumes.
Daily 2-5.

CRAIGHEAD JACKSON HOUSE
1000 State Street, Knoxville, Tennessee 37902
House (1818). 18th-19th century American and English furniture, mirrors, paintings. 17th-18th century English silver.
Tu.-Sa. 9.30-12, 1-5; Su. 1-5. Closed Thanksgiving, Christmas.

DULIN GALLERY OF ART
3100 Kingston Pike, Knoxville, Tennessee 37919
Paintings, graphics, by contemporary American artists.
Tu.-Su. 1-5. Closed public holidays.

FRANK H. McCLUNG MUSEUM
University of Tennessee, Knoxville, Tennessee 37916
History of Knoxville. Natural history. Anthropology. Ecology.
M.-F. 9-5; Sa. 9-12; Su. 2-5; Tu., Th. also 6.30-10.

GOVERNOR WILLIAM BLOUNT MANSION
200 W. Hill Avenue, Knoxville, Tennessee 37919
House (1792), former home of William Blount. Period furnishings. Glass. English silver. Documents. Reconstruction of Governor Blount's office.
May 1 - Oct. 31. M.-Sa. 9.30-5.

MARBLE SPRINGS
Neubert Springs Road, Knoxville, Tennessee 37920
House (1783-1815) was former farm home of Governor John Sevier. Pioneer furniture. Smokehouse.
M.-Sa. 10-12, 2-5; Su. 2-5.

RAMSEY HOUSE
Thorngrove Pike, Route 8, Knoxville, Tennessee 37914
House (1797). Period furnishings. Local history.
Apr. 1 - Oct. 31: Sa., Su. 1-5.

STUDENTS' MUSEUM
3816 Oakland Drive, Knoxville, Tennessee 37918
Children's museum. Geology. Mathematics. Weather. Light. Energy. Space exploration.
Tu.-Sa. 9-5.

JAMES WHITE'S FORT ASSOCIATION MUSEUM
205 E. Hill Avenue, Knoxville, Tennessee 37901
General White's home (1786) and White's Fort (1788). Furniture. Tools.
M.-Sa., public holidays 9.30-5; Su. 1-5. Closed Christmas.

KODIAK

KODIAK HISTORICAL SOCIETY MUSEUM
Box 1412, Kodiak, Alaska 99615
In log-house (1793-4), built by Alexander Baranof as a fur-warehouse. History of Russian settlement in Alaska. Collections from Kodiak and Aleutian Islands. Maritime history. Ethnography. Natural history.
June 10 - Labour Day, M.-F. 11-3; Sa., Su. 1-4. Labour Day - June 9, W., F.-Su. 1-3. Closed New Year, Christmas.

KOKOMO

HOWARD COUNTY HISTORICAL SOCIETY MUSEUM
Court House, Kokomo, Indiana 46901
Local history. Indian artifacts. Agriculture.
M., W., F. 1.30-4. Closed public holidays.

KOOSKIA

NEE MEE POO MUSEUM
Star Route, Kooskia, Idaho 83539
Indian history and artifacts. Arrowheads. Costumes.
June 1 - Sept. 30, M.-F. 9-5.

KOTZEBUE

KOTZEBUE MUSEUM
Box 73, Kotzebue, Alaska 99752
Archaeology. Anthropology. Eskimo and Indian arts and crafts. Costumes.
June 1 - Sept. 1, M.-Sa. 9-5, Su. 1-4. Closed July 4.

KURE BEACH

FORT FISHER STATE HISTORIC SITE, VISITOR CENTER
Kure Beach, North Carolina 28449
Local history. Civil War relics. Archaeology. Underwater archaeology.
Tu.-Sa. 9-5; Su. 1-5. Closed Thanksgiving, Dec. 24-6.

LACLEDE

GENERAL JOHN J. PERSHING BOYHOOD HOME MEMORIAL SHRINE
Laclede, Missouri 64651
House (1858) was Pershing's boyhood home. Period furnishings. Exhibits relating to Pershing's career.
Tu.-Sa. 10-4; Su. 12-5 (Memorial Day - Labour Day 12-6). Closed New Year, Easter, Thanksgiving, Christmas.

LACONIA

LACONIA HISTORICAL SOCIETY MUSEUM
P.O. Box 267, Laconia, New Hampshire 03246
Local history.
By appointment.

THOMPSON-AMES HISTORICAL SOCIETY OF GILFORD
Laconia, New Hampshire 03246
Local history.
By appointment.

LA CONNER

SKAGIT COUNTY HISTORICAL SOCIETY MUSEUM
P.O. Box 32, La Conner, Washington 98527
Local history. Indian artifacts. Agriculture. Anthropology.
W. 1-4: Su. 1-5.

LA CROSSE

POST ROCK MUSEUM
Rush County Historical Society, La Crosse, Kansas 67548
History and techniques of local post rock industry.
May 15 - Sept. 15, daily 8-9. Other times by appointment.

LA CROSSE COUNTY HISTORICAL SOCIETY MUSEUM
429 7th Street, La Crosse, Wisconsin 54601
In Hixon House (1857). Period furnishings. Paintings. Decorative arts. County history.
June 1 - Labour Day, daily 1-5.

VITERBO COLLEGE MUSEUM
815 S. 9th Street, La Crosse, Wisconsin 54601
Natural history. Ceramics. Stamps.
By appointment.

LAFAYETTE

LAFAYETTE ART CENTER
101 S. 9th Street, Lafayette, Indiana 47901
19th-20th century European and American paintings, prints, drawings. Paintings and prints by Midwestern artists.
Tu.-Su. 1-5. Closed Aug., public holidays.

PURDUE UNIVERSITY ARTHUR HERBARIUM
Dept. of Botany and Plant Pathology, Lafayette, Indiana 47907
Herbarium of fungi and flowering plants.
M.-Sa. 8.30-5. Closed public holidays.

TIPPECANOE COUNTY HISTORICAL MUSEUM
10th and S. Streets, Lafayette, Indiana 47901
Local history. Relics of Battle of Tippecanoe and site of Fort Oniatenon. Indian artifacts. Industry. Agriculture. Paintings by local artists. Dresden porcelain. Lustre-ware. Outdoor museum.
Moses Fowler House (1851-2) and Fort Oniatenon (1717), first European settlement in Indiana, are in the care of the Museum.
Tippecanoe County Museum: Tu.-Su. 1-5. Closed Dec. 10 - Jan. 10, public holidays. Fort Oniatenon: Tu.-Su. 1-5. Closed Nov. 1 - Apr. 15, a.m. public holidays.

LAFAYETTE MUSEUM
1122 Lafayette Street, Lafayette, Louisiana 70501
Building (c.1750). Furniture. Portraits. Documents. Indian artifacts. Costumes.
Tu.-Sa. 9-12, 2-5; Su. 2-5. Closed New Year, Mardi Gras, Easter, July 4, Christmas.

LAFAYETTE NATURAL HISTORY MUSEUM AND PLANETARIUM
637 Girard Park Drive, Lafayette, Louisiana 70501
Astronomy. Natural history.
Tu.-Sa. 9-5; Su. 1-5. Closed New Year, Good Friday, Easter, Thanksgiving, Christmas.

LA GRANDE

EASTERN OREGON COLLEGE
Walter Pierce Museum, College Library, 8th Street, La Grande, Oregon 97850
Works by American and European artists. Paintings. Prints. Drawings. Decorative arts.
M.-F. 8-5, 7-10; Sa. 9-12; Su. 7-10 p.m. Closed national holidays.

LA GRANGE

NATHANIEL W. FAISON HOME AND MUSEUM
822 N. Jefferson Street, La Grange, Texas 78945
House (1845), owned by Faison family since 1866. Original furnishings.
June 1 - Aug. 31: Tu.-Su. 1-5.

LA GRANGEVILLE

LA GRANGE HISTORICAL SOCIETY
Old School House, La Grangeville, New York 12540
Local history. Furniture.
By appointment.

LAGUNA BEACH

LAGUNA BEACH ART GALLERY
307 Cliff Drive, Laguna Beach, California 92651
Paintings by early Californian artists. Photographs by Paul Outerbridge. Contemporary American paintings, sculpture.
Daily, 11.30-4.30. Closed first four days of each month and New Year, Labor Day, Thanksgiving, Christmas.

LAHAINA

LAHAINA RESTORATION FOUNDATION
Dickenson and Chapel Streets, Lahaina, Hawaii 96761
Local history, based on 2 historic buildings and a ship: Baldwin Home Missionary Museum (1834), 'Carthaginian' Whaleship Museum (1920) and Hale Pa'i Printshop Museum (1833).
Daily 9.30-5.

LAIE

POLYNESIAN CULTURAL CENTER
Laie, Hawaii 96762
Living village display, showing Hawaiian culture, handicrafts, painting, decorative arts, costumes.
M.-Sa. 10.30-7. Closed Thanksgiving, Christmas.

LA JOLLA

LA JOLLA MUSEUM OF ART
700 Prospect Street, La Jolla, California 92037
19th and 20th century European and American paintings, sculpture, drawings, prints.
Tu.-F., 11-5; W. evening, 7-10; Sa., Su., 12.30-5. Closed New Year, Thanksgiving, Christmas.

T. WAYLAND VAUGHAN AQUARIUM AND MUSEUM
Scripps Institute of Oceanography, 8602 La Jolla Shores Drive, La Jolla, California 92037
Oceanography. Zoology.
M.-F., 8-5; Sa., Su. 9-5.

LA JUNTA

BENT'S OLD FORT NATIONAL HISTORIC SITE
La Junta, Colorado 81050
Local history. Material found during excavation of Fort site. 'Overland' stage coach.
June 1 - Aug. 30, daily 8-8. Sept. 1 - May 31, M.-F., 8-4.30; weekends, public holidays, 9.30-6.

KOSHARE INDIAN MUSEUM
18th and Santa Fe Streets, La Junta, Colorado 81050
Indian arts and crafts. Archaeology. Anthropology.
June 1 - Sept. 30, daily 9-5, 7-9; Oct. 1 - May 31, daily 1-5.

LAKE CHARLES

IMPERIAL CALCASIEU HISTORICAL MUSEUM
204 W. Sallier Street, Lake Charles, Louisiana 70601
Local history. Industry, especially timber, sulphur, rice. Costumes. Bottles.
W.-F. 10-12, 2-5; Sa. 10-12; Su. 2-5. Closed New Year, Easter, Christmas, June 1 - Aug. 31 Wednesdays.

LAKE CITY

MUSEUM OF WABASHA COUNTY HISTORICAL SOCIETY
Lake City, Minnesota 55041
In former school (1870). Local history. Agriculture.
June 15 - Sept. 30: Sa., Su. 2-5.

FORT SISSETON STATE PARK VISITOR CENTER
Lake City, South Dakota 57247
Local history. Indian artifacts.
Memorial Day - Labour Day, daily 9-5.

LAKE GEORGE

FORT WILLIAM HENRY MUSEUM
Canada Street, Lake George, New York 12845
Restored fort of French and Indian Wars. Military history. Maps. Plans. Documents. Aboriginal occupation of northern New York State.
May 1 - June 30, Sept. 1 - Nov. 30, daily 10-5. July 1 - Aug. 31, 9 a.m. - 10 p.m.

LAKE GEORGE INSTITUTE OF HISTORY, ART AND SCIENCE
Canada Street, Lake George, New York 12845
Building (1845). Local history. Natural history. Science. Paintings, sculpture by American artists. Indian artifacts.
May 1 - Sept. 30, Tu.-Su. 1-5. Labour Day - Memorial Day, M.-F. 1-5. Closed Christmas, New Year, Easter, July 4, Thanksgiving, public holidays.

OLD STONE SCHOOLHOUSE
Stone Schoolhouse Lane, Lake George, New York 12845
Arts and crafts of Adirondacks.
July 1 - Aug. 31, daily 10-8. Rest of year by appointment.

LAKE HOPATCONG

LAKE HOPATCONG HISTORICAL MUSEUM
Hopatcong State Park, P.O. Box 36, Lake Hopatcong, New Jersey 07849
House (1832). History of iron-ore industry and abandoned Morris Canal. Indian artifacts.
W. 1-4. Other times by appointment. Closed Christmas.

LAKE JACKSON

BRAZOSPORT MUSEUM OF NATURAL SCIENCES
101 This Way, Lake Jackson, Texas 77566
Natural sciences, with emphasis on conservation of local resources. Geology, shells, flora and fauna of the area.
Tu.-Sa. 10-5; Su. 2-5.

LAKE JUNALUSKA

MUSEUM OF COMMISSION ON ARCHIVES AND HISTORY, UNITED METHODIST CHURCH
World Methodist Building, Lakeshore Drive, Lake Junaluska, North Carolina 28745
History of Methodist Church. Portraits of Methodist leaders. Busts and statuettes of John Wesley.
M.-F. 8.30-4.30; Sa., Su. by appointment. Closed public holidays.

LAKELAND

POLK PUBLIC MUSEUM
800 E. Palmetto Street, Lakeland, Florida 33801
Paintings. Graphics. Sculpture.
M.-F. 9-5; Su., public holidays 1-4.

LAKE LINDEN

HOUGHTON COUNTY HISTORICAL MUSEUM
High M-26, Lake Linden, Michigan 49945
Local history.
June 1 - Aug. 31: Tu.-Sa. 9.30-4.30; Su. 12-5.

LAKE OF THE WOODS

FORT ST. CHARLES
Magnussen Island, Lake of the Woods, Minnesota 56745
Restored fort (1732). Local history.
Daily 10-5.

LAKE PLACID

JOHN BROWN FARM
Route 73, Lake Placid, New York 12946
Home and burial place of John Brown. Period furniture. Memorabilia of John Brown.
M.-Sa. 9-5; Su. 1-5.

LAKE PLACID AND NORTH ELBA HISTORICAL SOCIETY MUSEUM
Averyville Road, Lake Placid, New York 12946
House (1905). Local history. Replica of general store. Mounted animals and birds.
July 1 - Sept. 14: Tu.-Su. 12.30-5.30.

LAKEPORT

LAKE COUNTY MUSEUM
175 Third Street, Lakeport, California 95453
Local history. Geology.
M.-F., 1-4. Sa., 11-4. Closed public holidays.

LAKE VIEW

MUSEUM OF HISTORICAL SOCIETY OF LAKE VIEW
Lake View, Iowa 51450
In log cabin (1870). Local history.
June 1 - Aug. 31, Su. 2-5.

LAKEVIEW

PENROD'S MUSEUM
Lakeview, Arkansas 72642
57 hobby collections, including dolls, guns, stamps, coins, glass. Indian artifacts.
Apr. 1 - Nov. 1, daily 9-6.

SCHMINCK MEMORIAL MUSEUM
128 S. East Street, Lakeview, Oregon 97630
Local history. Indian artifacts. Prints. Drawings. Costumes.
M., W.-F. 9-5; Tu. 1.30-5; other times by appointment. Closed Thanksgiving, Dec. 23-8.

LAKEWOOD

JEFFERSON COUNTY PLANETARIUM
200 Kipling Street, Lakewood, Colorado 80226
Planetarium. Astronomy.
By appointment.

LAKEWOOD HISTORICAL SOCIETY MUSEUM
14710 Lake Avenue, Lakewood, Ohio 44107
In old Stone House (1838). Early 19th century pioneer and domestic equipment.
W.-Su. 2-5. Closed public holidays, Dec. 1 - Jan. 31.

LAMAR

BIG TIMBERS MUSEUM
North Santa Fe Trail, P.O. Box 362, Lamar, Colorado 81052
Local history.
M.-F., Su., 2-5. Closed New Year, July 4, Christmas.

HARRY S. TRUMAN BIRTHPLACE
Truman Avenue and 11th Street, Lamar, Missouri 64759
House (c.1880) was family home of President Truman. Period furnishings.
M.-Sa. 10-4; Su., Memorial Day, Labour Day, 12-6. Closed New Year, Easter, Thanksgiving, Christmas.

LAMESA

LAMESA-DAWSON COUNTY MUSEUM
S. 2nd and Avenue M, Lamesa, Texas 79331
Local history. Furniture. Domestic equipment.
Sept. 1 - May 31, Tu. 2-5, June 1 - Aug. 31, Su. 2-5.

LANCASTER

ANTELOPE VALLEY INDIAN MUSEUM
15701 East Avenue M, Lancaster, California 93534
Anthropology. Archaeology. Indian artifacts.
Daily, 10-5. Closed New Year, Thanksgiving, Christmas.

LANCASTER HISTORICAL SOCIETY MUSEUM
226 Main Street, Lancaster, New Hampshire 03246
In Holton House (1780). Local history.
July 1 - Aug. 31, daily 2-5, 7-9.

SHERMAN HOUSE STATE MEMORIAL
137 E. Main Street, Lancaster, Ohio 43130
Birthplace of Civil War General William T. Sherman. Period furnishings.
June 1 - Oct. 31: Tu.-Su. 9.30-5.

AMISH FARM AND HOUSE
2395 Lincoln Highway E., Lancaster, Pennsylvania 17602
Living museum, with replica of old Order Amish home and fully operating farm. Exhibits to show the Plain People's way of life, history, customs and religion.
June 1 - Sept. 30, 8.30-8. Oct. 1 - Nov. 14 and Apr. 1 - May 31, 8.30-5. Nov. 15 - Feb. 14, 8.30-4.

MUSEUM OF LANCASTER COUNTY HISTORICAL SOCIETY
230 N. President Avenue, Lancaster, Pennsylvania 17603
History of Lancaster County. Costumes. Pewter. Glass.
Tu.-Sa. 10-5; Su. 1-5. Closed public holidays.

NORTH MUSEUM
Franklin and Marshall College, College and Buchanan Avenues, Lancaster, Pennsylvania 17604
Geology. Mineralogy. Palaeontology. Conchology. Herbarium. Planetarium. Natural history. Anthropology. Ethnology. Archaeology. Indian material.
Sept. 1 - June 30: W.-Sa. 9-5; Su. 1.30-5. July 1 - Aug. 31: Sa., Su. 1.30-5. Closed Christmas, New Year, Easter.

PENNSYLVANIA FARM MUSEUM
2451 Kissell Hill Road, Lancaster, Pennsylvania 17601
Collections illustrating 19th century rural life. Agricultural implements. Craftsmen's tools. Vehicles. Furnished farmhouse (c.1815). Log town-house (1780). Blacksmith's shop. Print shop. Household equipment. Folk art gallery.
M.-Sa., public holidays, 8.30-5; Su. 1-5. Closed New Year, Good F., Easter, Thanksgiving, Christmas.

ROCK FORD
Rock Ford Road, Lancaster, Pennsylvania 17602
House (1810) was home of Surgeon - Gen. Edward Hand. Hand family furnishings and personal possessions. 18th-19th century paintings, portraits.
Apr. 10 - Oct. 14: M.-Sa. 10-5; Su. 12-5.

WHEATLAND
1120 Marietta Avenue, Lancaster, Pennsylvania 17603
House (1828), formerly home of President James Buchanan. Mid-19th century furnishings. Buchanan MSS. President's carriage.
Mar. 15 - Nov. 30: M.-Sa. 9-5; Su. 10-5.

THE CAROLINA MUSEUM
Gay Street, Lancaster, South Carolina 29720
History of the Carolinas. Civil War material. Indian artifacts.
First Presbyterian Church (1862) is in the care of the Museum.
Su. 2-6 and by appointment.

MARY BALL MEMORIAL MUSEUM AND LIBRARY
Lancaster, Virginia 22503
Local history and archaeology. Civil War history. Powhatan Indian artifacts. Glass of Colonial period. 18th-19th century furniture.
Old Jail (1742) is in the care of the Museum.
Tu., W., F. 10-3. Closed Christmas week.

LANDER

FREMONT COUNTY PIONEER MUSEUM
630 Lincoln Street, Lander, Wyoming 82520
Geology. Mineralogy. Pioneer life. Local and military history. Indian artifacts. Costumes.
Apr. 1 - Oct. 31: M.-Sa. 9-9; Su. 3-9. Rest of year by appointment.

LANGTRY

JUDGE ROY BEAN VISITOR CENTER
Langtry, Texas 78871
Local history and natural history. Includes building (1896) in which Judge Bean had his famous Jersey Lily Saloon.
June 1 - Aug. 31, daily 7-7. Sept. 1 - May 31, daily 8-5. Closed Dec. 24-6.

L'ANSE

MUSEUM OF BARAGA COUNTY HISTORICAL SOCIETY
L'Anse, Michigan 49946
In reconstructed James Oliver Curwood cabin. Local history. Indian artifacts.
June 1 - Nov. 31, daily 10-8.

LANSING

MICHIGAN HISTORICAL COMMISSION MUSEUM
505 N. Washington Avenue, Lansing, Michigan 48933
History of Michigan and its region. Natural resources. Agriculture. Tools, implements. Transport. Industry and technology. Furniture. Domestic equipment. Folklore.
Mann House (1884) is in the care of the Commission.
M.-F. 9-4.30; Sa., Su. 12-5; Public holidays 12-5. Closed New Year, Christmas.

MUSEUM OF CARL G. FENNER ARBORETUM
2020 E. Mount Hope Road, Lansing, Michigan 48910
Natural history. Indian artifacts. Children's museum.
Tu.-Su. 10-5.

LAONA

LUMBERJACK SPECIAL AND CAMP FIVE MUSEUM
Laona, Wisconsin 54541
Lumbercamp museum. Botany. Local history and industry. Farm implements. Coins. Railway equipment. Restored buildings include Cracker Barrel store (1903), farm buildings (1905) and slaughter house (1910).
June 14 - Sept. 2: M.-Sa. 10-4.15.

LA POINTE

MADELINE ISLAND HISTORICAL MUSEUM
La Pointe, Wisconsin 54850
House (c.1835). Local, military and maritime history. Entomology.
June 15 - Sept. 15, daily 11-4.

LA PORTE

LA PORTE COUNTY HISTORICAL MUSEUM
Court House Basement, Lincolnway, La Porte, Indiana 46350
Local history. Portraits. Guns.
Nov.-Mar., M.-F. 10-4.30. Apr.-Oct., Tu.-Sa. 10-4.30. Closed public holidays.

LARAMIE

LARAMIE PLAINS MUSEUM
1420 Grand Avenue, Laramie, Wyoming 82070
Local history. Pioneer furniture, domestic equipment. Indian artifacts.
May 1 - Oct. 31: Tu., Th. 2-4, 7-9. Nov. 1 - Apr. 30: Tu., Th. 2-4. Other times by appointment.

ROCKY MOUNTAIN HERBARIUM
University of Wyoming, Laramie, Wyoming 82070
Botany. Herbarium.
By appointment.

UNIVERSITY OF WYOMING ANTHROPOLOGICAL MUSEUM
Arts and Sciences Building, Laramie, Wyoming 82070
Anthropology. Ethnology. Archaeology. Indian material.
M.-F. 8-5. Closed university vacations.

UNIVERSITY OF WYOMING ART MUSEUM
Laramie, Wyoming 82070
American, European, Oriental paintings. Prints. Sculpture.
Tu.-Sa. 9-5, Su. 2-4.30. Closed public holidays.

UNIVERSITY OF WYOMING GEOLOGICAL MUSEUM
Laramie, Wyoming 82070
Geology. Mineralogy. Fossils. Skeletons of prehistoric animals. Anthropology.
M.-F. 8-5; Sa., Su., public holidays 2-5.

LAREDO

CAPITOL OF THE REPUBLIC OF THE RIO GRANDE MUSEUM
1000 Saragoza, Laredo, Texas 78040
History of Republic of the Rio Grande (1839-47).
W.-F. 9.30-11.30; Sa., Su. 9.30-11.30, 2.30-4.30. Closed national holidays.

LARNED

FORT LARNED NATIONAL HISTORIC SITE
Route 3, Larned, Kansas 67550
Museum based on barracks (1866-8). Guns of Indian Wars period. Pioneer life. Indian artifacts.
Sept. 1 - May 30: daily 9-5. Memorial Day - Labour Day: 7 a.m. - 8 p.m. Closed Christmas.

PAWNEE COUNTY HISTORICAL SOCIETY MUSEUM
Cummins Memorial Library, Larned, Kansas 67550
County history. Documents. Paintings. Photographs. Clothing. Guns.
Th., Sa. 1-5.

LAS ANIMAS

KIT CARSON MUSEUM
125 9th Street, Las Animas, Colorado 81054
Local history. Agriculture. Cattle industry. Railways. Indian material.
County jail (1876), schoolhouse (1922) and stage-coach station (1884) are in the care of the Museum.
Memorial Day - Labour Day, daily 1.15-5.

LAS CRUCES

NEW MEXICO STATE UNIVERSITY MUSEUM
Box 3564, Las Cruces, New Mexico 88001
Botany. Herbarium. Zoology. Entomology. Anthropology. Ethnology. Science. Local history. Archaeology. Architecture. Agriculture. Industry.
M.-F. by appointment. Closed university vacations.

LAS VEGAS

ROUGH RIDERS MEMORIAL AND CITY MUSEUM
Municipal Building, Las Vegas, New Mexico 87701
Pioneer life in S.W. Teddy Roosevelt Rough Rider collection.
M.-Sa. 9-4. Closed public holidays.

LAUGHLINTOWN

COMPASS INN MUSEUM
U.S. Route 30, Laughlintown, Pennsylvania 15655
Inn (1799). Furnished rooms, showing inn as it was in early 1800s.
Tu.-Su. 10-5.

LAUREL

MONTPELIER
Laurel-Bowie Road, Route 197, Laurel, Maryland 20810
House (1740). 18th century furniture.
M.-F. 9-4; Sa., Su. 12-8.

LAUREN ROGERS LIBRARY AND MUSEUM OF ART
5th Avenue and 7th Street, Laurel, Mississippi 39440
Indian, Chinese, Japanese artifacts. 19th-20th century European and American paintings, sculpture, prints. Japanese prints. 18th-19th century European and American furniture. Decorative arts.
Tu.-Sa. 10-12, 2-5; Su. 2-5. Closed public holidays.

LAURINBURG

ST. ANDREWS PRESBYTERIAN COLLEGE, ART GALLERY
Laurinburg, North Carolina 28352
Paintings, decorative arts by local artists and craftsmen.
M.-F. 8.30 a.m. - 10 p.m.; Sa. 8.30-5; Su. 1-5, during college year and summer sessions. Closed all holidays except July 4.

LAURIUM

YESTERYEAR HOUSE
Central Mine, Laurium, Michigan 49113
House (1860). History of local mining industry and of Laurium.
M.-Sa. 10-5. Closed Labour Day - July 1.

LA VETA

FORT FRANCISCO MUSEUM
Francisco Street, La Veta, Colorado 81055
Fort (1862). Replica of mountain homestead of 1880s. Furniture. Indian artifacts. Natural history.
The Ritter schoolhouse (1876) is in the care of the Museum.
Memorial Day - Oct. 1, daily 9-5.

LAWRENCE

MUSEUM OF ANTHROPOLOGY
University of Kansas, Lawrence, Kansas 66044
Archaeology. Anthropology. Ethnology. Indian artifacts.
M.-Sa. 8-5; Su. 2-5.

SNOW ENTOMOLOGICAL MUSEUM
University of Kansas, Lawrence, Kansas 66044
Entomology.
M.-F. 8.30-5; Sa. 9-12. Public holidays by appointment.

SYSTEMATICS MUSEUMS
University of Kansas, Dyche Hall, Lawrence, Kansas 66044
Natural history. Palaeontology.
M.-Sa. 8-4.45; Su., public holidays 1-4.45. Closed Christmas, New Year, July 4, Thanksgiving.

UNIVERSITY OF KANSAS MUSEUM OF ART
University of Kansas, Lawrence, Kansas 66044
European paintings, sculpture, especially 17th-18th century German, Austrian, American painting. Oriental art. Graphics. Ceramics. Textiles. Medals.
M.-Sa. 9-4.45; Su. 1.30-4.45. Closed New Year, Thanksgiving, July 4, Christmas.

WILCOX MUSEUM
University of Kansas, Fraser Hall, Lawrence, Kansas 66044
Greek, Roman, Etruscan antiquities.
M.-F. 7.30-5; Sa. 7.30-12. Closed holidays.

ROCK HALL
199 Broadway, Lawrence, New York 11559
House (1767). Period furnishings. Paintings.
Apr. 1 - Nov. 30: M., W., Sa., 10-5; Su. 12-5.

LAWRENCEBURG

DAVID CROCKETT MUSEUM
David Crockett State Park, Lawrenceburg, Tennessee 38464
Local history.
M.-Sa. 9-5; Su. 1-5.

LAWSON

WATKINS WOOLLEN MILL
Rural Route 2, Lawson, Missouri 64062
Mill (1860), containing museum of local agriculture and woollen industry. The Mill complex also includes outbuildings (1850-80), the W. L. Watkins house (1850), Franklin School (1856) and Mount Vernon Church (1871).
M.-Sa. 10-4. May 1 - Sept. 30, Su. 10-5; Oct. 1 - Apr. 30, Su. 11-4. Closed New Year, Easter, Thanksgiving, Christmas.

LAWTON

MUSEUM OF THE GREAT PLAINS
Elmer Thomas Park, Lawton, Oklahoma 73501
History of material culture of the Great Plains from earliest times to present day.
Daily 10-5; Su. 2-5. Tu., W., Th. also 7 p.m. - 10 p.m.

THE HOLY CITY
Wichita Mountains Wildlife Refuge, Lawton, Oklahoma 73501
Buildings and settings portraying physical aspects of ancient City of Jerusalem.
Daily, sunrise-sunset.

LEADVILLE

HEALY HOUSE - DEXTER CABIN
912 Harrison Avenue, Leadville, Colorado 80461
In Healy House (1878), with contemporary furnishings.
Dexter Cabin (1879) is in the care of the Museum.
May 15 - Sept. 30, daily 9-4.30.

HERITAGE MUSEUM AND ART GALLERY
9th and Harrison Streets, Leadville, Colorado 80461
Local history. Mining.
Daily 10-9.

LEADVILLE ASSEMBLY
Box 217, Leadville, Colorado 80461
At Matchless Mine (1879). Items illustrating history of mine.
May 31 - Labour Day, daily 9-4.30.

TABOR OPERA HOUSE MUSEUM
815 Harrison Avenue, Leadville, Colorado 80461
Local and theatre history. Costumes. Paintings.
June 1 - Oct. 31, Su.-F., 9-5.30; Nov. 1 - May 31, by appointment.

LEAVENWORTH

LEAVENWORTH HISTORICAL MUSEUM
334 5th Avenue, Leavenworth, Kansas 66084
Local history. Furniture and furnishings. Silver. China. Costumes. Bank, barber's shop, store of the 1870s.
Tu.-Su. 1-4. Closed New Year, Christmas.

LEBANON

NATURE INTERPRETIVE CENTER
Bennett Spring State Park, Lebanon, Missouri 65536
Botany. Zoology.
Mar. 1 - Oct. 31, daily 9-6: Nov. 1 - Feb. 28, Tu.-Su. 9-5. Closed New Year, Christmas.

GLENDOWER STATE MEMORIAL
U.S. Route 42, Lebanon, Ohio 45036
House (1836). Period furnishings.
Apr. 1 - Oct. 31: Tu.-Su. 9.30-5.

WARREN COUNTY HISTORICAL SOCIETY MUSEUM
Harmon Hall, S. Broadway, Lebanon, Ohio 45036
Geology. Mineralogy. Palaeontology. Archaeology. Replica of pioneer cabin, containing tools, agricultural implements, spinning and weaving equipment. Shaker material. Warren County furniture. Indian material. Folk art.
Tu.-Sa. 9-4; Su. 12-4. Closed Christmas.

MUSEUM OF LEBANON COUNTY HISTORICAL SOCIETY
6th and Walnut Streets, Lebanon, Pennsylvania 17042
County history.
M. 1-5, 7-9. Closed public holidays.

LEBEC

FORT TEJON STATE HISTORIC PARK
Grapevine Canyon, Highway 99, Lebec, Kern County, California 93243
U.S. Army Dragoon post, established 1854, abandoned 1864. Museum exhibits on army life, local history. Mock Civil War skirmish held 3rd Sunday each month.
Daily 8-5. Closed New Year, Thanksgiving, Christmas.

LEESBURG

JOHNSTON'S TAVERN
U.S. Route 19, Leesburg, Pennsylvania 17044
House (1831), built as stage-coach tavern. Period furnishings.
May-Oct., Tu.-Sa. 8.30-5; Su. 1-5. Nov.-Apr., Tu.-Sa. 9-4.30; Su. 1-4.30.

WESTMORELAND DAVIS MEMORIAL FOUNDATION
Route 2, Leesburg, Virginia 22075
House, Morven Park (1781, with later additions). Local history. Botany. Herbarium. Agriculture. Costumes.
Apr. 1 - Oct. 31: W.-Sa. 10-5; Su. 1-5.

LOUDOUN COUNTY MUSEUM
16 W. Loudoun Street, Leesburg, Virginia 22075
History of Loudoun County.
Log cabin (1763) is preserved by the Museum.
M.-F. 10-4.30; Sa. 10-5. Su. 1-5. Closed Thanksgiving, Christmas, New Year.

OATLANDS
Route 2, Box 352, Leesburg, Virginia 22075
House (1800). English and American period furnishings. Paintings. Porcelain.
Apr. 1 - Oct. 31: M.-Sa. 10-5; Su. 1-5. Rest of year by appointment. Closed Christmas.

LEHI

JOHN HUTCHINGS MUSEUM OF NATURAL HISTORY
678 N. 2nd Street W., Lehi, Utah 84043
Geology. Natural history. Anthropology. Pioneer history.
Feb. 1 - Dec. 31: Tu.-Su. 1-5. Closed public holidays.

LELAND

LEELAUNU HISTORICAL MUSEUM
P.O. Box 246, Leland, Michigan 49654
In Old Jail (1900). Local history. Great Lakes shipping. Agriculture. Industry. Clothing. Domestic equipment. Indian artifacts.
July 1 - Oct. 15: M., W., F. 10-12, 1-4. May 15 - June 30: Tu.-Th. 1-4.

LEMMON

PETRIFIED WOOD PARK MUSEUM
Lemmon, South Dakota 57638
Building (1931) of petrified wood. Furnishings. Household equipment. Tools. Farm implements. Costumes.
May 16 - Sept. 14, M.-Sa. 8-8; Su., public holidays 8-6.

LENHARTSVILLE

MUSEUM OF PENNSYLVANIA DUTCH FOLK CULTURE SOCIETY
U.S. Route 22, Lenhartsville, Pennsylvania 19534
In former schoolhouse (c.1888), in original condition. Life and customs of the area during woodstove period. Period rooms. Household items.
Apr. 1 - May 31, Sept. 1 - Oct. 31, Sa., Su. 10-5. July 1 - Aug. 31: daily 10-5.

LENOIR

FORT DEFIANCE
Route 5, Lenoir, North Carolina 28645
Fort (1788-90). Period furnishings.
Tu.-Sa. 9-5; Su. 1-5. Closed Thanksgiving, New Year, Christmas.

LEONIA

ENGLISH NEIGHBORHOOD HISTORICAL SOCIETY MUSEUM
130 Grand Avenue, Leonia, New Jersey 07605
House (1859) was Civil War armoury. Local history. Indian material.
By appointment.

LERNA

LINCOLN LOG CABIN STATE PARK
Route 2, Lerna, Illinois 62440
Homes of Thomas Lincoln and of Matilda Moore, Abraham Lincoln's step-sister.
Daily 8-5.

LE ROY

LE ROY HOUSE
23 E. Main Street, Le Roy, New York 14482
House (1815). Local history. Agriculture. Indian artifacts. Period furnishings. Paintings. Glass. Costumes.
July 1 - Aug. 31, daily 2-5. Other times by appointment.

LEWISTON

MUSEUM OF LEWIS-CLARK STATE COLLEGE
8th Avenue and 6th Street, Lewiston, Idaho 83501
Local history. Gold Rush. Missions.
By appointment. Closed Christmas, public holidays.

LEVELLAND

SOUTH PLAINS MUSEUM
606 Avenue H., Levelland, Texas 79336
Mounted specimens of N. American game animals. History and memorabilia of South Plains and cattle industry.
Tu.-Sa. 2-5. Other times by appointment.

LEWELLEN

MUSEUM OF ASH HOLLOW STATE HISTORIC PARK
Lewellen, Nebraska 69147
Palaeontology. Natural history. Anthropology. Indian artifacts. Archaeology.
May 1 - Sept. 30, daily 8-5.

LEWES

LEWES HISTORICAL SOCIETY MUSEUM
Lewes, Delaware 19958
Indian material. Children's museum. Early Sussex County furniture. Swedish log cabin, with pioneer furnishings.
May 1 - Sept. 30, 2-5.

ZWAASENDAEL MUSEUM
Kings Highway and Savannah Road, Lewes, Delaware 19958
In replica of Town Hall, at Hoorn, Netherlands. Local history and archaeology. Indian material.
Tu.-Sa., 10-5; Su., Easter, Memorial Day, July 4, 12.30-5. Closed other public holidays.

LEWISBURG

MUSEUMS OF UNION COUNTY HISTORICAL SOCIETY
Lewisburg, Pennsylvania 17837
In Rays Church (1801) and Union County Court House (1887). History of Union County.
New Berlin Court House (1815) is in the care of the Society.
Rays Church: June 1 - Aug. 31, Su. 2-5. Union County Court House: Su. 2-5.

DAYWOOD ART GALLERY
Lewisburg, West Virginia 24901
American paintings and prints of 19th and 20th centuries.
Daily 10-12, 2-4.

FORT SAVANNAH INN
204 N. Jefferson Street, Lewisburg, West Virginia 24901
Fort Savannah (1760). Barracks (c.1770). Local and military history exhibits. Early American sewing machines.
Daily 7 a.m. - 10 p.m. Closed Christmas.

GREENBRIER COUNTY LIBRARY AND MUSEUM
312 Church Street, Lewisburg, West Virginia 24901
Building (1834). Early history of the area.
Daily 10-1, 3-5. Closed Su. and Th. mornings.

LEWISTON

STANTON MUSEUM
Bates College, Department of Biology, Carnegie Hall, Lewiston, Maine 04240
Natural history, especially birds.
By appointment, during college terms only.

TREAT GALLERY
College Street, Lewiston, Maine 04240
Chinese art. American paintings, drawings, printings, especially by Maine artists. Drawings and sketches by Marsden Hartley. 16th-19th century prints, including one by Rembrandt; 17th-18th century English, Dutch, French, Italian landscapes, portraits.
M.-F. 8-12 by appointment, 1-5, 7-8; Su. 2-5. Closed public holidays.

ARCHES BRANCH MUSEUM
Lewiston, Minnesota 55952
Natural history. Local history. Windmill. Agricultural books. Domestic equipment. 1845 log house.
M.-Sa. 8-5; Su. 1-5. Closed New Year, Easter, Christmas.

LEWISTOWN

DICKSON MOUNDS MUSEUM
Lewistown, Illinois 61542
Indian burial mounds. Artifacts. Skeletons.
A one-room school (1903) is in the care of the Museum.
M.-Sa. 8.30-5; Su. 2-5. Closed New Yer, Easter, Thanksgiving, Christmas.

CENTRAL MONTANA MUSEUM
E. Main Street, Lewistown, Montana 59457
Geology. Local history and archaeology. Indian artifacts.
M.-F. 8-5; May 1 - Sept. 30, Sa., Su. 8-8.

MUSEUM OF MIFFLIN COUNTY HISTORICAL SOCIETY
17 N. Main Street, Lewistown, Pennsylvania 17044
House (1840). County history. Birthplace (1874) of General Frank Ross McCoy.
By appointment.

LEXINGTON

HENRY CLAY MEMORIAL FOUNDATION
E. Main Street and Sycamore Road, Lexington, Kentucky 40528
House 'Ashland' (1806-11) was home of Henry Clay, 1811-52. Original furnishings. Mementoes of Clay's travels in Europe and of his public career. Portraits.
Daily 9.30-4.30. Closed Christmas.

HUNT-MORGAN HOUSE
201 North Mill Street, Lexington, Kentucky 40502
House (1814), with period furniture.
Henry Clay Law Office (1803) is in the care of the same Trust.
Tu.-Sa., public holidays 10-4; Su. 2-5. Closed New Year, Christmas.

KENTUCKY LIFE MUSEUM
Higbee Mill Pike, Lexington, Kentucky 40503
Local history. Agriculture. Tools. Furniture and furnishings. Period rooms. Costumes. Portraits. Drawings.
Bryan Mansion (1847), with slave quarters, smoke house, blacksmith's shop, ice house and country store is in the care of the Museum.
Tu.-Sa. 9-4; Su. 1.30-4.30. Closed University vacations.

LIVING ARTS AND SCIENCE CENTER
362 Walnut Street, Lexington, Kentucky 40508
Children's art and science museum.
M.-Sa. 9-5. Closed July 4, Thanksgiving, Christmas, New Year.

MUSEUM OF ANTHROPOLOGY
Lafferty Hall, University of Kentucky, Lexington, Kentucky 40506
Anthropological and archaeological material.
M.-F. 8.30-4.30. Closed public holidays.

SHAKERTOWN, INC.
2220 Young Drive, Lexington, Kentucky 40505
Local history.
Apr.-Oct. daily 9-5.

TRANSYLVANIA MUSEUM
300 N. Broadway, Lexington, Kentucky 40508
History of science. Early 19th century scientific instruments.
Patterson Cabin (1780) and Old Morrison House (1833) are in the care of the Museum.
M.-Sa. by appointment. Closed public holidays.

UNIVERSITY OF KENTUCKY ART GALLERY
Fine Arts Building, Rose Street, Lexington, Kentucky 40506
19th century American and European paintings. Contemporary prints, drawings.
Tu.-F. 10-5; June 1 - Aug. 31, Sa., Su. 1-5.

WAVELAND STATE SHRINE
Higbee Mill Road, Lexington, Kentucky 40508
House (1847), with period furnishings. Exhibits illustrating Kentucky life from pioneer days to recent past. Country store. Early workshops. Farm and craftsmen's tools. Kitchen utensils. Clothing. Silver. China. Toys. Military relics.
Tu.-Sa. 9-4; Su. 1.30-4.30.

BUCKMAN TAVERN
Battlegreen, Lexington, Massachusetts 02173
House (1710), became Buckman Tavern, 1775. Period rooms.
Apr. 19 - Oct. 31, M.-Sa., public holidays, 10-5; Su. 1-5.

HANCOCK-CLARKE HOUSE
35 Hancock Street, Lexington, Massachusetts 02173
House (1698). Period rooms. Revolutionary war relics, including William Diamond's drum and Pitcairn's pistols.
Apr. 19 - Oct. 31, M.-Sa. 10-5; Su. 1-5. Nov. 1 - Apr. 18, M.-Sa. 10-4; Su. 1-4.

LEXINGTON HISTORICAL SOCIETY MUSEUM
1322 Massachusetts Avenue, Lexington, Massachusetts 02173
In Monroe Tavern (1695). Period rooms. Local history, especially relating to Battle of Lexington. Hancock-Clarke House (1698) and Buckman Tavern (c.1710) are in the care of the Society.
Apr. 19 - Oct. 31, M.-Sa. 10-5; Su. 1-5. Nov. 1 - Apr. 18, M.-Sa. 10-4; Su. 1-4.

ANDERSON HOUSE
Civil War Battle of Lexington State Historic Site, Lexington, Missouri 64067
House (1853) was used as hospital in Civil War. Period furnishings. Civil War relics.
Daily 10-4. Closed New Year, Easter, Thanksgiving, Christmas.

DAWSON COUNTY HISTORICAL SOCIETY MUSEUM
1505 N. Monroe Street, Lexington, Nebraska 68850
Local history.
Willow Island Railway Depot (1870) and Tom Reed School (1885) are in the care of the Society.
Apr.-Sept., Tu.-Sa. 2-4; Su. 2-5.

RICHLAND COUNTY MUSEUM
51 Church Street, Lexington, Ohio 44904
Building (1850). Local history. Agriculture. Indian material. Medical history. Children's museum.
Sa., Su. 1-4. Closed Jan. 1 - Mar. 31.

THE FOX HOUSE
Fox Street, Lexington, South Carolina 29072
House (1833-34). Museum showing life of small 19th century landowner. Local furniture.
May-Oct., Tu.-Sa. 10-5; Su. 2-5. Nov.-Apr., F., Sa. 10-4; Su. 2-4.

STONEWALL JACKSON MEMORIAL
8 E. Washington Street, Lexington, Virginia 24450
Jackson family furniture and personal possessions. Portraits and deathmask of General Jackson.
Daily 8.30-4.30 p.m.

LEE CHAPEL
Washington and Lee University, Lexington, Virginia 24450
In Chapel (1865-70). Robert E. Lee memorabilia. Local history. Paintings.
Lee-Jackson House (1842) and Lee's house (1869) are in the care of the university.
Apr. 1 - Sept. 30: M.-Sa. 9-5; Su. 2-5. Oct. 1 - Mar 31: M.-Sa. 9-4; Su. 2-5. Closed Thanksgiving, Christmas.

MUSEUM OF ROCKBRIDGE COUNTY HISTORICAL SOCIETY
7 Randolph Street, Lexington, Virginia 24450
In Campbell House (1830). Local history. Indian artifacts. Agriculture. Industry. Transport. Anthropology. Graphics. Decorative arts.
The Castle (1776) is in the care of the Society.
F. 10-12.

SALE PLANETARIUM
Virginia Military Institute, Lexington, Virginia 24450
Astronomy. Planetarium.
F. 8 p.m. Other times by appointment. Closed Institute vacations.

VMI MUSEUM
Virginia Military Institute, Jackson Memorial Hall, Lexington, Virginia 24450
Local, military and naval history. Costumes.
M.-F. 9-4.30; Sa. 9-12, 2-5; Su. 2-5. Closed New Year, Thanksgiving, Christmas.

LIBERTY

UNION COUNTY HISTORICAL SOCIETY MUSEUM
26 West Union, Liberty, Indiana 47353
County history. Furniture. Paintings. Clocks. Documents.
By appointment.

CLAY COUNTY HISTORICAL MUSEUM
Liberty, Missouri 64068
Building (1877) was former drug store. Local history. Tavern registers. Indian material.
Tu.-Su. 1-5. Closed public holidays.

JESSE JAMES BANK MUSEUM
104 E. Franklin Street, Liberty, Missouri 64068
In old Liberty Bank building (1858). History of local banking.
M.-Sa. 9-12, 1-5; Su. 1-5. Closed New Year, Thanksgiving, Christmas, weekdays Dec. 1 - Feb. 28.

WILLIAM JEWELL COLLEGE MUSEUM
Liberty, Missouri 64068
Geology. Fossils. Zoology. Local flora and fauna. Anthropology. Archaeology. Agriculture. Indian artifacts.
M.-F. 8-5. Closed public holidays, Aug. 1-31.

LIBERTY JAIL MUSEUM
Mississippi and Main Streets, Liberty, Missouri 64068
History of Latter-day Saints.
Daily 8-8.

LIBERTYVILLE

MUSEUM OF LIBERTYVILLE - MUNDELEIN HISTORICAL SOCIETY
413 North Milwaukee Avenue, Libertyville, Illinois 60048
In Ansel B. Cook Memorial Mansion (1878). Local history.
May 1 - Sept. 30, Su. 2-4. Oct. 1 - Apr. 30 by appointment.

LIGONIER

STONE'S TAVERN
State Road 5 and U.S.33, Ligonier, Indiana 46767
Tavern (1839). Local history.
May 1 - Sept. 30, Su. 1-5. Other times by appointment.

FORT LIGONIER MEMORIAL FOUNDATION
Ligonier, Pennsylvania 15658
Restored fort (1758). Museum contains early Americana and material from French and Indian wars.
Mar. 1 - Nov. 30, daily 9-dusk. Closed Christmas and Thanksgiving.

MUSEUM OF FORT LIGONIER MEMORIAL FOUNDATION
Market Street, Ligonier, Pennsylvania 15658
Restoration of Fort (1758). Relics of French and Indian War. Early American furnishings, tools, domestic utensils.
Mar. 1 - Nov. 30, daily 9-dusk.

LIHUE

KAUAI MUSEUM
4428 Rice Street, Lihue, Hawaii 96766
Local history, customs, handicrafts.
M.-Sa. 9.30-4.30.

LIMA

ALLEN COUNTY MUSEUM
620 W. Market Street, Lima, Ohio 45801
Geology. Mineralogy. Palaeontology. Archaeology. Local history, including railway collection of photographs, blueprints, documents. Indian material. Costumes.
Log House (1848), with pioneer furnishings, and MacDonell House (1890) are in the care of the museum.
Tu.-Su. 1.30-5. Closed public holidays.

LINCOLN

POSTVILLE COURT HOUSE AND MUSEUM
914 Fifth Street, Lincoln, Illinois 62656
Local history. Replica (1953) of the Court House, one of the circuit of 8 made famous by Abraham Lincoln 1840-8.
Daily 9-5. Closed New Year, Thanksgiving, Christmas.

CODMAN HOUSE
Codman Road, Lincoln, Massachusetts 01773
House (c.1730, with later additions). 18th-20th century Codman family furnishings.
June-Oct., Tu., Th., Sa. 1-5.

DE CORDOVA AND DANA MUSEUM AND PARK
Sandy Pond Road, Lincoln, Massachusetts 01773
20th century American paintings, drawings, prints, sculpture.
Tu.-Sa. 10-5; Su. 1.30-5.

ELDER ART GALLERY
Nebraska Wesleyan University, 50th and Western Streets, Lincoln, Nebraska 68504
Paintings. Sculpture. Graphics. Handicrafts.
M.-F. 10-5; Sa. 10-4; Su., public holidays 2-5. Closed M. May 15 - Aug. 25; Dec. 1-31, Thanksgiving.

FAIRVIEW MUSEUM
4900 Sumner Street, Lincoln, Nebraska 68506
House (1901-2), home of William Jennings Bryan. Memorabilia of Bryan. Bryan family furnishings and personal possessions, including material brought back from foreign travels.
M.-Sa. 1-4.30; Su. and holidays 2-4.30.

MUSEUM OF NEBRASKA STATE HISTORICAL SOCIETY
1500 R Street, Lincoln, Nebraska 68508
History of Nebraska and the Central Plains. Archaeology. Anthropology. Ethnology. Costumes.
Thomas P. Kennard house (1869), George W. Norris house (1886), Neligh Mills (1873) and Fort Robinson (1902) are in the care of the Society.
M.-Sa. 8-5; Su., public holidays 1.30-5. Closed New Year, Christmas.

NEBRASKA STATEHOOD MEMORIAL
1627 H. Street, Lincoln, Nebraska 68508
In Kennard House (1869), home of Nebraska's first Secretary of State, Thomas P. Kennard. Collections illustrating Nebraska history. Period furnishings.
Tu.-Sa. 9-4; Su., public holidays 2-5. Closed New Year, Christmas.

UNIVERSITY OF NEBRASKA ART GALLERIES
University of Nebraska, Lincoln, Nebraska 68508
20th century American painting, sculpture, graphics.
Tu. 10-10; W.-Sa. 10-5; Su. 2-5. Closed New Year, July 4, Thanksgiving, Christmas and Aug. 17-31.

UNIVERSITY OF NEBRASKA STATE MUSEUM
101 Morrill Hall, 14th and U Streets, Lincoln, Nebraska 68508
Geology. Palaeontology. Botany. Herbarium. Planetarium. Entomology. Zoology. Anthropology. Health sciences.
M.-Sa. 8-5; Su., holidays 1.30-5. W. evening 7-9. Closed Dec. 24-5, 31, Thanksgiving.

OLD LINCOLN COUNTY COURTHOUSE MUSEUM
Main Street, Lincoln, New Mexico 88338
Building (1874) was first store, then (1881) courthouse. Frontier history of Lincoln County. Indian artifacts.
May 1 - Sept. 30, 8-5.30. Oct. 1 - Apr. 30, daily 9-4.30. Closed Christmas.

TUNSTALL STORE
Main Street, Lincoln, New Mexico 88338
Building (c.1870), restored to give impression of store during second half of 19th century.
Daily, May 1 - Sept. 30, 8-5.30; Oct. 1 - Apr. 30, 9-4.30.

WORTLEY HOTEL
Main Street, Lincoln, New Mexico 88338
Building (c.1870), restored and furnished in character with hotel of the period.
Daily, May 1 - Sept. 30, 8-5.30; Oct. 1 - Apr. 30, 9-4.30.

ELEAZAR ARNOLD HOUSE
449 Great Road, Lincoln, Rhode Island 02865
House (1687). Period furnishings.
June-Oct., Tu., Th. 1-5.

MUSEUM OF BLACKSTONE VALLEY HISTORICAL SOCIETY
North Gate Louisquisset Pike, Lincoln, Rhode Island 02863
Local history.
By appointment.

LINCOLN CITY

LINCOLN BOYHOOD NATIONAL MEMORIAL
Lincoln City, Indiana 47552
Material relating to Abraham Lincoln. Outdoor museum.
June 1 - Aug. 31, daily 7-6. Sept. 1 - May 31, 8-5. Closed New Year, Christmas and M., Tu., Nov. 1 - Mar. 1.

LINCOLN PARK

LINCOLN PARK HISTORICAL MUSEUM
1382 Cleophus Street, Lincoln Park, Michigan 48146
Local history.
Sa., Su. 1-4. Other times by appointment.

LINCOLN'S NEW SALEM

LINCOLN'S NEW SALEM VILLAGE
Lincoln's New Salem, Illinois 62659
Wooden houses, shops, stores, workshops, school and Rutledge Tavern.
Oct. 15 - Apr. 15, daily 8.30-4.30. Apr. 16 - Oct. 14, daily 9-5. Closed New Year, Thanksgiving, Christmas.

LINCOLNTON

ELIJAH CLARK STATE PARK MUSEUM
Route 4, Lincolnton, Georgia 30817
Museum building is replica of home of Elijah Clark (c.1770). Local history. Uniforms.
June 1 - Aug. 31: F.-W. 10-6. Mar. 1 - May 30: Sa., Su. 10-6.

LIND

ADAMS COUNTY HISTORICAL SOCIETY MUSEUM
Phillips Building, 2nd Street, Lind, Washington 99341
Local history.
M., W., F. 1.30-3.

LINDENHURST

OLD VILLAGE HALL MUSEUM
215 S. Wellwood Avenue, Lindenhurst, New York 11757
Local history. Industry. Costumes. Photographs.
May 1 - Oct. 31: M., W. 2-4; F. 7-9. Nov. 1 - Apr. 30: W. 2-4; F. 7-9: Sa. and 1st Su. each month 2-4.

LINDSBORG

MCPHERSON COUNTY OLD MILL MUSEUM
120 Mill Street, Lindsborg, Kansas 67456
Geology. Natural history. Local history. Agriculture. Industry. Indian artifacts.
5 buildings. including water-powered flour-mill (1898), are in the care of the Museum.
May 1 - Oct. 31: Tu.-Sa. 9.30-5; Su. 1-5. Nov. 1 - Apr. 30: Tu.-Su. 1-5. Closed New Year, Thanksgiving, Christmas.

BIRGER SANDZEN MEMORIAL GALLERY
401 N. 1st Street, Lindsborg, Kansas 67456
Paintings and graphics by Birger Sandzen. Japanese bronzes. Paintings, watercolours, sculpture, prints, ceramics by other 20th century American artists.
Tu.-Su. 1-5. Closed New Year, Memorial Day, July 4, Christmas.

LINN CREEK

CAMDEN COUNTY MUSEUM
Linn Creek, Missouri 65052
County history.
May-Sept., daily 10-5.

LISBON

LISBON HISTORICAL SOCIETY MUSEUM
100 E. Washington Street, Lisbon, Ohio 44432
Museum building (1803). Furniture. Paintings. Local history. Indian artifacts. Domestic equipment. Harness-making tools.
Oct. 15 - May 31, Tu.-Su. 1-4; June 1 - Aug. 31, Tu.-Sa. 1-4; Sept. 1 - Oct. 14, Tu.-F. 1-4. Closed public holidays.

LITCHFIELD

LITCHFIELD HISTORICAL SOCIETY MUSEUM
On-the-Green, Litchfield, Connecticut 06759
Local history. Indian artifacts. Civil War material. Portraits. Miniatures. Lace. Needles. Bobbins. China. Costume. Archaeology. Folklore. Portraits and miniatures of people important in history of the County. Works by 18th-20th century Litchfield artists, including Ralph East and Austin Purves.
The Tapping Reeve House and the Law School (1774) are in the care of the Society.
May 16 - Labour Day, Tu.-Sa. 11-5; Su. 2-5. Labour Day - May 15, Tu.-Sa. 2-4. Closed public holidays.

LITCHFIELD NATURE CENTER AND MUSEUM
S. of Route 25, Litchfield, Connecticut 06759
Regional geology and botany. Natural history, Habitat groups of local flora and fauna.
June 15 - Labour Day: Tu.-Sa., 10-4.30; Su., 2-5. Apr. 15 - June 14, Labour Day - Oct. 31: Sa., Su., 2-5. Nov. 1 - Apr. 14: by appointment.

TAPPING REEVE HOUSE AND FIRST LAW SCHOOL
South Street, Litchfield, Connecticut 06759
Reeve was Chief Justice of Connecticut. House (1774), Law School (1784). Collection illustrating his life, work and times.
May 15 - Oct. 15, Tu.-Sa. 11-5; Su. 2-5. Closed public holidays.

G.A.R. HALL AND MUSEUM
318 N. Marshall Street, Litchfield, Minnesota 55355
In G.A.R. Hall (1885), with original furnishings. G.A.R. and Civil War material. Local history. Indian artifacts.
M.-Th. by appointment; F., Sa. 1-6; public holidays 10-6.

LITHOPOLIS

WAGNALLS MEMORIAL
150 E. Columbus Street, Lithopolis, Ohio 43136.
Contemporary American paintings. Letters from O. Henry.
M.-Sa. 1-5. Closed public holidays.

LITITZ

JOHANNES MUELLER HOUSE
137-9 Main Street, Lititz, Pennsylvania 17543
House (1792). Period furnishings. Early household items. Farm tools. Handicrafts.
M.-F. 9-5; Sa., Su. 1-5. Closed public holidays.

LITTLE COMPTON

MUSEUM OF LITTLE COMPTON HISTORICAL SOCIETY
West Road, Little Compton, Rhode Island 02837
In Wilbor House (1687-1750) and Wilbor Barn (1850). 17th-18th century furniture, household equipment. Agriculture.
Friends' Meeting House (1800) and Peggotty Studio (1850) are in the care of the Society.
May-Sept., Tu.-Su. 2-5.

LITTLE FALLS

CHARLES A. LINDBERGH HOUSE
Morrison County Road 52, Little Falls, Minnesota 56345
Restored house (1906), where Charles A. Lindbergh Jr. spent much of his boyhood. Exhibits relating to Lindbergh family.
May 1 - Oct. 31, daily 10-5.

MORRISON COUNTY HISTORICAL MUSEUM
Court House, 2nd Street S.E., Little Falls, Minnesota 56345
Local history.
W.-F. 10-12, 1-5. Closed public holidays.

HERKIMER HOME
Route 5S, Little Falls, New York 13365
House (c.1752) was home of Gen. Herkimer, who fought Battle of Oriskany (1777). Original furnishings. Personal possessions and other material illustrating career of Gen. Herkimer. History of Mohawk Valley.
Apr. 1 - Oct. 31, M.-Sa. 9-5; Su. 1-5.

LITTLE FALLS HISTORICAL MUSEUM
Little Falls, New York 13365
Local history.
By appointment.

LITTLE ROCK

ARKANSAS ARTS CENTER
MacArthur Park, Little Rock, Arkansas 72203
Paintings. Sculpture. Graphics. Decorative arts. Costumes. Children's museum. Open-air museum.
M.-Sa. 9-5; Su., public holidays, 12-5. Closed Christmas.

ARKANSAS FIRST STATE CAPITOL
300 W. Capitol Street, Little Rock, Arkansas 72201
In Old State House (1833-6). Furniture, furnishings and decorative arts illustrating history of Arkansas. Gowns worn by wives of State Governors at inauguration ceremony.
M.-F. 8-4. Closed holidays.

ARKANSAS TERRITORIAL CAPITOL RESTORATION
214 East Third Street, Little Rock, Arkansas 72201
13 houses (1824-36), with period furnishings.
Apr. 1 - Oct. 1, Tu.-Sa. 9.30-5; Su., M. 1-5; Oct. 1 - Apr. 1, Tu.-Sa. 10-4.30; Su., M. 1-4.30. Closed New Year, Easter, Thanksgiving, Christmas.

HISTORY MUSEUM
Arkansas History Commission, 300 West Markham Street, Little Rock, Arkansas 72201
In Old State House (1833-40). Portraits of people important in history of Arkansas. Civil War material. Pioneer relics. Indian artifacts.
M.-F. 8-4. Closed holidays.

MUSEUM OF SCIENCE AND NATURAL HISTORY
MacArthur Park, Little Rock, Arkansas 72202
In Tower Building (1838) of the old Little Rock Arsenal. Geology. Natural history. Botany. Anthropology. Local history. Textiles. Glass.
Tu.-Sa. 10-5; Su. 2-5. Closed public holidays.

RIVER MUSEUM
111 E. 3rd Street, Little Rock, Arkansas 72201
History of Arkansas river navigation. Steamboat, towboat and barge exhibits.
M.-Sa. 10-5; Su. 1-5. Closed Memorial Day, Thanksgiving, Christmas, New Year.

VILLE MARRE
1321 Scott Street, Little Rock, Arkansas 72202
House (1881) with period furnishings. Paintings. Decorative arts.
Tu., Th., Sa. 1-5. Closed public holidays.

LITTLETON

LITTLETON AREA HISTORICAL MUSEUM
6028 South Gallop, Littleton, Colorado 80120
Local history. Agriculture. Industry. Transport. Costume. Decorative arts. Medicine. Indian artifacts.
Log cabin schoolhouse (1863) is in the care of the Museum.
M.-F. 8-5; Sa., public holidays 10-5; Su. 1-5. Closed New Year, Easter, Thanksgiving, Christmas.

LIVERMORE

MUSEUM OF HUMBOLDT COUNTY OLD SETTLERS' ASSOCIATION
Livermore, Iowa 50558
In log cabin (1890). House equipment. Tools.
1st Saturday in Sept. 10-5. Other times by appointment.

LIVERPOOL

FRENCH FORT
Onondaga Lake Park, Liverpool, New York 13088
Replica of Jesuit Mission Fort. History of French and Jesuit settlement in area.
Daily 9-dusk.

SALT MUSEUM
P.O. Box 146, Onondaga Lake Park, Liverpool, New York 13088
History of local salt industry. Tools and equipment.
Daily 9-dusk.

LIVINGSTON

ALABAMA-COUSHATTA INDIAN MUSEUM
Alabama-Coushatta Indian Reservation, Route 3, Box 170, Livingston, Texas 77351
Natural history dioramas of Tripelo Gum Swamp and the Big Thicket. History of Texas Indians, especially Alabama and Coushatta tribes. Arrowheads. Basketry. Beadwork.
M.-F. 10-5; Sa., public holidays 9-6; Su. 12.30-6.

POLK COUNTY MEMORIAL MUSEUM
601 W. Church Street, Livingston, Texas 77351
History of Polk County. Geology. Indian material. Tools. Period room. Replica of country store.
Tu., W., F. 9.30-5; Th. 12.30-5; Sa. 9.30-12.30. Other times by appointment.

LLANO

LLANO COUNTY HISTORICAL MUSEUM
310 Bessemer Street, Llano, Texas 78643
History of Llano County. Minerals and gem stones of the region. Natural history. Indian artifacts. Texas Republic currency.
June 1 - Aug. 31: Tu.-Su. 1-6. Sept. 1 - May 31: F.-Su. 1-6.

LOCK HAVEN

HEISEY MUSEUM
E. Water Street, Lock Haven, Pennsylvania 17745
In Heisey House (c.1834). Local history. Indian material.
M.-F. 1-3; Sa., Su. 2-4. Closed Thanksgiving, Christmas, Good Friday, Easter.

LOCKPORT

MUSEUM OF NIAGARA COUNTY HISTORICAL SOCIETY
215 Niagara Street, Lockport, New York 14094
In former Washington Hunt Law office (1835). History of Niagara area. Iroquois Indian culture. Herbarium. Music.
Colonel Bond House (1824) is in the care of the Society.
Tu.-F. 10-5; Sa., Su. 1-5. Closed public holidays.

LOCUST GROVE

SERPENT MOUND
State Route 73, Locust Grove, Ohio
Indian museum at site of mound with serpent effigy. Adena artifacts.
Apr. 1 - Oct. 31, daily 9-5.

LODI

SAN JOAQUIN COUNTY HISTORICAL MUSEUM
11793 North Micke Grove Road, Lodi, California 95240
Anthropology. Local history. Agriculture. Transport. Industry. Indian artifacts.
W.-Su. 10-5. Closed New Year, Thanksgiving, Christmas.

LOGAN

CACHE VALLEY HISTORICAL MUSEUM
68 W. 2nd Street N., Logan, Utah 84321
Local history.
M.-F. 8-5.

INTERMOUNTAIN HERBARIUM
Utah State University, Logan, Utah 84321
Herbarium of vascular plants of the Intermountain Region.
M.-F. 8-5. Other times by appointment.

MAN AND HIS BREAD MUSEUM
Utah State University, Logan, Utah 84321
Agricultural tools, implements and equipment, 1750 onwards.
M.-F. 8-5. Closed public holidays.

LOGANSPORT

CASS COUNTY HISTORICAL SOCIETY MUSEUM
1004 E. Market Street, Logansport, Indian 46947
In Benjamin Long House (c.1851). Local history. Glass. Lustre-ware. Natural history.
Tu.-Sa. 1-5; 1st Su. in month 1-5. Closed public holidays.

LOMITA

KUSKA MUSEUM
24201 Walnut Street, Lomita, California 90717
Americana. Antiques. Jewellery. Dolls.
M.-Sa. 9-6; Su. 12-5.

LOMPOC

LA PURISMA MISSION STATE HISTORIC PARK
Casmalic Road, Lompoc, California 93436
Restoration of a California mission (1813-34). Exhibits illustrating mission life in early California and Indian life during Spanish period.
Nov. 1 - Apr. 30, daily 8-5. May 1 - Oct. 31, daily 9-6. Closed New Year, Thanksgiving, Christmas.

LOMPOC MUSEUM
200 South H Street, Lompoc, California 93436
Geology. Mineralogy. Zoology. Botany. Local history. Industry. Indian artifacts.
M.-F. by appointment; Sa., Su. 1-4.

LOMPOC VALLEY HISTORICAL SOCIETY MUSEUM
207 N. L. Street, Lompoc, California 93436
In Fabing House (1875). Furnishings. Local history. Horse-drawn vehicles.
By appointment.

LONDON

MOUNTAIN LIFE MUSEUM
Levi Jackson Wilderness Road State Park, London, Kentucky 40741
Local history. Indian artifacts. Transport. Costumes.
May 1 - Aug. 31, M.-Sa. 9-5. Sept. 1-30, Su. 9-5.

LONDONVILLE

MUSEUM OF MOHICAN HISTORICAL SOCIETY
R.D.2, Londonville, Ohio 44842
Restored log cabin (c.1835), with exhibits illustrating early pioneer life.
F.-Su. 1-5.

LONE JACK

JACKSON COUNTY CIVIL WAR MUSEUM AND BATTLEFIELD
Lone Jack, Missouri 64070
Civil War history and relics.
Daily 9-5. Closed New Year, Thanksgiving, Christmas.

LONG BEACH

CALIFORNIA STATE COLLEGE GALLERY
Long Beach, California 90801
Paintings. Prints. Sculpture. Drawings.
M.-F. 11-3; Su. 1-3. Closed college vacations.

LA CASA DE RANCHO LOS CERRITOS
4600 Virginia Road, Long Beach, California 90807
In ranchhouse (1844), with period furnishings. Clothing. Tools. Archaeology. Indian material.
W.-Su. 1-5. Closed New Year, Thanksgiving, Christmas.

LONG BEACH MUSEUM OF ART
2300 E. Ocean Boulevard, Long Beach, California 90803
Contemporary European and American, especially Southern Californian paintings, sculpture, prints.
Tu.-F. 10-5; Sa., Su., public holidays 1-5. Closed New Year, Thanksgiving, Christmas.

MUSEUM OF THE SEA ABOARD THE 'QUEEN MARY'
P.O. Box 20890, Pier J, Long Beach, California 90801
In former Cunard liner, 'Queen Mary'. History of Cunard Transatlantic services. Tours of ship. Photographs of Captains and famous passengers. 'Living Sea' exhibit, on past, present and future of the oceans, by Jacques Cousteau.
Daily 9-5.

LONG BRANCH

LONG BRANCH HISTORICAL MUSEUM
1260 Ocean Avenue, Long Branch, New Jersey 07740
In St. James's Chapel (1879). Religious and local history from Civil War to 1914.
By appointment.

LONG ISLAND

LONG ISLAND OLD FIRE ENGINE MUSEUM
2880 Grand Avenue, Baldwin, Long Island, New York 11100
Horse-drawn and motorised fire apparatus, 1837-1926.
Apr. 15 - Dec. 14, Tu.-Sa. 9-5.

LONG LAKE

MUSEUM OF WESTERN HENNEPIN COUNTY PIONEER ASSOCIATION
Long Lake, Minnesota 55356
Local history.
June 1 - Aug. 31, daily 2-5. Sept. 1 - May 31 also Su. 2-5. Other times by appointment.

LONGMEADOW

CODMAN HOUSE
Codman Road, Longmeadow, Massachusetts 01106
House (1734). Period furnishings.
By appointment.

MUSEUM OF LONGMEADOW HISTORICAL SOCIETY
697 Longmeadow Street, Longmeadow, Massachusetts 01106
Local history. 17th-18th century English and American furnishings. Folklore. Handicrafts
Storrs House (1786) is in the care of the Society.
June 1 - Sept. 15: F., Sa. 2-5. Rest of year by appointment.

LONGMIRE

MOUNT RAINIER NATIONAL PARK MUSEUM
Longmire, Washington 98397
Geology. Botany. Natural history. Local history. Indian artifacts.
Longmire cabin (1888) is within the Park area.
Daily 9-6.

LONGMONT

LONGMONT PIONEER MUSEUM
306 Kimbark Street, Longmont, Colorado 80501
History of the St. Vrain Valley. Agriculture. Costumes. Paintings.
M.-Sa. 9-5; Su. 1-5. Closed New Year, Easter, Thanksgiving, Christmas.

LONGVIEW

CADDO INDIAN MUSEUM
701 Hardy Street, Longview, Texas 75601
Caddo Indian material. 18th-19th century Spanish trade items.
Daily 9-6. Closed Christmas.

LOOKOUT MOUNTAIN

CRAVENS HOUSE
Cravens Terrace, Route 4, Lookout Mountain, Tennessee 37409
House (1856). Civil War relics. Period furniture.
Feb. 15 - Dec. 15, Tu.-Sa. 9-5; Su., public holidays 1-5.

LORTON

GUNSTON HALL PLANTATION
Route 282, Lorton, Virginia 22079
House (1755-8), formerly home of George Mason (1725-92). Mason family portraits. 18th century furniture and decorative arts.
Daily 9.30-5. Closed Christmas.

LOS ALAMOS

BANDELIER NATIONAL MONUMENT
Los Alamos, New Mexico 87544
Ruins of Indian cliff-dwellings (A.D. 1200-1500). Museum contains artifacts and other archaeological material from Bandelier and the surrounding Pueblo areas.
Daily 8-5. Closed Christmas.

LOS ALAMOS COUNTY HISTORICAL MUSEUM
1921 Juniper Street, Los Alamos, New Mexico 87544
In former guest cottage of Los Alamos Ranch School (1920). Geology. Mineralogy. Palaeontology. Archaeology. Open-air museum. Children's museum.
Tu.-Th. 12-5; Sa., Su. 1-5. Closed public holidays.

BRADBURY SCIENCE HALL
P.O. Box 1663, Los Alamos, New Mexico 87544
Science. Technology. Archaeology.
M.-F. 8-12, 1-5; Sa. 9-5; Su. 1-5.

LOS ALTOS HILLS

SPACE SCIENCE CENTER
12345 El Monte Road, Los Altos Hills, California 94022
Astronomy. Electricity and electronics. Planetarium. Memorabilia of Lee De Forest.
F. evening, 5-8.

LOS ANGELES

AVILA ADOBE
14 Olvera Street, Los Angeles, California 90012
House (1818), with period furnishings.
Daily, 10-5.

BARLOW SOCIETY FOR THE HISTORY OF MEDICINE
634 South Westlake Avenue, Los Angeles, California 90057
History of medicine. Doctors' equipment, instruments. Pharmacology. Memorabilia of members of Barlow Society.
M.-Sa. 9-5; M. and W. evenings, 5-9.

CALIFORNIA MUSEUM OF SCIENCE AND INDUSTRY
700 State Drive, Los Angeles, California 90037
Geology. Mineralogy. Science and technology. Industry. Transport. Medicine. Aeronautics.
Daily, 10-5. Closed Thanksgiving, Christmas.

EL PUEBLO DE LOS ANGELES STATE HISTORIC PARK
128 Plaza Street, Los Angeles 90060
Site of founding of City of Los Angeles. Exhibits of early California city life.
Daily 10-5. Closed New Year, Thanksgiving, Christmas.

FERNDELL RANGER STATION AND NATURE MUSEUM
5375 Red Oak Drive, Los Angeles, California 90028
Natural history and botany of Southern California.
W.-Su. 1-5. Closed Thanksgiving, Christmas.

FRANCES E. FOWLER JR. FOUNDATION MUSEUM
10884 Weyburn Avenue, Los Angeles, California 90024
Decorative arts. Carved ivory. Ship models. English silver.
M.-F. 1-5. Closed public holidays.

MUSEUM OF GRIFFITH OBSERVATORY
P.O. Box 27787, Los Angeles, California 90027
Geology. Astronomy. Planetarium.
June 15 - Sept. 16, M.-F. 2-10; Sa. 10.30-10; Su., public holidays 1-10. Rest of year Tu.-F. 2-10, Sa. 10.30-10, Su., public holidays 11-10. Closed Christmas.

LOS ANGELES ART ASSOCIATION AND GALLERIES
825 North La Cienga Boulevard, Los Angeles, California 90069
Paintings and sculpture by Southern Californian artists.
M. 7.30 p.m. - 10; Tu.-F. 12-5; Sa. 12-4; Su., 2-4. Closed New Year, July 4, Easter.

LOS ANGELES COUNTY MEDICAL ASSOCIATION LIBRARY AND MUSEUM
634 S. Westlake Avenue, Los Angeles, California 90057
Museum of 19th and early 20th century medical and surgical instruments.
W. 9-9; M., Tu., Th.-Sa. 9-5. Closed New Year, Thanksgiving, Christmas.

LOS ANGELES COUNTY MUSEUM OF ART
5905 Wilshire Boulevard, Los Angeles, California 90036
Archaeology. European and American paintings, sculpture, graphics, decorative arts. Costumes. Tapestries. Stained glass. Oriental glass, textiles.
Tu.-F. 10-5; Sa. 10-6; Su. 12-6.

LOS ANGELES COUNTY MUSEUM OF NATURAL HISTORY
900 Exposition Boulevard, Los Angeles, California 90007
American, especially Californian history. Geology. Palaeontology. Zoology. Natural history. Herbarium. Anthropology. Ethnology. Indian culture. Technology.
Tu.-Su. 10-5.

LOS ANGELES PUBLIC LIBRARY COLLECTIONS
630 W. Fifth Street, Los Angeles, California 90017
Japanese prints. Coloured plates of costumes, 1780-1880. Murals by Albert Herter and Dean Cornwell. Sculpture by Lee Lawrie.
M.-Sa. 10-9.

LUMMIS HOME: EL ALISAL
200 E. Avenue 43, Los Angeles, California 90031
House (1897-1912). Home of Charles F. Lummis, editor of *Los Angeles Times.* Books and personal possessions of Lummis, with his collections of archaeology, ethnology and Indian artifacts.
Su.-F. 1-4. Closed New Year, July 4, Thanksgiving, Christmas.

MUNICIPAL ART GALLERY
4804 Hollywood Boulevard, Los Angeles, California 90027
American and European paintings, sculpture and graphics.
Tu.-Su. 12-5. Closed New Year, July 4, Thanksgiving, Christmas.

MUSEUM OF CULTURAL HISTORY
Haines Hall, University of California, Los Angeles, California 90024
Primitive art and technology. Anthropology.
Tu.-Sa. 12-5; Su. 1-5. Closed University holidays.

NORTON SIMON MUSEUM OF ART
3440 Wilshire Boulevard, Los Angeles, California 90005
19th-20th century European paintings. Sculpture. Graphics. Decorative arts.
By appointment.

SKIRBALL MUSEUM
3077 University Avenue, Los Angeles, California 90007
Jewish history. Archaeology. Coins. Ceremonial art. Textiles. Paintings, sculpture, prints, drawings by Jewish artists.
M.-F. 9-5. Closed public and Jewish holidays.

SOUTHWEST MUSEUM
234 Museum Drive, Los Angeles, California 90065
Archaeology. Anthropology. Ethnology. Paintings. Decorative art. Indian art and artifacts.
Casa de Adobe (1915) is in the care of the Museum.
Tu.-Su. 1-4.45.
Casa de Adobe, W., Sa., Su. 1-4.45.
Museum and Casa de Adobe closed New Year, July 4, Thanksgiving, Christmas.

TOWER GALLERY
City Hall (top floor), 200 N. Spring Street, Los Angeles, California 90012
Paintings by contemporary American artists.
M.-Th. 10-10; F. 11-5; Sa., Su. 11-4. Closed holidays.

UNIVERSITY GALLERIES
University of Southern California, 823 Exposition Boulevard, Los Angeles, California 90007
Archaeology. Paintings. Sculpture. Graphics. Hancock Mansion (1880) and the Gamble House (1907) are in the care of the Galleries.
M.-F. 12-5. Closed August and Christmas and Easter vacation.

UNIVERSITY OF CALIFORNIA AT LOS ANGELES ART GALLERIES
405 Hilgard Avenue, Los Angeles, California 90024
Paintings. Sculpture. 19th and 20th century European and American prints and drawings.
M.-F. 11-5; Sa., Su. 1-5. Closed August.

UNIVERSITY OF CALIFORNIA AT LOS ANGELES BOTANICAL GARDEN AND HERBARIUM
Botany Building, Room 120, Los Angeles, California 90024
World-wide collections, mainly Phanerogam, with emphasis on sub-tropical ornamentals.
M.-Sa. 8-5; Su. 10-4.

LOS BANOS

RALPH LEROY MILLIKEN MUSEUM
City Hall, Los Banos, California 93635
Palaeontology. Local history and archaeology. Archives. Costumes. Ethnology. Indian artifacts.
Sa., Su. 1-5.

LOS GATOS

LOS GATOS MUSEUM
Main and Tait Streets, Los Gatos, California 95030
Geology. Palaeontology. Natural history. Botany. Local history. Costumes. Indian history.
M.-Sa. 1-5; Su. 2-4. Closed public holidays.

LOUISVILLE

LOUISVILLE MUSEUM AND ARCHIVES
Seventh Street, Louisville, Georgia 30434
Early history of Louisville area. Maps. Documents. Indian artifacts.
M.-F. 10-5.

CHURCHILL DOWNS MUSEUM
Louisville, Kentucky 40208
History of the Kentucky Derby.
Daily 9.30-4.30. Race days 9-11. Closed Easter, Christmas, New Year, Derby Day.

EISENBERG MUSEUM
Southern Baptist Seminary, 2825 Lexington Road, Louisville, Kentucky 40206
Biblical museum. Archaeology. Material from excavations at Caesarea and Machserus. Coins. Sculpture. Glass. Lamps.
M.-Sa. 7.30 a.m. - 10 p.m. Closed public holidays.

FARMINGTON
3033 Bardstown Road, Louisville, Kentucky 40205
House (1810). Early 19th century American and English furnishings and kitchen utensils. Working blacksmith's shop.
Tu.-Sa. 10-4.30; Su. 1.30-4.30.

FILSON CLUB
118 W. Breckinridge Street, Louisville, Kentucky 40203
Pioneer history. Domestic equipment. Portraits. Paintings. Indian artifacts. Early American silver. Steamboat pictures and memorabilia.
Oct. - June, M.-F. 9-5; Sa. 9-12. July 1 - Sept. 30, M.-F. 9-5. Closed public holidays.

ALLEN R. HITE ART INSTITUTE
3rd Street, Belknap Campus, University of Louisville, Louisville, Kentucky 40208
13th-20th century European and American paintings, prints, drawings.
M.-F. 8.30-5. Closed public holidays.

KENTUCKY RAILWAY MUSEUM
P.O. Box 295, Upper River Road, Louisville, Kentucky 40201
Transport, especially railways. Local history. Industry. Technology. Children's and junior museum.
May 1 - Sept. 30, Su. 1-5.

MUSEUM OF SCIENCE AND HISTORY
743 S. 5th Street, Louisville, Kentucky 40203
Geology. Mineralogy. Natural history. Science. Indian artifacts. Archaeology. Local history.
Monsarrat Public School (1857) is in the care of the Museum.
M.-F. 9-5. Closed public holidays.

JOSEPH RAUCH MEMORIAL PLANETARIUM
Belknap Campus, University of Louisville, Louisville, Kentucky 40208
Planetarium.
Shows W. 4, F. 8, Su. 3-5. Closed Aug., public holidays.

J. B. SPEED ART MUSEUM
2035 S. 3rd Street, Louisville, Kentucky 40208
European decorative arts of the medieval period and Renaissance. Kentucky portraits. Indian art. Sculpture. Tapestries. Furniture. Elizabethan hall. Miniatures. 18th century porcelain.
Tu.-Sa. 10-4; Su. 2-6. Closed public holidays, Kentucky Derby.

LOVELAND

LOVELAND MUSEUM
5th and Lincoln Streets, Loveland, Colorado 80537
Mineralogy. Natural history. Archaeology. Pioneer history. Paintings. Sculpture. Graphics.
May 1 - Sept. 30, M.-F. 9-8; Sa. 10-4; Su. 1-5. Oct. 1 - Apr. 30, M.-F. 9-4; Sa. 10-4; Su. 1-5. Closed public holidays.

LOWELL

LOWELL ART ASSOCIATION
243 Worthen Street, Lowell, Massachusetts 01852
In Whistler House (1823), birthplace of Whistler. Paintings, drawings by Whistler and his contemporaries. 19th-20th century American paintings, especially works relating to James M. Whistler.
Tu.-Su. 2-4.30. Closed public holidays.

MIDDLESEX CANAL MUSEUM
Alumni Library, Lowell Technical Institute, Textile Avenue, Lowell, Massachusetts 01854
History of Middlesex Canal.
M.-F. 9-4.

MUSEUM OF LOWELL HISTORICAL SOCIETY
401 Merrimack Street, Lowell, Massachusetts 01852
Local history. Indian artifacts. Paintings.
By appointment.

MUSEUM OF WEST CENTRAL MICHIGAN HISTORICAL SOCIETY
1043 Lincoln Lake Avenue, Lowell, Michigan 49331
Local history. Agricultural machinery and implements. Furniture. Glass. Indian artifacts.
July 4, 9-5. Other times by appointment.

LOWVILLE

LEWIS COUNTY HISTORICAL SOCIETY MUSEUM
Dayon Street, Lowville, New York 13367
Palaeontology. Natural history. Archaeology. Anthropology. Local history. Indian artifacts. Paintings. Industry. Coins.
M.-Sa. 2-5.30. Closed public holidays.

LUBBOCK

TEXAS TECHNICAL UNIVERSITY MUSEUM
4th Street and Indiana Avenue, Lubbock, Texas 79409
Regional palaeontology, archaeology, history, natural history. Costumes of Mexican Indians. Yaqui Indian artifacts. Costumes c.1880-1910.
M.-Sa. 9-5; Su., public holidays 2-5. Closed Thanksgiving, Christmas, New Year.

LUBEC

ROOSEVELT CAMPOBELLO INTERNATIONAL PARK COMMISSION
Lubec, Maine 04652
House, 'Campobello', was summer home of Franklin D. Roosevelt. Memorabilia of Roosevelt.
May 19 - Oct. 17, daily 9-5.

LUCAS

LOUIS BROMFIELD MALABAR FARM FOUNDATION
Route 1, Lucas, Ohio 44843
In The Big House, former home of the author and conservationist, Louis Bromfield. Material relating to his life, writings and farming experiments.
M.-Sa. 9-5; Su. 10-5. Closed Thanksgiving, Christmas.

LUDINGTON

ROSE HAWLEY MUSEUM
305 E. Filer Street, Ludington, Michigan 49431
Local history. Maritime history. Indian archaeology and artifacts.
Courthouse (1849) and a pioneer village (1852) are in the care of the Museum.
July 1 - Aug. 31: daily 10-12, 1-4. Apr. 1 - June 30, Sept. 1 - Dec. 31: W., F. 1-4. Other times by appointment. Closed public holidays.

LUNENBURG

MUSEUM OF LUNENBURG HISTORICAL SOCIETY
School Street, Lunenburg, Massachusetts 01462
Local history.
May 1 - Sept. 30: Sa. 2-4. Other days by appointment.

LURAY

CAR AND CARRIAGE CARAVAN
Luray, Virginia 22835
Old cars. Horse-drawn carriages. Costumes.
Daily, Mar. 1-15, 9-5. Mar. 16 - June 15, 9-7. June 16 - Labour Day, 9-9. Sept. 8 - Nov. 15, 9-7. Nov. 16-30, 9-5.

SHENANDOAH NATIONAL PARK
Dickley Ridge and Burd Visitor Center, Luray, Virginia 22835
Geology. Botany. Entomology. Herpetology. Local history.
Apr. 1 - Nov. 30, daily 9-5.

LUSK

LUSK MUSEUM
Fourth and Main Streets, Lusk, Wyoming 82225
Early Wyoming history. Indian artifacts. Stage coach.
May-Sept. daily 7 a.m. - 9 p.m., and by appointment.

LUTHERVILLE

FIRE MUSEUM OF MARYLAND
1301 York Road, Lutherville, Maryland 21093
Fire-fighting equipment, 1819-1927. Photographs.
Sa. 10-4; Su. 1-4.

LYME

LYME HISTORIANS
Conant Hall, Union Street, Lyme, New Hampshire 03768
Photographs and artifacts illustrating Lyme history.
July 4 - Labour Day: W. 1-5, 7-9; Sa. 1-5. Other days by appointment.

LYNCHBURG

LYNCHBURG HISTORICAL SOCIETY MUSEUM
971 Rothowood Road, Lynchburg, Virginia 24504
In old courthouse (1855). Local history. 18th century furnishings.
Miller-Clayton House (1796) is in the care of the Society.
Sa. 11-3.

RANDOLPH-MACON WOMAN'S COLLEGE ART GALLERY
2500 Rivermont Avenue, Lynchburg, Virginia 24504
Paintings, drawings, prints by American artists.
By appointment. Closed College vacations.

LYNDON

MUSEUM OF OSAGE COUNTY HISTORICAL SOCIETY
Courthouse, Lyndon, Kansas 66451
History of Osage County.
M.-F. 7.30-5. Other times by appointment.

LYNN

LYNN HISTORICAL SOCIETY MUSEUM
125 Green Street, Lynn, Massachusetts 01902
In Hyde-Mills House (1839). Local history.
M.-F. 1-4. Closed public holidays.

LYONS

RICE COUNTY HISTORICAL MUSEUM
221 E. Avenue, Lyons, Kansas 67554
Anthropology. Pioneer history. Indian artifacts.
M.-F. 8-5; Su. 2-5. Closed public holidays.

WAYNE COUNTY HISTORICAL MUSEUM
21 Butternut Street, Lyons, New York 14489
In former sheriff's house (1854). Criminology. Lyons pottery. Clyde glass. Agriculture. Transport. History of Erie Canal.
Daily 2-4. Closed public holidays.

MACHIAS

BURNHAM TAVERN
Main Street, Machias, Maine 04654
House (1770), with early 19th century furnishings. Local history.
June 1 - Sept., M.-F. 10-5; Sa. 10-3.

MACHIASPORT

GATES HOUSE
Machiasport, Maine 04655
House (1800). Local history.
By appointment.

MACKINAC ISLAND

FORT MICHILIMACKINAC
Straits Avenue, Mackinac Island, Michigan 49757
French fort (1715). Stockade, fort buildings and a French village have been reconstructed.
Daily 9-5.

MUSEUM OF MACKINAC ISLAND STATE PARK COMMISSION
Box 370, Mackinac Island, Michigan 49757
History of Mackinac Island. Archaeology. Costumes. Indian artifacts. Museum is based on 8 historic buildings (1715-1897), 2 of them reconstructed.
Usually (but enquire locally) May 16 - Sept. 30, daily 9-6.

STUART HOUSE MUSEUM OF ASTOR FUR POST
Market Street, Mackinac Island, Michigan 49757
Astor fur post agent's house. History of Post. Indian artifacts.
June 15 - Sept. 15: M.-F. 10.30-4.30; Sa., Su. 1-5.

MACON

MUSEUM OF ARTS AND SCIENCES
4182 Forsyth Road, Macon, Georgia 31204
Geology. Natural history. Anthropology. Archaeology. Transport. Paintings. Graphics.
Kingfisher Cabin (c.1928) is in the care of the Society.
M.-Sa. 9-5; Su. 2-5. Closed July 4, Labour Day, Thanksgiving, Christmas.

MUSEUM OF MIDDLE GEORGIA HISTORICAL SOCIETY
Macon Coliseum, Macon, Georgia 31201
Local history, based on preserved historic buildings.
The Ocmulgee National Monument and 4 local buildings, including restored Grand Opera House, are in the care of the Society.
Hay House: Tu.-Sa. 10.30-1.30, 2.30-5.30; Su. 2-5. Cannonball House: Tu.-Su. 2-5. Fort Hawkins: Apr. - Nov., Su. 2-6. Opera House: by appointment.

OCMULGEE NATIONAL MONUMENT
Jeffersonville Road, P.O. Box 4186, Macon, Georgia 31208
Indian history, archaeology, and artifacts.
Earth lodge (c.1015) is in the care of the Monument.
Daily 9-5. Closed Christmas.

MACOMB

UNIVERSITY OF WESTERN ILLINOIS ART GALLERY
Browne Hall, Macomb, Illinois 61455
Contemporary paintings, sculpture, graphics. Ceramics. Glass.
M.-F. 9-5. Closed university vacations.

MADAWASKA

MUSEUM OF MADAWASKA HISTORICAL SOCIETY
Library Building, Main Street, Madawaska, Maine 04756
Local history. Industry. Indian artifacts. Music.
M.-Sa. 3-8.

MADELIA

WATONWAN COUNTY HISTORICAL SOCIETY
P.O. Box 126, Madelia, Minnesota 56062
Local history.
By appointment.

MADISON

MADISON HISTORICAL SOCIETY MUSEUM
953 Boston Post Road, Madison, Connecticut 06443
In Nathaniel Allis House (1740). Local history. Tools and equipment used in agriculture, spinning, weaving, carpentry, shipbuilding. Maps, documents.
Lee Academy (1821) is in the care of the Society.
June 15 - Sept. 15, Tu.-Sa. 10-5.

HISTORIC MADISON
301 W. 1st Street, Madison, Indiana 47250
4 buildings (1818-43), including hospital. Original and period furnishings.
May-Oct., Su.-M. 1-4.30; Sa., Tu. 10-4.30.

JEREMIAH SULLIVAN HOUSE
304 W. 2nd Street, Madison, Indiana 47250
House (1818) with original furnishings.
May 1 - Nov. 1, M. 1-4.30; Tu.-Sa. 10-4.30; Su. 1-4.30. Public holidays by appointment.

J. F. D. LANIER MEMORIAL
W. 1st Street, Madison, Indiana 47250
Material relating to J. F. D. Lanier.
Apr. 1 - Oct. 31: daily, public holidays, 9-12, 1-4.30. Nov. 1 - Apr. 1: Tu.-Su. 9-12, 1-4.30. Closed New Year, Thanksgiving, Christmas.

SHREWSBURY HOUSE MUSEUM
301 W. 1st Street, Madison, Indiana 47250
House (1846-9), with period furnishings.
Mar. 1 - Dec. 31, daily 9-5. Jan., Feb., by appointment.

MUSEUM OF LAC QUI PARLE COUNTY HISTORICAL SOCIETY
Fairgrounds, Madison, Minnesota 56256
Indian and pioneer history. Textiles.
Log cabin (1872) and rural school museum (1900) are in the care of the Society.
Oct. 1 - Apr. 30: W., F. 1-4.

MADISON HISTORICAL SOCIETY MUSEUM
Main Street, Madison, New Hampshire 03849
Early Americana. Documents. Manuscripts.
July 7 - Aug. 25, Tu. 2-4.

LAKE COUNTY HISTORICAL MUSEUM
Madison, South Dakota 57042
County and State history. Farm implements. Household equipment. Indian artifacts. Coins.
Tu.-Th., Su. 2-5. Closed Thanksgiving, Christmas, New Year.

PRAIRIE VILLAGE
Highways 34 and 81 W, Box 256, Madison, South Dakota 57042
19th century buildings, including school. Period furnishings.
May-Sept., daily 8-8.

ELVEHJEM ART CENTER
800 University Avenue, Madison, Wisconsin 53706
Paintings. Sculpture. Prints. Drawings. Decorative arts. Archaeology.
M.-Sa. 9-4.45; Su. 1-4.45. Closed public holidays.

GRAND ARMY OF THE REPUBLIC, MEMORIAL HALL
State Capitol, 419N, Madison, Wisconsin 53702
Relics of Civil War and Spanish American War.
M.-F. 9-4. Closed public holidays.

MADISON ART CENTER
720 E. Gorham, Madison, Wisconsin 53703
Paintings. Sculpture. Graphics.
Daily 9.30-5.

MUSEUM OF STATE HISTORICAL SOCIETY OF WASHINGTON
816 State Street, Madison, Wisconsin 53706
History of Wisconsin from prehistoric to modern times. Indian material. Anthropology. Ethnology. Civil war relics. Handicrafts. Costumes. Theatre and circus history.
M.-F. 8-5. Closed public holidays.

UNIVERSITY OF WISCONSIN ZOOLOGICAL MUSEUM
Lowell Noland Building, Madison, Wisconsin 53706
Palaeontology. Molluscs. Fishes. Mammals. Spiders. Snakes. Birds.
M.-F. 9-5. Closed Aug. 1-31, public holidays.

WASHBURN OBSERVATORY
University of Wisconsin, Sterling Hall, North Charter Street (6), Madison, Wisconsin 53706
Planetarium. Astronomical instruments. Old Observatory (1878).
Telescope in old observatory: 1st and 3rd W. of each month, 2 hours after dark.
Planetarium: regular evening schedule during academic year.

THE WISCONSIN UNION
University of Wisconsin, University Art Gallery, 770 Langden Street, Madison, Wisconsin 53706
Paintings, drawings, prints by American, especially Wisconsin artists. Japanese prints.
Daily 9 a.m. - 10 p.m. Closed Christmas.

MADISONVILLE

YESTERYEAR
Interstate 45 at OSR Exit, Madisonville, Texas 77864
Reconstruction of 19th century Western town, with shops, bank, blacksmith's shop. Texas animals.
May 30 - Labour Day, daily 9-6.

MADRID

OLD COAL MINE MUSEUM
Madrid, New Mexico 87033
Local history. Industry. Technology. Transport.
Machine-shop and carpenter's shop (c.1890) are in the care of the Museum.
Daily 8-5.

MAHOMET

EARLY AMERICAN MUSEUM
Box 336, Mahomet, Illinois 61853
Local history. Indian artifacts. Agriculture. 18th century tools.
Easter - Thanksgiving: Tu.-F. 1-5; Sa., Su., public holidays 1-7. Closed Thanksgiving.

MAHWAH

MAHWAH HISTORICAL SOCIETY MUSEUM
Old Station Lane, Mahwah, New Jersey 07430
In old Erie Railroad Station (1871). Railway history.
Apr. 1 - Nov. 30, Su. 2-4.

MAITLAND

ART MUSEUM
Maitland Research Centre, 301 W. Packwood Avenue, Maitland, Florida 32751
Primitive and folk art.
By appointment.

MALDEN

MALDEN PUBLIC LIBRARY
36 Salem Street, Malden, Massachusetts 02148
American and European paintings. Sculpture. Etchings. Lithography.
M.-F. 9.30-9. Oct.-Apr., Sa. 9.30-6.

MALIBU

J. PAUL GETTY MUSEUM
17985 Pacific Coast Highway, Malibu, California 90265
Greek and Roman sculpture. 14th-20th century European paintings. 18th century French furniture and tapestries.
Tu.-F. 12-5; Sa. 9-5.

MONTEREY PENINSULA MUSEUM OF ART
559 Pacific Street, Malibu, California 93940
Early American paintings. Sculpture, paintings, graphics by California artists.
Tu.-F. 10-5; Sa., Su. 2-5.

MALONE

FRANKLIN HOUSE OF HISTORY
216 E. Main Street, Malone, New York 12953
Local history. Agriculture.
July 1 - Sept. 30: Tu.-Sa. 1-5.

MAMMOTH CAVE

MAMMOTH CAVE NATIONAL PARK
Mammoth Cave, Kentucky 44259
Geology. Archaeology.
May 1 - Sept. 30, daily 7.30 a.m. - 8 p.m. Oct. 1 - Apr. 30, daily 8-5.30.

MANASSA

JACK DEMPSEY MUSEUM
Main Street, Manassa, Colorado 81141
Birthplace of the boxer, Jack Dempsey. Items connected with his life and career.
May 1 - Sept. 30, daily 8-6.

MANASSAS

MANASSAS NATIONAL BATTLEFIELD PARK MUSEUM
P.O. Box 350, Manassas, Virginia 22110
House (1828). Civil War history and relics.
Daily 8.30-5.30. Closed Christmas.

MANCHESTER

LUTZ JUNIOR MUSEUM
126 Cedar Street, Manchester, Connecticut 06040
Natural history. Ethnography.
Tu.-Su. 2-5. School holidays 1-5. Closed Aug., public holidays.

MANCHESTER HISTORICAL SOCIETY MUSEUM
106 Hartford Road, Manchester, Connecticut 06040
History of Manchester.
The Cheney homestead (c.1780) is in the care of the Society.
Th., Su. 1-5. Closed public holidays.

CHAPEL ARTS CENTER
St. Anselm's College, Manchester, New Hampshire 03102
Paintings. Graphics. Sculpture.
M.-F. 10-4; Sa., Su. 1-5. Closed Mar. 25 - Apr. 6, June 1-15, Aug. 15 - Sept. 19, Dec. 17 - Jan. 6, Thanksgiving.

CURRIER GALLERY OF ART
192 Orange Street, Manchester, New Hampshire 03104
European and American painting and sculpture. 17th-19th century American furniture, glass, silver, pewter, textiles. 15th century Tournai tapestry.
M.-Sa. 10-5; Su. 2-5. Closed New Year, July 4, Thanksgiving, Christmas.

MUSEUM OF MANCHESTER HISTORIC ASSOCIATION
129 Amherst Street, Manchester, New Hampshire 03104
Local history. Business records. Photographs. Prints. Maps. Tools. Decorative arts. Costumes.
Tu.-F. 9-4; Sa. 10-4. Closed public holidays.

MANCHESTER HISTORIC ASSOCIATION
129 Amherst Street, Manchester, New Jersey 03104
Local history. Handicrafts. Industry. Agriculture. Indian artifacts. Household equipment. Furniture. Glass. Pewter. Maps. Paintings. Prints.
Tu.-F. 9-4; Sa. 10-4.

MUSEUM OF AMERICAN FLY FISHING
Manchester, Vermont 05254
Rods. Flies. Reels. Paintings.
Daily 9-5. Closed Christmas, New Year, July 4, Labour Day, Thanksgiving.

MANCHESTER HISTORICAL SOCIETY MUSEUM
Manchester, Vermont 05254
Local history.
Daily 10-5.

SOUTHERN VERMONT ART CENTER
Manchester, Vermont 05254
Works by 20th century Vermont artists. Paintings. Sculpture. Prints.
June 1 - Oct. 31: Tu., W.-Sa. 10-5; Su. 1-5.

MANDAN

MUSEUM OF FORT ABRAHAM LINCOLN STATE HISTORICAL PARK
Route 2, Mandan, North Dakota 58554
Material relating to General Custer and the 7th Cavalry. Mandan Indian artifacts.
May 1-31, Sept. 1 - Oct. 31, daily 9-5. June 1 - Aug. 31, daily, public holidays 9-9.

MANHASSET

MANHASSET VALLEY SCHOOL
Manhasset Valley Park, N. Hempstead Turnpike and Shore Road, Manhasset, New York 11030
One-roomed school (1826). Early American school books, school materials.
Apr. 1 - Oct. 31: W.-Su. 1-5.

MUSEUM OF HISTORICAL SOCIETY OF THE TOWN OF NORTH MANHASSET
320 Plandome Road, Manhasset, New York 11024
Botany. Herbarium. Agriculture. Local history. Indian artifacts. Transport.
By appointment.

MANHATTAN

GOODNOW HOUSE
Manhattan, Kansas 66502
Home of Isac Goodnow, the early Kansas educationist. Furnished in period style.
Tu.-Sa. 10-5.

KANSAS STATE UNIVERSITY HERBARIUM
Division of Biology, Manhattan, Kansas 66502
Herbarium.
M.-F. 8-5; Sa. by appointment. Closed public holidays.

RILEY COUNTY HISTORICAL MUSEUM
Memorial Auditorium Building, 11th Street and Poyntz Avenue, Manhattan, Kansas 66502
History of Riley County. Pioneer relics. Domestic and farm equipment. Indian relics. Weapons. Musical instruments.
Log Cabin (1915-16), with furniture and farm equipment, is in the care of the Museum.
Tu.-Sa. 1-5; Su. 2-4.30. Closed Thanksgiving, Dec. 24-26, Dec. 30 - Jan. 2, Good Friday, Easter.

MANISTEE

MANISTEE COUNTY HISTORICAL MUSEUM
425 River Street, Manistee, Michigan 49660
In Building (1883) of A. H. Lyman Drug Co. Local history. Logging, lumbering. Great Lakes shipping. Railways. Costumes. Country store. Barber's shop. Drug store.
Holly Water Works (1881) is in the care of the Museum.
M.-Sa. 10-5. Closed public holidays except July 4.

OLD WATERWORKS BUILDING MUSEUM
W. 1st Street, Manistee, Michigan 49660
Waterworks building (1881), now used as museum. Lumbering exhibits. Victorian parlours and kitchen. Barber's shop. Logging wheels.
M.-Sa. 10-5; closed public holidays, ex. July 4.

MANISTIQUE

IMOGENE HERBERT HISTORICAL MUSEUM
Deer Street, Manistique, Michigan 49854
Geology. Local history. Indian artifacts.
July 1 - Aug. 31: M.-F. 2-5.

INDIAN LAKE STATE PARK
Manistique, Michigan 49854
Indian artifacts.
May 15 - Sept. 30, daily 8-8.

SCHOOLCRAFT COUNTY POST MUSEUM
104 South Cedar Street, Manistique, Michigan 49854
Victorian house, with period rooms.
On request.

MANITON SPRINGS

CAMERON'S DOLL AND CARRIAGE MUSEUM
218 Becker's Lane, Maniton Springs, Colorado 80829
Dolls and dolls' houses. Horse-drawn carriages.
May 1 - Oct. 30, M.-Sa. 9-5; Su. 10.30-6.

MANITOWOC

MANITOWOC MARITIME MUSEUM
402 N. 8th Street, Manitowoc, Wisconsin 54220
Submarine 'Cobia' (1944). Models and equipment of Great Lakes ships and of submarines.
Daily 10-5. Closed Christmas, New Year.

RAHR CIVIC CENTER AND PUBLIC MUSEUM
610 N. 8th Street, Manitowoc, Wisconsin 54220
Local history. Pioneer collections. Indian archaeology. Maritime history of Great Lakes. Paintings. Drawings. Prints.
M.-F. 9-12, 1-5; Su. 2-5. Closed public holidays.

MANKATO

JEWELL COUNTY HISTORICAL MUSEUM
Mankato, Kansas 66956
Mineralogy. Local history. Industry. Glass.
Tu.-Sa. Closed public holidays.

BLUE EARTH COUNTY HISTORICAL SOCIETY MUSEUM
606 S. Broad Street, Mankato, Minnesota 56001
Local history. Transport. Indian and pioneer artifacts.
Hubbard House (1871), log cabin (1873) and carriage house (1895) are in the care of the Society.
Tu.-Su, 1-5. Closed public holidays.

MANSFIELD

MANSFIELD BATTLE PARK
Route 2, Box 252, Mansfield, Louisiana 71052
Local history, especially Civil War.
Tu.-Sa. 9-5; Su. 1-5. Closed Christmas.

FISHER-RICHARDSON HOUSE OF THE MANSFIELD HISTORICAL SOCIETY
534 Willow Street, Mansfield, Massachusetts 02048
House (1704). Furniture. Household equipment. Material relating to local straw hat industry. Agricultural implements.
June 15 - Sept. 15, Sa., Su. 2-5.

KINGWOOD CENTER
900 Park Avenue W., Mansfield, Ohio 44903
Mineralogy. Botany. Herbarium. Natural history. Paintings. Sculpture.
Easter - Oct. 31, Tu.-Sa. 8-5; Su. 1.30-4.30. Closed public holidays.

MANTEO

BODIE ISLAND VISITOR CENTER
P.O. Box 457, Manteo, North Carolina 27954
In Coast Guard Station (1872). Natural history. Local history.
June 15 - Labour Day, daily 9-6.

CAPE HATTERAS NATIONAL SEASHORE MUSEUM OF THE SEA
Manteo, North Carolina 27959
Formerly Cape Hatteras Lighthouse Keeper's house. Exhibits showing history and natural history of Cape Hatteras. Cape Hatteras Lighthouse (1870) is open to public.
June 15 - Labour Day, daily 8-5.

CAPE HATTERAS NATIONAL SEASHORE OCRACOKE VISITOR CENTER
Manteo, P.O. Box 457, North Carolina 27954
History and natural history of Ocracoke Island.
Daily 8-4.30.

FORT RALEIGH NATIONAL HISTORIC SITE
Manteo, North Carolina 27954
Site of first English colony in America (1585). History of colony. Restored fort (c.1590). Indian artifacts.
June 19 - Aug. 30, daily 8 a.m. - 8.15 p.m. Rest of year, 8-4.30.

ROANOAK ISLAND HISTORICAL PARK MUSEUM
P.O. Box 906, Manteo, North Carolina 27954
Indian village museum, with working exhibits.
Oct.-Apr., M.-Sa. 10-5; Su. 1-5. Rest of year, M., W., F. 10-5, 8.30-10. Closed Christmas, New Year.

WRIGHT BROTHERS NATIONAL MONUMENT
Box 457, Kill Devil Hills, Manteo, North Carolina 27954
Site of experimental flights made by Wilbur and Orville Wright (1900-03). History of the pioneering aircraft and flights. Full-scale reproduction of 1902 glider and 1903 flying machine. Reproduction of buildings where the Wrights lived and stored their aircraft.
Daily 8.30-4.30.

MAPLE VIEW

PUTNAM'S ANTIQUE MUSEUM
Route 11, Maple View, New York 13107
Ship models. Clocks. Butterflies and moths.
May 31 - Sept. 30, daily 10-5.

MAQUOKETA

JACKSON COUNTY HISTORICAL MUSEUM
Fairgrounds, P.O. Box 1335, Maquoketa, Iowa 52060
History of Jackson County. Farm implements. Schoolroom. Country store. Dolls.
May 1 - Oct. 1, daily 1-4. Closed public holidays.

SAGERS MUSEUM
Maquoketa, Iowa 52060
Archaeology. Natural history. Local history.
Apr. 15 - Oct. 31, daily 10-5.

MARBLE FALLS

MARBLE FALLS MUSEUM
Lois Anderson Memorial Library, Masonic Building, Highway 281, Marble Falls, Texas 78654
Natural history. Pioneer history. Household equipment. Guns. Prints. Photographs.
Tu., Th.-Sa.

MARBLEHEAD

ABBOT HALL
Marblehead Town Hall, Washington Street, Marblehead, Massachusetts 01945
House (1876). 19th century American paintings, furnishings.
M.-F. 8 a.m. - 9 p.m.; Sa. 8-12; Su. and holidays (June-Sept.) 1-5. Closed holidays in winter.

MARBLEHEAD ARTS ASSOCIATION
8 Hooper Street, Marblehead, Massachusetts 01945
In King Hooper Mansion (1728). Paintings by American artists.
Tu.-Su. 2-5.

MUSEUM OF MARBLEHEAD HISTORICAL SOCIETY
161 Washington Street, Marblehead, Massachusetts 01945
In Jeremiah Lee Mansion (1768). Local and maritime history. Paintings. Portraits. Furniture. Silver. Glass. Logbooks.
May 15 - Oct. 12: M.-Sa. 9.30-4. Closed Memorial Day.

MARBLETOWN

ULSTER COUNTY HISTORICAL SOCIETY
Route 209, Marbletown, New York 12457
In Bevin House (c.1700). 18th century furniture, paintings. Restored 18th century kitchen and scullery. Agricultural tools.
June-Sept. W.-Su. 1-5. Closed national holidays.

MARCELLUS

MARCELLUS HISTORICAL SOCIETY MUSEUM
1 Park Street, Marcellus, New York 13108
Local history.
By appointment.

MARTISCO RAILROAD STATION MUSEUM
Route 174, Marcellus, New York 13108
Restored railway depot (1870). Railway history.
May 3 - Oct. 25, Su. 2-5.

MARIETTA

KENNESAW MOUNTAIN NATIONAL BATTLEFIELD PARK MUSEUM
Marietta, Georgia 30060
Civil War park museum.
Kolb Farm House (1833) is in the care of the Museum.
Apr. 15 - Sept. 15: M.-Sa. 8.30-5; Su. 9.30-6.

CAMPUS MARTIUS MUSEUM
601 2nd Street, Marietta, Ohio 45750
Local history and archaeology. History of local river navigation. Paintings by Marietta artists. Decorative arts. Costumes. Furniture. Tools.
Ohio Company Land Office (1788) and Rufus Putnam House (1789) are in the care of the Museum.
M.-Sa. 9-5; Su. 1-5. Closed New Year, Thanksgiving, Christmas.

STEAMER 'W. P. SNYDER JR.'
Marietta, Ohio 45750
Steamboat museum in one of the last Ohio River sternwheelers (1918).
Apr. 1 - Oct. 31, daily 9-5.

MARILLA

MARILLA HISTORICAL SOCIETY MUSEUM
Bullis Road, Marilla, New York 14102
Local history.
M.-Sa., by appointment.

MARION

MUSEUM OF WILLIAMSON COUNTY HISTORICAL SOCIETY
South Market, Marion, Illinois 62959
Anthropology. Archaeology. Local history.
By appointment.

GRANT COUNTY HISTORICAL SOCIETY MUSEUM
205 N. Washington Street, Marion, Indiana 46952
Local history.
Su. 1-5.

OCTOGENARIAN MUSEUM
Matter Park, Marion, Indiana 46952
Local history. Furniture. Pioneer tools, household equipment. Indian artifacts.
May 30 - Labour Day, 12-6.

MUSEUM OF MARION COUNTY HISTORICAL SOCIETY
County Court House, Marion, Kansas 66861
Local history.
May 1 - Sept. 30: M.-Sa. 9-12, 2-5. Rest of year by appointment.

CARSON HOUSE
Route 4, Marion, North Carolina 28752
House (1790). Local history. Domestic equipment. Period furnishings. Indian artifacts.
M.-F. by appointment; Sa., Su. 2-5. Closed May 1, Dec. 1.

MUSEUM OF HARDING MEMORIAL ASSOCIATION
380 Mount Vernon Avenue, Marion, Ohio 43302
In President Harding's former home (1890). Original furnishings. Memorabilia of the President.
May 1 - Oct. 31: M.-Sa. 10-5; Su. 1-6. Nov. 1 - Apr. 30: Tu.-Su. 1-5. Other times by appointment. Closed New Year, Thanksgiving, Christmas.

SMYTH COUNTY HISTORICAL MUSEUM
230 N. Church Street, Marion, Virginia 24354
In former schoolhouse (1838). Local history and archaeology. Costumes.
By appointment.

MARIPOSA

MARIPOSA COUNTY HISTORICAL SOCIETY MUSEUM
Jessie Street, Mariposa, California 05338
Gold Rush history. Indian history and artifacts.
May 1 - Sept. 30, Tu.-Su. 10-4. Oct. 1 - Dec. 31, Feb. 1 - Apr. 30, 10-4. Closed Jan. 1 - 31, Easter Su., Christmas.

MARKSVILLE

MARKSVILLE PREHISTORIC INDIAN STATE MONUMENT
P.O. Box 336, Marksville, Louisiana 71351
History of man in Lower Mississippi Valley. Archaeology of mound-builder Indians. Indian artifacts and pottery.
M.-F. 10-4; Sa. 7-4; Su., public holidays 10-6. Closed New Year, Christmas.

MARLBORO

PETER RICE HOMESTEAD
377 Elm Street, Marlboro, Massachusetts 01752
House (1688). Local history. Industry. Indian artifacts.
Oct. 1 - May 31: 1st Sa. in month 10-1.

MARLIN

HIGHLANDS MANSION
Groesbeck Highway, Marlin, Texas 76661
House (1900). Ceilings decorated with gold leaf. Period furnishings.
M.-Sa. 10-4; Su. 1-4.

MARLINTON

POCAHANTAS COUNTY MUSEUM
Seneca Trail, Marlinton, West Virginia 24954
In log cabin (1862). County History. Indian artifacts.
June 1 - Labour Day: M.-Sa. 11-5; Su. 1-5.

MARQUETTE

JOHN BURT HOUSE
220 Craig Street, Marquette, Michigan 49855
House (1858), built by the surveyor and iron mine operator, John Burt. Pioneer and mining relics. Local history. Restored pioneer home.
July 1 - Aug. 31, daily 9-5.

MUSEUM OF BISHOP BARAGA ASSOCIATION
239 Baraga Avenue, Marquette, Michigan 49855
Local history. Indian affairs.
By appointment.

MUSEUM OF MARQUETTE COUNTY HISTORICAL SOCIETY
213 N. Front Street, Marquette, Michigan 49855
Geology. Mineralogy. History of Marquette County and its region. Archaeology. Indian material. Pioneer life. Logging. Shipping. Transport. Ethnology. Folklore. Technology.
John Burt House (c.1858) is in the care of the Society.
M.-F. 9-12, 1-4.30. Closed public holidays.

MARSHALL

CLARK COUNTY MUSEUM
502 S. Fourth Street, Marshall, Illinois 62441
History of Clark County.
W. 2-4; Su. 1.30-4.

HONOLULU HOUSE MUSEUM
P.O. Box 15, Marshall, Michigan 49068
Building (1860). Early settlement of Marshall. School books. Decorative arts. Folklore. Indian artifacts.
Capitol Hill School (1860) is in the care of the Museum.
June 1 - Sept. 30: Tu.-F. 2-5; Sa., Su. 2-6.

LYONS COUNTY HISTORICAL SOCIETY MUSEUM
Marshall Library Building, Marshall, Minnesota 56258
Geology. Natural history. Local history. Pioneer life. Indian artifacts. Civil War documents.
M.-F. 1-5.

MUSEUM OF SALINE COUNTY HISTORICAL SOCIETY
561 W. North Street, Marshall, Missouri 65340
Local history.
By appointment.

HARRISON COUNTY HISTORICAL MUSEUM
Old Courthouse, Peter Whetstone Square, Marshall, Texas 75670
History and development of County, from War of Independence onwards. Pioneer life. Caddo Indian material. Transport. Y.A. Tittle football memorabilia. Transport. Max Cole water colours.
Su.-F. 1.30-4.30. Closed public holidays, Christmas week.

MARSHALLTOWN

CENTRAL IOWA ART ASSOCIATION
Fisher Community Center, 709 S. Center Street, Marshalltown, Iowa 50158
19th century French paintings. 19th-20th century sculpture by American and European artists.
Daily 8.30-5.

MARSHFIELD

HISTORIC WINSLOW HOUSE
Webster and Carswell Streets, Marshfield, Massachusetts 02050
House (1699). Period furnishings. In the grounds is the original Daniel Webster law office, furnished with many of his belongings.
July-Aug. daily ex. Tu., 10-5.

MARTINEZ

JOHN MUIR NATIONAL HISTORIC SITE
4202 Alhambic Avenue, Martinez, California 94553
Local history. Museum complex includes John Muir House and outbuildings (1882-5), with Martinez adobe (1885).
Daily, 8-5. Closed New Year, Thanksgiving, Christmas.

MARTINSBURG

GENERAL ADAM STEPHEN HOUSE
Martinsburg, West Virginia 25401
House (1772-89). Period furniture.
By appointment.

MARYHILL

MARYHILL MUSEUM OF FINE ARTS
U.S. Highway 830, Maryhill, Washington 98620
Northwest Indian artifacts. European and American paintings, sculpture, ceramics, glass. Chessmen. Guns. 17th-20th century French drawings. Portraits of N.W. Indian chiefs. Dolls. Paintings by Sydney Lawrence.
Mar. 15-Nov. 14, daily 9-5.30.

MARYSVILLE

ORIGINAL PONY EXPRESS HOME STATION
809 N. Street, Marysville, Kansas 66508
Pony Express history and mementoes. Agricultural implements. Indian artifacts. Restored Pony Express Barn (1859).
May 1-Sept. 1: M.-Sa. 9-12, 1-5; Su. 2-5.

MUSEUM OF UNION COUNTY HISTORICAL SOCIETY
246 W. 6th Street, Marysville, Ohio 43040
In Henry W. Morey home (1870). Local history. Farm implements. Furniture. Domestic utensils. Military history. Indian arrowheads and tools.
Th. 1.30-5. Closed New Year, Thanksgiving, Christmas.

MARYVILLE

NORTHWEST MISSOURI STATE COLLEGE GALLERY
Maryville, Missouri 64468
American paintings, prints. American and European furniture, decorative arts.
M.-F. 9-5.

MARYVILLE COLLEGE FINE ARTS CENTER
Maryville, Tennessee 37801
Contemporary American and European prints.
M.-F. 8.30-4.30; Sa. 8.30-12.

MUSEUM OF SAM HOUSTON MEMORIAL ASSOCIATION
Box 368, Sam Houston Road, Maryville, Tennessee 37801
In schoolhouse (1794). Local and pioneer history. Stamps.
M.-Sa., 9-dusk.

MASON

MASON COUNTY MUSEUM
300 Moody Street, Mason, Texas 76856
In former schoolhouse (1876). Pioneer life. Material from Fort Mason site.
Apr. 1-Dec. 31, M.-F. 1-5. Sa., Su. 2-5. Jan. 1-Mar. 31, M.-F. 1-5. Other times by appointment.

MASON CITY

CHARLES H. MACNIDER MUSEUM
303 2nd Street S.E., Mason City, Iowa 50401
Paintings, prints, drawings, sculpture, decorative arts, by Iowa and American artists.
Tu., Th. 10-9; W., F., Sa. 10-5; Su. 2-5; Dec. 24, 31, 10-1. Closed public holidays.

MASSENA

MASSENA HISTORICAL CENTER AND MUSEUM
62 Main Street, Massena, New York 13062
Children's Museum. Farm tools. Domestic equipment. History of navigation of St. Lawrence Seaway.
M., W., F. 10-12, 1-4. Closed public holidays, Aug. 28-Sept. 15.

MASSILLON

MASSILLON MUSEUM
Public Library, 212 Lincoln Way E., Massillon, Ohio 44646
Oriental ivories. American and European paintings, sculpture, graphics. American folk art, furniture, decorative arts. European ivories and decorative arts. Indian artifacts. Military history.
M.-W., F., Sa. 10-5. Th. 10-5, 7-9. Closed Sept. 1-30, public holidays.

MATTAPOISETT

MATTAPOISETT HISTORICAL MUSEUM AND CARRIAGE HOUSE
5 Church Street, Mattapoisett, Massachusetts 02739
In Mattapoisett Meeting House (1821). Local history. Agriculture. Handicrafts. Kitchen and spinning equipment. Industry. Whaling. Costumes. Glass. Horse-drawn vehicles.
June 1-Aug. 31: Tu.-Sa. 10-12, 2-5. Other times by appointment.

MAUMEE

WOLCOTT HOUSE MUSEUM
1031 River Road, Maumee, Ohio 43537
House (1827). Local history. Indian artifacts.
Th. 1-4; Su. 2-4.

MAUSTON

BOORMAN HOUSE
211 N. Union Street, Mauston, Wisconsin 53948
House (1877). Local history. Furniture. Farm implements. Indian artifacts. Children's museum.
Oct. 1-Apr. 30, M.-Sa. by appointment. May 1-Sept. 30, 3rd Su. in month 2-4.

JUNEAU COUNTY HISTORICAL SOCIETY MUSEUM
211 N. Union Street, Mauston, Wisconsin 53948
Indian material. Military history.
Apr.-Oct., Su. 2-4. Other times by appointment.

MAXWELL

COMMUNITY HISTORICAL SOCIETY MUSEUM
Maxwell, Iowa 50161
Local history. Indian material. Agriculture. Transport. Costumes. Textiles. Coins. Children's Museum.
June 1-Oct. 31, Su. 2-5; public holidays 10-5.

MAYAGUEZ

MARINE STATION MUSEUM
Department of Marine Sciences, Mayaguez, Puerto Rico 00708
Marine algae herbarium. Fish. Marine invertebrates.
By appointment.

MAZOMANIE

MAZOMANIE HISTORICAL SOCIETY MUSEUM
9 W. Hudson Street, Mazomanie, Wisconsin 53560
Local history. Farm implements. Tools.
May 1-Aug. 31, Su., public holidays 1-5.

McALLEN

McALLEN INTERNATIONAL MUSEUM
2500 Quince Street, McAllen, Texas 78501
Mineralogy. Science.
Tu.-F. 9-5; Sa. 9-4; Su., public holidays 1-5.

McCAMEY

MENDOZA TRAIL MUSEUM AND ADRIAN HOUSE
U.S. 67 E., Santa Fe Park, McCamey, Texas 79752
Frontier history. Memorabilia of ranching and the oil industry. Fossils. Recorded memories of old people. Adrian House (c.1900) has period furnishings.
Tu.-Sa. 1.30-5. Other times by appointment.

McCLELLANVILLE

HAMPTON PLANTATION
McClellanville, South Carolina 29458
Mid 18th century plantation house. Period furnishings.
Nov.-May, daily 9-5.

McCOOK

HIGH PLAINS MUSEUM
423 Norris Avenue, McCook, Nebraska 69001
Local history. Costumes. Pictures painted by German prisoners in World War II.
Daily 1.30-4.30. Closed public holidays.

GEORGE W. NORRIS HOME
706 Norris Avenue, McCook, Nebraska 69001
House (1886), remodelled by Senator George Norris in 1931 as his own private relief act to help his home town during the great depression.
Tu.-Sa. 9-6; Su. 2-6.

McDADE

MCDADE MUSEUM
Main Street, McDade, Texas 78650
McDade history. Replica of kitchen (c.1900). Restorations of saloon (1875), post office, stagecoach stand.
By appointment.

McGREGOR

EFFIGY MOUNDS NATIONAL MONUMENT
P.O. Box K, McGregor, Iowa 52157
Archaeological site museum. Indian artifacts.
Nov. 1-May 31, daily 8-5. June 1-Oct. 31, daily 8-7. Closed Christmas.

McKINNEY

HEARD NATURAL SCIENCE MUSEUM
F.M. 1378, McKinney, Texas 75069
Natural history of N. Central Texas. Habitat groups. Seashells. Marine life. Nature prints.
Tu.-Sa. 9-5; Su. 1-5. Closed New Year, July 4, Thanksgiving, Christmas.

McLEAN

ALANREED-MCLEAN AREA MUSEUM
117 N. Main Street, McLean, Texas 79057
Period rooms. Pioneer relics, including clothing. Exhibit showing 19th century doctor's surgery.
M.-F. 9.30-5.

McNARY

COVERED WAGON TRADING POST
U.S. 80, McNary, Texas 79841
Pioneer, Mexican and Indian material.
M.-Sa. 7-5.

FORT QUITMAN REPLICA
Box 2, Interstate 10 and F.M. 34, McNary, Texas 79841
Scale model of Fort (1858). Weapons. Indian collection.
June 1-Sept. 31, daily 9-5. Oct. 1-May 31: Sa., Su. 9-5.

McPHERSON

McPHERSON MUSEUM
1130 E. Euclid Street, McPherson, Kansas 67460
Local history. Palaeontology. Anthropology. Indian artifacts. Oriental art.
Tu.-Su. 1-5. Closed public holidays.

MEADE

DALTON GANG HIDEOUT MUSEUM
U.S. Highways 54 and 160, Meade, Kansas 67864
Pioneer and Indian relics. Furnishings of 1880s. Guns. Escape tunnel.
Daily 8-5.30 (winter); 7-6 (summer).

MEADENHALL

PROJECT 400
Hillendale and Hickory Hill Roads, Meadenhall, Pennsylvania 19357
Local history and geography.
M.-Sa. 9.30-1, by appointment. Closed public holidays.

MEADVILLE

BALDWIN-REYNOLDS HOUSE MUSEUM
639 Terrace Street, Meadville, Pennsylvania 16335
House (1841-3). Mineralogy. Natural history. Local history. Indian artifacts. Costumes. Paintings. Glass. Coins.
June 1 - Aug. 31: W., Sa., Su. 2-5.

MEDFIELD

MEDFIELD HISTORICAL SOCIETY
Main Street, Medfield, Massachusetts 02052
In the Peak House (1680). Local history.
June-Aug., Su. 2-5.

MEDFORD

BARNUM MUSEUM
Tufts University, Medford, Massachusetts 02155
Circus material connected with P. T. Barnum. Skin of Barnum's elephant, 'Jumbo'. Jenny Lind collection.
M.-F. 9-5. Oct. 1 - Apr. 30: Sa., Su. 2-5.

MEDFORD HISTORICAL SOCIETY MUSEUM
10 Governors' Avenue, Medford, Massachusetts 02155
Local history. Copper utensils of Old Medford Rum Distillery. Wooden water-pipes. Civil War material. Silver. Lustre-ware.
W. 2-4.

MUSEUM OF ROYALL HOUSE ASSOCIATION
15 George Street, Medford, Massachusetts 02155
Late 17th - early 18th century house, with period furnishings. Local history.
May 1 - Oct. 15: Tu.-Th., Sa., Su. 2-5.

MEDICINE LODGE

MEDICINE LODGE STOCKADE
West Fremont, Medicine Lodge, Kansas 67104
Natural history. Local history. Indian artifacts.
M.-Sa. 10-6. Su., public holidays 1-6. Closed Thanksgiving, Christmas.

CARRY A. NATION HOME MEMORIAL
211 West Fowler Street, Medicine Lodge, Kansas 67104
House (1884), home of Carry A. Nation.
Daily 9-5.

MEDINA

MUNSON HOUSE
231 E. Washington Street, Medina, Ohio 44256
Local history. Indian material.
Mar., May, June, Oct., Dec., 2nd M. in month 8-10.

MEDORA

FUR TRADE AND WILD LIFE MUSEUM
Medora, North Dakota 58645
Indian material. Wild life. Fur trade. Costumes. Dioramas of Indian and pioneer life.
May 1 - Sept. 30, daily 9-8.

DE MORES HISTORIC SITE
U.S. Highway 10 and Interstate 94, Medora, North Dakota 58645
House (1883), formerly home of Marquis de Mores. Original furnishings. Ruins of meat-packing plant (1883).
Daily 8-5. Closed Thanksgiving, Christmas.

MEDORA DOLL HOUSE
Medora, North Dakota 58645
Dolls and dolls' furniture, mainly 19th century.
May 1 - Sept. 30, daily 9-8.

THEODORE ROOSEVELT NATIONAL MEMORIAL PARK, VISITOR CENTER
Medora, North Dakota 58645
In Maltese Cross Ranch Cabin (1883). Theodore Roosevelt's first ranch home. Original and period furnishings. Roosevelt memorabilia.
June 15 - Labour Day, daily 8-8. Labour Day - June 14, daily 8-5.

MEEKER

WHITE RIVER MUSEUM
565 Park Street, Meeker, Colorado 81641
Local history. Handicrafts. Tools. Indian artifacts.
Daily 10-12, 1-4. Closed New Year, Christmas.

MELROSE

UPHAM FAMILY SOCIETY
486 Main Street, Melrose, Massachusetts 02346
Owns Phineas Upham House (1703). 18th century furnishings.
M.-F. by appointment.

MEMPHIS

BROOKS MEMORIAL ART GALLERY
Overton Park, Memphis, Tennessee 38112
16th-17th century Italian paintings, sculpture. 18th-20th century American and English paintings, prints. Oriental and European porcelain. Textiles. Glass. Porcelain birds. African, pre-Columbian art.
Tu.-Sa. 10-5; Su. 2-5. Closed New Year, Christmas.

CLOUGH-HANSON GALLERY
Southwestern at Memphis, Department of Art, 2000 N. Parkway, Memphis, Tennessee 38112
Chinese ceramics. Japanese textiles and prints.
M.-Sa. 9-5.

FONTAINE HOUSE
690 Adams Avenue, Memphis, Tennessee 38105
House (1870). Costumes. Period furniture.
Daily 1-4. Closed July 4, Dec. 24-5.

LEE HOUSE
680 Adams Avenue, Memphis, Tennessee 38105
House (1870). Period furnishings.
Daily 1-4. Closed July 4, Dec. 24-5.

E. H. LITTLE GALLERY
Memphis State University Campus, Memphis, Tennessee 38111
Archaeology. Costumes. Paintings. Prints. Drawings.
Oct. 1 - Apr. 30, M.-F. 8-11, 12-4; Su. 2-5. Closed public holidays.

MAGEVNEY HOUSE
198 Adams Street, Memphis, Tennessee 38105
House (1832), was home of first Memphis schoolmaster. Period furniture.
Tu.-Sa. 10-4; Su. 1-4. Closed New Year, Thanksgiving, Dec. 24-5.

MEMPHIS PINK PALACE MUSEUM
232 Tilton Road, Memphis, Tennessee 38111
Astronomy. Palaeontology. Zoology. Ethnology. Local history and archaeology. Textiles.
Tu.-Sa. 9-5; Su. 2-5. Closed New Year, Thanksgiving, Dec. 24-5.

MUSEUM OF THE ASSOCIATION FOR THE PRESERVATION OF TENNESSEE ANTIQUITIES
680-690 Adams Avenue, Memphis, Tennessee 38105
In Fontaine House (1870). Period furniture. Costumes.
Daily 1-4. Closed July 4, Dec. 24-25.

C. H. NASH MUSEUM - CHUCALISSA
1987 Indian Village Drive, Memphis, Tennessee 38109
Archaeology of the mid-south. Reconstructed Indian village. Temple Mound. Burial exhibit.
Tu.-Sa. 9-5; Su. 1-5. Closed Thanksgiving, Dec. 17 - Jan. 7.

SOUTHWESTERN AT MEMPHIS ARBORETUM
2000 N. Parkway, Memphis, Tennessee 38112
Herbarium.
Daily, round-the-clock.

MENDHAM

RALSTON HISTORICAL ASSOCIATION MUSEUM
Route 24, Mendham, New Jersey 07945
Museum building (1732). Local history. Agricultural tools. Industry. Handicrafts. Glass. Herbarium.
June 1 - Nov. 30: Su., public holidays 2-5.

MENDOTA

SIBLEY HOUSE
Mendota, Minnesota 55050
House (1836) was home of 1st Governor of Minnesota. Furniture and personal possessions of Sibley family. Indian handicrafts.
Apr. 15 - Oct. 31: M.-Sa. 10-5; Su., public holidays 1-6. Closed M. from 3rd M. in June to end of Aug.

MENGES MILLS

COLONIAL VALLEY
Menges Mills, Pennsylvania 17346
Restored 18th century village. Water-powered sawmill (1740), grist-mill (1740). Blacksmith's shop. Craftsmen's tools of 1740-1840 period. Kitchen equipment. Period rooms. Farm implements. Transport. Country store.
May 1 - Oct. 31, daily 8-6.

MENLO PARK

EDISON MEMORIAL TOWER AND STATE PARK
Christie Street, Menlo Park, New Jersey 08817
Museum in entrance building to tower contains originals, replicas and models of some of Edison's inventions, and a model of his Menlo Park Laboratory, where he invented the electric light bulb (1879).
Tu.-Sa. 10-12, 1-5; Su. 12-5. Closed Thanksgiving, Christmas, New Year.

MENOMINEE

MYSTERY SHIP
Riverview Park, Menominee, Michigan 49858
Restored 19th century sailing ship, salvaged from Lake Michigan. Now ship museum, with period furnishings.
Daily 9-5.

MENOMONEE FALLS

OLD FALLS VILLAGE
County Line Road, Menomonee Falls, Wisconsin 53051
Local history museum based on Miller Davidson House (1858), log cabin and schoolhouse. 19th century furniture.
May-Oct., Sa., Su. 1-4.

MENOMONIE

ART CENTER GALLERY
University of Wisconsin, 4th Street, Menomonie, Wisconsin 54751
20th century American paintings, graphics, sculpture, ceramics.
M.-F. 9-12, 1-5; Sa., Su. 1-5. Closed public holidays.

DUNN COUNTY HISTORICAL SOCIETY MUSEUM
1020 9th Street, Menomonie, Wisconsin 54751
In Caddie Woodlawn (1857). Local history. Indian artifacts. Paintings. Theatre history.
Rural school (1873) and Mabel Tainter Playhouse (c.1885) are in the care of the Society.
By appointment.

MENTOR

LAKE COUNTY HISTORICAL SOCIETY MUSEUM
8095 Mentor Avenue, Mentor, Ohio 44060
In Lawnfield (1880), former home of President Garfield. Original furnishings. Local history. Decorative arts. Costumes. Memorabilia of the President.
Tu.-Sa. 9-5; Su., public holidays 1-5.

MERCER

JOHNSTON TAVERN
R.D.6, Mercer, Pennsylvania 16137
House (1831). Period furnishings.
May 1 - Oct. 31: Tu.-Sa. 8.30-5; Su. 1-5. Nov. 1 - Apr. 30: Tu.-Sa. 9-4.30; Su. 1-4.30. Closed public holidays.

MUSEUM OF MERCER COUNTY HISTORICAL SOCIETY
119 S. Pitt Street, Mercer, Pennsylvania 16137
In Magoffin House (1821). History of Mercer County. Indian archaeology and artifacts. Pioneer furniture and clothing.
Caldwell School (1880) is in the care of the Society.
Tu.-Th., Sa. 1-4.30; F. 1-4.30, 7-9. Closed public holidays.

MEREDITH

MEREDITH AUTO MUSEUM
Route 3, Meredith, New Hampshire 03523
Cars. Motorcycles. Bicycles. Fire-engines.
July 1 - Labour Day, daily 9-6.

MERIDEN

MERIDEN HISTORICAL SOCIETY MUSEUM
424 West Main Street, Meriden, Connecticut 06450
In Moses Andrew House (1760). Local history. Industry. Costumes. Glass.
Su., W. 2-5. Other times by appointment.

MERIDEN BIRD SANCTUARY AND MUSEUM OF BIRD CONSERVATION
P.O. Box 124, Meriden, New Hampshire 03770
Ornithology. Eggs. Nests. Mounted birds.
By appointment.

MERIDIAN

MERIDIAN MUSEUM OF ART
25th Avenue and 7th Street, Meridian, Mississippi 39301
European and American paintings, sculpture, graphics.
M.-F. 10-5; Sa., Su. 1-5. Closed New Year, July 4, Christmas.

MERION

BARNES FOUNDATION
North Latch's Lane and Lapsley Road, Merion, Pennsylvania 19066
15th-16th century European paintings. 20th century American paintings. Chinese art. African sculpture. American furniture.
Sept.-June, F., Sa. 9.30-4.30.

BUTEN MUSEUM OF WEDGWOOD
246 N. Bowman Avenue, Merion, Pennsylvania 19066
Wedgwood china. Steuber and Galle glass. Jensen silver. Jewish ceremonial art and utensils.
Oct. 1 - May 30: Tu.-Th. 2-5.

MESA VERDE

MESA VERDE NATIONAL PARK MUSEUM
Mesa Verde National Park, Colorado 81330
Park Museum. Dioramas showing life of prehistoric inhabitants of the area. Arts and crafts of modern Indians.
Sept. 1 - May 30, daily 8-5. June 1 - Aug. 31, daily 8-6.30.

MESILLA

GADSDEN MUSEUM
Mesilla, New Mexico 88046
Local history. Furnishings. Paintings.
W., Su. 3-5.

METAMORA

METAMORA COURTHOUSE LINCOLN MEMORIAL
113 E. Partridge, Metamora, Illinois 61548
Local history of the Abraham Lincoln period. Pioneer items.
Daily 9-5. Closed New Year, Thanksgiving, Christmas.

MEXICO

AUDRAIN COUNTY HISTORICAL SOCIETY MUSEUM
501 S. Muldrow Street, Mexico, Missouri 65365
In James Ross house (1857), with period furnishings. Local history. Indian artifacts. Agriculture. Industry. Medicine. Costumes. Currier and Ives prints. Saddle horse paintings, prints.
Dec. 1 - Feb. 28, Tu.-Sa. 2-5. Mar. 1 - Nov. 30, Tu.-Su. 2-5. Closed public holidays.

MIAMI

CAPE FLORIDA STATE RECREATION AREA
U.S. Highway 1, Key Biscayne, Miami, Florida 33100
Old Lighthouse (1846). Replicas of lighthouse-keeper's house and kitchen. History of lighthouse, especially during Seminole wars.
Daily 8-dusk.

HISTORICAL MUSEUM OF SOUTHERN FLORIDA
2010 North Bayshore Drive, Miami, Florida 33137
Local history. Anthropology. Aeronautics. Aviation.
M., F. 9-5, 7.30-10; Tu.-Th., Sa., 9-5; Su. 12.30-10. Closed public holidays, Christmas.

LYMAN ARCHAEOLOGICAL RESEARCH CENTER MUSEUM
Route 2, Miami, Missouri 65344
Oneonta culture site museum. Indian earthworks, burial mounds.
May 15 - Aug. 31, Tu.-Su. 8-5.

MARINE LABORATORY MUSEUM
10 Rickenbacker Causeway, Miami, Florida 33149
Research collection of marine animals, fishes and plants from the West Indies area.
M.-F. 8.30-5. Closed public holidays, university vacations.

MIAMI ART CENTER
7867 N. Kendall Drive, Miami, Florida 33156
Sculpture from Japan, Africa, France, S.E. Asia.
M.-Tu., Th.-F. 10-4.40; W. 10-4.40, 7-10; Sa., Su. 1-7. Closed Aug. 1-31, Memorial Day, July 4, Labour Day, Thanksgiving, Christmas, New Year.

MIAMI MUSEUM OF MODERN ART
381 Northeast 20th Street, Miami, Florida 33137
Contemporary paintings, sculpture, drawings, prints. Oriental art. Primitive art.
Tu.-Sa. 10-4.30. Closed July, Aug., public holidays.

MUSEUM OF SCIENCE
3280 South Miami Avenue, Miami, Florida 33125
Geology. Mineralogy. Astronomy. Planetarium. Natural history, especially birds of South Florida. Marine life. Anthropology. Ethnology. Culture of Florida Indians.
M., F. 9-5, 7.30-10; Tu.-Th., Sa. 9-5; Su. 1.30-10. Closed Christmas.

VISCAYA-DADE COUNTY ART MUSEUM
3251 South Miami Avenue, Miami, Florida 33129
House (1916), formerly James Deering estate, in Italian Renaissance style. 16th-19th century European decorative arts. Paintings. Sculpture.
Daily 9.30-5.30. Closed Christmas.

OTTAWA COUNTY HISTORICAL MUSEUM
Miami, Oklahoma 74354
Indian, western and mining collections.
Th. 2-5. Other times by appointment.

MIAMI BEACH

BASS MUSEUM OF ART
2100 Collins Avenue, Miami Beach, Florida 33139
15th-17th century European painting, sculpture, tapestries. French Impressionist drawings. Jewellery. Ecclesiastical vestments. Costumes. Tibetan bronzes.
M.-Sa. 10-4. Closed Su., public holidays.

MIDDLEBOROUGH

MUSEUM OF MIDDLEBOROUGH HISTORICAL ASSOCIATION
Jackson Street, Middleborough, Massachusetts 02346
Local history. Tom Thumb collection. Portraits. Costumes. Indian artifacts. Folklore. 18th century loom. Carriage house, with 19th century vehicles. 1790 law office.
June 15 - 30: Su. 1-5. July 1 - Aug. 31: W., F., Su. 1-5. Sept. 1 - Oct. 15: Su. 1-5. Closed public holidays.

MIDDLEBURY

JOHNSON GALLERY
Middlebury College, Middlebury, Vermont 05753
World-wide collection of paintings, graphics.
Daily 1-5. Closed public holidays.

SHELDON ART MUSEUM
1 Park Street, Middlebury, Vermont 05753
In the Judd House (1829). Early American furniture, domestic equipment, tools, lamps. Sewing machines. Country store. Tavern. Paintings.
June 1 - Oct. 15: M.-Sa. 10-5. Oct. 16 - May 31: Tu., Th. 1-5. Closed public holidays.

MIDDLEFIELD

MUSEUM OF TOWN OF MIDDLEFIELD HISTORY ASSOCIATION
Middlefield, New York 13405
In former schoolhouse (1875). Local history.
By appointment.

MIDDLESBORO

MUSEUM OF CUMBERLAND GAP NATIONAL HISTORICAL PARK
P.O. Box 840, Middlesboro, Kentucky 40965
History of Cumberland Gap, including its use as crossing by Indians and frontiersmen. Story of Daniel Boone and the Wilderness Road. Civil War actions. Hensley Settlement of Appalachian mountain community. Charcoal iron furnace (c.1815).
June 15 - Labour Day, daily 8-7. Rest of year, daily 8.30-5.

MIDDLETON

MIDDLETON HISTORICAL SOCIETY MUSEUM
King Street, Middleton, Massachusetts 01949
Local history. Craftsmen's tools, including those used by shoe-makers, blacksmiths, peat-cutters, lumber workers. Household equipment. Agricultural implements.
By appointment.

MIDDLETOWN

DAVISON ART CENTER OF WESLEYAN UNIVERSITY
301 High Street, Middletown, Connecticut 06457
In Alsop House (1830-40). 15th-20th century European prints, with strong collections of Dürer, Cranach, Rembrandt, Canaletto, Goya, Millet. 19th-20th century English, American prints. Japanese prints.
M.-F. 9-5; Sa. 9-12, 1-4; Su. 2-5.

MIDDLESEX COUNTY HISTORICAL SOCIETY MUSEUM
151 Main Street, Middletown, Connecticut 06457
In General Mansfield house (1810), with antique furnishings. Local history. Decorative arts.
W., 3-5.

MARLPIT HALL
137 King's Highway, Middletown, New Jersey 07748
House (1684), with 17th and 18th century furnishings, china and portraits.
Tu., Th., Sa. 11-5; Su. 2-5. Closed Jan. 1-31, Thanksgiving, Christmas.

CLOCK COLLECTION
Middletown Savings Bank, 4 South Street, Middletown, New York 10940
Antique clocks.
M.-Th. 9-3; F. 9-5.

MUSEUM OF HISTORICAL SOCIETY OF MIDDLETOWN AND THE WALKILL PRECINCT
Walkill Precinct, 25 E. Avenue, Middletown, New York 10940
Building (1886). Local history. Indian artifacts. Clothing. China.
Sept. 1 - June 30: W. 2-4.30; M., Tu., Th., F. by appointment.

BELLE GROVE
U.S Route 11, Box 57, Middletown, Virginia 22645
House (1794). Period furnishings.
Apr. 1 - Oct. 31: M.-Sa. 10-4; Su. 1-5. Rest of year by appointment.

MIDLAND

MIDLAND CENTER FOR THE ARTS
1801 W. St. Andrews Street, Midland, Michigan 48640
History and character of Midland County and its region.
M.-F. 1.30-3.30; Sa., Su. 1-5.

THE AEROPLANE MUSEUM
Midland-Odessa Air Terminal, Midland, Texas 79701
History of aviation in Midland-Odessa area from 1911 onwards. Restored Pliska aeroplane (1911-12) and other Pliska mementoes. Roberts 1911 aero-engine.
Daily, round-the-clock.

MIDLAND COUNTY HISTORICAL MUSEUM
301 W. Missouri Street, Midland, Texas 79701
Local history and archaeology. Indian artifacts. Taylor-Brown House (1899) is in the care of the Museum.
M.-Th. 12-6; Sa. 9-4. Closed New Year, July 4, Thanksgiving, Christmas.

MUSEUM OF THE SOUTHWEST
1705 W. Missouri Street, Midland, Texas 79701
Local history. Natural science. Planetarium. Paintings by Texas artists. Ceramics.
M.-Sa. 10-5; Su. 2-5. Closed New Year, Easter, July 4, Labour Day, Thanksgiving, Christmas.

PERMIAN BASIN PETROLEUM MUSEUM
408 Wilkinson-Foster Building, Midland, Texas 79701
Paintings of local historical scenes and oil industry. Early oil industry machinery. Geology. Palaeontology. Petroleum technology.
By appointment.

MIDWAY

MIDWAY MUSEUM
U.S. Highway 17, Midway, Georgia 31320
Local history. Furniture and furnishings of the Colonial period.
May 1 - Sept. 30: Tu.-Sa. 9-5.30; Su. 2-5.30. Oct. 1 - Apr. 30: Tu.-Sa. 9-5; Su. 2-5. Closed Thanksgiving, Christmas.

MILAN

THOMAS EDISON BIRTHPLACE MUSEUM
9 Edison Drive, Milan, Ohio 44846
House (1841) where Edison was born. Edison memorabilia and inventions. Photographs.
Apr. 1 - Nov. 30: Tu.-Sa. 9-5; Su. 1-5. Jan. 1 - Feb. 10: by appointment. Feb. 11 - Mar. 31: Sa., Su. 1-5 and by appointment.

MILAN HISTORICAL MUSEUM
10 Edison Drive, Milan, Ohio 44846
House (1840). Mineralogy. Natural history. Ethnology. Indian artifacts. Agriculture. Transport. Maritime history. Country store. Blacksmith's shop. Carriage house. Costumes. Textiles. Dolls. Early American glass. Coins. Children's and junior museum.
Apr. 1 - May 31, Sept. 1 - Oct. 31: Tu.-Su. 1-5. June 1 - Aug. 31: Tu.-Su. 10-5.

MILES CITY

FORT KEOGH MUSEUM
Highway 10, Bypass W., Miles City, Montana 59301
Officers' quarters of Fort Keogh (1877). Indian material.
May 15 - Oct. 30, daily 8-8.

MILFORD

EELLS-STOW HOUSE, MILFORD HISTORICAL SOCIETY
34 High Street, Milford, Connecticut 06460
House (c.1685). Furniture. Local history. Indian artifacts.
Ebenezer Downes House (1785) is also in the care of the Society.
May 30 - Labour Day, W., 1-5, Su., 2-5. Labour Day - May 24 by appointment.

MILFORD HISTORICAL SOCIETY MUSEUM
501 N.W. Front Street, Milford, Delaware 19963
In Parson Thorne house (1750). Local history. Decorative arts.
By appointment.

MUSEUM OF PIKE COUNTY HISTORICAL SOCIETY
Harford Street, Milford, Pennsylvania 18337
Local history.
May 1 - Oct. 31: M.-Th. by appointment; Sa. 2-5. Nov. 1 - Apr. 30: by appointment.

MILLERSBURG

HOLMES COUNTY HISTORICAL SOCIETY MUSEUM
Logsdon Memorial Park, Millersburg, Ohio 44654
History of Holmes County. Furniture. Portraits. Domestic equipment. China. Glass. Guns. Toys.
Sa., Su. 1-5; public holidays 10-4. Other times by appointment.

MILLVILLE

MILLVILLE HISTORICAL SOCIETY, INC.
Columbia Avenue, Millville, New Jersey 08332
In Mansion House (1804). Local history.
By appointment.

WHEATON HISTORICAL ASSOCIATION MUSEUM
Wheaton Village, Millville, New Jersey 08332
History and technology of glassmaking.
M.-Sa. 10-5, Su. 12-5. Closed Thanksgiving, Christmas.

MILTON

BLUE HILLS TRAILSIDE MUSEUM
1904 Canton Avenue, Milton, Massachusetts 01286
Geology. Natural history. Archaeology.
May-Sept., Tu.-Sa. 10-5; Su. 1-5. Rest of year, Th.-Sa. 10-5; Su. 1-5. Closed July 4, Thanksgiving, Christmas, New Year.

MUSEUM OF THE AMERICAN CHINA TRADE
215 Adams Street, Milton, Massachusetts 02186
In Captain R. B. Forbes House (1833). Material relating to China, the China Trade, Abraham Lincoln, the Civil War. Replica of Lincoln's cabin birthplace.
Tu.-Sa. 2-5. Closed public holidays.

SUFFOLK RESOLVES HOUSE
1370 Canton Avenue, Milton, Massachusetts 02186
House (1773). Documents.
W. 2-5.

MILTON HOUSE MUSEUM
Highway 26 and 59, Milton, Wisconsin 53563
Milton House (1844). Costumes. Period furnishings.
Log cabin (1837), Goodrich House (1867) and livery stable (1890) are in the care of the Museum.
May 1 - Oct. 16, daily 10-5.

MILWAUKEE

CHARLES ALLIS ART MUSEUM AND LIBRARY
1630 E. Royall Place, Milwaukee, Wisconsin 53202
In Allen House (1908). Egyptian and Greek terracotta. Phoenician, Greek, Roman and Syrian glass. Oriental ceramics. Chinese jade. American and European paintings. European graphics. French furniture. Decorative arts.
Tu., Th.-Su. 1-5; W. 1-5, 7-9.30. Closed public holidays.

ART HISTORY GALLERIES, UNIVERSITY OF WISCONSIN
Milwaukee, Wisconsin 53201
Paintings. Greek and Russian icons. Sculpture. Graphics. Archaeology.
M.-F. 9-4.30.

GREENE MEMORIAL MUSEUM, UNIVERSITY OF WISCONSIN
3409A N. Downer Avenue, Milwaukee, Wisconsin 53201
Geology. Mineralogy. Fossils from Illinois and Wisconsin.
W., Th. 2-5. Other days by appointment. Closed public holidays.

KILBOURNTOWN HOUSE
Estabrook Park, Milwaukee, Wisconsin 53202
House (1844). Period furnishings. Paintings.
Summer: Su. afternoons and by appointment.

LOWELL DAMON HOUSE
Wauwatosa Avenue and Rogers Street, Milwaukee, Wisconsin 53202
House (1847). Period furnishings.
Su. 2-4 and by appointment.

MARQUETTE UNIVERSITY GALLERY
Milwaukee, Wisconsin 53233
Renaissance religious art. Dürer collection.
Daily 8 a.m. - 10 p.m.

MILWAUKEE ART CENTRE
750 N. Lincoln Memorial Drive, Milwaukee, Wisconsin 53202
Late 19th - early 20th century American, European, paintings. Sculpture. Prints. Decorative arts.
M.-W., F.-Sa. 10-5; Th. 10-10; Su., public holidays 1-5. Closed New Year, Thanksgiving, Christmas.

MUSEUM OF MILWAUKEE COUNTY HISTORICAL SOCIETY
910 N. 3rd Street, Milwaukee, Wisconsin 52303
In former bank (1913). County history. Maritime history. Pioneer life. Transport. Industry and technology, especially brewing. Aviation. Decorative arts. Theatre history.
Kilbourntown House (1844), Lowell Damon House (1846) and Jeremiah Curtis House (1838) are in the care of the Society.
M.-Sa. 9-5; Su. 1-5. Closed public holidays.

MILWAUKEE PUBLIC MUSEUM
800 W. Wells Street, Milwaukee, Wisconsin 53233
Herbarium. Mineralogy. Geology. Palaeontology. Natural history of N., S. and Central America, Africa, Oceania, Asia, Europe. Primitive and folk art. Anthropology. Ethnology. American and European history. Decorative arts. Weapons. Armour. Children's museum. Furniture. Tapestry. Spanish Colonial art. Reconstructions of Mexican and Guatemalan markets.
Daily 9-5. Closed public holidays.

UNIVERSITY OF WISCONSIN FINE ARTS GALLERIES
3200 Downer Avenue, Milwaukee, Wisconsin 53201
20th century American prints, drawings.
M.-F. 12-4; Sa., Su. 1-5. Closed University vacations, public holidays.

MINDEN

KEARNEY COUNTY HISTORICAL SOCIETY MUSEUM
P.O. Box 3, Minden, Nebraska 68959
Local history.
Schoolhouse (1881) is in the care of the Society.
Tu.-Su. 2-4.

PIONEER VILLAGE
Highway 6, Minden, Nebraska 68959
20 buildings reassembled to form village, to show changes in living since 1830. Science and technology exhibits. Industry. Aviation. Agriculture. Paintings. Sculpture. Graphics. Folklore. Music.
Daily 10-5.

CARSON VALLEY HISTORICAL SOCIETY MUSEUM
Minden, Nevada 89423
Mementoes of early settlers. Washoe Indian baskets and other artifacts.
June-Sept., daily 11-5.

MINERAL

LOOMIS MUSEUM
Lassen Volcanic National Park, Mineral, California 96063
Geology. Herbarium. Natural history. Local and Indian history.
May 1 - Sept. 30, 8-8.

MINERAL POINT

MINERAL POINT HISTORICAL SOCIETY MUSEUM
311 High Street, Mineral Point, Wisconsin 53565
House (1855). Geology. Mineralogy. Lead and zinc mining tools. Local history. Costumes. Theatre history.
May 30 - Sept. 15, daily 9-5.

MINERVA

MUSEUM OF MINERVA AREA HISTORICAL SOCIETY
City Hall, Minerva, Ohio 44657
Local history. Household utensils. Clothing. Tools.
3rd Th. evening of each month and by appointment.

MINNEAPOLIS

OTTAWA COUNTY HISTORICAL MUSEUM
101 W. 2nd Street, Minneapolis, Kansas 67104
Local history.
Tu.-Sa. 10-12, 1-5; Su. 1-5.

JAMES FORD BELL MUSEUM OF NATURAL HISTORY
17th Street and University Avenue S.E., Minneapolis, Minnesota 55455
Palaeontology. Ichthyology. Natural history.
M.-Tu., Th.-Sa. 9-5; W. 9-9; Su. 2-5. Closed public holidays.

MINNEAPOLIS INSTITUTE OF ARTS
201 E. 24th Street, Minneapolis, Minnesota 55404
European paintings and sculpture. Period rooms. Decorative arts. Oriental art. Pre-Columbian art. Prints and drawings. Junior museum.
Burbank House, St. Paul (1862), with 17th-18th century period rooms, is is the care of the Institute.
Tu. 10-10; W.-Sa. 10-5; Su. 1-5. Closed Christmas.

MINNEAPOLIS PUBLIC LIBRARY SCIENCE MUSEUM AND PLANETARIUM
300 Nichollet Mall, Minneapolis, Minnesota 55401
Geology. Fossils. Natural history. Marine biology. Science. Egyptian mummies.
Oct. 1 - May 30: M.-Sa. 9-5; Su. 2-5. June 1 - Sept. 30: M.-F. 9-5; Sa., Su. 2-5. Closed public holidays.

MUSEUM OF AMERICAN SWEDISH INSTITUTE
2600 Park Avenue, Minneapolis, Minnesota 55407
Pioneer and immigrant life. 17th-18th century Swedish furnishings. Swedish bridal crowns. Värmland exhibit. Swedish and Swedish-American paintings, textiles, glass, silver, furniture. Porcelain tile fireplaces.
Tu.-Su. 2-5. Closed public holidays.

MUSEUM OF HENNEPIN COUNTY HISTORICAL SOCIETY
2303 3rd Avenue S., Minneapolis, Minnesota 55404
Pioneer life. Furniture. Period kitchen and schoolroom. Miniature village.
M.-F. 9-4.30; Sa., Su. 2-4.30. Closed Sa., June 1 - Aug. 31, public holidays.

UNIVERSITY GALLERY
University of Minnesota, 316 Northrop Memorial Auditorium, Minneapolis, Minnesota 55455
20th century American paintings, sculpture, prints. Decorative arts.
M.-F. 11-4; Su. 2-5. Closed public holidays.

WALKER ART CENTER
Vineland Place, Minneapolis, Minnesota 55403
16th-19th century European paintings. Chinese jades, bronzes, ceramics. Near Eastern, Greek, Roman glass. 20th century American and European paintings, sculpture, graphics.
May 1 - Sept. 30, Tu. Th. 10-9; W., F., Sa. 10-5; Su. 12-6. Oct. 1 - Apr. 30, Tu. 10-9; W.-Sa. 10-5. Closed public holidays.

MISHAWAKA

MISHAWAKA CHILDREN'S MUSEUM
410 Lincoln Way E., Mishawaka, Indiana 46544
Natural history. Archaeology. Local history. Indian artifacts. Costumes. Sculpture.
M.-F. 1-5, Sa. 2-4. Closed Christmas, Easter, school holidays.

MISSION

ZEITNER GEOLOGICAL MUSEUM
Box 67, Mission, South Dakota 57555
Mineralogy. Palaeontology. Sioux and Re Indian artifacts. Natural history.
By appointment.

WILLIAM JENNINGS BRYAN HOUSE
Bryan and Owen Council Roads, Mission, Texas 78572
House (1909), formerly home of Bryan. Period furnishings. Personal possessions of Bryan.
By appointment.

MISSION HILLS

SAN FERNANDO VALLEY HISTORICAL SOCIETY MUSEUM
10940 Sepulveda Boulevard, Mission Hills, California 91340
Local history. Indian artifacts. Paintings. Decorative arts. Costumes.
Andres Pico adobe (1834) is in the care of the museum.
Tu.-Su. 1-4. Closed Easter, Thanksgiving, Christmas.

MISSOULA

MONTANA STATE UNIVERSITY MUSEUM
Fine Arts Building, Missoula, Montana 59801
Frontier life. Guns, 1500 - present day. Oriental art. Montana Indian art, artifacts.
M.-Th. 3-5; Su. 1.30-4.30. Closed university holidays.

MITCHELL

FRIENDS OF THE MIDDLE BORDER PIONEER MUSEUM
1311 S. Duff Street, Mitchell, South Dakota 57301
Pioneer History. Indian artifacts. Transport. Ravenna schoolhouse (1885) and Dimock railway station (c.1905) are in the care of the Museum.
June 1 - Labour Day, M.-Sa. 8 a.m. - 9 p.m.; Su. 1-9.

MOAB

DEAD HORSE POINT STATE PARK MUSEUM
Box 187, Moab, Utah 84532
Geology. Mineralogy. Natural history. Anthropology. Ethnology. Indian artifacts. Local history and archaeology.
Apr. 1 - Dec. 15, daily 9-7.

MOAB MUSEUM
118 E. Center, Moab, Utah 84532
Geology. Gem stones. Uranium mining and milling. Local history. Indian material.
Daily 3-5, 7-9. Closed Christmas, New Year.

MUSEUM OF ARCHES NATIONAL PARK
Moab, Utah 84532
Geology. Botany. Herbarium. Natural history. Entomology. Local history and archaeology.
Turnbow Cabin (1906) forms part of the Monument.
Daily 8-5. Closed New Year, Thanksgiving, Christmas.

MOBILE

HISTORIC MOBILE PRESERVATION SOCIETY
350 Oakleigh Place, Mobile, Alabama 36604
In Oakleigh House (1833). Period furnishings. Local history. Costumes. Civil War relics.
M.-Sa. 10-3.30, Su. 2-4. Closed one week at Christmas, and on public holidays.

MOBILE ART GALLERY
Langan Park, Mobile, Alabama 36608
19th-20th century American and European paintings, sculpture, prints, decorative arts. Wood engravings.
M. 10-9; Tu.-Sa. 10-5; Su. 12-5. Closed New Year, Mardi Gras, July 4, Labour Day, Thanksgiving, Christmas.

MUSEUM OF THE CITY OF MOBILE
355 Government Street, Mobile, Alabama 36602
In 1854 town house. Archaeology. Local, military, marine and naval history. Transport. Gulf Coast Indian artifacts. The Museum is also responsible for the Carlen House (1840), Phoenix Fire Station (1859) and the Mule-Car House (1900).
Tu.-Sa. 10-5; Su. 1-5. Closed New Year, Thanksgiving, Christmas.

MOBRIDGE

LAND OF THE SIOUX MUSEUM
511 N. Main Street, Mobridge, South Dakota 57601
Indian artifacts.
Memorial Day - Labour Day, daily 1-6.

MOCCASIN

PARK MUSEUM
Pipe Spring National Monument, Arizona Highway 389, Moccasin, Arizona 86022
Mormon fort (1869). Mementoes and household equipment of early Mormon settlers.
Sept.-Apr. daily 8-5. June-Aug. daily 8-7.

MOLINE

DEERE AND COMPANY ADMINISTRATIVE CENTER MUSEUM
John Deere Road, Moline, Illinois 61265
History of agriculture and agricultural implements.
M.-F. 9-4.30. Closed public holidays.

MUSEUM OF ROCK ISLAND COUNTY HISTORICAL SOCIETY
822 11th Avenue, Moline, Illinois 61265
House (1880). Local history. Clothing. Agriculture. Indian artifacts.
Apr. 1 - Nov. 30, by appointment. Closed New Year, Christmas.

MONAHANS

SANDHILLS MUSEUM
Sandhills State Park, U.S. 80, Monahans, Texas 79756
Geology, botany, archaeology and history of State Park area.
May 30 - Labour Day, daily 9-6. Rest of year: Sa., Su. 9-6.

T. AND P. SECTION HOUSE MUSEUM
Monahans Sandhill State Park, P.O. Box 1495, Monahans, Texas 79756
Local history. Railway history. Indian artifacts.
By appointment.

MONCLAIR

MONCLAIR ART MUSEUM
3 S. Mountain Avenue, Monclair, New Jersey 07042
American paintings, graphics, sculpture. American Indian art. Chinese snuff bottles.
Sept.-June, Tu.-Sa. 10-5; Su. 2-5.30. Closed Thanksgiving, Christmas, New Year.

MONKTON

BREEZEWOOD FOUNDATION
80 Hess Road, Monkton, Maryland 21111
Oriental sculpture in stone and bronze. Buddhist art.
May 1 - Oct. 31, 1st Sunday in month.

MONROE

MONROE HISTORICAL SOCIETY MUSEUM
Monroe Center, Monroe, Connecticut 06468
Mineralogy. Archaeology. Agriculture. Local history. Folklore. Costumes.
Barn Hill East Village schoolhouse (1800) is also in the care of the Society.
By appointment.

MASUR MUSEUM OF ART
1400 S. Grand Street, Monroe, Louisiana 71201
American paintings, sculpture, graphics. Archaeology.
Tu.-F. 1-4. Sa.-Su., public holidays 2-5. Closed Easter, Thanksgiving, Christmas.

MONROE COUNTY HISTORICAL MUSEUM
320 E. Front Street, Monroe, Michigan 48161
House (1872). Period rooms. Pioneer exhibits. Musical instruments. History of Monroe County. Gen. George Armstrong Custer rooms. Indian history. Costumes. Music.
Bridge School (1830), Eby log cabin (1853), Papermill School Museum (1860) and Sawyer Memorial Building (1873) are in the care of the Museum.
Tu.-Su. 1-5. Closed public holidays.

OLD MUSEUM VILLAGE OF SMITH'S CLOVE
M.D.3, Monroe, New York 10940
39 19th century buildings, with collections illustrating American domestic life. Indian relics. Demonstrations of handicrafts. Workshops. Country store. Dress emporium. Toys. Furniture.
Apr. 15 - Oct. 31, daily 10-6.

MONROEVILLE

MONROE COUNTY MUSEUM AND HISTORICAL SOCIETY
P.O. Box 765, Public Square, Monroeville, Alabama 36400
In County Courthouse (1902). Regional archaeology and history. Agriculture. Geology. Natural history. Anatomy. Indian artifacts. Paintings, graphics, decorative arts, costumes.
M., W., F. 10-3.

MONTCLAIR

MONTCLAIR ART MUSEUM
3 S. Mountain Avenue, Montclair, New Jersey 07042
Greco-Roman pottery. American Indian art. American and European paintings and sculpture. Graphics. Decorative arts. Oriental snuff bottles. Tapestries. Needlepoint. Lace. Silver.
Sept. 1 - June 30: Tu.-Sa. 10-5; Su. 2-5.30. Closed public holidays.

MONTCLAIR HISTORICAL SOCIETY MUSEUM
110 Orange Road, Montclair, New Jersey 07042
Israel Crane House (1796). Period furnishings. Local history.
Sept. 1 - June 30, Su. 2-5.

MONTEREY

COLTON HALL
Monterey, California 93940
In first public building built in California under United States rule.
Californian history. Portraits of delegates to first Californian Constitutional Convention (1849).
Daily, 10-12, 1-5. Closed New Year, Thanksgiving, Christmas.

ALLEN KNIGHT MARITIME MUSEUM
550 Calle Principal, P.O. Box 805, Monterey, California 93940
Maritime history, especially Californian.
M.-F., 10-12, 1-4. Closed public holidays, M., Sept. 15 - June 15.

MUSEUM OF MONTEREY HISTORY AND ART ASSOCIATION
550 Calle Principal, P.O. Box 805, Monterey, California 93940
Maritime history. Paintings. Costume.
Serrano Adobe (1845), Fremont House (1845) and St. James Chapel Library (1876) are in the care of the Museum.
Sa., Su. 1-4. Closed Christmas.

MONTEREY PENINSULA MUSEUM OF ART
559 Pacific Street, Monterey, California 93940
Paintings. Sculpture. Graphics.
Tu.-F. 10-4; Sa., Su. 1-4. Closed public holidays.

MONTEREY STATE HISTORICAL PARK MUSEUM
10 Custom House Plaza, Monterey, California 93940
9 restored and preserved buildings, forming a museum of old Monterey. They include Casa Soberanes (1830), Casa Gutierrez (1841), Larkin House (c.1830), with original furnishings, Pacific Building (1847), with a museum of California history and Indian artifacts, California's first theatre (c.1847), Casa del Oro (c.1850), with trading exhibits, the Custom House (1846) and the Stevenson house (c.1840), with period rooms.
Daily 9-5. Closed New Year, Thanksgiving, Christmas.

ROBERT LOUIS STEVENSON HOUSE
530 Houston Street, Monterey, California 93940
House where Stevenson lived in 1879. Restored and furnished to its appearance at that period. Stevenson memorabilia and works.
Daily, June 10 - Sept. 10, 9-5. Sept. 11 - June 9, 10-5. Closed New Year, Thanksgiving, Christmas.

SAN CARLOS CATHEDRAL
550 Church Street, Monterey, California 93940
Art museum in Royal Presidio Chapel (1794). 18th and 19th century Spanish religious painting and sculpture.
Daily 6.30-9.

U.S. ARMY MUSEUM
Presidio, Monterey, California 93940
In former cavalry supply depot (1908). History of the Presidio and U.S. Cavalry.
W.-F. 11-1, 2-5.

MONTEVIDEO

MUSEUM OF CHIPPEWA COUNTY HISTORICAL SOCIETY
221 N. 1st Street, Montevideo, Minnesota 56265
Museum based on group of preserved and reconstructed buildings. Log cabin (1870), with exhibits of local history, agriculture, and Indian artifacts. Church and rural school (1882). Chippewa City Pioneer Village, replicas of mid-19th century buildings. Swennson House (1901), with furniture and furnishings.
May 17 - Sept. 27: Th.-Su. 1.30-5.30.

MONTGOMERY

ALABAMA DEPARTMENT OF ARCHIVES AND HISTORY
624 Washington Avenue, Montgomery, Alabama 36104
Archaeology. Anthropology. Indian artifacts. Industrial and military history. Costumes. Paintings, sculpture, decorative arts. Life of French and Colonial settlers.
M.-F. 8.4.30; Sa., Su., public holidays 8-11.30, 12.30-4.30. Closed New Year, Christmas.

FIRST WHITE HOUSE OF THE CONFEDERACY
Washington and Union Streets, Montgomery, Alabama 36104
Home of President Jefferson Davis, with his furniture and personal possessions. Civil War relics.
M.-F. 9-4.30; Sa., Su., public holidays 9-11.30, 12-30-4.30. Closed Christmas, New year, Easter Sunday a.m.

W. A. GAYLE PLANETARIUM
1010 Forest Avenue, Montgomery, Alabama 36106
Astronomy. Planetarium.
M.-Th. 8-5; Sa., Su. 2-4.30.

MONTGOMERY MUSEUM OF FINE ARTS
440 South McDonough Street, Montgomery, Alabama 36104
Mineralogy. Palaeontology. American Indian archaeology. Paintings, sculpture, graphic and decorative arts. Civil War relics. Ceramics. Early American lighting. Silver. Glass. Early American portraits.
Tu.-Sa. 10-5; Su. 2.30-5. Closed New Year, July 4, Labour Day, Thanksgiving, Christmas.

PIONEER HISTORICAL ASSOCIATION OF MONTGOMERY
Community Park, Fifth Street S.E., Montgomery, Minnesota 56069
Local history. Pioneer relics. Steam traction engines.
Sept., Oct., daily.

MONTICELLO

ILLINOIS PIONEER HERITAGE CENTER
315 West Main Street, Monticello, Illinois 61856
Local history. Indian artifacts.
Apr. 1 - Sept. 30, daily 9-5. Oct. 1 - Nov. 30, Sa., Su. 9-5.

SULLIVAN COUNTY MUSEUM
Bank Street, Monticello, New York 12701
Local history. Industry. Transport.
Sa. 9-12; W. evening 7-10. Closed national holidays.

MONTICELLO MUSEUM
Public Library, Main Street, Monticello, Utah 84535
Geology. Archaeology. Indian artifacts. History.
June 1 - Aug. 31: M.-F. 2-9. Closed public holidays.

MONTPELIER

WILLIAMS COUNTY HISTORICAL MUSEUM
E. Main Street, Williams County Fairgrounds, Montpelier, Ohio 43543
Local history. Agriculture. Anthropology. Archaeology. Indian artifacts. Railway history.
Lett log-cabin (1850) is in the care of the Museum.
Apr. 1 - Oct. 31, 1st Su. in month 2-4.

VERMONT HISTORICAL SOCIETY MUSEUM
Pavilion Hotel Building, Montpelier, Vermont 05602
Geology, flora and fauna of Vermont. Indian artifacts. Vermont history and archaeology, in exhibits and dioramas. Stephen Daye Press (1638), earliest surviving printing press in N. America.
M.-F. 8-4.30. July 1 - Aug. 31 also Sa., Su. 1-5.

THOMAS WATERMAN WOOD ART GALLERY
135 Main Street, Montpelier, Vermont 05602
Paintings by Thomas Waterman Wood and works by other contemporary American artists.
M.-F. 2-6. Closed public holidays.

MONTREAT

MUSEUM OF HISTORICAL FOUNDATION OF THE PRESBYTERIAN AND REFORMED CHURCHES
Box 847, Montreat, North Carolina 28757
History of Presbyterian and Reformed Churches. Paintings. Sculpture. Costume. Coins. Music.
Sept. 1 - June 30: M.-F. 8.30-4.30; Sa. 8.30-1. July 1 - Aug. 31: M.-Sa. 8.30-5.30. Closed public holidays.

MONTROSE

UTE INDIAN MUSEUM
135 N. 3rd Street, Montrose, Colorado 81401
History and ethnology of Ute Indians. Archaeology. Artifacts. Paintings. Costumes.
Memorial Day - July 3, Labour Day - Sept. 15, daily 9-6; July 4 - Labour Day, daily 9-8; April 15 - Memorial Day, Sept. 15 - last Sunday in Oct., daily 9-5.

MUSEUM OF SUSQUEHANNA COUNTY HISTORICAL SOCIETY
Monument Square, Montrose, Pennsylvania 18801
Local history.
Tu., F. 10-5. June 1 - Sept. 30, W., Th. 1-5, July 1 - Aug. 31, Sa. 2-5. Closed public holidays.

MONTVILLE

MONTVILLE HISTORICAL MUSEUM
Taylortown Road, Montville, New Jersey 07045
In former schoolhouse (1864). Geology. Local history. Agriculture. Indian artifacts. Costumes. Decorative arts. Children's and junior museum.
Sept. 1 - June 30: Sa. 2-4. Closed public holidays.

MOODUS

AMASA DAY HOUSE
Routes 149 and 151, Moodus, Connecticut 06469
House (1816), with Day family furniture and collections of ceramics, wrought iron, toys, mirrors, clocks.
Daily, May 15 - Oct. 15 1-5.

MOORHEAD

MUSEUM OF CLAY COUNTY HISTORICAL SOCIETY
Courthouse, Moorhead, Minnesota 56560
History of Clay County. Domestic equipment. Farm implements. Documents. Ulen Viking Sword.
May 1 - Sept. 30: M.-F. 10-12, 1-5; Su. 2-5.

RED RIVER OF THE NORTH ART CENTER
521 Main Avenue, Moorhead, Minnesota 56560
Contemporary paintings, sculpture, prints by local artists.
M. Tu. 10-5; Th.-Sa. 10-5; W. 10-5, 7-9; Su. 1-5. Closed public holidays.

MOOSE

GRAND TETON NATIONAL PARK MUSEUMS
P.O. Box 67, Moose, Wyoming 83012
Geology. Botany. Herbarium. Natural history. History of fur trade.
Fur Trade Museum: May 1 - Sept. 30, daily 8-7; Oct. 1 - Apr. 30, daily 8-5. Jenny Museum: June 7 - Sept. 15, daily 8-7. Colter Bay Visitor Center: Memorial Day - Sept. 30, daily 8-9.

MOREHEAD CITY

HAMPTON MUSEUM OF MARINE LIFE
U.S. Highway 70, Morehead City, North Carolina 28557
Mounted specimens of fish, birds, snakes, mammals.
Apr.-Oct. Tu.-Sa. 10-5; Su. 2-6.

MORGANTOWN

CREATIVE ARTS CENTER
West Virginia University, Morgantown, West Virginia 26506
Paintings by 20th century American artists. Costumes. Theatre history. Music.
M.-F. 9-12, 1-4. Closed public holidays.

NATURAL WILDLIFE MUSEUM
Morgantown, West Virginia 26506
Preserved water-fowl, reptiles, insects, marine and wild game.
Daily 9-5.

MORIARTY

LONGHORN RANCH AND MUSEUM OF THE OLD WEST
Highway 66, Moriarty, New Mexico 87035
Mining equipment. Horse-drawn vehicles. Indian artifacts. Guns. General store. Barber's shop. Saloon (1880).
Daily 7-6. Closed Christmas.

MORRILL

MUSEUM OF MORRILL HISTORICAL SOCIETY
Morrill, Maine 04952
Local history.
By appointment.

MORRILTON

MUSEUM OF AUTOMOBILES
Route 3, Morrilton, Arkansas 72110
Old cars.
Daily 10-5. Closed New Year, Christmas.

MORRIS

ILLINOIS VALLEY MUSEUM
RR 1, Morris, Illinois 60450
Village museum. Replicas of stores, Indian building. Agricultural implements. Fossils. Costumes.
Heritage House (1868) is in the care of the Museum.
Memorial Day, July 4, Labour Day and Sunday, 1-5. Closed from Labour Day to Memorial Day.

STEVENS COUNTY HISTORICAL MUSEUM
6th and Nevada Streets, Morris, Minnesota 56267
Natural history. Local history. Agriculture. Aviation. Costumes. Indian artifacts. County school.
Carnegie Library (1910) is in the care of the Museum.
Su., Memorial Day, 2-5.

MORRISON

THE FORT
Highway 8, Morrison, Colorado 80465
Local history. Indian artifacts. Katchina dolls and masks. Spanish and Indian medicinal herbs.
M.-Sa. 4.30-12; Su. 12-9. Closed Monday, Jan. 15 - May 1.

MORRISTOWN

MORRIS MUSEUM OF ARTS AND SCIENCES
Normandy Heights and Columbia Roads, Morristown, New Jersey 07960
Physical and earth sciences. Natural history. Archaeology. Industry. African, Oceanic and American Indian art and ethnology. Toys, dolls. 19th century Americana. Decorative arts.
Sept. 1 - June 30: M.-Sa. 10-5; Su. 2-5. July 1 - Aug. 31: Tu.-Sa. 10-4. Closed public holidays.

MORRISTOWN NATIONAL HISTORICAL PARK MUSEUM
230 Morris Street, Morristown, New Jersey 07960
Museum in Ford Mansion (c.1772). Furnishings of Colonial period, including many belonging to Ford family. Material relating to Washington. Reconstruction of Fort Nonsense (1777), Continental Army Hospital and officer's hut (1779-80). Site includes restored farmhouse, Wick House (1750), with period furnishings.
Daily 10-5. Closed Labour Day, Thanksgiving, Christmas, New Year.

SCUYLER-HAMILTON HOUSE
5 Olyphant Place, Morristown, New Jersey 07960
House (1760). Period furnishings.
Tu., Su. 2-5. Washington's birthday, 10-5.

DAVID CROCKETT TAVERN MUSEUM
U.S. Highway 11-E, Morristown, Tennessee 37814
Reconstruction of tavern which was David Crockett's boyhood home. Pioneer furnishings, household equipment.
Apr. 25 - Oct. 31, daily 9-5. Other times by appointment.

MORRISVILLE

PENNSBURY MANOR
R.D.9, Morrisville, Pennsylvania 19067
House was originally planned and built by William Penn (1683). Present buildings are 1945 reconstruction. They include Manor House, brewhouse, bakehouse and plantation office. Period furnishings. Local history and archaeology. Agriculture. Indian material.
May 1 - Oct. 31: M.-Sa. 8.30-5; Su. 1-5. Nov. 1 - Apr. 30: M.-Sa. 9-4.30; Su. 1-4.30. Closed public holidays.

MORRISTOWN HISTORICAL MUSEUM
1 W. High Street, Morrisville, Vermont 05661
Early 19th century costumes. Farm implements. Spinning and weaving equipment. Pitchers. Toby jugs. Clocks and watches. Indian Joe and Molly dolls. Mementoes of Walker family, first Vermont settlers.
Noyes House (1820), with period furnishings, is in the care of the Museum.
May-Oct. daily 2-5, and by appointment.

MORRO BAY

MORRO BAY MUSEUM OF NATURAL HISTORY
State Park Road, Morro Bay, California 93442
Herbarium. Archaeology. Natural history. Indian artifacts.
Daily, 10-5. Closed Monday and Labour Day - June 15.

MORTON

RENVILLE COUNTY HISTORICAL SOCIETY MUSEUM
Morton, Minnesota 56270
In country schoolhouse (1898). Agricultural implements and machinery.
Memorial Day - Labour Day, Su. 12-6.

COCHRAN COUNTY MUSEUM
206 S.W. 1st Street, Morton, Texas 79346
In Morton's first telephone exchange (1925), with early switchboard. History of Cochran County. Ranching industry.
Sa., Su. 2-5. Other times by appointment.

MORTON GROVE

SKOKIE HISTORICAL SOCIETY
7901 Golf Road, Morton Grove, Illinois 60053
Local history.
M.-Sa. 8-5. Closed public holidays.

MOSCOW

LATAH COUNTY PIONEER HISTORICAL MUSEUM
110 South Avenue, Moscow, Idaho 83843
In Governor McConnell Mansion (1893-6). Exhibits showing domestic life in Latah County up to 1914.
By appointment.

UNIVERSITY OF IDAHO MUSEUM
Pine and Idaho Streets, Moscow, Idaho 83843
Geology. Local and natural history. Ethnology. African masks, figurines. Arab textiles.
Daily 1-5. Closed Aug., University vacations.

MOSES LAKE

ADAM EAST MUSEUM
401 5th Street, Moses Lake, Washington 98837
Archaeology. Columbia River Indian artifacts.
May 1 - Aug. 31: Tu.-F. 9-5. Mar. 1 - Apr. 30, Sept. 1 - Oct. 31: Tu.-F. 1-5; Sa., Su. 2-5. Closed Easter, Memorial Day, July 4.

MOULTON

COMMUNITY HERITAGE HOUSE
South Street, Moulton, Texas 77975
House (1909), dedicated to John C. Mueller, local builder and contractor. Early history of Moulton.
1st and 3rd Su. in month, 2-5.

MOULTONBORO

THE OLD COUNTY STORE AND MUSEUM
Routes 25 and 109, Moultonboro, New Hampshire 03254
Building (c.1730) has been store since 1781. Old store furnishings and equipment. Peddler's cart (1841).
May 15 - Jan. 10, daily 9 a.m. - 10 p.m. Jan. 11 - May 14, Tu.-Su. 10-5.

MOUND CITY

LINN COUNTY HISTORICAL SOCIETY MUSEUM
Mound City, Kansas 66056
Local history. Agriculture.
By appointment.

MOUNDSVILLE

MOUND MUSEUM
10th Street and Tomlinson Avenue, Moundsville, West Virginia 26041
Grave Creek burial mound. Archaeology of West Virginia and upper Ohio valley.
Apr. 1 - Dec. 1, daily, dawn-dusk.

MOUNTAINAIR

GRAN QUIVIRA NATIONAL MONUMENT
Route 1, Mountainair, New Mexico 87036
On site of prehistoric Indian ruins. Botany. Herbarium. Natural history. Anthropology. Ethnology. Indian artifacts. San Isidrio Mission Church (c.1629) and San Buenaventura Mission Church (c.1659).
Daily 8-5.

MOUNTAINSIDE

TRAILSIDE NATURE AND SCIENCE CENTER AND PLANETARIUM
Coles Avenue and New Providence Road, Mountainside, New Jersey 07092
Geology. Mineralogy. Fossils. Shells. Natural history. Botany. Entomology. Herpetology. Indian artifacts.
M.-Th. 3-5; Sa., Su., public holidays 1-5. Closed Christmas.

MOUNTAINVILLE

STORM KING ART CENTER
Old Pleasant Hill Road, Mountainville, New York 10953
Sculpture by modern American and European artists.
Apr. 1 - Nov. 30: Tu.-Su. 2-5.30.

MOUNT AUBURN

HUDDLESTON HOUSE MUSEUM
U.S. Highway 40, Mount Auburn, Indiana 47327
In former Stagecoach Inn (1839). Period furnishings. Kitchen equipment.
Daily 10-4.

MOUNT AYR

RINGGOLD COUNTY HISTORICAL SOCIETY MUSEUM
Courthouse, Mount Ayr, Iowa 50854
County history.
Daily 8-5.

MOUNT CARROLL

JAMES SPENCER DICKERSON GALLERY
Shimer College, Mount Carroll, Illinois 61053
Paintings. Sculpture. Prints. Furniture.
Daily 3-5.

MOUNT CLEMENS

TRINITY HISTORICAL MUSEUM
47460 Sugar Bush Road, Mount Clemens, Michigan 48043
Local history.
Sa., Su. 10-1.

MOUNT GILEAD

TOWN CREEK INDIAN MOUND STATE HISTORIC SITE
Mount Gilead, North Carolina 27306
Reconstructions of Indian Temple mound, burial house and priest's house (1450-1550 A.D.). Interpretive exhibits on the site and its people.
Tu.-Sa. 9-5; Su. 2-5. Closed Dec. 24-6.

MOUNT HOLLY

HISTORIC BURLINGTON COUNTY PRISON MUSEUM
128 High Street, Mount Holly, New Jersey 08060
Prison building (1810). Prison history. Local history. Indian artifacts. Military and naval history. Paintings. Sculpture. Graphics.
Tu.-Sa. 10-12, 1-4. Closed public holidays.

JOHN WOOLMAN MEMORIAL
99 Branch Street, Mount Holly, New Jersey 08060
House (1783). Material relating to John Woolman. Period furnishings.
M.-Sa. 10-5, Su. 10-4.

MOUNT McGREGOR

GRANT COTTAGE
Mount McGregor, New York
Cottage in which Gen. U. S. Grant died. Memorabilia of Gen. Grant.
Tu.-Sa. 9-5; Su. 1-5.

MOUNT McKINLEY

MOUNT McKINLEY NATIONAL PARK MUSEUM
McKinley Park, Alaska 99755
Botany. Zoology. Geology. Local history. Open-air museum.
Daily 8-5.

MOUNT OLIVET

BLUE LICKS BATTLEFIELD MUSEUM
Blue Licks Battlefield State Park, Mount Olivet, Kentucky 41064
Mastodon bones. Natural history. Archaeology. Pioneer history. Costumes. Indian artifacts. Decorative arts. Artifacts from Fort Ancient.
Apr. 1 - Oct. 31, daily 9-5.

MOUNTON

COMMUNITY HERITAGE HOUSE MUSEUM
South Street, Mounton, Texas 77975
Social history of the region.
1st and 3rd Su. of each month, 2-5. Other times by appointment.

MOUNT PLEASANT

MUSEUM OF MIDWEST OLD SETTLERS AND THRESHERS ASSOCIATION
R.R.4, Box 46, Mount Pleasant, Indiana 52641
Village history museum, based on log cabin, church, schoolhouse, railway station, barber's shop. Agricultural implements. Furnishings.
M.-F., public holidays 9-4.

HARLAN-LINCOLN HOME
101 W. Broad Street, Mount Pleasant, Iowa 52641
House (1861), formerly home of Senator James Harlan. Original furnishings and family possessions.
Labour Day weekend, 10-5. Other times by appointment.

IOWA WESLEYAN COLLEGE MUSEUM
Mount Pleasant, Iowa 52641
Geology. Hebarium. Zoology. Archaeology.
By appointment.

CENTER FOR CULTURAL AND NATURAL HISTORY
S. Main Street, Mount Pleasant, Michigan 48858
Geology. Mineralogy. Palaeontology. Natural history. Anthropology. Indian artifacts.
M.-F. 12-5; Sa. 12-3. Su, public holidays 1-4. Closed Thanksgiving, Christmas.

MUSEUM OF HISTORICAL SOCIETY OF MOUNT PLEASANT
Union and Concord Streets, Mount Pleasant, Ohio 43939
Local and Quaker history.
May 1 - Oct. 31, M.-Sa. by appointment; Su. 1.30-5.

BOONE HALL
U.S. Highway 17, Mount Pleasant, South Carolina 29464
18th century plantation mansion. Period furnishings. Slaves' cabins.
M.-Sa. 9-5; Su. 1-5.

MOUNT PULASKI

MOUNT PULASKI COURT HOUSE
Mount Pulaski, Illinois 62548
Local history.
Daily 9-12, 1-5. Closed New Year, Thanksgiving, Christmas.

MOUNT VERNON

KNOX COUNTY HISTORICAL SOCIETY, OLD TOOL CRIB
Newark Road, Mount Vernon, Ohio 43050
Tools. Clocks. Steam engines. Musical instruments.
M.-F. 8-5; Sa., Su., public holidays, by appointment.

MOUNT VERNON
Mount Vernon, Virginia 22121
House (c.1690, with later additions), home of George Washington. Washington furnishings, paintings, personal possessions and memorabilia. Tombs of George and Martha Washington.
Mar. 1 - Sept. 30, daily 9-5. Oct. 1 - Feb. 28, daily 9-4.

POPE-LEIGHEY HOUSE
Richmond Highway, Mount Vernon, Virginia 22151
House (1940) designed by Frank Lloyd Wright. Original and period furnishings.
Apr. 1 - Oct. 31: Sa., Su. 9.30-4.30. Rest of year by appointment.

WOODLAWN PLANTATION
Richmond Highway, Mount Vernon, Virginia 22121
House (1803). Period furnishings.
Daily 9.30-4.30. Closed Christmas.

MOUNT WILSON

MOUNT WILSON OBSERVATORY
Mount Wilson, California 91023
26 m. north of Pasadena. Exhibit Hall, with photographs taken with instruments in the Observatory.
M.-F. 1.30-4.30; Sa., Su. 11-4.30. Closed Christmas.

MUNCIE

BALL STATE UNIVERSITY ART GALLERY
Muncie, Indiana 47306
18th-20th century European and American paintings. 20th century American prints, drawings. Roman glass.
M.-F. 10-4, 7-9; Sa., Su. 1.30-4.30. Closed public holidays, university vacations.

GRINTER HOUSE
Muncie, Kansas 66057
Home of Moses Grinter, furnished as it was in the early days of Kansas.
Tu.-Sa. 10-5.

MUNCY

MUNCY HISTORICAL MUSEUM
N. Main Street, Muncy, Pennsylvania 17756
House (1810). Early American and Victorian rooms. Local history and archaeology. Farm implements. Household utensils. Indian artifacts.
2nd F. each month 6-10. Other days by appointment.

MURDO

PIONEER AND AUTO MUSEUM
Murdo, South Dakota 57559
Old cars, tractors. Horse-drawn vehicles.
Apr.-Nov. daily 7 a.m. - 9 p.m.

MURFREESBORO

NORTH CAROLINA MUSEUM
P.O. Box 3, Murfreesboro, North Carolina 27855
In former William Rea store (1790). Local history. Indian artifacts. Gatling artifacts and memorabilia of Gatling family.
Tu.-Sa. 9-5; Su. 1-5. Closed Thanksgiving, July 4, Christmas, New Year.

OAKLANDS
N. Maney Avenue, Murfreesboro, Tennessee 37130
House (1800, with later additions). Period furnishings. Military history to 1865. Local history. Textiles. Medicine.
Apr. 1 - Oct. 31: M.-Sa., public holidays 10-4.30; Su. 1-4.30. Other times by appointment.

STONES RIVER NATIONAL BATTLEFIELD MUSEUM
P.O. Box 1039, Murfreesboro, Tennessee 37130
Civil War relics, especially relating to Battle of Stones River. Local history.
May 1 - Sept. 30, daily 8-6; Oct. 1 - Apr. 30, daily 8-4.30. Closed Christmas.

MURPHY

OWYHEE COUNTY HISTORICAL MUSEUM
Murphy, Idaho 83650
Geology. History of Owyhee County. Agriculture. Indian material.
Th. 9-5; Su. 1-4. Closed Christmas, Thanksgiving.

MURPHYS

OLD TIMER'S MUSEUM
Box 94, Murphys, California 95247
Local history. Anthropology. Indian artifacts.
June 1 - Oct. 31, W.-Su. 10-5.30; Nov. 1 - May 30, Sa., Su. 10-5.30. Closed Thanksgiving, Christmas.

MURRAY

TURTLE MOUND INDIAN MUSEUM
Murray, Nebraska 68409
Natural history. Anthropology. Archaeology. Indian material.
By appointment.

MURRELLS INLET

BROOKGREEN GARDENS
U.S. Highway 17, Murrells Inlet, South Carolina 29576
Outdoor museum of 19th-20th century American sculpture.
Daily 9-4.45. Closed Christmas.

MUSCATINE

LAURER MUSSER ART GALLERY AND MUSEUM
1314 Mulberry Avenue, Muscatine, Iowa 52761
Local history. Ethnology. Paintings. Graphics. Decorative arts.
Tu., Th. 2-5, 7-9; W., F.-Su. 2-5. Closed public holidays.

MUSKEGON

HACKLEY ART GALLERY
296 W. Webster Avenue, Muskegon, Michigan 49440
European, especially French Impressionist, and American paintings, sculpture, prints, decorative arts. Manuscripts. Persian miniatures. Japanese prints. Junior museum.
M.-Sa. 9-5; Su., public holidays 2-5.

MUSKEGON COUNTY MUSEUM
30 W. Muskegon Street, Muskegon, Michigan 49440
Geology. Natural history. Archaeology. Pioneer life. Lumbering. Indian artifacts.
Tu.-Sa. 10-5; Su. 2-5.

MUSKOGEE

BACONE COLLEGE INDIAN MUSEUM
Highways 62 and 16, Muskogee, Oklahoma 74401
Indian artifacts. Blankets. Pottery. Rugs. Birch bark canoe. Indian burial chest.
M.-F. 8-5, by appointment.

FIVE CIVILISED TRIBES MUSEUM
Agency Hill, Honor Heights Drive, Muskogee, Oklahoma 74401
House (1875). Paintings by artists of the Cherokee, Choctaw, Chickasaw, Creek and Seminole tribes. 19th-20th century American paintings, sculpture, decorative art.
M.-Sa. 10-5; Su. 1-5. Closed Christmas.

THOMAS-FOREMAN HOUSE
1419 W. Okmulgee Street, Muskogee, Oklahoma 74401
House (1898), was home of Grant and Carolyn Foreman, historians of Indians and Indian Territory. Original furnishings. Foreman family possessions.
Tu.-F. 9-5; Sa., Su. 2-5.

MYSTIC

DENISON HOMESTEAD
Mystic, Connecticut 06355
House (1717). Rooms furnished in successive periods to illustrate Connecticut life. Furniture and family possessions of eleven generations of Denisons.
May 31 - Oct. 14, Tu.-Su. 1-5; other months by appointment.

MARINE HISTORICAL SOCIETY MUSEUM
Greenmanville Avenue, Mystic, Connecticut 06355
Crafts connected with building, equipping and sailing 19th century ships. Workshops and shops, including sail and rigging lofts, chandler's shop. Paintings of marine subjects. Stamps.
4 ships, including the last wooden whaler, *Charles W. Morgan*, are in the care of the Society.
Oct. 31 - Mar. 29, M.-Su., public holidays 9-4. Mar. 30 - Oct. 30, daily, M.-Su., public holidays 9-5. Nov. 2 - Dec. 31, M.-Su., public holidays 9-4. Closed Christmas, Thanksgiving, New Year.

MYSTIC ART GALLERY
Mystic, Connecticut 06355
Paintings, sculpture, etchings by local artists.
Summer: M.-Sa. 10-5.30; Su. 2-5.

NATURAL HISTORY MUSEUM
Pequot-Sepos Wildlife Sanctuary, Pequot-Sepos Road, Mystic, Connecticut 06355
Birds. Nests. Eggs. Anatomy of birds.
Tu.-Sa. 10-5; Su. 1-5.

WHITEHALL MANSION
Whitehall Avenue, Mystic, Connecticut 06355
Mansion (1750). Local history. Period furniture, silver, pewter. Domestic equipment. Paintings.
Arcade Building, Stonington (1838). Stonington Lighthouse (1842) and Old Bank, Stonington (1851) are in the care of the Stonington Historical Society, associated with the Mansion.
M.-F. 1-4; Su. 1-4. Public holidays 1-4.

NACOGDOCHES

HOGAN MEMORIAL LIBRARY AND MUSEUM
211 S. Lanana Street, Nacogdoches, Texas 75961
Texas pioneer history. Furniture. Household equipment.
M.-Sa. 2-5. Closed public holidays.

OLD NACOGDOCHES UNIVERSITY BUILDING
High School Campus, Nacogdoches, Texas 75961
Original university building (1859). Now museum of local history.
June 1 - Aug. 31: M.-Sa. 10-12, 2-5; Su. 2-5. Rest of year by appointment.

STONE FORT MUSEUM
Stephen F. Austin University, College Drive and Griffith Boulevard, Nacogdoches, Texas 75961
Built (1779) as trading post. Agricultural equipment. Local history. Flags. Coins. Guns. Pottery. Dolls.
M.-Sa. 9-12, 1-5; Su. 1-5. Closed university vacations.

NANTUCKET

PETER FOULGER MUSEUM
Broad Street, Nantucket, Massachusetts 02554
Early Nantucket and New England life and history.
M.-Sa. 10-5.

HADWEN HOUSE-SATLER MEMORIAL
Main Street, Nantucket, Massachusetts 02554
House (c.1770). 18th century furnishings.
June-Sept., daily 10-5.

1800 HOUSE
Mill Street, Nantucket, Massachusetts 02554
House (1800). Folklore. Period furnishings. China. Costumes. Loom.
June 1 - Sept. 30, daily 10-5.

MARIA MITCHELL BIRTHPLACE
1 Vestal Street, Nantucket, Massachusetts 02554
House (1790), was birthplace of Maria Mitchell, pioneer astronomer and educator. Quaker furnishings. Toys. Herbarium. Observatory.
House: June 15 - Sept. 15, M.-F. 10-12, 2-5; Sa. 10-12. Observatory: June 15 - Sept. 15, 9-10.

MUSEUM OF NANTUCKET HISTORICAL ASSOCIATION
Old Town Building, Union Street, Nantucket, Massachusetts 02554
Anthropology. Agriculture. Local history. Maritime history. Whaling. Paintings of ships and ship-captains. Indian artifacts.
June 12 - Oct. 12: Daily 10-5.

NANTUCKET WHALING MUSEUM
Broad Street, Nantucket, Massachusetts 02554
History of local whaling industry. Portraits. Documents. Cooper's and blacksmith's shops. Completely rigged whale-boat.
May 30 - Oct. 12, daily 10-5.

OLD JAIL
Vestal Street, Nantucket, Massachusetts 02554
Building (1805). One of the oldest jails in the United States.
June 15 - Sept. 15, M.-Sa. 10-5.

OLD WINDMILL
Nantucket, Massachusetts 02554
Building (1746). Original wooden machinery and millstones.
June 15 - Sept. 15, M.-Sa. 10-5.

"OLDEST HOUSE", JETHRO COFFIN HOUSE
Sunset Hill, Nantucket, Massachusetts 02554
House (1686). Period furnishings.
June 15 - Sept. 15, daily 10-5.

KENNETH TAYLOR GALLERY
Straight Wharf, Nantucket, Massachusetts 02554
Contemporary paintings by local artists.
June 1 - Sept. 15: M.-Sa. 10-5.

NAMPA

CLEO'S FERRY MUSEUM
311 4th Avenue S., Nampa, Idaho 83651
In Ferry Hotel (1861). Local history. Music.
By appointment.

NAPLES

COLLIER COUNTY HISTORICAL SOCIETY MUSEUM
P.O. Box 201, Naples, Florida 33940
Local history. Indian material. Life of early settlers. Shells.
M.-F. 9-5.

NARROWSBURG

FORT DELAWARE
Route 97, Narrowsburg, New York 12764
Local history. Museum of pioneer life along Delaware River. Replica of stockade, with blockhouse, cabins, blacksmith's shop. 18th century furnishings. Early American farm tools and equipment.
July 1 - Labour Day: M.-Sa. 10-6; Su. 12-6.

NASHUA

CHICKASAW COUNTY HISTORICAL SOCIETY MUSEUM
Highway 346 E., Nashua, Iowa 50658
Local history. Agriculture. Indian artifacts. Folklore. Costumes.
Deerfield Church (1860), Dr. Pitt's surgery (1883) and Chickasaw Church (1890) are in the care of the Society.
Memorial Day - Labour Day, daily 9-5.30.

NASHVILLE

MUSEUM OF HISTORICAL SOCIETY OF WASHINGTON COUNTY
Nashville, Illinois 62263
Local history. Domestic equipment.
Su., M., public holidays 1.30-3.30; Tu., Sa. by appointment. Closed Thanksgiving, Christmas, New Year.

BROWN COUNTY ART GALLERY ASSOCIATION
Artist Square, One Artist Drive, Nashville, Indiana 47448
20th century American paintings, graphics, photographs. Pastels by Glen Cooper Henshaw.
Daily 10-5. Closed Sa. before Christmas - Feb. 14.

BAPTIST HISTORICAL MUSEUM
Dargan-Carver Library, 127 9th Avenue N., Nashville, Tennessee 37203
Baptistiana. Personal possessions of early American Baptists. Documents. Bibles.
M.-F. 7.30-4. Closed public holidays.

BELLE MEADE MANSION
Harding Road and Leake Avenue, Nashville, Tennessee 37205
House (1853), home of Harding and Jackson families. Original and period furnishings. Log cabin (1808) on estate. Paintings of thoroughbreds from Belle Meade stud.
Apr. 1 - Oct. 31, 9-5. Nov. 1 - Mar. 31, 10-4.30.

CHILDREN'S MUSEUM
2nd Avenue and Lindsley Street, Nashville, Tennessee 37210
In original university building (1853). Geology. Palaeontology. Science. Astronomy. Planetarium. Botany. Natural history. Anthropology. Ethnology. Local history and archaeology. Indian artifacts. Costumes.
Tu.-Sa. 10-5; Su. 2-5. Closed public holidays.

COUNTRY MUSIC HALL OF FAME AND MUSEUM
700 16th Avenue, Nashville, Tennessee 37203
History of rural music. Instruments. Memorabilia. Recordings.
Sept.-May, M.-F. 9-5; Sa., Su. 9-5.30. June-Aug., M.-W. 8.30-5; Th.-Su. 8.30-8. Closed Dec. 24-25, Dec. 31 - Jan. 1.

FORT NASHBOROUGH
170 1st Avenue N., Nashville, Tennessee 37201
Replica of Fort Nashborough (1779), first settlement at Nashville. Period furniture. Tools.
Daily 9-4. Closed Dec. 24-5, New Year.

JOHN F. KENNEDY MEMORIAL CENTER
1308 16th Avenue S., Nashville, Tennessee 37212
Kennedy memorabilia.
Daily 9-5.

NASHVILLE PARTHENON
Centennial Park, Nashville, Tennessee 37203
Exact, full-size reproduction of Parthenon and of Elgin marbles. Paintings.
M.-Sa. 8-4.30; Su. 8-12. Closed public holidays.

GEORGE PEABODY COLLEGE MUSEUM
21st Avenue, Nashville, Tennessee 37203
16th-19th century European paintings, sculpture. 20th century American paintings, sculpture. English china, silver. European and American furniture. Tapestries. Lace.
M.-F. 10-5; Sa., Su. 1-5. Closed college vacations.

TENNESSEE AGRICULTURAL MUSEUM
Ellington Agricultural Center, Hogan Road, Nashville, Tennessee 37311
Agricultural history of Tennessee. Farm implements. Craftsmen's tools. Domestic equipment.
M.-F. 9-5.

TENNESSEE BOTANICAL GARDENS AND FINE ARTS CENTER
Cheekwood, Cheek Road, Nashville, Tennessee 37205
Herbarium. 17th-20th century European and American paintings, sculpture, graphics. Chinese porcelain and snuff boxes.
Tu.-Sa. 10-5; Su., public holidays 1-5. Closed New Year, Labour Day, Christmas.

TENNESSEE HISTORICAL SOCIETY MUSEUM
403 7th Avenue N., Nashville, Tennessee 37219
Local history. Portraits. Paintings.
M.-Sa. 8-4.30. Closed public holidays.

TENNESSEE STATE MUSEUM
301 Capitol Boulevard, Nashville, Tennessee 37219
Geology. Mineralogy. Natural history. Local history. Indian artifacts. Portraits of Governors of Tennessee and leading State politicians. Coins. Stamps. Civil War relics. Relics from Battleship 'Tennessee'.
Tu.-F. 9-4. Sa. 12-4, Su. 2-4. Closed public holidays.

THE UPPER ROOM
1908 Grand Avenue, Nashville, Tennessee 37203
Religious art.
Daily 8-9.

THRUSTON COLLECTION
Vanderbilt University, Nashville, Tennessee 37203
Science. Paintings. Indian artifacts.
M.-F. 8-5. Closed Christmas.

TRAVELLERS' REST MUSEUM HOUSE
1125 Chickering Park Drive, Nashville, Tennessee 37220
House (1799, with later additions). Period furnishings and decorations. Indian collection in converted smokehouse.
M.-Sa. 8.30-5; Su. 1-5. Closed New Year, Christmas.

CARL VAN VECHLEN GALLERY OF FINE ARTS
18th Avenue and Jackson Street N., Nashville, Tennessee 37203
African sculpture. Afro-American paintings, graphics. 18th-20th century European and American paintings, drawings. Photography.
M.-F. 8.30-12, 2-5; Su. 4-6. Closed public holidays.

VANDERBILT UNIVERSITY GALLERY
23rd Street and West End Avenue, Nashville, Tennessee 37203
Paintings. Sculpture. Graphics.
Daily 1-5. Closed university vacations.

WATKINS INSTITUTE
6th and Church Streets, Nashville, Tennessee 37219
Paintings. Graphics. Sculpture.
M.-Th. 9-9; F. 9-1.30.

NATCHEZ

MOUNT LOCUST
Natchez Trace Parkway, Natchez, Mississippi 39120
House (1780). Period furnishings.
Mar. daily 9.30-6. Apr.-Sept. Sa., Su. 9.30-6.

'ROSALIE' STATE SHRINE
100 Orleans Street, Natchez, Mississippi 39120
House (1820). 18th-early 19th century furnishings.
Daily 9-5. Closed Thanksgiving, Christmas Eve, Christmas.

NATCHITOCHES

MUSEUM CONTENTS
424 Jefferson Street, Natchitoches, Louisiana 71457
In Rogue's House (1793). Local history. Folklore.
Mar. 1 - Oct., M.-Su. 1-5. Closed Christmas.

NATIONAL CITY

MUSEUM OF AMERICAN TREASURES
1315 East 4th Street, National City, California 92050
Americana. Indian artifacts. Ship models. Sculpture. Desert glass.
M.-F., by appointment. Su. 10-dusk.

NAUGATUCK

NAUGATUCK HISTORICAL SOCIETY MUSEUM
P.O. Box 317, Naugatuck, Connecticut 06770
Local history.
By appointment.

NAUVOO

NAUVOO HISTORICAL SOCIETY MUSEUM
P.O. Box 337, Nauvoo, Illinois 62354
Geology. Local history. Indian artifacts. Children's museum.
Apr. 15 - Oct. 15, M.-Sa. 1-5. Su., public holidays 12-5.

JOSEPH SMITH HISTORIC CENTER
Main and Water Streets, Nauvoo, Illinois 62354
Joseph Smith Homestead (1803-40) and Joseph Smith Nauvoo Mansion (1843), with period furnishings.
May 1 - Sept. 30, 8-8. Oct. 1 - Apr. 30, 8.30-5.

NAZARETH

MUSEUM OF MORAVIAN HISTORICAL SOCIETY
208 E. Center Street, Nazareth, Pennsylvania 18064
In Whitfield House (1740). History of Moravian Church. 18th century paintings, musical instruments, bells. Books printed by the Benjamin Franklin, Ephrata Cloister and Christopher Saur presses.
Tu., F., Sa and 2nd Su. in month, 2-5. Other times by appointment.

NEBRASKA CITY

ARBOR LODGE STATE HISTORICAL PARK MUSEUM
Nebraska City, Nebraska 68410
In Arbor Lodge (1871), former home of J. S. Morton. Carriage house and carriages. Period furnishings. Agriculture.
Apr. 15-June 4, daily 1-5; June 15-Sept. 14, daily 10-5; Sept. 15-Oct. 30, daily 1-5.30.

WILDWOOD CENTER
Steinhart Park Road, Nebraska City, Nebraska 68410
House (1869). Period furnishings.
Apr. 15-Oct. 15, Tu.-Su. 1-5.

NECHE

PATON ISLE OF MEMORIES
Neche, North Dakota 58265
Agriculture. Replica of pioneer village (c.1879).
June 1-Oct. 24, daily 10-8.

NEENAH

DOTY CABIN
Lincoln Street, Neenah, Wisconsin 54956
House (1847). Doty family furnishings. Indian artifacts.
June-Labour Day, Tu.-F. 9.30-11.30, 1.30-5; Sa., Su., holidays, 1.30-5.

JOHN NELSON BERGSTROM ART CENTER AND MUSEUM
165 N. Park Avenue, Neenah, Wisconsin 54956
Austrian and Bohemian glass. Glass paperweights. American paintings, graphics, decorative arts.
W., Th., Sa., Su. 1-5. June 1-Aug. 31 also Tu. 1-5. Closed New Year, Thanksgiving, Christmas.

NELIGH

ANTELOPE COUNTY HISTORICAL COLLECTION
Neligh, Nebraska 68756
In former jail. 19th century household equipment, clothing, utensils. Indian artifacts. Carpenter's tools. Guns.
Apr. 1-Nov. 30: F., Su. 2-5 and by appointment.

NELIGH MILLS
N. Street and Wylie Drive, Neligh, Nebraska 68756
In flour-mill (1874), operational until 1956. History of flour-milling in Nebraska.
M.-Sa. 9-5. June-Aug. also Su. 2-5. Apr.-May, Sept.-Oct., Sa., Su. 2-5.

NEVADA

BUSHWHACKER MUSEUM
231 N. Main Street, Nevada, Missouri 64772
In former Vernon County Jail (1871). Mineralogy. Archaeology. Indian artifacts. Medicine.
Apr. 15-Nov. 30, daily 1-5. Rest of year by appointment.

NEVADA CITY

MALAKOFF DIGGINS
North Bloomfield, Graniteville Star Route, Nevada City, California 95959
Hydraulic gold mining town. Museum exhibits on hydraulic mining. Chinese settlement.
Museum, daily 10-5.

NATIONAL HOTEL MUSEUM
Main Street, Nevada City, California 95959
Local history, especially mining. Furnishings, clothing, tools, vehicles used by miners.
On request.

NEVADA COUNTY HISTORICAL SOCIETY MUSEUM
214 Main Street, Nevada City, California 95959
Local history. Minerals. Relics of early gold mining. Costumes.
July-Sept. daily 11-4.30.

NEW ALMADEN

NEW ALMADEN MUSEUM
21570 Almaden Road, P.O. Box 1, New Almaden, California 95042
Local history. Archaeology. Indian artifacts. Coins. Children's Museum.
Carson and Bulmore houses (1854) are in the care of the Museum.
Feb. 1-Nov. 30, M., W.-F. 1-4. Closed Easter, Thanksgiving.

NEWARK

IRON HILL MUSEUM
Old Baltimore Pike, Newark, Delaware 19711
Natural history of Delaware.
Tu., Th. 7-9; Su. 1-5. Other times by appointment.

UNIVERSITY OF DELAWARE ART GALLERY
Student Center, Newark, Delaware 19711
American and European paintings, prints, sculpture.
M.-Sa. 8 a.m. - 10 p.m.; Su. 1-5, 7-10.

MUSEUM OF NEW JERSEY HISTORICAL SOCIETY
230 Broadway, Newark, New Jersey 07104
State and local history. Transport, especially railways. Costumes. Paintings. Graphics. Decorative arts. Furniture. Period rooms. New Jersey portraits.
Tu.-Sa. 10-4.30. Closed Thanksgiving, Christmas, New Year, July 4.

MUSEUM OF RAILROADIANS OF AMERICA
230 Broadway, Newark, New Jersey 07104
Railway and canal history.
Tu.-Sa. 10-4.

NEWARK MUSEUM
43-9 Washington Street, Newark, New Jersey 07102
American and European paintings, sculpture, decorative arts. Costumes. Textiles. Oriental, especially Tibetan, art. Greek and Roman art. Coins. Clocks and watches. Physical and earth sciences. Planetarium. Natural history. Archaeology. Ethnology. Indian artifacts. Pre-Columbian material. Crosses and crucifixes.
M.-Sa. 12-5; Su., public holidays 1-5. Closed July 4, Thanksgiving, Christmas.

NEW JERSEY BELL TELEPHONE COMPANY, PIONEER HISTORICAL MUSEUM
540 Broad Street, Newark, New Jersey 07102
Displays illustrating development of telephone equipment.
M.-F. 9-5.

HOFFMANN CLOCK MUSEUM
Newark, New York 14513
Clocks and watches.
M.-Sa. 10-5.

DAWES ARBORETUM
Route 5, Newark, Ohio 43055
Palaeontology. Nature center.
Pioneer cabin (1818), with smoke house and blacksmith's shop, and Dawes Arboretum Founder House (1845) are in the care of the Arboretum.
Daily, dawn-dusk.

MOUND BUILDERS EARTHWORKS
State Route 79, Newark, Ohio 43055
Prehistoric Indian ceremonial earthwork and effigy mound. Museum of Ohio Indian art.
Mar.-Nov., Tu.-Su. 9.30-5.

MUSEUM OF LICKING COUNTY HISTORICAL SOCIETY
P.O. Box 535, Newark, Ohio 43055
Museum building (1820) was former Sherwood-Davidson House. 18th-early 19th century furnishings, paintings. Local history and archaeology. Costumes. Indian artifacts. Early 19th century clocks, silver.
Feb. 1-Dec. 31: M., W., F. 9-5; Sa., Su. 1-4.

NEW BEDFORD

NEW BEDFORD FREE PUBLIC LIBRARY
613 Pleasant Street, New Bedford, Massachusetts 02741
Paintings by New Bedford artists. Prints and paintings of whaling scenes. Plates of Audubon's *Birds of America*. Paintings, watercolours, prints by New Bedford artists. Ship models.
M.-F. 9-9; Sa. 9-5. Closed public holidays.

NEW BEDFORD WHALING MUSEUM
18 Johnny Cake Hill, New Bedford, Massachusetts 02740
Whaling history. Paintings. Prints. Whaleship logbooks. Half-scale model of whaling-bark, 'Lagoda'. Whaling and fishing gear. Scrimshaw. Local history of old Dartmouth area. Pairpoint and other New Bedford glassware.
May 2-Sept. 30: M.-Sa. 9-5; Su., public holidays 1-5. Oct. 1-May 1: Tu.-Sa. 9-5; Su., public holidays 1-5.

NEWBERG

MINTHORN HOUSE
S. River and E. 2nd Streets, Newberg, Oregon 97132
House (1881) was boyhood home of Herbert Hoover. Original bedroom furnishings. Memorabilia of President Hoover.
By appointment.

NEW BERN

ATTMORE-OLIVER HOUSE
511 Broad Street, New Bern, North Carolina 28560
House (1791), with period furnishings. Museum of the Cayederate period. Documents. Maps. Clothing. Military relics.
Bright-Bishop House (1796) is in the care of the same authority.
Tu.-Su. 2.30-5. Closed public holidays.

NEW BERN FIREMEN'S MUSEUM
420-1 Broad Street, New Bern, North Carolina 28560
Old fire-fighting equipment. Civil War exhibit.
Tu.-Sa. 9.30-12, 1-5; Su. 1-5. Closed Thanksgiving, Christmas.

STEVENSON HOUSE
611 Pollock Street, New Bern, North Carolina 28560
House (1805). Period furnishings. Decorative arts.
Tu.-Sa. 9.30-4; Su. 1.30-4. Closed New Year, Thanksgiving, Dec. 24-6.

TRYON PALACE RESTORATION
613 Pollock Street, New Bern, North Carolina 28560
Reconstruction (1950s) of Governor Tryon's residence (1770). Period furnishings. Decorative arts. Portraits. Local history. Governor Tryon's library. Paintings, including works by Gainsborough, Richard Wilson, Claude Lorrain.
Tu.-Sa. 9.30-4; Su. 1.30-4. Closed New Year, Thanksgiving, Dec. 24-26.

NEW BRAUNFELS

SOPHIENBURG MEMORIAL MUSEUM
401 W. College Street, New Braunfels, Texas 78130
Pioneer life. Furniture. Clothing. Weapons. Musical instruments. Personal possessions of Prince Carl Salms. founder of New Braunfels.
May 1-Sept. 30: M.-Sa. 3-5; Su., public holidays 2-6. Oct. 1-Apr. 30: W., F. 3-6; Su. 2-6. Closed Christmas.

NEW BRIGHTON

MERRICK ART GALLERY
5th and 11th Streets, New Brighton, Pennsylvania 15066
20th century American paintings, drawings, prints.
M.-Sa. 9-4.

NEW BRITAIN

MUSEUM OF CENTRAL CONNECTICUT STATE COLLEGE
New Britain, Connecticut 06050
Archaeology. Anthropology. Folklore. Industry. Paintings. Sculpture. Graphics. Decorative arts. Architectural drawings and models.
By appointment, during College term.

NEW BRITAIN'S YOUTH MUSEUM
28 High Street, New Britain, Connecticut 06051
Natural history. Ethnology. Circus collection. Indian artifacts. Dolls.
M.-F. children 2-5, Sa., 10-4. Closed public holidays and Sa. June 1-Labour Day.

NEW BRITAIN MUSEUM OF AMERICAN ART
56 Lexington Street, New Britain, Connecticut 06052
American paintings, sculpture, graphics, from Colonial period to present day.
Tu.-Su., 1-5. Closed public holidays.

NEW BRUNSWICK

BUCCLEUCH MANSION
George Street, New Brunswick, New Jersey 08901
House (1739). Period furnishings and clothing.
Memorial Day-Labour Day: Su., public holidays 3-5. Other times by appointment.

DELAPLAINE ELECTRICAL MUSEUM
125 Georges Road, New Brunswick, New Jersey 08903
Electrical items from 1854. Electric cars.
May 1 - Oct. 31 by appointment.

HENRY GUEST HOUSE
58 Livingston Avenue, New Brunswick, New Jersey 08901
House (1760). Furnishings, personal possessions and correspondence of the Guest family.
M.-F. 9-5. Closed public holidays.

KILMER MUSEUM OF SURGICAL PRODUCTS
501 George Street, New Brunswick, New Jersey 08901
History of Johnson and Johnson Company. Surgical products, 1886 to present day.
By appointment.

RUTGERS UNIVERSITY, COLLEGE OF AGRICULTURE MUSEUM
Nichol Avenue, New Brunswick, New Jersey 08903
Agricultural history. Tools, implements. machinery and equipment. Catalogues, pamphlets, reports.
By appointment.

RUTGERS UNIVERSITY ART GALLERY
Vorhees Hall, Hamilton Street, New Brunswick, New Jersey 08903
15th-17th century Italian paintings. 17th century Dutch paintings. 18th-19th century English paintings. 18th-20th century American paintings.
Sept. 1 - May 30, M.-Sa. 9.30-4.30; Su. 1.30-4.30. June 1 - Aug. 31, M.-F. 10-4.30. Closed Sa., Su. at Easter, Thanksgiving, Christmas.

RUTGERS UNIVERSITY, GEOLOGY MUSEUM
Department of Geology, Queen's Campus, New Brunswick, New Jersey 08903
Mineralogy. Palaeontology. Mastodon. Sea shells. Egyptian mummy. Indian artifacts.
M.-F. 9-4; Sa. 9-2.

RUTGERS UNIVERSITY, SEROLOGICAL MUSEUM
University Heights, New Brunswick, New Jersey 08903
Animal bloods and sera. Blood testing and serology.
By appointment.

NEWBURGH

BETHLEHEM ART GALLERY
Jackson Avenue, Newburgh, New York 12550
Paintings, Sculpture. Tiles. Ceramics.
M.-Sa. 10-5; Tu. also 7-9.

JONATHAN HASBROUCK HOUSE
Library and Washington Streets, Newburgh, New York 12550
House (1750) was Washington's Headquarters (1782-3). Collection showing arms and equipment used in Revolutionary War.
W.-Sa. 9-5; Su. 1-5.

KNOX HEADQUARTERS
Route 94, Newburgh, New York 12550
House (1754), with late 18th century furniture. Civil War history.
M.-Sa. 9-4.30; Su. 1-4.30.

NEW WINDSOR CANTONMENT
Temple Hill Road, Newburgh, New York 12550
Restored Revolutionary War winter camp. Collections in reconstructed 'Publick Building' dealing with Colonial Freemasonry and the Continental Army.
May 1 - Nov. 1: W.-Su. 9.30-5.

NEWBURY

TRISTRAM COFFIN HOUSE
16 High Road, Newbury, Massachusetts 01950
House (c.1654), with late additions. 17th-20th century Coffin family furnishings.
June-Sept., Tu., Th., Sa. 1-5.

SHORT HOUSE
39 High Road, Newbury, Massachusetts 01950
House (c.1732). Furnishings of 1710-1740.
June-Sept., Tu., Th., Sa. 1-5.

NEWBURYPORT

MUSEUM OF HISTORICAL SOCIETY OF OLD NEWBURY
98 High Street, Newburyport, Massachusetts 01950
In Cushing House (1808). Local history. Maritime history. Paintings.
Tu.-Sa. 10-4; Su. 2-5.

NEW CANAAN

HANFORD-SILLIMAN HOUSE
Oenoke Avenue, New Canaan, Connecticut 06850
House (c.1770). Period furnishings.
Su., M., Tu., Th. 2-5.

NEW CANAAN HISTORICAL SOCIETY MUSEUM
13 Oenoke Ridge, New Canaan, Connecticut 06840
Local history. Costumes. Old tools.
4 buildings (1764-1878), including the Cody Drug Store, with its old printing press and collection of tools, are in the care of the Society.
Tu.-F., Su. 2-4.

SILVERMINE GUILD OF ARTISTS
1037 Silvermine Road, New Canaan, Connecticut 06840
20th century American graphics.
Daily 12.30-5.

NEW CASTLE

NEW CASTLE HISTORICAL SOCIETY MUSEUM
2 E. Fourth Street, New Castle, Delaware 19720
Dutch House (1700), Amsbel House (1730) both with period furnishings.
Dutch House: Tu.-Su. 11-5. Closed Nov. 1 - Mar. 31, Memorial Day, July 4, Labour Day.
Amsbel House: Tu.-Sa. 11-5. Closed public holidays.

HENRY COUNTY HISTORICAL SOCIETY MUSEUM
614 S. 14th Street, New Castle, Indiana 47362
House (1870), formerly home of General William Grose. Furniture. Tools. Household equipment. Documents. Natural history.
M.-Sa. 1-4.30. Closed public holidays, Good Friday.

NEWCASTLE

FORT BELKNAP MUSEUM
F.M. 61, Newcastle, Texas 76372
In former Commisary's store (1853) at Fort. Furnishings, tools, weapons used on Fort Belknap frontier. Photographs of officers once stationed at Fort. Women's clothing, including gowns worn by Mrs. Eisenhower, Mrs. MacArthur and Mrs. Lyndon B. Johnson.
M.-Th., Sa., Su. 9-5.

ANNA MILLER MUSEUM
Newcastle, Wyoming 82701
Mineralogy. Palaeontology. Natural history. Local history. Indian material.
Green Mountain School (1888) is in the care of the Museum.
May 1 - Sept. 30: M.-F. 9-7; Sa. 1-7. Oct. 1 - Apr. 30: F. 9-5. Closed public holidays.

NEWCOMERSTOWN

NEWCOMERSTOWN HISTORICAL SOCIETY MUSEUM
471 S. Goodrich Street, Newcomerstown, Ohio 43832
Local history. Indian artifacts.
Sa., Su. 2-4. Other times by appointment.

NEW FAIRFIELD

HIDDEN VALLEY NATURE CENTER
Gillotti Road, New Fairfield, Connecticut 06810
Geology. Natural history. Indian artifacts.
Weekdays by appointment; Su. 2-5. Closed Nov. 1 - Mar. 31.

NEWFANE

MUSEUM OF WINDHAM COUNTY HISTORICAL SOCIETY
Newfane, Vermont 05345
Local history. 18th-19th century furniture, domestic equipment, clothing. Indian artifacts. Farm tools.
Su., public holidays 2-5. Other times by appointment.

NEW GLARUS

CHALET OF THE GOLDEN FLEECE
618 2nd Street, New Glarus, Wisconsin 53574
Swiss-type chalet. Swiss furniture, carvings, dolls, prints. Early American furniture. Weapons.
Apr. 1 - Oct. 31, daily 9-5.

MUSEUM OF NEW GLARUS HISTORICAL SOCIETY
6th Avenue and 7th Street, New Glarus, Wisconsin 53574
Village museum, illustrating early settlers' life in New Glarus. Replicas of blacksmith's shop, country store, log church, log cabin, cheese factory, school.
May-Oct., daily 9-5.

NEWHALL

WILLIAM S. HART COUNTY PARK MUSEUM
24151 North Newhall Avenue, Newhall, California 91321
Paintings by American artists. Sculpture. Indian artifacts.
Hart's Horseshoe Ranch (1928), with period furniture, is in the care of the Park.
Tu.-Su. 10-5.

NEW HARMONY

COLONIAL DAMES RESTORED HARMONIST DWELLING
New Harmony, Indiana 47631
House (1814). Period furnishings. Harmonist history, artifacts.
Apr.-Oct., Tu.-Sa. 10-12, 1-5. Rest of year by appointment.

THE OLD FAUNTLEROY HOUSE
New Harmony, Indiana 47631
In pioneer frame-house, where Minerva Society was founded. Victorian furnishings.
By appointment.

WORKINGMEN'S INSTITUTE
West Tavern Street, New Harmony, Indiana 47631
History of New Harmony. Furniture, clothing, household equipment, tools used by first settlers. Geology. Shells.
May-Sept. Tu.-Sa. 10-4; Su. 2-5. Closed Memorial Day, July 4.

NEW HAVEN

HERBARIUM
Yale University, Osborn Memorial Laboratories, 167 Prospect Street, New Haven, Connecticut 06520
Herbarium. World collection of vascular plants, bryophytes, lichens.
M.-F. 9-5.

PAUL MELLON CENTER FOR BRITISH ART AND BRITISH STUDIES
Box 2120, Yale Station, New Haven, Connecticut 06520
British paintings, drawings, prints, illustrated books.
By appointment.

NEW HAVEN COLONY HISTORICAL SOCIETY MUSEUM
114 Whitney Avenue, New Haven, Connecticut 06510
Local history. Industry. Costumes. Paintings by local artists. Decorative arts. Silver. Glass.
Pardee's Old Morris House (1675) is in the care of the Society.
Tu.-F. 10-5; Sa., Su. 2-5.

OLD MORRIS HOUSE
325 Lighthouse Road, New Haven, Connecticut 06500
Mid-18th century house. Period furniture.
May-Oct., Tu.-F. 10-5; Su. 2-5.

PEABODY MUSEUM OF NATURAL HISTORY
170 Whitney Avenue, New Haven, Connecticut 06520
Geology. Mineralogy. Palaeontology. Dinosaur fossilised remains. Anthropology. Botany. Zoology. Meteorites. Scientific instruments.
M.-Sa. 9-5; Su., public holidays 1-5. Closed New Year, July 4, Thanksgiving, Christmas.

WINCHESTER GUN MUSEUM
275 Winchester Avenue, New Haven, Connecticut 06510
Firearms and accessories from 15th century onwards.
M.-Sa. 9-4. Closed public holidays.

YALE MEDICAL LIBRARY
333 Cedar Street, New Haven, Connecticut 06510
History of medicine and pharmacy. Medical instruments. Paintings of medical subjects. Weights and measures.
M.-F. 8.30 a.m. - midnight; Sa. 8.30 a.m. - 10 p.m.; Su., public holidays 11 a.m. - midnight. Closed Christmas.

YALE UNIVERSITY ART GALLERY
1111 Chapel Street, New Haven, Connecticut 06510
Archaeology. Pre-Columbian art. African sculpture. Near and Far Eastern art. Italian Renaissance paintings. 17th-19th century American furniture, silver, glass. 20th century European and American paintings and sculpture. Furniture. Miniatures.
Tu., Sa. 10-5; Su. 2-5. Sept. 1 - June 30 also Th. 6-9. Closed New Year, July 4, Thanksgiving, Christmas.

YALE UNIVERSITY COLLECTION OF MUSICAL INSTRUMENTS
15 Hillhouse Avenue, New Haven, Connecticut 06520
European and American instruments, 15th-20th century.
Tu., Th. 2-4; Su. 2-5. University vacations by appointment.

NEW IBERIA

SHADOWS-ON-THE-TECHE
117 E. Main Street, New Iberia, Louisiana 70560
House (1831-34), with period furniture, silver. Family portraits.
Daily 9-4.30. Closed Christmas.

NEWINGTON

AMERICAN RADIO RELAY LEAGUE
Museum of Amateur Radio, 225 North Main Street, Newington, Connecticut 06111
Old radio transmitting and receiving equipment, including early spark transmitter in operating condition.
M.-F. 8-4; Sa., Su. by appointment. Closed public holidays.

OLD PARSONAGE
Newington, New Hampshire 03801
House (1699), with period furnishings. Local history.
July 1 - Aug. 31, Sa. 2-5.

NEW IPSWICH

BARRETT HOUSE
Main Street, New Ipswich, New Hampshire 03071
House (1800). Family furniture, portraits.
June-Oct., Tu.-Sa. 11-5.

NEW LONDON

DESHON-ALLYN HOUSE
613 Williams Street, New London, Connecticut 06320
House (1829), with Federal period furnishings.
Tu.-Sa. 1-5; Su. 2-5. Closed public holidays.

THE HEMPSTEAD HOUSE
Hempstead and Jay Streets, New London, Connecticut 06320
House (1678), occupied by Hempstead family until 1937. Original family furniture and other possessions.
May 15 - Oct. 15, 1-5.

LYMAN ALLYN MUSEUM
100 Mohegan Avenue, New London, Connecticut 06320
American and European paintings, including work by Connecticut artists. European drawings. Chinese and American ceramics. American and English furniture and silver. 19th-20th century costumes. Dolls and toys. Antiquities from Mediterranean area.
Deshon-Allyn house (1829) is in the care of the Museum.
Tu.-Sa. 1-5; Su. 2-5. Closed public holidays.

NEW LONDON COUNTY HISTORICAL SOCIETY MUSEUM
11 Blinman Street, New London, Connecticut 06320
In Shaw Mansion (1756). Shaw family portraits, furniture, manuscripts. Local history. Documents relating to West Indian trade and early history of New London. Whaling
Tu.-Sa. 1-4. Closed public holidays.

THAMES SCIENCE CENTER
Gallows Lane, New London, Connecticut 06320
Children's museum. Minerals. Shells. Natural history. Fossils.
M.-F. 9-5; Sa. 1-5. Closed public holidays, last week June, first two weeks Sept.

NEW LONDON HISTORICAL SOCIETY MUSEUM
Little Sunapee Road, New London, New Hampshire 03257
Local history. Costumes. Agriculture. Folklore.
5 buildings (1800-30) are in the care of the Society.
Aug. 1-31, Sa. 2-4.30. Other times by appointment.

NEW LONDON PUBLIC MUSEUM
412 S. Pearl Street, New London, Wisconsin 54961
Geology. Mineralogy. Fossils. Mounted birds. Indian artifacts. Local history.
June 1 - Aug. 31: Tu.-F. 1-5. Rest of year, W.-F. 2.30-5. Sa. all year 11-4. Closed public holidays.

NEW MARKET

ENDLESS CAVERNS MUSEUM OF ART
Endless Caverns, New Market, Virginia 22844
Paintings by the American artist, William Starkweather.
Daily 9-5.

NEW MARKET BATTLEFIELD PARK MUSEUM
P.O. Box 1864, New Market, Virginia 22844
Civil War material.
The Park includes Bushong House (1830-50), with contemporary furnishings.
May 1 - Oct. 31, daily 9-6. Nov. 1 - Apr. 30, daily 9-5. Closed Christmas.

NEW MILFORD

NEW MILFORD HISTORICAL SOCIETY MUSEUM
6 Aspetuck Avenue, New Milford, Connecticut 06716
In former Litchfield County Bank (1800). Local history. Costumes. Portraits. Furnishings. Decorative arts.
W., Sa. 2-5. Closed public holidays.

OLD MILL VILLAGE MUSEUM
Route 848, New Milford, Pennsylvania 18834
Local history.
May 29 - Oct. 22, daily 11-4.

NEW ORLEANS

1850 HOUSE
Pontalba Building, 523 St. Ann Street, New Orleans, Louisiana 70116
Typical terrace house of the 1850s. Period rooms. Kitchen, with Victorian utensils. Exhibitions relating to the history of the Pontalba building and Jackson Square.
Tu.-Su. 9-5. Closed public holidays.

CASA HOVE
723 Toulouse Street, New Orleans, Louisiana 70130
House (1720), with family heirlooms and period furniture.
M.-F. 10-5; Sa., and public holidays 10-4.

CONFEDERATE MUSEUM
929 Camp Street, New Orleans, Louisiana 70130
Military history. Civil War relics.
M.-F. 10-4. Closed public holidays.

HISTORIC NEW ORLEANS COLLECTION
533 Royal Street, New Orleans, Louisiana 76130
In Merieult House (1792). Prints, paintings, drawings and other material illustrating Battle of New Orleans. Drawings of local subjects, including 1814 series of forts on Lower Mississippi. Privateer papers. Military letters.
Tu.-Sa. 1.30-4.30. Closed public holidays.

THE LOUISIANA LANDMARKS SOCIETY, INC.
203 Gallier Hall, St. Charles at Lafayette (12), New Orleans, Louisiana 70112
In Gallier Hall (c.1840), former New Orleans City Hall. Photographic collection of Louisiana plantation houses.
M., W., F. 1-4.

LOUISIANA STATE MUSEUM
751 Chartres Street, New Orleans, Louisiana 70116
Local history. Archaeology. Indian artifacts. Transport. Paintings. Sculpture. Graphics. Decorative arts. Textiles. Glass. Coins. Music. Children's Museum. Mardi Gras costumes.
The Presbytère (1791) and The Cabildo (1795) are in the care of the Museum.
Tu.-Su. 9-5. Closed public holidays.

LOUISIANA WILDLIFE MUSEUM
400 Royal Street, New Orleans, Louisiana 70130
Louisiana birds, mammals, reptiles. Habitat groups.
M.-F. 8.30-5. Closed public holidays.

NEW ORLEANS JAZZ MUSEUM
Royal Sonesta Hotel, Bourbon and Conti Streets, New Orleans, Louisiana 70116
History of Jazz. Recordings. Instruments used by famous musicians. Photographs.
M.-Sa. 10-5.

NEW ORLEANS MUSEUM OF ART
Lelong Avenue, City Park, New Orleans, Louisiana 70119
European painting and sculpture, 15th-18th centuries. Pre-Columbian and Colonial art of Latin America. 19th-20th century art of the U.S. and Louisiana. Late 19th-20th century European painting, sculpture, graphic art. Glass. Chinese jades. Greek and Roman vases. Silver.
Tu.-Sa. 10-5; Su. 1-6. Closed public holidays.

NEW ORLEANS RECREATION DEPARTMENT
Children's Museum, 1218 Burgundy Street (16), New Orleans, Louisiana 70116
Dolls. Toys.
M.-F. 9-5; Sa. 9-12.

LA PHARMACIE FRANÇAISE
514 Chartres Street, New Orleans, Louisiana 70130
History of pharmacy. 19th century pharmacy equipment. Soda fountain (1890). Natural sponges display.
Tu.-Sa. 10-5.

PRESBYTÈRE
Jackson Square, New Orleans, Louisiana 70116
Building (1791-1847). Collections illustrating Louisiana history. Paintings. Portraits. Mardi Gras section. 19th century fire-fighting equipment. History of Louisiana fashions. Toys.
Tu.-Su. 9-5. Closed public holidays.

THE CABILDO
Jackson Square, New Orleans, Louisiana 70116
Built (1795) to house the Spanish governing body. Displays illustrating French Colonial, Spanish Colonial and American periods of Louisiana history.
Exhibitions showing plantation life, steamboats and the Mississippi River.
Tu.-Su. 9-5. Closed public holidays.

NEW PALTZ

COLONEL JOSIAH HASBROUCK HOUSE
Route 32, New Paltz, New York 12561
House (1814). Furnishings of Federal period.
May 15 - Oct. 15: Tu.-Su. 10-5.

HUGUENOT HISTORICAL MUSEUM (JEAN HASBROUCK HOUSE)
6 Brodhead Avenue, New Paltz, New York 12561
Huguenot memorabilia. Rooms furnished in style of c.1714.
5 Huguenot houses (1692-1712) are in the care of the Museum.
Tu.-Su. 10-5.

STATE UNIVERSITY COLLEGE ART GALLERY
New Paltz, New York 12561
Paintings, mainly 20th century American. Pre-Columbian, African, Chinese, Japanese prints. Sculptures.
M.-F. 9-5. Closed Thanksgiving, University Spring and Winter vacations.

NEW PHILADELPHIA

SCHOENBRUNN VILLAGE STATE MEMORIAL
U.S. Route 250, New Philadelphia, Ohio 44663
Reconstructions of buildings of Moravian Mission (founded 1772), including church, school and 13 log cabins. Moravian and local history.
May 1 - Sept. 30, daily 9-6. Mar. 1 - Apr. 30, Oct. 1 - Nov. 30, daily 9-5.

NEWPORT

NEWPORT CLOCK MUSEUM
43 Park Street, Newport, New Hampshire 03773
Sundials. Clocks. Watches.
May 1 - Sept. 30: M.-Sa. 9-4; Su. 1-4. Rest of year by appointment.

LINCOLN COUNTY HISTORICAL MUSEUM
579 S.W. 9th Street, Newport, Oregon 97365
In Old Yaquina Bay lighthouse (1871). Palaeontology. Maritime history. Indian artifacts. Industry. Handicrafts.
June 1 - Sept. 30: Tu.-Su. 11-5. Oct. 1 - May 31: Tu.-Su. 11-11.

OREGON STATE UNIVERSITY, MARINE SCIENCE CENTER
Marine Science Drive, Newport, Oregon 97365
Marine biology. Local history. Junior museum.
Daily 10-4. Closed Christmas, New Year.

HISTORICAL SOCIETY OF PERRY COUNTY MUSEUM
129 North Second Street, Newport, Pennsylvania 17074
County history. Civil War material. Farm implements. Guns.
M.-F. 10-4. Closed holidays.

BELCOURT CASTLE
Bellevue Avenue, Newport, Rhode Island 02840
House (1894), replica of Louis XIII Castle. European and Oriental furniture, silver, paintings, rugs, carpets, objets d'art, armour.
Apr. 1 - Nov. 30, daily 10-5.

THE BREAKERS
Ochre Point Avenue, Newport, Rhode Island 02840
House (1895), built for Cornelius Vanderbilt. 70 rooms, with original furnishings. Carriage house and stable has collection of carriages, coaches, harness and livery.
House: Apr. 15 - Memorial Day, Sa., Su. 10-5. Memorial Day - Sept. 14, daily 10-5. July 1 - Sept. 30, Su. also to 9 p.m.
Carriage House: July 1 - Sept. 30, daily 10-5.

BULL-MAWDSLEY HOUSE
Spring and John Streets, Newport, Rhode Island 02841
House (1680, enlarged 1747). 17th-18th century Rhode Island furniture.
June-Sept., Tu., Th., Sa. 1-5.

CHÂTEAU-SUR-MER
Bellevue Avenue, Newport, Rhode Island 02840
House (1852, additions 1872) built by W. S. and G. P. Westmore. Original furnishings.
Apr. 15 - Memorial Day: Sa., Su. 10-5. Memorial Day - Sept. 14, daily 10-5. July 1 - Sept. 30, Su. also to 9 p.m.

THE ELMS
Bellevue Avenue, Newport, Rhode Island 02840
House (1901), built for Edward J. Berwind. Some original furnishings, others lent by museums and private collectors.
Apr. 15 - Memorial Day: Sa., Su. 10-5. Memorial Day - Sept. 14, daily 10-5. July 1 - Sept. 30, Su. also to 9 p.m.

HUNTER HOUSE
Washington Street, Newport, Rhode Island 02840
House (1748). 18th century Newport-made furniture, by the Townsends and Goddards. Newport silver.
June 1 - Sept. 30, daily 10-5. Rest of year by appointment.

MARBLE HOUSE
Bellevue Avenue, Newport, Rhode Island 02840
House (1892), Built for William H. Vanderbilt. Original furnishings.
Apr. 15 - Memorial Day: Sa., Su. 10-5. Memorial Day - Sept. 14, daily 10-5. July 1 - Sept. 30, Su. also to 9 p.m.

NATIONAL TENNIS HALL OF FAME AND TENNIS MUSEUM
Newport Casino, 194 Bellevue Avenue, Newport, Rhode Island 02840
Casino (1880). Site of first American Championship Tournament (1881). Tennis memorabilia. Trophies. Rackets. Photographs.
May 1 - Oct. 31: M.-Sa. 9.30-5; Su. 11-5.

NEWPORT ARTILLERY COMPANY MUSEUM
23 Clarke Street, Newport, Rhode Island 02840
In former Armoury (c.1836). History of the Company.
Apr.-Sept., Tu.-Su. 1-5. Sept.-Mar., Sa. 1-5.

NEWPORT HISTORICAL SOCIETY
82 Touro Street, Newport, Rhode Island 02840
In Seventh Day Baptist Church (c.1729). Maritime history. Newport scenes and portraits. Silver. China. Glass. Furniture.
Wanton-Lyman-Hazard House (c.1675) is also in the care of the Society.
Tu.-F. 9.30-4.30; Sa. 9.30-12.

OLD STATE HOUSE
Washington Square, Newport, Rhode Island 02840
Building (1739). Period furnishings.
July 1 - Labour Day, daily 9.30-4. Rest of year M.-F. 9.30-12, 1-4; Sa. 9.30-12.

REDWOOD LIBRARY AND ATHENAEUM
50 Bellevue Avenue, Newport, Rhode Island 02840
Early American portraits. Paintings by Charles B. King.
M.-Sa. 10-6. Closed public holidays.

SWANHURST
Bellevue Avenue and Webster Street, Newport, Rhode Island 02840
House (1851), with period furnishings.
By appointment.

WANTON-LYMAN-HAZARD HOUSE
17 Broadway, Newport, Rhode Island 02840
House (1675). Scene of Stamp Act Riot.
July 1 - Labour Day, daily 10-5.

WHITEHALL
Berkeley Avenue, Middletown, Newport, Rhode Island 02840
House (1729). 18th century furnishings.
July 1 - Labour Day, daily 10-5.

NEWPORT BEACH

NEWPORT HARBOR ART MUSEUM
2211 W. Balboa Boulevard, Newport Beach, California 92660
Paintings, sculpture by the contemporary artists, Joseph Albers, Ludwig Sander and James Wines.
Tu.-Su. 12-4. Closed Easter, Memorial Day, July 4, Thanksgiving, Christmas, New Year.

NEWPORT NEWS

JAMES RIVER GOLF MUSEUM
James River Country Club, U.S. Highway 60, Newport News, Virginia 23601
History of golf in United States and abroad. Golfing relics. Paintings. Photography.
Tu.-Su. 12-8.

THE MARINERS MUSEUM
Route 60 and J. Clyde Morris Boulevard, Newport News, Virginia 23606
In Causey's Mill (1870). History of Man's conquest of the sea. Ship models. Small craft. Navigation instruments. Ships' machinery and equipment. Dioramas. Paintings, drawings, prints with nautical themes. Sailors' handicrafts. Ships' papers.
M.-Sa. 9-5; Su. 12-5. Closed Christmas.

PENINSULA NATURE AND SCIENCE CENTER
524 J. Clyde Morris Boulevard, Newport News, Virginia 23601
Ecology. Mineralogy. Fossils. Natural history. Entomology. Science. Planetarium.
Museum: M.-Sa. 10-5; Su. 1-5. Closed public holidays.
Planetarium: Su. 3 and 4.

WAR MEMORIAL MUSEUM OF VIRGINIA
9285 Warwick Road, Newport News, Virginia 23607
War posters. Relics of wars in which U.S. forces have been engaged. Uniforms.
M.-Sa. 9-5; Su. 1-5. Closed Christmas.

NEW ROCHELLE

THOMAS PAINE MEMORIAL BUILDING
983 Paine Avenue, New Rochelle, New York 10804
Writings, portraits and personal possessions of Thomas Paine. Books, pamphlets, prints, maps dealing with history of Westchester County. Thomas Paine cottage, lived in by Paine, adjoins Memorial Building.
Tu.-Su. 2-5.

WILDCLIFF NATURAL SCIENCE CENTER
Wildcliff Road, New Rochelle, New York 10805
Ecology. History of Colonial period. Indian relics. Artifacts from Africa, Polynesia, Far East.
M.-Sa. 9-5; Su. 1-5. Closed Thanksgiving, Christmas.

NEW ROCKFORD

EDDY COUNTY MUSEUM
1st Avenue N., New Rockford, North Dakota 58356
Local history.
Su., public holidays 2-5.

NEW SMYRNA BEACH

NEW SMYRNA STATE HISTORIC SITE
New Smyrna Beach, Florida 32069
Ruins of sugar-mill (1830).
Daily 8-dusk.

NEW SWEDEN

MUSEUM OF NEW SWEDEN HISTORICAL SOCIETY
New Sweden, Maine 04762
Local history.
July 1 - Aug. 31; Su. 2-5. Other months, weekdays by appointment.

NEWTON

NEWTON PUBLIC LIBRARY AND MUSEUM
Newton, Illinois 62448
Local history. Indian material.
Daily 10-5. Closed public holidays.

JACKSON HOMESTEAD
527 Washington Street, Newton, Massachusetts 02158
House (1809). History of Newton. Maps. Costumes. Colonial kitchen.
M.-F. 2-4. Closed public holidays.

MUSEUM OF SUSSEX COUNTY HISTORICAL SOCIETY
82 Main Street, Newton, New Jersey 07860
Local history. Mastodon skeleton. Indian artifacts.
M.-F. 9-12. Closed public holidays.

CATAWBA COUNTY HISTORICAL MUSEUM
South Main Avenue, Newton, North Carolina 28658
History of Catawba County. Pioneer artifacts. Textiles and textile manufacturing equipment. Kitchen utensils. Carpenters' and cobblers' tools.
W., Su. 2.30-5.30; F. evening 7-9; holidays 9-11, 2.30-5.30. Closed Thanksgiving, Christmas, Easter.

NEWTON GROVE

BENTONVILLE BATTLEGROUND STATE HISTORIC SITE
Visitor Center, Box 27, Newton Grove, North Carolina 28366
Local and military history. Site also includes Harper House (c.1860), used as hospital in Civil War. Sections of original trench-work. Exhibits telling story of Battle of Bentonville (1865).
Tu.-Sa. 9-5; Sa., Su. 1-5. Closed Thanksgiving, Dec. 24-6.

NEWTON HIGHLANDS

NATIONAL FIRE MUSEUM
21 Endicott Street, Newton Highlands, Massachusetts 02161
Fire-fighting apparatus, from hand-truck onwards. Helmets. Badges.
Nov. 27 - Dec. 31, June 13 - Oct. 12: M.-Sa. 11-5.30; Su. 1-5.30. Closed Christmas.

NEWTOWN

MUSEUM OF NEWTOWN HISTORIC ASSOCIATION
Court Street and Center Avenue, Newtown, Pennsylvania 18940
In Court Inn (1733, 1792). Local and Bucks. County history. Early American furniture.
Su. 2-5. Other times by appointment.

NEW ULM

BROWN COUNTY HISTORICAL SOCIETY MUSEUM
Broadway and 1st North Street, New Ulm, Minnesota 56073
Local history. Pioneer history. Minnesota Indian war relics.
M.-Sa. 1-5. Closed public holidays.

NEW WINDSOR

SPRINGDALE SCHOOL
New Windsor, Maryland 21157
School building (1854). Period furnishings, equipment, school books.
May-Sept., by appointment.

KNOX HEADQUARTERS
Route 94, New Windsor, New York 12550
Local history.
W.-Sa. 9-5; Su. 1-5. Closed New Year, Easter, Thanksgiving, Christmas.

NEW YORK

AEROFLEX MUSEUM
560 W. 42nd Street, New York, New York 10004
History of military aviation, road transport.
By appointment.

AMERICAN ACADEMY OF ARTS AND LETTERS
633 W. 155th Street, New York, New York 10032
20th century paintings, sculpture, drawings by New York artists. Special collection of works by Childe Hassam and Eugene Speicher.
Oct.-Apr., Tu.-Su. 1-4. Closed public holidays.

AMERICAN MUSEUM, HAYDEN PLANETARIUM
81st Street and Central Park W., New York, New York 10024
Astronomy. Meteorology. Planetarium.
M.-F. 10-5; Sa. 10-6; Su. 12-6. Closed Thanksgiving, Christmas.

AMERICAN MUSEUM OF IMMIGRATION
Liberty Island, New York, New York 10004
In base of Statue of Liberty. History of immigration to United States.
Labour Day- Memorial Day, daily 9-5. Rest of year M.-F. 9-6; Sa., Su. 9-7.

AMERICAN MUSEUM OF NATURAL HISTORY
79th Street and Central Park W., New York, New York 10024
Geology. Mineralogy. Palaeontology. Astronomy. Halls of Man in Africa, Mexico, Central America. Indians of the Plains and Eastern woodland habitat groups of birds and mammals. Biology of man and invertebrates. Dinosaur Halls.
M.-Sa. 10-5; Su., public holidays 1-5. Closed Thanksgiving, Christmas.

ART COMMISSION OF THE CITY OF NEW YORK
City Hall, Broadway at Murray Street, New York, New York 10007
Portraits by American artists. Furniture of Federal period.
M.-F. 10-2. Closed public holidays.

ART GALLERY OF CENTER FOR INTER-AMERICAN RELATIONS
680 Park Avenue, New York, New York 10021
Contemporary Latin-American art.
Tu.-Su. 12-6.

BARTOW-PELL MANSION
Shore Road, Pelham Bay Park, New York, New York 10469
House (1836-42). Furniture, carpets, paintings and objets d'art of the period.
Tu., F., Su. 1-5.

BELL TELEPHONE LABORATORIES, INC.
463 West Street (14), New York, New York 10014
Development of the telephone.
By appointment.

BROOKLYN CHILDREN'S MUSEUM
1530 Bedford Avenue, Brooklyn, New York, New York 11216
Geology. Minerals. Fossils. Shells. Natural history. Planetarium. Anthropology. American Indian material. Prehistoric cultures. American and World history.
Oct. 1 - May 31: Tu.-F. 10-5; Sa., Su., public holidays 1-5. Jun. 1 - Sept. 30: M.-Sa. 10-5.

BROOKLYN MUSEUM
188 Eastern Parkway, Brooklyn, New York, New York 11238
American decorative arts and period rooms, including Brooklyn home (1675) of Jan Martense Shenck. European and American prints, drawings, paintings, sculpture. Primitive and African art. American Indian collections. Pre-Columbian Central and S. American art. Oriental, Middle Eastern and Islamic art. Greek and Roman art. American furniture, pewter, silver, ceramics.
W.-Sa. 10-5; Su. 11-5; public holidays 1-5. Closed Christmas.

CASSWELL-MASSEY PHARMACY
518 Lexington Avenue at 48th Street, New York, New York 10000
Pharmacy (1752). Display of old pharmacy equipment.
M.-F. 8.30-7; Sa. 10-6.

CHASE MANHATTAN BANK MONEY MUSEUM
1254 Avenue of the Americas, New York, New York 10020
Money from many countries and of many periods. Cheques signed by all U.S. Presidents.
Tu.-Sa. 10-5. Closed New Year, Thanksgiving, Christmas.

CHINESE MUSEUM
7 Moth Street, New York, New York 10000
Evolution of Chinese culture. Buddhist temple altars. Food display. Jade carvings.
Daily 10-10.

THE CITY COLLEGE ART GALLERY
139th Street and Convent Avenue (31), New York, New York 10031
16th-20th century European and American paintings, prints.
School days during school hours.

CLOISTERS
Fort Tryon Park, New York, New York 10040
European medieval art and architecture. Parts of 5 cloisters. 12th century apse. Sections of 12th century chapter house. Tapestries. Stained glass. Medieval religious art. Herbarium.
Tu.-Sa. 10-4.45; Su., public holidays 1-4.45.

CONFERENCE HOUSE
Conference House Park, 7455 Hylan Avenue, Tottenville, Staten Island, New York, New York 10307
House (c.1690) where unsuccessful conference to stop Revolutionary War was held.
Tu.-Su. 10-5.

COOPER-HEWITT MUSEUM OF DECORATIVE ARTS AND DESIGN
Andrew Carnegie Mansion, 190th Street and 5th Avenue, New York, New York 10028
Drawings and prints, especially 18th-19th century Italian designs for architecture and decoration; French designs for textiles and decoration: French ornamental prints; American wood engravings. 19th century American drawings. European and Oriental ceramics. Carved woodwork. Furniture. European, Oriental wallpaper. Oriental, Middle-Eastern and European textiles. Iron work. Silver. Glass.
Tu.-F. 12-9; Sa., Su., public holidays 1-5. Closed New Year, July 4, Thanksgiving, Christmas.

THE COOPER UNION MUSEUM
Cooper Square at 7th Street, New York, New York 10003
Decorative arts. Drawings. Prints.
Oct.-May, M.-Sa. 10-5.

DYCKMAN HOUSE
204th Street and Broadway, New York, New York 10053
Farmhouse (1788) and garden, restored to original condition. Period furnishings.
Tu.-Su. 11-5.

EL MUSEO DEL BARRIO
206 E. 116th Street, New York, New York 10029
Paintings, graphics, handicrafts by Puerto Rican artists.
M., Tu., Th. 10-5; W. 10-7; F. 10-2.

FEDERAL HALL NATIONAL MONUMENT
26 Wall Street, New York, New York 10005
Exhibits commemorating Washington's inauguration, Peter Zenger trial, Stamp Act Congress, Bill of Rights, first government under Articles of Confederation and first under U.S. Constitution.
Daily 9-5.

FINCH COLLEGE MUSEUM OF ART
62-4 E. 78th Street, New York, New York 10021
20th century paintings, sculpture, drawings, prints, posters.
Sept. 1 - June 30: Tu.-Su. 1-5. Closed New Year, Thanksgiving, Christmas.

JOHN H. FINLEY MUSEUM OF THE PRINTED WORD
***New York Times*, 229 W. 43rd Street, New York, New York 10038**
History of printing and of newspapers.
M.-F. 9-5. Closed public holidays.

FIRE DEPARTMENT MUSEUM
104 Duane Street, New York, New York 10007
Old apparatus and mementoes of New York City Fire Department.
M.-F. 9-4; Sa. 9-1. Closed public holidays.

FORT WADSWORTH MUSEUM
Fort Wadsworth, Staten Island, New York, New York 10000
History of Fort (1663) and of U.S. Army.
Sa., Su., public holidays 1-5. Other times by appointment.

FRAUNCES TAVERN MUSEUM
54 Pearl Street, New York, New York 10004
Revolutionary War relics. Art gallery.
M.-F. 10-4. Closed public holidays (except Washington's birthday).

FRICK COLLECTION
1 E. 70th Street, New York, New York 10021
House (1914) was formerly home of Henry C. Frick, steel industrialist. 14th-19th century European paintings, including works by Titian, El Greco, Renoir, Fragonard, Rembrandt, Goya. French 18th century furniture. Suites with Boucher, Fragonard decorations. Limoges enamels. 17th-18th century Chinese, French porcelain. 15th-18th century sculpture, especially Renaissance bronzes.
June 1 - Aug. 31: Th.-Sa. 10-6; W., Su. 1-6. Rest of year: Tu.-Sa. 10-6; Su. 1-6. Closed public holidays.

THE GARIBALDI AND MEUCCI MEMORIAL MUSEUM
420 Tomkins Avenue, Rosebank, Staten Island, New York, New York 10305
House (c.1810) was home of Antonio Meucci, inventor of the telephone. Working models of first telephone (1841). Relics of Italian Risorgimento wars.
Tu.-Sa. 10-5; Su. 1-5. Closed national holidays.

GENERAL GRANT NATIONAL MONUMENT
Riverside Drive and W. 122nd Street, New York, New York 10031
Memorabilia of Gen. Ulysses S. Grant. Military history.
W.-Su., public holidays 9-4.30.

SOLOMON R. GUGGENHEIM MUSEUM
5th Avenue between 88th and 89th Streets, New York, New York 10000
Museum building by Frank Lloyd Wright. 19th-20th century European and American paintings, sculpture, graphic arts. Includes works by Picasso, Chagall, Modigliani, Klee and Kandinsky.
W.-Sa. 10-6; Su., public holidays 12-6; Tu. 10-9. Closed July 4, Dec. 25.

HALLMARK GALLERY
720 5th Avenue, New York, New York 10019
Photography. Folk art. History of Hallmark Cards Inc.
M.-Sa. 9.30-7. Closed public holidays, Sa. July 1 - Aug. 31.

HALL OF FAME FOR GREAT AMERICANS
Campus of New York University, University Avenue and 181st Street, New York, New York 10028
Colonnade with 95 bronze busts and portrait plaques of prominent Americans.
Daily 9-5.

JOSPEH H. HIRSHHORN MUSEUM AND SCULPTURE GARDEN
135 E. 65th Street, New York, New York 10021
20th century American paintings, graphics. 19th-20th century American and European sculpture. 20th century European paintings.
By appointment.

JEWISH MUSEUM
1109 5th Avenue at 92nd Street, New York, New York 10028
In former Warburg Mansion (1908). Jewish ceremonial art. Sculpture garden.
M.-Th. 11-5; F. 11-3; Su. 11-6. Closed Jewish festivals.

JUNIOR MUSEUM OF THE METROPOLITAN MUSEUM OF ART
5th Avenue and 82nd Street, New York, New York 10028
Musical instruments. Arts and crafts of medieval Europe. 17th-18th century American period rooms.
Tu.-F. 10-9; W., Th., Sa. 10-5; Su., public holidays 11-5.

KING MANOR
Jamaica Avenue at 153rd Street, Jamaica, L.I., New York 10028
House (1750). Period furnishings.
M., W., Sa. 1.30-4.30.

KINGSBRIDGE HISTORICAL SOCIETY
144 W. 228th Street, Bronx (63), New York, New York 10463
History of Manhattan and the Bronx.
By appointment.

LEFFERTS HOMESTEAD
Prospect Park at Flatbush Avenue and Empire Boulevard, Brooklyn, New York, New York 11215
House (1776). Period furniture. Costumes.
Nov. 1 - May 31: W., F.-Su. 1-5. Closed 2nd Sa. each month.

JACQUES MARCHAIS CENTER OF TIBETAN ART
338 Lighthouse Avenue, Richmond, Staten Island, New York, New York 10306
Tibetan and other Buddhist art.
Apr. 1 - Oct. 31: Tu.-F., 2nd and 4th Sa. each month, 2-5.

MARINE MUSEUM OF THE CITY OF NEW YORK
1220 5th Avenue, New York, New York 10029
History of the Port of New York. Dioramas. Ship models.
Tu.-Sa. 10-5; Su., public holidays 1-5.

BRANDER MATTHEWS DRAMATIC MUSEUM
412 Low Library, New York, New York 10027
History of theatre arts. Architecture. Models. Playbills. Puppets. Costumes. Stage designs.
Oct. 1 - Aug. 15: M.-F. 1-5. Closed public holidays. Aug. 15-31 by appointment.

METROPOLITAN MUSEUM OF ART
5th Avenue and 82nd Street, New York, New York 10028
Art of Europe, America, Near and Far East, Greece, Rome. European period rooms. Costumes. European and Oriental arms and armour. Musical instruments. European decorative arts. Pre-Columbian art.
W.-Sa. 10-5; Tu. 10-9; Su., public holidays 11-5.

MUSEUM OF AMERICAN FOLK ART
49 W. 53rd Street, New York, New York 10019
Paintings and sculpture by self-taught American artists from Colonial times to the present, including portraits, weathervanes, figureheads, furniture, handicrafts.
Tu.-Su. 10.30-5.30. Closed New Year, Labour Day, Christmas.

MUSEUM OF THE AMERICAN INDIAN
Broadway and 155th Street, New York, New York 10032
Ethnology and archaeology of the Indians of N., S. and Central America and the W. Indies. Pre-Columbian art and archaeology.
Tu.-Su. 1-5. Closed public holidays, Aug. 1-31.

MUSEUM OF THE AMERICAN NUMISMATIC SOCIETY
Broadway and 155th Street, New York, New York 10032
Coins, medals, decorations of the world.
Tu.-Sa. 9-5; Su. 1-4. Closed public holidays.

MUSEUM OF THE CITY OF NEW YORK
5th Avenue and 103rd Street, New York, New York 10029
Social, economic, and political history of New York. Dioramas. Period rooms. Furniture. Costumes. Portraits. Prints. Decorative arts. Toys. Ship models and figureheads. Dutch Gallery, showing life in New Amsterdam. Views of New York City. Theatre and musical memorabilia. Maps. Photographs. Dolls and dolls-houses.
Tu.-Sa. 10-5; Su., public holidays 1-5.

MUSEUM OF CONTEMPORARY CRAFTS
29 W. 53rd Street, New York, New York 10019
National exhibition centre of American Crafts Council. American and foreign handicrafts, arranged to illustrate themes and stylistic development. Textiles. Metal. Ceramics. Wood.
M.-Sa. 11-6; Su., public holidays 1-6.

MUSEUM OF COURTSHIP, LOVE AND MARRIAGE
50 W. 57th Street, New York, New York 10019
History, psychology, sociology and folklore of family life. Dioramas. Paintings. Prints.
Daily 11-6.

MUSEUM OF FAMOUS PEOPLE
133 W. 50th Street, New York, New York 10019
Life-sized figures of celebrities, past and present. Recordings. Film.
Mar. 1 - Aug. 31: M.-F. 10 a.m. - 10.30 p.m. Sept. 1 - Feb. 28: M.-Th. 10-5.30.

MUSEUM OF GRAPHIC ART
245 W. 19th Street, New York, New York 10011
American graphics.
By appointment.

MUSEUM AND LIBRARY OF HISPANIC SOCIETY OF AMERICA
Broadway, between 155th and 156th Streets, New York, New York 10000
Art and literature of Spain. Spanish paintings, sculpture, decorative arts, representative of culture of Iberian peninsula from prehistoric times to the present.
Tu.-Sa. 10-4.30; Su. 2-5. Closed New Year, Feb. 12, Easter, May 30, July 4, Thanksgiving, Christmas.

MUSEUM OF LONG ISLAND HISTORICAL SOCIETY
128 Pierrepont Street at Clinton Street, Brooklyn, New York, New York 10000
Local history. Portraits. Prints. Costumes.
Tu.-Sa. 9-5. Closed public holidays, Aug. 1-31.

MUSEUM OF THE MEDIA
1 Union Square W., New York, New York 10003
History of media technology.
M.-F. 4-7; Sa., Su. 1-6. Closed public holidays.

MUSEUM OF MODERN ART
11 W. 54th Street, New York, New York 10000
World 20th century art. Paintings. Sculpture. Architecture. Photography. Industrial design. Prints. Drawings.
M.-W., F.-Sa. 11-6; Th. 11-9; Su. 12-6.

MUSEUM OF NEW YORK GENEALOGICAL AND BIOGRAPHICAL SOCIETY
122 E. 58th Street, New York, New York 10022
Genealogy. Portraits.
M.-F. 9.30-5. Oct. 1 - May 30, Sa. 9.30-5. Closed Aug. 1-31, public holidays.

MUSEUM OF NEW YORK HISTORICAL SOCIETY
170 Central Park W., 76th-77th Streets, New York, New York 10024
Collections relating to American history, especially New York City and New York State. Period rooms. Furniture. Paintings. Prints. Decorative arts. Folk arts. Ceramics. Silver. 433 original drawings from Audubon's *Birds of America.*
Tu.-F., Su. 1-5; Sa. 10-5.

MUSEUM OF PHARMACEUTICAL SCIENCES, COLUMBIA UNIVERSITY
115 W. 68th Street, New York, New York 10023
Apothecary's equipment. Patent medicines.
By appointment.

MUSEUM OF PHARMACY, BROOKLYN COLLEGE OF PHARMACY
600 Lafayette Avenue, Brooklyn, New York, New York 11216
Pharmaceutical equipment. History of drugs.
Nov. 1 - Mar. 31: M.-Th. 9-5; F. 9-4. Closed public holidays.

MUSEUM OF PRIMITIVE ART
15 W. 54th Street, New York, New York 10019
Native art of N. and S. America, Africa, Oceania. Sculpture. Mexican pottery. S. American textiles, featherwork. Wooden figures, masks from Africa and Oceania.
W.-F., public holidays 11-5; Sa. 12-5; Su. 1-5.

NATIONAL ACADEMY OF DESIGN
1083 5th Avenue, New York, New York 10028
Works by Academicians. Portraits.
Oct. 1 - Apr. 30, daily 1-5.

NATIONAL ART MUSEUM OF SPORT
Pennsylvania Plaza, New York, New York 10001
Paintings, graphics, sculpture with sporting subjects.
M.-F. 9-5.30; Sa., Su., public holidays 10-5.30. Closed Christmas, New Year.

NATIONAL INSTITUTE OF ARTS AND LETTERS
633 W. 155th Street, New York, New York 10032
Paintings, sculpture, drawings, prints by and about members of the Institute and of the American Academy of Arts and Letters.
Tu.-Su. 1-4. Closed public holidays.

NEW YORK CULTURAL CENTER
2 Columbus Circle, New York, New York 10019
19th-20th century American, European paintings, posters, sculpture.
Tu.-W., Sa.-Su., public holidays 11-6; Th. 11-9. Closed Christmas.

NEW YORK JAZZ MUSEUM
125 W. 55th Street, New York, New York 10019
Jazz memorabilia, paintings, posters, tapes, discs, films.
By appointment.

NEW YORK PUBLIC LIBRARY
5th Avenue and 42nd Street, New York, New York 10018
Early American paintings. Prints. U.S. postage stamps. Maps. Photographs. History of printing.
M.-F. 10-6.

NEW YORK STATE MARITIME MUSEUM
S. and Fulton Streets, New York, New York 10001
Building, Schermerhorn Block (1811-12). Maritime history of New York.
M.-Sa. 9-5.

NEW YORK UNIVERSITY ART COLLECTION
1 Washington Square Village, Suite 8S, New York, New York 10012
20th century American and European paintings, sculpture, graphics.
M.-F. 9.30-5.30.

OLD MERCHANT'S HOUSE
29 E. 4th Street, New York, New York 10003
House (1830). Original furniture. Costumes.
Tu.-Su. 2-5. Closed Aug. 1-31, public holidays.

PEN AND BRUSH
16 E. 10th Street, New York, New York 10003
Modern American paintings, sculpture.
M.-F. 9-5. Closed public holidays.

PIERPONT MORGAN LIBRARY
29 E. 36th Street, New York, New York 10016
Illuminated manuscripts. Autograph manuscripts. Early printed books. Book-binding. Paintings. Sculpture. Drawings. Objets d'art. Rembrandt etchings. 19th-20th century calligraphy.
June 1 - July 31: M.-F. 9.30-5. Rest of year: M.-Sa. 9.30-5. Closed public holidays, Aug. 1-31.

POE COTTAGE
Poe Park, 2640 Grand Concourse at Kingsbridge Road, New York, New York 10451
Home (1846-9) of Edgar Allan Poe, where he wrote many of his poems and where his wife died. Her bed and other furniture remain.
May 1 - Oct. 31: Tu.-Sa. 10-1, 2-5; Su. 1-5. Nov. 1 - Apr. 30: Sa. 10-1, 2-4; Su. 1-5.

POLICE ACADEMY AND MUSEUM
235 E. 20th Street, New York, New York 10003
Weapons. Uniforms. Narcotics. Gambling. Forging. Memorabilia of famous police incidents.
M.-F. 9-5.

RATSEY MUSEUM
E. Schofield Street, City Island, New York, New York 10000
Museum of sail-making, in sail-loft.
M.-Sa. 10-5.

RIVERSIDE MUSEUM
310 Riverside Drive at 103rd Street, New York, New York 10025
Contemporary American paintings, sculpture, photographs, graphics. American Indian paintings, crafts, artifacts. Japanese prints. Tibetan and Nepalese art.
Sept. 1 - June 30: Tu.-F., Su. 2-5. Closed public holidays.

NICHOLAS ROERICH MUSEUM
319 W. 107th Street, New York, New York 10025
Paintings by Nicholas Roerich of scenes in India, Tibet and Russia.
M.-F., Su. 2-5. Closed public holidays.

ROGER MORRIS JUMEL MANSION
W. 160th Street and Edgecombe Avenue, Washington Heights, New York, New York 10025
House (1765). 18th-early 19th century European and American furniture. Personal possessions of Jumel family. Portraits.
Tu.-Su. 11-5.

THEODORE ROOSEVELT BIRTHPLACE NATIONAL HISTORIC SITE
28 E. 20th Street, New York, New York 10003
Birthplace and boyhood home of President Theodore Roosevelt, furnished in style of 1850s. Mementoes of the President.
M.-F. 9-4.30. Closed New Year, Christmas.

SCALAMANDRE MUSEUM OF TEXTILES
201 E. 58th Street, New York, New York 10022
European and American textiles.
M.-F. 9-5; closed public holidays.

SOUTH STREET SEAPORT MUSEUM
16 Fulton Street, New York, New York 10038
Maritime history. Historic ships moored at pier; hull of square-rigged ship, 'Wavertree' (c.1885); iron schooner 'Pioneer' (1885); wooden fishing schooner 'Caviare' (1891); original Ambrose lightship (1907).
Daily 12-6.

STATEN ISLAND HISTORICAL SOCIETY
302 Center Street, Richmondtown, Staten Island, New York, New York 10306
Social, economic and political history of Staten Island community. Museum is part of a village restoration. Buildings completed include Voorlezer's house (c.1696), probably the earliest surviving elementary schoolhouse in the U.S., general store (1837), Lake-Tysen house (1840), carpenter's shop (1880) and carriage-house, with 19th century horse-drawn vehicles.
Tu.-Sa. 10-5; Su. 2-5.

STATEN ISLAND INSTITUTE OF ARTS AND SCIENCES
75 Stuyvesant Place, Staten Island, New York, New York 10301
Scientific and natural history material especially relevant to Staten Island. Geology. Ecology. Archaeology. Herbarium. Paintings. Prints.
Tu.-Sa. 10-5; Su., public holidays 2-5. Closed New Year, July 4, Labour Day, Thanksgiving, Christmas.

STATEN ISLAND MUSEUM
Stuyvesant Place and Wall Street, St. George, New York, New York 10306
Natural history. Science. Local history. American Indian and local archaeology. Photography.
Tu.-Sa. 10-5; Su. 2-5.

STATUE OF LIBERTY NATIONAL MONUMENT
Liberty Island, New York, New York 10004
Drawings, photographs, models, documents illustrating history of the Statue of Liberty.
Labour Day-Memorial Day: Tu. 9-4. Memorial Day-Labour Day: M.-F. 9-5; Sa., Su., public holidays 9-6.

STUDIO MUSEUM IN HARLEM
2033 5th Avenue, New York, New York 10035
African and Afro-American art.
M., W. 10-9; Tu., Th., F. 10-6; Sa., Su. 1-6. Closed public holidays.

TRAPHAGEN SCHOOL OF FASHION, MUSEUM COLLECTION
257 Park Avenue S., New York, New York 10010
National and period costumes and accessories. Dolls. Textiles and textile prints. American Indian pottery, baskets, blankets. Meissen, Chinese, Japanese porcelain.
By appointment.

VALENTINE-VARIAN HOUSE
Bainbridge Avenue and E. 207th Street, New York, New York 10467
House (c.1756). Bronx County Historical Museum. Natural history. Paintings. Prints. Photographs. Indian artifacts.
Su. 1-5.

VAN CORTLANDT HOUSE MUSEUM
Van Cortlandt Park, Broadway at 242nd Street, New York, New York 10471
House (1748). 17th-18th century furniture. Delftware. Pottery. Glass.
Tu.-Sa. 10-5; Su. 2-5. Closed Feb. 1-28.

WARSHAW COLLECTION OF BUSINESS AMERICANA
126 W. 97th Street (25), New York, New York 10025
19th-20th century history of American commerce. Advertisements. Posters. Catalogues. Packages. Labels. Trade cards.
By appointment.

WAVE HILL CENTER FOR ENVIRONMENTAL STUDIES
675 W. 252nd Street, Bronx, New York, New York 10471
House (1843-4). Botany. Environmental exhibits. Sculpture.
Daily 10-4.

WHITNEY MUSEUM OF AMERICAN ART
945 Madison Avenue at 75th Street, New York, New York 10021
Contemporary and historical American paintings, sculpture, prints.
M., W.-Sa. 11-6; Tu. 11-10; Su. 12-6.

WYCKOFF HOUSE
Canarsie Lane, Brooklyn, New York, New York 10000
17th century house. Dutch Colonial furniture.
By appointment.

NIAGARA

MUSEUM OF NIAGARA COMMUNITY HISTORICAL SOCIETY
Niagara, North Dakota 58266
Log cabin (1881). Pioneer history.
By appointment.

NIAGARA FALLS

NIAGARAMA ANIMATED HISTORICAL MUSEUM
18 W. Falls Street, Niagara Falls, New York 14301
Push-button displays of Niagara history.
Apr. 1 - Oct. 31, daily 9-midnight. Nov. 1 - Mar. 31, 9-6.

SCHOELLKOPJ GEOLOGICAL MUSEUM
Niagara Reservation, Niagara Falls, New York 14301
Audio-visual displays showing history of Falls from c.1790 to present day.
Daily 12-8.

NIANTIC

EAST LYME HISTORICAL SOCIETY
Romagna Court, Route 156, Niantic, Connecticut 06357
In Thomas Lee House (1660), with 17th-18th century furnishings. Local history.
Memorial Day - Columbus Day, M., W.-Su., 10-5.

NILES

FORT ST. JOSEPH MUSEUM
508 E. Main Street, Niles, Michigan 49120
Local history. Archaeology. Anthropology. Industry. Sioux Indian artifacts.
Tu.-Su. 1-5. Closed public holidays.

MUSEUM OF NATIONAL McKINLEY BIRTHPLACE MEMORIAL ASSOCIATION
40 N. Main Street, Niles, Ohio 44446
Furniture and memorabilia of President McKinley. Costumes. Military history. Glass.
M.-F. 10-8: Sa. 9.30-5.30; Su. 1-5. Closed Christmas, New Year, Memorial Day, July 4, Labour Day, Thanksgiving.

NOANK

NOANK HISTORICAL SOCIETY MUSEUM
17 Sylvan Street, Noank, Connecticut 06340
Local history. Indian artifacts. Maritime and naval history.
July-Aug., Sa., Su. 2-5. Sept.-June, W. 2-5. Other times by appointment.

NOBLESVILLE

CONNER PRAIRIE PIONEER SETTLEMENT AND MUSEUM
30 Conner Lane, Noblesville, Indiana 46060
Museum of local history and agriculture, based on group of early 19th century buildings, including log barn and cabin, trading post, schoolhouse and William Conner Homestead (1823).
Apr. 1 - Oct. 31, Tu.-Sa. 9.30-5; Su., public holidays 1-5. First 3 weekends in December, Sa., Su., 1-5.

INDIANA MUSEUM OF TRANSPORT AND COMMUNICATIONS
P.O. Box 83, Forest Park, Noblesville, Indiana 46060
In Hobbs Station (1930). Transport, especially railways. Indianapolis Traction terminal shed (1905) is in the care of the Museum.
May 1 - Oct. 31, M.-F. by appointment; Sa., Su., public holidays 1-6.

NOGALES

PETE KITCHEN MUSEUM
Pete Kitchen Ranch, Highway 89, Nogales, Arizona 85621
Furniture and armour of the Conquistador period. Mission relics. Navaho blankets. Branding irons. Guadalupe retable (1584). Mexican artifacts. Paintings. Pete Kitchen ranch house (1854) and Pete Kitchen fort (1860) are in the care of the Museum.
Tu.-Su., 10-5. Closed Christmas.

PIMERIA ALTA HISTORICAL SOCIETY MUSEUM
Grand Avenue, P.O. Box 2281, Nogales, Arizona 85611
Geology. Mineralogy. Archaeology. Indian artifacts. Costumes. History of medicine. Art collection.
W.-Su. 1-5. Closed public holidays.

NOME

NOME MUSEUM
Front Street, Nome, Alaska 99762
History of the Nome Gold Rush (1900). Indian artifacts. Archaeology. Contemporary art.
M., W.-F. 10-5.30; Tu. 10-5.30, 7.30-9; Sa. 1-4. Closed public holidays.

NORFOLK

NORFOLK HISTORICAL SOCIETY MUSEUM
Village Green, Norfolk, Connecticut 06058
Local history. Agriculture. Costumes. Crafts. Folklore.
June 16 - Sept. 14, Sa. 10-12, 2-5; Su. 2-5.

ELKHORN VALLEY HISTORICAL SOCIETY
104 E. Norfolk Street, Norfolk, Nebraska 68701
Local history.
Tu.-Su. 2-5; F. evening 7-9.

CHRYSLER MUSEUM
Mowbray Arch and Olney Road, Norfolk, Virginia 23510
History and archaeology of Norfolk. Natural history. Pre-Columbian art. Art of Africa, Middle East, Far East. European and American paintings, sculpture, drawings, prints, decorative arts. Glass. Furniture. Silver.
Adam Thoroughgood House (1630), Moses Myers house (1792) and Willoughby-Baylor House (1794) are in the care of the Museum.
Thanksgiving - Mar. 31, daily 12-5. Apr. 1 - Thanksgiving M.-Sa. 10-5; Su. 12-6. Closed New Year, Christmas.

HERMITAGE FOUNDATION MUSEUM
7637 N. Shore Road, Norfolk, Virginia 23505
Indian and Chinese art. Paintings. Sculpture. Decorative arts. Furniture. Coptic bronzes.
Daily 10-5. Closed Christmas.

HOTEL NANSEAMOND
236 W. Ocean View Avenue, Norfolk, Virginia 23503
Building where Gen. Patton planned invasion of Africa and Italy in World War II. Photographs of landings. Items of naval equipment.
Daily 8 a.m. - 11 p.m.

GENERAL DOUGLAS MacARTHUR MEMORIAL
City Hall Avenue and Bank Street, Norfolk, Virginia 23510
Personal papers and memorabilia of Gen. MacArthur.
M.-Sa. 10-5; Su., Apr 1-Thanksgiving, 11-6; Thanksgiving-Mar. 31, 12-5. Closed New Year, Christmas.

MUSEUM OF NORFOLK HISTORICAL SOCIETY
708 Professional Arts Building, Norfolk, Virginia 23510
Local history.
Nov. 1 - Apr. 30: M.-F. 10-2.

ADAM THOROUGHGOOD HOUSE
1635 Parrish Road, Bayside, Virginia Beach, Norfolk, Virginia 23455
House (1650). Early American furnishings. Local history.
M.-Sa. 10-5; Su. 12-5.

NORMAL

ILLINOIS STATE UNIVERSITY MUSEUMS
Normal, Illinois 61761
Mineralogy. Natural history. Agriculture. Pioneer and Indian life. Culture and artifacts of Illinois prehistoric Indians. Social history.

Eyestone Rural School (1899) is in the care of the Museums.
Funk Mineral Museum: M.-F. 8-11.30, 12.30-5; Sa. 9-12, 1-5; Su. 2-5.
Eyestone School, Hudelson Agricultural Museum: by appointment.
Stevenson Memorial Room: M. 1-5; Tu. 10-12, 3-5; W. 8-12, 1-5; Th. 10-12, 3-5. Closed University vacations.

NORMAN

BEBB HERBARIUM OF THE UNIVERSITY OF OKLAHOMA
770 Van Vleet Oval, Norman, Oklahoma 73069
Botany. Herbarium.
Daily 9-5.

MUSEUM OF ART, UNIVERSITY OF OKLAHOMA
410 W. Boyd Avenue, Norman, Oklahoma 73069
Chinese, Japanese, Indian art. Contemporary American paintings. American and European sculpture, graphics, design.
Tu.-F. 10-4; Sa. 10-1; Su. 1-4. Closed public holidays.

STOVALL MUSEUM OF SCIENCE AND HISTORY
University of Oklahoma, 1335 Asp Avenue, Norman, Oklahoma 73069
Earth sciences. Life sciences. Social sciences. Greek and Roman art and archaeology. Local history.
M.-F. 9-5; Sa., Su. 1-5. Closed Thanksgiving, Christmas, New Year.

NORRISTOWN

MUSEUM OF HISTORICAL SOCIETY OF NORRIS COUNTY
1654 DeKalb Street, Norristown, Pennsylvania 19401
Civil, political, religious history of Montgomery County. 18th - early 19th century American and English furniture. Household equipment. Coverlets, quilts. Needlework. Indian artifacts. Weapons. Civil War relics.
M.-F. 10-4; Sa. by appointment. Closed public holidays, Aug. 1-31.

NORTHAMPTON

CALVIN COOLIDGE MEMORIAL ROOM
Forbes Library, Northampton, Massachusetts 01060
Documents, recordings and photographs relating to Calvin Coolidge and his wife.
M.-Sa. 8-9.30; Su., public holidays 2-6. Closed Memorial Day, July 4, Thanksgiving, Christmas.

CORNET JOSEPH PARSON'S HOUSE
58 Bridge Street, Northampton, Massachusetts 01060
House (1658). 17th-18th century furnishings.
W., F., Su. 2-5. Other times by appointment.

ISAAC DAMON HOUSE
46 Bridge Street, Northampton, Massachusetts 01060
House (1820), formerly home of Isaac Damon, architect and bridge-builder.
Summer: W., Sa. 2-5. Closed holidays.

FORBES LIBRARY
West Street, Northampton, Massachusetts 01060
English miniatures. Paintings, drawings by local artists.
M.-Sa. 9-6.

NORTHAMPTON HISTORICAL SOCIETY MUSEUM
58 Bridge Street, Northampton, Massachusetts 01060
Local history.
Cornet Joseph Parsons House (1658) and Isaac Damon House (1812) are in the care of the Society.
W., F., Su. 2-4.30.

SMITH COLLEGE MUSEUM OF ART
McConnell Hall, Smith College, Northampton, Massachusetts 01060
18th-20th century European art, especially French. 20th century American art.
M.-Sa. 9-5; Su. 2.30-4.30. Closed New Year, July 4, Labour Day, Thanksgiving, Christmas.

NORTH ANDOVER

MERRIMACK VALLEY TEXTILE MUSEUM
Massachusetts Avenue, North Andover, Massachusetts 01845
History of American textile industry. Machinery. Tools. Implements, 18th-20th century. Textiles. Business records.
Daily 1-5. Closed New Year, Easter, Thanksgiving, Christmas.

MUSEUM OF NORTH ANDOVER HISTORICAL SOCIETY
153 Academy Road, North Andover, Massachusetts 01845
American furniture, textiles, silver. Tools. Domestic equipment. 17th-19th century decorative arts.
Parson Barnard House (c.1715) and 4 other houses are in the care of the Society.
Su. 1-5. July 4 1-7.

NORTH ATTLEBOROUGH

NORTH ATTLEBOROUGH HISTORICAL SOCIETY
South Washington Street, North Attleborough, Massachusetts 02762
Local history. Paintings. Documents.
By appointment.

NORTH BEND

COOS-CURRY MUSEUM
Simpson Park, North Bend, Oregon 97459
Indian material. Local history.
May 1 - Oct. 31: Tu.-Su. 11-5. Nov. 1 - Apr. 30: Tu.-Su. 1-5. Closed Christmas.

SNOQUALMIE VALLEY HISTORICAL MUSEUM
4th and Ballarat Streets, North Bend, Washington 98045
Local history. Indian artifacts. Pioneer life.
Tu. 7-9; Sa., Su. 1-5. Closed public holidays.

NORTH BENNINGTON

GOVERNOR McCULLOUGH MANSION
North Bennington, Vermont 05257
House (c.1855). Home of John G. McCullough, Governor of Vermont, 1902-4. Original furniture, paintings. Costumes and accessories.
July 1 - Oct. 31: Tu.-F., Su. 10-5; Sa. by appointment.

NORTHBOROUGH

MUSEUM OF NORTHBOROUGH HISTORICAL SOCIETY
52 Main Street, Northborough, Massachusetts 01532
Tools. Domestic equipment. Educational history.
May 17 - Oct. 11: W., 1-4. Other times by appointment.

NORTH BRUNSWICK

BOY SCOUTS OF AMERICA CONSERVATION EDUCATION CENTER
Routes 1 and 130, North Brunswick, New Jersey 08902
Geology. Soil. Water. Botany. Natural history.
M.-Sa. 9-5; Su. 1-5.

JOHNSTON HISTORICAL MUSEUM, BOY SCOUTS OF AMERICA
Route U.S.1 and 130, North Brunswick, New Jersey 08903
History of Boy Scouts of America. Paintings of Scouts by Norman Rockwell. Stamps.
M.-Sa. 9-5; Su. 1-5. Closed public holidays.

NORTH COLLINS

NORTH COLLINS HISTORICAL SOCIETY
North Collins Memorial Library, Center Street, North Collins, New York 14111
Local history. Period room (1850). Prints. Photographs. Military history. Indian relics.
May-Sept. by appointment.

NORTH CREEK

GARNET MINE
Gore Mountain, Route 28, North Creek, New York 12853
Open-pit mine. Tours showing geology, history and operating techniques of mine.
June 26 - Sept. 6: M.-Sa. 9-5; Su. 11-5.

NORTH EAST

MUSEUM OF LAKE SHORE RAILWAY HISTORICAL SOCIETY
Wall and Robinson Streets, North East, Pennsylvania 16428
In former railway station (1901). Local railway history.
Memorial Day - Labour Day, Su. 1-5.

NORTH EDGECOMB

FORT EDGECOMB STATE MEMORIAL
North Edgecomb, Maine 04556
Wooden blockhouse (1808). History of Fort Edgecomb.
By appointment.

NORTHFIELD

MUSEUM OF NORWEGIAN-AMERICAN HISTORICAL ASSOCIATION
St. Olaf College Library, Northfield, Minnesota 55057
Books, documents, personal papers and other material relating to the Norwegian immigration to America.
M.-F. 9-5; Sa., Su., College vacations by appointment.

MUSEUM OF HISTORICAL SOCIETY OF OLDE NORTHFIELD
Box 99, Northfield, Ohio 44067
Local history. Agriculture. Industry. Indian artifacts. Costumes.
Palmer House (1852) is in the care of the Society.
Daily 7 p.m. - 9. Closed New Year, Christmas.

NORWICH UNIVERSITY MUSEUM
Northfield, Vermont 05663
Local history. Globes (1811) made by James Wilson. Admiral George Dewey trophies. Weapons. Cadet uniforms, 1830-1890.
M.-F. 8.30-4.30; Sa. 8.30-11.30.

PRESIDENT CHESTER A. ARTHUR BIRTHPLACE
Northfield, Vermont 05663
Replica of President Chester's birthplace. Period furnishings. Memorabilia of the President.
Memorial Day - Oct. 15: Tu.-Su. 9-6.

NORTHFORD

NORTHFORD HISTORICAL SOCIETY MUSEUM
Northford, Colorado 06472
Local history. Products of 19th century local manufacturing industries.
By appointment.

NORTH FREEDOM

MID-CONTINENT RAILWAY HISTORICAL SOCIETY MUSEUM
North Freedom, Wisconsin 53951
In North Freedom Railway Depot (1884). Locomotives. Railway equipment. Tramway cars and equipment.
May 30 - Labour Day, daily 10-5.

NORTH GROTON

MARY BAKER EDDY HISTORICAL HOUSE
North Groton, New Hampshire 03582
Home of Mary Baker Eddy (1856-59). Memorabilia of Mrs. Eddy.
May 30 - Oct., M.-W., F., Sa. 10-5. Closed national holidays.

NORTH HACKENSACK

DEMAREST HOUSE
Main Street, North Hackensack, New Jersey 07661
House (1678), reconstructed on site next to Von Steuben House. Period furnishings.
By appointment.

VON STEUBEN HOUSE
Main Street, North Hackensack, New Jersey 07661
House (1739). Colonial furniture. China. Glass. History of Bergen County. Indian artifacts. Early industry.
Tu.-Sa. 10-12, 1-5; Su., public holidays 2-5. Closed New Year, Thanksgiving, Christmas.

NORTH HOLLYWOOD

CIVIC ARTS CENTER
Campo de Cahuenga, 3191 Lankershim Boulevard, North Hollywood, California 91604
Replica of house where treaty between Mexico and United States was signed. Portraits. Documents.
M.-F. 8-4, 7-10; Sa., Su. on permit.

NORTH INGLEWOOD

LA CASA DE LA CENTINELA ADOBE
7634 Midfield Avenue, North Inglewood, California 90301
Adobe built in the early 1800s, furnished with Victorian pieces.
Su., W. 2-4.

NORTH KINGSTON

CASEY FARM
Route A, North Kingston, Rhode Island 02881
House and farm buildings (c.1750), home of General T. L. Casey, supervising engineer for Washington Monument and Library of Congress. Casey family furnishings.
June-Oct., Tu., Th., Sa. 1-5.

NORTH KINGSTOWN

SOUTH COUNTY MUSEUM
Scrabbletown Road, Box 182, North Kingstown, Rhode Island 02852
History of Rhode Island. Agriculture. Transport. Household equipment.
June-Sept., Tu.-Su. 1-5.

NORTH MANCHESTER

MANCHESTER COLLEGE MUSEUM
North Manchester, Indiana 46962
Natural history.
By appointment.

NORTH MIAMI BEACH

MONASTERY CLOISTER OF ST. BERNARD
16711 West Dixie Highway, North Miami Beach, Florida 33160
Reconstruction, with original stones, of cloister and refectory of monastery (1154) at Segovia, Spain. Religious paintings, sculpture.
M.-Sa. 10-4; Su., public holidays, Ash Wednesday, Good Friday, Holy Saturday, Easter, 12-4. Closed Christmas.

NORTH NEWTON

KAUFFMAN MUSEUM
E. 27th Street, North Newton, Kansas 67117
Geology. Natural history. Anthropology. Agriculture. Indian material.
Pioneer home (1875) is in the care of the Museum.
M.-F. 8.30-5; Sa. 8.30-12; Su. 1-5. Closed Easter, Christmas.

MENNONITE LIBRARY
North Newton, Kansas 67117
Anabaptist and Mennonite history. Documents. Paintings, prints.
M.-F. 8-5; Sa. 8-12. Closed public holidays.

NORTH OXFORD

CLARA BARTON BIRTHPLACE
Clara Barton Road, North Oxford, Massachusetts 01537
House (1805), birthplace of Clara Barton, founder of the American Red Cross. Memorabilia and personal possessions of Clara Barton.
Tu.-Sa. 1-4; Su., public holidays 2-4.

NORTH PLAINS

MRS. JACOB VAN DOMELEN'S FARM
Mountaindale Road, North Plains, Oregon 97133
Indian artifacts.
By appointment.

NORTH PLATTE

BUFFALO BILL'S RANCH
State Historical Park, Route 1, North Platte, Nebraska 69109
In Buffalo Bill's scouts' rest ranch (1886). History of Buffalo Bill. Indian material.
May 1 - Sept. 30: M.-F. 9-9; Sa., Su. 9-10. Oct. 1 - Apr. 30: M.-Sa. 2-5; Su. 10-5.

SIOUX LOOKOUT
D.A.R. Log Cabin Museum, Memorial Park, North Platte, Nebraska 69101
Cabin (1868). Natural history. Local history. Indian artifacts. Costumes. Folklore. Music.
June 1 - Aug. 31: Daily 12-4.

NORTHPORT

NORTHPORT HISTORICAL SOCIETY MUSEUM
Box 545, Northport, New York 11768
Local history.
M.-F. 8.30-4.

NORTH SALEM

HAMMOND MUSEUM
Deveau Road, North Salem, New York 10560
History. Religious, Oriental, decorative and folk arts. Costumes.
May 15 - Dec. 31: W.-Su. 11-5. Closed Thanksgiving, Christmas.

NORTH SWANSEA

MARTIN HOUSE
Route 6, North Swansea, Massachusetts
Farmhouse (c.1750). 18th-early 19th century furnishings, household equipment. Needlework. Pewter. Family portraits. Indian relics.
May 1 - Nov. 1, daily 10-6.

NORTHUMBERLAND

JOSEPH PRIESTLEY HOUSE
472 Priestley Avenue, Northumberland, Pennsylvania 17857
House (1794). Home of Priestley. Period furnishings. Priestley memorabilia. 18th-early 19th century scientific equipment.
May 1 - Oct. 31: Tu.-Sa. 8.30-5; Su. 1-5. Nov. 1 - Apr. 30: Tu.-Sa. 9-4.30; Su. 1-4.30. Closed public holidays.

NORTH VASSALBORO

VASSALBORO HISTORICAL SOCIETY MUSEUM
North Vassalboro, Maine 04962
History of Vassalboro.
June 1 - Sept. 15: W., Su. 2-4. Other times by appointment.

NORTH WILKESBORO

WILKES COUNTY HISTORICAL SOCIETY
North Wilkesboro Town Hall, Main Street, North Wilkesboro, North Carolina 28659
Local history.
By appointment.

NORTON

STATION 15
200 Horace Greeley Avenue, Norton, Kansas 67654
Replica of stagecoach and waggontrain depot (1859), with costumed figures. Indian artifacts.
Daily, 24 hours.

WHEATON COLLEGE
Watson Gallery, Watson Hall, Norton, Massachusetts 02766
19th-20th century American, European paintings.
M.-F. 2-5, 7-9; Sa., Su. 2-5. Other times by appointment.

NORWALK

LOCKWOOD-MATHEWS MANSION MUSEUM
295 West Avenue, Norwalk, Connecticut 06850
House (c.1863). Victorian furnishings, domestic equipment.
Su. 2-5. Other times by appointment.

FIRELANDS MUSEUM
4 Case Avenue, Norwalk, Ohio 44857
Geology. Palaeontology. Local history and archaeology. Indian material. Weapons. Coins. Primitive paintings. Decorative arts. Primitive art.
May 1 - June 30, Sept. 1 - Oct. 31: Tu.-Su. 12-6. July 1 - Aug. 31: M.-Sa. 9-6; Su. 12-6. Apr. 1-30, Nov. 1-30: Sa., Su. 12-6. Dec. 1 - Mar. 31: by appointment.

NORWELL

JACOBS FARM
Main Street and Jacobs Lane, Assinippi, Norwell, Massachusetts 02061
Farmhouse (c.1750), with later additions. Period rooms. Local history. Early fire-fighting equipment.
June-Sept., Tu., Th., Sa. 1-5.

NORWICH

LEFFINGWELL INN
348 Washington Street, Norwich, Connecticut 06360
House (1675). Period furnishings. Norwich silver, pewter. Indian artifacts.
The Joseph Carpenter Silversmith Shop (1772-4) is also in the care of the Society of the Founders of Norwich.
May 16-31, Tu.-Su. 2-4; June 1 - Labour Day, Tu.-Su. 10-12, 2-4. Labour Day - Oct. 15, Tu.-Su. 2-4. Oct. 16 - May 14, Sa., Su. 2-4. Other times by appointment.

MUSEUM OF THE FAITH TRUMBULL CHAPTER OF THE DAUGHTERS OF THE AMERICAN REVOLUTION
42 Rockwell Green, Norwich, Connecticut 06360
Local history.
Nathanial Backus house (1750) and Rockwell House (1818) are in the care of the Chapter.
July 1 - Aug. 31, W. 2-5.

SLATER MEMORIAL MUSEUM
108 Crescent Street, Norwich, Connecticut 06360
17th-18th century Oriental ceramics, prints, woodcarvings, textiles, ivories. 17th-19th century American furniture, ceramics, pewter. 16th-18th century European furniture. 17th-18th century lace, jewellery. 19th-20th century American paintings, prints. Persian tiles. Egyptian bronzes, pottery. Greek pottery. Maritime history.
Sept.-May, M.-F. 9-4; Sa., Su. 2-5. June-Aug., Tu.-Su. 1-4. Closed public holidays.

CHENANGO COUNTY HISTORICAL SOCIETY MUSEUM
Silver and Rexford Streets, Norwich, New York 13815
County history. Agriculture. Settlers' handicrafts, artifacts. Tools. Indian artifacts.
June 1 - Sept. 30: Tu., W., Sa., Su. 2-5.

NORWOOD

NORWOOD HISTORICAL SOCIETY MUSEUM
93 Day Street, Norwood, Massachusetts 02062
In Day House (1859). Victorian furnishings. Toys.
By appointment.

NORWOOD MUSEUM
39 N. Main Street, Norwood, New York 13668
Local history. Industry. Railway history. Fire-fighting equipment.
Apr. 1 - Nov. 30: 2nd, 4th Tu. each month, 2-4. Other times by appointment.

MORTON MORTONSEN HOUSE
Darby Creek and Muckmipates Creek, Norwood, Pennsylvania 19074
House (1764). Folk art.
By appointment.

NOTRE DAME

UNIVERSITY OF NOTRE DAME ART GALLERY
O'Shaughnessy Hall, Notre Dame, Indiana 46556
Primitive art. Archaeology. Italian Renaissance paintings, sculpture. 17th-18th century European paintings. 20th century European and American paintings, sculpture, prints, drawings. Furniture. Tapestries. Ceramics. Glass.
M.-F. 10-5; Sa., Su. 1-5. Closed New Year, Thanksgiving, July 4, Christmas.

UNIVERSITY OF NOTRE DAME HERBARIA
Department of Biology, University of Notre Dame, Notre Dame, Indiana 46556
Herbaria of plants from the American West, Mid-west and Atlantic States.
By appointment.

NOVATO

NOVATO PREHISTORY MUSEUM
2200 Novato Boulevard, Novato, California 94947
Marin County archaeology. Palaeontology. Mineralogy. Ethnology.
Daily 9-5.

NUTLEY

NUTLEY HISTORICAL SOCIETY MUSEUM
65 Church Street, Nutley, New Jersey 07110
In former schoolhouse (1875). Mineralogy. Birds of New Jersey. Local history. Early Americana. Costumes. Circus history. Children's museum. Paintings, sculpture, graphics by local artists.
Vreeland Homestead (1702), Fire Department (1894) are in the care of the Society.
M.-Sa. by appointment; Su., public holidays 2-5. Closed Christmas.

OAK CREEK

OAK CREEK HISTORICAL SOCIETY MUSEUM
8500 S. 15th Street, Oak Creek, Wisconsin 53154
Local history.
Blacksmith's shop (1889) and Town Hall (1877) are in the care of the Society.
June 1 - Sept. 30, Su. 2-4.

OAKDALE

MUSEUM OF BAYARD CUTTING ARBORETUM
Montauk Highway, Route 27A, Great River, Oakdale, New York 11769
Geology. Mineralogy. Ornithology.
Apr. 15 - Oct. 15, daily 9-6. Rest of year, Sa., Su., public holidays 9-6. Closed Christmas, New Year.

OAK HILL

SHIRLEY DONNELLY MUSEUM
Pea Ridge Section, Oak Hill, West Virginia 25901
Mineralogy. Local history and archaeology. Indian artifacts. Folklore.
M.-Sa. 9-5.

OAKLAND

MILLS COLLEGE ART GALLERY
Seminary and MacArthur Boulevard, Oakland, California 94613
California paintings, prints. European and American prints, drawings. Guatemalan textiles.
W.-Su., 12-4. Closed College vacations.

OAKLAND MUSEUM
1000 Oak Street, Oakland, California 94607
Geology. Palaeontology. Natural history. Botany. Oceanography. Indian artifacts. Paintings. Sculpture. Graphics. Decorative arts. Gold Rush pictures. Sketches and paintings by California artist-explorers. Photographs of California subjects.
M.-Th., Sa., Su. 10-5; F., 10-10. Closed New Year, Thanksgiving, Christmas.

OAKLAND PUBLIC LIBRARY
Art and Picture Division, 125 14th Street, Oakland, California 94612
Paintings of California wild flowers by Kate Cole. Prints. Autographed photographs of eminent Californians.
M.-F. 9-9; Sa. 10-6.

ROTARY NATURAL SCIENCE CENTER
1520 Lakeside Drive, Oakland, California 94612
Natural history. Local history. Children's Museum.
Joaquin Miller's Abbey (1880) is in the care of the Center.
M. 12-5. Tu.-Su., public holidays 10-5.

GARRETT COUNTY HISTORICAL MUSEUM
Center Street, Oakland, Maryland 21550
Local history. Indian artifacts. Period rooms. Glass. Domestic utensils.
M.-F. 9-5.

OAKLEY

MUSEUM OF DAUGHTERS OF THE UTAH PIONEERS
105 W. Main Street, Oakley, Idaho 83346
Pioneer history. Household equipment. Arrowheads.
May-Sept., Sa., Su., public holidays 2-6. July 24-25, 9-9.

OAK PARK

FREEDOM HALL MUSEUM
1235 North Harlem Avenue, Oak Park, Illinois 60301
Local history. Americana.
Sept. 15 - June 15, Su. 1-5. Other days by appointment. Closed public holidays.

OAK RIDGE

AMERICAN MUSEUM OF ATOMIC ENERGY
Jefferson Circle, Oak Ridge, Tennessee 37830
Nuclear science. Exhibits showing peaceful uses of atomic energy.
M.-Sa. 9-5; Su. 12.30-6.30. Closed New Year, Thanksgiving, Christmas.

OBERLIN

LAST INDIAN RAID MUSEUM
258 S. Penn Avenue, Oberlin, Kansas 67749
Local history. Relics of 1878 Indian raid. Sod house.
May 1 - Sept. 30: M.-Sa. 9-9; Su., public holidays 1.30-9. Oct. 1 - Apr. 30: M.-Sa. 9-5; Su., public holidays 1.30-5. Closed Thanksgiving, Christmas.

ALLEN MEMORIAL ART MUSEUM, OBERLIN COLLEGE
Oberlin, Ohio 44074
Archaeology. Paintings. Sculpture. Graphics. Decorative arts.
M.-F. 9.30-12, 1.30-4.30, 7-9; Su. 1.30-5, 7-9.

LITTLE RED SCHOOLHOUSE
80 S. Main Street, Oberlin, Ohio 44074
Schoolhouse (1836). Period furnishings, books, equipment.
By appointment.

OBERLIN HISTORICAL SOCIETY MUSEUM
Vine Street, Oberlin, Ohio 44074
In restored 19th century schoolhouse. Pioneer school furnishings, equipment.
M., W., F. 2-4.

OCEAN CITY

OCEAN CITY HISTORICAL MUSEUM
409 Wesley Avenue, Ocean City, New Jersey 08226
Natural history. Local history. Victorian period rooms. Fashions.
June 15 - Sept. 14: M.-Sa. 10-4. Sept. 15 - June 14: Tu.-Sa. 1-4. Closed public holidays.

OCEANPORT

MUSEUM OF OCEANPORT HISTORICAL SOCIETY
Oceanport Municipal Building, Oceanport, New Jersey 07757
History of Oceanport.
By appointment.

OCEANSIDE

SAN LUIS REY HISTORICAL SOCIETY MUSEUM
1945 South Pacific Street, Oceanside, California 92054
Palaeontology. Ethnology. Local history. Indian artifacts.
By appointment.

OCONTO

BEYER HOME, OCONTO COUNTY HISTORICAL MUSEUM
917 Park Avenue, Oconto, Wisconsin 54153
House (1860). 18th-19th century furnishings.
Holt and Balcon Logging Camp (1880), with fur-trade and lumbering relics, is in the care of the Museum.
May 30 - Labour Day, M.-Sa. 9-5; Su., public holidays 12.30-6.

ODESSA

CORBIT-SHARP HOUSE
Main Street, Odessa, Delaware 19730
Restored house (1772), John Janvier stable (1791). 18th-19th century decorative arts, furniture. Local history.
Tu.-Sa., 10-5; Su., Easter, 2-5. Closed public holidays.

WILSON-WARNER HOUSE
Main Street, Odessa, Delaware 19730
Restored house (1745-69). Local history and archaeology. Decorative arts.
Tu.-Sa., 10-5; Su., Easter, 2-5. Closed public holidays.

MUSEUM OF SCHUYLER COUNTY HISTORICAL SOCIETY
Odessa, New York 14869
Local history and archaeology. Agriculture.
Tu., F., Sa. 2-5.

ODESSA COLLEGE MUSEUM
2300 Andrews Highway, Odessa, Texas 79760
History of West Texas. Indian artifacts.
M.-Sa. 9-5. Closed Thanksgiving, Christmas, Easter.

ODESSA METEORITE MUSEUM
U.S. 80, Odessa, Texas 79760
Site of U.S. second largest meteor crater. Photographs and fragments of meteorites.
Th.-M. 10-6. Closed Tu., W., Christmas Day.

PRESIDENTIAL MUSEUM
622 N. Lee Street, Odessa, Texas 79760
Raymer portraits of U.S. Presidents. Russell portraits of Presidents of Republic of Texas. Presidential campaign items. First Lady dolls.
May 1 - Sept. 30, M.-F. 9-5, Sa. 9-6.

OGALLALA

TRAILS MUSEUM
Route 2, Box 37, Ogallala, Nebraska 69153
Geology. Natural history. Local history. Indian material. Costumes. Transport. Music.
Country schoolhouse (1902) and J. W. Welpton home (1918) are in the care of the Museum.
Apr. 1 - Dec. 31, daily 9-9.

OGDEN

BROWNING GUN COLLECTION
National Guard Armoury, 625 E. and 5300 S. Streets, Ogden, Utah 34401
Guns invented by or associated with John M. Browning.
M.-F. 8-5. Closed public holidays, July 24.

PIONEER RELIC HALL AND MILES GOODYEAR CABIN
2148 Grant Avenue, Ogden, Utah 34403
Pioneer cabin (1841). Pioneer furnishings, costumes, painting, drawings, handicrafts.
June 10 - Sept. 10, 1-4.30.

WEBER STATE COLLEGE, MUSEUM OF NATURAL HISTORY
3750 Harrison Boulevard, Ogden, Utah 34403
Geology. Natural history.
M.-F. 8-5. Closed College vacations.

OGDENSBURG

REMINGTON ART MUSEUM
State and Washington Streets, Ogdensburg, New York 13669
In former Remington-Parish Mansion (1809). Paintings, bronzes, sketches of the Old West by Frederic Remington. Remington's personal library. 19th century American and European paintings. Belter furniture.
M.-Sa. 10-5. June 1 - Sept. 30, 1-5. Closed public holidays.

OGUNQUIT

BARN GALLERY ASSOCIATES
Shore Road and Bourne's Lane, Ogunquit, Maine 03907
20th century American paintings, sculpture, graphics.
June 15 - Sept. 15: M.-Sa. 10-5, 8-10; Su. 2-5.

MUSEUM OF ART OF OGUNQUIT
Shore Road, Ogunquit, Maine 03907
20th century American paintings, sculpture.
July 1 - Labour Day: M.-Sa. 10.30-5; Su. 1.30-5.

OKANOGAN

MUSEUM OF OKANOGAN COUNTY HISTORICAL SOCIETY
County Court House, Okanogan, Washington 98840
Natural history. History of Washington State and Okanogan County.
W. 1.30-4.30. Other times by appointment.

OKEMAH

INDIAN TERRITORY TOWN MUSEUM
1-40 at S4.48, Okemah, Oklahoma 74859
Indian Territory history. Civil War relics. Guns. Photographs. Documents.
Daily 8 a.m. - 9 p.m. Closed Christmas.

OKLAHOMA CITY

CONTEMPORARY ARTS FOUNDATION GALLERY
609 Robert S. Kerr Avenue, Oklahoma City, Oklahoma 73102
Works by contemporary American artists. Paintings. Sculpture. Prints. Drawings. Ceramics. Theatre history.
M.-Sa. 10-4; Su. 2-5.

MUSEUM OF OKLAHOMA SCIENCE AND ARTS FOUNDATION
3000 General Pershing Boulevard, Oklahoma City, Oklahoma 73107
Geology. Mineralogy. Astronomy. Planetarium. Science and petroleum models. 16th-17th century European paintings. Weapons. Coins. Stamps.
M.-Sa. 9-5; Su. 1-5. Closed public holidays.

NATIONAL COWBOY HALL OF FAME AND WESTERN HERITAGE CENTER
1700 N.E. 63rd Street, Oklahoma City, Oklahoma 73111
Rodeo Hall of Fame. Paintings of the American West. History and mementoes of cowboys and the cattle industry.
Daily 9.30-5.30. Closed Christmas, New Year.

OKLAHOMA ART CENTER
3113 Pershing Boulevard, Oklahoma City, Oklahoma 73107
18th-20th century American paintings, sculpture, prints, decorative arts. Early American glass.
Tu.-Sa. 10-5; Su. 2-5. Closed July 4, Memorial Day, Thanksgiving, Christmas, New Year.

OKLAHOMA FIREFIGHTERS MUSEUM
2716 N.E. 50th Street, Oklahoma City, Oklahoma 93111
In fire-station (1869). History of fire-fighting.
Daily 10-5.

OKLAHOMA HISTORICAL SOCIETY MUSEUM
Historical Building, Oklahoma City, Oklahoma 73105
State history from prehistoric times. Archaeology. Indian artifacts. Pioneer life. Paintings.
11 historic houses (1832-1920) are in the care of the Society.
M.-F. 8-9.30; Sa. 8-6; Su. 1.30-4.30. Closed public holidays.

OKLAHOMA MUSEUM OF ART
5500 N. Lincoln Boulevard, Oklahoma City, Oklahoma 73105
19th-20th century American paintings, graphics.
Tu.-Sa. 1-4; Su. 2-5.

TREBOR INTERIORS AND GALLERY
5105 N. Portland Street, Oklahoma City, Oklahoma 73100
20th century European and American graphics, including works by Picasso, Chagall, Dali.
M.-Sa. 9-5; Su. 1-5.

NORMAN WILKS GALLERY
3839 N.W. 63rd Street, Oklahoma City, Oklahoma 73100
American and European paintings, watercolours.
M.-F. 8-5; Sa. 8-12.

OKMULGEE

CREEK COUNCIL HOUSE AND MUSEUM
Creek Council House, Town Square, Okmulgee, Oklahoma 74447
In Indian Council House (1870). Indian history. Paintings of Creek Indian chiefs. Local pioneer history. Indian paintings.
June 1 - Aug. 31: M.-Sa. 9-5; Su. 1-5. Sept. 1 - May 31: Tu.-Sa. 9-5. Closed Christmas, New Year, Memorial Day, Thanksgiving.

OLD BENNINGTON

BENNINGTON MUSEUM
W. Main Street, Old Bennington, Vermont 05201
Local history. Bennington pottery. American furniture, glass. Paintings by Vermont artists. Grandma Moses paintings, memorabilia.
Grandma Moses Schoolhouse (1836) is in the care of the Museum.
May-Sept., daily 9-6. Oct.-Apr., daily 9.30-4.30. Closed Thanksgiving.

OLD BETHPAGE BR.

OLD BETHPAGE VILLAGE RESTORATION
Round Scamp Road, Old Bethpage Br., New York 11804
Restored farming village of pre-Civil War period. Outdoor museum with 25 re-assembled buildings, including houses, homesteads, workshops, tavern and church.
Dec. 1 - Feb. 28, 10-4. Closed Christmas, Thanksgiving, New Year.

OLD CHATHAM

SHAKER MUSEUM
95 Shaker Museum Road, Old Chatham, New York 12136
Shaker history. Furniture. Textiles. Decorative arts. Shaker laundry (c.1860), brought from Enfield, Connecticut.
May 1 - Oct. 31, daily 10-5.30.

OLD LYME

LYME HISTORICAL SOCIETY MUSEUM
Florence Griswold House, Lyme Street, Old Lyme, Connecticut 06371
House (1817). Paintings by American Impressionist painters who lived here 1900-35. Clara Champlain Toy Museum, showing American life in miniature, 1800 onwards. Local history. Agriculture. Costumes. Folklore.
June 15 - Sept. 6, Tu.-Su. 1-5.

OLD WESTBURY

OLD WESTBURY GARDENS, INC.
Old Westbury Road, Old Westbury, Long Island, New York 11568
Contains Westbury House (1906). 18th-19th century furniture, paintings.
May-Oct., W.-Su., holidays, 10-5.

OLIVET

ARMSTRONG MUSEUM OF ART AND ARCHAEOLOGY
Olivet College, Olivet, Michigan 49076
20th century American prints. Mesopotamian and Philippine artifacts.
By appointment.

OLUSTEE

OLUSTEE BATTLEFIELD HISTORIC MEMORIAL
Olustee, Florida 32072
Site of Civil War battle, 1865. Local and military history.
Daily 8-5.

OLYMPIA

BIGELOW HOUSE
918 Glass Street, Olympia, Washington 98506
House (1854). Period furnishings. Musical instruments.
By appointment.

DRY FALLS
P.O. Box 1128, Olympia, Washington 98504
Regional geology, archaeology, anthropology, ethnology.
Daily 9-5.

FORT CASEY INTERPRETIVE CENTER
P.O. Box 1128, Olympia, Washington 98504
In lighthouse (c.1900) at Fort Casey. Coastal artillery.
Daily 9-5.

FORT COLUMBIA STATE PARK HISTORICAL MUSEUM
P.O. Box 1128, Olympia, Washington 98504
In restored artillery barracks. Pioneer history. Indian artifacts. Material from shipwrecks.
Daily 9-5.

FORT OKANOGAN INTERPRETIVE CENTER
P.O. Box 1128, Olympia, Washington 98504
Indian and pioneer history. Crafts. Weapons.
Daily 9-5.

FORT SIMCOE
P.O. Box 1128, Olympia, Washington 98504
In former Commandant's quarters (1856). Collections illustrating life at the Fort. Indian material.
Daily 9-5.

MUSEUM OF WASHINGTON STATE BOARD OF PHARMACY
319 E. 7th Avenue, Olympia, Washington 98504
19th century pharmacy equipment. Patent medicine. Prescriptions.
M.-F. 8-5.

STATE CAPITOL MUSEUM
211 W. 21st Avenue, Olympia, Washington 98501
Mineralogy. Fossils. Natural history. Indian art and culture. Local history. Pioneer life. Transport. Forestry and logging. Northwest paintings, sculpture.
Tu.-F. 10-5; Sa. 12-5; Su. 1-5. Closed public holidays.

OMAHA

JOSLYN ART MUSEUM
2218 Dodge Street, Omaha, Nebraska 68102
European painting. American paintings by early frontier artists. 20th century American and European paintings, sculpture, graphics. Decorative arts. Archaeology. Indian artifacts.
Tu.-Sa. 10-5; Su. 1-5. Closed public holidays.

UNION PACIFIC HISTORICAL MUSEUM
1416 Dodge Street, Omaha, Nebraska 68102
History of building and operating Union Pacific lines. Photographs. Locomotive models. Furnishings from Abraham Lincoln's private coach (1864). Lincoln portraits and personal papers.
M.-F. 9-5; Sa. 9-1.

ONAMIA

MILLE LACS INDIAN MUSEUM
Onamia, Minnesota 56359
History of Chippewa Indians. Life-size dioramas showing Chippewa life in each of the four seasons. Crafts.
May 1 - Sept. 30, daily 10-4.

ONANCOCK

EASTERN SHORE OF VIRGINIA HISTORICAL SOCIETY, INC.
Market Street, Onancock, Virginia 23417
Local history.
By appointment.

ONCHIOTA

SIX NATIONS INDIAN MUSEUM
Onchiota, New York 12968
Indian material. Miniature Iroquois villages. Iroquois culture, history and artifacts.
June 1 - Oct. 31, daily 9-7.

ONEIDA

MADISON COUNTY HISTORICAL SOCIETY MUSEUM
435 Main Street, Oneida, New York 13421
House (1849). Madison County history. Agricultural implements, tools. Early American furnishings, glass, china, pewter. Indian artifacts. Civil War relics.
May 1 - Oct. 31, Tu.-Su. 2-5.

ONEONTA

BLOUNT COUNTY MEMORIAL MUSEUM
308 5th Avenue, Oneonta, Alabama 35121
Local, military and natural history.
Daily 2-4.

NATIONAL RAILROAD MUSEUM
1 Railroad Avenue, Oneonta, New York 13820
In Ulster and Delaware Station (1902). Railway history. Operating steam train.
Daily 9-5.

UPPER SUSQUEHANNA HISTORICAL SOCIETY MUSEUM
Municipal Building, 11 Ford Avenue, Oneonta, New York 13820
Delaware and Hudson history. Paintings. Prints. Maps. Indian artifacts. Glass. China. Toys.
July-Aug., Sa. 10-4.

YAGER MUSEUM
Hartwick College, Oneonta, New York 13820
N. and S. American Indian culture. Anthropology. Artifacts. Archaeology.
M.-F. 10-3; Sa. 10-12; Su. 2-4. Closed Dec. 23 - Jan. 2; Mar. 25-31; July 4; June 8-14.

ONSTED

FRONTIER CITY MUSEUM
Onsted, Michigan 49265
Pioneer history. Household equipment. Tools. Agricultural implements.
Memorial Day - Labour Day, daily 10-6; weekdays during Sept. and Oct.

ONTARIO

BROOKWOOD SCIENCE INFORMATION CENTER
Lake Road, Ontario, New York 14519
Peaceful uses of atomic energy.
W.-Su. 10-4.

ONTONAGON

ONTONAGON COUNTY HISTORICAL SOCIETY MUSEUM
319 River Street, Ontonagon, Michigan 49953
County history. Paintings. Prints. Minerals. Indian artifacts.
June 15 - Sept., M.-Sa. 9-6.

OPELOUSAS

JIM BOWIE HOUSE
163 West Landry Street, Opelousas, Louisiana 70570
Mementoes of the planter, Jim Bowie (1795-1836).
Tu.-Sa. 10-4.

ORADELL

HIRAM BLAUVELT WILDLIFE MUSEUM
637 Kinderkermack Road, Oradell, New Jersey 07649
Preserved wildlife from all over world.
Th. 10-3. Other times by appointment.

ORANGE

ORANGE JUNIOR MUSEUM
Community Center, 2111 W. Burton Avenue, Orange, Texas 77630
Early American furniture, household equipment. Geology. Zoology. Insects.
Sept.-May M.-F. 2-5; Sa. 10-12. Closed national holidays.

ORANGEBURG

ROCKLAND COUNTY HISTORICAL SOCIETY MUSEUM
King's Highway, Orangeburg, New York 10962
Local history. Furniture. Paintings. Folk art. Glass. Jewellery. Guns. Coins.
Su. 2-5.

TAPPAN ZEE HISTORICAL SOCIETY
Kings Highway, Orangeburg, New York 10962
History of Rockland County.
Su., W. 2-5.

ORCHARD PARK

ORCHARD PARK HISTORICAL SOCIETY MUSEUM
E. Quaker and Freeman Roads, Orchard Park, New York 14127
In former Quaker meeting house (1820). Local history. Agriculture. Indian artifacts. Costumes.
July 1 - Aug. 31: Tu. 2-4; Th. 7-9. Other times by appointment.

ORD

MUSEUM OF LOUP VALLEY HISTORICAL ASSOCIATION
Ord, Nebraska 68862
Local and military history.
Fort Harstuff (1875-6) is in the care of the Association.
By appointment.

ORDERVILLE

DAUGHTERS OF UTAH PIONEERS MUSEUM
Orderville, Utah 84758
Pioneer artifacts.
On request.

OREGON

OGLE COUNTY HISTORICAL MUSEUM
6th and Franklin Streets, Oregon, Illinois 61061
Local history. Domestic equipment. Agriculture.
May 21 - Oct. 8, Su. 2-5.

OREGON JERUSALEM HISTORICAL MUSEUM
Starr Avenue and City Road, Oregon, Ohio 43616
Local history. Agriculture. Replicas of country store and schoolroom. Costumes.
By appointment.

BERMANS AUTO AND ANTIQUE MUSEUM
Route 1, Oregon, Wisconsin 53575
Farm implements. Transport. Maritime history.
Mar. 1 - Nov. 30, daily 8-8.

OREGONIA

FORT ANCIENT MUSEUM
Interstate 71, Exit 29, Oregonia, Ohio 45054
Prehistoric Indian culture.
Mar. 1 - Nov. 30, Tu.-Su. 9.30-5. Dec., Feb., Su. 9.30-5.

OREGON CITY

CAPTAIN JOHN C. AINSWORTH HOUSE
19195 S. Leland Road, Oregon City, Oregon 97045
House (1850), built by steamboat and banking magnate. Period furnishings. Sea-chests from USS 'Constitution' ('Old Ironsides'), 1812.
Sa., Su. 10-4.

McLOUGHLIN HOUSE
713 Center Street, Oregon City, Oregon 97045
Former home of Dr. John McLoughlin, chief factor of Hudson's Bay Company and founder of Oregon City. Family furnishings. Pioneer relics.
May-Oct., Tu.-Su. 10-5. Nov.-Apr., Tu.-Su. 10-4. Closed Dec. 25.

MERTIE STEVENS HOUSE
603 6th Street, Oregon City, Oregon 97045
House (1908). Contains local history collections of Clackamas County Historical Society.
By appointment.

ORICK

PRAIRIE CREEK REDWOODS STATE PARK
Orick, California 95555
Natural history. Mining history.
May-Sept., daily 8 a.m. - 10 p.m. Oct.-Apr., daily 8-5. Closed Thanksgiving, Christmas, Jan. 1.

ORIENT

MUSEUM OF OYSTERPONDS HISTORICAL SOCIETY
Village Lane, Orient, New York 11957
Based on 6 buildings, representing early village of Orient. Village inn (1790) has period rooms, tools, Indian material and war relics. Schoolhouse, with original decorations, furnishings. 19th century house, with marine and fishing exhibits, handicrafts, farm implements, carpenter's shop. Dame school (1830), now children's museum. Carriage and waggon house also contains country store.
July 1 - Sept. 30: Tu., Th., Sa., Su. 2-5.

WEBB HOUSE
Village Lane, Orient, L.I., New York 11957
House (c.1720). Period furnishings.
July - Oct. 15, Tu., Th., Sa., Su. 2-5.

ORISKANY

ORISKANY HISTORICAL SOCIETY, INC.
R.F.D. 1, Oriskany, New York 13424
Paintings illustrating Battle of Oriskany. Revolutionary War relics.
By appointment.

ORLAND

ORLAND HISTORICAL SOCIETY
Box 435, Orland, Maine 04472
Local history.
Sa., Su. 1-5.

ORLANDO

CENTRAL FLORIDA MUSEUM AND PLANETARIUM
810 E. Rollins Avenue, Orlando, Florida 32803
Mineralogy. Palaeontology. Astronomy. Planetarium. Natural history. Shells. Archaeology. Anthropology. Ethnology. Indian material.
M., W., Th. 10-5; Tu., F. 10-5, 7.30-9; Sa., Su. 2-5. Closed public holidays, Aug. 31 - Sept. 14.

LOCH HAVEN ART CENTER
2416 N. Mills Avenue, Orlando, Florida 32803
Pre-Colombian art from Mexico and Costa Rica. 20th century paintings by American artists.
Tu.-Sa. 10-5; Su. 2-5. Closed July 4, Thanksgiving, Christmas, New Year.

ORANGE COUNTY HISTORICAL COMMISSION MUSEUM
27 E. Central Boulevard, Orlando, Florida 32801
Furniture. Household equipment and ornaments. Tools. Weapons. Clothing.
M., W., F. 2-5. Closed public holidays.

ORLEANS

OLD STONE HOUSE
Orleans, Vermont 05860
House (1836). Period furniture. Local and state history. Farm implements. Household equipment. Military history.
May 15 - Oct. 15, daily 9-5.

ORMOND BEACH

FRED DANA MARSH MUSEUM
Tomoka State Park, Ormond Beach, Florida 32074
Paintings and sculpture by Fred Dana Marsh, including the 45 foot 'Legend of Tomolkie'. Exhibits illustrating Florida geology, wildlife, history. Indian artifacts.
Daily 8-12, 1-5.

ORMOND BEACH WAR MEMORIAL ART GALLERY
78 E. Granada Avenue, Ormond Beach, Florida 32074
Paintings by Malcolm Fraser. History of automobile racing.
Daily 2-5.

OROFINO

CLEARWATER HISTORICAL SOCIETY MUSEUM
315 College Avenue, Orofino, Idaho 83544
Pioneer history. Indian material.
Tu.-Sa. 1.30-4.30. Public holidays by appointment only.

ORONO

ANTHROPOLOGY MUSEUM
University of Maine, Orono, Maine 04473
Palaeontology. Archaeology of the American N.E. Ethnology of Africa, N. and S. America, Oceania, N.E. Asia and the Arctic. Indian artifacts.
M.-F. 8-4.30. Closed Easter, Christmas.

UNIVERSITY OF MAINE ART GALLERY
Carnegie Hall, Orono, Maine 04473
Contemporary American paintings, sculpture. American and European graphics.
M.-F. 8-5; Sa. 9-12. Closed university vacations.

UNIVERSITY OF MAINE HERBARIUM
317 Deering Hall, University of Maine, Orono, Maine 04473
Plants of Maine and Canada. N. American fungi.
M.-F. 8-5. Closed New Year, Thanksgiving, Christmas.

ORWELL

DANIELS MUSEUM
Orwell, Vermont 05760
Revolutionary and Civil War relics. Guns. Indian material.
Tu.-Th., Sa., Su. 9-5.

OSAGE

MITCHELL COUNTY HISTORICAL MUSEUM
N. 6th Street, Osage, Iowa 50461
Local history. Indian material. Agriculture. Children's museum. Paintings, graphics by local artists. Horse-drawn vehicles.
Log-house (1854) and rural school-house (1878) are in the care of the Museum.
May 15 - Oct. 1, F.-Su. 2-5.

OSAWATOMIE

JOHN BROWN MUSEUM
John Brown Memorial Park, Osawatomie, Kansas 66064
Brown's cabin (1854), with much of the original furniture.
Tu.-Sa. 10-5; Su. 1.30-5.

OSCEOLA

POLK COUNTY HISTORICAL MUSEUM
Hawkeye Street, Osceola, Nebraska 68651
Local history. 17 period rooms, c.1900. Dress and millinery shop.
June 1 - Oct. 31, Su. 2-5.

OSHKOSH

MUSEUM OF HISTORICAL SOCIETY OF GARDEN COUNTY
W. 2nd and G Streets, Oshkosh, Nebraska 69514
In Rock Schoolhouse (1904-5). Natural history. Local history. Indian artifacts.
May 1 - Sept. 30: M.-Sa. 9-5; Su. 1-5.

OSHKOSH PUBLIC MUSEUM
1331 Algoma Boulevard, Oshkosh, Wisconsin 54901
Natural history. Regional and pioneer history. Firearms. River steamboat history. Indian archaeology of the Upper Great Lakes. Paintings. Sculpture.
Tu.-Sa. 9-5; Su. 1-5. Closed public holidays.

PAINE ART CENTER
1410 Algoma Boulevard, Oshkosh, Wisconsin 54901
American 19th - early 20th century paintings. French paintings of the Barbizon School. Persian rugs. 18th-19th century English furniture. Silver.
Tu., Th., Sa., Su. 2-5. June 1 - Aug. 31 also W., F. 2-5. Closed public holidays.

OSKALOOSA

NELSON PIONEER FARM AND CRAFTS MUSEUM
Rural Route 1, Oskaloosa, Iowa 52577
Local history. Agriculture. Indian material.
Nelson Home (1853), Nelson barn (1856) and Prine Schoolhouse (1861) are in the care of the Museum.
May 12 - Oct. 12, Tu.-F. 10-5; Su., public holidays 1-5.

OLD FRONTIER MUSEUM
Oskaloosa, Kansas 66066
Local history. Agriculture. Transport. Indian artifacts. Costumes. China. Glass.
1st Sunday in month, 12-5.

OLD JEFFERSON TOWN
Jefferson County Historical Society, Oskaloosa, Kansas 66066
Country store, school, chapel (all c.1880), with original furnishings.
May-Oct., Su., public holidays 12-5.

OSSINING

OSSINING HISTORICAL SOCIETY MUSEUM
196 Croton Avenue, Ossining, New York 10562
Local history. Indian artifacts. Costumes. Paintings.
M., W., Sa. 2-4. Other times by appointment. Closed school vacations.

OSWEGO

FORT ONTARIO
Oswego, New York 13126
Fortifications (1839-49), on site of British fort (1755-59). Exhibits of military and naval history. Paintings. Weapons. Uniforms.
Apr. 1 - Oct. 31, M.-Sa. 9-5; Su. 1-5. Closed Easter.

MUSEUM OF OSWEGO COUNTY HISTORICAL SOCIETY
135 E. 3rd Street, Oswego, New York 13126
In Bates-Richardson House (1890). Local history. Agriculture. Indian artifacts. Paintings. Costumes. Silver. Glass. Victorian furnishings.
May 1 - Oct. 31: W., Sa., Su. 1-5. Other times by appointment.

NIAGRA MOHAWK PROGRESS CENTER
Nine Mile Point Nuclear Station, Oswego, New York 13126
Techniques of generating nuclear power.
Tu.-Sa. 10-5; Su. 12-6.

OTTAWA

MUSEUM OF FRANKLIN COUNTY HISTORICAL SOCIETY
Box 145, Ottawa, Kansas 66067
In old Depot building (1888). Geology. Natural history. Local history. Agriculture. Transport. Aviation. Costumes. Indian artifacts.
Centennial Cabin (1859), a restored and furnished pioneer cabin, is in the care of the Society.
June 1 - Aug. 31, Su. 2-5.

OTTUMWA

WAPELLO COUNTY HISTORICAL MUSEUM
402 Chester Avenue, Ottumwa, Iowa 52501
Local history. Cigar industry in Ottumwa district.
Apr. 16 - Nov. 30, Sa., Su., public holidays 2-5. Other times by appointment.

OUTER BANKS

BODIE ISLAND VISITOR CENTER
Bodie Island, Outer Banks, North Carolina
Natural history.
July-Aug., daily 8.30-5.

OVERTON

MOAPA VALLEY ART GUILD
Overton, Nevada 89040
Paintings by contemporary Nevada artists.
By appointment.

OWEGO

TIOGA COUNTY HISTORICAL SOCIETY MUSEUM
110 Front Street, Owego, New York 13827
Pioneer life. Handicrafts. Indian artifacts. Relics of Colonial and Civil Wars. Tools. Pewter. Paintings.
Tu.-F. 10-12, 1.30-4.30; W. also 7-9; Sa., Su. 1.30-4.30. Closed public holidays.

OWENSBORO

OWENSBORO AREA MUSEUM
901 Frederica Street, Owensboro, Kentucky 42301
Geology. Mineralogy. Palaeontology. Botany. Natural history. Planetarium. Astronomy. Indian artifacts. Local history. Children's museum.
M.-F. 8-4; Su. 1-4. Closed public holidays.

OXFORD

OXFORD MUSEUM
Morris and Market Streets, Oxford, Maryland 21654
Local and maritime history.
Mar. 1 - Jan. 31: F.-Su. 2-5.

CHARLES LARNED MUSEUM
Main Street, Oxford, Massachusetts 01540
History of Oxford and early New England.
By appointment.

MARY BUIE MUSEUM
510 University Avenue, Oxford, Mississippi 38555
Paintings by Mary Buie. Local history. Costumes. Relics of Revolutionary and Civil Wars. Dolls. Fans.
Tu., W., Sa. 10-12, 1.30-4.30; Th., F. 1.30-4.30; Su. 2-5. Closed public holidays, Aug. 17-31.

WILLIAM HOLMES MCGUFFEY HOUSE AND MUSEUM
Spring and Oak Streets, Oxford, Ohio 45056
McGuffey House (1831), with period furnishings and personal memorabilia of W. H. McGuffey. 19th century school and children's books, especially those written and edited by McGuffey.
Tu. 2-4.30; Sa. 9-11, 2-4.30; Su. 2-4.30. Closed Aug. 1-31, University vacations.

MIAMI UNIVERSITY ART GALLERY
Oxford, Ohio 45056
Paintings by American, English and Italian artists.
M.-F. 8-5; Su. 2-5.

OXFORD MUSEUM ASSOCIATION
316 West High Street, Oxford, Ohio 45056
House (1850-80). Pioneer furnishings.
May-Nov., Sa., Su. 1.30-5.

PIONEER FARM AND HOUSE MUSEUM
Brown Road and Hueston Woods State Park, Oxford, Ohio 45056
Pioneer house and barn (1833). Period furnishings. Domestic equipment, utensils. Farm tools, implements.
May 1 - Oct. 31: Tu.-Su. 1-5.

WESTERN COLLEGE FOR WOMEN, ART COLLECTIONS
Oxford, Ohio 45056
19th century French and American paintings. Watercolours by Florence Robinson. Mound pottery. Fossils. Japanese prints.
By appointment.

OXON HILL

FORT WASHINGTON PARK
Indian Head Highway, Oxon Hill, Maryland 20021
Fort buildings (1817-24). Military history.
Daily 8 dusk.

JOHN HANSON MEMORIAL MUSEUM
6701 Oxon Hill Road, Oxon Hill, Maryland 20021
Pre-Columbian art. European art. Americana. Local history. Indian artifacts.
Su. 1-6. Weekdays by appointment.

OYSTER BAY, L.I.

THE OYSTER HISTORICAL SOCIETY
East Main Street, Oyster Bay, L.I., New York 11771
Local history.
By appointment.

RAYNHAM HALL
20 W. Main Street, Oyster Bay, L.I., New York 11771
Restored home (1738, with mid-19th century addition) of Townsend family. Victorian furnishings.
M., W.-Sa. 10-12, 1-5.

SAGAMORE HILL NATIONAL HISTORIC SITE
Cove Neck Road, Oyster Bay, L.I., New York 11771
House (1884), furnished as it was when President Theodore Roosevelt lived in it.
Daily 9-5. Closed New Year, Christmas.

THEODORE ROOSEVELT MEMORIAL SANCTUARY AND TRAILSIDE MUSEUM
Cove Road, Oyster Bay, L.I., New York 11771
Natural history. Children's museum.
May-Nov. M., W.-Sa. and holidays, 2-5.

OZONA

CROCKETT COUNTY MUSEUM
404 11th Street, Ozona, Texas 76943
County history. Ranching industry. Guns. Cattle brands. Photographs and memorabilia of early settlers. Indian collection.
Oct. 1 - Apr. 30, Tu., Th., Sa. 12.30-4.30. May 1 - Sept. 30: Tu.-Sa. 11-5. Closed Thanksgiving, Christmas, New Year.

FORT LANCASTER VISITOR CENTER
Fort Lancaster State Park, U.S. 290, Ozona, Texas 76943
Frontier Fort (1855). Exhibits illustrating frontier life. Archaeology.
Daily 8-5.

PACIFICA

SANCHEZ ADOBE
Linda Mar Boulevard and Adobe Drive, Pacifica, California 94044
House (1842-6), formerly home of Francisco Sanchez.
W.-Su. 10-4. Closed New Year, Christmas.

PACIFIC GROVE

PACIFIC GROVE MUSEUM OF NATURAL HISTORY
165 Forest Avenue, Pacific Grove, California 93950
Geology, botany and natural history of Monterey County. Herbarium. Ethnology.
Point Pinos lighthouse (1853) is in the care of the Museum.
Tu.-Su., public holidays, 10-5. Closed New Year, Christmas, Thanksgiving, Thursday before 3rd weekend in April.

PACIFIC PALISADES

WILL ROGERS STATE HISTORIC PARK
14253 Sunset Boulevard, Pacific Palisades, California 90212
In Will Rogers' Ranch House (1928). Personal possessions of Rogers. Indian artifacts. Cowboy souvenirs. Paintings by artists of the Western U.S.
Daily 10-5.

PAGE

GLEN CANYON NATIONAL RECREATION AREA MUSEUM
P.O. Box 1507, Page, Arizona 86040
Geology. Archaeology. Natural history. Botany. Anthropology. Ethnology. Indian artifacts. Local and industrial history.
Daily 8.30-5. Closed New Year, Christmas.

JOHN WESLEY POWELL MEMORIAL MUSEUM
6 N. Seventh Avenue, Page, Arizona 86040
Geology. Palaeontology. Zoology. Archaeology. Ethnology. Indian artifacts. Coins. Postage stamps.
Apr. 1-30, Oct. 1-31, daily 10-6; May 1 - Sept. 30, daily 10-10. Closed Christmas.

PAICINES

PINNACLES NATIONAL MONUMENT
Paicines, California 95043
Geology. Natural history. Herbarium.
Daily 8-5.

PAINTED POST

TOWN OF ERWIN MUSEUM
Town Hall, Painted Post, New York 14870
Local history. Indian relics. Replica of Painted Post. Pioneer life.
M.-F. 9-4. July 1 - Aug. 31: M.-Sa. 9.30-4. Closed public holidays.

PALA

MUSEUM OF MISSION SAN ANTONIO DE PALA
Highway 76, Pala, California 92059
Building (1810). Indian stone carvings, baskets, pottery, glass. Frescoes.
M.-Sa., holidays, 10-12, 1-4; Su. 12-4. Closed Christmas.

PALESTINE

HOWARD HOUSE MUSEUM
1011 N. Perry Street, Palestine, Texas 75801
House (c.1850). Period furnishings. Local history since 1850. Photographs of early settlers.
Sa., Su. 2-5.

PALM BEACH

HENRY MORRISON FLAGLER MUSEUM
Whitehall Way, Palm Beach, Florida 33480
In 'Whitehall' (1901). Furnishings. Flagler family memorabilia. Local history. Transport, especially East Coast railways. Paintings. Sculpture. Lace. China. 17th century fans.
Tu.-Su. 10-5. Closed Christmas.

PALM BEACH COUNTY HISTORICAL SOCIETY MUSEUM
in Henry Morrison Flagler Museum, Whitehall Way, Palm Beach, Florida 33480
Local history. Indian material. Furniture. Music.
Tu.-Th. 12-4. Closed Christmas.

SOCIETY OF THE FOUR ARTS
Four Arts Plaza, Palm Beach, Florida 33480
Paintings. Sculpture.
Dec. 1 - Apr. 15, M.-F. 10-5; Su. 2-5.

PALMER LAKE

MUSEUM OF PALMER LAKE HISTORICAL SOCIETY
Box 427, Palmer Lake, Colorado 80133
Local history.
M. 1.30-6.30; W. 1.30-8.30; Tu., Th. 1-5.30; F. 3.30-5.30; Sa. 9.30-4.30. Closed public holidays.

PALM SPRINGS

PALM SPRINGS DESERT MUSEUM
135 East Tahquitz Street and McCallum Way, P.O. Box 2288, Palm Springs, California 92262
Geology. Archaeology. Ethnology. Modern American, especially Californian, paintings, prints, sculpture.
Cornelia White House (early 1900s) is in the care of the Museum.
Tu.-Sa. 10-5; Su. 2-5. Closed June 1 - Aug. 31.

PALMYRA

JOSEPH SMITH HOME
Stafford Road, Palmyra, New York 14522
House (1825) was boyhood home of Joseph Fielding Smith, founder of Mormonism. Memorabilia of Smith.
Peter Whitmer house (1840-50) and Martin Harris house (1849-50) are in the care of the same governing authority.
Daily 8-6. Closed Christmas, New Year.

OLD STONE JAIL MUSEUM
Palmyra, Virginia 22963
Building (1829). Local history collection.
June 1 - Sept. 30: F., Sa. 11-4; Su. 2-5.

PALO ALTO

PALO ALTO JUNIOR MUSEUM
250 Hamilton Avenue, Palo Alto, California 94301
Natural history. History of Californian Indians.
Tu.-F. 10-5; Sa. 9-5; Su., public holidays 1-4.

PAMPA

WHITE DEER LAND MUSEUM
116 S. Cuyler Street, Pampa, Texas 79065
In former White Deer Land Company Building (1916). Records and documents of White Deer Company. Replica of first oil well on White Deer Lands. Pioneer furnishings, clothing. Items from pioneer churches and schools. Agricultural machinery. Barbed wire. Arrowheads.
Sa., Su. 3-5.

PANGUITCH

DAUGHTERS OF UTAH PIONEERS MUSEUM
100 E. Center, Panguitch, Utah 84759
Pioneer relics.
Daily 2-6.

PANHANDLE

CARSON COUNTY SQUARE HOUSE MUSEUM
5th and Elsie Streets, Panhandle, Texas 79068
History of area. Restored pioneer dug-out house, farm and ranch building. Windmill. Santa Fe railroad caboose. Agriculture. Costumes. Furniture. Folklore.
June 1 - Labour Day: M.-Sa. 10-12.30; Su. 1.30-5.30. Rest of year: F., Sa., Su. 1.30-5.30.

PARAMUS

BERGEN COMMUNITY MUSEUM
Ridgewood Avenue and Fairview Street, Paramus, New Jersey 07652
Geology. Science. Natural history. Local history. Paintings, sculpture, graphics by American artists.
W.-Sa. 1-5; Su. 2-6.

PARIS

CANE RIDGE SHRINE
Route 3, Paris, Kentucky 40361
Log meeting-house (1791), centre of the Christian Church (Disciples of Christ). Historical items relating to the Church.
Daily 9-dusk.

MUSEUM OF MONROE COUNTY HISTORICAL SOCIETY
Paris, Missouri 65275
History of Monroe County.
M.-F. 8-5; Sa. 8-12.

MAXEY MUSEUM
812 Church Street, Paris, Texas 75460
House (c.1840). Original furnishings. Memorabilia of General Maxey. Maxey family possessions.
Tu.-Sa. 10-12, 3-6; Su. 2-6.

PARISHVILLE

PARISHVILLE MUSEUM
Main Street, Parishville, New York 13672
House (c.1800). Early history of Parishville.
Apr. 1 - Nov. 30, 2nd and 4th W. in month. Other times by appointment.

PARKER

BUCKSKIN UNIT
Colorado River State Park, Parker, Arizona 85344
Anthropology. Spanish artifacts. Mining and transport history. Life and techniques of trappers.
Daily 9-4. Closed Christmas.

COLORADO RIVER INDIAN TRIBES MUSEUM
Route 1, Box 23-B, Parker, Arizona 85344
Indian anthropology and archaeology.
Old Presbyterian Indian Mission (1918) is in the care of the Museum.
M.-F. 9-6; Sa. 9-3.

PARKERSBURG

CENTENNIAL CABIN MUSEUM
City Park, Parkersburg, West Virginia 26101
House (1851). Farm implements. Handicrafts. Civil War and Spanish-American War relics. Costumes.
Summer: Su., holidays 1-9.

PARK RAPIDS

HUBBARD COUNTY HISTORICAL SOCIETY
Little Log Museum, Highway 34 and Riverside Avenue, Park Rapids, Minnesota 56470
Local history.
Summer: daily 9-12, 2-5, 7-9.

PARK RIDGE

WOOD LIBRARY AND MUSEUM OF ANAESTHESIOLOGY
515 Busse Highway, Park Ridge, Illinois 60068
History of medicine and anaesthetics.
M.-F. 9.30-4.30. Closed public holidays.

PASCACK HISTORICAL SOCIETY MUSEUM
19 Ridge Avenue, Park Ridge, New Jersey 07656
In former Congregational Church (1873). Local history. Costumes. Wampum drilling machine.
May 1 - Oct. 31, Su. 2-5. Rest of year by appointment.

PARKVILLE

PLATTE COUNTY HISTORICAL SOCIETY MUSEUM
603 Main Street, Parkville, Missouri 64152
Local history.
By appointment.

PARSONS

PARSONS MUSEUM
1808 Washington Avenue, Parsons, Kansas 67357
Local history. Agriculture. Transport, especially railways. Costumes. Paintings.
By appointment.

PASADENA

HALE OBSERVATORIES
813 Santa Barbara Street, Pasadena, California 91106
At Mount Wilson Observatory, Mount Wilson, California, 100 inch telescope (1918); astronomical photographs. At Palomar Observatory, Palomar, California, 200 inch telescope (1948); astronomical photographs.
Daily 10-5.

PASADENA ART MUSEUM
Colorado and Orange Grove Boulevards, Pasadena, California 91101
20th century European and American art. Scheyer 'Blue Form'. Collections of paintings by Jawlensky, Feininger, Kandinsky, Klee.
Tu.-Sa. 10-5; Su. 12-5. Closed New Year, Christmas.

PASADENA HISTORICAL SOCIETY MUSEUM
470 W. Walnut Street, Pasadena, California 91103
In Curtin-Paloheimo House (1905). Period furnishings. Local history. Clothing. Fans.
Tu., Th., 1-4. Closed public holidays.

PASAGOULA

OLD SPANISH FORT AND MUSEUM
4602 Fort Street, Pasagoula, Mississippi 39567
Fort (1718), built of timber, oyster shells, mud and moss. Farm implements. Household equipment. Furniture. Indian artifacts. Revolutionary and Civil War weapons. Coins.
Daily 9-5.

PASCO

SACAJAWEA MUSEUM
Route 1, Pasco, Washington 99301
Indian artifacts. Arrowheads. Tools.
May 1 - Sept. 30, daily 6.30-10. Oct. 1 - Apr. 30, daily 8-5.

PATAGONIA

STRADLING MUSEUM OF THE HORSE
McKeown Avenue, Patagonia, Arizona 85624
Types and uses of horses. Harness. Indian artifacts. Paintings. Sculpture.
Daily, including public holidays 9-6. Closed Thanksgiving, Christmas.

PATERSON

MUSEUM OF PASSAIC COUNTY HISTORICAL SOCIETY
P.O. Box 1729, Paterson, New Jersey 07509
In Lambert Castle (1892). Paintings, including local primitives. Sculpture. Indian artifacts. Spoons. Stamps.
W.-F. 1-4.30; Sa., Su. 11-4.30. Closed public holidays.

PATERSON MUSEUM
268 Summer Street, Paterson, New Jersey 07501
Mineralogy. Zoology. New Jersey Indian artifacts. John P. Holland's submarine.
M.-F. 1-5; Sa. 10-12, 1-5. Closed July 4, Labour Day, Thanksgiving, Christmas, New Year.

PATTEN

LUMBERMEN'S MUSEUM
Rogers Lane, Patten, Maine 04765
History of lumber industry. Replicas of lumbercamps. Tools and equipment. Dioramas. Models. Photographs.
Su. before Memorial Day - Nov. 1, Tu.-Sa. 9-4; Su. 1-5. Other times by appointment. Closed New Year, Memorial Day.

PAWHUSKA

OSAGE COUNTY HISTORICAL MUSEUM
700 Lynn Avenue, Pawhuska, Oklahoma 74056
In former Santa Fe Depot (1923). Indian and pioneer history. Development of local oil industry.
M.-F. 10-5; Sa., Su. 9.30-5.

PAWLING

MUSEUM OF HISTORICAL SOCIETY OF QUAKER HILL AND VICINITY
Akin Hall, Pawling, New York 12564
Material relating to Quaker settlement (early 1700s). Furniture. Textiles. Ceramics. Tools. Glass. Pewter. Farm implements. Costumes. Paintings of local scenes. Relics of Revolutionary War. Quaker Meeting House (1764).
June 1 - Aug. 31: M., W., Sa. 2-5.

MUSEUM OF NATURAL HISTORY
Quaker Hill, Pawling, New York 12564
Geology. Mineralogy. Natural history. Botany. Anatomy. Indian artifacts.
Apr. 1 - Dec. 31: Tu.-Th. 2-4.30; Sa. 10-4.30.

PAWNEE

PAWNEE BILL MUSEUM
W. Highway 64, Pawnee, Oklahoma 74058
House (1910) was home of Maj. Gordon Lillie (Pawnee Bill). Original furnishings. Mementoes of Pawnee Bill and Wild West Shows. Indian relics.
Daily 9-7. Closed Christmas.

PAWNEE CITY

PAWNEE CITY HISTORICAL SOCIETY AND MUSEUM
Pawnee City, Nebraska 68420
Local history.
Schoolhouse (1868) and Governor's house (1870) are in the care of the Society.
By appointment.

PAWTUCKET

JOHN DAGGETT HOUSE
Slater Park, Pawtucket, Rhode Island 02861
House (1685). Period furnishings. Household equipment.
June 15 - Sept. 30, Su. 2-5.

OLD SLATER MILL MUSEUM
Roosevelt Avenue, Pawtucket, Rhode Island 02865
Cotton Mill (1793). First successful cotton factory in N. America. American textile history. Early textile machinery. Work of Samuel Slater. Spinning and weaving techniques.
Tu.-Sa. 10-5; Su. 2-5. Closed public holidays, Jan. 1-31.

PEABODY

PEABODY HISTORICAL SOCIETY AND MUSEUM
Peabody, Kansas 66866
Local history.
Su. 2-5.

PEABODY HISTORICAL SOCIETY
35 Washington Street, Peabody, Massachusetts 01960
In General Gideon Foster House (1810). Local history.
By appointment. Closed national holidays.

PEACE DALE

MUSEUM OF PRIMITIVE CULTURES
604 Kingstown Road, Peace Dale, Rhode Island 02883
Archaeology, ethnology, especially of N. America.
M.-Sa. 9-5.

PEACHAM

PEACHAM HISTORICAL ASSOCIATION MUSEUM
Peacham, Vermont 05862
In Dr. Ernest Bogart House (c.1810). Local history. Paintings, drawings by Vermont artists. Carpentry tools.
May 1 - Sept. 30, Su. 12-4.

PEA RIDGE

PEA RIDGE NATIONAL MILITARY PARK
Pea Ridge, Arkansas 72751
Military history. Civil War relics. Open-air museum.
Daily 8-5. Closed New Year, Christmas.

PECOS

WEST OF THE PECOS MUSEUM
120 E. 1st Street, Pecos, Texas 79772
In old Orient Hotel. Restored lobby, dining room and saloon. Period furnishings. Local history. Rock and mineral display. Rodeo room.
Tu.-Sa. 10-4, Su. 1-6. Closed New Year, Thanksgiving, Christmas.

PEDRO

LAWRENCE COUNTY MUSEUM
Vesuvius Lake, Pedro, Ohio 45638
Local history. Geology. Indian artifacts. Industry, handicrafts.
May 1 - Oct. 31, Su. 1-5.

PEEBLES

SERPENT MOUND MUSEUM
State Route 73, Locust Grove, Peebles, Ohio 45660
Indian history and culture.
Apr. 1 - Oct. 31, daily 9-5.

PELLA

PELLA HISTORICAL SITE
505 Franklin Street, Pella, Iowa 50219
Museum of local history, based on 4 mid-19th century houses, including Wyatt Earp boyhood home.
M.-Sa. 9-11.30. Closed public holidays.

PEMAQUID

ANCIENT PEMAQUID RESTORATION
Pemaquid, Maine 04558
History of Pemaquid.
June 15 - Labour Day, daily 9-5.

HARRINGTON MEETING HOUSE
Old Harrington Road, Pemaquid, Maine 04558
In former Meeting House (1772). Furniture, tools. Clothing. Local history.
July-Aug., M., W., Sa. 2-5. Other times by appointment.

PEMAQUID BEACH

FORT WILLIAM HENRY STATE MEMORIAL
Pemaquid Beach, Maine 04559
Partial replica of 1692 fortification. Interpretative displays. Early American artifacts.
May 30 - Labour Day, daily 10-5.

PEMBINA

PEMBINA STATE MUSEUM
Pembina State Park, Pembina, North Dakota 58266
History of Red River Valley. Fur trade. Indian life. Agriculture. Transport. Domestic equipment. Costumes.
May 15 - Sept. 15, daily 9-5.

PEMBROKE

MUSEUM OF PEMBROKE HISTORICAL SOCIETY
Center Street, Pembroke, Massachusetts 02359
House (1695) is Adah F. Hall Memorial. Local history. Furnishings.
By appointment.

PENASCO

PICURIS PUEBLO MUSEUM
P.O. Box 228, Penasco, New Mexico 87553
Picuris Pueblo (c.A.D.1500) ruins. Archaeology. Anthropology. Indian artifacts.
Apr. 1 - Oct. 31, daily 9.30-4.

PENDLETON

ASHTABULA
U.S. Highway 76, Pendleton, South Carolina 29670
House (c.1828). Period furnishings. Servants' quarters.
June-Sept., Su. 2-5. Other times by appointment.

MUSEUM OF PENDLETON DISTRICT HISTORICAL AND RECREATIONAL COMMISSION
125 E. Queen Street, Pendleton, South Carolina 29670
In former Hunter's Store (1850). History of Anderson County. Farm tools. Civil War history.
Benson House (1800) and Stumphouse Railway Tunnel (1853) are in the care of the Commission.
M.-F. 9-4.30; Su. 1-4.30. Closed public holidays.

PENINSULA

JONATHAN HALE HOMESTEAD AND WESTERN RESERVE VILLAGE
2686 Oak Hill Road, Peninsula, Ohio 44210
Open-air museum, with 7 buildings (1825-52) from the Western Reserve reconstructed around the Hale Homestead (1825). Demonstrations of blacksmithing, spinning and other crafts.
May 1 - Oct. 31: Tu.-Sa. 10-5; Su., public holidays 1-5.

PENNSAUKEN

PENNSAUKEN HISTORICAL SOCIETY MUSEUM
Box 56, Pennsauken, New Jersey 08110
In Borough-Dover House (1710). Period furnishings. Local history.
By appointment.

PENNSBURG

SCHWENKFELDER MUSEUM
Seminary Avenue, Pennsburg, Pennsylvania 18073
History of Pennsburg region. Agricultural implements. Domestic equipment. Costumes. Indian material.
By appointment.

PENN YAN

YATES COUNTY HISTORICAL MUSEUM
200 Main Street, Penn Yan, New York 14527
Local history. Articles belonging to Jemima Wilkinson, the Publick Universal Friend.
July 1 - Aug. 31: Tu., Th., last Sa. in month, 2-4.

PENSACOLA

HISTORIC PENSACOLA PRESERVATION BOARD
200 Zaragoza Street, Pensacola, Florida 32501
In Commodity Warehouse (1870). Horse-drawn vehicles. Maps. Local history. Furniture and furnishings in historic houses; Lavalle House (c.1805), Walton House (1810), Hispanic Museum (c.1870), Lee House (c.1860).
M.-Sa. 9-5; Su. 12-5.

NAVAL AVIATION MUSEUM
U.S. Naval Air Station, Pensacola, Florida 32508
History of naval aviation and of aeronautics. Models. Equipment. Mementoes and relics.
Tu.-Sa. 8.30-4.30; Su. 12.30-4.30. Closed Thanksgiving, Christmas, New Year.

PENSACOLA ART ASSOCIATION MUSEUM
407 South Jefferson Street, Pensacola, Florida 32501
In old City Jail (1908). Paintings. Graphics. Sculpture.
Tu.-Sa. 9-5; Su. 2-5. Closed public holidays.

PENSACOLA HISTORICAL MUSEUM
405 S. Adams Street, Seville Square, Pensacola, Florida 32501
In old Christ Church (1832). History of Pensacola and Escambia County. Paintings of local subjects. Furniture. Decorative arts. Maps. Documents. Costumes.
Tu.-Sa. 10.30-4.30; Su. 2-4.30. Closed public holidays.

PENSACOLA HISTORICAL PRESERVATION SOCIETY MUSEUM
Alcaniz Street, Pensacola, Florida 32501
Local history. Doctor's surgery equipment. Walton House (c.1815) and Quina House (1815) are in the care of the Society.
May 16 - Aug. 31, Tu.-F. 10-4; Sa., Su. 1-4.

T. T. WENTWORTH JR. MUSEUM
P.O. Box 806, 7100 Palafox Highway, Pensacola, Florida 32502
History of Pensacola area. Agriculture. Archaeology. Anthropology. Mineralogy. Indian artifacts. Costumes. Natural history. Coins. Outdoor museum.
Sa., Su. 2-6.

PEORIA

BRADLEY UNIVERSITY GALLERY
Peoria, Illinois 61614
Contemporary American prints.
By appointment.

LAKEVIEW CENTER FOR THE ARTS AND SCIENCES
1125 West Lake Avenue, Peoria, Illinois 61614
Geology. Palaeontology. Planetarium. Anthropology. Archaeology. Paintings. Graphics.
Tu.-Sa. 9-5; Su. 1-6. Closed New Year, Thanksgiving, Christmas.

PEORIA HISTORICAL SOCIETY MUSEUM
942 N.E. Glen Oak Avenue, Peoria, Illinois 61603
In Morron House (1868). Victorian furniture, silver, glass. Carpentry tools. Late 19th century costumes.
Flanagan House (1837), with period furnishings, is also in the care of the Society.
Flanagan House: Sa., Su. 2-5. Morron House: 2nd and 4th Sunday each month 2-5. Closed public holidays.

PERKINSVILLE

WEATHERSFIELD HISTORICAL SOCIETY MUSEUM
Perkinsville, Vermont 05151
Local history. Furniture. Civil War relics. Farm implements. Paintings. Costumes.
June 24 - Oct. 31: W., Su., public holidays 2-5.

PERRIS

ORANGE EMPIRE TROLLEY MUSEUM
2201 South A Street, P.O. Box 548, Perris, California 92370
Electric railway and tramway vehicles, some operating on tracks.
Dugout Building (1880) and framehouse (1885) are in the care of the Museum.
M.-F. 10-4, Sa., Su., public holidays 9 - dusk. Closed July 4, Labour day.

PERRY

CHEROKEE STRIP HISTORICAL SOCIETY MUSEUM
W. Ditch Witch Road, Perry, Oklahoma 73077
In former County Schoolhouse (1896). Local history. Indian artifacts. Costumes. Medicine. Glass.
Daily 9-7. Closed New Year, July 4, Thanksgiving, Christmas.

PERRYOPOLIS

MUSEUM OF PERRYOPOLIS HISTORICAL SOCIETY
R.D.2, Box 15 M, Perryopolis, Pennsylvania 15473
In restored fulling mill (1814). Local history.
Washington Grist Mill (1774) and Providence Meeting House (1789) are in the care of the Society.
May 1 - Oct. 15, daily 1-5.

PERRYVILLE

PERRYVILLE BATTLEFIELD STATE SHRINE
Highways U.S. 68 and U.S. 150, Perryville, Kentucky 40468
Site of Civil War battle of Perryville (1842). Museum contains diorama and battle relics.
May-Sept., daily 9-5. Oct.-Apr., Tu.-Su. 9-5.

PERTH AMBOY

MUSEUM OF KEARNY COTTAGE HISTORICAL SOCIETY
39 Catalpa Avenue, Perth Amboy, New Jersey 08861
Furniture. Local history.
Tu., Th. 3-5.

PERU

MIAMI COUNTY HISTORICAL MUSEUM
Court House, U.S.24 and Business U.S.31, Peru, Indiana 46970
Natural history. Local history. Indian material. Transport. Circus history.
M.-Sa. 9-12. Closed public holidays.

PUTERBAUGH MUSEUM
11 North Huntington Street, Peru, Indiana 46970
Natural history. Pioneer history. Indian material. Circus history.
M.-Tu., Th.-Sa. 1-5. Closed public holidays.

PESHTIGO

PESHTIGO FIRE MUSEUM
400 Oconto Avenue, Peshtigo, Wisconsin 54157
Farm tools, equipment. Glass.
May 30 - Oct. 7, daily 9-5.

PETALUMA

PETALUMA ADOBE STATE HISTORIC PARK
3325 Adobe Road, Petaluma, California 94952
Ranch house (1834-8), belonging to General Vallejo. Period furnishings and equipment. Indian material. Exhibits illustrating early rancho life.
Daily 10-5. Closed New Year, Thanksgiving, Christmas.

PETERBOROUGH

"BLEAKHOUSE"
Route 101, Peterborough, New Hampshire 03458
House (1792). Period furnishings.
Members only, by appointment.

GOYETTE MUSEUM OF AMERICANA
Elm Street, Peterborough, New Hampshire 03458
Horse-drawn vehicles. Old cars. Craftsmen's workshops. Tavern. Chemist's and barber's shops. Dolls. Early flasks, bottles. Pewter. Brass. Pine and maple furniture. Staffordshire and Lowestoft china. Currier and Ives prints.
Tu.-Su. 1.30-4.30.

PETERBOROUGH HISTORICAL SOCIETY MUSEUM
Grove Street, P.O. Box 58, Peterborough, New Hampshire 03458
Local history. Indian artifacts. Industry. Decorative arts. Textiles. Junior Museum.
Phoenix Mill House (1805) and Brick End House (1830) are in the care of the Society.
July 1 - Aug. 31: M.-F. 2-4. Other times by appointment.

PETERSBURG

MUSEUM SOCIETY OF PETERSBURG
Front Street, Petersburg, Alaska 99833
Local history. Musical instruments.
May-Oct., daily 1-4.

LINCOLN'S NEW SALEM STATE PARK
Petersburg, Illinois 62675
Reproduction of 12 timber houses, 10 shops, stores, workshops, a school, a church and a tavern; furnished and equipped as they were in the 1830s, and commemorating Abraham Lincoln's years in New Salem.
Village: 24 hours daily.
Individual buildings: Apr. 15 - Oct. 15, 9-5.
Rutledge Tavern: Apr. 15 - Oct. 15, 9-5. Oct. 16 - Apr. 14, 8.30-4.30.

CENTRE HILL MANSION
Franklin Street, Petersburg, Virginia 23803
House (1823). Period furnishings. Local history.
Tu.-Sa. 10-1, 2-5; Su. 2.30-5. Closed Christmas, New Year.

PETERSBURG NATIONAL BATTLEFIELD PARK VISITOR CENTER
E. Washington Street, Box 549, Petersburg, Virginia 23803
Photographs, paintings, and audio-visual presentation of Civil War Siege of Petersburg.
Memorial Day - Labour Day 8-8. Rest of year, 8-5.

QUARTERMASTER MUSEUM
Lee Street and Avenue A, Petersburg, Virginia 23803
Exhibits illustrating history of U.S. Army Quartermaster Corps. Military uniforms. Gen. Pershing's office furniture. Memorabilia of Presidents Eisenhower and Kennedy.
M.-F. 8-5; Sa., Su. 1-5. Closed public holidays.

PETERSHAM

FISHER MUSEUM OF FORESTRY
Athol Road, Petersham, Massachusetts 01366
History of forestry and land-use. Forestry techniques. Indian tools.
Daily 9-5. Oct. 1 - Apr. 30, Sa., Su. by appointment only.

MUSEUM OF PETERSHAM HISTORICAL SOCIETY
North Main Street, Petersham, Massachusetts 01366
Local history. Paintings by local artists.
May 1 - Sept. 30, M.-Sa. by appointment; Su. 2-4.

SECOND EAST SCHOOL
East Street, Petersham, Massachusetts 01366
18th century school equipment. Maps. Schoolbooks.
By appointment.

PHARR

OLD CLOCK MUSEUM
929 E. Preston Street, Pharr, Texas 78577
History of early clock-making, and of different methods of time-keeping. Exhibits of 500 clocks from different countries.
Daily 9 a.m. - 10 p.m.

PHILADELPHIA

ACADEMY OF NATURAL SCIENCES OF PHILADELPHIA
19 Street and Parkway, Philadelphia, Pennsylvania 19103
Geology. Mineralogy. Palaeontology. Herbarium. Natural history. Habitat groups.
M.-Sa. 10-5; Su. 1-5. Closed public holidays.

AMERICAN-SWEDISH HISTORICAL FOUNDATION MUSEUM
1900 Pattison Avenue, Philadelphia, Pennsylvania 19145
History of Swedish immigration and culture in U.S. Special John Ericsson, Jenny Lind and Frederika Bremer collections.
M.-F. 10-5; Sa. 1-4. Closed 2 weeks July, 2 weeks Aug., public holidays.

ATHENAEUM OF PHILADELPHIA
219 S. 6th Street, E. Washington Square, Philadelphia, Pennsylvania 19106
Building (1847). Paintings. Fine and decorative arts, 1820-40. Manuscripts. Books and documents from libraries of Franklin, William Byrd, John Ross. 19th century social and cultural history.
M.-F. 9-4.

ATWATER KENT MUSEUM
15 S. Seventh Street, Philadelphia, Pennsylvania 19106
Local history and popular art. Prints of Philadelphia.
M.-Sa. 9-5; Su. 1-5.

BALCH INSTITUTE
123 S. Broad Street, Philadelphia, Pennsylvania 19109
American ethnic and racial history.
M.-F. 9-4.30. Closed public holidays.

BAYNTON HOUSE
5208 Germantown Avenue (44), Philadelphia, Pennsylvania 19144
House (1803). Period furnishings.
Tu. 2-5.

BECHTEL HOUSE
5226 Germantown Avenue (44), Philadelphia, Pennsylvania 19144
House (1760). Costume collection.
Tu., Th., Sa. 1-5.

BLUMHAVEN LIBRARY AND GALLERY
4651 Leiper Street, Philadelphia, Pennsylvania 19124
Local history. Industry. Lincoln memorabilia. Coptic and Incan fabrics.
By appointment.

CEDAR GROVE
Lansdowne Drive, Fairmount Park, Philadelphia, Pennsylvania 19130
House (c.1748). Period furnishings.
Daily 10-5.

CIVIC CENTER MUSEUM
Civic Center Boulevard and 34th Street, Philadelphia, Pennsylvania 19104
Oriental, African crafts, Musical instruments. Crafts of the Philippines, S. Pacific, Latin America, Siberia.
Tu.-Sa. 9-5; Su. 1-5. Closed public holidays.

CYCLORAMA OF LIFE
Lankenan Hospital, City Line and Lancaster Avenues, Philadelphia, Pennsylvania 19151
Anatomy. Medicine. Medical history. Human growth and development.
M.-F. 9-5. Closed public holidays.

DREXEL MUSEUM COLLECTION
Drexel University, 32nd and Chestnut Streets, Philadelphia 19104
Decorative arts of India, China, Japan, Europe. European textiles. Hand-printed Indian cottons. Sèvres and other ceramics. 19th century German, French paintings.
M.-F. 9-5; Sa. 9-1. Picture Gallery M.-F. 8-5. Closed public holidays.

FRANKFORD HISTORICAL SOCIETY
1507 Orthodox Street, Philadelphia, Pennsylvania 19124
Local history.
Tu. evenings, and by appointment.

FRANKLIN INSTITUTE SCIENCE MUSEUM
20th Street and Parkway, Philadelphia, Pennsylvania 19103
Astronomy. Planetarium. Maritime and naval history. Aviation. Space exploration. Industry. Transport. Technology.
M.-Sa. 10-5; Su. 12-5. Closed public holidays.

FREE LIBRARY OF PHILADELPHIA
Logan Square, Philadelphia, Pennsylvania 19103
Medieval illuminated manuscripts. Prints. Engravings. Lithographs. Original Elkins' illustrations to Dickens. Anthropology. Theatre history. Coins. Stamps. Greeting and tradesmen's cards. Cuneiform tablets, seals. Horn books.
M.-W. 9-9; Th., F. 9-6; Sa. 9-5. Nov. 1 - Apr. 30, also Su. 2-6. Closed public holidays.

STEPHEN GIRARD COLLECTION
Cornithian and Girard Avenues, Philadelphia, Pennsylvania 19121
Furniture. Silver. Glass. Porcelain. Decorative arts.
By appointment.

THE GWINN COLLECTION
Lombard and 27th Street, Philadelphia, Pennsylvania 19146
Dairy machinery and equipment.
By appointment.

HERBARIUM OF THE UNIVERSITY OF PENNSYLVANIA
38th Street and Hamilton Walk, Philadelphia, Pennsylvania 19104
Plants of Pennsylvania and the Atlantic coastal plain.
By appointment.

INDEPENDENCE NATIONAL HISTORICAL PARK
313 Walnut Street, Philadelphia, Pennsylvania 19106
Open-air museum, with 20 Pennsylvania buildings (1732-

1834). American portraits, 1770-1830. 18th century American period furnishings. Memorabilia of Revolutionary and Federal periods.
Daily 9-5.

LA SALLE STUDY COLLECTION OF ART
La Salle College, 20th Street and Olney Avenue, Philadelphia, Pennsylvania 19141
House (1880). American and European paintings, prints, sculpture.
By appointment. Closed College vacations.

LEMON HILL MANSION
E. River and Sedgeley Drives, Philadelphia, Pennsylvania 19130
House (1800), was home of Robert Morris. Local history. Decorative arts.
Th. 11-4; 2nd and 4th Su. each month 1-4. Other times by appointment.

LIBRARY COMPANY OF PHILADELPHIA
1314 Locust Street, Philadelphia, Pennsylvania 19107
Manuscripts, paintings, graphics, furniture of the Colonial period.
M.-F. 9-4.45. Closed public holidays.

'MAN FULL OF TROUBLE' TAVERN
127-9 Spruce Street, Philadelphia, Pennsylvania 19106
Building (1759). Period furnishings. Pewter. Delftware. Glass.
Apr. 1-Dec. 31: Tu.-Su. 1-4. Jan. 1-Mar. 31: Sa., Su. 1-4. Closed Christmas, Thanksgiving.

MOORE COLLEGE OF ART GALLERY
20th and Race Streets, Philadelphia, Pennsylvania 19130
House (1850). Paintings, graphics. Sculpture. Textiles. Decorative arts.
Daily 9-5. Closed Thanksgiving, Christmas, New Year.

MORRIS ARBORETUM
9414 Meadowbrook Avenue, Philadelphia, Pennsylvania 19118
Botany. Herbarium.
Daily 9-4. Closed Christmas.

MOUNT PLEASANT
Fairmount Park, Philadelphia, Pennsylvania 19130
House (1762). Period furnishings.
Daily 10-5. Closed national holidays.

MUETTER MUSEUM OF THE COLLEGE OF PHYSICIANS OF PHILADELPHIA
19 S. 22nd Street, Philadelphia, Pennsylvania 19103
Anatomy. Pathology. Anthropology. Fetishes. Medical history, biography. Instruments.
Sept. 1-May 30, M.-F. 9.30-12.30, 1.30-4.30. June 1-Aug. 31, Tu.-F., 10-12, 2-4. Closed public holidays, 1 week in May, 2 weeks in August.

MUSEUM OF AMERICAN CATHOLIC HISTORICAL SOCIETY
263 S. 4th Street, Philadelphia, Pennsylvania 19105
Building (1810). History of Catholic Church in U.S.
By appointment.

MUSEUM OF THE CARNEGIE INSTITUTE
4400 Forbes Avenue, Philadelphia, Pennsylvania 195213
American and European paintings, sculpture, prints, drawings. Watercolours, decorative arts. Oriental decorative arts. Furniture. Miniatures. Enamels. Fans.
M.-Sa. 10-5 (Oct. 20-Mar. 23, Tu. 10-9); Su. 1-5.

MUSEUMS OF GERMANTOWN HISTORICAL SOCIETY
5208, 5214, 5218, 5275-77 Germantown Avenue, Philadelphia, Pennsylvania 19144
Correspondence to 5214 Germantown Avenue
At 5208: Furniture. Kitchen equipment. Sleighs. Dolls houses. At 5214: Furniture. Weapons. China. At 5218: Toys. Textiles. At 5275-77: Costumes.
Tu., Th., Sa. 1-5.

MUSEUM OF THE HISTORICAL SOCIETY OF PENNSYLVANIA
1300 Locust Street, Philadelphia, Pennsylvania 19107
Local history. Portraits by Pennsylvania artists, Colonial period to 1860.
M.-F. 9-5. Closed public holidays, Aug. 1-31.

MUSEUM OF INSURANCE COMPANY OF NORTH AMERICA
1600 Arch Street, Philadelphia, Pennsylvania 19101
History of fire-fighting. Fire-engines and models. Documents. Paintings. Currier and Ives prints. Maritime history.
M.-F. 8-4. Closed public holidays.

MUSEUM OF PRESBYTERIAN HISTORICAL SOCIETY
425 Lombard Street, Philadelphia, Pennsylvania 19147
Portraits. Pewter. Silver. Early books, especially Bibles. Coins and tokens.
M.-F. 9-5. Closed public holidays.

MUSEUM OF THE SOCIETY OF ARCHITECTURAL HISTORIANS
1700 Walnut Street, Philadelphia, Pennsylvania 19103
Architectural history. Decorative arts. Archaeology.
M.-F. 9-5.

NATIONAL CARL SCHURZ ASSOCIATION
339 Walnut Street, Philadelphia, Pennsylvania 19106
German contributions to American culture. Prints, drawings by German artists.
M.-F. 9-5. Closed holidays.

PENNSYLVANIA ACADEMY OF THE FINE ARTS
Broad and Cherry Streets, Philadelphia, Pennsylvania 19602
Building (1876). European paintings, graphics, drawings. 18th-19th century American paintings, sculpture.
Tu.-Sa. 10-5; Su. 1-5.

PERELMAN ANTIQUE TOY MUSEUM
270 South 2nd Street, Philadelphia, Pennsylvania 19106
In Abercrombie House (1758). Toys. Mechanical banks. Toy pistols. Automatic toys.
Daily 9.30-5. Closed New Year, Thanksgiving, Christmas.

PHILADELPHIA MARITIME MUSEUM
321 Chestnut Street, Philadelphia, Pennsylvania 19106
Maritime history. Ship models. Paintings. Prints. Navigational equipment. Weapons. Figureheads.
M.-Sa. 10-4; Su. 12-5. Closed Thanksgiving, Christmas, New Year.

PHILADELPHIA METHODIST CONFERENCE HISTORICAL CENTER AND OLD ST. GEORGE METHODIST CHURCH
326 New Street and 235 N. Fourth Street, Philadelphia, Pennsylvania 19106
History of Methodism in New England.
Daily 10-4.

PHILADELPHIA MUSEUM OF ART
26th Street and Parkway, Philadelphia, Pennsylvania 19101
World art, from beginning of Christian era to present day. American and English period rooms. Architectural settings, including 12th century Burgundian Abbey, 14th century French Gothic Chapel, Japanese ceremonial tea house and garden. Nepalese, Tibetan and Persian art. European and Indian sculpture. Philadelphia furniture, silver. Stiegel glass. Pennsylvania folk art. Thomas Eakins paintings.
Daily 9-5. Closed public holidays.

RODIN MUSEUM
Benjamin Franklin Parkway and 22nd Street, Philadelphia, Pennsylvania 19101
Sculptures and drawings by Rodin.
Daily 9-5. Closed public holidays.

PHILIP H. AND A. S. W. ROSENBACH FOUNDATION MUSEUM
2010 DeLancey Place, Philadelphia, Pennsylvania 19103
Building (1863). Decorative arts. Manuscripts.
Sept. 1-May 30, Tu.-Su. 2-5; June 1-July 31, M.-F. 2-5. Closed Aug. 1-Aug. 31, Su., public holidays.

STRAWBERRY MANSION
33rd Street and Ridge Avenue, Fairmount Park, Philadelphia, Pennsylvania 19130
House (1797, c.1825). Late 18th-early 19th century furnishings. Tucker porcelain. Toys.
Tu.-Su. 11-5. Closed Jan. 1-31.

SWEETBRIAR MANSION
Fairmount Park W., Philadelphia, Pennsylvania 19131
House (1797). Period furnishings.
M.-Sa. 10.30-5. Closed July and national holidays.

UNIVERSITY MUSEUM
33rd and Spruce Streets, Philadelphia, Pennsylvania 19104
Archaeology, especially of Egypt, Greece and Rome. Anthropology. Ethnology of American Indians, Oceania, Africa. Negro art. Art of China, India, Persia.
Tu.-Sa. 10-5; Su. 1-5. Closed public holidays.

WAGNER FREE INSTITUTE OF SCIENCE
17th Street and Montgomery Avenue, Philadelphia, Pennsylvania 19121
Mineralogy. Palaeontology. Fossils. Shells. Natural history.
M.-F. 10-5. Closed public holidays.

WAR LIBRARY AND MUSEUM OF THE MILITARY ORDER OF THE LOYAL LEGION OF THE UNITED STATES
1805 Pine Street, Philadelphia, Pennsylvania 19103
Civil War history.
M.-F. 10-4. Closed public holidays.

NAOMI WOOD COLLECTION
33rd and Dauphin Streets, E. Fairmount Park, Philadelphia, Pennsylvania 19132
In Woodford Mansion (1759-90). Furnishings of the Colonial period. Decorative arts.
Tu.-Su. 1-5. Closed Aug. 1-31.

WOODMERE ART GALLERY
9201 Germantown Avenue, Philadelphia, Pennsylvania 19118
European and American paintings. Oriental rugs, furniture, porcelain. European and American sculpture. Contemporary American paintings, sculpture, graphics.
M.-Sa. 10-5; Su. 2-6. Closed public holidays.

PHILLIPS

MUSEUM OF PHILLIPS HISTORICAL SOCIETY
Pleasant Street, Phillips, Maine 04966
In house of 1832. Local history. Tools. Glass. Railway relics. Portland glass.
Aug. 1-31, Th., F., Su. 2-4. Other times by appointment.

PHILLIPSBURG

OLD FORT BISSELL
Phillipsburg, Kansas 67661
Guns.
2 log cabins (1872-3) are in the care of the Fort.
Memorial Day-Labour Day, daily 9-9.

PHIPPSBURG

MUSEUM OF PHIPPSBURG HISTORICAL SOCIETY
Phippsburg, Maine 04562
Building (1859). Local history. Agriculture. Shipbuilding. Paintings. Costumes. Furnishings. Indian and coloured period artifacts.
July 1-Labour Day, M.-F. 2-4.

PHOENIX

ARIZONA HISTORY ROOM
First National Bank of Arizona, 1st Avenue and Washington Street, Phoenix, Arizona 85002
History of early settlement of Arizona.
M.-F., 10-3. Closed public holidays.

ARIZONA MINERAL MUSEUM
State Fairgrounds, Phoenix, Arizona 85002
Geology. Petrology. Palaeontology.
M.-F., 9.30-5; Sa., Su. 12.30-4.30. Closed public holidays.

ARIZONA MUSEUM
1001 W. Van Buren Street, Phoenix, Arizona 85007
House (1843). Paintings. Sculpture. Archaeology. Costumes. Indian artifacts.
Nov.-Apr., Tu.-Su. 2-5. Closed Thanksgiving, Christmas.

DEPARTMENT OF LIBRARY AND ARCHIVES MUSEUM
3rd Floor, State Capitol, Phoenix, Arizona 85007
Archaeology. Anthropology. History of Arizona and the South-West. Minerals of Arizona. Indian artifacts.
M.-F. 8-5.

HEARD MUSEUM
22 E. Monte Vista Road, Phoenix, Arizona 85004
Indian art-Apache, Hopi, Papago, Pima, Hohokan. Primitive art from Africa, Asia, Oceania. Archaeology. Anthropology. Ethnology. Paintings. Sculpture.
M.-Sa., 10-5; Su., 1-5. Closed public holidays.

PHOENIX ART MUSEUM
1625 North Central Avenue, Phoenix, Arizona 85004
American, European and Oriental paintings. Sculpture. Decorative arts. Graphics. Costumes. Mexican art.
Tu., Th.-Sa. 10-5; W. 10-9; Su. 1-5. Closed August, public holidays.

PIONEER ARIZONA
N. Black Canyon Freeway and Pioneer Road, Phoenix, Arizona 85020
Open-air museum. 19th century houses, shops, school. Carpenter's and waggon-builder's shops. Miners' camp. Lumber-yard.
Daily 9-sunset.

PUEBLO GRANDE MUSEUM
4619 East Washington, Phoenix, Arizona 85034
Archaeological site museum. Palaeontology. Indian culture. Ethnology. Open-air museum.
M.-F., 9-5; Su. 1-5. Closed public holidays.

PIEDMONT

TIMBERS OF AGES PETRIFIED FOREST MUSEUM
Box 129, Piedmont, South Dakota 57769
Petrified wood. Animal fossils. Arrowheads. Minerals.
May 15 - Sept. 15, daily 7-7.

PIERRE

MUSEUM OF SOUTH DAKOTA STATE HISTORICAL SOCIETY
Soldiers' Memorial Building, Pierre, South Dakota 57501
Indian and pioneer life. Homestead claim shanty. General store. Parlour of c.1900. Sioux artifacts. Winter counts. Gold mining. Fur trading. Political history. Study collections of barbed wire, political buttons, trade tokens, World War I history.
Oahe mission chapel (1877) and Mentor Graham house (1890) are in the care of the Society.
M.-F. 8-5; Sa. 10-5; Su. 1-5. Closed public holidays.

PIMA

EASTERN ARIZONA MUSEUM AND HISTORICAL SOCIETY OF GRAHAM COUNTY
2 North Main Street, Pima, Arizona 85543
Local history. Pioneer and Indian artifacts.
Old Cluff Hall (1880) is in the care of the Society.
M.-F. 9-12, 1-6. Closed public holidays.

PINE BLUFF

SOUTH-EAST ARKANSAS ARTS AND SCIENCES CENTER
Civic Center, Pine Bluff, Arkansas 71601
Paintings. Sculpture.
M.-Sa. 10-5. Closed New Year, July 4, Labour Day, Christmas.

PINE CITY

CONNOR'S POST
Pine City, Minnesota 55063
Reconstructed trading post (1840).
May 1 - Sept. 30: daily 10-5. Oct. 1-31: Sa., Su. 1-5.

PINEVILLE

JAMES K. POLK BIRTHPLACE STATE HISTORIC SITE
Pineville, North Carolina 28134
In reconstructed log-house. Local history. Memorabilia of Polk, U.S. President, 1845-49. Early 19th century furnishings.
Tu.-Sa. 9-5; Su. 1-5. Closed Thanksgiving, Dec. 24-6.

WILMAN LAPIDARY MUSEUM
Pineville Road, Pineville, Pennsylvania 18946
Minerals. Gemstones.
Tu.-Sa. 10-5; Su. 1-5. Closed Christmas, New Year.

PINEY FLATS

ROCKY MOUNT
Piney Flats, Tennessee 37686
House (1790-2), first U.S. Territorial Capitol. 18th century furnishings. History of E. Tennessee. Outbuildings include kitchen, smokehouse, blacksmith's shop.
Apr. 1 - Oct. 31: M.-Sa. 10-5. Su. 2-6.

PIOCHE

LINCOLN COUNTY HISTORICAL MUSEUM
Main Street, Pioche, Nevada 89043
In Gottgredson Building (c.1870). County history.
Winter: M.-F. 2-6; Su. 3-5. Summer: M.-Sa. 10-6. Closed national holidays.

PIPESTONE

PIPESTONE NATIONAL MONUMENT
P.O. Box 727, Pipestone, Minnesota 56164
Pipestone quarries. Indian ceremonial pipes and pipestone artifacts.
May 1 - Sept. 30, daily 8 a.m. - 9 p.m. Oct. 1 - Apr. 30, daily 8-5. Closed New Year, Christmas.

PIQUA

PIQUA HISTORICAL AREA STATE MEMORIAL
9845 N. Hardin Road, Piqua, Ohio 45356
Restored farmstead (c.1812). Section of Miami-Erie Canal, including passenger boat.
Apr. 1 - Nov. 30: Tu.-Su. 9.30-5.

PISECO LAKE

PISECO LAKE MUSEUM
Route 8, Piseco, New York 12139
19th century tavern. Period furnishings. Adirondack tools, domestic equipment.
May 1 - Oct. 31, daily 9-5. Other times by appointment.

PITTSBURG

PITTSBURG HISTORICAL SOCIETY MUSEUM
Civic Avenue, Pittsburg, California 94565
Mineralogy. Natural history. Local history. Costumes. Industry and handicrafts.
Su., 2-5. Other days by appointment.

MUSEUM OF CRAWFORD COUNTY HISTORICAL SOCIETY
305-7 E. Madison Street, Pittsburg, Kansas 66762
Local history. Household equipment. Replica of coal mine. Transport.
A grocery store (1902) is in the care of the Society.
Sa., Su. 2-4. Other days by appointment.

PITTSBURGH

BLOCK HOUSE
Point State Park, Pittsburgh, Pennsylvania 15222
Remains of original Fort Pitt (1764).
Tu.-Sa. 9-5; Su. 2-5.

BUHL PLANETARIUM
Allegheny Square, Pittsburgh, Pennsylvania 15212
Science, astronomy, space exhibits. Planetarium.
M.-F. 1-5, 7-10; Sa. 10.45-5, 7-10; Su. 1-10.

CARNEGIE MUSEUM
4400 Forbes Avenue, Pittsburgh, Pennsylvania 15213
Geology. Mineralogy. Palaeontology. Dinosaur collection. Botany. Herbarium. Natural history. Anthropology. Ethnology. Costumes. Textiles. Transport. Clocks and watches. Dolls.
M.-Sa. 10-5; Su. 2-5.

CARNEGIE MUSEUM OF ART
4400 Forbes Avenue, Pittsburgh, Pennsylvania 15213
Oriental ivories, bronzes, sculpture, jades, paintings, textiles. European and American decorative arts, paintings, sculpture, drawings, prints. Special collection of paintings by Pittsburgh artists, 19th-early 20th century French artists, early American prints, drawings. European furniture, porcelain, silver.
Sept. 15 - May 30, M., W.-Sa. 10-5; Tu. 10-9; Su. 1-5. June 1 - Sept. 14, M.-Sa. 10-5, Su. 2-5. Closed public holidays.

FISHER COLLECTION
711 Forbes Avenue, Pittsburgh, Pennsylvania 15219
17th-18th century Dutch, Flemish paintings, prints on medical and scientific subjects. Exhibits illustrating life and work of Pasteur.
M.-F. 9-4. Closed public holidays.

FORT PITT MUSEUM
Point State Park, Pittsburgh, Pennsylvania 15222
In Fort Pitt Blockhouse (1764). Early Indian culture in Western Pennsylvania. Fur trade. Conflict between England and France for control of Ohio. Pittsburgh in 1800.
M.-Sa. 9.30-4.30, Su. 12-4.30. Closed Easter, Thanksgiving, Christmas.

FOSTER HALL COLLECTION
Pitt Campus, University of Pittsburgh, Pittsburgh, Pennsylvania 15213
Music and personal possessions of the composer, Stephen Foster.
M.-F. 9-5. Closed public holidays.

FRICK ART MUSEUM
7227 Reynolds Street, Point Breeze, Pittsburgh, Pennsylvania 15213
French, Flemish, Italian paintings. Tapestries. Sculpture. 18th century French period room.
W.-Sa. 10-4; Su. 1-5. Closed public holidays.

HISTORICAL SOCIETY OF WESTERN PENNSYLVANIA
4338 Bigelow Boulevard, Pittsburgh, Pennsylvania 15213
Early American glass and firearms. Furniture. Paintings.
Tu.-F. 10-4.30; Sa. 10-12. Closed Aug. 1-31, public holidays.

SCHENLEY PARK NATURE MUSEUM
Schenley Park, Pittsburgh, Pennsylvania 15213
Geology. Astronomy. Botany. Natural history. Archaeology. Indian material.
M.-F. 9-9, Sa. 9-5, Su. 1-5.

UNIVERSITY ART GALLERY
Henry Clay Frick Fine Arts Building, University of Pittsburgh, Pittsburgh, Pennsylvania 15213
17th-20th century paintings. 16th-20th century prints. 18th-20th century sculpture.
Tu.-Su. 1-5. Closed Thanksgiving, Christmas, New Year.

PITTSFIELD

BERKSHIRE MUSEUM
39 South Street, Pittsfield, Massachusetts 01201
Mineralogy. Palaeontology. Science. Zoology. Local history. Transport. Indian artifacts. 17th-18th century European paintings. 20th century American paintings and sculpture. 18th century American silver. 18th-19th century American portraits. Chinese art. Sledge with which Peary reached North Pole. William Stanley's original transformer.
Tu.-Sa. 10-5; Su. 2-5. Closed New Year, July 4, Thanksgiving, Christmas.

GOODRICH HOUSE
323 N. Street, Pittsfield, Massachusetts 01201
House (1792-1813). 18th-19th century furnishings. History of Berkshire County.
July 1 - Oct. 15, Tu.-Sa. 10-4; Su. 1-4.

MELVILLE MEMORIAL ROOM
Berkshire Athenaeum Public Library, 44 Bank Row, Pittsfield, Massachusetts 01201
Portraits and personal possessions of Herman Melville.
Oct. 1 - Apr. 30: M.-F. 9-9; Sa. 9-6. May 1 - Sept. 30: M., W., F. 9-9; Tu., Th., Sa. 9-6. Closed public holidays.

MUSEUM OF BERKSHIRE COUNTY HISTORICAL SOCIETY
113 E. Housatonic Street, Pittsfield, Massachusetts 01201
Building (1855-8). Local history. Costumes.
Butler Goodrich House (1792-1813) is in the care of the Society.
M.-F. 2-5. Butler Goodrich House, July 1 - Oct. 30, Tu.-Sa. 10-4; Su. 1-4. Closed public holidays.

PITTSFORD

HISTORIC PITTSFORD
4 S. Main Street, Pittsford, New York 14534
In The Little House (c.1820). Local history.
Sa. 11-2.

PLACERVILLE

EL DORADO COUNTY HISTORICAL SOCIETY MUSEUM
542 Main Street, Placerville, California 95667
In former Methodist Church (1851). Local history. Gold mining equipment. Indian artifacts.
M.-F. 8.30-12, 1-5. Closed public holidays.

PLAINFIELD

DRAKE HOUSE MUSEUM
602 W. Front Street, Plainfield, New Jersey 07060
In house (1745), with 18th-19th century furnishings. Americana. Indian relics. Local military history.
M., W., Sa. 2-5.

HERBERT LEWIS TAYLOR MUSEUM AND LIBRARY
739 W. 8th Street, Plainfield, New Jersey 07060
Anthropology. Ethnology. Indian artifacts. Archaeology.
M.-F. 2-5, Sa. 3-5.

PLAINS

TSA MO GA MEMORIAL MUSEUM
1109 Avenue H, Plains, Texas 79355
Pioneer history. Civil War mementoes.
By appointment.

PLAQUEMINE

CARRIAGE HOUSE MUSEUM
712 Eden Street, Plaquemine, Louisiana 70764
Material illustrating life in Iberville parish c.1900. Documents. Paintings. Photographs. Domestic equipment. Tools.
M.-Sa. 8.30-4. Closed public holidays.

PLATTSBURGH

KENT-DELORD HOUSE MUSEUM
17 Cumberland Avenue, Plattsburgh, New York 12901
House (1797) was British headquarters during War of 1812. Local history.
Jan. 15 - Dec. 15, M.-Sa. 9-5.

PLATTEVILLE

FORT VASQUEZ VISITOR CENTER
State Historical Society of Colorado, Route 2, Platteville, Colorado 80651
Archaeology. Local history. History of the fur trade.
Weld County Court House (1861) and the reconstructed Fort Vasquez (orig. 1835) are in the care of the Center.
Mar. 1 - Nov. 30, daily 9-5.

PLATTSMOUTH

CASS COUNTY HISTORICAL SOCIETY MUSEUM
644 Main Street, Plattsmouth, Nebraska 68048
Geology. Palaeontology. Pioneer life. Tools. Furnishings. Plains Indian artifacts. Civil War material. Schoolroom.
Apr. 1 - Nov. 15: Th.-Tu. 2-5. Other times by appointment.

PLEASANT HILL

DIABLO VALLEY COLLEGE MUSEUM
Golf Club Road, Pleasant Hill, California 94523
Mineralogy. Botany. Zoology. Anthropology. Physics.
M.-W. 9.30-4.30; F., Sa. 1.30-5. Closed August, public holidays.

MIAMI COUNTY ARCHAEOLOGICAL SOCIETY MUSEUM
Indian Hills 4-H Camp, Lauver Road, Pleasant Hill, Ohio 45359
Local archaeology.
Apr. 1 - Sept. 30, 4th Su. in month 2-4.

PLYMOUTH

MARSHALL COUNTY HISTORICAL MUSEUM
317 W. Monroe Street, Plymouth, Indiana 46563
Local history. Furniture. Tools. Household equipment.
M.-F., Su. 2-5.30. Closed public holidays and last two weeks Aug.

ANTIQUARIAN HOUSE
126 Water Street, Plymouth, Massachusetts 02360
House (1809-30). 19th century furniture, household equipment, ornaments. China. Dolls. Toys.
June 15 - Oct. 15, daily 10-5.

HARLOW-HOLMES MUSEUM
8 Winter Street, Plymouth, Massachusetts 02360
House (1649). Family furniture. Local history.
Daily 10-5.

HARLOW OLD FORT HOUSE
119 Sandwich Street, Plymouth, Massachusetts 02360
House (1677). 17th century furniture, household equipment.
June 15 - Oct. 15, daily 10-5.

JABEZ HOWLAND HOUSE
33 Sandwich Street, Plymouth, Massachusetts 02360
House (1667). Archaeology. Period furnishings.
May 15 - Oct. 15, daily 9.30-5.

MAYFLOWER SOCIETY HOUSE
4 Winslow Street, Plymouth, Massachusetts 02360
House (1754). 18th-19th century furnishings. Local history.
May 30 - Oct. 15, daily 10-5.

MUSEUM OF PLYMOUTH PLANTATION
Warren Avenue, Plymouth, Massachusetts 02360
History of 17th century settlers of Massachusetts. Furnishings. Costumes. Replicas of early settlers' houses. Replica of 'Mayflower'.
Apr. 1 - Nov. 30, daily 10-5.

PILGRIM HALL MUSEUM
75 Court Street, Plymouth, Massachusetts 02360
House (1824). Local history. Material relating to 17th century settlers of Massachusetts. Indian artifacts. Archaeology. Sculpture. Graphics. Costumes.
Daily 9-4.30. Closed New Year, Christmas.

PILGRIM JOHN HOWLAND SOCIETY
Clifford R.F.D.4, Plymouth, Massachusetts 02360
In John Howland House (1667). 17th century household equipment, furnishings.
May 15 - Oct. 15, daily 9.30-5.

PLYMOUTH ANTIQUARIAN SOCIETY
Spooner House, 27 North Street, Plymouth, Massachusetts 02360
Museum based on Spooner House (1747), Harlow House (1677), Antiquarian House (1809). Furnishings. Costumes. Household equipment. Dolls.
Daily 10-5.

RICHARD SPARROW HOUSE
42 Summer Street, Plymouth, Massachusetts 02360
House (1640). 17th century furnishings.
May-Sept., M.-Sa. 9-5.

SPOONER HOUSE
27 North Street, Plymouth, Massachusetts 02360
House (1750), occupied by Spooner family until 1950. 18th-19th century furnishings. Family possessions.
June 15 - Oct. 15, daily 10-5.

PLYMOUTH HISTORICAL SOCIETY MUSEUM
157 S. Main Street, Plymouth, Michigan 48170
History of Plymouth.
Sa., Su. 2-5.

CALVIN COOLIDGE HOMESTEAD
Route 100-A, Plymouth, Vermont 05056
Coolidge general store. Original Coolidge family furnishings, personal possessions. Wilder house and barn, with exhibition of early farm implements.
May 25 - Oct. 17, daily 9-6.

WILDER HOUSE INN
Route 100-A, Plymouth, Vermont 05056
Home of President Coolidge's mother. Original and period furnishings.
By appointment.

CALVIN COOLIDGE BIRTHPLACE
Plymouth, Vermont 05056
House in which Coolidge was born and in which he was sworn in by his father as U.S. President, August 3, 1923. Rooms furnished and arranged exactly as they were on that day.
May 25 - Oct. 15, daily 9-6.

JOHN G. VOIGT HOUSE
Route 1, Plymouth, Wisconsin 53073
House (1850). Period furnishings.
June 1 - Sept. 30: W.-Su. 1-5.

PMC COLLEGES

MUSEUM OF DELAWARE COUNTY HISTORICAL SOCIETY
PMC Colleges, Pennsylvania 19013
History of Delaware County. Costumes. Glass. Coins.
W. after Labour Day - July 31: M.-F. 1-4; Sa. 9-12. Closed public holidays.

POCATELLO

BANNOCK COUNTY HISTORICAL MUSEUM
Center and Carfield Streets, Pocatello, Idaho 83201
Local history.
Tu.-Su. 2-5. Closed public holidays.

IDAHO STATE UNIVERSITY MUSEUM
Box 96, Pocatello, Idaho 83201
Archaeology, ethnology and linguistics of N.W. Coast, Plateau and Great Basin. Ethnology of Amazon Basin. Polish, Anatolian textiles. Flintworking.
M.-F. 10-5, Su. 2-5. Closed University vacations.

POINT LOOKOUT

RALPH FOSTER MUSEUM
Point Lookout, Missouri 65726
Geology. Ozark history. Indian artifacts. Folklore. Kewpies. Cameos. Coins.
M.-Sa. 8-5; Su. 1-5.

POINT PLEASANT

GRANT'S BIRTHPLACE STATE MEMORIAL
State Route 232, Point Pleasant, Ohio 45163
House (1821), where Ulysses S. Grant was born. Period furnishings. Grant memorabilia. Civil War items.
Apr. 1 - Oct. 31: Tu.-Su. 9.30-5.

MANSION HOUSE MUSEUM
Point Pleasant, West Virginia 25550
Building (1796), erected as a tavern. Period furnishings. Large square piano, one of the first to be brought over the Alleghenies. Four-poster beds (19th century).
Daily 10-12, 2-4.

TUE-ENDI-WEI STATE PARK MUSEUM
Main Street, Point Pleasant, West Virginia 25550
Log house (1796). Colonial period furnishings.
May 1 - Nov. 30, daily 9-5.

POLAND SPRING

SHAKER MUSEUM
Sabbathday Lake, Poland Spring, Maine 04274
Based on village of 17 buildings. Furniture. Textiles. Tools. Farm implements. Paintings and drawings by Shaker artists. Metal and wooden ware.
May 30 - Sept. 30: Tu.-Sa. 10-4.30.

STATE OF MAINE BUILDING
Poland Spring, Maine 04274
Building originally erected at Chicago Columbian Exposition (1893). Geology. Botany. Paintings. State history.
Daily 9-5.

POLLOCK

LITTLE SALMON RIVER CANYON MUSEUM
Pollock, Idaho 83547
Natural history. Archaeology. Agriculture. Transport. Indian material. Paintings. Sculpture.
Tu.-Su. 9-9. Closed Dec. 1 - Jan. 31.

POMEROY

MEIGS COUNTY PIONEER AND HISTORICAL SOCIETY MUSEUM
144 Butternut Avenue, Pomeroy, Ohio 45769
Local history. Pioneer life.
By appointment.

POMONA

ADOBE DE PALOMARES
491 East Cucamonga Avenue, Pomona, California 91767
Ygnacio Palomares Adobe (1850-4), with furnishings and rancho equipment. Indian artifacts.
Tu.-Su. 2-5; public holidays, 1-5. Closed Thanksgiving, Christmas.

LENOX, INCORPORATED
Tilton Road, Pomona, New Jersey 08420
Early Lenox china, including services made for state, national, international dignitaries.
M.-Sa. 9-4.30.

PONCA CITY

PIONEER WOMAN STATUE AND MUSEUM
701 Monument Road, Ponca City, Oklahoma 74601
Mementoes of Oklahoma pioneer women. Domestic equipment, utensils from pioneer homes. Furnishings from 101 Ranch.
Oct. 1 - Apr. 30, M.-Sa. 9-5; Su. 1-5. May 1 - Sept. 30, M.-Sa. 9-7; Su. 1-7. Closed Christmas.

PONCA CITY CULTURAL CENTER AND INDIAN MUSEUM
1000 E. Grand Avenue, Ponca City, Oklahoma 74601
House (1916) was home of Governor of Oklahoma. Indian artifacts, paintings, costumes.
M., W.-Sa. 10-5; Su. 1-5. Closed Christmas.

PONCE

PONCE ART MUSEUM
Avenue Las Américas, P.O. Box 1492, Ponce, Puerto Rico 00731
Italian primitives. 15th-18th century Flemish, German, Spanish paintings. 17th century Dutch paintings. 18th - early 19th century French and English portraits. 18th-20th

century Puerto Rican paintings. Taino and Carib artifacts. European and American sculpture, c.1300 - present day.
Tu.-Su. 10-12, 2-5. Closed New Year, Good Friday, Three Kings Day, Christmas.

PONTIAC

MUSEUM OF OAKLAND COUNTY PIONEER AND HISTORICAL SOCIETY
405 Oakland Avenue, Pontiac, Michigan 48058
In Wisher House, Pine Grove (1845), former home of Governor Moses Wisher. Original and period furnishings. History of Oakland County, Drayton Plains School, etc.
Michigan week, July 1 - Aug. 31, Tu.-Sa. 1-4. Closed public holidays.

PORTAGE

FORT WINNEBAGO SURGEON'S QUARTERS
Rural Route 1, Portage, Wisconsin 53901
Surgeon's Quarters (1824) with period furnishings. Garrison School (1850). Military history. Indian artifacts.
Apr. 1 - Oct. 31, daily 9-5. Winter by appointment. Closed Christmas.

OLD INDIAN AGENCY HOUSE
Portage, Wisconsin 53901
House (1832). Decorative arts. Indian beadwork.
May 1 - Sept. 30, daily 9-5. Winter by appointment. Closed Christmas.

PORTALES

BLACKWATER DRAW MUSEUM
Highway 70, Portales, New Mexico 88130
Site museum. Palaeo-Indian geology, archaeology, anthropology.
Su. 1-5.

MILES MUSEUM
Eastern New Mexico University, Portales, New Mexico 88130
Geology. Mineralogy. Palaeontology. Archaeology. Ethnology.
M., W., F. 1-5. Closed university vacations.

PALAEO-INDIAN INSTITUTE AND MUSEUM
Eastern New Mexico University, Portales, New Mexico 88130
Palaeo-Indian archaeology and anthropology.
M.-F. 9-5. Closed university vacations.

ROOSEVELT COUNTY MUSEUM
Portales, New Mexico 88130
Anthropology. Ethnology. Archaeology. Technology. Folklore. Local history. Life of early settlers. Coins.
M.-F. 8-11.45, 1-4.30; Sa. 9-11.45, 1-4.30; Su. 1-4. Closed public holidays.

PORT ANGELES

CLALLAM COUNTY HISTORICAL SOCIETY MUSEUM
2800 Hurricane Ridge Road, Port Angeles, Washington 98362
Local history. 19th century furniture. Beaumont Cabin (1888).
By appointment.

PIONEER MEMORIAL MUSEUM
2800 Hurricane Ridge Road, Port Angeles, Washington 98362
Botany. Herbarium. Zoology. Anthropology.
May 1 - Sept. 30, daily 8 a.m. - 9 p.m. Oct. 1 - Apr. 30, daily 8.30-5. Closed New Year, Thanksgiving, Christmas.

PORT ARTHUR

PORT ARTHUR HISTORICAL MUSEUM
Merchants National Bank Building, 441 Austin Avenue, Port Arthur, Texas 77640
History of Port Arthur and Jefferson County.
By appointment.

PORT CHESTER

BUSH HOMESTEAD
479 King Street, Port Chester, New York 10573
House (1778). Period furnishings.
Th. 1.30-4.30.

PORT CLINTON

OTTAWA COUNTY HISTORICAL MUSEUM
City Hall, Adams and E. 2nd Streets, Port Clinton, Ohio 43452
Geology. Local history. Indian material. Pioneer relics.
W. 6.30-8.30; Th. 3-5. Sa. 3-5, 6.30-8.30. Closed New Year, Memorial Day, July 4, Thanksgiving, Christmas.

PORTERVILLE

PORTERVILLE MUSEUM
251 North D Street, Porterville, California 93257
Local history. Indian artifacts.
Th.-Sa., 10-5. Closed New Year, Christmas.

PORT GIBSON

GRAND GULF MILITARY PARK
Route 2, Box 140, Port Gibson, Mississippi 39150
Site of Civil War battles, 1862-3. Includes Forts Coburn and Wade. Original trenches and gun emplacements. Museum contains Civil War displays - maps, models, paintings, dioramas.
Tu.-Su. 9-dusk. Closed Christmas, Thanksgiving.

PORT HUENEME

CIVIL ENGINEERS CORPS SEEBEE MUSEUM
USN Construction Battalion Center, Port Hueneme, California 93041
History of U.S. Navy Construction Battalions. Weapons. Uniforms. Equipment. Several 1941 quonset huts are preserved.
M.-F. 8-4.30; Sa., 9-4.30. Closed New Year, Thanksgiving, Christmas.

PORT HURON

MUSEUM OF ARTS AND HISTORY
1115 6th Street, Port Huron, Michigan 48060
Port Huron history. Tools used by Alconquin Indians. Lumbering. Edison material. Civil War relics. American primitive paintings. Artifacts from wrecked and scrapped ships. Scale models of marine engines. Agricultural implements. 19th century American furniture. Geology. Wildlife.
W., Su. 1-4.30.

PORT JEFFERSON

MUSEUM OF HISTORICAL SOCIETY OF GREATER PORT JEFFERSON
Prospect Street, Port Jefferson, New York 11777
In John T. Mather homestead (c.1840). Local maritime history. Paintings. Half-models. Tools.
Mar. 15 - Nov. 15: Tu., Su. 1-4.

PORTLAND

BEACH MUSEUM
1245 Forest Avenue (5), Portland, Maine 04106
Fossils. Minerals. Shells. Birds. Indian artifacts.
By appointment.

MAINE HISTORICAL SOCIETY MUSEUM
485 Congress Street, Portland, Maine 04111
History of Maine. Furniture. Costumes.
June 1 - Sept. 30, M.-F. 10-5: Oct. 1 - May 31, Sa. 12-5.

MUSEUM OF NATURAL HISTORY
22 Elm Street, Portland, Maine 04111
Geology. Palaeontology. Natural history. Molluscs. Archaeology. Anthropology. Indian material. Costumes.
M.-F. 8.30-4.30. Closed public holidays.

PORTLAND MUSEUM OF ART
111 High Street, Portland, Maine 04103
In McLellan-Sweat Mansion (1800), with furnishings of the period. Contains Portland Museum of Art, with 20th century American paintings and sculpture. Portland glass. Japanese sword guards.
Tu.-Sa. 10-5; Su. 2-5. Closed public holidays.

TATE HOUSE
1270 Westbrook Street, Portland, Maine 04102
House (1755) with period furnishings.
July 1-3, Sept. 1-14: M.-Sa. 11-5; Su. 1.30-5.

VICTORIA MANSION (MORSE-LIBBY HOUSE)
Park and Danforth Streets, Portland, Maine 04101
House (1859). Period, including some original, furnishings. Fans. Portland glass.
June 15 - Oct. 15: Tu.-Sa. 11-4.30; Su. 2-4.30. Closed public holidays.

THE WADSWORTH-LONGFELLOW HOUSE
487 Congress Street, Portland, Maine 04111
House (1785), Longfellow's boyhood home. Wadsworth-Longfellow family furnishings, documents.
June 1 - Sept. 30, M.-F. 9.40-4.30. Closed public holidays.

MUSEUM OF CONTEMPORARY CRAFTS ASSOCIATION
3934 S.W. Corbett Avenue, Portland, Oregon 97201
Works by N.W. craftsmen. Sculpture. Pottery. Jewellery. Textiles.
M.-Sa. 11-5; Su. 1-5.

OLD CHURCH SOCIETY
1422 S.W. 11th Avenue, Portland, Oregon 97201
In Calvary Presbyterian Church (1882). Parlour, with Victorian furnishings. Pipe and chamber organs.
Tu.-Sa. 11-3. Closed Memorial Day, July 4, Thanksgiving, Christmas, New Year.

OREGON HISTORICAL SOCIETY MUSEUM
1230 S.W. Park Avenue, Portland, Oregon 97205
Indian relics. Pioneer life. Maritime and military history. Exploration of Pacific North West. Paintings, drawings, prints by artists of the North West.
Beekman Bank (1853), Fort Dalles (1856) and Bybee Howell House (1857) are in the care of the Society.
M.-Sa. 10-5; Su. 12-5. Closed public holidays.

OREGON MUSEUM OF SCIENCE AND INDUSTRY
4015 S.W. Canyon Road, Portland, Oregon 97221
Geology. Palaeontology. Anthropology. Northwest Indian artifacts. Physical sciences. Technology. Industry.
Sept. 15 - June 14: M.-Th. 9-5; F. 9-9; Sa., Su. 9-6. June 15 - Sept. 14: M.-Th. 9-6; F.-Su. 9-9. Closed Christmas.

PITTOCK MANSION
3229 N.W. Pittock Drive, Portland, Oregon 97204
House (1909-14). Period furnishings.
W.-Su. 1-5. Closed New Year, Thanksgiving, Christmas.

PORTLAND ART MUSEUM
1219 S.W. Park Avenue, Portland, Oregon 97205
Pre-Columbian and Northwest Indian art. Chinese sculpture, bronzes, ceramics. Greek and Roman antiquities. Persian and Hindu miniatures. Japanese prints. Italian Renaissance paintings, sculpture. English silver. Paintings, sculpture, drawings, prints by artists of the Pacific Northwest. English water-colours. 16th-20th century French paintings, sculpture. Cameroon art. Ethiopian crosses. Oriental rugs.
Tu.-Th. 12-5; F. 12-10; Sa., Su. 12-5. Closed public holidays.

PORTLAND CHILDREN'S MUSEUM
3037 S.W. 2nd Avenue, Portland, Oregon 97201
Minerals. Shells. Natural history. Anthropology. Archaeology. Dolls. Paintings. Sculpture.
June 1 - July 31: M.-F. 9-5. Rest of year: M.-F. 10-6. Closed public holidays.

WESTERN FORESTRY CENTER
4033 S.W. Canyon Road, Portland, Oregon 97221
Herbarium of forestry trees. Logging equipment.
Daily 10-5. Closed Christmas.

PORT LAVACA

JAIL MUSEUM
301 S. Ann Street, Port Lavaca, Texas 77979
In old Calhoun County Jail. County history. Furnishings, household equipment. Photographs.
Tu. 2-6; F. 10-2; Sa. 10-1.

PORT NECHES

D.A.R. MUSEUM
P.O. Box 444, Millard Park, Port Neches, Texas 77651
Local and military history.
Public holidays 9-5. Other times by appointment.

PORT ROYAL

JUNIATA COUNTY HISTORICAL SOCIETY
Tuscarora Academy, R.D.2, Port Royal, Pennsylvania 17082
Building (1816). Local history. Furniture. Paintings. Prints.
By appointment.

PORT ST. JOE

CONSTITUTION CONVENTION STATE MUSEUM
U.S. Highway 98, Port St. Joe, Florida 32456
Dioramas and exhibits telling story of Florida's first State Constitution Convention, 1838-39.
Daily 9-12, 1-5.

PORT SANILAC

MUSEUM OF SANILAC COUNTY HISTORICAL SOCIETY
228 S. Ridge Street, Port Sanilac, Michigan 48469
Agriculture. Maritime history. Medicine. Dolls. Glass.
Loop Harrison House (1873) is in the care of the Society.
June 15 - Sept. 4: Tu.-Su., public holidays 1-5.

PORTSMOUTH

THOMAS BAILEY ALDRICH MEMORIAL
386 Court Street, Portsmouth, New Hampshire 03801
House (c.1790). Early Victorian furniture, decorations, silver. Scene of Aldrich's *Story of a Bad Boy*. First editions. Autograph letters.
June 15 - Sept. 15: M.-Sa. 10-5.

RICHARD JACKSON HOUSE
Northwest Street, Portsmouth, New Hampshire 03801
House (1664), with period furnishings.
June 1 - Sept. 30: Tu.-Sa. 1-5.

GOVERNOR JOHN LANGDON MANSION
143 Pleasant Street, Portsmouth, New Hampshire 03801
House (1784). Wood-carving. Scenic wall-paper. Period furnishings.
June 1 - Oct. 31: Tu.-Sa. 10-4.

MOFFATT-LADD HOUSE
154 Market Street, Portsmouth, New Hampshire 03801
House (1763). 18th century furniture. Panelling.
May 15 - Oct. 15: M.-Sa. 10-5. Su. 2-5.

PORTSMOUTH ATHENAEUM
9 Market Square, Portsmouth, New Hampshire 03801
Building (1805). Portsmouth history. Paintings. Clipper ship models.
Th. 1-4.

PORTSMOUTH HISTORICAL SOCIETY MUSEUM
43 Middle Street, Portsmouth, New Hampshire 03801
In John Paul Jones House (1758). Local history. Period furniture. Portraits. China. Silver. Costumes.
May 15 - Sept. 30: M.-Sa. 10-5. July 1 - Aug. 30: also Su. 2-5. Closed Memorial Day.

STRAWBERY BANKE
Hancock, Washington, Court and Marcy Streets, Portsmouth, New Hampshire 03801
30 17th - early 19th century houses, restored, furnished and open to the public.
May 1 - Oct. 31: M.-Sa. 9.30-5; Su. 12-5. July 1 - Aug. 31: open until 7 p.m. Tu., Th.

WARNER HOUSE
Daniel and Chapel Streets, Portsmouth, New Hampshire 03801
House (c.1716). Period furnishings. Panelling. Early marbled finishes. Life-size mural paintings, 2 of Indian chiefs. Portraits by Joseph Blackburn of members of Warner family.
May 15 - Oct. 15: M.-Sa. 10-5; Su. 2-5.

WENTWORTH-COOLIDGE MANSION
State Highway 1A, Portsmouth, New Hampshire 03801
House (1741) was home of 1st Royal Governor of New Hampshire. Lilacs in garden were probably the first to be introduced to USA.
May 22 - Oct. 11, daily 10-5.

WENTWORTH-GARDNER MANSION
Marcy Street, Portsmouth, New Hampshire 03801
Early 18th century house. Wood-carving. Windmill spit. Dutch tiles. Spinning attic.
May 1 - Oct. 31: Tu.-Su. 10-5.

MUSEUM OF PORTSMOUTH HISTORICAL SOCIETY
E. Main Road and Union Street, Portsmouth, Rhode Island 02871
In former schoolhouse (1775). Furniture. Clothing. Tools. Agricultural equipment.
July-Aug., M., F.-Su. 2-5. May-June, Su. 2-5.

PORTSMOUTH NAVAL SHIPYARD MUSEUM
2 High Street, Portsmouth, Virginia 23705
History of Portsmouth, the Navy and the Naval Shipyard. The CSS 'Virginia'. Ship models. Uniforms. Flags. Weapons. Maps. Prints.
Tu.-Sa. 10-5; Su. 2-5. Closed Christmas, New Year.

PORT TOWNSEND

JEFFERSON COUNTY HISTORICAL SOCIETY MUSEUM
City Hall, Port Townsend, Washington 98368
Building (1892). Mineralogy. Local history. Agriculture. Costumes. Furniture. Indian artifacts.
Apr. 14 - May 31, F.-Su. 12-5. June 1 - Sept. 30, W.-Su. 11-5. Oct. 1-31, W., Su. 12-5. Nov. 1-30, Su. 12-5. Public holidays 12.30-5.

THE ROTHSCHILD HOUSE
Jefferson and Taylor Streets, Port Townsend, Washington 98368
House (1868). Period furnishings. Rothschild family personal possessions.
June-Sept., Tu.-Su. 10-5.

POTEAU

KERR MUSEUM
P.O. Box 588, Poteau, Oklahoma 74953
In former home (1960) of Senator Robert Kerr. Exhibits illustrating history and development of E. Oklahoma. Geology. Prehistoric Spiro Indian artifacts. Pioneer life. Coal mining. Barbed wire collection. History of Arkansas River. Development of rockets and space craft. Conservation of natural resources.
Oct. 1 - Apr. 30 daily 1-5. May 1 - Sept. 30, M.-F. 10-5, Sa., Su. 1-5. Closed New Year, Thanksgiving, Christmas.

POTOMAC

GREAT FALLS TAVERN MUSEUM
11710 MacArthur Boulevard, Potomac, Maryland 20854
In Crommelin House (1828). Canal history. Natural history. Indian artifacts.
Daily 9.30-5.30. Closed Christmas.

POTSDAM

POTSDAM PUBLIC MUSEUM
Civic Center, Elm and Park Streets, Potsdam, New York 13676
History of Lawrence County. English pottery. Glass. Decorative arts. Coverlets and quilts. Costumes.
Tu.-F. 2-5; Sa. 1-3. Closed public holidays.

POTTSTOWN

POTTSGROVE MANSION
W. King Street, Pottstown, Pennsylvania 19464
House (1752). Period furnishings. Home of the ironmaster, John Potts.
May 1 - Oct. 31: Tu.-Sa. 8.30-5; Su. 1-5. Nov. 1 - Apr. 30: Tu.-Sa. 9-4.30; Su. 1-4.30. Closed public holidays.

POTTSVILLE

OLD POTT'S TAVERN
Pottsville, Arkansas 72858
House (1845). Local history.
By appointment.

MUSEUM OF SCHUYLKILL COUNTY HISTORICAL SOCIETY
14 N. 3rd Street, Pottsville, Pennsylvania 17901
Railway history. History of anthracite coalfields. County history.
Tu., F. 11-5; Th. 1-9; Sa. 10-4. Closed public holidays.

POUGHKEEPSIE

CLINTON HOUSE
549 Main Street, Poughkeepsie, New York 12601
House (c.1767), associated with George Clinton, first New York State governor. Period furnishings.
Daily 9-5.

VASSAR COLLEGE ART GALLERY
Raymond Avenue, Poughkeepsie, New York 12601
Oriental porcelain, jade. Dürer and Rembrandt prints. Sculpture. 16th-20th century European paintings. Paintings of the Hudson River School. Archaeology. Decorative arts. 16th-20th European graphics, including works by Rembrandt, Picasso, Matisse, Braque.
M.-Sa. 9-4.45; Su. 2-5. During college vacations by appointment.

POULTNEY

EAST POULTNEY MUSEUM
The Green, Poultney, Vermont 05764
In former blacksmith's shop and Melodeon factory (1800). Local history. Agriculture. Household equipment.
June-Sept., Su. 1-5.

POYNETTE

MCKENZIE ENVIRONMENTAL CENTER
Route 1, Poynette, Wisconsin 53955
Ecology. Herbarium. Wildlife of Wisconsin. Exhibits illustrating conservation policy.
Apr. 1 - Oct. 31: M.-Sa. 8-4; Su., public holidays 9-5. Nov. 1 - Mar. 31: M.-F. 8-4.

POYNOR

MILNER'S MILL
S.H. 175, Poynor, Texas 75782
Restored and operating water-powered grist mill. Relics of early settlers.
Daily 8-5.

PRAIRIE CITY

DE WITT MUSEUM
Prairie City Council, Prairie City, Oregon 97860
History of gold-mining era in Grant County. Sawmilling. Ranching. Relics of Sumpter Valley Railway.
May 1 - Oct. 31, 10-4. Other times by appointment.

PRAIRIE DU CHIEN

MUSEUM OF MEDICAL PROGRESS
700 South Beaumont Road, Prairie du Chien, Wisconsin 53821
Medical history. In Old Fort Crawford Military Hospital (1829).
July 4 - Labour Day, daily 9-9. Labour Day - Oct. 30, Apr. 16 - July 3, daily 9-5.

SUN PRAIRIE HISTORICAL LIBRARY AND MUSEUM
115 E. Main Street, Prairie du Chien, Wisconsin 53821
Local history.
W., Su. 2-4.

VILLA LOUIS AND MUSEUM
721 N. Villa Louis Road, Prairie du Chien, Wisconsin 53821
Fur trader's house (1843), furnished in style of 1870s. History of Port Louis and of the fur-trade and early settlement of the area.
May 1 - Oct. 31, daily 9-5.

PRAIRIE DU ROCHER

FORT DE CHARTRES STATE PARK MUSEUM
Prairie du Rocher, Illinois 62277
Military history. The Museum comprises a barracks and fort of 1775.
W.-Su. 8.30-5.

PRATTSBURG

NARCISSA PRENTISS HOME
Prattsburg, New York 14873
Birthplace of one of first white women to cross Rockies (1836). Period furnishings.
Apr. 1 - Oct. 31: W.-Su. 1.30-5. Other times by appointment.

PRATTSVILLE

ZADOCK PRATT MUSEUM
Prattsville, New York 12468
Memorabilia of founder of village (1824).
May 30 - Oct. 1: W., Sa., Su. 2-5.

PRESCOTT

OLD GOVERNOR'S MANSION
West Gurley Street, Prescott, Arizona 86301
House (1864). Relics of early pioneers. Indian artifacts. Minerals.
Tu.-Sa., 9-12; Su., 1-5. Closed New Year, Memorial Day, Thanksgiving, Christmas.

SHARLOT HALL MUSEUM
Prescott Historical Society, West Gurley Street, Prescott, Arizona 86301
Indian artifacts. Costumes. Herbarium. Mineralogy.
In the care of the Museum are the Old Governor's Mansion (1864), Old Fort Misery (1864) and a replica of the first schoolhouse (1864) in the territory.
Tu.-Sa., 9-12, 1-5; Su., 1-5. Closed New Year, Memorial Day, Thanksgiving, Christmas.

SMOKI MUSEUM
North Arizona Avenue, Prescott, Arizona 86301
Indian artifacts, especially pottery, from ruins of local villages.
June-Aug. M.-Sa. 10-4.30; Su. 1-5. Other times by appointment.

PRESQUE ISLE

MUSEUM OF PRESQUE ISLE HISTORICAL SOCIETY
12 2nd Street, Presque Isle, Maine 04769
Local history.
W. 2-4.

OLD LIGHT HOUSE
Presque Isle, Michigan 49777
Gout Light House (1840). Maritime history.
June 1 - Sept. 30, daily 9-8.

PRESTON

MUSEUM OF FILLMORE COUNTY HISTORICAL SOCIETY
Fairgrounds, Preston, Minnesota 55965
In rural schoolhouse (1890). Geology. Local history, archaeology, costumes.
M., W., F. 1-4.30.

PRICE

CARBON COLLEGE PREHISTORIC MUSEUM
Price City Municipal Building, Price, Utah 84501
Utah geology. Dinosaur tracks, skeletons. Archaeology. 9th century Indian relics.
June-Sept., M.-Sa. 10-8; Su. 1-8.

PRINCESS ANNE

OLDE PRINCESS ANNE DAYS
Teackle Mansion, Mansion Street, Princess Anne, Maryland 21853
House (1801). Local history. Costumes. Children's museum.
M.-Sa. by appointment; Su. 2-4.

PRINCETON

BUREAU COUNTY HISTORICAL SOCIETY MUSEUM
109 Park Avenue, West Princeton, Illinois 61356
Local history.
Th., Sa., Su. 1-5. Closed Thanksgiving, Christmas.

MUSEUM OF MERCER COUNTY HISTORICAL SOCIETY
902 E. Oak Street, Princeton, Missouri 64673
Local history.
M.-Sa. 10-5. Closed public holidays.

ART MUSEUM
Princeton University, Princeton, New Jersey 08540
European and American paintings, graphics, sculpture. Archaeology. Coins. Pre-Colombian art. Far Eastern art.
Tu.-Sa. 10-4; Su. 2-4. Closed public holidays.

MORVEN
Route 206, Princeton, New Jersey 08540
House (1701). Original Stockton family furniture, portraits, with other 18th century furnishings.
By appointment.

MUSEUM OF HISTORICAL SOCIETY OF PRINCETON
158 Nassau Street, Princeton, New Jersey 08540
In William Bainbridge House (1766). Architecture. History of Princeton and New Jersey.
M.-F. 10-3; Sa. 1-3; Su. 2-4. Closed public holidays.

PRINCETON JUNIOR MUSEUM
Borough Hall, Princeton, New Jersey 08540
Rocks. Pottery. Stamps.
By appointment.

PRINCETON UNIVERSITY ART MUSEUM
Princeton, New Jersey 08540
Oriental, especially Chinese, art. Pre-Columbian paintings, sculpture. European and American paintings, sculpture, graphics. Archaeology. Coins.
Tu.-Sa. 10-4; Su. 2-4. Closed public holidays.

PRINCETON UNIVERSITY, MUSEUM OF NATURAL HISTORY
Princeton, New Jersey 08540
Geology. Mineralogy. Palaeontology. Ornithology. Indian artifacts.
M.-Sa. 9-5. Su., public holidays 2-5.

PRINEVILLE

A. R. BOWMAN MEMORIAL MUSEUM
3rd and N. Main Streets, Prineville, Oregon 97754
Material illustrating early settlement of Oregon. Indian artifacts. History of Crook County.
Apr. 15 - Oct. 15: Tu.-Sa. 11-6.30; Su., public holidays 11-7. Oct. 16 - Apr. 14, closed M.

PIONEER CABIN MUSEUM
Pioneer Park, Prineville, Oregon 97754
Restored cabin c.1850. Pioneer furnishings.
June 1 - Sept. 30: M.-Sa. 10-5; Su. 1-5. Other times by appointment.

PROCTOR

MARBLE EXHIBIT
Main Street, Proctor, Vermont 05765
Specimens of marble from all over the world. Marble busts of U.S. Presidents. Quarrying and processing of marble.
May 26 - Oct. 15, daily 9-6.

PROSPECT

PROSPECT HISTORICAL SOCIETY MUSEUM
Prospect, Connecticut 06712
Local history. Agriculture. Domestic life.
By appointment.

FORT KNOX STATE PARK
State Highway 174, Prospect, Maine 04981
Fort (1864). Military history.
May 1 - Oct. 31, daily 10-6.

PROSPECT PARK

MORTON HOMESTEAD
Route 420, Prospect Park, Pennsylvania 19076
House (c.1680). Early American furnishings.
May 1 - Oct. 31: Tu.-Sa. 8.30-5; Su. 1-5. Nov. 1 - Apr. 30: Tu.-Sa. 9-4.30; Su. 1-4.30. Closed public holidays.

PROSSER

BENTON COUNTY HISTORICAL MUSEUM
P.O. Box 591, Prosser, Washington 99350
Natural history. Crafts. Indian artifacts.
Tu.-Sa. 10-4; Su. 1-5. Closed Christmas, Thanksgiving.

PROVIDENCE

ANNMARY BROWN MEMORIAL
Brown University, 21 Brown Street, Providence, Rhode Island 02912
15th century printed books. 16th-18th century paintings. Exhibits illustrating art and history of the Renaissance.
May 1 - Oct. 31: M.-F. 9-5; Sa. 8.30-12. Closed public holidays. Rest of year M.-F. 9-5.

GOVERNOR STEPHEN HOPKINS HOUSE
Hopkins and Benefit Streets, Providence, Rhode Island 02903
House (1707). Home of Stephen Hopkins, signatory of Declaration of Independence. Period furnishings.
W., Sa. 1-4.

MUSEUM OF ART, RHODE ISLAND SCHOOL OF DESIGN
224 Benefit Street, Providence, Rhode Island 02903
Aboriginal and pre-Columbian art. European and American paintings, especially French Impressionists. European sculpture, including Rodin's 'Balzac'. Greek and Roman art. 18th century European porcelain figurines. Japanese prints. Modern Latin American paintings. 20th century American art. 18th century American furniture.
Tu.-Sa. 11-5; Su., public holidays 2-5. Closed July 4, Labour Day, Thanksgiving, New Year, Christmas.

MUSEUM OF WESTERN RHODE ISLAND CIVIC HISTORICAL SOCIETY
365 Plainfield Street, Providence, Rhode Island 02909
Local history. 18th century furnishings. Costumes. Tools. Domestic equipment.
May-Sept., Tu. 1-4.

PROVIDENCE ART CLUB GALLERY
11 Thomas Street, Providence, Rhode Island 02903
Houses (1787 and 1793). Paintings by American artists.
M.-F. 10-5; Su. 2-5.

RHODE ISLAND HISTORICAL SOCIETY
52 Power Street, Providence, Rhode Island 02906
In John Brown House (1788). Local history. 18th century Rhode Island furniture. Staffordshire pewter. Sandwich glass. Chinese export porcelain. Indian artifacts. Paintings by Rhode Island artists. Dolls.
Tu.-F. 11-4; Sa., Su. 2-4. Closed public holidays.

RHODE ISLAND STATE ARCHIVES
Room 314, State House, Smith Street, Providence, Rhode Island 02903
Rhode Island history. Indian artifacts.
M.-F. 9-4.30. Closed public holidays, Aug. 1-15.

BETSEY WILLIAMS COTTAGE
Roger Williams Park, Providence, Rhode Island 02905
Cottage (1773). Local history. Period furnishings.
M.-W., F., Sa. 10-4; Su. 2-5. Closed public holidays.

ROGER WILLIAMS PARK MUSEUM
Roger Williams Park, Providence, Rhode Island 02905
Geology. Mineralogy. Wildlife. Indian and Eskimo culture.
M.-Sa. 8.30-4.30; Su., public holidays 2-5. Closed Christmas, New Year.

PROVINCETOWN

CHRYSLER ART MUSEUM
Commercial and Center Streets, Provincetown, Massachusetts 02657
Greek, Roman, Egyptian, Near-Eastern, Oriental, Pre-Columbian, African sculpture. European and American paintings. New England furniture and glass.
June 15 - Sept. 14: daily 9-11. Sept. 15 - June 14: daily 9-6.

MUSEUM OF CAPE COD PILGRIM MEMORIAL ASSOCIATION
Town Hall, Provincetown, Massachusetts 02657
History of Cape Cod. Industry.
June 15 - Sept. 14: daily 9-9. Sept. 15 - July 14: daily 9-5. Closed New Year, Christmas.

PROVINCETOWN ART ASSOCIATION MUSEUM
460 Commercial Street, Provincetown, Massachusetts 02657
Contemporary American paintings, sculpture, graphics.
June 1 - Sept. 30: M.-Sa. 10-6, 8-11; Su. 2-6.

PROVO

BRIGHAM YOUNG UNIVERSITY, ARCHAEOLOGICAL COLLECTION
Maeser Building, Provo, Utah 84601
Archaeology of N. America, especially Utah.
By appointment.

BRIGHAM YOUNG UNIVERSITY, BOTANICAL COLLECTIONS
Plant Science Building, Provo, Utah 84601
Herbaria of N. and S. America.
Daily 9-5.

BRIGHAM YOUNG UNIVERSITY, EARTH SCIENCES MUSEUM
Provo, Utah 84601
Geology. Mineralogy. Palaeontology.
M.-F. 8-5. Closed public holidays.

BRIGHAM YOUNG UNIVERSITY, FINE ARTS COLLECTION
New Fine Arts Center, Provo, Utah 84601
Chinese ivories. Japanese prints. American and European paintings, prints, sculpture. Mormon and Utah art.
Daily 8-10.

BRIGHAM YOUNG UNIVERSITY, GEOLOGICAL COLLECTION
Science Building, Provo, Utah 84601
Geology. Mineralogy, fossils, especially of Utah.
Daily 9-4.

BRIGHAM YOUNG UNIVERSITY, LIFE SCIENCES MUSEUM
H. J. Grant Building, Provo, Utah 84601
Herbarium. Zoology. Marine biology. Entomology. Herpetology. Ichthyology.
M.-F. 9-6. Closed public holidays.

BRIGHAM YOUNG UNIVERSITY, ZOOLOGICAL AND ENTOMOLOGICAL COLLECTIONS
Provo, Utah 84601
Zoology. Entomology.
By appointment.

MUSEUM OF SONS AND DAUGHTERS OF UTAH PIONEERS OF PROVO
5th W. and 5th N. Streets, Provo, Utah 84601
Memorabilia of Mormon pioneers. Replicas of Mormon cabins. Children's museum.
June 1 - Aug. 31, daily 9-5. Other times by appointment.

PROUTS

STUDIO
Winslow Homer Road, Prouts, Maine 04074
House (1860). Paintings.
May 1 - Oct. 31, M. 10-4. Other times by appointment.

PRYOR

CHIEF PLENTY COUPS MEMORIAL VISITOR CENTER
Box 39, Pryor, Montana 59066
House (c.1900), home of Chief Plenty Coups. Original furnishings. Ethnography of the Crow Indians.
May 1 - Oct. 31, M.-F. 9-9; Sa. 10-9; Su. 12-6.

PUEBLO

EL PUEBLO MUSEUM
905 S. Prairie Avenue, Pueblo, Colorado 81005
History of Colorado. Development of local steel industry. Replica of El Pueblo adobe post (orig. 1842).
M.-F. 9-5; Sa., Su., public holidays 10-5. Closed New Year, Thanksgiving, Christmas.

PUEBLO METROPOLITAN MUSEUM
419 W. 14th Street, Pueblo, Colorado 81003
Mineralogy. Natural history. Archaeology. Local history. Indian artifacts.
June 1 - Aug. 31, Tu.-Sa. 9-5; Su., public holidays 1-4. Sept. 1 - May 31, Tu.-Su. 1-4. Closed New Year, Christmas.

PULLMAN

CHARLES R. CONNER MUSEUM
Washington State University, Pullman, Washington 99163
Zoology. Ornithology. Herpetology.
M.-F. 8-5; Sa. 8-12; public holidays 8-5.

MUSEUM OF ANTHROPOLOGY
Department of Anthropology, Washington State University, Pullman, Washington 99163
Anthropological collections from S. America, W. Africa, New Guinea, China. Archaeological material from Alaska and Washington State.
M.-Sa. 1-5. Closed University vacations.

WASHINGTON STATE UNIVERSITY HERBARIUM
Pullman, Washington 99163
Botany. Herbarium.
M.-F. 8-12, 1-5. Closed university vacations.

PUTNEY

PUTNEY HISTORICAL MUSEUM
Town Hall, Main Street, Putney, Vermont 05346
Local history. Geology, mineralogy of the area. Indian artifacts. Costumes. Folklore.
June 1 - Oct. 31: W., Sa. 2-5.

PUYALLUP

PAUL H. KARSHNER MEMORIAL MUSEUM
426 4th Street N.E., Puyallup, Washington 98371
Children's museum. Geology. Palaeontology. Natural history. Pioneer history. Indian artifacts.
Tu.-F. 9-3. Closed school vacations.

QUAKERTOWN

MUSEUM OF QUAKERTOWN HISTORICAL SOCIETY
44 S. Main Street, Quakertown, Pennsylvania 18951
Local history. Costumes. Glass.
By appointment.

QUANAH

MEDICINE MOUND TRADING POST
U.S.287 E., Quanah, Texas 79252
In former Santa Fe depot (1910), moved from Medicine Mound to Quanah in 1960. Railway equipment. Pioneer relics.
May 1 - Sept. 30: M.-Sa. 8-6. Oct. 1 - Apr. 30, 8-5.

QUANTICO

U.S. MARINE CORPS MUSEUM
Marine Corps Base, Quantico, Virginia 22134
History of Marine Corps. Development of weapons. Uniforms. Aviation. Coins. Stamps.
M.-F. 9-6; Sa. 9-5; Su., public holidays 12-4. Closed New Year, Christmas.

QUARRYVILLE

ROBERT FULTON BIRTHPLACE
R.D.1, Quarryville, Pennsylvania 17566
House (c.1780, with later additions). 18th - early 19th century furnishings. Early home of Robert Fulton, artist, inventor, engineer and pioneer steamship builder.
May 1 - Oct. 31: Tu.-Sa. 8.30-5; Su. 1-5. Nov. 1 - Apr. 30: Sa. 9-4.30; Su. 1-4.30. Closed public holidays.

QUEENS

HALL OF SCIENCE OF THE CITY OF NEW YORK
111th Street and 48th Avenue, Corona, Queens, New York 11352
Science and technology. Life sciences. Energy conversion. Communications. Housing. Space exploration. Aviation. Children's museum.
Tu.-Sa. 10-5; Su. 1-5.

QUINCY

PLUMAS COUNTY MUSEUM
586 Jackson Street, Quincy, California 95971
Geology. Local history. Costumes. Indian artifacts.
M.-F. 9-5; Sa., Su. 12-5. Closed public holidays.

HISTORICAL SOCIETY OF QUINCY AND ADAMS COUNTY
425 S. 12th Street, Quincy, Illinois 62301
John Wood Mansion (1835). Period furnishings. Local history.
Tu.-F. 11-5.30; Sa., Su. 2-5. Closed public holidays.

QUINCY ART CENTER
1515 Jersey Street, Quincy, Illinois 62301
In building (1888) designed by Frank Lloyd Wright's teacher, J. L. Sisbee. Paintings. Graphics. Sculpture. Handicrafts.
Tu.-Su. 2-5. Closed public holidays.

JOHN ADAMS BIRTHPLACE
133 Franklin Street, Quincy, Massachusetts 02169
House (1675), birthplace of President John Adams. Period furnishings.
Apr. 19 - Sept. 30, Tu.-Sa. 9-5; Su. and holidays 10-5.

ADAMS NATIONAL HISTORICAL SITE
135 Adams Street, Quincy, Massachusetts 02169
House (1731). Paintings. Sculpture. Graphics. Glass. Coins.
Apr. 19 - Nov. 10, daily 9-5.

THE QUINCY HOMESTEAD
34 Butler Road at Hancock Street, Quincy, Massachusetts 02169
House (1636), birthplace of Dorothy Quincy, wife of John Hancock. Period furnishings.
Apr. 19 - Oct. 31, Tu.-Su. 10-5.

QUINCY HOUSE
20 Muirhead Street, Wollaston, Quincy, Massachusetts 02169
House (1770). Quincy family furnishings.
June-Sept., Tu., Th., F. 1-5.

QUITMAN

GOVERNOR HOGG SHRINE
518 S. Main Street, Quitman, Texas 75783
House (1870) is former home of Governor J. S. Hogg. Hogg family furnishings and personal possessions.
Tu.-Su. 8-12, 1-5. Closed Christmas.

QUOGUE

OLD SCHOOLHOUSE MUSEUM
Quogue, New York 11959
Schoolhouse (1822). Local history exhibits.
July 1 - Aug. 31: M., W., F. 2-5; W., Sa. 10-12.

RACINE

RACINE ART ASSOCIATION WUSTUM MUSEUM OF FINE ARTS
2519 Northwestern Avenue, Racine, Wisconsin 53404
Works by contemporary American artists. Paintings. Sculpture. Drawings. Prints.
Su., Th. 11-9; F., Sa. 11-5. Closed New Year, July 4, Christmas.

RACINE COUNTY HISTORICAL MUSEUM
701 S. Main Street, Racine, Wisconsin 53403
Local history and archaeology. Industrial development. Natural history.
Log cabin (1837) is in the care of the Museum.
Tu.-Sa. 9-5; Su. 12-5. Closed public holidays.

RALEIGH

ANDREW JOHNSON MEMORIAL COMMISSION
P.O. Box 1881, Raleigh, North Carolina 27602
In Andrew Johnson House (c.1808). Period furnishings. Memorabilia of President Johnson, in the house where he was born.
M.-F., Su. 2-5. Closed Thanksgiving, Christmas.

JOEL LANE HOUSE
728 W. Hargett Street, Raleigh, North Carolina 27603
House, known also as Wakefield (1770). Period furnishings.
On request to the caretaker.

MUSEUM OF NORTH CAROLINA PRESBYTERIAN HISTORICAL SOCIETY
1015 Wade Avenue, Raleigh, North Carolina 27605
History of Presbyterian Church in North Carolina.
M.-F. 8.30-5. Closed public holidays.

MUSEUM OF NORTH CAROLINA STATE DEPARTMENT OF ARCHIVES AND HISTORY
109 E. Jones Street, Raleigh, North Carolina 27602
History and archaeology of N. Carolina. Naval and military history. Indian material. Folklore. Paintings. Sculpture. Graphics. Glass. Costumes. Medicine. Junior museum.
12 historic buildings, 1744 onwards, are in the care of the Department.
Sept. 1 - May 31: M.-Sa. 8.30-5.30. June 1 - Aug. 31: M.-Sa. 8-5.

NORTH CAROLINA MUSEUM OF ART
107 E. Morgan Street, Raleigh, North Carolina 27601
European and American paintings, sculpture, decorative arts, graphics. Tapestries. Furniture. N. Carolina pottery.
Tu.-Sa. 10-5; Su. 2-6. Closed Thanksgiving, Christmas, New Year.

NORTH CAROLINA MUSEUM OF HISTORY
109 E. Jones Street, Raleigh, North Carolina 27602
History of North Carolina. Furniture. Decorative arts. Costumes, uniforms. Paintings. Graphics. Photography. Coins. Anthropology. Archaeology. Industry. Transport. Military history.
Sept. 1 - May 31: M.-Sa. 8.30-5.30; Su. 2-5. June 1 - Aug. 31: M.-Sa. 8-5; Su. 2-5. Closed Thanksgiving, Christmas.

NORTH CAROLINA STATE MUSEUM
101 Halifax Street, Raleigh, North Carolina 27611
Natural history of N. Carolina. Geology. Mineralogy. Botany. Herbarium. Zoology. Herpetology. Archaeology.
M.-Sa., public holidays 9-5; Su. 2-5. Closed New Year, Christmas.

RALLS

RALLS HISTORICAL MUSEUM
Box 384, Ralls, Texas 79357
In First National Bank building (1918). Local history, archaeology, ethnography. Natural history.
June 1 - Aug. 1: M.-F., Su. 2-5. Sept. 1 - May 31: W., F., Su. 2-5.

RAMAH

EL MORRO NATIONAL MONUMENT
Ramah, New Mexico 87321
Local history. Indian and Spanish artifacts.
Daily 8-5. Closed Christmas.

RAMSEY

OLD STONE HOUSE MUSEUM
536 Island Road, Ramsey, New Jersey 07446
House (c.1750). Period rooms. Junior museum in separate building.
May 1 - Oct. 31: Su. 2-4.30.

RAMSEY HISTORICAL ASSOCIATION
536 Island Road, Ramsey, New Jersey 07446
Local history.
Th., Su. 2-4.30.

RANDLEMAN

NORTH RANDOLPH HISTORICAL SOCIETY MUSEUM
411 High Point Street, Randleman, North Carolina 27317
In former St. Paul's Church (1879). History of Randolph County. Agricultural tools and implements. Furniture. Paintings. Drawings. Photographs. Horse-drawn hearse.
By appointment.

RANDOLPH

RANDOLPH HISTORICAL MUSEUM
Main Street, Randolph, Vermont 05060
Local history. Photographs. Agricultural implements. Household utensils, equipment. Trade signs.
June 15 - Sept. 15: Su., July 4, 2-4.

RANDSBURG

DESERT MUSEUM
Butte Street, Randsburg, California 93554
Mineralogy.
Sa., Su., public holidays 9-5.

RANKIN

RANKIN MUSEUM
12th Avenue, Rankin, Texas 97998
Geology. Costumes. Local history.
F. 3-5; M.-Th., Sa. by appointment.

RAPID CITY

MINNILUSA PIONEER MUSEUM
West Boulevard, Rapid City, South Dakota 57701
Pioneer history. Fur trade. Trapping. Natural history.
Apr. 15 - Oct. 15, M.-Sa. 8-5; Su. 1-5.

MUSEUM OF GEOLOGY
South Dakota School of Mines and Technology, Rapid City, South Dakota 57701
Geology. Mineralogy. Fossils.
M.-F. 8-5; Sa. 8-12. Closed public holidays.

SIOUX INDIAN MUSEUM
P.O. Box 1504, Rapid City, South Dakota 57701
Arts of the Sioux. Costumes. Paintings. Drawings. Decorative arts.
June-Aug., M.-Sa. 8-5; Su. 1-5. Sept.-May, Tu.-Sa. 10-5; Su. 1-5. Closed M. from Sept.-May, also New Year, Thanksgiving, Christmas.

RATON

MUSEUM OF COLEFAX COUNTY SOCIETY OF ART, HISTORY AND ARCHAEOLOGY
430 Rio Grande, Raton, New Mexico 87740
Building (1882). Local history. Paintings, sculpture, graphics by local artists.
July 1 - Aug. 31, daily 2-5.

RAVENNA

MUSEUM OF PORTAGE COUNTY HISTORICAL SOCIETY
6459 N. Chestnut Street, Ravenna, Ohio 44266
In Charlotte Strickland House (1829). Local history and archaeology. Indian material. Glass.
Tu.-Th., Su. 2-5. Other times by appointment. Closed New Year, Christmas.

RAWLINS

CARBON COUNTY MUSEUM
Carbon County Courthouse, Fifth and Pine Streets, Rawlins, Wyoming 82301
County and Wyoming history. Indian artifacts.
Summer: Tu. 1-4; F. 1-4, and by appointment.

MUSEUM OF RAWLINS NATIONAL BANK
220 5th Street, Rawlins, Wyoming 82301
Natural history. Mineralogy. Local history. Guns. Indian material.
M.-Th. 9-3; F. 9-5. Closed public holidays.

RAYMOND

PACIFIC COUNTY HISTORICAL SOCIETY MUSEUM
P.O. Box 384, Raymond, Washington 98577
Pioneer history. Indian collection.
Daily 1-5. Closed Christmas.

READING

MUSEUM OF READING ANTIQUARIAN SOCIETY
26 Vine Street, Reading, Massachusetts 01867
House (1694). Local history, crafts.
May-Oct., Su. 2-5.

PARKER TAVERN
103 Washington Street, Reading, Massachusetts 01867
Farmhouse (1694), with 17th-19th century furnishings. History of Reading.
Apr. 30 - Oct. 31, Su. 2-5.

MUSEUM OF HISTORICAL SOCIETY OF BERKS COUNTY
940 Centre Avenue, Reading, Pennsylvania 19601
County history. Indian artifacts. Agriculture. Decorative arts.
Tu.-Sa. 9-4; Oct.-May also Su. 2-5. Closed public holidays.

PLANETARIUM
1211 Parkside Drive S., Reading, Pennsylvania 19602
Astronomy. Instruments. Meteorites.
M., Tu., F. 9-4; W.-Th. 9-4, 7-9; Su. 2-4. Closed Aug. 1-31, public holidays.

READING PUBLIC MUSEUM AND ART GALLERY
500 Museum Road, Reading, Pennsylvania 19601
Natural history. Local history. Indian artifacts. Agriculture. Decorative arts. Paintings by artists of the Hudson River School. Early American and Pennsylvania German art. African, Chinese, Japanese art.
M.-F. 9-5; Sa. 9-12; Su. 2-5. Closed public holidays.

READING HISTORICAL SOCIETY MUSEUM
Main Street, Reading, Vermont 05062
Local and military history. Photographs. Tools. Medicine. Textiles.
May 29 - Oct. 14: W. 2-5, 7-9; July 4 by appointment.

RED BLUFF

WILLIAM B. IDE ADOBE STATE HISTORIC PARK
Route 3, Adobe Road, Red Bluff, California 96080
Home of California pioneer, William B. Ide. Exhibits of pioneer life and artifacts. Indian camp.
Daily 8-5. Closed New Year, Thanksgiving, Christmas.

KELLY-GRIGGS HOUSE MUSEUM
311 Washington Street, Red Bluff, California 96080
House (1880). Period furnishings. Paintings. Sculpture. Indian artifacts. Pioneer collection. Victorian costumes.
Th.-Su. 2-5. Closed Easter, July 4, Thanksgiving, Christmas, New Year.

RED CLOUD

WILLA CATHER PIONEER MEMORIAL AND EDUCATIONAL FOUNDATION
329 N. Cedar Street, Red Cloud, Nebraska 68970
Letters, books and personal possessions of Willa Cather. 5 local buildings (1878-97), including Willa Cather childhood home, are in the care of the Foundation.
May 1 - Sept. 30, daily 10-5. Rest of year by appointment.

WEBSTER COUNTY HISTORICAL SOCIETY MUSEUM
741 W. 4th Avenue, Red Cloud, Nebraska 68970
Natural history. Local history. Agriculture. Indian artifacts.
May 1 - Sept. 30: Tu., Su. 2-4.30.

REDDING

REDDING MUSEUM AND ART CENTRE
Box 427, Redding, California 96001
Indian ethnology and archaeology. Basketry.
May 1 - Sept. 30, Tu.-Su. 10-5; Oct. 1 - Apr. 30, Tu.-F. 12-5; Sa. 10-5. Closed New Year, Thanksgiving, Christmas.

REDDING-BETHEL

COLONIAL MUSEUM
Putnam Memorial State Park, Route 58, Redding-Bethel, Connecticut 06896
Local history.
The site of the Revolutionary Encampment is in the care of the Museum.
Memorial Day - Labour Day, daily 12-4.

REDFIELD

SPINK COUNTY MEMORIAL MUSEUM
Sixth Avenue E. and Third Street E., Redfield, South Dakota 57469
County history. Mounted animals, birds, butterflies. Arrowheads. Coins. Farm implements.
June-Sept. daily 1-5.

REDLANDS

ASISTENCIA DE SAN GABRIEL
26930 Barton Road, Redlands, California 92373
House (1830-4). Local history. Indian and American pioneer artifacts.
Tu.-Su. 1-5. Closed public holidays.

LINCOLN MEMORIAL SHRINE
Fourth and Eureka Streets, Smiley Park, Redlands, California 92373
Paintings and sculpture illustrating Civil War period and life of Abraham Lincoln.
M.-Tu., Th.-F. 2-5; W. 9-5. Closed public holidays.

PEPPERS ART CENTER
University of Redlands, 1200 East Colton Avenue, Redlands, California 92373
Paintings. Sculpture. Graphics.
Tu.-F. 1-5; Sa., Su. 2-5.

UNIVERSITY OF REDLANDS PLANETARIUM
1200 East Colton Avenue, Redlands, California 92373
Planetarium.
By appointment.

RED LODGE

BIG SKY HISTORICAL MUSEUM
Red Lodge, Montana 59068
Pioneer history. Indian artifacts.
Daily 8 a.m. - 9 p.m.

RED WING

GOODHUE COUNTY HISTORICAL SOCIETY MUSEUM
1166 Oak Street, Red Wing, Minnesota 55066
Geology. Mineralogy. Palaeontology. Natural history. Local history. Indian artifacts. Immigration. Agriculture. Industry. Transport. Textiles. Medical history. Musical and theatrical history.
Tu.-Su. 1-5. Closed public holidays.

REDWOOD FALLS

REDWOOD FALLS MUSEUM
101 E. 4th Street, Redwood Falls, Minnesota 56283
Natural history. Local history. Indian material, including clothing.
May 1 - Sept. 30, F., Sa. 1-3; Su. 1-5. Oct. 1 - Apr. 30, F. 1-3.

REGENT

HETTINGER COUNTY HISTORICAL SOCIETY MUSEUM
Box 276, Regent, North Dakota 58650
Pioneer drug store (1911), with doctor's surgery and original furnishings. Early farm implements and tools. Clothing. Pictures.
W. 1-3. Other times by appointment.

REHOBOTH BEACH

REHOBOTH ART LEAGUE
Henlopen Acres, Rehoboth Beach, Delaware 19971
Paintings. Sculpture. Prints. Decorative arts. Paynter studio (1775), moved 4 miles to present site.
May 7-28, F.-M. 12.30-5; May 29 - Sept. 4, daily 9.30-5; Sept. 5 - Oct. 1, daily 12-5.

REIDSVILLE

CHINQUA-PENN PLANTATION HOUSE
Route 29, Box 437, Reidsville, North Carolina 27320
House (1925). European and Oriental furnishings, objets d'art.
May 1 - Dec. 14: W.-Sa. 10-4; Su. 1-4. Closed Thanksgiving.

REMSEN

BARON VON STEUBEN MEMORIAL
Starr Hill Road, Remsen, New York 13438
Replica of 2-room log-house (c.1780), home of Frederick William von Steuben, "drill-master of the American Revolution". Contains personal possessions of von Steuben.
Apr. 15 - Oct. 15: M.-Sa. 9-5; Su. 1-5.

RENFRO VALLEY

RENFRO VALLEY PIONEER MUSEUM
U.S. Highway 25, Renfro Valley, Kentucky 40473
Agricultural implements. Household equipment. Guns. Horse-drawn vehicles. Musical instruments. Printing shop. Country store.
May-Nov. daily 8.30-4.

RENO

HARRAH'S AUTOMOBILE COLLECTION
P.O. Box 10, Reno, Nevada 89504
Cars. Aeroplanes.
May 1 - Sept. 30, daily 9 a.m. - 10 p.m. Oct. 1 - Apr. 30, daily 9-6.

MACKAY SCHOOL OF MINES MUSEUM
University of Nevada, Reno, Nevada 89507
Geology. Mineralogy. Palaeontology. History of mining.
M.-F. 8-5; Sa. 1-5. Closed University vacations.

NEVADA ART GALLERY
643 Ralston Street, Reno, Nevada 89503
Works by American, especially local, artists. Paintings. Sculpture. Graphics. Decorative arts. Archaeology.
Tu.-Su. 1-4. Closed Aug. 1-31, public holidays.

NEVADA HISTORICAL SOCIETY MUSEUM
1650 N. Virginia Street, Reno, Nevada 89504
Natural history. Anthropology. Primitive art. Costumes. Textiles. Furniture. Indian baskets. Cattle brands. Nevada history.
M.-F. 8-5; Sa. 9-5. Closed public holidays, Oct. 31.

RENSSELAER

JASPER COUNTY HISTORICAL SOCIETY MUSEUM
Route 4, Rensselaer, Indiana 47978
Local history. Furniture. Clothing. Civil War relics.
Log cabin (1865) is in the care of the Society.
May 1-8 and last week Aug. daily 1-5. Remainder of period May 9 - Sept. 30 by appointment.

FORT CRAILO
Riverside Avenue, Rensselaer, New York 12144
Manor House (1729). Period furniture. Local history.
Tu.-Sa. 9-5; Su. 12-5.

RESERVE

SAN FRANCISCO PLANTATION HOUSE
Highway 44, River Road, Reserve, Louisiana 70084
House (1749). Frescoes. Period furnishings.
Daily 9-5.

REXBURG

UPPER SNAKE RIVER VALLEY HISTORICAL SOCIETY
Route 2, Box 12D, Rexburg, Idaho 83440
Idaho history.
M.-F. 9-5. Closed public holidays.

RHINEBECK

MONTGOMERY HOUSE
Livingston Street, Rhinebeck, New York 12572
House (c.1778). Period furnishings, china, kitchen equipment.
By appointment.

OLD RHINEBECK AERODROME
Stone Church Road, Rhinebeck, New York 12572
Collection of 1909-18 aeroplanes. Replica of World War I aerodrome.
May 1 - Oct. 31, daily 10-5.

RHINELANDER

RHINELANDER LOGGING MUSEUM
Pioneer Park, Martin Lynch Drive, Rhinelander, Wisconsin 54501
In replica of 19th century logging camp. Tools and equipment. Photographs of early logging industry in Wisconsin and Michigan.
June 15 - Labour Day: M.-Sa. 9-4; Su., public holidays 11-4.

RICHFIELD SPRINGS

PETRIFIED CREATURES
Route 20, Richfield Springs, New York 13439
Devonian fossils. Petrified wood. Dinosaur models.
May 1 - Oct. 31, 8 a.m. - dusk.

TOWN OF RICHFIELD HISTORICAL SOCIETY MUSEUMS
Public Library, W. Main Street, Richfield Springs, New York 13439
Local history. Paintings. Portraits.
M.-F. 11.30-4.30; M. 7-9. Closed public holidays.

RICHMOND

RICHMOND ART CENTER
Civic Center, 25th and Barrett Avenue, Richmond, California 94804
Contemporary paintings, drawings, prints, sculpture by Bay Area artists.
M., W.-F. 10-4.30; Th. also 4.30-9; Sa., Su. 12-4.30. Closed public holidays.

ART ASSOCIATION OF RICHMOND
McGuire Hall, Whitewater Boulevard, Richmond, Indiana 47374
Paintings. Graphic arts. Decorative arts. Sculpture.
Labour Day - June 6, M.-F. 9-4; Su., public holidays 2-5. Closed Christmas and following week.

JOSEPH MOORE MUSEUM
Earlham College, National Road West, Richmond, Indiana 47374
Palaeontology. Natural history. Indian artifacts.
Sept. 1 - June 30, M.-F. 9-5. All year, Su. 1-5.

WAYNE COUNTY HISTORICAL MUSEUM
1150 N. A Street, Richmond, Indiana 47374
In Hicksite Friends Meeting House (1864). Local history. Agriculture. Industry. Transport. Indian artifacts. Costumes. Folklore. Paintings by Wayne County artists.
Levi Coffin House (1839), Solomon Dickinson House (1823), Mansion House (1837) are in the care of the Museum.
Tu.-F. 12-4; Sa., Su. 1-5. School holidays, Tu.-Su. 1-5. Closed public holidays, Dec. 24 - Feb. 15.

JONATHAN TRUMAN DORRIS MUSEUM
Eastern Kentucky University, Richmond, Kentucky 40475
History of Kentucky. Ethnology. Archaeology. Domestic equipment. Surgical instruments.
M.-F. 10-4; Sa., Su. by appointment. Closed university vacations.

MUSEUM OF MADISON COUNTY HISTORICAL SOCIETY
120 W. Main Street, Richmond, Kentucky 40475
Local history. Material from Indian burial mounds.
White Hall State Shrine (1799) and Irvineton (1820) are in the care of the Society.
By appointment.

WHITE HALL STATE SHRINE
U.S. Highway 25, Richmond, Kentucky 40475
House (1799, remodelled c.1860), was home of the abolitionist Cassius Marcellus Clay (1810-1903). Original furnishings. Paintings. Ceremonial swords. Guns. Mementoes of Clay's daughter, Laura, active in feminist movement.
Daily 8-5. Closed Christmas, New Year.

AGECROFT HALL
Sulgrave Road, Richmond, Virginia 23211
15th century house, moved from England. Tudor furniture.
Tu.-F. 10-4.

ANDERSON GALLERY, SCHOOL OF THE ARTS
Virginia Commonwealth University, 901 West Franklin Street, Richmond, Virginia 23220
Paintings. Sculpture. Graphics. Costumes.
M.-F. 8-10. Closed New Year, Easter, Christmas.

DIVISION OF STATE PARKS MUSEUM
1201 State Office Building, Capitol Square, Richmond, Virginia 23219
Geology. Botany. Herbarium. Entomology. Herpetology.
June 1 - Sept. 1, daily 9-5.

ROBERT E. LEE HOUSE
707 E. Franklin Street, Richmond, Virginia 23219
House (1844). Period furnishings.
May 1 - Oct. 31: Tu.-Sa. 10-4; Su. 2-6. Nov. 1 - Apr. 30: M.-F. 10-4. Closed public holidays.

JOHN MARSHALL HOUSE
9th and Marshall Streets E., Richmond, Virginia 23219
House (1790), home of John Marshall, Chief Justice of United States, 1801-46. Marshall family furnishings and papers. Portraits.
M.-Sa. 10-5; Su. 2-5.

MUSEUM OF ARCHAEOLOGICAL SOCIETY OF VIRGINIA
1946 Lansing Avenue, Richmond, Virginia 23225
Archaeology of Virginia. Indian artifacts.
By appointment.

MUSEUM OF THE CONFEDERACY
1201 E. Clay Street, Richmond, Virginia 23219
In White House of the Confederacy (1817-18). Social and cultural history of the Confederate Period. Weapons. Uniforms. Civil War memorabilia.
M.-Sa. 9-5; Su. 2-5. Closed public holidays.

MUSEUM OF VIRGINIA HISTORICAL SOCIETY
428 N. Boulevard, Richmond, Virginia 23221
In Virginia House (c.1635). Local history. Paintings.
M.-F. 9-5; Sa., Su. 2-5. Closed public holidays.

EDGAR ALLAN POE MUSEUM
1914 E. Main Street, Richmond, Virginia 23223
House (c.1680), memorial museum to Edgar Allan Poe. Memorabilia and personal possessions of Poe. Illustrations to *The Raven*. Model of Richmond as it was in the early 19th century.
Tu.-Sa. 10-4.30; Su., M. 1.30-4.30. Closed Christmas.

RICHMOND NATIONAL BATTLEFIELD PARK MUSEUM
3215 E. Broad Street, Richmond, Virginia 23223
Civil War history and relics.
Watt House (c.1835) and Garthright House (c.1840) for part of the Park.
Daily 9-4.30. Closed Christmas, New Year.

VALENTINE MUSEUM
1015 E. Clay Street, Richmond, Virginia 23219
Prints and photographs illustrating Richmond and Virginia history. Historical portraits, landscapes. Indian artifacts. Handicrafts. Transport. Meerschaum and leather-root pipes. Costumes. Paintings. Sculpture. Decorative arts. Porcelain. Silver.
Wickham-Valentine House (1812), Edward V. Valentine sculpture studio (1835), Granville G. Valentine building (1870) and Bradford-Cecil House (1840) are in the care of the Museum.
Tu.-Sa. 10-4.45; Su. 1.30-5. Closed New Year, Easter, Labour Day, Dec. 24-5.

VIRGINIA MUSEUM OF FINE ARTS
Boulevard and Grove Street, Richmond, Virginia 23221
Early Greek vases. Chinese bronzes, jades, porcelain. Japanese prints, porcelain. Art of India, Nepal, Kashmir, Tibet. Fabergé jewellery. Portuguese, Italian, French, English furniture. European and American paintings, prints, sculpture. Tapestries. Silver. Greek, Roman, Egyptian art.
Tu.-Sa. 11-5; Su. 1-5. Closed public holidays.

VIRGINIA STATE MUSEUM
Finance Building, Capitol Square, Richmond, Virginia 23219
Mineral resources and wildlife of Virginia. State history. Replica of McCormick's first reaping machine.
M.-F. 8.15-5; Sa. 9-2.

WILTON
S. Wilton Road, Richmond, Virginia 23226
House (1753), home of William Randolph, moved to present site in 1935. Randolph family portraits. Period furniture.
May 1 - Oct. 31: M.-Sa. 9-5; Su. 3-5. Nov. 1 - Apr. 30: M.-Sa. 9-4; Su. 2.30-4.30. Closed Su. in July and Aug., public holidays.

RICHMOND HILL

FORT McALLISTER
P.O. Box 198, Richmond Hill, Georgia 31324
Restored earthworks of Confederate fort (1861). Military museum.
May 1 - Sept. 30: Tu.-Sa. 9-5.30; Su. 2-5.30. Oct. 1 - Apr. 30: Tu.-Sa. 9-5; Su. 2-5.

RICHWOOD

CRANBERRY MOUNTAIN VISITOR CENTER
Route 39, Richwood, Virginia 26261
Geology, botany and wildlife of the area. Forestry. Conservation.
June 1 - Aug. 31, daily 9.30-5.30. May 1-31, Sept. 1 - Oct. 31: Sa., Su. 9.30-5.30.

RIDGEFIELD

ALDRICH MUSEUM OF CONTEMPORARY ART
45 Main Street, Ridgefield, Connecticut 06877
Contemporary paintings, sculpture.
Sa., Su. 2-5.

KEELER TAVERN PRESERVATION SOCIETY MUSEUM
Main Street, Ridgefield, Connecticut 06877
Keeler Tavern (1750), with furnishings. Local history.
W., Sa., Su. 2-5.

RIDGEFIELD LIBRARY AND HISTORICAL ASSOCIATION MUSEUM
151 Main Street, Ridgefield, Connecticut 06877
Local history.
M.-F., Sa. 9-5. Closed public holidays.

RIDGELAND

RIDGELAND MUSEUM
P.O. Box 438, Ridgeland, Mississippi 39157
Local history.
Daily 8-5. Closed Christmas.

RIDGEWOOD

MUSEUM OF PARAMUS HISTORICAL AND PRESERVATION SOCIETY
650 E. Glen Avenue, Ridgewood, New Jersey 07450
17th-19th century history of Bergen County and New Jersey. Farm tools. Harness. Blacksmith's tools. Indian artifacts. Replicas of 18th century kitchen and Dutch room, and 19th century kitchen and parlour. One-roomed schoolhouse (1873).
W. 2.30-4.30; Su. 3-5.

RIFLE

RIFLE CREEK MUSEUM
Rural Route 1, Rifle, Colorado 81650
Natural history. Local history. Indian artifacts. Coins. Textiles. Children's museum.
Austin School (1916) is in the care of the Museum.
May 1 - Oct. 30, Th.-Su. 1-5.

RINGWOOD

RINGWOOD MANOR HOUSE MUSEUM
Ringwood State Park, P.O. Box 1304, Ringwood, New Jersey 07456
78 room house (1810), furnished to show living conditions of the 3 families who lived there, 1810 - 1930.
May 1 - Oct. 30: Tu.-F. 10-4; Sa.-Su., public holidays 10-5. Closed Thanksgiving, Christmas, New Year.

RIO PEDRAS

MUSEUM OF ARCHAEOLOGY, HISTORY AND ART
University of Puerto Rico, Rio Pedras, Puerto Rico 00931
Paintings by Puerto Rican artists. Archaeology. History.
M.-F. 9-9; Sa. 8-12, 1.30-5. Closed public holidays.

RIPLEY

RANKIN HOUSE STATE MEMORIAL
Ripley, Ohio 45167
Restored home of the Ohio abolitionist, Rev. John Rankin.
Apr. 1 - Oct. 31: Tu.-Su. 9.30-5.

RIPLEY-HANCOCK

ARCADIAN COPPER MINE
Ripley-Hancock, Michigan 49930
Copper mine, with tours of workings.
June 1 - Sept. 30, daily 8-6.

RIPON

RIPON HISTORICAL SOCIETY MUSEUM
508 Watson Street, Ripon, Wisconsin 54971
Local history. Costumes. Children's museum.
Sept. 1 - May 30: 3rd Th. in month 2-4. June 1 - Aug. 31: Sa. 1-5.

RISON

SMALLWOOD STATE PARK MUSEUM
P.O. Box 25, Rison, Maryland 20681
In house that was General Smallwood's Retreat. Natural history. Local history.
Mar. 1 - May 30: Sa., Su. 10-5; other times by appointment. May 30 - Labour Day, daily 10-6. Labour Day - Nov. 30, daily 10-5.

RITZVILLE

DR. FRANK R. BURROUGHS WHEATLAND MUSEUM
Ritzville, Washington 99169
House (c.1870). Displays illustrating history of wheat, wheat growing and wheat processing.
By appointment.

RIVER EDGE

BERGEN COUNTY HISTORICAL SOCIETY MUSEUM
River Edge, New Jersey 07666
History of Bergen County. Indian artifacts. Industry.
Tu.-Sa. 10-12, 1-5; Su. 2-5. Closed Christmas, New Year.

RIVER FALLS

AREA RESEARCH CENTER, WISCONSIN STATE UNIVERSITY
River Falls, Wisconsin 54022
History of Western Wisconsin. Farm, household and handicraft artifacts. Relics of the Civil War and of Ku Klux Klan.
M.-F. 9-10; Sa. 9-5. Closed university vacations.

RIVERHEAD

SUFFOLK COUNTY HISTORICAL SOCIETY MUSEUM
300 W. Main Street, Riverhead, New York 11901
Local history. Indian artifacts. Farm tools. Whaling history. China. Furniture. Civil War prints.
May 1 - Sept. 30: M.-Sa. 1-5. Oct. 1 - Apr. 30. Closed public holidays.

RIVERSIDE

BOOK OF LIFE MUSEUM (AFFILIATED TO CALIFORNIA BAPTIST COLLEGE)
8432 Magnolia Avenue, Riverside, California 92504
Archaeology. Coins. Postage stamps.
M.-F. 8.30-5; Sa. 8.30-12. Closed college vacations.

JURUPA MOUNTAINS CULTURAL CENTER
7621 Highway 60, Riverside, California 92509
Geology. Botany. Herbarium. Palaeontology. Archaeology. Natural history. Local and Indian history.
M.-Sa. 9-5. Closed July 4, Christmas.

RIVERSIDE ART CENTER AND MUSEUM
3425 Seventh Street, Riverside, California 92501
Paintings. Sculpture. Graphics. Porcelain.
Tu.-Sa., public holidays 10-5; Su. 1-5.

RIVERSIDE MUNICIPAL MUSEUM
3720 Orange Street, Riverside, California 92501
Geology. Palaeontology. Botany. Natural history. Local history. Indian artifacts.
Heritage House (1891) is in the care of the Museum.
M.-Sa. 9-5; Su. 1-5. Closed public holidays.

WESTERN CAMERA MUSEUM
3636 Main Street, Riverside, California 92501
Collection illustrating development of photographic equipment.
W., Sa. 9-5.

RIVIERA BEACH

CONTEMPORARY ART CENTER OF THE PALM BEACHES
301 Broadway, Riviera Beach, Florida 33404
Permanent collections of laser art and holograms.
Temporary exhibitions from permanent collection, as announced locally.

ROANOKE

MUSEUM OF NORTH CAROLINA MINERALS
Gillespie Gap, Blue Ridge Parkway, Roanoke, Virginia 24008
Minerals. Rocks. Gemstones. Exhibits showing commerical uses of North Carolina minerals.
May-Oct. daily 9-6.

ROANOKE FINE ARTS CENTER
301 23rd Street S.W., Roanoke, Virginia 24014
In Cherry Hall (1906). Works by 20th century American artists. Paintings. Prints. Drawings. Mediterranean archaeology.
M.-F. 10-5; Su. 3-5. Closed public holidays.

ROANOKE HISTORICAL SOCIETY MUSEUM
P.O. Box 1904, Roanoke, Virginia 24008
Local history. Replica of general store, 'Kefauver's Folly' (c.1880). Domestic crafts.
By appointment. Closed June 1 - Aug. 31.

TRANSPORTATION CENTER AND RAILWAY MUSEUM
Wiley Drive S.W., Roanoke, Virginia 24015
Horse-drawn vehicles. Railway coaches and equipment.
Daily 10-10. Closed Labour Day - Memorial Day.

ROCHESTER

MEADOW BROOK HALL
Oakland University Campus, Rochester, Michigan 48063
House contains 18th-19th century European and American furniture. European paintings, including Works by Van Dyck and Turner.
Su. 2-5. June 1 - Aug. 31: Th., F. 2-5.

UNIVERSITY ART GALLERY
Oakland University, Rochester, Michigan 48063
Art of Africa, Oceania and pre-Columbian America.
Sept. 1 - May 31: Tu.-Su. 1-5. Also 7 p.m. - 8.30 p.m. during Meadow Brook Theater season.

HEMP OLD VEHICLE MUSEUM
Hemp Farm, Country Club Road, Highway 34, Rochester, Minnesota 55901
Horse-drawn vehicles. Steam engines. Tractors. Cars. Old musical instruments.
Mar. 1 - Nov. 30, daily 8-8.

MAYO MEDICAL MUSEUM
200 1st Street S.W., Rochester, Minnesota 55901
Human biology, anatomy, physiology. Operative techniques and procedures.
M.-F. 9-9; Sa. 9-5; Su. 1-5. Closed New Year, Easter, Thanksgiving, Christmas.

MUSEUM OF OLMSTED COUNTY HISTORICAL SOCIETY
214 3rd Avenue S.W., Rochester, Minnesota 55901
Local history. Norwegian arts and crafts.
Log cabin and rural school (1862) and Mayowood (1910-11) are in the care of the Society.
M.-F. 9-5; Sa., Su. 12-4. Closed public holidays.

ROCHESTER ART CENTER
320 E. Center Street, Rochester, Minnesota 55901
In Dr. Henry Plummer House (1923). Paintings. Graphics. Decorative arts. Music.
Tu.-Sa. 10-4; Su. 1-5. Closed public holidays.

AMERICAN BAPTIST HISTORICAL SOCIETY MUSEUM
1106 S. Goodman Street, Rochester, New York 14620
History of Baptist Church in U.S.
M.-F. 9-4. Closed public holidays.

ANTHONY HOUSE
17 Madison Street, Rochester, New York 14607
Furniture, pictures and memorabilia of Susan B. Anthony, Women's Suffrage leader.
W.-Sa. 11-4.

CAMPBELL-WHITTLESEY HOUSE
123 S. Fitzhugh Street, Rochester, New York 14608
House (1836). Empire furnishings. Stencilled decorations.
Tu.-Sa. 10-5; Su. 2-5. Closed Dec. 1-31, public holidays.

HERVEY ELY HOUSE
11 Livingston Park, Rochester, New York 14608
House (1837). Period furnishings.
By appointment.

INTERNATIONAL MUSEUM OF PHOTOGRAPHY
900 E. Avenue, Rochester, New York 14607
House (1905) was birthplace of George Eastman. Has been moved here and restored and furnished to period (1846-61). History of photography. Films. Photographic equipment. George Eastman collection of 16th-18th century European paintings.
Museum: daily 10-5. Birthplace: July 1 - Aug. 31, daily 10-5.

MEMORIAL ART GALLERY, UNIVERSITY OF ROCHESTER
490 University Avenue, Rochester, New York 14607
Chinese and Near-Eastern art. Greek and Roman art. Italian, Flemish, Dutch paintings. Romanesque and Gothic painting and sculpture. 19th-20th century French painting. 18th-20th century American painting. Folk art. Decorative art. Contemporary sculpture. Furniture.
Tu., Sa. 10-10. W.-F. 10-5; Su. 2-6. Closed public holidays.

MONROE COUNTY PARKS HERBARIUM
375 Westall Road, Rochester, New York 14620
Geology. Herbarium. Natural history. Ethnology.
M.-F. 9-5. Other times by appointment.

MORTIMER AND RED CREEK RAILROAD MUSEUM
1329 Brighton-Henrietta Town Line Road, Rochester, New York 14607
Steam locomotive. Coaches. Equipment.
May 31 - Oct. 15, Sa. 1-5. Closed public holidays.

MUSEUM OF LANDMARK SOCIETY OF WESTERN NEW YORK
130 Spring Street, Rochester, New York 14608
In Brewster-Burke House (1849). Period furnishings. Decorative arts.
Campbell-Whittlesy House (1830) and Stone-Tolan House (1792) are in the care of the Society.
Tu.-Sa. 10-5; Su. 1-4. Closed public holidays.

MUSEUM OF NEW YORK STATE ARCHAEOLOGICAL ASSOCIATION
Rochester Museum and Science Center, 657 E. Avenue, Rochester, New York 14608
Archaeology, anthropology, ethnology of N.E. North America.
M.-Sa. 9-5; Su., public holidays 1-5. Closed Christmas.

MUSEUM OF PETRIFIED WOOD
106 Thomas Street, Rochester, New York 14621
Geology and mineralogy of western New York State. Palaeontology.
By appointment.

ROCHESTER HISTORICAL SOCIETY MUSEUM
485 E. Avenue, Rochester, New York 14607
In Woodside (1838). Local history. Furniture. Paintings. Costumes. Weapons. Medals. Pewter.
M.-F. 10-4.30. Closed New Year, Easter, July 4, Thanksgiving, Christmas.

ROCHESTER MUSEUM AND SCIENCE CENTER
657 E. Avenue, Rochester, New York 14604
Geology. Palaeontology. Mineralogy. Planetarium. Natural history. Anthropology. Ethnology. Indian and pioneer history. County store. Apothecary. Barber shop. Transport. History of technology. Machinery.
M.-Sa. 9-5; Su. 1-5. Closed Christmas, Thanksgiving, New Year, July 4, Labour Day, Memorial Day.

STRASENBURGH PLANETARIUM
663 E. Avenue, Rochester, New York 14607
Astronomy. Planetarium.
M.-F. 9-5, 7-9.30; Sa. 10-9.30; Su., public holidays 1-9.30. Closed Christmas, New Year.

THE STRONG MUSEUM
700 Allen Creek Road, Rochester, New York 14618
Dolls and dolls' house. Toys. Paintings. Prints. Miniatures. Circus history. Folk art.
By appointment.

TEMPLE B'RITH KODESH MUSEUM
2131 Elmwood Avenue, Rochester, New York 14618
Collections illustration history and practice of Jewish religion.
M.-Th., Sa. 9.30-5; F. 9.30 a.m. - 10.30 p.m.; Su. 9.30-12. Closed Rosh Hashana and Yom Kippur.

ROCKERVILLE

ROCKERVILLE GOLDTOWN
Rockerville, South Dakota 57701
Log cabin (1878). Period furnishings, equipment.
May-Nov., daily 7 a.m. - 8.30 p.m.

ROCKFORD

BURPEE ART MUSEUM
737 N. Main Street, Rockford, Illinois 61103
Contemporary American painting, sculpture, graphics.
Tu.-Sa. 9-5; Su. 1-4. Closed public holidays.

BURPEE NATURAL HISTORY MUSEUM
813 North Main Street, Rockford, Illinois 61103
Geology. Mineralogy. Palaeontology. Botany. Herbarium. Natural history. Anthropology. Archaeology. Indian artifacts.
Tu.-Sa. 1-5; Su. 2-5. Closed public holidays.

ERLANDER HOME MUSEUM
404 S. Third Street, Rockford, Illinois 61108
House (1871). Local history. Material relating to Swedish immigrants to America.
Su. 2-4. Closed Christmas.

MEMORIAL HALL
211 North Main Street, Rockford, Illinois 61101
Relics and weapons of Civil War, Spanish War, World Wars I and II.
M.-F. 10-12, 2-4. Closed public holidays.

MUSEUM OF ROCKFORD HISTORICAL SOCIETY
2703 Jackson Street, Rockford, Illinois 61107
Local history.
By appointment.

TINKER SWISS COTTAGE
411 Kent Street, Rockford, Illinois 61102
House (1865-69), with Robert Tinker's original furnishings, library.
W., Th., Sa., Su. 2-5.

ROCKHILL

RAILWAYS TO YESTERDAY
E. Broad Top Railroad, Rockhill, Pennsylvania 17249
Railway history.
June 1 - Oct. 31: Sa., Su., public holidays 11-5.

ROCK HILL

CHILDREN'S NATURE MUSEUM OF YORK COUNTY
Route 4, Box 211, Rock Hill, South Carolina 29730
Local history. Industry. Maritime history. Indian artifacts. Natural history.
Tu.-Sa. 10-5; Su. 2-5. Closed Easter, Christmas, New Year.

ROCKINGHAM

VERMONT COUNTRY STORES AND MUSEUM
Route 103, Rockingham, Vermont 05101
Store (1890). Vermont farm kitchen (1890). Victorian parlour. Water-powered grist mill. 19th century Vermont life illustrated by photographs, letters, pamphlets.
M.-Sa. 9-5. Closed New Year, Thanksgiving, Christmas.

ROCK ISLAND

BLACK HAWK STATE PARK
1500 47th Avenue, Rock Island, Illinois 61201
Archaeology. Ethnology. Indian paintings and artifacts. Blackhawk War material.
W.-Su., public holidays 9-5. Closed New Year, Christmas.

JOHN M. BROWNING MEMORIAL MUSEUM
U.S. Army Weapons Command, Rock Island, Illinois 61201
Weapons. Military equipment. Indian artifacts.
W.-Su. 11-4. Closed New Year, Thanksgiving, Christmas.

JOHN DEERE PLANETARIUM
Augustana College, Rock Island, Illinois 61201
Planetarium. Meteorites.
M.-F. 8-4.

FRYXELL GEOLOGY MUSEUM
New Science Building, Augustana College, Rock Island, Illinois 61201
Geology. Palaeontology. Archaeology.
M.-F. 8-5; Sa., Su., and June, July, Aug., by appointment only.

ROCKLAND

WILLIAM A. FARNSWORTH LIBRARY AND ART MUSEUM
19 Elm Street, Rockland, Maine 04841
In Farnsworth Homestead (c.1840). 18th-20th century American and European paintings, drawings, prints, with emphasis on contemporary works on Maine subjects. Local history. Maritime history.
M.-Sa. 10-5; Su. 1-5. Closed New Year, Memorial Day, Christmas, and M. Oct.-May.

ROCKPORT

LINCOLN PIONEER VILLAGE
City Park, Rockport, Indiana 47635
Reconstructed village, with 18 log cabins. Pioneer tools, furnishings. Horse-drawn vehicles.
Daily 8-5.

MAINE COAST ARTISTS
Russell Avenue, Rockport, Maine 04856
Maine history. Paintings. Sculpture. Graphics.
July-Sept., Tu.-Sa., public holidays 10-6; Su. 1-6.

MUSEUM OF SANDY BAY HISTORICAL SOCIETY
40 King Street, Rockport, Massachusetts 01966
In Sewall Scripture House (1832). Early American furniture and domestic equipment. Industry, especially granite quarrying. Archaeology. Maritime history. Atlantic cable room. Sewall Scripture House (1832) is in the care of the Society.
July 1 - Labour Day, daily 2-5.

THE OLD CASTLE
Castle Lane, Pigeon Cove, Rockport, Massachusetts 01966
House (1678). 17th-18th century American furniture, domestic equipment. Local history. Granite quarrying.
July-Aug., Sa., Su. 2-5.

ROCK SPRINGS

ROCK SPRINGS FINE ARTS CENTER
Rock Springs, Wyoming 82901
Paintings by local artists. Indian artifacts.
M.-Sa. 10-12, 2-5, 7-9; Su., public holidays 2-5, 7-9.

ROCKTON

STEPHEN MACK MUSEUM AND WHITMAN TRADING POST
Macktown Forest Preserve, Rockton, Illinois 61072
Local history museum, based on Stephen Mack House (1839) and Whitman Trading Post (1846).
June 1 - Sept. 30, W., Su. 1-4.30. Other days by appointment.

ROCKVILLE

JUDIAC MUSEUM
6125 Montrose Road, Rockville, Maryland 20852
Jewish history and culture.
M.-Th., Su. 9 a.m. - 11 p.m.; F. 9-5. Closed public and Jewish holidays.

MONTGOMERY COUNTY HISTORICAL SOCIETY MUSEUM
103 W. Montgomery Avenue, Rockville, Maryland 20850
In Beall-Dawson House (1815). Maryland history. Maps. Doctor's surgery.
Tu.-Sa. 12-4; 1st Su. in month 2-5. Closed Christmas week.

ROCKWELL CITY

CALHOUN COUNTY HISTORICAL SOCIETY MUSEUM
626 8th Street, Rockwell City, Iowa 50579
Local history.
June 1 - Aug. 31, Su. 2-4. Other days by appointment.

ROCKY FORD

ROCKY FORD HISTORICAL MUSEUM
Library basement, Rocky Ford, Colorado 81067
Local history. Archaeology.
On request.

ROCKY HILL

ACADEMY HALL MUSEUM OF THE ROCKY HILL HISTORICAL SOCIETY
785 Old Main Street, Rocky Hill, Connecticut 06067
Furniture. Domestic equipment. Agricultural implements. Indian artifacts. Clothing.
May 1 - Nov. 30, Su. 3-5. Closed Dec. - Apr.

ROCKINGHAM
Route 518, Rocky Hill, New Jersey 08553
House (1730-64), used as headquarters by Rockingham (1783). Period furnishings.
Tu.-Sa. 10-12, 1-5; Su., public holidays 2-5. Closed Thanksgiving, Christmas, New Year.

ROCKY MOUNT

ROCKY MOUNT CHILDREN'S MUSEUM
Sunset Park, Rocky Mount, North Carolina 27801
Geology. Herbarium. Natural sciences. Natural history.
M.-F. 10-12, 2-5; Sa., Su. 2-5.

ROEBUCK

WALNUT GROVE PLANTATION
Route 1, Roebuck, South Carolina 29376
Plantation house (1765). Period furnishings.
Mar.-Nov., Tu.-Sa. 11-5; Su. 2-5. Dec.-Feb., Su. 2-5.

ROGERS

DAISY INTERNATIONAL AIR GUN MUSEUM
U.S. Highway 71 S., Rogers, Arkansas 72756
Non-powder guns.
M.-F., 9-5.

ROLLA

ED CLARK MUSEUM OF MISSOURI GEOLOGY
Buehler Park, Rolla, Missouri 65401
Geology. Mineralogy. Palaeontology.
M.-F. 8-12, 1-5. Closed public holidays.

PHELPS COUNTY HISTORICAL SOCIETY MUSEUM
W. 3rd Street, Rolla, Missouri 65401
Local history.
By appointment.

ROLLA GEOLOGY MUSEUM
University of Missouri, Rolla, Missouri 65401
Geology. Mineralogy. Palaeontology.
M.-F. 8-5. Closed public holidays.

ROME

FORT STANWIX MUSEUM
112 Spring Street, Rome, New York 13440
History of area from prehistoric times to mid-19th century. Dioramas. Iroquois Indian artifacts.
Tu.-F. 9-4; Sa., Su. 1-4. Closed public holidays.

ROME CITY

GENE STRATTON PORTER STATE MEMORIAL
State Highway 9, Rome City, Indiana 46734
House (1914). Memorabilia of novelist, Gene Stratton Porter, and his wife.
M.-F. 9-12, 1-5.

ROOSEVELT

TONTO NATIONAL MONUMENT
P.O. Box 707, Roosevelt, Arizona 85545
Cliff dwellings, artifacts and utensils of the Salado Indians, 1100-1400.
Daily 8-5.

ROSAMOND

BURTONS' TROPICS GOLDMINE AND MUSEUM
Route 1, Box 98, Rosamond, California 93560
Goldmine. Mining museum.
Goldmine: Th.-M., 9.30-4. Museum: Oct. 1 - May 31, Sa., Su. 9.30-4. Closed Thanksgiving, Christmas.

KERN ANTELOPE HISTORICAL SOCIETY MUSEUM
Mojave Tropics Road, Box 325, Rosamond, California 93560
Local history. Indian artifacts.
Oct. 1 - May 31, Sa., Su. 10-4. Closed Thanksgiving, Christmas.

ROSEAU

ROSEAU COUNTY HISTORICAL MUSEUM
Roseau, Minnesota 56751
Natural history. Local history.
M.-F. 1-5. M.-Sa. mornings by appointment. Closed public holidays.

ROSEBURG

DOUGLAS COUNTY MUSEUM
Box 1550, County Fairgrounds, Roseburg, Oregon 97470
Logging. Agriculture. Pioneer life. Fur trade. Maritime history. Horse-drawn vehicles. Military equipment. Medical instruments. Indian artifacts.
Daily 8.30-5. Closed public holidays.

MUSEUM OF DOUGLAS COUNTY HISTORICAL SOCIETY
544 S.E. Douglas Avenue, Roseburg, Oregon 97570
In Lane House (1854). Period furnishings. Local history. Pioneer life.
Sa., Su. 1-5. Other times by appointment. Closed Christmas, Easter, Thanksgiving.

ROSLYN

OLD GRIST MILL
Route 25A, Hempstead Harbor, Roslyn, New York 11576
Mill (1701). Local history.
Feb. 1 - Dec. 31: Tu.-F. 12-5; Sa., Su. 12-8.

VALENTINE HOUSE, INC.
1 Paper Mill Road, Roslyn, New York 11576
House (1792). 18th century furniture.
M.-F. 9-4.30; evenings by appointment. Closed national holidays.

ROSWELL

ROSWELL MUSEUM AND ART CENTER
100 W. 11th Street, Roswell, New Mexico 88201
Geology. Botany. Herpetology. Aquarium. Rockets. Pre-Columbian art. Chinese paintings and jades. 19th-20th century European and American paintings, sculpture, drawings, lithographs. S.W. Indian art. Historical material from S.E. New Mexico.
M.-Sa. 9-5; Su., public holidays 1-5. Closed Christmas.

ROUND ROCK

EL MILAGRO; WASHINGTON ANDERSON-IRVIN HOME MUSEUM
Highway 79, Box 188, Round Rock, Texas 78664
House (1854-9). 18th-19th century American furniture. Oriental objets d'art.
By appointment.

ROUND TOP

UNIVERSITY OF TEXAS
Winedale Inn Properties, Box 11, Round Top, Texas 78954
Outdoor museum of cultural history. 8 restored 19th century farm buildings, housing local collections. 19th century Texas county furniture. Pennsylvanian German furnishings and decorative arts. 19th century cabinet maker's tools. Southern stoneware pottery.
May 1 - Sept. 30, Th.-Su. 10-6. Oct. 1 - Apr. 30, Th.-Su. 9-5. Closed New Year, Easter, July 4, Thanksgiving, Christmas.

ROWE

ROWE HISTORICAL MUSEUM
King's Highway, Rowe, Massachusetts 01367
In two former schoolhouses (1785, 1835). Local history.
July 4 - Oct. 15, Sa., Su., public holidays 2.30-5.30.

ROWLEY

PLATTS-BRADSTREET HOUSE
Main Street, Rowley, Massachusetts 01969
House (1677), with later remodelling. Local history. 18th century shoe shop.
June 25 - Sept. 3, Th. 2-5.

ROYALTON

DANFORTH MAPLE MUSEUM
Junction of Routes 14 and 107, Extension I-89, Royalton, Vermont 05068
Equipment for processing maple sugar.
Mar. 1 - Dec. 31, daily 10-4.

ROXBURY

ROXBURY HISTORICAL SOCIETY MUSEUM
The Manse, John Eliot Square, Roxbury, Massachusetts 02119
House (1750). Local and military history. Costumes.
July 1 - Aug. 31, M.-F. 10-4. Other times by appointment.

BURROUGHS MEMORIAL
Rosendale, Roxbury, New York 12474
Woodchuck Lodge (c.1850), summer cottage of author-naturalist, John Burroughs (1837-1921).
May 15 - Sept. 30, daily 9-5.

RUMNEY

MARY BAKER HISTORIC HOUSE
Stinson Lake Road, Rumney, New Hampshire 03266
Home of Mary Baker Eddy (1860-2), founder of Christian Science. Memorabilia of Mary Baker Eddy.
May 31 - Oct. 31: Tu.-Sa. 10-5; Su. 2-5.

RUSHFORD

RUSHFORD HISTORICAL SOCIETY
Main Street, Rushford, New York 14777
Local history.
May 29 - Sept. 7, Sa. 1-4.

RUSHVILLE

RUSH COUNTY HISTORICAL SOCIETY MUSEUM
619 N. Perkins Street, Rushville, Indiana 46173
History of Rush County.
M.-F., by appointment; Su. 1-5.

MUSEUM OF SHERIDAN COUNTY HISTORICAL SOCIETY
U.S. Highway 20, Rushville, Nebraska 69360
In Westover House (1890). Local history and archaeology. 5 local buildings (1884-90) are in the care of the Society.
May 1 - Sept. 30, daily 10-4.

NUNDAWAGA SOCIETY FOR HISTORY AND FOLKLORE
Rushville, New York 14544
Indian relics, especially costumes.
By appointment.

RUSSELL

FOSSIL STATION MUSEUM
331 Kansas Street, Russell, Kansas 67665
Local history. Agriculture. Indian artifacts.
F.-Su. 2-6.

RUSSELL SPRINGS

BUTTERFIELD TRAIL HISTORICAL MUSEUM
Russell Springs, Kansas 67755
Geology. Palaeontology. Local history. Agriculture. Indian artifacts.
May 1 - Sept. 30, Tu.-Sa. 9-5; Su., public holidays 9-6.

RUSSELLVILLE

MARCELLITE HARDY MEMORIAL MUSEUM
296 S. Main Street, Russellville, Kentucky 42276
In old Southern Bank of Kentucky. One of the first banks robbed by the Jesse James gang (1863). Original bank vaults. Mid 19th century furnishings. Artifacts relating to early Kentucky history and to Jesse James.
Sept., during local Tobacco Festival, 10-5. July, during Shaker Festival. Other times by appointment.

RUTHERFORD

RUTHERFORD MUSEUM
6 Ames Avenue, Rutherford, New Jersey 07070
Children's Museum. Mineralogy. Natural history. Local history. Indian material.
Th. 1.30-4.30; 1st and 3rd M. each month, 2-4. Closed public holidays.

DAVID CROCKETT CABIN
Highway 45 W., Rutherford, Tennessee 38369
Restored pioneer cabin (c.1820). Pioneer domestic equipment. Farming tools, utensils. Rocking chair made by David Crockett.
May 1 - Sept. 30: Tu.-Su., public holidays 9-5. Other times by appointment.

RUTLAND

CHAFFEE ART GALLERY
16 S. Main Street, Rutland, Vermont 05707
Contemporary paintings, prints, photographs by Vermont artists.
M.-Sa. 10.30-5.30; Su. 1-4.

RYE

RYE HISTORICAL SOCIETY MUSEUM
Purchase Street and Boston Post Road, Rye, New York 10580
In Square House (1710). Local and regional history. Tools. Domestic utensils. Costumes. Folklore. Indian artifacts.
M.-F., Su. 2.30-4.30. Closed public holidays, Dec. 25-31.

SABETHA

ALBANY HISTORICAL SOCIETY MUSEUM
Route 2, P.O. Box 96, Sabetha, Kansas 66534
Local history. Agriculture. Transport.
5 buildings (1866-7), including Rock Island Depot, are in the care of the Society.
June 1 - Nov. 30, daily 2-5. Dec. 1 - May 31, by appointment.

SACKETS HARBOR

PICKERING-BEACH HISTORICAL MUSEUM
503 W. Main Street, Sackets Harbor, New York 13685
House (1817). Period furniture. Regional history. Relics of War of 1812. Dolls.
June 1 - Aug. 31, daily 10-5.

SACKETS HARBOR BATTLEFIELD STATE PARK
Box 48, Sackets Harbor, New York 13685
Local history, based on 6 buildings (1818-50). Weapons. Uniforms. Equipment. 19th century furniture.
Daily 9-5.

SACO

YORK INSTITUTE MUSEUM
375 Main Street, Saco, Maine 04072
Mineralogy. Paintings and sculpture of the Colonial and Federal periods. Glass. Costumes.
Tu.-Sa. 1-4. Closed New Year, Thanksgiving, Christmas, 1 week in May, 1 week in Sept.

SACRAMENTO

CALIFORNIA STATE FAIR AND EXPOSITION ART SHOW
Sacramento, California 95813
Permanent collection of works by California artists. Paintings. Watercolours. Prints. Photographs. Ceramics. Enamels.
Aug. 21 - Sept. 9, 10-10.

E. B. CROCKER ART GALLERY
216 O Street, Sacramento, California 95814
European and American paintings, graphics, glass. Oriental sculpture and decorative arts.
Tu. 2-10; W.-Su. 10-5; Closed New Year, Christmas.

GOVERNORS' MANSION
16th and H Streets, Sacramento, California 95814
House (1877-8), home of Governors of California, 1903-67. Period furniture, furnishings, decorative arts.
Daily 10-5. Closed New Year, Thanksgiving, Christmas.

SACRAMENTO CITY AND COUNTY MUSEUM
1009 Seventh Street, Sacramento, California 95814
Local history. Transport.
Pioneer Hall (1869) is in the care of the Museum.
Daily 10-4.

SACRAMENTO SCIENCE CENTER AND JUNIOR MUSEUM INC.
4500 Y Street, Sacramento, California 95817
Science. Planetarium. Natural history.
M.-Sa. 9.30-5. Closed public holidays.

STATE INDIAN MUSEUM
1218 K Street, Sacramento, California 95816
Life and artifacts of Californian Indians. Archaeology. Basketry. Featherwork. Pottery. Dances and cermonies. House and fishing-boat types. Jewellery.
Daily 10-5. Closed New Year, Thanksgiving, Christmas.

SUTTER'S FORT STATE HISTORICAL MONUMENT
27th and L Streets, Sacramento, California 95816
Settlement founded 1839 by Captain John A. Sutter. Dioramas and furnished rooms, showing Californian life in the 1840s and 1850s. Blacksmith's, gunsmith's and carpenter's shop.
Daily 10-4.30. Closed New Year, Thanksgiving, Christmas.

SADDLE ROCK

SADDLE ROCK GRIST MILL
Grist Mill Lane, Saddle Rock, L.I., New York 11101
Operating tide-mill (c.1700).
Apr.-Oct., W.-Su. 9-5.

SAFETY HARBOR

MUSEUM OF SAFETY HARBOR AREA HISTORICAL SOCIETY
123 Main Street, Safety Harbor, Florida 33572
Local history. Palaeontology. Indian material. Archaeology.
Tu. 7-9. Other times by appointment.

SAFFORD

GRAHAM COUNTY HISTORICAL SOCIETY MUSEUM
808 Eight Avenue, Safford, Arizona 85546
Local archaeology. Pioneer history. Indian artifacts.
M.-Tu., Th. 2-5. Public holidays by appointment. Closed first two weeks in September, last week in December.

SAG HARBOR

SUFFOLK COUNTY WHALING MUSEUM
Main Street, Sag Harbor, New York 11963
History of local whaling industry. Whaleboat. Harpoons and other whaling equipment. Ships' figureheads. Scrimshaw.
Benjamin Hunting House (1845) is in the care of the Museum.
May 15 - Sept. 30: M.-Sa. 10-5; Su. 2-5.

SAGINAW

SAGINAW ART MUSEUM
1126 N. Michigan Avenue, Saginaw, Michigan 48602
Paintings, especially by contemporary Michigan artists. Sculpture. Prints. Indian artifacts.
Tu., Th. 10-5, 7-9; W., F., Sa. 10-5; Su. 1-5. Closed public holidays.

SAGUACHE

SAGUACHE COUNTY MUSEUM
Highway 285, Saguache, Colorado 81149
Geology. Natural history. Archaeology. Local history. Indian material. Open-air museum.
Blacksmith's shop (c.1880), school and jailer's residence (1870), County Jail (1906) are in the care of the Museums.
Memorial Day - Labour Day, daily, public holidays 10-5.

ST. AUGUSTINE

CASA DEL HIDALGO
Hypolita and St. George Streets, St. Augustine, Florida 32064
Late 16th century Spanish house. Local history. Furniture.
Tu.-Sa. 10-5.

CASTILLO DE SAN MARCOS NATIONAL MUSEUM
1 Castillo Drive, St. Augustine, Florida 32084
In Spanish fort (1672). Local and military history. Archaeology.
Daily 8.30-5.30. Closed Christmas.

FORT MATANZAS NATIONAL MONUMENT
Route 1, St. Augustine, Florida 32084
Spanish fort (1742). Local and military history. Archaeology.
Daily 8.30-5.30. Closed Christmas.

HISTORIC ST. AUGUSTINE
46 St. George Street, St. Augustine, Florida 32084
A group of 29 late 18th century buildings. Restored houses, furnished with 18th century Spanish antiques. Workshop, with demonstration. Museum (Pan American Center), with contemporary arts and crafts of Latin American countries, Spanish colonial painting, sculpture.
M.-Sa. 9-5.30; Su. 10-5.30. Closed Christmas.

LIGHTNER MUSEUM
70 King Street, St. Augustine, Florida 32084
In Alcazar Hotel (1848). Local history. Industry. Transport. 19th century Americana, antiques. Mineralogy. Coins. Dolls. Costumes. Folklore. Decorative arts.
M.-Sa. 9-5; Su. 11-5. Closed Christmas.

MARINELAND
Route 1, St. Augustine, Florida 32084
Marine animals, fishes, plants.
Daily 8-5.

MUSEUM OF ST. AUGUSTINE HISTORICAL SOCIETY
271 Charlotte Street, St. Augustine, Florida 32084
Local history.
Gonzalez-Alvarez House (c.1720) and Tovar House (c.1760) are in the care of the Society.
Daily 9-5.45.

MUSEUM OF WASHINGTON OAKS GARDENS STATE PARK
Route 1, St. Augustine, Florida 32084
Local history. Natural history.
Daily 8-5.

OLDEST HOUSE
14 St. Francis Street, St. Augustine, Florida 32084
House (1720), with period Spanish, English, and American furniture.
Daily 9-6.

ST. AUGUSTINE ART ASSOCIATION GALLERY
22 Marine Street, St. Augustine, Florida 32084
Paintings, watercolours, graphics by Florida artists.
Oct.-May, Tu.-Sa. 1-5; Su. 2-5.

TOVAR HOUSE
St. Francis Street, St. Augustine, Florida 32084
House (1730). Interpretative museum of crafts, building materials, tools and related items connected with everyday life in 18th - early 19th century St. Augustine.
Daily 9-6.

WEBB MUSEUM
271 Charlotte Street, St. Augustine, Florida 32084
Narrative museum of St. Augustine history.
Daily 9-6.

WOODEN SCHOOLHOUSE
14 St. George Street, St. Augustine, Florida 32084
19th century schoolhouse. Period furnishings.
Daily 8.30-5.

ST. BONAVENTURE

ST. BONAVENTURE ART COLLEGE MUSEUM
St. Bonaventure, New York 14778
Local history. Indian artifacts. Paintings. Sculpture. Coins. Postage stamps.
M.-Th. 8 a.m. - midnight; F. 8-5; Sa. 9.30-4.30; Su. 1-midnight. Public holidays 1-5. Closed Easter, Thanksgiving, Christmas.

ST. CHARLES

LITTLE RED SCHOOL HOUSE
County Fairgrounds, St. Charles, Minnesota 55972
Schoolhouse (1905). Exhibits illustrating history of rural education.
During County Fair only.

FIRST MISSOURI STATE CAPITOL
S. Main Street, St. Charles, Missouri 63301
Building (c.1818). Decorative arts. Archaeology.
M.-Sa. 10-4; May 1 - Sept. 30, Su. 12-6; Oct. 1 - Apr. 30, Su. 12-5. Closed New Year, Thanksgiving, Christmas.

MUSEUM OF ST. CHARLES COUNTY HISTORICAL SOCIETY
St. Charles, Missouri 63301
Local history. Costumes. Indian artifacts.
Tu.-F. 1-4; Sa., Su. 1-5. Closed public holidays.

ST. CLAIR

PHOEBE APPERSON HEARST HISTORICAL SOCIETY MUSEUM
St. Clair, Missouri 63077
Local history. Material illustrating life of Phoebe Apperson Hearst.
May 1 - Sept. 30: Sa., Su. 10-6. Other days by appointment.

PHOEBE APPERSON HEARST PIONEER SCHOOL
St. Clair, Missouri 63077
Mid-19th century school, with period furnishings and equipment.
Sa., Su., public holidays 10-6. Other times by appointment.

ST. CLOUD

STEARNS COUNTY HISTORICAL MUSEUM
123 S. 4th Avenue, St. Cloud, Minnesota 56301
Local history. Costumes. Handicrafts. Folk art. Porcelain. Silver. Coins.
Tu., Th. 1-5; Sa. 9-12.

ST. FRANCIS

BUECHEL MEMORIAL SIOUX INDIAN MUSEUM
St. Francis, South Dakota 57572
Botany. History and ethnology of the Sioux Indians.
June-Aug., daily 8-5. Other times by appointment.

ST. FRANCISVILLE

AUDUBON MEMORIAL STATE PARK
Louisiana State Highway 965, St. Francisville, Louisiana 70755
Oakley House (1795-9), home of John James Audubon. Period furnishings. Audubon prints.
M.-Sa. 9-4.45; Su. 1-4.45. Closed New Year, Thanksgiving, Christmas.

COTTAGE PLANTATION
U.S. Highway 61, St. Francisville, Louisiana 70775
House (1795), with original furnishings.
Daily 9-5.

ST. GEORGE

DAUGHTERS OF UTAH PIONEERS COLLECTION
St. George, Utah 84770
Pioneer relics of Utah's Dixie region.
May-Sept., daily 1-5.

ST. HELENA

THE SILVERADO MUSEUM
1347 Railroad Avenue, St. Helena, California 94574
R. L. Stevenson memorabilia. Manuscripts. Paintings. Photographs. Sculpture.
Tu.-Su. 12-4.

COLUMBIA COUNTY COURTHOUSE MUSEUM
45 S. 21st Street, St. Helena, Oregon 97051
Pioneer history. Indian artifacts. Furniture.
Th., F. 1-5. Other times by appointment.

ST. IGNACE

FORT ALGONQUIN
U.S. Highway 1, St. Ignace, Michigan 49781
Reproduction of Indian fort and trading post. Pioneer material. Logging relics. Indian artifacts.
June 30 - Sept. 10, daily 9-7.

TREASURE ISLAND MUSEUM
State and Marquette Streets, St. Ignace, Michigan 49781
Mineralogy. Archaeology. Indian artifacts. Material from sunken 17th century ships. Paintings. In mission church (1671), moved from original site on Moran Bay.
May 15 - Oct. 31, daily 8 a.m. - 10 p.m.

ST. JAMES

BEAVER ISLAND HISTORICAL SOCIETY MUSEUM
St. James, Michigan 49782
In former Mormon Print Shop (1856). Local history. Household articles.
July 1 - Aug. 31, daily 12-4. May 1 - June 30, Sept. 1 - Oct. 31, by appointment.

MARAMEC MUSEUM
P.O. Box 425, St. James, Missouri 65559
Geology. History of Maramec Ironworks (1826-76). Indian ethnography.
By appointment.

ST. JO

STONEWALL SALOON AND WESTERN MUSEUM
Public Square, St. Jo, Texas 76265
Farming and ranching implements and equipment. Early cattle brands. Household items. Guns.
Daily 8-6.

ST. JOHNSBURY

FAIRBANKS MUSEUM OF NATURAL SCIENCE
83 Main Street, St. Johnsbury, Vermont 05819
Geology. Mineralogy. Botany. Herbarium. Planetarium. Physical sciences. Electricity. American and European birds. Entomology. Native art of Africa and Polynesia. Anthropology. Archaeology. Indian artifacts.
M.-Sa. 9-4.30; Su. 1-5. Closed New Year, Thanksgiving, Christmas.

MAPLE MUSEUM
167 Portland Street, St. Johnsbury, Vermont 05819
Museum of Maple Grove Company. Displays showing development of maple-sugar making equipment.
June 10 - Oct. 15, M.-F. 8-5; Sa., Su., holidays 9-5.

ST. JOHNSBURY ATHENAEUM
30 Main Street, St. Johnsbury, Vermont 05819
Paintings, especially by artists of Hudson River School. Sculpture.
M., W., F. 10-9; Tu., Th., Sa. 10-5. Closed public holidays.

ST. JOHNSVILLE

MARGARET REANEY MEMORIAL LIBRARY
19 Kingsbury Avenue, St. Johnsville, New York 13452
Paintings. China. Glass. Military buttons. Indian artifacts.
M.-F. 1-5; Sa. 1-3; M., W., F. also 7-9.

ST. JOSEPH

BENEDICTA ARTS CENTER
College of St. Benedict, St. Joseph, Minnesota 56374
Art and handicrafts of the N. American Indians, Africa and the Far East. Contemporary American paintings, drawings, prints.
Daily 9-5. Closed Christmas, New Year, Easter.

ALBRECHT GALLERY AND MUSEUM OF ART
2818 Frederick Boulevard, St. Joseph, Missouri 64506
Building (1935) was formerly home of William Albrecht. 19th-20th century American paintings, drawings, prints, sculpture. 19th-20th century European prints. Children's and Junior Museums.
Tu.-F. 10-4; Sa., Su. 1-5. Closed New Year, Thanksgiving, Christmas.

JESSE JAMES HOUSE MUSEUM
U.S. Highways 59 and 69, St. Joseph, Missouri 64507
House (1879) where Jesse James was killed. Exhibits relating to James family.
M.-Sa. 9-5.30; Su. 10-6. Closed Dec. 1 - Jan. 31.

PONY EXPRESS STABLES MUSEUM
914 Penn Street, St. Joseph, Missouri 64503
In Stables (1858). History of Pony Express and St. Joseph.
May 1 - Sept. 15: M.-Sa. 9-5; Su., public holidays 2-5.

ST. JOSEPH HISTORICAL SOCIETY MUSEUM
402 Felix Street, St. Joseph, Missouri 64501
Local history.
M. 2-4.

ST. JOSEPH MUSEUM
11th and Charles Streets, St. Joseph, Missouri 64501
Geology. Zoology. Ethnology of the N. American Indians, Central America and the Philippines. Local history. Pony Express. Jesse James collection.
May 1 - Sept. 15, M.-Sa. 9-5; Su., public holidays 2-5. Sept. 16 - Apr. 30, Tu.-Sa. 1-5; Su., public holidays 2-5. Closed Dec. 24, 25, 31, Jan. 1.

ST. JOSEPH STATE HOSPITAL PSYCHIATRIC MUSEUM
3400 Frederick Avenue, St. Joseph, Missouri 64502
In Hospital ward (1893). Collections illustrating history of psychiatric treatment.
M.-F. 8-4.30. Closed public holidays.

ST. LOUIS

CAMPBELL HOUSE MUSEUM
1508 Locust Street, St. Louis, Missouri 63103
In Robert Campbell House (1851). Period furnishings.
Tu.-Sa. 10-4; Su. 12-5. Closed public holidays.

CHATILLON DE MENIL MANSION
3352 De Menil Place, St. Louis, Missouri 63118
House (1848, remodelled 1858-62). Local history. Indian artifacts. Decorative arts. Glass.
Tu.-Sa. 10-4. Su. 12-5. Closed Christmas, New Year.

CONCORDIA HISTORICAL INSTITUTE
801 DeMun Avenue, St. Louis, Missouri 63105
History of Lutheran Church. Medals. Coins. Paintings. Costumes.
M.-F. 8-5; Sa., Su. 2-5. Closed public holidays.

FALSTAFF INTERNATIONAL MUSEUM OF BREWING
1923 Shenandoah Avenue, St. Louis, Missouri 63104
History of local brewing industry. 19th century brewing equipment and tools. Bottles. Cooperage. Tavern furniture. Advertising material.
By appointment.

EUGENE FIELD MUSEUM
634 S. Broadway, St. Louis, Missouri 63102
House (1845) was birthplace of poet, Eugene Field. Period furniture. Items associated with Field and his family. Toys. Children's museum.
Tu.-Sa. 10-4. Su. 12-5. Closed New Year, Christmas, 1st Tu. in month, July 4, Thanksgiving.

GALLERY OF LORETTO-HILTON CENTER
130 Edgar Road, St. Louis, Missouri 63119
Paintings, sculpture, graphics by 20th century mid-western artists.
M.-Sa. 10-4; Su. 1.30-5. Closed Christmas.

JEFFERSON NATIONAL EXPANSION MEMORIAL
11 N. 4th Street, St. Louis, Missouri 63102
History of westward expansion 1800-1900. Transport. Indian artifacts. Industry. Military history.
Daily 9-5. Closed New Year, Christmas.

McDONNELL PLANETARIUM
5100 Clayton Road, Forest Park, St. Louis, Missouri 63110
Planetarium. Astronomy. Space science. Seismograph. Gemini VI and VII spacecraft.
Tu.-F. 10-5; Sa. 10-10; Su. 12-6. Closed New Year, Christmas.

MISSOURI BOTANICAL GARDEN
2315 Tower Grove Avenue, St. Louis, Missouri 63110
Herbarium.
May-Oct., daily 9-6. Nov.-Apr., daily 9-5. Closed Christmas, New Year.

MUSEUM OF JEWISH HISTORICAL ASSOCIATION OF GREATER ST. LOUIS
11001 Scheltz Road, St. Louis, Missouri 63141
Jewish history.
By appointment. Closed Jewish holidays.

MUSEUM OF MISSOURI HISTORICAL SOCIETY
Lindell and De Baliviere Streets, St. Louis, Missouri 63112
History of the St. Louis region. Indian archaeology and artifacts. Costumes. Industry. Medicine. Music. Paintings. Sculpture. Graphics.
Daily 9.30-4.45. Closed New Year, July 4, Thanksgiving, Christmas.

MUSEUM OF SCIENCE AND NATURAL HISTORY
Oak Knoll Park, St. Louis, Missouri 63105
Geology. Mineralogy. Natural history. Anthropology. Archaeology of Missouri Indians. Industry. Aviation. Technology.
Tu.-Sa. 9-5; Su. 1-5. Closed New Year, July 4, Labour Day, Thanksgiving, Christmas.

NATIONAL MUSEUM OF TRANSPORT
3015 Barrett Station Road, St. Louis, Missouri 63122
History of transport from primitive times to present day. Railway locomotives and coaches. City transport. Horse-drawn vehicles. Early automobiles. Pipelines.
Labour Day - May 29, daily 10-5. Memorial Day - Labour Day 10-8.

OLD CATHEDRAL MUSEUM
209 Walnut Street, St. Louis, Missouri 63102
Catholic Church (1850). History of the Church and of St. Louis.
M.-F. 10-6; Sa., Su., public holidays 10-7.

ST. LOUIS ARTISTS GUILD
812 N. Union Boulevard, St. Louis, Missouri 63108
Works by contemporary local artists. Paintings. Sculpture. Graphics. Decorative arts.
M., W.-Sa. 11-3; Su. 1-5. Closed New Year, Thanksgiving, June 15 - Aug. 31, Christmas.

ST. LOUIS ART MUSEUM
Forest Park, St. Louis, Missouri 63110
Chinese bronzes, porcelain. Oriental rugs. 15th-20th century European paintings, sculpture. 18th-20th century American paintings. Greek, Roman, Egyptian, Pre-Columbian, African art.
Tu. 2.30-9.30; W.-Su. 10-5. Closed New Year, Memorial Day, July 4, Christmas.

ST. LOUIS MEDICAL MUSEUM AND NATIONAL MUSEUM OF MEDICAL QUACKERY
3939 Lindell Boulevard, St. Louis, Missouri 63108
Medicine. Pharmacy. Nutrition. Dentistry. Quackery in these fields.
Daily 11-4. Easter-Labour Day.

SOLDIERS MEMORIAL
1315 Chestnut Street, St. Louis, Missouri 63103
Military history.
Daily 10-4.30.

WALTKE MUSEUM AND CONCORDIA HISTORICAL INSTITUTE
801 DeMun Avenue, St. Louis, Missouri 63105
Building (1830) is Saxon Lutheran Memorial. History of Lutheran Church. Paintings. Medals and coins of the Reformation period. Costumes.
M.-F. 8-5; Sa., Su. 2-5. Closed public holidays.

WASHINGTON UNIVERSITY GALLERY OF ART
Steinberg Hall, Forsyth and Skinker Campus, St. Louis, Missouri 63130
16th-20th century European and American paintings, sculpture, graphics, decorative arts. Archaeology. Aboriginal art. Coins. Greek vases, artifacts.
M.-F. 9-5; Sa. 10-4; Su. 1-5. Closed public holidays.

ST. MARKS

SAN MARCOS DE APALACHE STATE MUSEUM
State Highway 363, San Marcos de Apalache, St. Marks, Florida 32355
On site of former Fort Ward and Federal Marine Hospital. Museum illustrating history of area.
Daily 8-5.

ST. MARY'S

MUSEUM OF HISTORICAL SOCIETY OF ST. MARY'S AND BENZIGER TOWNSHIP
Municipal Building, Erie Avenue, St. Mary's, Pennsylvania 15857
Early history of St. Mary's. Photographs. Documents.
M.-Sa. 9-4; Su. by appointment. June 1 - Aug. 31, by appointment only.

ST. MARY'S CITY

ST. MARY'S CITY COMMISSION
St. Mary's City, Maryland 20686
In reconstructed State House (1676). Local history. Anthropology. Indian artifacts.
May 1 - Oct. 10, daily 10-5. Nov. 1 - Apr. 10, Tu.-Su. 10-4. Closed Christmas, New Year.

ST. MATTHEWS

CALHOUN COUNTY HISTORICAL MUSEUM
Railroad Avenue, St. Matthews, South Carolina 29135
In Clark-Cain House (1850). Local history. Archaeology. Agriculture.
M.-F. 10-5. Closed public holidays.

ST. MICHAEL'S

CHESAPEAKE BAY MARITIME MUSEUM
P.O. Box 636, St. Michael's, Maryland 21663
Museum based on 4 early 19th century buildings, including Hoopers Strait Lighthouse (1879). Local and maritime history. Aquarium. Vessels moored at waterfront.
May 1 - Sept. 30: Tu.-Su., public holidays 10-5. Oct. 1 - Apr. 30: Tu.-Su., public holidays 10-4.

ST. PAUL

HAMLINE UNIVERSITY GALLERIES
Snelling and Hewitt Streets, St. Paul, Minnesota 55104
Contemporary paintings, prints, sculpture. Archaeology.
M.-F. 8-5; Sa. 8-12. Closed Dec. 15 - Jan. 3, public holidays.

MINNESOTA HISTORICAL SOCIETY MUSEUM
690 Cedar Street, St. Paul, Minnesota 55101
Ethnology. Archaeology. Pioneer life. Victorian parlour. Country Store. Newspaper office. Log cabin. Indian life. Costumes.
11 historic sites and buildings (1740-1896) are in the care of the Society.
M.-F. 8.30-5; Sa. 10-4; Su. 2-4. Closed public holidays.

MINNESOTA MUSEUM OF ART
30 E. 10th Street, St. Paul, Minnesota 55101
20th century drawings, paintings, sculpture. Oriental paintings, drawings, sculpture, furniture, ceramics, textiles. Contemporary American, N.W. Coast Indian, African crafts.
M.-W. 9-5; Th.-Sa. 9 a.m. - 9.30 p.m.; Su. 11-9.30. Closed Thanksgiving, Christmas.

MUSEUM OF CATHOLIC HISTORICAL SOCIETY OF ST. PAUL
St. Paul Seminary, 2260 Summit Avenue, St. Paul, Minnesota 55101
Catholic church history.
M.-F. 9-3.30, by appointment. Closed public holidays, holy days, seminary vacations.

MUSICAL INSTRUMENT MUSEUM
1124 Dionne Street, St. Paul, Minnesota 55113
Musical instruments.
Daily 8 a.m. - 9 p.m., by appointment.

RAMSEY COUNTY HISTORICAL SOCIETY MUSEUM
2097 W. Larpenteur Museum, St. Paul, Minnesota 55113
Local history. Agricultural tools, implements, horse-drawn vehicles.
Gibbs Farm House (1854-74) and schoolhouse (1878) are in the care of the Society.
Museum: May 1-30, Sept. 1 - Oct. 31, Tu.-F., Su. 2-5. June 1 - Aug. 31, Tu.-F. 10-5. Su. 2-5; Dec. 15 - Mar. 15, Su. 2-5.

ST. PAUL PUBLIC LIBRARY
90 W. 4th Street, St. Paul, Minnesota 55102
Assyro-Babylonian cuneiform tablets. Arundel prints.
M., T. 9-9; W.-F. 9-5.30; Oct. 1 - Apr. 30, also Sa. 9-5.30. Closed public holidays.

SCIENCE MUSEUM OF MINNESOTA
30 E. 10th Street, St. Paul, Minnesota 55101
Geology. Palaeontology. Zoology. Ethnology. Archaeology. Physics. Astronomy. Chemistry. Biology. Technology.
M.-W. 9-5; Th., Sa. 9 a.m. - 9.30 p.m.; Su. 11-9.30. Closed public holidays.

ST. PETER

MUSEUM OF NICOLLET COUNTY HISTORICAL SOCIETY
100 W. Nassau Street, St. Peter, Minnesota 56082
Local history. Memorabilia of local artists, writers and musicians. Costumes. Portraits.
M.-F. 2-5.

ST. PETERSBURG

HAAS MUSEUM AND GRACE S. TURNER HOUSE AND VILLAGE
3511 2nd Avenue S., St. Petersburg, Florida 33711
Grace Turner House (1920). Antique furniture.
Tu.-Su. 1-5. Closed Christmas, Sept. 1-30.

MUSEUM OF FINE ARTS OF ST. PETERSBURG
255 Beach Drive North, St. Petersburg, Florida 33701
Far Eastern, especially Indian, sculpture. 19th century European and American paintings, graphic arts, sculpture, decorative arts. 17th-18th century French and English period rooms.
Tu., W., F., Sa. 10-5; Th. 10-9; Su. 1-5. Closed June 1-30, Christmas.

ST. PETERSBURG HISTORICAL MUSEUM
335 2nd Avenue Northeast, St. Petersburg, Florida 33701
Geology. Mineralogy. Natural history. History and archaeology of Florida. Culture of the Timucua Indians. Children's museum.
M.-Sa. 11-5; Su. 2-5. Closed Christmas.

SCIENCE CENTER OF PINELLAS COUNTY
7701 22nd Avenue North, St. Petersburg, Florida 33710
Geology. Palaeontology. Astronomy. Planetarium. Natural history. Botany. Anthropology. Anatomy. Astronautics.
June 1 - July 31: M.-F. 9-4. Oct. 1 - May 31: M.-Sa. 8.30-4.30. Closed Aug., Sept., New Year, Thanksgiving, Christmas.

ST. SIMONS

FORT FREDERICA NATIONAL MONUMENT
St. Simons, Georgia 31522
Site museum. Ruins of English fort and barracks. (1736-46). Local history.
Daily 8-5.

STE. GENEVIEVE

BOLDUC HOUSE
Main Street, Ste. Genevieve, Missouri 63670
House (1785), formerly home of Louis Bolduc. French Creole period furnishings.
Apr. 1 - Oct. 31, daily 10-4.

FELIX-VALLE HOUSE
Ste. Genevieve, Missouri 63670
House (1818). Period furnishings.
Apr.-Oct., daily 10-4.

STE. GENEVIEVE MUSEUM
Merchant Street, Ste. Genevieve, Missouri 63670
Local history. Indian artifacts. Folk art.
May 1 - Sept. 30: 9-11, 12-4. Oct. 1 - Apr. 30: 1-4.

SALADO

CENTRAL TEXAS AREA MUSEUM
Old U.S. 81, Salado, Texas 76571
History of Central Texas since 1825. Tonkawa artifacts.
M.-Sa. 10-5; Su. 11-5.

SALEM

WILLIAM JENNINGS BRYAN MUSEUM
408 S. Broadway, Salem, Illinois 62881
House (1852), birthplace of William Jennings Bryan. Original and period furnishings. Bryan's personal possessions.
Daily 10-5.

WASHINGTON COUNTY HISTORICAL SOCIETY MUSEUM
307 East Market Street, Salem, Indiana 47167
In John Hay birthplace (1824). Local history.
M.-Sa. 1-5, by appointment.

CROWNINSHIELD-BENTLEY HOUSE
120 Essex Street, Salem, Massachusetts 01970
House (1727). 18th century furnishings.
June 1 - Oct. 15, Tu.-Sa. 10-4; Su. 2-4.30.

HATHAWAY HOUSE
54 Turner Street, Salem, Massachusetts 01970
House (1682), former bakery. Now guest house.
July 1 - Labour Day, daily.

HOUSE OF THE SEVEN GABLES
54 Turner Street, Salem, Massachusetts 01970
House (1668). Material relating to Nathanial Hawthorne. Hathaway House (1682), Retire Beckett House (1655), Nathanial Hawthorne House (c.1750) are in the care of the same organisation.
July 1 - Labour Day, daily 9.30-7.30. Rest of year, 10-4.30. Closed Thanksgiving, Christmas, New Year.

INGREE HOUSE
128 Essex Street, Salem, Massachusetts 01970
House (1804). Period furnishings.
Tu.-Sa. 10-4. June 1 - Oct. 15, Su. 2-4.30.

PEABODY MUSEUM OF SALEM
161 Essex Street, Salem, Massachusetts 01970
In East India Marine Hall (1824). Local history. Maritime and naval history. Natural history. Ethnology. Folklore. Costumes. Primitive arts.
Mar. 1 - Oct. 31: M.-Sa. 9-5; Su. 2-5. Nov. 1 - Feb. 28: M.-Sa. 9-4. Closed Thanksgiving, Christmas, New Year.

PEIRCE-NICHOLS HOUSE
80 Federal Street, Salem, Massachusetts 01970
House (1782), furnished to show 18th century Salem merchant's home.
Tu.-Sa. 2-4.30.

PIONEERS' VILLAGE
Salem, Massachusetts 01970
Replica of the wilderness village of Salem (1630).
June 1 - Oct. 18, daily 9.30-6.30. Oct. 19 - May 1, daily 10-5.

RETIRE BECKETT HOUSE
54 Turner Street, Salem, Massachusetts 01970
House (1655). Period furnishings.
July - Labour Day, M.-Sa. 10-4.

ROPES MANSION
318 Essex Street, Salem, Massachusetts 01970
House (1719), with original furnishings. Chinese export porcelain.
May 1 - Oct. 31: M.-Sa. 10-4.30.

SALEM MARITIME NATIONAL HISTORIC SITE
Custom House, Derby Street, Salem, Massachusetts 01970
Museum of local and maritime history, based on 10 historic buildings (1760-1829).
Oct. 1 - Apr. 30, daily 8.30-5. May 1 - Sept. 30, daily 8.30-7. Closed New Year, Thanksgiving, Christmas.

JOHN WARD HOUSE
Essex Institute Gardens, 132-4 Essex Street, Salem, Massachusetts 01970
House (1684). 17th-18th century furnishings.
June 1 - Oct. 15, Tu.-Sa. 10-4; Su. 2-4.30.

THE WITCH HOUSE
310 Essex Street, Salem, Massachusetts 01970
House (1642), formerly home of Jonathan Curwin, witch trial judge. History of witchcraft and witch-trials.
June-Oct. daily 10-6.

WILDWOOD ART GALLERY
205 Rolla Street, Salem, Missouri 65560
Missouri landscapes. Portraits of early Missouri settlers. Paintings of Indians. European paintings, prints, drawings.
Daily 8.30 a.m. - 9 p.m.

MUSEUM OF SALEM HISTORICAL SOCIETY
Main Street, Salem, New Hampshire 03079
Local history. Agriculture.
M. 2-4.

MUSEUM OF SALEM COUNTY HISTORICAL SOCIETY
79-83 Market Street, Salem, New Jersey 08079
In Grant Building (1721). Local history and archaeology. Indian artifacts. Costumes. Glass. Agriculture. Children's Museum.
Law Office (1735) is in the care of the Society.
Sept. 1 - June 30: Tu.-F. 12-4. Other times by appointment.

OLD RED BARN MUSEUM
Greenwich Road (Star Route), Salem, New York 12865
Americana. Tools. Clocks and watches. Firearms. Glass.
June 1 - Oct. 31, daily 9-6.

BUSH HOUSE AND BUSH BARN ART CENTER
600 Mission Street S.E., Salem, Oregon 97301
House (1877-8). Period furnishings. Paintings, drawings, sculpture by local artists. Costumes. Decorative arts.
May 1 - Oct. 31: Tu.-Sa. 12-5. Nov. 1 - Apr. 30: Tu.-Su. 2-5. Closed public holidays.

SALIDA

SALIDA MUSEUM
Swimming Pool Building, 410 West Rainbow Boulevard, Salida, Colorado 81201
Mineralogy. Local history. Indian material. Textiles.
Tu.-Su. 7-9.

SALINA

SMOKY HILL HISTORICAL MUSEUM
Oakdale Park, Salina, Kansas 67401
Local history.
Tu.-Su. 1-5. Closed Christmas, New Year.

SALINAS

SALINAS VALLEY MUSEUM
1150 North Main Street, Salinas, California 93901
Natural history. Anthropology. Archaeology. Local history. Agriculture. Indian artifacts. Costume.
First Mayor's house (1868) is in the care of the Museum.
May 1 - Sept. 30, daily 12-4. Oct. 1 - Apr. 30, Sa., Su. 12-4.

YOUTH SCIENCE CENTER OF MONTEREY COUNTY
544 River Road, Salinas, California 93901
Natural history.
Tu.-F. 10-5; Sa. 10-4. Closed public holidays.

SALISBURY

WICOMICO HISTORICAL SOCIETY
309 Gay Street, Salisbury, Maryland 21801
History of Wicomico County. Furniture. Household equipment. China. Glass. Lace. Costumes.
By appointment.

MUSEUM OF CHARITON COUNTY HISTORICAL SOCIETY
South Weber Street, Salisbury, Missouri 65281
Local history. Archaeology. Agriculture.
Th.-Su. 2-5. M.-W. by appointment.

MUSEUM OF SALISBURY HISTORICAL SOCIETY
Salisbury, New Hampshire 03268
In former Baptist Church (1791). History of Salisbury.
May 1 - Oct. 31: Su., public holidays 2-5.

OLD STONE HOUSE
Granite Quarry, Highway 52, Salisbury, North Carolina 28144
Home (1766), furnished in period 1766-1810.
Oct.-Apr., daily 2-5. May-Sept., daily 3-6.

ROWAN MUSEUM
114 S. Jackson Street, Salisbury, North Carolina 28144
In Maxwell Chambers House (1819). Federal period furnishings. Local history. Indian material.
Tu.-Su. 2-5.

SALLISAW

SEQUOYAH'S LOG CABIN
State Highway 101, Sallisaw, Oklahoma 74955
Log-cabin (1828) was home of Sequoyah, inventor of Cherokee alphabet. Period furnishings. Indian material.
Tu.-F. 9-5; Sa., Su. 2-5.

SALMON

LEMHI COUNTY HISTORICAL MUSEUM
Salmon, Idaho 83467
Local history. Indian artifacts. Oriental collection.
M.-Sa. 10-12, 1-5. Closed Nov. 1 - Mar. 31, public holidays.

SALT LAKE CITY

BEEHIVE HOUSE
75 E. S. Temple Street, Salt Lake City, Utah 84111
Residence of Brigham Young and early Presidents of Mormon Church. Restored and furnished as it was in the 1850s.
M.-Sa. 9-5.

BRIGHAM YOUNG FARM HOME
732 Ashton Avenue, Salt Lake City, Utah 84106
Forest Farm, experimental farm established by Brigham Young in 1860s. Period rooms.
May-Oct., daily 9.30-4.30.

FORT DOUGLAS
East Bench of University of Utah, Salt Lake City, Utah 84113
Surviving buildings of stone fort (1847).
M.-F. 7.30-4.15.

HANSEN PLANETARIUM
15 S. State Street, Salt Lake City, Utah 84111
Planetarium. American Indian astronomy. Meteorites. Technology. History of mythology.
Tu., Th.-Sa. 9 a.m. - 9.30 p.m.; W. 9-5.30; Su. 1-5.30. Closed New Year, Easter, Christmas.

INFORMATION CENTER AND MUSEUM
Temple Square, Salt Lake City, Utah 84101
Pioneer history. Indian and Polynesian artifacts.
May 1 - Sept. 30, daily 6.30-9. Oct. 1 - Apr. 30, daily 8-6.

KEITH-BROWN MANSION
529 E. South Temple Street, Salt Lake City, Utah 84102
House (1900), built by mine-owner, David Keith. Now offices. Original decorations. Period furnishings.
By appointment.

LATTER DAY SAINTS (MORMON) CHURCH MUSEUM
Temple Square, Salt Lake City, Utah 84102
Personal possessions of early Mormon leaders. Indian relics. Paintings. Portraits of Mormon leaders.
May-Sept., 6.30 a.m. - 9 p.m. Oct.-Apr., 8-5.

LIBERTY PARK
6th E. and S. Streets, Salt Lake City, Utah 84102
Contains Old Chase Home, historical museum operated by Daughters of Utah Pioneers, and Old Chase Mill.
May 10 - Sept. 16, 10-6.

LION HOUSE
63 E. South Temple Street, Salt Lake City, Utah 84111
House (1855-6), formerly home of Brigham Young. Period furnishings. Now restaurant, and reception centre.
By appointment.

MUSEUM OF DAUGHTERS OF UTAH PIONEERS
300 N. Main Street, Salt Lake City, Utah 84103
Pioneer Relics, 1847-69. Indian artifacts. Paintings. Children's museum.
M.-Sa. 9-5. May 1 - Sept. 30 also Su. 1-5. Closed public holidays, July 24.

PIONEER MONUMENT STATE PARK HISTORY MUSEUM
Salt Lake City, Utah 84108
Mormon history.
By appointment.

RAILROAD MUSEUM
3000 Conmor Street, Salt Lake City, Utah 84109
In former Union Pacific railway station. Railway history. Indian collection.
May-Sept., Tu.-Sa. 9-5; Su. 2-5.

SALT LAKE ART CENTER
54 Finch Lane, Salt Lake City, Utah 84102
18th-20th century American and European paintings, drawings, prints. Works by artists from Utah and the surrounding region.
Sept. 15 - July 15, Tu.-Su. 1-5. Closed public holidays.

STATE CAPITOL
Capitol Hill, Salt Lake City, Utah 84102
Pioneer costumes. Industries and minerals of Utah.
Daily 8-5.

UNIVERSITY OF UTAH, MUSEUM OF ANTHROPOLOGY
East Bench, Salt Lake City, Utah 84102
Anthropology, especially of N. and S. America.
May-Sept., daily 9-4.

UNIVERSITY OF UTAH, MUSEUM OF EARTH SCIENCES
East Bench, Salt Lake City, Utah 84102
Geology. Palaeontology. Mineralogy. Geography.
M.-Sa. 8-4.30. Other times by arrangement.

UTAH MUSEUM OF FINE ARTS
Art and Architecture Center, University of Utah, Salt Lake City, Utah 84112
European and American paintings. Sculpture. 17th century tapestries. English and French furniture. Prints, drawings, decorative arts. Egyptian artifacts.
M.-F. 10-5; Su. 2-5. Closed public holidays.

UTAH MUSEUM OF NATURAL HISTORY
University of Utah, Salt Lake City, Utah 84112
Natural history. Dinosaurs.
Daily 9.30-5.30. Closed Thanksgiving, Christmas, New Year.

UTAH PIONEER VILLAGE
2998 Connor Street, Salt Lake City, Utah 84109
Pioneer buildings moved from Rockport and elsewhere in Utah. Horse-drawn vehicles. Period rooms and furnishings. Guns. Craft demonstrations.
Apr. 1 - Oct. 31: M.-Sa. 9-5; Su. 1-5.

UTAH STATE HISTORICAL SOCIETY MUSEUM
603 E. South Temple Street, Salt Lake City, Utah 84102
In former Thomas Kearns Mansion (1901). Governor's mansion 1937-57. History of Utah and adjoining territory. Journals and diaries of pioneers. Paintings. Documents. Photographs.
M.-F. 8-5. Closed public holidays.

WESTMINSTER COLLEGE MUSEUM
13th E. and 17th S. Streets, Salt Lake City, Utah 84102
Mineral collections, including specimens from famous gold mines of the Old West.
M.-F. 8-5.

WIRE MEMORIAL MUSEUM
668 S. 3rd Street E., Salt Lake City, Utah 84111
Memorabilia and personal possessions of Lester F. Wire, inventor of the electric traffic light. Collections of traffic signals and safety devices.
By appointment.

SAN ANDREAS

CALAVERAS COUNTY HISTORICAL MUSEUM
Old Government Center, Main Street, San Andreas, California 95249
Minerals, especially gold from local mines and streams. Pioneer relics. Indian artifacts.
Mar. 1 - Sept. 30, 10-5.30. Other times by appointment.

SAN ANGELO

ELMER H. DANNER MUSEUM OF TELEPHONY
2701 S. Johnson Street, San Angelo, Texas 76901
Development of the telephone. Historic telephone equipment.
M.-F. 8-5.

FORT CONCHO RESTORATION AND MUSEUM
716 Burges Street, Texas 76901
22 restored buildings of fort (1868-70). Geology, mineralogy and natural history of Texas. Collection illustrating history of W. Texas. Frontier history.
M.-Sa. 9-5; Su., public holidays 1-5. Closed Thanksgiving, Christmas, New Year.

SAN ANGELO ART CLUB
Kendall Art Gallery, 119 W. 1st Street, San Angelo, Texas 76901
Paintings by contemporary Texan artists.
Sept.-May, Su., W., Sa. 2-5. June-Aug., Sa., Su. 1-5.

SAN ANTONIO

BUCKHORN HALL OF HORNS AND HALL OF FINS
600 Lone Star Boulevard, San Antonio, Texas 78206
World collection of horns, started by Albert Friedrich in 1884. Includes at least one specimen from every kind of horned animal. Marine specimens.
Daily 10-6.

ESPADA MISSION
Espada Road, San Antonio, Texas 78221
Spanish Mission (c.1720). Period furnishings. Local history and archaeology.
Daily 10-6.

HANGER 9, EDWARD H. WHITE II MEMORIAL MUSEUM
Brooks Air Force Base, San Antonio, Texas 78235
Medical testing equipment developed by U.S. Air Force School of Aerospace Medicine. Testing equipment and training aids for pilots, instruments and flying clothing, 1917 to present day.
Closed Sa., Su., public holidays.

HERTZBERG CIRCUS COLLECTION
Public Library, 210 W. Market Street, San Antonio, Texas 78205
Circus history. Paintings. Posters. Route books. Photographs. Circus memorabilia.
M.-Sa. 9-5.30. Closed public holidays.

INSTITUTE OF TEXAN CULTURES, UNIVERSITY OF TEXAS
Hemisfair Plaza, San Antonio, Texas 78206
Exhibits on 24 ethnic groups, showing their contributions to the culture and history of Texas.
July 1 - Aug. 31: Tu.-Su. 1-6. Rest of year, Tu.-F. 10-4, Sa.-Su. 1-6. Closed public holidays.

MARION KOOGLER MCNAY ART INSTITUTE
6000 N. New Braunfels Street, San Antonio, Texas 78209
Modern, especially Post-Impressionist, paintings, drawings, including works by Picasso, Van Gogh, Gauguin, Renoir, Cezanne. Religious art and crafts of New Mexico. 19th-20th century American art. Medieval art. 18th-20th century European and American prints, drawings.
M.-Sa. 9-5; Su. 2-5. Closed July 4, Thanksgiving, Christmas.

MISSION NUESTRA DENORA DE LA PURISMA CONCEPCION
807 Mission Road, San Antonio, Texas 78210
Spanish mission (c.1730). Period furnishings.
Daily 10-6.

MISSION DE LA PURISIMA CONCEPCION DE ACUNA
Mission Road, San Antonio, Texas 78213
Mission building (1731-62). Religious art.
May-Labour Day, daily 9-5. Labour Day-Apr., Sa., Su. 9-5.

MISSION SAN JUAN CAPISTRANO
Graf Road, San Antonio, Texas 78221
Spanish mission (c.1730). Period furnishings.
Daily 10-6.

MUSEUM OF SAN ANTONIO CONSERVATION SOCIETY
511 Villita Street, San Antonio, Texas 78205
In Casa Villita (1855). Local history.
M.-Sa. 10-12, 2-4.

OFFICIAL GRAND LODGE INDEPENDENT ORDER OF ODD FELLOWS MUSEUM
Crockett Hotel, Bonham and Crockett Streets, San Antonio, Texas 78206
Material illustrating history of the I.O.O.F. in Texas.
M.-F. 10-4. Closed public holidays.

O. HENRY HOUSE
600 Lone Star Boulevard, San Antonio, Texas 78204
Restored house (1855), home of O. Henry (William Sydney Porter) 1894-5. Photostat file of Henry's newspaper *The Rolling Stone.* Copies of Henry's Texas pamphlets, booklets.
Daily 10-6. Closed New Year, Christmas.

OLD SAN ANTONIO MUSEUM
521 Villita Street, San Antonio, Texas 78205
Local history. Dioramas of historic events in Texas and San Antonio.
Daily 10-12, 2-4. Closed Christmas, New Year.

SAN JOSÉ MISSION
6539 San José Drive, San Antonio, Texas 78214
Spanish mission (c.1730). Exhibits related to history of the site and building.
Apr. 1 - Sept. 30, 9-8. Oct. 1 - Mar. 31, 9-6.

SPANISH GOVERNOR'S PALACE
105 Military Plaza, San Antonio, Texas 78205
Palace (1749). Period furnishings. Local history. Paintings. Sculpture. Graphic arts. Decorative arts.
M.-Sa. 9-5; Su. 10-5. Closed Christmas.

STEVES HOMESTEAD
509 King William Street, San Antonio, Texas 78204
House (1890). Period furnishings.
Daily 10-12, 2-4. Closed Christmas, New Year.

THE ALAMO
Alamo Plaza, San Antonio, Texas 78205
In former fort (1744). History of the Alamo and the Republic of Texas. Weapons. Maps. Portraits. Photographs.
M.-Sa. 9-5.30; Su. 10-5.30. Closed Dec. 24-5.

WITTE CONFLUENCE MUSEUM
Hemisfair Plaza, San Antonio, Texas 78209
Railway and tramway coaches and equipment. Old motorcars. Horse-drawn vehicles. Spanish, Italian, Mexican, Oriental decorative arts.
Daily 10-6.

WITTE MEMORIAL MUSEUM
3801 Broadway, Brackenridge Park, San Antonio, Texas 78209
Texas natural history and ecology. Anthropology. Archaeology. Texas history. Latin American cultures. Fiesta costumes. Arms, armour. Paintings. Porcelain. Glass. Coins. Minerals. Gems.
Ruiz House (1753) and Twohig House (1840) are in the care of the Museum.
M.-F. 9-5; Sa., Su., public holidays 10-6.

SAN AUGUSTINE

EZEKIEL CULLEN HOUSE
Congress Street, San Augustine, Texas 75972
House (1839). Period furnishings. Paintings by S. Seymour Thomas, native of San Augustine.
By appointment.

SAN DIEGO

CABRILLO NATIONAL MONUMENT
Catalina Boulevard, P.O. Box 6175, Point Loma, San Diego, California 92106
Point Loma Lighthouse (1855). Local history.
June 15 - Labour Day, daily 8.30-8. Remainder of year, daily 9-5.30.

CALIFORNIA STATE UNIVERSITY, DEPARTMENT OF GEOLOGY
5402 College Avenue, San Diego, California 92115
Geology. Palaeontology. Mineralogy.
M.-F. 8-4.30.

FINE ARTS GALLERY OF SAN DIEGO
Balboa Park, P.O. Box 2107, San Diego, California 92112
Chinese ceramics, scrolls and sculpture. Japanese prints and decorative arts. 15th-17th century Flemish paintings. 17th century Dutch paintings. 16th-18th century Italian and Spanish paintings. French and German Expressionist paintings. America and European graphic arts. American furniture, glass. English silver.
Tu.-Sa. 10-5; Su. 12.30-5. Closed New Year, July 4, Thanksgiving, Christmas.

HISTORIC SHRINE FOUNDATION OF SAN DIEGO COUNTY
2482 San Diego Avenue, San Diego, California 92110
Group of 5 buildings (1850-70) with original or period furnishings, including Theatre (1868) and drugstore (1868).
W.-Su. 10-4.30. Closed public holidays.

MISSION SAN DIEGO DE ALCALA
10818 San Diego Mission Road, San Diego, California 92120
Mission site (1769). Archaeology. Costume.
Daily 9-5.

NATURAL HISTORY MUSEUM
P.O. Box 1390, Balboa Park, San Diego, California 92112
Geology. Palaeontology. Botany. Herbarium. Natural history.
Daily 10-4.30. Closed New Year, Christmas.

NAVAL TRAINING CENTER HISTORICAL MUSEUM
USNTC Code 1900, San Diego, California 92133
Ship models. Equipment. History of U.S. and foreign navies and of early U.S. merchant navy.
M.-F. 8-4; Sa., Su., public holidays by appointment.

OLD TOWN SAN DIEGO STATE HISTORIC PARK
4016 Wallace Street, San Diego, California 92110
Casa de Estudillo (1829), Casa de Machado y Stewart (1829), Casa de Altimirano (1851), Mason Street School (1865). The Casa de Estudillo and the Casa de Machado y Stewart have period furnishings. The Park also includes the restored building (1868) of the San Diego Union, with period furnishings and printing office equipment.
Daily, May 1 - Sept. 30, 10-6; Oct. 1 - Apr. 30, 10-5. Closed New Year, Thanksgiving, Christmas.

SAN DIEGO AEROSPACE MUSEUM
1649 El Prado, Balboa Park, San Diego, California 92101
Aeronautics. History of civil and military aircraft.
Daily 10-4.30. Closed New Year, Thanksgiving, Christmas.

SAN DIEGO HALL OF SCIENCE
1875 El Prado, Balboa Park, San Diego, California 92101
Science. Technology. Industry. Planetarium.
Daily 10-10.

SAN DIEGO HISTORICAL SOCIETY
Serra Museum, Presidio Park, San Diego, California 92110
History of Pacific South-West, especially San Diego Company. Firearms. Indian and pioneer history.
Villa Montezuma (1887) is in the care of the Society.
Tu.-Su. 10-5. Closed New Year, Thanksgiving, Christmas.

SAN DIEGO MUSEUM OF MAN
1350 El Prado, Balboa Park, San Diego, California 92101
American ethnology and anthropology, especially California, the S.-W., Peru. Archaeology. Primitive weapons.
Daily 10-5. Closed New Year, Thanksgiving, Christmas.

SAN DIEGO STATE COLLEGE PLANETARIUM
5401 College Avenue, San Diego, California 92115
Planetarium.
M.-F. by appointment.

'STAR OF INDIA' MARITIME MUSEUM
Embarcadero, San Diego, California 92101
In former iron-hulled merchantman 'Star of India', launched 1863, as 'Euterpe'. Photographic display. Equipment.
Daily 9-8.

TIMKEN ART GALLERY
Balboa Park, San Diego, California 92101
Paintings of the Italian, Flemish, Dutch, Spanish and French schools. Icons.
Tu.-Sa. 10-4.30; Su. 1.30-4. Closed Sept., public holidays.

SAND LAKE

YESTERYEAR ANTIQUE DOLL MUSEUM
Sand Lake, New York 12153
Dolls. Dolls' houses. Miniature circus.
By appointment.

SANDPOINT

BONNER COUNTY MUSEUM
2nd and Alder Streets, Sandpoint, Idaho 83864
Geology. Mineralogy. Natural history. Local history. Indian artifacts.
By appointment.

SANDUSKY

ERIE COUNTY HISTORICAL SOCIETY
1507 Columbus Avenue, Sandusky, Ohio 44870
Local history. Civil War material.
3rd Su. in month, 1.30-5. Other times by appointment.

SANDWICH

SANDWICH HISTORICAL SOCIETY MUSEUM
704 N. Main Street, Sandwich, Illinois 60548
Geology. Archaeology. Local history. Houshold equipment. Furniture. Agriculture. Industry. Indian material.
Su. 1-5.

STONE MILL MUSEUM
E. Railroad Street, Sandwich, Illinois 60548
In former mill (1856). Blacksmith's shop. Agricultural tools, machinery. Barbed wire. Indian artifacts. 19th century kitchen.
Su. 1-5.

HERITAGE PLANTATION OF SANDWICH
Grove Street, Sandwich, Massachusetts 02563
Local and military history. Transport. Tools. American primitive paintings.
May 1 - Oct. 31, daily 10-4.30.

HOXIE HOUSE AND DEXTER'S GRIST MILL
Sandwich Historical Center, Sandwich, Massachusetts 02563
House (c.1637), owned by whaling captain, Abraham Hoxie, in mid-19th century. Furnishings of period 1680-90. Restored 17th century grist mill.
June 15 - Sept. 30, M.-Sa. 10-5; Su. 1-5.

SANDWICH GLASS MUSEUM
Route 130, Sandwich, Massachusetts 02563
Sandwich glass. Diorama of old glass factory.
Daily 10-5.

YESTERYEAR'S MUSEUM
Main and River Streets, Sandwich, Massachusetts 02563
In First Parish Meeting House (1638). Dolls, Western and Far Eastern, especially Japanese. Miniature Nuremberg kitchens, 1730-1900. Dolls' houses.
May 15 - Oct. 15: M.-Sa. 10-5; Su. 1-5.

SANDY CREEK

RAIL CITY, INC.
Sandy Creek, New York 13145
Railway history. Steam locomotives.
July-Aug. daily 10-6. Weekends during June and Sept.

SAN ELIZARIO

SAN ELIZARIO MUSEUM
San Elizario, Texas 79849
Pre-Columbian, Apache and Pueblo Indian artifacts. Memorabilia from Butterfield and Santa Fe Trails. Mexican Revolution collection. Spanish and Mexican spurs.
El Paso County Jail (1850), with jail records, is in the care of the Museum.
Sa., Su. 1-6. Other times by appointment.

SAN FELIPE

J. J. JOSEY GENERAL STORE MUSEUM
Stephen F. Austin State Park, San Felipe, Texas 77473
Building (1847). 19th century country store merchandise, furnishings.
Dec. 1 - Feb. 28: Sa., Su., public holidays 1-5. Mar. 1 - Nov. 30: Sa., Su., public holidays 9-5. Closed Christmas, New Year.

SAN FERNANDO

MISSION SAN FERNANDO
Rey de Espana, 5151 San Fernando Mission Boulevard, Mission Hills, San Fernando, California 91340
Restored Mission buildings (1797). Religious art. Crucifixion dioramas. Indian artifacts.
Daily 9-5.

SANFORD

PIKES STOCKADE
Route 1, Sanford, Colorado 81151
House (1807), with relics of pioneer period.
May 15 - Oct. 15, 9-dusk.

HOUSE IN THE HORSESHOE STATE HISTORIC SITE
Route 3, Box 503, Sanford, North Carolina 27330
House (1770). Period furnishings.
Tu.-Su. 2-5. Closed Christmas, New Year, Thanksgiving.

THE RAILROAD HOUSE
Hawkins Avenue and Carthage Street, Sanford, North Carolina 27330
House (1872), was home of first depot agent of Raleigh and Augusta Air Line Railroad Co. Period furnishings. Steam locomotive in grounds.
M.-F. 9-5; Sa. 9-12.

SAN FRANCISCO

CALIFORNIA HISTORICAL SOCIETY MUSEUM
2090 Jackson Street, San Francisco, California 94109
In Whittier Mansion (1894-6) and Library Building (1904). Interior decorations using woods and marbles from all over the world. Period furnishings. Paintings, drawings, prints by Californian artists.
Tu.-Sa. 10-4. Closed New Year, Thanksgiving, Christmas.

CENTER OF ASIAN ART AND CULTURE, AVERY BRUNDAGE COLLECTION
Golden Gate Park, San Francisco, California 94121
Art and culture of the Far and Near East from the neolithic period to modern times.
Daily 1-5.

EXPLORATORIUM
3601 Lyon Street, San Francisco, California 94123
Exhibits planned to develop understanding of science, technology and art. Tactile Gallery.
W. 10-5, 7-9.30; Th., F. 10-5; Sa., Su., public holidays 1-5.

FORT POINT MUSEUM
Sheridan and Ord Streets, Presidio of San Francisco, San Francisco, California 94129
Fort Point (1853-61). Military history of Spanish-American Wars, 1860-1906. Cannons of early - late 18th century.
Daily 1-4. Closed New Year, Thanksgiving, Christmas.

INTERNATIONAL MUSEUM OF EROTIC ART
Kronhausen Collection, 540 Powell Street, San Francisco, California 94108
Japanese erotic scrolls and woodblock prints; erotic paintings and sculpture from India; painted erotic scrolls and albums from China. Erotic art from France, Germany, Netherlands, Sweden, Denmark, Italy and Africa, including works by Picasso, Dali, Leonor Fini, Karel Appel and Andy Warhol.
Su., M. 11-5; Tu.-Th. 11-7; F., Sa. 11-9.

MISSION SAN FRANCISCO DE ASIS
Dolores Street and 16th Street, San Francisco, California 94101
Mission buildings (1776). Original altar, decorations.
May-Oct. daily 9-5. Nov.-Apr. daily 10-4.

ALEXANDER F. MORRISON PLANETARIUM
Golden Gate Park, San Francisco, California 94118
Astronomy. Space science. Planetarium.
M., Tu. 2-3; W., F. 2-3, 8-9; Sa., Su. 2-4.30, 8-9.

MUSEUM OF PACKAGING ANTIQUITIES
Pier 5, Ferryboat 'Klamatt', San Francisco, California 94111
Bottles. Tins. Cigarette cartons.
By appointment.

MUSEUM OF RUSSIAN CULTURE
2450 Sutter Street, San Francisco, California 94115
Russian history, especially relating to the Russian community in the Western U.S.
Sa. 1-3.

MUSEUM OF THE CALIFORNIA ACADEMY OF SCIENCE
Golden Gate Park, San Francisco, California 94118
Natural history, especially of North America and Africa. Skeletons and fossils of prehistoric animals. Herbarium. Aquarium. Clocks. Lamps.
May 1 - Sept. 30, daily 10-9. Rest of year daily 10-5.

MUSEUM OF THE CALIFORNIA DIVISION OF MINES AND GEOLOGY
Room 2022, Ferry Building, San Francisco, California 94111
Palaeontology. Rocks and minerals. Gold mining.
M.-F. 8-5; first Sa. of each month, 10-12. Closed public holidays.

OCTAGON HOUSE
2645 Gough Street, San Francisco, California 94123
House (1861). American Colonial furniture and domestic equipment. Lustreware. Leeds and Staffordshire china. Chinese export porcelain.
1st Sunday, 2nd and 4th Thursday each month, 1-4.

OLD MISSION SAN MIGUEL
U.S. Highway 101, San Miguel, California 93451
Mission buildings (1816-18), with original decorations. 16th century Spanish wood carving. Early 19th century furniture.
Daily, except Christmas 10-5.

JOSEPHINE D. RANDALL JUNIOR MUSEUM
199 Museum Way, San Francisco, California 94114
Geology. Natural history. Indian artifacts. Art and nature centre.
Tu.-Sa. 10-5; Su., public holidays 11-5. Closed New Year, Christmas.

SAN FRANCISCO AFRICAN AMERICAN HISTORICAL AND CULTURAL SOCIETY
680 McAllister Street, San Francisco, California 94102
Black history in the W. United States. Black national history in the Caribbean, S. America and Africa.
M.-F. 9-5; Sa. 12-4. Closed Christmas, New Year, Memorial Day, July 4, Labour Day.

SAN FRANCISCO FIRE DEPARTMENT PIONEER MEMORIAL MUSEUM
655 Presidio Avenue, San Francisco, California 94115
Old fire fighting equipment.
Daily 1-5.

SAN FRANCISCO MARITIME ASSOCIATION MUSEUM
Polk Street, San Francisco, California 94109
History of sea transport. Photographs. Paintings. Models. Sailing ship 'Balclutha' (1886), at Fisherman's Wharf, is maintained by the Association as a floating museum. The paddle-wheel tug, 'Eppleton Hall', is also preserved.
Museum: daily 10-5. 'Balclutha': daily 9.30-11.30.

SAN FRANCISCO MARITIME STATE HISTORICAL PARK
2905 Hide Street, San Francisco, California 94109
Local and maritime history.
The following ships form part of the Park: lumber schooner 'C. A. Thayer' (1895); steam lumber schooner 'Wapama' (1915); ferry boat 'Eureka' (1890); scow schooner 'Alma' (1891); together with Tubbs building (1900).
Su.-Th. 10-6; Sa. 10-10. Closed New Year, Thanksgiving, Christmas.

SAN FRANCISCO MUSEUM OF ART
McAllister Street at Van Ness Avenue, San Francisco, California 94102
European and American paintings, drawings, prints, sculpture, photography, 1900 - present day.
M.-F. 10-10; Sa. 10-5; Su. 1-5. Closed public holidays.

THE SOCIETY OF CALIFORNIA PIONEERS MUSEUM
456 McAllister Street, San Francisco, California 94102
Local history. Prints, paintings, lithographs showing development of San Francisco and California.
M.-F., 10-4. Closed national holidays and during August.

EMANUEL WALKER GALLERY
800 Chestnut Street, San Francisco, California 94133
19th and 20th century European and American paintings, sculpture, prints.
Daily 10-4. Closed public holidays.

WELLS FARGO BANK HISTORY ROOM
420 Montgomery Street, San Francisco, California 94104
History of Wells Fargo and Co. Relics of Gold Rush.
M.-F. 10-3. Closed public holidays.

M. H. DE YOUNG MEMORIAL MUSEUM
Golden Gate Park, San Francisco, California 94118
Primitive art of Africa, the Americas, Oceania. Art of ancient Egypt, Rome, Europe, America. Paintings. Sculpture. Period rooms. Furniture. Decorative arts. Brussels tapestries. Chinese bronzes, ceramics, jades. Chinese lacquerware, ceramics. Persian pottery, bronzes. Sculpture of China, Japan, S. E. Asia.
Daily 10-5.

SAN GABRIEL

MISSION SAN GABRIEL ARCHANGEL
537 W. Mission Drive, San Gabriel, California 91776
Mission Church (1791-1805). 18th century Spanish wooden statues. Original winery. Soap and tallow vats. Vestments. Indian paintings of Stations of the Cross.
Daily, except Christmas, 10-5.

SAN GERMÁN

PORTA COELI MUSEUM OF RELIGIOUS ARTS
San Germán, Puerto Rico 00753
17th century Spanish chapel. 16th-19th century religious art. Liturgical objects.
Daily 9-5.

SAN JACINTO

SAN JACINTO MUSEUM
181 East Main Street, San Jacinto, California 95126
Geology. Palaeontology. Local history. Indian archaeology.
Tu.-Su. 1-5. Closed Thanksgiving, Christmas.

SAN JACINTO MUSEUM OF HISTORY
San Jacinto Battleground State Park, San Jacinto, Texas 77536
Site, on Houston Ship Channel, where Texas Independence was won (1836). History of the region. Cultural development of Texas in Spanish-Mexican and Anglo-American periods.
Sept. 1 - May 31: Tu.-Sa. 9.30-5.30; Su. 10-6. June 1 - Labour Day: daily 9.30-5.30. Closed public holidays.

SAN JOSÉ

CALIFORNIA STATE UNIVERSITY ART GALLERY
Art Department, California State University, San José, California 95114
20th century American and European paintings, graphics, sculpture.
M.-F. 10-3. Closed Christmas, New Year, Easter, Aug. 1-31.

CIVIC ART GALLERY OF SAN JOSÉ
110 S. Market Street, San José, California 95113
Paintings by N. California artists.
Tu.-Sa. 10-4.30; Su., public holidays 12-4.

COLLEGE UNION ART GALLERY
211 S. Ninth Street, San José, California 95114
Paintings, drawings, prints, ceramics by contemporary artists.
M.-F. 10-5; Sa. 12-4. Closed College holidays and during July and Aug.

NEW ALMADEN QUICKSILVER MINES EXHIBIT
Annex, Statehouse Museum, Santa Clara County Fairgrounds, San José, California 95215
History and relics of New Almaden mines.
M.-F. 1-5.

ROSICRUCIAN EGYPTIAN MUSEUM AND ART GALLERY
Rosicrucian Park, San José, California 95114
Near Eastern archaeology, paintings, sculpture, graphics and decorative arts.
M., Sa. 12-5; Tu.-F. 9-5. Closed New Year, July 4, Aug. 2, Thanksgiving, Christmas.

ROSICRUCIAN SCIENCE MUSEUM AND PLANETARIUM
Rosicrucian Park, San José, California 95114
Astronomy. Aeronautics. Science. Planetarium.
Oct. 1-May 31, Sa., Su. 1-5; June 1-Sept. 30, W.-Su. 1-5. Closed New Year, Thanksgiving, Christmas.

SAN JOSÉ HISTORICAL MUSEUM
635 Phelan Avenue, San José, California 95112
Local history. Agriculture. Transport. Open-air museum. The Peralta Adobe (1804) and the Roberto Adobe (1839) are in the care of the Museum.
M.-F. 10-4.30; Sa., Su., public holidays 12-4.30. Closed New Year, Thanksgiving, Christmas.

TRITON MUSEUM OF ART
99 S. 2nd Street, San José, California 95513
In Jameson Brown House (1868). European and American paintings, including works by Turner, Hogarth, Oliver Clare and Theodore Wores.
M.-F. 12.30-4.30; Sa. 12.30-4.30. Closed New Year, Thanksgiving, Christmas.

YOUTH SCIENCE INSTITUTE
16260 Alum Rock Avenue, San José, California 95127
Junior museum. Geology. Natural history.
Tu.-F. 9-4.30; Sa. 10-5. Closed public holidays.

SAN JUAN

THE HOUSE OF THE BOOK
Calle del Cristo 255, San Juan, Puerto Rico 00903
In restored 18th century building. History of book-production. Typography. Printing. Papermaking. Binding.
M.-F. 11-5; Sa. 1-5. Closed public holidays.

INSTITUTE OF PUERTO RICAN CULTURE
Old Dominican Convent, Old San Juan, San Juan, Puerto Rico 00904
Collections illustrating Island culture. Restored 16th-17th century library.
Daily 9-12, 2-5.

MUSEUM OF FINE ARTS
Calle del Santo Cristo de la Salud 253, San Juan, Puerto Rico 00901
Paintings. Sculpture. Prints. Drawings. Archaeology.
M.-F. 8.30-4; Sa., Su., public holidays 9-5. Closed Good Friday, New Year, Christmas.

MUSEUM OF COLONIAL ARCHITECTURE
319 Fortaleza Street, Old San Juan, San Juan, Puerto Rico 00904
In restored 18th century building. Exhibits illustrating three centuries of Puerto Rico's Spanish colonial architecture.
M.-Sa. 9-5; Su. and holidays 2-6.

MUSEUM OF LATIN-AMERICAN ENGRAVINGS
Casa de los Contrafuertes, Plaza de San José, San Juan, Puerto Rico 00900
Engravings, mainly 19th-20th century, by artists from Puerto Rico and the other Latin American countries.
Daily 9-5.

MUSEUM OF MILITARY AND NAVAL HISTORY
Fort San Jeronimo, San Juan, Puerto Rico 00905
Displays illustrating military and naval history of Puerto Rico. Weapons. Paintings. Prints. Uniforms. Photographs. Models.
Su.-F., public holidays 9-5; Sa. 9-6. Closed Good Friday.

MUSEUM OF POPULAR RELIGIOUS ART
Casa de las Contrafuertes, Plaza de San José, San Juan, Puerto Rico 00900
Paintings. Figures of saints. Votive objects.
Daily 9-5.

MUSEUM OF THE PUERTO RICAN FAMILY
Casa del Callejon, San Juan, Puerto Rico 00900
Rooms furnished to show how a middle-class Puerto Rican family lived in the mid. 19th century.
Daily 9-12, 1-5.

PHARMACY MUSEUM
Casa de los Contrafuertes, Calle de San Sebastian, San Juan, Puerto Rico 00900
19th century pharmacy equipment, furnishings.
Daily 9-12, 1-5.

PUERTO RICAN ATHENEUM
Ponce de Léon Avenue, San Juan, Puerto Rico 00902
Paintings by Puerto Rican artists. Sculpture. History of Puerto Rico. Physical sciences.
M.-F. 9-9; Sa. 9-5. Closed public holidays.

SAN JUAN NATIONAL HISTORIC SITE
Old San Juan, Puerto Rico 00902
Military history and fort construction. Italian and German armour. Spanish medals. 16th century Spanish wooden statue of Santa Barbara, patron saint of artillerymen.
Daily 8-6.

SAN JUAN BAUTISTA

OLD MISSION SAN JUAN BAUTISTA
2nd and Mariposa Streets, San Juan Bautista, California 95045
Franciscan Mission buildings (1797). Furniture and religious items of Spanish colonial period. Indian wall decorations.
Daily 9.30-5.30. Closed New Year, Thanksgiving, Christmas.

SAN JUAN BAUTISTA STATE HISTORIC PARK
P.O. Box 116, San Juan Bautista, California 95045
Local history. Archaeology. Horse-drawn vehicles. Agriculture. Indian artifacts. Open-air museum. 5 historic buildings, including San Juan Bautista Mission (1797) and Castro House (1840) are in the care of the Park.
Nov. 1-Mar. 30, daily 8-5. Apr. 1-Oct. 31, daily 8-6. Closed 2nd Sunday in July, New Year, Thanksgiving, Christmas.

SAN JUAN CAPISTRANO

MISSION SAN JUAN CAPISTRANO
San Juan Capistrano, California 92675
18th century furniture used by founders of Mission. Pottery and other artifacts discovered during site excavation.
Daily 9-5. Closed New Year, Thanksgiving, Christmas.

SAN LUIS OBISPO

DALLIDET ADOBE
Pacific and Toro Streets, San Luis Obispo, California 93401
House (1853) was home of Pierre Hyppolite Dallidet. Original furnishings. Horse-drawn vehicles.
Apr.-Nov., Su. 1-4.30.

SAN LUIS OBISPO COUNTY HISTORICAL MUSEUM
696 Monterey Street, San Luis Obispo, California 93401
Local history and archaeology. Decorative arts. Indian artifacts. Costumes. Children's museum.
The Dana adobe (1830) and the Dallidet adobe (1853) are in the care of the Museum.
Tu.-Su. 10-12, 1-4. Closed public holidays.

SAN LUIS OBISPO MISSION
P.O. Box 241, San Luis Obispo, California 93401
Buildings (1772) of Franciscan mission. Religious art of Spanish colonial period.
House: M.-Sa. 9-12, 1-5; Su. 1-5. Museum: daily 10-12, 1-5.30.

SAN LUIS REY

OLD MISSION SAN LUIS REY
4050 Mission Avenue, San Luis Rey, California 92068
In Mission buildings (1798). Spanish paintings. Sculpture. Mission furnishings.
M.-Sa. 9.30-4.30; Su. 1.30-4.30. Closed Thanksgiving, Christmas.

SAN MARCOS

GENERAL EDWARD BURLESON HOUSE
Box 2330, Aquarena Springs, San Marcos, Texas 78666
Reproduction of original Burleson family cabin. Personal possessions and documents, photographs illustrating career of the famous frontiersman and political leader.
May 1-Sept. 30, M.-F. 8 a.m. 9 p.m. Sa., Su. 8 a.m. - 10 p.m. Closed Christmas.

DR. ELI T. MERRIMAN HOME
Loop 82, P.O. Box 2330, Texana Village, Aquarena, San Marcos, Texas 78666
One-room log cabin (c.1850). Period furnishings.
Oct. 1-Apr. 30. M.-F. 8.30-5.30; Sa. 8.30-6. May 1-Sept. 30, M.-F. 8 a.m. - 9 p.m.; Sa., Su. 8 a.m. - 10 p.m. Closed Christmas.

SAN MARINO

HENRY E. HUNTINGTON LIBRARY AND ART GALLERY
1151 Oxford Road, San Marino, California 91108
15th-16th century Italian and Flemish paintings. 18th century French sculpture. English and French 18th century decorative arts. 18th century British portraits. Renaissance bronzes. English and French furniture. French tapestries, porcelain. English miniatures, porcelain, silver, drawings.
Tu.-Su. 1-4.30. Closed New Year, Memorial Day, July 4, Thanksgiving, October, Christmas.

SAN MATEO

SAN MATEO COUNTY HISTORICAL ASSOCIATION MUSEUM
1700 West Hillsdale Boulevard, San Mateo, California 94402
Anthropology. Archaeology. Local and Indian history. Agriculture. Transport. Maritime history. Aviation. Music. Decorative arts.
4 historic buildings, including the Sanchez adobe (1835) are in the care of the Assocation.
M.-F. 9.30-4.30; Sa., Su. 10.30-4.30. Closed public holidays.

SAN MATEO COUNTY JUNIOR MUSEUM
Coyote Point Drive, Coyote Point, San Mateo, California 94401
Mineralogy. Botany. Natural history.
M.-Sa. 9-5; Su. 1-5. Closed New Year, Thanksgiving, Christmas.

SAN PEDRO

CABRILLO BEACH MARINE MUSEUM
3720 Stephen White Drive, San Pedro, California 90731
Palaeontology. Shells, birds, fish, whales, fossils. Ships. Nautical equipment.
Daily, May 1-Sept. 30. 10-6; Oct. 1-Apr. 30, 9-5.

SAN PEDRO MUNICIPAL ART GALLERY
638 South Beacon Street, San Pedro, California 90731
European and American paintings, sculpture, graphics.
Tu.-Sa. 12-5. Closed public holidays.

SAN RAFAEL

LOUISE A. BOYD MARIN MUSEUM OF SCIENCE
76 Albert Park Lane, San Rafael, California 94907
In Wooden Church (c.1850), built by Mormons. Natural history. Indian collection.
Tu.-Sa. 10-5; Su. 12-5. Closed Christmas, New Year, Thanksgiving.

PONY EXPRESS HISTORY AND ART GALLERY
75 Margarita Drive, San Rafael, California 94901
History of the Pony Express. Guns. Medals.
By appointment.

SAN SABA

SAN SABA COUNTY HISTORICAL MUSEUM
Mill Pond Park, San Saba, Texas 76877
In 2 log cabins (c.1870). County history. Ranch and farm implements, equipment, furnishings. Clothing. Blacksmith's tools.
Apr. 1-Aug. 31, Su. 3-5. Other times by appointment.

SAN SIMEON

HEARST SAN SIMEON STATE HISTORICAL MONUMENT
State Highway 1, San Simeon, California 93452
'La Cuesta Encantada' (1919), mansion and estate of William Randolph Hearst. Original furniture and furnishings. Tapestries. Persian rugs. Roman mosaics. Statuary. Wood carvings.
Daily 10-5. Closed New Year, Christmas, Thanksgiving.

SANTA ANA

CHARLES W. BOWERS MEMORIAL MUSEUM
2002 North Main Street, Santa Ana, California 92706
Mineralogy. Palaeontology. Natural history. Ethnology. Agriculture. Transport. Indian artifacts. 19th-20th century American paintings, decorative arts. Costumes.
Tu., F., Sa. 10-4.30; W., Th. 10-4.30, 7-9; Su. 1-5. Closed New Year, Thanksgiving, Christmas.

ORANGE COUNTY HISTORICAL SOCIETY MUSEUM
2002 North Main, Santa Ana, California 92706
Local history.
2nd Th. each month, 7.30-10. Closed July, August.

SANTA ANNA

OLD ROCK HOUSE
Box 335, Santa Anna, Texas 76878
Pioneer cabin (1873). Late 19th - early 20th century furnishings.
By appointment.

SANTA BARBARA

ART MUSEUM AND HISTORY MUSEUM
Mission Santa Barbara, Los Olivos and Laguna Streets, Santa Barbara, California 93105
Mission buildings (1786-1833). Spanish and Mexican paintings, sculpture, church furnishings.
M.-Sa. 9.30-5; Su. 1-5.

SANTA BARBARA HISTORICAL SOCIETY MUSEUM
136 E. De la Guerra Street, Santa Barbara, California 93102
Local history.
4 historic houses (1817-61) are in the care of the Society.
Tu.-F. 12-5; Sa.-Su., public holidays 12-5. Closed New Year, Easter, Thanksgiving, Christmas.

SANTA BARBARA MUSEUM OF ART
1130 State Street, Santa Barbara, California 93104
Egyptian, Greek, Roman antiquities. Oriental paintings, sculpture, porcelain, musical instruments. European paintings, sculpture, drawings. American paintings. Dolls. Tibetan, African, Pre-Columbian sculpture and other artifacts.
Tu.-Sa. 11-5; Su. 12-5. Closed public holidays.

SANTA BARBARA MUSEUM OF NATURAL HISTORY
2559 Puerta del Sol, Santa Barbara, California 93105
Geology. Natural history and prehistory of Pacific Coast. Botany. Archaeology. Anthropology. Astronomy.
M.-Sa. 9-5; Su., public holidays 1-5. Closed Christmas.

UNIVERSITY OF CALIFORNIA ART GALLERIES
Santa Barbara, California 93106
16th-18th century European paintings. 20th century American paintings. Archaeology. Architecture. Sculpture. Graphics.
M.-Sa. 10-4; Su., public holidays 1-5. Closed Christmas.

SANTA CLARA

DE SAISSET ART GALLERY AND MUSEUM
University of Santa Clara, Santa Clara, California 95053
Early Californian history. Chinese art. Sculpture. Graphics. Porcelain. Silver. Ivory.
Tu.-F. 10-5; Th. also 7-9 p.m.; Sa., Su. 1-5. Closed August, public holidays.

TRITON MUSEUM OF ART
1505 Warburton Avenue, Santa Clara, California 95050
16th-20th century European paintings, sculpture, graphics. 18th-19th century American art. Paintings by 19th-20th century California artists.
M.-F. 12.30-4.30; Sa., public holidays 10-5; Su. 1-5. Closed New Year, Christmas.

SANTA CRUZ

SANTA CRUZ ART LEAGUE MUSEUM
526 Broadway, Santa Cruz, California 95060
Contemporary American art.
Daily 1-5.

SANTA CRUZ MUSEUM
1305 East Cliff Drive, Santa Cruz, California 95060
Local history. Natural history. Anthropology.
Tu.-Su. 10-5. Closed New Year, Thanksgiving, Christmas.

SANTA FE

INSTITUTE OF AMERICAN INDIAN ARTS
Cerrillos Road, Santa Fe, New Mexico 87501
Indian artifacts, arts and crafts.
M.-F. 8-5; Sa., Su. by appointment. Closed public holidays.

MUSEUM OF HISTORICAL SOCIETY OF NEW MEXICO
Palace of the Governors, P.O. Box 2087, Santa Fe, New Mexico 87501
Local history. Archaeology. Indian artifacts. Paintings of New Mexico.
By appointment.

MUSEUM OF INTERNATIONAL INSTITUTE OF IBERIAN COLONIAL ARTS
Station 1, St. Michael's Drive, Santa Fe, New Mexico 87501
Paintings and sculpture of the Colonial period in Latin America and Philippines.
M.-F. 9-5; Sa. 1-4; Su. 2-5.

MUSEUM OF NAVAJO CEREMONIAL ART
704 Camino Lejo, Santa Fe, New Mexico 87501
Ceremonial objects. Sand paintings. Musical recordings. Paintings and drawings. Ethnology.
Tu.-Sa. 9-5; Su., public holidays 2-5. Closed New Year, Thanksgiving, Christmas.

MUSEUM OF NEW MEXICO
Palace of the Governors, P.O. Box 2087, Santa Fe, New Mexico 87501
Anthropology, archaeology and ethnology of the S.W. History. Folk art. Paintings. Sculpture. Drawings.
M.-Sa. 9-5; Su., public holidays 2-5. Closed M., Sept. 15- May 15.

NEW MEXICO MILITARY MUSEUM
Santa Fe, New Mexico 87501
Local history. Coins. Costumes. American army saddles. Aeronautics.
Oct.-Apr., Tu.-Sa. 8-4; May-Sept., Th., Su. 8-4. Closed public holidays.

OLD CIENEGA VILLAGE MUSEUM
614 Acequia Madre, Santa Fe, New Mexico 87501
Open-air museum, at former Las Golondrinas Ranch. The major buildings reassembled here include mills, a blacksmith's shop, a wheelwright's shop, large hacienda-type dwellings and a country store. There are also many smaller houses from N. New Mexico.
By appointment.

PALACE OF THE GOVERNORS
Palace Avenue, Santa Fe, New Mexico 87501
Building (1610). Exhibits covering the history of New Mexico, as a Spanish colony, a territory and a State.
M.-Sa. 9-5; Su., holidays, Nov. 1- Apr. 30, 2-4; May 1- Oct. 30, 2-5. Closed Christmas, New Year, Thanksgiving.

SANTA PAULA

CALIFORNIA OIL MUSEUM
1003 Main Street, Santa Paula, California 93060
History of Californian oil industry. Geology. Mineralogy. Early drilling equipment.
W.-Su. 10-4.

SANTA ROSA

CODDING MUSEUM
557 Summerfield Road, Santa Rosa, California 95405
Local history. Indian artifacts. Natural history.
Tu.-Th., Sa., Su. 1-5. Closed New Year, Christmas.

JESSE PETER MEMORIAL MUSEUM
Santa Rosa Junior College, Mendocrino Avenue, Santa Rosa, California 95401
Geology. Natural history. Local history. Indian artifacts.
Tu., Th. 12-4. Closed college vacations.

SANTA YNEZ

SANTA YNEZ VALLEY HISTORICAL SOCIETY MUSEUM
P.O. Box 181, Santa Ynez, California 93460
Local history.
Sa., Su. 1-4.30. Closed New Year, Christmas.

SARANAC LAKE

DICKERT MEMORIAL WILDLIFE COLLECTION
Saranac Lake, New York 12983
Mounted animals, birds, fish. Photographs. Maps.
July 1- Aug. 31: Tu.-F. 10-5; Sa. 10-1.

STEVENSON COTTAGE
Saranac Lake, New York 12983
House where Robert Louis Stevenson lived, 1887 8. Literary and personal memorabilia of Stevenson.
June 30- Sept. 30: Tu.-Su. 9-12, 1-5.

SARASOTA

ASOLO THEATER MUSEUM
P.O. Box 1838, Sarasota, Florida 33578
Theatre history. Paintings of Harlequin.
M.-F. 9-10; Sa. 9-5; Su., public holidays 1-5.

MUSEUM OF SARASOTA ART ASSOCIATION
Civic Center, P.O. Box 2077, Sarasota, Florida 33578
Paintings. Graphics. Sculpture.
Oct.-May, M.-F. 10-5; Sa., Su. 1-4. Closed Thanksgiving, Christmas, New Year.

RINGLING CIRCUS MUSEUM
6255 North Tamiami Trail, Sarasota, Florida 33578
Circus history. Posters. Programs. Mementoes of famous performers. Coach presented by Queen Victoria to Tom Thumb, sleigh presented by P. T. Barnum to Jenny Lind.
M.-F. 9 a.m. - 10 p.m.; Sa. 9-5; Su., public holidays. 1-5.

RINGLING MUSEUM OF ART
Sarasota, Florida 33578
14th-18th century European paintings and drawings, especially Baroque art and works by Rubens. Archaeology of Cyprus. 18th century decorative arts.
M.-F. 9-10; Sa. 9-5; Su. 1-5.

SARATOGA

MONTALVO CENTER FOR THE ARTS
14800 Montalvo Road, Saratoga, California 95070
Paintings. Sculpture. Graphics. Decorative arts. Children's museum.
Villa Montalvo (1912) is in the care of the Center.
Tu.-Su. 1-4. Closed New Year, Thanksgiving, Christmas.

SARATOGA SPRINGS

GRANT COTTAGE
Mount McGregor, Wilton, Saratoga Springs, New York 12866
House where President Grant died. Grant memorabilia.
Tu.-Sa. 9-5; Su. 1-5.

HATHORN GALLERY
Court Street, Saratoga Springs, New York 12866
Paintings, sculpture by contemporary American artists.
Sept. 21- May 31: M.-F. 9 a.m. - 10 p.m.; Sa., Su. 10-6.

NATIONAL MUSEUM OF RACING
Union Avenue, Saratoga Springs, New York 12866
History of horse-racing. Paintings. Prints. Trophies.
M.-F. 10-5; Sa. 12-5. June 15- Sept. 15, Su. 12-5. Aug. 2-28, daily 9.30-7.30.

SARATOGA HISTORICAL MUSEUM AND WALWORTH MEMORIAL MUSEUM
Congress Park, Saratoga Springs, New York 12866
Local history. Furnishings and personal possessions from home of Reuben Hyde Walworth.
June 1-30, Sept. 1- Oct. 31, daily 10-4. July 1- Aug. 31, daily 9.30-4.30.

SAUGERTIES

WEDE MARINE MUSEUM
Saugerties, New York 12477
Maritime history.
May 1- Sept. 30, daily 10-5.

SAUGUS

"SCOTCH" BOARDMAN HOUSE
17 Howard Street, Saugus, Massachusetts 01906
House (1651), built to house Scottish Covenanters brought to work at Saugus Ironworks.
June-Sept. M.-Th., Sa. 10-5. Other times by appointment.

SAUGUS IRON WORKS NATIONAL HISTORIC SITE
244 Central Street, Saugus, Massachusetts 01906
Reconstruction of 17th century iron-works. Ironmaster's house (1648).
Apr. 1- Oct. 31: daily 9-5. Nov. 1- Mar. 31, daily 9-4.

SAUK CENTER

SINCLAIR LEWIS MUSEUM
532 Main Street, Sauk Center, Minnesota 56378
House (c. 1880) was boyhood home of Sinclair Lewis. Family furnishings and personal possessions. Doctor's surgery.
Memorial Day- Labour Day, M.-Sa. 10-4; Su. 1-5.

SAUK CITY

SAUK PRAIRIE HISTORICAL SOCIETY MUSEUM
Sauk City, Wisconsin 53583
In Hahn House (c.1870). Household and other local items from the period 1830-80.
Memorial Day - Labour Day: Su., public holidays 2-5.

SAULT STE. MARIE

JOHN JOHNSON HOUSE
415 Park Place, Sault Ste. Marie, Michigan 49783
Reconstructed house of 1815. Pioneer furnishings, household equipment.
June - Labour Day, daily 10-5.

THE SCHOOLCRAFT INDIAN AGENCY HOUSE
715 E. Portage Avenue, Sault Ste. Marie, Michigan 49783
House, 'Elmwood' (1827), built by Indian agent, Henry Rowe Schoolcraft, whose *Algic Researches* inspired Longfellow's *Hiawatha*. Local history. Indian material.
June - Labour Day, daily 10-5.

SAUNDERSTOWN

GILBERT STUART MEMORIAL
Gilbert Stuart Road, Saunderstown, Rhode Island 02874
House (1755), with period furniture, birthplace of the artist, Gilbert Stuart. Intact 18th century grist mill and snuff mill.
Su.-Th. 11-5.

SAVANNAH

COLONIAL DAMES HOUSE
329 Abercorn Street, Savannah, Georgia 31401
House (1848) was formerly home of Low family, visited by Thackeray and Robert E. Lee. Period furnishings.
W., F., Sa. 10.30-5. Closed public holidays.

DAVENPORT HOUSE
Habersham and E. State Streets, Savannah, Georgia 31401
House (1821-2). Period furnishings from Savannah area. Furniture and other heirlooms of Davenport family. China, including Davenport, Spode, Chinese Export, Philadelphia Tucker.
M.-Sa. 10-5. Closed public holidays.

FACTORS WALK MILITARY MUSEUM
222 Factors Walk, Savannah, Georgia 31401
Civil War history. Documents. Pictures. Weapons.
M.-Sa. 9.30-5.30; Su. 2-5.

FORT JACKSON MARITIME MUSEUM
P.O. Box 2132, Savannah, Georgia 31402
Maritime history of Georgia, in Fort buildings (1842).
Oct. 1 - Apr. 30: Tu.-Sa. 9-5; Su. 2-5. May 1 - Sept. 30: Tu.-Sa. 9-5.30; Su. 2-5.30. Closed Thanksgiving, Christmas.

FORT SCREVEN AND TYBEE MUSEUM
Tybee Island, U.S. Highway 80E, Savannah, Georgia 31401
Fort (1875). Displays illustrating life on the Island in the Colonial and pre-Colonial periods.
May 1 - Sept. 30: daily 10-6. Oct. 1 - Apr. 30: daily, except Tu., 1-5.

GEORGIA SALZBURGER SOCIETY MUSEUM
Route 3, Box 631, Savannah, Georgia 31401
Material relating to history of the Salzburgers.
Sa.-Su. 3-5.

JULIETTE GORDON LOW BIRTHPLACE
142 Bull Street, Savannah, Georgia 31401
House (1812-21) was birthplace and girlhood home of Juliette Gordon Low, founder of Girl Scouting in USA. Family furniture and furnishings.
Weekdays, except W., 10-4; Su. 2-4.30. Closed Christmas, New Year, Thanksgiving.

MUSEUM OF GEORGIA HISTORICAL SOCIETY
501 Whitaker Street, Savannah, Georgia 31401
Georgia history.
M.-F. 10-6; Sa. 9.30-1. Closed public holidays.

OWENS-THOMAS HOUSE
124 Abercorn Street, Savannah, Georgia 31401
House (1816-19). Early 19th century American furniture. 18th century and Regency English furniture and furnishings. Decorative arts.
Tu.-Sa. 10-5; Su., M. 2-5. Closed Sept. 1-30.

SAVANNAH SCIENCE MUSEUM
4405 Paulsen Street, Savannah, Georgia 31401
Habitat groups of plants and animals. Science. Technology. Industry. Planetarium.
M.-Sa. 10-5; Su. 2-5.

SHIPS OF THE SEA MUSEUM
503 River Street, Savannah, Georgia 31401
Ship models. Ships in bottles. Figureheads. Ships' furniture. Early 19th century signs from London waterfront taverns. Walrus and whale teeth scrimshaw. Weapons. Mugs and figurines, including complete Royal Doulton 'Personages of the Sea' series. Charts. Logs. The 3-masted 'Cruz del Sur' is moored at the Museum.
Daily 10-6.

TELFAIR ACADEMY OF ARTS AND SCIENCES
121 Barnard Street, Savannah, Georgia 31401
18th-20th century American paintings, 19th-20th century American and English sculpture, graphic and decorative arts.
Tu.-Sa. 10-5; Su. 2-5. Closed Jan., public holidays.

SAVANNAH BEACH

FORT PULASKI NATIONAL MONUMENT
Savannah Beach, Georgia 31328
Fort (1829-47). Local and military history.
Daily 8.30-5.30. Closed Christmas.

SAXTONS RIVER

SAXTONS RIVER HISTORICAL MUSEUM
Main Street, Saxtons River, Vermont 05154
In former Congregational Church (1836). Local history.
July 1 - Sept. 15: Sa., Su. 2.30-5.

SAYNER

VILAS COUNTY MUSEUM
Sayner, Wisconsin 54560
Geology. Botany. Natural history. Local history and archaeology. Indian material. Costumes. Paintings. Sculpture. Graphics. Decorative arts.
May 8 - Sept. 15: Tu.-Su. 9.30-5.

SAYVILLE

SAYVILLE HISTORICAL SOCIETY MUSEUM
39 Edwards Street, Sayville, New York 11782
In Edwards homestead (1675). Agriculture. Maritime history. Indian artifacts. Costumes. Country store. Folklore. Children's museum.
June 1 - Aug. 31: W., Sa. 2-5. Other times by appointment.

SCARBOROUGH

SCARBOROUGH HISTORICAL MUSEUM
U.S. Route 1, Scarborough, Maine 04074
Local history. Furnishings, domestic equipment of Colonial farmhouse.
May 1 - Sept. 30, Tu. 2-4.30. Summer only.

SCARSDALE

MUSEUM OF MUSIC
34 Greenacres Avenue, Scarsdale, New York 10583
Musical instruments.
By appointment.

WAYSIDE COTTAGE
1039 Post Road, Scarsdale, New York 10583
Furniture, 1750-1850.
By appointment.

WERNBERG NATURE CENTER
455 Mamaroneck Road, Scarsdale, New York 10583
Geology. Botany. Natural history.
M.-Th., Sa. 9-5; Su. 1-5.

SCHAEFFERSTOWN

HISTORIC SCHAEFFERSTOWN
N. Market Street, Schaefferstown, Pennsylvania 17088
Early 19th century Pennsylvania Dutch life. Tools. Household equipment. Guns. Part of general store. Indian artifacts. Glass.
Mar. 1 - Oct. 31: Sa., Su. 1-4.30.

SCHAGHTICOKE

KNICKERBOCKER HISTORICAL SOCIETY MUSEUM
Schaghticoke, New York 12154
In Knickerbocker Mansion (1770). Knickerbocker family possessions. 18th-19th century furniture. Fashion books. Pottery. Glass.
June 1 - Sept. 30, Su. 2-5. Other times by appointment.

SCHENECTADY

MUSEUM OF SCHENECTADY COUNTY HISTORICAL SOCIETY
32 Washington Avenue, Schenectady, New York 12305
County history. Indian artifacts. Dolls. Toys. Early equipment of the General Electric Company. Paintings.
M.-Sa. 12.30-5.30; Su. 1-5. Closed public holidays.

SCHENECTADY MUSEUM
North Terrace Heights, Schenectady, New York 12308
Geology. Mineralogy. Natural history. Anthropology. Ethnology. Technology. Toys. Dolls. Costumes. Paintings. Graphics. Sculpture.
Tu.-Sa. 10-4.30; Su. 1-5. Closed July 4, Thanksgiving, Christmas, New Year.

SCHOFIELD BARRACKS

25th INFANTRY DIVISION MUSEUM
Trimble Road, Schofield Barracks, Hawaii 96786
Military history. Weapons. Photographs. Documents.
F.-Su. 12-6.

SCHOHARIE

OLD STONE FORT MUSEUM
North Main Street, Schoharie, New York 12157
Originally church (1772), fortified during Revolution. Local history. Early Americana. Indian artifacts.
June 1 - Aug. 31, daily 10-5. May 1-31, Sept. 1 - Oct. 31: Tu.-Su. 10-5.

SCHUYLER LAKE

EXETER HISTORICAL SOCIETY MUSEUM
Main Street, Schuyler Lake, New York 13457
Local history. Tools. Folklore.
By appointment.

SCHUYLERVILLE

GENERAL PHILIP SCHUYLER HOUSE
Saratoga National Park, Schuylerville, New York 12871
Country home (1762) of Gen. Schuyler (d.1804). Memorabilia of Gen. Schuyler.
June 1 - Sept. 6: M.-Sa. 10-5; Su. 12-7.

SCITUATE

SCITUATE HISTORICAL SOCIETY MUSEUM
121 Maple Street, Scituate, Massachusetts 02066
In Cudworth House (1797). Local history. Agriculture. Indian artifacts. Costumes.
Stockbridge Mill (1640), barn (1750), and lighthouse (1811) are in the care of the Society.
June 1 - Aug. 31: W.-Sa. 2-5.

OLD STOCKBRIDGE GRIST MILL
Scituate, Massachusetts 02066
Mill (1640), with original machinery.
On request.

SCOBEY

DANIELS COUNTY MUSEUM AND PIONEER TOWN
Scobey, Montana 59263
Reconstructed and restored buildings of pioneer period, including blacksmith's shop, general store and theatre.
Mar. 1 - Sept. 30, daily 1-5.

SCOTIA

PACIFIC LUMBER COMPANY MUSEUM
U.S. Highway 101, Scotia, California 95565
History of Pacific Lumber Company. Photographs and artifacts illustrating development of logging techniques. Steam engines. Ox-yokes. Axes. Products made from redwood.
M.-F. 7.30-4.30. Closed New Year, Thanksgiving, Christmas.

SCOTT

PLANTATION MUSEUM
Lakeshore Drive, Scott, Arkansas 72142
Plantation agriculture. Machinery and equipment. Steam tractors. Blacksmiths shop.
M.-F., groups only by appointment. Sa., Su. 1-5. Closed public holidays, except by appointment.

SCOTT CITY

EL QUARTELEJO KIVA INDIAN MUSEUM
Scott City, Kansas 67871
1 mile west of city. Indian history. Artifacts of Cheyenne and Pueblo cultures. Relics of Indian wars.
Daily 10-6; evenings during summer 6-9.

SCOTTDALE

WESTMORLAND-FAYETTE HISTORICAL SOCIETY MUSEUM
Scottdale, Pennsylvania 15683
Museum building (1859). Fossils. Mounted animals and birds. 18th-19th century farm implements, household equipment. China. Glass.
May 15 - Oct. 15: M.-F. by appointment; Sa., Su. 2-5.

SCOTTSDALE

HALL OF FLAME
3626 Civic Center Plaza, Scottsdale, Arizona 85251
History of Fire Service. Fire engines.
Sept. 5 - May 31, M.-F. 10-6; Sa., Su. 12-5.

SCOTTSVILLE

HOBBY CORNER MUSEUM
Commercial and Illinois Streets, Scottsville, Kansas 67477
Local history. Domestic utensils. Machinery.
Su. 9-9. Other times by appointment.

SCRANTON

EVERHART MUSEUM OF NATURAL HISTORY, SCIENCE AND ART
Nay Aug, Scranton, Pennsylvania 18510
Geology. Coal fossils. Shells. Herbarium. Pennsylvania fish, reptiles, animals, butterflies, insects. Planetarium. Ethnology. Primitive art of America, Africa, Oceania. Oriental art. American paintings, sculpture, decorative arts, glass.
Tu.-Sa. 10-5; Su. 2-5. Closed New Year, Thanksgiving, Christmas.

MUSEUM OF LACKAWANNA HISTORICAL SOCIETY
323 Monroe Avenue, Scranton, Pennsylvania 18510
House (1912). 18th-19th century furniture. Clothing. Household and farm equipment. Indian material. Civil War relics.
Tu.-F. 10-5; Sa. 10-12.

SEAFORD

NASSAU COUNTY MUSEUM OF NATURAL HISTORY
Washington Avenue, Seaford, New York 11783
Flora and fauna of coastal New York.
Sa. 10-5; Su., public holidays 1-5.

SEAGROVE

POTTERS MUSEUM
Seagrove Pottery, Highway 220, Seagrove, North Carolina 27341
History of pottery-making in North Carolina.
May-Sept., M.-Sa. 1-5. Oct.-Apr., W. 1-5.

SEARCY

WHITE COUNTY PIONEER MUSEUM
Route 1, Searcy, Arkansas 72143
Pioneer village, with original buildings (1850-1911). Includes mills, blacksmith's shop, schoolhouse, store and jail. Early farm implements.
M., W., Th., Sa., Su. 10-5.

SEARSPORT

MUSEUM OF SEARSPORT HISTORICAL SOCIETY
Searsport, Maine 04974
Local history. Costumes.
2nd and 4th Tu. each month.

PENOBSCOT MARINE MUSEUM
Church Street, Searsport, Maine 04975
Exhibits in Old Town Hall (1845), Merithew House (1825), Nickels-Concord Duncan House (c.1870) and Fowler-True-Ross House (1825). Maritime history of Maine. Ship models and half-models, charts, portraits, instruments. Whaling history. Early American pressed-glass butter dishes. Paintings and prints of ships built in Maine.
June 1 - Sept. 30: M.-Sa. 9-5; Su. 1-5.

SEATTLE

THOMAS BURKE MEMORIAL
Washington State Museum, Seattle, Washington 98105
Geology. Mineralogy. Palaeontology. Natural history and pre-history of State of Washington. Chinese gallery with 19th century street scene. Northwest Indian exhibits. History of science. Primitive art.
Tu.-Sa. 10-4.30.

CALKINS-SLATER METROPOLITAN MUSEUM OF ART
866 3rd Avenue, Seattle, Washington 98105
Paintings. Sculpture. Prints. Photography.
M.-F. 1-5. Closed public holidays, W. in July, Aug.

CHARLES AND EMMA FRYE ART MUSEUM
704 Terry Avenue, Seattle, Washington 98104
19th-20th century European and American paintings, especially Munich and Barbizon schools.
M.-Sa. 10-5; Su., public holidays 12-6. Closed Christmas.

HENRY ART GALLERY
University of Washington, Seattle, Washington 98105
19th-20th century European and American paintings. 20th century American prints, ceramics. Contemporary Japanese pottery.
Tu., W., F., Sa. 10-5; Th. 10-10; Su. 1-5.

MUSEUM OF HISTORY AND INDUSTRY
2161 E. Hamlin Street, Seattle, Washington 98102
Natural history and history of Pacific Northwest. Relics of early settlers. Maritime history. History of aviation on Pacific Coast. All-wood flying boat, Boeing B1. Miniature 14 room Colonial mansion. Transport, including Indian canoes.
Tu.-F. 11-5; Sa. 10-5; Su. 12-5. Closed M., Christmas, Thanksgiving, New Year, Memorial Day.

PACIFIC SCIENCE CENTER
200 2nd Avenue N., Seattle, Washington 98109
Life sciences. Radiation. N.W. Indian (Kwakiutl) House. Mathematics. Astronomy. Aerospace.
Sept. 1 - June 30, M.-F. 9-5; Sa., Su. 12-8. July 1 - Aug. 31, daily 11-8.

PUGET SOUND RAILWAY MUSEUM
Box 3801, Seattle, Washington 98124
Locomotives. Coaches. Freight cars. Trams.
July-Aug., Sa., Su. 11-5.

PULLEN ALASKA MUSEUM
Seattle Center, Seattle, Washington 98109
History of Klondike gold rush. Arts of N.W. Indians.
May 1 - Sept. 15, daily 12-8.

SEATTLE ART MUSEUM
14th E. and E. Prospect Streets, Seattle, Washington 98102
Egyptian, Greek and Roman art. Pre-Columbian and African art. Chinese, Japanese, Indian and Near Eastern art. 16th-18th century European paintings, sculpture. 18th century European porcelain. 19th - 20th century American paintings, sculpture.
Tu.-Sa. 10-5; Th. also 7 p.m. - 10; Su. 12-5. Closed New Year, Memorial Day, Thanksgiving, Christmas.

UNIVERSITY OF WASHINGTON, COSTUME AND TEXTILE STUDY CENTER
Seattle, Washington 98105
Textiles from all over the world. Special collections of Balkan embroideries, Italian velvets, brocades, damasks, contemporary Scandinavian fabrics.
By appointment.

UNIVERSITY OF WASHINGTON, SCHOOL OF MEDICINE
Seattle, Washington 98105
History of medicine.
M.-F. 8-10; Sa., Su. 8-5.

WASHINGTON STATE FIRE SERVICE HISTORICAL MUSEUM
16231 11th Avenue N.E., Seattle, Washington 98155
Firefighting equipment. Models of fire-boats. Uniforms. Badges.
Apr. 1 - June 10, W.-Su. 12-6. June 11 - Aug. 31, daily 11-8. Sept.-Oct., Sa., Su. 12-6.

SEBASTIAN

McLARTY STATE MUSEUM
Sebastian Inlet, Florida A1A, Sebastian, Florida 32958
Museum of material salvaged from Spanish treasure-fleet, sunk 1715. Dioramas illustrating history of area.
Daily 8-dusk.

SEBEWAING

LUCKHARD'S MUSEUM
Sebewaing, Michigan 49783
Indian Mission House (1849), built by Lutherans. Original furnishings. Indian artifacts.
June-Sept., 1st Su. of each month, and by appointment.

SEDALIA

PETTIS COUNTY MUSEUM
Courthouse, S. Ohio Street, Sedalia, Missouri 65301
Local history. Agriculture and rural life. Indian artifacts. Costumes.
McVey School (1883) is in the care of the Museum.
M.-F. 9-5. Closed public holidays.

SEDAN

EMMETT KELLY MUSEUM
Sedan, Kansas 67361
History of the circus.
By appointment.

SEDGWICK

MUSEUM OF SEDGWICK-BROOKLIN HISTORICAL SOCIETY
Sedgwick, Maine 04676
In Rev. Danial Merrill House (1790). Local history.
July 1 - Aug. 31, Su. 2-4.

SEGUIN

LOS NOGALES MUSEUM
S. River and Live Oak Streets, Seguin, Texas 78155
Building (1823) was originally a post office. Texas history. Furniture. Pictures.
By appointment.

SEBASTOPOL
704 Zorn Street, Seguin, Texas 78155
House (1853). Period furnishings. Costumes. Indian artifacts.
Su. 2-5.

SELINSGROVE

MUSEUM OF SNYDER COUNTY HISTORICAL SOCIETY
Susquehanna University, Selinsgrove, Pennsylvania 17870
Geology. Local history. Civil War relics. Indian material. Postal history.
M., W. 1-5; Th. 7-9.

SELKIRK

MUSEUM OF THE TOWN OF BETHLEHEM HISTORICAL ASSOCIATION
Clapper Road and Route 144, Selkirk, New York 12158
In former Cedar Hill school (1859). Dolls. Kitchen equipment. Agriculture. Ice-harvesting. Railways. Spinning wheels.
May 15 - Oct. 15, Su. 2-5.

SELMA

STURDIVANT MUSEUM
713 Mabry Street, Selma, Alabama 36701
18th - early 19th century furniture, decorative arts. Indian artifacts. History of the plantations and the South. Documents. Dolls. Bottles.
By appointment.

SENECA FALLS

SENECA FALLS HISTORICAL SOCIETY MUSEUM
55 Cayuga Street, Seneca Falls, New York 13148
In Becker House (1875). Local history. Indian artifacts. Industry. Circus history. Children's museum. Paintings by Carlos Bellows. Portraits.
Mar. 1 - Nov. 30: M., Tu., Th., F. 1-4.

SENEY

SENEY NATIONAL WILDLIFE REFUGE VISITOR CENTER
Seney, Michigan 49883
Geology. Natural history. Herbarium.
Apr. 1 - Oct. 31, daily 8 a.m. - 8.30 p.m.

SETAUKET

CUSTOMS HOUSE
Setauket, New York 11733
Building (c.1765). Period furnishings.
May 1 - Sept. 30: W.-M. 1-5.

MUSEUM OF SOCIETY FOR THE PRESERVATION OF LONG ISLAND ANTIQUITIES
North Country Road, Box 206, Setauket, New York 11733
The Society is responsible for the preservation of 4 historic houses, all with period furnishings.
Thompson House, Sherwood-Jayne House: May 1 - Oct. 15, W.-M. 1-5; Rock Hall: Apr. 1 - Nov. 30, M.-F. 10-5; Su. 12-5; Custom House: May 1 - Sept. 30, daily 10-5.

ROCK HALL
Setauket, New York 11733
House (c.1767). Period furnishings.
Apr. 1 - Nov. 30: M.-F. 10-5; Su. 12-5.

SAYRELANDS
Setauket, New York 11733
House (c.1734). Period furnishings.
May 1 - Sept. 30: F.-M. 2-5.

SHERWOOD-JAYNE HOUSE
Setauket, New York 11733
House (c.1730). Period furnishings.
May 1 - Oct. 15: W.-M. 1-5.

THOMPSON HOUSE
Setauket, New York 11733
House (c.1700), birthplace of Benjamin Thompson, historian of Long Island. 19th century furnishings.
May 1 - Oct. 15: W.-M. 1-5.

SEVERNA PARK

ANN ARUNDEL COUNTY HISTORICAL SOCIETY
Old Annapolis Boulevard and Jones Station Road, Severna Park, Maryland 21146
History of County. Household equipment. 19th century portraits. Maps.
By appointment.

SEWANEE

FINE ARTS GALLERY OF THE UNIVERSITY OF THE SOUTH
Sewanee, Tennessee 37375
Paintings. Graphics.
M.-F. 10-12, 2-5; Sa., Su. 2-5. Closed Thanksgiving, Christmas, University vacation.

SEWARD

KOENIG ART GALLERY
Concordia Teachers College, 800 N. Columbia Street, Seward, Nebraska 68934
Contemporary American art. Graphics. Glass. Ceramics.
M.-F. 8-5; Su. 1-5. Closed one week either side of Christmas and Easter.

SHAFTSBURY

SHAFTSBURY HISTORICAL MUSEUM
R.R.1, Box 101, Shaftsbury, Vermont 05262
In former Baptist Meeting House (1846). Local history. 19th century furnishings. Tools. Handicrafts. Costumes.
May 1 - Oct. 31: Sa., Su., public holidays 10-4.

TOPPING TAVERN MUSEUM
East Road, Shaftsbury, Vermont 05262
Restored stage coach tavern (1783) with period furnishings.
May 1 - Oct. 31: M.-Sa. 10-5. Rest of year by appointment.

SHAKER HEIGHTS

SHAKER HISTORICAL SOCIETY MUSEUM
3486 Lee Road, Shaker Heights, Ohio 44120
Shaker furniture. Tools. Household utensils and equipment.
M.-F. 1-3; Sept., Apr., also Su. 2-5. Closed public holidays.

SHARON

SHARON AUDUBON CENTER
Route 4, Sharon, Connecticut 06059
Natural history.
Tu.-Sa. 9-12, 1-5.

KENDALL WHALING MUSEUM
Everett Street, Sharon, Massachusetts 02067
History of whaling. Paintings. Prints.
Tu., W. 1-4. Closed public holidays.

SHARPSBURG

ANTIETAM NATIONAL BATTLEFIELD SITE
Visitor Center, Sharpsburg, Maryland 21782
Mementoes of Civil War and Battle of Antietam. Weapons and equipment. Documents. Photographs. Papers of Robert E. Lee. Maps.
Sherrick House (c.1840) and Piper House (c.1790) are in the care of the Center.
May 1 - Sept. 30, 8.30-6; Oct. 1 - Apr. 30, 8.30-5. Closed New Year, Christmas.

SHASTA

SHASTA STATE HISTORICAL MONUMENT
P.O. Box 507, Shasta, California 96087
Gold-mining area in 1850s. Local history. Mining. Indian artifacts. Guns. American paintings.
5 historic buildings, including Whaley Brewery (1855) are in the care of the Monument.
Daily 10-5. Closed New Year, Thanksgiving, Christmas.

SHAWANO

SHAWANO COUNTY HISTORICAL SOCIETY MUSEUM
524 N. Franklin Street, Shawano, Wisconsin 54166
In Heritage House (1871). Furnishings. Local history. Indian artifacts. Costumes.
June 15 - Sept. 14: Th., Su. 2-4.

SHAW ISLAND

MUSEUM OF SHAW ISLAND AND HISTORICAL SOCIETY
Shaw Island, Washington 98286
In log cabin (1870). Local history.
May 1 - Oct. 31, M., Sa. 2-4, W. 10-12.

SHAWNEE

JOHNSON COUNTY HISTORICAL MUSEUM
6305 Lackman Road, Shawnee, Kansas 66203
History of Johnson County 1880-1920. Period rooms. Country Store.
Tu.-Su. 1-5.

SHEBOYGAN

JOHN MICHAEL KOHLER ARTS CENTER
608 New York Avenue, Sheboygan, Wisconsin 53081
In J. M. Kohler House (1882). Prehistoric Wisconsin Indian artifacts. Prints. Ceramics. Glass.
M. 7-9; Tu.-Su. 1-5. Closed public holidays.

SHEBOYGAN COUNTY HISTORICAL SOCIETY MUSEUM
3110 Erie Avenue, Sheboygan, Wisconsin 53081
House (1848). County history. Indian material. Surgical instruments. Mounted birds.
Apr.-Sept. Tu.-Su., holidays 10-5.

SHEFFIELD

COL. ASHLEY HOUSE
Cooper Hill Road, Sheffield, Massachusetts 01257
House (1735). Period furniture. Pottery.
June 1 - Oct. 15: W.-Su. 1-5. Other times by appointment.

SHELBURNE

SHELBURNE MUSEUM
Route 7, Shelburne, Vermont 05482
Outdoor museum, in 35 early American buildings, including shops, railway station, inn, jail, barn, doctor's and dentist's surgeries. Paintings, prints, sculpture. Folk art. Tools. Vehicles. Household equipment. Agricultural implements.
May 15 - Oct. 15, daily 9-5.

SHELBY

MARIAS MUSEUM OF HISTORY AND ARTS
Maple Avenue, Shelby, Montana 59474
Geology. Local history. Indian artifacts. Costumes. Paintings.
May 1 - Sept. 30: M. 2-4.30; Th. 7-9.

SHELBYVILLE

SHELBY COUNTY HISTORICAL SOCIETY MUSEUM
Shelbyville, Missouri 63469
Local history.
By appointment.

SHELTER ISLAND HEIGHTS

SHELTER ISLAND HISTORICAL SOCIETY MUSEUM
Shelter Island Heights, New York 11965
In Jonathan Havens House (1742). Furniture. History of Shelter Island.
By appointment.

SHERBORN

SHERBORN HISTORICAL SOCIETY MUSEUM
Public Library, Main Street, Sherborn, Massachusetts 01770
Local history.
M., W., F. 1-9.

SHERBURNE

ROGERS ENVIRONMENTAL EDUCATION CENTER
New York State Route 80 W, Sherburne, New York 13460
Geology. Botany. Herbarium. Zoology.
M.-F. 8.30-4.45. Apr. 1 - Nov. 30: Sa., Su. 2-6. Closed New Year, Easter, Lincoln's Birthday, Thanksgiving, Christmas.

SHERIDAN

TRAIL END MUSEUM
400 Clarendon Street, Sheridan, Wyoming 82801
In Trail End Mansion (1908-10). Local history and archaeology. Indian material.
June 1 - Sept. 30, daily 9-5, 7-9.

SHILOH

SHILOH NATIONAL MILITARY PARK MUSEUM
Shiloh, Tennessee 38376
Pre-Columbian Indian mounds. Indian artifacts. Local, especially Civil War, history.
June 1 - Labour Day, daily 8-6. Rest of year, daily 8-5. Closed Christmas.

SHINER

EDWIN WOLTERS MEMORIAL MUSEUM
1609 E. Avenue, Shiner, Texas 77984
House (1900) was home of Edwin Wolters. Natural history. Period kitchen. Personal possessions of Wolters family. Weapons. Indian artifacts.
2nd, 4th Su. in month, 2-5.

SHIPPENSBURG

SHIPPENSBURG HISTORICAL SOCIETY MUSEUM
Library Building, W. King Street, Shippensburg, Pennsylvania 17257
Local history. Costumes. Indian artifacts.
M., Tu., Th.-Sa. 10-12, 1-6, 6.30-9. Closed public holidays.

SHIRLEY

MANOR OF ST. GEORGE MUSEUM
Neighborhood Road, Shirley, New York 11967
House (c.1825). Local history. Material related to Tangier Smith family.
May 15 - Oct. 31: W.-Su., public holidays 1-5.

SHREVEPORT

LOUISIANA STATE EXHIBIT MUSEUM
3015 Greenwood Road, Shreveport, Louisiana 71109
Geology. Herpetology. Local history. Industry. Paintings, sculpture, graphics by Louisiana artists.
M.-Sa. 9-5; Su. 1-5. Closed Christmas.

R. W. NORTON ART GALLERY
4700 Creswell Avenue, Shreveport, Louisiana 71106
European paintings, sculpture. American paintings, sculpture, glass, silver, miniatures. Wedgwood china. Dolls dressed in Louisiana clothes 1720-1920. Portraits of Confederate leaders. 16th century Flemish tapestries.
Tu.-Sa. 1-5; Su. 2-5. Closed public holidays.

SHRUB OAK

TOWN OF YORKTOWN MUSEUM
Curry House, Route 6, Shrub Oak, New York 10588
Local history. Archaeology. Costumes.
Tu.-Th., Su. 2-5. Closed Jan. 15 - Feb. 15.

SHULLSBURG

BADGER MINE AND MUSEUM
Shullsburg, Wisconsin 53586
19th century mining tools and equipment. History of local mining. Farm implements.
May 1 - Oct. 31, daily 9-5.

SIBLEY

MCCALLUM MUSEUM
City Park, Sibley, Iowa 51249
Civil War history. Agriculture. Domestic equipment. Indian artifacts. Dolls.
May 1 - Sept. 30, Su. 2-5. Other days by appointment.

SIDNEY

CHEYENNE COUNTY HISTORICAL ASSOCIATION MUSEUM
740 Illinois Street, Sidney, Nebraska 69162
In Gen. Morrow's house (1867), Fort Sidney. Local history. Indian artifacts.
M.-F. 8-5. Morrow house, May 1 - Sept. 30, daily 1-5.

MUSEUM OF SIDNEY HISTORICAL ASSOCIATION
Main Street, Box 173, Sidney, New York 13838
Local history. Archaeology. Indian artifacts.
M.-F. 12-9; Sa. 12-5. Closed public holidays.

SIERRA BLANCA

E. A. (DOGIE) WRIGHT COLLECTION
County Courthouse, Sierra Blanca, Texas 79851
Relics and memorabilia of Texas Rangers, sheriffs, border patrolmen and other peace officers. Photographs, 1865-1968, illustrating life along Mexican border.
M.-F. 8-5.

SIKESTON

GAY NINETIES VILLAGE
U.S. Highway 60, Sikeston, Missouri 63801
Restored player-pianos and nickelodeons.
M.-Sa., holidays, 8.30-5; Su. 8.30-4.

SILESIA

FORT WASHINGTON
Old Fort Drive, off State Route 210, Silesia, Maryland
Fort (1814-48) with guardroom. History of Fort.
June-Aug., Sa., Su., holidays 11-7.

SILVER CITY

GILA CLIFF DWELLINGS NATIONAL MONUMENT
Route 11, Silver City, New Mexico 88061
Ruins of Indian pit-houses (A.D.100-1000) and of Pueblo Indian cliff-dwellings and huts (A.D.1000-1400). Museum showing artifacts of both cultures.
June 1 - Aug. 31, 8-7. Sept. 1 - May 31, 8-5.

SILVER CITY MUSEUM
312 W. Broadway, Silver City, New Mexico 88061
In Ailman House (c.1881). Rock and minerals room. Prehistoric cultures section. Local history and artifacts, 1870-1930.
Tu.-F. 9-4; Sa. 9-1; Su. 1-4. Closed public holidays.

SILVER CLIFF

SILVER CLIFF MUSEUM
Silver Cliff, Colorado 81249
Local history.
Th.-Su. 1-4. Closed Sept. 1 - May 31.

SILVER PLUME

LOCAL MUSEUM
Silver Plume, Colorado 80476
Early pictures of the mining town. Mining tools, books. Uniforms. Antiques. Local history.
July-Aug., M.-F. 1-4; Sa., Su. 12-4.

SILVER SPRING

MARYLAND NATIONAL CAPITAL PARK AND PLANNING COMMISSION
8787 Georgia Avenue, Silver Spring, Maryland 20907
Park tramway museum.
The Commission is responsible for 8 historic houses (1732-1850) in Montgomery County.
M.-F. 9-5. Closed public holidays.

SILVER SPRINGS

EARLY AMERICAN MUSEUM
East Silver Springs Boulevard, Silver Springs, Florida 32688
Coaches and carriages. Automobiles. Fire-engines. Snowmobiles. Americana. Costumes. Dolls. Space and naval exhibits.
Daily 9-9.

SILVERTON

SAN JUAN COUNTY HISTORICAL SOCIETY MUSEUM
Courthouse Square, Silverton, Colorado 81433
Mineralogy. Mining. Transport. Costume.
Silverton Railroad Depot (1882) and old San Juan County Jail (1902) are in the care of the museum.
Daily 9-5. Closed Oct. 2 - Memorial Day.

SIMI

SIMI VALLEY HISTORICAL MUSEUM
1958 Third Street, Simi, California 93065
Local history. Agriculture. Indian artifacts.
W., Su. 2-5. Closed public holidays.

SIMI VALLEY

ROBERT P. STRATHEARN HISTORICAL PARK
137 Strathearn Place, Simi Valley, California 93065
In De La Guerra Adobe (c.1800, with late Victorian additions). Period furnishings, household equipment. Tools. Agriculture.
2nd Su. in month, 1-4.

SIMSBURY

SIMSBURY HISTORIC CENTER
800 Hopmeadow Street, Simsbury, Connecticut 06070
Preservation project showing 300 years of life in one community. Buildings include first Meeting House (1683), first Simsbury Schoolhouse (1740), Capt. Elisha Phelps house, barn, out-buildings (1771), Hendrick Cottage (1795) and Victorian carriage house are in the care of the Centre, together with related carriages, sleighs, tools and domestic equipment.
Tu.-Sa. 1-4. Closed New Year, Thanksgiving, Christmas. The Phelps Barn and out-buildings and the Victorian carriage house are closed Nov. 1 - Apr. 30.

SINTON

MUSEUM OF ROB AND BESSIE WELDER WILDLIFE FOUNDATION
Highway 77, Sinton, Texas 78387
Photographs, paintings, specimens of plants and wildlife in the Foundation's Wildlife Refuge.
Th. 3-5 p.m.

SIOUX CITY

SIOUX CITY ART CENTER
513 Nebraska Street, Sioux City, Iowa 51101
Paintings, sculpture, prints, drawings by contemporary artists of the Mid-West.
Sept. 1 - July 31: Tu.-Sa. 10-5; Su. 1-5. Closed public holidays.

SIOUX CITY PUBLIC MUSEUM
2901 Hackson Street, Sioux City, Iowa 51104
In Pierce Mansion (1891). Mineralogy. Palaeontology. Local archaeology and history. Indian artifacts. Costumes.
Tu.-Sa. 9-5; Su. 2-5. Closed public holidays.

SIOUX FALLS

CIVIC FINE ARTS ASSOCIATION
318 S. Main Street, Sioux Falls, South Dakota 57102
Paintings, drawings, prints, sculpture by contemporary American artists.
Tu.-Sa. 11.30-5; Su. 2-5.

PETTIGREW MUSEUM
131 N. Duluth Street, Sioux Falls, South Dakota 57104
In Pettigrew House (1875). Pioneer history. Rocks. Indian artifacts. Egyptian collections.
M.-Sa. 9-12, 1.30-5; Su. 2-5. Closed Christmas, New Year, Thanksgiving.

SIREN

BURNETT COUNTY HISTORICAL MUSEUM
Siren, Wisconsin 54872
Local history. Indian artifacts.
Daily, dawn-dusk.

SITKA

SHELDON JACKSON MUSEUM
Box 479, Sitka, Alaska 99835
Anthropology. Museum of Sheldon Jackson College. History and ethnology of Alaska. Haida slate carvings. Eskimo implements and handicrafts. Tlingit relics and totems. Religious objects of the Russian Orthodox Church.
June 1 - Aug. 31, M.-Sa. 10-12, 1-5, 7-9, Su. 1-5; Sept. 1 - May 31, M.-F. 2-4, Sa., Su. 1-4.

SITKA NATIONAL MONUMENT
Sitka, Alaska 99835
Visitor centre illustrates local Indian history and culture and describes life in Sitka when it was a Russian stronghold. Totem poles. House forts. Excavated site of Tlingit fort, burnt by Russians in 1802.
Daily 8-5. Closed New Year, Thanksgiving, Christmas.

SKAGWAY

TRAIL OF '98 MUSEUM
P.O. Box 415, Skagway, Alaska 99840
Building (1899-1900) was originally McCabe College. Material relating to the Trail of 1898.
May 1 - Oct. 15, 8.30-10, 3-8.

SKANEATELES

SKANEATELES LIBRARY ASSOCIATION
49 E. Genesee Street, Skaneateles, New York 13152
Paintings by American artists, especially John D. Barrow. Etchings by American and foreign artists.
M.-Sa. 10-5.

SLAYTON

MUSEUM OF MURRAY COUNTY HISTORICAL SOCIETY
2420 26th Street, Slayton, Minnesota 56172
Local history.
May 1 - Sept. 30: Sa. 2-5; Su., public holidays 1-5. Closed New Year, Christmas.

SLIPPERY ROCK

OLD STONE HOUSE
R.D.4, Slippery Rock, Pennsylvania 16057
Reconstructed inn of 1822. Period furnishings.
May 1 - Oct. 31: Tu.-Sa. 8.30-5; Su. 1-5. Nov. 1 - Apr. 30: Tu.-Sa. 9-4.30; Su. 1-4.30. Closed public holidays.

SMETHPORT

MCKEAN COUNTY HISTORICAL MUSEUM
The Courthouse, Smethport, Pennsylvania 16749
Local history. Pioneer household items. Civil War records and relics. Agriculture. Educational history. Indian artifacts. Local oil industry.
Tu., Th. 1-5. Other times by appointment.

SMITHDOWN

SMITHDOWN HISTORICAL SOCIETY
Route 25-A, Smithdown, New York 11787
Local history museum based on three houses (1700-1819).
June-Sept., Th., Su. 2-5.

SMITHLAND

SMITHLAND LOG CABIN MUSEUM
Smithland, Iowa 51056
Local history. Indian artifacts.
By appointment.

SMITHTOWN

SMITHTOWN HISTORICAL SOCIETY MUSEUM
Route 25-A, Smithtown, New York 11787
In Caleb Smith House (1819). Local history.
Obadiah Smith House (1700) and Hoyt House (1770) are in the care of the Society.
June 1 - Sept. 30: Th., Su. 2-5.

SMITHVILLE

PATERSON MEMORIAL MUSEUM
210 N. Bridge Street, Smithville, Missouri 64089
In Paterson House (1874-6). Period furnishings.
Apr. 1 - Dec. 31, Su. 1-5. Other days by appointment.

HISTORIC TOWNE OF SMITHVILLE
U.S. Route 9, Smithville, New Jersey 08201
45 reconstructed 19th century buildings. Folklore. Maritime history. Decorative arts.
Daily 10.30-dusk.

SMYRNA

MUSEUM OF SAM DAVIS MEMORIAL ASSOCIATION
Smyrna, Tennessee 37167
House (1810) was home of Sam Davis, Confederate hero. Period furnishings. Restored outbuildings and slave quarters. Davis personal possessions. Confederate Army weapons.
Mar. 1 - Oct. 31: M.-Sa. 9-5; Su. 1-5. Nov. 1 - Feb. 28: M.-Sa. 10-4; Su. 1-4.

SNOW HILL

JULIA A. PURNELL MUSEUM
Market Street, Snow Hill, Maryland 21863
American and European history, decorative arts.
Summer: daily 1-5. Winter: Su. 2-5.

SNYDER

THE AMERICAN HERITAGE MUSEUM
309 25th Street, Snyder, Texas 79549
Pioneer history. Tools. Household equipment. Costumes. Guns. Indian artifacts.
By appointment.

DIAMOND M. FOUNDATION MUSEUM
909 25th Street, Snyder, Texas 79257
Works by American artists. Paintings. Bronzes. China. Ivories. Jades.
By appointment.

SOLDOTNA

DAMON MEMORIAL HISTORICAL MUSEUM
P.O. Box 66, Soldotna, Alaska 99669
Geology. Archaeology. Anthropology. Regional and maritime history. Indian artifacts. Natural history. Open-air museum, including early homestead cabins.
May 1 - Sept. 30, by appointment.

SOLOMONS

CALVERT MARINE MUSEUM
Solomons, Maryland 20688
Zoology. Local, naval and maritime history.
Sa., Su. 10-5.

SOLVANG

OLD MISSION SANTA INES
1760 Mission Drive, Solvang, California 93463
Mission (1804). Furnishings. Religious items.
M.-Sa. 9.30-4.30; Su. 12-5. Closed Thanksgiving, p.m. Dec. 25.

SOMERS

SOMERS HISTORICAL SOCIETY MUSEUM
Elephant Hotel, Somers, New York 10589
Hotel (1825) was formerly patronised by circus propietors. Period rooms. Memorial to circus elephant, Old Bet. Barnum and Bailey memorabilia. Circus playbills.
F. 2-4; Sa. 10-12. Other times by appointment.

SOMERSET

PERRY COUNTY HISTORY MUSEUM
S. Columbus Street, Somerset, Ohio 43783
House (1816). Period furnishings. Local history.
June 1 - Aug. 31: F.-Su. 1-4.

MUSEUM OF HISTORICAL AND GENEALOGICAL SOCIETY OF SOMERSET COUNTY
Somerset, Pennsylvania 15501
Local history and archaeology. Agricultural implements, tools.
Group of pioneer log houses (1804) is in the care of the Society.
Tu.-F. 10-4; Sa., Su. 1-4. Closed public holidays.

SOMERSET HISTORICAL CENTER
R.D.2, Somerset, Pennsylvania 15501
Local history. Pioneer life. Agriculture. Indian artifacts. Outdoor exhibits include log house (1804), covered bridge (1850), sugar maple camp-house (1860).
M.-Sa. 9-5; Su. 1-5. Closed public holidays.

SOMERS POINT

MUSEUM OF ATLANTIC COUNTY HISTORICAL SOCIETY
905 Shore Road, Somers Point, New Jersey 08244
Local history.
Tu.-Sa. 10-12, 1-4. Closed New Year, Thanksgiving, Christmas.

SOMERVILLE

SOMERVILLE HISTORICAL SOCIETY MUSEUM
Central Street and Westwood Road, Somerville, Massachusetts 02143
Local history. Civil War mementoes. Union glass. Charles Bulfinch 'Flying Staircase'.
By appointment.

OLD DUTCH PARSONAGE
38 Washington Place, Somerville, New Jersey 08876
House (1751) was original building of Rutgers University. Dutch furnishings.
Tu.-Sa. 10-12, 1-5; Su., public holidays 2-5. Closed New Year, Thanksgiving, Christmas.

SOMERS POINT

SOMERS MANSION
907 Shore Road, Somers Point, New Jersey 08244
House (1720-30). Local history. 18th - early 19th century furnishings, clothing. Ship-models. Indian artifacts.
Tu.-Sa. 10-12, 1-4; Su., public holidays 2-5. Closed Thanksgiving, Christmas, New Year.

SOMERVILLE

WALLACE HOUSE
38 Washington Place, Somerville, New Jersey 08876
House (1778). Colonial period furniture and glass. Relics of Revolutionary War.
Tu.-Sa. 10-12, 1-5; Su., public holidays 2-5. Closed Thanksgiving, Christmas, New Year.

SOMESVILLE

MUSEUM OF MOUNT DESERT ISLAND HISTORICAL SOCIETY
Somesville, Maine 04660
Local history.
July 1 - Aug. 31: W., Su. 2-5.

SONOMA

SONOMA STATE HISTORIC PARK
Spain Street, Sonoma, California 95476
Consists of Vallejo Home (1852), with original furnishings, San Francisco Solano Mission (1823), furnished and decorated with mission period objects, and Sonoma Barracks (1837). Mission paintings.
Daily 10-5. Closed New Year, Thanksgiving, Christmas.

SONOMA VALLEY HISTORICAL SOCIETY MUSEUM
Sonoma, California 95476
Local history.
M.-F. 9-5. Closed public holidays.

SOUTHAMPTON

HALSEY HOMESTEAD
S. Main Street, Southampton, New York 11968
House (1648). Period furnishings.
June 12 - Sept. 12: Tu.-Sa. 11-4.30; Su. 2-4.30.

LONG ISLAND AUTOMOTIVE MUSEUM
Route 27, Museum Square, Southampton, New York 11968
Petrol, electric and steam cars. Buses. Taxis. Fire engines.
June 1 - Sept. 30, daily 9-5. May 15-30, Oct. 1-31: Sa., Su. 9-5.

PARRISH ART MUSEUM
25 Job's Lane, Southampton, New York 11968
Italian and American furniture. European art of the Renaissance. Sculpture. Prints. Drawings. Decorative arts.
Tu.-Sa. 10-4.45; Su. 2-4.45. Closed public holidays.

ELIAS PELLETREAU SILVERSMITH SHOP
80 Main Street, Southampton, New York 11968
Mid 19th century silversmith's shop and equipment.
Su. 1.30-4.30.

SOUTHAMPTON HISTORICAL MUSEUM
17 Meeting House Lane, Southampton, New York 11968
Local history, especially of Colonial period.
Shinnecock and Montauk Indian artifacts. Portraits of local sea-captains. Log-books and charts.
Rogers Homestead (1843) is in the care of the Museum.
June 12 - Sept. 12: Tu.-Sa. 11-4.30; Su. 2-4.30.

SOUTH BEND

NORTHERN INDIANA HISTORICAL SOCIETY MUSEUM
112 S. Lafayette Boulevard, South Bend, Indiana 46600
In former Courthouse (1855). Local history. Industry. Indian artifacts. Costumes. Paintings. Furniture. Decorative arts.
Tu.-Sa. 9-5. Closed New Year, Thanksgiving, Christmas.

SOUTH BEND ART CENTER
121 N. Lafayette Boulevard, South Bend, Indiana 46601
Contemporary American paintings, graphics, ceramics.
Tu.-Sa. 9-5; Su. 2-5. Closed New Year, Easter, Christmas.

SOUTH BERWICK

HAMILTON HOUSE
Routes 236 and 91, South Berwick, Maine 03908
House (c.1785). Setting of Sarah Orne Jewett's novel, *The Tory Lover.* Georgian and Federal Period furniture.
June-Sept., W.-Sa. 1-5.

SARAH ORNE JEWETT MEMORIAL
101 Portland Street, South Berwick, Maine 03908
House (1774). Birthplace of novelist, Sarah Orne Jewett. Antique furnishings. Early Jewett family wallpapers, carpets. Miss Jewett's bedroom-study has been left as she arranged it.
June 1 - Sept. 30, W.-Sa. 1-5.

SOUTH CARVER

EDAVILLE RAILROAD MUSEUM
Rochester Road, P.O. Box 7, South Carver, Massachusetts 02566
Railway history. Old fire-engines and motorcars.
Complicated opening hours (see local announcements), but approximately:
Apr. 19 - May 25, June 13 - Labour Day: M.-Sa. 10-5.30; Su. 12.30-5.30. Labour Day - Columbus Day: M.-Sa. 10.30-3; Su., public holidays 1-5.

NATIONAL FIRE MUSEUM
Edaville R.R., South Carver, Massachusetts 02566
Fire-fighting equipment. Helmets. Badges.
June 12 - Oct. 15, Nov. 24 - Jan. 1, M., Tu., Th., F., Sa. 11-5.30; Su., public holidays 1-5.30; W. 11-9. Closed Christmas, Thanksgiving.

SOUTH CHARLESTON

MUSEUM OF FORT SCAMMON HISTORICAL ASSOCIATION
421 1-2 Rosemont Avenue, Apartment 3, South Charleston, West Virginia 25303
Fort (1863). Local and military history, especially Civil War.
By appointment.

SOUTH COVENTRY

NATHAN HALE HOMESTEAD
South Street, South Coventry, Connecticut 06238
House (1776). Period furnishings.
May 15 - Oct. 15, daily 1-5.

SOUTHERN PINES

MUSEUM OF MOORE COUNTY HISTORICAL ASSOCIATION
Southern Pines, North Carolina 28387
In Shaw House (1840). Period furnishings. Local history.
Loom House (1790), House in the Horseshoe (1770) and Bryant House (1840) are in the care of the Association.
Feb. 1 - Apr. 30, daily 10-5.30. House in the Horseshoe, daily 10-5.30.

SOUTH HADLEY

DWIGHT ART MEMORIAL
Mount Holyoke College, South Hadley, Massachusetts 01075
Egyptian, Greek, Roman, Oriental art. Pompeian frescoes. Medieval sculpture. 18th-20th century European and American paintings, sculpture, drawings, prints.
M.-Sa. 9-5.30; Su. 2.30-4.30, during College sessions.

NASH DINOSAUR LAND
South Hadley, Massachusetts 01075
Local geology and history. Quarry with dinosaur footprints.
Apr.-Nov. daily.

SKINNER MUSEUM
35 Woodbridge Street, South Hadley, Massachusetts 01075
Geology. New England birds. Agriculture. Local history. Indian artifacts. New England furniture.
W., Su. 2-5. Closed Nov. 1 - Apr. 30.

SOUTH HAVEN

DR. LIBERTY HYDE BAILEY MEMORIAL MUSEUM
903 Bailey Avenue, South Haven, Michigan 49090
House (1856-58) was home of the botanist, Liberty Hyde Bailey. Personal possessions and memorabilia of Dr. Bailey.
Tu.-F. 2-4.30. Other times by appointment.

SOUTH LANCASTER

THAYER MUSEUM
Main Street, South Lancaster, Massachusetts 01561
Birds of North America.
M., W., Sa. 1-5.

SOUTH LEE

MERRELL TAVERN
Route 102, South Lee, Massachusetts 01260
House (1811-1838). Original tap-room, bar, locally made furnishings.
By appointment.

SOUTH NATICK

MUSEUM OF HISTORICAL, NATURAL HISTORY AND LIBRARY SOCIETY
Bacon Free Library Building, Eliot Street, South Natick, Massachusetts 01760
Local history. Indian artifacts. Material relating to Henry Wilson, U.S. Vice-President.
W., Sa. 2-5. Closed public holidays.

SOUTH MARQUETTE

JOHN BURT HOUSE
220 Craig House, South Marquette, Michigan
House (c.1850). Period furnishings.
July 1 - Aug. 31, daily 10-5.

SOUTHOLD

SOUTHOLD HISTORICAL SOCIETY MUSEUM
Main Street and Maple Lane, Southold, New York 11971
In Hallock Currie-Bell House (1899). Local history. Furniture. Spinning and other handicraft equipment. Farm carts and tools. Dairy equipment. Carriages. Sleighs. Bonnets and hats. Paintings. Decorative arts. Glass. Toys.
Pine-Neck barn (c.1750) and Thomas Moore house (c.1650) are in the care of the Society.
June 16 - Sept. 14: Tu., Th., Su. 2-5.

SOUTH ORANGE

NEW JERSEY FIRE MUSEUM
177 Valley Street, South Orange, New Jersey 07079
In reconstructed Fire House (1905). History of fire service. Costumes. Prints and drawings.
Nov. 1 - Apr. 30: M.-F. 9.30-5.30. Sa. 10-2.30, by appointment. Closed public holidays.

SETON HALL UNIVERSITY MUSEUM
Orange Avenue, South Orange, New Jersey 07079
Contemporary American art, especially graphics. Archaeology. Woodland Indian artifacts.
Daily 9 a.m. - 10 p.m.

SOUTH OTSELIC

GLADDING FISHING MUSEUM
Octagon House, South Otselic, New York 13155
History of fresh and salt water fishing.
May 1 - Oct. 30, daily 10-5.

SOUTHPORT

BRUNSWICK TOWN FORT ANDERSON STATE HISTORIC SITE
Visitor Center, 225 Pine Grove Drive, Southport, North Carolina 28461
Local and military history. Excavated for site (1726-76).
Tu.-Sa. 9-5; Su. 1.30-5.30. Closed Thanksgiving, Dec. 24-6.

BRUNSWICK TOWN HALL HISTORIC SITE
Visitor Center, Southport, North Carolina 28461
Ruins and excavated sites of the town of Brunswick, burned by British troops in 1776.
Tu.-Sa. 9-5; Su. 1-5.

FORT ANDERSON
Visitor Center, Southport, North Carolina 28461
Ruins of Confederate Fort (1862).
Tu.-Sa. 9-5; Su. 1-5.

SOUTH ST. PAUL

DAKOTA COUNTY HISTORICAL MUSEUM
125 3rd Avenue N., S. St. Paul, Minnesota 55075
Mineralogy. Palaeontology. Natural history. Agriculture. Handicrafts. Indian artifacts.
Industry. Lumbering. Railways. Pioneer kitchen, parlour and bedroom. Shops. Dentist's surgery.
Tu., Th., Su. 2-5. Closed public holidays.

SOUTH SOLON

SOUTH SOLON HISTORICAL SOCIETY MUSEUM
South Solon, Maine 04979
In early New England meeting house. Period furnishings. Local history.
Summer: M.

SOUTH WELLFLEET

CAPE COD NATIONAL SEASHORE VISITOR CENTERS
South Wellfleet, Massachusetts 02663
Local history. Natural history.
By local announcement.

SOUTH WOODSTOCK

GREEN MOUNTAIN ACADEMY HISTORICAL ASSOCIATION
South Woodstock, Vermont 05071
In Academy building (1848). Material illustrating academic education, 1848-98. Local history.
June-Sept. by appointment.

SPALDING

MUSEUM OF NEZ PERCE NATIONAL HISTORIC PARK
P.O. Box 93, Spalding, Idaho 83551
On early mission site. Local and Indian history. Crafts.
Oct.-Apr., M.-F. 8-4.30; Sa., Su. 9.30-6. May-Sept., daily 8-4.30. Closed Thanksgiving, Christmas, New Year.

SPARTANBURG

ARTS COUNCIL OF SPARTANBURG COUNTY
151 N. Fairview Avenue, Spartanburg, South Carolina 29302
20th century paintings by South-eastern artists.
Tu.-F. 10-5; Sa. 10-1; Su. 3-5.

PRICE HOUSE
Spartanburg, South Carolina 29302
House (c.1790). Period furnishings.
Mar. 1 - Nov. 30: Tu.-Sa. 11-5. All year, Su. 2-5.

SPARTANBURG COUNTY REGIONAL MUSEUM
501 Otis Boulevard, Spartanburg, South Carolina 29302
Local history. Indian artifacts. Maps. Dolls.
Tu.-Sa. 10-12, 3-5. Sept. 15 - May 31, Su. 3-5.

WALNUT GROVE PLANTATION
U.S. Highways 29 and 221, Spartanburg, South Carolina 29302
Restoration of 18th century plantation. Includes Manor House (c.1765), Drovers House, Rocky Spring Academy, Smoke House, Barn and Wheat House. Period furnishings. Kitchen equipment.
Mar.-May, Sept.-Nov., Tu.-Sa. 11-4. June-Aug., Tu.-Sa. 11-5; Su. 2-5.

SPENCER

MUSEUM OF PARKER HISTORICAL SOCIETY OF CLAY COUNTY
300 East 3rd Street, Spencer, Iowa 51301
Local history. Agriculture.
Su. 2-5. Other days by appointment.

SPENCERPORT

OGDEN HISTORICAL SOCIETY MUSEUM
568 Colby Road, Spencerport, New York 14559
In Pulver House (1811). Local history. Furniture.
Su. 2-5.

SPILLVILLE

BILY CLOCK EXHIBIT
Spillville, Iowa 52168
House (1865), formerly house of the composer, Antonin Dvořak. Hand-carved clocks.
May 1 - Oct. 30, daily 8.30-5.30. Dec. 1 - Feb. 28, Su. 8.30-5.30. Mar., Apr., Nov. by appointment.

SPOKANE

CHENEY COWLES MEMORIAL MUSEUM
W. 2316 1st Avenue, Spokane, Washington 99204
Geology. Local history and archaeology. Indian material. Paintings. Sculpture.
Grace Campbell Memorial House (1898) is in the care of the Museum.
Tu.-Sa. 10-5; Su. 2-5. Closed New Year, July 4, Thanksgiving, Christmas.

FORT WRIGHT COLLEGE HISTORICAL MUSEUM
W. 4000 Randolph Road, Spokane, Washington 99204
Local history.
St. Michael's Mission Church (1872) and Post Executive Officer's residence (1899) are in the care of the Museum.
Daily 1-5. Other times by appointment.

SPOKANE VALLEY PIONEER MUSEUM
E. 10303 Sprague Avenue, Spokane, Washington 99206
Pioneer history and relics.
M., Tu., Th. 1-5.

SPOTSYLVANIA

MUSEUM OF SPOTSYLVANIA HISTORICAL ASSOCIATION
Spotsylvania, Virginia 22534
Mineralogy. History and archaeology of Spotsylvania County. Agriculture. Indian artifacts. Decorative arts.
M.-Sa. 10-3; Su. 2-4. Closed New Year, Thanksgiving, Christmas.

SPRINGDALE

SHILOH MUSEUM
118 W. Johnson Avenue, Springdale, Arizona 72764
Local history. Furniture. Tools. Household equipment. Indian artifacts.
Tu.-Sa. 10-5. Closed public holidays.

HUNTER'S HOT SPRINGS MUSEUM
Box 132, Springdale, Montana 59082
Pioneer life in Montana. Domestic equipment. Tools. Indian artifacts.
Store and post office (1880) are in the care of the Museum.
May 1 - Aug. 31: Tu.-Su. 10-6.

ZION NATIONAL PARK MUSEUM
Park Headquarters, Springdale, Utah 84767
Geology. Herbarium. Natural history. Entomology. Herpetology. Local history.
May 1 - Oct. 31, daily 8-9. Nov. 1 - Apr. 30, daily 8-5.

SPRINGFIELD

EDWARDS PLACE, SPRINGFIELD ART ASSOCIATION
700 N. 4th Street, Springfield, Illinois 62702
House (c.1850). Some original furnishings, belonging to Edwards family. Other period furniture. 19th-20th century paintings, water-colours, prints.
Tu.-Sa. 9-5; Su. 2-5.

ILLINOIS STATE MUSEUM
Spring and Edward Streets, Springfield, Illinois 62706
Geology. Palaeontology. Botany. Herbarium. Natural history. Anthropology. Indian material. Paintings, sculpture, graphics by Illinois artists. Oriental porcelain textiles, bronzes. American and foreign firearms. Furniture, coverlets. Clocks. Miniature dioramas showing history of Illinois. Dolls.
M.-Sa. 8.30-5; Su. 2-5. Closed New Year, Easter, Thanksgiving, Christmas.

LINCOLN HOME STATE MEMORIAL
430 S. 8th Street, Springfield, Illinois 62702
House (1839) was home of Abraham Lincoln. Original and period furniture. Paintings.
Daily 9-5. Closed New Year, Thanksgiving, Christmas.

OLD STATE CAPITOL
5th and Adams Streets, Springfield, Illinois 62706
Former Statehouse (1839-76). Original and period furnishings.
Daily 9-5. Closed Christmas, New Year, Thanksgiving.

VACHEL LINDSAY ASSOCIATION
502 S. State Street, Springfield, Illinois 62704
House (1824) was home of Vachel Lindsay. First edition of Lindsay's poems. Recordings by him. Drawing.
June 1 - Sept. 11, daily 9-5. Other times by appointment.

LINCOLN HOMESTEAD STATE SHRINE
Rural Route 1, Springfield, Kentucky 40069
Museums based on Lincoln Home and Francis Berry House. Natural history. Local history. Blacksmith's shop. Open-air museum.
Apr. 30 - Oct. 1, daily 8-6.

CONNECTICUT VALLEY HISTORICAL MUSEUM
William Pynchon Memorial Building, Springfield, Massachusetts 01103
17th-18th century period rooms. 17th-19th century business records. Local history. Miniatures. China. Glass. Pewter.
Tu.-Sa. 1-5; Su. 2-5. Closed August and Su. July.

GEORGE WALTER VINCENT SMITH ART MUSEUM
222 State Street, Springfield, Massachusetts 01103
Chinese porcelain, enamels, jades, robes. Japanese porcelain, ivories, lacquers, weapons, armour, pottery. 19th-20th century American paintings, sculpture. European glass, furniture, textiles, paintings, armour.
Tu.-Sa. 1-5; Su. 2-5. Closed public holidays, Aug.

MUSEUM OF FINE ARTS
49 Chestnut Street, Springfield, Massachusetts 01103
14th-20th century European paintings, watercolours, prints, lithographs, wood engravings. 18th-20th century American paintings, watercolours. 17th-18th century European furniture, ceramics, silver. Japanese prints. Chinese bronzes, ceramics.
Tu.-Sa. 1-5; Su. 2-5. Closed Aug., public holidays.

NATIONAL BASKETBALL HALL OF FAME
Springfield College Campus, Springfield, Massachusetts 01100
History of basketball.
Sept.-June, M.-Sa. 10-5; Su. 1-5. July-Aug., M.-Sa. 10-5. Closed Thanksgiving, Dec. 25, Jan. 1.

SPRINGFIELD ARMOURY MUSEUM
Federal Street, Springfield, Massachusetts 01101
In Armoury (1847). History of American firearms.
M.-Sa. 10-5; Su., public holidays 1-5. Closed New Year, Thanksgiving, Christmas.

SPRINGFIELD SCIENCE MUSEUM
236 State Street, Springfield, Massachusetts 01103
Geology. Mineralogy. Astronomy. Planetarium. Natural history. Anthropology. Ethnology. Indian artifacts. Textiles.
Sept. 1 - June 30, Tu.-Sa. 1-5; Su. 2-5. July 1 - Aug. 31, Tu.-Sa. 2-5. Closed New Year, July 4, Thanksgiving, Christmas.

TRAILSIDE MUSEUM
Forest Park, Springfield, Massachusetts 01108
Geology. Mineralogy. Botany. Natural history. Indian artifacts. Children's Museum. Junior Museum.
Daily 11-4. Closed New Year, Thanksgiving, Christmas.

MUSEUM OF GREENE COUNTY HISTORICAL SOCIETY
397 E. Central Street, Springfield, Missouri 65802
Local history.
M.-F. 8.30 a.m. - 9 p.m.; Sa. 8.30-5. Closed public holidays.

SPRINGFIELD ART MUSEUM
111 E. Brookside Drive, Springfield, Missouri 65804
American paintings and sculpture. European and American prints and ceramics.
M. 8-5; Tu.-Th. 8-5, 6.30-9.30; F., Sa. 8-5; Su. 1-5. Closed public holidays.

MUSEUM OF SPRINGFIELD HISTORICAL SOCIETY
126 Morris Avenue, Springfield, New Jersey 07081
In Cannon Ball House (1760). Local history. Prints. Drawings. Decorative arts. Costumes. Coins.
Sept. 15 - June 30: Su. 2-4. Other days by appointment.

CLARK COUNTY HISTORICAL SOCIETY MUSEUM
Memorial Hall, 300 W. Main Street, Springfield, Ohio 45504
Mineralogy. Local history. Prehistoric Indian artifacts. Furniture. 19th century portraits of prominent Springfield citizens. Early tools, farm equipment.
M., Tu., Th. 1-4, W., Sa. 9-4, alternate Su. 2-4.30. Closed public holidays.

SPRINGFIELD ART CENTER
107 Cliff Park Road, Springfield, Ohio 45501
Paintings, drawings, prints, sculpture by contemporary Ohio artists.
Tu.-F. 9-5; Sa. 9-3; Su. 2-4. Closed Aug. 1-31 and week before Easter, Thanksgiving, Christmas.

EUREKA SCHOOL HOUSE
Route 11, Springfield, Vermont 05156
Oldest schoolhouse in Vermont (1790). Period furnishings.
June-Oct., daily 10-5.

SPRINGFIELD ART AND HISTORICAL SOCIETY
9 Elm Hill, Springfield, Vermont 05156
Primitive portraits. Bennington pottery. Richard Lee pewter. Dolls.
Apr. 1 - Jan. 30, M.-F. 12-4.30. Other times by appointment. Closed public holidays.

SPRINGFIELD CENTER

DENNY'S TOY MUSEUM
Springfield Center, New York 13468
Old toys.
May 15-Oct. 15, daily 9.30-8. Rest of year by appointment.

SPRING PLACE

VANN HOUSE
U.S. Highway 76, Spring Place, Georgia 30705
House (1804), with furniture and personal possessions of the Vann family.
May 1 - Sept. 30; Tu.-Sa. 9-5.30; Su. 2-5.30. Oct. 1 - Apr. 30: Tu.-Sa. 9-5; Su. 2-5. Closed Thanksgiving, Christmas.

SPRINGS

SPRINGS MUSEUM
Springs, Pennsylvania 15562
Fossils. Local history. Folklore. Pioneer tools. Furniture.
Memorial Day - Oct. 14: M.-Sa. 11-5.

SPRINGVILLE

MUSEUM OF CONCORD HISTORICAL SOCIETY MUSEUM
98 E. Main Street, Springville, New York 14141
Local history. Indian artifacts. Agriculture. Costume. Toys. Musical instruments.
M., Th. 2-5. Other times by appointment. Closed New Year, Thanksgiving, Christmas.

SPRINGVILLE HIGH SCHOOL ART GALLERY
4th Street S. and 1st Street E., Springville, Utah 84663
18th-20th century American paintings, sculpture.
Sept.-May, M.-F. 9-4.30. June-Aug. M.-F. 2-8.

SPRINGVILLE MUSEUM OF ART
Springville, Utah 84663
16th-18th century European paintings, sculpture, graphics. Contemporary American paintings.
Tu.-F. 10-5; Sa., Su. 2-5. Apr. 1-30, Feb. 1-28: M.-F. 10-9. Closed Mar. 18-31, Dec. 18-31.

SPRUCE

HALTINERS' HALL OF ANCIENT MAN
Spruce, Michigan 48762
Local history. Archaeology. Indian artifacts.
By appointment.

SPRUCE PINE

MUSEUM OF NORTH CAROLINA MINERALS
Blue Ridge Parkway, Gillespie Gap, Spruce Pine, North Carolina 28777
Geology. Mineralogy. Commercial uses of N. Carolina minerals.
June 1 - Labour Day, daily 9-5. Sept. 1 - Oct. 31, Sa., Su. 9-5.

STAATSBURG

MILLS MUSEUM
Ogden and Ruth Livingston Mills State Park, Route 9, Staatsburg, New York 12580
In Ogden Mills House (1775, remodelled in French Renaissance style 1895). Louis XIV and Louis XV furniture. Indian and Turkish carpets. Tapestries. Ming dynasty Chinese art.
Apr. 1 - Oct. 31, daily 10.30-4. Nov. 1 - Mar. 31: Sa., Su., public holidays 10.30-4. Closed Dec. 20 - Jan. 2.

STAFFORD

JUSTIN SMITH MORRILL HOMESTEAD
Stafford, Vermont 05672
House (c.1840). Original Morrill furnishings, and personal possessions.
Memorial Day - Oct. 15, Tu.-Su. 9-5.

STAMFORD

STAMFORD HISTORICAL SOCIETY MUSEUM
713 Bedford Street, Stamford, Connecticut 06901
In Hoyt Farmhouse (1700). Local history. Farm implements. Craft tools. 17th-18th century Americana. Furnishings. Household equipment. Costumes. Quilts. Fans.
By appointment.

STAMFORD MUSEUM AND NATURE CENTER
39 Scofieldtown Road, Stamford, Connecticut 06903
Geology. Conchology. Palaeontology. Botany. Natural history. Astronomy. Paintings. Sculpture. Graphics. Indian material.
M.-Sa. 9-5; Su., public holidays 2-6. Closed Thanksgiving, Christmas, New Year.

MAPLE SUGAR MUSEUM
Windy Ridge Road, Stamford, New York 12167
Equipment for making maple-sugar by old process.
June 15 - Sept. 1, daily 9-6. Sept. 2 - June 14: Sa., Su. 9-6.

STANDISH

DANIEL MARRETT HOUSE
Route 25, Standish, Maine 04084
House (1789). Period furnishings. Family portraits.
June 1 - Sept. 30: Tu., Th., Su. 1-5.

STANFORD

STANFORD UNIVERSITY MUSEUM AND ART GALLERY
Museum Way, Stanford, California 94305
Oriental art. Greek, Roman, Egyptian art. Cypriot antiquities. Primitive art. 16th-20th century European paintings, sculpture, graphics.
Tu.-F. 10-5; Sa., Su. 1-5.

WILLIAM WHITLEY STATE PARK AND SHRINE
Stanford, Kentucky 40484
William Whitley House (1792), with period furnishings. Built to make it impregnable to Indian attack, with thick walls, rifle posts, heavily shuttered windows.
June 1 - Aug. 31, daily 9-5. Sept. 1 - May 31, Tu.-Su. 9-5.

JUDITH BASIN MUSEUM
Stanford, Montana 59479
Local history. Indian artifacts.
June 1 - Aug. 31, M.-F. 9-5; Sa., Su. 1-5.

STANTON

STANTON COUNTY HISTORICAL MUSEUM
Stanton, Nebraska 68779
Local history. Indian artifacts.
Pilger Museum is also in the care of the Society.
May-Oct., Su., public holidays 2-4.

STARKE

MUSEUM OF THE NORTH AND THE SOUTH
Route 1, Kingsley Lake, Starke, Florida 32091
Material relating to the Revolutionary and Civil Wars. Weapons. Furniture and furnishings. Paintings. Documents. Friendship Estate House (1900) is in the care of the Museum.
M.-Sa. 9-6; Su. 1-7. Closed New Year, Easter, Thanksgiving, Christmas.

STATE COLLEGE

DUNN-SEILER MUSEUM
Dept. of Geology and Geography, Mississippi State University, State College, Mississippi 39762
Geology. Mineralogy. Palaeontology. Indian artifacts.
M.-F. 8-5. Closed public holidays, university vacations.

COLLEGE OF EARTH AND MINERAL SCIENCES MUSEUM
State College, Pennsylvania 16802
Geology. Mineralogy. Palaeontology. Natural history. Science. Technology.
M.-Sa. 9-5; Su. 1-5. Closed Easter, Thanksgiving, and Sa., Su. nearest to New Year, Memorial Day, July 4, Labour Day and Christmas.

JUNIOR MUSEUM OF CENTRAL PENNSYLVANIA
P.O. Box 134, State College, Pennsylvania 16801
Minerals. Fossils.
By appointment.

STATESVILLE

STATESVILLE ARTS AND SCIENCE MUSEUM
Pump Station Road, Statesville, North Carolina 28677
Geology. Anthropology. Works by North Carolina artists.
Su. 2-5. Other times by appointment.

STAUNTON

WOODROW WILSON BIRTHPLACE
24 N. Coalter Street, Staunton, Virginia 24401
House (1846). Wilson family furniture. Memorabilia of the President.
Mar. 1 - May 30, Sept. 1 - Nov. 30: daily 9-5; June 1 - Aug. 31, daily 8.30-6, Dec. 1 - Feb. 28, M.-Sa. 9-5. Closed New Year, Thanksgiving, Christmas.

STEAMBOAT SPRINGS

TREAD OF PIONEERS
505 Oak Street, Steamboat Springs, Colorado 80477
Local and mining history. Indian artifacts. Skiing history.
June 1 - Aug. 31, daily 1-9.

STEELES TAVERN

CYRUS H. McCORMICK MEMORIAL MUSEUM
Steeles Tavern, Virginia 24476
Agricultural history. Development of farm machinery. McCormick's workshop and gristmill.
May 1 - Oct. 14: M.-F. 9-5; Sa., Su. 1-5.

STEPHENVILLE

STEPHENVILLE HISTORICAL HOUSE MUSEUM
525 E. Washington Street, Stephenville, Texas 76401
In Berry House (1869). Period rooms. Local history. Geology. Indian arrowheads. Barbed wire. Photographs.
Sa., Su. 2-5.

STERLING

OVERLAND TRAIL MUSEUM
1320 S. 4th Avenue, Sterling, Colorado 80751
Palaeontology. Petrified wood. Archaeology. Pioneer and Indian history. Indian arrowheads. Blacksmith's work. Branding irons.
May 1 - Sept. 14, M.-Sa. 9.30-5. Su., public holidays 10.30-5.

STERLING AND ROCK FALLS HISTORICAL SOCIETY MUSEUM
212 3rd Avenue, Sterling, Illinois 61081
Local history. Industry. Indian material. Paintings.
Sa. 1-4.

STEVENSON

SKAMANIA COUNTY HISTORICAL SOCIETY
Stevenson, Washington 98648
Local history. Indian artifacts.
W. 1-4.

STEVENSVILLE

ST. MARY'S MISSION
Stevensville, Montana 59840
1st church in Montana (1841). Apothecary shop and hospital (1860). Archaeology. Agriculture. Indian artifacts.
May 1 - Sept. 30: daily 8-8. Oct. 1 - Apr. 30: dawn - dusk.

STILLWATER

WASHINGTON COUNTY HISTORICAL MUSEUM
602 N. Main Street, Stillwater, Minnesota 55082
Pioneer life. Indian artifacts. Costumes. Lumberjack tools. Children's museum.
Warden's house (1856) for Old State Prison is in the care of the Museum.
May 1 - Oct. 31: Tu., Th., Sa., Su. 2-5. Other times by appointment.

SARATOGA NATIONAL HISTORICAL PARK MUSEUM
R.D.1, Box 113-C, Stillwater, New York 12170
Material illustrating Burgoyne's campaign and Battle of Saratoga (1777). John Neilson house (1775), American headquarters during Battle of Saratoga.
Daily, public holidays 9-5. Closed Thanksgiving, Christmas, New Year.

GARDINER ART GALLERY
Whitehurst Hall, Oklahoma State University, Stillwater, Oklahoma 74074
Contemporary American drawings, prints.
M.-F. 8-5; Sa. 9-12; Su. 2-5. Closed public holidays.

OKLAHOMA STATE UNIVERSITY, HERBARIUM
104 Life Sciences E., Stillwater, Oklahoma 74074
Flora of United States, especially Oklahoma and Mexico.
M.-F. 8-5. Other times by appointment.

STILWELL

GOLDA'S OLD MILL
Oklahoma Route 51, Stilwell, Oklahoma 74960
Grist mill (c.1820), still operating.
Daily 8-5.

STOCKBRIDGE

CHESTERWOOD
Box 248, Stockbridge, Massachusetts 01262
Studio (1897) of the sculptor Danial Chester French. Works by French. Material illustrating his early days in Concord.
June 1 - Labour Day, daily 10-5. Labour Day - Columbus Day, Sa., Su. 10-5.

HISTORICAL ROOM
Stockbridge Library, Stockbridge, Massachusetts 01262
Local history. Personal possessions and memorabilia of Cyrus W. Field and Jonathan Edwards. Inventions by Anson Clark.
Tu.-Sa. 10-5. Closed public holidays.

MERWIN HOUSE
39 Main Street, Stockbridge, Massachusetts 01262
House (c.1825). European and American furniture, decorative arts.
June-Oct., Tu.-Sa. 10-12.

MISSION HOUSE
Main and Sergeant Streets, Stockbridge, Massachusetts 01262
House (1739), home of John Sergeant, first missionary to the Stockbridge Indians. 18th century furnishings, decorations, portraits. Indian relics.
May 30 - Oct. 30, M.-Sa. 10-6; Su. 2-6.

NAUMKEAG GARDENS
Prospect Street, Stockbridge, Massachusetts 01262
House (1880), former home of Joseph Choate, ambassador to England. Period furnishings. Formal gardens.
May 1 - Sept. 5, Tu.-Su. 10-5.30. Sept. 5 - Oct. 1, Sa., Su. 10-4.

OLD CORNER HOUSE
Main Street, Stockbridge, Massachusetts 01262
House (1810). Paintings, by Norman Rockwell.
Daily 10-5. Closed Thanksgiving, Christmas.

WATERLOO FARM MUSEUM
9998 Waterloo-Munith Road, Stockbridge, Michigan 49285
Mid-19th century farm, now restored as museum. Original furnishings. Agricultural implements. Early pioneer handicrafts.
June 1 - Sept. 30, Tu.-Su. 1-4.

STOCKTON

MUSEUM OF THE PACIFIC CENTER FOR WESTERN HISTORICAL STUDIES
University of the Pacific, Stockton, California 95204
Local history. Maps. Photographs.
M.-F. 8.30-5; Sa. 9-1; Su. by appointment. Closed public holidays.

PIONEER MUSEUM AND HAGGIN GALLERIES
1201 N. Pershing Avenue, Stockton, California 95203
California pioneer history. Furnishings, clothing, domestic equipment and other possessions of early settlers. Indian artifacts. 19th century French and American paintings. European, American and Oriental decorative arts. Textiles. Glass. Folk art.
Tu.-Su. 1.30-5. Closed New Year, Thanksgiving, Christmas.

BOTANICAL MUSEUM
University of the Pacific, Weber Hall, Stockton, California 95204
Herbarium.
Admission times dependent on class schedules.

STONEHAM

MUSEUM OF STONEHAM HISTORICAL SOCIETY
36 William Street, Stoneham, Massachusetts 02180
Building (1867), formerly shoe shop. Local history.
By appointment.

STONE MILLS

AGRICULTURAL MUSEUM
Route 180, Stone Mills, New York
Farm implements. Tools. Domestic equipment.
July 1 - Sept. 13: Tu., Th., Su. 1-4.

STONE MOUNTAIN

STONE MOUNTAIN PARK
Box 778, Stone Mountain, Georgia 30083
Indian arrowheads and artifacts. Civil War material.
Thornton house (1790), Kingston House (1815), Dickey house (1850) are in the care of the Park. Dickey house contains an Auto and Music museum.
May 1 - Sept. 30, 10-9. Oct. 1 - Apr. 30, 10-5. Closed Christmas.

STONEWALL

LYNDON B. JOHNSON NATIONAL HISTORIC SITE
State Park Road 49, Stonewall, Texas 78671
Reconstructed house of parents of President Johnson. President's birthplace. Family furnishings.
Daily 9-5. Closed Christmas.

LYNDON B. JOHNSON STATE PARK, VISITOR CENTER
Highway 290, Stonewall, Texas 78671
Exhibits on Indian tribes of Central Texas, Spanish colonists and priests, farmers and ranchers. Reconstruction of Behrens Cabin (c.1870).
May 1 - Sept. 30, daily 9-6. Oct. 1 - Apr. 30, daily 8-5.

STONINGTON

LIGHTHOUSE MUSEUM
Water Street, Stonington Point, Stonington, Connecticut 06378
Maritime history. Whaling. Sealing. Costumes. Paintings. Village and farm life since 1649. Relics of Battle of Stonington (1814). Early portraits.
July 1 - Sept. 30, Tu.-Su. 11-4.30.

STONINGTON HISTORICAL SOCIETY MUSEUM
P.O. Box 103, Stonington, Connecticut 06378
In Whitehall Mansion (1750). Furniture. Household equipment. Silver. Pewter. Paintings. Local history.
Su.-F. 2-4.

STONY BROOK

GRIST MILL
Stony Brook, New York 11778
Mill (1699).
M.-Sa. 10-5; Su. 2-5.

SUFFOLK MUSEUM AND CARRIAGE HOUSE
Christian Avenue, Stony Brook, New York 11778
Paintings by Mount family, with sketches, letters, diaries. Decorative arts. Natural history.
Archaeology. Horse-drawn vehicles.
Daily 10-5. Closed Christmas, Thanksgiving. Carriage House closed Nov. 1 - Apr. 15.

STONY POINT

STONY POINT BATTLEFIELD RESERVATION
Route 9W, Stony Point, New York 10980
Site of Revolutionary War battle (1779). Original earthworks Museum, with exhibits relating to the War.
May 1 - Oct. 31, daily 10-5.

STORRS

WILLIAM BENTON MUSEUM OF ART
University of Connecticut, Storrs, Connecticut 06268
American paintings. Prints and drawings by Käthe Kollwitz. Sculpture. Decorative arts.
M.-Sa. 10-4.30; Su. 1.30-5.30. Closed Aug., public holidays.

MANSFIELD HISTORICAL SOCIETY MUSEUM
Route 32 and South Eagleville Road, Storrs, Connecticut 06268
18th-19th century rural life. Agriculture. Industry. Costumes.
June 1 - Aug. 31, Th. 2-5. Closed Sept. - May.

STOUGHTON

MARY BAKER EDDY HISTORIC HOUSE
133 Central Street, Stoughton, Massachusetts 02072
Home (1868-70) of founder of Christian Science. Memorabilia of Mrs. Eddy.
May-Oct., Tu.-Su. 10-5.

MUSEUM OF STOUGHTON HISTORICAL SOCIETY
Lucius Clapp Memorial Building, 6 Park Street, Stoughton, Massachusetts 02072
History of Stoughton.
Su., public holidays 2-7. Other times by appointment.

STOUGHTON HISTORICAL SOCIETY MUSEUM
112 S. Page Street, Stoughton, Wisconsin 53589
In Former Universal Church (1858). Local history. Early settlement of area. Norwegian Rosemalling. Portraits. Costumes. Musical instruments. Local wagon-building industry.
May 15 - Sept. 30: Sa., Su., public holidays 1.30-4.30.

STOUTSVILLE

MARK TWAIN BIRTHPLACE MEMORIAL SHRINE
Route 2, Stoutsville, Missouri 65283
House (1834). Material relating to life and work of Mark Twain.
M.-Sa. 10-5; Sept. 1 - May 31, Su. 12-5. June 1 - Aug. 31, Su. 12-6.

STOW

MUSEUM OF RANDALL MEMORIAL LIBRARY
Stow, Massachusetts 01775
Local history. Antique furniture.
M., Tu., F. 1.30-8; W. 9-11, 1.30-8; Sa. 1.30-5. Closed public holidays, July 1 - Aug. 31.

STRAFFORD

JUSTIN SMITH MORRILL HOMESTEAD
Justin Smith Morrill Highway, Strafford, Vermont 05072
House (1841). Period furnishings. Justin Smith Morrill memorabilia.
Memorial Day-Mid Oct., Tu.-Su. 9-5.

STRASBURG

EAGLE AMERICAN SHOP AND GUN MUSEUM
R.D.1, Strasburg, Pennsylvania 17579
In former mill (1740). History of firearms. Local history. Indian material. Costumes. Medical history. Children's museum.
M.-F. 10-5; Sa., Su. 10-7. Closed Thanksgiving and Dec. 1 - Feb. 21.

RAILROAD MUSEUM OF PENNSYLVANIA
P.O. Box 15, Strasburg, Pennsylvania 17579
Railway history. Operational line. Locomotives. Coaches. Equipment. Mementoes.
M.-F. 9-5; Sa., Su. 10-7.

STRATFORD

STRATFORD HISTORICAL SOCIETY MUSEUM
967 Academy Hill, Stratford, Connecticut 06497
In Capt. David Judson house (1723). Local history. Period furnishings. 18th-19th century household equipment. Costumes. Decorative arts. Glass. China. Silver. Agricultural implements. Slave quarters.
W., Sa., Su. 11-5. Closed Dec. 1 - Mar. 31.

STRATFORD HALL
Stratford, Virginia 22558
House (1725-30), home of Robert E. Lee family. 18th century furniture, textiles, decorative arts, glass and china. Farm tools, implements.
Daily 9-4.30. Closed Christmas.

STROUDSBURG

MUSEUM OF MONROE COUNTY HISTORICAL SOCIETY
9th and Main Streets, Stroudsburg, Pennsylvania 18360
Local history. Furniture. Costumes. Indian artifacts.
Bell Schoolhouse (1871) is in the care of the Society.
Tu. 1-4. Other days by appointment.

STUART

ELLIOTT MUSEUM
Route 5, Hutchinson Island, Stuart, Florida 33494
Local history. Indian material. Circus history. Costumes. Transport. Natural history. Paintings. Sculpture. Graphics.
Daily 1-5.

HOUSE OF REFUGE MUSEUM
Route 5, Hutchinson Island, Stuart, Florida 33494
House (1875). Local history. Natural history. Aquarium.
Tu.-Sa. 1-5. Closed Christmas.

STURBRIDGE

OLD STURBRIDGE VILLAGE
Sturbridge, Massachusetts 01566
Recreated New England village, 1790-1840. Museum based on 35 old houses, shops and workshops. Furniture. Domestic equipment. Tools. Handicrafts. Costumes. Agriculture. Firearms. Early New England paintings.
Mar. 15 - Nov. 30, daily 9.30-5.30. Dec. 1 - Mar. 14, daily 10-4.

STURBRIDGE AUTO MUSEUM
Route 20, Sturbridge, Massachusetts 01566
Old automobiles, including steam and electric cars.
June 1 - Aug. 31: daily 10.30-9.30. Sept. 1 - Oct. 31: daily 10.30-5.30. Apr., May, Nov.: Sa., Su. 12.30-5.30.

STURGEON BAY

DOOR COUNTY HISTORICAL SOCIETY MUSEUM
4th and Michigan Streets, Sturgeon Bay, Wisconsin 54235
Local history. Maritime and agricultural history.
Eagle Lighthouse (1869) is in the care of the Society.
May 15 - Oct. 15: Tu.-Sa. 10-12, 1-5.

SUDBURY

LONGFELLOW'S WAYSIDE INN
Sudbury, Massachusetts 01776
Inn (1706). Colonial period furniture.
Redstone School (1787) and a replica of an 18th century water-driven cornmill are in the care of the Inn.
Daily 9-9. Closed Christmas.

SUFFIELD

HATHEWAY HOUSE
Main Street, Suffield, Connecticut 06078
House (1760). Hand blocked French wallpaper (c.1780). 18th century furniture.
Daily, May 15 - Oct. 15 1-5.

SUISUN

SOLANO COUNTY HISTORICAL SOCIETY MUSEUM
Route 1, Box 292, Suisun Valley Road, Suisun, California 94585
Local history.
By appointment.

SULLIVAN

MERAMEC STATE PARK NATURE MUSEUM
Sullivan, Missouri 63080
Botany. Zoology. Archaeology.
June-Aug., daily 8-5.

SULLIVAN'S ISLAND

FORT SUMTER NATIONAL MONUMENT
Box 428, Sullivan's Island, South Carolina 29482
Military history.
Daily 8.30-5. Closed Christmas.

SULPHUR

TRAVERTINE NATURE CENTER
P.O. Box 201, Sulphur, Oklahoma 73086
Herbarium.
May 1 - Oct. 31, daily 8-9. Nov. 1 - Apr. 30, daily 8-5. Closed New Year, Christmas.

SUMTER

MUSEUM OF SUMTER COUNTY HISTORICAL SOCIETY
Court House, Room 103, Sumter, South Carolina 29150
Local history.
W. 3.30-5.

SUNBURY

FORT AUGUSTA
1150 N. Front Street, Sunbury, Pennsylvania 17801
Outdoor scale model of Fort Augusta (1750). Indian artifacts. Military relics.
May 1 - Oct. 31: Tu.-Sa. 8.30-5; Su. 1-5. Nov. 1 - Apr. 30: Tu.-Sa. 9-4.30; Su. 1-4.30. Closed New Year, Good Friday, Easter, Thanksgiving, Christmas.

SUNCOCK

AUDUBON NATURE CENTER
Bear Brook State Park, Suncock, New Hampshire 03275
Geology, ecology and natural history of New Hampshire.
June 24 - Labour Day: Tu.-Su. 10-5.

SUN PRAIRIE

SUN PRAIRIE HISTORICAL LIBRARY AND MUSEUM
115 E. Main Street, Sun Prairie, Wisconsin 53590
Local history.
May 1 - Labour Day, W.-Su. 2-4.

SUNSET

OLD WEST MUSEUM
Route 1, Sunset, Texas 76270
Exhibits on early ranchers, settlers, cowboys. Wells Fargo Express. Paintings of local scenes. Documents of Republic of Texas.
Daily 8-6.

SUNSET TRADING POST AND OLD WEST MUSEUM
Route 1, Sunset, Texas 76270
Local history. Pioneer agriculture. Paintings. Graphics. Sculpture. Archaeology. Indian collection. Oil history.
Daily 8-6.

SUPERIOR

DOUGLAS COUNTY HISTORICAL MUSEUM
906 E. 2nd Street, Superior, Wisconsin 54880
In former Mark Pattison mansion (1890). Period furnishings. Local history. Indian artifacts. Sioux Indian portraits. Western American prints. Anthropology. Ethnology. Geology. Local flora. Japanese ceramics. Firearms. Costumes. Toys.
Tu.-F. 10-12; Sa. 1-5; Su. 2-5. Closed Dec. 15-25.

SURRY

ROLFE-WARREN HOUSE
Route 31, Surry, Virginia 23883
House (1652), on land given by Chief Powhatan to his daughter, Pocahantas, on her marriage to John Rolfe. 17th-18th century furnishings. Indian relics.
Apr. 1 - Oct. 31, daily 9.30-5.

SURRY NUCLEAR INFORMATION CENTER
Route 650, Surry County, Surry, Virginia 23883
Museum of nuclear energy.
M.-Sa. 10-4; Su. 1-6. Closed New Year, Christmas.

SUSANVILLE

LASSEN COUNTY HISTORICAL SOCIETY MUSEUM
North Weatherlow Street, Susanville, California 96130
History of Lassen County.
May 1 - Sept. 30, Tu.-Su. 10-6. Closed Oct.-Apr. 30.

SUSSEX

SPACE FARMS MUSEUM
Beemerville Road, Sussex, New Jersey 07461
Tools. Household equipment. Agriculture. Wildlife specimens. Musical instruments.
Daily 9-6.

SWAMPSCOTT

ATLANTIC 1
Burrill Street, Swampscott, Massachusetts 01907
History of fire-fighting.
Daily 8-8.

MARY BAKER EDDY HISTORIC HOUSE
23 Paradise Road, Swampscott, Massachusetts 01907
Home of Mary Baker Eddy at time of her discovery of Christian Science (1866). Memorabilia of Mrs. Eddy.
May 15 - Oct. 14, M.-Sa. 10-5; Su. 2-5. Oct. 15 - May 14, M.-Sa. 10-3.

SWAMPSCOTT HISTORICAL SOCIETY MUSEUM
99 Paradise Road, Swampscott, Massachusetts 01907
In John Humphrey House (1634). Local history.
M.-F. 2-5.

SWANSBORO

SWANSBORO HISTORICAL ASSOCIATION MUSEUM
21 Main Street, Swansboro, North Carolina 28584
Local and maritime history. Indian artifacts. Archaeology.
By appointment.

SWANSEA

MARTIN HOUSE
22 Stoney Hill Road, Swansea, Massachusetts 02777
House (1728). 17th-19th century furnishings, pewter, silver, paintings, prints.
May-Sept. daily 10-6.

MUSEUM OF SWANSEA HISTORICAL SOCIETY
Luthers Corners, Swansea Center, Massachusetts 02777
Building (1815) was formerly Luther General Store. Local history. Indian artifacts.
July 1 - Aug. 31, Su. 2-5.

SWARTHMORE

FRIENDS HISTORICAL LIBRARY OF SWARTHMORE COLLEGE
Swarthmore College, Swarthmore, Pennsylvania 19081
History of Society of Friends. Paintings, engravings, prints, relics of the Society. John Woolman's diary.
M.-F. 8.30-4.30; Sa. 9-12. Closed Aug. 1-31, Sa. during vacations.

SWEETWATER

NOLAN COUNTY HISTORICAL MUSEUM
219 W. 3rd Street, Sweetwater, Texas 79556
History of Nolan County. Furniture. Pioneer life. Early photographs of settlers.
W., Su. 2-5.

SYOSSET

NASSAU COUNTY HISTORICAL MUSEUM
Eisenhower Park, E. Meadow, Syosset, New York 11791
American history. Indian material. Agricultural implements. Domestic equipment. Handicrafts. Toys. Costumes. Aviation history.
17 historic buildings (1710-1934) are in the care of the Museum.
Museum: daily 9-5. Closed Christmas, New Year, Thanksgiving.

SYRACUSE

MUSEUM OF HAMILTON COUNTY HISTORICAL SOCIETY
E. Avenue A, Syracuse, Kansas 67878
Local history. Indian artifacts.
M.-Sa. 12-4; Su., public holidays 2-5. Closed Christmas.

CANAL MUSEUM
Weighlock Building, Erie Boulevard E., Syracuse, New York 13202
In former administrative building (1849-50) of Erie Canal. History of canals. Models. Photographs. Prints.
Tu., W., F. 12-5; Th. 12-9; Sa. 10-5; Su. 2-6. Other times by appointment. Closed public holidays.

EVERSON MUSEUM OF ART
401 Harrison Street, Syracuse, New York 13202
American paintings. 17th-19th century Chinese, English and American porcelain and pottery. 19th-20th century American and English sculpture. American prints and drawings.
Tu.-F., Su. 12-5; Sa. 10-5. Closed public holidays.

JOE AND EMILY LOWE ART CENTER
Syracuse University, 309 University Place, Syracuse, New York 13210
Japanese and Korean ceramics. 19th-20th century American paintings, sculpture, graphics. Art Nouveau. Scandinavian industrial design. European prints. Indian and African sculpture, textiles.
M.-F. 9-5, 7-10. Closed public holidays.

MUSEUM OF CANAL SOCIETY OF NEW YORK STATE
311 Montgomery Street, Syracuse, New York 13202
Canal history.
Daily 2-5.

MUSEUM OF GEORGE ARENTS RESEARCH LIBRARY
Syracuse University, Syracuse, New York 13210
Natural history. Science. Transport.
M.-F. 8.30-5; Sa. by appointment. Closed New Year, Labour Day, Thanksgiving, Christmas.

ONONDAGA HISTORICAL ASSOCIATION MUSEUM
311 Montgomery Street, Syracuse, New York 13202
History of Onondaga County and Syracuse. Iroquois Indian artifacts. Canal history. Paintings by local artists.
Daily 2-5. Other times by appointment.

DANIEL PARRISH WITTER AGRICULTURAL MUSEUM
New York State Fair Grounds, Syracuse, New York 13209
Agriculture and society in New York State before mechanisation. Farm implements and vehicles. Furnishings. Domestic equipment. Paintings.
W.-F. 9-12, Sa. 11-5, Su. 2-5.

TABLE ROCK

TABLE ROCK HISTORICAL SOCIETY MUSEUM
Table Rock, Nebraska 68447
Local history.
Log cabin (1854), St. John's Church (1877) and Table Rock Opera House (1893) are in the care of the Society.
May 1 - Sept. 30, Su. 2-5. Other times by appointment.

TACOMA

FORT NISQUALLY MUSEUM
Point Defiance Park, Tacoma, Washington 98407
Early Washington and Oregon relics and exhibits. History of Hudson Bay Company. Granary (1843). Factor's House (1853). Replicas of 7 buildings of old Fort Nisqually.
Nov. 1 - Mar. 30: Tu.-Sa. 1-4; Su., public holidays 1-4.30. Apr. 1 - May 30: Tu.-Sa. 1-5; Su., public holidays 1-6. June 1 - Oct. 31: M.-Sa. 1-6; Su., public holidays 1-7. Closed day after public holidays, Christmas.

HANDFORTH GALLERY
Public Library, 1102 S. Tacoma Avenue, Tacoma, Washington 98402
Paintings, drawings, etchings, lithographs by American and European artists.
M.-Th. 9-9; F., Sa. 9-6.

TACOMA ART MUSEUM
12th Street and Pacific Avenue, Tacoma, Washington 98402
19th-20th century American, European paintings. Sculpture. Prints. Drawings. Photographs. Decorative arts. Contemporary American glass, ceramics.
M.-F. 9-5; Sa. 10-4; Su. 2-5. Closed public holidays.

WASHINGTON STATE HISTORICAL SOCIETY MUSEUM
315 North Stadium Way (3), Tacoma, Washington 98403
Eskimo material. Natural history and history of Pacific North West. Indian and Alaskan paintings, documents, artifacts.
M.-F. 9-4. Closed national holidays.

TAHLEQUAH

MUSEUM OF NORTHEASTERN STATE COLLEGE
Tahlequah, Oklahoma 74464
Cherokee history and culture.
M.-F. 1-4; Sa., Su., public holidays 1-5, Easter week.

MURRELL HOME
Route 2, Tahlequah, Oklahoma 74464
House (1844). Original and period furnishings. Local history. Indian artifacts. Costumes. Paintings by contemporary American artists.
M.-F. 10-5; Sa., Su., public holidays 1-5.

TSA-LA-GI
Tahlequah, Oklahoma 74464
Living reconstruction of Cherokee village, c.1700.
May 1 - Sept. 6: Tu.-Su. 10-5.

TALLAHASSEE

FLORIDA STATE UNIVERSITY ART GALLERY
Fine Arts Building, Tallahassee, Florida 32306
Paintings. Sculpture. Graphics.
M.-F. 10-4; Sa., Su. 1-4. Closed college vacations.

LEMOYNE ART FOUNDATION
2321 Amelia Circle, Tallahassee, Florida 32301
Paintings. Sculpture.
Tu.-Sa. 11-5; Su. 2-5. Closed New Year, Christmas.

MUSEUM OF DIVISION OF ARCHIVES, HISTORY AND RECORDS MANAGEMENT
401 E. Gaines Street, Tallahassee, Florida 32304
History and archaeology of Florida.
M.-Sa. 10-5.

TALLAHASSEE JUNIOR MUSEUM
3945 Museum Drive, Tallahassee, Florida 32311
Natural history. Agriculture. Local history. Costumes. Pioneer farmhouse (1880) is in the care of the Museum.
Tu.-Sa. 9-5; Su. 2-5. Closed Easter, July 4, 2 weeks at Christmas.

TAMA

MUSEUM OF TAMA COUNTY HISTORICAL SOCIETY
111 E. 6th Street, Tama, Iowa 52339
Local history.
M.-F. 8-5; Sa. 8-12. Closed Court House holidays.

TAMPA

FLORIDA CENTER FOR THE ARTS
4202 E. Fowler Avenue, Tampa, Florida 33620
Contemporary American paintings, graphics, photography, sculpture. Folk art. Archaeology.
M.-Sa. 8-5; Su. 1-5. Closed University holidays.

MUSEUM OF HILLSBOROUGH COUNTY HISTORICAL COMMISSION
County Court House, Tampa, Florida 33604
Florida history, especially of Hillsborough County. Material relating to Spanish-American War.
M.-F. 9.30-4.30. Closed public holidays.

MUSEUM OF SCIENCE AND NATURAL HISTORY
1101 East River Cove, Tampa, Florida 33604
Geology. Astronomy. Botany. Entomology.
Tu.-Sa. 9.30-4; Su. 2-4.30.

TAMPA BAY ART CENTER
320 N. Boulevard, Tampa, Florida 33606
American painting and sculpture, with special emphasis on Latin-American art.
Tu.-Sa. 10-4.30.

TAMPA JUNIOR MUSEUM
1908 Dekle Avenue, Tampa, Florida 33606
Seminole Indian collection.
Day after Labour Day - July 31, Tu.-F. 9.30-4.30; Sa. 10-2. Closed Dec. 15 - Jan. 2, Gasparilla Day, Good F., Thanksgiving.

TAMWORTH

MUSEUM OF THE TAMWORTH HISTORICAL SOCIETY
Tamworth, New Hampshire 03886
Local history. Costumes.
May 1 - Oct. 31 by appointment.

TAOS

KIT CARSON MEMORIAL FOUNDATION
E. Kit Carson Street, Taos, New Mexico 87571
In Kit Carson and Blumenschein Home (1800). Mementoes of Carson's life and adventures. Furnishings. Personal possessions. Pioneer history.
The Museum also includes the Ferdinand Maxwell House (1860) and the Penitente Chapel, with exhibits illustrating prehistoric Indian culture in Taos and the S.W., Spanish Colonial Taos and the fur trade.
June 1 - Sept. 30, daily 7-8. Oct. 1-31, daily 7.30-6. Nov. 1 - Mar. 31, daily 8-5. Apr. 1 - May 30, daily 7.30-6.

GOVERNOR BENT MUSEUM
Bent Street, Taos, New Mexico 87571
In Governor Bent House (1825). Mineralogy. Anthropology. Archaeology. Indian artifacts. Paintings. Drawings. Prints.
Daily 9-5.

HARWOOD FOUNDATION
University of New Mexico, Taos, New Mexico 87571
Works by Taos artists. Primitive New Mexico wood sculpture, tinware. Persian miniatures.
M.-Sa. 10-5. Closed public holidays.

D. H. LAWRENCE RANCH
Taos, New Mexico 87571
Home of the novelist, D. H. Lawrence. Lawrence furnishings, memorabilia.
By appointment.

TAPPAN

GEORGE WASHINGTON MASONIC SHRINE
Route 9W, Tappan, New York 10983
De Windt House (1700) where Washington lived, 1780, 1783. Period rooms. Masonic material.
Daily 10-4.

TARENTUM

ALLE-KISKI MUSEUM
224 E. 7th Avenue and Lock Street, Tarentum, Pennsylvania 15084
Local history. Agriculture. Industry. Tarentum glass. 19th century furniture, tableware. Indian collection. Toys.
M.-F., Su. 1-4.

TARKIO

MULE BARN MUSEUM
Park Street, Tarkio, Missouri 64491
Natural history. Anthropology. Indian artifacts. Paintings by local artists. Theatre history.
May 1-Sept. 30, daily 10-6 Oct. 1-Apr. 30 by appointment.

TARRYTOWN

LYNDHURST
635 S. Broadway, Tarrytown, New York 10591
Early 19th century house, once home of Gen. William Paulding, George Merrit, Jay Gould. Victorian furnishings.
May 1 - Oct. 31, daily 10-5. Nov. 1 - Apr. 30, daily 10-4.

PHILIPSBURG MANOR
Route 9, Tarrytown, New York 10591
Manor House (1683). Early 18th century grist mill - trading complex. Operating grist mill.
Apr. 1 - Nov. 15, daily 10-5. Nov. 16 - Mar. 31, M.-F. 12-4; Sa., Su. 10-5.

MUSEUM OF HISTORICAL SOCIETY OF THE TARRYTOWNS
1 Grove Street, Tarrytown, New York 10591
Regional history. American Revolution. Costumes. Paintings. Washington Irving material.
Tu.-Sa. 2-4. Closed July 4, Thanksgiving, Christmas.

SUNNYSIDE
W. Sunnyside Lane, Tarrytown, New York 10591
House (1837-59) was home of Washington Irving. Period furnishings. Personal possessions of Irving, including his private library and manuscripts.
Apr. 1 - Nov. 15, daily 10-5. Nov. 16 - Mar. 31: M.-F. 12-4; Sa. 10-5.

TAUNTON

OLD COLONY HISTORICAL SOCIETY MUSEUM
66 Church Green, Taunton, Massachusetts 02780
18th century furniture, clothing, uniforms, guns, swords.
Oct.-June, M.-F. 10-4; Sa. 10-12. July-Sept., Tu.-Sa. 10-4; Su. 1-4.

TAVARES

LAKE COUNTY HISTORICAL SOCIETY MUSEUM
315 New Hampshire Avenue, Tavares, Florida 32778
Early history of Lake County. Furniture. Tools. Costumes.
M. and Sa. 2-5. Closed Aug.

TAWAS CITY

TAWAS HISTORIC INDIAN MUSEUM
1702 South Street, Tawas City, Michigan 48763
Indian history, artifacts.
Daily 10-5.

TAYLORSVILLE

JOHN EVANS HOUSE
Yohn Farm, Route 407, Taylorsville, Maryland
Log cabin (1764). Period furnishings.
By request.

TECUMSEH

MUSEUM OF JOHNSON COUNTY HISTORICAL SOCIETY
3rd and Lincoln Streets, Tecumseh, Nebraska 68450
Local history. Indian artifacts. Household equipment. World War I mementoes.
May-Oct., Su., public holidays 2-5.30. Other times by appointment.

TEKAMAH

BURT COUNTY MUSEUM
Tekamah, Nebraska 68061
Local history. Agriculture.
Sa. 12-5.

TELLURIDE

SAN MIGUEL HISTORICAL SOCIETY MUSEUM
Telluride, Colorado 81435
Geology. Mineralogy. Local and mining history. Costumes. Indian artifacts.
May 1 - Sept. 30, daily 1-5.

TEMPE

UNIVERSITY ART COLLECTIONS
Arizona State University, Matthews Center, Tempe, Arizona 85281
16th-20th century American paintings, sculpture, graphics, ceramics. 19th-20th century European paintings, graphics, sculpture. Mexican art. Photography.
M.-F. 8-5; Su. 1-5. Closed public holidays.

CENTER FOR METEORITE STUDIES
Arizona State University, Tempe, Arizona 85281
Meteorite collection.
M.-F. 8-5. Closed public holidays.

RAILROAD AND PIONEER MUSEUM
Cultural Activities Center, 318 W. Avenue G, Tempe, Texas 76501
In old Katy Depot. Railway relics. Pioneer memorabilia.
M.-F. 9-12, 2-5; Sa. 9-12. Closed Christmas week.

MUSEUM OF SLAVONIC BENEVOLENT ORDER OF THE STATE OF TEXAS
Main and French Streets, Tempe, Texas 76501
History of the Slavonic Order and community in Texas.
By appointment.

TEMPLETON

MUSEUM OF NARRAGANSETT HISTORICAL SOCIETY
The Common, Templeton, Massachusetts 01468
Building (1810). Local history.
Sa. 2-5.

TERRE HAUTE

EUGENE V. DEBS FOUNDATION
451 N. 8th Street, Terre Haute, Indiana 47808
Home of Eugene Debs (1890), furnished as it was during his occupancy, is in the care of the Foundation. Personal mementoes of Debs.
Su. 2-4.

GAR MEMORIAL HALL ASSOCIATION
219 Ohio Street, Terre Haute, Indiana 46618
House (1832) was first Land Bank in Western Indiana. Local history. Civil War material.
By appointment.

HISTORICAL MUSEUM OF THE WABASH VALLEY
1411 S. Sixth Street, Terre Haute, Indiana 47802
Paul Dresser, Eugene Debs and Chauncey Rose collections. Local history. Archaeology. Indian artifacts. Costumes. Textiles.
Paul Dresser birthplace (1850) is in the care of the Museum.
Su.-F. 1-4. Museum closed public holidays. Paul Dresser Birthplace closed Oct. - Apr.

INDIANA STATE UNIVERSITY
Turman Gallery, Terre Haute, Indiana 47809
Paintings. Sculpture.
M.-F. 8-5. Closed Aug. 17-31.

SHELDON SWOPE ART GALLERY
25 South 7th Street, Terre Haute, Indiana 47801
Archaeology. Primitive and Oriental drawings, decorative arts. 19th-20th century American paintings, sculpture. Renaissance and modern European art. Glass.
Sept. 9 - July 26, W.-Sa. 12-5; Tu, 12-5, 7-9.30; Su. 2-5. Closed public holidays.

TEXARKANA

TEXARKANA HISTORICAL SOCIETY MUSEUM
219 State Line Avenue, Texarkana, Texas 75501
Local history.
M.-F. 10-4. Closed Christmas, New Year, July 4, Labour Day, Thanksgiving.

THE DALLES

FORT DALLES MUSEUM
16th and Garrison Streets, The Dalles, Oregon 97058
In Fort Dalles Surgeon's quarters (1856). Local and military history. Furniture. Weapons. Pictures.
May 1 - Sept. 30: M., W.-Su. 9-5. Oct. 1 - Apr. 30: W.-Su. 12-4.

NICHOLS MUSEUM
601 Union Street, The Dalles, Oregon 97058
In Old St. Paul's Episcopal Church (1875). Geology. Mineralogy. Palaeontology.
May 15 - Nov. 30: Tu.-Sa. 1-5.

WINGUATT MUSEUM
Seufert Cannery, The Dalles, Oregon 97058
Natural history. Archaeology. Indian material.
May 1 - Sept. 30: M., W., Su. 9-5. Oct. 1 - Apr. 30: W., Su. 12-4. Closed public holidays.

THEODORE

BELLINGRATH GARDENS AND HOME
Theodore, Alabama 36582
Home (1936) containing the Bessie Morse collection of furniture, porcelain, china and silver.
Daily 8.30-5.

THERMOPOLIS

PIONEER MUSEUM
Springview Avenue, Thermopolis, Wyoming 82443
Pioneer furniture, household equipment, tools. Costumes. Musical instruments. Paintings.
Daily 8-6.

WYOMING PIONEER HOME
5 Pioneer Drive, Thermopolis, Wyoming 82443
Pioneer life. Indian material.
M.-F. 8-5; Sa., Su. 8-4.

THETFORD

THETFORD HISTORICAL SOCIETY MUSEUM
Thetford, Vermont 05074
Local history. Agricultural implements. Tradesmen's tools.
Last 2 Sundays in Aug. Other times by appointment.

THIBODAUX

EDWARD DOUGLASS WHITE COTTAGE
Highway 1, Thibodaux, Louisiana 70301
Memorial to Chief Justice White, furnished as in his youth.
Tu.-Sa. 9-5; Su. 1-5. Closed national holidays.

THIEF RIVER FALLS

PENNINGTON COUNTY HISTORICAL SOCIETY
County Court House, First and Main Streets, Thief River Falls, Minnesota 56701
Local history.
F. 12-5.

THIENSVILLE

OZAUKEE COUNTY HISTORICAL SOCIETY MUSEUM
Thiensville, Wisconsin 53092
Pioneer village of 10 buildings (1848-90), re-erected on site. Local and pioneer history. Agriculture.
1st Su. in June - 2nd Su. in Oct.: W. 10-5; Su. 1-6.

THOMASTON

MONTPELIER
High Street, Thomaston, Maine 04861
Reproduction (1929) of the original General Knox Mansion (1793). Period furnishings. Personal possessions of Gen. Knox, 1st U.S. Secretary of War.
June 1 - Sept. 30: daily 10-4.15.

THOMASVILLE

LAMPHAM-PATTERSON HOUSE
626 N. Dawson Street, Thomasville, Georgia 31792
House (1884). Victorian furnishings.
Oct.-Apr., Tu.-Sa. 9-5; Su. 2-5. May-Sept., Tu.-Sa. 9-5.30; Su. 2-5.30. Closed Christmas, Thanksgiving.

THOUSAND OAKS

STAGECOACH INN MUSEUM
Ventu Park Road and Susan Drive, Thousand Oaks, California 91360
Inn rebuilt (1970-1) after fire. Local history. Transport.
W., Su. 1.30-5.

TIBURON

ANGEL ISLAND STATE PARK
Tiburon, California 94920
Former Indian prison, duelling site and immigrant quarantine station.
May-Sept., daily 8 a.m. - 10 p.m. Oct.-Apr., daily 8-5; Closed Thanksgiving, Christmas, Jan. 1.

BELVEDERE TIBURON LANDMARKS SOCIETY MUSEUM
Old St. Hilary's Historic Reserve, Esperanza Street, Tiburon, California 94920
Local history. Botany.
Old St. Hilary's Church (1888) is in the care of the Society.
Apr. 1 - Sept. 30, W., Su., 1-4.

TICONDEROGA

FORT MOUNT HOPE
Burgoyne Road, Ticonderoga, New York 12883
Site of fort (1776). Museum has material relating to Revolutionary, French and Indian Wars.
May 28 - Oct. 15, daily 8-dusk.

FORT TICONDEROGA
Box 390, Ticonderoga, New York 12883
Restored Colonial fort (1775). Military museum. Weapon demonstrations. Local and regional history.
May 15 - Oct. 15, daily 8-6. (July 1 - Aug. 31, 8-7).

TIFFIN

JONES COLLECTION OF MINERALS AND BIOLOGY MUSEUM
Heidelberg College, Greenfield Street, Tiffin, Ohio 44883
Mineralogy. Natural history.
Th. 2-5. Other times by appointment. Closed college vacations.

SENECA COUNTY MUSEUM
28 Clay Street, Tiffin, Ohio 44883
Local history. Pioneer life. Costumes. Stamps. Glass.
Rezin W. Shawhan House and carriage house (1853) are in the care of the Museums.
Mar. 1 - Nov. 30: W., Su. 2-5. Other times by appointment.

TILDEN

MCMULLEN COUNTY MUSEUM
County Courthouse, Tilden, Texas 78072
Indian artifacts. Local history. Pioneer life.
By appointment.

TILLAMOOK

TILLAMOOK COUNTY PIONEER MUSEUM
2106 2nd Street, Tillamook, Oregon 97141
In old Courthouse (1905). Geology. Zoology. Natural history. Archaeology. Replica of pioneer home. Pioneer furniture, tools, utensils. Old cars. Stage coach.
May 1 - Sept. 30: M.-Sa. 9.30-5; Su. 1-5. Oct. 1 - Apr. 30: Tu.-Sa. 8.30-5; Su. 1-5.

TIPTON

TIPTON COUNTY HISTORICAL SOCIETY MUSEUM
233 W. Madison Street, Tipton, Indiana 46072
Local history. Agriculture. Furnishings. Costumes.
M.-F. 8-4; Sa. 8-12.

TITUSVILLE

MCKONKEY FERRY MUSEUM
Washington Crossing State Park, Titusville, New Jersey 08560
Mid-18th century building, formerly ferry-house and tavern. Now restored as Colonial inn, with taproom, kitchen and bedroom. Period furnishings and utensils.
Tu.-Sa. 10-12, 1-5; Su., public holidays 2-5. Closed Thanksgiving, Christmas, New Year.

DRAKE WELL MUSEUM
R.D.2, Titusville, Pennsylvania 16354
Site of beginning of Pennsylvania oil industry (1859). Replica of first derrick and engine house. Development of oil drilling equipment. Paintings and photographs of oil industry.
May 1 - Oct. 31: M.-Sa. 8-5; Su. 1-5. Nov. 1 - Apr. 30: M.-Sa. 9-4.30; Su. 1-4.30. Closed New Year, Good Friday, Easter, Thanksgiving, Christmas.

PITHOLE
Drake Well Memorial Park, Titusville, Pennsylvania 16354
Preserved site of oil-boom town (1865).
Daily 8.30-5.

TIVERTON

FORT BARTON
Tiverton, Rhode Island 02878
Restored Revolutionary War redoubt (1777). Revolutionary War relics.
At all times.

TIVERTON HISTORICAL SOCIETY MUSEUM
3908 Main Road, Tiverton, Rhode Island 02878
In Chace-Cory House (1730). Original furniture and utensils.
May 1 - Oct. 30, Su. 1-4.

TIVOLI

CLERMONT STATE PARK
County Route 6, Tivoli, New York 12583
Clermont (1778) was Livingston family mansion. Family possessions. Decorative arts.
Apr. 1 - Nov. 31, daily 9-5.

TOBIAS

MUSEUM OF TOBIAS HISTORICAL SOCIETY
Tobias, Nebraska 68453
Local history. Agriculture. Coins. Stamps.
May 1 - Sept. 30, Su. 2-4.30.

TOCCOA

HISTORIC TRAVELLER'S REST
Route 3, Toccoa, Georgia 30577
House (1825). Furnishings. Indian material. 19th century hotel registers, account books.
Oct. 1 - Apr. 30, Tu.-Sa. 9-5, Su. 2-5. May 1 - Sept. 30, Tu.-Sa. 9-5.30; Su. 2-5.30. Closed Thanksgiving, Christmas.

TOLEDO

BLAIR MUSEUM OF LITHOPANES AND WAX CARVINGS
2032 Robinwood Avenue, Toledo, Ohio 43620
17th-19th century wax carvings. Wax and plaster of paris moulds. Lithopanes.
By appointment.

TOLEDO-LUCAS COUNTY PUBLIC LIBRARY
325 Michigan Street, Toledo, Ohio 43624
Glass. Glass technology.
M.-Sa. 9-5. Closed public holidays.

TOLEDO MUSEUM OF ART
Monroe Street and Scottswood Avenue, Toledo, Ohio 43601
History of art, from ancient Egypt to 20th century. Egyptian mummies. Medieval cloister. European and American glass. 17th century Dutch and Flemish paintings. 17th-18th century French paintings. History of writing and printing. Stained glass. Ceramics.
Tu.-F. 9-5; Su., public holidays 1-5. Closed Christmas, New Year.

TOLEDO MUSEUM OF HEALTH AND NATURAL HISTORY
2700 Broadway, Toledo, Ohio 43609
Mineralogy. Anthropology. Natural history. Entomology. Herpetology. Industry.
M.-F. 1-5; Sa., Su., public holidays 10-5.

TOLLAND

TOLLAND HISTORICAL SOCIETY MUSEUM
Tolland, Connecticut 06084
Local history. Indian material.
Benton Homestead (1720) and Tolland State Jail (1856) are in the care of the Society.
Su. 1-4.

TOMBALL

GRIFFIN MEMORIAL HOUSE AND MAGDALENE CHARLTON MEMORIAL MUSEUM
Pine Street, Tomball, Texas 77375
In Griffin House (c.1860). 19th century furniture, tools, domestic equipment. Farm collection, illustrating early rural life in Texas. Horse-drawn cotton gin.
June 1 - Labour Day: F.-Su. 2-5. Mar. 1 - May 31, Sept. 1 - Oct. 31: Su. 2-5.

TOMBSTONE

PIONEER HOME MUSEUM
810 E. Fremont Street, Tombstone, Arizona 85638
Pioneer cabin, with original furnishings. Clothing.
Daily.

TOMBSTONE COURTHOUSE STATE HISTORIC PARK
219 Toughnut Street, Tombstone, Arizona 85638
Museum is former Courthouse (1882). Pioneer life and history.
Daily, except Christmas, 8-5.30.

TOMS RIVER

MUSEUM OF OCEAN COUNTY HISTORICAL SOCIETY
26 Stadley Avenue, Toms River, New Jersey 08753
Local history.
M.-F. by appointment.

TONALEA

NAVAJO NATIONAL MONUMENT
Tonalea, Arizona 86044
Indian archaeology and artifacts.
Daily 8-5.

TONAWANDA

MUSEUM OF HISTORICAL SOCIETY OF THE TONAWANDAS
113 Main Street, Tonawanda, New York 14150
Building (1870) was originally station of New York and Hudson River Railroad. Local history. Indian artifacts. Industry. Transport. Circus material.
Tu.-F. 10-5; Sa., Su. 1-5. Closed public holidays.

TONKAWA

MUSEUM OF NORTHERN OKLAHOMA COLLEGE
1220 E. Grand Street, Tonkawa, Oklahoma 74653
Geology. Mineralogy. Natural history. Archaeology. Indian artifacts.
May 1 - Oct. 31, daily 2-5.

TOPEKA

KANSAS STATE HISTORICAL SOCIETY MUSEUM
120 W. 10th Street, Topeka, Kansas 66612
Kansas, Western and Indian history. Archaeology. Period rooms. Stage coach. Early automobiles. Agriculture. Military history. Costumes.
10 historic buildings and sites, including a Pawnee Indian village, are in the care of the Society.
M.-F. 8.15-5; Sa. 8.15-4; Su. 1-4.30. Closed public holidays.

MULVANE ART CENTER
17th and Jewell Streets, Topeka, Kansas 66621
Modern and contemporary paintings, sculpture, prints, ceramics by Mid-Western artists.
Sept. 1 - July 31, M.-F. 9-5; Su. 2-5. Closed Easter, Thanksgiving, July 4, Christmas.

MUSEUM OF THE MEININGER FOUNDATION
5600 W. 6th Avenue, Topeka, Kansas 66601
History of psychiatry. Indian material. Geology. Shells. Paintings, prints, photographs.
M.-F. 8.45-4.30; Sa. 9.15-3.30.

NATURAL SCIENCE MUSEUM
Washburn University, 17th and College Streets (21), Topeka, Kansas 66621
Physical and biological sciences. Astronomy. Observatory.
By appointment.

TOPEKA ART GUILD, INC.
Topeka High School, Topeka, Kansas 66601
19th-20th century paintings by artists of the Mid-West.
M.-F., Su. 3-5.

TOPSFIELD

MUSEUM OF IPSWICH RIVER NATURE CENTER
Perkins Row, Topsfield, Massachusetts 01983
Natural history. Mineralogy.
Daily, dawn-dusk.

MUSEUM OF TOPSFIELD HISTORICAL SOCIETY
27 Prospect Street, Topsfield, Massachusetts 01983
In Parson Capen House (1683). Local history. Early American furniture.
June 16 - Sept. 14, daily 1-4.30.

TORREY

CAPITOL REEF NATIONAL MONUMENT VISITOR CENTER
Capitol Reef National Monument, Torrey, Utah 84775
Geology. Natural history. Local history and archaeology. Monument includes Old Fruita schoolhouse (c.1890).
May 1 - Oct. 31, daily 8-8. Nov. 1 - Apr. 30: M.-F. 8-12, 1-5.

TORRINGTON

TORRINGTON HISTORICAL SOCIETY MUSEUM
192 Main Street, Torrington, Connecticut 06790
Local history. Industry, 1750 onwards. Costumes. Agriculture.
M.-F. 8-4. Closed public holidays.

TURNER MUSEUM
36 Litchfield Street, Torrington, Connecticut 06790
Early American glass. China. Silver. Firearms.
Sa. 9-5. Other times by appointment.

TOWANDA

MUSEUM OF BRADFORD COUNTY HISTORICAL SOCIETY
Court Street, Towanda, Pennsylvania 18848
Local history. Primitive paintings. Portraits.
W., Th. 2-4; F. 7-9. Other times by appointment.

TOWER

MUSEUM OF TOWERSOUDAN HISTORICAL SOCIETY
Tower, Minnesota 55790
Local history. Indian artifacts.
May 30 - Sept. 2, daily 10-3.

TOWSON

HAMPTON NATIONAL HISTORIC SITE
535 Hampton Lane, Towson, Maryland 21204
House (c.1790) with period furnishings.
Tu.-Sa. 11-5; Su. 1-5. Closed public holidays.

TRAVERSE CITY

CON FOSTER MUSEUM
Grandview Parkway, Traverse City, Michigan 49684
Natural history. Agriculture. Transport. Indian artifacts. Costumes.
June 1 - Sept. 15, daily 9-9.

INDIAN DRUM LODGE MUSEUM
Camp Greilick, 6419 W. Bay Shore Road, Traverse City, Michigan 49684
In Camp Greilick, log-structure (1850). Natural history. Ethnology. Archaeology. Indian handicrafts. Costumes.
June 1 - Aug. 31: M.-F. 1-2, 6.30-8; Su. 2-5, 6.30-8.30. Rest of year by appointment.

TRENTON

TRENTON HISTORICAL MUSEUM
St. Joseph and 3rd Streets, Trenton, Michigan 48183
House (1881). Period furnishings. Local history.
Nov. 1 - Apr. 30: M.-Sa. by appointment; Su. 2-5.

HITCHCOCK COUNTY HISTORICAL MUSEUM
Trenton, Nebraska 69044
Local history.
Bank (1886) and store (1888) are in the care of the Museum.
May 1 - Oct. 31, Su. 2-5.

LENOX CHINA MUSEUM
Prince and Meade Streets, Trenton, New Jersey 08605
Lenox china.
M.-F. 8.30-5; Su. 9-3. Closed public holidays.

MUSEUM OF OLD BARRACKS ASSOCIATION
S. Willow Street, Trenton, New Jersey 08608
In old Barracks (1758). 18th century furnishings. Firearms. Washington mementoes and dioramas.
June 1 - Aug. 31: M.-Sa. 10-5. Sept. 1 - May 31: M.-Sa. 10-4. Closed public holidays.

NEW JERSEY STATE MUSEUM
205 W. State Street, Trenton, New Jersey 08625
State history and archaeology. Ecology. Ornithology. Ethnology. Anthropology. Indian artifacts. Printings, prints by New Jersey artists. Decorative arts. Planetarium. Junior museum.
M.-Sa., public holidays 9-5; Su. 2-5. Closed Christmas, New Year.

W2Z1 HISTORICAL WIRELESS MUSEUM
19 Blackwood Drive, Trenton, New Jersey 08628
Radio apparatus from 1899 onwards.
By appointment.

WILLIAM TRENT HOUSE
539 S. Warren Street, Trenton, New Jersey 08611
House (1719). Early 18th century furniture.
M.-Sa. 10-4; Su., public holidays 1-4. Closed Thanksgiving, Christmas, New Year.

TRINIDAD

PATRICK'S POINT STATE HISTORIC PARK
Trinidad, California 95570
Natural history. Indian life.
Daily 10-5. Closed New Year, Thanksgiving, Christmas.

BACA HOUSE
Main Street, Trinidad, Colorado 81082
Adobe house (1869) of Felipe Baca. Period furnishings.
May 15 - Oct. 15, 9-5.

BLOOM HOUSE
Main Street, Trinidad, Colorado 81082
House (1882) of Frank G. Bloom, with Victorian furnishings and Victorian garden.
May 15 - Oct. 15, daily 9-5.

PIONEER MUSEUM
Main Street, Trinidad, Colorado 81082
In former servants' quarters of the Baca house. History of Trinidad and Southern Colorado. Early ranching. Horse-drawn vehicles.
May 15 - Oct. 15 9-5.

TRINIDAD STATE JUNIOR COLLEGE MUSEUM
600 Prospect, Trinidad, Colorado 81082
Geology. Mineralogy. Palaeontology. Local history. Archaeology of South-East Colorado and North-East New Mexico.
M.-F. 8-5; Sa., Su. 1-5. Closed public holidays.

TROY

MUSEUM OF RENSSELAER COUNTY HISTORICAL SOCIETY
59 2nd Street, Troy, New York 12180
In Hart-Cluett mansion (1827). History of Rensselaer County and New York State. Period rooms. Portraits. Silver. Ceramics. Religious art.
Tu.-Sa. 10-4. Closed public holidays.

RENSSELAER COUNTY JUNIOR MUSEUM
108 2nd Avenue, Troy, New York 12180
Planetarium. Science. Herpetology. History.
June 1 - Sept. 30, M.-W. 9-12, 1-4. Rest of year, Tu.-Su. 9-12, 1-4. Closed New Year, Easter, Christmas.

RENSSELAER POLYTECHNIC INSTITUTE
Troy, New York 12180
Museum of engineering and local history.
M.-F. 9-5. Closed Institute vacations, public holidays.

OVERFIELD TAVERN
106 S. Plum Street, Troy, Ohio 45373
Overfield Tavern (1808). Late 18th - early 19th century primitive paintings. Pewter.
Th., 2nd, 4th Su. in month, 2-5.

TRUCKEE

EMIGRANT TRAIL MUSEUM
Donner Memorial State Park, Truckee, California 95734
Commemorates and illustrates journey of the Donner Party to California (1846). History of railways and the lumber industry.
Daily 10-4. Closed New Year, Thanksgiving, Christmas.

TUBAC

TUBAC PRESIDIO STATE HISTORIC PARK
P.O. Box 1296, Tubac, Arizona 85640
Material illustrating Spanish colonisation of Arizona. Life in 1770s shown by walk-through dioramas. Ruins of Spanish military fort (c.1752). Mining.
Daily, except Christmas, 8-5.30.

TUCKAHOE

HAMMOND HOUSE
Route 100 C, Eastview, Tuckahoe, New York 10707
Colonial farmhouse (1719). Period furnishings.
May 1 - Nov. 1: W.-Su. 2-5. Closed public holidays.

MUSEUM OF WESTCHESTER COUNTY HISTORICAL SOCIETY
43 Read Avenue, Tuckahoe, New York 10707
In Hammond House (1719). Local history. Period furniture.
May-Oct., W.-Su. 2-5.

TUCSON

ARIZONA HISTORICAL SOCIETY MUSEUM
949 East 2nd Street, Tucson, Arizona 85719
Local and military history. History of technology, including aviation. Weapons. Paintings. Decorative arts.
C. O. Brown Home (1868), John C. Fremont Home (1859), American Flag Ranch House (1880) and Oro Belle Mining Camp (1890) are in the care of the Society.
M.-F. 9-5; Sa. 9-1; Su. 2-5.

ARIZONA SONORA DESERT MUSEUM
Tucson Mountain Park, P.O. Box 5607, Tucson, Arizona 85703
Natural history. Botany. Geology.
Daily, 9 to sunset.

ARIZONA STATE MUSEUM
University of Arizona, Tucson, Arizona 85721
Archaeology. Anthropology. Indian culture. Arts and crafts of the Navajo, Pueblo, Desert and Apache Indians.
M.-Sa. 10-5; Su. 2-5. Closed public holidays.

MINERALOGICAL MUSEUM
Department of Geosciences, University of Arizona, Tucson, Arizona 85721
Geology. Mineralogy. Fossils.
M.-F. 8-5; Sa. 8-12. Closed public holidays.

MISSIAN SAN XAVIER DEL BAC
P.O. Box 6451, Route 11, Tucson, Arizona 85721
Mission church (1783-97). Items illustrating local social and religious history in late 18th century.
Daily 9-6. Closed Easter, Thanksgiving, New Year, Christmas.

SAGUARDO NATIONAL MONUMENT
P.O. Box 17210, Tucson, Arizona 85710
Zoology. Botany.
Daily 8-6.

SCIENCE MUSEUM
Kitt Peak National Observatory, 950 N. Cherry Avenue, Tucson, Arizona 85717
Astronomy. Anthropology and ethnology of the Papago Indians.
By appointment.

TUCSON ART CENTER
325 West Franklin, Tucson, Arizona 85705
Pre-Columbian and Spanish colonial painting. Latin-American folk-art. African and Oceanic art.
Sept. 1 - July 31, Tu.-Sa. 10-5; Su. 1-5. Closed August.

UNIVERSITY OF ARIZONA MUSEUM OF ART
Olive Road, Tucson, Arizona 85721
Italian art. 19th-20th century American and European paintings and sculpture. Graphics. Decorative arts. Furniture.
M.-Sa. 10-5; Su. 2-5. Closed New Year, July 4, Thanksgiving, Christmas.

TUCUMCARI

MUSEUM OF TUCUMCARI HISTORICAL RESEARCH INSTITUTE
416 S. Adams Street, Tucumcari, New Mexico 88401
Geology. Mineralogy. Palaeontology. Botany. Herbarium. Natural history. Local history. Agriculture. Industry. Transport. Anthropology. Folklore. Indian artifacts. Paintings, sculpture, drawings by regional artists.
M.-Sa. 9-12, 1-9; Su. 1-6.

TULELAKE

LAVA BEDS NATIONAL MONUMENT
Tulelake, California 96134
Geology of lava tubes. Natural history. Archaeology. Modoc Indian artifacts.
Daily 8-5.

TULSA

REBECCA AND GERSHON FENSTER GALLERY OF JEWISH ART
1719 S. Owasso Avenue, Tulsa, Oklahoma 74120
Jewish ceremonial art. Paintings. Sculpture. Decorative arts. Archaeology.
Su. 2-4. Other times by appointment. Closed public and Jewish holidays.

THOMAS GILCREASE INSTITUTE OF AMERICAN HISTORY AND ART
2500 W. Newton Street, Tulsa, Oklahoma 74127
History of westward migration. Cultures of the Five Civilised Tribes, and of the Plains and Central American Indians. American paintings, sculpture, Colonial period to present day.
M.-F. 9-5; Sa., Su., public holidays 1-5. Closed Christmas.

PHILBROOK ART CENTER
2727 S. Rockford Road, Tulsa, Oklahoma 74114
Oriental art. Japanese screens and scrolls. Archaeology of American Southwest. African sculpture. American Indian paintings, costumes, baskets, pottery. European paintings, sculpture, especially Italian 16th-17th century. American paintings, including paintings of oil industry.
Tu. 10-5, 7.30-9.30; W.-Sa. 10-5; Su. 1-5. Closed public holidays.

TUMACACORI

TUMACACORI NATIONAL MONUMENT
P.O. Box 67, Tumacacori, Arizona 85640
Spanish mission history in the South-West U.S.A. and North-West Mexico.
The Tumacacori Mission House (1800-22) is in the care of the Society.
Daily 9-5.

TUPELO

NATCHEZ TRACE PARKWAY, VISITOR CENTER
Rural Route 5, Tupelo, Mississippi 38801
Indian trails. Geology. Ethnology. Archaeology. Herbarium.
Daily 8-5. Closed Christmas.

TUPPER LAKE

JACKMAN GALLERY OF ART
Route 30, Tupper Lake, New York 12986
Paintings by Adirondack artists.
Daily 10-4.

TUSCALOOSA

GORGAS HOUSE
P.O. Box 1943, University, Tuscaloosa, Alabama 35486
House (1829) was the home of General Josiah Gorgas and of his son, Dr. William Crawford Gorgas, who helped to control yellow fever during the construction of the Panama Canal.
M.-Sa. 10-12, 2-5; Su. 3-5. Closed national holidys.

OLD TAVERN
Capitol Square, University Boulevard and 28th Avenue, Tuscaloosa, Alabama 35401
Old Tavern (1827). Local history.
The Friedman Home (1835), with a collection of period furniture, is under the same control.
Tu.-Su. 2-5. Closed Christmas.

UNIVERSITY OF ALABAMA ART GALLERY
University, Tuscaloosa, Alabama 35486
Paintings. Sculpture. Graphics. Drawings.
Daily 2-5, during University terms.

UNIVERSITY OF ALABAMA MUSEUM OF NATURAL HISTORY
University, Tuscaloosa, Alabama 35486
Mineralogy. Botany. Conchology. Ichthyology. Herpetology. Anthropology.
Daily 8-5. Closed Christmas.

TUSCUMBIA

IVY GREEN
300 West North Common, Tuscumbia, Alabama 35674
House (1820) was birthplace of Helen Keller. Her furniture and personal possessions.
M.-Su. 8.30-4.30.

TUSKEGEE

GEORGE WASHINGTON CARVER MUSEUM
Tuskegee Institute, Tuskegee, Alabama 36088
Material illustrating scientific work of George Washington Carver. Ethnology. Paintings. Sculpture. Graphics.
M.-Sa. 10-4; Su. 1-4.

TWENTYNINE PALMS

TWENTYNINE PALMS OASIS VISITORS CENTER
Joshua Tree National Monument, 74485 Palm Vista, Twentynine Palms, California 92277
Geology. Botany. Natural history. Archaeology.
Daily 8-5.

TWIN FALLS

HERRETT ARTS AND SCIENCE CENTER
1220 Kemberly Road, East Five Points, Twin Falls, Idaho 83301
Pre-Columbian Indian culture. Archaeology. Children's museum.
M.-Th., Sa. 9-5.30; F. 9-9. Closed public holidays.

TWINSBURG

TWINSBURG HISTORICAL SOCIETY MUSEUM
8996 Darrow Road, Twinsburg, Ohio 44087
Building (1865). Local history.
May 1 - Oct. 31, last Su. in month 2-5.

TWO HARBORS

MUSEUM OF LAKE COUNTY HISTORICAL SOCIETY
Depot Building, Two Harbors, Minnesota 55616
Mineral collection. Pictures of local railways and of iron ore and lumbering industries. Locomotives.
May 31 - Oct. 1: M.-Sa. 9-4; Su., public holidays 1-4.

TYLER

SMITH COUNTY HISTORICAL SOCIETY MUSEUM
624 N. Broadway, Tyler, Texas 75701
In Goodman House (1859). Furnishings of c.1900. Civil War material. Indian artifacts. Medical instruments.
Daily 1-5. Closed Christmas.

TYLER MUSEUM OF ART
1300 S. Mahon Avenue, Tyler, Texas 75701
Paintings. Graphics. Jewellery.
M.-Sa. 10-5; Su. 1-5. Closed public holidays.

TYRINGHAM

TYRINGHAM ART GALLERIES
Tyringham Road, Tyringham, Massachusetts 01264
In Gingerbread House Studio (1930). Sculpture. Graphics.
May 1 - Aug. 31, daily 10-5. Sept. 1 - Oct. 31, by appointment.

UKIAH

HELD-POAGE MEMORIAL HOME AND RESEARCH LABORATORY
603 West Perkins Street, Ukiah, California 95482
Local history. Indian artifacts.
Tu., Sa. 2-4. Other times by appointment.

UNCASVILLE

TANTAQUIDGEON INDIAN MUSEUM
1819 Norwich - New London Turnpike, Uncasville, Connecticut 06382
Indian handicrafts. Archaeology.
May 1 - Oct. 31, M.-Su., public holidays 10-6.

UNION

ILLINOIS RAILWAY MUSEUM
Olson Road, Union, Illinois 60180
Illinois railway history. Electric railway items.
Marengo C. and N.W. Depot (1851) is in the care of the Museum.
May 1 - Oct. 1, M.-F. 10.30-5; Sa. 12-6; Su. 12-7. Mar. and Nov., Su. 12-7.

MATTHEWS FARM MUSEUM
Union, Maine 04862
Agricultural history. Farm implements.
July 1 - Labour Day, Tu.-Su. 12-5.

ROSE HILL STATE HISTORICAL SITE
Union, South Carolina 29379
House (1832). Period furnishings.
By appointment.

UNION CITY

MUSEUM OF UNION CITY HISTORICAL SOCIETY
407 N. Broadway, Union City, Michigan 49094
Local history. Industry and handicrafts. Indian material.
May 1 - Sept. 30: M.-Sa. 10-5.

UNION MILLS

UNION MILLS HOMESTEAD
Westminster, Union Mills, Maryland 21157
Shriver Mill (1797). Original furnishings, household equipment. Paintings. Agriculture.
May 1 - Oct. 30: M.-Sa., public holidays 10-5; Su. 1-5.

UNIONTOWN

SEARIGHT'S TOLLHOUSE
U.S. Route 40 W., Uniontown, Pennsylvania 15401
National Road Toll House (1835). History of road transport in Pennsylvania.
May 1 - Oct. 31: Tu.-Sa. 8.30-5; Su. 1-5. Nov. 1 - Apr. 30: Tu.-Sa. 9-4.30; Su. 1-4.30. Closed New Year, Good Friday, Easter, Thanksgiving, Christmas.

UNIONVILLE

SHANDY HALL
Route 84, Unionville, Ohio 44088
House (1815), was home of Harper family, 1815-1935. Original furnishings and equipment.
Tu.-Sa. 10-5; Su. 2-6.

UNIVERSITY PARK

NEW MEXICO STATE UNIVERSITY MUSEUM
P.O. Box 157, University Park, New Mexico 88070
Herbarium. Zoology. Archaeology. Ethnology. Agricultural implements, machinery. Stoves and other domestic equipment. Guns. Coins. Costumes. Decorative arts.
By appointment.

ART GALLERY
Pennsylvania State University, The Hetzel Union Building, University Park, Pennsylvania 16802
American and European paintings, sculpture, prints, mainly 19th-20th centuries.
Daily 8 a.m. - 10 p.m.

FROST ENTOMOLOGICAL MUSEUM
Pennsylvania State University, Department of Entomology, University Park, Pennsylvania 16802
Entomology. Zoology.
By appointment.

UPLAND

CHAFFEY COMMUNITY CULTURAL CENTER
525 West 18th Street, Upland, California 91786
Local history. Indian artifacts. Agriculture.
M.-W., Sa. 1-4. Closed public holidays.

MUSEUM OF FRIENDS OF THE CALEB PUSEY HOUSE
15 Race Street, Upland, Pennsylvania 19015
Local history and archaeology.
Caleb Pusey House (1683), Pennock log house (1790), Lancaster County Barn (1810), Schoolhouse Museum (1849) and Mill Houses (1850) are in the care of the Friends.
Tu.-Su. 1-5.

UPPER SANDUSKY

INDIAN MILL MUSEUM STATE MEMORIAL
State Route 67, Upper Sandusky, Ohio 43351
Grist Mill (1861), restored and in working order.
May 1 - Oct. 31: W.-Su. 10-5.

MUSEUM OF WYANDOT COUNTY HISTORICAL SOCIETY
130 S. 7th Street, Upper Sandusky, Ohio 43351
Local history. Agriculture. Maritime history. Medicine. Indian artifacts. Costumes. Paintings. Glass. Musical instruments.
McCutcheonville Overland Inn (1829) is in the care of the Society.
Tu.-Sa. 10-12, 1-5; Su. 1-5. Closed Christmas.

URBANA

WORLD HERITAGE MUSEUM
University of Illinois, 484 Lincoln Hall, Urbana, Illinois 61801
Archaeology. History. Anthropology. Coins. Glass. Paintings. Sculpture. Decorative arts.
May 1 - Sept. 30: M.-F. 10-12, 1-3.30. Oct. 1 - Apr. 30: M.-F. 9-12, 1-5; Sa. 9-12; Su. 2-5.

MUSEUM OF NATURAL HISTORY
University of Illinois, Matthews and Green Streets, Urbana, Illinois 61801
Geology. Archaeology. Mammals. Snakes. Molluscs.
M.-Sa. 8-5. Closed public holidays.

UTICA

LASALLE COUNTY HISTORICAL SOCIETY MUSEUM
Utica, Illinois 61373
In former Warehouse (1842). Local history. Indian artifacts. Agriculture. Costumes. Outdoor museum.
Hitt Wellhouse (1873) is in the care of the Society.
Sa. 2-4; Su. 10-5. Other times by appointment. Closed Christmas, New Year.

FORT SCHUYLER MILITARY MUSEUM
Route 12, Utica, New York 13503
Reconstructed Colonial blockhouse (1758). Military equipment from time of French and Indian Wars to present day.
By appointment.

JUNIOR MUSEUM OF ONEIDA COUNTY
1703 Oneida Street, Utica, New York 13503
Natural history. Science. History. Planetarium. Indian artifacts.
Tu.-Sa. 10-5; Su. 1-4.

MUNSON-WILLIAMS-PROCTOR INSTITUTE
310 Genessee Street, Utica, New York 13502
18th-19th century American paintings. 20th century American and European paintings, sculpture. European, Japanese, American prints. American decorative arts. Fountain Elms (c.1850), next to the Institute, is house-museum of mid-19th century history and decorative arts.
M.-Sa. 10-5; Su. 1-5. Closed public holidays.

ONEIDA HISTORICAL SOCIETY MUSEUM
318 Genessee Street, Utica, New York 13502
History of Mohawk Valley and Oneida County.
M.-Sa. 10-5. Closed public holidays.

UTUADO

MUSEUM AND PARK OF ARCHAEOLOGY
Utuado, Puerto Rico 00761
On site of 12th century Indian ceremonial site. Religious and other artifacts discovered during excavations.
Daily 9-5.

UVALDE

GARNER MEMORIAL MUSEUM
333 N. Park Street, Uvalde, Texas 78801
House (1920) was home of Vice-President Garner. Local history. Garner memorabilia, including his collection of gavels. Pioneer clothing. Ranching equipment. Arrowheads.
M.-Sa. 9-12, 1-5. Su. 1-5. Closed public holidays.

VACHERIE

OAK ALLEY MANSION
State Highway 18, Vacherie, Louisiana 70090
House (c.1830). Period furnishings.
Daily 9-5.

VAILS GATE

NEW WINDSOR CANTONMENT AND TEMPLE HILL MONUMENT
Vails Gate, New York 12584
Final encampment of Revolutionary Army, 1782-83. Knox Headquarters house (1754). Reconstruction of typical buildings used by Continental Army. History of the campaign.
Apr. 16 - Oct. 31, W.-Su. 9.30-5.

VALENTINE

FORT NIOBRARA NATIONAL WILDLIFE REFUGE
Hidden Timber Route, Valentine, Nebraska 69201
Natural history. Fossils of large mammals and amphibians. Archaeology. Indian artifacts. Local historical photographs.
Daily 8-8.

MUSEUM OF CHERRY COUNTY HISTORICAL SOCIETY
Eleanor Drive, Valentine, Nebraska 69201
Natural history. Local history. Indian artifacts. Folklore. Costumes. Needlework. Recordings. Paintings. Drawings. Portraits.
Apr. 15 - Oct. 15: M.-Sa. 9-5. Closed public holidays.

VALLEY

MUSEUM OF VALLEY COMMUNITY HISTORICAL SOCIETY
218 W. Alexander Street, Valley, Nebraska 68064
In former Schoolhouse (1872). Pioneer life.
M.-Sa. by appointment. Apr. 1 - Oct. 31, Su. 2-5.

VALLEY CITY

BARNES COUNTY HISTORICAL MUSEUM
County Courthouse, Valley City, North Dakota 58072
Local and military history. Indian material. Costumes.
Tu., Th. 2-5. Closed public holidays.

GALE PRIVATE MUSEUM
300 Viking Drive, Valley City, North Dakota 58072
Pioneer and Indian relics. Weapons. Minerals.
By appointment.

VALLEY FORGE

MUSEUM OF VALLEY FORGE HISTORICAL SOCIETY
Valley Forge State Park, Valley Forge, Pennsylvania 19481
Mementoes of George Washington. Firearms of the Revolutionary period. Staffordshire china. 18th - early 19th century portraits.
M.-Sa. 9-4.30; Su. 1-5. Closed Christmas.

VALPARAISO

MUSEUM OF HISTORICAL SOCIETY OF POSTER COUNTY
Room 411, Court House, Valparaiso, Indiana 46383
Local history. Pioneer relics. Mastodon bones.
Tu., W., F. 9-4. Closed public holidays.

SLOAN GALLERIES OF AMERICAN PAINTINGS
Valparaiso University, Valparaiso, Indiana 46383
19th-20th century American paintings. Works by Junius R. Sloan.
M.-Th. 8-11; F. 8-10; Sa. 9-8; Su. 1-10. Closed Easter, July 4, Thanksgiving, Christmas.

VANCOUVER

CLARK COUNTY HISTORICAL MUSEUM
1511 Main Street, Vancouver, Washington 98660
Pioneer history. Prints. Drawings. Replica of early doctor's surgery. Indian artifacts.
Store (1890) is in the care of the Museum.
Tu.-Su. 1-5. Closed New Year, Easter, Thanksgiving, Christmas.

FORT VANCOUVER NATIONAL HISTORIC SITE
Vancouver, Washington 98661
Objects excavated from site of original Fort Vancouver. U.S. military relics (1849). Material from fur-trade period (1829-60).
May 1 - Sept. 30: M.-F. 8-4.30; Sa., Su. 9-5. Oct. 1 - Apr. 30: M.-F. 8-4.30; Sa., Su. 12-5. Closed New Year, Easter, Thanksgiving, Christmas.

ULYSSES S. GRANT MUSEUM
1106 E. Evergreen Boulevard, Vancouver, Washington 98663
House (1849). Furniture belonging to Grant. Local history. Artifacts of N.W. Indians.
Daily, except Th. 1-4.

VANDALIA

VANDALIA HISTORICAL SOCIETY MUSEUM
212 Gallatin Avenue, Vandalia, Illinois 62471
Material relating to the early pioneer period, 1820-40. Furniture. Costumes. Paintings. Glass.
Tu.-Sa. 1-5.

VANDALIA STATE HOUSE MEMORIAL
315 West Gallatin Street, Vandalia, Illinois 62471
State House offices and legislative rooms (1836), with original and period furnishings.
Daily 9-5. Closed New Year, Thanksgiving, Christmas.

VANTAGE

GINKGO PETRIFIED FOREST STATE PARK MUSEUM
U.S. Highway 10, Vantage, Washington 98950
Geology. Mineralogy. Palaeontology. Archaeology. Anthropology. Indian artifacts.
June-Sept., daily 8-6. Oct.-May, daily 9-6.

VAN WERT

MUSEUM OF VAN WERT COUNTY HISTORICAL SOCIETY
602 N. Washington Street, Van Wert, Ohio 45891
Natural history. Local history. Civil War history. Household equipment. Clothing. Reproductions of grocer's and barber's shops. Agriculture. Children's museum.
Su. 2-4.30. Other times by appointment.

VENTURA

SAN BUENAVENTURA MISSION MUSEUM
225 East Main Street, Ventura, California 93001
Local and Mission history. Religious paintings and statues. Wooden bells. Indian artifacts.
San Buenventura Mission Building (1782) and Adobe Settling Tank (1800) are in the care of the Museum.
Daily 10-5. Closed Christmas.

VENTURA COUNTY PIONEER MUSEUM
77 North California Street, Ventura, California 93001
Geology. Archaeology. Local history. Indian artifacts.
M.-F. 8-4.30; Sa. 12-4. Closed July 4, Thanksgiving, Christmas.

VERGENNES

BIXBY MEMORIAL LIBRARY
Vergennes, Vermont 05491
Local history. Furniture. Maps. Indian artifacts. Military relics.
M.-Th., Sa. 12.30-5 (not May 1 - Sept. 30); F. 12.30-9; May 1 - Sept. 30, W. 10-5. Closed public holidays, Town Meeting day, Aug. 16.

JOHN STRONG MANSION
RFD 3, Vergennes, Vermont 05491
House (1794-6). Period furniture. Paintings.
May 15 - Oct. 15, daily 10-5.

VERMILION

GREAT LAKES HISTORICAL SOCIETY MUSEUM
480 N. Main Street, Vermilion, Ohio 44089
History of Great Lakes Navigation. Ship models. Navigational equipment, instruments. Paintings. Working models of marine engines.
May 1 - Oct. 31, daily 10.30-9. Nov. 1 - Apr. 30, daily 10.30-5. Closed Dec. 15 - Jan. 15.

VERMILLION

ARNE B. LARSON MUSIC MUSEUM
Clark Street, Vermillion, South Dakota 57069
Worldwide collection of musical instuments. Ethnology.
M.-Sa. 8-5; Su., public holidays 1-4.30. Closed Christmas, New Year, Easter.

W. H. OVER DAKOTA MUSEUM
University of South Dakota, Vermillion, South Dakota 57069
South Dakota geology, archaeology, agrarian history. Ethnology of Plains Indians. Contemporary Sioux Indians. Chinese medical instruments.
M.-F. 8-4.30; Sa. 10-4.30; Su. 2-4.30. Closed public holidays.

VERMONTVILLE

VERMONTVILLE MUSEUM
Public Square, Vermontville, Michigan 49096
In former school building (1844). History of the Congregationalist colonists from Vermont who settled in Vermontville.
By appointment.

VERNAL

LEO THORNE'S MUSEUM
18 W. Main Street, Vernal, Utah 84078
Prehistory of Utah. Dinosaur bones.
Opening times published locally.

PIONEER MUSEUM
2nd S. and 5th W. Streets, Vernal, Utah 84078
In First Mormon Tithing House (1887), now Little Rock House. Pioneer life and history.
June 1 - Sept. 15, daily 9-5.

NATURAL HISTORY STATE MUSEUM
235 E. Main Street, Vernal, Utah 84078
Geology. Fluorescent minerals. Fossils. Natural history. Archaeology.
May-Sept., 8 a.m. - 9 p.m. Oct.-Apr., 9-6.

VERNFIELD

GOSCHENHOPPEN FOLKLIFE LIBRARY AND MUSEUM
Route 63, Vernfield, Pennsylvania 18973
Herbarium. Agriculture. Local history and archaeology. Folk culture. Costumes. Decorative arts.
May 1 - Oct. 31: Su. 1.30-4.

VERNON

RED RIVER VALLEY MUSEUM
Walbarger Memorial Auditorium, 2100 Yamparika Street, Vernon, Texas 67384
Indian artifacts.
M.-F. 9-5; Sa. 9-12.

VERNON HISTORIANS MUSEUM
Vernon, Vermont 05354
Local history. Indian artifacts. Costumes. Folklore.
Pond Road Chapel (1860) and Lieut.-Governor Jonathan Hunt house (1779) are in the care of the Historians.
By appointment.

VERONIA

COLUMBIA COUNTY MUSEUM
Veronia, Oregon 97064
Mineralogy. Natural history. Local history. Indian artifacts. Archaeology. Folklore.
Tu.-F. 1-5; Sa., Su. 10-5. Closed Christmas.

VERSAILLES

MUSEUM OF RIPLEY COUNTY HISTORICAL SOCIETY
Versailles, Indiana 47042
Local history. Indian artifacts.
May 30 - Labour Day. Sa., Su. 2-5.

MORGAN COUNTY HISTORICAL SOCIETY MUSEUM
118 N. Monroe Street, Versailles, Missouri 65084
Local history.
June-Oct., daily 1-5.

VEVAY

MUSEUM OF SWITZERLAND COUNTY HISTORICAL SOCIETY
Main Street, Vevay, Indiana 47043
Local history. Indian material. Costumes. Pioneer relics. Archaeology.
May 1 - Sept. 30, Sa., Su. 1-5.

VICKSBURG

CEDAR GROVE
2200 Oak Street, Vicksburg, Mississippi 39180
House (1840-52). Period furnishings.
M.-Sa. 9-4.30; Su. 1-5. Closed Dec. 1 - Jan. 31.

McRAVEN
1503 Harrison Street, Vicksburg, Mississippi 39180
House (1797-1849), with period furnishings.
M.-Sa. 9-4.30; Su. 2-4.30. Closed Thanksgiving, Christmas.

OLD COURT HOUSE MUSEUM
Cherry, Jackson, Grove and Monroe Streets, Vicksburg, Mississippi 39180
Building (1858). History of Southern states before Civil War. Civil War material. Indian artifacts. Glass negatives and prints of steamboats.
M.-Sa. 9.30-4.30; Su. 1.30-4.30. Closed Thanksgiving, Dec. 24-5.

STEAMER 'SPRAGUE' MUSEUM
City Waterfront, Vicksburg, Mississippi 39180
'Sprague' (1900), sternwheeler. History of Mississippi navigation.
Daily 8-5.

VICKSBURG NATIONAL MILITARY PARK
Box 349, Vicksburg, Mississippi 39180
Civil War relics and displays.
Daily 8-5. Closed Christmas.

VICTOR

LOWELL THOMAS BOYHOOD HOME
225 South Sixth Street, Victor, Colorado 80860
House (1897). Original furniture. Photographs and other personal possessions of Lowell Thomas.
May 30 - Labour Day, daily 10-5.

VICTOR MUSEUM AND COUNTRY STORE
Third and Victor Avenue, Victor, Colorado 80860
House (1748). Indian artifacts. Civil War relics. Colonial period furnishings.
June-Sept. daily 9-5.

VICTORIA

MCNAMARA-O'CONNOR HISTORICAL AND FINE ARTS MUSEUM
502 N. Liberty Street, Victoria, Texas 77901
House (1869). Period furnishings. Photographs of local subjects. Volunteer Fire Department relics.
W. 10-12; Su. 3-5.

VIENNA

JOHNSON COUNTY HISTORICAL SOCIETY MUSEUM
Vienna, Illinois 62995
Local history. Agriculture.
M.-Th. 9-3; F. 9-12. Closed Christmas.

OLD JAIL MUSEUM AND FELKER HOUSE
Vienna, Missouri 65084
Natural history. Local history. Indian material. Civil War relics. Furniture. Glass. Jewellery. Coins. Costumes. Children's museum.
Daily 8-5.

VINALHAVEN

VINALHAVEN HISTORICAL SOCIETY MUSEUM
High Street, Vinalhaven, Maine 04863
In former church (1871), later used as Town Hall. Local history. Industry. Maritime history. Folklore. Indian artifacts. Costumes.
July 4 - Labour Day: M.-Sa., public holidays 11-2; Su. 1-4. Other times by appointment.

VINCENNES

WILLIAM HENRY HARRISON MANSION
3 W. Scott Street, Vincennes, Indiana 47591
House, 'Grouselands' (1803-4), formerly home of W. H. Harrison, Governor of Indiana and 9th President of U.S. Period furniture and furnishings.
Daily 9-5. Closed Thanksgiving, New Year, Christmas.

INDIANA TERRITORY STATE MEMORIAL
Harrison and Park Streets, Vincennes, Indiana 47591
In Capitol building (1800). Local history. Offices of *The Western Sun*, containing Ramage press of the kind used by Elihu Stout to print the Territory's first newspaper, 1804.
Daily 9-5.

OLD STATE BANK OF INDIANA
112-14 N. 2nd Street, Vincennes, Indiana 47591
Former Bank building (1836-8).
Now houses Northwest Territory Art Guild and Gallery, with displays of contemporary American paintings, sculpture, handicrafts.
Tu.-Su. 1-4.

MAURICE THOMPSON BIRTHPLACE
Harrison Street, Vincennes, Indiana 47591
One-room house, birthplace (1844) of author of *Alice of Old Vincennes*. Material relating to Thompson's life and work.
Daily 9-5.

VINELAND

MUSEUM OF VINELAND HISTORICAL AND ANTIQUARIAN SOCIETY
108 S. 7th Street, Vineland, New Jersey 08360
19th century domestic equipment. Woodworking tools. Weapons. Books, portraits, furniture from home of Charles K. Landis. Paintings of Indians. Indian artifacts.
Tu.-Sa. 2-5.

VIRGINIA BEACH

SKICOAK LIVING MUSEUM OF THE AMERICAN INDIAN
4439 Southern Boulevard, Virginia Beach, Virginia 23462
History and culture of the Indians of Virginia and America. Handicrafts. Archaeology.
M.-F. 9-4; Sa. 1-4. Closed Dec. 20 - Mar. 15.

VIRGINIA CITY

NEVADA CITY
Virginia City, Montana 59755
19th century ghost town, with restored buildings refurnished in period style.
May 15 - Sept. 30, daily 8-8.

RANK DRUG STORE MUSEUM
Wallace Street, Virginia City, Montana 49755
Medicines. Prescriptions. Bottles.
June 1 - Sept. 15, daily 8 a.m. - 10 p.m.

THOMPSON-HICKMAN MEMORIAL MUSEUM
Wallace Street, Virginia City, Montana 59755
Local history.
Daily 8-6.

VIRGINIA CITY MADISON COUNTY HISTORICAL MUSEUM
Wallace Street, Virginia City, Montana 59755
Local, State and Western history. Minerals. Natural history. Indian artifacts. Costumes. Coins.
June 1 - Oct. 15, daily 8-6.

VIROQUA

VERNON COUNTY HISTORICAL MUSEUM
W. Broadway, Viroqua, Wisconsin 54665
History of Vernon County.
Tu.-Su. 1-5.

VISALIA

TULARE COUNTY MUSEUM
27000 Mooney Boulevard, Visalia, California 93277
Pioneer history. Household equipment. Agricultural equipment. Horse-drawn vehicles. Clothing. Indian material.
Log cabin (1854), Jail (1872), School (1893) are in the care of the Museum.
M.-F. 9-5. Closed public holidays and Saturday, Sunday Oct. 15 - Apr. 15.

VOLCANO

INDIAN GRINDING ROCK STATE HISTORIC PARK
Volcano, California 95689
Site of Miwok Indian village, with Indian petroglyphs and bed-rock mortars.
May-Sept., daily 8 a.m. - 10 p.m. Oct.-Apr., daily 8-5. Closed Thanksgiving, Christmas, Jan. 1.

THOMAS A. JAGGAR MEMORIAL MUSEUM
Hawaii Volcanoes National Park, Volcano, Hawaii 96718
Geology. Archaeology. Biology.
Daily 7.30-5.

VONORE

MUSEUM OF FORT LOUDOUN ASSOCIATION
Route 1, Vonore, Tennessee 37885
Botany. Archaeology. Cherokee Indian artifacts. Agriculture.
Daily 9-5. Closed Thanksgiving, Christmas.

WABASH

WABASH COUNTY HISTORICAL MUSEUM
Memorial Hall, Miami and Hill Streets, Wabash, Indiana 46992
County history. Maps. Documents. Civil War material. Indian history, especially of Miami and Powatomi tribes.
Tu., Th. 9-12, 1-4.30; Sa. 9-12.

WACO

BAYLOR ART MUSEUM
Baylor University, Waco, Texas 76703
European, American prints. Texas paintings. African, New Guinea sculpture.
M.-F. 8-5; Sa. 8-12.

EARLE-HARRISON HOUSE
1901 N. 5th Street, Waco, Texas 76701
House (1858). Empire and early Victorian furnishings. China. Glass. Paintings.
Sa., Su. 2-5.

EARLE-NAPIER-KINNARD HOUSE
Waco, Texas 76701
House (1858, 1866-7). Period furnishings include Duncan Phyfe sofa and John Talman pianoforte of c.1812.
M.-F. 9-5; Sa. 9-12.

EAST TERRACE
100 Hill Street, Waco, Texas 76701
House (1878). Period furnishings. Collection of Cotton Palace gowns and crowns, relics of annual crowning of Cotton Palace Queen.
Sa., Su. 2-5. Other times by appointment.

FORT FISHER AND HOMER GARRISON MEMORIAL MUSEUM
Box 1370, Lake Brazos Park, Waco, Texas 76703
In replica of Texas frontier fort, on site where old Fort Fisher, a Texas Ranger outpost, was established in 1837. History of Texas Rangers.
M.-Sa. 9-6; Su. 1-6.

FORT HOUSE
503 S. 4th Street, Waco, Texas 76701
House (1868). Period furnishings. Maps. Documents.
Sa., Su. 2-5.

HERITAGE SOCIETY OF WACO
Mill Street and Brazos River, Waco, Texas 76704
Furniture. Costumes of Texas Cotton Palace queens.
By appointment.

MUSEUM OF GRAND LODGE OF TEXAS
715 Columbus Street, Waco, Texas 76703
History of the Masons of Texas.
M.-F. 8-4.30.

SIMS CABIN
1219 N. 64th Street, Waco, Texas 76701
Log-house (1852), originally in Freestone County. Early Texan furnishings. Indian arrowheads. Pioneer memorabilia and tools used to build the cabin.
By appointment.

STRECKER MUSEUM
Sid Richardson Science Building, Baylor University, Waco, Texas 76703
Geology. Palaeontology. Botany. Natural history. Amphibians. Reptiles. Molluscs. Birds' eggs, nests and skins.
M.-F. 9-5; Sa. 9-12. Closed public holidays.

TEXAS COLLECTION
Carroll Library Building, Baylor University, Waco, Texas 76703
History of Texas. Weapons. Portraits. Artifacts.
M.-F. 10-5; Sa. 8-12.

WACONIA

MUSEUM OF CARVER COUNTY HISTORICAL SOCIETY
119 Cherry Street, Waconia, Minnesota 55387
Pioneer life. Indian artifacts. Costumes. Tools. Musical instruments.
Tu., F., Su. 1-4.30.

WADESBORO

MUSEUM OF ANSON COUNTY HISTORICAL SOCIETY
210 E. Wade Street, Wadesboro, North Carolina 28170
In Boggan-Hammond House (1783, 1839). Colonial period furniture. Local history. Agriculture. Paintings.
4 historic houses (1790-1872), including Cedar Creek Meeting House (1872) are in the care of the Society.
W.-Su. 3-5.

WAHPETON

FORT ABERCROMBIE
State Highway 81, Wahpeton, North Dakota 58075
Military post (1858). Restored buildings and museum illustrating history and importance of the Fort.
Apr.-Oct., Tu., Sa. 10-6; Su. 2-6.

RICHLAND COUNTY HISTORICAL MUSEUM
2nd Street and 7th Avenue N., Wahpeton, North Dakota 58075
Local history. Indian artifacts.
June 1 - Oct. 20: Tu.-Su. 2-5. Oct. 20 - June 1: F.-Su. 2-5. Other days by appointment. Closed New Year, Easter, July 4, Christmas.

WAILUKU

HALE HOIKEIKE
Iao Road, Wailuku, Hawaii 96793
In Bailey House (1833-50). Period furnishings. Pre-missionary artifacts. Decorative arts. Silver coronation gifts. Paintings by E. H. Bailey.
M.-Sa. 10-3.30. Closed public holidays.

WAIMANALO

SEA LIFE PARK
Makapuku Point, Waimanalo, Hawaii 96795
Maritime history. Natural history. Zoology. Technology.
Daily 10-5.

WAIMEA

KAMUELA MUSEUM
Kawaihae-Kohala Junction, Route 25 and 26, Waimea, Hawaii 96796
History of Hawaii. Military history.
Daily 9-5.

WAITSFIELD

BUNDY ART GALLERY
Waitsfield, Vermont 05673
Paintings, sculpture by contemporary American artists.
Jul. 1 - Aug. 31: M., W.-Sa. 10-5; Su. 1-5. Closed public holidays.

WAKEFIELD

COL. JAMES HARTSHORNE HOUSE
41 Church Street, Wakefield, Massachusetts 01880
House (1681 and 1742). Period furnishings.
By appointment.

WAKEFIELD HISTORICAL SOCIETY MUSEUM
21 Chestnut Street, Wakefield, Massachusetts 01880
Local history.
By appointment.

WALKER

WALKER MUSEUMS
Minnesota Avenue, Walker, Minnesota 56484
Geology. Mineralogy. Natural history. Butterflies. Indian, mainly Chippewa, handicrafts. Anthropology. Local history.
Memorial Day - Labour Day: M.-F. 9-5; Sa., public holidays 9-9; Su. 9-5.

WALLACE

CHAMBER OF COMMERCE MUSEUM
715-719 Bank Street, Wallace, Idaho 83873
History and natural history of the area. Relics of early pioneers. Indian material.
May-Oct., M.-Sa. 9-5. Nov.-Apr. M.-Sa. 10-4. Su. by appointment.

COEUR D'ALENE DISTRICT MINING MUSEUM
517 Bank Street, Wallace, Idaho 83873
History of local mining industry.
June 1 - Aug. 31, M.-Sa. 9-6; Sept. 1 - May 31, M.-F. 10-4. Closed public holidays.

FORT WALLACE MEMORIAL MUSEUM
U.S. Highway 40, Wallace, Kansas 67761
History of old Fort Wallace. Pioneer relics.
Summer: daily. Winter: Su.

WALLA WALLA

FORT WALLA WALLA MUSEUM COMPLEX
Fort Walla Walla Park, P.O. Box 1616, Walla Walla, Washington 99362
Pioneer village. 19th century buildings moved to site include log cabin, Union School, Country store, Babcock railway station, and blacksmith's shop. Tools, machinery, furnishings. Reconstruction of early blockhouse.
June 1 - Aug. 31, Su. 1-5.

WHITMAN MISSION NATIONAL HISTORIC SITE
Route 2, Walla Walla, Washington 99362
Exhibits illustrating work of Marcus Whitman and of missionary period in Pacific Northwest.
May 1 - Sept. 30, daily 8-8. Rest of year, daily 8-5. Closed New Year, Thanksgiving, Christmas.

WALLINGFORD

WALLINGFORD HISTORICAL SOCIETY
180 S. Main Street, Wallingford, Connecticut 06492
Local history. Costumes.
Parsons House (1759) is in the care of the Society.
Su. and July 4, 2-5.

WALNUT CREEK

ALEXANDER LINDSAY JUNIOR MUSEUM
1901 First Avenue, Walnut Creek, California 94596
Geology. Palaeontology. Botany. Natural history. Anthropology. Astronomy.
Tu.-F. 1-5, Sa. 10-5. Closed public holidays.

CIVIC ARTS GALLERY
1641 Locust Street, Walnut Creek, California 94596
Paintings. 20th century tapestries.
Tu.-Th., Sa.-Su. 12-5; F. 12-5, 7-9. Closed New Year, Thanksgiving, Christmas.

WALTHAM

GORE PLACE SOCIETY MUSEUM
52 Gore Street, Waltham, Massachusetts 02154
In Gore Mansion (1805). Period furnishings, including some original items.
Apr. 15 - Nov. 15: Tu.-Sa. 10-5; Su. 2-5.

LYMAN HOUSE
Lyman and Beaver Streets, Waltham, Massachusetts 02154
House (1793). Original and period furnishings.
July-Aug., Th.-Sa. 11-5.

MUSEUM OF AMERICAN JEWISH HISTORICAL SOCIETY
2 Thornton Road, Waltham, Massachusetts 02154
American-Jewish history. Portraits and memorabilia of 18th century families. Liturgical objects. Yiddish theatre programmes and posters.
Sept. 1 - May 31, M.-F. 9-5, Su. 2-5. Closed Jewish and public holidays.

THE ROSE ART MUSEUM
Brandeis University, 415 South Street, Waltham, Massachusetts 02154
19th-20th century American, European paintings, sculpture. Oceanic art. Ceramics.
Daily 1-5. Closed Christmas, New Year, July 4, Labour Day, Thanksgiving.

WALTHAM HISTORICAL SOCIETY MUSEUM
185 Lyman Street, Waltham, Massachusetts 02154
In The Vale (1793). Waltham history. Local watch industry. Costumes.
By appointment.

WAPAKONETA

NEIL ARMSTRONG MUSEUM
Fisher Road and Interstate 75, Wapakoneta, Ohio 45895
Ohio air and space museum.
Daily 9-5.

WAREHOUSE POINT

MUSEUM OF CONNECTICUT ELECTRIC RAILWAY ASSOCIATION
North Road, East Windsor, Warehouse Point, Connecticut 06088
Trams and tramway equipment, 1895-1947. 1 miles of operational track.
May 30 - Oct. 30, Sa., 1-5. Also Mar. 1 - Dec. 31, Su. 1-dusk. Closed Christmas and Jan., Feb., except by appointment.

SCANTIC ACADEMY MUSEUM
East Windsor Historical Society, Scantic Road, Route 191, Warehouse Point, Connecticut 06088
In former Academy building (1817). Local agriculture, industry, Transport. Paintings.
May-June, Sept.-Oct., Su. 2-5. Other days by appointment.

WARM SPRINGS

FRANKLIN D. ROOSEVELT WARM SPRINGS MEMORIAL COMMISSION
Warm Springs, Georgia 31830
Museum illustrating life and political achievements of Franklin Roosevelt.
Roosevelt's Little White House (1932), where he died, is in the care of the Commission.
Daily 9-5. Closed Christmas morning.

WARNER

CONNORS STATE COLLEGE MUSEUM
Warner, Oklahoma 74469
Geology. Local history. Indian artifacts. Coins.
M.-F. 8-4. Closed College vacations.

WARREN

MUSEUM OF WARREN HISTORICAL SOCIETY
Warren, Maine 04864
History and development of Warren.
By appointment.

MARSHALL COUNTY HISTORICAL SOCIETY MUSEUM
Warren, Minnesota 56762
Local history museum based on log-house (1882), school-house (1900) and church (1901).
By appointment.

MORSE MUSEUM
Main Street, Warren, New Hampshire 03279
Mounted specimens of Indian and African game animals. Hunting equipment. Native shoes.
May 15 - Oct. 15, daily 10-5.

MUSEUM OF CONFEDERATE MEMORIAL HISTORIC RESEARCH COUNCIL
254 King George Road, Warren, New Jersey 07060
Civil War history.
By appointment.

THE TRUMBULL COUNTY HISTORICAL SOCIETY
259 South Street, S.E., Warren, Ohio 44481
In John Stark Edwards House (1807). Early history of the Western Reserve. Furniture.
Daily: afternoons or by appointment.

MUSEUM OF WARREN COUNTY HISTORICAL SOCIETY
210 4th Avenue, Warren, Pennsylvania 16365
Pennsylvania and local history. Documents. Photographs. Victorian furniture.
W., Th. 1-5. Closed public holidays.

WARREN MILITARY MUSEUM
Building 211, Randall Avenue, F. E. Warren Air Force Base, Wyoming 82001
Local and military history. Aviation.
Su., public holidays 1-5.

WARRENSBURG

CENTRAL MISSOURI STATE MUSEUM
Central Missouri State College, Warrensburg, Missouri 64093
Natural history. Anthropology. Archaeology.
M.-F. 9.30-4.30. Closed College vacations.

JOHNSON COUNTY HISTORICAL SOCIETY MUSEUM
Main and Gay Streets, Warrensburg, Missouri 64093
In Old Courthouse (1838-41). Local history. Indian material. Folklore.
June 1 - Sept. 14: Sa., Su. 1-5.

WARRENTON

OLD JAIL MUSEUM
Warrenton, Virginia 22186
Jail (1778, with later additions). History of Fauquier County.
By appointment.

WARSAW

BENTON COUNTY MUSEUM
Warsaw, Missouri 65355
Local history.
Apr.-Oct., daily 9-5.

WARSAW HISTORICAL MUSEUM
15 Perry Avenue, Warsaw, New York 14569
In Gates House (1824). Period furniture. Local history.
By appointment and special announcement.

WARWICK

MUSEUM OF OLD BOHEMIA HISTORICAL SOCIETY
St. Francis Xavier House, Warwick, Maryland 21912
House (1797). Local history. Agriculture.
June 1 - Sept. 30, Th. 9-1. 3rd Sunday in month 11-6.

SHINGLE HOUSE
Forester Avenue, Warwick, New York 10990
House and barn (1764). Period furnishings. Tools. Carriages. Sleighs. Farm machinery and implements.
July 1 - Sept. 15: Tu., Sa. 2-4.

WARWICK HISTORICAL SOCIETY MUSEUM
Main Street, Warwick, New York 10990
House (1810). 18th-19th century furniture by local makers. Sports equipment of W. H. Herbert (Frank Forester), author during 1830s. Local history.
Tu., Sa. 2-4.

WARWICK HISTORICAL SOCIETY MUSEUM
70 Warwick Neck Avenue, Warwick, Rhode Island 02887
Local history.
By appointment.

WASECA

MUSEUM OF WASECA COUNTY HISTORICAL SOCIETY
4th Street and 2nd Avenue N.E., Waseca, Minnesota 56093
Agriculture. Costumes. Decorative arts.
Sa.-Su. 1-5. Other times by appointment.

WASHINGTON

PIONEER WASHINGTON RESTORATION FOUNDATION
Washington, Arkansas 71862
Archaeology. Indian artifacts. Weapons. Paintings. Sculpture.
Three houses (1828-45), and a reconstructed 19th century tavern and blacksmith's shop, are in the care of the Foundation.
M.-Sa. 9-5; Su. 1-5. Closed Christmas.

HISTORICAL MUSEUM OF THE GUNN MEMORIAL LIBRARY
Wykeham Road, Washington, Connecticut 06793
Building (1780). Local history. Mementoes of Revolutionary, Civil and 1914-18 wars. Letters of George Washington and Thomas Jefferson. Indian material. Portraits. Dolls. Glass.
Tu., Th. 2-5. Sa. 1-4.

AGRA GALLERY
1721 De Sales Street N.W., Washington D.C. 20036
Paintings. Sculpture. Graphics.
Tu.-Sa. 10-6.

AGRICULTURAL HISTORY SOCIETY MUSEUM
U.S. Department of Agriculture, Economics Research Service, 12th Street S.W., Washington D.C. 20250
History of agriculture in U.S.A.
Daily 8.30-5. Closed public holidays.

AMERICAN HAND
1214 31st Street N.W., Washington D.C. 20007
Sculpture. Graphics. Decorative arts. Ceramics.
Tu.-F. 11-6; Sa. 10-6. Closed public holidays.

AMERICAN PSYCHIATRIC MUSEUM
1811 R Street N.W., Washington D.C. 20009
Collections illustrating history of mental illness and its treatment.
By appointment.

ANACOSTIA NEIGHBORHOOD MUSEUM
2405 Nichols Avenue S.E., Washington D.C. 20020
Afro-American history and art. Urban social problems.
M.-F. 10-6; Sa., Su., public holidays 1-6. Closed Christmas.

ANDERSON HOUSE MUSEUM
2118 Massachusetts Avenue N.W., Washington D.C. 20008
Weapons and other relics of the American Revolution. Japanese screens, bronzes, ceramics, jade. 16th-17th century Flemish tapestries. Sculptures. 18th-19th century furniture, paintings.
Tu.-Su. 2-4.

BARNETT ADEN GALLERY
127 Randolph Place, N.W. (1), Washington, District of Columbia 20001
Paintings, sculpture, prints by contemporary American artists.
M.-Sa. 12-7; Su. 2-5.

COLUMBIA HISTORICAL SOCIETY MUSEUM
1307 New Hampshire Avenue N.W., Washington D.C. 20030
In Christian Neurich Memorial Mansion (1892-4). History of the Federal District. 19th century furniture.
M.-F. 10-4; Sa. 1-4.

CORCORAN GALLERY OF ART
17th Street and New York Avenue N.W., Washington D.C. 20006
18th-20th century American paintings, sculpture, drawings. 18th century English paintings. Dutch, Flemish and French paintings, sculpture, decorative arts. 18th century French salon. Majolica. Tapestries. Greek antiquities.
Tu.-Su. 11-5.

DAUGHTERS OF THE AMERICAN REVOLUTION MUSEUM
1776 D Street N.W., Washington D.C. 20006
American history. Furniture. Decorative arts. Costumes. Paintings. 17th-19th century period rooms.
M.-F. 9-4. Closed public holidays and one week in April (variable).

DECATUR HOUSE
748 Jackson Place N.W., Washington D.C. 20006
House (1818). Furniture and personal possessions of successive owners of the house.
Daily 10-4. Closed Christmas.

DIMOCK GALLERY
George Washington University, Washington D.C. 20037
Paintings, sculpture, graphics relating to George Washington and to Washington. Photographs.
M.-F. 10-5. Closed Sa., Su., public holidays.

DUMBARTON HOUSE
2715 Que Street N.W., Washington D.C. 20007
House (1799). Early Federal period furnishings.
M.-Sa. 9-12. Closed July 1 - Aug. 31, government holidays.

DUMBARTON OAKS RESEARCH LIBRARY AND COLLECTION
1703 32nd Street N.W., Washington D.C. 20007
Byzantine and pre-Columbian art. European and American paintings, decorative arts. Exhibition of rare books on gardening and landscaping.
Day following Labour Day - June 30, Tu.-Su. 2-4.45. Closed rest of year, public holidays.

FORD'S THEATRE AND LINCOLN MUSEUM
511 10th Street N.W., Washington D.C. 20004
Theatre (1863) where Lincoln was assassinated (1865), restored as it was on that evening. Material associated with Lincoln.
Theatre: M., Tu., Th., F. 9-5; W., Sa. 9-12; Su. 9-1. May 1 - Sept. 30, daily 9-5. Museum: daily 9-5. Closed Christmas.

FRANCISCAN MONASTERY (HOLY LAND OF AMERICA)
Biblical Museum, 1400 Quincy Street N.E., Washington D.C. 20017
Replicas of chapels, shrines, catacombs. Frescoes. Jewellery.
Daily 8-5. Closed New Year, Good Friday, Thanksgiving, Christmas.

FREER GALLERY OF ART
12th Street and Jefferson Drive S.W., Washington D.C. 20560
Near and Far Eastern art. Paintings, drawings, watercolours by Whistler and his contemporaries.
Daily 10-5.30. Closed Christmas.

GALLERY OF AFRICAN ART
1621 21st Street N.W., Washington D.C. 20009
Folk art. Traditional African sculpture. Contemporary graphics and sculpture. Tapestry.
W. 6-9; Sa. 11-5; Su. 1-7.

GEORGETOWN UNIVERSITY MUSEUM
Box 1595 Hoya Station, 37th and O Streets N.W., Washington D.C. 20007
Archaeology. European and American paintings. Sculpture. Graphics. Portraits.
M.-F., usually 10-4. Closed public holidays.

THE HOUSE WHERE LINCOLN DIED
516 10th Street N.W., Washington D.C. 20004
Petersen House (1849), to which Lincoln was taken after the shooting in Ford's Theatre. Period furnishings. Lincoln memorabilia.
Daily 9-5. Closed Christmas.

HOWARD UNIVERSITY GALLERY OF ART
2455 6th Street N.W., Washington D.C. 20001
African sculpture. European, especially Italian, and American, paintings, sculpture, graphic art.
M.-F. 9-5. Closed public holidays.

INDIAN ARTS AND CRAFTS BOARD
U.S. Department of the Interior, Washington D.C. 20240
Contemporary United States Indian and Eskimo arts and crafts.
M.-F. 7.45-4.15. Closed public holidays.

INSTITUTE OF CONTEMPORARY ARTS
The Meridian House, 1630 Crescent Place N.W., Washington D.C. 20009
Contemporary paintings, sculpture, graphics, ceramics by American and foreign artists.
M.-Sa. 12-6.

THE ISLAMIC CENTER
2551 Massachusetts Avenue N.W., Washington D.C. 20008
Islamic religious art. Calligraphy. Copies of the Koran.
By appointment.

KLUTZNICK EXHIBITION HALL
1640 Rhode Island Avenue N.W., Washington D.C. 20336
American-Jewish history. Ethnology. Folk art.
M.-F. 1.30-5. Closed public and Jewish holidays.

LIBRARY OF THE SUPREME COUNCIL, 33 DEGREES
1733 16th Street N.W., Washington D.C. 20009
Masonic medals, jewels, documents.
M.-F. 9-4; Sa. 9-12. Closed public holidays.

MEDICAL MUSEUM OF THE ARMED FORCES INSTITUTE OF PATHOLOGY
6825 16th Street N.W., Washington D.C. 20305
Medical and military history. Pathology. Medical and surgical instruments and techniques.
Daily 9-5.

MUSEUM OF AFRICAN ART
316-8 A Street N.E., Washington D.C. 20002
In Frederick Douglass house (1871). Works by African and Afro-American artists. Sculpture. Decorative arts. Musical instruments. Textiles. History. Ethnology.
M.-F. 10-5.30; Sa., Su. 2-5.30. Closed New Year, Thanksgiving, Christmas.

MUSEUM OF THE NATIONAL ARCHIVES
Washington D.C. 20408
Historic documents, including Declaration of Independence, Constitution, Bill of Rights.
M.-Sa. 9-10; Su., holidays 1-10. Closed Christmas, New Year.

MUSEUM OF THE SOCIETY OF THE CINCINNATI-ANDERSON HOUSE
2118 Massachusetts Avenue N.W., Washington D.C. 20008
History of the American Revolution. Drawings. Relics. Documents. Art collection of sculpture, paintings, decorative arts.
Anderson House (1903-5) is in the care of the Society.
Tu.-Su. 2-4. Closed Thanksgiving, Christmas.

MUSEUM OF THE UNITED STATES CAPITOL HISTORICAL SOCIETY
200 Maryland Avenue N.E., Washington D.C. 20515
Local history.
M.-F. 8.30-5. Closed public holidays.

MUSEUM OF THE U.S. DEPARTMENT OF THE INTERIOR
C Street, between 18th and 19th Streets N.W., Washington D.C. 20240
Paintings of early American explorers, wildlife, Western conservation scenes, the Antarctic. Miniature dioramas. Indian, Eskimo, Virgin Islands and South Sea Islands arts and crafts.
M.-F. 8-4.

NATIONAL AIR AND SPACE MUSEUM
900 Jefferson Drive S.W., Washington D.C. 20560
History of aviation. Original aircraft. Engines, equipment, accessories. Models. Instruments. Astronautics. Space travel.
Daily 10-5.30. Closed Christmas.

NATIONAL COLLECTION OF FINE ARTS
8th and G Streets N.W., Washington D.C. 20560
In Old Patent office (1836). Paintings. Sculpture. Decorative arts. Graphics.
Renwick Gallery (1859) and Barney Studio House (1906) are in the care of the same governing authority, the Smithsonian Institution.
Daily 10-5.30. Closed Christmas.

NATIONAL GALLERY OF ART
Constitution Avenue at 6th Street, Washington D.C. 20565
12th-20th century European and American paintings, sculpture, decorative arts, graphics. Special features include French Impressionist and post-impressionist paintings, American primitive paintings, Renaissance bronzes, Chinese porcelain. 18th century French period rooms and decorative arts. American folk art.
Day after Labour Day - Mar. 31, M.-Sa. 10-5; Su. 12-9. Apr. 1 - Labour Day, M.-Sa. 10-9; Su. 12-9. Closed Christmas, New Year.

NATIONAL GEOGRAPHIC SOCIETY
Explorers' Hall, 17th and M Streets N.W., Washington D.C. 20036
Material relating to land, sea and space exploration, especially expeditions sponsored by the National Geographic Society.
M.-F. 9-6; Sa. 9-5; Su. 12-5. Closed Christmas.

NATIONAL MUSEUM OF HISTORY AND TECHNOLOGY
Part of the Smithsonian Institution, 14th Street and Constitution Avenue N.W., Washington D.C. 20560
Aeronautics. Anatomy. Anthropology. Ethnology. Archaeology. Astronomy. Industry. Technology. Maritime history. Medicine. Music. Military and naval history. Transport. Textiles. Toys.
Oct.-Apr., daily 10-5. May-Sept., daily 10-6. Closed Christmas.

NATIONAL MUSEUM OF NATURAL HISTORY
Part of the Smithsonian Institution, 10th Street and Constitution Avenue N.W., Washington D.C. 20560
Anthropology. Botany. Zoology. Entomology. Mineralogy. Petrology. Palaeontology. Ethnology, especially of American Indians. Archaeology.
Daily 10-5.30. Closed Christmas.

NATIONAL PORTRAIT GALLERY
8th and F Streets N.W., Washington D.C. 20560
In Old Patent Office (1836). Paintings, especially portraits of people eminent in American history. Portrait busts and sculpture.
Daily 10-5.30. Closed Christmas.

NATIONAL RIFLE ASSOCIATION FIREARMS MUSEUM
1600 Rhode Island Avenue N.W., Washington D.C. 20036
History of firearms. American and foreign shotguns, rifles, pistols.
Daily 10-4. Closed New Year, Easter, Christmas.

NATIONAL SOCIETY OF CHILDREN OF AMERICAN REVOLUTION MUSEUM
1776 D Street N.W., Washington D.C. 20006
Children's museum. Applied arts. Decorative arts.
M.-F. 9-4. Closed public holidays, Dec. 24, 30, 31.

OCTAGON
1799 New York Avenue N.W., Washington D.C. 20006
Building (1798-1800). History of architecture. Decorative arts, especially early 19th century furniture.
Tu.-Sa. 10-4; Su. 1-4. Closed New Year, Thanksgiving, Christmas.

OLD STONE HOUSE
3051 M Street, N.W., Washington D.C. 20405
House (1764-65), built as home and cabinet-maker's shop by Christopher Layhman. Period furnishings.
W.-Su., holidays 1-5.

ORGANISATION OF AMERICAN STATES
General Secretariat, 17th Street and Constitution Avenue N.W., Washington D.C. 20006
In Pan American Union building (1910). Contemporary art of Latin America.
M.-F. 9-5.30; Sa. 9-4. Closed public holidays.

PHILLIPS COLLECTION
1600-1612 21st Street N.W., Washington D.C. 20001
Paintings, especially contemporary, by European and American artists.
Tu.-Sa. 10-5; Su. 2-7. Closed July 4, Christmas.

PIERCE MILL
Washington D.C. 20025
Water-powered grist mill (c.1820), with much original machinery and equipment.
June 20 - Aug. 30, Sa. 9-5; Su. 1-5. Sept. 1 - June 14, F. 9-5; Su. 1-5.

RENWICK GALLERY
Pennsylvania Avenue and 17th Street N.W., Washington D.C. 20560
In Corcoran Gallery of Art (1859). American crafts, designs.
Daily 10-5.30. Closed Christmas.

ROCK GREEN NATURE CENTER
Military and Glover Roads N.W., Washington D.C. 20015
Children's nature centre. Geology. Botany. Entomology.
M.-Sa., public holidays 9.30-5; Su. 12-6. Closed Christmas, New Year.

SMITH-MASON GALLERY OF ART
1207 Rhode Island Avenue N.W., Washington D.C. 20005
Ethnology. Paintings. Sculpture. Graphics. Decorative arts.
Tu.-F. 12-4; Sa. 10-4; Su. 2-5. Closed July 1 - Sept. 15.

TEXTILE MUSEUM
2320 S. Street N.W., Washington D.C. 20008
Fabrics from the Mediterranean, the Far East, Africa, Oceania, and the Americas. Rugs from the Near East, Spain and Portugal.
Tu.-F. 1-5; Sa. 10-5. Closed public holidays.

THE AMERICAN UNIVERSITY, WATKINS GALLERY
Massachusetts and Nebraska Avenues N.W., Washington D.C. 20016
20th century paintings and drawings, with emphasis on American paintings. Exhibits include works by Modigliani, Matisse and Ben Nicholson.
M.-F. 9-12, 1-5; Su. 2-5. Closed public holidays.

TRUXTUN-DECATUR NAVAL MUSEUM
1610 H Street N.W., Washington D.C. 20006
Naval history. Paintings on naval subjects.
Tu.-Su., public holidays 10.30-4. Closed Christmas, public holidays.

THE UNITED STATES CAPITOL
Capitol Hill, Washington D.C. 20201
Sculpture, paintings, furnishings (mainly 19th century), illustrating history of the Capital.
M.-Sa. 9-4.30. Guided tours every 15 minutes.

UNITED STATES DEPARTMENT OF JUSTICE
Federal Bureau of Investigation, Department of Justice Building, 9th Street and Pennsylvania Avenue N.W., Washington D.C. 20535
Exhibition illustrating celebrated criminal and espionage cases dealt with by the Bureau.
M.-F. 9.15-4.15. Closed public holidays.

UNITED STATES NATIONAL ARBORETUM
Washington D.C. 20002
Herbarium. Outdoor museum of horticulture and agriculture.
Nov. 1 - Apr. 30, M.-F. 8-5; Sa., Su., public holidays 10-5. May 1 - Oct. 31, M.-F. 8-7; Sa., Su. public holidays 10-7.

U.S. NAVY MEMORIAL MUSEUM
Building 76, Washington Navy Yard, Washington D.C. 20390
In part of former Naval Gun Factory (1828). Naval history and technology. Paintings. Weapons. Memorabilia.
M.-F. 9-4; Sa., Su., public holidays, 10-5. Closed New Year, Thanksgiving, Christmas.

WASHINGTON CITY MUSEUM
Guardian Building, 1369 Connecticut Avenue, N.W. (6), Washington D.C. 20006
Local history, illustrated by paintings, prints, manuscripts, letters, books.
M.-Th. 9-4; F. 9-6. Closed national holidays.

WASHINGTON GALLERY OF MODERN ART
1503 21st Street N.W., Washington D.C. 20006
Works by 20th century American and foreign artists. Paintings. Drawings. Prints. Sculpture.
Tu.-Sa. 10-5; Su. 2-6.

WHITE HOUSE
1600 Pennsylvania Avenue N.W., Washington D.C. 20500
The Presidential residence (1800). Furniture. Decorative arts. Paintings. Sculpture.
Tu.-F., public holidays 10-12; May 1 - Sept. 30, Tu.-Sa. 10-2. Closed New Year, Thanksgiving, Christmas.

WOODROW WILSON HOUSE
2340 S. Street N.W., Washington D.C. 20008
Retirement home (1915) of president Wilson. Wilson family furniture. Mementoes related to his period of office.
Daily 10-4. Closed Christmas.

WASHINGTON-WILKES HISTORICAL MUSEUM
308 East Robert Toombs Avenue, Washington, Georgia 30673
In Barnett-Slaton House (1836). Period furnishings. Civil War relics.
Oct. 1 - Apr. 30, Tu.-Sa. 9-5; Su. 2-5. May 1 - Sept. 30, Tu.-Sa. 9-5.30. Su. 2-5.30. Closed Thanksgiving, Christmas.

WASHINGTON MUSEUM
Washington, New Hampshire 03280
Horse-drawn carriages, sleighs.
By appointment.

ARDEN TROLLEY MUSEUM
N. Main Street, Washington, Pennsylvania 15301
Tram cars, including 'The Streetcar Named Desire'. Steam, electric, diesel locomotives. Railway.
May 30 - Oct. 31: Su., public holidays 1-6.

DAVID BRADFORD HOUSE
175 S. Main Street, Washington, Pennsylvania 15301
House (1788), built by David Bradford, leader of Whisky Rebellion. Period furnishings.
May 1 - Oct. 31: Tu.-Sa. 8.30-5; Su. 1-5. Nov. 1 - Apr. 30: Tu.-Sa. 9-4.30; Su. 1-4.30. Closed public holidays.

MUSEUM OF WASHINGTON COUNTY HISTORICAL SOCIETY
49 E. Maiden Street, Washington, Pennsylvania 15301
In Le Moyne House (1812). History of Washington County.
M.-F. 1-5.

BARRINGTON
Washington-on-the-Brazos State Park, Washington, Texas 77880
House (1844-5) was home of Anson Jones, last President of Republic of Texas. Period furnishings. Jones family memorabilia. Medical equipment.
W.-Su. 10-5.

STAR OF THE REPUBLIC MUSEUM
P.O. Box 317, Washington-on-the-Brazos State Park, Washington, Texas 77880
Natural history. Texas history and archaeology. Decorative arts. Maps.
June 1 - Aug. 31, daily 10-6. Sept. 1 - May 31, W.-Su. 10-5. Closed Christmas, New Year.

RAPPAHANNOCK COUNTY HISTORICAL SOCIETY MUSEUM
Avon Hall, Washington, Virginia 22747
House (1790). Local history and archaeology. Indian artifacts. Transport. Anthropology.
By appointment.

WASHINGTON CROSSING

WASHINGTON CROSSING STATE PARK MUSEUM
Washington Crossing, Pennsylvania 18977
In Taylor Mansion (1812). Botany. Local and military history. Paintings, including Leutze's 'Washington Crossing the Delaware'.
Daily 9.30-5.

WASHINGTON'S BIRTHPLACE

GEORGE WASHINGTON BIRTHPLACE NATIONAL MONUMENT
Washington's Birthplace, Virginia 22575
House (1730-50). Furnishings of Colonial period. Local history. Agriculture. Costumes.
Daily 9-5.

WASHINGTON ISLAND

JACOBSEN'S MUSEUM
Washington Island, Wisconsin 54246
Indian relics.
June-Sept., daily 10-3.

WATERBURY

MATTATUCK MUSEUM OF THE MATTATUCK HISTORICAL SOCIETY
119 West Main Street, Waterbury, Connecticut 06702
Local history. Colonial period arts and crafts. Industry. Furniture. Decorative arts. Paintings by Connecticut artists. Baseball. Junior museum, with apothecary shop and post office.
Sept. 1 - June 30; Tu.-Sa. 12-5; Su. 2-5. July 1 - Aug. 31; Tu.-Sa. 12-5. Closed Sunday in July, Aug.

WATERBURY HISTORICAL MUSEUM
30 N. Main Street, Waterbury, Vermont 05676
Geology. Natural history. Local history.
M.-W., F., Sa. 1-5, 7-9. Closed public holidays.

WATERFORD

HARKNESS MEMORIAL STATE PARK MUSEUM
275 Great Neck Road, Waterford, Connecticut 06385
Botany. Paintings.
May 31 - Oct. 12, daily 10-5. Closed Oct. 13 - May 30.

WATERFORD MUSEUM
2 Museum Lane, Waterford, New York 12188
History of Waterford.
Sa., Su. 2-4. Closed New Year, Easter, Christmas.

FORT LE BOEUF MEMORIAL
Box 16, Waterford, Pennsylvania 16441
In Amos Judson House (1816-20), on site of French Fort Le Boeuf. Period furnishings. Local history. especially period of French occupation.
Tu.-Sa. 9-5; Su. 1-5.

WATERFORD FOUNDATION MUSEUM
Waterford, Virginia 22190
Local history. 18th-19th century agricultural and trade tools, implements.
Old Mill and Weaver's Cottage, Waterford, are in the care of the Foundation.
Daily 9-5.

WATERLOO

CEDAR VALLEY HISTORICAL SOCIETY
503 South Street, Waterloo, Iowa 50701
Local history.
By appointment.

MUSEUM OF HISTORY AND SCIENCE
Park Avenue and South Street, Waterloo, Iowa 50701
Early American handicrafts. Indian artifacts. Buildings and displays illustrating pioneer life, including blacksmith's and carpenter's shop, apothecary's shop and country store.
Tu.-F. 1-5; Sa. 10-4; Su. 1-4. Closed public holidays.

MUSEUM OF WATERLOO HISTORICAL SOCIETY
31 E. Williams Street, Waterloo, New York 13165
Building (1880). Period rooms. Local history. Country store. Indian artifacts.
F. 7-9; Sa. 2-5. Closed public holidays.

WATER MILL

OLD WATER MILL MUSEUM
Old Mill Road, Water Mill, New York 11976
Early American tools.
June 1 - Sept. 30: M., W.-Sa. 11-5; Su. 1-4. May 1-31, Oct. 1-31, by appointment.

WATERSTOWN

JEFFERSON COUNTY HISTORICAL SOCIETY MUSEUM
228 Washington Street, Waterstown, New York 13601
In Edwin L. Paddock house (1874). Local history. Indian artifacts. Steamboat paintings. Water turbines. Coverlets. Tools and implements of early settlers. Military uniforms, insignia. Carriages.
Hart Massey house (1807-10) is in the care of the Society.
Tu.-F. 12-5; Sa. 10-5.

WATERTOWN

WATERTOWN HISTORICAL SOCIETY MUSEUM
22 DeForest Street, Watertown, Connecticut 06795
Local history. Tools. Watertown furniture.
W. 2-4; Th. 7-9. Other times by appointment.

ABRAHAM BROWNE HOUSE
562 Main Street, Watertown, Massachusetts. 02172
House (c.1698). Parlour furnished to reflect 17th century interior, as reconstructed from inventories.
June-Oct., M., W., F. 2-5.

HISTORICAL SOCIETY OF WATERTOWN MUSEUM
26 Marshall Street, Watertown, Massachusetts 02172
In Fowle House (c.1742). Local history.
By appointment.

MUSEUM ON THE HISTORY OF BLINDNESS
Perkins School for the Blind, 175 North Beacon Street, Watertown, Massachusetts 02172
Pictures showing history of blindness.
M.-F. 8.30-12, 1-5. Closed school vacations.

ROSWELL P. FLOWER MEMORIAL LIBRARY
229 Washington Street, Watertown, New York 13601
American paintings, sculpture, New York furniture. Japanese prints.
Daily 9-9.

MELLETTE HOUSE
421 5th Avenue N.W., Watertown, South Dakota 57201
House (1883). Mellette family portraits, furnishings.
May-Oct., Tu.-Su. 1-5.

WATERTOWN HISTORICAL SOCIETY MUSEUM
919 Charles Street, Watertown, Wisconsin 53094
Early Watertown history.
Octagon House (1854), with original Victorian furnishings, and Margarette Meyer Schurz kindergarten (1856) are in the care of the Society.
May 1 - Oct. 31, daily 10-5.

WATERVILLE

COLBY COLLEGE ART MUSEUM
Waterville, Maine 04901
European and American paintings, sculpture, graphics. Pre-Columbian Mexican art. Chinese, Japanese ceramics. Etruscan art.
June 1 - Aug. 31: M.-Sa. 10-12, 1-5.

REDINGTON MUSEUM
64 Silver Street, Waterville, Maine 04901
Museum building (1814). Local history. Indian artifacts.
May 15 - Oct. 31, Tu.-Sa. 2-6. Closed public holidays.

MUSEUM OF LE SUEUR COUNTY HISTORICAL SOCIETY
306 W. Lake Street, Waterville, Minnesota 56096
Agriculture. Archaeology. Indian artifacts.
May-Sept., W.-M. 1.30-5.30.

WATERVILLE HISTORICAL MUSEUM
191-2 N. 3rd Street, Waterville, Ohio 43566
Local history. Furnishings.
May 1 - Sept. 30, 1st Su. in month 1-5.

MUSEUM OF DOUGLAS COUNTY HISTORICAL SOCIETY
P.O. Box 308, Waterville, Washington 38858
Local history. Natural history. Animal holes. Minerals. Meteorites. Guns.
June-Sept., daily 11-5.

WATKINS GLEN

MUSEUM OF AMERICAN LIFE FOUNDATION AND STUDY INSTITUTE
Old Irelandville, Watkins Glen, New York 14891
Building (1833). Paintings. Costumes. Decorative arts. Folklore. Music. Dolls. Toys.
June 1 - Aug. 31: Tu.-Sa. 9.30-4.30; Su. 1.30-5.30.

MUSEUM OF SCHUYLER COUNTY HISTORICAL SOCIETY
R.D.1, Watkins Glen, New York 14891
Local history. Agriculture. Furnishings. Costumes.
Tu., F. 2-4.30. Closed public holidays.

YORKER YANKEE VILLAGE
Irelandville Road, Watkins Glen, New York 14891
19th century village of buildings moved to site. Shops. Workshops. School. Chapel. Meeting house. Stores. Manor house. White Pump Tavern (used 1799-1829), contains collections of dolls, toys, china, glass, primitive paintings and Currier and Ives prints.
June-Aug., Tu.-Sa. 9-5; Su. 12.30-6.30.

WATKINSVILLE

EAGLE TAVERN
U.S. Highway 129, Watkinsville, Georgia 30677
Building (1820). Local history, especially exhibits on early travel in Georgia. Period furnishings.
Oct. 1 - Apr. 30, Tu.-Sa. 9-5; Su. 2-5. May 1 - Sept. 30, Tu.-Sa. 9-5.30; Su. 2-5.30. Closed Thanksgiving, Christmas.

WATROUS

FORT UNION NATIONAL MONUMENT
Watrous, New Mexico 87753
Museum showing history of Fort Union, 1851-91, and its importance during the Civil War and settlement of the West.
Oct. 1 - Apr. 30, daily 8-4.30. May 1 - Sept. 30, daily 8-7. Closed Christmas.

WATSEKA

IROQUOIS COUNTY HISTORICAL MUSEUM
Old Court House, Watseka, Illinois 60970
County history. One-room school. Old jail. Works by Iroquois County artists.
June 1 - Aug. 31: M.-Sa. 9-5, Su. 1-5. Sept. 1 - May 31: daily 1-5.

WATSON

LAC QUI PARLE INDIAN MISSION CHURCH
Rural Route 1, Watson, Minnesota 56295
House (1835). Local history. Indian material.
Apr. 1 - Dec. 31: M.-Sa. 8-5; Su., public holidays 10-6.

WATSONVILLE

PAJARO VALLEY HISTORICAL ASSOCIATION MUSEUM
P.O. Box 960, Watsonville, California 95076
History of Pajaro Valley.
W., Sa., Su. 2-4. Other times by appointment.

WAUKEGAN

WAUKEGAN HISTORICAL SOCIETY
428 Franklin Street, Waukegan, Illinois 60085
Local history.
M., W., F. 1-4.

WAUKESHA

WAUKESHA COUNTY HISTORICAL SOCIETY MUSEUM
101 W. Main Street, Waukesha, Wisconsin 53186
Local history.
M.-F. 9-4.30. Closed public holidays.

WAUPACA

HUTCHINSON HOUSE
South Park, Waupaca, Wisconsin 54981
House (1854) furnished in style of 1850-1900.
May 30 - Labour Day, Sa., Su., holidays 2-5. Other times by appointment.

WAURIKA

CHISHOLM TRAIL HISTORICAL MUSEUM
107 West E. Street, Waurika, Oklahoma 73573
Material illustrating history of Chisholm Trail, cattle industry and pioneer life.
M.-F. 9-5; Sa., Su. 1-5.

WAUSAU

MARATHON COUNTY HISTORICAL SOCIETY MUSEUM
403 McIndoe Street, Wausau, Wisconsin 54401
Local history. Logging industry.
M.-F. 9-5; Su. 2-5. Closed New Year, Veterans' Day, Christmas.

WAUSEON

MUSEUM OF FULTON COUNTY HISTORICAL SOCIETY
229 Monroe Street, Wauseon, Ohio 43567
History of Fulton County. Domestic equipment, utensils. Tools.
Su. 2-5.

WAUZEKA

PHETTEPLACE MUSEUM
Wauzeka, Wisconsin 53826
Mineralogy. Palaeontology. Local and maritime history. Paintings. Furniture. Pietre Dure inlays.
Apr. 15 - Oct. 14, daily 9-5.

WAVERLY

MUSEUM OF BREMER COUNTY HISTORICAL SOCIETY
402 West Bremer Avenue, Waverly, Iowa 50677
Museum building (1863-4). Local history. Agriculture.
May 1 - Oct. 30, Tu., Th., Su. 1-5.

WAXAHACHIE

ELLIS COUNTY HISTORICAL MUSEUM AND ART GALLERY
604 W. Main Street, Waxahachie, Texas 75165
History of Ellis County. Paintings, sculpture, prints by local artists.
W. 10-5; Sa., Su. 2-5.

WAYCROSS

OKEFENOKEE SWAMP PARK MUSEUM
U.S. Highway 1, Waycross, Georgia 31501
History of the Park area. Fossils. Indian relics. Photographs.
Daily 8-sunset.

WAYLAND

WAYLAND HISTORICAL SOCIETY MUSEUM
182 Concord Road, Wayland, Massachusetts 01778
In Grout-Heard House (1800). Local history. Indian artifacts. Costumes.
Oct. 1 - May 30: Tu., Th. 2-4. Other times by appointment.

WAYNE

WAYNE HISTORICAL MUSEUM
3747 Old Wayne Road, Wayne, Michigan 48184
In old Village Hall (1878). Local history.
F., Sa. 1-5.

WAYNE COUNTY HISTORICAL MUSEUM
Wayne, Nebraska 68787
Pioneer life in mid-West.
By appointment.

DEY MANSION
199 Totowa Road, Wayne, New Jersey 07470
House (1740). Period furnishings. Local history. Herbarium.
Tu., W., F. 1-5; Sa. 10-12, 1-5. Su. 10-5. Closed Thanksgiving, Christmas, New Year.

VAN RIPER-HOPPER HOUSE AND WAYNE MUSEUM
533 Berdan Avenue, Wayne, New Jersey 07470
House (1786). Period furnishings. Local history.
Tu., F.-Su. 1-5. Closed New Year, Thanksgiving, Christmas.

RADNOR HISTORICAL SOCIETY MUSEUM
113 W. Beech Tree Lane, Wayne, Pennsylvania 19087
In Fenley House (1789). Mineralogy. Local history. Transport.
Tu. 2-5. Other times by appointment.

WAYNESBORO

WAYNESBORO HISTORICAL MUSEUM
536 Liberty Street, Waynesboro, Georgia 30830
Building (c.1855). Local history.
By appointment.

WAYNESBURG

GREENE COUNTY HISTORICAL SOCIETY MUSEUM
R.D.2, Waynesburg, Pennsylvania 15370
Local history and archaeology. Indian artifacts.
W.-Su. 1-4.30. Closed Christmas, Thanksgiving, Su. Nov. 1 - Apr. 30.

WAYNESVILLE

PULASKI COUNTY MUSEUM
County Courthouse, Waynesville, Missouri 65583
Local history.
By appointment.

WEATHERFORD

TEXAS RAILROAD MUSEUM
Santa Fe Depot, Fort Worth Street, Weatherford, Texas 76086
Collection of railway lamps. Menus from dining cars. Timetables. Two-man handcar. Trolley Car from San Francisco. Private Presidential Coach. Street car from New Orleans. Steam engine. Milk cans. Mailbags. Luggage waggon.
June 10 - Aug. 10, M.-Sa. 9-6; Su. 1-5. Rest of year, Sa. 10-5; Su. 1-5.

WEATHERLY

ANTHRACITE MUSEUM, ECKLEY VILLAGE
R.D.2, Weatherly, Pennsylvania 18255
In original building of Glen Burn Mine. Working mine. Miners' houses (1854-60). History of local mining industry.
May 1 - Oct. 31: Sa., Su., public holidays 10-6.

WEAVERVILLE

J. J. JACKSON MEMORIAL MUSEUM
Main Street, Box 333, Weaverville, California 96093
Local history. Indian artifacts.
Daily 10-5. Closed Dec. 1 - Apr. 30.

WEAVERVILLE JOSS HOUSE STATE HISTORIC PARK
Main and Oregon Streets, Weaverville, California 93960
Chinese temple (1874-5) and furnishings. Temple attendant's quarters. Chinese art objects, pictures, mining tools. Wrought iron weapons used in 1854 tong war. Chinese life and contribution to development of California.
Daily 10-5. Closed New Year, Thanksgiving, Christmas.

ZEBULON B. VANCE BIRTHPLACE
Weaverville, North Carolina 28787
Group of restored buildings (1795), including slave cabin, smoke house, spring house, loom house, and tool house. Local history. Memorabilia of Vance family. Farm tools. Log-house (1795), birthplace of Senator Z. B. Vance (1830).
Tu.-Sa. 9-5; Su. 1-5. Closed Thanksgiving, Dec. 24-6.

WEBSTER

DAY COUNTY MUSEUM
Day County Court House, Webster, South Dakota 57274
Local history. Indian artifacts. Costumes. Music.
M., W., F. 2-4.

WEEPING WATER

HERITAGE HOUSE MUSEUM
Weeping Water, Nebraska 68663
Heritage House (1862). Geology. Archaeology. Medicine. Anthropology. Prehistoric Indian artifacts.
Doctor's surgery (1865) is in the care of the Museum.
May 1 - Oct. 31: Sa., Su., public holidays 1-5.

WEISER

WASHINGTON COUNTY MUSEUM AND FIDDLERS' HALL OF FAME
46 Commercial Street, Weiser, Idaho 83672
Geology. Local history and folklore. Fiddlers' museum. Costumes. Glass. Children's museum.
June 1 - Labour Day, Th.-Sa. 10-5.

WELLESLEY

WELLESLEY COLLEGE MUSEUM
Jewett Arts Center, Wellesley, Massachusetts 02181
European, American and Oriental paintings, drawings, sculpture. African sculpture.
M.-Sa. 8.30-5; Su. 2-5. Closed New Year, Thanksgiving, Christmas, June 15 - Aug. 31.

WELLESLEY HISTORICAL SOCIETY MUSEUM
210 Washington Street, Wellesley, Massachusetts 02181
Local history. Civil War collection.
M.-Sa. (not July-Aug.), 2-4.30.

WELLFLEET

WELLFLEET HISTORICAL SOCIETY
Main Street, Wellfleet, Massachusetts 02667
History of Cape Cod area.
W., F., Sa. 2-5. Closed last week in June - 1st week in Sept.

WELLINGTON

CHISHOLM TRAIL MUSEUM
502 N. Washington Street, Wellington, Kansas 67152
Local history. Agriculture. Tools. Domestic equipment. Costumes.
Sept. 1 - May 31: Sa., Su. 2-4. June 1 - Aug. 31: Tu., W., Th., Sa., Su. 2-7.

HARBAUGH MUSEUM
National Bank of Commerce Building, Wellington, Kansas 67152
Agricultural implements. Horse-drawn vehicles. Guns. Arrowheads. Clocks.
Daily 9.30-3.

WELLS FARGO

CASS COUNTY HISTORICAL SOCIETY
Box 719, Wells Fargo, North Dakota 58078
Local history. Replica of pioneer village. Indian artifacts. Crafts. Household equipment.
Tu.-Su. 9-5.

WELLSVILLE

RIVER MUSEUM
1607 Buckeye Avenue, Wellsville, Ohio 43968
In Henry Aten Mansion (1811). Early transport on the Ohio River. Local history. Railway history. Civil War material. Indian artifacts.
Memorial Day - Labour Day, Tu.-Su., afternoons.

WENATCHEE

NORTH CENTRAL WASHINGTON MUSEUM
2 S. Chelan Street, Wenatchee, Washington 98801
Local history. N. American Indian material. Philippine items. Natural history of central Washington.
M.-F. 10-5; Sa. 1-5. Closed Christmas, New Year, Thanksgiving.

WENHAM

WENHAM HISTORICAL ASSOCIATION MUSEUM
Main Street, Wenham, Massachusetts 01984
In Claplin-Richards House (c.1662). Domestic equipment and crafts. Costumes. Dolls. Shoes. Quilts. Fans. Agricultural implements.
Merrill shoe shop (1840), Winslow shoe shop (1840) are in the care of the Association.
M.-F. 1-4. Closed public holidays, Feb. 1-28.

WEOTT

HUMBOLDT REDWOODS STATE PARK
Weott, California 95571
Exhibits on redwoods and local history.
May-Sept., daily 8 a.m. - 10 p.m. Oct.-Apr., daily 8-5. Closed Thanksgiving, Christmas, Jan. 1.

WESLACO

WESLACO'S WORLD'S SMALLEST MUSEUM
500 S. Kansas Street, Weslaco, Texas 78596
In old Texas Ranger's building (1921). Local history, with exhibits viewed from outside building.
Daily, round-the-clock.

WEST ALLIS

WEST ALLIS HISTORICAL SOCIETY MUSEUM
8405 W. National Avenues, West Allis, Wisconsin 53227
Local history. Agricultural implements. Costumes.
School (1887) and dentists's surgery (1898) are in the care of the Society.
Tu. 7-9; Su. 2-4. Closed New Year, Memorial Day, July 4, Thanksgiving, Christmas.

WEST BEND

WASHINGTON COUNTY HISTORICAL MUSEUM
340 5th Avenue, West Bend, Wisconsin 53095
In former County Jail (1886). Geology. Local history Indian artifacts. Costumes.
Tu., 2nd Su. in month, 2-4.

WEST BOOTHBAY HARBOR

MUSEUM OF U.S. NATIONAL MARINE FISHERIES SERVICE
McKown Point, West Boothbay Harbor, Maine 04575
Aquarium. Oceanography. Natural history. Charts and maps.
May 31 - Sept. 30, M.-Sa. 8-5.

WESTBOROUGH

WESTBOROUGH HISTORICAL SOCIETY
7 Parkman Street, Westborough, Massachusetts 01581
Local history.
By appointment.

WEST BRANCH

HERBERT HOOVER PRESIDENTIAL LIBRARY
234 S. Downey Street, West Branch, Iowa 52358
Library and personal possessions of Hoover. Material relating to his life and times.
Hoover's birthplace (1871), Meeting House (1871), blacksmith's shop (1871) and schoolhouse are in the care of the Library.
May 1 - Labour Day: M.-Sa. 9-6; Su., public holidays 10-6. Labour Day - Apr. 30: M.-Sa. 9-5; Su., public holidays 2-5. Closed New Year, Thanksgiving, Christmas.

WEST CHESTER

MUSEUM OF CHESTER COUNTY HISTORICAL SOCIETY
225 N. High Street, West Chester, Pennsylvania 19380
Mineralogy. Local history and archaeology. Indian material. Agriculture. Costumes. Paintings, sculpture, graphics by Pennsylvania artists. Coins. Stamps. Children's museum.
Brinton House (1704) and David Townsend House (1830) are in the care of the Society.
M., Tu. 1-5; W. 1-9; Th., F. 10-5. Closed Aug. 1 - Labour Day, public holidays.

WEST CHESTER STATE COLLEGE MUSEUM
West Chester, Pennsylvania 19380
Geology. Botany. Herbarium. Ornithology. Local history and archaeology.
M.-F. 8-5; Sa. 8-12. Closed college holidays.

WEST CHESTERFIELD

MUSEUM OF OLD DOLLS AND TOYS
Chesterfield Road, West Chesterfield, New Hampshire 03466
18th-19th century dolls and toys.
July 1 - Aug. 31, daily 10-5. June, Sept., by appointment.

WEST COLUMBIA

VARNER-HOGG PLANTATION HOUSE
F.M. 2852, West Columbia, Texas 77486
House (1835), was home of Texas Governor, James S. Hogg. Mid-19th century period furniture. Exhibits relating to Governor Hogg, Sam Houston and Zachary Taylor.
Tu., Th., F., Sa. 10-12, 1-5. Su. 1-5.

WEST DE PERE

DE PERE HISTORICAL SOCIETY MUSEUM
366 Main Avenue, West De Pere, Wisconsin 54178
In Pillons House (1836). Local history. Junior museum.
M.-F. 2-5.

WESTERLY

WESTERLY PUBLIC LIBRARY
Broad Street, Westerly, Pennsylvania 02891
19th century American paintings. Civil War relics. Lustreware. Bronzes. Minerals.
M.-F. 9-9; Sa. 9-5.30.

WESTERVILLE

HANBY HOUSE
Main Street, Westerville, Ohio 43081
House (1857). Home of composer and author, Benjamin R. Hanby. Hanby manuscripts and memorabilia.
June 1 - Sept. 30: W.-Su. 10-5. Apr., May, Oct. by appointment.

OTTERBEIN COLLEGE
Weitkamp Observatory and Planetarium, Westerville, Ohio 43081
Astronomy. Planetarium.
By appointment.

USA JINJA AND KYOTO TEA HOUSE
Plum and State Streets, Westerville, Ohio 43081
Japanese and Chinese art.
Tea House: M.-F. by appointment only. Usa Jinja: May-Sept., Sa., Su. 11-4.

WEST FALMOUTH

SACONESSET HOMESTEAD AND SHIP'S BOTTOM ROOF HOUSE
Route 28A, West Falmouth, Massachusetts 02574
House (1676). Early agricultural implements, dairying equipment. Americana, 1670-present day.
May 25 - Oct. 24, daily 10-6.

WESTFIELD

JASPER RAND ART MUSEUM
6 Elm Street, Westfield, Massachusetts 01085
Paintings and drawings by American artists.
M., Tu., Th., F. 9-9; W., Sa. 9-6. Closed public holidays.

EDWIN SMITH HISTORICAL MUSEUM
6 Elm Street, Westfield, Massachusetts 01085
Local glass. Indian artifacts. Costumes. Glass. Decorative arts.
M., Sa. 1-5; F. 1-5, 7-9. Closed public holidays.

HISTORY CENTER AND MUSEUM
Main and Portage Streets, Center of Village Park, Westfield, New York 14787
Local history. Archaeology. Agriculture. Indian artifacts. Costumes. Children's museum.
Apr. 15 - Oct. 31: Tu.-Sa. 10-12, 1-4. Closed Decoration Day, Labour Day.

WEST GLACIER

GLACIER NATIONAL PARK
Glacier Natural History Association Museum, West Glacier, Montana 59936
Geology. Botany. Natural history. Ethnology. Archaeology.
M.-F. 8-5.

WEST HARTFORD

CHILDREN'S MUSEUM OF HARTFORD
950 Trout Brook Drive, West Hartford, Connecticut 06119
Natural history. Material illustrating the culture of the Pacific Islands, Colonial America, the Far East and North American Indians.
M.-Sa. 9-5; Su., public holidays 1-5. Closed July 4, Labour Day weekend, Thanksgiving, Christmas.

WESTLAND

NANKIN MILLS NATURE CENTER
33175 Ann Arbor Trail, Westland, Michigan 48185
In Miller's House (1868). Natural history. Children's Museum.
Oct. 1 - Apr. 30: Tu.-Su. 1-5. May 1 - Sept. 30: Tu.-F. 1-4; Sa., Su. 1-5. Closed New Year, Easter, Thanksgiving, Christmas.

WEST LIBERTY

PIATT CASTLES
Rural Route 2, West Liberty, Ohio 43357
Castle Piatt Mac-A-Cheek (1864). French-style castle. Original furnishings. American and French furniture. Castle

Mac-O-Chee. Flemish-style castle. 14th-18th century European paintings, sculpture, decorative arts, furnishings.
Daily 8-7.

WESTMINISTER

WESTMINISTER HISTORICAL SOCIETY MUSEUM
Westminister, Vermont 05158
Local history.
July 1 - Sept. 30, Su. 2-4.

WESTMINSTER

CARROLL COUNTY FARM MUSEUM
Route 6, P.O. Box 412, Westminster, Maryland 21157
Farm house (1850) with outbuildings. Period rooms. Horse-drawn vehicles and equipment. Early threshing machines. 19th century handicrafts.
Apr. 1 - Oct. 31: Tu.-F. 10-4; Sa., Su., public holidays 12-5.

WEST NEWBURY

WEST NEWBURY HISTORICAL SOCIETY MUSEUM
409 Main Street, West Newbury, Massachusetts 01985
In Hills House. Local history.
By appointment.

WESTON

BARN MUSEUM OF THE WESTON HISTORICAL SOCIETY
Weston Road, Weston, Connecticut 06880
In old Barn (1835). Agricultural implements. Indian material.
By appointment.

CARDINAL SPELLMAN PHILATELIC MUSEUM
Regis College, Wellesley Street, Weston, Massachusetts 02193
World postage stamps.
Tu., Th. 9.30-1.30; Su. 2-5. W. 7.30-10.30. Other times by appointment.

SMITH TAVERN
Boston Post Road, Weston, Massachusetts 02193
Building (c.1750), now used as town offices and for community events. Local history collections.
W. 2-4.

WESTON HISTORICAL SOCIETY MUSEUM
626 Boston Post Road, Weston, Massachusetts 02193
Local history. Costumes.
Isaac Fiske law office (c.1805) is in the care of the Society.
By appointment.

WESTON HISTORICAL MUSEUM
Main at Spring Street, Weston, Missouri 64098
Local history. Pioneer relics. Indian artifacts.
Tu.-Sa. 2-5; Su. 1.30-5.30. Closed New Year, Thanksgiving, Christmas.

FARRAR-MANSUR HOUSE
On the Common, Weston, Vermont 05161
House (1797), originally built as inn. 19th century furniture by Vermont makers. Primitive portraits.
June 26 - Columbus Day: Tu.-F. 1-5; Sa. 10-5; Su. 1-5.

JACKSON'S MILL MUSEUM
Weston, West Virginia 26452
In McWhorter Cabin (c.1820). Period furnishings. Civil War relics. Farm tools, implements.
June 15 - Sept. 30: M., W.-Sa. 10.30-5.30; Su. 1.30-5.30.

WEST ORANGE

EDISON NATIONAL HISTORIC SITE
Main Street and Lakeside Avenue, West Orange, New Jersey 07052
In Glenmot (1880), home of Thomas Edison. Edison's study and original laboratories. Material illustrating his life and inventions. Research notebooks, personal and business papers. First phonographs. Cylinder and disc recordings.
M.-Sa. 10-4. Closed New Year, Thanksgiving, Christmas.

WEST PALM BEACH

NORTON GALLERY AND SCHOOL OF ART
1451 South Olive Avenue, West Palm Beach, Florida 33402
16th-20th century European paintings and sculpture. 19th-20th century American paintings. Chinese jade, bronzes, decorative arts.
Tu.-Sa. 10-5; Su., public holidays 1.30-5.30. Closed Labour Day, Christmas.

SCIENCE MUSEUM AND PLANETARIUM OF PALM BEACH COUNTY
1141 West Lakewood Road, West Palm Beach, Florida 33405
Geology. Palaeontology. Astronomy. Local history. Ethnology.
Tu., Th. 10-5, 6.30-10; W., F., Sa. 10-5; Su. 1-5. Closed Easter, Thanksgiving, Christmas.

WEST PARK

SLABSIDES
West Park, New York 12493
House (1895-6) was home of the naturalist, John Burroughs. Natural history. Material relating to John Burroughs.
By appointment.

WEST POINT

MUSEUM OF CONSTITUTION ISLAND ASSOCIATION
P.O. Box 41, West Point, New York 10996
In Warner House (1800). Original furnishings. Warner family memorabilia.
May 1 - Sept. 30, by appointment.

MUSEUM OF UNITED STATES MILITARY ACADEMY
West Point, New York 10996
Military history. American and foreign guns, uniforms, equipment. Paintings. Prints. Posters.
Daily 10.30-4.15. Closed New Year, Christmas.

WESTPORT

MID-FAIRFIELD COUNTY YOUTH MUSEUM
10 Woodside Lane, Westport, Connecticut 06880
Geology. Natural history. Astronomy. Paintings.
M.-Sa. 9-5; Su., public holidays 2-5. Closed New Year, Christmas.

WEST ROXBURY

WEST ROXBURY HISTORICAL SOCIETY MUSEUM
Library, Centre Street, West Roxbury, Massachusetts 02132
History of Roxbury. Paintings of the area.
Library hours.

WEST SAYVILLE

SUFFOLK MARINE MUSEUM
Montauk Highway, West Sayville, New York 11796
Local history. Maritime and naval history.
W.-Sa. 10-3; Su. 10-4. Closed public holidays.

WEST SCARBOROUGH

SCARBOROUGH HISTORICAL SOCIETY MUSEUM
U.S. Route 1, West Scarborough, Maine 04074
History of Scarborough.
July-Aug., Tu. 2-4, 7-9.

WEST SPRINGFIELD

RAMAPOGUE HISTORICAL SOCIETY MUSEUM
70 Park Street, West Springfield, Massachusetts 01089
In old Day House (1754). Local history. 18th century furnishings.
W.-Su., public holidays 1-5. Closed New Year, Thanksgiving, Christmas.

STORROWTON VILLAGE MUSEUM
Eastern States Exposition Grounds, West Springfield, Massachusetts 01089
Museum of local history, based on 9 historic buildings (1794-1822).
June 15 - Labour Day: Tu.-Su. 1-5.

WETHERSFIELD

BUTTOLPH-WILLIAMS HOUSE
Broad and Marsh Streets, Wethersfield, Connecticut 06109
House (1692), with 17th century furniture, kitchen equipment, pewter and pottery.
Daily, May 15 - Oct. 15 1-5.

COVE WAREHOUSE
Wethersfield Cove, Wethersfield, Connecticut 06109
Local history.
By appointment.

SILAS DEANE HOUSE
215 Main Street, Wethersfield, Connecticut 06109
House (1766). Period furnishings.
By appointment.

OLD ACADEMY MUSEUM
150 Main Street, Wethersfield, Connecticut 06109
Local and maritime history. Agricultural implements. Tools. Domestic equipment.
Capt. James Francis house (1793) and Capt. John Hurlbut house (1804) are in the care of the Museum and the Wethersfield Historical Society.
May 15 - Oct., Tu., Th., Sa. 1-4. Other times by appointment.

ISAAC STEVENS HOUSE
Wethersfield, Connecticut 06109
House (1788). Original and period furnishings. Stevens family possessions. Ladies' caps. Toys.
By appointment.

JOSEPH WEBB HOUSE
211 Main Street, Wethersfield, Connecticut 06109
House (1752), where General Washington and Count de Rochambeau planned the Yorktown campaign. Revolutionary War history. Period furnishings.
By appointment.

WEYMOUTH

ABIGAIL ADAMS HOUSE
North and Pearl Streets, Weymouth, Massachusetts 02188
House (c.1730). Period furnishings.
June-Sept., Tu.-F. 1-4. Other times by appointment.

WHEATLAND

ROCK MUSEUM
806 10th Street, Wheatland, Wyoming 82201
Geology. Mineralogy. Indian artifacts.
Daily 8-9. Closed Christmas.

WHEATON

CANTIGNY WAR MEMORIAL MUSEUM OF THE FIRST DIVISION
Winfield Road, Wheaton, Illinois 60187
History of First Division from 1917 onwards. Trench and bunker replicas. Weapons and equipment. Dioramas. Films. Photographs. Tanks. Artillery.
May 1 - Sept. 30, 9-5. Oct. 1 - Apr. 30, 10-4.

DUPAGE COUNTY HISTORICAL MUSEUM
102 E. Wesley Street, Wheaton, Illinois 60187
Museum building (1890). Parlour and bedroom settings. Replica of early cabin. Country store. Farm implements. Barber's shop. Furnishings. Quilts. Glass. Silver. Staffordshire china. Fans. Doctor's surgery.
M., W., F., Sa. 10-4.

ROBERT R. McCORMICK MUSEUM
Cantigny Estate, Wheaton, Illinois 61087
House (1896) was formerly residence of Col. McCormick, publisher of *Chicago Tribune*. Furniture. Sabres. Miniature cannon.
W.-Su. 1-4.30. Closed Dec. 24-5, New Year, Thanksgiving.

WHEATRIDGE

WESTERNAIRE MUSEUM OF RIDING AND DRIVING HISTORY
3876 Robb Street, Wheatridge, Colorado 80033
History of riding and driving. Types of horse. Equipment.
By appointment.

WHEELER

WHEELER COUNTY HISTORICAL MUSEUM
Courthouse Square, Wheeler, Texas 79096
In old County jail (1908). Local history
June 1 - Aug. 31: M.-Sa. 1-4. Sept. 1 - May 31: M., W., Sa. 1-4.

WHEELING

BENNETT MEMORIAL MUSEUM
Wheeling, West Virginia 26003
Costumes from foreign countries. Old firearms. Musical instruments.
By appointment.

OGLEBAY INSTITUTE AND MANSION MUSEUM
Oglebay Park, Wheeling, West Virginia 26003
House (1835). Period rooms. Early Wheeling glass. China. Pewter. Firearms.
Sept. 1 - May 31: M.-Sa. 9.30-5; Su. 1.30-5. June 1 - Aug. 31: 9.30-8. Closed public holidays.

WHITEHALL

SKENESBOROUGH MUSEUM
Whitehall, New York 12887
Model of 1776 harbour. Reconstructed canal locks. Hull of U.S.S. Ticonderoga (1811). Scale model of U.S.S. Saratoga (1814). Railway caboose. Ship and shipyard models.
June 15 - Labour Day, daily 10-5.

WHITE PLAINS

HAMMOND HOUSE
Route 100C, Eastview, White Plains, New York 10601
Farmhouse (1719). Local history. Colonial display.
May 1 - Nov. 1: F.-Su. 2-5.

MILLER HILL RESTORATION
White Plains, New York 10601
Restored earthworks of Washington's troops at Battle of White Plains. Diagrams. Marked trails.
Feb. 22 - Dec. 15: W.-F. 10-4; Sa., Su. 1-4.

ELIJAH MILLER HOUSE
North White Plains, New York 10601
House (1738), used as headquarters by Washington. Demonstrations of domestic crafts of Colonial period.
Feb. 22 - Dec. 15: W.-F. 10-4; Sa., Su. 1-4.

PURDY HOUSE
P.O. Box 1776, White Plains, New York 10602
House (1727), once Washington's headquarters. Farm tools and implements.
Tu.-Sa. 10-5. Closed public holidays.

WHITE SPRINGS

STEPHEN FOSTER MEMORIAL
P.O. Box 265, White Springs, Florida 32096
State Park Museum. Musical instruments. Paintings. Folklore. Dioramas illustrating Stephen Foster's folk songs.
Daily 9-5.30. Closed Christmas.

WHITESTOWN

ORISKANY HISTORICAL SOCIETY MUSEUM
Route 69, Whitestown, New York
Regional history.
M.-Sa. 1-5.

WHITE SWAN

FORT SIMCOE
Fort Simcoe State Park, Route 1, White Swan, Washington 98952
Restored buildings of Fort (1856). Blockhouse. Commanding officer's house. Captains' quarters.
Apr. 1 - Oct. 31: Tu.-Su. 9-6.

WHITTIER

PIO PICO STATE HISTORIC PARK
6003 Pioneer Boulevard, Whittier, California 90606
House (1852-5), formerly home of Pio Pico, last Mexican Governor of California. Period furnishings.
Daily 10-5. Closed New Year, Thanksgiving, Christmas.

WICHITA

FELLOW-REEVE MUSEUM
Friends University, University and Hiram Avenues, Wichita, Kansas 67213
Pioneer history. Indian material. African and North American game animals. African artifacts.
M.-F. 2-4. Other times by appointment.

HISTORIC WICHITA COW TOWN
1717 Sion Park Drive, Wichita, Kansas 67203
Local history. Agriculture. Indian artifacts. History of medicine. Replica of village of 1870-80, Horse Thief Cabin (1865) and 4 other buildings of the 1870s are in the care of the Museum.
Mar. 21 - Nov. 30, Tu.-Su. 9-5.

WICHITA ART ASSOCIATION
9112 E. Central Street, Wichita, Kansas 67206
Paintings. Sculpture. Graphic arts. Ceramics. Enamels. Mosaics. Silver. Glass.
Sept. 1 - July 15, Tu.-Su. 1-5. Closed public holidays.

WICHITA ART MUSEUM
619 Stackman Drive, Wichita, Kansas 67203
American paintings. American and European sculpture, prints, drawings. Decorative arts. Oriental art.
Tu.-F. 10-5; Sa., Su. 1-5. Closed public holidays.

WICHITA HISTORICAL MUSEUM
3751 E. Douglas Street, Wichita, Kansas 67210
In C. M. Beachy Mansion (1909). Geology. Mineralogy. Natural history. Archaeology. Local history. Industry. Transport. Indian material. Costumes. Glass. History of medicine. Children's museum.
Tu.-Sa. 11-5; Su. 1-5. Closed public holidays.

WICHITA FALLS

WICHITA FALLS MUSEUM AND ART CENTER
2 Eureka Circle, Wichita Falls, Texas 76308
Science. Planetarium. Local history.
M.-Sa. 9.30-4.30; Th. 7-9; Su. 2-5. Closed public holidays.

WICKENBURG

DESERT CABALLEROS WESTERN MUSEUM
Frontier Street, Wickenburg, Arizona 85358
Local and Indian history. Period rooms. Replica of street in mining town.
M.-F., 9-11.30, 1-4.30; Sa. 10-4; Su. 1-4. Closed public holidays.

WICKFORD

COCUMSCUSSOC ASSOCIATION
Post Road, Wickford, Rhode Island 02852
House, Smiths's Castle (1678). 17th-19th century furnishings, costumes.
Mar. 16 - Dec. 15, F.-W. 11-5. Other times by appointment.

WICKLIFFE

ANCIENT BURIED CITY
P.O. Box 155, Wickliffe, Kentucky 42087
Minerals. Fossils. Material from mound excavations.
M.-Sa. 8-6; Su. 12-6.

WIDENER COLLEGE

MUSEUM OF DELAWARE COUNTY HISTORICAL SOCIETY
Box 1036, Widener College, Pennsylvania 19013
Local history.
Sept.-June, college library hours.

WILBER

WILBER CZECH MUSEUM
Wilber, Nebraska 68465
History of Czech community. Paintings. Costumes. Decorative arts. Textiles. Glass. Agriculture.
Su. 2-5. Other times by appointment.

WILBERFORCE

WILBERFORCE UNIVERSITY, CARNEGIE LIBRARY
Wilberforce, Ohio 45384
Negro art. Memorabilia of William Wilberforce.
M., Tu., Th., F. 9-4; W. 9-11, 1-4; Sa. 9-12; Su. 5-7.30; M.-F. evenings 6-9.

WILD ROSE

PIONEER MUSEUM
Highway A, Wild Rose, Wisconsin 54984
Agricultural tools, implements. Medicine. Children's museum.
5 buildings (1860-1900) including Elisha Stewart House and blacksmith's and cobbler's shops, are in the care of the Museum.
June 16 - Labour Day: W., Sa., Su. 1-4.

WILDWOOD

WILDWOOD HISTORICAL COMMISSION MUSEUM
4400 New Jersey Avenue, Wildwood, New Jersey 08260
Local and state history.
M.-F. 9-4. Closed public holidays.

WILKES-BARRE

MUSEUM OF WYOMING HISTORICAL AND GEOLOGICAL SOCIETY
69 S. Franklin Street, Wilkes-Barre, Pennsylvania 18701
Geology. Mineralogy. Palaeontology. Local history and archaeology. Indian artifacts. Costumes.
Swetland Homestead (1797) is in the care of the Society.
Tu.-Sa. 10-5. Closed public holidays.

WILLCOX

CHIRICAHUA NATIONAL MONUMENT
Dos Cabezas Star Route, Willcox, Arizona 85643
Local history. Natural history. Herbarium.
Daily 8-5.

WILLIAMS

SACRAMENTO VALLEY MUSEUM
1491 E. Street, Williams, California 95987
Local history. Agriculture. Costume. Yahi Indian artifacts.
M.-W., F.-Su. 10-5. Closed Christmas.

WILLIAMSBURG

CARTER'S GROVE PLANTATION
P.O. Box GP, Williamsburg, Virginia 23185
House (c.1750). 18th century English and American furnishings.
Mar. 1 - Nov. 30, daily 9-5.

COLONIAL WILLIAMSBURG
Goodwin Building, Williamsburg, Virginia 23185
Recreation of 18th century Williamsburg. Restored and reconstructed public buildings, shops, tavern, houses, craft workshops. In the the buildings are 18th century American and English furnishings, tools, paintings.
Jan. 1 - Mar. 20: M.-F. 9-4; Sa., Su. 9-5. Mar. 21 - Nov. 1: daily 9-5. Nov. 2 - Dec. 31: M.-F. 9-4; Sa., Su. 9-5.

JAMESTOWN FESTIVAL PARK MUSEUM
P.O. Drawer J.F., Williamsburg, Virginia 23185
Virginia history, archaeology. Indian history.
Daily 9-5. Closed Christmas, New Year.

ABBY ALDRICH ROCKEFELLER FOLK ART COLLECTION
S. England Street, Williamsburg, Virginia 23185
Paintings and sculpture by American folk artists.
M.-Sa. 10-9; Su 12-9.

WILLIAMSPORT

LYCOMING COUNTY HISTORICAL MUSEUM
858 W. 4th Street, Williamsport, Pennsylvania 17701
Natural history. Civil War relics. Indian artifacts. Industry and handicrafts. Lumbering. Agricultural implements. Household equipment. Transport. Newman School (1841).
Tu.-Sa. 10-4; Su. 2-5. Closed public holidays.

WILLIAMSTOWN

STERLING AND FRANCINE CLARK ART INSTITUTE
South Street, Williamstown, Massachusetts 01267
14th-16th century Italian, Dutch paintings. 17th-19th century American, European (especially 19th century French) paintings. English silver. 19th century French sculpture.
Tu.-Su., public holidays 10-5.

WILLIAMS COLLEGE MUSEUM OF ART
Main Street, Williamstown, Massachusetts 01267
In Lawrence Hall (1846). Assyrian sculpture. Egyptian art. Italian Renaissance paintings, sculpture. 15th-18th century Spanish painting, furniture. 18th-20th century European painting, sculpture, graphics. 18th-19th century British and American portraits. 19th-20th century American paintings, sculpture. 18th-19th century American furniture.
M.-F. 9-12, 1-4; Sa. 10-12, 2-4; Su. 2-5. Closed public holidays.

WILLIAMSTOWN HISTORICAL SOCIETY MUSEUM
Williamstown, Vermont 05679
Local history.
By appointment.

WILLIAMSVILLE

WILLIAMSVILLE WATER MILLS
56 Spring Street, Williamsville, New York 14221
Restored and operating mill (1811). Museum of early Americana.
M., Tu., Th.-Sa. 9-11.30, 12.15-5.

WILLISTON

FRONTIER MUSEUM
714 4th Avenue E., Williston, North Dakota 58801
Local history. Archaeology. Transport. Paintings. Drawings. Decorative arts. Stamps. Coins.
Log Cabin (1890), judge's house (1906) and school (1914) are in the care of the Museum Society.
May 1 - Sept. 30; M.-Sa. by appointment, Su. 2-5.

WILLITS

MENDOCINO COUNTY MUSEUM
400 E. Commercial Street, Willits, California 95490
Agricultural implements. Stagecoaches. Waggons. Pomo Indian artifacts. Ship chandlery.
By appointment.

WILLMAR

MUSEUM OF KANDIYOHI COUNTY HISTORICAL SOCIETY
610 Highway 71 N.E., Willmar, Minnesota 56201
Pioneer history. Indian artifacts. Transport.
Lars Enreson log cabin (1858) is in the care of the Society.
Memorial Day - Labour Day, daily 2-5.

WILMETTE

WILMETTE HISTORICAL MUSEUM
825 Green Bay Road, Wilmette, Illinois 60091
Local history. Costumes. Paintings.
M.-Sa. 9-3. Closed public holidays.

WILMINGTON

DELAWARE ART MUSEUM
2301 Kentmere Parkway, Wilmington, Delaware 19806
American and European paintings, sculpture, graphics. English Pre-Raphaelite paintings.
M.-Sa. 10-5; Su. 2-6. Closed Thanksgiving, Christmas, New Year, July 4.

HAGLEY MUSEUM
Greenville, Wilmington, Delaware 19807
19th century industry on the Brandywine river. Restored gunpowder mills of Du Pont Company, the Eleutherian Mills (1803).
Tu.-Sa. 9.30-4.30. Closed New Year, Thanksgiving, Christmas.

MUSEUM OF THE HISTORICAL SOCIETY OF DELAWARE
509 Market Street, Wilmington, Delaware 19801
In Old Town Hall (1798). Delaware history. Decorative arts. Costumes. Delaware silver.
Tu.-F. 10-4. Closed July 4, Aug. 1 - Labour Day, Thanksgiving, Christmas.

BURGWIN-WRIGHT HOUSE AND GARDEN
3rd and Market Streets, Wilmington, North Carolina 28401
House (1771). Panelling. 18th century furnishings. Reproduction of 18th century garden.
M.-F. 9-4; Apr. 1 - May 31, Sa., Su. 9-4.

BRUNSWICK TOWN
225 Pine Grove Drive, Wilmington, North Carolina 28401
Site museum of 18th century port. English artifacts.
Daily 7-6.

CORNWALLIS HOUSE
224 Market Street, Wilmington, North Carolina 28401
House (1771). Colonial period furniture.
May - Mar. 14, M.-F. 9-4. Mar. 15 - Apr., M.-F. 9-4; Sa. 11-4; Su. 2-4. Closed holidays.

MUSEUM OF LOWER CAPE FEAR HISTORICAL SOCIETY
118 S. 4th Street, Wilmington, North Carolina 28401
Local history. Decorative arts. Period furnishings.
Latimer House (1852) is in the care of the Society.
By appointment.

ST. JOHN'S ART GALERY
114 Orange Street, Wilmington, North Carolina 28401
In St. John's Masonic Lodge (1805). Contemporary American paintings, glass, pottery.
M.-Sa. 10-5; Su. 2-5. Closed Christmas, Thanksgiving, July 4.

USS 'NORTH CAROLINA' BATTLESHIP MEMORIAL
Eagles Island, Cape Fear River, Wilmington, North Carolina 28401
Ship 'North Carolina'. Naval history. Paintings. Equipment. Relics of World War II.
Daily.

WILMINGTON-NEW HANOVER MUSEUM
814 Market Street, Wilmington, North Carolina 28401
History of the Lower Cape Fear area. Natural science and natural history displays relating to Cape Fear. Anthropology. Congo handicrafts. Oriental and Near Eastern bronzes, pottery.
Tu.-Sa. 10-5; Su. 2-5. Closed public holidays.

THE CLINTON COUNTY HISTORICAL SOCIETY
149 E. Locust Street, Wilmington, Ohio 45177
In Rombach Place (1835). Furniture and decorative arts, 1620-1820. Tools.
May-Oct., Th., Su. 1-5; closed national holidays.

ST. JOHN'S ART GALLERY
114 Orange Street, Wilmington, Ohio 28401
Paintings by Elizabeth Chant. Jugtown pottery. Glass scent bottles. Contemporary American paintings.
M.-Sa. 10-5; Su. 2-5. June-Aug. Closed Sa., Su.

WILSON

NODENA SITE
Nodena Plantation, Wilson, Arizona 72395
On site of Moundbuilder burials and dwellings. Material from excavations.
By appointment.

HENRY CLAY HAMPSON II MEMORIAL MUSEUM OF ARCHAEOLOGY
Lake Drive at Highway 61, Wilson, Arkansas 72395
Local archaeology.
Tu.-Sa. 10-5; Su. 1-5. Closed July 4, Thanksgiving, Christmas.

WILTON

CRAFT CENTER MUSEUM
78 Danbury Road, Wilton, Connecticut 06897
17th-19th century American crafts in iron, copper, lead, brass wood.
Mar. 1 - Dec. 31, M.-F. 10-4. Closed public holidays.

WILTON HISTORICAL SOCIETY MUSEUM
150 Danbury Road, Wilton, Connecticut 06897
In Lambert house (c.1726) and Sloan house (c.1760). Local history. Costumes. 18th-19th century furniture.
Lambert House: Tu.-F. 10-5. Closed July 1 - Aug. 31, public holidays. Sloan House: Sa.-Su. 2-5. Closed Aug. 1-31, public holidays.

WIMBERLEY

PIONEER TOWN
7-A Ranch Resort, Wimberley, Texas 78676
Restoration and reproduction of 19th century Texas village. Buildings include gunshop, bank, barber's shop and jail.
May 1 - Sept. 30, daily 9-10. Oct. 1 - Apr. 30, Sa., Su. 2-5.

WINCHESTER

RANDOLPH COUNTY INDIANA HISTORICAL MUSEUM
416 S. Meridian Street, Winchester, Indiana 47394
Local history. Glass.
May 1 - Sept. 30, M.-F. by appointment; Su. 1-5.

STONEWALL JACKSON'S HEADQUARTERS
415 North Braddock Street, Winchester, Virginia 22601
House occupied by General Jackson 1861-62. Military history. Jackson memorabilia.
Daily 9-5.

WINCHESTER AND FREDERICK COUNTY, HISTORICAL SOCIETY
Winchester, Virginia 22601
Local history.
George Washington's office (1746) and Hollingsworth House (1754) are in the care of the Society.
Apr. 30 - Oct. 31: M.-Sa. 9-5; Su. 2-5.

WINDMILL ISLAND

DE ZWAAN
Columbia Avenue and 4th Street, Windmill Island, Michigan
18th century Dutch windmill, brought from Holland in 1964.
Daily 9-5.

WINDOM

MUSEUM OF COTTONWOOD COUNTY HISTORICAL SOCIETY
9th Street and 5th Avenue, Windom, Minnesota 56101
County history. Pioneer life. Civil War guns.
May 1 - Sept. 30: W., Sa. 1-5.

WINDOW ROCK

NAVAJO TRIBAL MUSEUM
P.O. Box 797, Window Rock, Arizona 86515
Navajo history, ethnology, handicrafts (especially textiles). Costumes. Geology. Palaeontology. Botany. Herbarium. Archaeology of the South-West. Open-air museum, showing family life of the Navajo tribe.
Daily 8-5.

WINDSOR

OLIVER ELLSWORTH HOMESTEAD
Windsor, Connecticut 06095
Homestead (1690-1783). Ellsworth family furnishings.
May-Oct., Tu.-Sa. 1-6.

HISTORIC HOPE FOUNDATION
Windsor, North Carolina 27983
House (1798). Period furniture. Decorative arts.
Tu.-Sa. 10-5; Su. 2-5. Closed public holidays.

CHRIST CHURCH WINDSOR MILLS
Wiswell Street and Maryfield Road, Windsor, Ohio 44099
Christ Church (1832). Local history.
Apr. 1 - Nov. 30: M.-F. by appointment; Sa., Su. 2-5.

AMERICAN PRECISION MUSEUM
Main Street, Windsor, Vermont 05089
In former Robbins and Lawrence Armory and Machine Shop (1846). Original machines and hand-tools of this firearms and machine-tool factory. Guns.
June 1 - Oct. 15, daily 12-5.

OLD CONSTITUTION HOUSE
N. Main Street, Windsor, Vermont 05089
Building originally inn, in which Vermont Constitution was framed (1777). 18th-19th century furniture Colonial and Civil War relics. Firearms. Pottery.
Memorial Day - Oct. 15, daily 10-6.

WINDSOR LOCKS

CONNECTICUT AERONAUTICAL HISTORICAL ASSOCIATION
Bradley Air Museum, Bradley International Airport, Windsor Locks, Connecticut 06096
History of aviation. Aircraft collection.
Mar 16 - Dec. 14, Sa., Su., public holidays 9-6.

WINFIELD

MUSEUM OF COWLEY COUNTY HISTORICAL SOCIETY
1011 Mansfield Street, Winfield, Kansas 67156
Local history. Glass.
Sa., Su. 2-5.

MORGAN'S MUSEUM
Route 17, Winfield, West Virginia 25213
House (1840). Mounted animals.
Daily, dawn-dusk.

WINLOCK

JOHN R. JACKSON HOUSE
Route 1, Box 520, Winlock, Washington 98596
House (1844). Jackson's library, personal possessions.
By appointment.

WINONA

MUSEUM OF WINONA COUNTY HISTORICAL SOCIETY
165 W. 5th Street, Winona, Minnesota 55987
Local history. Pioneer tools, household furnishings. Logging and lumbering. Indian, mainly Shippewa, artifacts. Glass.
Bunnell House, Homer (1850) is in the care of the Society.
Sept. 1 - July 31: M.-F. 1-5. Closed public holidays.

STEAMBOAT MUSEUM
Levee Park, Winona, Minnesota 55987
In Sternwheeler, 'Julius C. Wilke' (1898). Steamboat and Mississippi river history. Models. Prints.
May 1 - Sept. 30: M.-Sa. 9-5; Su., public holidays 10-6.

WINNSBORO

FAIRFIELD COUNTY HISTORICAL SOCIETY
Walnut and Hudson Streets, Winnsboro, South Carolina 29180
Farm implements. Clothing.
By appointment.

WINSLOW

METEOR CRATER MUSEUM
P.O. Box AC, Winslow, Arizona 86047
Meteorites.
Daily 8-dusk.

FORT HALIFAX
Bay Street, Winslow, Maine 04901
Early settlers' fort (1754).
Daily.

WINSTON-SALEM

BOYS SCHOOL
Old Salem, Winston-Salem, North Carolina 27108
Wachovia Historical Society's collection of antiquities.
M.-Sa. 9.30-4.30; Su. 1.30-4.30. Closed Christmas.

HISTORIC BETHABARA
2141 Bethabara Road, Winston-Salem, North Carolina 27108
Archaeological park on site of first Moravian settlement in North Carolina.
By appointment.

MARKET HOUSE AND FIRE HOUSE
Old Salem, Winston-Salem, North Carolina 27108
Building (1803). Early fire-fighting equipment.
M.-Sa. 9.30-4.30; Su. 1.30-4.30. Closed Christmas.

MIKSCH TOBACCO SHOP
Old Salem, Winston-Salem, North Carolina 27108
Shop (1771), with period fittings and furnishings.
M.-Sa. 9.30-4.30; Su. 1.30-4.30. Closed Christmas.

MUSEUM OF EARLY SOUTHERN DECORATIVE ARTS
924 S. Main Street, Old Salem, Winston-Salem, North Carolina 27108
15 period rooms (mid 17th century - 1820) rebuilt from Southern homes. Paintings. Furniture. Ceramics. Textiles. Metal work.
M.-Sa. 11-6; Su. 1.30-4.30. Closed Christmas.

MUSEUM OF MAN
Wake Forest University, Renolda Station, Winston-Salem, North Carolina 27109
Archaeology. Ethnology. Anthropology. Indian artifacts.
M.-F. 9-5; Sa. 9-12.

NATURE-SCIENCE CENTER
Reynolda Village, Winston-Salem, North Carolina 27106
Geology. Palaeontology. Botany. Natural history. Planetarium.
M.-Sa. 9-5. Closed public holidays.

REYNOLDA HOUSE
Reynolda Road, Winston-Salem, North Carolina 27106
House (1915-17) was home of R. J. Reynolds, founder of R. J. Reynolds Tobacco Co. Period furnishings. 19th-20th century American paintings. Complete collection of Dorothy Doughty's *American Birds.*
Tu.-Sa., public holidays 9.30-4.30. Su. 1.30-4.30. Closed Christmas, Jan. 1-31.

SALEM TAVERN AND TAVERN BARN
Old Salem, Winston-Salem, North Carolina 27108
Tavern and Barn (1784). Collection of early farm implements.
M.-Sa. 9.30-4.30; Su. 1.30-4.30. Closed Christmas.

SINGLE BROTHERS HOUSE
Old Salem, Winston-Salem, North Carolina 27108
House (1769-86), where unmarried men lived and had their workshops.
M.-Sa. 9.30-4.30; Su. 1.30-4.30. Closed Christmas.

JOHN VOGLER HOUSE
Winston-Salem, North Carolina 27108
House (1819) was home and workshop of silversmith and clockmaker. Clockmaking demonstrations.
M.-Sa. 9.30-4.30; Su. 1.30-4.30. Closed Christmas.

WINKLER BAKERY
Old Salem, Winston-Salem, North Carolina 27108
Building (1800). Bakery equipment. Demonstrations of early baking methods.
M.-Sa. 9.30-4.30; Su. 1.30-4.30. Closed Christmas.

WINTER HAVEN

FLORIDA CITRUS MUSEUM
3rd Street at Avenue E., N.E., Winter Haven, Florida 33880
History of citrus industry. Displays showing packing and processing of citrus fruit.
Daily 9-4.

MUSEUM OF OLD TOYS AND DOLLS
1530 6th Street N.W., Winter Haven, Florida 33880
European and American dolls. Dolls' houses. Tin and iron toys.
M.-Sa. 10-5; Su. 1-5. Closed Thanksgiving, Christmas, New Year.

WINTER PARK

BEAL-MALTBIE SHELL MUSEUM OF ROLLINS COLLEGE
Holt Avenue, Winter Park, Florida 32789
Mollusc shells.
Tu. 1-9; W.-Sa. 1-5; Su., public holidays 1-5. Closed July 4, Aug. 1 - Sept. 8, 10 days at Christmas.

MUSEUM OF ART
Rollins College, 208 Interlaken Avenue, Winter Park, Florida 32789
American and European paintings, sculpture, graphics, decorative arts.
M.-F. 1-4.30. Closed College vacations.

WINTERTHUR

HENRY FRANCIS DU PONT WINTERTHUR MUSEUM
Winterthur, Delaware 19735
Period rooms. American decorative arts and furniture, 1640-1840. 17th-19th century European decorative arts and furnishings. English and Oriental carpets. Chinese export porcelain. Herbarium.
4 Historic houses (1769-1822) in Odessa are in the care of the Museum.
Main part of Museum, Tu.-Sa. 9.30-4, by appointment only. 10 rooms: Tu.-Sa. 9.30-4. Mid-Apr. - May 31: 16 rooms, 9.30-4. Closed public holidays.

WINTHROP

WINTHROP IMPROVEMENT AND HISTORICAL ASSOCIATION
40 Shirley Street, Winthrop, Massachusetts 02152
In Deane Winthrop House (1637). 17th-18th century furnishings.
M., W., F. 3-5.

WISDOM

BIG HOLE NATIONAL BATTLEFIELD
Wisdom, Montana 59761
Indian and pioneer items of the 1870 period. Firearms.
Daily 8-5.

WISCASSET

LINCOLN COUNTY FIRE MUSEUM
Federal Street, Wiscasset, Maine 04578
Old fire-fighting equipment. Stagecoach. Horse-drawn hearse.
July 1 - Aug. 31: M.-Sa. 10-5; Su. 12-5.

LINCOLN COUNTY MUSEUM
Federal Street, Wiscasset, Maine 04578
History of Lincoln County. Indian artifacts. Textiles.
Old Lincoln County Jail (1809-11), with jailer's hous (1837) is in the care of the Museum.
May 1 - Sept. 30: M.-Sa. 10-5; Su. 12.30-5. Winter b appointment.

MAINE ART GALLERY
Warren Street, Wiscasset, Maine 04578
In former academy building (1807). Paintings by Mair artists.
M.-Sa. 10-5; Su. 12.30-5.

MUSIC MUSEUM
18 High Street, Wiscasset, Maine 04578
Mechanical musical instruments.
June 1 - Labour Day: M.-Sa. 10-5; Su., public holiday 1-5.

NICKELS SORTWELL HOUSE
Maine and Federal Streets, Wiscasset, Maine 04578
House (1807). Sortwell family furnishings.
June 1 - Sept. 30: Tu.-Sa. 11-5.

WOBURN

MUSEUM OF RUMFORD HISTORICAL ASSOCIATION
90 Elm Street, Woburn, Massachusetts 01801
House (1700-26) was Count Rumford's birthplace. Loca history. Science.
Daily 1-4.30. Closed Thanksgiving, Christmas.

WOLFEBORO

LIBBY MUSEUM
Route 109 N., Wolfeboro, New Hampshire 03894
Geology. Mineralogy. Palaeontology. Botany. Entomology. Natural history. Coins. Indian material. Junio museum.
June 23 - Labour Day: Tu.-Su. 10-5.

MUSEUM OF WOLFEBORO HISTORICAL SOCIETY
S. Main Street, Wolfeboro, New Hampshire 03894
In Clark House (1778). Local history. Furniture. Costumes China. Pewter.
July 4 - Labour Day: M.-Sa. 1-5.

WOLFORD

DALE HAWK MUSEUM
Wolford, North Dakota 58385
Agriculture. Indian artifacts.
Apr. 1 - Nov. 30: M.-Sa. 9-5; Su. 1-6. Closed Easter, July 4.

WOLF POINT

MUSEUM OF WOLF POINT AREA HISTORICAL SOCIETY
Wolf Point, Montana 59201
Indian clothing, tools, arrow-heads. History of fur-trade Pioneer life. Guns. Indian and Western American art.
June 1 - Sept. 30, daily 1-5.

WOLMESDORF

CONRAD WEISER HOMESTEAD
R.D.1, Wolmesdorf, Pennsylvania 19567
House (1729). Period furnishings. Local history. Indian material. Documents relating to Weiser, Indian affairs expert of Colonial period.
May 1 - Oct. 31: Tu.-Sa. 8.30-5; Su. 1-5. Nov. 1 - Apr. 30 Tu.-Sa. 9-4.30; Su. 1-4.30. Closed New Year, Good Friday, Easter, Thanksgiving, Christmas.

WOODBRIDGE

AMITY AND WOODBRIDGE HISTORICAL SOCIETY MUSEUM
Woodbridge Town Library, Woodbridge, Connecticut 06525
Local history.
By appointment.

WOODBURY

GLEBE HOUSE
Hollow Road, Woodbury, Connecticut 06798
House (1690). Early American furniture. Documents relating to Samuel Seabury, founder of American episcopacy.
W.-Sa. 11-5; Su. 1-5.

MUSEUM OF GLOUCESTER COUNTY HISTORICAL SOCIETY
58 N. Broad Street, Woodbury, New Jersey 08096
Local history. Indian artifacts. Costumes. Glass. Children's museum.
Hunter-Lawrence house (1765) and Moravian Church (1786) are in the care of the Society.
W. 2-4; last Su. in month, Nov. 1 - Apr. 30, 2-5. Closed public holidays.

WOODSIDE

WOODSIDE STORE
471 King's Mountain Road, Woodside, California 94062
Grocery store (1853). Guns. Logging equipment. Dentist's room, with original furnishings and equipment.
W.-Su. 10-12, 1-5. Closed public holidays.

WOODSTOCK

HENRY C. BOWEN HOUSE
(Roseland Cottage), Woodstock, Connecticut 06281
House (1846), built for the New York publisher and newspaper owner, Henry C. Bowen. Original furnishings.
June-Oct., Tu., Th., Sa. 1-5.

QUASSET SCHOOL
R.F.D.1, Woodstock, Connecticut 06281
Community school (1748). Restored and furnished to give original appearance.
By appointment.

WOODSTOCK HISTORICAL SOCIETY MUSEUM
Woodstock, Connecticut 06281
In the Red-White school (1851). Local history. Agriculture.
By appointment.

McHENRY COUNTY HISTORICAL SOCIETY MUSEUM
205 E. Main Street, Woodstock, Illinois 60098
Local history. Clothing. Log cabin (1847).
F. 10-4.30.

TITUS HUTCHINSON HOUSE
5 The Green, Woodstock, Vermont 05091
House (1825). Period furnishings.
June 1 - Oct. 31: M.-Sa. 10-5; Su. 2-5.30.

WOODSTOCK HISTORICAL SOCIETY MUSEUM
26 Elm Street, Woodstock, Vermont 05091
In Charles Dana House (1807). Period furnishings. Costumes. Early Woodstock portraits. History of Woodstock.
June 1 - Oct. 31: M.-Sa. 10-5; Su. 2-5.30.

WOODVILLE

ALLAN SHIVERS MUSEUM
302 N. Charlton Street, Woodville, Texas 75979
House (1800). 19th century furniture. Mementoes and personal possessions of Governor Allan Shivers.
M., W., F. 12-5; Tu. 8-5; Th. 12-8; Sa. 8-12, 2-4; Su. 2-4.

HERITAGE GARDEN VILLAGE
Highway 190, P.O. Box 666, Woodville, Texas 75979
Living museum of pioneer life. 31 buildings include operating grist-mill, whiskey still, blacksmith's shop and school. Art, handicrafts and life of early Texas.
Daily 9-6. Closed Christmas, Thanksgiving.

WOODWARD

PIONEER MUSEUM
2009 Williams Avenue, Woodward, Oklahoma 73801
Indian art artifacts. Pioneer life. Early 20th century fashions.
Tu.-Sa. 12-5; Su. 2-5. Closed public holidays.

WOOSTER

COLLEGE OF WOOSTER MUSEUM
E. University Street, Wooster, Ohio 44691
Chinese paintings. Oriental bronzes. American, European, Oriental graphic arts. Archaeology. Decorative arts.
M.-F. 9-12, 1-5; Su. 2-5. Closed public holidays, June 20 - Sept. 15.

WAYNE COUNTY HISTORICAL SOCIETY MUSEUM
546 E. Bowman Street, Wooster, Ohio 44691
In Gen. Reasin Beall House (1817). Local history. Pioneer furnishings, tools. Indian material.
Log cabin (c.1850) and schoolhouse (1873) are in the care of the Society.
Tu.-Su. 2-4.30. Closed public holidays.

WORCESTER

JOHN WOODMAN HIGGINS ARMORY
100 Barber Avenue, Worcester, Massachusetts 01606
Weapons. Armour. Wrought iron. Stained glass. Tapestries. Paintings. Wood carvings. Armorial banners. Furniture.
M.-F. 8.30-4.30; Sa. 8.30-12. Closed public holidays.

WORCESTER ART MUSEUM
55 Salisbury Street, Worcester, Massachusetts 01608
Egyptian, Mesopotamian, Greek, Roman sculpture. Greek vases. Antioch mosaics. Persian, Indian sculpture, miniatures. Chinese bronzes, ceramics, paintings, sculpture. Japanese prints, bronzes. Pre-Columbian pottery, sculpture, gold. Medieval, Renaissance, European sculptures. European, American paintings, prints, drawings. Italian, French, English furniture, ceramics. Flemish, French, Norwegian tapestries. Early American furniture, silver.
M.-Sa. 10-5; Su., public holidays 2-5. Oct.-Apr. also 10-10. Closed July 4, Thanksgiving, Christmas.

WORCESTER HISTORICAL SOCIETY MUSEUM
39 Salisbury Street, Worcester, Massachusetts 01608
Local history. Architecture. Costumes.
Tu.-Sa. 1-4. Closed Aug., public holidays.

WORCESTER SCIENCE CENTER
222 Harrington Way, Worcester, Massachusetts 01604
Natural and physical science.
M.-Sa. 10-5; Su. 12-5. Closed public holidays.

WORLAND

WASHAKIE COUNTY MUSEUM
1100 Coburn Street, Worland, Wyoming 82401
Natural history. Indian artifacts. Costumes. Children's museum.
June 1 - Labour Day: M.-Sa. 2-5.

WORTHINGTON

MUSEUM OF NOBLES COUNTY HISTORICAL SOCIETY
416 12th Street, Worthington, Minnesota 56187
Local history. Agriculture. Replica of pioneer village.
M., W., F. 2-4.30. Closed public holidays.

OHIO RAILWAY MUSEUM
990 Proprietors Road, Worthington, Ohio 43085
Ohio railway history. Locomotives. Coaches. Equipment. Operating steam and electric trains.
May 1-31, Oct. 1-31: Su. 12.30-5.30. June 1 - July 31, Sept. 1-30: Sa. 1-5; Su. 12.30-5.30. Aug. 1-31: M.-Sa. 1-3.

ORANGE JOHNSON HOUSE
956 High Street, Worthington, Ohio 43085
House (1816). Local history. Dolls.
Su. 2-5. Other times by appointment.

WRANGELL

TRIBAL HOUSE OF THE BEAR
Wrangell, Alaska 99928
Archaeology. Paintings. Decorative arts. Indian houses and totems. Wood carvings. Costumes. Open-air museum.
By appointment.

WRAY

WRAY MUSEUM
140 W. 4th Street, Wray, Colorado 80758
Local history. Agriculture.
Tu., Th., Sa. 1-5; M., W., F., Su., by appointment. Closed public holidays.

WYANDOTTE

WYANDOTTE HISTORICAL SOCIETY MUSEUM
301 Maple Street, Wyandotte, Michigan 48192
Local history.
M.-F. by appointment; Sa. 9.30-12.30; Oct. 1 - June 30, Su. 2-5. Closed public holidays.

WYMORE

MUSEUM OF WYMORE HISTORICAL SOCIETY
100 N. 14th Street, Wymore, Nebraska 68466
In former Schoolhouse (1878). School books and equipment.
May 1 - Sept. 30: Tu.-Th., Sa., Su. 11-5.

WYOMING

MIDDLEBURY ACADEMY MUSEUM
32 S. Academy Street, Wyoming, New York 14591
Local history.
July 1 - Oct. 31, Su. 2-5.

MIDDLEBURY HISTORICAL SOCIETY MUSEUM
22 S. Academy Street, Wyoming, New York 14591
Geology. Farm tools. Military equipment. Indian artifacts. Women's clothing. Musical instruments.
Middlebury Academy (1817) is in the care of the Society.
July 1 - Oct. 31, Su. 2-5.

XENIA

GALLOWAY CABIN
S. Monroe Street, Xenia, Ohio 45385
Early 19th century house, with period furniture.
By appointment.

YAKIMA

FORT SIMCOE HISTORICAL MUSEUM
Fort Simcoe State Park, Yakima, Washington 98901
Museum based on 5 houses from Old Fort Simcoe. Local history.
Apr. 15 - Sept. 30, Tu.-Su. 6.30 a.m. - 10 p.m.

YAKIMA FRONTIER MUSEUM
102 N. 1st Street, Yakima, Washington 98901
Local history. Agriculture. Indian artifacts. Transport.
Apr. 1 - Sept. 30, daily 10-7. Oct. 1 - Mar. 31: Th.-Su. 12-5. Other times by appointment. Closed Christmas.

YAKIMA VALLEY MUSEUM
2105 Tilton Drive, Yakima, Washington 98902
Geology. Mineralogy. Archaeology. Yakima Indian material. Agriculture. Costumes. Porcelain. Postal history of central Washington.
W., F. 10-4; Su. 2-5.

YANKTON

YANKTON COLLEGE, DURAND COLLECTION OF ART
Forbes Hall, Douglas Avenue, Yankton, South Dakota 57078
Paintings, sculpture, prints by European and American artists. Geology. Zoology. Archaeology. Indian material.
M.-F. 8-6.

YARDLEY

ALEXANDER RAILROAD MUSEUM
Upper River Road, Yardley, Pennsylvania 19067
19th-20th century railway models. Railway relics. Model steam-powered operating railway.
Sa., Su. 2-5. Other times by appointment.

YARMOUTH

YARMOUTH HISTORICAL SOCIETY MUSEUM
Merrill Memorial Library Building, Yarmouth, Maine 04096
History of Yarmouth.
May 1 - Nov. 30: W., Sa. 2-4.

YARMOUTH PORT

THACHER HOUSE
Kings Highway and Thacher Lane, Yarmouth Port, Massachusetts 02675
Mid-17th century house, with later additions. 17th-19th century furnishings.
June-Sept., Tu.-Sa. 11-4.

WINSLOW CROCKER HOUSE
King's Highway, Yarmouth Port, Massachusetts 02675
House (c.1780), moved from West Barnstable. Furniture collection.
June-Sept., Tu.-Sa. 11-4.

YATES CENTER

MUSEUM OF WOODSON COUNTY HISTORICAL SOCIETY
411 N. State Street, Yates Center, Kansas 66783
Building (1877). Local history. Agriculture. Indian material.
Apr. 15 - Nov. 14, Tu.-Su. 1-5.

YELLOW SPRINGS

TRAILSIDE MUSEUM
Glen Helen, Yellow Springs, Ohio 45387
Natural history. Museum includes Grinnell Mill (1814).
Tu.-Su. 1.30-5.30. Closed New Year, Christmas.

YELLOWSTONE PARK

YELLOWSTONE NATIONAL PARK MUSEUM
Yellowstone National Park, Wyoming 82190
Museum at 5 centres. Geology. Mineralogy. Botany. Herbarium. Natural history. Ecology. Anthropology. Ethnology. Indian life.
Grant Village, Fishing Bridge, Canyon: June 1 - Labour Day, daily 8-8. Old Faithful: May 1-31, Sept. 1-30, daily 8-12, 1-5. June 1 - Labour Day, daily 8-8. Norris: June 1 - Labour Day, daily 8-6. Mammoth: June 1 - Labour Day, daily 8-8. Rest of year, daily 8-12, 1-5.

YONKERS

HUDSON RIVER MUSEUM
511 Warburton Avenue, Yonkers, New York 10701
Regional history. 19th century and contemporary American paintings, sculpture, drawings. Paintings of Hudson River School. Planetarium. Indian artifacts. 19th century furniture, objets d'art.
Tu.-Sa. 10-5; W. also 7-10 p.m.; Su. 1-6. Closed public holidays.

MUSEUM OF UNITED STATES CATHOLIC HISTORICAL SOCIETY
Dumwoodie, Yonkers, New York 10704
History of Catholic Church, especially in USA.
By appointment.

PHILIPSE MANOR
Warburton Avenue and Dock Street, Yonkers, New York 10701
House (1682-1740). 18th century furniture. Portraits of famous Americans, including all Presidents.
Daily 9-5.

SHERWOOD HOUSE
Tuckahoe Road and Sprain Brook Parkway, Yonkers, New York 10701
Restored farmhouse (1740). Period furnishings.
May 1 - Oct. 1: Th., Su. 2-5. Other times by appointment.

YORK

EMERSON-WILCOX HOUSE
Route 1A, York, Maine 03909
House (1740). Period furnishings.
June 1 - Sept. 30: M.-Sa. 9.30-5; Su. 1.30-5.

JEFFERD'S TAVERN
Lindsay Road, York, Maine 03909
Tavern (1760), furnished in period style.
May 29 - Sept. 12: M.-Sa. 9.30-5; Su. 1.30-5.

JOHN HANCOCK WAREHOUSE
Lindsay Road and York River, York, Maine 03909
Owned by Hancock at the time of his death (1794). Old tools. Ship's models.
June 26 - Sept. 12: M.-Sa. 9.30-5; Su. 1-30-5.

GEORGE MARSHALL STORE
Lindsay Road and York River, York, Maine 03909
Country store (1870). Now shop-museum, displaying goods of the period.
May 29 - Sept. 12: M.-Sa. 9.30-5; Su. 1.30-5.

OLD GAOL MUSEUM
Route 1A, York Street, York, Maine 03909
Old Gaol (1720) is oldest English public building in USA. Dungeons. Colonial furniture. China. Household equipment. Crewel bedhangings.
June 1 - Sept. 30: M.-Sa. 9.30-5; Su. 1.30-5.

OLD SCHOOL HOUSE
Lindsay Road, York, Maine 03909
School house (1745). Displays with models of schoolmaster and children in period dress.
May 29 - Sept. 12: M.-Sa. 9.30-5; Su. 1.30-5.

ELIZABETH PERKINS HOUSE
South Side Road, York, Maine 03909
House (1730). 18th-19th century furniture, china, prints.
June 26 - Sept. 12: M.-Sa. 9.30-5; Su. 1.30-5.

DAUGHTERS OF AMERICAN REVOLUTION MUSEUM
222 W. Tenth Street, York, Nebraska 68467
Pioneer history. Collections relating to Spanish-American War, Civil War and World War I.
One Sa. afternoon each month.

MUSEUM OF YORK COUNTY HISTORICAL ASSOCIATION
Route 1, York, Nebraska 68467
House (1869). History of York County.
Th. 7.30-9 p.m.

ANNA BEMIS PALMER MUSEUM
211 E. 7th Street, York, Nebraska 68467
History of York County. Early farm implements. Victorian bedroom and living room. Sod house, with 1860-70 furnishings.
M.-Sa. 10-5.

HISTORICAL SOCIETY OF YORK COUNTY
250 E. Market Street, York, Pennsylvania 17403
Local history. Early settlement of County. Natural history. Period rooms. Musical instruments, including Tannenberg organ (1804). Street of shops. Costumes. Circus history. Golden Plough tavern (1741), General Horatio Gale house (1751), Log house (1812), Bonham house (c.1870) are in the care of the Society.
Museum and 1st 3 houses: M.-Sa. 9-5; Su. 1-5. Bonham House: M.-Sa. 10-4; Su. 1-5. Closed New Year, Good Friday, Easter, Thanksgiving, Christmas.

YORKTOWN

COLONIAL NATIONAL HISTORICAL PARK MUSEUM
P.O. Box 210, Yorktown, Virginia 23490
18th century weapons and artifacts.
8 18th century houses are within the area of the Park.
Daily 8-5.

YORKTOWN
Moore House, Moore House Road, Yorktown, Virginia 23490
House (c.1725) where British Army's surrender was arranged. Furnishings of 1725-81, including some Moore family pieces.
Apr. 1 - Oct. 31, daily 9.30-5.30.

YORKTOWN VISITOR CENTER
Colonial National Historical Park, Yorktown, Virginia 23490
Paintings and relics relating to American Revolution, especially Battle of Yorktown.
May 1 - Sept. 30, daily 8-6. Oct. 1 - Apr. 30, 8.30-5. Closed Christmas.

YORKTOWN HEIGHTS

TOWN OF YORKTOWN MUSEUM
1886 Hanover Road, Yorktown Heights, New York 10598
Local history. Household equipment. Agriculture. Indian artifacts. Costumes.
Su.-Tu., Th. 2-5. Closed Christmas, Easter, Thanksgiving.

YOSEMITE

YOSEMITE NATIONAL PARK MUSEUM
Yosemite National Park, P.O. Box 545, California 95389
Geology. Botany. Natural history. Archaeology. Anthropology. Local history.
A number of buildings (1880-1930) of historic interest are in the care of the Museum.
May 1 - Sept. 30, 8 a.m. - 9.30 p.m.; Oct. 1 - Apr. 30, 8-6.

YOUNGSTOWN

MUSEUM OF OLD FORT NIAGARA ASSOCIATION
Old Fort Niagara, Box 248, Youngstown, New York 14174
Military history, in restored French fort (1679).
Daily 9-dusk. Closed Christmas, New Year, Thanksgiving.

ARMS MUSEUM
648 Wick Avenue, Youngstown, Ohio 44502
Local history. Personal possessions of Arms family. 19th - early 20th century furnishings. Early American farm tools and household equipment.
W.-F. 1-4; Sa., Su. 1.30-5. Closed public holidays.

BUTLER INSTITUTE OF AMERICAN ART
524 Wick Avenue, Youngstown, Ohio 44502
17th-20th century American paintings. Paintings, drawings of Indians. Miniatures of Presidents. Pictures and models of clipper ships. Glass bells. Sculpture. China, pottery.
Tu.-Sa. 10-4.30; Su. 1-5. Closed Thanksgiving, Christmas.

OLD MILL MUSEUM
Canfield Road, Youngstown, Ohio 44511
In former grist mill (1846). Geology. Mineralogy. Palaeontology. Local history. Indian artifacts. Natural history. Entomology.
May 1 - Oct. 31: Tu.-Su. 10-6. Nov. 1 - Apr. 30: Sa., Su. 10-6. Closed New Year, Thanksgiving, Christmas.

YPSILANTI

YPSILANTI HISTORICAL SOCIETY MUSEUM
220 N. Huron Street, Ypsilanti, Michigan 48197
Local history.
F., Sa. 1-5.

YREKA

SISKIYOU COUNTY MUSEUM
910 South Main Street, Yreka, California 96097
Geology. Local history, especially 1850 Gold Rush. Portraits and other paintings. Replicas of blacksmith's shop, store, schoolroom, miner's cabin. Costumes. Archaeology. Indian artifacts. Open-air museum.
Tu.-Sa. 9-5; Su. 1-5. Closed public holidays.

YUCAIPA

MOUSLEY MUSEUM OF NATURAL HISTORY
11555 Bryant Street, Yucaipa, California 92399
Minerals. Natural history. Shells.
Jan. 1-31, June 1-30, Sept.-Dec., M., Tu., F.-Su. 1-5. Closed Christmas.

SEPULVEDA ADOBE
32183 Kentucky Street, Yucaipa, California 92399
House (1842) with period furnishings.
Tu.-Su. 1-5.

YUCCA VALLEY

HI-DESERT NATURE MUSEUM
55680 Onaga Trail, Yucca Valley, California 92284
Butterflies. Fossils. Minerals. Desert wild flowers. Pottery. Indian artifacts.
W.-F. 1-5; Sa. 10.30-5; Su. 1-5. Closed Sept. 15-30, Oct. 1-14, Christmas, Thanksgiving.

YUKON

ADDINGTON GALLERY
430 W. Main Street, Yukon, Oklahoma 73099
Paintings by Oklahoma artists.
M.-Sa. 9-5; Su. 2-5.

HENSON GALLERY
446 W. Main Street, Yukon, Oklahoma 73099
Works by Oklahoma and Indian artists. Paintings. Drawings. Sculpture. Pottery. Woodcarving.
M.-Sa. 9-6; Su. 2-5. Closed Christmas, New Year.

YUMA

YUMA COUNTY HISTORICAL SOCIETY MUSEUM
240 Madison Avenue, Yuma, Arizona 85364
Local history. Agriculture. Transport. Indian artifacts.
House (1870) is in the care of the Society.
Tu.-Su. 1.30-4.30. Closed June 1 - Sept. 30, public holidays.

YUMA FINE ARTS ASSOCIATION
248 Madison Avenue, Yuma, Arizona 85364
Contemporary American paintings, sculpture, pottery, graphics.
Tu.-F. 12-5; Sa., Su. 2-5. Closed June 1 - Oct. 15, public holidays.

YUMA TERRITORIAL PRISON STATE HISTORIC PARK
Yuma, Arizona 85364
Museum in former prison (1876). Contains material illustrating history of State penal system, with some Indian artifacts. Cells, including some cut into hillside, can be visited.
Daily, except Christmas, 8-5.30.

ZANESFIELD

MUSEUM OF LOGAN COUNTY HISTORICAL SOCIETY
P.O. Box 45, Zanesfield, Ohio 43360
Household equipment. Threshers. Tools. Clothing. Weapons. Uniforms.
Su. 2-4. Other times by appointment.

ZANESVILLE

ART INSTITUTE OF ZANESVILLE
1145 Maple Avenue, Zanesville, Ohio 43701
Local history. Pre-Columbian, African and Oriental sculpture, paintings, drawings. European and American paintings, sculpture, prints, drawings, decorative arts. Children's art. Ceramics. Glass. Objets d'art. English panelled room (c.1700).
M., Th. 9.30-5, 7.30-10; Tu., W., Sa. 9.30-5; Su. 2-5. Closed public holidays, Aug. 1-31.

ZAVALA

'REMEMBERING', A LOG MUSEUM
Route 1, Zavala, Texas 75980
Log House (c.1853), moved to present site from Neches River log landing. Pioneer furnishings and relics.
Daily, June 1 - Oct. 31 8-5.

ZION

ZION HISTORICAL SOCIETY MUSEUM
1300 Shiloh Boulevard, Zion, Illinois 60099
In Shiloh House (1902). Local history. Religious history.
Memorial Day - Labour Day, Sa., Su. 2-5. Public holidays 10-5. Other times by appointment.

ZOAR

ZOAR STATE MEMORIAL
Zoar, Ohio 44697
Restored buildings (c.1820) of German Pietist community. Zoar handicrafts.
Apr. 1 - Oct. 31: Tu.-Su. 9.30-5.

ZOLFO SPRINGS

PIONEER PARK MUSEUM
Highway and State Road 64, Zolfo Springs, Florida 33890
Paintings. Decorative arts. Aeronautics. Agriculture. Anthropology. Archaeology. Industry. Indian artifacts. Transport. Natural history. Circus costumes.
M.-F. by appointment. Sa., Su. 2-6.

Upper Volta

The Republic of Upper Volta became independent in 1960. It has a considerable manganese and gold-mining activity and is a substantial exporter of agricultural produce. The National Museum is not, however, directly concerned with the country's economy, and concentrates its attentions on the traditional native way of life.

OUAGADOUGOU

NATIONAL MUSEUM OF UPPER VOLTA
Avenue Outbritenga, P.O. Box 6, Ouagadougou
Ethnography of the Upper Volta. Costumes. Domestic equipment.
Daily ex. Su. 7.30-12, 3-5.

Uruguay

The museums of Uruguay are not numerous, but they reflect in a reasonably satisfactory manner the past and present of this still largely rural and agricultural country. There are several comprehensive collections of geology, botany and zoology and the several Indian cultures are also well represented. The art galleries concentrate mainly on modern works by Uruguayan artists. There is a single maritime museum, which also deals with oceanography, but as yet Uruguay has no museum of technology, to provide a helpful background to the country's industrial development.

CHUY

MUSEUM
Fortress, Chuy
Local history.
Daily ex. M. and Sa., 1.30-6.30.

COLONIA DEL SACRAMENTO

MUNICIPAL MUSEUM
House of Almirante Brown, Colonia del Sacramento
History of Colonia del Sacramento and the surrounding area. Ethnography.
Daily ex. M. and Sa., 1.30-6.30.

MERCEDES

EUSEBIO GIMENEZ MUSEUM
Mercedes
Paintings, mainly by Uruguayan artists.
Daily ex. M. and Sa., 1.30-6.30.

PALAEONTOLOGY AND NATURAL SCIENCES MUSEUM
Mercedes
Palaeontology. Geology. Natural history of Uruguay.
Daily ex. M. and Sa., 1.30-6.30.

MONTEVIDEO

BOTANICAL MUSEUM
19 de Abril 1179, Montevideo
Plants, especially of Uruguay.
Daily ex. M. and Sa., 1.30-6.30.

MUNICIPAL FINE ARTS MUSEUM
Avenida Millan 4015, Montevideo
Paintings. Drawings. Woodcarvings. Sculptures. Section devoted to the work of Juan M. Blanes.
Daily ex. M. and Sa., 1.30-6.30.

MUNICIPAL MUSEUM OF HISTORY AND ARCHIVES
Calle Juan Carlos Gomez 1362, Montevideo
Furniture. Icons. Paintings. Jewellery. Maps.
Daily ex. M. and Sa., 1.30-6.30.

NATIONAL HISTORICAL MUSEUM
Casa Rivera, Rincon 437. Also at Casa Lavalleja, Zabala 1469 and Museo Romantico, 25 de Mayo 428, Montevideo
Local Indian cultures. Development and political history of the country. Portraits, relics, arms, documents, coins, medals relating to the Wars of Independence, British invasion and early revolutions. Musicology. Social history.
Daily ex. M. and Sa., 1.30-6.30.

NATIONAL MUSEUM OF DECORATIVE ARTS
Solis 1446, Montevideo
European paintings. Mediterranean and Persian crafts.
Daily ex. M. 3-7.

NATIONAL MUSEUM OF FINE ARTS
El Prado Park, Montevideo
Paintings by Uruguayan artists, including Juan Manuel Blanes, Carlos Federico Sáez, Rafael Barradas, Pedro Figari, Joaquín Torres Garcia, Alfredo de Simone, José Cúneo, Carlos González. Sculpture.
Daily ex. M. and Sa. 6-10 p.m. (winter 2-6).

NATURAL HISTORY MUSEUM
Buenos Aires 652, Montevideo
Archaeology. Native cultures. Flora and fauna of Uruguay. Zoology. Geology, mineralogy, palaeontology. Ethnography.
Daily ex. M. and Sa., 1.30-6.30.

OCEANOGRAPHIC AND MARITIME MUSEUM
Rambla Republica de Chile 4215, Puerto Buceo, Montevideo
Maritime history. Fishing. Ships' models. Charts, maps.
Daily ex. M. and Sa. 1.30-6.30.

ZOOLOGICAL MUSEUM
Rambla Republica de Chile 4215, Montevideo
Collections of fauna and molluscs.
Daily ex. M. and Sa., 1.30-6.30.

SAN JOSÉ DE MAYO

REGIONAL MUSEUM
Calle Dr. Julian Becerro de Bengoa 493, San José de Mayo
Paintings. Drawings. Ceramics. Sculpture.
Daily ex. M. and Sa., 1.30-6.30.

TACUAREMBÓ

INDIAN MUSEUM
Calle 25 de Mayo 315, Tacuarembó
Ancient native crafts. Weapons and other implements of the aboriginal Indians and Gauchos.
Daily ex. M. and Sa., 1.30-6.30.

Venezuela

However good they may be in other ways, the museums of Venezuela certainly live in the past, so far as the subject-matter of their collections is concerned. This is a country with one of the largest systems of inland waterways in the world, an important petroleum industry, and a considerable amount of manufacturing industry. None of these aspects of the nation's life is represented at all adequately in museum collections. Nor, for that matter, is agriculture. What we do find, however, are some good collections of the arts and crafts of the colonial period and the nineteenth century, of natural history and of items relating to the nineteenth-century movement for national independence. This is still Bolivár country.

BARCELONA

LOCAL MUSEUM
Calle Juncal 3-45, Barcelona, Estado Anzoátegui
Colonial art and crafts.
Daily 8-12, 3-6.

CARACAS

BOLIVÁR'S HOUSE
San Jacinto a Trapazos, Caracas 101
Murals by Tito Salas depicting events of the Independence Movement. Correspondence and official documents written by Bolivár during the Wars of Independence.
Tu.-F. 9-12, 3-6; Su. 10-1, 3.30-6.

BOLIVÁR MUSEUM
San Jacinto a Trapazos, Caracas 101
Mementoes, portraits, personal relics and historical paintings of Simon Bolivár and his fellow-workers in the Independence Movement.
Tu.-F. 9-12, 3-6; Su. 10-1, 3.30-6.

FOLKLORE MUSEUM
Calle California con Monterrey, Quinta Luisa, Urbanización Las Mercedes, Caracas 106
Folklore, especially of Venezuela.
By appointment only.

ARTURO MICHELENA MUSEUM
La Pastora, Caracas 101
19th century house, home of the painter Arturo Michelena, with documents and personal possessions.
Tu.-Th., Sa., Su. 9-12, 3-5.

MUSEUM OF COLONIAL ART
Quinta Anauco, Avenida Panteón y Calle Gamboa, San Bernardino, Caracas 101
House (1720). Colonial arts and crafts.
W., Th., Sa. 9-12, 3-5; Su. 9-5.30.

MUSEUM OF FINE ARTS
Plaza de Los Museos, Los Caobos, Caracas 105
19th and 20th century Venezuelan paintings. European paintings. Sculpture from Rodin to the present day. 15th-20th century drawings and prints. Latin American paintings. Kinetics and Geometrics. Chinese and European porcelain.
Tu.-Sa. 9-12, 3-5.30; Su. 10-5.

MUSEUM OF TRANSPORT
Frente Parque del Este, Distribuidor La Casona, Caracas 107
Transport collections. Horse-drawn vehicles. Early automobiles. Railway history.
W., Sa., Su. 9-12, 3-5.

NATURAL SCIENCE MUSEUM
Plaza de Los Museos, Los Caobos, Caracas 105
Palaeontology. Geology. Zoology. Archaeology. Ethnography. Gold 'guaca' (funeral treasure) of the Tairona culture. Artificially deformed prehistoric crania.
Tu.-Sa. 9-12, 3-5.30; Su. 10-5.

PHELPS ORNITHOLOGICAL COLLECTION
Avenida Paez, Apdo. 2009, Caracas 102
Natural history collections.
M.-Sa. 9-12, 3-5.30.

'RAUL SANTANA' MUSEUM
Concejo Municipal del Dto. Federal, Esquina de Las Monjas, Caracas 101
Historical collections, mostly relating to Caracas and Venezuela.
Tu., Th., 9-12, 3-5.

CIUDAD BOLIVÁR

'JESUS SOTO' MUSEUM OF MODERN ART
Avenida Germania, Ciudad Bolivár, Estado Bolivár
19th-20th century paintings, sculpture, drawings and prints, mostly by Venezuelan artists.
Tu.-Su. 9.30-1, 3-6.

TALAVERA MUSEUM
Calle Bolivár 103, Ciudad Bolivár, Estado Bolivár
Pre-Columbian and Colonial period exhibits. Religious art. Natural sciences. Numismatics.
Tu.-Su. 9.30-1, 3-6.

CIUDAD DE EL TOCUYO

HISTORICAL MUSEUM
Ciudad de El Tocuyo
Historical collections, illustrating life in the Colonial period.
Tu.-Su. 9.30-1, 3-6.

CORO

LUCAS GUILLERMO CASTILLO DIOCESAN MUSEUM
Calle Zamora, Coro, Estado Falcón
Colonial art and crafts.
Su., Tu. 9-12; W.-F. 4-7.

LA ASUNCIÓN

NEW CADIZ MUSEUM AND LIBRARY
Calle Independencia, La Asunción, Estado Neuva Esparta
Historical collections, mostly 18th-19th century material.
Daily 8-12, 2-5.

LA GUAIRA

JOHN BOULTON MUSEUM
Calle Bolivár 180, La Guaira, Dto. Federal
History of La Guaira.
Tu.-Su. 9.30-1, 3-6.

MARACAIBO

MUSEUM OF MILITARY HISTORY
Calle 91A No. 7A-70, Maracaibo, Estado Zulia
Military history of Venezuela.
Tu.-F. 9-12, 3-6; Su. 9-3.

NATURAL SCIENCE MUSEUM
Maracaibo, Estado Zulia
Natural science collections, mostly zoology, botany.
Tu.-F. 9-12, 3-6; Su. 9-3.

MARACAY

AVIATION MUSEUM
Base Logistica 'Aragua', Maracay, Estado Aragua
Aviation and aeronautical history.
Su. 8-6.

INSTITUTE OF ANTHROPOLOGY AND HISTORY MUSEUM
Maracay, Estado Aragua
Anthropology and history of Venezuela.
Tu.-Su. 9-12, 3-5.30.

MÉRIDA

MUSEUM OF HISTORY, SCIENCE AND ARTS
Avenida 2 Lora, Mérida, Estado Mérida
Local history. Natural history. Paintings, sculpture by Venezuelan artists.
M.-F. 9-12, 3-6.

MUSEUM OF MODERN ART OF MÉRIDA
Plaza Beethoven, Urbanización Santa Maria, Mérida, Estado Mérida
Modern Venezuelan paintings, sculpture, drawings and prints.
Tu.-F. 9-12, 3-7; Sa. 3-8; Su. 10-12, 3-8.

TRUJILLO

'CRISTÓBAL MENDOZA' MUSEUM
(Historical Museum), Trujillo
Historical collections, mostly relating to Venezuela in the 18th-19th centuries.
Tu.-Su. 9.30-1, 3-6.

Vietnam, Democratic Republic of

The severe American bombing of North Vietnam in December 1972 caused immense damage, especially in the areas of Hanoi and Haiphong. It has not, so far, been possible to establish what destruction was caused to museums, and the information given below should therefore be used with great caution.

DIEN-BIEN-PHU

DIEN-BIEN-PHU MUSEUM
Dien-Bien-Phu
Political, cultural and economic history of Dien-Bien-Phu and its region.
Daily 9-5.

HAIPHONG

HAIPHONG MUSEUM
Haiphong
Local and maritime history.
Daily 9-5.

HANOI

FINE ARTS MUSEUM
Hanoi
Paintings, drawings, sculpture by European and Vietnamese artists.
Tu.-Su. 10-5.

HISTORICAL MUSEUM
Hanoi
History and archaeology of North Vietnam. Folk art. Handicrafts.
Daily 9-6.

MUSEUM OF THE NAVY
Hanoi
History of the North Vietnamese navy. Documents. Photographs. Models. Equipment.
Daily 9-5.

MUSEUM OF THE REVOLUTION
Hanoi
Documents, photographs, military relics and other material illustrating the political history of North Vietnam.
Daily 9-5.

HONG-GAI

HONG QUANG MUSEUM
Hong-Gai
History of the Hong-Gai region.
Daily 9-5.

HUNG YEN

HUNG YEN MUSEUM
Hung Yen
Local history, archaeology
Tu.-Su. 10-6.

THAI-NGUYEN

VIET BAC MUSEUM
Thai-Nguyen
History of local workers' movement.
Daily 9-5.

VINH

SOVIET NGHE-TINH MUSEUM
Vinh
History of Soviet military and economic assistance to Vietnam.
Daily 9-5.

Vietnam, Republic of (South)

The museums of South Vietnam are essentially non-political. They deal almost entirely with archaeological and artistic material, much of it from North Vietnam, which shows, as in Ireland, the absurdity of drawing political lines across a natural cultural unit.

DA-NANG

ARCHAEOLOGICAL MUSEUM
Da-Nang
Cham sculpture. Objects from holy city of Mi-son. 12th century sandstone sculpture. Sculptured altars, Buddhas and Diarapalas from 9th century Buddhist monastery.
Daily ex. M. and F., 10-1, 2-5.

HUÉ

ARCHAEOLOGICAL MUSEUM
Hué
Furniture. Vases, statues. Bronzes. Ivories. Lacquer-ware. Weapons. Drawings and paintings on glass. Embroidery. Jewellery. Ceremonial dresses of princes and mandarins. Ingots and coins. Religious objects. Domestic equipment. Chinese porcelain.
Daily ex. M. and F., 10-1, 2-5.

NHATRANG

OCEANOGRAPHIC MUSEUM
Nhatrang
Science. Oceanography.
Daily ex. M. and F., 10-1, 2-5.

SAIGON

NATIONAL MUSEUM OF VIET-NAM
Botanical Garden, Saigon
Ethnography. History. Arts. Numismatics. Archaeology. Cham and Khmer sculptures. Japanese, Chinese and Vietnamese art, including swords, masks, bronzes, porcelain, ceramics. Ethnography. Traditional musical instruments. Objects from the Han tombs in North Vietnam.
Daily ex. M. and F., 10-1, 2-5.

Yemen, People's Democratic Republic of

No great changes, apart from military coups, have occurred in the Yemen for a long time, and it is therefore perfectly reasonable for the museums to enshrine the traditional way of life, which they do very well.

ADEN

NATIONAL ARCHAEOLOGICAL MUSEUM
Tawahee, Aden, 1st Governate
Finds from excavations of the sites of the ancient kingdoms of Qataban, Ausan, Himyar and Hadramut. Alabaster statues and statuettes of kings. Bronzes. Gold and silver jewellery. Seals of the kingdom of Qataban.
M.-Sa. 8-7.

FINE ARTS HALL
Front Bay, Crater, Aden, 1st Governate
National art collections.
Daily 8-6.

NATIONAL ETHNOGRAPHICAL MUSEUM
Taweela, Crater, Aden, 1st Governate
Ethnography of different parts of the country. Costumes, especially those worn at festivals. Tools used in traditional industries: weaving, leather-work, metal decoration. Traditional dhow making.
Daily ex. F. 8-6.

BEIHAN

BEIHAN MUSEUM
Beihan, 4th Governate
Excavated material from the city and from Hajar bin Kholan and Hajar bim Humeid, including large spherical bronze bowl with Himyarite inscriptions.
Daily ex. F. 8-2.

MUKALLA

MUKALLA MUSEUM
Mukalla, 5th Governate
Archaeological exhibits from nearby sites. Coins. Wall inscriptions. Ethnography.
Daily ex. F. 8-2.

Yugoslavia

The list of Yugoslav museums shows a good balance between the ancient and the modern world and between the capital and the provinces. There is an abundance of Greek and Roman material, the Turks have no reason to feel neglected, and there are some splendid exhibits, both indoors and out, which preserve the buildings, tools and arts and crafts of the old rural culture. Few countries have ecclesiastical collections as rich as those of Yugoslavia, and there are remarkable works of art, too, in the now state-owned palaces and castles which formerly belonged to the nobility and landowners of the old Austro-Hungarian Empire. A number of these great houses also contain notable collections of weapons and hunting trophies.

Among the places which tell the story of Yugoslavia's maritime activities and prowess is the naval museum housed in the technical school where Peter the Great sent his princes and boyars to learn the principles of navigation. Shipping and navigation have a privileged position, however. The other industries are not given the same degree of attention as in the other Communist countries, although post-war industrial development in Yugoslavia has been quite as remarkable as elsewhere in Eastern Europe.

In general, however, the history of the nineteenth and twentieth centuries is well covered in Yugoslav museums, the period since 1939 especially. The visitor is offered, for instance, a museum of the Illyric movement, which fought for the introduction of the Croatian language into public life, a wartime partisan hospital, partly underground, and a museum illustrating President Tito's apprenticeship to a blacksmith, the exhibits including a wrought-iron fence he made while he was learning the trade. Most towns of any size have a museum celebrating the revolution which established the present régime and, within the same field, there is a string of museums commemorating the annual Party Conferences, one museum for each conference. This appears to be a peculiarly Yugoslav custom.

Among the many art museums there is one in the former studio of the sculptor, Meštrović. It contains, as the catalogue says, with a frankness unusual in these matters, "miscellaneous objects too large to be exhibited elsewhere".

BAKAR

LOCAL MUSEUM
Bakar
Navigation instruments. Maps. Collection of old maritime laws, including those of Grotius.
Tu.-Su. 8-12, 4-7.

BANJA LUKA

MUSEUM OF BASANSKA KRAJINA REGION
Banja Luka
Regional museum for north-west Bosnia. Archaeology. History. Ethnology. National Revolution.
Daily ex. M. 8-12, 4-7.

BELGRADE

BELGRADE CITY ART GALLERY
Zmaj Jovina St. 1, Belgrade
Paintings, drawings, sculpture, especially by 19th-20th century Yugoslav artists.
Tu.-Sa., 9-6. Su. 9-5.

BELGRADE NATURAL HISTORY MUSEUM
Ivana Milutinovica 57, Belgrade
Botany. Geology. Mineralogy. Palaeontology. Petrology. Zoology. Fossilised mammals and fauna from the areas of Veles and Jastrebac.
May-Sept., Tu.-Su. 9-8. Oct.-Apr., Tu.-Su. 10-5.

CITY MUSEUM
Zmaj Jovina St. 1, P.O. Box 87, Belgrade
History of Belgrade.
Tu.-Sa. 9-6, Su. 9-1.

ETHNOGRAPHICAL MUSEUM
Studentski trt. 13, Belgrade
Costumes and textiles. Social life. Houses and other buildings. Customs. Documents. Embroidery. Tools. Pottery. Metalware. Crafts. Folk costumes from different regions. Ceramics.
May-Sept., Tu.-Su. 9-8. Oct.-Apr. Tu.-Su. 10-5.

HISTORICAL MUSEUM OF SERBIA
Prince Milosh's Cottage, Konak kneza Milosa, Topčider Park, Belgrade
Story of the 1804 uprising by the Serbs against the Turks. Personal effects of the leader of the first uprising, Dord Petrović (Black George), including his armour, seal and standard. 19th century paintings by Serbian artists of famous personalities of the period.
Su., W. 10-5.

JULY 4, 1941 MUSEUM
10a Bulevar Oktobarske Revolucije, Belgrade
Commemorates the meeting here in 1941 at which it was decided to incite general revolt in Yugoslavia. Tito's room, with his furniture, medicine box and small radio receiver. Documents, including the party archives.
Tu.-Su. 11-5.

MANAK'S HOUSE
Crnilovic's Collection, 10 Kraljevica Marka Street, Belgrade
19th century house built in Serbo-Balkan style, containing ethnographical collections. On the ground floor is the Belgrade Collectors Club, where information is available about private collections in Belgrade.
W., Sa. 11-7; Su. 9-2.

MAY 25th MUSEUM
8 Botićeva Street, Belgrade
Commemorates 70th birthday of Josip Broz Tito. Presents he received, including a harp from Mandalay, Burma; model of Dubrovnik cannon (17th century); antique vase dating from 4th century B.C. Yugoslav national costumes. Collection of batons, 1945 - present day.
Tu.-Su. 10-5.

MILITARY MUSEUM OF THE YUGOSLAV PEOPLE'S ARMY
Belgrade-Kalemegdan, Belgrade
Military history of the Yugoslav peoples until the present day. Ancient arms. Documents. Weapons from the Turkish period (14th-18th centuries), including two Turkish spears and the armour of a Turkish vizir, from the Battle of Kosovo.
May-Sept., Tu.-Su. 9-8. Oct.-Apr. Tu.-Su. 10-6.

MUSEUM OF APPLIED ART
Vuka Karadžíca 18, Belgrade
Development of applied arts from 12th century to the present day. Ceramics, glass and porcelain by Emile Galle. Glass produced in Serbian glassworks. 19th century glass. Metalwork. Jewellery (early Middle Ages - 19th century). Old Serbian and Greek coins. Crosses (8th-19th centuries). Icons of reed-mace (16th-18th centuries). Furniture, including Serbian furniture of 19th century. Sundials (17th-18th centuries). Clocks.
Tu.-Sa. 10-1, 4-7; Su. 10-1.

MUSEUM OF CONTEMPORARY ART
Novi Beograd kod Ušca, Belgrade
Modern art in Yugoslavia from 1900 to present day.
May-Sept., M.-Sa. 9-8. Oct.-Apr. M.-Sa. 10-5.

MUSEUM OF FORESTRY AND HUNTING
Stambol kapija 1, Kalemegdan, Belgrade
Hunting weapons and their development, from prehistoric tools and weapons to an 1894 carbine. Plastic replicas of birds and animals, in particular the swamp birds of Obedska Bara. Forestry. Trophies. Paintings.
Daily 9-7.

MUSEUM OF FRESCOES
20 Ulica Cara Uroša, Belgrade
Life-sized copies of frescoes from Serbian monasteries (11th-15th centuries). Plaster copies of church portals.
May-Sept., Tu.-Su. 9-8. Oct.-Apr. Tu.-Su. 9-4.

MUSEUM OF POST AND TELECOMMUNICATIONS
Majke Jevrosime 13, Belgrade
Development of postal communications in Yugoslavia. Metal strong-boxes. Postage stamps, domestic and foreign. Postmen's uniforms. 4-horse carriage used in Istria during 19th century. Means used to prevent spread of plague and cholera by postal services.
M., W., Th. 9-3; Tu., F. 11-7; Sa. 8-2; Su. 9-11.

MUSEUM OF THE SERBIAN ORTHODOX CHURCH
Ulica 7 juia, 5, Belgrade
In Patriarch's Palace. Items from monasteries. Religious objects plundered by the Ustashas. Embroidery by the nun Jefimija. Bowl belonging to the Russian Tsar, Ivan the Terrible. Icons, including two from the Monastery of Krušedol: a Virgin and Child from 16th century and an icon of Johan the Baptist, the work of the Metropolitan Ilarion (1644).
Daily ex. M. and holidays 9-12. Su. 11-1.

MUSEUM OF THEATRE ARTS
Gospodar Jevremova 19, Belgrade
Collections illustrating the development of the theatre arts in Serbia from the earliest times.
M.-Sa. 9-2.

MUSEUM OF THE YUGOSLAV PEOPLE'S REVOLUTION
Trg Marksa i Engelsa 11, Belgrade
History of the 50-year-old struggle of the Yugoslav Communist Party. Documents. Photographs. Sculptures by Yugoslav artists on the theme of revolution.
Tu.-Su. 10-5.

NATIONAL MUSEUM
Trg Republike 1, Belgrade
Archaeological exhibits of the prehistoric period. Yugoslav and foreign paintings and sculpture. Medieval frescoes. Serbian portraits and icons. Coin collection. Inscribed stones. 18th-20th Serbian art. Modern sculptures. French and other Impressionists (Renoir, Degas, Van Gogh, Matisse, Picasso, Utrillo). Works by modern Dutch, Flemish and German masters.
Tu.-Su. 10-1; Tu. and F. also 5-9.

RAILWAY MUSEUM OF F.S.R. OF YUGOSLAVIA
6 Nemanjina ul., Belgrade
Development of railways inside and outside Yugoslavia. Locomotive dating from 1861. First locomotive built in Yugoslavia, 1882.
M., W., Th., Sa., Su. 9-2; Tu., F. 9-6.

NIKOLA TESLA MUSEUM
Proleterskih brigada 51, Belgrade
Collections illustrating the life and scientific work of Nikola Tesla. Letters, books. Plans and models of his experiments in the field of electronics. Urn containing Tesla's ashes.
Tu.-Sa. 10-12, 4-6; Su. 9-1.

VUK AND DOSITEJ MUSEUM
21 Gospodar Jevremova Ulica, Belgrade
Collections illustrating the life and work of the Serbian writers, Obradović Dositej and Karadžić Vuk (reformer of the written Serbian language).
Daily 9-3.

BITOLA

MUNICIPAL MUSEUM
Trg Mali Ploštad, Bitola
Local history, including finds from Heracleia.
Daily 10-1.

BOL

DOMINICAN MONASTERY
Bol
Paintings, including an icon of the Adoration of the Magi and a copy of Titian's *St. John the Baptist.* Numismatic collections. In the treasury is a Baroque chalice from Florence (1666).
On request.

BREŽICE

PROVINCIAL MUSEUM
Brežice
Archaeological exhibits from Neolithic times to the early Middle Ages. Ethnography. History of the Slovene-Croat peasants' revolt, 1573, and Slovene national struggle for liberation, 1941-45. Baroque painting and frescoes.
Daily ex. M. 8-12, 4-7.

BUDVA

TOWN MUSEUM
Franciscan Monastery, Budva
Phoenician, Greek and Roman archaeological finds from a necropolis on the site of the Hotel Avala.
Daily 8-11, 2-5.

BUZET

TOWN MUSEUM
Buzet
Lapidary collection, Ethnography.
On request.

CAVTAT

VLAHO BUKOVAC'S HOUSE
Cavtat
House and studio of Vlaho Bukovac (1855-1922), a native of Cavtat, now housing his paintings.
On request.

MUSEUM
Kapetanov dvor, Cavtat
House (1555-58), containing collections bequeathed by Baltazar Bogišić (1834-1908), lawyer and bibliophile. Engravings, including works by Lucas Cranach the Younger, Martin Rota-Kolunić, Andrea Medulić, Stefano della Bella, Chodowiecki and Natale Bonifazio.
Daily ex. M. 9-12, 4-7.

CELJE

LOCAL MUSEUM
Muzejski trg 1, 63000 Celje
Archaeology. Art and cultural history. Ethnography. History. Lapidarium, including the 'Noric Warrior', a late-Roman marble figure.
Daily ex. M. 9-12, 4-7.

CETINJE

ETHNOGRAPHICAL MUSEUM
Biljarda, Cetinje
Ethnography of the region.
Daily ex. M. 8-1.

MUSEUM OF THE LIBERATION STRUGGLE
Biljarda Palace, Cetinje
History of the National Liberation Struggle, 1941-45.
Daily ex. M. 8-1.

NJEGOS MUSEUM
Biljarda, Cetinje
Local history.
Daily ex. M. 8-1.

STATE MUSEUM
Titov trg., Cetinje
Housed in former palace of King Nikola, in its original state. History. Ethnography. Archaeology. Arts. Portraits. Furniture. War trophies. Oriental weapons.
Daily ex. M. 8-12, 4-7.

TREASURY
Monastery, Cetinje
Icons. Vestments. Gospel of 1493, one of the first books to be printed in the Cyrillic alphabet.
On request.

DEČANI

TREASURY
Monastery of Visoki Dečani, Dečani
Manuscripts (13th-20th century), especially a biography of Decanski by Camblack, c.1402. Icons. Crosses. 15th century bells. Sacerdotal ornaments.
On request.

DOBRINJ

TREASURY
Church of St. Stjepan, Dobrinj, nr. Krk
14th century altar frontal embroidered with gold and silver thread; 15th century silvered crosses; 16th century ciborium; gold reliquary of St. Ursula.
On request.

DOBROTA

TREASURY
Church of Sv. Stasija, Ljuta, Dobrota
Trophies captured from the Turks in battle. Vestments. Local lace.
On request.

DUBROVNIK

CATHEDRAL TREASURY
Katedrala, Poljana Marina Držića, Dubrovnik
138 reliquaries. Reliefs. Silver crosses. Ewer and basin of silver by W. Jamnitzer of Nuremberg (c.1550). Baroque caskets containing relics. Bronze English lectern.
Tu. and Th. 11-12.

ETHNOGRAPHICAL MUSEUM
St. John's Fortress, Dubrovnik
Folk costumes, musical instruments and bygones illustrating the life of the surrounding countryside.
Daily ex. M. 9-12, 5-7.

LAPIDARY COLLECTION
Rupa, Ul. od Rupa, Dubrovnik
Annexe of the Gradski Muzej, housed in 16th century granary. Fragments from churches damaged by earthquake. Pre-Romanesque stone carving. Roman pieces from Cavtat.
Daily 9-12, 5-7.

MARITIME MUSEUM
St. John's Fortress, Dubrovnik
Dubrovnik's maritime history; the Republican period; the age of steam; the Second World War; techniques of sailing and navigation.
Daily ex. M. 9-12, 5-7.

MUSEUM OF THE SERBIAN ORTHODOX CHURCH
Od Puća 2, Dubrovnik
Collection of portraits, and over 170 icons from Serbia, Crete, Corfu, Venice, Russia, Greece, Dubrovnik, Boka-Kotorska.
Daily 10-12.

TOWN MUSEUM
Knežev dvor, Prid Dvorom, Dubrovnik
In Rector's Palace. State Rooms with Baroque and Rococo furniture, portraits of Republican notables, and faience. Louis XVI furniture, and paintings by Annibale Carracci (1560-1609). Former state seals and keys of the city gates. Coins (1350-1803). Copies of the city statutes, registers of the nobility and state decrees. Robes of officials, mainly 17th-18th century.
Daily 9-11.30.

TREASURY
Dominican Church and Monastery, Put Medju Vratima od Ploca, Dubrovnik
Silver crosses. Relief. Paintings. Illuminated manuscripts. 239 incunabula, notably the illustrated chronicle of Pleydenwurff and Wolgemut (1493) and the speeches of Savonarola (1497).
On request.

TREASURY
Franciscan Monastery, Poljana Paskoje Mili Čevića, Dubrovnik
In Chapter House. 15th century silver-gilt cross and silver thurible. Display from Monastery's library. Paintings include one by Rudjer Bosković, painted in London in 1760.
The adjoining Pharmacy (1317), the oldest to survive in Europe, has been restored, with early ceramic jars (faience and Delft), apparatus, furniture and 16th century pharmacy registers.
Daily 8-12, 4-8.

GROZNJAN

ART GALLERY
Palača Biriani, Groznjan, nr. Buje
Modern paintings by Slovene and Croatian artists.
On request.

HERCEGNOVI

TOWN MUSEUM
Topla, Hercegnovi
History and ethnography of the National Liberation Struggle. Icons of the Boka Kotorska school (mainly 18th century), notably by the Dimitrijević-Rafailović family of Risan. Pre-Romanesque stone relief (11th century).
Weekdays 8-11, 5-7.

TREASURY
Serbian Orthodox Monastery of Savina, nr. Hercegnovi
Silver crosses and plate. Chalices. Reliquaries. Vestments and frontals, including a Brocade embroidered with scenes of the Passion in silver and gold thread (1659). Library contains historical manuscripts. Pictures, including portraits of Peter the Great and Catherine the Great of Russia. Icons by painters of the Boka Kotorska school (17th-18th century).
Daily 9-12, 4-7.

HLEBINE

HLEBINE GALLERY
Hlebine
Primitive paintings by Podravina artists.
Daily ex. M. 10-12, 3-7.

HRASTOVLJE

CHURCH OF ST. TROJICE
Hrastovlje
Building in Romanesque style (13th century). Frescoes of the Istrian school, in a rustic Gothic style, illustrating the history of the world in terms of Old and New Testaments. The sacristy contains 15th and 17th century reliquaries.
Daily 10-5.

HVAR

REFECTORY
Franciscan Monastery, Promenade, Hvar
Last Supper, attributed to Matteo Rosselli but now thought to be by Matteo Ingoli. 16th-18th century paintings. Illuminated church books. A Ptolemy atlas (1524). Coins. Plates. Vestments. Lace.
On request.

TREASURY OF THE CATHEDRAL
Bishop's Palace, Hvar
Ornamented Pastoral Staff of Bishop Pritić (Patrizius, 1509-22) in gilt brass, the work of Pavao Dubravčić, a local silversmith. Church plate. Baroque vessels and chalices. Lace garments (16th-18th centuries). 16th century figure of St. Michael in stone.
Daily 9-11, 5-6.

JAJCE

LOCAL MUSEUM
Jajce
In house where the fundamental principles of the federal constitution of the new Yugoslavia were laid down in 1943. Memorabilia of that meeting.
On request.

JASENOVAC

MEMORIAL MUSEUM
Jasenovac
On the site of the former concentration camp. Exhibits relating to life in the camp. Documents.
Apr.-Oct., daily 7 a.m. - 8 p.m. Nov.-Mar. daily 9-5.

JELSA

TREASURY
Church of St. Fabujan i Sebastijan, Jelsa
Gothic crucifixion in wood. Late Renaissance crucifixion in silver-gilt. Vestments (16th-18th centuries).
On request.

JESENICE NA DOLENJSKOM

CASTLE MUSEUM
Mokrice Castle, Jesenice na Dolenjskom
Material relating to Matija Gubec, leader of the Croatian and Slovenian Peasant Revolt, who was incarcerated here in 1573.
Daily ex. M. 9-12.

KARLOVAC

CITY MUSEUM
Strossmayerov trg 7, Karlovac
Collections illustrate the development of the town.
Su. 10-1; Tu. 4-6; F. 9-1; Sa. 10-12.

VJEKOSLAV KARAS GALLERY
Marinkovićeva bb, Karlovac
Paintings. Sculpture.
Enquire locally.

KLIS

CASTLE MUSEUM
Klis
Pictures and documents. Local history. The castle also contains a small Turkish mosque, later converted to Christian worship.
On request: ask for key in village.

KOMIŽA

ART GALLERY
Kastel, Komiža
Paintings of Djuro Tiljak (1895-1965), a former pupil of Kandinsky.
Daily 10-12, 7-8.

MUSEUM
Church of Sv. Nikola (Mustar), Komiža
16th-17th century vestments. Baroque paintings and statuary. Ethnographical collection.
On request.

KOPER

ART AND HISTORICAL MUSEUM
Palača Belgramoni-Tacco, Muzejski trg., Koper
Lapidary collection. Roman mosaics. 16th-18th century paintings, including works by Correggio, Padovanino, Fiamminghini and Romanino. Venetian icons, porcelain figurines. Modern Slovene and Italian paintings. Reconstructed Istrian kitchen (18th century). Armoury. Local history.
Daily 9-12, 3-6.

CATHEDRAL OF ST. NAZARIUS AND TREASURY
Titov trg., Koper
16th century sarcophagus of St. Nazarius. Walnut choir stalls. Bishop's throne. Paintings by Vittoria Carpaccio. The Treasury includes 12th century Byzantine casket, silver crucifixes and a silver monstrance (15th century).
Treasury: apply to the Sacristan.

KORČULA

ALL SAINTS CHURCH MUSEUM
Korčula
Religious art. Gold and silversmiths' work.
When the church is open.

CATHEDRAL TREASURY
Biskupska palača, Trg. Sv. Marka, Korčula
Drawings by Italian and German artists (17th-18th centuries), notably by Tiepolo, Carracci and Palma Giovane. Church plate and jewellery (15th-18th centuries). Medals. Works by Dalmatian painters. Lapidary collection. Works by Italian painters of the Renaissance. Reliefs. Bishops' portraits. Embroidered vestments.
Daily 7-11, 3-7.

ICON MUSEUM
Trg Marsala Tita, Korčula
14th-17th century icons. Paintings by Croatian masters. 17th-18th century silver and gold. Ornamental candles (17th-20th centuries). 15th century Byzantine cross.
Daily 8.30-1, 2.30-7.

TOWN MUSEUM
Palača Gabrielis, Trg. Sv. Marka, Korčula
Building (early 16th century). Plaster cast (original in Zagreb) of a Greek inscription (4th century B.C.). Ethnographic, lapidary and maritime displays. Room devoted to the wartime resistance movement, including photographs of the British military mission to Korčula. Maritime history.
Daily 8-12, 5-7.

KOŠLJUN

MONASTIC MUSEUM
Chapel of St. Bernadin, Franciscan Monastery, Košljun, nr. Punat
Well-head. Roman child's sarcophagus. Gravestones. Paintings (16th-17th century Venetian) including works by Franjo Juričić (1671-1718), a local artist. Krk folk costumes. The *Library* contains an early copy of Ptolemy's atlas (1511); the Papal bull granting Košljun to the Franciscans; a fragment of one of the earliest printed books in Croatian (1483); Katerina Frankopan's will (1520); incunabula; manuscripts in Glagolitic and Latin dating back to the 11th century.
Daily 9-12, 4-6. Library: on request.

KOTOR

CATHEDRAL OF SV. NIKOLA TREASURY
Trg bratstva-jedinstva, Kotor
Collection of ancient icons. 14th-17th century silver reliquaries. 15th century silver cross belonging to Bishop Kontaren of Kotor. Renaissance paintings.
Enquire locally.

CATHEDRAL OF SV. TRIPUN TREASURY
Trg pobune mornara, Kotor
Chalices. Monstrances. Pastoral crosses. Paintings. Sarcophagi. 17th century Venetian casket. 16th century crystal cross. Reliquaries.
On request.

LAPIDARY COLLECTION
Trg Oktobarske Revolucije, Kotor
Original 12th century wheel-window from cathedral. Inlaid marble reredos with a relief of St. Tryphon. Pre-Romanesque stone sarcophagus decorated in low relief.
Daily ex. M. 9-12, 4-7.

MARITIME MUSEUM
Palata Grgurina, Trg Bokeljske mornarice, Kotor
History of the Kotor Sailors' Guild (later the Boka Kotorska Navy). Armoury. Ships models. Traditional costumes of the Kotor sailors.
Daily ex. M. 8-1.

KRAPINA

GAJ'S MUSEUM
Gajeva 14, Krapina
Exhibits connected with the work of Ljudevit Gaj, the leader of Illyric Movement, which in the last century fought for the introduction of Croatian language into public life.
Daily ex. M. 8-12.

MUSEUM OF EVOLUTION
Krapina
Exhibits include the remains of the Krapina Neolithic man and of prehistoric animals at Hušnjakevo, near Krapina.
Daily ex. M. 8-12.

KROPA

LOCAL MUSEUM
Kropa
History of local metalworking activities. Specimens of wrought iron.
On request.

KUMROVEC

MARSHAL TITO MEMORIAL MUSEUM
Kumrovec
House in which Josip Broz (Tito) was born, May 1892. Furnishings. Documents. Wrought iron fence made by Broz. Photographs. Exhibition of Tito's life and work.
Daily ex. M. 8-6. Summer: daily 8-6.

LABIN

TOWN MUSEUM
Palača Battiala-Lazzarini, Labin
Building (1717). Local history. Reconstruction of a mining gallery.
Daily 10-4.

LASTOVO

CHURCH TREASURY
Church of Sv. Kuzma i Damjan, Lastovo
15th-16th century objects of Ragusan workmanship, including a silver-gilt processional cross by Marul Ivaneo (1574). Reliquaries. Monstrances.
Apply to the Sacristan.

LESKOVAC

TOWN MUSEUM
2 Včetelja Josifa Street, Leskovac
Archaeological finds from excavations at Stublje, Gradac, Hisar and Kopašnica. Lapidarium. Ethnography, including regional costumes and domestic articles. Mementoes of the War of Liberation.
Tu.-Su. 8-12, 4-7.

LJUBLJANA

ARCHIVES OF SLOVENIA
Levstikov trg 3, Ljubljana
Collection of archives, especially those connected with the territory populated by Slovenes from 13th century onwards.
Tu.-Su. 8-12, 4-7.

ETHNOGRAPHICAL MUSEUM
Presernova cesta 20, Ljubljana
Slovene and non-European ethnographic collections.
Tu.-Su. 9-12, 4-7.

GEOGRAPHICAL MUSEUM OF SLOVENIA
Trg francoske revolucije 7, Ljubljana
Maps of Slovenia. Geographical collections.
Tu.-Su. 9-12, 4-7.

MODERN ART GALLERY
Cankarjeva 15, Ljubljana
Slovene (Yugoslav) art from the Impressionists to the present day.
Tu.-Su. 8-12, 4-7.

MUNICIPAL MUSEUM
Gosposka 15, Ljubljana
Cultural history collections. Furniture from the Gothic period to the Biedermeier period. Arts and crafts. Topography. Archaeology, including articles from lake-dwellings of the Celtic-Illyrian period and period of Roman domination.
Tu.-Su. 8-12, 4-7.

NATIONAL ART GALLERY
Ljubljana Prezihova 1, Ljubljana
Gothic sculptural arts. Medieval frescoes and imitations of Gothic frescoes from Slovenia. Renaissance, Baroque and 19th century paintings and sculptures. Paintings by Slovene Impressionists. Slovenian graphic arts from 18th - early 20th century. Photographs.
Tu.-Su. 10-1.

NATIONAL LIBERATION MUSEUM
Celovska c. 23, Ljubljana
Archives, museum objects and library material from the War of Liberation, 1941-45. Exhibition showing the struggle of the Slovene people for liberation.
Tu.-Su. 8-12, 4-7.

NATIONAL MUSEUM
Presernova ul. 20, P.O. Box 529-X, Ljubljana
Archaeology and prehistory. Applied arts. Coins and medals. Graphic arts. Peasants' costumes. Old and modern paintings by Slovenian artists. Ethnography. Natural science.
Tu.-Su. 10-1.

SLOVENIAN NATURAL HISTORY MUSEUM
Presernova 20, Ljubljana
Zoological, botanical and palaeontological dioramas.
Tu.-Su. 9-12, 4-7.

SLOVENIAN SCHOOL MUSEUM
Poljanska 28, Ljubljana
Development of schools in Slovenia. School documents and pedagogic books from 12th century onwards. Records of teachers killed during 1941-45 war.
Tu.-Su. 9-12, 4-7.

MAKARSKA

MUSEUM OF MALACOLOGY
Franciscan Monastery, Put žrtava fašizma, Makarska
Seashells from all parts of the world.
Daily 10-12, 5-7.

MARIBOR

REGIONAL MUSEUM
Grajska ul. 2, Maribor
Archaeology. Ethnography. History. Topography. Art. Coins. Weapons.
Daily ex. M. 9-12, 4-7.

MOTOVUN

CHURCH OF ST. STJEPAN
Motovun
Building 1614, attributed to Palladio. 18th century Baroque choir stalls. Treasury contains silver processional cross and gold chalice (both 15th century); 14th century altar cloth, once the property of Bartolomeo. Colleoni.
Treasury: apply to the sacristan.

NIN

MUSEUM
Church of St. Anzelm, Nin, nr. Zadar
Prehistoric and Roman ornaments. Copies of objects found at Nin but since removed.
On request: ask for the cuvar.

NIŠ

OCHRID NATIONAL MUSEUM
Tzar Samuel Street, Niš
Prehistory. Antique and medieval history. Folklore. Roman, Byzantine and Turkish coins. Jewellery. Embroideries. Tools and weapons.
Tu.-Su. 10-5.

NOVI SAD

ART GALLERY OF MATIČA SRPSKA (SERBIAN CULTURAL ASSOCIATION)
Novi Sad
Collection of Serbian art from 18th century.
On request.

GALLERY OF THE DIOCESE OF BAČKA
Novi Sad
Portraits by Serbian 18th and 19th century painters.
Tu.-Su. 9-12, 4-7.

MUSEUM OF VOJVODINA
Petrovaradinska tvrdjava, Novi Sad
Archaeology. Ethnography. History of the Socialist Movement. History of the town and its crafts. Natural sciences.
Daily ex. M. 9-12, 4-7.

NOVI VINODOL

TOWN MUSEUM
Novi Vinodol
Local history. Ethnography. Mementoes of the Mažuranić family. Early Baroque altar frontal. Folk costumes of Novi Vinodolski. Weapons.
M. and Th. 9-11.

OHRID

LOCAL MUSEUM
Tsar Samuilo Street, Ohrid
Collections of material from excavations in the region. Local traditions.
On request.

OMIS

TOWN MUSEUM
Omis
Lapidary collection, including Roman relief of Diomysus and 13th century memorial slab of Prince Miroslav Kačić. Historical documents. Folk costumes. Relics of the second World War.
Evenings, 5-7.

OREBIĆ

CAPTAINS' HOUSES
Orebić
18th century villa, containing collection of furniture by Chippendale and Biedermeier, pottery by Wedgwood and the Russian court potter. Kuznetsov. Copper and pewter. House reproducing conditions of life in 18th-19th centuries, with displays of icons and 19th century costumes.
Enquire locally.

MARITIME MUSEUM
Orebić
History of Orebić's merchant fleet, illustrated by models, paintings and documents.
Daily 8-11, 4-7.

OSIJEK

ART GALLERY
4 August-Cesarec Street, Osijek
Works by 18th-19th century Austrian painters, and Slavonic landscape painters, including Hetzendorf and Waldinger. Paintings by Croat and Serbian artists.
Tu.-Su. 9-12, 4-7.

MUNICIPAL MUSEUM
Castle, Osijek
Local history. Coins. Old furniture, Renaissance - present day.
Tu.-Su. 10-5.

OSOR

MUSEUM
former Town Hall, Osor
Fragments of masonry. Roman busts. Burial urns. Pottery. Illyrian jewellery, pottery and weapons from local excavations.
On request.

PANCEVO

LOCAL MUSEUM
Pancevo
Local history and archaeology.
On request.

PAZIN

ETHNOGRAPHIC AND HISTORICAL MUSEUM
Kaštel, Pazin
History of the city. Ethnography. Collection of bells of 12th-18th centuries.
Daily 10-1, 4-6.

PEĆ

TREASURY OF THE PATRIARCHATE OF PEĆ
Peć
Icons, sacred books, religious ornaments, dating from 16th century.
On request.

PERAST

MUSEUM
Palača Viskovic, Main Street, Perast
Palace (1718). Portraits. Weapons.
By appointment.

NAVAL MUSEUM
Perast
Housed in school where, in 1689, Marko Martinović taught the principles of navigation to the Russian princes and boyars of Peter I. Paintings. Weapons. Documents.
Tu.-Su. 9-12, 4-7.

TREASURY
Church of Sv. Nikola, Town Square, Perast
Plate includes large Renaissance silver Cross of Abp. Zmajevic; silver tablet depicting the Battle of Perast against the Turks (1654); large silver censer. Vestments include robes of Abp. Zmajevic. Lace of 16th-19th centuries. Oriental silk canopy.
Apply to parish priest.

PETROVA GORA

CENTRAL PARTISAN HOSPITAL
Memorial Park, Petrova Gora
Rebuilt hospital, with operating theatres, underground shelters, auxiliary installations and a cemetery with the graves of about 1060 partisans.
Daily 7-7.

PIRAN

ART GALLERY AND CITY MUSEUM
Tartinijev trg., Piran
History of Piran salt mines. Lapidary collection, including three 15th-16th century well-heads. Archaeological remains from prehistoric to early Slavonic times. 17th century engravings and paintings. Memorabilia of the composer Tartini, including a copy of his violin and the Baroque Paduan furniture (1720) of his bedroom. 18th-20th century paintings and statues.
July-Aug. daily 8-11, 4-7. Apr.-June and Sept.-Oct., daily 8-11, 4-6.

MARITIME MUSEUM
Gabrielli Mansion, Tartinijev trg., Piran
Ships' models, including a 17th century Venetian galley. 18th century seascapes. Local Istrian sea chests. Relics of early Piranian notables, little votive pictures painted at sea by mariners and given to local churches. Wooden figure of St. Anne (c.1500). 17th century ship's figurehead depicting the Virgin. Slovene maritime history of the past hundred years.
July-Aug. daily 8-11, 4-7. Apr.-June and Sept.-Oct., daily 8-11, 4-6.

POREČ

TOWN MUSEUM
Palača Sinčič, Dekumanska, Poreč
Roman architectural fragments. Early Bronze Age and Etruscan pottery. Roman and Greek objects, including mosaics. Paintings of local nobility. Istrian ethnography.
Daily 9-12, 5-8.

POSTOJNA

COLLECTIONS OF THE INSTITUTE OF SPELEOLOGY
Postojna
Large collections from the caves (Postojnska Jama) on the outskirts of the town. Models, plans, specimens and photographs of all the caves in the region.
On request.

PREDJAMA

CASTLE MUSEUM
Predjama, nr. Postojna
Archaeological finds. Furniture. Armour. 15th century Gothic *Pietà*.
Daily ex. M. 8-12, 4-7.

PTUJ

CASTLE MUSEUM
Kastel, Ptuj
Prehistory. Arts and crafts.
Tu.-Su. 8-12, 4-7.

REGIONAL MUSEUM
Muzejski trg 1, Ptuj
Archaeology. Art. History and ethnography of the prehistoric, Roman, Old Slavonic and Feudal periods. Ecclesiastical art. Folklore. Local history. Three temples of Mithras.
Daily ex. M. 8-12, 4-7.

PULA

ARCHAEOLOGICAL MUSEUM
Twin Gates, Trg. Bratstva i Jedinstva, Pula
Prehistoric, Roman and medieval collections.
Daily ex. M. 8-12, 4-7.

MUSEUM OF THE NATIONAL LIBERATION MOVEMENT
Kastel, Pula
Mementoes of the National Liberation Movement.
Daily 8-7.

RAB

MUSEUM
Knezev dvor, Rab
Lapidary collections.
On request.

TREASURY
Cathedral of Sveta Marija Velika, Trg Maršala Tita, Rab
Reliquary of silver parcel-gilt with gabled lid containing head of St. Christopher. The skull inside bears a crown said to have been the gift of Queen Elizabeth the Younger of Hungary. 4 copper plates bearing champlevé enamels of saints.
Rarely open.

RIJEKA

DIOCESAN MUSEUM
Uzarska ul., Rijeka
Church ornaments and vestments. Documents. Gold and silverware.
Daily 8-12, 4-6.

MARITIME AND HISTORICAL MUSEUM
Guvernerova palaca, Zrtava fasizma 18, Rijeka
Building (1896). Public rooms have been restored and arranged as they were when the governors were in residence. Violins by Franjo Kresnik, a local maker. Piano of Ivan Zajc. Ships' models, documents and portraits.
Daily 9-1, 2-5; Sa. and Su. 9-12. Closed M.

MUSEUM OF MODERN YUGOSLAV ART
Reference and Lending Library, Trg republike and Dolac, Rijeka
Modern paintings by Yugoslav and foreign artists.
Daily 9-12, 5-7.

MUSEUM OF THE NATIONAL REVOLUTION
Rijeka Zrinskog 12, Rijeka
Series of documents illustrating the development of the working people from 1918 to the beginning of the second World War. Documents and photographs of the National Revolution (1941-45).
Daily 9-12, 2-4; Su. 9-12.

NATURAL HISTORY MUSEUM
Šetalište Vladimira Nazora 3, Rijeka
Natural history collections. Aquarium. Geology. Palaeontology. Entomology.
Daily 9-12, 2-4; Su. 9-12.

ROVINJ

ETHNOGRAPHICAL MUSEUM
Ul. Silvano Chiurco, Rovinj
Housed in former bakery. Ethnographical collections.
Daily ex. M. 9-12, 4-7.

TOWN MUSEUM
Vrata Sv. Križa, Trg. Maršala Tita, Rovinj
Paintings by Bonifazio. Portraits of the Hütteroth family. Furniture. Paintings by modern Yugoslav artists.
Daily 9 11, 6-9.

SARAJEVO

ART GALLERY
Trg Oslobodenja 1, Sarajevo
Paintings, sculptures and works of graphic art by Bosnian and Herzogovinian artists.
Daily ex. M. 9-12, 2-5.

DESPIĆ'S HOUSE
Obala Ognjena Price, Sarajevo
A completely furnished Serbian patrician home of the 17th century.
May 1 - Oct. 15, daily ex. Su. 9-12, 2-5.

JEWISH MUSEUM
Ulica Marsala Tita, Sarajevo
Located in old synagogue. Documents, photographs and art objects illustrating the life and history of Jews in Sarajevo.
Daily ex. M. 9-2; Su. 9-1. Apr. 15 - Oct. 15, daily ex. M. 9-12, 2-5.

MUSEUM OF THE CITY OF SARAJEVO
Remzije Omanovic 31, Sarajevo
Political, economic and cultural history of Sarajevo from ancient times to the present day. Archaeology. History. Art. Ethnography.
Daily ex. Tu. 9-2; Su. 9-1. Apr. 15 - Oct. 15, 9-12, 4-7.

MUSEUM COLLECTION OF THE OLD ORTHODOX CHURCH
Ulica Maršala Tita 83, Sarajevo
Rich collection of icons, old frescoes, medieval manuscripts, gold and silver objects and other items of church furnishings.
Daily 9-5.

MUSEUM OF THE REVOLUTION
Ulica Vojvode Putnika 9, Sarajevo
Collections illustrating the struggle of the people of Bosnia and Herzegovinia for national and social liberation (1875-1945).
Daily ex. M. 9-12, 4-7.

MUSEUM OF YOUNG BOSNIA
Vojvode Stepe Obala 36, Sarajevo
Documents, photographs, art objects and personal belongings of Gavrilo Princip and his companions from the Young Bosnia revolutionary movement give a complete account of the assassination of Archduke Franz Ferdinand. The museum is on the ground-floor of the building in front of which Princip shot the archduke on June 28, 1914.
Daily ex. Tu. 9-2; Su. 9-1. Apr. 15 - Oct. 15, 9-12, 4-7.

STATE MUSEUM
Vojvode Putnika 7, Sarajevo
Prehistoric, ancient and medieval archaeology. Ethnography. Natural sciences: zoology, botany, geology, mineralogy. Collection of Bogomil tombstones.
Daily ex. M. 9-1. Apr. 15 - Oct. 15, also W., Th., F. 4-7.

SVRSO'S HOUSE
Jovana Kršića 6, Sarajevo
Moslem dwelling-house, a classic example of the Turkish-influenced architecture of the area. Furnishings and furniture.
May 1 - Oct. 15, daily ex. Su. 9-12, 2-5.

SENJ

DIOCESAN MUSEUM
Palača Carina, Senj
Gothic Kaptolski kriz in silver and wood. Gothic cross in beaten silver. Silver votive tablets. Church plate and vestments. Lapidary collection.
Summer: daily 9-12, 4-7. Winter: Th. and Su. 10-12.

TOWN MUSEUM
Palača Vukasovic, Senj
Lapidary collection. Archaeology. Partisan relics. History of literature in Glagolitic.
Summer: daily 9-12, 4-7. Winter: Th. and Su. 10-12.

USKOK MUSEUM
Kastel Nehaj, Senj
Castle (1538-58). Local history. Period furnishings.
Summer: daily 9-12, 5-8.

ŠIBENIK

TOWN MUSEUM
Kneževa palača, Šibenik
Archaeological collections and exhibits devoted to the history of Šibenik and the Partisan movement.
Daily ex. M. 9-12, 5-7.

SINJ

ALKARI MUSEUM
Sinj
Costumes used by the Alkari, or knights of Sinj, who won a famous victory over the Turks in 1715. 18th century costumes. Horses' harness. Weapons. Turkish weapons and the saddle of Serašcer Mehmet Pasha, the defeated Turkish general.
Daily ex. M. 9-12, 4-7.

MUSEUM
Franciscan Monastery, nr. Sinj
Finds from the neighbouring Roman site of Aequum (now Čitluk). Roman gravestones. Sculpture, reliefs and coins. Folk costumes, musical instruments, jewellery and bygones.
On request.

TOWN MUSEUM
Sinj
Local history. Section devoted to the National Liberation Struggle. Persian furniture, including inlaid games table and a rich trellis screen.
Daily ex. M. 9-12, 4-7.

SISAK

MUSEUM OF THE REVOLUTION
tomislavova 10, Sisak
Memorial collection illustrating Marshal Tito's apprenticeship in one of Sisak's workshops, 1907-10.
Summer: daily 10-12, 5-7. Winter: daily 10-12, 4-6.

MUSEUM OF SISAK
Trg Slobode 8, Sisak
Material illustrating the origin and development of the town.
Summer: daily 10-12, 5-7. Winter: daily 10-12, 4-6.

STARI GRAD MUSEUM
Kastel, Sisak
Collections illustrating historic events at Sisak. Ethnography.
May 1 - Oct. 1, daily 10-12, 5-7. Winter: daily 10-12, 4-6.

SKOFJA LOKA

MUSEUM
Skofja Lok Castle, Skofja Loka
Exhibits relating to the Freising dominion (973-1803). Ethnographic, topographic, natural history and historical exhibits. Records of altars from 17th century. Exhibits of medieval guilds. Relics of the struggle for national liberation. Art Gallery. Open air museum.
Early ex. M. 9-12, 4-7.

SKOPJE

ARCHAEOLOGICAL MUSEUM
Kursumlihan, Skopje
Statues. Sarcophagi. Tombstones. Mosaics. Coins.
Tu.-Su. 9-12, 4-7.

ART GALLERY
Skopje
Yugoslav medieval and modern art, in former Turkish baths. Icons. Copies of old frescoes.
Tu.-Su. 9-12, 4-7.

ETHNOLOGICAL MUSEUM
Plostad Maršala Titoa 18 III, Skopje
Ethnographical collections.
Damaged by earthquake: temporarily closed.

NATURAL HISTORY MUSEUM
Ul. Bulevar Ilinden, 91000 Skopje
Natural history collections. Botany. Zoology. Mineralogy. Palaeontology.
Tu.-Su. 9-12, 4-7.

SOMOBOR

MUSEUM OF SOMOBOR
Livadic Hall, Somobor
Historical material relating to prominent personalities, and illustrating the origin and development of the Panonic Lowlands.
Daily ex. Th. 9-1.

SPLIT

ARCHAEOLOGICAL MUSEUM
Zrinjsko-Frankopanska 25, Split
Prehistoric collections. Relics from Greek colonies on east shore of Adriatic. Roman and Christian relics from Salonae and Dalmatia. Croatian medieval monuments from 9th-13th centuries.
Daily ex. M. 8-1; Su. 10-12.

ART GALLERY
Lovretska 11, Split
Ancient and modern paintings and sculptures. 15th-19th century icons. Works by Andrea Meldola 'Schiavone', Aleši, Federiko Benković. Local painters' work (19th and 20th centuries). Drawings by Kokoschka and George Grosz. Venetian Gothic, Renaissance and Baroque masters.
Daily 9-12, 5-7; Su. 9-12.

CITY MUSEUM OF SPLIT
Papalićeva 1, Split
Political and cultural history of Split. 15th-18th century weapons. Turkish and European small arms, including two rare examples of guns with wicks, the forerunners of flintlocks. History of the city, 12th-16th century. Models. Drawings. Plans. Original sculptures from the Cathedral. Coins.
Daily 9-1; Su. 10-12; Tu. and Th. 5-8.

ETHNOGRAPHICAL MUSEUM
Narodni trg 1, Split
National costumes. Jewels. Weapons. Technological objects from Dalmatia. Basketwork. Furniture. Household utensils. Wood-carving. Wool production.
Daily 8-1; Su. 10-12; Th. 6-8 p.m. July-Aug. also daily 6-8 p.m.

MARITIME MUSEUM
Palača Milesi, 7 Trg braće Radića, Split
Collections and models illustrating the maritime history of Dalmatia. Ship models, paintings, documents and objects. Ship building. Development of the War for Independence (1941-45).
Daily ex. M. 9-12.

MEŠTROVIĆ GALLERY
Moše Pijade 46, Split
Former villa of the sculptor Ivan Meštrović (1883-1962), containing exhibitions of his work. Religious subjects, including two colossal unfinished figures of Adam and Eve. Private apartments of the sculptor. Miscellaneous objects too large to be exhibited elsewhere.
Daily 10-7 (May 15 - Sept. 15).

MUSEUM OF CROATIAN MEDIEVAL ANTIQUITIES
7 Obala J.N.A., Split
Croatian archaeological finds, mainly pre-Romanesque from the period of early Croatian independence (9th-12th century). Ciboria. Jewellery. 8th century censer found at Stara Vrlika. Oldest document cut in stone, dating from 9th century A.D.
Daily ex. M. 9-12; Su. 10-12.

MUSEUM OF NATIONAL REVOLUTION
10 Šetalište 1, Maja, Split
Development of the working class revolutionary movement and of the Communist Party in the Littoral region from the earliest period to the outbreak of World War I. Over 50,000 pictures illustrating the history of the Movement.
Daily ex. Sa. 7-2; Tu. 4-7.

MUSEUM OF NATURAL SCIENCES
Marjanske stube, Split
Mineralogical, palaeontological and zoological specimens from Dalmatia and the Adriatic Sea. Collections of colleoptera, shells and birds (mostly Dalmatian). Dioramas.
Daily 8-sunset.

NAVAL MUSEUM
4 Klaićeva Poljana, Split
Naval history of Split, especially events from the Yugoslav Liberation War. Ship models, weapons, large relief of the Adriatic coast. Photographs and documents.
Daily ex. M. 9-12; Th. afternoon by arrangement.

STUDIO OF EMANUEL VIDOVIĆ
19 ul. Maksima Gorkog, Split
Former studio of Emanuel Vidović (1897-1953), the landscape painter, housing examples of his work.
Daily ex. M., 9-12, 4-7.

TREASURY
Cathedral of the Blessed Virgin Mary, Split
Collection of codices, including the Evangeliarum Spalatense, a rare 8th century copy of the Gospels. Silver monstrances. Jewellery. Gilt cross (12th century). 15th century chalices. Vestments. Collection of lace.
June - mid.Sept., daily 9-12, 4-7.

SREMSKA MITROVICA

ARCHAEOLOGICAL MUSEUM
Sremska Mitrovica
Items from Roman excavations in the area.
On request.

SREMSKI KARLOVCI

TOWN MUSEUM
Palace of the Serb Patriarch Rajacic, Sremski Karlovci
Archaeology. Prehistoric tools. Manuscripts and mementoes of the patriarchs. Ethnography, including traditional crafts of the Karlovci region. Works of art, including portraits by local painters, especially Djurković, Bakalović, Simić and Predić. 18th-19th century furniture.
Tu.-Su. 9-12, 4-7.

STARI GRAD

ETHNOGRAPHICAL MUSEUM
Tvrdalj, Stari Grad
Building (c.1520). Ethnographical collection.
Daily ex. M. 9-12, 4-7.

MARITIME MUSEUM AND ART GALLERY
Tvrdalj, Stari Grad
Maritime collections. Paintings by Meštrović, Rendić, and Juraj Plančić (1899-1930), who was born in Stari Grad.
Daily ex. M. 9-12, 4-7.

STUDENICA

MONASTERY TREASURY
Studenica
Religious books, icons, vases, chasubles and sacerdotal ornaments (17th-18th century).
On request.

SUBOTICA

TOWN MUSEUM
Subotica
Archaeology, local history, art and ethnography (Slav and Hungarian). Coins.
Daily ex. M. 8-1.

SVETI STEFAN

TREASURY
Church of Sv. Nikola, Sveti Stefan
16th century copy of the gospels, with engraved silver covers and miniature reliefs. Silver-gilt chalice presented by Tsar Paul of Russia (18th century). Large 16th century icon.
On request.

SV. FUMIJA

LIBRARY
Monastery of Sv. Fumija, nr. Rab
14th-15th century illuminated codices. Incunabula. Small Roman statue of Diana. Gothic figure of St. Francis in wood.
M.-Sa. 9-12, 4-7.

TITOVO UŽICE

MUSEUM OF THE INSURRECTION OF 1941
Corner Marshal Tito and Hero Dejovic Streets, Titovo Užice
In headquarters of the People's Army of Liberation. History of the struggle for liberation.
Tu.-Su. 9-12, 4-7.

TRAKOŠČAN

CASTLE MUSEUM
Trakoščan
16th century castle, surrounded by a 2 km. long lake. Furniture. Works of art. Weapons.
May 1 - Oct. 1, daily ex. M. 9-5. Oct. 1 - Mar. 31, daily ex. M. 9-1.

TROGIR

TOWN MUSEUM
Palača Gagarnin-Fanfogna, Ul. Rade Koncara, Trogir
History of Trogir. Paintings.
Daily 8-12, 5-7.

TREASURY
Benedictine Nunnery, Palača Vituri, Trogir
Marble Relief of Kairos, the Greek god of luck (1st century B.C.). Icons. Paintings. Wooden polyptych (c.1400), Gothic paintings, sculpture.
Daily 8.30-11.30, 3.30-5.30.

TREASURY
Cathedral of Sv. Lovrijenac, Narodni trg, Trogir
Paintings, including a polyptych in Gothic frame (15th century). Two painted doors from an organ case by Gentile Bellini. The plate includes a 14th century silver-gilt ewer with a lid in the shape of the crown of Hungary. Monstrances. Reliquaries. Jewelled mitre (14th century). Ecclesiastical robes.
On application to the Sacristan.

VARAŽDIN

STARI GRAD MUSEUM
Strossmayerovo šetalište 7, Varaždin
In castle, which has original furnishings and furniture. Works of art. Weapons.
M.-Sa. 8-12; Su. and holidays 10-12.

VELIKA GORICA

MUSEUM OF TUROPOLJE
Trg Slobode 1, Velika Gorica
History of Turopolje. Ethnography, including timber architecture. People's Revolution section.
Daily 9-1.

VISOVAC

FRANCISCAN MONASTERY AND SEMINARY
Visovac
17th-18th century pictures. Madonna (1576). Annunciation (17th century) in mother-of-pearl inlay. Library has one of three known copies of an illustrated translation of Aesop's fables, published by Boninus de Boninis (Dobrić Dobrićević) of Dubrovnik in 1487.
Occasionally on request.

VRBA

HOUSE-MUSEUM
Vrba, near Zirovnica
House in which the Slovene poet, Fr. Prešeren was born. Memorabilia of Prešeren.
Tu.-Su. 9-12, 4-7.

VRBOVSKA

FORTIFIED CHURCH
Vrbovska
Paintings by Titian and Veronese. Works by the sculptor Peri. Hvar laces.
On request.

ZADAR

ARCHAEOLOGICAL MUSEUM
Filozofski fakultet, University of Zagreb, Nova obala, Zadar
Prehistoric jewellery, pottery and utensils. Mosaic and sculpture from Roman times. Medieval Croatian items.
On request: collection scattered.

ETHNOGRAPHICAL MUSEUM
Loža gradske straže, Narodni trg, Zadar
Ethnography. Collection of folk costumes. Wood-work.
Daily ex. M. 8-11, 6-8.

GALLERY OF MODERN ART
Ul. Andrije Medulića, Zadar
Collection of icons and other works by modern Yugoslav painters.
Daily 8-12.

NATIONAL MUSEUM
Trg Vladimira Gortana, Zadar
Mementoes of the second World War.
Daily ex. M. 8-12, 4-7.

NATURAL HISTORY MUSEUM
Ul. Andrije Medulića, Zadar
Collection of Mediterranean fish and birds.
Daily 8-12.

TREASURY OF THE CATHEDRAL AND OF THE BENEDICTINE NUNNERY OF SV. MARIJA
Slavensko sjemenište, Trg 27 marta, Zadar
Pre-Romanesque cross of gilded copper; 12th century processional cross with miniatures; 14th-15th century Reliquary of the Holy Cross and Sponge; Gothic Pastoral Staff (1460) of Abp. Maffeo Valaresso. Reliquaries. Jewels. Precious stones. Busts. Mitre of St. Sylvester. 12th century silver gilt Pax of Pope Gregory. Embroideries and vestments (14th-17th centuries), including Dalmatian lace.
By special permission only.

ZAGREB

ARCHAEOLOGICAL MUSEUM
Zrinjski trg 19, Zagreb
Croatian history from Neolithic times to the 13th century, from Celtic, Illyrian and Roman times, and relics from Italy and Egypt. Mummy with Etruscan text. Statues from S. Italy, Dalmatia and Croatia. Coins.
Daily ex. M. 9-1.

ARCHIVES OF CROATIA
Marulićev trg 21, 41000 Zagreb
Documents dating from 10th century, concerning mainly the history of Northern Croatia and Slavonia. Eleven charters from the time of Croatian kings. King Bela IV's Golden Bull by which Zagreb was proclaimed a royal free city in 1242.
By appointment.

ARCHIVES OF THE HISTORY OF THE CROATIAN WORKERS' MOVEMENT
8 Opatička Ulica, Zagreb
Documents relating to the history of the Croatian workers' movement and of the Communist Party of Croatia.
By appointment.

ARCHIVES OF THE YUGOSLAV ACADEMY OF SCIENCES AND ARTS
11 Zrinjski Trg., Zagreb
Original manuscripts by Croatian writers and scholars. Glagolitic and Cryllic manuscripts. Medieval Latin documents, rolls and codexes. Byzantine sculptures of 9th-10th centuries. 15th-18th century icons. Italian paintings, 15th-18th centuries. Works by artists of the Flemish and Dutch schools and by painters from Dubrovnik and Dalmatia.
By appointment.

ATELIER IVAN MEŠTROVIĆ
Mletačka 8, Zagreb
Studio of the late Croatian sculptor Ivan Meštrović. Works by the artist - in stone, marble, bronze and wood.
By appointment.

CITY MUSEUM OF ZAGREB
Opatička 20, Zagreb
Collections depicting Zagreb from prehistoric times to 1835. Popular liberation struggle, 1919-45. Church art. Guilds. Theatre. Illyrian movement.
Daily 9-1; Sa. 10-1; Tu. and Th. also 4-7.

COLLECTION OF GRAPHICS
National University Library, 21 Marulicev trg., Zagreb
Drawings and watercolours by Croatian artists of the beginning of the 20th century. Wood-carvings, copper-plate engravings and lithographs by Yugoslav and foreign masters from 17th century to the present day.
Daily 7-2.

CROATIAN NATIONAL ZOOLOGICAL MUSEUM
1 Demetrova Ulica, Zagreb
Mammals. Birds. Reptiles. Amphibians. Fish.
Daily 9-1; Tu. and Th. also 2-6.

CROATIAN SCHOOLS' MUSEUM
Trg Maršala Tita 4, Zagreb
History of schools and education in Croatia. Teaching-aids, hand-work, specimens of copy-books, drawing-pads, text-books. Documents and photographs.
Weekdays 8-2.

DIOCESAN MUSEUM
28 Kaptol, Zagreb
Ecclesiastical vestments. Silver and gold church vessels. Paintings. Statues.
By appointment.

ETHNOGRAPHICAL MUSEUM
Mažuranićev trg 14, Zagreb
Ethnographic material from all over Yugoslavia: national costumes, lace, carpets, peasant implements. Various products of peasant crafts and cottage industries made of wood, earthenware, metal. Interiors of Croat peasant houses from various regions. Musical instruments. Foreign folk art.
Daily ex. M. 9-1.

GALLERY OF CONTEMPORARY ARTS
Katarinski trg 2, Zagreb
Works by contemporary Yugoslav artists.
Daily 11-1, 5-8.

GALLERY OF MODERN ART
Braće Kavurića 1, Zagreb
Development of Croatian painting during 19th and 20th centuries. Works by the sculptors Ivan Meštrović, Antun Augustinčić and Vanja Radauš. Paintings by foreign artists, including works by Renoir and Dégas.
Daily ex. M. 10-1.

GALLERY OF NATIVE ARTS
Cirilometodska 3, Zagreb
Works by Yugoslav primitive painters and sculptors.
Daily 11-1, 5-8.

GEOLOGICAL AND PALAEONTOLOGICAL MUSEUM
Demetrova 1, Zagreb
Geology. Palaeontology. Remains of a diluvial man of the Neanderthal type, *homo crapiniensis.*
Daily 9-12. Tu. and F. also 4-6.

IVAN GERESDORFER COLLECTION OF MUSICAL AUTOMATA
7 Demetrova Ulica, Zagreb
Musical automata dating from the Biedermeier period to the 1920s.
By appointment.

HISTORICAL MUSEUM OF CROATIA
Matoševa 9, Zagreb
Historical material from 14th century to the present day. Weapons. Flags. Historical portraits. Prints. Social and cultural development of the Slavs. Russian incunabula. Handwritten books. Church vestments and vessels.
Daily ex. M. 10-5.

HUNTING MUSEUM
63 Nazorova Ulica, Zagreb
Stuffed specimens of all kinds of Yugoslav small and big game. Nests. Eggs. Specimens of deer, roe-buck and chamois antlers. Guns and hunting equipment.
Daily ex. M. and F., 9-12.30.

LITERARY MUSEUM
18 Opatička Ulica, Zagreb
Books, manuscripts, letters, photographs and documents from the life and work of various Croatian writers.
Daily ex. Sa. 8-2.

LUBIENSKY-DURIEUX COLLECTION OF OBJETS D'ART
Jurjevska Ulica, Zagreb
Paintings by Rosa, Waldmüller, Bukovac, Brueghel, Chagall, Klee. Artifacts of Mycenean, Etruscan, Persian, Chinese and Japanese cultures.
Su. 10-1.

MEMORIAL EXHIBITION, "600th ANNIVERSARY OF ZAGREB PHARMACEUTICS"
9 Kamenita Ulica, Zagreb
Medieval laboratories, with a hearth with bellows and other equipment for heating and distilling; vessels; mortars; poisons. Stuffed alligators.
By appointment.

MUSEUM OF APPLIED ARTS
Trg maršala Tita 10, Zagreb
Applied arts from 14th-20th centuries. Furniture. Tapestries. Textiles. Ceramics. Glass. Gold and silver work. Sculpture. Paintings. Miniatures. Costumes. Samples of industrial design. Antique clocks.
Daily ex. M. 10-1; Th. also 6 a.m. - 8 p.m.

MUSEUM OF THE BLIND
80/11 Draškovićeva, Zagreb
Methods of educating the blind, their rehabilitation, work, and social and recreational life. Specialist library of braille books.
Daily ex. M. 8-2.

MUSEUM OF THE EIGHTH CONFERENCE OF THE ZAGREB ORGANISATION OF THE COMMUNIST PARTY OF YUGOSLAVIA
178a Pantovčak, Zagreb
Struggle of the Communist Party of Yugoslavia at the end of King Aleksandar's dictatorship. Documents relating to the Party Conference held 25-26 February 1968, at which Comrade Tito was elected chairman of the local committee.
Daily ex. M. 10-12.

MUSEUM OF THE FIFTH NATIONAL CONFERENCE OF THE COMMUNIST PARTY OF YUGOSLAVIA
Ulica Pete Konferencije KPJ, Zagreb
Documents of the Fifth National Party Conference held from October 19-23, 1940, at which the new party leadership headed by Tito was elected.
Daily ex. M. 9-1, 4-7.

MUSEUM OF THE FIRST NATIONAL CONFERENCE OF THE COMMUNIST PARTY OF CROATIA
205 Ulica Prosinačkih Žrtava, Zagreb
Documents relating to the work of the Communist Party of Croatia immediately before the beginning of the Second World War.
Daily ex. M. 9-1, 4-7; Su. 9-1.

MUSEUM OF MINERALOGY AND PETROGRAPHY
Demetrova ul. 1, Zagreb
Minerals from all over the world. Yugoslav minerals, stones and ores.
Daily ex. M. 9-12.

NATURAL HISTORY MUSEUM
Radićev Trg, Zagreb
Natural history collections, including remains of the early-diluvial man (*Homo crapiniensis*), excavated in 1895-1905 at Krapinske Toplice, nr. Krapina.
Th., Su. 9-1.

PICTURE GALLERY
Yugoslav Academy of Sciences and Arts, Medvedgradska 2, Zagreb
Collection of medieval frescoes and plaster casts of ancient, medieval and recent sculptures and architecture. Originals of sculptures of 19th and 20th centuries in the S.R. of Croatia.
Daily ex. Sa. 10-1.

THE PEOPLE'S REVOLUTION MUSEUM
Trg. Zrtava Fašizma, Zagreb
The national liberation struggle of the peoples of Yugoslavia, depicted by means of photographs, paintings, drawings, documents and weapons. The people's revolution in Croatia.
Daily ex. M. 9-1, 4-7.

PRINT ROOM
Braće Kavurića 1, Zagreb
Collection of prints, drawings and posters.
By appointment.

STROSSMAYER'S GALLERY OF OLD MASTERS
Zrinski trg 11/II, Zagreb
13th-19th century paintings, predominantly Italian Renaissance, as well as works by 16th-19th century Flemish, Dutch, French and German artists.
Daily ex. M. 10-1.

STUDY COLLECTION OF THE HISTORY OF THE CROATIAN THEATRE
3/1 Demetrova Ulica, Zagreb
Collection of documents relating to the history of Croatian theatrical art.
By appointment.

TECHNICAL MUSEUM
Savska c.18, Zagreb
Collections illustrating scientific and technical development in Yugoslavia.
Group visits: daily 8-1. Individual visits: Th. 4-7; Su. 10-1.

ZAGREB MUNICIPAL ARCHIVES
29 Opatička Ulica, Zagreb
Archive material from 19th century to the present day, including material on municipal administration, schools, enterprises, clubs and societies, chambers of commerce, banks and some court archives.
By appointment.

Zaire, Republic of

Zaire, the Democratic Republic of the Congo, has a complex population structure, with three sorts of Negroes, Pygmies, Hamites and a miscellaneous lot of Europeans, of whom the Belgians are much the most numerous. Although agriculture is important, mining has been the great attraction for European interests for many years. The museums of Zaire, however, are concerned mainly with the geology and the mining activities of the country, with several comprehensive collections of art and handicrafts, and of displays illustrating the non-mining ways in which the Congolese people earn their living. There is, as yet, no National Museum to present the history of Zaire.

BUKAVU

MUSEUM OF PREHISTORY AND GEOLOGY
Bukavu
Mineralogical and geological specimens, especially of Zaire.
M.-Sa. 9-12, 2-5.

KANANGA

NATIONAL MUSEUM
Kananga
Ethnography. History. Handicrafts. One room only open to visitors. The remainder of the museum is closed for reorganisation and is expected to re-open in 1974-75.
M.-Sa. 9-12, 2-5.

KANGU

MAYOMBE MUSEUM
Kangu
Private collection of ethnography of Zaire.
By appointment.

KIMPESE

PRIVATE COLLECTION
Mission Protestante, Kimpese, Zone Songololo, Région du Bas-Zaire
Ethnography of Zaire.
By appointment.

KINSHASA

FINE ARTS ACADEMY
Avenue des Victimes de la Rébellion, B.P. 8249, Kinshasa
Art and modern sculptures.
Su. 10-12.

MUSEUM OF ANTHROPOLOGY
Université Lovanium, B.P. 139, Kinshasa
Handicrafts. Coins. Musical instruments. Pottery. Woodcarvings. Sculpture. Traditional agricultural, hunting and fishery methods of the people of Zaire.
Daily ex. Su. 8.30-12, 1.30-3.30. Sa. 8.30-12.

KOLWESI

MINERALOGICAL MUSEUM
Kolwesi
Mineralogy and geology, especially of Zaire.
By appointment.

LIKASI

SENGIER-COUSIN GEOLOGICAL MUSEUM
Génerale Congolaise des Minerais (GECOMIN), Likasi
Geology, and economic minerals of Katanga.
By appointment.

MBENDAKA

NATIONAL MUSEUM
Mbendaka
History and ethnography of the district.
M.-Sa. 9-12, 2-5.

MUSHENGE

ART COLLECTION
École d'Art, Mushenge
Art and ethnography of the Kasai region.
By appointment.

Zambia

It is interesting to observe the differences, and to a lesser extent the similarities, of the museums of Zambia and Rhodesia. Both pay a good deal of attention to geology and mining, but Zambia somewhat naturally plays down the past and present culture of the white man in the area and places correspondingly more stress on the culture of the Zambian peoples. David Livingstone, however, features in museums on both sides of the border.

LIVINGSTONE

LIVINGSTONE MUSEUM
Mosi-oa-Tunya Road, P.O. Box 498, Livingstone
Natural history. Archaeology. Ethnography, especially material culture of the Zambian people. Recent history of Zambia, including relics of David Livingstone. African art. Metallurgy.
Daily 10-6.

OPEN-AIR MUSEUM
nr. Livingstone
Between Livingstone and the Victoria Falls. Traditional buildings. Handicrafts.
Daily 9-5.

LUSAKA

THE ART CENTRE FOUNDATION
74 Independence Avenue, P.O. Box 1986, Lusaka
Art collections.
Daily ex. M. 10-8.

NDOLA

COPPERBELT MUSEUM ASSOCIATION
P.O. Box 61, Ndola
Ecology. Geology. Mineralogy. Mining history of the Copperbelt. Local history.
By appointment.

VICTORIA FALLS

EASTERN CATARACT FIELD MUSEUM
(National Monuments Commission of Zambia), Victoria Falls, nr. Livingstone
Archaeology. Geology. Illustrations of the formation of the Victoria Falls and the Stone Age sequence in the area.
Daily ex. F. 10-5. Closed Th. afternoon.

Classified Index of Specialised and Outstanding Collections

This index has been compiled in order to make it easier to identify museums and collections within museums which are exceptionally important or interesting within a particular field. Some museums will consequently appear under more than one classification, one entry for agriculture, another for forestry, and so on. No attempt has been made to index local history collections as such, since it can be assumed that the great majority of museums outside major urban centres will be local history museums. Where, however, the local material is also of interest to specialists, as, for instance, in the case of mining, textiles or transport, it is put under these headings.

In making our selection, we have done our best to be fair, fully recognising that there is room for argument as to what makes one collection more significant than another.

Group A
THE ARTS

Fine art

ALBANIA

ELBASAN
LOCAL MUSEUM
TIRANA
MUSEUM OF ARCHAEOLOGY AND ETHNOGRAPHY

ALGERIA

ALGIERS
NATIONAL MUSEUM OF FINE ART
CHERCHELL (EL-ASNAM)
CHERCHELL MUSEUM

ARGENTINA

BOLIVAR
FLORENTINO AMEGHINO MUSEUM
BUENOS AIRES
ISAAC FERNÁNDEZ BLANCO MUSEUM OF SPANISH-AMERICAN ART
DE LA BOCA MUSEUM OF FINE ART
ENRIQUE LARRETA MUSEUM OF SPANISH ART
MUSEUM OF ENGRAVINGS
MUSEUM OF FINE ARTS
MUSEUM OF MARITIME ART
MUSEUM OF MODERN ART
NATIONAL MUSEUM OF FINE ART
NATIONAL MUSEUM OF ORIENTAL ART
SAN ROQUE MUSEUM
EDUARDO SIVORI MUSEUM OF THE PLASTIC ARTS
YRURTIA HOUSE
CÓRDOBA
HISTORICAL MUSEUM OF THE HOUSE OF THE VICEROY SOBREMONTE
MUSEUM OF FINE ARTS
ENTRE RIOS
PROVINCIAL MUSEUM OF FINE ART
GODOY CRUZ
FERNANDO FADER MUNICIPAL MUSEUM OF FINE ART
GUALEGUAYCHÚ
MAGNASCO MUSEUM OF FINE ART
LA PLATA
PROVINCIAL MUSEUM OF FINE ART
LA RIOJA
PROVINCIAL HISTORICAL MUSEUM
LAS HERAS
MUSEUM OF FINE ART
LOSA CORRAL
FERNANDO FADER HOUSE- MUSEUM
LÚJAN
MUSEUM OF FINE ART
MAR DEL PLATA
MUSEUM OF FINE ART
MENDOZA
MUSEUM OF THE ANCIENT PROVINCE
MUSEUM OF MODERN ART
MORENO
MUSEUM OF THE PLASTIC ARTS
MORÓN
GENERAL SAN MARTIN MUSEUM OF HISTORY AND ART
PARANÁ
DR. PEDRO MARTINEZ MUSEUM OF FINE ART
RAFAELA
MUNICIPAL MUSEUM OF FINE ART
ROSARIO
MUNICIPAL MUSEUM
MUSEUM OF FINE ARTS
SAN RAFAEL
MUSEUM OF FINE ART
SANTA FÉ
ROSA GALISTEO DE RODRIGUEZ MUSEUM OF FINE ARTS
PROVINCIAL MUSEUM OF HISTORY
SANTIAGO DEL ESTERO
MUSEUM OF FINE ART
TANDIL
MUNICIPAL MUSEUM OF FINE ARTS
TUCUMÁN
MUSEUM OF FINE ART
VICENTE LOPEZ
MUSEUM OF FINE ART

AUSTRALIA

ADELAIDE
ART GALLERY OF SOUTH AUSTRALIA
CONTEMPORARY ART SOCIETY
ARMIDALE
ART GALLERY
BALLARAT
BALLARAT ART GALLERY
BATHURST
THE REGIONAL GALLERY
BENDIGO
BENDIGO ART GALLERY
BRISBANE
QUEENSLAND NATIONAL ART GALLERY AND MUSEUM
ROYAL HISTORICAL SOCIETY OF QUEENSLAND MUSEUM
BUNBURY
ART GALLERY
CASTLEMAINE
CASTLEMAINE ART GALLERY AND HISTORICAL MUSEUM
FORTITUDE VALLEY
QUEENSLAND ART GALLERY
FRANKSTON
McCLELLAND GALLERY
GEELONG
GEELONG ART GALLERY
GRAFTON
SCHAEFFER HOUSE
HOBART
ALLPORT LIBRARY AND MUSEUM OF FINE ARTS
LAUNCESTON
QUEEN VICTORIA MUSEUM AND ART GALLERY
MELBOURNE
UNIVERSITY MUSEUM
MILDURA
MILDURA ARTS CENTRE ART GALLERY
MORWELL
LATROBE VALLEY ARTS CENTRE
NEWCASTLE
CITY ART GALLERY
PERTH
WESTERN AUSTRALIAN ART GALLERY
SYDNEY
ART GALLERY OF NEW SOUTH WALES
WILLIAM DIXSON GALLERY AND MITCHELL LIBRARY
TAMWORTH
TAMWORTH ART GALLERY AND MUSEUM
TOOWOOMBA
CREATIVE 92 ART CENTRE
LIONEL LINDSAY ART GALLERY
TIA GALLERY
TOOWOOMBA ART GALLERY

AUSTRIA

ADMONT
MUSEUM OF ART HISTORY
AIGEN
COLLECTIONS OF SCHLÄGL MONASTERY
ALTENBURG
COLLECTIONS OF BENEDICTINE MONASTERY
ARNFELS
MUSEUM OF CLOCKS, MUSICAL INSTRUMENTS AND FOLKLORE
BAD DEUTSCH ALTENBURG
CARL LEOPOLD HOLLITZER MUSEUM
BADEN
ROLLETT MUSEUM
BAD GOISERN
GOISERN REGIONAL MUSEUM
BAD ISCHL
LÉHAR VILLA
MUSEUM OF THE HAENEL AND PANCERA FAMILIES
VILLA OF THE EMPEROR
BAD VOSLAU
REGIONAL MUSEUM
BEZAU
REGIONAL MUSEUM
BLEIBURG
WERNER BERG GALERIE
BLUDENZ
REGIONAL MUSEUM
BREGENZ
VORARLBERG MUSEUM
EFERDING
MUNICIPAL MUSEUM, STARHEMBERG FAMILY MUSEUM, REGIONAL MUSEUM
ELBIGENALP
FALGER MUSEUM
ENNS
MUNICIPAL MUSEUM
FELDKIRCH
REGIONAL MUSEUM IN THE SCHATTENBURG
FRIESACH
REGIONAL MUSEUM
GLEISDORF
REGIONAL MUSEUM
GMUNDEN
TOWN MUSEUM
GOBELSBURG
PALACE MUSEUM
GÖTTWEIG
MONASTERY GRAPHICS COLLECTION
GRAZ
BAROQUE MUSEUM
DIOCESAN MUSEUM
JOANNEUM PROVINCIAL MUSEUM OF CULTURAL HISTORY AND APPLIED ART
JOANNEUM MUSEUM OF THE HISTORY OF GRAZ
JOANNEUM PROVINCIAL MUSEUM: NEW GALLERY
JOANNEUM PROVINCIAL MUSEUM: OLD GALLERY
GRAZ-MARIA TROST
MAURACH MUSEUM
GRIEFENSTEIN
CASTLE MUSEUM
GRESTEN
REGIONAL MUSEUM
GUTENBRUNN
BAROQUE MUSEUM
HEILIGENKREUZ
MONASTERY COLLECTIONS
HERZOGENBURG
COLLECTIONS OF THE MONASTERY
HOCHOSTERWITZ
CASTLE COLLECTIONS
HOHENAU
REGIONAL MUSEUM
HOHENBRUNN
HUNTING MUSEUM OF UPPER AUSTRIA
HOLLENEGG
PALACE COLLECTION

HORN
HÖBARTH MUSEUM
IMST
REGIONAL MUSEUM
INNSBRUCK
AMBRAS CASTLE COLLECTION
ART COLLECTION OF THE SERVITEN MONASTERY
'FERDINANDEUM', TIROL MUSEUM
MUSEUM OF THE WILTEN PRAEMONSTRATENSIAN CHORAL FOUNDATION
PALACE, SILVER CHAPEL AND PALACE CHURCH
JUDENBURG
TOWN AND DISTRICT MUSEUM
KLAGENFURT
CARINTHIAN GALLERY
KLEINENGERSDORF
"DER BISAMBERG UND DER WEINVIERTLER" MUSEUM
KLOSTERNEUBURG
MUSEUM OF THE AUGUSTINIAN MONASTERY
KREMS
MUNICIPAL MUSEUM
KREMSMUNSTER
MONASTERY COLLECTIONS
KREUZENSTEIN
CASTLE AND CASTLE COLLECTIONS
KUFSTEIN
REGIONAL MUSEUM
LAMBACH
COLLECTIONS OF THE BENEDICTINE MONASTERY
LANGENLOIS
REGIONAL MUSEUM
LANGENZERSDORF
REGIONAL MUSEUM
LEOBEN
MUNICIPAL MUSEUM
LIENZ
EAST TIROL REGIONAL MUSEUM
LILIENFELD
MONASTERY COLLECTIONS
LINZ
DIOCESAN MUSEUM
MUSEUM OF THE CITY OF LINZ
NEW GALLERY OF THE TOWN OF LINZ AND WOLFGANG GURLITT MUSEUM
UPPER AUSTRIA PROVINCIAL MUSEUM
MARIA STEIN
PALACE MUSEUM
MARIA TAFERL
TREASURY OF THE PILGRIMAGE CHURCH
MARIAZELL
TREASURY OF THE BASILICA OF GOD'S GRACE
MELK
BENEDICTINE ABBEY COLLECTION
MICHAELBEUERN
ABBEY REGIONAL MUSEUM
MIESENBACH
GAUERMANN MEMORIAL MUSEUM
MISTELBACH
MUNICIPAL MUSEUM OF REGIONAL LIFE
MÖDLING
MUNICIPAL MUSEUM
MONDSEE
REGIONAL MUSEUM
MOOSHAM
PALACE COLLECTIONS
NEULENGBACH
REGIONAL MUSEUM
NIEDERLEIS
CASTLE MUSEUM
OBERNBERG
REGIONAL MUSEUM
RABENSTEIN
PIELACHTAL REGIONAL MUSEUM
REICHERSBERG
MONASTERY MUSEUM
RETZ
MUSEUM OF TOWN HISTORY
REUTTE
REGIONAL MUSEUM
RIED
ETHNOLOGICAL MUSEUM OF THE INNVIERTEL
RIEGERSBURG
CASTLE MUSEUM
ROHRAU
FAMILY COLLECTION OF COUNT HARRACH
ROSENBURG
CASTLE MUSEUM
SALZBURG
COLLECTIONS OF THE BENEDICTINE ABBEY OF ST. PETER
COLLECTION OF THE NONNBERG BENEDICTINE MONASTERY
RESIDENZ GALERIE
SALZBURGER MUSEUM, CAROLINO AUGUSTEUM
ST. FLORIAN
COLLECTIONS OF THE AUGUSTIAN MONASTERY
ST. GEORGEN
PALACE MEMORIAL MUSEUM
ST. LAMBRECHT
COLLECTIONS OF THE BENEDICTINE MONASTERY
ST. MARGARETHEN
OPEN-AIR MUSEUM IN ROMAN QUARRY
ST. PAUL
MONASTERY ART COLLECTIONS
ST. PÖLTEN
DIOCESAN MUSEUM
SCHÄRDING
MUNICIPAL MUSEUM
SCHLÄGL
COLLECTIONS OF THE PREMONSTRATENSIAN ABBEY
SCHLAINING
CASTLE MUSEUM
SCHWARZENBERG
COMMUNITY MUSEUM
SEEBENSTEIN
CASTLE MUSEUM
SEEKIRCHEN
REGIONAL MUSEUM
SEITENSTETTEN
COLLECTIONS OF THE BENEDICTINE ABBEY
SPITTAL
MUSEUM OF LOCAL LIFE
STEYR
REGIONAL MUSEUM
STOCKERAU
DISTRICT MUSEUM
STRASSBURG
DIOCESAN AND REGIONAL MUSEUM
TAMSWEG
LUNGAU REGIONAL MUSEUM
TELFS
REGIONAL MUSEUM
TULLN
REGIONAL MUSEUM
VILLACH
MUNICIPAL MUSEUM
VÖCKLABRUCK
REGIONAL HOUSE
VIENNA
ALBERTINA GRAPHICS COLLECTION
ALSERGRUND DISTRICT MUSEUM
ART COLLECTIONS OF THE SCHWARZENBERG PALACE
AUSTRIAN GALLERY: AUSTRIAN BAROQUE MUSEUM
AUSTRIAN GALLERY: MUSEUM OF MEDIEVAL AUSTRIAN ART
AUSTRIAN GALLERY OF THE 19th AND 20th CENTURIES
CABINET OF ENGRAVINGS OF THE ACADEMY OF FINE ARTS
CATHEDRAL AND DIOCESAN MUSEUM
COUNT HARRACH'S PICTURE GALLERY
FIRST AUSTRIAN-SILESIAN MUSEUM IN VIENNA
GALLERY OF PAINTINGS OF THE ACADEMY OF FINE ARTS
HERNALS DISTRICT MUSEUM
HISTORICAL MUSEUM OF THE CITY OF VIENNA
LIESING DISTRICT MUSEUM
MEIDLING DISTRICT MUSEUM
MUSEUM OF THE BÖHMERWALD
MUSEUM OF THE HISTORY OF ART: EGYPTIAN AND ORIENTAL COLLECTION
MUSEUM OF THE HISTORY OF ART: GALLERY OF PAINTINGS
MUSEUM OF THE HISTORY OF ART: SCULPTURE AND APPLIED ART COLLECTION
MUSEUM OF THE MARIAHILF DISTRICT
MUSEUM OF THE PROVINCE OF LOWER AUSTRIA
MUSEUM OF THE 20th CENTURY
NEW GALLERY OF THE MUSEUM OF THE HISTORY OF ART
PENZING DISTRICT MUSEUM
PRATERMUSEUM
SCHOTTEN ABBEY COLLECTION
ADALBERT STIFTER MUSEUM
UNIVERSITY MUSEUM
WALCHEN
PAULI HANREICH-LUDWIG COLLECTION
WEISSENKIRCHEN
WACHAU MUSEUM
WELS
MUNICIPAL MUSEUM
WIENER NEUSTADT
MUNICIPAL MUSEUM
WILHERING
MONASTERY COLLECTION
ZWETTL
ANTON MUSEUM
ZWICKLEDT
KUBIN HOUSE

BANGLADESH

DACCA
DACCA MUSEUM
LALBAGH FORT SITE MUSEUM

BARBADOS

BARBADOS
BARBADOS MUSEUM

BELGIUM

AALST
LOCAL MUSEUM
ANTWERP
ARCHIVES AND MUSEUM OF FLEMISH CULTURAL LIFE
CITY PRINT-ROOM
MAAGDENHUIS MUSEUM
MAYER VAN DEN BERGH MUSEUM
OPEN-AIR MUSEUM OF SCULPTURE
PLANTIN-MORETUS MUSEUM
RIDDER SMIDT VAN GELDER MUSEUM
ROCKOX'S HOUSE
ROYAL MUSEUM OF FINE ARTS
RUBENS' HOUSE
ATTRE
LOCAL MUSEUM
BELOEIL
CASTLE MUSEUM
BRUGES
ARCHERS GUILD OF ST. SEBASTIAN
BRANGWYN MUSEUM
CATHEDRAL MUSEUM
GRUUTHUSE MUSEUM
MEMLING MUSEUM
MUNICIPAL ART GALLERY
MUSEUM OF THE COURTS OF JUSTICE
MUSEUM OF THE HOLY BLOOD
MUSEUM OF THE POTTERY HOSTEL
STORIE HOUSE
BRUSSELS
BREUGHEL MUSEUM
CHARLIER MUSEUM
ERASMUS' HOUSE
IXELLES FINE ARTS GALLERY
CONSTANTIN MEUNIER MUSEUM
MUSEUM OF ART
MUSEUM OF MODERN ART
MUSEUM OF THE POOR LAW ADMINISTRATION
SCHOTT MUSEUM
WIERTZ MUSEUM
CHARLEROI
MUNICIPAL PICTURE AND SCULPTURE GALLERY

COURTRAI

MUSEUM OF PAINTING

DENDERMONDE

PICTURE GALLERY

GAASBEEK

CHÂTEAU MUSEUM

GHENT

FINE ARTS MUSEUM
MUSEUM OF ANTIQUITIES
MUSEUM OF THE TREATY OF GHENT

HANZINELLE

CHÂTEAU

HASSELT

PROVINCIAL MUSEUM

HERENTALS

FRAIKIN MUSEUM

JABBEKE

LOCAL MUSEUM

LAVAUX-SAINTE-ANNE

BELGIAN MUSEUM OF HUNTING AND NATURAL CONSERVATION

LIÈGE

CABINET OF PRINTS AND DRAWINGS
DIOCESAN MUSEUM AND CATHEDRAL TREASURY
MUSEUM OF FINE ART
MUSEUM OF WALLOON ART
WITTERT MUSEUM

LIERRE

WUYTS VAN CAMPEN MUSEUM

LOUVAIN

MUSEUM OF ART AND ARCHAEOLOGY
SPOELBERCH DE LOVENJOEL MUSEUM
TOWN HALL MUSEUM

MARIEMONT- MORLANWELZ

MUSEUM OF ART AND OF THE HISTORY OF ARCHAEOLOGY

MECHELEN (MALINES)

MUSEUM OF ART AND ARCHAEOLOGY

MONS

CANON PUISSANT MUSEUM
ICONOGRAPHIC MUSEUM OF MONS
MUSEUM OF FINE ART

NAMUR

THE DE CROIX MUSEUM
NAMUR MUSEUM OF ARTS AND CRAFTS

NIEUWPOORT

PIETER-BRAECKE MUSEUM

OSTEND

CITY ART GALLERY
JAMES ENSOR MUSEUM

SPA

DISTRICT MUSEUM

SPONTIN

CASTLE

TONGRES

ARCHAEOLOGICAL MUSEUM

TOURNAI

FINE ARTS MUSEUM

VERVIERS

MUSEUM OF FINE ART

BERMUDA

HAMILTON

PAR-LA-VILLE MUSEUM

BOLIVIA

LA PAZ

MUNICIPAL ART GALLERY
NAIRA GALLERY
NATIONAL MUSEUM OF ART

POTOSI

NATIONAL MUSEUM OF THE POTOSI MINT
PALACE OF THE MARQUESS OF VILLAVERDE

SUCRE

ART GALLERY
MUSEUM OF FINE ART

BRAZIL

ARAXÁ

DONA BEJA REGIONAL MUSEUM OF ART

AREIA

PEDRO AMÉRICO MUSEUM

BATATAIS

DR. WASHINGTON LUIZ HISTORICAL MUSEUM

BELEM

MUNICIPAL ART GALLERY

BELO HORIZONTE

MUSEUM OF ART
MUSEUM OF COLONIAL ART

BRODÓSQUI

PORTINARI HOUSE-MUSEUM

CACHOEIRA

NOBRE HOUSE MUSEUM

CAMPINAS

MUSEUM OF CONTEMPORARY ART

CAMPOS DO JORDÃO

GOVERNOR'S PALACE MUSEUM

CATAGUESES

MUSEUM OF FINE ART

CURITIBA

ALFREDO ANDERSEN MUSEUM
DAVID CARNEIRO MUSEUM

FEIRA DE SANTANA

REGIONAL MUSEUM

FLORIANÓPOLIS

VITOR MEIRLES HOUSE MUSEUM
MUSEUM OF MODERN ART

FORTALEZA

UNIVERSITY MUSEUM OF ART

GOIÂNIA

MUSEUM OF MODERN ART

ITAPORANGA D'AJUDA

MUSEUM OF ART AND POPULAR TRADITIONS

ITU

MUSEUM OF THE REPUBLICAN CONVENTION

JAGUARÃO

ALFREDO VARELA MUSEUM

JUIZ DE FORA

MARIANO PROCÓPIO MUSEUM

MACEIÓ

COMMERCIAL AND ARCHAEOLOGICAL MUSEUM OF THE COMMERCIAL EMPLOYEES' SYNDICATE

MANAUS

ART GALLERY

MARIANA

ARCHDIOCESAN MUSEUM

MIRACATU

PEDRO LARAGNOIT MUSEUM

NITERÓI

ANTÓNIO PARREIRAS MUSEUM

OLINDA

PERNAMBUCO MUSEUM OF CONTEMPORARY ART

PINDAMONHANGABA

LOCAL MUSEUM

PÔRTO ALEGRE

RIO GRANDE DO SUL MUSEUM OF ART
STATE ART GALLERIES

RECIFE

STATE MUSEUM

RESENDE

MUSEUM OF MODERN ART

RIO DE JANEIRO

ITAMARTY MUSEUM OF HISTORY AND DIPLOMACY
MUSEUM OF THE CITY OF RIO DE JANEIRO
MUSEUM OF PICTURES OF THE UNCONSCIOUS
MUSEUM OF THE RAYMUNDO OTTONI DE CASTRO FOUNDATION
NATIONAL MUSEUM OF FINE ART
RIO DE JANEIRO MUSEUM OF MODERN ART
SANTA CASA DA MISERICÓRDIA DO RIO DE JANEIRO: MUSEUM OF RELIGIOUS ART

SALVADOR

BAHIA MUSEUM OF ART
BAHIA MUSEUM OF MODERN ART
MUSEUM OF ART
MUSEUM OF THE CARLOS COSTA PINTO FOUNDATION
MUSEUM OF THE CARMELITE CONVENT
NELSON DE SOUSA OLIVEIRA COLLECTION

SANTA LEOPOLDINA

COLONIAL MUSEUM

SANTANA DO IPANEMA

MUNICIPAL MUSEUM OF HISTORY AND ART

SÃO PAULO

ART MUSEUM OF SÃO PAOLO
ECCLESIASTICAL MUSEUM
MUSEUM OF CONTEMPORARY ART
PAULISTA MUSEUM
REPUBLICAN CONVENTION MUSEUM
SÃO PAULO MUSEUM OF MODERN ART
STATE ART GALLERY

SÃO VICENTE

MUSEUM OF ART

VASSOURAS

CASA DA HERA MUSEUM

BULGARIA

KAZANLUK

NATIONAL MUSEUM

KJUSTENDIL

VLADIMIR DIMITROV-MAJSTORA GALLERY

PAZARDŽIK

STANISLAV DOSPEVSKY MUSEUM

PLEVEN

NATIONAL ART GALLERY

PLOVDIV

ART GALLERY

RILA

RILA MONASTERY NATIONAL MUSEUM

RUSE

REGIONAL MUSEUM OF HISTORY

SOFIA

BOYANA CHURCH NATIONAL MUSEUM
NATIONAL ART GALLERY

TRJAVNA

TRJAVNA MUSEUM

TROJAN

MUSEUM OF APPLIED ARTS AND CRAFTS

VARNA

ART GALLERY
MUSEUM OF ICON-PAINTING
GEORGI VELČEV HOUSE- MUSEUM

BURMA

MANDALAY

STATE LIBRARY AND MUSEUM

RANGOON

NATIONAL MUSEUM OF ART AND ARCHAEOLOGY

CAMEROUN

YAOUNDÉ

MUSEUM OF CAMEROUN ART

CANADA

ALMONTE

MILL OF KINTAIL MUSEUM

BRAMPTON

PEEL COUNTY MUSEUM AND ART GALLERY

BRANTFORD

ART GALLERY OF BRANT

BURNABY

BURNABY ART GALLERY

CALGARY

ART GALLERY OF THE UNIVERSITY OF CALGARY
CALGARY ALLIED ARTS CENTRE
GALLERY OF ALBERTA COLLEGE OF ART

CHARLOTTETOWN

CONFEDERATION ART GALLERY AND MUSEUM

COBOURG

COBOURG PUBLIC LIBRARY ART GALLERY

COWANSVILLE

COWANSVILLE ART CENTRE

DAWSON CREEK

DAWSON CREEK MUSEUM AND ART GALLERY

DOON

HOMER WATSON GALLERY

EDMONTON

EDMONTON ART GALLERY
UNIVERSITY ART GALLERY AND MUSEUM

FREDERICTON

BEAVERBROOK ART GALLERY
PROVINCIAL PORTRAIT GALLERY
UNIVERSITY OF NEW BRUNSWICK ART CENTRE

GRAFTON

BARNUM HOUSE MUSEUM

HALIFAX

CENTENNIAL ART GALLERY
DALHOUSIE ART GALLERY

HAMILTON

ART GALLERY OF HAMILTON

JOLIETTE

JOLIETTE ART MUSEUM

KINGSTON

AGNES ETHERINGTON ART CENTRE

KITCHENER

KITCHENER-WATERLOO ART GALLERY

KLEINBERG

MCMICHAEL CONSERVATION COLLECTION OF ART

LONDON

LONDON PUBLIC LIBRARY AND ART MUSEUM
MCINTOSH MEMORIAL ART GALLERY

MEDICINE HAT

MEDICINE HAT ART CLUB

MONCTON

UNIVERSITY OF MONCTON ART GALLERY

MONTREAL

ART GALLERY OF SIR GEORGE WILLIAMS UNIVERSITY
ART NOVA ET VETERA GALLERY
MCCORD MUSEUM
MONTREAL MUSEUM OF FINE ART
MUSEUM OF CONTEMPORARY ART
MUSEUM OF QUEBEC FEDERATION OF CULTURAL CENTRES

MOOSE JAW

MOOSE JAW ART MUSEUM

OSHAWA

ROBERT MCLAUGHLIN GALLERY

OTTAWA

NATIONAL GALLERY OF CANADA

OWEN SOUND

TOM THOMSON MEMORIAL GALLERY AND MUSEUM OF FINE ART

QUEBEC

LAVAL UNIVERSITY
MUSEUM OF QUEBEC
QUEBEC SEMINARY MUSEUM
MUSEUM OF THE ARCHIVES OF QUEBEC

REGINA

NORMAN MACKENZIE ART GALLERY

SACKVILLE

OWENS ART GALLERY

ST. JOHNS

MEMORIAL UNIVERSITY ART GALLERY

SAINT-LAURENT

NOVA ET VETERA GALLERY

SARNIA

SARNIA PUBLIC LIBRARY AND ART GALLERY

SASKATOON

MARQUIS HALL ART GALLERY
NUTANA COLLEGIATE LIBRARY AND ART GALLERY
SASKATOON GALLERY AND CONSERVATORY

SHERBROOKE

SHERBROOKE UNIVERSITY ART GALLERY

SIMCOE

EVA BROOK DONLY MUSEUM

STRATFORD

ROTHMANS ART GALLERY OF STRATFORD

SUDBURY

SUDBURY CENTENNIAL MUSEUM AND ART GALLERY

TORONTO

ART GALLERY OF ONTARIO
SIGMUND SAMUEL CANADIANA MUSEUM

VANCOUVER

LIPSETT COLLECTION
THE VANCOUVER ART GALLERY

VICTORIA

ART GALLERY OF GREATER VICTORIA

WATERLOO

GALLERY OF THE THEATRE OF THE ARTS

WINDSOR

WILLISTEAD ART GALLERY OF WINDSOR

WINNIPEG

GALLERY 111, UNIVERSITY OF MANITOBA
WINNIPEG ART GALLERY

WOLFVILLE

ACADIA UNIVERSITY ART GALLERY
WOLFVILLE HISTORICAL MUSEUM

CHILE

SANTIAGO

CONTEMPORARY ART MUSEUM
NATIONAL MUSEUM OF FINE ARTS

VALPARAISO

MUSEUM OF FINE ARTS

CHINA, P.R.

CHENG TU (CHENG DU)

FU'S COTTAGE

CHINCHOW (JINZHOW)

PROVINCIAL MUSEUM

CHINGTEHCHEN (TSINGTAO)

CERAMICS MUSEUM

HANGCHOW (HANG ZHOU)

CHEKIANG PROVINCIAL MUSEUM

HARBIN

PROVINCIAL MUSEUM

KAIFENG

PROVINCIAL MUSEUM

KUEILIN

PROVINCIAL MUSEUM

LANCHOW (LANZHOU)

PROVINCIAL MUSEUM

LUO YANG

TOWN MUSEUM

MUKDEN (SHENYIANG)

IMPERIAL PALACE

NAN CHANG

BA DA SHAN REN MUSEUM
QING YUN PU MONASTERY

PEKING

HSU PEI HUNG MUSEUM
IMPERIAL PALACE
TEMPLE OF THE SOURCE OF THE LAW

QU FU

RESIDENCES OF THE DESCENDANTS OF CONFUCIUS
TEMPLE OF CONFUCIUS

SHANGHAI

ART AND HISTORY MUSEUM

SUCHOW (SU ZHOU)

HISTORY MUSEUM

TIENSIN (TIANJING)

PROVINCIAL MUSEUM

REPUBLIC OF CHINA

TAIPEI

NATIONAL ART GALLERY OF TAIWAN
NATIONAL MUSEUM OF HISTORY
NATIONAL PALACE MUSEUM AND NATIONAL CENTRAL MUSEUM
RAN-IN-TING MUSEUM

COLOMBIA

BOGOTA

MUSEUM OF COLONIAL ART
MUSEUM OF CONTEMPORARY ART
MUSEUM OF FINE ART
MUSEUM OF GRAPHIC ART
MUSEUM OF MODERN ART
MERCEDES SIERRA DE PEREZ MUSEUM
SANTA CLARA MUSEUM

BUCARAMANGA

GARCÍA ROVIRA HOUSE- MUSEUM

CALI

LA TERTULIA MUSEUM OF ART

CARTAGENA

COLONIAL MUSEUM

CENTROS CULTURALES

MUSEUM OF THE SCHOOL OF FINE ART

MEDELLÍN

COLTEJER MUSEUM OF MODERN ART

MONTERIA

UNIVERSITY MUSEUM

POPAYAN

COLONIAL MUSEUM
MARTÍNEZ MUSEUM
MUSEUM OF COLONIAL HISTORY AND ART
MUSEUM OF RELIGIOUS ART
VALENCIA HOUSE-MUSEUM

RIOHACHA

GUAJIRO MUSEUM OF PRE- COLOMBIAN ART AND CULTURE

TUNJA

HOUSE OF JERONIMO DE HOLGUIN

VILLA DE LEYVA

COLONIAL MUSEUM

COSTA RICA

SAN JOSÉ

ART GALLERY
GALLERY OF THE FACULTY OF FINE ARTS

CUBA

HABANA

MUSEUM OF COLONIAL ART
NATIONAL MUSEUM

CYPRUS

NICOSIA

MUSEUM OF BYZANTINE ICONS

CZECHOSLOVAKIA

BARDEJOV

ŠARIŠ MUSEUM

BETLIAR

STATE PALACE

BOJNICE

REGIONAL MUSEUM

BOUZOV

REGIONAL CENTRE

BRATISLAVA

MUNICIPAL MUSEUM

BŘEZNICE

MUNICIPAL MUSEUM AND LUDVÍKA KUBA GALLERY

BRNO

MUSEUM OF THE CITY OF BRNO

ČECHY POD KOSÍŘEM

JOSEF MÁNESA MEMORIAL MUSEUM

ČELÁKOVICE

MUNICIPAL MUSEUM

ČERVENÝ KAMEŇ

MUSEUM OF FURNITURE

ČESKA SKALICE

BOŽENY NĚMCOVA MUSEUM

ČESKE BUDĚJOVICE
MUSEUM OF SOUTHERN CZECHOSLOVAKIA

ČESKÝ KRUMLOV
REGIONAL MUSEUM

CHOMUTOV
REGIONAL MUSEUM

CHOTĚBOŘ
JINDŘICH PRUCHY GALLERY

DAČICE
MUNICIPAL MUSEUM

DOMAŽLICE
DOMAŽLICE MUSEUM
JINDŘICHA JINDŘICHA MUSEUM

DUCHOV
MANOR HOUSE MUSEUM

HAVLÍČKŮV BROD
OTAKAR ŠTÁFLY MEMORIAL

HLINSKO
REGIONAL MUSEUM AND ART GALLERY

HOSTINNÉ
MUSEUM OF ANTIQUE ART

JAROMĚŘ
MUNICIPAL MUSEUM AND ART GALLERY

JEMNICE
JEMNICE MUSEUM

JILEMNICE
KRKONOŠ MUSEUM

JINDŘICHŮV HRODEC
REGIONAL MUSEUM

KARLOVY VARY
KARLOVY MUSEUM

KAŠPERSKÉ HORY
ŠUMAVY MUSEUM

KLADNO
DISTRICT MUSEUM

KOMÁRNO
PODUNAJSKA REGIONAL MUSEUM

KRNOV
MUNICIPAL MUSEUM

KUTNÁ HORA
DISTRICT MUSEUM: JENEWEIN GALLERY

LEVICE
TEKOV MUSEUM

LEVOČA
SPIŠ MUSEUM

LIBEREC
MUSEUM OF NORTHERN CZECHOSLOVAKIA

LIPNÍK NAD BEČVOU
ZÁHOŘÍ MUSEUM

LIPTOVSKÝ MIKULÁŠ
PETER MICHAL BOHÚŇ GALLERY

LYSÁ NAD LABEM
MUSEUM OF ANCIENT ORIENTAL CULTURE

MANĚTÍN
REGIONAL MUSEUM

MORAVSKÁ TŘEBOVA
MUNICIPAL MUSEUM

NÁCHOD
NÁCHOD GALLERY

NÁMEŠŤ NA HANÉ
REGIONAL MUSEUM

NEPOMUK
LOCAL MUSEUM

OLOMORIC
REGIONAL ART GALLERY

OLOMOUC
ART GALLERY
GALLERY OF FINE ART

OPAVA
SILESIAN MUSEUM: ETHNOGRAPHY AND ART COLLECTIONS

ORAVSKY PODZÁMOK
ORAVA MUSEUM

OSTRAVA
ART GALLERY

OSTROV NAD OHRI
ART GALLERY

PARDUBICE
ART GALLERY OF EASTERN CZECHOSLOVAKIA

PEZINOK
JAN KUPECKÝ HOUSE-MUSEUM

PÍSEK
REGIONAL MUSEUM

PLZEŇ
ART GALLERY OF WESTERN CZECHOSLOVAKIA

PODĚBRADY
DISTRICT MUSEUM

POLIČKA
MUNICIPAL MUSEUM AND ART GALLERY

POLNÁ
LOCAL MUSEUM

PRACHATICE
DISTRICT MUSEUM

PRAGUE
MUSEUM OF THE CITY OF PRAGUE

PŘEROV
J. A. KOMENSKY MUSEUM

RONOV NAD DOUBRAVOU
ANTONÍN CHITTUSSIKY MEMORIAL MUSEUM

ROŠTEJN
VYSOČINY MUSEUM

ROUDNICE NAD LABEM
DISTRICT GALLERY OF FINE ART

RUMBURK
REGIONAL MUSEUM

RUŽOMBEROK
LIPTOV MUSEUM

RYCHNOV NAD KNĚŽNOU
ORLICKÁ GALLERY

SLANÝ
REGIONAL MUSEUM

SOBĚSLAV
MUSEUM OF SOUTHERN CZECHOSLOVAKIA

ŠTERNBERK
ŠTERNBERK STATE CASTLE

TELČ
TELČ MUSEUM

TEPLICE
REGIONAL MUSEUM

TRHANOV
JAROSLAV ŠPILLAR GALLERY

TRNAVA
MUSEUM OF WESTERN SLOVAKIA

UHERSKÉ HRADIŠTĚ
GALLERY OF FINE ART

VRCHLABÍ
KRKONOŠ MUSEUM (ASSOCIATED WITH KRKONOŠSKÝ NATIONAL PARK)

VYŠKOV
VYŠKOV MUSEUM

VYSOKÉ NAD JIZEROU
REGIONAL MUSEUM

ZÁBŘEH NA MORAVĚ
REGIONAL MUSEUM

ŽĎÁR NAD SÁZAVOU
ŽĎÁR MUSEUM AND ART GALLERY

ZELEZNICE
MUNICIPAL MUSEUM AND T. F. SIMON ART GALLERY

ŽILINA
POVAŽIA MUSEUM AND ART GALLERY

DENMARK

ABENRÅ
ÅBENRÅ MUSEUM

ALBORG
ÅLBORG ART GALLERY

ÅRHUS
ÅRHUS KUNSTMUSEUM
ÅRHUS MUSEUM

AUNING
GAMMEL ESTRUP

BOVBJERG
JENS SØNDERGAARD MUSEUM

COPENHAGEN
AMAGER MUSEUM
CHRISTIANSBORG PALACE
C. L. DAVID'S COLLECTION
HIRSCHSPRUNG COLLECTION
MUSEUM OF DECORATIVE ART
NEW CARLSBERG GALLERY
ORDRUPGAARD
ROSENBORG PALACE
ROYAL MUSEUM OF FINE ARTS
THORVALDSEN MUSEUM

DRONNINGMØLLE
RUDOLPH TEGNER MUSEUM

ESBJERG
ESBJERG ART GALLERY

FAABORG
FAABORG MUSEUM

FERRING
SØNDERGAARD'S MUSEUM

FREDENSBORG
PALACE OF FREDENSBORG

FREDERICIA
FREDERICIA MUSEUM

FREDERIKSHAVN
BANGSBO MUSEET

FREDERIKSSUND
J. F. WILLUMSEN MUSEUM

GAMMEL ESTRUP
JYLLANDS HERREGAARDSMUSEUM

GAVNØ
GAVNØ CASTLE

HELSINGØR
HELSINGØR TOWN AND HAMLET MUSEUM

HILLERØD
NATIONAL HISTORICAL MUSEUM

HJØRRING
VENDSYSSEL HISTORICAL MUSEUM

HORNBAEK
RUDOLPH TEGNER'S MUSEUM

HORNSLET
ROSENHOLM

HORSENS
HORSENS MUSEUM

HUMLEBAEK
LOUISIANA ART GALLERY

KERTEMINDE
KERTEMINDE MUSEUM

KILDEKROG
MUSEUM

KOLDING
KOLDING ART GALLERY

MARIBO
LOLLAND AND FALSTER MUSEUM

NIVAA
NIVAAGAARD ART GALLERY

NYBORG
NYBORG CASTLE

ODENSE
ODENSE MUNICIPAL MUSEUMS

PEDERSTRUP
REVENTLOW MUSEUM

PRAESTØ
THORVALDSEN COLLECTION

RANDERS
RANDERS ART GALLERY

RIBE
RIBE ART MUSEUM

ROSENHOLM
ROSENHOLM CASTLE

RØNNE
BORNHOLM MUSEUM

SAEBY
VOERGÅRD CASTLE

SILKEBORG
SILKEBORG MUSEUM

SKAGEN
SKAGEN MUSEUM

SKIVE
SKIVE MUSEUM
SORØ
SORØ ART GALLERY
SORØ DISTRICT MUSEUM
SØNDERBORG
SCHOOL OF ATHLETICS
TINGBAEK
BUNDGÅRD MUSEUM
UDBY
GRUNDTVIG MEMORIAL MUSEUM
VARDE
VARDE AND DISTRICT MUSEUM
VEJEN
VEJEN MUSEUM
VEJLE
VEJLE MUSEUM
VIBORG
SKOVGAARD MUSEUM

DOMINICAN REPUBLIC

SANTO DOMINGO
NATIONAL FINE ARTS GALLERY
NATIONAL MUSEUM

ECUADOR

GUAYAQUIL
TOWN MUSEUM
QUITO
CIVIC MUSEUM OF ARTS AND HISTORY
FRANCISCAN MUSEUM
MUSEUM OF ARCHAEOLOGY AND ETHNOLOGY
NATIONAL MUSEUM OF COLONIAL ART

EGYPT, ARAB REPUBLIC OF

ALEXANDRIA
FINE ARTS MUSEUM AND CULTURAL CENTRE
GRECO-ROMAN MUSEUM
CAIRO
AL GAWHARA PALACE MUSEUM
ANDERSON MUSEUM
COPTIC MUSEUM
MUSEUM OF EGYPTIAN CIVILISATION
MUSEUM OF ISLAMIC ART
MUSEUM OF MODERN ART

ETHIOPIA

ADDIS ABABA
INSTITUTE OF ETHIOPIAN STUDIES MUSEUM
NATIONAL MUSEUM

FINLAND

ESPOO
GALLEN-KALLELAN MUSEUM
HÄMEENLINNA
ART MUSEUM
HELSINKI
AMOS ANDERSON MUSEUM OF ART
ATENEUM ART GALLERY
CYGNAEUKSEN GALLERY
DIDRICHSEN MUSEUM OF ART
GALLEN-KALLELA MUSEUM
PAUL AND FANNY SINEBRIJ CHOFFIN ART COLLECTION
HYVINKÄÄ
ART GALLERY
IMATRA
MUSEUM OF ART
JOENSUU
ART GALLERY
MUNICIPAL MUSEUM AND KARELIA HOUSE
JYVÄSKYLÄ
MUSEUM OF CENTRAL FINLAND
KAJAANI
KAINUU MUSEUM
KEMI
ART GALLERY
KOKKOLA
K. H. RENLUNDIN MUSEUM
LAHTI
ART GALLERY
MAARIANHAMINA
ÅLANDS MUSEUM OF ART
MÀNTTÄ
MUSEUM OF THE GÖSTA SERLACHIUKSEN ART INSTITUTE
OULU
MUSEUM OF ART
PORVOO
ALBERT EDELFELT MUSEUM
SÄÄKSMÄKI
EMIL WIKSTRÖMIN MUSEUM
TAMPERE
ART GALLERY
GALLERY OF MODERN ART
HIEKKA MUSEUM OF ART
TURKU
ART GALLERY
CITY MUSEUM
"ETT HEM" MUSEUM
VAASA
EAST BOTHNIA MUSEUM
TIKANOJA ART GALLERY

FRANCE

ABBEVILLE
BOUCHER-DE-PERTHES MUSEUM
AGEN
MUNICIPAL MUSEUM
AIX-EN-PROVENCE
GRANET MUSEUM
MUSEUM OF TAPESTRY AND FURNITURE
SAINT-SAUVEUR CATHEDRAL
AIX-LES-BAINS
DOCTEUR FAURE MUSEUM
AJACCIO
FESCH MUSEUM
ALBERTVILLE
CONFLANS MUSEUM
ALBI
TOULOUSE-LAUTREC MUSEUM
ALENÇON
MUSEUM OF PAINTING
D'OZÉ MUSEUM
ALÈS
ALÈS MUSEUM
ALTKIRCH
SUNDGAU MUSEUM
AMBOISE
TOWN HALL MUSEUM
AMIENS
PICARDY MUSEUM
ANCY-LE-FRANC
CHÂTEAU
ANGERS
MUSEUM OF FINE ART
TURPIN DE CRISSÉ MUSEUM
ANGOULÊME
MUNICIPAL MUSEUM
MUSEUM OF THE CHARENTE ARCHAEOLOGICAL AND HISTORICAL SOCIETY
ANNECY
CHÂTEAU D'ANNECY
CHÂTEAU DE MONTROTTIER
ANTIBES
GRIMALDI MUSEUM
ANZIN
THÉOPHILE JOUGLET MUSEUM
ARLES
LAPIDARY MUSEUM OF CHRISTIAN ART
LAPIDARY MUSEUM OF PAGAN ART
REATTU MUSEUM
ARRAS
MUSEUM OF THE FORMER ABBEY OF SAINT-VAAST
AUCH
MUSEUM OF ART AND ARCHAEOLOGY
AURILLAC
HIPPOLYTE DE PARIEU MUSEUM
AUTUN
ROLIN MUSEUM
AUXERRE
MUSEUM OF ART AND HISTORY
SAINT-GERMAIN ABBEY
AVALLON
AVALLON MUSEUM
AVESNES-SUR-HELPE
ARCHAEOLOGICAL SOCIETY MUSEUM
AVIGNON
CALVET MUSEUM
LAPIDARY MUSEUM
AZAY-LE-FERRON
CHÂTEAU MUSEUM
BAGNOLS-SUR-CÈZE
LÉON ALÈGRE MUSEUM
BARBIZON
AUBERGE GANNE MUSEUM
BAYEUX
MUSEUM OF PAINTING
BAYONNE
BASQUE MUSEUM
BONNAT MUSEUM
BEAULIEU-SUR-MER
THÉODORE REINACH FOUNDATION
BEAUMONT-EN-AUGE
LAPLACE MUSEUM AND MUSEUM OF PAINTING
BEAUNE
HÔTEL-DIEU
MUSEUM OF BURGUNDIAN CRAFTS
MUSEUM OF FINE ART
BEAUVAIS
CATHEDRAL TREASURY
MUSEUM OF THE OISE DEPARTMENT
BERGUES
MUNICIPAL MUSEUM
BERNAY
MUNICIPAL MUSEUM
BESANCON
HISTORICAL MUSEUM
MUSEUM OF FINE ART
BÉZIERS
MUSEUM OF FINE ART
BIOT
FERNAND LÉGER MUSEUM
BLOIS
CHÂTEAU MUSEUM
ROBERT HOUDIN MUSEUM
BORDEAUX
MUSEUM OF FINE ART
TREASURY OF CATHEDRAL OF SAINT-ANDRÉ
BORMES-LES-MIMOSAS
CHARLES CAZIN MUSEUM
BOULOGNE-SUR-MER
MUSEUM OF FINE ART AND ARCHAEOLOGY
BOULOGNE BILLANCOURT
PAUL LANDOWSKY MUSEUM
BOURBON LANCY
MUNICIPAL MUSEUM
BOURG-EN-BRESSE
AIN MUSEUM
BOURGES
DU BERRY MUSEUM
HÔTEL JACQUES COEUR
BOURGOIN-JALLIEU
VICTOR CHARRETON MUSEUM
BOUSSY-SAINT-ANTOINE
DUNOYER DE SEGONZAC MUSEUM
BOUXWILLER
BOUXWILLER MUSEUM
BRANTÔME
FERNAND DESMOULINS MUSEUM
BRIVE-LA-GAILLARDE
ERNEST RUPIN MUSEUM
CAEN
MUSEUM OF FINE ART

CAGNES-SUR-MER
RENOIR HOUSE-MUSEUM

CAHORS
MUNICIPAL MUSEUM

CALAIS
NEW MUSEUM

CAMBRAI
MUNICIPAL MUSEUM

CANNES
LYCKLAMA MUSEUM

CARCASSONNE
CATHEDRAL MUSEUM
MUSEUM OF FINE ARTS
MUSEUM OF THE WALLED CITY

CARPENTRAS
COMTADIN MUSEUM
DUPLESSIS MUSEUM

CASTRES
GOYA MUSEUM

LE CATEAU
HENRI MATISSE MUSEUM

CÉRET
MUSEUM OF MODERN ART

CHAÂLIS
JACQUEMART-ANDRÉ MUSEUM

CHÂLONS-SUR-MARNE
CATHEDRAL OF ST. ETIENNE
MUNICIPAL MUSEUM

CHALON-SUR-SAÔNE
DENON MUSEUM

CHAMBÉRY
CHARMETTES MUSEUM
MUSEUM OF FINE ART

CHAMBORD
CHÂTEAU DE CHAMBORD

CHAMPLITTE- ET-LE-PRÉLOT
DEPARTMENTAL MUSEUM OF HISTORY AND ETHNOGRAPHY

CHAMPS-SUR-MARNE
CHÂTEAU DE CHAMPS- SUR-MARNE

CHANTILLY
CONDÉ MUSEUM

CHAROLLES
RENÉ DAVOINE MUSEUM
JEAN LARONZE MUSEUM

CHARROUX
ABBEY MUSEUM

CHARTRES
MUNICIPAL MUSEUM

CHÂTEAUDUN
CHÂTEAU DE CHÂTEAUDUN

CHÂTEAU-GONTIER
MUNICIPAL MUSEUM

CHÂTELLERAULT
PAUL CHÉRON DE LA MARTINIÈRE MUSEUM

CHAUMONT
CHAUMONT MUSEUM

CHERBOURG
THOMAS HENRY MUSEUM

CLAMECY
MUNICIPAL MUSEUM

CLOS-LUCÉ
LEONARDO DA VINCI MUSEUM

COGNAC
MUNICIPAL MUSEUM

COLMAR
BARTHOLDI MUSEUM

COMPIÈGNE
COMPIÈGNE PALACE NATIONAL MUSEUM
VIVENEL MUSEUM

CONDÉ-SUR-L'ÉSCAUT
MUNICIPAL MUSEUM

COSSÉ-LE-VIVIEN
ROBERT TATIN MUSEUM

COULOMMIERS
MUNICIPAL MUSEUM

COURBEVOIE
ROYBET-FOULD MUSEUM

COUR-CHEVERNY
CHÂTEAU COLLECTIONS

DIEPPE
CHÂTEAU MUSEUM

DIJON
CHAMPMOL CHARTERHOUSE
MAGNIN MUSEUM
MUSEUM OF FINE ART

DOLE
MUSEUM OF FINE ART

DOUAI
MUNICIPAL MUSEUM

DOULLENS
LOMBARD MUSEUM

DREUX
MUNICIPAL MUSEUM

DUNKERQUE
DUNKERQUE MUSEUM

ÉPERNAY
MUSEUM OF FINE ART

ÉPINAL
VOSGES MUSEUM

EQUEURDREVILLE- HAINNEVILLE
TOWN-HALL MUSEUM

ÉTAMPES
MUNICIPAL MUSEUM

ÉVREUX
MUNICIPAL MUSEUM

FÉCAMP
MUNICIPAL MUSEUM

LA FÈRE
JEANNE D'ABOVILLE MUSEUM

FONTENAY-LE-COMTE
VENDÉE MUSEUM

GORDES
CHÂTEAU MUSEUM

GRASSE
FRAGONARD MUSEUM

GRAY
BARON MARTIN MUSEUM

GRENOBLE
FANTIN LATOUR MUSEUM
MUSEUM OF PAINTING AND SCULPTURE

GROSBOIS
CHÂTEAU DE GROSBOIS

GUÉRET
MUNICIPAL MUSEUM

LE HAVRE
GRAVILLE ABBEY
MUSEUM OF FINE ART
MUSEUM OF OLD LE HAVRE

HÉRICOURT
MINAL MUSEUM

HONFLEUR
EUGÈNE BOUDIN MUSEUM

HYERES
MUNICIPAL MUSEUM

L'ISLE-ADAM
MUSÉE SEULECQ

LAON
MUNICIPAL MUSEUM OF ARCHAEOLOGY

LAVAL
HENRI ROUSSEAU MUSEUM OF PRIMITIVE ART

LIBOURNE
RENÉ PRINCETEAU MUSEUM

LILLE
MUSEUM OF THE COMTESSE HOSPICE
PALACE OF FINE ART

LIMOGES
ADRIEN DUBOUCHE NATIONAL MUSEUM
MUNICIPAL MUSEUM

LISIEUX
MUSEUM OF PAINTINGS

LOCHES
LANSYER MUSEUM

LOCRONAN
MUNICIPAL MUSEUM

LONS-LE-SAUNIER
MUSEUM OF FINE ART AND PREHISTORY

LUXEUIL-LES-BAINS
MUSEUM OF THE ECHEVINS TOWER

LUZ-SAINT-SAUVEUR
LOCAL MUSEUM

LYON
MUSEUM OF FINE ART
MUSEUM OF THE HISTORY OF LYON

MÂCON
MUNICIPAL MUSEUM OF THE URSULINES

MAGNY-LES-HAMEAUX
NATIONAL MUSEUM OF THE GRANGES DE PORT-ROYAL

MAISONS-LAFFITTE
CHÂTEAU

MANDELIEU-LA NAPOULE
CHÂTEAU DE MANDELIEU-LA NAPOULE

LE MANS
DE TESSÉ MUSEUM

MARCIGNY
RÉGIONAL MUSEUM

MARSEILLE
CANTINI MUSEUM
GROBET-LABADIE MUSEUM
MUSEUM OF FINE ART

MARTIGUES
MUSEUM OF OLD MARTIGUES
FÉLIX ZIEM MUSEUM

MAUBEUGE
FERCOT DELMOTTE MUSEUM

MEAUX
BOSSUET MUSEUM

LE MÉE-SUR-SEINE
CHAPU MUSEUM

MELUN
MELUN MUSEUM

MENTON
COCTEAU MUSEUM
MARRIAGE HALL
MUNICIPAL MUSEUM

METZ
CENTRAL MUSEUM

MEUDON
RODIN MUSEUM

MILLY-LA-FORÊT
CHAPELLE

MIRANDE
MUSEUM OF THE MINOR PAINTERS OF MIRANDE

LE- MONASTIER-SUR-GAZEILLE
ABBEY CHURCH

MONTAIGU
MUSEUM OF THE NORTHERN VENDÉE

MONTARGIS
GIRODET MUSEUM

MONTAUBAN
INGRÈS MUSEUM

MONTBARD
MUSEUM

MONTPELLIER
ATGER MUSEUM
FABRE MUSEUM
HÔTEL DE CABRIÈRES-SABATIER D'ESPEYRAN

MONTPEZAT-DE-QUERCY
CHURCH MUSEUM

MONT-SAINT-MICHEL
MUSEUM OF HISTORY

MOREZ
JOURDAIN MUSEUM

MORLAIX
MUSÉE MUNICIPAL

MORTAGNE-AU-PERCHE
PERCHERON MUSEUM

MOULINS
CATHEDRAL
MUNICIPAL AND REGIONAL MUSEUM

MULHOUSE
MUSEUM OF FINE ART
SAINT-JEAN CHAPEL MUSEUM

NANCY
CHURCH OF THE CORDELIERS
LORRAINE MUSEUM OF HISTORY
MUSEUM OF DECORATIVE ARTS
MUSEUM OF FINE ART

NANTES
DOBRÉE MUSEUM
MUSEUM OF FINE ART
MUSEUM OF REGIONAL POPULAR ART

NARBONNE
MUNICIPAL MUSEUM

NEMOURS
CHÂTEAU MUSEUM

NEVERS
FAIENCE MUSEUM
NIÈVRE MUSEUM OF ARCHAEOLOGY

NICE
CHÉRET MUSEUM
MASSÉNA MUSEUM
MATISSE MUSEUM
VIEUX-LOGIS PRIORY MUSEUM

NÎMES
MUSEUM OF FINE ART

NOGENT-LE-ROTROU
MUNICIPAL MUSEUM

NOGENT-SUR-MARNE
MUSEUM OF THE SMITH- LESOUËF FOUNDATION

NOGENT-SUR-SEINE
PAUL DUBOIS AND ALFRED BOUCHER MUSEUM

ORLÉANS
MUSEUM OF FINE ART

ORNANS
GUSTAVE COURBET'S BIRTHPLACE
COURBET MUSEUM

PARAY-LE-MONIAL
HIÉRON EUCHARISTIC MUSEUM

PARIS
JACQUEMART ANDRÉ MUSEUM
ANTOINE BOURDELLE MUSEUM
CARNAVALLET MUSEUM
CERNUSCHI MUSEUM
CITY OF PARIS MUSEUM OF MODERN ART
CLUNY MUSEUM
COGNACQ JAY MUSEUM
EUGÈNE DELACROIX MUSEUM
FORNEY LIBRARY
GUIMET MUSEUM
JEAN-JACQUES HENNER MUSEUM
HÔTEL DE CLUNY MUSEUM
PAUL LANDOWSKI MUSEUM
THE LOUVRE
MARMOTTAN MUSEUM
GUSTAVE MOREAU MUSEUM
MUSEUM OF THE HIGHER SCHOOL OF FINE ART
MUSEUM OF IMPRESSIONNISM
MUSEUM OF JEWISH ART
MUSEUM OF SWEDISH ART
NATIONAL MUSEUM OF MODERN ART
ORANGERIE MUSEUM
PETIT PALAIS MUSEUM
RODIN MUSEUM
TENNIS COURT MUSEUM

PAU
MUSEUM OF FINE ART

PAUILLAC
MOUTON-ROTHSCHILD MUSEUM OF WINE

PÉRIGUEUX
PÉRIGORD MUSEUM

PERPIGNAN
HYACINTHE RIGAUD MUSEUM

PÉZENAS
VULLIOD SAINT-GERMAIN MUSEUM

PLOMBIÈRES-LES-BAINS
LOUIS FRANÇAIS MUSEUM

POITIERS
MUSEUM OF FINE ART

PONS
ARCHAEOLOGICAL MUSEUM

PONT-AVEN
PONT-AVEN MUSEUM

PONT-DE-VAUX
CHINTREUIL MUSEUM

PONTOISE LES NOYON
TAVET-DELACOUR MUSEUM

PROVINS
TITHE-BARN MUSEUM

LE PUY-EN-VELAY
CATHEDRAL OF NOTRE DAME TREASURY
CROZATIER MUSEUM

QUIMPER
BRITTANY MUSEUM
MUSEUM OF FINE ART

RAMBOUILLET
CHÂTEAU DE RAMBOUILLET

REMIREMONT
MUNICIPAL MUSEUM

RENNES
BRITTANY MUSEUM
MUSEUM OF ARCHAEOLOGY AND FINE ART

RHEIMS
OLD RHEIMS MUSEUM
SAINT-DENIS MUSEUM

RIBEAUVILLÉ
HOSPICE MUSEUM

RICHELIEU
MUSEUM OF THE 17th CENTURY

RIOM
FRANCISQUE MANDET MUSEUM

ROANNE
JOSEPH DECHELETTE MUSEUM

ROCHEFORT
MUSEUM OF FINE ART

LA ROCHELLE
MUSEUM OF FINE ART

RODEZ
FÉNAILLE MUSEUM
MUSEUM OF FINE ART

ROMANÈCHE-THORINS
GUILLON MUSEUM

ROMENAY-EN-BRESSE
MUSEUM OF BRESSAN FOLKLORE

ROUEN
MUSEUM OF FINE ARTS AND CERAMICS

RUEIL-MALMAISON
MALMAISON NATIONAL CHÂTEAU

RUMILLY
CHÂTEAU DE CLERMONT- EN-GENEVOIS

SAINT- AMAND-MONTROND
SAINT VIC MUSEUM

SAINT-AMARIN
SERRET MUSEUM

SAINT BRIEUC
HÔTEL DE VILLE MUSEUM

SAINT-DENIS
MUNICIPAL MUSEUM

SAINTES
MUSEUM OF FINE ART

ST. ÉTIENNE
MUSEUM OF ART AND INDUSTRY

SAINT-FLOUR
HAUTE-AUVERGNE MUSEUM

SAINT-GERMAIN-EN-LAYE
MUNICIPAL MUSEUM

SAINT-JEAN-CAP-FERRAT
EPHRUSSI DE ROTHSCHILD FOUNDATION

SAINT-LÔ
SAINT-LÔ MUSEUM

SAINT-MAUR-DES-FOSSÉS
MUNICIPAL MUSEUM

SAINT-MIHIEL
LIGIER RICHIER MUSEUM

SAINT-OMER
HÔTEL SANDELIN MUSEUM

SAINT-PAUL-DE-VENCE
MAEGHT FOUNDATION

SAINT-QUENTIN
A. LÉCUYER MUSEUM

SAINT- SAVIN-SUR-GARTEMPE
ABBEY CHURCH
LOCAL MUSEUM

SAINT-TROPEZ
MUSEUM OF THE ANNUNCIATION

SARREBOURG
REGIONAL MUSEUM

SAULIEU
FRANÇOIS POMPON MUSEUM

SAUMUR
MUSEUM OF DECORATIVE ARTS AND MUSEUM OF THE HORSE

SAVERNE
MUNICIPAL MUSEUM

SCEAUX
ILE-DE-FRANCE MUSEUM

SEMUR-EN-AUXOIS
SEMUR MUSEUM

SENLIS
MUSEUM

SENS
CATHEDRAL TREASURY
MUNICIPAL MUSEUM
OFFICIALITÉ

SÈTE
PAUL VALÉRY MUNICIPAL MUSEUM

SOISSONS
MUNICIPAL MUSEUM

STRASBOURG
ALSACE MUSEUM
CHÂTEAU DES ROHAN
MUSEUM OF CASTS
MUSEUM OF THE CATHEDRAL WORKSHOPS
MUSEUM OF FINE ART
MUSEUM OF THE FORMER CUSTOMS HOUSE

TANLAY
CHÂTEAU TANLAY

THONON-LES-BAINS
CHABLAIS MUSEUM OF FOLKLORE

TOULON
MUSEUM OF ART AND ARCHAEOLOGY

TOULOUSE
PAUL DUPUY MUSEUM
GEORGES LABIT MUSEUM
MUSEUM OF THE AUGUSTINIANS
OLD TOULOUSE MUSEUM
SAINT-RAYMOND MUSEUM

TOURCOING
MUNICIPAL MUSEUM OF FINE ART

TOURNUS
GREUZE MUSEUM

TOURS
ESPELOSIN MUSEUM
MUSEUM OF FINE ART
MUSEUM OF MEDIEVAL ART AND OF THE RESISTANCE

TROUVILLE-SUR-MER
MUSEUM OF LOCAL AND REGIONAL ART

TROYES
MUSEUM OF FINE ART
MUSEUM OF THE HISTORY OF TROYES AND CHAMPAGNE

VALENÇAY
GALLERY OF MEMENTOES OF PRINCE DE TALLEYRAND

VALENCE
MUSEUM OF FINE ART AND NATURAL HISTORY

VALENCIENNES
MUSEUM OF FINE ART

VALLAURIS
NATIONAL MUSEUM

VANNES
LIMUR MUSEUM

VARZY
MUNICIPAL MUSEUM

VAUX-LE-VICOMTE
CHÂTEAU

VENCE
CHAPEL OF THE ROSARY

VENDÔME
MUNICIPAL MUSEUM

VERSAILLES
CHÂTEAU
GRAND TRIANON
LAMBINET MUSEUM
MUSEUM OF HISTORY

VESOUL
GARRET MUSEUM

VIENNE
LAPIDARY MUSEUM
MUSEUM OF FINE ART

VILLEFRANCHE-SUR-MER
CHAPEL OF SAINT-PIERRE

VILLENEUVE-SUR-LOT
GASTON RAPIN MUSEUM

VILLENEUVE-DE-MARSAN
CHÂTEAU DE RAVIGNAN

VILLIERS-SAINT-BENOÎT
MUNICIPAL MUSEUM

VOIRON
MAINSSIEUX COLLECTION

WISSEMBOURG
WESTERCAMP MUSEUM

FRENCH POLYNESIA

TAHITI
PAUL GAUGUIN MUSEUM

GDR

ALTENBURG
LINDENAU STATE MUSEUM

BAUTZEN
MUSEUM OF ART AND CULTURAL HISTORY

BERLIN
BODE MUSEUM: COLLECTION OF EARLY CHRISTIAN AND BYZANTINE ART
BODE MUSEUM: COLLECTION OF PAINTINGS
BODE MUSEUM: DEPARTMENT OF PRINTS AND DRAWINGS
BODE MUSEUM: EGYPTIAN MUSEUM
BODE MUSEUM: SCULPTURE COLLECTION
MUSEUM OF CULTURAL HISTORY
NATIONAL GALLERY
PERGAMON MUSEUM: COLLECTION OF GREEK AND ROMAN ANTIQUITIES
PERGAMON MUSEUM: FAR EASTERN COLLECTION
PERGAMON MUSEUM: ISLAMIC MUSEUM
PERGAMON MUSEUM: NEAR EASTERN MUSEUM
OLD MUSEUM

BRANDENBURG
DISTRICT MUSEUM

COTTBUS
BLECHEN MEMORIAL

DEMMIN
DISTRICT MUSEUM

DESSAU
LUISIUM CASTLE
STATE GALLERY: GEORGIUN PALACE

DRESDEN
INSTITUTE AND MUSEUM OF THE HISTORY OF THE CITY OF DRESDEN
KRASZEWSKI HOUSE
LEONHARDI MUSEUM
STATE ART COLLECTIONS: DEPARTMENT OF PRINTS AND DRAWINGS
STATE ART COLLECTIONS: GALLERY OF MODERN PAINTINGS
STATE ART COLLECTIONS: OLD MASTERS GALLERY
STATE ART COLLECTION: SCULPTURE GALLERY

EISENACH
REUTER HOUSE
SCULPTURE COLLECTION
THURINGIA MUSEUM
WARTBURG

ERFURT
ANGER MUSEUM OF ART

FRANKFURT AN DER ODER
GALLERY OF MODERN ART

FRAUENSTEIN
REGIONAL MUSEUM

GERA
MUSEUM OF CULTURAL HISTORY

GLAUCHAU
MUNICIPAL MUSEUM AND ART COLLECTION

GNANDSTEIN
REGIONAL MUSEUM

GÖRLITZ
KAISERTRUTZ: STATE ART COLLECTION
STATE ART MUSEUM: HAUS NEISSSTRASSE MUSEUM

GOTHA
CASTLE MUSEUM

GREIFSWALD
GREIFSWALD MUNICIPAL MUSEUM

GREIZ
STATE COLLECTION OF BOOKS AND ENGRAVINGS

GRIMMA
GÖSCHEN HOUSE

GÜSTROW
ERNST BARLACH MEMORIAL

HALBERSTADT
CATHEDRAL COLLECTION
MUNICIPAL MUSEUM

HALDENSLEBEN
DISTRICT MUSEUM

HEILIGENSTADT
EICHFELD REGIONAL MUSEUM

JENA
MUNICIPAL MUSEUM

KARL MARX STADT
MUNICIPAL ART COLLECTION
SCHLOSSBERG MUSEUM: MUNICIPAL AND CULTURAL HISTORY COLLECTION

LEIPZIG
MUSEUM OF PICTORIAL ART

LÜBBENAU
LÜBBENAU MUSEUM IN THE SPREEWALD

MAGDEBURG
MUSEUM OF CULTURAL HISTORY

MARIENBERG
REGIONAL MUSEUM

MEININGEN
MEININGEN MUSEUM

MITTWEIDA
REGIONAL MUSEUM

MORITZBURG
MORITZBURG CASTLE BAROQUE MUSEUM

NAUMBURG
FRITZ RENTSCH MEMORIAL

NAUMBURG-GROSSJENA
MAX KLINGER MEMORIAL

NEUBRANDENBURG
MUSEUM OF CULTURAL HISTORY

PLAUEN
HERMANN VOGEL HOUSE

POTSDAM
SANSSOUCI PALACE: CHARLOTTENHOF PALACE
SANSSOUCI PALACE: NEW PALACE
SANSSOUCI PALACE: NEW ROOMS
SANSSOUCI PALACE: ORANGERY
SANSSOUCI PALACE: PARK SCULPTURE
SANSSOUCI PALACE: PICTURE GALLERY
SANSSOUCI PALACE: ROMAN BATHS

QUEDLINBURG
CASTLE MUSEUM

RADEBURG
REGIONAL MUSEUM

RIBNITZ-DAMGARTEN
DISTRICT MUSEUM

ROSTOCK
MUSEUM OF CULTURAL HISTORY

RUDOLSTADT
HEIDECKSBURG STATE MUSEUM

SAALFELD
THURINGIA REGIONAL MUSEUM

SALZWEDEL
JOHANN FRIEDRICH DANNEIL MUSEUM

SCHWERIN
SCHWERIN STATE MUSEUM

SONDERHAUSEN
STATE REGIONAL AND CASTLE MUSEUM

STENDAL
ALTMARK MUSEUM: COLLECTION AT THE CATHEDRAL
ALTMARK MUSEUM: MÖNCHSKIRCHOF COLLECTION
WINCKELMANN MEMORIAL MUSEUM

STRALSUND
MUSEUM OF CULTURAL HISTORY

WALDENBURG
REGIONAL MUSEUM AND NATURAL HISTORY COLLECTION

WEIMAR
BELVEDERE PALACE ROCOCO MUSEUM
CASTLE MUSEUM
NATIONAL GOETHE MUSEUM

WERNIGERODE
FEUDAL MUSEUM

WISMAR
SCHABBELT HOUSE REGIONAL MUSEUM

WÖRLITZ
STATE PALACES

ZEITZ
MUNICIPAL MUSEUM

ZITTAU
MUNICIPAL MUSEUM

ZWICKAU
MUNICIPAL MUSEUM

GFR

AACHEN
CATHEDRAL TREASURY
SUERMONDT MUSEUM

AHRENSBURG
AHRENSBURG CASTLE MUSEUM

ANHOLT
CASTLE MUSEUM

ANSBACH
ANSBACH MANSION
RESIDENZ STATE ART GALLERY

AROLSEN
KAULBACH MUSEUM

ASCHAFFENBURG
STATE COLLECTION OF GRAPHICS

AUGSBURG
GERMAN GALLERY OF THE BAROQUE
GRAPHICS COLLECTION
MAXIMILIAN MUSEUM
STATE GALLERY

BADEN-BADEN
ZÄHRINGER MUSEUM

BAD DRIBURG
ST. XAVIER MISSION MUSEUM

BAD REICHENHALL
MUNICIPAL MUSEUM

BAD WALDSEE
SMALL GALLERY

BAD WILDUNGEN
ASIATIC MUSEUM

BAMBERG
BAMBERG STATE GALLERY
J. HELLER COLLECTION OF GRAPHICS
HISTORICAL MUSEUM
NEW RESIDENCE

BAUSCHLOTT
GALLERY OF THE BUSLAT GUILD OF ARTISTS

BAYREUTH
BRANCH GALLERY OF THE BAVARIAN STATE COLLECTIONS OF PAINTINGS
NEW PALACE

BEBENHAUSEN
STATE COLLECTION OF MEDIEVAL ART IN CISTERCIAN ABBEY

BERCHTESGADEN
PALACE MUSEUM

BERLEBURG
BERLEBURG PALACE

BERLIN
BELLEVUE PALACE COLLECTIONS
BRÜCKE MUSEUM
CHARLOTTENBURG PALACE
DEPARTMENT OF ENGRAVINGS
DEPARTMENT OF SCULPTURE
EGYPTIAN MUSEUM
GALLERY OF PAINTINGS
GRUNEWALD HUNTING LODGE COLLECTIONS
GEORG KOLBE MUSEUM
MUSEUM OF APPLIED ART
MUSEUM OF FAR EASTERN ART
MUSEUM OF INDIAN ART
MUSEUM OF ISLAMIC ART

NATIONAL GALLERY
SPANDAU LOCAL MUSEUM
TEGEL PALACE
ZILLE EXHIBITION

BERSENBRÜCK

DISTRICT MUSEUM

BERTOLDSHEIM

PICTURE GALLERY

BIBERACH

BRAITH-MALI MUSEUM

BIELEFELD

BIELEFELD MUNICIPAL ART GALLERY
MUSEUM OF CULTURAL HISTORY

BLAUBEUREN

REGIONAL MUSEUM

BOCHUM

BOCHUM MUSEUM

BOGENBERG

REGIONAL MUSEUM

BONN

BONN MUSEUM OF PAINTINGS: KASIMIR HAGEN COLLECTION
ERNST MORITZ ARNDT HOUSE MUSEUM
MUNICIPAL ART COLLECTIONS
RHINELAND MUSEUM

BRAUNSCHWEIG

COUNT ANTON ULRICH MUSEUM
DANKWARDEROBE CASTLE

BREMEN

BREMEN MUSEUM OF THE ARTS
COLLECTION OF PAINTINGS IN THE PAULA BECKER MODERSOHN HOUSE
GERHARD MARCKS FOUNDATION
LUDWIG ROSELIUS COLLECTION

BRUCHSAL

PALACE

BÜCKEBURG

GALLERY OF PAINTINGS

BÜDINGEN

PALACE MUSEUM

BURGHAUSEN

CASTLE
BURGHAUSEN STATE GALLERY

BURG-WUPPER

MUSEUM OF THE COUNTS VON BERG

COBURG

DR. OTTO BLOSS MEMORIAL COLLECTION
MUNICIPAL ART COLLECTIONS

COESFELD

REGIONAL MUSEUM

DACHAU

REGIONAL MUSEUM

DARMSTADT

ART GALLERY
HESSE MUSEUM
PALACE MUSEUM

DEGGENDORF

REGIONAL MUSEUM

DETMOLD

PALACE OF THE PRINCES OF LIPPE

DIEZ/LAHN

ORANIENSTEIN NASSAU MUSEUM

DILLENBURG

MUSEUM OF ORANGE-NASSAU

DINGOLFING

REGIONAL MUSEUM

DONAUESCHINGEN

COLLECTIONS OF THE PRINCES OF FÜRSTENBERG

DORTMUND

KHAYON FOUNDATION FOR INDO-ASIAN RESEARCH
MUSEUM ON THE EAST WALL

DREVENACK

OTTO PANKOK MUSEUM

DUISBURG

WILHELM LEHMBRUCK MUSEUM

DÜREN

LEOPOLD HOESCH MUSEUM

DÜSSELDORF

ART COLLECTION OF NORDRHEIN-WESTFALEN
CITY MUSEUM OF ART
CONZEN COLLECTION
HALL OF THE ARTS
LÖBBECKE MUSEUM
MUSEUM OF THE HISTORY OF DÜSSELDORF

EHINGEN

REGIONAL MUSEUM

EICHSTÄTT

BENEDICTINE ABBEY OF ST. WALBURG
DIOCESAN MUSEUM
WILLIBALD CASTLE MUSEUM

ELLWANGEN

PALACE MUSEUM

EMDEN

LAND MUSEUM OF OSTFRISIEN
MUNICIPAL MUSEUM

EMMENDINGEN

REGIONAL MUSEUM

EPPSTEIN

REGIONAL MUSEUM

ERDING

REGIONAL MUSEUM

ERLANGEN

CITY ART COLLECTIONS
CITY MUSEUM
GRAPHICS COLLECTION OF THE LIBRARY OF THE UNIVERSITY OF ERLANGEN-NÜRNBERG
PAINTINGS COLLECTION OF THE UNIVERSITY OF ERLANGEN- NÜRNBERG
TEACHING COLLECTION OF PAINTINGS OF ERLANGEN FOLK HIGH SCHOOL

ESSEN

FOLKWANG MUSEUM
VILLA HÜGEL

EUTIN

EUTIN PALACE

FALLERSLEBEN

HOFFMANN VON FALLERSLEBEN MUSEUM

FLENSBURG

FLENSBURG MUNICIPAL MUSEUM

FRANKENTHAL

ERKENBERT MUSEUM

FRANKFURT

GOETHE HOUSE AND MUSEUM
HISTORY MUSEUM
LIEBIGHAUS MUNICIPAL GALLERY
MUSEUM OF APPLIED ART
STÄDEL INSTITUTE OF ART

FRAUENWÖRTH

FRAUENCHIEMSEE EXHIBITION OF PAINTINGS

FREIBURG IM BREISGAU

AUGUSTINER MUSEUM

FREISING

CATHEDRAL TREASURY
MUSEUM OF FREISING HISTORICAL ASSOCIATION
SEMINARY ART COLLECTION

FREYUNG

WOLFSTEIN DISTRICT MUSEUM

FRIEDBERG (SCHWABEN)

REGIONAL MUSEUM

FRITZLAR

CATHEDRAL MUSEUM

FULDA

CATHEDRAL MUSEUM
VONDERAU MUSEUM

FÜRTH

TOWN MUSEUM

FÜRTH IM WALD

TOWN TOWER MUSEUM

FÜSSEN

FÜSSEN STATE GALLERY
REGIONAL MUSEUM

GARMISCH-PARTENKIRCHEN

WERDENFELSER MUSEUM

GELSENKIRCHEN

MUNICIPAL ART COLLECTION

GIESSEN

UPPER HESSE MUSEUM

GOCH

GATE-HOUSE MUSEUM

GÖPPINGEN

MUNICIPAL MUSEUM

GÖTTINGEN

ART COLLECTION OF THE UNIVERSITY OF GÖTTINGEN
MUNICIPAL MUSEUM

GOSLAR

CATHEDRAL ANTECHAMBER
COLLECTION ILLUSTRATING THE CULTURAL HISTORY OF GERMANY AND EUROPE
HALL OF HOMAGE

GRAFENWÖHR

REGIONAL MUSEUM

GÜNZBURG

REGIONAL MUSEUM

GÜTERSLOH

REGIONAL MUSEUM

HAGEN

KARL ERNST OSTHAUS REGIONAL MUSEUM

HAMBURG

ALTONA MUSEUM
ERNST BARLACH HOUSE
HAMBURG HALL OF THE ARTS
MUSEUM OF ARTS AND CRAFTS

HAMBURG-BRUNSBÜTTEL

BRUNSBÜTTEL REGIONAL MUSEUM

HAMM

GUSTAV LÜBCKE MUNICIPAL MUSEUM

HANAU

HISTORY MUSEUM

HANNOVER

WILHELM BUSCH MUSEUM
CITY ART GALLERY AND LAND ART GALLERY OF LOWER SAXONY
HERRENHAUSEN MUSEUM
KESTNER MUSEUM

HASLACH

HANSJAKOB AND REGIONAL MUSEUM

HEIDE

MUSEUM OF DITHMARSCHEN PREHISTORY

HEIDELBERG

COLLECTIONS OF GREEK AND ROMAN MINOR ART AND SCULPTURE CASTS
EGYPTOLOGY COLLECTION OF HEIDELBERG UNIVERSITY
PALATINE MUSEUM

HEINSBERG

REGIONAL MUSEUM

HELMSTEDT

DISTRICT MUSEUM
MUSEUM OF ST. MARIENBERG MONASTERY

HERRENCHIEMSEE

NEW PALACE AND LUDWIG II MUSEUM

HILDESHEIM

ROEMER-PELIZAEUS MUSEUM

HIRSAU

MONASTERY MUSEUM

HOF

MUNICIPAL MUSEUM

HOFGEISMAR

REGIONAL MUSEUM

HOHENLIMBURG

REGIONAL MUSEUM

HOMBURG

REGIONAL MUSEUM

HUSUM

NISSEN HOUSE

IMMENSTADT

REGIONAL MUSEUM

INGOLSTADT

MUNICIPAL MUSEUM

KAISERSLAUTERN

PALACE GALLERY AND ARTS AND CRAFTS COLLECTION

KALKAR

ART COLLECTION OF THE NICOLAI CHURCH

KARLSRUHE

BADEN MUSEUM
CITY ART COLLECTION
STATE HALL OF ARTS

KASSEL

MUNICIPAL ART COLLECTION

KAUFBEUREN

REGIONAL MUSEUM

KAUFBEUREN-NEUGABLONZ

GABLONZ GALLERY

KELHEIM

HALL OF LIBERATION

KEMPEN

KRAMER MUNICIPAL MUSEUM

KEMPTEN
ALLGAU REGIONAL MUSEUM
KEVELAER
FOLKLORE MUSEUM OF THE LOWER RHINE
KIEL
HISTORY COLLECTION OF THE SCHLESWIG-HOLSTEIN LAND LIBRARY
PICTURE GALLERY AND GRAPHICS COLLECTION OF THE KIEL KUNSTHALLE
KLEVE
HAUS KOEKKOEK MUNICIPAL MUSEUM
KNITTLINGEN
FAUST MEMORIAL
KOBLENZ
MUSEUM OF THE MIDDLE RHINE
RHINE MUSEUM
KÖLN
MUSEUM OF THE CITY OF COLOGNE
MUSEUM OF ORIENTAL ART
RAUTENSTRANCH-JOEST MUSEUM
SCHNÜTGEN MUSEUM
WALLROF RICHARTZ MUSEUM
KÖNIGHEIM
DR. ARTHUR BECHTOLD'S COLLECTION OF PAINTINGS
KONSTANZ
VON WESSENBERG PICTURE GALLERY
KRANENBURG
KATHARINENHOF MUSEUM
KREFELD
KAISER WILHELM MUSEUM
KRONACH
FRANKENWALD REGIONAL MUSEUM
KRONBERG
FASANERIE PALACE MUSEUM
KULMBACH-PLASSENBURG
PLASSENBURG STATE GALLERY
LANDSHUT
LANDSHUT RESIDENCE
TOWN AND DISTRICT MUSEUM
LAUF AN DER PEGNITZ
MUNICIPAL COLLECTIONS
LAUINGEN
REGIONAL HOUSE
LEER
REGIONAL MUSEUM
LEINSWEILER
SLEVOGTHOF NEUCASTEL
LEVERKUSEN
MUNICIPAL MUSEUM
LICHTENSTEIN
PALACE MUSEUM
LIESBORN
BECKUM DISTRICT MUSEUM
LIMBURG (LAHN)
LIMBURG CATHEDRAL TREASURY
LIMBURG DIOCESAN MUSEUM
LINDAU
MUNICIPAL ART COLLECTIONS
LIPPSTADT
DISTRICT MUSEUM
LÖRRACH
REGIONAL MUSEUM
LORSCH
HOUSE OF THE ELECTORAL PRINCES
LÜBECK
BEHNHAUS MUSEUM
ST. ANNEN MUSEUM
LUDWIGSBURG
PALACE MUSEUM
REGIONAL MUSEUM
LUDWIGSHAFEN
MUNICIPAL ART COLLECTIONS
LÜNE
ART COLLECTIONS OF LÜNE MONASTERY
LÜNEBURG
MUSEUM OF THE PRINCIPALITY OF LÜNEBURG
LÜNEN
MUSEUM OF ART AND CULTURAL HISTORY OF DORTMUND
MAINZ
CATHEDRAL AND DIOCESAN MUSEUM
KUPPERBERG COLLECTION
LAND MUSEUM OF THE MIDDLE RHINE
PRINZ JOHANN GEORG MUSEUM
MANNHEIM
MANNHEIM CITY HALL OF THE ARTS
REISS CITY MUSEUM
MARBACH
NATIONAL SCHILLER MUSEUM AND GERMAN LITERARY ARCHIVES
MARBURG
UNIVERSITY COLLECTION OF MATERIAL RELATING TO RELIGION
UNIVERSITY OF MARBURG MUSEUM OF ART AND CULTURAL HISTORY
MAULBRONN
ART COLLECTIONS
MEERSBURG
MEERSBURG PALACE
MELDORF
DITHMARSCH LAND MUSEUM
MEMMINGEN
MUNICIPAL MUSEUM
MINDELHEIM
MINDELHEIM REGIONAL MUSEUM
MÖNCHENGLADBACH
MUNICIPAL MUSEUM
MÜNCHEN
BAVARIAN NATIONAL MUSEUM
EXHIBITION COLLECTIONS OF THE BAVARIAN STATE LIBRARY
GLYPOTHEK
KRAUSS-MAFFEI COMPANY ART EXHIBITIONS AND COLLECTION
LENBACH HOUSE MUNICIPAL GALLERY
MODERN ART MUSEUM
MUNICH CITY MUSEUM
NEW GALLERY
NEW STATE GALLERY
OLD GALLERY
PROBST COLLECTION
RESIDENCE MUSEUM
SCHACK GALLERY
STATE COLLECTIONS OF CLASSICAL ART
STATE GRAPHICS COLLECTION
STUCK MUSEUM OF ART NOUVEAU
VALENTIN MUSEUM
MÜNSTER
CATHEDRAL MUSEUM AND TREASURY
LAND MUSEUM OF ART AND CULTURAL HISTORY
UNIVERSITY OF MÜNSTER MUSEUM OF ARCHAEOLOGY
MÜNSTERSCHWARZACH
BENEDICTINE ABBEY
NECKARMÜHLBACH
GUTTENBERG CASTLE
NEHEIM-HÜSTEN
GERMAN MUSEUM OF BIRDCAGES
NEUBURG
REGIONAL MUSEUM
STATE GALLERY
NEUSCHWANSTEIN
PALACE
NEUSS
CLEMENS SELS MUSEUM
NEUWIED
DISTRICT MUSEUM
NIEDERALTAICH
BENEDICTINE ABBEY
NIEDERMARSBERG
REGIONAL MUSEUM
NÖRDLINGEN
TOWN MUSEUM
NORDEN
REGIONAL MUSEUM
NÜRNBERG
CITY ART COLLECTIONS
FEMBO HOUSE CITY MUSEUM
GERMAN NATIONAL MUSEUM
NÜRNBERG IMPERIAL CASTLE
OBERAMMERGAU
OBERAMMERGAU REGIONAL MUSEUM
OBERGÜNZBURG
REGIONAL MUSEUM
OBERHAUSEN
MUNICIPAL GALLERY
OBERSTDORF
REGIONAL MUSEUM
OFFENBURG
MUNICIPAL GALLERY
OLDENBURG
LAND MUSEUM OF ART AND CULTURAL HISTORY
MUNICIPAL ART COLLECTIONS
OSNABRÜCK
MUNICIPAL MUSEUM
PASSAU
NEW COLLECTION
OBERHAUS MUSEUM
STATE GALLERY
POMMERSFELDEN
WEISSENSTEIN PALACE
PRIEN
REGIONAL MUSEUM
PRUNN
PALACE
RASTATT
PALACE
RATZEBURG
ERNST BARLACH MEMORIAL
RAVENSBURG
REGIONAL MUSEUM
RECKLINGHAUSEN
ICON MUSEUM
MUNICIPAL HALL OF THE ARTS
VESTISCH MUSEUM
REGENSBURG
EAST GERMAN FOUNDATION GALLERY
GALLERY OF THE 20th CENTURY
MUSEUM OF THE PALACE OF THE PRINCES OF THURN AND TAXIS
REGENSBURG CITY MUSEUM
STATE GALLERY
REINFELD
REINFELD REGIONAL MUSEUM
REKEN
MUSEUM IN THE OLD CHURCH
REUTLINGEN
SPENDHAUS ART EXHIBITION
RHEINE
FALKENHOF MUSEUM
RHEYDT
MUNICIPAL MUSEUM
ROSENHEIM
MUNICIPAL ART COLLECTIONS
ROTHENBURG OB DER TAUBER
ROTHENBURG AND WASSE GALLERIES
ROTTHALMÜNSTER
REGIONAL MUSEUM
ROTTWEIL
ART COLLECTION OF THE LORENZKAPELLE
ROTTWEIL MUNICIPAL MUSEUM
ROXEL
DROSTE ZU HÜLSHOFF MUSEUM
SAARBRÜCKEN
SAARLAND MUSEUM
SÄCKINGEN
UPPER RHINE MUSEUM
SCHLEISSHEIM
SCHLEISSHEIM NEW PALACE AND STATE GALLERY
SCHLESWIG
LAND MUSEUM OF SCHLESWIG- HOLSTEIN
MUNICIPAL MUSEUM
SCHLOSS MESPELBRUNN
PALACE MUSEUM
SCHONGAU
TOWN MUSEUM
SCHWABACH
TOWN MUSEUM
SCHWÄBISCH-GMÜND
SCHWÄBISCH-GMÜND MUSEUM
SCHWABMÜNCHEN
REGIONAL MUSEUM
SCHWETZINGEN
PALACE
SEEBÜLL
ADA AND EMIL NOLDE SEEBÜLL FOUNDATION

SIEGBURG
SIEGBURG REGIONAL MUSEUM
SIEGEN
SIEGERLAND MUSEUM
SIGMARINGEN
HOHENZOLLERN MUSEUM
SINZIG
REGIONAL MUSEUM
SOEST
WILHELM MORGNER HOUSE
STRAUBING
GÄUBODEN AND STRAUBING MUSEUM
STUTTGART
OSKAR SCHLEMMER COLLECTION
STATE GALLERY
STUTTGART CITY GALLERY
WÜRTTEMBERG MUSEUM
TRABEN-TRARBACH
MUSEUM OF THE CENTRAL MOSEL AREA
TRAUNSTEIN
REGIONAL MUSEUM
TRECHTLINGHAUSEN
RHEINSTEIN PALACE ART COLLECTIONS
TRIER
CATHEDRAL AND DIOCESAN MUSEUM
MUNICIPAL MUSEUM
RHINELAND MUSEUM
TROSTBERG
TROSTBERG MUNICIPAL MUSEUM
TÜBINGEN
COLLECTIONS OF THE UNIVERSITY INSTITUTE OF THE HISTORY OF ART
THEODOR HEARING HOUSE
ÜBERLINGEN
REGIONAL MUSEUM
ULM
ULM MUSEUM
VEITSHÖCHHEIM
SUMMER PALACE
VILLINGEN
VILLINGEN MUSEUM
WALDSHUT
REGIONAL MUSEUM
WALDSRODE
REGIONAL MUSEUM
WARTHAUSEN
PALACE MUSEUM
WASSERBURG
WASSERBURG REGIONAL MUSEUM
WEILBURG
PALACE
WEILER
WEST ALLGAU REGIONAL MUSEUM
WEILHEIM
TOWN MUSEUM
WEINSBERG
JUSTINUS KERNER HOUSE
WEISSENHORN
REGIONAL MUSEUM
WERTACH
REGIONAL MUSEUM
WERTINGEN
REGIONAL MUSEUM
WETZLAR
MUNICIPAL MUSEUM
WEWELSBURG
DISTRICT MUSEUM
WIESBADEN
WIESBADEN MUNICIPAL MUSEUM
WILFINGEN
PALACE MUSEUM
WITTEN
REGIONAL MUSEUM
WITTMUND
KARL BÖSCH COLLECTION
WOLFACH
WOLFACH REGIONAL MUSEUM
WOLFEGG
WOLFEGG PALACE
WOLFENBÜTTEL
WOLFENBÜTTEL DISTRICT MUSEUM
WORMS
HEYLSHOF GALLERY
WUPPERTAL
VON DER HEYDT MUSEUM
WÜRZBURG
CITY GALLERY
FRANKISH MUSEUM
MARIENBERG CASTLE
RESIDENCE
MARTIN VON WAGNER MUSEUM OF THE UNIVERSITY OF WÜRZBURG
XANTEN
CATHEDRAL MUSEUM
ZWIESEL
TOWN MUSEUM

GIBRALTAR

GIBRALTAR
GIBRALTAR MUSEUM

GREAT BRITAIN

ABERDEEN
ABERDEEN ART GALLERY AND MUSEUM
ABERYSTWYTH
UNIVERSITY COLLEGE OF WALES GALLERY
ABINGDON
GUILDHALL
ACCRINGTON
HAWORTH ART GALLERY
ALCESTER
RAGLEY HALL
ANNAN
ANNAN MUSEUM
AYLESBURY
WADDESDON MANOR
AYLSHAM
BLICKLING HALL
BADMINTON
BADMINTON HOUSE
BAKEWELL
CHATSWORTH
BANBURY
SULGRAVE MANOR
BARNARD CASTLE
BOWES MUSEUM
BARNSLEY
COOPER ART GALLERY
BASINGSTOKE
WILLIS MUSEUM
BATH
HOLBURNE OF MENSTRIE MUSEUM
VICTORIA ART GALLERY
BATLEY
ART GALLERY
BEDFORD
CECIL HIGGINS ART GALLERY
BELFAST
ULSTER MUSEUM
BEMBRIDGE
RUSKIN GALLERY
BERKELEY
BERKELEY CASTLE
BERWICK- ON-TWEED
BERWICK-ON-TWEED MUSEUM AND ART GALLERY
BEVERLEY
BEVERLEY ART GALLERY AND MUSEUM
BIRKENHEAD
WILLIAMSON ART GALLERY AND MUSEUM
BIRMINGHAM
BARBER INSTITUTE OF FINE ARTS
BIRMINGHAM CITY MUSEUM AND ART GALLERY
BLACKPOOL
GRUNDY ART GALLERY
BLAIR ATHOLL
BLAIR CASTLE AND ATHOLL MUSEUM
BODMIN
LANYDROCK
BOSTON SPA
BRAMHALL PARK
BOURNEMOUTH
RUSSELL-COTES ART GALLERY AND MUSEUM
BRADFORD
CITY ART GALLERY AND MUSEUM
BRIDLINGTON
BURTON AGNES HALL
BRIGHOUSE
BRIGHOUSE ART GALLERY
BRIGHTON
BRIGHTON MUSEUM AND ART GALLERY
BRISTOL
BRISTOL CITY ART GALLERY
DYRHAM PARK
BURNLEY
TOWNELEY HALL ART GALLERY AND MUSEUM
BURTON- ON-TRENT
HOAR CROSS HALL
CAMBO
WALLINGTON
CAMBRIDGE
ANGLESEY ABBEY
FITZWILLIAM MUSEUM
CARDIFF
NATIONAL MUSEUM OF WALES
CARLISLE
MUSEUM AND ART GALLERY
CAWTHORNE
CANNON HALL
CHELTENHAM
CHELTENHAM ART GALLERY AND MUSEUM
CHICHESTER
GOODWOOD HOUSE
CHIPPENHAM
CORSHAM COURT
CHORLEY
ASTLEY HALL, ART GALLERY AND MUSEUM
CONWY
ROYAL CAMBRIAN ACADEMY OF ART
COOKHAM- ON-THAMES
STANLEY SPENCER GALLERY
COVENTRY
HERBERT ART GALLERY AND MUSEUM
CULROSS
DUNIMARLE MUSEUM
DARLINGTON
DARLINGTON ART GALLERY
RABY CASTLE
DEDHAM
CASTLE HOUSE
DERBY
DERBY MUSEUM AND ART GALLERY
KEDLESTON HALL
DIDSBURY
FLETCHER MOSS
DORKING
POLESDEN LACEY
DOUGLAS
MANX MUSEUM
DUDLEY
DUDLEY MUSEUM AND ART GALLERY
DUNDEE
DUNDEE CITY MUSEUM AND ART GALLERIES
ORCHAR ART GALLERY
DURHAM
GULBENKIAN MUSEUM OF ORIENTAL ART AND ARCHAEOLOGY

EASTBOURNE
TOWNER ART GALLERY

EDENBRIDGE
CHIDDINGSTONE CASTLE
HEVER CASTLE

EDINBURGH
NATIONAL GALLERY OF SCOTLAND
ROYAL SCOTTISH MUSEUM
SCOTTISH NATIONAL GALLERY OF MODERN ART
SCOTTISH NATIONAL PORTRAIT GALLERY

EXETER
ROYAL ALBERT MEMORIAL MUSEUM AND ART GALLERY

FIFE
CULROSS PALACE

FORDINGBRIDGE
BREAMORE HOUSE
HALE PARK

GLASGOW
CITY OF GLASGOW CORPORATION ART GALLERY AND MUSEUM
HUNTERIAN MUSEUM
OLD GLASGOW MUSEUM
POLLOK HOUSE

GRANTHAM
BELVOIR CASTLE

GUILDFORD
WATTS GALLERY

HATFIELD
HATFIELD HOUSE

HEREFORD
KENTCHURCH COURT

HUDDERSFIELD
HUDDERSFIELD ART GALLERY

HULL
FERENS ART GALLERY

INGATESTONE
INGATESTONE HALL

IPSWICH
CHRISTCHURCH MANSION

KENDAL
SIZERGH CASTLE

KETTERING
ALFRED EAST ART GALLERY

KIDDERMINSTER
ART GALLERY

KILMARNOCK
DICK INSTITUTE MUSEUM

KIRKCALDY
KIRKCALDY MUSEUMS AND ART GALLERY

KNEBWORTH
KNEBWORTH HOUSE

KNUTSFORD
TATTON PARK

LAMBOURN
ASHDOWN HOUSE

LEAMINGTON SPA
LEAMINGTON SPA ART GALLERY AND MUSEUM

LEEDS
CITY ART GALLERY
HAREWOOD HOUSE
TEMPLE NEWSAM HOUSE

LEEK
LEEK ART GALLERY

LEWES
BARBICAN HOUSE MUSEUM
FIRLE PLACE
GLYNDE PLACE

LINCOLN
USHER GALLERY

LITTLE GADDESDEN
THE MANOR HOUSE

LIVERPOOL
CITY OF LIVERPOOL MUSEUMS
SPEKE HALL
SUDLEY ART GALLERY AND MUSEUM
WALKER ART GALLERY

LLANDUDNO
RAPALLO HOUSE MUSEUM AND ART GALLERY

LLANELLI
PARC HOWARD MUSEUM AND ART GALLERY

LLANFAIR P.G.
PLAS NEWYDD

LONDON
APSLEY HOUSE
BETHNAL GREEN MUSEUM
BRITISH MUSEUM
BUCKINGHAM PALACE
COURTAULD INSTITUTE GALLERIES
DULWICH COLLEGE PICTURE GALLERY
FOUNDLING HOSPITAL ART TREASURES
GUNNERSBURY PARK MUSEUM
HAM HOUSE
HAMPTON COURT PALACE
HOGARTH'S HOUSE
THE IVEAGH BEQUEST
JOHN EVELYN SOCIETY'S MUSEUM
KENSINGTON PALACE
KEW PALACE
LEIGHTON HOUSE ART GALLERY AND MUSEUM
NATIONAL GALLERY
NATIONAL PORTRAIT GALLERY
ORLEANS HOUSE GALLERY
OSTERLEY PARK HOUSE
SIR JOHN SOANE'S MUSEUM
SOUTH LONDON ART GALLERY
VALENCE HOUSE MUSEUM
VICTORIA AND ALBERT MUSEUM
WALLACE COLLECTION
WILLIAM MORRIS GALLERY

LUTON
WERNHER COLLECTION

MACCLESFIELD
CAPESTHORNE
WEST PARK MUSEUM AND ART GALLERY

MAIDENHEAD
HENRY REITLINGER BEQUEST

MAIDSTONE
THE FRIARS

MANCHESTER
CITY ART GALLERY
FLETCHER MOSS MUSEUM
HEATON HALL
QUEEN'S PARK ART GALLERY
WHITWORTH ART GALLERY
WYTHENSHAWE HALL

MERE
STOURHEAD

NEWCASTLE- UPON-TYNE
HIGHAM PLACE GALLERY
LAING ART GALLERY AND MUSEUM
UNIVERSITY OF NEWCASTLE- UPON-TYNE

NEWPORT
NEWPORT MUSEUM AND ART GALLERY

NORTHAMPTON
ALTHORP
CASTLE ASHBY

NORWICH
NORWICH CASTLE MUSEUM

NOTTINGHAM
NOTTINGHAM CITY MUSEUM AND ART GALLERY

OLDHAM
ART GALLERY AND MUSEUM

OXFORD
ASHMOLEAN MUSEUM OF ART AND ARCHAEOLOGY
CHRIST CHURCH PICTURE GALLERY
MUSEUM OF MODERN ART

PAISLEY
PAISLEY MUSEUM AND ART GALLERIES

PENARTH
TURNER HOUSE GALLERY

PERTH
PERTH ART GALLERY AND MUSEUM

PETWORTH
PETWORTH HOUSE

PLYMOUTH
CITY MUSEUM AND ART GALLERY
SALTRAM HOUSE

PORTSMOUTH
CITY MUSEUM AND ART GALLERY

PORT SUNLIGHT
THE LADY LEVER ART GALLERY

PRESTON
HARRIS MUSEUM AND ART GALLERY

PRESTWICH
HEATON HALL

PULBOROUGH
PARHAM

RAVENGLASS
MUNCASTER CASTLE

RIPON
NEWBY HALL

SALFORD
MUSEUM AND ART GALLERY

SALISBURY
WILTON HOUSE

SCARBOROUGH
SCARBOROUGH ART GALLERY
SCARBOROUGH MUSEUM OF NATURAL HISTORY

SCUNTHORPE
NORMANBY HALL

SEVENOAKS
KNOLE

SHEFFIELD
GRAVES ART GALLERY
MAPPIN ART GALLERY

SHERBORNE
SHERBORNE CASTLE

SHIFNAL
WESTON PARK

SHUGBOROUGH
STAFFORDSHIRE COUNTY MUSEUM AND MANSION HOUSE

SOUTHAMPTON
SOUTHAMPTON ART GALLERY

STAMFORD
BURGHLEY HOUSE

STEEPLE ASTON
ROUSHAM HOUSE

STOCKPORT
WAR MEMORIAL ART GALLERY

STOKE-ON-TRENT
CITY MUSEUM AND ART GALLERY

SUDBURY
GAINSBOROUGH'S HOUSE
MELFORD HALL

SUNDERLAND
SUNDERLAND CENTRAL MUSEUM AND ART GALLERY

SWANSEA
GLYNN VIVIAN ART GALLERY

TEESSIDE
MIDDLESBROUGH ART GALLERY

TETBURY
LASBOROUGH MANOR

THETFORD
DULEEP SINGH COLLECTION

TORPOINT
ANTONY HOUSE

TUNBRIDGE WELLS
PENSHURST PLACE

WADDESDON
WADDESDON MANOR

WAKEFIELD
HEATH HALL

WALSALL
E. M. FLINT ART GALLERY

WARMINSTER
LONGLEAT HOUSE

WARWICK
WARWICK CASTLE

WELLINGBOROUGH
HINWICK HOUSE

WELLS
HOLKHAM HALL

WELSHPOOL
POWIS CASTLE

WESTERHAM
SQUERRYES COURT

WHITBY
WHITBY MUSEUM AND ART GALLERY

WINCHCOMBE
SUDELEY CASTLE

WINCHESTER
WINCHESTER COLLEGE MUSEUM

WINDSOR
THE GUILDHALL EXHIBITIONS
WINDSOR CASTLE

WING
ASCOTT

WOBURN
WOBURN ABBEY

WOLVERHAMPTON
MUNICIPAL ART GALLERY AND MUSEUM
WIGHTWICK MANOR

WOODSTOCK
BLENHEIM PALACE

WORTHING
WORTHING MUSEUM AND ART GALLERY

WREXHAM
CHIRK CASTLE

YORK
CITY OF YORK ART GALLERY

GREECE

AEGINA
MUSEUM

AGIASSOS
CHURCH OF THE PANAGIA

AGION OROS
MONASTERY SACRISTY

AGRINION
ARCHAEOLOGICAL MUSEUM

AIANI
ARCHAEOLOGICAL AND FOLKLORE COLLECTION

AIGINA
ARCHAEOLOGICAL MUSEUM

ALEXANDROUPOLIS
ARCHAEOLOGICAL COLLECTION

ALMYROS
MUSEUM

AMFISSA
EXHIBITION OF CONTEMPORARY GREEK PAINTERS

AMORGOS
CHOZOVIOTISSA MONASTERY

AMPHIARAION
SITE MUSEUM

ANO KARDAMYLA
KARDAMYLA CULTURAL CENTRE OF MICHAEL AND STAMATIA XYLAS

ANTISSA
MONASTERY OF ST. JOHN THE DIVINE, YPSILOU

ARGOS
ARCHAEOLOGICAL MUSEUM

ARGOSTOLION
ARCHAEOLOGICAL MUSEUM
E. BASSIAS HISTORICAL AND FOLKLORE MUSEUM
COLLECTION OF THE MTROPOLIS OF KEFALLINIA

ARTA
ARCHAEOLOGICAL COLLECTION

ATHENS
ACROPOLIS MUSEUM
AGORA MUSEUM
R. ANDREADIS PRIVATE COLLECTION
D. ARTEMIS PRIVATE COLLECTION
BENAKI MUSEUM
L. BENAKIS PRIVATE COLLECTION
BYZANTINE MUSEUM
M. DAPERGOLAS PRIVATE COLLECTION
D. ECONOMIDIS PRIVATE COLLECTION
A. GOULANDRIS PRIVATE COLLECTION
HISTORICAL AND ETHNOLOGICAL MUSEUM
A. IOLAS PRIVATE COLLECTION
P. KANELLOPOULOS PRIVATE COLLECTION
E. KOUTLIDIS PRIVATE COLLECTION
LOVERDO MUSEUM
A. MELAS PRIVATE COLLECTION
MUSEUM OF SACRED ICONS OF THE ARCHBISHOPRIC OF ATHENS
NATIONAL ARCHAEOLOGICAL MUSEUM
NATIONAL HISTORICAL MUSEUM
NATIONAL PICTURE GALLERY AND ALEXANDROS SOUTSOS MUSEUM
I. AND D. PASSAS MUSEUM OF EUROPEAN AND ORIENTAL ART

BATSI
MONASTERY OF THE ZOODOCHOS PIGI OR AGIA

CAVALA
ARCHAEOLOGICAL MUSEUM

CHAIRONEIA
ARCHAEOLOGICAL MUSEUM

CHALKIS
ARCHAEOLOGICAL MUSEUM
BYZANTINE COLLECTION

CHIOS
ARCHAEOLOGICAL MUSEUM
NEA MONI MONASTERY

CHORA
ARCHAEOLOGICAL COLLECTION
MONASTERY OF ST. JOHN THE DIVINE

COMOTINI
ARCHAEOLOGICAL MUSEUM

CORFU
ARCHAEOLOGICAL MUSEUM
BYZANTINE COLLECTION
ECCLESIASTICAL MUSEUM
R. EVELPIDIS PRIVATE COLLECTION
HISTORICAL MUSEUM
SINO-JAPANESE MUSEUM

CORINTH
ANCIENT CORINTH MUSEUM

DELOS
ARCHAEOLOGICAL MUSEUM

DELPHI
ARCHAEOLOGICAL MUSEUM

DIMITSANA
ARCHAEOLOGICAL COLLECTION

DION
ARCHAEOLOGICAL MUSEUM

DRAMA
ARCHAEOLOGICAL COLLECTION

ELASSON
OLYMPIOTISSA MONASTERY

ELEFSIS
ARCHAEOLOGICAL MUSEUM

ELEUSIS
ELEUSIS MUSEUM

EPIDAVROS
ARCHAEOLOGICAL MUSEUM

ERESSOS
ARCHAEOLOGICAL MUSEUM

ERETRIA
ARCHAEOLOGICAL MUSEUM

ERMOUPOLIS
ARCHAEOLOGICAL COLLECTION

FLORINA
ARCHAEOLOGICAL MUSEUM

GYTHION
ARCHAEOLOGICAL COLLECTION

IERAPETRA
ARCHAEOLOGICAL COLLECTION

IOANNINA
MUSEUM

IRAKLION
HISTORICAL MUSEUM OF CRETE

KALAMATA
HISTORICAL AND FOLKLORE MUSEUM

KALAMOS
ARCHAEOLOGICAL MUSEUM

KALAVRYTA
AGIA LAVRA MONASTERY
MEGA SPILEON MONASTERY

KALLONI
MONASTERY OF ST. IGNATIOS, LIMONOS

KALYMNOS
THE VOUVALINA MANSION

KAMPOS
ARCHAEOLOGICAL MUSEUM

KARDITSA
KORONI MONASTERY

KARYSTOS
ARCHAEOLOGICAL MUSEUM

KASTELLORIZON
ARCHAEOLOGICAL MUSEUM

KASTRON AGIOU GEORGIOU
CHURCH OF THE EVANGELISTRIA

KAVALA
ARCHAEOLOGICAL MUSEUM

KOLYMVARI
MONASTERY OF THE ODIGITRIA, CHANIA

KOS
ARCHAEOLOGICAL MUSEUM
FOLK ART MUSEUM OF THE METROPOLIS OF KOS

KOSMITI, XANTHI
ARCHAEOLOGICAL COLLECTION

LAMIA
ARCHAEOLOGICAL COLLECTION

LARISSA
G. GOURYOTIS PRIVATE COLLECTION
G. KATSIGRAS PRIVATE COLLECTION

LEFKAS
ARCHAEOLOGICAL COLLECTION
COLLECTION OF ECCLESIASTICAL PAINTINGS AND RELICS OF ORTHODOXY

LINDOS
ARCHAEOLOGICAL COLLECTION

LIXOURI
ARCHAEOLOGICAL COLLECTION

LYKOSOURA
ARCHAEOLOGICAL MUSEUM

MANDRAKI
ARCHAEOLOGICAL COLLECTION

MESOLONGION
ART GALLERY OF THE MUNICIPALITY AND TOWN OF MESOLONGION

METEORA
MONASTERY OF AGION PANTON (VARLAAM)
MONASTERY OF THE METAMORPHOSIS SOTIROS (METEORON)

METSOVON
MUSEUM OF EPIROT FOLK ART

MONEMVASSIA
ARCHAEOLOGICAL COLLECTION

MYKONOS
ARCHAEOLOGICAL MUSEUM

MYRINA
ARCHAEOLOGICAL MUSEUM

MYTILINI (MYTILENE)
ARCHAEOLOGICAL COLLECTION

NAFPLION
ARCHAEOLOGICAL MUSEUM

NAOUSSA
ECCLESIASTICAL COLLECTION

NAXOS
ARCHAEOLOGICAL MUSEUM

NEAPOLIS
ARCHAEOLOGICAL COLLECTION

NEAPOLIS, VOION
ARCHAEOLOGICAL COLLECTION

NEMEA
ARCHAEOLOGICAL COLLECTION

NIKOPOLIS
ARCHAEOLOGICAL COLLECTION

OINOUSSAI
NAUTICAL MUSEUM

OLYMPIA
ARCHAEOLOGICAL MUSEUM

OLYMPOS
ARCHAEOLOGICAL COLLECTION

PALAIA KORINTHOS
ARCHAEOLOGICAL MUSEUM

PANAGITSA PELLIS
CHURCH OF THE KOIMISSIS TIS THEOTOKOU

PAROS
ARCHAEOLOGICAL MUSEUM
BYZANTINE COLLECTION OF KATAPOLIANI

PATMOS
MONASTERY OF ST. JOHN

PATRAI
ARCHAEOLOGICAL MUSEUM

PELLA
ARCHAEOLOGICAL COLLECTION

PERATATA
MONASTERY OF AGIOS ANDREAS

PIRAEUS
ARCHAEOLOGICAL MUSEUM

PLAKA
ARCHAEOLOGICAL MUSEUM

PLATANOS
ARCHAEOLOGICAL COLLECTION
POLYGYROS
ARCHAEOLOGICAL MUSEUM
PYLOS
ANTONOPOULEION ARCHAEOLOGICAL MUSEUM
PYRGOS
MONASTERY OF PROFITIS ILIAS
P. NOMIKOS PRIVATE COLLECTION
MONASTERY OF THE KOIMISSIS TIS THEOTOKOU, KECHROVOUNI
RETHYMNON
ARCHAEOLOGICAL MUSEUM
ARKADI MONASTERY
MONASTERY OF AGIOS IOANNIS PREVELIS
RHODES
ARCHAEOLOGICAL MUSEUM
PALACE OF THE GRAND MASTERS (KASTELLO)
SALAMIS
ARCHAEOLOGICAL MUSEUM
SAMARINA, GREVENA
CHURCH OF THE PANAGIA
SAMOS
ARCHAEOLOGICAL MUSEUM
BYZANTINE MUSEUM OF THE METROPOLIS OF SAMOS AND IKARIA
SAMOTHRAKI
ARCHAEOLOGICAL MUSEUM
SERRAI
ARCHAEOLOGICAL COLLECTION
SIKYON
ARCHAEOLOGICAL MUSEUM
SKIATHOS
MONASTERY OF THE EVANGELISMOS TIS THEOTOKOU
SKOPELOS
MONASTERY OF THE EVANGELISTRIA
SKYROS
ARCHAEOLOGICAL MUSEUM
SOLOMOS
SOLOMOS AND EMINENT ZANTIANS MUSEUM
SPARTI
ARCHAEOLOGICAL MUSEUM
SYMI
ARCHAEOLOGICAL COLLECTION
TANAGRA
ARCHAEOLOGICAL COLLECTION
TEGEA
ARCHAEOLOGICAL MUSEUM
THASSOS
ARCHAEOLOGICAL MUSEUM
THEBES
THEBES MUSEUM
THESSALONIKI
ARCHAEOLOGICAL MUSEUM
BYZANTINE MUSEUM OF THE ROTUNDA OF ST. GEORGE
I. PAPAILIAKIS PRIVATE COLLECTION
I. VASSILIOU PRIVATE COLLECTION
THIRA
ARCHAEOLOGICAL MUSEUM
THIVAI
ARCHAEOLOGICAL MUSEUM
THYRREION
ARCHAEOLOGICAL MUSEUM
TINOS
ARCHAEOLOGICAL MUSEUM
BYZANTINE MUSEUM
CHURCH OF THE PANAGIA EVANGELISTRIA
MUSEUM OF A. SOHOS
MUSEUM OF TINIAN ARTISTS
I. PAPADOPOULOS PICTURE GALLERY
'THEOMITORIKI' EXHIBITION
TRAIANOUPOLIS (LOUTROS)
ARCHAEOLOGICAL COLLECTION
TRIKALA
ARCHAEOLOGICAL COLLECTION
ECCESIASTICAL MUSEUM OF THE METROPOLIS OF TRIKKI AND STAGOI
MONASTERY OF AGIOS VISSARION (DOUSSIKOU)
VAREIA
THEOPHILOS MUSEUM
VEROIA
ARCHAEOLOGICAL MUSEUM
VOLOS
ATHANASSAKEION ARCHAEOLOGICAL MUSEUM
A. BASTIS PRIVATE COLLECTION
K. A. MAKRIS PRIVATE COLLECTION
MUNICIPAL ART GALLERY
SEFEL PRIVATE COLLECTION
VRAVRON
ARCHAEOLOGICAL MUSEUM
YPATI
AGATHONOS MONASTERY
ZAKYNTHOS
BYZANTINE MUSEUM
ZANTE
POST-BYZANTINE MUSEUM
ZAVORDA
MONASTERY OF OSSIOS NIKANOR
ZERBITSA
MONASTERY OF THE KOIMISSIS TIS THEOTOKOU

GUATEMALA

GUATEMALA CITY
MUSEUM OF HISTORY AND FINE ARTS

HAITI

PORT-AU-PRINCE
ARTS CENTRE

HONG KONG

HONG KONG
CITY MUSEUM AND ART GALLERY
FUNG PING SHAN MUSEUM
SHA TIN
ART GALLERY OF THE INSTITUTE OF CHINESE STUDIES

HUNGARY

BAJA
ISTVÁN TÜRR MUSEUM
BÉKÉSCSABA
MIHÁLY MUNKÁCSY MUSEUM
BUDAPEST
CHINESE MUSEUM
HUNGARIAN NATIONAL GALLERY
MUSEUM OF FINE ART
MUSEUM OF THE HISTORY OF BUDAPEST: DEPARTMENT OF MODERN HISTORY
DEBRECEN
DÉRI MUSEUM
ESZTERGOM
MUSEUM OF CHRISTIANITY
FERTÖD
CHÂTEAU MUSEUM
HÓDMEZÖVÁSARHELY
JÁNOS TORNYAI MUSEUM
KAPOSVÁR
RIPPL-RÓNAI MUSEUM
KESZTHELY
BALATON MUSEUM
NYÍREGYHÁZA
ANDRÁS JÓSA MUSEUM
PANNONHALMA
ECCLESIASTICAL MUSEUM
PÉCS
JANUS PANNONIUS MUSEUM
SOMOGYTÚR
KUNFFY GALLERY
SZADA
BERTALAN SZÉKELY MEMORIAL MUSEUM
SZEGED
FERENC MÓRA MUZEUM
SZÉKESFEHÉRVÁR
ISTVÁN CSÓK GALLERY
KING ISTVÁN MUSEUM
SZENTENDRE
COLLECTION OF SERBIAN CHURCH HISTORY
KÁROLY FERENCZY MUSEUM
SCULPTURE GARDEN
SZENTES
JÓZSEF KOSZTA MUSEUM
SZOLNOK
JÁNOS DAMJANICH MUSEUM
SZOMBATHELY
GYULA DERKOVITS MEMORIAL MUSEUM
ZEBEGÉNY
ISTVÁN SZŐNYI MUSEUM

ICELAND

REYKJAVIK
GALLERY OF ÁSGRÍMUR JÓNSSON'S PAINTINGS
EINAR JONSSON ART MUSEUM
NATIONAL ART GALLERY
NATIONAL MUSEUM OF ANTIQUITIES

INDIA

AGRA
ST. JOHN'S COLLEGE MUSEUM
AHMEDABAD
GUJARAT MUSEUM SOCIETY
AJMER
RAJPUTANA MUSEUM
ALLAHABAD
ALLAHABAD MUSEUM
ALWAR
GOVERNMENT MUSEUM
AMRITSAR
CENTRAL SIKH MUSEUM
AUNDH
SRI BHAVANI MUSEUM
BARODA
MUSEUM AND PICTURE GALLERY
BELKHANDI
BELKHANDI MUSEUM
BENARES
MUSEUM OF INDIAN ARTS AND ARCHAEOLOGY
BHARATPUR
STATE MUSEUM
BHOPAL
CENTRAL MUSEUM
BHUBANESHWAR
ORISSA STATE MUSEUM
BHUJ
KUTCH MUSEUM
BIJAPUR
ARCHAEOLOGICAL MUSEUM
BIKANER
GANGA GOLDEN JUBILEE MUSEUM
BOMBAY
HERAS INSTITUTE OF INDIAN HISTORY AND CULTURE
JEHANGIR ART GALLERY
MUSEUM OF THE INDIAN HISTORICAL RESEARCH INSTITUTE
PRINCE OF WALES MUSEUM OF WESTERN INDIA
CALCUTTA
ART IN INDUSTRY MUSEUM
ASIATIC SOCIETY OF BENGAL MUSEUM
ASUTOSH MUSEUM OF INDIAN ART
BIRLA ACADEMY OF ART AND CULTURE
CRAFTS MUSEUM
GURUSADAY MUSEUM
INDIAN MUSEUM
MUSEUM OF THE BANGIYA SAHITYA PARISHAD
VICTORIA MEMORIAL HALL
CHAMBA
BHURI SINGH MUSEUM
CHANDIGARH
GOVERNMENT MUSEUM AND ART GALLERY
DHARWAR
MUSEUM OF ART AND ARCHAEOLOGY
DHULIA
I.V.K. RAJWADE SANSHODHAN MANDAL MUSEUM
GAUHATI
ASSAM STATE MUSEUM
GAYA
GAYA MUSEUM
GURUKUL JHAJJAR
HARYANA PRANTIYA PURATATVA SANGRAHALAYA

GWALIOR
STATE MUSEUM
HARDWAR
GURUKULA MUSEUM
HYDERABAD
SALARJUNG MUSEUM
STATE ARCHAEOLOGICAL MUSEUM
IMPHAL
MANIPUR STATE MUSEUM
INDORE
CENTRAL MUSEUM
JAIPUR
CENTRAL MUSEUM
THE MAHARAJA OF JAIPUR MUSEUM
JAMMU
DOGRA ART GALLERY
JAMNAGAR
JAMNAGAR MUSEUM OF ANTIQUITIES, LAKHOTE BUILDING
JHALAWAR
ARCHAEOLOGICAL MUSEUM
JODHPUR
SARDAR MUSEUM
STATE MUSEUM
JUNAGADH
DARBAR HALL MUSEUM
KALPI
MAHATMA GANDHI HINDI SANGRAHALAYA
KONARAK
ARCHAEOLOGICAL MUSEUM
KOLHAPUR
KOLHAPUR MUSEUM
KOTAH
MUSEUM AND SARASWATI BHANDAR
LUCKNOW
STATE MUSEUM
MADRAS
FORT ST. GEORGE MUSEUM
THE GOVERNMENT MUSEUM AND NATIONAL ART GALLERY
MADANAPALLE
MADANAPALLE COLLEGE MUSEUM
MALDA
B. R. SEN MUSEUM
MANGALORE
GOVERNMENT MUSEUM
MAHATMA GANDHI MUSEUM
MATHURA
ARCHAEOLOGICAL MUSEUM
MYSORE
SRI CHAMRAJENDRA ART GALLERY
NAGPUR
CENTRAL MUSEUM
NEW DELHI
NATIONAL GALLERY OF MODERN ART
NATIONAL MUSEUM OF INDIA
RABINDRA BHAVAN ART GALLERY
TIBET HOUSE MUSEUM
NOWGONG
STATE MUSEUM
PADMANABHAPURAM
MUSEUM OF ANTIQUITIES
PATIALA
STATE MUSEUM
PATNA
PATNA MUSEUM
POONA
BHARTIYA ITIHASA SAMSHODHAKA MANDALA MUSEUM
PUDDUKKOTTAI
GOVERNMENT MUSEUM
RAIPUR
MAHANT GHASI DASS MEMORIAL MUSEUM
SANGARIA
SIR CHOTURAM MUSEUM
SANTINIKETAN
KALA BHAVAN
SIKAR
SIKAR MUSEUM
SRINAGAR
S.P.S. MUSEUM
SRIRANGAM
DEVASTHANAMS MUSEUM
SURAT
SARDAR V. PATEL MUSEUM
TAL. KHATAV
SHRI BHAVANI MUSEUM AND LIBRARY
TANJORE
THE TANJORE ART GALLERY
TRIVANDRUM
ART MUSEUM
SRI CHITRA ART GALLERY
VALLABH VIDYANAGAR
MUSEUM OF ART AND ARCHAEOLOGY
VARANASI
BHARAT KALA BHAVAN
MAHARAJA BANARAS MUSEUM
VIDISHA
DISTRICT ARCHAEOLOGICAL MUSEUM
VIJAYAWADA
VICTORIA JUBILEE MUSEUM

INDONESIA

DJAKARTA
SEDJARAH MUSEUM
SANUR
MEMORIAL MUSEUM
SURAKARTA
ART MUSEUM
UBUD
MUSEUM PURI LUKISAN RATNAWARTHA

IRAN

ISFAHAN
CHEHEL SOTOUN MUSEUM
TEHERAN
ARCHAEOLOGICAL MUSEUM
GOLESTAN PALACE
NATIONAL ARTS MUSEUM

IRAQ

BAB-AL-SHARQUI
PICTURE GALLERY
BAGHDAD
BAGHDADI MUSEUM
NATIONAL MUSEUM OF MODERN ART

IRELAND

ADARE
ADARE MANOR
BANTRY
BANTRY HOUSE
CELBRIDGE
CASTLETOWN HOUSE
DUBLIN
MUNICIPAL GALLERY OF MODERN ART
NATIONAL GALLERY OF IRELAND
MAYNOOTH
CARTON
SLIGO
COUNTY SLIGO MUSEUM

ISRAEL

ASHDOT YA'AKOV
MUSEUM OF ART
BEERSHEBA
NEGEV MUSEUM
EILAT
MUSEUM OF MODERN ART
EIN-HAROD
MUSEUM OF ART
HAIFA
MUSEUM OF ANCIENT ART
MUSEUM OF MODERN ART
TIKOTIN MUSEUM OF JAPANESE ART
HAZOREA
WILFRID ISRAEL HOUSE FOR ORIENTAL ART AND STUDIES
JERUSALEM
BEIT HA'OMANIM
BEZALEL NATIONAL ART MUSEUM
BILLY ROSE ART GARDEN
L. A. MAYER MEMORIAL INSTITUTE FOR ISLAMIC ART
MUSEUM DOR VADOR
POLOMBO MUSEUM
NAHARIYA
MUSEUM OF ARCHAEOLOGY, HISTORY AND ART
NIR-DAVID
MUSEUM OF MEDITERRANEAN ARCHAEOLOGY
POST EMEK SOREK
SHEPHELA REGIONAL MUSEUM
SAFED
GILCENSTEIN MUSEUM

ITALY

ACIREALE
ART GALLERY
AGRIGENTO
MUNCIPAL MUSEUM
ANCONA
PODESTI PICTURE GALLERY
ANGERA
THE ROCCA
AQUILEIA
ARCHAEOLOGICAL MUSEUM
AREZZO
PICTURE GALLERY AND MUSEUM OF MEDIEVAL AND MODERN ART
VASARI'S HOUSE
ASCOLI PICENO
PICTURE GALLERY
ASSISI
MUNICIPAL ART GALLERY
BARI
REGIONAL ART GALLERY
BARLETTA
MUSEUM AND PICTURE GALLERY
BASSANO DEL GRAPPA
MUNICIPAL MUSEUM AND PICTURE GALLERY
BELLUNO
MUNICIPAL MUSEUM
BERGAMO
GALLERY OF CARRARA ACADEMY
BOLOGNA
COMMUNAL ART COLLECTIONS
DAVIA BARGELLINI ART GALLERY AND MUSEUM OF INDUSTRIAL ART
GALLERY OF MODERN ART
MUSEUM OF SANTO STEFANO
NATIONAL PICTURE GALLERY
BRESCIA
GALLERY OF MODERN ART
MUSEUM OF CHRISTIAN ART
TOSIO MARTINENGO PICTURE GALLERY
BRESSANONE
LIBRARY AND PICTURE GALLERY
BUDRIO
INZAGHI MUNICIPAL ART GALLERY
CADENABBIA
VILLA CARLOTTA
CAGLIARI
MUNICIPAL ART GALLERY
NATIONAL ARCHAEOLOGICAL MUSEUM
CAPRESE
MICHELANGELO MUSEUM
CAPUA
CAMPANO MUSEUM
CARRARA
MARMO MUSEUM
CASTELFIORENTINO
ART GALLERY

CATANIA
MUNICIPAL MUSEUM AND PICTURE GALLERY

CATANZARO
REGIONAL MUSEUM

CEFALÙ
MENDRALISCA MUSEUM

CITTÀ DI CASTELLO
MUNICIPAL ART GALLERY

CIVIDALE DEL FRIULI
NATIONAL ARCHAEOLOGICAL MUSEUM

COL DI RODI
RAMBALDI ART GALLERY

CORTONA
DIOCESAN MUSEUM
MUSEUM OF EGYPTIAN AND ETRUSCAN ANTIQUITIES

CREMONA
CATHEDRAL
ST. AUGUSTINE'S CHURCH

EMPOLI
ART GALLERY

ERICE
CORDICI CATALDO MUSEUM

FAENZA
MUNICIPAL MUSEUM AND PICTURE GALLERY

FELTRE
ART MUSEUM
RIZZARDA MUSEUM

FERRARA
CATHEDRAL MUSEUM
PICTURE GALLERY

FIESOLE
BANDINI MUSEUM

FLORENCE
"A. DELLA RAGIONE" MODERN ART COLLECTIONS
ARCHAEOLOGICAL MUSEUM
BARDINI MUSEUM AND CORSI GALLERY
BOBOLI GARDENS
CORSINI GALLERY
"FLORENCE AS IT WAS"
GALLERY OF THE ACADEMY
GALLERY OF THE OSPEDALE DEGLI INNOCENTI
HOUSE OF MICHELANGELO BUONARROTI
LOGGIA DELLA SIGNORIA
MEDICI MUSEUM
MODERN ART GALLERY
MONASTERY OF SANTA APOLLONIA
MUSEUM OF THE CATHEDRAL DI SANTA MARIA DEL FIORE
MUSEUM OF THE HORNE FOUNDATION
MUSEUM OF THE OLD FLORENTINE HOUSE
MUSEUM OF SAN MARCO
NATIONAL MUSEUM
ORSANMICHELE (TABERNACOLO)
PALATINE GALLERY
PALAZZO VECCHIO AND MONUMENTAL APARTMENTS
PERUGINO COLLECTION
SAN SALVI MONASTERY
SILVER MUSEUM
STIBBERT MUSEUM
UFFIZI GALLERY

FOGGIA
MUNICIPAL MUSEUM

FOLIGNO
ARCHAEOLOGICAL MUSEUM AND PICTURE GALLERY

FORLI
MUSEUM AND PICTURE GALLERY

GENOA
ART GALLERY
ART GALLERY
CHIOSSONE MUSEUM
LIGURIAN MUSEUM OF ARCHITECTURE AND SCULPTURE
MUSEUM OF MODERN ART
ROYAL PALACE (NOW BALBI- DURAZZO PALACE)
SPINOLA PALACE GALLERY
TREASURY

GUBBIO
MUSEUM AND PICTURE GALLERY

ISOLA BELLA
PALACE

JESI
PICTURE GALLERY

L'AQUILA
ABBRUZZO NATIONAL MUSEUM
DIOCESAN MUSEUM

LA VERNA
MONASTERY OF LA VERNA

LECCE
CASTROMEDIANO MUSEUM

LORETO
APOSTOLIC PALACE
TREASURY

LOVERE
TADINI MUSEUM

LUCCA
CIVIC MUSEUM
PICTURE GALLERY OF THE PALAZZO DUCALE

LUGANO
PICTURE GALLERY

MANTUA
CATHEDRAL
CAVRIANI PALACE
DUCAL PALACE
REGGIA DEI GONZAGA
MUSEUM OF MEDIEVAL AND MODERN ART

MESSINA
NATIONAL MUSEUM

MILAN
AMBROSIAN GALLERY
ARCHAEOLOGICAL MUSEUM
ACHILLE BERTARELLI COLLECTION
BRERA PICTURE GALLERY
CATHEDRAL MUSEUM
CONVENT REFECTORY
GALLERY OF CONTEMPORARY SACRED ART
GALLERY OF MODERN ART
MUSEUM OF ANCIENT ART
MUSEUM OF THE BASILICA OF SANT-AMBROGIO
MUSEUM OF FAR EASTERN ART AND ETHNOGRAPHY
POLDI-PEZZOLI MUSEUM

MODENA
CAMPORI GALLERY
CATHEDRAL LAPIDARY MUSEUM
CITY MUSEUM
ESTE GALLERY
LAPIDARY MUSEUM
POLETTI GALLERY

MONSELICE
ART COLLECTION

MONTALCINO
MUNICIPAL MUSEUM

MONTEPULCIANO
MUNICIPAL MUSEUM

MONZA
CATHEDRAL AND TREASURY
MUNICIPAL ART GALLERY

NAPLES
FILANGERI MUSEUM
GALLERY OF THE ACADEMY OF FINE ART
MUSEUM OF THE CARTHUSIAN MONASTERY OF ST. MARTIN
NATIONAL CERAMICS MUSEUM
NATIONAL GALLERY OF NAPLES
NATIONAL MUSEUM OF SAN MARTINO
PAGLIARA ART COLLECTION
ROYAL PALACE

NERVI
GALLERY OF MODERN ART

ORTE
MUSEUM OF SACRED ART

OSTIA ANTICA
DELLA ROCCA CASTLE AND MUSEUM

PADUA
MUNICIPAL MUSEUM

PALERMO
CASINA CINESE
DIOCESAN MUSEUM
GALLERY OF MODERN ART
NATIONAL GALLERY OF SICILY

PARMA
MUSEUM OF CHINESE ART
MUSEUM OF CHINESE ETHNOGRAPHY
NATIONAL GALLERY
PALATINE GALLERY
STUARD ART GALLERY

PAVIA
CARTHUSIAN MONASTERY MUSEUM
GALLERY OF MODERN ART
MALASPINA ART GALLERY
MUNICIPAL MUSEUM

PERUGIA
CHAPTERHOUSE MUSEUM
NATIONAL GALLERY OF UMBRIA

PESARO
MUNICIPAL MUSEUM

PESCIA
MUNICIPAL MUSEUM

PIACENZA
ALBERONI GALLERY
GIUSEPPE RICCI ODDI GALLERY OF MODERN ART
MUNICIPAL MUSEUM

PIENZA
MUSEUM

PIEVE DI CADORE
MUSEUM

PISA
CEMETERY
NATIONAL MUSEUM OF SAN MATTEO

PORDENONE
ART GALLERY

POSSAGNO
CANOVA MUSEUM

PRATO
MUNICIPAL GALLERY

RAVENNA
GALLERY OF THE ACADEMY OF FINE ART
NATIONAL MUSEUM OF ANTIQUITIES

RECANATI
DIOCESAN MUSEUM

REGGIO CALABRIA
NATIONAL MUSEUM

REGGIO EMILIA
CIVIC MUSEUM
PARMEGGIANI GALLERY

RIETI
MUNICIPAL MUSEUM

RIMINI
MUNICIPAL MUSEUM AND ART GALLERY

ROME
ACADEMY OF SAN LUCA
AURORA PALLAVICINI GALLERY
BARRACCO MUSEUM
BASILICA OF S. PAOLO FUORI LE MURA
BORGHESE GALLERY
BRACCIO NUOVO MUSEUM (VATICAN MUSEUMS)
CAPITOLINO MUSEUM
CHIARAMONTE MUSEUM (VATICAN MUSEUMS)
COLONNA GALLERY
CRISTIANO MUSEUM (VATICAN MUSEUMS)
DORIA PAMPHILJ GALLERY
EGIZIANO MUSEUM (VATICAN MUSEUMS)
ETRUSCAN MUSEUM (VATICAN MUSEUMS)
MEDIEVAL MUSEUM
MUSEUM OF THE PALAZZO DEI CONSERVATORI
MUSEUM OF THE PALAZZO VENEZIA
MUSEUM OF ROME
NATIONAL GALLERY OF ANCIENT ART
NATIONAL GALLERY OF MODERN ART
NATIONAL MUSEUM OF CASTEL SANT'ANGELO
NATIONAL MUSEUM OF ENGRAVINGS
NATIONAL MUSEUM OF ORIENTAL ART
NATIONAL MUSEUM OF VILLA GIULIA
PAOLINO MUSEUM (VATICAN MUSEUM)
PICTURE GALLERY (VATICAN MUSEUMS)
PIO-CLEMENTINO MUSEUM (VATICAN MUSEUMS)
RAPHAËL ROOMS (VATICAN MUSEUMS)
ROMAN NATIONAL MUSEUM
ST. PETER'S BASILICA, SACRISTY AND TREASURY
SISTINE CHAPEL (VATICAN MUSEUM)
SPADA GALLERY
TORLONIA MUSEUM
VILLA ALBANI MUSEUM

ROSSANO
DIOCESAN MUSEUM

ROVIGO
ART GALLERY OF THE CONCORDI ACADEMY

SAN GIMIGNANO
ART GALLERY
MUSEUM OF SACRED ART

SANSEPOLCRO
PICTURE GALLERY

SESTRI LEVANTE
RIZZI ART GALLERY

SIENA
ART MUSEUM
AURELIO CASTELLI MUSEUM
CATHEDRAL MUSEUM
GALLERY OF TUSCAN PAINTING
MUNICIPAL MUSEUM AND APARTMENTS
PICTURE GALLERY
PUBLIC LIBRARY

SORRENTO
CORREALE MUSEUM

SPOLETO

PICTURE GALLERY

STRA

VILLA NAZIONALE

SYRACUSE

MUSEUM OF ANCIENT AND MODERN ART

TERLIZZI

'DE NAPOLI' ART GALLERY

TERNI

MUSEUM AND ART GALLERY

TOLENTINO

INTERNATIONAL MUSEUM OF CARICATURES

TRAPANI

PEPOLI MUSEUM

TREMEZZO

VILLA CARLOTTA

TRENT

DIOCESAN MUSEUM
NATIONAL MUSEUM

TREVI

MUNICIPAL ART GALLERY

TREVISO

BAILO MUSEUM

TRIESTE

GALLERY OF ANCIENT ART
MUSEUM OF HISTORY AND ART
MUSEUM OF RELIGIOUS ART
REVOLTELLA MUSEUM

TURIN

ALBERTINA GALLERY
MUNICIPAL GALLERY OF MODERN ART
MUSEUM OF ANCIENT ART
ROYAL PALACE
SABAUDA GALLERY

UDINE

CASTLE MUSEUM AND PICTURE GALLERY

URBINO

NATIONAL GALLERY OF THE MARCHES
RAPHAËL'S HOUSE

VENICE

ACADEMY OF FINE ARTS
ARMENIAN MONASTERY
ART COLLECTION, SS. GIORGIO E TRIFONE
ART COLLECTION, SANTA MARIA
ART COLLECTION, SAN GIOUANNI
CORRER MUSEUM
DIPINTI MUSEUM OF SACRED BYZANTINE ART
THE FRANCHETTI GALLERY
PEGGY GUGGENHEIM COLLECTION
MANFREDIANA PICTURE GALLERY
MARCIANA LIBRARY
SCUOLA GRANDE DI SAN ROCCO
SETTECENTO MUSEUM

VERONA

MODERN ART GALLERY

VERRUCHIO

COMMUNAL GALLERY OF MODERN ART

VICENZA

MUNICIPAL MUSEUM
VILLA VALMARANA

VINCI

VINCIANO MUSEUM

VITERBO

MUNICIPAL MUSEUM

VOLTERRA

MUSEUM OF SACRED ART

JAMAICA

HALF-WAY TREE

DEVON HOUSE

KINGSTON

EXHIBITION GALLERY
WEST INDIA REFERENCE LIBRARY HISTORICAL GALLERY

JAPAN

AKASHI-SHI

MEMORIAL HALL OF THE EMPEROR MEIJI'S TEMPORARY HEADQUARTERS AT AKASHI

ATAMI-SHI

ATAMI ART MUSEUM

BEPPU

ANCIENT CULTURE MUSEUM, BEPPU UNIVERSITY

BEPPU-SHI

BEPPU MUNICIPAL MUSEUM OF ART
KINSUIEN ART MUSEUM

CHIKUFUJIMA

TREASURE HOUSE ON SHIKUFUJIMA ISLANDS

FUEDA

ART GALLERY OF THE TOKIWAYAMA FOUNDATION

HAKONE-MACHI

HAKONE ART MUSEUM
OPEN AIR MUSEUM

HIKONE-SHI

I'I ART MUSEUM

IWAKI-SHI

NAKASO ART MUSEUM

KAGOSHIMA-SHI

KAGOSHIMA MUNICIPAL MUSEUM OF ART

KAMAKURA-SHI

KAMAKURA NATIONAL TREASURE HOUSE
MODERN ART MUSEUM OF KANAGAWA PREFECTURE

KANAZAWA-MACHI

KANAZAWA BUNKO MUSEUM

KOBE-SHI

HAKUTSURU ART MUSEUM
KOBE MUNICIPAL MUSEUM OF ART

KORIYAMA-SHI

WATANABE SHINPO MEMORIAL HALL

KOYA-SAN

TREASURE HOUSE OF THE TEMPLES ON MT. KOYA

KURASHIKI-SHI

OHARA ART MUSEUM

KYOTO

FUJI'I COLLECTION
IKENO TAIGA ART MUSEUM
KYOTO MUNICIPAL MUSEUM OF ART
KYOTO NATIONAL MUSEUM
NATIONAL MUSEUM OF MODERN ART
SUMITOMO COLLECTION
YOGEN'IN TEMPLE
YURINKAN COLLECTION

MINAMIAZUMI-GUN

ROKUZAN ART MUSEUM

MITO-SHI

IBARAKI PREFECTURAL MUSEUM OF ART

NAGASAKI-SHI

NAGASAKI MUNICIPAL MUSEUM

NARA-SHI

HORYUJI TEMPLE
NARA NATIONAL MUSEUM
YAMATO CULTURAL HOUSE

ODAWARA-SHI

MATSUNAGA MEMORIAL HALL

OSAKA

FUJITA ART MUSEUM
ITSUO ART MUSEUM
MUNICIPAL ART MUSEUM
MUNICIPAL MUSEUM

OTARU-SHI

OTARU CITY MUSEUM

OTSU

SHIGA PREFECTURAL MUSEUM

SAKATA-SHI

HONMA ART MUSEUM

SENDAI-SHI

KAWAGUCHI TIBETAN COLLECTION OF TOHUKU UNIVERSITY

SUWA-SHI

SUWA MUNICIPAL MUSEUM OF ART

TAKAMATSU-SHI

TAKAMATSU MUNICIPAL MUSEUM OF ART

TAKAOKA-SHI

TAKAOKA MUNICIPAL MUSEUM OF ART

TOKYO

BRIDGESTONE MUSEUM OF ART
EXHIBITION HALL OF TOKYO UNIVERSITY OF ARTS LIBRARY AND MASAKI MEMORIAL HALL
GOTO ART MUSEUM
GYOKUDO ART MUSEUM
HATAKEYAMA COLLECTION
IDEMITSU ART GALLERY
KOMABA HIGH SCHOOL MUSEUM
MEIJI THE GREAT MEMORIAL GALLERY
MEIJI THE GREAT MEMORIAL HALL OF TAMA
MEIJI SHRINE TREASURE MUSEUM
METROPOLITAN KOMABA HIGH SCHOOL ART MUSEUM
MIAGEIKAN MUSEUM OF MODERN ART
MUSEUM OF ART AND HISTORY OF THE UNIVERSITY OF TOKYO
NATIONAL MUSEUM
NATIONAL MUSEUM OF MODERN ART
NATIONAL MUSEUM OF WESTERN ART
NEZU ART MUSEUM
OKURA MUSEUM
OKURA MUSEUM
PROFESSOR AIZU MEMORIAL EXHIBITION ROOM OF ORIENTAL ARTS
RYUSHI KAWABABA MUSEUM

TOYKO

TAKANAWA ART MUSEUM

TOKYO

TOKYO METROPOLITAN ART GALLERY
UMEZAWA MUSEUM
VISCOUNT KURODA MEMORIAL ROOM
YAMATANE MUSEUM OF ART

TOYOTA-GUN

KOZOJI TEMPLE MUSEUM

URAWA-SHI

SAITAMA PREFECTURAL MUSEUM OF ART

YOKOGOSHIMURA

HOPPO BUNKA MUSEUM

YOKOSUKA-SHI

YOKOSUKA CITY MUSEUM

YONEZAWA-SHI

TREASURE HOUSE OF THE UESUGI SHRINE

KENYA

NAIROBI

PAA-YA-PAA ART GALLERY

KOREA, DEMO. PEOPLE'S REP.

PYONGYANG

STATE CENTRAL FINE ARTS MUSEUM

KOREA, REPUBLIC OF

PUSAN

NATONAL UNIVERSITY MUSEUM

PUYO

NATIONAL MUSEUM

SEOUL

MUSEUM
NATIONAL MUSEUM
UNIVERSITY MUSEUM

TAEGU

UNIVERSITY MUSEUM

KUWAIT

KUWAIT

KUWAIT MUSEUM

LIECHTENSTEIN

VADUZ

STATE ART COLLECTION

LUXEMBOURG

LUXEMBOURG

STATE MUSEUM
JEAN-PIERRE PESCATORE MUSEUM

MALAGASY REPUBLIC

TANANARIVE

MUSEUM OF ART AND ARCHAEOLOGY

MALAYSIA

KUALA LUMPUR
NATIONAL MUSEUM

PENANG
PENANG MUSEUM AND ART GALLERY

MALTA

MDINA
CATHEDRAL MUSEUM

VALLETTA
NATIONAL MUSEUM
ST. JOHN'S MUSEUM AND CATHEDRAL

MEXICO

CULIACAN
SINALOA REGIONAL MUSEUM

GUADALAJARA
GUADALAJARA REGIONAL MUSEUM

GUANAJUATO
GUANAJUATO REGIONAL MUSEUM

MATAMOROS
MEXICAN MUSEUM

MEXICO CITY
CARMEL MUSEUM OF COLONIAL HISTORY
CONVENT OF SANTA MARIA DE LOS ANGELES
DIEGO RIVERA MUSEUM OF ANAHUACALLI
FRIDA KAHLO MUSEUM
MUNICIPAL SCULPTURE GALLERY
MUSEUM OF THE SCHOOL OF FINE ARTS
MUSEUM OF WESTERN MEXICAN CULTURE
NATIONAL HISTORICAL MUSEUM
NATIONAL MUSEUM OF MODERN ART
PALACE OF FINE ARTS
SAN CARLOS MUSEUM
SAN DIEGO MUSEUM OF MEXICAN (OOLONIAL) PAINTING

OAXACA
JUÁREZ HOUSE

PATZUCARO
MUSEUM OF FOLK ARTS AND CRAFTS

PUEBLA
MUSEUM OF THE ACADEMY OF FINE ART
JOSÉ LUIS BEELO Y GONZALEZ MUSEUM
PUEBLA REGIONAL MUSEUM
SANTA MONICA COLONIAL MUSEUM

QUERETARO
QUERETARO REGIONAL MUSEUM

SAN CRISTOBAL ECATEPEC
CASA DE MORELOS

TAXIO
LOCAL MUSEUM

TEPOZOTLAN
COLONIAL ART MUSEUM

TOLUCA
MUSEUM OF NATURAL HISTORY AND ARCHAEOLOGY

VILLAHERMOSA
PARK MUSEUM
TABASCO REGIONAL MUSEUM

MONACO

MONACO
ROYAL PALACE

MONTE CARLO
NATIONAL FINE ARTS MUSEUM
VILLA ISPAHAN

MOZAMBIQUE

LOURENÇO MARQUES
HISTORICAL MUSEUM

NEPAL

BHAKTAPUR
PICTURE GALLERY

KATHMANDU
NATIONAL MUSEUM OF NEPAL

NETHERLANDS

ALKMAAR
MUNICIPAL MUSEUM

ALPHEN AAN DEN RIJN
OLD ALPHEN MUSEUM

ALMEN
A. BONGER COLLECTION

AMERONGEN
COLLECTION OF THE HEIRS OF COUNT VAN ALDENBURG BENTINCK

AMSTERDAM
CITY MUSEUM
COLLECTION OF BARON VAN HEECKEREN VAN WALIEN
E. A. KLATTE COLLECTION
MUSEUM AMSTELKRING
NATIONAL MUSEUM: DEPARTMENT OF DUTCH HISTORY
NATIONAL MUSEUM: DEPARTMENT OF FAR-EASTERN ART
NATIONAL MUSEUM: DEPARTMENT OF PAINTINGS
NATIONAL MUSEUM: DEPARTMENT OF SCULPTURE AND INDUSTRIAL ART
NATIONAL MUSEUM: NATIONAL CABINET OF PRINTS AND DRAWINGS
E. PROEHL COLLECTION
REMBRANDT HOUSE
A. SCHWARTZ COLLECTION
SIX COLLECTION
DR. B. SLINGENBERG'S COLLECTION

ANGERLO
VAN WEEDE COLLECTION

APELDOORN
MOERMAN HISTORICAL MUSEUM

ARNHEM
LOCAL MUSEUM
VAN SIMMEREN VAN DER WEERD COLLECTION

BEETSTERZWAAG
VAN HARINXMA THOE SLOETEN FOUNDATION

BERGEN OP ZOOM
DISTRICT MUSEUM

BERLICUM
VAN RIJCKEVORSEL COLLECTION

BREDA
DIOCESAN MUSEUM
MUNICIPAL MUSEUM

BREUKELEN
GUNTERSTEIN RESIDENCE

BUSSUM
E. A. VELTMAN COLLECTION

COTTEN
BARON VAN HARDENBROEK COLLECTION

CULEMBORG
CULEMBORG AND DISTRICT MUSEUM OF LOCAL HISTORY

DALFSEN
VON MARTELS DANKERN AND RÖELL VAN HAZERWOUDE COLLECTION
VAN RECHTEREN LIMPURG COLLECTION

DELFT
PAUL TETAR VAN ELVEN MUSEUM
HET PRINSENHOF MUNICIPAL MUSEUM
MUSEUM OF THE HOUSE OF ORANGE-NASSAU

DENEKAMP
SINGRAVEN

DE STEEG
MIDDACHTEN CASTLE

DOORN
DOORN HOUSE

DOORNENBURG
DOORNENBURG CASTLE

DORDRECHT
BILDERBEEK-LAMAISON NATIONAL MUSEUM
DORDRECHTS MUSEUM

DRACHTEN
THE BLEACH HOUSE

EDAM
NIEUWENKAMP MUSEUM

EINDHOVEN
KEMPENLAND MUSEUM
VAN ABBE MUNICIPAL MUSEUM

ENKHUIZEN
NATIONAL ZUIDERZEE MUSEUM

ENSCHEDE
TWENTE NATIONAL MUSEUM

FRANEKER
DR. COOPMAN'S HOUSE MUNICIPAL MUSEUM

GOUDA
CATHARINA INN MUNICIPAL MUSEUM

'S GRAVENHAGE
D. H. G. BOLTEN COLLECTION
BREDIUS MUSEUM
HENDRIK WILLEM MESDAG NATIONAL MUSEUM
MESDAG PANORAMA
MUNICIPAL MUSEUM
ROYAL GALLERY OF PAINTINGS: MAURITSHUIS
THURKOW COLLECTION

HAARLEM
DIOCESAN MUSEUM OF RELIGIOUS ART
FRANS HALS MUSEUM
TEYLER'S MUSEUM
TOWN HALL

HAARZUILENS
VAN ZUYLEN VAN NIJVELT VAN DE HAAN COLLECTION

'S HEERENBERG
BERGH HOUSE

HEEZE
VAN TUYLL VAN SEROOSKERKEN VAN HEEZE EN LEENDE COLLECTION

HEINO
HANNEMA-DE STUERS FOUNDATION

LAREN
SINGER MUSEUM

LEEUWARDEN
FRISIAN MUSEUM
PIER PANDER MUSEUM
PIER PANDER TEMPLE
HET PRINCESSEHOF LOCAL MUSEUM

LEIDEN
LAKENHAL MUNICIPAL MUSEUM
MEERMANSBURG
PRINT CABINET OF THE NATIONAL UNIVERSITY

LOOSDRECHT
SYPESTEYN CASTLE MUSEUM

MAASTRICHT
BONNEFANTEN MUSEUM
T. J. BOTKE COLLECTION
TREASURY OF THE BASILICA OF OUR LADY
TREASURY OF ST. SERVAAS CHURCH

MARSSUM
HERINGA STATE

MIDDELBURG
ZEALAND MUSEUM

MUIDEN
MUIDEN CASTLE NATIONAL MUSEUM

NAALDWIJK
WESTLAND DISTRICT MUSEUM

OSS
JAN CUNEN MUSEUM

OTTERLOO
KROLLER-MULLER NATIONAL MUSEUM

OUD-ZUILEN
ZUYLEN CASTLE

ROSENDAAL
MUSEUM OF THE GOLDEN ROSE

ROTTERDAM
ATLAS VAN STOCK FOUNDATION
BOYMANS AND VAN BEUNIGEN MUSEUM
CHABOT MUSEUM
HISTORICAL MUSEUM
WILLEM VAN DER VORM FOUNDATION

SCHIEDAM
MUNICIPAL MUSEUM

SCHIPLUIDEN
H. JUNGELING COLLECTION

SCHOONHAVEN
MUNICIPAL COLLECTIONS OF ANTIQUITIES

SLUIS
TOWN LOCAL HISTORY COLLECTION

SOMMELSDIJK
GOEREE AND OVERFLAKEE DISTRICT MUSEUM

TIEL
TIEL AND DISTRICT LOCAL HISTORY MUSEUM

UTRECHT
VAN BAAREN MUSEUM
CENTRAL MUSEUM
DIOCESAN MUSEUM

MUSEUM OF MODERN RELIGIOUS ART

VENLO

GOLTZIUS MUSEUM

VLIELAND

TROMP HOUSE

VLISSINGEN

MUNICIPAL MUSEUM

VOORSCHOTEN

DUIVENSVOORDE CASTLE

VORDEN

VICTOR DE STUERS COLLECTION

ZOELEN

SOELEN CASTLE

ZWOLLE

OVERIJSSEL PROVINCIAL MUSEUM

NEW ZEALAND

AUCKLAND

AUCKLAND CITY ART GALLERY

CHRISTCHURCH

CANTERBURY MUSEUM
CANTERBURY PUBLIC LIBRARY
ROBERT MCDOUGALL ART GALLERY

DUNEDIN

DUNEDIN PUBLIC ART GALLERY
DUNEDIN PUBLIC LIBRARY
HOCKEN LIBRARY
OTAGO EARLY SETTLERS' ASSOCIATION (INC)
THE THEOMIN GALLERY (OLVESTON)

GISBORNE

ART GALLERY AND MUSEUM

HAMILTON

WAIKATO GALLERY

INVERCARGILL

INVERCARGILL PUBLIC ART GALLERY

LOWER HUTT

THE DOWSE ART GALLERY

MASTERTON

WAIRARAPA ARTS CENTRE

MATAKOHE

OTAMATEA KAURI AND PIONEER MUSEUM

NAPIER

HAWKE'S BAY ART GALLERY AND MUSEUM

NEW PLYMOUTH

GOVETT-BREWSTER ART GALLERY

PAIHIA

TREATY HOUSE

PALMERSTON NORTH

PALMERSTON NORTH ART GALLERY

TIMARU

AIGANTIGHE ART GALLERY

WANGANUI

SARJEANT ART GALLERY
WANGANUI PUBLIC MUSEUM

WELLINGTON

ALEXANDER TURNBULL LIBRARY
NATIONAL ART GALLERY

NIGERIA

BENIN CITY

BENIN MUSEUM

ESIE

ESIE MUSEUM

IFE

IFE MUSEUM

KANO

MAKAMA'S HOUSE

LAGOS

NIGERIAN MUSEUM

ORON

ORON MUSEUM

OWO

OWO MUSEUM

NORWAY

BERGEN

BERGEN ART GALLERY
HISTORICAL MUSEUM
MUNICIPAL ART MUSEUM

DRAMMEN

ART GALLERY

HAUGESUND

HAUGESUND GALLERY

HORNINDAL

THE ANDERS SVOR MUSEUM

HØVIKODDEN

SONJA HENIE AND NIELS ONSTAD FOUNDATION

KAUPANGER

HEIBERG COLLECTION

KRAGERØ

BERG-KRAGERØ MUSEUM

LILLEHAMMER

LILLEHAMMER MUNICIPAL ART GALLERY

MANDAL

MANDAL MUSEUM

OSLO

HISTORICAL MUSEUM
MUNCH MUSEUM
NATIONAL GALLERY
VIGELAND SCULPTURE PARK AND MUSEUM

ØYSTESE

INGEBRIGT VIK MUSEUM

STAVANGER

ART GALLERY

TRONDHEIM

TRONDHEIM ART ASSOCIATION GALLERY

VANSE

LISTA MUSEUM

PAKISTAN, WEST

KARACHI

AIWEN-E-RIFAF MUSEUM AND ART GALLERY
NATIONAL MUSEUM OF PAKISTAN

LAHORE

LAHORE MUSEUM
LAHORE FORT MUSEUM

RAWALPINDI

RAWALPINDI GALLERY OF MODERN ART

PARAGUAY

ASUNCION

MONSEÑOR SINFORIANO BAGARIN MUSEUM
MUSEUM OF FINE ARTS AND ANTIQUITIES

ITAUGUÁ

MUSEUM OF ICONOGRAPHY

PERU

AREQUIPA

CATALINA CONVENT

LIMA

MUNICIPAL ART GALLERY
MUSEUM OF ART
MUSEUM OF ITALIAN ART
MUSEUM OF MILITARY HISTORY
MUSEUM OF SAN FRANCISCO THE GREAT

RIMAC

COLONIAL MUSEUM

SACSAYHUAMAN

ARCHAEOLOGICAL MUSEUM

PHILIPPINES

PASAY CITY

LOPEZ MEMORIAL MUSEUM

QUEZON CITY

ATENEO ART GALLERY

POLAND

BYDGOSZCZ

LEON WYCZÓŁKOWSKI MEMORIAL MUSEUM

BYTOM

MUSEUM OF UPPER SILESIA

CHORZÓW

CHORZÓW MUSEUM

CZĘSTOCHOWA

MUNICIPAL MUSEUM

GDAŃSK

POMERANIAN MUSEUM

GLIWICE

GLIWICE MUSEUM

GOŁUCHÓW

GOŁUCHÓW MUSEUM

GRUDZIĄDZ

MUNICIPAL MUSEUM

ISTEBNA NA KUBALONCE

MUSEUM OF RELIGIOUS ART

JELENIA GÓRA

REGIONAL MUSEUM

KĘTRZYN

KĘTRZYN MUSEUM

KIELCE

MUSEUM OF THE HOLY CROSS
ŚWIĘTOKRZYKIE MUSEUM

KÓRNIK

KÓRNIK MUSEUM

KRAKÓW

CLOTH-HALL MUSEUM
CZAPSKI MUSEUM
CZARTORYSKI MUSEUM
GRAPHICS COLLECTION OF THE POLISH ACADEMY OF SCIENCES
MUSEUM OF THE JAGELLONIAN LIBRARY
NATIONAL ART COLLECTIONS
NEW BUILDING
SZOŁAYSKI HOUSE
UNIVERSITY MUSEUM OF FINE ART

KROŚNIEWICE

COLLECTIONS OF JERZY DUNIN- BORKOWSKI

ŁAŃCUT

REGIONAL MUSEUM

LEGNICA

REGIONAL MUSEUM

ŁÓDŹ

MUSEUM OF FINE ART

NIDZICA

REGIONAL MUSEUM

NIEBORÓW I ARKADIA

NIEBORÓW PALACE

NOWY SĄCZ

REGIONAL MUSEUM

NYSA

REGIONAL MUSEUM

OPOLE

SILESIAN MUSEUM

PELPIN

DIOCESAN MUSEUM

PŁOCK

DIOCESAN MUSEUM

PODDĘBICE

REGIONAL MUSEUM

POZNAŃ

DIOCESAN MUSEUM
MUSEUM OF DECORATIVE ARTS
POZNAŃ NATIONAL MUSEUM
POZNAŃ HISTORICAL MUSEUM

PRZEMYŚL

DIOCESAN MUSEUM

PSZCZYNA

PALACE MUSEUM

PUŁAWY

REGIONAL MUSEUM

PUŁTUSK

REGIONAL MUSEUM

RACIBÓRZ
MUNICIPAL MUSEUM
RADOM
MUNICIPAL MUSEUM
RADZYN CHEŁMIŃSKI
REGIONAL MUSEUM
ROGALIN
LOCAL MUSEUM
SANDOMIERZ
DIOCESAN MUSEUM
SANOK
SANOK MUSEUM
SIERADZ
SIERADZ MUSEUM
SZCZYRZYC
LOCAL MUSEUM
TARNÓW
DIOCESAN MUSEUM
TARNOW
MUNICIPAL MUSEUM
TORUŃ
MUSEUM OF ART
REGIONAL MUSEUM
SCULPTURE GALLERY
WARSAW
CABINET OF PRINTS AND ENGRAVINGS OF THE UNIVERSITY OF WARSAW
WARREN XAVIER DUNIKOWSKI MUSEUM
GRAPHICS COLLECTION OF THE NATIONAL LIBRARY
ŁAZIENKACH MUSEUM
ADAM MICKIEWICZ MUSEUM
MUSEUM OF THE HISTORY OF THE CITY OF WARSAW
NATIONAL MUSEUM
WROCŁAW
ARCHIDIOCESAN MUSEUM
CABINET OF PRINTS AND DRAWINGS
NATIONAL MUSEUM
WSCHOWA
REGIONAL MUSEUM

PORTUGAL

ALPIARÇA
MUSEUM
AMARANTE
MUSEUM
AVEIRO
REGIONAL MUSEUM
BEJA
REGIONAL MUSEUM
BRAGA
MUSEUM OF RELIGIOUS ART
TREASURY
CALDAS DA RAINHA
MALHOA MUSEUM
CARAMULO
ART MUSEUM
COIMBRA
MACHADO DE CASTRO MUSEUM
OLD CATHEDRAL
ELVAS
REGIONAL MUSEUM
ÉVORA
MUSEUM OF ANCIENT ART
FUNCHAL
MUSEUM OF RELIGIOUS ART
GUIMARÃES
PALACE OF THE DUKES OF BRAGANCA
LAMEGO
REGIONAL MUSEUM
LISBON
CALOUSTE GULBENKIAN MUSEUM
MUSEUM OF CONTEMPORARY ART
MUSEUM OF RELIGIOUS ART
NATIONAL MUSEUM OF ANCIENT ART
LISON
RAFAEL BORDALO PINHEIRO MUSEUM
OPORTO
SOARES DOS REIS MUSEUM
SETUBAL
MUNICIPAL MUSEUM
VIANA DO CASTELO
MUNICIPAL MUSEUM
VILA REAL DE SANTO ANTONIO
DUCAL PALACE
VISEU
GRÃO VASCO MUSEUM

RÉUNION

SAINT-DENIS
LÉON DIERX FINE ARTS MUSEUM

RHODESIA

SALISBURY
RHODES NATIONAL GALLERY

ROMANIA

ARAD
ARAD MUSEUM
BABADAG
LOCAL MUSEUM
BACĂU
MUSEUM OF ART
BAIA MARE
MARAMUREŞ DISTRICT MUSEUM
BEREVOIEŞTI
BEREVOIEŞTI MUSEUM
BRAŞOV
BRAŞOV MUSEUM
ST. NICOLAE SCHOOL MUSEUM
BUCHAREST
THEODOR AMAN MUSEUM
ART MUSEUM
'BUCHAREST AS SEEN BY ARTISTS'
CABINET OF PRINTS AND ENGRAVINGS
ELENA AND DR. I. N. DONA COLLECTION
I. ISER COLLECTION OF PAINTINGS
CORNEL MEDREA MUSEUM
ING. MINOVICI MUSEUM OF MEDIEVAL ART
ION MINULESCU COLLECTION
MOGOŞOAIA MUSEUM OF THE ART OF THE BRÂNCOVEANU PERIOD
G. OPRESCU COLLECTION
MARIA AND DR. G. SEVEREANU COLLECTION
ANASTASE SIMU ART MUSEUM
STATE ARCHIVES MUSEUM
TOMA STELIAN MUSEUM
CECILIA AND FREDERIC STORCK MUSEUM
G. L. TATTARESCU MEMORIAL MUSEUM
MOISE M. WEINBURG COLLECTION
ZAMBACCIAN MUSEUM
CARACAL
CARACAL MUSEUM
CÎMPINA
NICOLAE GRIGORESCU MUSEUM
CÎMPULUNG
CÎMPULUNG-MUSCEL MUSEUM
CLUJ
ART MUSEUM
CONSTANŢA
DUBROGEA MUSEUM OF ART
CRAIOVA
ART MUSEUM
FĂLTICENI
FĂLTICENI MUSEUM
FILIAŞI
BRANCUSI MUSEUM
FOCŞANI
HISTORY MUSEUM
GALAŢI
MUSEUM OF MODERN AND CONTEMPORARY ROMANIAN ART
IAŞI
MUSEUM OF ART
LIMANU
LOCAL MUSEUM
MANGALIA
ARCHAEOLOGICAL MUSEUM
MEDGIDIA
LOCAL MUSEUM
ORADEA
ORIŞANA MUSEUM
PIATRA NEAMŢ
MUSEUM OF ARCHAEOLOGY
PITEŞTI
ARGES DISTRICT MUSEUM
PITEŞTI MUSEUM
PLOIEŞTI
MUSEUM OF ART
HAGI PRODAN HOUSE
RIMNICU SARAT
RIMNICU SARAT MUSEUM
RÎMNICU VILCEA
RÎMNICU VILCEA MUSEUM
ROMAN
ROMAN MUSEUM
SATU MARE
SATU MARE MUSEUM
SFINTU GHEORGHE
SFINTU GHEORGHE MUSEUM
SIBIU
BRUKENTHAL MUSEUM
SINAIA
PELEŞ MUSEUM
TIMIŞOARA
BANAT MUSEUM
TÎRGU MUREŞ
MUSEUM OF ART
TÎRGU NEAMŢ
MONASTERY MUSEUM
TOPALU
LOCAL MUSEUM
URLAŢI
MUSEUM OF ETHNOGRAPHY
VĂLENII DE MUNTE
NICOLAE IORGA MUSEUM
ZALĂU
ZALĂU MUSEUM

RWANDA

NYUNDO/GISENYI
NYUNDO SCHOOL OF ART

SAN MARINO, REPUBLIC OF

SAN MARINO
GOVERNMENT MUSEUM AND PICTURE-GALLERY
SAN FRANCESCO ART GALLERY

SINGAPORE

SINGAPORE
ART MUSEUM AND EXHIBITION GALLERY
NATIONAL MUSEUM

SOUTH AFRICA, REPUBLIC OF

ALICE
E. S. MALAN ETHNOGRAPHICAL MUSEUM
CAPE TOWN
GROOT CONSTANTIA MANOR HOUSE
CAPETOWN
KOOPMANS DE WET HOUSE
CAPE TOWN
MICHAELIS COLLECTION
RUST EN VREUGD
SOUTH AFRICAN CULTURAL HISTORY MUSEUM
SOUTH AFRICAN NATIONAL GALLERY
DURBAN
DURBAN MUSEUM AND ART GALLERY
WILLIAM CAMPBELL MUSEUM
EAST LONDON
ANN BRYANT ART GALLERY

GRAAFF-REINET
HESTER RUPERT ART MUSEUM

GRAHAMSTOWN
ALBANY MUSEUM

JOHANNESBURG
AFRICANA MUSEUM
JOHANNESBURG ART GALLERY

KIMBERLEY
WILLIAM HUMPHREYS ART GALLERY

PIETERMARITZBURG
TATHAM ART GALLERY

PORT ELIZABETH
KING GEORGE VI ART GALLERY

PRETORIA
PRETORIA ART MUSEUM

RIVERSDALE
JULIUS GORDON AFRICANA CENTRE

SOUTH-WEST AFRICA (NAMIBIA)

WINDHOEK
ART GALLERY

SPAIN

ALBARRACIN
CATHEDRAL

ALBOCACER
PAROCHIAL MUSEUM

AMPUDIA
FONTANEDA COLLECTION

ARANJUEZ
ROYAL PALACE

ARCOS DE LA FRONTERA
PARISH MUSEUM AND TREASURY

ASTORGA
DIOCESAN AND CATHEDRAL MUSEUM

AVILA
CATHEDRAL MUSEUM
MUSEUM OF ORIENTAL ART
PROVINCIAL MUSEUM

AYLLON
MUNICIPAL MUSEUM

BADAJOZ
DIOCESAN AND CATHEDRAL MUSEUM
PROVINCIAL MUSEUM OF FINE ART

BALSARENY
COLLECTION OF PAINTING AND HISTORY

BARCELONA
AMATLLER INSTITUTE OF SPANISH ART
CAMBÓ COLLECTION AND MUSEUM OF DECORATIVE ART
CATHEDRAL MUSEUM
CLARÁ MUSEUM
DIOCESAN MUSEUM
FEDERICO MARES MUSEUM
MONASTERY OF SANTA MARIA DE PEDRALBES
MUSEUM OF CATALONIAN ART
MUSEUM OF ETHNOLOGY
MUSEUM OF THE HISTORY OF THE CITY OF BARCELONA
MUSEUM OF MODERN ART
PALACIO DE PEDRALBES
PICASSO MUSEUM

BARCO DE AVILA
PAROCHIAL MUSEUM

BEJAR
MUNICIPAL MUSEUM

BILBAO
MUSEUM OF FINE ART
MUSEUM OF MODERN ART
MUSEUM OF REPRODUCTIONS OF WORKS OF ART

BURGO DE OSMA
CATHEDRAL MUSEUM

BURGOS
DIOCESAN AND CATHEDRAL MUSEUM
MARCELIANO SANTA MARIA MUSEUM
PROVINCIAL ARCHAEOLOGICAL MUSEUM

CADIZ
CATHEDRAL MUSEUM
PROVINCIAL MUSEUM OF FINE ART

CALAHORRA
CATHEDRAL AND DIOCESAN MUSEUM AND TREASURY

CASTELLON
PROVINCIAL MUSEUM OF FINE ART

COLMENAR DE OREJA
CHECA MUNICIPAL MUSEUM

CORDOBA
CATHEDRAL MUSEUM AND TREASURY
JULIO ROMERO DE TORRES MUSEUM
PALACE OF THE MARQUISES OF VIANA
PROVINCIAL ARCHAEOLOGICAL MUSEUM
PROVINCIAL MUSEUM OF FINE ART

LA CORUÑA
PROVINCIAL MUSEUM OF FINE ART

COVARRUBIAS
PAROCHIAL MUSEUM

CREVILLENTE
MUNICIPAL MUSEUM

CUENCA
CASA COLGADAS

EL ESCORIAL
MONASTERY OF SAN LORENZO DE EL ESCORIAL

ESTELLA
GUSTAVO DE MAEZTU MUSEUM

FIGUERAS
MUSEUM OF THE AMPURDÁN

GERONA
CATHEDRAL MUSEUM AND TREASURY
DIOCESAN MUSEUM
PROVINCIAL ARCHAEOLOGICAL MUSEUM

GIJON
JOVELLANOS MUSEUM

GRANADA
ART COLLECTION
BASILICA OF SAN JUAN DE DIOS
CHARTERHOUSE OF THE ASSUMPTION
MUSEUM OF THE CATHOLIC KINGS
PROVINCIAL MUSEUM OF FINE ART

ILLESCAS
HOSPITAL AND SANCTUARY OF OUR LADY OF CHARITY

JAÉN
PROVINCIAL MUSEUM

LAS PALMAS
COLUMBUS HOUSE-MUSEUM
PROVINCIAL MUSEUM OF FINE ART

LEÓN
CATHEDRAL MUSEUM
DIOCESAN MUSEUM OF RELIGIOUS ART

LERIDA
CATHEDRAL MUSEUM
DIOCESAN MUSEUM
JAIME MORERA MUSEUM OF MODERN ART

LOGROÑO
PROVINCIAL MUSEUM

LUGO
CATHEDRAL MUSEUM AND TREASURY

MADRID
ABBEY OF SAN ANTONIO
CABINET OF ANTIQUITIES
CERRALBO MUSEUM
COLLECTION OF THE FACULTY OF PHILOSOPHY AND LETTERS
COLLECTION OF THE HOUSE OF ALBA
COLLECTION OF PAINTINGS
CONVENT OF LAS DESCALZAS REALES
LAZARO GALDIANO MUSEUM
MUNICIPAL COLLECTION
MUNICIPAL MUSEUM
MUSEUM OF ICONOGRAPHY
MUSEUM OF THE ROMANTIC PERIOD
NATIONAL MUSEUM OF CONTEMPORARY ENGRAVING
NATIONAL MUSEUM OF PAINTING AND SCULPTURE
PALACIO DE ORIENTE
PANTEON DE GOYA
ROYAL LIBRARY
ROYAL PALACE
SAN FERNANDO FINE ARTS ACADEMY MUSEUM
SOROLLA MUSEUM
SPANISH MUSEUM OF CONTEMPORARY ART
ZULOAGA'S STUDIO

MALAGA
PROVINCIAL MUSEUM OF FINE ART

MARCHENA
PAROCHIAL MUSEUM

MARTIN MUÑOZ DE LAS POSADAS
CARDINAL ESPINOSA MUSEUM

MONTSERRAT
MUSEUM

MURCIA
PROVINCIAL MUSEUM OF FINE ART
SALZILLO MUSEUM

OLOT
MUSEUM OF MODERN ART
PAROCHIAL MUSEUM AND TREASURY

PALMA DE MALLORCA
DIOCESAN MUSEUM
KREKOVIC COLLECTION
VIVOT COLLECTION

PAMPLONA
NAVARRA MUSEUM

PARADAS
PAROCHIAL MUSEUM

PERELADA
MATEU COLLECTION

POLLENSA
HOUSE AND STUDIO OF THE PAINTER, HERMENE ANGLADA CAMARASA

PONTEVEDRA
PONTEVEDRA MUSEUM

QUESADA
ZABALETA MUSEUM

RODA DE ISABENA
PAROCHIAL MUSEUM

RONCESVALLES
MUSEUM OF ART

SALAMANCA
DIOCESAN MUSEUM
MUSEUM OF THE CONVENT OF ST. URSULA
PROVINCIAL MUSEUM OF FINE ART

SAN JUAN DE VILASAR
MONJÓ GALLERY

SAN SEBASTIAN
CASA DE UQUENDO
MUNICIPAL MUSEUM OF SAN TELMO

SANTA CRUZ
PROVINCIAL MUSEUM OF FINE ART

SANTA EULALIA DEL RIO
BARRAU MUSEUM

SANTANDER
MUNICIPAL MUSEUM OF FINE ART

SEGORBE
DIOCESAN AND CATHEDRAL MUSEUM

SEGOVIA
CATHEDRAL MUSEUM
PALACIO DE RIOFRIO
PROVINCIAL MUSEUM OF FINE ART

SEO DE URGEL
DIOCESAN MUSEUM

SEVILLE
ALCAZAR
CATHEDRAL MUSEUM
HOLY WEEK MUSEUM
MUSEUM OF CONTEMPORARY ART
OSUNA COLLECTION
PROVINCIAL MUSEUM OF FINE ART

SIGÜENZA
CATHEDRAL MUSEUM

SITGES
MUSEUM OF CAU FERRAT

SOLSONA
DIOCESAN ARCHAEOLOGICAL MUSEUM

TARRAGONA
DIOCESAN MUSEUM
MUSEUM OF FOLK ART AND CUSTOMS
PROVINCIAL ARCHAEOLOGICAL MUSEUM

TARRASA
BIOSCA TEXTILE MUSEUM

TOLEDO
EL GRECO MUSEUM
MUSEUM OF THE DUKE OF LERMA'S FOUNDATION
MUSEUM OF THE PARISH OF SANTO TOME
SANTA CRUZ MUSEUM
VICTORIO MACHO HOUSE MUSEUM

TOSSA
MUNICIPAL MUSEUM

TUDELA
DIOCESAN MUSEUM

VALDEPEÑAS
GREGORIO PRIETO MILL- MUSEUM

VALENCIA

BENLLIURE HOUSE-MUSEUM
DIOCESAN AND CATHEDRAL MUSEUM
MUSEUM OF THE PATRIARCH
PROVINCIAL MUSEUM OF FINE ART

VALLADOLID

HOUSE OF ZORRILLA
MUSEUM OF THE MISSIONS
MUSEUM OF PAINTINGS
NATIONAL MUSEUM OF SCULPTURE
PROVINCIAL MUSEUM OF ARCHAEOLOGY

VICH

EPISCOPAL MUSEUM OF ART AND ARCHAEOLOGY

VILLAGARCIA DE CAMPOS

MUSEUM OF THE COLLEGIATE CHURCH

VILLANUEVA Y GELTRU

VICTOR BALAGUER MUSEUM

VITORIA

ALAVA PROVINCIAL MUSEUM

ZAMORA

CATHEDRAL MUSEUM
PROVINCIAL MUSEUM OF FINE ART

ZARAGOZA

BASILICA OF NOSTRA SENORA DEL PILAR
CATHEDRAL MUSEUM
PROVINCIAL MUSEUM OF FINE ART

SRI LANKA, REPUBLIC OF

ANURADHAPURA

FOLK MUSEUM

COLOMBO

NATIONAL MUSEUM

RATNAPURA

NATIONAL MUSEUM

SWEDEN

ASKERSUND

STJERNSUND CASTLE

BORÅS

BORÅS MUSEUM OF ART

ESKILSTUNA

ESKILSTUNA MUSEUM OF ART

GÄVLE

GÄVLE MUSEUM

GÖTEBORG

GÖTEBORG ART GALLERY
HISTORICAL MUSEUM

HÄLSINGBORG

VIKINGSBERG ART MUSEUM

HÄRNÖSAND

MUSEUM OF CULTURAL HISTORY

HUDIKSVALL

HÄLSINGLANDS MUSEUM

JÖNKÖPING

JÖNKÖPING MUSEUM

LINKÖPING

LINKÖPING MUSEUM

LUND

ARCHIVES OF DECORATIVE ART
UNIVERSITY ART GALLERY

MALMÖ

MALMÖ MUSEUM

MARIEFRED

GRIPSHOLM CASTLE

MORA

ZORN HOUSE-MUSEUM
ZORN MUSEUM

NORRKÖPING

NORRKÖPING MUSEUM

NYKÖPING

SÖDERMANLAND COUNTY MUSEUM

ÖREBRO

ÖREBRO MUSEUM

ÖSTERSUND

MUNICIPAL MUSEUM AND OLOF AHLBERGS GALLERY

ROTHNEROS

ROTHNEROS PARK

SKOKLOSTER

SKOKLOSTER CASTLE

STOCKHOLM

DROTTNINGHOLM PALACE
ELDH'S STUDIO-MUSEUM
GUSTAV III'S COLLECTION OF ANTIQUITIES
HALLWYL MUSEUM
KARL-JOHAN'S MUSEUM
MILLES MUSEUM
MUSEUM OF MODERN ART
NATIONAL MUSEUM
PRINCE EUGEN'S HOUSE
THIEL ART GALLERY

SUNDBORN

CARL LARSSON HOUSE-MUSEUM

UDDEVALLA

UDDEVALLA MUSEUM

UMEA

VÄSTERBOTTEN MUSEUM

VÄNERSBORG

VÄNERSBORG MUSEUM

YSTAD

ART MUSEUM

SWITZERLAND

AARAU

AARGAU ART MUSEUM

ALTDORF

URI HISTORICAL MUSEUM

APPENZELL

REGIONAL MUSEUM

ASCONA

MARIANNE WEREFKIN MUSEUM

BADEN

HISTORICAL MUSEUM

BASEL

ART GALLERY
HISTORICAL MUSEUM
MUSEUM OF GREEK AND ROMAN ART
PUBLIC ART COLLECTION

BERN

ART MUSEUM
BERN HISTORICAL MUSEUM

BRIEG

CASTLE OF THE STOCKALPERS

BRUGG

STÄBLIS MUSEUM

BULLE

MUSEUM OF THE GRUYÈRE DISTRICT

BURGDORF

HISTORICAL MUSEUM OF THE BURGDORF HALL OF THE KNIGHTS SOCIETY

CASTAGNOLA

SCHLOSS ROHONCZ COLLECTION

CHÂTEAU D'OEX

MUSEUM OF THE FORMER PAYS D'ENHAUT AND OF THE AUGUST COTTIER FOUNDATION

LA CHAUX- DE-FONDS

MUSEUM OF FINE ART AND MUSEUM OF ETHNOGRAPHY
MUSEUM OF HISTORY, COINS AND MEDALS

CHUR

ART COLLECTION
MUNICIPAL MUSEUM

COPPET

CHÂTEAU COPPET AND MUSEUM OF THE SWISS WHO SERVED ABROAD

DAVOS

ERNST LUDWIG KIRCHNER HOUSE

DELÉMONT

JURA MUSEUM

DIESSENHOFEN

LOCAL MUSEUM

DISENTIS

COLLECTION OF THE BENEDICTINE ABBEY

EBNAT-KAPPEL

ALBERT EDELMANN FOUNDATION

ENGELBERG

ANTIQUITIES COLLECTION OF THE BENEDICTINE ABBEY

EVOLÈNE

FOLKLORE MUSEUM

FRAUENFELD

CANTON THURGAU MUSEUM
PUBLIC ART COLLECTION

FRIBOURG

FINE ART GALLERY
MUSEUM OF ART AND HISTORY
PRINT COLLECTION

GELFINGEN

HEIDEGG CASTLE

GENEVA

ARIANA MUSEUM
BAUR COLLECTION
COLLECTION OF PRINTS AND ENGRAVINGS
MUSEUM OF ART AND HISTORY
MUSEUM OF THE ATHENEUM
PETIT PALAIS

GLARUS

ART GALLERY

GRUYÈRES

CHÂTEAU

JEGENSTORF

SCHLOSS JEGENSTORF

KÖLLIKEN

ICON COLLECTION

LAUSANNE

CANTONAL MUSEUM OF FINE ART
CATHEDRAL MUSEUM
HISTORICAL MUSEUM OF THE OLD BISHOPRIC
MON REPOS MUSEUM
MUSEUM OF DECORATIVE ARTS

LENZBURG

CANTONAL HISTORICAL COLLECTION
REGIONAL MUSEUM

LICHTENSTEIG

TOGGENBURG REGIONAL MUSEUM

LIESTAL

BASEL-LAND CANTONAL MUSEUM

LIGORNETTO

VELA MUSEUM

LOCARNO

MUNICIPAL MUSEUM

LE LOCLE

FINE ART MUSEUM
ALEXANDRE GIROD MUSEUM

LOCO

MUSEUM OF THE ONSERNONE VALLEY

LUGANO

MUSEUM OF FINE ART, CACCIA FOUNDATION
MUSEUM OF HISTORY AND ARCHAEOLOGY

LUZERN

ART MUSEUM
HISTORICAL MUSEUM

MÖRIKEN

WILDEGG CASTLE

MORGES

ALEXIS FOREL MUSEUM

MOUDON

EUGÈNE BURNAND MUSEUM
MUSEUM OF OLD MOUDON

MOUTIER

MUSEUM OF FINE ART

MÜSTAIR

MUSEUM OF THE MONASTERY

NEUCHÂTEL

MUSEUM OF ART AND HISTORY

OBERHOFEN AM THUNERSEE

CASTLE

OLTEN

MUSEUM OF ART

ORBE

MUSEUM OF OLD ORBE

ORON-LE-CHATEL

CHÂTEAU

PAYERNE

MUSEUM

PULLY

MUSEUM

RANCATE

GIOVANNI ZÜST CANTONAL ART GALLERY

RAPPERSWIL

REGIONAL MUSEUM

RIGGISBERG

MUSEUM OF THE ABEGG FOUNDATION, BERN

RORSCHACH

REGIONAL MUSEUM

SAINTE-CROIX

MUSEUM

ST. GALLEN

NEW MUSEUM
OLD MUSEUM
REGIONAL MUSEUM

ST. MORITZ

SEGANTINI MUSEUM

SALENSTEIN

NAPOLEON MUSEUM

SAN VITTORE

MOESANO MUSEUM

SARNEN

REGIONAL MUSEUM

LA SARRAZ

CHÂTEAU

SCHAFFHAUSEN

ALL SAINTS' MUSEUM

SCHWYZ

DIOCESAN MUSEUM
TOWER MUSEUM

SEEDORF

À PRO CASTLE

SION

CANTONAL MUSEUM OF FINE ART
VALÈRE CANTONAL MUSEUM

SOLOTHURN

CASTLE BLUMENSTEIN HISTORICAL MUSEUM
SOLOTHURN MUNICIPAL MUSEUM

STAMPA

CIÄSE GRANDA

STANS

HISTORICAL MUSEUM

THUN

ART COLLECTION OF THUN
SCHADAU GALLERY

UZNACH

MUSEUM OF LOCAL LIFE AND HISTORY

VEVEY

JENISCH MUSEUM
MUSEUM OF OLD VEVEY

WIL

MUNICIPAL MUSEUM

WINTERTHUR

MUSEUM OF ART
OSKAR REINHART COLLECTION
OSKAR REINHART FOUNDATION

ZOFINGEN

MUSEUM

ZURICH

COLLECTION OF THE E. G. BÜHRLE FOUNDATION
GRAPHICS COLLECTION OF THE FEDERAL TECHNICAL UNIVERSITY
HERMANN HALLER'S STUDIO
MURALTENGUT HOUSE
MUSEUM OF ART
MUSEUM RIETBERG
SWISS NATIONAL MUSEUM

THAILAND

AYUDHYA

CHAO SAM PHYA NATIONAL MUSEUM

BANGKOK

NATIONAL MUSEUM
SUAN PAKKAD PALACE
JIM THOMPSON HOUSE

LOPBURI

LOPBURI MUSEUM

TUNISIA

CARTHAGE

BATHS OF ANTONIUS
NATIONAL MUSEUM OF CARTHAGE

TUNIS

LE BARDO NATIONAL MUSEUM

TURKEY

ANKARA

ETHNOGRAPHICAL MUSEUM

ISTANBUL

ARCHAEOLOGICAL MUSEUM OF ISTANBUL
MUSEUM OF PAINTING AND SCULPTURE
MUSEUM OF TURKISH AND ISLAMIC ART
TOPKAPI PALACE MUSEUM

PERGAMUM

ARCHAEOLOGICAL MUSEUM

UGANDA

KAMPALA

ART MUSEUM
NOMMO GALLERY

USSR

ASHKHABAD

STATE FINE ART MUSEUM OF THE REPUBLIC OF TURKMENISTAN

BAKU

R. MUSTAFAEV STATE ART MUSEUM

CHUGUYEV

REPIN MUSEUM

DUSHANBE (formerly STALINABAD)

MUSEUM OF THE REPUBLIC OF TADZHIKISTAN

EREVAN

MUSEUM OF LITERATURE AND ART OF THE ACADEMY OF SCIENCES
STATE PICTURE GALLERY OF THE ARMENIAN S.S.R.

FEODOSIJA

J. K. AJVAZOVSKOGO ART GALLERY

GORKI

GORKI STATE MUSEUM OF ART

GRODNO

MUSEUM OF HISTORY AND ARCHAEOLOGY

IRKUTSK

MUSEUM OF ART

JAROSLAVL

MUSEUM OF FINE ART

KALININ

MUSEUM OF FINE ART

KAUNAS

M. K. CHIURLENIS STATE ART MUSEUM
PRINCE VYTANSAS MUSEUM
STATE MUSEUM

KAZBEGI

LOCAL MUSEUM

KHARKOV

KHARKOV STATE ART MUSEUM

KIEV

KIEV NATIONAL MUSEUM OF WESTERN AND ORIENTAL ART
STATE MUSEUM OF RUSSIAN ART
STATE MUSEUM OF UKRAINIAN ART

KISHINEV

MUSEUM OF FINE ART

KISLOVODSK

YAROSHENKO MUSEUM

KRASNODAR

MUSEUM OF HISTORY, FOLKLORE AND ART
A. V. LUNACHARSKY KRASNODAR REGIONAL ART MUSEUM

KUIBYSHEV

MUSEUM OF FINE ART

LENINGRAD

BRODSKY MUSEUM
HERMITAGE MUSEUM
MUSEUM OF ST. ISAAC'S CATHEDRAL
MUSEUM OF URBAN SCULPTURE
NATIONAL RUSSIAN MUSEUM
PERMANENT EXHIBITION OF LENINGRAD ARTISTS
I. R. REPIN HOUSE-MUSEUM

LOMONOSOV (formerly ORANIENBAUM)

FINE ART MUSEUM

LVOV

ART GALLERY
MUSEUM OF UKRAINIAN ART

MINSK

BYELORUSSIAN MUSEUM OF ART
STATE GALLERY OF BYELORUSSIA

MOSCOW

ARKHANGELSKOYE ESTATE MUSEUM
18th CENTURY KUSKOVO ESTATE AND CERAMICS MUSEUM
EXHIBITION GALLERY OF THE PAINTERS OF THE RUSSIAN FEDERATION
MUSEUM OF DECORATIVE ARTS
MUSEUM OF ORIENTAL ART
ANDREI RUBIEV MUSEUM OF ANCIENT RUSSIAN ART
STATE PUSHKIN MUSEUM OF THE FINE ARTS
TRETJAKOV NATIONAL GALLERY
VICTOR VASNETSOV HOUSE- MUSEUM

NALCHIK

MUSEUM OF FINE ARTS

NOVGOROD

GRANOVITAYA PALACE MUSEUM

NOVOCHERKASSK

GREKHOV MUSEUM

NOVOGRUDOK

ADAM MICKIEWICZ MEMORIAL MUSEUM

ODESSA

MUSEUM OF WESTERN AND EASTERN ART
NATIONAL ART GALLERY

ORDZHONIKIDZE

MUSEUM OF ART

OREL

REGIONAL MUSEUM

OSTANKINO

ART GALLERY

OSTROG

REGIONAL MUSEUM

PAVLOVSK

MUSEUM OF FINE ARTS

PERESLAYL-ZALESSKIY

GORITSKI MONASTERY

PERM (formerly MOLOTOV)

GALLERY OF FINE ART

PETROVORETZ (formerly PETERHOF)

MUSEUM OF FINE ART

PITSUNDA

CATHEDRAL OF ST. SOPHIA

POLTAVA

MUSEUM OF FINE ART

PUSHKINO

MUSEUM OF FINE ART

RIGA

NATIONAL MUSEUM OF FINE ARTS
NATIONAL MUSEUM OF LATVIAN AND RUSSIAN ART

ROSTOV-ON-DON

FINE ARTS MUSEUM

ROSTOV VELIKI

LOCAL MUSEUM

SARATOV

A. N. RADISHCHEV NATIONAL MUSEUM OF ART

SERPUKHOV

MUSEUM OF FINE ART
MUSEUM OF HISTORY AND ART

SEVASTOPOL

MUSEUM OF FINE ART

SIMFEROPOL

MUSEUM OF FINE ART

SMOLENSK

MUSEUM OF ART

SVERDLOVSK

SVERDLOVSK ART GALLERY

TALASHKINO

LOCAL MUSEUM

TALLINN

ESTONIAN MUSEUM OF FINE ART
MUSEUM OF HISTORY

TARTU

MUSEUM OF FINE ART

TASHKENT

NATIONAL ART MUSEUM OF UZBEKISTAN

TBILISI

GEORGIAN ART MUSEUM

NATIONAL MUSEUM OF ART OF GEORGIA

TULA

REGIONAL MUSEUM OF ART

ULAN-BATOR

FINE ARTS MUSEUM
PALACE MUSEUM

ULYANOVSK

MUSEUM OF FINE ART

UZHGOROD

MUSEUM OF ART

VILNIUS (formerly WILNO)

MANOR-HOUSE MUSEUM
NATIONAL MUSEUM OF FINE ART

YALTA

ALUPKA PALACE MUSEUM

ZAGORSK

METROPOLITAN'S HOUSE MUSEUM
NATIONAL MUSEUM-PARK OF THE HISTORY OF ART

UNITED STATES

ABILENE

ABILENE FINE ARTS MUSEUM
HARDIN-SIMMONS UNIVERSITY ART GALLERY

AKRON

AKRON ART INSTITUTE

ALBANY

ALBANY INSTITUTE OF HISTORY AND ART

ALBUQUERQUE

THE CLASSICAL SCHOOL GALLERY
JONSON GALLERY, UNIVERSITY OF NEW MEXICO
ALBERT K. MITCHELL COLLECTION OF WESTERN ART
NEW MEXICO ART LEAGUE OLD TOWN GALLERY
UNIVERSITY ART MUSEUM

ALLENTOWN

ALLENTOWN ART MUSEUM

AMERICUS

GEORGIA SOUTHWESTERN COLLEGE

AMHERST

MEAD ART BUILDING
UNIVERSITY OF MASSACHUSETTS ART COLLECTION

ANDERSON

ALFORD HOUSE AND ANDERSON FINE ARTS CENTER

ANDOVER

ADDISON GALLERY OF AMERICAN ART
JOHN-ESTHER ART GALLERY

ANN ARBOR

MUSEUM OF ART

ATHENS

GEORGIA MUSEUM OF ART, UNIVERSITY OF GEORGIA

ATLANTA

HIGH MUSEUM OF ART

ATTLEBORO

ATTLEBORO MUSEUM

AUGUSTA

GERTRUDE HERBERT MEMORIAL INSTITUTE OF ART

AUSTIN

ELISABET NEY MUSEUM
LAGUNA GLORIA ART MUSEUM
UNIVERSITY OF TEXAS ART MUSEUM

BAKERSFIELD

KERN COUNTY MUSEUM

BALTIMORE

BALTIMORE MUSEUM OF ART
GALLERY OF ART
JOHNS HOPKINS UNIVERSITY ART GALLERY
JOHNS HOPKINS UNIVERSITY, MUSEUM OF CLASSICAL ART
MARYLAND INSTITUTE COLLEGE OF ART
MOUNT CLARE MANSION
MUSEUM OF MARYLAND HISTORICAL SOCIETY
PEALE MUSEUM
WALTERS ART GALLERY

BANDERA

FRONTIER TIMES MUSEUM

BATON ROUGE

ANGLO-AMERICAN ART MUSEUM

BATTLE CREEK

BATTLE CREEK CIVIC ART CENTER

BEAUMONT

BEAUMONT ART MUSEUM

BELHAVEN

FANNIE MEBANE RALPH LIBRARY AND GALLERY

BELOIT

THEODORE LYMON WRIGHT ART CENTER

BENNINGTON

BENNINGTON MUSEUM

BERKELEY

UNIVERSITY ART MUSEUM

BETHLEHEM

ANNIE S. KEMERER MUSEUM
LEHIGH UNIVERSITY COLLECTIONS

BEVERLY HILLS

FRANCIS E. FOWLER, JR., FOUNDATION MUSEUM

BILLINGS

YELLOWSTONE COUNTY FINE ARTS CENTER

BINGHAMPTON

UNIVERSITY ART GALLERY

BIRMINGHAM

BIRMINGHAM MUSEUM OF ART

BLOOMFIELD HILLS

GALLERIES OF CRANBROOK ACADEMY OF ART

BLOOMINGTON

INDIANA UNIVERSITY ART MUSEUM

BOALSBURG

BOAL MANSION AND MUSEUM, CHRISTOPHER COLUMBUS FAMILY CHAPEL

BOSTON

BOSTON ATHENAEUM
INSTITUTE OF CONTEMPORARY ART
MUSEUM OF FINE ARTS
ISABELLA STEWART GARDNER MUSEUM

BOWLING GREEN

KENTUCKY MUSEUM
WESTERN KENTUCKY UNIVERSITY ART GALLERY

BRIDGEPORT

HOUSATONIC MUSEUM OF ART
MUSEUM OF ART, SCIENCE AND INDUSTRY

BROCKTON

BROCKTON ART CENTER
BROCKTON PUBLIC LIBRARY AND ART GALLERY

BROOKINGS

SOUTH DAKOTA MEMORIAL ART CENTER

BRUNSWICK

BOWDOIN MUSEUM OF ART

BUFFALO

ALBRIGHT-KNOX ART GALLERY

CAMBRIDGE

BUSCH-REISINGER MUSEUM
FOGG ART MUSEUM
HAYDEN GALLERY

CANAJOHARIE

CANAJOHARIE ART GALLERY

CANTON

CANTON ART INSTITUTE

CARBONDALE

UNIVERSITY GALLERIES

CEDAR RAPIDS

COE COLLEGE ART GALLERIES
COE COLLEGE, THOMAS W. SINCLAIR MEMORIAL ART GALLERY

CENTERPORT

VANDERBILT MUSEUM AND PLANETARIUM

CENTERVILLE

CAPE COD MUSEUM OF HISTORY AND ART

CHAMPAIGN

KRANNERT ART MUSEUM

CHAPEL HILL

WILLIAM HAYES ACKLAND MEMORIAL ART CENTER

CHARLESTON

GIBBS ART GALLERY
CHARLESTON ART GALLERY OF SUNRISE

CHARLOTTE

MINT MUSEUM OF ART

CHATTANOOGA

GEORGE THOMAS HUNTER GALLERY OF ART
UNIVERSITY GALLERY

CHERRY VALLEY

EDWARD DEAN MUSEUM OF DECORATIVE ARTS

CHESTER

DESHONG MEMORIAL ART GALLERY

CHEYENNE

WYOMING STATE ART GALLERY

CHICAGO

ART INSTITUTE OF CHICAGO
MUSEUM OF CHICAGO HISTORICAL SOCIETY
MUSEUM OF CONTEMPORARY ART
ORIENTAL INSTITUTE MUSEUM
LORADO TAFT MIDWAY STUDIOS

CINCINNATI

CINCINNATI ART MUSEUM
TAFT MUSEUM

CLAREMONT

MONTGOMERY ART CENTER

CLEARWATER

FLORIDA GULF COAST ART CENTER

CLEMSON

RUDOLPH LEE GALLERY

CLEVELAND

ART GALLERY OF CLEVELAND PUBLIC LIBRARY
CLEVELAND MUSEUM OF ART
SALVADOR DALI MUSEUM
GUND COLLECTION OF WESTERN ART

CLINTON

FINE ARTS CENTRE OF CLINTON
HUNTERDON ART CENTER

COLLEGE PARK

ART GALLERY OF UNIVERSITY OF MARYLAND

COLORADO SPRINGS

COLORADO SPRINGS FINE ARTS CENTER

COLUMBIA

MUSEUM OF ART AND ARCHAEOLOGY
MUSEUM OF STATE HISTORICAL SOCIETY OF MISSOURI
COLUMBIA MUSEUM OF ART

COLUMBUS

COLUMBUS MUSEUM OF ARTS AND CRAFTS
MISSISSIPPI STATE COLLEGE FOR WOMEN
COLUMBUS GALLERY OF FINE ARTS

COOPERSTOWN

MUSEUM OF NEW YORK STATE HISTORICAL ASSOCIATION

CORAL GABLES

LOWE ART MUSEUM

CORNISH

SAINT-GAUDENS NATIONAL HISTORICAL SITE

CORVALLIS

OREGON STATE UNIVERSITY MEMORIAL UNION BUILDING

COURTLAND

WALTER C. RAWLS MUSEUM

DALLAS

DALLAS MUSEUM OF FINE ARTS
MEADOWS MUSEUM AND SCULPTURE COURT
POLLOCK GALLERIES

DAVENPORT

DAVENPORT MUNICIPAL ART GALLERY
DAVENPORT MUSEUM

DAVIDSON

CUNNINGHAM FINE ARTS CENTER

DAVIS

MEMORIAL UNION ART GALLERY

DAYTON

DAYTON ART INSTITUTE

DAYTONA BEACH

HALIFAX HISTORICAL SOCIETY MUSEUM
MUSEUM OF ART AND SCIENCES

DECATUR

KIRKLAND FINE ARTS CENTER

DEERFIELD

HILSON GALLERY

DE LAND

STETSON UNIVERSITY GALLERY OF ART

DENVER

DENVER ART MUSEUM

DES MOINES

DES MOINES ART CENTER
SALISBURY HOUSE

DETROIT

DETROIT INSTITUTE OF ARTS
McGREGOR MEMORIAL

DORCHESTER

MUSEUM OF THE NATIONAL CENTER OF AFRO-AMERICAN ARTISTS

DOWNEY

DOWNEY MUSEUM OF ART

DUBUQUE

MUSEUM OF DUBUQUE ART ASSOCIATION

DULUTH
TWEED MUSEUM OF ART
DURHAM
SCUDDER GALLERY
DUKE UNIVERSITY MUSEUM OF ART
EASTON
ACADEMY OF THE ARTS
EL PASO
EL PASO MUSEUM OF ART
ENID
GRACE PHILLIPS JOHNSON ART GALLERY
EUGENE
MUSEUM OF ART
EVANSVILLE
EVANSVILLE MUSEUM OF ARTS AND SCIENCES
EXETER
THE LAMONT ART GALLERY OF THE PHILLIPS EXETER ACADEMY
FARMINGTON
HILL-STEAD MUSEUM
FAYETTE
FAYETTE ART MUSEUM
FLAGSTAFF
NORTHERN ARIZONA UNIVERSITY ART GALLERY
FLINT
FLINT INSTITUTE OF ARTS
FLUSHING
QUEEN'S COLLEGE ART COLLECTION
FORT DODGE
BLANDEN ART GALLERY
FORT LAUDERDALE
FORT LAUDERDALE MUSEUM OF THE ARTS
UNIVERSITY GALLERY
FORT SMITH
FORT SMITH ART CENTER
FORT WORTH
AMON CARTER MUSEUM OF WESTERN ART
FORT WORTH ART CENTER MUSEUM
KIMBELL ART MUSEUM
FREDERICK
MUSEUM OF HISTORICAL SOCIETY OF FREDERICK COUNTY
FREDONIA
MICHAEL C. ROCKEFELLER ARTS CENTER
FRESNO
FRESNO ARTS CENTER
GAINESVILLE
UNIVERSITY GALLERY
GALVESTON
ROSENBERG LIBRARY
GARNETT
BRIDGET WALKER ART COLLECTION
GLENDALE
CALIFORNIA NATIONAL WATER COLOR SOCIETY
GLENS FALLS
HYDE COLLECTION
GLOUCESTER
CAPTAIN ELIAS DAVIS HOUSE AND MUSEUM
GORHAM
ART GALLERY OF UNIVERSITY OF MAINE
GRAND RAPIDS
GRAND RAPIDS ART MUSEUM
GREAT FALLS
C. H. RUSSELL MUSEUM
GREENSBORO
WEATHERSPOON ART GALLERY
GREENVILLE
GREENVILLE ART CENTER
GREENVILLE COUNTY MUSEUM OF ART
HAGERSTOWN
WASHINGTON COUNTY MUSEUM OF FINE ARTS
HANOVER
HOPKINS CENTER ART GALLERIES
HARPER
HARPER ART ASSOCIATION
HARTFORD
WADSWORTH ATHENEUM
HARVARD
FRUITLANDS MUSEUMS
HAVERHILL
HAVERHILL PUBLIC LIBRARY
HEMPSTEAD
EMILY LOWE GALLERY
HICKORY
HICKORY MUSEUM OF ART
HOLLY SPRINGS
KATE FREEMAN CLARK ART GALLERY
HONOLULU
HONOLULU ACADEMY OF ARTS
TENNENT ART FOUNDATION GALLERY
HOUSTON
CONTEMPORARY ARTS MUSEUM
INSTITUTE FOR THE ARTS
MUSEUM OF FINE ARTS
HUDSON
OLANA
HUNTINGTON
HECKSCHER MUSEUM
HUNTINGTON GALLERIES
INDIANAPOLIS
CLOWES FUND COLLECTION
HOOSIER SALON
INDIANAPOLIS MUSEUM OF ART
INDIANA STATE MUSEUM
IOWA CITY
UNIVERSITY OF IOWA MUSEUM OF ART
ITHACA
ITHACA COLLEGE MUSEUM OF ART
HERBERT F. JOHNSON MUSEUM OF ART
MARTHA VAN RENSSELAER ART GALLERY
WILLARD STRAIGHT HALL
JACKSON
MISSISSIPPI ART ASSOCIATION
MUNICIPAL ART GALLERY
JACKSONVILLE
CUMNER GALLERY OF ART
JACKSONVILLE ART MUSEUM
JAMAICA
STORE FRONT MUSEUM
JAMESTOWN
JAMES PRENDERGAST LIBRARY ASSOCIATION ART GALLERY
JONESBORO
ARKANSAS STATE UNIVERSITY ART GALLERY
JOPLIN
SPIVA ART CENTER
KALAMAZOO
GENEVIEVE AND DONALD GILMORE ART CENTER
KALISPELL
HOCKADAY CENTER FOR THE ARTS
KANSAS CITY
ART RESEARCH CENTER
CHARLOTTE CROSBY KEMPER GALLERY
WILLIAM ROCKHILL NELSON GALLERY AND ATKINS MUSEUM OF FINE ARTS
KATONAH
KATONAH GALLERY
KENNEBUNK
BRICK STORE MUSEUM
KENT
SCHOOL OF ART GALLERY
KEY WEST
MARTELLO GALLERY AND MUSEUM
KNOXVILLE
CRAIGHEAD JACKSON HOUSE
DULIN GALLERY OF ART
LAFAYETTE
LAFAYETTE ART CENTER
LAGUNA BEACH
LAGUNA BEACH ART GALLERY
LA JOLLA
LA JOLLA MUSEUM OF ART
LARAMIE
UNIVERSITY OF WYOMING ART MUSEUM
LAUREL
LAUREN ROGERS LIBRARY AND MUSEUM OF ART
LAWRENCE
UNIVERSITY OF KANSAS MUSEUM OF ART
WILCOX MUSEUM
LEWISBURG
DAYWOOD ART GALLERY
LEWISTON
TREAT GALLERY
LEXINGTON
UNIVERSITY OF KENTUCKY ART GALLERY
LINCOLN
DE CORDOVA AND DANA MUSEUM AND PARK
UNIVERSITY OF NEBRASKA ART GALLERIES
LINDSBORG
BIRGER SANDZEN MEMORIAL GALLERY
LITCHFIELD
LITCHFIELD HISTORICAL SOCIETY MUSEUM
LITHOPOLIS
WAGNALLS MEMORIAL
LONG BEACH
CALIFORNIA STATE COLLEGE GALLERY
LONG BEACH MUSEUM OF ART
LOS ANGELES
LOS ANGELES ART ASSOCIATION AND GALLERIES
LOS ANGELES COUNTY MUSEUM OF ART
LOS ANGELES PUBLIC LIBRARY COLLECTIONS
MUNICIPAL ART GALLERY
NORTON SIMON MUSEUM OF ART
TOWER GALLERY
UNIVERSITY GALLERIES
UNIVERSITY OF CALIFORNIA AT LOS ANGELES ART GALLERIES
LOUISVILLE
ALLEN R. HITE ART INSTITUTE
J. B. SPEED ART MUSEUM
LOWELL
LOWELL ART ASSOCIATION
LYNCHBURG
RANDOLPH-MACON WOMAN'S COLLEGE ART GALLERY
MACOMB
UNIVERSITY OF WESTERN ILLINOIS ART GALLERY
MADISON
MADISON ART CENTER
THE WISCONSIN UNION
MALDEN
MALDEN PUBLIC LIBRARY
MALIBU
J. PAUL GETTY MUSEUM
MONTEREY PENINSULA MUSEUM OF ART
MANCHESTER
CURRIER GALLERY OF ART
SOUTHERN VERMONT ART CENTER
MARSHALLTOWN
CENTRAL IOWA ART ASSOCIATION
MARYHILL
MARYHILL MUSEUM OF FINE ARTS
MARYVILLE
NORTHWEST MISSOURI STATE COLLEGE GALLERY
MARYVILLE COLLEGE FINE ARTS CENTER
MASSILLON
MASSILLON MUSEUM
MEMPHIS
BROOKS MEMORIAL ART GALLERY
MENOMONIE
ART CENTER GALLERY
MERIDIAN
MERIDIAN MUSEUM OF ART
MERION
BARNES FOUNDATION
MIAMI
MIAMI MUSEUM OF MODERN ART
VISCAYA-DADE COUNTY ART MUSEUM
MIAMI BEACH
BASS MUSEUM OF ART
MIDDLETOWN
DAVISON ART CENTER OF WESLEYAN UNIVERSITY
MIDLAND
MUSEUM OF THE SOUTHWEST
MILWAUKEE
CHARLES ALLIS ART MUSEUM AND LIBRARY
ART HISTORY GALLERIES, UNIVERSITY OF WISCONSIN
MARQUETTE UNIVERSITY GALLERY
MILWAUKEE ART CENTRE
MILWAUKEE PUBLIC MUSEUM
UNIVERSITY OF WISCONSIN FINE ARTS GALLERIES
MINNEAPOLIS
MINNEAPOLIS INSTITUTE OF ARTS
UNIVERSITY GALLERY
WALKER ART CENTER
MOBILE
MOBILE ART GALLERY
MONCLAIR
MONCLAIR ART MUSEUM

MONKTON
BREEZEWOOD FOUNDATION
MONROE
MASUR MUSEUM OF ART
MONTCLAIR
MONTCLAIR ART MUSEUM
MONTEREY
MONTEREY PENINSULA MUSEUM OF ART
MONTGOMERY
MONTGOMERY MUSEUM OF FINE ARTS
MONTPELIER
THOMAS WATERMAN WOOD ART GALLERY
MOORHEAD
RED RIVER OF THE NORTH ART CENTER
MORGANTOWN
CREATIVE ARTS CENTER
MOUNTAINVILLE
STORM KING ART CENTER
MUNCIE
BALL STATE UNIVERSITY ART GALLERY
MURRELLS INLET
BROOKGREEN GARDENS
MUSCATINE
LAURER MUSSER ART GALLERY AND MUSEUM
MUSKEGON
HACKLEY ART GALLERY
MUSKOGEE
FIVE CIVILISED TRIBES MUSEUM
NASHVILLE
BROWN COUNTY ART GALLERY ASSOCIATION
GEORGE PEABODY COLLEGE MUSEUM
TENNESSEE BOTANICAL GARDENS AND FINE ARTS CENTER
CARL VAN VECHLEN GALLERY OF FINE ARTS
VANDERBILT UNIVERSITY GALLERY
WATKINS INSTITUTE
NEENAH
JOHN NELSON BERGSTROM ART CENTER AND MUSEUM
NEWARK
UNIVERSITY OF DELAWARE ART GALLERY
NEWARK MUSEUM
NEW BEDFORD
NEW BEDFORD FREE PUBLIC LIBRARY
NEW BERN
TRYON PALACE RESTORATION
NEW BRIGHTON
MERRICK ART GALLERY
NEW BRITAIN
NEW BRITAIN MUSEUM OF AMERICAN ART
NEW BRUNSWICK
RUTGERS UNIVERSITY ART GALLERY
NEW CANAAN
SILVERMINE GUILD OF ARTISTS
NEW HAVEN
PAUL MELLON CENTER FOR BRITISH ART AND BRITISH STUDIES
YALE UNIVERSITY ART GALLERY
NEW LONDON
LYMAN ALLYN MUSEUM
NEW MARKET
ENDLESS CAVERNS MUSEUM OF ART
NEW ORLEANS
NEW ORLEANS MUSEUM OF ART
NEW PALTZ
STATE UNIVERSITY COLLEGE ART GALLERY
NEWPORT
REDWOOD LIBRARY AND ATHENAEUM
NEW YORK
AMERICAN ACADEMY OF ARTS AND LETTERS
ART COMMISSION OF THE CITY OF NEW YORK
BROOKLYN MUSEUM
CHINESE MUSEUM
THE CITY COLLEGE ART GALLERY
CLOISTERS
COOPER-HEWITT MUSEUM OF DECORATIVE ARTS AND DESIGN
THE COOPER UNION MUSEUM
FINCH COLLEGE MUSEUM OF ART
FRICK COLLECTION
SOLOMON R. GUGGENHEIM MUSEUM
JOSEPH H. HIRSHHORN MUSEUM AND SCULPTURE GARDEN
JUNIOR MUSEUM OF THE METROPOLITAN MUSEUM OF ART
JACQUES MARCHAIS CENTER OF TIBETAN ART
METROPOLITAN MUSEUM OF ART
MUSEUM OF GRAPHIC ART
MUSEUM AND LIBRARY OF HISPANIC SOCIETY OF AMERICA
MUSEUM OF MODERN ART
MUSEUM OF NEW YORK HISTORICAL SOCIETY
NATIONAL ART MUSEUM OF SPORT
NEW YORK CULTURAL CENTER
NEW YORK PUBLIC LIBRARY
NEW YORK UNIVERSITY ART COLLECTION
PIERPONT MORGAN LIBRARY
RIVERSIDE MUSEUM
NICHOLAS ROERICH MUSEUM
STUDIO MUSEUM IN HARLEM
WHITNEY MUSEUM OF AMERICAN ART
NORFOLK
CHRYSLER MUSEUM
HERMITAGE FOUNDATION MUSEUM
NORMAN
MUSEUM OF ART, UNIVERSITY OF OKLAHOMA
NORTHAMPTON
FORBES LIBRARY
SMITH COLLEGE MUSEUM OF ART
NORTH MIAMI BEACH
MONASTERY CLOISTER OF ST. BERNARD
NORTON
WHEATON COLLEGE
NORWICH
SLATER MEMORIAL MUSEUM
NOTRE DAME
UNIVERSITY OF NOTRE DAME ART GALLERY
OAKLAND
MILLS COLLEGE ART GALLERY
OAKLAND MUSEUM
OAKLAND PUBLIC LIBRARY
OGDENSBURG
REMINGTON ART MUSEUM
OGUNQUIT
MUSEUM OF ART OF OGUNQUIT
OKLAHOMA CITY
CONTEMPORARY ARTS FOUNDATION GALLERY
OKLAHOMA ART CENTER
OKLAHOMA MUSEUM OF ART
TREBOR INTERIORS AND GALLERY
NORMAN WILKS GALLERY
OLD BENNINGTON
BENNINGTON MUSEUM
OLD LYME
LYME HISTORICAL SOCIETY MUSEUM
OLIVET
ARMSTRONG MUSEUM OF ART AND ARCHAEOLOGY
OMAHA
JOSLYN ART MUSEUM
ORLANDO
LOCH HAVEN ART CENTER
ORMOND BEACH
FRED DANA MARSH MUSEUM
ORMOND BEACH WAR MEMORIAL ART GALLERY
ORONO
UNIVERSITY OF MAINE ART GALLERY
OSHKOSH
PAINE ART CENTER
OXFORD
MIAMI UNIVERSITY ART GALLERY
WESTERN COLLEGE FOR WOMEN, ART COLLECTIONS
PACIFIC PALISADES
WILL ROGERS STATE HISTORIC PARK
PALM SPRINGS
PALM SPRINGS DESERT MUSEUM
PARAMUS
BERGEN COMMUNITY MUSEUM
PASADENA
PASADENA ART MUSEUM
PEORIA
BRADLEY UNIVERSITY GALLERY
PHILADELPHIA
DREXEL MUSEUM COLLECTION
MUSEUM OF THE CARNEGIE INSTITUTE
MUSEUM OF THE HISTORICAL SOCIETY OF PENNSYLVANIA
PENNSYLVANIA ACADEMY OF THE FINE ARTS
PHILADELPHIA MUSEUM OF ART
RODIN MUSEUM
UNIVERSITY MUSEUM
WOODMERE ART GALLERY
PHOENIX
HEARD MUSEUM
PHOENIX ART MUSEUM
PITTSBURGH
CARNEGIE MUSEUM OF ART
FRICK ART MUSEUM
UNIVERSITY ART GALLERY
PITTSFIELD
BERKSHIRE MUSEUM
POLAND SPRING
SHAKER MUSEUM
PONCE
PONCE ART MUSEUM
PORTLAND
PORTLAND MUSEUM OF ART
OREGON HISTORICAL SOCIETY MUSEUM
PORTLAND ART MUSEUM
POUGHKEEPSIE
VASSAR COLLEGE ART GALLERY
PRINCETON
ART MUSEUM
PRINCETON UNIVERSITY ART MUSEUM
PROVIDENCE
ANNMARY BROWN MEMORIAL
MUSEUM OF ART, RHODE ISLAND SCHOOL OF DESIGN
RHODE ISLAND HISTORICAL SOCIETY
PROVINCETOWN
CHRYSLER ART MUSEUM
PROVINCETOWN ART ASSOCIATION MUSEUM
PROVO
BRIGHAM YOUNG UNIVERSITY, FINE ARTS COLLECTION
QUINCY
QUINCY ART CENTER
RACINE
RACINE ART ASSOCIATION WUSTUM MUSEUM OF FINE ARTS
RALEIGH
NORTH CAROLINA MUSEUM OF ART
READING
READING PUBLIC MUSEUM AND ART GALLERY
RENO
NEVADA ART GALLERY
RICHMOND
RICHMOND ART CENTER
ANDERSON GALLERY, SCHOOL OF THE ARTS
VIRGINIA MUSEUM OF FINE ARTS
RIDGEFIELD
ALDRICH MUSEUM OF CONTEMPORARY ART
RIO PEDRAS
MUSEUM OF ARCHAEOLOGY, HISTORY AND ART
RIVIERA BEACH
CONTEMPORARY ART CENTER OF THE PALM BEACHES
ROANOKE
ROANOKE FINE ARTS CENTER
ROCHESTER
MEADOW BROOK HALL
MEMORIAL ART GALLERY, UNIVERSITY OF ROCHESTER
ROCKFORD
BURPEE ART MUSEUM
ROCKLAND
WILLIAM A. FARNSWORTH LIBRARY AND ART MUSEUM
ROSWELL
ROSWELL MUSEUM AND ART CENTER
RUTLAND
CHAFFEE ART GALLERY
SACO
YORK INSTITUTE MUSEUM
SACRAMENTO
CALIFORNIA STATE FAIR AND EXPOSITION ART SHOW
E. B. CROCKER ART GALLERY
SAGINAW
SAGINAW ART MUSEUM
ST. JOHNSBURY
ST. JOHNSBURY ATHENAEUM
ST. JOSEPH
ALBRECHT GALLERY AND MUSEUM OF ART
ST. LOUIS
GALLERY OF LORETTO-HILTON CENTER
ST. LOUIS ART MUSEUM
WASHINGTON UNIVERSITY GALLERY OF ART
ST. PAUL
HAMLINE UNIVERSITY GALLERIES
MINNESOTA MUSEUM OF ART
ST. PETERSBURG
MUSEUM OF FINE ARTS OF ST. PETERSBURG

SALEM

WILDWOOD ART GALLERY

SALT LAKE CITY

SALT LAKE ART CENTER
UTAH MUSEUM OF FINE ARTS

SAN ANTONIO

MARION KOOGLER McNAY ART INSTITUTE

SAN DIEGO

FINE ARTS GALLERY OF SAN DIEGO
TIMKEN ART GALLERY

SAN FRANCISCO

CALIFORNIA HISTORICAL SOCIETY MUSEUM
CENTER OF ASIAN ART AND CULTURE, AVERY BRUNDAGE COLLECTION
EXPLORATORIUM
INTERNATIONAL MUSEUM OF EROTIC ART
SAN FRANCISCO MUSEUM OF ART
EMANUEL WALKER GALLERY
M. H. DE YOUNG MEMORIAL MUSEUM

SAN GERMÁN

PORTA COELI MUSEUM OF RELIGIOUS ARTS

SAN JOSÉ

CALIFORNIA STATE UNIVERSITY ART GALLERY
COLLEGE UNION ART GALLERY
TRITON MUSEUM OF ART

SAN JUAN

MUSEUM OF FINE ARTS
MUSEUM OF LATIN-AMERICAN ENGRAVINGS
PUERTO RICAN ATHENEUM

SAN LUIS OBISPO

SAN LUIS OBISPO MISSION

SAN MARINO

HENRY E. HUNTINGTON LIBRARY AND ART GALLERY

SAN PEDRO

SAN PEDRO MUNICIPAL ART GALLERY

SANTA BARBARA

ART MUSEUM AND HISTORY MUSEUM
SANTA BARBARA MUSEUM OF ART
UNIVERSITY OF CALIFORNIA ART GALLERIES

SANTA CLARA

DE SAISSET ART GALLERY AND MUSEUM
TRITON MUSEUM OF ART

SANTA CRUZ

SANTA CRUZ ART LEAGUE MUSEUM

SANTA FE

MUSEUM OF HISTORICAL SOCIETY OF NEW MEXICO
MUSEUM OF INTERNATIONAL INSTITUTE OF IBERIAN COLONIAL ARTS
MUSEUM OF NEW MEXICO

SARASOTA

RINGLING MUSEUM OF ART

SARATOGA

MONTALVO CENTER FOR THE ARTS

SARATOGA SPRINGS

HATHORN GALLERY

SAVANNAH

TELFAIR ACADEMY OF ARTS AND SCIENCES

SEATTLE

CALKINS-SLATER METROPOLITAN MUSEUM OF ART
CHARLES AND EMMA FRYE ART MUSEUM
HENRY ART GALLERY
SEATTLE ART MUSEUM

SEWANEE

FINE ARTS GALLERY OF THE UNIVERSITY OF THE SOUTH

SEWARD

KOENIG ART GALLERY

SHREVEPORT

R. W. NORTON ART GALLERY

SIOUX CITY

SIOUX CITY ART CENTER

SIOUX FALLS

CIVIC FINE ARTS ASSOCIATION

SKANEATELES

SKANEATELES LIBRARY ASSOCIATION

SNYDER

DIAMOND M. FOUNDATION MUSEUM

SOUTHAMPTON

PARRISH ART MUSEUM

SOUTH BEND

SOUTH BEND ART CENTER

SOUTH HADLEY

DWIGHT ART MEMORIAL

SPRINGFIELD

EDWARDS PLACE, SPRINGFIELD ART ASSOCIATION
ILLINOIS STATE MUSEUM
GEORGE WALTER VINCENT SMITH ART MUSEUM
MUSEUM OF FINE ARTS
SPRINGFIELD ART CENTER
SPRINGFIELD ART MUSEUM

SPRINGVILLE

SPRINGVILLE HIGH SCHOOL ART GALLERY
SPRINGVILLE MUSEUM OF ART

STAATSBURG

MILLS MUSEUM

STANFORD

STANFORD UNIVERSITY MUSEUM AND ART GALLERY

STATESVILLE

STATESVILLE ARTS AND SCIENCE MUSEUM

STILLWATER

GARDINER ART GALLERY

STOCKBRIDGE

CHESTERWOOD

STOCKTON

PIONEER MUSEUM AND HAGGIN GALLERIES

STONY BROOK

SUFFOLK MUSEUM AND CARRIAGE HOUSE

STORRS

WILLIAM BENTON MUSEUM OF ART

SYRACUSE

EVERSON MUSEUM OF ART
JOE AND EMILY LOWE ART CENTER

TACOMA

HANDFORTH GALLERY
TACOMA ART MUSEUM

TAHLEQUAH

MURRELL HOME

TALLAHASSEE

FLORIDA STATE UNIVERSITY ART GALLERY
LEMOYNE ART FOUNDATION

TAMPA

FLORIDA CENTER FOR THE ARTS
TAMPA BAY ART CENTER

TEMPE

UNIVERSITY ART COLLECTIONS

TERRE HAUTE

INDIANA STATE UNIVERSITY
SHELDON SWOPE ART GALLERY

TOLEDO

TOLEDO MUSEUM OF ART

TOPEKA

MULVANE ART CENTER
TOPEKA ART GUILD, INC.

TROY

MUSEUM OF RENSSELAER COUNTY HISTORICAL SOCIETY

TUCSON

TUCSON ART CENTER
UNIVERSITY OF ARIZONA MUSEUM OF ART

TUCUMCARI

MUSEUM OF TUCUMCARI HISTORICAL RESEARCH INSTITUTE

TULSA

THOMAS GILCREASE INSTITUTE OF AMERICAN HISTORY AND ART
PHILBROOK ART CENTER

TUPPER LAKE

JACKMAN GALLERY OF ART

TUSCALOOSA

UNIVERSITY OF ALABAMA

TYRINGHAM

TYRINGHAM ART GALLERIES

UNIVERSITY PARK

ART GALLERY

UTICA

MUNSON-WILLIAMS-PROCTOR INSTITUTE

VALLEY FORGE

MUSEUM OF VALLEY FORGE HISTORICAL SOCIETY

VALPARAISO

SLOAN GALLERIES OF AMERICAN PAINTINGS

VINCENNES

OLD STATE BANK OF INDIANA

WACO

BAYLOR ART MUSEUM

WAITSFIELD

BUNDY ART GALLERY

WALNUT CREEK

CIVIC ARTS GALLERY

WALTHAM

THE ROSE ART MUSEUM

WASHINGTON

AGRA GALLERY
ANDERSON HOUSE MUSEUM
BARNETT ADEN GALLERY
CORCORAN GALLERY OF ART
DAUGHTERS OF THE AMERICAN REVOLUTION MUSEUM
DIMOCK GALLERY
DUMBARTON OAKS RESEARCH LIBRARY AND COLLECTION
FREER GALLERY OF ART
GALLERY OF AFRICAN ART
HOWARD UNIVERSITY GALLERY OF ART
INSTITUTE OF CONTEMPORARY ARTS
MUSEUM OF AFRICAN ART
MUSEUM OF THE SOCIETY OF THE CINCINNATI-ANDERSON HOUSE
MUSEUM OF THE U.S. DEPARTMENT OF THE INTERIOR
NATIONAL COLLECTION OF FINE ARTS
NATIONAL GALLERY OF ART
NATIONAL PORTRAIT GALLERY
ORGANISATION OF AMERICAN STATES
PHILLIPS COLLECTION
SMITH-MASON GALLERY OF ART
THE AMERICAN UNIVERSITY, WATKINS GALLERY
THE UNITED STATES CAPITOL
WASHINGTON GALLERY OF MODERN ART

WATERTOWN

ROSWELL P. FLOWER MEMORIAL LIBRARY

WATERVILLE

COLBY COLLEGE ART MUSEUM

WATKINS GLEN

YORKER YANKEE VILLAGE

WELLESLEY

WELLESLEY COLLEGE MUSEUM

WESTERLY

WESTERLY PUBLIC LIBRARY

WESTFIELD

JASPER RAND ART MUSEUM

WEST LIBERTY

PIATT CASTLES

WEST PALM BEACH

NORTON GALLERY
NORTON GALLERY AND SCHOOL OF ART

WICHITA

WICHITA ART ASSOCIATION
WICHITA ART MUSEUM

WILLIAMSBURG

COLONIAL WILLIAMSBURG

WILLIAMSTOWN

STERLING AND FRANCINE CLARK ART INSTITUTE
WILLIAMS COLLEGE MUSEUM OF ART

WILMINGTON

DELAWARE ART MUSEUM
ST. JOHN'S ART GALLERY

WINTER PARK

MUSEUM OF ART

WISCASSET

MAINE ART GALLERY

WOOSTER

COLLEGE OF WOOSTER MUSEUM

WORCESTER

WORCESTER ART MUSEUM

YANKTON

YANKTON COLLEGE, DURAND COLLECTION OF ART

YONKERS

HUDSON RIVER MUSEUM
PHILIPSE MANOR

YOUNGSTOWN

BUTLER INSTITUTE OF AMERICAN ART

YUKON

ADDINGTON GALLERY
HENSON GALLERY

YUMA

YUMA FINE ARTS ASSOCIATION

ZANESVILLE

ART INSTITUTE OF ZANESVILLE

URUGUAY

MERCEDES

EUSEBIO GIMENEZ MUSEUM

MONTEVIDEO

MUNICIPAL FINE ARTS MUSEUM

MUNICIPAL MUSEUM OF HISTORY AND ARCHIVES
NATIONAL MUSEUM OF DECORATIVE ARTS
NATIONAL MUSEUM OF FINE ARTS

SAN JOSÉ DE MAYO

REGIONAL MUSEUM

VENEZUELA

CARACAS

ARTURO MICHELENA MUSEUM
MUSEUM OF COLONIAL ART
MUSEUM OF FINE ARTS

CIUDAD BOLIVÁR

'JESUS SOTO' MUSEUM OF MODERN ART
TALAVERA MUSEUM

MÉRIDA

MUSEUM OF MODERN ART OF MÉRIDA

VIETNAM, DEMOCRATIC REPUBLIC OF

HANOI

FINE ARTS MUSEUM

VIETNAM, REPUBLIC OF

HUÉ

ARCHAEOLOGICAL MUSEUM

SAIGON

NATIONAL MUSEUM OF VIET- NAM

YEMEN, PEOPLE'S DEMOCRATIC REPUBLIC OF

ADEN

FINE ARTS HALL

YUGOSLAVIA

BELGRADE

HISTORICAL MUSEUM OF SERBIA
MUSEUM OF CONTEMPORARY ART
MUSEUM OF FRESCOES
NATIONAL MUSEUM

BOL

DOMINICAN MONASTERY

BREŽICE

PROVINCIAL MUSEUM

CAVTAT

VLAHO BUKOVAC'S HOUSE
MUSEUM

CETINJE

STATE MUSEUM

DUBROVNIK

MUSEUM OF THE SERBIAN ORTHODOX CHURCH
TOWN MUSEUM
TREASURY

GROZNJAN

ART GALLERY

HERCEGNOVI

TOWN MUSEUM
TREASURY

HLEBINE

HLEBINE GALLERY

HRASTOVLJE

CHURCH OF ST. TROJICE

HVAR

REFECTORY
TREASURY OF THE CATHEDRAL

KOMIŽA

ART GALLERY
MUSEUM

KOPER

ART AND HISTORICAL MUSEUM
CATHEDRAL OF ST. NAZARIUS AND TREASURY

KORČULA

CATHEDRAL TREASURY

KOŠLJUN

MONASTIC MUSEUM

KOTOR

CATHEDRAL OF SV. NIKOLA TREASURY

LJUBLJANA

MODERN ART GALLERY
NATIONAL ART GALLERY
NATIONAL MUSEUM

NOVI SAD

ART GALLERY OF MATIČA SRPSKA (SERBIAN CULTURAL ASSOCIATION)
GALLERY OF THE DIOCESE OF BAČKA

OREBIĆ

CAPTAINS' HOUSES

OSIJEK

ART GALLERY

PIRAN

ART GALLERY AND CITY MUSEUM

POREČ

TOWN MUSEUM

PREDJAMA

CASTLE MUSEUM

PTUJ

REGIONAL MUSEUM

RIJEKA

MUSEUM OF MODERN YUGOSLAV ART

ROVINJ

TOWN MUSEUM

SARAJEVO

ART GALLERY
MUSEUM COLLECTION OF THE OLD ORTHODOX CHURCH

SKOFJA LOKA

MUSEUM

SKOPJE

ART GALLERY

SPLIT

ART GALLERY
MEŠTROVIĆ GALLERY
STUDIO OF EMANUEL VIDOVIĆ

SREMSKI KARLOVCI

TOWN MUSEUM

STARI GRAD

MARITIME MUSEUM AND ART GALLERY

TRAKOŠĆAN

CASTLE MUSEUM

TROGIR

TREASURY

VARAŽDIN

STARI GRAD MUSEUM

VISOVAC

FRANCISCAN MONASTERY AND SEMINARY

VRBOVSKA

FORTIFIED CHURCH

ZADAR

GALLERY OF MODERN ART
TREASURY OF THE CATHEDRAL AND OF THE BENEDICTINE NUNNERY OF SV. MARIJA

ZAGREB

ARCHIVES OF THE YUGOSLAV ACADEMY OF SCIENCES AND ARTS
ATELIER IVAN MEŠTROVIĆ
COLLECTION OF GRAPHICS
DIOCESAN MUSEUM
GALLERY OF CONTEMPORARY ARTS
GALLERY OF MODERN ART
GALLERY OF NATIVE ARTS
HISTORICAL MUSEUM OF CROATIA
LUBIENSKY-DURIEUX COLLECTION OF OBJETS D'ART
MUSEUM OF APPLIED ARTS
PICTURE GALLERY
PRINT ROOM
STROSSMAYER'S GALLERY OF OLD MASTERS

ZAIRE, REPUBLIC OF

KANGU

MAYOMBE MUSEUM

KINSHASA

FINE ARTS ACADEMY
MUSEUM OF ANTHROPOLOGY

ZAMBIA

LIVINGSTONE

LIVINGSTONE MUSEUM

Applied art

ALBANIA

ELBASAN

LOCAL MUSEUM

TIRANA

MUSEUM OF ARCHAEOLOGY AND ETHNOGRAPHY

ALGERIA

ALGIERS

MUSEUM OF POPULAR ARTS AND TRADITIONS
NATIONAL MUSEUM OF ANTIQUITIES

ANGOLA

LUANDA

ANGOLA MUSEUM

ARGENTINA

BOLIVAR

FLORENTINO AMEGHINO MUSEUM

BUENOS AIRES

ISAAC FERNÁNDEZ BLANCO MUSEUM OF SPANISH-AMERICAN ART
DE LA BOCA MUSEUM OF FINE ART
JOSÉ HERNÁNDEZ MUSEUM OF POPULAR ART
ENRIQUE LARRETA MUSEUM OF SPANISH ART
NATIONAL MUSEUM OF DECORATIVE ART
NATIONAL MUSEUM OF FINE ART
NATIONAL MUSEUM OF ORIENTAL ART
CORNELIO SAAVEDRA HISTORICAL MUSEUM

CÓRDOBA

HISTORICAL MUSEUM OF THE HOUSE OF THE VICEROY SOBREMONTE

ENTRE RIOS

PROVINCIAL MUSEUM

LA RIOJA

PROVINCIAL HISTORICAL MUSEUM

MORÓN

GENERAL SAN MARTIN MUSEUM OF HISTORY AND ART

ROSARIO

MUNICIPAL MUSEUM

SANTA FÉ

PROVINCIAL MUSEUM OF HISTORY

VICENTE LOPEZ

MUSEUM OF FINE ART

AUSTRALIA

ADELAIDE

ART GALLERY OF SOUTH AUSTRALIA

ALBANY

PATRICK TAYLOR COTTAGE MUSEUM

ALBURY

MUSEUM OF APPLIED ARTS AND SCIENCES, ALBURY BRANCH

BALLARAT

BALLARAT ART GALLERY

BATHURST

MUSEUM OF APPLIED ARTS AND SCIENCES

BATTERY POINT

VAN DIEMEN'S LAND MEMORIAL FOLK MUSEUM

BENDIGO

BENDIGO ART GALLERY

BROKEN HILL

MUSEUM OF APPLIED ARTS AND SCIENCES

GOULBURN

MUSEUM OF APPLIED ARTS AND SCIENCES

HOBART

ALLPORT LIBRARY AND MUSEUM OF FINE ARTS

INNISFAIL

CHINESE JOSS HOUSE

MAITLAND

FOLK MUSEUM

PERTH

WESTERN AUSTRALIAN ART GALLERY

SYDNEY

ART GALLERY OF NEW SOUTH WALES
MUSEUM OF APPLIED ARTS AND SCIENCES

TAMWORTH

TAMWORTH ART GALLERY AND MUSEUM

TINGHA

SMITH'S MINING AND NATURAL HISTORY MUSEUM

TOOWOOMBA

CREATIVE 92 ART CENTRE

AUSTRIA

ADMONT

MUSEUM OF ART HISTORY

ARNFELS

MUSEUM OF CLOCKS, MUSICAL INSTRUMENTS AND FOLKLORE

BADEN

EMPEROR FRANZ JOSEPH MUSEUM

BAD ISCHL

MUSEUM OF THE HAENEL AND PANCERA FAMILIES
VILLA OF THE EMPEROR

BEZAU

REGIONAL MUSEUM

BRAMBERG

REGIONAL MUSEUM

BREGENZ

VORARLBERG MUSEUM

DÖLLACH

REGIONAL AND GOLDMINING MUSEUM

EGGENBURG

KRAHULETZ MUSEUM

EIBISWALD

REGIONAL MUSEUM

EISBACH

COLLECTION OF REIN CISTERCIAN MONASTERY

EISENERZ

REGIONAL MUSEUM

ELBIGENALP

FALGER MUSEUM

ENNS

MUNICIPAL MUSEUM

FELDKIRCH

REGIONAL MUSEUM IN THE SCHATTENBURG

GMUND

MUSEUM OF GLASS

GMUNDEN

TOWN MUSEUM

GNAS

REGIONAL MUSEUM

GOBELSBURG

PALACE MUSEUM

GRAZ

BAROQUE MUSEUM
DIOCESAN MUSEUM
JOANNEUM PROVINCIAL MUSEUM OF CULTURAL HISTORY AND APPLIED ART

GRESTEN

REGIONAL MUSEUM

GUTENBRUNN

BAROQUE MUSEUM

HALLEIN

MUNICIPAL MUSEUM

HEILIGENKREUZ

MONASTERY COLLECTIONS

HERMAGOR

GAITAL REGIONAL MUSEUM

HERZOGENBURG

COLLECTIONS OF THE MONASTERY

HOLLABRUNN

MUNICIPAL MUSEUM

HORN

HÖBARTH MUSEUM

IMST

REGIONAL MUSEUM

INNSBRUCK

AMBRAS CASTLE COLLECTION
ART COLLECTION OF THE SERVITEN MONASTERY
'FERDINANDEUM', TIROL MUSEUM
MUSEUM OF THE WILTEN PRAEMONSTRATENSIAN CHORAL FOUNDATION
PALACE, SILVER CHAPEL AND PALACE CHURCH
SCHWARZKOPF COLLECTION

KINDBERG

HUNGARIAN MUSEUM IN WESTERN EUROPE

KLAGENFURT

DIOCESAN MUSEUM

KLAM

KLAM CASTLE MUSEUM

KLEINENGERSDORF

"DER BISAMBERG UND DER WEINVIERTLER" MUSEUM

KLOSTERNEUBURG

MUSEUM OF THE AUGUSTINIAN MONASTERY

KREMS

MUNICIPAL MUSEUM

KREMSMUNSTER

MONASTERY COLLECTIONS

KREUZENSTEIN

CASTLE AND CASTLE COLLECTIONS

KUFSTEIN

REGIONAL MUSEUM

LANGENLOIS

REGIONAL MUSEUM

LEOBEN

MUNICIPAL MUSEUM

LIENZ

EAST TIROL REGIONAL MUSEUM

LINZ

DIOCESAN MUSEUM
UPPER AUSTRIA PROVINCIAL MUSEUM

LOOSDORF

CASTLE COLLECTIONS

LUNZ

AMON HOUSE MUSEUM

MARIA LANGEGG

TREASURY OF THE PILGRIMAGE CHURCH

MARIA SAAL

MONASTERY CHURCH MUSEUM

MARIA STEIN

PALACE MUSEUM

MARIA TAFERL

TREASURY OF THE PILGRIMAGE CHURCH

MARIAZELL

TREASURY OF THE BASILICA OF GOD'S GRACE

MATTSEE

REGIONAL MUSEUM

MICHAELBEUERN

ABBEY REGIONAL MUSEUM

MITTERNDORF

MUSEUM OF REGIONAL LIFE

MÖDLING

MUNICIPAL MUSEUM

MONDSEE

REGIONAL MUSEUM

MOOSHAM

PALACE COLLECTIONS

MURAU

MUNICIPAL MUSEUM OF LOCAL LIFE

NIEDERLEIS

CASTLE MUSEUM

OTTMANACH

MUSEUM OF THE MAGDALENSBERG EXCAVATIONS

PETRONELL

MUSEUM OF APPLIED ART

PÖLS-ENZERSDORF

HUSSLIK REGIONAL MUSEUM

RETZ

MUNICIPAL MUSEUM
MUSEUM OF TOWN HISTORY

REUTTE

REGIONAL MUSEUM

RIED

ETHNOLOGICAL MUSEUM OF THE INNVIERTEL

RIEGERSBURG

CASTLE MUSEUM

ROHRAU

FAMILY COLLECTION OF COUNT HARRACH

ROSENBURG

CASTLE MUSEUM

SALZBURG

CASTLE MUSEUM
COLLECTIONS OF THE BENEDICTINE ABBEY OF ST. PETER
COLLECTION OF THE NONNBERG BENEDICTINE MONASTERY
MUSEUM OF ETHNOLOGY
SALZBURGER MUSEUM, CAROLINO AUGUSTEUM

ST. PAUL

MONASTERY ART COLLECTIONS

ST. PÖLTEN

DIOCESAN MUSEUM

SCHÄRDING

MUNICIPAL MUSEUM

SCHLAINING

CASTLE MUSEUM

SCHWARZENBERG

COMMUNITY MUSEUM

SEEBENSTEIN

CASTLE MUSEUM

SEEKIRCHEN

REGIONAL MUSEUM

SEITENSTETTEN

COLLECTIONS OF THE BENEDICTINE ABBEY

SONNTAGBERG

TREASURY OF THE PILGRIMS' CHURCH

STRASSBURG

DIOCESAN AND REGIONAL MUSEUM

TAMSWEG

LUNGAU REGIONAL MUSEUM

TELFS

REGIONAL MUSEUM

VIENNA

ALSERGRUND DISTRICT MUSEUM
AUSTRIAN GALLERY: AUSTRIAN BAROQUE MUSEUM
AUSTRIAN MUSEUM OF APPLIED ART
AUSTRIAN MUSEUM OF ETHNOLOGY
CATHEDRAL AND DIOCESAN MUSEUM
EXHIBITION OF THE FORMER COURT COLLECTIONS OF TABLEWARE AND SILVER
FIRST AUSTRIAN-SILESIAN MUSEUM IN VIENNA
HISTORICAL MUSEUM OF THE CITY OF VIENNA
LIESING DISTRICT MUSEUM
MUSEUM OF ETHNOLOGY
MUSEUM OF THE HISTORY OF ART: COLLECTION OF ANTIQUES
MUSEUM OF THE HISTORY OF ART: EGYPTIAN AND ORIENTAL COLLECTION
MUSEUM OF THE HISTORY OF ART: SCULPTURE AND APPLIED ART COLLECTION
MUSEUM OF THE HISTORY OF ART: TREASURY
MUSEUM OF THE PROVINCE OF LOWER AUSTRIA
TREASURY OF THE GERMAN ORDER

WAIDHOFEN AN DER YBBS

REGIONAL MUSEUM

WALCHEN

PAULI HANREICH LUDWIG COLLECTION

WELS

MUNICIPAL MUSEUM

WIENER NEUSTADT

MUNICIPAL MUSEUM

BANGLADESH

DACCA

DACCA MUSEUM
MUSEUM OF ART AND ARCHAEOLOGY

BARBADOS

BARBADOS

BARBADOS MUSEUM

BELGIUM

ANDENNE

LOCAL MUSEUM

ANTWERP

MAAGDENHUIS MUSEUM
MAYER VAN DEN BERGH MUSEUM
OLD BUTCHERS' HALL
PLANTIN-MORETUS MUSEUM
PROVINCIAL MUSEUM OF INDUSTRIAL ART
RIDDER SMIDT VAN GELDER MUSEUM

ARLON

ARCHAEOLOGICAL MUSEUM

BELOEIL

CASTLE MUSEUM

BRUGES

ARCHERS GUILD OF ST. SEBASTIAN
CATHEDRAL MUSEUM
GRUUTHUSE MUSEUM
MUSEUM OF FOLKLORE
MUSEUM OF THE HOLY BLOOD
MUSEUM OF THE POTTERY HOSTEL

BRUSSELS

CHINESE PAVILION
ERASMUS' HOUSE
MUNICIPAL MUSEUM OF THE CITY OF BRUSSELS
SCHOTT MUSEUM

COURTRAI

MUSEUM OF ARCHAEOLOGY AND INDUSTRIAL ART

GAASBEEK

CHÂTEAU MUSEUM

GHENT

FINE ARTS MUSEUM
FOLKLORE MUSEUM
MUSEUM OF ANTIQUITIES
MUSEUM OF DECORATIVE ARTS AND INDUSTRIAL DESIGN
MUSEUM OF THE TREATY OF GHENT

HANZINELLE

CHÂTEAU

HOOGSTRATEN

SAINT-SANG MUSEUM OF FOLK- LORE AND FOLK-ART

HUY

TREASURY OF THE COLLEGIATE CHURCH OF NOTRE-DAME

LIÈGE

ANSEMBOURG MUSEUM
CURTIUS MUSEUM
DIOCESAN MUSEUM AND CATHEDRAL TREASURY
GLASS MUSEUM
MUSEUM OF WALLOON LIFE

LIERRE

WUYTS VAN CAMPEN MUSEUM

LOUVAIN

MUSEUM OF ART AND ARCHAEOLOGY
SPOELBERCH DE LOVENJOEL MUSEUM

MAASEIK

CHURCH TREASURY

MARIEMONT- MORLANWELZ

MUSEUM OF ART AND OF THE HISTORY OF ARCHAEOLOGY

MECHELEN (MALINES)

MUSEUM OF APPLIED ART

MONS

CANON PUISSANT MUSEUM
CERAMICS MUSEUM
JEAN LESCARTS MUSEUM
MUSEUM OF FINE ART

NAMUR

ARCHAEOLOGICAL MUSEUM
THE DE CROIX MUSEUM
DIOCESAN MUSEUM
NAMUR MUSEUM OF ARTS AND CRAFTS
THE HUGO D'OIGNIES GOLD PLATE COLLECTION

OUDENARDE

ARCHAEOLOGICAL MUSEUM

SPA

DISTRICT MUSEUM

TERVUEREN

ROYAL CENTRAL AFRICAN MUSEUM

TONGRES

TREASURY OF THE BASILICA OF ONZE LIEVE VROUW

TOURNAI

CATHEDRAL TREASURY
FOLKLORE MUSEUM
MUSEUM OF HISTORY AND ARCHAEOLOGY

VERVIERS

MUSEUM OF ARCHAEOLOGY AND FOLKLORE
MUSEUM OF FINE ART
RENIER MUSEUM

BOLIVIA

LA PAZ

NATIONAL MUSEUM OF ART

SUCRE

COLONIAL MUSEUM

BRAZIL

BELEM

EMÍLIO GOELDI PARÁ MUSEUM

CAMPOS DO JORDÃO

GOVERNOR'S PALACE MUSEUM

CURITIBA

DAVID CARNEIRO MUSEUM

FORTALEZA

DIAS DA ROCHA MUSEUM
ARTUR RAMOS MUSEUM

JAGUARÃO

ALFREDO VARELA MUSEUM

JUIZ DE FORA

MARIANO PROCÓPIO MUSEUM

MIRACATU

PEDRO LARAGNOIT MUSEUM

PINDAMONHANGABA

LOCAL MUSEUM

RECIFE

STATE MUSEUM
SUGAR MUSEUM

RIO DE JANEIRO

ITAMARTY MUSEUM OF HISTORY AND DIPLOMACY
MUSEUM OF THE CITY OF RIO DE JANEIRO
MUSEUM OF THE RAYMUNDO OTTONI DE CASTRO FOUNDATION
NATIONAL MUSEUM OF FINE ART
SANTA CASA DA MISERICÓRDIA DO RIO DE JANEIRO: MUSEUM OF RELIGIOUS ART

SALVADOR

BAHIA MUSEUM OF ART
MUSEUM OF ART
MUSEUM OF THE CARLOS COSTA PINTO FOUNDATION
MUSEUM OF THE CARMELITE CONVENT
MUSEUM OF POPULAR ART
NELSON DE SOUSA OLIVEIRA COLLECTION

SANTA LEOPOLDINA

COLONIAL MUSEUM

SÃO PAULO

ECCLESIASTICAL MUSEUM
ETHNOGRAPHICAL MUSEUM OF THE FACULTY OF PHILOSOPHY, SCIENCE AND LETTERS
PAULISTA MUSEUM

VASSOURAS

CASA DA HERA MUSEUM

BULGARIA

SOFIA

BOYANA CHURCH NATIONAL MUSEUM
NATIONAL ART GALLERY
NATIONAL ETHNOGRAPHICAL MUSEUM

TARNOVO

PROVINCIAL MUSEUM

TRJAVNA

MUSEUM OF WOOD CARVING AND MURAL PAINTINGS

TROJAN

MUSEUM OF APPLIED ARTS AND CRAFTS

VARNA

MUSEUM OF ICON-PAINTING

BURMA

MANDALAY

STATE LIBRARY AND MUSEUM

MOULMEIN

STATE LIBRARY AND MUSEUM

RANGOON

NATIONAL MUSEUM OF ART AND ARCHAEOLOGY

CAMEROUN

DSCHANG

BAMILIKE MUSEUM

FOUMBAN

MUSEUM OF THE BAMOUN ROYAL PALACE

YAOUNDÉ

MUSEUM OF CAMEROUN ART
MUSEUM OF NEGRO ART

CANADA

CHARLOTTETOWN

CONFEDERATION ART GALLERY AND MUSEUM

HALIFAX

DALHOUSIE ART GALLERY

MONTREAL

CANADIAN GUILD OF CRAFTS
McCORD MUSEUM
MONTREAL MUSEUM OF FINE ART
MUSEUM OF THE INSTITUTE OF APPLIED ARTS

QUEBEC

MUSEUM OF QUEBEC
QUEBEC SEMINARY MUSEUM

SAINT-LAURENT

NOVA ET VETERA GALLERY

TORONTO

SIGMUND SAMUEL CANADIANA MUSEUM

VICTORIA

ART GALLERY OF GREATER VICTORIA
MALTWOOD MEMORIAL MUSEUM OF HISTORIC ART, UNIVERSITY OF VICTORIA

CHILE

LA SERENA

LA SERENA ARCHAEOLOGICAL MUSEUM

SANTIAGO

MUSEUM OF THE ART OF THE AMERICAN PEOPLES

CHINA, P.R.

AMOY (XIAMEN)

OVERSEAS CHINESE MUSEUM

CANTON (GUANG DONG)

HISTORY MUSEUM

CHANG SHA (ZHENG ZHOU)

PROVINCIAL MUSEUM

CHINCHOW (JINZHOW)

PROVINCIAL MUSEUM

CHINGTEHCHEN (TSINGTAO)

CERAMICS MUSEUM

HANGCHOW (HANG ZHOU)

CHEKIANG PROVINCIAL MUSEUM

HARBIN

PROVINCIAL MUSEUM

KUEILIN

PROVINCIAL MUSEUM

KUN MING
PROVINCIAL MUSEUM

LANCHOW (LANZHOU)
PROVINCIAL MUSEUM

LUO YANG
TOWN MUSEUM

MUKDEN (SHENYIANG)
IMPERIAL PALACE

NANKING (NAN JING)
KIANG SU PROVINCIAL MUSEUM

PEKING
IMPERIAL PALACE
TEMPLE OF THE SOURCE OF THE LAW

QU FU
RESIDENCES OF THE DESCENDANTS OF CONFUCIUS
TEMPLE OF CONFUCIUS

SHANGHAI
ART AND HISTORY MUSEUM
THE INDUSTRIAL EXHIBITION

SIAN (XIAN)
SHENSI PROVINCIAL MUSEUM

SUCHOW (SU ZHOU)
HISTORY MUSEUM

TAI YUAN
SHAN XI MUSEUM

TIENSIN (TIANJING)
CITY MUSEUM OF HISTORY

URUMCHI (WULUMUCHI)
REGIONAL MUSEUM

REPUBLIC OF CHINA

TAIPEI
NATIONAL ART GALLERY OF TAIWAN
NATIONAL MUSEUM OF HISTORY
NATIONAL PALACE MUSEUM AND NATIONAL CENTRAL MUSEUM

COLOMBIA

BOGOTA
ETHNOGRAPHICAL MUSEUM OF THE CARO AND CUERVO INSTITUTE
MUSEUM OF COLONIAL ART
MUSEUM OF ETHNOGRAPHY
MUSEUM OF GOLD
MUSEUM OF MUSEUMS
MUSEUM OF POPULAR ARTS AND TRADITIONS
MUSEUM OF PRE-COLOMBIAN CERAMICS
NATIONAL MUSEUM
SANTA CLARA MUSEUM

CARTAGENA
COLONIAL MUSEUM

CENTROS CULTURALES
MUSEUM OF THE SCHOOL OF FINE ART

COLOSO
PRIVATE MUSEUM

MANIZALES
MUSEUM OF ANTHROPOLOGY
MUSEUM OF PRE-COLOMBIAN CERAMICS

MEDELLÍN
INDIAN MUSEUM
MUSEUM OF ANTHROPOLOGY
MUSEUM OF ETHNOGRAPHY
MUSEUM OF FOLKLORE
MUSEUM OF PRE-COLOMBIAN CERAMICS

NEIVA
DEPARTMENTAL MUSEUM

POPAYAN
COLONIAL MUSEUM
MUSEUM OF COLONIAL HISTORY AND ART
MUSEUM OF RELIGIOUS ART

RIOHACHA
GUAJIRO MUSEUM OF PRE- COLOMBIAN ART AND CULTURE

SOCORRO
MUSEUM OF PRE-COLOMBIAN ART

VILLA DE LEYVA
COLONIAL MUSEUM

VILLANUEVA
MUSEUM OF NATIVE ART AND CULTURE

COSTA RICA

SAN JOSÉ
GOLD MUSEUM

CUBA

HABANA
MUSEUM OF COLONIAL ART
MUSEUM OF DECORATIVE ARTS

CYPRUS

KYRENIA
FOLK ART MUSEUM

NICOSIA
THE MUSEUM OF FOLK ART

CZECHOSLOVAKIA

AŠ
MUNICIPAL MUSEUM

BANSKÁ BYSTRICA
MUSEUM OF THE HISTORY OF SLOVAKIA

BARDEJOV
ŠARIŠ MUSEUM

BETLIAR
STATE PALACE

BLANSKO
BLANSKO REGIONAL MUSEUM

BRATISLAVA
MUNICIPAL MUSEUM
SLOVAKIAN NATIONAL MUSEUM: HISTORICAL COLLECTIONS

BRNO
MUSEUM OF THE CITY OF BRNO

ČÁSLAV
MUNICIPAL MUSEUM

ČERVENÝ KAMEŇ
MUSEUM OF FURNITURE

ČESKA SKALICE
BOŽENY NĚMCOVA MUSEUM

DĚČÍN
DISTRICT MUSEUM

DOMAŽLICE
JINDŘICHA JINDŘICHA MUSEUM

HLINSKO
REGIONAL MUSEUM AND ART GALLERY

HOLICE V ČECHÁCH
AFRICA MUSEUM; DR. EMIL HOLUB MEMORIAL

HRADEC KRÁLOVÉ
REGIONAL MUSEUM: DEPARTMENT OF ARCHAEOLOGY AND HISTORY

HRANICE NA MORAVĚ
MUSEUM OF CENTRAL MORAVIA

JABLONEC NAD NISOU
MUSEUM OF GLASS AND JEWELLERY

JEMNICE
JEMNICE MUSEUM

JESENÍK
REGIONAL MUSEUM

JINDŘICHŮV HRODEC
REGIONAL MUSEUM

KAMENICE NAD LIPOU
REGIONAL MUSEUM

KAMENICKÝ ŠENOV
MUSEUM OF GLASS

KARLOVY VARY - BŘEZOV
MUSEUM OF KARLOVY PORCELAIN

KARLOVY VARY - DVORY
MUSEUM OF GLASS

KLÁŠTEREC NAD OHŘÍ
MUSEUM OF CZECH PORCELAIN

KOMÁRNO
MUSEUM OF RELIGIOUS ART
PODUNAJSKA REGIONAL MUSEUM

KOMÁROV
MUSEUM OF IRON

KOPŘIVNICE
TECHNICAL MUSEUM

KOŠICE
MUSEUM OF EASTERN SLOVAKIA

KOSTELEC NAD ČERNÝMI LESY
CENTRAL CZECHOSLOVAKIAN MUSEUM OF POTTERY AND CERAMICS

KRÁSNA HÔRKA
CASTLE MUSEUM

LEVOČA
SPIŠ MUSEUM

LIBEREC
MUSEUM OF NORTHERN CZECHOSLOVAKIA

LIPNÍK NAD BEČVOU
ZÁHOŘÍ MUSEUM

LITOVEL
REGIONAL MUSEUM

LOŠTICE
REGIONAL MUSEUM

LYSÁ NAD LABEM
MUSEUM OF ANCIENT ORIENTAL CULTURE

MARIANSKÁ TYNICE - KRALOVICE
DISTRICT MUSEUM

MARIÁNSKE LÁZNĚ
MUNICIPAL MUSEUM

MARKUŠOVCE
MUSEUM OF FURNITURE

MARTIN
SLOVAKIAN NATIONAL MUSEUM: ETHNOGRAPHICAL COLLECTIONS

MĚLNÍK
DISTRICT MUSEUM

MICHALOVCE
ZEMPLIN MUSEUM

NOVÝ BOR
MUSEUM OF GLASS

OLOMUČANY
CERAMICS MUSEUM AND MUSEUM OF THE WORKERS' MOVEMENT

OPAVA
SILESIAN MUSEUM: ETHNOGRAPHY AND ART COLLECTIONS

OSTRAVA
OSTRAVA MUSEUM

PELHŘIMOV
DISTRICT MUSEUM

PIEŠTANY
SPA MUSEUM

PÍSEK
REGIONAL MUSEUM

POLIČKA
MUNICIPAL MUSEUM AND ART GALLERY

POLNÁ
LOCAL MUSEUM

PRAGUE
ETHNOLOGICAL COLLECTIONS
MUSEUM OF THE CITY OF PRAGUE

PŘEROV
J. A. KOMENSKY MUSEUM

RIMAVSKÁ SOBOTA
GEMER MUSEUM

ROŠTEJN
VYSOČINY MUSEUM

RUMBURK
REGIONAL MUSEUM

RUŽOMBEROK
LIPTOV MUSEUM

SÁZAVA
MUSEUM OF GLASS TECHNOLOGY

SLANÝ
REGIONAL MUSEUM

SOBĚSLAV
MUSEUM OF SOUTHERN CZECHOSLOVAKIA

ŠTERNBERK
ŠTERNBERK STATE CASTLE

STRÁŽNICI
REGIONAL MUSEUM OF FOLK ART

TEPLICE
REGIONAL MUSEUM
TOVAČOV
MUSEUM OF ETHNOGRAPHY
TRENČÍN
TRENČÍN MUSEUM
TRNAVA
MUSEUM OF WESTERN SLOVAKIA
TÝNEC NAD SÁZAVOU
TÝNEC MUSEUM OF CERAMICS
VIMPERK
MUNICIPAL MUSEUM AND ŠUMAVY GALLERY
VRCHLABÍ
KRKONOŠ MUSEUM (ASSOCIATED WITH KRKONOŠSKÝ NATIONAL PARK)
VYŠKOV
VYŠKOV MUSEUM
ZÁBŘEH NA MORAVĚ
REGIONAL MUSEUM
ŽELEZNÁ RUDA
ŠUMAVY MUSEUM
ŽIROVNICE
REGIONAL MUSEUM

DENMARK

COPENHAGEN
C. L. DAVID'S COLLECTION
MUSEUM OF DECORATIVE ART
NEW CARLSBERG GALLERY
ROSENBORG PALACE
ROYAL LIBRARY
DRAGØR
AMAGER MUSEUM
GILLELEJE
GILLELEJE MUSEUM
HILLERØD
NATIONAL HISTORICAL MUSEUM
HORNSLET
ROSENHOLM
HUMLEBAEK
LOUISIANA ART GALLERY
KOLDING
KOLDINGHUS MUSEUM
NYKØBING
ANNEBERG COLLECTION
FALSTERS MINDER MUSEUM
ODDER
MUSEUM
ODENSE
ODENSE MUNICIPAL MUSEUMS
PEDERSTRUP
REVENTLOW MUSEUM
RØNNE
BORNHOLM MUSEUM
SAEBY
VOERGÅRD CASTLE
SILKEBORG
SILKEBORG MUSEUM
TØNDER
TØNDER MUSEUM
VARDE
VARDE AND DISTRICT MUSEUM

DOMINICAN REPUBLIC

SANTO DOMINGO
NATIONAL MUSEUM

ECUADOR

QUITO
FRANCISCAN MUSEUM
MUSEUM OF ARCHAEOLOGY AND ETHNOLOGY

EGYPT, ARAB REPUBLIC OF

ALEXANDRIA
GRECO-ROMAN MUSEUM
CAIRO
AL GAWHARA PALACE MUSEUM
ANDERSON MUSEUM
COPTIC MUSEUM
MUSEUM OF EGYPTIAN CIVILISATION
MUSEUM OF ISLAMIC ART

EQUATORIAL GUINEA

SANTA ISABEL
MUSEUM OF ETHNOGRAPHY

ETHIOPIA

ADDIS ABABA
INSTITUTE OF ETHIOPIAN STUDIES MUSEUM
MUSEUM OF THE HOLY TRINITY CHURCH OF ETHIOPIA

FINLAND

HELSINKI
ARABIA MUSEUM
DIDRICHSEN MUSEUM OF ART
PAUL AND FANNY SINEBRIJ CHOFFIN ART COLLECTION
JOENSUU
MUNICIPAL MUSEUM AND KARELIA HOUSE
JYVÄSKYLÄ
MUSEUM OF CENTRAL FINLAND
KARHULA
MUSEUM OF GLASS
LAHTI
MUSEUM OF HISTORY
RIIHIMÄKI
FINNISH GLASS MUSEUM
TURKU
CITY MUSEUM
"ETT HEM" MUSEUM
MONASTERY MUSEUM OF HANDICRAFTS
URJALA
NUUTAJÄRVI GLASS MUSEUM
VAASA
EAST BOTHNIA MUSEUM
VAMMALA
TYRVÄA MUSEUM

FRANCE

ABBEVILLE
BOUCHER-DE-PERTHES MUSEUM
AIX-EN-PROVENCE
PAUL ARBAUD MUSEUM
GRANET MUSEUM
ALLAUCH
MUSEUM OF OLD ALLAUCH
ANGERS
CATHEDRAL TREASURY
SAINT-JEAN MUSEUM OF ARCHAEOLOGY
TURPIN DE CRISSÉ MUSEUM
ANGOULÊME
MUNICIPAL MUSEUM
MUSEUM OF THE CHARENTE ARCHAEOLOGICAL AND HISTORICAL SOCIETY
ANNECY
CHÂTEAU DE MONTROTTIER
ANNONAY
OLD ANNONAY MUSEUM
ANTIBES
GRIMALDI MUSEUM
ARLANC-EN-LIBRADOIS
MUSEUM OF HANDMADE LACE
ARLES
LAPIDARY MUSEUM OF CHRISTIAN ART
ARRAS
MUSEUM OF THE FORMER ABBEY OF SAINT-VAAST
AUCH
MUSEUM OF ART AND ARCHAEOLOGY
AUVILLAR
OLD AUVILLAR MUSEUM
AUXERRE
LEBLANC-DUVERNOY MUSEUM
AVIGNON
CALVET MUSEUM
AZAY-LE-FERRON
CHÂTEAU MUSEUM
AZAY-LE-RIDEAU
CHÂTEAU
BAILLEUL
BENOÎT DE PUYDT MUSEUM
BARR
LA FOLIE MARCO MUSEUM
BAYEUX
MUSEUM OF PAINTING
BEAUNE
CHARITÉ HOSPICE
HÔTEL-DIEU
MUSEUM OF FINE ART
BEAUVAIS
CATHEDRAL TREASURY
MUSEUM OF THE OISE DEPARTMENT
BELFORT
BELFORT MUSEUM
BERNAY
MUNICIPAL MUSEUM
BÉZIERS
MUSEUM OF FINE ART
BIOT
FERNAND LÉGER MUSEUM
BLOIS
CHÂTEAU MUSEUM
BORDEAUX
AQUITAINE MUSEUM
MUSEUM OF DECORATIVE ARTS
TREASURY OF CATHEDRAL OF SAINT-ANDRÉ
BORMES-LES-MIMOSAS
CHARLES CAZIN MUSEUM
BOULOGNE-SUR-MER
MUSEUM OF FINE ART AND ARCHAEOLOGY
BOURBON LANCY
MUNICIPAL MUSEUM
BOURGES
DU BERRY MUSEUM
HÔTEL JACQUES COEUR
HÔTEL LALLEMANT
BRANTÔME
FERNAND DESMOULINS MUSEUM
BRICQEBEC
MUNICIPAL MUSEUM
CANNES
LYCKLAMA MUSEUM
CARCASSONNE
CATHEDRAL MUSEUM
CARPENTRAS
DUPLESSIS MUSEUM
MUSEUM OF RELIGIOUS ART
SOBIRATS MUSEUM
CASSEL
MONT CASSEL MUSEUM OF LOCAL LIFE
CHÂLONS-SUR-MARNE
CATHEDRAL OF ST. ETIENNE
MUNICIPAL MUSEUM
CHAMBÉRY
MUSEUM OF FINE ART
CHANCELADE
DIOCESAN MUSEUM OF ART
CHARTRES
MUNICIPAL MUSEUM
TREASURY
CHÂTELLERAULT
PAUL CHÉRON DE LA MARTINIÈRE MUSEUM
CHAUNY
LOCAL MUSEUM
CLAMECY
MUNICIPAL MUSEUM

CLUNY
OCHIER MUSEUM

COMMERCY
LOCAL MUSEUM

COMPIÈGNE
VIVENEL MUSEUM

CONQUES
CONQUES ABBEY MUSEUM

CORCELLE
FRANCHE-COMTÉ MUSEUM

CORTE
MUSEUM OF CORSICAN HISTORY

DIEPPE
CHÂTEAU MUSEUM

DIJON
MUSEUM OF FINE ART

DOULLENS
LOMBARD MUSEUM

EMBRUN
CATHEDRAL OF NOTRE-DAME

ÉPERNAY
MUSEUM OF FINE ART

ÉTAMPES
MUNICIPAL MUSEUM

ÉVREUX
MUNICIPAL MUSEUM

FORCALQUIER
MUNICIPAL MUSEUM

GRASSE
FRAGONARD MUSEUM

GROSBOIS
CHÂTEAU DE GROSBOIS

GUÉRET
MUNICIPAL MUSEUM

LE HAVRE
MUSEUM OF OLD LE HAVRE

L'HAY-LES-ROSES
MUSEUM OF THE ROSE

LANGRES
HÔTEL DU BREUIL DE SAINT- GERMAIN MUSEUM

LAON
MUNICIPAL MUSEUM OF ARCHAEOLOGY

LEZOUX
MUSEUM OF GALLO-ROMAN POTTERY

LILLE
MUSEUM OF THE COMTESSE HOSPICE
PALACE OF FINE ART

LILLEBONNE
MUNICIPAL MUSEUM

LIMOGES
MUNICIPAL MUSEUM

LOCHES
LANSYER MUSEUM

LONS-LE-SAUNIER
PHARMACY

LOURDES
MUSEUM OF THE PYRENEES

LOUVIERS
MUNICIPAL MUSEUM

LOVAGNY- GORGES-DU-FIER
LÉON MARÈS COLLECTION

LUNÉVILLE
MUNICIPAL MUSEUM

LUZ-SAINT-SAUVEUR
LOCAL MUSEUM

LYON
LYON MUSEUM OF DECORATIVE ARTS
MUSEUM OF THE CIVILIAN HOSPITALS OF LYON
MUSEUM OF FINE ART
MUSEUM OF THE HISTORY OF LYON

MÂCON
MUNICIPAL MUSEUM OF THE URSULINES

LE MANS
QUEEN BERENGARIA MUSEUM
DE TESSÉ MUSEUM

MARCIGNY
RÉGIONAL MUSEUM

MARSEILLE
CANTINI MUSEUM
GROBET-LABADIE MUSEUM
MUSEUM OF PROVENÇAL ART

MAUBEUGE
FERCOT DELMOTTE MUSEUM

MEHUN-SUR-YEVRE
CHÂTEAU CHARLES VII MUSEUM

MELUN
MELUN MUSEUM

MENDE
MUSEUM OF THE LOZÈRE SOCIETY OF LETTERS, SCIENCES AND ARTS

MENTON
COCTEAU MUSEUM

MEUDON
MEUDON MUSEUM

MIRANDE
MUSEUM OF THE MINOR PAINTERS OF MIRANDE

MONTLUCON
MUNICIPAL MUSEUM

MONTPELLIER
ARCHAEOLOGICAL SOCIETY MUSEUM
HÔTEL DE CABRIÈRES-SABATIER D'ESPEYRAN

MONTPEZAT-DE-QUERCY
CHURCH MUSEUM

MOULINS
MUNICIPAL AND REGIONAL MUSEUM

MOUSTIERS- SAINTE-MARIE
FAIENCE MUSEUM

MOUTIERS
MUSEUM OF THE ACADEMY OF THE VAL D'ISÈRE

NANCY
LORRAINE MUSEUM OF HISTORY
MUSEUM OF DECORATIVE ARTS

NANTES
DOBRÉE MUSEUM
MUSEUM OF DECORATIVE ARTS

NARBONNE
MUNICIPAL MUSEUM

NEUFCHÂTEL-EN-BRAY
MATHON MUSEUM

NEVERS
FAIENCE MUSEUM

NICE
MASSÉNA MUSEUM
PALAIS LASCARIS

NOGENT-LE-ROTROU
MUNICIPAL MUSEUM

NOGENT-SUR-MARNE
MUSEUM OF THE SMITH- LESOUËF FOUNDATION

NOIRMOUTIER EN L'ILE
CHÂTEAU MUSEUM

OIRON
CHÂTEAU

ORLÉANS
MUSEUM OF HISTORY AND ARCHAEOLOGY

PARIS
JACQUEMART ANDRÉ MUSEUM
ARMENIAN MUSEUM IN FRANCE
CABINET OF COINS
CERNUSCHI MUSEUM
CLUNY MUSEUM
COGNACQ JAY MUSEUM
ENNERY MUSEUM
FORNEY LIBRARY
GUIMET MUSEUM
THE LOUVRE
MUSEUM OF DECORATIVE ARTS
MUSEUM OF IMPRESSIONNISM
MUSEUM OF JEWISH ART
NATIONAL CONSERVATORY OF ARTS AND CRAFTS
NATIONAL MUSEUM OF AFRICAN AND OCEANIC ART
NISSIM DE CAMONDO MUSEUM
PETIT PALAIS MUSEUM
TREASURY OF NOTRE DAME

PAUILLAC
MOUTON-ROTHSCHILD MUSEUM OF WINE

PÉROUGES
OLD PÉROUGES MUSEUM

PERPIGNAN
HYACINTHE RIGAUD MUSEUM

PÉZENAS
VULLIOD SAINT-GERMAIN MUSEUM

POITIERS
RUPERT DE CHIÈVRES MUSEUM

PONT-L'ABBÉ
BIGOUDEN MUSEUM

PONT-DE-VAUX
CHINTREUIL MUSEUM

PROVINS
TITHE-BARN MUSEUM

LE PUY-EN-VELAY
CATHEDRAL OF NOTRE DAME TREASURY
CROZATIER MUSEUM

QUIMPER
BRITTANY MUSEUM

RAMBOUILLET
CHÂTEAU DE RAMBOUILLET

RENNES
BRITTANY MUSEUM
MUSEUM OF ARCHAEOLOGY AND FINE ART

RHEIMS
SAINT-DENIS MUSEUM
TREASURY

RICHELIEU
MUSEUM OF THE 17th CENTURY

RIOM
FRANCISQUE MANDET MUSEUM

ROANNE
JOSEPH DECHELETTE MUSEUM

ROCHECHOUART
A. ET P. MASFRAND MUNICIPAL MUSEUM

ROCHEFORT
MUSEUM OF FINE ART

LA ROCHELLE
MUSEUM OF FINE ART
ORBIGNY MUSEUM

ROUEN
MUSEUM OF ANTIQUITIES OF THE DEPARTMENT OF THE SEINE MARITIME

RUEIL-MALMAISON
MALMAISON NATIONAL CHÂTEAU

RUMILLY
CHÂTEAU DE CLERMONT- EN-GENEVOIS
MUNICIPAL MUSEUM

SAINT-AMAND-LES-EAUX
CARILLON MUSEUM

SAINT-AMARIN
SERRET MUSEUM

SAINT-CLOUD
MUSEUM OF LOCAL HISTORY

SAINT-DENIS
MUNICIPAL MUSEUM

SAINTES
MUSEUM OF FINE ART

ST. ÉTIENNE
MUSEUM OF ART AND INDUSTRY

SAINT-FLOUR
HAUTE-AUVERGNE MUSEUM
MUSEUM OF THE CONSULAR HOUSE ALFRED DOUET

SAINT-JEAN-CAP-FERRAT
EPHRUSSI DE ROTHSCHILD FOUNDATION

SAINT LAURENT DE LA PLAINE
MUSEUM OF THE OLD TRADES OF ANJOU

SAINT-OMER
HÔTEL SANDELIN MUSEUM

SAINT-PAUL-DE-VENCE
MAEGHT FOUNDATION

SAINT-QUENTIN
A. LÉCUYER MUSEUM

SAINT- RAMBERT-SUR-LOIRE
SAINT-RAMBERT-SUR-LOIRE MUSEUM

SAINT- SAVIN-SUR-GARTEMPE
LOCAL MUSEUM

SALINS-LES-BAINS
HOSPITAL

SAMADET
MUSEUM OF FAIENCE

SARREBOURG
REGIONAL MUSEUM

SARS-POTERIES
GLASS MUSEUM

SAULIEU
FRANÇOIS POMPON MUSEUM

SAUMUR
MUSEUM OF DECORATIVE ARTS AND MUSEUM OF THE HORSE

SCEAUX
ILE-DE-FRANCE MUSEUM

SENS
CATHEDRAL TREASURY

SEPT-FONTAINES
SEPT-FONTAINES ABBEY MUSEUM

SÈVRES
SÈVRES NATIONAL MUSEUM OF CERAMICS

SIGEAN
MUNICIPAL MUSEUM

STRASBOURG
ALSACE MUSEUM
CHÂTEAU DES ROHAN
MUSEUM OF ARCHAEOLOGY
MUSEUM OF THE CATHEDRAL WORKSHOPS
MUSEUM OF DECORATIVE ARTS
MUSEUM OF THE FORMER CUSTOMS HOUSE

THOUARS
LOCAL MUSEUM

TOULOUSE
PAUL DUPUY MUSEUM
GEORGES LABIT MUSEUM
SAINT-RAYMOND MUSEUM

TOURCOING
MUNICIPAL MUSEUM OF FINE ART

TOURS
MUSEUM OF FINE ART

TOURS-LA-RICHE
CHÂTEAU DE PLESSIS- LÈS-TOURS

TROYES
CATHEDRAL OF SAINT- PIERRE-ET-SAINT-PAUL
MUSEUM OF FINE ART
MUSEUM OF THE HISTORY OF TROYES AND CHAMPAGNE

UZÈS
LOCAL MUSEUM

VAISON-LA-ROMAINE
ARCHAEOLOGICAL MUSEUM

VALENÇAY
GALLERY OF MEMENTOES OF PRINCE DE TALLEYRAND

VALENCIENNES
MUSEUM OF FINE ART

VARZY
MUNICIPAL MUSEUM

VENDÔME
MUNICIPAL MUSEUM

VERDUN
PRINCERIE MUSEUM

VERSAILLES
CHÂTEAU
GRAND TRIANON
LAMBINET MUSEUM
PETIT TRIANON

VIENNE
LAPIDARY MUSEUM
MUSEUM OF FINE ART

VILLIERS-SAINT-BENOÎT
MUNICIPAL MUSEUM

WISSEMBOURG
WESTERCAMP MUSEUM

FRENCH POLYNESIA

TAHITI
PAPEETE MUSEUM

GDR

ALTENBURG
CASTLE MUSEUM AND PLAYING CARDS MUSEUM
LINDENAU STATE MUSEUM

ARNEBURG
REGIONAL MUSEUM

ARNSTADT
PALACE MUSEUM
REGIONAL MUSEUM

BAD ELSTER
REGIONAL ROOM

BAD FRANKENHAUSEN
DISTRICT MUSEUM

BAD FREIENWALDE
ODERLAND MUSEUM

BAUTZEN
MUSEUM OF ART AND CULTURAL HISTORY

BERLIN
BODE MUSEUM: COLLECTION OF EARLY CHRISTIAN AND BYZANTINE ART
BODE MUSEUM: EGYPTIAN MUSEUM
MUSEUM OF CULTURAL HISTORY
PERGAMON MUSEUM: COLLECTION OF GREEK AND ROMAN ANTIQUITIES
PERGAMON MUSEUM: FAR EASTERN COLLECTION
PERGAMON MUSEUM: ISLAMIC MUSEUM
PERGAMON MUSEUM: MUSEUM OF ETHNOGRAPHY
PERGAMON MUSEUM: NEAR EASTERN MUSEUM
STATE MUSEUM OF ARTS AND CRAFTS

BERNBURG
BERNBURG CASTLE MUSEUM

BLANKENBURG
REGIONAL MUSEUM

BLANKENHAIN
REGIONAL MUSEUM

BRANDENBURG
DISTRICT MUSEUM

BÜRGEL
CERAMICS MUSEUM

COLDITZ
REGIONAL MUSEUM

COSWIG
CERAMICS FACTORY MUSEUM

COTTBUS
DISTRICT MUSEUM

CRIMMITSCHAU
REGIONAL MUSEUM

DEMMIN
DISTRICT MUSEUM

DERMBACH
DISTRICT MUSEUM

DESSAU
MOGIŠKAU PALACE STATE MUSEUM
MUSEUM OF NATURAL HISTORY AND PREHISTORY

DORNBURG
DORNBURG CASTLES

DRESDEN
INSTITUTE AND MUSEUM OF THE HISTORY OF THE CITY OF DRESDEN
MUSEUM OF POPULAR ART
STATE ART COLLECTIONS: GREEN VAULT
STATE ART COLLECTIONS: MUSEUM OF ARTS AND CRAFTS
STATE ART COLLECTIONS: PEWTER COLLECTION
STATE ART COLLECTIONS: PORCELAIN COLLECTION
STATE ART COLLECTION: SCULPTURE GALLERY

EBERSBACK
REGIONAL MUSEUM

EIBAU
REGIONAL AND HUMBOLDT MUSEUM

EISENACH
TEA-HOUSE IN THE KARTAUSGARTEN
THURINGIA MUSEUM
WARTBURG

EISFELD
OTTO LUDWIG REGIONAL MUSEUM

ERFURT
ANGER MUSEUM OF ART
FOLK-LORE MUSEUM
MUNICIPAL HISTORY MUSEUM

FREIBERG
MUNICIPAL AND MINING MUSEUM

GERA
MUSEUM OF CULTURAL HISTORY

GEYER
REGIONAL MUSEUM

GLAUCHAU
MUNICIPAL MUSEUM AND ART COLLECTION

GÖRLITZ
KAISERTRUTZ: STATE ART COLLECTION
STATE ART MUSEUM: HAUS NEISSSTRASSE MUSEUM

GOTHA
CASTLE MUSEUM

GREIFSWALD
GREIFSWALD MUNICIPAL MUSEUM

GREIZ
STATE COLLECTION OF BOOKS AND ENGRAVINGS

GROSSROHRSDORF
REGIONAL MUSEUM

HAINICHEN
REGIONAL MUSEUM

HALBERSTADT
CATHEDRAL COLLECTION

HALLE
HALLOREN MUSEUM

JENA
MUNICIPAL MUSEUM

KAMENZ
WEST LAUSITZ MUSEUM

KARL MARX STADT
MUNICIPAL ART COLLECTION
SCHLOSSBERG MUSEUM: MUNICIPAL AND CULTURAL HISTORY COLLECTION

KÖTHEN
REGIONAL MUSEUM

KOHREN-SAHLIS
POTTERY MUSEUM

LEIPZIG
EGYPTIAN MUSEUM
MUSEUM OF ARTS AND CRAFTS
MUSEUM OF THE HISTORY OF THE CITY OF LEIPZIG

LÖBAU
MUNICIPAL MUSEUM

LÜBBENAU
LÜBBENAU MUSEUM IN THE SPREEWALD

MAGDEBURG
MUSEUM OF CULTURAL HISTORY

MEISSEN
ALBRECHTSBURG
MUNICIPAL AND DISTRICT MUSEUM

MORITZBURG
MORITZBURG CASTLE BAROQUE MUSEUM

MÜHLHAUSEN
DISTRICT MUSEUM

NERCHAU
REGIONAL ROOM

NEUBRANDENBURG
MUSEUM OF CULTURAL HISTORY

NORDHAUSEN
MEYENBURG MUSEUM

NOSSEN
REGIONAL MUSEUM

OHRDRUF
REGIONAL MUSEUM

PARCHIN
REGIONAL MUSEUM

POTSDAM
DISTRICT MUSEUM
SANSSOUCI PALACE: CHARLOTTENHOF PALACE
SANSSOUCI PALACE: CHINESE TEAHOUSE
SANSSOUCI PALACE: NEW PALACE
SANSSOUCI PALACE: NEW ROOMS
SANSSOUCI PALACE: ORANGERY
SANSSOUCI PALACE: ROMAN BATHS

ROCHLITZ
REGIONAL MUSEUM

RODEWISCH
GÖLTZSCH MUSEUM

RUDOLSTADT
HEIDECKSBURG STATE MUSEUM

RUHLA
REGIONAL MUSEUM

SAALFELD
THURINGIA REGIONAL MUSEUM

SALZWEDEL
JOHANN FRIEDRICH DANNEIL MUSEUM

SCHMALKALDEN
DISTRICT MUSEUM

SCHÖNBERG
REGIONAL MUSEUM

SCHWERIN
SCHWERIN STATE MUSEUM

SEBNITZ
REGIONAL MUSEUM
SENFTENBERG
DISTRICT MUSEUM
SONDERHAUSEN
STATE REGIONAL AND CASTLE MUSEUM
SONNEBERG
GERMAN TOY MUSEUM
STENDAL
ALTMARK MUSEUM: COLLECTION AT THE CATHEDRAL
STRALSUND
MUSEUM OF CULTURAL HISTORY
WALDENBURG
REGIONAL MUSEUM AND NATURAL HISTORY COLLECTION
WEIMAR
BELVEDERE PALACE ROCOCO MUSEUM
CASTLE MUSEUM
KIRMS KRACKOW HOUSE
NATIONAL GOETHE MUSEUM
RÖMISCHES HOUSE
TIEFURT PALACE
WERDAU
REGIONAL MUSEUM
WERNIGERODE
FEUDAL MUSEUM
WÖRLITZ
STATE PALACES
ZEITZ
MUNICIPAL MUSEUM
ZEULENRODA
MUNICIPAL MUSEUM OF INDUSTRIAL ART AND REGIONAL LIFE
ZITTAU
MUNICIPAL MUSEUM
ZWICKAU
MUNICIPAL MUSEUM

GFR

AACHEN
CATHEDRAL TREASURY
REGIONAL MUSEUM AND COLLECTION OF INDUSTRIAL ART
SUERMONDT MUSEUM
AHRENSBURG
AHRENSBURG CASTLE MUSEUM
ALTENA
MUSEUM OF THE COUNTY OF MARK, WITH THE GERMAN BLACKSMITH'S MUSEUM AND WIRE MUSEUM
ALZEY
ALZEY MUSEUM
ANHOLT
CASTLE MUSEUM
ANSBACH
ANSBACH MANSION
COLLECTION OF ANSBACH PORCELAIN
ASCHAFFENBURG
ASCHAFFENBURG MUNICIPAL MUSEUM
AUGSBURG
MAXIMILIAN MUSEUM
AUTENRIED
ICON MUSEUM
BABENHAUSEN
FUGGER MUSEUM
BADEN-BADEN
ZÄHRINGER MUSEUM
BAD DRIBURG
ST. XAVIER MISSION MUSEUM
BAD GANDERSHEIM
REGIONAL MUSEUM
BAD SEGEBERG
OLD SEGEBERG TOWN HOUSE
BAD WIESSEE
CERAMICS MUSEUM
BAD WILDUNGEN
ASIATIC MUSEUM
BALDERN
CERAMICS COLLECTION
BAMBERG
BÖTTINGER HOUSE MUSEUM
HISTORICAL MUSEUM
HISTORY MUSEUM
BAYREUTH
MUNICIPAL MUSEUM
BEBENHAUSEN
STATE COLLECTION OF MEDIEVAL ART IN CISTERCIAN ABBEY
BENSHEIM-AUERBACH
FÜRSTENLAGER TOWN PARK
BERCHTESGADEN
PALACE MUSEUM
BERLEBURG
BERLEBURG PALACE
BERLIN
BELLEVUE PALACE COLLECTIONS
CHARLOTTENBURG PALACE
DEPARTMENT OF ENGRAVINGS
EGYPTIAN MUSEUM
GREEK AND ROMAN DEPARTMENT
MUSEUM OF APPLIED ART
MUSEUM OF FAR EASTERN ART
MUSEUM OF INDIAN ART
MUSEUM OF ISLAMIC ART
STATE PORCELAIN FACTORY
TEGEL PALACE
BERTOLDSHEIM
PICTURE GALLERY
BIELEFELD
MUSEUM OF CULTURAL HISTORY
BLAUBEUREN
REGIONAL MUSEUM
BONN
RHINELAND MUSEUM
UNIVERSITY MUSEUM OF ART
BRAUNSCHWEIG
COLLECTION OF THE SCHOOL OF DESIGN
COUNT ANTON ULRICH MUSEUM
DANKWARDEROBE CASTLE
BREMEN
LUDWIG ROSELIUS COLLECTION
BUCHEN
STEINERNES HOUSE REGIONAL MUSEUM
BÜCKEBURG
GALLERY OF PAINTINGS
BÜDINGEN
HEUSON MUSEUM
PALACE MUSEUM
BURGAU
REGIONAL MUSEUM
BUXTEHUDE
REGIONAL MUSEUM
COBURG
EHRENBURG PALACE MUSEUM
MUNICIPAL ART COLLECTIONS
COESFELD
REGIONAL MUSEUM
CREUSSEN
MUSEUM OF CREUSSEN JUGS
DARMSTADT
BAUHAUS COLLECTIONS
HESSE MUSEUM
PALACE MUSEUM
PORCELAIN COLLECTION OF THE GRAND DUKES
DEGGENDORF
REGIONAL MUSEUM
DEIDESHEIM
MUSEUM OF MODERN CERAMICS
DETMOLD
PALACE OF THE PRINCES OF LIPPE
DIEZ/LAHN
SCHAUMBURG PALACE
DILLENBURG
MUSEUM OF ORANGE-NASSAU
DONAUESCHINGEN
PALACE OF THE PRINCES OF FÜRSTENBERG
DORTMUND
KHAYON FOUNDATION FOR INDO-ASIAN RESEARCH
DÜREN
LEOPOLD HOESCH MUSEUM
DÜSSELDORF
BENRATH PALACE
CITY MUSEUM OF ART
GOETHE MUSEUM
HETJENS MUSEUM
MUSEUM OF THE HISTORY OF DÜSSELDORF
DR. ERNST SCHNEIDER COLLECTION
EICHSTÄTT
BENEDICTINE ABBEY OF ST. WALBURG
CATHEDRAL TREASURY
DIOCESAN MUSEUM
WILLIBALD CASTLE MUSEUM
ELLWANGEN
PALACE MUSEUM
EMDEN
LAND MUSEUM OF OSTFRISIEN
EPPSTEIN
REGIONAL MUSEUM
ERBACH
ERBACH IVORY MUSEUM
ERFELDEN
REGIONAL MUSEUM
ESSEN
FOLKWANG MUSEUM
GERMAN POSTER MUSEUM
VILLA HÜGEL
EUTIN
EUTIN PALACE
FEUCHTWANGEN
REGIONAL MUSEUM
FISCHERHUDE
IRMINTRUT REGIONAL MUSEUM
FLENSBURG
FLENSBURG MUNICIPAL MUSEUM
FRANKENTHAL
ERKENBERT MUSEUM
MUNICIPAL PORCELAIN COLLECTION
FRANKFURT
LIEBIGHAUS MUNICIPAL GALLERY
MUSEUM OF APPLIED ART
MUSEUM OF PREHISTORY AND EARLY HISTORY
FREIBURG IM BREISGAU
AUGUSTINER MUSEUM
MINSTER MUSEUM
PEWTER-FIGURES ROOM
FREISING
CATHEDRAL TREASURY
SEMINARY ART COLLECTION
FREYUNG
WOLFSTEIN DISTRICT MUSEUM
FRIEDBERG (HESSEN)
FRIEDBERG CASTLE
FRIEDBERG (SCHWABEN)
REGIONAL MUSEUM
FRITZLAR
CATHEDRAL MUSEUM
FULDA
CATHEDRAL MUSEUM
EXHIBITION COLLECTION OF THE HESSE LAND LIBRARY AT FULDA
VONDERAU MUSEUM
FÜRTH
TOWN MUSEUM
GARMISCH-PARTENKIRCHEN
WERDENFELSER MUSEUM
GEROLSTEIN
DAUN DISTRICT MUSEUM
GERSFELD
PALACE MUSEUM
GLÜCKSBURG
PALACE MUSEUM
GOCH
GATE-HOUSE MUSEUM
GÖPPINGEN
MUNICIPAL MUSEUM
GÖTTINGEN
COLLECTIONS OF THE ARCHAEOLOGICAL INSTITUTE OF THE UNIVERSITY OF GÖTTINGEN
MUNICIPAL MUSEUM
GOSLAR
HALL OF HOMAGE
GRAFENWÖHR
REGIONAL MUSEUM
GÜNZBURG
REGIONAL MUSEUM

GUNZENHAUSEN
REGIONAL MUSEUM

GÜTERSLOH
REGIONAL MUSEUM

HALLIG HOOGE
THE KING'S PARLOUR

HAMBURG
MUSEUM OF ARTS AND CRAFTS

HAMBURG-BRUNSBÜTTEL
BRUNSBÜTTEL REGIONAL MUSEUM

HAMM
GUSTAV LÜBCKE MUNICIPAL MUSEUM

HANAU
HISTORY MUSEUM
HOUSE OF GERMAN GOLDSMITHS' WORK

HANNOVER
KESTNER MUSEUM

HARBURG
LIBRARY AND ART COLLECTION OF THE PRINCES OF OETTINGEN-WALLERSTEIN

HASLACH
HANSJAKOB AND REGIONAL MUSEUM

HEIDELBERG
EGYPTOLOGY COLLECTION OF HEIDELBERG UNIVERSITY
PALATINE MUSEUM

HEINSBERG
REGIONAL MUSEUM

HELMSTEDT
MUSEUM OF ST. MARIENBERG MONASTERY

HERRENCHIEMSEE
NEW PALACE AND LUDWIG II MUSEUM

HITZACKER
REGIONAL MUSEUM

HOF
MUNICIPAL MUSEUM

HOHENLIMBURG
REGIONAL MUSEUM

HOHENSCHWANGAU
HOHENSCHWANGAU PALACE

HÖHR-GRENZHAUSEN
GRENZAU CASTLE

HÜCKESWAGEN
REGIONAL MUSEUM

HÜLLHORST
REGIONAL MUSEUM

ILLEBEUREN
FARMHOUSE MUSEUM

IMMENSTADT
REGIONAL MUSEUM

INGOLSTADT
MUNICIPAL MUSEUM

JEVER
PALACE AND REGIONAL MUSEUM

KAISERSLAUTERN
PALACE GALLERY AND ARTS AND CRAFTS COLLECTION

KALKAR
ART COLLECTION OF THE NICOLAI CHURCH

KARLSRUHE
BADEN MUSEUM

KAUFBEUREN
REGIONAL MUSEUM

KELLINGHUSEN
REGIONAL MUSEUM

KEMPEN
KRAMER MUNICIPAL MUSEUM

KEVELAER
FOLKLORE MUSEUM OF THE LOWER RHINE

KIRCHHEIMBOLANDEN
REGIONAL MUSEUM

KÖLN
CUTLERY MUSEUM
DIOCESAN MUSEUM
MUSEUM OF ARTS AND CRAFTS
MUSEUM OF ORIENTAL ART
RAUTENSTRANCH-JOEST MUSEUM
SCHNÜTGEN MUSEUM
TREASURY

KÖLN-BIKKENDORF
HERBIG HAARHAUS MUSEUM OF LACQUERWARE

KOMMERN
LAND MUSEUM OF FOLKLORE

KRONACH
FRANKENWALD REGIONAL MUSEUM

KRONBERG
FASANERIE PALACE MUSEUM

KRUMBACH
REGIONAL MUSEUM

LANDAU (ISAR)
REGIONAL MUSEUM

LANDAU IN DER PFALZ
LANDAU REGIONAL MUSEUM

LANDSHUT
LANDSHUT RESIDENCE
TOWN AND DISTRICT MUSEUM
TRAUSNITZ CASTLE

LANGENBURG
PALACE MUSEUM

LANGERWEHE
POTTERY MUSEUM

LAUDENBACH
PALACE MUSEUM

LAUTERBACH
HOHLHAUS MUSEUM

LEMBECK ÜBER DORSTEN
LEMBECK PALACE MUSEUM

LEUTKIRCH
REGIONAL MUSEUM

LICHTENSTEIN
PALACE MUSEUM

LIMBURG (LAHN)
LIMBURG CATHEDRAL TREASURY
LIMBURG DIOCESAN MUSEUM

LINDAU
MUNICIPAL ART COLLECTIONS

LOHR AM MAIN
REGIONAL AND SPESSART MUSEUM

LÖRRACH
REGIONAL MUSEUM

LÜBECK
ST. ANNEN MUSEUM

LUDWIGSBURG
PALACE MUSEUM

LUDWIGSHAFEN
K. O. BRAUN REGIONAL MUSEUM

LÜNE
ART COLLECTIONS OF LÜNE MONASTERY

LÜNEBURG
MUSEUM OF THE PRINCIPALITY OF LÜNEBURG

LÜNEN
MUNICIPAL MUSEUM
MUSEUM OF ART AND CULTURAL HISTORY OF DORTMUND

MAINBURG
HOLLEDAU REGIONAL MUSEUM

MAINZ
CATHEDRAL AND DIOCESAN MUSEUM
CENTRAL MUSEUM OF ROMAN AND GERMANIC ANTIQUITIES
LAND MUSEUM OF THE MIDDLE RHINE
PRINZ JOHANN GEORG MUSEUM

MANNHEIM
REISS CITY MUSEUM

MARBURG
PHILIPPS UNIVERSITY COLLECTION OF GREEK AND ROMAN SCULPTURE AND CASTS
UNIVERSITY COLLECTION OF MATERIAL RELATING TO RELIGION

MAULBRONN
ART COLLECTIONS

MEERSBURG
MEERSBURG PALACE

MELDORF
DITHMARSCH LAND MUSEUM

MELLE
GRÖNEGAU MUSEUM

MEMMINGEN
MUNICIPAL MUSEUM

MILTENBERG
REGIONAL MUSEUM

MINDELHEIM
MINDELHEIM REGIONAL MUSEUM

MINDEN
CATHEDRAL TREASURY AND ARCHITECTURAL MUSEUM OF THE OLD CATHEDRAL

MÖNCHENGLADBACH
MUNICIPAL MUSEUM

MONSCHAU
MUSEUM OF THE SCHEIBLER FOUNDATION

MONTABAUR
DISTRICT MUSEUM

MOOSBURG
REGIONAL MUSEUM

MÜNCHEN
BAVARIAN NATIONAL MUSEUM
MUNICH CITY MUSEUM
THE NEW COLLECTION
RESIDENCE MUSEUM
STATE COLLECTIONS OF CLASSICAL ART
STATE COLLECTION OF EGYPTIAN ART
STUCK MUSEUM OF ART NOUVEAU
TREASURY OF THE MUNICH RESIDENCE

MÜNNERSTADT
REGIONAL MUSEUM

MÜNSTER
CATHEDRAL MUSEUM AND TREASURY
LAND MUSEUM OF ART AND CULTURAL HISTORY
UNIVERSITY OF MÜNSTER MUSEUM OF ARCHAEOLOGY

MÜNSTERSCHWARZACH
BENEDICTINE ABBEY

NECKARMÜHLBACH
GUTTENBERG CASTLE

NENTERSHAUSEN
TANNENBERG MUSEUM

NEUBURG
REGIONAL MUSEUM

NEUNBURG VOR WALD
DISTRICT MUSEUM

NEUSCHWANSTEIN
PALACE

NEUWIED
DISTRICT MUSEUM

NIEDERALTAICH
BENEDICTINE ABBEY

NIEDERBÜHL-FÖRCH
FAVORITE PALACE

NIEDERMARSBERG
REGIONAL MUSEUM

NÜMBRECHT
MUSEUM OF THE OBERBERG REGION

NÜRNBERG
GERMAN NATIONAL MUSEUM
MUSEUM OF APPLIED ARTS

ÖHRINGEN
WEYGANG MUSEUM

OETTINGEN
REGIONAL MUSEUM

OLDENBURG
LAND MUSEUM OF ART AND CULTURAL HISTORY

OSNABRÜCK
MUNICIPAL MUSEUM

PASSAU
OBERHAUS MUSEUM

PFARRKIRCHEN
ROTTAL REGIONAL MUSEUM

PLÖN
PLÖN DISTRICT MUSEUM

POMMERSFELDEN
WEISSENSTEIN PALACE

POTTENSTEIN
REGIONAL MUSEUM

PRIEN
REGIONAL MUSEUM

RATINGEN
MUSEUM OF THE HISTORY OF RATINGEN

RECKLINGHAUSEN
ICON MUSEUM

REGENSBURG
MUSEUM OF THE PALACE OF THE PRINCES OF THURN AND TAXIS
REGENSBURG CITY MUSEUM

REINFELD
REINFELD REGIONAL MUSEUM

REKEN
MUSEUM IN THE OLD CHURCH
REMAGEN
ROMAN AND FRANKISH MUSEUM
RENDSBURG
REGIONAL MUSEUM
RHEINBACH
GLASS MUSEUM
RHEINHAUSEN
HEHL COLLECTION
RHEYDT
MUNICIPAL MUSEUM
ROTH
REGIONAL MUSEUM
ROTTWEIL
ROTTWEIL MUNICIPAL MUSEUM
ROXEL
DROSTE ZU HÜLSHOFF MUSEUM
SAARBRÜCKEN
SAARLAND MUSEUM
SCHLESWIG
LAND MUSEUM OF SCHLESWIG- HOLSTEIN
MUNICIPAL MUSEUM
SCHLOSS MESPELBRUNN
PALACE MUSEUM
SCHLÜCHTERN
BERGWINKEL MUSEUM
SCHWÄBISCH-GMÜND
SCHWÄBISCH-GMÜND MUSEUM
SCHWANDORF
REGIONAL MUSEUM
SIEGBURG
SIEGBURG REGIONAL MUSEUM
SIEGEN
SIEGERLAND MUSEUM
SINSHEIM
REGIONAL MUSEUM
SINZIG
REGIONAL MUSEUM
STARNBERG
MUNICIPAL MUSEUM
STRAUBING
GÄUBODEN AND STRAUBING MUSEUM
STUTTGART
WÜRTTEMBERG MUSEUM
TITTMONING
REGIONAL MUSEUM
TRABEN-TRARBACH
MUSEUM OF THE CENTRAL MOSEL AREA
TRIBERG
REGIONAL MUSEUM
TRIER
CATHEDRAL AND DIOCESAN MUSEUM
CATHEDRAL TRESURY
TROSTBERG
TROSTBERG MUNICIPAL MUSEUM
TÜBINGEN
COLLECTION OF THE UNIVERSITY INSTITUTE OF ARCHAEOLOGY
COLLECTION OF THE UNIVERSITY INSTITUTE OF EGYPTOLOGY
THEODOR HEARING HOUSE
UFFENHEIM
REGIONAL MUSEUM
UNTERRODACH
FLÖSSER MUSEUM
VELBERT
GERMAN MUSEUM OF LOCKS AND FASTENINGS
VILLINGEN
VILLINGEN MUSEUM
VILSIBURG
REGIONAL MUSEUM
VOLKACH
SCHELF HOUSE
WALDSHUT
REGIONAL MUSEUM
WALDSRODE
REGIONAL MUSEUM
WALLDÜRN
WALLDÜRN MUSEUM OF IVORY
WARTHAUSEN
PALACE MUSEUM
WASSERBURG
WASSERBURG REGIONAL MUSEUM
WASSERTRÜDINGEN
SCHWARZKOPF COLLECTION
WEIDEN
TOWN MUSEUM
WEIKERSHEIM
PALACE MUSEUM
WEILBURG
PALACE
WEILER
WEST ALLGAU REGIONAL MUSEUM
WEISMAIN
REGIONAL MUSEUM
WEISSENHORN
REGIONAL MUSEUM
WETZLAR
MUNICIPAL MUSEUM
PAPIUS MANSION
WEWELSBURG
DISTRICT MUSEUM
WIESBADEN
WIESBADEN MUNICIPAL MUSEUM
WILHELMSTHAL
PALACE
WOLFACH
WOLFACH REGIONAL MUSEUM
WOLFHAGEN
REGIONAL MUSEUM
WORMS
HEYLSHOF GALLERY
WÜRZBURG
FRANKISH MUSEUM
MARTIN VON WAGNER MUSEUM OF THE UNIVERSITY OF WÜRZBURG
XANTEN
CATHEDRAL MUSEUM
ZWIESEL
TOWN MUSEUM

GHANA

KUMASI
PREMPEH II JUBILEE MUSEUM

GIBRALTAR

GIBRALTAR
GIBRALTAR MUSEUM

GREAT BRITAIN

ABERDEEN
ABERDEEN ART GALLERY AND MUSEUM
ABINGDON
GUILDHALL
ACCRINGTON
HAWORTH ART GALLERY
ALCESTER
RAGLEY HALL
AYLESBURY
WADDESDON MANOR
AYLSHAM
BLICKLING HALL
BARNARD CASTLE
BOWES MUSEUM
BARNSLEY
CANNON HALL ART GALLERY AND MUSEUM
BATH
AMERICAN MUSEUM IN BRITAIN
HOLBURNE OF MENSTRIE MUSEUM
VICTORIA ART GALLERY
BEDFORD
CECIL HIGGINS ART GALLERY
BELFAST
ULSTER MUSEUM
BERKELEY
BERKELEY CASTLE
BERWICK- ON-TWEED
BERWICK-ON-TWEED MUSEUM AND ART GALLERY
BIBURY
ARLINGTON MILL
BIRKENHEAD
WILLIAMSON ART GALLERY AND MUSEUM
BIRMINGHAM
THE ASSAY OFFICE
BIRMINGHAM CITY MUSEUM AND ART GALLERY
BOOTLE
BOOTLE MUSEUM AND ART GALLERY
BRIDLINGTON
BURTON AGNES HALL
BRIGHTON
BRIGHTON MUSEUM AND ART GALLERY
PRESTON MANOR
BRISTOL
BLAISE CASTLE HOUSE MUSEUM
BRISTOL CITY ART GALLERY
BURNLEY
TOWNELEY HALL ART GALLERY AND MUSEUM
CALSTOCK
COTEHELE HOUSE
CAMBRIDGE
ANGLESEY ABBEY
FITZWILLIAM MUSEUM
CARDIFF
NATIONAL MUSEUM OF WALES
CARLISLE
MUSEUM AND ART GALLERY
CASTLEFORD
CASTLEFORD PUBLIC LIBRARY AND MUSEUM
CHARD
FORDE ABBEY
CHELTENHAM
CHELTENHAM ART GALLERY AND MUSEUM
CHESTERFIELD
HARDWICK HALL
CHICHESTER
GOODWOOD HOUSE
CHORLEY
ASTLEY HALL, ART GALLERY AND MUSEUM
CLACTON
ST. OSYTH'S PRIORY
CLEVEDON
CLEVEDON COURT
COVENTRY
HERBERT ART GALLERY AND MUSEUM
CULROSS
DUNIMARLE MUSEUM
DRIFFIELD
SLEDMERE HOUSE
DUDLEY
BRIERLEY HILL GLASS MUSEUM AND ART GALLERY
DURHAM
GULBENKIAN MUSEUM OF ORIENTAL ART AND ARCHAEOLOGY
EDENBRIDGE
CHIDDINGSTONE CASTLE
EDGEHILL
UPTON HOUSE
EDINBURGH
HUNTLY HOUSE
LAURISTON CASTLE
ROYAL SCOTTISH MUSEUM
EXETER
ROYAL ALBERT MEMORIAL MUSEUM AND ART GALLERY
GLASGOW
CITY OF GLASGOW CORPORATION ART GALLERY AND MUSEUM
POLLOK HOUSE
HEREFORD
KENTCHURCH COURT

HOVE
HOVE MUSEUM OF ART
IPSWICH
CHRISTCHURCH MANSION
KENDAL
SIZERGH CASTLE
KNUTSFORD
TATTON PARK
LEAMINGTON SPA
LEAMINGTON SPA ART GALLERY AND MUSEUM
LECHLADE
KELMSCOTT MANOR
LEEDS
CITY ART GALLERY
HAREWOOD HOUSE
LOTHERTON HALL
TEMPLE NEWSAM HOUSE
LEWES
FIRLE PLACE
GLYNDE PLACE
LINCOLN
LINCOLN CATHEDRAL TREASURY
USHER GALLERY
LINDISFARNE
LINDISFARNE PRIORY
LIVERPOOL
CITY OF LIVERPOOL MUSEUMS
SPEKE HALL
SUDLEY ART GALLERY AND MUSEUM
LLANDUDNO
RAPALLO HOUSE MUSEUM AND ART GALLERY
LLANELLI
PARC HOWARD MUSEUM AND ART GALLERY
LLANFAIR P.G.
PLAS NEWYDD
LONDON
ABBEY ART CENTRE AND MUSEUM
APSLEY HOUSE
BETHNAL GREEN MUSEUM
BRITISH MUSEUM
BUCKINGHAM PALACE
FENTON HOUSE
GOLDSMITHS' HALL
GUILDHALL MUSEUM
MARTINWARE POTTERY COLLECTION
PERCIVAL DAVID FOUNDATION OF CHINESE ART
SIR JOHN SOANE'S MUSEUM
VICTORIA AND ALBERT MUSEUM
WALLACE COLLECTION
WILLIAM MORRIS GALLERY
LUTON
WERNHER COLLECTION
LUTON MUSEUM AND ART GALLERY
MAIDENHEAD
HENRY REITLINGER BEQUEST
MAIDSTONE
THE FRIARS
MANCHESTER
ATHENAEUM ANNEXE
CITY ART GALLERY
WHITWORTH ART GALLERY
WYTHENSHAWE HALL
MANSFIELD
MANSFIELD MUSEUM AND ART GALLERY
MELTON MOWBRAY
STAPLEFORD PARK
MERE
STOURHEAD
NEWCASTLE- UPON-TYNE
LAING ART GALLERY AND MUSEUM
UNIVERSITY OF NEWCASTLE- UPON-TYNE
NEWPORT
NEWPORT MUSEUM AND ART GALLERY
NORTHAMPTON
ABINGTON MUSEUM
ALTHORP
NORTHENDEN
WYTHENSHAWE HALL
NOTTINGHAM
NOTTINGHAM CITY MUSEUM AND ART GALLERY
OLDHAM
ART GALLERY AND MUSEUM
OXFORD
ASHMOLEAN MUSEUM OF ART AND ARCHAEOLOGY
PADIHAM
GAWTHORPE HALL
PERTH
SCONE PALACE
PETERSFIELD
UPPARK
PETWORTH
PETWORTH HOUSE
PLYMOUTH
CITY MUSEUM AND ART GALLERY
SALTRAM HOUSE
PORTSMOUTH
CITY MUSEUM AND ART GALLERY
PORT SUNLIGHT
THE LADY LEVER ART GALLERY
PRESTON
HARRIS MUSEUM AND ART GALLERY
PULBOROUGH
PARHAM
RAVENGLASS
MUNCASTER CASTLE
READING
MUSEUM AND ART GALLERY
RIPON
NEWBY HALL
ROTHERHAM
ROTHERHAM MUSEUM AND ART GALLERY
RUFFORD
RUFFORD OLD HALL
RYE
RYE MUSEUM
ST. HELENS
PILKINGTON GLASS MUSEUM
SEVENOAKS
KNOLE
SHERBORNE
SHERBORNE CASTLE
SHIFNAL
WESTON PARK
SHUGBOROUGH
STAFFORDSHIRE COUNTY MUSEUM AND MANSION HOUSE
STOKE-ON-TRENT
CITY MUSEUM AND ART GALLERY
SPODE-COPELAND MUSEUM AND ART GALLERY
THE WEDGWOOD MUSEUM
STOWMARKET
THE ABBOT'S HALL MUSEUM OF RURAL LIFE OF EAST ANGLIA
SUDBURY
MELFORD HALL
SUNDERLAND
SUNDERLAND CENTRAL MUSEUM AND ART GALLERY
SWANSEA
GLYNN VIVIAN ART GALLERY
TUNBRIDGE WELLS
PENSHURST PLACE
WADDESDON
WADDESDON MANOR
WAKEFIELD
CITY MUSEUM
HEATH HALL
WALSALL
E. M. FLINT ART GALLERY
MUSEUM OF LEATHERCRAFT
WELLINGBOROUGH
HINWICK HOUSE
WELSHPOOL
POWIS CASTLE
WINCHESTER
WINCHESTER COLLEGE MUSEUM
WINDSOR
WINDSOR CASTLE
WING
ASCOTT
WOBURN
WOBURN ABBEY
WOLVERHAMPTON
BANTOCK HOUSE
MUNICIPAL ART GALLERY AND MUSEUM
WIGHTWICK MANOR
WOODSTOCK
BLENHEIM PALACE
WORCESTER
THE DYSON PERRINS MUSEUM OF WORCESTER PORCELAIN
WREXHAM
CHIRK CASTLE
YEOVIL
MONTACUTE HOUSE
YORK
CASTLE HOWARD
CITY OF YORK ART GALLERY
THE YORKSHIRE MUSEUM

GREECE

AEGINA
MUSEUM
AGIA
ARCHAEOLOGICAL COLLECTION
AGIASSOS
CHURCH OF THE PANAGIA
AGION OROS
MONASTERY SACRISTY
AGIOS KIRYKOS
ARCHAEOLOGICAL COLLECTION
AGIOS NIKOLAOS
ARCHAEOLOGICAL MUSEUM
AGRINION
ARCHAEOLOGICAL MUSEUM
AIANI
ARCHAEOLOGICAL AND FOLKLORE COLLECTION
AIGINA
ARCHAEOLOGICAL MUSEUM
AIGION
MONASTERY OF THE TAXIARCHS
ALEXANDROUPOLIS
E. FILIPPIDIS PRIVATE COLLECTION
ALMYROS
MONASTERY OF THE PANAGIA XENIA
AMBELAKIA
THE G. SCHWARZ MANSION
AMORGOS
CHOZOVIOTISSA MONASTERY
ANO KARDAMYLA
KARDAMYLA CULTURAL CENTRE OF MICHAEL AND STAMATIA XYLAS
ANO MERA
MONASTERY OF THE PANAGIA TOURLIANI
ANTISSA
MONASTERY OF ST. JOHN THE DIVINE, YPSILOU
APEIRANTHOS
ARCHAEOLOGICAL COLLECTION
ARGOS
ARCHAEOLOGICAL MUSEUM
ARGOSTOLION
ARCHAEOLOGICAL MUSEUM
E. BASSIAS HISTORICAL AND FOLKLORE MUSEUM
ATHENS
AGORA MUSEUM
R. ANDREADIS PRIVATE COLLECTION
D. ARTEMIS PRIVATE COLLECTION
BENAKI MUSEUM
L. BENAKIS PRIVATE COLLECTION
BYZANTINE MUSEUM
M. DAPERGOLAS PRIVATE COLLECTION
D. ECONOMIDIS PRIVATE COLLECTION
A. GOULANDRIS PRIVATE COLLECTION
GREEK FOLKLORE SOCIETY MUSEUM COLLECTION
A. HADJIDIMOU PRIVATE COLLECTION
A. IOLAS PRIVATE COLLECTION
P. KANELLOPOULOS PRIVATE COLLECTION
I. KONSTANDOGLOU PRIVATE COLLECTION
A. MELAS PRIVATE COLLECTION
MUSEUM OF GREEK POPULAR ART
MUSEUM OF SACRED ICONS OF THE ARCHBISHOPRIC OF ATHENS
NATIONAL ARCHAEOLOGICAL MUSEUM
NATIONAL HISTORICAL MUSEUM
I. AND D. PASSAS MUSEUM OF EUROPEAN AND ORIENTAL ART
AVLON
ZYGOMALA MUSEUM

AXIOKASTRON
ARCHAEOLOGICAL COLLECTION

BATSI
MONASTERY OF THE ZOODOCHOS PIGI OR AGIA

CHAIRONEIA
ARCHAEOLOGICAL MUSEUM

CHALKIS
ARCHAEOLOGICAL MUSEUM
BYZANTINE COLLECTION

CHANIA
ARCHAEOLOGICAL MUSEUM

CHIOS
ARCHAEOLOGICAL MUSEUM
ETHNOLOGICAL AND FOLKLORE MUSEUM OF THE A. KORAIS LIBRARY
NEA MONI MONASTERY

CHORA
ARCHAEOLOGICAL MUSEUM
MONASTERY OF ST. JOHN THE DIVINE

CHORA TRIFYLIAS
ARCHAEOLOGICAL MUSEUM

COMOTINI
ARCHAEOLOGICAL MUSEUM

CORFU
ARCHAEOLOGICAL MUSEUM
R. EVELPIDIS PRIVATE COLLECTION
SINO-JAPANESE MUSEUM

CORINTH
ANCIENT CORINTH MUSEUM

DELOS
ARCHAEOLOGICAL MUSEUM

DELPHI
ARCHAEOLOGICAL MUSEUM

DIMITSANA
ARCHAEOLOGICAL COLLECTION

ELASSON
OLYMPIOTISSA MONASTERY

ELEFSIS
ARCHAEOLOGICAL MUSEUM

ELEUSIS
ELEUSIS MUSEUM

ERESSOS
ARCHAEOLOGICAL MUSEUM

ERETRIA
ARCHAEOLOGICAL MUSEUM

ERMOUPOLIS
ARCHAEOLOGICAL COLLECTION

FALIKA
PANACHRANTOS MONASTERY

FLORINA
ARCHAEOLOGICAL MUSEUM

GALAXIDI
ARCHAEOLOGICAL COLLECTION

IERAPETRA
ARCHAEOLOGICAL COLLECTION

IOANNINA
FOLKLORE MUSEUM AND ARCHIVES OF THE IOANNINA FACULTY OF PHILOSOPHY
MUNICIPAL MUSEUM
MUSEUM

IRAKLION
HISTORICAL MUSEUM OF CRETE
N. METAXES PRIVATE COLLECTION
MONASTERY OF ST. GEORGE EPANOSIFIS

KALAMATA
ARCHAEOLOGICAL MUSEUM

KALAVRYTA
AGIA LAVRA MONASTERY
MEGA SPILEON MONASTERY

KALLONI
MONASTERY OF ST. IGNATIOS, LIMONOS

KAMMENA VOURLA
KARANASSOS PRIVATE COLLECTION

KAMPOS
ARCHAEOLOGICAL MUSEUM

KARDAMYLI, MESSINIA
ARCHAEOLOGICAL COLLECTION

KARDITSA
KORONI MONASTERY

KARPENISSION
TATARNA MONASTERY

KARYSTOS
ARCHAEOLOGICAL MUSEUM

KASTELLI KISAMOU
ARCHAEOLOGICAL COLLECTION

KASTELLORIZON
ARCHAEOLOGICAL MUSEUM

KASTRO
ARCHAEOLOGICAL COLLECTION

KAVALA
ARCHAEOLOGICAL MUSEUM

KOLYMVARI
MONASTERY OF THE ODIGITRIA, CHANIA

KOMOTINI
FOLKLORE MUSEUM OF THRACE

KOS
ARCHAEOLOGICAL MUSEUM
FOLK ART MUSEUM OF THE METROPOLIS OF KOS

KOZANI
ARCHAEOLOGICAL COLLECTION

LAMIA
ARCHAEOLOGICAL COLLECTION
A. KOUNOUPIS PRIVATE COLLECTION
G. PLATIS PRIVATE COLLECTION

LARISSA
G. GOURYOTIS PRIVATE COLLECTION

LEFKAS
ARCHAEOLOGICAL COLLECTION
COLLECTION OF ECCLESIASTICAL PAINTINGS AND RELICS OF ORTHODOXY

LIMENARIA
I. PAPAGEORGIOU PRIVATE COLLECTION

LINDOS
ARCHAEOLOGICAL COLLECTION
H. GEORGIOU PRIVATE COLLECTION
P. IOANNIDIS PRIVATE COLLECTION
E. KASKINES PRIVATE COLLECTION

LIXOURI
ARCHAEOLOGICAL COLLECTION

MAKRYNITSA
D. MAVROS PRIVATE COLLECTION

MANDRAKI
ARCHAEOLOGICAL COLLECTION

MAVRADZEI
MONASTERY OF THE TIMIOS STAVROS

MELOS (MILOS)
MELOS MUSEUM

METEORA
MONASTERY OF AGION PANTON (VARLAAM)
MONASTERY OF AGIOS STEPHANOS
MONASTERY OF THE METAMORPHOSIS SOTIROS (METEORON)

MYKONOS
ARCHAEOLOGICAL MUSEUM
FOLKLORE COLLECTION

MYRINA
ARCHAEOLOGICAL MUSEUM

MYTILINI (MYTILENE)
ARCHAEOLOGICAL COLLECTION
NATIONAL FOLK MUSEUM OF LESVOS

NAFPLION
ARCHAEOLOGICAL MUSEUM

NAOUSSA
ECCLESIASTICAL COLLECTION

NAXOS
ARCHAEOLOGICAL MUSEUM

NEA ANCHIALOS
ARCHAEOLOGICAL COLLECTION

NEAPOLIS
ARCHAEOLOGICAL COLLECTION

OLYMPIA
ARCHAEOLOGICAL MUSEUM

OLYMPOS
ARCHAEOLOGICAL COLLECTION

PALAIA KORINTHOS
ARCHAEOLOGICAL MUSEUM

PANAGITSA PELLIS
CHURCH OF THE KOIMISSIS TIS THEOTOKOU

PAROS
ARCHAEOLOGICAL MUSEUM
BYZANTINE COLLECTION OF KATAPOLIANI

PATMOS
MONASTERY OF ST. JOHN

PATRAI
ARCHAEOLOGICAL MUSEUM

PELLA
ARCHAEOLOGICAL COLLECTION

PERACHORA
ARCHAEOLOGICAL COLLECTION

PERATATA
MONASTERY OF AGIOS ANDREAS

PIRAEUS
ARCHAEOLOGICAL MUSEUM

PLAKA
ARCHAEOLOGICAL MUSEUM

PLATANOS
ARCHAEOLOGICAL COLLECTION

POLYGYROS
ARCHAEOLOGICAL MUSEUM
I. LAMBROPOULOS PRIVATE COLLECTION

PYLOS
ANTONOPOULEION ARCHAEOLOGICAL MUSEUM

PYRGOS
MONASTERY OF PROFITIS ILIAS
P. NOMIKOS PRIVATE COLLECTION

RETHYMNON
ARCHAEOLOGICAL MUSEUM
ARKADI MONASTERY
COLLECTION OF THE LIKION TON ELLINIDON
MONASTERY OF AGIOS IOANNIS PREVELIS

RHODES
ARCHAEOLOGICAL MUSEUM
DECORATIVE ARTS COLLECTION OF THE MUSEUM OF RHODES

SALAMIS
ARCHAEOLOGICAL MUSEUM

SAMARINA, GREVENA
CHURCH OF THE PANAGIA

SAMOS
ARCHAEOLOGICAL MUSEUM
BYZANTINE MUSEUM OF THE METROPOLIS OF SAMOS AND IKARIA

SAMOTHRAKI
ARCHAEOLOGICAL MUSEUM

SIKYON
ARCHAEOLOGICAL MUSEUM

SKIATHOS
MONASTERY OF THE EVANGELISMOS TIS THEOTOKOU

SKOPELOS
MONASTERY OF THE EVANGELISTRIA

SKYROS
ARCHAEOLOGICAL MUSEUM

SOLOMOS
SOLOMOS AND EMINENT ZANTIANS MUSEUM

SPARTI
ARCHAEOLOGICAL MUSEUM

SPETSAI
MUSEUM

STAVROS
ARCHAEOLOGICAL MUSEUM

SYMI
ARCHAEOLOGICAL COLLECTION

TANAGRA
ARCHAEOLOGICAL COLLECTION

TEGEA
ARCHAEOLOGICAL MUSEUM

THASSOS
ARCHAEOLOGICAL MUSEUM

THEBES
THEBES MUSEUM

THERMON
ARCHAEOLOGICAL MUSEUM

THESSALONIKI
ARCHAEOLOGICAL MUSEUM
FOLKLORE MUSEUM AND ARCHIVES
FOLKLORE MUSEUM OF NORTHERN GREECE
V. KYRIAZOPOULOS PRIVATE COLLECTION
I. PAPAILIAKIS PRIVATE COLLECTION
G. PARALIS PRIVATE COLLECTION
G. PHILIPPOU PRIVATE COLLECTION
I. VASSILIOU PRIVATE COLLECTION

THIRA
ARCHAEOLOGICAL MUSEUM

THIVAI
ARCHAEOLOGICAL MUSEUM

TINOS

ARCHAEOLOGICAL MUSEUM
CHURCH OF THE PANAGIA EVANGELISTRIA

TRIKALA

ARCHAEOLOGICAL COLLECTION
ECCESIASTICAL MUSEUM OF THE METROPOLIS OF TRIKKI AND STAGOI
MONASTERY OF AGIOS VISSARION (DOUSSIKOU)

VEROIA

ARCHAEOLOGICAL MUSEUM

VOLOS

ATHANASSAKEION ARCHAEOLOGICAL MUSEUM
K. A. MAKRIS PRIVATE COLLECTION

VRAVRON

ARCHAEOLOGICAL MUSEUM

YPATI

AGATHONOS MONASTERY

ZAKYNTHOS

BYZANTINE MUSEUM

ZAVORDA

MONASTERY OF OSSIOS NIKANOR

ZERBITSA

MONASTERY OF THE KOIMISSIS TIS THEOTOKOU

GUATEMALA

GUATEMALA CITY

NATIONAL MUSEUM OF ART AND HANDICRAFTS

HONG KONG

HONG KONG

CITY MUSEUM AND ART GALLERY
FUNG PING SHAN MUSEUM

HUNGARY

BUDAPEST

CHINESE MUSEUM
FERENC HOPP MUSEUM OF ORIENTAL ART
HUNGARIAN NATIONAL MUSEUM
JÓKAI MEMORIAL ROOM
MUSEUM OF APPLIED ARTS
MUSEUM OF FINE ART
MUSEUM OF THE HISTORY OF BUDAPEST: DEPARTMENT OF MODERN HISTORY
MUSEUM OF THE HISTORY OF BUDAPEST: MEDIEVAL DEPARTMENT
NAGYTÉTÉNY PALACE MUSEUM

DEBRECEN

DÉRI MUSEUM

ESZTERGOM

BÁLINT BALASSI MUSEUM
MUSEUM OF CHRISTIANITY
TREASURY OF ESZTERGOM CATHEDRAL

FERTÖD

CHÂTEAU MUSEUM

HEREND

PORCELAIN FACTORY MUSEUM

HÓDMEZÖVÁSARHELY

JÁNOS TORNYAI MUSEUM

HOLLÓKÖ

VILLAGE MUSEUM

MOSONMAGYARÓVAR

HANSÁG MUSEUM

PANNONHALMA

ECCLESIASTICAL MUSEUM

PÁPA

LOCAL HISTORY MUSEUM

SÁRVÁR

FERENC NADASDY CASTLE MUSEUM

SIKLÓS

CASTLE MUSEUM

SZENTENDRE

COLLECTION OF SERBIAN CHURCH HISTORY

SZERENCS

PICTURE-POSTCARD MUSEUM

SZOLNOK

JÁNOS DAMJANICH MUSEUM

INDIA

ALLAHABAD

ALLAHABAD MUSEUM

ALWAR

GOVERNMENT MUSEUM

AUNDH

SRI BHAVANI MUSEUM

BARIPADA

BARIPADA MUSEUM

BARODA

MUSEUM AND PICTURE GALLERY

BENARES

MUSEUM OF INDIAN ARTS AND ARCHAEOLOGY
SARNATH MUSEUM

BHAWANAGAR

GANDHI SMRITI MUSEUMS

BHOPAL

CENTRAL MUSEUM

BHUBANESHWAR

ORISSA STATE MUSEUM

BHUJ

KUTCH MUSEUM

BIJAPUR

ARCHAEOLOGICAL MUSEUM

BIKANER

GANGA GOLDEN JUBILEE MUSEUM

BOMBAY

HERAS INSTITUTE OF INDIAN HISTORY AND CULTURE
JEHANGIR ART GALLERY
PRINCE OF WALES MUSEUM OF WESTERN INDIA
VICTORIA AND ALBERT MUSEUM

CALCUTTA

ART IN INDUSTRY MUSEUM
CRAFTS MUSEUM
GURUSADAY MUSEUM
INDIAN MUSEUM
MUSEUM OF THE BANGIYA SAHITYA PARISHAD
VICTORIA MEMORIAL HALL

DHAR

DHAR DISTRICT MUSEUM

GAUHATI

ASSAM STATE MUSEUM

GAYA

GAYA MUSEUM

GURUKUL JHAJJAR

HARYANA PRANTIYA PURATATVA SANGRAHALAYA

GWALIOR

STATE MUSEUM

HYDERABAD

CHOW MAHALLA PALACE
SALARJUNG MUSEUM
STATE ARCHAEOLOGICAL MUSEUM

INDORE

CENTRAL MUSEUM

JAIPUR

CENTRAL MUSEUM

JAMNAGAR

JAMNAGAR MUSEUM OF ANTIQUITIES, LAKHOTE BUILDING

JUNAGADH

DARBAR HALL MUSEUM

KALPI

MAHATMA GANDHI HINDI SANGRAHALAYA

LUCKNOW

STATE MUSEUM

MADRAS

FORT ST. GEORGE MUSEUM
THE GOVERNMENT MUSEUM AND NATIONAL ART GALLERY
VICTORIA TECHNICAL INSTITUTE

MADURAI

GANDHI SMARAK SANGRAHALAYA

MALDA

B. R. SEN MUSEUM

MANGALORE

GOVERNMENT MUSEUM
MAHATMA GANDHI MUSEUM

MATHURA

ARCHAEOLOGICAL MUSEUM

NAGPUR

CENTRAL MUSEUM

NEW DELHI

ARCHAEOLOGICAL MUSEUM
CRAFTS MUSEUM
NATIONAL MUSEUM OF INDIA
RABINDRA BHAVAN ART GALLERY
TIBET HOUSE MUSEUM

NOWGONG

STATE MUSEUM

PADMANABHAPURAM

MUSEUM OF ANTIQUITIES

POONA

BHARTIYA ITIHASA SAMSHODHAKA MANDALA MUSEUM
DECCAN COLLEGE MUSEUM

RAIPUR

MAHANT GHASI DASS MEMORIAL MUSEUM

SANGARIA

SIR CHOTURAM MUSEUM

SANTINIKETAN

KALA BHAVAN

SIKAR

SIKAR MUSEUM

SIROHI

STATE MUSEUM

SRINAGAR

S.P.S. MUSEUM

SRIRANGAM

DEVASTHANAMS MUSEUM

SURAT

SARDAR V. PATEL MUSEUM

TAL. KHATAV

SHRI BHAVANI MUSEUM AND LIBRARY

TAMLUK

HAMILTON HIGH SCHOOL MUSEUM

TRICHUR

STATE MUSEUM

TRIVANDRUM

ART MUSEUM

VALLABH VIDYANAGAR

MUSEUM OF ART AND ARCHAEOLOGY

VARANASI

BHARAT KALA BHAVAN
MAHARAJA BANARAS MUSEUM

INDONESIA

DENPASAR

BALI MUSEUM

DJAKARTA

MUSEUM OF INDONESIAN CULTURE
SEDJARAH MUSEUM

SURAKARTA

ART MUSEUM

IRAN

BANDAR ABBAS

MOHITSHENASI MUSEUM

ISFAHAN

CHEHEL SOTOUN MUSEUM

TEHERAN

ARCHAEOLOGICAL MUSEUM
GOLESTAN PALACE
MUSEUM OF DECORATIVE ARTS
NATIONAL ARTS MUSEUM
TREASURY OF THE CROWN JEWELS

IRAQ

BAGHDAD

AL-MUSTANSIRIYIA SCHOOL MUSEUM
THE ARAB MUSEUM

IRELAND

BANTRY

BANTRY HOUSE

CELBRIDGE

CASTLETOWN HOUSE

CLONFERT

CLONFERT MUSEUM

DUBLIN

NATIONAL MUSEUM OF IRELAND

KILKENNY

ROTHE HOUSE MUSEUM

MAYNOOTH

CARTON
MUSEUM OF ECCLESIOLOGY AND PHYSICS

WESTPORT

WESTPORT HOUSE

ISRAEL

AKKO (ACRE)

AKKO MUNICIPAL MUSEUM

HAIFA

ETHNOLOGICAL MUSEUM AND FOLKLORE ARCHIVES
MUSEUM OF ANCIENT ART
MUSEUM OF MODERN ART
TIKOTIN MUSEUM OF JAPANESE ART

JERUSALEM

BEZALEL NATIONAL ART MUSEUM
MUSEUM DOR VADOR
I. WOLFSON MUSEUM

NIR-DAVID

MUSEUM OF MEDITERRANEAN ARCHAEOLOGY

SEDOT YAM

CAESAREA MUSEUM

TEL-AVIV

CERAMICS MUSEUM
GLASS MUSEUM
MUSEUM OF ETHNOGRAPHY AND FOLKLORE

ITALY

AGRIGENTO

DIOCESAN MUSEUM

ALBISOLA SUPERIORE

VILLA GAVOTTI

AOSTA

CATHEDRAL TREASURY

AQUILEIA

ARCHAEOLOGICAL MUSEUM

AQUINO

CATHEDRAL TREASURY

AREZZO

PICTURE GALLERY AND MUSEUM OF MEDIEVAL AND MODERN ART

BENEVENTO

SANNIO MUSEUM

BERGAMO

DONIZETTI MUSEUM

BOLOGNA

COMMUNAL ART COLLECTIONS
DAVIA BARGELLINI ART GALLERY AND MUSEUM OF INDUSTRIAL ART
POMPEO ARIA ETRUSCAN MUSEUM

BRESCIA

MUSEUM OF CHRISTIAN ART

CAGLIARI

NATIONAL ARCHAEOLOGICAL MUSEUM

CALTAGIRONE

MUNICIPAL MUSEUM
MUSEUM OF CERAMICS

CASTEL SANT'ELIA

MUSEUM OF SACRED ART

CATANIA

MUNICIPAL MUSEUM AND PICTURE GALLERY

CATANZARO

REGIONAL MUSEUM

CHIETI

NATIONAL MUSEUM OF ANTIQUITIES

CITTÀ DI CASTELLO

CHAPTER HOUSE MUSEUM
MUNICIPAL ART GALLERY

CIVIDALE DEL FRIULI

CHAPTER MUSEUM
NATIONAL ARCHAEOLOGICAL MUSEUM

CORTONA

DIOCESAN MUSEUM
MUSEUM OF EGYPTIAN AND ETRUSCAN ANTIQUITIES

CREMONA

CATHEDRAL

ENNA

ALESSI MUSEUM

ESTE

ATESTINO NATIONAL MUSEUM

FAENZA

INTERNATIONAL CERAMICS MUSEUM

FELTRE

RIZZARDA MUSEUM

FERRARA

SPINA NATIONAL ARCHAEOLOGICAL MUSEUM

FIESOLE

MISSIONARY MUSEUM

FLORENCE

ARCHAEOLOGICAL MUSEUM
BARDINI MUSEUM AND CORSI GALLERY
MEDICI CHAPELS
MUSEUM OF THE CATHEDRAL DI SANTA MARIA DEL FIORE
MUSEUM OF SAN MARCO
NATIONAL MUSEUM OF DECORATIVE ARTS
SILVER MUSEUM
STIBBERT MUSEUM

FORLI

MUSEUM OF CERAMICS
MUSEUM AND PICTURE GALLERY

GELA

NATIONAL MUSEUM

GENOA

CATALDI PALACE
CHIOSSONE MUSEUM
TREASURY

GRADARA

THE ROCCA

GUBBIO

DUCAL PALACE
MUSEUM AND PICTURE GALLERY

L'AQUILA

ABBRUZZO NATIONAL MUSEUM
DIOCESAN MUSEUM

LECCE

CASTROMEDIANO MUSEUM

LORETO

TREASURY

LORETO APRUTINO

MUSEUM OF ANCIENT ABRUZZI CERAMICS

LOVERE

TADINI MUSEUM

LUCERA

FIORELLI MUSEUM

MANTUA

CATHEDRAL
CAVRIANI PALACE
DUCAL PALACE

MASER

VILLA BARBARO (or VILLA MASER)

MILAN

CATHEDRAL MUSEUM
MUSEUM OF ANCIENT ART
MUSEUM OF THE BASILICA OF SANT-AMBROGIO
POLDI-PEZZOLI MUSEUM

MODENA

CITY MUSEUM

MONZA

CATHEDRAL AND TREASURY

MURANO

MUSEUM OF GLASSWARE

NAPLES

FILANGERI MUSEUM
MUSEUM OF THE CARTHUSIAN MONASTERY OF ST. MARTIN
MUSEUM OF THE STATE INSTITUTE OF ART
NATIONAL CERAMICS MUSEUM
NATIONAL GALLERY OF NAPLES
PAGLIARA ART COLLECTION
ROYAL PALACE

OSTIA ANTICA

DELLA ROCCA CASTLE AND MUSEUM

PADUA

BASILICA OF SANT'ANTONIO

PALERMO

CASINA CINESE
PITRÉ ETHNOGRAPHICAL MUSEUM

PALMI

CALABRESE MUSEUM OF ETHNOGRAPHY AND FOLK-LORE

PARMA

MUSEUM OF CHINESE ART
MUSEUM OF CHINESE ETHNOGRAPHY

PAVIA

CARTHUSIAN MONASTERY MUSEUM

PERUGIA

CHAPTERHOUSE MUSEUM
NATIONAL GALLERY OF UMBRIA

PESARO

MUSEUM OF MAJOLICA

PISA

NATIONAL MUSEUM OF SAN MATTEO

RAVENNA

BASILICA OF SANT'APOLLINARE IN CLASSE
CHURCH OF SAN VITALE AND MAUSOLEUM OF GALLA PLACIDA

RECANATI

DIOCESAN MUSEUM

REGGIO CALABRIA

NATIONAL MUSEUM

ROME

BARRACCO MUSEUM
BASILICA OF S. PAOLO FUORI LE MURA
CRISTIANO MUSEUM (VATICAN MUSEUMS)
DORIA PAMPHILJ GALLERY
ETRUSCAN MUSEUM (VATICAN MUSEUMS)
MAP GALLERY AND CANDELABRA GALLERY (VATICAN MUSEUMS)
MEDIEVAL MUSEUM
MUSEUM OF THE PALAZZO VENEZIA
NATIONAL MUSEUM OF CASTEL SANT'ANGELO
NATIONAL MUSEUM OF ORIENTAL ART
PAOLINO MUSEUM (VATICAN MUSEUM)
PICTURE GALLERY (VATICAN MUSEUMS)
PROFANO MUSEUM (VATICAN MUSEUMS)
ST. PETER'S BASILICA, SACRISTY AND TREASURY

ROSSANO

DIOCESAN MUSEUM

SALERNO

CATHEDRAL MUSEUM

SAN GIMIGNANO

MUSEUM OF SACRED ART

SIENA

CATHEDRAL MUSEUM
MUNICIPAL MUSEUM AND APARTMENTS
PUBLIC LIBRARY

SORRENTO

CORREALE MUSEUM

TARANTO

NATIONAL MUSEUM

TARQUINIA

NATIONAL MUSEUM

TOLENTINO

MUNICIPAL MUSEUM

TORCELLO

MUSEO DELL'ESTUARIO

TRAPANI

PEPOLI MUSEUM

TRENT

NATIONAL MUSEUM

TRIESTE

MUSEUM OF HISTORY AND ART
MUSEUM OF RELIGIOUS ART

TURIN

MUNICIPAL GALLERY OF MODERN ART
MUSEUM OF ANCIENT ART
ROYAL PALACE

UDINE

CASTLE MUSEUM AND PICTURE GALLERY

URBINO

NATIONAL GALLERY OF THE MARCHES

VENICE

CORRER MUSEUM
MARCIANA LIBRARY
MUSEUM OF ORIENTAL ART
SCUOLA GRANDE DI SAN ROCCO
SETTECENTO MUSEUM
TREASURY OF THE BASILICA SAN MARCO

JAMAICA

HALF-WAY TREE

AFRICAN MUSEUM

KINGSTON

WEST INDIA REFERENCE LIBRARY HISTORICAL GALLERY

JAPAN

AKASHI-SHI

MEMORIAL HALL OF THE EMPEROR MEIJI'S TEMPORARY HEADQUARTERS AT AKASHI

AKITA-SHI

AKITA CITY MUSEUM OF ART

ARITA-MACHI

ARITA CHINA-WARE ART MUSEUM

ATAMI-SHI

ATAMI ART MUSEUM

BEPPU

ANCIENT CULTURE MUSEUM, BEPPU UNIVERSITY

BEPPU-SHI

KINSUIEN ART MUSEUM

CHIKUFUJIMA

TREASURE HOUSE ON SHIKUFUJIMA ISLANDS

FUEDA

ART GALLERY OF THE TOKIWAYAMA FOUNDATION

FUKUI-SHI

FUKUI HISTORY HALL

HAKONE-MACHI

HAKONE ART MUSEUM

HANAMAKI-SHI

TIBETAN COLLECTION ATTACHED TO THE KOTOKUJI TEMPLE

HIKONE-SHI

I'I ART MUSEUM

HIRAIZUMI-MACHI

TREASURE HOUSE OF THE CHUSONJI TEMPLE

HIRATA-SHI

TREASURE HOUSE OF THE WANIBUCHIJI TEMPLE

IKARUGA-MACHI

TREASURE HOUSE OF THE HORYUJI TEMPLE

ISE-SHI

JINGU HISTORICAL AND AGRICULTURAL MUSEUM

ISHINOMAKI-SHI

ENDO-MORI ARCHAEOLOGICAL COLLECTION OF ISHINOMAKI

IWAKI-SHI

NAKASO ART MUSEUM

KAMAKURA-SHI

KAMAKURA NATIONAL TREASURE HOUSE
TREASURE HOUSE OF THE TSURUGAOKA-HACHIMAN SHRINE

KAMIYAMA-SHI

KANISENDO MUSEUM

KAMO-GUN

CHOHACHI MEMORIAL COLLECTION

KANAZAWA-MACHI

KANAZAWA BUNKO MUSEUM

KAWANISHI-CHO

KIKUSUI HANDICRAFT MUSEUM

KIBI-GUN

KIBI ARCHAEOLOGICAL COLLECTION

KOBE-SHI

HAKUTSURU ART MUSEUM
KOBE MUNICIPAL MUSEUM OF ART

KOYA-SAN

TREASURE HOUSE OF THE TEMPLES ON MT. KOYA

KURASHIKI-SHI

KURASHIKI HANDICRAFT MUSEUM
OHARA ART MUSEUM

KUSHIRO-SHI

KUSHIRO MUNICIPAL MUSEUM

KYOTO

FUJI'I COLLECTION
KYOTO MUNICIPAL MUSEUM OF ART
KYOTO NATIONAL MUSEUM
NATIONAL MUSEUM OF MODERN ART
TREASURE HOUSE OF THE TOYOKUNI SHRINE
YURINKAN COLLECTION

MITO-SHI

IBARAKI PREFECTURAL MUSEUM OF ART

NAGASAKI-SHI

NAGASAKI MUNICIPAL MUSEUM

NAKA KOMATSU

KIKUSUI KOGEIKAN

NARA-SHI

HORYUJI TEMPLE
NARA NATIONAL MUSEUM
NEIRAKU ART MUSEUM
SHOSOIN TREASURE HOUSE
TREASURE HOUSE OF THE KASUGA SHRINE
TREASURE HALL OF THE TODAIJI TEMPLE
YAMATO CULTURAL HOUSE

NIKKO-SHI

TREASURE HOUSE OF THE JOKODO, RINNOJI TEMPLE

ODAWARA-SHI

MATSUNAGA MEMORIAL HALL

OSAKA

FUJITA ART MUSEUM
ITSUO ART MUSEUM
JAPAN HANDICRAFT MUSEUM
MUNICIPAL MUSEUM

OTSU

SHIGA PREFECTURAL MUSEUM

RIKUZENTAKADA-SHI

RIKUZENTAKADA MUNICIPAL MUSEUM

SAKATA-SHI

HONMA ART MUSEUM

SUWA-SHI

SUWA MUNICIPAL MUSEUM OF ART

TAJIMI-SHI

TAJIMI MUNICIPAL OLD CHINA- WARE EXHIBITION HALL

TAKAMATSU-SHI

TAKAMATSU MUNICIPAL MUSEUM OF ART

TAKAOKA-SHI

TAKAOKA MUNICIPAL MUSEUM OF ART

TAMANO-SHI

TAMANO MARINE MUSEUM

TOKONAME-SHI

TOKONAME CHINA-WARE HALL

TOKYO

BRIDGESTONE MUSEUM OF ART
EXHIBITION HALL OF TOKYO UNIVERSITY OF ARTS LIBRARY AND MASAKI MEMORIAL HALL
FOLK ART MUSEUM
FOLK MUSEUM OF SETAGAYA
GOTO ART MUSEUM
IDEMITSU ART GALLERY
JAPANESE FOLK CRAFT MUSEUM
MEIJI SHRINE TREASURE MUSEUM
MIAGEIKAN MUSEUM OF MODERN ART
MUSEUM OF CALLIGRAPHY
NATIONAL MUSEUM
NATIONAL MUSEUM OF ANTIQUES
NATIONAL MUSEUM OF MODERN ART
NEZU ART MUSEUM
PROFESSOR AIZU MEMORIAL EXHIBITION ROOM OF ORIENTAL ARTS
SUNTORY ART GALLERY
TENRI GALLERY

TOYKO

TAKANAWA ART MUSEUM

TOKYO

UMEZAWA MUSEUM
YAMATANE MUSEUM OF ART

TOTTORI-SHI

TOTTORI HANDICRAFT MUSEUM

TOYOTA-GUN

KOZOJI TEMPLE MUSEUM

URAWA-SHI

SAITAMA PREFECTURAL MUSEUM OF ART

YAMATO-MURA

TREASURE HALL OF THE RAKUHOJI TEMPLE

YOKOGOSHIMURA

HOPPO BUNKA MUSEUM

YOKOSUKA-SHI

YOKOSUKA CITY MUSEUM

KENYA

MOMBASA

NATIONAL MUSEUM

KOREA, REPUBLIC OF

PUSAN

NATONAL UNIVERSITY MUSEUM

PUYO

NATIONAL MUSEUM

SEOUL

MUSEUM
MUSEUM OF CHANG-DUK PALACE
NATIONAL MUSEUM

KUWAIT

KUWAIT

KUWAIT MUSEUM

LEBANON

BEIRUT

ARCHAEOLOGICAL MUSEUM

LUXEMBOURG

LUXEMBOURG

STATE MUSEUM

MALAGASY REPUBLIC

TANANARIVE

MUSEUM OF ART AND ARCHAEOLOGY

MALAYSIA

ALOR STAR

MUSEUM NEGERI KEDAH

KUALA LUMPUR

NATIONAL MUSEUM

MALACCA

MALACCA MUSEUM

PENANG

PENANG MUSEUM AND ART GALLERY

PERAK

TAIPING MUSEUM

SARAWAK

SARAWAK MUSEUM

MALTA

MDINA

CATHEDRAL MUSEUM

VALLETTA

NATIONAL MUSEUM
ST. JOHN'S MUSEUM AND CATHEDRAL

MEXICO

CHIAPA DE CORZO

MUSEUM OF LACQUER-WARE

CULIACAN

SINALOA REGIONAL MUSEUM

DOLORES HIDALGO

CASA DE HIDALGO

DZIBILCHALTUN

DZIBILCHALTUN REGIONAL ARCHAEOLOGICAL MUSEUM

GUADALUPE

GUADALUPE REGIONAL MUSEUM

GUANAJUATO

GUANAJUATO REGIONAL MUSEUM

MEXICO CITY

CARMEL MUSEUM OF COLONIAL HISTORY
CONVENT OF SANTA MARIA DE LOS ANGELES
DIEGO RIVERA MUSEUM OF ANAHUACALLI
MUSEUM OF RURAL LIFE (CHARRERIA)
MUSEUM OF WESTERN MEXICAN CULTURE
NATIONAL HISTORICAL MUSEUM

OAXACA

JUÁREZ HOUSE

PATZUCARO

MUSEUM OF FOLK ARTS AND CRAFTS

PUEBLA

JOSÉ LUIS BEELO Y GONZALEZ MUSEUM
MUSEUM OF HANDICRAFTS
PUEBLA REGIONAL MUSEUM
SANTA MONICA COLONIAL MUSEUM

SAN LUIS POTOSI

SAN LUIS POTOSI REGIONAL MUSEUM

TLAQUEPAQUE

REGIONAL CERAMICS MUSEUM

TOLUCA

MUSEUM OF NATURAL HISTORY AND ARCHAEOLOGY

MOROCCO

FEZ

BATHA MUSEUM

MARRAKESH

DAR SI SAID MUSEUM
MUSEUM OF THE MENARA

MEKMES

DAR JAMAÏ MUSEUM

TANGIER

KASBAH MUSEUM

TETOUAN

TETOUAN MUSEUM

MOZAMBIQUE

LOURENÇO MARQUES

HISTORICAL MUSEUM

NEPAL

BHAKTAPUR

WOODWORK MUSEUM

KATHMANDU

NATIONAL MUSEUM OF NEPAL

NETHERLANDS

ALPHEN AAN DEN RIJN

OLD ALPHEN MUSEUM

AMERONGEN

COLLECTION OF THE HEIRS OF COUNT VAN ALDENBURG BENTINCK

AMERSFOORT

MUSEUM FLEHITE

AMSTERDAM

CITROEN COLLECTION
CITY MUSEUM
COLLECTION OF BARON VAN HEECKEREN VAN WALIEN
FAN MUSEUM
E. A. KLATTE COLLECTION
MUSEUM AMSTELKRING
NATIONAL MUSEUM: DEPARTMENT OF DUTCH HISTORY
NATIONAL MUSEUM: DEPARTMENT OF FAR-EASTERN ART
NATIONAL MUSEUM: DEPARTMENT OF SCULPTURE AND INDUSTRIAL ART
E. PROEHL COLLECTION
A. SCHWARTZ COLLECTION
SIX COLLECTION
DR. B. SLINGENBERG'S COLLECTION

ANGERLO

VAN WEEDE COLLECTION

ARNHEM

LOCAL MUSEUM
VAN SIMMEREN VAN DER WEERD COLLECTION

ASSELT

ASSELT MUSEUM OF FOLKLORE

BERGEN OP ZOOM

DISTRICT MUSEUM

BERLICUM

VAN RIJCKEVORSEL COLLECTION

BREDA

DIOCESAN MUSEUM
MUNICIPAL MUSEUM

BREUKELEN

GUNTERSTEIN RESIDENCE

BUSSUM

E. A. VELTMAN COLLECTION

CADIER EN KEER

CADIER EN KEER AFRICA CENTRE

COTTEN

BARON VAN HARDENBROEK COLLECTION

CULEMBORG

CULEMBORG AND DISTRICT MUSEUM OF LOCAL HISTORY

DALFSEN

VON MARTELS DANKERN AND ROËLL VAN HAZERWOUDE COLLECTION
VAN RECHTEREN LIMPURG COLLECTION

DELFT

PAUL TETAR VAN ELVEN MUSEUM
HET PRINSENHOF MUNICIPAL MUSEUM
MUSEUM OF THE HOUSE OF ORANGE-NASSAU
NATIONAL MUSEUM: LAMBERT VAN MEERTEN HOUSE

DENEKAMP

SINGRAVEN

DE STEEG

MIDDACHTEN CASTLE

DEVENTER

WEIGH HOUSE MUSEUM

DIEVER

SCHULTE HOUSE

DOKKUM

'ADMIRALTY HOUSE' DISTRICT MUSEUM

DOORN

DOORN HOUSE

DORDRECHT

BILDERBEEK-LAMAISON NATIONAL MUSEUM
SIMON VAN GIJN MUSEUM

ENKHUIZEN

NATIONAL ZUIDERZEE MUSEUM

ENSCHEDE

TWENTE NATIONAL MUSEUM

FRANEKER

DR. COOPMAN'S HOUSE MUNICIPAL MUSEUM

GORREDIJK

'DE ZUID OSTHOCK' MUSEUM OF LOCAL HISTORY AND NATURAL HISTORY

GOUDA

CATHARINA INN MUNICIPAL MUSEUM
GOUDA STAINED GLASS
DE MORIAAN PIPE AND POTTERY MUSEUM

'S GRAVENHAGE

D. H. G. BOLTEN COLLECTION
BREDIUS MUSEUM
HENDRIK WILLEM MESDAG NATIONAL MUSEUM
MUNICIPAL MUSEUM
H. H. F. SALOMON COLLECTION
THURKOW COLLECTION

HAARLEM

DIOCESAN MUSEUM OF RELIGIOUS ART
FRANS HALS MUSEUM

HAARZUILENS

VAN ZUYLEN VAN NIJVELT VAN DE HAAN COLLECTION

HARDEWIJK

MUSEUM OF THE HISTORY OF THE VELUWE

HEEMSTEDE

DE RAAF BRAND VAN STRAATER COLLECTION

'S HEERENBERG

BERGH HOUSE

HEINENOORD

HOEKSCHE WARD DISTRICT MUSEUM

HEINO

HANNEMA-DE STUERS FOUNDATION

HELVERSUM

DE VAART MUSEUM OF ART

'S HERTOGENBOSCH

NORTH BRABANT MUSEUM

HOORN

WEST FRISIAN MUSEUM

LAREN

VERWOLDE HOUSE

LEERDAM

LEERDAM NATIONAL GLASS MUSEUM

LEEUWARDEN

FRISIAN MUSEUM

LEIDEN

LAKENHAL MUNICIPAL MUSEUM
NATIONAL MUSEUM OF ETHNOLOGY

LOOSDRECHT

SYPESTEYN CASTLE MUSEUM

MAASTRICHT

BONNEFANTEN MUSEUM
T. J. BOTKE COLLECTION
TREASURY OF THE BASILICA OF OUR LADY
TREASURY OF ST. SERVAAS CHURCH

MAKKUM

FRISIAN POTTERY MUSEUM IN THE WEIGH HOUSE

MARSSUM

HERINGA STATE

MONNIKENDAM

THE WEIGH-HOUSE

MUIDEN

MUIDEN CASTLE NATIONAL MUSEUM

NIJMEGEN

LOCAL HISTORY MUSEUM

OLDENZAAL

TREASURY OF THE BASILICA OF ST. PLECHELMUS

OPHEMERT

OPHEMERT CASTLE

OTTERLOO

'IT NOFLIK STÊ' TILE MUSEUM
KROLLER-MULLER NATIONAL MUSEUM

OUD-ZUILEN

ZUYLEN CASTLE

OVERWEEN

KLATTE- DE WAAL COLLECTION

RHENEN

RHENEN DISTRICT MUSEUM

ROSENDAAL

MUSEUM OF THE GOLDEN ROSE

ROTTERDAM

BOYMANS AND VAN BEUNIGEN MUSEUM
HISTORICAL MUSEUM
MUSEUM OF ETHNOLOGY
WILLEM VAN DER VORM FOUNDATION

SCHEVENINGEN

H. M. KNIGHT COLLECTION

SCHIEDAM

MUNICIPAL MUSEUM

SLUIS

TOWN LOCAL HISTORY COLLECTION

SPANKEREN

J. G. WURFBAIN COLLECTION

TEGELEN

TEGELEN LOCAL HISTORY MUSEUM

TIEL

TIEL AND DISTRICT LOCAL HISTORY MUSEUM

UTRECHT

VAN BAAREN MUSEUM
CENTRAL MUSEUM
DIOCESAN MUSEUM
MUSEUM OF MODERN RELIGIOUS ART
NETHERLANDS GOLD, SILVER AND CLOCK MUSEUM

VAASSEN

CANNENBURCH CASTLE

VENLO

GOLTZIUS MUSEUM

VLISSINGEN

MUNICIPAL MUSEUM

VOORSCHOTEN

DUIVENSVOORDE CASTLE

VORDEN

VICTOR DE STUERS COLLECTION

WESTERBORK

NETHERLANDS MUSEUM OF PAPER-CUTTING

ZIERIKZEE

LOCAL MUSEUM

ZOELEN

SOELEN CASTLE

ZUTPHEN
MUNICIPAL MUSEUM
ZWOLLE
OVERIJSSEL PROVINCIAL MUSEUM

NEW ZEALAND

AUCKLAND
AUCKLAND CITY ART GALLERY
CHRISTCHURCH
CANTERBURY MUSEUM
ROBERT McDOUGALL ART GALLERY
DUNEDIN
OTAGO MUSEUM
THE THEOMIN GALLERY (OLVESTON)
NAPIER
HAWKE'S BAY ART GALLERY AND MUSEUM
NELSON
ISEL HOUSE
ROTORUA
MAORI PA
TIMARU
AIGANTIGHE ART GALLERY

NICARAGUA

MANAGUA
NATIONAL MUSEUM OF NICARAGUA
NINDIRÍ
ARCHAEOLOGICAL MUSEUM

NIGERIA

KANO
MAKAMA'S HOUSE
LAGOS
NIGERIAN MUSEUM

NORWAY

BERGEN
HISTORICAL MUSEUM
WESTERN NORWAY MUSEUM OF APPLIED ART
FLEKKEFJORD
FLEKKEFJORD TOWN MUSEUM
KAUPANGER
HEIBERG COLLECTION
KRAGERØ
BERG-KRAGERØ MUSEUM
NESBYEN
HALLINGDAL FOLK MUSEUM
OSLO
HISTORICAL MUSEUM
MUSEUM OF APPLIED ARTS
RÖROS
RÖROS MUSEUM
TROMSØ
TROMSØ MUSEUM
TRONDHEIM
MUSEUM OF THE ROYAL NORWEGIAN SOCIETY OF SCIENCES AND LETTERS
NORTH NORWAY MUSEUM OF APPLIED ARTS
TRONDHEIM AND TRØNDELAG FOLK MUSEUM

PAKISTAN, WEST

KARACHI
NATIONAL MUSEUM OF PAKISTAN
LAHORE
INDUSTRIAL AND COMMERCIAL MUSEUM
LAHORE MUSEUM
LAHORE FORT MUSEUM
PESHAWAR
PESHAWAR MUSEUM

PARAGUAY

ASUNCION
MONSEÑOR SINFORIANO BAGARIN MUSEUM
ITAUGUÁ
MUSEUM OF ICONOGRAPHY

PERU

LIMA
ARCHAEOLOGICAL MUSEUM
RAFAEL LARCO HERRERA MUSEUM
MUSEUM OF ART
MUSEUM OF THE PRE-HISPANIC ANTHROPOLOGY AND AGRICULTURE INSTITUTE
MUSEUM OF SAN FRANCISCO THE GREAT
NATIONAL MUSEUM OF PERUVIAN CULTURE
THE PERUVIAN GOLD MUSEUM
RIMAC
COLONIAL MUSEUM
TRUJILLO
ARCHAEOLOGICAL MUSEUM

PHILIPPINES

MANILA
MUSEUM OF ARTS AND SCIENCES
SANTA ANA ARCHAEOLOGICAL SITE AND LITURGICAL ARTS MUSEUM
MARAWI CITY
AGA KHAN MUSEUM OF MUSLIM ARTS
TACLOBAN CITY
LEYTE-SAMAR MUSEUM

POLAND

BOLISTAWIEC
LOCAL MUSEUM
BYTOM
MUSEUM OF UPPER SILESIA
DUKLA
LOCAL MUSEUM
GDAŃSK
POMERANIAN MUSEUM
GLIWICE
GLIWICE MUSEUM
GOŁUCHÓW
GOŁUCHÓW MUSEUM
ISTEBNA NA KUBALONCE
MUSEUM OF RELIGIOUS ART
JELENIA GÓRA
REGIONAL MUSEUM
KARTUZY
KASUBIAN MUSEUM
KĘTRZYN
KĘTRZYN MUSEUM
KOLBUSZOWA
LASOWIAKOW REGIONAL MUSEUM
KÓRNIK
KÓRNIK MUSEUM
KRAKÓW
CZAPSKI MUSEUM
CZARTORYSKI MUSEUM
MUSEUM OF THE JAGELLONIAN LIBRARY
NATIONAL ART COLLECTIONS
UNIVERSITY MUSEUM OF FINE ART
KROŚNIEWICE
COLLECTIONS OF JERZY DUNIN- BORKOWSKI
ŁAŃCUT
REGIONAL MUSEUM
LIDZBARK WARMIŃSKI
LOCAL MUSEUM
ŁÓDŹ
ARCHAEOLOGICAL AND ETHNOGRAPHICAL MUSEUM
MUSEUM OF ARCHAEOLOGY AND ETHNOGRAPHY
LUBLIN
NATIONAL MUSEUM
NIEBORÓW I ARKADIA
NIEBORÓW PALACE
OLIWA
REGIONAL MUSEUM OF ETHNOGRAPHY
OPOLE
SILESIAN MUSEUM
OSTROWIEC ŚWIĘLKRZYSKI
REGIONAL MUSEUM
PELPIN
DIOCESAN MUSEUM
PODDĘBICE
REGIONAL MUSEUM
POZNAŃ
DIOCESAN MUSEUM
MUSEUM OF DECORATIVE ARTS
MUSEUM OF RURAL CULTURE AND HANDICRAFTS
POZNAŃ NATIONAL MUSEUM
PRZEMYŚL
DIOCESAN MUSEUM
PSZCZYNA
PALACE MUSEUM
RABKA ZDROJ
REGIONAL MUSEUM 'WŁADYSŁAW ORKAN'
RADOM
MUNICIPAL MUSEUM
ROGALIN
LOCAL MUSEUM
RZESZOW
REGIONAL MUSEUM
SANDOMIERZ
DIOCESAN MUSEUM
SANOK
SANOK MUSEUM
SIERADZ
SIERADZ MUSEUM
SKLARSKA PORĘBA
MUSEUM OF CUT GLASS
SZCZYRZYC
LOCAL MUSEUM
TARNÓW
DIOCESAN MUSEUM
TARNOW
MUNICIPAL MUSEUM
TATARY POD KADZIDŁEM
KURPIE MUSEUM
TORUŃ
MUSEUM OF ART
REGIONAL MUSEUM
WAŁBRZYCH
REGIONAL MUSEUM
WARSAW
ŁAZIENKACH MUSEUM
MUSEUM OF APPLIED ARTS
MUSEUM OF THE HISTORY OF THE CITY OF WARSAW
NATIONAL MUSEUM
POSTER MUSEUM
WILANÓW MUSEUM
WROCŁAW
ARCHIDIOCESAN MUSEUM
COLLECTIONS OF THE ACADEMY OF PLASTIC ARTS
ETHNOGRAPHICAL MUSEUM
NATIONAL MUSEUM

PORTUGAL

ALPIARÇA
MUSEUM
BARCELOS
MUNICIPAL ARCHAEOLOGICAL MUSEUM
BEJA
REGIONAL MUSEUM
BRAGA
MUSEUM OF RELIGIOUS ART
TREASURY
COIMBRA
MACHADO DE CASTRO MUSEUM
OLD CATHEDRAL
ELVAS
REGIONAL MUSEUM
ÉVORA
MUSEUM OF ANCIENT ART
TREASURY

FUNCHAL

THE CROSSES' QUINTA
MUSEUM OF RELIGIOUS ART

GUIMARÃES

ALBERTO SAMPAIO MUSEUM
MARTINS SARMENTO MUSEUM
PALACE OF THE DUKES OF BRAGANCA

ILHAVO

CERAMICS MUSEUM
LOCAL MUSEUM

LAMEGO

REGIONAL MUSEUM

LISBON

ARCHAEOLOGICAL MUSEUM
CALOUSTE GULBENKIAN MUSEUM
MUSEUM OF DECORATIVE ART
MUSEUM OF POPULAR ART
MUSEUM OF RELIGIOUS ART
NATIONAL MUSEUM OF ANCIENT ART
NATIONAL MUSEUM OF ARCHAEOLOGY AND ETHNOLOGY

LISON

RAFAEL BORDALO PINHEIRO MUSEUM

OPORTO

GUERRA JUNQUEIRO MUSEUM
SOARES DOS REIS MUSEUM

VIANA DO CASTELO

MUNICIPAL MUSEUM

VILA REAL DE SANTO ANTONIO

DUCAL PALACE

VISEU

GRÃO VASCO MUSEUM

ROMANIA

AGNITA

AGNITA MUSEUM

ALBA IULIA

ALBA IULIA MUSEUM

ARAD

ARAD MUSEUM

BUCHAREST

ART MUSEUM
ELENA AND DR. I. N. DONA COLLECTION
DR. N. MINOVICI MUSEUM OF FOLK ART
ING. MINOVICI MUSEUM OF MEDIEVAL ART
ION MINULESCU COLLECTION
MOGOŞOAIA MUSEUM OF THE ART OF THE BRÂNCOVEANU PERIOD
MUSEUM OF FOLK ART
NATIONAL MUSEUM OF ANTIQUITIES
G. OPRESCU COLLECTION
MARIA AND DR. G. SEVEREANU COLLECTION
SLATINEANU COLLECTION
MOISE M. WEINBURG COLLECTION

CÎMPULUNG

CÎMPULUNG-MUSCEL MUSEUM

CÎMPULUNG- MOLDOVENESC

MOLDOVENIAN MUSEUM

CLUJ

ART MUSEUM
HISTORY MUSEUM
TRANSYLVANIAN MUSEUM OF ETHNOGRAPHY

CRAIOVA

ART MUSEUM
OLTENIEI MUSEUM

FOCŞANI

HISTORY MUSEUM

GALAŢI

MUSEUM OF MODERN AND CONTEMPORARY ROMANIAN ART

MANGALIA

ARCHAEOLOGICAL MUSEUM

MIERCUREA CIUC

MIERCUREA CIUC MUSEUM

NĂSĂUD

NĂSĂUD MUSEUM

NEGREŞTI

OPEN-AIR MUSEUM

ORLEA

LOCAL MUSEUM

RIMETEA

LOCAL MUSEUM

SIBIU

BRUKENTHAL MUSEUM

SINAIA

PELEŞ MUSEUM

TIMIŞOARA

BANAT MUSEUM

TÎRGU JIU

TIRGU JIU MUSEUM

TÎRGU NEAMŢ

MONASTERY MUSEUM

TURNU SEVERIN

IRON GATE (PORŢILE DE FIER) MUSEUM

URLAŢI

MUSEUM OF ETHNOGRAPHY

SINGAPORE

SINGAPORE

ART MUSEUM AND EXHIBITION GALLERY
NATIONAL MUSEUM

SOUTH AFRICA, REPUBLIC OF

ADELAIDE

"OUR HERITAGE" MUSEUM

BEAUFORT WEST

BEAUFORT WEST MUSEUM

CAPE TOWN

CASTLE OF GOOD HOPE
GROOT CONSTANTIA MANOR HOUSE

CAPETOWN

KOOPMANS DE WET HOUSE

CAPE TOWN

SOUTH AFRICAN CULTURAL HISTORY MUSEUM

DURBAN

DURBAN MUSEUM AND ART GALLERY
WILLIAM CAMPBELL MUSEUM

GRAHAMSTOWN

ALBANY MUSEUM

JOHANNESBURG

JOHANNESBURG ART GALLERY

KIMBERLEY

WILLIAM HUMPHREYS ART GALLERY

PAARL

OLD PARSONAGE MUSEUM

PIETERMARITZBURG

TATHAM ART GALLERY

PORT ELIZABETH

KING GEORGE VI ART GALLERY

PRETORIA

ENGELENBURG HOUSE ART COLLECTION
NATIONAL CULTURAL HISTORY AND OPEN-AIR MUSEUM

STELLENBOSCH

THE BURGERHUIS
STELLENBOSCH MUSEUM

WORCESTER

WORCESTER MUSEUM

SOUTH-WEST AFRICA (NAMIBIA)

LÜDERITZ

LÜDERITZ MUSEUM

SPAIN

ALBARRACIN

CATHEDRAL

ALBOCACER

PAROCHIAL MUSEUM

ALICANTE

PROVINCIAL ARCHAEOLOGICAL MUSEUM

ARCOS DE LA FRONTERA

PARISH MUSEUM AND TREASURY

ASTORGA

DIOCESAN AND CATHEDRAL MUSEUM

AVILA

MUSEUM OF ORIENTAL ART
PROVINCIAL MUSEUM

BADAJOZ

DIOCESAN AND CATHEDRAL MUSEUM

BAÑOLAS

DISTRICT ARCHAEOLOGICAL MUSEUM

BARCELONA

AMATLLER INSTITUTE OF SPANISH ART
CAMBÓ COLLECTION AND MUSEUM OF DECORATIVE ART
CATHEDRAL MUSEUM
DIOCESAN MUSEUM
FEDERICO MARES MUSEUM
MIGUEL SOLDEIRA MUSEUM
MONASTERY OF SANTA MARIA DE PEDRALBES
MUSEUM OF CATALONIAN ART
MUSEUM OF CERAMICS
MUSEUM OF DECORATIVE ARTS
MUSEUM OF THE HISTORY OF THE CITY OF BARCELONA
PALACIO DE PEDRALBES
PICASSO MUSEUM

BARCO DE AVILA

PAROCHIAL MUSEUM

BILBAO

MUSEUM OF FINE ART

BURGO DE OSMA

CATHEDRAL MUSEUM

BURGOS

DIOCESAN AND CATHEDRAL MUSEUM
MARCELIANO SANTA MARIA MUSEUM
PROVINCIAL ARCHAEOLOGICAL MUSEUM

CADIZ

CATHEDRAL MUSEUM

CALAHORRA

CATHEDRAL AND DIOCESAN MUSEUM AND TREASURY

CASTELLON

PROVINCIAL MUSEUM OF FINE ART

CORDOBA

CATHEDRAL MUSEUM AND TREASURY
MUNICIPAL MUSEUM OF ART AND BULLFIGHTING
PROVINCIAL ARCHAEOLOGICAL MUSEUM

LA CORUÑA

PROVINCIAL MUSEUM OF FINE ART

COVARRUBIAS

PAROCHIAL MUSEUM

CREVILLENTE

MUNICIPAL MUSEUM

GERONA

CATHEDRAL MUSEUM AND TREASURY
DIOCESAN MUSEUM

GRANADA

LA ALHAMBRA
MUSEUM OF THE CATHOLIC KINGS
NATIONAL MUSEUM OF SPANISH-MOSLEM ART
PROVINCIAL ARCHAEOLOGICAL MUSEUM
PROVINCIAL MUSEUM OF FINE ART

ILLESCAS

HOSPITAL AND SANCTUARY OF OUR LADY OF CHARITY

LEÔN

CATHEDRAL MUSEUM

LERIDA

CATHEDRAL MUSEUM
DIOCESAN MUSEUM

LLUCH

LLUCH TREASURY AND MUSEUM

LOGROÑO

PROVINCIAL MUSEUM

LUGO

CATHEDRAL MUSEUM AND TREASURY

MADRID

CERRALBO MUSEUM
COLLECTION OF THE HOUSE OF ALBA
CONVENT OF LAS DESCALZAS REALES
LAZARO GALDIANO MUSEUM
MUNICIPAL COLLECTION
MUSEUM OF ICONOGRAPHY
MUSEUM OF THE SPANISH VILLAGE
NATIONAL MUSEUM OF DECORATIVE ART
NATIONAL MUSEUM OF PAINTING AND SCULPTURE
PALACIO DE ORIENTE
ROYAL PALACE

MANISES

CASANOVA DALFO-SANCHIS CAUSA MUNICIPAL MUSEUM

MARCHENA

PAROCHIAL MUSEUM

MEDINA DE RIOSECO

INTERPAROCHIAL MUSEUM AND TREASURY

MORELLA
ETHNOLOGICAL MUSEUM OF MORELLA AND THE MAESTRAZGO

ORIHUELA
JOSÉ MA. SOLER PROVINCIAL ARCHAEOLOGICAL MUSEUM

OVIEDO
CÁMARA SANTA

PADRON
PADRON MUSEUM OF RELIGIOUS ART

PALMA DE MALLORCA
CATHEDRAL MUSEUM
DIOCESAN MUSEUM

PARADAS
PAROCHIAL MUSEUM

PERELADA
MATEU COLLECTION

PONTEVEDRA
PONTEVEDRA MUSEUM

SAN FELIU DE GUIXOLS
MUNICIPAL MUSEUM

SEGORBE
DIOCESAN AND CATHEDRAL MUSEUM

SEGOVIA
CATHEDRAL MUSEUM
PROVINCIAL MUSEUM OF FINE ART
ZULOAGA MUSEUM

SEVILLE
HOLY WEEK MUSEUM
MUSEUM AND TREASURY OF THE BASILICA OF THE MACARENA
OSUNA COLLECTION
PROVINCIAL MUSEUM OF FINE ART

SITGES
MARICEL DE MAR MUSEUM
MUSEUM OF CAU FERRAT

TALAVERA DE LA REINA
RUIZ DE LUNA MUSEUM OF CERAMICS

TARRAGONA
CITY MUSEUM
DIOCESAN MUSEUM
MUSEUM OF FOLK ART AND CUSTOMS
MUSEUM OF THE ROMANTIC PERIOD
PROVINCIAL ARCHAEOLOGICAL MUSEUM

TOLEDO
SANTA CRUZ MUSEUM
TALLER DEL MORO

VALENCIA
DIOCESAN AND CATHEDRAL MUSEUM
GONZALEZ MARTI NATIONAL MUSEUM OF CERAMICS
MUSEUM OF THE PATRIARCH
PROVINCIAL MUSEUM OF FINE ART

VALLADOLID
MUSEUM OF THE MISSIONS

VILLAGARCIA DE CAMPOS
MUSEUM OF THE COLLEGIATE CHURCH

VILLANUEVA Y GELTRU
VICTOR BALAGUER MUSEUM

ZAMORA
CATHEDRAL MUSEUM
PROVINCIAL MUSEUM OF FINE ART

ZARAGOZA
BASILICA OF NOSTRA SENORA DEL PILAR
CATHEDRAL MUSEUM
PROVINCIAL MUSEUM OF FINE ART

SRI LANKA, REPUBLIC OF

ANURADHAPURA
FOLK MUSEUM

COLOMBO
NATIONAL MUSEUM

KANDY
NATIONAL MUSEUM

RATNAPURA
NATIONAL MUSEUM

SWEDEN

GÄVLE
GÄVLE MUSEUM

GÖTEBORG
HISTORICAL MUSEUM
RÖHSS MUSEUM OF ARTS AND CRAFTS

HALMSTAD
HALLANDS MUSEUM

HÄLSINGBORG
TOWN MUSEUM

HÄRNÖSAND
MUSEUM OF CULTURAL HISTORY

HUDIKSVALL
HÄLSINGLANDS MUSEUM

JOKKMOKK
JOKKMOKK MUSEUM

KARLSTAD
VÄRMLAND MUSEUM

LINKÖPING
LINKÖPING MUSEUM

LUND
MUSEUM OF CULTURAL HISTORY

MALMÖ
MALMÖ MUSEUM

MARIEFRED
GRIPSHOLM CASTLE

MÖLNDAL
GUNNEBO

MORA
ZORN MUSEUM

ÖREBRO
ÖREBRO MUSEUM

ÖSTERSUND
JÄMTLAND MUSEUM

SKARA
WEST GÖTLAND MUSEUM

SKELLEFTEÅ
SKELLEFTEÅ MUSEUM

SKOKLOSTER
SKOKLOSTER CASTLE

STOCKHOLM
CHINESE PAVILION
DROTTNINGHOLM PALACE
HALLWYL MUSEUM
MILLES MUSEUM
MUSEUM OF FAR EASTERN ANTIQUITIES
MUSEUM OF MEDITERRANEAN AND NEAR EASTERN ANTIQUITIES
NATIONAL MUSEUM
NORDIC MUSEUM
PRINCE EUGEN'S HOUSE
ROYAL PALACE
STUREHOV MANOR
SVINDERSVIK MANOR

SUNDBORN
CARL LARSSON HOUSE-MUSEUM

SUNDSVALL
SUNDSVALL MUSEUM OF HANDICRAFTS

UPPSALA
UPPLAND MUSEUM

VÄXJÖ
SMÅLAND MUSEUM

VISBY
GOTLAND HISTORICAL MUSEUM

SWITZERLAND

ALTDORF
URI HISTORICAL MUSEUM

ALTSTÄTTEN
HISTORICAL MUSEUM

APPENZELL
REGIONAL MUSEUM

BADEN
HISTORICAL MUSEUM

BALSTHAL
REGIONAL MUSEUM OF OLD FALKENSTEIN

BASEL
HISTORICAL MUSEUM
KIRSCHGARTEN
MUSEUM OF GREEK AND ROMAN ART
MUSEUM OF SWISS FOLKLORE

BERN
BERN HISTORICAL MUSEUM
CANTONAL MUSEUM OF APPLIED ART
SWISS TECHNICAL MUSEUM OF BOOKBINDING

BOURG-SAINT-PIERRE
MUSEUM OF THE GREAT ST. BERNARD SHELTER FOR TRAVELLERS

BULLE
MUSEUM OF THE GRUYÈRE DISTRICT

BURGDORF
HISTORICAL MUSEUM OF THE BURGDORF HALL OF THE KNIGHTS SOCIETY

CHÂTEAU D'OEX
MUSEUM OF THE FORMER PAYS D'ENHAUT AND OF THE AUGUST COTTIER FOUNDATION

LA CHAUX-DE-FONDS
MUSEUM OF HISTORY, COINS AND MEDALS

CHUR
CATHEDRAL TREASURY AND MUSEUM
MUNICIPAL MUSEUM

COPPET
CHÂTEAU COPPET AND MUSEUM OF THE SWISS WHO SERVED ABROAD

DELÉMONT
JURA MUSEUM

ENGELBERG
ANTIQUITIES COLLECTION OF THE BENEDICTINE ABBEY

ESTAVAYER-LE-LAC
MUSEUM

FRAUENFELD
CANTON THURGAU MUSEUM

FRIBOURG
MUSEUM OF ART AND HISTORY

GELFINGEN
HEIDEGG CASTLE

GENEVA
ARIANA MUSEUM
BAUR COLLECTION
MUSEUM OF ART AND HISTORY
MUSEUM AND INSTITUTE OF ETHNOGRAPHY

GRUYÈRES
CHÂTEAU

JEGENSTORF
SCHLOSS JEGENSTORF

KILCHBERG
LOCAL HISTORY COLLECTION

LE LANDERON
MUSEUM

LANGNAU IM EMMENTAL
REGIONAL MUSEUM

LAUSANNE
HISTORICAL MUSEUM OF THE OLD BISHOPRIC
MON REPOS MUSEUM
MUSEUM OF DECORATIVE ARTS

LENZBURG
CANTONAL HISTORICAL COLLECTION
REGIONAL MUSEUM

LIESTAL
BASEL-LAND CANTONAL MUSEUM

LUGANO
MUSEUM OF HISTORY AND ARCHAEOLOGY

LUZERN
HISTORICAL MUSEUM
TREASURY OF ST. LEODEGAR'S FOUNDATION

MORGES
ALEXIS FOREL MUSEUM

MOUDON
EUGÈNE BURNAND MUSEUM

NEUCHÂTEL
MUSEUM OF ART AND HISTORY

LA NEUVEVILLE
HISTORICAL MUSEUM

NYON
HISTORICAL MUSEUM

OBERHOFEN AM THUNERSEE
CASTLE

OLTEN
HISTORICAL MUSEUM

RAPPERSWIL
REGIONAL MUSEUM

RHEINFELDEN
FIRCKTALER MUSEUM

RIGGISBERG

MUSEUM OF THE ABEGG FOUNDATION, BERN

SAINTE-CROIX

MUSEUM

ST. GALLEN

MUSEUM OF INDUSTRIAL AND APPLIED ARTS
NEW MUSEUM

SAINT-MAURICE

ABBEY TREASURY

ST. MORITZ

ENGADINE MUSEUM

SAN VITTORE

MOESANO MUSEUM

SARNEN

REGIONAL MUSEUM

LA SARRAZ

CHÂTEAU

SCHAFFHAUSEN

ALL SAINTS' MUSEUM

SCHINZNACH-DORF

REGIONAL MUSEUM

SCHÖNENWERD

BALLY MUSEUM FOUNDATION

SION

VALÈRE CANTONAL MUSEUM

SOLOTHURN

CASTLE BLUMENSTEIN HISTORICAL MUSEUM
CATHEDRAL TREASURY

STANS

HISTORICAL MUSEUM

STEIN AM RHEIN

MUSEUM OF ST. GEORGEN MONASTERY

TARASP

CASTLE

THUN

HISTORICAL MUSEUM

UZNACH

MUSEUM OF LOCAL LIFE AND HISTORY

VALANGIN

MUSEUM

VEVEY

MUSEUM OF OLD VEVEY

WANGEN AN DER AARE

LOCAL COLLECTION

WIEDLISBACH

HISTORICAL MUSEUM

WIL

MUNICIPAL MUSEUM

WINTERTHUR

LINDENGUT REGIONAL MUSEUM
MUSEUM OF APPLIED ART

WINTERTHUR- MÖRSBURG

MÖRSBURG CASTLE

YVERDON

MUSEUM OF OLD YVERDON

ZOFINGEN

MUSEUM

ZURICH

CERAMICS COLLECTION
MUSEUM BELLERIVE
MUSEUM OF APPLIED ART
MUSEUM RIETBERG
SWISS NATIONAL MUSEUM

SYRIAN ARAB REPUBLIC

DAMASCUS

DAMASCUS NATIONAL MUSEUM
MUSEUM OF ARAB CALLIGRAPHY
MUSEUM OF POPULAR ARTS AND TRADITIONS

HAMA

HAMA MUSEUM

THAILAND

AYUDHYA

CHAO SAM PHYA NATIONAL MUSEUM

BANGKOK

NATIONAL MUSEUM
SUAN PAKKAD PALACE
JIM THOMPSON HOUSE

LOPBURI

LOPBURI MUSEUM

TUNISIA

CARTHAGE

NATIONAL MUSEUM OF CARTHAGE

JERBA

JERBA MUSEUM

KAIROUAN

KAIROUAN MUSEUM

MAHDIA

MAHDIA MUSEUM

MONASTIR

ALI BOURGUIBA MUSEUM

SFAX

MUSEUM OF POPULAR ARTS AND TRADITIONS (JELLOULI MUSEUM)

TUNIS

ARAB MUSEUM
LE BARDO NATIONAL MUSEUM
MUSELMAN DE SIDI- BOU-KRISSAN LAPIDARY MUSEUM
MUSEUM OF ISLAMIC ART
MUSEUM OF MOSLEM ART

TURKEY

ANKARA

ETHNOGRAPHICAL MUSEUM

ISTANBUL

ARCHAEOLOGICAL MUSEUM OF ISTANBUL
MUSEUM OF MOSAICS
MUSEUM OF TURKISH AND ISLAMIC ART
TOPKAPI PALACE MUSEUM

KONYA

MEVLÂNA MUSEUM
TURKISH CERAMICS MUSEUM

UGANDA

KAMPALA

NOMMO GALLERY

USSR

ARCHANGEL

MANOR-HOUSE MUSEUM

BAKU

MUSEUM OF THE HISTORY OF AZERBAIJAN
R. MUSTAFAEV STATE ART MUSEUM

BOKHARA

HISTORICAL AND ETHNOGRAPHICAL MUSEUM OF BOKHARA

GRODNO

MUSEUM OF HISTORY AND ARCHAEOLOGY

KALININ

MUSEUM OF FINE ART

KAUNAS

PRINCE VYTANSAS MUSEUM
STATE MUSEUM

KIEV

KIEV NATIONAL MUSEUM OF WESTERN AND ORIENTAL ART
STATE MUSEUM OF POPULAR AND DECORATIVE ART
STATE MUSEUM OF RUSSIAN ART
STATE MUSEUM OF UKRAINIAN ART

KISHINEV

REGIONAL MUSEUM OF THE REPUBLIC OF MOLDAVIA

KUSKOVO

NATIONAL CERAMIC MUSEUM

LENINGRAD

HERMITAGE MUSEUM
MUSEUM OF THE COLLEGE OF DECORATIVE ARTS
MUSEUM OF PORCELAIN
MUSEUM OF URBAN SCULPTURE
NATIONAL MUSEUM OF ETHNOGRAPHY OF THE PEOPLES OF THE U.S.S.R.
NATIONAL MUSEUM OF THE HISTORY OF LENINGRAD
NATIONAL RUSSIAN MUSEUM
SUMMER PALACE MUSEUM

LERMONTOVO

M. Y. LERMONTOV MUSEUM

LOMONOSOV (formerly ORANIENBAUM)

FINE ART MUSEUM

MINSK

BYELORUSSIAN MUSEUM OF ART

MOSCOW

ARKHANGELSKOYE ESTATE MUSEUM
18th CENTURY KUSKOVO ESTATE AND CERAMICS MUSEUM
KOLOMENSKOYE ESTATE MUSEUM
MUSEUM OF DECORATIVE ARTS
MUSEUM OF ORIENTAL ART
NATIONAL ARMOURY
NOVODEVICHY MONASTERY
OSTAKINO MUSEUM OF SERF ART

NOVGOROD

GRANOVITAYA PALACE MUSEUM

ODESSA

MUSEUM OF WESTERN AND EASTERN ART

PALEKH

MUSEUM OF HANDICRAFTS

PAVLOVSK

MUSEUM OF FINE ARTS

PETROZAVODSK

NATIONAL HISTORICAL MUSEUM

PITSUNDA

CATHEDRAL OF ST. SOPHIA

PUSHKINO

YEKATERINSKI PALACE

RIGA

LATVIAN HISTORICAL MUSEUM
NATIONAL MUSEUM OF FINE ARTS

ROSTOV VELIKI

LOCAL MUSEUM

TALASHKINO

LOCAL MUSEUM

TASHKENT

MUSEUM OF APPLIED ART
NATIONAL ART MUSEUM OF UZBEKISTAN

TBILISI

GEORGIAN ART MUSEUM

ULAN-BATOR

FINE ARTS MUSEUM

VILNIUS (formerly WILNO)

MANOR-HOUSE MUSEUM

YALTA

ALUPKA PALACE MUSEUM

ZAGORSK

METROPOLITAN'S HOUSE MUSEUM

UNITED STATES

AKRON

AKRON ART INSTITUTE

ALBANY

ALBANY INSTITUTE OF HISTORY AND ART
NEW YORK STATE MUSEUM

ALBUQUERQUE

MAXWELL MUSEUM OF ANTHROPOLOGY
UNIVERSITY ART MUSEUM

ANN ARBOR

MUSEUM OF ART

BALTIMORE

BALTIMORE MUSEUM OF ART
SAMUEL KIRK MUSEUM
MARYLAND INSTITUTE COLLEGE OF ART
MUSEUM OF MARYLAND HISTORICAL SOCIETY
WALTERS ART GALLERY

BATON ROUGE

ANGLO-AMERICAN ART MUSEUM

BELOIT

THEODORE LYMON WRIGHT ART CENTER

BEVERLY HILLS
FRANCIS E. FOWLER, JR., FOUNDATION MUSEUM
BINGHAMPTON
UNIVERSITY ART GALLERY
BIRMINGHAM
BIRMINGHAM MUSEUM OF ART
BLOOMFIELD HILLS
GALLERIES OF CRANBROOK ACADEMY OF ART
BLOOMINGTON
INDIANA UNIVERSITY ART MUSEUM
BOSTON
MUSEUM OF FINE ARTS
ISABELLA STEWART GARDNER MUSEUM
BROCKTON
BROCKTON ART CENTER
BROOKINGS
SOUTH DAKOTA MEMORIAL ART CENTER
BRUNSWICK
BOWDOIN MUSEUM OF ART
CAMBRIDGE
FOGG ART MUSEUM
HAYDEN GALLERY
CAMDEN
CAMPBELL MUSEUM
CEDAR RAPIDS
COE COLLEGE, THOMAS W. SINCLAIR MEMORIAL ART GALLERY
CHARLOTTE
MINT MUSEUM OF ART
CHATTANOOGA
HOUSTON ANTIQUE MUSEUM
CHICAGO
ART INSTITUTE OF CHICAGO
MUSEUM OF CHICAGO HISTORICAL SOCIETY
ORIENTAL INSTITUTE MUSEUM
CINCINNATI
CINCINNATI ART MUSEUM
TAFT MUSEUM
CLEARWATER
FLORIDA GULF COAST ART CENTER
CLEVELAND
CLEVELAND MUSEUM OF ART
DUNHAM TAVERN MUSEUM
COLUMBUS
COLUMBUS MUSEUM OF ARTS AND CRAFTS
CONCORD
CONCORD ANTIQUARIAN SOCIETY MUSEUM
COOPERSTOWN
MUSEUM OF HISTORICAL SOCIETY OF EARLY AMERICAN DECORATION
COSHOCTON
JOHNSON-HUMRICKHOUSE MEMORIAL MUSEUM
DANBURY
DANBURY SCOTT-FANTON MUSEUM
DAVENPORT
DAVENPORT MUNICIPAL ART GALLERY
DAYTON
DAYTON ART INSTITUTE
DAYTONA BEACH
MUSEUM OF ART AND SCIENCES
DEERFIELD
PARKER AND RUSSELL SILVER SHOP
DES MOINES
SALISBURY HOUSE
DETROIT
DETROIT INSTITUTE OF ARTS
EVANSVILLE
EVANSVILLE MUSEUM OF ARTS AND SCIENCES
FARMINGTON
HILL-STEAD MUSEUM
FITCHBURG
FITCHBURG ART MUSEUM
FLINT
FLINT INSTITUTE OF ARTS
FLUSHING
QUEEN'S COLLEGE ART COLLECTION
FORT WORTH
KIMBELL ART MUSEUM
FRANKFORT
LIBERTY HALL MUSEUM
GALVESTON
ROSENBERG LIBRARY
GAUTIER
GAUTIER'S PLANTATION HOUSE
GLENS FALLS
HYDE COLLECTION
HAGERSTOWN
WASHINGTON COUNTY MUSEUM OF FINE ARTS
HANOVER
HOPKINS CENTER ART GALLERIES
HARTFORD
WADSWORTH ATHENEUM
HELENA
ARCHIE BRAY FOUNDATION
HICKORY
HICKORY MUSEUM OF ART
HONOLULU
HONOLULU ACADEMY OF ARTS
HOUSTON
BAYOU BEND COLLECTION
INSTITUTE FOR THE ARTS
MUSEUM OF AMERICAN ARCHITECTURE AND DECORATIVE ARTS
MUSEUM OF FINE ARTS
HUNTINGTON
HUNTINGTON GALLERIES
INDIANAPOLIS
INDIANAPOLIS MUSEUM OF ART
INDIANA STATE MUSEUM
ITHACA
ITHACA COLLEGE MUSEUM OF ART
JACKSONVILLE
CUMNER GALLERY OF ART
KANSAS CITY
FOLGER COFFEE COMPANY MUSEUM
WILLIAM ROCKHILL NELSON GALLERY AND ATKINS MUSEUM OF FINE ARTS
KNOXVILLE
CRAIGHEAD JACKSON HOUSE
LAUREL
LAUREN ROGERS LIBRARY AND MUSEUM OF ART
LAWRENCE
UNIVERSITY OF KANSAS MUSEUM OF ART
WILCOX MUSEUM
LOS ANGELES
LOS ANGELES COUNTY MUSEUM OF ART
LOUISVILLE
J. B. SPEED ART MUSEUM
MANCHESTER
CURRIER GALLERY OF ART
MARYHILL
MARYHILL MUSEUM OF FINE ARTS
MARYVILLE
NORTHWEST MISSOURI STATE COLLEGE GALLERY
MASSILLON
MASSILLON MUSEUM
MEMPHIS
BROOKS MEMORIAL ART GALLERY
MERION
BUTEN MUSEUM OF WEDGWOOD
MIAMI
VISCAYA-DADE COUNTY ART MUSEUM
MIAMI BEACH
BASS MUSEUM OF ART
MILWAUKEE
CHARLES ALLIS ART MUSEUM AND LIBRARY
MILWAUKEE ART CENTRE
MILWAUKEE PUBLIC MUSEUM
MINNEAPOLIS
MINNEAPOLIS INSTITUTE OF ARTS
UNIVERSITY GALLERY
WALKER ART CENTER
MOBILE
MOBILE ART GALLERY
MONCLAIR
MONCLAIR ART MUSEUM
MONTCLAIR
MONTCLAIR ART MUSEUM
MONTGOMERY
MONTGOMERY MUSEUM OF FINE ARTS
MUSCATINE
LAURER MUSSER ART GALLERY AND MUSEUM
NASHVILLE
GEORGE PEABODY COLLEGE MUSEUM
TENNESSEE BOTANICAL GARDENS AND FINE ARTS CENTER
NEENAH
JOHN NELSON BERGSTROM ART CENTER AND MUSEUM
NEWARK
NEWARK MUSEUM
NEW HAVEN
PAUL MELLON CENTER FOR BRITISH ART AND BRITISH STUDIES
YALE UNIVERSITY ART GALLERY
NEW LONDON
LYMAN ALLYN MUSEUM
NEW ORLEANS
NEW ORLEANS MUSEUM OF ART
NEWPORT
HUNTER HOUSE
NEW YORK
BROOKLYN MUSEUM
CHINESE MUSEUM
COOPER-HEWITT MUSEUM OF DECORATIVE ARTS AND DESIGN
THE COOPER UNION MUSEUM
FRICK COLLECTION
JUNIOR MUSEUM OF THE METROPOLITAN MUSEUM OF ART
JACQUES MARCHAIS CENTER OF TIBETAN ART
METROPOLITAN MUSEUM OF ART
MUSEUM OF CONTEMPORARY CRAFTS
MUSEUM AND LIBRARY OF HISPANIC SOCIETY OF AMERICA
MUSEUM OF NEW YORK HISTORICAL SOCIETY
PIERPONT MORGAN LIBRARY
TRAPHAGEN SCHOOL OF FASHION, MUSEUM COLLECTION
NORFOLK
CHRYSLER MUSEUM
HERMITAGE FOUNDATION MUSEUM
NORWICH
SLATER MEMORIAL MUSEUM
NOTRE DAME
UNIVERSITY OF NOTRE DAME ART GALLERY
OKLAHOMA CITY
OKLAHOMA ART CENTER
OLD BENNINGTON
BENNINGTON MUSEUM
OMAHA
JOSLYN ART MUSEUM
PHILADELPHIA
DREXEL MUSEUM COLLECTION
STEPHEN GIRARD COLLECTION
MUSEUM OF THE CARNEGIE INSTITUTE
MUSEUM OF THE SOCIETY OF ARCHITECTURAL HISTORIANS
PHILADELPHIA MUSEUM OF ART
PHILIP H. AND A. S. W. ROSENBACH FOUNDATION MUSEUM
WOODMERE ART GALLERY
PITTSBURGH
CARNEGIE MUSEUM OF ART
PITTSFIELD
BERKSHIRE MUSEUM
POMONA
LENOX, INCORPORATED
PONCE
PONCE ART MUSEUM
PORTLAND
PORTLAND MUSEUM OF ART
MUSEUM OF CONTEMPORARY CRAFTS ASSOCIATION
PORTLAND ART MUSEUM
POUGHKEEPSIE
VASSAR COLLEGE ART GALLERY
PRINCETON
ART MUSEUM
PRINCETON UNIVERSITY ART MUSEUM
PROVIDENCE
MUSEUM OF ART, RHODE ISLAND SCHOOL OF DESIGN
RHODE ISLAND HISTORICAL SOCIETY
PROVINCETOWN
CHRYSLER ART MUSEUM
PROVO
BRIGHAM YOUNG UNIVERSITY, FINE ARTS COLLECTION
QUINCY
QUINCY ART CENTER

RALEIGH
NORTH CAROLINA MUSEUM OF ART

RICHMOND
VIRGINIA MUSEUM OF FINE ARTS

ROCHESTER
MEMORIAL ART GALLERY, UNIVERSITY OF ROCHESTER
MUSEUM OF LANDMARK SOCIETY OF WESTERN NEW YORK

ROSWELL
ROSWELL MUSEUM AND ART CENTER

SACRAMENTO
E. B. CROCKER ART GALLERY

ST. AUGUSTINE
HISTORIC ST. AUGUSTINE

ST. LOUIS
ST. LOUIS ART MUSEUM
WASHINGTON UNIVERSITY GALLERY OF ART

ST. PAUL
MINNESOTA MUSEUM OF ART

SALT LAKE CITY
UTAH MUSEUM OF FINE ARTS

SAN DIEGO
FINE ARTS GALLERY OF SAN DIEGO

SAN FRANCISCO
CENTER OF ASIAN ART AND CULTURE, AVERY BRUNDAGE COLLECTION
OCTAGON HOUSE
M. H. DE YOUNG MEMORIAL MUSEUM

SAN GERMÁN
PORTA COELI MUSEUM OF RELIGIOUS ARTS

SAN LUIS OBISPO
SAN LUIS OBISPO MISSION

SAN MARINO
HENRY E. HUNTINGTON LIBRARY AND ART GALLERY

SANTA BARBARA
SANTA BARBARA MUSEUM OF ART

SANTA CLARA
DE SAISSET ART GALLERY AND MUSEUM

SEATTLE
HENRY ART GALLERY
SEATTLE ART MUSEUM

SEWARD
KOENIG ART GALLERY

SHREVEPORT
R. W. NORTON ART GALLERY

SNYDER
DIAMOND M. FOUNDATION MUSEUM

SOUTH HADLEY
DWIGHT ART MEMORIAL

SPRINGFIELD
ILLINOIS STATE MUSEUM
GEORGE WALTER VINCENT SMITH ART MUSEUM
MUSEUM OF FINE ARTS
SPRINGFIELD ART AND HISTORICAL SOCIETY
SPRINGFIELD ART MUSEUM

STAATSBURG
MILLS MUSEUM

STOCKTON
PIONEER MUSEUM AND HAGGIN GALLERIES

STORRS
WILLIAM BENTON MUSEUM OF ART

SYRACUSE
EVERSON MUSEUM OF ART
JOE AND EMILY LOWE ART CENTER

TEMPE
UNIVERSITY ART COLLECTIONS

TERRE HAUTE
SHELDON SWOPE ART GALLERY

THEODORE
BELLINGRATH GARDENS AND HOME

TOLEDO
TOLEDO-LUCAS COUNTY PUBLIC LIBRARY
TOLEDO MUSEUM OF ART

TORRINGTON
TURNER MUSEUM

TRENTON
LENOX CHINA MUSEUM

TROY
MUSEUM OF RENSSELAER COUNTY HISTORICAL SOCIETY

TUCSON
TUCSON ART CENTER

TULSA
PHILBROOK ART CENTER

UTICA
MUNSON-WILLIAMS-PROCTOR INSTITUTE

WALTHAM
THE ROSE ART MUSEUM

WASHINGTON
ANDERSON HOUSE MUSEUM
CORCORAN GALLERY OF ART
DAUGHTERS OF THE AMERICAN REVOLUTION MUSEUM
FREER GALLERY OF ART
INSTITUTE OF CONTEMPORARY ARTS
NATIONAL COLLECTION OF FINE ARTS
NATIONAL GALLERY OF ART
RENWICK GALLERY
SMITH-MASON GALLERY OF ART

WATERVILLE
COLBY COLLEGE ART MUSEUM

WESTERLY
WESTERLY PUBLIC LIBRARY

WEST PALM BEACH
NORTON GALLERY
NORTON GALLERY AND SCHOOL OF ART

WICHITA
WICHITA ART ASSOCIATION
WICHITA ART MUSEUM

WILLIAMSTOWN
STERLING AND FRANCINE CLARK ART INSTITUTE

WILMINGTON
MUSEUM OF THE HISTORICAL SOCIETY OF DELAWARE
ST. JOHN'S ART GALLERY

WILTON
CRAFT CENTER MUSEUM

WINSTON-SALEM
MUSEUM OF EARLY SOUTHERN DECORATIVE ARTS

WINTERTHUR
HENRY FRANCIS DU PONT WINTERTHUR MUSEUM

WOOSTER
COLLEGE OF WOOSTER MUSEUM

WORCESTER
JOHN WOODMAN HIGGINS ARMORY
WORCESTER ART MUSEUM

YONKERS
HUDSON RIVER MUSEUM

YOUNGSTOWN
BUTLER INSTITUTE OF AMERICAN ART

YUKON
HENSON GALLERY

YUMA
YUMA FINE ARTS ASSOCIATION

ZANESVILLE
ART INSTITUTE OF ZANESVILLE

URUGUAY

MONTEVIDEO
MUNICIPAL FINE ARTS MUSEUM
MUNICIPAL MUSEUM OF HISTORY AND ARCHIVES
NATIONAL MUSEUM OF DECORATIVE ARTS

SAN JOSÉ DE MAYO
REGIONAL MUSEUM

VENEZUELA

CARACAS
MUSEUM OF COLONIAL ART
MUSEUM OF FINE ARTS

CIUDAD BOLIVÁR
TALAVERA MUSEUM

VIETNAM, REPUBLIC OF

HUÉ
ARCHAEOLOGICAL MUSEUM

SAIGON
NATIONAL MUSEUM OF VIET- NAM

YUGOSLAVIA

BELGRADE
ETHNOGRAPHICAL MUSEUM
MUSEUM OF APPLIED ART
NATIONAL MUSEUM

BOL
DOMINICAN MONASTERY

DUBROVNIK
TOWN MUSEUM
TREASURY
TREASURY

HERCEGNOVI
TREASURY

HRASTOVLJE
CHURCH OF ST. TROJICE

HVAR
REFECTORY
TREASURY OF THE CATHEDRAL

KOMIŽA
MUSEUM

KOPER
ART AND HISTORICAL MUSEUM
CATHEDRAL OF ST. NAZARIUS AND TREASURY

KORČULA
CATHEDRAL TREASURY

KOŠLJUN
MONASTIC MUSEUM

KOTOR
CATHEDRAL OF SV. NIKOLA TREASURY
CATHEDRAL OF SV. TRIPUN TREASURY

LJUBLJANA
MUNICIPAL MUSEUM
NATIONAL MUSEUM

NIŠ
OCHRID NATIONAL MUSEUM

OREBIĆ
CAPTAINS' HOUSES

PERAST
TREASURY

PIRAN
ART GALLERY AND CITY MUSEUM

PTUJ
REGIONAL MUSEUM

RAB
TREASURY

SARAJEVO
MUSEUM COLLECTION OF THE OLD ORTHODOX CHURCH

SENJ
DIOCESAN MUSEUM

SKOFJA LOKA
MUSEUM

SPLIT
ETHNOGRAPHICAL MUSEUM
TREASURY

SREMSKI KARLOVCI
TOWN MUSEUM

SVETI STEFAN
TREASURY

TROGIR
TREASURY

VARAŽDIN
STARI GRAD MUSEUM

ZADAR
ETHNOGRAPHICAL MUSEUM
TREASURY OF THE CATHEDRAL AND OF THE BENEDICTINE NUNNERY OF SV. MARIJA

ZAGREB
DIOCESAN MUSEUM
ETHNOGRAPHICAL MUSEUM
HISTORICAL MUSEUM OF CROATIA
LUBIENSKY-DURIEUX COLLECTION OF OBJETS D'ART
MUSEUM OF APPLIED ARTS

ZAIRE, REPUBLIC OF

KINSHASA
MUSEUM OF ANTHROPOLOGY

Folk art, popular art, advertising

ALGERIA

ALGIERS
LE BARDO MUSEUM OF ETHNOGRAPHY AND PREHISTORY

ANGOLA

LUANDA
ANGOLA MUSEUM

ARGENTINA

BUENOS AIRES
DE LA BOCA MUSEUM OF FINE ART
JOSÉ HERNÁNDEZ MUSEUM OF POPULAR ART
SANTA FÉ
MUSEUM OF ETHNOGRAPHY
TUCUMÁN
MUSEUM OF ARGENTINE FOLKLORE AND HANDICRAFTS

AUSTRALIA

BRISBANE
QUEENSLAND ABORIGINAL CREATIONS GALLERY
MELBOURNE
UNIVERSITY MUSEUM

AUSTRIA

ALTAUSSEE
SALTMINE
ARNFELS
MUSEUM OF CLOCKS, MUSICAL INSTRUMENTS AND FOLKLORE
BAD AUSSEE
AUSSEE REGIONAL MUSEUM
BRAUNAU AM INN
DISTRICT MUSEUM
BREITENAU
VOTIVE COLLECTION OF ST. ERHARD'S CHURCH
EGG
REGIONAL MUSEUM
GOBELSBURG
PALACE MUSEUM
GRAZ
JOANNEUM PROVINCIAL MUSEUM OF THE ETHNOLOGY AND FOLKLORE OF STEIERMARK
HOLLERSBACH
REGIONAL MUSEUM
KREMS
MUNICIPAL MUSEUM
LANGENLOIS
REGIONAL MUSEUM
MARIA LANGEGG
TREASURY OF THE PILGRIMAGE CHURCH
MARIA STEIN
PALACE MUSEUM
MARIA TAFERL
TREASURY OF THE PILGRIMAGE CHURCH
MARIAZELL
TREASURY OF THE BASILICA OF GOD'S GRACE
MICHAELBEUERN
ABBEY REGIONAL MUSEUM
MITTERNDORF
MUSEUM OF REGIONAL LIFE
NEUNKIRCHEN
REGIONAL MUSEUM
PINKAFELD
REGIONAL MUSEUM
RABENSTEIN
PIELACHTAL REGIONAL MUSEUM
REUTTE
REGIONAL MUSEUM
RIED
ETHNOLOGICAL MUSEUM OF THE INNVIERTEL
SAALFELDEN
MUSEUM OF LOCAL LIFE AND OF CRIBS
SALZBURG
MUSEUM OF ETHNOLOGY
ST. ERHARD
VOTIVE COLLECTION IN THE PILGRIMS' CHURCH
ST. LAMBRECHT
COLLECTIONS OF THE BENEDICTINE MONASTERY
ST. MARTIN
VOTIVES COLLECTION OF THE PILGRIMS' CHURCH OF MARIA KIRCHENTAL
ST. ULRICH
LAVANTTAL MUSEUM OF LOCAL LIFE
SCHEIBBS
HOTTENROTH COLLECTION
SCHRUNS
MONTAFON REGIONAL MUSEUM
SONNTAGBERG
TREASURY OF THE PILGRIMS' CHURCH
TELFS
REGIONAL MUSEUM
VIENNA
AUSTRIAN MUSEUM OF ETHNOLOGY
COLLECTION OF POPULAR RELIGIOUS ART
MUSEUM OF ETHNOLOGY
MUSEUM OF THE HISTORY OF ART: COLLECTION OF ANTIQUES
MUSEUM OF THE MARIAHILF DISTRICT
MUSEUM OF THE PROVINCE OF LOWER AUSTRIA
WAIDHOFEN AN DER YBBS
REGIONAL MUSEUM
WELS
MUNICIPAL MUSEUM

BANGLADESH

CHITTAGONG
ETHNOLOGICAL MUSEUM
DACCA
BANGLA ACADEMY MUSEUM
DACCA MUSEUM
MUSEUM OF ART AND ARCHAEOLOGY

BELGIUM

ANTWERP
ETHNOGRAPHICAL MUSEUM
FOLK-LORE MUSEUM
BRUGES
MUSEUM OF FOLKLORE
BRUSSELS
ROYAL MUSEUM OF ART AND HISTORY
GHENT
FOLKLORE MUSEUM
LIÈGE
MUSEUM OF WALLOON LIFE
WITTERT MUSEUM
TERVUEREN
ROYAL CENTRAL AFRICAN MUSEUM
TOURNAI
FOLKLORE MUSEUM
TURNHOUT
TAXANDRIA MUSEUM OF ARCHAEOLOGY

BOLIVIA

LA PAZ
"CASA DE MURILLO" MUSEUM

BRAZIL

CARUARU
MUSEUM OF POPULAR ART
CAXIAS DO SUL
MUSEUM OF POPULAR TRADITIONS
CURITIBA
MUSEUM OF MAN
FLORIANÓPOLIS
FOLKLORE MUSEUM
FORTALEZA
ARTUR RAMOS MUSEUM
ITAPORANGA D'AJUDA
MUSEUM OF ART AND POPULAR TRADITIONS
JUAZEIRO DO NORTE
FATHER CÍCERO MUSEUM
MACEIÓ
COMMERCIAL AND ARCHAEOLOGICAL MUSEUM OF THE COMMERCIAL EMPLOYEES' SYNDICATE
MANAUS
MUSEUM OF INDIAN CULTURE
NATAL
MUSEUM OF THE HISTORICAL AND GEOGRAPHICAL INSTITUTE
MUSEUM OF POPULAR ART
PENEDO
MUSEUM OF FOLK ART AND FOLK CULTURE
RECIFE
MUSEUM OF POPULAR ART
RIO DE JANEIRO
MUSEUM OF POPULAR ART AND TRADITIONS
SALVADOR
MUSEUM OF MODERN ART
SANTANA DO IPANEMA
MUNICIPAL MUSEUM OF HISTORY AND ART

BULGARIA

BATAK
MUSEUM OF HISTORY AND ARCHAEOLOGY
KJUSTENDIL
DISTRICT MUSEUM
PLOVDIV
DISTRICT NATIONAL MUSEUM
REGIONAL MUSEUM OF ETHNOLOGY
RAJKOVO
NATIONAL MUSEUM OF THE RHODOPE
RILA
RILA MONASTERY NATIONAL MUSEUM
ŠČRAKLEVO
MUSEUM OF REGIONAL HISTORY AND ETHNOGRAPHY
SLIVEN
NATIONAL MUSEUM
SOFIA
NATIONAL ETHNOGRAPHICAL MUSEUM
TARGOVIŠČE
PROVINCIAL HISTORICAL MUSEUM
TRJAVNA
MUSEUM OF WOOD CARVING AND MURAL PAINTINGS
TRJAVNA MUSEUM

BURUNDI

BUJUMBURA
MUSEUM OF AFRICAN CIVILISATION

CAMEROUN

DOUALA
DOUALA MUSEUM
DSCHANG
BAMILIKE MUSEUM

FOUMBAN
MUSEUM OF ETHNOGRAPHY AND ART
YAOUNDÉ
MUSEUM OF NEGRO ART

CANADA

HALIFAX
DALHOUSIE ART GALLERY
KLEINBERG
McMICHAEL CONSERVATION COLLECTION OF ART
MONTREAL
ART GALLERY OF SIR GEORGE WILLIAMS UNIVERSITY
ART NOVA ET VETERA GALLERY
MONTREAL MUSEUM OF PRIMITIVE ART
NELSON
KOOTENAY MUSEUM
SARNIA
SARNIA PUBLIC LIBRARY AND ART GALLERY
SASKATOON
SASKATOON GALLERY AND CONSERVATORY
VICTORIA
PROVINCIAL MUSEUM
YELLOWKNIFE
MUSEUM OF THE NORTH

CENTRAL AFRICAN REPUBLIC

BANGUI
BARTHÉLÉMY BOGANDA MUSEUM

CHAD

FORT LAMY
CHAD NATIONAL MUSEUM

CHILE

HUALPEN
MUSEO DE HUALPEN
SANTIAGO
MUSEUM OF THE ART OF THE AMERICAN PEOPLES
TEMUCO
ARAUCANIAN MUSEUM

CHINA, P.R.

HANGCHOW (HANG ZHOU)
CHEKIANG PROVINCIAL MUSEUM

COLOMBIA

BOGOTA
ETHNOGRAPHICAL MUSEUM OF THE CARO AND CUERVO INSTITUTE
MUSEUM OF ETHNOGRAPHY
NATIONAL MUSEUM
MEDELLÍN
INDIAN MUSEUM
MUSEUM OF FOLKLORE
NEIVA
DEPARTMENTAL MUSEUM
RIOHACHA
GUAJIRO MUSEUM OF PRE- COLOMBIAN ART AND CULTURE
SOCORRO
MUSEUM OF PRE-COLOMBIAN ART
VILLANUEVA
MUSEUM OF NATIVE ART AND CULTURE

CYPRUS

KYRENIA
FOLK ART MUSEUM
LIMASSOL
MUNICIPAL FOLK ART MUSEUM
NICOSIA
THE MUSEUM OF FOLK ART

CZECHOSLOVAKIA

BANSKÁ BYSTRICA
MUSEUM OF THE HISTORY OF SLOVAKIA
BECHYNĚ
CERAMICS MUSEUM
BRATISLAVA
SLOVAKIAN NATIONAL MUSEUM: HISTORICAL COLLECTIONS
ČESKÝ KRUMLOV
REGIONAL MUSEUM
DOBŘÍŠ
MUNICIPAL MUSEUM
HLINSKO
REGIONAL MUSEUM AND ART GALLERY
HOLICE V ČECHÁCH
AFRICA MUSEUM; DR. EMIL HOLUB MEMORIAL
JIHLAVA
VYSOČINY MUSEUM
JINDŘICHŮV HRODEC
REGIONAL MUSEUM
KAŠPERSKÉ HORY
ŠUMAVY MUSEUM
KOŠICE
MUSEUM OF EASTERN SLOVAKIA
MARTIN
SLOVAKIAN NATIONAL MUSEUM: ETHNOGRAPHICAL COLLECTIONS
NOVÝ JIČIN
DISTRICT MUSEUM
OSTRAVA
OSTRAVA MUSEUM
PARDUBICE
MUSEUM OF EASTERN CZECHOSLOVAKIA
PELHŘIMOV
DISTRICT MUSEUM
PÍSEK
REGIONAL MUSEUM
POLIČKA
MUNICIPAL MUSEUM AND ART GALLERY
PRAGUE
ETHNOLOGICAL COLLECTIONS
PŘEROV NAD LABEM
MUSEUM OF ETHNOGRAPHY
ROŽNOV POD RADHOŠTĚM
VALASKIAN MUSEUM OF ETHNOGRAPHY
SLANÝ
REGIONAL MUSEUM
SOBĚSLAV
MUSEUM OF SOUTHERN CZECHOSLOVAKIA
ŠTERNBERK
ŠTERNBERK STATE CASTLE
TELČ
TELČ MUSEUM
UHLIŘSKÉ JANOVICE
MUSEUM OF HISTORY
VYSOKÉ NAD JIZEROU
REGIONAL MUSEUM
ZELEZNICE
MUNICIPAL MUSEUM AND T. F. SIMON ART GALLERY

DENMARK

NYBORG
MADS LERCHES HOUSE
REBILD BAKKER
FOLK ART AND SPILLEMAEND MUSEUM
RINGKØBING
RINGKØBING MUSEUM
SØNDERBORG
MUSEUM
VORDINGBORG
SOUTH ZEALAND MUSEUM

EQUATORIAL GUINEA

SANTA ISABEL
MUSEUM OF ETHNOGRAPHY

FIJI

SUVA
FIJI MUSEUM

FINLAND

HELSINKI
DIDRICHSEN MUSEUM OF ART
JUVA
REGIONAL MUSEUM

FRANCE

AIX-EN-PROVENCE
MUSEUM OF OLD AIX
ANGOULÊME
MUSEUM OF THE CHARENTE ARCHAEOLOGICAL AND HISTORICAL SOCIETY
ANNECY
CHÂTEAU D'ANNECY
AVALLON
AVALLON MUSEUM
AVESNES-SUR-HELPE
ARCHAEOLOGICAL SOCIETY MUSEUM
BOURGES
DU BERRY MUSEUM
BOUXWILLER
BOUXWILLER MUSEUM
CHAMPLITTE- ET-LE-PRÉLOT
DEPARTMENTAL MUSEUM OF HISTORY AND ETHNOGRAPHY
FOIX
ARIÈGE MUSEUM
KERJEAN
BRETON MUSEUM
LAGHET
SANCTUARY MUSEUM
LOURDES
MUSEUM OF THE PYRENEES
LYON
MUSEUM OF THE LYON AFRICAN MISSIONS
MARSEILLE
MUSEUM OF OLD MARSEILLE
MONTIGNAC-LASCAUX
LASCAUX GROTTO
MULHOUSE
MUSEUM OF HISTORY
NANTES
MUSEUM OF REGIONAL POPULAR ART
NÎMES
MUSEUM OF OLD NÎMES
PARIS
MUSEUM OF MAN
NATIONAL MUSEUM OF AFRICAN AND OCEANIC ART
RIOM
AUVERGNE REGIONAL MUSEUM OF FOLKLORE
LA ROCHELLE
LAFAILLE AND FLEURIAU MUSEUM
SAINT- AMAND-MONTROND
SAINT VIC MUSEUM
SAINT-GERMAIN-EN-LAYE
MUSEUM OF NATIONAL ANTIQUITIES
SAINT- SYMPHORIEN-SUR-COISE
LA NEYLIÈRE OCEANIC MUSEUM
SAMADET
MUSEUM OF FAIENCE

WALDERSBACH
OBERLIN MUSEUM

GDR

AUE
REGIONAL COLLECTION
BAD ELSTER
REGIONAL ROOM
BERLIN
PERGAMON MUSEUM: MUSEUM OF ETHNOGRAPHY
DORFCHEMNITZ, KREIS STOLBERG
BONE-MILL CULTURAL CENTRE
DRESDEN
MUSEUM OF POPULAR ART
GREIZ
DISTRICT AND REGIONAL MUSEUM
LEIPZIG
ETHNOLOGICAL MUSEUM
MÜLLROSE
REGIONAL MUSEUM
OEDERAN
REGIONAL MUSEUM
RADEBEUL
INDIAN MUSEUM
SCHNEEBERG
MUSEUM FOR POPULAR ART OF THE MINING COMMUNITY
SCHWERIN
SCHWERIN STATE MUSEUM
WUSTERHAUSEN
KYRITZ DISTRICT MUSEUM

GFR

BABENHAUSEN
FUGGER MUSEUM
BAD DRIBURG
ST. XAVIER MISSION MUSEUM
BAD REICHENHALL
MUNICIPAL MUSEUM
BAD TÖLZ
BAD TÖLZ MUSEUM
BAYREUTH
GERMAN MUSEUM OF FREEMASONRY
BERCHTESGADEN
REGIONAL MUSEUM
BERLIN
MUSEUM OF FREEMASONRY
MUSEUM OF GERMAN FOLKLORE
BERSENBRÜCK
DISTRICT MUSEUM
BIELEFELD
FARMHOUSE OPEN-AIR MUSEUM
BOCHUM
LOCAL HISTORY COLLECTIONS
BOGENBERG
REGIONAL MUSEUM
BOXBERG
REGIONAL MUSEUM
BRAUNFELS
PALACE MUSEUM
BRILON
REGIONAL MUSEUM
BUCHEN
STEINERNES HOUSE REGIONAL MUSEUM
BÜDINGEN
HEUSON MUSEUM
BÜHL
REGIONAL MUSEUM
BÜNDE
DISTRICT MUSEUM
BURGAU
REGIONAL MUSEUM
BURGHAUSEN
MUSEUM OF THE HISTORY OF BURGHAUSEN
BUXTEHUDE
REGIONAL MUSEUM
CALW
CALW REGIONAL MUSEUM AND HERMANN HESSE MEMORIAL
CELLE
BOMANN MUSEUM
DACHAU
REGIONAL MUSEUM
DIESSEN-AM-AMMERSEE
REGIONAL MUSEUM
DINGOLFING
REGIONAL MUSEUM
DINKELSBÜHL
MUSEUM OF HISTORY
DONAUWÖRTH
REGIONAL MUSEUM
DÜSSELDORF
HALL OF THE ARTS
EBERMANNSTADT
REGIONAL MUSEUM
EBINGEN
EBINGEN REGIONAL MUSEUM
EICHSTÄTT
WILLIBALD CASTLE MUSEUM
ELLWANGEN
PALACE MUSEUM
ERDING
REGIONAL MUSEUM
ESSEN
FOLKWANG MUSEUM
GERMAN POSTER MUSEUM
FEUCHTWANGEN
REGIONAL MUSEUM
FLADUNGEN
RHÖN MUSEUM
FLENSBURG
FLENSBURG MUNICIPAL MUSEUM
FRIEDBERG (HESSEN)
WETTERAU MUSEUM
FRIEDBERG (SCHWABEN)
REGIONAL MUSEUM
FÜRSTENFELDBRUCK
REGIONAL MUSEUM
FÜRTH
TOWN MUSEUM
FURTH IM WALD
TOWN TOWER MUSEUM
HAMBURG
ALTONA MUSEUM
HAMBURG MUSEUM OF ETHNOLOGY AND PREHISTORY
HANNOVER
KESTNER MUSEUM
HATTINGEN
SIEBENBURG REGIONAL ROOMS
HEIDELBERG
UNIVERSITY COLLECTION OF FOLK ART
HEIDENHEIM
REGIONAL MUSEUM
HELMSTEDT
DISTRICT MUSEUM
HOHENBURG
SPÖRER MUSEUM OF CULTURAL HISTORY
HOLZMINDEN
REGIONAL MUSEUM
ILSFELD
LIEBENSTEIN CASTLE
IMMENSTADT
REGIONAL MUSEUM
ISERLOHN
REGIONAL HOUSE
ISNY
ISNY REGIONAL MUSEUM
KALKAR
ART COLLECTION OF THE NICOLAI CHURCH
KAUFBEUREN
REGIONAL MUSEUM
KEITUM-SYLT
SYLT REGIONAL MUSEUM
KEMPTEN
ALLGAU REGIONAL MUSEUM
KIEL
MUSEUM OF ETHNOGRAPHY
KITZINGEN
GERMAN FASCHING MUSEUM
KÖLN
RAUTENSTRANCH-JOEST MUSEUM
KONSTANZ
ROSGARTEN MUSEUM
KRANENBURG
REGIONAL MUSEUM
KREFELD
KAISER WILHELM MUSEUM
KRUMBACH
REGIONAL MUSEUM
KULMBACH-PLASSENBURG
UPPER MAIN REGIONAL MUSEUM
LADENBURG
LOBDENGAU MUSEUM
LANDAU (ISAR)
REGIONAL MUSEUM
LAUINGEN
REGIONAL HOUSE
LUDWIGSHAFEN
K. O. BRAUN REGIONAL MUSEUM
LÜNEN
MUSEUM OF ART AND CULTURAL HISTORY OF DORTMUND
MAINBURG
HOLLEDAU REGIONAL MUSEUM
MANNHEIM
REISS CITY MUSEUM
MARKTOBERDORF
COLLECTIONS OF LOCAL LIFE AND HISTORY
RIESENGEBIRGE COLLECTION
MINDELHEIM
MINDELHEIM REGIONAL MUSEUM
MOOSBURG
REGIONAL MUSEUM
MÜHLDORF
DISTRICT MUSEUM
MÜNCHEN
BAVARIAN NATIONAL MUSEUM
MUNICH CITY MUSEUM
STATE COLLECTION OF EGYPTIAN ART
STATE MUSEUM OF ETHNOGRAPHY
MÜNNERSTADT
REGIONAL MUSEUM
NEUNBURG VOR WALD
DISTRICT MUSEUM
NEUNHOF
KNOBLAUCHLAND REGIONAL MUSEUM
NEUSS
CLEMENS SELS MUSEUM
NEUSTADT AN DER WALDNAAB
LOCAL MUSEUM
NEU-ULM
NEU-ULM REGIONAL MUSEUM
NEUWIED
DISTRICT MUSEUM
OBERAMMERGAU
OBERAMMERGAU REGIONAL MUSEUM
OBERGÜNZBURG
REGIONAL MUSEUM
OBERHEINING
BRECHELBAD MUSEUM
OBERSTDORF
REGIONAL MUSEUM
OFFENBURG
HOUSE OF THE KNIGHTS MUSEUM
PFAFFENHOFEN
REGIONAL MUSEUM
PFARRKIRCHEN
ROTTAL REGIONAL MUSEUM
PRIEN
REGIONAL MUSEUM
RATZEBURG
DISTRICT MUSEUM

RECKLINGHAUSEN
VESTISCH MUSEUM
REGENSBURG
REGENSBURG CITY MUSEUM
ROTTHALMÜNSTER
REGIONAL MUSEUM
RÖTZ
RÖTZ REGIONAL MUSEUM
RUHPOLDING
BARTHOLOMÄUS SCHMUCKER REGIONAL MUSEUM
SALZGITTER-SALDER
TOWN MUSEUM
SCHWABACH
TOWN MUSEUM
SCHWEINFURT
MUNICIPAL MUSEUM
SESSLACH
REGIONAL MUSEUM
SIMBACH
TOWN MUSEUM
STARNBERG
MUNICIPAL MUSEUM
STRAUBING
GÄUBODEN AND STRAUBING MUSEUM
STUTTGART
WÜRTTEMBERG MUSEUM
TEGERNSEE
TEGERNSEE REGIONAL MUSEUM
TELGTE
MÜNSTERLAND REGIONAL HOUSE
TRAUNSTEIN
REGIONAL MUSEUM
VOHENSTRAUSS
VOHENSTRAUSS REGIONAL MUSEUM
WALLDÜRN
REGIONAL AND PILGRIMAGES MUSEUM
WANGEN
WANGEN REGIONAL MUSEUM
WASSERBURG
WASSERBURG REGIONAL MUSEUM
WEISMAIN
REGIONAL MUSEUM
WERTINGEN
REGIONAL MUSEUM
WESTRHAUDERFEHN
OSTFRIESLAND AND SATERLAND FEN AND SHIPPING MUSEUM
WETTELSHEIM
LOCAL COLLECTION
WUPPERTAL
MUSEUM OF KITSCH

GREAT BRITAIN

BIRCHINGTON
POWELL-COTTON MUSEUM
CAMBRIDGE
THE SCOTT POLAR RESEARCH INSTITUTE
HEMEL HEMPSTEAD
PICCOTTS END MEDIAEVAL MURALS
LONDON
BRITISH MUSEUM
WINCHCOMBE
SUDELEY CASTLE

GREECE

ALEXANDROUPOLIS
E. FILIPPIDIS PRIVATE COLLECTION
AMBELAKIA
THE G. SCHWARZ MANSION
ATHENS
BENAKI MUSEUM
BYZANTINE MUSEUM
HISTORICAL AND ETHNOLOGICAL MUSEUM
MUSEUM OF GREEK POPULAR ART
NATIONAL HISTORICAL MUSEUM
CHANIA
HISTORICAL MUSEUM AND CRETAN CORNER
CORFU
HISTORICAL MUSEUM
DIMITSANA
GREEK FOLK MUSEUM
KARDAMYLI, MESSINIA
ARCHAEOLOGICAL COLLECTION
KARDITSA
COLLECTION OF THE KARDITSA FOLKLORE SOCIETY
LAMIA
A. KOUNOUPIS PRIVATE COLLECTION
PETRA
T. ELEFTHERIADIS PRIVATE COLLECTION
SPARTI
ARCHAEOLOGICAL MUSEUM
SYMI
ARCHAEOLOGICAL COLLECTION
TINOS
CHURCH OF THE PANAGIA EVANGELISTRIA
VOLOS
K. A. MAKRIS PRIVATE COLLECTION

HUNGARY

BALASSAGYARMAT
PALÓC MUSEUM
DEBRECEN
DÉRI MUSEUM
DUNAPATAJ
LOCAL HISTORY COLLECTION
GYÖNGYÖS
MÁTRA MUSEUM
HÓDMEZÖVÁSARHELY
JÁNOS TORNYAI MUSEUM
MOHÁCS
DOROTHYA KANIZSAI MUSEUM
PÉCS
JANUS PANNONIUS MUSEUM
SÁROSPATAK
MUSEUM OF THE REFORMED CHURCH
SIÓFOK
JÓZSEF BESZÉDES MUSEUM
ZALAEGERSZEG
GÖCSEJ MUSEUM
ZIRC
ANTAL REGULY MUSEUM

INDIA

BHAWANAGAR
GANDHI SMRITI MUSEUMS
CALCUTTA
ASUTOSH MUSEUM OF INDIAN ART
CRAFTS MUSEUM
GOVERNMENT INDUSTRIAL AND COMMERCIAL MUSEUM
GAUHATI
COTTAGE INDUSTRIES MUSEUM
JAMNAGAR
JAMNAGAR MUSEUM OF ANTIQUITIES, LAKHOTE BUILDING

INDONESIA

DENPASAR
BALI MUSEUM

ISRAEL

TEL-AVIV
HISTORICAL FOLK MUSEUM OF THE LAND OF ISRAEL
KADMAN NUMISMATIC MUSEUM
MUSEUM OF ETHNOGRAPHY AND FOLKLORE

ITALY

CAGLIARI
MUNICIPAL ART GALLERY
GENOA
MUNICIPAL ETHNOGRAPHICAL MUSEUM
LA FAVORITA
PITRÉ MUSEUM OF SICILIAN ETHNOGRAPHY
PALERMO
PITRÉ ETHNOGRAPHICAL MUSEUM
PARMA
MUSEUM OF CHINESE ETHNOGRAPHY
PERUGIA
NATIONAL GALLERY OF UMBRIA
ROME
NATIONAL MUSEUM OF ARTS AND POPULAR TRADITIONS
LUIGI PIGORINI MUSEUM OF PREHISTORY AND ETHNOGRAPHY
TOLMEZZO
CARNICO MUSEUM OF ARTS AND POPULAR TRADITIONS
UDINE
FRIULANO MUSEUM OF POPULAR ARTS AND TRADITIONS

IVORY COAST

ABIDJAN
MUSEUM OF THE CENTRE DES SCIENCES HUMAINES

JAMAICA

HALF-WAY TREE
AFRICAN MUSEUM

JAPAN

AKITA-SHI
AKITA CITY MUSEUM OF ART
ASAHIKAWA-SHI
ASAHIKAWA LOCAL MUSEUM
CHIYODA-MACHI
GEIHOKU ETHNOGRAPHICAL MUSEUM
HATANO-SHI
KOAN COLLECTION
ITOIGAWA-SHI
GYOFU SOMA MEMORIAL COLLECTION
KUSHIRO-SHI
KUSHIRO MUNICIPAL MUSEUM
MATSUMOTO-SHI
MATSUMOTO MUNICIPAL MUSEUM
NARA-SHI
ORIENTAL FOLK MUSEUM
SHOSOIN TREASURE HOUSE
OSAKA
MUNICIPAL MUSEUM
OTARU-SHI
OTARU CITY MUSEUM
OTSU
SHIGA PREFECTURAL MUSEUM
SHINOHARA-MACHI
BUSO ARCHAEOLOGICAL COLLECTION
TENRI-SHI
TENRI MUSEUM
TOKYO
FOLK ART MUSEUM
TENRI GALLERY

MEXICO

CHIHUAHUA
CHIHUAHUA REGIONAL MUSEUM
DOLORES HIDALGO
CASA DE HIDALGO
GUADALAJARA
GUADALAJARA REGIONAL MUSEUM

GUANAJUATO
GUANAJUATO REGIONAL MUSEUM
MEXICO CITY
MUSEUM OF RURAL LIFE (CHARRERIA)
NATIONAL MUSEUM OF ARTS AND CRAFTS
NATIONAL MUSEUM OF MODERN ART
TOLUCA
NATIONAL MUSEUM OF FOLK ART
XALAPA
VERACRUZ MUSEUM OF ANTHROPOLOGY

NETHERLANDS

ASSEN
DRENTHE PROVINCIAL MUSEUM
CADIER EN KEER
CADIER EN KEER AFRICA CENTRE
EERNEWOUDE
JAN EN SJUT'S COOK-SHOP
KRIMPEN AAN DEN IJSSEL
CRIMPENERHOF DISTRICT MUSEUM
MIDDEN- BEEMSTER
BETJE WOLFF HOUSE
VLIELAND
TROMP HOUSE
WEST- TERSCHELLING
LOCAL MUSEUM

NEW ZEALAND

NEW PLYMOUTH
TARANAKI MUSEUM
THAMES
THAMES MINERALOGICAL MUSEUM

NIGERIA

ORON
ORON MUSEUM
OWO
OWO MUSEUM

NORWAY

BERGEN
HISTORICAL MUSEUM
HALLINGDAL
HALLINGDAL FOLK MUSEUM
KRISTIANSUND
KRISTIANSUND MUSEUM
MELBU
VESTERÅL COLLECTION OF BUILDINGS
NESBYEN
HALLINGDAL FOLK MUSEUM
SKIEN
TELEMARK AND GRENLAND FOLK MUSEUM
TROMSØ
TROMSØ MUSEUM
TRONDHEIM
MUSEUM OF THE ROYAL NORWEGIAN SOCIETY OF SCIENCES AND LETTERS
TRONDHEIM AND TRØNDELAG FOLK MUSEUM

PERU

LIMA
POPULAR ART COLLECTION

POLAND

BIELINY
MUSEUM OF ETHNOGRAPHY
KIELCE
ŚWIĘTOKRZYKIE MUSEUM
KOLBUSZOWA
LASOWIAKOW REGIONAL MUSEUM
ŁÓDŹ
MUSEUM OF ARCHAEOLOGY AND ETHNOGRAPHY
ŁOWICZ
REGIONAL MUSEUM
OLSZTYN
OPEN-AIR MUSEUM
OPOCZNO
REGIONAL MUSEUM
PŁOCK
DIOCESAN MUSEUM
PODEGRODZIE
REGIONAL MUSEUM
POZNAŃ
POZNAŃ HISTORICAL MUSEUM
POZNAŃ NATIONAL MUSEUM
PUŁKOWO WIELKIE
REGIONAL MUSEUM
RZESZOW
REGIONAL MUSEUM
SLAKÓW BOROWY
ŁOWICK MUSEUM OF ART
SŁUPSK
REGIONAL MUSEUM OF ETHNOGRAPHY
SMOLNIK
OPEN-AIR MUSEUM
TARNÓW
DIOCESAN MUSEUM
TORUŃ
TORUŃ ETHNOGRAPHICAL MUSEUM
WARSAW
NATIONAL ETHNOGRAPHICAL MUSEUM
POSTER MUSEUM
WISŁA-ZDRÓJ
BESKIDZKI MUSEUM
WROCŁAW
ETHNOGRAPHICAL MUSEUM
NATIONAL MUSEUM
ZAKOPANE
TATRA MUSEUM AND T. CHAŁUBIŃSKI MEMORIAL
ZBĄSZIN
REGIONAL MUSEUM
ZŁOTÓW
ETHNOGRAPHICAL PARK

PORTUGAL

LISBON
FOLK ART MUSEUM
PORTUGUESE NUMISMATIC MUSEUM

ROMANIA

BUCHAREST
KARADJA COLLECTION
DR. N. MINOVICI MUSEUM OF FOLK ART
MUSEUM OF FOLK ART
VILLAGE MUSEUM
GOLEŞTI
MUSEUM OF HISTORY AND ETHNOGRAPHY
ORĂŞTIE
ORĂŞTIE MUSEUM
PLOIEŞTI
HISTORY MUSEUM
HAGI PRODAN HOUSE
POIANA SIBIULUI
LOCAL MUSEUM
SATU MARE
SATU MARE MUSEUM

SINGAPORE

SINGAPORE
NATIONAL MUSEUM

SOUTH AFRICA, REPUBLIC OF

DURBAN
WILLIAM CAMPBELL MUSEUM
GRAHAMSTOWN
ALBANY MUSEUM
JOHANNESBURG
ARCHAEOLOGICAL MUSEUM
KIMBERLEY
ALEXANDER MCGREGOR MEMORIAL MUSEUM
PRETORIA
ANTHROPOLOGICAL MUSEUM OF THE UNIVERSITY OF SOUTH AFRICA

SOUTH-WEST AFRICA (NAMIBIA)

LÜDERITZ
LÜDERITZ MUSEUM

SPAIN

ARENYS DE MAR
FIDEL FITA MUNICIPAL MUSEUM
AVILA
PROVINCIAL MUSEUM
BADALONA
MUNICIPAL MUSEUM
BARCELONA
MUSEUM OF ETHNOLOGY
MUSEUM OF INDUSTRY AND POPULAR ARTS
BEJAR
MUNICIPAL MUSEUM
GERONA
PROVINCIAL ARCHAEOLOGICAL MUSEUM
JEREZ DE LA FRONTERA
FLAMENCO MUSEUM
LLUCH
LLUCH TREASURY AND MUSEUM
LUGO
PROVINCIAL MUSEUM
MADRID
MUNICIPAL MUSEUM
PALMA DE MALLORCA
MALLORCA MUSEUM
PONTEVEDRA
PONTEVEDRA MUSEUM
SABADELL
MUSEUM OF HISTORY
SAN LORENZO DE MORUNYS
MUSEUM OF THE PATRONATO OF VALL DE LORD

SRI LANKA, REPUBLIC OF

ANURADHAPURA
FOLK MUSEUM

SWEDEN

FALUN
DALARNAS MUSEUM
HUDIKSVALL
HÄLSINGLANDS MUSEUM
KRISTIANSTAD
KRISTIANSTAD MUSEUM
LULEÅ
NORBOTTEN MUSEUM
MORA
ZORN HOUSE-MUSEUM
ZORN MUSEUM
ÖSTERSUND
JÄMTLAND MUSEUM
SUNDBORN
CARL LARSSON HOUSE-MUSEUM
UPPSALA
UPPLAND MUSEUM

SWITZERLAND

APPENZELL
REGIONAL MUSEUM

BASEL
MUSEUM OF ETHNOLOGY
MUSEUM OF SWISS FOLKLORE

BERN
BERN HISTORICAL MUSEUM
CANTONAL MUSEUM OF APPLIED ART

BOURG- SAINT-PIERRE
MUSEUM OF THE GREAT ST. BERNARD SHELTER FOR TRAVELLERS

BRIEG
CASTLE OF THE STOCKALPERS

CEVIO
MUSEUM OF THE VALLEMAGGIA

CHUR
MUNICIPAL MUSEUM

EBNAT-KAPPEL
ALBERT EDELMANN FOUNDATION

GENEVA
MUSEUM OF THE HISTORY OF SCIENCE
MUSEUM AND INSTITUTE OF ETHNOGRAPHY

HERISAU
MUSEUM

LICHTENSTEIG
TOGGENBURG REGIONAL MUSEUM

LUZERN
HISTORICAL MUSEUM

ST. GALLEN
NEW MUSEUM

SCHWYZ
TOWER MUSEUM

ZURICH
MUSEUM OF APPLIED ART
MUSEUM RIETBERG

USSR

BREST-LITOVSK
REGIONAL MUSEUM OF FOLK ART

CHERNOVTSY
MUSEUM OF UKRAINIAN FOLKLORE

DNEPROPETROVSK (formerly JEKATERINOSLAV)
MUSEUM OF ART

DUSHANBE (formerly STALINABAD)
MUSEUM OF THE REPUBLIC OF TADZHIKISTAN

KIEV
STATE MUSEUM OF POPULAR AND DECORATIVE ART

KOLONNA
MUSEUM OF POPULAR ART OF THE GOUTZOULES

LENINGRAD
HERMITAGE MUSEUM
NATIONAL MUSEUM OF ETHNOGRAPHY OF THE PEOPLES OF THE U.S.S.R.
NATIONAL RUSSIAN MUSEUM

MOSCOW
HOUSE-MUSEUM OF K. S. STANISLAVSKI
MUSEUM OF FOLK ART

MSTERA
MUSEUM OF HANDICRAFTS

TASHKENT
CENTRAL REGIONAL MUSEUM

ULAN-BATOR
FINE ARTS MUSEUM

UNITED STATES

AKRON
AKRON ART INSTITUTE

AMERICUS
GEORGIA SOUTHWESTERN COLLEGE

ANADARKO
SOUTHERN PLAINS INDIAN MUSEUM AND CRAFTS CENTER

ANCHORAGE
ANCHORAGE HISTORICAL AND FINE ARTS MUSEUM

ATHENS
GEORGIA MUSEUM OF ART, UNIVERSITY OF GEORGIA

ATLANTA
HIGH MUSEUM OF ART

BALTIMORE
BALTIMORE MUSEUM OF ART

BELLINGHAM
WHATCOM MUSEUM OF HISTORY AND ART

BIRMINGHAM
BIRMINGHAM MUSEUM OF ART

BLOOMFIELD HILLS
GALLERIES OF CRANBROOK ACADEMY OF ART

BLOOMINGTON
INDIANA UNIVERSITY ART MUSEUM

BURLINGTON
ROBERT HULL FLEMING MUSEUM

CAMBRIDGE
FOGG ART MUSEUM

CHAMPAIGN
KRANNERT ART MUSEUM

CHARLESTON
OLD SLAVE MART MUSEUM

CHICAGO
ART INSTITUTE OF CHICAGO

CINCINNATI
CINCINNATI ART MUSEUM

CLEVELAND
CLEVELAND MUSEUM OF ART

COLORADO SPRINGS
COLORADO SPRINGS FINE ARTS CENTER

COLUMBIA
MUSEUM OF ART AND ARCHAEOLOGY

COLUMBUS
COLUMBUS GALLERY OF FINE ARTS

COOPERSTOWN
MUSEUM OF NEW YORK STATE HISTORICAL ASSOCIATION

DALLAS
DALLAS MUSEUM OF FINE ARTS

DAVENPORT
DAVENPORT MUNICIPAL ART GALLERY
DAVENPORT MUSEUM

DAYTON
DAYTON ART INSTITUTE

DELAWARE
OHIO WESLEYAN UNIVERSITY

DENTON
TEXAS WOMEN'S UNIVERSITY ART GALLERIES

DENVER
DENVER ART MUSEUM

DETROIT
DETROIT INSTITUTE OF ARTS
INTERNATIONAL INSTITUTE OF METROPOLITAN DETROIT

DULUTH
MUSEUM OF ST. LOUIS COUNTY HISTORICAL SOCIETY

EAGLE BRIDGE
GRANDMA MOSES SCHOOLHOUSE

EL PASO
EL PASO MUSEUM OF ART

FLAGSTAFF
MUSEUM OF NORTHERN ARIZONA

FORT LAUDERDALE
FORT LAUDERDALE MUSEUM OF THE ARTS

FORT WORTH
KIMBELL ART MUSEUM

FRESNO
FRESNO ARTS CENTER

GALLUP
GALLUP MUSEUM OF INDIAN ARTS AND CRAFTS

GREENSBURG
WESTMORELAND COUNTY MUSEUM OF ART

HAINES
SHELDON'S MUSEUM

HEMPSTEAD
EMILY LOWE GALLERY

HONOLULU
HONOLULU ACADEMY OF ARTS

HOUSTON
MUSEUM OF FINE ARTS

INDIANAPOLIS
INDIANAPOLIS MUSEUM OF ART

ITHACA
ITHACA COLLEGE MUSEUM OF ART

JACKSONVILLE
DAVID STRAWN ART GALLERY

JOPLIN
SPIVA ART CENTER

KANSAS CITY
WILLIAM ROCKHILL NELSON GALLERY AND ATKINS MUSEUM OF FINE ARTS

KATONAH
KATONAH GALLERY

LOS ANGELES
MUSEUM OF CULTURAL HISTORY

LOUISVILLE
J. B. SPEED ART MUSEUM

MAITLAND
ART MUSEUM

MASSILLON
MASSILLON MUSEUM

MEMPHIS
BROOKS MEMORIAL ART GALLERY

MIAMI
MIAMI MUSEUM OF MODERN ART

MILWAUKEE
MILWAUKEE PUBLIC MUSEUM

MINNEAPOLIS
MINNEAPOLIS INSTITUTE OF ARTS

MUSKOGEE
FIVE CIVILISED TRIBES MUSEUM

NASHVILLE
CARL VAN VECHLEN GALLERY OF FINE ARTS

NEWARK
NEWARK MUSEUM

NEW BERN
TRYON PALACE RESTORATION

NEW HAVEN
YALE UNIVERSITY ART GALLERY

NEW ORLEANS
NEW ORLEANS MUSEUM OF ART

NEW PALTZ
STATE UNIVERSITY COLLEGE ART GALLERY

NEWPORT
BELCOURT CASTLE

NEW YORK
BROOKLYN MUSEUM
JUNIOR MUSEUM OF THE METROPOLITAN MUSEUM OF ART
METROPOLITAN MUSEUM OF ART
MUSEUM OF AMERICAN FOLK ART
MUSEUM OF NEW YORK HISTORICAL SOCIETY
MUSEUM OF PRIMITIVE ART
RIVERSIDE MUSEUM
WARSHAW COLLECTION OF BUSINESS AMERICANA

NOTRE DAME
UNIVERSITY OF NOTRE DAME ART GALLERY

OLD BENNINGTON
BENNINGTON MUSEUM

ORLANDO
LOCH HAVEN ART CENTER

OXON HILL
JOHN HANSON MEMORIAL MUSEUM

PHILADELPHIA
PHILADELPHIA MUSEUM OF ART
UNIVERSITY MUSEUM

PHOENIX
HEARD MUSEUM
PHOENIX ART MUSEUM

PORTLAND
PORTLAND ART MUSEUM

PRINCETON
PRINCETON UNIVERSITY ART MUSEUM

PROVIDENCE
MUSEUM OF ART, RHODE ISLAND SCHOOL OF DESIGN

PROVINCETOWN
CHRYSLER ART MUSEUM
RAPID CITY
SIOUX INDIAN MUSEUM
READING
READING PUBLIC MUSEUM AND ART GALLERY
ROCHESTER
UNIVERSITY ART GALLERY
MUSEUM OF OLMSTED COUNTY HISTORICAL SOCIETY
MEMORIAL ART GALLERY, UNIVERSITY OF ROCHESTER
ROSWELL
ROSWELL MUSEUM AND ART CENTER
ST. JOHNSBURY
FAIRBANKS MUSEUM OF NATURAL SCIENCE
ST. JOSEPH
BENEDICTA ARTS CENTER
ST. LOUIS
ST. LOUIS ART MUSEUM
WASHINGTON UNIVERSITY GALLERY OF ART
ST. PAUL
MINNESOTA MUSEUM OF ART
SAN ANTONIO
MARION KOOGLER MCNAY ART INSTITUTE
SAN FRANCISCO
M. H. DE YOUNG MEMORIAL MUSEUM
SAN JUAN
MUSEUM OF POPULAR RELIGIOUS ART
SANTA BARBARA
SANTA BARBARA MUSEUM OF ART
SANTA FE
MUSEUM OF NEW MEXICO
SEATTLE
PULLEN ALASKA MUSEUM
SEATTLE ART MUSEUM
SPRINGFIELD
SPRINGFIELD ART AND HISTORICAL SOCIETY
STANFORD
STANFORD UNIVERSITY MUSEUM AND ART GALLERY
STOCKTON
PIONEER MUSEUM AND HAGGIN GALLERIES
TACOMA
WASHINGTON STATE HISTORICAL SOCIETY MUSEUM
TAOS
HARWOOD FOUNDATION
TEMPE
UNIVERSITY ART COLLECTIONS
TERRE HAUTE
SHELDON SWOPE ART GALLERY
TOWANDA
MUSEUM OF BRADFORD COUNTY HISTORICAL SOCIETY
TROY
OVERFIELD TAVERN
TUCSON
TUCSON ART CENTER
TULSA
PHILBROOK ART CENTER
WACO
BAYLOR ART MUSEUM
WALTHAM
THE ROSE ART MUSEUM
WASHINGTON
DUMBARTON OAKS RESEARCH LIBRARY AND COLLECTION
GALLERY OF AFRICAN ART
HOWARD UNIVERSITY GALLERY OF ART
INDIAN ARTS AND CRAFTS BOARD
MUSEUM OF AFRICAN ART
NATIONAL GALLERY OF ART
WATERVILLE
COLBY COLLEGE ART MUSEUM
WATKINS GLEN
YORKER YANKEE VILLAGE
WELLESLEY
WELLESLEY COLLEGE MUSEUM
WESTON
FARRAR-MANSUR HOUSE
WILBERFORCE
WILBERFORCE UNIVERSITY, CARNEGIE LIBRARY
WILLIAMSBURG
ABBY ALDRICH ROCKEFELLER FOLK ART COLLECTION
WOLF POINT
MUSEUM OF WOLF POINT AREA HISTORICAL SOCIETY
WORCESTER
WORCESTER ART MUSEUM
YUKON
HENSON GALLERY
ZANESVILLE
ART INSTITUTE OF ZANESVILLE

VIETNAM, DEMOCRATIC REPUBLIC OF

HANOI
HISTORICAL MUSEUM

YUGOSLAVIA

CETINJE
ETHNOGRAPHICAL MUSEUM
SREMSKI KARLOVCI
TOWN MUSEUM
ZAGREB
ETHNOGRAPHICAL MUSEUM

Architecture, including village museums and open-air museums of buildings

AUSTRALIA

BALLARAT
SOVEREIGN HILL HISTORICAL PARK
BRISBANE
EARLY STREET
BURNIE
THE PIONEER VILLAGE MUSEUM
GRIFFITH
PIONEER PARK MUSEUM
HILL END
NATIONAL PARKS AND WILDLIFE VISITATION CENTRE
MOE
FOLK MUSEUM
MORPHETT VALE
PIONEER VILLAGE MUSEUM
SWAN HILL
SWAN HILL FOLK MUSEUM
WILBERFORCE
AUTHENTICATED AUSTRALIAN SETTLERS VILLAGE

AUSTRIA

ASPARN
LOWER AUSTRIA MUSEUM OF PREHISTORY
BAD TATZMANNSDORF
BURGENLAND OPEN-AIR MUSEUM
GNAS
REGIONAL MUSEUM
HERBERTSTEIN
PALACE MUSEUM
LIENZ
KLÖSTERLE SMITHY OPEN-AIR MUSEUM
MARIA SAAL
CARINTHIAN OPEN-AIR MUSEUM
MONDSEE
'MONDSEE RAUCHHAUS' OPEN- AIR MUSEUM
RAURIS
RAURIS GOLD-MINING MUSEUM
STUBING
AUSTRIAN OPEN-AIR MUSEUM
VIENNA
CABINET OF ENGRAVINGS OF THE ACADEMY OF FINE ARTS
MUSEUM OF THE BÖHMERWALD
MUSEUM OF THE HISTORY OF ART: EGYPTIAN AND ORIENTAL COLLECTION
MUSEUM OF THE PROVINCE OF LOWER AUSTRIA
MUSEUM OF THE 20th CENTURY

BELGIUM

ANTWERP
OPEN-AIR MUSEUM OF SCULPTURE
BRUGES
ARCHERS GUILD OF ST. SEBASTIAN
BRUSSELS
THE OLD BÉGUINAGE AT ANDERLECHT
HASSELT
OPEN-AIR MUSEUM
LOUVAIN
TOWN HALL MUSEUM

BRAZIL

VASSOURAS
CASA DA HERA MUSEUM

BULGARIA

ETARA
OPEN-AIR MUSEUM
RILA
RILA MONASTERY NATIONAL MUSEUM

BURMA

MANDALAY
STATE LIBRARY AND MUSEUM
MOULMEIN
STATE LIBRARY AND MUSEUM
RANGOON
NATIONAL MUSEUM OF ART AND ARCHAEOLOGY

CANADA

AUSTIN
MANITOBA AGRICULTURAL MUSEUM
BARKERVILLE
BARKERVILLE HISTORIC PARK
BROUGHAM
PICKERING TOWNSHIP MUSEUM
CALGARY
HERITAGE PARK
DOWNSVIEW
BLACK CREEK PIONEER VILLAGE
EDMONTON
FORT EDMONTON HISTORIC PARK
ELK ISLAND
ELK ISLAND NATIONAL PARK
FANSHAWE
FANSHAWE PIONEER VILLAGE
FORT STEELE
FORT STEELE HISTORIC PARK

FORT WILLIAM
LOGGING MUSEUM
HUNTSVILLE
MUSKOKA MUSEUM
JORDAN
BALL'S FALLS MUSEUM
KITCHENER
DOON PIONEER VILLAGE
LANG
CENTURY VILLAGE
MIDLAND
HURON INDIAN VILLAGE
SAINTE MARIE AMONG THE HURONS
MORRISBURG
UPPER CANADA VILLAGE
OKANAGAN MISSION
FATHER PANDESY MISSION INDIAN VILLAGE
PETERBOROUGH
CENTURY VILLAGE
PICKERING
PICKERING TOWNSHIP MUSEUM
PINCHER CREEK
PINCHER CREEK HISTORICAL PARK
PORCUPINE
PORCUPINE MINING MUSEUM
RIMBEY
PAS-KA-POO HISTORICAL PARK
ROCKTON
WESTFIELD PIONEER VILLAGE
ROSSLAND
ROSSLAND HISTORICAL MUSEUM
SHERBROOKE
SHERBROOKE VILLAGE PROJECT
STEINBACH
MENNONITE VILLAGE MUSEUM
TORONTO
TODMORDEN MILLS MUSEUM PARK
TROIS RIVIÈRES
VILLAGE OF ST. MAURICE IRONWORKS
VICTORIA
PROVINCIAL MUSEUM
WILLINGDON
HISTORIC VILLAGE AND PIONEER MUSEUM

CUBA

HABANA
MUSEUM OF COLONIAL ART

CZECHOSLOVAKIA

BARDEJOV
OPEN-AIR MUSEUM OF FOLK-ARCHITECTURE
KRAVAŘE
PALACE MUSEUM
MARTIN
SLOVAKIAN NATIONAL MUSEUM: ETHNOGRAPHICAL COLLECTIONS
NOVÝ JIČIN
DISTRICT MUSEUM
PRAGUE
ETHNOLOGICAL COLLECTIONS
MUSEUM OF THE CITY OF PRAGUE
PŘEROV NAD LABEM
MUSEUM OF ETHNOGRAPHY
ROŽNOV POD RADHOŠTĚM
VALASKIAN MUSEUM OF ETHNOGRAPHY
RTYNĚ Y PODKRKONOŠÍ
MEMORIAL OF THE PEASANT REVOLT OF 1777
TRENČÍN
TRENČÍN MUSEUM

DENMARK

ARHUS
DEN GAMLE BY
COPENHAGEN
NYBODEN MUSEUM
GLUD
GLUD MUSEUM
HADERSLEV
HADERSLEV MUSEUM
HERNING
HERNING MUSEUM
LYNGBY
OPEN-AIR MUSEUM
MARIBO
LOLLAND AND FALSTER MUSEUM
ODENSE
THE FUNEN VILLAGE
RØMØ
COMMANDER'S HOUSE
SKAGEN
SKAGEN BYGONES
TÓRSHAVN
FAROES HISTORICAL MUSEUM

EGYPT, ARAB REPUBLIC OF

ALEXANDRIA
MONTAZAH PALACE MUSEUM
CAIRO
ABDINE PALACE MUSEUM
AL GAWHARA PALACE MUSEUM
AL MANIAL PALACE MUSEUM
HELWAN PALACE MUSEUM

FINLAND

ARTJÄRVI
DISTRICT MUSEUM
EVIJÄRVI
LAKE MUSEUM
HAUHO
HAUHO MUSEUM
HELSINKI
ARCHITECTURAL MUSEUM OF FINLAND
SEURASAARI OPEN-AIR MUSEUM
INARI
LAPP OPEN-AIR MUSEUM
ISOKYRÖ
REGIONAL MUSEUM
JANAKKALA
REGIONAL MUSEUM
JUVA
REGIONAL MUSEUM
KALANTI
OSKARI RAULAN REGIONAL MUSEUM
KEMIÖ
REGIONAL MUSEUM
KESÄLAHTI
LOCAL MUSEUM
KIURUVESI
REGIONAL MUSEUM
KOKEMÄKI
OPEN-AIR MUSEUM
KULLAA
LOCAL MUSEUM
KUOREVESI
REGIONAL MUSEUM
KUORTANE
MUSEUM OF BUILDINGS
LAMONI
LOCAL MUSEUM
LAPINJÄRVI
PORLAMMI REGIONAL MUSEUM
LAUKAA
VILLAGE MUSEUM
LEPPÄVIRTA
REGIONAL MUSEUM
LIEKSA
MUSEUM OF HISTORY
LIETO
VANHALINNA MUSEUM
LUHANKA
PELTOLA MOUNTAIN VILLAGE MUSEUM
LUOPIOINEN
LOCAL MUSEUM
MUHOS
REGIONAL MUSEUM
NAANTALI
LOCAL MUSEUM
NÄRPIÖ
REGIONAL MUSEUM
NASTOLA
REGIONAL MUSEUM
NIVALA
LOCAL MUSEUM
NOKIA
REGIONAL MUSEUM
NURMIJÄRVI
REGIONAL MUSEUM
ORWESI
DISTRICT MUSEUM
OULU
TURKANSAARI OPEN-AIR MUSEUM
PARAINEN
REGIONAL MUSEUM
PÖYTYÄ
MUSEUM OF THE PÖYTYÄ HISTORICAL SOCIETY
PUNKAHARJU
REGIONAL MUSEUM
PUNKALAIDUN
LOCAL MUSEUM
PYHÄJOKI
REGIONAL MUSEUM
RANTASALMI
REGIONAL MUSEUM
ROVANIEMI
REGIONAL MUSEUM
RUOKOLAHTI
REGIONAL MUSEUM
RUOVESI
REGIONAL MUSEUM
SÄKYLÄ
LOCAL MUSEUM
SEINÄJOKI
MUSEUM OF SOUTH OSTROBOTHNIA
SOMERO
LOCAL MUSEUM
VAASA
BRAGE OPEN-AIR MUSEUM
VALKEAKOSKI
KAIPPILANMÄKI
ÄHTÄRI
LOCAL MUSEUM

FRANCE

BORDEAUX
AQUITAINE MUSEUM
COMMANA
OPEN-AIR MUSEUM
DIJON
CHAMPMOL CHARTERHOUSE
PERRIN DE PUYCOUSIN MUSEUM
FONTAINEBLEAU
PALACE OF FONTAINEBLEAU
LE HAVRE
GRAVILLE ABBEY
MARQUÈZE
OPEN-AIR MUSEUM OF THE LANDES DE GASCOIGNE
METZ
CENTRAL MUSEUM
NEUFCHÂTEL-EN-BRAY
MATHON MUSEUM
NICE
VIEUX-LOGIS PRIORY MUSEUM

OUESSANT
OPEN-AIR MUSEUM
PARIS
MUSEUM OF MATERIALS
QUIMPER
BRITTANY MUSEUM
SAINT-PAUL-DE-VENCE
MAEGHT FOUNDATION

GDR

BERLIN
PERGAMON MUSEUM: NEAR EASTERN MUSEUM
GREIFSWALD
GREIFSWALD MUNICIPAL MUSEUM
HAVELBERG
PRIGNITZ MUSEUM
LEHDE
OPEN-AIR MUSEUM
LEIPZIG
MUSEUM OF THE HISTORY OF THE CITY OF LEIPZIG
MITTWEIDA
REGIONAL MUSEUM
RUDOLSTADT
MUSEUM OF ETHNOLOGY: THURINGIAN PEASANT HOUSES
STENDAL
ALTMARK MUSEUM: MÖNCHSKIRCHOF COLLECTION

GFR

BERLIN
STUCCO MUSEUM
BIELEFELD
FARMHOUSE OPEN-AIR MUSEUM
BREMEN
OVERSEAS MUSEUM
BREMERHAVEN
SPECKENBÜTTEL OPEN-AIR MUSEUM
CLOPPENBURG
VILLAGE MUSEUM
DARMSTADT
BAUHAUS COLLECTIONS
DETMOLD
OPEN AIR MUSEUM
FREIBURG IM BREISGAU
MINSTER MUSEUM
GOSLAR
CATHEDRAL ANTECHAMBER
GUTACH
BAILIFF'S FARM OPEN-AIR MUSEUM
HAMBURG
KIEKEBERG OPEN-AIR MUSEUM
RIECK HOUSE: VIERLAND OPEN- AIR MUSEUM
VOLKSDORF VILLAGE MUSEUM
HUSUM
OSTENFELD FARMHOUSE OPEN- AIR MUSEUM
KIEL
SCHLESWIG-HOLSTEIN OPEN- AIR MUSEUM
KIRCHHEIMBOLANDEN
REGIONAL MUSEUM
KOMMERN
RHINE OPEN-AIR MUSEUM
MINDEN
CATHEDRAL TREASURY AND ARCHITECTURAL MUSEUM OF THE OLD CATHEDRAL
MÜNCHEN
ARCHITECTURAL COLLECTION OF THE TECHNICAL UNIVERSITY
OERLINGHAUSEN
GERMANIC FARMHOUSE OPEN- AIR MUSEUM
PERSCHEN
PEASANT MUSEUM OF THE UPPER PALATINATE
PEWSUM
EAST FRISIAN OPEN-AIR MUSEUM
RAHDEN
RAHDEN FARM MUSEUM

REKEN
MUSEUM IN THE OLD CHURCH
SCHWARZENAHER
OPEN-AIR ROMAN MUSEUM
STADE
OPEN-AIR MUSEUM
UNTERUHLDINGEN
OPEN-AIR MUSEUM OF GERMAN PREHISTORY

GREAT BRITAIN

ASHWELL
ASHWELL VILLAGE MUSEUM
AYLSHAM
BLICKLING HALL
BAKEWELL
CHATSWORTH
OLD HOUSE MUSEUM
BATH
NO. 1 ROYAL CRESCENT
BELFAST
ULSTER FOLK MUSEUM
BICTON
BICTON COUNTRYSIDE MUSEUM
BIRMINGHAM
ASTON HALL
BLAKESLEY HALL
WEOLEY CASTLE
BLACKBURN
SAMLESBURY HALL
BRAMHALL
BRAMALL HALL
BRIDLINGTON
BURTON AGNES HALL
BRISTOL
BLAISE CASTLE HOUSE MUSEUM
THE RED LODGE
BROMSGROVE
AVONCROFT MUSEUM OF BUILDINGS
CALSTOCK
COTEHELE HOUSE
CAMBO
WALLINGTON
CAMBRIDGE
ANGLESEY ABBEY
CARDIFF
ST. FAGANS CASTLE
CHESTERFIELD
HARDWICK HALL
CHICHESTER
GOODWOOD HOUSE
THE WEALD AND DOWNLAND OPEN AIR MUSEUM
CHIPPENHAM
CORSHAM COURT
CHIPPING SODBURY
DODINGTON HOUSE
CHIRK
CHIRK CASTLE
COLCHESTER
COLCHESTER AND ESSEX MUSEUM
CREGNEASH
MANX VILLAGE FOLK MUSEUM
DERBY
KEDLESTON HALL
DISLEY
LYME PARK
DORKING
POLESDEN LACEY
DOUGLAS
MANX MUSEUM
DUDLEY
BLACK COUNTRY MUSEUM
EDINBURGH
LAURISTON CASTLE
GAINSBOROUGH
GAINSBOROUGH OLD HALL
GLOUCESTER
BISHOP HOOPER'S LODGING

GORDON
MELLERSTAIN
GREENHAM
COTHAY MANOR
HATFIELD
HATFIELD HOUSE
HUTTON-LE-HOLE
RYEDALE FOLK MUSEUM
INGATESTONE
INGATESTONE HALL
KILBARCHAN
WEAVER'S COTTAGE
KNEBWORTH
KNEBWORTH HOUSE
KNUTSFORD
TATTON PARK
LEEDS
TEMPLE NEWSAM HOUSE
LETCHWORTH
LETCHWORTH MUSEUM AND ART GALLERY
LIVERPOOL
SPEKE HALL
LONDON
CHISWICK HOUSE
GEFFRYE MUSEUM
GUNNERSBURY PARK MUSEUM
HAM HOUSE
HAMPTON COURT PALACE
KENSINGTON PALACE
KEW PALACE
LANCASTER HOUSE
MARBLE HILL HOUSE
ORLEANS HOUSE GALLERY
OSTERLEY PARK HOUSE
SIR JOHN SOANE'S MUSEUM
VALENCE HOUSE MUSEUM
MACCLESFIELD
CAPESTHORNE
MAIDENHEAD
CLIVEDEN
MAIDSTONE
ALLINGTON CASTLE
MANCHESTER
HEATON HALL
MERE
STOURHEAD
NORTHAMPTON
CASTLE ASHBY
NOTTINGHAM
NATURAL HISTORY MUSEUM
WOLLATON HALL
PLYMOUTH
SALTRAM HOUSE
PORTMEIRION
PORTMEIRION
PORTSMOUTH
CITY MUSEUM AND ART GALLERY
ST. FAGANS
WELSH FOLK MUSEUM
SALISBURY
WILTON HOUSE
SCUNTHORPE
NORMANBY HALL
SEVENOAKS
KNOLE
SHERBORNE
SHERBORNE CASTLE
SINGLETON
WEALD AND DOWNLAND OPEN AIR MUSEUM
STAMFORD
BURGHLEY HOUSE
STEEPLE ASTON
ROUSHAM HOUSE
STOKE-ON-TRENT
FORD GREEN HALL
STRATFORD- UPON-AVON
HALL'S CROFT
TELFORD
IRONBRIDGE GORGE MUSEUM

TENBY
TUDOR MERCHANT'S HOUSE
TETBURY
LASBOROUGH MANOR
TORPOINT
ANTONY HOUSE
TORQUAY
TORRE ABBEY
TROUTBECK
TOWNEND
WARMINSTER
LONGLEAT HOUSE
WARWICK
WARWICK CASTLE
WELLS
HOLKHAM HALL
WEST BROMWICH
OAK HOUSE MUSEUM
WIMBORNE ST. GILES
ST. GILES' HOUSE
WINDSOR
WINDSOR CASTLE
WOODSTOCK
BLENHEIM PALACE
YEOVIL
MONTACUTE HOUSE
YORK
CASTLE HOWARD
THE YORKSHIRE MUSEUM

GREECE

AGIA
ARCHAEOLOGICAL COLLECTION
AIGINA
ARCHAEOLOGICAL MUSEUM
AMBELAKIA
THE G. SCHWARZ MANSION
AMPHIARAION
SITE MUSEUM
ATHENS
BYZANTINE MUSEUM
DELOS
ARCHAEOLOGICAL MUSEUM
ELASSON
OLYMPIOTISSA MONASTERY
EPIDAVROS
ARCHAEOLOGICAL MUSEUM
GERAKI
ARCHAEOLOGICAL COLLECTION
KALAMOS
ARCHAEOLOGICAL MUSEUM
KALYMNOS
THE VOUVALINA MANSION
KARDAMYLI, MESSINIA
ARCHAEOLOGICAL COLLECTION
KAVALA
ARCHAEOLOGICAL MUSEUM
LYKOSOURA
ARCHAEOLOGICAL MUSEUM
NAFPLION
ARCHAEOLOGICAL MUSEUM
NEA ANCHIALOS
ARCHAEOLOGICAL COLLECTION
NEMEA
ARCHAEOLOGICAL COLLECTION
NIKOPOLIS
ARCHAEOLOGICAL COLLECTION
OLYMPIA
ARCHAEOLOGICAL MUSEUM
PELLA
ARCHAEOLOGICAL COLLECTION
PYRGOS
KARDAMITSIS PRIVATE COLLECTION
SAMOTHRAKI
ARCHAEOLOGICAL MUSEUM
SIKYON
ARCHAEOLOGICAL MUSEUM
SKYROS
ARCHAEOLOGICAL MUSEUM
SPARTI
ARCHAEOLOGICAL MUSEUM
TANAGRA
ARCHAEOLOGICAL COLLECTION
TEGEA
ARCHAEOLOGICAL MUSEUM
THASSOS
ARCHAEOLOGICAL MUSEUM
THERMON
ARCHAEOLOGICAL MUSEUM
THESSALONIKI
ARCHAEOLOGICAL MUSEUM
BYZANTINE MUSEUM OF THE ROTUNDA OF ST. GEORGE
VEROIA
ARCHAEOLOGICAL MUSEUM

HUNGARY

SZENTENDRE
OPEN-AIR MUSEUM
ZALAEGERSZEG
GÖCSEJ VILLAGE MUSEUM

ICELAND

REYKJAVIK
ARBOER FOLK MUSEUM

INDIA

BELKHANDI
BELKHANDI MUSEUM
BENARES
SARNATH MUSEUM
INDORE
CENTRAL MUSEUM
KONDAPUR
ARCHAEOLOGICAL MUSEUM

IRAQ

BAGHDAD
THE ABBASID PALACE MUSEUM
AL-MUSTANSIRIYIA SCHOOL MUSEUM
BAGHDAD GOVERNORATE MUSEUM OF COSTUMES AND ETHNOGRAPHY

IRELAND

BUNRATTY
BUNRATTY CASTLE AND FOLK PARK
DUBLIN
STATE APARTMENTS
GLENCOLUMBKILLE
AN CLACHAN

ITALY

BERGAMO
DONIZETTI MUSEUM
BOLOGNA
POMPEO ARIA ETRUSCAN MUSEUM
ERICE
CORDICI CATALDO MUSEUM
GENOA
LIGURIAN MUSEUM OF ARCHITECTURE AND SCULPTURE
GUBBIO
DUCAL PALACE
PALERMO
DIOCESAN MUSEUM
PAVIA
MUNICIPAL MUSEUM
POGGIO A CAIANO
VILLA MEDICEA
SALUZZO
CAVASSA HOUSE
TARQUINIA
NATIONAL MUSEUM

JAMAICA

SPANISH TOWN
FOLK MUSEUM

JAPAN

ASAHI-MACHI
MIYAZAKI OPEN-AIR MUSEUM
IKARUGA-MACHI
TREASURE HOUSE OF THE HORYUJI TEMPLE
KYOTO
THE SILVER TEMPLE
NARA-SHI
HORYUJI TEMPLE
NARA NATIONAL MUSEUM
OSAKA
MUSEUM OF JAPANESE FARMHOUSES
TOKYO
HACHIOJI CITY MUSEUM
NATIONAL MUSEUM
TOYONAKA-SHI
THE MUSEUM OF JAPANESE FOLK DWELLINGS
TOYOTA-GUN
KOZOJI TEMPLE MUSEUM
YAMAGUCHI-SHI
YAMAGUCHI PREFECTURAL MUSEUM

MALTA

MDINA
THE NORMAN HOUSE

MEXICO

MEXICO CITY
DIEGO RIVERA MUSEUM OF ANAHUACALLI
MUSEUM OF RURAL LIFE (CHARRERIA)
VILLAHERMOSA
PARK MUSEUM

NETHERLANDS

ARNHEM
NATIONAL MUSEUM OF ETHNOLOGY: NETHERLANDS OPEN-AIR MUSEUM
ROZENDAAL
MUSEUM OF THE INTERNATIONAL CASTLES INSTITUTE

NEW ZEALAND

AUCKLAND
MUSEUM OF TRANSPORT AND TECHNOLOGY
WAIMATE
THE CUDDY
WAIMATE NORTH
WAIMATE MISSION HOUSE

NIGERIA

JOS
JOS MUSEUM

NORWAY

AALESUND
SUNNMØRE MUSEUM
AKERSHUS FYLKE
SKEDSMO MUSEUM OF BUILDINGS
ÅL
ÅL MUSEUM OF BUILDINGS
AMLA
THE HEIBERG COLLECTIONS
ASKIM
ASKIM HISTORICAL MUSEUM
BAGN
ISLANDMOEN FARM
BERG
KRAGERØ MUSEUM
BERGEN
GAMLE BERGEN (OLD BERGEN)
BRYNE
ROGALAND FOLK MUSEUM
DAGALI
DAGALI MUSEUM
ELVERUM
GLOMDAL MUSEUM
FAGERNES
VALDRE FOLK MUSEUM
FLEKKEFJORD
FLEKKEFJORD DISTRICT MUSEUM
FØRDE
SUNNIFJORD FOLK MUSEUM
HALLINGDAL
HALLINGDAL FOLK MUSEUM
HAMAR
OPEN-AIR MUSEUM
INDRØY
INDRØY MUSEUM
KAUPANGER
HEIBERG COLLECTION
KRISTIANSAND
VEST-AGDER FOLK MUSEUM
KRISTIANSUND
KRISTIANSUND MUSEUM
LANDE
DOKKA MUSEUM
LÅRDAL
LOCAL MUSEUM
LILLEHAMMER
DE SANDVIGSKE SAMLINGER
LOM
OPEN-AIR MUSEUM
MANDAL
MANDAL AND DISTRICT FOLK MUSEUM
MELBU
VESTERÅL COLLECTION OF BUILDINGS
MELDAL
MELDAL MUSEUM OF BUILDINGS
MO I RANA
MO AND NORTH-RANA MUSEUM OF BUILDINGS
MOLDE
ROMSDAL MUSEUM
MOSJØEN
VEFSN LOCAL COLLECTION
NAMSOS
NAMDAL MUSEUM
NESBYEN
HALLINGDAL FOLK MUSEUM
NOTODDEN
HEDDAL AND NOTODDEN MUSEUM
OSLO
AKERSHUS PALACE AND FORTRESS
NORWEGIAN FOLK MUSEUM
MUSEUM OF CITY PLANNING AUTHORITY
ØYSTESE
KVAM MUSEUM OF BUILDINGS
RAKKESTAD
RAKKESTAD OPEN-AIR MUSEUM
RJUKAN
TINN MUSEUM
SANDANE
NORDFJORD FOLK MUSEUM
SARPSBORG
FOLK MUSEUM FOR ØSTFOLD
SKIEN
TELEMARK AND GRENLAND FOLK MUSEUM
SUNNDAL
LEIKVIN MUSEUM OF BUILDINGS
TINGELSTAD
HADELAND FOLK MUSEUM
TØNSBERG
VESTFOLD FOLK MUSEUM
TRØGSTAD
TRØGSTAD OPEN-AIR MUSEUM
TRONDHEIM
TRONDHEIM AND TRØNDELAG FOLK MUSEUM
UTNE
HARDANGER MUSEUM OF BUILDINGS
VÅGÅ
OPEN-AIR MUSEUM
VARDAL OG SNERTINGDAL
OPEN-AIR MUSEUM
VERDAL
VERDAL MUSEUM
VOLDA
VOLDA MUSEUM OF BUILDINGS
VOSS
VOSS FOLK MUSEUM

PERU

AREQUIPA
CATALINA CONVENT

POLAND

KLUKI
FARM MUSEUM
OLESNO
REGIONAL MUSEUM
OLSZTYNEK
MUSEUM OF RURAL BUILDINGS
OLSZTYN
OPEN-AIR MUSEUM
OPOLE-BIERKOWICE
OPEN-AIR MUSEUM
OSTRÓW LEDNICKI
LOCAL MUSEUM
PUŁKOWO WIELKIE
REGIONAL MUSEUM
SANOK
OPEN-AIR MUSEUM
SMOLNIK
OPEN-AIR MUSEUM
STARA ŚWIĘTA
OPEN-AIR MUSEUM
TORUŃ
TORUŃ ETHNOGRAPHICAL MUSEUM
WARSAW
MUSEUM OF ARCHITECTURE
MUSEUM OF THE HISTORY OF THE CITY OF WARSAW
WDZYDZE KISZEWSKIE
OPEN-AIR MUSEUM
WROCŁAW
MUSEUM OF ARCHITECTURE AND RECONSTRUCTION
ZAKOPANE
CHATA 'TEA' (TEA COTTAGE)
TATRA MUSEUM AND T.CHAŁUBIŃSKI MEMORIAL
ZŁOTÓW
ETHNOGRAPHICAL PARK
ZUBRZYCA GORNA
OPEN-AIR MUSEUM

ROMANIA

BUCHAREST
VILLAGE MUSEUM
CLUJ
OPEN-AIR MUSEUM
TRANSYLVANIAN MUSEUM OF ETHNOGRAPHY
CONSTANȚA
ARCHAEOLOGICAL MUSEUM OF THE DOBRUDSCHA
EFORIE SUD
ARCHAEOLOGICAL MUSEUM
MANGALIA
ARCHAEOLOGICAL MUSEUM
NEGREȘTI
OPEN-AIR MUSEUM
REGHIN
REGHIN MUSEUM
SIBIU
OPEN-AIR MUSEUM OF PRE- INDUSTRIAL TECHNOLOGY
TÎRGU JIU
TIRGU JIU MUSEUM

SOUTH AFRICA, REPUBLIC OF

KIMBERLEY
KIMBERLEY MINE MUSEUM
PIETERMARITZBURG
NATAL MUSEUM
PRETORIA
VOORTREKKER MONUMENT MUSEUM

SOUTH-WEST AFRICA (NAMIBIA)

FISCHFLUSS CANYON
OPEN-AIR MUSEUM
MUKEROB
OPEN-AIR MUSEUM

SPAIN

BILBAO
MUSEUM OF REPRODUCTIONS OF WORKS OF ART
GERONA
PROVINCIAL ARCHAEOLOGICAL MUSEUM
GRANADA
LA ALHAMBRA
NATIONAL MUSEUM OF SPANISH-MOSLEM ART
MADRID
NATIONAL MUSEUM OF ARCHITECTURE
MARTORELL
L'ENREJOLADA SANTACANA PROVINCIAL MUSEUM
PAMPLONA
NAVARRA MUSEUM
SEGOVIA
ALCAZÁR

SWEDEN

ARVIKA
ARVIKA MUSEUM
BORÅS
BORÅS MUSEUM
BUNGE
BUNGE MUSEUM
ESKILSTUNA
DJURGÅRDEN MUSEUM
HALMSTAD
HALLANDSGÅRDEN MUSEUM
HÄLSINGBORG
FREDRIKSDAL OPEN-AIR MUSEUM
HÄRNÖSAND
MUSEUM OF CULTURAL HISTORY
JÖNKÖPING
MUNICIPAL PARK OPEN-AIR MUSEUM

JULITA
OPEN-AIR MUSEUM
KARLSKRONA
VÄMÖ PARK
KARLSTAD
MARIEBERGSSKOGEN
LULEA
UDDEN OPEN-AIR MUSEUM
LUND
MUSEUM OF CULTURAL HISTORY
MÖLNDAL
GUNNEBO
MORA
ZORN MUSEUM OF OLD BUILDINGS
NORBERG
NORBERGS MUSEUM OF VERNACULAR BUILDINGS
ÖRNSKÖLDSVIK
ÖRNSKÖLDSVIK MUSEUM
ÖSTERSUND
JAMTLI MUSEUM
SÄTER
ÅSGÅRD MUSEUM
SKELLEFTEÅ
SKELLEFTEÅ MUSEUM
STOCKHOLM
SKANSEN
SWEDISH MUSEUM OF ARCHITECTURE
SUNDSVALL
MEDELPAD MUSEUM
SVEG
MUSEUM OF OLD BUILDINGS
UMEA
VÄSTERBOTTEN MUSEUM
UPPSALA
OPEN-AIR MUSEUM
VÄSTERÅS
VALLBY OPEN-AIR MUSEUM
VETLANDA
OPEN-AIR MUSEUM

SWITZERLAND

BASEL
CITY AND MINSTER MUSEUM IN THE LITTLE KLINGENTAL
MUSEUM OF APPLIED ARTS
BULLE
MUSEUM OF THE GRUYÈRE DISTRICT
JEGENSTORF
SCHLOSS JEGENSTORF
LAUSANNE
CATHEDRAL MUSEUM
LUGANO
MUSEUM OF HISTORY AND ARCHAEOLOGY
LUZERN
GLACIER GARDEN AND GLACIER MUSEUM
RHEINFELDEN
FIRCKTALER MUSEUM
WOHLENSCHWIL
PEASANT MUSEUM
ZURICH
LE CORBUSIER-HEIDI WEBER CENTRE

TANZANIA

DAR ES SALAAM
VILLAGE MUSEUM

THAILAND

BANGKOK
KAMTHIENG HOUSE MUSEUM

TUNISIA

CARTHAGE
NATIONAL MUSEUM OF CARTHAGE
TOPHET OF SALAMBÔ
JERBA
JERBA MUSEUM

USSR

ARCHANGEL
MANOR-HOUSE MUSEUM
BAKU
ARCHITECTURAL MUSEUM
BARAGKHAN
VILLAGE MUSEUM
KIZHI
OPEN-AIR MUSEUM
MOSCOW
ARCHITECTURAL MUSEUM
CATHEDRAL OF THE INTERCESSION
KOLOMENSKOYE ESTATE MUSEUM
MUSEUM OF HISTORY AND OF THE RECONSTRUCTION OF MOSCOW
OSTAKINO MUSEUM OF SERF ART
PARK OF ETHNOGRAPHY (ETHNOPARK)
A. V. SHCHUSEV NATIONAL MUSEUM OF RUSSIAN ARCHITECTURE
PEREYASLAV-KHMEL'NITSKIY
HISTORICAL MUSEUM
RIGA
OPEN-AIR MUSEUM OF ETHNOGRAPHY
TALLINN
ESTONIAN STATE PARK MUSEUM
PETER THE GREAT'S COTTAGE
YEKABPILS
OPEN-AIR MUSEUM

UNITED STATES

ACCOKEEK
NATIONAL COLONIAL FARM
ADA
NORMAN COUNTY MUSEUM
ALLAIRE
ALLAIRE STATE PARK
ANADARKO
INDIAN CITY, U.S.A.
ANNAPOLIS
HISTORIC ANNAPOLIS
APPOMATOX
MUSEUM OF APPOMATOX COURT HOUSE NATIONAL HISTORIC PARK
ARDMORE
TUCKER TOWER MUSEUM
ARROW ROCK
ARROW ROCK STATE PARK
AUBURN
CAYUGA MUSEUM OF HISTORY AND ART
OWASCO STOCKADED INDIAN VILLAGE
BATON ROUGE
RURAL LIFE MUSEUM
BETHLEHEM
HISTORIC BETHLEHEM INCORPORATED
BISHOP HILL
BISHOP HILL STATE MEMORIAL
BLUE MOUNDS
LITTLE NORWAY
BLUE MOUNTAIN LAKE
ADIRONDACK MUSEUM
BLUE RIDGE PARKWAY
HUMPBACK ROCKS VISITOR CENTER AND MUSEUM
BLUE SPRINGS
MISSOURI TOWN 1855
BOURNE
APTUXCET TRADING POST
BRACKETTVILLE
ALAMO VILLAGE
BRAINERD
LUMBERTOWN USA
BUTTE
WORLD MUSEUM OF MINING
CABOOL
OZARKS HILLBILLY VILLAGE
CALHOUN
NEW ECHOTA
CAMBRIDGE
BUSCH-REISINGER MUSEUM
CAPE MAY
VICTORIAN VILLAGE MUSEUM
CASHMERE
WILLIS CAREY HISTORICAL MUSEUM
CASSVILLE
STONEFIELD
CEDARBURG
OZAUKEE COUNTY HISTORICAL SOCIETY MUSEUM
CHEROKEE
OCONALUFTEE INDIAN VILLAGE
CHESTER
LIBERTY COUNTY MUSEUM
CHICAGO
ART INSTITUTE OF CHICAGO
MUSEUM OF CHICAGO SCHOOL OF ARCHITECTURE FOUNDATION
COLBY
SOD TOWN PRAIRIE PIONEER MUSEUM
COLEMAN
COLEMAN COUNTY MUSEUM
COLOMA
JAMES W. MARSHALL GOLD DISCOVERY MUSEUM
COLUMBIA
MUSEUM OF COLUMBIA STATE HISTORIC PARK
COOPERSTOWN
FARMERS MUSEUM
COPPER HARBOR
FORT WILKINS STATE PARK
CORSICANA
PIONEER VILLAGE
COSHOCTON
JOHNSON-HUMRICKHOUSE MEMORIAL MUSEUM
COXSACKIE
BRONCK HOUSE MUSEUM
CRESWELL
SOMERSET PLACE STATE HISTORIC SITE
DANVILLE
CONSTITUTION SQUARE STATE PARK MUSEUM
DARIEN
MILESTONE VILLAGE MUSEUM
DETROIT
FORT WAYNE MILITARY MUSEUM
INDIAN VALLEY HISTORIC DISTRICT
DODGE CITY
HISTORIC OLD FRONT STREET
ELVERSON
HOPEWELL VILLAGE
FALLSINGTON
HISTORIC FALLSINGTON
FARGO
CASS COUNTY HISTORICAL MUSEUM
FARMINGTON
VILLAGE OF ST. FRANÇOIS
FORT MYERS
EDISON HOME MUSEUM
FORT RANSOM
FORT RANSOM HISTORICAL SOCIETY MUSEUM
FORT WORTH
LOG CABIN VILLAGE
FULTON
WINSTON CHURCHILL MEMORIAL
GALVESTON
BISHOP'S PALACE
GATLINBURG
CADES COVE OPEN AIR MUSEUM
HOMESPUN VALLEY MOUNTAINEER VILLAGE
GLOUCESTER
BEAUPORT
HAMMOND MUSEUM
GREENSBORO
GREENSBORO HISTORICAL MUSEUM

HAINES
ALASKA INDIAN ARTS
HAMMONTON
BATSO VILLAGE
HANCOCK
HANCOCK SHAKER VILLAGE
HARPERS FERRY
HARPERS FERRY NATIONAL HISTORICAL PARK
HARRODSBURG
SHAKERTOWN
HARVARD
FRUITLANDS MUSEUMS
HAYWARD
HISTORYLAND
HOGANSBURG
AKWESASNE MOHAWK INDIAN VILLAGE
HOUSTON
HARRIS COUNTY HERITAGE SOCIETY MUSEUM
MUSEUM OF AMERICAN ARCHITECTURE AND DECORATIVE ARTS
HURON CITY
PIONEER HURON CITY
JAMESTOWN
JAMESTOWN FESTIVAL PARK
JEKYLL ISLAND
JEKYLL ISLAND MUSEUM (ROCKEFELLER COTTAGE)
KANEOHE
ULU MAU VILLAGE
KINGMAN
MOHAVE MUSEUM OF HISTORY AND ARTS
LAIE
POLYNESIAN CULTURAL CENTER
LANCASTER
AMISH FARM AND HOUSE
PENNSYLVANIA FARM MUSEUM
LAWTON
THE HOLY CITY
LEXINGTON
KENTUCKY LIFE MUSEUM
LINCOLN'S NEW SALEM
LINCOLN'S NEW SALEM VILLAGE
MADISONVILLE
YESTERYEAR
MANTEO
ROANOAK ISLAND HISTORICAL PARK MUSEUM
MENGES MILLS
COLONIAL VALLEY
MINDEN
PIONEER VILLAGE
MONROE
OLD MUSEUM VILLAGE OF SMITH'S CLOVE
MONTEREY
MONTEREY STATE HISTORICAL PARK MUSEUM
MONTEVIDEO
MUSEUM OF CHIPPEWA COUNTY HISTORICAL SOCIETY
MORRIS
ILLINOIS VALLEY MUSEUM
MOUNT PLEASANT
MUSEUM OF MIDWEST OLD SETTLERS AND THRESHERS ASSOCIATION
BOONE HALL
MOUNT VERNON
POPE-LEIGHEY HOUSE
NASHVILLE
NASHVILLE PARTHENON
NECHE
PATON ISLE OF MEMORIES
NEW GLARUS
MUSEUM OF NEW GLARUS HISTORICAL SOCIETY
NEW ORLEANS
1850 HOUSE
NEW YORK
CLOISTERS
COOPER-HEWITT MUSEUM OF DECORATIVE ARTS AND DESIGN
SOLOMON R. GUGGENHEIM MUSEUM
MUSEUM OF MODERN ART
STATEN ISLAND HISTORICAL SOCIETY
NOBLESVILLE
CONNER PRAIRIE PIONEER SETTLEMENT AND MUSEUM
NORTH MIAMI BEACH
MONASTERY CLOISTER OF ST. BERNARD
OLD BETHPAGE BR.
OLD BETHPAGE VILLAGE RESTORATION
ORIENT
MUSEUM OF OYSTERPONDS HISTORICAL SOCIETY
PENINSULA
JONATHAN HALE HOMESTEAD AND WESTERN RESERVE VILLAGE
PETERSBURG
LINCOLN'S NEW SALEM STATE PARK
PHILADELPHIA
INDEPENDENCE NATIONAL HISTORICAL PARK
MUSEUM OF THE SOCIETY OF ARCHITECTURAL HISTORIANS
PHOENIX
PIONEER ARIZONA
POLAND SPRING
SHAKER MUSEUM
QUINCY
QUINCY ART CENTER
RICHMOND
AGECROFT HALL
ROCKPORT
LINCOLN PIONEER VILLAGE
ROEBUCK
WALNUT GROVE PLANTATION
ROUND TOP
UNIVERSITY OF TEXAS
RUSSELLVILLE
MARCELLITE HARDY MEMORIAL MUSEUM
ST. AUGUSTINE
HISTORIC ST. AUGUSTINE
SALEM
PIONEERS' VILLAGE
SALT LAKE CITY
UTAH PIONEER VILLAGE
SAN DIEGO
OLD TOWN SAN DIEGO STATE HISTORIC PARK
SAN JUAN
MUSEUM OF COLONIAL ARCHITECTURE
SANTA FE
OLD CIENEGA VILLAGE MUSEUM
SCOBEY
DANIELS COUNTY MUSEUM AND PIONEER TOWN
SEARCY
WHITE COUNTY PIONEER MUSEUM
SHELBURNE
SHELBURNE MUSEUM
SOLDOTNA
DAMON MEMORIAL HISTORICAL MUSEUM
SOMERSET
MUSEUM OF HISTORICAL AND GENEALOGICAL SOCIETY OF SOMERSET COUNTY
SPARTANBURG
WALNUT GROVE PLANTATION
STURBRIDGE
OLD STURBRIDGE VILLAGE
TAHLEQUAH
TSA-LA-GI
THIENSVILLE
OZAUKEE COUNTY HISTORICAL SOCIETY MUSEUM
TOPEKA
KANSAS STATE HISTORICAL SOCIETY MUSEUM
VIRGINIA CITY
NEVADA CITY
WALLA WALLA
FORT WALLA WALLA MUSEUM COMPLEX
WASHINGTON
OCTAGON
WATKINS GLEN
YORKER YANKEE VILLAGE
WELLS FARGO
CASS COUNTY HISTORICAL SOCIETY
WEST LIBERTY
PIATT CASTLES
WICHITA
HISTORIC WICHITA COW TOWN
WICKENBURG
DESERT CABALLEROS WESTERN MUSEUM
WILLIAMSBURG
COLONIAL WILLIAMSBURG
WIMBERLEY
PIONEER TOWN
WINDOW ROCK
NAVAJO TRIBAL MUSEUM
WOODVILLE
HERITAGE GARDEN VILLAGE
WORTHINGTON
MUSEUM OF NOBLES COUNTY HISTORICAL SOCIETY
WRANGELL
TRIBAL HOUSE OF THE BEAR

YUGOSLAVIA

SARAJEVO
SVRSO'S HOUSE
SKOFJA LOKA
MUSEUM
VELIKA GORICA
MUSEUM OF TUROPOLJE

ZAMBIA

LIVINGSTONE
OPEN-AIR MUSEUM

Furniture, furnishings, domestic equipment

ALBANIA

TIRANA
MUSEUM OF ARCHAEOLOGY AND ETHNOGRAPHY

ALGERIA

ALGIERS
LE BARDO MUSEUM OF ETHNOGRAPHY AND PREHISTORY
MUSEUM OF POPULAR ARTS AND TRADITIONS
NATIONAL MUSEUM OF ANTIQUITIES

ANGOLA

LUANDA
ANGOLA MUSEUM

ARGENTINA

BOLIVAR
FLORENTINO AMEGHINO MUSEUM
BUENOS AIRES
ARCHITECTURAL MUSEUM
NATIONAL MUSEUM OF DECORATIVE ART
CORNELIO SAAVEDRA HISTORICAL MUSEUM
CÓRDOBA
HISTORICAL MUSEUM OF THE HOUSE OF THE VICEROY SOBREMONTE

LA RIOJA
PROVINCIAL HISTORICAL MUSEUM
MENDOZA
MUSEUM OF THE ANCIENT PROVINCE
ROSARIO
MUNICIPAL MUSEUM

AUSTRALIA

ADELAIDE
ART GALLERY OF SOUTH AUSTRALIA
ALBANY
PATRICK TAYLOR COTTAGE MUSEUM
ARMIDALE
ARMIDALE FOLK MUSEUM
BALLARAT
BALLARAT ART GALLERY
BATHURST
FOLK MUSEUM
BATTERY POINT
VAN DIEMEN'S LAND MEMORIAL FOLK MUSEUM
BEXLEY
LYDHAM HALL
BOWRAVILLE
FOLK MUSEUM
BRISBANE
MIEGUNYAH
ROYAL HISTORICAL SOCIETY OF QUEENSLAND MUSEUM
WOLSTON HOUSE
GOULBURN
RIVERSDALE
GRAFTON
SCHAEFFER HOUSE
GRENFELL
HISTORICAL MUSEUM
GUNDAGAI
HISTORICAL MUSEUM
HADSPEN
ENTALLY HOUSE
HOBART
ALLPORT LIBRARY AND MUSEUM OF FINE ARTS
KADINA
NATIONAL TRUST MUSEUM
KEMPSEY
GILL'S BOTTLE MUSEUM
KYNETON
KYNETON HISTORICAL MUSEUM
MILLTHORPE
HISTORICAL MUSEUM
PARRAMATTA
OLD GOVERNMENT HOUSE
SINGLETON
HISTORICAL MUSEUM
SWAN HILL
SWAN HILL FOLK MUSEUM
SYDNEY
MUSEUM OF APPLIED ARTS AND SCIENCES
TANUNDA
BAROSSA VALLEY MUSEUM
TOOWOOMBA
TAWA PIONEER COTTAGE
VAUCLUSE
VAUCLUSE HOUSE
WALCHA
FOLK MUSEUM
WILBERFORCE
AUTHENTICATED AUSTRALIAN SETTLERS VILLAGE

AUSTRIA

ALTENBURG
COLLECTIONS OF BENEDICTINE MONASTERY
ARZBERG
REGIONAL MUSEUM
BAD GOISERN
GOISERN REGIONAL MUSEUM
BAD HALL
REGIONAL MUSEUM
BAD ISCHL
LÉHAR VILLA
REGIONAL MUSEUM
VILLA OF THE EMPEROR
BAD VOSLAU
REGIONAL MUSEUM
BEZAU
REGIONAL MUSEUM
BRAMBERG
REGIONAL MUSEUM
BRANDHOF
ARCHDUKE JOHANN HUNTING MUSEUM
BRAUNAU AM INN
DISTRICT MUSEUM
BRUCK AN DER LEITHA
REGIONAL MUSEUM
DÖLLACH
REGIONAL AND GOLDMINING MUSEUM
DREISTETTEN
SCHERRER INN REGIONAL MUSEUM
DÜRNSTEIN
DÜRNSTEIN REGIONAL MUSEUM
EBENAU
REGIONAL MUSEUM
EGG
REGIONAL MUSEUM
EGGENBURG
KRAHULETZ MUSEUM
EIBISWALD
REGIONAL MUSEUM
ENNS
MUNICIPAL MUSEUM
ERNSTBRUNN
PALACE MUSEUM
GLEISDORF
REGIONAL MUSEUM
GMUND
REGIONAL MUSEUM
GOBELSBURG
PALACE MUSEUM
GRAZ
BAROQUE MUSEUM
JOANNEUM PROVINCIAL MUSEUM OF CULTURAL HISTORY AND APPLIED ART
JOANNEUM PROVINCIAL MUSEUM OF THE ETHNOLOGY AND FOLKLORE OF STEIERMARK
GRIEFENSTEIN
CASTLE MUSEUM
GRESTEN
REGIONAL MUSEUM
GUNDORF
MUSEUM OF LOCAL LIFE
HALLEIN
MUNICIPAL MUSEUM
HARD
MITTELWEIBERBURG REGIONAL MUSEUM
HERBERTSTEIN
PALACE MUSEUM
HERMAGOR
GAITAL REGIONAL MUSEUM
HOHENAU
REGIONAL MUSEUM
HOLLENEGG
PALACE COLLECTION
HOLLERSBACH
REGIONAL MUSEUM
INNSBRUCK
PALACE, SILVER CHAPEL AND PALACE CHURCH
KLAGENFURT
CARINTHIA PROVINCIAL MUSEUM
KLAM
KLAM CASTLE MUSEUM
KLEINENGERSDORF
"DER BISAMBERG UND DER WEINVIERTLER" MUSEUM
KREMS
MUNICIPAL MUSEUM
KREUZENSTEIN
CASTLE AND CASTLE COLLECTIONS
KUCHL
REGIONAL MUSEUM
KUFSTEIN
REGIONAL MUSEUM
LANGENLOIS
REGIONAL MUSEUM
LIENZ
EAST TIROL REGIONAL MUSEUM
LINZ
MUSEUM OF THE CITY OF LINZ
UPPER AUSTRIA PROVINCIAL MUSEUM
LOICH
LOICH REGIONAL ROOM
LOOSDORF
CASTLE COLLECTIONS
LUNZ
AMON HOUSE MUSEUM
MATTSEE
REGIONAL MUSEUM
MELK
REGIONAL MUSEUM
MITTERNDORF
MUSEUM OF REGIONAL LIFE
MÖDLING
MUNICIPAL MUSEUM
MOOSHAM
PALACE COLLECTIONS
MURAU
MUNICIPAL MUSEUM OF LOCAL LIFE
NEUNKIRCHEN
REGIONAL MUSEUM
NIEDERLEIS
CASTLE MUSEUM
OBERNBERG
REGIONAL MUSEUM
OBERNDORF
REGIONAL MUSEUM
ORTH
REGIONAL MUSEUM
PETRONELL
MUSEUM OF APPLIED ART
PINKAFELD
REGIONAL MUSEUM
PISCHELSDORF
REGIONAL MUSEUM
PÖCHLARN
REGIONAL MUSEUM
PÖGGSTALL
REGIONAL MUSEUM
PÖLS-ENZERSDORF
HUSSLIK REGIONAL MUSEUM
POPPENDORFBERG
VINTNER'S HOUSE
POYSDORF
REGIONAL MUSEUM
PRESSBAUM
REGIONAL MUSEUM
RABENSTEIN
PIELACHTAL REGIONAL MUSEUM
RAURIS
RAURIS GOLD-MINING MUSEUM
RENNWEG
VILLAGE MUSEUM
RETZ
MUNICIPAL MUSEUM
MUSEUM OF TOWN HISTORY
REUTTE
REGIONAL MUSEUM
RIED
ETHNOLOGICAL MUSEUM OF THE INNVIERTEL
RIEGERSBURG
CASTLE MUSEUM
ROHRAU
FAMILY COLLECTION OF COUNT HARRACH
SAALFELDEN
MUSEUM OF LOCAL LIFE AND OF CRIBS

SALZBURG
CASTLE MUSEUM
MUSEUM OF ETHNOLOGY
SALZBURGER MUSEUM, CAROLINO AUGUSTEUM

ST. PÖLTEN
DIOCESAN MUSEUM

ST. ULRICH
LAVANTTAL MUSEUM OF LOCAL LIFE

SCHÄRDING
MUNICIPAL MUSEUM

SCHEIBBS
HOTTENROTH COLLECTION

SCHLAINING
CASTLE MUSEUM

SCHRUNS
MONTAFON REGIONAL MUSEUM

SCHWARZENBERG
COMMUNITY MUSEUM

SEEBENSTEIN
CASTLE MUSEUM

SEEKIRCHEN
REGIONAL MUSEUM

SPARBEREGG
REGIONAL MUSEUM

SPITAL
REGIONAL MUSEUM

SPITTAL
MUSEUM OF LOCAL LIFE

STADL-PAURA
MUSEUM OF SHIPPING

STANS
PALACE COLLECTION

STEGERSBACH
SOUTH BURGENLAND COUNTRYSIDE MUSEUM

STEYR
REGIONAL MUSEUM

STRASSBURG
DIOCESAN AND REGIONAL MUSEUM

TAMSWEG
LUNGAU REGIONAL MUSEUM

TAUFKIRCHEN
REGIONAL ROOM

TELFS
REGIONAL MUSEUM

TRAUN
REGIONAL HOUSE

TRAUTENFELS
COUNTRYSIDE MUSEUM

VIGAUN
REGIONAL MUSEUM

VÖCKLABRUCK
REGIONAL HOUSE

WAIDHOFEN AN DER THAYA
REGIONAL MUSEUM

VIENNA
ART COLLECTIONS OF THE SCHWARZENBERG PALACE
AUSTRIAN MUSEUM OF APPLIED ART
AUSTRIAN MUSEUM OF ETHNOLOGY
FEDERAL COLLECTION OF PERIOD FURNITURE
FIRST AUSTRIAN-SILESIAN MUSEUM IN VIENNA
FLORISDORF DISTRICT MUSEUM
HERNALS DISTRICT MUSEUM
HISTORICAL MUSEUM OF THE CITY OF VIENNA
MUSEUM OF THE BÖHMERWALD
MUSEUM OF THE PROVINCE OF LOWER AUSTRIA
OTTAKRING DISTRICT MUSEUM
PENZING DISTRICT MUSEUM
SIMMERING DISTRICT MUSEUM
SOBEK COLLECTION
TREASURY OF THE GERMAN ORDER

VÖCKLAMARKT
WALCHEN CASTLE

WAIDHOFEN AN DER YBBS
PIATY PRIVATE COLLECTION
REGIONAL MUSEUM

WALCHEN
PAULI HANREICH-LUDWIG COLLECTION

WALDING
LOCAL MUSEUM

WARTBERG
REGIONAL MUSEUM AT THE RUINS OF LICHTENEGG CASTLE

WEIKENDORF
MARCHFELD MUSEUM

WELS
CASTLE MUSEUM

WENIGZELL
REGIONAL HOUSE

WIENERBRUCK
TRÜBENBACH SCHOOL MUSEUM

WIENER NEUSTADT
MUNICIPAL MUSEUM

WILDALPEN
FORESTRY MUSEUM

ZELL AM MOOS
IRRSEE REGIONAL MUSEUM

ZWETTL
ANTON MUSEUM

BARBADOS

BARBADOS
BARBADOS MUSEUM

BELGIUM

ANTWERP
FLAT IRON MUSEUM
OLD BUTCHERS' HALL
PLANTIN-MORETUS MUSEUM
POLDER MUSEUM
RIDDER SMIDT VAN GELDER MUSEUM
ROCKOX'S HOUSE
RUBENS' HOUSE

ATTRE
LOCAL MUSEUM

BELOEIL
CASTLE MUSEUM

BRUGES
FOLKLORE MUSEUM
MEMLING MUSEUM
MUSEUM OF THE COURTS OF JUSTICE
MUSEUM OF THE POTTERY HOSTEL

BRUSSELS
MUSEUM OF THE POOR LAW ADMINISTRATION
SCHOTT MUSEUM

ECAUSSINNES
CASTLE

FRANC-WARET
CHÂTEAU

GAASBEEK
CHÂTEAU MUSEUM

GHENT
CASTLE OF THE COUNTS OF FLANDERS
FOLKLORE MUSEUM
MUSEUM OF ANTIQUITIES
MUSEUM OF DECORATIVE ARTS AND INDUSTRIAL DESIGN
MUSEUM OF THE TREATY OF GHENT

LAVAUX-SAINTE-ANNE
BELGIAN MUSEUM OF HUNTING AND NATURAL CONSERVATION

LIÈGE
ANSEMBOURG MUSEUM
DIOCESAN MUSEUM AND CATHEDRAL TREASURY
TCHANTCHÈS MUSEUM

LOUVAIN
MUSEUM OF ART AND ARCHAEOLOGY
SPOELBERCH DE LOVENJOEL MUSEUM

NAMUR
THE DE CROIX MUSEUM

NEDER- OVER-HEEMBEEK
FOLKLORE MUSEUM

NIEUWPOORT
MUSEUM OF HISTORY AND FOLKLORE

SAINT-VITH
REGIONAL MUSEUM

SPONTIN
CASTLE

TOURNAI
FOLKLORE MUSEUM

VERVIERS
MUSEUM OF ARCHAEOLOGY AND FOLKLORE

VIRTON
GAUMAIS MUSEUM

BERMUDA

ST. GEORGE'S
THE CONFEDERATE MUSEUM
PRESIDENT HENRY TUCKER HOUSE
ST. GEORGE'S HISTORICAL SOCIETY MUSEUM

SMITH'S PARISH
VERDMONT

BOLIVIA

LA PAZ
NATIONAL MUSEUM OF ART

SUCRE
COLONIAL MUSEUM

BRAZIL

CAMPOS DO JORDÃO
GOVERNOR'S PALACE MUSEUM

ITU
MUSEUM OF THE REPUBLICAN CONVENTION

JOINVILLE
NATIONAL MUSEUM OF IMMIGRATION AND COLONISATION

JUIZ DE FORA
MARIANO PROCÓPIO MUSEUM

LIMOEIRO
SEVERINO ARAGÃO RURAL MUSEUM

NATAL
MUSEUM OF POPULAR ART

PENEDO
MUSEUM OF FOLK ART AND FOLK CULTURE

PINDAMONHANGABA
LOCAL MUSEUM

RIO DE JANEIRO
ITAMARTY MUSEUM OF HISTORY AND DIPLOMACY
MUSEUM OF THE CITY OF RIO DE JANEIRO
MUSEUM OF THE RAYMUNDO OTTONI DE CASTRO FOUNDATION
NATIONAL MUSEUM OF FINE ART

SALVADOR
BAHIA MUSEUM OF ART
MUSEUM OF ART
MUSEUM OF THE CARMELITE CONVENT

SANTA LEOPOLDINA
COLONIAL MUSEUM

VASSOURAS
CASA DA HERA MUSEUM

BULGARIA

KARNOBAT
NATIONAL MUSEUM

KJUSTENDIL
DISTRICT MUSEUM

KOPRIVSHTIŹA
OSLEKOV ETHNOGRAPHICAL MUSEUM

KOPRIVŠTICA
DIMČO DEBELJANOV HOUSE- MUSEUM

PLOVDIV
BUKURESCHLIEV HOUSE- MUSEUM
REGIONAL MUSEUM OF ETHNOLOGY

RAJKOVO
NATIONAL MUSEUM OF THE RHODOPE

ŠČRAKLEVO
MUSEUM OF REGIONAL HISTORY AND ETHNOGRAPHY

SLIVEN
NATIONAL MUSEUM

SOFIA
NATIONAL ETHNOGRAPHICAL MUSEUM

TARGOVIŠČE
PROVINCIAL HISTORICAL MUSEUM

TARNOVO
PROVINCIAL MUSEUM

TROJAN
MUSEUM OF APPLIED ARTS AND CRAFTS

CANADA

AYLESFORD
AYLESFORD MUSEUM OF CANADIANA

MONCTON
UNIVERSITY OF MONCTON MUSEUM

MONTREAL
MCCORD MUSEUM
MUSEUM OF THE INSTITUTE OF APPLIED ARTS
WISER'S CANADIAN MUSEUM

NIAGARA FALLS
OAK HALL

QUEBEC
MUSEUM OF QUEBEC
QUEBEC SEMINARY MUSEUM

SAINT-LAURENT
NOVA ET VETERA GALLERY

SAINT-LIN
LAURIER HOUSE

TADOUSSAC
CHAUVIN HOUSE

TORONTO
SIGMUND SAMUEL CANADIANA MUSEUM

VICTORIA
ART GALLERY OF GREATER VICTORIA
MALTWOOD MEMORIAL MUSEUM OF HISTORIC ART, UNIVERSITY OF VICTORIA

WOLFVILLE
WOLFVILLE HISTORICAL MUSEUM

CHILE

HUALPEN
MUSEO DE HUALPEN

CHINA, P.R.

KAIFENG
PROVINCIAL MUSEUM

LANCHOW (LANZHOU)
PROVINCIAL MUSEUM

LUCHOU
LOCAL MUSEUM

MUKDEN (SHENYIANG)
IMPERIAL PALACE

NANKING (NAN JING)
KIANG SU PROVINCIAL MUSEUM

PEKING
IMPERIAL PALACE

QU FU
RESIDENCES OF THE DESCENDANTS OF CONFUCIUS

TIENSIN (TIANJING)
PROVINCIAL MUSEUM

COLOMBIA

BOGOTA
ETHNOGRAPHICAL MUSEUM OF THE CARO AND CUERVO INSTITUTE
MUSEUM OF COLONIAL ART
MUSEUM OF LITERATURE
MUSEUM OF THE URBAN DEVELOPMENT OF BOGOTA

BUCARAMANGA
GARCÍA ROVIRA HOUSE- MUSEUM

PASTO
TAMINANGO MUSEUM

TUNJA
HOUSE OF THE FOUNDER
HOUSE OF RUIZ DE MANCIPE

CUBA

GUANABACOA
HISTORICAL MUSEUM

HABANA
MUSEUM OF COLONIAL ART
MUSEUM OF DECORATIVE ARTS

SANCTI-SPIRITUS
PALACIO VALLE IZNAGA COLONIAL MUSEUM

SANTIAGO DE CUBA
COLONIAL MUSEUM

CYPRUS

KYRENIA
FOLK ART MUSEUM

CZECHOSLOVAKIA

ANTOL
FORESTRY AND HUNTING MUSEUM

AŠ
MUNICIPAL MUSEUM

BARDEJOV
ŠARIŠ MUSEUM

BETLIAR
STATE PALACE

BOJNICE
REGIONAL MUSEUM

BOUZOV
REGIONAL CENTRE

BRATISLAVA
ETHNOGRAPHICAL MUSEUM
MUNICIPAL MUSEUM

BRNO
MUSEUM OF THE CITY OF BRNO

ČERVENÝ KAMEŇ
MUSEUM OF FURNITURE

ČERVENÝ KLÁŠTOR
MONASTERY MUSEUM

DĚČÍN
DISTRICT MUSEUM

DOLNI DOMASLOVICE
DOMASLOVICE AND DISTRICT MUSEUM

DOMAŽLICE
DOMAŽLICE MUSEUM
JINDŘICHA JINDŘICHA MUSEUM

HOŘOVICE
MUNICIPAL MUSEUM

JEMNICE
JEMNICE MUSEUM

JILEMNICE
KRKONOŠ MUSEUM

KAMENICE NAD LIPOU
REGIONAL MUSEUM

KLATOVY
REGIONAL MUSEUM

KRÁSNA HŌRKA
CASTLE MUSEUM

KRAVAŘE
PALACE MUSEUM

LEVOČA
SPIŠ MUSEUM

LIBEREC
MUSEUM OF NORTHERN CZECHOSLOVAKIA

LIPNÍK NAD BEČVOU
ZÁHOŘÍ MUSEUM

MARKUŠOVCE
MUSEUM OF FURNITURE

NÁMEŠŤ NA HANÉ
REGIONAL MUSEUM

OPAVA
SILESIAN MUSEUM: ETHNOGRAPHY AND ART COLLECTIONS

ORAVSKY PODZÁMOK
ORAVA MUSEUM

PELHŘIMOV
DISTRICT MUSEUM

PRACHATICE
DISTRICT MUSEUM

PRAGUE
ETHNOLOGICAL COLLECTIONS

PŘEROV NAD LABEM
MUSEUM OF ETHNOGRAPHY

RIMAVSKÁ SOBOTA
GEMER MUSEUM

ROŽNOV POD RADHOŠTĚM
VALASKIAN MUSEUM OF ETHNOGRAPHY

RTYNĚ Y PODKRKONOŠÍ
MEMORIAL OF THE PEASANT REVOLT OF 1777

ŠTERNBERK
ŠTERNBERK STATE CASTLE

DENMARK

ÅRHUS
DEN GAMLE BY

ALS
LOCAL HISTORY MUSEUM

AUNING
GAMMEL ESTRUP

BREGNINGE
HJEMSTAVNMUSEUM

CLAUSHOLM
CLAUSHOLM CASTLE

COPENHAGEN
AMAGER MUSEUM
CHRISTIANSBORG PALACE
MUSEUM OF DECORATIVE ART
NYBODEN MUSEUM
ROSENBORG PALACE

DRAGØR
AMAGER MUSEUM

FAABORG
KALEKO MILL MUSEUM

FREDENSBORG
PALACE OF FREDENSBORG

GUMMERUP
VESTFYNS HJEMSTAVNSGÅRDEN

HELSINGØR
KRONBORG CASTLE

HILLERØD
NATIONAL HISTORICAL MUSEUM
NORDSJAELLANDSK MUSEUMSFORENING

HOLSTEBRO
HOLSTEBRO MUSEUM

HORNSLET
ROSENHOLM

HORSENS
HORSENS MUSEUM

HØJBY SJ.
STENSTRUP MUSEUM

HØJERUP
STEVNS MUSEUM

HØVE
LOCAL HISTORY MUSEUM

KALUNDBORG
KALUNDBORG AND DISTRICT MUSEUM

LERCHENBORG
LERCHENBORG MANOR

LYNGBY
OPEN-AIR MUSEUM

LYSGÅRD
BLIONER MEMORIAL MUSEUM

NYBORG
MADS LERCHES HOUSE
NYBORG CASTLE

NYKØBING
FALSTERS MINDER MUSEUM
MORSLAND HISTORICAL MUSEUM
ODSHERRED FOLK MUSEUM

ODDER
MUSEUM

ODENSE
THE FUNEN VILLAGE

ØLGOD
ØLGOD MUSEUM

PEDERSTRUP
REVENTLOW MUSEUM
RANDERS
MUSEUM OF CULTURAL HISTORY
ROSENHOLM
ROSENHOLM CASTLE
ROSKILDE
ROSKILDE MUSEUM
RØMØ
COMMANDER'S HOUSE
RØNNE
BORNHOLM MUSEUM
SAEBY
VOERGÅRD CASTLE
SLEGE
SLEGE MUSEUM
SORØ
SORØ DISTRICT MUSEUM
SPØTTRUP
SPØTTRUP CASTLE
STRUER
STRUER MUSEUM
TRANEBJERG
SAMSØ MUSEUM
TØNDER
TØNDER MUSEUM
UDBY
GRUNDTVIG MEMORIAL MUSEUM
VAERLØSE
VAERLØSE MUSEUM
VARDE
VARDE AND DISTRICT MUSEUM

EGYPT, ARAB REPUBLIC OF

ALEXANDRIA
MONTAZAH PALACE MUSEUM
CAIRO
ABDINE PALACE MUSEUM
AL GAWHARA PALACE MUSEUM
AL MANIAL PALACE MUSEUM
HELWAN PALACE MUSEUM

FINLAND

HELSINKI
ARMFELT MUSEUM
JOKIOINEN
PARSONAGE MUSEUM
JYVÄSKYLÄ
MUSEUM OF CENTRAL FINLAND
KAUHAJOKI
LOCAL MUSEUM
KEMI
KEMI MUSEUM
LAHTI
MUSEUM OF HISTORY
TAMMISAARI
MUNICIPAL MUSEUM
TURKU
CITY MUSEUM
MONASTERY MUSEUM OF HANDICRAFTS
UUSIKAARLEPYY
ZACHARIAS TOPELIUS HOUSE- MUSEUM
VAASA
EAST BOTHNIA MUSEUM

FRANCE

ABBEVILLE
BOUCHER-DE-PERTHES MUSEUM
AIX-EN-PROVENCE
DOBLER MUSEUM
GRANET MUSEUM
MUSEUM OF TAPESTRY AND FURNITURE
ALBERTVILLE
CONFLANS MUSEUM
AMBIERLE
FORÈZE MUSEUM
AMBOISE
LEONARDO DA VINCI MUSEUM
AMIENS
MUSEUM OF REGIONAL ART AND HISTORY
ANCY-LE-FRANC
CHÂTEAU
ANDILLAC
EUGÉNIE AND MAURICE DE GUÉRIN MUSEUM
ANNECY
CHÂTEAU DE MONTROTTIER
AUTUN
ROLIN MUSEUM
AVALLON
AVALLON MUSEUM
AZAY-LE-FERRON
CHÂTEAU MUSEUM
AZAY-LE-RIDEAU
CHÂTEAU
BARR
LA FOLIE MARCO MUSEUM
BEAUGENCY
DUNOIS MUSEUM
BEAUNE
CHARITÉ HOSPICE
HÔTEL-DIEU
MUSEUM OF FINE ART
BEAUVAIS
MUSEUM OF THE OISE DEPARTMENT
BORDEAUX
MUSEUM OF DECORATIVE ARTS
BOUGES-LE-CHÂTEAU
COLLECTION OF CARRIAGES AND HARNESS
BOURG-EN-BRESSE
AIN MUSEUM
BOURGES
HÔTEL LALLEMANT
BOURGNEUF-EN-RETZ
RETZ REGIONAL MUSEUM
BOURGOIN-JALLIEU
VICTOR CHARRETON MUSEUM
BOUXWILLER
BOUXWILLER MUSEUM
BRICQEBEC
MUNICIPAL MUSEUM
LA BUSSIÈRE
MUSEUM OF FISHING
CARPENTRAS
SOBIRATS MUSEUM
CASSEL
MONT CASSEL MUSEUM OF LOCAL LIFE
CHAÂLIS
JACQUEMART-ANDRÉ MUSEUM
CHÂLONS-SUR-MARNE
SCHILLER-GOETHE MEMORABILIA
CHAMBÉRY
CHARMETTES MUSEUM
CHAMPLITTE- ET-LE-PRÉLOT
DEPARTMENTAL MUSEUM OF HISTORY AND ETHNOGRAPHY
CHAMPS-SUR-MARNE
CHÂTEAU DE CHAMPS- SUR-MARNE
CHAUMONT-SUR-LOIRE
MUSEUM IN THE STABLES
COMPIÈGNE
COMPIÈGNE PALACE NATIONAL MUSEUM
VIVENEL MUSEUM
CORCELLE
FRANCHE-COMTÉ MUSEUM
COUR-CHEVERNY
CHÂTEAU COLLECTIONS
CREIL
GALLÉ JUILLET MUSEUM
CROIX-DE-VIE
MARAICHIN MUSEUM
DIJON
MUSEUM OF FINE ART
PERRIN DE PUYCOUSIN MUSEUM
DREUX
MUNICIPAL MUSEUM
ÉPERNAY
MUSEUM OF FINE ART
ÉVREUX
MUNICIPAL MUSEUM
FONTAINEBLEAU
PALACE OF FONTAINEBLEAU
FORCALQUIER
MUNICIPAL MUSEUM
GRASSE
FRAGONARD MUSEUM
GROSBOIS
CHÂTEAU DE GROSBOIS
HAGUENAU
HAGUENAU MUSEUM
HONFLEUR
NORMANDY MUSEUM OF ETHNOGRAPHY AND FOLK ART
KERJEAN
BRETON MUSEUM
LANGEAIS
CHÂTEAU
LANGRES
HÔTEL DU BREUIL DE SAINT- GERMAIN MUSEUM
LANQUAIS
CHÂTEAU DE LANQUAIS
LILLE
MUSEUM OF THE COMTESSE HOSPICE
LOVAGNY- GORGES-DU-FIER
LÉON MARÈS COLLECTION
LYON
MUSEUM OF THE CIVILIAN HOSPITALS OF LYON
MUSEUM OF THE HISTORY OF LYON
MARLY-LE-ROI
OLD MARLY MUSEUM
MARSEILLE
GROBET-LABADIE MUSEUM
MUSEUM OF OLD MARSEILLE
MUSEUM OF PROVENÇAL ART
MAZÉ
CHÂTEAU DE MONTGEOFFROY
MEAUX
BOSSUET MUSEUM
MELUN
MELUN MUSEUM
MOLSHEIM
MUSEUM OF ART AND HISTORY
MONTPELLIER
HÔTEL DE CABRIÈRES-SABATIER D'ESPEYRAN
NANCY
MUSEUM OF DECORATIVE ARTS
NANTES
DOBRÉE MUSEUM
MUSEUM OF DECORATIVE ARTS
MUSEUM OF REGIONAL POPULAR ART
NICE
VIEUX-LOGIS PRIORY MUSEUM
NOGENT-SUR-MARNE
MUSEUM OF THE SMITH- LESOUËF FOUNDATION
ORANGE
LOCAL MUSEUM
PARIS
JACQUEMART ANDRÉ MUSEUM
COGNACQ JAY MUSEUM
COSTUME MUSEUM
GUIMET MUSEUM
MARMOTTAN MUSEUM
GUSTAVE MOREAU MUSEUM
MUSEUM OF DECORATIVE ARTS
MUSEUM OF IMPRESSIONNISM
NISSIM DE CAMONDO MUSEUM
PAU
HENRI IV NATIONAL MUSEUM
PÉROUGES
OLD PÉROUGES MUSEUM
PONT-L'ABBÉ
BIGOUDEN MUSEUM
PONTÉCOULANT
CHÂTEAU DE PONTÉCOULANT MUSEUM
QUIMPER
BRITTANY MUSEUM

RENNES
BRITTANY MUSEUM
RICHELIEU
MUSEUM OF THE 17th CENTURY
ROANNE
JOSEPH DECHELETTE MUSEUM
ROQUEBRUNE- CAP-MARTIN
CHÂTEAU DE ROQUEBRUNE
RUEIL-MALMAISON
MALMAISON NATIONAL CHÂTEAU
RUMILLY
CHÂTEAU DE CLERMONT- EN-GENEVOIS
MUNICIPAL MUSEUM
SAINT-DENIS
MUNICIPAL MUSEUM
SAINT ETIENNE LE MOLARD
BASTIE D'URFÉ MUSEUM
SAINT-FLOUR
MUSEUM OF THE CONSULAR HOUSE ALFRED DOUET
ST. GERMAIN LAVAL
MUNICIPAL MUSEUM
SAINT-JEAN-CAP-FERRAT
EPHRUSSI DE ROTHSCHILD FOUNDATION
SAINT-OMER
HENRI DUPUIS MUSEUM
SAMADET
MUSEUM OF FAIENCE
SAUMUR
MUSEUM OF DECORATIVE ARTS AND MUSEUM OF THE HORSE
SEPT-FONTAINES
SEPT-FONTAINES ABBEY MUSEUM
SIGEAN
MUNICIPAL MUSEUM
STRASBOURG
CHÂTEAU DES ROHAN
MUSEUM OF THE CATHEDRAL WORKSHOPS
TALCY
CHÂTEAU DE TALCY
TANLAY
CHÂTEAU TANLAY
THIERS
FONTENILLE MONDIÈRE MUSEUM
TOURNUS
PERRIN DE PUYCOUSIN MUSEUM
TOURS
ESPELOSIN MUSEUM
MUSEUM OF FINE ART
VAISON-LA-ROMAINE
ARCHAEOLOGICAL MUSEUM
VALENÇAY
GALLERY OF MEMENTOES OF PRINCE DE TALLEYRAND
VARZY
MUNICIPAL MUSEUM
VAUX-LE-VICOMTE
CHÂTEAU
VERSAILLES
CHÂTEAU
GRAND TRIANON
LAMBINET MUSEUM
PETIT TRIANON
VILLEDIEU-LES-POELES
LOCAL MUSEUM
VILLESAVIN
COLLECTION OF HORSE-DRAWN VEHICLES
WISSEMBOURG
WESTERCAMP MUSEUM

GDR

ALTENBURG
CASTLE MUSEUM AND PLAYING CARDS MUSEUM
ANNABERG-BUCHHOLZ
ERZGEBIRG MUSEUM: DEPARTMENT OF CULTURAL HISTORY
ASCHERSLEBEN
REGIONAL MUSEUM
BAD FREIENWALDE
ODERLAND MUSEUM
BALLENSTEDT
REGIONAL MUSEUM
BAUTZEN
MUSEUM OF ART AND CULTURAL HISTORY
BERLIN
MUSEUM OF CULTURAL HISTORY
PERGAMON MUSEUM: COLLECTION OF GREEK AND ROMAN ANTIQUITIES
PERGAMON MUSEUM: ISLAMIC MUSEUM
PERGAMON MUSEUM: MUSEUM OF ETHNOGRAPHY
STATE MUSEUM OF ARTS AND CRAFTS
BERNBURG
BERNBURG CASTLE MUSEUM
BLANKENBURG
REGIONAL MUSEUM
BLANKENHAIN
REGIONAL MUSEUM
BRANDENBURG
DISTRICT MUSEUM
BÜTZOW
REGIONAL MUSEUM
BURGK
REGIONAL AND CASTLE MUSEUM
BUTTSTADT
REGIONAL MUSEUM
COTTBUS
DISTRICT MUSEUM
DAHME
REGIONAL MUSEUM
DELITZSCH
DISTRICT MUSEUM
DEMMIN
DISTRICT MUSEUM
DESSAU
MOGISKAU PALACE STATE MUSEUM
DÖMITZ
REGIONAL MUSEUM
DORNBURG
DORNBURG CASTLES
DRESDEN
INSTITUTE AND MUSEUM OF THE HISTORY OF THE CITY OF DRESDEN
MUSEUM OF POPULAR ART
STATE ART COLLECTIONS: MUSEUM OF ARTS AND CRAFTS
EBERSBACK
REGIONAL MUSEUM
EHRENFRIEDERSDORF
GREIFENSTEIN MUSEUM
EIBAU
REGIONAL AND HUMBOLDT MUSEUM
EISENACH
TEA-HOUSE IN THE KARTAUSGARTEN
THURINGIA MUSEUM
WARTBURG
EISENBERG
DISTRICT AND REGIONAL MUSEUM
EISFELD
OTTO LUDWIG REGIONAL MUSEUM
ERFURT
ANGER MUSEUM OF ART
FOLK-LORE MUSEUM
MOLSDORF MUSEUM
FREIBERG
MUNICIPAL AND MINING MUSEUM
GEISA
REGIONAL MUSEUM
GERA
MUSEUM OF CULTURAL HISTORY
GERSTUNGEN
REGIONAL MUSEUM
GLAUCHAU
MUNICIPAL MUSEUM AND ART COLLECTION
GNANDSTEIN
REGIONAL MUSEUM
GÖRLITZ
STATE ART MUSEUM: HAUS NEISSSTRASSE MUSEUM
GREIZ
DISTRICT AND REGIONAL MUSEUM
STATE COLLECTION OF BOOKS AND ENGRAVINGS
GRIMMA
DISTRICT MUSEUM
GÖSCHEN HOUSE
GROSSENGOTTERN
REGIONAL ROOM
GROSSENHAIN
DISTRICT MUSEUM
GÜSTROW
DISTRICT MUSEUM
HALBERSTADT
MUNICIPAL MUSEUM
HALDENSLEBEN
DISTRICT MUSEUM
HEILIGENSTADT
EICHFELD REGIONAL MUSEUM
HERRNHUT
'ALT HERRNHUTER STUBE' REGIONAL MUSEUM
HILDBURGHAUSEN
REGIONAL MUSEUM
HINZDORF
REGIONAL ROOM
KAHLA
LEUCHTERBURG REGIONAL MUSEUM
KAMENZ
WEST LAUSITZ MUSEUM
KARL MARX STADT
MUNICIPAL ART COLLECTION
SCHLOSSBERG MUSEUM: MUNICIPAL AND CULTURAL HISTORY COLLECTION
KÖTHEN
REGIONAL MUSEUM
LANDWÜST
VOGTLAND PEASANT MUSEUM
LAUENSTEIN
CASTLE AND REGIONAL MUSEUM
LEHDE
OPEN-AIR MUSEUM
LEIPZIG
MUSEUM OF ARTS AND CRAFTS
LEISNIG
MILDENSTEIN CASTLE DISTRICT MUSEUM
LÖBAU
MUNICIPAL MUSEUM
LUCKAU
REGIONAL MUSEUM
MEININGEN
BAUMBACH HOUSE
MEININGEN MUSEUM
MEISSEN
MUNICIPAL AND DISTRICT MUSEUM
MORITZBURG
MORITZBURG CASTLE BAROQUE MUSEUM
MÜHLHAUSEN
RAVENS' TOWER AND PARAPET WALK
MÜLLROSE
REGIONAL MUSEUM
NIEDER-NEUNDORF
REGIONAL ROOM
NEUHAUS-SCHIERSCHNITZ
REGIONAL ROOM
NEUKIRCH
REGIONAL MUSEUM
NORDHAUSEN
MEYENBURG MUSEUM
NOSSEN
REGIONAL MUSEUM
OSCHATZ
REGIONAL ROOM
PERLEBERG
DISTRICT MUSEUM
PLAUEN
HERMANN VOGEL HOUSE
VOGTLAND DISTRICT MUSEUM
POSTERSTEIN
DISTRICT MUSEUM
POTSDAM
DISTRICT MUSEUM
SANSSOUCI PALACE: CHARLOTTENHOF PALACE
SANSSOUCI PALACE: CHINESE TEAHOUSE
SANSSOUCI PALACE: NEW PALACE
SANSSOUCI PALACE: NEW ROOMS
SANSSOUCI PALACE: ORANGERY
SANSSOUCI PALACE: ROMAN BATHS

ROCHSBURG
CASTLE MUSEUM

ROSSLA
REGIONAL MUSEUM

RUDOLSTADT
HEIDECKSBURG STATE MUSEUM
MUSEUM OF ETHNOLOGY: THURINGIAN PEASANT HOUSES

RUHLA
REGIONAL MUSEUM

SAALFELD
THURINGIA REGIONAL MUSEUM

SCHLETTAU
CASTLE MUSEUM

SCHLEUSINGEN
REGIONAL MUSEUM

SCHMALKALDEN
DISTRICT MUSEUM

SCHMÖLLN
REGIONAL MUSEUM

SCHÖNBERG
REGIONAL MUSEUM

SCHÖNEBECK
DISTRICT MUSEUM

SCHWERIN
SCHWERIN STATE MUSEUM

SEIFHENNERSDORF
NATURAL HISTORY AND REGIONAL MUSEUM

SENFTENBERG
DISTRICT MUSEUM

SONDERHAUSEN
STATE REGIONAL AND CASTLE MUSEUM

STADTILM
REGIONAL MUSEUM

STENDAL
ALTMARK MUSEUM: COLLECTION AT THE CATHEDRAL

STOLBERG
OLD STOLBERG TOWN-HOUSE

TANGERMÜNDE
REGIONAL MUSEUM

UMMENDORF
WANZLEBEN DISTRICT MUSEUM

WALDENBURG
REGIONAL MUSEUM AND NATURAL HISTORY COLLECTION

WALTERSDORF
REGIONAL MUSEUM

WALTERSHAUSEN
REGIONAL MUSEUM

WANDLITZ
REGIONAL MUSEUM

WEESENSTEIN
CASTLE MUSEUM

WEIMAR
BELVEDERE PALACE ROCOCO MUSEUM
KIRMS KRACKOW HOUSE
REGIONAL MUSEUM OF NATURAL HISTORY, HISTORY AND POPULAR ART
RÖMISCHES HOUSE
TIEFURT PALACE
WITHUM PALACE

WERDAU
REGIONAL MUSEUM

WERNIGERODE
FEUDAL MUSEUM
HARZ MUSEUM

WÖRLITZ
STATE PALACES

ZITTAU
MUNICIPAL MUSEUM

GFR

AACHEN
COUVEN MUSEUM
SUERMONDT MUSEUM

AHRENSBURG
AHRENSBURG CASTLE MUSEUM

ALTENHOF
ALTENHOF MANORHOUSE

ALTÖTTING
MUNICIPAL MUSEUM OF REGIONAL LIFE

AMBERG
REGIONAL MUSEUM

ANHOLT
CASTLE MUSEUM

ANSBACH
ANSBACH MANSION

AUGSBURG
MAXIMILIAN MUSEUM

BADEN-BADEN
ZÄHRINGER MUSEUM

BAD GANDERSHEIM
REGIONAL MUSEUM

BAD REICHENHALL
MUNICIPAL MUSEUM

BAD SEGEBERG
OLD SEGEBERG TOWN HOUSE

BAD TÖLZ
BAD TÖLZ MUSEUM

BAD WALDSEE
BAD WALDSEE REGIONAL MUSEUM

BAD WIMPFEN
STEINHAUS MUSEUM

BALINGEN
REGIONAL MUSEUM

BAMBERG
BÖTTINGER HOUSE MUSEUM
NEW RESIDENCE

BAYREUTH
HERMITAGE
MUNICIPAL MUSEUM
NEW PALACE
SANSPAREIL

BENSHEIM-AUERBACH
FÜRSTENLAGER TOWN PARK

BERCHTESGADEN
PALACE MUSEUM

BERLEBURG
BERLEBURG PALACE

BERLIN
BELLEVUE PALACE COLLECTIONS
GLIENICKE PALACE
GRUNEWALD HUNTING LODGE COLLECTIONS
MUSEUM OF GERMAN FOLKLORE
MUSEUM OF ISLAMIC ART
SPANDAU LOCAL MUSEUM

BERSENBRÜCK
DISTRICT MUSEUM

BERTOLDSHEIM
PICTURE GALLERY

BOGENBERG
REGIONAL MUSEUM

BORTFELD
FARM-HOUSE MUSEUM

BRAUBACH
MARKSBURG CASTLE MUSEUM

BRAUNFELS
PALACE MUSEUM

BRAUNSCHWEIG
DANKWARDEROBE CASTLE
MUNICIPAL MUSEUM

BREMEN
LUDWIG ROSELIUS COLLECTION

BREMERHAVEN
SPECKENBÜTTEL OPEN-AIR MUSEUM

BRUCHSAL
PALACE

BRÜHL
AUGUSTUSBERG PALACE

BUCHEN
STEINERNES HOUSE REGIONAL MUSEUM

BÜCKEBURG
GALLERY OF PAINTINGS
REGIONAL MUSEUM OF SCHAUMBURG-LIPPISCH

BÜDINGEN
PALACE MUSEUM

BÜHL
REGIONAL MUSEUM

BÜNDE
DISTRICT MUSEUM

BÜNZEN
THE OLD HOUSE

BURGHAUSEN
CASTLE

BURG-WUPPER
MUSEUM OF THE COUNTS VON BERG

CALW
CALW REGIONAL MUSEUM AND HERMANN HESSE MEMORIAL

CELLE
DUCAL PALACE

CHAM
REGIONAL MUSEUM

CLOPPENBURG
VILLAGE MUSEUM

COBURG
EHRENBURG PALACE MUSEUM

COESFELD
REGIONAL MUSEUM

CUXHAVEN
CUXHAVEN REGIONAL MUSEUM

DARMSTADT
BAUHAUS COLLECTIONS
PALACE MUSEUM

DEGGENDORF
REGIONAL MUSEUM

DETMOLD
OPEN AIR MUSEUM

DIEZ/LAHN
SCHAUMBURG PALACE

DINKELSBÜHL
MUSEUM OF HISTORY

DONAUESCHINGEN
PALACE OF THE PRINCES OF FÜRSTENBERG

DONAUWÖRTH
REGIONAL MUSEUM

DREIEICHENHAIN
DREIEICH MUSEUM

DUDERSTADT
EICHSFELD REGIONAL MUSEUM

DUISBURG
KÖNIGSBERG HOUSE

DÜREN
REGIONAL MUSEUM

DÜSSELDORF
BENRATH PALACE
HOUSE OF THE EASTERN GERMAN TERRITORIES
MUSEUM OF THE HISTORY OF DÜSSELDORF

ELLINGEN
ELLINGEN PALACE

ELMSHORN
KONRAD STRUVE MUSEUM

EMDEN
LAND MUSEUM OF OSTFRISIEN

EPPSTEIN
REGIONAL MUSEUM

ERDING
REGIONAL MUSEUM

EUTIN
DISTRICT MUSEUM
EUTIN PALACE

FEUCHTWANGEN
REGIONAL MUSEUM

FISCHERHUDE
IRMINTRUT REGIONAL MUSEUM

FLADUNGEN
RHÖN MUSEUM

FREYUNG
WOLFSTEIN DISTRICT MUSEUM

FRIEDBERG (HESSEN)
FRIEDBERG CASTLE

FRIEDBERG (SCHWABEN)
REGIONAL MUSEUM

FRITZLAR
FRITZLAR MUSEUM

FULDA
VONDERAU MUSEUM

FÜSSEN
REGIONAL MUSEUM

GARMISCH-PARTENKIRCHEN
WERDENFELSER MUSEUM
GEROLSTEIN
DAUN DISTRICT MUSEUM
GERSFELD
PALACE MUSEUM
GLÜCKSBURG
PALACE MUSEUM
GOCH
GATE-HOUSE MUSEUM
GÖTTINGEN
MUNICIPAL MUSEUM
GROSS-GERAU
REGIONAL MUSEUM
GUNZENHAUSEN
REGIONAL MUSEUM
GÜTERSLOH
REGIONAL MUSEUM
HALLIG HOOGE
THE KING'S PARLOUR
HAMBURG
JENISCH HOUSE
KIEKEBERG OPEN-AIR MUSEUM
MILK MUSEUM AND WILHELMSBURG REGIONAL MUSEUM
MUSEUM OF ARTS AND CRAFTS
RIECK HOUSE: VIERLAND OPEN- AIR MUSEUM
VOLKSDORF VILLAGE MUSEUM
HAMM
GUSTAV LÜBCKE MUNICIPAL MUSEUM
HANNOVER
HERRENHAUSEN MUSEUM
HASELÜNNE
REGIONAL MUSEUM
HEILSBRONN
REGIONAL MUSEUM
HEINSBERG
REGIONAL MUSEUM
HERSBRUCK
REGIONAL AND HUNTING MUSEUM
HITZACKER
REGIONAL MUSEUM
HOF
MUNICIPAL MUSEUM
HOHENLIMBURG
REGIONAL MUSEUM
HOHENSCHWANGAU
HOHENSCHWANGAU PALACE
HOMBERG
REGIONAL MUSEUM
HORB
HORB PEASANT MUSEUM
HÜCKESWAGEN
REGIONAL MUSEUM
HÜLLHORST
REGIONAL MUSEUM
HUSUM
OSTENFELD FARMHOUSE OPEN- AIR MUSEUM
IGGELHEIM
REGIONAL MUSEUM
ILLEBEUREN
FARMHOUSE MUSEUM
JEVER
PALACE AND REGIONAL MUSEUM
KASSEL
GERMAN TAPESTRY MUSEUM
KAUFBEUREN
REGIONAL MUSEUM
KEITUM-SYLT
OLD FRISIAN HOUSE
KELLINGHUSEN
REGIONAL MUSEUM
KITZINGEN
MUNICIPAL ARCHIVES
KOHLGRUB
REGIONAL MUSEUM
KÖLN-BIKKENDORF
HERBIG HAARHAUS MUSEUM OF LACQUERWARE
KOMMERN
LAND MUSEUM OF FOLKLORE

KÖNIGSHOFEN
REGIONAL MUSEUM
KORBACH
KORBACH REGIONAL MUSEUM
KREMPE
TOWN HALL
KRONACH
FRANKENWALD REGIONAL MUSEUM
KRONBERG
FASANERIE PALACE MUSEUM
KRUMBACH
REGIONAL MUSEUM
KULMBACH-PLASSENBURG
PLASSENBURG
UPPER MAIN REGIONAL MUSEUM
KÜNTZELSAU
REGIONAL MUSEUM
KÜRNBACH
THATCHED HOUSE
LADBERGEN
REGIONAL MUSEUM
LANDAU (ISAR)
REGIONAL MUSEUM
LANDAU IN DER PFALZ
LANDAU REGIONAL MUSEUM
LANDSHUT
LANDSHUT RESIDENCE
TOWN AND DISTRICT MUSEUM
TRAUSNITZ CASTLE
LANGENAU
REGIONAL MUSEUM
LANGENBURG
PALACE MUSEUM
HALLIG LANGENESS
HONKENSWARF FRISIAN ROOM
LANGERWEHE
POTTERY MUSEUM
LAUDENBACH
PALACE MUSEUM
LAUTERBACH
HOHLHAUS MUSEUM
LEER
REGIONAL MUSEUM
LEIHGESTERN
HÜTTENBERG REGIONAL MUSEUM
LEMBECK ÜBER DORSTEN
LEMBECK PALACE MUSEUM
LEUTKIRCH
REGIONAL MUSEUM
LINDAU
MUNICIPAL ART COLLECTIONS
LOHR AM MAIN
REGIONAL AND SPESSART MUSEUM
LOSSBURG
BLACK FOREST MUSEUM
LÜBECK
ST. ANNEN MUSEUM
LUDWIGSHAFEN
K. O. BRAUN REGIONAL MUSEUM
LÜNE
ART COLLECTIONS OF LÜNE MONASTERY
LÜNEBURG
MUSEUM OF THE PRINCIPALITY OF LÜNEBURG
MAINBURG
HOLLEDAU REGIONAL MUSEUM
MANNHEIM
MANNHEIM PALACE
REISS CITY MUSEUM
MARL
REGIONAL MUSEUM
MARQUARTSTEIN
MARQUARTSTEIN CASTLE
MASSING
FARM MUSEUM OF LOWER BAVARIA
MEERSBURG
MEERSBURG PALACE
NEW PALACE
MELDORF
DITHMARSCH FARMHOUSE MUSEUM
DITHMARSCH LAND MUSEUM

MELLE
GRÖNEGAU MUSEUM
METTINGEN
TÜÖTTEN MUSEUM
MICHELSTADT
ODENWALD MUSEUM
REGIONAL MUSEUM
MIESBACH
REGIONAL MUSEUM
MILTENBERG
REGIONAL MUSEUM
MINDELHEIM
MINDELHEIM REGIONAL MUSEUM
MITTENWALD
REGIONAL MUSEUM AND MUSEUM OF VIOLIN MAKING
MONSCHAU
MUSEUM OF THE SCHEIBLER FOUNDATION
MONTABAUR
DISTRICT MUSEUM
MOOSBURG
REGIONAL MUSEUM
MÜNCHEN
RESIDENCE MUSEUM
MÜNNERSTADT
REGIONAL MUSEUM
NECKARMÜHLBACH
GUTTENBERG CASTLE
NEUBURG
REGIONAL MUSEUM
NEUENBURG
RAUCHKATE REGIONAL MUSEUM
NEUENSTEIN
HOHENLOHE MUSEUM
NEUNBURG VOR WALD
DISTRICT MUSEUM
NEUNHOF
NEUNHOF PALACE
NEUSCHWANSTEIN
PALACE
NEUSTADT AN RÜBENBERGE
DISTRICT MUSEUM
NEUSTADT (HOLSTEIN)
DISTRICT MUSEUM
NEUSTADT (SCHWARZWALD)
REGIONAL ROOMS
NEU-ULM
NEU-ULM REGIONAL MUSEUM
NEUWIED
DISTRICT MUSEUM
NIEDERBÜHL-FÖRCH
FAVORITE PALACE
NÖRDLINGEN
TOWN MUSEUM
NORDEN
REGIONAL MUSEUM
NÜMBRECHT
MUSEUM OF THE OBERBERG REGION
NÜRNBERG
FEMBO HOUSE CITY MUSEUM
GERMAN NATIONAL MUSEUM
NÜRNBERG IMPERIAL CASTLE
OBERHEINING
BRECHELBAD MUSEUM
OBERNDORF
REGIONAL MUSEUM
OBERSTDORF
REGIONAL MUSEUM
ÖHRINGEN
WEYGANG MUSEUM
OETTINGEN
REGIONAL MUSEUM
OSTHEIM
REGIONAL MUSEUM
OTTOBEUREN
ABBEY MUSEUM
PASSAU
OBERHAUS MUSEUM
PFARRKIRCHEN
ROTTAL REGIONAL MUSEUM

POMMERSFELDEN
WEISSENSTEIN PALACE
POTTENSTEIN
REGIONAL MUSEUM
PRIEN
REGIONAL MUSEUM
PRUNN
PALACE
RASTATT
PALACE
RATINGEN
MUSEUM OF THE HISTORY OF RATINGEN
RATZEBURG
DISTRICT MUSEUM
RAVENSBURG
REGIONAL MUSEUM
RECKLINGHAUSEN
VESTISCH MUSEUM
REGENSBURG
MUSEUM OF THE PALACE OF THE PRINCES OF THURN AND TAXIS
REGENSBURG CITY MUSEUM
REMSCHEID
REGIONAL MUSEUM
REUTLINGEN
REGIONAL MUSEUM
ROTENBURG-WÜMME
REGIONAL MUSEUM
ROTH
REGIONAL MUSEUM
ROTHENBURG OB DER TAUBER
MUSEUM OF THE IMPERIAL CITY
ROTTHALMÜNSTER
REGIONAL MUSEUM
ROXEL
DROSTE ZU HÜLSHOFF MUSEUM
RUHPOLDING
BARTHOLOMÄUS SCHMUCKER REGIONAL MUSEUM
RUNKEL
RUNKEL CASTLE
RÜSSELSHEIM
LOCAL MUSEUM
SAFFERSTETTEN
MUSEUM OF PEASANT LIFE
ST. GEORGEN
REGIONAL MUSEUM
SCHACHEN-GARMISCH PARTENKIRCHEN
HUNTING PALACE
SCHIFFERSTADT
REGIONAL MUSEUM
SCHLESWIG
LAND MUSEUM OF SCHLESWIG- HOLSTEIN
SCHLIERSEE
REGIONAL MUSEUM
SCHLITZ
REGIONAL MUSEUM
SCHLOSS MESPELBRUNN
PALACE MUSEUM
SCHNAITTACH
REGIONAL MUSEUM
SCHONGAU
TOWN MUSEUM
SCHUSSENRIED
FARMHOUSE MUSEUM
SCHWÄBISCH-GMÜND
SCHWÄBISCH-GMÜND MUSEUM
SCHWABMÜNCHEN
REGIONAL MUSEUM
SCHWANDORF
REGIONAL MUSEUM
SCHWEINFURT
MUNICIPAL MUSEUM
SCHWELM
SCHWELM MUNICIPAL MUSEUM
SCHWETZINGEN
PALACE
SESSLACH
REGIONAL MUSEUM
SIEGBURG
SIEGBURG REGIONAL MUSEUM
SIGMARINGEN
HOHENZOLLERN MUSEUM
SIMBACH
TOWN MUSEUM
SIMMERN
HUNSRÜCK MUSEUM
SINZIG
REGIONAL MUSEUM
SOLINGEN
GERMAN MUSEUM OF CUTTING IMPLEMENTS
SONTHOFEN
REGIONAL MUSEUM
STADE
OPEN-AIR MUSEUM
STARNBERG
MUNICIPAL MUSEUM
STEINAU
PALACE MUSEUM
STRAUBING
GÄUBODEN AND STRAUBING MUSEUM
TAUBERBISCHOFSHEIM
TAUBERFRANKEN REGIONAL MUSEUM
TELGTE
MÜNSTERLAND REGIONAL HOUSE
TITTMONING
REGIONAL MUSEUM
TRABEN-TRARBACH
MUSEUM OF THE CENTRAL MOSEL AREA
TRAUNSTEIN
REGIONAL MUSEUM
TROSTBERG
TROSTBERG MUNICIPAL MUSEUM
TÜBINGEN
THEODOR HEARING HOUSE
UFFENHEIM
REGIONAL MUSEUM
VEITSHÖCHHEIM
SUMMER PALACE
VILLINGEN
VILLINGEN MUSEUM
VOLKACH
SCHELF HOUSE
WALDBURG
CASTLE MUSEUM
WALLDÜRN
REGIONAL AND PILGRIMAGES MUSEUM
WARBURG
REGIONAL MUSEUM
WARTHAUSEN
PALACE MUSEUM
WASSERBURG
WASSERBURG REGIONAL MUSEUM
WEENER
REGIONAL MUSEUM
WEIDEN
TOWN MUSEUM
WEIKERSHEIM
PALACE MUSEUM
WEILBURG
MUNICIPAL AND MINING MUSEUM
PALACE
WEILER
WEST ALLGAU REGIONAL MUSEUM
WEINHEIM
REGIONAL MUSEUM
WEISSENBURG
REGIONAL MUSEUM
WEISSENHORN
REGIONAL MUSEUM
WEMDING
REGIONAL MUSEUM
WERTINGEN
REGIONAL MUSEUM
WETTELSHEIM
LOCAL COLLECTION
WETZLAR
FURNITURE COLLECTION
MUNICIPAL MUSEUM
PAPIUS MANSION
WEWELSBURG
DISTRICT MUSEUM
WIESBADEN
WIESBADEN MUNICIPAL MUSEUM
WILFINGEN
PALACE MUSEUM
WILHELMSTHAL
PALACE
WOLFACH
WOLFACH REGIONAL MUSEUM
WOLFEGG
WOLFEGG PALACE
WOLFENBÜTTEL
WOLFENBÜTTEL DISTRICT MUSEUM
WUNSIEDEL
WUNSIEDEL MUSEUM OF THE FICHTELGEBIRG REGION
WÜRZBURG
MARIENBERG CASTLE
RESIDENCE
ZIEGENHAIN
SCHWALM MUSEUM

GREAT BRITAIN

ABERGAVENNY
ABERGAVENNY AND DISTRICT MUSEUM
ALCESTER
RAGLEY HALL
AYLSHAM
BLICKLING HALL
BADMINTON
BADMINTON HOUSE
BAKEWELL
CHATSWORTH
BANBURY
SULGRAVE MANOR
BANCHORY
CRATHES CASTLE
BARNARD CASTLE
BOWES MUSEUM
BARNSLEY
CANNON HALL ART GALLERY AND MUSEUM
BATH
AMERICAN MUSEUM IN BRITAIN
HOLBURNE OF MENSTRIE MUSEUM
NO. 1 ROYAL CRESCENT
BELFAST
ULSTER FOLK MUSEUM
BERKELEY
BERKELEY CASTLE
BIBURY
ARLINGTON MILL
BIRCHINGTON
POWELL-COTTON MUSEUM
BIRMINGHAM
ASTON HALL
BLACKBURN
SAMLESBURY HALL
BOSTON
BOSTON MUSEUM
BRADFORD
BOLLING HALL
BRAMHALL
BRAMALL HALL
BRIGHTON
PRESTON MANOR
ROYAL PAVILION
BRISTOL
BLAISE CASTLE HOUSE MUSEUM
DYRHAM PARK
GEORGIAN HOUSE
THE RED LODGE
BUCKFASTLEIGH
BUCKFASTLEIGH FARM MUSEUM
BURTON- ON-TRENT
HOAR CROSS HALL
BURY ST. EDMUNDS
ICKWORTH

CALSTOCK
COTEHELE HOUSE
CAMBO
WALLINGTON
CARDIFF
NATIONAL MUSEUM OF WALES
CHARD
FORDE ABBEY
CHELTENHAM
CHELTENHAM ART GALLERY AND MUSEUM
CHESTERFIELD
HARDWICK HALL
CHICHESTER
GOODWOOD HOUSE
CHIPPENHAM
CORSHAM COURT
CHIRK
CHIRK CASTLE
CHORLEY
ASTLEY HALL, ART GALLERY AND MUSEUM
COLCHESTER
MINORIES ART GALLERY
CULROSS
DUNIMARLE MUSEUM
DERBY
KEDLESTON HALL
DISLEY
LYME PARK
DORKING
POLESDEN LACEY
DRIFFIELD
SLEDMERE HOUSE
DUMFRIES
OLD BRIDGE HOUSE MUSEUM
EDGEHILL
UPTON HOUSE
EDINBURGH
HUNTLY HOUSE
LAURISTON CASTLE
FILKINS
FILKINS AND BROUGHTON POGGS MUSEUM
FIFE
CULROSS PALACE
FORDINGBRIDGE
BREAMORE HOUSE
GAINSBOROUGH
GAINSBOROUGH OLD HALL
GLAMIS
ANGUS FOLK COLLECTION
GLASGOW
CITY OF GLASGOW CORPORATION ART GALLERY AND MUSEUM
OLD GLASGOW MUSEUM
GORDON
MELLERSTAIN
GREAT HAYWOOD
SHUGBOROUGH
GREAT YARMOUTH
MUSEUM OF DOMESTIC LIFE
OLD MERCHANT'S HOUSE
GREENHAM
COTHAY MANOR
GUILDFORD
CLANDON PARK
HALESWORTH
HEVENINGHAM HALL
HALIFAX
WEST YORKSHIRE FOLK MUSEUM
HATFIELD
HATFIELD HOUSE
HIGH WYCOMBE
ART GALLERY AND MUSEUM
PARKER-KNOLL LIMITED
HOLLINGBOURNE
EYHORNE MANOR
HONITON
HONITON AND ALLHALLOWS PUBLIC MUSEUM
HULL
WILBERFORCE HOUSE

ILFRACOMBE
CHAMBERCOMBE MANOR
KENDAL
ABBOT HALL ART GALLERY
ABBOT HALL MUSEUM OF LAKELAND LIFE AND INDUSTRY
SIZERGH CASTLE
KINGSBRIDGE
WILLIAM COOKWORTHY MUSEUM
KINGUSSIE
HIGHLAND FOLK MUSEUM
KNEBWORTH
KNEBWORTH HOUSE
KNUTSFORD
TATTON PARK
LEEDS
HAREWOOD HOUSE
LOTHERTON HALL
TEMPLE NEWSAM HOUSE
LEWES
ANNE OF CLEVES HOUSE
FIRLE PLACE
LINGFIELD
PUTTENDEN MANOR
LITTLE GADDESDEN
THE MANOR HOUSE
LIVERPOOL
SPEKE HALL
LLANDUDNO
RAPALLO HOUSE MUSEUM AND ART GALLERY
LLANFAIR P.G.
PLAS NEWYDD
LLANRWST
GWYDIR CASTLE
LLANVAPLEY
RURAL CRAFTS MUSEUM
LONDON
BUCKINGHAM PALACE
CHISWICK HOUSE
DANOR ENGINEERING LIMITED
FENTON HOUSE
GEFFRYE MUSEUM
HAM HOUSE
HAMPTON COURT PALACE
KEW PALACE
LANCASTER HOUSE
MARBLE HILL HOUSE
LEIGHTON HOUSE ART GALLERY AND MUSEUM
LONDON MUSEUM
OSTERLEY PARK HOUSE
SIR JOHN SOANE'S MUSEUM
VICTORIA AND ALBERT MUSEUM
WALLACE COLLECTION
WILLIAM MORRIS GALLERY
LUTON
WERNHER COLLECTION
LUTON MUSEUM AND ART GALLERY
MACCLESFIELD
CAPESTHORNE
MAIDENHEAD
CLIVEDEN
MAIDSTONE
ALLINGTON CASTLE
MANCHESTER
HEATON HALL
WYTHENSHAWE HALL
NORTHAMPTON
ABINGTON MUSEUM
ALTHORP
CASTLE ASHBY
NORWICH
STRANGERS' HALL
NOTTINGHAM
WOLLATON HALL
PERTH
SCONE PALACE
PETERSFIELD
UPPARK
PLYMOUTH
SALTRAM HOUSE
PORTSMOUTH
CUMBERLAND HOUSE MUSEUM AND ART GALLERY
PORT SUNLIGHT
THE LADY LEVER ART GALLERY

PRESTWICH
HEATON HALL
PULBOROUGH
PARHAM
RAVENGLASS
MUNCASTER CASTLE
RIPON
NEWBY HALL
RUFFORD
RUFFORD OLD HALL
RUGBY
STANFORD HALL
SALISBURY
WILTON HOUSE
SANDFORD ORCAS
THE MANOR HOUSE
SCUNTHORPE
BOROUGH MUSEUM AND ART GALLERY
NORMANBY HALL
SEVENOAKS
KNOLE
SHERBORNE
SHERBORNE CASTLE
SHUGBOROUGH
STAFFORDSHIRE COUNTY MUSEUM AND MANSION HOUSE
STAMFORD
BURGHLEY HOUSE
STEEPLE ASTON
ROUSHAM HOUSE
STOKE-ON-TRENT
FORD GREEN HALL
STRANGFORD
CASTLE WARD
STRATFORD- UPON-AVON
ANNE HATHAWAY'S COTTAGE
HARVARD HOUSE
HALL'S CROFT
SUDBURY
MELFORD HALL
SULGRAVE
SULGRAVE MANOR
SUNDERLAND
GRINDON CLOSE BRANCH MUSEUM
TEESSIDE
PRESTON HALL MUSEUM
TENBY
TUDOR MERCHANT'S HOUSE
TETBURY
LASBOROUGH MANOR
TONBRIDGE
PENSHURST PLACE
TORPOINT
ANTONY HOUSE
TROUTBECK
TOWNEND
TUNBRIDGE WELLS
PENSHURST PLACE
WADDESDON
WADDESDON MANOR
WAKEFIELD
CITY MUSEUM
HEATH HALL
NOSTELL PRIORY
WARMINSTER
LONGLEAT HOUSE
WARWICK
WARWICK CASTLE
WELLINGBOROUGH
HINWICK HOUSE
WELLS
HOLKHAM HALL
WELSHPOOL
POWIS CASTLE
WEST BROMWICH
OAK HOUSE MUSEUM
WESTERHAM
CHARTWELL
SQUERRYES COURT
WEYMOUTH
NO. 3 TRINITY STREET

WIMBORNE ST. GILES
ST. GILES' HOUSE
WINCHCOMBE
SUDELEY CASTLE
WINDSOR
WINDSOR CASTLE
WING
ASCOTT
WINSLOW
CLAYDON HOUSE
WOBURN
WOBURN ABBEY
WOLVERHAMPTON
MOSELEY OLD HALL
WIGHTWICK MANOR
WOODBRIDGE
GLEMHEM HALL
WOODSTOCK
OXFORD CITY AND COUNTY MUSEUM
WORCESTER
TUDOR HOUSE FOLK MUSEUM
WREXHAM
CHIRK CASTLE
YORK
CASTLE HOWARD
YORK CASTLE MUSEUM

GREECE

ATHENS
AGORA MUSEUM
IRAKLION
HISTORICAL MUSEUM OF CRETE
KALAMATA
HISTORICAL AND FOLKLORE MUSEUM
KALYMNOS
THE VOUVALINA MANSION
METSOVON
MUSEUM OF EPIROT FOLK ART
MYTILINI (MYTILENE)
H. BINOS PRIVATE COLLECTION
M. NIKOU PRIVATE COLLECTION
M. VLACHOS PRIVATE COLLECTION
RHODES
DECORATIVE ARTS COLLECTION OF THE MUSEUM OF RHODES
PALACE OF THE GRAND MASTERS (KASTELLO)

HUNGARY

BUDAPEST
HUNGARIAN NATIONAL MUSEUM
JÓKAI MEMORIAL ROOM
MUSEUM OF APPLIED ARTS
MUSEUM OF THE HISTORY OF BUDAPEST: DEPARTMENT OF MODERN HISTORY
MUSEUM OF THE HISTORY OF BUDAPEST: MEDIEVAL DEPARTMENT
NAGYTÉTÉNY PALACE MUSEUM
DUNAPATAJ
LOCAL HISTORY COLLECTION
GYÖNGYÖS
MÁTRA MUSEUM
MOSONMAGYARÓVAR
HANSÁG MUSEUM
NAGYVÁZSONY
OPEN-AIR MUSEUM OF ETHNOLOGY
SÁROSPATAK
RÁKOCZI MUSEUM
SIKLÓS
CASTLE MUSEUM
SUKORÓ
SUKORÓ FOLKLORE MUSEUM
TIHANY
OPEN-AIR FOLKLORE MUSEUM
TISZACSEGE
VILLAGE HOUSE
VAJA
ADAM VAY MUSEUM
ZALAEGERSZEG
GÖCSEJ VILLAGE MUSEUM

ICELAND

REYKJAVIK
ARBOER FOLK MUSEUM

INDIA

CALCUTTA
INDIAN MUSEUM
HYDERABAD
CHOW MAHALLA PALACE
SALARJUNG MUSEUM
PADMANABHAPURAM
MUSEUM OF ANTIQUITIES

INDONESIA

DJAKARTA
SEDJARAH MUSEUM

IRAN

TEHERAN
PAHLAVI MUSEUM

IRAQ

BAGHDAD
AL-MUSTANSIRIYIA SCHOOL MUSEUM

IRELAND

ADARE
ADARE MANOR
BANTRY
BANTRY HOUSE
BUNRATTY
BUNRATTY CASTLE AND FOLK PARK
CASTLEPOLLARD
TULLYNALLY CASTLE
CASTLEREA
CLONALIS HOUSE
CELBRIDGE
CASTLETOWN HOUSE
DERRYNAMUCK
DWYER-MACALLISTER COTTAGE
DUBLIN
STATE APARTMENTS
GLENCOLUMBKILLE
AN CLACHAN
KILKENNY
ROTHE HOUSE MUSEUM
KILLARNEY
MUCKROSS HOUSE
LISSADELL
LISSADELL HOUSE

ITALY

ANACAPRI
VILLA SAN MICHELE
ANGERA
THE ROCCA
BOLOGNA
DAVIA BARGELLINI ART GALLERY AND MUSEUM OF INDUSTRIAL ART
BRACCIANO
CASTLE
CAPRESE
MICHELANGELO MUSEUM
CASERTA
PALAZZO REALE
COLLODI
CHÂTEAU
FÉNIS
THE FORTRESS
FERRARA
PALAZZINA MARFISA D'ESTE
FLORENCE
BARDINI MUSEUM AND CORSI GALLERY
MUSEUM OF THE HORNE FOUNDATION
MUSEUM OF THE OLD FLORENTINE HOUSE
NATIONAL MUSEUM OF DECORATIVE ARTS
FONTANELLATO
MUSEUM OF THE ROCCA DEI SANVITALE
GENOA
CATALDI PALACE
ROYAL PALACE (NOW BALBI- DURAZZO PALACE)
SPINOLA PALACE GALLERY
GRADARA
THE ROCCA
ISOLA BELLA
PALACE
MERANO
PRINCIPESCO CASTLE
NAPLES
MUSEUM OF THE CARTHUSIAN MONASTERY OF ST. MARTIN
NUORO
REGIONAL MUSEUM OF COSTUME AND POPULAR TRADITIONS
PALERMO
CASINA CINESE
PITRÉ ETHNOGRAPHICAL MUSEUM
PAVIA
CARTHUSIAN MONASTERY MUSEUM
REGGIO EMILIA
PARMEGGIANI GALLERY
ROME
NATIONAL MUSEUM OF ARTS AND POPULAR TRADITIONS
PAOLINO MUSEUM (VATICAN MUSEUM)
SALUZZO
CAVASSA HOUSE
STRA
VILLA NAZIONALE
TURIN
MUSEUM OF ANCIENT ART
ROYAL PALACE
UDINE
FRIULANO MUSEUM OF POPULAR ARTS AND TRADITIONS
VENICE
SETTECENTO MUSEUM
VERRÈS
CASTLE OF ISSOGNE

JAMAICA

HALF-WAY TREE
DEVON HOUSE

JAPAN

HIKONE-SHI
HIKONE CASTLE COLLECTION
KURASHIKI-SHI
KURASHIKI HISTORICAL MUSEUM
MATSUMOTO-SHI
MATSUMOTO MUNICIPAL MUSEUM
MATSUSHIMA-MACHI
MATSUSHIMA MUSEUM, KANRANTEI
OSAKA
MUSEUM OF JAPANESE FARMHOUSES
TOKYO
FOLKLORE COLLECTION OF IGUSA HACHIMAN-GU SHRINE
SUNTORY ART GALLERY
TOYONAKA-SHI
THE MUSEUM OF JAPANESE FOLK DWELLINGS

YOKOGOSHIMURA
HOPPO BUNKA MUSEUM

KOREA, REPUBLIC OF

SEOUL
MUSEUM OF CHANG-DUK PALACE
MUSEUM OF KOREAN FOLKLORE

KUWAIT

FAILAKA ISLAND
FAILAKA ETHNOGRAPHICAL MUSEUM
KUWAIT
BAIT AL-BADER
KUWAIT MUSEUM

LUXEMBOURG

VIANDEN
MUSEUM OF RURAL ARTS

MALAGASY REPUBLIC

TANANARIVE
MUSEUM OF FINE ART AND HISTORY

MALAYSIA

MALACCA
MALACCA MUSEUM
PENANG
PENANG MUSEUM AND ART GALLERY

MALTA

VITTORIOSA
INQUISITOR'S PALACE

MEXICO

DOLORES HIDALGO
CASA DE HIDALGO
GUANAJUATO
GUANAJUATO REGIONAL MUSEUM
MEXICO CITY
CARMEL MUSEUM OF COLONIAL HISTORY
MUSEUM OF RURAL LIFE (CHARRERIA)
MORELIA
MICHOACAN REGIONAL MUSEUM
OAXACA
JUÁREZ HOUSE
PATZUCARO
MUSEUM OF FOLK ARTS AND CRAFTS
PUEBLA
JOSÉ LUIS BEELO Y GONZALEZ MUSEUM
SANTA MONICA COLONIAL MUSEUM
SAN CRISTOBAL ECATEPEC
CASA DE MORELOS
TLAQUEPAQUE
REGIONAL CERAMICS MUSEUM
TOLUCA
NATIONAL MUSEUM OF FOLK ART

MOROCCO

MARRAKESH
DAR SI SAID MUSEUM
MEKMES
DAR JAMAÏ MUSEUM
RABAT
MUSEUM OF THE OUDAIAS
TETOUAN
TETOUAN MUSEUM

MOZAMBIQUE

LOURENÇO MARQUES
HISTORICAL MUSEUM

NETHERLANDS

ALPHEN AAN DEN RIJN
OLD ALPHEN MUSEUM
AMERONGEN
COLLECTION OF THE HEIRS OF COUNT VAN ALDENBURG BENTINCK
AMERSFOORT
MUSEUM FLEHITE
AMSTERDAM
CITY MUSEUM
HERENGRACHT 524
MUSEUM AMSTELKRING
NATIONAL MUSEUM: DEPARTMENT OF SCULPTURE AND INDUSTRIAL ART
ANGERLO
VAN WEEDE COLLECTION
ARNHEM
NATIONAL MUSEUM OF ETHNOLOGY: NETHERLANDS OPEN-AIR MUSEUM
ASSEN
DRENTHE PROVINCIAL MUSEUM
AXEL
AXEL MUSEUM OF RURAL LIFE
BERGEN OP ZOOM
DISTRICT MUSEUM
BERLICUM
VAN RIJCKEVORSEL COLLECTION
BORCULO
DE LEBBENBRUUGE FARM
BORGER
FARM MUSEUM
BORNE
BUSSEMAKER HOUSE
BREUKELEN
GUNTERSTEIN RESIDENCE
COTTEN
BARON VAN HARDENBROEK COLLECTION
DALFSEN
VON MARTELS DANKERN AND RÖELL VAN HAZERWOUDE COLLECTION
VAN RECHTEREN LIMPURG COLLECTION
DELFT
PAUL TETAR VAN ELVEN MUSEUM
NATIONAL MUSEUM: LAMBERT VAN MEERTEN HOUSE
DENEKAMP
SINGRAVEN
DE STEEG
MIDDACHTEN CASTLE
DEVENTER
THE THREE HERRINGS
WEIGH HOUSE MUSEUM
DIEVER
SCHULTE HOUSE
DOKKUM
ADMIRALTY HOUSE' DISTRICT MUSEUM
DOORN
DOORN HOUSE
DOORNENBURG
DOORNENBURG CASTLE
DORDRECHT
SIMON VAN GIJN MUSEUM
EDAM
EDAM'S MUSEUM
EDE
OLD EDE
EERSEL
LOCAL HISTORY MUSEUM
EINDHOVEN
KEMPENLAND MUSEUM
ELSLOO
SHIPPING EXCHANGE REGIONAL MUSEUM
ENKHUIZEN
NATIONAL ZUIDERZEE MUSEUM
ETTEN-LEUR
JAN OUTEN HOUTE MUSEUM OF LOCAL HISTORY AND FOLKLORE
FRANEKER
DR. COOPMAN'S HOUSE MUNICIPAL MUSEUM
GEERTRUIDENBERG
MUNICIPAL MUSEUM OF LOCAL HISTORY
GEERVLIET
GEERVLIET LOCAL HISTORY MUSEUM
GELDROP
LOCAL HISTORY MUSEUM
GOIRLE
HET SMISKE MUSEUM OF LOCAL HISTORY
GOUDA
CATHARINA INN MUNICIPAL MUSEUM
GRAMSBERGEN
TOWN HISTORICAL MUSEUM
'S GRAVELAND
H. L. HOUTHOFF COLLECTION
'S GRAVENHAGE
MUNICIPAL MUSEUM
H. H. F. SALOMON COLLECTION
THURKOW COLLECTION
HAARLEM
FRANS HALS MUSEUM
HAARZUILENS
VAN ZUYLEN VAN NIJVELT VAN DE HAAN COLLECTION
HAASTRECHT
MUSEUM OF THE BISDOM VAN VLIET FOUNDATION
HARDEWIJK
MUSEUM OF THE HISTORY OF THE VELUWE
HEEMSTEDE
DE RAAF BRAND VAN STRAATER COLLECTION
'S HEERENBERG
BERGH HOUSE
HEERENVEEN
HEERENVEEN LOCAL MUSEUM
HEEZE
VAN TUYLL VAN SEROOSKERKEN VAN HEEZE EN LEENDE COLLECTION
HEINO
HANNEMA-DE STUERS FOUNDATION
HOORN
DE VISSER COLLECTION
KRIMPEN AAN DEN IJSSEL
CRIMPENERHOF DISTRICT MUSEUM
LAREN
VERWOLDE HOUSE
LEENS
OMMELAND MUSEUM OF AGRICULTURE AND HISTORY
LEEUWARDEN
FRISIAN MUSEUM
HET PRINCESSEHOF LOCAL MUSEUM
LEIDEN
LAKENHAL MUNICIPAL MUSEUM
LOENEN
F. DUYVENZ COLLECTION
LOOSDRECHT
SYPESTEYN CASTLE MUSEUM
MAASTRICHT
BONNEFANTEN MUSEUM
T. J. BOTKE COLLECTION
TREASURY OF ST. SERVAAS CHURCH
MIDDEN- BEEMSTER
BETJE WOLFF HOUSE
MUIDEN
MUIDEN CASTLE NATIONAL MUSEUM
OLDENZAAL
PALTHE HOUSE HISTORICAL MUSEUM
OOSTBURG
CADANZE ROOM
OPHEMERT
OPHEMERT CASTLE
OSS
JAN CUNEN MUSEUM
OTTERLOO
KROLLER-MULLER NATIONAL MUSEUM

ROTTERDAM
BOYMANS AND VAN BEUNIGEN MUSEUM
HISTORICAL MUSEUM

SCHOONHAVEN
MUNICIPAL COLLECTIONS OF ANTIQUITIES

SCHOONOORD
THE SEVEN MARKS

SOMMELSDIJK
GOEREE AND OVERFLAKEE DISTRICT MUSEUM

SPANKEREN
J. G. WURFBAIN COLLECTION

STAPHORST
OLD STAPHORST FARMHOUSE

RUINERWOLD
RUINERWOLD FARM MUSEUM

TILBURG
NETHERLANDS MUSEUM OF ETHNOLOGY

UTRECHT
CENTRAL MUSEUM
CENTRAL MUSEUM

VAASSEN
CANNENBURCH CASTLE

VEENKLOSTER
FOGELSANGH STATE

VENLO
GOLTZIUS MUSEUM

VLISSINGEN
MUNICIPAL MUSEUM

VOORSCHOTEN
DUIVENSVOORDE CASTLE

VORDEN
VICTOR DE STUERS COLLECTION

VRIEZENVEEN
VRIEZENVEEN MUSEUM OF ANTIQUITIES

WARFFUM
HET HOGELAND MUSEUM

WEST-TERSCHELLING
LOCAL MUSEUM

ZUTPHEN
MUNICIPAL MUSEUM

ZWOLLE
OVERIJSSEL PROVINCIAL MUSEUM

NEW ZEALAND

AKAROA
LANGLOIS-ETEVENEAUX HOUSE

AUCKLAND
EWELME COTTAGE
FENCIBLE COTTAGE
'JOURNEY'S END' COTTAGE AND MUSEUM
MUSEUM OF TRANSPORT AND TECHNOLOGY

BLENHEIM
RIVERLANDS COB COTTAGE

CHRISTCHURCH
CANTERBURY MUSEUM

CLYDE
VINCENT COUNTY AND DUNSTAN GOLDFIELDS MUSEUM

DUNEDIN
OTAGO MUSEUM
THE THEOMIN GALLERY (OLVESTON)

MATAKOHE
OTAMATEA KAURI AND PIONEER MUSEUM

NAPIER
HAWKE'S BAY ART GALLERY AND MUSEUM

NASEBY
MANIOTOTO EARLY SETTLERS' MUSEUM

NELSON
ISEL HOUSE

NEW PLYMOUTH
RICHMOND COTTAGE
TARANAKI MUSEUM

NORSEWOOD
NORSEWOOD PIONEER MUSEUM

OAMARU
NORTH OTAGO PIONEER GALLERY

PICTON
RAI VALLEY PIONEER HOUSE

PUKEKOHE
PIONEER MEMORIAL COTTAGE

QUEENSTOWN
THE OLD HOUSE

RUSSELL
CAPTAIN COOK MEMORIAL MUSEUM
POMPALLIER HOUSE

WAIMATE NORTH
WAIMATE MISSION HOUSE

NIGERIA

LAGOS
NIGERIAN MUSEUM

NORWAY

AKERSHUS FYLKE
EIDSVOLL WORKS

ARENDAL
MERDØ HOUSE

BERG
KRAGERØ MUSEUM

BERGEN
GAMLE BERGEN (OLD BERGEN)
HANSEATIC MUSEUM
HISTORICAL MUSEUM
MUNICIPAL ART MUSEUM
WESTERN NORWAY MUSEUM OF APPLIED ART

DRAMMEN
DRAMMENS MUSEUM
MARIENLYST MANOR AND MARITIME MUSEUM

EGERSUND
DALANE FOLK MUSEUM

FARSUND
FARSUND MUSEUM

FLEKKEFJORD
FLEKKEFJORD TOWN MUSEUM

FØRDE
SUNNIFJORD FOLK MUSEUM

KRAGERØ
BERG-KRAGERØ MUSEUM

MANDAL
MANDAL AND DISTRICT FOLK MUSEUM

MELBU
VESTERÅL COLLECTION OF BUILDINGS

MOLDE
ROMSDAL MUSEUM

MOSJØEN
VEFSN LOCAL COLLECTION

NES
OLD HVAM

OSLO
CITY MUSEUM

RAKKESTAD
RAKKESTAD OPEN-AIR MUSEUM

RØROS
RÓROS MUSEUM

SANDANE
NORDFJORD FOLK MUSEUM

SANDEFJORD
TOWN MUSEUM

SARPSBORG
FOLK MUSEUM FOR ØSTFOLD

SKIEN
TELEMARK AND GRENLAND FOLK MUSEUM

STAVANGER
MANOR HOUSE

TOTEN
TOTEN MUSEUM

TRØGSTAD
TRØGSTAD OPEN-AIR MUSEUM

TRONDHEIM
NORTH NORWAY MUSEUM OF APPLIED ARTS

VANSE
LISTA MUSEUM

VERDAL
VERDAL MUSEUM

PARAGUAY

ASUNCION
MUSEUM OF THE HOUSE WHERE INDEPENDENCE WAS BORN

YAGUARÓN
DOCTOR FRANCIA MUSEUM

PERU

AREQUIPA
CATALINA CONVENT

LIMA
MUSEUM OF ART

RIMAC
COLONIAL MUSEUM

POLAND

BYSTRZYCA KŁODZKIA
MUSEUM OF LIGHTING

BYTOM
MUSEUM OF UPPER SILESIA

DARŁOWO
REGIONAL MUSEUM

DUKLA
LOCAL MUSEUM

KOLBUSZOWA
LASOWIAKOW REGIONAL MUSEUM

KÓRNIK
KÓRNIK MUSEUM

KRAKÓW
CZAPSKI MUSEUM
CZARTORYSKI MUSEUM

KROŚNIEWICE
COLLECTIONS OF JERZY DUNIN-BORKOWSKI

ŁAŃCUT
REGIONAL MUSEUM

ŁÓDŹ
MUSEUM OF ARCHAEOLOGY AND ETHNOGRAPHY

ŁOWICZ
REGIONAL MUSEUM

LUBLIN
NATIONAL MUSEUM

NIDZICA
REGIONAL MUSEUM

NIEBORÓW I ARKADIA
NIEBORÓW PALACE

OLESNO
REGIONAL MUSEUM

OLIWA
REGIONAL MUSEUM OF ETHNOGRAPHY

OLSZTYN
OPEN-AIR MUSEUM

OPOLE-BIERKOWICE
OPEN-AIR MUSEUM

PELPIN
DIOCESAN MUSEUM

PODDĘBICE
REGIONAL MUSEUM

POZNAŃ
MUSEUM OF DECORATIVE ARTS
MUSEUM OF RURAL CULTURE AND HANDICRAFTS
POZNAŃ NATIONAL MUSEUM

PSZCZYNA
PALACE MUSEUM

RADZYN CHEŁMIŃSKI
REGIONAL MUSEUM

RZESZOW
REGIONAL MUSEUM

SANOK
OPEN-AIR MUSEUM

ŚRODA SLĄSKA
MUNICIPAL MUSEUM

TARNOW
MUNICIPAL MUSEUM
TATARY POD KADZIDŁEM
KURPIE MUSEUM
TORUŃ
MUSEUM OF ART
REGIONAL MUSEUM
WARSAW
ŁAZIENKACH MUSEUM
MUSEUM OF THE HISTORY OF THE CITY OF WARSAW
NATIONAL MUSEUM
WILANÓW MUSEUM
WSCHOWA
REGIONAL MUSEUM
ZAKOPANE
CHATA 'TEA' (TEA COTTAGE)
TATRA MUSEUM AND T.CHAŁUBIŃSKI MEMORIAL

PORTUGAL

FUNCHAL
THE CROSSES' QUINTA
LISBON
CALOUSTE GULBENKIAN MUSEUM
MUSEUM
MUSEUM OF DECORATIVE ART
OPORTO
GUERRA JUNQUEIRO MUSEUM
VIANA DO CASTELO
MUNICIPAL MUSEUM

ROMANIA

BRAN
BRAN CASTLE MUSEUM
BUCHAREST
THEODOR AMAN MUSEUM
DR. N. MINOVICI MUSEUM OF FOLK ART
ING. MINOVICI MUSEUM OF MEDIEVAL ART
MUSEUM OF FOLK ART
SLATINEANU COLLECTION
VILLAGE MUSEUM
CLUJ
OPEN-AIR MUSEUM
TRANSYLVANIAN MUSEUM OF ETHNOGRAPHY
CRAIOVA
OLTENIEI MUSEUM
FOCŞANI
MUSEUM OF ETHNOGRAPHY
GOLEŞTI
MUSEUM OF HISTORY AND ETHNOGRAPHY
NEGREŞTI
OPEN-AIR MUSEUM
PLOIEŞTI
HAGI PRODAN HOUSE
RĂDĂUŢI
RĂDĂUŢI MUSEUM OF ETHNOGRAPHY
REGHIN
REGHIN MUSEUM
RIMETEA
LOCAL MUSEUM
SIBIU
BRUKENTHAL MUSEUM
TIMIŞOARA
BANAT MUSEUM
URLAŢI
MUSEUM OF ETHNOGRAPHY
VĂLENII DE MUNTE
NICOLAE IORGA MUSEUM

SOUTH AFRICA, REPUBLIC OF

ADELAIDE
"OUR HERITAGE" MUSEUM
BEAUFORT WEST
BEAUFORT WEST MUSEUM
BLOEMFONTEIN
NATIONAL MUSEUM
BREDASDORP
BREDASDORP MUSEUM
CAPE TOWN
CASTLE OF GOOD HOPE
GROOT CONSTANTIA MANOR HOUSE
CAPETOWN
KOOPMANS DE WET HOUSE
CRADOCK
ZEBRA NATIONAL PARKS MUSEUM
DURBAN
MUSEUM OF LOCAL HISTORY
THE OLD HOUSE
WILLIAM CAMPBELL MUSEUM
EAST LONDON
GATELY HOUSE
ESHOWE
ZULULAND HISTORICAL MUSEUM
FRANSCHHOEK
HUGUENOT MEMORIAL MUSEUM
GRAAFF-REINET
GRAAFF-REINET MUSEUM
GRAHAMSTOWN
ALBANY MUSEUM
IRENE
GENERAL SMUTS MUSEUM
JOHANNESBURG
JOHANNESBURG ART GALLERY
KIMBERLEY
ALEXANDER MCGREGOR MEMORIAL MUSEUM
KING WILLIAM'S TOWN
THE KAFFRARIAN MUSEUM
MODDERFONTEIN
MODDERFONTEIN DYNAMITE FACTORY MUSEUM
PAARL
OLD PARSONAGE MUSEUM
PIETERMARITZBURG
VOORTREKKER MUSEUM
PORT ELIZABETH
NO. 7 CASTLE HILL
PORT ELIZABETH MUSEUM
PRETORIA
ENGELENBURG HOUSE ART COLLECTION
MELROSE HOUSE
NATIONAL CULTURAL HISTORY AND OPEN-AIR MUSEUM
VOORTREKKER MONUMENT MUSEUM
RIVERSDALE
JULIUS GORDON AFRICANA CENTRE
STELLENBOSCH
THE BURGERHUIS
STELLENBOSCH MUSEUM
SWELLENDAM
DROSTDY MUSEUM
TULBAGH
OUDEKERK VOLKSMUSEUM
UITENHAGE
UITENHAGE AFRICANA MUSEUM
VRYHEID
NIEUWE REPUBLIEK MUSEUM
WORCESTER
WORCESTER MUSEUM

SPAIN

ALCANTARILLA
MUNICIPAL MUSEUM OF ETHNOLOGY
ASTORGA
DIOCESAN AND CATHEDRAL MUSEUM
BALSARENY
COLLECTION OF PAINTING AND HISTORY
BARCELONA
GAUDI HOUSE MUSEUM
MUSEUM OF DECORATIVE ARTS
PALACIO DE PEDRALBES
BURGOS
MARCELIANO SANTA MARIA MUSEUM
CORDOBA
PALACE OF THE MARQUISES OF VIANA
EL PARDO
HOUSE OF THE PRINCE
FIGUERAS
MUSEUM OF THE AMPURDÁN
IGUALADA
MUSEUM OF LEATHER
LEÓN
CATHEDRAL MUSEUM
LLUCH
LLUCH TREASURY AND MUSEUM
MADRID
CERRALBO MUSEUM
COLLECTION OF THE HOUSE OF ALBA
LAZARO GALDIANO MUSEUM
MUSEUM OF THE ROMANTIC PERIOD
MUSEUM OF THE SPANISH VILLAGE
ROYAL CARPET FACTORY
ROYAL PALACE
PALMA DE MALLORCA
PALACIO MORELL
VIVOT COLLECTION
PIEDRAFITA DE EL CEBRERO
MUSEUM OF FOLK ARTS AND CUSTOMS
SAN SEBASTIAN
CASA DE UQUENDO
SEGOVIA
ALCAZÁR
PALACIO DE RIOFRIO
SEVILLE
OSUNA COLLECTION
PROVINCIAL MUSEUM OF FINE ART
SITGES
MUSEUM OF CAU FERRAT
PROVINCIAL MUSEUM OF THE ROMANTIC PERIOD
TOLEDO
MUSEUM OF THE DUKE OF LERMA'S FOUNDATION
VALENCIA
MUSEUM OF THE PATRIARCH

SWEDEN

ÄLVDALEN
ROTS SKANS FORT AND HOMESTEAD MUSEUM
ASKERSUND
STJERNSUND CASTLE
FALUN
DALARNAS MUSEUM
GÖTEBORG
HISTORICAL MUSEUM
RÖHSS MUSEUM OF ARTS AND CRAFTS
HALMSTAD
HALLANDS MUSEUM
HALLANDSGÅRDEN MUSEUM
HÄLSINGBORG
TOWN MUSEUM
VIKINGSBERG ART MUSEUM
HAMMARBY
LINNAEUS MUSEUM
JOKKMOKK
JOKKMOKK MUSEUM
JULITA
OPEN-AIR MUSEUM
KARLSTAD
VÄRMLAND MUSEUM
KRISTIANSTAD
KRISTIANSTAD MUSEUM
LÖFSTAD
LÖFSTAD PALACE
LULEA
UDDEN OPEN-AIR MUSEUM
MARIEFRED
GRIPSHOLM CASTLE
MÖLNDAL
GUNNEBO
MORA
ZORN HOUSE-MUSEUM
NYKÖPING
SÖDERMANLAND COUNTY MUSEUM
ÖRNSKÖLDSVIK
ÖRNSKÖLDSVIK MUSEUM
SÄTER
ÅSGÅRD MUSEUM

SIMRISHAMN
ÖSTERLEN MUSEUM
SKOKLOSTER
SKOKLOSTER CASTLE
STJÄRNSUND
STJÄRNSUND CASTLE
STOCKHOLM
CHINESE PAVILION
DROTTNINGHOLM PALACE
GUSTAV III'S PAVILION
HALLWYL MUSEUM
KARL-JOHAN'S MUSEUM
NORDIC MUSEUM
PRINCE EUGEN'S HOUSE
ROYAL PALACE
STUREHOV MANOR
SVINDERSVIK MANOR
THIEL ART GALLERY
SUNDBORN
CARL LARSSON HOUSE-MUSEUM
TYRESÖ
TYRESÖ CASTLE
VÄSTERÄS
VALLBY OPEN-AIR MUSEUM
YSTAD
CHARLOTTE BERLIN MUSEUM

SWITZERLAND

AARAU
OLD AARAU MUSEUM
AARBURG
REGIONAL MUSEUM
AESCH BEI BIRMENSDORF
VILLAGE MUSEUM
ALTDORF
URI HISTORICAL MUSEUM
ALTSTÄTTEN
HISTORICAL MUSEUM
APPENZELL
REGIONAL MUSEUM
AROSA
SCHANFIGGER REGIONAL MUSEUM
ATTISWIL
REGIONAL MUSEUM
BALSTHAL
REGIONAL MUSEUM OF OLD FALKENSTEIN
BASEL
HISTORICAL MUSEUM
KIRSCHGARTEN
MUSEUM OF APPLIED ARTS
MUSEUM OF SWISS FOLKLORE
BERN
BERN HISTORICAL MUSEUM
BISSONE
TENCALLA HOUSE
BOSCO-GURIN
GURIN HOUSE OF THE WAISERS
BRIEG
CASTLE OF THE STOCKALPERS
BULLE
MUSEUM OF THE GRUYÈRE DISTRICT
CHÂTEAU D'OEX
MUSEUM OF THE FORMER PAYS D'ENHAUT AND OF THE AUGUST COTTIER FOUNDATION
LA CHAUX- DE-FONDS
MUSEUM OF HISTORY, COINS AND MEDALS
CHUR
MUNICIPAL MUSEUM
COLOMBIER
MILITARY MUSEUM AND MUSEUM OF PAINTED BLINDS
COPPET
CHÂTEAU COPPET AND MUSEUM OF THE SWISS WHO SERVED ABROAD
DAVOS
REGIONAL MUSEUM
DELÉMONT
JURA MUSEUM
ELGG
REGIONAL MUSEUM
ESTAVAYER- LE-LAC
MUSEUM
EVOLÈNE
FOLKLORE MUSEUM
FLEURIER
MUSEUM
FRAUENFELD
CANTON THURGAU MUSEUM
FRIBOURG
MUSEUM OF ART AND HISTORY
GELFINGEN
HEIDEGG CASTLE
GENEVA
ARIANA MUSEUM
GRANDSON
CHÂTEAU
GRANDVAUX
BUTTIN-DE LOËS HOUSE
GRANDVILLARD
BANNERET HOUSE
GRINDELWALD
REGIONAL MUSEUM
GRUYÈRES
CHÂTEAU
HALLAU
REGIONAL MUSEUM
HALTEN
HALTEN TOWER
HEIDEN
MUSEUM
HILTERFINGEN
SCHLOSS HÜNEGG
HINWIL
LOCAL MUSEUM
JEGENSTORF
SCHLOSS JEGENSTORF
KLOSTERS
NUTLI-HÜSLI REGIONAL MUSEUM
KYBURG
CASTLE
KYBURG-BUCHEGG
BUCHEGGBERGISCHES REGIONAL MUSEUM
LE LANDERON
MUSEUM
LAUFEN
LAUFENTAL REGIONAL MUSEUM
LAUSANNE
HISTORICAL MUSEUM OF THE OLD BISHOPRIC
MON REPOS MUSEUM
LENZBURG
CANTONAL HISTORICAL COLLECTION
LICHTENSTEIG
TOGGENBURG REGIONAL MUSEUM
LOCARNO
MUNICIPAL MUSEUM
LUGANO
MUSEUM OF HISTORY AND ARCHAEOLOGY
LUZERN
GLACIER GARDEN AND GLACIER MUSEUM
MEIRINGEN
MUSEUM OF HASLI COUNTY
MONTHEY
OLD MONTHEY MUSEUM
MONTREUX- VEYTAUX
CHÂTEAU DE CHILLON
MÖRIKEN
WILDEGG CASTLE
MORGES
ALEXIS FOREL MUSEUM
MOUDON
MUSEUM OF OLD MOUDON
MÜSTAIR
MUSEUM OF THE MONASTERY
LA NEUVEVILLE
HISTORICAL MUSEUM
NYON
HISTORICAL MUSEUM
OBERDORF
HISTORICAL COLLECTION OF THE TEACHER TRAINING COLLEGE
OBERHOFEN AM THUNERSEE
CASTLE
OLTEN
HISTORICAL MUSEUM
ORBE
MUSEUM OF OLD ORBE
ORON-LE-CHATEL
CHÂTEAU
PFÄFFIKON
LOCAL MUSEUM
POSCHIAVO
VALLIGIANO POSCHIAVINO MUSEUM
RATZ
LOCAL MUSEUM
RAPPERSWIL
REGIONAL MUSEUM
REINACH
REGIONAL MUSEUM
RHEINFELDEN
FIRCKTALER MUSEUM
RICKENBACH BEI WINTERTHUR
HANNSELI GRANARY
RORSCHACH
REGIONAL MUSEUM
ST. GALLEN
NEW MUSEUM
ST. MORITZ
ENGADINE MUSEUM
SALENSTEIN
NAPOLEON MUSEUM
SAN VITTORE
MOESANO MUSEUM
SARGANS
CASTLE
SARNEN
REGIONAL MUSEUM
LA SARRAZ
CHÂTEAU
SCHAFFHAUSEN
ALL SAINTS' MUSEUM
SCUOL-SCHULS
LOWER ENGADINE MUSEUM
SEENGEN
HALLWIL CASTLE
SION
VALÈRE CANTONAL MUSEUM
SISSACH
REGIONAL MUSEUM
SOLOTHURN
CASTLE BLUMENSTEIN HISTORICAL MUSEUM
SPIEZ
CASTLE
STAMPA
PALAZZO CASTELMUR
STANS
HISTORICAL MUSEUM
STECKBORN
UNTERSEE REGIONAL MUSEUM
STEIN AM RHEIN
MUSEUM OF ST. GEORGEN MONASTERY
SUHR
REGIONAL MUSEUM
TARASP
CASTLE
THUN
HISTORICAL MUSEUM
TRUN/TRUNS
SURSILVAN MUSEUM
UNTERSTAMMHEIM
STAMMHEIMERTAL REGIONAL MUSEUM
UTZENSTORF
LANDSHUT CASTLE
UZNACH
MUSEUM OF LOCAL LIFE AND HISTORY
VALANGIN
MUSEUM
VALS
GANDA HOUSE

VEVEY
MUSEUM OF OLD VEVEY
WÄDENSWIL
LOCAL MUSEUM
WETZIKON
LOCAL MUSEUM
WIESENDANGEN
LOCAL MUSEUM
WINTERTHUR
LINDENGUT REGIONAL MUSEUM
WINTERTHUR-HEGI
HEGI CASTLE
WINTERTHUR- MÖRSBURG
MÖRSBURG CASTLE
WITTENBACH
LOCAL MUSEUM
ZERMATT
ALPINE MUSEUM
ZOFINGEN
MUSEUM
ZURICH
MURALTENGUT HOUSE
SWISS NATIONAL MUSEUM

SYRIAN ARAB REPUBLIC

DAMASCUS
MUSEUM OF POPULAR ARTS AND TRADITIONS

TUNISIA

MAHDIA
MAHDIA MUSEUM
SFAX
MUSEUM OF POPULAR ARTS AND TRADITIONS (JELLOULI MUSEUM)
TUNIS
MUSEUM OF ISLAMIC ART

TURKEY

ANKARA
ETHNOGRAPHICAL MUSEUM
ISTANBUL
TOPKAPI PALACE MUSEUM

USSR

ARCHANGEL
MANOR-HOUSE MUSEUM
BARAGKHAN
VILLAGE MUSEUM
BOKHARA
HISTORICAL AND ETHNOGRAPHICAL MUSEUM OF BOKHARA
CHERNOVTSY
MUSEUM OF UKRAINIAN FOLKLORE
DUSHANBE (formerly STALINABAD)
MUSEUM OF THE REPUBLIC OF TADZHIKISTAN
KAUNAS
PRINCE VYTANSAS MUSEUM
STATE MUSEUM
KISHINEV
REGIONAL MUSEUM OF THE REPUBLIC OF MOLDAVIA
KIZHI
OPEN-AIR MUSEUM
LENINGRAD
HERMITAGE MUSEUM
LERMONTOVO
M. Y. LERMONTOV MUSEUM
MOSCOW
ARKHANGELSKOYE ESTATE MUSEUM
18th CENTURY KUSKOVO ESTATE AND CERAMICS MUSEUM
MUSEUM OF DECORATIVE ARTS
MUSEUM OF FOLK ART
OSTAKINO MUSEUM OF SERF ART
OREL
REGIONAL MUSEUM
OSTANKINO
ART GALLERY
PAVLOVSK
MUSEUM OF FINE ARTS
PETROVORETZ (formerly PETERHOF)
MUSEUM OF FINE ART
PETROZAVODSK
NATIONAL HISTORICAL MUSEUM
PUSHKINO
YEKATERINSKI PALACE
TALLINN
PETER THE GREAT'S COTTAGE
YALTA
ALUPKA PALACE MUSEUM

UNITED STATES

ALBANY
ALBANY COUNTY HISTORICAL ASSOCIATION MUSEUM
ALBEMARLE
STANLY HISTORICAL KITCHEN MUSEUM
ALBION
GARDNER HOUSE MUSEUM
ALMA
MILL CREEK MUSEUM AND CAMP GROUND
AMHERST
MEAD ART BUILDING
ANDOVER
ANDOVER MUSEUM
ANSONIA
MANSFIELD HOUSE
ASHLEY FALLS
COLONEL ASHLEY HOUSE
AUSTIN
FRENCH LEGATION
BAKERSFIELD
KERN COUNTY MUSEUM
BALTIMORE
BALTIMORE MUSEUM OF ART
PEALE MUSEUM
WALTERS ART GALLERY
BARNSTABLE
CROCKER HOUSE
BAYAMÓN
JOSE CELSO BARBOSA MUSEUM
BELOIT
THEODORE LYMON WRIGHT ART CENTER
BENNINGTON
BENNINGTON MUSEUM
BETHLEHEM
ANNIE S. KEMERER MUSEUM
MORAVIAN MUSEUM
BEVERLY
JOHN BALCH HOUSE
BOSTON
HARRISON GRAY OTIS HOUSE
ISABELLA STEWART GARDNER MUSEUM
WOMEN'S CITY CLUB OF BOSTON
CAMBRIDGE
BUSCH-REISINGER MUSEUM
CAMDEN
CAMPBELL MUSEUM
CAPE MAY
VICTORIAN VILLAGE MUSEUM
CHAMPAIGN
KRANNERT ART MUSEUM
CHARLESTON
THOMAS ELFE WORKSHOP
HEYWARD-WASHINGTON HOUSE
CHATTANOOGA
HOUSTON ANTIQUE MUSEUM
CHICAGO
GLESSNER HOUSE
MUSEUM OF CHICAGO HISTORICAL SOCIETY
CHINOOK
D.A.R. HOUSE MUSEUM
CINCINNATI
CINCINNATI ART MUSEUM
TAFT MUSEUM
CLEVELAND
CLEVELAND MUSEUM OF ART
DUNHAM TAVERN MUSEUM
THE SHAKER HISTORICAL SOCIETY MUSEUM
WESTERN RESERVE HISTORICAL SOCIETY AND FREDERICK C. CRAWFORD AUTO-AVIATION MUSEUM
COHOES
VAN SCHAICK MANSION
COLBY
SOD TOWN PRAIRIE PIONEER MUSEUM
COOPERSTOWN
MUSEUM OF HISTORICAL SOCIETY OF EARLY AMERICAN DECORATION
COSHOCTON
JOHNSON-HUMRICKHOUSE MEMORIAL MUSEUM
DANVERS PORT
SAMUEL FOWLER HOUSE
DE BARY
DE BARY HALL STATE MUSEUM
DELHI
FRISBEE HOUSE MUSEUM
DENTON
STATE MUSEUM OF THE D.A.R.
DENVER
DENVER ART MUSEUM
DETROIT
DETROIT INSTITUTE OF ARTS
EDGEFIELD
EDGEFIELD COUNTY HISTORICAL SOCIETY
EL PASO
EL PASO MUSEUM OF ART
ESSEX
PRATT HOUSE
FARMINGTON
HILL-STEAD MUSEUM
FRANKFORT
LIBERTY HALL MUSEUM
FREDERICK
MUSEUM OF HISTORICAL SOCIETY OF FREDERICK COUNTY
GAUTIER
GAUTIER'S PLANTATION HOUSE
GEORGETOWN
HOTEL DE PARIS
GLENS FALLS
HYDE COLLECTION
GLOUCESTER
BEAUPORT
GREENSBURG
WESTMORELAND COUNTY MUSEUM OF ART
GUILFORD
THOMAS GRISWOLD HOUSE
HAGERSTOWN
WASHINGTON COUNTY MUSEUM OF FINE ARTS
HANCOCK
HANCOCK SHAKER VILLAGE
HARTFORD
WADSWORTH ATHENEUM
HARVARD
FRUITLANDS MUSEUMS
HIGH POINT
SPRINGFIELD MUSEUM OF OLD DOMESTIC ARTS
HOLLAND
BAKER FURNITURE MUSEUM
HOLLIDAYSBURG
BAKER MANSION MUSEUM
HOLYOKE
HOLYOKE MUSEUM - WISTARIAHURST
HOUSTON
BAYOU BEND COLLECTION
MUSEUM OF AMERICAN ARCHITECTURE AND DECORATIVE ARTS
MUSEUM OF FINE ARTS
HYDE PARK
VANDERBILT MANSION NATIONAL HISTORIC SITE
INDIANAPOLIS
INDIANAPOLIS MUSEUM OF ART
IOWA CITY
UNIVERSITY OF IOWA MUSEUM OF ART

JACKSONVILLE
CUMNER GALLERY OF ART
JEKYLL ISLAND
JEKYLL ISLAND MUSEUM (ROCKEFELLER COTTAGE)
KANSAS CITY
FOLGER COFFEE COMPANY MUSEUM
WILLIAM ROCKHILL NELSON GALLERY AND ATKINS MUSEUM OF FINE ARTS
KELSO
COWLITZ COUNTY HISTORICAL MUSEUM
KNOXVILLE
CRAIGHEAD JACKSON HOUSE
LAUGHLINTOWN
COMPASS INN MUSEUM
LAUREL
LAUREN ROGERS LIBRARY AND MUSEUM OF ART
LEXINGTON
THE FOX HOUSE
LOUISVILLE
J. B. SPEED ART MUSEUM
MALIBU
J. PAUL GETTY MUSEUM
MARYVILLE
NORTHWEST MISSOURI STATE COLLEGE GALLERY
MERION
BARNES FOUNDATION
MIAMI
VISCAYA-DADE COUNTY ART MUSEUM
MILWAUKEE
CHARLES ALLIS ART MUSEUM AND LIBRARY
MINNEAPOLIS
MINNEAPOLIS INSTITUTE OF ARTS
MONTCLAIR
MONTCLAIR ART MUSEUM
MONTGOMERY
MONTGOMERY MUSEUM OF FINE ARTS
MOUNT PLEASANT
BOONE HALL
MUNCIE
GRINTER HOUSE
MUSCATINE
LAURER MUSSER ART GALLERY AND MUSEUM
MYSTIC
DENISON HOMESTEAD
NASHVILLE
GEORGE PEABODY COLLEGE MUSEUM
NEW HAVEN
YALE UNIVERSITY ART GALLERY
NEW LONDON
LYMAN ALLYN MUSEUM
NEWPORT
BELCOURT CASTLE
THE BREAKERS
BULL-MAWDSLEY HOUSE
HUNTER HOUSE
NEW YORK
ART COMMISSION OF THE CITY OF NEW YORK
BROOKLYN MUSEUM
CLOISTERS
COOPER-HEWITT MUSEUM OF DECORATIVE ARTS AND DESIGN
JUNIOR MUSEUM OF THE METROPOLITAN MUSEUM OF ART
MUSEUM OF NEW YORK HISTORICAL SOCIETY
ROGER MORRIS JUMEL MANSION
NOGALES
PETE KITCHEN MUSEUM
NORFOLK
HERMITAGE FOUNDATION MUSEUM
NORRISTOWN
MUSEUM OF HISTORICAL SOCIETY OF NORRIS COUNTY
NORTH ANDOVER
MUSEUM OF NORTH ANDOVER HISTORICAL SOCIETY
NORWICH
SLATER MEMORIAL MUSEUM
NOTRE DAME
UNIVERSITY OF NOTRE DAME ART GALLERY
OAKLAND
OAKLAND MUSEUM
OLD CHATHAM
SHAKER MUSEUM
OMAHA
JOSLYN ART MUSEUM
OSCEOLA
POLK COUNTY HISTORICAL MUSEUM
OSHKOSH
PAINE ART CENTER
PHILADELPHIA
DREXEL MUSEUM COLLECTION
STEPHEN GIRARD COLLECTION
INDEPENDENCE NATIONAL HISTORICAL PARK
MUSEUM OF THE CARNEGIE INSTITUTE
PHILADELPHIA MUSEUM OF ART
PHILIP H. AND A. S. W. ROSENBACH FOUNDATION MUSEUM
NAOMI WOOD COLLECTION
WOODMERE ART GALLERY
PHOENIX
PHOENIX ART MUSEUM
PITTSBURGH
CARNEGIE MUSEUM OF ART
POLAND SPRING
SHAKER MUSEUM
PORTLAND
PORTLAND MUSEUM OF ART
PORTSMOUTH
WENTWORTH-GARDNER MANSION
POUGHKEEPSIE
VASSAR COLLEGE ART GALLERY
PROVIDENCE
MUSEUM OF ART, RHODE ISLAND SCHOOL OF DESIGN
RHODE ISLAND HISTORICAL SOCIETY
PROVINCETOWN
CHRYSLER ART MUSEUM
RALEIGH
NORTH CAROLINA MUSEUM OF ART
RALLS
RALLS HISTORICAL MUSEUM
READING
READING PUBLIC MUSEUM AND ART GALLERY
RICHMOND
VIRGINIA MUSEUM OF FINE ARTS
RINGWOOD
RINGWOOD MANOR HOUSE MUSEUM
ROCHESTER
MEADOW BROOK HALL
MEMORIAL ART GALLERY, UNIVERSITY OF ROCHESTER
MUSEUM OF LANDMARK SOCIETY OF WESTERN NEW YORK
ROEBUCK
WALNUT GROVE PLANTATION
SACRAMENTO
E. B. CROCKER ART GALLERY
ST. LOUIS
ST. LOUIS ART MUSEUM
ST. PETERSBURG
MUSEUM OF FINE ARTS OF ST. PETERSBURG
SALEM
PEIRCE-NICHOLS HOUSE
SALT LAKE CITY
UTAH MUSEUM OF FINE ARTS
SAN DIEGO
FINE ARTS GALLERY OF SAN DIEGO
OLD TOWN SAN DIEGO STATE HISTORIC PARK
SAN FRANCISCO
OCTAGON HOUSE
M. H. DE YOUNG MEMORIAL MUSEUM
SAN JUAN
MUSEUM OF THE PUERTO RICAN FAMILY
SAN MARINO
HENRY E. HUNTINGTON LIBRARY AND ART GALLERY
SANTA BARBARA
ART MUSEUM AND HISTORY MUSEUM
SARASOTA
RINGLING MUSEUM OF ART
SARATOGA
MONTALVO CENTER FOR THE ARTS
SAVANNAH
TELFAIR ACADEMY OF ARTS AND SCIENCES
SELMA
STURDIVANT MUSEUM
SHAKER HEIGHTS
SHAKER HISTORICAL SOCIETY MUSEUM
SHREVEPORT
R. W. NORTON ART GALLERY
SOMERVILLE
SOMERVILLE HISTORICAL SOCIETY MUSEUM
SOUTHAMPTON
PARRISH ART MUSEUM
SOUTH LEE
MERRELL TAVERN
SPARTANBURG
WALNUT GROVE PLANTATION
SPRINGFIELD
ILLINOIS STATE MUSEUM
GEORGE WALTER VINCENT SMITH ART MUSEUM
MUSEUM OF FINE ARTS
STAATSBURG
MILLS MUSEUM
STOCKTON
PIONEER MUSEUM AND HAGGIN GALLERIES
STORRS
WILLIAM BENTON MUSEUM OF ART
TERRE HAUTE
SHELDON SWOPE ART GALLERY
THEODORE
BELLINGRATH GARDENS AND HOME
TOLEDO
TOLEDO MUSEUM OF ART
TROY
MUSEUM OF RENSSELAER COUNTY HISTORICAL SOCIETY
TUCSON
UNIVERSITY OF ARIZONA MUSEUM OF ART
UTICA
MUNSON-WILLIAMS-PROCTOR INSTITUTE
WALNUT CREEK
CIVIC ARTS GALLERY
WARWICK
WARWICK HISTORICAL SOCIETY MUSEUM
WASHINGTON
ANDERSON HOUSE MUSEUM
CORCORAN GALLERY OF ART
DAUGHTERS OF THE AMERICAN REVOLUTION MUSEUM
DECATUR HOUSE
MUSEUM OF AFRICAN ART
MUSEUM OF THE SOCIETY OF THE CINCINNATI-ANDERSON HOUSE
NATIONAL COLLECTION OF FINE ARTS
NATIONAL GALLERY OF ART
OCTAGON
OLD STONE HOUSE
RENWICK GALLERY
SMITH-MASON GALLERY OF ART
THE UNITED STATES CAPITOL
WATERTOWN
ROSWELL P. FLOWER MEMORIAL LIBRARY
WEST LIBERTY
PIATT CASTLES
WESTON
FARRAR-MANSUR HOUSE
WEST PALM BEACH
NORTON GALLERY AND SCHOOL OF ART
WICHITA
WICHITA ART ASSOCIATION
WICHITA ART MUSEUM
WILLIAMSBURG
COLONIAL WILLIAMSBURG
WILLIAMSTOWN
WILLIAMS COLLEGE MUSEUM OF ART
WILMINGTON
MUSEUM OF THE HISTORICAL SOCIETY OF DELAWARE
WINDSOR
OLIVER ELLSWORTH HOMESTEAD
WINSTON-SALEM
MUSEUM OF EARLY SOUTHERN DECORATIVE ARTS
WINTERTHUR
HENRY FRANCIS DU PONT WINTERTHUR MUSEUM
WOODBURY
GLEBE HOUSE
WOOSTER
COLLEGE OF WOOSTER MUSEUM
WORCESTER
JOHN WOODMAN HIGGINS ARMORY
WORCESTER ART MUSEUM

YARMOUTH PORT
WINSLOW CROCKER HOUSE
YONKERS
HUDSON RIVER MUSEUM
ZANESVILLE
ART INSTITUTE OF ZANESVILLE

URUGUAY

MONTEVIDEO
MUNICIPAL MUSEUM OF HISTORY AND ARCHIVES

YUGOSLAVIA

BELGRADE
MUSEUM OF APPLIED ART
CETINJE
STATE MUSEUM
DUBROVNIK
ETHNOGRAPHICAL MUSEUM
TOWN MUSEUM
KOPER
ART AND HISTORICAL MUSEUM
LESKOVAC
TOWN MUSEUM
LJUBLJANA
MUNICIPAL MUSEUM
OREBIĆ
CAPTAINS' HOUSES
PREDJAMA
CASTLE MUSEUM
RIJEKA
MARITIME AND HISTORICAL MUSEUM
ROVINJ
TOWN MUSEUM
SARAJEVO
DESPIĆ'S HOUSE
SVRSO'S HOUSE
SINJ
TOWN MUSEUM
SPLIT
ETHNOGRAPHICAL MUSEUM
SREMSKI KARLOVCI
TOWN MUSEUM
TRAKOŠĆAN
CASTLE MUSEUM
VARAŽDIN
STARI GRAD MUSEUM
ZAGREB
ETHNOGRAPHICAL MUSEUM
MUSEUM OF APPLIED ARTS

Coins, medals, paper currency

ALGERIA

ALGIERS
MUSEUM OF POPULAR ARTS AND TRADITIONS
NATIONAL MUSEUM OF ANTIQUITIES

ARGENTINA

BUENOS AIRES
ARGENTINE NATIONAL BANK MUSEUM OF HISTORY AND NUMISMATICS
BANK OF LONDON AND SOUTH AMERICA MUSEUM
HISTORICAL MUSEUM OF THE BANK OF THE PROVINCE OF BUENOS AIRES
NUMISMATICS MUSEUM OF THE CENTRAL BANK
MENDOZA
MUSEUM OF THE ANCIENT PROVINCE
MORÓN
GENERAL SAN MARTIN MUSEUM OF HISTORY AND ART

AUSTRALIA

ADELAIDE
ART GALLERY OF SOUTH AUSTRALIA
ALBURY
MUSEUM OF APPLIED ARTS AND SCIENCES, ALBURY BRANCH
BATHURST
MUSEUM OF APPLIED ARTS AND SCIENCES
SYDNEY
WILLIAM DIXSON GALLERY AND MITCHELL LIBRARY
TAMWORTH
TAMWORTH ART GALLERY AND MUSEUM
TOOWOOMBA
ART GALLERY AND GEM COLLECTION

AUSTRIA

ADMONT
MUSEUM OF ART HISTORY
BADGASTEIN
REGIONAL MUSEUM
EGG
REGIONAL MUSEUM
ENNS
MUNICIPAL MUSEUM
GRAZ
JOANNEUM PROVINCIAL MUSEUM OF PREHISTORY AND EARLY HISTORY
HEILIGENKREUZ
MONASTERY COLLECTIONS
HERZOGENBURG
COLLECTIONS OF THE MONASTERY
HOLLABRUNN
MUNICIPAL MUSEUM
INNSBRUCK
AMBRAS CASTLE COLLECTION
JUDENBURG
TOWN AND DISTRICT MUSEUM
KLEINENGERSDORF
"DER BISAMBERG UND DER WEINVIERTLER" MUSEUM
MURAU
MUNICIPAL MUSEUM OF LOCAL LIFE
PFAFFSTÄTTEN
REGIONAL MUSEUM
RENNWEG
VILLAGE MUSEUM
SALZBURG
SALZBURGER MUSEUM, CAROLINO AUGUSTEUM
ST. PAUL
MONASTERY ART COLLECTIONS
ST. PÖLTEN
DIOCESAN MUSEUM
STOCKERAU
DISTRICT MUSEUM
VIENNA
AUSTRIAN MUSEUM OF INDUSTRY AND COMMERCE
MUSEUM OF THE AUSTRIAN POST OFFICE SAVINGS BANK
MUSEUM OF THE FIRST AUSTRIAN SAVINGS BANK
MUSEUM OF THE HISTORY OF ART: COIN, MEDAL AND CURRENCY COLLECTIONS
MUSEUM OF THE HISTORY OF ART: EGYPTIAN AND ORIENTAL COLLECTION
WILHERING
MONASTERY COLLECTION

BANGLADESH

DACCA
DACCA MUSEUM
POSTAL MUSEUM

BELGIUM

ANTWERP
OLD BUTCHERS' HALL
PROVINCIAL MUSEUM OF INDUSTRIAL ART
RIDDER SMIDT VAN GELDER MUSEUM
ATH
ARCHAEOLOGICAL SOCIETY MUSEUM
BRUGES
GRUUTHUSE MUSEUM
BRUSSELS
MUNICIPAL MUSEUM OF THE CITY OF BRUSSELS
MUSEUM OF THE POOR LAW ADMINISTRATION
GHENT
MUSEUM OF THE TREATY OF GHENT
HASSELT
PROVINCIAL MUSEUM
LIÈGE
CURTIUS MUSEUM
DIOCESAN MUSEUM AND CATHEDRAL TREASURY
WITTERT MUSEUM
LOUVAIN
MUSEUM OF ART AND ARCHAEOLOGY
MARIEMONT-MORLANWELZ
MUSEUM OF ART AND OF THE HISTORY OF ARCHAEOLOGY
MONS
MUSEUM OF NUMISMATICS AND PREHISTORY
TOURNAI
FOLKLORE MUSEUM
VERVIERS
RENIER MUSEUM

BOLIVIA

POTOSI
NATIONAL MUSEUM OF THE POTOSI MINT

BRAZIL

JUIZ DE FORA
MUSEUM OF THE ROYAL BANK OF MINAS GERAIS
MANAUS
MUSEUM OF NUMISMATICS
RIO DE JANEIRO
COIN AND POSTAGE STAMP MUSEUM
CURRENCY MUSEUM OF THE BANK OF BRAZIL
MUSEUM OF THE BANK OF BRAZIL
MUSEUM OF THE CITY OF RIO DE JANEIRO
MUSEUM OF NUMISMATICS AND PHILATELY
NATIONAL MUSEUM OF FINE ART
SALVADOR
MUSEUM OF ART
MUSEUM OF THE CARLOS COSTA PINTO FOUNDATION
MUSEUM OF POPULAR ART
NELSON DE SOUSA OLIVEIRA COLLECTION
TATUÍ
MARQUÊS DE MONTE ALEGRE HISTORICAL MUSEUM

BULGARIA

RAJKOVO
NATIONAL MUSEUM OF THE RHODOPE

CAMEROUN

YAOUNDÉ
MUSEUM OF NEGRO ART

CANADA

MONTREAL
BANK OF MONTREAL MUSEUM
QUEBEC
QUEBEC SEMINARY MUSEUM

CHILE

HUALPEN
MUSEO DE HUALPEN

COLOMBIA

BOGOTA
MUSEUM OF GRAPHIC ART

CZECHOSLOVAKIA

BANSKÁ ŠTIAVNICA
MINING MUSEUM
HRANICE NA MORAVĚ
MUSEUM OF CENTRAL MORAVIA
JABLONEC NAD NISOU
MUSEUM OF GLASS AND JEWELLERY
KELČ
KELČ MUSEUM
KOMÁRNO
PODUNAJSKA REGIONAL MUSEUM
KREMNICA
MUNICIPAL MUSEUM
LEVICE
TEKOV MUSEUM
MARIÁNSKE LÁZNĚ
MUNICIPAL MUSEUM
NOVÁ PAKA
MUSEUM OF GEM-STONES
OPAVA
SILESIAN MUSEUM: HISTORY COLLECTIONS
ORAVSKY PODZÁMOK
ORAVA MUSEUM
PIEŠTANY
SPA MUSEUM
PODĚBRADY
DISTRICT MUSEUM
POPRAD
TATRA MUSEUM
PRACHATICE
DISTRICT MUSEUM
PRAGUE
NATIONAL MUSEUM: MUSEUM OF HISTORY
PŘEROV
J. A. KOMENSKY MUSEUM
RIMAVSKÁ SOBOTA
GEMER MUSEUM
SOBĚSLAV
MUSEUM OF SOUTHERN CZECHOSLOVAKIA
STRAKONICE
MUSEUM OF HISTORY AND ETHNOGRAPHY

DENMARK

COPENHAGEN
NATIONAL MUSEUM
ROSENBORG PALACE
VARDE
VARDE AND DISTRICT MUSEUM

DOMINICAN REPUBLIC

SANTO DOMINGO
NATIONAL MUSEUM

ECUADOR

GUAYAQUIL
TOWN MUSEUM

ETHIOPIA

ADDIS ABABA
INSTITUTE OF ETHIOPIAN STUDIES MUSEUM

FINLAND

HELSINKI
MUSEUM OF THE CO-OPERATIVE BANK
MUSEUM OF THE NATIONAL BANK
MUSEUM OF THE UNITED BANK
TAMMISAARI
MUNICIPAL MUSEUM

FRANCE

BORDEAUX
MUNICIPAL COLLECTION OF COINS AND MEDALS
BOURGOIN-JALLIEU
VICTOR CHARRETON MUSEUM
HÉRICOURT
MINAL MUSEUM
LAON
MUNICIPAL MUSEUM OF ARCHAEOLOGY
LILLE
MUSEUM OF INDUSTRY, COMMERCE, TECHNOLOGY AND AGRICULTURE
LYON
MUSEUM OF FINE ART
MUSEUM OF PRINTING AND PAPER-MONEY
MEAUX
BOSSUET MUSEUM
MENDE
MUSEUM OF THE LOZÈRE SOCIETY OF LETTERS, SCIENCES AND ARTS
MONTPELLIER
HÔTEL DE CABRIÈRES-SABATIER D'ESPEYRAN
MOUTIERS
MUSEUM OF THE ACADEMY OF THE VAL D'ISÈRE
MUROL
ARCHAEOLOGICAL MUSEUM
NEMOURS
CHÂTEAU MUSEUM
NICE
MASSÉNA MUSEUM
PARIS
CABINET OF COINS
COGNACQ JAY MUSEUM
MUSEUM OF THE BIBLE AND THE HOLY LAND
MUSEUM OF COINS AND MEDALS
MUSEUM OF THE LEGION OF HONOUR
MUSEUM OF THE PARIS MINT
PÉRONNE
DANICOURT MUSEUM
PERPIGNAN
JOSEPH PUIG MUSEUM OF NUMISMATICS
POITIERS
RUPERT DE CHIÈVRES MUSEUM
RIBEAUVILLÉ
HOSPICE MUSEUM
RUMILLY
MUNICIPAL MUSEUM
SAINT-DENIS
MUNICIPAL MUSEUM
SEPT-FONTAINES
SEPT-FONTAINES ABBEY MUSEUM
STRASBOURG
COIN CABINET
MUSEUM OF ARCHAEOLOGY
THOUARS
LOCAL MUSEUM
TOULOUSE
PAUL DUPUY MUSEUM
SAINT-RAYMOND MUSEUM
TOURCOING
MUNICIPAL MUSEUM OF FINE ART
VAISON-LA-ROMAINE
ARCHAEOLOGICAL MUSEUM
VIENNE
MUSEUM OF FINE ART

GDR

BERLIN
BODE MUSEUM: COIN COLLECTION
DEMMIN
DISTRICT MUSEUM
DRESDEN
INSTITUTE AND MUSEUM OF THE HISTORY OF THE CITY OF DRESDEN
STATE ART COLLECTIONS: DEPARTMENT OF COINS
STATE ART COLLECTIONS: GREEN VAULT
ERFURT
MUNICIPAL HISTORY MUSEUM
GENTHIN
DISTRICT AND REGIONAL MUSEUM
GÖRLITZ
STATE ART MUSEUM: HAUS NEISSSTRASSE MUSEUM
GOTHA
CASTLE MUSEUM
GROSSROHRSDORF
REGIONAL MUSEUM
JENA
COLLECTION OF THE ARCHAEOLOGICAL DEPARTMENT OF THE FRIEDRICH SCHILLER UNIVERSITY
LEIPZIG
MUSEUM OF ARTS AND CRAFTS
POTSDAM
DISTRICT MUSEUM
SONDERHAUSEN
STATE REGIONAL AND CASTLE MUSEUM
STOLBERG
REGIONAL MUSEUM
STRALSUND
MUSEUM OF CULTURAL HISTORY
WEIMAR
CASTLE MUSEUM

GFR

BREMEN
LUDWIG ROSELIUS COLLECTION
DIEZ/LAHN
ORANIENSTEIN NASSAU MUSEUM
EICHSTÄTT
BERGÉR MUSEUM
ERLANGEN
GRAPHICS COLLECTION OF THE LIBRARY OF THE UNIVERSITY OF ERLANGEN-NÜRNBERG
FRANKFURT
COIN COLLECTION OF THE GERMAN FEDERAL BANK
HISTORY MUSEUM
FULDA
VONDERAU MUSEUM
FÜRTH
TOWN MUSEUM
GOSLAR
GOSLAR MUSEUM
GRAFENWÖHR
REGIONAL MUSEUM
HAMBURG
HAMBURG HALL OF THE ARTS
MUSEUM OF THE HISTORY OF HAMBURG
HAMM
GUSTAV LÜBCKE MUNICIPAL MUSEUM
HANNOVER
KESTNER MUSEUM
HEIDELBERG
PALATINE MUSEUM
HELMSTEDT
DISTRICT MUSEUM
HILDESHEIM
ROEMER-PELIZAEUS MUSEUM

HÜLLHORST
REGIONAL MUSEUM

IDAR-OBERSTEIN
REGIONAL MUSEUM

KEMPTEN
ALLGAU REGIONAL MUSEUM

KIEL
HISTORY COLLECTION OF THE SCHLESWIG-HOLSTEIN LAND LIBRARY
PICTURE GALLERY AND GRAPHICS COLLECTION OF THE KIEL KUNSTHALLE

KÖLN
MUSEUM OF THE CITY OF COLOGNE

KONSTANZ
ROSGARTEN MUSEUM

LAUTERBACH
HOHLHAUS MUSEUM

LINDAU
MUNICIPAL ART COLLECTIONS

LÖFFINGEN
REGIONAL MUSEUM

LÜBECK
MUNICIPAL COLLECTION OF COINS AND MEDALS

LUDWIGSHAFEN (RHEIN)
CITY MUSEUM

MAINZ
COIN CABINET

MICHELSTADT
ODENWALD MUSEUM

MÜNCHEN
EXHIBITION COLLECTIONS OF THE BAVARIAN STATE LIBRARY
HUNTING MUSEUM
MUNICH CITY MUSEUM
STATE COLLECTION OF COINS
TREASURY OF THE MUNICH RESIDENCE

MÜNSTER
LAND MUSEUM OF ART AND CULTURAL HISTORY

NEUWIED
DISTRICT MUSEUM

NIEDERMARSBERG
REGIONAL MUSEUM

NÜMBRECHT
MUSEUM OF THE OBERBERG REGION

NÜRNBERG
GERMAN NATIONAL MUSEUM

OLDENBURG
LAND MUSEUM OF ART AND CULTURAL HISTORY

PFORZHEIM
JEWELLERY MUSEUM

SCHWERTE
MUSEUM OF THE RUHR VALLEY

STUTTGART
WÜRTTEMBERG MUSEUM

TRABEN-TRARBACH
MUSEUM OF THE CENTRAL MOSEL AREA

TRAUNSTEIN
REGIONAL MUSEUM

WALDSRODE
REGIONAL MUSEUM

WEISMAIN
REGIONAL MUSEUM

GHANA

KUMASI
PREMPEH II JUBILEE MUSEUM

GIBRALTAR

GIBRALTAR
GIBRALTAR MUSEUM

GREAT BRITAIN

BASINGSTOKE
WILLIS MUSEUM

BATH
VICTORIA ART GALLERY

BIRMINGHAM
THE ASSAY OFFICE

BRIGHTON
BRIGHTON MUSEUM AND ART GALLERY

DURHAM
GULBENKIAN MUSEUM OF ORIENTAL ART AND ARCHAEOLOGY

EDINBURGH
EDINBURGH CASTLE
NATIONAL MUSEUM OF ANTIQUITIES OF SCOTLAND

GLASGOW
HUNTERIAN MUSEUM

GREENHAM
COTHAY MANOR

LIVERPOOL
CITY OF LIVERPOOL MUSEUMS

LONDON
BRITISH MUSEUM
GOLDSMITHS' HALL
TOWER OF LONDON

OXFORD
ASHMOLEAN MUSEUM OF ART AND ARCHAEOLOGY

ROTHERHAM
ROTHERHAM MUSEUM AND ART GALLERY

TAMWORTH
TAMWORTH CASTLE

GREECE

AGIOS NIKOLAOS
ARCHAEOLOGICAL MUSEUM

AIANI
ARCHAEOLOGICAL AND FOLKLORE COLLECTION

ARGOS
ARCHAEOLOGICAL MUSEUM

ATHENS
AGORA MUSEUM
D. ARTEMIS PRIVATE COLLECTION
ATHENS NUMISMATIC COLLECTION
BENAKI MUSEUM
BYZANTINE MUSEUM
D. ECONOMIDIS PRIVATE COLLECTION
R. EVELPIDIS PRIVATE COLLECTION
A. IOLAS PRIVATE COLLECTION
P. KANELLOPOULOS PRIVATE COLLECTION
A. KYROU PRIVATE COLLECTION
NATIONAL ARCHAEOLOGICAL MUSEUM
I. PAPANDONIOU PRIVATE COLLECTION

AXIOKASTRON
ARCHAEOLOGICAL COLLECTION

CAVALA
ARCHAEOLOGICAL MUSEUM

CHIOS
ARCHAEOLOGICAL MUSEUM

CHORA TRIFYLIAS
ARCHAEOLOGICAL MUSEUM

CORFU
ARCHAEOLOGICAL MUSEUM
R. EVELPIDIS PRIVATE COLLECTION

FLORINA
ARCHAEOLOGICAL MUSEUM

IOANNINA
MUSEUM

IRAKLION
HISTORICAL MUSEUM OF CRETE
N. METAXES PRIVATE COLLECTION

KAMMENA VOURLA
KARANASSOS PRIVATE COLLECTION

KASTELLI KISAMOU
ARCHAEOLOGICAL COLLECTION

KAVALA
ARCHAEOLOGICAL MUSEUM

KOZANI
ARCHAEOLOGICAL COLLECTION

LAMIA
A. KOUNOUPIS PRIVATE COLLECTION

LIMENARIA
I. PAPAGEORGIOU PRIVATE COLLECTION

NAXOS
ARCHAEOLOGICAL MUSEUM

NEA ANCHIALOS
ARCHAEOLOGICAL COLLECTION

NEAPOLIS
ARCHAEOLOGICAL COLLECTION

PALAIA KORINTHOS
ARCHAEOLOGICAL MUSEUM

PATRAI
ARCHAEOLOGICAL MUSEUM

PELLA
ARCHAEOLOGICAL COLLECTION

PIRAEUS
ARCHAEOLOGICAL MUSEUM

RETHYMNON
ARCHAEOLOGICAL MUSEUM
MONASTERY OF AGIOS IOANNIS PREVELIS

RHODES
ARCHAEOLOGICAL MUSEUM

SAMOTHRAKI
ARCHAEOLOGICAL MUSEUM

THASSOS
ARCHAEOLOGICAL MUSEUM

THEBES
THEBES MUSEUM

THESSALONIKI
ARCHAEOLOGICAL MUSEUM
I. PAPAILIAKIS PRIVATE COLLECTION
G. PHILIPPOU PRIVATE COLLECTION
I. VASSILIOU PRIVATE COLLECTION

THIVAI
ARCHAEOLOGICAL MUSEUM

VOLOS
ATHANASSAKEION ARCHAEOLOGICAL MUSEUM
A. BASTIS PRIVATE COLLECTION
K. A. MAKRIS PRIVATE COLLECTION

VRAVRON
ARCHAEOLOGICAL MUSEUM

HUNGARY

BUDAPEST
HUNGARIAN NATIONAL MUSEUM

DEBRECEN
DÉRI MUSEUM

ESZTERGOM
BÁLINT BALASSI MUSEUM

ICELAND

REYKJAVIK
NATIONAL MUSEUM OF ANTIQUITIES

INDIA

AJMER
RAJPUTANA MUSEUM

AMRITSAR
CENTRAL SIKH MUSEUM

BANGALORE
MYSORE GOVERNMENT MUSEUM

BARIPADA
BARIPADA MUSEUM

BARODA
MUSEUM AND PICTURE GALLERY

BENARES
MUSEUM OF INDIAN ARTS AND ARCHAEOLOGY

BHARATPUR
STATE MUSEUM

BHAWANAGAR
GANDHI SMRITI MUSEUMS

BHUJ
KUTCH MUSEUM

BOMBAY
MUSEUM OF THE INDIAN HISTORICAL RESEARCH INSTITUTE

CALCUTTA
ASIATIC SOCIETY OF BENGAL MUSEUM
INDIAN MUSEUM

DHARWAR
MUSEUM OF ART AND ARCHAEOLOGY

GAUHATI
ASSAM STATE MUSEUM

GAYA
GAYA MUSEUM

GURUKUL JHAJJAR
HARYANA PRANTIYA PURATATVA SANGRAHALAYA

GWALIOR
STATE MUSEUM

HYDERABAD
STATE ARCHAEOLOGICAL MUSEUM

INDORE
CENTRAL MUSEUM

JAMNAGAR
JAMNAGAR MUSEUM OF ANTIQUITIES, LAKHOTE BUILDING

JHALAWAR
ARCHAEOLOGICAL MUSEUM

KALPI
MAHATMA GANDHI HINDI SANGRAHALAYA

KOLHAPUR
KOLHAPUR MUSEUM

LUCKNOW
STATE MUSEUM

MADRAS
FORT ST. GEORGE MUSEUM
THE GOVERNMENT MUSEUM AND NATIONAL ART GALLERY

MALDA
B. R. SEN MUSEUM

NEW DELHI
CRAFTS MUSEUM

NOWGONG
STATE MUSEUM

PADMANABHAPURAM
MUSEUM OF ANTIQUITIES

PATNA
PATNA MUSEUM

POONA
BHARTIYA ITIHASA SAMSHODHAKA MANDALA MUSEUM

SANGARIA
SIR CHOTURAM MUSEUM

SRIRANGAM
DEVASTHANAMS MUSEUM

TAMLUK
HAMILTON HIGH SCHOOL MUSEUM

INDONESIA

DJAKARTA
SEDJARAH MUSEUM

IRAN

TEHERAN
MUSEUM OF DECORATIVE ARTS
TREASURY OF THE CROWN JEWELS

IRAQ

BAGHDAD
THE IRAQ MUSEUM

IRELAND

CORK
CORK PUBLIC MUSEUM

SLIGO
COUNTY SLIGO MUSEUM

ISRAEL

BETH SHE'AN
BETH SHE'AN MUSEUM

HAIFA
ETHNOLOGICAL MUSEUM AND FOLKLORE ARCHIVES
MUSEUM OF ANCIENT ART

TEL-AVIV
MUSEUM OF ETHNOGRAPHY AND FOLKLORE

ITALY

AREZZO
PICTURE GALLERY AND MUSEUM OF MEDIEVAL AND MODERN ART

BELLUNO
MUNICIPAL MUSEUM

BRESCIA
MUSEUM OF CHRISTIAN ART

CEFALÙ
MENDRALISCA MUSEUM

CROTONE
MUNICIPAL MUSEUM

ENNA
ALESSI MUSEUM

ESTE
ATESTINO NATIONAL MUSEUM

FLORENCE
NATIONAL MUSEUM
STIBBERT MUSEUM

GELA
NATIONAL MUSEUM

MANTUA
CAVRIANI PALACE

MILAN
MUNICIPAL NUMISMATIC COLLECTION

MODENA
MEDAL CABINET

PARMA
MUSEUM OF CHINESE ART

PAVIA
ARCHAEOLOGICAL MUSEUM

RIMINI
MUNICIPAL MUSEUM AND ART GALLERY

ROME
BASILICA OF S. PAOLO FUORI LE MURA
COLLECTIONS OF THE ITALIAN INSTITUTE OF NUMISMATICS
HISTORICAL MUSEUM OF BANKING
NATIONAL MUSEUM OF ORIENTAL ART
NUMISMATIC MUSEUM OF THE ZECCA

TARANTO
NATIONAL MUSEUM

UDINE
CASTLE MUSEUM AND PICTURE GALLERY

JAPAN

NARA-SHI
SHOSOIN TREASURE HOUSE

TOKYO
MUSEUM OF CALLIGRAPHY
PROFESSOR AIZU MEMORIAL EXHIBITION ROOM OF ORIENTAL ARTS

KOREA, REPUBLIC OF

SEOUL
MUSEUM OF CHANG-DUK PALACE
NATIONAL MUSEUM

KUWAIT

KUWAIT
KUWAIT MUSEUM

LEBANON

BEIRUT
ARCHAEOLOGICAL MUSEUM

MALAGASY REPUBLIC

TANANARIVE
MUSEUM OF FINE ART AND HISTORY

MALAYSIA

PENANG
PENANG MUSEUM AND ART GALLERY

MOROCCO

RABAT
MUSEUM OF THE OUDAIAS

TANGIER
KASBAH MUSEUM

NEPAL

KATHMANDU
NUMISMATIC MUSEUM

NETHERLANDS

AMSTERDAM
CITY MUSEUM
NATIONAL MUSEUM: DEPARTMENT OF DUTCH HISTORY

DELFT
HET PRINSENHOF MUNICIPAL MUSEUM
MUSEUM OF THE HOUSE OF ORANGE-NASSAU

ENKHUIZEN
TOWN HALL MUSEUM

GELDROP
LOCAL HISTORY MUSEUM

'S GRAVENHAGE
MUNICIPAL MUSEUM
MUSEUM OF THE CHANCERY OF THE ORDERS OF THE NETHERLANDS
ROYAL CABINET OF COINS, MEDALS AND CARVED STONES

HAARLEM
FRANS HALS MUSEUM
TEYLER'S MUSEUM

HARDEWIJK
MUSEUM OF THE HISTORY OF THE VELUWE

'S HERTOGENBOSCH
NORTH BRABANT MUSEUM

LEEUWARDEN
FRISIAN MUSEUM

LEIDEN
COIN AND MEDAL CABINET OF THE NATIONAL UNIVERSITY

MIDDELBURG
ZEALAND MUSEUM

ROTTERDAM
CABINET OF MEDALS RELATING TO THE DUTCH ECONOMY
H. REMKES COLLECTION

TIEL
TIEL AND DISTRICT LOCAL HISTORY MUSEUM

UTRECHT
CABINET OF COINS AND MEDALS OF THE ROYAL MINT

VENLO
GOLTZIUS MUSEUM

VLISSINGEN
MUNICIPAL MUSEUM

ZUTPHEN
MUNICIPAL MUSEUM

NEW ZEALAND

CHRISTCHURCH

CANTERBURY MUSEUM

NICARAGUA

MANAGUA

NATIONAL MUSEUM OF NICARAGUA
NUMISMATICS COLLECTION

NORWAY

BERGEN

HISTORICAL MUSEUM

OSLO

CABINET OF COINS AND MEDALS
HISTORICAL MUSEUM
NORGES BANK MUSEUM COLLECTION

TRONDHEIM

MUSEUM OF THE ROYAL NORWEGIAN SOCIETY OF SCIENCES AND LETTERS

PAKISTAN, WEST

LAHORE

LAHORE MUSEUM
LAHORE FORT MUSEUM

PARAGUAY

ASUNCION

NUMISMATIC COLLECTION OF THE CENTRAL BANK OF PARAGUAY

PERU

LIMA

NATIONAL MUSEUM OF PERUVIAN CULTURE
NUMISMATIC MUSEUM

PHILIPPINES

MANILA

MUSEUM OF ARTS AND SCIENCES

MARAWI CITY

AGA KHAN MUSEUM OF MUSLIM ARTS

POLAND

KRAKÓW

CZAPSKI MUSEUM

KROŚNIEWICE

COLLECTIONS OF JERZY DUNIN- BORKOWSKI

ŁÓDŹ

ARCHAEOLOGICAL AND ETHNOGRAPHICAL MUSEUM
MUSEUM OF ARCHAEOLOGY AND ETHNOGRAPHY

LUBLIN

NATIONAL MUSEUM

PŁOCK

DIOCESAN MUSEUM

POZNAŃ

DIOCESAN MUSEUM
MUSEUM OF DECORATIVE ARTS
POZNAŃ NATIONAL MUSEUM

PRZEMYŚL

DIOCESAN MUSEUM

PSZCZYNA

PALACE MUSEUM

SIERADZ

SIERADZ MUSEUM

STRZEZÓW

JULIAN PUVOWARSKI COLLECTION

TORUŃ

REGIONAL MUSEUM

WARSAW

NATIONAL MUSEUM
NUMISMATICS MUSEUM

WROCŁAW

COIN COLLECTION
MUSEUM OF MEDALS
SEALS AND NUMISMATICS COLLECTION OF THE NATIONAL BIBLIOGRAPHICAL INSTITUTE

PORTUGAL

COIMBRA

MACHADO DE CASTRO MUSEUM

ELVAS

REGIONAL MUSEUM

ROMANIA

ALBA IULIA

ALBA IULIA MUSEUM

BRAŞOV

FORTRESS MUSEUM

BUCHAREST

COIN CABINET OF THE ACADEMY LIBRARY
COIN COLLECTION
MARIA AND DR. G. SEVEREANU COLLECTION

CLUJ

HISTORY MUSEUM

CRISTURUL

CRISTURUL MUSEUM

FOCŞANI

HISTORY MUSEUM

ORLEA

LOCAL MUSEUM

PLOIEŞTI

HISTORY MUSEUM

SIBIU

BRUKENTHAL MUSEUM

TULCEA

MUSEUM OF THE DANUBE DELTA

TURNU SEVERIN

IRON GATE (PORŢILE DE FIER) MUSEUM

SAN MARINO, REPUBLIC OF

SAN MARINO

GOVERNMENT MUSEUM AND PICTURE-GALLERY

SOUTH AFRICA, REPUBLIC OF

CAPE TOWN

SOUTH AFRICAN CULTURAL HISTORY MUSEUM

GEORGE

GEORGE MUSEUM

PRETORIA

MUSEUM OF THE SOUTH AFRICAN MINT

STELLENBOSCH

STELLENBOSCH MUSEUM

VRYHEID

NIEUWE REPUBLIEK MUSEUM

SPAIN

BARCELONA

COIN CABINET OF CATALONIA

BURGOS

PROVINCIAL ARCHAEOLOGICAL MUSEUM
ROYAL CONVENT OF LAS HUELGAS

CADIZ

ARCHAEOLOGICAL MUSEUM

MADRID

LAZARO GALDIANO MUSEUM
MUNICIPAL MUSEUM
MUSEUM OF THE MINT AND STAMP PRINTING WORKS
NATIONAL MUSEUM OF PAINTING AND SCULPTURE
ROYAL LIBRARY

SITGES

MARICEL DE MAR MUSEUM

TARRAGONA

CITY MUSEUM
DIOCESAN MUSEUM

SRI LANKA, REPUBLIC OF

COLOMBO

NATIONAL MUSEUM

RATNAPURA

NATIONAL MUSEUM

SWEDEN

GÖTEBORG

HISTORICAL MUSEUM

LUND

UNIVERSITY OF LUND HISTORICAL MUSEUM

NORRKÖPING

NORRKÖPING MUSEUM

ÖREBRO

ÖREBRO MUSEUM

ÖRNSKÖLDSVIK

ÖRNSKÖLDSVIK MUSEUM

STOCKHOLM

BANK MUSEUM
MUSEUM OF NATIONAL ANTIQUITIES AND ROYAL COIN CABINET
ROYAL PALACE

UPPSALA

UNIVERSITY COIN CABINET

VÄNERSBORG

VÄNERSBORG MUSEUM

SWITZERLAND

ALTSTÄTTEN

HISTORICAL MUSEUM

BADEN

HISTORICAL MUSEUM

BASEL

HISTORICAL MUSEUM

BRIEG

CASTLE OF THE STOCKALPERS

LA CHAUX- DE-FONDS

MUSEUM OF HISTORY, COINS AND MEDALS

FRIBOURG

MUSEUM OF ART AND HISTORY

GENEVA

MUSEUM OF ART AND HISTORY

LAUSANNE

CANTONAL CABINET OF COINS AND MEDALS
HISTORICAL MUSEUM OF THE OLD BISHOPRIC

LUZERN

HISTORICAL MUSEUM

MOUDON

EUGÈNE BURNAND MUSEUM

NEUCHÂTEL

MUSEUM OF ART AND HISTORY

OLTEN

HISTORICAL MUSEUM

SARNEN

REGIONAL MUSEUM

SION

VALÈRE CANTONAL MUSEUM

SOLOTHURN

CATHEDRAL TREASURY

WINTERTHUR

WINTERTHUR MUNICIPAL COLLECTION OF COINS AND MEDALS

ZOFINGEN

MUSEUM

SYRIAN ARAB REPUBLIC

DAMASCUS
MUSEUM OF POPULAR ARTS AND TRADITIONS

TUNISIA

MOKNINE
MOKNINE MUSEUM
MONASTIR
ALI BOURGUIBA MUSEUM
SFAX
MUSEUM OF POPULAR ARTS AND TRADITIONS (JELLOULI MUSEUM)
TUNIS
MUSEUM OF THE MINT
NATIONAL MUSEUM OF POSTS AND TELECOMMUNICATIONS

TURKEY

ANKARA
ARCHAEOLOGICAL MUSEUM
ISTANBUL
ARCHAEOLOGICAL MUSEUM OF ISTANBUL
TOPKAPI PALACE MUSEUM

USSR

LENINGRAD
HERMITAGE MUSEUM
NATIONAL RUSSIAN MUSEUM
MOSCOW
NATIONAL ARMOURY
TALLINN
MUSEUM OF HISTORY

UNITED STATES

ANNAPOLIS
OLD TREASURY BUILDING
ATTLEBORO
ATTLEBORO MUSEUM
BALTIMORE
JOHNS HOPKINS UNIVERSITY, MUSEUM OF CLASSICAL ART
CINCINNATI
CINCINNATI ART MUSEUM
CLEVELAND
CLEVELAND MUSEUM OF ART
COLORADO SPRINGS
MUSEUM OF THE AMERICAN NUMISMATIC ASSOCIATION
COLUMBUS
COLUMBUS MUSEUM OF ARTS AND CRAFTS
DALTON
CRANE MUSEUM
DETROIT
NATIONAL BANK OF DETROIT MONEY MUSEUM
ELMHURST
LIZZADRO MUSEUM OF LAPIDARY ART
FOSTORIA
EMERINE COLLECTION
LIBERTY
JESSE JAMES BANK MUSEUM
NEW YORK
CHASE MANHATTAN BANK MONEY MUSEUM
MUSEUM OF THE AMERICAN NUMISMATIC SOCIETY
PORTLAND
MUSEUM OF CONTEMPORARY CRAFTS ASSOCIATION
PRINCETON
ART MUSEUM
RICHMOND
VIRGINIA MUSEUM OF FINE ARTS

YUGOSLAVIA

BELGRADE
NATIONAL MUSEUM
BOL
DOMINICAN MONASTERY
DUBROVNIK
TOWN MUSEUM
KORČULA
CATHEDRAL TREASURY
LJUBLJANA
NATIONAL MUSEUM
NIŠ
OCHRID NATIONAL MUSEUM
SPLIT
ETHNOGRAPHICAL MUSEUM
ZAGREB
MUSEUM OF APPLIED ARTS

Philately

AUSTRALIA

SYDNEY
WILLIAM DIXSON GALLERY AND MITCHELL LIBRARY

AUSTRIA

BAD VOSLAU
REGIONAL MUSEUM
VIENNA
MUSEUM OF POSTAL AND TELECOMMUNICATION SERVICES

BELGIUM

BRUSSELS
POSTAL MUSEUM

BRAZIL

RIO DE JANEIRO
COIN AND POSTAGE STAMP MUSEUM
MUSEUM OF NUMISMATICS AND PHILATELY

CANADA

QUEBEC
QUEBEC SEMINARY MUSEUM
TROIS RIVIÈRES
INTERNATIONAL PHILATELIC GALLERIES

REPUBLIC OF CHINA

TAIPEI
POSTAL MUSEUM

COLOMBIA

BOGOTA
MUSEUM OF GRAPHIC ART
MUSEUM OF NUMISMATICS

CUBA

HABANA
POSTAL MUSEUM

CZECHOSLOVAKIA

PRAGUE
MUSEUM OF POSTAL SERVICES AND TELECOMMUNICATIONS

DENMARK

COPENHAGEN
DANISH POST AND TELEGRAPH MUSEUM

ECUADOR

QUITO
MUSEUM OF ARCHAEOLOGY AND ETHNOLOGY

EGYPT, ARAB REPUBLIC OF

CAIRO
POSTAL MUSEUM

FINLAND

HELSINKI
MUSEUM OF POSTAL SERVICES AND COMMUNICATIONS

FRANCE

AMBOISE
POSTAL MUSEUM
LIMERAY
MUSEUM OF POSTAL HISTORY
PARIS
FRENCH POSTAL MUSEUM

GDR

BERLIN
MUSEUM OF POSTAL HISTORY

GFR

BERLIN POSTAL AND TELECOMMUNICATIONS MUSEUM
HAMBURG
POSTAL MUSEUM
HOHENBURG
SPÖRER MUSEUM OF CULTURAL HISTORY
KOBLENZ
POSTAL MUSEUM OF THE MIDDLE RHINE
NÜRNBERG
NÜRNBERG MUSEUM OF TRANSPORT
STUTTGART
POSTAL MUSEUM

GREAT BRITAIN

LONDON
BRITISH MUSEUM
BRUCE CASTLE MUSEUM
NATIONAL POSTAL MUSEUM

GREECE

OLYMPIA
OLYMPIC GAMES MUSEUM

HUNGARY

BALATONSZEMES
POSTAL MUSEUM
BUDAPEST
MUSEUM OF POSTAGE STAMPS

INDIA

MADRAS
THE GOVERNMENT MUSEUM AND NATIONAL ART GALLERY
NEW DELHI
NATIONAL PHILATELIC MUSEUM

ITALY

CASTELLO
VILLA DI CASTELLO
CREMONA
MUNICIPAL MUSEUM AND PICTURE GALLERY
ROME
NATIONAL STAMP COLLECTION
URBINO
BOTANICAL COLLECTION

JAPAN

TOKYO
COMMUNICATIONS AND POSTAL SERVICE MUSEUM

LIECHTENSTEIN

VADUZ
POSTAL MUSEUM

MEXICO

MEXICO CITY
POSTAL MUSEUM

NEW ZEALAND

CHRISTCHURCH
CANTERBURY MUSEUM

NORWAY

OSLO
POST OFFICE MUSEUM

PARAGUAY

ASUNCION
MUSEUM OF POSTAL HISTORY

PERU

LIMA
PHILATELIC MUSEUM

PHILIPPINES

MANILA
MUSEUM OF ARTS AND SCIENCES

POLAND

WROCŁAW
MUSEUM OF POSTS AND TELECOMMUNICATIONS

SOUTH AFRICA, REPUBLIC OF

CAPE TOWN
SOUTH AFRICAN CULTURAL HISTORY MUSEUM
KIMBERLEY
ALEXANDER MCGREGOR MEMORIAL MUSEUM

SPAIN

BARCELONA
POSTAL MUSEUM

SWEDEN

STOCKHOLM
POSTAL MUSEUM

SWITZERLAND

BERN
SWISS POSTAL, TELEPHONE AND TELEGRAPH MUSEUM

USSR

LENINGRAD
A. S. POPOV CENTRAL MUSEUM OF COMMUNICATIONS

UNITED STATES

NEW YORK
NEW YORK PUBLIC LIBRARY
WESTON
CARDINAL SPELLMAN PHILATELIC MUSEUM
YAKIMA
YAKIMA VALLEY MUSEUM

Group B

THE SCIENCES

Geology, mineralogy, palaeontology

ALBANIA

TIRANA
MUSEUM OF NATURAL HISTORY

ANGOLA

LUANDA
ANGOLA MUSEUM
MUSEUM OF GEOLOGY, PALAEONTOLOGY AND MINERALOGY
MUSEUM OF MINERALOGY AND GEOLOGY

ARGENTINA

BUENOS AIRES
MUSEUM OF GEOLOGY AND MINERALOGY
MUSEUM OF THE INSTITUTE OF THE ANTARCTIC
MUSEUM OF MINERALS
BERNARDINO RIVODAVIA MUSEUM OF NATURAL SCIENCES
CORRIENTES
NATURAL HISTORY MUSEUM
LA PLATA
LA PLATA MUSEUM OF NATURAL SCIENCES
LOMAS DE ZÁMORA
AMERICAN MUSEUM OF ANTHROPOLOGY, HISTORY, NUMISMATICS AND NATURAL SCIENCE
MENDOZA
MOYANO MUSEUM OF NATURAL HISTORY
ROSARIO
A. GALLARDO MUSEUM OF NATURAL SCIENCES
SANTA FÉ
NATURAL HISTORY MUSEUM

AUSTRALIA

ADELAIDE
THE SOUTH AUSTRALIAN MUSEUM
BROKEN HILL
MUSEUM OF APPLIED ARTS AND SCIENCES
FORTITUDE VALLEY
QUEENSLAND MUSEUM
GOULBURN
MUSEUM OF APPLIED ARTS AND SCIENCES
JENOLAN CAVES
JENOLAN CAVES MUSEUM
KALBARRI
SHELL, MARINE AND MINERAL MUSEUM
KOROIT
NATURAL HISTORY CENTRE
LIGHTNING RIDGE
MICK'S MUSEUM
MELBOURNE
GEOLOGICAL MUSEUM
MOUNT YORK
NATURAL MUSEUM
NELSON BAY
GEMSTONE HOUSE
PERTH
WESTERN AUSTRALIAN MUSEUM
SYDNEY
AUSTRALIAN MUSEUM
MINING AND GEOLOGICAL MUSEUM
TEMORA
ROCK AND MINERAL MUSEUM
TOOWOOMBA
ART GALLERY AND GEM COLLECTION
URALLA
ROCK HUNTER'S RENDEZVOUS
ZEEHAN
WEST COAST PIONEERS' MEMORIAL MUSEUM

AUSTRIA

ADMONT
NATURAL HISTORY MUSEUM
ASPARN
WEINLAND MUSEUM
BADEN
ROLLETT MUSEUM
BADGASTEIN
REGIONAL MUSEUM
BAD VOSLAU
REGIONAL MUSEUM
BAD WIMSBACH- NEYDHARTING
INTERNATIONAL PEAT-BOG MUSEUM
DÖLLACH
REGIONAL AND GOLDMINING MUSEUM
DORNBIRN
LANDSCAPE AND ECOLOGY OF THE VORARLBERG

DREISTETTEN
SCHERRER INN REGIONAL MUSEUM
EGGENBURG
KRAHULETZ MUSEUM
EIBENSTEIN
OPEN-AIR MUSEUM
EISENSTADT
BURGENLAND MUSEUM
GRAZ
JOANNEUM PROVINCIAL MUSEUM OF MINERALOGY
JOANNEUM PROVINCIAL MUSEUM OF MINING, GEOLOGY AND TECHNOLOGY
HOHENAU
REGIONAL MUSEUM
HOLLABRUNN
MUNICIPAL MUSEUM
HOLLERSBACH
REGIONAL MUSEUM
HORN
HÖBARTH MUSEUM
INNSBRUCK
'FERDINANDEUM', TIROL MUSEUM
KLAGENFURT
CARINTHIA PROVINCIAL MUSEUM
KREMSMUNSTER
MONASTERY COLLECTIONS
KUFSTEIN
REGIONAL MUSEUM
LIENZ
EAST TIROL REGIONAL MUSEUM
LINZ
UPPER AUSTRIA PROVINCIAL MUSEUM
MATTSEE
REGIONAL MUSEUM
MISTELBACH
MUNICIPAL MUSEUM OF REGIONAL LIFE
MITTERNDORF
MUSEUM OF REGIONAL LIFE
MITTERSILL
REGIONAL MUSEUM
MÖDLING
MUNICIPAL MUSEUM
NEUNKIRCHEN
REGIONAL MUSEUM
OBERZEIRING
DEMONSTRATION MINE AND MUSEUM
ORTH
REGIONAL MUSEUM
RETZ
MUNICIPAL MUSEUM
SALZBURG
NATURE HOUSE
ST. PÖLTEN
DIOCESAN MUSEUM
SEITENSTETTEN
COLLECTIONS OF THE BENEDICTINE ABBEY
SPITAL
REGIONAL MUSEUM
STEGERSBACH
SOUTH BURGENLAND COUNTRYSIDE MUSEUM
STOCKERAU
DISTRICT MUSEUM
TRAUTENFELS
COUNTRYSIDE MUSEUM
TULLN
REGIONAL MUSEUM
VIGAUN
REGIONAL MUSEUM
VIENNA
FLORISDORF DISTRICT MUSEUM
HIETZING DISTRICT MUSEUM
MUSEUM OF THE FEDERAL GEOLOGICAL INSTITUTE
MUSEUM OF THE PROVINCE OF LOWER AUSTRIA
NATURAL HISTORY MUSEUM: GEOLOGY AND PALAEONTOLOGY COLLECTIONS
NATURAL HISTORY MUSEUM: MINERALOGICAL-PETROGRAPHICAL SECTION
WAIDHOFEN AN DER YBBS
REGIONAL MUSEUM
WELS
MUNICIPAL MUSEUM

BANGLADESH

DACCA
GEOLOGY MUSEUM
SOIL SCIENCE MUSEUM

BELGIUM

ANTWERP
MUSEUM OF CONCHOLOGY
BRUSSELS
MUSEUM OF THE ROYAL BELGIAN INSTITUTE OF NATURAL SCIENCES
HAN-SUR-LESSE
GROTTO MUSEUM
MONS
MUSEUM OF NATURAL HISTORY
TERVUEREN
ROYAL CENTRAL AFRICAN MUSEUM
TOURNAI
MUSEUM OF NATURAL HISTORY
MUSEUM OF PALAEONTOLOGY AND PREHISTORY

BRAZIL

ARACAJU
MUSEUM OF THE HISTORICAL AND GEOGRAPHICAL INSTITUTE
CAMPINAS
MUNICIPAL MUSEUM
CAXIAS DO SUL
MUSEUM OF POPULAR TRADITIONS
FLORIANÓPOLIS
SAMBAGUI MUSEUM OF MAN
FORTALEZA
DIAS DA ROCHA MUSEUM
IJUÍ
MUSEUM OF ANTHROPOLOGY
PÔRTO ALEGRE
NATURAL HISTORY MUSEUM
RIO GRANDE MUSEUM OF THE NATURAL SCIENCES
RECIFE
MUSEUM OF NATURAL SCIENCES OF THE FEDERAL RURAL UNIVERSITY OF PERNAMBUCO
RIO CLARO
ARGEMIRO M. DIAS MUSEUM
RIO DE JANEIRO
MUSEUM OF THE GEOLOGICAL AND MINERALOGICAL DIVISION OF THE MINISTRY OF MINES AND ENERGY
NATIONAL MUSEUM
SÃO PAULO
GEOGRAPHICAL AND GEOLOGICAL MUSEUM

BULGARIA

BOURGAS
REGIONAL MUSEUM OF HISTORY
KAZANLUK
NATIONAL MUSEUM
KOBEL
NATURAL HISTORY MUSEUM
PLOVDIV
NATURAL SCIENCE MUSEUM
RUSE
REGIONAL MUSEUM OF HISTORY
SOFIA
NATIONAL ZOOLOGICAL MUSEUM
VARNA
NATURAL HISTORY MUSEUM

BURMA

RANGOON
NATURAL HISTORY MUSEUM

CANADA

ALGONQUIN
ALGONQUIN PROVINCIAL PARK VISITOR CENTRE
ATIKOKAN
QUETICO PROVINCIAL PARK MUSEUM
BONAVENTURE
BONAVENTURE ACADIAN MUSEUM
CALGARY
CALGARY ZOOLOGICAL GARDENS, PALAEONTOLOGICAL PARK
EASTEND
EASTEND SCHOOL MUSEUM
EDMONTON
MINERALOGY AND PALAEONTOLOGY MUSEUM OF THE UNIVERSITY OF ALBERTA
UNIVERSITY OF ALBERTA GEOLOGY MUSEUM
GRANDE PRAIRIE
GRANDE PRAIRIE PIONEER MUSEUM
HALIFAX
SCIENCE MUSEUM
HANEY
DYCH'S DINOSAUR PARK
KINGSTON
GEOLOGICAL MUSEUM
LACHINE
SAINTE-ANNE MUSEUM
MONTREAL
REDPATH MUSEUM
OTTAWA
NATIONAL MUSEUM OF NATURAL SCIENCES
PATRICIA
DINOSAUR PROVINCIAL PARK
QUEBEC
MUSEUM OF MINERALOGY AND GEOLOGY
REGINA
SASKATCHEWAN MUSEUM OF NATURAL HISTORY
ROSE BAY
THE OVENS NATURAL PARK AND MUSEUM
SAINT JOHN
THE NEW BRUNSWICK MUSEUM
SAINT-LAURENT
MUSEUM OF THE NUNS OF THE HOLY CROSS
TORONTO
ROYAL ONTARIO MUSEUM
TROIS RIVIÈRES
MUSEUM OF PREHISTORIC ARCHAEOLOGY
VANCOUVER
CENTENNIAL MUSEUM
M. Y. WILLIAMS GEOLOGICAL MUSEUM
VICTORIA
BRITISH COLUMBIA MINERAL MUSEUM
WINNIPEG
MANITOBA MUSEUM OF MAN AND NATURE
UNIVERSITY OF MANITOBA, MINERALOGY MUSEUM
YELLOWKNIFE
MUSEUM OF THE NORTH

CHAD

FORT LAMY
CHAD NATIONAL MUSEUM

CHILE

SANTIAGO
MUSEUM OF NATURAL HISTORY
NATIONAL MUSEUM OF NATURAL HISTORY
NATURAL HISTORY MUSEUM
EMILIO AND DUNCAN WAGNER ARCHAEOLOGICAL MUSEUM
VALPARAISO
NATURAL HISTORY MUSEUM

CHINA, P.R.

HANGCHOW (HANG ZHOU)
CHEKIANG PROVINCIAL MUSEUM
LUO YANG
TOWN MUSEUM
PEKING
CULTURAL PALACE OF THE MINORITIES
NATURAL HISTORY MUSEUM
SHANGHAI
MUSEUM OF NATURAL SCIENCES
TIENSIN (TIANJING)
PEOPLE'S HALL OF SCIENCE

COLOMBIA

BOGOTA
MUSEUM OF NATURAL HISTORY
CALI
MUSEUM OF NATURAL HISTORY
MEDELLÍN
MINERALOGICAL MUSEUM
MUSEUM OF NATURAL SCIENCES

CONGO, POPULAR REPUBLIC OF

BRAZZAVILLE
MUSEUM OF EARTH SCIENCES

CUBA

HABANA
FELIPE POEY MUSEUM
SANTIAGO DE CUBA
SCIENCE MUSEUM

CZECHOSLOVAKIA

AŠ
MUNICIPAL MUSEUM
BANSKÁ ŠTIAVNICA
MINING MUSEUM
BARDEJOV
ŠARIŠ MUSEUM
BECHYNĚ
CERAMICS MUSEUM
BENÁTKY NAD JIZEROU
MUNICIPAL MUSEUM
BOJKOVICE
LOCAL MUSEUM
BOJNICE
REGIONAL MUSEUM
BRANDÝS NAD LABEM- STANÁ BOLESLAV
PRAGUE-VÝCHOD DISTRICT MUSEUM
BRATISLAVA
SLOVAKIAN NATIONAL MUSEUM: NATURAL HISTORY COLLECTIONS
BRNO
MORAVIAN MUSEUM: ANTHROPOLOGICAL MUSEUM
MORAVIAN MUSEUM: NATURAL HISTORY AND HISTORY COLLECTIONS
ČELČICE
ČELČICE MUSEUM
ČERVENÝ KLÁŠTOR
MONASTERY MUSEUM
ČESKE BUDĚJOVICE
MUSEUM OF SOUTHERN CZECHOSLOVAKIA
ČESKÝ DUB
KAROLINY SVĚTLÉ MUSEUM
ČESKÝ KRUMLOV
REGIONAL MUSEUM
CHOELŇ
ORLICKÝ MUSEUM
CHOMUTOV
REGIONAL MUSEUM
DĚČÍN
DISTRICT MUSEUM
GOTTWALDOV
GOTTWALDOV MUSEUM OF SOUTHERN MORAVIA
HLINSKO
REGIONAL MUSEUM AND ART GALLERY
HLUBOKÁ NAD VLTAVOU
MUSEUM OF THE COUNTRYSIDE
HOŘOVICE
MUNICIPAL MUSEUM
HRADEC KRÁLOVÉ
REGIONAL MUSEUM: DEPARTMENT OF NATURAL HISTORY
HRANICE NA MORAVĚ
MUSEUM OF CENTRAL MORAVIA
JÁCHYMOV
MUNICIPAL MUSEUM
JAVOŘÍČKO
CAVE MUSEUM
JIČÍN
DISTRICT MUSEUM
JIHLAVA
VYSOČINY MUSEUM
KAMENICE NAD LIPOU
REGIONAL MUSEUM
KARLOVY VARY
KARLOVY MUSEUM
KAŠPERSKÉ HORY
ŠUMAVY MUSEUM
KELČ
KELČ MUSEUM
KLADNO
DISTRICT MUSEUM
KLATOVY
REGIONAL MUSEUM
KOŠICE
MUSEUM OF EASTERN SLOVAKIA
LIBEREC
MUSEUM OF NORTHERN CZECHOSLOVAKIA
LIPOVÁ LÁZNĚ
REGIONAL MUSEUM
LIPTOVSKÝ MIKULÁŠ
MUSEUM OF THE SLOVAKIAN LIMESTONE FORMATION
LITOMĚŘICE
DISTRICT MUSEUM
MARIÁNSKE LÁZNĚ
MUNICIPAL MUSEUM
MICHALOVCE
ZEMPLIN MUSEUM
MLADEČ
CAVE MUSEUM
OPAVA
SILESIAN MUSEUM: NATURAL HISTORY COLLECTIONS
ORAVSKY PODZÁMOK
ORAVA MUSEUM
OSTRAVA
OSTRAVA MUSEUM
PARDUBICE
MUSEUM OF EASTERN CZECHOSLOVAKIA
PLZEŇ
MUSEUM OF WESTERN CZECHOSLOVAKIA: NATURAL HISTORY COLLECTIONS
PODĚBRADY
DISTRICT MUSEUM
POPRAD
TATRA MUSEUM
PRAGUE
NATIONAL MUSEUM: MUSEUM OF NATURAL HISTORY
PREŠOV
MUSEUM OF THE SLOVAK REPUBLIC
PŘIBRAM
DISTRICT MUSEUM
ROŽŇAVA
MINING AND METALWORKING MUSEUM
RUŽOMBEROK
LIPTOV MUSEUM
SOBĚSLAV
MUSEUM OF SOUTHERN CZECHOSLOVAKIA
SOKOLOV
MINING MUSEUM
TATRANSKÁ LOMNICA
MUSEUM OF THE TATRA NATIONAL PARK (TANAP)
TEPLICE NAD BEČVOU
REGIONAL MUSEUM
TRENČÍN
TRENČÍN MUSEUM
TRNAVA
MUSEUM OF WESTERN SLOVAKIA
VRCHLABÍ
KRKONOŠ MUSEUM (ASSOCIATED WITH KRKONOŠSKÝ NATIONAL PARK)
ŽILINA
POVAŽIA MUSEUM AND ART GALLERY

DENMARK

ÅRHUS
NATURAL HISTORY MUSEUM
COPENHAGEN
MINERALOGICAL MUSEUM
ZOOLOGICAL MUSEUM

ECUADOR

GUAYAQUIL
TOWN MUSEUM
QUITO
NATURAL HISTORY MUSEUM

EGYPT, ARAB REPUBLIC OF

CAIRO
GEOLOGICAL MUSEUM

FINLAND

ESPOO
MUSEUM OF THE GEOLOGICAL INSTITUTE
HELSINKI
UNIVERSITY MUSEUM OF ZOOLOGY
JYVÄSKYLÄ
UNIVERSITY MUSEUM
PALLASTUNTURI
NATURAL HISTORY MUSEUM
PORVOO
MUSEUM OF NATURAL HISTORY
TAMPERE
NATURAL HISTORY MUSEUM
VAASA
EAST BOTHNIA AUSTRALIS MUSEUM

FRANCE

ALÈS
ALÈS MUSEUM
ALLAUCH
MUSEUM OF OLD ALLAUCH
ANGERS
MUSEUM OF PALAEONTOLOGY AND NATURAL HISTORY
ARUDY
OSSAU MUSEUM
AUTUN
AUTUN NATURAL HISTORY MUSEUM
AVIGNON
RÉQUIEN MUSEUM OF NATURAL HISTORY
BÉZIERS
MUSEUM OF NATURAL HISTORY
BOUXWILLER
BOUXWILLER MUSEUM
CHAMBÉRY
MUSEUM OF NATURAL HISTORY
CHERBOURG
MUSEUM OF NATURAL HISTORY AND ETHNOGRAPHY

CLERMONT-FERRAND
LECOQ MUSEUM
DIJON
MUSEUM OF NATURAL HISTORY
GAILLAC
NATURAL HISTORY MUSEUM
LE HAVRE
MUSEUM OF NATURAL HISTORY
JARVILLE- LA-MALGRANGE
MUSEUM OF THE HISTORY OF IRON
LANGRES
SAINT-DIDIER MUSEUM
LILLE
MUSEUM OF NATURAL HISTORY
LODÈVE
MUSEUM OF NATURAL HISTORY
LYON
MUSEUM OF NATURAL HISTORY
MENDE
MUSEUM OF THE LOZÈRE SOCIETY OF LETTERS, SCIENCES AND ARTS
MONTAUBAN
VICTOR BRUN MUSEUM OF NATURAL HISTORY
MOUTIERS
MUSEUM OF THE ACADEMY OF THE VAL D'ISÈRE
NANCY
MUSEUM OF EARTH SCIENCES
NANTES
MUSEUM OF NATURAL HISTORY
NICE
INTERNATIONAL MUSEUM OF MALACOLOGY
NATURAL HISTORY MUSEUM
ORLÉANS
MUSEUM OF NATURAL SCIENCE
PARIS
MUSEUM OF THE HIGHER SCHOOL OF MINES
MUSEUM OF MINERALOGY
MUSEUM OF NATURAL HISTORY
LE PUY-EN-VELAY
CROZATIER MUSEUM
SAINT- ANTONIN-NOBLE-VAL
MUSEUM OF PREHISTORY, ARCHAEOLOGY AND ETHNOGRAPHY
SAINT-OMER
HENRI DUPUIS MUSEUM
SEMUR-EN-AUXOIS
SEMUR MUSEUM
TOULON
NATURAL HISTORY MUSEUM
TOULOUSE
MUSEUM OF NATURAL HISTORY
TRÉGASTEL
MUSEUM OF PREHISTORY
VALENCE
MUSEUM OF FINE ART AND NATURAL HISTORY

GDR

ALLSTEDT
REGIONAL MUSEUM
ALTENBURG
'MAURITIANUM' MUSEUM OF NATURAL HISTORY
ANNABERG-BUCHHOLZ
ERZGEBIRG MUSEUM: DEPARTMENT OF NATURAL HISTORY
ASCHERSLEBEN
REGIONAL MUSEUM
AUE
REGIONAL COLLECTION
BAD DURRENBERG
BORLACH MUSEUM
BERLIN
CENTRAL COLLECTION OF THE STATE GEOLOGICAL MUSEUM
HUMBOLDT UNIVERSITY: MUSEUM OF MINERALOGY AND PETROGRAPHY
HUMBOLDT UNIVERSITY: MUSEUM OF PALAEONTOLOGY
BITTERFELD
DISTRICT MUSEUM
BRAND-ERBISDORF
REGIONAL MINING MUSEUM
DERMBACH
DISTRICT MUSEUM
DESSAU
MUSEUM OF NATURAL HISTORY AND PREHISTORY
DRESDEN
STATE MUSEUM OF MINERALOGY AND GEOLOGY
EISFELD
OTTO LUDWIG REGIONAL MUSEUM
EISLEBEN
NATURAL HISTORY COLLECTION
ERFURT
NATURAL SCIENCE MUSEUM
FALKENSEE
REGIONAL ROOM
FREIBERG
GEOLOGICAL INSTITUTE
INSTITUTE OF FUEL
MUSEUM OF NATURAL HISTORY
SCIENTIFIC COLLECTION OF FREIBERG MINING ACADEMY
FREITAL
REGIONAL HOUSE
GERA
NATURAL HISTORY MUSEUM
GEYER
REGIONAL MUSEUM
GLAUCHAU
MUNICIPAL MUSEUM AND ART COLLECTION
GÖRLITZ
STATE MUSEUM OF NATURAL HISTORY
GOLDBERG
DISTRICT MUSEUM
GOTHA
NATURAL HISTORY MUSEUM
GREIFSWALD
COLLECTION OF THE ERNST MORITZ ARNDT UNIVERSITY: GEOLOGICAL AND PALAEONTOLOGICAL INSTITUTE
COLLECTION OF THE ERNST MORITZ ARNDT UNIVERSITY: MINERALOGICAL AND PETROGRAPHICAL INSTITUTE
HALLE
COLLECTION OF THE DEPARTMENT OF MINERALOGY AND PETROLOGY OF MARTIN LUTHER UNIVERSITY
HIDDENSEE
BIOLOGICAL RESEARCH INSTITUTE OF THE ERNST MORITZ ARNDT UNIVERSITY, GREIFSWALD: BIRD-WATCHING STATION
HIDDENSEE ISLAND REGIONAL MUSEUM
HOHENLEUBEN
HOHENLEUBEN - REICHSFELS MUSEUM
ILMENAU
REGIONAL MUSEUM
JENA
COLLECTION OF THE DEPARTMENT OF GEOLOGY AND PALAEONTOLOGY OF THE FRIEDRICH SCHILLER UNIVERSITY
COLLECTION OF THE DEPARTMENT OF MINERALOGY AND PETROGRAPHY OF THE FRIEDRICH SCHILLER UNIVERSITY
PHYLETIC MUSEUM
KAMENZ
WEST LAUSITZ MUSEUM
KARL MARX STADT
NATURAL HISTORY MUSEUM
LEIPZIG
INSTITUTE OF GEOLOGY AND PALAEONTOLOGY
INSTITUTE OF MINERALOGY AND PETROGRAPHY
MUSEUM OF NATURAL SCIENCES
LIEBSTADT
CASTLE KUCKUCKSTEIN REGIONAL MUSEUM
MAGDEBURG
LIFE AND RESOURCES OF THE WELTALL
MARKRANSTÄDT
REGIONAL MUSEUM
MEERANE
REGIONAL MUSEUM
MÜHLHAUSEN
DISTRICT MUSEUM
MYLAU
REGIONAL MUSEUM
ROSTOCK
COLLECTION OF THE DEPARTMENT OF GEOLOGY AND PALAEONTOLOGY
COLLECTION OF THE DEPARTMENT OF MINERALOGY AND PETROGRAPHY
ROTTLEBEN
BARBAROSSA CAVERN
RÜBELAND
RÜBELAND STALACTITE CAVERNS
SANGERHAUSEN
SPENGLER MUSEUM
SCHMALKALDEN
DISTRICT MUSEUM
SCHNEEBERG
MUSEUM FOR POPULAR ART OF THE MINING COMMUNITY
SEIFHENNERSDORF
NATURAL HISTORY AND REGIONAL MUSEUM
SENFTENBERG
DISTRICT MUSEUM
WALDENBURG
REGIONAL MUSEUM AND NATURAL HISTORY COLLECTION
WEIMAR
MUSEUM OF NATURAL HISTORY
MUSEUM OF THE PREHISTORY AND EARLY HISTORY OF THURINGIA
WEISSENFELS
MUNICIPAL MUSEUM
WERDER
ORCHARD MUSEUM
ZITTAU
DR. CURT HEINKE MUSEUM
ZWICKAU
MUNICIPAL MUSEUM

GFR

ASCHAFFENBURG
NATURAL HISTORY MUSEUM
AUGSBURG
NATURAL HISTORY MUSEUM
BAD KREUZNACH
KARL GEIB MUSEUM
BAD ORB
SPESSART MUSEUM
BAMBERG
NATURAL HISTORY MUSEUM
BANZ
COLLECTION OF PETRIFIED OBJECTS
BIELEFELD
NATURAL HISTORY MUSEUM
BOCHUM
GEOLOGICAL MUSEUM OF THE RUHR MINING DISTRICT
BONN
UNIVERSITY MUSEUM OF MINERALOGY AND PETROLOGY
BREMEN
OVERSEAS MUSEUM
BREMERVÖRDE
DISTRICT MUSEUM
BÜNDE
DISTRICT MUSEUM
CLAUSTHAL-ZELLERFELD
COLLECTIONS OF THE GEOLOGICAL INSTITUTE: CLAUSTHAL TECHNICAL UNIVERSITY
MINERAL COLLECTION OF THE ACADEMY OF MINES
COBURG
MUSEUM OF NATURAL SCIENCE
COESFELD
REGIONAL MUSEUM
DARMSTADT
HESSE MUSEUM
DATTELN
HERMANN GROCHTMANN MUSEUM
DAUN
REGIONAL MUSEUM
DONAUESCHINGEN
COLLECTIONS OF THE PRINCES OF FÜRSTENBERG
DÜSSELDORF
LÖBBECKE MUSEUM

EICHSTÄTT
NATURAL SCIENCE COLLECTIONS

ERLANGEN
GEOLOGICAL COLLECTION OF THE UNIVERSITY OF ERLANGEN-NÜRNBERG
MINERALOGICAL COLLECTION OF THE UNIVERSITY OF ERLANGEN-NÜRNBERG

ESSEN
RUHR AND REGIONAL MUSEUM

FRANKFURT
SENCKENBERG NATURAL HISTORY MUSEUM AND RESEARCH INSTITUTE

FREIBURG IM BREISGAU
NATURAL HISTORY MUSEUM

GEILENKIRCHEN
REGIONAL MUSEUM

GEROLSTEIN
DAUN DISTRICT MUSEUM

GIFHORN
DISTRICT MUSEUM

GLADBECK
GLADBECK TOWN MUSEUM

GÖPPINGEN
DR. ENGEL MUSEUM

GOSLAR
COLLECTION ILLUSTRATING THE CULTURAL HISTORY OF GERMANY AND EUROPE

GREVENBROICH
GEOLOGICAL MUSEUM

HAMBURG
ALTONA MUSEUM
HELMS MUSEUM

HANNOVER
LAND MUSEUM OF LOWER SAXONY: DEPARTMENT OF NATURAL HISTORY

HELMSTEDT
DISTRICT MUSEUM

HERNE
EMSCHERTAL MUSEUM

HILDESHEIM
ROEMER-PELIZAEUS MUSEUM

HOFGEISMAR
REGIONAL MUSEUM

HUSUM
NISSEN HOUSE

IDAR-OBERSTEIN
EXHIBITION OF GEM-STONES
MINERAL MUSEUM
REGIONAL MUSEUM

KARLSRUHE
LAND NATURAL HISTORY COLLECTIONS

KASSEL
NATURAL HISTORY MUSEUM

KEHL
HANAU MUSEUM

KIEL
INSTITUTE AND MUSEUM OF MINERALOGY, PETROLOGY, GEOLOGY AND PALAEONTOLOGY
SCHLESWIG-HOLSTEIN TRAVELLING MUSEUM

KÖNIGSLUTTER
KLAGES COLLECTION

KÖNIGSWINTER
SIEBENGEBIRGE MUSEUM

KONSTANZ
LAKE CONSTANCE MUSEUM OF NATURAL HISTORY

KORBACH
KORBACH REGIONAL MUSEUM

KULMBACH-PLÄSSENBURG
UPPER MAIN REGIONAL MUSEUM

LAICHINGEN
LAICHINGEN CAVE MUSEUM

LEONBERG
MUSEUM OF GEOLOGY AND PALAEONTOLOGY

LÖRRACH
REGIONAL MUSEUM

LÜBECK
NATURAL HISTORY MUSEUM

LUDWIGSBURG
STATE MUSEUM OF NATURAL HISTORY

LÜNEN
MUNICIPAL MUSEUM

MAINZ
NATURAL HISTORY MUSEUM

MARL
REGIONAL MUSEUM

MAXBERG
SOLENHOFER COMPANY MUSEUM

MAYEN
EIFEL MUSEUM

MENDEN
MENDEN REGIONAL MUSEUM

MINDEN
MINDEN MUSEUM OF HISTORY, ETHNOLOGY AND REGIONAL STUDIES

MÖRNSHEIM
MUSEUM OF PETRIFIED OBJECTS

MÜNCHEN
BAVARIAN STATE COLLECTIONS OF GENERAL AND APPLIED GEOLOGY
BAVARIAN STATE COLLECTION OF PALAEONTOLOGY AND HISTORICAL GEOLOGY
GERMAN MUSEUM
MINERALOGY COLLECTION

MÜNSTER
MUSEUM OF CRYSTALS AND ROCKS
UNIVERSITY OF MÜNSTER MUSEUM OF GEOLOGY AND PALAEONTOLOGY

NEUSTADT-WEISTRASSE
NATURAL HISTORY MUSEUM

NÜMBRECHT
MUSEUM OF THE OBERBERG REGION

NÜRNBERG
MAN AND NATURE MUSEUM

OBERKIRCHEN
MINERALOGICAL MUSEUM

OLDENBURG
STATE MUSEUM OF NATURAL HISTORY AND PREHISTORY

OSNABRÜCK
MUNICIPAL MUSEUM

PADERBORN
REGIONAL MUSEUM OF NATURAL HISTORY

REGENSBURG
NATURAL HISTORY MUSEUM

RÜSSELSHEIM
LOCAL MUSEUM

SÄCKINGEN
UPPER RHINE MUSEUM

SCHÖNINGEN
REGIONAL MUSEUM

SCHWÄBISCH-GMÜND
SCHWÄBISCH-GMÜND MUSEUM

SCHWABMÜNCHEN
REGIONAL MUSEUM

SCHWENNINGEN
SCHWENNINGEN REGIONAL MUSEUM

SCHWERTE
MUSEUM OF THE RUHR VALLEY

SPAICHINGEN
MUSEUM OF GEOLOGY AND PREHISTORY

STADE
MUSEUM OF PREHISTORY

STUTTGART
STATE MUSEUM OF NATURAL HISTORY

TÜBINGEN
COLLECTION OF THE UNIVERSITY INSTITUTE OF GEOLOGY AND PALAEONTOLOGY
MUSEUM OF THE UNIVERSITY INSTITUTE OF MINERALOGY AND PETROGRAPHY

VON DER HEYDT
GEOLOGICAL COLLECTION OF THE SAARBRÜCKEN SCHOOL OF MINING

WANNE-EICKEL
REGIONAL MUSEUM

WEWELSBURG
DISTRICT MUSEUM

WIESBADEN
NATURAL SCIENCES COLLECTION

WILHELMSHAVEN
COASTAL AND SHIPPING MUSEUM

WITTEN
REGIONAL MUSEUM

WÜLFRATH
NIEDERBERG REGIONAL MUSEUM

WÜRZBURG
UNIVERSITY OF WÜRZBURG COLLECTION OF MINERALOGY AND PETROGRAPHY

GIBRALTAR

GIBRALTAR
GIBRALTAR MUSEUM

GREAT BRITAIN

ABINGDON
BOROUGH MUSEUM

BELFAST
QUEEN'S UNIVERSITY

BIRMINGHAM
GEOLOGICAL DEPARTMENT MUSEUM

BLACKBURN
BLACKBURN MUSEUM AND ART GALLERY

BOURNEMOUTH
BOURNEMOUTH NATURAL SCIENCE SOCIETY'S MUSEUM

BUXTON
BUXTON MUSEUM

CAMBRIDGE
UNIVERSITY MUSEUM OF MINERALOGY AND PETROLOGY

CARDIFF
NATIONAL MUSEUM OF WALES

CARLISLE
MUSEUM AND ART GALLERY

CHEDDAR
GOUGH'S CAVES MUSEUM

CROMARTY
HUGH MILLER'S COTTAGE

DEVIZES
DEVIZES MUSEUM

DUDLEY
DUDLEY MUSEUM AND ART GALLERY

EDINBURGH
ROYAL SCOTTISH MUSEUM

ELGIN
ELGIN MUSEUM

ETON
ETON COLLEGE NATURAL HISTORY SOCIETY MUSEUM

FORRES
FALCONER MUSEUM

GLASGOW
CITY OF GLASGOW CORPORATION ART GALLERY AND MUSEUM
HUNTERIAN MUSEUM

LIVERPOOL
CITY OF LIVERPOOL MUSEUMS

LONDON
BRITISH MUSEUM (NATURAL HISTORY)
GEOLOGICAL MUSEUM

MANCHESTER
MANCHESTER MUSEUM

NEWCASTLE-UPON-TYNE
UNIVERSITY OF NEWCASTLE-UPON-TYNE
UNIVERSITY OF NEWCASTLE-UPON-TYNE

NOTTINGHAM
NATURAL HISTORY MUSEUM

OXFORD
OXFORD UNIVERSITY MUSEUM

REIGATE
HOLMESDALE NATURAL HISTORY CLUB MUSEUM

SANDOWN
MUSEUM OF ISLE OF WIGHT GEOLOGY

SETTLE
PIG YARD CLUB MUSEUM

TEESSIDE
DORMAN MUSEUM

TRURO
COUNTY MUSEUM AND ART GALLERY

WELLS
WELLS MUSEUM

GREECE

ATHENS
GEOLOGICAL AND PALAEONTOLOGICAL MUSEUM

GUATEMALA

GUATEMALA CITY
MUSEUM OF NATURAL HISTORY

HUNGARY

BUDAPEST
NATURAL HISTORY MUSEUM
MISKOLC-HÁMOR
CENTRAL MUSEUM OF METALLURGY
SÜMEG
KISFALUDY MEMORIAL MUSEUM

ICELAND

REYKJAVIK
MUSEUM OF NATURAL HISTORY

INDIA

AGRA
ST. JOHN'S COLLEGE MUSEUM
ANNAMALAINAGAR
ZOOLOGY MUSEUM
BANGALORE
CENTRAL COLLEGE MUSEUMS
MYSORE GOVERNMENT MUSEUM
BHAWANAGAR
GANDHI SMRITI MUSEUMS
BHUBANESHWAR
ORISSA STATE MUSEUM
BHUJ
KUTCH MUSEUM
BOMBAY
VICTORIA AND ALBERT MUSEUM
CALCUTTA
INDIAN MUSEUM
COIMBATORE
AGRICULTURAL COLLEGE MUSEUM
SOUTHERN FOREST RANGERS COLLEGE AND RESEARCH CENTRE
GAUHATI
COMMERCIAL MUSEUM
GWALIOR
STATE MUSEUM
IMPHAL
MANIPUR STATE MUSEUM
JAMMU
DOGRA ART GALLERY
JODHPUR
STATE MUSEUM
LUCKNOW
UNIVERSITY OF LUCKNOW MUSEUMS
MADRAS
CENTRAL INDUSTRIAL MUSEUM
THE GOVERNMENT MUSEUM AND NATIONAL ART GALLERY
NAGPUR
CENTRAL MUSEUM
PATIALA
STATE MUSEUM
PATNA
PATNA MUSEUM
PUDDUKKOTTAI
GOVERNMENT MUSEUM
TAMLUK
HAMILTON HIGH SCHOOL MUSEUM
TIRUCHIRAPALLI
NATURAL HISTORY MUSEUM
TRICHUR
STATE MUSEUM
TRIVANDRUM
NATURAL HISTORY MUSEUM

INDONESIA

BANDUNG
GEOLOGICAL MUSEUM

IRAQ

BAGHDAD
IRAQ NATURAL HISTORY MUSEUM

ISRAEL

DAN
USSISHKIN HOUSE
DEGANIA
A. D. GORDON MUSEUM
HAIFA
MUSEUM OF NATURAL HISTORY AND PREHISTORY
JERUSALEM
MUSEUM OF NATURAL HISTORY
POST EMEK SOREK
SHEPHELA REGIONAL MUSEUM

ITALY

BARI
COLLECTIONS OF THE INSTITUTE OF GEOLOGY AND PALAEONTOLOGY
COLLECTIONS OF THE INSTITUTE OF PETROGRAPHY AND MINERALOGY
BESOZZO
BRUNELLA GEOLOGICAL MUSEUM
BIELLA
COLLECTIONS OF THE ITALIAN ALPINE CLUB
QUINTINO SELLA INSTITUTE COLLECTIONS
BOLOGNA
CAPELLINI MUSEUM
MUSEUM OF THE INSTITUTE OF MINERALOGY AND PETROGRAPHY
BORGO GROTTA GIGANTE
MUSEUM OF SPELEOLOGY AND GROTTOS
CAGLIARI
MUSEUM OF THE INSTITUTE OF GEOLOGY AND PALAEONTOLOGY
MUSEUM OF MINERALOGY AND PETROGRAPHY
CALTANISSETTA
MUSEUM OF MINERALOGY AND PALAEONTOLOGY
CAMERINO
COLLECTION OF FOSSILS, MINERALS AND ROCKS
CASTELL'ARQUATA
FOSSIL COLLECTION OF THE PIACENZA DISTRICT
CATANIA
COLLECTIONS OF THE INSTITUTE OF GEOLOGY
FABRIANO
CANAVARI MUSEUM OF MINERALOGY
FIESOLE
MUSEUM OF STONES AND FOSSILS
FLORENCE
MUSEUM OF GEOLOGY AND PALAEONTOLOGY
MUSEUM OF MINERALOGY
SCIENTIFIC COLLECTIONS
GENOA
COLLECTIONS OF THE INSTITUTE OF GEOLOGY
COLLECTIONS OF NATURAL HISTORY
COLLECTIONS OF THE UNIVERSITY INSTITUTE OF MINERALOGY
NATURAL HISTORY MUSEUM
PETROGRAPHIC MUSEUM
GORLA MINORA
MUSEUM OF NATURAL HISTORY
GROSSETO
MUSEUM OF NATURAL HISTORY
IGLESIAS
MUSEUM OF THE TECHNICAL INSTITUTE
L'AQUILA
PALAEONTOLOGICAL MUSEUM
LA SPEZIA
MUSEUM OF NATURAL HISTORY AND ETHNOGRAPHY
LIVORNO
MUNICIPAL MUSEUM OF NATURAL HISTORY
LUCCA
NATURAL HISTORY MUSEUM
MASSA MARITIMA
MINERALOGICAL COLLECTION
MILAN
CIVIC MUSEUM OF NATURAL HISTORY
COLLECTIONS OF THE INSTITUTE OF GEOLOGY
COLLECTION OF THE INSTITUTE OF MINERALOGY, PETROGRAPHY AND GEOCHEMISTRY
MUNICIPAL MUSEUM OF NATURAL HISTORY
MODENA
CITY MUSEUM
MUSEUM OF THE INSTITUTE OF MINERALOGY
MUSEUM OF THE INSTITUTE OF PALAEONTOLOGY
MONFORTE D'ALBA
ORNITHOLOGICAL AND MALACOLOGICAL COLLECTION
MONTEVARCHI
PALAEONTOLOGICAL MUSEUM
NAPLES
MUSEUM OF GEOLOGY AND PALAEONTOLOGY
NARNI
MELI PALAEONTOLOGICAL COLLECTION
PADUA
MUSEUM OF THE INSTITUTE OF GEOLOGY
MUSEUM OF THE INSTITUTE OF PETROGRAPHY AND MINERALOGY
PALERMO
MUSEUM OF MINERALOGY
MUSEUM OF PALAEONTOLOGY AND GEOLOGY
PARMA
COLLECTIONS OF THE INSTITUTE OF MINERALOGY
MUSEUM OF PALAEONTOLOGY
PAVIA
MUSEUM OF THE INSTITUTE OF GEOLOGY
MUSEUM OF THE INSTITUTE OF MINERALOGY AND PETROGRAPHY
PERTICARTA
MUSEUM OF THE HISTORY OF MINERALS
PERUGIA
NATURAL HISTORY COLLECTION
PISA
MUSEUM OF GEOLOGY AND PALAEONTOLOGY
POMPEI
VESUVIAN MUSEUM
REGGIO EMILIA
CIVIC MUSEUM
LAZZARO SPALLANZANI MUSEUM OF NATURAL HISTORY
ROME
COLLECTIONS OF THE ITALIAN INSTITUTE OF HUMAN PALAEONTOLOGY
MUSEUM OF THE GEOLOGICAL SERVICE
MUSEUM OF THE INSTITUTE OF MINERALOGY
ZOOLOGICAL MUSEUM
SASSARI
COLLECTION OF THE INSTITUTE OF MINERALOGY
SIENA
GEO-MINERALOGICAL MUSEUM
TERMINI IMERESE
NATURAL HISTORY COLLECTION
TRIESTE
MUSEUM OF MINERALOGY
NATURAL HISTORY MUSEUM
TRULLI
CASTELLANA CAVES
TURIN
MUSEUM OF GEOLOGY AND PALAEONTOLOGY
SCIENTIFIC COLLECTIONS OF THE MUNICIPAL MUSEUM
UDINE
FOSSIL COLLECTION
VERONA
MUSEUM OF NATURAL HISTORY
VESTENANUOVA
FOSSIL MUSEUM
VICENZA
NATURAL HISTORY MUSEUM

JAPAN

AKKESHI-MACHI
AKKESHI MUSEUM OF HOKKAIDO UNIVERSITY

ASAHI-MACHI
MIYAZAKI OPEN-AIR MUSEUM

FUKUI-SHI
FUKUI MUNICIPAL NATURAL HISTORY MUSEUM

FUTTSU
FUTTSU OCEANOGRAPHIC MUSEUM OF CHIBA PREFECTURE

HAKODATE-SHI
HAKODATE MUNICIPAL MUSEUM

HAKONE-MACHI
GORA PARK HAKONE NATURAL HISTORY MUSEUM

HIWA-MACHI
HIWA MUSEUM OF NATURAL HISTORY

HOROBETSU-MACHI
NOBORIBETSU HOT SPRING MUSEUM

IBURI-SHICHO
THE VOLCANO MUSEUM

KAGOSHIMA-SHI
KAGOSHIMA PREFECTURAL MUSEUM

KOMATSU-SHI
KOMATSU MUNICIPAL MUSEUM

MINOBU-MACHI
THE YAMANASHI PREFECTURAL MUSEUM OF FUJI NATIONAL PARK

MIYAZAKI-SHI
AGRICULTURAL MUSEUM OF MIYAZAKI UNIVERSITY

NAGOYA
MUNICIPAL SCIENCE MUSEUM

NARA-SHI
THE AYAMEIKE MUSEUM OF NATURAL HISTORY

NIKKO-SHI
NIKKO MUSEUM OF NATURAL HISTORY

NOGAMI-MACHI
CHICHIBU MUSEUM OF NATURAL HISTORY

OSAKA
NATURAL SCIENCE MUSEUM

SAIJO-SHI
SAIJO LOCAL MUSEUM

SAPPORO-SHI
NATURAL HISTORY MUSEUM OF HOKKAIDO UNIVERSITY

SAWADA-MACHI
SADO MUSEUM

SHIOBARA-MACHI
MUSEUM OF FOSSILISED LEAVES

SHUHO-MACHI
AKIYOSHIDAI MUSEUM OF NATURAL HISTORY

TAMANO-SHI
TAMANO MARINE MUSEUM

TOKYO
MEMORIAL HALL OF THE RECONSTRUCTION OF TOKYO
MUSEUM OF ART AND HISTORY OF THE UNIVERSITY OF TOKYO
NATIONAL SCIENCE MUSEUM
TOKYO-TO TAKAO MUSEUM OF NATURAL HISTORY

TOSAYAMADA-MACHI
THE RYUGADO MUSEUM

UME-MACHI
UME LOCAL MUSEUM

UOZU-SHI
UOZU BURIED FOREST MUSEUM

YAMAGUCHI-SHI
YAMAGUCHI PREFECTURAL MUSEUM

KENYA

NAIROBI
NATIONAL MUSEUM

LEBANON

BEIRUT
GEOLOGICAL MUSEUM

LIBYAN ARAB REPUBLIC

TRIPOLI
NATURAL HISTORY MUSEUM

MALTA

BIRZEBBUGA
GHAR DALAM CAVE AND MUSEUM

MEXICO

MEXICO CITY
MUSEUM OF NATURAL HISTORY
NATURAL HISTORY MUSEUM
UNIVERSITY MUSEUM OF SCIENCE AND ART

UNIVERSITY CITY
NATURAL HISTORY MUSEUM

MOZAMBIQUE

BEIRA
MUNICIPAL MUSEUM

LOURENÇO MARQUES
FREIRE DE ANDRADE MUSEUM

MANICA
MOSTRUÁRO DE MANICA MUSEUM

NETHERLANDS

AARDENBURG
DISTRICT MUSEUM

AMSTERDAM
GEOLOGICAL INSTITUTE OF THE UNIVERSITY OF AMSTERDAM

APPELSCHA
NATURAL HISTORY MUSEUM

DENEKAMP
'NATURE TEACHER' MUSEUM

ENSCHEDE
NATURAL HISTORY MUSEUM

FREDERIKSVORD
MIRAMAR MUSEUM OF THE SEA

'S GRAVENHAGE
'IN DER SCHULP' SHELL MUSEUM

GRONINGEN
GRONINGEN MUSEUM OF NATURAL HISTORY
NATIONAL UNIVERSITY: INSTITUTE OF BIOLOGY AND ARCHAEOLOGY

HAARLEM
TEYLER'S MUSEUM

HEERLEN
SOUTH LIMBURG GEOLOGICAL MUSEUM

LEEUWARDEN
FRISIAN MUSEUM OF NATURAL HISTORY

LEIDEN
NATIONAL MUSEUM OF GEOLOGY AND MINERALOGY
NATIONAL MUSEUM OF NATURAL HISTORY

LELYSTAD
LELYSTAD HARBOUR EXHIBITION BUILDING

MAASTRICHT
NATURAL HISTORY MUSEUM

ST. MICHIELSGESTEL
NATURAL HISTORY MUSEUM OF THE ROMAN CATHOLIC SCHOOL AND SEMINARY 'BEEKOLIET'

DEN OEVER
ZUIDERZEE WORKS INFORMATION CENTRE

ROTTERDAM
DIORAMA BUILDING OF THE NATURAL HISTORY MUSEUM
NATURAL HISTORY MUSEUM

SCHOKLAND
IJSSELMEER POLDER MUSEUM

SCHOONOORD
THE SEVEN MARKS

TILBURG
NATURAL HISTORY MUSEUM

NEW ZEALAND

AUCKLAND
AUCKLAND WAR MEMORIAL MUSEUM

CHRISTCHURCH
CANTERBURY MUSEUM
DEPARTMENTS OF BOTANY, GEOLOGY AND ZOOLOGY

CLYDE
VINCENT COUNTY AND DUNSTAN GOLDFIELDS MUSEUM

DUNEDIN
OTAGO MUSEUM
UNIVERSITY OF OTAGO

LOWER HUTT
NEW ZEALAND GEOLOGICAL SURVEY

MURCHISON
MURCHISON MUSEUM

NASEBY
MANIOTOTO EARLY SETTLERS' MUSEUM

NELSON
ISEL HOUSE
NELSON PROVINCIAL MUSEUM

OAMARU
NORTH OTAGO PIONEER GALLERY

THAMES
THAMES MINERALOGICAL MUSEUM

WANGANUI
WANGANUI PUBLIC MUSEUM

WELLINGTON
DOMINION MUSEUM
VICTORIA UNIVERSITY OF WELLINGTON

NICARAGUA

MANAGUA
MUSEUM OF NATURAL SCIENCE

NIGERIA

KADUNA
GEOLOGICAL SURVEY MUSEUM

NORWAY

BERGEN
GEOLOGICAL MUSEUM
MUSEUM OF NATURAL HISTORY

OSLO
MINERALOGICAL-GEOLOGICAL MUSEUM
PALAEONTOLOGY MUSEUM

TRONDHEIM
MUSEUM OF THE ROYAL NORWEGIAN SOCIETY OF SCIENCES AND LETTERS

PAKISTAN, WEST

PESHAWAR
PESHAWAR MUSEUM

QUETTA
GEOLOGICAL SURVEY OF PAKISTAN MUSEUM

PARAGUAY

ASUNCION
NATURAL SCIENCE MUSEUM OF THE INTERNATIONAL COLLEGE

PERU

LIMA
GEOLOGICAL MUSEUM OF THE NATIONAL UNIVERSITY OF ENGINEERING
JAVIER PRADO NATURAL HISTORY MUSEUM

PHILIPPINES

BAGUIO CITY
ST. LOUIS UNIVERSITY MUSEUM
CEBU CITY
UNIVERSITY MUSEUM
MANILA
MUSEUM OF ARTS AND SCIENCES
NATIONAL MUSEUM OF THE PHILIPPINES

POLAND

BYTOM
MUSEUM OF UPPER SILESIA
CIEPLICE ŚLĄSKIE ZDRÓJ
REGIONAL MUSEUM OF NATURAL HISTORY
DĄBROWA GÓRNICZA
REGIONAL MUSEUM OF GEOLOGY
KAMIENNA GÓRA
MUNICIPAL MUSEUM
KĘTRZYN
KĘTRZYN MUSEUM
KRAKÓW
GEOLOGICAL MUSEUM
MUSEUM OF THE IRON AND STEEL INDUSTRY
MUSEUM OF NATURAL HISTORY
KRÓSCIENKO
PIENIN MUSEUM
MALBORK
CASTLE MUSEUM
MIĘDZYZDROJ
NATURAL HISTORY MUSEUM
POZNAŃ
NATURAL HISTORY MUSEUM OF THE INSTITUTE OF ZOOLOGY
SOBIESZÓW
KARKONOSKI PARK MUSEUM
SOSNOWIEC
MINING MUSEUM
WARSAW
MUSEUM OF EARTH SCIENCES
MUSEUM OF THE GEOLOGICAL INSTITUTE
WŁVEŁAWEK
KUJAWSKI MUSEUM
ZAWOJA
BABIEJ GÓRY NATIONAL PARK MUSEUM

PORTUGAL

FUNCHAL
MUNICIPAL MUSEUM
LISBON
GEOLOGICAL AND MINERALOGICAL MUSEUM

REUNION

SAINT-DENIS
MUSEUM OF NATURAL HISTORY

RHODESIA

MARANDELLOS
CHILDREN'S MUSEUM
SALISBURY
GEOLOGICAL SURVEY MUSEUM
QUEEN VICTORIA MUSEUM
UMTALI
UMTALI MUSEUM

ROMANIA

AIUD
NATURAL HISTORY MUSEUM
BACĂU
NATURAL HISTORY MUSEUM
BUCHAREST
COLLECTION OF THE GEOLOGY COMMITTEE
GRIGORE ANTIPA MUSEUM OF NATURAL HISTORY
CLUJ
ARDELEAN MUSEUM
DEVA
DEVA MUSEUM
IAŞI
NATURAL HISTORY MUSEUM
PIATRA NEAMŢ
NATURAL HISTORY MUSEUM
PITEŞTI
ARGES DISTRICT MUSEUM
PITEŞTI MUSEUM
REŞIŢA
LOCAL MUSEUM
SIBIU
BRUKENTHAL MUSEUM
NATURAL HISTORY MUSEUM
SIGHET
SIGHET MUSEUM
TINCA
NATURAL HISTORY MUSEUM
TULCEA
MUSEUM OF THE DANUBE DELTA
TURNU SEVERIN
IRON GATE (PORŢILE DE FIER) MUSEUM

RWANDA

RUHENGERI
MUSEUM OF PETROGRAPHY AND MINERALOGY

ST. HELENA

GEORGETOWN
FORT HAYES MUSEUM

SENEGAL

DAKAR
MUSEUM OF AFRICAN GEOLOGY

SOUTH AFRICA, REPUBLIC OF

BLOEMFONTEIN
NATIONAL MUSEUM
CAPE TOWN
SOUTH AFRICAN MUSEUM
MUSEUMS OF THE UNIVERSITY OF CAPE TOWN
DUNDEE
DEPARTMENT OF MINES MUSEUM
DURBAN
DURBAN MUSEUM AND ART GALLERY
EAST LONDON
EAST LONDON MUSEUM
JOHANNESBURG
BERNARD PRICE INSTITUTE FOR PALAEONTOLOGICAL RESEARCH
BLELOCH MUSEUM
GEOLOGICAL MUSEUM
MUSEUMS OF THE UNIVERSITY OF THE WITWATERSRAND
OUDTSHOORN
CANGO CAVES MUSEUM
PIETERMARITZBURG
MINES DEPARTMENT MUSEUM
PORT ELIZABETH
PORT ELIZABETH MUSEUM
PRETORIA
MUSEUM OF THE GEOLOGICAL SURVEY
MUSEUM OF SCIENCE AND INDUSTRY
TRANSVAAL MUSEUM
SKUKUZA
STEVENSON-HAMILTON MEMORIAL LIBRARY
VICTORIA WEST
VICTORIA WEST MUSEUM
VEREENIGING
VEREENIGING MUSEUM

SOUTH-WEST AFRICA (NAMIBIA)

LÜDERITZ
LÜDERITZ MUSEUM
WINDHOEK
STATE MUSEUM

SPAIN

AMBRONA
MUSEUM OF THE EXCAVATIONS AT TORRALBA
AVILES
MUSEUM OF THE NATURAL SCIENCES
BARCELONA
GEOLOGICAL MUSEUM OF THE SEMINARY
MUSEUM OF GEOLOGY (MARTORELL MUSEUM)
MADRID
MUSEUM OF THE MUNICIPAL ARCHAEOLOGICAL INSTITUTE
NATIONAL MUSEUM OF GEOLOGY
NATIONAL MUSEUM OF NATURAL SCIENCE
NATURAL SCIENCE MUSEUM
ONDA
MUSEUM OF THE NATURAL SCIENCES
SABADELL
MUSEUM OF HISTORY
PROVINCIAL INSTITUTE AND MUSEUM OF PALAEONTOLOGY
SANTIAGO DE COMPOSTELA
LUIS IGLESIAS MUSEUM OF NATURAL HISTORY
VALENCIA
MUNICIPAL MUSEUM OF PALAEONTOLOGY
VILAJUIGA
GEOLOGICAL MUSEUM

SRI LANKA, REPUBLIC OF

COLOMBO
NATIONAL MUSEUM
RATNAPURA
NATIONAL MUSEUM

SUDAN

KHARTOUM
GEOLOGICAL SURVEY MUSEUM

SWEDEN

FALUN
MINING MUSEUM
GÖTEBORG
NATURAL HISTORY MUSEUM
STOCKHOLM
NATURAL HISTORY MUSEUM

SWITZERLAND

AARAU
MUSEUM OF NATURAL HISTORY AND LOCAL LIFE
AROSA
SCHANFIGGER REGIONAL MUSEUM
BASEL
NATURAL HISTORY MUSEUM
BERN
NATURAL HISTORY MUSEUM
SWISS ALPINE MUSEUM
BOURG- SAINT-PIERRE
MUSEUM OF THE GREAT ST. BERNARD SHELTER FOR TRAVELLERS
LA CHAUX- DE-FONDS
MUSEUM OF NATURAL HISTORY

CHUR

BÜNDER NATURAL HISTORY AND NATURAL PARK MUSEUM

DORNACH

REGIONAL MUSEUM OF SCHWAZBUBENLAND

FLEURIER

MUSEUM

FRAUENFELD

CANTON THURGAU MUSEUM

FRIBOURG

MUSEUM OF NATURAL HISTORY

GENEVA

NATURAL HISTORY MUSEUM

GLARUS

NATURAL SCIENCE COLLECTIONS OF CANTON GLARUS

GRENCHEN

MUSEUM SOCIETY'S COLLECTION

HEIDEN

MUSEUM

KLOSTERS

NUTLI-HÜSLI REGIONAL MUSEUM

LANGENTHAL

REGIONAL MUSEUM

LAUSANNE

CANTONAL GEOLOGICAL MUSEUM

LIESTAL

BASEL-LAND CANTONAL MUSEUM

LOCARNO

MUNICIPAL MUSEUM

LUZERN

GLACIER GARDEN AND GLACIER MUSEUM
NATURAL HISTORY MUSEUM

MEIRINGEN

MUSEUM OF HASLI COUNTY

OLTEN

MUSEUM OF NATURAL HISTORY

SAINTE-CROIX

MUSEUM

ST. GALLEN

OLD MUSEUM
REGIONAL MUSEUM

SARNEN

REGIONAL MUSEUM

SCHAFFHAUSEN

MUSEUM STEMMLER

SION

CANTONAL MUSEUM OF NATURAL HISTORY

SOLOTHURN

SOLOTHURN MUNICIPAL MUSEUM

VEVEY

JENISCH MUSEUM

WINTERTHUR

NATURAL SCIENCE COLLECTION OF THE TOWN OF WINTERTHUR

YVERDON

MUSEUM OF OLD YVERDON

ZERMATT

ALPINE MUSEUM

ZOFINGEN

MUSEUM

ZURICH

GEOLOGICAL AND MINERALOGICAL- PETROGRAPHICAL COLLECTIONS OF THE FEDERAL TECHNICAL UNIVERSITY

TANZANIA

DAR ES SALAAM

NATIONAL MUSEUM OF TANZANIA

DODOMA

GEOLOGICAL MUSEUM

MWEKA

NATURAL HISTORY MUSEUM

THAILAND

BANGKOK

MUSEUM OF MINERALOGY

UGANDA

ENTEBBE

GEOLOGICAL MUSEUM

KAMPALA

UGANDA MUSEUM

USSR

ARBYOMOVSK

GEOLOGICAL MUSEUM

ASKANIA-NOVA

NATURAL HISTORY MUSEUM

ASTRAKHAN

MUSEUM OF THE NATIONAL PARK OF ASTRAKHAN

KHERSON

NATURAL HISTORY MUSEUM

KIEV

UKRAINIAN GEOLOGICAL MUSEUM OF THE ACADEMY OF SCIENCES
ZOOLOGICAL MUSEUM OF THE STATE UNIVERSITY OF THE UKRAINE

KROTOSK

KROTOSK NATIONAL PARK MUSEUM

LENINGRAD

ACADEMICIAN F. N. CHERNYSCHEV CENTRAL SCIENTIFIC GEOLOGICAL AND PROSPECTING MUSEUM
V. V. DOKUCHAYEV CENTRAL MUSEUM OF SOIL SCIENCE
GEOLOGICAL MUSEUM, A. P. KARPINSKY

LVOV

NATURAL HISTORY MUSEUM

MIASS

MUSEUM OF THE ILMEN MINERAL PARK

MINSK

GEOLOGICAL-MINERALOGICAL MUSEUM OF THE BYELORUSSIAN ACADEMY OF SCIENCES

MOSCOW

MINERALOGICAL MUSEUM
PALAEONTOLOGICAL MUSEUM OF THE ACADEMY OF SCIENCE
PAVLOV MUSEUM OF GEOLOGY AND PALAEONTOLOGY

ODESSA

REGIONAL MUSEUM

ORDZHONIKIDZE

ORDZHONIKIDZE MUSEUM: NATURAL HISTORY COLLECTIONS

SIMFEROPOL

MUSEUM OF NATURAL HISTORY

SVERDLOVSK

V. V. VAKHRUSEHV GEOLOGICAL MUSEUM

TALLINN

MUSEUM OF NATURAL HISTORY

TASHKENT

CENTRAL REGIONAL MUSEUM
NATURAL HISTORY MUSEUM OF THE ACADEMY OF SCIENCES

TBILISI

NATURAL HISTORY MUSEUM OF GEORGIA

ULAN-BATOR

STATE CENTRAL MUSEUM

UNITED STATES

ALBUQUERQUE

MUSEUM OF GEOLOGY
MUSEUM OF UNIVERSITY OF NEW MEXICO BIOLOGY DEPARTMENT

AMERICAN FALLS

MASSACRE ROCKS STATE PARK MUSEUM

ANN ARBOR

MUSEUM OF PALAEONTOLOGY

ARCO

CRATERS OF THE MOON NATIONAL MONUMENT

ASHEVILLE

COLBURN MEMORIAL MINERAL MUSEUM

BALTIMORE

MUSEUM OF MARYLAND ACADEMY OF SCIENCES

BATON ROUGE

MUSEUM OF GEOSCIENCE

BERKELEY

MUSEUM OF PALAEONTOLOGY

BOSTON

MUSEUM OF SCIENCE

BOULDER

UNIVERSITY OF COLORADO MUSEUM

BOWLING GREEN

KENTUCKY MUSEUM

BREWSTER

DINOSAUR LAND

BUFFALO

BUFFALO MUSEUM OF SCIENCE

BUTTE

MINERAL MUSEUM

CAMBRIDGE

GEOLOGICAL MUSEUM
MINERALOGICAL MUSEUM OF HARVARD UNIVERSITY

CARLSBAD

CARLSBAD CAVERNS NATIONAL PARK

CHARLOTTE

CHARLOTTE NATURE MUSEUM

CHICAGO

CHICAGO ACADEMY OF SCIENCES

CINCINNATI

CINCINNATI MUSEUM OF NATURAL HISTORY
ALFRED K. NIPPERT NATURE MUSEUM
UNIVERSITY OF CINCINNATI GEOLOGY MUSEUM

CLEVELAND

CLEVELAND MUSEUM OF NATURAL HISTORY

COLUMBIA

MUSEUM OF DEPARTMENT OF GEOLOGY
UNIVERSITY OF MISSOURI MUSEUM

COLUMBUS

ORTON MUSEUM

CORTLAND

SCIENCE MUSEUM

CORVALLIS

HORNER MUSEUM

COVINGTON

BEHRINGER-CRAWFORD MEMORIAL MUSEUM OF NATURAL HISTORY

DE LAND

GILLESPIE MUSEUM OF MINERALS

DES MOINES

DES MOINES CENTER OF SCIENCE AND INDUSTRY

DURHAM

NORTH CAROLINA MUSEUM OF LIFE AND SCIENCE

EAST LANSING

MICHIGAN STATE UNIVERSITY MUSEUM

FLAGSTAFF

GREAT METEOR CRATER MUSEUM OF ASTROGEOLOGY

FLORISANT

COLORADO PETRIFIED FOREST

FORT PECK

FORT PECK PROJECT

FRUITA

COLORADO NATIONAL MONUMENT

GLEN COVE

NASSAU MUSEUM OF NATURAL HISTORY

HAMPTON

KENNETH E. RICE MEMORIAL MUSEUM

HANOVER

BRADLEY-CAMPBELL GEOLOGICAL MUSEUM

HARRISONBURG

EASTERN MENNONITE COLLEGE MUSEUM

HELLERTOWN

GILMAN MUSEUM

HENDERSON

SOUTHERN NEVADA MUSEUM

HOLBROOK

RAINBOW FOREST MUSEUM

HOT SPRINGS

QUARTZ CRYSTAL CAVE AND MUSEUM

HOUGHTON

A. E. SEAMAN MINERALOGICAL MUSEUM

HOUSTON

HOUSTON MUSEUM OF NATURAL SCIENCE
MUSEUM OF UNIVERSITY OF HOUSTON

HUNTINGTON

GEOLOGY MUSEUM, MARSHALL UNIVERSITY

INTERIOR
BADLANDS NATIONAL MONUMENT

IRAAN
IRAAN ARCHAEOLOGICAL MUSEUM

ITHACA
PALAEONTOLOGICAL RESEARCH INSTITUTION

JONESBORO
ARKANSAS STATE UNIVERSITY MUSEUM

JOPLIN
SCHIFFERDECKER MINERAL MUSEUM

KANSAS CITY
KANSAS CITY MUSEUM OF HISTORY AND SCIENCE

LAKE JACKSON
BRAZOSPORT MUSEUM OF NATURAL SCIENCES

LANCASTER
NORTH MUSEUM

LARAMIE
UNIVERSITY OF WYOMING GEOLOGICAL MUSEUM

LINCOLN
UNIVERSITY OF NEBRASKA STATE MUSEUM

LITCHFIELD
LITCHFIELD NATURE CENTER AND MUSEUM

LLANO
LLANO COUNTY HISTORICAL MUSEUM

LOS ANGELES
CALIFORNIA MUSEUM OF SCIENCE AND INDUSTRY
LOS ANGELES COUNTY MUSEUM OF NATURAL HISTORY

LOS GATOS
LOS GATOS MUSEUM

LOUISVILLE
MUSEUM OF SCIENCE AND HISTORY

MADISON
UNIVERSITY OF WISCONSIN ZOOLOGICAL MUSEUM

MIAMI
MUSEUM OF SCIENCE

MILWAUKEE
GREENE MEMORIAL MUSEUM, UNIVERSITY OF WISCONSIN
MILWAUKEE PUBLIC MUSEUM

MINNEAPOLIS
JAMES FORD BELL MUSEUM OF NATURAL HISTORY
MINNEAPOLIS PUBLIC LIBRARY SCIENCE MUSEUM AND PLANETARIUM

MORRISTOWN
MORRIS MUSEUM OF ARTS AND SCIENCES

MOSCOW
UNIVERSITY OF IDAHO MUSEUM

MOUNTAINSIDE
TRAILSIDE NATURE AND SCIENCE CENTER AND PLANETARIUM

MOUNT McKINLEY
MOUNT McKINLEY NATIONAL PARK MUSEUM

MOUNT PLEASANT
CENTER FOR CULTURAL AND NATURAL HISTORY

NEW BRUNSWICK
RUTGERS UNIVERSITY, GEOLOGY MUSEUM

NEW HAVEN
PEABODY MUSEUM OF NATURAL HISTORY

NEW YORK
AMERICAN MUSEUM OF NATURAL HISTORY

NORMAL
ILLINOIS STATE UNIVERSITY MUSEUMS

NORMAN
STOVALL MUSEUM OF SCIENCE AND HISTORY

OAKLAND
OAKLAND MUSEUM

ODESSA
ODESSA METEORITE MUSEUM

OGDEN
WEBER STATE COLLEGE, MUSEUM OF NATURAL HISTORY

OKLAHOMA CITY
MUSEUM OF OKLAHOMA SCIENCE AND ARTS FOUNDATION

ORLANDO
CENTRAL FLORIDA MUSEUM AND PLANETARIUM

PACIFIC GROVE
PACIFIC GROVE MUSEUM OF NATURAL HISTORY

PHILADELPHIA
ACADEMY OF NATURAL SCIENCES OF PHILADELPHIA

PHOENIX
ARIZONA MINERAL MUSEUM

PIEDMONT
TIMBERS OF AGES PETRIFIED FOREST MUSEUM

PINEVILLE
WILMAN LAPIDARY MUSEUM

PORTLAND
MUSEUM OF NATURAL HISTORY
OREGON MUSEUM OF SCIENCE AND INDUSTRY

PRICE
CARBON COLLEGE PREHISTORIC MUSEUM

PRINCETON
PRINCETON UNIVERSITY, MUSEUM OF NATURAL HISTORY

PROCTOR
MARBLE EXHIBIT

PROVO
BRIGHAM YOUNG UNIVERSITY, EARTH SCIENCES MUSEUM
BRIGHAM YOUNG UNIVERSITY, GEOLOGICAL COLLECTION

QUEENS
HALL OF SCIENCE OF THE CITY OF NEW YORK

RALEIGH
NORTH CAROLINA STATE MUSEUM

RANDSBURG
DESERT MUSEUM

RAPID CITY
MUSEUM OF GEOLOGY

RENO
MACKAY SCHOOL OF MINES MUSEUM

RICHFIELD SPRINGS
PETRIFIED CREATURES

RICHMOND
VIRGINIA STATE MUSEUM

ROANOKE
MUSEUM OF NORTH CAROLINA MINERALS

ROCHESTER
MUSEUM OF PETRIFIED WOOD
ROCHESTER MUSEUM AND SCIENCE CENTER

ROCKFORD
BURPEE NATURAL HISTORY MUSEUM

ROCK ISLAND
FRYXELL GEOLOGY MUSEUM

ROLLA
ED CLARK MUSEUM OF MISSOURI GEOLOGY
ROLLA GEOLOGY MUSEUM

ST. JOHNSBURY
FAIRBANKS MUSEUM OF NATURAL SCIENCE

ST. LOUIS
MUSEUM OF SCIENCE AND NATURAL HISTORY

ST. PAUL
SCIENCE MUSEUM OF MINNESOTA

ST. PETERSBURG
SCIENCE CENTER OF PINELLAS COUNTY

SALT LAKE CITY
UNIVERSITY OF UTAH, MUSEUM OF EARTH SCIENCES
WESTMINSTER COLLEGE MUSEUM

SAN ANDREAS
CALAVERAS COUNTY HISTORICAL MUSEUM

SAN DIEGO
CALIFORNIA STATE UNIVERSITY, DEPARTMENT OF GEOLOGY
NATURAL HISTORY MUSEUM

SAN FRANCISCO
MUSEUM OF THE CALIFORNIA DIVISION OF MINES AND GEOLOGY

SANTA BARBARA
SANTA BARBARA MUSEUM OF NATURAL HISTORY

SCRANTON
EVERHART MUSEUM OF NATURAL HISTORY, SCIENCE AND ART

SOUTH HADLEY
NASH DINOSAUR LAND

SPRUCE PINE
MUSEUM OF NORTH CAROLINA MINERALS

STAMFORD
STAMFORD MUSEUM AND NATURE CENTER

STATE COLLEGE
DUNN-SEILER MUSEUM
COLLEGE OF EARTH AND MINERAL SCIENCES MUSEUM

STATESVILLE
STATESVILLE ARTS AND SCIENCE MUSEUM

SUNCOCK
AUDUBON NATURE CENTER

TAMPA
MUSEUM OF SCIENCE AND NATURAL HISTORY

TEMPE
CENTER FOR METEORITE STUDIES

TIFFIN
JONES COLLECTION OF MINERALS AND BIOLOGY MUSEUM

TOLEDO
TOLEDO MUSEUM OF HEALTH AND NATURAL HISTORY

TUCSON
ARIZONA SONORA DESERT MUSEUM

TULELAKE
LAVA BEDS NATIONAL MONUMENT

TUSCALOOSA
UNIVERSITY OF ALABAMA MUSEUM OF NATURAL HISTORY

VALENTINE
FORT NIOBRARA NATIONAL WILDLIFE REFUGE

VANTAGE
GINKGO PETRIFIED FOREST STATE PARK MUSEUM

VERNAL
LEO THORNE'S MUSEUM
NATURAL HISTORY STATE MUSEUM

WASHINGTON
NATIONAL MUSEUM OF NATURAL HISTORY

WAUSAU
MARATHON COUNTY HISTORICAL SOCIETY MUSEUM

WEST PALM BEACH
SCIENCE MUSEUM AND PLANETARIUM OF PALM BEACH COUNTY

WILMINGTON
WILMINGTON-NEW HANOVER MUSEUM

WINSTON-SALEM
NATURE-SCIENCE CENTER

WOLFEBORO
LIBBY MUSEUM

YELLOWSTONE PARK
YELLOWSTONE NATIONAL PARK MUSEUM

YOSEMITE
YOSEMITE NATIONAL PARK MUSEUM

YUCAIPA
MOUSLEY MUSEUM OF NATURAL HISTORY

YUCCA VALLEY
HI-DESERT NATURE MUSEUM

URUGUAY

MERCEDES
PALAEONTOLOGY AND NATURAL SCIENCES MUSEUM

MONTEVIDEO
NATURAL HISTORY MUSEUM

VENEZUELA

CARACAS
NATURAL SCIENCE MUSEUM

MARACAIBO
NATURAL SCIENCE MUSEUM

YUGOSLAVIA

BELGRADE
BELGRADE NATURAL HISTORY MUSEUM

LJUBLJANA
SLOVENIAN NATURAL HISTORY MUSEUM

POSTOJNA
COLLECTIONS OF THE INSTITUTE OF SPELEOLOGY

RIJEKA
NATURAL HISTORY MUSEUM

SARAJEVO
STATE MUSEUM

SKOPJE
NATURAL HISTORY MUSEUM

SPLIT

MUSEUM OF NATURAL SCIENCES

ZAGREB

GEOLOGICAL AND PALAEONTOLOGICAL MUSEUM
MUSEUM OF MINERALOGY AND PETROGRAPHY
NATURAL HISTORY MUSEUM
TECHNICAL MUSEUM

ZAIRE, REPUBLIC OF

BUKAVU

MUSEUM OF PREHISTORY AND GEOLOGY

KOLWESI

MINERALOGICAL MUSEUM

LIKASI

SENGIER-COUSIN GEOLOGICAL MUSEUM

ZAMBIA

VICTORIA FALLS

EASTERN CATARACT FIELD MUSEUM

Mathematics, physical sciences, geography, exploration

ARGENTINA

BUENOS AIRES

MUSEUM OF THE INSTITUTE OF THE ANTARCTIC

AUSTRALIA

LAUNCESTON

QUEEN VICTORIA MUSEUM AND ART GALLERY

LUCAS HEIGHTS

AUSTRALIAN ATOMIC ENERGY COMMISSION RESEARCH ESTABLISHMENT VISITORS CENTRE

MELBOURNE

SCIENCE MUSEUM OF VICTORIA

AUSTRIA

GLEISDORF

REGIONAL MUSEUM

KREMSMUNSTER

MONASTERY COLLECTIONS

LINZ

UPPER AUSTRIA PROVINCIAL MUSEUM

VILLACH

MUNICIPAL MUSEUM

VIENNA

ELECTROPATHOLOGICAL MUSEUM
MUSEUM OF INDUSTRY AND TECHNOLOGY
NATURAL HISTORY MUSEUM: MINERALOGICAL-PETROGRAPHICAL SECTION

BANGLADESH

DACCA

GEOGRAPHY MUSEUM
SOIL SCIENCE MUSEUM

BELGIUM

BRUSSELS

ATOMIUM

GHENT

MUSEUM OF THE HISTORY OF SCIENCE

SINT-NIKLAAS WAAS

ARCHAEOLOGICAL MUSEUM

BRAZIL

RIO DE JANEIRO

NATIONAL MUSEUM

SÃO PAULO

MUNICIPAL PLANETARIUM
MUSEUM OF SCIENCE

BULGARIA

PLOVDIV

NATURAL SCIENCE MUSEUM

CANADA

CALGARY

CALGARY CENTENNIAL PLANETARIUM

EDMONTON

QUEEN ELIZABETH PLANETARIUM

HALIFAX

SCIENCE MUSEUM

HAMILTON

MCMASTER UNIVERSITY PLANETARIUM

LACHINE

SAINTE-ANNE MUSEUM

MONTREAL

DOW PLANETARIUM

OTTAWA

MUSEUM OF NATIONAL HISTORIC SITES SERVICE
NATIONAL MUSEUM OF SCIENCE AND TECHNOLOGY

TORONTO

MCLAUGHLIN PLANETARIUM
ONTARIO SCIENCE CENTRE

WINNIPEG

MANITOBA MUSEUM OF MAN AND NATURE

CHINA, P.R.

CANTON (GUANG DONG)

HISTORY MUSEUM

HANGCHOW (HANG ZHOU)

CHEKIANG PROVINCIAL MUSEUM

PEKING

OLD OBSERVATORY
PLANETARIUM

TIENSIN (TIANJING)

PEOPLE'S HALL OF SCIENCE

REPUBLIC OF CHINA

TAIPEI

NATIONAL TAIWAN SCIENCE HALL

COLOMBIA

BOGOTA

MUSEUM OF NATURAL HISTORY
NATIONAL MUSEUM

CUBA

HABANA

FELIPE POEY MUSEUM

SANTIAGO DE CUBA

SCIENCE MUSEUM

CZECHOSLOVAKIA

JÁCHYMOV

MUNICIPAL MUSEUM

KOŠICE

TECHNICAL MUSEUM

MORAVSKÝ KRUMLOV

MUNICIPAL MUSEUM

PRAGUE

NATIONAL TECHNICAL MUSEUM

DENMARK

COPENHAGEN

ASTRONOMY MUSEUM
TS MUSEUM

HELSINGØR

DANISH TECHNICAL MUSEUM

SORØ

ACADEMY MUSEUM

EGYPT, ARAB REPUBLIC OF

CAIRO

SCIENCE MUSEUM

FRANCE

BEAUMONT-EN-AUGE

LAPLACE MUSEUM AND MUSEUM OF PAINTING

CLERMONT-FERRAND

LECOQ MUSEUM
RANQUET MUSEUM

LILLE

MUSEUM OF INDUSTRY, COMMERCE, TECHNOLOGY AND AGRICULTURE

LYON

AMPÈRE MUSEUM

MEUDON

MEUDON MUSEUM

PARIS

ASTRONOMICAL MUSEUM OF THE PARIS OBSERVATORY
BRANLY MUSEUM
NATIONAL TECHNICAL MUSEUM
PALACE OF DISCOVERY

POLEYMIEUX AU MONT D'OR

AMPÈRE HOUSE AND MUSEUM OF ELECTRICITY

GDR

BAD FREIENWALDE

ODERLAND MUSEUM

DRESDEN

POLYTECHNIC MUSEUM

ERFURT

NATURAL SCIENCE MUSEUM

FREIBERG

MUSEUM OF NATURAL HISTORY

LEIPZIG

GEOGRAPHICAL MUSEUM OF THE GERMAN ACADEMY OF SCIENCES, BERLIN
GERMAN GEOGRAPHICAL INSTITUTE
MUSEUM OF NATURAL SCIENCES

MAGDEBURG

LIFE AND RESOURCES OF THE WELTALL

ORANIENBURG

DISTRICT MUSEUM

STRALSUND

MUSEUM OF THE SEA

GFR

BAMBERG

HISTORICAL MUSEUM

DUISBURG

MUSEUM OF THE LOWER RHINE

ERLANGEN

GEOGRAPHICAL AND ETHNOLOGICAL COLLECTIONS OF THE UNIVERSITY OF ERLANGEN- NÜRNBERG

ESSEN

RUHR AND REGIONAL MUSEUM

GIESSEN

LIEBIG MUSEUM

GOSLAR

COLLECTION ILLUSTRATING THE CULTURAL HISTORY OF GERMANY AND EUROPE

HAMBURG

EXHIBITION IN THE PLANETARIUM

KIEL

SCHLESWIG-HOLSTEIN TRAVELLING MUSEUM

KIRCHHEIMBOLANDEN

REGIONAL MUSEUM

KOBLENZ

RHINE MUSEUM

LUDWIGSHAFEN (RHEIN)

CITY MUSEUM

MÜNCHEN

BAVARIAN STATE SCIENCE COLLECTIONS
GERMAN MUSEUM
WERNER VON SIEMENS INSTITUTE FOR THE HISTORY OF THE HOUSE OF SIEMENS

NEHEIM-HÜSTEN

LIGHTING MUSEUM

REGENSBURG

KEPLER HOUSE MEMORIAL

REMSCHEID

GERMAN X-RAY MUSEUM

WEIL DER STADT

KEPLER MUSEUM

GREAT BRITAIN

CAMBRIDGE

THE SCOTT POLAR RESEARCH INSTITUTE

EDINBURGH

ROYAL SCOTTISH MUSEUM

JODRELL BANK

MUSEUM OF DEPARTMENT OF RADIO ASTRONOMY

LIVERPOOL

CITY OF LIVERPOOL MUSEUMS

LONDON

COMMONWEALTH INSTITUTE
DOLLOND AND AITCHISON LIMITED
OLD ROYAL OBSERVATORY
SCIENCE MUSEUM

NEWCASTLE- UPON-TYNE

UNIVERSITY OF NEWCASTLE- UPON-TYNE

PETERHEAD

ARBUTHNOT MUSEUM

SELBORNE

GILBERT WHITE MUSEUM

SELKIRK

SELKIRK MUSEUM

TEESSIDE

CAPTAIN COOK MUSEUM

WHITBY

WHITBY MUSEUM AND ART GALLERY

INDIA

BANGALORE

VISVESVARAYA INDUSTRIAL AND TECHNOLOGICAL MUSEUM

BHUBANESHWAR

ORISSA STATE MUSEUM

CALCUTTA

BIRLA INDUSTRIAL AND TECHNOLOGICAL MUSEUM
BIRLA PLANETARIUM AND ASTRONOMICAL RESEARCH CENTRE

DEHRA DUN

GEODETIC BRANCH MUSEUM (SURVEY OF INDIA)

NEW DELHI

ARCHAEOLOGICAL MUSEUM
SCIENCE MUSEUM

PATIALA

STATE MUSEUM

PILANI

CENTRAL MUSEUM

POONA

LORD REAY MAHARASHTRA INDUSTRIAL MUSEUM
MAHATMA PHULE VASTU SANGRAHALAYA

IRELAND

DUBLIN

EGESTORFF COLLECTION

MAYNOOTH

MUSEUM OF ECCLESIOLOGY AND PHYSICS

ISRAEL

REHOVOT

WEIZMANN ARCHIVES

TEL-AVIV

MUSEUM OF SCIENCE AND TECHNOLOGY

ITALY

FAENZA

TORRICELLI MUSEUM

FLORENCE

CARTOGRAPHY AND INSTRUMENTS MUSEUM

MILAN

LEONARDO DA VINCI MUSEUM OF SCIENCE AND TECHNOLOGY

PISA

DOMUS GALILEIANA

ROME

ASTRONOMICAL AND COPERNICUS MUSEUM
COLLECTION OF THE ITALIAN GEOGRAPHICAL SOCIETY
MUSEUM OF HISTORICAL APPARATUS FOR THE REPRODUCTION OF SOUND

TURIN

MUSEUM OF NATURAL SCIENCE

JAPAN

AKASHI-SHI

AKASHI CITY PLANETARIUM & SCIENCE HALL

FUKUI-SHI

FUKUI MUNICIPAL NATURAL HISTORY MUSEUM

GIFU-SHI

GIFU CHILDREN'S SCIENCE HALL

HIROSHIMA-SHI

HIROSHIMA PEACE MEMORIAL MUSEUM

IKOMASAN

ASTRONOMICAL MUSEUM

KYOTO

KYOTO BOARD OF EDUCATION SCIENCE ROOM

MITO-SHI

IBARAKI PREFECTURAL MUSEUM OF ATOMIC ENERGY

NAGAOKA-SHI

SNOW MUSEUM

NAGASAKI-SHI

NAGASAKI MUNICIPAL CHILDREN'S SCIENCE HALL

NAGOYA

MUNICIPAL SCIENCE MUSEUM

OSAKA

ELECTRIC SCIENCE MUSEUM
IKOMASAN ASTRONOMICAL MUSEUM

OTARU-SHI

OTARU CITY MUSEUM

RIKUZENTAKADA-SHI

RIKUZENTAKADA MUNICIPAL MUSEUM

SAGAMIKO-MACHI

SAGAMIKO ELECTRIC SCIENCE MUSEUM

SENDAI-SHI

THE SCIENCE ROOM, LEISURE CENTRE OF SENDAI

TOKYO

ELECTRICAL SCIENCE MUSEUM OF TOKYO METROPOLITAN ELECTROTECHNICAL LABORATORY
GOTOH PLANETARIUM AND ASTRONOMICAL MUSEUM
SCIENCE MUSEUM

TOTTORI-SHI

TOTTORI PREFECTURAL SCIENCE MUSEUM

YAMAGUCHI-SHI

YAMAGUCHI PREFECTURAL MUSEUM

LUXEMBOURG

LUXEMBOURG

STATE MUSEUM

MEXICO

MEXICO CITY

UNIVERSITY MUSEUM OF SCIENCE AND ART

NETHERLANDS

AMSTERDAM

NETHERLANDS INSTITUTE OF SCIENCE AND TECHNOLOGY

DELFT

ELECTRO-TECHNOLOGY STUDY COLLECTION

EINDHOVEN

EVOLUON

FRANEKER

EISE EISINGA PLANETARIUM

LEIDEN

NATIONAL MUSEUM OF THE HISTORY OF THE NATURAL SCIENCES

NEW ZEALAND

AUCKLAND

MUSEUM OF TRANSPORT AND TECHNOLOGY

NORWAY

OSLO

NORWEGIAN SCIENCE AND INDUSTRY MUSEUM

POLAND

BYSTRZYCA KŁODZKIA

MUSEUM OF LIGHTING

FROMBORK

MIKOŁAJA KOPERNIKA (COPERNICUS) MUSEUM

KRAKÓW

UNIVERSITY MUSEUM OF FINE ART

TORUŃ

MIKOŁAJ KOPERNIKI (COPERNICUS) MUSEUM

WARSAW

MARIE-SKŁODOWSKA CURIE MUSEUM
METEOROLOGICAL MUSEUM (MIAR MUSEUM)
TECHNICAL MUSEUM

ROMANIA

BACĂU

NATURAL HISTORY MUSEUM

BUCHAREST

NATIONAL OBSERVATORY AND MUSEUM OF EXPERIMENTAL SCIENCE

CLUJ

ARDELEAN MUSEUM

SENEGAL

ILE DE GORÉE

MARITIME MUSEUM

SOUTH AFRICA, REPUBLIC OF

PRETORIA

MUSEUM OF SCIENCE AND INDUSTRY

SPAIN

MADRID

COLLECTION OF THE NATIONAL OBSERVATORY
NATURAL SCIENCE MUSEUM

SWEDEN

NORRKÖPING

FÄRGAR HOUSE

STOCKHOLM

TECHNICAL MUSEUM

SWITZERLAND

ARTH

AVALANCHE MUSEUM

BERN

SWISS ALPINE MUSEUM

GENEVA

MUSEUM OF THE HISTORY OF SCIENCE

NYON

LAKE LÉMAN MUSEUM

SCHÖNENWERD

BALLY MUSEUM FOUNDATION

UGANDA

KAMPALA

UGANDA MUSEUM

USSR

LENINGRAD

LENINGRAD PLANETARIUM
M. V. LOMONOSOV MUSEUM
MUSEUM OF ANTHROPOLOGY AND ETHNOLOGY
MUSEUM OF THE ARCTIC AND THE ANTARCTIC
MUSEUM OF SCIENTIFIC RESEARCH

MOSCOW

MUSEUM OF EARTH SCIENCES
PLANETARIUM
POLYTECHNICAL MUSEUM

SVERDLOVSK

HOUSE OF TECHNOLOGY

VOYKOVO

METEOROLOGICAL MUSEUM OF THE CENTRAL GEOPHYSICAL OBSERVATORY

UNITED STATES

ANN ARBOR

ARGUS PLANETARIUM

AUSTIN

AUSTIN NATURAL SCIENCE CENTER

BALTIMORE

MUSEUM OF MARYLAND ACADEMY OF SCIENCES

BOSTON

MUSEUM OF SCIENCE

BUFFALO

BUFFALO MUSEUM OF SCIENCE

CHAPEL HILL

MOREHEAD PLANETARIUM

CHARLOTTE

CHARLOTTE NATURE MUSEUM

CHEROKEE

SANFORD MUSEUM AND PLANETARIUM

CHESAPEAKE

CHESAPEAKE PLANETARIUM

CHICAGO

ADLER PLANETARIUM
MUSEUM OF SCIENCE AND INDUSTRY

CINCINNATI

CINCINNATI MUSEUM OF NATURAL HISTORY
CINCINNATI SCIENCE CENTER

CLEVELAND

CLEVELAND MUSEUM OF NATURAL HISTORY

COLUMBIA

COLUMBIA SCIENCE MUSEUM

CORTLAND

SCIENCE MUSEUM

CORVALLIS

HORNER MUSEUM

DE LAND

L. L. RICE PLANETARIUM AND MONROE HEATH MUSEUM

DES MOINES

DES MOINES CENTER OF SCIENCE AND INDUSTRY

EAST LANSING

ABRAMS PLANETARIUM
MICHIGAN STATE UNIVERSITY MUSEUM

ERIE

ERIE PUBLIC MUSEUM AND PLANETARIUM

FLINT

ROBERT T. LONGWAY PLANETARIUM

FLUSHING

HALL OF SCIENCE OF THE CITY OF NEW YORK

FOLSOM

FOLSOM POWERHOUSE

FORT WORTH

FORT WORTH MUSEUM OF SCIENCE AND HISTORY

GAINESVILLE

UNIVERSITY OF FLORIDA PLANETARIUM

GRAND RAPIDS

GRAND RAPIDS PUBLIC MUSEUM

HARRISBURG

WILLIAM PENN MEMORIAL MUSEUM

HARRISONBURG

M. T. BRACKBILL PLANETARIUM
MADISON COLLEGE PLANETARIUM

HILTON HEAD ISLAND

HARBOUR TOWN MUSEUM

HOUSTON

HOUSTON MUSEUM OF NATURAL SCIENCE

LAFAYETTE

LAFAYETTE NATURAL HISTORY MUSEUM AND PLANETARIUM

LAKEWOOD

JEFFERSON COUNTY PLANETARIUM

LANCASTER

NORTH MUSEUM

LEXINGTON

TRANSYLVANIA MUSEUM
SALE PLANETARIUM

LINCOLN

UNIVERSITY OF NEBRASKA STATE MUSEUM

LOS ALAMOS

BRADBURY SCIENCE HALL

LOS ALTOS HILLS

SPACE SCIENCE CENTER

LOS ANGELES

CALIFORNIA MUSEUM OF SCIENCE AND INDUSTRY
MUSEUM OF GRIFFITH OBSERVATORY

LOUISVILLE

MUSEUM OF SCIENCE AND HISTORY
JOSEPH RAUCH MEMORIAL PLANETARIUM

MADISON

WASHBURN OBSERVATORY

MENLO PARK

EDISON MEMORIAL TOWER AND STATE PARK

MIAMI

MUSEUM OF SCIENCE

MIDLAND

MUSEUM OF THE SOUTHWEST

MINNEAPOLIS

MINNEAPOLIS PUBLIC LIBRARY SCIENCE MUSEUM AND PLANETARIUM

MONTGOMERY

W. A. GAYLE PLANETARIUM

MORRISTOWN

MORRIS MUSEUM OF ARTS AND SCIENCES

MOSCOW

UNIVERSITY OF IDAHO MUSEUM

MOUNT WILSON

MOUNT WILSON OBSERVATORY

NEWARK

NEWARK MUSEUM

NEW BRUNSWICK

DELAPLAINE ELECTRICAL MUSEUM

NEWPORT NEWS

PENINSULA NATURE AND SCIENCE CENTER

NEW YORK

AMERICAN MUSEUM, HAYDEN PLANETARIUM

NORMAN

STOVALL MUSEUM OF SCIENCE AND HISTORY

OAK RIDGE

AMERICAN MUSEUM OF ATOMIC ENERGY

OKLAHOMA CITY

MUSEUM OF OKLAHOMA SCIENCE AND ARTS FOUNDATION

ONTARIO

BROOKWOOD SCIENCE INFORMATION CENTER

ORLANDO

CENTRAL FLORIDA MUSEUM AND PLANETARIUM

OSWEGO

NIAGRA MOHAWK PROGRESS CENTER

OWENSBORO

OWENSBORO AREA MUSEUM

PACIFIC GROVE

PACIFIC GROVE MUSEUM OF NATURAL HISTORY

PASADENA

HALE OBSERVATORIES

PEORIA

LAKEVIEW CENTER FOR THE ARTS AND SCIENCES

PHILADELPHIA

FRANKLIN INSTITUTE SCIENCE MUSEUM

PITTSBURGH

BUHL PLANETARIUM

PORTLAND

OREGON MUSEUM OF SCIENCE AND INDUSTRY

QUEENS

HALL OF SCIENCE OF THE CITY OF NEW YORK

RALEIGH

NORTH CAROLINA STATE MUSEUM

READING

PLANETARIUM

REDLANDS

UNIVERSITY OF REDLANDS PLANETARIUM

ROCHESTER

ROCHESTER MUSEUM AND SCIENCE CENTER
STRASENBURGH PLANETARIUM

ST. JOHNSBURY

FAIRBANKS MUSEUM OF NATURAL SCIENCE

ST. LOUIS

MCDONNELL PLANETARIUM
MUSEUM OF SCIENCE AND NATURAL HISTORY

ST. PAUL

SCIENCE MUSEUM OF MINNESOTA

ST. PETERSBURG

SCIENCE CENTER OF PINELLAS COUNTY

SALT LAKE CITY

HANSEN PLANETARIUM

SAN DIEGO

SAN DIEGO HALL OF SCIENCE
SAN DIEGO STATE COLLEGE PLANETARIUM

SAN FRANCISCO

EXPLORATORIUM

SANTA BARBARA

SANTA BARBARA MUSEUM OF NATURAL HISTORY

SCRANTON

EVERHART MUSEUM OF NATURAL HISTORY, SCIENCE AND ART

SEATTLE

PACIFIC SCIENCE CENTER

STATE COLLEGE

COLLEGE OF EARTH AND MINERAL SCIENCES MUSEUM

SURRY

SURRY NUCLEAR INFORMATION CENTER

TAMPA

MUSEUM OF SCIENCE AND NATURAL HISTORY

TEMPE

CENTER FOR METEORITE STUDIES

TOPEKA

NATURAL SCIENCE MUSEUM

TRENTON

NEW JERSEY STATE MUSEUM

TUCSON

ARIZONA SONORA DESERT MUSEUM
SCIENCE MUSEUM

WASHINGTON

NATIONAL MUSEUM OF HISTORY AND TECHNOLOGY

WESTERVILLE

OTTERBEIN COLLEGE

WEST PALM BEACH

SCIENCE MUSEUM AND PLANETARIUM OF PALM BEACH COUNTY

WICHITA FALLS

WICHITA FALLS MUSEUM AND ART CENTER

WINSLOW

METEOR CRATER MUSEUM

YONKERS

HUDSON RIVER MUSEUM

VIETNAM, REPUBLIC OF

NHATRANG

OCEANOGRAPHIC MUSEUM

YUGOSLAVIA

BELGRADE

NIKOLA TESLA MUSEUM

LJUBLJANA

GEOGRAPHICAL MUSEUM OF SLOVENIA

Biology, zoology, natural history

ALBANIA

TIRANA

MUSEUM OF NATURAL HISTORY

ALGERIA

ALGIERS

ZOOLOGICAL PARK

BENI-ABBES

BOTANICAL ET ZOOLOGICAL COLLECTIONS

BOU ISMAIL

AQUARIUM

ORAN

MUNICIPAL MUSEUM

ANGOLA

LUANDA

ANGOLA MUSEUM

LUNDA

DUNDO MUSEUM

ARGENTINA

BUENOS AIRES

MUSEUM OF THE INSTITUTE OF THE ANTARCTIC
MUSEUM OF THE NATIONAL INSTITUTE OF MICROBIOLOGY
BERNARDINO RIVODAVIA MUSEUM OF NATURAL SCIENCES

CORRIENTES

NATURAL HISTORY MUSEUM

LA PLATA

LA PLATA MUSEUM OF NATURAL SCIENCES

LOMAS DE ZÁMORA

AMERICAN MUSEUM OF ANTHROPOLOGY, HISTORY, NUMISMATICS AND NATURAL SCIENCE

MENDOZA

MOYANO MUSEUM OF NATURAL HISTORY

ROSARIO

A. GALLARDO MUSEUM OF NATURAL SCIENCES
MUSEUM OF MARINE BIOLOGY

SANTA FÉ

NATURAL HISTORY MUSEUM

TUCUMÁN

MUSEUM OF NATURAL HISTORY AND ANTHROPOLOGY

AUSTRALIA

ADELAIDE

APPLIED SCIENCE MUSEUM
BOTANIC MUSEUM
MUSEUM OF NATURAL HISTORY
SHELL MUSEUM
THE SOUTH AUSTRALIAN MUSEUM

BRISBANE

QUEENSLAND NATIONAL ART GALLERY AND MUSEUM
SHELL BUNGALOW

CAIRNS

HOUSE OF 10,000 SHELLS

CANBERRA

AUSTRALIAN INSTITUTE OF ANATOMY

HOBART

TASMANIAN MUSEUM AND ART GALLERY

KALBARRI

SHELL, MARINE AND MINERAL MUSEUM

KOROIT

NATURAL HISTORY CENTRE

LAUNCESTON

QUEEN VICTORIA MUSEUM AND ART GALLERY

LONG JETTY

WONDERS OF THE SEA AND GEMSTONE HOUSE

MELBOURNE

O. W. TIEGS MUSEUM

PERTH

WESTERN AUSTRALIAN MUSEUM

PORT DOUGLAS

BARRIER REEF SHELL COLLECTION

SYDNEY

AUSTRALIAN MUSEUM
MACLEAY MUSEUM OF NATURAL HISTORY
J. L. SHELLSHEAR MUSEUM OF COMPARATIVE ANATOMY AND PHYSICAL ANTHROPOLOGY

AUSTRIA

ADMONT

NATURAL HISTORY MUSEUM

ASPARN

WEINLAND MUSEUM

BAD DEUTSCH ALTENBURG

AFRICAN MUSEUM

BADEN

ROLLETT MUSEUM

DORNBIRN

LANDSCAPE AND ECOLOGY OF THE VORARLBERG

GRAZ

JOANEUM PROVINCIAL MUSEUM FOR ZOOLOGY AND BOTANY

HALLSTATT

LOCAL MUSEUM

KLAGENFURT

CARINTHIA PROVINCIAL MUSEUM

KREMSMUNSTER

MONASTERY COLLECTIONS

LILIENFELD

MUSEUM OF LOCAL LIFE

LINZ

UPPER AUSTRIA PROVINCIAL MUSEUM

MÖDLING

MUNICIPAL MUSEUM

NEUSIEDL

LAKE MUSEUM

PRESSBAUM

REGIONAL MUSEUM

REICHENAU AN DER RAX

REICHENAU NATURAL HISTORY MUSEUM

SALZBURG

NATURE HOUSE

SEITENSTETTEN

COLLECTIONS OF THE BENEDICTINE ABBEY

STEYR

REGIONAL MUSEUM

TRAUTENFELS

COUNTRYSIDE MUSEUM

VIENNA

DOG MUSEUM
HOUSE OF THE SEA
NATURAL HISTORY MUSEUM: DEPARTMENT OF ZOOLOGY

WAIDHOFEN AN DER YBBS

REGIONAL MUSEUM

BANGLADESH

BARISAL

BARISAL MEDICAL COLLEGE MUSEUM

CHITTAGONG

MEDICAL COLLEGE MUSEUM

DACCA

MEDICAL COLLEGE MUSEUM
SALIMULLAH MEDICAL COLLEGE MUSEUM
ZOOLOGY MUSEUM

DINAJPUR

TAXIDERMY MUSEUM

BELGIUM

ANTWERP

MUSEUM OF CONCHOLOGY
MUSEUM OF NATURAL HISTORY

BRUSSELS

MUSEUM OF THE ROYAL BELGIAN INSTITUTE OF NATURAL SCIENCES

LAVAUX-SAINTE-ANNE

BELGIAN MUSEUM OF HUNTING AND NATURAL CONSERVATION

LIÈGE

ZOOLOGICAL MUSEUM

MONS

MUSEUM OF NATURAL HISTORY

NIEUWPOORT

MUSEUM OF ORNITHOLOGY

TERVUEREN

ROYAL CENTRAL AFRICAN MUSEUM

TOURNAI

MUSEUM OF NATURAL HISTORY
MUSEUM OF PALAEONTOLOGY AND PREHISTORY

BRAZIL

BELEM

EMÍLIO GOELDI PARÁ MUSEUM

CAMPINAS
MUNICIPAL MUSEUM
CURITIBA
MUSEUM OF MAN
FLORIANÓPOLIS
SAMBAGUI MUSEUM OF MAN
FORTALEZA
DIAS DA ROCHA MUSEUM
GOIÂNIA
MUSEUM OF ORNITHOLOGY
ITATAIA
REGIONAL MUSEUM OF ITATAIA NATIONAL PARK
JUAZEIRO DO NORTE
FATHER CÍCERO MUSEUM
MACAPÁ
JOAQUIM CAETANO DA SILVA MUSEUM
NATAL
MUSEUM OF THE INSTITUTE OF MARINE BIOLOGY
MUSEUM OF THE PÂMPONO SPORTING CLUB
PIRACICABA
MUSEUM OF THE AGRICULTURAL HIGH SCHOOL
PÔRTO ALEGRE
NATURAL HISTORY MUSEUM
RIO GRANDE MUSEUM OF THE NATURAL SCIENCES
RECIFE
MUSEUM OF NATURAL SCIENCES OF THE FEDERAL RURAL UNIVERSITY OF PERNAMBUCO
RIO CLARO
NAVARRO DE ANDRADE FORESTRY MUSEUM
RIO DE JANEIRO
CARPOLOGICAL MUSEUM
MUSEUM OF DENDROLOGY
MUSEUM OF FAUNA
NATIONAL MUSEUM
SÃO PAULO
DR. JOÃO BARBOSA RODRIGUES BOTANICAL MUSEUM
MUSEUM OF THE BUTANTÃ INSTITUTE
MUSEUM OF THE OSCAR FREIRE INSTITUTE
ZOOLOGICAL MUSEUM

BRUNEI

KOTA BATU
BRUNEI MUSEUM

BULGARIA

BOURGAS
REGIONAL MUSEUM OF HISTORY
KAZANLUK
NATIONAL MUSEUM
KOBEL
NATURAL HISTORY MUSEUM
PLOVDIV
NATURAL SCIENCE MUSEUM
RUSE
REGIONAL MUSEUM OF HISTORY
SOFIA
NATIONAL ZOOLOGICAL MUSEUM
VARNA
NATURAL HISTORY MUSEUM

BURMA

RANGOON
NATURAL HISTORY MUSEUM

CANADA

ALGONQUIN
ALGONQUIN PROVINCIAL PARK VISITOR CENTRE
ATIKOKAN
QUETICO PROVINCIAL PARK MUSEUM
BADDECK
ALEXANDER GRAHAM BELL MUSEUM
BANFF
BANFF NATIONAL PARK NATURAL HISTORY MUSEUM
BRANDON
B. J. HALES MUSEUM OF NATURAL HISTORY
CALGARY
MUSEUM OF ZOOLOGY
CHATHAM
MIRAMICHI NATURAL HISTORY MUSEUM
GRANDE PRAIRIE
GRANDE PRAIRIE PIONEER MUSEUM
HALIFAX
SCIENCE MUSEUM
KINGSTON
GEOLOGICAL MUSEUM
LACHINE
SAINTE-ANNE MUSEUM
MCBRIDE
OSCAR'S WILDLIFE MUSEUM
MONTREAL
REDPATH MUSEUM
OTTAWA
COLLECTIONS OF PLANT RESEARCH INSTITUTE
MUSEUM OF NATIONAL HISTORIC SITES SERVICE
NATIONAL MUSEUM OF NATURAL SCIENCES
PRINCE ALBERT
LUND WILDLIFE EXHIBIT
REGINA
SASKATCHEWAN MUSEUM OF NATURAL HISTORY
SAINT JOHN
THE NEW BRUNSWICK MUSEUM
SAINT-LAURENT
MUSEUM OF THE NUNS OF THE HOLY CROSS
SWIFT CURRENT
SWIFT CURRENT MUSEUM
TORONTO
ROYAL ONTARIO MUSEUM
VANCOUVER
CENTENNIAL MUSEUM
PACIFIC NATIONAL EXHIBITION
UNIVERSITY OF BRITISH COLUMBIA, VERTEBRATE MUSEUM
M. Y. WILLIAMS GEOLOGICAL MUSEUM
VICTORIA
PROVINCIAL MUSEUM
WASKESIU
PRINCE ALBERT NATIONAL PARK MUSEUM
WINNIPEG
MANITOBA MUSEUM OF MAN AND NATURE
UNIVERSITY OF MANITOBA, NATURAL HISTORY MUSEUM
YELLOWKNIFE
MUSEUM OF THE NORTH

CHAD

FORT LAMY
CHAD NATIONAL MUSEUM

CHILE

ANGOL
DILLMAN S. BULLOCK MUSEUM
SANTIAGO
MUSEUM OF NATURAL HISTORY
NATIONAL MUSEUM OF NATURAL HISTORY
NATURAL HISTORY MUSEUM
VALPARAISO
NATURAL HISTORY MUSEUM
VIÑA DEL MAR
INSTITUTE OF OCEANOGRAPHY
MUSEUM OF COMPARATIVE MARINE ZOOLOGY

CHINA, P.R.

HANGCHOW (HANG ZHOU)
CHEKIANG PROVINCIAL MUSEUM
PEKING
CULTURAL PALACE OF THE MINORITIES
NATURAL HISTORY MUSEUM
SHANGHAI
MUSEUM OF NATURAL SCIENCES
TIENSIN (TIANJING)
PEOPLE'S HALL OF SCIENCE

REPUBLIC OF CHINA

TAIPEI
NATIONAL TAIWAN SCIENCE HALL
TAIWAN PROVINCIAL MUSEUM

COLOMBIA

BOGOTA
MUSEUM OF NATURAL HISTORY
NATIONAL MUSEUM
CALI
MUSEUM OF NATURAL HISTORY
MANIZALES
MUSEUM OF NATURAL SCIENCES
MEDELLÍN
MUSEUM OF NATURAL SCIENCES
SANTA FÉ MUSEUM
POPAYAN
NATURAL HISTORY MUSEUM

COSTA RICA

SAN JOSÉ
NATIONAL MUSEUM

CUBA

GIBARA
NATURAL HISTORY MUSEUM
HABANA
FELIPE POEY MUSEUM
HOLGUÍN
CARLOS DE LA TORRE NATURAL HISTORY MUSEUM
PINAR DEL RIO
MUSEUM OF MARINE FAUNA
SANTIAGO DE CUBA
SCIENCE MUSEUM

CYPRUS

LIMASSOL
NATURAL HISTORY MUSEUM

CZECHOSLOVAKIA

AŠ
MUNICIPAL MUSEUM
BANSKÁ BYSTRICA
MUSEUM OF THE HISTORY OF SLOVAKIA
BARDEJOV
ŠARIŠ MUSEUM
BENÁTKY NAD JIZEROU
MUNICIPAL MUSEUM
BOJKOVICE
LOCAL MUSEUM
BRANDÝS NAD LABEM- STANÁ BOLESLAV
PRAGUE-VÝCHOD DISTRICT MUSEUM
BRATISLAVA
SLOVAKIAN NATIONAL MUSEUM: NATURAL HISTORY COLLECTIONS
BRNO
MORAVIAN MUSEUM: BOTANICAL AND ENTOMOLOGICAL COLLECTIONS
MORAVIAN MUSEUM: GREGOR MENDEL MEMORIAL MUSEUM
MORAVIAN MUSEUM: NATURAL HISTORY AND HISTORY COLLECTIONS
BROUMOV
REGIONAL MUSEUM
ČELÁKOVICE
MUNICIPAL MUSEUM

ČERVENÝ KLÁŠTOR
MONASTERY MUSEUM
ČESKE BUDĚJOVICE
MUSEUM OF SOUTHERN CZECHOSLOVAKIA
ČESKÝ BROD
MUSEUM OF LOWER LIPAN
CHEB
REGIONAL MUSEUM
CHOELŇ
ORLICKÝ MUSEUM
HLUBOKÁ NAD VLTAVOU
MUSEUM OF THE COUNTRYSIDE
HOLICE V ČECHÁCH
AFRICA MUSEUM; DR. EMIL HOLUB MEMORIAL
HOŘOVICE
MUNICIPAL MUSEUM
HRADEC KRÁLOVÉ
REGIONAL MUSEUM: DEPARTMENT OF NATURAL HISTORY
HYNIČE-VRAŽNÉ
J. GREGOR MENDEL MEMORIAL
KAMENICE NAD LIPOU
REGIONAL MUSEUM
KARLOVY VARY
KARLOVY MUSEUM
KAŠPERSKÉ HORY
ŠUMAVY MUSEUM
KLATOVY
REGIONAL MUSEUM
KOŠICE
MUSEUM OF EASTERN SLOVAKIA
LEVOČA
SPIŠ MUSEUM
LIBEREC
MUSEUM OF NORTHERN CZECHOSLOVAKIA
LITOMĚŘICE
DISTRICT MUSEUM
MICHALOVCE
ZEMPLIN MUSEUM
OPAVA
SILESIAN MUSEUM: NATURAL HISTORY COLLECTIONS
ORAVSKY PODZÁMOK
ORAVA MUSEUM
OSTRAVA
OSTRAVA MUSEUM
PARDUBICE
MUSEUM OF EASTERN CZECHOSLOVAKIA
PLZEŇ
MUSEUM OF WESTERN CZECHOSLOVAKIA: NATURAL HISTORY COLLECTIONS
PODĚBRADY
DISTRICT MUSEUM
POPRAD
TATRA MUSEUM
PRAGUE
NATIONAL MUSEUM: MUSEUM OF NATURAL HISTORY
PREŠOV
MUSEUM OF THE SLOVAK REPUBLIC
PŘIMĚTICE
PROKOP DIVIŠ MEMORIAL
RUŽOMBEROK
LIPTOV MUSEUM
SLATIŇANY
MUSEUM OF THE HORSE
SOBĚSLAV
MUSEUM OF SOUTHERN CZECHOSLOVAKIA
TATRANSKÁ LOMNICA
MUSEUM OF THE TATRA NATIONAL PARK (TANAP)
TRENČÍN
TRENČÍN MUSEUM
TRNAVA
MUSEUM OF WESTERN SLOVAKIA
ÚSOV
REGIONAL MUSEUM
VRCHLABÍ
KRKONOŠ MUSEUM (ASSOCIATED WITH KRKONOŠSKÝ NATIONAL PARK)
ŽAMBERK
PROKOP DIVIŠ MEMORIAL MUSEUM
MUNICIPAL MUSEUM
ŽILINA
POVAŽIA MUSEUM AND ART GALLERY

DAHOMEY

PARAKOU
OPEN-AIR MUSEUM OF ETHNOGRAPHY AND NATURAL SCIENCES

DENMARK

ÅRHUS
NATURAL HISTORY MUSEUM
COPENHAGEN
BIOLOGICAL COLLECTION
ZOOLOGICAL MUSEUM
GILLELEJE
GILLELEJE MUSEUM
SORØ
ACADEMY MUSEUM
SVENDBORG
ZOOLOGICAL MUSEUM

ECUADOR

QUITO
NATURAL HISTORY MUSEUM

EGYPT, ARAB REPUBLIC OF

ALEXANDRIA
OCEANOGRAPHY AND AQUARIUM MUSEUM
CAIRO
AGRICULTURE MUSEUM
SCIENCE MUSEUM

EL SALVADOR

SAN SALVADOR
NATURAL HISTORY MUSEUM

ETHIOPIA

ADDIS ABABA
NATURAL HISTORY MUSEUM

FINLAND

FORSSA
NATURAL HISTORY MUSEUM
HELSINKI
UNIVERSITY MUSEUM OF ZOOLOGY
JYVÄSKYLÄ
UNIVERSITY MUSEUM
OULU
UNIVERSITY ZOOLOGICAL MUSEUM
PALLASTUNTURI
NATURAL HISTORY MUSEUM
PORVOO
MUSEUM OF NATURAL HISTORY
ROVANIEMI
MUNICIPAL NATURAL HISTORY MUSEUM
TAMPERE
NATURAL HISTORY MUSEUM
TURKU
BIOLOGICAL MUSEUM
MUSEUM OF BIOLOGY
VAASA
EAST BOTHNIA AUSTRALIS MUSEUM

FRANCE

ALLAUCH
MUSEUM OF OLD ALLAUCH
ANGERS
MUSEUM OF PALAEONTOLOGY AND NATURAL HISTORY
ARCACHON
ARCACHON AQUARIUM MUSEUM
ARUDY
OSSAU MUSEUM
AUTUN
AUTUN NATURAL HISTORY MUSEUM
AVIGNON
RÉQUIEN MUSEUM OF NATURAL HISTORY
BAYONNE
NATURAL HISTORY MUSEUM
BERGUES
MUNICIPAL MUSEUM
BÉZIERS
MUSEUM OF NATURAL HISTORY
BIARRITZ
MUSEUM OF THE SEA
LE BLANC
MUSEUM OF BIRDS
LE BRUSC
MUSEUM OF THE MARINE OBSERVATORY
CHAMBÉRY
MUSEUM OF NATURAL HISTORY
LA CHÂTRE
MUSEUM OF GEORGE SAND AND OF THE VALLÉE NOIRE
CHERBOURG
MUSEUM OFNATURAL HISTORY AND ETHNOGRAPHY
CONCARNEAU
MUSEUM OF FISHING
DIJON
MUSEUM OF NATURAL HISTORY
GAILLAC
NATURAL HISTORY MUSEUM
LE HAVRE
MUSEUM OF NATURAL HISTORY
LILLE
MUSEUM OF NATURAL HISTORY
LODÈVE
MUSEUM OF NATURAL HISTORY
LYON
MUSEUM OF NATURAL HISTORY
MARSEILLE
NATURAL HISTORY MUSEUM
LE MAS D'AZIL
LADEVÈZE MUSEUM
MONTAUBAN
VICTOR BRUN MUSEUM OF NATURAL HISTORY
MONTBARD
BUFFON MUSEUM
MONTBÉLIARD
HISTORICAL MUSEUM OF OLD MONTBELIARD
MONTLUCON
MUNICIPAL MUSEUM
NANCY
UNIVERSITY AND CITY MUSEUM OF ZOOLOGY
NANTES
MUSEUM OF NATURAL HISTORY
NEMOURS
CHÂTEAU MUSEUM
NICE
INTERNATIONAL MUSEUM OF MALACOLOGY
NATURAL HISTORY MUSEUM
NOIRMOUTIER EN L'ILE
CHÂTEAU MUSEUM
ORLÉANS
MUSEUM OF NATURAL SCIENCE
PARIS
MUSEUM OF THE DUKE OF ORLEANS
MUSEUM OF MAN
MUSEUM OF NATURAL HISTORY
ORFILA MUSEUM
ROUEN
MUSEUM OF NATURAL HISTORY, ETHNOGRAPHY AND PREHISTORY

SAINTES- MARIES-DE-LA-MER
CAMARGUE MUSEUM

ST. GILLES DU GARD
ARCHAEOLOGICAL MUSEUM

SAINT-OMER
HENRI DUPUIS MUSEUM

SAUMUR
MUSEUM OF DECORATIVE ARTS AND MUSEUM OF THE HORSE

SÉRIGNAN-DU-COMTAT
HENRI FABRE MUSEUM

TOULON
NATURAL HISTORY MUSEUM

TOULOUSE
MUSEUM OF NATURAL HISTORY

TRÉGASTEL
MUSEUM OF PREHISTORY

UZÈS
LOCAL MUSEUM

VALENCE
MUSEUM OF FINE ART AND NATURAL HISTORY

FRENCH POLYNESIA

TAHITI
PAPEETE MUSEUM

GDR

ALTENBURG
'MAURITIANUM' MUSEUM OF NATURAL HISTORY

ANNABERG-BUCHHOLZ
ERZGEBIRG MUSEUM: DEPARTMENT OF NATURAL HISTORY

ARNEBURG
REGIONAL MUSEUM

ARNSTADT
REGIONAL MUSEUM

AUGUSTUSBURG
REGIONAL MUSEUM

BEESKOW
REGIONAL MUSEUM OF BIOLOGY

BERLIN
HUMBOLDT UNIVERSITY: ZOOLOGICAL MUSEUM

BITTERFELD
DISTRICT MUSEUM

BÜTZOW
REGIONAL MUSEUM

COLDITZ
REGIONAL MUSEUM

CRIMMITSCHAU
REGIONAL MUSEUM

DELITZSCH
DISTRICT MUSEUM

DERMBACH
DISTRICT MUSEUM

DESSAU
MUSEUM OF NATURAL HISTORY AND PREHISTORY

DORFCHEMNITZ, KREIS STOLBERG
BONE-MILL CULTURAL CENTRE

DRESDEN
STATE MUSEUM OF ZOOLOGY
ZOOLOGICAL INSTITUTE OF DRESDEN TECHNICAL UNIVERSITY

EISFELD
OTTO LUDWIG REGIONAL MUSEUM

EISLEBEN
NATURAL HISTORY COLLECTION

ERFURT
NATURAL SCIENCE MUSEUM

FALKENSEE
REGIONAL ROOM

FREIBERG
MUSEUM OF NATURAL HISTORY

GERA
NATURAL HISTORY MUSEUM

GLAUCHAU
MUNICIPAL MUSEUM AND ART COLLECTION

GÖRLITZ
STATE MUSEUM OF NATURAL HISTORY

GOTHA
NATURAL HISTORY MUSEUM

GREIFSWALD
COLLECTIONS OF THE ERNST MORITZ ARNDT UNIVERSITY: ANATOMICAL INSTITUTE AND MUSEUM
COLLECTIONS OF THE ERNST MORITZ ARNDT UNIVERSITY: ZOOLOGICAL INSTITUTE AND MUSEUM

HALLE
MUSEUM OF THE DEPARTMENT OF ZOOLOGY OF MARTIN LUTHER UNIVERSITY
WALDKATER REGIONAL MUSEUM

HIDDENSEE
BIOLOGICAL RESEARCH INSTITUTE OF THE ERNST MORITZ ARNDT UNIVERSITY, GREIFSWALD: BIRD-WATCHING STATION
HIDDENSEE ISLAND REGIONAL MUSEUM

HOHENLEUBEN
HOHENLEUBEN - REICHSFELS MUSEUM

JENA
ERNST HAECKEL HOUSE
PHYLETIC MUSEUM

KAMENZ
WEST LAUSITZ MUSEUM

KÖTHEN
JOHANN FRIEDRICH NAUMANN MUSEUM

LEIPZIG
GEOGRAPHICAL MUSEUM OF THE GERMAN ACADEMY OF SCIENCES, BERLIN
INSTITUTE OF ZOOLOGY
MUSEUM OF NATURAL SCIENCES

LIEBSTADT
CASTLE KUCKUCKSTEIN REGIONAL MUSEUM

LUCKAU
REGIONAL MUSEUM

MAGDEBURG
MUSEUM OF CULTURAL HISTORY

MARIENBERG
REGIONAL MUSEUM

MEININGEN
TEACHING DISPLAY FOR THE PROTECTION OF BIRDS

MOLCHOW-STENDENITZ
MUSEUM IN THE FOREST

MORITZBURG
MUSEUM OF BIRDS AND BIRD PROTECTION

MÜHLHAUSEN
DISTRICT MUSEUM

MYLAU
REGIONAL MUSEUM

NESCHWITZ
BIRD PROTECTION STATION

NEUBRANDENBURG
MUSEUM OF CULTURAL HISTORY

NOSSEN
REGIONAL MUSEUM

QUEDLINBURG
MUSEUM BEHIND THE KLOPSTOCK HOUSE

ROSTOCK
COLLECTION OF THE DEPARTMENT OF ZOOLOGY

SANGERHAUSEN
SPENGLER MUSEUM

SEEBACH
SEEBACH BIRD-PROTECTION STATION

SEIFHENNERSDORF
NATURAL HISTORY AND REGIONAL MUSEUM

SERRAHN
SERRAHN BIOLOGICAL STATION

SIEBENLEHN
REGIONAL MUSEUM

STECKBY
STECKBY BIRD PROTECTION STATION

STRALSUND
MUSEUM OF THE SEA

THARANDT
INSTITUTE OF FORESTRY ZOOLOGY

WALDENBURG
REGIONAL MUSEUM AND NATURAL HISTORY COLLECTION

WEIMAR
GERMAN BEE MUSEUM
MUSEUM OF NATURAL HISTORY
MUSEUM OF THE PREHISTORY AND EARLY HISTORY OF THURINGIA

WEISSENFELS
MUNICIPAL MUSEUM

GFR

ASCHAFFENBURG
NATURAL HISTORY MUSEUM

AUGSBURG
NATURAL HISTORY MUSEUM

BAD SCHWARTAU
REGIONAL MUSEUM

BAMBERG
NATURAL HISTORY MUSEUM

BERUMERFEHN
WOODLAND AND MOOR MUSEUM

BIELEFELD
NATURAL HISTORY MUSEUM

BONN
INSTITUTE OF ZOOLOGICAL RESEARCH AND ALEXANDER KOENIG MUSEUM

BOPPARD
FOREST AND TIMBER MUSEUM

BRAUNFELS
DR. KANNGIESSER'S WOODLAND MUSEUM

BRAUNSCHWEIG
STATE MUSEUM OF NATURAL HISTORY

BREMEN
OVERSEAS MUSEUM: CHILDREN'S MUSEUM

BREMERHAVEN
NORTH SEA MUSEUM

BREMERVÖRDE
DISTRICT MUSEUM

BURG-DITHMARSCHEN
WOODLAND MUSEUM

BÜSUM
WILDLIFE PARADISE

COBURG
MUSEUM OF NATURAL SCIENCE

DARMSTADT
HESSE MUSEUM

DATTELN
HERMANN GROCHTMANN MUSEUM

DORTMUND
NATURAL HISTORY MUSEUM

DÜSSELDORF
BENRATH NATURAL HISTORY MUSEUM
LÖBBECKE MUSEUM

EICHSTÄTT
BERGÉR MUSEUM
NATURAL SCIENCE COLLECTIONS

ERLANGEN
ZOOLOGICAL COLLECTION OF THE UNIVERSITY OF ERLANGEN- NÜRNBERG

FLADUNGEN
RHÖN MUSEUM

FLENSBURG
REGIONAL MUSEUM OF NATURAL HISTORY

FRANKFURT
SENCKENBERG NATURAL HISTORY MUSEUM AND RESEARCH INSTITUTE

FREIBURG IM BREISGAU
NATURAL HISTORY MUSEUM

FREYUNG
WOLFSTEIN DISTRICT MUSEUM

FULDA
VONDERAU MUSEUM

GEILENKIRCHEN
REGIONAL MUSEUM

GIFHORN
DISTRICT MUSEUM

GLADBECK
GLADBECK TOWN MUSEUM

GÖTTINGEN
COLLECTIONS OF THE ZOOLOGICAL INSTITUTE OF THE UNIVERSITY OF GÖTTINGEN

GOSLAR
GOSLAR MUSEUM
MUSEUM OF NATURAL HISTORY

GRAFENWÖHR
REGIONAL MUSEUM

HAMBURG
ALTONA MUSEUM
ZOOLOGY MUSEUM

HANNOVER
LAND MUSEUM OF LOWER SAXONY: DEPARTMENT OF NATURAL HISTORY

HEIDELBERG
UNIVERSITY MUSEUM OF ZOOLOGY

HERNE
EMSCHERTAL MUSEUM

HILDESHEIM
ROEMER-PELIZAEUS MUSEUM

HUSUM
NISSEN HOUSE

IDAR-OBERSTEIN
REGIONAL MUSEUM

INGELHEIM
CARLO FREIHERR VON ERLANGER MUSEUM

JUIST
COASTAL MUSEUM

KARLSRUHE
LAND NATURAL HISTORY COLLECTIONS

KASSEL
NATURAL HISTORY MUSEUM

KEITUM-SYLT
SYLT REGIONAL MUSEUM

KIEL
SCHLESWIG-HOLSTEIN TRAVELLING MUSEUM
ZOOLOGY MUSEUM OF THE UNIVERSITY OF KIEL

KIRCHHEIMBOLANDEN
REGIONAL MUSEUM

KÖLN-MERHEIM
GERMAN MUSEUM OF HEALTH

KONSTANZ
LAKE CONSTANCE MUSEUM OF NATURAL HISTORY

KORBACH
KORBACH REGIONAL MUSEUM

KULMBACH-PLASSENBURG
UPPER MAIN REGIONAL MUSEUM

LAICHINGEN
LAICHINGEN CAVE MUSEUM

LEER
REGIONAL MUSEUM

LEMBRUCK
DÜMMER MUSEUM

LIMBURG (LAHN)
MISSION MUSEUM

LÜBECK
NATURAL HISTORY MUSEUM

LUDWIGSBURG
STATE MUSEUM OF NATURAL HISTORY

MAINZ
NATURAL HISTORY MUSEUM

MAXBERG
SOLENHOFER COMPANY MUSEUM

MÖRNSHEIM
MUSEUM OF PETRIFIED OBJECTS

MÜNCHEN
STATE ANTHROPOLOGICAL COLLECTION

MÜNSTER
LAND MUSEUM OF NATURAL HISTORY

MURRHARDT
CARL SCHWEIZER MUSEUM

NEBEL
AMRUNER MUSEUM

NEUSTADT AN DER AISCH
MUSEUM OF THE LOCAL HISTORY SOCIETY

NEUSTADT-WEISTRASSE
NATURAL HISTORY MUSEUM

NIEBÜLL
NIEBÜLL FRISIAN MUSEUM

NÜMBRECHT
MUSEUM OF THE OBERBERG REGION

NÜRNBERG
MAN AND NATURE MUSEUM

OBERGÜNZBURG
SOUTH SEAS COLLECTION

OEVENTROP
SOUTH SEAS MUSEUM

OFFENBURG
HOUSE OF THE KNIGHTS MUSEUM

OLDENBURG
STATE MUSEUM OF NATURAL HISTORY AND PREHISTORY

OSNABRÜCK
MUNICIPAL MUSEUM

OTTOBEUREN
ABBEY MUSEUM

PADERBORN
REGIONAL MUSEUM OF NATURAL HISTORY

PASSAU
OBERHAUS MUSEUM

POTTENSTEIN
REGIONAL MUSEUM

REGENSBURG
NATURAL HISTORY MUSEUM

REUTLINGEN
MUSEUM OF NATURAL HISTORY

ROTTHALMÜNSTER
REGIONAL MUSEUM

ST. OTTILIEN
MISSION MUSEUM

SCHWÄBISCH-GMÜND
SCHWÄBISCH-GMÜND MUSEUM

SPAICHINGEN
MUSEUM OF GEOLOGY AND PREHISTORY

STUTTGART
STATE MUSEUM OF NATURAL HISTORY

SURWOLD
WOODLAND MUSEUM

TIENGEN
NATURAL HISTORY MUSEUM

TRAUNSTEIN
REGIONAL MUSEUM

TÜBINGEN
MUSEUM OF THE UNIVERSITY INSTITUTE OF ZOOLOGY

TUTZING
G. FREY MUSEUM

VON DER HEYDT
GEOLOGICAL COLLECTION OF THE SAARBRÜCKEN SCHOOL OF MINING

WERTACH
REGIONAL MUSEUM

WESTRHAUDERFEHN
OSTFRIESLAND AND SATERLAND FEN AND SHIPPING MUSEUM

WIESBADEN
NATURAL SCIENCES COLLECTION

WIESMOOR
MOOR MUSEUM

WILHELMSHAVEN
COLLECTION OF THE INSTITUTE FOR ORNITHOLOGICAL RESEARCH

WÜLFRATH
NIEDERBERG REGIONAL MUSEUM

WÜRZBURG
MACROSCOPIC ANATOMY COLLECTION

GHANA

ACCRA
MUSEUM OF SCIENCE AND TECHNOLOGY

KUMASI
MUSEUM OF NATURAL HISTORY

GIBRALTAR

GIBRALTAR
GIBRALTAR MUSEUM

GREAT BRITAIN

ABERDEEN
ABERDEEN UNIVERSITY NATURAL HISTORY MUSEUM

BIRCHINGTON
POWELL-COTTON MUSEUM

BIRMINGHAM
BIRMINGHAM CITY MUSEUM AND ART GALLERY
CANNON HILL MUSEUM
UNIVERSITY MEDICAL SCHOOL MUSEUM

BRAMBER
POTTER'S MUSEUM

BRIGHTON
BOOTH MUSEUM OF BRITISH BIRDS

BROKERSWOOD
THE PHILLIPS COUNTRYSIDE MUSEUM OF NATURAL HISTORY AND FORESTRY

BURTON- ON-TRENT
MUSEUM AND ART GALLERY

CAMBRIDGE
UNIVERSITY MUSEUM OF ZOOLOGY AND COMPARATIVE ANATOMY

CARDIFF
NATIONAL MUSEUM OF WALES

CARLISLE
MUSEUM AND ART GALLERY

CHELMSFORD
CHELMSFORD AND ESSEX MUSEUM

COLCHESTER
COLCHESTER AND ESSEX MUSEUM

EDINBURGH
ROYAL SCOTTISH MUSEUM

ELGIN
ELGIN MUSEUM

ETON
ETON COLLEGE NATURAL HISTORY SOCIETY MUSEUM

EXETER
ROYAL ALBERT MEMORIAL MUSEUM AND ART GALLERY

GLASGOW
CITY OF GLASGOW CORPORATION ART GALLERY AND MUSEUM

LEEDS
CITY MUSEUM

LIVERPOOL
CITY OF LIVERPOOL MUSEUMS

LONDON
BRITISH MUSEUM: NATURAL HISTORY
BUTLER MUSEUM
DARWIN MUSEUM
EPPING FOREST MUSEUM
HORNIMAN MUSEUM

MANCHESTER
MANCHESTER MUSEUM

MILLPORT
ROBERTSON MUSEUM AND AQUARIUM

NEWCASTLE- UPON-TYNE
UNIVERSITY OF NEWCASTLE- UPON-TYNE

NORTHAMPTON
ABINGTON MUSEUM

NOTTINGHAM
NATURAL HISTORY MUSEUM
WOLLATON HALL

OXFORD
OXFORD UNIVERSITY MUSEUM

PERTH
PERTH ART GALLERY AND MUSEUM

POOLE
POOLE MUSEUM

PORT ERIN
MARINE BIOLOGICAL STATION

READING
COLE MUSEUM OF ZOOLOGY

REIGATE
HOLMESDALE NATURAL HISTORY CLUB MUSEUM

SCARBOROUGH
SCARBOROUGH MUSEUM OF NATURAL HISTORY

SELBORNE
GILBERT WHITE MUSEUM

STIRLING
UNIVERSITY OF STIRLING

TEESSIDE
DORMAN MUSEUM

TRING
ZOOLOGICAL MUSEUM

GREECE

ATHENS
ANTHROPOLOGICAL AND ETHNOLOGICAL MUSEUM
ZOOLOGICAL MUSEUM

GUATEMALA

GUATEMALA CITY
MUSEUM OF NATURAL HISTORY

HUNGARY

ÁBRAHÁMHEGY
ORNITHOLOGICAL COLLECTION

BALASSAGYARMAT
PALÓC MUSEUM

BUDAPEST
NATURAL HISTORY MUSEUM

MISKOLC-LILLAFÜRED
OTTÓ HERMAN MEMORIAL MUSEUM

SZEGED
FERENC MÓRA MUZEUM

SZÉKESFEHÉRVÁR
KING ISTVÁN MUSEUM

ZIRC
ANTAL REGULY MUSEUM

ICELAND

REYKJAVIK
ICELANDIC STUFFED ANIMALS COLLECTION
MUSEUM OF NATURAL HISTORY

INDIA

AGRA
ST. JOHN'S COLLEGE MUSEUM

AHMEDABAD
B. J. MEDICAL COLLEGE MUSEUMS

ALLAHABAD
UNIVERSITY MUSEUMS

ANNAMALAINAGAR
ZOOLOGY MUSEUM

BANGALORE
CENTRAL COLLEGE MUSEUMS
MYSORE GOVERNMENT MUSEUM

BOMBAY
GRANT MEDICAL COLLEGE MUSEUMS
NATURAL HISTORY MUSEUM
PRINCE OF WALES MUSEUM OF WESTERN INDIA
SETH GORDHANDAS SUNDERDAS MEDICAL COLLEGE MUSEUM
VICTORIA AND ALBERT MUSEUM

CALCUTTA
MUSEUM

COIMBATORE
AGRICULTURAL COLLEGE MUSEUM
SOUTHERN FOREST RANGERS COLLEGE AND RESEARCH CENTRE

DARJEELING
NATURAL HISTORY MUSEUM

ERNAKULAM
ZOOLOGY AND BOTANY MUSEUM

GAUHATI
GAUHATI MEDICAL COLLEGE

HOSHIARPUR
MUSEUM OF THE ZOOLOGY DEPARTMENT

IMPHAL
MANIPUR STATE MUSEUM

JODHPUR
STATE MUSEUM

LUCKNOW
UNIVERSITY OF LUCKNOW MUSEUMS

MADRAS
THE GOVERNMENT MUSEUM AND NATIONAL ART GALLERY
STANLEY MEDICAL COLLEGE MUSEUM

MANDAPAM CAMP
CENTRAL MARINE FISHERIES RESEARCH STATION REFERENCE MUSEUM

MANGALORE
MAHATMA GANDHI MUSEUM

MYSORE
MEDICAL COLLEGE MUSEUMS

NAGPUR
CENTRAL MUSEUM

NEW DELHI
LADY HARDINGE MEDICAL COLLEGE MUSEUMS

PATNA
PATNA MUSEUM

PUDDUKKOTTAI
GOVERNMENT MUSEUM

RAIPUR
MAHANT GHASI DASS MEMORIAL MUSEUM

SRINAGAR
S.P.S. MUSEUM

SURAT
SARDAR V. PATEL MUSEUM

TAMBARAM
ZOOLOGICAL MUSEUM

TAMLUK
HAMILTON HIGH SCHOOL MUSEUM

TIRUCHIRAPALLI
NATURAL HISTORY MUSEUM

TRICHUR
STATE MUSEUM

TRIVANDRUM
NATURAL HISTORY MUSEUM

VIJAYAWADA
VICTORIA JUBILEE MUSEUM

VISAKHAPATNAM
ANDHRA MEDICAL COLLEGE MUSEUMS

INDONESIA

BANDUNG
ZOOLOGICAL MUSEUM

BOGOR
BOGOR ZOOLOGICAL MUSEUM

IRAN

KARAJ
ZOOLOGICAL MUSEUM

IRAQ

BAGHDAD
IRAQ NATURAL HISTORY MUSEUM

IRELAND

DUBLIN
NATIONAL MUSEUM OF IRELAND

ISRAEL

DAN
USSISHKIN HOUSE

DEGANIA
A. D. GORDON MUSEUM

EILAT
RED SEA MARITIME MUSEUM

HAIFA
MUSEUM OF NATURAL HISTORY AND PREHISTORY

JERUSALEM
MUSEUM OF NATURAL HISTORY

PETAH-TIQVA
MUSEUM OF THE HUMAN BODY

TEL-AVIV
ZOOLOGICAL MUSEUM

ITALY

BOLOGNA
MUSEUM OF THE ZOOLOGICAL INSTITUTE
ZOOLOGICAL COLLECTIONS

BORDIGHERA
BICKNELL MUSEUM
GARIBALDI ORNITHOLOGICAL COLLECTION

BRA
NATURAL HISTORY COLLECTIONS OF THE CRAVERI MUSEUM

BRESCIA
RAGAZZONI NATURAL HISTORY MUSEUM

BUIA
MARANGOLI ORNITHOLOGICAL COLLECTION

CAGLIARI
ZOOLOGICAL MUSEUM

CAMERINO
MUSEUM OF COMPARATIVE ANATOMY
ZOOLOGICAL MUSEUM

CATANIA
MUSEUM OF ZOOLOGY AND COMPARATIVE ANATOMY

CATANZARO
ENTOMOLOGICAL COLLECTION

COMO
BARI ENTOMOLOGICAL COLLECTION
POZZI MONTANDON ENTOMOLOGICAL COLLECTION

FALCONARA MARITTIMA
MORODER ENTOMOLOGICAL COLLECTION

FLORENCE
LA SPECOLA MUSEUM OF ZOOLOGY

GAIOLI IN CHIANTI
MALACOLOGICAL COLLECTION

GENOA
COLLECTION OF THE INSTITUTE OF COMPARATIVE ANATOMY
COLLECTIONS OF THE INSTITUTE OF ZOOLOGY
COLLECTIONS OF NATURAL HISTORY
NATURAL HISTORY MUSEUM

GORLA MINORA
MUSEUM OF NATURAL HISTORY

GROSSETO
MUSEUM OF NATURAL HISTORY
NATURAL HISTORY COLLECTIONS

LA SPEZIA
MUSEUM OF NATURAL HISTORY AND ETHNOGRAPHY

LIVORNO
MUNICIPAL MUSEUM OF NATURAL HISTORY

LUCCA
MASSAGLI ORNITHOLOGICAL COLLECTION
NATURAL HISTORY MUSEUM

MESSINA
MUSEUM OF THE INSTITUTE OF ZOOLOGY

MILAN
CIVIC MUSEUM OF NATURAL HISTORY
COLLECTION OF THE INSTITUTE OF ENTOMOLOGY
COLLECTION OF THE INSTITUTE OF MICROBIOLOGY
COLLECTIONS OF THE INSTITUTE OF ZOOLOGY
MUNICIPAL MUSEUM OF NATURAL HISTORY
ZOOLOGICAL MUSEUM

MODENA
MUSEUM OF THE INSTITUTE OF ZOOLOGY

NAPLES
COLLECTION OF NAPLES ZOOLOGICAL STATION
ZOOLOGICAL MUSEUM
ZOOLOGICAL MUSEUM

PADUA
MUSEUM OF THE INSTITUTE OF ZOOLOGY, COMPARATIVE ANATOMY AND GENETICS

PARMA
"VITTORIO BOTTEGO" ERYTHREAN ZOOLOGICAL MUSEUM
GENERAL COLLECTIONS
PIOLA CONGOLESE COLLECTION

PERUGIA
COLLECTION OF THE INSTITUTE OF BIOLOGY
NATURAL HISTORY COLLECTION

PESCASSEROLI

MUSEUM OF THE ABRUZZO NATIONAL PARK

PORTICI

FILIPPO SILVESTRI MUSEUM

PORTOGRUARO

FAVERO ORNITHOLOGICAL COLLECTION

REGGIO EMILIA

CIVIC MUSEUM
LAZZARO SPALLANZANI MUSEUM OF NATURAL HISTORY

ROME

COLLECTION OF THE NATIONAL INSTITUTE OF ENTOMOLOGY
ZOOLOGICAL MUSEUM

SAN PANCRAZIO DI RUSSI

ORNITHOLOGICAL MUSEUM

SASSARI

COLLECTION OF THE INSTITUTE OF BIOLOGY AND ZOOLOGY
SCIENTIFIC COLLECTIONS

TARANTO

NATURAL HISTORY COLLECTION

TEMPIO PAUSANIA

STAZZA COLLECTION

TREVISO

SCARPA ZOOLOGICAL MUSEUM

TRIESTE

NATURAL HISTORY MUSEUM
SAULI ENTOMOLOGICAL COLLECTION

TURIN

MUSEUM OF NATURAL SCIENCE
ZOOLOGICAL MUSEUM

UDINE

ORNITHOLOGY MUSEUM
ZOOLOGICAL COLLECTION

VARALLO SESIA

MUSEUM OF ZOOLOGY

VARENNA

ORNITHOLOGICAL MUSEUM
SCANAGATTA COLLECTION

VARESE

SAVERI COLLECTION

VENICE

CADAMURO MORGANTE COLLECTION
ENTOMOLOGY COLLECTION
LEVRINI COLLECTION
MEGGIOLARO COLLECTION
MUSEUM OF NATURAL HISTORY
TOLOTTI COLLECTION
ZOOLOGICAL COLLECTION

VERBANIA

NATURAL HISTORY COLLECTION

VERCELLI

BORGOGNA MUSEUM

VERONA

MUSEUM OF NATURAL HISTORY

VICENZA

NATURAL HISTORY MUSEUM

JAMAICA

KINGSTON

NATURAL HISTORY MUSEUM

JAPAN

AKKESHI-MACHI

AKKESHI MUSEUM OF HOKKAIDO UNIVERSITY

ASAHIKAWA-SHI

ASAHIKAWA LOCAL MUSEUM

FUKUI-SHI

FUKUI MUNICIPAL NATURAL HISTORY MUSEUM

FUTTSU

FUTTSU OCEANOGRAPHIC MUSEUM OF CHIBA PREFECTURE

HAKODATE-SHI

HAKODATE MUNICIPAL MUSEUM

HIWA-MACHI

HIWA MUSEUM OF NATURAL HISTORY

IBURI-SHICHO

FOREST MUSEUM OF TOYA NATIONAL PARK

KOMATSU-SHI

KOMATSU MUNICIPAL MUSEUM

KYOTO

MT. HIEI NATURAL HISTORY MUSEUM AND ROCK GARDEN
THE ZOOLOGICAL SPECIMEN GALLERY OF DOSHISHA HIGH SCHOOL

MINOBU-MACHI

THE YAMANASHI PREFECTURAL MUSEUM OF FUJI NATIONAL PARK

MINO'O-SHI

MINO'O PARK ENTOMOLOGICAL MUSEUM

MIYAKO-SHI

FISHERIES MUSEUM OF MIYAKO FISHERIES HIGH SCHOOL

MIYAZAKI-SHI

AGRICULTURAL MUSEUM OF MIYAZAKI UNIVERSITY

NAGAOKA-SHI

NAGAOKA MUNICIPAL MUSEUM OF NATURAL SCIENCE

NAGASAKI-SHI

NAGASAKI MUNICIPAL CHILDREN'S SCIENCE HALL

NARA-SHI

THE AYAMEIKE MUSEUM OF NATURAL HISTORY

NATORI-GUN

HORSEMANSHIP MUSEUM OF TAKEKOMA SHRINE

NI'IGATA-SHI

NI'IGATA SCIENCE AND TECHNOLOGY MUSEUM

NIKKO-SHI

NIKKO MUSEUM OF NATURAL HISTORY
OKUNIKKO MUSEUM OF NATURAL HISTORY

NOGAMI-MACHI

CHICHIBU MUSEUM OF NATURAL HISTORY

NO'O-MACHI

NO'O MARINE AND MARITIME MUSEUM

OARAI-MACHI

OARAI MARINE MUSEUM

OSAKA

MUSEUM OF INSECTS
NATURAL SCIENCE MUSEUM

OTARU-SHI

OTARU CITY MUSEUM

SAIJO-SHI

SAIJO LOCAL MUSEUM

SAPPORO-SHI

NATURAL HISTORY MUSEUM OF HOKKAIDO UNIVERSITY

SAWADA-MACHI

SADO MUSEUM

SHUHO-MACHI

AKIYOSHIDAI MUSEUM OF NATURAL HISTORY

TAKANOSU-MACHI

AGRICULTURAL MUSEUM OF TAKANOSU PREFECTURAL AGRICULTURAL AND FORESTRY HIGH SCHOOL

TAMANO-SHI

TAMANO MARINE MUSEUM

TESHIKAGA-MACHI

AKAN WAGOTO MUSEUM

TOKYO

THE LABOUR MUSEUM OF LABOUR SCIENCE INSTITUTE
MEGURO PARASITOLOGICAL MUSEUM
MUSEUM OF ART AND HISTORY OF THE UNIVERSITY OF TOKYO
NATIONAL SCIENCE MUSEUM
ODAWARA CARCINOLOGICAL MUSEUM
TOKYO-TO TAKAO MUSEUM OF NATURAL HISTORY
TOSHIMAEN INSECTARIUM
YAMASHINA INSTITUTE OF ORNITHOLOGY

TOTTORI-SHI

TOTTORI PREFECTURAL SCIENCE MUSEUM

TOWADA-MACHI

TOWADA MUSEUM OF NATURAL HISTORY

YAMAGUCHI-SHI

YAMAGUCHI PREFECTURAL MUSEUM

YOKOSUKA-SHI

YOKOSUKA CITY MUSEUM

KENYA

KITALE

STONEHAM MUSEUM AND RESEARCH CENTRE

NAIROBI

NATIONAL MUSEUM

KOREA, REPUBLIC OF

SEOUL

NATIONAL SCIENCE MUSEUM

KUWAIT

KUWAIT

KUWAIT MUSEUM
KUWAIT NATURAL HISTORY MUSEUM

LESOTHO

MORIJA

MUSEUM OF MORIJA

LIBYAN ARAB REPUBLIC

TRIPOLI

NATURAL HISTORY MUSEUM

MALAYSIA

ALOR STAR

MUSEUM NEGERI KEDAH

KUALA LUMPUR

NATIONAL MUSEUM

SARAWAK

SARAWAK MUSEUM

MALTA

MDINA

MUSEUM OF NATURAL HISTORY AND FOLKLORE

NAXXAR

BIRD MUSEUM

MAURITIUS

PORT LOUIS

NATURAL HISTORY MUSEUM

MEXICO

MEXICO CITY

MUSEUM OF NATURAL HISTORY
NATURAL HISTORY MUSEUM

UNIVERSITY CITY

NATURAL HISTORY MUSEUM

MOZAMBIQUE

BEIRA

MUNICIPAL MUSEUM

INHACA ISLAND

MUSEUM OF MARINE BIOLOGY

MANICA

MOSTRUÁRO DE MANICA MUSEUM

NETHERLANDS

AMSTERDAM

NATURAL HISTORY COLLECTION
ZOOLOGICAL MUSEUM OF THE UNIVERSITY OF AMSTERDAM

APPELSCHA

NATURAL HISTORY MUSEUM

BAKKUM
WAYSIDE MUSEUM
DENEKAMP
'NATURE TEACHER' MUSEUM
ELBURG
'SEEING IS KNOWING' NATURAL HISTORY MUSEUM
ENSCHEDE
NATURAL HISTORY MUSEUM
FREDERIKSVORD
MIRAMAR MUSEUM OF THE SEA
'S GRAVENHAGE
'IN DER SCHULP' SHELL MUSEUM
GRONINGEN
GRONINGEN MUSEUM OF NATURAL HISTORY
NATIONAL UNIVERSITY: INSTITUTE OF BIOLOGY AND ARCHAEOLOGY
HOLTEN
'PIET BOS' MUSEUM OF NATURAL HISTORY
LEEUWARDEN
FRISIAN MUSEUM OF NATURAL HISTORY
MAASTRICHT
NATURAL HISTORY MUSEUM
ST. MICHIELSGESTEL
NATURAL HISTORY MUSEUM OF THE ROMAN CATHOLIC SCHOOL AND SEMINARY 'BEEKOLIET'
NUNSPEET
VELUWE DIORAMA
OUDEMIRDUM
KLIF EN GAAST DISTRICT MUSEUM OF NATURAL HISTORY
ROTTERDAM
DIORAMA BUILDING OF THE NATURAL HISTORY MUSEUM
NATURAL HISTORY MUSEUM
ST. GEERTRUD
SAVELSBOS VISITOR CENTRE
SCHIERMONNIKOOG
NATURAL HISTORY MUSEUM
SCHOKLAND
IJSSELMEER POLDER MUSEUM
STEYL
STEYL MISSION MUSEUM
TILBURG
NATURAL HISTORY MUSEUM
VLIELAND
NATURAL HISTORY MUSEUM
WEST- TERSCHELLING
BRANDARIS MUSEUM OF BIRDS
DISTRICT MUSEUM OF NATURAL HISTORY
ZWARTSLUIS
SCHOONEWELLE NATURAL HISTORY MUSEUM

NEW ZEALAND

ARTHUR'S PASS
ARTHUR'S PASS NATIONAL PARK MUSEUM
AUCKLAND
AUCKLAND WAR MEMORIAL MUSEUM
AVARUA (RAROTONGA)
COOK ISLANDS LIBRARY AND MUSEUM
CHRISTCHURCH
CANTERBURY MUSEUM
DEPARTMENTS OF BOTANY, GEOLOGY AND ZOOLOGY
DUNEDIN
OTAGO MUSEUM
UNIVERSITY OF OTAGO
LOWER HUTT
ANIMAL ECOLOGY DIVISION
NAPIER
HAWKE'S BAY ART GALLERY AND MUSEUM
NELSON
ENTOMOLOGY DIVISION
NEW PLYMOUTH
TARANAKI MUSEUM
WANGANUI
WANGANUI PUBLIC MUSEUM
WELLINGTON
DOMINION MUSEUM
NEW ZEALAND OCEANOGRAPHIC INSTITUTE
VICTORIA UNIVERSITY OF WELLINGTON
WHANGAREI
WHANGAREI CITY COUNCIL MUSEUM

NICARAGUA

MANAGUA
MUSEUM OF NATURAL SCIENCE
NATIONAL MUSEUM OF NICARAGUA

NORWAY

AALESUND
SUNNMØRE MUSEUM
BERGEN
BERGEN AQUARIUM
MUSEUM OF NATURAL HISTORY
ZOOLOGICAL MUSEUM
OSLO
ZOOLOGICAL MUSEUM
TRONDHEIM
MUSEUM OF THE ROYAL NORWEGIAN SOCIETY OF SCIENCES AND LETTERS

PAKISTAN, WEST

LAHORE
ZOOLOGICAL MUSEUM

PARAGUAY

ASUNCION
MUSEUM OF NATURAL HISTORY
NATURAL SCIENCE MUSEUM OF THE INTERNATIONAL COLLEGE

PERU

IQUITOS
MUSEUM
LIMA
JAVIER PRADO NATURAL HISTORY MUSEUM

PHILIPPINES

BAGUIO CITY
ST. LOUIS UNIVERSITY MUSEUM
CEBU CITY
UNIVERSITY MUSEUM
MANILA
MUSEUM OF ARTS AND SCIENCES
NATIONAL MUSEUM OF THE PHILIPPINES
MARAWI CITY
AGA KHAN MUSEUM OF MUSLIM ARTS
NAGA CITY
UNIVERSITY MUSEUM
NUEVA VIZCAYA
DALTON FIELD STATION

POLAND

BYTOM
MUSEUM OF UPPER SILESIA
CIEPLICE ŚLĄSKIE ZDRÓJ
REGIONAL MUSEUM OF NATURAL HISTORY
GDYNIA
OCEANOGRAPHICAL MUSEUM
KAMIENNA GÓRA
MUNICIPAL MUSEUM
KĘTRZYN
KĘTRZYN MUSEUM
KRAKÓW
MUSEUM OF NATURAL HISTORY
UNIVERSITY MUSEUM OF NATURAL HISTORY
KRÓSCIENKO
PIENIN MUSEUM
KRYNICA
NATURAL HISTORY MUSEUM
LESKO
LOCAL MUSEUM
ŁÓDŹ
UNIVERSITY OF **ŁÓDŹ MUSEUM OF EVOLUTION**
LUBLIN
UNIVERSITY ZOOLOGICAL MUSEUM
MALBORK
CASTLE MUSEUM
MIĘDZYZDROJ
NATURAL HISTORY MUSEUM
OJCÓW
NATURAL HISTORY MUSEUM
POZNAŃ
NATURAL HISTORY MUSEUM OF THE INSTITUTE OF ZOOLOGY
PUSZCZYKOWO
NATURAL HISTORY MUSEUM
SOBIESZÓW
KARKONOSKI PARK MUSEUM
SZCZECIN
MARINE MUSEUM OF THE BALTIC INSTITUTE
TATARY POD KADZIDŁEM
KURPIE MUSEUM
WARSAW
ZOOLOGICAL MUSEUM OF THE POLISH ACADEMY OF SCIENCES
WROCŁAW
UNIVERSITY MUSEUM OF ZOOLOGY
ZAWOJA
BABIEJ GÓRY NATIONAL PARK MUSEUM

PORTUGAL

FUNCHAL
MUNICIPAL MUSEUM
LISBON
ZOOLOGICAL AND ANTHROPOLOGICAL MUSEUM

RÉUNION

SAINT-DENIS
MUSEUM OF NATURAL HISTORY

RHODESIA

MARANDELLOS
CHILDREN'S MUSEUM
SALISBURY
QUEEN VICTORIA MUSEUM
UMTALI
UMTALI MUSEUM

ROMANIA

AIUD
NATURAL HISTORY MUSEUM
BACĂU
NATURAL HISTORY MUSEUM
BUCHAREST
GRIGORE ANTIPA MUSEUM OF NATURAL HISTORY
CÎMPULUNG
CÎMPULUNG-MUSCEL MUSEUM
CÎMPULUNG- MOLDOVENESC
MOLDOVENIAN MUSEUM
CLUJ
ARDELEAN MUSEUM
ZOOLOGICAL MUSEUM
CORABIA
CORABIA MUSEUM
CRAIOVA
OLTENIEI MUSEUM
DEJ
DEJ MUSEUM

DEVA
DEVA MUSEUM
FOÇŞANI
NATURAL HISTORY MUSEUM
GALAŢI
NATURAL HISTORY MUSEUM
IAŞI
NATURAL HISTORY MUSEUM
MEDIAŞ
MEDIAŞ MUSEUM
MIERCUREA CIUC
MIERCUREA CIUC MUSEUM
NĂSĂUD
NĂSĂUD MUSEUM
ORADEA
ORIŞANA MUSEUM
ORLEA
LOCAL MUSEUM
PIATRA NEAMŢ
NATURAL HISTORY MUSEUM
PITEŞTI
ARGES DISTRICT MUSEUM
ROMAN
NATURAL HISTORY MUSEUM
SFÎNTU GHEORGHE
SFÎNTU GHEORGHE MUSEUM
SIBIU
NATURAL HISTORY MUSEUM
SUCEAVA
SUCEAVA MUSEUM
TIMIŞOARA
BANAT MUSEUM
TINCA
NATURAL HISTORY MUSEUM
TÎRGU MUREŞ
REGIONAL MUSEUM
TULCEA
MUSEUM OF THE DANUBE DELTA
TURNU SEVERIN
IRON GATE (PORŢILE DE FIER) MUSEUM
VATRA DORNEI
VATRA DORNEI MUSEUM

ST HELENA

GEORGETOWN
FORT HAYES MUSEUM

SOUTH AFRICA, REPUBLIC OF

CAPE TOWN
SOUTH AFRICAN MUSEUM
MUSEUMS OF THE UNIVERSITY OF CAPE TOWN
DURBAN
DURBAN MUSEUM AND ART GALLERY
EAST LONDON
EAST LONDON MUSEUM
GEORGE
GEORGE MUSEUM
JOHANNESBURG
MUSEUMS OF THE UNIVERSITY OF THE WITWATERSRAND
KING WILLIAM'S TOWN
THE KAFFRARIAN MUSEUM
MOSSEL BAY
MOSSEL BAY MUSEUM
PIETERMARITZBURG
NATAL MUSEUM
PORT ELIZABETH
PORT ELIZABETH MUSEUM
PRETORIA
TRANSVAAL MUSEUM
QUEENSTOWN
QUEENSTOWN AND FRONTIER MUSEUM
SKUKUZA
STEVENSON-HAMILTON MEMORIAL LIBRARY

SOUTH-WEST AFRICA (NAMIBIA)

LÜDERITZ
LÜDERITZ MUSEUM

SPAIN

ARTA
REGIONAL MUSEUM
AVILES
MUSEUM OF THE NATURAL SCIENCES
BARCELONA
MUNICIPAL INSTITUTE OF NATURAL SCIENCE
MUSEUM OF ZOOLOGY
BURGOS
SEMINARY MUSEUM
MADRID
ANATOMY COLLECTION
NATIONAL MUSEUM OF NATURAL SCIENCE
NATURAL SCIENCE MUSEUM
MOTRIL
EXOTICUARIUM
ONDA
MUSEUM OF THE NATURAL SCIENCES
SANTIAGO DE COMPOSTELA
LUIS IGLESIAS MUSEUM OF NATURAL HISTORY
ZARAGOZA
ARAGON MUSEUM OF ETHNOLOGY AND NATURAL SCIENCES

SUDAN

KHARTOUM
NATURAL HISTORY MUSEUM

SWEDEN

GÖTEBORG
NATURAL HISTORY MUSEUM
HAMMARBY
LINNAEUS MUSEUM
LUND
ZOOLOGICAL MUSEUM
MALMÖ
MALMÖ MUSEUM
STOCKHOLM
BIOLOGICAL MUSEUM
NATURAL HISTORY MUSEUM
UPPSALA
LINNAEUS MUSEUM
VÄNERSBORG
VÄNERSBORG MUSEUM

SWITZERLAND

AARAU
MUSEUM OF NATURAL HISTORY AND LOCAL LIFE
BASEL
ANATOMICAL MUSEUM
NATURAL HISTORY MUSEUM
BERN
NATURAL HISTORY MUSEUM
BOUDRY
L'AREUSE MUSEUM
BOURG- SAINT-PIERRE
MUSEUM OF THE GREAT ST. BERNARD SHELTER FOR TRAVELLERS
LA CHAUX- DE-FONDS
MUSEUM OF NATURAL HISTORY
CHUR
BÜNDER NATURAL HISTORY AND NATURAL PARK MUSEUM
EBIKON
WILDLIFE PANORAMA
FRAUENFELD
CANTON THURGAU MUSEUM
FRIBOURG
MUSEUM OF THE INSTITUTE OF ANATOMY
MUSEUM OF NATURAL HISTORY
GENEVA
MUSEUM OF THE HISTORY OF SCIENCE
NATURAL HISTORY MUSEUM
GLARUS
NATURAL SCIENCE COLLECTIONS OF CANTON GLARUS
HEIDEN
MUSEUM
LE LANDERON
MUSEUM
LAUSANNE
CANTONAL ZOOLOGICAL MUSEUM
LIESTAL
BASEL-LAND CANTONAL MUSEUM
LOCARNO
MUNICIPAL MUSEUM
LUZERN
NATURAL HISTORY MUSEUM
NEUCHÂTEL
MUSEUM OF NATURAL HISTORY
NYON
LAKE LÉMAN MUSEUM
OLTEN
MUSEUM OF NATURAL HISTORY
RORSCHACH
REGIONAL MUSEUM
SAINTE-CROIX
MUSEUM
ST. GALLEN
OLD MUSEUM
REGIONAL MUSEUM
SARNEN
REGIONAL MUSEUM
SCHAFFHAUSEN
MUSEUM STEMMLER
SEMPACH
TOWN HALL MUSEUM
SION
CANTONAL MUSEUM OF NATURAL HISTORY
SOLOTHURN
SOLOTHURN MUNICIPAL MUSEUM
VEVEY
JENISCH MUSEUM
WINTERTHUR
NATURAL SCIENCE COLLECTION OF THE TOWN OF WINTERTHUR
YVERDON
MUSEUM OF OLD YVERDON
ZERMATT
ALPINE MUSEUM
ZOFINGEN
MUSEUM
ZUG
FISHERY MUSEUM
ZURICH
UNIVERSITY MUSEUM OF ZOOLOGY AND PALAEONTOLOGY

TANZANIA

MBEYA
GAME MUSEUM
MWANZA
GAME MUSEUM
MWEKA
NATURAL HISTORY MUSEUM

THAILAND

BANGKOK
MUSEUM OF MOUNTED ANIMALS

TUNISIA

CARTHAGE

OCEANOGRAPHIC MUSEUM

SALAMBO

MUSEUM AND AQUARIUM

UGANDA

KAMPALA

KAWANDA AGRICULTURAL RESEARCH STATION
UGANDA MUSEUM
ZOOLOGICAL MUSEUM

MWEYA

QUEEN ELIZABETH NATIONAL PARK MUSEUM

PARAA

MURCHISON FALLS NATIONAL PARK MUSEUM

USSR

ASKANIA-NOVA

NATURAL HISTORY MUSEUM

ASTRAKHAN

MUSEUM OF THE NATIONAL PARK OF ASTRAKHAN

KHERSON

NATURAL HISTORY MUSEUM

KIEV

ZOOLOGICAL MUSEUM OF THE ACADEMY OF SCIENCES
ZOOLOGICAL MUSEUM OF THE STATE UNIVERSITY OF THE UKRAINE

KROTOSK

KROTOSK NATIONAL PARK MUSEUM

LENINGRAD

ACADEMICIAN I. P. PAVLOV MUSEUM
BOTANICAL MUSEUM OF THE V. L. KOMAROV BOTANICAL INSTITUTE
HOUSE-MUSEUM OF ACADEMICIAN I. P. PAVLOV
LESGAFT MUSEUM OF HUMAN MORPHOLOGY
D. I. MENDELEYEV HOUSE- MUSEUM
D. I. MENDELEYEV MUSEUM
MUSEUM OF ANTHROPOLOGY AND ETHNOLOGY
MUSEUM OF THE EVOLUTION OF THE NERVOUS SYSTEM
MUSEUM OF HYGIENE
MUSEUM OF SCIENTIFIC RESEARCH
ZOOLOGICAL MUSEUM OF THE ACADEMY OF SCIENCES

LVOV

NATURAL HISTORY MUSEUM

MINSK

UNIVERSITY MUSEUM OF ZOOLOGY

MOSCOW

MOSCOW STATE UNIVERSITY ZOOLOGICAL MUSEUM
STATE MUSEUM OF DARWINISM
TIMIRYAZEV STATE BIOLOGICAL MUSEUM

ODESSA

REGIONAL MUSEUM

ORDZHONIKIDZE

ORDZHONIKIDZE MUSEUM: NATURAL HISTORY COLLECTIONS

RYAZAN

PAVLOV MUSEUM

SEVASTOPOL

MUSEUM OF KOVALEVSKI BIOLOGICAL STATION

SIMFEROPOL

MUSEUM OF NATURAL HISTORY

SOCHI

SOCHI MUSEUM

TALLINN

MUSEUM OF NATURAL HISTORY

TARTU

ZOOLOGICAL MUSEUM

TASHKENT

CENTRAL REGIONAL MUSEUM
NATURAL HISTORY MUSEUM OF THE ACADEMY OF SCIENCES

TBILISI

NATURAL HISTORY MUSEUM OF GEORGIA

ULAN-BATOR

STATE CENTRAL MUSEUM

UNITED STATES

ABIQUIU

GHOST RANCH MUSEUM

ALAMAGORDO

WHITE SANDS NATIONAL MONUMENT VISITOR CENTER

ALBANY

NEW YORK STATE MUSEUM

ALBUQUERQUE

MUSEUM OF UNIVERSITY OF NEW MEXICO BIOLOGY DEPARTMENT

AMHERST

MUSEUM OF ZOOLOGY

ANCHORAGE

ANCHORAGE LOG CABIN MUSEUM

ANN ARBOR

MUSEUM OF ZOOLOGY

ANNISTON

REGAR MEMORIAL MUSEUM OF NATURAL HISTORY

ASHLAND

SOUTHERN OREGON COLLEGE MUSEUM OF VERTEBRATE NATURAL HISTORY

AUGUSTA

MAINE STATE MUSEUM

AUSTIN

AUSTIN NATURAL SCIENCE CENTER

BALTIMORE

MUSEUM OF MARYLAND ACADEMY OF SCIENCES
THE MUSEUM OF NATURAL HISTORY

BATON ROUGE

MUSEUM OF NATURAL SCIENCE

BATTLE CREEK

KINGMAN MUSEUM OF NATURAL HISTORY

BEAUFORT

HAMPTON MARINE MUSEUM

BERKELEY

ENTOMOLOGICAL COLLECTIONS
MUSEUM OF VERTEBRATE ZOOLOGY

BIG BASIN

MUSEUM OF BIG BASIN REDWOODS

BOSTON

MUSEUM OF SCIENCE

BOULDER

UNIVERSITY OF COLORADO MUSEUM

BRIGHAM CITY

BEAR RIVER MIGRATORY BIRD REFUGE

BROWNING

SCRIVER MUSEUM OF MONTANA WILDLIFE

BUFFALO

BUFFALO MUSEUM OF SCIENCE

BURLINGTON

MCDADE WILDLIFE MUSEUM

BUXTON

CAPE HATTERAS NATIONAL SEASHORE

CAMBRIDGE

MUSEUM OF COMPARATIVE ZOOLOGY

CANON CITY

CANON CITY MUNICIPAL MUSEUM

CARLSBAD

CARLSBAD CAVERNS NATIONAL PARK

CEDAR CITY

MUSEUM OF NATURAL HISTORY

CENTERPORT

VANDERBILT MUSEUM AND PLANETARIUM

CHANUTE

MARTIN AND OSA JOHNSON SAFARI MUSEUM

CHARLESTON

MUSEUM OF WEST VIRGINIA DEPARTMENT OF ARCHIVES AND HISTORY

CHICAGO

CHICAGO ACADEMY OF SCIENCES
FIELD MUSEUM OF NATURAL HISTORY

CINCINNATI

CINCINNATI MUSEUM OF NATURAL HISTORY
ALFRED K. NIPPERT NATURE MUSEUM

CLEVELAND

CLEVELAND MUSEUM OF NATURAL HISTORY

COLORADO SPRINGS

MAY NATURAL HISTORY MUSEUM

COLUMBIA

UNIVERSITY OF MISSOURI MUSEUM
COLUMBIA SCIENCE MUSEUM

CORTLAND

SCIENCE MUSEUM

CORVALLIS

OREGON STATE UNIVERSITY NATURAL HISTORY MUSEUM

COVINGTON

BEHRINGER-CRAWFORD MEMORIAL MUSEUM OF NATURAL HISTORY

CRESSON

HAL S. SMITH FARM MACHINERY MUSEUM

DALLAS

DALLAS MUSEUM OF NATURAL HISTORY

DAVIS

MUSEUM OF ENTOMOLOGY

DAYTON

AULLWOOD AUDUBON CENTER
DAYTON MUSEUM OF NATURAL HISTORY

DENVER

DENVER MUSEUM OF NATURAL HISTORY

DES MOINES

DES MOINES CENTER OF SCIENCE AND INDUSTRY

ELGIN

AUDUBON MUSEUM

EL PASO

EL PASO CENTENNIAL MUSEUM

EUGENE

MUSEUM OF NATURAL HISTORY

EVANSVILLE

EVANSVILLE MUSEUM OF ARTS AND SCIENCES

FAIRFIELD

AUDUBON SOCIETY OF THE STATE OF CONNECTICUT
BIRDCRAFT MUSEUM

FLAMINGO

EVERGLADES NATIONAL PARK

FORT MYERS

FLORIDA MARINE MUSEUM

FORT WORTH

FORT WORTH MUSEUM OF SCIENCE AND HISTORY

FRANKFORT

MUSEUM OF EXPERIMENTAL GAME FARM

FRESNO

FRESNO MUSEUM OF NATURAL HISTORY AND JUNIOR MUSEUM

FRUITA

COLORADO NATIONAL MONUMENT

GALVESTON

CENTRE ON THE STRAND

GARDEN CITY

NANKIN MILLS NATURE CENTER

GASTONIA

SCHIELE MUSEUM OF NATURAL HISTORY AND PLANETARIUM

GAYLORD

CALL OF THE WILD MUSEUM

GLEN COVE

NASSAU MUSEUM OF NATURAL HISTORY

GRAND FORKS

UNIVERSITY OF NORTH DAKOTA ZOOLOGY MUSEUM

GREENVILLE

DELAWARE MUSEUM OF NATURAL HISTORY

HAMPTON

KENNETH E. RICE MEMORIAL MUSEUM

HARRISONBURG

D. RALPH HOSTETTER MUSEUM OF NATURAL HISTORY

HELLERTOWN

GILMAN MUSEUM

HENDERSON

JOHN JAMES AUDUBON MUSEUM

HEREFORD

CORONADO NATIONAL MEMORIAL

HOLBROOK

RAINBOW FOREST MUSEUM

HOMESTEAD

EVERGLADES NATIONAL PARK

HOT SPRINGS

NATURAL SCIENCE MUSEUM

HOUSTON
HOUSTON MUSEUM OF NATURAL SCIENCE
IOWA CITY
MUSEUM OF NATURAL HISTORY
IRVINE
MUSEUM OF SYSTEMATIC BIOLOGY
ITHACA
L. H. BAILEY HORTORIUM
JACKSON
MISSISSIPPI MUSEUM OF NATURAL SCIENCE
JUNEAU
ALASKA STATE MUSEUM
KANE
MUSEUM OF LOBO WOLF PARK
KANSAS CITY
KANSAS CITY MUSEUM OF HISTORY AND SCIENCE
KINGSTON
UNIVERSITY OF RHODE ISLAND
LAFAYETTE
LAFAYETTE NATURAL HISTORY MUSEUM AND PLANETARIUM
LA JOLLA
T. WAYLAND VAUGHAN AQUARIUM AND MUSEUM
LAKE JACKSON
BRAZOSPORT MUSEUM OF NATURAL SCIENCES
LANCASTER
NORTH MUSEUM
LAS CRUCES
NEW MEXICO STATE UNIVERSITY MUSEUM
LAWRENCE
SNOW ENTOMOLOGICAL MUSEUM
LEHI
JOHN HUTCHINGS MUSEUM OF NATURAL HISTORY
LEVELLAND
SOUTH PLAINS MUSEUM
LEWISTON
STANTON MUSEUM
LINCOLN
UNIVERSITY OF NEBRASKA STATE MUSEUM
LITCHFIELD
LITCHFIELD NATURE CENTER AND MUSEUM
LOS ANGELES
FERNDELL RANGER STATION AND NATURE MUSEUM
LOS ANGELES COUNTY MUSEUM OF NATURAL HISTORY
LOS GATOS
LOS GATOS MUSEUM
MADISON
UNIVERSITY OF WISCONSIN ZOOLOGICAL MUSEUM
MAYAGUEZ
MARINE STATION MUSEUM
MCKINNEY
HEARD NATURAL SCIENCE MUSEUM
MIAMI
MARINE LABORATORY MUSEUM
MUSEUM OF SCIENCE
MILWAUKEE
MILWAUKEE PUBLIC MUSEUM
MINNEAPOLIS
JAMES FORD BELL MUSEUM OF NATURAL HISTORY
MINNEAPOLIS PUBLIC LIBRARY SCIENCE MUSEUM AND PLANETARIUM
MOREHEAD CITY
HAMPTON MUSEUM OF MARINE LIFE
MORGANTOWN
NATURAL WILDLIFE MUSEUM
MORRISTOWN
MORRIS MUSEUM OF ARTS AND SCIENCES
MORRO BAY
MORRO BAY MUSEUM OF NATURAL HISTORY
MOSCOW
UNIVERSITY OF IDAHO MUSEUM
MOUNTAINSIDE
TRAILSIDE NATURE AND SCIENCE CENTER AND PLANETARIUM
MOUNT MCKINLEY
MOUNT MCKINLEY NATIONAL PARK MUSEUM
MOUNT PLEASANT
CENTER FOR CULTURAL AND NATURAL HISTORY
MYSTIC
NATURAL HISTORY MUSEUM
NEWARK
IRON HILL MUSEUM
NEW HAVEN
PEABODY MUSEUM OF NATURAL HISTORY
NEW ORLEANS
LOUISIANA WILDLIFE MUSEUM
NEWPORT
OREGON STATE UNIVERSITY, MARINE SCIENCE CENTER
NEW YORK
AMERICAN MUSEUM OF NATURAL HISTORY
STATEN ISLAND INSTITUTE OF ARTS AND SCIENCES
NORMAL
ILLINOIS STATE UNIVERSITY MUSEUMS
NORMAN
STOVALL MUSEUM OF SCIENCE AND HISTORY
OAKLAND
OAKLAND MUSEUM
OGDEN
WEBER STATE COLLEGE, MUSEUM OF NATURAL HISTORY
ORADELL
HIRAM BLAUVELT WILDLIFE MUSEUM
ORLANDO
CENTRAL FLORIDA MUSEUM AND PLANETARIUM
PACIFIC GROVE
PACIFIC GROVE MUSEUM OF NATURAL HISTORY
PATAGONIA
STRADLING MUSEUM OF THE HORSE
PHILADELPHIA
ACADEMY OF NATURAL SCIENCES OF PHILADELPHIA
PITTSBURGH
FISHER COLLECTION
PORTLAND
MUSEUM OF NATURAL HISTORY
OREGON MUSEUM OF SCIENCE AND INDUSTRY
PROVO
BRIGHAM YOUNG UNIVERSITY, LIFE SCIENCES MUSEUM
BRIGHAM YOUNG UNIVERSITY, ZOOLOGICAL AND ENTOMOLOGICAL COLLECTIONS
PULLMAN
CHARLES R. CONNER MUSEUM
QUEENS
HALL OF SCIENCE OF THE CITY OF NEW YORK
RALEIGH
NORTH CAROLINA STATE MUSEUM
RICHMOND
VIRGINIA STATE MUSEUM
ROCHESTER
ROCHESTER MUSEUM AND SCIENCE CENTER
ROCKFORD
BURPEE NATURAL HISTORY MUSEUM
ST. AUGUSTINE
MARINELAND
ST. JOHNSBURY
FAIRBANKS MUSEUM OF NATURAL SCIENCE
ST. LOUIS
MUSEUM OF SCIENCE AND NATURAL HISTORY
ST. PAUL
SCIENCE MUSEUM OF MINNESOTA
ST. PETERSBURG
SCIENCE CENTER OF PINELLAS COUNTY
SALT LAKE CITY
UTAH MUSEUM OF NATURAL HISTORY
SAN ANTONIO
BUCKHORN HALL OF HORNS AND HALL OF FINS
SAN DIEGO
NATURAL HISTORY MUSEUM
SAN FRANCISCO
MUSEUM OF THE CALIFORNIA ACADEMY OF SCIENCE
SAN PEDRO
CABRILLO BEACH MARINE MUSEUM
SAN RAFAEL
LOUISE A. BOYD MARIN MUSEUM OF SCIENCE
SARANAC LAKE
DICKERT MEMORIAL WILDLIFE COLLECTION
SAVANNAH
SAVANNAH SCIENCE MUSEUM
SCRANTON
EVERHART MUSEUM OF NATURAL HISTORY, SCIENCE AND ART
SEAFORD
NASSAU COUNTY MUSEUM OF NATURAL HISTORY
SEATTLE
PACIFIC SCIENCE CENTER
SHARON
SHARON AUDUBON CENTER
SOUTH LANCASTER
THAYER MUSEUM
SOUTH WELLFLEET
CAPE COD NATIONAL SEASHORE VISITOR CENTERS
SPRINGDALE
ZION NATIONAL PARK MUSEUM
STAMFORD
STAMFORD MUSEUM AND NATURE CENTER
STATE COLLEGE
COLLEGE OF EARTH AND MINERAL SCIENCES MUSEUM
SUNCOCK
AUDUBON NATURE CENTER
TAMPA
MUSEUM OF SCIENCE AND NATURAL HISTORY
TIFFIN
JONES COLLECTION OF MINERALS AND BIOLOGY MUSEUM
TOLEDO
TOLEDO MUSEUM OF HEALTH AND NATURAL HISTORY
TOPEKA
NATURAL SCIENCE MUSEUM
TUCSON
ARIZONA SONORA DESERT MUSEUM
TUSCALOOSA
UNIVERSITY OF ALABAMA MUSEUM OF NATURAL HISTORY
UNIVERSITY PARK
FROST ENTOMOLOGICAL MUSEUM
URBANA
MUSEUM OF NATURAL HISTORY
VERNAL
NATURAL HISTORY STATE MUSEUM
WASHINGTON
NATIONAL MUSEUM OF NATURAL HISTORY
WILMINGTON
WILMINGTON-NEW HANOVER MUSEUM
WINSTON-SALEM
NATURE-SCIENCE CENTER
WOLFEBORO
LIBBY MUSEUM
YELLOW SPRINGS
TRAILSIDE MUSEUM
YELLOWSTONE PARK
YELLOWSTONE NATIONAL PARK MUSEUM
YOSEMITE
YOSEMITE NATIONAL PARK MUSEUM
YUCAIPA
MOUSLEY MUSEUM OF NATURAL HISTORY
YUCCA VALLEY
HI-DESERT NATURE MUSEUM

URUGUAY

MERCEDES
PALAEONTOLOGY AND NATURAL SCIENCES MUSEUM
MONTEVIDEO
NATURAL HISTORY MUSEUM
ZOOLOGICAL MUSEUM

VENEZUELA

CARACAS
NATURAL SCIENCE MUSEUM
PHELPS ORNITHOLOGICAL COLLECTION
MARACAIBO
NATURAL SCIENCE MUSEUM

YUGOSLAVIA

BELGRADE
BELGRADE NATURAL HISTORY MUSEUM
KRAPINA
MUSEUM OF EVOLUTION
LJUBLJANA
SLOVENIAN NATURAL HISTORY MUSEUM
MAKARSKA
MUSEUM OF MALACOLOGY
RIJEKA
NATURAL HISTORY MUSEUM
SARAJEVO
STATE MUSEUM
SKOPJE
NATURAL HISTORY MUSEUM
SPLIT
MUSEUM OF NATURAL SCIENCES
ZADAR
NATURAL HISTORY MUSEUM
ZAGREB
CROATIAN NATIONAL ZOOLOGICAL MUSEUM
HUNTING MUSEUM

Botany

ALBANIA

TIRANA
MUSEUM OF NATURAL HISTORY

ALGERIA

ALGIERS
ZOOLOGICAL PARK
BENI-ABBES
BOTANICAL ET ZOOLOGICAL COLLECTIONS
ORAN
MUNICIPAL MUSEUM

ANGOLA

LUANDA
ANGOLA MUSEUM
LUNDA
DUNDO MUSEUM

ARGENTINA

BUENOS AIRES
MUSEUM OF BOTANY AND PHARMACOLOGY
BERNARDINO RIVADAVIA MUSEUM OF NATURAL SCIENCES
CÓRDOBA
BOTANICAL MUSEUM
CORRIENTES
NATURAL HISTORY MUSEUM
LA PLATA
LA PLATA MUSEUM OF NATURAL SCIENCES
LOMAS DE ZÁMORA
AMERICAN MUSEUM OF ANTHROPOLOGY, HISTORY, NUMISMATICS AND NATURAL SCIENCE
MENDOZA
MOYANO MUSEUM OF NATURAL HISTORY
ROSARIO
A. GALLARDO MUSEUM OF NATURAL SCIENCES
SANTA FÉ
NATURAL HISTORY MUSEUM

AUSTRALIA

KOROIT
NATURAL HISTORY CENTRE
TOWNSVILLE
KENNEDY ANTHROPOLOGICAL MUSEUM

AUSTRIA

ASPARN
WEINLAND MUSEUM
BADEN
ROLLETT MUSEUM
DORNBIRN
LANDSCAPE AND ECOLOGY OF THE VORARLBERG
GRAZ
JOANEUM PROVINCIAL MUSEUM FOR ZOOLOGY AND BOTANY
KLAGENFURT
CARINTHIA PROVINCIAL MUSEUM
LIENZ
EAST TIROL REGIONAL MUSEUM
MÖDLING
MUNICIPAL MUSEUM
NEUSIEDL
LAKE MUSEUM
PRESSBAUM
REGIONAL MUSEUM
REICHENAU AN DER RAX
REICHENAU NATURAL HISTORY MUSEUM
SALZBURG
NATURE HOUSE
VIENNA
COLLECTIONS OF THE MARKETS AUTHORITY OF THE CITY OF VIENNA
WAIDHOFEN AN DER YBBS
REGIONAL MUSEUM

BANGLADESH

DACCA
BOTANY MUSEUM

BELGIUM

BRUSSELS
MUSEUM OF THE ROYAL BELGIAN INSTITUTE OF NATURAL SCIENCES
MONS
MUSEUM OF NATURAL HISTORY
TOURNAI
MUSEUM OF NATURAL HISTORY

BRAZIL

BELEM
EMÍLIO GOELDI PARÁ MUSEUM
FORTALEZA
DIAS DA ROCHA MUSEUM
ITATAIA
REGIONAL MUSEUM OF ITATAIA NATIONAL PARK
JUAZEIRO DO NORTE
FATHER CÍCERO MUSEUM
PÔRTO ALEGRE
RIO GRANDE MUSEUM OF THE NATURAL SCIENCES
RIO DE JANEIRO
KUHLMANN BOTANICAL MUSEUM
SÃO PAULO
BOTANICAL MUSEUM

BRUNEI

KOTA BATU
BRUNEI MUSEUM

BULGARIA

KOBEL
NATURAL HISTORY MUSEUM
VARNA
NATURAL HISTORY MUSEUM

BURMA

RANGOON
NATURAL HISTORY MUSEUM

CANADA

ATIKOKAN
QUETICO PROVINCIAL PARK MUSEUM
BANFF
BANFF NATIONAL PARK NATURAL HISTORY MUSEUM
CALGARY
HERBARIUM
CALUMET
CIP NATURE CENTRE
EDMONTON
HERBARIUM
HAMILTON
ROYAL BOTANICAL GARDENS
LACHINE
SAINTE-ANNE MUSEUM
MONTREAL
MONTREAL BOTANICAL GARDEN
NIAGARA FALLS
SCHOOL OF HORTICULTURE HERBARIUM
OTTAWA
COLLECTIONS OF PLANT RESEARCH INSTITUTE
NATIONAL MUSEUM OF NATURAL SCIENCES
SAINT-LAURENT
MUSEUM OF THE NUNS OF THE HOLY CROSS
SASKATOON
W. P. FRASER MEMORIAL HERBARIUM
VANCOUVER
UNIVERSITY OF BRITISH COLUMBIA, HERBARIUM
WASKESIU
PRINCE ALBERT NATIONAL PARK MUSEUM
WINNIPEG
MANITOBA MUSEUM OF MAN AND NATURE

CHILE

ANGOL
DILLMAN S. BULLOCK MUSEUM
SANTIAGO
MUSEUM OF NATURAL HISTORY
NATIONAL MUSEUM OF NATURAL HISTORY
NATURAL HISTORY MUSEUM
VALPARAISO
NATURAL HISTORY MUSEUM

CHINA, P.R.

HANGCHOW (HANG ZHOU)
CHEKIANG PROVINCIAL MUSEUM
PEKING
CULTURAL PALACE OF THE MINORITIES
NATURAL HISTORY MUSEUM
SHANGHAI
MUSEUM OF NATURAL SCIENCES
TIENSIN (TIANJING)
PEOPLE'S HALL OF SCIENCE

REPUBLIC OF CHINA

TAIPEI

TAIWAN PROVINCIAL MUSEUM

COLOMBIA

CALI

MUSEUM OF NATURAL HISTORY

MANIZALES

MUSEUM OF NATURAL SCIENCES

MEDELLÍN

MUSEUM OF NATURAL SCIENCES

POPAYAN

NATURAL HISTORY MUSEUM

COSTA RICA

SAN JOSÉ

NATIONAL MUSEUM

CYPRUS

LIMASSOL

NATURAL HISTORY MUSEUM

CZECHOSLOVAKIA

BARDEJOV

ŠARIŠ MUSEUM

BENÁTKY NAD JIZEROU

MUNICIPAL MUSEUM

BRATISLAVA

SLOVAKIAN NATIONAL MUSEUM: NATURAL HISTORY COLLECTIONS

BRNO

MORAVIAN MUSEUM: BOTANICAL AND ENTOMOLOGICAL COLLECTIONS

ČELÁKOVICE

MUNICIPAL MUSEUM

KARLOVY VARY

KARLOVY MUSEUM

KLATOVY

REGIONAL MUSEUM

LEVOČA

SPIŠ MUSEUM

LITOMĚŘICE

DISTRICT MUSEUM

MICHALOVCE

ZEMPLIN MUSEUM

OPAVA

SILESIAN MUSEUM: NATURAL HISTORY COLLECTIONS

ORAVSKY PODZÁMOK

ORAVA MUSEUM

PARDUBICE

MUSEUM OF EASTERN CZECHOSLOVAKIA

PODĚBRADY

DISTRICT MUSEUM

POPRAD

TATRA MUSEUM

PRAGUE

NATIONAL MUSEUM: MUSEUM OF NATURAL HISTORY

PREŠOV

MUSEUM OF THE SLOVAK REPUBLIC

RUŽOMBEROK

LIPTOV MUSEUM

SOBĚSLAV

MUSEUM OF SOUTHERN CZECHOSLOVAKIA

TATRANSKÁ LOMNICA

MUSEUM OF THE TATRA NATIONAL PARK (TANAP)

VRCHLABÍ

KRKONOŠ MUSEUM (ASSOCIATED WITH KRKONOŠSKÝ NATIONAL PARK)

ŽILINA

POVAŽIA MUSEUM AND ART GALLERY

DAHOMEY

PARAKOU

OPEN-AIR MUSEUM OF ETHNOGRAPHY AND NATURAL SCIENCES

DENMARK

GILLELEJE

GILLELEJE MUSEUM

EGYPT, ARAB REPUBLIC OF

CAIRO

AGRICULTURE MUSEUM

EL SALVADOR

SAN SALVADOR

NATURAL HISTORY MUSEUM

ETHIOPIA

ADDIS ABABA

NATURAL HISTORY MUSEUM

FINLAND

FORSSA

NATURAL HISTORY MUSEUM

HELSINKI

UNIVERSITY MUSEUM OF BOTANY

JYVÄSKYLÄ

UNIVERSITY MUSEUM

OULU

UNIVERSITY BOTANICAL COLLECTIONS

PALLASTUNTURI

NATURAL HISTORY MUSEUM

PORVOO

MUSEUM OF NATURAL HISTORY

ROVANIEMI

MUNICIPAL NATURAL HISTORY MUSEUM

TAMPERE

NATURAL HISTORY MUSEUM

TURKU

WÄINÖ AALTOSEN MUSEUM
UNIVERSITY BOTANICAL MUSEUM

VAASA

EAST BOTHNIA AUSTRALIS MUSEUM

FRANCE

AVIGNON

RÉQUIEN MUSEUM OF NATURAL HISTORY

CHAMBÉRY

MUSEUM OF NATURAL HISTORY

CHERBOURG

MUSEUM OFNATURAL HISTORY AND ETHNOGRAPHY

NANTES

MUSEUM OF NATURAL HISTORY

PARIS

MUSEUM OF NATURAL HISTORY

UZÈS

LOCAL MUSEUM

FRENCH POLYNESIA

TAHITI

PAPEETE MUSEUM

GDR

ANNABERG-BUCHHOLZ

ERZGEBIRG MUSEUM: DEPARTMENT OF NATURAL HISTORY

ARNEBURG

REGIONAL MUSEUM

DRESDEN

BOTANICAL INSTITUTE OF DRESDEN TECHNICAL UNIVERSITY

EISFELD

OTTO LUDWIG REGIONAL MUSEUM

EISLEBEN

NATURAL HISTORY COLLECTION

FREIBERG

MUSEUM OF NATURAL HISTORY

GERA

NATURAL HISTORY MUSEUM

GLAUCHAU

MUNICIPAL MUSEUM AND ART COLLECTION

GÖRLITZ

STATE MUSEUM OF NATURAL HISTORY

GREIFSWALD

COLLECTIONS OF THE ERNST MORITZ ARNDT UNIVERSITY: INSTITUTE OF AGRICULTURAL BIOLOGY
COLLECTIONS OF THE ERNST MORITZ ARNDT UNIVERSITY: BOTANICAL INSTITUTE
COLLECTIONS OF THE ERNST MORITZ ARNDT UNIVERSITY: ZOOLOGICAL INSTITUTE AND MUSEUM

HALLE

WALDKATER REGIONAL MUSEUM

JENA

HAUSKNECHT HERBARIUM: COLLECTION OF THE BOTANICAL DEPARTMENT OF THE FRIEDRICH SCHILLER UNIVERSITY

KAMENZ

WEST LAUSITZ MUSEUM

LEIPZIG

BOTANICAL INSTITUTE
KARL SUDHOFF INSTITUTE FOR THE HISTORY OF MEDICINE AND THE NATURAL SCIENCES

LIEBSTADT

CASTLE KUCKUCKSTEIN REGIONAL MUSEUM

MOLCHOW-STENDENITZ

MUSEUM IN THE FOREST

QUEDLINBURG

MUSEUM BEHIND THE KLOPSTOCK HOUSE

ROSTOCK

COLLECTION OF THE DEPARTMENT OF BOTANY

SIEBENLEHN

REGIONAL MUSEUM

STRALSUND

MUSEUM OF THE SEA

THARANDT

INSTITUTE OF FORESTRY ZOOLOGY

UMMENDORF

WANZLEBEN DISTRICT MUSEUM

WALDENBURG

REGIONAL MUSEUM AND NATURAL HISTORY COLLECTION

WEISSENFELS

MUNICIPAL MUSEUM

GFR

ASCHAFFENBURG

NATURAL HISTORY MUSEUM

AUGSBURG

NATURAL HISTORY MUSEUM

BAMBERG

NATURAL HISTORY MUSEUM

BERLIN

BOTANICAL GARDEN AND MUSEUM

BERUMERFEHN

WOODLAND AND MOOR MUSEUM

BIELEFELD

NATURAL HISTORY MUSEUM

BOPPARD

FOREST AND TIMBER MUSEUM

BRAUNFELS

DR. KANNGIESSER'S WOODLAND MUSEUM

BREMEN
OVERSEAS MUSEUM: CHILDREN'S MUSEUM
BREMERHAVEN
NORTH SEA MUSEUM
BURG-DITHMARSCHEN
WOODLAND MUSEUM
DÜSSELDORF
BENRATH NATURAL HISTORY MUSEUM
EICHSTÄTT
NATURAL SCIENCE COLLECTIONS
FREIBURG IM BREISGAU
NATURAL HISTORY MUSEUM
HAMBURG
ALTONA MUSEUM
UNIVERSITY OF HAMBURG: ECONOMIC BOTANY COLLECTION
HILDESHEIM
ROEMER-PELIZAEUS MUSEUM
KARLSRUHE
LAND NATURAL HISTORY COLLECTIONS
KASSEL
NATURAL HISTORY MUSEUM
KONSTANZ
LAKE CONSTANCE MUSEUM OF NATURAL HISTORY
LÜBECK
NATURAL HISTORY MUSEUM
LUDWIGSBURG
STATE MUSEUM OF NATURAL HISTORY
MAINZ
NATURAL HISTORY MUSEUM
MAXBERG
SOLENHOFER COMPANY MUSEUM
MÖRNSHEIM
MUSEUM OF PETRIFIED OBJECTS
MÜNCHEN
STATE BOTANICAL COLLECTION
NEBEL
AMRUNER MUSEUM
NEUSTADT-WEISTRASSE
NATURAL HISTORY MUSEUM
NÜMBRECHT
MUSEUM OF THE OBERBERG REGION
OEVENTROP
SOUTH SEAS MUSEUM
OLDENBURG
STATE MUSEUM OF NATURAL HISTORY AND PREHISTORY
OSNABRÜCK
MUNICIPAL MUSEUM
PADERBORN
REGIONAL MUSEUM OF NATURAL HISTORY
ST. OTTILIEN
MISSION MUSEUM
SPAICHINGEN
MUSEUM OF GEOLOGY AND PREHISTORY
STUTTGART
STATE MUSEUM OF NATURAL HISTORY
SURWOLD
WOODLAND MUSEUM
TIENGEN
NATURAL HISTORY MUSEUM
WIESBADEN
NATURAL SCIENCES COLLECTION
WIESMOOR
MOOR MUSEUM

GHANA

ACCRA
MUSEUM OF SCIENCE AND TECHNOLOGY

GIBRALTAR

GIBRALTAR
GIBRALTAR MUSEUM

GREAT BRITAIN

BIRMINGHAM
BIRMINGHAM CITY MUSEUM AND ART GALLERY
LONDON
BRITISH MUSEUM (NATURAL HISTORY)
BUTLER MUSEUM
ROYAL BOTANIC GARDENS
MANCHESTER
MANCHESTER MUSEUM
NOTTINGHAM
NATURAL HISTORY MUSEUM
REIGATE
HOLMESDALE NATURAL HISTORY CLUB MUSEUM
STIRLING
UNIVERSITY OF STIRLING
THURSO
THURSO MUSEUM

GREECE

ATHENS
BOTANICAL MUSEUM
GOULANDRI BOTANICAL MUSEUM

GUATEMALA

GUATEMALA CITY
MUSEUM OF NATURAL HISTORY

HUNGARY

BUDAPEST
NATURAL HISTORY MUSEUM

ICELAND

REYKJAVIK
MUSEUM OF NATURAL HISTORY

INDIA

AGRA
ST. JOHN'S COLLEGE MUSEUM
ALLAHABAD
UNIVERSITY MUSEUMS
AMRITSAR
MUSEUM OF THE BOTANY DEPARTMENT
BANGALORE
CENTRAL COLLEGE MUSEUMS
MYSORE GOVERNMENT MUSEUM
BOMBAY
NATURAL HISTORY MUSEUM
PRINCE OF WALES MUSEUM OF WESTERN INDIA
COIMBATORE
AGRICULTURAL COLLEGE MUSEUM
SOUTHERN FOREST RANGERS COLLEGE AND RESEARCH CENTRE
ERNAKULAM
ZOOLOGY AND BOTANY MUSEUM
MADRAS
THE GOVERNMENT MUSEUM AND NATIONAL ART GALLERY
PUDDUKKOTTAI
GOVERNMENT MUSEUM
TAMBARAM
ZOOLOGICAL MUSEUM

IRAQ

BAGHDAD
IRAQ NATURAL HISTORY MUSEUM

IRELAND

DUBLIN
NATIONAL MUSEUM OF IRELAND

ISRAEL

EILAT
RED SEA MARITIME MUSEUM
JERUSALEM
MUSEUM OF NATURAL HISTORY
TEL-AVIV
TEL-AVIV MUSEUM

ITALY

CAGLIARI
COLLECTION OF THE BOTANICAL INSTITUTE
CUGGIONO
STUCCHI BOTANICAL COLLECTION
FLORENCE
BOTANICAL MUSEUM
GENOA
COLLECTIONS OF THE HAMBURY BOTANICAL INSTITUTE
COLLECTIONS OF NATURAL HISTORY
NATURAL HISTORY MUSEUM
LUCCA
PUCCINELLI MUSEUM AND HERBARIUM
MILAN
INSTITUTE OF BOTANY HERBARIUM
LUZZATTO HERBARIUM
MODENA
BOTANICAL COLLECTION AND HERBARIUM
PALERMO
BORZI BOTANICAL MUSEUM
BOTANICAL COLLECTION
PERUGIA
COLLECTIONS OF THE INSTITUTE OF BOTANY
NATURAL HISTORY COLLECTION
PESCASSEROLI
MUSEUM OF THE ABRUZZO NATIONAL PARK
PESCIA
BOTANICAL COLLECTION
PISA
COLLECTION OF THE INSTITUTE OF BOTANY
PORTOGRUARO
GAMBARINI BOTANICAL COLLECTION
REGGIO EMILIA
LAZZARO SPALLANZANI MUSEUM OF NATURAL HISTORY
ROME
COLLECTIONS OF THE INSTITUTE OF BOTANY
COLLECTION OF THE NATIONAL INSTITUTE OF ENTOMOLOGY
SASSARI
COLLECTION OF THE INSTITUTE OF BOTANY
SENIGALLIA
BOTANICAL MUSEUM
SIENA
BOTANICAL MUSEUM
STRESA
BOTANICAL MUSEUM
BOTANICAL MUSEUM
TARANTO
NATURAL HISTORY COLLECTION
TRIESTE
NATURAL HISTORY MUSEUM
VALDOTTAVO
FLORA LUCENSIS HERBARIUM
VENICE
MARCELLO BOTANICAL COLLECTION
ZOOLOGICAL COLLECTION
VERONA
MUSEUM OF ART
MUSEUM OF NATURAL HISTORY

JAMAICA

KINGSTON

NATURAL HISTORY MUSEUM

JAPAN

AKKESHI-MACHI

AKKESHI MUSEUM OF HOKKAIDO UNIVERSITY

ASAHIKAWA-SHI

ASAHIKAWA LOCAL MUSEUM

FUKUI-SHI

FUKUI MUNICIPAL NATURAL HISTORY MUSEUM

FUTTSU

FUTTSU OCEANOGRAPHIC MUSEUM OF CHIBA PREFECTURE

GIFU-SHI

NAWA INSECT MUSEUM

HAKODATE-SHI

HAKODATE MUNICIPAL MUSEUM

HIWA-MACHI

HIWA MUSEUM OF NATURAL HISTORY

KOMATSU-SHI

KOMATSU MUNICIPAL MUSEUM

KYOTO

MT. HIEI NATURAL HISTORY MUSEUM AND ROCK GARDEN

MINOBU-MACHI

THE YAMANASHI PREFECTURAL MUSEUM OF FUJI NATIONAL PARK

MIYAZAKI-SHI

AGRICULTURAL MUSEUM OF MIYAZAKI UNIVERSITY

NAGAOKA-SHI

NAGAOKA MUNICIPAL MUSEUM OF NATURAL SCIENCE

NAGASAKI-SHI

NAGASAKI MUNICIPAL CHILDREN'S SCIENCE HALL

NICHINAN-SHI

THE HATTORI BOTANICAL LABORATORY

NI'IGATA-SHI

NI'IGATA SCIENCE AND TECHNOLOGY MUSEUM

NIKKO-SHI

NIKKO MUSEUM OF NATURAL HISTORY
OKUNIKKO MUSEUM OF NATURAL HISTORY

NOGAMI-MACHI

CHICHIBU MUSEUM OF NATURAL HISTORY

OSAKA

NATURAL SCIENCE MUSEUM

OTARU-SHI

OTARU CITY MUSEUM

SAIJO-SHI

SAIJO LOCAL MUSEUM

SAPPORO-SHI

NATURAL HISTORY MUSEUM OF HOKKAIDO UNIVERSITY

SAWADA-MACHI

SADO MUSEUM

TAMANO-SHI

TAMANO MARINE MUSEUM

TESHIKAGA-MACHI

AKAN WAGOTO MUSEUM

TOKYO

THE CICADA MUSEUM OF THE KATO INSTITUTE FOR ENTOMOLOGY
NATIONAL SCIENCE MUSEUM
TOKYO-TO TAKAO MUSEUM OF NATURAL HISTORY

TOSAYAMADA-MACHI

THE RYUGADO MUSEUM

TOTTORI-SHI

TOTTORI PREFECTURAL SCIENCE MUSEUM

YAMAGUCHI-SHI

YAMAGUCHI PREFECTURAL MUSEUM

KENYA

KITALE

STONEHAM MUSEUM AND RESEARCH CENTRE

LIBYAN ARAB REPUBLIC

TRIPOLI

NATURAL HISTORY MUSEUM

MALTA

MDINA

MUSEUM OF NATURAL HISTORY AND FOLKLORE

MEXICO

MEXICO CITY

MUSEUM OF NATURAL HISTORY
NATURAL HISTORY MUSEUM

UNIVERSITY CITY

NATURAL HISTORY MUSEUM

MOROCCO

RABAT

MUSEUM OF THE CHÉRIF SCIENTIFIC INSTITUTE

NETHERLANDS

AMSTERDAM

BOTANICAL MUSEUM
NATURAL HISTORY COLLECTION

ENSCHEDE

NATURAL HISTORY MUSEUM

FRANEKER

DR. COOPMAN'S HOUSE MUNICIPAL MUSEUM

LEEUWARDEN

FRISIAN MUSEUM OF NATURAL HISTORY

LEIDEN

NATIONAL HERBARIUM

MAASTRICHT

NATURAL HISTORY MUSEUM

ST. MICHIELSGESTEL

NATURAL HISTORY MUSEUM OF THE ROMAN CATHOLIC SCHOOL AND SEMINARY 'BEEKOLIET'

OUDEMIRDUM

KLIF EN GAAST DISTRICT MUSEUM OF NATURAL HISTORY

TILBURG

NATURAL HISTORY MUSEUM

VLIELAND

NATURAL HISTORY MUSEUM

WEST-TERSCHELLING

DISTRICT MUSEUM OF NATURAL HISTORY

NEW ZEALAND

ARTHUR'S PASS

ARTHUR'S PASS NATIONAL PARK MUSEUM

AUCKLAND

AUCKLAND WAR MEMORIAL MUSEUM
PLANT DISEASES DIVISION

CHRISTCHURCH

BOTANY DIVISION
DEPARTMENTS OF BOTANY, GEOLOGY AND ZOOLOGY

DUNEDIN

OTAGO MUSEUM

WELLINGTON

DOMINION MUSEUM
VICTORIA UNIVERSITY OF WELLINGTON

WHANGAREI

WHANGAREI CITY COUNCIL MUSEUM

NICARAGUA

MANAGUA

MUSEUM OF NATURAL SCIENCE
NATIONAL MUSEUM OF NICARAGUA

NORWAY

BERGEN

MUSEUM OF NATURAL HISTORY

OSLO

BOTANICAL MUSEUM OF THE UNIVERSITY

TRONDHEIM

MUSEUM OF THE ROYAL NORWEGIAN SOCIETY OF SCIENCES AND LETTERS

PARAGUAY

ASUNCION

MUSEUM OF NATURAL HISTORY
NATURAL SCIENCE MUSEUM OF THE INTERNATIONAL COLLEGE

PERU

LIMA

JAVIER PRADO NATURAL HISTORY MUSEUM

POLAND

BYTOM

MUSEUM OF UPPER SILESIA

CIEPLICE ŚLĄSKIE ZDRÓJ

REGIONAL MUSEUM OF NATURAL HISTORY

KRÓSCIENKO

PIENIN MUSEUM

LESKO

LOCAL MUSEUM

MIĘDZYZDROJ

NATURAL HISTORY MUSEUM

OJCÓW

NATURAL HISTORY MUSEUM

POZNAŃ

NATURAL HISTORY MUSEUM OF THE INSTITUTE OF ZOOLOGY

PUSZCZYKOWO

NATURAL HISTORY MUSEUM

SOBIESZÓW

KARKONOSKI PARK MUSEUM

WARSAW

MUSEUM OF EARTH SCIENCES

ZAWOJA

BABIEJ GÓRY NATIONAL PARK MUSEUM

PORTUGAL

FUNCHAL

MUNICIPAL MUSEUM

RHODESIA

UMTALI

UMTALI MUSEUM

ROMANIA

BACĂU

NATURAL HISTORY MUSEUM

CLUJ

BOTANICAL GARDEN AND HERBARIUM

FĂLTICENI

FĂLTICENI MUSEUM

FOCŞANI

NATURAL HISTORY MUSEUM

GALAŢI

NATURAL HISTORY MUSEUM

IAŞI

NATURAL HISTORY MUSEUM

NĂSĂUD

NĂSĂUD MUSEUM

ODORHEI
ODORHEI MUSEUM
PIATRA NEAMŢ
NATURAL HISTORY MUSEUM
SIBIU
BRUKENTHAL MUSEUM
TULCEA
MUSEUM OF THE DANUBE DELTA
TURNU SEVERIN
IRON GATE (PORŢILE DE FIER) MUSEUM

ST. HELENA

GEORGETOWN
FORT HAYES MUSEUM

SOUTH AFRICA, REPUBLIC OF

CAPE TOWN
COMPTON HERBARIUM
SOUTH AFRICAN MUSEUM
DURBAN
NATAL HERBARIUM
GRAHAMSTOWN
ALBANY MUSEUM
JOHANNESBURG
MOSS HERBARIUM
SKUKUZA
STEVENSON-HAMILTON MEMORIAL LIBRARY

SPAIN

BARCELONA
BOTANICAL INSTITUTE
MUNICIPAL INSTITUTE OF NATURAL SCIENCE
MADRID
BOTANICAL GARDEN
ZARAGOZA
ARAGON MUSEUM OF ETHNOLOGY AND NATURAL SCIENCES

SWEDEN

HÄLSINGBORG
FREDRIKSDAL OPEN-AIR MUSEUM
HAMMARBY
LINNAEUS MUSEUM
STOCKHOLM
MUSEUM OF MEDITERRANEAN AND NEAR EASTERN ANTIQUITIES
NATURAL HISTORY MUSEUM

SWITZERLAND

AROSA
SCHANFIGGER REGIONAL MUSEUM
BERN
SWISS ALPINE MUSEUM
BRISSAGO
CANTONAL BOTANICAL GARDEN AND MUSEUM OF AFRICAN ETHNOGRAPHY
CHUR
BÜNDER NATURAL HISTORY AND NATURAL PARK MUSEUM
ESTAVAYER- LE-LAC
MUSEUM
FRAUENFELD
CANTON THURGAU MUSEUM
LAUSANNE
CANTON BOTANICAL MUSEUM
LUZERN
NATURAL HISTORY MUSEUM
NYON
LAKE LÉMAN MUSEUM
ST. GALLEN
REGIONAL MUSEUM
SION
CANTONAL MUSEUM OF NATURAL HISTORY
ZERMATT
ALPINE MUSEUM
ZURICH
BOTANICAL GARDEN AND MUSEUM

TANZANIA

MWEKA
NATURAL HISTORY MUSEUM

UGANDA

KAMPALA
KAWANDA AGRICULTURAL RESEARCH STATION

USSR

ASKANIA-NOVA
NATURAL HISTORY MUSEUM
ASTRAKHAN
MUSEUM OF THE NATIONAL PARK OF ASTRAKHAN
KHERSON
NATURAL HISTORY MUSEUM
KROTOSK
KROTOSK NATIONAL PARK MUSEUM
LVOV
NATURAL HISTORY MUSEUM
ODESSA
REGIONAL MUSEUM
ORDZHONIKIDZE
ORDZHONIKIDZE MUSEUM: NATURAL HISTORY COLLECTIONS
SIMFEROPOL
MUSEUM OF NATURAL HISTORY
SOCHI
SOCHI MUSEUM
TASHKENT
CENTRAL REGIONAL MUSEUM
NATURAL HISTORY MUSEUM OF THE ACADEMY OF SCIENCES
TBILISI
NATURAL HISTORY MUSEUM OF GEORGIA
ULAN-BATOR
STATE CENTRAL MUSEUM

UNITED STATES

ALBUQUERQUE
MUSEUM OF UNIVERSITY OF NEW MEXICO BIOLOGY DEPARTMENT
ANN ARBOR
HERBARIUM OF THE UNIVERSITY OF MICHIGAN
MATTHAEI BOTANICAL GARDENS
ARCADIA
LOS ANGELES STATE AND COUNTY ARBORETUM
BATON ROUGE
LOUISIANA STATE UNIVERSITY HERBARIUM
BERKELEY
UNIVERSITY OF CALIFORNIA HERBARIUM
BOTTINEAU
NORTH DAKOTA SCHOOL OF FORESTRY
BOULDER
UNIVERSITY OF COLORADO MUSEUM
BOZEMAN
MONTANA STATE UNIVERSITY HERBARIUM
BREWSTER
CAPE COD MUSEUM OF NATURAL HISTORY
BRONX
NEW YORK BOTANICAL GARDEN
BUFFALO
BUFFALO MUSEUM OF SCIENCE
BURLINGTON
PRINGLE HERBARIUM
CAMBRIDGE
BOTANICAL MUSEUM OF HARVARD UNIVERSITY
GRAY HERBARIUM
CINCINNATI
CINCINNATI MUSEUM OF NATURAL HISTORY
CLAREMONT
MUSEUM OF RANCHO SANTA ANA BOTANIC GARDENS
CLEVELAND
CLEVELAND MUSEUM OF NATURAL HISTORY
CORTLAND
SCIENCE MUSEUM
DAYTON
AULLWOOD AUDUBON CENTER
DENVER
DENVER BOTANIC GARDENS
EAST LANSING
BEAL-DARLINGTON HERBARIUM
HOLBROOK
RAINBOW FOREST MUSEUM
ITHACA
L. H. BAILEY HORTORIUM
JACKSON
MISSISSIPPI MUSEUM OF NATURAL SCIENCE
JUNEAU
ALASKA STATE MUSEUM
KENNETT SQUARE
LONGWOOD GARDENS
LAFAYETTE
PURDUE UNIVERSITY ARTHUR HERBARIUM
LAKE JACKSON
BRAZOSPORT MUSEUM OF NATURAL SCIENCES
LANCASTER
NORTH MUSEUM
LARAMIE
ROCKY MOUNTAIN HERBARIUM
LAS CRUCES
NEW MEXICO STATE UNIVERSITY MUSEUM
LINCOLN
UNIVERSITY OF NEBRASKA STATE MUSEUM
LITCHFIELD
LITCHFIELD NATURE CENTER AND MUSEUM
LOGAN
INTERMOUNTAIN HERBARIUM
LOS ANGELES
FERNDELL RANGER STATION AND NATURE MUSEUM
LOS ANGELES COUNTY MUSEUM OF NATURAL HISTORY
UNIVERSITY OF CALIFORNIA AT LOS ANGELES BOTANICAL GARDEN AND HERBARIUM
LOS GATOS
LOS GATOS MUSEUM
MANHATTAN
KANSAS STATE UNIVERSITY HERBARIUM
MAYAGUEZ
MARINE STATION MUSEUM
MEMPHIS
SOUTHWESTERN AT MEMPHIS ARBORETUM
MIAMI
MARINE LABORATORY MUSEUM
MUSEUM OF SCIENCE
MORRISTOWN
MORRIS MUSEUM OF ARTS AND SCIENCES
MORRO BAY
MORRO BAY MUSEUM OF NATURAL HISTORY
MOUNT MCKINLEY
MOUNT MCKINLEY NATIONAL PARK MUSEUM
NASHVILLE
TENNESSEE BOTANICAL GARDENS AND FINE ARTS CENTER
NEW HAVEN
HERBARIUM
PEABODY MUSEUM OF NATURAL HISTORY
NEW YORK
AMERICAN MUSEUM OF NATURAL HISTORY
CLOISTERS
NORMAN
BEBB HERBARIUM OF THE UNIVERSITY OF OKLAHOMA
NOTRE DAME
UNIVERSITY OF NOTRE DAME HERBARIA
OAKLAND
OAKLAND MUSEUM

ORONO
UNIVERSITY OF MAINE HERBARIUM
PHILADELPHIA
ACADEMY OF NATURAL SCIENCES OF PHILADELPHIA
HERBARIUM OF THE UNIVERSITY OF PENNSYLVANIA
MORRIS ARBORETUM
PROVO
BRIGHAM YOUNG UNIVERSITY, BOTANICAL COLLECTIONS
BRIGHAM YOUNG UNIVERSITY, LIFE SCIENCES MUSEUM
PULLMAN
WASHINGTON STATE UNIVERSITY HERBARIUM
RALEIGH
NORTH CAROLINA STATE MUSEUM
ROCHESTER
MONROE COUNTY PARKS HERBARIUM
ROCKFORD
BURPEE NATURAL HISTORY MUSEUM
ST. JOHNSBURY
FAIRBANKS MUSEUM OF NATURAL SCIENCE
ST. LOUIS
MISSOURI BOTANICAL GARDEN
ST. PETERSBURG
SCIENCE CENTER OF PINELLAS COUNTY
SAN DIEGO
NATURAL HISTORY MUSEUM
SAVANNAH
SAVANNAH SCIENCE MUSEUM
SEAFORD
NASSAU COUNTY MUSEUM OF NATURAL HISTORY
STILLWATER
OKLAHOMA STATE UNIVERSITY, HERBARIUM
SULPHUR
TRAVERTINE NATURE CENTER
TUSCALOOSA
UNIVERSITY OF ALABAMA MUSEUM OF NATURAL HISTORY
WASHINGTON
NATIONAL MUSEUM OF NATURAL HISTORY
UNITED STATES NATIONAL ARBORETUM
WINSTON-SALEM
NATURE-SCIENCE CENTER
WOLFEBORO
LIBBY MUSEUM
YELLOWSTONE PARK
YELLOWSTONE NATIONAL PARK MUSEUM
YOSEMITE
YOSEMITE NATIONAL PARK MUSEUM
YUCCA VALLEY
HI-DESERT NATURE MUSEUM

URUGUAY

MONTEVIDEO
BOTANICAL MUSEUM
NATURAL HISTORY MUSEUM

VENEZUELA

MARACAIBO
NATURAL SCIENCE MUSEUM

YUGOSLAVIA

BELGRADE
BELGRADE NATURAL HISTORY MUSEUM
LJUBLJANA
SLOVENIAN NATURAL HISTORY MUSEUM
SARAJEVO
STATE MUSEUM
SKOPJE
NATURAL HISTORY MUSEUM

Anthropology, ethnology

ALBANIA

ELBASAN
LOCAL MUSEUM
TIRANA
MUSEUM OF ARCHAEOLOGY AND ETHNOGRAPHY

ALGERIA

ALGIERS
LE BARDO MUSEUM OF ETHNOGRAPHY AND PREHISTORY
EL OUED
EL OUED MUSEUM
GHARDAIA
GHARDAIA MUSEUM OF FOLKLORE
ORAN
MUNICIPAL MUSEUM
OUARGLA
SAHARA MUSEUM
SÉTIF
SÉTIF MUSEUM

ANGOLA

LUANDA
ANGOLA MUSEUM
LUNDA
DUNDO MUSEUM

ARGENTINA

AZUL
ENRIQUE SQUIRRU ETHNOGRAPHICAL MUSEUM
BUENOS AIRES
JUAN B. AMBROSETTI MUSEUM OF ETHNOGRAPHY
ENTRE RIOS
PROVINCIAL MUSEUM
LA PLATA
LA PLATA MUSEUM OF NATURAL SCIENCES
OLAVARRIA
DÁMASO ARCE ETHNOGRAPHICAL MUSEUM
SAN CARLOS DE BARILOCHE
DR. FRANCISCO MORENO PATAGONIAN MUSEUM
SANTA FÉ
MUSEUM OF ETHNOGRAPHY
TILCARA
ARCHAEOLOGICAL MUSEUM
TUCUMÁN
MUSEUM OF ANTHROPOLOGY
MUSEUM OF NATURAL HISTORY AND ANTHROPOLOGY

AUSTRALIA

ADELAIDE
APPLIED SCIENCE MUSEUM
MUSEUM OF NATURAL HISTORY
THE SOUTH AUSTRALIAN MUSEUM
ALBANY
ALBANY OLD JAIL
CANBERRA
AUSTRALIAN INSTITUTE OF ANATOMY
FORTITUDE VALLEY
QUEENSLAND MUSEUM
INNISFAIL
CHINESE JOSS HOUSE
LAKES ENTRANCE
ABORIGINAL ART MUSEUM
LAUNCESTON
QUEEN VICTORIA MUSEUM AND ART GALLERY
MELBOURNE
UNIVERSITY MUSEUM
MOORA
BERKSHIRE VALLEY FOLK MUSEUM
MORPHETT VALE
PIONEER VILLAGE MUSEUM
PENNESHAW
NATIONAL TRUST MUSEUM
PERTH
WESTERN AUSTRALIAN MUSEUM
SYDNEY
AUSTRALIAN MUSEUM
MACLEAY MUSEUM OF NATURAL HISTORY
J. L. SHELLSHEAR MUSEUM OF COMPARATIVE ANATOMY AND PHYSICAL ANTHROPOLOGY
TINGHA
SMITH'S MINING AND NATURAL HISTORY MUSEUM
TOWNSVILLE
KENNEDY ANTHROPOLOGICAL MUSEUM

AUSTRIA

ASPARN
WEINLAND MUSEUM
BAD DEUTSCH ALTENBURG
AFRICAN MUSEUM
BAD ISCHL
MUSEUM OF ETHNOLOGY
BAD LEONFELDEN
REGIONAL MUSEUM
BAD WIMSBACH- NEYDHARTING
PENTAGRAM MUSEUM
BLUDENZ
REGIONAL MUSEUM
BRAUNAU AM INN
DISTRICT MUSEUM
EGGENBURG
KRAHULETZ MUSEUM
EISENERZ
REGIONAL MUSEUM
EISENSTADT
BURGENLAND MUSEUM
GMUNDEN
TOWN MUSEUM
HAAG
HAAG MUSEUM OF LOCAL LIFE AND HISTORY
HALLSTATT
LOCAL MUSEUM
KINDBERG
HUNGARIAN MUSEUM IN WESTERN EUROPE
KREMSMUNSTER
MONASTERY COLLECTIONS
LIEFERING
MISSION MUSEUM
MÖDLING
ST. GABRIEL'S MISSION MUSEUM
SCHÄRDING
MUNICIPAL MUSEUM
SCHWARZENBERG
COMMUNITY MUSEUM
SPITTAL
MUSEUM OF LOCAL LIFE
STEGERSBACH
SOUTH BURGENLAND COUNTRYSIDE MUSEUM
STEYR
REGIONAL MUSEUM
TULLN
REGIONAL MUSEUM

VIENNA

FRIEDRICH JULIUS BIEBER MUSEUM
FIRST AUSTRIAN-SILESIAN MUSEUM IN VIENNA
HIETZING DISTRICT MUSEUM
HOUSE OF THE SEA
MUSEUM OF ETHNOLOGY

WARTBERG

REGIONAL MUSEUM AT THE RUINS OF LICHTENEGG CASTLE

WATTENS

REGIONAL MUSEUM

BAHAMAS

NASSAU

BAHAMIA MUSEUM

BANGLADESH

CHITTAGONG

ETHNOLOGICAL MUSEUM

DACCA

DACCA MUSEUM
SOCIOLOGY MUSEUM

BELGIUM

AALST

LOCAL MUSEUM

AARSCHOT

REGIONAL MUSEUM

ANTWERP

ETHNOGRAPHICAL MUSEUM
FOLK-LORE MUSEUM
POLDER MUSEUM

BLANKENBERGE

FOLK MUSEUM

BOUILLON

BOUILLON MUSEUM

BRUGES

MUSEUM OF FOLKLORE

BRUSSELS

BELLONA HOUSE
MUSEUM OF THE ROYAL BELGIAN INSTITUTE OF NATURAL SCIENCES
ROYAL MUSEUM OF ART AND HISTORY

HASSELT

PROVINCIAL MUSEUM

HOOGSTRATEN

SAINT-SANG MUSEUM OF FOLK- LORE AND FOLK-ART

LIÈGE

MUSEUM OF WALLOON LIFE

LIERRE

ASTRONOMICAL CLOCK

MALMEDY

ABBEY MUSEUM

MONS

JEAN LESCARTS MUSEUM

NIEUWPOORT

MUSEUM OF HISTORY AND FOLKLORE

NISMES

FOLKLORE MUSEUM

OSTEND

FOLKLORE MUSEUM

OUDENARDE

ARCHAEOLOGICAL MUSEUM

SINT-NIKLAAS WAAS

ARCHAEOLOGICAL MUSEUM

TERVUEREN

ROYAL CENTRAL AFRICAN MUSEUM

VERVIERS

MUSEUM OF ARCHAEOLOGY AND FOLKLORE
RENIER MUSEUM

BOLIVIA

LA PAZ

NATIONAL MUSEUM OF ARCHAEOLOGY

POTOSI

NATIONAL MUSEUM OF THE POTOSI MINT

SUCRE

ANTHROPOLOGICAL MUSEUM

BRAZIL

BAGÉ

PATRICIO CORREA DA CAMARA MUSEUM
MUSEUM OF THE FORTE DE SANTA TECLA

BELEM

EMÍLIO GOELDI PARÁ MUSEUM

CAMPINAS

MUNICIPAL MUSEUM

CATANDUVA

GOVERNOR PEDRO DE TOLEDO HISTORICAL MUSEUM

CURITIBA

MUSEUM OF MAN
PARANÁ MUSEUM

FLORIANÓPOLIS

SAMBAGUI MUSEUM OF MAN

FORTALEZA

DIAS DA ROCHA MUSEUM
ARTUR RAMOS MUSEUM
UNIVERSITY MUSEUM OF ANTHROPOLOGY

GUARAPUAVA

VISCONDE DE GUARAPUAVA MUNICIPAL MUSEUM

IJUÍ

MUSEUM OF ANTHROPOLOGY

ITAPORANGA D'AJUDA

MUSEUM OF ART AND POPULAR TRADITIONS

JOINVILLE

SAMBAQUI MUSEUM

JUAZEIRO DO NORTE

FATHER CÍCERO MUSEUM

MANAUS

MUSEUM OF INDIAN CULTURE

PENEDO

MUSEUM OF FOLK ART AND FOLK CULTURE

RIO DE JANEIRO

MUSEUM OF THE BRAZILIAN HISTORICAL AND GEOGRAPHICAL INSTITUTE
MUSEUM OF FOLK-LORE
MUSEUM OF THE INDIAN
NATIONAL MUSEUM

SÃO PAULO

ETHNOGRAPHICAL MUSEUM OF THE FACULTY OF PHILOSOPHY, SCIENCE AND LETTERS
PAULISTA MUSEUM
UNIVERSITY MUSEUM OF ARCHAEOLOGY AND ETHNOGRAPHY

BRUNEI

KOTA BATU

BRUNEI MUSEUM

BULGARIA

ASENOVGRAD

NATIONAL MUSEUM

BATAK

MUSEUM OF HISTORY AND ARCHAEOLOGY

BOURGAS

REGIONAL MUSEUM OF HISTORY

ETARA

OPEN-AIR MUSEUM

GORA LIPNICA

ZORA MUSEUM

KAZANLUK

NATIONAL MUSEUM

KOPRIVSHTIŽA

OSLEKOV ETHNOGRAPHICAL MUSEUM

KOPRIVŠTICA

DIMČO DEBELJANOV HOUSE- MUSEUM

LOVEČ

REGIONAL MUSEUM OF HISTORY

PANAGIOURISTE

RAJNA KNIAGJANIA REGIONAL MUSEUM

PLEVEN

REGIONAL MUSEUM OF HISTORY

PLOVDIV

DISTRICT NATIONAL MUSEUM
REGIONAL MUSEUM OF ETHNOLOGY

RAJKOVO

NATIONAL MUSEUM OF THE RHODOPE

RUSE

REGIONAL MUSEUM OF HISTORY

SOFIA

NATIONAL ETHNOGRAPHICAL MUSEUM

STARA ZAGORA

REGIONAL MUSEUM OF HISTORY

VARNA

REGIONAL MUSEUM OF HISTORY

VIDIN

REGIONAL MUSEUM OF HISTORY

VRATSA

NATIONAL MUSEUM

BURMA

RANGOON

NATIONAL MUSEUM OF ART AND ARCHAEOLOGY

BURUNDI

ASTRIDA

ETHNOGRAPHIC MUSEUM

BUJUMBURA

MUSEUM OF AFRICAN CIVILISATION

KITEGA

NATIONAL MUSEUM

CAMEROUN

DOUALA

DOUALA MUSEUM

FOUMBAN

MUSEUM OF ETHNOGRAPHY AND ART

MOKOLO

MUNICIPAL MUSEUM

CANADA

ALERT BAY

ALERT BAY PUBLIC LIBRARY AND MUSEUM
KWAKWALA ARTS AND CRAFTS ASSOCIATION MUSEUM

BANFF

LUXTON MUSEUM

CAMPBELL RIVER

CAMPBELL RIVER CENTENNIAL MUSEUM

CAUGHNAWAGA

MUSEUM OF THE MISSION OF FORT ST. LOUIS

CHURCHILL

ESKIMO MUSEUM

EDMONTON

UKRAINIAN ARTS AND CRAFTS MUSEUM

GILFORD ISLAND

NA WA LA GWA TSI

GOLDEN LAKE

ALGONQUIN MUSEUM

HAZELTON

KSAN INDIAN VILLAGE AND MUSEUM

LONDON

MUSEUM OF INDIAN ARCHAEOLOGY AND PIONEER LIFE

MANITOULIN ISLAND

LITTLE CURRENT - HOWLAND CENTENNIAL MUSEUM

MIDLAND
HURON INDIAN VILLAGE
MINESING
SIMCOE COUNTY MUSEUM
ODANAK
ODANAK MUSEUM
OKANAGAN MISSION
INDIAN VILLAGE
OTTAWA
NATIONAL MUSEUM OF MAN
PICTON
MIC MAC MUSEUM
REGINA
SASKATCHEWAN MUSEUM OF NATURAL HISTORY
ST. JOHNS
NEWFOUNDLAND MUSEUM
SASKATOON
MUSEUM OF UKRAINIAN CULTURE
VIGFUSSON MUSEUM
TORONTO
ROYAL ONTARIO MUSEUM
UKRAINIAN ARTS AND CRAFTS MUSEUM
TROIS RIVIÈRES
MUSEUM OF PREHISTORIC ARCHAEOLOGY
VANCOUVER
CENTENNIAL MUSEUM
LIPSETT COLLECTION
UKRAINIAN FOLK ART MUSEUM
UNIVERSITY OF BRITISH COLUMBIA, ANTHROPOLOGY MUSEUM
VERNON
VERNON MUSEUM
VICTORIA
PROVINCIAL MUSEUM
THUNDERBIRD PARK
WINNIPEG
MANITOBA MUSEUM OF MAN AND NATURE
MUSEUM OF UKRAINIAN WOMEN'S ASSOCIATION
YELLOWKNIFE
MUSEUM OF THE NORTH

CENTRAL AFRICAN REPUBLIC

BANGUI
BARTHÉLÉMY BOGANDA MUSEUM

CHAD

FORT ARCHAMBAULT
CHAD NATIONAL MUSEUM
FORT LAMY
CHAD NATIONAL MUSEUM

CHILE

LA SERENA
LA SERENA ARCHAEOLOGICAL MUSEUM
PUNTA ARENAS
SALESIAN REGIONAL MUSEUM
SANTIAGO
INDIAN HISTORIC MUSEUM
MUSEUM OF THE ART OF THE AMERICAN PEOPLES
MUSEUM OF NATURAL HISTORY
EMILIO AND DUNCAN WAGNER ARCHAEOLOGICAL MUSEUM
TEMUCO
ARAUCANIAN MUSEUM

CHINA, P.R.

PEKING
CULTURAL PALACE OF THE MINORITIES
TSINAN (JI NAN)
PROVINCIAL MUSEUM
URUMCHI (WULUMUCHI)
REGIONAL MUSEUM

REPUBLIC OF CHINA

TAIPEI
TAIWAN PROVINCIAL MUSEUM

COLOMBIA

BOGOTA
ETHNOGRAPHICAL MUSEUM OF THE CARO AND CUERVO INSTITUTE
NATIONAL MUSEUM
NATIONAL MUSEUM OF ANTHROPOLOGY
CARTAGENA
ANTHROPOLOGICAL MUSEUM
MANIZALES
MUSEUM OF ANTHROPOLOGY
MEDELLÍN
INDIAN MUSEUM
MUSEUM OF ANTHROPOLOGY
MUSEUM OF ETHNOGRAPHY
POPAYAN
MUSEUM OF COLONIAL HISTORY AND ART
SANTA MARIA
ETHNOGRAPHICAL MUSEUM
VILLANUEVA
MUSEUM OF NATIVE ART AND CULTURE

COSTA RICA

SAN JOSÉ
NATIONAL MUSEUM

CUBA

BANES
MUSEUM OF THE CUBAN INDIANS
GUANABACOA
HISTORICAL MUSEUM
HABANA
AGRICULTURAL MUSEUM
MONTANÉ ANTHROPOLOGICAL MUSEUM
SANTIAGO DE CUBA
SCIENCE MUSEUM

CZECHOSLOVAKIA

BĚLÁ POD BEZDĚZEM
REGIONAL MUSEUM
BENÁTKY NAD JIZEROU
MUNICIPAL MUSEUM
BRANDÝS NAD LABEM- STANÁ BOLESLAV
PRAGUE-VÝCHOD DISTRICT MUSEUM
BRATISLAVA
SLOVAKIAN NATIONAL MUSEUM: NATURAL HISTORY COLLECTIONS
BRNO
MORAVIAN MUSEUM: ANTHROPOLOGICAL MUSEUM
MORAVIAN MUSEUM: ETHNOGRAPHICAL COLLECTIONS
BROUMOV
REGIONAL MUSEUM
ČERVENÝ KLÁŠTOR
MONASTERY MUSEUM
ČESKE BUDĚJOVICE
MUSEUM OF SOUTHERN CZECHOSLOVAKIA
ČESKÝ BROD
MUSEUM OF LOWER LIPAN
ČESKÝ KRUMLOV
REGIONAL MUSEUM
CHOELŇ
ORLICKÝ MUSEUM
CHROPYNĚ
DR. EMIL AXMAN MEMORIAL
DOBŘÍŠ
MUNICIPAL MUSEUM
DOLNI DOMASLOVICE
DOMASLOVICE AND DISTRICT MUSEUM
DOMAŽLICE
DOMAŽLICE MUSEUM
JINDŘICHA JINDŘICHA MUSEUM
GOTTWALDOV
GOTTWALDOV MUSEUM OF SOUTHERN MORAVIA
HLINSKO
REGIONAL MUSEUM AND ART GALLERY
HOLICE V ČECHÁCH
AFRICA MUSEUM; DR. EMIL HOLUB MEMORIAL
HOŘOVICE
MUNICIPAL MUSEUM
HORŠOVSKY TÝN
REGIONAL MUSEUM
HRANICE NA MORAVĚ
MUSEUM OF CENTRAL MORAVIA
JAROMĚŘ
MUNICIPAL MUSEUM AND ART GALLERY
JIČÍN
DISTRICT MUSEUM
JIHLAVA
VYSOČINY MUSEUM
KAMENICE NAD LIPOU
REGIONAL MUSEUM
KEŽMAROK
MUNICIPAL MUSEUM
KLADNO
DISTRICT MUSEUM
KLATOVY
REGIONAL MUSEUM
KOPŘIVNICE
TECHNICAL MUSEUM
KOŠICE
MUSEUM OF EASTERN SLOVAKIA
KRAVAŘE
PALACE MUSEUM
LEVICE
TEKOV MUSEUM
LITOMĚŘICE
DISTRICT MUSEUM
LYSÁ NAD LABEM
MUSEUM OF ANCIENT ORIENTAL CULTURE
MARIANSKÁ TYNICE - KRALOVICE
DISTRICT MUSEUM
MARTIN
SLOVAKIAN NATIONAL MUSEUM: ETHNOGRAPHICAL COLLECTIONS
OSTRAVA
OSTRAVA MUSEUM
PARDUBICE
MUSEUM OF EASTERN CZECHOSLOVAKIA
PLZEŇ
MUSEUM OF WESTERN CZECHOSLOVAKIA: ETHNOGRAPHICAL COLLECTION
PODĚBRADY
DISTRICT MUSEUM
POLIČKA
MUNICIPAL MUSEUM AND ART GALLERY
PRAGUE
ETHNOLOGICAL COLLECTIONS
MUSEUM OF ANTHROPOLOGY
MUSEUM OF THE CULTURES OF ASIA, AFRICA AND AMERICA
NATIONAL MUSEUM: MUSEUM OF NATURAL HISTORY
RUŽOMBEROK
LIPTOV MUSEUM
SLANÝ
REGIONAL MUSEUM
SOBĚSLAV
MUSEUM OF SOUTHERN CZECHOSLOVAKIA
STRAKONICE
MUSEUM OF HISTORY AND ETHNOGRAPHY
TATRANSKÁ LOMNICA
MUSEUM OF THE TATRA NATIONAL PARK (TANAP)
TOVAČOV
MUSEUM OF ETHNOGRAPHY
TRNAVA
MUSEUM OF WESTERN SLOVAKIA
UHERSKÉ HRADIŠTĚ
SLOVAK MUSEUM
UHLIŘSKÉ JANOVICE
MUSEUM OF HISTORY

ÚJEZD
J. S. KOZINY MEMORIAL MUSEUM
VAMBERK
MUNICIPAL MUSEUM
VRCHLABÍ
KRKONOŠ MUSEUM (ASSOCIATED WITH KRKONOŠSKÝ NATIONAL PARK)

DAHOMEY

PARAKOU
OPEN-AIR MUSEUM OF ETHNOGRAPHY AND NATURAL SCIENCES
PORTO-NOVO
ETHNOGRAPHICAL MUSEUM

DENMARK

ÅBENRÅ
ÅBENRÅ MUSEUM
ÅRHUS
MUSEUM OF PREHISTORY
CHRISTIANSFELD
BRØDREMENIGHEDENS MUSEUM
COPENHAGEN
NATIONAL MUSEUM
EBELTOFT
POST HOUSE
ESBJERG
ESBJERG MUSEUM
SORØ
ACADEMY MUSEUM
SØNDERBORG
MUSEUM
VORDINGBORG
SOUTH ZEALAND MUSEUM

DOMINICAN REPUBLIC

SANTO DOMINGO
NATIONAL MUSEUM

ECUADOR

GUAYAQUIL
TOWN MUSEUM
QUITO
ANTONIO SANTIANA ANTHROPOLOGICAL MUSEUM

EGYPT, ARAB REPUBLIC OF

CAIRO
MUSEUM OF EGYPTIAN CIVILISATION

EL SALVADOR

SAN SALVADOR
NATIONAL MUSEUM DAVID J. GUZMAN

EQUATORIAL GUINEA

SANTA ISABEL
MUSEUM OF ETHNOGRAPHY

ETHIOPIA

ADDIS ABABA
INSTITUTE OF ETHIOPIAN STUDIES MUSEUM

FIJI

SUVA
FIJI MUSEUM

FINLAND

HELSINKI
FINNISH NATIONAL MUSEUM
MISSIONARY MUSEUM
JOENSUU
MUNICIPAL MUSEUM AND KARELIA HOUSE
JYVÄSKYLÄ
UNIVERSITY MUSEUM
LAPPEENRANTA
MUSEUM OF SOUTHERN KARELIA
OULU
MUSEUM OF NORTH OSTROBOTHNIA
TORNIO
TORNIO VALLEY MUSEUM

FRANCE

AGDE
AGDE MUSEUM
AIGUILLES
OLD QUEYRAS MUSEUM
AIX (ÎLE D')
AFRICAN MUSEUM
AIX-EN-PROVENCE
MUSEUM OF OLD AIX
ALBERTVILLE
CONFLANS MUSEUM
ALENÇON
D'OZÉ MUSEUM
AMBERT
PEASANT MUSEUM OF THE VALLORGUE AND 'FOURME' MUSEUM
AMBIERLE
FORÈZE MUSEUM
ANGOULÊME
MUNICIPAL MUSEUM
ANNONAY
OLD ANNONAY MUSEUM
ARGENTEUIL
OLD ARGENTEUIL MUSEUM
ARLES
ARLES MUSEUM
AUXONNE
BONAPARTE MUSEUM
AVRANCHES
LOCAL MUSEUM
BAGNÈRES-DE-LUCHON
LUCHON REGIONAL MUSEUM
BASTIA
MUSEUM OF CORSICAN ETHNOGRAPHY
BEAUGENCY
DUNOIS MUSEUM
BEAUJEU
MARIUS AUDIN MUSEUM OF POPULAR TRADITIONS
BEAUMONT-EN-AUGE
LAPLACE MUSEUM AND MUSEUM OF PAINTING
BERGUES
MUNICIPAL MUSEUM
BESANÇON
FOLK MUSEUM
BIARRITZ
MUSEUM OF THE SEA
BORDEAUX
AQUITAINE MUSEUM
BOURBON- L'ARCHAMBAULT
AUGUSTIN BERNARD MUSEUM
BOURG-EN-BRESSE
AIN MUSEUM
BOURGNEUF-EN-RETZ
RETZ REGIONAL MUSEUM
BOURGOIN-JALLIEU
VICTOR CHARRETON MUSEUM
BRICQEBEC
MUNICIPAL MUSEUM
BRIVE-LA-GAILLARDE
ERNEST RUPIN MUSEUM
CABRERETS
MUSEUM OF PREHISTORY AND AFRICAN ETHNOLOGY
CAGNES-SUR-MER
CASTLE MUSEUM
CANNES
LYCKLAMA MUSEUM
CARPENTRAS
COMTADIN MUSEUM
CHAMBÉRY
MUSEUM OF SAVOY
CHAMPLITTE- ET-LE-PRÉLOT
DEPARTMENTAL MUSEUM OF HISTORY AND ETHNOGRAPHY
LA CHARITÉ-SUR-LOIRE
LOCAL MUSEUM
CHARLEVILLE-MÉZIÈRES
ARDENNES AND RIMBAUD MUSEUM
CHAUVIGNY
FOLKLORE AND ETHNOGRAPHIC MUSEUM
CLAMECY
MUNICIPAL MUSEUM
CLERMONT-FERRAND
RANQUET MUSEUM
COGNAC
MUNICIPAL MUSEUM
COMMANA
OPEN-AIR MUSEUM
CONFLANS- SAINTE-HONORINE
MUSEUM OF WATER TRANSPORT
CROIX-DE-VIE
MARAICHIN MUSEUM
DIJON
PERRIN DE PUYCOUSIN MUSEUM
DOULLENS
LOMBARD MUSEUM
ÉPINAL
VOSGES MUSEUM
ÉVIAN-LES-BAINS
MUSEUM OF SAVOY
FOIX
ARIÈGE MUSEUM
FONTENAY-LE-COMTE
VENDÉE MUSEUM
GAP
MUSEUM OF THE HAUTES-ALPES DEPARTEMENT
GRANVILLE
MUSEUM OF OLD GRANVILLE
GRENOBLE
DAUPHINÉ MUSEUM
LE HAVRE
MUSEUM OF NATURAL HISTORY
ISSOUDUN
MISSION MUSEUM
LILLE
MUSEUM OF THE COMTESSE HOSPICE
LOCHES
LANSYER MUSEUM
LOCRONAN
MUNICIPAL MUSEUM
LOURDES
MUSEUM OF THE PYRENEES
LUZ-SAINT-SAUVEUR
LOCAL MUSEUM
LYON
MUSEUM OF THE LYON AFRICAN MISSIONS
MUSEUM OF THE PROPAGATION OF THE FAITH
MÂCON
MUNICIPAL MUSEUM OF THE URSULINES
LE MANS
QUEEN BERENGARIA MUSEUM
MARTAINVILLE EPREVILLE
DEPARTMENTAL MUSEUM OF HAUTE-NORMANDIE

MARZY
FOLKLORE MUSEUM
MAUBEUGE
FERCOT DELMOTTE MUSEUM
MAUVEZIN
CHÂTEAU MUSEUM
MEAUX
BOSSUET MUSEUM
MENDE
MUSEUM OF THE LOZÈRE SOCIETY OF LETTERS, SCIENCES AND ARTS
MENTON
MUNICIPAL MUSEUM
MOISSAC
MUSEUM OF THE POPULAR ARTS AND TRADITIONS OF BAS- QUERCY
MOLSHEIM
MUSEUM OF ART AND HISTORY
MONTAIGU
MUSEUM OF THE NORTHERN VENDÉE
MONTBÉLIARD
HISTORICAL MUSEUM OF OLD MONTBELIARD
MONT-DE-MARSAN
DAUBALEN MUSEUM
MONTLUCON
MUNICIPAL MUSEUM
MONTRICHARD
PORT-CHER CASTLE MUSEUM
MORLAIX
MUNICIPAL MUSEUM
MUROL
ARCHAEOLOGICAL MUSEUM
NANTES
MUSEUM OF DECORATIVE ARTS
MUSEUM OF REGIONAL POPULAR ART
NARBONNE
MUSEUM OF NARBONNE PREHISTORY AND ANTIQUITIES
NICE
CHÉRET MUSEUM
NÎMES
MUSEUM OF OLD NÎMES
NIORT
MUSEUM OF FINE ART
POITEVIN MUSEUM OF COSTUME
PARIS
ARMENIAN MUSEUM IN FRANCE
HÔTEL DE CLUNY MUSEUM
MUSEUM OF THE FRENCH OVERSEAS TERRITORIES
MUSEUM OF MAN
MUSEUM OF POPULAR ARTS AND TRADITIONS
NATIONAL MUSEUM OF AFRICAN AND OCEANIC ART
PAU
BÉARNAIS MUSEUM
PÉZENAS
VULLIOD SAINT-GERMAIN MUSEUM
PITHIVIERS
MUNICIPAL MUSEUM
POITIERS
RUPERT DE CHIÈVRES MUSEUM
PONT-DE-VAUX
CHINTREUIL MUSEUM
REMIREMONT
MUNICIPAL MUSEUM
RIBEAUVILLÉ
HOSPICE MUSEUM
RIOM
AUVERGNE REGIONAL MUSEUM OF FOLKLORE
RIQUEWIHR
MUSEUM OF HISTORY AND ARCHAEOLOGY
ROCHEFORT
MUSEUM OF FINE ART
LA ROCHELLE
LAFAILLE AND FLEURIAU MUSEUM
ROMORANTIN- LANTHENAY
SOLOGNE MUSEUM
ROQUEBRUNE- CAP-MARTIN
CHÂTEAU DE ROQUEBRUNE
ROUEN
MUSEUM OF NATURAL HISTORY, ETHNOGRAPHY AND PREHISTORY
SAINT- AMAND-MONTROND
SAINT VIC MUSEUM
SAINT BRIEUC
HÔTEL DE VILLE MUSEUM
SAINT-ÉMILION
ARCHAEOLOGICAL MUSEUM
SAINTES
DUPUY-MESTREAU MUSEUM
SAINTES- MARIES-DE-LA-MER
CAMARGUE MUSEUM
SAINT-OMER
HENRI DUPUIS MUSEUM
SAINT- RAMBERT-SUR-LOIRE
SAINT-RAMBERT-SUR-LOIRE MUSEUM
SAINT- SYMPHORIEN-SUR-COISE
LA NEYLIÈRE OCEANIC MUSEUM
SAMADET
MUSEUM OF FAIENCE
SAULIEU
FRANÇOIS POMPON MUSEUM
SAVERNE
MUNICIPAL MUSEUM
THONON-LES-BAINS
CHABLAIS MUSEUM OF FOLKLORE
TOULOUSE
PAUL DUPUY MUSEUM
MUSEUM OF NATURAL HISTORY
OLD TOULOUSE MUSEUM
TOURNON-SUR-RHÔNE
RHÔNE MUSEUM
TOURNUS
PERRIN DE PUYCOUSIN MUSEUM
TOURS-LA-RICHE
CHÂTEAU DE PLESSIS- LÈS-TOURS
VILLEFRANCHE- DE-ROUERGUE
CABROL MUSEUM
VILLENEUVE-SUR-LOT
GASTON RAPIN MUSEUM

FRENCH POLYNESIA

TAHITI
PAPEETE MUSEUM

GDR

ALT SCHWERIN
OPEN-AIR MUSEUM OF AGRICULTURAL HISTORY
AUE
REGIONAL COLLECTION
BERLIN
ANTHROPOLOGICAL COLLECTION OF HUMBOLDT UNIVERSITY
BODE MUSEUM: EGYPTIAN MUSEUM
MUSEUM OF PREHISTORY AND EARLY HISTORY
BLANKENSEE
VILLAGE MUSEUM
DRESDEN
STATE MUSEUM OF ETHNOLOGY
GREIFSWALD
COLLECTIONS OF THE ERNST MORITZ ARNDT UNIVERSITY: ANATOMICAL INSTITUTE AND MUSEUM
HERRNHUT
ETHNOGRAPHICAL MUSEUM
JENA
COLLECTION OF THE ANTHROPOLOGICAL AND ETHNOLOGICAL DEPARTMENTS, FRIEDRICH SCHILLER UNIVERSITY
KAPELLENDORF
CASTLE MUSEUM
LANDWÜST
VOGTLAND PEASANT MUSEUM
LEIPZIG
ETHNOLOGICAL MUSEUM
INSTITUTE OF ZOOLOGY
KARL SUDHOFF INSTITUTE FOR THE HISTORY OF MEDICINE AND THE NATURAL SCIENCES
LUCKAU
REGIONAL MUSEUM
MEERANE
REGIONAL MUSEUM
MÜHLHAUSEN
DISTRICT MUSEUM
NERCHAU
REGIONAL ROOM
NORDHAUSEN
MEYENBURG MUSEUM
QUEDLINBURG
MUSEUM BEHIND THE KLOPSTOCK HOUSE
RADEBEUL
INDIAN MUSEUM
SAALFELD
THURINGIA REGIONAL MUSEUM
STENDAL
WINCKELMANN MEMORIAL MUSEUM
WAREN AN DER MÜRITZ
MÜRITZ MUSEUM
WEIMAR
MUSEUM OF THE PREHISTORY AND EARLY HISTORY OF THURINGIA
WERNIGERODE
HARZ MUSEUM
WITTENBERG LUTHERSTADT
JULIUS RIEMER MUSEUM OF NATURAL HISTORY AND ETHNOLOGY
WUSTERHAUSEN
KYRITZ DISTRICT MUSEUM

GFR

AACHEN
REGIONAL MUSEUM AND COLLECTION OF INDUSTRIAL ART
AALEN
REGIONAL AND SCHUBART MUSEUM
AICHACH
REGIONAL MUSEUM
ALTÖTTING
MUNICIPAL MUSEUM OF REGIONAL LIFE
ALTWIEDERMUS
RONNEBURG CASTLE MUSEUM
AMBERG
REGIONAL MUSEUM
BAD DRIBURG
MISSION MUSEUM
ST. XAVIER MISSION MUSEUM
BAD MERGENTHEIM
MUSEUM OF THE TEUTONIC ORDER AND REGIONAL MUSEUM
BAD ROTHENFELDE
REGIONAL MUSEUM
BAD WIMPFEN
STEINHAUS MUSEUM
BAD WINDSHEIM
REGIONAL MUSEUM
BAMBERG
KARL MAY MUSEUM
BARMSTEDT
RANTZAU COUNTY MUSEUM
BERCHTESGADEN
REGIONAL MUSEUM
SALT MUSEUM
BERGEN
RÖMSTEDT HOUSE REGIONAL MUSEUM
BERLIN
EGYPTIAN MUSEUM
MUSEUM OF ETHNOLOGY
MUSEUM OF GERMAN FOLKLORE
MUSEUM OF INDIAN ART
MUSEUM OF PREHISTORY AND EARLY HISTORY
BOCHUM
BOCHUM MUSEUM
MINING MUSEUM
BORKUM
REGIONAL MUSEUM
BOTTROP
REGIONAL MUSEUM
BOXBERG
REGIONAL MUSEUM

BRAUNFELS
PALACE MUSEUM
BRAUNSCHWEIG
BRUNSWICK PROVINCIAL MUSEUM OF HISTORY AND LOCAL LIFE
MUNICIPAL MUSEUM
BREMEN
FOCKE MUSEUM
OVERSEAS MUSEUM
VEGESACK REGIONAL MUSEUM
BREMERHAVEN
MORGENSTEIN MUSEUM
SPECKENBÜTTEL OPEN-AIR MUSEUM
BREMERVÖRDE
DISTRICT MUSEUM
BUCHEN
STEINERNES HOUSE REGIONAL MUSEUM
BÜDINGEN
HEUSON MUSEUM
BÜHL
REGIONAL MUSEUM
BÜNDE
DISTRICT MUSEUM
BURG-FEHMARN
FEHMARN REGIONAL MUSEUM
BURGHAUSEN
MUSEUM OF THE HISTORY OF BURGHAUSEN
CASTROP-RAUXEL
CASTROP-RAUXEL REGIONAL MUSEUM
CELLE
BOMANN MUSEUM
CLOPPENBURG
VILLAGE MUSEUM
COESFELD
REGIONAL MUSEUM
DACHAU
REGIONAL MUSEUM
DARMSTADT
HESSE MUSEUM
DETMOLD
LIPPE MUSEUM
OPEN AIR MUSEUM
DIEBURG
DIEBURG AND DISTRICT MUSEUM
DIESSEN-AM-AMMERSEE
REGIONAL MUSEUM
DIEZ/LAHN
NASSAU REGIONAL MUSEUM
DILLINGEN AN DER DONAU
MUSEUM OF DILLINGEN HISTORICAL SOCIETY
DONAUWÖRTH
REGIONAL MUSEUM
DORTMUND
KHAYON FOUNDATION FOR INDO-ASIAN RESEARCH
DREIEICHENHAIN
DREIEICH MUSEUM
DUDERSTADT
EICHSFELD REGIONAL MUSEUM
ERLANGEN
GEOGRAPHICAL AND ETHNOLOGICAL COLLECTIONS OF THE UNIVERSITY OF ERLANGEN- NÜRNBERG
PREHISTORY AND EARLY HISTORY COLLECTION OF THE UNIVERSITY OF ERLANGEN- NÜRNBERG
ESCHWEGE
REGIONAL MUSEUM
EUTIN
DISTRICT MUSEUM
FEUCHTWANGEN
REGIONAL MUSEUM
FLADUNGEN
RHÖN MUSEUM
FRANKFURT
MUSEUM OF ETHNOGRAPHY
FREIBURG IM BREISGAU
MUSEUM OF ETHNOGRAPHY
FREISING
MUSEUM OF FREISING HISTORICAL ASSOCIATION
FÜRTH
TOWN MUSEUM
GEILENKIRCHEN
REGIONAL MUSEUM

GIESSEN
UPPER HESSE MUSEUM
GIFHORN
DISTRICT MUSEUM
GLADBECK
GLADBECK TOWN MUSEUM
GLÜCKSTADT
DETLEFSEN MUSEUM
GÖPPINGEN
MUNICIPAL MUSEUM
GÖTTINGEN
COLLECTIONS OF THE ETHNOGRAPHICAL INSTITUTE OF THE UNIVERSITY OF GÖTTINGEN
GRAFENWÖHR
REGIONAL MUSEUM
HAMBURG
ALTONA MUSEUM
HAMBURG MUSEUM OF ETHNOLOGY AND PREHISTORY
MUSEUM OF THE HISTORY OF HAMBURG
HANNOVER
HISTORY MUSEUM ON THE HIGH BANK
LAND MUSEUM OF LOWER SAXONY: DEPARTMENT OF ETHNOLOGY
HEIDE
MUSEUM OF DITHMARSCHEN PREHISTORY
HEIDELBERG
ETHNOLOGY MUSEUM OF THE J. AND E. VON PORTHEIM FOUNDATION
UNIVERSITY COLLECTION OF FOLK ART
HEIDENHEIM
REGIONAL MUSEUM
HELMBRECHTS
REGIONAL MUSEUM
HELMSTEDT
DISTRICT MUSEUM
HERMANNSBURG
MISSIONARY AND REGIONAL MUSEUM
HERNE
EMSCHERTAL MUSEUM
HILTRUP
COLLECTIONS OF THE HILTRUP MISSION HOUSE
HOFGEISMAR
REGIONAL MUSEUM
HOHENBURG
SPÖRER MUSEUM OF CULTURAL HISTORY
HOISDORF
STORMARN VILLAGE MUSEUM
HOMBERG
REGIONAL MUSEUM
HUSUM
NISSEN HOUSE
ITZEHOE
PRINZESSHOF REGIONAL MUSEUM
KAISERLAUTERN
THEODOR ZINK MUSEUM
KARLSRUHE
BADEN MUSEUM
KAUFBEUREN-NEUGABLONZ
GABLONZ ARCHIVES AND MUSEUM
KEITUM-SYLT
SYLT REGIONAL MUSEUM
KEVELAER
FOLKLORE MUSEUM OF THE LOWER RHINE
KIEL
MUSEUM OF ETHNOGRAPHY
KITZINGEN
GERMAN FASCHING MUSEUM
KOBLENZ
STATE COLLECTIONS OF PREHISTORY AND FOLKLORE
KÖLN
MUSEUM OF THE CITY OF COLOGNE
RAUTENSTRANCH-JOEST MUSEUM
KOMMERN
LAND MUSEUM OF FOLKLORE
KREFELD
REGIONAL MUSEUM OF THE LOWER RHINE
LADBERGEN
REGIONAL MUSEUM
LAHR (SCHWARZWALD)
MUSEUM IN THE TOWN PARK

LANDSHUT
TOWN AND DISTRICT MUSEUM
LANGENAU
REGIONAL MUSEUM
LAUDA
REGIONAL MUSEUM
LAUF AN DER PEGNITZ
MUNICIPAL COLLECTIONS
LAUTERBACH
HOHLHAUS MUSEUM
LEMGO
HOUSE OF THE WITCHES' MAYOR
LETMATHE
REGIONAL MUSEUM
LIMBURG (LAHN)
MISSION MUSEUM
LIPPSTADT
DISTRICT MUSEUM
LÜBECK
ETHNOGRAPHY COLLECTION
LUCHOW
REGIONAL MUSEUM
LUDWIGSHAFEN
K. O. BRAUN REGIONAL MUSEUM
MANNHEIM
REISS CITY MUSEUM
MARBURG
ETHNOGRAPHICAL COLLECTION OF MARBURG UNIVERSITY
MARKTOBERDORF
COLLECTIONS OF LOCAL LIFE AND HISTORY
RIESENGEBIRGE COLLECTION
MARL
REGIONAL MUSEUM
MARNE
SKAT CLUB MUSEUM
MAYEN
EIFEL MUSEUM
MENDEN
MENDEN REGIONAL MUSEUM
MICHELSTADT
ODENWALD MUSEUM
REGIONAL MUSEUM
MIESBACH
REGIONAL MUSEUM
MINDEN
MINDEN MUSEUM OF HISTORY, ETHNOLOGY AND REGIONAL STUDIES
MÖLLN
REGIONAL MUSEUM
MOSBACH
REGIONAL MUSEUM
MÜNCHEN
STATE ANTHROPOLOGICAL COLLECTION
STATE MUSEUM OF ETHNOGRAPHY
MÜSEN
MINING AND REGIONAL MUSEUM
NEUSTADT AN DER WALDNAAB
LOCAL MUSEUM
NEUSTADT (ODENWALD)
BREUBERG MUSEUM
NIEBÜLL
NIEBÜLL FRISIAN MUSEUM
NORDESEIF
FISHERMAN'S HOUSE MUSEUM
NÜRNBERG
MAN AND NATURE MUSEUM
OBERGÜNZBURG
REGIONAL MUSEUM
SOUTH SEAS COLLECTION
OBERHEINING
BRECHELBAD MUSEUM
OBERKAUFUNGEN
REGIONAL MUSEUM
OBERNDORF
REGIONAL MUSEUM
OBERSTDORF
REGIONAL MUSEUM
OEVENTROP
SOUTH SEAS MUSEUM

OFFENBURG
HOUSE OF THE KNIGHTS MUSEUM

OLDENBURG
LAND MUSEUM OF ART AND CULTURAL HISTORY
STATE MUSEUM OF NATURAL HISTORY AND PREHISTORY

OTTERNDORF
KRANICH HOUSE DISTRICT MUSEUM

PADERBORN
MUSEUM OF THE HISTORICAL SOCIETY

PARSBERG
REGIONAL MUSEUM

PASSAU
OBERHAUS MUSEUM

PRIEN
REGIONAL MUSEUM

REGENSBURG
REGENSBURG CITY MUSEUM

RENDSBURG
REGIONAL MUSEUM

RHEINE
FALKENHOF MUSEUM

RIEDENBURG
MUNICIPAL MUSEUM

RIETBERG
MISSION MUSEUM

ROSENHEIM
REGIONAL MUSEUM

ROTENBURG-WÜMME
REGIONAL MUSEUM

ROTTENBURG AM NECKAR
SÜLCHGAU MUSEUM

RÖTZ
RÖTZ REGIONAL MUSEUM

ST. OTTILIEN
MISSION MUSEUM

ST. PETER-ORDING
EIDERSTEDT REGIONAL MUSEUM

ST. WENDEL
ETHNOLOGICAL COLLECTION OF THE STEYL MISSIONARIES

SCHLESWIG
LAND MUSEUM OF SCHLESWIG- HOLSTEIN

SCHWANDORF
REGIONAL MUSEUM

SIEGBURG
SIEGBURG REGIONAL MUSEUM

SIMBACH
TOWN MUSEUM

SIMMERN
HUNSRÜCK MUSEUM

SINDELFINGEN
TOWN MUSEUM

SÖGEL
EMSLAND MUSEUM

STADE
REGIONAL MUSEUM

STEINHEIM-MURR
MUSEUM OF PRIMITIVE MAN

STUTTGART
LINDEN MUSEUM

SYKE
DISTRICT MUSEUM

TAUBERBISCHOFSHEIM
TAUBERFRANKEN REGIONAL MUSEUM

TEGERNSEE
TEGERNSEE REGIONAL MUSEUM

TRECHTLINGHAUSEN
RHEINSTEIN PALACE ART COLLECTIONS

TÜBINGEN
STUDY-COLLECTIONS OF THE UNIVERSITY INSTITUTE OF ANTHROPOLOGY
COLLECTION OF THE UNIVERSITY INSTITUTE OF ETHNOLOGY

TUTTLINGEN
REGIONAL MUSEUM

ÜBERLINGEN
REGIONAL MUSEUM

UNNA
HELLWEG MUSEUM

USINGEN
WILHELM AND REGIONAL MUSEUM

VERINGENSTADT
REGIONAL MUSEUM

VILLINGEN
BLACK FOREST COLLECTION

WALDSHUT
REGIONAL MUSEUM

WALLERSHAUSEN
REGIONAL COLLECTION

WANGEN
WANGEN REGIONAL MUSEUM

WASSERBURG
WASSERBURG REGIONAL MUSEUM

WEISSENBURG
REGIONAL MUSEUM

WERL
MISSION MUSEUM

WINSEN
MUSEUM ST. GEORG

WITTEN
REGIONAL MUSEUM

WOLFACH
WOLFACH REGIONAL MUSEUM

WOLFHAGEN
REGIONAL MUSEUM

WÜLFRATH
NIEDERBERG REGIONAL MUSEUM

WUPPERTAL
MISSION MUSEUM

WYK
FÖHR ISLAND MUSEUM SOCIETY

ZIEGENHAIN
SCHWALM MUSEUM

GHANA

ACCRA
DEPARTMENT OF ARCHAEOLOGY
ETHNOGRAPHIC COLLECTION

GREAT BRITAIN

ABERDEEN
ABERDEEN UNIVERSITY ANTHROPOLOGICAL MUSEUM

ABERGAVENNY
ABERGAVENNY AND DISTRICT MUSEUM

ABERYSTWYTH
CEREDIGION MUSEUM

ACHARN
LOCHTAYSIDE CRAFTS

ASHWELL
ASHWELL VILLAGE MUSEUM

BIRCHINGTON
POWELL-COTTON MUSEUM

BIRMINGHAM
UNIVERSITY MEDICAL SCHOOL MUSEUM

BISHOP'S STORTFORD
RHODES MEMORIAL MUSEUM

BRIGHTON
GRANGE ART GALLERY AND MUSEUM

CAMBRIDGE
UNIVERSITY MUSEUM OF ARCHAEOLOGY AND ETHNOLOGY

DUMFRIES
FOLK MATERIAL COLLECTION

ETON
ETON COLLEGE NATURAL HISTORY SOCIETY MUSEUM

EXETER
ROYAL ALBERT MEMORIAL MUSEUM AND ART GALLERY

FILKINS
FILKINS AND BROUGHTON POGGS MUSEUM

GAINSBOROUGH
GAINSBOROUGH OLD HALL

GLASGOW
CITY OF GLASGOW CORPORATION ART GALLERY AND MUSEUM
HUNTERIAN MUSEUM

IPSWICH
IPSWICH MUSEUM

LEEDS
ABBEY HOUSE MUSEUM
CITY MUSEUM

LONDON
ABBEY ART CENTRE AND MUSEUM
BRITISH MUSEUM
CUMING MUSEUM
HORNIMAN MUSEUM
MUSEUM OF MANKIND

LOOE
THE CORNISH MUSEUM

NEWCASTLE- UPON-TYNE
UNIVERSITY OF NEWCASTLE- UPON-TYNE
UNIVERSITY OF NEWCASTLE- UPON-TYNE

NORTHAMPTON
ABINGTON MUSEUM

OXFORD
PITT RIVERS MUSEUM

READING
MUSEUM OF ENGLISH RURAL LIFE

ST. FAGANS
WELSH FOLK MUSEUM

SALFORD
MUSEUM AND ART GALLERY

WOODSTOCK
OXFORD CITY AND COUNTY MUSEUM

WORCESTER
TUDOR HOUSE FOLK MUSEUM

ZENNOR
WAYSIDE MUSEUM

GREECE

ATHENS
ANTHROPOLOGICAL AND ETHNOLOGICAL MUSEUM
RESEARCH CENTRE OF GREEK FOLKLORE

KOMOTINI
FOLKLORE MUSEUM OF THRACE

GUATEMALA

GUATEMALA CITY
ARCHAEOLOGICAL MUSEUM

GUINEA

KISSIDOUGOU
KISSIDOUGOU MUSEUM

KOUNDARA
FEDERAL MUSEUM

N'ZEREKORE
LOCAL MUSEUM

HUNGARY

ABONY
LAJOS ABONYI VILLAGE MUSEUM

BAJA
ISTVÁN TÜRR MUSEUM

BÉKÉSCSABA
MIHÁLY MUNKÁCSY MUSEUM

BONYHÁD
LOCAL HISTORY COLLECTION

BUDAPEST
MUSEUM OF ETHNOGRAPHY
NATURAL HISTORY MUSEUM

DEBRECEN
DÉRI MUSEUM

DUNAPATAJ
LOCAL HISTORY COLLECTION

EGERÁG
VILLAGE MUSEUM

HÓDMEZÖVÁSARHELY
JÁNOS TORNYAI MUSEUM

JÁSZBERÉNY
JÁSZ MUSEUM

KAPOSVÁR
RIPPL-RÓNAI MUSEUM

KESZTHELY
BALATON MUSEUM

MÁTÉSZALKA
SZATMÁR ETHNOLOGICAL COLLECTION

MOHÁCS
DOROTHYA KANIZSAI MUSEUM

NAGYHORTOBÁGY
SHEPHERDS' MUSEUM

NYÍREGYHÁZA
ANDRÁS JÓSA MUSEUM

PÁPA
LOCAL HISTORY MUSEUM

PARÁD
PÁLOC HOUSE

SELLYE
GÉZA KISS MUSEUM

SZEGED
FERENC MÓRA MUZEUM

SZÉKESFEHÉRVÁR
KING ISTVÁN MUSEUM

SZEKSZÁRD
ADÁM BALOGH MUSEUM

SZENTENDRE
KÁROLY FERENCZY MUSEUM

SZENTES
JÓZSEF KOSZTA MUSEUM

VÁSÁROSNAMÉNY
VÁSÁROSNAMÉNY REGIONAL MUSEUM

VESZPRÉM
BAKONY MUSEUM

ZALAEGERSZEG
GÖCSEJ MUSEUM

ICELAND

REYKJAVIK
NATIONAL MUSEUM OF ANTIQUITIES

INDIA

AHMEDABAD
GUJARAT MUSEUM SOCIETY
TRIBAL RESEARCH AND TRAINING INSTITUTE

BHUBANESHWAR
ORISSA STATE MUSEUM

CALCUTTA
BIRLA ACADEMY OF ART AND CULTURE
CULTURAL RESEARCH INSTITUTE MUSEUM
INDIAN MUSEUM

CHAMBA
BHURI SINGH MUSEUM

CHHINDWARA
TRIBAL RESEARCH INSTITUTE MUSEUM

COIMBATORE
SOUTHERN FOREST RANGERS COLLEGE AND RESEARCH CENTRE

GAUHATI
ASSAM STATE MUSEUM

GURUKUL JHAJJAR
HARYANA PRANTIYA PURATATVA SANGRAHALAYA

IMPHAL
MANIPUR STATE MUSEUM

JAIPUR
CENTRAL MUSEUM

LUCKNOW
STATE MUSEUM
UNIVERSITY OF LUCKNOW MUSEUMS

MADRAS
THE GOVERNMENT MUSEUM AND NATIONAL ART GALLERY

MANGALORE
MAHATMA GANDHI MUSEUM

NAGPUR
CENTRAL MUSEUM

NEW DELHI
ANTHROPOLOGY DEPARTMENT MUSEUM
NATIONAL MUSEUM OF INDIA

PATIALA
STATE MUSEUM

PATNA
PATNA MUSEUM

POONA
MAHATMA PHULE VASTU SANGRAHALAYA
RAJA KELKAR MUSEUM

PUDDUKKOTTAI
GOVERNMENT MUSEUM

RAIPUR
MAHANT GHASI DASS MEMORIAL MUSEUM

RANCHI
BIHAR TRIBAL WELFARE RESEARCH INSTITUTE

SHILLONG
CENTRAL MUSEUM

SHIVPURI
SHIVPURI DISTRICT MUSEUM

SRINAGAR
S.P.S. MUSEUM

TRIVANDRUM
NATURAL HISTORY MUSEUM

UDAIPUR
VICTORIA HALL MUSEUM

VAISALI
VAISALI MUSEUM

VISAKHAPATNAM
ANDHRA MEDICAL COLLEGE MUSEUMS

INDONESIA

DJAKARTA
MUSEUM OF INDONESIAN CULTURE
SEDJARAH MUSEUM

IRAN

ISFAHAN
CHEHEL SOTOUN MUSEUM

RASHT
RASHT MUSEUM

TEHERAN
MUSEUM OF ETHNOLOGY

IRAQ

BAGHDAD
BAGHDADI MUSEUM
MUSEUM OF ARAB ANTIQUITIES
MUSEUM OF ETHNOGRAPHY

IRELAND

SLIGO
COUNTY SLIGO MUSEUM

ISRAEL

AKKO (ACRE)
AKKO MUNICIPAL MUSEUM

BEERSHEBA
NEGEV MUSEUM

HAIFA
ETHNOLOGICAL MUSEUM AND FOLKLORE ARCHIVES

JERUSALEM
BEZALEL NATIONAL ART MUSEUM
MUSEUM DOR VADOR

TEL-AVIV
HISTORICAL FOLK MUSEUM OF THE LAND OF ISRAEL
MUSEUM OF ETHNOGRAPHY AND FOLKLORE

ITALY

BOLOGNA
MUSEUM OF THE INSTITUTE OF ANTHROPOLOGY

CAGLIARI
MUNICIPAL ART GALLERY
SARDO MUSEUM OF ANTHROPOLOGY AND ETHNOGRAPHY

FLORENCE
ANTHROPOLOGICAL AND ETHNOGRAPHICAL MUSEUM
SCIENTIFIC COLLECTIONS

FORLI
ETHNOGRAPHICAL MUSEUM
MUSEUM AND PICTURE GALLERY

FRASCATI
ETHIOPIAN MUSEUM

GALATINA
PIETRO CAVOTI MUSEUM OF ART

GENOA
COLLECTION OF THE INSTITUTE OF COMPARATIVE ANATOMY
MUNICIPAL ETHNOGRAPHICAL MUSEUM
MUSEUM OF THE INSTITUTE OF HUMAN ANATOMY
MUSEUM OF THE INSTITUTE OF MEDICINE

ISCHIA
ISLAND MUSEUM

LA FAVORITA
PITRÉ MUSEUM OF SICILIAN ETHNOGRAPHY

LA SPEZIA
MUSEUM OF NATURAL HISTORY AND ETHNOGRAPHY

MILAN
COLLECTIONS OF THE INSTITUTE OF ZOOLOGY
MUSEUM OF ANCIENT ART
MUSEUM OF FAR EASTERN ART AND ETHNOGRAPHY

NAPLES
ETHNOGRAPHICAL COLLECTION
MUSEUM OF ANTHROPOLOGY

NOVARA
FARAGGIANA MUSEUM OF NATURAL HISTORY AND ETHNOGRAPHY AND FERRANDI ETHNOGRAPHICAL MUSEUM

NUORO
REGIONAL MUSEUM OF COSTUME AND POPULAR TRADITIONS

PADUA
MUSEUM OF THE INSTITUTE OF ANTHROPOLOGY

PALERMO
MUSEUM OF ANATOMY AND PATHOLOGY
MUSEUM OF THE INSTITUTE OF HUMAN ANATOMY
PITRÉ ETHNOGRAPHICAL MUSEUM

PALMI
CALABRESE MUSEUM OF ETHNOGRAPHY AND FOLKLORE

PARMA
COLLECTION OF THE INSTITUTE OF HUMAN ANATOMY
MUSEUM OF CHINESE ETHNOGRAPHY
PIOLA CONGOLESE COLLECTION

PAVIA
MUSEUM OF THE INSTITUTE OF COMPARATIVE ANATOMY
MUSEUM OF THE INSTITUTE OF HUMAN ANATOMY

PEGLI
ARCHAEOLOGICAL AND ETHNOGRAPHICAL MUSEUM OF AMERICA

PESCIA
MUNICIPAL MUSEUM

PISA
MUSEUM OF THE INSTITUTE OF HUMAN ANATOMY

REGGIO EMILIA
LAZZARO SPALLANZANI MUSEUM OF NATURAL HISTORY

ROME
AFRICAN MUSEUM
COLLECTION OF THE INSTITUTE OF COMPARATIVE ANATOMY
GENIO MUSEUM
MUSEUM OF ANTHROPOLOGY
PAOLINO MUSEUM (VATICAN MUSEUM)
LUIGI PIGORINI MUSEUM OF PREHISTORY AND ETHNOGRAPHY

SCORRANO
CAGGIUOLA ETHNOGRAPHICAL COLLECTION

SIENA
MUSEUM OF ANATOMY

TODI
FRANCESCAN MISSIONARY MUSEUM

TOLENTINO

ETHNOGRAPHICAL MUSEUM

TOLMEZZO

CARNICO MUSEUM OF ARTS AND POPULAR TRADITIONS

TREBISACCE

ETHNOGRAPHICAL COLLECTION

TRENT

NATIONAL MUSEUM

TURIN

MUSEUM OF ANTHROPOLOGY AND ETHNOLOGY
MUSEUM OF HUMAN ANATOMY
SCIENTIFIC COLLECTIONS OF THE MUNICIPAL MUSEUM

UDINE

FRIULANO MUSEUM OF POPULAR ARTS AND TRADITIONS

VENEGAZZÙ DI VOLPAGO DEL MONTELLO

GASPERINI COLLECTIONS

IVORY COAST

ABIDJAN

MUSEUM OF THE CENTRE DES SCIENCES HUMAINES

JAMAICA

WHITE MARL

ARAWAK MUSEUM

JAPAN

ABASHIRI-SHI

ABASHIRI MUNICIPAL MUSEUM

AKITA-SHI

AKITA CITY MUSEUM OF ART

ASAHI-MACHI

MIYAZAKI OPEN-AIR MUSEUM

CHIYODA-MACHI

GEIHOKU ETHNOGRAPHICAL MUSEUM

HAKODATE-SHI

HAKODATE MUNICIPAL MUSEUM

KAGOSHIMA-SHI

KAGOSHIMA PREFECTURAL MUSEUM

MATSUMOTO-SHI

MATSUMOTO MUNICIPAL MUSEUM

OSAKA

MUSEUM OF JAPANESE FARMHOUSES

OTSU

SHIGA PREFECTURAL MUSEUM

SAPPORO-SHI

AINU MUSEUM
SAPPORO COLLECTION OF LOCAL HISTORY

TESHIKAGA-MACHI

AKAN WAGOTO MUSEUM

TOKYO

ETHNOGRAPHICAL MUSEUM OF HOYA
HATAKEYAMA COLLECTION
MIAGEIKAN MUSEUM OF MODERN ART
MUSEUM OF ART AND HISTORY OF THE UNIVERSITY OF TOKYO
TENRI GALLERY

TOYONAKA-SHI

THE MUSEUM OF JAPANESE FOLK DWELLINGS

KENYA

KITALE

STONEHAM MUSEUM AND RESEARCH CENTRE

LAMU

NATIONAL MUSEUM

NAIROBI

NATIONAL MUSEUM

KOREA, DEMO. PEOPLE'S REP.

PYONGYANG

STATE CENTRAL ETHNOGRAPHIC MUSEUM

KOREA, REPUBLIC OF

SEOUL

MUSEUM OF KOREAN FOLKLORE
UNIVERSITY MUSEUM
UNIVERSITY MUSEUM

KUWAIT

FAILAKA ISLAND

FAILAKA ETHNOGRAPHICAL MUSEUM

KUWAIT

KUWAIT MUSEUM

LESOTHO

MORIJA

MUSEUM OF MORIJA

LIBYAN ARAB REPUBLIC

TRIPOLI

ETHNOGRAPHICAL MUSEUM

LUXEMBOURG

LUXEMBOURG

STATE MUSEUM

MALAGASY REPUBLIC

TANANARIVE

MUSEUM OF ART AND ARCHAEOLOGY

MALAWI

BLANTYRE

MUSEUM OF MALAWI

MALAYSIA

PERAK

TAIPING MUSEUM

SARAWAK

SARAWAK MUSEUM

MALTA

BIRZEBBUGA

GHAR DALAM CAVE AND MUSEUM

MEXICO

CAMPECHE

CAMPECHE ARCHAEOLOGICAL MUSEUM

CHIAPAS

CHIAPAS REGIONAL MUSEUM

GUADALAJARA

REGIONAL MUSEUM OF ANTHROPOLOGY AND HISTORY

MADERO

MUSEUM OF THE HUASTECA CULTURE

MERIDA

YUCATAN MUSEUM OF ANTHROPOLOGY

MEXICO CITY

ETHNOGRAPHICAL MUSEUM
MUSEUM OF WORLD CULTURES
NATIONAL ANTHROPOLOGICAL MUSEUM

MOROCCO

FEZ

BATHA MUSEUM

TETOUAN

TETOUAN MUSEUM

MOZAMBIQUE

BEIRA

MUNICIPAL MUSEUM

LOURENÇO MARQUES

DR. ALVARO DE CASTRO PROVINCIAL MUSEUM

NEPAL

KATHMANDU

NATIONAL MUSEUM OF NEPAL

NETHERLANDS

ARNHEM

NATIONAL MUSEUM OF ETHNOLOGY: NETHERLANDS OPEN-AIR MUSEUM

ASSELT

ASSELT MUSEUM OF FOLKLORE

BREDA

JUSTINUS VAN NASSAU MUSEUM OF ETHNOLOGY

CADIER EN KEER

CADIER EN KEER AFRICA CENTRE

DELFT

ETHNOGRAPHICAL MUSEUM

DEVENTER

MUSEUM OF TROPICAL AGRICULTURE AND ETHNOLOGY

EDAM

NIEUWENKAMP MUSEUM

GRONINGEN

MUSEUM OF THE GRONINGEN REGION
NATIONAL UNIVERSITY: INSTITUTE OF BIOLOGY AND ARCHAEOLOGY

LEIDEN

NATIONAL MUSEUM OF ETHNOLOGY

LIEVELDE

KOTS OPEN-AIR MUSEUM

NIJMEGEN

AFRICA MUSEUM

ROTTERDAM

MUSEUM OF ETHNOLOGY

STEYL

STEYL MISSION MUSEUM

TILBURG

NETHERLANDS MUSEUM OF ETHNOLOGY

NEW ZEALAND

AKAROA

LANGLOIS-ETEVENEAUX HOUSE

AUCKLAND

AUCKLAND WAR MEMORIAL MUSEUM
MELANESIAN MISSION MUSEUM

CAMBRIDGE

MUSEUM OF THE CAMBRIDGE HISTORICAL SOCIETY

CHRISTCHURCH

CANTERBURY MUSEUM

DUNEDIN

OTAGO MUSEUM

HAMILTON

WAIKATO MUSEUM

NAPIER

HAWKE'S BAY ART GALLERY AND MUSEUM

NELSON

NELSON PROVINCIAL MUSEUM

OBAN

RAKIURA MUSEUM

PAIHIA

TREATY HOUSE

ROTORUA
ROTORUA CITY MUSEUM
TE AMORANGI MUSEUM
RUSSELL
CAPTAIN COOK MEMORIAL MUSEUM
TE AWAMUTU
GAVIN GIFFORD MEMORIAL MUSEUM
WAIPU
PIONEERS' MEMORIAL MUSEUM
WANGANUI
WANGANUI PUBLIC MUSEUM
WELLINGTON
ALEXANDER TURNBULL LIBRARY
DOMINION MUSEUM

NIGERIA

KANO
MAKAMA'S HOUSE

NORWAY

AALESUND
SUNNMØRE MUSEUM
AMLA
THE HEIBERG COLLECTIONS
ARENDAL
MERDØ HOUSE
ASKIM
ASKIM HISTORICAL MUSEUM
BERGEN
HISTORICAL MUSEUM
GRUE FINNSKOG
FINNISH VILLAGE
HALLINGDAL
HALLINGDAL FOLK MUSEUM
KARASJOK
LOCAL MUSEUM
KAUPANGER
HEIBERG COLLECTION
MO I RANA
MO AND NORTH-RANA MUSEUM OF BUILDINGS
NAMSOS
NAMDAL MUSEUM
OSLO
COLLECTION OF ANTIQUITIES
ETHNOGRAPHICAL MUSEUM
HISTORICAL MUSEUM
RÓROS
RÓROS MUSEUM
SARPSBORG
FOLK MUSEUM FOR ØSTFOLD
SETESDAL
SETESDAL MUSEUM
STAVANGER
STAVANGER MUSEUM
TINGELSTAD
HADELAND FOLK MUSEUM
TROMSØ
TROMSØ MUSEUM
TRONDHEIM
MUSEUM OF THE ROYAL NORWEGIAN SOCIETY OF SCIENCES AND LETTERS
TRONDHEIM AND TRØNDELAG FOLK MUSEUM

PAKISTAN, WEST

KARACHI
NATIONAL MUSEUM OF PAKISTAN

PAPUA AND NEW GUINEA, TERRITORY OF

PORT MORESBY
PAPUA AND NEW GUINEA PUBLIC MUSEUM

PARAGUAY

ASUNCION
ETHNOGRAPHICAL COLLECTION
ETHNOGRAPHICAL MUSEUM
MUSEUM OF NATURAL HISTORY

PERU

LIMA
MUSEUM OF THE PRE-HISPANIC ANTHROPOLOGY AND AGRICULTURE INSTITUTE
MUSEUM OF THE SUMMER LINGUISTIC INSTITUTE
NATIONAL MUSEUM OF ANTHROPOLOGY AND ARCHAEOLOGY
NATIONAL MUSEUM OF PERUVIAN CULTURE
PACHACAMAC
PACHACAMAC MUSEUM

PHILIPPINES

CAGAYAN DE ORO CITY
XAVIER FOLKLIFE MUSEUM
CEBU CITY
ST. THERESA'S COLLEGE MUSEUM
UNIVERSITY MUSEUM
DUMAGUETE CITY
SILLIMAN UNIVERSITY CULTURAL RESEARCH CENTRE
MANILA
THE BEYER COLLECTION
MUSEUM OF ARTS AND SCIENCES
NAGA CITY
UNIVERSITY MUSEUM
QUEZON CITY
MUSEUM OF ANTHROPOLOGY

POLAND

BRZEG
PRASTÓW SILESIAN MUSEUM
CHORZÓW
CHORZÓW MUSEUM
DARŁOWO
REGIONAL MUSEUM
JASŁO
REGIONAL MUSEUM
JAWORZYNKA ŚLĄSKA
REGIONAL MUSEUM
KONARZEWO
ADAM MICKIEWICZ MUSEUM
KRAKÓW
ETHNOGRAPHICAL MUSEUM
UNIVERSITY MUSEUM OF ANTHROPOLOGY
ŁÓDŹ
UNIVERSITY OF ŁÓDŹ MUSEUM OF EVOLUTION
ŁOWICZ
REGIONAL MUSEUM
NOWY SĄCZ
REGIONAL MUSEUM
NOWY TARG
REGIONAL MUSEUM
OLESNO
REGIONAL MUSEUM
OLIWA
REGIONAL MUSEUM OF ETHNOGRAPHY
OLSZTYNEK
MUSEUM OF RURAL BUILDINGS
OPOCZNO
REGIONAL MUSEUM
POZNAŃ
MUSEUM OF RURAL CULTURE AND HANDICRAFTS
PRZEMYŚL
REGIONAL MUSEUM
MUSEUM OF RURAL LIFE
RABKA ZDROJ
REGIONAL MUSEUM 'WŁADYSŁAW ORKAN'
RADOM
MUNICIPAL MUSEUM
SANDOMIERZ
REGIONAL MUSEUM
SŁUPSK
REGIONAL MUSEUM OF ETHNOGRAPHY
SMOLNIK
OPEN-AIR MUSEUM
STARA ŚWIĘTA
OPEN-AIR MUSEUM
TARNOW
MUNICIPAL MUSEUM
TORUŃ
REGIONAL MUSEUM
TORUŃ ETHNOGRAPHICAL MUSEUM
WARSAW
NATIONAL ETHNOGRAPHICAL MUSEUM
WDZYDZE KISZEWSKIE
OPEN-AIR MUSEUM
WISŁA-ZDRÓJ
BESKIDZKI MUSEUM
WŁVEŁAWEK
KUJAWSKI MUSEUM
WROCŁAW
ANTHROPOLOGICAL MUSEUM OF THE UNIVERSITY OF WROCŁAW
ETHNOGRAPHICAL MUSEUM
ZAKOPANE
CHATA 'TEA' (TEA COTTAGE)
ZŁOTÓW
ETHNOGRAPHICAL PARK
ZUBRZYCA GORNA
OPEN-AIR MUSEUM

PORTUGAL

LISBON
NATIONAL MUSEUM OF ARCHAEOLOGY AND ETHNOLOGY
OVERSEAS ETHNOGRAPHY MUSEUM
ZOOLOGICAL AND ANTHROPOLOGICAL MUSEUM
OPORTO
ETHNOGRAPHICAL MUSEUM
SANTARÉM
ARCHAEOLOGICAL MUSEUM

RHODESIA

MARANDELLOS
CHILDREN'S MUSEUM
SALISBURY
QUEEN VICTORIA MUSEUM
UMTALI
UMTALI MUSEUM

ROMANIA

ALBA IULIA
ALBA IULIA MUSEUM
BRĂILA
LOCAL HISTORY MUSEUM
BRAN
BRAN CASTLE MUSEUM
BUCHAREST
KARADJA COLLECTION
MUSEUM OF ANTHROPOLOGY
VILLAGE MUSEUM
CARACAL
CARACAL MUSEUM
CÎMPULUNG
CÎMPULUNG-MUSCEL MUSEUM
CÎMPULUNG- MOLDOVENESC
MOLDOVENIAN MUSEUM
CIUCEA
OCTAVIAN GOGA MEMORIAL MUSEUM
CLUJ
TRANSYLVANIAN MUSEUM OF ETHNOGRAPHY
CORABIA
CORABIA MUSEUM

CRAIOVA
OLTENIEI MUSEUM
CRISTURUL
CRISTURUL MUSEUM
DEJ
DEJ MUSEUM
DEVA
DEVA MUSEUM
DURĂU
DURĂU MUSEUM
FOCŞANI
MUSEUM OF ETHNOGRAPHY
GALAŢI
HISTORY MUSEUM
GHERLA
HISTORY MUSEUM
GOLEŞTI
MUSEUM OF HISTORY AND ETHNOGRAPHY
IAŞI
MOLDAVIAN MUSEUM OF ETHNOLOGY
LIPOVA
LIPOVA MUSEUM
LUGOJ
LUGOJ MUSEUM
MEDIAŞ
MEDIAŞ MUSEUM
MIERCUREA CIUC
MIERCUREA CIUC MUSEUM
NĂSĂUD
NĂSĂUD MUSEUM
ODORHEI
ODORHEI MUSEUM
ORĂŞTIE
ORĂŞTIE MUSEUM
PĂULEŞTI
LOCAL MUSEUM
POIANA SIBIULUI
LOCAL MUSEUM
RĂDĂUŢI
RĂDĂUŢI MUSEUM OF ETHNOGRAPHY
REGHIN
REGHIN MUSEUM
RETEAG
ION POP RETEGANUL MUSEUM
RÎMNICU VILCEA
RÎMNICU VILCEA MUSEUM
SATU MARE
SATU MARE MUSEUM
SFÎNTU GHEORGHE
SFÎNTU GHEORGHE MUSEUM
SIGHET
SIGHET MUSEUM
TIMIŞOARA
BANAT MUSEUM
TÎRGU JIU
TIRGU JIU MUSEUM
TÎRGU MUREŞ
REGIONAL MUSEUM
TÎRGU NEAMŢ
ŞTEFAN CEL MARE MUSEUM
TULCEA
MUSEUM OF THE DANUBE DELTA
TURNU SEVERIN
IRON GATE (PORŢILE DE FIER) MUSEUM
VATRA DORNEI
VATRA DORNEI MUSEUM
ZALĂU
ZALĂU MUSEUM

RWANDA

BUTARE
RWANDA NATIONAL MUSEUM
KABGAYI
KABGAYI MUSEUM

SENEGAL

DAKAR
ETHNOGRAPHICAL MUSEUM

SIERRA LEONE

FREETOWN
SIERRA LEONE NATIONAL MUSEUM

SINGAPORE

SINGAPORE
NATIONAL MUSEUM

SOUTH AFRICA, REPUBLIC OF

ALICE
E. S. MALAN ETHNOGRAPHICAL MUSEUM
BLOEMFONTEIN
NATIONAL MUSEUM
CAPE TOWN
SOUTH AFRICAN MUSEUM
MUSEUMS OF THE UNIVERSITY OF CAPE TOWN
DURBAN
DURBAN MUSEUM AND ART GALLERY
EAST LONDON
EAST LONDON MUSEUM
ESHOWE
ZULULAND HISTORICAL MUSEUM
GRAHAMSTOWN
ALBANY MUSEUM
GREYTOWN
UMVOTI MUSEUM
JOHANNESBURG
AFRICANA MUSEUM
ARCHAEOLOGICAL MUSEUM
ETHNOLOGICAL MUSEUM OF THE DEPARTMENT OF SOCIAL ANTHROPOLOGY
MUSEUM OF MAN AND SCIENCE
KIMBERLEY
ALEXANDER MCGREGOR MEMORIAL MUSEUM
DUGGAN-CRONIN BANTU GALLERY
OUDTSHOORN
CANGO CAVES MUSEUM
PIETERMARITZBURG
NATAL MUSEUM
PRETORIA
ANTHROPOLOGICAL MUSEUM OF THE UNIVERSITY OF SOUTH AFRICA
NATIONAL CULTURAL HISTORY AND OPEN-AIR MUSEUM
TRANSVAAL MUSEUM
SKUKUZA
STEVENSON-HAMILTON MEMORIAL LIBRARY
UPINGTON
MUNICIPAL LIBRARY MUSEUM

SOUTH-WEST AFRICA (NAMIBIA)

FISCHFLUSS CANYON
OPEN-AIR MUSEUM
LÜDERITZ
LÜDERITZ MUSEUM
WINDHOEK
STATE MUSEUM

SPAIN

ALBARRACIN
CATHEDRAL
ALCANTARILLA
MUNICIPAL MUSEUM OF ETHNOLOGY
ALCAZAR DE SAN JUAN
FRAY JUAN COBO ARCHAEOLOGICAL MUSEUM
ANTEQUERA
MUNICIPAL MUSEUM
ARTA
REGIONAL MUSEUM
ASTORGA
MUSEUM OF JOURNEYS (DE LOS CAMINOS)
BARCELONA
MUSEUM OF ETHNOLOGY
MUSEUM OF INDUSTRY AND POPULAR ARTS
BEJAR
MUNICIPAL MUSEUM
BILBAO
VIZCAYA HISTORICAL MUSEUM
BURRIANA
MUNICIPAL HISTORICAL MUSEUM
CACERES
MUSEO PROVINCIAL
CADIZ
ARCHAEOLOGICAL MUSEUM
CAPDEPERA
TORRE DE CANYAMEL
CAZORLA
MUSEUM OF FOLK ART AND CUSTOMS
CERVERA
MUSEUM DEL BLAT Y DE LA PAGESIA
IBIZA
ARCHAEOLOGICAL MUSEUM
MADRID
AFRICAN MUSEUM
AMERICAN MUSEUM
COLLECTION OF AMERICAN ARCHAEOLOGY AND ETHNOGRAPHY
MUSEUM OF THE SPANISH VILLAGE
NATIONAL ARCHAEOLOGICAL MUSEUM
NATIONAL MUSEUM OF ANTHROPOLOGY AND ETHNOLOGY
MAHON
PROVINCIAL MUSEUM OF FINE ART
MARTIN MUÑOZ DE LAS POSADAS
CARDINAL ESPINOSA MUSEUM
MURIEDAS
ETHNOGRAPHICAL MUSEUM OF CANTABRIA
ONDA
MUSEUM OF THE NATURAL SCIENCES
PALMA DE MALLORCA
KREKOVIC COLLECTION
MALLORCA MUSEUM
PAMPLONA
ETHNOLOGICAL MUSEUM
PIEDRAFITA DE EL CEBRERO
MUSEUM OF FOLK ARTS AND CUSTOMS
RIBADAVIA
MUSEUM OF FOLK ART AND CUSTOMS
RIPOLL
PAROCHIAL MUSEUM AND ARCHIVE OF FOLKLORE
SAN SEBASTIAN
MUNICIPAL MUSEUM OF SAN TELMO
SANTA CRUZ
MUSEUM OF ETHNOGRAPHY AND NATURAL HISTORY
SANTA CRUZ DE TENERIFE
ARCHAEOLOGICAL MUSEUM
SIERRA DE YEGUAS
MUSEO DEL COMPO
SOLSONA
DISTRICT MUSEUM OF ETHNOGRAPHY
TARRAGONA
MUSEUM OF FOLK ART AND CUSTOMS
VALENCIA
MUNICIPAL MUSEUM OF PALAEONTOLOGY
ZARAGOZA
ARAGON MUSEUM OF ETHNOLOGY AND NATURAL SCIENCES

SRI LANKA, REPUBLIC OF

COLOMBO
NATIONAL MUSEUM
KANDY
NATIONAL MUSEUM

SUDAN

EL OBEID
SHIEKAN MUSEUM
KHARTOUM
ETHNOGRAPHICAL MUSEUM
MEROWE
MEROWE MUSEUM

SWEDEN

ARVIKA
ARVIKA MUSEUM
BORÅS
BORÅS MUSEUM
FALUN
DALARNAS MUSEUM
GÄVLE
GÄVLE MUSEUM
GÖTEBORG
ETHNOGRAPHICAL MUSEUM
HALMSTAD
HALLANDS MUSEUM
HÄRNÖSAND
MUSEUM OF CULTURAL HISTORY
HÄSSLEHOLM
MUSEUM OF ETHNOGRAPHY
HUSKVARNA
HUSKVARNA MUSEUM
JOKKMOKK
JOKKMOKK MUSEUM
JÖNKÖPING
MUNICIPAL PARK OPEN-AIR MUSEUM
KALMAR
KALMAR MUSEUM
KARLSKRONA
VÄMÖ PARK
KARLSTAD
MARIEBERGSSKOGEN
KIRUNA
JUKKASJÄRVI ETHNOGRAPHICAL MUSEUM
LAHOLM
SOUTH HALLAND MUSEUM OF HISTORY AND ETHNOGRAPHY
LINKÖPING
LINKÖPING MUSEUM
LULEÅ
NORBOTTEN MUSEUM
UDDEN OPEN-AIR MUSEUM
NORBERG
NORBERGS MUSEUM OF VERNACULAR BUILDINGS
NORRKÖPING
NORRKÖPING MUSEUM
SKARA
WEST GÖTLAND MUSEUM
SKELLEFTEÅ
SKELLEFTEÅ MUSEUM
STOCKHOLM
NATIONAL MUSEUM OF ETHNOGRAPHY
NORDIC MUSEUM
SUNDSVALL
MEDELPAD MUSEUM
SVEG
MUSEUM OF OLD BUILDINGS
UMEÅ
VÄSTERBOTTEN MUSEUM
UPPSALA
OPEN-AIR MUSEUM
VÄNERSBORG
VÄNERSBORG MUSEUM
VÄXJÖ
SMÅLAND MUSEUM
VETLANDA
OPEN-AIR MUSEUM

SWITZERLAND

BASEL
EXHIBITION OF BASEL MISSION
MUSEUM OF ETHNOLOGY
MUSEUM OF SWISS FOLKLORE
BERN
BERN HISTORICAL MUSEUM
NATURAL HISTORY MUSEUM
SWISS ALPINE MUSEUM
BOUDRY
L'AREUSE MUSEUM
BRIEG
CASTLE OF THE STOCKALPERS
BRISSAGO
CANTONAL BOTANICAL GARDEN AND MUSEUM OF AFRICAN ETHNOGRAPHY
BULLE
MUSEUM OF THE GRUYÈRE DISTRICT
BURGDORF
ETHNOGRAPHICAL COLLECTION
LA CHAUX- DE-FONDS
MUSEUM OF FINE ART AND MUSEUM OF ETHNOGRAPHY
FLEURIER
MUSEUM
FRAUENFELD
CANTON THURGAU MUSEUM
FRIBOURG
ETHNOGRAPHICAL COLLECTION
GANDRIA
CUSTOMS MUSEUM
GENEVA
MUSEUM AND INSTITUTE OF ETHNOGRAPHY
GRENCHEN
MUSEUM SOCIETY'S COLLECTION
HEIDEN
MUSEUM
LIESTAL
BASEL-LAND CANTONAL MUSEUM
MOUDON
EUGÈNE BURNAND MUSEUM
NEUCHÂTEL
MUSEUM OF ETHNOGRAPHY AND INSTITUTE OF ETHNOLOGY
ST. GALLEN
NEW MUSEUM
SOLOTHURN
SOLOTHURN MUNICIPAL MUSEUM
STANS
HISTORICAL MUSEUM
WINTERTHUR
NATURAL SCIENCE COLLECTION OF THE TOWN OF WINTERTHUR
ZURICH
COLLECTION OF THE CULTURE OF THE NORTH AMERICAN INDIANS
ETHNOLOGICAL COLLECTION OF THE UNIVERSITY OF ZURICH

TANZANIA

BWERANYANGE
BWERENYANGE MUSEUM
DAR ES SALAAM
NATIONAL MUSEUM OF TANZANIA
VILLAGE MUSEUM
MWANZA
BUJORA MUSEUM

THAILAND

BANGKOK
HILL TRIBE MUSEUM
CHIENGMAI
MUSEUM OF THE TRIBAL INSTITUTE
NATIONAL MUSEUM
CHIENG-SAEN
CHIENG-SAEN MUSEUM
KAMPHAENGPHET
NATIONAL MUSEUM

TUNISIA

JERBA
JERBA MUSEUM
MOKNINE
MOKNINE MUSEUM

TURKEY

KONYA
ATATÜRK MUSEUM
PERGAMUM
ETHNOGRAPHY MUSEUM
SAMSUN
REGIONAL MUSEUM

UGANDA

KAMPALA
UGANDA MUSEUM
ZOOLOGICAL MUSEUM
MBARARA
FOLK MUSEUM
SOROTI
ITESO MUSEUM

USSR

BAKU
MUSEUM OF ETHNOGRAPHY
BREST-LITOVSK
REGIONAL MUSEUM OF FOLK ART
CHERNOVTSY
MUSEUM OF UKRAINIAN FOLKLORE
DNEPROPETROVSK (formerly JEKATERINOSLAV)
MUSEUM OF ART
DUSHANBE (formerly STALINABAD)
MUSEUM OF THE REPUBLIC OF TADZHIKISTAN
EREVAN
MUSEUM OF ETHNOGRAPHY
GORI
MUSEUM OF HISTORY AND ETHNOGRAPHY
IZYUM
LOCAL MUSEUM
JAROSLAVL
REGIONAL MUSEUM
KISHINEV
MOLDAVIAN MUSEUM
REGIONAL MUSEUM OF THE REPUBLIC OF MOLDAVIA
KRASNODAR
MUSEUM OF HISTORY, FOLKLORE AND ART
LENINGRAD
HERMITAGE MUSEUM
NATIONAL MUSEUM OF ETHNOGRAPHY OF THE PEOPLES OF THE U.S.S.R.
LVOV
MUSEUM OF ETHNOGRAPHY AND INDUSTRIAL ARTS
MOSCOW
D. N. ANUCHIN ANTHROPOLOGICAL INSTITUTE AND MUSEUM
MUSEUM OF ANTHROPOLOGY
ORDZHONIKIDZE
ORDZHONIKIDZE MUSEUM: HISTORY COLLECTIONS
PETROZAVODSK
NATIONAL HISTORICAL MUSEUM
RIGA
OPEN-AIR MUSEUM OF ETHNOGRAPHY
SOCHI
SOCHI MUSEUM
TALLINN
MUSEUM OF HISTORY
TARTU
MUSEUM OF ETHNOGRAPHY
TASHKENT
CENTRAL REGIONAL MUSEUM
TBILISI
DZHANASHIYA GEORGIAN MUSEUM
MUSEUM OF HISTORY AND ETHNOGRAPHY
VILNIUS (formerly WILNO)
HISTORICAL AND ETHNOGRAPHICAL MUSEUM OF THE LITHUANIAN REPUBLIC

UNITED STATES

ALAMAGORDO
MUSEUM OF TULAROSA BASIN HISTORICAL SOCIETY

ALBANY
NEW YORK STATE MUSEUM

ALBUQUERQUE
MAXWELL MUSEUM OF ANTHROPOLOGY

AMSTERDAM
WALTER ELWOOD MUSEUM

ANADARKO
ANADARKO MUSEUM
INDIAN CITY, U.S.A.

ANCHORAGE
ANCHORAGE HISTORICAL AND FINE ARTS MUSEUM

ANDOVER
ROBERT S. PEABODY FOUNDATION FOR ARCHAEOLOGY

ANN ARBOR
MUSEUM OF ANTHROPOLOGY

ARKANSAS CITY
CHEROKEE STRIP LIVING MUSEUM

ASHAWAY
TOMAQUAG INDIAN MEMORIAL MUSEUM

AUGUSTA
MAINE STATE MUSEUM

AURIESVILLE
KATERI MUSEUM

AUSTIN
MEMORIAL MUSEUM

AZTEC
AZTEC RUINS NATIONAL MONUMENT

BALTIMORE
MUSEUM OF MARYLAND ACADEMY OF SCIENCES

BANNING
MALKI MUSEUM

BARTLESVILLE
WOOLAROC MUSEUM

BELOIT
LOGAN MUSEUM OF ANTHROPOLOGY

BERKELEY
ROBERT H. LOWRIE MUSEUM OF ANTHROPOLOGY

BERNANILLO
CORONADO STATE MONUMENT

BETHEL
BETHEL MUSEUM

BLOOMINGTON
INDIANA UNIVERSITY MUSEUM

BOULDER
UNIVERSITY OF COLORADO MUSEUM

BRENTWOOD
BUCKLAND MUSEUM OF WITCHCRAFT AND MAGICK

BRIDGEPORT
MUSEUM OF ART, SCIENCE AND INDUSTRY
RUSSELL CAVE NATIONAL MONUMENT

BRISTOL
HAFFENREFFER MUSEUM OF ANTHROPOLOGY

BROCKVILLE
E. M. PARKER INDIAN MUSEUM

BROKEN BOW
MEMORIAL INDIAN MUSEUM

BROWNING
MUSEUM OF THE PLAINS INDIAN

BROWNS VALLEY
SAM BROWN LOG HOUSE

BUFFALO
BUFFALO MUSEUM OF SCIENCE

CAMBRIDGE
PEABODY MUSEUM OF ARCHAEOLOGY AND ETHNOLOGY

CANTERBURY
PRUDENCE CRANDALL MEMORIAL MUSEUM

CARBONDALE
UNIVERSITY MUSEUM

CARTERSVILLE
ETOWAH MOUNDS ARCHAEOLOGICAL AREA

CEDAR CITY
PIUTE INDIAN MUSEUM

CHAPEL HILL
MUSEUM OF RESEARCH LABORATORIES OF ANTHROPOLOGY

CHARLESTON
OLD SLAVE MART MUSEUM

CHARLOTTE
CHARLOTTE NATURE MUSEUM

CHEROKEE
MUSEUM OF THE CHEROKEE INDIAN
OCONALUFTEE INDIAN VILLAGE

CHEYENNE
BLACK KETTLE MUSEUM

CHICAGO
BALZEKAS MUSEUM OF LITHUANIAN CULTURE
THE POLISH MUSEUM OF AMERICA

CINCINNATI
CINCINNATI MUSEUM OF NATURAL HISTORY
ALFRED K. NIPPERT NATURE MUSEUM
HARRIET B. STOWE HOUSE STATE MEMORIAL

COLUMBIA
MUSEUM OF ANTHROPOLOGY
MUSEUM OF ART AND ARCHAEOLOGY
UNIVERSITY OF MISSOURI MUSEUM

COOPERSTOWN
INDIAN MUSEUM

CROSS VILLAGE
GREAT LAKES INDIAN MUSEUM

CUYAMACA
CUYAMACA STATE PARK MUSEUM

DECORAH
NORWEGIAN-AMERICAN MUSEUM

DEERFIELD
INDIAN HOUSE MEMORIAL

DEKALB
ANTHROPOLOGY MUSEUM

DENVER
COLORADO STATE MUSEUM

DESERT HOT SPRINGS
CABOT YERXA OLD INDIAN PUEBLO MUSEUM

DETROIT
MUSEUM OF ANTHROPOLOGY
WAYNE STATE UNIVERSITY MUSEUM OF ANTHROPOLOGY

EAST LANSING
MICHIGAN STATE UNIVERSITY MUSEUM

EXIRA
AUDUBON COUNTY HISTORICAL SOCIETY MUSEUM

FAIRBANKS
UNIVERSITY OF ALASKA MUSEUM

FLAGSTAFF
MUSEUM OF NORTHERN ARIZONA

FORT LAUDERDALE
FORT LAUDERDALE MUSEUM OF THE ARTS

FRUITA
COLORADO NATIONAL MONUMENT

GALVESTON
KARANKAWA INDIAN MUSEUM
TIMEWEALTH CORPORATION KARANKAWA INDIAN MUSEUM

GILA HOT SPRINGS
GILA CLIFF DWELLINGS NATIONAL MONUMENT

HAINES
ALASKA INDIAN ARTS

HAMPTON
COLLEGE MUSEUM

HANOVER
DARTMOUTH COLLEGE MUSEUM

HARVARD
FRUITLANDS MUSEUMS

HARWOOD
TEXAS INDIAN MUSEUM

HOGANSBURG
AKWESASNE MOHAWK INDIAN VILLAGE

HOMER
HOMER MUSEUM

HOMESTEAD
EVERGLADES NATIONAL PARK

INDIANAPOLIS
MUSEUM OF INDIAN HERITAGE

INDIAN SPRINGS
INDIAN CREEK MUSEUM

INTERIOR
BADLANDS NATIONAL MONUMENT

JEFFERSON
AZTALAN MUSEUM

JEFFERSON CITY
GRAHAM CAVE STATE PARK

JONESBORO
ARKANSAS STATE UNIVERSITY MUSEUM

JUNEAU
ALASKA STATE MUSEUM

KALAMAZOO
KALAMAZOO PUBLIC MUSEUM

KANEOHE
ULU MAU VILLAGE

KEY BISCAYNE
CAPE FLORIDA STATE PARK MUSEUM

KOOSKIA
NEE MEE POO MUSEUM

KOTZEBUE
KOTZEBUE MUSEUM

LANCASTER
NORTH MUSEUM

LARAMIE
UNIVERSITY OF WYOMING ANTHROPOLOGICAL MUSEUM

LAS CRUCES
NEW MEXICO STATE UNIVERSITY MUSEUM

LAWRENCE
MUSEUM OF ANTHROPOLOGY

LEXINGTON
MUSEUM OF ANTHROPOLOGY

LINCOLN
UNIVERSITY OF NEBRASKA STATE MUSEUM

LIVINGSTON
ALABAMA-COUSHATTA INDIAN MUSEUM

LONGVIEW
CADDO INDIAN MUSEUM

LOS ALAMOS
BANDELIER NATIONAL MONUMENT

LOS ANGELES
LOS ANGELES COUNTY MUSEUM OF NATURAL HISTORY
MUSEUM OF CULTURAL HISTORY
SOUTHWEST MUSEUM

LOS GATOS
LOS GATOS MUSEUM

MACON
OCMULGEE NATIONAL MONUMENT

MANISTIQUE
INDIAN LAKE STATE PARK

MANTEO
ROANOAK ISLAND HISTORICAL PARK MUSEUM

MARKSVILLE
MARKSVILLE PREHISTORIC INDIAN STATE MONUMENT

MESA VERDE
MESA VERDE NATIONAL PARK MUSEUM

MIAMI
LYMAN ARCHAEOLOGICAL RESEARCH CENTER MUSEUM
MUSEUM OF SCIENCE

MILWAUKEE
MILWAUKEE PUBLIC MUSEUM

MONTROSE
UTE INDIAN MUSEUM

MORRISTOWN
MORRIS MUSEUM OF ARTS AND SCIENCES

MOSCOW
UNIVERSITY OF IDAHO MUSEUM

MOUNTAINSIDE
TRAILSIDE NATURE AND SCIENCE CENTER AND PLANETARIUM

MOUNT PLEASANT
CENTER FOR CULTURAL AND NATURAL HISTORY

MURRAY
TURTLE MOUND INDIAN MUSEUM

MUSKOGEE
BACONE COLLEGE INDIAN MUSEUM

NEWARK
NEWARK MUSEUM

NEW YORK
AMERICAN MUSEUM OF NATURAL HISTORY
BROOKLYN MUSEUM
MUSEUM OF THE AMERICAN INDIAN
MUSEUM OF PRIMITIVE ART

TRAPHAGEN SCHOOL OF FASHION, MUSEUM COLLECTION

NOGALES

PETE KITCHEN MUSEUM

NORMAL

ILLINOIS STATE UNIVERSITY MUSEUMS

NORTH BEND

COOS-CURRY MUSEUM

OAKLAND

OAKLAND MUSEUM

ONAMIA

MILLE LACS INDIAN MUSEUM

ONCHIOTA

SIX NATIONS INDIAN MUSEUM

ONEONTA

YAGER MUSEUM

OREGONIA

FORT ANCIENT MUSEUM

ORLANDO

CENTRAL FLORIDA MUSEUM AND PLANETARIUM

PACIFIC GROVE

PACIFIC GROVE MUSEUM OF NATURAL HISTORY

PALA

MUSEUM OF MISSION SAN ANTONIO DE PALA

PALO ALTO

PALO ALTO JUNIOR MUSEUM

PARKER

COLORADO RIVER INDIAN TRIBES MUSEUM

PASCO

SACAJAWEA MUSEUM

PEACE DALE

MUSEUM OF PRIMITIVE CULTURES

PEEBLES

SERPENT MOUND MUSEUM

PENASCO

PICURIS PUEBLO MUSEUM

PHILADELPHIA

UNIVERSITY MUSEUM

PHOENIX

HEARD MUSEUM
PUEBLO GRANDE MUSEUM

PIPESTONE

PIPESTONE NATIONAL MONUMENT

PITTSBURGH

FORT PITT MUSEUM

PORTALES

PALAEO-INDIAN INSTITUTE AND MUSEUM

PORTLAND

MUSEUM OF NATURAL HISTORY
OREGON MUSEUM OF SCIENCE AND INDUSTRY

PRINCETON

PRINCETON UNIVERSITY, MUSEUM OF NATURAL HISTORY

PROVIDENCE

ROGER WILLIAMS PARK MUSEUM

REDDING

REDDING MUSEUM AND ART CENTRE

ROCHESTER

MUSEUM OF OLMSTED COUNTY HISTORICAL SOCIETY
MUSEUM OF NEW YORK STATE ARCHAEOLOGICAL ASSOCIATION
ROCHESTER MUSEUM AND SCIENCE CENTER

ROCKFORD

BURPEE NATURAL HISTORY MUSEUM

ROCK ISLAND

BLACK HAWK STATE PARK

ROOSEVELT

TONTO NATIONAL MONUMENT

RUSHVILLE

NUNDAWAGA SOCIETY FOR HISTORY AND FOLKLORE

SACRAMENTO

STATE INDIAN MUSEUM

ST. FRANCIS

BUECHEL MEMORIAL SIOUX INDIAN MUSEUM

ST. JOHNSBURY

FAIRBANKS MUSEUM OF NATURAL SCIENCE

ST. JOSEPH

BENEDICTA ARTS CENTER
ST. JOSEPH MUSEUM

ST. LOUIS

MUSEUM OF SCIENCE AND NATURAL HISTORY

ST. PETERSBURG

ST. PETERSBURG HISTORICAL MUSEUM
SCIENCE CENTER OF PINELLAS COUNTY

SALT LAKE CITY

UNIVERSITY OF UTAH, MUSEUM OF ANTHROPOLOGY

SAN ANTONIO

INSTITUTE OF TEXAN CULTURES, UNIVERSITY OF TEXAS

SAN DIEGO

SAN DIEGO MUSEUM OF MAN

SAN ELIZARIO

SAN ELIZARIO MUSEUM

SAN FRANCISCO

CENTER OF ASIAN ART AND CULTURE, AVERY BRUNDAGE COLLECTION
SAN FRANCISCO AFRICAN AMERICAN HISTORICAL AND CULTURAL SOCIETY

SANTA FE

MUSEUM OF NAVAJO CEREMONIAL ART
MUSEUM OF NEW MEXICO

SCOTT CITY

EL QUARTELEJO KIVA INDIAN MUSEUM

SHILOH

SHILOH NATIONAL MILITARY PARK MUSEUM

SITKA

SHELDON JACKSON MUSEUM
SITKA NATIONAL MONUMENT

STAMFORD

STAMFORD MUSEUM AND NATURE CENTER

STATESVILLE

STATESVILLE ARTS AND SCIENCE MUSEUM

STONEWALL

LYNDON B. JOHNSON STATE PARK, VISITOR CENTER

TAHLEQUAH

MUSEUM OF NORTHEASTERN STATE COLLEGE

TAWAS CITY

TAWAS HISTORIC INDIAN MUSEUM

THOUSAND OAKS

STAGECOACH INN MUSEUM

TOLEDO

TOLEDO MUSEUM OF ART
TOLEDO MUSEUM OF HEALTH AND NATURAL HISTORY

TONALEA

NAVAJO NATIONAL MONUMENT

TUCSON

ARIZONA STATE MUSEUM
SCIENCE MUSEUM

TULSA

THOMAS GILCREASE INSTITUTE OF AMERICAN HISTORY AND ART
PHILBROOK ART CENTER

TWIN FALLS

HERRETT ARTS AND SCIENCE CENTER

UNCASVILLE

TANTAQUIDGEON INDIAN MUSEUM

VANTAGE

GINKGO PETRIFIED FOREST STATE PARK MUSEUM

VERMILLION

W. H. OVER DAKOTA MUSEUM

VIRGINIA BEACH

SKICOAK LIVING MUSEUM OF THE AMERICAN INDIAN

WABASH

WABASH COUNTY HISTORICAL MUSEUM

WASHINGTON

GALLERY OF AFRICAN ART
MUSEUM OF AFRICAN ART
MUSEUM OF THE U.S. DEPARTMENT OF THE INTERIOR
NATIONAL MUSEUM OF HISTORY AND TECHNOLOGY
NATIONAL MUSEUM OF NATURAL HISTORY
SMITH-MASON GALLERY OF ART

WASHINGTON ISLAND

JACOBSEN'S MUSEUM

WELLS FARGO

CASS COUNTY HISTORICAL SOCIETY

WENATCHEE

NORTH CENTRAL WASHINGTON MUSEUM

WINDOW ROCK

NAVAJO TRIBAL MUSEUM

WINSTON-SALEM

MUSEUM OF MAN

WOLF POINT

MUSEUM OF WOLF POINT AREA HISTORICAL SOCIETY

WRANGELL

TRIBAL HOUSE OF THE BEAR

YELLOWSTONE PARK

YELLOWSTONE NATIONAL PARK MUSEUM

YOSEMITE

YOSEMITE NATIONAL PARK MUSEUM

URUGUAY

COLONIA DEL SACRAMENTO

MUNICIPAL MUSEUM

MONTEVIDEO

NATIONAL HISTORICAL MUSEUM
NATURAL HISTORY MUSEUM

TACUAREMBÓ

INDIAN MUSEUM

VENEZUELA

CARACAS

FOLKLORE MUSEUM
NATURAL SCIENCE MUSEUM

CIUDAD BOLIVÁR

TALAVERA MUSEUM

MARACAY

INSTITUTE OF ANTHROPOLOGY AND HISTORY MUSEUM

VIETNAM, DEMOCRATIC REPUBLIC OF

HANOI

HISTORICAL MUSEUM

VIETNAM, REPUBLIC OF

SAIGON

NATIONAL MUSEUM OF VIET- NAM

YEMEN, PEOPLE'S DEMOCRATIC REPUBLIC OF

ADEN

NATIONAL ETHNOGRAPHICAL MUSEUM

YUGOSLAVIA

BANJA LUKA

MUSEUM OF BASANSKA KRAJINA REGION

BELGRADE

ETHNOGRAPHICAL MUSEUM
MANAK'S HOUSE

BREŽICE

PROVINCIAL MUSEUM

CETINJE

ETHNOGRAPHICAL MUSEUM

DUBROVNIK

ETHNOGRAPHICAL MUSEUM

HERCEGNOVI

TOWN MUSEUM

KOMIŽA

MUSEUM

KORČULA

TOWN MUSEUM

KRAPINA

MUSEUM OF EVOLUTION

LESKOVAC

TOWN MUSEUM

LJUBLJANA

ETHNOGRAPHICAL MUSEUM
NATIONAL MUSEUM

NIŠ

OCHRID NATIONAL MUSEUM

NOVI VINODOL

TOWN MUSEUM

PTUJ
REGIONAL MUSEUM
ROVINJ
ETHNOGRAPHICAL MUSEUM
SKOFJA LOKA
MUSEUM
SREMSKI KARLOVCI
TOWN MUSEUM
VELIKA GORICA
MUSEUM OF TUROPOLJE
ZADAR
ETHNOGRAPHICAL MUSEUM
ZAGREB
ETHNOGRAPHICAL MUSEUM
GEOLOGICAL AND PALAEONTOLOGICAL MUSEUM
HISTORICAL MUSEUM OF CROATIA
NATURAL HISTORY MUSEUM

ZAIRE, REPUBLIC OF

KANANGA
NATIONAL MUSEUM
KIMPESE
PRIVATE COLLECTION
KINSHASA
MUSEUM OF ANTHROPOLOGY
MBENDAKA
NATIONAL MUSEUM

ZAMBIA

LIVINGSTONE
LIVINGSTONE MUSEUM

Medical sciences

ARGENTINA

BUENOS AIRES
MUSEUM OF BOTANY AND PHARMACOLOGY

AUSTRALIA

MELBOURNE
SCIENCE MUSEUM OF VICTORIA

AUSTRIA

EIBISWALD
KLOEPFER MUSEUM
INNSBRUCK
APOTHECARY MUSEUM
KREMS
MUNICIPAL MUSEUM
LICHTENEGG
JOHANN JAKOB TSCHUDI MEMORIAL MUSEUM
OBERNBERG
REGIONAL MUSEUM
VIENNA
COLLECTION OF THE INSTITUTE OF THE HISTORY OF MEDICINE
COLLECTION OF POPULAR RELIGIOUS ART
MUSEUM OF THE FARRIER'S ART
MUSEUM OF THE INSTITUTE OF FORENSIC MEDICINE
MUSEUM OF THE VIENNA VETERINARY INSTITUTE

BAHAMAS

NASSAU
BAHAMIA MUSEUM

BANGLADESH

BARISAL
BARISAL MEDICAL COLLEGE MUSEUM
CHITTAGONG
MEDICAL COLLEGE MUSEUM
DACCA
MEDICAL COLLEGE MUSEUM
SALIMULLAH MEDICAL COLLEGE MUSEUM

BELGIUM

GHENT
MUSEUM OF THE HISTORY OF SCIENCE

BRAZIL

BELO HORIZONTE
MUSEUM OF THE FACULTY OF MEDICINE
NITERÓI
MUSEUM OF PUBLIC HEALTH
OURO PRÊTO
MUSEUM OF PHARMACY
RIO DE JANEIRO
ANTÔNIO LAGO MUSEUM
MUSEUM OF THE INSTITUTE OF FORENSIC MEDICINE
MUSEUM OF THE NATIONAL ACADEMY OF MEDICINE
MUSEUM OF PICTURES OF THE UNCONSCIOUS
PATHOLOGY MUSEUM
SANTA CASA DA MISERICÓRDIA: MUSEUM OF PHARMACY
SÃO PAULO
OSWALDO CRUZ MUSEUM
MUSEUM OF THE BUTANTÃ INSTITUTE

CANADA

OTTAWA
NATIONAL MUSEUM OF SCIENCE AND TECHNOLOGY
PONOKA
ALBERTA HOSPITAL MUSEUM

CHINA, P.R.

CANTON (GUANG DONG)
HISTORY MUSEUM

CUBA

HABANA
CARLOS J. FINLAY MUSEUM OF MEDICAL SCIENCE
MATANZAS
MUSEUM OF PHARMACY

CZECHOSLOVAKIA

BRATISLAVA
MUSEUM OF PHARMACY
KLATOVY
REGIONAL MUSEUM
PIEŠTANY
SPA MUSEUM
PRAGUE
CZECH MUSEUM OF MEDICINE AND HEALTH
PHARMACEUTICAL MUSEUM
PŘIBOR
PŘIBOR MUSEUM AND SIGMUND FREUD MEMORIAL

DENMARK

COPENHAGEN
MUSEUM OF THE HISTORY OF MEDICINE
HELSINGØR
MUSEUM

EGYPT, ARAB REPUBLIC OF

CAIRO
MUSEUM OF HYGIENE
SCIENCE MUSEUM

FINLAND

HELSINKI
SAFETY AT WORK MUSEUM
UNIVERSITY MUSEUM OF THE HISTORY OF MEDICINE
TURKU
MUSEUM OF PHARMACOLOGY

FRANCE

BESANÇON
SAINT-JACQUES HOSPITAL
BOURBON- L'ARCHAMBAULT
AUGUSTIN BERNARD MUSEUM
ISSOUDUN
SAINT-ROCH HOSPITAL MUSEUM
LONS-LE-SAUNIER
PHARMACY
LYON
MUSEUM OF THE CIVILIAN HOSPITALS OF LYON
MUSEUM OF FORENSIC MEDICINE
MAISONS-ALFORT
ANATOMICAL MUSEUM OF THE SCHOOL OF VETERINARY SCIENCE
NICE
PALAIS LASCARIS
ORNANS
HOSPITAL PHARMACY
PARIS
FAUCHARD DENTAL MUSEUM
VALENTIN HAÜY MUSEUM
MUSEUM OF THE ARMY MEDICAL SERVICES
MUSEUM OF THE FACULTY OF PHARMACY
MUSEUM OF THE HOSPITALS OF PARIS
MUSEUM OF PUBLIC ASSISTANCE
ORFILA MUSEUM
PASTEUR MUSEUM
VAL DE GRACE MUSEUM
PÉZENAS
VULLIOD SAINT-GERMAIN MUSEUM
LA ROCHELLE
ORBIGNY MUSEUM
SAINT- JULIEN-EN-BEAUJOLAIS
CLAUDE BERNARD MUSEUM
SALINS-LES-BAINS
HOSPITAL
TOURNUS
HÔTEL-DIEU

GDR

BERLIN
ROBERT KOCH MUSEUM
DRESDEN
GERMAN MUSEUM OF HEALTH EDUCATION
JENA
PHYLETIC MUSEUM

LEIPZIG

KARL SUDHOFF INSTITUTE FOR THE HISTORY OF MEDICINE AND THE NATURAL SCIENCES

QUEDLINBURG

KLOPSTOCK MUSEUM

GFR

BARMSTEDT

RANTZAU COUNTY MUSEUM

DÜSSELDORF

VESTER'S ARCHIVE

HEIDELBERG

GERMAN APOTHECARY MUSEUM

MÜNCHEN

GERMAN MUSEUM

REMSCHEID

GERMAN X-RAY MUSEUM

SINSHEIM

REGIONAL MUSEUM

UFFENHEIM

REGIONAL MUSEUM

GREAT BRITAIN

ALDERSHOT

ROYAL ARMY DENTAL CORPS MUSEUM

EDINBURGH

MUSEUM OF THE ROYAL COLLEGE OF SURGEONS OF EDINBURGH

LIVERPOOL

DENTAL HOSPITAL MUSEUM
MUSEUM OF THE SCHOOL OF HYGIENE

LONDON

BLINDIANA MUSEUM
BRITISH DENTAL ASSOCIATION MUSEUM
GORDON MEDICAL MUSEUM
HEALTH EXHIBITION CENTRE
INDUSTRIAL HEALTH AND SAFETY CENTRE
INSTITUTE OF OPHTHALMOLOGY
PHARMACEUTICAL SOCIETY'S MUSEUM
ROYAL COLLEGE OF SURGEONS' MUSEUM
ST. BARTHOLOMEW'S HOSPITAL PATHOLOGICAL MUSEUM
ST. GEORGE'S HOSPITAL MEDICAL SCHOOL PATHOLOGICAL MUSEUM
UNIVERSITY COLLEGE ANATOMY MUSEUM
UNIVERSITY COLLEGE MUSEUM OF ZOOLOGY AND COMPARATIVE ANATOMY
WELLCOME INSTITUTE OF THE HISTORY OF MEDICINE

REDHILL

ROYAL EARLSWOOD HOSPITAL MUSEUM

SUNDERLAND

GRINDON CLOSE BRANCH MUSEUM

WINSLOW

CLAYDON HOUSE

HUNGARY

BUDAPEST

MUSEUM OF THE HISTORY OF BUDAPEST: DEPARTMENT OF MODERN HISTORY
SEMMELWEIS MUSEUM OF THE HISTORY OF MEDICINE

INDIA

AHMEDABAD

B. J. MEDICAL COLLEGE MUSEUMS

BARODA

HEALTH MUSEUM
MEDICAL COLLEGE MUSEUMS

BOMBAY

GRANT MEDICAL COLLEGE MUSEUMS

CALCUTTA

R. G. KAR MEDICAL COLLEGE (PATHOLOGY) MUSEUM
MEDICAL COLLEGE MUSEUMS
MUNICIPAL MUSEUM
MUSEUM

GAUHATI

GAUHATI MEDICAL COLLEGE
MUSEUM OF ANIMAL HUSBANDRY AND VETERINARY SCIENCE

GUNTUR

MEDICAL COLLEGE MUSEUMS

HYDERABAD

HEALTH MUSEUM

LUCKNOW

PROVINCIAL HYGIENE INSTITUTE MUSEUM
UNIVERSITY OF LUCKNOW MUSEUMS

MADRAS

MEDICAL COLLEGE MUSEUMS
STANLEY MEDICAL COLLEGE MUSEUM

MYSORE

MEDICAL COLLEGE MUSEUMS

NEW DELHI

LADY HARDINGE MEDICAL COLLEGE MUSEUMS

POONA

B.J. MEDICAL COLLEGE MUSEUM

VISAKHAPATNAM

ANDHRA MEDICAL COLLEGE MUSEUMS

IRAQ

BAGHDAD

AL-MUSTANSIRIYIA SCHOOL MUSEUM

ISRAEL

PETAH-TIQVA

MUSEUM OF THE HUMAN BODY

ITALY

BOLOGNA

COLLECTION OF THE INSTITUTE OF HUMAN ANATOMY
COLLECTION OF THE ORTHOPAEDIC CLINIC
MUSEUM OF THE INSTITUTE OF COMPARATIVE ANATOMY
MUSEUM OF OBSTETRICS
VETERINARY MUSEUM

CAMERINO

MUSEUM OF AUTOPSY
MUSEUM OF COMPARATIVE ANATOMY

CASTIGLIONE DELLA STIVIERE

INTERNATIONAL MUSEUM OF THE RED CROSS

FLORENCE

LA SPECOLA MUSEUM OF ZOOLOGY

GENOA

HOSPITAL MUSEUM
MUSEUM OF THE INSTITUTE OF HUMAN ANATOMY
MUSEUM OF THE INSTITUTE OF MEDICINE
UNIVERSITY MEDICAL MUSEUM

MILAN

LEONARDO DA VINCI MUSEUM OF SCIENCE AND TECHNOLOGY

MODENA

MUSEUM OF THE INSTITUTE OF HUMAN ANATOMY
MUSEUM OF THE INSTITUTE OF TROPICAL MEDICINE

PADUA

MEDICAL MUSEUM
MUSEUM OF THE INSTITUTE OF ZOOLOGY, COMPARATIVE ANATOMY AND GENETICS
UNIVERSITY MUSEUM

PALERMO

MUSEUM OF ANATOMY AND PATHOLOGY

PAVIA

HISTORICAL COLLECTION
MEDICAL MUSEUM
MUSEUM OF THE INSTITUTE OF COMPARATIVE ANATOMY
MUSEUM OF THE INSTITUTE OF HUMAN ANATOMY

PISA

ANATOMY MUSEUM
MUSEUM OF THE INSTITUTE OF HUMAN ANATOMY

ROME

COLLECTION OF THE INSTITUTE OF CLINICAL NEUROPSYCHIATRY
COLLECTION OF THE INSTITUTE OF COMPARATIVE ANATOMY
COLLECTION OF THE INSTITUTE OF MEDICAL RADIOLOGY
COLLECTION OF THE INSTITUTE OF PARASITOLOGY
COLLECTION OF THE INSTITUTE OF PATHOLOGICAL ANATOMY
COLLECTION OF THE INSTITUTE OF TROPICAL DISEASES
COLLECTION OF THE INSTITUTE OF UROLOGY
COLLECTIONS OF THE INSTITUTE OF ZOOLOGY
MUSEUM OF THE INSTITUTE OF HEALTH
MUSEUM OF THE INSTITUTE OF THE HISTORY OF MEDICINE
NATIONAL MUSEUM OF THE HISTORY OF MEDICINE

SIENA

MUSEUM OF ANATOMY

TURIN

HISTORICAL MUSEUM
MUSEUM OF FORENSIC SCIENCE
MUSEUM OF HUMAN ANATOMY

VENICE

MUSEUM OF THE CONVENTO DEI MINORI CAPPUCCINI

JAPAN

TOKYO

HIDEYO NOGUCHI MUSEUM
THE LABOUR MUSEUM OF LABOUR SCIENCE INSTITUTE
MEGURO PARASITOLOGICAL MUSEUM
ODAWARA CARCINOLOGICAL MUSEUM
RED CROSS MUSEUM

NETHERLANDS

AMSTERDAM

MUSEUM OF THE HISTORY OF MEDICINE AND PHARMACY

GOUDA

CATHARINA INN MUNICIPAL MUSEUM

OLDENZAAL

PALTHE HOUSE HISTORICAL MUSEUM

UTRECHT

MUSEUM OF UTRECHT UNIVERSITY: DEPARTMENT OF DENTISTRY
MUSEUM OF UTRECHT UNIVERSITY: VETERINARY DEPARTMENT

NORWAY

BERGEN

LEPROSY MUSEUM

GRIMSTAD

IBSEN HOUSE AND GRIMSTAD MUSEUM

PAKISTAN, WEST

BAHAWALPUR

VETERINARY MUSEUM

POLAND

KARPACZ

MUSEUM OF RURAL MEDICINE

KRAKÓW

MUSEUM OF PHARMACY

ŁÓDŹ

MUSEUM OF PHARMACY

WARSAW

MARIE-SKŁODOWSKA CURIE MUSEUM
MEDICAL MUSEUM
TECHNICAL MUSEUM

WOLSZTYN

ROBERT KOCH MUSEUM

ROMANIA

BUCHAREST

PROF. DR. VICTOR BABEŞ MEMORIAL MUSEUM
PROF. DR. GH. MARINESCU MUSEUM
MUSEUM OF ANATOMY

CLUJ

HISTORY MUSEUM

SOUTH AFRICA, REPUBLIC OF

JOHANNESBURG

MUSEUM OF THE HISTORY OF MEDICINE
MUSEUMS OF THE UNIVERSITY OF THE WITWATERSRAND

SPAIN

CARDEDEU

BALVEY MUSEUM AND ARCHIVES

LLIVIA

PHARMACY MUSEUM

MADRID

ANATOMY COLLECTION
CAJAL MUSEUM
MUSEUM OF DR. OLAVIDE
MUSEUM OF SPANISH PHARMACY
PHARMACEUTICAL COLLECTION
ROYAL PHARMACY (OFICINA DE FARMACIA)

MASNOU

MUSEUM OF THE HISTORY OF PHARMACY AND MEDICINE

PALMA DE MALLORCA

MALLORCA MUSEUM

PENARANDA DE DUERO

PHARMACEUTICAL MUSEUM

SANTO DOMINGO DE SITOS

MUSEUM OF ARCHAEOLOGY AND NATURAL HISTORY

TOLEDO

MUSEUM OF THE DUKE OF LERMA'S FOUNDATION

VALLDEMOSA

ROYAL CHARTERHOUSE

SUDAN

KHARTOUM

GRAPHIC MUSEUM

SWEDEN

STOCKHOLM

MUSEUM OF MEDICAL HISTORY

SWITZERLAND

BASEL

ANATOMICAL MUSEUM
MUSEUM OF THE HISTORY OF PHARMACY
NATURAL HISTORY MUSEUM

FRIBOURG

MUSEUM OF THE INSTITUTE OF ANATOMY

LANGENTHAL

REGIONAL MUSEUM

LANGNAU IM EMMENTAL

REGIONAL MUSEUM

ZURICH

ZURICH UNIVERSITY COLLECTION OF THE HISTORY OF MEDICINE

UGANDA

KAMPALA

MEDICAL SCHOOL MUSEUM

USSR

LENINGRAD

ACADEMICIAN I. P. PAVLOV MUSEUM
MUSEUM OF THE EVOLUTION OF THE NERVOUS SYSTEM
MUSEUM OF HYGIENE
MUSEUM OF MILITARY MEDICINE

MOSCOW

MUSEUM OF HYGIENE
PHARMACEUTICAL MUSEUM OF THE CENTRAL DRUG RESEARCH INSTITUTE

RIGA

P. STRADIN MUSEUM OF THE HISTORY OF MEDICINE

UNITED STATES

ALEXANDRIA

STABLER-LEADBEATER APOTHECARY MUSEUM

BAILEY

COUNTRY DOCTOR MUSEUM

BALTIMORE

PATHOLOGY MUSEUM
UNIVERSITY OF MARYLAND DENTAL SCHOOL MUSEUM
WELCH LIBRARY

BLOOMFIELD

HISTORICAL MUSEUM OF ACADEMY OF MEDICINE OF NEW JERSEY

BOSTON

MUSEUM OF SCIENCE

CAMBRIDGE

HENRY COUNTY HISTORICAL SOCIETY MUSEUM

CHICAGO

AMERICAN INSTITUTE OF RADIOLOGY
ILLINOIS FUNERAL SERVICE FOUNDATION MUSEUM
MUSEUM OF SCIENCE AND INDUSTRY

CLEVELAND

CLEVELAND HEALTH MUSEUM AND EDUCATION CENTER
CLEVELAND MUSEUM OF NATURAL HISTORY
HOWARD DITTRICK MUSEUM OF HISTORICAL MEDICINE

COLUMBUS

DR. JOHN HARRIS DENTAL MUSEUM

DALLAS

BAYLOR DENTAL MUSEUM
DALLAS HEALTH AND SCIENCE MUSEUM

DANVILLE

MCDOWELL HOUSE AND APOTHECARY SHOP

DODGE CITY

BEESON MUSEUM

DURHAM

TRENT COLLECTION IN THE HISTORY OF MEDICINES

EVANSVILLE

EVANSVILLE MUSEUM OF ARTS AND SCIENCES

FORT WORTH

FORT WORTH MUSEUM OF SCIENCE AND HISTORY

FREDERICKSBURG

HUGH MERCER APOTHECARY SHOP

GAIL

BORDEN COUNTY HISTORICAL MUSEUM

HALSTEAD

KANSAS HEALTH MUSEUM

HAMILTON

RICKETTS MEMORIAL MUSEUM

HINSDALE

HINSDALE HEALTH MUSEUM

HOUSTON

MUSEUM OF MEDICAL SCIENCE

INDIANAPOLIS

ELI LILLY AND CO.

JEFFERSON

CRAWFORD W. LONG MEDICAL MUSEUM

LINCOLN

UNIVERSITY OF NEBRASKA STATE MUSEUM

LOS ANGELES

BARLOW SOCIETY FOR THE HISTORY OF MEDICINE
CALIFORNIA MUSEUM OF SCIENCE AND INDUSTRY
LOS ANGELES COUNTY MEDICAL ASSOCIATION LIBRARY AND MUSEUM

MADISON

HISTORIC MADISON

MCLEAN

ALANREED-MCLEAN AREA MUSEUM

NEW BRUNSWICK

KILMER MUSEUM OF SURGICAL PRODUCTS
RUTGERS UNIVERSITY, SEROLOGICAL MUSEUM

NEW HAVEN

YALE MEDICAL LIBRARY

NEW ORLEANS

LA PHARMACIE FRANÇAISE

NEW YORK

CASSWELL-MASSEY PHARMACY
MUSEUM OF PHARMACEUTICAL SCIENCES, COLUMBIA UNIVERSITY
MUSEUM OF PHARMACY, BROOKLYN COLLEGE OF PHARMACY

OLYMPIA

MUSEUM OF WASHINGTON STATE BOARD OF PHARMACY

PARK RIDGE

WOOD LIBRARY AND MUSEUM OF ANAESTHESIOLOGY

PHILADELPHIA

CYCLORAMA OF LIFE
MUETTER MUSEUM OF THE COLLEGE OF PHYSICIANS OF PHILADELPHIA

PITTSBURGH

FISHER COLLECTION

PRAIRIE DU CHIEN

MUSEUM OF MEDICAL PROGRESS

REGENT

HETTINGER COUNTY HISTORICAL SOCIETY MUSEUM

ROCHESTER

MAYO MEDICAL MUSEUM

ST. JOSEPH

ST. JOSEPH STATE HOSPITAL PSYCHIATRIC MUSEUM

ST. LOUIS

ST. LOUIS MEDICAL MUSEUM AND NATIONAL MUSEUM OF MEDICAL QUACKERY

SAN ANTONIO

HANGER 9, EDWARD H. WHITE II MEMORIAL MUSEUM

SAN JUAN

PHARMACY MUSEUM

SEATTLE

UNIVERSITY OF WASHINGTON, SCHOOL OF MEDICINE

TOPEKA

MUSEUM OF THE MEININGER FOUNDATION

TUSCALOOSA

GORGAS HOUSE

VIRGINIA CITY

RANK DRUG STORE MUSEUM

WASHINGTON

AMERICAN PSYCHIATRIC MUSEUM
MEDICAL MUSEUM OF THE ARMED FORCES INSTITUTE OF PATHOLOGY
NATIONAL MUSEUM OF HISTORY AND TECHNOLOGY

WATERTOWN

MUSEUM ON THE HISTORY OF BLINDNESS

WOODSIDE

WOODSIDE STORE

YUGOSLAVIA

DUBROVNIK

TREASURY

PETROVA GORA

CENTRAL PARTISAN HOSPITAL

ZAGREB

MEMORIAL EXHIBITION, "600th ANNIVERSARY OF ZAGREB PHARMACEUTICS"

Aeronautics

ARGENTINA

BUENOS AIRES

NATIONAL AVIATION MUSEUM

AUSTRALIA

BEVERLEY

BEVERLEY AERONAUTICAL MUSEUM

BRISBANE

ROYAL HISTORICAL SOCIETY OF QUEENSLAND MUSEUM

CAMDEN

CAMDEN MUSEUM OF AVIATION

FORTITUDE VALLEY

QUEENSLAND MUSEUM

SYDNEY

MUSEUM OF APPLIED ARTS AND SCIENCES

BRAZIL

PETRÓPOLIS
SANTOS DUMONT'S HOUSE
PÔRTO ALEGRE
VARIG MUSEUM
SANTOS DUMONT
SANTOS DUMONT MUSEUM
SÃO PAULO
MUSEUM OF AERONAUTICS

CANADA

BADDECK
ALEXANDER GRAHAM BELL MUSEUM
GANDER
CONQUEST OF THE ATLANTIC MUSEUM
OTTAWA
MUSEUM OF NATIONAL HISTORIC SITES SERVICE
NATIONAL AERONAUTICAL COLLECTION
NATIONAL MUSEUM OF SCIENCE AND TECHNOLOGY

COLOMBIA

BOGOTA
MUSEUM OF AVIATION

CZECHOSLOVAKIA

KOŠICE
TECHNICAL MUSEUM
PRAGUE
NATIONAL TECHNICAL MUSEUM

DENMARK

HELSINGØR
DANISH TECHNICAL MUSEUM

FRANCE

ANNONAY
OLD ANNONAY MUSEUM
MEUDON
MEUDON MUSEUM
MUSEUM OF AVIATION
MURET
CLÉMENT ADER MUSEUM
PARIS
AVIATION MUSEUM
NATIONAL TECHNICAL MUSEUM

GDR

ANKLAM
REGIONAL MUSEUM
BAD FREIENWALDE
ODERLAND MUSEUM

GFR

BERLIN
AVIATION MUSEUM
BERLIN TRANSPORT MUSEUM
FRANKFURT
AIRPORT EXHIBITION OF MODELS
FRIEDRICHSHAFEN
MUNICIPAL MUSEUM OF LAKE CONSTANCE
HAMBURG
AIRPORT EXHIBITION OF MODELS
MÜNCHEN
GERMAN MUSEUM
UETERSEN
MUSEUM OF MILITARY AVIATION
WEILBURG
MUNICIPAL AND MINING MUSEUM

GREAT BRITAIN

BIGGLESWADE
SHUTTLEWORTH COLLECTION
BRIDLINGTON
BRIDLINGTON ART GALLERY AND MUSEUM
CANTERBURY
BATTLE OF BRITAIN MUSEUM
CHELTENHAM
SKYFRAME AIRCRAFT MUSEUM
CRANFIELD
COLLEGE OF AERONAUTICS
DERBY
MUSEUM OF INDUSTRY AND TECHNOLOGY
LITTLE RISSINGTON
CENTRAL FLYING SCHOOL MUSEUM
LONDON
ROYAL AIR FORCE MUSEUM
LONDON COLNEY
PROTOTYPE DE HAVILLAND MOSQUITO
OLD WARDEN (see Biggleswade)
THE SHUTTLEWORTH COLLECTION
PAIGNTON
TORBAY AIRCRAFT MUSEUM
RUGBY
STANFORD HALL
SCARBOROUGH
SCARBOROUGH MUSEUM OF LOCAL HISTORY AND BYGONES
SOUTHEND
HISTORIC AIRCRAFT MUSEUM

HUNGARY

BUDAPEST
HUNGARIAN TRANSPORT MUSEUM

INDIA

BANGALORE
VISVESVARAYA INDUSTRIAL AND TECHNOLOGICAL MUSEUM
CALCUTTA
BIRLA INDUSTRIAL AND TECHNOLOGICAL MUSEUM
NEW DELHI
SCIENCE MUSEUM

ISRAEL

TEL-AVIV
MUSEUM OF SCIENCE AND TECHNOLOGY

ITALY

MILAN
LEONARDO DA VINCI MUSEUM OF SCIENCE AND TECHNOLOGY
ROME
CAPRONI DI TALIEDO AERONAUTICAL MUSEUM
VARESE
AERONAUTICAL MUSEUM
VENEGONO SUPERIORE
CAPRONI DI TALIEDO AERONAUTICAL MUSEUM

JAPAN

TOKYO
MUSEUM OF TRANSPORT

NETHERLANDS

ROTTERDAM
MUSEUM OF THE NATIONAL TECHNICAL INSTITUTE OF SHIPPING AND AVIATION
SCHIPHOL- CENTRUM
AVIODROME

NEW ZEALAND

AUCKLAND
MUSEUM OF TRANSPORT AND TECHNOLOGY
CHRISTCHURCH
THE FERRYMEAD TRUST

NORWAY

OSLO
NORWEGIAN SCIENCE AND INDUSTRY MUSEUM

PERU

LIMA
MUSEUM OF MILITARY HISTORY

POLAND

KRAKÓW
AVIATION MUSEUM
WARSAW
TECHNICAL MUSEUM

PORTUGAL

LISBON
MARITIME MUSEUM

ROMANIA

AUREL VLAICU
AUREL VLAICU MUSEUM

SPAIN

MADRID
MUSEUM OF AERONAUTICS AND ASTRONAUTICS

SWEDEN

GÖTEBORG
MARITIME MUSEUM
GRÄNNA
ANDRÉE MUSEUM
LANDSKRONA
LANDSKRONA MUSEUM
STOCKHOLM
TECHNICAL MUSEUM

USSR

G. GAGARIN (formerly GZHATSK)
YURI GAGARIN MEMORIAL MUSEUM
KALUGA
K. E. TSIOLKOVSKI MUSEUM
KHERSON
YURI GAGARIN PLANETARIUM

KURSK
UFIMTSEV MUSEUM
MOSCOW
M. V. FRUNZE CENTRAL MUSEUM OF AVIATION AND ASTRONAUTICS
N. E. ZHUKOVKSKI MEMORIAL MUSEUM

UNITED STATES

BOSTON
MUSEUM OF SCIENCE
BROOKS AIR FORCE BASE
EDWARD H. WHITE MEMORIAL MUSEUM
CHICAGO
MUSEUM OF SCIENCE AND INDUSTRY
ELMIRA
NATIONAL SOARING MUSEUM
FLUSHING
HALL OF SCIENCE OF THE CITY OF NEW YORK
FRANKLIN
EXPERIMENTAL AIRCRAFT ASSOCIATION
HAMMONDSPORT
GLEN H. CURTISS MUSEUM
HARLINGEN
CONFEDERATE AIR FORCE FLYING MUSEUM
HOUSTON
HOUSTON MUSEUM OF NATURAL SCIENCE
INDIANAPOLIS
MUSEUM OF ROSCOE TURNER AVIATION FOUNDATION
LOS ALTOS HILLS
SPACE SCIENCE CENTER
LOS ANGELES
CALIFORNIA MUSEUM OF SCIENCE AND INDUSTRY
MANTEO
WRIGHT BROTHERS NATIONAL MONUMENT
MIDLAND
THE AEROPLANE MUSEUM
NEW YORK
AEROFLEX MUSEUM
PENSACOLA
NAVAL AVIATION MUSEUM
PHILADELPHIA
FRANKLIN INSTITUTE SCIENCE MUSEUM
PITTSBURGH
BUHL PLANETARIUM
QUEENS
HALL OF SCIENCE OF THE CITY OF NEW YORK
RHINEBECK
OLD RHINEBECK AERODROME
ST. PETERSBURG
SCIENCE CENTER OF PINELLAS COUNTY
SAN ANTONIO
HANGER 9, EDWARD H. WHITE II MEMORIAL MUSEUM
SAN DIEGO
SAN DIEGO AEROSPACE MUSEUM
SAN FRANCISCO
ALEXANDER F. MORRISON PLANETARIUM
SAN JOSÉ
ROSICRUCIAN SCIENCE MUSEUM AND PLANETARIUM
SEATTLE
MUSEUM OF HISTORY AND INDUSTRY
PACIFIC SCIENCE CENTER
SYOSSET
NASSAU COUNTY HISTORICAL MUSEUM
WAPAKONETA
NEIL ARMSTRONG MUSEUM
WARREN
WARREN MILITARY MUSEUM
WASHINGTON
NATIONAL AIR AND SPACE MUSEUM
WINDSOR LOCKS
CONNECTICUT AERONAUTICAL HISTORICAL ASSOCIATION

VENEZUELA

MARACAY
AVIATION MUSEUM

Group C

INDUSTRY AND TECHNOLOGY

Agriculture, horticulture

ANGOLA

LUANDA
COFFEE MUSEUM

ARGENTINA

LOS CORRALES
CREOLE MUSEUM
POSTA DE SINSACATE
MUSEUM OF RURAL LIFE

AUSTRALIA

ADELAIDE
BOTANIC MUSEUM
ALBANY
THE OLD FARM
ARMIDALE
ARMIDALE FOLK MUSEUM
BATHURST
FOLK MUSEUM
BOWRAVILLE
FOLK MUSEUM
BRISBANE
EARLY STREET
ORMISTON HOUSE
REDLANDS MUSEUM
CASINO
HISTORICAL MUSEUM
FRANKSTON
BALLAM PARK HOMESTEAD AND HISTORICAL MUSEUM
GOULBURN
MUSEUM OF APPLIED ARTS AND SCIENCES
GRIFFITH
PIONEER PARK MUSEUM
GUNDAGAI
HISTORICAL MUSEUM
JEPARIT
AGRICULTURAL MUSEUM
KADINA
NATIONAL TRUST MUSEUM
KATANNING
KATANNING HISTORICAL MUSEUM
PARRAMATTA
EXPERIMENT FARM COTTAGE
PORT LINCOLN
OLD MILL MUSEUM
SWAN HILL
SWAN HILL FOLK MUSEUM
TANUNDA
BAROSSA VALLEY MUSEUM
TINGHA
SMITH'S MINING AND NATURAL HISTORY MUSEUM
TOODYAY
TOODYAY GAOL HISTORICAL MUSEUM
WILBERFORCE
AUTHENTICATED AUSTRALIAN SETTLERS VILLAGE

AUSTRIA

ANZENAU
ANZENAU MILL OPEN-AIR MUSEUM
ARNFELS
MUSEUM OF CLOCKS, MUSICAL INSTRUMENTS AND FOLKLORE
ASPARN
WEINLAND MUSEUM
BAD HALL
REGIONAL MUSEUM
BAD TATZMANNSDORF
BURGENLAND OPEN-AIR MUSEUM
BAD VOSLAU
REGIONAL MUSEUM
BRAMBERG
REGIONAL MUSEUM
DORNBIRN
LANDSCAPE AND ECOLOGY OF THE VORARLBERG
EGG
REGIONAL MUSEUM
FELDBACH
REGIONAL MUSEUM
FISCHAMEND
REGIONAL MUSEUM
GMUND
REGIONAL MUSEUM
GRAZ
JOANNEUM PROVINCIAL MUSEUM OF THE ETHNOLOGY AND FOLKLORE OF STEIERMARK
KLEINENGERSDORF
"DER BISAMBERG UND DER WEINVIERTLER" MUSEUM
KREMS
WINE MUSEUM
MARIA SAAL
CARINTHIAN OPEN-AIR MUSEUM
MONDSEE
'MONDSEE RAUCHHAUS' OPEN- AIR MUSEUM
NEUNKIRCHEN
REGIONAL MUSEUM
OBERNDORF
REGIONAL MUSEUM
OTTMANACH
MUSEUM OF THE MAGDALENSBERG EXCAVATIONS
PFAFFSTÄTTEN
REGIONAL MUSEUM
PINKAFELD
REGIONAL MUSEUM
RAABS
DR. JOSEF GRASSL REGIONAL MUSEUM
RETZ
MUNICIPAL MUSEUM
SCHÄRDING
MUNICIPAL MUSEUM
SCHEIBBS
HOTTENROTH COLLECTION
SCHWANENSTADT
REGIONAL MUSEUM
SEEKIRCHEN
REGIONAL MUSEUM
SPARBEREGG
REGIONAL MUSEUM
SPITTAL
MUSEUM OF LOCAL LIFE
STÜBING
AUSTRIAN OPEN-AIR MUSEUM
TAUFKIRCHEN
REGIONAL ROOM
TRAUTENFELS
COUNTRYSIDE MUSEUM

WAIDHOFEN AN DER THAYA
REGIONAL MUSEUM
VIENNA
MUSEUM OF INDUSTRY AND TECHNOLOGY
MUSEUM OF THE PROVINCE OF LOWER AUSTRIA
SCHLUMBERGER WINE MUSEUM
WAIDHOFEN AN DER YBBS
PIATY PRIVATE COLLECTION
WEIKENDORF
MARCHFELD MUSEUM
WELS
CASTLE MUSEUM
WENIGZELL
REGIONAL HOUSE

BARBADOS

BARBADOS
BARBADOS MUSEUM

BELGIUM

HASSELT
OPEN-AIR MUSEUM
HUY
DISTRICT MUSEUM

BRAZIL

CAXIAS DO SUL
MUSEUM OF POPULAR TRADITIONS
LIMOEIRO
SEVERINO ARAGÃO RURAL MUSEUM
RIBEIRÃO PRÊTO
FRANCESCO SCHMIDTH MUSEUM

BULGARIA

ETARA
OPEN-AIR MUSEUM
PLOVDIV
REGIONAL MUSEUM OF ETHNOLOGY
VIDIN
REGIONAL MUSEUM OF HISTORY

CANADA

ALBERTA BEACH
GARDEN PARK FARM MUSEUM
AUSTIN
MANITOBA AGRICULTURAL MUSEUM
BARRINGTON
OLD WOOLLEN MILL MUSEUM
BONSHAW
CAR LIFE MUSEUM
CALGARY
CALGARY BREWERY HORSEMAN'S HALL OF FAME
CARBON
SIR JOHN A. MACDONALD MUSEUM
COMBER
TILBURY WEST AGRICULTURAL MUSEUM
ELKHORN
MANITOBA AUTOMOBILE MUSEUM
FORT LANGLEY
BRITISH COLUMBIA FARM MACHINERY MUSEUM
FORT WILLIAM
FOUNDERS MUSEUM
FRANKVILLE
KITLEY HISTORICAL SOCIETY MUSEUM
KAMLOOPS
FORT KAMLOOPS
NEW ROSS
ROSS FARM AGRICULTURAL MUSEUM
OTTAWA
NATIONAL MUSEUM OF SCIENCE AND TECHNOLOGY
PORT ROWAN
THE BACKHOUSE (BACKUS) MILL AND BACKUS AGRICULTURAL MUSEUM
RENFREW
MCDOUGALL MILL MUSEUM
ROCANVILLE
ROCANVILLE AND DISTRICT MUSEUM
ROSE BAY
THE OVENS NATURAL PARK AND MUSEUM
STANSTEAD
BARN MUSEUM
STAVELY
WILLOW CREEK HISTORICAL MUSEUM
STRATFORD
MINNIE THOMSON MEMORIAL MUSEUM
VERNON
HISTORIC O'KEEFE RANCH

CHINA, P.R.

ANTUNG (ANDONG)
PROVINCIAL MUSEUM
CHUNKING
MUNICIPAL MUSEUM
HARBIN
PROVINCIAL MUSEUM
KAIFENG
PROVINCIAL MUSEUM
LANCHOW (LANZHOU)
PROVINCIAL MUSEUM
NANKING (NAN JING)
KIANG SU PROVINCIAL MUSEUM
PEKING
CULTURAL PALACE OF THE MINORITIES

CZECHOSLOVAKIA

BRATISLAVA
MUNICIPAL MUSEUM
BRNO
MORAVIAN MUSEUM: ETHNOGRAPHICAL COLLECTIONS
ČERVENÝ KLÁŠTOR
MONASTERY MUSEUM
KAČINA U NOVÝCH DVORŮ
MUSEUM OF AGRICULTURE
LEDNICE NA MORAVĚ
MUSEUM OF AGRICULTURE
LITOMĚŘICE
DISTRICT MUSEUM
MĚLNÍK
DISTRICT MUSEUM
MICHALOVCE
ZEMPLIN MUSEUM
NITRA
AGRICULTURAL MUSEUM
PRAGUE
CZECH MUSEUM OF AGRICULTURE
ETHNOLOGICAL COLLECTIONS
PŘEROV NAD LABEM
MUSEUM OF ETHNOGRAPHY
RUŽOMBEROK
LIPTOV MUSEUM
SLATIŇANY
MUSEUM OF THE HORSE

DENMARK

ALS
LOCAL HISTORY MUSEUM
COPENHAGEN
AGRICULTURAL MUSEUM
AMAGER MUSEUM
HADERSLEV
HADERSLEV MUSEUM
HERNING
HERNING MUSEUM
HILLERØD
NORDSJAELLANDSK MUSEUMSFORENING
HJERL HEDE
HJERL HEDE OPEN-AIR MUSEUM
LYNGBY
AGRICULTURAL MUSEUM
NYKØBING
MORSLAND HISTORICAL MUSEUM
ODENSE
THE FUNEN VILLAGE
ØLGOD
ØLGOD MUSEUM
VARDE
VARDE AND DISTRICT MUSEUM

EGYPT, ARAB REPUBLIC OF

CAIRO
AGRICULTURE MUSEUM
COTTON MUSEUM
MUSEUM OF EGYPTIAN CIVILISATION

FINLAND

ARTJÄRVI
DISTRICT MUSEUM
ASIKKALA
URAJÄRVI FARM MUSEUM
ASKAINEN
LOUHISAAREN FARM MUSEUM
ESPOO
DISTRICT MUSEUM
EVIJÄRVI
LAKE MUSEUM
HELSINKI
SEURASAARI OPEN-AIR MUSEUM
UNIVERSITY AGRICULTURAL MUSEUM
JUVA
REGIONAL MUSEUM
KOKEMÄKI
AGRICULTURAL MUSEUM
LAMONI
LOCAL MUSEUM
LAPINJÄRVI
PORLAMMI REGIONAL MUSEUM
LIETO
VANHALINNA MUSEUM
ORIMATTILA
AGRICULTURAL MUSEUM
PUNKALAIDUN
LOCAL MUSEUM
SAMMATTI
LOHILAMPI MUSEUM
SUND
JAN KARLS FARM
TAMMELA
MUSTRALA MUSEUM OF AGRICULTURAL HISTORY
URJALA
FARMHOUSE MUSEUM
VALTIMO
MURTOVAARA HOUSE MUSEUM

FRANCE

ANGERS
WINE MUSEUM
BEAUGENCY
DUNOIS MUSEUM
BEAUNE
MUSEUM OF THE WINE OF BURGUNDY
BESANÇON
FOLK MUSEUM
BORDEAUX
HISTORICAL COLLECTION OF THE CONSEIL INTERPROFESSIONAL DU VIN DE BORDEAUX
CAGNES-SUR-MER
CASTLE MUSEUM

COGNAC
MUNICIPAL MUSEUM
CONDOM
ARMAGNAC MUSEUM
CORCELLE
FRANCHE-COMTÉ MUSEUM
LILLE
MUSEUM OF INDUSTRY, COMMERCE, TECHNOLOGY AND AGRICULTURE
MARQUÈZE
OPEN-AIR MUSEUM OF THE LANDES DE GASCOIGNE
MARSAC-EN-LIVRADOIS
JASSERIE DU COQ NOIR
MARSEILLE
MUSEUM OF PROVENÇAL ART
MIRABEL
OLIVIER DE SERRES MUSEUM
PAUILLAC
MOUTON-ROTHSCHILD MUSEUM OF WINE
ST. ÉMILION
MUSEUM OF WINE
ST. PIERRE D'OLÉRON
ALIENOR D'AQUITAINE MUSEUM
STRASBOURG
ALSACE MUSEUM
SURESNES
MUNICIPAL MUSEUM
TIGY
MUSEUM OF RURAL CRAFTS
TOURS
ESPELOSIN MUSEUM

GDR

ALT SCHWERIN
OPEN-AIR MUSEUM OF AGRICULTURAL HISTORY
BERLIN
PERGAMON MUSEUM: MUSEUM OF ETHNOGRAPHY
DELITZSCH
DISTRICT MUSEUM
DIESDORF
ALTMARK REGIONAL MUSEUM
GARDELEGEN
REGIONAL MUSEUM
GENTHIN
DISTRICT AND REGIONAL MUSEUM
GERSTUNGEN
REGIONAL MUSEUM
JARMEN
MILL MUSEUM
KAPELLENDORF
CASTLE MUSEUM
LEHDE
OPEN-AIR MUSEUM
ODERBERG
REGIONAL MUSEUM
PRENZLAU
DISTRICT MUSEUM
RUDOLSTADT
MUSEUM OF ETHNOLOGY: THURINGIAN PEASANT HOUSES
SCHÖNBERG
REGIONAL MUSEUM
UMMENDORF
WANZLEBEN DISTRICT MUSEUM
WERDER
ORCHARD MUSEUM

GFR

ALTWIEDERMUS
RONNEBURG CASTLE MUSEUM
AMBERG
REGIONAL MUSEUM
BAD KREUZNACH
MAX PLANCK INSTITUTE FOR AGRICULTURE AND AGRICULTURAL TECHNOLOGY
BAYREUTH
COLLECTION OF AGRICULTURAL IMPLEMENTS AND EQUIPMENT
BERGEN
RÖMSTEDT HOUSE REGIONAL MUSEUM
BERLIN
SUGAR MUSEUM
BINGEN
REGIONAL MUSEUM
BLAUBEUREN
REGIONAL MUSEUM
BORTFELD
FARM-HOUSE MUSEUM
BREMEN
VEGESACK REGIONAL MUSEUM
BREMERHAVEN
SPECKENBÜTTEL OPEN-AIR MUSEUM
BURGAU
REGIONAL MUSEUM
DETMOLD
OPEN AIR MUSEUM
FÜRSTENFELDBRUCK
REGIONAL MUSEUM
GARMISCH-PARTENKIRCHEN
WERDENFELSER MUSEUM
GREBENSTEIN
DIEMEL HOUSE AGRICULTURAL MUSEUM
GUTACH
BAILIFF'S FARM OPEN-AIR MUSEUM
HAMBURG
MILK MUSEUM AND WILHELMSBURG REGIONAL MUSEUM
RIECK HOUSE: VIERLAND OPEN- AIR MUSEUM
UNIVERSITY OF HAMBURG: ECONOMIC BOTANY COLLECTION
VOLKSDORF VILLAGE MUSEUM
HEILBRONN
HISTORY MUSEUM
HEINSBERG
REGIONAL MUSEUM
HERMANNSBURG
MISSIONARY AND REGIONAL MUSEUM
HÖCHSTADT-AISCH
REGIONAL MUSEUM
HORB
HORB PEASANT MUSEUM
HÜCKESWAGEN
REGIONAL MUSEUM
KIRCHHEIMBOLANDEN
REGIONAL MUSEUM
KITZINGEN
MUNICIPAL MUSEUM
KORBACH
KORBACH REGIONAL MUSEUM
KÜRNBACH
THATCHED HOUSE
LEMKENHAFEN
MUSEUM OF WINDMILLS AND AGRICULTURE
LENNGRIES
REGIONAL MUSEUM
LIPPSTADT
DISTRICT MUSEUM
MALENTE-GREMSMÜHLEN
REGIONAL HOUSE
MASSING
FARM MUSEUM OF LOWER BAVARIA
MELDORF
DITHMARSCH FARMHOUSE MUSEUM
MÜNCHEN
GERMAN MUSEUM
MÜNSTER
MILL MUSEUM
OBERKAUFUNGEN
REGIONAL MUSEUM
PERSCHEN
PEASANT MUSEUM OF THE UPPER PALATINATE
PEWSUM
EAST FRISIAN OPEN-AIR MUSEUM
RECKLINGHAUSEN
VESTISCH MUSEUM
ROCKENHAUSEN
NORTH PALATINATE REGIONAL MUSEUM
SCHÖNINGEN
REGIONAL MUSEUM
SCHWENNINGEN
SCHWENNINGEN REGIONAL MUSEUM
SESSLACH
REGIONAL MUSEUM
SPEYER
MUSEUM OF THE HISTORY OF THE PALATINATE
STADE
OPEN-AIR MUSEUM
STARNBERG
MUNICIPAL MUSEUM
STUTTGART
HOHENHEIM MODEL COLLECTION
THAINING
REGIONAL HOUSE
TITTMONING
REGIONAL MUSEUM
TRABEN-TRARBACH
MUSEUM OF THE CENTRAL MOSEL AREA
VERDEN
GERMAN MUSEUM OF THE HORSE
WAIBLINGEN
REGIONAL MUSEUM
WALDERBACH
REGIONAL MUSEUM
WALLDÜRN
REGIONAL AND PILGRIMAGES MUSEUM
WASSERBURG
WASSERBURG REGIONAL MUSEUM
WERTACH
REGIONAL MUSEUM
WEWELSBURG
DISTRICT MUSEUM
WIESMOOR
MOOR MUSEUM
WINDECK
WINDECK REGIONAL MUSEUM
ZIEGENHAIN
SCHWALM MUSEUM

GREAT BRITAIN

ANDOVER
TASKERS OF ANDOVER LIMITED
ASHFORD
WYE COLLEGE AGRICULTURAL MUSEUM
ASTON MUNSLOW
WHITE HOUSE COUNTRY LIFE MUSEUM
BICTON
BICTON COUNTRYSIDE MUSEUM
BUCKFASTLEIGH
BUCKFASTLEIGH FARM MUSEUM
BUCKLAND ABBEY
BUCKLAND ABBEY
CORSLEY
THE LONGHEDGE COLLECTION
DOUGLAS
MANX MUSEUM
DURSLEY
R. A. LISTER AND COMPANY LIMITED
EVESHAM
ALMONRY MUSEUM
GLAMIS
ANGUS FOLK COLLECTION
HAILSHAM
MICHELHAM PRIORY
HALIFAX
WEST YORKSHIRE FOLK MUSEUM
HORSHAM
HORSHAM MUSEUM
KINGUSSIE
HIGHLAND FOLK MUSEUM
LACOCK
LACKHAM COLLEGE OF AGRICULTURE

LEICESTER
BELGRAVE HALL
LLANVAPLEY
RURAL CRAFTS MUSEUM
NETHER ALDERLEY
ALDERLEY OLD MILL
NORWICH
BRIDEWELL MUSEUM
POLEGATE
WILMINGTON PRIORY MUSEUM OF AGRICULTURAL IMPLEMENTS
READING
MUSEUM OF ENGLISH RURAL LIFE
STOWMARKET
THE ABBOT'S HALL MUSEUM OF RURAL LIFE OF EAST ANGLIA
STRATFORD- UPON-AVON
MARY ARDEN'S HOUSE
TILFORD
OLD KILN AGRICULTURAL MUSEUM
WILMINGTON
WILMINGTON MUSEUM
WOODSTOCK
OXFORD CITY AND COUNTY MUSEUM
WYE
AGRICULTURAL MUSEUM
YORK
YORK CASTLE MUSEUM

HUNGARY

BADACSONY
IRODALMI MUSEUM
BORJÁD
PETŐFI MEMORIAL APIARY
BUDAPEST
HUNGARIAN AGRICULTURAL MUSEUM
GYÖNGYÖS
MÁTRA MUSEUM
NAGYVÁZSONY
OPEN-AIR MUSEUM OF ETHNOLOGY
TIHANY
OPEN-AIR FOLKLORE MUSEUM
TOKAJ
LOCAL HISTORY MUSEUM
ZALAEGERSZEG
GÖCSEJ VILLAGE MUSEUM

INDIA

AGRA
ST. JOHN'S COLLEGE MUSEUM
BOMBAY
VICTORIA AND ALBERT MUSEUM
COIMBATORE
AGRICULTURAL COLLEGE MUSEUM
GAUHATI
COMMERCIAL MUSEUM
MADRAS
CENTRAL INDUSTRIAL MUSEUM
POONA
LORD REAY MAHARASHTRA INDUSTRIAL MUSEUM
MAHATMA PHULE VASTU SANGRAHALAYA

IRELAND

BUNRATTY
BUNRATTY CASTLE AND FOLK PARK
GLENCOLUMBKILLE
AN CLACHAN

ISRAEL

HAIFA
DAGON COLLECTION

ITALY

LA FAVORITA
PITRÉ MUSEUM OF SICILIAN ETHNOGRAPHY
MILAN
LEONARDO DA VINCI MUSEUM OF SCIENCE AND TECHNOLOGY
ROME
NATIONAL MUSEUM OF ARTS AND POPULAR TRADITIONS

JAPAN

ISE-SHI
JINGU HISTORICAL AND AGRICULTURAL MUSEUM
MATSUMOTO-SHI
MATSUMOTO MUNICIPAL MUSEUM
MIYAZAKI-SHI
AGRICULTURAL MUSEUM OF MIYAZAKI UNIVERSITY
NI'IGATA-SHI
NI'IGATA SCIENCE AND TECHNOLOGY MUSEUM
ODAWARA-SHI
TREASURE HOUSE OF THE HOTOKU NINOMIYA SHRINE
OSAKA
MUSEUM OF JAPANESE FARMHOUSES
TAKANOSU-MACHI
AGRICULTURAL MUSEUM OF TAKANOSU PREFECTURAL AGRICULTURAL AND FORESTRY HIGH SCHOOL
TOKYO
FOLKLORE COLLECTION OF IGUSA HACHIMAN-GU SHRINE
TEXTILE MUSEUM
YOKOHAMA
SILK MUSEUM

MALAYSIA

PENANG
PENANG MUSEUM AND ART GALLERY

MEXICO

PUEBLA
MUSEUM OF HANDICRAFTS

MOROCCO

MEKMES
DAR JAMAÏ MUSEUM

NETHERLANDS

AMSTELVEEN
AEMSTELLE
BORCULO
DE LEBBENBRUUGE FARM
BORGER
FARM MUSEUM
BUREN
THE FARM WAGGON
DEVENTER
MUSEUM OF TROPICAL AGRICULTURE AND ETHNOLOGY
EDE
OLD EDE
EERSEL
LOCAL HISTORY MUSEUM
ELSLOO
SHIPPING EXCHANGE REGIONAL MUSEUM
ENKHUIZEN
NATIONAL ZUIDERZEE MUSEUM
ETTEN-LEUR
JAN OUTEN HOUTE MUSEUM OF LOCAL HISTORY AND FOLKLORE
GORREDIJK
'DE ZUID OSTHOCK' MUSEUM OF LOCAL HISTORY AND NATURAL HISTORY
HEERENVEEN
HEERENVEEN LOCAL MUSEUM
HEINENOORD
HOEKSCHE WARD DISTRICT MUSEUM
HELLENDOORN
LOCAL HISTORY MUSEUM
HOORN
WEST FRISIAN MUSEUM
HULST
'DE VIER AMBACHTEN' LOCAL HISTORY MUSEUM
LEENS
OMMELAND MUSEUM OF AGRICULTURE AND HISTORY
LELYSTAD
LELYSTAD HARBOUR EXHIBITION BUILDING
LIMMEN
MUSEUM OF BULB GROWING
NOORDWIJK AAN ZEE
OLD NOORDWIJK FARMHOUSE MUSEUM
NIJ BEETS
DAMHÛS PEAT MUSEUM
OENKERK
STANIA STATE AGRICULTURAL MUSEUM
DEN OEVER
WIERING FARM MUSEUM
ZUIDERZEE WORKS INFORMATION CENTRE
OSPEL
MIJL OP ZEVEN VISITOR CENTRE
ROSENDAAL
MUSEUM OF THE GOLDEN ROSE
SLIEDRECHT
SLIEDRECHT MUSEUM
STAPHORST
OLD STAPHORST FARMHOUSE
RUINERWOLD
RUINERWOLD FARM MUSEUM
TILBURG
NATURAL HISTORY MUSEUM
VIJFHUIZEN
CRUQUIUS MUSEUM
ZIERIKZEE
LOCAL MUSEUM

NEW ZEALAND

AKAROA
LANGLOIS-ETEVENEAUX HOUSE
AUCKLAND
MUSEUM OF TRANSPORT AND TECHNOLOGY
NAPIER
HAWKE'S BAY ART GALLERY AND MUSEUM
NORSEWOOD
NORSEWOOD PIONEER MUSEUM

NORWAY

AALESUND
SUNNMØRE MUSEUM
BAGN
ISLANDMOEN FARM
BERGEN
HORDALAND AGRICULTURAL MUSEUM
HILL FARM MUSEUM
BODØ
NORDLAND FOLK MUSEUM
BRYNE
ROGALAND FOLK MUSEUM
DAGALI
DAGALI MUSEUM
DRAMMEN
DRAMMENS MUSEUM
EGERSUND
DALANE FOLK MUSEUM
ELVERUM
GLOMDAL MUSEUM
FLEKKEFJORD
FLEKKEFJORD DISTRICT MUSEUM

HAMAR
OPEN-AIR MUSEUM
INDRØY
INDRØY MUSEUM
KAUPANGER
HEIBERG COLLECTION
KONGSBERG
LÅGDAL MUSEUM
KRISTIANSAND
VEST-AGDER FOLK MUSEUM
KRISTIANSUND
KRISTIANSUND MUSEUM
MELBU
VESTERÅL COLLECTION OF BUILDINGS
MOLDE
ROMSDAL MUSEUM
NAMSOS
NAMDAL MUSEUM
NES
OLD HVAM
OSLO
NORWEGIAN FOLK MUSEUM
SETESDAL
SETESDAL MUSEUM
SUNNDAL
LEIKVIN MUSEUM OF BUILDINGS
TINGELSTAD
HADELAND FOLK MUSEUM
TØNSBERG
VESTFOLD FOLK MUSEUM
TOTEN
TOTEN MUSEUM

PARAGUAY

ASUNCION
EXHIBITION OF NATIONAL PRODUCTS

PERU

LIMA
MUSEUM OF THE PRE-HISPANIC ANTHROPOLOGY AND AGRICULTURE INSTITUTE

POLAND

CIECHANOWIEC
REGIONAL MUSEUM OF AGRICULTURE
KARTUZY
KASUBIAN MUSEUM
KLUCZBORK
KLUCZBORK MUSEUM
KLUKI
FARM MUSEUM
ŁÓDŹ
MUSEUM OF ARCHAEOLOGY AND ETHNOGRAPHY
NOWY JASIENIC
AGRICULTURAL MUSEUM
OLIWA
REGIONAL MUSEUM OF ETHNOGRAPHY
OLSZTYNEK
MUSEUM OF RURAL BUILDINGS
OPOLE-BIERKOWICE
OPEN-AIR MUSEUM
PODEGRODZIE
REGIONAL MUSEUM
RABKA ZDROJ
REGIONAL MUSEUM 'WŁADYSŁAW ORKAN'
SANOK
OPEN-AIR MUSEUM
SMOLNIK
OPEN-AIR MUSEUM
STARA ŚWIĘTA
OPEN-AIR MUSEUM
SZRENIAWA
AGRICULTURAL MUSEUM
WARSAW
HENRYKA MARII FUKIERA MUSEUM OF WINE
TECHNICAL MUSEUM
WILKOŁAZ
MEMORIAL MUSEUM
WŁVEŁAWEK
KUJAWSKI MUSEUM
WROCŁAW
MUSEUM OF AGRICULTURE
ZIELONA GÓRA
ZIELONA GÓRA MUSEUM
ZŁOTÓW
ETHNOGRAPHICAL PARK
ZUBRZYCA GORNA
OPEN-AIR MUSEUM

PORTUGAL

LISBON
MUSEUM OF OVERSEAS AGRICULTURE

ROMANIA

BUCHAREST
VILLAGE MUSEUM
CLUJ
OPEN-AIR MUSEUM
TRANSYLVANIAN MUSEUM OF ETHNOGRAPHY
FOCŞANI
MUSEUM OF ETHNOGRAPHY
GOLEŞTI
MUSEUM OF HISTORY AND ETHNOGRAPHY
RĂDĂUŢI
RĂDĂUŢI MUSEUM OF ETHNOGRAPHY
REGHIN
REGHIN MUSEUM
TULCEA
MUSEUM OF THE DANUBE DELTA

SOUTH AFRICA, REPUBLIC OF

ADELAIDE
"OUR HERITAGE" MUSEUM
BREDASDORP
BREDASDORP MUSEUM
CAPE TOWN
GROOT CONSTANTIA MANOR HOUSE
CRADOCK
ZEBRA NATIONAL PARKS MUSEUM
GRAAFF-REINET
GRAAFF-REINET MUSEUM
GRAHAMSTOWN
ALBANY MUSEUM
MOORREESBURG
WHEAT INDUSTRY MUSEUM
PAARL
OLD PARSONAGE MUSEUM
STELLENBOSCH
STELLENBOSCH MUSEUM
SWELLENDAM
DROSTDY MUSEUM

SPAIN

CANDUELA
VALLES DE CAMPOO ETHNOGRAPHICAL MUSEUM
CERVERA
MUSEUM DEL BLAT Y DE LA PAGESIA
VILAFRANCA DEL PANADES
VILAFRANCA MUSEUM

SWEDEN

BUNGE
BUNGE MUSEUM
HUDIKSVALL
HÄLSINGLANDS MUSEUM
ÖRNSKÖLDSVIK
ÖRNSKÖLDSVIK MUSEUM
SIMRISHAMN
ÖSTERLEN MUSEUM
STOCKHOLM
MUSEUM OF MEDITERRANEAN AND NEAR EASTERN ANTIQUITIES
NORDIC MUSEUM
SKANSEN
UPPSALA
OPEN-AIR MUSEUM

SWITZERLAND

AESCH BEI BIRMENSDORF
VILLAGE MUSEUM
AIGLE
WINE MUSEUM
AROSA
SCHANFIGGER REGIONAL MUSEUM
BASEL
MUSEUM OF SWISS FOLKLORE
BOSCO-GURIN
GURIN HOUSE OF THE WAISERS
BOUDRY
MUSEUM OF WINE AND THE VINE
BULLE
MUSEUM OF THE GRUYÈRE DISTRICT
BURGDORF
HISTORICAL MUSEUM OF THE BURGDORF HALL OF THE KNIGHTS SOCIETY
CEVIO
MUSEUM OF THE VALLEMAGGIA
CHÂTEAU D'OEX
MUSEUM OF THE FORMER PAYS D'ENHAUT AND OF THE AUGUST COTTIER FOUNDATION
CHUR
MUNICIPAL MUSEUM
COFFRANE
AGRICULTURAL MUSEUM
DAVOS
REGIONAL MUSEUM
DISENTIS
COLLECTION OF THE BENEDICTINE ABBEY
DORNACH
REGIONAL MUSEUM OF SCHWAZBUBENLAND
GRINDELWALD
REGIONAL MUSEUM
HALTEN
HALTEN TOWER
HINWIL
LOCAL MUSEUM
ISÉRABLES
MUSEUM
LANGNAU IM EMMENTAL
REGIONAL MUSEUM
LICHTENSTEIG
TOGGENBURG REGIONAL MUSEUM
LIESTAL
BASEL-LAND CANTONAL MUSEUM
LOCO
MUSEUM OF THE ONSERNONE VALLEY
MEIRINGEN
MUSEUM OF HASLI COUNTY
MOUDON
MUSEUM OF OLD MOUDON
LA NEUVEVILLE
HISTORICAL MUSEUM
OBERDORF
HISTORICAL COLLECTION OF THE TEACHER TRAINING COLLEGE
OBERHOFEN AM THUNERSEE
CASTLE
OLTEN
HISTORICAL MUSEUM
PFÄFFIKON
LOCAL MUSEUM

POSCHIAVO
VALLIGIANO POSCHIAVINO MUSEUM
RATZ
LOCAL MUSEUM
REINACH
REGIONAL MUSEUM
RICKENBACH BEI WINTERTHUR
HANNSELI GRANARY
SAN VITTORE
MOESANO MUSEUM
SARNEN
REGIONAL MUSEUM
SCHINZNACH-DORF
REGIONAL MUSEUM
SCHLIEREN
LOCAL MUSEUM
SCUOL-SCHULS
LOWER ENGADINE MUSEUM
SIERRE-SIDERS
VILLA MANOR
SISSACH
REGIONAL MUSEUM
TWANN (DOUANNE)
VINEYARD MUSEUM
UNTERSTAMMHEIM
STAMMHEIMERTAL REGIONAL MUSEUM
UTZENSTORF
LANDSHUT CASTLE
WALTENSBURG/VUORZ
ARCUN DA TRADIZIUN
WETZIKON
LOCAL MUSEUM
WIEDLISBACH
HISTORICAL MUSEUM
WIESENDANGEN
LOCAL MUSEUM
ZERMATT
ALPINE MUSEUM
ZUG
COLLECTION OF THE GERMAN- SWISS BEE-KEEPERS ASSOCIATION
ZURZACH
FAIR AND DISTRICT MUSEUM

SYRIAN ARAB REPUBLIC

DAMASCUS
DAMASCUS AGRICULTURAL MUSEUM

THAILAND

BANGKOK
KAMTHIENG HOUSE MUSEUM

TUNISIA

MOKNINE
MOKNINE MUSEUM

USSR

BARAGKHAN
VILLAGE MUSEUM
KIZHI
OPEN-AIR MUSEUM
LENINGRAD
V. V. DOKUCHAYEV CENTRAL MUSEUM OF SOIL SCIENCE
TOS
PEAT MUSEUM

UNITED STATES

ABILENE
DICKINSON COUNTY HISTORICAL SOCIETY MUSEUM
HERITAGE MUSEUM
ACCOKEEK
NATIONAL COLONIAL FARM
ALAMO
LIVE STEAM MUSEUM
ALBANY
LEDBETTER PICKET HOUSE MUSEUM
ALMA
MILL CREEK MUSEUM AND CAMP GROUND
ARKANSAS CITY
CHEROKEE STRIP LIVING MUSEUM
AURORA
AURORA HISTORICAL SOCIETY MUSEUM
BAGLEY
MUSEUM OF CLEARWATER COUNTY HISTORICAL SOCIETY
BATON ROUGE
RURAL LIFE MUSEUM
BELOIT
BARTLETT MEMORIAL HISTORICAL MUSEUM
BENKELMAN
MUSEUM OF DUNDY COUNTY HISTORICAL SOCIETY
BLUE MOUNDS
LITTLE NORWAY
BLUE RIDGE PARKWAY
HUMPBACK ROCKS VISITOR CENTER AND MUSEUM
BONNER SPRINGS
AGRICULTURAL HALL OF FAME AND NATIONAL CENTER
BUFFALO
MUSEUM OF BUFFALO AND ERIE COUNTY HISTORICAL SOCIETY
BUNNELL
BULOW PLANTATION STATE HISTORIC SITE
CALDWELL
VAN SLYKE MUSEUM
CANYON
PANHANDLE-PLAINS HISTORICAL MUSEUM
CARPENTER
HOMESTEAD MUSEUM
CEDARBURG
OZAUKEE COUNTY HISTORICAL SOCIETY MUSEUM
CHERRY VALLEY
CHERRY VALLEY MUSEUM
CHESTER
LIBERTY COUNTY MUSEUM
CHEYENNE
WYOMING STATE MUSEUM
CHICAGO
MUSEUM OF SCIENCE AND INDUSTRY
CLAYTON
MUSEUM OF NORTHERN NEW YORK AGRICULTURAL HISTORICAL SOCIETY
CLINTON
CLINTON HISTORICAL MUSEUM
COOPERSTOWN
FARMERS MUSEUM
COXSACKIE
BRONCK HOUSE MUSEUM
CRESSON
HAL S. SMITH FARM MACHINERY MUSEUM
CULBERTSON
MUSEUM OF NORTHEASTERN MONTANA THRESHERS AND ANTIQUE ASSOCIATION
DAYTON
AULLWOOD AUDUBON FARM
DEARBORN
GREENFIELD VILLAGE AND HENRY FORD MUSEUM
DEKALB
ELLWOOD HOUSE MUSEUM
DEXTER
DEXTER HISTORICAL SOCIETY MUSEUM
DILWORTHTOWN
1704 BRINTON HOUSE
DODGE CITY
HARDESTY HOUSE
DOUGLAS
WYOMING PIONEER ASSOCIATION MUSEUM
ENCINO
MUSEUM OF LOS ENCINOS STATE HISTORICAL PARK
FLORENCE
MUSEUM OF PINAL COUNTY HISTORICAL SOCIETY
GEORGETOWN
THE RICE MUSEUM
GUILFORD
THOMAS GRISWOLD HOUSE
HADLEY
MUSEUM OF HADLEY FARM MUSEUM ASSOCIATION
HAMMONDSPORT
GREYTON H. TAYLOR WINE MUSEUM
HEREFORD
DEAF SMITH COUNTY MUSEUM
JOHNSON CITY
TIPTON-HAYNES LIVING HISTORICAL FARM
KERMIT
COMANCHE TRAILS MUSEUM
KINGSVILLE
JOHN E. CONNER MUSEUM
LAKE CHARLES
IMPERIAL CALCASIEU HISTORICAL MUSEUM
LANCASTER
PENNSYLVANIA FARM MUSEUM
LAS CRUCES
NEW MEXICO STATE UNIVERSITY MUSEUM
LEVELLAND
SOUTH PLAINS MUSEUM
LOGAN
MAN AND HIS BREAD MUSEUM
LOWELL
MUSEUM OF WEST CENTRAL MICHIGAN HISTORICAL SOCIETY
MOLINE
DEERE AND COMPANY ADMINISTRATIVE CENTER MUSEUM
MORTON
RENVILLE COUNTY HISTORICAL SOCIETY MUSEUM
NASHVILLE
TENNESSEE AGRICULTURAL MUSEUM
NECHE
PATON ISLE OF MEMORIES
NEW BRUNSWICK
RUTGERS UNIVERSITY, COLLEGE OF AGRICULTURE MUSEUM
OKLAHOMA CITY
NATIONAL COWBOY HALL OF FAME AND WESTERN HERITAGE CENTER
OZONA
CROCKETT COUNTY MUSEUM
PETALUMA
PETALUMA ADOBE STATE HISTORIC PARK
PHILADELPHIA
THE GWINN COLLECTION
PIERRE
MUSEUM OF SOUTH DAKOTA STATE HISTORICAL SOCIETY
PLYMOUTH
CALVIN COOLIDGE HOMESTEAD
POTEAU
KERR MUSEUM
RENO
NEVADA HISTORICAL SOCIETY MUSEUM
RICHMOND
VIRGINIA STATE MUSEUM
RITZVILLE
DR. FRANK R. BURROUGHS WHEATLAND MUSEUM
ROSEBURG
DOUGLAS COUNTY MUSEUM
SAINT JO
STONEWALL SALOON AND WESTERN MUSEUM
SALT LAKE CITY
BRIGHAM YOUNG FARM HOME
SAN SABA
SAN SABA COUNTY HISTORICAL MUSEUM
SCOTT
PLANTATION MUSEUM
SOUTHOLD
SOUTHOLD HISTORICAL SOCIETY MUSEUM
SPARTANBURG
WALNUT GROVE PLANTATION

SPENCER
MUSEUM OF PARKER HISTORICAL SOCIETY OF CLAY COUNTY
STAMFORD
STAMFORD HISTORICAL SOCIETY MUSEUM
STEELES TAVERN
CYRUS H. MCCORMICK MEMORIAL MUSEUM
STEPHENVILLE
STEPHENVILLE HISTORICAL HOUSE MUSEUM
STERLING
OVERLAND TRAIL MUSEUM
STEVENSVILLE
ST. MARY'S MISSION
STOCKBRIDGE
WATERLOO FARM MUSEUM
STONE MILLS
AGRICULTURAL MUSEUM
STORRS
MANSFIELD HISTORICAL SOCIETY MUSEUM
SUNSET
OLD WEST MUSEUM
SYRACUSE
DANIEL PARRISH WITTER AGRICULTURAL MUSEUM
TOMBALL
GRIFFIN MEMORIAL HOUSE AND MAGDALENE CHARLTON MEMORIAL MUSEUM
UNION
MATTHEWS FARM MUSEUM
WARWICK
SHINGLE HOUSE
WASHINGTON
AGRICULTURAL HISTORY SOCIETY MUSEUM
NATIONAL MUSEUM OF HISTORY AND TECHNOLOGY
UNITED STATES NATIONAL ARBORETUM
WATERFORD
WATERFORD FOUNDATION MUSEUM
WEST FALMOUTH
SACONESSET HOMESTEAD AND SHIP'S BOTTOM ROOF HOUSE
WESTMINSTER
CARROLL COUNTY FARM MUSEUM
WESTON
BARN MUSEUM OF THE WESTON HISTORICAL SOCIETY
WINSTON-SALEM
SALEM TAVERN AND TAVERN BARN
WINTER HAVEN
FLORIDA CITRUS MUSEUM
WOLFORD
DALE HAWK MUSEUM
ZANESFIELD
MUSEUM OF LOGAN COUNTY HISTORICAL SOCIETY

YUGOSLAVIA

SPLIT
ETHNOGRAPHICAL MUSEUM
ZAGREB
ETHNOGRAPHICAL MUSEUM

ZAIRE, REPUBLIC OF

KINSHASA
MUSEUM OF ANTHROPOLOGY

Food, drink, tobacco

ANGOLA

LUANDA
COFFEE MUSEUM

AUSTRALIA

ADELAIDE
APPLIED SCIENCE MUSEUM
ATHERTON
FRANKIE'S BOTTLE BONANZA
BERRIMA
MUSEUM OF BAKING
MOORA
BERKSHIRE VALLEY FOLK MUSEUM
PERTH
OLD MILL

AUSTRIA

FELDBACH
REGIONAL MUSEUM
FISCHAMEND
REGIONAL MUSEUM
HAINBURG
MUNICIPAL MUSEUM
HOLLABRUNN
MUNICIPAL MUSEUM
KREMS
WINE MUSEUM
LEOBEN-GÖSS
GÖSS BREWERY MUSEUM
LINZ
UPPER AUSTRIA PROVINCIAL MUSEUM
MISTELBACH
MUNICIPAL MUSEUM OF REGIONAL LIFE
OBERNBERG
REGIONAL MUSEUM
POYSDORF
REGIONAL MUSEUM
RETZ
MUNICIPAL MUSEUM
VIENNA
COLLECTIONS OF THE MARKETS AUTHORITY OF THE CITY OF VIENNA
FLORISDORF DISTRICT MUSEUM
MUSEUM OF THE HISTORY OF ART: MUSEUM OF AUSTRIAN CULTURE
MUSEUM OF INDUSTRY AND TECHNOLOGY
MUSEUM OF THE JOSEFSTADT DISTRICT, 'OLD BAKEHOUSE'
MUSEUM OF THE PROVINCE OF LOWER AUSTRIA
MUSEUM OF THE TOBACCO MONOPOLY
SCHLUMBERGER WINE MUSEUM
ZELL AM MOOS
IRRSEE REGIONAL MUSEUM

BARBADOS

BARBADOS
BARBADOS MUSEUM

BELGIUM

ANTWERP
BREWERS' HOUSE
BRUSSELS
BREWERY MUSEUM
GHENT
FOLKLORE MUSEUM
HASSELT
OPEN-AIR MUSEUM
HUY
DISTRICT MUSEUM
VRESSE-SUR-SEMOIS
TOBACCO MUSEUM

BRAZIL

RECIFE
SUGAR MUSEUM

CANADA

BALMORAL
BALMORAL GRIST MILL
BARRINGTON
OLD WOOLLEN MILL MUSEUM
GODERICH
HURON COUNTY PIONEER MUSEUM
KITCHENER
DOON PIONEER VILLAGE
LANG
LANG MILL MUSEUM
MANOTICK
LONG ISLAND MILL
PORT ROWAN
THE BACKHOUSE (BACKUS) MILL AND BACKUS AGRICULTURAL MUSEUM
RENFREW
MCDOUGALL MILL MUSEUM

CHINA, P.R.

FOOCHOW (FUZHOU)
PROVINCIAL MUSEUM

CUBA

GUANABACOA
HISTORICAL MUSEUM

CYPRUS

KYRENIA
SHIPWRECK MUSEUM

CZECHOSLOVAKIA

BRATISLAVA
MUNICIPAL MUSEUM
KAČINA U NOVÝCH DVORŮ
MUSEUM OF AGRICULTURE
MĚLNÍK
DISTRICT MUSEUM
MICHALOVCE
ZEMPLIN MUSEUM
PLZEŇ
MUSEUM OF WESTERN CZECHOSLOVAKIA: MUSEUM OF BREWING
PRAGUE
ETHNOLOGICAL COLLECTIONS
RUŽOMBEROK
LIPTOV MUSEUM

DENMARK

COPENHAGEN
CARLSBERG MUSEUM
FAABORG
KALEKO MILL MUSEUM
HADERSLEV
HADERSLEV MUSEUM

FINLAND

NURMIJÄRVI
INDUSTRIAL MUSEUM
PIETARSAARI
STRENGBERG'S TOBACCO MUSEUM
UUSIKAUPUNKI
WINDMILLS MUSEUM

FRANCE

AGDE
AGDE MUSEUM
ANGERS
WINE MUSEUM
BEAUGENCY
DUNOIS MUSEUM
BEAUNE
MUSEUM OF THE WINE OF BURGUNDY
BERGERAC
TOBACCO MUSEUM
BORDEAUX
HISTORICAL COLLECTION OF THE CONSEIL INTERPROFESSIONAL DU VIN DE BORDEAUX
COGNAC
MUNICIPAL MUSEUM
COLMAR
UNTERLINDEN MUSEUM
ÉPERNAY
CHAMPAGNE MUSEUM
LILLE
MUSEUM OF INDUSTRY, COMMERCE, TECHNOLOGY AND AGRICULTURE
MARSAC-EN-LIVRADOIS
JASSERIE DU COQ NOIR
NEUFCHÂTEL-EN-BRAY
MATHON MUSEUM
OUARVILLE
MILL MUSEUM
PAUILLAC
MOUTON-ROTHSCHILD MUSEUM OF WINE
ROCHECORBON
ESPELOSIN MUSEUM
ST. ÉMILION
MUSEUM OF WINE
SAINT LAURENT DE LA PLAINE
MUSEUM OF THE OLD TRADES OF ANJOU
ST. PIERRE D'OLÉRON
ALIENOR D'AQUITAINE MUSEUM
SAULIEU
FRANÇOIS POMPON MUSEUM
TOURS
ESPELOSIN MUSEUM
MUSEUM OF THE WINES OF TOURAINE
VALOGNES
CIDER MUSEUM
VILLENEUVE-LOUBET
MUSEUM OF THE ART OF COOKERY

GDR

BAD DÜBEN
DÜBEN HEATH MUSEUM
DIESDORF
ALTMARK REGIONAL MUSEUM
GRIMMA
MILL MUSEUM
JARMEN
MILL MUSEUM
KRAKOW AM SEE
MILL MUSEUM
MEISSEN
MUNICIPAL AND DISTRICT MUSEUM
RADEBEUL
REGIONAL MUSEUM
RUHLA
REGIONAL MUSEUM
WALTERSDORF
REGIONAL MUSEUM
WEISSENBERG
'OLD SPICE BREAD BAKERY' REGIONAL MUSEUM

GFR

BAD NAUHEIM
SALT MUSEUM
BAD ORB
BAD ORB REGIONAL MUSEUM
BAD SALZUFLEN
MUSEUM OF THE SPA AND THE TOWN
BAMBERG
BEER MUSEUM
BAYREUTH
COLLECTION OF AGRICULTURAL IMPLEMENTS AND EQUIPMENT
BERLIN
SUGAR MUSEUM
BINGEN
REGIONAL MUSEUM
BÜNDE
GERMAN TOBACCO AND CIGAR MUSEUM
DETMOLD
BREAD MUSEUM
DORTMUND
NATURAL HISTORY MUSEUM
EINBECK
MUNICIPAL MUSEUM
HAMBURG
REEMTSMA COLLECTION OF THE HISTORY OF TOBACCO
HEILBRONN
HISTORY MUSEUM
HINDELANG
REGIONAL COLLECTION
ILLEBEUREN
FARMHOUSE MUSEUM
KITZINGEN
MUNICIPAL MUSEUM
KÖLN
CUTLERY MUSEUM
LAUDA
REGIONAL MUSEUM
LEMKENHAFEN
MUSEUM OF WINDMILLS AND AGRICULTURE
MAINZ
KUPPERBERG COLLECTION
MOLLENFELDE
BREAD AND CAKE MUSEUM
MÜNCHEN
GERMAN MUSEUM
GERMAN MUSEUM OF BREWING
NEUSTADT-WEINSTRASSE
REGIONAL AND WINE MUSEUM
OBERRIEXINGEN
ROMAN WINE CELLAR
OPPENAU
RENCHTAL REGIONAL MUSEUM
OSTERHOLZ-SCHARMBECK
REGIONAL MUSEUM
PEWSUM
EAST FRISIAN OPEN-AIR MUSEUM
RÜDESHEIM
RHEINGAU AND WINE MUSEUM
SPEYER
MUSEUM OF THE HISTORY OF THE PALATINATE
TRABEN-TRARBACH
MUSEUM OF THE CENTRAL MOSEL AREA
ULM
GERMAN BREAD MUSEUM

GREAT BRITAIN

BIBURY
ARLINGTON MILL
BIRMINGHAM
SAREHOLE MILL
BRISTOL
BLAISE CASTLE HOUSE MUSEUM
HARVEYS WINE MUSEUM
BROKERSWOOD
THE PHILLIPS COUNTRYSIDE MUSEUM OF NATURAL HISTORY AND FORESTRY
GREAT HAYWOOD
SHUGBOROUGH
HALSTEAD
BLUE BRIDGE HOUSE
INNERLEITHEN
TRAQUAIR HOUSE
KIDDERMINSTER
WORCESTERSHIRE COUNTY MUSEUM
LIVERPOOL
TATE AND LYLE REFINERIES LIMITED
MANCHESTER
MANCHESTER MUSEUM
NARBERTH
BLACKPOOL MILL
NETHER ALDERLEY
ALDERLEY OLD MILL
SHUGBOROUGH
STAFFORDSHIRE COUNTY MUSEUM AND MANSION HOUSE

HUNGARY

BUDAPEST
HUNGARIAN AGRICULTURAL MUSEUM
TOKAJ
LOCAL HISTORY MUSEUM

IRELAND

DUBLIN
GUINNESS MUSEUM
TUAM
MILL MUSEUM

ISRAEL

HAIFA
DAGON COLLECTION

ITALY

ONEGLIA
MUSEUM OF THE HISTORY OF SPAGHETTI
PONTEDASSIO
MUSEUM OF THE HISTORY OF SPAGHETTI

JAPAN

KARIHA-GUN
TEA CULT MUSEUM
OKANO
MEISHO TEIKAN-EN HURETSU CHADO BIJUTSUKAN

NETHERLANDS

AMSTERDAM
LUCAS BOLS MUSEUM
GUILD HOUSE OF THE WINE COOPERS
MUSEUM OF CULINARY HISTORY
NIEMEYER DUTCH TOBACCO MUSEUM
DELFZIJL
MUSEUM IN THE ADAM MILL
GOUDA
DE MORIAAN PIPE AND POTTERY MUSEUM
HAELEN
VISITOR CENTRE AT THE ST. URSULA MILL, LEUDAL
KOOG AAN DE ZAAN
HET PINK OIL-MILL
ZAAN MILL MUSEUM
LEIDEN
DE VALK MILL MUSEUM
MIDDELSTUM
MENDEL BAKERY MUSEUM
NIEUW- VOSSEMEER
ASSUMBURG MILL MUSEUM
OENKERK
STANIA STATE AGRICULTURAL MUSEUM

OMMEN
OMMEN LOCAL HISTORY MUSEUM
SCHIEDAM
LIQUEUR MUSEUM, WITH B. J. DE JONGH'S COLLECTION
NATIONAL MUSEUM OF DISTILLED LIQUOR
UTRECHT
MUSEUM OF PIPES, COFFEE AND TEA
ZWOLLE
PASSION FLOWER MILL

NEW ZEALAND

HAVELOCK
HAVELOCK MILLING MUSEUM
NORSEWOOD
NORSEWOOD PIONEER MUSEUM

NORWAY

AALESUND
SUNNMØRE MUSEUM

POLAND

JĘDRZEJOW
PRYZPKOWSKICH NATIONAL MUSEUM
TATARY POD KADZIDŁEM
KURPIE MUSEUM
WARSAW
HENRYKA MARII FUKIERA MUSEUM OF WINE
TECHNICAL MUSEUM
ZIELONA GÓRA
ZIELONA GÓRA MUSEUM

ROMANIA

GOLEŞTI
MUSEUM OF HISTORY AND ETHNOGRAPHY
IAŞI
MOLDAVIAN MUSEUM OF ETHNOLOGY
SIBIU
OPEN-AIR MUSEUM OF PRE- INDUSTRIAL TECHNOLOGY

SOUTH AFRICA, REPUBLIC OF

MOORREESBURG
WHEAT INDUSTRY MUSEUM
OUDTSHOORN
C.P. NEL MUSEUM

SPAIN

FALSET
MUSEUM AND ARCHIVES OF FALSET AND DISTRICT
VILAFRANCA DEL PANADES
VILAFRANCA MUSEUM

SWEDEN

STOCKHOLM
BREWERY MUSEUM
TOBACCO MUSEUM
WINE AND SPIRIT MUSEUM

SWITZERLAND

AIGLE
WINE MUSEUM
BOUDRY
MUSEUM OF WINE AND THE VINE
BURGDORF
HISTORICAL MUSEUM OF THE BURGDORF HALL OF THE KNIGHTS SOCIETY
CHÂTEAU D'OEX
MUSEUM OF THE FORMER PAYS D'ENHAUT AND OF THE AUGUST COTTIER FOUNDATION
DISENTIS
COLLECTION OF THE BENEDICTINE ABBEY
LANGNAU IM EMMENTAL
REGIONAL MUSEUM
LUZERN
SWISS MUSEUM OF BREAD AND CAKES
LA NEUVEVILLE
HISTORICAL MUSEUM
REINACH
REGIONAL MUSEUM
SAXON
MUSEUM OF OLD SAXON
SCHINZNACH-DORF
REGIONAL MUSEUM
SIERRE-SIDERS
VILLA MANOR
TWANN (DOUANNE)
VINEYARD MUSEUM
VEVEY
MUSEUM OF THE FRATERNITY OF WINE PRODUCERS
ZURICH-HÖNGG
MUSEUM OF LOCAL HISTORY

UNITED STATES

ALLEY SPRING
THE OLD RED MILL
ATLANTA
ATLANTA MUSEUM
AUSTIN
OLD BAKERY
BALTIMORE
MCCORMICK AND COMPANY'S TEA HOUSE AND MUSEUM
BARDSTOWN
BARTON MUSEUM OF WHISKEY HISTORY
BELLOWS FALLS
ADAMS OLD STONE GRIST MILL MUSEUM
BERRYVILLE
MUSEUM OF CARROLL COUNTY HISTORICAL SOCIETY
BOURNE
APTUXCET TRADING POST
BUNNELL
BULOW PLANTATION STATE HISTORIC SITE
CLINTON
CLINTON HISTORICAL MUSEUM
COLORADO SPRINGS
PIONEERS' MUSEUM
DANVILLE
NATIONAL TOBACCO AND TEXTILE MUSEUM
DEXTER
DEXTER HISTORICAL SOCIETY MUSEUM
DURHAM
DUKE HOMESTEAD
EAST HAMPTON
HOOK MILL
EAST ROCKAWAY
OLD GRIST MILL MUSEUM
EUREKA SPRINGS
HATCHET HALL MUSEUM
FREMONT
WINDMILL GARDENS
GARDEN CITY
NANKIN MILLS NATURE CENTER
GREENBUSH
OLD WADE HOUSE
HAMMONDSPORT
GREYTON H. TAYLOR WINE MUSEUM
HINSDALE
THE OLD GRAUE MILL AND MUSEUM
HOMOSASSA
YULEE SUGAR MILL
LINDSBORG
McPHERSON COUNTY OLD MILL MUSEUM
MEDORA
DE MORES HISTORIC SITE
MILWAUKEE
MUSEUM OF MILWAUKEE COUNTY HISTORICAL SOCIETY
NANTUCKET
OLD WINDMILL
NELIGH
NELIGH MILLS
NEW SMYRNA BEACH
NEW SMYRNA STATE HISTORIC SITE
POYNOR
MILNER'S MILL
ROCKINGHAM
VERMONT COUNTRY STORES AND MUSEUM
ROSEBURG
DOUGLAS COUNTY MUSEUM
ROSLYN
OLD GRIST MILL
ROYALTON
DANFORTH MAPLE MUSEUM
SADDLE ROCK, L.I.
SADDLE ROCK GRIST MILL
ST. JOHNSBURY
MAPLE MUSEUM
ST. LOUIS
FALSTAFF INTERNATIONAL MUSEUM OF BREWING
SANDWICH
HOXIE HOUSE AND DEXTER'S GRIST MILL
SAUNDERSTOWN
GILBERT STUART MEMORIAL
SCITUATE
OLD STOCKBRIDGE GRIST MILL
SHASTA
SHASTA STATE HISTORICAL MONUMENT
SOMERSET
SOMERSET HISTORICAL CENTER
STAMFORD
MAPLE SUGAR MUSEUM
STEELES TAVERN
CYRUS H. MCCORMICK MEMORIAL MUSEUM
STILWELL
GOLDA'S OLD MILL
STONY BROOK
GRIST MILL
SUDBURY
LONGFELLOW'S WAYSIDE INN
TARRYTOWN
PHILIPSBURG MANOR
WASHINGTON
PIERCE MILL
WILLIAMSVILLE
WILLIAMSVILLE WATER MILLS
WINDMILL ISLAND
DE ZWAAN
WINSTON-SALEM
WINKLER BAKERY

ZAIRE, REPUBLIC OF

KINSHASA
MUSEUM OF ANTHROPOLOGY

Fishing, hunting

ANGOLA

MOÇAMEDES
MUSEUM OF THE FISHING INDUSTRY

AUSTRALIA

CASINO
HISTORICAL MUSEUM
EDEN
EDEN MUSEUM
FREMANTLE
MARITIME AND HISTORICAL MUSEUM
KALBARRI
SHELL, MARINE AND MINERAL MUSEUM
VICTOR HARBOR
WHALERS HAVEN MUSEUM

AUSTRIA

BAD VOSLAU
REGIONAL MUSEUM
BRANDHOF
ARCHDUKE JOHANN HUNTING MUSEUM
FORCHTENSTEIN
COLLECTIONS AT FORCHTENSTEIN CASTLE
GRAZ
STEIERMARK HUNTING MUSEUM
GUTENSTEIN
HUNTING COLLECTION
HOHENBRUNN
HUNTING MUSEUM OF UPPER AUSTRIA
MARCHEGG
HUNTING MUSEUM OF LOWER AUSTRIA
MATTSEE
REGIONAL MUSEUM
MONDSEE
REGIONAL MUSEUM
ORTH
FISHING MUSEUM
PETRONELL
DANUBE MUSEUM
SEEKIRCHEN
REGIONAL MUSEUM
SPITTAL
MUSEUM OF LOCAL LIFE
TAUFKIRCHEN
REGIONAL ROOM
TRAUN
REGIONAL HOUSE
WELS
CASTLE MUSEUM

BAHAMAS

NASSAU
BAHAMIA MUSEUM

BELGIUM

LAVAUX-SAINTE-ANNE
BELGIAN MUSEUM OF HUNTING AND NATURAL CONSERVATION
OSTEND
FISHERY MUSEUM

BRAZIL

RIO DE JANEIRO
MUSEUM OF THE HUNTERS' CLUB
SÃO PAULO
MUSEUM OF HUNTING AND FISHING

CANADA

ATIKOKAN
ATIKOKAN CENTENNIAL MUSEUM
MARGAREE CENTRE
MARGAREE SALMON MUSEUM
ST. JOHNS
NEWFOUNDLAND MUSEUM
SAULT STE. MARIE
WOSGUHAEGUN
SELKIRK
LOWER FORT GARRY NATIONAL HISTORIC PARK
WILLIAMSTOWN
NORTH WEST AND LOYALIST MUSEUM
YELLOWKNIFE
MUSEUM OF THE NORTH

CZECHOSLOVAKIA

ANTOL
FORESTRY AND HUNTING MUSEUM
BETLIAR
STATE PALACE
ČERVENÝ KAMEŇ
MUSEUM OF FURNITURE
HLUBOKÁ NAD VLTAVOU
MUSEUM OF THE COUNTRYSIDE
LEDNICE NA MORAVĚ
MUSEUM OF AGRICULTURE
RUŽOMBEROK
LIPTOV MUSEUM
ÚSOV
REGIONAL MUSEUM

DENMARK

COPENHAGEN
FISHERIES MUSEUM
DRAGØR
DRAGØR MUSEUM
ESBJERG
ESBJERG MUSEUM
FISHING AND MARITIME MUSEUM
FREDERIKSHAVN
BANGSBO MUSEET
GILLELEJE
GILLELEJE MUSEUM
HUNDESTED
KNUD RASMUSSEN'S COTTAGE
HØRSHOLM
HUNTING AND FORESTRY MUSEUM
SKAGEN
SKAGEN BYGONES
TÓRSHAVN
FAROES HISTORICAL MUSEUM
VARDE
VARDE AND DISTRICT MUSEUM

FINLAND

HELSINKI
SEURASAARI OPEN-AIR MUSEUM
KALAJOKI
HISTORICAL MUSEUM
KOTKA
CZAR'S FISHING LODGE

FRANCE

BIARRITZ
MUSEUM OF THE SEA
LA BUSSIÈRE
MUSEUM OF FISHING
CONCARNEAU
MUSEUM OF FISHING
COUR-CHEVERNY
CHÂTEAU COLLECTIONS
GIEN
INTERNATIONAL MUSEUM OF HUNTING
MARTIGUES
MUSEUM OF OLD MARTIGUES
PARIS
MUSEUM OF HUNTING
SENLIS
MUSEUM

GDR

ARENDSEE
REGIONAL MUSEUM
AUGUSTUSBURG
REGIONAL MUSEUM
BAD DOBERAN
DISTRICT MUSEUM
BAD ELSTER
REGIONAL ROOM
GRAUPA
RICHARD WAGNER AND REGIONAL MUSEUM
GROSSROHRSDORF
REGIONAL MUSEUM
HAVELBERG
PRIGNITZ MUSEUM
KAHLA
LEUCHTERBURG REGIONAL MUSEUM
PREROW
DARSS REGIONAL MUSEUM
RERIK
REGIONAL MUSEUM
ROSTOCK-WARNEMÜNDE
WARNEMÜNDE REGIONAL MUSEUM
STRALSUND
MUSEUM OF CULTURAL HISTORY
THARANDT
GRILLENBURG CASTLE
WAREN AN DER MÜRITZ
MÜRITZ MUSEUM
WEESENSTEIN
CASTLE MUSEUM
WITTENBERGE
REGIONAL MUSEUM

GFR

BERLEBURG
BERLEBURG PALACE
BERLIN
GRUNEWALD HUNTING LODGE COLLECTIONS
BORKUM
REGIONAL MUSEUM
DARMSTADT
KRANICHSTEIN PALACE MUSEUM OF HUNTING
FLENSBURG
REGIONAL MUSEUM OF NATURAL HISTORY
GLÜCKSTADT
DETLEFSEN MUSEUM
GOSLAR
MÖNCHEHAUS HUNTING AND FORESTRY MUSEUM
HAMBURG
ALTONA MUSEUM
HANNOVER
LAND MUSEUM OF LOWER SAXONY: DEPARTMENT OF NATURAL HISTORY
HERSBRUCK
REGIONAL AND HUNTING MUSEUM
HITZACKER
REGIONAL MUSEUM
MEERSBURG
MEERSBURG PALACE
MÜNCHEN
HUNTING MUSEUM
NEUNHOF
NEUNHOF PALACE
NEUSTADT (HOLSTEIN)
DISTRICT MUSEUM
NORDESEIF
FISHERMAN'S HOUSE MUSEUM
NÜRNBERG
GERMAN NATIONAL MUSEUM

OFFENBURG
HOUSE OF THE KNIGHTS MUSEUM
PAPENBURG
SHIPPING AND MOOR MUSEUM
PRIEN
REGIONAL MUSEUM
ST. PETER-ORDING
EIDERSTEDT REGIONAL MUSEUM
SÖGEL
EMSLAND MUSEUM
WYK
FÖHR ISLAND MUSEUM SOCIETY

GREAT BRITAIN

ANSTRUTHER
SCOTTISH FISHERIES MUSEUM
BIRMINGHAM
CANNON HILL MUSEUM
BRIDPORT
BRIDPORT MUSEUM AND ART GALLERY
BRIXHAM
BRIXHAM MUSEUM
GLOUCESTER
BISHOP HOOPER'S LODGING
GREAT YARMOUTH
MARITIME MUSEUM FOR EAST ANGLIA
HULL
MARITIME MUSEUM
PETERHEAD
ARBUTHNOT MUSEUM
SANDRINGHAM
THE SANDRINGHAM ESTATE MUSEUM
STAFFORD
IZAAK WALTON COTTAGE
TEESSIDE
TEESSIDE MUSEUMS AND ART GALLERIES SERVICE

HUNGARY

BUDAPEST
HUNGARIAN AGRICULTURAL MUSEUM

INDIA

MANDAPAM CAMP
CENTRAL MARINE FISHERIES RESEARCH STATION REFERENCE MUSEUM

IRELAND

BUNRATTY
BUNRATTY CASTLE AND FOLK PARK

ITALY

ROME
NATIONAL MUSEUM OF CASTEL SANT'ANGELO
TRIESTE
MARITIME MUSEUM

JAPAN

AKO-MACHI
NATIONAL PEARL RESEARCH INSTITUTE EXHIBITION ROOM
FUTTSU
FUTTSU OCEANOGRAPHIC MUSEUM OF CHIBA PREFECTURE
ISE-SHI
JINGU HISTORICAL AND AGRICULTURAL MUSEUM
KESEN'NUMA-SHI
KESEN'NUMA MUSEUM OF MARINE PRODUCTS
MIYAKO-SHI
FISHERIES MUSEUM OF MIYAKO FISHERIES HIGH SCHOOL
NO'O-MACHI
NO'O MARINE AND MARITIME MUSEUM
NUMAZU-SHI
MITO PEARL MUSEUM
OARAI-MACHI
OARAI MARINE MUSEUM
OJIKA-MACHI
MUSEUM OF WHALING
TAMANO-SHI
TAMANO MARINE MUSEUM
YOKOSUKA-SHI
KANNONZAKI NATURAL HISTORY MUSEUM

MALAYSIA

PENANG
PENANG MUSEUM AND ART GALLERY

NETHERLANDS

BRUINISSE
LOCAL HISTORY MUSEUM
ENKHUIZEN
NATIONAL ZUIDERZEE MUSEUM
HARDEWIJK
MUSEUM OF THE HISTORY OF THE VELUWE
MODDERGAT
THE FISHERMAN'S HOUSE
MONNIKENDAM
'T HAVENLAND GOUWZEE MUSEUM
NOORDWIJK AAN ZEE
OLD NOORDWIJK FARMHOUSE MUSEUM
DE RIJP
'IN THE WOODEN HOUSE' MUSEUM OF DE RIJP
SOMMELSDIJK
GOEREE AND OVERFLAKEE DISTRICT MUSEUM
TILBURG
NATURAL HISTORY MUSEUM
VEENKLOSTER
FOGELSANGH STATE
VLAARDINGEN
MUSEUM OF THE NETHERLANDS FISHING INDUSTRY
WEST- TERSCHELLING
LOCAL MUSEUM
ZIERIKZEE
LOCAL MUSEUM

NEW ZEALAND

CHRISTCHURCH
CANTERBURY MUSEUM
HAMILTON
WAIKATO MUSEUM
KAIKOURA
KAIKOURA MUSEUM
OBAN
RAKIURA MUSEUM
ROTORUA
TE AMORANGI MUSEUM
RUSSELL
CAPTAIN COOK MEMORIAL MUSEUM

NORWAY

AALESUND
AALESUND MUSEUM
SUNNMØRE MUSEUM
BERGEN
FISHERY MUSEUM
DRAMMEN
DRAMMENS MUSEUM
FAGERNES
VALDRE FOLK MUSEUM
HJERTØYA
FISHERY MUSEUM
KABELVÅG
MUSEUM OF FISHERIES AND THE LOFOTEN ISLANDS
MOLDE
HJERTØYA FISHERIES MUSEUM
SANDEFJORD
COMMANDER CHR. CHRISTENSEN'S WHALING MUSEUM
SUNNDAL
LEIKVIN MUSEUM OF BUILDINGS
TØNSBERG
VESTFOLD FOLK MUSEUM

POLAND

DARŁOWO
REGIONAL MUSEUM
HEL
MUSEUM OF FISHING
SZCZECIN
MARINE MUSEUM OF THE BALTIC INSTITUTE
WARSAW
HUNTING MUSEUM
NATIONAL ETHNOGRAPHICAL MUSEUM

PORTUGAL

FARO
MARITIME MUSEUM
ILHAVO
LOCAL MUSEUM

ROMANIA

CLUJ
TRANSYLVANIAN MUSEUM OF ETHNOGRAPHY
FOCŞANI
MUSEUM OF ETHNOGRAPHY
GOLEŞTI
MUSEUM OF HISTORY AND ETHNOGRAPHY
RIMNICU SARAT
RIMNICU SARAT MUSEUM
TULCEA
MUSEUM OF THE DANUBE DELTA

SOUTH AFRICA, REPUBLIC OF

OUDTSHOORN
C.P. NEL MUSEUM

SPAIN

RIOFRIO
NATIONAL HUNTING MUSEUM

SWEDEN

BUNGE
BUNGE MUSEUM
GÖTEBORG
MARITIME MUSEUM
HUDIKSVALL
HÄLSINGLANDS MUSEUM
SIMRISHAMN
ÖSTERLEN MUSEUM
STOCKHOLM
NORDIC MUSEUM
UDDEVALLA
UDDEVALLA MUSEUM

SWITZERLAND

BERN
SWISS MUSEUM OF SHOOTING
GELFINGEN
HEIDEGG CASTLE
KILCHBERG
LOCAL HISTORY COLLECTION
RHEINFELDEN
FIRCKTALER MUSEUM
SARGANS
CASTLE
SIERRE-SIDERS
VILLA MANOR
UTZENSTORF
LANDSHUT CASTLE
ZUG
FISHERY MUSEUM

THAILAND

BANGKOK
KAMTHIENG HOUSE MUSEUM

UGANDA

KAMPALA
FOREST DEPARTMENT UTILISATION DIVISION AND MUSEUM

USSR

ODESSA
MARITIME MUSEUM
VLADIVOSTOK
MUSEUM OF THE INSTITUTE OF THE PACIFIC

UNITED STATES

AMAGANSETT
EAST HAMPTON TOWN MARINE MUSEUM
BOOTHBAY HARBOR
MUSEUM OF BOOTHBAY REGION HISTORICAL SOCIETY
CHADRON
MUSEUM OF THE FUR TRADE
CHANUTE
MARTIN AND OSA JOHNSON SAFARI MUSEUM
CHINCOTEAGUE
OYSTER MUSEUM
COLD SPRING HARBOR
WHALING MUSEUM
EDGARTOWN
DUKES COUNTY HISTORICAL SOCIETY MUSEUM
FALMOUTH
FALMOUTH HISTORICAL SOCIETY MUSEUM
GLOUCESTER
CAPTAIN ELIAS DAVIS HOUSE AND MUSEUM
HIGHLANDS
TWIN LIGHT MUSEUM
LAHAINA
LAHAINA RESTORATION FOUNDATION
NANTUCKET
MUSEUM OF NANTUCKET HISTORICAL ASSOCIATION
NANTUCKET WHALING MUSEUM
NEW BEDFORD
NEW BEDFORD WHALING MUSEUM
PARKER
BUCKSKIN UNIT
PIERRE
MUSEUM OF SOUTH DAKOTA STATE HISTORICAL SOCIETY
PITTSBURGH
FORT PITT MUSEUM
PLATTEVILLE
FORT VASQUEZ VISITOR CENTER
PRAIRIE DU CHIEN
VILLA LOUIS AND MUSEUM
ROSEBURG
DOUGLAS COUNTY MUSEUM
SAG HARBOR
SUFFOLK COUNTY WHALING MUSEUM
SHARON
KENDALL WHALING MUSEUM
SOUTH OTSELIC
GLADDING FISHING MUSEUM
STONINGTON
LIGHTHOUSE MUSEUM
WARREN
MORSE MUSEUM
WEST BOOTHBAY HARBOR
MUSEUM OF U.S. NATIONAL MARINE FISHERIES SERVICE

YUGOSLAVIA

BELGRADE
MUSEUM OF FORESTRY AND HUNTING
ZAGREB
HUNTING MUSEUM

Forestry

AUSTRALIA

BOWRAVILLE
FOLK MUSEUM

AUSTRIA

BAD AUSSEE
AUSSEE REGIONAL MUSEUM
BAD WIMSBACH- NEYDHARTING
BUDWEIS COLLECTION
DORNBIRN
LANDSCAPE AND ECOLOGY OF THE VORARLBERG
GUTENSTEIN
'ALTE HOFMÜHLE' REGIONAL MUSEUM
PFAFFSTÄTTEN
REGIONAL MUSEUM

BELGIUM

NAMUR
FORESTRY MUSEUM

BRAZIL

MACAPÁ
JOAQUIM CAETANO DA SILVA MUSEUM
RIO CLARO
NAVARRO DE ANDRADE FORESTRY MUSEUM
RIO DE JANEIRO
FORESTRY MUSEUM
MUSEUM OF THE TECHNOLOGICAL DEPARTMENT OF THE FORESTRY SERVICE
SÃO PAULO
FORESTRY MUSEUM

CANADA

ALGONQUIN
ALGONQUIN PIONEER LOGGING EXHIBIT
ATIKOKAN
ATIKOKAN CENTENNIAL MUSEUM
BALDWIN TOWNSHIP
BEAVER VALLEY MUSEUM
BLIND RIVER
TIMBER VILLAGE MUSEUM
COURTENAY
COURTENAY AND DISTRICT MUSEUM
DUNCAN
COWICHAN VALLEY FOREST MUSEUM
FORT WILLIAM
LOGGING MUSEUM
GODERICH
HURON COUNTY PIONEER MUSEUM
LADYSMITH
CROWN ZELLERBACH CANADA ARBORETUM AND MUSEUM
MADOC
O'HARA MILL
PORT ARTHUR
LOGGING MUSEUM
ST. JOHNS
NEWFOUNDLAND MUSEUM
SAYWARD
LINK AND PIN LOGGING AND PIONEER MUSEUM
VICTORIA
BRITISH COLUMBIA FOREST SERVICE MUSEUM

CHINA, P.R.

ANTUNG (ANDONG)
PROVINCIAL MUSEUM

CZECHOSLOVAKIA

ANTOL
FORESTRY AND HUNTING MUSEUM
HLUBOKÁ NAD VLTAVOU
MUSEUM OF THE COUNTRYSIDE
ÚSOV
REGIONAL MUSEUM

DENMARK

HØRSHOLM
HUNTING AND FORESTRY MUSEUM

FINLAND

KEMI
KEMI MUSEUM
LAMONI
LOCAL MUSEUM
PUNKALAIDUN
LOCAL MUSEUM

GDR

PLAUEN
VOGTLAND DISTRICT MUSEUM
PREROW
DARSS REGIONAL MUSEUM
THARANDT
INSTITUTE OF FORESTRY BOTANY
INSTITUTE OF FORESTRY ZOOLOGY

GFR

BAYREUTH
COLLECTION OF AGRICULTURAL IMPLEMENTS AND EQUIPMENT
BOPPARD
FOREST AND TIMBER MUSEUM
ERBACH
COLLECTIONS OF COUNT ZU ERBACH-ERBACH
GOSLAR
MÖNCHEHAUS HUNTING AND FORESTRY MUSEUM
NIENBERGE
DROSTE MUSEUM
ZWIESEL
TOWN MUSEUM

GREAT BRITAIN

BROKERSWOOD
THE PHILLIPS COUNTRYSIDE MUSEUM OF NATURAL HISTORY AND FORESTRY

HUNGARY

BUDAPEST
HUNGARIAN AGRICULTURAL MUSEUM

INDIA

COIMBATORE
SOUTHERN FOREST RANGERS COLLEGE AND RESEARCH CENTRE
DEHRA DUN
MUSEUMS OF THE FOREST RESEARCH INSTITUTE AND COLLEGES
GAUHATI
ASSAM FOREST MUSEUM
COMMERCIAL MUSEUM
GWALIOR
STATE MUSEUM
POONA
LORD REAY MAHARASHTRA INDUSTRIAL MUSEUM
MAHATMA PHULE VASTU SANGRAHALAYA
SHIVPURI
FOREST SCHOOL

JAPAN

IBURI-SHICHO
FOREST MUSEUM OF TOYA NATIONAL PARK
TAKANOSU-MACHI
AGRICULTURAL MUSEUM OF TAKANOSU PREFECTURAL AGRICULTURAL AND FORESTRY HIGH SCHOOL

NETHERLANDS

TILBURG
NATURAL HISTORY MUSEUM

NEW ZEALAND

MATAKOHE
OTAMATEA KAURI AND PIONEER MUSEUM

NORWAY

ELVERUM
NORWEGIAN FORESTRY MUSEUM

PAKISTAN, WEST

PESHAWAR
FOREST MUSEUM
PESHAWAR MUSEUM

PORTUGAL

LISBON
MUSEUM OF OVERSEAS AGRICULTURE

ROMANIA

CÎMPULUNG- MOLDOVENESC
MOLDOVENIAN MUSEUM

SOUTH AFRICA, REPUBLIC OF

GEORGE
GEORGE MUSEUM

SWEDEN

SUNDSVALL
SUNDSVALL MUSEUM
VÄXJÖ
SMÅLAND MUSEUM

SWITZERLAND

AARAU
MUSEUM OF NATURAL HISTORY AND LOCAL LIFE
RHEINFELDEN
FIRCKTALER MUSEUM
SAXON
MUSEUM OF OLD SAXON

UNITED STATES

ASHLAND
ASHLAND LOGGING MUSEUM
BAGLEY
MUSEUM OF CLEARWATER COUNTY HISTORICAL SOCIETY
BANGOR
PENOBSCOT HERITAGE MUSEUM
BELLINGHAM
WHATCOM MUSEUM OF HISTORY AND ART
BIG RAPIDS
MECOSTA COUNTY HISTORICAL MUSEUM
BIRDSBORO
DANIEL BOONE HOMESTEAD
BLUE MOUNTAIN LAKE
ADIRONDACK MUSEUM
BRAINERD
LUMBERTOWN USA
CASPIAN
IRON COUNTY MUSEUM
CATHLAMET
MUSEUM OF WAHKIAKUM COUNTY HISTORICAL SOCIETY
CEDAR KEY
ST. CLAIR WHITMAN MUSEUM
COLOMA
JAMES W. MARSHALL GOLD DISCOVERY MUSEUM
CRESCENT CITY
MUSEUM OF DEL NORTE COUNTY HISTORICAL SOCIETY
EAU CLAIRE
PAUL BUNYAN CAMP
ELIZABETHTOWN
ADIRONDACK CENTER MUSEUM
FORT BRAGG
BOISE CASCADE CORPORATION MUSEUM
GALETON
PENNSYLVANIA LUMBER MUSEUM
GARBERVILLE
RICHARDSON GROVE STATE PARK
GRAYLING
HARTWICK PINES STATE PARK
HAYWARD
HISTORYLAND
HILLSBORO
FOX STATE FOREST MUSEUM
HURON CITY
WILLIAM LYON PHELPS MUSEUM
IRON RIVER
IRON COUNTY MUSEUM
KLAMATH FALLS
COLLIER STATE PARK LOGGING MUSEUM
LAKE CHARLES
IMPERIAL CALCASIEU HISTORICAL MUSEUM
LAONA
LUMBERJACK SPECIAL AND CAMP FIVE MUSEUM
MANISTEE
OLD WATERWORKS BUILDING MUSEUM
OCONTO
BEYER HOME, OCONTO COUNTY HISTORICAL MUSEUM
PATTEN
LUMBERMEN'S MUSEUM
PETERSHAM
FISHER MUSEUM OF FORESTRY
PHOENIX
PIONEER ARIZONA
PORTLAND
WESTERN FORESTRY CENTER
PRAIRIE CITY
DE WITT MUSEUM
RHINELANDER
RHINELANDER LOGGING MUSEUM
ROSEBURG
DOUGLAS COUNTY MUSEUM
SCOTIA
PACIFIC LUMBER COMPANY MUSEUM
TRINIDAD
PIONEER MUSEUM
TRUCKEE
EMIGRANT TRAIL MUSEUM
WEOTT
HUMBOLDT REDWOODS STATE PARK

Mining, quarrying, oil

AUSTRALIA

ALBURY
MUSEUM OF APPLIED ARTS AND SCIENCES, ALBURY BRANCH
ARMIDALE
ARMIDALE FOLK MUSEUM
BALLARAT
MONTROSE COTTAGE AND EUREKA MILITARY MUSEUM
SOVEREIGN HILL HISTORICAL PARK
BATHURST
FOLK MUSEUM
MUSEUM OF APPLIED ARTS AND SCIENCES
BEECHWORTH
BURKE MEMORIAL MUSEUM
BENDIGO
CENTRAL DEBORAH GOLD MINE
COBB & COMPANY HISTORICAL FOLK MUSEUM
BRIGHT
BRIGHT AND DISTRICT HISTORICAL SOCIETY MUSEUM
CASTLEMAINE
CASTLEMAINE ART GALLERY AND HISTORICAL MUSEUM
COBAR
COBAR PASTORAL, MINING AND TECHNOLOGICAL MUSEUM
COOLGARDIE
GOLDFIELDS EXHIBITION

GULGONG
PIONEERS' MUSEUM
GUNDAGAI
HISTORICAL MUSEUM
GYMPIE
GYMPIE AND DISTRICT HISTORICAL MUSEUM
KADINA
NATIONAL TRUST MUSEUM
KYNETON
KYNETON HISTORICAL MUSEUM
LIGHTNING RIDGE
MICK'S MUSEUM
MOONTA
NATIONAL TRUST MUSEUM
MOUNT MORGAN
MOUNT MORGAN HISTORICAL MUSEUM
SYDNEY
MINING AND GEOLOGICAL MUSEUM
TINGHA
SMITH'S MINING AND NATURAL HISTORY MUSEUM
WILLIAMSTOWN
MUNICIPAL MUSEUM
ZEEHAN
WEST COAST PIONEERS' MEMORIAL MUSEUM

AUSTRIA

ALTAUSSEE
SALTMINE
ARZBERG
REGIONAL MUSEUM
BADGASTEIN
REGIONAL MUSEUM
BAD ISCHL
REGIONAL MUSEUM
DÖLLACH
REGIONAL AND GOLDMINING MUSEUM
EIBENSTEIN
OPEN-AIR MUSEUM
EIBISWALD
REGIONAL MUSEUM
EISENERZ
MINING MUSEUM
REGIONAL MUSEUM
GMUND
MUSEUM OF GLASS
GRAZ
JOANNEUM PROVINCIAL MUSEUM OF MINING, GEOLOGY AND TECHNOLOGY
HAAG
HAAG MUSEUM OF LOCAL LIFE AND HISTORY
HABACH
EMERALD MINING MUSEUM
HALLEIN
MUNICIPAL MUSEUM
HALLSTATT
LOCAL MUSEUM
IMST
REGIONAL MUSEUM
KITZBÜHEL
REGIONAL MUSEUM
KLAGENFURT
CARINTHIA PROVINCIAL MUSEUM
LEOBEN
MINING MUSEUM
MUNICIPAL MUSEUM
LILIENFELD
MUSEUM OF LOCAL LIFE
LOICH
LOICH REGIONAL ROOM
MURAU
PALACE MUSEUM
OBERNBERG
REGIONAL MUSEUM
OBERZEIRING
DEMONSTRATION MINE AND MUSEUM
RAURIS
RAURIS GOLD-MINING MUSEUM
REICHENAU AN DER RAX
MUSEUM OF MINING AND REGIONAL LIFE
RENNWEG
VILLAGE MUSEUM
ST. MARGARETHEN
OPEN-AIR MUSEUM IN ROMAN QUARRY
SCHÄRDING
MUNICIPAL MUSEUM
SOLBAD HALL
MINING MUSEUM
MUNICIPAL MUSEUM
VILLACH
MUNICIPAL MUSEUM
VIENNA
MUSEUM OF THE HISTORY OF ART: MUSEUM OF AUSTRIAN CULTURE
MUSEUM OF INDUSTRY AND TECHNOLOGY
MUSEUM OF THE PROVINCE OF LOWER AUSTRIA
WIENERBRUCK
TRÜBENBACH SCHOOL MUSEUM

BRAZIL

DIAMANTINA
DIAMOND MUSEUM
NATAL
MUSEUM OF THE CAMARA CASCUDO INSTITUTE OF ANTHROPOLOGY
SABARÁ
MUSEUM OF GOLD MINING

BULGARIA

SOFIA
NATIONAL POLYTECHNIC MUSEUM

CANADA

ATIKOKAN
ATIKOKAN CENTENNIAL MUSEUM
BARKERVILLE
BARKERVILLE HISTORIC PARK
BRUCE MINES
BRUCE MINES MUSEUM
COBALT
NORTHERN ONTARIO MINING MUSEUM
ELLIOT LAKE
ELLIOT LAKE MINING AND NUCLEAR MUSEUM
GLACE BAY
MINERS' MUSEUM
KIRKLAND LAKE
MUSEUM OF NORTHERN HISTORY
LETHBRIDGE
SIR ALEXANDER GALT MUSEUM
MONTREAL
ALCAN MUSEUM
OIL SPRINGS
OIL MUSEUM OF CANADA
OTTAWA
NATIONAL MUSEUM OF SCIENCE AND TECHNOLOGY
PORCUPINE
PORCUPINE MINING MUSEUM
PRINCETON
PRINCETON AND DISTRICT PIONEER MUSEUM
ROSE BAY
THE OVENS NATURAL PARK AND MUSEUM
ROSSLAND
ROSSLAND HISTORICAL MUSEUM
STELLARTON
MINERS' MUSEUM
VICTORIA
BRITISH COLUMBIA MINERAL MUSEUM
VIKING
VIKING HISTORICAL SOCIETY MUSEUM

CHINA, P.R.

SUCHOW (SU ZHOU)
HISTORY MUSEUM

CUBA

HABANA
AGRICULTURAL MUSEUM

CZECHOSLOVAKIA

BANSKÁ ŠTIAVNICA
MINING MUSEUM
BOJKOVICE
LOCAL MUSEUM
GELNICA
MINING MUSEUM
JÁCHYMOV
MUNICIPAL MUSEUM
JEMNICE
JEMNICE MUSEUM
JILOVÉ U PRAHY
MUSEUM OF THE PRODUCTION AND PROCESSING OF GOLD
KAŠPERSKÉ HORY
ŠUMAVY MUSEUM
KOMÁRNO
PODUNAJSKA REGIONAL MUSEUM
KOŠICE
TECHNICAL MUSEUM
KUTNÁ HORA
DISTRICT MUSEUM: HRADKU COLLECTIONS
PRAGUE
NATIONAL TECHNICAL MUSEUM
PŘIBRAM
DISTRICT MUSEUM
ROŽŇAVA
MINING AND METALWORKING MUSEUM
RUŽOMBEROK
LIPTOV MUSEUM
SOKOLOV
MINING MUSEUM
STŘÍBRO
REGIONAL MUSEUM
TŘEBENICE
MUSEUM OF GARNETS
VLASTĚJOVICE
LOCAL MUSEUM

FRANCE

JARVILLE- LA-MALGRANGE
MUSEUM OF THE HISTORY OF IRON
PARIS
MUSEUM OF MATERIALS
ST. ÉTIENNE
MUSEUM OF ART AND INDUSTRY
SAINT LAURENT DE LA PLAINE
MUSEUM OF THE OLD TRADES OF ANJOU

GDR

ALTENBURG
ORE-CRUSHING AND TINWASHING PLANT
ANNABERG-BUCHHOLZ
ERZGEBIRG MUSEUM: DEPARTMENT OF CULTURAL HISTORY
ASBACH
FINSTERTAL DEMONSTRATION MINE IN THE KOHLBERG
ASCHERSLEBEN
REGIONAL MUSEUM
AUE
REGIONAL COLLECTION
BAD DURRENBERG
BORLACH MUSEUM

BAD KOSEN
REGIONAL MUSEUM
BAD SCHANDAU
REGIONAL MUSEUM
BAD SULZA
SALTWORKS MUSEUM
BAD SULZE
SALT MUSEUM
BERNBURG
BERNBURG CASTLE MUSEUM
BITTERFELD
DISTRICT MUSEUM
BORNA
REGIONAL MUSEUM
BRAND-ERBISDORF
REGIONAL MINING MUSEUM
EHRENFRIEDERSDORF
GREIFENSTEIN MUSEUM
EISLEBEN
DISTRICT AND REGIONAL MUSEUM
FALKENSTEIN
REGIONAL MUSEUM
FREIBERG
INSTITUTE OF FUEL
SCIENTIFIC COLLECTION OF FREIBERG MINING ACADEMY
FREITAL
REGIONAL HOUSE
GEYER
REGIONAL MUSEUM
HALLE
HALLOREN MUSEUM
MARTIN LUTHER UNIVERSITY MUSEUM OF THE GEISEL VALLEY
HARTENSTEIN
REGIONAL MUSEUM
ILSENBURG
REGIONAL MUSEUM
KARL MARX STADT
RABENSTEIN UNDERGROUND ROCK CATHEDRAL
LEIPZIG
MUSEUM OF NATURAL SCIENCES
MARIENBERG
REGIONAL MUSEUM
MARKRANSTÄDT
REGIONAL MUSEUM
MITTWEIDA
REGIONAL MUSEUM
NEUHAUS-SCHIERSCHNITZ
REGIONAL ROOM
PLAUEN
VOGTLAND DISTRICT MUSEUM
POBERSHAU
DEMONSTRATION MINE
SANGERHAUSEN
SPENGLER MUSEUM
SCHNEEBERG
MUSEUM FOR POPULAR ART OF THE MINING COMMUNITY
SENFTENBERG
DISTRICT MUSEUM
STOLBERG
REGIONAL MUSEUM
WALLDORF
QUARRY
WASCHLEITHE
HERKULES FRISCH GLÜCK DEMONSTRATION MINE
WORBIS
REGIONAL MUSEUM
ZWICKAU
MUNICIPAL MUSEUM

GFR

BAD SEGEBERG
OLD SEGEBERG TOWN HOUSE
BERCHTESGADEN
SALT MUSEUM
BEXBACH
REGIONAL AND MINING MUSEUM
BOCHUM
MINING MUSEUM
BÜCKEBURG
REGIONAL MUSEUM OF SCHAUMBURG-LIPPISCH
CLAUSTHAL-ZELLERFELD
UPPER HARZ REGIONAL AND MINING MUSEUM
KAMEN
MUNICIPAL MUSEUM
MÜNCHEN
GERMAN MUSEUM
MÜSEN
MINING AND REGIONAL MUSEUM
PAPENBURG
SHIPPING AND MOOR MUSEUM
ST. ANDREASBERG
REGIONAL MUSEUM AND HISTORIC SILVER MINE
SIEGEN
SIEGERLAND MUSEUM
SULZBACH-ROSENBERG
REGIONAL MUSEUM
WEILBURG
MUNICIPAL AND MINING MUSEUM
WOLFACH
WOLFACH REGIONAL MUSEUM
WÜLFRATH
NIEDERBERG REGIONAL MUSEUM

GREAT BRITAIN

BURFORD
TOLSEY MUSEUM
CAMBORNE
CAMBORNE SCHOOL OF METALLIFEROUS MINING MUSEUM
CORNISH ENGINES
HOLMAN BROTHERS LIMITED
CARDIFF
NATIONAL MUSEUM OF WALES
ECCLES
PROTECTOR LAMP AND LIGHTING COMPANY LIMITED
EDINBURGH
ROYAL SCOTTISH MUSEUM
GREAT YARMOUTH
MARITIME MUSEUM FOR EAST ANGLIA
KINGSBRIDGE
WILLIAM COOKWORTHY MUSEUM
LLANBERIS
NORTH WALES QUARRYING MUSEUM
LONDON
SCIENCE MUSEUM
MORWELLHAM
MORWELLHAM QUAY
NEWCASTLE- UPON-TYNE
MUSEUM OF SCIENCE AND ENGINEERING
UNIVERSITY OF NEWCASTLE- UPON-TYNE
PENZANCE
PENZANCE NATURAL HISTORY AND ANTIQUARIAN MUSEUM
REDRUTH
TOLGUS TIN
SALFORD
SCIENCE MUSEUM
TELFORD
IRONBRIDGE GORGE MUSEUM
ZENNOR
WAYSIDE MUSEUM

HUNGARY

KOMLÓ
KOMLÓ MUSEUM
RUDABÁNYA
ORE AND MINERAL MINING MUSEUM
SALGÓRTARJÁN
MUSEUM OF UNDERGROUND MINING
SOPRON
CENTRAL MINING MUSEUM
MINERS' MEMORIAL MUSEUM AT THE BRENNBERG MINE

INDIA

CALCUTTA
BIRLA INDUSTRIAL AND TECHNOLOGICAL MUSEUM

ITALY

FLORENCE
SEMI-PRECIOUS STONE WORKSHOP MUSEUM
MILAN
LEONARDO DA VINCI MUSEUM OF SCIENCE AND TECHNOLOGY
TRIESTE
MUSEUM OF MINERALOGY

JAPAN

AIKAWA-MACHI
AIKAWA LOCAL MUSEUM
AKITA-SHI
MUSEUM OF AKITA UNIVERSITY, FACULTY OF MINING
UME-MACHI
UME LOCAL MUSEUM

MALAYSIA

PENANG
PENANG MUSEUM AND ART GALLERY

NETHERLANDS

TILBURG
NATURAL HISTORY MUSEUM

NEW ZEALAND

ALEXANDRA
ALEXANDRA MUSEUM
ARROWTOWN
LAKES DISTRICT CENTENNIAL MUSEUM
CLYDE
VINCENT COUNTY AND DUNSTAN GOLDFIELDS MUSEUM
HOKITIKA
WEST COAST HISTORICAL MUSEUM
MURCHISON
MURCHISON MUSEUM
NASEBY
MANIOTOTO EARLY SETTLERS' MUSEUM
OBAN
RAKIURA MUSEUM
QUEENSTOWN
THE OLD HOUSE
REEFTON
BLACK'S POINT MUSEUM
THAMES
THAMES MINERALOGICAL MUSEUM
WAIHI
WAIHI ARTS CENTRE AND MUSEUM

NORWAY

KONGSBERG
SILVER MINE MUSEUM
OSLO
MINERALOGICAL-GEOLOGICAL MUSEUM
NORWEGIAN SCIENCE AND INDUSTRY MUSEUM
RÔROS
MINING MUSEUM

POLAND

BÓBRKA
LOCAL MUSEUM
KRAKÓW
MUSEUM OF THE IRON AND STEEL INDUSTRY
PŁOCK
MAZOVIAN MUSEUM
SOSNOWIEC
MINING MUSEUM
TARNOWSKIE GÓRY
SILVER-MINE MUSEUM
WARSAW
TECHNICAL MUSEUM
WIELICZKA
ROCK-SALT MUSEUM
ZABRZE
MINING MUSEUM
REGIONAL MUSEUM
ZŁOTY STOK
LOCAL MUSEUM

RHODESIA

BULAWAYO
RHODESIAN MINING ANTIQUARIA

ROMANIA

BAIA MARE
MARAMUREŞ DISTRICT MUSEUM
BRAD
GOLD MUSEUM
DEVA
DEVA MUSEUM
LUPŞA
VILLAGE MUSEUM
PETROŞENI
MUSEUM OF THE INSTITUTE OF MINING
PLOIEŞTI
PROVINCIAL PETROLEUM MUSEUM
RIMETEA
LOCAL MUSEUM

SOUTH AFRICA, REPUBLIC OF

BARBERTON
BARBERTON MUSEUM
DUNDEE
DEPARTMENT OF MINES MUSEUM
JOHANNESBURG
BLELOCH MUSEUM
KIMBERLEY
KIMBERLEY MINE MUSEUM
LYDENBURG
VOORTREKKER CHURCH AND SCHOOL
PIETERMARITZBURG
MINES DEPARTMENT MUSEUM
PRETORIA
MUSEUM OF THE GEOLOGICAL SURVEY

SOUTH-WEST AFRICA (NAMIBIA)

LÜDERITZ
LÜDERITZ MUSEUM

SPAIN

MADRID
MUSEUM OF THE SCHOOL OF MINES

SWEDEN

FALUN
MINING MUSEUM
STOCKHOLM
TECHNICAL MUSEUM

SWITZERLAND

HORGEN
LOCAL MUSEUM
NYON
LAKE LÉMAN MUSEUM
SCHLEITHEIM
GYPSUM MUSEUM

USSR

BAKU
MUSEUM OF THE PETROLEUM INDUSTRY AND OF INDUSTRIAL SAFETY
LENINGRAD
MUSEUM OF THE G. V. PLEKHANOV MINING INSTITUTE

UNITED STATES

ALAMO
LIVE STEAM MUSEUM
ALBANY
LEDBETTER PICKET HOUSE MUSEUM
AMADOR CITY
GOLD RUSH MUSEUM
ASPEN
ASPEN HISTORICAL SOCIETY MUSEUM
AUBURN
PLACER COUNTY MUSEUM
BARTLESVILLE
PHILLIPS PETROLEUM EXHIBIT HALL
BEAUMONT
SPINDLETOP MUSEUM
BECKLEY
BECKLEY EXHIBITION MINE
BLAIRSDEN
PLUMAS EUREKA STATE PARK MUSEUM
BREWSTER
DINOSAUR LAND
BRIDGEPORT
BODIE STATE HISTORIC PARK
BUTTE
WORLD MUSEUM OF MINING
CANYON CITY
HERMAN AND ELIZA OLIVER MUSEUM
CASPIAN
IRON COUNTY MUSEUM
CENTRAL CITY
CENTRAL GOLD MINE AND MUSEUM
CHICAGO
MUSEUM OF SCIENCE AND INDUSTRY
CHISHOLM
MINNESOTA MUSEUM OF MINING
CLAYTON
CUSTER MUSEUM
COLOMA
JAMES W. MARSHALL GOLD DISCOVERY MUSEUM
COLORADO SPRINGS
PIKES PEAK GHOST TOWN
WESTERN MUSEUM OF MINING AND INDUSTRY
COLUMBIA
MUSEUM OF COLUMBIA STATE HISTORIC PARK
CORSICANA
PETROLEUM INDUSTRY PARK
CRYSTAL FALLS
CRYSTAL FALLS IRON MINE
DAHLONEGA
GOLD HILLS OF OLD DAHLONEGA
DENVER
MUSEUM OF THE STATE HISTORICAL SOCIETY OF COLORADO
DOWNIEVILLE
SIERRA COUNTY MUSEUM
DRUMRIGHT
DRUMRIGHT COMMUNITY HISTORICAL MUSEUM
EAST GRANBY
OLD NEW-GATE PRISON AND COPPER MINE
ELIZABETHTOWN
ADIRONDACK CENTER MUSEUM
ENCINO
MUSEUM OF LOS ENCINOS STATE HISTORICAL PARK
EPHRATA
WANAPUM DAM TOUR CENTER
FRANCESTOWN
THE FRANCESTOWN VILLAGE IMPROVEMENT SOCIETY MUSEUM
GALENA
VINEGAR HILL LEAD MINE
GRANGEVILLE
IDAHO COUNTY HISTORICAL SOCIETY
GRANTS
GRANTS AND WEST VALENCIA COUNTY CHAMBER OF COMMERCE MUSEUM
HARTFORD
OLD NEWGATE PRISON AND COPPER MINE
HILL CITY
OIL MUSEUM
HUGOTON
STEVENS COUNTY GAS AND HISTORICAL MUSEUM
IRON MOUNTAIN
IRON MOUNTAIN IRON MINE
IRON RIVER
IRON COUNTY MUSEUM
JACKSONVILLE
JACKSONVILLE MUSEUM
JASPER
JASPER COUNTY MUSEUM
JEROME
JEROME STATE HISTORIC PARK
JOPLIN
TRI-STATE MINERAL MUSEUM
LA CROSSE
POST ROCK MUSEUM
LAKE CHARLES
IMPERIAL CALCASIEU HISTORICAL MUSEUM
LAKE HOPATCONG
LAKE HOPATCONG HISTORICAL MUSEUM
LAURIUM
YESTERYEAR HOUSE
LEADVILLE
HEALY HOUSE - DEXTER CABIN
LEADVILLE ASSEMBLY
MARQUETTE
JOHN BURT HOUSE
MIDLAND
PERMIAN BASIN PETROLEUM MUSEUM
MOAB
MOAB MUSEUM
NEVADA CITY
MALAKOFF DIGGINS
NATIONAL HOTEL MUSEUM
NEVADA COUNTY HISTORICAL SOCIETY MUSEUM
NORTH CREEK
GARNET MINE
PAMPA
WHITE DEER LAND MUSEUM
PARKER
BUCKSKIN UNIT
PAWHUSKA
OSAGE COUNTY HISTORICAL MUSEUM
PHOENIX
PIONEER ARIZONA
PIERRE
MUSEUM OF SOUTH DAKOTA STATE HISTORICAL

SOCIETY

PITTSBURG
MUSEUM OF CRAWFORD COUNTY HISTORICAL SOCIETY

PLACERVILLE
EL DORADO COUNTY HISTORICAL SOCIETY MUSEUM

POTEAU
KERR MUSEUM

POTTSVILLE
MUSEUM OF SCHUYLKILL COUNTY HISTORICAL SOCIETY

PRAIRIE CITY
DE WITT MUSEUM

PROCTOR
MARBLE EXHIBIT

PUEBLO
EL PUEBLO MUSEUM

RENO
MACKAY SCHOOL OF MINES MUSEUM

RIPLEY-HANCOCK
ARCADIAN COPPER MINE

ROCKPORT
MUSEUM OF SANDY BAY HISTORICAL SOCIETY
THE OLD CASTLE

ROSAMOND
BURTONS' TROPICS GOLDMINE AND MUSEUM

SAN FRANCISCO
MUSEUM OF THE CALIFORNIA DIVISION OF MINES AND GEOLOGY
WELLS FARGO BANK HISTORY ROOM

SAN JOSÉ
NEW ALMADEN QUICKSILVER MINES EXHIBIT

SANTA PAULA
CALIFORNIA OIL MUSEUM

SEATTLE
PULLEN ALASKA MUSEUM

SHASTA
SHASTA STATE HISTORICAL MONUMENT

SHULLSBURG
BADGER MINE AND MUSEUM

SILVER PLUME
LOCAL MUSEUM

SMETHPORT
MCKEAN COUNTY HISTORICAL MUSEUM

STEAMBOAT SPRINGS
TREAD OF PIONEERS

TITUSVILLE
DRAKE WELL MUSEUM
PITHOLE

VIRGINIA CITY
NEVADA CITY

WALLACE
COEUR D'ALENE DISTRICT MINING MUSEUM

WASHINGTON
NATIONAL MUSEUM OF HISTORY AND TECHNOLOGY

WEATHERLY
ANTHRACITE MUSEUM, ECKLEY VILLAGE

YUGOSLAVIA

LABIN
TOWN MUSEUM

PIRAN
ART GALLERY AND CITY MUSEUM

ZAMBIA

NDOLA
COPPERBELT MUSEUM ASSOCIATION

Manufacturing, handicrafts, business

AFGHANISTAN

KABUL
KABUL MUSEUM

ALBANIA

TIRANA
MUSEUM OF ARCHAEOLOGY AND ETHNOGRAPHY

ALGERIA

ALGIERS
LE BARDO MUSEUM OF ETHNOGRAPHY AND PREHISTORY

EL OUED
EL OUED MUSEUM

OUARGLA
SAHARA MUSEUM

ANGOLA

LUANDA
ANGOLA MUSEUM

ARGENTINA

AZUL
ENRIQUE SQUIRRU ETHNOGRAPHICAL MUSEUM

BUENOS AIRES
JOSÉ HERNÁNDEZ MUSEUM OF POPULAR ART
ENRIQUE LARRETA MUSEUM OF SPANISH ART
MUSEUM OF TECHNOLOGY

ENTRE RIOS
PROVINCIAL MUSEUM

SANTA FÉ
MUSEUM OF ETHNOGRAPHY

TUCUMÁN
MUSEUM OF ARGENTINE FOLKLORE AND HANDICRAFTS

AUSTRALIA

ARMIDALE
ARMIDALE FOLK MUSEUM

ATHERTON
FRANKIE'S BOTTLE BONANZA

BATHURST
MUSEUM OF APPLIED ARTS AND SCIENCES

BURNIE
THE PIONEER VILLAGE MUSEUM

KADINA
NATIONAL TRUST MUSEUM

SWAN HILL
SWAN HILL FOLK MUSEUM

TANUNDA
BAROSSA VALLEY MUSEUM

TOOWOOMBA
CREATIVE 92 ART CENTRE

AUSTRIA

ANZENAU
ANZENAU MILL OPEN-AIR MUSEUM

ARZBERG
REGIONAL MUSEUM

BADEN
EMPEROR FRANZ JOSEPH MUSEUM

BAD GOISERN
GOISERN REGIONAL MUSEUM

BAD HALL
REGIONAL MUSEUM

BAD LEONFELDEN
REGIONAL MUSEUM

BAD TATZMANNSDORF
BURGENLAND OPEN-AIR MUSEUM

BAD VOSLAU
REGIONAL MUSEUM

BEZAU
REGIONAL MUSEUM

BRAMBERG
REGIONAL MUSEUM

BRAUNAU AM INN
DISTRICT MUSEUM

BRUCK AN DER LEITHA
REGIONAL MUSEUM

DÖLLACH
REGIONAL AND GOLDMINING MUSEUM

DROSENDORF
FRANZ KIESSLING MUSEUM

DÜRNSTEIN
DÜRNSTEIN REGIONAL MUSEUM

EBENAU
REGIONAL MUSEUM

EIBISWALD
REGIONAL MUSEUM

EISENERZ
MINING MUSEUM

FELDBACH
REGIONAL MUSEUM

FISCHAMEND
REGIONAL MUSEUM

GLEISDORF
REGIONAL MUSEUM

GMUND
MUNICIPAL MUSEUM
MUSEUM OF GLASS

GNAS
REGIONAL MUSEUM

GRESTEN
REGIONAL MUSEUM

GUNDORF
MUSEUM OF LOCAL LIFE

GÜSSING
REGIONAL AND CASTLE MUSEUM

HAAG
HAAG MUSEUM OF LOCAL LIFE AND HISTORY

HALLSTATT
LOCAL MUSEUM

HARD
MITTELWEIBERBURG REGIONAL MUSEUM

HASLACH
MUSEUM OF LOCAL HISTORY AND FOLKLORE

HOHENAU
REGIONAL MUSEUM

IMST
REGIONAL MUSEUM

JUDENBURG
TOWN AND DISTRICT MUSEUM

KAPFENBERG
CAVE MUSEUM

KLAGENFURT
CARINTHIA PROVINCIAL MUSEUM

KREMS
MUNICIPAL MUSEUM

KUFSTEIN
REGIONAL MUSEUM

LANGENLOIS
REGIONAL MUSEUM

LANGENZERSDORF
REGIONAL MUSEUM

LIENZ
KLÖSTERLE SMITHY OPEN-AIR MUSEUM
EAST TIROL REGIONAL MUSEUM

LINZ
MUSEUM OF THE CITY OF LINZ
UPPER AUSTRIA PROVINCIAL MUSEUM

LOICH
LOICH REGIONAL ROOM

LOSENSTEIN
REGIONAL MUSEUM

LUNZ
AMON HOUSE MUSEUM

MICHAELBEUERN
ABBEY REGIONAL MUSEUM

MONDSEE
REGIONAL MUSEUM

MURAU
MUNICIPAL MUSEUM OF LOCAL LIFE
PALACE MUSEUM

MURAU-KENDLBRUCK
SMELTER

NEUNKIRCHEN
REGIONAL MUSEUM

OBERNDORF
REGIONAL MUSEUM

PINKAFELD
REGIONAL MUSEUM

PISCHELSDORF
REGIONAL MUSEUM

PÖGGSTALL
REGIONAL MUSEUM

RAABS
DR. JOSEF GRASSL REGIONAL MUSEUM

RABENSTEIN
PIELACHTAL REGIONAL MUSEUM

SAALFELDEN
MUSEUM OF LOCAL LIFE AND OF CRIBS

SALZBURG
CASTLE MUSEUM

ST. PÖLTEN
MUNICIPAL MUSEUM

ST. ULRICH
LAVANTTAL MUSEUM OF LOCAL LIFE

SCHÄRDING
MUNICIPAL MUSEUM

SCHEIBBS
HOTTENROTH COLLECTION

SCHWANENSTADT
REGIONAL MUSEUM

SEEKIRCHEN
REGIONAL MUSEUM

SPITAL
REGIONAL MUSEUM

STEGERSBACH
SOUTH BURGENLAND COUNTRYSIDE MUSEUM

STEYR
REGIONAL MUSEUM

STEYRERMÜHL
STEYRERMÜHL PAPER-MILL MUSEUM

STRASSBURG
DIOCESAN AND REGIONAL MUSEUM

STUBING
AUSTRIAN OPEN-AIR MUSEUM

TAMSWEG
LUNGAU REGIONAL MUSEUM

TAUFKIRCHEN
REGIONAL ROOM

TELFS
REGIONAL MUSEUM

TRAISMAUER
REGIONAL MUSEUM

TRAUTENFELS
COUNTRYSIDE MUSEUM

TULLN
REGIONAL MUSEUM

VORDERNBERG
WATER-POWERED IRONWORKS AND FORGE

WAIDHOFEN AN DER THAYA
REGIONAL MUSEUM

VIENNA
ALSERGRUND DISTRICT MUSEUM
AUSTRIAN MUSEUM OF INDUSTRY AND COMMERCE
LIESING DISTRICT MUSEUM
MEIDLING DISTRICT MUSEUM
MUSEUM OF THE AUSTRIAN POST OFFICE SAVINGS BANK
MUSEUM OF ETHNOLOGY
MUSEUM OF THE HISTORY OF ART: MUSEUM OF AUSTRIAN CULTURE
MUSEUM OF INDUSTRY AND TECHNOLOGY
MUSEUM OF THE PROVINCE OF LOWER AUSTRIA
OTTAKRING DISTRICT MUSEUM
PENZING DISTRICT MUSEUM
SIMMERING DISTRICT MUSEUM

WAIDHOFEN AN DER YBBS
PIATY PRIVATE COLLECTION

WEIKENDORF
MARCHFELD MUSEUM

WELS
CASTLE MUSEUM

WENIGZELL
REGIONAL HOUSE

WIENERBRUCK
TRÜBENBACH SCHOOL MUSEUM

WIENER NEUSTADT
MUNICIPAL MUSEUM

WILDALPEN
FORESTRY MUSEUM

BAHAMAS

NASSAU
BAHAMIA MUSEUM

BANGLADESH

CHITTAGONG
ETHNOLOGICAL MUSEUM

BELGIUM

AARSCHOT
REGIONAL MUSEUM

ANTWERP
COOPERS' MUSEUM
ETHNOGRAPHICAL MUSEUM
FOLK-LORE MUSEUM
PROVINCIAL MUSEUM OF INDUSTRIAL ART

BRUSSELS
MUNICIPAL MUSEUM OF THE CITY OF BRUSSELS

GHENT
CASTLE OF THE COUNTS OF FLANDERS
FOLKLORE MUSEUM
MUSEUM OF ANTIQUITIES
MUSEUM OF THE TREATY OF GHENT

HOOGSTRATEN
TOWN HALL MUSEUM

HUY
DISTRICT MUSEUM

LIÈGE
ANSEMBOURG MUSEUM
MUSEUM OF WALLOON LIFE
TCHANTCHÈS MUSEUM

MALMEDY
ABBEY MUSEUM

MONS
INDUSTRIAL MUSEUM

NAMUR
THE DE CROIX MUSEUM

NEDER- OVER-HEEMBEEK
FOLKLORE MUSEUM

ROCLENGE-SUR-GEER
STRAW MUSEUM

STAVELOT
TANNERY MUSEUM

TERVUEREN
ROYAL CENTRAL AFRICAN MUSEUM

TURNHOUT
TAXANDRIA MUSEUM OF ARCHAEOLOGY

VIRTON
GAUMAIS MUSEUM

BOLIVIA

LA PAZ
NATIONAL MUSEUM OF ARCHAEOLOGY

SUCRE
COLONIAL MUSEUM

BRAZIL

CARUARU
MUSEUM OF POPULAR ART

CAXIAS DO SUL
MUSEUM OF POPULAR TRADITIONS

CURITIBA
MUSEUM OF MAN

FLORIANÓPOLIS
FOLKLORE MUSEUM

ITABIRITO
MUSEUM OF THE IRON AND STEEL INDUSTRY

MANAUS
MUSEUM OF INDIAN CULTURE

NATAL
MUSEUM OF THE CAMARA CASCUDO INSTITUTE OF ANTHROPOLOGY

PENEDO
MUSEUM OF FOLK ART AND FOLK CULTURE

SALVADOR
MUSEUM OF MODERN ART

BULGARIA

KARNOBAT
NATIONAL MUSEUM

KJUSTENDIL
DISTRICT MUSEUM

PANAGIOURISTE
RAJNA KNIAGJANIA REGIONAL MUSEUM

PLOVDIV
DISTRICT NATIONAL MUSEUM
REGIONAL MUSEUM OF ETHNOLOGY

RAJKOVO
NATIONAL MUSEUM OF THE RHODOPE

ŠČRAKLEVO
MUSEUM OF REGIONAL HISTORY AND ETHNOGRAPHY

SLIVEN
NATIONAL MUSEUM

SOFIA
NATIONAL ETHNOGRAPHICAL MUSEUM
NATIONAL POLYTECHNIC MUSEUM

TARNOVO
PROVINCIAL MUSEUM

CAMEROUN

FOUMBAN
MUSEUM OF THE BAMOUN ROYAL PALACE

CANADA

ARICHAT
LENOIR FORGE

BALDWIN TOWNSHIP
BEAVER VALLEY MUSEUM

CHETICAMP
ACADIAN MUSEUM

GODERICH
HURON COUNTY PIONEER MUSEUM

MONCTON
UNIVERSITY OF MONCTON MUSEUM

MONTREAL
ALCAN MUSEUM
CANADIAN GUILD OF CRAFTS

NELSON
KOOTENAY MUSEUM

OTTAWA
MUSEUM OF NATIONAL HISTORIC SITES SERVICE
NATIONAL MUSEUM OF SCIENCE AND TECHNOLOGY

QUEBEC
MUSEUM OF THE ARCHIVES OF QUEBEC

ST. JOHNS
NEWFOUNDLAND MUSEUM

SASKATOON
MUSEUM OF THE UKRAINIAN WOMEN'S ASSOCIATION

TORONTO
UKRAINIAN ARTS AND CRAFTS MUSEUM

TROIS RIVIÈRES
VILLAGE OF ST. MAURICE IRONWORKS

VANCOUVER
UKRAINIAN FOLK ART MUSEUM

VICTORIA
MALTWOOD MEMORIAL MUSEUM OF HISTORIC ART, UNIVERSITY OF VICTORIA

CHAD

FORT LAMY
CHAD NATIONAL MUSEUM

CHINA, P.R.

AMOY (XIAMEN)
OVERSEAS CHINESE MUSEUM

CANTON (GUANG DONG)
HISTORY MUSEUM

CHANGCHUN
PROVINCIAL MUSEUM

CHINCHOW (JINZHOW)
PROVINCIAL MUSEUM

HANGCHOW (HANG ZHOU)
CHEKIANG PROVINCIAL MUSEUM

HARBIN
PROVINCIAL MUSEUM

KUEILIN
PROVINCIAL MUSEUM

KWEIYANG (GUIJANG)
PROVINCIAL MUSEUM

LANCHOW (LANZHOU)
PROVINCIAL MUSEUM

LUCHOU
LOCAL MUSEUM

MUKDEN (SHENYIANG)
INDUSTRIAL EXHIBITION
NORTH EAST MUSEUM

NANKING (NAN JING)
KIANG SU PROVINCIAL MUSEUM

SHANGHAI
THE INDUSTRIAL EXHIBITION

SUCHOW (SU ZHOU)
HISTORY MUSEUM

TIENSIN (TIANJING)
CITY MUSEUM OF HISTORY
PEOPLE'S HALL OF SCIENCE
PROVINCIAL MUSEUM

TSINAN (JI NAN)
PROVINCIAL MUSEUM

URUMCHI (WULUMUCHI)
REGIONAL MUSEUM

REPUBLIC OF CHINA

NANKING
EXHIBITION ROOM OF THE ARCHAEOLOGICAL SECTION

COLOMBIA

BOGOTA
MUSEUM OF ETHNOGRAPHY
MUSEUM OF POPULAR ARTS AND TRADITIONS

COLOSO
PRIVATE MUSEUM

MEDELLÍN
INDIAN MUSEUM
MUSEUM OF ETHNOGRAPHY
MUSEUM OF FOLKLORE

POPAYAN
COLONIAL MUSEUM

COSTA RICA

SAN JOSÉ
GOLD MUSEUM

CYPRUS

KYRENIA
FOLK ART MUSEUM

CZECHOSLOVAKIA

BANSKÁ BYSTRICA
MUSEUM OF THE HISTORY OF SLOVAKIA

BARDEJOV
MUSEUM OF URBAN HANDICRAFTS
ŠARIŠ MUSEUM

BLANSKO
BLANSKO REGIONAL MUSEUM

BOJNICE
REGIONAL MUSEUM

BOUZOV
REGIONAL CENTRE

ČERVENÝ KLÁŠTOR
MONASTERY MUSEUM

DOBŘÍV
FORGE MUSEUM

DOLNI DOMASLOVICE
DOMASLOVICE AND DISTRICT MUSEUM

DOMAŽLICE
JINDŘICHA JINDŘICHA MUSEUM

DVUR KRÁLOVÉ NAD LABEM
TEXTILE MUSEUM

GOTTWALDOV
MUSEUM OF SHOE-MAKING

HORŠOVSKY TÝN
REGIONAL MUSEUM

JEMNICE
JEMNICE MUSEUM

KARLOVY VARY - BŘEZOV
MUSEUM OF KARLOVY PORCELAIN

KARLOVY VARY - DVORY
MUSEUM OF GLASS

KAŠPERSKÉ HORY
ŠUMAVY MUSEUM

KEŽMAROK
MUNICIPAL MUSEUM

KOMÁRNO
PODUNAJSKA REGIONAL MUSEUM

KOMÁROV
MUSEUM OF IRON

KOPŘIVNICE
TECHNICAL MUSEUM

KOŠICE
MUSEUM OF EASTERN SLOVAKIA
TECHNICAL MUSEUM

LITOMĚŘICE
DISTRICT MUSEUM

LITVINOV
LOCAL MUSEUM

LOMNICE NAD POPELKOU
MUNICIPAL MUSEUM

MARTIN
SLOVAKIAN NATIONAL MUSEUM: ETHNOGRAPHICAL COLLECTIONS

MORAVSKÁ TŘEBOVA
MUNICIPAL MUSEUM

MORAVSKÉ BUDĚJOVICE
MUSEUM OF WESTERN MORAVIA

NOVÝ BOR
MUSEUM OF GLASS

NOVÝ JIČIN
DISTRICT MUSEUM
MUSEUM OF HAT-MAKING
MUSEUM OF LIGHTING AND REFRIGERATION

OLOMUČANY
CERAMICS MUSEUM AND MUSEUM OF THE WORKERS' MOVEMENT

OPAVA
SILESIAN MUSEUM: ETHNOGRAPHY AND ART COLLECTIONS

OSTRAVA
OSTRAVA MUSEUM

OSTRAVA-VÍTKNOVICE
MUSEUM OF THE VÍTKOVICE IRON-WORKS

POTŠTEJN
JIRÁSKŮV 'POKLAD' MEMORIAL MUSEUM

PRAGUE
ETHNOLOGICAL COLLECTIONS
NATIONAL TECHNICAL MUSEUM

PŘEROV NAD LABEM
MUSEUM OF ETHNOGRAPHY

RIMAVSKÁ SOBOTA
GEMER MUSEUM

SÁZAVA
MUSEUM OF GLASS TECHNOLOGY

SKUTEČ
MUNICIPAL MUSEUM

SLANÝ
REGIONAL MUSEUM

TOVAČOV
MUSEUM OF ETHNOGRAPHY

TRENČÍN
TRENČÍN MUSEUM

TÝNEC NAD SÁZAVOU
TÝNEC MUSEUM OF CERAMICS

UHLIŘSKÉ JANOVICE
MUSEUM OF HISTORY

VIMPERK
MUNICIPAL MUSEUM AND ŠUMAVY GALLERY

VRCHLABÍ
KRKONOŠ MUSEUM (ASSOCIATED WITH KRKONOŠSKÝ NATIONAL PARK)

ŽELEZNÁ RUDA
ŠUMAVY MUSEUM

ŽILINA
POVAŽIA MUSEUM AND ART GALLERY

DENMARK

ÅRHUS
DEN GAMLE BY

ALS
LOCAL HISTORY MUSEUM

BOGENSE
MUSEUM OF NORTH FUNEN

COPENHAGEN
BURMEISTER AND WAIN MUSEUM
GUNPOWDER FACTORY MUSEUM
MUSEUM OF DECORATIVE ART

EBELTOFT
DYER'S HOUSE

FREDERIKSVAERK
FREDERIKSVAERK AND DISTRICT MUSEUM

GUMMERUP
VESTFYNS HJEMSTAVNSGÅRDEN

HELSINGØR
DANISH TECHNICAL MUSEUM

HILLERØD
NORDSJAELLANDSK MUSEUMSFORENING

HOLSTEBRO
HOLSTEBRO MUSEUM

NYKØBING
FALSTERS MINDER MUSEUM
ØLGOD
ØLGOD MUSEUM

EGYPT, ARAB REPUBLIC OF

CAIRO
MUSEUM OF EGYPTIAN CIVILISATION
SCIENCE MUSEUM

FINLAND

BILLNÄS
IRON MUSEUM
HELSINKI
ARABIA MUSEUM
MUSEUM OF THE CO-OPERATIVE SOCIETY
PAPER MUSEUM
JYVÄSKYLÄ
MUSEUM OF CENTRAL FINLAND
KARHULA
MUSEUM OF GLASS
KAUHAJOKI
LOCAL MUSEUM
KEMI
KEMI MUSEUM
KOKEMÄKI
AGRICULTURAL MUSEUM
KOKKOLA
K. H. RENLUNDIN MUSEUM
KUHMOINEN
HISTORICAL MUSEUM
LAHTI
MUSEUM OF HISTORY
LAPINJÄRVI
PORLAMMI REGIONAL MUSEUM
OULU
MUSEUM OF NORTH OSTROBOTHNIA
PIETARSAARI
STRENGBERG'S TOBACCO MUSEUM
RIIHIMÄKI
FINNISH GLASS MUSEUM
RUOTSINPYHTÄA
STRÖMFORS MUSEUM
SEINÄJOKI
GUNPOWDER MUSEUM
TAMPERE
TECHNICAL MUSEUM
TURKU
CITY MUSEUM
VAMMALA
TYRVÄA MUSEUM

FRANCE

AMBERT
MUSEUM OF THE HISTORY OF PAPER-MAKING
BAYONNE
BASQUE MUSEUM
BEAUNE
CHARITÉ HOSPICE
BRICQEBEC
MUNICIPAL MUSEUM
CALAIS
NEW MUSEUM
CHÂTELLERAULT
PAUL CHÉRON DE LA MARTINIÈRE MUSEUM
LA CHÂTRE
MUSEUM OF GEORGE SAND AND OF THE VALLÉE NOIRE
COMMANA
OPEN-AIR MUSEUM
CONDOM
ARMAGNAC MUSEUM
HYERES
MUNICIPAL MUSEUM
JARVILLE- LA-MALGRANGE
MUSEUM OF THE HISTORY OF IRON
LILLE
MUSEUM OF INDUSTRY, COMMERCE, TECHNOLOGY AND AGRICULTURE
LYON
CANUT MUSEUM
MARSEILLE
GROBET-LABADIE MUSEUM
MEUDON
MEUDON MUSEUM
MONTLUCON
MUNICIPAL MUSEUM
MOUSTIERS- SAINTE-MARIE
FAIENCE MUSEUM
NANTES
MUSEUM OF DECORATIVE ARTS
SALORGES MUSEUM
NARBONNE
MUSEUM OF NARBONNE PREHISTORY AND ANTIQUITIES
PARIS
FORNEY LIBRARY
MUSEUM OF MATERIALS
NATIONAL CONSERVATORY OF ARTS AND CRAFTS
PLESSIS-LES-TOURS
MUSEUM CHÂTEAU
LE PUY-EN-VELAY
CROZATIER MUSEUM
ROUEN
LE SECQ DES TOURNELLES MUSEUM
SAINT-DENIS
MUNICIPAL MUSEUM
ST. ÉTIENNE
MUSEUM OF ART AND INDUSTRY
FOLKLORE MUSEUM
SAINT LAURENT DE LA PLAINE
MUSEUM OF THE OLD TRADES OF ANJOU
ST. PIERRE D'OLÉRON
ALIENOR D'AQUITAINE MUSEUM
SAMADET
MUSEUM OF FAIENCE
SARS-POTERIES
GLASS MUSEUM
SAULIEU
FRANÇOIS POMPON MUSEUM
STRASBOURG
MUSEUM OF THE CATHEDRAL WORKSHOPS
TIGY
MUSEUM OF RURAL CRAFTS
TOURS
MUSEUM OF THE COMPAGNONNAGE
TOURS-LA-RICHE
CHÂTEAU DE PLESSIS- LÈS-TOURS
TROYES
MUSEUM OF THE HISTORY OF TROYES AND CHAMPAGNE
LE VIGAN
CÉVENNE MUSEUM
VILLEDIEU-LES-POELES
LOCAL MUSEUM

GDR

ADORF
REGIONAL MUSEUM
AKEN
REGIONAL MUSEUM
ALTENBURG
CASTLE MUSEUM AND PLAYING CARDS MUSEUM
ANKLAM
REGIONAL MUSEUM
ANNABERG-BUCHHOLZ
ERZGEBIRG MUSEUM: DEPARTMENT OF CULTURAL HISTORY
APOLDA
BELL AND REGIONAL MUSEUM
ARNEBURG
REGIONAL MUSEUM
ARNSTADT
PALACE MUSEUM
REGIONAL MUSEUM
AUGUSTUSBURG
REGIONAL MUSEUM
BAD DÜBEN
DÜBEN HEATH MUSEUM
BAD FRANKENHAUSEN
DISTRICT MUSEUM
BALLENSTEDT
REGIONAL MUSEUM
BERLIN
PERGAMON MUSEUM: MUSEUM OF ETHNOGRAPHY
BERNBURG
BERNBURG CASTLE MUSEUM
BLANKENBURG
REGIONAL MUSEUM
BLANKENHAIN
REGIONAL MUSEUM
BLANKENSEE
VILLAGE MUSEUM
BÜRGEL
CERAMICS MUSEUM
BÜTZOW
REGIONAL MUSEUM
BUTTSTADT
REGIONAL MUSEUM
COLDITZ
REGIONAL MUSEUM
COSWIG
CERAMICS FACTORY MUSEUM
COTTBUS
DISTRICT MUSEUM
CRIMMITSCHAU
REGIONAL MUSEUM
CROSTAU
REGIONAL ROOM
DAHME
REGIONAL MUSEUM
DELITZSCH
DISTRICT MUSEUM
DERMBACH
DISTRICT MUSEUM
DESSAU
MUSEUM OF NATURAL HISTORY AND PREHISTORY
DOBERLUG-KIRCHHAIN
TAWERS' MUSEUM
DÖMITZ
REGIONAL MUSEUM
DORFCHEMNITZ, KREIS BRAND-EIBISDORF
DORFCHEMNITZ FORGE HAMMER
DORFCHEMNITZ, KREIS STOLBERG
BONE-MILL CULTURAL CENTRE
EIBENSTOCK
MUNICIPAL EXHIBITION OF REGIONAL LIFE
EISENACH
THURINGIA MUSEUM
EISENBERG
DISTRICT AND REGIONAL MUSEUM
EISFELD
OTTO LUDWIG REGIONAL MUSEUM
EISLEBEN
DISTRICT AND REGIONAL MUSEUM
ERFURT
FOLK-LORE MUSEUM
FALKENSTEIN
REGIONAL MUSEUM
FREIBERG
MUNICIPAL AND MINING MUSEUM
FROHBURG
ALTE FARBE REGIONAL MUSEUM
FROHNAU
FROHNAU FORGE
GARDELEGEN
REGIONAL MUSEUM
GEISA
REGIONAL MUSEUM
GENTHIN
DISTRICT AND REGIONAL MUSEUM

GERA
MUSEUM OF CULTURAL HISTORY
GERSTUNGEN
REGIONAL MUSEUM
GEYER
REGIONAL MUSEUM
GLAUCHAU
MUNICIPAL MUSEUM AND ART COLLECTION
GNANDSTEIN
REGIONAL MUSEUM
GÖRLITZ
KAISERTRUTZ: STATE ART COLLECTION
STATE ART MUSEUM: HAUS NEISSSTRASSE MUSEUM
GOLDBERG
DISTRICT MUSEUM
GRAUPA
RICHARD WAGNER AND REGIONAL MUSEUM
GRIMMA
DISTRICT MUSEUM
GROSSENGOTTERN
REGIONAL ROOM
GROSSROHRSDORF
REGIONAL MUSEUM
GROSSSCHÖNAU
OBERLAURITZ REGIONAL AND DAMASK MUSEUM
HAINICHEN
REGIONAL MUSEUM
HALBERSTADT
MUNICIPAL MUSEUM
HALDENSLEBEN
DISTRICT MUSEUM
HEILIGENSTADT
EICHFELD REGIONAL MUSEUM
HILDBURGHAUSEN
REGIONAL MUSEUM
HOHENLEUBEN
HOHENLEUBEN - REICHSFELS MUSEUM
JARMEN
MILL MUSEUM
JENA
MUNICIPAL MUSEUM
OPTICAL MUSEUM
KARL MARX STADT
SCHLOSSBERG MUSEUM: MUNICIPAL AND CULTURAL HISTORY COLLECTION
KÖTHEN
REGIONAL MUSEUM
KOHREN-SAHLIS
POTTERY MUSEUM
LANDWÜST
VOGTLAND PEASANT MUSEUM
LAUCHA
BELL MUSEUM
LAUENSTEIN
CASTLE AND REGIONAL MUSEUM
LAUSCHA
GLASS MUSEUM
LEHDE
OPEN-AIR MUSEUM
LEIPZIG
ETHNOLOGICAL MUSEUM
MUSEUM OF NATURAL SCIENCES
LEISNIG
MILDENSTEIN CASTLE DISTRICT MUSEUM
LIMBACH-OBERFROHNA
REGIONAL MUSEUM
LÖBAU
MUNICIPAL MUSEUM
LÜBBENAU
LÜBBENAU MUSEUM IN THE SPREEWALD
LUCKAU
REGIONAL MUSEUM
LUCKENWALDE
DISTRICT MUSEUM
MEISSEN
ALBRECHTSBURG
DISPLAY HALL OF THE MEISSEN STATE PORCELAIN FACTORY
MORITZBURG
MORITZBURG CASTLE BAROQUE MUSEUM
MÜHLHAUSEN
DISTRICT MUSEUM
MÜLLROSE
REGIONAL MUSEUM
MUTZSCHEN
REGIONAL ROOM
MYLAU
REGIONAL MUSEUM
NERCHAU
REGIONAL ROOM
NEUBRANDENBURG
MUSEUM OF CULTURAL HISTORY
NEUHAUS-SCHIERSCHNITZ
REGIONAL ROOM
NEUKIRCH
REGIONAL MUSEUM
NEUSTADT
REGIONAL MUSEUM
ODERBERG
REGIONAL MUSEUM
OEDERAN
REGIONAL MUSEUM
OELSNITZ
REGIONAL MUSEUM
OHRDRUF
REGIONAL MUSEUM
OLBERNHAU
ALTHAMMER
REGIONAL HOUSE
ORANIENBAUM
DISTRICT MUSEUM
ORANIENBURG
DISTRICT MUSEUM
PERLEBERG
DISTRICT MUSEUM
PIRNA
DISTRICT MUSEUM AND POLYTECHNIC MUSEUM OF ARTIFICIAL SILK
PLAUEN
VOGTLAND DISTRICT MUSEUM
POSTERSTEIN
DISTRICT MUSEUM
QUEDLINBURG
CASTLE MUSEUM
RABENAU
REGIONAL COLLECTION
RIESA
REGIONAL MUSEUM
ROCHLITZ
REGIONAL MUSEUM
RODEWISCH
GÖLTZSCH MUSEUM
ROSTOCK
MUSEUM OF CULTURAL HISTORY
MUSEUM OF SHIP BUILDING
RUDOLSTADT
MUSEUM OF ETHNOLOGY: THURINGIAN PEASANT HOUSES
RUHLA
REGIONAL MUSEUM
SAALFELD
THURINGIA REGIONAL MUSEUM
SALZWEDEL
JOHANN FRIEDRICH DANNEIL MUSEUM
SCHLEUSINGEN
REGIONAL MUSEUM
SCHMALKALDEN
DISTRICT MUSEUM
SCHMÖLLN
REGIONAL MUSEUM
SCHNEEBERG
MUSEUM FOR POPULAR ART OF THE MINING COMMUNITY
SCHÖNBERG
REGIONAL MUSEUM
SCHÖNEBECK
DISTRICT MUSEUM
SCHWARZENBERG
MUSEUM OF THE ERZGEBIRGE IRON INDUSTRY
SCHWERIN
SCHWERIN STATE MUSEUM
SEBNITZ
REGIONAL MUSEUM
SEIFFEN
ERZGEBIRGE TOY MUSEUM
SONNEBERG
GERMAN TOY MUSEUM
STADTILM
REGIONAL MUSEUM
STADT WEHLEN
REGIONAL MUSEUM
STENDAL
WINCKELMANN MEMORIAL MUSEUM
STOLBERG
REGIONAL MUSEUM
STRALSUND
MUSEUM OF CULTURAL HISTORY
STUTZERBACH
GOETHE HOUSE AND GLASS MUSEUM
SUHL
REGIONAL AND WEAPONS MUSEUM
TANGERMÜNDE
REGIONAL MUSEUM
THEMAR
REGIONAL MUSEUM
TORGAU
DISTRICT MUSEUM
UMMENDORF
WANZLEBEN DISTRICT MUSEUM
VELTEN
MUNICIPAL AND CERAMICS MUSEUM
WANDLITZ
REGIONAL MUSEUM
WAREN AN DER MÜRITZ
MÜRITZ MUSEUM
WEIMAR
REGIONAL MUSEUM OF NATURAL HISTORY, HISTORY AND POPULAR ART
WEISSENFELS
MUNICIPAL MUSEUM
WERDAU
REGIONAL MUSEUM
WERNIGERODE
HARZ MUSEUM
WILTHEN
REGIONAL ROOM
WURZEN
DISTRICT MUSEUM
ZEITZ
MUNICIPAL MUSEUM
ZEULENRODA
MUNICIPAL MUSEUM OF INDUSTRIAL ART AND REGIONAL LIFE

GFR

ALTENA
MUSEUM OF THE COUNTY OF MARK, WITH THE GERMAN BLACKSMITH'S MUSEUM AND WIRE MUSEUM
ALTWIEDERMUS
RONNEBURG CASTLE MUSEUM
AMBERG
REGIONAL MUSEUM
BAD HERSFELD
MUNICIPAL MUSEUM
BAD HOMBURG
LOCAL HISTORY AND HAT MUSEUM
BALINGEN
MUSEUM OF WEIGHING EQUIPMENT
REGIONAL MUSEUM
BARMSTEDT
RANTZAU COUNTY MUSEUM
BAYREUTH
COLLECTION OF AGRICULTURAL IMPLEMENTS AND EQUIPMENT
BENEDIKTBEUERN
FRAUNHOFER GLASSWORKS

BENSBERG
TOWN MUSEUM

BERGEN
RÖMSTEDT HOUSE REGIONAL MUSEUM

BEXBACH
REGIONAL AND MINING MUSEUM

BRAUNFELS
PALACE MUSEUM

BRAUNSCHWEIG
COLLECTION OF THE SCHOOL OF DESIGN

BRILON
REGIONAL MUSEUM

BÜDINGEN
HEUSON MUSEUM

BURGAU
REGIONAL MUSEUM

CELLE
BOMANN MUSEUM

CUXHAVEN
CUXHAVEN REGIONAL MUSEUM

DEGGENDORF
REGIONAL MUSEUM

DETMOLD
OPEN AIR MUSEUM

DIESSEN-AM-AMMERSEE
REGIONAL MUSEUM

DREIEICHENHAIN
DREIEICH MUSEUM

DÜSSELDORF
LAND MUSEUM OF THE PEOPLE AND THE ECONOMY
MUSEUM OF THE HISTORY OF DÜSSELDORF

EINBECK
MUNICIPAL MUSEUM

EMMENDINGEN
REGIONAL MUSEUM

ERDING
REGIONAL MUSEUM

ESCHWEGE
REGIONAL MUSEUM

ESSEN
VILLA HÜGEL

EUTIN
DISTRICT MUSEUM

FEUCHTWANGEN
REGIONAL MUSEUM

FREYUNG
WOLFSTEIN DISTRICT MUSEUM

FRITZLAR
FRITZLAR MUSEUM

FÜRSTENFELDBRUCK
REGIONAL MUSEUM

FULDA
VONDERAU MUSEUM

FURTH IM WALD
TOWN TOWER MUSEUM

FÜSSEN
REGIONAL MUSEUM

GARMISCH-PARTENKIRCHEN
WERDENFELSER MUSEUM

GIFHORN
DISTRICT MUSEUM

GLADBECK
GLADBECK TOWN MUSEUM

GLÜCKSTADT
DETLEFSEN MUSEUM

GOSLAR
COLLECTION ILLUSTRATING THE CULTURAL HISTORY OF GERMANY AND EUROPE

GRAFENWÖHR
REGIONAL MUSEUM

GREBENSTEIN
DIEMEL HOUSE AGRICULTURAL MUSEUM

GUNZENHAUSEN
REGIONAL MUSEUM

GÜTERSLOH
REGIONAL MUSEUM

HAGEN
WESTPHALIAN OPEN-AIR MUSEUM OF TECHNICAL MONUMENTS

HAMBURG
VOLKSDORF VILLAGE MUSEUM

HEIDE
MUSEUM OF DITHMARSCHEN PREHISTORY

HEIDENHEIM
REGIONAL MUSEUM

HEINSBERG
REGIONAL MUSEUM

HELMBRECHTS
REGIONAL MUSEUM

HELMSTEDT
DISTRICT MUSEUM

HERRENALB
REGIONAL ROOM

HERSBRUCK
REGIONAL AND HUNTING MUSEUM

HINDELANG
REGIONAL COLLECTION

HÖCHSTADT-AISCH
REGIONAL MUSEUM

HÖCHSTÄDT-DONAU
REGIONAL MUSEUM

HÖHR-GRENZHAUSEN
GRENZAU CASTLE

HUSUM
NISSEN HOUSE
OSTENFELD FARMHOUSE OPEN- AIR MUSEUM

IGGELHEIM
REGIONAL MUSEUM

ILLEBEUREN
FARMHOUSE MUSEUM

ITZEHOE
PRINZESSHOF REGIONAL MUSEUM

KASSEL
RHEINSTAHL-HENSCHEL WORKS MUSEUM

KAUFBEUREN
REGIONAL MUSEUM

KAUFBEUREN-NEUGABLONZ
GABLONZ ARCHIVES AND MUSEUM

KITZINGEN
MUNICIPAL ARCHIVES

KÖLN
MUSEUM OF ARTS AND CRAFTS
MUSEUM OF THE CITY OF COLOGNE

KONSTANZ
ROSGARTEN MUSEUM

KORBACH
KORBACH REGIONAL MUSEUM

KRONACH
FRANKENWALD REGIONAL MUSEUM

KRUMBACH
REGIONAL MUSEUM

KULMBACH-PLASSENBURG
UPPER MAIN REGIONAL MUSEUM

KÜNTZELSAU
REGIONAL MUSEUM

LADBERGEN
REGIONAL MUSEUM

LAGE
LOCAL, REGIONAL AND TILE- MAKING MUSEUM

LANDAU IN DER PFALZ
LANDAU REGIONAL MUSEUM

LANGENAU
REGIONAL MUSEUM

LANGERWEHE
POTTERY MUSEUM

LAUDA
REGIONAL MUSEUM

LAUF AN DER PEGNITZ
MUNICIPAL COLLECTIONS

LAUTERBACH
HOHLHAUS MUSEUM

LEMBRUCK
DÜMMER MUSEUM

LENNGRIES
REGIONAL MUSEUM

LETMATHE
REGIONAL MUSEUM

LEUTKIRCH
REGIONAL MUSEUM

LIESBORN
BECKUM DISTRICT MUSEUM

LIMBURG (LAHN)
REGIONAL MUSEUM

LÖFFINGEN
REGIONAL MUSEUM

LOHR AM MAIN
REGIONAL AND SPESSART MUSEUM

LOSSBURG
BLACK FOREST MUSEUM

LÜNEN
MUSEUM OF ART AND CULTURAL HISTORY OF DORTMUND

MAINBURG
HOLLEDAU REGIONAL MUSEUM

MAINZ
RESEARCH INSTITUTE FOR THE HISTORY OF PAPER

MALENTE-GREMSMÜHLEN
REGIONAL HOUSE

MELLE
GRÖNEGAU MUSEUM

MEMMINGEN
MUNICIPAL MUSEUM

METTINGEN
TÜÖTTEN MUSEUM

MICHELAU
BASKETRY AND WICKERWORK MUSEUM

MICHELSTADT
ODENWALD MUSEUM
REGIONAL MUSEUM

MIESBACH
REGIONAL MUSEUM

MINDELHEIM
MINDELHEIM REGIONAL MUSEUM

MITTENWALD
REGIONAL MUSEUM AND MUSEUM OF VIOLIN MAKING

MÖLLN
REGIONAL MUSEUM

MÖNCHENGLADBACH
MUNICIPAL MUSEUM

MOOSBURG
REGIONAL MUSEUM

MOSBACH
REGIONAL MUSEUM

MÜHLDORF
DISTRICT MUSEUM

MÜLHEIM
MUNICIPAL MUSEUM

MÜNCHBERG
REGIONAL MUSEUM

MÜNCHEN
GERMAN MUSEUM
STATE MUSEUM OF ETHNOGRAPHY
WERNER VON SIEMENS INSTITUTE FOR THE HISTORY OF THE HOUSE OF SIEMENS

MÜNSTER
LAND MUSEUM OF ART AND CULTURAL HISTORY

NEHEIM-HÜSTEN
GERMAN MUSEUM OF BIRDCAGES

NEUENBURG
RAUCHKATE REGIONAL MUSEUM

NEUMÜNSTER
TEXTILE MUSEUM

NEUNHOF
KNOBLAUCHLAND REGIONAL MUSEUM

NEUSTADT AN DER AISCH
MUSEUM OF THE LOCAL HISTORY SOCIETY

NEUSTADT AN RÜBENBERGE
DISTRICT MUSEUM

NEUSTADT (SCHWARZWALD)
REGIONAL ROOMS

NÖRDLINGEN
TOWN MUSEUM

OBERKAUFUNGEN
REGIONAL MUSEUM

OBERNDORF
REGIONAL MUSEUM

OBERNZELL
REGIONAL MUSEUM
OBER-RAMSTADT
REGIONAL MUSEUM
OBERSTDORF
REGIONAL MUSEUM
OFFENBACH
GERMAN MUSEUM OF LEATHER
PASSAU
OBERHAUS MUSEUM
PFAFFENHOFEN
REGIONAL MUSEUM
PFARRKIRCHEN
ROTTAL REGIONAL MUSEUM
PLÖN
PLÖN DISTRICT MUSEUM
RAHDEN
RAHDEN FARM MUSEUM
REMSCHEID
GERMAN TOOL MUSEUM
RENDSBURG
MUSEUM OF ARTISTIC CASTS
REUTLINGEN
REGIONAL MUSEUM
RHEINBACH
GLASS MUSEUM
RINTELN
SCHAUMBURG REGIONAL MUSEUM
ROCKENHAUSEN
NORTH PALATINATE REGIONAL MUSEUM
ROSENHEIM
REGIONAL MUSEUM
ROTH
REGIONAL MUSEUM
ROTHENBURG OB DER TAUBER
MUSEUM OF THE IMPERIAL CITY
ROTTENBURG AM NECKAR
SÜLCHGAU MUSEUM
ROTTHALMÜNSTER
REGIONAL MUSEUM
RUHPOLDING
BARTHOLOMÄUS SCHMUCKER REGIONAL MUSEUM
SAARLOUIS
REGIONAL MUSEUM
ST. PETER-ORDING
EIDERSTEDT REGIONAL MUSEUM
SCHLESWIG
LAND MUSEUM OF SCHLESWIG- HOLSTEIN
SCHLITZ
REGIONAL MUSEUM
SCHLÜCHTERN
MUSEUM OF WOODEN TOOLS AND EQUIPMENT
SCHONGAU
TOWN MUSEUM
SCHÖNINGEN
REGIONAL MUSEUM
SCHWABACH
TOWN MUSEUM
SCHWÄBISCH-GMÜND
SCHWÄBISCH-GMÜND MUSEUM
SCHWENNINGEN
SCHWENNINGEN REGIONAL MUSEUM
SESSLACH
REGIONAL MUSEUM
SINSHEIM
REGIONAL MUSEUM
STUTTGART
WÜRTTEMBERG MUSEUM
TELGTE
MÜNSTERLAND REGIONAL HOUSE
THAINING
REGIONAL HOUSE
TITTMONING
REGIONAL MUSEUM
TRAUNSTEIN
REGIONAL MUSEUM
TRIBERG
REGIONAL MUSEUM
TUTTLINGEN
REGIONAL MUSEUM
UNNA
HELLWEG MUSEUM
UNTERRODACH
FLÖSSER MUSEUM
VELBERT
GERMAN MUSEUM OF LOCKS AND FASTENINGS
VILLINGEN
VILLINGEN MUSEUM
VOHENSTRAUSS
VOHENSTRAUSS REGIONAL MUSEUM
WAIBLINGEN
REGIONAL MUSEUM
WALDERBACH
REGIONAL MUSEUM
WALDSRODE
REGIONAL MUSEUM
WALLDÜRN
REGIONAL AND PILGRIMAGES MUSEUM
WEENER
REGIONAL MUSEUM
WEIDEN
TOWN MUSEUM
WEILBURG
MUNICIPAL AND MINING MUSEUM
WEILHEIM
TOWN MUSEUM
WEISMAIN
REGIONAL MUSEUM
WEISSENBURG
REGIONAL MUSEUM
WEISSENHORN
REGIONAL MUSEUM
WERTINGEN
REGIONAL MUSEUM
WETTELSHEIM
LOCAL COLLECTION
WEWELSBURG
DISTRICT MUSEUM
WINDECK
WINDECK REGIONAL MUSEUM
WOCKLUM
LUISENHÜTTE IRONWORKS MUSEUM
WUNSIEDEL
WUNSIEDEL MUSEUM OF THE FICHTELGEBIRG REGION
ZWIESEL
TOWN MUSEUM

GHANA

ACCRA
DEPARTMENT OF ARCHAEOLOGY

GREAT BRITAIN

BAKEWELL
OLD HOUSE MUSEUM
BASINGSTOKE
WILLIS MUSEUM
BATTLE
BATTLE MUSEUM
BEAMISH
NORTH OF ENGLAND OPEN AIR MUSEUM
BELFAST
ULSTER MUSEUM
BEWDLEY
BEWDLEY MUSEUM
BIBURY
ARLINGTON MILL
BIGGAR
GLADSTONE COURT
BIRMINGHAM
MUSEUM OF SCIENCE AND INDUSTRY
SAREHOLE MILL
BOLTON
HALL I'TH'WOOD MUSEUM
TONGE MOOR TEXTILE MACHINERY MUSEUM
BRADFORD
BRADFORD INDUSTRIAL MUSEUM
BRIDPORT
BRIDPORT MUSEUM AND ART GALLERY
BRISTOL
BRISTOL CITY MUSEUM
G. B. BRITTON AND SONS LIMITED
CARDIFF
NATIONAL MUSEUM OF WALES
ST. FAGANS CASTLE
COALBROOKDALE
MUSEUM OF IRONFOUNDING
CREGNEASH
MANX VILLAGE FOLK MUSEUM
DERBY
MUSEUM OF INDUSTRY AND TECHNOLOGY
DUDLEY
BLACK COUNTRY MUSEUM
DUDLEY MUSEUM AND ART GALLERY
FORT WILLIAM
WEST HIGHLAND MUSEUM
GLOUCESTER
BISHOP HOOPER'S LODGING
GOLCAR
COLNE VALLEY MUSEUM
HAILSHAM
MICHELHAM PRIORY
HALIFAX
BANKFIELD MUSEUM AND ART GALLERY
WEST YORKSHIRE FOLK MUSEUM
HARTLEBURY
WORCESTERSHIRE COUNTY MUSEUM
HAWICK
WILTON LODGE MUSEUM
HIGH WYCOMBE
PARKER-KNOLL LIMITED
HOLLINWOOD
FERRANTI LIMITED
HONITON
HONITON AND ALLHALLOWS PUBLIC MUSEUM
HORSHAM
HORSHAM MUSEUM
HUTTON-LE-HOLE
RYEDALE FOLK MUSEUM
KEIGHLEY
KEIGHLEY ART GALLERY AND MUSEUM
KENDAL
ABBOT HALL MUSEUM OF LAKELAND LIFE AND INDUSTRY
KESWICK
PENCIL MUSEUM
KETTERING
WESTFIELD MUSEUM
KIDDERMINSTER
WORCESTERSHIRE COUNTY MUSEUM
KILBARCHAN
WEAVER'S COTTAGE
KIRKCALDY
INDUSTRIAL MUSEUM
KIRKCALDY MUSEUMS AND ART GALLERY
LEEDS
ABBEY HOUSE MUSEUM
LEEK
CHEDDLETON FLINT MILL
LEICESTER
NEWARKE HOUSES MUSEUM
LEIGH
PENNINGTON HALL MUSEUM AND ART GALLERY
LIVERPOOL
CITY OF LIVERPOOL MUSEUMS
TATE AND LYLE REFINERIES LIMITED
LLANVAPLEY
RURAL CRAFTS MUSEUM
LONDON
SCIENCE MUSEUM
LUTON
LUTON MUSEUM AND ART GALLERY

MANCHESTER
MANCHESTER MUSEUM OF SCIENCE AND TECHNOLOGY
NEWCASTLE-UPON-TYNE
THE BAGPIPE MUSEUM
MUSEUM OF SCIENCE AND ENGINEERING
NEWTOWN
THE ROBERT OWEN MEMORIAL MUSEUM
NORWICH
BRIDEWELL MUSEUM
NOTTINGHAM
INDUSTRIAL MUSEUM
ST. ALBANS
CITY MUSEUM
ST. FAGANS
WELSH FOLK MUSEUM
ST. HELENS
PILKINGTON GLASS MUSEUM
PUBLIC ART GALLERY AND MUSEUM
SHEFFIELD
ABBEYDALE INDUSTRIAL HAMLET
SHEFFIELD CITY MUSEUM
SHEPHERD WHEEL
SHERBORNE
SHERBORNE MUSEUM
STAFFORD
STAFFORD MUSEUM
STICKLEPATH
STICKLEPATH MUSEUM OF RURAL INDUSTRY
STOWMARKET
THE ABBOT'S HALL MUSEUM OF RURAL LIFE OF EAST ANGLIA
STREET
SHOE MUSEUM
SUNDERLAND
GRINDON CLOSE BRANCH MUSEUM
SUNDERLAND CENTRAL MUSEUM AND ART GALLERY
SWANSEA
INDUSTRIAL MUSEUM OF SOUTH WALES
TELFORD
IRONBRIDGE GORGE MUSEUM
WIGAN
WIGAN ART GALLERY AND MUSEUM
WILLENHALL
UNION WORKS
WOLVERHAMPTON
BILSTON MUSEUM AND ART GALLERY
WOODSTOCK
OXFORD CITY AND COUNTY MUSEUM
WORCESTER
THE DYSON PERRINS MUSEUM OF WORCESTER PORCELAIN
YORK
YORK CASTLE MUSEUM
ZENNOR
WAYSIDE MUSEUM

GREECE

ATHENS
BENAKI MUSEUM
NATIONAL HISTORICAL MUSEUM
RESEARCH CENTRE OF GREEK FOLKLORE
CHANIA
HISTORICAL MUSEUM AND CRETAN CORNER
DIMITSANA
GREEK FOLK MUSEUM
HORA
ARCHAEOLOGICAL MUSEUM
IOANNINA
FOLKLORE MUSEUM AND ARCHIVES OF THE IOANNINA FACULTY OF PHILOSOPHY
MAKRYNITSA
D. MAVROS PRIVATE COLLECTION
MYTILINI (MYTILENE)
NATIONAL FOLK MUSEUM OF LESVOS
M. VLACHOS PRIVATE COLLECTION
THESSALONIKI
FOLKLORE MUSEUM AND ARCHIVES
FOLKLORE MUSEUM OF NORTHERN GREECE

HUNGARY

BUDAPEST
HUNGARIAN HOTEL AND CATERING MUSEUM
MUSEUM OF APPLIED ARTS
HEREND
PORCELAIN FACTORY MUSEUM
KALOCSA
KÁROLY VISKI MUSEUM
MEZŐKÖVESD
MATYÓ MUSEUM
MISKOLC-HÁMOR
CENTRAL MUSEUM OF METALLURGY
NAGYVÁZSONY
OPEN-AIR MUSEUM OF ETHNOLOGY
PÁPA
MUSEUM OF INDIGO-DYEING
SZEGED
FERENC MÓRA MUZEUM
SZENDRŐ
SZENDRŐ DYE-HOUSE
TIHANY
OPEN-AIR FOLKLORE MUSEUM
VERPELÉT
BLACKSMITH'S SHOP
VÉRTES
JÁNOS IRINYI MEMORIAL ROOM

INDIA

AGRA
ST. JOHN'S COLLEGE MUSEUM
AHMEDABAD
CALICO MUSEUM OF TEXTILES
BANGALORE
VISVESVARAYA INDUSTRIAL AND TECHNOLOGICAL MUSEUM
BENARES
MUSEUM OF INDIAN ARTS AND ARCHAEOLOGY
BHOPAL
CENTRAL MUSEUM
CALCUTTA
ART IN INDUSTRY MUSEUM
BIRLA INDUSTRIAL AND TECHNOLOGICAL MUSEUM
CRAFTS MUSEUM
GOVERNMENT INDUSTRIAL AND COMMERCIAL MUSEUM
INDIAN MUSEUM
GAUHATI
COMMERCIAL MUSEUM
COTTAGE INDUSTRIES MUSEUM
HARDWAR
GURUKULA MUSEUM
JODHPUR
SARDAR MUSEUM
MADRAS
CENTRAL INDUSTRIAL MUSEUM
VICTORIA TECHNICAL INSTITUTE
NEW DELHI
BHARTIYA ADIM JATI SEVAK SANGH MUSEUM
CRAFTS MUSEUM
SCIENCE MUSEUM
POONA
LORD REAY MAHARASHTRA INDUSTRIAL MUSEUM
MAHATMA PHULE VASTU SANGRAHALAYA
SANTINIKETAN
KALA BHAVAN
SIKAR
SIKAR MUSEUM
SIROHI
STATE MUSEUM
SRINAGAR
S.P.S. MUSEUM
TRICHUR
STATE MUSEUM
TRIVANDRUM
ART MUSEUM
SRI MOOLAM SHASTYABDAPURTI MEMORIAL INSTITUTE MUSEUM
VIJAYAWADA
VICTORIA JUBILEE MUSEUM
WARDHA
MAGAN SANGRAHAYALA

IRAN

TEHERAN
MUSEUM OF DECORATIVE ARTS

IRAQ

BAGHDAD
BAGHDAD GOVERNORATE MUSEUM OF COSTUMES AND ETHNOGRAPHY

IRELAND

DUBLIN
NATIONAL MUSEUM OF IRELAND
GLENCOLUMBKILLE
AN CLACHAN

ISRAEL

TEL-AVIV
MUSEUM "ADAM VA'AMALO"

ITALY

LA FAVORITA
PITRÉ MUSEUM OF SICILIAN ETHNOGRAPHY
MILAN
LEONARDO DA VINCI MUSEUM OF SCIENCE AND TECHNOLOGY
PALERMO
PITRÉ ETHNOGRAPHICAL MUSEUM
ROME
COLLECTION OF THE INSTITUTE OF MERCEOLOGY
TRAPANI
PEPOLI MUSEUM
TRIESTE
HISTORICAL INSURANCE DISPLAY OF THE RIUNIONE ADRIATICA DI SICURTA COMPANY
MERCANTILE MUSEUM

JAMAICA

HALF-WAY TREE
AFRICAN MUSEUM

JAPAN

ABASHIRI-SHI
ABASHIRI MUNICIPAL MUSEUM
AKASHI-SHI
AKASHI CITY PLANETARIUM & SCIENCE HALL
AKITA-SHI
AKITA CITY MUSEUM OF ART
ASAHIKAWA-SHI
ASAHIKAWA LOCAL MUSEUM
FUEDA
ART GALLERY OF THE TOKIWAYAMA FOUNDATION
KOBE-SHI
HAKUTSURU ART MUSEUM
KURASHIKI-SHI
KURASHIKI HANDICRAFT MUSEUM
OHARA ART MUSEUM
KUSHIRO-SHI
KUSHIRO MUNICIPAL MUSEUM

KYOTO
KYOTO MUNICIPAL MUSEUM OF ART
KYOTO SCIENCE AND ENGINEERING INSTITUTE
NATIONAL MUSEUM OF MODERN ART

NARA-SHI
YAMATO CULTURAL HOUSE

NI'IGATA-SHI
NI'IGATA SCIENCE AND TECHNOLOGY MUSEUM

OKAYA-SHI
OKAYA SILK-THREAD MEMORIAL COLLECTION

OSAKA
JAPAN HANDICRAFT MUSEUM
MUNICIPAL MUSEUM

SASEHO-SHI
SASEHO CULTURAL MUSEUM

SAWADA-MACHI
SADO MUSEUM

SHUHO-MACHI
AKIYOSHIDAI MUSEUM OF NATURAL HISTORY

SUWA-SHI
KATAKURA MEMORIAL COLLECTION
SUWA MUNICIPAL MUSEUM OF ART

TAMANO-SHI
TAMANO MARINE MUSEUM

TOKONAME-SHI
TOKÓNAME CHINA-WARE HALL

TOKYO
FIBRE MUSEUM
FOLK MUSEUM OF SETAGAYA
GAS MUSEUM
HACHIOJI CITY MUSEUM
JAPANESE FOLK CRAFT MUSEUM
MEIJI UNIVERSITY MUSEUM OF TRADE AND COMMERCE
MUSEUM OF THE PATENT OFFICE
NATIONAL MUSEUM OF ANTIQUES
NATIONAL MUSEUM OF MODERN ART
NATIONAL SCIENCE MUSEUM
PAPER MUSEUM

TOTTORI-SHI
TOTTORI HANDICRAFT MUSEUM

TSU-SHI
MIE PREFECTURAL MUSEUM

YAMAGUCHI-SHI
YAMAGUCHI PREFECTURAL MUSEUM

YASUKI-SHI
WAKO MEMORIAL HALL

YOKOHAMA
SILK MUSEUM

MALAWI

BLANTYRE
MUSEUM OF MALAWI

MEXICO

ACTOPAN
ACTOPAN MUSEUM OF THE COLONIAL PERIOD

MEXICO CITY
MUSEUM OF RURAL LIFE (CHARRERIA)

PUEBLA
MUSEUM OF HANDICRAFTS

SAN LUIS POTOSI
SAN LUIS POTOSI REGIONAL MUSEUM

TOLUCA
NATIONAL MUSEUM OF FOLK ART

MOROCCO

FEZ
BATHA MUSEUM

MEKMES
DAR JAMAÏ MUSEUM

TANGIER
KASBAH MUSEUM

TETOUAN
TETOUAN MUSEUM

NETHERLANDS

ARNHEM
NATIONAL MUSEUM OF ETHNOLOGY: NETHERLANDS OPEN-AIR MUSEUM

AXEL
AXEL MUSEUM OF RURAL LIFE

BUREN
THE FARM WAGGON

DELFSHAVEN
THE ZAKKENDRAGEN HOUSE

DORDRECHT
MUSEUM OF LIPS' SAFE AND LOCK COMPANY

EDE
OLD EDE

EINDHOVEN
KEMPENLAND MUSEUM

ENSCHEDE
TWENTE AND GELDER TEXTILE MUSEUM

ETTEN-LEUR
JAN OUTEN HOUTE MUSEUM OF LOCAL HISTORY AND FOLKLORE

GELDROP
LOCAL HISTORY MUSEUM

GOIRLE
HET SMISKE MUSEUM OF LOCAL HISTORY

GORREDIJK
'DE ZUID OSTHOCK' MUSEUM OF LOCAL HISTORY AND NATURAL HISTORY

GOUDA
DE MORIAAN PIPE AND POTTERY MUSEUM

HEINENOORD
HOEKSCHE WARD DISTRICT MUSEUM

HELLENDOORN
LOCAL HISTORY MUSEUM

HEUSDEN
HEUSDEN DISTRICT MUSEUM

HOORN
WEST FRISIAN MUSEUM

HULST
'DE VIER AMBACHTEN' LOCAL HISTORY MUSEUM

KOOG AAN DE ZAAN
HET PINK OIL-MILL

KRIMPEN AAN DEN IJSSEL
CRIMPENERHOF DISTRICT MUSEUM

LEENS
OMMELAND MUSEUM OF AGRICULTURE AND HISTORY

LEERDAM
GATEHOUSE MUSEUM

LIEVELDE
KOTS OPEN-AIR MUSEUM

MONNIKENDAM
'T HAVENLAND GOUWZEE MUSEUM

ROSENDAAL
MUSEUM OF THE GOLDEN ROSE

ROTTERDAM
HISTORICAL MUSEUM
PROF. DR. VAN DEN POEL MUSEUM OF TAXATION, DUTY AND EXCISE

TIEL
TIEL AND DISTRICT LOCAL HISTORY MUSEUM

TILBURG
NETHERLANDS TEXTILE MUSEUM

VEENKLOSTER
FOGELSANGH STATE

VLISSINGEN
MUNICIPAL MUSEUM

VRIES
CHURCH MUSEUM AND BELL- FOUNDRY

WAALWIJK
NETHERLANDS MUSEUM OF SHOES, LEATHER AND LEATHER GOODS

ZIERIKZEE
LOCAL MUSEUM

ZWOLLE
PASSION FLOWER MILL

NEW ZEALAND

CHRISTCHURCH
THE FERRYMEAD TRUST

KAITAIA
FAR NORTH REGIONAL MUSEUM

NEW PLYMOUTH
TARANAKI MUSEUM

OBAN
RAKIURA MUSEUM

ROTORUA
MAORI PA

NICARAGUA

NINDIRÍ
ARCHAEOLOGICAL MUSEUM

NIGERIA

KANO
MAKAMA'S HOUSE

NORWAY

AKERSHUS FYLKE
EIDSVOLL WORKS

ARENDAL
MERDØ HOUSE

BERGEN
GAMLE BERGEN (OLD BERGEN)

BODØ
NORDLAND FOLK MUSEUM

BRYNE
ROGALAND FOLK MUSEUM

EGERSUND
DALANE FOLK MUSEUM

KAUPANGER
HEIBERG COLLECTION

KONGSBERG
LÅGDAL MUSEUM

KRISTIANSAND
VEST-AGDER FOLK MUSEUM

LILLEHAMMER
DE SANDVIGSKE SAMLINGER

NAMSOS
NAMDAL MUSEUM

OSLO
NORWEGIAN FOLK MUSEUM
NORWEGIAN SCIENCE AND INDUSTRY MUSEUM

SANDANE
NORDFJORD FOLK MUSEUM

TRONDHEIM
TRONDHEIM AND TRØNDELAG FOLK MUSEUM

PAKISTAN, WEST

LAHORE
INDUSTRIAL AND COMMERCIAL MUSEUM

PESHAWAR
PESHAWAR MUSEUM

PARAGUAY

ASUNCION
EXHIBITION OF NATIONAL PRODUCTS

PERU

LIMA
MUSEUM OF THE PRE-HISPANIC ANTHROPOLOGY AND AGRICULTURE INSTITUTE

POLAND

BYTOM
MUSEUM OF UPPER SILESIA

CHLEWISKA
FOUNDRY MUSEUM
DUSZNIKI ZDRÓJ
MUSEUM OF PAPER-MAKING
GDAŃSK
MUSEUM OF SHIPBUILDING
GLIWICE
GLIWICE MUSEUM
GŁOGOW
REGIONAL MUSEUM
JELENIA GÓRA
REGIONAL MUSEUM
KAMIENNA GÓRA
MUNICIPAL MUSEUM
KLUKI
FARM MUSEUM
KOLBUSZOWA
LASOWIAKOW REGIONAL MUSEUM
KONIAKÓW
LACE MUSEUM
KRAKÓW
MUSEUM OF THE IRON AND STEEL INDUSTRY
KWIDZYN
REGIONAL MUSEUM
LEGNICA
REGIONAL MUSEUM
ŁÓDŹ
ARCHAEOLOGICAL AND ETHNOGRAPHICAL MUSEUM
MUSEUM OF THE HISTORY OF TEXTILES
LUBARTÓW
REGIONAL MUSEUM
LUBLIN
NATIONAL MUSEUM
ŁUKOW
REGIONAL MUSEUM
MALBORK
CASTLE MUSEUM
MALENIEC
HISTORIC IRON-WORKS
OLIWA
FORGE MUSEUM
REGIONAL MUSEUM OF ETHNOGRAPHY
OLSZTYN
OPEN-AIR MUSEUM
OPOLE-BIERKOWICE
OPEN-AIR MUSEUM
OSTROWIEC ŚWIĘLKRZYSKI
REGIONAL MUSEUM
POZNAŃ
H. CEGIELSKI FACTORY MUSEUM
MUSEUM OF RURAL CULTURE AND HANDICRAFTS
PRZEMYŚL
REGIONAL MUSEUM
PUŁKOWO WIELKIE
REGIONAL MUSEUM
RABKA ZDROJ
REGIONAL MUSEUM 'WŁADYSŁAW ORKAN'
RZESZOW
REGIONAL MUSEUM
SAMSANÓW
EARLY BLAST-FURNACE
SANOK
OPEN-AIR MUSEUM
SIELPIA WIELKA
OLD LAKE MUSEUM
SKLARSKA PORĘBA
MUSEUM OF CUT GLASS
SŁAKÓW BOROWY
ŁOWICK MUSEUM OF ART
SŁUPIA NOWA
ANCIENT FOUNDRIES MUSEUM
SŁUPSK
REGIONAL MUSEUM OF ETHNOGRAPHY
SMOLNIK
OPEN-AIR MUSEUM
STARY SĄCZ
ART MUSEUM
SWIDNICA
MUSEUM OF TRADE
TORUŃ
TORUŃ ETHNOGRAPHICAL MUSEUM
URSUS
INDUSTRIAL MUSEUM
WARSAW
MUSEUM OF APPLIED ARTS
MUSEUM OF ARTISTIC AND PRECISION HANDICRAFTS
TECHNICAL MUSEUM
WISŁA-ZDRÓJ
BESKIDZKI MUSEUM
WŁVEŁAWEK
KUJAWSKI MUSEUM
WROCŁAW
ETHNOGRAPHICAL MUSEUM
NATIONAL MUSEUM
ZABRZE
REGIONAL MUSEUM
ZAKOPANE
TATRA MUSEUM AND T. CHAŁUBIŃSKI MEMORIAL
ZBĄSZIN
REGIONAL MUSEUM
ZŁOTÓW
ETHNOGRAPHICAL PARK

PORTUGAL

ILHAVO
CERAMICS MUSEUM
LISBON
FOLK ART MUSEUM
MUSEUM OF POPULAR ART

ROMANIA

BAIA MARE
MARAMUREŞ DISTRICT MUSEUM
BRAN
BRAN CASTLE MUSEUM
BRAŞOV
FORTRESS MUSEUM
BUCHAREST
KARADJA COLLECTION
MUSEUM OF FOLK ART
MARIA AND DR. G. SEVEREANU COLLECTION
VILLAGE MUSEUM
CÎMPULUNG- MOLDOVENESC
MOLDOVENIAN MUSEUM
CLUJ
OPEN-AIR MUSEUM
TRANSYLVANIAN MUSEUM OF ETHNOGRAPHY
CRAIOVA
OLTENIEI MUSEUM
DEVA
DEVA MUSEUM
GHEORGHE GHEORGHIU-DEJ
MUNICIPAL MUSEUM
GOLEŞTI
MUSEUM OF HISTORY AND ETHNOGRAPHY
IAŞI
MOLDAVIAN MUSEUM OF ETHNOLOGY
POLYTECHNIC MUSEUM
LUPŞA
VILLAGE MUSEUM
NĂSĂUD
NĂSĂUD MUSEUM
NEGREŞTI
OPEN-AIR MUSEUM
PLOIEŞTI
HISTORY MUSEUM
RĂDĂUŢI
RĂDĂUŢI MUSEUM OF ETHNOGRAPHY
REŞIŢA
LOCAL MUSEUM
RIMETEA
LOCAL MUSEUM
RIMNICU SARAT
RIMNICU SARAT MUSEUM
SIBIU
OPEN-AIR MUSEUM OF PRE- INDUSTRIAL TECHNOLOGY
SIGHET
SIGHET MUSEUM
TIMIŞOARA
BANAT MUSEUM
TURNU SEVERIN
IRON GATE (PORŢILE DE FIER) MUSEUM
URLAŢI
MUSEUM OF ETHNOGRAPHY

SOUTH AFRICA, REPUBLIC OF

MODDERFONTEIN
MODDERFONTEIN DYNAMITE FACTORY MUSEUM
PAARL
OLD PARSONAGE MUSEUM
PRETORIA
MUSEUM OF SCIENCE AND INDUSTRY
STELLENBOSCH
STELLENBOSCH MUSEUM
SWELLENDAM
DROSTDY MUSEUM

SPAIN

ALCANTARILLA
MUNICIPAL MUSEUM OF ETHNOLOGY
BARCELONA
TECHNICAL MUSEUM
TEXTILE MUSEUM
CAPELLADES
PAPERMILL MUSEUM
MURCIA
PROVINCIAL MUSEUM OF ARCHAEOLOGY
SAN LORENZO DE MORUNYS
MUSEUM OF THE PATRONATO OF VALL DE LORD
SOLSONA
DISTRICT MUSEUM OF ETHNOGRAPHY
VALENCIA
MUSEUM OF THE VALENCIA SILK INDUSTRY
VILLANUEVA Y GELTRU
VICTOR BALAGUER MUSEUM

SWEDEN

BORÅS
BORÅS MUSEUM
BUNGE
BUNGE MUSEUM
ESKILSTUNA
DJURGÅRDEN MUSEUM
GÄVLE
GÄVLE MUSEUM
GÒTEBORG
MUSEUM FOR THE HISTORY OF INDUSTRY
HÄLSINGBORG
TOWN MUSEUM
HÄRNÖSAND
MUSEUM OF CULTURAL HISTORY
JOKKMOKK
JOKKMOKK MUSEUM
JÖNKÖPING
JÖNKÖPING MUSEUM
MUNICIPAL PARK OPEN-AIR MUSEUM
KARLSTAD
VÄRMLAND MUSEUM
KRISTIANSTAD
KRISTIANSTAD MUSEUM
LANDSKRONA
LANDSKRONA MUSEUM
LULEÅ
NORBOTTEN MUSEUM
UDDEN OPEN-AIR MUSEUM
ÖREBRO
ÖREBRO MUSEUM
ÖRNSKÖLDSVIK
ÖRNSKÖLDSVIK MUSEUM

ÖSTERSUND
JÄMTLAND MUSEUM
SÄTER
ÅSGÅRD MUSEUM
SKARA
WEST GÖTLAND MUSEUM
SÖDERHAMN
SÖDERHAMN MUSEUM
STOCKHOLM
SKANSEN
TECHNICAL MUSEUM
SUNDSVALL
SUNDSVALL MUSEUM OF HANDICRAFTS
UPPSALA
UPPLAND MUSEUM
VÄSTERÅS
ALMÄNNA SVENSKA ELEKTRISKA AKTIEBOLAGET (ASEA)
VÄXJÖ
SMÅLAND MUSEUM
YSTAD
FRIARY WITH ST. PETER'S CHURCH

SWITZERLAND

AARBURG
REGIONAL MUSEUM
AESCH BEI BIRMENSDORF
VILLAGE MUSEUM
ALTDORF
URI HISTORICAL MUSEUM
ARBON
HISTORICAL MUSEUM
ATTISWIL
REGIONAL MUSEUM
BASEL
MUSEUM OF SWISS FOLKLORE
PAPER MUSEUM
BOSCO-GURIN
GURIN HOUSE OF THE WAISERS
BULLE
MUSEUM OF THE GRUYÈRE DISTRICT
BURGDORF
HISTORICAL MUSEUM OF THE BURGDORF HALL OF THE KNIGHTS SOCIETY
CEVIO
MUSEUM OF THE VALLEMAGGIA
CHÂTEAU D'OEX
MUSEUM OF THE FORMER PAYS D'ENHAUT AND OF THE AUGUST COTTIER FOUNDATION
CHUR
MUNICIPAL MUSEUM
COFFRANE
AGRICULTURAL MUSEUM
COLOMBIER
MILITARY MUSEUM AND MUSEUM OF PAINTED BLINDS
DIESSENHOFEN
LOCAL MUSEUM
DIETIKON
LOCAL MUSEUM
DORNACH
REGIONAL MUSEUM OF SCHWAZBUBENLAND
ELGG
REGIONAL MUSEUM
ESTAVAYER- LE-LAC
MUSEUM
EVOLÈNE
FOLKLORE MUSEUM
GRINDELWALD
REGIONAL MUSEUM
HALLAU
REGIONAL MUSEUM
HERISAU
MUSEUM
HINWIL
LOCAL MUSEUM
HORGEN
LOCAL MUSEUM
KYBURG-BUCHEGG
BUCHEGGBERGISCHES REGIONAL MUSEUM
LANGNAU IM EMMENTAL
REGIONAL MUSEUM
LAUFEN
LAUFENTAL REGIONAL MUSEUM
LENZBURG
REGIONAL MUSEUM
MONTHEY
OLD MONTHEY MUSEUM
MORGES
ALEXIS FOREL MUSEUM
MOUDON
MUSEUM OF OLD MOUDON
NÄFELS
MUSEUM OF GLARUS CANTON
OLTEN
HISTORICAL MUSEUM
POSCHIAVO
VALLIGIANO POSCHIAVINO MUSEUM
RATZ
LOCAL MUSEUM
REINACH
REGIONAL MUSEUM
RHEINFELDEN
FIRCKTALER MUSEUM
RICKENBACH BEI WINTERTHUR
HANNSELI GRANARY
SAINTE-CROIX
MUSEUM
ST. GALLEN
NEW MUSEUM
SAN VITTORE
MOESANO MUSEUM
SCHAFFHAUSEN
ALL SAINTS' MUSEUM
SCHINZNACH-DORF
REGIONAL MUSEUM
SCHLIEREN
LOCAL MUSEUM
SCHLEITHEIM
GYPSUM MUSEUM
SEENGEN
HALLWIL CASTLE
STECKBORN
UNTERSEE REGIONAL MUSEUM
SUHR
REGIONAL MUSEUM
TRUN/TRUNS
SURSILVAN MUSEUM
UNTERSTAMMHEIM
STAMMHEIMERTAL REGIONAL MUSEUM
VEVEY
MUSEUM OF OLD VEVEY
WÄDENSWIL
LOCAL MUSEUM
WALTENSBURG/VUORZ
ARCUN DA TRADIZIUN
WINTERTHUR
INDUSTRIAL SAFETY EXHIBITION OF THE FEDERAL LABOUR INSPECTORATE
WITTENBACH
LOCAL MUSEUM
WOHLENSCHWIL
PEASANT MUSEUM

TANZANIA

DAR ES SALAAM
VILLAGE MUSEUM

TUNISIA

JERBA
JERBA MUSEUM
MOKNINE
MOKNINE MUSEUM

TURKEY

ANKARA
ETHNOGRAPHICAL MUSEUM
KÜTAHYA
ARCHAEOLOGICAL MUSEUM
PERGAMUM
ETHNOGRAPHY MUSEUM

UGANDA

KAMPALA
UGANDA MUSEUM

USSR

BREST-LITOVSK
REGIONAL MUSEUM OF FOLK ART
CHERNOVTSY
INDUSTRIAL MUSEUM
DNEPROPETROVSK (formerly JEKATERINOSLAV)
MUSEUM OF ART
KHARKOV
HOUSE OF TECHNOLOGY
KIEV
STATE MUSEUM OF POPULAR AND DECORATIVE ART
KIROVSK
HOUSE OF TECHNOLOGY
LENINGRAD
HERMITAGE MUSEUM
HOUSE OF SCIENTIFIC AND TECHNICAL PROPAGANDA
MUSEUM OF PORCELAIN
NATIONAL MUSEUM OF ETHNOGRAPHY OF THE PEOPLES OF THE U.S.S.R.
LVOV
MUSEUM OF ETHNOGRAPHY AND INDUSTRIAL ARTS
MOSCOW
EXHIBITION OF SOVIET ECONOMIC ACHIEVEMENT
MUSEUM OF FOLK ART
MSTERA
MUSEUM OF HANDICRAFTS
NOVOKUZNETZK (formerly STALINSK)
TECHNICAL MUSEUM OF THE METALLURGICAL INDUSTRY
ODESSA
MUSEUM OF WESTERN AND EASTERN ART
PALEKH
MUSEUM OF HANDICRAFTS
RIGA
OPEN-AIR MUSEUM OF ETHNOGRAPHY
TASHKENT
CENTRAL REGIONAL MUSEUM
NATIONAL ART MUSEUM OF UZBEKISTAN
ZAGORSK
METROPOLITAN'S HOUSE MUSEUM

UNITED STATES

AKRON
GOODYEAR RUBBER EXHIBIT
ALAMO
LIVE STEAM MUSEUM
ALLAIRE
ALLAIRE STATE PARK
ALPINE
MUSEUM OF THE BIG BEND
APPLETON
DARD HUNTER PAPER MUSEUM
ARROW ROCK
JOHN SITES GUNSHOP
ATTICA
ATTICA HISTORICAL SOCIETY MUSEUM
AUGUSTA
MACKAY HOUSE
BALTIMORE
MOUNT VERNON MUSEUM OF INCANDESCENT LIGHTING

BEAUMONT
FRENCH TRADING POST MUSEUM

BEREA
WALLACE NUTTING MUSEUM

BUFFALO
MUSEUM OF BUFFALO AND ERIE COUNTY HISTORICAL SOCIETY

CHADRON
MUSEUM OF THE FUR TRADE

CHARLESTON
THOMAS ELFE WORKSHOP

CHEYENNE
BLACK KETTLE MUSEUM

CHICAGO
MUSEUM OF SCIENCE AND INDUSTRY

CLINTON
CLINTON HISTORICAL MUSEUM

COLD SPRING
FOUNDRY SCHOOL MUSEUM

CORNING
CORNING MUSEUM OF GLASS AND CORNING GLASS CENTER

CORNWALL
CORNWALL FURNACE

DALTON
CRANE MUSEUM

DANBURY
DANBURY SCOTT-FANTON MUSEUM

DAYTON
DAYTON POWER AND LIGHT COMPANY MUSEUM

DEARBORN
GREENFIELD VILLAGE AND HENRY FORD MUSEUM

DEATH VALLEY
DEATH VALLEY MUSEUM

DOVER-FOXCROFT
BLACKSMITH SHOP MUSEUM

DOYLESTOWN
MERCER MUSEUM

DRESDEN
INGERSOLL MEMORIAL HOUSE

EAST AURORA
ELBERT HUBBARD LIBRARY MUSEUM

ELVERSON
HOPEWELL VILLAGE

ESSEX
ESSEX HISTORICAL SOCIETY MUSEUM

EVERGREEN
BELLS OF GRANITE GLEN MUSEUM

FAYETTE
FAYETTE STATE PARK

GLOUCESTER
BABSON HISTORICAL ASSOCIATION

GREENBUSH
OLD WADE HOUSE

HAMMONTON
BATSO VILLAGE

HARPERS FERRY
HARPERS FERRY NATIONAL HISTORICAL PARK

HARRODSBURG
SHAKERTOWN

HARTFORD
SLOANE-STANLEY MUSEUM AND KENT FURNACE

HIGH POINT
JOHN HALEY HOUSE
HIGH POINT HISTORICAL SOCIETY MUSEUM

HOPEDALE
LITTLE RED SHOP

ISLE DE LA MOTTE
MUSEUM OF ISLE DE LA MOTTE HISTORICAL SOCIETY

JACKSON
BUCKEYE FURNACE

KATAHDIN
KATAHDIN IRON WORKS

LAWSON
WATKINS WOOLLEN MILL

LOS ANGELES
CALIFORNIA MUSEUM OF SCIENCE AND INDUSTRY

LOUISVILLE
MUSEUM OF SCIENCE AND HISTORY

MANSFIELD
FISHER-RICHARDSON HOUSE OF THE MANSFIELD HISTORICAL SOCIETY

MIDDLESBORO
MUSEUM OF CUMBERLAND GAP NATIONAL HISTORICAL PARK

MILLVILLE
WHEATON HISTORICAL ASSOCIATION MUSEUM

NEWTON
CATAWBA COUNTY HISTORICAL MUSEUM

NEW YORK
JUNIOR MUSEUM OF THE METROPOLITAN MUSEUM OF ART
MUSEUM OF CONTEMPORARY CRAFTS
RATSEY MUSEUM

NORTH ANDOVER
MERRIMACK VALLEY TEXTILE MUSEUM

OTTUMWA
WAPELLO COUNTY HISTORICAL MUSEUM

PAWTUCKET
OLD SLATER MILL MUSEUM

PHOENIX
PIONEER ARIZONA

ST. JAMES
MARAMEC MUSEUM

ST. PAUL
MINNESOTA MUSEUM OF ART

SANDWICH
SANDWICH GLASS MUSEUM

SAUGUS
"SCOTCH" BOARDMAN HOUSE
SAUGUS IRON WORKS NATIONAL HISTORIC SITE

SEAGROVE
POTTERS MUSEUM

SOUTHAMPTON
ELIAS PELLETREAU SILVERSMITH SHOP

TOLEDO
TOLEDO-LUCAS COUNTY PUBLIC LIBRARY

WASHINGTON
NATIONAL MUSEUM OF HISTORY AND TECHNOLOGY
RENWICK GALLERY

WATERLOO
MUSEUM OF HISTORY AND SCIENCE

WATER MILL
OLD WATER MILL MUSEUM

WILLIAMSBURG
COLONIAL WILLIAMSBURG

WILMINGTON
HAGLEY MUSEUM

WILTON
CRAFT CENTER MUSEUM

WINDSOR
AMERICAN PRECISION MUSEUM

WINSTON-SALEM
MIKSCH TOBACCO SHOP
JOHN VOGLER HOUSE

ZOAR
ZOAR STATE MEMORIAL

VENEZUELA

CIUDAD BOLIVÁR
TALAVERA MUSEUM

VIETNAM, DEMOCRATIC REPUBLIC OF

HANOI
HISTORICAL MUSEUM

YUGOSLAVIA

BELGRADE
ETHNOGRAPHICAL MUSEUM

CETINJE
ETHNOGRAPHICAL MUSEUM

DUBROVNIK
ETHNOGRAPHICAL MUSEUM

KROPA
LOCAL MUSEUM

SKOFJA LOKA
MUSEUM

SPLIT
ETHNOGRAPHICAL MUSEUM

ZADAR
ETHNOGRAPHICAL MUSEUM

ZAGREB
ETHNOGRAPHICAL MUSEUM

ZAMBIA

LIVINGSTONE
OPEN-AIR MUSEUM

Engineering, technology

ARGENTINA

BUENOS AIRES
MUSEUM OF TECHNOLOGY

AUSTRALIA

COBAR
COBAR PASTORAL, MINING AND TECHNOLOGICAL MUSEUM

FORTITUDE VALLEY
QUEENSLAND MUSEUM

GOULBURN
MUSEUM OF APPLIED ARTS AND SCIENCES
MUSEUM OF HISTORIC ENGINES

MELBOURNE
SCIENCE MUSEUM OF VICTORIA

PERTH
WESTERN AUSTRALIAN MUSEUM

SYDNEY
MUSEUM OF APPLIED ARTS AND SCIENCES

AUSTRIA

BADEN
EMPEROR FRANZ JOSEPH MUSEUM

KUFSTEIN
REGIONAL MUSEUM

MAUTHAUSEN
REGIONAL MUSEUM

MURZZUSCHLAG
WINTER SPORTS AND REGIONAL MUSEUM

VIENNA
MUSEUM OF INDUSTRY AND TECHNOLOGY

BULGARIA

SOFIA
NATIONAL POLYTECHNIC MUSEUM

CANADA

CORNWALL
UNITED COUNTIES MUSEUM

FORT WILLIAM
FOUNDERS MUSEUM
GODERICH
HURON COUNTY PIONEER MUSEUM
KINGSTON
PUMP HOUSE AND STEAM MUSEUM
NIAGARA FALLS
HYDRO HALL OF MEMORY
OTTAWA
MUSEUM OF NATIONAL HISTORIC SITES SERVICE
NATIONAL MUSEUM OF SCIENCE AND TECHNOLOGY
ROCANVILLE
ROCANVILLE AND DISTRICT MUSEUM
TORONTO
ONTARIO SCIENCE CENTRE

CHINA, P.R.

GUAN XIAN
DAM MUSEUM
TIENSIN (TIANJING)
PEOPLE'S HALL OF SCIENCE

CZECHOSLOVAKIA

BRNO
TECHNICAL MUSEUM
KOPŘIVNICE
TECHNICAL MUSEUM
KOŠICE
TECHNICAL MUSEUM
PRAGUE
NATIONAL TECHNICAL MUSEUM

DENMARK

HELSINGØR
DANISH TECHNICAL MUSEUM
HØJBY SJ.
STENSTRUP MUSEUM

EGYPT, ARAB REPUBLIC OF

CAIRO
SCIENCE MUSEUM

FRANCE

LYON
SEWING MACHINE MUSEUM
MEUDON
MEUDON MUSEUM
PARIS
NATIONAL CONSERVATORY OF ARTS AND CRAFTS
NATIONAL TECHNICAL MUSEUM
PALACE OF DISCOVERY

GDR

BAUTZEN
OLD WATERWORKS TECHNICAL MUSEUM
DRESDEN
INSTITUTE OF PRECISION INSTRUMENT-MAKING OF THE TECHNICAL UNIVERSITY OF DRESDEN
POLYTECHNIC MUSEUM
EIBENSTOCK
MUNICIPAL EXHIBITION OF REGIONAL LIFE
FROHNAU
FROHNAU FORGE
JENA
OPTICAL MUSEUM
LAUSCHA
GLASS MUSEUM
MAGDEBURG
MUSEUM OF CULTURAL HISTORY
OLBERNHAU
ALTHAMMER
ORANIENBAUM
DISTRICT MUSEUM
PLAUEN
VOGTLAND DISTRICT MUSEUM
STUTZERBACH
GOETHE HOUSE AND GLASS MUSEUM
ZIEGENRÜCK
MUSEUM OF WATER-POWER

GFR

BERLIN
GERMAN CARBURETTOR MUSEUM
ESSEN
VILLA HÜGEL
HAGEN
WESTPHALIAN OPEN-AIR MUSEUM OF TECHNICAL MONUMENTS
MÜNCHEN
GERMAN MUSEUM
WERNER VON SIEMENS INSTITUTE FOR THE HISTORY OF THE HOUSE OF SIEMENS
NEHEIM-HÜSTEN
LIGHTING MUSEUM
WOCKLUM
LUISENHÜTTE IRONWORKS MUSEUM

GHANA

ACCRA
MUSEUM OF SCIENCE AND TECHNOLOGY

GREAT BRITAIN

BIRMINGHAM
MUSEUM OF SCIENCE AND INDUSTRY
BRADFORD
BRADFORD INDUSTRIAL MUSEUM
BRISTOL
BRISTOL CITY MUSEUM
BRISTOL WATERWORKS COMPANY
CARDIFF
NATIONAL MUSEUM OF WALES
DARLINGTON
DARLINGTON MUSEUM
DURSLEY
R. A. LISTER AND COMPANY LIMITED
ECCLES
MONKS HALL MUSEUM
EDINBURGH
ROYAL SCOTTISH MUSEUM
GREENOCK
GREENOCK MUSEUM AND ART GALLERY
HOLLINWOOD
FERRANTI LIMITED
HULL
HULL CORPORATION WATER DEPARTMENT
KINGSBRIDGE
WILLIAM COOKWORTHY MUSEUM
LINCOLN
MUSEUM OF LINCOLNSHIRE LIFE
LLANBERIS
NORTH WALES QUARRYING MUSEUM
LONDON
SCIENCE MUSEUM
MANCHESTER
MANCHESTER MUSEUM OF SCIENCE AND TECHNOLOGY
NEWCASTLE- UPON-TYNE
MUSEUM OF SCIENCE AND ENGINEERING
NEWPORT
CARISBROOKE CASTLE MUSEUM
NORWICH
BRIDEWELL MUSEUM
LAWRENCE SCOTT AND ELECTROMOTORS LIMITED
PORTSMOUTH
NEW BEAM ENGINE HOUSE
RYHOPE
RYHOPE PUMPING STATION AND MUSEUM
SHREWSBURY
COLEHAM PUMPING STATION

HUNGARY

BUDAPEST
MUSEUM OF THE HISTORY OF BUDAPEST: DEPARTMENT OF MODERN HISTORY

INDIA

BANGALORE
VISVESVARAYA INDUSTRIAL AND TECHNOLOGICAL MUSEUM
CALCUTTA
BIRLA INDUSTRIAL AND TECHNOLOGICAL MUSEUM
MADRAS
MUSEUM OF THE COLLEGE OF ENGINEERING
NEW DELHI
ENGINEERING MUSEUM
SCIENCE MUSEUM
PILANI
CENTRAL MUSEUM

IRELAND

DUBLIN
EGESTORFF COLLECTION
MAYNOOTH
MUSEUM OF ECCLESIOLOGY AND PHYSICS
STRADBALLY
STRADBALLY STEAM MUSEUM

ITALY

COMO
VOLTA MUSEUM
MILAN
LEONARDO DA VINCI MUSEUM OF SCIENCE AND TECHNOLOGY
TRIESTE
TECHNICAL MUSEUM
VINCI
VINCIANO MUSEUM

JAPAN

AKASHI-SHI
AKASHI CITY PLANETARIUM & SCIENCE HALL
KYOTO
KYOTO BOARD OF EDUCATION SCIENCE ROOM
KYOTO SCIENCE AND ENGINEERING INSTITUTE
MITO-SHI
IBARAKI PREFECTURAL MUSEUM OF ATOMIC ENERGY
OSAKA
ELECTRIC SCIENCE MUSEUM
SAGAMIKO-MACHI
SAGAMIKO ELECTRIC SCIENCE MUSEUM
TOKUSHIMA-SHI
ATTACHED SCIENCE ROOM FOR CHILDREN OF TOKUSHIMA LIBRARY
TOKYO
GAS MUSEUM
NATIONAL SCIENCE MUSEUM
SCIENCE MUSEUM
TOKYO DENRYOKU IKEBUKURO SERVICE CENTRE WITH HISTORICAL MATERIALS OF ELECTRIC ENTERPRISE
YASUKI-SHI
WAKO MEMORIAL HALL

KUWAIT

KUWAIT
KUWAIT MUSEUM

MEXICO

MERIDA
ARCHAEOLOGICAL MUSEUM

NETHERLANDS

AMSTERDAM
NETHERLANDS INSTITUTE OF SCIENCE AND TECHNOLOGY
EINDHOVEN
EVOLUON
HAELEN
VISITOR CENTRE AT THE ST. URSULA MILL, LEUDAL
KAMPERZEEDIJK
MASTENBROEK STEAM-ENGINE
NIEUW- VOSSEMEER
ASSUMBURG MILL MUSEUM
VIJFHUIZEN
CRUQUIUS MUSEUM

NEW ZEALAND

AUCKLAND
MUSEUM OF TRANSPORT AND TECHNOLOGY
CHRISTCHURCH
THE FERRYMEAD TRUST
DUNEDIN
OTAGO MUSEUM

NORWAY

OSLO
NORWEGIAN SCIENCE AND INDUSTRY MUSEUM

PHILIPPINES

DUMAGUETE CITY
SILLIMAN UNIVERSITY CULTURAL RESEARCH CENTRE

POLAND

OLIWA
FORGE MUSEUM
WARSAW
TECHNICAL MUSEUM
WATER-SUPPLY MUSEUM

ROMANIA

BICAZ
BICAZ MUSEUM
BUCHAREST
ING. D. LEONIDA MUSEUM OF THE CENTRE FOR TECHNICAL DOCUMENTATION
IAŞI
POLYTECHNIC MUSEUM

SOUTH AFRICA, REPUBLIC OF

PRETORIA
MUSEUM OF SCIENCE AND INDUSTRY

SPAIN

BARCELONA
TECHNICAL MUSEUM

SWEDEN

HUSKVARNA
HUSKVARNA MUSEUM
NORRKÖPING
FÄRGAR HOUSE
STOCKHOLM
TECHNICAL MUSEUM

SWITZERLAND

STECKBORN
MUSEUM OF SEWING MACHINES
WINTERTHUR
SWISS TECHNORAMA

USSR

KHARKOV
HOUSE OF TECHNOLOGY
KIROVSK
HOUSE OF TECHNOLOGY
LENINGRAD
HOUSE OF SCIENTIFIC AND TECHNICAL PROPAGANDA
MOSCOW
PERMANENT EXHIBITION OF THE SOVIET CONSTRUCTION INDUSTRY
POLYTECHNICAL MUSEUM
NOVOKUZNETZK (formerly STALINSK)
TECHNICAL MUSEUM OF THE METALLURGICAL INDUSTRY
SVERDLOVSK
HOUSE OF TECHNOLOGY

UNITED STATES

BRIDGE HAMPTON
CORWITH HOMESTEAD
CHICAGO
MUSEUM OF SCIENCE AND INDUSTRY
CODY
BUFFALO BILL HISTORICAL CENTER
DEARBORN
GREENFIELD VILLAGE AND HENRY FORD MUSEUM
DES MOINES
DES MOINES CENTER OF SCIENCE AND INDUSTRY
DOVER
WARTHER MUSEUM
EXTON
THOMAS NEWCOMEN MEMORIAL LIBRARY AND MUSEUM
FOLSOM
FOLSOM POWERHOUSE
IRONVILLE
PENFIELD HOMESTEAD MUSEUM
LOS ANGELES
CALIFORNIA MUSEUM OF SCIENCE AND INDUSTRY
MENLO PARK
EDISON MEMORIAL TOWER AND STATE PARK
NEW BRUNSWICK
DELAPLAINE ELECTRICAL MUSEUM
SAN FRANCISCO
EXPLORATORIUM
SCHENECTADY
MUSEUM OF SCHENECTADY COUNTY HISTORICAL SOCIETY
TROY
RENSSELAER POLYTECHNIC INSTITUTE
WASHINGTON
NATIONAL MUSEUM OF HISTORY AND TECHNOLOGY
WEST ORANGE
EDISON NATIONAL HISTORIC SITE

YUGOSLAVIA

ZAGREB
TECHNICAL MUSEUM

Transport

ARGENTINA

LÚJAN
TRANSPORT MUSEUM
ENRIQUE UDSONDO MUSEUM OF HISTORY AND THE COLONIAL PERIOD
QUILMES
MUSEUM OF THE HISTORY OF TRANSPORT

AUSTRALIA

ADELAIDE
RAILWAY MUSEUM
BENDIGO
COBB & COMPANY HISTORICAL FOLK MUSEUM
BRIGHT
BRIGHT AND DISTRICT HISTORICAL SOCIETY MUSEUM
BRISBANE
EARLY STREET
REDBANK RAILWAY MUSEUM
REDLANDS MUSEUM
CANBERRA
BILLABONG PARK HORSE ERA MUSEUM
COOLANGATTA
VINTAGE AND VETERAN CAR MUSEUM
FRANKSTON
BALLAM PARK HOMESTEAD AND HISTORICAL MUSEUM
GOULBURN
MUSEUM OF APPLIED ARTS AND SCIENCES
ILFRACOMBE
ILFRACOMBE FOLK MUSEUM
KEMPSEY
GILL'S BOTTLE MUSEUM
KIRRA
GILLTRAP'S AUTO MUSEUM
KYNETON
KYNETON HISTORICAL MUSEUM
LITTLEHAMPTON
BADERLOO COACH AND RAILWAY MUSEUM
LOFTUS
TRAMWAY MUSEUM
MANNUM
MARION PADDLEWHEEL MUSEUM
MELBOURNE
RAILWAY MUSEUM
SCIENCE MUSEUM OF VICTORIA
TRAMWAY MUSEUM SOCIETY OF VICTORIA LTD.
PARRAMATTA
STEAM TRAM AND RAILWAY MUSEUM
PERTH
VINTAGE CAR MUSEUM
ST. KILDA
ELECTRICAL TRANSPORT MUSEUM
SWAN HILL
SWAN HILL FOLK MUSEUM
SYDNEY
RAIL TRANSPORT MUSEUM
TOOWOOMBA
COBB & COMPANY AUSTRALIAN MUSEUM
WATSON'S BAY
BRONKS MOTOR MUSEUM

AUSTRIA

BAD WIMSBACH- NEYDHARTING
TRANSPORT MUSEUM
DEUTSCH WAGRAM
REGIONAL MUSEUM

LINZ
UPPER AUSTRIA PROVINCIAL MUSEUM
MONDSEE
REGIONAL MUSEUM
MOOSHAM
PALACE COLLECTIONS
OBERNDORF
REGIONAL MUSEUM
PETRONELL
DANUBE MUSEUM
SALZBURG
MUSEUM OF ETHNOLOGY
SPITTAL
MUSEUM OF LOCAL LIFE
SPITZ
MUSEUM OF NAVIGATION
STADL-PAURA
MUSEUM OF SHIPPING
VIENNA
AUSTRIAN MUSEUM OF ETHNOLOGY
AUSTRIAN RAILWAY MUSEUM
COLLECTION OF HISTORIC CARRIAGES
FLORISDORF DISTRICT MUSEUM
MUSEUM OF HARNESS AND SADDLERY
MUSEUM OF THE HISTORY OF ART: MUSEUM OF AUSTRIAN CULTURE
MUSEUM OF HORSE-DRAWN CABS

BELGIUM

BRUSSELS
BELGIAN RAILWAYS MUSEUM
TRAMWAY MUSEUM
VEHICLE MUSEUM
HOUTHALEN
PROVINCIAL AUTOMUSEUM

BERMUDA

ST. GEORGE'S
THE CARRIAGE MUSEUM

BRAZIL

CAMPINAS
RAILWAY MUSEUM
FRANCA
HISTORICAL MUSEUM
JOINVILLE
NATIONAL MUSEUM OF IMMIGRATION AND COLONISATION
PARAIBUNA
PARAIBUNA MUSEUM OF ROAD TRANSPORT
PÔRTO VELHO
HISTORICAL MUSEUM OF THE MADEIRA-MAMORÉ RAILWAY
RIO DE JANEIRO
MUSEUM OF THE AUTOMOBILE

BULGARIA

SOFIA
NATIONAL POLYTECHNIC MUSEUM

CANADA

BONSHAW
CAR LIFE MUSEUM
EAR FALLS
EAR FALLS HISTORICAL MUSEUM
EDMUNTON
AUTOS OF YESTERYEAR MUSEUM
ELKHORN
MANITOBA AUTOMOBILE MUSEUM
KAMLOOPS
FORT KAMLOOPS
MONTREAL
CANADA RAILWAY MUSEUM
NEW WESTMINSTER
ANTIQUE AUTO MUSEUM
OSHAWA
CANADIAN AUTOMOTIVE MUSEUM
OTTAWA
BYTOWN MUSEUM
ST. CATHERINES
ST. CATHERINES HISTORICAL MUSEUM
ST. CONSTANT
CANADIAN RAILWAY MUSEUM
SARNIA
BAYVIEW RAILROAD MUSEUM
SASKATOON
WESTERN DEVELOPMENT MUSEUM
STANSTEAD
BARN MUSEUM
STRATFORD
MINNIE THOMSON MEMORIAL MUSEUM

CHINA, P.R.

SUCHOW (SU ZHOU)
HISTORY MUSEUM

CZECHOSLOVAKIA

PRAGUE
NATIONAL TECHNICAL MUSEUM
SLATIŇANY
MUSEUM OF THE HORSE
STUDÉNKA
CARRIAGE MUSEUM

DENMARK

COPENHAGEN
RAILWAY MUSEUM
HELSINGØR
DANISH TECHNICAL MUSEUM

EGYPT, ARAB REPUBLIC OF

CAIRO
STATE RAILWAYS MUSEUM

FINLAND

HELSINKI
RAILWAY MUSEUM
LAMONI
LOCAL MUSEUM

FRANCE

AMBOISE
POSTAL MUSEUM
BARENTIN
MUNICIPAL MUSEUM
BOUGES-LE-CHÂTEAU
COLLECTION OF CARRIAGES AND HARNESS
CHALON-SUR-SAÔNE
DENON MUSEUM
CLÈRES
MOTOR MUSEUM
COMPIÈGNE
NATIONAL MUSEUM OF ROAD TRANSPORT AND TOURISM
CONFLANS- SAINTE-HONORINE
MUSEUM OF WATER TRANSPORT
COSNE-SUR-LOIRE
MUNICIPAL MUSEUM
LYON
BERLIET MUSEUM
FRENCH MOTOR MUSEUM
LE MANS
AUTOMOBILE MUSEUM
MARTIGUES
MUSEUM OF OLD MARTIGUES
MULHOUSE
RAILWAY MUSEUM
PARIS
HERMES MUSEUM
MUSEUM OF URBAN, INTERURBAN AND RURAL TRANSPORT
NATIONAL MUSEUM OF ROAD TRANSPORT AND TOURISM
NATIONAL TECHNICAL MUSEUM
PITHIVIERS
TRANSPORT MUSEUM
RENNES
AUTOMOBILE MUSEUM OF BRITTANY
RIQUEWIHR
REGIONAL POSTAL AND TELECOMMUNICATIONS MUSEUM
LA ROCHE-TAILLÉE
AUTOMOBILE MUSEUM
SAINT- RAMBERT-SUR-LOIRE
SAINT-RAMBERT-SUR-LOIRE MUSEUM
SCEAUX
ILE-DE-FRANCE MUSEUM
SERRIÈRES
MUSEUM OF RHÔNE SHIPPING
TOURNON-SUR-RHÔNE
RHÔNE MUSEUM
UZÈS
DI RODO MUSEUM
VERSAILLES
MUSEUM OF HORSE-DRAWN VEHICLES
VILLESAVIN
COLLECTION OF HORSE-DRAWN VEHICLES

GDR

AKEN
REGIONAL MUSEUM
ARNEBURG
REGIONAL MUSEUM
AUGUSTUSBURG
GERMAN TWO-STROKE MOTOR CYCLE MUSEUM
BAD SCHANDAU
REGIONAL MUSEUM
DÖMITZ
REGIONAL MUSEUM
DRESDEN
TRANSPORT MUSEUM
MORITZBURG
MORITZBURG CASTLE BAROQUE MUSEUM
ODERBERG
REGIONAL MUSEUM
ORANIENBURG
DISTRICT MUSEUM
PEGAU
REGIONAL MUSEUM
PREROW
DARSS REGIONAL MUSEUM
RIBNITZ-DAMGARTEN
DISTRICT MUSEUM
RIESA
REGIONAL MUSEUM
ROSTOCK
SHIPPING MUSEUM
ROSTOCK-WARNEMÜNDE
WARNEMÜNDE REGIONAL MUSEUM
RUDOLSTADT
HEIDECKSBURG STATE MUSEUM
SCHÖNEBECK
DISTRICT MUSEUM
STADT WEHLEN
REGIONAL MUSEUM

STRALSUND
MUSEUM OF CULTURAL HISTORY
TANGERMÜNDE
REGIONAL MUSEUM
WEIMAR
ORANGERY
WITTENBERGE
REGIONAL MUSEUM
ZINGST
REGIONAL HOUSE

GFR

BERLIN
BERLIN TRANSPORT MUSEUM
BRAKE
MUSEUM OF SHIPPING AND NAVIGATION OF THE OLDENBURG RIVER PORTS
DARMSTADT
PALACE MUSEUM
FRANKFURT
MODEL RAILWAY MUSEUM
HAMBURG
MUSEUM OF THE HISTORY OF HAMBURG
HEIDENHEIM
REGIONAL MUSEUM
KOBLENZ
POSTAL MUSEUM OF THE MIDDLE RHINE
RHINE MUSEUM
LAUENBURG
ELBE SHIPPING MUSEUM
LÜDENSCHEID
MUNICIPAL MUSEUM
MINDEN
MINDEN TOWN LOCKS EXHIBITION HALL
MÜHLDORF
DISTRICT MUSEUM
MÜNCHEN
BMW MUSEUM
GERMAN MUSEUM
ROYAL STABLES
NECKARSULM
GERMAN BICYCLE MUSEUM
NÜRNBERG
NÜRNBERG MUSEUM OF TRANSPORT
REGENSBURG
STABLES MUSEUM OF THE PRINCES OF THURN AND TAXIS
SAARLOUIS
REGIONAL MUSEUM
SIGMARINGEN
HOHENZOLLERN MUSEUM
STUTTGART
DAIMLER BENZ MUSEUM
TREMSBÜTTEL
HILLERS MUSEUM OF AUTOMOBILES
TRIBERG
REGIONAL MUSEUM
VERDEN
GERMAN MUSEUM OF THE HORSE
WEILBURG
MUNICIPAL AND MINING MUSEUM

GREAT BRITAIN

BANGOR
PENRHYN CASTLE
BEAULIEU
NATIONAL MOTOR MUSEUM
BECKINGTON
THE MIN LEWIS PERAMBULATOR MUSEUM
BELFAST
TRANSPORT MUSEUM
ULSTER MUSEUM
BRADFORD
BRADFORD INDUSTRIAL MUSEUM
BRENTFORD
LONDON TRANSPORT COLLECTION OF HISTORIC VEHICLES
BRISTOL
BRISTOL CITY MUSEUM
BURY
BURY TRANSPORT MUSEUM
CHEDDAR
CHEDDAR MOTOR AND TRANSPORT MUSEUM
CHIPPING SODBURY
DODINGTON HOUSE
CORRIS
CORRIS RAILWAY MUSEUM
CRICH
TRAMWAY MUSEUM
DERBY
DERBY MUSEUM AND ART GALLERY
DUDLEY
BLACK COUNTRY MUSEUM
EDINBURGH
TRANSPORT MUSEUM
FALKIRK
SCOTTISH RAILWAY PRESERVATION COLLECTION
GLASGOW
MUSEUM OF TRANSPORT
GREAT YARMOUTH
CAISTER CASTLE
HARTLEBURY
WORCESTERSHIRE COUNTY MUSEUM
HULL
TRANSPORT AND ARCHAEOLOGY MUSEUM
KIDDERMINSTER
WORCESTERSHIRE COUNTY MUSEUM
KIRKCALDY
KIRKCALDY MUSEUMS AND ART GALLERY
LEICESTER
BELGRAVE HALL
MUSEUM OF TECHNOLOGY
RAILWAY MUSEUM
LINGFIELD
PUTTENDEN MANOR
LIVERPOOL
CITY OF LIVERPOOL MUSEUMS
LLANDRINDOD WELLS
AUTOMOBILE PALACE VETERAN CYCLE COLLECTION
LONDON
GUNNERSBURY PARK MUSEUM
MUSEUM OF BRITISH TRANSPORT
ROYAL MEWS
SCIENCE MUSEUM
LOWESTOFT
EAST ANGLIA TRANSPORT MUSEUM
LUTON
VAUXHALL MOTORS LIMITED
MANCHESTER
MANCHESTER SHIP CANAL COMPANY MUSEUM
NORWICH
BRIDEWELL MUSEUM
NOTTINGHAM
NOTTINGHAM CITY MUSEUM AND ART GALLERY
OLD WARDEN
THE SHUTTLEWORTH COLLECTION
PEMBROKE DOCK
PEMBROKESHIRE MOTOR MUSEUM
PORTHMADOG
FESTINIOG RAILWAY MUSEUM
RUGBY
STANFORD HALL
RUGELEY
BLITHFIELD HALL
SANDRINGHAM
THE SANDRINGHAM ESTATE MUSEUM
SANDTOFT
SANDTOFT TRANSPORT CENTRE
SCARBOROUGH
SCARBOROUGH MUSEUM OF LOCAL HISTORY AND BYGONES
SHUGBOROUGH
STAFFORDSHIRE COUNTY MUSEUM AND MANSION HOUSE
STOKE BRUERNE
WATERWAYS MUSEUM
SUNDERLAND
MONKWEARMOUTH STATION MUSEUM
SWANSEA
INDUSTRIAL MUSEUM OF SOUTH WALES
SWINDON
GREAT WESTERN RAILWAY MUSEUM
TEESSIDE
STOCKTON AND DARLINGTON RAILWAY MUSEUM
TELFORD
IRONBRIDGE GORGE MUSEUM
TYWYN
NARROW GAUGE RAILWAY MUSEUM
WAKEFIELD
NOSTELL PRIORY
YORK
RAILWAY MUSEUM

HUNGARY

BUDAPEST
HUNGARIAN TRANSPORT MUSEUM

INDIA

BANGALORE
VISVESVARAYA INDUSTRIAL AND TECHNOLOGICAL MUSEUM
CALCUTTA
BIRLA INDUSTRIAL AND TECHNOLOGICAL MUSEUM
PILANI
CENTRAL MUSEUM

IRELAND

ASHFORD
MOUNT USHER MUSEUM
CELBRIDGE
CELBRIDGE MOTOR MUSEUM

ITALY

DOMODOSSOLA
SIMPLON MUSEUM
FLORENCE
COLLECTION OF CARRIAGES
MASER
CAR MUSEUM
MILAN
LEONARDO DA VINCI MUSEUM OF SCIENCE AND TECHNOLOGY
ROME
MUSEUM OF THE ROAD TO OSTIA
MUSEUM OF TRANSPORTATION
SAN MARTINO IN RIO
COLLECTION OF VINTAGE CARS
SYRACUSE
MUSEUM OF ANCIENT AND MODERN ART
TURIN
CARLO BISCARETTI DI RUFFIA MOTOR MUSEUM

JAPAN

NAGOYA
MUNICIPAL SCIENCE MUSEUM
NATORI-GUN
HORSEMANSHIP MUSEUM OF TAKEKOMA SHRINE
TOKYO
MUSEUM OF TRANSPORT
OME RAILWAY PARK
TRANSPORT MUSEUM

MALAYSIA

PENANG
PENANG MUSEUM AND ART GALLERY

MEXICO

MEXICO CITY
CONVENT OF SANTA MARIA DE LOS ANGELES

NETHERLANDS

HEERENVEEN
BATAVUS MUSEUM
LEEK
NATIONAL CARRIAGE MUSEUM
UTRECHT
NETHERLANDS RAILWAY MUSEUM
VEENKLOSTER
FOGELSANGH STATE
WEERT
NETHERLANDS TRAM MUSEUM

NEW ZEALAND

CHRISTCHURCH
THE FERRYMEAD TRUST
DUNEDIN
OTAGO EARLY SETTLERS' ASSOCIATION (INC)

NORWAY

HAMAR
RAILWAY MUSEUM
OSLO
NORWEGIAN SCIENCE AND INDUSTRY MUSEUM

POLAND

AUGUSTÓW
REGIONAL MUSEUM
ŁAŃCUT
CARRIAGE MUSEUM
SMOLNIK
OPEN-AIR MUSEUM
WARSAW
RAILWAY MUSEUM
TECHNICAL MUSEUM

PORTUGAL

CARAMULO
CAR MUSEUM
LISBON
MUSEUM OF ROYAL COACHES
VILA REAL DE SANTO ANTONIO
DUCAL PALACE

RHODESIA

BULAWAYO
RHODESIA RAILWAYS MUSEUM

ROMANIA

BUCHAREST
RAILWAY MUSEUM
SLATINEANU COLLECTION

SOUTH AFRICA, REPUBLIC OF

CRADOCK
ZEBRA NATIONAL PARKS MUSEUM
JOHANNESBURG
JAMES HALL MUSEUM OF TRANSPORT
SOUTH AFRICAN RAILWAY MUSEUM
OUDTSHOORN
C.P. NEL MUSEUM
PRETORIA
KRUGER HOUSE MUSEUM
SWELLENDAM
DROSTDY MUSEUM

SPAIN

CANDUELA
VALLES DE CAMPOO ETHNOGRAPHICAL MUSEUM
MADRID
MUSEUM OF CARRIAGES
RAILWAY MUSEUM
ROYAL PALACE

SWEDEN

MALMÖ
CARRIAGE MUSEUM
ÖRNSKÖLDSVIK
ÖRNSKÖLDSVIK MUSEUM
STOCKHOLM
HALLWYL MUSEUM
RAILWAY MUSEUM
TECHNICAL MUSEUM
TRAMWAY MUSEUM

SWITZERLAND

AMRISWIL
ROBERT SALLMANN CARRIAGE COLLECTION
BASEL
RHINE NAVIGATION MUSEUM, 'OUR WAY TO THE SEA'
CHUR
MUNICIPAL MUSEUM
FLEURIER
MUSEUM
HORGEN
LOCAL MUSEUM
LUZERN
SWISS MUSEUM OF TRANSPORT
UTZENSTORF
LANDSHUT CASTLE

TURKEY

ISTANBUL
TOPKAPI PALACE MUSEUM

USSR

GORKI
MUSEUM OF TRANSPORT
LENINGRAD
MUSEUM OF RAILWAY HISTORY
MOSCOW
NATIONAL ARMOURY

UNITED STATES

ARCADE
ARCADE AND ATTICA RAILROAD MUSEUM
ARCADIA
LOS ANGELES STATE AND COUNTY ARBORETUM
ASHLAND
SANTA FE MUSEUM
ASKOV
PINE COUNTY HISTORICAL SOCIETY MUSEUM
AUSABLE CHASM
AUSABLE CHASM ANTIQUE CAR MUSEUM
AUSTIN
MOWER COUNTY PIONEER AND HISTORICAL CENTER
BALTIMORE
BALTIMORE AND OHIO TRANSPORTATION MUSEUM
MOUNT CLARE RAILROAD STATION AND TRANSPORTATION MUSEUM
BARABOO
SAUK COUNTY HISTORICAL MUSEUM
BARBOURSVILLE
DAR TOLL HOUSE MUSEUM
BATAVIA
BATAVIA HISTORICAL SOCIETY MUSEUM
BELLOWS FALLS
STEAMTOWN U.S.A.
BILLERICA
MIDDLESEX CANAL MUSEUM
BILLINGS
YELLOWSTONE COUNTY MUSEUM
BLOOMINGTON
SAN BERNADINO COUNTY MUSEUM
BLOOMSBURG
MAGEE TRANSPORTATION MUSEUM
BLUE MOUNTAIN LAKE
ADIRONDACK MUSEUM
BONNER SPRINGS
AGRICULTURAL HALL OF FAME AND NATIONAL CENTER
BOOTHBAY
BOOTHBAY RAILWAY MUSEUM
BOWLING GREEN
MUSEUM OF WOOD COUNTY HISTORICAL SOCIETY
BOYERTOWN
BOYERTOWN MUSEUM OF HISTORIC VEHICLES
BRIDGE HAMPTON
CORWITH HOMESTEAD
BRIDGEWATER
UPSTATE ANTIQUE AUTO MUSEUM
BROOKLINE
MUSEUM OF TRANSPORTATION
BROWNVILLE
BROWNVILLE RAILROAD MUSEUM
BUCKSPORT
BUCKSPORT HISTORICAL SOCIETY MUSEUM
BUFFALO
MUSEUM OF BUFFALO AND ERIE COUNTY HISTORICAL SOCIETY
CAMDENTON
KELSEY'S ANTIQUE AUTOMOBILES
CANANDAIGUA
GRANGER HOMESTEAD AND CARRIAGE MUSEUM
CANASTOTA
CANAL TOWN MUSEUM
CASS
CIVIL WAR MUSEUM
CHATHAM
CHATHAM RAILROAD MUSEUM
CHATTANOOGA
TENNESSEE VALLEY RAILROAD MUSEUM, INC.
CHICAGO
MUSEUM OF CHICAGO HISTORICAL SOCIETY
MUSEUM OF SCIENCE AND INDUSTRY
CLEVELAND
WESTERN RESERVE HISTORICAL SOCIETY AND FREDERICK C. CRAWFORD AUTO-AVIATION MUSEUM
CLINTONVILLE
MUSEUM OF FOUR WHEEL DRIVE FOUNDATION
COLORADO SPRINGS
CARRIAGE HOUSE MUSEUM
CONCORD
MANN HOUSE
CONNEAUT
CONNEAUT RAILROAD HISTORICAL MUSEUM
CONNERSVILLE
HENRY H. BLOMMEL HISTORIC AUTOMOTIVE DATA COLLECTION
COOPERSTOWN
CARRIAGE AND HARNESS MUSEUM
CORINNE
RAILROAD MUSEUM
CRESSON
ALLEGHENY PORTAGE RAILROAD NATIONAL HISTORIC SITE
CRIPPLE CREEK
CRIPPLE CREEK DISTRICT MUSEUM

CUYAHOGA FALLS
RAILWAYS OF AMERICA
DALLAS
'AGE OF STEAM' RAILROAD MUSEUM
DAYTON
DEEDS CARILLON AND CELESTRON
U.S. AIR FORCE MUSEUM
DEARBORN
GREENFIELD VILLAGE AND HENRY FORD MUSEUM
DE LEON
TEXAS CENTRAL RAILROAD MUSEUM
DENVER
COLORADO TRANSPORTATION MUSEUM
FORNEY TRANSPORTATION MUSEUM
MUSEUM OF THE STATE HISTORICAL SOCIETY OF COLORADO
VETERAN CAR MUSEUM
DETROIT
DETROIT HISTORICAL MUSEUM
DILWORTHTOWN
1704 BRINTON HOUSE
EAST HAVEN
BRANFORD TROLLEY MUSEUM
EAST WINDSOR
CONNECTICUT ELECTRIC RAILWAY ASSOCIATION MUSEUM
ELLENVILLE
HARRY RESNICK MOTOR MUSEUM AND DOLL HOUSE
EL RENO
CANADIAN COUNTY HISTORICAL SOCIETY MUSEUM
EUGENE
WAGON MUSEUM
EVANSVILLE
EVANSVILLE MUSEUM OF ARTS AND SCIENCES
FLINT
SLOAN MUSEUM
SLOAN PANORAMA OF TRANSPORTATION
FORT LEAVENWORTH
FORT LEAVENWORTH MUSEUM
FORT WORTH
PATE MUSEUM OF TRANSPORTATION
FRESNO
MUSEUM OF FRESNO COUNTY HISTORICAL SOCIETY
GETTYSBURG
LINCOLN TRAIN MUSEUM
GILLETT
WELTNER WONDER MUSEUM
GLENCOE
MUSEUM OF WABASH, FRISCO AND PACIFIC ASSOCIATION
GLENWOOD
MUSEUM OF OREGON ELECTRIC RAILWAY HISTORICAL SOCIETY
GOLDEN
COLORADO RAILROAD MUSEUM
GOTHENBURG
PONY EXPRESS STATION
GREEN BAY
NATIONAL RAILROAD MUSEUM
GREENBUSH
JUNG CARRIAGE MUSEUM
GROSSE ILE
GROSSE ILE HISTORICAL MUSEUM
HASKELL
HASKELL RAILROAD MUSEUM
HEREFORD
DEAF SMITH COUNTY MUSEUM
HILL CITY
BLACK HILLS CENTRAL RAILROAD
HILLIARD
TRAINS OF YESTERDAY MUSEUM
HINSDALE
THE OLD GRAUE MILL AND MUSEUM
HOLLAND
POLL MUSEUM
HOLLIDAYSBURG
BAKER MANSION MUSEUM
HONESDALE
WAYNE COUNTY HISTORICAL SOCIETY MUSEUM
HOUSTON
CLASSIC CAR SHOWCASE
HUNTINGDON
SWIGART MUSEUM
JACKSON
CASEY JONES' HOME AND RAILROAD MUSEUM
JAMESTOWN
JAMESTOWN MUSEUM
JEFFERSON
JAY GOULD PRIVATE RAILROAD CAR
JOHNSTOWN
ALLEGHENY PORTAGE RAILROAD
KENNEBUNKPORT
SEASHORE TROLLEY MUSEUM
KENNESAW
BIG SHANTY MUSEUM
KEOKUK
KEOKUK RIVER MUSEUM
KEY WEST
OLD COFFEE MILL MUSEUM AND FLORIDA RAILROAD MUSEUM
KINGSTON
SENATE HOUSE
KIT CARSON
KIT CARSON HISTORICAL SOCIETY MUSEUM
LAKE HOPATCONG
LAKE HOPATCONG HISTORICAL MUSEUM
LIMA
ALLEN COUNTY MUSEUM
LOS ANGELES
CALIFORNIA MUSEUM OF SCIENCE AND INDUSTRY
LOUISVILLE
KENTUCKY RAILWAY MUSEUM
LOWELL
MIDDLESEX CANAL MUSEUM
LURAY
CAR AND CARRIAGE CARAVAN
LYONS
WAYNE COUNTY HISTORICAL MUSEUM
MAHWAH
MAHWAH HISTORICAL SOCIETY MUSEUM
MANITON SPRINGS
CAMERON'S DOLL AND CARRIAGE MUSEUM
MARCELLUS
MARTISCO RAILROAD STATION MUSEUM
MARIETTA
CAMPUS MARTIUS MUSEUM
STEAMER 'W. P. SNYDER JR.'
MARYSVILLE
ORIGINAL PONY EXPRESS HOME STATION
MEREDITH
MEREDITH AUTO MUSEUM
MONTGOMERY
PIONEER HISTORICAL ASSOCIATION OF MONTGOMERY
MORRILTON
MUSEUM OF AUTOMOBILES
MURDO
PIONEER AND AUTO MUSEUM
NEWARK
MUSEUM OF RAILROADIANS OF AMERICA
NEW BRUNSWICK
DELAPLAINE ELECTRICAL MUSEUM
NEW ORLEANS
THE CABILDO
NEWPORT
THE BREAKERS
NOBLESVILLE
INDIANA MUSEUM OF TRANSPORT AND COMMUNICATIONS
NORTH EAST
MUSEUM OF LAKE SHORE RAILWAY HISTORICAL SOCIETY
NORTH FREEDOM
MID-CONTINENT RAILWAY HISTORICAL SOCIETY MUSEUM
NORTON
STATION 15
OMAHA
UNION PACIFIC HISTORICAL MUSEUM
ONEONTA
NATIONAL RAILROAD MUSEUM
OSHKOSH
OSHKOSH PUBLIC MUSEUM
PALM BEACH
HENRY MORRISON FLAGLER MUSEUM
PERRIS
ORANGE EMPIRE TROLLEY MUSEUM
PIQUA
PIQUA HISTORICAL AREA STATE MEMORIAL
POTOMAC
GREAT FALLS TAVERN MUSEUM
POTTSVILLE
MUSEUM OF SCHUYLKILL COUNTY HISTORICAL SOCIETY
PRAIRIE CITY
DE WITT MUSEUM
QUANAH
MEDICINE MOUND TRADING POST
RALLS
RALLS HISTORICAL MUSEUM
ROANOKE
TRANSPORTATION CENTER AND RAILWAY MUSEUM
ROCHESTER
HEMP OLD VEHICLE MUSEUM
MORTIMER AND RED CREEK RAILROAD MUSEUM
ROCKHILL
RAILWAYS TO YESTERDAY
SABETHA
ALBANY HISTORICAL SOCIETY MUSEUM
ST. JOSEPH
PONY EXPRESS STABLES MUSEUM
ST. LOUIS
NATIONAL MUSEUM OF TRANSPORT
SALT LAKE CITY
RAILROAD MUSEUM
SAN ANTONIO
WITTE CONFLUENCE MUSEUM
SANDY CREEK
RAIL CITY, INC.
SAN FRANCISCO
WELLS FARGO BANK HISTORY ROOM
SAN RAFAEL
PONY EXPRESS HISTORY AND ART GALLERY
SEATTLE
MUSEUM OF HISTORY AND INDUSTRY
PUGET SOUND RAILWAY MUSEUM
SILVER SPRING
MARYLAND NATIONAL CAPITAL PARK AND PLANNING COMMISSION
SILVER SPRINGS
EARLY AMERICAN MUSEUM
SILVERTON
SAN JUAN COUNTY HISTORICAL SOCIETY MUSEUM
SOUTHAMPTON
LONG ISLAND AUTOMOTIVE MUSEUM
SOUTH CARVER
EDAVILLE RAILROAD MUSEUM
STONE MOUNTAIN
STONE MOUNTAIN PARK
STONY BROOK
SUFFOLK MUSEUM AND CARRIAGE HOUSE
STOUGHTON
STOUGHTON HISTORICAL SOCIETY MUSEUM
STRASBURG
RAILROAD MUSEUM OF PENNSYLVANIA
STURBRIDGE
STURBRIDGE AUTO MUSEUM
SYRACUSE
CANAL MUSEUM
MUSEUM OF CANAL SOCIETY OF NEW YORK STATE
TEMPE
RAILROAD AND PIONEER MUSEUM
TONAWANDA
MUSEUM OF HISTORICAL SOCIETY OF THE TONAWANDAS
TRUCKEE
EMIGRANT TRAIL MUSEUM
TWO HARBORS
MUSEUM OF LAKE COUNTY HISTORICAL SOCIETY
UNION
ILLINOIS RAILWAY MUSEUM

UNIONTOWN
SEARIGHT'S TOLLHOUSE
WAREHOUSE POINT
MUSEUM OF CONNECTICUT ELECTRIC RAILWAY ASSOCIATION
WARWICK
SHINGLE HOUSE
WASHINGTON
NATIONAL MUSEUM OF HISTORY AND TECHNOLOGY
WASHINGTON MUSEUM
ARDEN TROLLEY MUSEUM
WEATHERFORD
TEXAS RAILROAD MUSEUM
WELLSVILLE
RIVER MUSEUM
WHITEHALL
SKENESBOROUGH MUSEUM
WORTHINGTON
OHIO RAILWAY MUSEUM
YARDLEY
ALEXANDER RAILROAD MUSEUM

VENEZUELA

CARACAS
MUSEUM OF TRANSPORT

YUGOSLAVIA

BELGRADE
RAILWAY MUSEUM OF F.S.R. OF YUGOSLAVIA

Communications, including postal services

ARGENTINA

BUENOS AIRES
POSTAL MUSEUM

AUSTRALIA

MELBOURNE
SCIENCE MUSEUM OF VICTORIA

AUSTRIA

VIENNA
MUSEUM OF INDUSTRY AND TECHNOLOGY
MUSEUM OF POSTAL AND TELECOMMUNICATION SERVICES

BANGLADESH

DACCA
POSTAL MUSEUM

BELGIUM

BRUSSELS
POSTAL MUSEUM

BULGARIA

SOFIA
NATIONAL POLYTECHNIC MUSEUM

CANADA

BADDECK
ALEXANDER GRAHAM BELL MUSEUM
BRANTFORD
BELL HOMESTEAD
EDMONTON
ALBERTA GOVERNMENT TELEPHONES HISTORIC EXHIBIT
HALIFAX
TELEPHONE MUSEUM
KINGSTON
ROYAL CANADIAN SIGNALS MUSEUM
OTTAWA
NATIONAL MUSEUM OF SCIENCE AND TECHNOLOGY
REGINA
TELORAMA
ST. JOHNS
SIGNAL HILL NATIONAL HISTORIC PARK
TORONTO
ONTARIO SCIENCE CENTRE

REPUBLIC OF CHINA

TAIPEI
POSTAL MUSEUM

CUBA

HABANA
POSTAL MUSEUM

CZECHOSLOVAKIA

KOŠICE
TECHNICAL MUSEUM
PRAGUE
MUSEUM OF POSTAL SERVICES AND TELECOMMUNICATIONS
NATIONAL TECHNICAL MUSEUM

DENMARK

COPENHAGEN
DANISH POST AND TELEGRAPH MUSEUM
TS MUSEUM
HELSINGØR
DANISH TECHNICAL MUSEUM

EGYPT, ARAB REPUBLIC OF

CAIRO
POSTAL MUSEUM
SCIENCE MUSEUM

FINLAND

HELSINKI
HELSINKI TELEPHONE MUSEUM
MUSEUM OF POSTAL SERVICES AND COMMUNICATIONS

FRANCE

AMBOISE
POSTAL MUSEUM
LIMERAY
MUSEUM OF POSTAL HISTORY
PARIS
FRENCH POSTAL MUSEUM
NATIONAL TECHNICAL MUSEUM
RIQUEWIHR
REGIONAL POSTAL AND TELECOMMUNICATIONS MUSEUM

GDR

BERLIN
MUSEUM OF POSTAL HISTORY
PEGAU
REGIONAL MUSEUM

GFR

BERLIN
BERLIN POSTAL AND TELECOMMUNICATIONS MUSEUM
GERMAN RADIO AND TELEVISION MUSEUM
FRANKFURT
MUSEUM OF THE FEDERAL POSTAL SERVICES
FRIEDRICHSDORF
PHILIPP REIS MEMORIAL
HAMBURG
POSTAL MUSEUM
HEILBRONN
HISTORY MUSEUM
MÜNCHEN
GERMAN MUSEUM
SCHWERTE
MUSEUM OF THE RUHR VALLEY
STUTTGART
POSTAL MUSEUM

GREAT BRITAIN

BRIGHTON
CREED AND COMPANY LIMITED
HALIFAX
WEST YORKSHIRE FOLK MUSEUM
LONDON
FLEET BUILDING TELECOMMUNICATIONS MUSEUM
I.T.A. TELEVISION GALLERY
SCIENCE MUSEUM
NEWPORT
CARISBROOKE CASTLE MUSEUM
SPALDING
BRITISH VINTAGE WIRELESS MUSEUM

HUNGARY

BALATONSZEMES
POSTAL MUSEUM
BUDAPEST
POSTAL MUSEUM

INDIA

BANGALORE
VISVESVARAYA INDUSTRIAL AND TECHNOLOGICAL MUSEUM
CALCUTTA
BIRLA INDUSTRIAL AND TECHNOLOGICAL MUSEUM
NEW DELHI
SCIENCE MUSEUM

ITALY

MILAN
LEONARDO DA VINCI MUSEUM OF SCIENCE AND TECHNOLOGY

ROME
MUSEUM OF POSTAL HISTORY AND TELECOMMUNICATIONS

JAPAN

GIFU-SHI
GIFU CHILDREN'S SCIENCE HALL

OSAKA
ELECTRIC SCIENCE MUSEUM

TAKEDA-SHI
HISOKA MAEJIMA MEMORIAL COLLECTION

TOKYO
BROADCASTING MUSEUM
COMMUNICATIONS AND POSTAL SERVICE MUSEUM
N.H.K. MUSEUM OF BROADCASTING

TSUDAKA-MACHI
SAKANO MEMORIAL HALL ATTACHED COMMUNICATION MUSEUM

MALAWI

NAMAKA
MTENGATENGA POSTAL MUSEUM

MEXICO

MEXICO CITY
POSTAL MUSEUM

NETHERLANDS

DELFT
ELECTRO-TECHNOLOGY STUDY COLLECTION

'S GRAVENHAGE
NETHERLANDS POSTAL MUSEUM

NEW ZEALAND

OAMARU
NORTH OTAGO PIONEER GALLERY

NORWAY

OSLO
NORWEGIAN SCIENCE AND INDUSTRY MUSEUM
POST OFFICE MUSEUM

PERU

LIMA
PHILATELIC MUSEUM

POLAND

STARY SĄCZ
ART MUSEUM

WROCŁAW
MUSEUM OF POSTS AND TELECOMMUNICATIONS

PORTUGAL

LISBON
POST OFFICE MUSEUM

ST. HELENA

GEORGETOWN
FORT HAYES MUSEUM

SOUTH AFRICA, REPUBLIC OF

PRETORIA
MUSEUM OF SCIENCE AND INDUSTRY

SWEDEN

STOCKHOLM
MUSEUM OF TELECOMMUNICATIONS
POSTAL MUSEUM
TECHNICAL MUSEUM

SWITZERLAND

BERN
SWISS POSTAL, TELEPHONE AND TELEGRAPH MUSEUM

TUNISIA

TUNIS
NATIONAL MUSEUM OF POSTS AND TELECOMMUNICATIONS

USSR

KIROVSK
HOUSE OF TECHNOLOGY

LENINGRAD
A. S. POPOV CENTRAL MUSEUM OF COMMUNICATIONS

UNITED STATES

ALBUQUERQUE
TELEPHONE PIONEER MUSEUM

ANDOVER
MUSEUM OF COMMUNICATIONS SATELLITE CORPORATION

BAR HARBOR
SONOGEE MANSION

CHICAGO
ILLINOIS BELL PIONEER HISTORICAL MUSEUM
MUSEUM OF SCIENCE AND INDUSTRY

CLE ELREM
CLE ELREM HISTORICAL MUSEUM

DES MOINES
DES MOINES CENTER OF SCIENCE AND INDUSTRY

ELGIN
MUCHOW'S ANTIQUE RADIO MUSEUM

FLUSHING
HALL OF SCIENCE OF THE CITY OF NEW YORK

FORT MYERS
EDISON HOME MUSEUM

HOLCOMB
ANTIQUE WIRELESS ASSOCIATION MUSEUM

MENLO PARK
EDISON MEMORIAL TOWER AND STATE PARK

MILAN
THOMAS EDISON BIRTHPLACE MUSEUM

MORTON
COCHRAN COUNTY MUSEUM

NEWARK
NEW JERSEY BELL TELEPHONE COMPANY, PIONEER HISTORICAL MUSEUM

NEWINGTON
AMERICAN RADIO RELAY LEAGUE

NEW YORK
BELL TELEPHONE LABORATORIES, INC.
THE GARIBALDI AND MEUCCI MEMORIAL MUSEUM
MUSEUM OF THE MEDIA

QUEENS
HALL OF SCIENCE OF THE CITY OF NEW YORK

ROCKPORT
MUSEUM OF SANDY BAY HISTORICAL SOCIETY

SALT LAKE CITY
WIRE MEMORIAL MUSEUM

SAN ANGELO
ELMER H. DANNER MUSEUM OF TELEPHONY

TRENTON
W2Z1 HISTORICAL WIRELESS MUSEUM

WASHINGTON
NATIONAL MUSEUM OF HISTORY AND TECHNOLOGY

WEST ORANGE
EDISON NATIONAL HISTORIC SITE

YUGOSLAVIA

BELGRADE
MUSEUM OF POST AND TELECOMMUNICATIONS

Textiles, clothing, costumes, hairdressing

AFGHANISTAN

KABUL
KABUL MUSEUM

ALBANIA

TIRANA
MUSEUM OF ARCHAEOLOGY AND ETHNOGRAPHY

ALGERIA

ALGIERS
MUSEUM OF POPULAR ARTS AND TRADITIONS
NATIONAL MUSEUM OF ANTIQUITIES

AUSTRALIA

ARMIDALE
ARMIDALE FOLK MUSEUM

BATTERY POINT
VAN DIEMEN'S LAND MEMORIAL FOLK MUSEUM

BRISBANE
MIEGUNYAH

BROKEN HILL
MUSEUM OF APPLIED ARTS AND SCIENCES

SYDNEY
ART GALLERY OF NEW SOUTH WALES
MUSEUM OF APPLIED ARTS AND SCIENCES

AUSTRIA

BAD AUSSEE
AUSSEE REGIONAL MUSEUM

BADGASTEIN
REGIONAL MUSEUM

BAD LEONFELDEN
REGIONAL MUSEUM

DREISTETTEN
SCHERRER INN REGIONAL MUSEUM
DÜRNSTEIN
DÜRNSTEIN REGIONAL MUSEUM
EBENAU
REGIONAL MUSEUM
EGG
REGIONAL MUSEUM
FRIESACH
REGIONAL MUSEUM
GMUND
REGIONAL MUSEUM
GRAZ
JOANNEUM PROVINCIAL MUSEUM OF CULTURAL HISTORY AND APPLIED ART
JOANNEUM PROVINCIAL MUSEUM OF THE ETHNOLOGY AND FOLKLORE OF STEIERMARK
GUTENBRUNN
BAROQUE MUSEUM
HALLSTATT
LOCAL MUSEUM
HASLACH
MUSEUM OF LOCAL HISTORY AND FOLKLORE
HEILIGENKREUZ
MONASTERY COLLECTIONS
HERMAGOR
GAITAL REGIONAL MUSEUM
HOHENBRUNN
HUNTING MUSEUM OF UPPER AUSTRIA
HOLLERSBACH
REGIONAL MUSEUM
INNSBRUCK
AMBRAS CASTLE COLLECTION
PALACE, SILVER CHAPEL AND PALACE CHURCH
SCHWARZKOPF COLLECTION
KLEINENGERSDORF
"DE. ISAMBERG UND DER WEINVIERTLER" MUSEUM
KUCHL
REGIONAL MUSEUM
LIENZ
EAST TIROL REGIONAL MUSEUM
LINZ
MUSEUM OF THE CITY OF LINZ
MITTERNDORF
MUSEUM OF REGIONAL LIFE
RAABS
DR. JOSEF GRASSL REGIONAL MUSEUM
RABENSTEIN
PIELACHTAL REGIONAL MUSEUM
RAURIS
RAURIS GOLD-MINING MUSEUM
RIED
ETHNOLOGICAL MUSEUM OF THE INNVIERTEL
SCHRUNS
MONTAFON REGIONAL MUSEUM
SCHWARZENBERG
COMMUNITY MUSEUM
STEYR
REGIONAL MUSEUM
VIENNA
AUSTRIAN MUSEUM OF APPLIED ART
AUSTRIAN MUSEUM OF ETHNOLOGY
CATHEDRAL AND DIOCESAN MUSEUM
COSTUME COLLECTION OF THE ACADEMY OF FINE ARTS
HETZENDORF PALACE COLLECTION
MUSEUM OF THE VIENNA HAIRDRESSERS' ASSOCIATION
WEIKENDORF
MARCHFELD MUSEUM
WENIGZELL
REGIONAL HOUSE

BAHAMAS

NASSAU
BAHAMIA MUSEUM

BELGIUM

ANTWERP
PROVINCIAL MUSEUM OF INDUSTRIAL ART
BRUGES
GRUUTHUSE MUSEUM
MUSEUM OF THE POTTERY HOSTEL
STORIE HOUSE
BRUSSELS
MANNEKIN PIS COSTUME COLLECTION
MUSEUM OF THE POOR LAW ADMINISTRATION
TOWN HALL
COURTRAI
MUSEUM OF PAINTING
EUPEN
REGIONAL MUSEUM
FRANC-WARET
CHÂTEAU
GAASBEEK
CHÂTEAU MUSEUM
GHENT
MUSEUM OF ANTIQUITIES
HOOGSTRATEN
SAINT-SANG MUSEUM OF FOLK- LORE AND FOLK-ART
LIÈGE
ANSEMBOURG MUSEUM
DIOCESAN MUSEUM AND CATHEDRAL TREASURY
TCHANTCHÈS MUSEUM
MARIEMONT- MORLANWELZ
MUSEUM OF ART AND OF THE HISTORY OF ARCHAEOLOGY
MODAVE
CASTLE MUSEUM
MONS
CANON PUISSANT MUSEUM
SPONTIN
CASTLE
TOURNAI
FOLKLORE MUSEUM
MUSEUM OF HISTORY AND ARCHAEOLOGY
VERVIERS
RENIER MUSEUM

BRAZIL

CAXIAS DO SUL
MUSEUM OF POPULAR TRADITIONS
NATAL
MUSEUM OF POPULAR ART
RIO DE JANEIRO
ITAMARTY MUSEUM OF HISTORY AND DIPLOMACY
MUSEUM OF THE RAYMUNDO OTTONI DE CASTRO FOUNDATION
SALVADOR
BAHIA MUSEUM OF MODERN ART
MUSEUM OF ART
VASSOURAS
CASA DA HERA MUSEUM

BULGARIA

KARNOBAT
NATIONAL MUSEUM
PANAGIOURISTE
RAJNA KNIAGJANIA REGIONAL MUSEUM
RAJKOVO
NATIONAL MUSEUM OF THE RHODOPE
SOFIA
BOYANA CHURCH NATIONAL MUSEUM
NATIONAL ETHNOGRAPHICAL MUSEUM

CAMEROUN

FOUMBAN
MUSEUM OF THE BAMOUN ROYAL PALACE
MOKOLO
MUNICIPAL MUSEUM

CANADA

MONTREAL
McCORD MUSEUM
OWEN SOUND
COUNTY OF GREY AND OWEN SOUND MUSEUM
QUEBEC
MUSEUM OF THE ARCHIVES OF QUEBEC
SASKATOON
MUSEUM OF THE UKRAINIAN WOMEN'S ASSOCIATION
TORONTO
ROYAL ONTARIO MUSEUM

CHINA, P.R.

NANKING (NAN JING)
KIANG SU PROVINCIAL MUSEUM
PEKING
IMPERIAL PALACE
QU FU
RESIDENCES OF THE DESCENDANTS OF CONFUCIUS

CUBA

HABANA
MUSEUM OF DECORATIVE ARTS

CYPRUS

KYRENIA
FOLK ART MUSEUM
NICOSIA
THE MUSEUM OF FOLK ART

CZECHOSLOVAKIA

BANSKÁ BYSTRICA
MUSEUM OF THE HISTORY OF SLOVAKIA
BRATISLAVA
MUNICIPAL MUSEUM
BRNO
MUSEUM OF THE CITY OF BRNO
ČERVENÝ KLÁŠTOR
MONASTERY MUSEUM
ČESKÝ DUB
KAROLINY SVĚTLÉ MUSEUM
CHOMUTOV
REGIONAL MUSEUM
DOLNI DOMASLOVICE
DOMASLOVICE AND DISTRICT MUSEUM
DVUR KRÁLOVÉ NAD LABEM
TEXTILE MUSEUM
GOTTWALDOV
MUSEUM OF SHOE-MAKING
HLINSKO
REGIONAL MUSEUM AND ART GALLERY
JILEMNICE
KRKONOŠ MUSEUM
KLADNO
DISTRICT MUSEUM
LITVINOV
LOCAL MUSEUM
LOMNICE NAD POPELKOU
MUNICIPAL MUSEUM
MARIANSKÁ TYNICE - KRALOVICE
DISTRICT MUSEUM
MARTIN
SLOVAKIAN NATIONAL MUSEUM: ETHNOGRAPHICAL COLLECTIONS
MICHALOVCE
ZEMPLIN MUSEUM
MORAVSKÁ TŘEBOVA
MUNICIPAL MUSEUM
OPAVA
SILESIAN MUSEUM: ETHNOGRAPHY AND ART COLLECTIONS
PELHŘIMOV
DISTRICT MUSEUM
PIEŠTANY
SPA MUSEUM

PÍSEK
REGIONAL MUSEUM
POTŠTEJN
JIRÁSKŮV 'POKLAD' MEMORIAL MUSEUM
PŘEROV NAD LABEM
MUSEUM OF ETHNOGRAPHY
RUŽOMBEROK
LIPTOV MUSEUM
ŠTERNBERK
ŠTERNBERK STATE CASTLE
STRÁŽNICI
REGIONAL MUSEUM OF FOLK ART
TRENČÍN
TRENČÍN MUSEUM
VAMBERK
MUNICIPAL MUSEUM
VARNSDORF
MUNICIPAL MUSEUM
VIMPERK
MUNICIPAL MUSEUM AND ŠUMAVY GALLERY
ZÁBŘEH NA MORAVĚ
REGIONAL MUSEUM
ŽĎÁR NAD SÁZAVOU
ŽĎÁR MUSEUM AND ART GALLERY

DENMARK

AUNING
GAMMEL ESTRUP
BOGENSE
MUSEUM OF NORTH FUNEN
BREGNINGE
HJEMSTAVNMUSEUM
COPENHAGEN
AMAGER MUSEUM
MUSEUM OF DECORATIVE ART
DRAGØR
AMAGER MUSEUM
FREDENSBORG
PALACE OF FREDENSBORG
GAMMEL ESTRUP
JYLLANDS HERREGAARDSMUSEUM
GUMMERUP
VESTFYNS HJEMSTAVNSGÅRDEN
HELSINGØR
KRONBORG CASTLE
HERNING
HERNING MUSEUM
HORNSLET
ROSENHOLM
HUNDESTED
KNUD RASMUSSEN'S COTTAGE
HØJBY SJ.
STENSTRUP MUSEUM
HØJERUP
STEVNS MUSEUM
HØVE
LOCAL HISTORY MUSEUM
KALUNDBORG
KALUNDBORG AND DISTRICT MUSEUM
NYKØBING
FALSTERS MINDER MUSEUM
ODDER
MUSEUM
ODENSE
ODENSE MUNICIPAL MUSEUMS
ROSKILDE
ROSKILDE MUSEUM
SLEGE
SLEGE MUSEUM
STRUER
STRUER MUSEUM
VAERLØSE
VAERLØSE MUSEUM
VARDE
VARDE AND DISTRICT MUSEUM

EGYPT, ARAB REPUBLIC OF

CAIRO
AL GAWHARA PALACE MUSEUM
COTTON MUSEUM

ETHIOPIA

ADDIS ABABA
INSTITUTE OF ETHIOPIAN STUDIES MUSEUM

FINLAND

HELSINKI
ARABIA MUSEUM

FRANCE

ABBEVILLE
BOUCHER-DE-PERTHES MUSEUM
AIX-EN-PROVENCE
GRANET MUSEUM
MUSEUM OF TAPESTRY AND FURNITURE
SAINT-SAUVEUR CATHEDRAL
ALENÇON
MUSEUM OF PAINTING
AMBOISE
TOWN HALL MUSEUM
ANCY-LE-FRANC
CHÂTEAU
ANGERS
CATHEDRAL TREASURY
TAPESTRY MUSEUM
ANGLARDS-DE-SALERS
CHÂTEAU
ANGOULÊME
MUNICIPAL MUSEUM
ANNECY
CHÂTEAU DE MONTROTTIER
ARLANC-EN-LIBRADOIS
MUSEUM OF HANDMADE LACE
AUXERRE
LEBLANC-DUVERNOY MUSEUM
AZAY-LE-RIDEAU
CHÂTEAU
BAILLEUL
BENOÎT DE PUYDT MUSEUM
BAYEUX
MUSEUM OF PAINTING
QUEEN MATHILDA'S MUSEUM
BEAUGENCY
DUNOIS MUSEUM
BEAUNE
CATHEDRAL TREASURY
COLLÈGE OF NOTRE-DAME
HÔTEL-DIEU
MUSEUM OF THE WINE OF BURGUNDY
BEAUVAIS
CATHEDRAL TREASURY
MUSEUM OF THE OISE DEPARTMENT
BESANÇON
HISTORICAL MUSEUM
BIOT
FERNAND LÉGER MUSEUM
BLOIS
CHÂTEAU MUSEUM
BORDEAUX
HISTORICAL COLLECTION OF THE CONSEIL INTERPROFESSIONAL DU VIN DE BORDEAUX
BOURGES
HÔTEL JACQUES COEUR
HÔTEL LALLEMANT
BOURGNEUF-EN-RETZ
RETZ REGIONAL MUSEUM
BOURGOIN-JALLIEU
VICTOR CHARRETON MUSEUM
BOUXWILLER
BOUXWILLER MUSEUM
CARCASSONNE
CATHEDRAL MUSEUM
CHAÂLIS
JACQUEMART-ANDRÉ MUSEUM
CHALON-SUR-SAÔNE
DENON MUSEUM
CHAMBORD
CHÂTEAU DE CHAMBORD
CHARTRES
MUNICIPAL MUSEUM
CHÂTEAUDUN
CHÂTEAU DE CHÂTEAUDUN
CHÂTEAU-GOMBERT
MUSEUM OF PROVENÇAL ART
LA CHÂTRE
MUSEUM OF GEORGE SAND AND OF THE VALLÉE NOIRE
CHAUMONT-SUR-LOIRE
MUSEUM IN THE STABLES
COUR-CHEVERNY
CHÂTEAU COLLECTIONS
CROIX-DE-VIE
MARAICHIN MUSEUM
DIJON
MUSEUM OF FINE ART
PERRIN DE PUYCOUSIN MUSEUM
FONTAINEBLEAU
PALACE OF FONTAINEBLEAU
FRESNAY-SUR-SARTHE
MUSEUM OF HEADDRESSES
GRANVILLE
MUSEUM OF OLD GRANVILLE
GRASSE
FRAGONARD MUSEUM
GUÉRET
MUNICIPAL MUSEUM
HESDIN
TOWN HALL
HONFLEUR
EUGÈNE BOUDIN MUSEUM
NORMANDY MUSEUM OF ETHNOGRAPHY AND FOLK ART
LANGEAIS
CHÂTEAU
LILLE
MUSEUM OF THE COMTESSE HOSPICE
LOVAGNY- GORGES-DU-FIER
LÉON MARÈS COLLECTION
LYON
CANUT MUSEUM
LYON MUSEUM OF DECORATIVE ARTS
MUSEUM OF THE CIVILIAN HOSPITALS OF LYON
MUSEUM OF THE HISTORY OF TEXTILES
MÂCON
MUNICIPAL MUSEUM OF THE URSULINES
MAISONS-LAFFITTE
CHÂTEAU
MARSEILLE
GROBET-LABADIE MUSEUM
MUSEUM OF PROVENÇAL ART
MENTON
COCTEAU MUSEUM
LE- MONASTIER-SUR-GAZEILLE
ABBEY CHURCH
MONTPELLIER
HÔTEL DE CABRIÈRES-SABATIER D'ESPEYRAN
MONTPEZAT-DE-QUERCY
CHURCH MUSEUM
MOULINS
MUNICIPAL AND REGIONAL MUSEUM
MULHOUSE
MUSEUM OF TEXTILE PRINTING
NANCY
LORRAINE MUSEUM OF HISTORY
NANTES
MUSEUM OF DECORATIVE ARTS
NEVERS
FAIENCE MUSEUM
NIORT
MUSEUM OF FINE ART
POITEVIN MUSEUM OF COSTUME

NOGENT-LE-ROTROU
MUNICIPAL MUSEUM

PARIS
CLUNY MUSEUM
COSTUME MUSEUM
GOBELINS MUSEUM
HÔTEL DE CLUNY MUSEUM
THE LOUVRE
MARMOTTAN MUSEUM
MUSEUM OF SWEDISH ART
NATIONAL MUSEUM OF MODERN ART
NISSIM DE CAMONDO MUSEUM
PETIT PALAIS MUSEUM

PAU
HENRI IV NATIONAL MUSEUM

PÉZENAS
VULLIOD SAINT-GERMAIN MUSEUM

PONT-L'ABBÉ
BIGOUDEN MUSEUM

PONT-DE-VAUX
CHINTREUIL MUSEUM

QUIMPER
BRITTANY MUSEUM

RAMBOUILLET
CHÂTEAU DE RAMBOUILLET

RENNES
BRITTANY MUSEUM

RHEIMS
SAINT-DENIS MUSEUM

RICHELIEU
MUSEUM OF THE 17th CENTURY

ROMANS-SUR-ISÈRE
REGIONAL MUSEUM AND INTERNATIONAL MUSEUM OF FOOTWEAR

SAINT-AMARIN
SERRET MUSEUM

ST. ÉTIENNE
MUSEUM OF ART AND INDUSTRY

SAINT ETIENNE LE MOLARD
BASTIE D'URFÉ MUSEUM

SAINT-FLOUR
MUSEUM OF THE CONSULAR HOUSE ALFRED DOUET

ST. GERMAIN LAVAL
MUNICIPAL MUSEUM

SAINT-JEAN-CAP-FERRAT
EPHRUSSI DE ROTHSCHILD FOUNDATION

SAINT-LÔ
SAINT-LÔ MUSEUM

ST. PIERRE D'OLÉRON
ALIENOR D'AQUITAINE MUSEUM

SAUMUR
CHURCH OF NOTRE DAME DE NANTILLY
MUSEUM OF DECORATIVE ARTS AND MUSEUM OF THE HORSE

SCEAUX
ILE-DE-FRANCE MUSEUM

SENS
CATHEDRAL TREASURY
OFFICIALITÉ

STRASBOURG
ALSACE MUSEUM

TALCY
CHÂTEAU DE TALCY

TORIGNI-SUR-VIRE
LOCAL MUSEUM

TOULOUSE
PAUL DUPUY MUSEUM

TOURNUS
PERRIN DE PUYCOUSIN MUSEUM

TOURS-LA-RICHE
CHÂTEAU DE PLESSIS- LÈS-TOURS

VALENCIENNES
MUSEUM OF FINE ART

VAUX-LE-VICOMTE
CHÂTEAU

VILLENEUVE-DE-MARSAN
CHÂTEAU DE RAVIGNAN

VIZILLE
CHÂTEAU DE VIZILLE

WISSEMBOURG
WESTERCAMP MUSEUM

GDR

ALTENBURG
CASTLE MUSEUM AND PLAYING CARDS MUSEUM

ARNSTADT
PALACE MUSEUM

BAUTZEN
MUSEUM OF ART AND CULTURAL HISTORY

BERLIN
BODE MUSEUM: COLLECTION OF EARLY CHRISTIAN AND BYZANTINE ART
PERGAMON MUSEUM: FAR EASTERN COLLECTION
PERGAMON MUSEUM: MUSEUM OF ETHNOGRAPHY
STATE MUSEUM OF ARTS AND CRAFTS

BLANKENSEE
VILLAGE MUSEUM

BUTTSTADT
REGIONAL MUSEUM

COTTBUS
DISTRICT MUSEUM

CRIMMITSCHAU
REGIONAL MUSEUM

CROSTAU
REGIONAL ROOM

DAHME
REGIONAL MUSEUM

DRESDEN
MUSEUM OF POPULAR ART

EBERSBACK
REGIONAL MUSEUM

EISENBERG
DISTRICT AND REGIONAL MUSEUM

EISFELD
OTTO LUDWIG REGIONAL MUSEUM

EISLEBEN
DISTRICT AND REGIONAL MUSEUM

ERFURT
FOLK-LORE MUSEUM

FALKENSTEIN
REGIONAL MUSEUM

GARDELEGEN
REGIONAL MUSEUM

GNANDSTEIN
REGIONAL MUSEUM

GOTHA
MUSEUM OF REGIONAL HISTORY AND FOLKLORE

GREIZ
DISTRICT AND REGIONAL MUSEUM

GROSSSCHÖNAU
OBERLAURITZ REGIONAL AND DAMASK MUSEUM

HALBERSTADT
MUNICIPAL MUSEUM

HALDENSLEBEN
DISTRICT MUSEUM

HEILIGENSTADT
EICHFELD REGIONAL MUSEUM

LEHDE
OPEN-AIR MUSEUM

LEIPZIG
ETHNOLOGICAL MUSEUM
MUSEUM OF ARTS AND CRAFTS

LENGENFELD
REGIONAL ROOM

LIMBACH-OBERFROHNA
REGIONAL MUSEUM

LÜBBENAU
LÜBBENAU MUSEUM IN THE SPREEWALD

NERCHAU
REGIONAL ROOM

NEUHAUS-SCHIERSCHNITZ
REGIONAL ROOM

NEUKIRCH
REGIONAL MUSEUM

PIRNA
DISTRICT MUSEUM AND POLYTECHNIC MUSEUM OF ARTIFICIAL SILK

PLAUEN
VOGTLAND DISTRICT MUSEUM

QUEDLINBURG
CASTLE MUSEUM

RUHLA
REGIONAL MUSEUM

SCHMALKALDEN
DISTRICT MUSEUM

SCHÖNBERG
REGIONAL MUSEUM

SCHWERIN
SCHWERIN STATE MUSEUM

SONDERHAUSEN
STATE REGIONAL AND CASTLE MUSEUM

WEIMAR
BELVEDERE PALACE ROCOCO MUSEUM
REGIONAL MUSEUM OF NATURAL HISTORY, HISTORY AND POPULAR ART

WERDAU
REGIONAL MUSEUM

WISMAR
SCHABBELT HOUSE REGIONAL MUSEUM

ZEITZ
MUNICIPAL MUSEUM

GFR

BAD HOMBURG
LOCAL HISTORY AND HAT MUSEUM

BAD SEGEBERG
OLD SEGEBERG TOWN HOUSE

BAD TÖLZ
BAD TÖLZ MUSEUM

BAD WINDSHEIM
REGIONAL MUSEUM

BAMBERG
TEXTILE MUSEUM

BERLIN
MUSEUM OF GERMAN FOLKLORE

BLAUBEUREN
REGIONAL MUSEUM

BONN
UNIVERSITY MUSEUM OF ART

BRAUNSCHWEIG
COUNT ANTON ULRICH MUSEUM

BRUCHSAL
PALACE

BUCHEN
STEINERNES HOUSE REGIONAL MUSEUM

BÜCKEBURG
REGIONAL MUSEUM OF SCHAUMBURG-LIPPISCH

BÜNDE
DISTRICT MUSEUM

BURGAU
REGIONAL MUSEUM

COESFELD
REGIONAL MUSEUM

DARMSTADT
PALACE MUSEUM

DETMOLD
PALACE OF THE PRINCES OF LIPPE

DINKELSBÜHL
MUSEUM OF HISTORY

DUDERSTADT
EICHSFELD REGIONAL MUSEUM

EBERMANNSTADT
REGIONAL MUSEUM

EICHSTÄTT
CATHEDRAL TREASURY

FREIBURG IM BREISGAU
PEWTER-FIGURES ROOM

GARMISCH-PARTENKIRCHEN
WERDENFELSER MUSEUM

GIFHORN
DISTRICT MUSEUM

GÜTERSLOH
REGIONAL MUSEUM

HAMBURG
ALTONA MUSEUM
SCHWARZKOPF COLLECTION

HARBURG
LIBRARY AND ART COLLECTION OF THE PRINCES OF OETTINGEN-WALLERSTEIN

HASLACH
HANSJAKOB AND REGIONAL MUSEUM
HEILSBRONN
REGIONAL MUSEUM
HELMSTEDT
DISTRICT MUSEUM
HERMANNSBURG
MISSIONARY AND REGIONAL MUSEUM
HÜLLHORST
REGIONAL MUSEUM
KASSEL
GERMAN TAPESTRY MUSEUM
KEHL
HANAU MUSEUM
KELLINGHUSEN
REGIONAL MUSEUM
KÖLN
MUSEUM OF ARTS AND CRAFTS
KÖNIGSHOFEN
REGIONAL MUSEUM
KORBACH
KORBACH REGIONAL MUSEUM
KREFELD
CENTRAL RESEARCH INSTITUTE FOR THE RESTORATION OF HISTORIC TEXTILES
TEXTILE COLLECTION
KÜNTZELSAU
REGIONAL MUSEUM
LANDSHUT
TRAUSNITZ CASTLE
LANGENAU
REGIONAL MUSEUM
HALLIG LANGENESS
HONKENSWARF FRISIAN ROOM
LAUTERBACH
HOHLHAUS MUSEUM
LEIHGESTERN
HÜTTENBERG REGIONAL MUSEUM
LENNGRIES
REGIONAL MUSEUM
LÖFFINGEN
REGIONAL MUSEUM
LOSSBURG
BLACK FOREST MUSEUM
LUCHOW
REGIONAL MUSEUM
LÜDENSCHEID
MUNICIPAL MUSEUM
LÜNE
ART COLLECTIONS OF LÜNE MONASTERY
MAINZ
CATHEDRAL AND DIOCESAN MUSEUM
MARL
REGIONAL MUSEUM
MELDORF
DITHMARSCH LAND MUSEUM
MELLE
GRÖNEGAU MUSEUM
MINDELHEIM
MINDELHEIM REGIONAL MUSEUM
MÖNCHENGLADBACH
MUNICIPAL MUSEUM
MÜLHEIM
MUNICIPAL MUSEUM
MÜNCHEN
BAVARIAN NATIONAL MUSEUM
MUNICH CITY MUSEUM
RESIDENCE MUSEUM
NEUMÜNSTER
TEXTILE MUSEUM
NEUNHOF
KNOBLAUCHLAND REGIONAL MUSEUM
NÖRDLINGEN
TOWN MUSEUM
NÜRNBERG
GERMAN NATIONAL MUSEUM
OBERGÜNZBURG
REGIONAL MUSEUM
OEVENTROP
SOUTH SEAS MUSEUM
OFFENBACH
GERMAN SHOE MUSEUM
OSTHEIM
REGIONAL MUSEUM
PIRMASENS
SHOE MUSEUM
PRUNN
PALACE
RAHDEN
RAHDEN FARM MUSEUM
REUTLINGEN
REGIONAL MUSEUM
RINTELN
SCHAUMBURG REGIONAL MUSEUM
RÖTZ
RÖTZ REGIONAL MUSEUM
ST. GEORGEN
REGIONAL MUSEUM
SCHLITZ
REGIONAL MUSEUM
SCHWANDORF
REGIONAL MUSEUM
SESSLACH
REGIONAL MUSEUM
SIMMERN
HUNSRÜCK MUSEUM
SONTHOFEN
REGIONAL MUSEUM
STARNBERG
MUNICIPAL MUSEUM
STAUFEN
REGIONAL AND COSTUME MUSEUM
TRIBERG
REGIONAL MUSEUM
TRIER
MUNICIPAL MUSEUM
VEITSHÖCHHEIM
SUMMER PALACE
WASSERTRÜDINGEN
SCHWARZKOPF COLLECTION
WEIDEN
TOWN MUSEUM
WEIKERSHEIM
PALACE MUSEUM
WEILER
WEST ALLGAU REGIONAL MUSEUM
WETTELSHEIM
LOCAL COLLECTION
WOLFACH
WOLFACH REGIONAL MUSEUM
WUNSIEDEL
WUNSIEDEL MUSEUM OF THE FICHTELGEBIRG REGION
WÜRZBURG
RESIDENCE
ZIEGENHAIN
SCHWALM MUSEUM

GHANA

KUMASI
PREMPEH II JUBILEE MUSEUM

GREAT BRITAIN

BATH
MUSEUM OF COSTUME
BIRMINGHAM
BIRMINGHAM CITY MUSEUM AND ART GALLERY
BLACKBURN
LEWIS MUSEUM OF TEXTILE MACHINERY
BLITHFIELD
MUSEUM OF CHILDHOOD AND COSTUME
BOLTON
TONGE MOOR TEXTILE MACHINERY MUSEUM
BRISTOL
G. B. BRITTON AND SONS LIMITED
CASTLE HOWARD
CASTLE HOWARD COSTUME GALLERY
COOKSTOWN
WELLBROOK BEETLING MILL
DORKING
POLESDEN LACEY
DUNFERMLINE
PITTENCRIEFF HOUSE MUSEUM
DURHAM
GULBENKIAN MUSEUM OF ORIENTAL ART AND ARCHAEOLOGY
EARDISLAND
BURTON COURT
EDGEHILL
UPTON HOUSE
EDINBURGH
CANONGATE TOLBOOTH
EDINBURGH CASTLE
LAURISTON CASTLE
MUSEUM GALLERY
RUSSELL COLLECTION OF HARPSICHORDS AND CLAVICHORDS
FORDINGBRIDGE
BREAMORE HOUSE
HALE PARK
GLAMIS
ANGUS FOLK COLLECTION
GRANTHAM
BELVOIR CASTLE
HALIFAX
BANKFIELD MUSEUM AND ART GALLERY
HAWICK
WILTON LODGE MUSEUM
IPSWICH
CHRISTCHURCH MANSION
KETTERING
WESTFIELD MUSEUM
KINGUSSIE
HIGHLAND FOLK MUSEUM
LEIGH
PENNINGTON HALL MUSEUM AND ART GALLERY
LONDON
BETHNAL GREEN MUSEUM
GUILDHALL MUSEUM
HAMPTON COURT PALACE
MUSEUM OF LEATHERCRAFT
MELTONIAN WREN LIMITED
MANCHESTER
GALLERY OF ENGLISH COSTUME
WHITWORTH ART GALLERY
MARKET HARBOROUGH
SYMINGTON MUSEUM OF PERIOD CORSETRY
NEWTOWN
NEWTOWN WOOLLEN INDUSTRY MUSEUM
NORTHAMPTON
CENTRAL MUSEUM AND ART GALLERY
NORWICH
BRIDEWELL MUSEUM
NOTTINGHAM
INDUSTRIAL MUSEUM
NOTTINGHAM CITY MUSEUM AND ART GALLERY
PADIHAM
GAWTHORPE HALL
PAISLEY
PAISLEY MUSEUM AND ART GALLERIES
RUSHOLME
PLATT HALL
SHERBORNE
SHERBORNE MUSEUM
SHIFNAL
WESTON PARK
STREET
SHOE MUSEUM
WADDESDON
WADDESDON MANOR
WALSALL
MUSEUM OF LEATHERCRAFT
WELLS
HOLKHAM HALL

WELSHPOOL
POWIS CASTLE
WIMBORNE ST. GILES
ST. GILES' HOUSE
WOODSTOCK
BLENHEIM PALACE
WREXHAM
CHIRK CASTLE
YEOVIL
BOROUGH MUSEUM
YORK
CASTLE HOWARD
YORK CASTLE MUSEUM

GREECE

AGION OROS
MONASTERY SACRISTY
AIANI
ARCHAEOLOGICAL AND FOLKLORE COLLECTION
AIGION
MONASTERY OF THE TAXIARCHS
ALEXANDROUPOLIS
E. FILIPPIDIS PRIVATE COLLECTION
AMORGOS
CHOZOVIOTISSA MONASTERY
ANO KARDAMYLA
KARDAMYLA CULTURAL CENTRE OF MICHAEL AND STAMATIA XYLAS
ANO MERA
MONASTERY OF THE PANAGIA TOURLIANI
ARGOSTOLION
E. BASSIAS HISTORICAL AND FOLKLORE MUSEUM
COLLECTION OF THE MTROPOLIS OF KEFALLINIA
ATHENS
BENAKI MUSEUM
BYZANTINE MUSEUM
COLLECTION OF THE LIKION TON ELLINIDON (LYCEUM CLUB OF GREEK WOMEN)
GREEK FOLKLORE SOCIETY MUSEUM COLLECTION
LOVERDO MUSEUM
MUSEUM OF GREEK POPULAR ART
MUSEUM OF SACRED ICONS OF THE ARCHBISHOPRIC OF ATHENS
NATIONAL HISTORICAL MUSEUM
I. PAPANDONIOU PRIVATE COLLECTION
AVLON
ZYGOMALA MUSEUM
BATSI
MONASTERY OF THE ZOODOCHOS PIGI OR AGIA
CHIOS
ETHNOLOGICAL AND FOLKLORE MUSEUM OF THE A. KORAIS LIBRARY
NEA MONI MONASTERY
DIMITSANA
GREEK FOLK MUSEUM
FALIKA
PANACHRANTOS MONASTERY
IOANNINA
MUNICIPAL MUSEUM
NISI MUSEUM OF THE PREREVOLUTIONARY PERIOD
IRAKLION
HISTORICAL MUSEUM OF CRETE
E. KASTRINOYANNIS PRIVATE COLLECTION
KALAMATA
ARCHAEOLOGICAL MUSEUM
KALAVRYTA
MEGA SPILEON MONASTERY
KALLONI
MONASTERY OF ST. IGNATIOS, LIMONOS
KARDITSA
COLLECTION OF THE KARDITSA FOLKLORE SOCIETY
KARPENISSION
TATARNA MONASTERY
KASTELLORIZON
ARCHAEOLOGICAL MUSEUM
KOMOTINI
FOLKLORE MUSEUM OF THRACE
KOS
FOLK ART MUSEUM OF THE METROPOLIS OF KOS
LACHANAS
MUSEUM
LIMENARIA
I. PAPAGEORGIOU PRIVATE COLLECTION
METEORA
MONASTERY OF AGION PANTON (VARLAAM)
MONASTERY OF AGIOS STEPHANOS
MYTILINI (MYTILENE)
H. BINOS PRIVATE COLLECTION
NATIONAL FOLK MUSEUM OF LESVOS
M. VLACHOS PRIVATE COLLECTION
PANAGITSA PELLIS
CHURCH OF THE KOIMISSIS TIS THEOTOKOU
PAROS
BYZANTINE COLLECTION OF KATAPOLIANI
PERATATA
MONASTERY OF AGIOS ANDREAS
PYRGOS
P. NOMIKOS PRIVATE COLLECTION
RETHYMNON
ARKADI MONASTERY
COLLECTION OF THE LIKION TON ELLINIDON
MONASTERY OF AGIOS IOANNIS PREVELIS
RHODES
DECORATIVE ARTS COLLECTION OF THE MUSEUM OF RHODES
PALACE OF THE GRAND MASTERS (KASTELLO)
SAMARINA, GREVENA
CHURCH OF THE PANAGIA
SKOPELOS
MONASTERY OF THE EVANGELISTRIA
SPETSAI
MUSEUM
SYMI
ARCHAEOLOGICAL COLLECTION
THESSALONIKI
FOLKLORE MUSEUM AND ARCHIVES
FOLKLORE MUSEUM OF NORTHERN GREECE
TINOS
CHURCH OF THE PANAGIA EVANGELISTRIA
TRIKALA
ECCESIASTICAL MUSEUM OF THE METROPOLIS OF TRIKKI AND STAGOI
MONASTERY OF AGIOS VISSARION (DOUSSIKOU)
VOLOS
K. A. MAKRIS PRIVATE COLLECTION
XANTHI
FOLKLORE MUSEUM
YPATI
AGATHONOS MONASTERY
ZAKYNTHOS
MUSEUM OF SOMOMOS AND OTHER ILLUSTRIOUS ZAKYNTHIANS
ZAVORDA
MONASTERY OF OSSIOS NIKANOR
ZERBITSA
MONASTERY OF THE KOIMISSIS TIS THEOTOKOU

GUATEMALA

GUATEMALA CITY
NATIONAL MUSEUM OF ART AND HANDICRAFTS

HUNGARY

BALASSAGYARMAT
PALÓC MUSEUM
BUDAPEST
CHINESE MUSEUM
FERENC HOPP MUSEUM OF ORIENTAL ART
MUSEUM OF APPLIED ARTS
ESZTERGOM
MUSEUM OF CHRISTIANITY
GYÖNGYÖS
MÁTRA MUSEUM
KALOCSA
KÁROLY VISKI MUSEUM
KISKUNHALAS
JÁNOS THORMA MUSEUM
MEZŐKÖVESD
MATYÓ MUSEUM

INDIA

AHMEDABAD
CALICO MUSEUM OF TEXTILES
GUJARAT MUSEUM SOCIETY
BHAWANAGAR
GANDHI SMRITI MUSEUMS
BHOPAL
CENTRAL MUSEUM
BHUJ
KUTCH MUSEUM
BIJAPUR
ARCHAEOLOGICAL MUSEUM
BIKANER
GANGA GOLDEN JUBILEE MUSEUM
BOMBAY
PRINCE OF WALES MUSEUM OF WESTERN INDIA
CALCUTTA
ASUTOSH MUSEUM OF INDIAN ART
BIRLA ACADEMY OF ART AND CULTURE
CRAFTS MUSEUM
INDIAN MUSEUM
CHAMBA
BHURI SINGH MUSEUM
GAUHATI
ASSAM STATE MUSEUM
GAYA
GAYA MUSEUM
GURUKUL JHAJJAR
HARYANA PRANTIYA PURATATVA SANGRAHALAYA
HARDWAR
GURUKULA MUSEUM
HYDERABAD
SALARJUNG MUSEUM
STATE ARCHAEOLOGICAL MUSEUM
IMPHAL
MANIPUR STATE MUSEUM
JAIPUR
THE MAHARAJA OF JAIPUR MUSEUM
JAMMU
DOGRA ART GALLERY
JUNAGADH
DARBAR HALL MUSEUM
LUCKNOW
STATE MUSEUM
MADRAS
VICTORIA TECHNICAL INSTITUTE
MADURAI
GANDHI SMARAK SANGRAHALAYA
NEW DELHI
BHARTIYA ADIM JATI SEVAK SANGH MUSEUM
CRAFTS MUSEUM
TIBET HOUSE MUSEUM
PATIALA
STATE MUSEUM
POONA
BHARTIYA ITIHASA SAMSHODHAKA MANDALA MUSEUM
MAHATMA PHULE VASTU SANGRAHALAYA
RAJA KELKAR MUSEUM
PUDDUKKOTTAI
GOVERNMENT MUSEUM
SHILLONG
CENTRAL MUSEUM
SURAT
SARDAR V. PATEL MUSEUM
TAL. KHATAV
SHRI BHAVANI MUSEUM AND LIBRARY
VARANASI
BHARAT KALA BHAVAN
MAHARAJA BANARAS MUSEUM

INDONESIA

DJAKARTA
SEDJARAH MUSEUM

IRAN

BANDAR ABBAS
MOHITSHENASI MUSEUM
KASHAN
KASHAN MUSEUM
MASHHAD
ASTANE QODS MUSEUM
TEHERAN
MUSEUM OF DECORATIVE ARTS

IRAQ

BAGHDAD
BAGHDAD GOVERNORATE MUSEUM OF COSTUMES AND ETHNOGRAPHY
BAGHDADI MUSEUM
MUSEUM OF ETHNOGRAPHY

IRELAND

BANTRY
BANTRY HOUSE
CASTLEREA
CLONALIS HOUSE
KILKENNY
ROTHE HOUSE MUSEUM

ISRAEL

HAIFA
MUSEUM OF ANCIENT ART
TEL-AVIV
MUSEUM OF ETHNOGRAPHY AND FOLKLORE

ITALY

ANAGNI
CATHEDRAL TREASURY
BENEVENTO
SANNIO MUSEUM
BOLOGNA
NATIONAL HISTORIC AND EDUCATIONAL MUSEUM OF UPHOLSTERY AND FURNISHING TEXTILES
COMO
SILK MUSEUM
CREMONA
CATHEDRAL
FABRIANO
MUNICIPAL ART GALLERY AND ARAZZI MUSEUM
FLORENCE
BARDINI MUSEUM AND CORSI GALLERY
SILVER MUSEUM
GENOA
ART GALLERY
CHIOSSONE MUSEUM
ROYAL PALACE (NOW BALBI- DURAZZO PALACE)
GIGNESE (STRESA)
MUSEUM OF UMBRELLAS AND PARASOLS
ISOLA BELLA
PALACE
LA FAVORITA
PITRÉ MUSEUM OF SICILIAN ETHNOGRAPHY
LORETO
APOSTOLIC PALACE
MANTUA
CATHEDRAL
DUCAL PALACE
MILAN
MUSEUM OF THE BASILICA OF SANT-AMBROGIO
POLDI-PEZZOLI MUSEUM
MODENA
CITY MUSEUM
NAPLES
ROYAL PALACE
NUORO
REGIONAL MUSEUM OF COSTUME AND POPULAR TRADITIONS
PADUA
MUNICIPAL MUSEUM
PIACENZA
ALBERONI GALLERY
PIENZA
MUSEUM
RAVENNA
NATIONAL MUSEUM OF ANTIQUITIES
RECANATI
DIOCESAN MUSEUM
ROME
NATIONAL MUSEUM OF ARTS AND POPULAR TRADITIONS
SAN GIMIGNANO
MUSEUM OF SACRED ART
TOLMEZZO
CARNICO MUSEUM OF ARTS AND POPULAR TRADITIONS
TRENT
DIOCESAN MUSEUM
UDINE
FRIULANO MUSEUM OF POPULAR ARTS AND TRADITIONS
URBINO
NATIONAL GALLERY OF THE MARCHES
VENICE
THE FRANCHETTI GALLERY
SETTECENTO MUSEUM

JAPAN

KYOTO
TEXTILE MUSEUM
NARA-SHI
YAMATO CULTURAL HOUSE
NIKKO-SHI
NIKKO TREASURE HOUSE
SAKATA-SHI
HONMA ART MUSEUM
SAPPORO-SHI
AINU MUSEUM
TOKYO
COSTUME MUSEUM
FIBRE MUSEUM
SUGINO GAKUEN COSTUME MUSEUM
TEXTILE MUSEUM
YOKOHAMA
SILK MUSEUM

KOREA, REPUBLIC OF

SEOUL
MUSEUM OF CHANG-DUK PALACE

KUWAIT

KUWAIT
KUWAIT MUSEUM

MALTA

MDINA
CATHEDRAL MUSEUM
VALLETTA
ST. JOHN'S MUSEUM AND CATHEDRAL

MEXICO

CHIHUAHUA
CHIHUAHUA REGIONAL MUSEUM
MEXICO CITY
NATIONAL ANTHROPOLOGICAL MUSEUM
XALAPA
VERACRUZ MUSEUM OF ANTHROPOLOGY

MOROCCO

FEZ
BATHA MUSEUM
MARRAKESH
DAR SI SAID MUSEUM
RABAT
MUSEUM OF THE OUDAIAS
TANGIER
KASBAH MUSEUM

NETHERLANDS

AMSTERDAM
NATIONAL MUSEUM: DEPARTMENT OF DUTCH HISTORY
NATIONAL MUSEUM: DEPARTMENT OF SCULPTURE AND INDUSTRIAL ART
ARNHEM
NATIONAL MUSEUM OF ETHNOLOGY: NETHERLANDS OPEN-AIR MUSEUM
ASSEN
DRENTHE PROVINCIAL MUSEUM
AXEL
AXEL MUSEUM OF RURAL LIFE
BERGEN OP ZOOM
DISTRICT MUSEUM
BREUKELEN
GUNTERSTEIN RESIDENCE
DELFT
PAUL TETAR VAN ELVEN MUSEUM
DENEKAMP
SINGRAVEN
DE STEEG
MIDDACHTEN CASTLE
DEVENTER
THE THREE HERRINGS
EINDHOVEN
KEMPENLAND MUSEUM
ENKHUIZEN
NATIONAL ZUIDERZEE MUSEUM
GOIRLE
HET SMISKE MUSEUM OF LOCAL HISTORY
'S GRAVENHAGE
NETHERLANDS COSTUME MUSEUM: CABINET OF FASHION AND TASTE
HAARLEM
TOWN HALL
HARDEWIJK
MUSEUM OF THE HISTORY OF THE VELUWE
HOORN
DE VISSER COLLECTION
LEEUWARDEN
FRISIAN MUSEUM
LEIDEN
LAKENHAL MUNICIPAL MUSEUM
MAASTRICHT
TREASURY OF ST. SERVAAS CHURCH
MIDDELBURG
ZEALAND MUSEUM
OOSTBURG
CADANZE ROOM
OSS
JAN CUNEN MUSEUM
OUD-ZUILEN
ZUYLEN CASTLE
ROSENDAAL
MUSEUM OF THE GOLDEN ROSE
ROTTERDAM
HISTORICAL MUSEUM
SLUIS
TOWN LOCAL HISTORY COLLECTION
TILBURG
NETHERLANDS TEXTILE MUSEUM
VLISSINGEN
HAIRDRESSING MUSEUM
WAALWIJK
NETHERLANDS MUSEUM OF SHOES, LEATHER AND LEATHER GOODS

ZUTPHEN

MUNICIPAL MUSEUM

NEW ZEALAND

CLYDE

VINCENT COUNTY AND DUNSTAN GOLDFIELDS MUSEUM

NORWAY

BERGEN

HISTORICAL MUSEUM
WESTERN NORWAY MUSEUM OF APPLIED ART

NESBYEN

HALLINGDAL FOLK MUSEUM

RÖROS

RÖROS MUSEUM

PERU

LIMA

ARCHAEOLOGICAL MUSEUM
RAFAEL LARCO HERRERA MUSEUM
MUSEUM OF ART
NATIONAL MUSEUM OF PERUVIAN CULTURE

POLAND

ANDRYCHOW

TEXTILES MUSEUM

BIAŁYSTOK

TEXTILES MUSEUM

BYTOM

MUSEUM OF UPPER SILESIA

KAMIENNA GÓRA

MUNICIPAL MUSEUM

KONIAKÓW

LACE MUSEUM

KRAKÓW

CZARTORYSKI MUSEUM
NATIONAL ART COLLECTIONS

ŁÓDŹ

MUSEUM OF ARCHAEOLOGY AND ETHNOGRAPHY
MUSEUM OF THE HISTORY OF TEXTILES

POZNAŃ

DIOCESAN MUSEUM

PRZEMYŚL

DIOCESAN MUSEUM

TARNÓW

DIOCESAN MUSEUM

TORUŃ

MUSEUM OF ART
TORUŃ ETHNOGRAPHICAL MUSEUM

WARSAW

NATIONAL ETHNOGRAPHICAL MUSEUM
WILANÓW MUSEUM

WILKOŁAZ

MEMORIAL MUSEUM

WŁVEŁAWEK

KUJAWSKI MUSEUM

WROCŁAW

ARCHIDIOCESAN MUSEUM
ETHNOGRAPHICAL MUSEUM

ZAKOPANE

TATRA MUSEUM AND T. CHAŁUBIŃSKI MEMORIAL

PORTUGAL

ALPIARÇA

MUSEUM

BEJA

REGIONAL MUSEUM

COIMBRA

MACHADO DE CASTRO MUSEUM

GUIMARÃES

PALACE OF THE DUKES OF BRAGANCA

LAMEGO

REGIONAL MUSEUM

LISBON

MUSEUM OF POPULAR ART
MUSEUM OF RELIGIOUS ART

VILA REAL DE SANTO ANTONIO

DUCAL PALACE

ROMANIA

BUCHAREST

ART MUSEUM
ELENA AND DR. I. N. DONA COLLECTION
ING. MINOVICI MUSEUM OF MEDIEVAL ART
MUSEUM OF FOLK ART
G. OPRESCU COLLECTION
MOISE M. WEINBURG COLLECTION

CLUJ

ART MUSEUM
TRANSYLVANIAN MUSEUM OF ETHNOGRAPHY

CRAIOVA

OLTENIEI MUSEUM

IAŞI

MOLDAVIAN MUSEUM OF ETHNOLOGY

LUPŞA

VILLAGE MUSEUM

NĂSĂUD

NĂSĂUD MUSEUM

ODORHEI

ODORHEI MUSEUM

PLOIEŞTI

HAGI PRODAN HOUSE

RĂDĂUŢI

RĂDĂUŢI MUSEUM OF ETHNOGRAPHY

RIMETEA

LOCAL MUSEUM

RIMNICU SARAT

RIMNICU SARAT MUSEUM

SIBIU

BRUKENTHAL MUSEUM

SIGHET

SIGHET MUSEUM

SINAIA

PELEŞ MUSEUM

TIMIŞOARA

BANAT MUSEUM

TÎRGU JIU

TIRGU JIU MUSEUM

TÎRGU NEAMŢ

MONASTERY MUSEUM

URLAŢI

MUSEUM OF ETHNOGRAPHY

VĂLENII DE MUNTE

NICOLAE IORGA MUSEUM

SINGAPORE

SINGAPORE

ART MUSEUM AND EXHIBITION GALLERY

SOUTH AFRICA, REPUBLIC OF

ADELAIDE

"OUR HERITAGE" MUSEUM

BLOEMFONTEIN

NATIONAL MUSEUM

DURBAN

MUSEUM OF LOCAL HISTORY

KING WILLIAM'S TOWN

THE KAFFRARIAN MUSEUM

PIETERMARITZBURG

TATHAM ART GALLERY
VOORTREKKER MUSEUM

PRETORIA

NATIONAL CULTURAL HISTORY AND OPEN-AIR MUSEUM

TULBAGH

OUDEKERK VOLKSMUSEUM

UITENHAGE

UITENHAGE AFRICANA MUSEUM

SPAIN

ALBARRACIN

CATHEDRAL

BARCELONA

CAMBÓ COLLECTION AND MUSEUM OF DECORATIVE ART
FEDERICO MARES MUSEUM
TEXTILE MUSEUM

BURGOS

DIOCESAN AND CATHEDRAL MUSEUM
ROYAL CONVENT OF LAS HUELGAS

CADIZ

PROVINCIAL MUSEUM OF FINE ART

CARDEDEU

BALVEY MUSEUM AND ARCHIVES

CASTELLON

PROVINCIAL MUSEUM OF FINE ART

CORDOBA

CATHEDRAL MUSEUM AND TREASURY
PALACE OF THE MARQUISES OF VIANA

COVARRUBIAS

PAROCHIAL MUSEUM

EPILA

COLLECTION OF THE HOUSE OF ALBA

GERONA

CATHEDRAL MUSEUM AND TREASURY

IGUALADA

MUSEUM OF LEATHER

JEREZ DE LA FRONTERA

FLAMENCO MUSEUM

LEÓN

ROYAL COLLEGE OF SAN ISIDORO

LERIDA

CATHEDRAL MUSEUM

LLUCH

LLUCH TREASURY AND MUSEUM

MADRID

CERRALBO MUSEUM
COLLECTION OF THE HOUSE OF ALBA
CONVENT OF LAS DESCALZAS REALES
LAZARO GALDIANO MUSEUM
MUNICIPAL COLLECTION
MUSEUM OF THE SPANISH VILLAGE
ROYAL CARPET FACTORY

MORELLA

ETHNOLOGICAL MUSEUM OF MORELLA AND THE MAESTRAZGO

ONCALA

MUSEUM OF TAPESTRIES

PALMA DE MALLORCA

CATHEDRAL MUSEUM
DIOCESAN MUSEUM

PASTRANA

PAROCHIAL MUSEUM

RIPOLL

PAROCHIAL MUSEUM AND ARCHIVE OF FOLKLORE

SANTA MARIA DEL CAMPO

PAROCHIAL MUSEUM

SANTIAGO DE COMPOSTELA

CATHEDRAL MUSEUM

SEGOVIA

CATHEDRAL MUSEUM
PALACIO DE LA GRANJA DE SAN ILDEFONSO

SEO DE URGEL

DIOCESAN MUSEUM

SEVILLE

ALCAZAR
HOLY WEEK MUSEUM
MUSEUM AND TREASURY OF THE BASILICA OF THE MACARENA
OSUNA COLLECTION

SIGÜENZA

CATHEDRAL MUSEUM

TARRAGONA

DIOCESAN MUSEUM

TARRASA
BIOSCA TEXTILE MUSEUM

VALENCIA
GONZALEZ MARTI NATIONAL MUSEUM OF CERAMICS
MUSEUM OF THE PATRIARCH
MUSEUM OF THE VALENCIA SILK INDUSTRY

ZAMORA
CATHEDRAL MUSEUM

ZARAGOZA
ARAGON MUSEUM OF ETHNOLOGY AND NATURAL SCIENCES
CATHEDRAL MUSEUM

SWEDEN

GÖTEBORG
ETHNOGRAPHICAL MUSEUM

LINKÖPING
LINKÖPING MUSEUM

LULEĄ
NORBOTTEN MUSEUM

LUND
MUSEUM OF CULTURAL HISTORY

MARIEFRED
GRIPSHOLM CASTLE

MORA
ZORN HOUSE-MUSEUM
ZORN MUSEUM

ÖRNSKÖLDSVIK
ÖRNSKÖLDSVIK MUSEUM

ÖSTERSUND
JÄMTLAND MUSEUM

SKARA
WEST GÖTLAND MUSEUM

SKOKLOSTER
SKOKLOSTER CASTLE

STOCKHOLM
HALLWYL MUSEUM
NORDIC MUSEUM
ROYAL ARMOURY
ROYAL PALACE

SWITZERLAND

ALLSCHWIL
REGIONAL MUSEUM

BASEL
MUSEUM OF APPLIED ARTS
MUSEUM OF ETHNOLOGY

BELLINZONA
MUSEUM OF COSTUMES OF THE TICINO

BERN
BERN HISTORICAL MUSEUM
CANTONAL MUSEUM OF APPLIED ART

BURGDORF
HISTORICAL MUSEUM OF THE BURGDORF HALL OF THE KNIGHTS SOCIETY

COPPET
CHÂTEAU COPPET AND MUSEUM OF THE SWISS WHO SERVED ABROAD

DELÉMONT
JURA MUSEUM

DIESSENHOFEN
LOCAL MUSEUM

DISENTIS
COLLECTION OF THE BENEDICTINE ABBEY

EVOLÈNE
FOLKLORE MUSEUM

FLEURIER
MUSEUM

FRIBOURG
FINE ART GALLERY
MUSEUM OF ART AND HISTORY

GENEVA
ARIANA MUSEUM

GRUYÈRES
CHÂTEAU

HALLAU
REGIONAL MUSEUM

HALTEN
HALTEN TOWER

HORGEN
LOCAL MUSEUM

LANGENTHAL
REGIONAL MUSEUM

LAUSANNE
COLLECTIONS OF THE INTERNATIONAL CENTRE OF ANCIENT AND MODERN TAPESTRIES
MON REPOS MUSEUM
MUSEUM OF DECORATIVE ARTS

LICHTENSTEIG
TOGGENBURG REGIONAL MUSEUM

LIESTAL
BASEL-LAND CANTONAL MUSEUM

LOCO
MUSEUM OF THE ONSERNONE VALLEY

LUGANO
MUSEUM OF HISTORY AND ARCHAEOLOGY

LUZERN
GLACIER GARDEN AND GLACIER MUSEUM
HISTORICAL MUSEUM
SWISS MUSEUM OF COSTUMES AND REGIONAL LIFE
TREASURY OF ST. LEODEGAR'S FOUNDATION

MORGES
ALEXIS FOREL MUSEUM

OLTEN
HISTORICAL MUSEUM

RIGGISBERG
MUSEUM OF THE ABEGG FOUNDATION, BERN

SAINT-MAURICE
ABBEY TREASURY

ST. MORITZ
ENGADINE MUSEUM

SCHAFFHAUSEN
ALL SAINTS' MUSEUM

SCHÖNENWERD
SHOE MUSEUM

SION
VALÈRE CANTONAL MUSEUM

SISSACH
REGIONAL MUSEUM

SOLOTHURN
CASTLE BLUMENSTEIN HISTORICAL MUSEUM
CATHEDRAL TREASURY

STANS
HISTORICAL MUSEUM

THUN
HISTORICAL MUSEUM

VEVEY
MUSEUM OF OLD VEVEY

WIESENDANGEN
LOCAL MUSEUM

ZURICH
MURALTENGUT HOUSE
SWISS NATIONAL MUSEUM

THAILAND

BANGKOK
NATIONAL MUSEUM

TUNISIA

MAHDIA
MAHDIA MUSEUM

MOKNINE
MOKNINE MUSEUM

MONASTIR
ALI BOURGUIBA MUSEUM

SFAX
MUSEUM OF POPULAR ARTS AND TRADITIONS (JELLOULI MUSEUM)

TUNIS
ARAB MUSEUM
MUSEUM OF ISLAMIC ART

TURKEY

ANKARA
ETHNOGRAPHICAL MUSEUM

ISTANBUL
MUNICIPAL MUSEUM
MUSEUM OF TURKISH AND ISLAMIC ART

KONYA
ATATÜRK MUSEUM
MEVLÂNA MUSEUM

PERGAMUM
ETHNOGRAPHY MUSEUM

USSR

ASHKHABAD
STATE FINE ART MUSEUM OF THE REPUBLIC OF TURKMENISTAN

BAKU
MUSEUM OF THE HISTORY OF AZERBAIJAN

BOKHARA
HISTORICAL AND ETHNOGRAPHICAL MUSEUM OF BOKHARA

BREST-LITOVSK
REGIONAL MUSEUM OF FOLK ART

CHERNOVTSY
MUSEUM OF UKRAINIAN FOLKLORE

KIEV
STATE MUSEUM OF POPULAR AND DECORATIVE ART

MOSCOW
NATIONAL ARMOURY
NOVODEVICHY MONASTERY

MSTERA
MUSEUM OF HANDICRAFTS

OREL
REGIONAL MUSEUM

PALEKH
MUSEUM OF HANDICRAFTS

ZAGORSK
METROPOLITAN'S HOUSE MUSEUM

UNITED STATES

ATLANTA
ATLANTA MUSEUM

BOSTON
MUSEUM OF FINE ARTS
ISABELLA STEWART GARDNER MUSEUM

CINCINNATI
TAFT MUSEUM

DALLAS
DALLAS MUSEUM OF FASHION

DANVILLE
NATIONAL TOBACCO AND TEXTILE MUSEUM

DEERFIELD
HELEN GEIER FLYNT FABRIC HALL

DENTON
STATE MUSEUM OF THE D.A.R.

GALENA
J. R. GRANT LEATHER STORE

GRAND MARAIS
GRANT PORTAGE NATIONAL MONUMENT

GUILFORD
THOMAS GRISWOLD HOUSE

HOPEDALE
LITTLE RED SHOP

HUNTINGTON
HUNTINGTON GALLERIES

JENNER
FORT ROSS STATE HISTORIC PARK

KENNESAW
BIG SHANTY MUSEUM

KODIAK
KODIAK HISTORICAL SOCIETY MUSEUM

LUBBOCK
TEXAS TECHNICAL UNIVERSITY MUSEUM

MACKINAC ISLAND
STUART HOUSE MUSEUM OF ASTOR FUR POST

NEW LONDON
LYMAN ALLYN MUSEUM

NEW ORLEANS
LOUISIANA STATE MUSEUM
PRESBYTÈRE

NEW YORK
COOPER-HEWITT MUSEUM OF DECORATIVE ARTS AND DESIGN
METROPOLITAN MUSEUM OF ART
SCALAMANDRE MUSEUM OF TEXTILES
TRAPHAGEN SCHOOL OF FASHION, MUSEUM COLLECTION

NORTH ANDOVER
MERRIMACK VALLEY TEXTILE MUSEUM

OAKLAND
MILLS COLLEGE ART GALLERY

PAWTUCKET
OLD SLATER MILL MUSEUM

PHILADELPHIA
BLUMHAVEN LIBRARY AND GALLERY
DREXEL MUSEUM COLLECTION

PHOENIX
PHOENIX ART MUSEUM

PORTLAND
MUSEUM OF NATURAL HISTORY

RAPID CITY
SIOUX INDIAN MUSEUM

RUSHVILLE
NUNDAWAGA SOCIETY FOR HISTORY AND FOLKLORE

SEATTLE
UNIVERSITY OF WASHINGTON, COSTUME AND TEXTILE STUDY CENTER

SHREVEPORT
R. W. NORTON ART GALLERY

WACO
EAST TERRACE
HERITAGE SOCIETY OF WACO

WASHINGTON
NATIONAL MUSEUM OF HISTORY AND TECHNOLOGY
RENWICK GALLERY
TEXTILE MUSEUM

WINSTON-SALEM
MUSEUM OF EARLY SOUTHERN DECORATIVE ARTS

WOODWARD
PIONEER MUSEUM

YUGOSLAVIA

BELGRADE
ETHNOGRAPHICAL MUSEUM
MAY 25th MUSEUM

DUBROVNIK
TOWN MUSEUM

HERCEGNOVI
TREASURY

HVAR
REFECTORY
TREASURY OF THE CATHEDRAL

JELSA
TREASURY

KOMIŽA
MUSEUM

KOPER
ART AND HISTORICAL MUSEUM

KORČULA
CATHEDRAL TREASURY

KOŠLJUN
MONASTIC MUSEUM

LESKOVAC
TOWN MUSEUM

LJUBLJANA
NATIONAL MUSEUM

NIŠ
OCHRID NATIONAL MUSEUM

PERAST
TREASURY

SENJ
DIOCESAN MUSEUM

SINJ
ALKARI MUSEUM

SPLIT
TREASURY

TROGIR
TREASURY

ZADAR
ETHNOGRAPHICAL MUSEUM
TREASURY OF THE CATHEDRAL AND OF THE BENEDICTINE NUNNERY OF SV. MARIJA

ZAGREB
ETHNOGRAPHICAL MUSEUM
HISTORICAL MUSEUM OF CROATIA
MUSEUM OF APPLIED ARTS

Printing, photography

AUSTRIA

AIGEN
COLLECTIONS OF SCHLÄGL MONASTERY

DROSENDORF
FRANZ KIESSLING MUSEUM

EISBACH
COLLECTION OF REIN CISTERCIAN MONASTERY

SALZBURG
FRANK COLLECTION OF THE HISTORY OF PHOTOGRAPHY

VIENNA
HERNALS DISTRICT MUSEUM
MUSEUM OF INDUSTRY AND TECHNOLOGY

BELGIUM

ANTWERP
PLANTIN-MORETUS MUSEUM

BRUSSELS
INTERNATIONAL PRESS MUSEUM

GHENT
FOLKLORE MUSEUM
MUSEUM OF THE HISTORY OF SCIENCE

BRAZIL

RIO DE JANEIRO
MUSEUM OF THE NATIONAL PRINTING WORKS
PRESS MUSEUM

BULGARIA

RILA
RILA MONASTERY NATIONAL MUSEUM

CANADA

OTTAWA
NATIONAL FILM BOARD MUSEUM

TORONTO
MACKENZIE HOUSE

COLOMBIA

BOGOTA
MUSEUM OF GRAPHIC ART

CZECHOSLOVAKIA

JÁCHYMOV
MUNICIPAL MUSEUM

KOŠICE
TECHNICAL MUSEUM

OPAVA
SILESIAN MUSEUM: COLLECTIONS OF PREHISTORY AND PHOTOGRAPHY

PRAGUE
NATIONAL TECHNICAL MUSEUM

VIMPERK
MUNICIPAL MUSEUM AND ŠUMAVY GALLERY

ŽĎÁR NAD SÁZAVOU
MUSEUM OF THE BOOK

DENMARK

ARHUS
DANISH PRESS MUSEUM

COPENHAGEN
ROYAL LIBRARY

FRANCE

BEAUNE
MUSEUM OF FINE ART

BIÈVRES
MUSEUM OF PHOTOGRAPHY

CHALON-SUR-SAÔNE
DENON MUSEUM

LANGRES
HÔTEL DU BREUIL DE SAINT- GERMAIN MUSEUM

LILLE
MUSEUM OF INDUSTRY, COMMERCE, TECHNOLOGY AND AGRICULTURE

LYON
MUSEUM OF PRINTING AND PAPER-MONEY

NICE
INTERNATIONAL MUSEUM OF MALACOLOGY

PARIS
VALENTIN HAÜY MUSEUM
NATIONAL TECHNICAL MUSEUM

VINCENNES
KODAK MUSEUM

GDR

BAUTZEN
MUSEUM OF ART AND CULTURAL HISTORY

BITTERFELD
DISTRICT MUSEUM

DRESDEN
INSTITUTE OF PRECISION INSTRUMENT-MAKING OF THE TECHNICAL UNIVERSITY OF DRESDEN
MUSEUM OF PHOTOGRAPHY
POLYTECHNIC MUSEUM
STATE ART COLLECTIONS: DEPARTMENT OF PRINTS AND DRAWINGS

HILDBURGHAUSEN
REGIONAL MUSEUM

LEIPZIG
BOOK AND WRITING MUSEUM OF THE GERMAN BOOK-TRADE
ISKRA MEMORIAL
LENIN MEMORIAL
MUSEUM OF THE HISTORY OF THE CITY OF LEIPZIG

SCHLEUSINGEN
REGIONAL MUSEUM

GFR

AACHEN
AACHEN MUSEUM OF THE INTERNATIONAL PRESS

BAD HOMBURG
LOCAL HISTORY AND HAT MUSEUM

BAYREUTH
MUSEUM OF HISTORIC TYPEWRITERS

BERLIN
MUSEUM OF THE BLIND
DÜSSELDORF
DÜSSELDORF MUSEUM OF PHOTOGRAPHY
ELLWANGEN
PALACE MUSEUM
ESCHWEGE
REGIONAL MUSEUM
FRANKFURT
MUSEUM OF APPLIED ART
FULDA
EXHIBITION COLLECTION OF THE HESSE LAND LIBRARY AT FULDA
HACHTEL
OTTMAR MERGENTHALER'S BIRTHPLACE
INGOLSTADT
MUNICIPAL MUSEUM
LÜNEBURG
MUSEUM OF THE PRINCIPALITY OF LÜNEBURG
MAINZ
BOOK-BINDERS' MUSEUM
GUTENBERG MUSEUM
MAXBERG
SOLENHOFER COMPANY MUSEUM
MÜNCHEN
FILM AND PHOTOGRAPHY MUSEUM IN MUNICH CITY MUSEUM
GERMAN MUSEUM
OFFENBACH
KLINGSPOR MUSEUM
REGENSBURG
MUSEUM OF THE PALACE OF THE PRINCES OF THURN AND TAXIS
SCHWABACH
TOWN MUSEUM

GREAT BRITAIN

BOURNEMOUTH
BRITISH TYPEWRITER MUSEUM
CAMBRIDGE
UNIVERSITY COLLECTION OF AERIAL PHOTOGRAPHS
LIVERPOOL
HORNBY LIBRARY
LONDON
KINGSTON-UPON-THAMES MUSEUM AND ART GALLERY
KODAK MUSEUM
SCIENCE MUSEUM
ST. IVES
BARNES MUSEUM OF CINEMATOGRAPHY
STRABANE
PRINTING PRESS

HUNGARY

GYOMA
IMRE KNER MUSEUM

ISRAEL

SAFED
MUSEUM OF THE PRINTING ARTS

ITALY

RIVA DEL GARDA
CIVIC MUSEUM
SIENA
PUBLIC LIBRARY
STUPINIGI
PALAZZINA DI STUPINIGI
VENICE
ARMENIAN MONASTERY

JAPAN

TOKYO
OBUNSHA CENTER OF PUBLISHING CULTURE
PENTAX GALLERY
PUBLICATION CENTRE OF OBUNSHA COMPANY

NETHERLANDS

AMSTERDAM
COLLECTION OF THE NETHERLANDS TYPEFOUNDRY AND PRINTING MACHINERY COMPANY
NETHERLANDS MUSEUM OF THE PRESS
'S GRAVENHAGE
INTERNATIONAL PRESS MUSEUM
HAARLEM
ENSCHEDÉ MUSEUM
LEIDEN
PRINT CABINET OF THE NATIONAL UNIVERSITY
TILBURG
TYPEWRITING AND WRITING MUSEUM
UTRECHT
DIOCESAN MUSEUM

NEW ZEALAND

AUCKLAND
MUSEUM OF TRANSPORT AND TECHNOLOGY
DUNEDIN
OTAGO EARLY SETTLERS' ASSOCIATION (INC)
RUSSELL
POMPALLIER HOUSE

ROMANIA

BUCHAREST
ART MUSEUM
G. OPRESCU COLLECTION
SLATINA
LOCAL MUSEUM
TÎRGAVISTE
MUSEUM OF PRINTING AND EARLY PRINTED BOOKS

SOUTH AFRICA, REPUBLIC OF

CAPE TOWN
SOUTH AFRICAN MUSEUM
JOHANNESBURG
PHOTOGRAPHIC MUSEUM
PAARL
OLD PARSONAGE MUSEUM

SPAIN

MADRID
MUSEUM OF SPANISH BOOKS
NATIONAL ENGRAVING WORKS
ROYAL LIBRARY
VILLAGARCIA DE CAMPOS
MUSEUM OF THE COLLEGIATE CHURCH

SWEDEN

KARLSTAD
VÄRMLAND MUSEUM
STOCKHOLM
TECHNICAL MUSEUM

SWITZERLAND

BASEL
MUSEUM OF APPLIED ARTS
PUBLIC ART COLLECTION
BERN
SWISS TECHNICAL MUSEUM OF BOOKBINDING
BEROMÜNSTER
REGIONAL MUSEUM
LAUFEN
LAUFENTAL REGIONAL MUSEUM
VEVEY
MUSEUM OF OLD VEVEY

USSR

KISHINEV
ISKRA MUSEUM
MOSCOW
UNDERGROUND PRESS OF THE C. C. R.S.D.L.P. (B) 1905-6

UNITED STATES

CALHOUN
NEW ECHOTA
DEERFIELD
WILSON PRINTING HOUSE
GALENA
'GALENA GAZETTE' MUSEUM
HAMPTON
MEETING HOUSE GREEN MEMORIAL AND HISTORICAL ASSOCIATION MUSEUM
MONTPELIER
VERMONT HISTORICAL SOCIETY MUSEUM
NEW YORK
JOHN H. FINLEY MUSEUM OF THE PRINTED WORD
RIVERSIDE
WESTERN CAMERA MUSEUM
ROCHESTER
INTERNATIONAL MUSEUM OF PHOTOGRAPHY
SAN JUAN
THE HOUSE OF THE BOOK
SEATTLE
CALKINS-SLATER METROPOLITAN MUSEUM OF ART
TEMPE
UNIVERSITY ART COLLECTIONS
VINCENNES
INDIANA TERRITORY STATE MEMORIAL
WASHINGTON
NATIONAL MUSEUM OF HISTORY AND TECHNOLOGY

Clocks, watches, instruments, including weighing and measuring equipment

AUSTRALIA

MONTVILLE
ELANDS OLD CLOCK DISPLAY AND MINI MUSEUM
WEST GOSFORD
KENDALL COTTAGE

AUSTRIA

ARNFELS
MUSEUM OF CLOCKS, MUSICAL INSTRUMENTS AND FOLKLORE

BAD ISCHL
MUSEUM OF THE HAENEL AND PANCERA FAMILIES
GRAZ
JOANNEUM PROVINCIAL MUSEUM OF CULTURAL HISTORY AND APPLIED ART
KLOSTERNEUBURG
MUSEUM OF THE AUGUSTINIAN MONASTERY
KREMSMUNSTER
MONASTERY COLLECTIONS
LANGENLOIS
REGIONAL MUSEUM
OBERPERFUSS
ANICH-HUEBER MUSEUM
PÖLS-ENZERSDORF
HUSSLIK REGIONAL MUSEUM
REUTTE
REGIONAL MUSEUM
VIENNA
CLOCK MUSEUM OF THE CITY OF VIENNA
MUSEUM OF THE HISTORY OF ART: SCULPTURE AND APPLIED ART COLLECTION
MUSEUM OF INDUSTRY AND TECHNOLOGY
SOBEK COLLECTION
TREASURY OF THE GERMAN ORDER

BELGIUM

ANTWERP
PROVINCIAL MUSEUM OF INDUSTRIAL ART
GHENT
MUSEUM OF ANTIQUITIES
MUSEUM OF THE HISTORY OF SCIENCE
LIERRE
ASTRONOMICAL CLOCK
SAINT-TROND
BÉGUINAGE MUSEUM

BRAZIL

GOIÁS
MUSEUM OF THE BANDEIRAS

BULGARIA

SOFIA
NATIONAL POLYTECHNIC MUSEUM

CHINA, P.R.

PEKING
IMPERIAL PALACE
OLD OBSERVATORY
PLANETARIUM
TIENSIN (TIANJING)
PEOPLE'S HALL OF SCIENCE

CZECHOSLOVAKIA

BRATISLAVA
MUNICIPAL MUSEUM
KOŠICE
TECHNICAL MUSEUM
ORAVSKY PODZÁMOK
ORAVA MUSEUM
PRAGUE
NATIONAL TECHNICAL MUSEUM
PŘEROV
J. A. KOMENSKY MUSEUM

FINLAND

ESPOO
CLOCK MUSEUM

FRANCE

BESANÇON
MUSEUM OF CLOCKS AND WATCHES
BORDEAUX
MUNICIPAL COLLECTION OF COINS AND MEDALS
BOURGES
HÔTEL LALLEMANT
LAVAUR
VAURAIS MUSEUM
MOLSHEIM
MUSEUM OF ART AND HISTORY
MONT-SAINT-MICHEL
MUSEUM OF HISTORY
PARIS
ASTRONOMICAL MUSEUM OF THE PARIS OBSERVATORY
THE LOUVRE
NATIONAL CONSERVATORY OF ARTS AND CRAFTS
NATIONAL TECHNICAL MUSEUM
STRASBOURG
MUSEUM OF DECORATIVE ARTS
TOULOUSE
PAUL DUPUY MUSEUM

GDR

DELITZSCH
DISTRICT MUSEUM
DRESDEN
STATE HALL OF MATHEMATICS AND PHYSICS
MEISSEN
MUNICIPAL AND DISTRICT MUSEUM

GFR

BAMBERG
HISTORICAL MUSEUM
FRIEDBERG (SCHWABEN)
REGIONAL MUSEUM
FURTWANGEN
HISTORIC CLOCK COLLECTION
GRAFENWÖHR
REGIONAL MUSEUM
JEVER
PALACE AND REGIONAL MUSEUM
JUIST
COASTAL MUSEUM
LOSSBURG
BLACK FOREST MUSEUM
MICHELSTADT
ODENWALD MUSEUM
MÜNCHEN
BAVARIAN NATIONAL MUSEUM
NEUSTADT (SCHWARZWALD)
REGIONAL ROOMS
NEUWIED
DISTRICT MUSEUM
ST. GEORGEN
REGIONAL MUSEUM
SCHWABMÜNCHEN
REGIONAL MUSEUM
SCHWEINFURT
MUNICIPAL MUSEUM
SCHWENNINGEN
HELLMT KIENZLE CLOCK MUSEUM
SCHWENNINGEN REGIONAL MUSEUM
STUTTGART
WÜRTTEMBERG MUSEUM
WUPPERTAL
WUPPERTAL CLOCK MUSEUM

GREAT BRITAIN

BASINGSTOKE
WILLIS MUSEUM
BIRMINGHAM
AVERY HISTORICAL MUSEUM
MUSEUM OF SCIENCE AND INDUSTRY
BURY ST. EDMUNDS
GERSHOM-PARKINGTON MEMORIAL COLLECTION OF CLOCKS AND WATCHES
CAMBRIDGE
WHIPPLE MUSEUM OF THE HISTORY OF SCIENCE
LEICESTER
NEWARKE HOUSES MUSEUM
LINCOLN
USHER GALLERY
LIVERPOOL
CITY OF LIVERPOOL MUSEUMS
MORATH BROS.
LONDON
CLOCKMAKERS' COMPANY MUSEUM
DOLLOND AND AITCHISON LIMITED
OLD ROYAL OBSERVATORY
SCIENCE MUSEUM
MANCHESTER
MANCHESTER MUSEUM OF SCIENCE AND TECHNOLOGY
NORWICH
BRIDEWELL MUSEUM
OXFORD
MUSEUM OF THE HISTORY OF SCIENCE
ROTHERHAM
ROTHERHAM CORPORATION DEPARTMENT OF TRADING STANDARDS
TIVERTON
TIVERTON CASTLE
WINCHESTER
THE WESTGATE MUSEUM

HUNGARY

SÁROSPATAK
MUSEUM OF THE REFORMED CHURCH

INDIA

CALCUTTA
BIRLA INDUSTRIAL AND TECHNOLOGICAL MUSEUM
DHULIA
I.V.K. RAJWADE SANSHODHAN MANDAL MUSEUM
NEW DELHI
ARCHAEOLOGICAL MUSEUM

IRELAND

DUBLIN
EGESTORFF COLLECTION

ITALY

BOLOGNA
MUSEUM OF THE INSTITUTE OF ASTRONOMY
FLORENCE
CARTOGRAPHY AND INSTRUMENTS MUSEUM
NATIONAL MUSEUM FOR THE HISTORY OF SCIENCE
ROME
ASTRONOMICAL AND COPERNICUS MUSEUM
COLLECTION OF THE ASTRONOMICAL OBSERVATORY
TIVOLI
MENSA PONDERARIA

JAPAN

KYOTO
KYOTO BOARD OF EDUCATION SCIENCE ROOM
NI'IGATA-SHI
NI'IGATA SCIENCE AND TECHNOLOGY MUSEUM
TOKYO
MUSEUM OF THE NATIONAL RESEARCH LABORATORY OF METROLOGY
MUSEUM OF THE PATENT OFFICE

TOTTORI-SHI
TOTTORI PREFECTURAL SCIENCE MUSEUM

NETHERLANDS

BUSSUM
E. A. VELTMAN COLLECTION
DELFT
ELECTRO-TECHNOLOGY STUDY COLLECTION
ENKHUIZEN
WEIGH-HOUSE AND SURGEON'S ROOM
ENSCHEDE
TWENTE NATIONAL MUSEUM
'S GRAVELAND
H. L. HOUTHOFF COLLECTION
'S GRAVENHAGE
MUSEUM OF THE DEPARTMENT OF WEIGHTS AND MEASURES
GRONINGEN
UNIVERSITY MUSEUM
HAARLEM
TEYLER'S MUSEUM
HOORN
WEST FRISIAN MUSEUM
LEIDEN
NATIONAL MUSEUM OF THE HISTORY OF THE NATURAL SCIENCES
LOOSDRECHT
SYPESTEYN CASTLE MUSEUM
OLDENZAAL
PALTHE HOUSE HISTORICAL MUSEUM
OUDEWATER
WITCHES WEIGH-HOUSE
RIJNSBURG
SPINOZA HOUSE
ROTTERDAM
HISTORICAL MUSEUM
UTRECHT
MUSEUM OF UTRECHT UNIVERSITY
NETHERLANDS GOLD, SILVER AND CLOCK MUSEUM

NEW ZEALAND

OAMARU
NORTH OTAGO PIONEER GALLERY
WHANGAREI
CLAPHAM CLOCK COLLECTION MUSEUM

POLAND

KRAKÓW
UNIVERSITY MUSEUM OF FINE ART
ŁAŃCUT
REGIONAL MUSEUM
ROZEWIE
MUSEUM OF LIGHTHOUSES
TORUŃ
MIKOŁAJ KOPERNIKI (COPERNICUS) MUSEUM
WARSAW
MARIE-SKŁODOWSKA CURIE MUSEUM
METEOROLOGICAL MUSEUM (MIAR MUSEUM)
MUSEUM OF ARTISTIC AND PRECISION HANDICRAFTS
WŁOCŁAWEK
JOZEF ARENTOWICZ COLLECTION OF MEASURING INSTRUMENTS

ROMANIA

BUCHAREST
COIN COLLECTION
PLOIEŞTI
MUSEUM OF CLOCKS

SOUTH AFRICA, REPUBLIC OF

RIVERSDALE
JULIUS GORDON AFRICANA CENTRE
VRYHEID
NIEUWE REPUBLIEK MUSEUM

SPAIN

CORDOBA
MUNICIPAL MUSEUM OF ART AND BULLFIGHTING
LA CORUÑA
CLOCK MUSEUM

SWEDEN

STOCKHOLM
TECHNICAL MUSEUM

SWITZERLAND

ALTDORF
URI HISTORICAL MUSEUM
BASEL
KIRSCHGARTEN
LA CHAUX- DE-FONDS
WATCH AND CLOCK MUSEUM
DELÉMONT
JURA MUSEUM
FRAUENFELD
CANTON THURGAU MUSEUM
GENEVA
MUSEUM OF ART AND HISTORY
MUSEUM OF THE HISTORY OF SCIENCE
JEGENSTORF
SCHLOSS JEGENSTORF
LE LOCLE
MUSEUM OF HISTORY AND CLOCKMAKING
NEUCHÂTEL
MUSEUM OF ART AND HISTORY
SAINTE-CROIX
MUSEUM
LA SARRAZ
CHÂTEAU
WINTERTHUR
JAKOB BRYNER AND KONRAD KELLENBERGER COLLECTION
LINDENGUT REGIONAL MUSEUM
WINTERTHUR- MÖRSBURG
MÖRSBURG CASTLE

SYRIAN ARAB REPUBLIC

DAMASCUS
DAMASCUS NATIONAL MUSEUM

USSR

MOSCOW
MUSEUM OF THE HISTORY OF MICROSCOPY

UNITED STATES

BEVERLY
BEVERLY HISTORICAL SOCIETY MUSEUM
BRISTOL
AMERICAN CLOCK AND WATCH MUSEUM
CHICAGO
ADLER PLANETARIUM
COLUMBIA
COLUMBIA MUSEUM OF HOROLOGICAL ANTIQUITIES
FARMINGTON
HILL-STEAD MUSEUM
GRAFTON
WILLARD HOUSE AND CLOCK SHOP
MIDDLETOWN
CLOCK COLLECTION
NEWARK
HOFFMANN CLOCK MUSEUM
NEWPORT
NEWPORT CLOCK MUSEUM
PHARR
OLD CLOCK MUSEUM
SPILLVILLE
BILY CLOCK EXHIBIT
WALTHAM
WALTHAM HISTORICAL SOCIETY MUSEUM
WINSTON-SALEM
JOHN VOGLER HOUSE

YUGOSLAVIA

BAKAR
LOCAL MUSEUM
BELGRADE
MUSEUM OF APPLIED ART

Group D
HISTORY

Archaeology

AFGHANISTAN

KABUL
KABUL MUSEUM

ALBANIA

BRITRINTI
BRITRINTI MUSEUM (REGIONAL)
DURRËSI
LOCAL MUSEUM
ELBASAN
LOCAL MUSEUM
POJANI (APOLONIA)
POJANI MUSEUM
TIRANA
MUSEUM OF ARCHAEOLOGY AND ETHNOGRAPHY

ALGERIA

ALGIERS
LE BARDO MUSEUM OF ETHNOGRAPHY AND PREHISTORY
ANNABA
HIPPONE MUSEUM
BEDJAIA (Formerly BOUJIE)
BEDJAIA MUSEUM

CHERCHELL (EL-ASNAM)
CHERCHELL MUSEUM
OPEN-AIR MUSEUM
CONSTANTINE
CONSTANTINE MUSEUM
DJEMILA
DJEMILA MUSEUM
LAMBERE
TAZOULT SITE MUSEUM
ORAN
MUNICIPAL MUSEUM
SÉTIF
SÉTIF MUSEUM
SKIKDA
SKIKDA MUSEUM
TEBESSA (THEVESTE)
MUSEUM OF THE TEMPLE OF MINERVA
TIMGAD
TIMGAD MUSEUM
TIPASA
ANTIQUARIAN MUSEUM OF THE TIPASA EXCAVATIONS

ARGENTINA

BUENOS AIRES
JUAN B. AMBROSETTI MUSEUM OF ETHNOGRAPHY
CARMEN DE PATAGONES
FRANCISCO DE VIEDMA REGIONAL HISTORICAL MUSEUM
LA PLATA
LA PLATA MUSEUM OF NATURAL SCIENCES
MENDOZA
MOYANO MUSEUM OF NATURAL HISTORY
MORÓN
GENERAL SAN MARTIN MUSEUM OF HISTORY AND ART
SAN JUAN
INCA HOUSE MUSEUM
SANTIAGO DEL ESTERO
WAGNER ARCHAEOLOGICAL MUSEUM
TILCARA
ARCHAEOLOGICAL MUSEUM
TRENQUE LAUQUEN
REGIONAL HISTORICAL MUSEUM

AUSTRALIA

ADELAIDE
THE SOUTH AUSTRALIAN MUSEUM
SYDNEY
NICHOLSON MUSEUM OF ANTIQUITIES

AUSTRIA

AMSTETTEN
MUNICIPAL COLLECTION
ASPARN
LOWER AUSTRIA MUSEUM OF PREHISTORY
WEINLAND MUSEUM
BAD DEUTSCH ALTENBURG
CARNUNTIUM MUSEUM
BADEN
ROLLETT MUSEUM
BAD WIMSBACH- NEYDHARTING
INTERNATIONAL PEAT-BOG MUSEUM
REGIONAL MUSEUM
BERNSTEIN
PALACE MUSEUM
BREGENZ
VORARLBERG MUSEUM
BRUCK AN DER LEITHA
REGIONAL MUSEUM
DOLSACH
AGUNTINUM MUSEUM
EFERDING
MUNICIPAL MUSEUM, STARHEMBERG FAMILY MUSEUM, REGIONAL MUSEUM
EGGENBURG
KRAHULETZ MUSEUM
EISENSTADT
BURGENLAND MUSEUM
ENNS
MUNICIPAL MUSEUM
FISCHAMEND
REGIONAL MUSEUM
FRAUENBERG
ROMAN MUSEUM
GLEISDORF
REGIONAL MUSEUM
GRAZ
JOANNEUM PROVINCIAL MUSEUM OF PREHISTORY AND EARLY HISTORY
HADERSDORF
REGIONAL MUSEUM
HAINBURG
MUNICIPAL MUSEUM
HALLSTATT
LOCAL MUSEUM
HERRNBAUMGARTEN
LOCAL MUSEUM
HERZOGENBURG
COLLECTIONS OF THE MONASTERY
HOHENAU
REGIONAL MUSEUM
HOLLABRUNN
MUNICIPAL MUSEUM
IMST
REGIONAL MUSEUM
INNSBRUCK
MUSEUM OF THE WILTEN PRAEMONSTRATENSIAN CHORAL FOUNDATION
UNIVERSITY ARCHAEOLOGICAL COLLECTION
KAPFENBERG
CAVE MUSEUM
KLAGENFURT
CARINTHIA PROVINCIAL MUSEUM
KLEINENGERSDORF
"DER BISAMBERG UND DER WEINVIERTLER" MUSEUM
KREMS
MUNICIPAL MUSEUM
KUCHL
REGIONAL MUSEUM
LANGENLOIS
REGIONAL MUSEUM
LIENZ
EAST TIROL REGIONAL MUSEUM
LINZ
MUSEUM OF THE CITY OF LINZ
UPPER AUSTRIA PROVINCIAL MUSEUM
MATTSEE
REGIONAL MUSEUM
MAUTERN
TOWN MUSEUM
MAUTHAUSEN
REGIONAL MUSEUM
MELK
REGIONAL MUSEUM
MÖDLING
MUNICIPAL MUSEUM
NEUNKIRCHEN
REGIONAL MUSEUM
OTTMANACH
MUSEUM OF THE MAGDALENSBERG EXCAVATIONS
PEGGAU
MUSEUM OF THE LUR CAVES
PETRONELL
CARNUNTUM OPEN-AIR MUSEUM
DANUBE MUSEUM
PFAFFSTÄTTEN
REGIONAL MUSEUM
PISCHELSDORF
REGIONAL MUSEUM
PÖCHLARN
REGIONAL MUSEUM
PURGSTALL
REGIONAL MUSEUM
RADKERSBURG
TOWN MUSEUM OF REGIONAL LIFE
RANKWEIL
OPEN-AIR MUSEUM
RENNWEG
VILLAGE MUSEUM
SALZBURG
SALZBURGER MUSEUM, CAROLINO AUGUSTEUM
ST. PETER
TEURNIA MUSEUM
ST. PÖLTEN
DIOCESAN MUSEUM
MUNICIPAL MUSEUM
SCHÄRDING
MUNICIPAL MUSEUM
SCHWANENSTADT
REGIONAL MUSEUM
SEITENSTETTEN
COLLECTIONS OF THE BENEDICTINE ABBEY
SPITAL
REGIONAL MUSEUM
STEYR
REGIONAL MUSEUM
STILLFRIED
MUSEUM OF PREHISTORY AND EARLY HISTORY
TAMSWEG
LUNGAU REGIONAL MUSEUM
TELFS
REGIONAL MUSEUM
TRAISMAUER
REGIONAL MUSEUM
TULLN
REGIONAL MUSEUM
VIGAUN
REGIONAL MUSEUM
VILLACH
MUNICIPAL MUSEUM
VILLACH-WARMBAD
ARCHAEOLOGICAL COLLECTION
VÖCKLABRUCK
REGIONAL HOUSE
VIENNA
DÖBLING DISTRICT MUSEUM
HERNALS DISTRICT MUSEUM
HISTORICAL MUSEUM OF THE CITY OF VIENNA
LANDSTRASSE LOCAL MUSEUM
LIESING DISTRICT MUSEUM
MEIDLING DISTRICT MUSEUM
MUSEUM OF THE PROVINCE OF LOWER AUSTRIA
NATURAL HISTORY MUSEUM: PREHISTORIC DEPARTMENT
REMAINS OF ROMAN BUILDINGS
ROMAN RUINS
SIMMERING DISTRICT MUSEUM
WAIDHOFEN AN DER YBBS
REGIONAL MUSEUM
WALDING
LOCAL MUSEUM
WATTENS
REGIONAL MUSEUM
WELS
MUNICIPAL MUSEUM
WIENER NEUSTADT
MUNICIPAL MUSEUM
WIESELBURG
STEFAN MEMORIAL COLLECTION
ZWENTENDORF
LOCAL MUSEUM

BAHRAIN STATE

MANAMA
BAHRAIN NATIONAL MUSEUM

BANGLADESH

CHITTAGONG
UNIVERSITY HISTORY MUSEUM

DACCA
DACCA MUSEUM
MUSEUM OF ART AND ARCHAEOLOGY
DINAJPUR
DINAJPUR MUSEUM

BARBADOS

BARBADOS
BARBADOS MUSEUM

BELGIUM

AALST
LOCAL MUSEUM
ANTWERP
OLD BUTCHERS' HALL
ARLON
ARCHAEOLOGICAL MUSEUM
BOUILLON
BOUILLON MUSEUM
BRUSSELS
MUNICIPAL MUSEUM OF THE CITY OF BRUSSELS
MUSEUM OF THE ROYAL BELGIAN INSTITUTE OF NATURAL SCIENCES
ROYAL MUSEUM OF ART AND HISTORY
COURTRAI
MUSEUM OF ARCHAEOLOGY AND INDUSTRIAL ART
MUSEUM OF PAINTING
LIÈGE
ARCHAEOLOGICAL BASEMENT
CURTIUS MUSEUM
LAPIDARY GALLERY
LOUVAIN
MUSEUM OF ART AND ARCHAEOLOGY
MARIEMONT- MORLANWELZ
MUSEUM OF ART AND OF THE HISTORY OF ARCHAEOLOGY
MONS
JEAN LESCARTS MUSEUM
MUSEUM OF FINE ART
NAMUR
ARCHAEOLOGICAL MUSEUM
NIVELLES
ARCHAEOLOGICAL MUSEUM
OUDENARDE
ARCHAEOLOGICAL MUSEUM
SINT-NIKLAAS WAAS
ARCHAEOLOGICAL MUSEUM
TIRLEMONT
ARCHAEOLOGICAL MUSEUM
TONGRES
GALLO-ROMAN MUSEUM
TURNHOUT
TAXANDRIA MUSEUM OF ARCHAEOLOGY
VERVIERS
MUSEUM OF ARCHAEOLOGY AND FOLKLORE
RENIER MUSEUM

BOLIVIA

LA PAZ
NATIONAL MUSEUM OF ARCHAEOLOGY
POTOSI
NATIONAL MUSEUM OF THE POTOSI MINT
SUCRE
ANTHROPOLOGICAL MUSEUM

BRAZIL

CUIABÁ
RAMIS BUCAIR MUSEUM
CURITIBA
PARANÁ MUSEUM
FLORIANÔPOLIS
SAMBAGUI MUSEUM OF MAN
FORTALEZA
DIAS DA ROCHA MUSEUM
ARTUR RAMOS MUSEUM
JOINVILLE
SAMBAQUI MUSEUM
RECIFE
MUSEUM OF ARCHAEOLOGY
SÃO PAULO
UNIVERSITY MUSEUM OF ARCHAEOLOGY AND ETHNOGRAPHY

BULGARIA

ARTEMIDA
ARTEMIDA MUSEUM
BATAK
MUSEUM OF HISTORY AND ARCHAEOLOGY
BLOGOEVGRAD
BLOGOEVGRAD MUSEUM
BOTEVGRAD
HISTORY MUSEUM
BOURGAS
REGIONAL MUSEUM OF HISTORY
BRACIGOVO
HISTORICAL MUSEUM
DIMOVO
MAGURATA CAVE MUSEUM
HISARJA
DISTRICT MUSEUM
KARNOBAT
NATIONAL MUSEUM
KAZANLUK
NATIONAL MUSEUM
LOVEČ
REGIONAL MUSEUM OF HISTORY
MADARA
RAFAIL POPOV MUSEUM
PLEVEN
REGIONAL MUSEUM OF HISTORY
PLOVDIV
REGIONAL MUSEUM OF ARCHAEOLOGY
PRESLAV
ARCHAEOLOGICAL MUSEUM
RAZGRAD
NATIONAL MUSEUM
RUSE
REGIONAL MUSEUM OF HISTORY
SAMOKOV
NATIONAL MUSEUM
SANDANSKI
REGIONAL MUSEUM
ŠČRAKLEVO
MUSEUM OF REGIONAL HISTORY AND ETHNOGRAPHY
SOFIA
MUSEUM OF SOFIA'S HISTORY
NATIONAL ARCHAEOLOGICAL MUSEUM
NATIONAL MUSEUM OF ECCLESIASTICAL HISTORY AND ARCHAEOLOGY
STARA ZAGORA
ARCHAEOLOGICAL MUSEUM
REGIONAL MUSEUM OF HISTORY
TARGOVIŠČE
PROVINCIAL HISTORICAL MUSEUM
TRJAVNA
TRJAVNA MUSEUM
VARNA
ARCHAEOLOGICAL MUSEUM
REGIONAL MUSEUM OF HISTORY
VIDIN
ARCHAEOLOGICAL MUSEUM
REGIONAL MUSEUM OF HISTORY
VRATSA
NATIONAL MUSEUM
YAMBOL
NATIONAL MUSEUM

BURMA

PAGAN
ARCHAEOLOGY MUSEUM
RANGOON
INTERNATIONAL INSTITUTE OF ADVANCED BUDDHIC STUDIES MUSEUM

CAMEROUN

YAOUNDÉ
MUSEUM OF NEGRO ART

CANADA

MINESING
SIMCOE COUNTY MUSEUM
PICTON
MIC MAC MUSEUM
SASKATOON
VIGFUSSON MUSEUM
TORONTO
ROYAL ONTARIO MUSEUM
TROIS RIVIÈRES
MUSEUM OF PREHISTORIC ARCHAEOLOGY

CHAD

FORT ARCHAMBAULT
CHAD NATIONAL MUSEUM
FORT LAMY
CHAD NATIONAL MUSEUM

CHILE

HUALPEN
MUSEO DE HUALPEN
SANTIAGO
HISTORICAL MUSEUM
EMILIO AND DUNCAN WAGNER ARCHAEOLOGICAL MUSEUM

CHINA, P.R.

ANTUNG (ANDONG)
PROVINCIAL MUSEUM
CANTON (GUANG DONG)
HISTORY MUSEUM
CHANGCHUN
PROVINCIAL MUSEUM
CHANG SHA (ZHENG ZHOU)
PROVINCIAL MUSEUM
CHINCHOW (JINZHOW)
PROVINCIAL MUSEUM
CHOUKOUTIEN
MUSEUM OF PALAEONTOLOGY
CHUNKING
MUNICIPAL MUSEUM
FOOCHOW (FUZHOU)
PROVINCIAL MUSEUM
HARBIN
PROVINCIAL MUSEUM
HO FEI
PROVINCIAL MUSEUM
KAIFENG
PROVINCIAL MUSEUM
KUEILIN
PROVINCIAL MUSEUM
KUN MING
PROVINCIAL MUSEUM
KWANCHOW
MUSEUM OF THE HISTORY OF KWANCHOW FOREIGN TRADE
KWEIYANG (GUIJANG)
PROVINCIAL MUSEUM

LANCHOW (LANZHOU)
PROVINCIAL MUSEUM
MUKDEN (SHENYIANG)
NORTH EAST MUSEUM
SHANGHAI
ART AND HISTORY MUSEUM
SIAN (XIAN)
PANPO VILLAGE
SHENSI PROVINCIAL MUSEUM
SUCHOW (SU ZHOU)
HISTORY MUSEUM
TAI YUAN
SHAN XI MUSEUM
TIENSIN (TIANJING)
PROVINCIAL MUSEUM
TSINAN (JI NAN)
PROVINCIAL MUSEUM
WACHANG (WU HAN)
PROVINCIAL MUSEUM

REPUBLIC OF CHINA

NANKING
EXHIBITION ROOM OF THE ARCHAEOLOGICAL SECTION

COLOMBIA

ARMENIA
ARCHAEOLOGICAL MUSEUM
BARRANQUILLA
ARCHAEOLOGICAL MUSEUM
CALI
MUSEUM OF NATURAL HISTORY
INZA
MUSEUM OF ARCHAEOLOGY
PEREIRA
ARCHAEOLOGICAL MUSEUM
SOGAMOSO
ARCHAEOLOGICAL PARK

COSTA RICA

SAN JOSÉ
NATIONAL MUSEUM

CUBA

BANES
MUSEUM OF THE CUBAN INDIANS
HABANA
MONTANÉ ANTHROPOLOGICAL MUSEUM
MATAZANAS
ARCHAEOLOGICAL MUSEUM
SANTIAGO DE CUBA
SCIENCE MUSEUM

CYPRUS

EPISKOPI
CURIUM MUSEUM
FAMAGUSTA
FAMAGUSTA ARCHAEOLOGICAL MUSEUM
NICOSIA
THE CYPRUS MUSEUM
PALAEPAPHOS
PALAEPAPHOS MUSEUM
PAPHOS
PAPHOS MUSEUM

CZECHOSLOVAKIA

BETLIAR
STATE PALACE
BOJNICE
REGIONAL MUSEUM
BRANDÝS NAD LABEM- STANÁ BOLESLAV
PRAGUE-VÝCHOD DISTRICT MUSEUM
BRATISLAVA
SLOVAKIAN NATIONAL MUSEUM: HISTORICAL COLLECTIONS
BŘECLAV-POHANSKO
POHANSKO ARCHAEOLOGICAL MUSEUM
BRNO
MORAVIAN MUSEUM: ETHNOGRAPHICAL COLLECTIONS
ČELČICE
ČELČICE MUSEUM
ČESKE BUDĚJOVICE
MUSEUM OF SOUTHERN CZECHOSLOVAKIA
ČESKÝ BROD
MUSEUM OF LOWER LIPAN
ČESKÝ KRUMLOV
REGIONAL MUSEUM
CHOMUTOV
REGIONAL MUSEUM
GOTTWALDOV
GOTTWALDOV MUSEUM OF SOUTHERN MORAVIA
JAROMĚŘ
MUNICIPAL MUSEUM AND ART GALLERY
JAVOŘÍČKO
CAVE MUSEUM
JIČÍN
DISTRICT MUSEUM
KELČ
KELČ MUSEUM
KLADNO
DISTRICT MUSEUM
KOMÁRNO
DANUBE MUSEUM
PODUNAJSKA REGIONAL MUSEUM
KUTNÁ HORA
DISTRICT MUSEUM: KAMENNÝ HOUSE
LIPTOVSKÝ MIKULÁŠ
MUSEUM OF THE SLOVAKIAN LIMESTONE FORMATION
MICHALOVCE
ZEMPLIN MUSEUM
MIKULČICE
NATIONAL CULTURAL MEMORIAL
MLADEČ
CAVE MUSEUM
OPAVA
SILESIAN MUSEUM: COLLECTIONS OF PREHISTORY AND PHOTOGRAPHY
SILESIAN MUSEUM: HISTORY COLLECTIONS
OSTRAVA
OSTRAVA MUSEUM
PIEŠTANY
SPA MUSEUM
PLZEŇ
MUSEUM OF WESTERN CZECHOSLOVAKIA: ARCHAEOLOGICAL COLLECTIONS
POHANSKO U BŘECLAVĚ
ARCHAEOLOGICAL SITE MUSEUM
POPRAD
TATRA MUSEUM
PRAGUE
MUSEUM OF THE CITY OF PRAGUE
NATIONAL MUSEUM: MUSEUM OF HISTORY
PREŠOV
MUSEUM OF THE SLOVAK REPUBLIC
SEZIMOVO ÚSTI
JOSEF ŠVEHLY MEMORIAL
STARÉ MĚSTO
LOCAL MUSEUM
STRAKONICE
MUSEUM OF HISTORY AND ETHNOGRAPHY

DENMARK

ÅLBORG
ÅLBORG HISTORICAL MUSEUM
ÅRHUS
ÅRHUS MUSEUM
MUSEUM OF PREHISTORY
ÅRS
VESTHIMMERLAND MUSEUM
COPENHAGEN
NATIONAL MUSEUM
THORVALDSEN MUSEUM
EBELTOFT
POST HOUSE
ESBJERG
ESBJERG MUSEUM
HADERSLEV
HADERSLEV MUSEUM
HJERL HEDE
HJERL HEDE OPEN-AIR MUSEUM
HJØRRING
VENDSYSSEL HISTORICAL MUSEUM
HØJBY SJ.
STENSTRUP MUSEUM
LADBY
VIKING SHIP
LEJRE
RESEARCH CENTRE FOR HISTORY AND ARCHAEOLOGY
ODDER
MUSEUM
ODENSE
ODENSE MUNICIPAL MUSEUMS
OTTERUP
OTTERUP MUSEUM
RANDERS
MUSEUM OF CULTURAL HISTORY
RIBE
HANS TAUSEN'S HOUSE
RINGKØBING
RINGKØBING MUSEUM
RUDKØBING
LANGELAND MUSEUM
RØNNE
BORNHOLM MUSEUM
SAMSØ
SAMSØ MUSEUM
SKIVE
SKIVE MUSEUM
THISTED
THISTED MUSEUM
TÓRSHAVN
FAROES HISTORICAL MUSEUM
VIBORG
VIBORG MUSEUM

DOMINICAN REPUBLIC

SANTO DOMINGO
NATIONAL MUSEUM

ECUADOR

QUITO
JIJÓN Y CAAMAÑO ARCHAEOLOGICAL AND HISTORICAL MUSEUM

EGYPT, ARAB REPUBLIC OF

ALEXANDRIA
GRECO-ROMAN MUSEUM
CAIRO
EGYPTIAN NATIONAL MUSEUM
GEZIRA MUSEUM

EL SALVADOR

SAN SALVADOR
NATIONAL MUSEUM DAVID J. GUZMAN

ETHIOPIA

ASMARA
ARCHAEOLOGICAL MUSEUM
ADDIS ABABA
NATIONAL MUSEUM

FINLAND

HELSINKI
FINNISH NATIONAL MUSEUM

FRANCE

ABBEVILLE
BOUCHER-DE-PERTHES MUSEUM
AGDE
AGDE MUSEUM
AGEN
MUNICIPAL MUSEUM
AIME
ARCHAEOLOGICAL MUSEUM
AIX-EN-PROVENCE
GRANET MUSEUM
AIX-LES-BAINS
MUSEUM OF ARCHAEOLOGY
ALÉRIA
JÉRÔME CARCOPINO MUSEUM OF ARCHAEOLOGY
ALÈS
ALÈS MUSEUM
ALISE-SAINTE-REINE
MUNICIPAL AND ALÉSIA MUSEUM
ALLAUCH
MUSEUM OF OLD ALLAUCH
ALTKIRCH
SUNDGAU MUSEUM
AMIENS
PICARDY MUSEUM
ANGERS
SAINT-JEAN MUSEUM OF ARCHAEOLOGY
TURPIN DE CRISSÉ MUSEUM
ANGOULÊME
MUSEUM OF THE CHARENTE ARCHAEOLOGICAL AND HISTORICAL SOCIETY
ANNECY
CHÂTEAU D'ANNECY
ANTIBES
GRIMALDI MUSEUM
MUSEUM OF LAND AND UNDERWATER ARCHAEOLOGY
AOSTE
MUSEUM OF GALLO-ROMAN ANTIQUITIES
APT
ARCHAEOLOGICAL MUSEUM
ARLES
LAPIDARY MUSEUM OF PAGAN ART
AURILLAC
JEAN-BAPTISTE RAMES MUSEUM
AUTUN
ROLIN MUSEUM
SAINT-NICOLAS LAPIDARY MUSEUM
AUXERRE
LAPIDARY AND ARCHAEOLOGICAL MUSEUM
MUSEUM OF ART AND HISTORY
AUXONNE
BONAPARTE MUSEUM
AVALLON
AVALLON MUSEUM
AVESNES-SUR-HELPE
ARCHAEOLOGICAL SOCIETY MUSEUM
AVIGNON
CALVET MUSEUM
BAGNÈRES-DE-LUCHON
LUCHON REGIONAL MUSEUM
BAR-LE-DUC
BARROIS MUSEUM
BASTIA
MUSEUM OF CORSICAN ETHNOGRAPHY
BAVAY
ARCHAEOLOGICAL MUSEUM
BAYONNE
BASQUE MUSEUM
NATURAL HISTORY MUSEUM
BEAULIEU-SUR-MER
THÉODORE REINACH FOUNDATION
BEAUVAIS
MUSEUM OF THE OISE DEPARTMENT
BESANÇON
MUSEUM OF FINE ART
BÉZIERS
LAPIDARY MUSEUM
MUSEUM OF ARCHAEOLOGY
BONNIÈRES-SUR-SEINE
MUSEUM OF BURIALS
BORDEAUX
AQUITAINE MUSEUM
BOURBON LANCY
MUNICIPAL MUSEUM
BOURBON- L'ARCHAMBAULT
AUGUSTIN BERNARD MUSEUM
BOURBONNE-LES-BAINS
MUNICIPAL MUSEUM
BOURGES
DU BERRY MUSEUM
BRANTÔME
FERNAND DESMOULINS MUSEUM
BRIVE-LA-GAILLARDE
ERNEST RUPIN MUSEUM
LE BUGUE-SUR-VÉZÈRE
BARA-BOU CAVE
CABRERETS
MUSEUM OF PREHISTORY AND AFRICAN ETHNOLOGY
CANNES
LYCKLAMA MUSEUM
CARCASSONNE
MUSEUM OF THE WALLED CITY
CARNAC
MUSEUM OF PREHISTORY
CARPENTRAS
MUSEUM OF ARCHAEOLOGY
CASSIS
MUNICIPAL MUSEUM
CHÂLONS-SUR-MARNE
MUNICIPAL MUSEUM
CHALON-SUR-SAÔNE
DENON MUSEUM
CHAMBÉRY
MUSEUM OF SAVOY
CHÂTEAU-DU-LOIR
HEURTELOUP-CHEVALLIER MUSEUM
CHÂTEAUMEILLANT
ÉMILE CHENON MUSEUM OF ARCHAEOLOGY
CHÂTEAUPONSAC
LOCAL MUSEUM
CHÂTEAUROUX
MUSEUM OF ARCHAEOLOGY
CHÂTILLON-SUR-SEINE
MUSEUM OF ARCHAEOLOGY
CHAUMONT
CHAUMONT MUSEUM
CHAUNY
LOCAL MUSEUM
CHELLES
ALFRED BONNO MUSEUM
COGNAC
MUNICIPAL MUSEUM
COULOMMIERS
MUNICIPAL MUSEUM
DIE
MUNICIPAL MUSEUM
DOLE
JULIEN FEUVRIER MUSEUM OF ARCHAEOLOGY
ENSÉRUNE
ARCHAEOLOGICAL MUSEUM
ÉPERNAY
REGIONAL MUSEUM OF PREHISTORY
ÉPINAL
VOSGES MUSEUM
ÉTAMPES
MUNICIPAL MUSEUM
ETAPLES
MUNICIPAL MUSEUM
ÉVREUX
MUNICIPAL MUSEUM
LES EYZIES-DE-TAYAC
NATIONAL MUSEUM OF PRE- HISTORY
FOIX
ARIÈGE MUSEUM
FONTENAY-LE-COMTE
VENDÉE MUSEUM
FRÉJUS
ARCHAEOLOGICAL MUSEUM
LE GRAND-PRESSIGNY
MUSEUM OF PREHISTORY
GUIRY-EN-VEXIN
ARCHAEOLOGICAL MUSEUM
HAGUENAU
HAGUENAU MUSEUM
LE HAVRE
MUSEUM OF OLD LE HAVRE
HYERES
MUNICIPAL MUSEUM
IZERNORE
MUSEUM OF ARCHAEOLOGY
LAON
MUNICIPAL MUSEUM OF ARCHAEOLOGY
LAVAL
CHÂTEAU MUSEUM
LECTOURE
EUGÈNE CAMOREYT MUSEUM
LEZOUX
MUSEUM OF GALLO-ROMAN POTTERY
LIBOURNE
RENÉ PRINCETEAU MUSEUM
LILLEBONNE
MUNICIPAL MUSEUM
LIMOGES
MUNICIPAL MUSEUM
LIMOUX
PETIET MUSEUM
LISLE-SUR-TARN
RAIMOND LAFAGE MUSEUM
LODÈVE
MUSEUM OF NATURAL HISTORY
LONS-LE-SAUNIER
MUSEUM OF FINE ART AND PREHISTORY
LUXEUIL-LES-BAINS
MUSEUM OF THE ECHEVINS TOWER
LUZECH
ARCHAEOLOGICAL MUSEUM
LUZ-SAINT-SAUVEUR
LOCAL MUSEUM
LYON
FOURVIÈRE MUSEUM OF ARCHAEOLOGY
LE PUYLATA MUSEUM
MÂCON
MUNICIPAL MUSEUM OF THE URSULINES
MARSEILLE
MUSEUM OF ARCHAEOLOGY
ROMAN DOCKS MUSEUM
MARTEL
LOCAL MUSEUM
MARTIGUES
MUSEUM OF OLD MARTIGUES
LE MAS D'AZIL
LADEVÈZE MUSEUM
LES MATELLES
MUSEUM OF THE CENTRE FOR PREHISTORIC STUDIES AT THE UNIVERSITY OF MONTPELLIER
MAUBEUGE
FERCOT DELMOTTE MUSEUM
MELUN
MELUN MUSEUM

MENDE
MUSEUM OF THE LOZÈRE SOCIETY OF LETTERS, SCIENCES AND ARTS
MENTON
MUNICIPAL MUSEUM
METZ
CENTRAL MUSEUM
MILLAU
GRAUFESENQUE MUSEUM
MIRANDE
MUSEUM OF THE MINOR PAINTERS OF MIRANDE
MOLSHEIM
MUSEUM OF ART AND HISTORY
MONTAIGU
MUSEUM OF THE NORTHERN VENDÉE
MONTAUBAN
VICTOR BRUN MUSEUM OF NATURAL HISTORY
INGRÈS MUSEUM
MONTBARD
MUSEUM
MONTBÉLIARD
CHÂTEAU MUSEUM
MONTCARET
PIERRE TAUZIAC MUSEUM
MONT-DE-MARSAN
DAUBALEN MUSEUM
MONTIGNAC-LASCAUX
LASCAUX GROTTO
MONTMAURIN
ARCHAEOLOGICAL MUSEUM
MONTPELLIER
ARCHAEOLOGICAL SOCIETY MUSEUM
MORTAGNE-AU-PERCHE
PERCHERON MUSEUM
MOUTIERS
MUSEUM OF THE ACADEMY OF THE VAL D'ISÈRE
MULHOUSE
MUSEUM OF HISTORY
MUROL
ARCHAEOLOGICAL MUSEUM
MURVIEL- LÈS-MONTPELLIER
ARCHAEOLOGICAL MUSEUM
NANTES
DOBRÉE MUSEUM
NARBONNE
LAPIDARY MUSEUM
MUNICIPAL MUSEUM
MUSEUM OF NARBONNE PREHISTORY AND ANTIQUITIES
NEMOURS
CHÂTEAU MUSEUM
NÉRAC
CHÂTEAU HENRI IV MUSEUM
NÉRIS-LES-BAINS
RIECKOTTER MUNICIPAL MUSEUM
NEVERS
NIÈVRE MUSEUM OF ARCHAEOLOGY
NICE
MUSEUM OF ARCHAEOLOGY
NÎMES
ARCHAEOLOGICAL MUSEUM
MUSEUM OF ANTIQUITIES
NISSAN-LEZ-ENSÉRUNE
LOCAL MUSEUM
NOGENT-LE-ROTROU
MUNICIPAL MUSEUM
NOGENT-SUR-MARNE
MUSEUM OF THE SMITH- LESOUËF FOUNDATION
NOIRMOUTIER EN L'ILE
CHÂTEAU MUSEUM
ORANGE
LOCAL MUSEUM
ORLÉANS
MUSEUM OF HISTORY AND ARCHAEOLOGY
PARIS
MUSEUM OF THE BIBLE AND THE HOLY LAND
PÉRIGUEUX
PÉRIGORD MUSEUM
PÉROUGES
OLD PÉROUGES MUSEUM
PERPIGNAN
HYACINTHE RIGAUD MUSEUM
POITIERS
L'ÉCHEVINAGE MUSEUM
HYPOGEUM OF THE DUNES
MUSEUM OF THE BAPTISTRY OF ST. JOHN
PONS
ARCHAEOLOGICAL MUSEUM
PONT-DE-VAUX
CHINTREUIL MUSEUM
PROVINS
TITHE-BARN MUSEUM
RENNES
BRITTANY MUSEUM
MUSEUM OF ARCHAEOLOGY AND FINE ART
RHEIMS
SAINT-RÉMI MUSEUM
RIBEAUVILLÉ
HOSPICE MUSEUM
ROCHECHOUART
A. ET P. MASFRAND MUNICIPAL MUSEUM
LA ROCHE-SUR-YON
MUSEUM OF ART AND ARCHAEOLOGY
RODEZ
FÉNAILLE MUSEUM
ROUEN
MUSEUM OF ANTIQUITIES OF THE DEPARTMENT OF THE SEINE MARITIME
SAINT- AMAND-MONTROND
SAINT VIC MUSEUM
SAINT- BERTRAND-DE-COMMINGES
COMMINGES MUSEUM
SAINT-CYR-SUR-MER
ARCHAEOLOGICAL MUSEUM
SAINT-DENIS
MUNICIPAL MUSEUM
SAINT-DIZIER
MUNICIPAL MUSEUM
SAINT-ÉMILION
ARCHAEOLOGICAL MUSEUM
SAINTES
ARCHAEOLOGICAL MUSEUM
SAINTES- MARIES-DE-LA-MER
CAMARGUE MUSEUM
SAINT-FLOUR
HAUTE-AUVERGNE MUSEUM
SAINT-GERMAIN-EN-LAYE
MUSEUM OF NATIONAL ANTIQUITIES
SAINT- GUÉNOLÉ-PENMARCH
FINISTÈRE MUSEUM OF PREHISTORY
SAINT-MAUR-DES-FOSSÉS
MUNICIPAL MUSEUM
SAINT-OMER
HÔTEL SANDELIN MUSEUM
SAINT-PAULIEN
MUSEUM OF ANTIQUITIES
SAINT-PÈRE
REGIONAL ARCHAEOLOGICAL MUSEUM
SAINT- RAMBERT-SUR-LOIRE
SAINT-RAMBERT-SUR-LOIRE MUSEUM
SAINT-RAPHAEL
MUSEUM OF UNDER-WATER ARCHAEOLOGY
SAINT- RÉMY-DE-PROVENCE
ARCHAEOLOGICAL CENTRE
SARREBOURG
REGIONAL MUSEUM
SAULGES
PREHISTORIC CAVE DWELLINGS AND ROCKPAINTINGS
SAVERNE
MUNICIPAL MUSEUM
SEDAN
SEDAN MUSEUM
SEMUR-EN-AUXOIS
SEMUR MUSEUM
SENLIS
HAUBERGIER MUSEUM
SENS
MUNICIPAL MUSEUM
OFFICIALITÉ
SOISSONS
MUNICIPAL MUSEUM
SOLUTRÉ-POUILLY
MUSEUM OF PREHISTORY
SOYONS
MUSEUM OF ARCHAEOLOGY
STRASBOURG
MUSEUM OF ARCHAEOLOGY
THÉSÉE-LA-ROMAINE
EXCAVATIONS MUSEUM
THONON-LES-BAINS
CHABLAIS MUSEUM OF FOLKLORE
TOULON
MUSEUM OF ART AND ARCHAEOLOGY
TOULOUSE
GEORGES LABIT MUSEUM
MUSEUM OF NATURAL HISTORY
TOURS
MUSEUM OF ARCHAEOLOGY AND ANCIENT ART
TRÉGASTEL
MUSEUM OF PREHISTORY
UZÈS
LOCAL MUSEUM
VAISON-LA-ROMAINE
ARCHAEOLOGICAL MUSEUM
VARZY
MUNICIPAL MUSEUM
VERDUN
PRINCERIE MUSEUM
VERVINS
MUSEUM OF ARCHAEOLOGY AND HISTORY
VESOUL
GARRET MUSEUM
VICHY
MUSEUM OF ART AND HISTORY
VIENNE
LAPIDARY MUSEUM
MUSEUM OF FINE ART
VILLEFRANCHE- DE-ROUERGUE
CABROL MUSEUM
VILLENEUVE-SUR-LOT
GASTON RAPIN MUSEUM
VILLEVENARD
MARAIS DE SAINT-GOND MUSEUM OF PREHISTORY

GDR

ANKLAM
REGIONAL MUSEUM
BARLEBEN
COLLECTION OF PREHISTORY AND EARLY HISTORY
BERLIN
BODE MUSEUM: EGYPTIAN MUSEUM
MUSEUM OF PREHISTORY AND EARLY HISTORY
BLANKENBURG
REGIONAL MUSEUM
DRESDEN
PROVINCIAL MUSEUM OF PREHISTORY
FRANKFURT AN DER ODER
DISTRICT MUSEUM
GREIFSWALD
COLLECTIONS OF THE ERNST MORITZ ARNDT UNIVERSITY: INSTITUTE FOR PREHISTORY AND EARLY HISTORY
GROSSENGOTTERN
REGIONAL ROOM
HINZDORF
REGIONAL ROOM
JENA
HILPRECHT COLLECTION OF NEAR EASTERN ANTIQUITIES OF THE FRIEDRICH SCHILLER UNIVERSITY
KARL MARX STADT
RABENSTEIN CASTLE
KÖTHEN
REGIONAL MUSEUM

LEIPZIG
ARCHAEOLOGICAL MUSEUM
EGYPTIAN MUSEUM

LENZEN
REGIONAL MUSEUM

OSCHATZ
REGIONAL ROOM

OSTERBURG
DISTRICT MUSEUM

POTSDAM-BABELSBERG
MUSEUM OF PREHISTORY AND EARLY HISTORY

RANIS
DISTRICT MUSEUM

SCHMÖLLN
REGIONAL MUSEUM

SCHÖNEBECK
DISTRICT MUSEUM

SCHWERIN
MUSEUM OF PREHISTORY AND EARLY HISTORY

STENDAL
WINCKELMANN MEMORIAL MUSEUM

SUHL
REGIONAL AND WEAPONS MUSEUM

THEMAR
REGIONAL MUSEUM

WEIMAR
MUSEUM OF THE PREHISTORY AND EARLY HISTORY OF THURINGIA

WEISSENBERG
'OLD SPICE BREAD BAKERY' REGIONAL MUSEUM

WITTENBERG LUTHERSTADT
JULIUS RIEMER MUSEUM OF NATURAL HISTORY AND ETHNOLOGY

ZITTAU
DR. CURT HEINKE MUSEUM

GFR

AALEN
LIMES MUSEUM
REGIONAL AND SCHUBART MUSEUM

ALZEY
ALZEY MUSEUM

ASCHAFFENBURG
ASCHAFFENBURG MUNICIPAL MUSEUM

BAD VILBEL
REGIONAL AND MINERAL SPRINGS MUSEUM

BALVE
REGIONAL MUSEUM OF PREHISTORY AND CAVE ARCHAEOLOGY

BERLIN
EGYPTIAN MUSEUM
GREEK AND ROMAN DEPARTMENT
MUSEUM OF PREHISTORY AND EARLY HISTORY

BLAUBEUREN
MUSEUM OF PREHISTORY

BOCHUM
LOCAL HISTORY COLLECTIONS

BONN
RHINELAND MUSEUM
UNIVERSITY MUSEUM OF ART

BREMEN
LUDWIG ROSELIUS HOUSE OF PREHISTORY

BUCHAU
FEDERSEE MUSEUM

BUXTEHUDE
REGIONAL MUSEUM

DARMSTADT
HESSE MUSEUM

DIEBURG
DIEBURG AND DISTRICT MUSEUM

DONAUESCHINGEN
COLLECTIONS OF THE PRINCES OF FÜRSTENBERG

DORTMUND
MUSEUM OF THE HISTORY OF ART AND CULTURE

DUISBURG
MUSEUM OF THE LOWER RHINE

EICHSTÄTT
WILLIBALD CASTLE MUSEUM

ERLANGEN
PREHISTORY AND EARLY HISTORY COLLECTION OF THE UNIVERSITY OF ERLANGEN- NÜRNBERG

ESSEN
RUHR AND REGIONAL MUSEUM

FLENSBURG
FLENSBURG MUNICIPAL MUSEUM

FRANKFURT
HISTORY MUSEUM
MUSEUM OF PREHISTORY AND EARLY HISTORY

FREIBURG IM BREISGAU
MUSEUM OF PREHISTORY AND EARLY HISTORY

FREISING
MUSEUM OF FREISING HISTORICAL ASSOCIATION

FRIEDRICHSHAFEN
MUNICIPAL MUSEUM OF LAKE CONSTANCE

FRITZLAR
FRITZLAR MUSEUM

GEILENKIRCHEN
REGIONAL MUSEUM

GELNHAUSEN
REGIONAL MUSEUM

GEROLSTEIN
VILLA SARABODIS MUSEUM

GLADENBACH
REGIONAL MUSEUM

GOCH
GATE-HOUSE MUSEUM

GÖPPINGEN
MUNICIPAL MUSEUM

GÖTTINGEN
COLLECTIONS OF THE ARCHAEOLOGICAL INSTITUTE OF THE UNIVERSITY OF GÖTTINGEN

GOSLAR
GOSLAR MUSEUM

GROSS-GERAU
REGIONAL MUSEUM

GÜNZBURG
REGIONAL MUSEUM

GUNZENHAUSEN
REGIONAL MUSEUM

GÜTERSLOH
REGIONAL MUSEUM

HALTERN
ROMAN AND GERMANIC MUSEUM

HAMBURG
HAMBURG MUSEUM OF ETHNOLOGY AND PREHISTORY
HELMS MUSEUM
MUSEUM OF ARTS AND CRAFTS

HANAU
HISTORY MUSEUM

HANNOVER
LAND MUSEUM OF LOWER SAXONY: DEPARTMENT OF PREHISTORY

HASELÜNNE
REGIONAL MUSEUM

HEIDE
MUSEUM OF DITHMARSCHEN PREHISTORY

HEIDENHEIM
REGIONAL MUSEUM

HILDESHEIM
ROEMER PELIZAEUS MUSEUM

HOISDORF
STORMARN VILLAGE MUSEUM

HOLZMADEN-TECK
HAUFF MUSEUM

HOMBURG
REGIONAL MUSEUM

HÖXTER
HÖXTER-CORVEY MUSEUM

INGOLSTADT
MUNICIPAL MUSEUM

ITZEHOE
GERMANIC GRAVE
PRINZESSHOF REGIONAL MUSEUM

JÜLICH
ROMAN AND GERMANIC MUSEUM

KEITUM-SYLT
SYLT REGIONAL MUSEUM

KEMPTEN
CAMBODUNUM ROMAN COLLECTION AND NATURAL SCIENCES COLLECTION

KEVELAER
FOLKLORE MUSEUM OF THE LOWER RHINE

KIRCHHEIM
REGIONAL MUSEUM

KIRCHHEIMBOLANDEN
REGIONAL MUSEUM

KITZINGEN
MUNICIPAL MUSEUM

KOBLENZ
STATE COLLECTIONS OF PREHISTORY AND FOLKLORE

KÖLN
ROMAN AND GERMANIC MUSEUM

KONSTANZ
ROSGARTEN MUSEUM

KORBACH
KORBACH REGIONAL MUSEUM

KREFELD
REGIONAL MUSEUM OF THE LOWER RHINE

KRUMBACH
REGIONAL MUSEUM

LADENBURG
LOBDENGAU MUSEUM

LAGE
LOCAL, REGIONAL AND TILE- MAKING MUSEUM

LAHR (SCHWARZWALD)
LOWER BREISGAU MUSEUM OF PREHISTORY AND EARLY HISTORY

LAUTERBACH
HOHLHAUS MUSEUM

LEMBRUCK
DÜMMER MUSEUM

LORSCH
REGIONAL MUSEUM

LUDWIGSHAFEN
K. O. BRAUN REGIONAL MUSEUM

LUDWIGSHAFEN (RHEIN)
CITY MUSEUM

LÜNEBURG
MUSEUM OF THE PRINCIPALITY OF LÜNEBURG

MAINBURG
HOLLEDAU REGIONAL MUSEUM

MAINHARDT
REGIONAL MUSEUM

MAINZ
CENTRAL MUSEUM OF ROMAN AND GERMANIC ANTIQUITIES
PRINZ JOHANN GEORG MUSEUM

MANNHEIM
REISS CITY MUSEUM

MENDEN
MENDEN REGIONAL MUSEUM

METTMANN
NEANDERTAL MUSEUM

MINDEN
MINDEN MUSEUM OF HISTORY, ETHNOLOGY AND REGIONAL STUDIES

MOOSBURG
REGIONAL MUSEUM

MOSBACH
REGIONAL MUSEUM

MÜNCHEN
STATE COLLECTION OF EGYPTIAN ART
STATE PREHISTORICAL COLLECTION

MÜNNERSTADT
REGIONAL MUSEUM

MÜNSTER
LAND MUSEUM OF PREHISTORY AND EARLY HISTORY

NENNIG
ROMAN VILLA

NEUENSTEIN
HOHENLOHE MUSEUM

NEUSS
CLEMENS SELS MUSEUM

NEUWIED
DISTRICT MUSEUM

NIEBÜLL
NIEBÜLL FRISIAN MUSEUM

NIEDERMARSBERG
REGIONAL MUSEUM
NIENBURG
MUSEUM OF THE COUNTIES OF HOYA, DIEPHOLZ, WÖLPE
NÖRDLINGEN
TOWN MUSEUM
OBERNBURG
ROMAN HOUSE
OBER-RAMSTADT
REGIONAL MUSEUM
OBERRIEXINGEN
ROMAN WINE CELLAR
ÖHRINGEN
WEYGANG MUSEUM
OERLINGHAUSEN
GERMANIC FARMHOUSE OPEN- AIR MUSEUM
REGIONAL MUSEUM
OETTINGEN
REGIONAL MUSEUM
OFFENBURG
HOUSE OF THE KNIGHTS MUSEUM
PADERBORN
MUSEUM OF THE HISTORICAL SOCIETY
PFAFFENHOFEN
REGIONAL MUSEUM
POTTENSTEIN
REGIONAL MUSEUM
RADOLFZELL
REGIONAL MUSEUM
REMAGEN
ROMAN AND FRANKISH MUSEUM
RENDSBURG
REGIONAL MUSEUM
RHEINHAUSEN
MUNICIPAL COLLECTIONS
RHEYDT
MUNICIPAL MUSEUM
RIEDLINGEN
REGIONAL MUSEUM
RINTELN
SCHAUMBURG REGIONAL MUSEUM
RISSTISSEN
ROMAN FORT MUSEUM
ROCKENHAUSEN
NORTH PALATINATE REGIONAL MUSEUM
ROSENHEIM
REGIONAL MUSEUM
ROTENBURG-WÜMME
REGIONAL MUSEUM
ROTTWEIL
ROTTWEIL MUNICIPAL MUSEUM
SAALBURG-KASTELL
SAALBURG MUSEUM
SAARBRÜCKEN
LAND MUSEUM OF PREHISTORY AND EARLY HISTORY
SÄCKINGEN
UPPER RHINE MUSEUM
ST. GOAR
REGIONAL COLLECTION
SCHLESWIG
SCHLESWIG-HOLSTEIN MUSEUM OF PREHISTORY AND EARLY HISTORY
SCHWARZENAHER
OPEN-AIR ROMAN MUSEUM
SINZIG
REGIONAL MUSEUM
SPEYER
MUSEUM OF THE HISTORY OF THE PALATINATE
STADE
MUSEUM OF PREHISTORY
STEINHEIM AM MAIN
MUNICIPAL MUSEUM
STEINHEIM-MURR
MUSEUM OF PRIMITIVE MAN
STRAUBING
GÄUBODEN AND STRAUBING MUSEUM
STUTTGART
WÜRTTEMBERG MUSEUM
TAUBERBISCHOFSHEIM
TAUBERFRANKEN REGIONAL MUSEUM
TRIER
CATHEDRAL AND DIOCESAN MUSEUM
RHINELAND MUSEUM
TÜBINGEN
COLLECTION OF THE UNIVERSITY INSTITUTE OF ARCHAEOLOGY
COLLECTION OF THE UNIVERSITY INSTITUTE OF EGYPTOLOGY
COLLECTIONS OF THE UNIVERSITY INSTITUTE OF PREHISTORY AND EARLY HISTORY
UELZEN
REGIONAL MUSEUM
UNTERUHLDINGEN
OPEN-AIR MUSEUM OF GERMAN PREHISTORY
USINGEN
WILHELM AND REGIONAL MUSEUM
VERINGENSTADT
REGIONAL MUSEUM
WARBURG
REGIONAL MUSEUM
WEINGARTEN
WEINGARTEN MUSEUM OF PREHISTORY
WEINHEIM
REGIONAL MUSEUM
WESTRHAUDERFEHN
OSTFRIESLAND AND SATERLAND FEN AND SHIPPING MUSEUM
WILHELMSHAVEN
COASTAL AND SHIPPING MUSEUM
WOLFENBÜTTEL
LAND MUSEUM OF HISTORY AND TRADITION
WORPSWEDE
MUSEUM AMONG THE TREES
ZÜLPICH
ZÜLPICH REGIONAL MUSEUM

GHANA

ACCRA
DEPARTMENT OF ARCHAEOLOGY

GREAT BRITAIN

ABERDEEN
ABERDEEN UNIVERSITY ANTHROPOLOGICAL MUSEUM
ABERYSTWYTH
CEREDIGION MUSEUM
ABINGDON
BOROUGH MUSEUM
ALDBOROUGH
ALDBOROUGH ROMAN MUSEUM
ALDEBURGH
THE MOOT HALL
AVEBURY
ALEXANDER KEILLER MUSEUM
BARROW- IN-FURNESS
BARROW-IN-FURNESS MUSEUM
BATH
BATH ROMAN MUSEUM
BATTLE
BATTLE MUSEUM
BIGNOR
BIGNOR ROMAN VILLA COLLECTION
BIRCHOVER
HEATHCOTE MUSEUM
BIRMINGHAM
BIRMINGHAM CITY MUSEUM AND ART GALLERY
BLAKESLEY HALL
BODIAM
BODIAM CASTLE MUSEUM
BRADING
ROMAN VILLA
CAERLEON
LEGIONARY MUSEUM
CAERNARVON
SEGONTIUM ROMAN FORT AND MUSEUM
CAMBRIDGE
FITZWILLIAM MUSEUM
UNIVERSITY MUSEUM OF ARCHAEOLOGY AND ETHNOLOGY
CANTERBURY
ROMAN PAVEMENT
CARLISLE
MUSEUM AND ART GALLERY
CARMARTHEN
COUNTY MUSEUM
CASTLEFORD
CASTLEFORD PUBLIC LIBRARY AND MUSEUM
CHEDDAR
GOUGH'S CAVES MUSEUM
CHEDWORTH
CHEDWORTH ROMAN VILLA AND MUSEUM
CHELMSFORD
CHELMSFORD AND ESSEX MUSEUM
CHESTER
GROSVENOR MUSEUM
CHESTERS
CLAYTON COLLECTION
CHICHESTER
CHICHESTER CITY MUSEUM
ROMAN PALACE
CIRENCESTER
CORINIUM MUSEUM
COLCHESTER
COLCHESTER AND ESSEX MUSEUM
CORBRIDGE
CORBRIDGE ROMAN SITE
COVENTRY
LUNT ROMAN FORT
DEVIZES
DEVIZES MUSEUM
DONCASTER
DONCASTER MUSEUM AND ART GALLERY
DORCHESTER
DORSET COUNTY MUSEUM
DOUGLAS
MANX MUSEUM
DURHAM
GULBENKIAN MUSEUM OF ORIENTAL ART AND ARCHAEOLOGY
EDINBURGH
NATIONAL MUSEUM OF ANTIQUITIES OF SCOTLAND
ELGIN
ELGIN MUSEUM
ETON
ETON COLLEGE NATURAL HISTORY SOCIETY MUSEUM
EVESHAM
ALMONRY MUSEUM
EXETER
ROUGEMONT HOUSE MUSEUM
FARNHAM
PITT RIVERS MUSEUM
FAVERSHAM
MAISON DIEU
FORRES
FALCONER MUSEUM
GLASGOW
CITY OF GLASGOW CORPORATION ART GALLERY AND MUSEUM
GLASTONBURY
GLASTONBURY LAKE VILLAGE MUSEUM
GUERNSEY
LUKIS AND ISLAND MUSEUM
GUILDFORD
GUILDFORD MUSEUM
HARLYN BAY
HARLYN BAY PREHISTORIC BURIAL GROUND AND MUSEUM
HERNE BAY
HERNE BAY MUSEUM
HONITON
HONITON AND ALLHALLOWS PUBLIC MUSEUM
HOUSESTEADS
HOUSESTEADS MUSEUM

HULL
TRANSPORT AND ARCHAEOLOGY MUSEUM
IPSWICH
IPSWICH MUSEUM
KETTERING
WESTFIELD MUSEUM
LANCASTER
LANCASTER MUSEUM
LEEDS
CITY MUSEUM
LEICESTER
JEWRY WALL MUSEUM
LEWES
BARBICAN HOUSE MUSEUM
LINCOLN
LINCOLN CITY AND COUNTY MUSEUM
LLANDRINDOD WELLS
RADNORSHIRE COUNTY MUSEUM
LONDON
BRITISH MUSEUM
CUMING MUSEUM
GUILDHALL MUSEUM
KINGSTON-UPON-THAMES MUSEUM AND ART GALLERY
PASSMORE EDWARDS MUSEUM
ST. BRIDE'S CRYPT MUSEUM
SIR JOHN SOANE'S MUSEUM
UNIVERSITY COLLEGE DEPARTMENT OF EGYPTOLOGY MUSEUM
LUDLOW
LUDLOW MUSEUM
LUTON
LUTON MUSEUM AND ART GALLERY
MACCLESFIELD
WEST PARK MUSEUM AND ART GALLERY
MALTON
ROMAN MALTON MUSEUM
MANCHESTER
MANCHESTER MUSEUM
MARGAM
MUSEUM OF STONES
NEWCASTLE- UPON-TYNE
UNIVERSITY OF NEWCASTLE- UPON-TYNE
NEWPORT
NEWPORT MUSEUM AND ART GALLERY
NORWICH
NORWICH CASTLE MUSEUM
OXFORD
PITT RIVERS MUSEUM
PONTEFRACT
CASTLE MUSEUM
READING
MUSEUM AND ART GALLERY
RIBCHESTER
RIBCHESTER MUSEUM OF ROMAN ANTIQUITIES
RICHBOROUGH
RICHBOROUGH CASTLE
ROTHERHAM
ROTHERHAM MUSEUM AND ART GALLERY
RUDDINGTON
RUDDINGTON AND DISTRICT LOCAL HISTORY SOCIETY VILLAGE MUSEUM
ST. ALBANS
CITY MUSEUM
VERULAMIUM MUSEUM
ST. ANDREWS
ST. ANDREWS CATHEDRAL MUSEUM
SALISBURY
SALISBURY AND SOUTH WILTSHIRE MUSEUM
SCARBOROUGH
SCARBOROUGH MUSEUM OF LOCAL HISTORY AND BYGONES
SCUNTHORPE
BOROUGH MUSEUM AND ART GALLERY
SHAFTESBURY
ABBEY RUINS MUSEUM
SHEPTON MALLET
SHEPTON MALLET MUSEUM
SHREWSBURY
ROWLEY'S HOUSE MUSEUM
SKIPTON
CRAVEN MUSEUM
SOUTH SHIELDS
ROMAN FORT AND MUSEUM
TAUNTON
SOMERSET COUNTY MUSEUM
TORQUAY
TORQUAY NATURAL HISTORY SOCIETY MUSEUM
WALL
LETOCETUM MUSEUM
WELLS
WELLS MUSEUM
WHITBY
WHITBY LITERARY AND PHILOSOPHICAL SOCIETY MUSEUM
WHITHORN
WHITHORN PRIORY MUSEUM
WINCHESTER
WINCHESTER CITY MUSEUM
WOOKEY HOLE
WOOKEY HOLE
WROXETER
VIROCONIUM MUSEUM
YORK
THE YORKSHIRE MUSEUM
ZENNOR
WAYSIDE MUSEUM

GREECE

AEGINA
MUSEUM
AGIOS NIKOLAOS
ARCHAEOLOGICAL MUSEUM
AGRINION
ARCHAEOLOGICAL MUSEUM
AIGINA
ARCHAEOLOGICAL MUSEUM
ALEXANDROUPOLIS
ARCHAEOLOGICAL COLLECTION
ALMYROS
MUSEUM
ARGOSTOLION
ARCHAEOLOGICAL MUSEUM
ARTA
ARCHAEOLOGICAL COLLECTION
ATHENS
ACROPOLIS MUSEUM
AGORA MUSEUM
ATHENS EPIGRAPHICAL COLLECTION
KERAMEIKOS MUSEUM
Z. VAOS PRIVATE COLLECTION
I. YEROULANOS PRIVATE COLLECTION
CAVALA
ARCHAEOLOGICAL MUSEUM
CHALKIS
BYZANTINE COLLECTION
CHANIA
ARCHAEOLOGICAL MUSEUM
CHIOS
ARCHAEOLOGICAL MUSEUM
CHORA
ARCHAEOLOGICAL COLLECTIONS
ARCHAEOLOGICAL MUSEUM
MONASTERY OF ST. JOHN THE DIVINE
CHORA TRIFYLIAS
ARCHAEOLOGICAL MUSEUM
CORFU
ARCHAEOLOGICAL MUSEUM
BYZANTINE COLLECTION
CORINTH
ANCIENT CORINTH MUSEUM
DELPHI
ARCHAEOLOGICAL MUSEUM
DION
ARCHAEOLOGICAL MUSEUM
DIROS
CAVES OF DIROS
DISPILION, KASTORIA
ARCHAEOLOGICAL COLLECTION
ELEFSIS
ARCHAEOLOGICAL MUSEUM
ELEUSIS
ELEUSIS MUSEUM
ERESSOS
ARCHAEOLOGICAL MUSEUM
FILIPPI
ARCHAEOLOGICAL MUSEUM
IOANNINA
MUSEUM
IOS
ARCHAEOLOGICAL COLLECTION
IRAKLION
ARCHAEOLOGICAL MUSEUM
HISTORICAL MUSEUM OF CRETE
N. METAXES PRIVATE COLLECTION
ISTHMIA
ARCHAEOLOGICAL COLLECTION
KALAMATA
ARCHAEOLOGICAL MUSEUM
KALYMNOS
ARCHAEOLOGICAL MUSEUM
KALYVIA ILIDOS
ARCHAEOLOGICAL COLLECTION
KAVALA
ARCHAEOLOGICAL MUSEUM
KOMOTINI
ARCHAEOLOGICAL MUSEUM
KOS
ARCHAEOLOGICAL MUSEUM
CASA ROMANA
KOZANI
ARCHAEOLOGICAL COLLECTION
LARISSA
ARCHAEOLOGICAL MUSEUM
D. TLOUPAS PRIVATE COLLECTION
LEFKAS
ARCHAEOLOGICAL COLLECTION
LEMNOS
LEMNOS ISLAND MUSEUM
LOUTRA AIDIPSOU
ARCHAEOLOGICAL COLLECTION
MARONEIA
ARCHAEOLOGICAL COLLECTION
MAVROMATION, MESSINIA
ARCHAEOLOGICAL COLLECTION
MELOS (MILOS)
MELOS MUSEUM
MYTILINI (MYTILENE)
ARCHAEOLOGICAL COLLECTION
NAFPAKTOS
ARCHAEOLOGICAL COLLECTION
NAFPLION
ARCHAEOLOGICAL MUSEUM
PALAIA KORINTHOS
ARCHAEOLOGICAL MUSEUM
PAROS
ARCHAEOLOGICAL MUSEUM
PATRAI
ARCHAEOLOGICAL MUSEUM
PELLA
ARCHAEOLOGICAL COLLECTION
RHODES
ARCHAEOLOGICAL MUSEUM
SALAMIS
ARCHAEOLOGICAL MUSEUM
SAMOTHRAKI
ARCHAEOLOGICAL MUSEUM
SPARTI
ARCHAEOLOGICAL MUSEUM
THERA
THERA MUSEUM
THESSALONIKI
ARCHAEOLOGICAL MUSEUM
THIVAI
ARCHAEOLOGICAL MUSEUM

THYRREION
ARCHAEOLOGICAL MUSEUM
TRAIANOUPOLIS (LOUTROS)
ARCHAEOLOGICAL COLLECTION
VATHY
ARCHAEOLOGICAL MUSEUM
VEROIA
ARCHAEOLOGICAL MUSEUM
VOLOS
ATHANASSAKEION ARCHAEOLOGICAL MUSEUM

GUATEMALA

GUATEMALA CITY
ARCHAEOLOGICAL MUSEUM

HONDURAS

COMAYAGUA
REGIONAL MUSEUM OF ARCHAEOLOGY AND COLONIAL EXHIBITS OF THE COMAYAGUA VALLEY
COPAN
REGIONAL MUSEUM OF MAYAN ARCHAEOLOGY

HONG KONG

HONG KONG
CITY MUSEUM AND ART GALLERY
KOWLOON
LEI CHENG UK TOMB SITE MUSEUM
SHA TIN
ART GALLERY OF THE INSTITUTE OF CHINESE STUDIES

HUNGARY

ABONY
LAJOS ABONYI VILLAGE MUSEUM
BAJA
ISTVÁN TÜRR MUSEUM
BALASSAGYARMAT
PALÓC MUSEUM
BÉKÉSCSABA
MIHÁLY MUNKÁCSY MUSEUM
BUDAPEST
HERCULES VILLA
HUNGARIAN NATIONAL MUSEUM
MUSEUM OF THE HISTORY OF BUDAPEST: DEPARTMENT OF PREHISTORY AND ANTIQUITY
ROMAN BATH
TABORVAROS MUSEUM OF RUINS
DUNAÚJVÁROS
DUNAÚJVÁROS MUSEUM
ESZTERGOM
BÁLINT BALASSI MUSEUM
HÓDMEZÖVÁSARHELY
JÁNOS TORNYAI MUSEUM
JÁSZBERÉNY
JÁSZ MUSEUM
KAPOSVÁR
RIPPL-RÓNAI MUSEUM
KESZTHELY
BALATON MUSEUM
KOMÁROM
GYÖRGY KLAMPKA MUSEUM
NYÍREGYHÁZA
ANDRÁS JÓSA MUSEUM
PENC
VILLAGE MUSEUM
SZÉKESFEHÉRVÁR
KING ISTVÁN MUSEUM
SZEKSZÁRD
ADÁM BALOGH MUSEUM
SZENTES
JÓZSEF KOSZTA MUSEUM
SZOMBATHELY
RUINS OF ISTVÁN PAULOVICS VILLA
RUINS OF TEMPLE OF ISIS
TÁC
GORSIUM MUSEUM
VÉRTESSZÖLLŐS
VÉRTESSZÖLLŐS EXHIBITION
VESZPRÉM
BAKONY MUSEUM

ICELAND

REYKJAVIK
NATIONAL MUSEUM OF ANTIQUITIES

INDIA

AGRA
TAJ MUSEUM
AHAR
ARCHAEOLOGICAL MUSEUM
AHMEDABAD
GUJARAT MUSEUM SOCIETY
ALAMPUR
ARCHAEOLOGICAL SITE MUSEUM
ALLAHABAD
UNIVERSITY MUSEUMS
AMARAVATI
ARCHAEOLOGICAL MUSEUM
AMBER
ARCHAEOLOGICAL MUSEUM
BANGALORE
MYSORE GOVERNMENT MUSEUM
BARIPADA
BARIPADA MUSEUM
BARODA
MUSEUM OF THE DEPARTMENT OF ARCHAEOLOGY
BENARES
SARNATH MUSEUM
BHARATPUR
STATE MUSEUM
BHAWANAGAR
GANDHI SMRITI MUSEUMS
BHUBANESHWAR
ORISSA STATE MUSEUM
BODHGAYA
ARCHAEOLOGICAL MUSEUM
BOMBAY
HERAS INSTITUTE OF INDIAN HISTORY AND CULTURE
BUDDH GAYA
ARCHAEOLOGICAL MUSEUM
CALCUTTA
GURUSADAY MUSEUM
INDIAN MUSEUM
STATE ARCHAEOLOGICAL GALLERY
CHAMBA
BHURI SINGH MUSEUM
DHAR
DHAR DISTRICT MUSEUM
DHARWAR
MUSEUM OF ART AND ARCHAEOLOGY
GUNTUR
ARCHAEOLOGICAL MUSEUM
GURUKUL JHAJJAR
HARYANA PRANTIYA PURATATVA SANGRAHALAYA
GWALIOR
CENTRAL ARCHAEOLOGICAL MUSEUM
HALEBID
ARCHAEOLOGICAL MUSEUM
HAMPI
ARCHAEOLOGICAL MUSEUM
IMPHAL
MANIPUR STATE MUSEUM
INDORE
CENTRAL MUSEUM
JAMNAGAR
JAMNAGAR MUSEUM OF ANTIQUITIES, LAKHOTE BUILDING
JHALAWAR
ARCHAEOLOGICAL MUSEUM
JUNAGADH
DARBAR HALL MUSEUM
KALPI
MAHATMA GANDHI HINDI SANGRAHALAYA
KHAJURAHO
ARCHAEOLOGICAL MUSEUM
KHICHING
KHICHING MUSEUM
KONARAK
ARCHAEOLOGICAL MUSEUM
KOLHAPUR
KOLHAPUR MUSEUM
KONDAPUR
ARCHAEOLOGICAL MUSEUM
LUCKNOW
STATE MUSEUM
MADRAS
THE GOVERNMENT MUSEUM AND NATIONAL ART GALLERY
MATHURA
ARCHAEOLOGICAL MUSEUM
NAGARJUNKONDA
ARCHAEOLOGICAL MUSEUM
NAGPUR
CENTRAL MUSEUM
NALANDA
ARCHAEOLOGICAL MUSEUM
NEW DELHI
NATIONAL MUSEUM OF INDIA
PATIALA
STATE MUSEUM
PATNA
PATNA MUSEUM
POONA
DECCAN COLLEGE MUSEUM
MAHATMA PHULE VASTU SANGRAHALAYA
RAJA KELKAR MUSEUM
PUDDUKKOTTAI
GOVERNMENT MUSEUM
RAIPUR
MAHANT GHASI DASS MEMORIAL MUSEUM
SANCHI
ARCHAEOLOGICAL MUSEUM
SARNATH
SARNATH MUSEUM
SHILLONG
CENTRAL MUSEUM
SIKAR
SIKAR MUSEUM
SONAGIR
DIGAMBER JAIN MUSEUM
SRINAGAR
S.P.S. MUSEUM
SURAT
SARDAR V. PATEL MUSEUM
TAL. KHATAV
SHRI BHAVANI MUSEUM AND LIBRARY
TAMLUK
HAMILTON HIGH SCHOOL MUSEUM
TRICHUR
ARCHAEOLOGICAL MUSEUM AND PICTURE GALLERY
UDAIPUR
VICTORIA HALL MUSEUM
VARANASI
ARCHAEOLOGICAL MUSEUM
VIDISHA
DISTRICT ARCHAEOLOGICAL MUSEUM
VIJAYAWADA
VICTORIA JUBILEE MUSEUM

INDONESIA

DJAKARTA
MUSEUM OF INDONESIAN CULTURE
GIANJAR
MUSEUM GEDONG ARTJA

IRAN

TEHERAN
ARCHAEOLOGICAL MUSEUM

IRAQ

AQER QUF
LOCAL MUSEUM
BABYLON
LOCAL MUSEUM
BAGHDAD
AL-MADA'IN MUSEUM
THE IRAQ MUSEUM
ERBIL
ERBIL MUSEUM
KIRKUK
KIRKUK MUSEUM
MOSUL
LOCAL MUSEUM
SAMARRA
LOCAL MUSEUM
SULAIMANIYA
AL-SULAIMANIYA MUSEUM

IRELAND

CLONFERT
CLONFERT MUSEUM
CORK
CORK PUBLIC MUSEUM
DUBLIN
NATIONAL MUSEUM OF IRELAND
LIMERICK
LIMERICK CITY MUSEUM
NEWGRANGE
NEWGRANGE TOURIST OFFICE
ROSSNOWLAGH
MUSEUM OF THE COUNTY DONEGAL HISTORICAL SOCIETY

ISRAEL

ASHKELON
LOCAL MUSEUM
AVEDAT
LOCAL MUSEUM
BEERSHEBA
NEGEV MUSEUM
BETH SHE'AN
BETH SHE'AN MUSEUM
GVULOT
LOCAL MUSEUM
HAIFA
MUSEUM OF NATURAL HISTORY AND PREHISTORY
HAZOREA
WILFRID ISRAEL HOUSE FOR ORIENTAL ART AND STUDIES
JERUSALEM
BRONFMAN BIBLICAL AND ARCHAEOLOGICAL MUSEUM
MUSEUM OF PREHISTORY
ROCKEFELLER ARCHAEOLOGICAL MUSEUM
SHRINE OF THE BOOK
Y.M.C.A. "HERBERT E. CLARK" COLLECTION OF NEAR EASTERN ANTIQUITIES
MA'AYAN BARUCH
MA'AYAN BARUCH PREHISTORIC MUSEUM OF THE HULEH VALLEY
MEGIDDO
SITE MUSEUM
NAHARIYA
MUSEUM OF ARCHAEOLOGY, HISTORY AND ART
NAZARETH
TERRA SANCTA MUSEUM
NIR-DAVID
MUSEUM OF MEDITERRANEAN ARCHAEOLOGY
SEDOT YAM
CAESAREA MUSEUM
SH'AR HA-GOLAN
MUSEUM OF PREHISTORY
TEL-AVIV
MUSEUM OF TEL-QUASILA EXCAVATIONS
TIBERIAS
MUNICIPAL MUSEUM OF ANTIQUITIES

ITALY

ADRIA
ARCHAEOLOGICAL MUSEUM
AGRIGENTO
DIOCESAN MUSEUM
NATIONAL ARCHAEOLOGICAL MUSEUM
ALBA
EUSEBIO ARCHAEOLOGICAL MUSEUM
ALBENGA
ROMAN MARITIME MUSEUM
ANCONA
NATIONAL MUSEUM OF THE MARCHES
AOSTA
ARCHAEOLOGICAL MUSEUM
AQUILEIA
ARCHAEOLOGICAL MUSEUM
PALEOCHRISTIAN MUSEUM
AREZZO
ARCHAEOLOGICAL MUSEUM
ASCIANO
ETRUSCAN MUSEUM
ASTI
ARCHAEOLOGICAL MUSEUM
BACOLI
PISCINA MIRABILE
BARI
ARCHAEOLOGICAL MUSEUM
BOLOGNA
MUNICIPAL ARCHAEOLOGICAL MUSEUM
BRESCIA
MUSEUM OF ROMAN ANTIQUITIES
BRINDISI
FRANCESCO RIBEZZO REGIONAL MUSEUM
CANNE DELLA BATTAGLIA
ANTIQUARIUM
CANOSA DI PUGLIA
MUNICIPAL MUSEUM
CAPUA
CAMPANO MUSEUM
CASTIGLIONCELLO
NATIONAL ARCHAEOLOGICAL MUSEUM
CATANZARO
REGIONAL MUSEUM
CERVETERI
CERITE NATIONAL MUSEUM
CHIETI
NATIONAL MUSEUM OF ANTIQUITIES
CHIUSI
ETRUSCAN MUSEUM
CIVITACASTELLANA
ANTIQUARIUM
CORBETTA
PISANI-DOSSI ARCHAEOLOGICAL COLLECTION
CORTONA
MUSEUM OF EGYPTIAN AND ETRUSCAN ANTIQUITIES
DOMODOSSOLA
SILVA MUSEUM
ESTE
ATESTINO NATIONAL MUSEUM
FERRARA
LAPIDARY MUSEUM
SPINA NATIONAL ARCHAEOLOGICAL MUSEUM
FIESOLE
MUSEUM OF STONES AND FOSSILS
FLORENCE
MUSEUM OF PREHISTORY
FOGGIA
MUNICIPAL MUSEUM
FOLIGNO
ARCHAEOLOGICAL MUSEUM AND PICTURE GALLERY
FORLI
MUSEUM AND PICTURE GALLERY
FRASCATI
TUSCANY MUSEUM
GALLARATE
MUSEUM OF THE GALLARATE SOCIETY FOR NATIONAL STUDIES
GELA
NATIONAL MUSEUM
GENOA
LIGURIAN MUSEUM OF ARCHITECTURE AND SCULPTURE
HERCULANEUM
ARCHAEOLOGICAL SITE
L'AQUILA
ABBRUZZO NATIONAL MUSEUM
LENTINI
ARCHAEOLOGICAL MUSEUM
LIPARI
ARCHAEOLOGICAL MUSEUM
LUCERA
FIORELLI MUSEUM
MARZABOTTO
POMPEO ARIA ETRUSCAN MUSEUM
MILAN
ARCHAEOLOGICAL MUSEUM
MOTYA
ARCHAEOLOGICAL MUSEUM
NAPLES
NATIONAL ARCHAEOLOGICAL MUSEUM
NEMI
MUSEUM OF THE SHIPS OF NEMI
NOVARA
ARCHAEOLOGICAL MUSEUM
ORTONOVO
NATIONAL ARCHAEOLOGICAL MUSEUM
ORVIETO
CLAUDIO FAINA MUSEUM
OSTIA
OLD TOWN
PADUA
MUNICIPAL MUSEUM
PAESTUM
NATIONAL MUSEUM
PALERMO
NATIONAL ARCHAEOLOGICAL MUSEUM
PARMA
NATIONAL MUSEUM OF ANTIQUITIES
PAVIA
ARCHAEOLOGICAL MUSEUM
PEGLI
ARCHAEOLOGICAL MUSEUM OF LIGURIA
ARCHAEOLOGICAL AND ETHNOGRAPHICAL MUSEUM OF AMERICA
PERUGIA
MUSEUM OF PREHISTORY OF CENTRAL ITALY
NATIONAL ARCHAEOLOGICAL MUSEUM OF UMBRIA
PESARO
OLIVERI ARCHAEOLOGICAL MUSEUM
PIACENZA
MUNICIPAL MUSEUM
PIAZZA ARMERINA
IMPERIAL VILLA
PISA
CEMETERY
POMPEI
ARCHAEOLOGICAL SITE
POPULONIA
ETRUSCAN MUSEUM
PORTO D'ISCHIA
MUSEUM OF THE ISLAND OF ISCHIA
PORTOGRUARO
ARCHAEOLOGICAL MUSEUM
POTENZA
LUCANO REGIONAL MUSEUM
RIMINI
MUNICIPAL MUSEUM AND ART GALLERY
ROME
ANTIQUARIUM OF THE FORUM
ANTIQUARIUM OF THE PALATINE
CAPITOLINO MUSEUM
EGIZIANO MUSEUM (VATICAN MUSEUMS)
MUSEUM OF PREHISTORY AND ARCHAEOLOGY

NATIONAL MUSEUM OF VILLA GIULIA
PAOLINO MUSEUM (VATICAN MUSEUM)
PICTURE GALLERY (VATICAN MUSEUMS)
LUIGI PIGORINI MUSEUM OF PREHISTORY AND ETHNOGRAPHY
PIO-CLEMENTINO MUSEUM (VATICAN MUSEUMS)
ROMAN NATIONAL MUSEUM
TORLONIA MUSEUM

SALERNO
PROVINCIAL ARCHAEOLOGICAL MUSEUM

SARZINA
SARZINA ARCHAEOLOGICAL MUSEUM

SAVIGNANO SUL RUBICONE
ROMAN-GALLIC-ETRUSCAN MUSEUM

SIENA
ETRUSCAN ARCHAEOLOGICAL MUSEUM

SORRENTO
CORREALE MUSEUM

SPERLONGA
ARCHAEOLOGICAL MUSEUM

SPÉZIA
ARCHAEOLOGICAL MUSEUM

SYRACUSE
NATIONAL ARCHAEOLOGICAL MUSEUM

TAORMINA
ANTIQUARIUM

TARANTO
NATIONAL MUSEUM

TARQUINIA
NECROPOLIS

TOLENTINO
MUNICIPAL MUSEUM

TORCELLO
MUSEO DELL'ESTUARIO

TRENT
NATIONAL MUSEUM

TREVISO
BAILO MUSEUM

TRIESTE
MUSEUM OF HISTORY AND ART

TRIORA
REGIONAL MUSEUM

TUORO SUL TRASIMENTO
ANTIQUARIUM

TURIN
DUCAL CASTLE
EGYPTIAN MUSEUM
MUSEUM OF ANTIQUITIES

VENICE
ARCHAEOLOGICAL MUSEUM
MANFREDIANA PICTURE GALLERY
MUSEUM OF NATURAL HISTORY

VENTIMIGLIA
GIROLAMO ROSSI MUNICIPAL MUSEUM OF ARCHAEOLOGY

VIBO VALENTIA
MUSEUM
NATIONAL ARCHAEOLOGICAL MUSEUM

VITERBO
MUNICIPAL MUSEUM

VOLTERRA
ETRUSCAN MUSEUM

JAMAICA

WHITE MARL
ARAWAK MUSEUM

JAPAN

ABASHIRI-SHI
ABASHIRI MUNICIPAL MUSEUM

AKAHO-SHI
UNE ARCHAEOLOGICAL COLLECTION

CHINO-SHI
TOGARI'ISHI ARCHAEOLOGICAL MUSEUM

EBINA-MACHI
EBINA ARCHAEOLOGICAL COLLECTION

FUKUI-SHI
FUKUI HISTORY HALL

HAMAMATSU-SHI
HAMAMATSU CITY MUSEUM

ICHINOMIYA-SHI
MAMIZUKA ARCHAEOLOGICAL COLLECTION

ISHIKAWA-GUN
ABUKUMA ARCHAEOLOGICAL COLLECTION

ISHINOMAKI-SHI
ENDO-MORI ARCHAEOLOGICAL COLLECTION OF ISHINOMAKI

ITOIGAWA-SHI
GYOFU SOMA MEMORIAL COLLECTION

KISARAZU-SHI
EXCAVATED COLLECTION OF KINREIZUKA

KOMATSU-SHI
KOMATSU MUNICIPAL MUSEUM

KYOTO
ARCHAEOLOGICAL & HISTORICAL COLLECTION

NAGAOKA-SHI
NAGAOKA MUNICIPAL MUSEUM OF NATURAL SCIENCE

NAKA-GUN
SANNOMUJA ARCHAEOLOGICAL MUSEUM

NARA-SHI
NARA NATIONAL MUSEUM

NARITA-SHI
NARITASAN REIKO MUSEUM

RIKUZENTAKADA-SHI
RIKUZENTAKADA MUNICIPAL MUSEUM

SAIJO-SHI
SAIJO LOCAL MUSEUM

SENDAI-SHI
ARCHAEOLOGICAL COLLECTION OF TOHOKU UNIVERSITY

SHIMOSUWA-MACHI
SHIMOSUWA PUBLIC MUSEUM

SHINOHARA-MACHI
BUSO ARCHAEOLOGICAL COLLECTION

SHUHO-MACHI
AKIYOSHIDAI MUSEUM OF NATURAL HISTORY

SUWA-SHI
KATAKURA MEMORIAL COLLECTION

TOKYO
ARCHAEOLOGICAL COLLECTION
ARCHAEOLOGICAL COLLECTION OF KOKUBUNJI
ARCHAEOLOGICAL COLLECTION OF KOKUGAKUIN UNIVERSITY
ARCHAEOLOGICAL COLLECTION OF MEIJI UNIVERSITY
HACHIOJI CITY MUSEUM
NATIONAL MUSEUM
NEZU ART MUSEUM

TOSAYAMADA-MACHI
THE RYUGADO MUSEUM

TSURUOKA-SHI
CHIDO MUSEUM

UEDA-SHI
UEDA MUNICIPAL MUSEUM

YOKOSUKA-SHI
YOKOSUKA CITY MUSEUM

YONAGO-SHI
SAN'IN HISTORICAL COLLECTION

JORDAN

AMMAN
JORDAN ARCHAEOLOGICAL MUSEUM

IRBID
IRBID MUSEUM

KERAK
KERAK MUSEUM

MADABA
MADABA MUSEUM

PETRA
PETRA MUSEUM

KENYA

GEDI
NATIONAL MUSEUM

LAMU
NATIONAL MUSEUM

MOMBASA
NATIONAL MUSEUM

KHMER REPUBLIC

KAMPONG THOM
ARCHAEOLOGICAL MUSEUM

KOREA, DEMO. PEOPLE'S REP.

PYONGYANG
STATE CENTRAL HISTORICAL MUSEUM

KOREA, REPUBLIC OF

KYONGJU CITY
NATIONAL MUSEUM

PUSAN
NATONAL UNIVERSITY MUSEUM

PUYO
NATIONAL MUSEUM

SEOUL
NATIONAL MUSEUM
UNIVERSITY MUSEUM

TAEGU
UNIVERSITY MUSEUM

KUWAIT

KUWAIT
KUWAIT MUSEUM

LEBANON

BEIRUT
ARCHAEOLOGICAL MUSEUM
NATIONAL MUSEUM OF LEBANON
PREHISTORIC MUSEUM

LESOTHO

MORIJA
MUSEUM OF MORIJA

LIBYAN ARAB REPUBLIC

APOLLONIA
SUSA MUSEUM

CYRENE
SITE MUSEUM

GASR LEBIA
SITE MUSEUM

GERMA
GERMA MUSEUM

LEPCIS MAGNA
SITE MUSEUM

SABRATHA
SABRATHA MUSEUM

TOCRA
SITE MUSEUM

TRIPOLI
ARCHAEOLOGICAL MUSEUM
MUSEUM OF PREHISTORY

LUXEMBOURG

LUXEMBOURG
STATE MUSEUM

MALAGASY REPUBLIC

TANANARIVE
MUSEUM OF ART AND ARCHAEOLOGY
MUSEUM OF ART AND ARCHAEOLOGY

MALAWI

BLANTYRE
MUSEUM OF MALAWI
MANGOCHE
LAKE MALAWI MUSEUM

MALAYSIA

ALOR STAR
MUSEUM NEGERI KEDAH
SARAWAK
SARAWAK MUSEUM

MALTA

BIRZEBBUGA
GHAR DALAM CAVE AND MUSEUM
MGARR
TA' HAGRAT NEOLITHIC TEMPLES
PAOLA
HAL SAFLIENI HYPOGEUM
QRENDI
HAGAR QIM AND MNAJDRA NEOLITHIC TEMPLES
RABAT
ROMAN HOUSE AND MUSEUM OF ANTIQUITIES
THE ST. AGATHA CATACOMBS
ST. PAUL'S CATACOMBS
TARXIEN
NEOLITHIC TEMPLES
VALLETTA
NATIONAL MUSEUM
VICTORIA (GOZO)
THE GOZO MUSEUM
XAGHRA (GOZO)
GGANTIJA NEOLITHIC TEMPLES

MEXICO

CAMPECHE
CAMPECHE ARCHAEOLOGICAL MUSEUM
CHIHUAHUA
CHIHUAHUA REGIONAL MUSEUM
CHOLULA
CHOLULA MUSEUM OF ARCHAEOLOGY
GUADALAJARA
GUADALAJARA REGIONAL MUSEUM
JALAPA
ARCHAEOLOGICAL MUSEUM
MATAMOROS
MEXICAN MUSEUM
MEXICO CITY
DIEGO RIVERA MUSEUM OF ANAHUACALLI
MUSEUM OF WORLD CULTURES
NATIONAL ANTHROPOLOGICAL MUSEUM
MITLA
SITE MUSEUM
OAXACA
OAXACA REGIONAL MUSEUM
PALENQUE
ARCHAEOLOGICAL MUSEUM OF THE PALENQUE REGION
TEOTIHUACAN
TEOTIHUACAN MUSEUM
TEPEXPAN
PREHISTORIC MUSEUM OF THE VALLE DE MEXICO
TULA
ARCHAEOLOGICAL SITE MUSEUM
TUXTLA GUTIERREZ
STATE ARCHAEOLOGICAL MUSEUM
VILLAHERMOSA
PARK MUSEUM
TABASCO REGIONAL MUSEUM
XALAPA
VERACRUZ MUSEUM OF ANTHROPOLOGY

MONACO

MONTE CARLO
MUSEUM OF PREHISTORIC ANTHROPOLOGY

MOROCCO

RABAT
MUSEUM OF ANTIQUITIES
TANGIER
MUSEUM OF ANTIQUITIES
TETOUAN
TETOUAN ARCHAEOLOGICAL MUSEUM

MOZAMBIQUE

BEIRA
MUNICIPAL MUSEUM

NETHERLANDS

AARDENBURG
DISTRICT MUSEUM
ALPHEN
REGIONAL MUSEUM OF ANTIQUITIES
AMSTERDAM
ALLARD PIERSON MUSEUM
MUSEUM OF BIBLICAL ANTIQUITIES
ASSEN
DRENTHE PROVINCIAL MUSEUM
EGMOND-BINNEN
MUSEUM OF THE ABBEY OF EGMOND
ELSLOO
SHIPPING EXCHANGE REGIONAL MUSEUM
ELST
MUSEUM UNDER THE N.H. CHURCH
GRAMSBERGEN
TOWN HISTORICAL MUSEUM
'S GRAVENHAGE
NATIONAL MEERMAN AND WESTREENEN MUSEUM
HEEMSTEDE
DE RAAF BRAND VAN STRAATER COLLECTION
HEERLEN
LOCAL HISTORY MUSEUM
LEIDEN
NATIONAL MUSEUM OF ANTIQUITIES
LELYSTAD
LELYSTAD HARBOUR EXHIBITION BUILDING
LIEVELDE
KOTS OPEN-AIR MUSEUM
MAASTRICHT
BONNEFANTEN MUSEUM
MIDDELBURG
ZEALAND MUSEUM
NAALDWIJK
WESTLAND DISTRICT MUSEUM
NIJMEGEN
G. M. KAM NATIONAL MUSEUM
DEN OEVER
ZUIDERZEE WORKS INFORMATION CENTRE
OLDENZAAL
PALTHE HOUSE HISTORICAL MUSEUM
OSS
JAN CUNEN MUSEUM
ST. GEERTRUD
SAVELSBOS VISITOR CENTRE
ST. MICHIELSGESTEL
LOCAL HISTORY MUSEUM
SANTPOORT
BREDERODE RUINS
SCHOKLAND
IJSSELMEER POLDER MUSEUM
STEIN
ARCHAEOLOGICAL RESERVE
UTRECHT
ARCHAEOLOGICAL INSTITUTE
PROVINCIAL MUSEUM OF ANTIQUITIES
VEENDAM
PEAT SETTLEMENT MUSEUM
VENRAY
LOCAL HISTORY MUSEUM
WIJCHEN
FRANS BLOEMEN MUSEUM OF ANTIQUITIES

NEW ZEALAND

CHRISTCHURCH
CANTERBURY MUSEUM
DUNEDIN
OTAGO MUSEUM

NICARAGUA

GRANADA
ARCHAEOLOGICAL MUSEUM
MANAGUA
NATIONAL MUSEUM OF NICARAGUA
NINDIRÍ
ARCHAEOLOGICAL MUSEUM

NIGERIA

JOS
JOS MUSEUM

NORWAY

HAMAR
HEDMARK MUSEUM
OSLO
COLLECTION OF ANTIQUITIES
HISTORICAL MUSEUM
SARPSBORG
FOLK MUSEUM FOR ØSTFOLD
TROMSØ
TROMSØ MUSEUM
TRONDHEIM
MUSEUM OF THE ROYAL NORWEGIAN SOCIETY OF SCIENCES AND LETTERS
VANSE
LISTA MUSEUM

PAKISTAN, WEST

BANBHORE
ARCHAEOLOGICAL MUSEUM
HARAPPA
ARCHAEOLOGICAL MUSEUM
KARACHI
NATIONAL MUSEUM OF PAKISTAN
MOENJODARO
ARCHAEOLOGICAL MUSEUM
PESHAWAR
ARCHAEOLOGICAL MUSEUM
TAXILA
ARCHAEOLOGICAL MUSEUM

PARAGUAY

ASUNCION
ETHNOGRAPHICAL MUSEUM
MUSEUM OF NATURAL HISTORY

PERU

ANCASH
ARCHAEOLOGICAL MUSEUM
ATE
PURUCHUCO SITE MUSEUM
CUZCO
MUSEUM AND ARCHAEOLOGICAL INSTITUTE
HUANCAYO
ARCHAEOLOGICAL MUSEUM
LAMBAYEQUE
"BRUNING" ARCHAEOLOGICAL MUSEUM
LIMA
ARCHAEOLOGICAL MUSEUM
RAFAEL LARCO HERRERA MUSEUM
NATIONAL MUSEUM OF ANTHROPOLOGY AND ARCHAEOLOGY
PACHACAMAC
PACHACAMAC MUSEUM
SAN ISIDRO
HUALLAMARCA SITE MUSEUM

PHILIPPINES

MANILA
THE BEYER COLLECTION
SANTA ANA ARCHAEOLOGICAL SITE AND LITURGICAL ARTS MUSEUM
NAGA CITY
UNIVERSITY MUSEUM
PALAWAN ISLAND
TABON FIELD STATION
PANGASINAN
BOLINAO FIELD STATION
QUEZON CITY
MUSEUM OF ANTHROPOLOGY
TACLOBAN CITY
LEYTE-SAMAR MUSEUM

POLAND

BISKUPIN
LOCAL MUSEUM
CZĘSTOCHOWA
ARCHAEOLOGICAL SITE MUSEUM
GDAŃSK
ARCHAEOLOGICAL MUSEUM
GIECZ
MUSEUM OF ARCHAEOLOGY
KĘTRZYN
KĘTRZYN MUSEUM
KRAKÓW
ARCHAEOLOGICAL MUSEUM
UNIVERSITY MUSEUM OF FINE ART
KRZEMIONKI OPATOWSKIE
ARCHAEOLOGICAL SITE MUSEUM
ŁÓDŹ
ARCHAEOLOGICAL AND ETHNOGRAPHICAL MUSEUM
NOWA HUTA
NOWA HUTA ARCHAEOLOGICAL MUSEUM
NOWY SĄCZ
REGIONAL MUSEUM
OLEŚNICA
ARCHAEOLOGICAL MUSEUM
OSTRÓW LEDNICKI
LOCAL MUSEUM
POZNAŃ
ARCHAEOLOGICAL MUSEUM
PRZEMYŚL
REGIONAL MUSEUM
SKÓRCZ
MUSEUM OF ARCHAEOLOGY
SŁUPIA NOWA
ANCIENT FOUNDRIES MUSEUM
SURAŻ
REGIONAL MUSEUM
WARSAW
NATIONAL MUSEUM
NATIONAL MUSEUM OF ARCHAEOLOGY
WROCŁAW
ANTHROPOLOGICAL MUSEUM OF THE UNIVERSITY OF WROCŁAW
ARCHAEOLOGICAL MUSEUM
ZOFIPOLE
ARCHAEOLOGICAL SITE MUSEUM

PORTUGAL

BARCELOS
MUNICIPAL ARCHAEOLOGICAL MUSEUM
GUIMARÃES
MARTINS SARMENTO MUSEUM
LISBON
ARCHAEOLOGICAL MUSEUM
GEOLOGICAL AND MINERALOGICAL MUSEUM
NATIONAL MUSEUM OF ARCHAEOLOGY AND ETHNOLOGY
SANTARÉM
ARCHAEOLOGICAL MUSEUM

RHODESIA

BULAWAYO
KHAMI RUINS SITE MUSEUM
FORT VICTORIA
ZIMBABWE RUINS SITE MUSEUM
INYANGA
NYAHOKWE RUINS SITE MUSEUM
MARANDELLOS
CHILDREN'S MUSEUM

ROMANIA

AGNITA
AGNITA MUSEUM
AIUD
AIUD HISTORICAL MUSEUM
ALBA IULIA
ALBA IULIA MUSEUM
ARAD
ARAD MUSEUM
BACĂU
BACĂU HISTORICAL MUSEUM
BICAZ
BICAZ MUSEUM
BOTOŞANI
BOTOŞANI MUSEUM
BRĂILA
LOCAL HISTORY MUSEUM
BRAŞOV
BRAŞOV MUSEUM
BUCHAREST
NATIONAL MUSEUM OF ANTIQUITIES
MARIA AND DR. G. SEVEREANU COLLECTION
BUZĂU
MUSEUM OF THE HISTORY OF BUZĂU
CĂLĂRAŞI
CĂLĂRAŞI MUSEUM
CARACAL
CARACAL MUSEUM
CÎMPULUNG
CÎMPULUNG-MUSCEL MUSEUM
CLUJ
ARDELEAN MUSEUM
HISTORY MUSEUM
CONSTANŢA
ARCHAEOLOGICAL MUSEUM OF THE DOBRUDSCHA
CORABIA
CORABIA MUSEUM
CRISTURUL
CRISTURUL MUSEUM
EFORIE SUD
ARCHAEOLOGICAL MUSEUM
FĂLTICENI
FĂLTICENI MUSEUM
GALAŢI
HISTORY MUSEUM
GHEORGHE GHEORGHIU-DEJ
MUNICIPAL MUSEUM
GHERLA
HISTORY MUSEUM
IAŞI
MOLDAVIAN MUSEUM OF HISTORY
LIPOVA
LIPOVA MUSEUM
MANGALIA
ARCHAEOLOGICAL MUSEUM
MEDIAŞ
MEDIAŞ MUSEUM
ODORHEI
ODORHEI MUSEUM
OLTENIŢA
OLTENIŢA MUSEUM
PIATRA NEAMŢ
MUSEUM OF ARCHAEOLOGY
PITEŞTI
PITEŞTI MUSEUM
PLOIEŞTI
HISTORY MUSEUM
RÎMNICU VILCEA
RÎMNICU VILCEA MUSEUM
ROMAN
ROMAN MUSEUM
SARMIZEGETUSA
MUSEUM OF HISTORY AND ARCHAEOLOGY
SATU MARE
SATU MARE MUSEUM
SFÎNTU GHEORGHE
SFÎNTU GHEORGHE MUSEUM
SIBIU
BRUKENTHAL MUSEUM
SLATINA
LOCAL MUSEUM
SUCEAVA
SUCEAVA MUSEUM
TÎRGOVIŞTE
DÎMBOVITA DISTRICT MUSEUM
TÎRGU MUREŞ
REGIONAL MUSEUM
TULCEA
MUSEUM OF THE DANUBE DELTA
TURDA
TURDA MUSEUM
TURNU SEVERIN
IRON GATE (PORŢILE DE FIER) MUSEUM
ZALĂU
ZALĂU MUSEUM

SAN MARINO, REPUBLIC OF

SAN MARINO
GOVERNMENT MUSEUM AND PICTURE-GALLERY

SENEGAL

DAKAR
HISTORICAL MUSEUM OF GORÉE
ILE DE GORÉE
HISTORICAL MUSEUM OF WEST AFRICA AT GORÉE

SINGAPORE

SINGAPORE
NATIONAL MUSEUM

SOUTH AFRICA, REPUBLIC OF

CAPE TOWN
SOUTH AFRICAN MUSEUM
SOUTH AFRICAN CULTURAL HISTORY MUSEUM
DUNDEE
DEPARTMENT OF MINES MUSEUM

EAST LONDON
EAST LONDON MUSEUM

GRAHAMSTOWN
ALBANY MUSEUM

JOHANNESBURG
ARCHAEOLOGICAL MUSEUM
GEOLOGICAL MUSEUM
MUSEUM OF MAN AND SCIENCE

KIMBERLEY
ALEXANDER MCGREGOR MEMORIAL MUSEUM

PIETERMARITZBURG
MINES DEPARTMENT MUSEUM

PORT ELIZABETH
PORT ELIZABETH MUSEUM

PRETORIA
ANTHROPOLOGICAL MUSEUM OF THE UNIVERSITY OF SOUTH AFRICA
NATIONAL CULTURAL HISTORY AND OPEN-AIR MUSEUM

VICTORIA WEST
VICTORIA WEST MUSEUM

VEREENIGING
VEREENIGING MUSEUM

SPAIN

ALBACETE
PROVINCIAL ARCHAEOLOGICAL MUSEUM

ALCAZAR DE SAN JUAN
FRAY JUAN COBO ARCHAEOLOGICAL MUSEUM

ALCOY
MUNICIPAL ARCHAEOLOGICAL MUSEUM

ALCUDIA
MUNICIPAL ARCHAEOLOGICAL MUSEUM

ALICANTE
PROVINCIAL ARCHAEOLOGICAL MUSEUM

ALMERIA
LUIS SIRET PROVINCIAL ARCHAEOLOGICAL MUSEUM

AMBRONA
MUSEUM OF THE EXCAVATIONS AT TORRALBA

AMPUDIA
FONTANEDA COLLECTION

AMPURIAS
LA ESCALA

ANTEQUERA
MUNICIPAL MUSEUM

AROCHE
MUNICIPAL MUSEUM

ARTA
REGIONAL MUSEUM

ASTORGA
MUSEUM OF JOURNEYS (DE LOS CAMINOS)

BADAJOZ
ARCHAEOLOGICAL MUSEUM

BADALONA
MUNICIPAL MUSEUM

BAÑOLAS
DISTRICT ARCHAEOLOGICAL MUSEUM

BARCELONA
ARCHAEOLOGICAL MUSEUM

BENALMADENA
MUNICIPAL ARCHAEOLOGICAL MUSEUM

BESALU
MUNICIPAL ARCHAEOLOGICAL COLLECTION

BILBAO
VIZCAYA HISTORICAL MUSEUM

BURGOS
PROVINCIAL ARCHAEOLOGICAL MUSEUM

BURRIANA
MUNICIPAL HISTORICAL MUSEUM

CACERES
MUSEO PROVINCIAL

CADIZ
PROVINCIAL MUSEUM OF FINE ART

CALAHORRA
CATHEDRAL AND DIOCESAN MUSEUM AND TREASURY

CALDAS DE MONTBUY
ARCHAEOLOGICAL MUSEUM

CAPELLADES
AMADOR ROMANI ARCHAEOLOGICAL MUSEUM

CARDEDEU
BALVEY MUSEUM AND ARCHIVES

CARMONA
MUSEUM OF THE ROMAN NECROPOLIS

CARTAGENA
MUNICIPAL MUSEUM OF ARCHAEOLOGY

CIUDAD REAL
ARCHAEOLOGICAL COLLECTION

CLUNIA
MUSEUM OF THE EXCAVATIONS

CORDOBA
MUSEUM OF THE EXCAVATIONS OF MEDINA AZ-ZAHARA
PROVINCIAL ARCHAEOLOGICAL MUSEUM

LA CORUÑA
HISTORICAL AND ARCHAEOLOGICAL MUSEUM

CUENCA
PROVINCIAL MUSEUM

LA ESCALA
MUSEO MONOGRAFICO DE AMPURIAS

GRANADA
PROVINCIAL ARCHAEOLOGICAL MUSEUM

LA GUARDIA
MUSEUM OF THE CITANIA OF SANTA TECLA

HUELVA
PROVINCIAL MUSEUM

IBIZA
ARCHAEOLOGICAL MUSEUM
MONOGRAPHIC MUSEUM AND PUNIC NECROPOLIS OF PUIG DES MOLINS

JAÉN
PROVINCIAL MUSEUM

JEREZ DE LA FRONTERA
MUNICIPAL ARCHAEOLOGICAL MUSEUM

JUMILLA
MUNICIPAL MUSEUM

LEÓN
PROVINCIAL ARCHAEOLOGICAL MUSEUM

LERIDA
ARCHAEOLOGICAL MUSEUM OF THE INSTITUTE OF ILERDIAN STUDIES

LINARES
ARCHAEOLOGICAL MUSEUM

LLUCH
LLUCH TREASURY AND MUSEUM

LOGROÑO
PROVINCIAL MUSEUM

MADRID
CABINET OF ANTIQUITIES
COLLECTION OF THE FACULTY OF PHILOSOPHY AND LETTERS
MUSEUM OF ANCIENT HISTORY
MUSEUM OF THE MUNICIPAL ARCHAEOLOGICAL INSTITUTE
NATIONAL ARCHAEOLOGICAL MUSEUM

MAHON
PROVINCIAL MUSEUM OF FINE ART

MALAGA
PROVINCIAL ARCHAEOLOGICAL MUSEUM

MANACOR
MUNICIPAL ARCHAEOLOGICAL MUSEUM

MERIDA
ARCHAEOLOGICAL MUSEUM

MURCIA
MUSEUM OF THE ARAB WALL
PROVINCIAL MUSEUM OF ARCHAEOLOGY

ORENSE
PROVINCIAL MUSEUM OF ARCHAEOLOGY

ORIHUELA
JOSÉ MA. SOLER PROVINCIAL ARCHAEOLOGICAL MUSEUM

OSUNA
MUSEUM OF ARCHAEOLOGY

OVIEDO
PROVINCIAL MUSEUM

PALENCIA
PROVINCIAL ARCHAEOLOGICAL MUSEUM

PALMA DE MALLORCA
DIOCESAN MUSEUM
MALLORCA MUSEUM

PAMPLONA
NAVARRA MUSEUM

SABADELL
MUSEUM OF HISTORY

SAGUNTO
ARCHAEOLOGICAL MUSEUM

SANTA CRUZ DE TENERIFE
ARCHAEOLOGICAL MUSEUM

SANTANDER
PROVINCIAL MUSEUM OF PREHISTORY AND ARCHAEOLOGY

SANTILLANA DEL MAR
ALTAMIRA CAVES

SANTIPONCE
ITALICA ARCHAEOLOGICAL MUSEUM

SEGOVIA
ARCHAEOLOGICAL MUSEUM

SEVILLE
HOUSE OF THE COUNTESS OF LEBRIJA
PAROCHIAL MUSEUM
PROVINCIAL ARCHAEOLOGICAL MUSEUM

SORIA
CELTIBERIAN MUSEUM
NUMANCIA MUSEUM
SAN JUAN EPIGRAPHIC MUSEUM

TARRAGONA
DIOCESAN MUSEUM
MUSEUM OF EARLY CHRISTIANITY
PROVINCIAL ARCHAEOLOGICAL MUSEUM

TERUEL
PROVINCIAL ARCHAEOLOGICAL MUSEUM

TOLEDO
MUSEUM OF THE COUNCILS AND OF VISIGOTH CULTURE
SANTA CRUZ MUSEUM

ULLASTRET
MUSEUM OF THE EXCAVATIONS

VALENCIA
MUSEUM OF PREHISTORY

VALLADOLID
PROVINCIAL MUSEUM OF ARCHAEOLOGY

VILLENA
JOSE MARIA SOLER MUNICIPAL MUSEUM OF ARCHAEOLOGY

VITORIA
ALAVA PROVINCIAL MUSEUM

YECLA
ARCHAEOLOGICAL COLLECTION

ZAMORA
PROVINCIAL MUSEUM OF FINE ART

SRI LANKA, REPUBLIC OF

ANURADHAPURA
FOLK MUSEUM

COLOMBO
NATIONAL MUSEUM

DEDIGAMA
ARCHAEOLOGICAL MUSEUM

SUDAN

EL OBEID
SHIEKAN MUSEUM

KHARTOUM
SUDAN ARCHAEOLOGICAL MUSEUM

MEROWE
MEROWE MUSEUM

SWEDEN

ARVIKA
ARVIKA MUSEUM

GÄVLE
GÄVLE MUSEUM

GÖTEBORG
ARCHAEOLOGICAL MUSEUM

HÄLSINGBORG
TOWN MUSEUM

LAHOLM

SOUTH HALLAND MUSEUM OF HISTORY AND ETHNOGRAPHY

LUND

MUSEUM OF CULTURAL HISTORY
UNIVERSITY OF LUND HISTORICAL MUSEUM

SKARA

WEST GÖTLAND MUSEUM

STOCKHOLM

MILLES MUSEUM
MUSEUM OF MEDITERRANEAN AND NEAR EASTERN ANTIQUITIES
MUSEUM OF NATIONAL ANTIQUITIES AND ROYAL COIN CABINET

SUNDSVALL

SUNDSVALL MUSEUM

UPPSALA

UNIVERSITY MUSEUM OF NATIONAL ANTIQUITIES
VICTORIA MUSEUM

VÄNERSBORG

VÄNERSBORG MUSEUM

VARBERG

VARBERG MUSEUM

VISBY

GOTLAND HISTORICAL MUSEUM

YSTAD

FRIARY WITH ST. PETER'S CHURCH

SWITZERLAND

AGNO

TOWN MUSEUM

ALLSCHWIL

REGIONAL MUSEUM

APPENZELL

REGIONAL MUSEUM

ARBON

HISTORICAL MUSEUM

ATTISWIL

REGIONAL MUSEUM

AUGST

ROMAN HOUSE AND MUSEUM

AVENCHES

ROMAN MUSEUM

BADEN

HISTORICAL MUSEUM

BALSTHAL

REGIONAL MUSEUM OF OLD FALKENSTEIN

BASEL

HISTORICAL MUSEUM
MUSEUM OF GREEK AND ROMAN ART

BAULMES

MUSEUM OF OLD BAULMES

BEINWIL AM SEE

PFAHLBAUSAMMLUNG

BELLINZONA

MUNICIPAL MUSEUM

BERN

BERN HISTORICAL MUSEUM

BEROMÜNSTER

REGIONAL MUSEUM

BIEL

SCHWAB MUSEUM

BOUDRY

L'AREUSE MUSEUM

BOURG-SAINT-PIERRE

MUSEUM OF THE GREAT ST. BERNARD SHELTER FOR TRAVELLERS

BRUGG

VINDONISSA MUSEUM

CASTANEDA

PREHISTORIC COLLECTION

CHUR

MUNICIPAL MUSEUM

DELÉMONT

JURA MUSEUM

DIETIKON

LOCAL MUSEUM

DORNACH

REGIONAL MUSEUM OF SCHWAZBUBENLAND

ESTAVAYER-LE-LAC

MUSEUM

FRAUENFELD

CANTON THURGAU MUSEUM

HERISAU

MUSEUM

HERZOGENBUCHSEE

LOCAL MUSEUM

HITZKIRCH

PREHISTORIC COLLECTION

KÖLLIKEN

PREHISTORIC AND HISTORICAL COLLECTION

LE LANDERON

MUSEUM

LAUFEN

LAUFENTAL REGIONAL MUSEUM

LAUSANNE

CANTONAL MUSEUM OF ART AND HISTORY
HISTORICAL MUSEUM OF THE OLD BISHOPRIC
VIDY ROMAN MUSEUM

LENZBURG

REGIONAL MUSEUM

LIESTAL

MUNZACH ROMAN VILLA

LOCARNO

MUNICIPAL MUSEUM

LUGANO

MUSEUM OF HISTORY AND ARCHAEOLOGY

LUZERN

GLACIER GARDEN AND GLACIER MUSEUM
HISTORICAL MUSEUM
NATURAL HISTORY MUSEUM

MOUDON

MUSEUM OF OLD MOUDON

NÄFELS

MUSEUM OF GLARUS CANTON

NEUCHÂTEL

CANTONAL MUSEUM OF ARCHAEOLOGY
MUSEUM OF ETHNOGRAPHY AND INSTITUTE OF ETHNOLOGY

LA NEUVEVILLE

HISTORICAL MUSEUM

NYON

HISTORICAL MUSEUM

OBERDORF

HISTORICAL COLLECTION OF THE TEACHER TRAINING COLLEGE

OBERRIET

MONTLINGEN MUSEUM

ORBE

MUSEUM OF OLD ORBE

PAYERNE

MUSEUM

PFÅFFIKON

LOCAL MUSEUM

PFYN

LOCAL MUSEUM

RAPPERSWIL

REGIONAL MUSEUM

REIGOLDSWIL

LOCAL HISTORY COLLECTION

REINACH

COLLECTION OF PREHISTORY AND EARLY HISTORY

RORSCHACH

REGIONAL MUSEUM

SAINTE-CROIX

MUSEUM

ST. GALLEN

REGIONAL MUSEUM

ST. MORITZ

ENGADINE MUSEUM

SARNEN

REGIONAL MUSEUM

SCHAFFHAUSEN

ALL SAINTS' MUSEUM

SCHÖNENWERD

BALLY MUSEUM FOUNDATION

SCHÖTZ

WIGGERTAL REGIONAL MUSEUM

SEENGEN

HALLWIL CASTLE

SION

VALÈRE CANTONAL MUSEUM

SISSACH

REGIONAL MUSEUM

SOLOTHURN

SOLOTHURN MUNICIPAL MUSEUM

STECKBORN

UNTERSEE REGIONAL MUSEUM

STEIN AM RHEIN

MUSEUM OF ST. GEORGEN MONASTERY

THUN

HISTORICAL MUSEUM

UZNACH

MUSEUM OF LOCAL LIFE AND HISTORY

VALANGIN

MUSEUM

WETZIKON

LOCAL MUSEUM

WIL

MUNICIPAL MUSEUM

WOHLEN

COLLECTION OF THE FREIAMT HISTORICAL SOCIETY

YVERDON

MUSEUM OF OLD YVERDON

ZUG

CANTONAL MUSEUM FOR PREHISTORY

ZURICH

SWISS NATIONAL MUSEUM
UNIVERSITY ARCHAEOLOGICAL COLLECTION

SYRIAN ARAB REPUBLIC

ALEPPO

ALEPPO NATIONAL MUSEUM

BOSRA

BOSRA MUSEUM

CHAHBA

MOSAICS MUSEUM

DAMASCUS

DAMASCUS NATIONAL MUSEUM

HAMA

HAMA MUSEUM

PALMYRA

PALMYRA MUSEUM

SOUEIDA

SOUEIDA MUSEUM

TARTOUS

TARTOUS MUSEUM

TANZANIA

DAR ES SALAAM

NATIONAL MUSEUM OF TANZANIA

THAILAND

AYUDHYA

AYUDHYA MUSEUM
CHAO SAM PHYA NATIONAL MUSEUM

CHIENGMAI

NATIONAL MUSEUM

CHIENG-SAEN

CHIENG-SAEN MUSEUM

KAMPHAENGPHET

NATIONAL MUSEUM

LOPBURI

LOPBURI MUSEUM

SUKHOTHAI

RAMKHAMHAENG NATIONAL MUSEUM

U-THONG

U-THONG NATIONAL MUSEUM

TUNISIA

CARTHAGE

ANTIQUARIUM

BATHS OF ANTONIUS
NATIONAL MUSEUM OF CARTHAGE
TOPHET OF SALAMBÔ

EL JEM (THYSDRUS)
EL-JEM MUSEUM

KAIROUAN
KAIROUAN MUSEUM

MACTAR
MACTAR MUSEUM

MOKNINE
MOKNINE MUSEUM

SFAX
MUSEUM OF ANTIQUITIES

SOUSSE
ARCHAEOLOGICAL MUSEUM

TUNIS
LE BARDO NATIONAL MUSEUM

UTICA
UTICA MUSEUM

TURKEY

ADANA
ADANA MUSEUM

AFYON
ARCHAEOLOGICAL MUSEUM

AKŞEHIR
ARCHAEOLOGICAL MUSEUM

ALACAHÖYÜK
ARCHAEOLOGICAL MUSEUM

AMASRA
ARCHAEOLOGICAL MUSEUM

ANKARA
ARCHAEOLOGICAL MUSEUM

ANTALYA
ARCHAEOLOGICAL MUSEUM

BERGAMA
PERGAMON MUSEUM

BURDUR
ARCHAEOLOGICAL MUSEUM

ÇANAKKALE
ARCHAEOLOGICAL MUSEUM

DIYARBAKIR
ARCHAEOLOGICAL MUSEUM

GAZIANTEP
ARCHAEOLOGICAL MUSEUM

HACIBEKTAŞ
ARCHAEOLOGICAL MUSEUM

HATAY
HATAY MUSEUM

ISTANBUL
ARCHAEOLOGICAL MUSEUM OF ISTANBUL
MUSEUM OF MOSAICS

IZMIR
ARCHAEOLOGICAL MUSEUM

KARAKASU
APHRODISIAS ARCHAEOLOGICAL MUSEUM

KASTAMONU
ARCHAEOLOGICAL MUSEUM

KONYA
CLASSICAL MUSEUM

KÜLTEPE
ARCHAEOLOGICAL MUSEUM

MALATYA
ARCHAEOLOGICAL MUSEUM

MARAS
ARCHAEOLOGICAL MUSEUM

PERGAMUM
ARCHAEOLOGICAL MUSEUM

SAMSUN
REGIONAL MUSEUM

TARSUS
ARCHAEOLOGICAL MUSEUM

TRABZON
ARCHAEOLOGICAL MUSEUM

TRUVA
ARCHAEOLOGICAL MUSEUM

UGANDA

KAMPALA
UGANDA MUSEUM

USSR

ARMAVIR
LOCAL MUSEUM

BAKHCHISARAI
MUSEUM OF HISTORY AND ARCHAEOLOGY

EREVAN
ARIN-BERD MUSEUM

GRODNO
MUSEUM OF HISTORY AND ARCHAEOLOGY

KAUNAS
STATE MUSEUM

KHERSON
HISTORICAL AND ARCHAEOLOGICAL MUSEUM

KIEV
STATE HISTORICAL MUSEUM

KORSUN
HERSONES MUSEUM

MOSCOW
D. N. ANUCHIN ANTHROPOLOGICAL INSTITUTE AND MUSEUM

ODESSA
ARCHAEOLOGICAL MUSEUM

OLVIA
ARCHAEOLOGICAL MUSEUM

ORDZHONIKIDZE
ORDZHONIKIDZE MUSEUM: HISTORY COLLECTIONS

PANTIKAPEL
ARCHAEOLOGICAL MUSEUM

PETROZAVODSK
NATIONAL HISTORICAL MUSEUM

RIGA
LATVIAN HISTORICAL MUSEUM

SEVASTOPOL
KHERSONES MUSEUM OF HISTORY AND ARCHAEOLOGY
SAPUN-GORA MUSEUM

SIMFEROPOL
LOCAL MUSEUM

SMOLENSK
MUSEUM OF HISTORY

SUKHUMI
DMITRI GULUYA STATE MUSEUM

TALLINN
MUSEUM OF HISTORY

TBILISI
DZHANASHIYA GEORGIAN MUSEUM

VILNIUS (formerly WILNO)
HISTORICAL AND ETHNOGRAPHICAL MUSEUM OF THE LITHUANIAN REPUBLIC

YALTA
MUSEUM OF HISTORY AND ARCHAEOLOGY

UNITED STATES

ANCHORAGE
COOK INLET HISTORICAL SOCIETY MUSEUM

ANDOVER
ROBERT S. PEABODY FOUNDATION FOR ARCHAEOLOGY

ANN ARBOR
KELSEY MUSEUM OF ANCIENT AND MEDIEVAL ARCHAEOLOGY

ATTLEBORO
BRONSON MUSEUM

AZTEC
AZTEC RUINS NATIONAL MONUMENT

BERKELEY
PALESTINE INSTITUTE MUSEUM

BLAKELY
KOLOMOKI MOUNDS MUSEUM

BLOOMFIELD
CHACO CANYON NATIONAL MONUMENT

CAMBRIDGE
SEMITIC MUSEUM

CARTERSVILLE
ETOWAH MOUNDS ARCHAEOLOGICAL AREA

CHILLICOTHE
MOUND CITY GROUP NATIONAL MONUMENT

CHINLE
CANYON DE CHELLY NATIONAL MONUMENT

CINCINNATI
CINCINNATI MUSEUM OF NATURAL HISTORY
HEBREW UNION COLLEGE MUSEUM
ALFRED K. NIPPERT NATURE MUSEUM

CLARKDALE
TUZIGOOT NATIONAL MONUMENT

COLUMBIA
MUSEUM OF ART AND ARCHAEOLOGY

COOLIDGE
CASA GRANDE RUINS NATIONAL MONUMENT

COVINGTON
BEHRINGER-CRAWFORD MEMORIAL MUSEUM OF NATURAL HISTORY

CRYSTAL RIVER
CRYSTAL RIVER HISTORIC MEMORIAL

DENVER
COLORADO STATE MUSEUM

EAST PRAIRIE
TOWOSAHGY

FLAGSTAFF
WALNUT CANYON NATIONAL MONUMENT

FONDA
MOHAWK-CAUGHNAWAGO MUSEUM

GILA HOT SPRINGS
GILA CLIFF DWELLINGS NATIONAL MONUMENT

GRAND CANYON
TUSAYAN MUSEUM

GRAND RAPIDS
GRAND RAPIDS PUBLIC MUSEUM

GUNNISON
CLARENCE T. HURST MUSEUM

HEAVENER
CLEM HAMILTON HEAVENER RUNESTONE STATE PARK

HOMER
HOMER MUSEUM

IRAAN
IRAAN ARCHAEOLOGICAL MUSEUM

JEFFERSON
AZTALAN MUSEUM

JEFFERSON CITY
GRAHAM CAVE STATE PARK

JONESBORO
ARKANSAS STATE UNIVERSITY MUSEUM

JUNEAU
ALASKA STATE MUSEUM

KALAMAZOO
KALAMAZOO PUBLIC MUSEUM

KATMAI
KATMAI NATIONAL MONUMENT

KURE BEACH
FORT FISHER STATE HISTORIC SITE, VISITOR CENTER

LAWRENCE
WILCOX MUSEUM

LEXINGTON
MUSEUM OF ANTHROPOLOGY

LOCUST GROVE
SERPENT MOUND

LOS ALAMOS
BANDELIER NATIONAL MONUMENT

LOS ANGELES
UNIVERSITY GALLERIES

MCGREGOR
EFFIGY MOUNDS NATIONAL MONUMENT

MEMPHIS
C. H. NASH MUSEUM - CHUCALISSA

MIAMI
LYMAN ARCHAEOLOGICAL RESEARCH CENTER MUSEUM

MONTGOMERY
MONTGOMERY MUSEUM OF FINE ARTS

MORRO BAY
MORRO BAY MUSEUM OF NATURAL HISTORY

MOUNDSVILLE
MOUND MUSEUM

MOUNT GILEAD
TOWN CREEK INDIAN MOUND STATE HISTORIC SITE
NEWARK
MOUND BUILDERS EARTHWORKS
NEW YORK
MUSEUM OF THE AMERICAN INDIAN
NORMAN
STOVALL MUSEUM OF SCIENCE AND HISTORY
OREGONIA
FORT ANCIENT MUSEUM
OSHKOSH
OSHKOSH PUBLIC MUSEUM
PARKER
COLORADO RIVER INDIAN TRIBES MUSEUM
PEACE DALE
MUSEUM OF PRIMITIVE CULTURES
PEEBLES
SERPENT MOUND MUSEUM
PENASCO
PICURIS PUEBLO MUSEUM
PHILADELPHIA
UNIVERSITY MUSEUM
PHOENIX
HEARD MUSEUM
PUEBLO GRANDE MUSEUM
PORTALES
PALAEO-INDIAN INSTITUTE AND MUSEUM
PRESCOTT
SMOKI MUSEUM
PRICE
CARBON COLLEGE PREHISTORIC MUSEUM
PRINCETON
ART MUSEUM
PROVO
BRIGHAM YOUNG UNIVERSITY, ARCHAEOLOGICAL COLLECTION
REDDING
REDDING MUSEUM AND ART CENTRE
RICHMOND
MUSEUM OF ARCHAEOLOGICAL SOCIETY OF VIRGINIA
ROCHESTER
MUSEUM OF NEW YORK STATE ARCHAEOLOGICAL ASSOCIATION
ST. LOUIS
MUSEUM OF SCIENCE AND NATURAL HISTORY
ST. PAUL
ST. PAUL PUBLIC LIBRARY
SANTA BARBARA
SANTA BARBARA MUSEUM OF NATURAL HISTORY
SARASOTA
RINGLING MUSEUM OF ART
SHEBOYGAN
JOHN MICHAEL KOHLER ARTS CENTER
SHILOH
SHILOH NATIONAL MILITARY PARK MUSEUM
SILVER CITY
GILA CLIFF DWELLINGS NATIONAL MONUMENT
SOUTHPORT
BRUNSWICK TOWN HALL HISTORIC SITE
SPALDING
MUSEUM OF NEZ PERCE NATIONAL HISTORIC PARK
UNCASVILLE
TANTAQUIDGEON INDIAN MUSEUM
UTUADO
MUSEUM AND PARK OF ARCHAEOLOGY
VIRGINIA BEACH
SKICOAK LIVING MUSEUM OF THE AMERICAN INDIAN
VOLCANO
INDIAN GRINDING ROCK STATE HISTORIC PARK
WASHINGTON
NATIONAL MUSEUM OF NATURAL HISTORY
WICKLIFFE
ANCIENT BURIED CITY
WILSON
NODENA SITE
WINDOW ROCK
NAVAJO TRIBAL MUSEUM
WOOSTER
COLLEGE OF WOOSTER MUSEUM
YOSEMITE
YOSEMITE NATIONAL PARK MUSEUM

VENEZUELA

CARACAS
NATURAL SCIENCE MUSEUM

VIETNAM, DEMOCRATIC REPUBLIC OF

HANOI
HISTORICAL MUSEUM

VIETNAM, REPUBLIC OF

ĐA-NANG
ARCHAEOLOGICAL MUSEUM
HUÉ
ARCHAEOLOGICAL MUSEUM

YEMEN, PEOPLE'S DEMOCRATIC REPUBLIC OF

ADEN
NATIONAL ARCHAEOLOGICAL MUSEUM
BEIHAN
BEIHAN MUSEUM

YUGOSLAVIA

BANJA LUKA
MUSEUM OF BASANSKA KRAJINA REGION
BELGRADE
NATIONAL MUSEUM
BREŽICE
PROVINCIAL MUSEUM
BUDVA
TOWN MUSEUM
CETINJE
STATE MUSEUM
KOŠLJUN
MONASTIC MUSEUM
LJUBLJANA
MUNICIPAL MUSEUM
NIŠ
OCHRID NATIONAL MUSEUM
OHRID
LOCAL MUSEUM
OSOR
MUSEUM
PIRAN
ART GALLERY AND CITY MUSEUM
POREČ
TOWN MUSEUM
PREDJAMA
CASTLE MUSEUM
PTUJ
REGIONAL MUSEUM
PULA
ARCHAEOLOGICAL MUSEUM
SARAJEVO
STATE MUSEUM
ŠIBENIK
TOWN MUSEUM
SKOPJE
ARCHAEOLOGICAL MUSEUM
SPLIT
ARCHAEOLOGICAL MUSEUM
MUSEUM OF CROATIAN MEDIEVAL ANTIQUITIES
SREMSKI KARLOVCI
TOWN MUSEUM
ZADAR
ARCHAEOLOGICAL MUSEUM
ZAGREB
ARCHAEOLOGICAL MUSEUM
ARCHIVES OF THE YUGOSLAV ACADEMY OF SCIENCES AND ARTS
LUBIENSKY-DURIEUX COLLECTION OF OBJETS D'ART

ZAIRE, REPUBLIC OF

MBENDAKA
NATIONAL MUSEUM

ZAMBIA

LIVINGSTONE
LIVINGSTONE MUSEUM

National and international history

ALBANIA

TIRANA
MUSEUM OF THE STRUGGLE FOR NATIONAL LIBERATION

ALGERIA

ALGIERS
MUSEUM OF THE PALACE OF THE DEY
MUSEUM OF THE REVOLUTION
EL BIAR
MUSEUM OF THE REVOLUTION, 1954-62

ARGENTINA

BUENOS AIRES
MUSEUM OF THE GOVERNOR'S HOUSE
NATIONAL HISTORICAL MUSEUM
NATIONAL HISTORICAL MUSEUM OF THE MAY REVOLUTION
NATIONAL SAN MARTIN MUSEUM
ROCA MUSEUM
ESPERANZA
MUSEUM OF THE COLONIES
MENDOZA
SAN MARTIN HISTORICAL MUSEUM
SALTA
HOUSE OF PRESIDENT JOSÉ E. URIBURU
SAMAY HUASI
REGIONAL MUSEUM "MIS MONTAÑAS"
SAN ANTONIO DE ARECO
RICARDO GUIRALDES GAUCHO MUSEUM
SAN JOSÉ
REGIONAL MUSEUM
SAN MIGUEL DE TUCUMÁN
MUSEUM OF THE HISTORIC HOUSE OF THE INDEPENDENCE
SAN NICOLAS DE LOS ARROYOS
HOUSE OF THE AGREEMENT (CASA DEL ACUERDO) MUSEUM
TIGRE
MUSEUM OF THE RECONQUEST

TRENQUE LAUQUEN
REGIONAL HISTORICAL MUSEUM
TUCUMÁN
BISHOP COLOMBRES' HOUSE
MUSEUM OF HISTORY: HOUSE OF INDEPENDENCE

AUSTRALIA

BRUNI ISLAND
BLIGH MUSEUM OF PACIFIC EXPLORATION
CANBERRA
NATIONAL LIBRARY OF AUSTRALIA
KATANNING
KATANNING HISTORICAL MUSEUM
KINGSCOTE
NATIONAL TRUST MUSEUM
KURNELL
CAPTAIN COOK'S LANDING PLACE MUSEUM

AUSTRIA

BAD ISCHL
VILLA OF THE EMPEROR
BRANDHOF
ARCHDUKE JOHANN HUNTING MUSEUM
FISCHAMEND
REGIONAL MUSEUM
KINDBERG
HUNGARIAN MUSEUM IN WESTERN EUROPE
VIENNA
TREASURY OF THE GERMAN ORDER

BELGIUM

ANTWERP
ARCHIVES AND MUSEUM OF FLEMISH CULTURAL LIFE
BELOEIL
CASTLE MUSEUM
BRUSSELS
ERASMUS' HOUSE
MUSEUM OF THE DYNASTY
GHENT
MUSEUM OF THE TREATY OF GHENT

BERMUDA

FORT ST. CATHERINE
FORT ST. CATHERINE
HAMILTON
PAR-LA-VILLE MUSEUM
ST. GEORGE'S
THE CONFEDERATE MUSEUM

BOLIVIA

SUCRE
HISTORICAL MUSEUM

BRAZIL

BAGÉ
DIOGO DE SOUZA MUSEUM
BATATAIS
DR. WASHINGTON LUIZ HISTORICAL MUSEUM
IGARAÇU
COLLECTIONS OF THE HISTORICAL INSTITUTE
LAGUNA
ANITA GARIBALDI MUSEUM
ORLEANS
MUSEUM OF IMMIGRATION
OURO PRÊTO
MUSEUM OF THE HISTORY OF DEMOCRATIC IDEALS AND CULTURE IN MINAS GERAIS
PETRÓPOLIS
IMPERIAL MUSEUM
PIRACICABA
PRUDENTE DE MORAES HISTORICAL MUSEUM
PÔRTO ALEGRE
JULIO DE CASTILHOS STATE HISTORICAL MUSEUM
RECIFE
MUSEUM OF THE ABOLITION
RIO DE JANEIRO
MUSEUM OF THE REPUBLIC
MUSEUM OF THE RUI BARBOSA FOUNDATION
NATIONAL HISTORICAL MUSEUM
SANTA LUZIA
DOLABELA MUSEUM
SÃO CARLOS
HISTORICAL MUSEUM
SÃO PAULO
JOSÉ BONIFACIO MUSEUM
PAULISTA MUSEUM
REPUBLICAN CONVENTION MUSEUM
SOROCABA
BRIGADIER RAFAEL TOBIAS DE AGUIAR HISTORICAL MUSEUM

BULGARIA

KOLAROVGRAD
LAJOS KOSSUTH MUSEUM
LOVEČ
VASIL LEVSKI MUSEUM
REGIONAL MUSEUM OF HISTORY
PLOVDIV
MUSEUM OF SOCIALIST CONSTRUCTION
REGIONAL MUSEUM OF ARCHAEOLOGY
RILA
RILA MONASTERY NATIONAL MUSEUM
SOFIA
GEORGI DIMITROV CENTRAL MUSEUM
GEORGI DIMITROV MUSEUM
VASSIL KOLAROV MUSEUM
MUSEUM OF THE REVOLUTIONARY MOVEMENT
MUSEUM OF THE REVOLUTIONARY MOVEMENT IN BULGARIA
NATIONAL MUSEUM OF BULGARIAN-SOVIET FRIENDSHIP
ALEXANDER STAMBOLISKY MUSEUM
VARNA
MUSEUM OF THE NATIONAL REBIRTH
NAVAL MUSEUM

BURMA

RANGOON
BOGYOKE AUNG SAN MUSEUM

CANADA

ADOLPHUSTOWN
UNITED EMPIRE LOYALIST MUSEUM
ANNAPOLIS ROYAL
FORT ANNE NATIONAL HISTORIC PARK
BURLINGTON
JOSEPH BRANT MUSEUM
CRAIK
PRAIRIE PIONEER MUSEUM
FORT LANGLEY
FORT LANGLEY NATIONAL HISTORIC PARK
FORT QU'APPELLE
FORT QU'APPELLE MUSEUM
GRAND PRÉ
GRAND PRÉ NATIONAL HISTORIC PARK MUSEUM
LAURENTIDE
SIR WILFRED LAURIER HOUSE
OTTAWA
PUBLIC ARCHIVES OF CANADA
PLACENTIA
CASTLE HILL MUSEUM
ST. JOHNS
NEWFOUNDLAND MUSEUM
ST. GEORGE
ADELAIDE HUNTER HOODLESS HOMESTEAD
TORONTO
ROYAL ONTARIO MUSEUM

CENTRAL AFRICAN REPUBLIC

BANGUI
BARTHÉLÉMY BOGANDA MUSEUM

CHILE

SANTIAGO
NATIONAL HISTORICAL MUSEUM
HISTORICAL MUSEUM

CHINA, P.R.

AMOY (XIAMEN)
OVERSEAS CHINESE MUSEUM
ANTUNG (ANDONG)
PROVINCIAL MUSEUM
CANTON (GUANG DONG)
HISTORY MUSEUM
CHANG SHA (ZHENG ZHOU)
MUSEUM OF THE COMMUNIST PARTY COMMITTEE
OLD NORMAL SCHOOL
JING GANG SHEN
REVOLUTIONARY BASE MUSEUM
KWANCHOW
MUSEUM OF THE INSTITUTE OF THE PEASANT MOVEMENT
LHASA
LHASA MUSEUM
NANKING (NAN JING)
MUSEUM OF THE HEAVENLY KINGDOM OF GREAT PEACE
PEKING
CULTURAL PALACE OF THE MINORITIES
MILITARY MUSEUM OF THE CHINESE PEOPLE'S REVOLUTION
MUSEUM OF CHINESE HISTORY
MUSEUM OF THE REVOLUTION
SUN YAT SEN MUSEUM
QIU JIN
REVOLUTIONARY BASE MUSEUM
QU FU
TEMPLE OF CONFUCIUS
SHAO SHAN
MAO TSE TUNG MUSEUM
YENAN (YAN AN)
MAO'S HOUSE
MUSEUM OF THE REVOLUTION
ZUN YI
MAO TSE TUNG MUSEUM

COLOMBIA

BOGOTA
BOLÍVAR MUSEUM
JORGE ELIECER GAITAN MUSEUM
HISTORICAL MUSEUM
MUSEUM OF THE 20TH OF JULY, or HOUSE OF THE FLOWER VASE
ANTONIO NARIÑO MUSEUM
NATIONAL MUSEUM
CARTAGENA
COLONIAL MUSEUM
GUADUAS
LA POLA HOUSE-MUSEUM
POPAYAN
MUSEUM OF COLONIAL HISTORY AND ART
SAN PEDRO ALEJANDRINO
LOCAL MUSEUM
MUSEUM OF THE REVOLUTION

COSTA RICA

SAN JOSÉ

NATIONAL MUSEUM

CUBA

HABANA

MUSEUM OF COLONIAL ART
NAPOLEONIC MUSEUM

SANTA CLARA

HISTORICAL MUSEUM

CZECHOSLOVAKIA

BRATISLAVA

SLOVAKIAN NATIONAL MUSEUM: HISTORICAL COLLECTIONS

BRNO

MUSEUM OF HISTORICAL MOVEMENTS

ČERVENÝ HRÁDEK

MEMORIAL TO THE STRUGGLE AGAINST FASCISM

DĚČÍN

DISTRICT MUSEUM

DĚDICE U VYŠKOVA

KLEMENT GOTTWALD HOUSE- MUSEUM

FRÝDLANT V ČECHÁCH

MUNICIPAL MUSEUM

HRADEC KRÁLOVÉ

REGIONAL MUSEUM: DEPARTMENT OF ARCHAEOLOGY AND HISTORY

KARLOVY VARY

KARL MARX MUSEUM

KOMÁRNO

PODUNAJSKA REGIONAL MUSEUM

KOŠICE

MUSEUM OF EASTERN SLOVAKIA

KOŽLANY

MUNICIPAL MUSEUM

PLZEŇ

MUSEUM OF WESTERN CZECHOSLOVAKIA

PRACE

MOHYLA MIRU (MOUND OF PEACE) MEMORIAL

PRAGUE

KLEMENT GOTTWALD MUSEUM
V. I. LENIN MUSEUM
MUSEUM OF THE DEFENCE OF THE CZECH FRONTIER
NATIONAL MUSEUM: MUSEUM OF HISTORY

PREŠOV

MUSEUM OF THE SLOVAK REPUBLIC

ROUSÍNOV

KLEMENT GOTTWALD MEMORIAL

RUŽINOV

MUSEUM OF THE ILLEGAL SLOVAKIAN COMMUNIST PARTY

SLAVKOV

MUSEUM OF THE NAPOLEONIC WARS

SVIDNÍK

MUSEUM OF THE BATTLE OF DUKLA

TÁBOR

MUSEUM OF THE HUSSITE REVOLT

TEREZÍN

MEMORIAL OF THE NATIONAL SUFFERING

TRENČÍN

TRENČÍN MUSEUM

UHROVEC

STÚR MUSEUM

VRÚTKY

KLEMENT GOTTWALD MUSEUM OF THE REVOLUTIONARY PRESS

DAHOMEY

OUIDAH

HISTORICAL MUSEUM

DENMARK

COPENHAGEN

MUSEUM OF THE DANISH RESISTANCE MOVEMENT
STATE ARCHIVES MUSEUM

HILLERØD

NATIONAL HISTORICAL MUSEUM

MARIBO

LOLLAND AND FALSTER MUSEUM

REBILD BAKKER

THE LINCOLN LOG CABIN MUSEUM

SØNDERBORG

MUSEUM

ECUADOR

GUAYAQUIL

TOWN MUSEUM

QUITO

JIJÓN Y CAAMAÑO ARCHAEOLOGICAL AND HISTORICAL MUSEUM

EGYPT, ARAB REPUBLIC OF

ALEXANDRIA

MONTAZAH PALACE MUSEUM

CAIRO

ABDINE PALACE MUSEUM
AL MANIAL PALACE MUSEUM
ARAB POST MUSEUM
EGYPTIAN NATIONAL MUSEUM
HELWAN PALACE MUSEUM
MOHAMED MAHMRUD KHALIL MUSEUM
MOUSTAFA KAMEL MUSEUM

EL SALVADOR

SAN SALVADOR

NATIONAL MUSEUM DAVID J. GUZMAN

FINLAND

HELSINKI

FINNISH NATIONAL MUSEUM

TAMPERE

LENIN MUSEUM

FRANCE

AIX (ÎLE D')

NAPOLEONIC MUSEUM

AJACCIO

NAPOLEONIC MUSEUM
NATIONAL MUSEUM OF THE HOUSE OF THE BONAPARTES

AMBOISE

TOWN HALL MUSEUM

AMIENS

MUSEUM OF REGIONAL ART AND HISTORY

AUCH

MUSEUM OF ART AND ARCHAEOLOGY

AUXERRE

MUSEUM OF ART AND HISTORY

AUXONNE

BONAPARTE MUSEUM

BESANÇON

MUSEUM OF THE RESISTANCE

BLÉRANCOURT

NATIONAL MUSEUM OF FRANCO-AMERICAN FRIENDSHIP

BRIENNE-LE-CHÂTEAU

NAPOLEONIC MUSEUM

CASTRES

JAURÈS MUSEUM

CHÂTEAUROUX

BERTRAND MUSEUM

CHAUNY

LOCAL MUSEUM

CHAUVIGNY

FOLKLORE AND ETHNOGRAPHIC MUSEUM

CHERBOURG

MUSEUM OF THE WAR AND THE LIBERATION

CHINON

JEAN D'ARC MUSEUM

DOMRÉMY LA PUCELLE

JEANNE D'ARC MUSEUM

FIXIN

NOISOT NAPOLEONIC MUSEUM

LE HAVRE

MUSEUM OF OLD LE HAVRE

LIMOUX

PETIET MUSEUM

LYON

MUSEUM OF THE RESISTANCE

LE MAS-SOUBEYRAN

DESERT MUSEUM

MONTAUBAN

INGRÈS MUSEUM

MONTREUIL

MUSEUM OF LIVING HISTORY

MOROSAGLIA

PASCAL PAOLI MUSEUM

NÉRAC

CHÂTEAU HENRI IV MUSEUM

PARIS

ARMENIAN MUSEUM IN FRANCE
BOIS-PRÉAU NATIONAL MUSEUM
CLEMENCEAU MUSEUM
HÔTEL DE CLUNY MUSEUM
FRÉDÉRIC MASSON MUSEUM
MUSEUM OF THE FRENCH OVERSEAS TERRITORIES
MUSEUM OF THE HISTORY OF FRANCE
TREASURY OF NOTRE DAME

PAU

HENRI IV NATIONAL MUSEUM

PLESSIS-LES-TOURS

MUSEUM CHÂTEAU

RICHELIEU

MUSEUM OF THE 17th CENTURY

RIOM

JOAN OF ARC MUSEUM

RUEIL-MALMAISON

CHÂTEAU DE BOIS-PRÉAU
MALMAISON NATIONAL CHÂTEAU

ST. PIERRE D'OLÉRON

ALIENOR D'AQUITAINE MUSEUM

SAINT VINCENT- SUR-JARD

PRESIDENT CLEMENCEAU HOUSE-MUSEUM

VALENÇAY

GALLERY OF MEMENTOES OF PRINCE DE TALLEYRAND

VAUCOULEURS

MUNICIPAL MUSEUM

VERSAILLES

LAMBINET MUSEUM
MUSEUM OF HISTORY

VINCENNES

HISTORICAL MUSEUM OF THE CHÂTEAU DE VINCENNES

FRENCH POLYNESIA

TAHITI

PAPEETE MUSEUM

GDR

ALLSTEDT

THOMAS MÜNTZER MEMORIAL

BERLIN

BODE MUSEUM: PAPYRUS COLLECTION
MUSEUM OF GERMAN HISTORY
MUSEUM OF PREHISTORY AND EARLY HISTORY

BIRKENWERDER

CLARA ZETKIN MEMORIAL

BUCHENWALD DEI WEIMAR

NATIONAL BUCHENWALD MEMORIAL

DRESDEN

MARCOLINI PALACE

EISENACH
1869 EISENACH PARTY CONGRESS MEMORIAL
LUTHER HOUSE
ERFURT
MEMORIAL TO THE ERFURT PARTY CONGRESS OF 1891
GOTHA
1875 GOTHA PARTY CONGRESS MEMORIAL
HOHNSTEIN
CONCENTRATION CAMP MEMORIAL IN HOHNSTEIN CASTLE
JENA
HILPRECHT COLLECTION OF NEAR EASTERN ANTIQUITIES OF THE FRIEDRICH SCHILLER UNIVERSITY
KARL LIEBKNECHT HOUSE
LEIPZIG
GEORGI DIMITROFF MUSEUM
ISKRA MEMORIAL
LENIN MEMORIAL
MUSEUM OF THE HISTORY OF THE CITY OF LEIPZIG
MUSEUM OF THE HISTORY OF THE LEIPZIG WORKERS' MOVEMENT
MARKRANSTÄDT
PEACE ROOM
NEIDERLEHME-ZIEGENHALS
ERNST THÄLMANN MEMORIAL
POTSDAM
CECILIENHOF PALACE
RAVENSBRÜCK
NATIONAL RAVENSBRÜCK MEMORIAL
SACHSENHAUSEN BEI ORANIENBURG
NATIONAL MEMORIAL
SALZWEDEL
JENNY MARX MUSEUM
WERMSDORF
REGIONAL ROOM, WITH BEBEL AND LIEBKNECHT MEMORIALS
WIEDERAU
CLARA ZETKIN MEMORIAL
WILHELM PIECK STADT (formerly GUBEN)
WILHELM PIECK MEMORIAL

GFR

AALEN
LIMES MUSEUM
AHLEN
REGIONAL MUSEUM
AUMÜHLE-FRIEDRICHSRUH
BISMARCK MUSEUM
BAD MERGENTHEIM
MUSEUM OF THE TEUTONIC ORDER AND REGIONAL MUSEUM
BERLIN
PLÖTZENSEE MEMORIAL
STAUFFENBERGSTRASSE MEMORIAL
DACHAU
CONCENTRATION CAMP MEMORIAL
DÜSSELDORF
HOUSE OF THE EASTERN GERMAN TERRITORIES
ELLINGEN
ELLINGEN PALACE
FRANKFURT
HISTORY MUSEUM
FREUDENSTADT
TAXATION MUSEUM
FRIEDRICHSRUH
BISMARCK MUSEUM
GELNHAUSEN
REGIONAL MUSEUM
GOSLAR
COLLECTION ILLUSTRATING THE CULTURAL HISTORY OF GERMANY AND EUROPE
HALTERN
ROMAN AND GERMANIC MUSEUM
HAUSEN
BISMARCK'S RESIDENCE
HECHINGEN
HOHENZOLLERN LAND- COLLECTION
HOHENZOLLERN MUSEUM
KARLSRUHE
CARPATHIAN ROOM
KELHEIM
HALL OF LIBERATION
KÖLN
CUSTOMS MUSEUM
LINDERHOF
PALACE
MEMMINGEN
REGIONAL ROOM
MÜNCHEN
STATE PREHISTORICAL COLLECTION
MÜNSTER
HALL OF THE PEACE
REGENSBURG
PARLIAMENT MUSEUM
SIEGBURG
COLLECTION OF THE HISTORY OF TAXATION
TRIER
KARL MARX HOUSE
TÜBINGEN
COLLECTION OF THE UNIVERSITY INSTITUTE OF EGYPTOLOGY
WETZLAR
MUNICIPAL MUSEUM
WOLFENBÜTTEL
LESSING HOUSE
WUPPERTAL
FRIEDRICH ENGELS MEMORIAL

GIBRALTAR

GIBRALTAR
GIBRALTAR MUSEUM

GREAT BRITAIN

ABERYSTWYTH
NATIONAL LIBRARY OF WALES
ALCESTER
COUGHTON COURT
BANBURY
BROUGHTON CASTLE
BISHOP'S STORTFORD
RHODES MEMORIAL MUSEUM
BLAIR ATHOLL
BLAIR CASTLE AND ATHOLL MUSEUM
BLANTYRE
SCOTTISH NATIONAL MEMORIAL TO DAVID LIVINGSTONE
BUCKLAND ABBEY
BUCKLAND ABBEY
CHATHAM
ROYAL ENGINEERS MUSEUM
COLNE
BRITISH IN INDIA MUSEUM
DUNFERMLINE
ANDREW CARNEGIE BIRTHPLACE MEMORIAL
EDINBURGH
MUSEUM GALLERY
NATIONAL MUSEUM OF ANTIQUITIES OF SCOTLAND
PALACE OF HOLYROOD HOUSE
GLASGOW
HUNTERIAN MUSEUM
GRANTHAM
BELTON HOUSE
HIGH WYCOMBE
DISRAELI MUSEUM
HUNTINGDON
CROMWELL MUSEUM
INVERNESS
INVERNESS MUSEUM AND ART GALLERY
ISLE OF MULL
DUART CASTLE
JEDBURGH
MARY, QUEEN OF SCOTS' HOUSE
JERSEY
ST. PETER'S BUNKER MUSEUM OF NAZI GERMAN EQUIPMENT AND OCCUPATION RELICS
KENDAL
SIZERGH CASTLE
LEWES
FIRLE PLACE
LINCOLN
LINCOLN CATHEDRAL TREASURY
LLANYSTUMDWY
LLOYD GEORGE MEMORIAL MUSEUM
LONDON
BRITISH MUSEUM
PUBLIC RECORD OFFICE AND MUSEUM
ST. JOHN'S GATE
TOWER OF LONDON
MIDHURST
RICHARD COBDEN COLLECTION
MONMOUTH
NELSON MUSEUM
NEWTONMORE
CLAN MACPHERSON HOUSE AND MUSEUM
NEWTOWN
THE ROBERT OWEN MEMORIAL MUSEUM
ROCHDALE
ROCHDALE CO-OPERATIVE MUSEUM
SCUNTHORPE
BOROUGH MUSEUM AND ART GALLERY
SELBORNE
GILBERT WHITE MUSEUM
SHIFNAL
WESTON PARK
STRATFORD- UPON-AVON
NEW PLACE AND NASH'S HOUSE
SULGRAVE
SULGRAVE MANOR
WESTERHAM
CHARTWELL
WESTER ROSS
EILEAN DONAN CASTLE
WINCHCOMBE
SUDELEY CASTLE
WOLVERHAMPTON
MOSELEY OLD HALL

GREECE

ATHENS
BENAKI MUSEUM
HISTORICAL AND ETHNOLOGICAL MUSEUM
NATIONAL HISTORICAL MUSEUM
CHANIA
HISTORICAL MUSEUM AND CRETAN CORNER
HYDRA
HISTORICAL ARCHIVES OF HYDRA
KALAVRYTA
AGIA LAVRA MONASTERY
KOZANI
ARCHAEOLOGICAL COLLECTION
LACHANAS
MUSEUM

HONDURAS

COMAYAGUA
REGIONAL MUSEUM OF ARCHAEOLOGY AND COLONIAL EXHIBITS OF THE COMAYAGUA VALLEY

HUNGARY

BUDAPEST
HUNGARIAN NATIONAL MUSEUM
MIHÁLY KÁROLYI MEMORIAL MUSEUM
MUSEUM OF THE HISTORY OF BUDAPEST: MEDIEVAL DEPARTMENT
MUSEUM OF THE HISTORY OF THE HUNGARIAN COMMUNIST PARTY
MUSEUM OF THE WORKERS' MOVEMENT
PESTERZSÉBETI MÚZEUM
CEGLÉD
KOSSUTH MUSEUM

MONOK
KOSSUTH MEMORIAL MUSEUM
PÁPA
LOCAL HISTORY MUSEUM

INDIA

AHMEDABAD
GANDHI MEMORIAL MUSEUM
BHAWANAGAR
GANDHI SMRITI MUSEUMS
BOMBAY
MANI BHAVAN SANGRAHALAYA
CALCUTTA
INDIAN MUSEUM
VICTORIA MEMORIAL HALL
MADRAS
FORT ST. GEORGE MUSEUM
MADURAI
GANDHI SMARAK SANGRAHALAYA
NEW DELHI
BHARTIYA ADIM JATI SEVAK SANGH MUSEUM
GANDHI MEMORIAL MUSEUM AND LIBRARY
NATIONAL MUSEUM OF INDIA
NEHRU MEMORIAL MUSEUM
PARGANAS
GANDHI SMARAK SANGRAHALAYA
PATNA
GANDHI MEMORIAL MUSEUM
POONA
DECCAN COLLEGE MUSEUM
SERINGAPATAM
TIPU SULTAN PALACE
SEVAGRAM
GANDHI MEMORIAL MUSEUM

INDONESIA

DJAKARTA
SEDJARAH MUSEUM

IRAQ

BAB-AL-SHARQUI
MEMORIAL MUSEUM OF HIS MAJESTY THE LATE KING OF IRAQ, FAISAL I
BAGHDAD
AL-BAATH SOCIALIST PARTY MUSEUM
MUSEUM OF ETHNOGRAPHY
ERBIL
ERBIL MUSEUM

IRELAND

AVONDALE
PARNELL MUSEUM
CASTLEREA
CLONALIS HOUSE
CORK
CORK PUBLIC MUSEUM
DERRYNAMUCK
DWYER-MACALLISTER COTTAGE
DUBLIN
KILMAINHAM JAIL MUSEUM
NATIONAL MUSEUM OF IRELAND
SLIGO
COUNTY SLIGO MUSEUM

ISRAEL

AKKO (ACRE)
MUSEUM HAGEVURA
CAESAREA
LOCAL MUSEUM
JERUSALEM
HERZL MUSEUM
MUSEUM OF TAXES
MUSEUM YAD VASHEM
LOHAME-HAGETA'OT
GHETTO FIGHTERS' MEMORIAL MUSEUM
REHOVOT
WEIZMANN ARCHIVES
TEL-AVIV
JABOTINSKY MUSEUM

ITALY

BERGAMO
MUSEUM OF THE RISORGIMENTO
BRESCIA
MUSEUM OF THE RISORGIMENTO
CAPRERA
CASA BIANCA
COMO
GARIBALDI MUSEUM
FERRARA
MUSEUM OF THE RISORGIMENTO
GARDONE DI SOPRA
MUSEUM
GARDONE RIVIERA
VITTORIALE ESTATE
GENOA
DORIA TURSI PALACE (NOW PALAZZO MUNICIPALE)
MAZZINI HOUSE
MUSEUM OF THE RISORGIMENTO
LECCO
HISTORICAL MUSEUM
MENTANA
GARIBALDI MUSEUM
MILAN
MUSEUM OF THE NATIONAL RISORGIMENTO
MODENA
MUSEUM OF THE RISORGIMENTO
NAPLES
MUSEUM OF THE CARTHUSIAN MONASTERY OF ST. MARTIN
PADUA
MUNICIPAL MUSEUM
PARMA
LOMBARDI MUSEUM
PAVIA
MUSEUM OF THE RISORGIMENTO
PISA
DOMUS MAZZINIANA
POGGIO A CAIANO
VILLA MEDICEA
PORTOFERRAIO
NAPOLEONIC MUSEUM
ROME
CENTRAL MUSEUM OF THE RISORGIMENTO
MUSEUM OF THE LIBERATION OF ROME
MUSEUM OF ROMAN CIVILISATION
NAPOLEONIC MUSEUM
NATIONAL MUSEUM OF CASTEL SANT'ANGELO
SANTENA
CAVOUR MUSEUM
TRIESTE
MUSEUM OF THE RISORGIMENTO
TURIN
ABRUZZI MUSEUM
NATIONAL MUSEUM OF THE ITALIAN RISORGIMENTO
UDINE
CASTLE MUSEUM AND PICTURE GALLERY
URBISAGLIA
NAPOLEONIC ROOM
VENICE
MUSEUM OF THE RISORGIMENTO
VERONA
RISORGIMENTO MUSEUM

JAMAICA

KINGSTON
WEST INDIA REFERENCE LIBRARY HISTORICAL GALLERY
WHITE MARL
ARAWAK MUSEUM
PORT ROYAL
PORT ROYAL MUSEUM

JAPAN

AIZUWAKAMATSU-SHI
BYAKKOTAI MEMORIAL COLLECTION
FUKUI-SHI
FUKUI HISTORY HALL
HIKONE-SHI
ECONOMIC DOCUMENT COLLECTION
HIRADO-SHI
MATSURA HISTORICAL MUSEUM
HIROSHIMA-SHI
HIROSHIMA PEACE MEMORIAL MUSEUM
KYOTO
HISTORICAL MUSEUM
MUSEUM OF THE HISTORY OF THE RESTORATION
MINAMIARIMA-MACHI
HARA CASTLE MEMORIAL HALL
NAGASAKI-SHI
ATOMIC BOMB MEMORIAL ROOM
NAGASAKI MUNICIPAL MUSEUM
OARI-MACHI
JOYO MEMORIAL MUSEUM OF MEIJI THE GREAT
SAGAWA-MACHI-KO
SEIZAN BUNKO HISTORICAL COLLECTION
SHIMODA-MACHI
GYOKUSENJI COLLECTION
OKICHI MEMORIAL HALL
RYOSENJI COLLECTION
SHIMODA MEMORIAL COLLECTION OF OPENING JAPAN TO COMMERCE
SHIMONOSEKI-SHI
JAPAN-CHINA PEACE NEGOTIATIONS MEMORIAL HALL
TENRI-SHI
TENRI MUSEUM
TOKYO
ETHNOGRAPHICAL MUSEUM OF HOYA
MEIJI THE GREAT MEMORIAL GALLERY
MEIJI THE GREAT MEMORIAL HALL OF TAMA
MEIJI MEMORIAL MUSEUM
MEIJI SHRINE TREASURE MUSEUM
MEIJI UNIVERSITY MUSEUM OF CRIMINOLOGY
MUSEUM OF ART AND HISTORY OF THE UNIVERSITY OF TOKYO
TREASURE HOUSE OF THE MEIJI SHRINE
TSUKUI-MACHI
GAKUDO OZAKI MEMORIAL HALL

KOREA, DEMO. PEOPLE'S REP.

PYONGYANG
KOREAN REVOLUTIONARY MUSEUM
STATE CENTRAL HISTORICAL MUSEUM
STATE CENTRAL LIBERATION STRUGGLE MUSEUM

LEBANON

BEIT-ED-DINE
LEBANESE MUSEUM

LIBYAN ARAB REPUBLIC

TRIPOLI
MUSEUM OF THE LIBYAN NATIONAL RESISTANCE

MALAGASY REPUBLIC

TANANARIVE
MUSEUM OF FINE ART AND HISTORY

MALAWI

BLANTYRE

MUSEUM OF MALAWI

MALAYSIA

ALOR STAR

MUSEUM NEGERI KEDAH

PENANG

PENANG MUSEUM AND ART GALLERY

SARAWAK

SARAWAK MUSEUM

MALTA

VALLETTA

NATIONAL MUSEUM

MEXICO

CUAUTLA

MORELOS HOUSE

MATAMOROS

MEXICAN MUSEUM

MEXICO CITY

NATIONAL HISTORICAL MUSEUM
NATIONAL HISTORICAL MUSEUM

MORELIA

MICHOACAN REGIONAL MUSEUM

OAXACA

JUÁREZ HOUSE

SAN CRISTOBAL ECATEPEC

CASA DE MORELOS

TOLUCA

MUSEUM OF NATURAL HISTORY AND ARCHAEOLOGY

NETHERLANDS

AMERSFOORT

MUSEUM FLEHITE

AMSTERDAM

MUSEUM OF THE WERKSPOOR COMPANY
NATIONAL MUSEUM: DEPARTMENT OF DUTCH HISTORY

DELFT

HET PRINSENHOF MUNICIPAL MUSEUM
MUSEUM OF THE HOUSE OF ORANGE-NASSAU

DOORN

DOORN HOUSE

'S GRAVENHAGE

ROYAL ARCHIVE

LEIDEN

PILGRIM FATHERS HOUSE

OUD-ZUILEN

ZUYLEN CASTLE

ROTTERDAM

ERASMUS ROOM
H. REMKES COLLECTION

ZAANDAM

CZAR PETER'S COTTAGE

NEW ZEALAND

AUCKLAND

THE TREATY HOUSE

WELLINGTON

DOMINION MUSEUM

WHANGAREI

WHANGAREI CITY COUNCIL MUSEUM

NIGERIA

ARGUNGU

KANTA'S MUSEUM

NORWAY

AKERSHUS FYLKE

EIDSVOLL WORKS

OSLO

AKERSHUS PALACE AND FORTRESS
NORWAY'S RESISTANCE MUSEUM

PAKISTAN, WEST

LAHORE

PUNJAB GOVERNMENT RECORD OFFICE MUSEUM

PARAGUAY

ASUNCION

MUSEUM OF THE HOUSE WHERE INDEPENDENCE WAS BORN

PERU

LIMA

MUSEUM OF THE CONGRESS
MUSEUM OF MILITARY HISTORY
MUSEUM OF THE VICEROYALTY
NATIONAL MUSEUM OF HISTORY

PACHACAMAC

PACHACAMAC MUSEUM

PHILIPPINES

BATANGAS

LEON APACIBLE MUSEUM AND LIBRARY
JOSÉ P. LAUREL MEMORIAL MUSEUM
TALAGA MABINI SHRINE

CALAMBA

RIZAL SHRINE

CAVITE

AGUINALDO SHRINE

DAPITAN

RIZAL SHRINE

MANILA

PANDACAN MABINI SHRINE
PRESIDENTIAL MUSEUM
QUEZONIANA
RIZAL SHRINE

PASAY CITY

LOPEZ MEMORIAL MUSEUM

RIZAL

GENERAL CARLOS P. ROMULO'S MEMORABILIA AND LIBRARY
MUSEUM OF PHILIPPINE HISTORY AND ICONOGRAPHIC ARCHIVE

TACLOBAN CITY

LEYTE-SAMAR MUSEUM

POLAND

BIAŁY DUNAJEC

LENIN HOUSE MUSEUM

GUBIN

WILHELM PIECK MUSEUM

KRAKÓW

LENIN MUSEUM

KROSNO

REGIONAL MUSEUM

ŁAMBINOWICE

MUSEUM OF THE MARTYROLOGY OF PRISONERS OF WAR

ŁÓDŹ

MUSEUM OF THE HISTORY OF THE RUSSIAN REVOLUTION

LUBLIN

MEMORIAL MUSEUM OF THE MAJDAN CONCENTRATION CAMP

NAŁĘCZÓW

MUSEUM OF THE POLISH SYNDICATIST MOVEMENT

OŚWIĘCIM

MUSEUM OF THE MARTYRS

POLICE

CAMP MEMORIAL

PORONIN

LENIN MUSEUM

POZNAŃ

MUSEUM OF THE HISTORY OF THE WORKERS' MOVEMENT

SKOCZOW

GUSTAW MORCINEK MUSEUM

SZTUTOWO

STUTTHOF MUSEUM

WARKA-WINIARY

WARKA MUSEUM

WARSAW

KROLIKARNI PALACE MUSEUM
LENIN MUSEUM
MARTYRS' MUSEUM
MUSEUM OF THE HISTORY OF THE REVOLUTIONARY MOVEMENT
MUSEUM IN THE X PAVILION OF THE WARSAW CITADEL
'PARVIAK' PRISON MUSEUM

WILKOŁAZ

MEMORIAL MUSEUM

WROCŁAW

NATIONAL MUSEUM

ZAGAŃ

MARTYRS' MUSEUM

ZAMOŚĆ

ROSA LUXEMBURG MUSEUM
MARTYRS' MUSEUM

RHODESIA

BULAWAYO

NATIONAL MUSEUM OF RHODESIA

SALISBURY

NATIONAL ARCHIVES
QUEEN VICTORIA MUSEUM

ROMANIA

BUCHAREST

NATIONAL MUSEUM OF THE HISTORY OF THE ROMANIAN PEOPLE
STATE ARCHIVES MUSEUM

CERNEŢI

TUDOR VLADIMIRESCU HOUSE- MUSEUM

IAŞI

MUSEUM OF THE UNIFICATION OF ROMANIA

TÎRGU NEAMŢ

MONASTERY MUSEUM

VLADIMIR

TUDOR VLADIMIRESCU MUSEUM

SAN MARINO, REPUBLIC OF

SAN MARINO

GOVERNMENT MUSEUM AND PICTURE-GALLERY

SIERRA LEONE

FREETOWN

SIERRA LEONE NATIONAL MUSEUM

SOUTH AFRICA, REPUBLIC OF

BEAUFORT WEST

BEAUFORT WEST MUSEUM

CAPETOWN

KOOPMANS DE WET HOUSE

CAPE TOWN

SOUTH AFRICAN CULTURAL HISTORY MUSEUM

ESHOWE

ZULULAND HISTORICAL MUSEUM

GRAHAMSTOWN
ALBANY MUSEUM

GREYTOWN
UMVOTI MUSEUM

GRIQUATOWN
MARY MOFFAT MUSEUM

HARTENBOS
HARTENBOS MUSEUM

IRENE
GENERAL SMUTS MUSEUM

JOHANNESBURG
AFRICANA MUSEUM

LYDENBURG
VOORTREKKER CHURCH AND SCHOOL

PIETERMARITZBURG
VOORTREKKER MUSEUM

POTGIETERSRUS
AREND DIEPERINK MUSEUM

PRETORIA
KRUGER HOUSE MUSEUM
NATIONAL CULTURAL HISTORY AND OPEN-AIR MUSEUM
VOORTREKKER MONUMENT MUSEUM

TULBAGH
OUDEKERK VOLKSMUSEUM

SOUTH-WEST AFRICA (NAMIBIA)

SWAKOPMUND
SWAKOPMUND MUSEUM

WINDHOEK
ALTE FESTE

SPAIN

ALCALA DE HENARES
MUSEUM OF THE HISTORY OF PUBLIC ADMINISTRATION IN SPAIN

LAS PALMAS
COLUMBUS HOUSE-MUSEUM

MADRID
AMERICAN MUSEUM
COLLECTION OF AMERICAN ARCHAEOLOGY AND ETHNOGRAPHY
MUSEUM OF ANCIENT HISTORY

LA RABIDA
MONASTERIO DE SANTA MARIA

SEVILLE
CATHEDRAL MUSEUM

VALLADOLID
HOUSE-MUSEUM OF COLUMBUS

SRI LANKA, REPUBLIC OF

COLOMBO
NATIONAL MUSEUM

SUDAN

OMDURMAN
KHALIFA'S HOUSE MUSEUM

SWEDEN

KARLSTAD
VÄRMLAND MUSEUM

NORRKÖPING
NORRKÖPING MUSEUM

STJÄRNSUND
STJÄRNSUND CASTLE

STOCKHOLM
CITY MUSEUM

TYRESÖ
TYRESÖ CASTLE

SWITZERLAND

BUBIKON
MUSEUM OF THE ORDER OF THE JOHANNITER

BÜRGLEN
TELL MUSEUM

CEVIO
MUSEUM OF THE VALLEMAGGIA

COPPET
CHÂTEAU COPPET AND MUSEUM OF THE SWISS WHO SERVED ABROAD

GENEVA
VOLTAIRE INSTITUTE AND MUSEUM

SALENSTEIN
NAPOLEON MUSEUM

SCHWYZ
FEDERAL ARCHIVES

TANZANIA

BAGAMOYO
BAGAMOYO MUSEUM

THAILAND

CHIENGMAI
NATIONAL MUSEUM

CHIENG-SAEN
CHIENG-SAEN MUSEUM

TURKEY

ANKARA
ANIT KABIR MUSEUM
MUSEUM OF THE NATIONAL ASSEMBLY

KASTAMONU
ARCHAEOLOGICAL MUSEUM

KONYA
ATATÜRK MUSEUM

SAMSUN
REGIONAL MUSEUM

SIVAS
INKILÂP MUSEUM

UŞAK
ARCHAEOLOGICAL MUSEUM

USSR

ALTAN-BULAG
D. SUHE-BATOR HOUSE MUSEUM

BAKU
V. I. LENIN MUSEUM

GORI
STALIN MUSEUM

ILYICHOVO
LENIN HOUSE-MUSEUM

KAUNAS
STATE MUSEUM

KHARKOV
KHARKOV STATE HISTORICAL MUSEUM

KIEV
V. I. LENIN MUSEUM
STATE HISTORICAL MUSEUM

KISHINEV
ISKRA MUSEUM

KRASNODAR
MUSEUM OF THE HEROES OF THE YOUNG GUARD

KUIBYSHEV
LENIN MUSEUM

KUTAISI
TSULUKIDZE MUSEUM

LENINGRAD
CRUISER 'AURORA'
LENIN MEMORIAL APARTMENTS
V. I. LENIN MUSEUM
MUSEUM OF THE GREAT OCTOBER SOCIALIST REVOLUTION
MUSEUM OF THE OCTOBER REVOLUTION
PETER THE GREAT'S COTTAGE
SHED AND BARN MUSEUMS

LVOV
V. I. LENIN MUSEUM

MINSK
MUSEUM OF THE FIRST CONGRESS OF THE RUSSIAN SOCIAL DEMOCRATIC PARTY

MOSCOW
EXHIBITION OF SOVIET ECONOMIC ACHIEVEMENT
KRASNAYA PRESNYA MUSEUM
V. I. LENIN CENTRAL MUSEUM
MUSEUM OF HISTORY AND OF THE RECONSTRUCTION OF MOSCOW
MUSEUM OF KARL MARX AND FRIEDRICH ENGELS
NATIONAL HISTORICAL MUSEUM
NATIONAL M. J. KALININ MUSEUM
NATIONAL MUSEUM OF THE REVOLUTION

ORDZHONIKIDZE
KIROV AND ORDZHONIKIDZE MUSEUM

PERESLAYL-ZALESSKIY
GORITSKI MONASTERY

PODOLSK
V. I. LENIN HOUSE-MUSEUM
LENIN MUSEUM

RIGA
MUSEUM OF THE REVOLUTION

SHUSHENSKOYE
V. I. LENIN MUSEUM

TALLINN
MUSEUM OF HISTORY
PETER THE GREAT'S COTTAGE

TASHKENT
HISTORICAL MUSEUM

TBILISI
DZHANASHIYA GEORGIAN MUSEUM
V. I. LENIN MUSEUM

UFA
V. I. LENIN HOUSE-MUSEUM

ULAN-BATOR
V. I. LENIN MUSEUM
PALACE MUSEUM
REVOLUTIONARY MUSEUM

ULYANOVSK
V. I. LENIN HOUSE-MUSEUM

VILNIUS (formerly WILNO)
HISTORICAL AND ETHNOGRAPHICAL MUSEUM OF THE LITHUANIAN REPUBLIC

VOLGOGRAD (formerly STALINGRAD)
STALIN MEMORIAL MUSEUM

UNITED STATES

ABILENE
DWIGHT D. EISENHOWER CENTER
WESTERN MUSEUM

ACTON
HISTORICAL MUSEUM OF THE NORTH AND SOUTH

ALAMAGORDO
MUSEUM OF TULAROSA BASIN HISTORICAL SOCIETY

ANCHORAGE
COOK INLET HISTORICAL SOCIETY MUSEUM

ARCOLA
PRAIRIE HERITAGE MUSEUM

ASHLAND
PIONEER MUSEUM

ASTORIA
FORT CLATSOP NATIONAL MEMORIAL

ATTICA
ATTICA HISTORICAL SOCIETY MUSEUM

AUSTIN
TEXAS CONFEDERATE MUSEUM
DAUGHTERS OF THE REPUBLIC OF TEXAS MUSEUM
UNIVERSITY OF TEXAS

BALTIMORE
STAR-SPANGLED BANNER FLAG HOUSE AND MUSEUM

BEATRICE
HOMESTEAD NATIONAL MONUMENT

BENNINGTON
BENNINGTON MUSEUM

BEREA
BEREA COLLEGE MUSEUMS
BETHLEHEM
MORAVIAN MUSEUM
BIGFOOT
BIGFOOT WALLACE MUSEUM
BONHAM
SAM RAYBURN LIBRARY
BOSTON
STATE ARCHIVES MUSEUM
BRADENTON
CONQUISTADOR HISTORICAL FOUNDATION
BREWSTER
DRUMMER BOY MUSEUM
BUFFALO
THEODORE ROOSEVELT INAUGURATION NATIONAL HISTORIC SITE
CARROLLTON
MCCOOK HOUSE STATE MEMORIAL
CHARLESTON
FORT SUMTER
OLD SLAVE MART MUSEUM
CHARLOTTE COUNTY
PATRICK HENRY MEMORIAL FOUNDATION
CHARLOTTESVILLE
MONTICELLO
CHICAGO
CHICAGO PUBLIC LIBRARY MEMORIAL HALL
DUSABLE MUSEUM OF AFRICAN AMERICAN HISTORY
THE POLISH MUSEUM OF AMERICA
SWEDISH PIONEER HISTORICAL SOCIETY
CIMARRON
OLD MILL MUSEUM
CINCINNATI
WILLIAM HOWARD TAFT NATIONAL HISTORIC SITE
CODY
BUFFALO BILL HISTORICAL CENTER
DECORAH
NORWEGIAN-AMERICAN MUSEUM
DEERFIELD
INDIAN HOUSE MEMORIAL
DIAMOND
GEORGE WASHINGTON CARVER NATIONAL MONUMENT
EXETER
CINCINNATI MEMORIAL HALL
EXIRA
AUDUBON COUNTY HISTORICAL SOCIETY MUSEUM
FORT WAYNE
LINCOLN NATIONAL LIFE FOUNDATION
FULTON
WINSTON CHURCHILL MEMORIAL
GETTYSBURG
LINCOLN MUSEUM
PRESIDEO LA BAHIA
REFUGIO HIGHWAY
HARROGATE
LINCOLN MEMORIAL UNIVERSITY MUSEUM
HOLLAND
NETHERLANDS MUSEUM
HONOLULU
HAWAIAN WAX MUSEUM
HYDE PARK
FRANKLIN D. ROOSEVELT LIBRARY AND MUSEUM
INDEPENDENCE
HARRY S. TRUMAN LIBRARY AND MUSEUM
KAILUA-KONA
HULIHEE PALACE
KEYTESVILLE
GENERAL STERLING PRICE MUSEUM
KODIAK
KODIAK HISTORICAL SOCIETY MUSEUM
LINCOLN CITY
LINCOLN BOYHOOD NATIONAL MEMORIAL
MARION
MUSEUM OF HARDING MEMORIAL ASSOCIATION
MEDORA
FUR TRADE AND WILD LIFE MUSEUM
MIDDLESBORO
MUSEUM OF CUMBERLAND GAP NATIONAL HISTORICAL PARK
MINNEAPOLIS
MUSEUM OF AMERICAN SWEDISH INSTITUTE
NASHVILLE
JOHN F. KENNEDY MEMORIAL CENTER
NEW ROCHELLE
THOMAS PAINE MEMORIAL BUILDING
NEW YORK
AMERICAN MUSEUM OF IMMIGRATION
FEDERAL HALL NATIONAL MONUMENT
HALL OF FAME FOR GREAT AMERICANS
MUSEUM OF NEW YORK HISTORICAL SOCIETY
STATUE OF LIBERTY NATIONAL MONUMENT
WARSHAW COLLECTION OF BUSINESS AMERICANA
NORTHAMPTON
CALVIN COOLIDGE MEMORIAL ROOM
NORTH BRUNSWICK
JOHNSTON HISTORICAL MUSEUM, BOY SCOUTS OF AMERICA
NORTHFIELD
MUSEUM OF NORWEGIAN- AMERICAN HISTORICAL ASSOCIATION
PHILADELPHIA
AMERICAN-SWEDISH HISTORICAL FOUNDATION MUSEUM
BLUMHAVEN LIBRARY AND GALLERY
NATIONAL CARL SCHURZ ASSOCIATION
PITTSBURGH
FORT PITT MUSEUM
REDLANDS
LINCOLN MEMORIAL SHRINE
RICHMOND
MUSEUM OF THE CONFEDERACY
RIVER FALLS
AREA RESEARCH CENTER, WISCONSIN STATE UNIVERSITY
ROCKFORD
ERLANDER HOME MUSEUM
ST. LOUIS
JEFFERSON NATIONAL EXPANSION MEMORIAL
SAN FRANCISCO
MUSEUM OF RUSSIAN CULTURE
SAN FRANCISCO AFRICAN AMERICAN HISTORICAL AND CULTURAL SOCIETY
TERRE HAUTE
EUGENE V. DEBS FOUNDATION
HISTORICAL MUSEUM OF THE WABASH VALLEY
VALLEY FORGE
MUSEUM OF VALLEY FORGE HISTORICAL SOCIETY
WARM SPRINGS
FRANKLIN D. ROOSEVELT WARM SPRINGS MEMORIAL COMMISSION
WARREN
MUSEUM OF CONFEDERATE MEMORIAL HISTORIC RESEARCH COUNCIL
WASHINGTON
ANACOSTIA NEIGHBORHOOD MUSEUM
FORD'S THEATRE AND LINCOLN MUSEUM
MUSEUM OF THE NATIONAL ARCHIVES
MUSEUM OF THE SOCIETY OF THE CINCINNATI-ANDERSON HOUSE
THE UNITED STATES CAPITOL
WEAVERVILLE
WEAVERVILLE JOSS HOUSE STATE HISTORIC PARK
WILBER
WILBER CZECH MUSEUM

URUGUAY

COLONIA DEL SACRAMENTO
MUNICIPAL MUSEUM
MONTEVIDEO
NATIONAL HISTORICAL MUSEUM

VENEZUELA

CARACAS
BOLIVÁR'S HOUSE
BOLIVÁR MUSEUM
MARACAY
INSTITUTE OF ANTHROPOLOGY AND HISTORY MUSEUM
TRUJILLO
'CRISTÓBAL MENDOZA' MUSEUM

VIETNAM, DEMOCRATIC REPUBLIC OF

HANOI
MUSEUM OF THE REVOLUTION

YUGOSLAVIA

BELGRADE
HISTORICAL MUSEUM OF SERBIA
JULY 4, 1941 MUSEUM
MAY 25th MUSEUM
MUSEUM OF THE YUGOSLAV PEOPLE'S REVOLUTION
CETINJE
MUSEUM OF THE LIBERATION STRUGGLE
JAJCE
LOCAL MUSEUM
JASENOVAC
MEMORIAL MUSEUM
JESENICE NA DOLENJSKOM
CASTLE MUSEUM
KORČULA
TOWN MUSEUM
KRAPINA
GAJ'S MUSEUM
KUMROVEC
MARSHAL TITO MEMORIAL MUSEUM
LJUBLJANA
NATIONAL LIBERATION MUSEUM
PULA
MUSEUM OF THE NATIONAL LIBERATION MOVEMENT
RIJEKA
MUSEUM OF THE NATIONAL REVOLUTION
SARAJEVO
MUSEUM OF THE REVOLUTION
MUSEUM OF YOUNG BOSNIA
SINJ
ALKARI MUSEUM
SISAK
MUSEUM OF THE REVOLUTION
SPLIT
MUSEUM OF NATIONAL REVOLUTION
TITOVO UŽICE
MUSEUM OF THE INSURRECTION OF 1941
ZADAR
NATIONAL MUSEUM
ZAGREB
ARCHIVES OF CROATIA
ARCHIVES OF THE HISTORY OF THE CROATIAN WORKERS' MOVEMENT
ARCHIVES OF THE YUGOSLAV ACADEMY OF SCIENCES AND ARTS
HISTORICAL MUSEUM OF CROATIA
MUSEUM OF THE EIGHTH CONFERENCE OF THE ZAGREB ORGANISATION OF THE COMMUNIST PARTY OF YUGOSLAVIA
MUSEUM OF THE FIFTH NATIONAL CONFERENCE OF THE COMMUNIST PARTY OF YUGOSLAVIA
MUSEUM OF THE FIRST NATIONAL CONFERENCE OF THE COMMUNIST PARTY OF CROATIA
THE PEOPLE'S REVOLUTION MUSEUM

ZAIRE, REPUBLIC OF

KANANGA
NATIONAL MUSEUM

ZAMBIA

LIVINGSTONE
LIVINGSTONE MUSEUM

Historic-site museums

BANGLADESH

DACCA
LALBAGH FORT SITE MUSEUM

BULGARIA

VARNA
PARK-MUSEUM OF THE BROTHERHOOD OF ARMS

CANADA

BATOCHE
BATOCHE NATIONAL HISTORIC SITE
EDMONTON
JOHN WALTER HISTORICAL SITE
PLACENTIA
CASTLE HILL MUSEUM

CHINA, P.R.

CHOUKOUTIEN
MUSEUM OF PALAEONTOLOGY

GDR

LEIPZIG
MEMORIAL TO THE PEOPLE'S BATTLE
LÜTZEN
GUSTAVUS ADOLPHUS MEMORIAL

GFR

MÜNSTER
HALL OF THE PEACE

UNITED STATES

ARLINGTON
CURTIS-LEE MANSION, ROBERT E. LEE MEMORIAL
BALTIMORE
FORT MCHENRY NATIONAL MONUMENT AND HISTORIC SHRINE
BLOOMINGTON
INDIANA UNIVERSITY MUSEUM
BURLINGTON
ALAMANCE BATTLEGROUND STATE HISTORIC SITE
BUSHNELL
DADE BATTLEFIELD HISTORIC MONUMENT
CAPARRA
MUSEUM OF CONQUEST AND COLONISATION OF PUERTO RICO
CHADDS FORD
BRANDYWINE BATTLEFIELD PARK
CHARLESTON
FORT SUMTER
CHICAGO
ORIENTAL INSTITUTE MUSEUM
CROW AGENCY
CUSTER BATTLEFIELD NATIONAL MONUMENT
EAST HUBBARDTON
HUBBARDTON BATTLEFIELD AND MUSEUM
ELLENDALE
WHITESTONE BATTLEFIELD HISTORIC PARK
FORT BUFORD
FORT BUFORD HISTORIC SITE MUSEUM
FORT RALEIGH
FORT RALEIGH NATIONAL HISTORIC SITE
FORT RECOVERY
FORT RECOVERY HISTORICAL SOCIETY, INC.
GETTYSBURG
GETTYSBURG NATIONAL MILITARY PARK
HANCOCK'S BRIDGE
HANCOCK HOUSE
HARPERS FERRY
HARPERS FERRY NATIONAL HISTORICAL PARK
JAMESTOWN
JAMESTOWN FESTIVAL PARK
JEANNETTE
BUSHY RUN BATTLEFIELD MUSEUM
LOCUST GROVE
SERPENT MOUND
MANTEO
FORT RALEIGH NATIONAL HISTORIC SITE
MARIETTA
KENNESAW MOUNTAIN NATIONAL BATTLEFIELD PARK MUSEUM
McGREGOR
EFFIGY MOUNDS NATIONAL MONUMENT
NEWTON GROVE
BENTONVILLE BATTLEGROUND STATE HISTORIC SITE
OLUSTEE
OLUSTEE BATTLEFIELD HISTORIC MEMORIAL
PERRYVILLE
PERRYVILLE BATTLEFIELD STATE SHRINE
PORT GIBSON
GRAND GULF MILITARY PARK
RICHMOND
RICHMOND NATIONAL BATTLEFIELD PARK MUSEUM
ST. SIMONS
FORT FREDERICA NATIONAL MONUMENT
SHARPSBURG
ANTIETAM NATIONAL BATTLEFIELD SITE
STONY POINT
STONY POINT BATTLEFIELD RESERVATION
TITUSVILLE
PITHOLE
VANCOUVER
FORT VANCOUVER NATIONAL HISTORIC SITE
WHITE PLAINS
MILLER HILL RESTORATION
WILMINGTON
BRUNSWICK TOWN
WINSTON-SALEM
HISTORIC BETHABARA
WISDOM
BIG HOLE NATIONAL BATTLEFIELD

Local history

ARGENTINA

BUENOS AIRES
NATIONAL MUSEUM OF THE CITY HALL OF BUENOS AIRES
LA RIOJA
PROVINCIAL HISTORICAL MUSEUM
SALTA
NORTHERN HISTORICAL MUSEUM
SAN CARLOS DE BARILOCHE
DR. FRANCISCO MORENO PATAGONIAN MUSEUM

AUSTRALIA

ADVANCETOWN
PIONEER HOUSE
BATHURST
FOLK MUSEUM
BEECHWORTH
BURKE MEMORIAL MUSEUM
BRISBANE
EARLY STREET
QUEENSLAND NATIONAL ART GALLERY AND MUSEUM
CAMPERDOWN
CAMPERDOWN HISTORICAL MUSEUM
CANBERRA
REGATTA POINT MUSEUM
CHILTERN
CHILTERN ATHENAEUM AND MUSEUM
COOKTOWN
JAMES COOK HISTORICAL MUSEUM
FORTITUDE VALLEY
QUEENSLAND MUSEUM
FREMANTLE
MARITIME AND HISTORICAL MUSEUM
GRAFTON
SCHAEFFER HOUSE
HOBART
TASMANIAN MUSEUM AND ART GALLERY
JINDERA
PIONEER MUSEUM
KEMPSEY
MACLEAY RIVER HISTORICAL MUSEUM
KYNETON
KYNETON HISTORICAL MUSEUM
LANE COVE
CARISBROOK HISTORIC HOUSE AND MUSEUM
LAUNCESTON
QUEEN VICTORIA MUSEUM AND ART GALLERY
LISMORE
RICHMOND RIVER HISTORICAL SOCIETY MUSEUM
MILDURA
MUSEUM OF LOCAL HISTORY
MILLTHORPE
HISTORICAL MUSEUM
PENNESHAW
NATIONAL TRUST MUSEUM
PERTH
OLD MILL
STIRLING HOUSE MUSEUM
PORT ARTHUR
PORT ARTHUR MUSEUM
PORT LINCOLN
OLD MILL MUSEUM
SINGLETON
HISTORICAL MUSEUM
SWANSEA
GOOD OLD DAYS FOLK MUSEUM
TANUNDA
BAROSSA VALLEY MUSEUM
TENTERFIELD
SIR HENRY PARKES MEMORIAL MUSEUM
WARRNAMBOOL
HISTORY HOUSE
WELLINGTON
WELLINGTON MUSEUM
WEST GOSFORD
KENDALL COTTAGE
WILLIAMSTOWN
MUNICIPAL MUSEUM

AUSTRIA

BADEN
ROLLETT MUSEUM

BADGASTEIN
REGIONAL MUSEUM
BAD ISCHL
REGIONAL MUSEUM
EFERDING
MUNICIPAL MUSEUM, STARHEMBERG FAMILY MUSEUM, REGIONAL MUSEUM
GMUND
MUNICIPAL MUSEUM
REGIONAL MUSEUM
GRAZ
JOANNEUM PROVINCIAL MUSEUM OF CULTURAL HISTORY AND APPLIED ART
JOANNEUM MUSEUM OF THE HISTORY OF GRAZ
HAINBURG
MUNICIPAL MUSEUM
IMST
REGIONAL MUSEUM
JUDENBURG
TOWN AND DISTRICT MUSEUM
KLEINENGERSDORF
"DER BISAMBERG UND DER WEINVIERTLER" MUSEUM
LIENZ
EAST TIROL REGIONAL MUSEUM
OBERNBERG
REGIONAL MUSEUM
SALZBURG
SALZBURGER MUSEUM, CAROLINO AUGUSTEUM
SOLBAD HALL
MUNICIPAL MUSEUM
VIENNA
BRIGITTENAU DISTRICT MUSEUM
COLLECTIONS OF THE MARKETS AUTHORITY OF THE CITY OF VIENNA
DÖBLING DISTRICT MUSEUM
HERNALS DISTRICT MUSEUM
HIETZING DISTRICT MUSEUM
HISTORICAL MUSEUM OF THE CITY OF VIENNA
LANDSTRASSE LOCAL MUSEUM
LEOPOLDSTADT DISTRICT MUSEUM
MEIDLING DISTRICT MUSEUM
MUSEUM OF THE HISTORY OF ART: MUSEUM OF AUSTRIAN CULTURE
MUSEUM OF THE JOSEFSTADT DISTRICT
PRATERMUSEUM

BELGIUM

AARSCHOT
REGIONAL MUSEUM
ARLON
ARCHAEOLOGICAL MUSEUM
BOUILLON
BOUILLON MUSEUM
BRUGES
MUSEUM OF THE CROSS GATE
BRUSSELS
BELLONA HOUSE
MUNICIPAL MUSEUM OF THE CITY OF BRUSSELS
GAASBEEK
CHÂTEAU MUSEUM
HASSELT
PROVINCIAL MUSEUM
LIÈGE
CURTIUS MUSEUM
MUSEUM OF WALLOON LIFE
MONS
JEAN LESCARTS MUSEUM
NIEUWPOORT
MUSEUM OF HISTORY AND FOLKLORE
OUDENARDE
ARCHAEOLOGICAL MUSEUM
TURNHOUT
TAXANDRIA MUSEUM OF ARCHAEOLOGY

BRAZIL

BAGÉ
PATRICIO CORREA DA CAMARA MUSEUM
BELO HORIZONTE
ANTHROPOLOGICAL MUSEUM OF THE FACULTY OF PHILOSOPHY
ABILIO BARRETO HISTORICAL MUSEUM
HISTORICAL MUSEUM OF BELO HORIZONTE
CURITIBA
PARANÁ MUSEUM
MACEIÓ
MUSEUM OF THE ALAGOAS HISTORICAL INSTITUTE
NATAL
MUSEUM OF THE HISTORICAL AND GEOGRAPHICAL INSTITUTE
RECIFE
STATE MUSEUM
RIO DE JANEIRO
MUSEUM OF THE PORT OF RIO
VALENÇA
ESTÊVES ESTATE (FAZENDA) MUSEUM

BULGARIA

ASENOVGRAD
NATIONAL MUSEUM
BATAK
'ANTON IVANOV' MUSEUM
BLOGOEVGRAD
BLOGOEVGRAD MUSEUM
BOTEVGRAD
HISTORY MUSEUM
BOURGAS
REGIONAL MUSEUM OF HISTORY
BRACIGOVO
HISTORICAL MUSEUM
HASKOVO
NATIONAL MUSEUM
KARNOBAT
NATIONAL MUSEUM
KOPRIVSHTIŹA
GEORGI BENKOVSKI HOUSE- MUSEUM
MIHAJLOVGRAD
MUSEUM OF THE SEPTEMBER UPRISING
PAZARDŽIK
REGIONAL MUSEUM OF HISTORY
PLEVEN
REGIONAL MUSEUM OF HISTORY
PLOVDIV
REGIONAL MUSEUM OF THE REVOLUTIONARY MOVEMENT
RUSE
REGIONAL MUSEUM OF HISTORY
SAMOKOV
NATIONAL MUSEUM
SANDANSKI
REGIONAL MUSEUM
ŠČRAKLEVO
MUSEUM OF REGIONAL HISTORY AND ETHNOGRAPHY
SOFIA
MUSEUM OF SOFIA'S HISTORY
STARA ZAGORA
REGIONAL MUSEUM OF HISTORY
TARGOVIŠČE
PROVINCIAL HISTORICAL MUSEUM
TARNOVO
PROVINCIAL MUSEUM
TRJAVNA
TRJAVNA MUSEUM
VARNA
MUSEUM OF THE REVOLUTIONARY MOVEMENT
REGIONAL MUSEUM OF HISTORY
VIDIN
MUSEUM OF THE REVOLUTIONARY YOUTH MOVEMENT
VRATSA
NATIONAL MUSEUM
YAMBOL
NATIONAL MUSEUM

BURMA

MANDALAY
STATE LIBRARY AND MUSEUM
MOULMEIN
STATE LIBRARY AND MUSEUM

CANADA

CARIK
PRAIRIE PIONEER MUSEUM
CHARLOTTETOWN
PRINCE EDWARD ISLAND HERITAGE FOUNDATION
EDMONTON
HISTORICAL EXHIBITS BUILDING
PROVINCIAL MUSEUM AND ARCHIVES OF ALBERTA
GRAVENHURST
WOODWINDS HISTORICAL MUSEUM
HALIFAX
NOVA SCOTIA MUSEUM
HAVELOCK
TRENT RIVER MUSEUM
HIGH PRAIRIE
CENTENNIAL LIBRARY AND MUSEUM
KAMLOOPS
FORT KAMLOOPS
MILTON
HALTON COUNTY MUSEUM
MOOSE FACTORY
MOOSE FACTORY MUSEUM PARK
NORWICH
NORWICH AND DISTRICT HISTORICAL SOCIETY MUSEUM
OSOYOOS
OSOYOOS MUSEUM
ST. JOHNS
NEWFOUNDLAND MUSEUM
ST. PETER'S
NICOLAS DENYS MUSEUM
SASKATOON
WESTERN DEVELOPMENT MUSEUM
TORONTO
TODMORDEN MILLS MUSEUM PARK
TROIS RIVIÈRES
MUSEUM OF PREHISTORIC ARCHAEOLOGY
VANCOUVER
CENTENNIAL MUSEUM
WINNIPEG
PROVINCIAL ARCHIVES OF MANITOBA
WOODSTOCK
OXFORD MUSEUM

CHINA, P.R.

CHANGCHUN
PROVINCIAL MUSEUM
CHANG SHA (ZHENG ZHOU)
PROVINCIAL MUSEUM
CHINCHOW (JINZHOW)
PROVINCIAL MUSEUM
CHUNKING
MUNICIPAL MUSEUM
HARBIN
PROVINCIAL MUSEUM
HO FEI
PROVINCIAL MUSEUM
KUN MING
PROVINCIAL MUSEUM
KWANCHOW
MUSEUM OF THE HISTORY OF KWANCHOW FOREIGN TRADE
MUSEUM OF KWANCHOW'S FAMOUS MEN
KWEIYANG (GUIJANG)
PROVINCIAL MUSEUM
LANCHOW (LANZHOU)
PROVINCIAL MUSEUM
LUCHOU
LOCAL MUSEUM
LUO YANG
TOWN MUSEUM
MUKDEN (SHENYIANG)
NORTH EAST MUSEUM

NAN CHANG
MUSEUM OF THE NAN CHANG RISING
NANKING (NAN JING)
MUSEUM OF THE HEAVENLY KINGDOM OF GREAT PEACE
SHANGHAI
MEMORIAL HALL OF REVOLUTIONARY HISTORY
SHAO SHING
QIU JIN MUSEUM
TIENSIN (TIANJING)
CITY MUSEUM OF HISTORY
PROVINCIAL MUSEUM
TSINAN (JI NAN)
PROVINCIAL MUSEUM
URUMCHI (WULUMUCHI)
REGIONAL MUSEUM
WACHANG (WU HAN)
PROVINCIAL MUSEUM

COLOMBIA

BOGOTA
MUSEUM OF THE URBAN DEVELOPMENT OF BOGOTA
GUADUAS
EZPELETA MUSEUM

CUBA

HABANA
MUSEUM OF THE CITY OF HABANA

CZECHOSLOVAKIA

AŠ
MUNICIPAL MUSEUM
BANSKÁ BYSTRICA
MUSEUM OF THE HISTORY OF SLOVAKIA
BRNO
MUSEUM OF THE CITY OF BRNO
BROUMOV
REGIONAL MUSEUM
CHEB
REGIONAL MUSEUM
CHLUMEC NAD CIDLINOU
MUSEUM OF THE PEASANTS' REVOLT AND V. K. KLICPERA MEMORIAL
DAŠICE
JOSEF HYBEŠE MEMORIAL MUSEUM
GOTTWALDOV
GOTTWALDOV MUSEUM OF SOUTHERN MORAVIA
KAMENICE NAD LIPOU
REGIONAL MUSEUM
KARLOVY VARY
KARL MARX MUSEUM
LEŠKOVICE
LOCAL MUSEUM
LEŽÁKY
MUSEUM OF THE STRUGGLE AGAINST FASCISM
LIBEREC
MUSEUM OF NORTHERN CZECHOSLOVAKIA
LIDICE
MEMORIAL TO THE TRAGEDY OF LIDICE
LIPOVÁ LÁZNĚ
REGIONAL MUSEUM
LITEŇ
MEMORIAL TO THE MASSACRE AT LITEŇ AND TO V. B. TŘEBÍZSKY
MARIANSKÁ TYNICE - KRALOVICE
DISTRICT MUSEUM
OLOMUČANY
CERAMICS MUSEUM AND MUSEUM OF THE WORKERS' MOVEMENT
OPAVA
SILESIAN MUSEUM: HISTORY COLLECTIONS
OSTRAVA
MUSEUM OF SOCIALISM AND THE REVOLUTION
PRAGUE
MUSEUM OF THE CITY OF PRAGUE
SKUTEČ
MUNICIPAL MUSEUM

DENMARK

COPENHAGEN
MUSEUM OF THE CITY OF COPENHAGEN
HOLBAEK
HOLBAEK AND DISTRICT MUSEUM
KØGE
KØGE MUSEUM
ROSKILDE
ROSKILDE MUSEUM

ECUADOR

QUITO
CIVIC MUSEUM OF ARTS AND HISTORY

FINLAND

HANKO
HANKO MUSEUM
HEINOLA
HEINOLA MUSEUM
HELSINKI
HELSINKI MUNICIPAL MUSEUM
TORNIO
TORNIO VALLEY MUSEUM

FRANCE

ALTKIRCH
SUNDGAU MUSEUM
ANGOULÊME
MUNICIPAL MUSEUM
AUCH
MUSEUM OF ART AND ARCHAEOLOGY
MUSEUM OF THE GERS DEPARTMENTAL ARCHIVES
AVESNES-SUR-HELPE
ARCHAEOLOGICAL SOCIETY MUSEUM
BESANÇON
HISTORICAL MUSEUM
BOURGNEUF-EN-RETZ
RETZ REGIONAL MUSEUM
CORDES
CHARLES PORTAL MUSEUM
CORTE
MUSEUM OF CORSICAN HISTORY
DREUX
MUNICIPAL MUSEUM
ETAPLES
MUNICIPAL MUSEUM
LILLE
MUSEUM OF THE COMTESSE HOSPICE
LILLEBONNE
MUNICIPAL MUSEUM
LYON
MUSEUM OF THE HISTORY OF LYON
MÂCON
MUNICIPAL MUSEUM OF THE URSULINES
LE MANS
QUEEN BERENGARIA MUSEUM
MARLY-LE-ROI
OLD MARLY MUSEUM
MARSEILLE
MUSEUM OF OLD MARSEILLE
MARTEL
LOCAL MUSEUM
MARZY
FOLKLORE MUSEUM
MENTON
MUNICIPAL MUSEUM
MEUDON
MEUDON MUSEUM
MOLSHEIM
MUSEUM OF ART AND HISTORY
MONTLUCON
MUNICIPAL MUSEUM
MONTREUIL
MUSEUM OF LIVING HISTORY
MORTAGNE-AU-PERCHE
PERCHERON MUSEUM
MOUTIERS
MUSEUM OF THE ACADEMY OF THE VAL D'ISÈRE
MULHOUSE
MUSEUM OF HISTORY
NANCY
LORRAINE MUSEUM OF HISTORY
NANTES
DOBRÉE MUSEUM
NOIRMOUTIER EN L'ILE
CHÂTEAU MUSEUM
PARIS
CARNAVALLET MUSEUM
MUSEUM OF OLD MONTMARTRE
PAU
BÉARNAIS MUSEUM
PÉROUGES
OLD PÉROUGES MUSEUM
PHALSBOURG
MUSEUM OF HISTORY AND ART
PLOMBIÈRES-LES-BAINS
LOUIS FRANÇAIS MUSEUM
POITIERS
RUPERT DE CHIÈVRES MUSEUM
PONTOISE LES NOYON
TAVET-DELACOUR MUSEUM
LA ROCHELLE
ORBIGNY MUSEUM
ROQUEBRUNE- CAP-MARTIN
CHÂTEAU DE ROQUEBRUNE
SAINT-AMARIN
SERRET MUSEUM
SAINT-GERMAIN-EN-LAYE
MUNICIPAL MUSEUM
SAINT-JEAN-DE-LUZ
HOUSE OF MEMORIES
SAINT-MALO
QUIC-EN-GROIGNE GALLERY
SAINT- RAMBERT-SUR-LOIRE
SAINT-RAMBERT-SUR-LOIRE MUSEUM
SCEAUX
ILE-DE-FRANCE MUSEUM
SENS
JEAN COUSIN MUSEUM
STRASBOURG
HISTORICAL MUSEUM
SURESNES
MUNICIPAL MUSEUM
TOULON
OLD TOULON MUSEUM
TOULOUSE
PAUL DUPUY MUSEUM
OLD TOULOUSE MUSEUM
TROUVILLE-SUR-MER
MUSEUM OF LOCAL AND REGIONAL ART
VICHY
MUSEUM OF ART AND HISTORY
YZEURE
HISTORICAL MUSEUM OF THE BOURBONNAIS

GDR

ADORF
REGIONAL MUSEUM
AKEN
REGIONAL MUSEUM
ALTENBURG
CASTLE MUSEUM AND PLAYING CARDS MUSEUM

ANKLAM
REGIONAL MUSEUM
ARNSTADT
REGIONAL MUSEUM
ASCHERSLEBEN
REGIONAL MUSEUM
BAD DÜBEN
DISTRICT MUSEUM
BAD DÜBEN
DÜBEN HEATH MUSEUM
BAD LAUCHSTADT
GOETHE THEATRE AND PAVILION
BALLENSTEDT
REGIONAL MUSEUM
BRANDENBURG
DISTRICT MUSEUM
CAMBURG
REGIONAL MUSEUM
DESSAU
MUSEUM OF NATURAL HISTORY AND PREHISTORY
DIESDORF
ALTMARK REGIONAL MUSEUM
DOHNA
REGIONAL MUSEUM
DRESDEN
INSTITUTE AND MUSEUM OF THE HISTORY OF THE CITY OF DRESDEN
EISENACH
THURINGIA MUSEUM
EISENBERG
DISTRICT AND REGIONAL MUSEUM
EISLEBEN
BÜRGERGARTEN MEMORIAL TO THE MANSFELD WORKERS' MOVEMENT
DISTRICT AND REGIONAL MUSEUM
ERFURT
MEMORIAL TO THE ERFURT PARTY CONGRESS OF 1891
MUNICIPAL HISTORY MUSEUM
FRANKFURT AN DER ODER
DISTRICT MUSEUM
FREIBERG
MUNICIPAL AND MINING MUSEUM
GERA
MUSEUM OF CULTURAL HISTORY
GOTHA
1875 GOTHA PARTY CONGRESS MEMORIAL
MUSEUM OF REGIONAL HISTORY AND FOLKLORE
GROSSENHAIN
DISTRICT MUSEUM
HARTENSTEIN
REGIONAL MUSEUM
HEILIGENSTADT
EICHFELD REGIONAL MUSEUM
JENA
MUNICIPAL MUSEUM
KARL MARX STADT
"THE FIGHTER" MEMORIAL
SCHLOSSBERG MUSEUM: MUNICIPAL AND CULTURAL HISTORY COLLECTION
KÖTHEN
REGIONAL MUSEUM
LEIPZIG
MUSEUM OF THE HISTORY OF THE CITY OF LEIPZIG
LÖBAU
MUNICIPAL MUSEUM
LÜBBENAU
LÜBBENAU MUSEUM IN THE SPREEWALD
LUCKENWALDE
DISTRICT MUSEUM
MAGDEBURG
LIFE AND RESOURCES OF THE WELTALL
MUSEUM OF CULTURAL HISTORY
MEERANE
REGIONAL MUSEUM
MÜHLHAUSEN
RAVENS' TOWER AND PARAPET WALK
MUTZSCHEN
REGIONAL ROOM
NAUMBURG
REGIONAL MUSEUM
NEUBRANDENBURG
MUSEUM OF CULTURAL HISTORY
NEUGERSDORF
REGIONAL MUSEUM
NOSSEN
REGIONAL MUSEUM
OEDERAN
REGIONAL MUSEUM
OSCHATZ
REGIONAL ROOM
POTSDAM-BABELSBERG
MUSEUM OF PREHISTORY AND EARLY HISTORY
ROSTOCK
MUSEUM OF CULTURAL HISTORY
RUDOLSTADT
HEIDECKSBURG STATE MUSEUM
SAALFELD
THURINGIA REGIONAL MUSEUM
SALZWEDEL
JOHANN FRIEDRICH DANNEIL MUSEUM
SANGERHAUSEN
SPENGLER MUSEUM
SCHWERIN
MUSEUM OF PREHISTORY AND EARLY HISTORY
SCHWERIN HISTORICAL MUSEUM
SENFTENBERG
DISTRICT MUSEUM
WAREN AN DER MÜRITZ
MÜRITZ MUSEUM
WEIMAR
MUSEUM OF THE PREHISTORY AND EARLY HISTORY OF THURINGIA
WERMSDORF
REGIONAL ROOM, WITH BEBEL AND LIEBKNECHT MEMORIALS
WERNIGERODE
FEUDAL MUSEUM
WITTENBERG LUTHERSTADT
JULIUS RIEMER MUSEUM OF NATURAL HISTORY AND ETHNOLOGY

GFR

BAD DÜRKHEIM
REGIONAL MUSEUM
BERLIN
BERLIN MUSEUM
SPANDAU LOCAL MUSEUM
BOCHUM
BOCHUM MUSEUM
LOCAL HISTORY COLLECTIONS
BONN
ERNST MORITZ ARNDT HOUSE MUSEUM
MUNICIPAL ART COLLECTIONS
BOTTROP
REGIONAL MUSEUM
BRAUBACH
MARKSBURG CASTLE MUSEUM
BRAUNSCHWEIG
BRUNSWICK PROVINCIAL MUSEUM OF HISTORY AND LOCAL LIFE
MUNICIPAL MUSEUM
BREMERHAVEN
MORGENSTEIN MUSEUM
BÜCKEBURG
REGIONAL MUSEUM OF SCHAUMBURG-LIPPISCH
BÜDINGEN
HEUSON MUSEUM
BURG-FEHMARN
FEHMARN REGIONAL MUSEUM
BURG-WUPPER
MUSEUM OF THE COUNTS VON BERG
BUXTEHUDE
REGIONAL MUSEUM
CELLE
BOMANN MUSEUM
DUCAL PALACE
CLAUSTHAL-ZELLERFELD
UPPER HARZ REGIONAL AND MINING MUSEUM
CUXHAVEN
CUXHAVEN REGIONAL MUSEUM
KARL WALLER MUSEUM
DACHAU
REGIONAL MUSEUM
DARMSTADT
DARMSTADT MUSEUM
HESSE MUSEUM
DETMOLD
LIPPE MUSEUM
DIEBURG
DIEBURG AND DISTRICT MUSEUM
DIEZ/LAHN
ORANIENSTEIN NASSAU MUSEUM
DILLENBURG
MUSEUM OF ORANGE-NASSAU
DILLINGEN AN DER DONAU
MUSEUM OF DILLINGEN HISTORICAL SOCIETY
DINGOLFING
REGIONAL MUSEUM
DINKELSBÜHL
MUSEUM OF HISTORY
DONAUWÖRTH
REGIONAL MUSEUM
DORSTEN
REGIONAL MUSEUM
DORTMUND
MUSEUM OF THE HISTORY OF ART AND CULTURE
DREIEICHENHAIN
DREIEICH MUSEUM
DUISBURG
KÖNIGSBERG HOUSE
MUSEUM OF THE LOWER RHINE
DÜLKEN
DÜLKEN REGIONAL MUSEUM
DURBACH
STAUFENBERG PALACE
DÜREN
REGIONAL MUSEUM
DÜSSELDORF
CONZEN COLLECTION
KALKUM PALACE MUSEUM
EBERMANNSTADT
REGIONAL MUSEUM
EHINGEN
REGIONAL MUSEUM
EICHENZELL
FASANERIE PALACE MUSEUM
EINBECK
MUNICIPAL MUSEUM
EMDEN
LAND MUSEUM OF OSTFRISIEN
MUNICIPAL MUSEUM
EMMENDINGEN
REGIONAL MUSEUM
ENGER
WIDUKIND MEMORIAL MUSEUM
EPPSTEIN
REGIONAL MUSEUM
ERDING
REGIONAL MUSEUM
ERLANGEN
BRIX-KOMOTEN REGIONAL MUSEUM
CITY MUSEUM
ESCHWEGE
REGIONAL MUSEUM
ESSEN
RUHR AND REGIONAL MUSEUM
FLADUNGEN
RHÖN MUSEUM
FLENSBURG
FLENSBURG MUNICIPAL MUSEUM
FRANKENTHAL
ERKENBERT MUSEUM
FRIEDBERG (HESSEN)
FRIEDBERG CASTLE
WETTERAU MUSEUM
FRIEDBERG (SCHWABEN)
REGIONAL MUSEUM

FRITZLAR
FRITZLAR MUSEUM

GEILENKIRCHEN
REGIONAL MUSEUM

GELSENKIRCHEN
MUNICIPAL MUSEUM

GEROLSTEIN
DAUN DISTRICT MUSEUM

GEROLZHOFEN
REGIONAL MUSEUM

GIESSEN
UPPER HESSE MUSEUM

GLADBECK
GLADBECK TOWN MUSEUM

GLADENBACH
REGIONAL MUSEUM

GLÜCKSBURG
PALACE MUSEUM

GÖPPINGEN
MUNICIPAL MUSEUM

GOSLAR
COLLECTION ILLUSTRATING THE CULTURAL HISTORY OF GERMANY AND EUROPE
GOSLAR MUSEUM
IMPERIAL PALACE

GÜNZBURG
REGIONAL MUSEUM

GUNZENHAUSEN
REGIONAL MUSEUM

HAMBURG
BERGEDORF AND VIERLAND MUSEUM
HAMBURG STATE ARCHIVES: COLLECTION OF SEALS AND COATS OF ARMS
HELMS MUSEUM
MILK MUSEUM AND WILHELMSBURG REGIONAL MUSEUM
MUSEUM OF THE HISTORY OF HAMBURG

HANAU
HISTORY MUSEUM

HANNOVER
HISTORY MUSEUM ON THE HIGH BANK

HANNOVERSCH MÜNDEN
REGIONAL MUSEUM

HEILBRONN
HISTORY MUSEUM

HEILIGENHAFEN
REGIONAL MUSEUM

HERFORD
MUNICIPAL MUSEUM

HERNE
EMSCHERTAL MUSEUM

HERSBRUCK
REGIONAL AND HUNTING MUSEUM

HINDELANG
REGIONAL COLLECTION

HÖCHSTÄDT-DONAU
REGIONAL MUSEUM

HOF
MUNICIPAL MUSEUM

HOFGEISMAR
REGIONAL MUSEUM

HOHENBURG
SPÖRER MUSEUM OF CULTURAL HISTORY

HOHENLIMBURG
REGIONAL MUSEUM

HÖHR-GRENZHAUSEN
GRENZAU CASTLE

HOISDORF
STORMARN VILLAGE MUSEUM

HOLZMINDEN
REGIONAL MUSEUM

HOMBERG
REGIONAL MUSEUM

HOMBURG
REGIONAL MUSEUM

HÜLLHORST
REGIONAL MUSEUM

HUSUM
NISSEN HOUSE

IDAR-OBERSTEIN
REGIONAL MUSEUM

ILSFELD
LIEBENSTEIN CASTLE

IMMENSTADT
REGIONAL MUSEUM

INGOLSTADT
MUNICIPAL MUSEUM

ISNY
ISNY REGIONAL MUSEUM

ITZEHOE
PRINZESSHOF REGIONAL MUSEUM

KAISERLAUTERN
THEODOR ZINK MUSEUM

KAMEN
MUNICIPAL MUSEUM

KAPELLEN-STOLZENFELS
STOLZENFELS CASTLE

KARLSRUHE
PFINZGAU MUSEUM

KASSEL
WILLHELMSHÖHE PALACE AND STATE PARK

KAUFBEUREN
REGIONAL MUSEUM

KEHL
HANAU MUSEUM

KELLINGHUSEN
REGIONAL MUSEUM

KEMPTEN
ALLGAU REGIONAL MUSEUM

KIEL
HISTORY COLLECTION OF THE SCHLESWIG-HOLSTEIN LAND LIBRARY

KIRCHHEIM
REGIONAL MUSEUM

KIRCHHEIMBOLANDEN
REGIONAL MUSEUM

KITZINGEN
MUNICIPAL MUSEUM

KOBLENZ
STATE COLLECTIONS OF PREHISTORY AND FOLKLORE

KÖLN
MUSEUM OF THE CITY OF COLOGNE

KÖNIGSHOFEN
REGIONAL MUSEUM

KÖNIGSWINTER
SIEBENGEBIRGE MUSEUM

KONSTANZ
ROSGARTEN MUSEUM

KORBACH
KORBACH REGIONAL MUSEUM

KREFELD
REGIONAL MUSEUM OF THE LOWER RHINE

KREMPE
TOWN HALL

KRUMBACH
REGIONAL MUSEUM

KÜNTSELSAU
REGIONAL MUSEUM

LAGE
LOCAL, REGIONAL AND TILE- MAKING MUSEUM

LAHR (SCHWARZWALD)
MUSEUM IN THE TOWN PARK

LANDAU (ISAR)
REGIONAL MUSEUM

LANDAU IN DER PFALZ
LANDAU REGIONAL MUSEUM

LANDSHUT
TOWN AND DISTRICT MUSEUM

LANGENAU
REGIONAL MUSEUM

LAUDA
REGIONAL MUSEUM

LAUF AN DER PEGNITZ
MUNICIPAL COLLECTIONS

LAUINGEN
REGIONAL HOUSE

LAUTERBACH
HOHLHAUS MUSEUM

LEER
REGIONAL MUSEUM

LENNGRIES
REGIONAL MUSEUM

LEUTKIRCH
REGIONAL MUSEUM

LIESBORN
BECKUM DISTRICT MUSEUM

LIMBURG (LAHN)
REGIONAL MUSEUM

LINDAU
MUNICIPAL ART COLLECTIONS

LIPPSTADT
DISTRICT MUSEUM

LOHR AM MAIN
REGIONAL AND SPESSART MUSEUM

LORSCH
REGIONAL MUSEUM

LOSSBURG
BLACK FOREST MUSEUM

LÜBECK
HOLSTENTOR MUSEUM
STUDY COLLECTION OF THE CITY OF LÜBECK DEPARTMENT OF PREHISTORY AND EARLY HISTORY

LUCHOW
REGIONAL MUSEUM

LUDWIGSBURG
REGIONAL MUSEUM

LUDWIGSHAFEN (RHEIN)
CITY MUSEUM

LÜNEBURG
MUSEUM OF THE PRINCIPALITY OF LÜNEBURG
REGIONAL MUSEUM

LÜNEN
MUNICIPAL MUSEUM

MAINBURG
HOLLEDAU REGIONAL MUSEUM

MANNHEIM
MANNHEIM PALACE
REISS CITY MUSEUM

MARL
REGIONAL MUSEUM

MARNE
SKAT CLUB MUSEUM

MARQUARTSTEIN
MARQUARTSTEIN CASTLE

MAYEN
EIFEL MUSEUM

MELLE
GRÖNEGAU MUSEUM

MEMMINGEN
MUNICIPAL MUSEUM
REGIONAL ROOM

MILTENBERG
REGIONAL MUSEUM

MINDELHEIM
MINDELHEIM REGIONAL MUSEUM

MINDEN
MINDEN MUSEUM OF HISTORY, ETHNOLOGY AND REGIONAL STUDIES

MÖLLN
REGIONAL MUSEUM

MOOSBURG
REGIONAL MUSEUM

MÜLHEIM
MUNICIPAL MUSEUM

MÜNCHBERG
REGIONAL MUSEUM

MÜNCHEN
MUNICH CITY MUSEUM

MÜNNERSTADT
REGIONAL MUSEUM

MÜNSTER
LAND MUSEUM OF ART AND CULTURAL HISTORY
LAND MUSEUM OF PREHISTORY AND EARLY HISTORY

NEBEL
AMRUNER MUSEUM

NENTERSHAUSEN
TANNENBERG MUSEUM

NEUBURG
REGIONAL MUSEUM

NEUNBURG VOR WALD
DISTRICT MUSEUM
NEUNHOF
KNOBLAUCHLAND REGIONAL MUSEUM
NEUSS
CLEMENS SELS MUSEUM
NEUSTADT AN DER AISCH
MUSEUM OF THE LOCAL HISTORY SOCIETY
NEUSTADT AN RÜBENBERGE
DISTRICT MUSEUM
NEUSTADT AN DER WALDNAAB
LOCAL MUSEUM
NEUSTADT (HOLSTEIN)
DISTRICT MUSEUM
NEUSTADT (ODENWALD)
BREUBERG MUSEUM
NEU-ULM
NEU-ULM REGIONAL MUSEUM
NIEDERMARSBERG
REGIONAL MUSEUM
NIENBURG
MUSEUM OF THE COUNTIES OF HOYA, DIEPHOLZ, WÖLPE
NÖRDLINGEN
TOWN MUSEUM
NORDESEIF
FISHERMAN'S HOUSE MUSEUM
NÜMBRECHT
MUSEUM OF THE OBERBERG REGION
NÜRNBERG
FEMBO HOUSE CITY MUSEUM
OBERKAUFUNGEN
REGIONAL MUSEUM
OBERNDORF
REGIONAL MUSEUM
OBER-RAMSTADT
REGIONAL MUSEUM
OBERSTDORF
REGIONAL MUSEUM
OETTINGEN
REGIONAL MUSEUM
OFFENBURG
HOUSE OF THE KNIGHTS MUSEUM
OLDENBURG
LAND MUSEUM OF ART AND CULTURAL HISTORY
OSNABRÜCK
MUNICIPAL MUSEUM
OSTERODE
OSTERODE REGIONAL MUSEUM
OTTERNDORF
KRANICH HOUSE DISTRICT MUSEUM
PADERBORN
MUSEUM OF THE HISTORICAL SOCIETY
PARSBERG
REGIONAL MUSEUM
PFAFFENHOFEN
REGIONAL MUSEUM
PIDING
STAUFENECK PALACE
PLÖN
PLÖN DISTRICT MUSEUM
POTTENSTEIN
REGIONAL MUSEUM
PRESSATH
PRESSATH MUSEUM OF THE REGIONAL PROTECTION SOCIETY
RATINGEN
MUSEUM OF THE HISTORY OF RATINGEN
RAVENSBURG
REGIONAL MUSEUM
REMSCHEID
REGIONAL MUSEUM
REUTLINGEN
REGIONAL MUSEUM
RHEINE
FALKENHOF MUSEUM
RIEDENBURG
MUNICIPAL MUSEUM
RIEDLINGEN
REGIONAL MUSEUM
RINTELN
SCHAUMBURG REGIONAL MUSEUM
ROCKENHAUSEN
NORTH PALATINATE REGIONAL MUSEUM
ROSENHEIM
REGIONAL MUSEUM
ROTENBURG-WÜMME
REGIONAL MUSEUM
ROTH
REGIONAL MUSEUM
ROTHENBURG OB DER TAUBER
HISTORY MUSEUM
MUSEUM OF THE IMPERIAL CITY
ROTTENBURG AM NECKAR
SÜLCHGAU MUSEUM
ROTTWEIL
ROTTWEIL MUNICIPAL MUSEUM
RÜDESHEIM
RHEINGAU AND WINE MUSEUM
RÜSSELSHEIM
LOCAL MUSEUM
SÄCKINGEN
UPPER RHINE MUSEUM
SALZGITTER-SALDER
TOWN MUSEUM
ST. ANDREASBERG
REGIONAL MUSEUM AND HISTORIC SILVER MINE
ST. GOAR
REGIONAL COLLECTION
SCHIFFERSTADT
REGIONAL MUSEUM
SCHLESWIG
MUNICIPAL MUSEUM
SCHLITZ
REGIONAL MUSEUM
SCHONGAU
TOWN MUSEUM
SCHÖNINGEN
REGIONAL MUSEUM
SCHWANDORF
REGIONAL MUSEUM
SCHWELM
SCHWELM MUNICIPAL MUSEUM
SIEGEN
SIEGERLAND MUSEUM
SIGMARINGEN
HOHENZOLLERN MUSEUM
SOEST
BURGHOF MUSEUM
SÖGEL
EMSLAND MUSEUM
SPAICHINGEN
MUSEUM OF GEOLOGY AND PREHISTORY
SPEYER
MUSEUM OF THE HISTORY OF THE PALATINATE
STADE
MUSEUM OF PREHISTORY
REGIONAL MUSEUM
STARNBERG
MUNICIPAL MUSEUM
STAUFEN
REGIONAL AND COSTUME MUSEUM
STEINHEIM AM MAIN
MUNICIPAL MUSEUM
STEINHEIM-MURR
MUSEUM OF PRIMITIVE MAN
STRAUBING
GÄUBODEN AND STRAUBING MUSEUM
STUTTGART
MUSEUM OF THE HISTORY OF STUTTGART
REGIONAL MUSEUM
SULZBACH-ROSENBERG
REGIONAL MUSEUM
SYKE
DISTRICT MUSEUM
TEGERNSEE
TEGERNSEE REGIONAL MUSEUM
TETTNANG
MONTFORT MUSEUM
TRAUNSTEIN
REGIONAL MUSEUM
TRECHTLINGHAUSEN
RHEINSTEIN PALACE ART COLLECTIONS
TRIER
MUNICIPAL MUSEUM
RHINELAND MUSEUM
TROSTBERG
TROSTBERG MUNICIPAL MUSEUM
TÜBINGEN
COLLECTIONS OF THE UNIVERSITY INSTITUTE OF PREHISTORY AND EARLY HISTORY
THEODOR HEARING HOUSE
UELZEN
REGIONAL MUSEUM
URACH
URACH CASTLE ALPINE MUSEUM
USINGEN
WILHELM AND REGIONAL MUSEUM
VERINGENSTADT
REGIONAL MUSEUM
WANGEN
WANGEN REGIONAL MUSEUM
WANNE-EICKEL
REGIONAL MUSEUM
WASSERBURG
WASSERBURG REGIONAL MUSEUM
WEENER
REGIONAL MUSEUM
WEILER
WEST ALLGAU REGIONAL MUSEUM
WEILHEIM
TOWN MUSEUM
WEINGARTEN
WEINGARTEN MUSEUM OF PREHISTORY
WEINHEIM
REGIONAL MUSEUM
WEISSENBURG
REGIONAL MUSEUM
WEMDING
REGIONAL MUSEUM
WERTINGEN
REGIONAL MUSEUM
WESTRHAUDERFEHN
OSTFRIESLAND AND SATERLAND FEN AND SHIPPING MUSEUM
WETZLAR
MUNICIPAL MUSEUM
WEWELSBURG
DISTRICT MUSEUM
WILHELMSHAVEN
COASTAL AND SHIPPING MUSEUM
WITTEN
REGIONAL MUSEUM
WOLFENBÜTTEL
LAND MUSEUM OF HISTORY AND TRADITION
WOLFENBÜTTEL DISTRICT MUSEUM
WOLFHAGEN
REGIONAL MUSEUM
WORPSWEDE
MUSEUM AMONG THE TREES
WYK
FÖHR ISLAND MUSEUM SOCIETY
ZÜLPICH
ZÜLPICH REGIONAL MUSEUM

GHANA

CAPE COAST
CAPE COAST HISTORICAL MUSEUM

GREAT BRITAIN

ALNWICK
ALNWICK CASTLE
ASHWELL
ASHWELL VILLAGE MUSEUM

BANGOR
MUSEUM OF WELSH ANTIQUITIES
BIRMINGHAM
BLAKESLEY HALL
BODMIN
PASSMORE EDWARDS PUBLIC LIBRARY AND MUSEUM
BRADFORD
BOLLING HALL
BRIGHTON
BRIGHTON MUSEUM AND ART GALLERY
BRISTOL
BRISTOL CITY MUSEUM
BURFORD
TOLSEY MUSEUM
CHESTER
KING CHARLES'S TOWER
WATER TOWER
CHICHESTER
CHICHESTER CITY MUSEUM
DORCHESTER
DORSET COUNTY MUSEUM
DUMFRIES
OLD BRIDGE HOUSE MUSEUM
EXETER
ROUGEMONT HOUSE MUSEUM
FORT WILLIAM
WEST HIGHLAND MUSEUM
GLASGOW
OLD GLASGOW MUSEUM
GUILDFORD
GUILDFORD MUSEUM
ILKLEY
MANOR HOUSE MUSEUM
LEICESTER
NEWARKE HOUSES MUSEUM
LETCHWORTH
LETCHWORTH MUSEUM AND ART GALLERY
LONDON
GREENWICH BOROUGH MUSEUM
GUILDHALL MUSEUM
JOHN EVELYN SOCIETY'S MUSEUM
LONDON MUSEUM
WALTHAMSTOW MUSEUM
"WOODLANDS" LOCAL HISTORY CENTRE AND ART GALLERY
LOOE
THE CORNISH MUSEUM
LUTON
LUTON MUSEUM AND ART GALLERY
NEWTOWN
NEWTOWN WOOLLEN INDUSTRY MUSEUM
ROTHESAY
BUTESHIRE NATURAL HISTORY SOCIETY MUSEUM
SALFORD
MUSEUM AND ART GALLERY
SALTCOATS
NORTH AYRSHIRE MUSEUM
TRURO
COUNTY MUSEUM AND ART GALLERY
WARWICK
LORD LEYCESTER HOSPITAL
WINCHESTER
THE WESTGATE MUSEUM
WISBECH
WISBECH AND FENLAND MUSEUM
WOLVERHAMPTON
BILSTON MUSEUM AND ART GALLERY
WORCESTER
CITY MUSEUM
TUDOR HOUSE FOLK MUSEUM

GREECE

CORFU
HISTORICAL MUSEUM
CORINTH
ANCIENT CORINTH MUSEUM
RETHYMNON
ARKADI MONASTERY
SPETSAI
MUSEUM
ZAKYNTHOS
MUSEUM OF SOMOMOS AND OTHER ILLUSTRIOUS ZAKYNTHIANS

HONG KONG

KOWLOON
LEI CHENG UK TOMB SITE MUSEUM

HUNGARY

BUDAPEST
PESTERZSÉBETI MÚZEUM
DUNAÚJVÁROS
DUNAÚJVÁROS MUSEUM
KESZTHELY
BALATON MUSEUM
NYÍREGYHÁZA
ANDRÁS JÓSA MUSEUM
SZEGED
FERENC MÓRA MUZEUM
VESZPRÉM
BAKONY MUSEUM

INDIA

AMRITSAR
CENTRAL SIKH MUSEUM
BARIPADA
BARIPADA MUSEUM
PADMANABHAPURAM
MUSEUM OF ANTIQUITIES

IRELAND

DUBLIN
DUBLIN CIVIC MUSEUM
ENNISCORTHY
CASTLE MUSEUM
KILLARNEY
MUCKROSS HOUSE
KINSALE
KINSALE REGIONAL MUSEUM
ROSSNOWLAGH
MUSEUM OF THE COUNTY DONEGAL HISTORICAL SOCIETY
SLIGO
COUNTY SLIGO MUSEUM
YOUGHAL
CLOCK TOWER MUSEUM

ISRAEL

HAZOR
LOCAL MUSEUM
TEL-AVIV
HISTORICAL MUSEUM OF TEL- AVIV
MUSEUM OF THE ANTIQUITIES OF TEL-AVIV-YAFO

ITALY

BRESCIA
MUSEUM OF THE RISORGIMENTO
FLORENCE
"FLORENCE AS IT WAS"
GENOA
DORIA TURSI PALACE (NOW PALAZZO MUNICIPALE)
GUBBIO
MUSEUM AND PICTURE GALLERY
ISCHIA
ISLAND MUSEUM
MILAN
ARCHAEOLOGICAL MUSEUM
THE MILAN MUSEUM
NAPLES
NATIONAL MUSEUM OF SAN MARTINO
PALESTRINA
NATIONAL ARCHAEOLOGICAL MUSEUM
PERUGIA
TOPOGRAPHICAL AND HISTORICAL MUSEUM OF THE CITY AND TERRITORY OF PERUGIA
PINEROLO
MUNICIPAL MUSEUM
RIVA DEL GARDA
CIVIC MUSEUM
ROME
MUSEUM OF ROME
TRIESTE
HISTORICAL MUSEUM
MORPURGO MUSEUM OF NATIONAL HISTORY AND THE STAVROPULOS ART COLLECTIONS
MUSEUM OF THE RISORGIMENTO

JAPAN

KAGOSHIMA-SHI
SHOKO SHUSEI-KAN MEMORIAL COLLECTION
KYOTO
HISTORICAL MUSEUM
SENDAI-SHI
SAITO HO'ONKAI MUSEUM
TOKYO
MEMORIAL HALL OF THE RECONSTRUCTION OF TOKYO

KOREA, DEMO. PEOPLE'S REP.

BOCHUN COUNTY
STATE HISTORICAL MUSEUM
CHUNGJIN
STATE HISTORICAL MUSEUM
HAEJU
STATE HISTORICAL MUSEUM
HAMHEUNG
STATE HISTORICAL MUSEUM
HESAN
STATE HISTORICAL MUSEUM
KAESONG
STATE HISTORICAL MUSEUM
KANGGE
STATE HISTORICAL MUSEUM
MYOHYANG MT.
STATE HISTORICAL MUSEUM
SARIWON
STATE HISTORICAL MUSEUM
SHINCHUN COUNTY
STATE HISTORICAL MUSEUM
SHINUIJU
STATE HISTORICAL MUSEUM
WONSAN
STATE HISTORICAL MUSEUM

MOZAMBIQUE

LOURENÇO MARQUES
MUNICIPAL MUSEUM
MUSEUM OF MILITARY HISTORY

NETHERLANDS

AMSTERDAM
MUSEUM OF THE HISTORY OF AMSTERDAM
APPINGEDAM
REGIONAL HISTORICAL MUSEUM
ARNHEM
LOCAL MUSEUM
ASSEN
DRENTHE PROVINCIAL MUSEUM

DEVENTER
WEIGH HOUSE MUSEUM
GRAMSBERGEN
TOWN HISTORICAL MUSEUM
'S GRAVENHAGE
MUNICIPAL MUSEUM
GRONINGEN
MUSEUM OF THE GRONINGEN REGION
GROUW
LOCAL MUSEUM
LEIDEN
LAKENHAL MUNICIPAL MUSEUM
LELYSTAD
LELYSTAD HARBOUR EXHIBITION BUILDING
MAASTRICHT
BONNEFANTEN MUSEUM
OSS
JAN CUNEN MUSEUM
SCHOKLAND
IJSSELMEER POLDER MUSEUM
SCHOONOORD
THE SEVEN MARKS
VEENDAM
PEAT SETTLEMENT MUSEUM
VLISSINGEN
MUNICIPAL MUSEUM

NEW ZEALAND

ARTHUR'S PASS
ARTHUR'S PASS NATIONAL PARK MUSEUM
AUCKLAND
'JOURNEY'S END' COTTAGE AND MUSEUM
CAMBRIDGE
MUSEUM OF THE CAMBRIDGE HISTORICAL SOCIETY
HAMILTON
WAIKATO MUSEUM
KAITAIA
FAR NORTH REGIONAL MUSEUM
NELSON
ISEL HOUSE
NELSON PROVINCIAL MUSEUM
NEW PLYMOUTH
RICHMOND COTTAGE
NORSEWOOD
NORSEWOOD PIONEER MUSEUM
PUKEKOHE
PIONEER MEMORIAL COTTAGE
RANGIORA
RANGIORA AND DISTRICT EARLY RECORDS SOCIETY MUSEUM
RUSSELL
CAPTAIN COOK MEMORIAL MUSEUM
WAIPU
PIONEERS' MEMORIAL MUSEUM

NORWAY

BERGEN
HANSEATIC MUSEUM
HALDEN
MEMORIES OF HALDEN MUSEUM
KARASJOK
LOCAL MUSEUM
MO I RANA
MO AND NORTH-RANA MUSEUM OF BUILDINGS
OSLO
CITY MUSEUM
SETESDAL
SETESDAL MUSEUM
STAVANGER
STAVANGER MUSEUM
TRONDHEIM
MUSEUM OF THE ROYAL NORWEGIAN SOCIETY OF SCIENCES AND LETTERS

PHILIPPINES

MANILA
MUSEUM OF THE CITY OF MANILA

POLAND

BRZEG
PRASTÓW SILESIAN MUSEUM
CHORZÓW
CHORZÓW MUSEUM
GDAŃSK
MUSEUM OF THE HISTORY OF GDAŃSK
GDYNIA
MUSEUM OF THE CITY OF GDYNIA
KATOWICE-JANÓW ŚLĄSKI
JÓZEF WIECZORKI MUSEUM
KRAKÓW
MUSEUM OF KRAKÓW
LEŚNICA
MUSEUM OF THE UPRISING
MYSŁOWICE
MARTYRS' MEMORIAL MUSEUM
OSTROW LUBELSKI
LOCAL MUSEUM
POLICHNO
MUSEUM OF THE RESISTANCE
POZNAŃ
MUSEUM OF THE LIBERATION
MUSEUM OF THE MARTYRS
POZNAŃ HISTORICAL MUSEUM
PRZEMYŚL
REGIONAL MUSEUM
SZCZECIN
MEMORIAL MUSEUM
WARSAW
MUSEUM OF THE HISTORY OF THE CITY OF WARSAW
WOLSZTYN
MARCIN ROZKI MUSEUM
WROCŁAW
NATIONAL MUSEUM

PORTUGAL

LISBON
MUNICIPAL MUSEUM

ROMANIA

AIUD
AIUD HISTORICAL MUSEUM
ALBA IULIA
ALBA IULIA MUSEUM
ARAD
ARAD MUSEUM
BACĂU
BACĂU HISTORICAL MUSEUM
BOTOŞANI
BOTOŞANI MUSEUM
BRAŞOV
BRAŞOV MUSEUM
FORTRESS MUSEUM
BUCHAREST
'BUCHAREST AS SEEN BY ARTISTS'
MUSEUM OF THE HISTORY OF BUCHAREST
MARIA AND DR. G. SEVEREANU COLLECTION
BUZĂU
MUSEUM OF THE HISTORY OF BUZĂU
CĂLĂRAŞI
CĂLĂRAŞI MUSEUM
CLUJ
HISTORY MUSEUM
CRAIOVA
OLTENIEI MUSEUM
TRIAL OF THE RAILWAYMEN AND PETROLEUM WORKERS, JUNE-JULY 1934, MUSEUM
CRISTURUL
CRISTURUL MUSEUM
FĂLTICENI
FĂLTICENI MUSEUM
FOCŞANI
HISTORY MUSEUM
GALAŢI
HISTORY MUSEUM
GOLEŞTI
MUSEUM OF HISTORY AND ETHNOGRAPHY
IAŞI
ILIE PINTILIE MUSEUM
LUGOJ
LUGOJ MUSEUM
MIERCUREA CIUC
MIERCUREA CIUC MUSEUM
ORADEA
ORIŞANA MUSEUM
PITEŞTI
ARGES DISTRICT MUSEUM
PITEŞTI MUSEUM
POIANA SIBIULUI
LOCAL MUSEUM
REŞIŢA
LOCAL MUSEUM
RÎMNICU VILCEA
RÎMNICU VILCEA MUSEUM
ROMAN
ROMAN MUSEUM
SĂCELE
MUSEUM OF THE SEVEN VILLAGES
SATU MARE
SATU MARE MUSEUM
SFÎNTU GHEORGHE
SFÎNTU GHEORGHE MUSEUM
SIGHIŞOARA
SIGHIŞOARA MUSEUM
TÎRGU NEAMŢ
ŞTEFAN CEL MARE MUSEUM

SENEGAL

DAKAR
HISTORICAL MUSEUM OF GORÉE
SAINT-LOUIS
MICHEL ADANSON MUSEUM

SOUTH AFRICA, REPUBLIC OF

BEAUFORT WEST
BEAUFORT WEST MUSEUM
BURGERSDORP
BURGERSDORP CULTURAL HISTORY MUSEUM
DURBAN
MUSEUM OF LOCAL HISTORY
OUDTSHOORN
C.P. NEL MUSEUM
PIETERMARITZBURG
NATAL MUSEUM
PORT ELIZABETH
PORT ELIZABETH MUSEUM
POTCHEFSROOM
MUNICIPAL MUSEUM
VICTORIA WEST
VICTORIA WEST MUSEUM
VRYHEID
NIEUWE REPUBLIEK MUSEUM

SPAIN

BALSARENY
COLLECTION OF PAINTING AND HISTORY
BARCELONA
MUSEUM OF THE HISTORY OF THE CITY OF BARCELONA
BILBAO
VIZCAYA HISTORICAL MUSEUM

LA CORUÑA
HISTORICAL AND ARCHAEOLOGICAL MUSEUM
GERONA
TOWN HISTORICAL MUSEUM
LAS PALMAS
MUSEUM OF THE CANARY ISLANDS
MADRID
MUNICIPAL MUSEUM
SABADELL
MUSEUM OF HISTORY
TARRAGONA
CITY MUSEUM
VALENCIA
CITY HISTORICAL MUSEUM

SWEDEN

YSTAD
FRIARY WITH ST. PETER'S CHURCH

SWITZERLAND

AARAU
OLD AARAU MUSEUM
AARBURG
REGIONAL MUSEUM
BAULMES
MUSEUM OF OLD BAULMES
BERN
BERN HISTORICAL MUSEUM
BOSCO-GURIN
GURIN HOUSE OF THE WAISERS
BURGDORF
HISTORICAL MUSEUM OF THE BURGDORF HALL OF THE KNIGHTS SOCIETY
LE LANDERON
MUSEUM
LANGENTHAL
REGIONAL MUSEUM
LUZERN
GLACIER GARDEN AND GLACIER MUSEUM
NEUCHÂTEL
MUSEUM OF ART AND HISTORY
RORSCHACH
REGIONAL MUSEUM

TURKEY

ISTANBUL
MUNICIPAL MUSEUM

USSR

ASHAGA-STAL
SULEIMAN STAL HOUSE- MUSEUM
BAKU
MUSEUM OF THE HISTORY OF AZERBAIJAN
BATUM
MUSEUM OF THE REVOLUTION
STATE MUSEUM OF THE REVOLUTION
BREST-LITOVSK
REGIONAL MUSEUM
KAKHOVA
LOCAL MUSEUM
KAUNAS
STATE MUSEUM
KURSK
REGIONAL MUSEUM
LENINGRAD
NATIONAL MUSEUM OF THE HISTORY OF LENINGRAD
LVOV
LVOV HISTORICAL MUSEUM
MINSK
MUSEUM OF LOCAL HISTORY AND FOLKLORE
STATE MUSEUM OF THE BYELORUSSIAN S.S.R.
ORDZHONIKIDZE
ORDZHONIKIDZE MUSEUM: HISTORY COLLECTIONS
PETROZAVODSK
NATIONAL HISTORICAL MUSEUM
RIGA
LATVIAN HISTORICAL MUSEUM
SMOLENSK
MUSEUM OF HISTORY
TALLINN
CITY MUSEUM
TARTU
MUSEUM OF THE CITY OF TARTU
TBILISI
MUSEUM OF HISTORY AND ETHNOGRAPHY
VIBORG
FORTRESS MUSEUM
YALTA
MUSEUM OF HISTORY AND ARCHAEOLOGY

UNITED STATES

ABINGDON
MUSEUM OF HISTORICAL SOCIETY OF VIRGINIA
ALTUS
MUSEUM OF THE WESTERN PRAIRIE
ANDOVER
ANDOVER HISTORICAL SOCIETY MUSEUM
ANNAPOLIS
HALL OF RECORDS COMMISSION
ANN ARBOR
HISTORICAL SOCIETY OF MICHIGAN MUSEUM
ANSTED
MUSEUM OF FAYETTE COUNTY HISTORICAL SOCIETY
ANTIGO
LANGLADE COUNTY HISTORICAL SOCIETY MUSEUM
ARCADE
WYOMING HISTORICAL PIONEER ASSOCIATION MUSEUM
ASHBURNHAM
ASHBURNHAM HISTORICAL SOCIETY MUSEUM
ASTORIA
CLATSOP COUNTY HISTORICAL CENTER
ATLANTA
ATLANTA HISTORICAL SOCIETY MUSEUM
ATWOOD
MUSEUM OF RAWLINS COUNTY HISTORICAL SOCIETY
AUGUSTA
AUGUSTA RICHMOND COUNTY MUSEUM
BAIRD
CALLAHAN COUNTY PIONEER MUSEUM
BALTIMORE
MUSEUM OF MARYLAND HISTORICAL SOCIETY
MUSEUM OF UNITED METHODIST HISTORICAL SOCIETY OF THE BALTIMORE CONFERENCE
PEALE MUSEUM
BAR HARBOR
ISLEFORD MUSEUM
BARNEGAT LIGHT
BARNEGAT LIGHT HISTORICAL SOCIETY MUSEUM
BATAVIA
HOLLAND LAND OFFICE MUSEUM
BATON ROUGE
OLD ARSENAL MUSEUM
BAY CITY
MUSEUM OF THE GREAT LAKES
BIG HORN
BRADFORD BRINTON MEMORIAL MUSEUM
BIG STONE GAP
SOUTH-WEST VIRGINIA MUSEUM
BILLINGS
YELLOWSTONE COUNTY MUSEUM
BIRDSBORO
DANIEL BOONE HOMESTEAD
BISMARCK
CAMP HANCOCK MUSEUM
STATE HISTORICAL SOCIETY MUSEUM
BLOOMINGTON
SAN BERNADINO COUNTY MUSEUM
INDIANA UNIVERSITY MUSEUM
BOISE
IDAHO STATE HISTORICAL MUSEUM
BOSTON
BOSTON ATHENAEUM
MASSACHUSETTS HISTORICAL SOCIETY MUSEUM
OLD SOUTH MEETING HOUSE
OLD STATE HOUSE
BOULDER
PIONEER MUSEUM
BOURNE
APTUXCET TRADING POST
BOWLING GREEN
KENTUCKY MUSEUM
BOZEMAN
MUSEUM OF THE ROCKIES
BRACKETTVILLE
JOHN FRITTER MEMORIAL MUSEUM
BRADENTON
SOUTH FLORIDA MUSEUM AND BISHOP PLANETARIUM
BRAINERD
MUSEUM OF CROW WING COUNTY HISTORICAL SOCIETY
BRONX
VALENTINE-VARIAN HOUSE MUSEUM OF BRONX HISTORY
BUENA PARK
WESTERN TRAILS MUSEUM
BUFFALO
JOHNSON COUNTY, JIM GATCHELL MEMORIAL MUSEUM
BUFFALO GAP
ERNIE WILSON MUSEUM
CAPE MAY
CAPE MAY COUNTY HISTORICAL MUSEUM
CASPER
FORT CASPAR HISTORIC SITE AND MUSEUM
CATHLAMET
MUSEUM OF WAHKIAKUM COUNTY HISTORICAL SOCIETY
CHADRON
MUSEUM OF THE FUR TRADE
CHARLESTON
CHARLESTON MUSEUM
MUSEUM OF WEST VIRGINIA DEPARTMENT OF ARCHIVES AND HISTORY
CHERRYVALE
BENDER MUSEUM
CHEYENNE
MUSEUM OF WYOMING STATE ARCHIVES AND HISTORICAL DEPARTMENT
WYOMING STATE MUSEUM
CHICAGO
MUSEUM OF CHICAGO HISTORICAL SOCIETY
CHILLICOTHE
ROSS COUNTY HISTORICAL SOCIETY MUSEUM
CINCINNATI
MUSEUM OF CINCINNATI HISTORICAL SOCIETY
HARRIET B. STOWE HOUSE STATE MEMORIAL
CLEVELAND
WESTERN RESERVE HISTORICAL SOCIETY AND FREDERICK C. CRAWFORD AUTO-AVIATION MUSEUM
COLUMBIA
SOUTH CAROLINA CONFEDERATE RELIC ROOM AND MUSEUM
SOUTH CAROLINA STATE HISTORICAL MUSEUM
COLUMBUS
CONFEDERATE MEMORIAL MUSEUM
CORNWALL- ON-HUDSON
MUSEUM OF THE HUDSON HIGHLANDS
CROSBYTON
CROSBYTON COUNTY PIONEER MEMORIAL MUSEUM
CURRIE
MOORES CREEK NATIONAL MILITARY PARK MUSEUM
DALLAS
DALLAS HISTORICAL SOCIETY
DANVERS
REBECCA NOURSE HOUSE
DAVENPORT
DAVENPORT MUSEUM
DEARBORN
DEARBORN HISTORICAL MUSEUM
DEER PARK
SAN JACINTO MUSEUM OF HISTORY

DENVER
MUSEUM OF THE STATE HISTORICAL SOCIETY OF COLORADO

DOVER
DELAWARE STATE MUSEUM

EDENTON
MUSEUM OF HISTORIC EDENTON

FAIRBANKS
PIONEER MUSEUM

FILLMORE
TERRITORIAL STATEHOUSE

FLAGSTAFF
NORTHERN ARIZONA PIONEER HISTORICAL SOCIETY MUSEUM

FORT HUACHUCA
FORT HUACHUCA HISTORICAL MUSEUM

FORT RANSOM
FORT RANSOM HISTORICAL SOCIETY MUSEUM

FORT WORTH
HERITAGE HALL

FREDERICKSBURG
PIONEER MEMORIAL MUSEUM

GERING
OREGON TRAIL MUSEUM

GLENDIVE
FRONTIER GATEWAY MUSEUM

HARRIS COUNTY
SAN JACINTO MUSEUM OF HISTORY

HAWK'S STATE PARK
HAWK'S NEST MUSEUM

HILLSBOROUGH
ORANGE COUNTY HISTORICAL MUSEUM

HOHENWALD
MERIWETHER LEWIS NATIONAL MONUMENT, VISITOR CENTER

HOLYOKE
HOLYOKE MUSEUM - WISTARIAHURST

HOPEWELL
HOPEWELL MUSEUM

HOPKINTON
NEW HAMPSHIRE ANTIQUARIAN SOCIETY MUSEUM

HOUSTON
MUSEUM OF TEXAS GULF COAST HISTORICAL ASSOCIATION

HUNTSVILLE
SAM HOUSTON MEMORIAL MUSEUM

ISLEFORD
ISLEFORD MUSEUM

JACKSON
MISSISSIPPI STATE HISTORICAL MUSEUM

JOHNSON CITY
CARROLL REECE MUSEUM

KINGS CREEK
KINGS MOUNTAIN NATIONAL MILITARY PARK

KINGSTON
SENATE HOUSE

LAFAYETTE
TIPPECANOE COUNTY HISTORICAL MUSEUM

LANCASTER
THE CAROLINA MUSEUM

LANSING
MICHIGAN HISTORICAL COMMISSION MUSEUM

LAREDO
CAPITOL OF THE REPUBLIC OF THE RIO GRANDE MUSEUM

LAWTON
MUSEUM OF THE GREAT PLAINS

LEBANON
WARREN COUNTY HISTORICAL SOCIETY MUSEUM

LENHARTSVILLE
MUSEUM OF PENNSYLVANIA DUTCH FOLK CULTURE SOCIETY

LEXINGTON
WAVELAND STATE SHRINE

LITTLE ROCK
ARKANSAS FIRST STATE CAPITOL

LOS ANGELES
EL PUEBLO DE LOS ANGELES STATE HISTORIC PARK
SOUTHWEST MUSEUM

MADISON
MUSEUM OF STATE HISTORICAL SOCIETY OF WASHINGTON

MCCAMEY
MENDOZA TRAIL MUSEUM AND ADRIAN HOUSE

MINNEAPOLIS
MINNEAPOLIS INSTITUTE OF ARTS

MONTEREY
COLTON HALL

MONTPELIER
VERMONT HISTORICAL SOCIETY MUSEUM

MORRISTOWN
MORRISTOWN NATIONAL HISTORICAL PARK MUSEUM

MUNCIE
GRINTER HOUSE

NANTUCKET
PETER FOULGER MUSEUM

NASHVILLE
TENNESSEE STATE MUSEUM

NEWARK
MUSEUM OF NEW JERSEY HISTORICAL SOCIETY

NEW BRAUNFELS
SOPHIENBURG MEMORIAL MUSEUM

NEW HARMONY
WORKINGMEN'S INSTITUTE

NEW LONDON
NEW LONDON COUNTY HISTORICAL SOCIETY MUSEUM

NEW ORLEANS
PRESBYTÈRE
THE CABILDO

NEWPORT NEWS
PENINSULA NATURE AND SCIENCE CENTER

NEW YORK
KINGSBRIDGE HISTORICAL SOCIETY
MUSEUM OF THE CITY OF NEW YORK
MUSEUM OF NEW YORK HISTORICAL SOCIETY
STATEN ISLAND INSTITUTE OF ARTS AND SCIENCES

NIAGARA FALLS
SCHOELLKOPJ GEOLOGICAL MUSEUM

OGDENSBURG
REMINGTON ART MUSEUM

OKLAHOMA CITY
OKLAHOMA HISTORICAL SOCIETY MUSEUM

OLD CHATHAM
SHAKER MUSEUM

OLYMPIA
STATE CAPITOL MUSEUM

PECOS
WEST OF THE PECOS MUSEUM

PHOENIX
ARIZONA HISTORY ROOM

PLYMOUTH
MUSEUM OF PLYMOUTH PLANTATION
PILGRIM HALL MUSEUM

PORTLAND
MAINE HISTORICAL SOCIETY MUSEUM

PORT ST. JOE
CONSTITUTION CONVENTION STATE MUSEUM

POTEAU
KERR MUSEUM

PRINCETON
MUSEUM OF HISTORICAL SOCIETY OF PRINCETON

RALEIGH
MUSEUM OF NORTH CAROLINA STATE DEPARTMENT OF ARCHIVES AND HISTORY
NORTH CAROLINA MUSEUM OF HISTORY

RICHMOND
VALENTINE MUSEUM

RIDGEWOOD
MUSEUM OF PARAMUS HISTORICAL AND PRESERVATION SOCIETY

SACRAMENTO
SUTTER'S FORT STATE HISTORICAL MONUMENT

ST. AUGUSTINE
TOVAR HOUSE

ST. PAUL
MINNESOTA HISTORICAL SOCIETY MUSEUM

SALT LAKE CITY
UTAH STATE HISTORICAL SOCIETY MUSEUM

SAN ANGELO
FORT CONCHO RESTORATION AND MUSEUM

SAN ANTONIO
WITTE MEMORIAL MUSEUM

SAN DIEGO
SAN DIEGO HISTORICAL SOCIETY

SAN FRANCISCO
THE SOCIETY OF CALIFORNIA PIONEERS MUSEUM

SAN JACINTO
SAN JACINTO MUSEUM OF HISTORY

SAVANNAH
MUSEUM OF GEORGIA HISTORICAL SOCIETY

SEATTLE
THOMAS BURKE MEMORIAL
MUSEUM OF HISTORY AND INDUSTRY

SELMA
STURDIVANT MUSEUM

SEVERNA PARK
ANN ARUNDEL COUNTY HISTORICAL SOCIETY

SIMSBURY
HISTORIC CENTER

SITKA
SITKA NATIONAL MONUMENT

STANFORD
WILLIAM WHITLEY STATE PARK AND SHRINE

STARKE
MUSEUM OF THE NORTH AND THE SOUTH

STOCKTON
PIONEER MUSEUM AND HAGGIN GALLERIES

TACOMA
WASHINGTON STATE HISTORICAL SOCIETY MUSEUM

TALLAHASSEE
MUSEUM OF DIVISION OF ARCHIVES, HISTORY AND RECORDS MANAGEMENT

THOUSAND OAKS
STAGECOACH INN MUSEUM

TUBAC
TUBAC PRESIDIO STATE HISTORIC PARK

WASHINGTON
COLUMBIA HISTORICAL SOCIETY MUSEUM
WASHINGTON CITY MUSEUM

YORK
HISTORICAL SOCIETY OF YORK COUNTY

URUGUAY

MONTEVIDEO
MUNICIPAL MUSEUM OF HISTORY AND ARCHIVES

VENEZUELA

CARACAS
'RAUL SANTANA' MUSEUM

CIUDAD DE EL TOCUYO
HISTORICAL MUSEUM

LA GUAIRA
JOHN BOULTON MUSEUM

VIETNAM, DEMOCRATIC REPUBLIC OF

DIEN-BIEN-PHU
DIEN-BIEN-PHU MUSEUM

YUGOSLAVIA

BANJA LUKA
MUSEUM OF BASANSKA KRAJINA REGION

BELGRADE
CITY MUSEUM

BREŽICE
PROVINCIAL MUSEUM

HERCEGNOVI
TOWN MUSEUM

LJUBLJANA
ARCHIVES OF SLOVENIA

SARAJEVO
MUSEUM OF THE CITY OF SARAJEVO

ŠIBENIK
TOWN MUSEUM
SKOFJA LOKA
MUSEUM
SPLIT
CITY MUSEUM OF SPLIT
ZAGREB
CITY MUSEUM OF ZAGREB
ZAGREB MUNICIPAL ARCHIVES

Historic houses

ARGENTINA

FLORENCIA VARELA
BIRTHPLACE OF W. H. HUDSON
SALTA
HOUSE OF PRESIDENT JOSÉ E. URIBURU
SAMAY HUASI
REGIONAL MUSEUM ''MIS MONTAÑAS''
SAN ANTONIO DE ARECO
RICARDO GUIRALDES GAUCHO MUSEUM
SAN ISIDRO
BRIGADIER GENERAL JUAN MARTIN DE PUEYRREDÓN MUSEUM
SAN MIGUEL DE TUCUMÁN
MUSEUM OF THE HISTORIC HOUSE OF THE INDEPENDENCE
SAN NICOLAS DE LOS ARROYOS
HOUSE OF THE AGREEMENT (CASA DEL ACUERDO) MUSEUM

AUSTRIA

ALPL
PETER ROSEGGEN'S BIRTHPLACE
ARNSDORF
FRANZ XAVIER GRUBER MUSEUM
BAD ISCHL
LÉHAR VILLA
VILLA OF THE EMPEROR
EISENSTADT
HAYDN MUSEUM
KRIEGLACH
PETER ROSEGGER MUSEUM
LICHTENEGG
JOHANN JAKOB TSCHUDI MEMORIAL MUSEUM
RAIDING
FRANZ LISZT MUSEUM
ROHRAU
HAYDN MUSEUM
SALZBURG
MOZART MUSEUM
MOZART'S HOUSE
VIENNA
BEETHOVEN MEMORIAL ROOMS
HAYDN MUSEUM
HOUSE WHERE SCHUBERT DIED
MOZART MEMORIAL ROOM
WAIZENKIRCHEN
WILHELM KIENZ BIRTHPLACE
ZWICKLEDT
KUBIN HOUSE

BELGIUM

ANTWERP
RUBENS' HOUSE
BRUGES
STORIE HOUSE
BRUSSELS
CONSTANTIN MEUNIER MUSEUM
LIÈGE
GRÉTRY MUSEUM

BRAZIL

CARUARU
VITALINO HOUSE MUSEUM
FLORIANÓPOLIS
VITOR MEIRLES HOUSE MUSEUM
LENÇÓIS
AFRÂNIO PEIXOTO HOUSE OF CULTURE
NITERÓI
ANTÓNIO PARREIRAS MUSEUM
PALMEIRA DOS ÍNDIOS
GRACILIANO RAMOS HOUSE MUSEUM
RIO DE JANEIRO
BENJAMIN CONSTANT HOUSE- MUSEUM
MUSEUM OF THE REPUBLIC
SALVADOR
RUI BARBOSA HOUSE-MUSEUM
SANTOS DUMONT
SANTOS DUMONT MUSEUM
TRAMANDAÍ
GENERAL OSÓRIO MUSEUM
VICOSA DO CEARA
AMELIA BEVILACQUA MUSEUM

BULGARIA

BANSHO
NIKOLA VAPKAROV HOUSE- MUSEUM
BIALA CERKOVA
MEMORIAL MUSEUM OF THE POET ZANKO ZERKOVSKY
KALOFER
HRISTO BOLEV HOUSE-MUSEUM
KOLAROVGRAD
LAJOS KOSSUTH MUSEUM
KOPRIVSHTIŽA
GEORGI BENKOVSKI HOUSE- MUSEUM
TODOR KABLEŠOV HOUSE- MUSEUM
LJUBEN KARAVELOV HOUSE- MUSEUM
OSLEKOV ETHNOGRAPHICAL MUSEUM
KOPRIVŠTICA
DIMČO DEBELJANOV HOUSE- MUSEUM
JAKO DOROSSIEV HOUSE- MUSEUM
NAJDEN GEROV HOUSE-MUSEUM
LOVEČ
VASIL LEVSKI MUSEUM
MIHAJLOVGRAD
HRISTO MIHALJOV HOUSE- MUSEUM
PAZARDŽIK
STANISLAV DOSPEVSKY MUSEUM
HADJI STOIANOVATA HOUSE- MUSEUM
PLOVDIV
BUKURESCHLIEV HOUSE- MUSEUM
RAZLOG
NAKOLAJ PARAPUNOV HOUSE- MUSEUM
SOFIA
DIMITER BLAGOEV MUSEUM
GEORGI DIMITROV MUSEUM
P. K. JAVOROV HOUSE-MUSEUM
NIKOLA VAPTSAROV MUSEUM
IVAN VASOV MUSEUM
SVIŠTOV
HISTORY MUSEUM
VARNA
GEORGI VELČEV HOUSE- MUSEUM
VASOVGRAD (formerly SOPOT)
IVAN VAZOV HOUSE-MUSEUM
VIDIN
MUSEUM OF THE REVOLUTIONARY YOUTH MOVEMENT
ZHERAVNA
TORDAN YOVKOV HOUSE- MUSEUM

CANADA

ARTHABASKA
LAURIER MUSEUM
BRANTFORD
BELL HOMESTEAD
CAMPOBELLO
ROOSEVELT SUMMER HOUSE AND PARK
CARDSTON
C.O. CARD HOME AND MUSEUM
GUELPH
COLONEL JOHN McCREA MUSEUM
HAMILTON
DUNDURN CASTLE
KINGSTON
'BELLEVUE HOUSE' NATIONAL HISTORIC PARK
KITCHENER
WOODSIDE NATIONAL HISTORIC PARK
LAURENTIDE
SIR WILFRED LAURIER HOUSE
LIVERPOOL
SIMEON PERKINS HOUSE
MONTREAL
CHÂTEAU DE RAMEZAY
VILLA MARIA
NIAGARA FALLS
OAK HALL
NIAGARA-ON-THE-LAKE
NAVY HALL
OTTAWA
LAURIER HOUSE
REGINA
DIEFENBAKER HOMESTEAD
SABREVOIS
MUSEUM OF RICHELIEU VALLEY HISTORICAL SOCIETY
ST. GEORGE
ADELAIDE HUNTER HOODLESS HOMESTEAD
SAINT-LIN
LAURIER HOUSE
TADOUSSAC
CHAUVIN HOUSE
TORONTO
COLBORNE LODGE
MACKENZIE HOUSE
WHITEHORSE
MCBRIDE CENTENNIAL MUSEUM

CHINA, P.R.

CHANG SHA (ZHENG ZHOU)
MUSEUM OF THE COMMUNIST PARTY COMMITTEE
OLD NORMAL SCHOOL
JING GANG SHEN
REVOLUTIONARY BASE MUSEUM
KWANCHOW
MUSEUM OF THE INSTITUTE OF THE PEASANT MOVEMENT
NAN CHANG
MUSEUM OF THE NAN CHANG RISING
PEKING
HSU PEI HUNG MUSEUM
SHANGHAI
LU XUN (LU HSUN) MUSEUM
SHAO SHAN
BIRTHPLACE OF MAO TSE TUNG
SHAO SHING
LU HSUN MUSEUM
SIAN (XIAN)
MUSEUM OF HEADQUARTERS OF 8TH ROUTE ARMY
PANPO VILLAGE
YENAN (YAN AN)
MAO'S HOUSE
ZUN YI
MAO TSE TUNG MUSEUM

COLOMBIA

BUCARAMANGA
BOLÍVAR HOUSE-MUSEUM
PERU DE LA CROIX HOUSE- MUSEUM
GARCÍA ROVIRA HOUSE- MUSEUM

CARTAGENA
RAFAEL NUÑEZ HOUSE-MUSEUM

SAN PEDRO ALEJANDRINO
LOCAL MUSEUM

TUNJA
JUAN DE VARGAS HOUSE MUSEUM

CUBA

BAYAMO
CARLOS MANUEL DE CESPEDES BIRTHPLACE

HABANA
JOSÉ MARTI BIRTHPLACE

SANTIAGO DE CUBA
FRANK PAIS BIRTHPLACE

CZECHOSLOVAKIA

ČÁSLAVICE
DR. BEDŘICH VÁKLAV MEMORIAL MUSEUM

ČECHY POD KOSÍŘEM
JOSEF MÁNESA MEMORIAL MUSEUM

DĚDICE U VYŠKOVA
KLEMENT GOTTWALD HOUSE- MUSEUM

DIVÁKY
MEMORIAL MUSEUM TO THE MRŠTÍKŮ BROTHERS

HAVLÍČKOVA BOROVA
KARL HAVLÍCKY BOROVSKY MEMORIAL

HAVLÍČKŮV BROD
KARL HAVLÍCKY BOROVSKY MEMORIAL

HODSLAVICE
FRANTIŠEK PALACKY MEMORIAL

HORNI PLANÁ
ADALBERT STIFTER MEMORIAL

HUDLICE
JOSEF JUNGMANN MEMORIAL

HUSINEC
JAN HUS MEMORIAL

JUR PRI BRATISLAVE
PETRA JILEMNICKÝ MUSEUM

KREČOVICE U SEDLČAN
JOSEF SUK MEMORIAL

LETOHRAD
PETR JILEMNICKÝ MEMORIAL

MALEČ
FRANTIŠEK PALACKÝ AND FRANTIŠEK RIEGER MEMORIAL

MILETÍN
KARL JAROMÍR ERBEN MEMORIAL

NELAHOZEVES
ANTON DVOŘÁK MUSEUM

SOBOTKA
FRA. ŠRÁMEK HOUSE-MUSEUM

STARÁ HUŤ U DOBŘŮŠE
KAREL ČAPEK MEMORIAL MUSEUM

STRAKONICE
FR. L. ČELAKOVSKÝ HOUSE MUSEUM

TŘEBÍČ
DR. BOHUMÍR ŠMERALA MEMORIAL MUSEUM

TŘEBÍZ
V. B. TŘEBIZSKY MEMORIAL MUSEUM

VŠEBOŘICE
ZDEŇKO FIBICH MEMORIAL MUSEUM

VYSOKÁ U PŘIBRAMI
ANTON DVOŘÁK MEMORIAL MUSEUM

ZÁHLINICE
FR. SKOPALÍK MEMORIAL MUSEUM

ŽAMBERK
PROKOP DIVIŠ MEMORIAL MUSEUM

DENMARK

BOVBJERG
JENS SØNDERGAARD MUSEUM

COPENHAGEN
BAKKE HOUSE MUSEUM
WESSEL MUSEUM

FREDENSBORG
OLAF POULSEN MUSEUM

NØRRE LYNDELSE
CARL NEILSEN'S HOUSE

ODENSE
H.C. ANDERSEN'S CHILDHOOD HOME
HANS ANDERSEN'S HOUSE
CARL NIELSEN'S CHILDHOOD HOME

STRUER
STRUER MUSEUM

UDBY
GRUNDTVIG MEMORIAL MUSEUM

FINLAND

HELSINKI
MANNERHEIM MUSEUM

JÄRVENPÄÄ
AINOLA

KUORTANE
KLEMETTI MUSEUM

PORVOO
ALBERT EDELFELT MUSEUM
J. L. RUNEBERG HOUSE-MUSEUM

SAMMATTI
PAIKKARI FARM

UUSIKAARLEPYY
ZACHARIAS TOPELIUS HOUSE- MUSEUM

FRANCE

AJACCIO
NATIONAL MUSEUM OF THE HOUSE OF THE BONAPARTES

AMBOISE
LEONARDO DA VINCI MUSEUM

ARBOIS
MUSEUM OF THE PASTEUR FAMILY HOME

AUXERRE
MUSEUM OF ART AND HISTORY

BOUXWILLER
BOUXWILLER MUSEUM

LA CÔTE-SAINT-ANDRÉ
BERLIOZ MUSEUM

DOLE
PASTEUR MUSEUM

ILLIERS COMBRAY
MARCEL PROUST HOUSE- MUSEUM

LOURDES
BOLY MILL

LYON
AMPÈRE MUSEUM

MAILLANE
FRÉDÉRIC MISTRAL MUSEUM

LE MAS-SOUBEYRAN
DESERT MUSEUM

MONTMORENCY
JEAN-JACQUES ROUSSEAU MUSEUM

NOHANT-VIC
GEORGE SAND HOUSE-MUSEUM

ORNANS
GUSTAVE COURBET'S BIRTHPLACE

PARIS
BALZAC MUSEUM
CLEMENCEAU MUSEUM
EUGÈNE DELACROIX MUSEUM
JEAN-JACQUES HENNER MUSEUM
VICTOR HUGO MUSEUM
GUSTAVE MOREAU MUSEUM
PASTEUR MUSEUM

PAU
BERNADOTTE MUSEUM

LE PETIT-COURONNE
CORNEILLE MUSEUM

PLOMBIÈRES-LES-BAINS
LOUIS FRANÇAIS MUSEUM

ROUEN
CORNEILLE MUSEUM
FLAUBERT MUSEUM

RUEIL-MALMAISON
MALMAISON NATIONAL CHÂTEAU

SACHÉ
BALZAC MUSEUM

SAINT-POINT
CHÂTEAU

SAINT VINCENT- SUR-JARD
PRESIDENT CLEMENCEAU HOUSE-MUSEUM

SÉRIGNAN-DU-COMTAT
HENRI FABRE MUSEUM

SEUILLY-LA-DEVINIÈRE
RABELAIS MUSEUM

TARBES
BIRTHPLACE OF MARSHAL FOCH

TOURS-LA-RICHE
CHÂTEAU DE PLESSIS- LÈS-TOURS

TRÉGUIER
ERNEST RENAN'S BIRTHPLACE

VILLENEUVE-LOUBET
MUSEUM OF THE ART OF COOKERY

GDR

BAD KOSTRITZ
HEINRICH SCHÜTZ MEMORIAL

BAUERBACH
SCHILLERHAUS

BERLIN
JOHANNES R. BECHER HOUSE
ROBERT KOCH MUSEUM

BIRKENWERDER
CLARA ZETKIN MEMORIAL

DRESDEN
MARTIN ANDERSEN NEXÖ MEMORIAL
LEONHARDI MUSEUM
MARCOLINI PALACE
SCHILLER'S COTTAGE

EISENACH
BACH HOUSE
REUTER HOUSE

EISLEBEN
HOUSE WHERE LUTHER DIED
LUTHER'S BIRTHPLACE

FREYBURG
JAHN MUSEUM

GOTHA-SIEBLEBEN
GUSTAV FREYTAG MEMORIAL

GRIMMA
GÖSCHEN HOUSE

HALLE
HÄNDEL HOUSE

HIDDENSEE
GERHART HAUPTMANN MEMORIAL

JENA
GOETHE MEMORIAL
ERNST HAECKEL HOUSE
SCHILLER MEMORIAL

LEIPZIG
ISKRA MEMORIAL
KARL LIEBKNECHT HOUSE

MAGDEBURG
ERICH WEINERT MEMORIAL

MEININGEN
BAUMBACH HOUSE

OSSMANNSTEDT
WIELAND MEMORIAL

POTSDAM
CECILIENHOF PALACE

POTSDAM-BABELSBERG
BRUNO H. BÜRGEL MEMORIAL

REICHENBACH/VOGTLAND
NEUBER MEMORIAL

RENTHENDORF
BREHM MEMORIAL
REUTERSTADT STAVENHAGEN
FRITZ REUTER LITERATURE MUSEUM
SEEBAD HERINGSDORF
MAXIM GORKI MEMORIAL
WEIMAR
GOETHE'S GARDEN HOUSE
LISZT HOUSE
NATIONAL GOETHE MUSEUM
SCHILLER'S HOUSE
WEISSENFELS
HEINRICH SCHÜTZ MEMORIAL
WIEDERAU
CLARA ZETKIN MEMORIAL
WITTENBERG LUTHERSTADT
LUTHER MUSEUM
REGIONAL MUSEUM AND MELANCTHON HOUSE
ZWICKAU
ROBERT SCHUMANN HOUSE

GFR

ALHAUSEN
WEBER'S BIRTHPLACE
ASCHHAUSEN
COUNT VON ZEPPELIN MUSEUM
AUGSBURG
MOZART MEMORIAL
BAMBERG
E.T.A. HOFFMAN HOUSE AND MUSEUM
BAYREUTH
JEAN PAUL ROOM
BERLIN
GEORG KOLBE MUSEUM
TEGEL PALACE
BODENWERDER
BARON MÜNCHHAUSEN MUSEUM
BONN
BEETHOVEN HOUSE - MUSEUM
ERNST MORITZ ARNDT HOUSE MUSEUM
BRAUNSCHWEIG
WILHELM RAABE HOUSE - MEMORIAL
COBURG
EHRENBURG PALACE MUSEUM
DONAUESCHINGEN
COLLECTIONS OF THE PRINCES OF FÜRSTENBERG
DREVENACK
OTTO PANKOK MUSEUM
ESCHERSHAUSEN
RAABE MEMORIAL MUSEUM
GARDING
THEODOR MOMMSEN MEMORIAL
GIESSEN
LIEBIG MUSEUM
GROSS-GERAU
REGIONAL MUSEUM
HAUSEN
BISMARCK'S RESIDENCE
HEIDE
KLAUS GROTH MUSEUM
ISERLOHN
REGIONAL HOUSE
LEINSWEILER
SLEVOGTHOF NEUCASTEL
MARBACH
SCHILLER'S BIRTHPLACE
NEUSES
RÜCKERT MEMORIAL
NÜRNBERG
ALBRECHT DÜRER HOUSE
RATZEBURG
ERNST BARLACH MEMORIAL
REGENSBURG
KEPLER HOUSE MEMORIAL
ROXEL
DROSTE ZU HÜLSHOFF MUSEUM
SEEBÜLL
ADA AND EMIL NOLDE SEEBÜLL FOUNDATION
TRIER
KARL MARX HOUSE
WARBURG
REGIONAL MUSEUM
WETZLAR
LOTTE'S HOUSE

GREAT BRITAIN

ABERDEEN
ABERDEEN ART GALLERY AND MUSEUM
ALLOWAY
BURNS' COTTAGE AND MUSEUM
ALNWICK
ALNWICK CASTLE
AMBLESIDE
RYDAL MOUNT
ARUNDEL
ARUNDEL CASTLE
AYOT ST. LAWRENCE
SHAW'S CORNER
BAKEWELL
CHATSWORTH
BANBURY
SULGRAVE MANOR
BLANTYRE
SCOTTISH NATIONAL MEMORIAL TO DAVID LIVINGSTONE
BOLTON
HALL I'TH'WOOD MUSEUM
BOSTON
BOSTON MUSEUM
BRIDGWATER
ADMIRAL BLAKE MUSEUM
BRIGHTON
ROYAL PAVILION
BRISTOL
CHATTERTON HOUSE
BURWASH
BATEMAN'S, RUDYARD KIPLING'S HOME
CHALFONT ST. GILES
MILTON'S COTTAGE
CHAWTON
JANE AUSTEN'S HOME
CHIPPENHAM
CORSHAM COURT
COCKERMOUTH
WORDSWORTH HOUSE
CONISTON
ART GALLERY MUSEUM
DEDHAM
CASTLE HOUSE
DUMFRIES
FOLK MATERIAL COLLECTION
DUNFERMLINE
ANDREW CARNEGIE BIRTHPLACE MEMORIAL
EAST COWES
OSBORNE HOUSE
ECCLEFECHAN
CARLYLE'S BIRTHPLACE
EDINBURGH
CANONGATE TOLBOOTH
PALACE OF HOLYROOD HOUSE
GRASMERE
DOVE COTTAGE
GUERNSEY
HAUTEVILLE HOUSE
HALSTEAD
BLUE BRIDGE HOUSE
HATFIELD
HATFIELD HOUSE
HAWORTH
BRONTE PARSONAGE MUSEUM
HEREFORD
KENTCHURCH COURT
HIGH WYCOMBE
DISRAELI MUSEUM
HULL
WILBERFORCE HOUSE
KENDAL
SIZERGH CASTLE
KIRRIMUIR
BARRIE'S BIRTHPLACE
LECHLADE
KELMSCOTT MANOR
LICHFIELD
DR. JOHNSON'S BIRTHPLACE
LONDON
APSLEY HOUSE
CARLYLE'S HOUSE
DARWIN MUSEUM
DICKENS HOUSE
GUNNERSBURY PARK MUSEUM
HOGARTH'S HOUSE
DR. JOHNSON'S HOUSE
KEATS HOUSE AND MUSEUM
KENSINGTON PALACE
LEIGHTON HOUSE ART GALLERY AND MUSEUM
SIR JOHN SOANE'S MUSEUM
WILLIAM MORRIS GALLERY
"WOODLANDS" LOCAL HISTORY CENTRE AND ART GALLERY
MELROSE
ABBOTSFORD HOUSE
NEAR SAWREY
HILL TOP
NETHER STOWEY
COLERIDGE COTTAGE
NOTTINGHAM
NEWSTEAD ABBEY
PLYMOUTH
BUCKLAND ABBEY
PORTSMOUTH
DICKENS' BIRTHPLACE MUSEUM
SCARBOROUGH
SCARBOROUGH MUSEUM OF NATURAL HISTORY
STAFFORD
IZAAK WALTON COTTAGE
STOKE-ON-TRENT
ARNOLD BENNETT MUSEUM
STRATFORD- UPON-AVON
HARVARD HOUSE
MARY ARDEN'S HOUSE
SHAKESPEARE'S BIRTHPLACE
SUDBURY
GAINSBOROUGH'S HOUSE
SULGRAVE
SULGRAVE MANOR
TARBOLTON
BACHELORS CLUB
WESTERHAM
CHARTWELL
QUEBEC HOUSE
WINSLOW
CLAYDON HOUSE
WOODSTOCK
BLENHEIM PALACE

GREECE

IOANNINA
NISI MUSEUM OF THE PREREVOLUTIONARY PERIOD

HUNGARY

BADACSONY
IRODALMI MUSEUM
KISKŐRÖS
PETŐFI MEMORIAL MUSEUM

INDIA

KANTHALPARA
RISHI BANKIM MUSEUM AND LIBRARY
NEW DELHI
INDIAN WAR MEMORIAL MUSEUM

ITALY

AGRIGENTO
BIRTHPLACE OF PIRANDELLO
ANACAPRI
VILLA SAN MICHELE
AREZZO
VASARI'S HOUSE
ARQUA PETRARCA
PETRARCH'S HOUSE
ASTI
ALFIERI MUSEUM
BORGO
ARTURO TOSCANINI'S BIRTHPLACE
CAPRERA
CASA BIANCA
CAPRESE
MICHELANGELO MUSEUM
CATANIA
BELLINI MUSEUM
CERTALDO
MUSEUM OF BOCCACCIO
FERRARA
ARIOSTO'S HOUSE
PALAZZINA MARFISA D'ESTE
GARDONE RIVIERA
VITTORIALE ESTATE
GENOA
MAZZINI HOUSE
MUSEUM OF THE RISORGIMENTO
LECCO
VILLA DI ALESSANDRO MANZONI
LE RONCOLE-VERDI
HOUSE OF GIUSEPPE VERDI
MILAN
NATIONAL CENTRE OF MANZONI STUDIES
PESARO
ROSSINI'S HOUSE
PESCARA
HOUSE OF GABRIELE D'ANNUNZIO
PIEVE DI CADORE
MUSEUM
PISA
DOMUS GALILEIANA
DOMUS MAZZINIANA
PORTOFERRAIO
NAPOLEONIC MUSEUM
POSSAGNO
CANOVA MUSEUM
RIESE PIO X
S. PIO X HOUSE AND MUSEUM
ROME
JOHN KEATS' HOUSE
PIRANDELLO'S HOUSE
SAN MAURO PASCOLI
BIRTHPLACE OF G. PASCOLI
URBINO
RAPHAËL'S HOUSE
VENICE
CASA GOLDONI

MALTA

MDINA
THE NORMAN HOUSE
VITTORIOSA
INQUISITOR'S PALACE

MAURITIUS

SOUILLAC
R. E. HART MUSEUM

MEXICO

CUAUTLA
MORELOS HOUSE
DOLORES HIDALGO
CASA DE HIDALGO
MEXICO CITY
V. CARRANZA HOUSE AND MUSEUM OF THE REVOLUTION
OAXACA
JUÁREZ HOUSE
SAN CRISTOBAL ECATEPEC
CASA DE MORELOS

NETHERLANDS

AMSTERDAM
FERDINAND DOMELA NIEUWENHUIS MUSEUM
RIJNSBURG
SPINOZA HOUSE
ZAANDAM
CZAR PETER'S COTTAGE

NORWAY

OSLO
"AMUNDSEN"

PARAGUAY

ASUNCION
MUSEUM OF THE HOUSE WHERE INDEPENDENCE WAS BORN

PHILIPPINES

BATANGAS
LEON APACIBLE MUSEUM AND LIBRARY
TALAGA MABINI SHRINE
MANILA
PANDACAN MABINI SHRINE

POLAND

JAGNIĄTKÓW
GERHARDT HAUPTMANN HOUSE-MUSEUM
KRAKÓW
JAN MATEJKO HOUSE MUSEUM
KRZESLAWICE
JAN MATEJKO MUSEUM
NAŁĘCZOW
STEFAN ŻEROMSKI MUSEUM
TORUŃ
MIKOŁAJ KOPERNIKI (COPERNICUS) MUSEUM

ROMANIA

AUREL VLAICU
AUREL VLAICU MUSEUM
AVRAM IANCU
AVRAM IANCU MUSEUM
BUCHAREST
THEODOR AMAN MUSEUM
GEORGE ENESCU MUSEUM
CÎMPINA
HASCLEU MUSEUM
VĂLENII DE MUNTE
NICOLAE IORGA MUSEUM
VÎNĂTORI
MIHAIL SADOVEANU MUSEUM
VLADIMIR
TUDOR VLADIMIRESCU MUSEUM

SOUTH AFRICA, REPUBLIC OF

IRENE
GENERAL SMUTS MUSEUM
PRETORIA
KRUGER HOUSE MUSEUM
MELROSE HOUSE
STELLENBOSCH
D. F. MALAN MUSEUM

SPAIN

ALCALA DE HENARES
BIRTHPLACE OF CERVANTES
AVILA
BIRTHPLACE OF ST. TERESA DE JESUS
AZPEITIA
GÁRATE HOUSE-MUSEUM
BARCELONA
GAUDI HOUSE MUSEUM
PALACIO DE PEDRALBES
BURGOS
ISLA PALACE
JAVIER
CASTILLO
LOYOLA
BIRTHPLACE OF SAN IGNACIO
MADRID
HOUSE OF LOPE DE VEGA
MADRIGAL DE LAS ALTAS TORRES
BIRTHPLACE OF ISABEL LA CATOLICA
SALAMANCA
UNAMUNO HOUSE-MUSEUM
SANTANDER
MENÉNDEZ PELAYO HOUSE- MUSEUM
SEGOVIA
ANTONIO MACHADO HOUSE- MUSEUM
SEVILLE
HOUSE OF THE DUEÑAS
TELDE
LEON Y CASTILLO HOUSE MUSEUM
TOLEDO
EL GRECO MUSEUM
VALLADOLID
HOUSE OF CERVANTES
VILLANUEVA Y GELTRU
VICTOR BALAGUER MUSEUM
ZUMARRAGA
LEGAZPI HOUSE MUSEUM

SWEDEN

HAMMARBY
LINNAEUS MUSEUM
MÅRBACKA
THE MANOR HOUSE
RANSÄTER
GEIJERS HOUSE-MUSEUM

SWITZERLAND

ASCONA
MARIANNE WEREFKIN MUSEUM
MÔTIERS
JEAN-JACQUES ROUSSEAU MUSEUM
SALENSTEIN
NAPOLEON MUSEUM

USSR

ALTAN-BULAG
D. SUHE-BATOR HOUSE MUSEUM
ASHAGA-STAL
SULEIMAN STAL HOUSE- MUSEUM
GORI
STALIN MUSEUM
GORKI
KASHIRIK MUSEUM

ILYICHOVO
LENIN HOUSE-MUSEUM
LENINGRAD
HOUSE-MUSEUM OF ACADEMICIAN I. P. PAVLOV
S. M. KIROV MUSEUM
LENIN MEMORIAL APARTMENTS
D. I. MENDELEYEV HOUSE- MUSEUM
D. I. MENDELEYEV MUSEUM
MELIKHOVASKYA
HOUSE MUSEUM OF A. P. CHEKHOV
MINSK
MUSEUM OF THE FIRST CONGRESS OF THE RUSSIAN SOCIAL DEMOCRATIC PARTY
MOSCOW
A. P. CHEKHOV HOUSE-MUSEUM
KOLOMENSKOYE ESTATE MUSEUM
KRASNAYA PRESNYA MUSEUM
MUSEUM OF DECORATIVE ARTS
A. N. SCRIABIN MUSEUM
STATE V. V. MAYAKOVSKI LIBRARY AND MUSEUM
K. A. TIMIRYAZEV HOUSE- MUSEUM
LEO TOLSTOY HOUSE MUSEUM
VICTOR VASNETSOV HOUSE- MUSEUM
PODOLSK
V. I. LENIN HOUSE-MUSEUM
LENIN MUSEUM
SHUSHENSKOYE
V. I. LENIN MUSEUM
SPASSKOYE-LUTOVINOVO
TURGENEV ESTATE-MUSEUM
TAGANROG
A. P. CHEKHOV HOUSE-MUSEUM
TBILISI
GEORGIAN ART MUSEUM
UFA
V. I. LENIN HOUSE-MUSEUM
ULYANOVSK
V. I. LENIN HOUSE-MUSEUM
YALTA
A. P. CHEKHOV MUSEUM
YASNAYA POLYANA
TOLSTOY MUSEUM

UNITED STATES

ABILENE
DWIGHT D. EISENHOWER CENTER
ALBANY
SCHUYLER MANSION
ALBUQUERQUE
ERNIE PYLE MEMORIAL
ALDIE
OAK HILL
ALEXANDRIA
ROBERT E. LEE'S BOYHOOD HOME
MUSEUM OF HISTORIC ALEXANDRIA FOUNDATION
AMESBURY
JOHN GREENLEAF WHITTIER HOME
ANNAPOLIS
CHASE-LLOYD HOUSE
ASHEVILLE
BILTMORE HOUSE
THOMAS WOLFE MEMORIAL
ASHLAND
SCOTCHTOWN
AUBURN
SEWARD HOUSE
AUSTIN
ELISABET NEY MUSEUM
FRENCH LEGATION
BALTIMORE
EDGAR ALLAN POE HOUSE
STAR-SPANGLED BANNER FLAG HOUSE AND MUSEUM
BAR HARBOR
SONOGEE MANSION
BARRANQUITOS
LUIS MUÑOZ RIVERA LIBRARY AND MUSEUM
BILOXI
JEFFERSON DAVIS SHRINE
BLACKSBURG
SMITHFIELD PLANTATION
BLUNT
MENTOR GRAHAM MUSEUM
BOSTON
PAUL REVERE HOUSE
BROOKLINE
JOHN F. KENNEDY NATIONAL HISTORIC SITE
BROOKNEAL
RED HILL
BROWNS VALLEY
SAM BROWN LOG HOUSE
BUFFALO
THEODORE ROOSEVELT INAUGURATION NATIONAL HISTORIC SITE
BYRDSTOWN
CORDELL HULL BIRTHPLACE MEMORIAL
CALDWELL
GROVER CLEVELAND BIRTHPLACE
CANANDAIGUA
GRANGER HOMESTEAD AND CARRIAGE MUSEUM
CHARLES CITY
BERKELEY PLANTATION
SHERWOOD FOREST
SHIRLEY PLANTATION
CHARLESTON
THOMAS ELFE WORKSHOP
CHARLOTTE COUNTY
PATRICK HENRY MEMORIAL FOUNDATION
CHARLOTTESVILLE
ASH LAWN
MONTICELLO
CHICAGO
LORADO TAFT MIDWAY STUDIOS
CINCINNATI
WILLIAM HOWARD TAFT NATIONAL HISTORIC SITE
CODY
BUFFALO BILL HISTORICAL CENTER
COHOES
VAN SCHAICK MANSION
COLUMBIA
HISTORIC COLUMBIA FOUNDATION, INC.
SOUTH CAROLINA GOVERNOR'S MANSION
SOUTH CAROLINA STATE HISTORICAL MUSEUM
WOODROW WILSON HOME
JAMES K. POLK ANCESTRAL HOME
CONCORD
THE OLD MANSE
ORCHARD HOUSE
CONDORD
RALPH WALDO EMERSON MEMORIAL MUSEUM
CONCORD
FRANKLIN PIERCE HOUSE
CORNISH
SAINT-GAUDENS NATIONAL HISTORICAL SITE
CUMBERLAND
GEORGE WASHINGTON'S HEADQUARTERS
DE BARY
DE BARY HALL STATE MUSEUM
DEERFIELD
MEMORIAL HALL COLONIAL MUSEUM
DEFIANCE
DANIEL BOONE HOME
DENISON
EISENHOWER BIRTHPLACE STATE PARK
DETROIT
U. S. GRANT HOUSE
DODGE CITY
HARDESTY HOUSE
DRESDEN
INGERSOLL MEMORIAL HOUSE
DURHAM
DUKE HOMESTEAD
EAST HADDAN
GILLETTE CASTLE
EAST HAMPTON
'HOME, SWEET HOME' HOUSE
EASTON
GEORGE TAYLOR HOME
EDENTON
JAMES IREDELL HOUSE
ELLENTON
GAMBLE MANSION HISTORIC MEMORIAL
ELLIS
BOYHOOD HOME OF WALTER P. CHRYSLER
EUREKA SPRINGS
HATCHET HALL MUSEUM
FAIRFIELD
MOODY-BRADLEY HOUSE
PRESIDENT CHESTER A. ARTHUR BIRTHPLACE
FORT LYON
KIT CARSON MEMORIAL CHAPEL
FREDERICKSBURG
FREDERICKSBURG NATIONAL MILITARY PARK
JAMES MONROE MUSEUM AND MEMORIAL LIBRARY
RISING SUN TAVERN
MARY WASHINGTON HOUSE
FREMONT
RUTHERFORD B. HAYES LIBRARY AND MUSEUM
GALENA
ULYSSES S. GRANT HOME STATE MEMORIAL
GENEVA
LIMBERLOST STATE MEMORIAL
GLEN ELLEN
JACK LONDON STATE HISTORIC PARK
GREENEVILLE
ANDREW JOHNSON NATIONAL HISTORIC SITE
GREENFIELD
JAMES WHITCOMB RILEY OLD HOME
GREENSBORO
MAGNOLIA GROVE HOBSON MEMORIAL SHRINE
GREENWICH
PUTNAM COTTAGE
HANNIBAL
MARK TWAIN BOYHOOD HOME
HARBOR SPRINGS
CHIEF ANDREW J. BLACKBIRD MUSEUM
HARDY
WASHINGTON T. BOOKER NATIONAL MONUMENT
HARTFORD
MARK TWAIN MEMORIAL
HAVERHILL
JOHN GREENLEAF WHITTIER HOMESTEAD
HEAVENER
PETER CONSER HOUSE
HERMITAGE
LADIES HERMITAGE ASSOCIATION
HILLSBORO
FRANKLIN PIERCE HOMESTEAD
HODGENVILLE
ABRAHAM LINCOLN BIRTHPLACE NATIONAL HISTORIC SITE
HONOLULU
QUEEN EMMA SUMMER PALACE
HUNTINGTON
WALT WHITMAN HOUSE
HUNTSVILLE
SAM HOUSTON MEMORIAL MUSEUM
HYDE PARK
FRANKLIN D. ROOSEVELT NATIONAL HISTORIC SITE
VANDERBILT MANSION NATIONAL HISTORIC SITE
INDIANAPOLIS
PRESIDENT BENJAMIN HARRISON MEMORIAL HOME
INDIAN SPRINGS
INDIAN CHIEF WILLIAM MCINTOSH HOME
IRONVILLE
PENFIELD HOMESTEAD MUSEUM
JACKSON
CASEY JONES' HOME AND RAILROAD MUSEUM
JAMAICA
KING MANOR HOUSE
JEKYLL ISLAND
JEKYLL ISLAND MUSEUM (ROCKEFELLER COTTAGE)
JOHNSON CITY
LYNDON B. JOHNSON NATIONAL HISTORIC SITE
JOHNSTOWN
JOHNSON HALL
KATONAH
JOHN JAY HOUSE
KEY WEST
HEMINGWAY HOME AND MUSEUM

KNOXVILLE
GOVERNOR WILLIAM BLOUNT MANSION

KODIAK
KODIAK HISTORICAL SOCIETY MUSEUM

LACLEDE
GENERAL JOHN J. PERSHING BOYHOOD HOME MEMORIAL SHRINE

LAKE PLACID
JOHN BROWN FARM

LAMAR
HARRY S. TRUMAN BIRTHPLACE

LANCASTER
SHERMAN HOUSE STATE MEMORIAL
WHEATLAND

LANGTRY
JUDGE ROY BEAN VISITOR CENTER

LEWISTOWN
MUSEUM OF MIFFLIN COUNTY HISTORICAL SOCIETY

LEXINGTON
HENRY CLAY MEMORIAL FOUNDATION
STONEWALL JACKSON MEMORIAL
LEE CHAPEL

LINCOLN
FAIRVIEW MUSEUM
NEBRASKA STATEHOOD MEMORIAL

LITTLE FALLS
CHARLES A. LINDBERGH HOUSE
HERKIMER HOME

LOS ANGELES
LUMMIS HOME: EL ALISAL

LOWELL
LOWELL ART ASSOCIATION

LUBEC
ROOSEVELT CAMPOBELLO INTERNATIONAL PARK COMMISSION

LUCAS
LOUIS BROMFIELD MALABAR FARM FOUNDATION

MARSHFIELD
HISTORIC WINSLOW HOUSE

McCLELLANVILLE
HAMPTON PLANTATION

MCCOOK
GEORGE W. NORRIS HOME

MEDORA
THEODORE ROOSEVELT NATIONAL MEMORIAL PARK, VISITOR CENTER

MENTOR
LAKE COUNTY HISTORICAL SOCIETY MUSEUM

MILAN
THOMAS EDISON BIRTHPLACE MUSEUM

MISSION
WILLIAM JENNINGS BRYAN HOUSE

MONTEREY
ROBERT LOUIS STEVENSON HOUSE

MONTGOMERY
FIRST WHITE HOUSE OF THE CONFEDERACY

MORRISTOWN
DAVID CROCKETT TAVERN MUSEUM

MORRISVILLE
PENNSBURY MANOR

MOUNT MCGREGOR
GRANT COTTAGE

MOUNT VERNON
MOUNT VERNON
POPE-LEIGHEY HOUSE

MUSKOGEE
THOMAS-FOREMAN HOUSE

NANTUCKET
MARIA MITCHELL BIRTHPLACE

NEWBERG
MINTHORN HOUSE

NEWBURGH
JONATHAN HASBROUCK HOUSE

NEW HARMONY
THE OLD FAUNTLEROY HOUSE

NEWPORT
THE BREAKERS
MARBLE HOUSE
WANTON-LYMAN-HAZARD HOUSE

NEW YORK
CONFERENCE HOUSE
THE GARIBALDI AND MEUCCI MEMORIAL MUSEUM
THEODORE ROOSEVELT BIRTHPLACE NATIONAL HISTORIC SITE

NILES
MUSEUM OF NATIONAL MCKINLEY BIRTHPLACE MEMORIAL ASSOCIATION

NORTHAMPTON
ISAAC DAMON HOUSE

NORTH BENNINGTON
GOVERNOR MCCULLOUGH MANSION

NORTHFIELD
PRESIDENT CHESTER A. ARTHUR BIRTHPLACE

NORTH KINGSTON
CASEY FARM

NORTH OXFORD
CLARA BARTON BIRTHPLACE

NORTHUMBERLAND
JOSEPH PRIESTLEY HOUSE

OREGON CITY
CAPTAIN JOHN C. AINSWORTH HOUSE
MCLOUGHLIN HOUSE

OSAWATOMIE
JOHN BROWN MUSEUM

OYSTER BAY, L.I.
SAGAMORE HILL NATIONAL HISTORIC SITE

PACIFICA
SANCHEZ ADOBE

PALMYRA
JOSEPH SMITH HOME

PELLA
PELLA HISTORICAL SITE

PETALUMA
PETALUMA ADOBE STATE HISTORIC PARK

PINEVILLE
JAMES K. POLK BIRTHPLACE STATE HISTORIC SITE

PLYMOUTH
CALVIN COOLIDGE HOMESTEAD
CALVIN COOLIDGE BIRTHPLACE

POINT PLEASANT
GRANT'S BIRTHPLACE STATE MEMORIAL

PORTAGE
OLD INDIAN AGENCY HOUSE

PROVIDENCE
GOVERNOR STEPHEN HOPKINS HOUSE

QUARRYVILLE
ROBERT FULTON BIRTHPLACE

QUINCY
JOHN ADAMS BIRTHPLACE
ADAMS NATIONAL HISTORICAL SITE

RALEIGH
ANDREW JOHNSON MEMORIAL COMMISSION

REMSEN
BARON VON STEUBEN MEMORIAL

RICHMOND
WHITE HALL STATE SHRINE
JOHN MARSHALL HOUSE
MUSEUM OF THE CONFEDERACY

RIPLEY
RANKIN HOUSE STATE MEMORIAL

ROCHESTER
INTERNATIONAL MUSEUM OF PHOTOGRAPHY

RUTHERFORD
DAVID CROCKETT CABIN

SACRAMENTO
GOVERNORS' MANSION

ST. FRANCISVILLE
AUDUBON MEMORIAL STATE PARK

ST. JOSEPH
JESSE JAMES HOUSE MUSEUM

SALEM
WILLIAM JENNINGS BRYAN MUSEUM
HOUSE OF THE SEVEN GABLES
THE WITCH HOUSE

SALLISAW
SEQUOYAH'S LOG CABIN

SALT LAKE CITY
BEEHIVE HOUSE
LION HOUSE

SAN MARCOS
GENERAL EDWARD BURLESON HOUSE

SAN SIMEON
HEARST SAN SIMEON STATE HISTORICAL MONUMENT

SARANAC LAKE
STEVENSON COTTAGE

SARATOGA SPRINGS
GRANT COTTAGE

SAULT STE. MARIE
THE SCHOOLCRAFT INDIAN AGENCY HOUSE

SCHAGHTICOKE
KNICKERBOCKER HISTORICAL SOCIETY MUSEUM

SCHUYLERVILLE
GENERAL PHILIP SCHUYLER HOUSE

SMYRNA
MUSEUM OF SAM DAVIS MEMORIAL ASSOCIATION

SOUTH BERWICK
SARAH ORNE JEWETT MEMORIAL

SOUTH HAVEN
DR. LIBERTY HYDE BAILEY MEMORIAL MUSEUM

SPILLVILLE
BILY CLOCK EXHIBIT

SPRINGFIELD
LINCOLN HOME STATE MEMORIAL

STAFFORD
JUSTIN SMITH MORRILL HOMESTEAD

STANFORD
WILLIAM WHITLEY STATE PARK AND SHRINE

STAUNTON
WOODROW WILSON BIRTHPLACE

STOCKBRIDGE
CHESTERWOOD
NAUMKEAG GARDENS

STONEWALL
LYNDON B. JOHNSON NATIONAL HISTORIC SITE

STOUTSVILLE
MARK TWAIN BIRTHPLACE MEMORIAL SHRINE

STRATFORD
STRATFORD HALL

SURRY
ROLFE-WARREN HOUSE

SWAMPSCOTT
MARY BAKER EDDY HISTORIC HOUSE

TAOS
KIT CARSON MEMORIAL FOUNDATION
D. H. LAWRENCE RANCH

TARRYTOWN
LYNDHURST

TERRE HAUTE
EUGENE V. DEBS FOUNDATION

THOMASTON
MONTPELIER

TUSCUMBIA
IVY GREEN

VANCOUVER
ULYSSES S. GRANT MUSEUM

VICTOR
LOWELL THOMAS BOYHOOD HOME

WARM SPRINGS
FRANKLIN D. ROOSEVELT WARM SPRINGS MEMORIAL COMMISSION

WASHINGTON
FORD'S THEATRE AND LINCOLN MUSEUM
THE HOUSE WHERE LINCOLN DIED
WHITE HOUSE
WOODROW WILSON HOUSE
DAVID BRADFORD HOUSE
BARRINGTON

WASHINGTON'S BIRTHPLACE
GEORGE WASHINGTON BIRTHPLACE NATIONAL MONUMENT

WEAVERVILLE
ZEBULON B. VANCE BIRTHPLACE

WEST BRANCH
HERBERT HOOVER PRESIDENTIAL LIBRARY

WEST ORANGE
EDISON NATIONAL HISTORIC SITE

WEST PARK
SLABSIDES

WETHERSFIELD
JOSEPH WEBB HOUSE
WHEATON
ROBERT R. MCCORMICK MUSEUM
WINSTON-SALEM
REYNOLDA HOUSE
WOBURN
MUSEUM OF RUMFORD HISTORICAL ASSOCIATION
WOODSTOCK
HENRY C. BOWEN HOUSE

VENEZUELA

CARACAS
ARTURO MICHELENA MUSEUM

YUGOSLAVIA

TITOVO UŽICE
MUSEUM OF THE INSURRECTION OF 1941

Religious history, magic, superstition, Masonry, fraternities

ARGENTINA

BUENOS AIRES
JEWISH MUSEUM
CORRIENTES
FATHER JOSÉ DE LA QUINTANA MUSEUM
JESUS MARIA
JESUIT MUSEUM

AUSTRALIA

BROKEN HILL
AFGHAN MOSQUE

AUSTRIA

EISENSTADT
BURGENLAND MUSEUM
FRESACH
EVANGELICAL DIOCESAN MUSEUM
MELK
BENEDICTINE ABBEY COLLECTION
VIENNA
FRANCISCAN MONASTERY MUSEUM
JEWISH MUSEUM
MECHINARIST MUSEUM

BARBADOS

BARBADOS
BARBADOS MUSEUM

BELGIUM

BRUGES
BÉGUINE'S HOUSE
BRUSSELS
THE OLD BÉGUINAGE AT ANDERLECHT

BRAZIL

CAMPINAS
ARCHDIOCESAN MUSEUM
RIO DE JANEIRO
MUSEUM OF BLACK MAGIC
MUSEUM OF THE BRAZILIAN HISTORICAL AND GEOGRAPHICAL INSTITUTE
MUSEUM OF THE ORDER OF ST. FRANCIS
SÃO MIGUEL
MUSEUM OF THE JESUIT MISSIONS

BULGARIA

BĂCKOV
MUSEUM OF THE MONASTERY
SAMOKOV
SAMOKOV MOSQUE (BAJRAKLI DŽAMIJA)
SOFIA
BOYANA CHURCH NATIONAL MUSEUM
NATIONAL MUSEUM OF ECCLESIASTICAL HISTORY AND ARCHAEOLOGY

BURMA

RANGOON
INTERNATIONAL INSTITUTE OF ADVANCED BUDDHIC STUDIES MUSEUM

CANADA

BOTHWELL
FAIRFIELD MUSEUM
CARAQUET
ACADIAN MUSEUM
CASTLEGAR
CASTLEGAR AND DISTRICT MUSEUM
CAUGHNAWAGA
KATERI TEKAKWITHA MUSEUM
CHETICAMP
ACADIAN MUSEUM
EDMONTON
GEORGE McDOUGALL MUSEUM AND SHRINE
MONCTON
FREE MEETING HOUSE
UNIVERSITY OF MONCTON MUSEUM
MONTREAL
MARGUERITE BOURGEOYS MUSEUM
DOCUMENTATION CENTRE OF SAINT-JOSEPH ORATORY
ST. ALBERT
FATHER LACOMBE MUSEUM
SAINT BONIFACE
SAINT BONIFACE MUSEUM
SAINTE- ANNE-DE-DEAUPRÉ
HISTORICAL MUSEUM AND ART GALLERY
SHARON
TEMPLE OF PEACE

CHINA, P.R.

PEKING
TEMPLE OF THE SOURCE OF THE LAW
QU FU
TEMPLE OF CONFUCIUS

COLOMBIA

CALI
MUSEUM OF THE FRANCISCAN FATHERS
DUITAMA
MUSEUM OF RELIGIOUS ART

CYPRUS

NICOSIA
TEKKÉ OF THE MEVLEVI DERVISHES

CZECHOSLOVAKIA

HUSINEC
JAN HUS MEMORIAL
KOMÁRNO
MUSEUM OF RELIGIOUS ART
NÁMĚŠŤ NA HANÉ
REGIONAL MUSEUM
PRAGUE
HUSSITE COLLECTION
JEWISH MUSEUM
TÁBOR
MUSEUM OF THE HUSSITE REVOLT
ŽLUTICE
MUSEUM OF THE HUSSITE REVOLT

DENMARK

COPENHAGEN
MUSEUM OF THE MOSAIC CONGREGATION
RANDERS
MUSEUM OF CULTURAL HISTORY
STRUER
STRUER MUSEUM

FINLAND

JOKIOINEN
PARSONAGE MUSEUM
KUOPIO
MUSEUM OF THE ORTHODOX CHURCH

FRANCE

ANGERS
CATHEDRAL TREASURY
CAVAILLON
SYNAGOGUE
CLUNY
FLOUR-MERCHANT'S MUSEUM
OCHIER MUSEUM
CONQUES
CONQUES ABBEY MUSEUM
ÉPINAL
INTERNATIONAL MUSEUM OF RELIGIOUS IMAGES
ISSOUDUN
MISSION MUSEUM
LOURDES
BERNADETTE MUSEUM
BOLY MILL
MUSEUM OF OUR LADY OF LOURDES
MAGNY-LES-HAMEAUX
NATIONAL MUSEUM OF THE GRANGES DE PORT-ROYAL
MARSAC-EN-LIVRADOIS
CHAPEL-MUSEUM OF THE WHITE PENITENTS
MARSEILLE
MUSEUM OF THE BLACK PENITENTS
MARTIGUES
MUSEUM OF OLD MARTIGUES
MEAUX
BOSSUET MUSEUM

NARBONNE

MUSEUM OF NARBONNE PREHISTORY AND ANTIQUITIES

NÎMES

MUSEUM OF OLD NÎMES

NOYON

CALVIN MUSEUM
NOYON REGIONAL MUSEUM

PARIS

MUSEUM OF THE BIBLE AND THE HOLY LAND
MUSEUM OF THE HISTORY OF FRENCH PROTESTANTISM
TREASURY OF NOTRE DAME

POËT-LAVAL

MUSEUM OF PROTESTANTISM IN THE DAUPHINÉ

POITIERS

HYPOGEUM OF THE DUNES
MUSEUM OF THE BAPTISTRY OF ST. JOHN

PORT-ROYAL DES CHAMPS

LOCAL MUSEUM

LE PUY-EN-VELAY

CATHEDRAL OF NOTRE DAME TREASURY

LA ROCHELLE

PROTESTANT MUSEUM

SAINT- PIERRE-DE-CHARTREUSE

LA CORRERIE CHARTERHOUSE MUSEUM

SAINT- SYMPHORIEN-SUR-COISE

COLIN MUSEUM
LA NEYLIÈRE OCEANIC MUSEUM

TOURS-LA-RICHE

CHÂTEAU DE PLESSIS- LÈS-TOURS

VIENNE

MUSEUM OF CHRISTIAN ART

GDR

ALLSTEDT

THOMAS MÜNTZER MEMORIAL

BERLIN

HUGUENOT MUSEUM

DÖMITZ

REGIONAL MUSEUM

EISENACH

LUTHER HOUSE

EISLEBEN

HOUSE WHERE LUTHER DIED
LUTHER'S BIRTHPLACE

GEISA

REGIONAL MUSEUM

GEORGENTHAL

GEORGENTHAL REGIONAL MUSEUM

GRÖBZIG

LOCAL COLLECTION

HALBERSTADT

GLEIN HOUSE

LÜBBENAU

LÜBBENAU MUSEUM IN THE SPREEWALD

OSTERWIECK

REGIONAL MUSEUM

WITTENBERG LUTHERSTADT

LUTHER MUSEUM
REGIONAL MUSEUM AND MELANCTHON HOUSE

GFR

ALT-FRESENBURG

MENNONITE AND MENNO SIMONS MEMORIAL

ALTÖTTING

MUNICIPAL MUSEUM OF REGIONAL LIFE

BAYREUTH

GERMAN MUSEUM OF FREEMASONRY

BERLIN

MUSEUM OF FREEMASONRY

BEURON

BIBLE MUSEUM

BRETTEN

MELANCTHON MUSEUM

COBURG

MUNICIPAL ART COLLECTIONS

DETMOLD

PALACE OF THE PRINCES OF LIPPE

HILTRUP

COLLECTIONS OF THE HILTRUP MISSION HOUSE
COLLECTIONS OF THE HOUSE OF MISSIONARY NUNS

LIMBURG (LAHN)

MISSION MUSEUM

MARBURG

UNIVERSITY COLLECTION OF MATERIAL RELATING TO RELIGION

OELDE

GÖTZ ARCHIVES

REKEN

MUSEUM IN THE OLD CHURCH

ST. OTTILIEN

MISSION MUSEUM

ST. WENDEL

ETHNOLOGICAL COLLECTION OF THE STEYL MISSIONARIES

TRIER

CATHEDRAL AND DIOCESAN MUSEUM
CATHEDRAL TRESURY

WALLDÜRN

REGIONAL AND PILGRIMAGES MUSEUM

WEIL DER STADT

KEPLER MUSEUM

WOLFHAGEN

REGIONAL MUSEUM

WUPPERTAL

MISSION MUSEUM

GREAT BRITAIN

BEDFORD

BUNYAN COLLECTION
BUNYAN MEETING LIBRARY AND MUSEUM
ELSTOW MOOT HALL

DUNBLANE

DUNBLANE CATHEDRAL MUSEUM

DUNDEE

ST. MARY'S TOWER

DURHAM

DORMITORY MUSEUM

LINDISFARNE

LINDISFARNE PRIORY

LONDON

CUMING MUSEUM
JEWISH MUSEUM
WESLEY'S HOUSE AND MUSEUM

LOOE

THE CORNISH MUSEUM

MEIGLE

MEIGLE MUSEUM

SCUNTHORPE

BOROUGH MUSEUM AND ART GALLERY

SHERBORNE

SHERBORNE MUSEUM

TALGARTH

HYWEL HARRIS MUSEUM

WHITHORN

WHITHORN PRIORY MUSEUM

GREECE

AIGION

MONASTERY OF THE TAXIARCHS

ALMYROS

MONASTERY OF THE PANAGIA XENIA

HUNGARY

BUDAPEST

GÜL BABA'S TOMB
JEWISH HISTORY COLLECTIONS
MEDIEVAL JEWISH PRAYER HOUSE
PASTOR JÁNOS MEMORIAL MUSEUM

PANNONHALMA

ECCLESIASTICAL MUSEUM

INDIA

NEW DELHI

TIBET HOUSE MUSEUM

IRELAND

CLONFERT

CLONFERT MUSEUM

MAYNOOTH

MUSEUM OF ECCLESIOLOGY AND PHYSICS

ISRAEL

BAR'AM

LOCAL MUSEUM

BEIT ALPHA

LOCAL MUSEUM

BEIT SHEARIM

LOCAL MUSEUM

JERUSALEM

SHRINE OF THE BOOK

ITALY

BOLOGNA

CAPUCIN FRIARS MUSEUM AND ART GALLERY

FLORENCE

MUSEUM OF SAN MARCO

GENOA

FRANCISCAN MISSIONARY MUSEUM

PADUA

BASILICA OF SANT'ANTONIO

RIESE PIO X

S. PIO X HOUSE AND MUSEUM

ROME

FRANCISCAN MUSEUM OF THE CAPUCIN BROTHERS
HISTORY MUSEUM OF THE BROTHERHOOD OF SAN GIOVANNI DECOLLATO
NATIONAL MUSEUM OF ARTS AND POPULAR TRADITIONS
PAOLINO MUSEUM (VATICAN MUSEUM)

TODI

FRANCESCAN MISSIONARY MUSEUM

VENICE

MUSEUM OF THE ISRAELITE COMMUNITY
TREASURY OF THE BASILICA SAN MARCO

IVORY COAST

ABIDJAN

MUSEUM OF THE CENTRE DES SCIENCES HUMAINES

JAPAN

HANAMAKI-SHI

TIBETAN COLLECTION ATTACHED TO THE KOTOKUJI TEMPLE

HIRAIZUMI-MACHI

TREASURE HOUSE OF THE CHUSONJI TEMPLE

HIRATA-SHI

TREASURE HOUSE OF THE WANIBUCHIJI TEMPLE

IKARUGA-MACHI

TREASURE HOUSE OF THE HORYUJI TEMPLE

KOJIMA-SHI

GORYU BUDDHISTIC MUSEUM

KOYA-SAN

TREASURE HOUSE OF THE TEMPLES ON MT. KOYA

KYOTO

CHILDREN'S BUDDHIST MUSEUM
THE SILVER TEMPLE

NAGASAKI-SHI

NAGASAKI MUNICIPAL MUSEUM

NARA-SHI

TREASURE HALL OF THE TODAIJI TEMPLE

NARITA-SHI

NARITASAN REIKO MUSEUM

NIKKO-SHI
TREASURE HOUSE OF THE CHUZENJI TEMPLE
TREASURE HOUSE OF THE JOKODO, RINNOJI TEMPLE

YAMATO-MURA
TREASURE HALL OF THE RAKUHOJI TEMPLE

LESOTHO

MASITISE
MISSION CAFE HOUSE

MALTA

RABAT
ST. PAUL'S GROTTO

MEXICO

DOLORES HIDALGO
CASA DE HIDALGO

GUADALUPE
GUADALUPE REGIONAL MUSEUM

MOROCCO

RABAT
MUSEUM OF THE OUDAIAS

NETHERLANDS

AMSTERDAM
MUSEUM OF BIBLICAL ANTIQUITIES
MUSEUM OF JEWISH HISTORY
ROOTHAAN MUSEUM

NIJMEGEN
BIBLICAL OPEN-AIR MUSEUM

VALKENBURG- HOUTHEM
MUSEUM OF THE CATACOMBS FOUNDATION

WITTEM
CARDINAL VAN ROSSUM MUSEUM

NEW ZEALAND

AUCKLAND
MELANESIAN MISSION MUSEUM

ROTORUA
TE AMORANGI MUSEUM

RUSSELL
POMPALLIER HOUSE

TAURANGA
THE ELMS OR THE MISSION HOUSE

WAIMATE NORTH
WAIMATE MISSION HOUSE

POLAND

KRAKÓW
MUSEUM OF JEWISH CULTURE

ŁAŃCUT
JEWISH MUSEUM

WARSAW
MUSEUM OF THE INSTITUTE OF JEWISH HISTORY

PORTUGAL

ÉVORA
OSSUARY CHAPEL

SOUTH AFRICA, REPUBLIC OF

CAPE TOWN
JEWISH MUSEUM

ESHOWE
ZULULAND HISTORICAL MUSEUM

FRANSCHHOEK
HUGUENOT MEMORIAL MUSEUM

JOHANNESBURG
JEWISH MUSEUM

PIETERMARITZBURG
VOORTREKKER MUSEUM

SPAIN

ASTORGA
MUSEUM OF JOURNEYS (DE LOS CAMINOS)

AVILA
BIRTHPLACE OF ST. TERESA DE JESUS
VIRGEN DE LA PORTERÍA MUSEUM

CIUDAD REAL
CATHEDRAL MUSEUM

CORDOBA
ALCAZAR OF THE CHRISTIAN KINGS

LEÓN
ROYAL COLLEGE OF SAN ISIDORO

LOYOLA
BIRTHPLACE OF SAN IGNACIO

MADRID
AMERICAN MUSEUM

SAN SADURNI DE NOYA
MUSEUM OF THE ORDER OF LOS HOMENAJES A LA VEJEZ

SANTIAGO DE COMPOSTELA
MUSEUM OF PILGRIMAGES

SEVILLE
MUSEUM AND TREASURY OF THE BASILICA OF THE MACARENA

TARRAGONA
MUSEUM OF EARLY CHRISTIANITY

TOLEDO
SEPHARDIC MUSEUM

VALENCIA
BIRTHPLACE OF SAN VICENTE FERRER

VALLADOLID
MUSEUM OF THE MISSIONS

VERDU
SANCTUARY OF SAN PEDRO CLAVES

YUSTE
MUSEUM OF HISTORY AND ART

ZAMORA
MUSEUM OF HOLY WEEK

SWEDEN

JÖNKÖPING
JÖNKÖPING MUSEUM

KARLSTAD
VÄRMLAND MUSEUM

SWITZERLAND

BASEL
SWISS JEWISH MUSEUM

BEROMÜNSTER
CHURCH TREASURY OF THE CHORAL FOUNDATION

GENEVA
MUSEUM OF THE HISTORY OF THE REFORMATION

SURSEE
MUSEUM OF THE SWISS PROVINCE OF CAPUCHINS

ZURICH
CENTRAL LIBRARY

TURKEY

MARAS
ARCHAEOLOGICAL MUSEUM

USSR

LENINGRAD
MUSEUM OF THE HISTORY OF RELIGION AND ATHEISM

MOSCOW
CATHEDRAL OF THE INTERCESSION

ROSTOV-ON-DON
MUSEUM OF HISTORY

UNITED STATES

ALEXANDRIA
GEORGE WASHINGTON NATIONAL MASONIC MEMORIAL

ALTENBURG
MUSEUM OF PERRY COUNTY LUTHERAN HISTORICAL SOCIETY

AMBRIDGE
OLD ECONOMY VILLAGE

AMESBURY
ROCKY HILL MEETING-HOUSE

BALTIMORE
LLOYD STREET SYNAGOGUE
LOVELY LANE MUSEUM
MASONIC MUSEUM

BAY SHORE
BUCKLAND MUSEUM OF WITCHCRAFT AND MAGICK

BERKELEY
JUDAH L. MAGNES MEMORIAL MUSEUM

BETHLEHEM
HISTORIC BETHLEHEM INCORPORATED
MORAVIAN MUSEUM

BRENTWOOD
BUCKLAND MUSEUM OF WITCHCRAFT AND MAGICK

BROOKLINE
MARY BAKER EDDY MUSEUM

CALDWELL
ODDFELLOWS HISTORICAL BUILDING

CHATTANOOGA
HARRIS SWIFT MUSEUM OF RELIGIOUS AND CEREMONIAL ARTS

CHICAGO
MAURICE SPERTUS MUSEUM OF JUDAICA

CINCINNATI
HEBREW UNION COLLEGE MUSEUM

CLEVELAND
TEMPLE MUSEUM OF JEWISH RELIGIOUS ART AND MUSIC

CLINTON
MUSEUM OF MISSISSIPPI BAPTIST HISTORICAL COMMISSION

COLUMBIA
MISSOURI SCHOOL OF RELIGION MUSEUM

DULUTH
MUSEUM OF NORTHERN BIBLE SOCIETY

EPHRATA
EPHRATA CLOISTER

FREMONT
MISSION SAN JOSE DE GUADALUPE

GLOUCESTER
OPEN-CHURCH FOUNDATION BIBLE MUSEUM

GOLIAD
MISSION ESPIRITU SANTO DE ZUNIGA

GREENSBORO
GREENSBORO MASONIC MUSEUM

GREENVILLE
BOB JONES UNIVERSITY COLLECTION OF SACRED ART

HAVERFORD
QUAKER COLLECTION

HONOLULU
MISSION HOUSES MUSEUM

INDEPENDENCE
HERITAGE HALL

JOLON
SAN ANTONIO MISSION

LAHAINA
LAHAINA RESTORATION FOUNDATION

LAKE JUNALUSKA
MUSEUM OF COMMISSION ON ARCHIVES AND HISTORY, UNITED METHODIST CHURCH

LIBERTY
LIBERTY JAIL MUSEUM
LIVERPOOL
FRENCH FORT
LOMPOC
LA PURISMA MISSION STATE HISTORIC PARK
LOS ANGELES
SKIRBALL MUSEUM
LOUISVILLE
EISENBERG MUSEUM
MOCCASIN
PARK MUSEUM
MONTREAT
MUSEUM OF HISTORICAL FOUNDATION OF THE PRESBYTERIAN AND REFORMED CHURCHES
MOUNT HOLLY
JOHN WOOLMAN MEMORIAL
MOUNT PLEASANT
MUSEUM OF HISTORICAL SOCIETY OF MOUNT PLEASANT
NASHVILLE
BAPTIST HISTORICAL MUSEUM
NEW PHILADELPHIA
SCHOENBRUNN VILLAGE STATE MEMORIAL
NEW YORK
JEWISH MUSEUM
NORTH GROTON
MARY BAKER EDDY HISTORICAL HOUSE
NORTH MIAMI BEACH
MONASTERY CLOISTER OF ST. BERNARD
NORTH NEWTON
MENNONITE LIBRARY
OLD CHATHAM
SHAKER MUSEUM
PALMYRA
JOSEPH SMITH HOME
PARIS
CANE RIDGE SHRINE
PAWLING
MUSEUM OF HISTORICAL SOCIETY OF QUAKER HILL AND VICINITY
PHILADELPHIA
MUSEUM OF AMERICAN CATHOLIC HISTORICAL SOCIETY
MUSEUM OF PRESBYTERIAN HISTORICAL SOCIETY
PHILADELPHIA METHODIST CONFERENCE HISTORICAL CENTER AND OLD ST. GEORGE METHODIST CHURCH
PROVO
MUSEUM OF SONS AND DAUGHTERS OF UTAH PIONEERS OF PROVO
RALEIGH
MUSEUM OF NORTH CAROLINA PRESBYTERIAN HISTORICAL SOCIETY
ROCHESTER
AMERICAN BAPTIST HISTORICAL SOCIETY MUSEUM
TEMPLE B'RITH KODESH MUSEUM
ROCKVILLE
JUDIAC MUSEUM
RUMNEY
MARY BAKER HISTORIC HOUSE
ST. LOUIS
CONCORDIA HISTORICAL INSTITUTE
MUSEUM OF JEWISH HISTORICAL ASSOCIATION OF GREATER ST. LOUIS
OLD CATHEDRAL MUSEUM
WALTKE MUSEUM AND CONCORDIA HISTORICAL INSTITUTE
ST. PAUL
MUSEUM OF CATHOLIC HISTORICAL SOCIETY OF ST. PAUL
SALT LAKE CITY
LATTER DAY SAINTS (MORMON) CHURCH MUSEUM
PIONEER MONUMENT STATE PARK HISTORY MUSEUM
SAN ANTONIO
OFFICIAL GRAND LODGE INDEPENDENT ORDER OF ODD FELLOWS MUSEUM
SAN GABRIEL
MISSION SAN GABRIEL ARCHANGEL
SONOMA
SONOMA STATE HISTORIC PARK
STOCKBRIDGE
MISSION HOUSE
STOUGHTON
MARY BAKER EDDY HISTORIC HOUSE
SWAMPSCOTT
MARY BAKER EDDY HISTORIC HOUSE
SWARTHMORE
FRIENDS HISTORICAL LIBRARY OF SWARTHMORE COLLEGE
TUCSON
MISSIAN SAN XAVIER DEL BAC
TULSA
REBECCA AND GERSHON FENSTER GALLERY OF JEWISH ART
TUMACACORI
TUMACACORI NATIONAL MONUMENT
VENTURA
SAN BUENAVENTURA MISSION MUSEUM
WALLA WALLA
WHITMAN MISSION NATIONAL HISTORIC SITE
WALTHAM
MUSEUM OF AMERICAN JEWISH HISTORICAL SOCIETY
WASHINGTON
FRANCISCAN MONASTERY (HOLY LAND OF AMERICA)
THE ISLAMIC CENTER
LIBRARY OF THE SUPREME COUNCIL, 33 DEGREES
YONKERS
MUSEUM OF UNITED STATES CATHOLIC HISTORICAL SOCIETY
ZION
ZION HISTORICAL SOCIETY MUSEUM
ZOAR
ZOAR STATE MEMORIAL

YUGOSLAVIA

BELGRADE
MUSEUM OF THE SERBIAN ORTHODOX CHURCH
SARAJEVO
JEWISH MUSEUM

Maritime and naval history

ANGOLA

MOÇAMEDES
MUSEUM OF THE FISHING INDUSTRY

ARGENTINA

BERNAL
ADMIRAL BROWN MUSEUM
BUENOS AIRES
FRIGATE 'PRESIDENTE SARMIENTO' NAVAL MUSEUM
NATIONAL NAVAL MUSEUM
TIGRE
NAVAL MUSEUM

AUSTRALIA

ADELAIDE
NAUTICAL MUSEUM
ALBANY
ALBANY OLD JAIL
BATTERY POINT
VAN DIEMEN'S LAND MEMORIAL FOLK MUSEUM
BRISBANE
ROYAL HISTORICAL SOCIETY OF QUEENSLAND MUSEUM
BRUNI ISLAND
BLIGH MUSEUM OF PACIFIC EXPLORATION
FREMANTLE
MARITIME AND HISTORICAL MUSEUM
GOULBURN
MUSEUM OF APPLIED ARTS AND SCIENCES
MANNUM
MARION PADDLEWHEEL MUSEUM
PORT ADELAIDE
PORT ADELAIDE NAUTICAL MUSEUM
WILLIAMSTOWN
MUNICIPAL MUSEUM

AUSTRIA

OBERNDORF
REGIONAL MUSEUM
SPITZ
MUSEUM OF NAVIGATION
STADL-PAURA
MUSEUM OF SHIPPING
VIENNA
FLORISDORF DISTRICT MUSEUM

BELGIUM

ANTWERP
NATIONAL MARITIME MUSEUM
OPEN-AIR MARITIME MUSEUM
OSTEND
'MERCATOR'

BERMUDA

ST. GEORGE'S
THE "DELIVERANCE" REPLICA
SOUTHAMPTON
MARINE MUSEUM

BRAZIL

RIO DE JANEIRO
MUSEUM OF THE NAVAL SCHOOL
MUSEUM OF THE PORT OF RIO
NAVAL MUSEUM

BULGARIA

VARNA
NAVAL MUSEUM

CANADA

COLLINGWOOD
COLLINGWOOD MUSEUM
CORUNNA
PILOT HOUSE MUSEUM
DAWSON CITY
S.S. 'KENO'
GRAVENHURST
'SEGWUN' STEAMBOAT MUSEUM
HARTSPORT
CHURCHILL HOUSE AND MARINE MEMORIAL ROOM
KASLO
KOOTENAY LAKE HISTORICAL SOCIETY MUSEUM
LUNENBURG
LUNENBURG FISHERIES MUSEUM
OTTAWA
MUSEUM OF NATIONAL HISTORIC SITES SERVICE

ST. JOHNS
NEWFOUNDLAND NAVAL AND MILITARY MUSEUM
SARNIA
PILOT HOUSE MUSEUM
SOUTH BAY
MARINERS MEMORIAL LIGHTHOUSE PARK
TORONTO
H.M.C.S. 'HAIDA'
MARINE MUSEUM OF UPPER CANADA
VANCOUVER
MARITIME MUSEUM
VICTORIA
MARITIME MUSEUM OF BRITISH COLUMBIA
WASAGA BEACH
MUSEUM OF THE UPPER LAKES
WHITEHORSE
S.S. 'KLONDIKE'
YARMOUTH
YARMOUTH COUNTY HISTORICAL SOCIETY MUSEUM

CHILE

VIÑA DEL MAR
MUSEUM OF NAVAL HISTORY

CHINA, P.R.

CHINCHOW (JINZHOW)
PROVINCIAL MUSEUM
FOOCHOW (FUZHOU)
PROVINCIAL MUSEUM
HARBIN
PROVINCIAL MUSEUM
KWANCHOW
MUSEUM OF THE HISTORY OF KWANCHOW FOREIGN TRADE
TSINGTAO (QINGDAO)
MARITIME MUSEUM

CYPRUS

KYRENIA
SHIPWRECK MUSEUM

DENMARK

ABENRÅ
ÅBENRÅ MUSEUM
ASSENS
WILLEMOES MEMORIAL ROOMS
COPENHAGEN
BURMEISTER AND WAIN MUSEUM
ROYAL NAVAL MUSEUM
DRAGØR
DRAGØR MUSEUM
EBELTOFT
FRIGATE 'JYLLAND'
ESBJERG
FISHING AND MARITIME MUSEUM
FREDERIKSHAVN
BANGSBO MUSEET
HELSINGØR
DANISH MARITIME MUSEUM
HØJBY SJ.
STENSTRUP MUSEUM
LADBY
VIKING SHIP
LEMVIG
LEMVIG AND DISTRICT MUSEUM
MARSTAL
MARSTAL AND DISTRICT MUSEUM
ROSKILDE
VIKING SHIP MUSEUM
RØMØ
COMMANDER'S HOUSE
SVENDBORG
SVENDBORG DISTRICT MUSEUM
TÓRSHAVN
FAROES HISTORICAL MUSEUM
TROENSE
MARITIME MUSEUM
AERØSKØBING
COLLECTIONS OF BOTTLE AND MODEL SHIPS

EGYPT, ARAB REPUBLIC OF

ALEXANDRIA
MARITIME MUSEUM

FALKLAND ISLANDS

PORT STANLEY
FALKLAND ISLANDS MUSEUM

FIJI

SUVA
FIJI MUSEUM

FINLAND

HELSINKI
NAVAL MUSEUM
KOKKOLA
K. H. RENLUNDIN MUSEUM
MAARIANHAMINA
MARITIME MUSEUM
OULU
MUSEUM OF NORTH OSTROBOTHNIA
RAUMA
TOWN MUSEUM
TURKU
MARITIME MUSEUM

FRANCE

ANTIBES
NAVAL AND NAPOLEONIC MUSEUM
BENDOR
MARITIME MUSEUM
BÉZIERS
MUSEUM OF ARCHAEOLOGY
BORDEAUX
MARITIME MUSEUM
BREST
MARITIME MUSEUM
CAMARET-SUR-MER
MARITIME MUSEUM
CHÂTEAUNEUF- SUR-LOIRE
MUNICIPAL MUSEUM
CONCARNEAU
MUSEUM OF FISHING
CONDÉ-SUR-L'ÉSCAUT
MUNICIPAL MUSEUM
DIEPPE
CHÂTEAU MUSEUM
DINARD
MARITIME MUSEUM
FÉCAMP
MUNICIPAL MUSEUM
GRASSE
ADMIRAL DE GRASSE MEMORIAL MUSEUM
GUIDEL
MARITIME MUSEUM
HONFLEUR
NORMANDY MUSEUM OF ETHNOGRAPHY AND FOLK ART
LORIENT
NAVAL MUSEUM
MARSEILLE
MARSEILLE MARITIME MUSEUM
MUSEUM OF OLD MARSEILLE
MORLAIX
MUSÉE MUNICIPAL
NANTES
SALORGES MUSEUM
NICE
MARITIME MUSEUM
PARIS
MARITIME MUSEUM
PONT-L'ABBÉ
BIGOUDEN MUSEUM
PORT-LOUIS
MARITIME MUSEUM
ROCHEFORT
NAVAL MUSEUM
SAINT-MALO
INTERNATIONAL MUSEUM OF THE CAPE HORN ROUTE
SAINT-MALO MUSEUM
SAINT-MARTIN-DE-RÉ
MARITIME MUSEUM
SAINT-TROPEZ
MARITIME MUSEUM
SERRIÈRES
MUSEUM OF RHÔNE SHIPPING
SÈTE
PAUL VALÉRY MUNICIPAL MUSEUM
TOULON
NAVAL MUSEUM

GDR

AKEN
REGIONAL MUSEUM
ARNEBURG
REGIONAL MUSEUM
BAD SCHANDAU
REGIONAL MUSEUM
HAVELBERG
PRIGNITZ MUSEUM
ODERBERG
REGIONAL MUSEUM
ORANIENBURG
DISTRICT MUSEUM
PREROW
DARSS REGIONAL MUSEUM
RIBNITZ-DAMGARTEN
DISTRICT MUSEUM
RIESA
REGIONAL MUSEUM
ROSTOCK
MUSEUM OF CULTURAL HISTORY
MUSEUM OF SHIP BUILDING
SHIPPING MUSEUM
ROSTOCK-WARNEMÜNDE
WARNEMÜNDE REGIONAL MUSEUM
SCHÖNEBECK
DISTRICT MUSEUM
STADT WEHLEN
REGIONAL MUSEUM
STRALSUND
MUSEUM OF CULTURAL HISTORY
TANGERMÜNDE
REGIONAL MUSEUM
WITTENBERGE
REGIONAL MUSEUM
ZINGST
REGIONAL HOUSE

GFR

BORKUM
REGIONAL MUSEUM
BRAKE
MUSEUM OF SHIPPING AND NAVIGATION OF THE OLDENBURG RIVER PORTS

BREMEN
FOCKE MUSEUM
BREMERHAVEN
GERMAN MUSEUM OF SHIPPING AND NAVIGATION
MORGENSTEIN MUSEUM
CUXHAVEN
CUXHAVEN REGIONAL MUSEUM
DORSTEN
REGIONAL MUSEUM
DÜSSELDORF
MUSEUM OF THE HISTORY OF DÜSSELDORF
EMMERICH
RHINE MUSEUM
EUTIN
EUTIN PALACE
FLENSBURG
FLENSBURG MUNICIPAL MUSEUM
GLÜCKSTADT
DETLEFSEN MUSEUM
HAMBURG
ALTONA MUSEUM
HITZACKER
REGIONAL MUSEUM
JUIST
COASTAL MUSEUM
KEITUM-SYLT
SYLT REGIONAL MUSEUM
KOBLENZ
RHINE MUSEUM
LABOE
NAVAL MEMORIAL
LAUENBURG
ELBE SHIPPING MUSEUM
LEER
REGIONAL MUSEUM
LÜBECK
HOLSTENTOR MUSEUM
MELDORF
DITHMARSCH LAND MUSEUM
MÜHLDORF
DISTRICT MUSEUM
NEUSTADT (HOLSTEIN)
DISTRICT MUSEUM
PAPENBURG
SHIPPING AND MOOR MUSEUM
PASSAU
OBERHAUS MUSEUM
ROSENHEIM
REGIONAL MUSEUM
ST. PETER-ORDING
EIDERSTEDT REGIONAL MUSEUM
WESTRHAUDERFEHN
OSTFRIESLAND AND SATERLAND FEN AND SHIPPING MUSEUM
WILHELMSHAVEN
COASTAL AND SHIPPING MUSEUM
WYK
FÖHR ISLAND MUSEUM SOCIETY

GREAT BRITAIN

ALDEBURGH
THE MOOT HALL
ANSTRUTHER
SCOTTISH FISHERIES MUSEUM
BAMBURGH
GRACE DARLING MUSEUM
BARROW- IN-FURNESS
BARROW-IN-FURNESS MUSEUM
BEAULIEU
MARITIME MUSEUM
BIRKENHEAD
WILLIAMSON ART GALLERY AND MUSEUM
BRIXHAM
BRIXHAM MUSEUM
BUCKLAND ABBEY
BUCKLAND ABBEY
CASTLETOWN
NAUTICAL MUSEUM
DUNDEE
BARRACK STREET MUSEUM
BROUGHTY CASTLE MUSEUM
EASTBOURNE
ROYAL NATIONAL LIFEBOAT INSTITUTION MUSEUM
EDINBURGH
ROYAL SCOTTISH MUSEUM
EXETER
EXETER MARITIME MUSEUM
TOPSHAM MUSEUM
GOSPORT
SUBMARINE MUSEUM
GREAT YARMOUTH
MARITIME MUSEUM FOR EAST ANGLIA
GREENOCK
GREENOCK MUSEUM AND ART GALLERY
GRIMSBY
DOUGHTY MUSEUM
HARTLEPOOL
HARTLEPOOL MARITIME MUSEUM
HASTINGS
THE FISHERMAN'S MUSEUM
HULL
MARITIME MUSEUM
LONDON
THE "CUTTY SARK"
"GIPSY MOTH IV"
HMS BELFAST
NATIONAL MARITIME MUSEUM
MONMOUTH
NELSON MUSEUM
MORWELLHAM
MORWELLHAM QUAY
PLYMOUTH
BUCKLAND ABBEY
CITY MUSEUM AND ART GALLERY
POOLE
OLD TOWN HOUSE
POOLE MUSEUM
PORTSMOUTH
PORTSMOUTH ROYAL NAVAL MUSEUM
RYE
RYE MUSEUM
SOUTHAMPTON
MARITIME MUSEUM
SOUTH SHIELDS
SOUTH SHIELDS LIBRARY AND MUSEUM
TEESSIDE
CAPTAIN COOK MUSEUM
TEESSIDE MUSEUMS AND ART GALLERIES SERVICE
TRESCO
VALHALLA MARITIME MUSEUM
WHITBY
WHITBY MUSEUM AND ART GALLERY
WINCHELSEA
WINCHELSEA MUSEUM

GREECE

GALAXIDI
NAUTICAL MUSEUM
MYKONOS
FOLKLORE COLLECTION
PIRAEUS
MARITIME MUSEUM
SPETSAI
MUSEUM

HUNGARY

SIÓFOK
JÓZSEF BESZÉDES MUSEUM

IRELAND

WEXFORD
MARITIME MUSEUM

ISRAEL

HAIFA
IMMIGRATION AND MARINE MUSEUM
NATIONAL MARITIME MUSEUM

ITALY

BOLOGNA
COLLECTION OF ANCIENT MAPS
MARITIME MUSEUM
GENOA
COLLECTIONS OF THE ISTITUTO NAVALE DELLA FACOLTA DI INGEGNERIA
MARITIME MUSEUM
LA SPEZIA
NAVAL MUSEUM
MARENGO
MUSEUM OF THE BATTLE OF MARENGO
MILAN
NAVAL MUSEUM
NEMI
MUSEUM OF THE SHIPS OF NEMI
PEGLI
MARITIME MUSEUM
ROME
NATIONAL MUSEUM OF ARTS AND POPULAR TRADITIONS
SPÉZIA
MARITIME MUSEUM
TRIESTE
MARITIME MUSEUM
TUORO SUL TRASIMENO
ANTIQUARIUM
VENICE
MARITIME MUSEUM

JAMAICA

PORT ROYAL
PORT ROYAL MUSEUM

JAPAN

KOBE-SHI
INTERNATIONAL PORTS AND HARBOURS MUSEUM
NO'O-MACHI
NO'O MARINE AND MARITIME MUSEUM
OTARU-SHI
OTARU CITY MUSEUM
TOKYO
JAPANESE FOUNDATION FOR THE PROMOTION OF MARITIME SCIENCE
MUSEUM OF TRANSPORT
YOKOSUKA-SHI
KANNONZAKI NATURAL HISTORY MUSEUM

KUWAIT

KUWAIT
KUWAIT MUSEUM

MALAWI

MANGOCHE
LAKE MALAWI MUSEUM

MEXICO

CAMPECHE
NAVAL AND MILITARY MUSEUM

MOROCCO

TETOUAN
TETOUAN MUSEUM

NETHERLANDS

AMSTERDAM
NATIONAL MUSEUM: DEPARTMENT OF DUTCH HISTORY
NETHERLANDS MARITIME MUSEUM
DELFZIJL
MUSEUM IN THE ADAM MILL
ENKHUIZEN
NATIONAL ZUIDERZEE MUSEUM
GRONINGEN
NORTHERN MUSEUM OF SHIPS AND NAVIGATION
DEN HELDER
HELDER NAVAL MUSEUM
KETELHAVEN
IJSSELMEERPOLDER MUSEUM OF MARINE ARCHAEOLOGY
DE RIJP
'IN THE WOODEN HOUSE' MUSEUM OF DE RIJP
ROTTERDAM
MUSEUM OF THE NATIONAL TECHNICAL INSTITUTE OF SHIPPING AND AVIATION
PRINCE HENDRIK MARITIME MUSEUM
SCHEVENINGEN
LOCAL HISTORY AND FISHERY MUSEUM
SNEEK
FRISIAN SHIPPING MUSEUM AND SNEEK LOCAL HISTORY MUSEUM
SOMMELSDIJK
GOEREE AND OVERFLAKEE DISTRICT MUSEUM
WEST- TERSCHELLING
LOCAL MUSEUM

NEW ZEALAND

AUCKLAND
AUCKLAND WAR MEMORIAL MUSEUM

NORWAY

BERGEN
BERGEN MARITIME MUSEUM
DRAMMEN
MARIENLYST MANOR AND MARITIME MUSEUM
EGERSUND
DALANE FOLK MUSEUM
GRIMSTAD
IBSEN HOUSE AND GRIMSTAD MUSEUM
HORTEN
NAVAL MUSEUM
KABELVÅG
MUSEUM OF FISHERIES AND THE LOFOTEN ISLANDS
KRISTIANSAND
KRISTIANSAND MARITIME MUSEUM
OSLO
FRAM
KON-TIKI MUSEUM
NORWEGIAN MARITIME MUSEUM
VIKING SHIPS MUSEUM
SANDANE
NORDFJORD FOLK MUSEUM
SANDEFJORD
SANDEFJORD MARITIME MUSEUM
STAVANGER
MARITIME MUSEUM
STAVERN
THE BLOCK HOUSE
TRONDHEIM
MARITIME MUSEUM
VANSE
LISTA MUSEUM

PERU

CALLAO
PERUVIAN NAVAL MUSEUM

POLAND

GDAŃSK
MARITIME MUSEUM
MUSEUM OF SHIPBUILDING
GDYNIA
'BURZA' NAVAL MUSEUM
NAVAL MUSEUM
ROZEWIE
MUSEUM OF LIGHTHOUSES
SZCZECIN
MARINE MUSEUM OF THE BALTIC INSTITUTE

PORTUGAL

FARO
MARITIME MUSEUM
ILHAVO
LOCAL MUSEUM
LISBON
MARITIME MUSEUM

ST. HELENA

GEORGETOWN
FORT HAYES MUSEUM

SOUTH AFRICA, REPUBLIC OF

MOSSEL BAY
MOSSEL BAY MUSEUM
QUEENSTOWN
QUEENSTOWN AND FRONTIER MUSEUM

SPAIN

ARANJUEZ
CASA DE MARINOS
ARENYS DE MAR
FIDEL FITA MUNICIPAL MUSEUM
BARCELONA
MARITIME MUSEUM
BUEU
MASSÓ NAVAL MUSEUM
LA CORUÑA
HISTORICAL AND ARCHAEOLOGICAL MUSEUM
LAS PALMAS
COLUMBUS HOUSE-MUSEUM
LUANCO
MARITIME MUSEUM OF THE ASTURIAS
MADRID
NAVAL MUSEUM
PALMA DE MALLORCA
MARITIME MUSEUM OF THE BALEARICS
LA RABIDA
MONASTERIO DE SANTA MARIA
SAN SEBASTIAN
NAVAL MUSEUM
SEVILLE
MUSEUM OF THE GOLDEN TOWER
VISO DEL MARQUES
DON ALVARO DE BAZÁN MUSEUM AND ARCHIVES

SWEDEN

GÄVLE
GÄVLE MUSEUM
GÖTEBORG
MARITIME MUSEUM
HALMSTAD
HALLANDS MUSEUM
KALMAR
KALMAR MUSEUM
KARLSHAMN
KARLSHAMN MUSEUM
KARLSKRONA
NAVAL DOCKYARD MUSEUM
SIMRISHAMN
ÖSTERLEN MUSEUM
STOCKHOLM
NATIONAL MARITIME MUSEUM
WASA DOCKYARD

SWITZERLAND

BASEL
MUSEUM OF ETHNOLOGY
RHINE NAVIGATION MUSEUM, 'OUR WAY TO THE SEA'
NYON
LAKE LÉMAN MUSEUM
RHEINFELDEN
FIRCKTALER MUSEUM

TUNISIA

CARTHAGE
OCEANOGRAPHIC MUSEUM
JERBA
JERBA MUSEUM

TURKEY

ISTANBUL
MARITIME MUSEUM

USSR

LENINGRAD
CENTRAL NAVAL MUSEUM
CRUISER 'AURORA'
MUSEUM OF THE ARCTIC AND THE ANTARCTIC
ODESSA
MARITIME MUSEUM
RIGA
LATVIAN HISTORICAL MUSEUM
SEVASTOPOL
MUSEUM OF THE BLACK SEA FLEET
TALLINN
MARITIME MUSEUM
VESKOVO
BOTIK MUSEUM
VLADIVOSTOK
MUSEUM OF THE INSTITUTE OF THE PACIFIC

UNITED STATES

ANNAPOLIS
U.S. NAVAL ACADEMY MUSEUM
ASTORIA
COLUMBIA RIVER MARITIME MUSEUM
ATLANTA
GEORGIA STATE MUSEUM OF SCIENCE AND INDUSTRY
BALTIMORE
'DRAGONFISH' SUBMARINE MUSEUM
MUSEUM OF MARYLAND HISTORICAL SOCIETY
U.S. FRIGATE 'CONSTELLATION'
BAR HARBOR
ISLEFORD MUSEUM

BARNSTABLE
DONALD G. TRAYSER MEMORIAL MUSEUM
BATH
BATH MARINE MUSEUM
BATTLESHIP COVE
MARINE MUSEUM AT FALL RIVER
BAY CITY
MUSEUM OF THE GREAT LAKES
BEACH HAVEN
SCHOONER 'LUCY EVELYN'
BEAUFORT
ALPHONSO WHALING MUSEUM
BELHAVEN
BELHAVEN MEMORIAL MUSEUM
BEVERLY
BEVERLY HISTORICAL SOCIETY MUSEUM
BOSTON
U.S.S. CONSTITUTION
BREMERTON
NAVAL SHIPYARD MUSEUM
BUFFALO
MUSEUM OF BUFFALO AND ERIE COUNTY HISTORICAL SOCIETY
BURLINGTON
LAWRENCE HOUSE
CAMBRIDGE
FRANCIS RUSSELL HART NAUTICAL MUSEUM
CAROLINA BEACH
BLOCKDALE RUNNER MUSEUM
CHARLESTON
HUNLEY MUSEUM
POWDER MAGAZINE
CLINTON
SHOWBOAT 'RHODODENDRON' HISTORICAL MUSEUM
COHASSET
COHASSET MARITIME MUSEUM
COLD SPRING HARBOR
WHALING MUSEUM
COLUMBUS
CONFEDERATE NAVAL MUSEUM
DETROIT
DOSSIN GREAT LAKES MUSEUM
EAST GREENWICH
VARNUM MILITARY AND NAVAL MUSEUM
EDGARTOWN
DUKES COUNTY HISTORICAL SOCIETY MUSEUM
ERIE
FLAGSHIP 'NIAGARA'
FAIRPORT HARBOR
FAIRPORT MARINE MUSEUM
FALL RIVER
MARINE MUSEUM
FREDERICKSBURG
ADMIRAL NIMITZ CENTER
GLOUCESTER
CAPTAIN ELIAS DAVIS HOUSE AND MUSEUM
GROSSE ILE
GROSSE ILE HISTORICAL MUSEUM
GROTON
SUBMARINE FORCE LIBRARY AND MUSEUM
HATTERAS ISLAND
CAPE HATTERAS NATIONAL SEASHORE MUSEUM OF THE SEA
HIGHLANDS
TWIN LIGHT MUSEUM
HILTON HEAD ISLAND
HARBOUR TOWN MUSEUM
HONOLULU
BERNICE PAUAHI BISHOP MUSEUM
HOUSTON
BATTLESHIP 'TEXAS'
WEATHERBY ARMS MUSEUM
ISLEBORO
SAILORS MEMORIAL MUSEUM
KENNEBUNK
BRICK STORE MUSEUM
KEY BISCAYNE
CAPE FLORIDA STATE PARK MUSEUM
KEY WEST
LIGHTHOUSE MILITARY MUSEUM
KINSTON
CASWELL-NEUSE STATE HISTORIC SITE, VISITOR CENTER
LITTLE ROCK
RIVER MUSEUM
LONG BEACH
MUSEUM OF THE SEA ABOARD THE 'QUEEN MARY'
MANITOWOC
MANITOWOC MARITIME MUSEUM
MASSENA
MASSENA HISTORICAL CENTER AND MUSEUM
MENOMINEE
MYSTERY SHIP
MONTEREY
ALLEN KNIGHT MARITIME MUSEUM
MYSTIC
MARINE HISTORICAL SOCIETY MUSEUM
NANTUCKET
MUSEUM OF NANTUCKET HISTORICAL ASSOCIATION
NANTUCKET WHALING MUSEUM
NEW BEDFORD
NEW BEDFORD WHALING MUSEUM
NEWPORT NEWS
THE MARINERS MUSEUM
NEW YORK
MARINE MUSEUM OF THE CITY OF NEW YORK
NEW YORK STATE MARITIME MUSEUM
RATSEY MUSEUM
SOUTH STREET SEAPORT MUSEUM
PHILADELPHIA
PHILADELPHIA MARITIME MUSEUM
PORT JEFFERSON
MUSEUM OF HISTORICAL SOCIETY OF GREATER PORT JEFFERSON
PORTSMOUTH
PORTSMOUTH ATHENAEUM
PORTSMOUTH NAVAL SHIPYARD MUSEUM
ST. MICHAEL'S
CHESAPEAKE BAY MARITIME MUSEUM
SALEM
PEABODY MUSEUM OF SALEM
SALEM MARITIME NATIONAL HISTORIC SITE
SAN DIEGO
NAVAL TRAINING CENTER HISTORICAL MUSEUM
'STAR OF INDIA' MARITIME MUSEUM
SAN FRANCISCO
SAN FRANCISCO MARITIME ASSOCIATION MUSEUM
SAN FRANCISCO MARITIME STATE HISTORICAL PARK
SAN JUAN
MUSEUM OF MILITARY AND NAVAL HISTORY
SAN PEDRO
CABRILLO BEACH MARINE MUSEUM
SAUGERTIES
WEDE MARINE MUSEUM
SAVANNAH
FORT JACKSON MARITIME MUSEUM
SHIPS OF THE SEA MUSEUM
SEARSPORT
PENOBSCOT MARINE MUSEUM
SEATTLE
MUSEUM OF HISTORY AND INDUSTRY
SOLOMONS
CALVERT MARINE MUSEUM
SOUTHAMPTON
SOUTHAMPTON HISTORICAL MUSEUM
STONINGTON
LIGHTHOUSE MUSEUM
VERMILION
GREAT LAKES HISTORICAL SOCIETY MUSEUM
VICKSBURG
OLD COURT HOUSE MUSEUM
STEAMER 'SPRAGUE' MUSEUM
WASHINGTON
TRUXTUN-DECATUR NAVAL MUSEUM
U.S. NAVY MEMORIAL MUSEUM
WEST SAYVILLE
SUFFOLK MARINE MUSEUM
WHITEHALL
SKENESBOROUGH MUSEUM
WILMINGTON
USS 'NORTH CAROLINA' BATTLESHIP MEMORIAL
WINONA
STEAMBOAT MUSEUM
YORK
JOHN HANCOCK WAREHOUSE

URUGUAY

MONTEVIDEO
OCEANOGRAPHIC AND MARITIME MUSEUM

VIETNAM, DEMOCRATIC REPUBLIC OF

HAIPHONG
HAIPHONG MUSEUM
HANOI
MUSEUM OF THE NAVY

YEMEN, PEOPLE'S DEMOCRATIC REPUBLIC OF

ADEN
NATIONAL ETHNOGRAPHICAL MUSEUM

YUGOSLAVIA

BAKAR
LOCAL MUSEUM
DUBROVNIK
MARITIME MUSEUM
KORČULA
TOWN MUSEUM
KOTOR
MARITIME MUSEUM
OREBIĆ
MARITIME MUSEUM
PERAST
NAVAL MUSEUM
PIRAN
MARITIME MUSEUM
RIJEKA
MARITIME AND HISTORICAL MUSEUM
SPLIT
MARITIME MUSEUM
NAVAL MUSEUM
STARI GRAD
MARITIME MUSEUM AND ART GALLERY

Military history, weapons

ALBANIA

KRUJA
LOCAL MUSEUM

ARGENTINA

BUENOS AIRES

GENERAL SAN MARTIN MUSEUM OF THE REGIMENT OF MOUNTED GRENADIERS
NATIONAL MUSEUM OF WEAPONS

EL PALOMAR DE CASEROS

HISTORICAL MUSEUM

MENDOZA

MUSEUM OF THE ANCIENT PROVINCE

SAN CARLOS DE BARILOCHE

GENERAL VINTTER MUSEUM

SAN ISIDRO

BRIGADIER GENERAL JUAN MARTIN DE PUEYRREDÓN MUSEUM

SAN JOSÉ

REGIONAL MUSEUM

SAN MARTIN (JUJUY)

ROOM OF HISTORIC FLAGS

AUSTRALIA

ALBANY

ALBANY OLD JAIL

BALLARAT

MONTROSE COTTAGE AND EUREKA MILITARY MUSEUM

BURRADOO

BARBICAN MUSEUM

CANBERRA

AUSTRALIAN WAR MEMORIAL

PARRAMATTA

LINDEN HOUSE

SWAN HILL

INTERNATIONAL MILITARY MUSEUM

SYDNEY

FORT DENISON

AUSTRIA

ARNFELS

MUSEUM OF CLOCKS, MUSICAL INSTRUMENTS AND FOLKLORE

BAD WIMSBACH- NEYDHARTING

JUNGSCHÜTZEN MUSEUM

BERNSTEIN

PALACE MUSEUM

BREGENZ

VORARLBERG MUSEUM

DEUTSCH WAGRAM

REGIONAL MUSEUM

DREISTETTEN

SCHERRER INN REGIONAL MUSEUM

EBENAU

REGIONAL MUSEUM

ENNS

MUNICIPAL MUSEUM

FELDKIRCH

REGIONAL MUSEUM IN THE SCHATTENBURG

FORCHTENSTEIN

COLLECTIONS AT FORCHTENSTEIN CASTLE

FRIESACH

REGIONAL MUSEUM

FROHNLEITEN

RABENSTEIN CASTLE COLLECTIONS

GRAZ

JOANNEUM PROVINCIAL MUSEUM OF WEAPONS AND ARMOUR

GRIEFENSTEIN

CASTLE MUSEUM

GÜSSING

REGIONAL AND CASTLE MUSEUM

HERBERTSTEIN

PALACE MUSEUM

HERZOGENBURG

COLLECTIONS OF THE MONASTERY

HOCHOSTERWITZ

CASTLE COLLECTIONS

HOHENBRUNN

HUNTING MUSEUM OF UPPER AUSTRIA

INNSBRUCK

AMBRAS CASTLE COLLECTION
BERG ISEL MUSEUM OF THE TYROLEAN KAISERJÄGER REGIMENT
'FERDINANDEUM', TIROL MUSEUM
MUSEUM OF THE KAISERSCHÜTZEN REGIMENT

KLAM

KLAM CASTLE MUSEUM

KLEINWETZDORF

HEROES' MEMORIAL

KREMSMUNSTER

MONASTERY COLLECTIONS

KREUZENSTEIN

CASTLE AND CASTLE COLLECTIONS

KUCHL

REGIONAL MUSEUM

KUFSTEIN

REGIONAL MUSEUM

LANGENLOIS

REGIONAL MUSEUM

LINZ

UPPER AUSTRIA PROVINCIAL MUSEUM

MURAU

MUNICIPAL MUSEUM OF LOCAL LIFE

PISCHELSDORF

REGIONAL MUSEUM

RAABS

DR. JOSEF GRASSL REGIONAL MUSEUM

REICHERSBERG

MONASTERY MUSEUM

RETZ

MUSEUM OF TOWN HISTORY

RIEGERSBURG

CASTLE MUSEUM

ROSENBURG

CASTLE MUSEUM

SALZBURG

RAINER REGIMENT MUSEUM

SCHEIBBS

REGIONAL MUSEUM

SEEBENSTEIN

CASTLE MUSEUM

STANS

PALACE COLLECTION

VIENNA

HISTORICAL MUSEUM OF THE CITY OF VIENNA
MUSEUM OF THE HISTORY OF ART: WEAPONS COLLECTION
MUSEUM OF MILITARY HISTORY

WAIDHOFEN AN DER YBBS

REGIONAL MUSEUM

WALDING

LOCAL MUSEUM

WEISSENKIRCHEN

WACHAU MUSEUM

WIENER NEUSTADT

MUSEUM OF THE THERESIAN MILITARY ACADEMY

BANGLADESH

DACCA

DACCA MUSEUM

BELGIUM

ANTWERP

OLD BUTCHERS' HALL

BRUGES

MUSEUM OF THE CROSS GATE

BRUSSELS

PANORAMA OF WATERLOO MUSEUM
PORTE DE HAL MUSEUM
ROYAL ARMY MUSEUM

DINANT

MUSEUM OF ARMS AND ARMOUR

GHENT

MUSEUM OF ANTIQUITIES

LIÈGE

MUSEUM OF WEAPONS

MODAVE

CASTLE MUSEUM

MONS

WAR MUSEUM

NAMUR

MUSEUM OF WEAPONS

NIEUWPOORT

WAR MUSEUM "NIEUWPOORT 1914-1918"

OSTEND

WAR MUSEUM

TOURNAI

WAR MUSEUM

WATERLOO

MUSEUM OF CAILLIOU

YPRES

SALIENT MUSEUM

YZERTOREN

MUSEUM OF THE YSER BATTLE

ZEEBRUGGE

ZEEBRUGGE MUSEUM

BERMUDA

FORT ST. CATHERINE

FORT ST. CATHERINE

BOLIVIA

POTOSI

NATIONAL MUSEUM OF THE POTOSI MINT

BRAZIL

BELO HORIZONTE

MUSEUM OF THE 5th BATALLION OF CACADORES

CAÇAPAVA

MUSEUM OF THE IPIRANGHA BATALLION OF THE 1/6th REGIMENT

FLORIANÓPOLIS

MAJOR LARA RIBAS MUSEUM

FORTAZELA

GUSTAVO BAIROSO MUSEUM

JAGUARÃO

ALFREDO VARELA MUSEUM, Avenida 20 de setembro 348, Jaguarão, Rio Grande do Sul

PÔRTO ALEGRE

GENERAL OSÓRIO ARMOURY MUSEUM

RESENDE

MUSEUM OF THE MILITARY ACADEMY

RIO DE JANEIRO

MUSEUM OF THE INDEPENDENT COMPANY OF GUARDS OF THE PALACE OF GUANABARA
MUSEUM OF MILITARY HEROES
MUSEUM OF THE NATIONAL WAR MEMORIAL

SALVADOR

MUSEUM OF CAMPAIGN TROPHIES

SÃO JOÃO DEL REI

MUSEUM OF THE WAR VETERANS OF BRAZIL

BULGARIA

PLEVEN

MUSEUM OF MILITARY HISTORY

SOFIA

NATIONAL MUSEUM OF MILITARY HISTORY

VARNA

PARK-MUSEUM OF THE BROTHERHOOD OF ARMS

CANADA

ANNAPOLIS ROYAL

FORT ANNE NATIONAL HISTORIC PARK

BORDEN
CANADIAN FORCES INTELLIGENCE AND SECURITY MUSEUM
ROYAL CANADIAN ARMY SERVICE CORPS MUSEUM
WORTHINGTON MUSEUM
CALGARY
LORD STRATHCONA'S HORSE (ROYAL CANADIAN MUSEUM)
THE QUEEN'S OWN RIFLES OF CANADA REGIMENTAL MUSEUM
REGIMENTAL MUSEUM OF PRINCESS PATRICIA'S CANADIAN LIGHT INFANTRY
CHAMBLY
FORT CHAMBLY NATIONAL HISTORIC PARK
CHURCHILL
FORT PRINCE OF WALES NATIONAL HISTORIC PARK
COTEAU-DU-LAC
FORT COTEAU-DU-LAC
EDMONTON
OBLATE ARCHIVES
PRINCESS PAT'S LIGHT INFANTRY REGIMENTAL MUSEUM
ELK POINT
FORT GEORGE MUSEUM
FORT ERIE
OLD FORT ERIE
FREDERICTON
MILITARY COMPOUND
YORK SUNBURY HISTORICAL MUSEUM
HALIFAX
THE ARMY MUSEUM
HALIFAX CITADEL NATIONAL HISTORIC PARK
YORK REDOUBT NATIONAL HISTORIC SITE
KINGSTON
OLD FORT HENRY
ROYAL CANADIAN SIGNALS MUSEUM
ROYAL MILITARY COLLEGE MUSEUM
LONDON
ROYAL CANADIAN REGIMENT MUSEUM
LOUISBOURG
FORTRESS OF LOUISBOURG NATIONAL HISTORIC PARK
MONTREAL
MUSEUM OF THE MILITARY AND MARITIME SOCIETY OF MONTREAL
ROYAL CANADIAN ORDNANCE CORPS MUSEUM
MUNDARE
MUSEUM OF THE BAZILIAN FATHERS
NIAGARA FALLS
LUNDY'S LANE HISTORICAL MUSEUM
NIAGARA-ON-THE-LAKE
FORT GEORGE
NAVY HALL
OROMOCTO
CANADIAN FORCES BASE, GAGETOWN MUSEUM
OTTAWA
CANADIAN WAR MUSEUM
GOVERNOR GENERAL'S FOOTGUARDS MUSEUM
PENETANGUISHENE
BRITISH NAVAL AND MILITARY ESTABLISHMENT MUSEUM
QUEBEC
MUSEUM OF THE ROYAL 22ND REGIMENT
ST. ANDREWS
BLOCK HOUSE HISTORIC SITE AND CENTENNIAL PARK
SAINT-JEAN
ROYAL MILITARY COLLEGE
SAINT JOHN
MARTELLO TOWER
ST. JOHNS
NEWFOUNDLAND NAVAL AND MILITARY MUSEUM
SHILO
ROYAL CANADIAN ARTILLERY MUSEUM
TORONTO
HISTORIC FORT YORK
ROYAL CANADIAN MILITARY INSTITUTE
VEDDER CROSSING
R.C.E. MILITARY MUSEUM
VEREGIN
VEREGIN DOUKHOBOR PRAYER HOUSE

CHINA, P.R.

SHANGHAI
ART AND HISTORY MUSEUM
SIAN (XIAN)
MUSEUM OF HEADQUARTERS OF 8TH ROUTE ARMY
SHENSI PROVINCIAL MUSEUM
YENAN (YAN AN)
MUSEUM OF THE REVOLUTION

REPUBLIC OF CHINA

TAINAN CITY
CHIHKAN TOWER MUSEUM

COLOMBIA

BOGOTA
HISTORICAL MUSEUM

CUBA

SANTIAGO DE CUBA
SIBONEY BARN

CZECHOSLOVAKIA

BETLIAR
STATE PALACE
CHLUM
MUSEUM OF THE WAR OF 1866
FIL'AKOVO
MUNICIPAL MUSEUM
KRÁSNA HÔRKA
CASTLE MUSEUM
LEVOČA
SPIŠ MUSEUM
PRAGUE
MILITARY MUSEUM
SVIDNÍK
MUSEUM OF THE BATTLE OF DUKLA
TRNAVA
MUSEUM OF WESTERN SLOVAKIA

DENMARK

COPENHAGEN
ROYAL ARSENAL MUSEUM
FREDERICIA
FREDERICIA MUSEUM
FREDERIKSHAVN
KRUDTTÅRN MUSEUM
FREDERIKSVAERK
FREDERIKSVAERK AND DISTRICT MUSEUM
GILLELEJE
GILLELEJE MUSEUM
HOLSTEBRO
DRAGOON AND FREEDOM MUSEUM
KOLDING
KOLDINGHUS MUSEUM
NYBORG
NYBORG CASTLE
SPØTTRUP
SPØTTRUP CASTLE
SØNDERBORG
MUSEUM

EGYPT, ARAB REPUBLIC OF

CAIRO
MILITARY MUSEUM

FINLAND

ELIMÄKI
MUSEUM OF THE CORPS OF PIONEERS
HÄMEENLINNA
MILITARY MUSEUM
HATTULA
MUSEUM OF ARMOURED VEHICLES
HELSINKI
MANNERHEIM MUSEUM
MILITARY MUSEUM
TUUSULA
MUSEUM OF ANTI-AIRCRAFT DEFENCE

FRANCE

AIX (ÎLE D')
NAPOLEONIC MUSEUM
AJACCIO
NATIONAL MUSEUM OF THE HOUSE OF THE BONAPARTES
ALISE-SAINTE-REINE
MUNICIPAL AND ALÉSIA MUSEUM
AMIENS
MUSEUM OF REGIONAL ART AND HISTORY
ANTIBES
NAVAL AND NAPOLEONIC MUSEUM
ARGENTEUIL
OLD ARGENTEUIL MUSEUM
ARROMANCHES- LES-BAINS
MUSEUM OF THE NORMANDY LANDINGS
BAZEILLES
MUSEUM OF THE LAST CARTRIDGE
BORDEAUX
JEAN MOULIN MUSEUM
BOURGOIN-JALLIEU
VICTOR CHARRETON MUSEUM
BUSSY-LE-GRAND
CHÂTEAU DE BUSSY-RABUTIN
CARENTAN
WAR MUSEUM
CASSEL
MONT CASSEL MUSEUM OF LOCAL LIFE
CHARTRES
MUNICIPAL MUSEUM
CHÂTEAUROUX
BERTRAND MUSEUM
CHERBOURG
MUSEUM OF THE WAR AND THE LIBERATION
LA CLUSE-ET-MIJOUX
CHÂTEAU DE JOUX MUSEUM
DIORS
BERRICHON MUSEUM OF THREE WARS
FIXIN
NOISOT NAPOLEONIC MUSEUM
LA FLÈCHE
SOUVENOR BRUTION MUSEUM
FONTAINEBLEAU
MUNICIPAL MUSEUM OF MILITARY UNIFORMS AND EQUIPMENT
GRAVELOTTE
MILITARY MUSEUM
HAGUENAU
HAGUENAU MUSEUM
LILLE
MUSEUM OF THE LILLE BATALLION OF CANONNIERS SÉDENTAIRES
LIMOGES
MUNICIPAL MUSEUM
LOVAGNY- GORGES-DU-FIER
LÉON MARÈS COLLECTION
LUNÉVILLE
MUNICIPAL MUSEUM
LYON
MUSEUM OF THE RESISTANCE
MARS LA TOUR
FALLER MILITARY MUSEUM
MIALET
'DESERT' MUSEUM
MONSIREIGNE
MUSEUM OF PROTESTANTISM IN WESTERN FRANCE
MONT-SAINT-MICHEL
MUSEUM OF HISTORY

MONTSOREAU
GOUMS MUSEUM
MOUILLERON-EN-PAREDS
MUSEUM OF THE TWO VICTORIES
MURET
CLÉMENT ADER MUSEUM
NANCY
LORRAINE MUSEUM OF HISTORY
NICE
MASSÉNA MUSEUM
PARIS
ARC DE TRIOMPHE MUSEUM
ARMY MUSEUM
BOIS-PRÉAU NATIONAL MUSEUM
FOCH MUSEUM
FRÉDÉRIC MASSON MUSEUM
MEMORIAL OF THE ORDER OF THE LIBERATION
MUSEUM OF THE ARMY MEDICAL SERVICES
MUSEUM OF JEWISH ART
MUSEUM OF PLANS AND MODELS
MUSEUM OF SWEDISH ART
MUSEUM OF THE TWO WORLD WARS
VAL DE GRACE MUSEUM
PAU
BERNADOTTE MUSEUM
PÉRIGUEUX
MILITARY MUSEUM
PÉROUGES
OLD PÉROUGES MUSEUM
PLESSIS-LES-TOURS
MUSEUM CHÂTEAU
RHEIMS
HALL OF SURRENDER
RIQUEWIHR
MUSEUM OF HISTORY AND ARCHAEOLOGY
ROQUEBRUNE- CAP-MARTIN
CHÂTEAU DE ROQUEBRUNE
RUMILLY
MUNICIPAL MUSEUM
SAINT-AMARIN
SERRET MUSEUM
SAINTE- MARIE-DU-MONT-UTAH-BEACH
LOCAL MUSEUM
SAINTE-MÈRE-EGLISE
AIRBORNE TROOPS MUSEUM
ST. ÉTIENNE
MUSEUM OF ART AND INDUSTRY
SAINT-OMER
HÔTEL SANDELIN MUSEUM
SALON-DE-PROVENCE
L'EMPÉRI MUSEUM
SEDAN
SEDAN MUSEUM
STRASBOURG
HISTORICAL MUSEUM
MUSEUM OF ARCHAEOLOGY
TARBES
BIRTHPLACE OF MARSHAL FOCH
MASSEY MUSEUM
THOUARS
LOCAL MUSEUM
LA TURBIE
MUSEUM OF THE ALPINE VICTORY MONUMENT
VALENÇAY
GALLERY OF MEMENTOES OF PRINCE DE TALLEYRAND
VERDUN
UNDERGROUND CITADEL
FORT DE VAUX AND FORT DE DOUAUMONT
WAR MUSEUM
WISSEMBOURG
WESTERCAMP MUSEUM

GDR

BERNAU
REGIONAL MUSEUM
BURGK
REGIONAL AND CASTLE MUSEUM
COSPEDA
1806 MEMORIAL
DRESDEN
INSTITUTE AND MUSEUM OF THE HISTORY OF THE CITY OF DRESDEN
STATE ART COLLECTIONS: HISTORICAL MUSEUM
ECKARTSBERGA
MUSEUM OF REGIONAL LIFE
GÖRLITZ
REICHENBACK TOWER
GOTHA
MUSEUM OF REGIONAL HISTORY AND FOLKLORE
GROSSBEEREN
GROSSBEEREN 1813 MEMORIAL
HALDENSLEBEN
DISTRICT MUSEUM
HARTENSTEIN
REGIONAL MUSEUM
HOHENLEUBEN
HOHENLEUBEN - REICHSFELS MUSEUM
KÖNIGSTEIN
KÖNIGSTEIN FORTRESS
LEIPZIG
MEMORIAL TO THE PEOPLE'S BATTLE
LEISNIG
MILDENSTEIN CASTLE DISTRICT MUSEUM
LÜTZEN
GUSTAVUS ADOLPHUS MEMORIAL
REGIONAL MUSEUM
PEGAU
REGIONAL MUSEUM
POTSDAM
GERMAN ARMY MUSEUM
ROSTOCK
MUSEUM OF CULTURAL HISTORY
SCHLETTAU
CASTLE MUSEUM
SCHMALKALDEN
DISTRICT MUSEUM
SUHL
REGIONAL AND WEAPONS MUSEUM
TORGAU
DISTRICT MUSEUM
WEIMAR
REGIONAL MUSEUM OF NATURAL HISTORY, HISTORY AND POPULAR ART
WEISSENFELS
GUSTAVUS ADOLPHUS MEMORIAL
WERNIGERODE
FEUDAL MUSEUM
ZITTAU
MUNICIPAL MUSEUM

GFR

ALTENA
MUSEUM OF THE COUNTY OF MARK, WITH THE GERMAN BLACKSMITH'S MUSEUM AND WIRE MUSEUM
BABENHAUSEN
FUGGER MUSEUM
BERCHTESGADEN
PALACE MUSEUM
BRAUNSCHWEIG
DANKWARDEROBE CASTLE
BREMEN
WEAPON COLLECTION OF THE BÖTTCHERSTRASSE COMPANY
BÜDINGEN
PALACE MUSEUM
COBURG
MUNICIPAL ART COLLECTIONS
DAHLENBURG
REGIONAL MUSEUM
DILLENBURG
MUSEUM OF ORANGE-NASSAU
EMDEN
MUNICIPAL MUSEUM
EPPSTEIN
REGIONAL MUSEUM
ERBACH
COLLECTIONS OF COUNT ZU ERBACH-ERBACH
GEROLZHOFEN
REGIONAL MUSEUM
GRAFENWÖHR
REGIONAL MUSEUM
HARBER
GERMAN ARMY MUSEUM
HECHINGEN
TOWN MILITIA MUSEUM
HÖCHSTÄDT-DONAU
REGIONAL MUSEUM
HOFGEISMAR
REGIONAL MUSEUM
HOHENBURG
SPÖRER MUSEUM OF CULTURAL HISTORY
HOHENLIMBURG
REGIONAL MUSEUM
IDSTEDT
IDSTEDT MEMORIAL HALL
INGOLSTADT
BAVARIAN ARMY MUSEUM
KARLSRUHE
BADEN MUSEUM
KAUB-RHEIN
BLÜCHERMUSEUM
KIEL
HISTORY COLLECTION OF THE SCHLESWIG-HOLSTEIN LAND LIBRARY
KULMBACH-PLASSENBURG
PLASSENBURG
LICHTENSTEIN
PALACE MUSEUM
LÖFFINGEN
REGIONAL MUSEUM
LOHR AM MAIN
REGIONAL AND SPESSART MUSEUM
LÖRRACH
REGIONAL MUSEUM
LOSSBURG
BLACK FOREST MUSEUM
LUDWIGSHAFEN
K. O. BRAUN REGIONAL MUSEUM
MARL
REGIONAL MUSEUM
MEERSBURG
MEERSBURG PALACE
MONTABAUR
DISTRICT MUSEUM
MOOSBURG
REGIONAL MUSEUM
MÜHLDORF
DISTRICT MUSEUM
NEUBURG
REGIONAL MUSEUM
NÜMBRECHT
MUSEUM OF THE OBERBERG REGION
NÜRNBERG
GERMAN NATIONAL MUSEUM
NÜRNBERG IMPERIAL CASTLE
OETTINGEN
REGIONAL MUSEUM
OSNABRÜCK
MUNICIPAL MUSEUM
RASTATT
MUSEUM OF MILITARY HISTORY
RECKLINGHAUSEN
VESTISCH MUSEUM
RHEINE
FALKENHOF MUSEUM
RÖTZ
RÖTZ REGIONAL MUSEUM
RUNKEL
RUNKEL CASTLE
SCHIFFERSTADT
REGIONAL MUSEUM
SCHLITZ
REGIONAL MUSEUM
SCHLOSS MESPELBRUNN
PALACE MUSEUM

SCHWEINFURT
MUNICIPAL MUSEUM

SIGMARINGEN
HOHENZOLLERN MUSEUM

SINSHEIM
REGIONAL MUSEUM

SOLINGEN
GERMAN MUSEUM OF CUTTING IMPLEMENTS

STEINHUDE
PALACE MUSEUM

STUTTGART
WÜRTTEMBERG MUSEUM

TRABEN-TRARBACH
MUSEUM OF THE CENTRAL MOSEL AREA

UETERSEN
MUSEUM OF MILITARY AVIATION

URACH
URACH CASTLE ALPINE MUSEUM

VOHENSTRAUSS
VOHENSTRAUSS REGIONAL MUSEUM

WEISMAIN
REGIONAL MUSEUM

WERTACH
REGIONAL MUSEUM

WOLFACH
WOLFACH REGIONAL MUSEUM

WOLFEGG
WOLFEGG PALACE

GHANA

KUMASI
MILITARY MUSEUM

GIBRALTAR

GIBRALTAR
GIBRALTAR MUSEUM

GREAT BRITAIN

ABERDEEN
THE GORDON HIGHLANDERS SERVICE MUSEUM

ALDERSHOT
AIRBORNE FORCES MUSEUM
ARMY PHYSICAL TRAINING CORPS MUSEUM
QUEEN ALEXANDRA'S ROYAL ARMY NURSING CORPS SERVICE MUSEUM
ROYAL ARMY DENTAL CORPS MUSEUM
ROYAL ARMY MEDICAL CORPS HISTORICAL MUSEUM
ROYAL ARMY VETERINARY CORPS MUSEUM
ROYAL CORPS OF TRANSPORT MUSEUM

ALTON
C. G. VOKES GALLERY OF SPORTING FIREARMS

ARBORFIELD
ROYAL ELECTRICAL AND MECHANICAL ENGINEERS MUSEUM

ARMAGH
THE ROYAL IRISH FUSILIERS MUSEUM

ASHFORD
THE INTELLIGENCE CORPS MUSEUM

AYR
AYRSHIRE YEOMANRY SERVICE MUSEUM

BAGSHOT
ROYAL ARMY CHAPLAINS' DEPARTMENT CENTRE

BARNSLEY
CANNON HALL ART GALLERY AND MUSEUM

BATTLE
BATTLE MUSEUM

BELFAST
THE ROYAL ULSTER RIFLES MUSEUM

BERWICK-ON-TWEED
THE KING'S OWN SCOTTISH BORDERERS SERVICE MUSEUM

BEVERLEY
THE EAST YORKSHIRE REGIMENT SERVICE MUSEUM

BLAIR ATHOLL
BLAIR CASTLE AND ATHOLL MUSEUM

BLANDFORD FORUM
ROYAL SIGNALS MUSEUM

BODMIN
THE DUKE OF CORNWALL'S LIGHT INFANTRY SERVICE MUSEUM

BRECON
THE SOUTH WALES BORDERERS MUSEUM

BRENTWOOD
THE ESSEX REGIMENT SERVICE MUSEUM

BRIDGWATER
ADMIRAL BLAKE MUSEUM

BURNLEY
TOWNELEY HALL ART GALLERY AND MUSEUM

BURTON-ON-TRENT
HOAR CROSS HALL

BURY
THE LANCASHIRE FUSILIERS SERVICE MUSEUM

BURY ST. EDMUNDS
THE SUFFOLK REGIMENT MUSEUM

CAERNARVON
THE ROYAL WELCH FUSILIERS MUSEUM

CAMBERLEY
NATIONAL ARMY MUSEUM
ROYAL ARMY ORDNANCE CORPS MUSEUM

CANTERBURY
BATTLE OF BRITAIN MUSEUM
THE BUFFS REGIMENTAL MUSEUM
THE QUEEN'S REGIMENT MUSEUM
THE WESTGATE

CARDIFF
THE WELCH REGIMENT MUSEUM

CARLISLE
THE BORDER REGIMENT SERVICE MUSEUM

CARRICKFERGUS
5TH ROYAL INNISKILLING DRAGOON GUARDS MUSEUM
NORTH IRISH HORSE SERVICE MUSEUM
QUEEN'S ROYAL IRISH HUSSARS SERVICE MUSEUM

CAWTHORNE
CANNON HALL

CHATHAM
ROYAL ENGINEERS MUSEUM

CHESTER
THE CHESHIRE REGIMENT SERVICE MUSEUM
3RD CARABINIERS (PRINCE OF WALES'S DRAGOON GUARDS) SERVICE MUSEUM

CHICHESTER
CORPS OF ROYAL MILITARY POLICE SERVICE MUSEUM
THE ROYAL SUSSEX REGIMENT MUSEUM

CRICKHOWELL
WELSH BRIGADE MUSEUM

DEVIZES
THE WILTSHIRE REGIMENT MUSEUM

DORCHESTER
THE DORSET MILITARY MUSEUM

DUNKELD
THE SCOTTISH HORSE MUSEUM

DURHAM
DURHAM LIGHT INFANTRY MUSEUM AND ARTS CENTRE

EASTBOURNE
TOWER 73 (THE WISH TOWER)

EDENBRIDGE
CHIDDINGSTONE CASTLE

EDINBURGH
EDINBURGH CASTLE
HUNTLY HOUSE
NATIONAL MUSEUM OF ANTIQUITIES OF SCOTLAND
THE ROYAL SCOTS (THE ROYAL REGIMENT) MUSEUM
SCOTTISH UNITED SERVICES MUSEUM

ENNISKILLEN
THE ROYAL INNISKILLING FUSILIERS MUSEUM

EXETER
THE DEVONSHIRE REGIMENT SERVICE MUSEUM

FORT GEORGE
SEAFORTH HIGHLANDERS; THE QUEEN'S OWN CAMERON HIGHLANDERS AND QUEEN'S OWN HIGHLANDERS (SEAFORTH AND CAMERONS) MUSEUM

GLASGOW
THE ROYAL HIGHLAND FUSILIERS MUSEUM

GLOUCESTER
THE GLOUCESTER REGIMENT SERVICE MUSEUM

GRANTHAM
17TH/21ST LANCERS SERVICE MUSEUM

GUERNSEY
GUILLE ALLES MUSEUM

HALIFAX
THE DUKE OF WELLINGTON'S REGIMENT SERVICE MUSEUM

HAMILTON
THE CAMERONIANS (SCOTTISH RIFLES) SERVICE MUSEUM

HEREFORD
HEREFORDSHIRE LIGHT INFANTRY REGIMENTAL MUSEUM

HULL
4TH BATTALION THE EAST YORKSHIRE REGIMENT (T.A.) SERVICE MUSEUM

JERSEY
ST. PETER'S BUNKER MUSEUM OF NAZI GERMAN EQUIPMENT AND OCCUPATION RELICS

KILMARNOCK
DICK INSTITUTE MUSEUM

KINGSTON-UPON-THAMES
THE QUEEN'S ROYAL SURREY REGIMENT SERVICE MUSEUM

LANCASTER
THE KING'S OWN REGIMENTAL MUSEUM

LEICESTER
THE ROYAL LEICESTERSHIRE REGIMENT SERVICE MUSEUM

LICHFIELD
THE STAFFORDSHIRE REGIMENT (THE PRINCE OF WALES'S) MUSEUM

LINCOLN
ROYAL ANGLIAN REGIMENT (LINCOLNSHIRE) SERVICE MUSEUM

LISS
ARMY TRANSPORTATION AND MOVEMENT CONTROL MUSEUM

LIVERPOOL
THE KING'S REGIMENT COLLECTIONS

LLANDUDNO
RAPALLO HOUSE MUSEUM AND ART GALLERY

LONDON
APSLEY HOUSE
ARTILLERY MUSEUM
BADEN-POWELL HOUSE
HONOURABLE ARTILLERY COMPANY SERVICE MUSEUM
LONDON IRISH RIFLES MUSEUM (T.A.)
LONDON SCOTTISH REGIMENTAL MUSEUM (T.A.)
NATIONAL ARMY MUSEUM
ROYAL ARTILLERY REGIMENTAL MUSEUM
THE ROYAL FUSILIERS MUSEUM
ROYAL HOSPITAL MUSEUM
TOWER OF LONDON

LUDLOW
LUDLOW MUSEUM

MAIDSTONE
THE QUEEN'S OWN ROYAL WEST KENT REGIMENTAL MUSEUM

MANCHESTER
THE MANCHESTER REGIMENT SERVICE MUSEUM

NEWCASTLE-UPON-TYNE
THE ROYAL NORTHUMBERLAND FUSILIERS MUSEUM

NORTHAMPTON
THE NORTHAMPTONSHIRE REGIMENT SERVICE MUSEUM
ROYAL PIONEER CORPS MUSEUM

NORWICH
THE ROYAL NORFOLK REGIMENT MUSEUM

NOTTINGHAM
THE SHERWOOD FORESTERS MUSEUM

PENICUIK
SCOTTISH INFANTRY DEPOT (GLENCORSE) MUSEUM

PERTH
THE BLACK WATCH (R.H.R.) SERVICE MUSEUM

PONTEFRACT
CASTLE MUSEUM
THE KING'S OWN YORKSHIRE LIGHT INFANTRY SERVICE MUSEUM

PORTSMOUTH
SOUTHSEA CASTLE

PRESTON
THE EAST LANCASHIRE REGIMENT SERVICE MUSEUM
THE LANCASTRIAN BRIGADE MUSEUM
THE LOYAL REGIMENT (NL) SERVICE MUSEUM

READING
THE ROYAL BERKSHIRE REGIMENT

RICHMOND
THE GREEN HOWARDS SERVICE MUSEUM

SHEFFIELD
THE YORK AND LANCASTER REGIMENT MUSEUM
SHREWSBURY
1ST THE QUEEN'S DRAGOON GUARDS SERVICE MUSEUM
THE KING'S SHROPSHIRE LIGHT INFANTRY SERVICE MUSEUM
SHROPSHIRE YEOMANRY MUSEUM
SOUTHSEA
ROYAL MARINES MUSEUM
STIRLING
ARGYLL AND SUTHERLAND HIGHLANDERS SERVICE MUSEUM
STRATFORD- UPON-AVON
THE QUEEN'S OWN WARWICKSHIRE AND WORCESTERSHIRE YEOMANRY SERVICE MUSEUM
STRENSALL
YORKSHIRE REGIMENT'S MUSEUM
TAUNTON
SOMERSET LIGHT INFANTRY MUSEUM
TUNBRIDGE WELLS
PENSHURST PLACE
TWICKENHAM
ROYAL MILITARY SCHOOL OF MUSIC MUSEUM
WAREHAM
ROYAL ARMOURED CORPS TANK MUSEUM
WARRINGTON
THE LANCASHIRE REGIMENT (P.W.V.) SERVICE MUSEUM
WARWICK
THE QUEEN'S OWN HUSSARS SERVICE MUSEUM
THE ROYAL WARWICKSHIRE REGIMENT MUSEUM
WESTERHAM
KENT AND COUNTY OF LONDON YEOMANRY (SHARPSHOOTERS) SERVICE MUSEUM
QUEBEC HOUSE
SQUERRYES COURT
WINCHESTER
THE ROYAL GREEN JACKETS MUSEUM
THE ROYAL HAMPSHIRE REGIMENT SERVICE MUSEUM
WINDSOR
THE HOUSEHOLD CAVALRY MUSEUM
WORCESTER
THE WORCESTERSHIRE REGIMENT MUSEUM
YEOVIL
BOROUGH MUSEUM
YEOVILTON
FLEET AIR ARM SERVICE MUSEUM
YORK
YORK CASTLE MUSEUM

GREECE

AGIOS NIKOLAOS
ARCHAEOLOGICAL MUSEUM
ARGOS
ARCHAEOLOGICAL MUSEUM
ATHENS
BENAKI MUSEUM
NATIONAL HISTORICAL MUSEUM
WAR MUSEUM
CHAIRONEIA
ARCHAEOLOGICAL MUSEUM
CHANIA
ARCHAEOLOGICAL MUSEUM
CORFU
SINO-JAPANESE MUSEUM
GREVENA
ARCHAEOLOGICAL COLLECTION
KALAMATA
HISTORICAL AND FOLKLORE MUSEUM
KASTELLI KISAMOU
ARCHAEOLOGICAL COLLECTION
LAMIA
A. KOUNOUPIS PRIVATE COLLECTION
METSOVON
MUSEUM OF EPIROT FOLK ART
NAFPLION
ARCHAEOLOGICAL MUSEUM
NAXOS
ARCHAEOLOGICAL MUSEUM
RETHYMNON
MONASTERY OF AGIOS IOANNIS PREVELIS
ZAKYNTHOS
MUSEUM OF SOMOMOS AND OTHER ILLUSTRIOUS ZAKYNTHIANS

HUNGARY

BUDAPEST
HUNGARIAN NATIONAL MUSEUM
MUSEUM OF MILITARY HISTORY
SÁRVÁR
FERENC NADASDY CASTLE MUSEUM
SIKLÓS
CASTLE MUSEUM

INDIA

AJMER
RAJPUTANA MUSEUM
AMRITSAR
CENTRAL SIKH MUSEUM
BHUJ
KUTCH MUSEUM
BIJAPUR
ARCHAEOLOGICAL MUSEUM
BIKANER
GANGA GOLDEN JUBILEE MUSEUM
CALCUTTA
VICTORIA MEMORIAL HALL
GWALIOR
STATE MUSEUM
JAIPUR
THE MAHARAJA OF JAIPUR MUSEUM
JAMMU
DOGRA ART GALLERY
NEW DELHI
NATIONAL MUSEUM OF INDIA
WAR MEMORIAL MUSEUM
SANGARIA
SIR CHOTURAM MUSEUM
SIKAR
SIKAR MUSEUM

IRAN

TEHERAN
MILITARY ACADEMY MUSEUM
MUSEUM OF DECORATIVE ARTS

IRAQ

BAGHDAD
IRAQI MILITARY MUSEUM
MUSEUM OF ARMS

IRELAND

CURRAGH CAMP
CURRAGH CAMP MILITARY MUSEUM
MULLINGAR
MUSEUM OF THE 4TH ARTILLERY REGIMENT
ROSSNOWLAGH
MUSEUM OF THE COUNTY DONEGAL HISTORICAL SOCIETY

ISRAEL

AVIHAIL
ARMY MUSEUM
TEL-AVIV
HAGANAH MUSEUM

ITALY

ENNA
ALESSI MUSEUM
FERRARA
MUSEUM OF THE RISORGIMENTO
FLORENCE
STIBBERT MUSEUM
FORLI
MUSEUM AND PICTURE GALLERY
GENOA
CHIOSSONE MUSEUM
MUSEUM OF THE RISORGIMENTO
ISOLA MAGGIORE
ARMY MUSEUM
LOVERE
TADINI MUSEUM
MILAN
MUSEUM OF ANCIENT WEAPONS
MUSEUM OF ANCIENT ART
MUSEUM OF CONTEMPORARY HISTORY
POLDI-PEZZOLI MUSEUM
MODENA
CITY MUSEUM
MUSEUM OF THE RISORGIMENTO
NAPLES
FILANGERI MUSEUM
PAVIA
MUSEUM OF THE RISORGIMENTO
RIVA DEL GARDA
CIVIC MUSEUM
ROME
GENIO MUSEUM
HISTORICAL MUSEUM OF THE CARABINIERI
HISTORICAL MUSEUM OF THE ITALIAN INFANTRY
HISTORICAL MUSEUM OF THE SARDINIAN GRENADIERS
NATIONAL MILITARY MUSEUM
NATIONAL MUSEUM OF CASTEL SANT'ANGELO
ODESCALCHI COLLECTION OF WEAPONS
ROVERETO
MUSEUM OF THE HISTORY OF THE WAR
SALÒ
ADOLFO BATTISTI MUSEUM
SAN MARTINO DELLA BATTAGLIA
MILITARY MUSEUM
SESTO FIORENTINO
VILLA STIBBERT
SOLFERINO
MUSEUM OF THE 1859 WAR
TURIN
ARTILLERY MUSEUM
NATIONAL CAVALRY MUSEUM
PIETRO MICCA MUSEUM
ROYAL ARMOURY
VERONA
RISORGIMENTO MUSEUM
VITTORIO VENETO
MUSEUM OF THE BATTLE

JAMAICA

UP PARK CAMP
FORCES MUSEUM

JAPAN

BEPPU-SHI
KINSUIEN ART MUSEUM
CHIKUFUJIMA
TREASURE HOUSE ON SHIKUFUJIMA ISLANDS
HIKONE-SHI
HIKONE CASTLE COLLECTION
HIROSHIMA-SHI
HIROSHIMA PEACE MEMORIAL MUSEUM
IWAKI-SHI
NAKASO ART MUSEUM
KAMIYAMA-SHI
KANISENDO MUSEUM
KURASHIKI-SHI
KURASHIKI HISTORICAL MUSEUM
KYOTO
GENERAL NOGI MEMORIAL COLLECTION
MATSUE-SHI
MATSUE CASTLE TOWER

MATSUSHIMA-MACHI
MATSUSHIMA MUSEUM, KANRANTEI

MINOBU-MACHI
THE YAMANASHI PREFECTURAL MUSEUM OF FUJI NATIONAL PARK

NAGASAKI-SHI
ATOMIC BOMB MEMORIAL ROOM

NARA-SHI
TREASURE HOUSE OF THE KASUGA SHRINE

OMISHIMA-MACHI
TREASURE HOUSE OF THE OYAMAZUMI SHRINE

SAKATA-SHI
HONMA ART MUSEUM

SEKIGAHARA-MACHI
SEKIGAHARA PUBLIC MUSEUM

SHIMOSUWA-MACHI
SHIMOSUWA PUBLIC MUSEUM

TOKYO
JAPANESE SWORD MUSEUM
MEIJI THE GREAT MEMORIAL HALL OF TAMA
TREASURE HOUSE OF THE YASUKUNI SHRINE

YASUKI-SHI
WAKO MEMORIAL HALL

YONAGO-SHI
SAN'IN HISTORICAL COLLECTION

YONEZAWA-SHI
TREASURE HOUSE OF THE UESUGI SHRINE

YOSHINO-MACHI
TREASURE HOUSE OF THE NYOIRINJI TEMPLE

KOREA, REPUBLIC OF

SEOUL
MUSEUM OF CHANG-DUK PALACE

MALAYSIA

MALACCA
MALACCA MUSEUM

PERAK
TAIPING MUSEUM

MALTA

VALLETTA
PALACE ARMOURY

MARTINIQUE

FORT-DE-FRANCE
FORT SAINT-LOUIS MUSEUM

MEXICO

CAMPECHE
NAVAL AND MILITARY MUSEUM

CULIACAN
SINALOA REGIONAL MUSEUM

TOLUCA
MUSEUM OF NATURAL HISTORY AND ARCHAEOLOGY

MOROCCO

FEZ
BORDJ NORD MUSEUM OF WEAPONS

MARRAKESH
DAR SI SAID MUSEUM

TETOUAN
TETOUAN MUSEUM

MOZAMBIQUE

BOANE
MILITARY MUSEUM

LOURENÇO MARQUES
HISTORICAL MUSEUM

NETHERLANDS

ARNHEM
MUSEUM OF THE HISTORY OF THE GRENADIERS AND JAGERS

DELFT
STUDY COLLECTION OF THE GENERAL HOEFER MILITARY MUSEUM

'S HEERENBERG
BERGH HOUSE

LEIDEN
DUTCH ARMY AND WEAPONS MUSEUM

MUIDEN
MUIDEN CASTLE NATIONAL MUSEUM

OVERLOON
NETHERLANDS NATIONAL MUSEUM OF WAR AND THE RESISTANCE MOVEMENT

RENKUM
AIRBORNE MUSEUM

ROTTERDAM
MUSEUM OF ETHNOLOGY

VEENWOUDEN
DANTUMADEEL MUSEUM OF ANTIQUITIES

VENLO
MUSEUM OF THE LIMBURG JAGER REGIMENT

NEW ZEALAND

AUCKLAND
AUCKLAND WAR MEMORIAL MUSEUM

BURNHAM
MEDICAL CORPS MUSEUM

CHRISTCHURCH
CANTERBURY MUSEUM

GREYMOUTH
GREYMOUTH RETURNED SERVICES ASSOCIATION WAR MUSEUM

TE AWAMUTU
GAVIN GIFFORD MEMORIAL MUSEUM

WAIOURU
ARMY MUSEUM

NORWAY

STAVERN
THE BLOCK HOUSE

TRONDHEIM
HOME FRONT MUSEUM
MILITARY MUSEUM

PAKISTAN, WEST

LAHORE
LAHORE FORT MUSEUM

RAWALPINDI
ARMY MUSEUM

PARAGUAY

ASUNCION
MUSEUM OF MILITARY HISTORY

PERU

LIMA
MUSEUM OF MILITARY HISTORY

POLAND

GOZDOWICE
MUSEUM OF THE POLISH CORPS OF ENGINEERS

GRANICA
MUSEUM OF THE KAMPINOS NATIONAL PARK

KOŁOBRZEG
MUSEUM OF THE LIBERATION OF CENTRAL POMERANIA

KUTNO
COMMEMORATIVE MUSEUM OF THE BATTLE ON THE BZURA

LEGNICKÍE POLE
MUSEUM OF THE BATTLE OF LEGNICKÍE

POZNAŃ
POLISH MILITARY MUSEUM

STĘBARK
GRUNWALD MUSEUM

SZCZYRZYC
LOCAL MUSEUM

TORUŃ
HALL OF THE TEUTONIC KNIGHTS

WARSAW
MUSEUM OF THE POLISH ARMY

WOLA GUŁOWSKA
LOCAL MUSEUM

WSCHOWA
REGIONAL MUSEUM

PORTUGAL

BATALHA
UNKNOWN SOLDIER'S MUSEUM

BUÇACO
MILITARY MUSEUM

LISBON
MILITARY MUSEUM
MUSEUM OF THE VETERANS' ASSOCIATION

VILA REAL DE SANTO ANTONIO
DUCAL PALACE

RHODESIA

GWELO
ARMY MUSEUM

ROMANIA

BRAN
BRAN CASTLE MUSEUM

BRAŞOV
FORTRESS MUSEUM

BUCHAREST
CENTRAL MILITARY MUSEUM
NATIONAL MUSEUM OF ANTIQUITIES
SLATINEANU COLLECTION

CÎMPULUNG- MOLDOVENESC
MOLDOVENIAN MUSEUM

FOCŞANI
HISTORY MUSEUM

NĂSĂUD
NĂSĂUD MUSEUM

SINAIA
PELEŞ MUSEUM

SUCEAVA
SUCEAVA MUSEUM

TURNU SEVERIN
IRON GATE (PORŢILE DE FIER) MUSEUM

SAN MARINO, REPUBLIC OF

SAN MARINO
STATE ARMS MUSEUM

SOUTH AFRICA, REPUBLIC OF

BLOEMFONTEIN
WAR MUSEUM
CAPE TOWN
CASTLE OF GOOD HOPE
SOUTH AFRICAN CULTURAL HISTORY MUSEUM
EAST LONDON
EAST LONDON MUSEUM
FORT BEAUFORT
FORT BEAUFORT (HISTORICAL) MUSEUM
GREYTOWN
UMVOTI MUSEUM
JOHANNESBURG
SOUTH AFRICAN NATIONAL WAR MUSEUM
KING WILLIAM'S TOWN
THE KAFFRARIAN MUSEUM
LADYSMITH
LADYSMITH MUSEUM
POTCHEFSROOM
MUNICIPAL MUSEUM
PRETORIA
FORT KLAPPERKOP
KRUGER HOUSE MUSEUM
MELROSE HOUSE

SPAIN

BARCELONA
MILITARY MUSEUM OF THE CASTLE OF MONTJUICH
BURGOS
ISLA PALACE
ROYAL CONVENT OF LAS HUELGAS
GERONA
TOWN HISTORICAL MUSEUM
MADRID
ARMY MUSEUM
CERRALBO MUSEUM
LAZARO GALDIANO MUSEUM
ROYAL ARMOURY
RIPOLL
PAROCHIAL MUSEUM AND ARCHIVE OF FOLKLORE
SALLENT
BIRTHPLACE OF SAN ANTONIO MARIA CLARET
SAN SEBASTIAN
MUSEUM OF MILITARY HISTORY
SEGOVIA
ALCAZÁR
SEVILLE
PROVINCIAL MUSEUM OF FINE ART
TOLEDO
MUSEUM OF THE SIEGE
VITORIA
ALAVA PROVINCIAL MUSEUM
MUSEUM OF THE BATTLE OF VITORIA

SRI LANKA, REPUBLIC OF

COLOMBO
NATIONAL MUSEUM

SUDAN

EL OBEID
SHIEKAN MUSEUM

SWEDEN

ÄLVDALEN
ROTS SKANS FORT AND HOMESTEAD MUSEUM
GÖTEBORG
SKANSEN KRONAN MILITARY MUSEUM
KALMAR
KALMAR MUSEUM
KRISTIANSTAD
KRISTIANSTAD MUSEUM
NYKÖPING
SÖDERMANLAND COUNTY MUSEUM
SKOKLOSTER
SKOKLOSTER CASTLE
STOCKHOLM
ROYAL ARMOURY
ROYAL ARMY MUSEUM
UDDEVALLA
UDDEVALLA MUSEUM
VISBY
GOTLAND HISTORICAL MUSEUM
YSTAD
DRAGOON MUSEUM

SWITZERLAND

ALTSTÄTTEN
HISTORICAL MUSEUM
BASEL
HISTORICAL MUSEUM
BELLINZONA
MUNICIPAL MUSEUM
BERN
SWISS MUSEUM OF SHOOTING
BUBIKON
MUSEUM OF THE ORDER OF THE JOHANNITER
LA CHAUX- DE-FONDS
MUSEUM OF HISTORY, COINS AND MEDALS
COLOMBIER
MILITARY MUSEUM AND MUSEUM OF PAINTED BLINDS
COPPET
CHÂTEAU COPPET AND MUSEUM OF THE SWISS WHO SERVED ABROAD
DORNACH
REGIONAL MUSEUM OF SCHWAZBUBENLAND
GENEVA
MUSEUM OF ART AND HISTORY
GRANDSON
CHÂTEAU
HEIDEN
MUSEUM
HERISAU
MUSEUM
HORGEN
LOCAL MUSEUM
KYBURG
CASTLE
LE LANDERON
MUSEUM
LOCO
MUSEUM OF THE ONSERNONE VALLEY
MONTREUX- VEYTAUX
CHÂTEAU DE CHILLON
MÖRIKEN
WILDEGG CASTLE
MORGES
VAUD MILITARY MUSEUM
MOUDON
EUGÈNE BURNAND MUSEUM
MUSEUM OF OLD MOUDON
NÄFELS
MUSEUM OF GLARUS CANTON
NEUCHÂTEL
MUSEUM OF ART AND HISTORY
LA NEUVEVILLE
HISTORICAL MUSEUM
OBERHOFEN AM THUNERSEE
CASTLE
PAYERNE
MUSEUM
RAPPERSWIL
MUSEUM OF THE SWISS CASTLE ASSOCIATION
SCHWYZ
TOWER MUSEUM
SOLOTHURN
KOSCIUSZKO MUSEUM
WEAPON AND UNIFORM COLLECTION
THUN
HISTORICAL MUSEUM
VALANGIN
MUSEUM
VEVEY
MUSEUM OF OLD VEVEY
WINTERTHUR-HEGI
HEGI CASTLE
WINTERTHUR- MÖRSBURG
MÖRSBURG CASTLE
YVERDON
MUSEUM OF OLD YVERDON
ZOFINGEN
MUSEUM

SYRIAN ARAB REPUBLIC

DAMASCUS
DAMASCUS MILITARY MUSEUM
MUSEUM OF POPULAR ARTS AND TRADITIONS

TURKEY

ISTANBUL
MUSEUM OF THE FORTRESS OF RUMELI
MUSEUM OF THE JANISSARIES
KONYA
MEVLÂNA MUSEUM

UGANDA

JINJA
THE UGANDA RIFLES MUSEUM

USSR

BORISOV
MUSEUM OF HISTORY AND ETHNOGRAPHY
BREST-LITOVSK
FORTRESS DEFENCE MUSEUM
KAUNAS
MILITARY MUSEUM
KOBRIN
SUVOROV MUSEUM OF MILITARY HISTORY
KONCHANSKOYE- SUVOROVSKOYE
A. V. SUVOROV MEMORIAL MUSEUM
LENINGRAD
MUSEUM OF THE ARTILLERY, SIGNAL CORPS AND CORPS OF ENGINEERS
MUSEUM OF MILITARY MEDICINE
PETER THE GREAT'S COTTAGE
A. V. SUVOROV MUSEUM
MALOYAROSLAVETS
MUSEUM OF THE MILITARY HISTORY OF 1812
MINSK
BYELORUSSIAN MUSEUM OF THE GREAT PATRIOTIC WAR
MOSCOW
CENTRAL MUSEUM OF THE SOVIET ARMY
KUTUZOV HUT
MUSEUM OF THE BATTLE OF BORODINO
MOZHAISK
BORODINO MUSEUM
NOVOCHERKASSK
MUSEUM OF THE HISTORY OF THE DON COSSACKS
NOVYE PETROVCY
MEMORIAL MUSEUM OF THE RED ARMY
ODESSA
MUSEUM OF THE SIEGE OF ODESSA
POLTAVA
BATTLE OF POLTAVA MUSEUM
SEVASTOPOL
MUSEUM OF THE BATTLE FOR THE DEFENCE OF SEVASTOPOL, 1941-44
SUJA
N. B. FRUNZI MUSEUM
TALLINN
MUSEUM OF HISTORY

TULA
MUSEUM OF HISTORY OF WEAPONS

VIBORG
FORTRESS MUSEUM

VINNITSA
A. V. SUVOROV MUSEUM

VOLGOGRAD (formerly STALINGRAD)
MUSEUM OF THE SIEGE OF STALINGRAD

UNITED STATES

ABERCROMBIE
FORT ABERCROMBIE STATE PARK MUSEUM

ABERDEEN PROVING GROUND
U.S. ARMY ORDNANCE MUSEUM

ALBANY
ALBANY COUNTY HISTORICAL ASSOCIATION MUSEUM
STATE CAPITOL

ALBUQUERQUE
SANDIA ATOMIC MUSEUM
SANDIA LABORATORIES EXHIBIT CENTER

ALEXANDRIA
FORT WARD MUSEUM

ATLANTA
ATLANTA MUSEUM
GEORGIA STATE MUSEUM OF SCIENCE AND INDUSTRY

BEAUMONT
TEMPLE OF THE BRAVE

BEDFORD
FORT BEDFORD MUSEUM

BENNINGTON
BENNINGTON BATTLE MONUMENT

BERRYVILLE
SAUNDERS MEMORIAL MUSEUM

BOALSBURG
PENNSYLVANIA MILITARY MUSEUM

BOSTON
BUNKER HILL MONUMENT
MUSEUM OF ANCIENT AND HONORABLE ARTILLERY COMPANY OF MASSACHUSETTS

BUCKNER
FORT OSAGE

BUFFALO
MUSEUM OF BUFFALO AND ERIE COUNTY HISTORICAL SOCIETY

BURNET
FORT CROGHAN MUSEUM

BUSHNELL
DADE BATTLEFIELD HISTORIC MONUMENT

CAMP VERDE
FORT VERDE STATE HISTORIC PARK

CARLISLE
HESSIAN GUARDHOUSE MUSEUM

CASTINE
FORT GEORGE STATE MEMORIAL

CHADDS FORD
BRANDYWINE BATTLEFIELD PARK

CHARLESTON
FORT SUMTER

CHEYENNE
BLACK KETTLE MUSEUM
FORT BRIDGER STATE MUSEUM
FORT FETTERMAN STATE MUSEUM
WARREN MILITARY MUSEUM

CLAREMORE
J. M. DAVIS GUN COLLECTION

CLAYTON
GENERAL DANIEL BISSELL HOME AND JEFFERSON BARRACKS HISTORICAL PARK

COHOES
VAN SCHAICK MANSION

COLD SPRING
FOUNDRY SCHOOL MUSEUM

COLUMBIA
SOUTH CAROLINA CONFEDERATE RELIC ROOM AND MUSEUM

CONCORD
CONCORD ANTIQUARIAN SOCIETY MUSEUM

COPPER HARBOR
FORT WILKINS STATE PARK

CORDELE
WORLD WAR I AND II MUSEUM

COULEE DAM
FORT SPOKANE MUSEUM

CRAWFORD
FORT ROBINSON MUSEUM

CROW AGENCY
CUSTER BATTLEFIELD NATIONAL MONUMENT

CROWN POINT
CROWN POINT RESERVATION

CURRIE
MOORES CREEK NATIONAL MILITARY PARK MUSEUM

DARIEN
FORT KING GEORGE

DAVISTON
HORSESHOE BEND NATIONAL MILITARY PARK

DAYTON
U.S. AIR FORCE MUSEUM

DEARBORN
COMMANDANT'S QUARTERS

DETROIT
DETROIT INSTITUTE OF ARTS
FORT WAYNE MILITARY MUSEUM

DURANT
OKLAHOMA HISTORICAL SOCIETY MUSEUM

EAST GREENWICH
VARNUM MILITARY AND NAVAL MUSEUM

EDGEWOOD ARSENAL
EDGEWOOD ARSENAL MUSEUM

ELLENDALE
WHITESTONE BATTLEFIELD HISTORIC PARK

EUREKA
FORT HUMBOLDT STATE HISTORIC PARK

FAIRFIELD
STAGE COACH INN

FORT ASHBY
FORT ASHBY

FORT BELVOIR
U.S. ARMY CORPS OF ENGINEERS MUSEUM

FORT BENNING
U.S. ARMY INFANTRY MUSEUM

FORT BLISS
FORT BLISS REPLICA MUSEUM

FORT BRAGG
82nd AIRBORNE DIVISION WAR MEMORIAL

FORT CAMPBELL
FORT CAMPBELL MUSEUM

FORT CARSON
FORT CARSON MUSEUM

FORT DAVIS
FORT DAVIS NATIONAL HISTORIC SITE

FORT EUSTIS
U.S. ARMY TRANSPORTATION MUSEUM

FORT FISHER
FORT FISHER STATE HISTORIC SITE

FORT GARLAND
OLD FORT GARLAND

FORT KNOX
PATTON MUSEUM OF CAVALRY AND ARMOR

FORT LARAMIE
FORT LARAMIE NATIONAL HISTORIC SITE

FORT LEAVENWORTH
FORT LEAVENWORTH MUSEUM

FORT LEE
U.S. ARMY QUARTERMASTER CORPS MUSEUM

FORT LEWIS
FORT LEWIS MILITARY MUSEUM

FORT McCLELLAN
EDITH NOURSE ROGERS MUSEUM

FORT GEORGE G. MEADE
FIRST U.S. ARMY MUSEUM

FORT MONMOUTH
U.S. ARMY SIGNAL CORPS MUSEUM

FORT MONROE
FORT MONROE CASEMATE MUSEUM

FORT OGLETHORPE
CHICKAMAUGA-CHATTANOOGA NATIONAL MILITARY PARK

FORT RILEY
U.S. CAVALRY MUSEUM

FORT SILL
FORT SILL MUSEUM

FORT SMITH
FORT SMITH NATIONAL HISTORIC SITE

FORT TOTTEN
FORT TOTTEN HISTORIC SITE MUSEUM

FRANKLIN
HARDING MUSEUM
CARTER HOUSE

FREDERICKSBURG
FREDERICKSBURG NATIONAL MILITARY PARK

GOLIAD
GOLIAD STATE PARK MUSEUM

GREENSBORO
GUILFORD COURTHOUSE NATIONAL MILITARY PARK

HERMOSA
CUSTER STATE PARK MUSEUM

HILLSBORO
CONFEDERATE RESEARCH CENTER AND GUN MUSEUM

HOUSTON
WEATHERBY ARMS MUSEUM

ILION
REMINGTON GUN MUSEUM

INDEPENDENCE
HARRY S. TRUMAN LIBRARY AND MUSEUM

JENNER
FORT ROSS STATE HISTORIC PARK

KANOPOLIS
FORT HARKER MUSEUM

KANSAS CITY
LIBERTY MEMORIAL

KEARNEY
FORT KEARNEY STATE HISTORICAL PARK MUSEUM

KEY WEST
FORT JEFFERSON NATIONAL MONUMENT
LIGHTHOUSE MILITARY MUSEUM

KING
CARL L. BROSIUS MILITARY MUSEUM

KINGS MOUNTAIN
MUSEUM OF KINGS MOUNTAIN NATIONAL MILITARY PARK

KITTERY POINT
FORT MCCLARY STATE MEMORIAL

KNOXVILLE
JAMES WHITE'S FORT ASSOCIATION MUSEUM

LAKE GEORGE
FORT WILLIAM HENRY MUSEUM

LARNED
FORT LARNED NATIONAL HISTORIC SITE

LEBEC
FORT TEJON STATE HISTORIC PARK

LEWISBURG
FORT SAVANNAH INN

LEXINGTON
VMI MUSEUM

LIGONIER
MUSEUM OF FORT LIGONIER MEMORIAL FOUNDATION
FORT LIGONIER MEMORIAL FOUNDATION

LONE JACK
JACKSON COUNTY CIVIL WAR MUSEUM AND BATTLEFIELD

MACKINAC ISLAND
FORT MICHILIMACKINAC

MADISON
GRAND ARMY OF THE REPUBLIC, MEMORIAL HALL

MANASSAS
MANASSAS NATIONAL BATTLEFIELD PARK MUSEUM

MANDAN
MUSEUM OF FORT ABRAHAM LINCOLN STATE HISTORICAL PARK

MANSFIELD
MANSFIELD BATTLE PARK

MARIETTA
KENNESAW MOUNTAIN NATIONAL BATTLEFIELD PARK MUSEUM

MONTEREY
U.S. ARMY MUSEUM

NEWBURGH
JONATHAN HASBROUCK HOUSE
KNOX HEADQUARTERS
NEW WINDSOR CANTONMENT

NEWCASTLE
FORT BELKNAP MUSEUM

NEW HAVEN
WINCHESTER GUN MUSEUM

NEW MARKET
NEW MARKET BATTLEFIELD PARK MUSEUM

NEW ORLEANS
CONFEDERATE MUSEUM
HISTORIC NEW ORLEANS COLLECTION

NEWPORT NEWS
WAR MEMORIAL MUSEUM OF VIRGINIA

NEWTON GROVE
BENTONVILLE BATTLEGROUND STATE HISTORIC SITE

NEW YORK
FORT WADSWORTH MUSEUM
FRAUNCES TAVERN MUSEUM
GENERAL GRANT NATIONAL MONUMENT

NORFOLK
HOTEL NANSEAMOND
GENERAL DOUGLAS MACARTHUR MEMORIAL

NORTHFIELD
NORWICH UNIVERSITY MUSEUM

NORTH PLATTE
BUFFALO BILL'S RANCH

OGDEN
BROWNING GUN COLLECTION

OLUSTEE
OLUSTEE BATTLEFIELD HISTORIC MEMORIAL

ORISKANY
ORISKANY HISTORICAL SOCIETY, INC.

ORWELL
DANIELS MUSEUM

OSWEGO
FORT ONTARIO

OXON HILL
FORT WASHINGTON PARK

PARIS
MAXEY MUSEUM

PEMAQUID BEACH
FORT WILLIAM HENRY STATE MEMORIAL

PERRYVILLE
PERRYVILLE BATTLEFIELD STATE SHRINE

PETERSBURG
PETERSBURG NATIONAL BATTLEFIELD PARK VISITOR CENTER
QUARTERMASTER MUSEUM

PHILADELPHIA
WAR LIBRARY AND MUSEUM OF THE MILITARY ORDER OF THE LOYAL LEGION OF THE UNITED STATES

PLATTSBURGH
KENT-DELORD HOUSE MUSEUM

PORTAGE
FORT WINNEBAGO SURGEON'S QUARTERS

PORT GIBSON
GRAND GULF MILITARY PARK

PORT HUENEME
CIVIL ENGINEERS CORPS SEEBEE MUSEUM

PRAIRIE DU ROCHER
FORT DE CHARTRES STATE PARK MUSEUM

PROSPECT
FORT KNOX STATE PARK

QUANTICO
U.S. MARINE CORPS MUSEUM

RICHMOND
RICHMOND NATIONAL BATTLEFIELD PARK MUSEUM

RICHMOND HILL
FORT MCALLISTER

ROCK ISLAND
JOHN M. BROWNING MEMORIAL MUSEUM

ROGERS
DAISY INTERNATIONAL AIR GUN MUSEUM

SACKETS HARBOR
SACKETS HARBOR BATTLEFIELD STATE PARK

SAN ANGELO
FORT CONCHO RESTORATION AND MUSEUM

SAN JUAN
MUSEUM OF MILITARY AND NAVAL HISTORY
SAN JUAN NATIONAL HISTORIC SITE

SANTA FE
NEW MEXICO MILITARY MUSEUM

SAVANNAH
FACTORS WALK MILITARY MUSEUM

SCHOFIELD BARRACKS
25th INFANTRY DIVISION MUSEUM

SCHUYLERVILLE
GENERAL PHILIP SCHUYLER HOUSE

SHARPSBURG
ANTIETAM NATIONAL BATTLEFIELD SITE

SOUTHPORT
BRUNSWICK TOWN FORT ANDERSON STATE HISTORIC SITE

SPRINGFIELD
ILLINOIS STATE MUSEUM
SPRINGFIELD ARMOURY MUSEUM

STARKE
MUSEUM OF THE NORTH AND THE SOUTH

STILLWATER
SARATOGA NATIONAL HISTORICAL PARK MUSEUM

STONINGTON
LIGHTHOUSE MUSEUM

STONY POINT
STONY POINT BATTLEFIELD RESERVATION

STRASBURG
EAGLE AMERICAN SHOP AND GUN MUSEUM

SULLIVAN'S ISLAND
FORT SUMTER NATIONAL MONUMENT

SUNBURY
FORT AUGUSTA

THE DALLES
FORT DALLES MUSEUM

THOMASTON
MONTPELIER

TICONDEROGA
FORT MOUNT HOPE
FORT TICONDEROGA

TIVERTON
FORT BARTON

UTICA
FORT SCHUYLER MILITARY MUSEUM

VAILS GATE
NEW WINDSOR CANTONMENT AND TEMPLE HILL MONUMENT

VICKSBURG
VICKSBURG NATIONAL MILITARY PARK

WAHPETON
FORT ABERCROMBIE

WARREN
WARREN MILITARY MUSEUM

WASHINGTON
ANDERSON HOUSE MUSEUM
MEDICAL MUSEUM OF THE ARMED FORCES INSTITUTE OF PATHOLOGY
NATIONAL RIFLE ASSOCIATION FIREARMS MUSEUM

WASHINGTON CROSSING
WASHINGTON CROSSING STATE PARK MUSEUM

WEST POINT
MUSEUM OF UNITED STATES MILITARY ACADEMY

WETHERSFIELD
JOSEPH WEBB HOUSE

WHEATON
CANTIGNY WAR MEMORIAL MUSEUM OF THE FIRST DIVISION

WINCHESTER
STONEWALL JACKSON'S HEADQUARTERS

WINDSOR
AMERICAN PRECISION MUSEUM

WORCESTER
JOHN WOODMAN HIGGINS ARMORY

YORK
DAUGHTERS OF AMERICAN REVOLUTION MUSEUM

YORKTOWN
YORKTOWN VISITOR CENTER

YOUNGSTOWN
MUSEUM OF OLD FORT NIAGARA ASSOCIATION

VENEZUELA

MARACAIBO
MUSEUM OF MILITARY HISTORY

VIETNAM, REPUBLIC OF

SAIGON
NATIONAL MUSEUM OF VIET- NAM

YUGOSLAVIA

BELGRADE
MILITARY MUSEUM OF THE YUGOSLAV PEOPLE'S ARMY

CETINJE
STATE MUSEUM

KOPER
ART AND HISTORICAL MUSEUM

NIŠ
OCHRID NATIONAL MUSEUM

NOVI VINODOL
TOWN MUSEUM

PREDJAMA
CASTLE MUSEUM

SPLIT
CITY MUSEUM OF SPLIT

TRAKOŠĆAN
CASTLE MUSEUM

VARAŽDIN
STARI GRAD MUSEUM

ZADAR
NATIONAL MUSEUM

ZAGREB
HISTORICAL MUSEUM OF CROATIA

Group E

EDUCATION, SOCIAL CONTROL

Schools, educational techniques

AUSTRALIA

ARMIDALE
ARMIDALE MUSEUM OF EDUCATION

AUSTRIA

GRAZ
GRAZ SCHOOL MUSEUM

SALZBURG
CASTLE MUSEUM

SPITTAL
MUSEUM OF LOCAL LIFE

VIENNA
MUSEUM OF THE LIFE OF THE BLIND

BARBADOS

BARBADOS
BARBADOS MUSEUM

BULGARIA

VARNA
MUSEUM OF THE NATIONAL REBIRTH

CANADA

CHEAPSIDE
WILSON MACDONALD MEMORIAL SCHOOL MUSEUM
ISLAY
MORRISON MUSEUM OF THE COUNTRY SCHOOL
ROCK FOREST
MUSEUM OF PICE DORÉS NATURALIST YOUTH CLUB
SAINT JOHN
THE NEW BRUNSWICK MUSEUM
SASKATOON
VICTORIA SCHOOLHOUSE
VICTORIA
OLD CRAIGFLOWER SCHOOLHOUSE MUSEUM

CHILE

SANTIAGO
PEDAGOGICAL MUSEUM

CUBA

MARIANAO
MUSEUM OF LITERACY

CZECHOSLOVAKIA

BÍLÁ TŘEMEŠNÁ
JAN AMOS KOMENSKY (COMENIUS) MEMORIAL MUSEUM
ČESKA SKALICE
BOŽENY NÉMCOVA MUSEUM
FULNEK
JAN AMOS KOMENSKY (COMENIUS) MEMORIAL
HORNÍ BRANNÁ
JAN AMOS KOMENSKY (COMENIUS) MEMORIAL MUSEUM
PRAGUE
J. B. KOMENSKY (COMENIUS) MUSEUM OF EDUCATION
PŘEROV
J. A. KOMENSKY MUSEUM
UHERSKÝ BROD
JAN AMOS KOMENSKY (COMENIUS) MUSEUM

DENMARK

KØGE
KØGE MUSEUM
ØLGOD
ØLGOD MUSEUM
THISTED
THISTED MUSEUM

FINLAND

PIETARSAARI
J. L. RUNEBERG MUSEUM
TAMPERE
FINNISH SCHOOL MUSEUM

FRANCE

EPINEUIL-LE-FLEURIEL
ALAIN-FOURNIER MUSEUM
FÉCAMP
MUSEUM OF CHILDHOOD
PARIS
MUSEUM OF THE HISTORY OF EDUCATION

GDR

BAD BLANKENBURG
FRIEDRICH FRÖBEL MUSEUM
WALTERSHAUSEN- SCHNEPPENTHAL
GUTSMUTH MEMORIAL
WEISSENFELS
MUNICIPAL MUSEUM
ZEULENRODA
MUNICIPAL MUSEUM OF INDUSTRIAL ART AND REGIONAL LIFE

GFR

DORTMUND
WESTPHALIAN SCHOOL MUSEUM

GREAT BRITAIN

LEEDS
MUSEUM OF THE HISTORY OF EDUCATION
REPTON
REPTON SCHOOL MUSEUM
WINCHESTER
WINCHESTER COLLEGE MUSEUM

IRAQ

BAGHDAD
AL-MUSTANSIRIYIA SCHOOL MUSEUM

JAPAN

MATSUE-SHI
LAFCADIO HEARN MEMORIAL HALL
TOKYO
DOCUMENTARY COLLECTION OF THE MINISTRY OF EDUCATION

MEXICO

MEXICO CITY
NATIONAL MUSEUM OF EDUCATION

NETHERLANDS

GRONINGEN
NORTHERN INSTITUTE OF EDUCATION AND INSTRUCTION
LEEUWARDEN
FRIESLAND SCHOOL MUSEUM
NAARDEN
NETHERLANDS COMENIUS MUSEUM

NEW ZEALAND

ONGAONGA
ONGAONGA OLD SCHOOL MUSEUM

POLAND

LEZNO
REGIONAL MUSEUM

SOUTH AFRICA, REPUBLIC OF

LYDENBURG
VOORTREKKER CHURCH AND SCHOOL

SWEDEN

GÖTEBORG
SCHOOL MUSEUM
HALMSTAD
HALLANDSGÅRDEN MUSEUM

SWITZERLAND

FRIBOURG
SWISS PEDAGOGICAL MUSEUM
GENEVA
HISTORY OF EDUCATION
VOLTAIRE INSTITUTE AND MUSEUM
SAXON
MUSEUM OF OLD SAXON
ZURICH
PESTALOZZI COLLECTION

USSR

TAGANROG
TAGANROG SCHOOL MUSEUM

UNITED STATES

BELOIT
LITTLE RED SCHOOL HOUSE
BEMIDJI
MUSEUM OF BELTRAMI COUNTY HISTORICAL SOCIETY
BENKELMAN
MUSEUM OF DUNDY COUNTY HISTORICAL SOCIETY
BORDENTOWN
OLD CLARA BARTON SCHOOL
CHAMBERSBURG
OLD BROWN'S MILL SCHOOL
CHARLOTTE
EATON COUNTY HISTORICAL MUSEUM
CLARION
4-H HISTORICAL BUILDING
EASTHAM
EASTHAM HISTORICAL SOCIETY MUSEUM
EAST LYME
LITTLE BOSTON SCHOOLHOUSE
ENFIELD
LOCKEHAVEN SCHOOLHOUSE MUSEUM
FORT MADISON
NORTH LEE COUNTY HISTORICAL SOCIETY
HAZELWOOD
LITTLE RED SCHOOLHOUSE
KALAMAZOO
KALAMAZOO NATURE CENTER
MANHASSET
MANHASSET VALLEY SCHOOL
MASSENA
MASSENA HISTORICAL CENTER AND MUSEUM
NEW WINDSOR
SPRINGDALE SCHOOL
OBERLIN
LITTLE RED SCHOOLHOUSE
OBERLIN HISTORICAL SOCIETY MUSEUM
PETERSHAM
SECOND EAST SCHOOL
ROCKY MOUNT
ROCKY MOUNT CHILDREN'S MUSEUM
ST. AUGUSTINE
WOODEN SCHOOLHOUSE
ST. CHARLES
LITTLE RED SCHOOL HOUSE

ST. CLAIR
PHOEBE APPERSON HEARST PIONEER SCHOOL
SAN FRANCISCO
JOSEPHINE D. RANDALL JUNIOR MUSEUM
SPRINGFIELD
TRAILSIDE MUSEUM
EUREKA SCHOOL HOUSE
WOODSTOCK
QUASSET SCHOOL
WYMORE
MUSEUM OF WYMORE HISTORICAL SOCIETY
YORK
OLD SCHOOL HOUSE

YUGOSLAVIA

ZAGREB
CROATIAN SCHOOLS' MUSEUM
MUSEUM OF THE BLIND

Junior and children's museums

ALGERIA

ALGIERS
MONT RIANT CHILDREN'S MUSEUM

BELGIUM

BRUGES
GRUUTHUSE MUSEUM

CANADA

DRUMHELLER
DRUMHELLER AND DISTRICT MUSEUM
EDMONTON
EDMONTON ART GALLERY
MONTREAL
DEAF-MUTE MUSEUM
SAINT JOHN
LOYALIST HOUSE
TORONTO
ROYAL ONTARIO MUSEUM
VANCOUVER
CENTENNIAL MUSEUM

CHINA, P.R.

CANTON (GUANG DONG)
PALACE OF SCIENCE

FRANCE

SAINT-QUENTIN
CHILDREN'S MUSEUM

GREAT BRITAIN

GLASGOW
TOLLCROSS MUSEUM
KILMARNOCK
DICK INSTITUTE MUSEUM
LONDON
BETHNAL GREEN MUSEUM

INDIA

AMRELI
SHRI GIRDHARBHAI CHILDREN'S MUSEUM
BHAWANAGAR
GANDHI SMRITI MUSEUMS
JAMNAGAR
JAMNAGAR MUSEUM OF ANTIQUITIES, LAKHOTE BUILDING
LUCKNOW
MOTILAL NEHRU BAL SANGRAHALAYA

JAPAN

GIFU-SHI
GIFU CHILDREN'S SCIENCE HALL
KASAMATSU-MACHI
KASAMATSU JUNIOR HIGH SCHOOL SCIENCE MUSEUM
NAGASAKI-SHI
NAGASAKI MUNICIPAL CHILDREN'S SCIENCE HALL
TOKUSHIMA-SHI
ATTACHED SCIENCE ROOM FOR CHILDREN OF TOKUSHIMA LIBRARY

USSR

TBILISI
MUSEUM OF TOYS
ZAGORSK
TOY MUSEUM

UNITED STATES

AKRON
AKRON MUSEUM OF NATURAL HISTORY
BOSTON
CHILDREN'S MUSEUM
BRYAN
JUNIOR MUSEUM OF NATURAL HISTORY
CHARLESTON
CHILDREN'S MUSEUM AND PLANETARIUM OF SUNRISE
DARTMOUTH
CHILDREN'S MUSEUM
DETROIT
CHILDREN'S MUSEUM
DURHAM
DURHAM CHILDREN'S MUSEUM
FREEHOLD
MUSEUM OF MONMOUTH COUNTY HISTORICAL ASSOCIATION
FRESNO
FRESNO MUSEUM OF NATURAL HISTORY AND JUNIOR MUSEUM
GREENSBORO
NATURAL SCIENCE CENTER
GROTON
MONUMENT HOUSE
HONOLULU
CHILDREN'S MUSEUM OF NATURAL HISTORY
INDIANAPOLIS
CHILDREN'S MUSEUM OF INDIANAPOLIS
JACKSONVILLE
JACKSONVILLE CHILDREN'S MUSEUM
KINGMAN
KINGMAN COUNTY MUSEUM
KINGSPORT
ANDREW JACKSON SCHOOL CHILDREN'S MUSEUM
KNOXVILLE
STUDENTS' MUSEUM
LEWES
LEWES HISTORICAL SOCIETY MUSEUM
LEXINGTON
LIVING ARTS AND SCIENCE CENTER
LOUISVILLE
KENTUCKY RAILWAY MUSEUM
MANCHESTER
LUTZ JUNIOR MUSEUM
MAUSTON
BOORMAN HOUSE
MAXWELL
COMMUNITY HISTORICAL SOCIETY MUSEUM
MILAN
MILAN HISTORICAL MUSEUM
MISHAWAKA
MISHAWAKA CHILDREN'S MUSEUM
MONTVILLE
MONTVILLE HISTORICAL MUSEUM
MUSKEGON
HACKLEY ART GALLERY
NASHVILLE
CHILDREN'S MUSEUM
NEW ALMADEN
NEW ALMADEN MUSEUM
NEW BRITAIN
NEW BRITAIN'S YOUTH MUSEUM
NEW LONDON
THAMES SCIENCE CENTER
NEW ORLEANS
LOUISIANA STATE MUSEUM
NEW ORLEANS RECREATION DEPARTMENT
NEW ROCHELLE
WILDCLIFF NATURAL SCIENCE CENTER
NEW YORK
BROOKLYN CHILDREN'S MUSEUM
OAKLAND
ROTARY NATURAL SCIENCE CENTER
OBERLIN
LITTLE RED SCHOOLHOUSE
OYSTER BAY, L.I.
THEODORE ROOSEVELT MEMORIAL SANCTUARY AND TRAILSIDE MUSEUM
PORTLAND
PORTLAND CHILDREN'S MUSEUM
PRINCESS ANNE
OLDE PRINCESS ANNE DAYS
PRINCETON
PRINCETON JUNIOR MUSEUM
PROVO
MUSEUM OF SONS AND DAUGHTERS OF UTAH PIONEERS OF PROVO
RALEIGH
MUSEUM OF NORTH CAROLINA STATE DEPARTMENT OF ARCHIVES AND HISTORY
RAMSEY
OLD STONE HOUSE MUSEUM
RIFLE
RIFLE CREEK MUSEUM
RIPON
RIPON HISTORICAL SOCIETY MUSEUM
RUTHERFORD
RUTHERFORD MUSEUM
SACRAMENTO
SACRAMENTO SCIENCE CENTER AND JUNIOR MUSEUM INC.
ST. JOSEPH
ALBRECHT GALLERY AND MUSEUM OF ART
ST. PETERSBURG
ST. PETERSBURG HISTORICAL MUSEUM
SALINAS
YOUTH SCIENCE CENTER OF MONTEREY COUNTY
SALT LAKE CITY
MUSEUM OF DAUGHTERS OF UTAH PIONEERS
SAN JOSÉ
YOUTH SCIENCE INSTITUTE
SAN MATEO
SAN MATEO COUNTY JUNIOR MUSEUM
SARATOGA
MONTALVO CENTER FOR THE ARTS

SENECA FALLS
SENECA FALLS HISTORICAL SOCIETY MUSEUM
STATE COLLEGE
JUNIOR MUSEUM OF CENTRAL PENNSYLVANIA
STRASBURG
EAGLE AMERICAN SHOP AND GUN MUSEUM
TAMPA
TAMPA JUNIOR MUSEUM
TRENTON
NEW JERSEY STATE MUSEUM
TROY
RENSSELAER COUNTY JUNIOR MUSEUM
TWIN FALLS
HERRETT ARTS AND SCIENCE CENTER
UTICA
JUNIOR MUSEUM OF ONEIDA COUNTY
WALNUT CREEK
ALEXANDER LINDSAY JUNIOR MUSEUM
WASHINGTON
NATIONAL SOCIETY OF CHILDREN OF AMERICAN REVOLUTION MUSEUM
WATERBURY
MATTATUCK MUSEUM OF THE MATTATUCK HISTORICAL SOCIETY
WEISER
WASHINGTON COUNTY MUSEUM AND FIDDLERS' HALL OF FAME
WESTFIELD
HISTORY CENTER AND MUSEUM
WEST HARTFORD
CHILDREN'S MUSEUM OF HARTFORD
WESTPORT
MID-FAIRFIELD COUNTY YOUTH MUSEUM
WOLFEBORO
LIBBY MUSEUM
WOODBURY
MUSEUM OF GLOUCESTER COUNTY HISTORICAL SOCIETY
WORLAND
WASHAKIE COUNTY MUSEUM

Colleges, universities

AUSTRIA

VIENNA
UNIVERSITY MUSEUM

CHILE

SANTIAGO
PEDAGOGICAL MUSEUM

FINLAND

JYVÀSKYLÄ
UNIVERSITY MUSEUM

GDR

GREIFSWALD
GREIFSWALD MUNICIPAL MUSEUM
JENA
MUNICIPAL MUSEUM

GFR

GÖTTINGEN
MUNICIPAL MUSEUM
TÜBINGEN
THEODOR HEARING HOUSE

GREAT BRITAIN

CAMBRIDGE
UNIVERSITY ARCHIVES

IRAN

TEHERAN
CADET COLLEGE MUSEUM

ITALY

BOLOGNA
HISTORICAL MUSEUM
CATANIA
STUDY MUSEUM
PADUA
UNIVERSITY MUSEUM
PAVIA
HISTORICAL MUSEUM

JAPAN

KYOTO
NI'IJIMA MEMORIAL ROOM

MEXICO

MEXICO CITY
NATIONAL MUSEUM OF EDUCATION

NETHERLANDS

AMSTERDAM
HISTORICAL COLLECTION OF THE UNIVERSITY OF AMSTERDAM
GRONINGEN
UNIVERSITY MUSEUM
HARDEWIJK
MUSEUM OF THE HISTORY OF THE VELUWE
LEIDEN
HISTORICAL MUSEUM OF THE NATIONAL UNIVERSITY
UTRECHT
MUSEUM OF THE UTRECHT STUDENT CORPS
MUSEUM OF UTRECHT UNIVERSITY

UNITED STATES

SOMERVILLE
OLD DUTCH PARSONAGE
SOUTH WOODSTOCK
GREEN MOUNTAIN ACADEMY HISTORICAL ASSOCIATION
WAREHOUSE POINT
SCANTIC ACADEMY MUSEUM
WYOMING
MIDDLEBURY HISTORICAL SOCIETY MUSEUM

Crime, police

ARGENTINA

BUENOS AIRES
FORENSIC MUSEUM
POLICE MUSEUM
LA PLATA
POLICE MUSEUM

AUSTRALIA

ALBANY
ALBANY OLD JAIL
BROOME
MUSEUM OF FIREARMS
MELBOURNE
OLD MELBOURNE GAOL AND PENAL MUSEUM

AUSTRIA

GREILLENSTEIN
CRIMINAL LAW COLLECTION OF THE PROVINCIAL MUSEUM OF LOWER AUSTRIA

BRAZIL

BELO HORIZONTE
POLICE MUSEUM OF CRIMINOLOGY
FLORIANÓPOLIS
POLICE DEPARTMENT MUSEUM
NITERÓI
CRIME MUSEUM
PÔRTO ALEGRE
MUSEUM OF THE POLICE ACADEMY
RIO DE JANEIRO
MUSEUM OF THE INSTITUTE OF FORENSIC MEDICINE
MUSEUM OF THE POLICE ACADEMY

BULGARIA

TARNOVO
TURKISH PRISON

CANADA

BATTLEFORD
FORT BATTLEFORD NATIONAL HISTORIC PARK
FORT MACLEOD
FORT MACLEOD HISTORICAL MUSEUM
REGINA
ROYAL CANADIAN MOUNTED POLICE MUSEUM

COLOMBIA

BOGOTA
POLICE MUSEUM

FRANCE

LYON
CRIME MUSEUM
PARIS
CONCIÉRGERIE MUSEUM
MUSEUM OF FORGERY
POLICE MUSEUM

SAINT- CYR-AU-MONT-D'OR
NATIONAL POLICE MUSEUM

GFR

NÜRNBERG
DUNGEON PRISON IN THE OLD TOWN HALL
ROTHENBURG OB DER TAUBER
HISTORICAL COLLECTION OF MEDIEVAL LAW ENFORCEMENT

IRAN

TEHERAN
CRIMINOLOGICAL MUSEUM

ITALY

ROME
CRIMINOLOGY MUSEUM
HISTORICAL MUSEUM OF THE CARABINIERI

JAPAN

TOKYO
CORRECTIONAL MUSEUM
CRIMINAL MUSEUM OF MEIJI UNIVERSITY

MAURITIUS

PORT LOUIS
MUSEUM OF THE MAURITIUS POLICE

NETHERLANDS

'S GRAVENHAGE
NATIONAL PRISON MUSEUM
POLICE MUSEUM
ROTTERDAM
FOUNDATION OF THE HISTORICAL MUSEUM OF THE ROYAL MOUNTED POLICE

NEW ZEALAND

ROTORUA
TE AMORANGI MUSEUM

NORWAY

OSLO
MUSEUM OF CRIME AND CRIMINALS

POLAND

WARSAW
'PARVIAK' PRISON MUSEUM

ROMANIA

DOFTANA
DOFTANA MUSEUM

SOUTH AFRICA, REPUBLIC OF

PRETORIA
SOUTH AFRICAN POLICE MUSEUM

SPAIN

BARCELONA
MUSEUM OF CRIME
MADRID
MUSEUM OF THE GENERAL POLICE SCHOOL
PENITENTIARY MUSEUM
TOLEDO
MUSEUM OF THE SANTA HERMANDAD

SWITZERLAND

GANDRIA
CUSTOMS MUSEUM

USSR

LENINGRAD
PETER AND PAUL FORTRESS

UNITED STATES

CHARLESTON
THE PROVOST DUNGEON
EAST GRANBY
OLD NEW-GATE PRISON AND COPPER MINE
FALFURRIAS
TEXAS RANGER MUSEUM
MOUNT HOLLY
HISTORIC BURLINGTON COUNTY PRISON MUSEUM
NEW YORK
POLICE ACADEMY AND MUSEUM
ST. JOSEPH
ST. JOSEPH MUSEUM
SAN ELIZARIO
SAN ELIZARIO MUSEUM
SIERRA BLANCA
E. A. (DOGIE) WRIGHT COLLECTION
WACO
FORT FISHER AND HOMER GARRISON MEMORIAL MUSEUM
WASHINGTON
UNITED STATES DEPARTMENT OF JUSTICE
YUMA
YUMA TERRITORIAL PRISON STATE HISTORIC PARK

YUGOSLAVIA

LJUBLJANA
SLOVENIAN SCHOOL MUSEUM

Fire-fighting, industrial safety

AUSTRIA

MISTELBACH
MUNICIPAL MUSEUM OF REGIONAL LIFE
MURAU
MUNICIPAL MUSEUM OF LOCAL LIFE
POYSDORF
REGIONAL MUSEUM
VIENNA
MUSEUM OF INDUSTRY AND TECHNOLOGY

BELGIUM

ANTWERP
PROVINCIAL INSTITUTE FOR SAFETY

BRAZIL

RIO DE JANEIRO
MUSEUM OF THE FIRE BRIGADE

CANADA

YARMOUTH
FIREMEN'S MUSEUM

CZECHOSLOVAKIA

BRATISLAVA
MUNICIPAL MUSEUM

GDR

BUTTSTADT
REGIONAL MUSEUM
STOLPEN
STOLPEN CASTLE

GFR

BREMERHAVEN
SPECKENBÜTTEL OPEN-AIR MUSEUM
FEUCHTWANGEN
REGIONAL MUSEUM
FULDA
GERMAN MUSEUM OF FIRE- FIGHTING
KIEL
KIEL MUSEUM OF FIRE PREVENTION
KÖLN
MUSEUM OF FIRE-FIGHTING
PASSAU
LOWER BAVARIA MUSEUM OF FIRE-FIGHTING

GREAT BRITAIN

LONDON
CHARTERED INSURANCE INSTITUTE'S MUSEUM

HUNGARY

BUDAPEST
MUSEUM OF FIRE-FIGHTING

JAPAN

TOKYO
COLLECTION OF FIRE-FIGHTING EQUIPMENT
INDUSTRIAL SAFETY MUSEUM

NETHERLANDS

AMSTERDAM
MUSEUM OF THE INSTITUTE OF SAFETY
BORCULO
FIREFIGHTING MUSEUM
HELLEVOETSLUIS
NATIONAL FIRE-FIGHTING MUSEUM
ROTTERDAM
FIRE-FIGHTING MUSEUM OF THE CITY OF ROTTERDAM

PORTUGAL

FUNCHAL
FIREMEN'S MUSEUM

ROMANIA

BUCHAREST
MUSEUM OF FIRE-FIGHTING

SWITZERLAND

BASEL
SWISS MUSEUM OF FIREFIGHTING

UNITED STATES

BALTIMORE
BALTIMORE FIREMAN'S MUSEUM
CHICAGO
NATIONAL HISTORICAL FIRE FOUNDATION MUSEUM
GALENA
OLD FIREHOUSE
HUDSON
AMERICAN MUSEUM OF FIRE- FIGHTING
LONG ISLAND
LONG ISLAND OLD FIRE ENGINE MUSEUM
LUTHERVILLE
FIRE MUSEUM OF MARYLAND
NEW BERN
NEW BERN FIREMEN'S MUSEUM
NEW ORLEANS
PRESBYTÈRE
NEWTON HIGHLANDS
NATIONAL FIRE MUSEUM
NEW YORK
FIRE DEPARTMENT MUSEUM
OKLAHOMA CITY
OKLAHOMA FIREFIGHTERS MUSEUM
PHILADELPHIA
MUSEUM OF INSURANCE COMPANY OF NORTH AMERICA
SAN FRANCISCO
SAN FRANCISCO FIRE DEPARTMENT PIONEER MEMORIAL MUSEUM
SCOTTSDALE
HALL OF FLAME
SEATTLE
WASHINGTON STATE FIRE SERVICE HISTORICAL MUSEUM
SOUTH CARVER
EDAVILLE RAILROAD MUSEUM
NATIONAL FIRE MUSEUM
SOUTH ORANGE
NEW JERSEY FIRE MUSEUM
SWAMPSCOTT
ATLANTIC 1
WINSTON-SALEM
MARKET HOUSE AND FIRE HOUSE
WISCASSET
LINCOLN COUNTY FIRE MUSEUM

Group F

LEISURE, ENTERTAINMENT

Theatre, circus, film

ARGENTINA

BUENOS AIRES
COLÓN THEATRE MUSEUM

AUSTRALIA

BUDERIM
MOVIE MUSEUM

AUSTRIA

GRAZ
JOANNEUM MUSEUM OF THE HISTORY OF GRAZ
JOANNEUM PROVINCIAL MUSEUM OF THE ETHNOLOGY AND FOLKLORE OF STEIERMARK
LAMBACH
COLLECTIONS OF THE BENEDICTINE MONASTERY
ST. PÖLTEN
MUNICIPAL MUSEUM
VIENNA
HISTORICAL MUSEUM OF THE CITY OF VIENNA
LEOPOLDSTADT DISTRICT MUSEUM
MEIDLING DISTRICT MUSEUM
MUSEUM OF THE MARIAHILF DISTRICT

BELGIUM

ANTWERP
ARCHIVES AND MUSEUM OF FLEMISH CULTURAL LIFE
BRUSSELS
MARIONETTE MUSEUM
LE PÉRUCHET
GHENT
MUSEUM OF THE HISTORY OF SCIENCE
LIÈGE
TCHANTCHÈS MUSEUM

BRAZIL

RIO DE JANEIRO
THEATRE MUSEUM

CANADA

DAWSON CITY
PALACE GRAND
MONTREAL
MUSEUM OF QUEBEC FEDERATION OF CULTURAL CENTRES
OTTAWA
CANADIAN FILM ARCHIVES

CHINA, P.R.

SHANGHAI
ART AND HISTORY MUSEUM

COSTA RICA

SAN JOSÉ
NATIONAL THEATRE GALLERY

CZECHOSLOVAKIA

CHLUMEC NAD CIDLINOU
MUSEUM OF THE PEASANTS' REVOLT AND V. K. KLICPERA MEMORIAL

DENMARK

COPENHAGEN
DANISH FILM MUSEUM
THEATRE MUSEUM
FREDENSBORG
OLAF POULSEN MUSEUM
HELSINGØR
HELSINGØR TOWN AND HAMLET MUSEUM

FINLAND

HELSINKI
HELSINKI THEATRE MUSEUM

FRANCE

BESANÇON
FOLK MUSEUM
COUILLY PONT- AUX-DAMES
THEATRE MUSEUM
FONTAINEBLEAU
PALACE OF FONTAINEBLEAU
LYON
PUPPET MUSEUM
PARIS
COMÉDIE FRANÇAISE MUSEUM
NATIONAL OPERA MUSEUM
OPERA MUSEUM

GDR

BAD LAUCHSTADT
GOETHE THEATRE AND PAVILION
BERLIN
MUSEUM OF CULTURAL HISTORY
BITTERFELD
DISTRICT MUSEUM
DRESDEN
PUPPET THEATRE COLLECTION
STATE ART COLLECTIONS: DEPARTMENT OF PRINTS AND DRAWINGS
GOTHA
EKHOF THEATRE
GÜSTROW
DISTRICT MUSEUM
KAMENZ
LESSING MUSEUM
MEININGEN
MEININGEN MUSEUM
REICHENBACH/VOGTLAND
NEUBER MEMORIAL

GFR

ANSBACH
DISTRICT AND MUNICIPAL MUSEUM

BAYREUTH

MUNICIPAL MUSEUM
RICHARD WAGNER MEMORIAL

DÜSSELDORF

DUMONT-LINDEMANN COLLECTION

ESSEN

GERMAN POSTER MUSEUM

HAMBURG

ALTONA MUSEUM
THEATRE COLLECTION OF THE UNIVERSITY OF HAMBURG

HAMBURG-BRUNSBÜTTEL

BRUNSBÜTTEL REGIONAL MUSEUM

HERRENCHIEMSEE

NEW PALACE AND LUDWIG II MUSEUM

KASSEL

NATURAL HISTORY MUSEUM

KIEL

COLLECTION OF THEATRE HISTORY AND HEBBEL COLLECTION

MANNHEIM

REISS CITY MUSEUM

MÜNCHEN

FILM AND PHOTOGRAPHY MUSEUM IN MUNICH CITY MUSEUM
PUPPET THEATRE COLLECTION
THEATRE MUSEUM

NEUSTADT BEI COBURG

MUSEUM OF COSTUMES AND DOLLS

PORZ-WAHN

THEATRE MUSEUM

GREAT BRITAIN

BOURNEMOUTH

RUSSELL-COTES ART GALLERY AND MUSEUM

LONDON

BRITISH THEATRE MUSEUM
KODAK MUSEUM

ST. IVES

BARNES MUSEUM OF CINEMATOGRAPHY

STRATFORD- UPON-AVON

HALL'S CROFT
NEW PLACE AND NASH'S HOUSE
ROYAL SHAKESPEARE THEATRE PICTURE GALLERY
SHAKESPEARE'S BIRTHPLACE

TENTERDEN

ELLEN TERRY MEMORIAL MUSEUM

GREECE

ATHENS

THEATRICAL MUSEUM

HUNGARY

BUDAPEST

NATIONAL THEATRE MUSEUM

INDONESIA

DENPASAR

BALI MUSEUM

ITALY

AGRIGENTO

BIRTHPLACE OF PIRANDELLO

ASOLO

MUNICIPAL MUSEUM

FAENZA

THEATRE MUSEUM

FERRARA

PALAZZINA MARFISA D'ESTE

FORLI

MUSEUM OF THE TEATRO ROMAGNOLO

L'AQUILA

INTERNATIONAL MUSEUM OF PUPPETS AND MARIONETTES

MILAN

THE SCALA THEATRE MUSEUM

PIACENZA

THEATRE MUSEUM

ROME

BURCARDO MUSEUM
PIRANDELLO'S HOUSE

TRIESTE

TEATRO VERDI MUSEUM

TURIN

NATIONAL MUSEUM OF THE CINEMA

VENICE

CASA GOLDONI

JAPAN

HIKONE-SHI

I'I ART MUSEUM

KAMAKURA-SHI

TREASURE HOUSE OF THE TSURUGAOKA-HACHIMAN SHRINE

NARA-SHI

SHOSOIN TREASURE HOUSE
TREASURE HOUSE OF THE KASUGA SHRINE

TOKYO

TSUBOUCHI MEMORIAL MUSEUM OF WASEDA UNIVERSITY

MALAYSIA

KUALA LUMPUR

NATIONAL MUSEUM

MALTA

VALLETTA

MANOEL THEATRE

NETHERLANDS

AMSTERDAM

NETHERLANDS FILM MUSEUM
THEATRE MUSEUM

POLAND

KRAKÓW

MUSEUM OF THE HISTORY OF THE KRAKÓW THEATRE

WARSAW

THEATRE MUSEUM

WROCŁAW

CABINET OF PRINTS AND DRAWINGS

PORTUGAL

ROMEU

MUSEUM OF CURIOSITIES

ROMANIA

BUCHAREST

I. L. CARAGIALE MUSEUM OF THE NATIONAL THEATRE
C. I. AND C. C. NOTTARA MUSEUM

SPAIN

BARCELONA

MUSEUM OF THE INSTITUTE OF THEATRE

MADRID

SPANISH THEATRE MUSEUM

SWEDEN

GÖTEBORG

THEATRE MUSEUM

MARIEFRED

GRIPSHOLM CASTLE

STOCKHOLM

DANCE MUSEUM
DROTTNINGHOLM COURT THEATRE AND MUSEUM

SWITZERLAND

BERN

SWISS THEATRE COLLECTION

USSR

BAKU

NATIONAL MUSEUM OF THE DZABARLY THEATRE

EREVAN

ARMENIAN MUSEUM OF THE THEATRE

KIEV

UKRAINIAN STATE MUSEUM OF THEATRICAL, MUSICAL AND CINEMA ART

LENINGRAD

KIROV THEATRE MUSEUM
MUSEUM OF THE GORKI THEATRE
MUSEUM OF THE MALY OPERA THEATRE
STATE CIRCUS MUSEUM
THEATRE MUSEUM

MELIKHOVASKYA

HOUSE MUSEUM OF A. P. CHEKHOV

MOSCOW

APARTMENT-MUSEUM OF V. I. NEMIROVICH-DANCHENKO
ARKHANGELSKOYE ESTATE MUSEUM
BOLSHOI THEATRE MUSEUM
CENTRAL THEATRE MUSEUM OF THE A. A. BAKHRUSIN THEATRE
A. P. CHEKHOV HOUSE-MUSEUM
HOUSE-MUSEUM OF K. S. STANISLAVSKI
MUSEUM OF THE STATE ACADEMIC MALY THEATRE
MUSEUM OF THE ARTS THEATRE OF THE U.S.S.R., 'M. GORKI'
OSTAKINO MUSEUM OF SERF ART
PUPPET MUSEUM
B. V. SHCHUKIN MEMORIAL MUSEUM
E. B. VAKHTANGOV MUSEUM
VAKHTANGOV THEATRE MUSEUM

TALLINN

MUSEUM OF MUSIC AND THE THEATRE

VILNIUS (formerly WILNO)

MUSEUM OF MUSIC AND THE THEATRE

UNITED STATES

ANDERSON

ALFORD HOUSE AND ANDERSON FINE ARTS CENTER

BARABOO

CIRCUS WORLD MUSEUM
SAUK COUNTY HISTORICAL MUSEUM

BOOTHBAY

BOOTHBAY PLAYHOUSE THEATRE MUSEUM

BRIDGEPORT

BARNUM MUSEUM
MUSEUM OF ART, SCIENCE AND INDUSTRY

CENTRAL CITY

CENTRAL CITY OPERA HOUSE ASSOCIATION THEATER MUSEUM

CLAREMORE

WILL ROGERS MEMORIAL

CODY

BUFFALO BILL HISTORICAL CENTER

COLUMBUS

MERLE EVANS CIRCUS MUSEUM

CUYAHOGA FALLS

RAILWAYS OF AMERICA

DALLAS

McCORD THEATER MUSEUM AND LIBRARY

DEWEY

TOM MIX MUSEUM

GOLDEN
BUFFALO BILL MEMORIAL MUSEUM
KEARNEY
FORT KEARNEY MUSEUM
LEADVILLE
TABOR OPERA HOUSE MUSEUM
MADISON
MUSEUM OF STATE HISTORICAL SOCIETY OF WASHINGTON
MEDFORD
BARNUM MUSEUM
NEW YORK
BRANDER MATTHEWS DRAMATIC MUSEUM
NUTLEY
NUTLEY HISTORICAL SOCIETY MUSEUM
PACIFIC PALISADES
WILL ROGERS STATE HISTORIC PARK
PAWNEE
PAWNEE BILL MUSEUM
PERU
MIAMI COUNTY HISTORICAL MUSEUM
PUTERBAUGH MUSEUM
SAN ANTONIO
HERTZBERG CIRCUS COLLECTION
SAND LAKE
YESTERYEAR ANTIQUE DOLL MUSEUM
SARASOTA
ASOLO THEATER MUSEUM
RINGLING CIRCUS MUSEUM
SEDAN
EMMETT KELLY MUSEUM
SOMERS
SOMERS HISTORICAL SOCIETY MUSEUM
TONAWANDA
MUSEUM OF HISTORICAL SOCIETY OF THE TONAWANDAS
ZOLFO SPRINGS
PIONEER PARK MUSEUM

YUGOSLAVIA

BELGRADE
MUSEUM OF THEATRE ARTS
ZAGREB
STUDY COLLECTION OF THE HISTORY OF THE CROATIAN THEATRE

Toys, dolls

AUSTRALIA

EUNGELLA
DOLL MUSEUM

AUSTRIA

EISENERZ
REGIONAL MUSEUM
POTTENBRUNN
MUSEUM OF TIN FIGURES
ST. LAMBRECHT
COLLECTIONS OF THE BENEDICTINE MONASTERY
VIENNA
AUSTRIAN MUSEUM OF ETHNOLOGY

BELGIUM

GHENT
FOLKLORE MUSEUM

FINLAND

TAMPERE
HAIHARA DOLL MUSEUM

FRANCE

BEAUJEU
MARIUS AUDIN MUSEUM OF POPULAR TRADITIONS
COMPIÈGNE
MUSEUM OF HISTORIC MODEL FIGURES
FÉCAMP
MUSEUM OF CHILDHOOD
NANTES
MUSEUM OF DECORATIVE ARTS

GDR

ARNSTADT
PALACE MUSEUM
DRESDEN
MUSEUM OF POPULAR ART
ERFURT
FOLK-LORE MUSEUM
GRIMMA
DISTRICT MUSEUM
OHRDRUF
REGIONAL MUSEUM
SEIFFEN
ERZGEBIRGE TOY MUSEUM
SONNEBERG
GERMAN TOY MUSEUM
WALTERSHAUSEN
REGIONAL MUSEUM

GFR

ERLANGEN
CITY MUSEUM
KOMMERN
LAND MUSEUM OF FOLKLORE
KULMBACH-PLASSENBERG
GERMAN MUSEUM OF TIN FIGURES
MELDORF
DITHMARSCH LAND MUSEUM
MEMMINGEN
MUNICIPAL MUSEUM
MICHELSTADT
ODENWALD MUSEUM
NÜRNBERG
GERMAN NATIONAL MUSEUM
TOY MUSEUM
ROTH
REGIONAL MUSEUM
SCHLESWIG
LAND MUSEUM OF SCHLESWIG- HOLSTEIN
ÜBERLINGEN
REGIONAL MUSEUM

GREAT BRITAIN

BLITHFIELD
MUSEUM OF CHILDHOOD AND COSTUME
BRIGHTON
GRANGE ART GALLERY AND MUSEUM
BROMSGROVE
PLAYTHINGS PAST MUSEUM
BURFORD
TOLSEY MUSEUM
EDINBURGH
MUSEUM OF CHILDHOOD
GLASGOW
TOLLCROSS MUSEUM
HOVE
HOVE MUSEUM OF ART
KEIGHLEY
KEIGHLEY ART GALLERY AND MUSEUM
LINGFIELD
PUTTENDEN MANOR
LLANDRINDOD WELLS
RADNORSHIRE COUNTY MUSEUM
OXFORD
THE ROTUNDA
RUGELEY
BLITHFIELD HALL
SALISBURY
WILTON HOUSE
TONBRIDGE
PENSHURST PLACE
TUNBRIDGE WELLS
PENSHURST PLACE
WAREHAM
SMEDMORE
WARWICK
DOLL MUSEUM
WINDSOR
WINDSOR CASTLE
YORK
YORK CASTLE MUSEUM

INDIA

BHOPAL
CENTRAL MUSEUM
HYDERABAD
SALARJUNG MUSEUM
NEW DELHI
INTERNATIONAL DOLLS MUSEUM
NATIONAL CHILDREN'S MUSEUM

IRELAND

MOUNTRATH
ROUNDWOOD

JAPAN

TOKYO
THE CICADA MUSEUM OF THE KATO INSTITUTE FOR ENTOMOLOGY
TENRI GALLERY

NETHERLANDS

DEVENTER
THE THREE HERRINGS
GOUDA
CATHARINA INN MUNICIPAL MUSEUM
VEENKLOSTER
FOGELSANGH STATE

SOUTH AFRICA, REPUBLIC OF

QUEENSTOWN
QUEENSTOWN AND FRONTIER MUSEUM

SPAIN

SITGES
PROVINCIAL MUSEUM OF THE ROMANTIC PERIOD

SWITZERLAND

BASEL
MUSEUM OF SWISS FOLKLORE
MORGES
ALEXIS FOREL MUSEUM
SUHR
REGIONAL MUSEUM

USSR

TBILISI
MUSEUM OF TOYS
ZAGORSK
TOY MUSEUM

UNITED STATES

CHICAGO
MUSEUM OF SCIENCE AND INDUSTRY
DOUGLASSVILLE
MARY MERRITT DOLL MUSEUM
FOSTORIA
EMERINE COLLECTION
GREENVILLE
GARST MUSEUM
KINGSTON
MAJOR JOHN BRADFORD HOUSE
MANITON SPRINGS
CAMERON'S DOLL AND CARRIAGE MUSEUM
MEDORA
MEDORA DOLL HOUSE
NEW LONDON
LYMAN ALLYN MUSEUM
NEW ORLEANS
NEW ORLEANS RECREATION DEPARTMENT
OLD LYME
LYME HISTORICAL SOCIETY MUSEUM
PHILADELPHIA
PERELMAN ANTIQUE TOY MUSEUM
ROCHESTER
THE STRONG MUSEUM
SAND LAKE
YESTERYEAR ANTIQUE DOLL MUSEUM
SANDWICH
YESTERYEAR'S MUSEUM
SHREVEPORT
R. W. NORTON ART GALLERY
SPRINGFIELD CENTER
DENNY'S TOY MUSEUM
WEST CHESTERFIELD
MUSEUM OF OLD DOLLS AND TOYS
WINTER HAVEN
MUSEUM OF OLD TOYS AND DOLLS

Sports, pastimes, scouting and other youth movements

AUSTRIA

INNSBRUCK
AMBRAS CASTLE COLLECTION
KITZBÜHEL
REGIONAL MUSEUM
MURZZUSCHLAG
WINTER SPORTS AND REGIONAL MUSEUM

BELGIUM

MALMEDY
ABBEY MUSEUM

BRAZIL

RIO DE JANEIRO
JOCKEY CLUB COLLECTION

CANADA

AYLMER EAST
CANADIAN GOLF MUSEUM
BANFF
MUSEUM OF ARCHIVES OF THE CANADIAN ROCKIES
HULL
CANADIAN GOLF MUSEUM
OTTAWA
MUSEUM OF CANADIAN SCOUTING

CHINA, P.R.

SIAN (XIAN)
SHENSI PROVINCIAL MUSEUM

COLOMBIA

BOGOTA
MUSEUM OF BULL-FIGHTING

CZECHOSLOVAKIA

PRAGUE
MUSEUM OF SPORT
TATRANSKÁ LOMNICA
MUSEUM OF THE TATRA NATIONAL PARK (TANAP)

FINLAND

HELSINKI
MUSEUM OF SPORT

FRANCE

BAYONNE
BASQUE MUSEUM
CRÉPY-EN-VALOIS
MUSEUM OF THE VALOIS AND OF ARCHERY
LOURDES
MUSEUM OF THE PYRENEES
LE MANS
AUTOMOBILE MUSEUM
NÎMES
MUSEUM OF OLD NÎMES
SAUMUR
MUSEUM OF DECORATIVE ARTS AND MUSEUM OF THE HORSE
TROUVILLE-SUR-MER
MUSEUM OF LOCAL AND REGIONAL ART

GDR

ALTENBURG
CASTLE MUSEUM AND PLAYING CARDS MUSEUM
AUGUSTUSBURG
GERMAN TWO-STROKE MOTOR CYCLE MUSEUM

GFR

BIELEFELD
GERMAN PLAYING CARD MUSEUM
HAGEN
PLAYING CARD COLLECTION
LEINFELDEN BEI STUTTGART
MUSEUM OF THE ASSOCIATED ALTENBURG AND STRALSUND PLAYING CARD FACTORIES
LEMBRUCK
DÜMMER MUSEUM
MÜNCHEN
BMW MUSEUM
SCHWERTE
MUSEUM OF THE RUHR VALLEY
VERDEN
GERMAN MUSEUM OF THE HORSE

GREAT BRITAIN

BOSTON SPA
BRAMHALL PARK
DUNDEE
SPALDING GOLF MUSEUM
ISLE OF MULL
DUART CASTLE
LONDON
BADEN-POWELL HOUSE
THE CRICKET MEMORIAL GALLERY
NEWENT
THE FALCONRY CENTRE MUSEUM
NOTTINGHAM
NATURAL HISTORY MUSEUM

GREECE

OLYMPIA
OLYMPIC GAMES MUSEUM

ITALY

TURIN
NATIONAL MOUNTAIN MUSEUM

JAPAN

OMACHI-SHI
OMACHI ALPINE MUSEUM
TOKYO
BASEBALL HALL OF FAME AND MUSEUM
THE MEMORIAL SPORT MUSEUM OF PRINCE CHICHIBU
PRINCE CHICHIBU MEMORIAL SPORTS MUSEUM
SUMO MUSEUM

MEXICO

TLALPAN
CHARRERIA MUSEUM

NETHERLANDS

'S GRAVENHAGE
MUSEUM OF SCOUTING

NORWAY

HØVIKODDEN
SONJA HENIE AND NIELS ONSTAD FOUNDATION
OSLO
SKI MUSEUM

PERU

LIMA
MUSEUM OF THE BULLFIGHTING ART
RIMAC
MESON BULLFIGHTING MUSEUM

POLAND

CHOJNICE
REGIONAL MUSEUM
ŁOPUSZNA
MUSEUM OF THE HISTORY OF MOUNTAINEERING
WARSAW
MUSEUM OF PHYSICAL CULTURE AND TOURISM

PORTUGAL

LISBON
MUSEUM OF BULLFIGHTING

SPAIN

BARCELONA
MUSEUM OF BULL-FIGHTING
CORDOBA
MUNICIPAL MUSEUM OF ART AND BULLFIGHTING
GERENA
BULL-FIGHTING COLLECTION
MADRID
BULLFIGHTING MUSEUM
VALENCIA
MUSEUM OF BULL-FIGHTING
VITORIA
MUSEUM OF BULLFIGHTING
MUSEUM OF PLAYING-CARDS

SWITZERLAND

AROSA
SCHANFIGGER REGIONAL MUSEUM
BASEL
SWISS MUSEUM OF GYMNASTICS AND SPORT
BERN
SWISS ALPINE MUSEUM
GRINDELWALD
REGIONAL MUSEUM
ZERMATT
ALPINE MUSEUM

UNITED STATES

BUENA PARK
BOXING MUSEUM
COOPERSTOWN
BASEBALL HALL OF FAME AND MUSEUM
DALLAS
TEXAS SPORTS HALL OF FAME
DODGE CITY
HISTORIC OLD FRONT STREET
GOSHEN
HALL OF FAME OF THE TROTTER
GRAND PRAIRIE
TEXAN SPORTS HALL OF FAME
INDIANAPOLIS
INDIANAPOLIS MOTOR SPEEDWAY MUSEUM
ISHPEMING
NATIONAL SKI HALL OF FAME
LOUISVILLE
CHURCHILL DOWNS MUSEUM
MANASSA
JACK DEMPSEY MUSEUM
MANCHESTER
MUSEUM OF AMERICAN FLY FISHING
NEWPORT
NATIONAL TENNIS HALL OF FAME AND TENNIS MUSEUM
NEWPORT NEWS
JAMES RIVER GOLF MUSEUM
ORMOND BEACH
ORMOND BEACH WAR MEMORIAL ART GALLERY
SARATOGA SPRINGS
NATIONAL MUSEUM OF RACING
SAVANNAH
JULIETTE GORDON LOW BIRTHPLACE
SPRINGFIELD
NATIONAL BASKETBALL HALL OF FAME
STEAMBOAT SPRINGS
TREAD OF PIONEERS
WHEATRIDGE
WESTERNAIRE MUSEUM OF RIDING AND DRIVING HISTORY

Waxworks

FRANCE

MARZY
FOLKLORE MUSEUM
PARIS
GRÉVIN MUSEUM

UNITED STATES

HONOLULU
HAWAIAN WAX MUSEUM

Music

ARGENTINA

ALTA GRACIA
MANUEL DE FALLA MUSEUM

AUSTRALIA

SYDNEY
MUSEUM OF APPLIED ARTS AND SCIENCES
TOWNSVILLE
KENNEDY ANTHROPOLOGICAL MUSEUM

AUSTRIA

ARNSDORF
FRANZ XAVIER GRUBER MUSEUM
BADEN
ROLLETT MUSEUM
BREGENZ
VORARLBERG MUSEUM
EISBACH
COLLECTION OF REIN CISTERCIAN MONASTERY
EISENERZ
REGIONAL MUSEUM
EISENSTADT
HAYDN MUSEUM
GAADEN
FERDINAND RAIMUND MEMORIAL MUSEUM
GMUNDEN
TOWN MUSEUM
GRAZ
JOANNEUM PROVINCIAL MUSEUM OF CULTURAL HISTORY AND APPLIED ART
JOANNEUM PROVINCIAL MUSEUM OF THE ETHNOLOGY AND FOLKLORE OF STEIERMARK
HALLEIN
MUNICIPAL MUSEUM
HALLSTATT
LOCAL MUSEUM
HERBERTSTEIN
PALACE MUSEUM
HERMAGOR
GAITAL REGIONAL MUSEUM
HERZOGENBURG
COLLECTIONS OF THE MONASTERY
INNSBRUCK
AMBRAS CASTLE COLLECTION
KLAGENFURT
KOSCHAT MUSEUM
RAIDING
FRANZ LISZT MUSEUM
ROHRAU
HAYDN MUSEUM
SALZBURG
MOZART MUSEUM
MOZART'S HOUSE
ST. FLORIAN
COLLECTIONS OF THE AUGUSTIAN MONASTERY
SCHLAINING
CASTLE MUSEUM
VÖCKLABRUCK
REGIONAL HOUSE
VIENNA
ALSERGRUND DISTRICT MUSEUM
BEETHOVEN MEMORIAL ROOMS
FLORISDORF DISTRICT MUSEUM
HAYDN MUSEUM
HOUSE WHERE SCHUBERT DIED
MOZART MEMORIAL ROOM
MUSEUM OF THE HISTORY OF ART: COLLECTION OF OLD MUSICAL INSTRUMENTS
MUSEUM OF INDUSTRY AND TECHNOLOGY
MUSEUM OF THE JOSEFSTADT DISTRICT
TREASURY OF THE GERMAN ORDER
UNIVERSITY MUSEUM
WAIZENKIRCHEN
WILHELM KIENZ BIRTHPLACE
WEIKENDORF
MARCHFELD MUSEUM

BANGLADESH

DACCA
BANGLA ACADEMY MUSEUM
COLLEGE OF MUSIC MUSEUM

BELGIUM

ANTWERP
ARCHIVES AND MUSEUM OF FLEMISH CULTURAL LIFE
BRUGES
GRUUTHUSE MUSEUM

BRUSSELS
ROYAL CONSERVATORY OF MUSIC: COLLECTION OF MUSICAL INSTRUMENTS

LIÈGE
GRÉTRY MUSEUM
YSAYE'S STUDIO

MONS
ROYAL CONSERVATORY OF MUSIC

TOURNAI
CATHEDRAL TREASURY

BRAZIL

CAMPINAS
CARLOS GOMES MUSEUM

RIO DE JANEIRO
MUSEUM OF MUSICAL INSTRUMENTS
MUSEUM OF PICTURES AND SOUND
VILLA LOBOS MUSEUM

SANTA LEOPOLDINA
COLONIAL MUSEUM

SANTA RITA DO PASSA QUATRO
ZEQUINHA DE ABREU HISTORICAL MUSEUM

BULGARIA

PLOVDIV
BUKURESCHLIEV HOUSE- MUSEUM

BURUNDI

KITEGA

CANADA

OTTAWA
NATIONAL MUSEUM OF MAN

CENTRAL AFRICAN REPUBLIC

BANGUI
BARTHÉLÉMY BOGANDA MUSEUM

CHAD

FORT LAMY
CHAD NATIONAL MUSEUM

CHINA, P.R.

PEKING
IMPERIAL PALACE
MUSEUM OF THE INSTITUTE OF MUSICOLOGY

QU FU
TEMPLE OF CONFUCIUS

CZECHOSLOVAKIA

BRATISLAVA
J. N. HUMMEL MUSEUM
MUNICIPAL MUSEUM

BRNO
MORAVIAN MUSEUM: MUSICAL COLLECTIONS

DĚČÍN
DISTRICT MUSEUM

DUCHOV
MANOR HOUSE MUSEUM

HUKVALDY
LEOŠ JANÁČEK MEMORIAL

JABKENICE
SMETANA MEMORIAL MUSEUM

KRÁSNA HÔRKA
CASTLE MUSEUM

NELAHOZEVES
ANTON DVOŘÁK MUSEUM

OBŘÍSTVI
BEDŘICH SMETANA MEMORIAL MUSEUM

OPAVA
SILESIAN MUSEUM: HISTORY COLLECTIONS

PASEKY NAD JIZEROU
ZAPADLÝ VLASTENCA MUSEUM

PLZEŇ
MUSEUM OF WESTERN CZECHOSLOVAKIA: JULIUS FUČIK MEMORIAL COLLECTION

PRAGUE
ANTONÍN DVOŘÁK MUSEUM
NATIONAL MUSEUM: COLLECTIONS OF THE HISTORY OF MUSIC
BEDŘICH SMETANA MUSEUM

SEDLČANY
MUNICIPAL MUSEUM

SKUTEČ
VITĚZSLAV NOVAK MUSEUM

ŠTERNBERK
MUSEUM OF MUSIC

STRÁŽNICI
REGIONAL MUSEUM OF FOLK ART

TEPLICE
REGIONAL MUSEUM

TÝN NAD VLTAVOU
MUNICIPAL MUSEUM

ÚPICE
MUNICIPAL MUSEUM

VŠEBOŘICE
ZDEŇKO FIBICH MEMORIAL MUSEUM

VYSOKÁ U PŘIBRAMI
ANTON DVOŘÁK MEMORIAL MUSEUM

ZLONICE
DVOŘÁK MEMORIAL MUSEUM

DENMARK

COPENHAGEN
CARL CLAUDIUS' MUSICAL COLLECTION
MUSEUM OF THE HISTORY OF MUSIC
TS MUSEUM

NØRRE LYNDELSE
CARL NEILSEN'S HOUSE

ODENSE
CARL NIELSEN'S CHILDHOOD HOME

REBILD BAKKER
FOLK ART AND SPILLEMAEND MUSEUM

ETHIOPIA

ADDIS ABABA
INSTITUTE OF ETHIOPIAN STUDIES MUSEUM

FINLAND

JÄRVENPÄÄ
AINOLA
PEKKA HALONEN HOUSE- MUSEUM

FRANCE

LA CÔTE-SAINT-ANDRÉ
BERLIOZ MUSEUM

LA COUTURE-BOUSSEY
MUSEUM OF INDUSTRY AND INSTRUMENTS

DIEPPE
CHÂTEAU MUSEUM

LILLE
MUSEUM OF INDUSTRY, COMMERCE, TECHNOLOGY AND AGRICULTURE

MARLY-LE-ROI
OLD MARLY MUSEUM

MARSEILLE
GROBET-LABADIE MUSEUM

MONTFORT-L'AMAURY
MAURICE RAVEL MUSEUM

MONTLUCON
MUNICIPAL MUSEUM

NICE
MUSEUM OF MUSICAL INSTRUMENTS

PARIS
MUSEUM OF THE HIGHER NATIONAL CONSERVATORY OF MUSIC
MUSEUM OF MUSICAL INSTRUMENTS

SAINT-AMAND-LES-EAUX
CARILLON MUSEUM

VARZY
MUNICIPAL MUSEUM

VENDÔME
MUNICIPAL MUSEUM

GDR

APOLDA
BELL AND REGIONAL MUSEUM

ARNSTADT
BACH MEMORIAL

AUGUSTUSBURG
REGIONAL MUSEUM

BAD KOSTRITZ
HEINRICH SCHÜTZ MEMORIAL

BERLIN
MUSEUM OF CULTURAL HISTORY

BURGK
REGIONAL AND CASTLE MUSEUM

HALLE
HÄNDEL HOUSE

LAUCHA
BELL MUSEUM

LEIPZIG
BACH MUSEUM
ETHNOLOGICAL MUSEUM
KARL MARX UNIVERSITY MUSEUM OF MUSICAL INSTRUMENTS
MUSEUM OF THE HISTORY OF THE CITY OF LEIPZIG

MARKNEUKIRCHEN
MUSEUM OF MUSICAL INSTRUMENTS

MEININGEN
MEININGEN MUSEUM

SONDERHAUSEN
STATE REGIONAL AND CASTLE MUSEUM

WEIMAR
LISZT HOUSE

WEISSENFELS
MUNICIPAL MUSEUM
HEINRICH SCHÜTZ MEMORIAL

WERDAU
REGIONAL MUSEUM

ZITTAU
MUNICIPAL MUSEUM

ZWICKAU
ROBERT SCHUMANN HOUSE

GFR

AUGSBURG
MOZART MEMORIAL

BAMBERG
E.T.A. HOFFMAN HOUSE AND MUSEUM

BAYREUTH
RICHARD WAGNER MEMORIAL

BERLIN
MUSEUM OF MUSICAL INSTRUMENTS

BINGEN
REGIONAL MUSEUM

BONN
BEETHOVEN HOUSE - MUSEUM

DARMSTADT
EXHIBITION OF LITERARY AND MUSICAL MANUSCRIPTS

ERDING
REGIONAL MUSEUM
ERLANGEN
MUSICAL INSTRUMENTS COLLECTION OF THE UNIVERSITY OF ERLANGEN-NÜRNBERG
FREIBURG IM BREISGAU
GERMAN LIBRARY AND MUSEUM OF FOLKSONG
GARMISCH-PARTENKIRCHEN
RICHARD STRAUSS MUSEUM
HEIDE
MUSEUM OF DITHMARSCHEN PREHISTORY
HEIDELBERG
COLLECTION OF THE UNIVERSITY SEMINAR OF MUSIC
ETHNOLOGY MUSEUM OF THE J. AND E. VON PORTHEIM FOUNDATION
HEILBRONN
HEILBRONN COLLECTION OF MUSIC
INGOLSTADT
BAVARIAN ARMY MUSEUM
KASSEL
LOUIS SPOHR MEMORIAL AND RESEARCH INSTITUTE
MITTENWALD
REGIONAL MUSEUM AND MUSEUM OF VIOLIN MAKING
MÜNCHEN
CITY COLLECTION OF MUSICAL INSTRUMENTS
NÜRNBERG
GERMAN NATIONAL MUSEUM
NEUPERT PIANO MUSEUM
REGENSBURG
REGENSBURG CITY MUSEUM
SIEGBURG
SIEGBURG REGIONAL MUSEUM
TÜBINGEN
THEODOR HEARING HOUSE
WEIDEN
TOWN MUSEUM
WOLFACH
WOLFACH REGIONAL MUSEUM

GREAT BRITAIN

BRENTFORD
BRITISH PIANO MUSEUM
EDINBURGH
RUSSELL COLLECTION OF HARPSICHORDS AND CLAVICHORDS
LITTLE GADDESDEN
THE MANOR HOUSE
LONDON
BRITISH PIANO MUSEUM
FENTON HOUSE
FOUNDLING HOSPITAL ART TREASURES
HORNIMAN MUSEUM
ROYAL COLLEGE OF MUSIC
NEWCASTLE- UPON-TYNE
THE BAGPIPE MUSEUM
OXFORD
PITT RIVERS MUSEUM
TWICKENHAM
ROYAL MILITARY SCHOOL OF MUSIC MUSEUM

GREECE

ATHENS
F. ANOYANAKIS PRIVATE COLLECTION
RESEARCH CENTRE OF GREEK FOLKLORE
IOANNINA
FOLKLORE MUSEUM AND ARCHIVES OF THE IOANNINA FACULTY OF PHILOSOPHY

HUNGARY

BALASSAGYARMAT
PALÓC MUSEUM
BUDAPEST
MUSEUM OF THE HISTORY OF BUDAPEST: DEPARTMENT OF MODERN HISTORY
MARTONVÁSÁR
BEETHOVEN MUSEUM
SOPRON
FERENC LISZT MUSEUM
SZÉKESFEHÉRVÁR
KING ISTVÁN MUSEUM

INDIA

ALLAHABAD
ALLAHABAD MUSEUM
BHAWANAGAR
GANDHI SMRITI MUSEUMS
TRIVANDRUM
ART MUSEUM

IRELAND

LIMERICK
LIMERICK CITY MUSEUM

ISRAEL

HAIFA
MUSIC MUSEUM
JERUSALEM
MUSEUM OF MUSICAL INSTRUMENTS

ITALY

BERGAMO
MUSEUM
BOLOGNA
MUNICIPAL MUSEUM OF MUSICAL BIBLIOGRAPHY
BORGO
ARTURO TOSCANINI'S BIRTHPLACE
CATANIA
BELLINI MUSEUM
CREMONA
STRADIVARIUS MUSEUM
FLORENCE
MUSEUM OF MUSICAL INSTRUMENTS
GENOA
ART GALLERY
LA FAVORITA
PITRÉ MUSEUM OF SICILIAN ETHNOGRAPHY
LE RONCOLE-VERDI
HOUSE OF GIUSEPPE VERDI
MILAN
MUSEUM OF ANCIENT MUSICAL INSTRUMENTS
MODENA
CITY MUSEUM
NAPLES
MUSIC MUSEUM
PALERMO
PITRÉ ETHNOGRAPHICAL MUSEUM
PESARO
ROSSINI'S HOUSE
RECANATI
GIGLI MUSEUM
ROME
MUSEUM OF HISTORICAL APPARATUS FOR THE REPRODUCTION OF SOUND
MUSEUM OF MUSICAL INSTRUMENTS
NATIONAL MUSEUM OF ARTS AND POPULAR TRADITIONS
NATIONAL MUSEUM OF MUSICAL INSTRUMENTS
SIENA
GALLERY OF TUSCAN PAINTING

IVORY COAST

ABIDJAN
MUSEUM OF THE CENTRE DES SCIENCES HUMAINES

JAPAN

HIKONE-SHI
I'I ART MUSEUM
MATSUE-SHI
SHIMANE PREFECTURAL MUSEUM
NARA-SHI
SHOSOIN TREASURE HOUSE
TOKYO
MUSEUM OF MUSICAL INSTRUMENTS

MALAYSIA

MALACCA
MALACCA MUSEUM

MEXICO

MEXICO CITY
NATIONAL MUSEUM OF ARTS AND CRAFTS

NETHERLANDS

ASTEN
BELL AND CARILLON MUSEUM
'S GRAVENHAGE
MUNICIPAL MUSEUM
HEEMSTEDE
DE RAAF BRAND VAN STRAATER COLLECTION
ROTTERDAM
H. REMKES COLLECTION
UTRECHT
PIEREMENT MUSICAL BOX MUSEUM

NEW ZEALAND

WELLINGTON
THE ZILLAH AND RONALD CASTLE COLLECTION OF EARLY AND UNIQUE INSTRUMENTS AND MUSIC

NORWAY

BERGEN
"TROLDHAUGEN"
TRONDHEIM
RINGVE MUSICAL HISTORY MUSEUM

POLAND

ANTONIN
CHOPIN MEMORIAL MUSEUM
BARCZEWO
FELIX NOWOWIEJSKI MUSEUM
CZARNOLAS
JAN KOCHANOWSKI MUSEUM
CZĘSTOCHOWA
TREASURY
DUBIECKO
IGNAZ KRASICKI MUSEUM
GOŁOTCZYZNA
LOCAL MUSEUM
GORZEŃ GÓRNY
EMIL ZEGADŁOWICZ MUSEUM
KARTUZY
KASUBIAN MUSEUM
ŁÓDŹ
MUSEUM OF MUSIC
OPINOGÓRA
MUSEUM OF ROMANTICISM
POZNAŃ
MUSEUM OF MUSICAL INSTRUMENTS
PRANIE
K. I. GAŁCZYŃSKI MUSEUM

SIOŁKOWICE
JAKUB KANIA MUSEUM
SŁUŻEWO
LOCAL MUSEUM
SZAFARNIA
MEMORIAL ROOM
WARSAW
FRYDERYK CHOPIN MUSEUM
MUSEUM OF THE WARSAW MUSICAL ASSOCIATION
WEJHEROWO
MUSEUM OF MUSIC
ZACHEŁMIE
LUDOMIR ROZYCKI HOUSE- MUSEUM
ZBĄSZIN
REGIONAL MUSEUM
ŻELAZOWA WOLA
FRYDERYK CHOPIN MUSEUM

PORTUGAL

COIMBRA
MACHADO DE CASTRO MUSEUM
LISBON
MUSEUM OF THE NATIONAL CONSERVATORY OF MUSIC
MUSEUM OF POPULAR ART
ROMEU
MUSEUM OF CURIOSITIES

ROMANIA

BUCHAREST
GEORGE ENESCU MUSEUM
DR. N. MINOVICI MUSEUM OF FOLK ART
C. I. AND C. C. NOTTARA MUSEUM
VILLAGE MUSEUM
DOROHOI
GEORGE ENESCU MEMORIAL MUSEUM
GEORGE ENESCU
GEORGE ENESCU MUSEUM
IAŞI
MOLDAVIAN MUSEUM OF ETHNOLOGY
SUCEAVA
SUCEAVA MUSEUM

SOUTH AFRICA, REPUBLIC OF

TULBAGH
OUDEKERK VOLKSMUSEUM

SPAIN

AVILA
CATHEDRAL MUSEUM
BARCELONA
MUNICIPAL MUSEUM OF MUSIC
GIJON
NATIONAL GUITAR MUSEUM
GRANADA
MANUEL DE FALLA HOUSE- MUSEUM
JEREZ DE LA FRONTERA
FLAMENCO MUSEUM
MADRID
COLLECTION OF THE LIBRARY OF MUSIC
MUSEUM OF SPANISH BOOKS
PAMPLONA
SARASATE MUSEUM
VALLDEMOSA
ROYAL CHARTERHOUSE

SWEDEN

STOCKHOLM
MUSIC MUSEUM
NATIONAL MUSEUM OF ETHNOGRAPHY
STRINDBERG MUSEUM

SWITZERLAND

BADEN
HISTORICAL MUSEUM
BASEL
COLLECTION OF OLD MUSICAL INSTRUMENTS
EBNAT-KAPPEL
ALBERT EDELMANN FOUNDATION
GENEVA
MUSEUM OF ART AND HISTORY
MUSEUM AND INSTITUTE OF ETHNOGRAPHY
MUSEUM OF OLD MUSICAL INSTRUMENTS
HINWIL
LOCAL MUSEUM
LICHTENSTEIG
TOGGENBURG REGIONAL MUSEUM
LUZERN
RICHARD WAGNER MUSEUM
NEUCHÂTEL
MUSEUM OF ETHNOGRAPHY AND INSTITUTE OF ETHNOLOGY
SAINTE-CROIX
MUSEUM OF OLD MECHANICAL MUSICAL INSTRUMENTS
WETZIKON
LOCAL MUSEUM
WITTENBACH
LOCAL MUSEUM
ZURICH
MUSEUM OF APPLIED ART

THAILAND

BANGKOK
NATIONAL MUSEUM

TUNISIA

TUNIS
ARAB MUSEUM
MUSEUM OF THE CONSERVATOIRE

TURKEY

ANKARA
ETHNOGRAPHICAL MUSEUM

UGANDA

KAMPALA
UGANDA MUSEUM

USSR

CHERNIGOV
MUSEUM OF MUSICAL INSTRUMENTS
KLIN
P. J. TCHAIKOVSKY MEMORIAL MUSEUM
LENINGRAD
MUSEUM OF MUSICAL INSTRUMENTS
MOSCOW
CENTRAL MUSEUM OF MUSICAL CULTURE, 'M. J. GLINKA'
A. N. SCRIABIN MUSEUM
TCHAIKOVSKI MUSEUM
TALLINN
MUSEUM OF MUSIC AND THE THEATRE
TIKHVIN
RIMSKY-KORSAKOV HOUSE- MUSEUM
VILNIUS (formerly WILNO)
MUSEUM OF MUSIC AND THE THEATRE
VOTKINSK
TCHAIKOVSKY MEMORIAL MUSEUM

UNITED STATES

ANN ARBOR
STEARNS COLLECTION OF MUSICAL INSTRUMENTS
BARDSTOWN
MY OLD KENTUCKY HOME STATE PARK
BOLTON LANDING
MARCELLA SEMBRICK MEMORIAL STUDIO
BOSTON
MUSEUM OF FINE ARTS
CHICAGO
GEORGE F. HARDING MUSEUM
DEANSBORO
MUSICAL MUSEUM
DODGE CITY
BOOT HILL MUSEUM
EAST POULTNEY
POULTNEY HISTORICAL SOCIETY MUSEUM
FUQUAY-VARINA
JOHNSON GOURD MUSEUM
KALAMAZOO
KALAMAZOO PUBLIC MUSEUM
NASHVILLE
COUNTRY MUSIC HALL OF FAME AND MUSEUM
NEW HAVEN
YALE UNIVERSITY COLLECTION OF MUSICAL INSTRUMENTS
NEW ORLEANS
NEW ORLEANS JAZZ MUSEUM
NEW YORK
JUNIOR MUSEUM OF THE METROPOLITAN MUSEUM OF ART
METROPOLITAN MUSEUM OF ART
NEW YORK JAZZ MUSEUM
PITTSBURGH
FOSTER HALL COLLECTION
ST. PAUL
MUSICAL INSTRUMENT MUSEUM
SCARSDALE
MUSEUM OF MUSIC
SIKESTON
GAY NINETIES VILLAGE
STONE MOUNTAIN
STONE MOUNTAIN PARK
VERMILLION
ARNE B. LARSON MUSIC MUSEUM
WESTERVILLE
HANBY HOUSE
WHITE SPRINGS
STEPHEN FOSTER MEMORIAL
WISCASSET
MUSIC MUSEUM

YUGOSLAVIA

DUBROVNIK
ETHNOGRAPHICAL MUSEUM
PAZIN
ETHNOGRAPHIC AND HISTORICAL MUSEUM
PIRAN
ART GALLERY AND CITY MUSEUM
RIJEKA
MARITIME AND HISTORICAL MUSEUM
ZAGREB
IVAN GERESDORFER COLLECTION OF MUSICAL AUTOMATA

Literature

ARGENTINA

BUENOS AIRES
RICARDO ROJAS HOUSE
CÓRDOBA
LEOPOLDO LUGONES MUSEUM
FLORENCIA VARELA
BIRTHPLACE OF W. H. HUDSON
GUALEGUAYCHÚ
ANDRADE HOUSE-MUSEUM
SAN ANTONIO DE ARECO
RICARDO GUIRALDES GAUCHO MUSEUM
SAN MARTIN
JOSÉ HERNÁNDEZ-CHACRA DE PUEYRREDÓN MUSEUM

AUSTRALIA

BROKEN BAY
HENRY KENDALL'S COTTAGE
GOSFORD WEST
KENDALL COTTAGE
GRENFELL
HISTORICAL MUSEUM
TAMWORTH
TAMWORTH ART GALLERY AND MUSEUM

AUSTRIA

ALPL
PETER ROSEGGEN'S BIRTHPLACE
BADEN
ROLLETT MUSEUM
BAD ISCHL
LÉHAR VILLA
KIRCHBERG AM WALDE
HAMERLING MEMORIAL MUSEUM
KITZBÜHEL
REGIONAL MUSEUM
KLEINENGERSDORF
"DER BISAMBERG UND DER WEINVIERTLER" MUSEUM
LINZ
STIFTER MEMORIAL ROOM
LOSENSTEIN
REGIONAL MUSEUM
MÖDLING
MUNICIPAL MUSEUM
NEULENGBACH
REGIONAL MUSEUM
ST. GEORGEN
PALACE MEMORIAL MUSEUM
STOCKERAU
DISTRICT MUSEUM
VIENNA
FLORISDORF DISTRICT MUSEUM
MUSEUM OF THE BÖHMERWALD
MUSEUM OF THE MARIAHILF DISTRICT
VIENNA GOETHE MUSEUM

BELGIUM

BRUSSELS
ALBERT I ROYAL LIBRARY
CAMILLE LEMONNIER MUSEUM
DAMME
VAN MAERLANT MUSEUM

BRAZIL

CARUARU
VITALINO HOUSE MUSEUM
LENÇÓIS
AFRÂNIO PEIXOTO HOUSE OF CULTURE
MESSEJANA
ALENCAR MUSEUM
MURITIBA
MUSEUM OF THE CASTRO ALVES HISTORICAL PARK
PALMEIRA DOS ÍNDIOS
GRACILIANO RAMOS HOUSE MUSEUM
SALVADOR
CASTRO ALVES MUSEUM
SÃO JOSÉ DO RIO PARDO
EUCLIDES DA CUNHA MUSEUM

BULGARIA

BANSHO
NIKOLA VAPKAROV HOUSE- MUSEUM
KOPRIVŠTICA
DIMČO DEBELJANOV HOUSE- MUSEUM
SOFIA
V. KOLAROV NATIONAL LIBRARY
IVAN VASOV MUSEUM
P. K. YAVOROV MUSEUM
SVIŠTOV
HISTORY MUSEUM
VASOVGRAD (formerly SOPOT)
IVAN VAZOV HOUSE-MUSEUM

CANADA

CHATHAM
CHATHAM-KENT MUSEUM
DRESDEN
UNCLE TOM'S CABIN
MIDDLEPORT
CHIEFSWOOD
OAKVILLE
TARAS H. SHEVCHENKO MUSEUM
ORILLIA
STEPHEN LEACOCK MEMORIAL HOME
PERIBOUKA
LOUIS HÉMON - MARIA CHAPDELAINE MUSEUM
WHITEHORSE
MCBRIDE CENTENNIAL MUSEUM
WINDSOR
HALIBURTON MEMORIAL MUSEUM

CHILE

VICUNA
GABRIELA MISTRAL MUSEUM

CHINA, P.R.

CHENG TU (CHENG DU)
CINNAMON TREE LAKE MEMORIAL
FU'S COTTAGE
SHANGHAI
LU XUN (LU HSUN) MUSEUM
SHAO SHING
LU HSUN MUSEUM
TSINAN (JI NAN)
LI QING ZHAO MUSEUM
WACHANG (WU HAN)
PROVINCIAL MUSEUM

COLOMBIA

BOGOTA
MUSEUM OF LITERATURE
EL CERRITO
EL PARAISEO
POPAYAN
VALENCIA HOUSE-MUSEUM
TUNJA
JUAN DE VARGAS HOUSE MUSEUM

CUBA

HABANA
HEMINGWAY MUSEUM

CZECHOSLOVAKIA

BRATISLAVA
JANKO JESENSKÝ MUSEUM
ČERVENÝ KOSTELEA
BOŽENA NEMCOVA MEMORIAL MUSEUM
ČESKA SKALICE
BOŽENY NÉMCOVA MUSEUM
ČESKE BUDĚJOVICE
MUSEUM OF SOUTHERN CZECHOSLOVAKIA
ČESKÝ DUB
KAROLINY SVĚTLÉ MUSEUM
CHUDENICE
JOSEF DOBROVSKY AND JAROSLAV KVAPILA MUSEUM
DOLÍNEK
VÍTEZSLAV HÁLEK MEMORIAL MUSEUM
DOLNÝ KUBÍN
P.O. HVIEZDOSLAVA MUSEUM
JINDŘICHŮV HRODEC
REGIONAL MUSEUM
JUR PRI BRATISLAVE
PETRA JILEMNICKÝ MUSEUM
KOSTELNEC NA HANÉ
PETR BEZRUČ MEMORIAL
LIPTOVSKÝ MIKULÁŠ
JANKO KRÁL MUSEUM OF LITERATURE
MALÉ SVATOŇOVICE
MUSEUM OF THE BROTHERS ČAPEK
MARIÁNSKE LÁZNĚ
MUNICIPAL MUSEUM
OPAVA
PETR BEZRUČ MEMORIAL
PÍSEK
ADOLF HEYDUK MEMORIAL
POČÁTKY
OTOKARA BŘEZINY HOUSE- MUSEUM
PRAGUE
MUSEUM OF CZECH LITERATURE
PROSEČ U SKUTČE
TERÉZA NOVÁKOVÁ MEMORIAL MUSEUM
ROŽĎALOVICE
JIŘÍ MELANTRICH MEMORIAL MUSEUM
SKÁLY
ALOIS JIRÁSEK MEMORIAL MUSEUM
SOBOTKA
MUSEUM OF LITERARY HISTORY
FRA. ŠRÁMEK HOUSE-MUSEUM
STARÁ HUŤ U DOBŘÚŠE
KAREL ČAPEK MEMORIAL MUSEUM
STRAKONICE
FR. L. ČELAKOVSKÝ HOUSE MUSEUM
TŘEBÍZ
V. B. TŘEBIZSKY MEMORIAL MUSEUM
VODŇANY
MUNICIPAL MUSEUM AND ART GALLERY
VRCHOTOVY JANOVICE
R. M. RILKE MEMORIAL MUSEUM

DENMARK

COPENHAGEN
BAKKE HOUSE MUSEUM
LITERARY MUSEUM
WESSEL MUSEUM

LERCHENBORG
LERCHENBORG MANOR
LYSGARD
BLIONER MEMORIAL MUSEUM
ODENSE
H.C. ANDERSEN'S CHILDHOOD HOME
HANS ANDERSEN'S HOUSE
SORØ
SORØ DISTRICT MUSEUM
TERSLØSE
TERSLØSE HOUSE
THISTED
THISTED MUSEUM
UDBY
GRUNDTVIG MEMORIAL MUSEUM
VORDINGBORG
SOUTH ZEALAND MUSEUM

FINLAND

IISALMI
JUHANI AHO MUSEUM
PORVOO
J. L. RUNEBERG HOUSE-MUSEUM
TURKU
SIBELIUS MUSEUM
UUSIKAARLEPYY
ZACHARIAS TOPELIUS HOUSE- MUSEUM

FRANCE

AIX-EN-PROVENCE
PAUL ARBAUD MUSEUM
MUSEUM OF OLD AIX
AMIENS
MUSEUM OF REGIONAL ART AND HISTORY
ARGENTEUIL
OLD ARGENTEUIL MUSEUM
AUMONT
HENRI BARBUSSE MUSEUM
AURIOLLES
ALPHONSE DAUDET COLLECTION
BERGUES
MUNICIPAL MUSEUM
BESANÇON
HISTORICAL MUSEUM
CAMBO-LES-BAINS
EDMOND ROSTAND MUSEUM
CARCASSONNE
MUSEUM OF FINE ARTS
CHÂLONS-SUR-MARNE
GARINET MUSEUM
SCHILLER-GOETHE MEMORABILIA
CHAMBÉRY
CHARMETTES MUSEUM
CHARLEVILLE-MÉZIÈRES
ARDENNES AND RIMBAUD MUSEUM
CHÂTEAU-THIERRY
JEAN DE LA FONTAINE MUSEUM
LA CHÂTRE
MUSEUM OF GEORGE SAND AND OF THE VALLÉE NOIRE
CHAUNY
LOCAL MUSEUM
EPINEUIL-LE-FLEURIEL
ALAIN-FOURNIER MUSEUM
FONTAINE-DE-VAUCLUSE
PETRARCH MUSEUM
FONTVIEILLE
ALPHONSE DAUDET MUSEUM
GAILLAC
CHÂTEAU MUSEUM
GARGILESSE DAMPIERRE
GEORGE-SAND HOUSE-MUSEUM
GRENOBLE
STENDHAL MUSEUM
HASPARREN
MUSEUM FRANCIS JAMMES
ILLIERS COMBRAY
PIÉ-CATELAN
MARCEL PROUST HOUSE- MUSEUM
LANGRES
HÔTEL DU BREUIL DE SAINT- GERMAIN MUSEUM
LIRÉ
JOACHIM DU BELLAY MUSEUM
MÂCON
LAMARTINE MUSEUM
MAGNY-LES-HAMEAUX
NATIONAL MUSEUM OF THE GRANGES DE PORT-ROYAL
MAILLANE
FRÉDÉRIC MISTRAL MUSEUM
MONTMORENCY
JEAN-JACQUES ROUSSEAU MUSEUM
NANTES
JULES VERNE MUSEUM
NOHANT-VIC
GEORGE SAND HOUSE-MUSEUM
ORLÉANS
PÉGUY MUSEUM
PARIS
BALZAC MUSEUM
CARNAVALLET MUSEUM
VICTOR HUGO MUSEUM
ADAM MICKIEWICZ MUSEUM
LE PETIT-COURONNE
CORNEILLE MUSEUM
RICHELIEU
MUSEUM OF THE 17th CENTURY
ROUEN
CORNEILLE MUSEUM
FLAUBERT MUSEUM
SACHÉ
BALZAC MUSEUM
SAINT-DENIS
MUNICIPAL MUSEUM
ST. PIERRE D'OLÉRON
ALIENOR D'AQUITAINE MUSEUM
SAINT-POINT
CHÂTEAU
SAINT- SAUVIER-LE-VICOMTE
BARBEY-D'AUREVILLY MUSEUM
SESSENHEIM
GOETHE MEMORIAL
SÈTE
PAUL VALÉRY MUNICIPAL MUSEUM
SEUILLY-LA-DEVINIÈRE
RABELAIS MUSEUM
SOLLIÉS-PONT
JEAN AICARD MUSEUM
TRÉGUIER
ERNEST RENAN'S BIRTHPLACE
UZÈS
LOCAL MUSEUM
VILLEQUIER
VICTOR HUGO MUSEUM
VILLERS-COTTERETS
ALEXANDRE DUMAS MUSEUM
WALDERSBACH
OBERLIN MUSEUM

GDR

BAUERBACH
SCHILLERHAUS
BAUTZEN
MUSEUM OF SORBIAN LITERATURE
BERLIN
JOHANNES R. BECHER HOUSE
BODE MUSEUM: PAPYRUS COLLECTION
HUGUENOT MUSEUM
MUSEUM OF CULTURAL HISTORY
DORNBURG
DORNBURG CASTLES
DRESDEN
CARL MARIA VON WEBER MEMORIAL
SCHILLER'S COTTAGE
STATE ART COLLECTIONS: MUSEUM OF ARTS AND CRAFTS
EISENACH
BACH HOUSE
REUTER HOUSE
ERKNER
GERHART HAUPTMANN MEMORIAL
FRANKFURT AN DER ODER
KLEIST MEMORIAL
GARZ
ERNST MORITZ ARNDT MUSEUM
GNANDSTEIN
REGIONAL MUSEUM
GOTHA-SIEBLEBEN
GUSTAV FREYTAG MEMORIAL
GRAUPA
RICHARD WAGNER AND REGIONAL MUSEUM
GROSSKOCHBERG
GOETHE MEMORIAL
HAINICHEN
REGIONAL MUSEUM
HALBERSTADT
GLEIN HOUSE
HIDDENSEE
GERHART HAUPTMANN MEMORIAL
ILMENAU
REGIONAL MUSEUM
JENA
GOETHE MEMORIAL
SCHILLER MEMORIAL
KAMENZ
LESSING MUSEUM
LEIPZIG
SCHILLER'S COTTAGE
LÜBBENAU
LÜBBENAU MUSEUM IN THE SPREEWALD
MAGDEBURG
ERICH WEINERT MEMORIAL
MEININGEN
BAUMBACH HOUSE
MORITZBURG
MORITZBURG CASTLE BAROQUE MUSEUM
NEUBRANDENBURG
MUSEUM OF CULTURAL HISTORY
NEURUPPIN
DISTRICT MUSEUM
OSSMANNSTEDT
WIELAND MEMORIAL
QUEDLINBURG
KLOPSTOCK MUSEUM
RAMMENAU
FICHTE MUSEUM
REUTERSTADT STAVENHAGEN
FRITZ REUTER LITERATURE MUSEUM
SEEBAD HERINGSDORF
MAXIM GORKI MEMORIAL
STUTZERBACH
GOETHE HOUSE AND GLASS MUSEUM
THALE
WALPURGIS HALL
WEIMAR
GOETHE'S GARDEN HOUSE
KIRMS KRACKOW HOUSE
NATIONAL GOETHE MUSEUM
SCHILLER'S HOUSE
WÖBBELIN
KÖRNER MEMORIAL

GFR

AALEN
REGIONAL AND SCHUBART MUSEUM
ALHAUSEN
WEBER'S BIRTHPLACE
BAMBERG
E.T.A. HOFFMAN HOUSE AND MUSEUM
KARL MAY MUSEUM

BAYREUTH
JEAN PAUL ROOM
BIBERACH
WIELAND MUSEUM
BODENWERDER
BARON MÜNCHHAUSEN MUSEUM
BONN
ERNST MORITZ ARNDT HOUSE MUSEUM
BRAUNSCHWEIG
WILHELM RAABE HOUSE - MEMORIAL
CALW
CALW REGIONAL MUSEUM AND HERMANN HESSE MEMORIAL
DARMSTADT
EXHIBITION OF LITERARY AND MUSICAL MANUSCRIPTS
DÜSSELDORF
GOETHE MUSEUM
HEINE COLLECTION
EMMENDINGEN
REGIONAL MUSEUM
ESCHERSHAUSEN
RAABE MEMORIAL MUSEUM
FRANKFURT
GOETHE HOUSE AND MUSEUM
GARDING
THEODOR MOMMSEN MEMORIAL
HAMELN
REGIONAL MUSEUM
HEIDE
KLAUS GROTH MUSEUM
HEILIGENHAFEN
REGIONAL MUSEUM
HILCHENBACH-GRUND
JUNG-STILLING MEMORIAL ROOM
HÖXTER
HÖXTER-CORVEY MUSEUM
KARLSRUHE
WRITERS' MUSEUM OF THE UPPER RHINE
KASSEL
MUSEUM OF THE BROTHERS GRIMM
KELLINGHUSEN
REGIONAL MUSEUM
KNITTLINGEN
FAUST MEMORIAL
LUDWIGSHAFEN
SCHILLER HOUSE MUSEUM
MARBACH
NATIONAL SCHILLER MUSEUM AND GERMAN LITERARY ARCHIVES
SCHILLER'S BIRTHPLACE
MEERSBURG
DROSTE MUSEUM
MEERSBURG PALACE
MÖLLN
REGIONAL MUSEUM
NIENBERGE
DROSTE MUSEUM
NÜRNBERG
ALBRECHT DÜRER HOUSE
PASSAU
MUSEUM OF THE BÖHMERWALD
ROXEL
DROSTE ZU HÜLSHOFF MUSEUM
SCHLÜCHTERN
BERGWINKEL MUSEUM
SCHÖPPENSTEDT
TILL EULENSPIEGEL MUSEUM
STEINAU
PALACE MUSEUM
TÜBINGEN
THEODOR HEARING HOUSE
HÖLDERLIN MEMORIAL
WANGEN
GUSTAV FREYTAG MUSEUM AND ARCHIVES
WESSELBUREN
HEBBEL MUSEUM
WETZLAR
JERUSALEM HOUSE
LOTTE'S HOUSE
WOLFENBÜTTEL
LESSING HOUSE

GREAT BRITAIN

ALEXANDRIA
CAMERON HOUSE
ALLOWAY
BURNS' COTTAGE AND MUSEUM
AMBLESIDE
RYDAL MOUNT
AYOT ST. LAWRENCE
SHAW'S CORNER
BEDFORD
BUNYAN COLLECTION
BUNYAN MEETING LIBRARY AND MUSEUM
ELSTOW MOOT HALL
BEMBRIDGE
RUSKIN GALLERY
BRIGHTON
GRANGE ART GALLERY AND MUSEUM
BRISTOL
CHATTERTON HOUSE
BROADSTAIRS
DICKENS HOUSE MUSEUM
BURWASH
BATEMAN'S, RUDYARD KIPLING'S HOME
CHALFONT ST. GILES
MILTON'S COTTAGE
CHAWTON
JANE AUSTEN'S HOME
COCKERMOUTH
WORDSWORTH HOUSE
CONISTON
ART GALLERY MUSEUM
RUSKIN MUSEUM
DORCHESTER
DORSET COUNTY MUSEUM
ECCLEFECHAN
CARLYLE'S BIRTHPLACE
EDINBURGH
LADY STAIR'S HOUSE
GRASMERE
DOVE COTTAGE
WORDSWORTH MUSEUM
GUERNSEY
HAUTEVILLE HOUSE
HAWORTH
BRONTE PARSONAGE MUSEUM
KESWICK
FITZ PARK MUSEUM AND ART GALLERY
KILMARNOCK
BURNS' MONUMENT AND MUSEUM
KIRKCUDBRIGHT
BROUGHTON HOUSE
KIRKOSWALD
SOUTER JOHNNIE'S HOUSE
KIRRIMUIR
BARRIE'S BIRTHPLACE
LICHFIELD
DR. JOHNSON'S BIRTHPLACE
LINBY
NEWSTEAD ABBEY
LONDON
CARLYLE'S HOUSE
DICKENS HOUSE
DR. JOHNSON'S HOUSE
KEATS HOUSE AND MUSEUM
MELROSE
ABBOTSFORD HOUSE
NEAR SAWREY
HILL TOP
NETHER STOWEY
COLERIDGE COTTAGE
NEWPORT
CARISBROOKE CASTLE MUSEUM
NOTTINGHAM
NEWSTEAD ABBEY
NUNEATON
NUNEATON MUSEUM AND ART GALLERY
OLNEY
COWPER AND NEWTON MUSEUM
OXFORD
CHRIST CHURCH LIBRARY
PORTSMOUTH
DICKENS' BIRTHPLACE MUSEUM
ROCHESTER
ROCHESTER PUBLIC MUSEUM
SCARBOROUGH
SCARBOROUGH MUSEUM OF NATURAL HISTORY
SELKIRK
SELKIRK MUSEUM
STAFFORD
IZAAK WALTON COTTAGE
STOKE-ON-TRENT
ARNOLD BENNETT MUSEUM
STRATFORD- UPON-AVON
ANNE HATHAWAY'S COTTAGE
MARY ARDEN'S HOUSE
SWINDON
RICHARD JEFFERIES MUSEUM
TARBOLTON
BACHELORS CLUB
WISBECH
WISBECH AND FENLAND MUSEUM

GREECE

CHIOS
ADAMANTIOS KORAIS LIBRARY
CORFU
SOLOMOS MUSEUM

HUNGARY

ÁLMOSD
KÖLCSEY HOUSE MUSEUM
BADACSONY
IRODALMI MUSEUM
BAKONSZEG
GYÖRGY BESSENYEI HOUSE MUSEUM
BALATONFÜRED
JÓKAI MEMORIAL MUSEUM
BALATONSZÁRSZÓ
ATTILA JÓZSEF MEMORIAL MUSEUM
BUDAPEST
JÓKAI MEMORIAL ROOM
ATTILA JÓZSEF MEMORIAL ROOM
PETŐFI MUSEUM OF LITERATURE
DÖMSÖD
PETŐFI MEMORIAL MUSEUM
EGER
GÉZA GÁRDONYI MEMORIAL MUSEUM
ESZTERGOM
BÁLINT BALASSI MUSEUM
KISKŐRÖS
PETŐFI MEMORIAL MUSEUM
NAGYKŐRÖS
JÁNOS ARANY MEMORIAL MUSEUM
NAGYKŐRÖS
JÁNOS ARANY MUSEUM
NILKA
DÁNIEL BERZENYI MEMORIAL MUSEUM
SÜMEG
KISFALUDY MEMORIAL MUSEUM
SZEGED
FERENC MÓRA MUZEUM

ICELAND

REYKJAVIK
NATIONAL LIBRARY AND ARCHIVES

INDIA

CALCUTTA
MUSEUM OF THE BANGIYA SAHITYA PARISHAD
KANTHALPARA
RISHI BANKIM MUSEUM AND LIBRARY
SANTINIKETAN
TAGORE MEMORIAL MUSEUM

IRELAND

EDGEWORTHSTOWN
EDGEWORTH SOCIETY MUSEUM
GORT
THOOR BALLYLEE
LISSADELL
LISSADELL HOUSE
SANDYCOVE
JAMES JOYCE MUSEUM
SLIGO
COUNTY SLIGO MUSEUM
THOOR BALLYLEE
YEATS MUSEUM

ISRAEL

LOHAME-HAGETA'OT
BEIT KATZNELSON MUSEUM

ITALY

ANACAPRI
VILLA SAN MICHELE
ARQUA PETRARCA
PETRARCH'S HOUSE
ASOLO
MUNICIPAL MUSEUM
ASTI
ALFIERI MUSEUM
BOLOGNA
CARDUCCI HOUSE AND LIBRARY
MARSILIANA MUSEUM
CERTALDO
MUSEUM OF BOCCACCIO
COLLODI
CHÂTEAU
FERRARA
ARIOSTO'S HOUSE
PALAZZINA MARFISA D'ESTE
GARDONE DI SOPRA
MUSEUM
GARDONE RIVIERA
VITTORIALE ESTATE
LECCO
VILLA DI ALESSANDRO MANZONI
MILAN
NATIONAL CENTRE OF MANZONI STUDIES
PESCARA
HOUSE OF GABRIELE D'ANNUNZIO
RAVENNA
DANTE MUSEUM
MUSEUM AND TOMB OF DANTE
RECANATI
LEOPARDI PALACE
ROME
JOHN KEATS' HOUSE
PIRANDELLO'S HOUSE
TASSIANO MUSEUM
VATICAN LIBRARY
SAN MAURO PASCOLI
BIRTHPLACE OF G. PASCOLI

JAPAN

KISO-GUN
TOSON SHIMAZAKI MEMORIAL HALL
OSAKA
FUJITA ART MUSEUM
TOKYO
ICHI-YO MEMORIAL MUSEUM
MUSEUM OF MODERN JAPANESE LITERATURE
UENO-SHI
BASHO MEMORIAL HALL
YONEZAWA-SHI
TREASURE HOUSE OF THE UESUGI SHRINE

LUXEMBOURG

VIANDEN
VICTOR HUGO MUSEUM

MAURITIUS

SOUILLAC
R. E. HART MUSEUM

NETHERLANDS

AMSTERDAM
BILDERDIJK MUSEUM
MULTATULI MUSEUM
VONDEL MUSEUM
DOORN
MAARTEN MAARTENS HOUSE
'S GRAVENHAGE
NETHERLANDS MUSEUM OF LITERATURE
LEEUWARDEN
MUSEUM OF FRISIAN LITERATURE
NIEUW- VOSSEMEER
A. M. DE JONG MUSEUM

NORWAY

GAUSDAL
AULESTAD
GRIMSTAD
IBSEN HOUSE AND GRIMSTAD MUSEUM
RINGERIKE
RINGERIKE MUSEUM
SKIEN
TELEMARK AND GRENLAND FOLK MUSEUM
VENSTØP FARM

POLAND

EŁK
REGIONAL MUSEUM
JAGNIĄTKÓW
GERHARDT HAUPTMANN HOUSE-MUSEUM
KIELCE
STEFAN ZEROMSKI MEMORIAL MUSEUM
KONARZEWO
ADAM MICKIEWICZ MUSEUM
KOTACZKOWO
REGIONAL MUSEUM
KROŚNIEWICE
COLLECTIONS OF JERZY DUNIN- BORKOWSKI
ŁÓDŹ
JULIAN TUWIM MEMORIAL MUSEUM
LUBLIN
JOZEF CZECHOWICZ MUSEUM
MORĄG
JOHANN GOTTFRIED HERDER MUSEUM
NAŁECZOW
BOLESŁAW PRUS MUSEUM
OBLĘGOREK
HENRYK SIENKIEWICZ MUSEUM
OPINOGÓRA
MUSEUM OF ROMANTICISM
PIŁA
STANISŁAW STASZIC MUSEUM
PORĘBA WIELKA
WŁADYSŁAW ORKAN MUSEUM
ŚMIEŁOW
REGIONAL MUSEUM
SULEJÓW
REGIONAL MUSEUM
WARSAW
ŁADISLAUS BRONIEWSKI MUSEUM
ADAM MICKIEWICZ MUSEUM
WOLA OKRZEJSKA
HENRYK SIENKIEWICZ MUSEUM
ZAKOPANE
JAN KASPROWICZ MEMORIAL MUSEUM
K. MAKUSZYŃSKI MEMORIAL MUSEUM
ŻARNOWIEC
MARIA KONOPNICKI MUSEUM

ROMANIA

ADY ENDRE
ADY ENDRE MUSEUM
AGAPIA
ALEXANDRU VLAHUŢĂ HOUSE- MUSEUM
ALBEŞTI
SANDOR PETŐFI MUSEUM
BRĂILA
LOCAL HISTORY MUSEUM
BUCHAREST
ION MINULESCU COLLECTION
MUSEUM OF ROMANIAN LITERATURE
CLUJ
EMIL ISAC MUSEUM
COŞBUC
GEORGE COŞBUC MUSEUM
CRAIOVA
TRAIAN DEMETRESCU MUSEUM
DRAGOSLOVENI
ALEXANDRU VLAHUŢĂ MUSEUM
HUMULEŞTI
ION CREANGĂ MUSEUM
IAŞI
ION CREANGĂS HOUSE- MEMORIAL
IPOTEŞTI
MIHAIL EMINESCU MUSEUM
LENAUHEIM
LENAU MUSEUM
LIVIU REBREANU
LIVIU REBREANU MUSEUM
MIRCEŞTI
VASILE ALECSANDRI MUSEUM
NĂMĂEŞTI
G. TOPÎRCEANU MUSEUM
ORADEA
ADY ENDRE MUSEUM
IOSIF VULCAN MUSEUM
PIATRA NEAMŢ
CALISTRAT HOGAŞ MUSEUM
PLOIEŞTI
I. L. CARAGIALE MUSEUM
RÎMNICU VILCEA
ANTON PANN MEMORIAL HOUSE
SALONTA
JÁNOS ARANY MUSEUM
SIRIA
ION SLAVICI MUSEUM
TÎRGOVISTE
MUSEUM OF TÎRGOVISTE WRITERS
VÎNĂTORI
MIHAIL SADOVEANU MUSEUM

SPAIN

ALCALA DE HENARES
BIRTHPLACE OF CERVANTES
BARCELONA
VERDAGUER MUSEUM
EL TOBOSO
HOUSE OF DULCINEA

LAS PALMAS
PÉREZ GALDOS HOUSE-MUSEUM

MADRID
HOUSE OF LOPE DE VEGA
MESONERO ROMANOS MUSEUM
MUSEUM OF THE ROMANTIC PERIOD
MUSEUM OF SPANISH BOOKS
ROYAL LIBRARY

MOGUER
ZENOBIA-JUAN RAMON HOUSE- MUSEUM

MONOVAR
AZORIN HOUSE MUSEUM

SANTANDER
MENÉNDEZ PELAYO HOUSE- MUSEUM
MUNICIPAL MUSEUM OF FINE ART

SEGOVIA
ANTONIO MACHADO HOUSE- MUSEUM

VALLADOLID
HOUSE OF CERVANTES

VALLDEMOSA
ROYAL CHARTERHOUSE

VILLANUEVA Y GELTRU
VICTOR BALAGUER MUSEUM

SWEDEN

MARBACKA
THE MANOR HOUSE

RANSÄTER
GEIJERS HOUSE-MUSEUM

SWITZERLAND

GENEVA
JEAN-JACQUES ROUSSEAU MUSEUM

KILCHBERG
LOCAL HISTORY COLLECTION

LIESTAL
POETS' MUSEUM

LUCENS
CONAN DOYLE FOUNDATION

MÔTIERS
JEAN-JACQUES ROUSSEAU MUSEUM

SIERRE-SIDERS
VILLA MANOR

ZURICH
CENTRAL LIBRARY
THOMAS MANN COLLECTION

TURKEY

AKŞEHIR
ARCHAEOLOGICAL MUSEUM

USSR

ABOVYAN
TCHAVTCHAVADZÉ HOUSE- MUSEUM

ABRAMTSEVO
AKSAKOV HOUSE-MUSEUM

ALUSHTA
C. N. SERGEEV-TSENSKY HOUSE- MUSEUM

BAKU
STATE MUSEUM OF AZERBAIJAN LITERATURE

BELINSKIY
V. G. BELINSKIY MUSEUM

CHERNOVTSY
FEDKOVICH LITERARY MUSEUM
KOBILYANSKA MUSEUM OF LITERATURE

EREVAN
MUSEUM OF LITERATURE AND ART OF THE ACADEMY OF SCIENCES

GORKI
KASHIRIK MUSEUM
STATE LITERARY MUSEUM A. M. GORKI

KAMENSK URALSK
A. S. PUSHKIN MEMORIAL MUSEUM

KIEV
SHEVCHENKO HOUSE-MUSEUM
T. G. SHEVCHENKO STATE MUSEUM

KISHINEV
PUSHKIN HOUSE-MUSEUM

KISLOVODSK
SERGO ORDZHONIKIDZE MUSEUM

KRASNOYARSK
V. I. SURIKOV MEMORIAL MUSEUM

LENINGRAD
MUSEUM OF THE INSTITUTE OF RUSSIAN LITERATURE
NATIONAL PUSHKIN MUSEUM
N. A. NEKRASOV HOUSE- MUSEUM
G. V. PLEKHANOV MUSEUM
A. S. PUSHKIN HOUSE-MUSEUM

LVOV
IVAN FRANKO MUSEUM
YAROSLAV GALAN MUSEUM

MELIKHOVASKYA
HOUSE MUSEUM OF A. P. CHEKHOV

MINSK
YAKUB KOLAS MUSEUM

MOSCOW
APARTMENT-MUSEUM OF F. M. DOSTOIEVSKI
APARTMENT-MUSEUM OF N. A. OSTROVSKI
A. P. CHEKHOV HOUSE-MUSEUM
MAXIM GORKI MUSEUM
MEMORIAL MUSEUM IN THE FLAT OF THE ACTRESS, M. N. ERMOLOVA
NATIONAL MUSEUM OF LITERATURE
ALEXANDER PUSHKIN MUSEUM
STATE V. V. MAYAKOVSKI LIBRARY AND MUSEUM
STATE MUSEUM OF THE WRITER, N. A. OSTROVSKI
LEO TOLSTOY HOUSE MUSEUM
L. N. TOLSTOY MUSEUM

ORDZHONIKIDZE
KOSTA KHETAGUROV MUSEUM

OREL
MUSEUM OF LOCAL WRITERS
I. G. TURGENEV MUSEUM

PIATIGORSK
LERMONTOV MUSEUM

POLENOVO
V. D. POLENOV NATIONAL HOUSE-MUSEUM

POLTAVA
KOROLENKO MUSEUM OF LITERATURE
REGIONAL MUSEUM AND KOTLYAREVSKY LITERARY MUSEUM

PUSHKIN
ALL-UNION PUSHKIN MUSEUM
LYCÉE IN PUSHKIN

PUSHKINSKIYE GORY
PUSHKIN ESTATE

RIGA
J. RAINU MUSEUM OF LITERATURE

SARATOV
P. S. CHERNICHEVSKI MEMORIAL MUSEUM
A. S. SERAFIMOVICH HOUSE- MUSEUM

SHEVCHENKO
T. G. SHEVCHENKO MUSEUM

SOCHI
N. A. OSTROVSKI MUSEUM

SPASSKOYE-LUTOVINOVO
TURGENEV ESTATE-MUSEUM

SVERDLOVSK
BAZHOV LITERARY MUSEUM

TAGANROG
A. P. CHEKHOV HOUSE-MUSEUM
TAGANROG SCHOOL MUSEUM

TALLINN
EDUARD VILDE MEMORIAL MUSEUM

TBILISI
CHAVCHAVADZE HOUSE- MUSEUM
LITERARY MUSEUM OF GEORGIA

TULA
POLENEV HOUSE-MUSEUM

ULAN-BATOR
NATSAGDORZH MUSEUM

VINNITSA
PIROGOV HOUSE-MUSEUM

YALTA
A. P. CHEKHOV MUSEUM
MUSEUM OF LITERATURE

YASNAYA POLYANA
TOLSTOY MUSEUM
WRITERS' MUSEUM

UNITED STATES

AMESBURY
JOHN GREENLEAF WHITTIER HOME

ASHEVILLE
THOMAS WOLFE MEMORIAL

ATHENS
TIOGA POINT MUSEUM

BARDSTOWN
MY OLD KENTUCKY HOME STATE PARK

BRANSON
SHEPHERD OF THE HILLS FARM

CAMDEN
WALT WHITMAN HOUSE

CLAREMORE
LYNN RIGGS MEMORIAL

CONCORD
CONCORD ANTIQUARIAN SOCIETY MUSEUM
ORCHARD HOUSE

CONDORD
RALPH WALDO EMERSON MEMORIAL MUSEUM

COOPERSTOWN
MUSEUM OF NEW YORK STATE HISTORICAL ASSOCIATION

CRAWFORDSVILLE
GENERAL LEW WALLACE STUDY

CUMMINGTON
WILLIAM CULLEN BRYANT HOMESTEAD

DANBURY
DANBURY SCOTT-FANTON MUSEUM

DAYTON
PAUL L. DUNBAR HOUSE

GAINESVILLE
MARJORIE KINNAN RAWLINGS STATE MUSEUM

GALESBURG
CARL SANDBURG BIRTHPLACE

GALION
LOUIS BROMFIELD MALABAR FARM FOUNDATION

GENEVA
LIMBERLOST STATE MEMORIAL

GLEN ELLEN
JACK LONDON STATE HISTORIC PARK

GREENSBORO
GREENSBORO HISTORICAL MUSEUM

HANNIBAL
MARK TWAIN BOYHOOD HOME
MARK TWAIN HOME BOARD MUSEUM

HARTFORD
MARK TWAIN MEMORIAL

HAVERHILL
JOHN GREENLEAF WHITTIER HOMESTEAD

HUNTINGTON
WALT WHITMAN HOUSE

INDIANAPOLIS
LOCKERBIE STREET HOME OF JAMES WHITCOMB RILEY

KEY WEST
HEMINGWAY HOME AND MUSEUM

LITHOPOLIS
WAGNALLS MEMORIAL

LUCAS
LOUIS BROMFIELD MALABAR FARM FOUNDATION

MONTEREY
ROBERT LOUIS STEVENSON HOUSE

NEW YORK
POE COTTAGE

OXFORD
WILLIAM HOLMES MCGUFFEY HOUSE AND MUSEUM

PHILADELPHIA
FREE LIBRARY OF PHILADELPHIA

PITTSFIELD
MELVILLE MEMORIAL ROOM

PORTLAND
THE WADSWORTH- LONGFELLOW HOUSE

PORTSMOUTH
THOMAS BAILEY ALDRICH MEMORIAL

PROVIDENCE
ANNMARY BROWN MEMORIAL

RICHMOND
EDGAR ALLAN POE MUSEUM

ROME CITY
GENE STRATTON PORTER STATE MEMORIAL

ST. HELENA
THE SILVERADO MUSEUM

ST. LOUIS
EUGENE FIELD MUSEUM

SALEM
HOUSE OF THE SEVEN GABLES

SAN ANTONIO
O. HENRY HOUSE

SARANAC LAKE
STEVENSON COTTAGE

SAUK CENTER
SINCLAIR LEWIS MUSEUM

SAULT STE. MARIE
THE SCHOOLCRAFT INDIAN AGENCY HOUSE

SOUTH BERWICK
HAMILTON HOUSE
SARAH ORNE JEWETT MEMORIAL

SPRINGFIELD
VACHEL LINDSAY ASSOCIATION

STOUTSVILLE
MARK TWAIN BIRTHPLACE MEMORIAL SHRINE

TAOS
D. H. LAWRENCE RANCH

TARRYTOWN
MUSEUM OF HISTORICAL SOCIETY OF THE TARRYTOWNS
SUNNYSIDE

YUGOSLAVIA

BELGRADE
VUK AND DOSITEJ MUSEUM

KOŠLJUN
MONASTIC MUSEUM

VISOVAC
FRANCISCAN MONASTERY AND SEMINARY

VRBA
HOUSE-MUSEUM

ZAGREB
LITERARY MUSEUM

Select Bibliography of National Museum Directories and Articles

The literature relating to museums is enormous, and there is inevitably much duplication. We have listed below those general articles and guides which we have found particularly helpful in compiling and checking the present work. They are normally arranged under countries, but in the case of more comprehensive publications we have put them under the headings of continents or areas. There is also a heading for Specialised Subjects.

AFRICA

Directory of Museums in Tropical Africa (UNESCO/ICOM, 1966).

Reynolds, Barrie, *Directory of Museums of Ethnography in Africa* (ICOM, 1966).

Seidenspinner, Gundolf, *African Museums 1969* (Deutsche Afrika–Gesellschaft).

ALBANIA

Adhami, Stilian, 'Museums in Albania', *Museum*, XIII no. 2 (1960) 67-73.

ALGERIA

Arts et Musées d'Algérie (Alger: Ministére de l'Éducation Nationale).

ASIAN/PACIFIC

Fitzgerald, W. H., Force, Roland W., and Kaeppler, Adrienne L., *Directory of Asian-Pacific Museums* (Honolulu: Bishop Museum Press, 1969).

AUSTRALIA

Bryden, W., 'Museums in Australia', *Museum*, VIX no. 3 (1961) 133-41.

White, Omar, *Guide to Australia* (Heinemann, 1968).

AUSTRIA

Österreichische Museen Unveränderter Fortdruck aus dem Jahrbuch der Österreichischen Wissenschaft (Wien: Österreichischer Bundesverlag für Unterricht, Wissenschaft und Kunst, 1957-8).

Museen und Sammlungen in Österreich (Wien und München: Verlag Anton Schroll, 1968).

Handbuch der Museen (Verlag Dokumentation, 1971) I.

Musées et Monuments en Autriche (Bundesministerium für Handel und Wiederaufbau, 1963).

BANGLADESH

Haque, Enamul, *Survey of Museums and Archaeological Education and Training in East Pakistan* (Bureau of National Reconstruction, 1970).

BULGARIA

Atanassov, Néno, 'Natural History Museums, *Museum*, XVI no. 2 (1963) 63-6.

Djambov, Christo, 'Archaeological museums and archaeological sections of national museums, *Museum*, XVI no. 2 (1963) 74-7.

Peeva, Guinka, 'Museums in the People's Republic of Bulgaria', *Museum*, XVI no. 2 (1963) 54-8.

Velcov, Velizar, 'Museological sites and museums', *Museum*, XVI no. 2 (1963) 67-73.

CAMEROUN

Paré, Isaac, 'The museums of Cameroun', *Museum*, XVIII no. 3 (1965) 144-9.

CANADA

Canadian Museums and Related Institutions (Canadian Museums Association, 1968).

REPUBLIC OF CHINA

Lin-Ts'an, Li, 'New light on the development of the museums in the Republic of China', *Museum*, XIX no. 4 (1966), 230-6.

Pao, Ignatius T. P., *A History of Chinese Museums* (Taipei, Taiwan: National Historical Museum, 1964).

CZECHOSLOVAKIA

Drobna, Zoroslava, 'Principles, Projects and Achievements of History Museums in Czechoslovakia', *Museum*, XIV, no. 4 (1961) 186-94.

Musées et galeries de Prague (Prague: Editions Olympia, 1967).

Pubal, Vaclav, *Muzea a galerie v CSR* (Muzeologicky Kabinet při Národním Muzeu v Přaze, 1970).

Slovenské Muzéa (Slovenské Narodné Muzeum', 1968).

DENMARK

Bocsen, Gudmund, *Danish Museums* (Committee for Danish Cultural Activities Abroad, 1966).

Larsen, Svend, 'Local Museums of Cultural History in Denmark', *Museum*, XIII no. 2 (1960) 74-8.

FINLAND

Suomen Museot (Suomen Museoliiton, Julkaisuja 9, 1969).

FRANCE

Barnaud, Germaine, *Guide des Musées de Paris* (Paris: Arts et Métiers Graphiques, 1968).

Guide des Musées de France (Office du Livre, 1970).

The Museums of Paris, trs. James Brockway, text by Raymond Charmet (London: Oldbourne Press, 1968).

Poisson, Georges, *Les Musées de France* (Presses Universitaires de France, 1965).

GERMANY, DEMOCRATIC REPUBLIC

Handbuch der Museen (Verlag Dokumentation, 1971) II.

GERMANY, FEDERAL REPUBLIC

Handbuch der Bayerischen Museen und Sammlungen (Regensburg: Verlag Friedrich Pustet, 1968).

Handbuch der Museen (Verlag Dokumentation, 1971) I.

Hentzen, Alfred, 'German museums and the art of our time'. *Museum*, XXI no. 2 (1968) 148-57.

Jantzen, E., 'The modernisation of the museums of Hamburg', *Museum*, XV no. 3 (1962) 158-63.

Jedding, Hermann, *Führer durch Museen und Sammlungen* (Keysersche Verlagsbuchhandlung, 1961).

Museen In Hessen (Kassel: Hessischer Museumsverband eV, 1970).

State Museums Berlin (Prussian Cultural Foundation, 1964).

GREAT BRITAIN

Corbett, E. V., *The Libraries, Museums and Art Galleries Year Book 1971* (James Clarke & Co. Ltd., 1971).

Museums and Galleries of Great Britain and Ireland (Index Publications, 1971-2).

'Museums of the United Kingdom of Great Britain and Northern Ireland', *Museum*, XXIII no. 2 (1970-1) 87-90.

GREECE

Museums and Collections in Greece (National Bank of Greece, 1970).

HUNGARY

Balassa, I., and Szolnoky, L., *Ethnographische Sammlungen der Museen in Ungarn*, Révia Nyomda (Budapest, 1964).

Bodrogi, Tibor, 'Ethnographical Museums', *Museum*, XV no. 4 (1962) 212-15.

Fülep, Ferenc, 'History Museums', *Museum*, XV no. 4 (1962) 201-6.

Korek, J., and Kovrig, I., *Archaeological Collections in Hungary* (Budapest: Révai Nyomda, 1966).

Korek, J., 'Provincial Museums', *Museum*, XV no. 4 (1962) 243-6.

Magyar Múzeumok (Budapest: Népmúvelési Propaganda Iroda, 1969).

Mezaros, Vince, 'Technical Museums', *Museum*, XV no. 4 (1962) 220-3.

Székessy, Vilmos, 'Natural History Museums', *Museum*, XV no. 4 (1962) 216-19.

Weiner, M., and Horvath, Tibor, 'Museums of Applied Art', *Museum*, XV no. 4 (1962) 235-8.

INDIA

Anthropological Collections in the Museums of India (Indian National Committee of ICOM, 1967).

Brief Directory of Museums in India, 1944-69 (Museums Association of India, 1969).

Indian Museums Review 1961-64 (Ministry of Education, New Delhi).

Morley, Grace, 'Museums in India', *Museum*, XVIII no. 4 (1965) 191-250.

Sivaramamurti, C., *Directory of Museums in India* (Ministry of Scientific Research and Cultural Affairs, 1959).

ISRAEL

Biran, A., 'Museums in Israel', *Museum*, XX no. 1 (1967) 2-4.

Efron, Zusia, 'Museums in the Kibbutzim', *Museum*, XX no. 1 (1967) 42-8.

Hestrin, Ruth, 'Local and Regional Museums', *Museum*, XX no. 1 (1967) 34-41.

Museum Guide for Israel (Government Printer, Jerusalem, 1964).

Provisional List of the Museums of Israel (Israel National Committee for ICOM, 1970).

ITALY

Brea, Luigi Bernabo, 'From ancient art to history in Italian archaeological museums', *Museum*, XIV no. 4 (1961) 202-14.

I Musei di Lombardia (Milan: Instituto Lombardo di Scienze e Lettere, 1957).

Repertorio dei musei e raccolte scientifiche italiane, Comitato Italiano dell' ICOM/Associazone Nazionale dei Musei Italiani (Rome: Istituto Grafico Tiberino, 1967).

JAPAN

Art Museums in Japan (1960).

Guide to Art in Japan (Mayuyama, 1970).

'Museums and places of interest in Japan visited during the Tokyo Regional Seminar', *Museum*, XVI no. 4 (1963) 247-60.

Museums in Japan (UNESCO, 1960).

Museums in Tokyo (1970).

KENYA

Carcasson, R. H., 'The Coryndon Museum, Nairobi, and the role of natural history museums in Tropical Africa', *Museum*, XVI no. 3 (1963) 182-7.

LATIN AMERICA

Guiá de los Collecciones Publicas de Arte en la America Latina (Washington, D.C.: Union Panamerican, 1956) I.

Guiá de museos de America Latina (UNESCO, 1963).

Guiá de los museos de Costa Rica, Chile, Ecuador, Guatemala, Haiti, Honduras, Paraguay, Uraguay, Venezuela (UNESCO, 1961).

MALAYA

Bin Yahaya, Abdul Aziz, 'Museums in Malaya', *Museum*, XIX no. 4 (1966) 237-41.

MEXICO

Anzures, Miguel Salas, 'The Museums of the National Institute of Fine Arts', *Museum*, XV, no. 1 (1962) 34-7.

Hurtado, Eusebio Davalos, 'The Museums of the National Institute of Anthropology and History', *Museum*, XV no. 1 (1962) 15-21.

MOROCCO

Les Musées du Maroc (Rabat: Direction des Musées et des Antiquités, 1970).

NETHERLANDS

Balkenstein, J. M., 'Bourgeois and regional costumes in Dutch museums', *Museum*, xv no. 2 (1962) 99-103.

Bernet Kempers, A. J. 'Regional ethnography museums', *Museum*, xv no. 2 (1962) 114-19.

Braat, W. C., 'Archaeology Museums', *Museum*, xv no. 2 (1962) 95-8.

Engel, H., 'Natural history museums', *Museum*, xv no. 2 (1962) 120-8.

Frese, H. H., 'General ethnography museums', *Museum*, xv no. 2 (1962) 108-13.

de Nederlandse musea (Staatsvitgeverij 's-Gravenhage, 1970).

Scheurleer, D. F. Lunsingh, 'Small museums and cabinets of antiquities', *Museum*, xv no. 2 (1962) 128-31.

Van Luttervelt, R., 'Maritime museums', *Museum*, xv no. 2 (1962) 104-7.

Wijsenbeek, L. J. F., 'Art museums', *Museum*, xv no. 2 (1962) 79-83.

NEW ZEALAND

Gamble, Brenda, and Cooper, Robert C., *Art Galleries and Museums of New Zealand* (Art Galleries and Museums Association of New Zealand Inc., 1969).

NIGERIA

Fagg, Bernard, 'The museums of Nigeria', *Museum*, xvi no. 3 (1963) 124-48.

NORWAY

Engelstad, Eivind S., *Norwegian Museums: Museums of Art and Social History* (Oslo: Royal Norwegian Ministry of Foreign Affairs, 1959).

Natural History Museums in Norway (Universitetsforlagets Trykningssentral, 1960).

PAKISTAN

Kamul, Ahmad A., 'Museums in Pakistan', *Museum*, xix no. 4 (1966) 242-7.

PHILIPPINES

Tantoco, Mrs Rosario B., *Directory of Museums in the Philippines* (National Museum of the Philippines, 1970)

POLAND

Brzostowski, Stanisław, and Orysiak, Stanisław, *Muzea w Polsce* (Warszawa: Wydawniciwo Zwiazkowe Crzz, 1968).

Durko, Janusz, 'The historical museums', *Museum*, xix no. 2 (1966) 82-9.

Lorentz, Stanisław, 'The museums of Poland', *Museum*, xix no. 2 (1966), 70-81.

Lorentz, Stanisław, *Museen und Sammlungen in Polen* (Warschau: Polonia-Verlag, 1956).

Prufferowa, E., 'The ethnographical museums', *Museum*, xix no. 2 (1966) 107-16.

Smolen, Ks. Władysław, 'The diocesan museums', *Museum*, xix no. 2 (1966) 98-106.

PORTUGAL

Gonçalves, António Manuel, *Museus de Lisboa* (Guiá Turístico de Lisboa, 1960).

ROMANIA

Mihalache, Marin, *Die Museen von Bukarest* (Bucharest: Verlag Meridiane, 1963).

Rumänien Reiseführer (Bucharest: Verlag Meridiane, 1968).

SCANDINAVIA

Nordens Museer 1965-67: Danmark, Finland, Island, Norge och Sverige (Stockholm: Boktryckeriet P.A. Norstedt & Söner, 1968).

SENEGAL

Girard, Jean, 'The Museums of Senegal', *Museum*, xviii no. 3 (1965) 130-7.

SOUTH AFRICA

Fransen, H., *Guide to the Museums of Southern Africa* (Cape Town: South African Museums Association, 1969).

SPAIN

Museos y Colecciones de España (Madrid: Dirección General de Bellas Artes, 1972).

SPECIALISED SUBJECTS

Atkinson, Frank, 'New Open-air Museums', *Museum*, xxiii no. 2 (1970-1) 99-107.

Bibliothèques et Musées des Arts du Spectacle dans le Monde (Centre Nationale de la Recherche Scientifique, 1960).

Directory of Meteorite Collections and Meteorite Research (UNESCO, 1968).

Directory of Zoological (and Entomological) Specimen Collections of Tropical Institutions (UNESCO, 1962).

La Faience en Europe (Cadmus, 1964).

Hawcroft, Francis, 'University Museums', *Museum*, xxiii no. 2 (1970-1) 118-24.

Hiatt, Robert W., *World Directory of Hydrobiological and Fisheries Institutions* (American Institute of Biological Sciences, 1963).

La Porcelaine en Europe (Cadmus, 1964).

Museums of Science and Technology (Committee of ICOM, 1963).

'Les Musées du Vin: Europe', *La Revue Vinicole Internationale* (Nov/Dec. 1963).

Nicholson, T. R., *The World's Motor Museums* (J. M. Dent & Sons, 1970).

Repertoire International des Musées et Collections du Verre (ICOM, 1966).

Repertoire des Musées de la Mer (ICOM, 1965).

Repertory of Museums of Arms and Military History (Association of Museums of Arms and Military History, 1960).

Van Beylen, J., *Repertory of Maritime Museums and their Collections* (Antwerp: National Maritime Museum, 1969).

Veinstein, André, 'The world's theatrical museums', *Museum*, xix no. 1 (1966) 52-61.

SRI LANKA

de Silva, P. H. D. H., 'Museums in Ceylon', *Museum*, xix, no. 4 (1966) 219-30.

SWEDEN

A Key to the Museums of Sweden (Stockholm: The Swedish Institute, 1960).

SWITZERLAND

Handbuch der Museen (Verlag Dokumentation, 1971) ii.

Lapaire, Claude, *Guide des Musées Suisses* (Bern: Verlag Paul Haupt, 1969).

Musées et Bibliothèques de Genève (1965).

SYRIA

Zouhdi, Bachir, *Repertoire Sommaire des Musées de la République Arab Syrienne* (1971).

THAILAND

The Development of Museums and Archaeological Activities in Thailand (Bangkok: Fine Arts Department, 1965).

TUNISIA

Les musées de Tunisie (Comité Tunisien pour les Musées, ICOM, 1970).

U.S.S.R.

Bespalov, Nikolai, 'Tolstoy Museums in the U.S.S.R.', *Museum*, XVI no. 1 (1963) 12-17.

Doroshenko, E. P., 'The Shevchenko Museums in the Ukraine', *Museum*, XIX no. 3 (1966) 163-7.

Ignatieva, Vera, 'Museums of the Russian Soviet Federal Socialist Republic', *Museum*, XVI no. 1 (1963), 18-25.

Kiriljuk, G., 'The establishment of people's museums in the Ukraine', *Museum*, XIX no. 3 (1966) 152-5.

Kiriljuk, G., 'Museums of the Ukraine', *Museum*, XVI no. 1 (1963) 26-9.

Kozlov, G. P., 'The Polytechnic Museum, Moscow', *Museum*, XX no. 4 (1967) 195-9.

'Les Musées en U.R.S.S.', *Notes et Etudes Documentaires*, no. 3753 (12 Jan. 1971).

Tarasenko, Anatoli, 'Lenin Museums in the Soviet Union', *Museum*, XXII no. 3/4 (1969) 213-21.

Tuček, Karel, *Práce Museí v Sovětském Svazu* (Prague: Orbis, 1956).

Vinogradova, Klavdia Mikhailovna, 'The Chekhov Museums in the U.S.S.R.', *Museum*, XIII no. 2 (1960) 85-91.

U.S.A.

Cartwright, Aubrey W., *A Guide to Art Museums in the United States* (Duell, Sloan & Pearce, 1958).

Hunter, John E., *Inventory of Ethnological Collections in Museums in the United States and Canada* (Committee on Anthropological Research in Museums of the American Anthropological Association and the Wenner-Gren Foundation for Anthropological Research, 1967).

McDurrah, Fred. W., *Museums in New York* (New York: E. P. Dulton & Co. Inc., 1967).

The Official Museum Directory (American Association of Museums, 1973).

Taylor, Frank A., 'The museums of science and technology in the United States', *Museum*, XX no. 4 (1967) 158-63.

VIETNAM, REPUBLIC OF

Nguyễn-Bá-Lăng, 'The museums of the Republic of Vietnam', *Museum*, XIX no. 4 (1966) 253-8.

YUGOSLAVIA

Han, Verena, 'Regional and local museums in Yugoslavia', *Museum*, XIV no. 3 (1961) 150-60.

Muzeji Jugoslavije (Beograd: Savez Muzehskih Društava Jugoslavije, 1962).